The STANDARD CATALOG of® COMIC BOOKS

JOHN JACKSON MILLER
MAGGIE THOMPSON
PETER BICKFORD
BRENT FRANKENHOFF

Published by

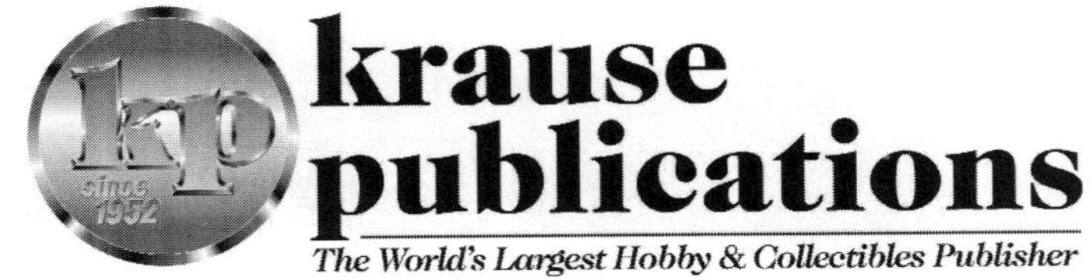

700 E. State St. • Iola, WI 54990-0001
Telephone: (715) 445-2214 • www.krause.com

Please, call or write us for our free catalog of collectibles publications.
To place an order or receive our free catalog, call (800) 258-0929.
For editorial comment and further information,
use our regular business telephone at (715) 445-2214.

ISBN: 0-87341-916-2 - Softcover
ISBN: 0-87349-585-3 - Hardcover
Library of Congress Catalog Number: 2001096292
Printed in the United States of America

"Libraries are not made; they grow."

— Augustine Birrell, 1850-1933

(The first comic book came out the following year. Little did he know...)

EDGAR RICE BURROUGHS'
TARZAN
and THE MEN OF A-LUR
AMERICA'S TYPICAL TEEN-AGER
Archie comics
IS THERE ANYONE IN THE CLASS WHO IS GOOD ON DATES?
DONALD DUCK
68 PAGES
Full Color
SUPERMAN
64 PAGES IN ACTION!
ALL IN FULL COLOR
THE COMPLETE STORY OF THE DARING EXPLOITS OF THE ONE AND ONLY SUPERMAN

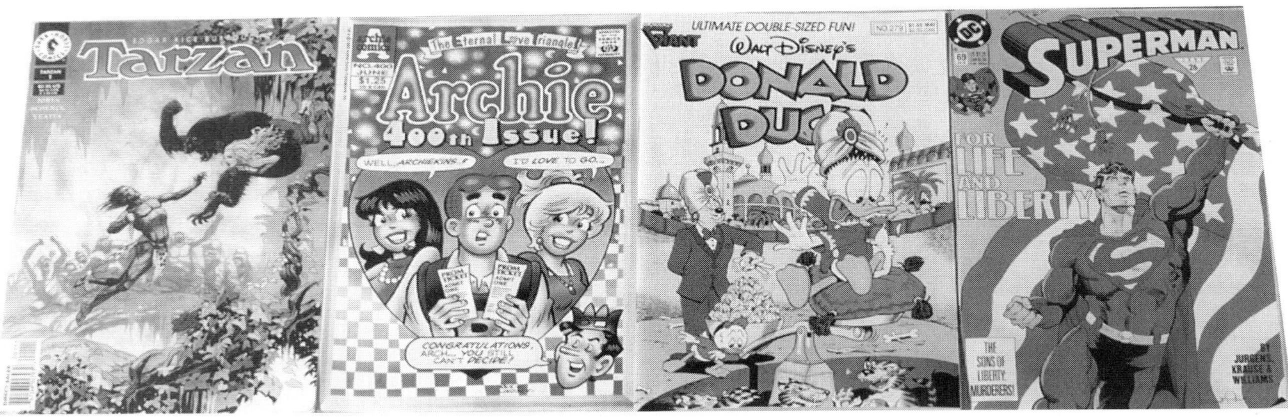
Tarzan
The Eternal Love Triangle!
Archie
400th Issue!
WELL, ARCHIEKINS...!
I'D LOVE TO GO...
CONGRATULATIONS, ARCH... YOU STILL CAN'T DECIDE!
ULTIMATE DOUBLE-SIZED FUN!
WALT DISNEY'S
DONALD DUCK
SUPERMAN
FOR LIFE AND LIBERTY
THE SONS OF LIBERTY MURDERERS!
BY JURGENS, KRAUSE & WILLIAMS

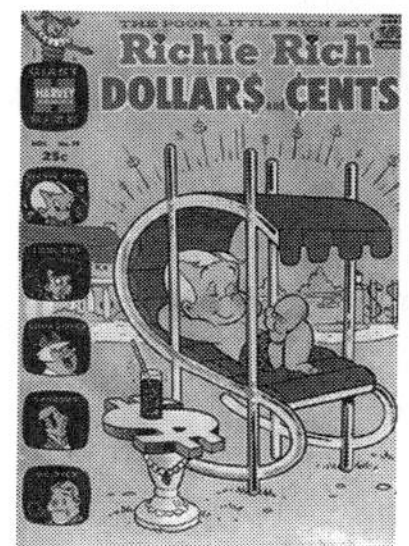

Mom or Dad or some kind soul brought a comic book home once.

Maybe some *Richie Rich* or *Archie* comic book. Maybe a Disney comic book or some super-hero title. You read it. Hopefully, you liked it.

And you kept it.

And you bought more.

And you read *them*. And you kept *them*.

And before long...

...you're dealing with a *collection*.

A collection that costs more to store than it did to buy.

A collection that causes floors to creak.

Professional movers to blanch.

Wives to walk out.

And you don't know quite how it happened — but, then again, you do. Because you love comic books, because comic books are the one kind of magazine that nobody throws away. (At least, not any more!)

But that's OK. We're here for you.

Consider us your support group. We've put our lives into publishing *Comics Buyer's Guide* magazine, the *ComicBase* CD-ROM, and other utilities to help you make sense out of your collection. We think this **Standard Catalog** will go a long way to help. This expansion of Krause Publications' signature line (which supports, not replaces, our annual, more portable ***CBG Checklist and Price Guide***) is designed to help answer your needs.

To help you spend *less* time figuring out what you have, what it's worth, and where it is — and *more* time doing something *really* important. Like reading your comic books.

Because, well, we know you. At least, we're just like you!

— John Jackson Miller
June 2002

Acknowledging those who helped make it all happen!

We've got four names on the cover, but the joint effort beyond the **Standard Catalog of Comic Books** extends far beyond.

Appreciation goes first and foremost to **Peter Bickford** and the skilled staff at his **Human Computing**, whose *ComicBase* provided much data for this edition. He and its contributors are responsible for many of the descriptions and images found herein.

The genesis for the Krause Publications contribution to the **Standard Catalog** database came from a price guide it and **Alex Malloy** developed for *Comics Collector* in 1983. Krause bought the rights to the database when that publication folded, and much credit for its growth goes to one who's no longer with us: **Don Thompson** edited *Comics Buyer's Guide* from 1983 until his untimely death in 1994. Don maintained and developed the database during that decade, and it's no surprise to anyone who knew Don that no other database has as much information from that era as the one he helped develop.

In more recent times, **Tammy Kuhnle** and **Jeff Kenton** were charged with helping to integrate the *ComicBase* and *Comics Buyer's Guide* databases. We greatly appreciate their help. **Bonnie Tetzlaff** and our book department were marvelous in helping work the database into a printable form. **Shawn "Slick" Williams** gave us our graphics, and the ever-patient **Debbie Bradley** helped smooth the way with the book department. And publisher **Mark Williams** helped make it all happen.

Denise Janec's contributions to the Standard Catalog are almost too many to name. Our local computer guru, she helped us capture more than 100,000 online auction results for comics and turned them into something recognizable. Taking an eBay auction titled "AMAZING SPIEDEY 4 VFN GREAT SHAPE WOW" and turning it into something that could be connected with *Amazing Spider-Man* Vol. 1, #4 in Very Fine in our database *sounds* simple, but doing it week after week sure isn't!

Denise aided us in confirming the existence of thousands of comics through her online research, referring to photo samples in auctions for information on cover price, publication date, and content. She also helped reconcile many of the comics listed in the CGC Population Report with the items in our database for this edition. Finally, she helped a lot with our photo database.

Believe it or not, she's still talking to us!

Special thanks go to the intrepid **Meredith Miller**, who spent hundreds of hours adding information about comic books to the **Standard Catalog** database and who helped locate many of the photographs used herein.

Meredith also helped match up comics listed in the CGC Population Report with the items in our database. She added many of the Capital City sales figures that appear in this edition. She also proved to be an exceptionally able troubleshooter — and still managed to put up with husband and author John Jackson Miller in the meantime. There are no words.

Special thanks go to **Milton Griepp** and **John Davis**, who in 1996 donated historical records from their **Capital City Distribution** to our archives for posterity. Both have contributed a lot to comics industry, and the records published here definitely illustrate the role that Capital and other direct-market distributors played in "saving" the comics industry in the 1980s, while comics were declining in exposure at mass-market newsstands.

Heading toward modern times, thanks go, of course, to **Diamond Comic Distributors**, which regularly supplies the comics industry, not only with comics, but plenty of information about how many comics it sells. Special thanks go to **Roger Fletcher, Lance Woods**, **Andrew Smith**, and others at Diamond who've been willing to find us answers on what we'll readily admit have often been trivial points about numbers.

Interested readers can find out a lot more about Diamond, its publications, and the stores it serves, at *www.diamondcomics.com*. Thanks, guys!

Thanks go to the **Audit Bureau of Circulation**, which opened its microfilm archives in 1997 so **Russ Maheras** could provide insight into comic-book circulation figures from before World War II. We're appreciative of *all* of Maheras' assistance over the years, but this extra effort deserves extra recognition. (And we're *really* sorry his car hit that deer on the way back from our offices. Glad you're OK, Russ!)

Big thanks go to **Comics Guaranty LLC**, which, from the start, has worked with us to provide readers with not only an introduction to third-party grading, but explanations of a lot of what goes on behind the scenes. CGC has also regularly provided us with our own version of its Population Report, listing how many comics it's graded and what grades they've appeared in, for dissemination to our readers. We've been able to do a lot of research using these figures in *Comics Buyer's Guide*, and we're pleased that we were able to reconfigure some of this information for this edition.

For a lot more population details for individual comic books — and information about CGC and its services — be sure to visit the company's website at *www.cgccomics.com*. Tell 'em we sent you!

Our appreciation goes to the large number of retail stores whose physical and catalog inventory we consulted over the years for information as this project was coming together. There are far too many to name — especially so, when it comes to the online vendors whose auctions and listings provided confirmation that specific issues existed. Of particular help was the website of *Comics Buyer's Guide* columnist Chuck Rozanski, whose **Mile High Comics** has the largest inventory around and whose website demonstrated on more than one occasion that comic books we were *sure* hadn't come out actually had! To prove it to youself, be sure to check *www.milehigh-comics.com*.

A number of people have come through with specific information on individual titles they've been directly involved with now or in the past. Knowledge about the long-running *Adventures of the Big Boy* series came from publishers **Manfred Bernhard** and **Craig Yoe**. **John Lustig**, whose *Last Kiss* work has given him access to much information on romance comics, shared a lot with us. Many active publishers shared information about their past and current comics works, including **Donna Barr; Central Park Media; CrossGen; Dark Horse Comics; DC Comics; Fantagraphics Books; Gemstone Publishing; Heavy Metal Publishing Group; Image Comics; Marvel Enterprises; Shanda Fantasy Arts; Viz Communications**; and many more.

We also extend our thanks to *Classics Illustrated* authority **Dan Malan**, who painstakingly determined the distinguishing characteristics of each printing and who has generously allowed us to use his information here.

Howard Michaels has painstakingly checked and rechecked information over the years in the *CBG Checklist & Price Guide*; we've incorporated much of his research here.

Comics Buyer's Guide (and its predecessor, *The Buyer's Guide for Comic Fandom*) have literally been using contributions from readers for 30+ years to compile annual lists of publishers' Statements of Ownership, and all the material gathered there over the years appears in this edition. It wasn't until the end of 1995, however, in *Comics Buyer's Guide* #1155, that we launched a formal "Circulation Scavenger Hunt" — and that's when the data really started to pour in. Some of the helpful collectors appear in the larger list below.

Thanks go as well to **Harold Buchholz, Michael Uslan**, and all the others who've expressed particular interest in seeing our comics circulation research come to fruition over the years. We always promised to publish all our research one day, but this edition has been so very long in coming, we wouldn't have blamed anyone for doubting it was going to happen — we weren't always sure ourselves! We hope this edition is a pleasant surprise for everyone.

Our appreciation also goes to the sponsors whose advertisements can be found in the back of this edition. They've directly contributed to our being able to add many pages to this volume without increasing the planned price, and for that we're most thankful. Pay 'em a visit!

Finally, our appreciation goes to you, the readers who've supported our research over the years by buying our publications and sending information. (And don't stop now! You can help us make our database even better by sending your additions and corrections to the Standard Catalog at *allcomics@krause.com.)*

Thanks, everyone!

Just *some* of the folks who provided specific information on individual comic books...

Michael Agnelli
Aaron Atwood
Bruce Bergeron
Daryl Broussard
Johanna Draper Carlson
Kurt Culler
Daryl Danforth
Shad Z. Daly
Mark Drummond
Mike Fanning
Dana Gabbard
Howie Gold
Randall A. Golden
Ronald Haar
Merlin V. Haas
Bill Helsel
Steve Horton
Rob Kirby
George Kochel
Dan Kocher
Tony Kolodiej
Tony Kowalik
Jeff Krell
J.P. Lang
John Lucas
Sean Meiers
Nathan Melby
Tom Michael
Scott Micheel
Stan Molson
Michael Pemberton
Roger Perez
Randy Phillips
Bob Reed
Steven Rowe
Craig J. Satterlee
Steve Shaw
Craig Shutt
Wally Stoelting
Preston Sweet
Mike Tiefenbacher
Bill Turok
Donald A. Whyte
Bob Youhouse
The Comic Warehouse
Super Giant Comics & Music
and many more!

Creating The Standard

How we hunted down info on 145,514 comic books

by John Jackson Miller

In coins, in records, in sports — the Krause Publications **Standard Catalog** line represents the ultimate resource for the hobby. Creating something worthy of the title for the comics field not only required the efforts of many people knowledgeable about the hobby; it took the fusion of two of the larger ongoing efforts in the field.

Krause Publications' ***Comics Buyer's Guide Price Guide*** has been in development since 1983, updates appearing over the years in *Comics Collector* and ***Comics Buyer's Guide*** magazines, in its own dedicated magazine, and most recently in the annual ***CBG Checklist and Price Guide*** book series. (The latter series continues to this day and serves as a portable, Silver-Age-to-present version of the volume you're holding.) The database is more complete than any other resource when it comes to independent comic books from the 1980s and 1990s, which competing guides dropped when they lost resale value. Since we offer collection management utilities, **lack of resale value is no reason to drop a comic book's listing**.

Meanwhile, Human Computing's ***ComicBase*** has been the leader, by far, among CD-ROM collection utilities for years, containing much information about individual titles and reviews and photographs for thousands of comic books. ***ComicBase*** has, by far, more entries than any other resource in comics — including this work, because, in addition to all the North American comics found here, it includes data on long-running foreign titles such as Britain's *Bunty*.

CBG and ***ComicBase*** joined forces in 2000, intent on developing, between them, the most complete archive of information about comic books ever seen. Far from its humble beginnings — ***CBG***'s guide was first on a typesetting system that was obsolete at the time — the combined database now exists on a vast, searchable server. Krause Publications hope to use it for a variety of publishing and research applications, and there's even the prospect of making it available to users online. And ***ComicBase*** customers will have access to the information that's in this volume on CD-ROM.

So where'd all the information come from? Research, both old-fashioned and high-tech!

Research into the comics

There is information about 145,514 North American comic books in the **Standard Catalog of Comic Books**, ranging from the beginning of the Golden Age to the beginning of 2002. Currently, the **Standard Catalog** database includes:

- **Cover prices** for about **95%** of all comic books;
- **Cover dates** for about **83%** of all comic books;
- **Story titles** for about **15%** of all comic books;
- **Writer names** for about **26%** of all comic books;
- **Artist names** for about **30%** of all comics books;

as well as information about character appearances, crossover storylines, production errors, and many more miscellaneous facts. In addition, there are descriptions and reviews for hundreds of the titles herein.

To such a Herculean task, we brought to bear a range of research strategies:

Firsthand hands-on research: First and foremost, we obviously looked at the comics themselves. Among the authors personal collections examined for this work is the Don and Maggie Thompson Collection, now recognized as a pedigree by Comics Guaranty LLC. The authors' joint archives amount to close to a quarter of a million comic books, many of which were examined in detail for this editon.

We have also benefited from the aid of many others who have searched their own collections over the years and provided information to *Comics Buyer's Guide* and *ComicBase.* If you'd like to help provide additional information from your collection, send an e-mail to us at *allcomics@krause.com* and tell us what you've got!

Firsthand remote research: While we had direct access to a large number of the comic books described in this edition, we couldn't find them all. In some cases, we looked at publicly available cover reproductions to confirm the existence of and additional details about comic books.

We eyeballed thousands of comic books, from the dawn of comics through last year, on **online auction sites,** including eBay. By 2001, there were more than 60,000 different comics auctioned online daily on eBay, and it was infrequent that we were able to "stump" it on a comic book we were looking for information about. With the cover depicted in most cases, we were usually able to glean publication dates and cover prices.

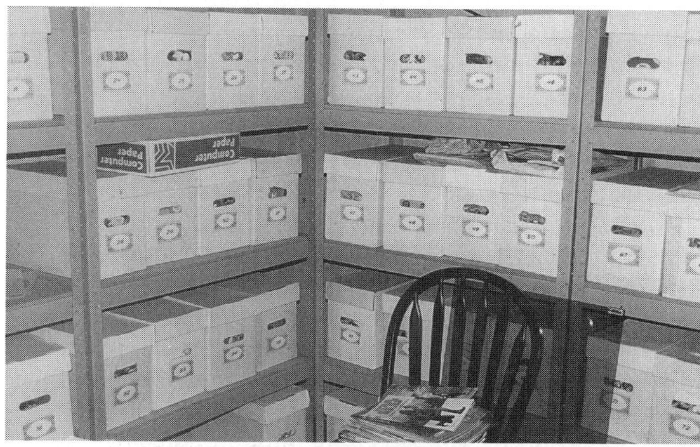

We also looked at comic-book covers in **retail advertisements and catalogs**, both online and print, from a variety of back-issue dealers to confirm the existence of many older comics. Depictions from these same public resources also conveyed information about the comics themselves, ranging from cover price and publication dates to information about content.

Secondhand hands-on research: Then there were instances in which we knew a comic book existed, even though we couldn't find a visual depiction of it anywhere. In these cases, we turned to information from others who had actually seen the comics.

A major new resource for such information can be found in the **grading service**, Comics Guaranty Corp., or CGC. CGC maintains an online "Census" or population report recording every comic book it has graded, along with publisher and cover dates drawn from the actual comics themselves. We regarded CGC's handling of a comic book as confirmation of the first order of the information it details — and the fact that people sending comics to CGC tend to send older and hard-to-find comics is definitely a good thing for anyone interested in proving their existence! Details for the more than 120,000

The authors' joint archives amount to close to a quarter of a million comic books, many of which were examined in detail for this editon.

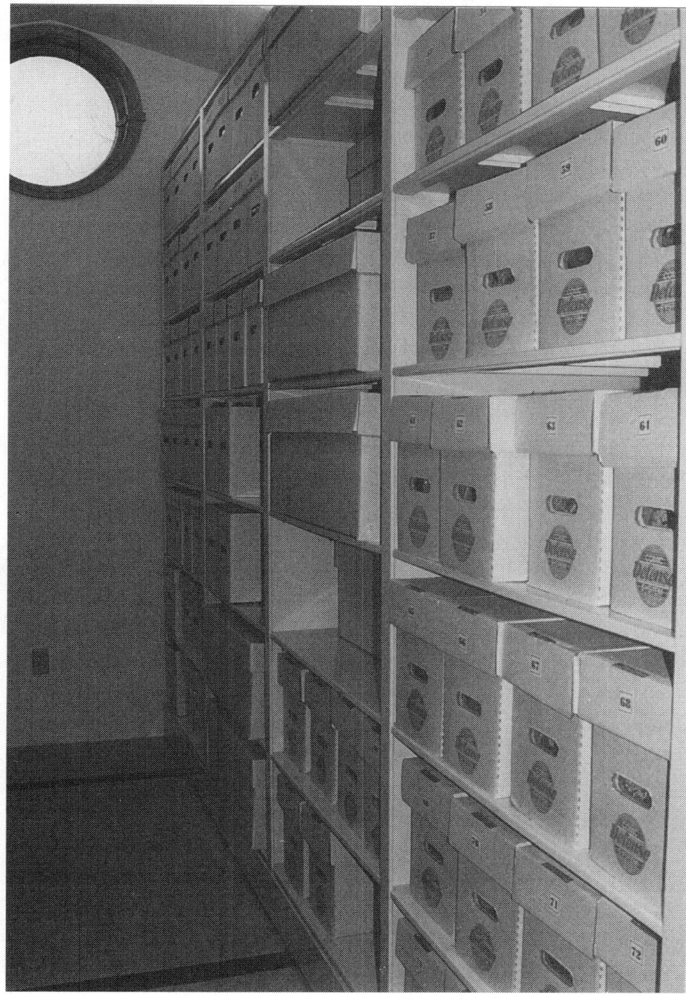

comics CGC has examined are available to the public at *www.cgccomics.com*.

For newer comics, we went to the **publishers** themselves, many of whom were able to provide partial or complete publishing histories (and some even provided the comics themselves). Our confidence in information provided by these publishers was generally very high.

We also consulted our own archives of **distributor catalogs** and **solicitations from publishers**. We maintain near-complete libraries of distribution catalogs and order-books from Diamond Comic Distributors, Capital City Distribution, Heroes World Distribution, Styx International, FM International, and more than a dozen other comic-book distributors, past and present. We also have data from the publishers themselves, put into permanent form in our "Comics In Your Future" and "CBG Calendar" columns in ***Comics Buyer's Guide*** since the mid-1980s. These provided helpful hints about publication dates, cover prices, story titles, and content. In no case were these resources allowed to be the *primary* confirmation of a comic book's existence, since we all know that many, many comics don't ship as solicited — or at all.

The **auction and retail resources** mentioned above often were able to provide additional information about the content of the comics being offered. A dealer has an obvious financial interest in telling as much as he or she can about a comic book — and a similar one in getting the information right.

*The **Standard Catalog** includes listings not just for comic books, but almost all graphic novels and trade paperback collections published in North America.*

In many cases, the sellers provided additional information as to creative teams, story titles, and character appearances. We did only include information that we felt was sound from these resources. It's sadly not unheard of for amateur auctioners to get things wrong about what they're selling, so we tended to place more faith in information from dealers who appeared to be better informed. When the details about the interiors of comics were ambiguous, incomplete, or otherwise open to question, we left them out.

Past printed resources: While the **Standard Catalog** is an original work, we cannot fail to acknowledge the debt owed to past chroniclers of comics history. Dozens of publications over the years have contributed to *everyone*'s knowledge of comic-book history, ourselves included. We first learned to look for, say, the 35-cent *Star Wars* #1 from Robert Overstreet years before the project you're holding began — and while we've certainly done our own research on prices and content, some portion of *everyone*'s knowledge of trivia gets its start somewhere else.

Not being able to parse out every source from decades of reading about comics, we've included a "Suggested Reading" on page 1219.

Ungraded-copy price research

This volume includes a Near-Mint price for **each** of the comic books listed herein. The prices are the result of a combined effort by Human Computing, producers of *ComicBase,* and the staff of *Comics Buyer's Guide*.

Human Computing has set more than 1 million prices for comic books over the years. It's investigated every title at least once, usually multiple times over the years, rechecking whenever a new trend surfaces. Convention sales, mail-order sales, and shop prices throughout the United States are gathered on a continual basis.

Comics Buyer's Guide has used many of the same methods, including making reference to the largest sortable database of actual online transactions ever assembled in comics. Each week since 2000, the *Comics Buyer's Guide* staff has downloaded thousands of completed transactions from the eBay auction service, including every single auction involving comic books graded by CGC. These transactions are sorted by publisher, title, issue number, and grade, and a range of prices is determined. These transactions have been used to **inform**, rather than set, the prices seen herein. One or two transactions, even for a high-profile rare comic book, can't always be solely counted on to estimate the typical going rate everywhere else.

The price ratios for each grade found at the bottom of the listing pages are based on many observations and, while the breakdowns for individual issues may vary, are representative of how the prices for the *typical* comic book have tended to break down.

There are many price guides available for comics, some

of which rely on each other so much that the prices all seem the same. Those accustomed to that will find that prices in the **Standard Catalog** will look different, and often considerably different. Our philosophy isn't to publish the highest prices we can find to make people feel better about their collections, but rather to publish the prices that smart collectors shopping at a variety of retail, convention, and online venues are likely to find. If you're in a remote area with only one shop or the Internet to rely on, the prices you're likely to find will be higher.

Likewise, a comic book with some pedigree — having come from a famous collection — may also sell for more.

Graded-copy price research

When it comes to comics graded by CGC, the **Standard Catalog** is the first price guide to systematically address after-market prices, drawing on the research done weekly in *Comics Buyer's Guide* since 2000.

It is not yet possible to publish a price guide listing going prices at each CGC grade for each issue. The reason is that CGC has, as of this printing, graded fewer than 150,000 copies — not much different from the number of different kinds of comic books there are! In very few cases has it graded one of *every* issue within a series; and in still fewer are there samples of each of those comics in *each* of the key grades. And even then, those comics may not all have come to market to establish a price.

Simply toughening grading standards and raising NM prices to reflect the high prices CGC-slabbed comics fetch is not a solution. From our observations, we can say that it is *not* generally the case that the high CGC prices have exerted upward influence on identical unslabbed copies. Rather, there seem to be developing two separate markets with two separate sets of valuations.

Fortunately, our research demonstrates that the two prices are related. For two years, we've compared a random sampling of comics in each CGC grade auctioned on eBay every day with our latest prices for ungraded comics. After tens of thousands of comparisons, we can say with some confidence that buyers are attaching a premium to the CGC labels, not the comics themselves; and that the premium is a function of both the CGC grade and what the comic book sells for without a slab.

For example, the presence of a CGC slab and a Near-Mint grade label on a Near Mint comic book made that comic book *tend* to fetch **five** times our NM value in online auctions in the three months immediately prior to the publication of the **Standard Catalog**. The comic book on the border between Near Mint and Mint, **16 times**. Consult the bottom of right-hand pages in this edition for the ratios for grades 9.0 VF/NM and above; look for insets elsewhere with other grades.

These ratios, while stable from week to week, do tend to move over longer periods. Each week's issue of *Comics Buyer's Guide* publishes ratios from the latest week's online auctions. And our ratios reflect the median sale of all comics within a grade; variance will occur due to the specific title and issue, the age of the comic book, the reputation of the seller, the professionalism and the number of other copies already available in slabbed form from CGC.

Which is why we also include...

Population research

For many issues, the number of comics graded by CGC and the best copy yet graded appears in the Standard Catalog. CGC provided the information, which is the most recent available before press time. We're most appreciative for it!

Circulation research

CGC's Census says how many copies it has seen. How many were originally out there and may be yet to be found? To begin to answer that question, this volume includes:

- **Statement of Ownership** circulation figures for about **14%** of all comic books;
- **Capital City Distribution** sales figures for about **17%** of all comic books;
- **Diamond Comic Distributors** retailer preorders for about **9%** of all comic books;

and several hundred more circulation figures from a variety of authorities. More details about where we found the figures that appear in the **Standard Catalog** appear in the section beginning on page 8.

Help us out!

Even in the unprecedented assemblage that is the **Standard Catalog,** there are a great many facts that remain to be added. Even after years of adding data from our own comic books, we still have many we haven't gotten to yet.

We'll continue to make additions and revisions to the database, but we'd love to have your help. If you have any of the following information for any comic book in (or not in) this directory, send it in:

- Title and issue number
- Publisher
- Publication date (as listed in the indicia)
- Cover price
- Page count (do not include covers)
- Whether it's color or black-and-white
- Titles of stories inside (note if any are text only)
- Writers whose works appear
- Artists whose works appear
- Cover artist
- Names of any people appearing on photo covers

Please send your findings (Excel files are acceptable) along with your name, address, and phone number to:

allcomics@krause.com

or to Standard Catalog of Comic Books, 700 E. State St., Iola, WI 54990. All submissions become the property of Krause Publications. Please state the source of your information and provide only what you can find through your own original research.

Tradition

What comics are, and how people collect them!

by Maggie Thompson

In the late 1800s, comic strips began to appear in American newspapers. There had been heavily illustrated stories before, and some histories of comics take note of everything from Egypt's *Book of the Dead* to medieval accounts of the crimes and punishment of criminals to William Hogarth's *The Rake's Progress.*

But modern collectors look on Richard Outcault's "Yellow Kid" as the first major modern comic-strip character. The strip first appeared in the New York *Journal* on Oct. 18, 1896 — and gave its name to "yellow journalism."

The evolution from comic strips to comic books took a bit longer. *Famous Funnies* #1 (with a cover date of July) went on sale in May 1934. It was begun by Eastern Color salesman Max C. Gaines, ran for 218 issues over the next 21 years, was the first monthly comic book, and sold for 10¢.

10¢ was the standard cover price for comics for more than 25 years after that, and millions of children — and adults — bought them regularly. As comic books became established, *types* of comic books emerged as typical. Comic-strip reprints were the first, but comic-book readers soon found themselves with a variety of subject matter from which to choose. The variety included Westerns,

Highlights from the last century-plus in comics

Oct. 18, 1896: Richard Outcault's "Yellow Kid," recognized as the first major modern comic-strip character, first appeared in the New York *Journal*. In late 1902, William Randolph Hearst's *New York Journal* released five 50¢ books with cardboard covers reprinting Sunday comic strips in full color, referring to them as "the best comic books that have ever been published."

1932: *The Adventures of Dick Tracy*, published by Whitman, was the first Big Little Book.

May 1934: *Famous Funnies* #1 (dated July) went on sale. Begun by Eastern Color salesman Max C. Gaines, it ran for 218 issues over the next 21 years, was the first monthly comic book, and sold for 10¢.

1935: *New Fun* was the first DC comic book.

March 1937: The first issue of DC's *Detective Comics* was published. Though Batman didn't make his debut in its pages until #27, this title is now the longest-running comic-book series in the world.

June 1938: *Action* #1 had this as its cover date; the issue featured the first appearance of Superman.

October-November 1939: This was the cover date for *Marvel Comics* #1, one of the comic-book issues bringing the highest prices as a collector's item today. The company became known as Timely through most of the Golden Age — not adopting the "Marvel Comics" imprint until the 1960s.

May 8, 1940: *Chicago Daily News* Literary Editor Sterling North denounced comic books as "a poisonous mushroom growth of the last two years," adding that comics were "guilty of a cultural slaughter of the innocents."

1942: Stan Lee became editor at Timely, when Simon and Kirby left for DC.

Fall 1942: E.C. started — with *Picture Stories from the Bible*.

March 1948: In a *Town Meeting of the Air* radio broadcast, *Saturday Review of Literature* drama critic John Mason Brown described comic books as "the marijuana of the nursery; the bane of the bassinet; the horror of the house; the curse of the kids; and a threat to the future."

Spring 1954: Sen. Estes Kefauver's Senate Subcommittee on Juvenile Delinquency holds hearings on comics, mostly focusing on distributors and exploring their ties to organized crime. Fredric Wertham, author of the *Seduction of the Innocent*, testifies against comics and their influence on children, while E.C.'s William Gaines comes to their defense in separate testimony.

October 1954: The Comics Magazine Association of America started to censor comics before publication.

crime, funny-animal, jungle, romance, and super-hero comics. Though super-hero characters had appeared in popular fiction — and even comic strips — before, *Action Comics* #1 is considered to be the starting point for super-hero comics. It was in that issue that Superman made his first appearance.

While many other types of comic books are collected today — and a few of them in near-perfect condition command prices of more than $1,000 — the most-collected comic books today are those devoted to super- or costume-heroes. Many collectors criticize this facet of the marketplace, because countless comics do *not* feature such characters but are still delightful and well worth collecting. Other comics fans are grateful that back-issue prices of other types of comics have not escalated as wildly as have the prices of many early super-hero comics.

Comic books were especially popular and widely circulated during World War II. They made quick, cheap, portable, disposable entertainment for service-men as well as children. Comic-book stories were easy to understand, and almost all stores had a comic-book rack, so comics were easy to find.

After the war came the baby boom — and an increasing number of potential readers. At the same time, parents had more leisure in which to supervise what their children read — and more and more parents became uneasy with the picture-story medium. As alarmists complained about comics that emphasized violence and bad taste, pressure mounted to prevent children from reading comic books *at all*.

There were even comic-book burnings in some areas. Such events — combined with paper drives that had been conducted during World War II — meant that few copies remained by the time hysteria had cooled and comics were "cleaned up" by the Comics Code in the autumn of 1954. (Not all comics carried the Code. Dell's titles and those in the *Classics Illustrated* line were not submitted for Code approval; other surviving comics, however, were.) Sequential art *as an art form* was looked upon as suitable only for children's reading — and unfashionable children's reading, at that.

Today, comic books have acquired a new popularity, as children who grew up with and loved them have become adults. Many doctors, lawyers, and college professors collect comics, and many other adults are ready as never before to accept the medium as a legitimate, creative form. At the same time, children continue to read comic books as cheap entertainment — though comics are no longer available for a dime.

Collecting comics then

As comic books became popular, some readers saved them. Most readers were children and treated comic books as disposable entertainment. Many children traded comics, and one issue might be read, reread, and handled

September-October 1956: *Showcase* with this cover date (issue #4) reintroduced The Flash, a DC super-hero from the '40s. The issue marked the start of The Silver Age.

Spring 1961: The world of wide-spread comics fandom emerged with the (almost simultaneous) publication of two amateur magazines devoted to comics: *Alter Ego* and *Comic Art*.

Fall 1961: *Fantastic Four* #1 was published with a cover date of November; it was the start of the so-called "Marvel Age of Comics."

July 27, 1964: Fan Bernie Bubnis put together a Monday-afternoon event in New York City that is usually acknowledged as the first comics convention, and by 1966, there was a two-day July event that followed much of the same format as today's comics conventions.

November 1967: *Zap Comix* #1 was printed, with a run of 5,000 for the 25¢, 24-page underground comic book.

November 1970: The first edition of what came to be known as *The Official Overstreet Comic Book Price Guide* was published; the print run was about 1,800, and a Mint copy of the eight-year-old *Amazing Fantasy* #15 was listed at $16, more than 100 times its original price of 12¢.

Spring 1971: High-school student Alan Light began publication of *The Buyer's Guide*, a comics collectors' publication which evolved into the weekly *Comics Buyer's Guide.*

September 5, 1972: Comics & Comix was founded in Berkeley, Calif. Store spokespeople estimated later that there were fewer than 25 stores of the type in the country at the time. By 1978, the line had expanded to six locations.

1974: Jack Katz's *The First Kingdom* began from Bud Plant: an independent, non-anthology, non-"underground" title.

1975: Phil Seuling began (non-returnable) direct distribution of Marvel and DC comics to comics specialty shops, later incorporating with partner Jonni Levas as Sea Gate Distributors, Inc.

December 1977: *Cerebus* by Dave Sim began with this date — a comic book that became so immensely popular that copies of the first issue were eventually forged. Sim's initial print-run was 2,000; it grew to 10 times that within a decade.

March 1978: *Fantasy Quarterly* carried this date — and the first installment of Wendy and Richard Pini's *ElfQuest*, one of the success stories in self-published comics.

September 30, 1978: Independent publisher Eclipse published *Sabre*, its first title. Eclipse would become a pioneer in the "graphic novel" format.

November 1982: Independent publisher First published its first comic book: *Warp* #1, dated March 1983.

roughly by five or more of them. Comic-book paper was newsprint, vulnerable to heat, light, and moisture, with a sulfur content so high that chemical reactions aged it rapidly. Despite this, some readers preserved their issues carefully — only to have them donated to paper drives or otherwise destroyed when their owners left home.

The few readers who preserved what they loved had to limit their source of back issues to thrift shops or the few second-hand book stores that bothered to stock comic books.

Earlier (in the '30s and '40s) among science-fiction readers, a tradition had sprung up of collecting (science-fiction and fantasy) magazines, of producing amateur fan magazines (fanzines) in which to discuss SF, and of holding gatherings at which fellow SF fans could meet. In that tradition, some fans in the early '50s produced fanzines devoted to E.C.'s line of comics — but those died with E.C.

At the World Science-Fiction Convention (Labor Day weekend 1960), SF fans Dick and Pat Lupoff gave away copies of the first issue of their fanzine, *Xero*. In that issue was the first installment of the continuing feature "All in Color for a Dime" — devoted to comics of the '40s. *Without* seeing *Xero*, several other comics aficionados — some SF fans, some not — decided to produce their *own* amateur magazines devoted to comic books and comic strips.

The time was right for comics collecting across America.

Since then, comics collecting has grown steadily. At first, comics collectors were few compared to the total number of people who read comic books. Comics publishing companies were distantly polite to (and a bit bewildered by) comics collectors — but comic books were not tailored to suit collector interests.

Over the years, comic-book circulations have shrunk, the comics-collector population has increased, and many comic books today do very well selling solely to the collector market.

Collecting comics now

Someone who wants to begin collecting comics or contact others who collect comics has an easier time of it today than did comics collectors in previous decades. More research material is available; specialty shops abound; reprints are being published at a rapid clip; professionals are accessible; comics companies respond to collectors' desires; and *Comics Buyer's Guide* is the weekly newspaper which brings the latest news and ads to comics collectors and professionals on an up-to-the minute basis. (Visit *www.comicsbuyersguide.com* for more details.)

On the other hand, prices are high and (on many back issues) going higher. As recently as 1961, a newsstand comic book cost only 10¢, and there were only a few titles of direct interest to collectors, even at those prices.

December 1, 1982: Krause Publications took over *The Buyer's Guide*, which became *Comics Buyer's Guide* and introduced a newspaper format. The comics publishing field had its own trade journal, one that served creators, publishers, distributors, shops, and collectors.

December 1982: The first issue of *Camelot 3000* appeared. It was a 12-issue maxi-series, the first DC produced exclusively for the direct-sales market.

April 6, 1984: Peter A. Laird and Kevin B. Eastman placed an ad in *Comics Buyer's Guide* to sell 3,000 copies of their *Teenage Mutant Ninja Turtles* #1. The title's success led to a black-and-white explosion of titles in the comics field.

Late 1986: New World, a TV production firm, bought Marvel.

February 1987: Four publishers cut off comics-shop distributor Glenwood, and that distributor ceased business by May.

1988: Andrews Group, Inc., bought Marvel for $82.5 million.

August 1988: Bud Plant sold his distribution company to national comics-shop distributor Diamond Comic Distribution, Inc.

1989: In *Illinois v. Correa* (familiarly known in the comics community as the "Friendly Frank's case"), a comics shop manager was charged with a crime for having material for adults in his shop. Out of the case was born the Comic Book Legal Defense Fund to help fight legal problems for comics creators and retailers. Cases continue to this day.

July 1990: *Spider-Man* #1 by Todd McFarlane set what was the highest recorded paid circulation for a comic book to that point. The first printing had sales of 2,350,000. When all editions were added, the total paid circulation was approximately 2,650,000 copies.

Summer 1991: MacAndrews and Forbes sold 40% of Marvel to the public, launching one of the most lucrative stocks of the early '90s.

June 1991: *X-Force* #1 by Fabian Nicieza and Rob Liefeld beat the record set by *Spider-Man* #1. Thanks in part to a marketing gimmick in which collector's cards were bagged with the issue, the paid circulation came to approximately 3,900,000.

July 1991: *X-Men* #1 by Chris Claremont, Jim Lee, and Scott Williams beat the paid circulation record set by *X-Force* #1. Marvel released the issue in five editions with variant covers. Estimated paid circulation was approximately 7,500,000.

February 1992: Several hot creators left top series at Marvel to form their own imprint, Image. Initially solicited and distributed by Malibu, the titles were eventually completely taken over by the creators.

July 4, 1992: Marvel announced it would acquire trading-card maker Fleer Corp. for $265 million.

A price of $1,000 for any out-of-print comic book was unheard of.

Today, there is a network of comics shops that spans America — a network supported by comics and games specialty distributors that provide comics on a nonreturnable basis. This so-called "direct-sales market" has been so profitable that even publishers which did well for years with returnable titles increasingly publish collector-oriented titles which are not sold on general newsstands (since newsstands handle only returnable products).

Customers who enter a comic-book shop today do so with much the same attitude as customers who enter a book store: They expect to find a full spectrum of reading material — from comics aimed at children just learning to read, to comics aimed at adults with college degrees.

When *Comics Buyer's Guide* polled its readers, it found that its audience was largely affluent, educated, and male. (More than 2/3 came from households with an annual income of $26,000 or more. Nearly 55% had had at least some college education. And nearly 96% were male.) Women are increasingly involved with comics today, and industry professionals are looking for more ways to get women to buy comics. However, one problem has been that comics are not as easily found today as they were in the '40s.

The ideal place to purchase comics is a specialty shop that carries both newsstand and independent comics. Collectors in rural areas may have to travel some distance to find such a shop and may choose, instead, to use a shopping service by mail. In urban areas, would-be comics buyers can check *Yellow Pages* for "bookstores," "used bookstores," and "periodicals," as well as "comic books." Comics shops are located across the country, and major cities have several.

Depending on the would-be customer's location, comics shops can also be located by ZIP code by calling (toll-free) to (888) 266-4226. Addresses and phone numbers may also be found by city using *www.yahoo.com* and its "Yellow Pages" service looking for "Comics."

Finally, eBay acts as a clearing-house for a wide variety of comics and related merchandise.

Nov. 17, 1992: DC shipped between 2.5 million and 3 million copies of Superman #75, featuring the death of Superman. They vanished from stores, as the issue brought more new customers into comics stores than ever before. In Detroit alone, more than 175,000 copies sold in one day.

Mid-1993: The glut of new comic books caused by a speculator bubble hit more than 700 per month.

Dec. 28, 1994: Marvel bought Heroes World, the third-largest direct-market distributor.

March 3, 1995: Marvel announced that, beginning with July-shipping product, Heroes World would become the exclusive distributor of Marvel products, eventually leading to the dissolution of the International Association for Direct Distribution, Inc.

March 9, 1995: Marvel bought SkyBox for about $150 million.

April 30, 1995: DC announced its product would be distributed exclusively by Diamond Comic Distribution, Inc. On July 24, Image and Dark Horse announced they would be exclusive with Diamond. Many other companies followed suit, with ensuing jockeying for exclusivity between national distributors Diamond and Capital City Distribution, the second-largest national comics distributor, in the months that followed. Capital exclusives eventually included Kitchen Sink and TSR.

Sept. 22, 1995: Marvel and DC announced their entire universes would cross over for the first time in a joint publishing project.

Dec. 14, 1995: Marvel announced it had hired two Image founders to reshape The Avengers, Captain America, Fantastic Four, and Iron Man.

July 1996: Diamond bought Capital City, making Diamond the last remaining major distributor for comic books to direct-market comics shops.

September 1996: Rob Liefeld left the Image group.

October 1996: Superman married Lois Lane.

Dec. 27, 1996: Marvel filed for Chapter 11 bankruptcy protection.

June 2000: CrossGen began publication with its monthly *Scion, Sigil, Meridian*, and *Mystic* titles.

2000: Bill Jemas took over Marvel Comics operations, and Joe Quesada was hired as Editor in Chief.

October 2000: Marvel launched its "Ultimate" line with *Ultimate Spider-Man*.

May 16, 2001: After nearly half a century, Marvel dropped the Comics Code and launched a mature-readers line.

May 4, 2002: One day after the record-setting opening of the Spider-Man film, publishers and retailers hosted Free Comic Book Day, an unprecedented effort to expand comics readership.

Circulation

How many comics were originally out there, anyway?

by John Jackson Miller

It's a question comics collectors have asked for decades. Now, for the first time, the **Standard Catalog** offers the largest repository of comics sales data ever gathered in one place.

It's useful for scholars of comics history and interesting to the curious — and it may well form the basis for a new kind of market analysis based on supply, once graders like Comics Guaranty Corp. gather enough data to help us determine comic-book "survival rates."

Publishers have been historically protective of their sales figures, usually in order to preserve their "sales story" before advertisers. Sales of past issues pose little concern, however, and while we don't want to embarass anyone, we feel that **it is absolutely in the collector's interest to know how many comics might be out there.** Would the comics boom of the early 1990s have gone differently if every price guide listing for *X-Men*, Vol. 2 #1 also said there were originally 7.1 million copies? Perhaps not — but then again, the crash might not have been as bad as it was. Those who understood the laws of supply and demand would have had part of the equation to work from.

So, the **Standard Catalog** has circulation information from several different sources:

- **Statements of Ownership**, filed by many publishers beginning in 1960 and continuing to the present;
- **Capital City Distribution**, covering comic books it sold between 1985 and 1995;
- **Diamond Comic Distributors**, covering comic books preordered from it from 1996 to present;
- and **alternative sources**, such as smaller distributors and the publishers themselves.

We also have a handful of circulation figures from the **Audit Bureau of Circulation** to provide an example of how comics in the Golden Age sold.

A caveat: Remember that these estimates indicate the number of comic books that were in circulation **when they came out**. It can be safely assumed that every copy of *Fantastic Four* released in 2002 still exists, and in high-grade. But of the hundreds of thousands of copies of *Fantastic Four* released in 1962, only a handful exist in the highest grades, and many don't exist at all. Again, we hope that once CGC has had the chance to grade more comics, resources like its population report can be compared with our figures to determine "mortality rates" for individual comic books.

Statements of Ownership

For the first few decades of comics fandom, the only time comic-book fans ever learned how their favorite (or least favorite) comics were selling was late in the year. Then, an alien-looking box suddenly appeared in many comic books, usually stuffed onto the letters page or hidden away under some house advertisement. For some reason, it seemed, the United States federal government wanted everyone to know how comics were selling!

Well, not really. Since the 19th Century (and far predating comic books), Section 4369, Title 39 of the U.S. Code has been requiring publishers who send periodicals through the mail at the special Second Class Rate to file a Statement of Ownership and Management. The intention was to make publishers — who were often controlled by a maze of holding companies and sold under a variety of imprints — to identify their owners and let the public know exactly who had applied for and received the preferential rates.

In 1960, the law was revised to require publishers to print their average paid circulations, including the portion of their magazine's print run that was sent by Second Class Mail — and the portion sent by mail that was sent for free. This permitted the Postal Service to monitor usage of the Second Class rate, making sure that the copies sent through the mail were mostly ones that people had asked for, rather than unsolicited junk mail.

As years passed, the government began asking publishers to supply ever more information, such as the

There are 58,631 circulation numbers of various types for comic books in the Standard Catalog.

number of copies printed for office use and a separate set of figures for the "issue closest to filing date." Even the name of the mail class changed, in the mid-1990s, to Periodical Class. Some comic-book publishers stopped sending subscription copies at this rate, either because they shifted to another mailing class (as DC did in 1988) or dropped subsrciptions altogether. By 2002, only Marvel and Archie, among major publishers, were still filing the forms — but for them, we have an unbroken record of sales information stretching back to 1960.

We have found Statements of Ownership in 357 titles from the following 20 publishers:

Publishers who've filed Statements of Ownership:

ACG • **Archie** • **Big Entertainment** • **Catholic Guild** (*Treasure Chest* only)• **Charlton** • **DC** • **Dell/Gold Key** • **Disney** • **E.C.** (*Mad* only) • **Fawcett** **First** • **Gemstone/Russ Cochran** **Gladstone** • **Globe** (*Cracked* only) **Harvey** • **Heavy Metal** **Kitchen Sink** • **Marvel** **Page One** (*Comic Relief* only) • **Warren**

How reliable are the numbers? That's been a point of contention since the 1960s, when fans began collecting the published numbers and circulating them (no pun intended) in fanzines.

In theory, since the figures are mandated by federal law, falsifying them would be a crime. But while there have been cases where the authorities have intervened to make a procrastinating publisher print its filings — and, evidently, one case in which a publisher was ordered to print revised forms — we've never heard of anyone in comics doing time on a Statement of Ownership rap!

And even if there were no falsification — at least one publisher in the 1970s was suspected of making its numbers up — there have certainly been some horrendous errors. In 2001, for example, the figures published for *Ultimate X-Men* were the exact same as those for *Uncanny X-Men*. Marvel also once accidentally ran the previous year's form in *Iron Man*. Math errors also consistenly appear, growing ironically more frequent in the computer age.

And at times publishers have apparently misread the requirements. In the early 1960s, Dell only ran its sales by subscription and no other figures. From 1963 to 1965, many Statements in DC comics (but curiously, not all of them) were just like the ones from before 1960 — no figures. In 1966, in fact, DC ran a second set of Statements months later that *did* have the required data.

As publishers who have to file such Statements ourselves, we suspect that, in general, no malice was intended. It's an afterthought each year, and publishers usually rush to find data to fill the spaces. "Hiding the truth" behind a publisher's sales might have some competitive or public relations value, but in fact it's the *advertisers* who publishers worried more about — and they could see much more detailed sales figures from the audit bureaus.

But while not always the most reliable source of information, these Statement of Ownership figures *are* from the publishers — and have tended to reflect what we believe to be the true sales trends over the years. When compared with some of the other figures available (such as the sales from Capital City Distribution and Diamond Comic Distributors), most Statement of Ownership figures do tend to be reasonably trustworthy.

In the **Standard Catalog**, when a figure is clearly out of the ballpark or suspect in any way, we try to note that.

Anatomy of a Statement. All statements of ownership — and the earliest we've found in any comic book is from the 1940s — have some or all of the following facts:

• *Title and publication number.* All Statements list the current title of a comic book being sent by Second Class Mail, but that's not necessarily the *only* title a Statement is reporting about. *Web of Spider-Man*, for example, picks up the subscribers from *Marvel Team-Up*. The **Standard Catalog** notes most situations where two different titles have the same publication number.

These switches also explain why Statement of Ownership figures, which, at least until the 1990s, were rarely reported before a title had run for two or three years, can appear for the first issues of a title.

• *Filing date.* Current regulations require that circulation figures for the preceding year be filed **on or before Oct. 1**. The deadline has generally been around then for the last 60 years.

It's useful to the comics archivist in determining *which* issues a Statement is reporting sales for. **Statements do not report sales for the issue they're in — and usually not the two or three issues before.** That's because publishers who sell comics returnably — and that's most publishers who have ever shipped comics Second Class — have little idea what their sales are until returns from newsstands come in, several months later. If they filed their most recent numbers (and some mistakenly have) sales would equal the print runs — which never happens on comics sold through newsstands!

There are Statement of Ownership circulation figures for 20,492 different comic books in the Standard Catalog.

STATEMENT OF OWNERSHIP, MANAGEMENT AND CIRCULATION (Act of October 23, 1962: Section 4369, Title 39, United States Code).

1. Date of filing: September 28, 1966.

2. Title of publication: MARGE'S LITTLE LULU.

3. Frequency of issue: Quarterly.

4. Location of known office of publication: North Road, Poughkeepsie, Dutchess County, New York 12601.

5. Location of the headquarters or general business offices of the publishers: North Road, Poughkeepsie, New York 12601.

6. Names and addresses of publisher, editor and managing editor. Publisher: K. K. Publications, Inc., North Road, Poughkeepsie, N.Y. 12601.
Editor: Marquis M. Morse, Staatsburg, N.Y.
Managing Editor: Marquis M. Morse, Staatsburg, N.Y.

7. The owner is K.K. Publications, Inc., Poughkeepsie, N.Y. (Western Publishing Company, Racine, Wisconsin). Stockholders at Racine, Wisconsin: H. M. Benstead Trust, Carif & Company, Arthur J. Christiansen Rev. Trust, C. W. DeWitt Rev. Trust, Firec & Co., Henry J. Haumersen, Gilbert Hoffman, Herman E. Johnson, John W. Kaiser, James B. Lyle, Paul Lyle, A. C. Naleid Rev. Trust, B. Howard Schaffer, Henry VanWingen, E. G. Voigt Estate, Ralph Voigt, W. R. Wadewitz Rev. Trust, Western Profit Sharing Trust Plan, Trust under Will of John Wiechers, Jerome C. Wiechers; Stockholders at Poughkeepsie, N.Y.: Charles Bruse, Harold D. Spencer; Stockholders at New York, N.Y.: Georges Duplaix, Leslie & Co., Pocket Books, Inc., Tepe & Co.; Stockholder at St. Louis, Mo.: John M. Wolff; Stockholders at Los Angeles, California: Robert S. Callender, Sopen & Co.; Stockholder at Boston, Mass.: Lot & Co.: Stockholder at Milwaukee, Wisconsin: Band & Co.; Stockholder at Minneapolis, Minn.: Var & Co.; Stockholder at Akron, Ohio: Parcol & Co.

8. The known bondholders, mortgagees, and other security holders owning or holding 1 per cent or more of total amount of bonds, mortgages or other securities are: at Racine, Wisconsin: H. M. Benstead Trust, Jesse I. Benstead, Alma C. Boernke, Arthur J. Christiansen Term. Trust, C. W. DeWitt Rev. Trust, James and Marie Drinkwater, Henry J. Haumersen, M. O. Lawson Rev. Trust, Roy W. Maher Estate, B. Howard Schaffer, Jessie Mignon Spencer Trust, Henry VanWingen, E. G. Voigt Estate, Nellie Voigt, Ralph Voigt, E. H. Wadewitz Trust #1, Robert Wadewitz Marital Trust, W. R. Wadewitz Rev. Trust, Western Profit Sharing Trust Plan, Western P. & L. Co. Retirement Trust, Western Welfare Association, Benton T. Wiechers, Jerome C. Wiechers, Trust Under Will of John Wiechers; Richard J. Wiechers; at Evanston, Illinois: Alice Schulte.

9. Paragraphs 7 and 8 include, in cases where the stockholder or security holder appears upon the books of the company as trustee or in any other fiduciary relation, the name of the person or corporation for whom such trustee is acting, also the statements in the two paragraphs show the affiant's full knowledge and belief as to the circumstances and conditions under which stockholders and security holders who do not appear upon the books of the company as trustees, hold stock and securities in a capacity other than that of a bona fide owner. Names and addresses of individuals who are stockholders of a corporation which itself is a stockholder or holder of bonds, mortgages or other securities of the publishing corporation have been included in paragraphs 7 and 8 when the interests of such individuals are equivalent to 1 per cent or more of the total amount of the stock or securities of the publishing corporation.

10. This item must be completed for all publications except those which do not carry advertising other than the publisher's own and which are named in sections 132.231, 132.232, and 132.233, postal manual (Sections 435a, 4355a, and 4356 of Title 39, United States Code).

	Average no. copies each issue during preceding 12 months.	Single issue nearest to filing date.
A. Total No. Copies Printed	393,371	362,210
B. Paid Circulation		
1. Sales through dealers and carriers, street vendors and counter sales	243,875	226,000
2. Mail Subscriptions	1,125	1,101
C. Total Paid Circulation	245,000	227,101
D. Free Distribution (including samples) by mail, carrier or other means	568	576
E. Total Distribution (Sum of C and D)	245,568	227,677
F. Office Use, Left-over, Unaccounted, Spoiled after Printing	147,803	134,533
G. Total (Sum of E & F—should equal net press run shown in A)	393,371	362,210

I CERTIFY THAT THE STATMENTS MADE BY ME ABOVE ARE CORRECT AND COMPLETE.
H. L. ANDERSON
Business Manager

*Statements of Ownership have ranged in appearance from very small to half a page or more, as seen in this 1967 report for **Little Lulu**.*

So, in general, the **Standard Catalog** tracks back three to four months to find the year being reported. If the filing takes place in early October, the period being measured is usually July to June or August to July.

Just to confuse you further, most publishers have long **post-dated** their comics — so an October filing will appear in a November-shipping issue appearing in an issue with an April cover date! In a convenient coincidence, though, the post-dating and the return period tend to cancel each other out. So a 1969 Statement published in an April or May 1970 issue probably really does cite sales for all the 1969-cover dated issues — even though some of those were sold in 1968!

• *Issue frequency.* The number of issues in the year being reported appears here, although publishers have tended to alternate between stating the number of issues that were promised and those that were really published; and between the number of issues published in the year being reported and the current frequency as of the lastest issue.

• *Annual subscription price.* We have not reported these in the **Standard Catalog**. Often, they are the highest rate available, and not the rates being offered in the issue's house ads. Also, they are usually the latest rates, and not what prevailed in the year being reported.

• *Owner identification.* Names and addresses of the publisher, editor, and managing editor appear, as do those of any owner or partial owners. Later on, forms also asked publishers to say whether they're a nonprofit organization. (Comics publishing just *seems* like it's nonprofit some years!)

Finally, for many decades, the figures appear divided in two columns, between the **averages** for the year and **the most recent issue published**. The distinction is important. Due to the nature of returnable publishing — which tends to make data for the most recent issues the most inaccurate — **the Standard Catalog only reports the average sales figures from Statements of Ownership. "Closest to filing date" data has, historically, been much less reliable.**

Depending on the year, Statements publish none, some, or all of the following:

• *Total print run.* Where this figure is given, it appears in the **Standard Catalog** entry coinciding with the issue the form Statement appears in.

• *Paid and/or requested circulation:* Originally, this represented only sales to newsstands; by 2002, it was mostly sales to comics shops. Regard that newsstand and direct-market sales are lumped together in this entry.

Where this figure is given, it also appears in the **Standard Catalog** entry for that issue.

• *Paid or requested mail subscriptions:* The major concern of the law, here the copies actually shipping by mail are reported.

"Requested" mail subscriptions are distinct from "free copies distributed by mail" in that the publisher has a signed request on file from the recipient. As such, free magazines — like our own *Comics & Games Retailer* — must still establish to the Postal Service that readers have actually asked for the magazine to receive the better rate.

It is enlightening to note that, despite retailer fears of publishers selling directly to customers, subscriptions have never been a major factor in comics, with the share tending to average around 5%. Exceptions are titles with heavy youth or teen marketing appeal and many crossover subscription deals, such as Marvel's *Barbie*.

Many Harvey titles in the 1960s sometimes had no subscribers reported at all, leading us to wonder why they bothered to get Second Class permits to begin with.

Figures from more than 2,350 Statements of Ownership since 1960 are reported in the Standard Catalog.

Where this figure is given, it appears in the **Standard Catalog** entry coinciding with the issue the form Statement appears in.

• *Total paid/requested circulation:* This is the figure most hobbyists have focused on over the decades. It is not, as we will see, the figure which best states the number of issues likely to have circulated, but it does tend to be the best measure of a title's relative health. (Add to that, of course, that it's the most frequently reported figure by publishers in Statements. Only Dell ever skipped it, and only for a while.)

Where this figure is given, it appears in the **Standard Catalog** entry coinciding with the issue the form Statement appears in. It **also** appears with the entries for each of the issues we believe the Statement reports, for comparison with sales figures we already know through other channels, where available.

There are some incidences in the **Standard Catalog** where total paid circulation figures appear with a year's worth of comics, but there is no listing for the contents of the full statement. That's because, while we were able to find many forms, in some cases the record of the figure comes from an aggregate report in *Comics Buyer's Guide*, its precursor *The Buyer's Guide for Comic Fandom*, or some fanzine. Most of those appear to be accurate reports, with only a few instances where rounding is suspected. We hope to obtain the actual Statements for these in the future.

• *Free distribution:* Statements list the number of copies given away, sometimes dividing between those sent by mail (as in the publisher's "comp list") or by hand (such as "freebies" given away at shows).

In the **Standard Catalog,** we list the **total** number of free copies with the corresponding Statement listing.

• *Office use, leftovers, spoiled:* Comics publishers often keep cases of comics for themselves for use as reference and to fill reorders.

Spoilage — ruined copies at the printer — is counted here as well, but since publishers historically have filled in the exact same number here for all their titles in a given year, it's doubtful that any meaningful information about any single issue's print run being partially spoiled has ever been reported.

Where this figure is given, it appears in the **Standard Catalog** entry coinciding with the issue the form Statement appears in.

• *Returns from news agents:* Today lumped together with office use copies under "copies not distributed," this figure records the number of copies that newsstand distributors could not sell.

The copies aren't really "returned." In general, "returned" copies no longer exist. The practice in newsstand distribution is for unsold copies to be "stripped" — to have the logo-bearing portion of their covers removed — and send back to the distributor, who files for a credit with the publisher. The stripped copies are then supposed to be destroyed. Most comic-book indicias, in fact, indicate that the issues are not to be sold in a stripped condition.

However, some are, as we've all seen a few in junk stores. Their impact on the market is minimal, though, existing only as reading copies with only the key issues having any resale value.

There is one case in which copies reported "returned" may still exist intact, and that's through good old-fashioned fraud. Magazine distribution was wild and woolly in the old days. Some say the main reason Sen. Estes Kefauver's Subcommittee on Juvenile Delinquency investigated comics in the 1950s in the first place was not because comics were naughty, but because it suspected organized crime ties to distribution.

In one celebrated case, an East Coast newsstand distributor filed "affadavit returns" with Marvel, stating that it had gotten covers from millions of comic books back from retailers and being paid for them. In fact, the comics were still sitting in its warehouse, presumably for later sale. They were still abandoned in the warehouse years later, when retailer Chuck Rozanski found them — more than 10 million high-grade comics, known today as the Mile High II collection.

In practice, though, it's next to impossible to know how many reported "returned" copies still exist. We're reporting figures in the **Standard Catalog** under the assumption that they don't.

Where this figure is given, it appears in the **Standard Catalog** entry coinciding with the issue the form Statement appears in. We have also figured and reported the **percentage of print run returned unsold**, which is indicative of sales trends in the business. Ratios crept ever higher through the 1960s and 1970s, as comics become harder to sell on the newsstands. More recently, they've dropped, as the portion of a comic book's print run — thus available to be returned — has dropped. "Direct-only" comics have no returns beyond those shipped back to the publisher due to lateness or damage.

We have added one more calculation of our own to Statement listings, adding free and office use copies to the average number of sold copies reported. That amounts to the **"maximum number existent"** figure, abbreviated in the **Standard Catalog** as "max existent".

• *Percentage paid/requested:* In the 1990s, the Postal Service began asking publishers to provide the ratio of "desired" copies as a portion of the whole run. These figures have generally been close to 99%, although publishers have occasionally fudged the math.

Statements of Ownership reported in the Standard Catalog account for more than 4,000,000,000 individual comic books.

While Statements of Ownership do tell us what the sales were for an average issue during a given year, they aren't exact. Particular issues with higher distribution are blended into the lot. For help on specific issues sold since 1985, we can turn to the sales of two distributors who sold to comics shops: Capital City Distribution and Diamond Comic Distributors.

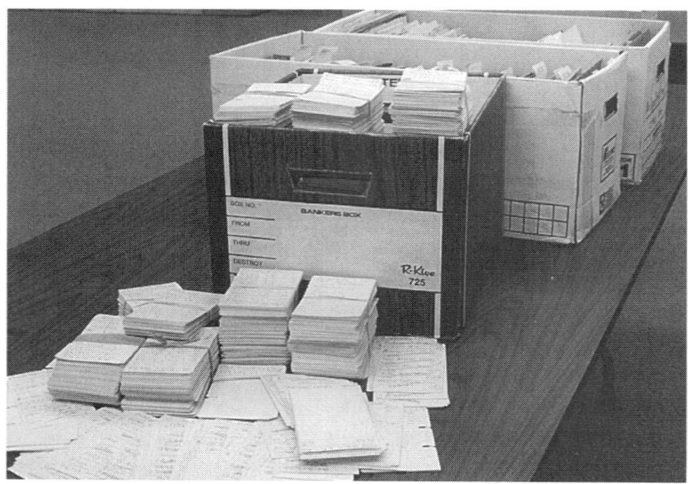

Capital City's historical data now in the ***Standard Catalog*** *archives exists both in the form of spreadsheet printouts and in thousands of index cards.*

Capital City Distribution sales

Founded by Milton Griepp and John Davis, Capital City Distribution was, at one time, the largest distributor of comic books to comics shops.

Capital City started out in the spring of 1980 with only 17 retail accounts and a half-dozen vendors. Expansion came quickly in the mid-1980s, with the company distributing comics from most publishers through a string of warehouses across the United States. By 1991, the company employed 300 and had a 65,000-square-foot distribution center in Sparta, Ill., close to World Color Press, where many comic books were printed.

The sales downturn of the mid-1990s brought turmoil to comics distribution, with Marvel pulling its business away from Capital City in the summer of 1995. Other publishers during the "exclusivity wars" took their offerings to competitor Diamond Comic Distributors, and on July 26, 1996, Griepp and Davis sold the company to Diamond.

Capital City's Madison, Wis., headquarters in 1992.

Before the end came, Griepp and Davis donated a massive amount of paper records from Capital City's cavernous Madison, Wis., headquarters, to the Krause Publications archives. In addition to copies of all the firm's support publications over the years, included were records of Capital City's actual sales from 1985 to 1996.

The data came in both high-tech and low-tech forms; computer printouts from later years, and index cards for each title kept by Davis since 1985. This latter material proved the most interesting, covering both the mid-1980s indepdendent comics boom and the color comics boom of the early 1990s — both periods in which Capital City was a key supplier.

Through considerable effort, the data from "The Caiptal Cards" appears in the Standard Catalog. Great efforts were made to reconcile Davis' notes with specific comics within the database. Correlation was generally very high. In the small number of cases where ambiguity existed as to which issue a sales figure belonged to, the figure was left out.

The figures appear to represent retailer orders — more specifically, the number of copies that Capital City ordered from the publisher once it knew how many copies its customers wanted. That interpretation is supported by a few facts. First, many of the earlier Capital City records are in round numbers, suggesting comics ordered by the case. Secondly, there are a few occasions where it's clear from the cards that a title was canceled and resolicited. (In these cases, we included the latest number listed for the *Standard Catalog* as the likely true order level for the title.) Finally, there are a few sales figures noted for comics known never to have been released, suggesting, again, that these figures represent not comics having arrived in Capital City's warehouses but rather, those it had ordered.

As such, there's one caveat in looking at the Capital City figures; in a small percentage of cases, the distributor may have received fewer than the number of comics it ordered. It also could have received *more*; there's no record of reorder activity until the very late years. That data exists, but has yet to be added to the *Standard Catalog* database.

Using the Capital City figures. The most important thing to remember when examining the "CapCity" figures in the *Standard Catalog* is that ***they are only part of the total number of copies that were actually sold overall,*** and that ***the fraction of the actual total varies from publisher to publisher and year to year***. By comparing the Capital City figures with the Statement of Ownership figures, we find that Capital City went from selling

There are Capital City Distribution sales figures for 24,248 different comic books in the Standard Catalog.

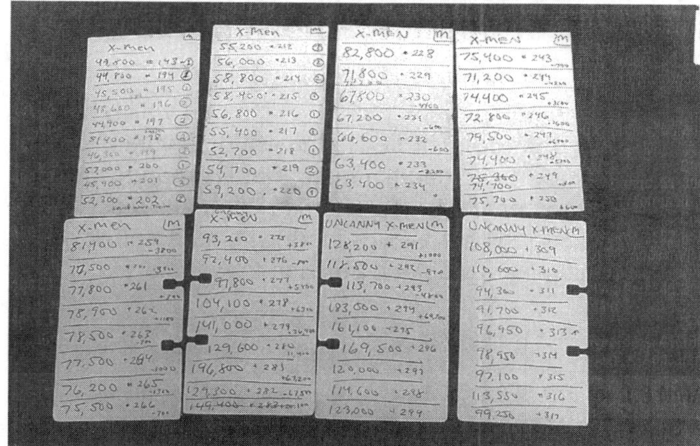

*Some actual handwritten Capital City sales reports for Marvel's **Uncanny X-Men** series.*

around 8% of all Marvel Comics sold in 1985 to an estimated 24% in 1995. Capital's share of DC's sales grew more quickly, from an estimated 8% in 1985 to 21% in 1988.

The two major factors determining whether a Capital City sales figure represents a little or a lot of what was actually sold are whether the comic book was sold on the mass-market newsstand or not, and the year. A Capital City sales figure will reflect much more of the total sales for a comic book not sold on the newsstands, such as *Cerebus the Aardvark* — than of a comic book sold through newsstand channels, such as most comics from Marvel, DC, Image, or Dark Horse. And among comics sold on the newsstands, Capital's share grew in later years for most titles as the role of mass-market distributors declined.

In later years, too, Capital City had grown from a regional distributor to a nationwide seller — lending more stability to figures that once saw major seasonal shifts due to retailers ordering fewer comics from Capital during Midwestern winters.

On its own, the Capital City data provides an invaluable — and heretofore unavailable — look at month-to-month sales for a wide variety of comics publishers in the 1980s and 1990s. By consulting Capital City's estimated market shares from year to year below, they can also help the reader formulate a good guess as to the total number of comics originally in circulation.

Diamond Comic Distributor preorders

Diamond Comic Distributors currently handles almost all comic book distribution to comics shops. In an age when four out of five comics are sold at comics shops, Diamond order information is of obvious importance to collectors.

Founded by Steve Geppi in 1982 to get comics to shops in the Baltimore and Washington D.C. area, Diamond was once one of the smallest comics distributors in America — like Capital City, initially serving only 17 accounts.

Quick growth came through the purchase of other distributors or the assumption of their accounts, such as in the case of Bud Plant in the summer of 1988. The early 1990s comics boom found Diamond the leader in a highly competitive field, with a market share approaching 50%.

But in 1995, Marvel announced it was going to distribute its comics on its own, leaving Diamond and other distributors in the lurch. In response, Diamond sought and signed exclusive distribution arrangements with DC, Image, Dark Horse, and other comics publishers that year, effectively gaining a lock on the comics distribution market and insuring its future as the largest distributor. Diamond bought failing Capital City in 1996, and Marvel returned to the Diamond fold in early 1997. By 2002, was doing more than $200 million in gross annual volume.

Like Capital City, Diamond has made considerable amounts of information about its sales public. Every month for the last few years, Diamond has published a Top 300 list ranking new comic books by the number of

Share of comics sold represented by Capital City

Through comparison of 4,358 comics for which both Capital City sales and a Statement of Ownership figure are known, we can estimate that Capital City sold the following percentages of these company's comics in the years indicated. Publishers with an asterisk also had significant newsstand sales in these years:

DC*

1985	7.9%
1986	9.1%
1987	15.5%
1988	21.5%

Disney*

1991	9.7%
1993	3.0%

First

1985	17.5%

Gladstone*

1987	6.3%
1988	7.6%
1989	9.1%
1995	5.7%

Kitchen Sink

1985	22.9%

Marvel*

1985	8.1%
1986	10.8%
1987	11.2%
1988	13.5%
1989	15.7%
1990	17.0%
1991	22.1%
1992	19.9%
1993	19.0%
1994	20.1%
1995	24.2%

Russ Cochran/ Gemstone

1992	20.9%
1993	21.6%
1994	27.4%
1995	29.5%

Tekno

1995	17.5%

retailer preorders it has received. Diamond does not publish its exact figures, but rather a number for each issue indicating how that issue's sales compare to that month's *Batman*, Diamond's benchmark title.

But that information is enough to unlock an estimate for the preorders for every comic book on Diamond's list — if you've got some of the actual preorders that Diamond placed with publishers that month to refer to. Since 1996, *Comics & Games Retailer*, a sister publication to the **Standard Catalog**, has led the field in obtaining actual preorders for a large fraction of titles appearing on Diamond's monthly list, and then applying them to the list to estimating the rest of the Diamond titles' preorders from them.

The Standard Catalog includes almost all the data we've compiled from Diamond's monthly charts since September 1996. We have a high level of confidence in the reliability of these figures, given the large sample of actual title sales we use to estimate for the population. While hobbyists online and elsewhere have fashioned their own estimates of Diamond's preorders from years past, they've tended to use only a few (or even one) title to form their estimates. **Standard Catalog** estimates are generated such that the margin of error is generally less than 2%.

Using the Diamond data. The first important thing to remember when consulting the Diamond figures in this book is that they're all estimates of preorders, not the number of comics that Diamond eventually sold. Retailers preorder comics two months in advance, then can place advance reorders, then can place reorders after the comics are released. Diamond does not publish any data helpful in determining the number of reordered comics.

Historically, reorder levels tend to be between 5%-8%. They tend to be slightly higher for major publishers, and can spike dramatically for particular high-demand issues, occasionally approaching or passing the number of preordered copies. It's an infrequent phenomenon, however, since publishers seldom print enough extra comics to permit retailers to keep reordering comics *ad infinitum*. (In fact, being able to print to a number of preorders is what makes the comics shop market attractive for publishers.) And in some cases, such as Marvel beginning in 2001, publishers have deliberately refused to set aside extra copies for reorders — meaning the estimated Diamond preoreder numbers here for its titles can be considered very close to Diamond's final sales.

Another thing to remember is that, as with Capital City, the Diamond figures are not everything that's out there in every case. Publishers sales on mass-market newsstands are not included, nor are publishers' sales by subscription or through such channels as alternative bookstores and record stores. But for publishers that don't have those other channels — and this probably accounts for most of the independent publishers Diamond handles — the Diamond preorder figure is not going to be far off the total number of comics in circulation.

Share of comics sold represented by Diamond preorders

Through comparison of 964 comics for which both Diamond preorders and a Statement of Ownership figure are known, we can estimate that Diamond sold the following percentages of these company's comics in the years indicated. Publishers with an asterisk also had significant newsstand sales in these years:

Archie*

1997	11.0%
1998	9.9%
2001	11.7%

Gemstone

1985	83.0%

Gladstone*

1997	31.9%

Marvel*

1997	61.9%
1998	74.0%
1999	68.4%
2000	68.4%
2001	72.7%

Explaining anomalies. Looking at the data, readers will note that there are a handful of situations where the Capital or Diamond figure is very close to, or even above, the "average total paid circulation" noted for an issue by the year's Statement of Ownership. The reason can be found in the word "average." Particularly in the high-flying early 1990s, there were occasions where a special issue of a title sold several times what other issues of the series did that year. Since Statements of Ownership deal in averages for an entire year, these individual outliers can be hidden. The true total sales for the individual issue are certainly beyond what the distributor sold.

Audit Bureau of Circulation reports

There are, of course, people who are in the business of tracking the actual sales of publishers, including comic-book publishers. The largest such entity is the Audit Bureau of Circulation, a non-profit organization founded in 1914.

The Audit Bureau works for advertisers and advertising agencies, and the media they use, to independently verify that publishers are telling the truth about the size and make-up of their readerships. The data for current member magazines is also made available to the public at *http://abcas1.accessabc.com/ecirc/.*

The Audit Bureau also keeps archives of its past reports accessible to the public at its Schaumburg, Ill.,

There are Diamond Comic Distributor sales figures for 13,322 different comic books in the Standard Catalog.

headquarters. Sales figures for old magazines aren't of much use to advertisers, but they're of great help in resolving one of the great disputes in comics collecting — namely, how lofty the legendary comics-book circulations of the 1930s and 1940s really were. In 1997, long-time *Comics Buyer's Guide* reader Russ Maheras visited the Audit Bureau offices and researched the question, consulting the micorfilmed records.

Sadly, the Audit Bureau tended to lump together titles from one publisher into a group. The January 1939 sales of 709,879 copies for the Detective Comics Group actually covers the month's issues of *Action Comics, Adventure Comics, Detective Comics*, and *More Fun Comics*. The Audit Bureau knows that Quality Comics Group had sales in January 1941 of 1,114,935 copies — but that that group includes issues from any of the titles that shipped that month from the list of *Feature Comics, Smash Comics, Crack Comics, Hit Comics, National Comics, Police Comics, Doll Man Quarterly,* and *Uncle Sam Quarterly.*

Data for single series are not impossible to find, however; *Famous Funnies*, for example, counted as its own "group" and had sales ranging from 485,136 copies in January 1937 to 175,561 copies in June 1941, according to the Audit Bureau. It's clear, however, from the figures of this series — and from some of the groups — that pre-World War II comic-book circulations weren't *that* far from what we're familiar with today.

To illustrate that point and demonstrate seasonal variances, we've included a handful of Audit Bureau data points for just three pre-war titles in this edition: *Famous Funnies*, from 1937-41; *Feature Funnies,* from 1938-40; and *Tip Top Comics*, from 1937-1939. We think the contrast is vital knowledge for any student of comics history, but we've only included the minimum necessary to make the point.

Other resources

We've also included some other circulation data in this edition, including estimates from other reliable sources and, occasionally, actual print runs as named by the publishers themselves.

Future research

Barring the publishers opening their records — or any mass publication of historical data from the various audit bureaus — there are a few more directions that can be taken to flesh out the circulation histories of comics.

We've projected that there are about 1,400 more **Statements of Ownership** that probably should exist, given their availability by Second-Class Subscription. The reader will note we're even shy some from more recent years. Just the numbers alone can be sent to us at *allcomics@krause.com*; simply provide the same details we list in this volume. Photocopies of the forms themselves are also helpful; send them to **Standard Catalog of Comic Books, 700 E. State St., Iola, WI 54990**. Make sure to say what issues you found them in.

There is some more **Capital City** information in our files, mostly from near the end when the distributor's share of comics sold had declined. We'll get around to adding that to the database in the future.

We still have a few **Diamond** figures from 1996 to present to add to the database, and we have in our archives enough records to reconstruct preorders from before 1996. We expect that work will be ongoing. There are also fragmentary records from other distributors, such as the pre-Marvel Heroes World, Styx International, and others that await further examination.

Not used here but interesting are the ***N.W. Ayers & Sons Directory*** volumes, huge tomes detailing publisher circulations from the 1940s and 1950s. These tend to lump together individual title sales, as well, but they are credible resources when it comes to learning who owned what publisher and when.

*The **Standard Catalog** archives represents the single largest repositiory of publications of Diamond, Capital, and other comic-book distributors past and present, many of which have information as to their sales.*

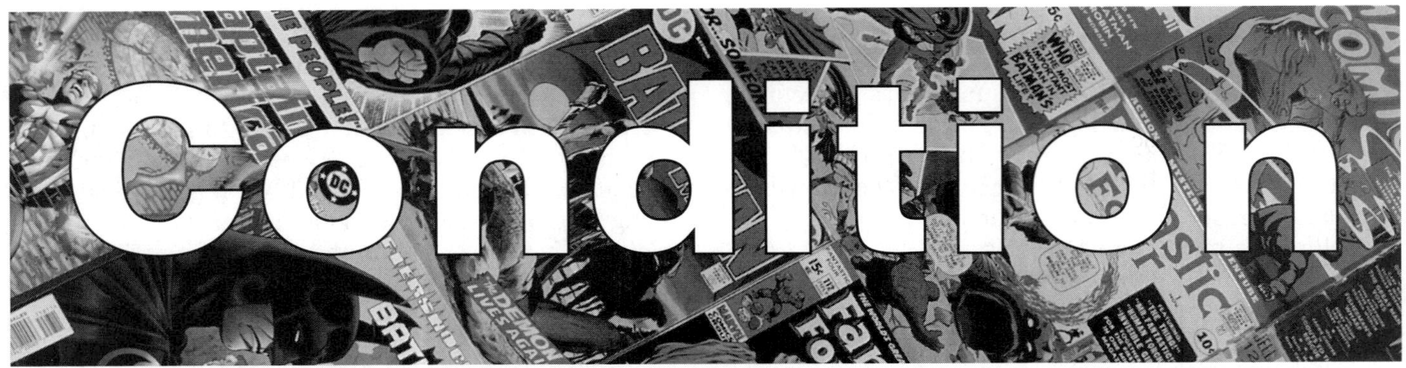

Condition

How much difference tender-loving care makes...

Why are comics from the 1940s, 1950s, and 1960s generally considered sound investment material, when comics from last Tuesday aren't? Part of that is because comics are literally living things — they were once trees, after all — and their natural inclination over the years is to decompose. So even if (as noted in the previous chapter) the number of copies around to begin with can be determined, there's a mortality factor at work, meaning comics in great shape are going to be harder and harder to find over time. Even if they haven't been loved to death through multiple readings and spine folds, comics are still going to try to turn yellow and brittle.

Collectors can slow that process with storage devices, ranging from the very expensive to the makeshift. The most common archival storage solution involves products made from Mylar, a transparent chemically inert substance. Much more common are bags made from plastic, most commonly polypropylene, of varying thicknesses and backing boards with coated surfaces. In general, the cheaper the method, the less protection it tends to afford.

Grading

For the last few decades, back-issue comic books have been sold with a designation indicating their condition. The eight grades recognized by the **Standard Catalog**, *Comics Buyer's Guide*, and *ComicBase* appear at the bottom of this and the next three pages.

The terms seen below have universal acceptance, even if different price guides — and, indeed, individual collectors and dealers — may not fully agree when it comes to

Mint

Abbreviated: **M, Mt.**

We believe this grade is roughly equivalent to **CGC's 10.0 grade.**

This is a perfect comic book.

Its cover has full luster, with edges sharp and pages like new. There are no signs of wear or aging.

It is not imperfectly printed or off-center.

"Mint" means just what it says.

Near Mint

Abbreviated: **NM**

We believe this grade is roughly equivalent to **CGC's 9.4 grade.**

This is a nearly perfect comic book.

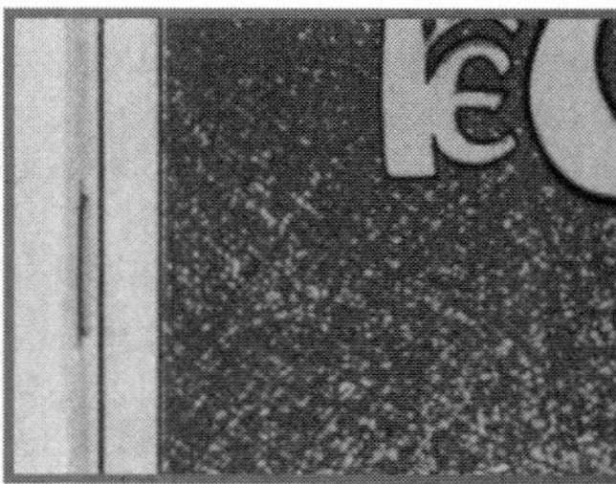

Its cover shows barely perceptible signs of wear. Its spine is tight, and its cover has only minor loss of luster and only minor printing defects. Some discoloration is acceptable in older comics — as are signs of aging.

what the attributes a comic book in each grade should have. It's that difference of opinion, in fact, that led to...

Third-party grading

Since the early 1990s, firms in the coin-collecting and sportscard-collecting hobbies have been attempting to standardize grading by certifying items and then "slabbing" them in plastic cases, along with a label stating their grade. That has led to several firms with competing standards — but has also made it easier for those items to be sold by mail-order.

One of those coin-grading firms, Numismatic Guaranty Corp., entered the comics hobby in 2000 with Comics Guaranty LLC (called "CGC" even by the company itself). The firm grades comics sent to it and places them in large protective "wells," along with their certification mark and grade label. These "slabs" and their grades facilitate the sale of comics through such venues as eBay and can, despite a popular misconception to the contrary, be opened to retrieve the comic book inside.

The effects of the introduction of CGC to the comics market were several and shocking. CGC never announced exactly what its standards were for each of its numeric grades (seen at right), and many longtime dealers were forced to change their own grading standards or fight against the current. And the current was fast: Auction prices for "slabbed" comics shot up, since a subset of each title now existed — in effect, making a new class of collectibles from existing comics.

CGC grades

CGC uses its own numeric grading scale and definitions; the grades appear at right. Fewer than 200 comics have yet received the top 10.0 grade; the oldest, a *Thor* #156 from 1968 (below), came from the Mile High II collection.

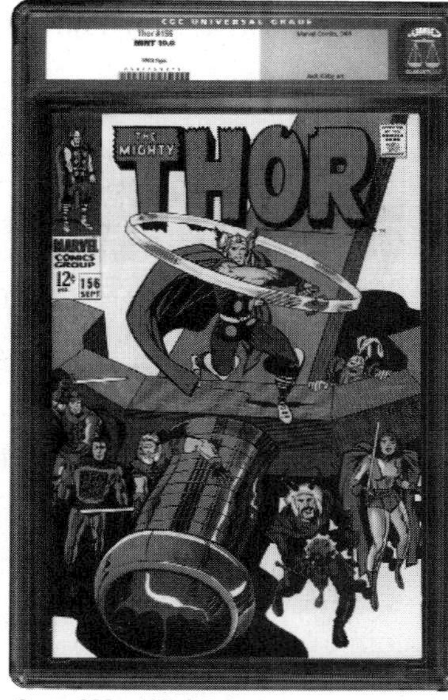

Source: CGC and Mile High Comics

10.0 Mint
9.9 Mint
9.8 Near Mint/Mint
9.6 Near Mint+
9.4 Near Mint
9.2 Near Mint-
9.0 Very Fine/Near Mint
8.5 Very Fine+
8.0 Very Fine
7.5 Very Fine-
7.0 Fine/Very Fine
6.5 Fine+
6.0 Fine
5.5 Fine-
5.0 Very Good/Fine
4.5 Very Good+
4.0 Very Good
3.5 Very Good-
3.0 Good/Very Good
2.5 Good+
2.0 Good
1.8 Good-
1.5 Fair/Good
1.0 Fair
0.5 Poor

Very Fine

Abbreviated: **VF**

We believe this grade is roughly equivalent to **CGC's 8.0 grade.**

A **Very Fine** copy is a nice comic book with beginning signs of wear.

There can be slight creases and wrinkles at the staples, but it is a flat, clean issue with definite signs of being read a few times. There is some loss of the original gloss, but it is in general an attractive comic book.

Fine

Abbreviated: **F, Fn**

We believe this grade is roughly equivalent to **CGC's 6.0 grade.**

A **Fine** comic book is a good-looking copy at first glance.

This comic book's cover is worn but flat and clean with no defacement. There is usually no writing on the cover or tape repair.

Stress lines around the staples and more rounded corners are permitted.

There are several different labels for CGC-graded comic books. **Universal** labels are blue and are applied to all comics with no restoration or signature. **Restored** labels are purple and indicate the comic book has restoration. Yellow labels belong to CGC's **Signature Series** and indicate an issue autographed in the presence of a CGC representative. **Qualified** labels are green and indicate a defect that may or may not argue against the item's given grade, such as an autograph that cannot be confirmed as authentic. **Modern** labels are red and were what CGC initially used for comic books from after 1975. Such comics now receive blue Universal labels.

All CGC populations reported in this edition are of Universal-label comic books and are from the most recent report provided to us by CGC before press time. Check *www.cgccomics.com* for updated "CGC Census" numbers.

To find the median price offered on eBay at press time for pre-1990 **CGC-graded comics**, multiply our **Standard Catalog** unslabbed NM prices by:

9.9 (M): **33**	8.5 (VF+): **1.25**
9.8(NM/M): **16**	8.0 (VF): **0.85**
9.6 (NM+): **7**	7.5 (VF-): **0.6**
9.4 (NM): **5**	7.0 (F/VF): **0.5**
9.2 (NM-): **2.5**	6.5 (F+): **0.4**
9.0 (VF/NM): **1.5**	6.0 (F-): **0.33**

These are median prices of all CGC comics auctioned on eBay; prices for individual issues will vary.

Based on extensive research into closed auctions for CGC-graded comics, the **Standard Catalog** recommends the application of the ratios appearing at left to project the estimated value of a slabbed comic book. As the ratios change over time, check current *Comics Buyer's Guide* issues for the most recent ones.

No one knows what the long-term influence of CGC will be — or what will happen if a competing third-party grader joins the fray. Regardless, most agree that what happens with this small and growing subset of existing comic books will surely affect the rest of the hobby.

Restoration

For years, individuals and services have made repairs to comic books, visibly improving their conditions. Fixes range from repairing small tears to color touches on covers to more intensive, far-reaching repairs. Such comics were often sold alongside unaltered issues, and seldom identified as restored.

When CGC began offering its third-party grading service in 2000, all that changed. A restoration check is included in CGC's grading service, and the firm puts a purple label on slabs for restored comics, indicating the **"Apparent"** grade and noting both whether the repairs are **amateur (A)** or professional **(P)** and whether the repairs are **Slight (S)**, **Moderate (M)**, or **Extensive (E)**.

The result was a collapse in prices for restored comics. Restored issues noted as such by CGC tend to close in online auctions for one-third to one-quarter what unrestored issues in the same grade do. Opinions differ as to why. Our theory holds that, since most of the early interest in CGC-graded comics came from investors in coin and sportscards, where restored items are disdained, it's no surprise that a gap between restored and untouched editions opened up.

Very Good

Abbreviated: **VG, VGd.**

We believe this grade is roughly equivalent to **CGC's 4.0 grade.**

A **Very Good** comic book is well-read and has some problems, but it's still nice.

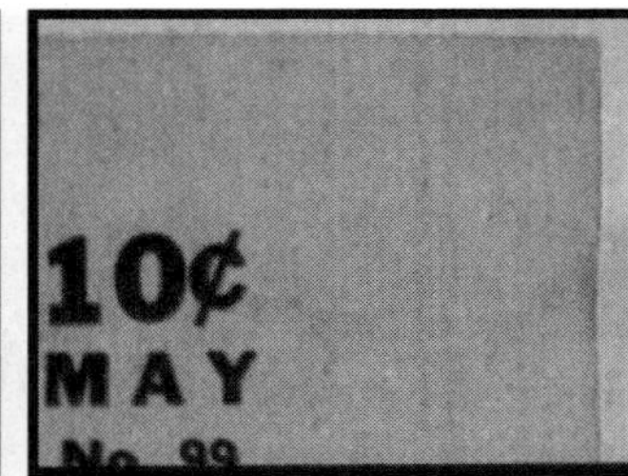

Most of the original gloss is gone. There are minor markings, discoloration, and/or heavier stress lines around the staples and spine. The cover may have minor tears and/or corner creases, and spine-rolling is permissible.

Good

Abbreviated: **G, Gd**

We believe this grade is roughly equivalent to **CGC's 2.0 grade.**

A **Good** copy is a very worn comic book with nothing missing.

Creases, minor tears, rolled spine, and cover flaking are permissible. in this grade.

Older Golden Age comic books often come in this condition.

Defects

Theoretically, given a set of rules, determining the condition of a comic book should be simple. But flaws vary from item to item, and it can be difficult to pin one label on a particular issue — as with a sharp issue with a coupon removed.

The examples shown here represent the specific defects listed. The condition of the individual issue as a whole is *not* necessarily that of the specific defect. (For example, the copy with stamped arrival date, off-center staple is *not* in mint condition aside from those defects.)

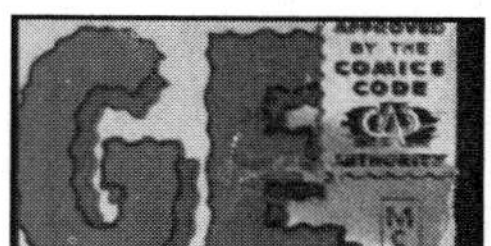

Tape. This extreme example of tape damage is used to show *why* tape shouldn't be used on a comic book — or *any* book — for repairs. *All* tape ages badly — as does rubber cement. Use of tape usually means "Fair," at best.

Rusty staple. Caused by dampness during storage, rust stains around staples may be minor — or more apparent. No better than "Very Good."

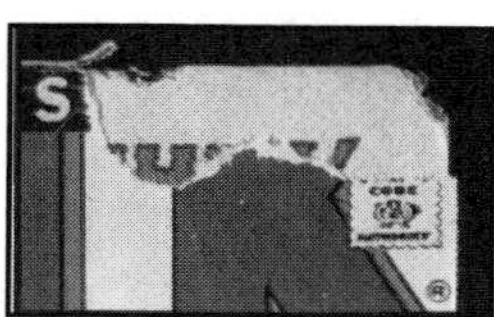

Chunk missing. Sizable piece missing. Issue can be no better than "Fair."

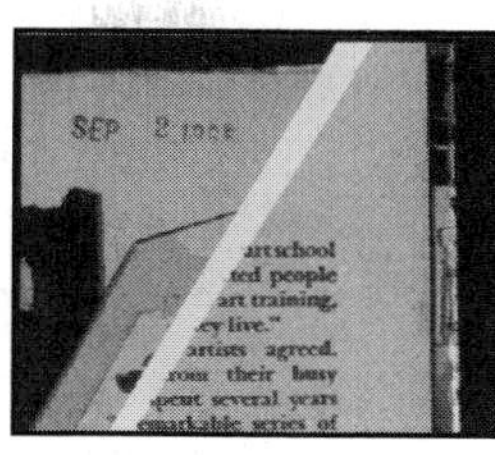

Stamped arrival date and **off-center cover** and **off-center stapling**. Minor defects. Some will not call it "Mint"; some will.

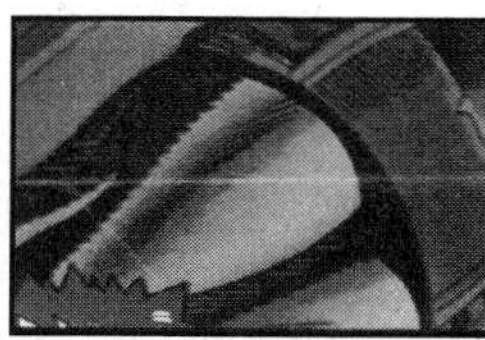

Subscription crease. Comic books sent by mail were often folded down the middle, leaving a permanent crease. Definitely no better than "Very Good"; probably no better than "Good."

Water damage. Varies from simple page-warping to staining shown here. Less damage than this could be "Very Good"; this is no better than "Good."

Writing defacing cover. Marking can include filling in light areas or childish scribbling. Usually no better than "Good."

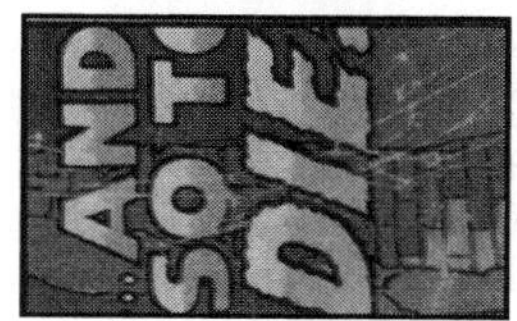

Multiple folds and wrinkles. Issues can be in no better than "Fair" condition.

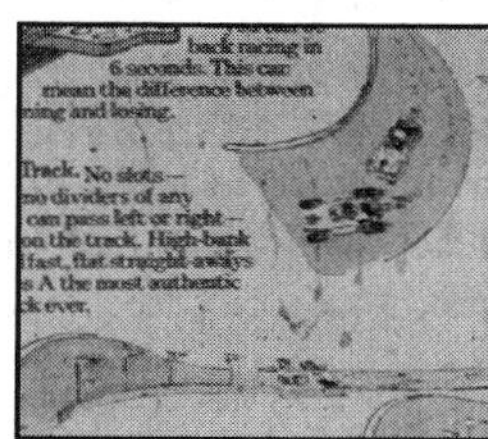

Stains. Can vary widely, depending on cause. These look like mud — but food, grease, and the like also stain. No better than "Good."

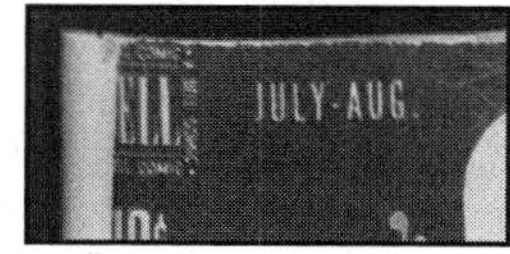

Rolled Spine. Caused by folding back each page while reading — rather than opening the issue flat. Repeated folding permanently bent the spine. The issue is no better than "Very Good."

Fair

Abbreviated: **FA, Fr.**

We believe this grade is roughly equivalent to **CGC's 1.0 grade.**

A **Fair** copy has multiple problems but is structurally intact.

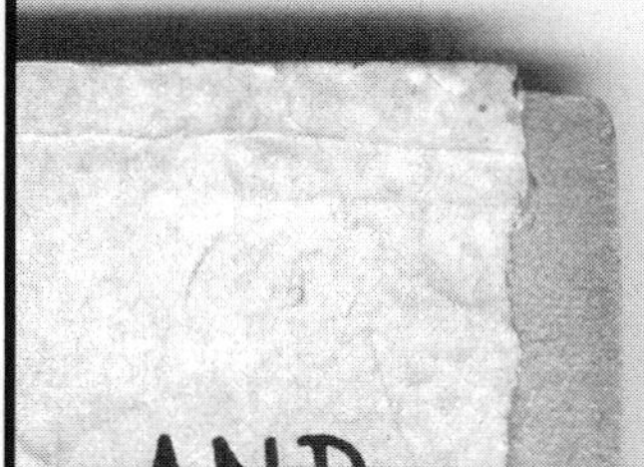

Copies may have a soiled, slightly damaged cover, a badly rolled spine, cover flaking, corners gone, and tears.

Tape may be present and is always considered a defect.

Poor

Abbreviated: **P, Pr.**

We believe this grade is roughly equivalent to **CGC's 0.5 grade.**

A **Poor** comic book is damaged and generally considered unsuitable for collecting.

While the copy may still contain some readable stories, major defects get in the way.

Copies may be in the process of disintegrating and may do so with even light handling.

Using the Standard Catalog

What's in the Standard Catalog

- All English-language **comic books published and offered for sale in North America** for which we've been able to confirm existence. (This includes, for example, the reprints of Fleetway's British comics that the publisher repackaged for the American market.)
- Many English-language **giveaway comic books** published in North America. (Included are such major titles as *Adventures of the Big Boy* and *March of Comics*, as well as giveaways published by Marvel and DC.)
- Every English-language **graphic novel** published in North America, hardcover and softcover, whose existence we've been able to confirm.
- Every English-language **collection of comic book reprints**, hardcover and softcover, published in North America whose existence we've been able to confirm.
- **Magazines** that have a high percentage of comics content (suc as *Mad, Cracked*, and *Heavy Metal*).
- **Certain reference works** in comic-book size. (Such heavily illustrated encyclopedias as *The Official Handbook to the Marvel Universe* and *Who's Who in the DC Universe* are included.)
- Select other works of peculiar interest to comics collectors (such as *FOOM, Seduction of the Innocent, Newstime*, and *Marvel Age*.)

What's not the Standard Catalog

- Some comic books released close to press time. (Issues are entered into our database *en masse* according to publisher; our listings for, say, Marvel titles have issues more current than listings for some other publishers might.)
- Comic books whose existence we have not been able to confirm.
- Comics in languages other than English.
- Comics not published in North America.
- Paperback or hardcover reprints of comic strips not published in the dimensions of a comic book; *e.g.*, Fawcett *Peanuts* reprints.
- Certain reference works in comic-book size. (Works that are mostly prose, such as indexes to series, are generally excluded.)
- Newspaper strips, with the exception of the *Spirit* series of stand-alone pull-outs.

Finding a title

The real, legal name of any comic book appears in its **indicia**, the block of small print usually found on the first or last inside page of most comics. **It does not necessarily match what's on the cover**; comics publishers have been known to relabel a single (or several) issues within a series for an editorial stunt, while never *really* changing the names of their series.

Drop proper names

Many titles have the name of one of their creators or the owner of a studio in their proper titles, such as *Kurt Busiek's Astro City*. In most cases, we have listed these comics in this manner: ***Astro City (Kurt Busiek's...).***

There are a handful of cases where the series has only ever been identified by the name of a creator or studio, and in those few cases, such as ***Walt Disney's Comics & Stories***, we've left the title alone.

Alphabetization

We alphabetize titles as if there were no spaces in their names. Numbers are spelled out.

Multiple series with identical titles from the same publisher

When a publisher has used the same name for a series more than once, such as in the case of ***Amazing Spider-Man Vol. 1*** and ***Amazing Spider-Man Vol. 2***, we list those different titles in order of release with some indicator to differentiate them from each other. We generally, but not always, run them uninterrupted in order of their release.

Where the volume number is a function of the turning of the year (as it was with some titles in the 1940s), we generally list them all under one header, with distinct subgroupings for each volume.

Multiple series with identical titles from multiple publishers

When two or more publishers have published distinct and unrelated series with the same name, we generally label them with their publisher name in parentheses. These are generally run alphabetically, except when collector interest is far higher in one series than the others; in such cases, the "major" series may appear first and with no publisher name following.

Another exception is made when a series changes publishers but does not interrupt its numbering. Such series may appear as a single title, with the name of their first publisher appearing at top; they may also appear as separate listings but in consecutive chronological order.

Inside a Catalog listing

Each title is identified by a unique **title** (upper left) and by a **publisher name** (upper right).

Many titles have **essays and pictures**. Essays include descriptive and historical information, and some evaluate the entertainment value of the series.

Essay authors are indicated:
Maggie: **Maggie Thompson**
Brent: **Brent Frankenhoff**
JJM: **John Jackson Miller**

Unsigned essays are by **Peter Bickford** and Human Computing freelancers, but all have been edited (and a few have been expanded upon) by the whole team.

Issues are listed in numerical order, meaning "#0" and "negative number" issues appear out of sequence and at the top.

Multiple printings are noted by a hyphen and the printing number following the issue number: **21-2**, **21-3**, and so on.

Multiple covers are noted by a slash and letter following the issue number: **1/A**, **1/B**, and so on.

Oddball versions of an issue are noted with the abbreviations at far right: Here, **1/GR** is the Golden Records variant of *Amazing Spider-Man* Vol. 1, #1. These are almost always explained in the text of the listing itself.

AMAZING SPIDER-MAN, THE **Marvel**

After being bitten by a radioactive spider, Peter Parker, a shy high school student, suddenly finds himself with the ability to sense danger, stick to walls, and possessed of the proportional strength of a spider. When his uncle is killed by a burglar, Peter resolves to use his new powers to fight crime. Thus is born the Amazing Spider-Man, Marvel's most popular character of all time.

The Amazing Spider-Man is the flagship of the Spider-Man titles — a list which has included Marvel Team-Up, Spectacular Spider-Man, Spidey Super Stories, Web of Spider-Man, and (just plain old) Spider-Man. Since its first issue in 1963, it has featured the wisecracking arachnid in many of his greatest adventures and has introduced such famous super-villains as the Green Goblin, Doctor Octopus, The Kingpin, The Vulture, and Venom.

Years later, Marvel restarted the series at #1, hungry for first-issue orders but irritating many long-time collectors.

-1 ❑ Jul 1997 Cover: 1.99 **NM** value: **2.50**
Circ: Diamd. preorders: **74,425**
• Flashback

1 ❑ Mar 1963 Cover: 0.12 **NM** value: **25000.00**
• **CGC:** 213 graded, best 9.8
🕮 Spider-Man; Spider-Man vs. the Chameleon; A Personal Message from Spider-Man **A:** Steve Ditko; Jack Kirby **W:** Steve Ditko; Stan Lee ★ Origin of Spider-Man. ★ 1st Appearance of John Jameson, J. Jonah Jameson, Chameleon. ★ Appearance of Fantastic Four.

1/GR❑ **NM** value: **250.00**
• **CGC:** 18 graded, best 9.8
• Golden Records reprint: No number or cover price.

2 ❑ May 1963 Cover: 0.12 **NM** value: **3200.00**
• **CGC:** 108 graded, best 9.4
🕮 Duel to the Death with the Vulture; The Uncanny Threat of the Terrible Tinkerer **A:** Steve Ditko **W:** Steve Ditko; Stan Lee ★ 1st Appearance of Mysterio (as "alien"), Tinkerer, Vulture.

3 ❑ Jul 1963 Cover: 0.12 **NM** value: **2500.00**
• **CGC:** 108 graded, best 9.6
🕮 Spider-Man Versus Doctor Octopus **A:** Steve Ditko **W:** Steve Ditko; Stan Lee ★ Origin of Doctor Octopus. ★ 1st Appearance of Doctor Octopus.

4 ❑ Sep 1963 Cover: 0.12 **NM** value: **1900.00**
• **CGC:** 107 graded, best 9.4
🕮 Nothing Can Stop the Sandman **A:** Steve Ditko **W:** Steve Ditko; Stan Lee ★ Origin of Sandman (Marvel). ★ 1st Appearance of Betty Brant, Sandman (Marvel).

5 ❑ Oct 1963 Cover: 0.12 **NM** value: **1600.00**
• **CGC:** 114 graded, best 9.6
🕮 Marked for Destruction by Dr. Doom **A:** Steve Ditko **W:** Steve Ditko; Stan Lee ★ Versus Doctor Doom.

Abbreviations appearing with issue numbers

Most are explained in their listings.

ACE	Wizard Ace Edition
AE	American Entertainment edition
AUT	Autographed
BL	Blue variation
AIM	Aim toothpaste giveaway
Anl	Annual
ASH	Ashcan
Bk	Book
Dlx	Deluxe
DM	Direct Market edition
DOT	Dept. of Transportation giveaway
FAN	Fan magazine giveaway
GF	Gold foil edition
GIVE	Giveaway
GN	Graphic novel
GO	Gold edition
GR	Golden Records variant
GS	Giant Size
HC	Hardcover
Hero	Hero magazine giveaway
HOL	Hologram edition
HS	Holiday Special
KS	King Size
LE	Limited edition
NT	New Testament
Nude	"Nude" edition
OT	Old Testament
PL	Platinum
PLND	Platinum "nude" edition
PR	Prestige edition
SC	Special cover
SD	Signed edition
SE	Special edition
SI	Silver edition
Smr	Summer
Spr	Spring
YB	Yearbook

Most issues list a **month and year**. This is not the true publication date but the date labeled on the comic book. Usually, it's the date in the indicia; occasionally, it's the date found on the cover. Where it's estimated but not known, we indicate with **ca.** for "circa."

(In a handful of cases, such as with Viz comics, we have been able to figure out true publication dates for issues which have no other such information.)

Cover prices are listed and are in U.S. dollars. So are **NM values**, which are our estimate for what loose Near-Mint copies of this issue can be found for. Use the indexes at the bottom of pages for different grades or to estimate values of CGC comics.

CGC notes indicate the number of **Universal-label copies** graded by CGC at press time and the grade of the best copy (or copies) graded by press time.

Circ: **Statement** notes the estimated number of copies sold of that issue according to the Statement of Ownership.

Circ: CapCity is the number of copies sold by Capital City Distributors.

Circ: Diamd preorders is an estimate of how many copies comics shops ordered in advance from Diamond Comic Distributors.

The book symbol (🕮) notes **story titles** and/or ongoing storylines.

Stars (★) denote important **character appearances**, deaths, and events.

Creators for each issue are noted:
A: Artists (pencillers and inkers)
W: Writers (scripters and plotters)
C: Cover artists

Dell giants and movie comics

At least one reference work has grouped the giant-sized and movie-adaptation comics produced by Dell as if there really were an ongoing *Dell Giant* or *Dell Movie* series. There wasn't any such series, and, to avoid confusion we have sorted these comics by their real names, found in their indicias (and, usually, their covers).

A note on consistency

While the **Standard Catalog** is the first comics work of its size based on a modern computer database (which can be revised, resorted, and updated over time), not all the fields now available were when data entry took place. So you may, for example, see "cover artists" grouped under **A:** for artist. We're working to fix that.

A A' — Viz

1 ❑ b&w Cover: 15.95 **NM** value: **Cover or less**

A-1 COMICS — Life's Romances / Epic

0 ❑ ca. 1944 Cover: 0.10 **NM** value: **185.00**
No number on cover.
1 ❑ Cover: 0.10 **NM** value: **95.00**
Mr. Ex; Rocky the Stone-Age Kid; Lew Loyal; Bush Berry; Dotty Dripple **A:** Bert Whitman; Evans Krehbel; Frank Engli; Milt Youngren **W:** Bert Whitman; Evans Krehbel; Frank Engli; Milt Youngren
2 ❑ Cover: 0.10 **NM** value: **40.00**
3 ❑ Cover: 0.10 **NM** value: **40.00**
4 ❑ Cover: 0.10 **NM** value: **40.00**
5 ❑ Cover: 0.10 **NM** value: **34.00**
6 ❑ Cover: 0.10 **NM** value: **34.00**
Texas Slim and Dirty Dalton; The Corsair Plays Home to a Ghost!; George and the Dragon; Mr. In-Between; Tugboat Tim; Tommy Tinker; Sheriff Shudders **A:** Charles M. Quinlan; Dale McFeatters; Macphail; Vernon Henkel **W:** Charles M. Quinlan; Dale McFeatters; Macphail; Vernon Henkel
7 ❑ Cover: 0.10 **NM** value: **34.00**
8 ❑ Cover: 0.10 **NM** value: **34.00**
9 ❑ Cover: 0.10 **NM** value: **34.00**
10 ❑ Cover: 0.10 **NM** value: **30.00**
11 ❑ Cover: 0.10 **NM** value: **30.00**
12 ❑ Cover: 0.10 **NM** value: **30.00**
13 ❑ Cover: 0.10 **NM** value: **125.00**
• Guns of Fact or Fiction
15 ❑ Cover: 0.10 **NM** value: **30.00**
A-1 covers continue until #17, but later issues are listed under their own title names..

A1 TRUE LIFE BIKINI CONFIDENTIAL, THE — Atomeka

1 ❑ b&w Cover: 1.00 **NM** value: **6.95**
Mr. Monster's Most Wanted!; Parcels of Events; Zi **A:** John Higgins; William Simpson; Bob Burden; Brian Bolland; Michael T. Gilbert; Gary Leach; Steve Parkhouse; Jamie Hewlett; Dougie Braithwaite; Carol Swain; David Jackson **C:** Brian Bolland **W:** Bob Burden; Brian Bolland; Michael T. Gilbert; Dave Elliott; Melinda Gebbie; Pedro Henry; Peter Milligan; Steve Moore; Alan Martin; Alan Moore

A1 (VOL. 1) — Atomeka

1 ❑ 1989 Cover: 9.95 **NM** value: **Cover or less**
The Big Button; Warpsmith: Ghostdance; Deadface: The Fall of Angels and Other Misfits; Bad Bread; The Ear of Seeing; Survivor; The Actress and the Bishop G **A:** Dave Gibbons; Bill Sienkiewicz; Barry Windsor-Smith **C:** Brian Bolland **W:** Eddie Campbell; Phil Elliott; Ted McKeever; Bob Burden; Glenn Fabry; Alan Moore; Dominic Regan; Neil Gaiman; Paul Behrer
2 ❑ 1989 Cover: 9.95 **NM** value: **10.00**
A: Matt Wagner; Dave Gibbons; Barry Windsor-Smith; Brian Bolland **W:** Eddie Campbell; Phil Elliott; Ted McKeever; Bob Burden; Glenn Fabry; Alan Moore; Dominic Regan; Neil Gaiman; Paul Behrer
3 ❑ 1990 Cover: 5.95 **NM** value: **6.00**
The American; Deadface: The Book-Keeper from Atlantis **A:** Eddie Campbell; Warren Pleece; Dave McKean; Brian Bolland; Moebius; Glenn Fabry; Dougie Braithwaite; Chris Smith; Gary Pleece **C:** Brian Bolland **W:** Warren Pleece; Brian Bolland; Glenn Fabry; Mark Verheiden; Chris Smith; Gary Pleece; Grant Morrison; Alan Moore; John Kaine
4 ❑ 1990 Cover: 5.95 **NM** value: **6.00**
A: Bill Sienkiewicz; Moebius **W:** Warren Pleece; Brian Bolland; Glenn Fabry; Mark Verheiden; Chris Smith; Gary Pleece; Grant Morrison; Alan Moore; John Kaine
5 ❑ 1991 Cover: 7.95 **NM** value: **8.00**
Cover Story; Bricktop: Sunglasses; In the Penal Colony; The Contact; Tor: Food Chai **A:** Roger Langridge; David Lloyd; Brett Ewins; Joe Kubert; Steve Dillon; Jeff Jones; Glenn Fabry; Trevor Goring; Steve Leialoha; Bambos Georgiou; Jim Sullivan; Kelly Jones; Nick Abadzis; William Stout; Ed Hillyer; Shaky Kane; William Stout(cover) **W:** Brett Ewins; Joe Kubert; Steve Dillon; Bill Mumy; Jeff Jones; Bruce Jones; Chris Smith; Nick Abadzis; Peter Milligan; Bambos Georgiou; Cornelius Stone; Ed Hillyer; Miguel Ferrer; Neil Gaiman; Ramsey Campbell; Sydney Jordan
6 ❑ 1992 Cover: 4.95 **NM** value: **5.00**
Tankgirl: She's F*cking Great!; Rescue; The Competition; The Happy Angel of Death; Harlequin Bones: Dada 331; Paris is a Ball; Alec MacGarry: Obsession; Bricktop: Fish; And they Never Get Drunk But Stay Sober **A:** Eddie Campbell; Bob Burden; Steve Dillon; Phil Winslade; Glenn Fabry; Jamie Hewlett; Doug Rice; Martin Hand; Serge Clerc; D'Israeli **W:** Eddie Campbell; Bob Burden; Warren Ellis; Hilary Barta; Jamie Hewlett; Chris Smith; Martin Hand; Serge Clerc; Archie Goodwin; Garth Ennis
7 ❑ Cover: 7.95 **NM** value: **8.00**
W: Eddie Campbell; Bob Burden; Warren Ellis; Hilary Barta; Jamie Hewlett; Chris Smith; Martin Hand; Serge Clerc; Archie Goodwin; Garth Ennis

A1 (VOL. 2) — Marvel / Epic

1 ❑ Cover: 5.95 **NM** value: **Cover or less**
Circ: CapCity orders: **3,200**
Along For The Ride; Cyrano De Bergerac's Voyage To The Moon; Goofing; Fanciable Headcase; Frankenstein Meets Shirley Temple, Part 1; Wonderful Life **A:** Roger Langridge; P. Craig Russell; Glenn Fabry; Ilya; Steve White **W:** Roger Langridge; Frank Miller; Scott Hampton; Ilya; Steve White; Igor Goldkind
2 ❑ Cover: 5.95 **NM** value: **Cover or less**
Circ: CapCity orders: **3,450**
Max Zillion and Alto Ego: Pawn Shop; Deadline; Cheeky Wee Budgie Boy: The Castafiore Affair; Saccharine Fools; Wonderful Life; Frankenstein Meets Shirley Temple, Part 2; King Leon, Part 1 **A:** Roger Langridge; Philip Bond; George Pratt; Jamie Hewlett; Hunt Emerson; Jon Beeston; Nick Abadzis; Steve White **W:** Roger Langridge; Philip Bond; Frank Miller; George Pratt; Scott Hampton; Ilya; Hunt Emerson; Jon Beeston; Nick Abadzis; Peter Milligan; Steve White; Igor Goldkind
3 ❑ Cover: 5.95 **NM** value: **Cover or less**
Circ: CapCity orders: **2,650**
Axel Pressbutton: The Movie; Pale Horses; Stripey: Social Victim Fashion Frenzy; Where Is It, Wonderful Life; Frankenstein Meets Shirley Temple, Part 3; King Leon, Part 2 **A:** Roger Langridge; Gary Erskine; Simon Bisley; Colin MacNeil; Kent Williams; Jamie Hewlett; Martin Edmond; Roddy MacNeil; Una Fricker **W:** Roger Langridge; Philip Bond; George Pratt; Kent Williams; Hunt Emerson; Jon Beeston; Nick Abadzis; Pedro Henry; Peter Milligan; Steve White; Una Fricker; Dan Abnett
4 ❑ Cover: 5.95 **NM** value: **Cover or less**
Circ: CapCity orders: **2,550**
Frankenstein Meets Shirley Temple, Part 4; King Leon, Part 3; The Edge, Uptown Ruler, Wonderful Life **A:** Roger Langridge; Dave McKean; Dave Dorman; Jamie Hewlett; Una Fricker **W:** Roger Langridge; Dave McKean; Dave Dorman; Kent Williams; Pedro Henry; Peter Milligan; Steve White; Una Fricker; Dan Abnett

ÄARDWOLF — Aardwolf

1 ❑ Dec 1994 Cover: 2.95 **NM** value: **Cover or less**
I, Gezheh; Stiffed; Street **A:** Paty Cockrum; Dave Cockrum **W:** William Messner-Loebs; Clifford Lawrence
2 ❑ Feb 1995 Cover: 2.95 **NM** value: **Cover or less**

AARON STRIPS — Image

1 ❑ Apr 1997 Cover: 2.95 **NM** value: **Cover or less**
Circ: Diamd. preorders: **8,834**
A: Aaron Warner **W:** Aaron Warner
2 ❑ Jun 1997 Cover: 2.95 **NM** value: **Cover or less**
Circ: Diamd. preorders: **6,732**
A: Aaron Warner **W:** Aaron Warner
3 ❑ Aug 1997 Cover: 2.95 **NM** value: **Cover or less**
Circ: Diamd. preorders: **4,721**
A: Aaron Warner **W:** Aaron Warner
4 ❑ Oct 1997 Cover: 2.95 **NM** value: **Cover or less**
• has "Aaron Warner's Year of the Monkey" back-up; goes to Amazing Aaron Productions **A:** Aaron Warner **W:** Aaron Warner
5 ❑ Jan 1999 Cover: 2.95 **NM** value: **Cover or less**
• continued numbering from Image series **A:** Aaron Warner **W:** Aaron Warner
6 ❑ Mar 1999 Cover: 2.95 **NM** value: **Cover or less**
A: Aaron Warner **W:** Aaron Warner

ABBIE AN' SLATS — United Feature

The newspaper strip was created in 1937 by Al Capp (1909-1979) and drawn by Reuben Van Buren (1891-1987) and, though it appeared as a continuing feature in a number of anthology comic-book titles, it also had a brief run on its own. Later written by Capp's brother, Eliot Caplin, the soap-opera strip dealt with a city youth living with spinster Abbie in a small town. — Maggie

1 ❑ Mar 1948 Cover: 0.10 **NM** value: **100.00**
2 ❑ Apr 1948 Cover: 0.10 **NM** value: **75.00**
3 ❑ Jun 1948 Cover: 0.10 **NM** value: **60.00**
4 ❑ Aug 1948 Cover: 0.10 **NM** value: **50.00**

ABBOTT & COSTELLO (CHARLTON) — Charlton

1 ❑ Feb 1968 Cover: 0.12 **NM** value: **25.00**
• **CGC:** 1 graded, best 9.6
2 ❑ Apr 1968 Cover: 0.12 **NM** value: **18.00**
3 ❑ Jun 1968 Cover: 0.12 **NM** value: **18.00**
4 ❑ Aug 1968 Cover: 0.12 **NM** value: **12.00**
There's No Business; Flowers of the Business World; Growth; Way of All Fish; When Swallows Come Back; The Gong and I; Ask Any Lamp; My Fellow Americans **A:** Henry Scarpelli
5 ❑ Oct 1968 Cover: 0.12 **NM** value: **12.00**
6 ❑ Dec 1968 Cover: 0.12 **NM** value: **12.00**
7 ❑ Feb 1969 Cover: 0.12 **NM** value: **12.00**
8 ❑ Apr 1969 Cover: 0.12 **NM** value: **12.00**
9 ❑ Jun 1969 Cover: 0.12 **NM** value: **12.00**
10 ❑ Aug 1969 Cover: 0.15 **NM** value: **12.00**
11 ❑ Oct 1969 Cover: 0.15 **NM** value: **10.00**
12 ❑ Dec 1969 Cover: 0.15 **NM** value: **10.00**
The Spooky Past Cleaned-Out Fast!; Famous Kitchens We Have Known; Boss and Groovey in Nobody Home; A TV Fix for Rodney's Sticks!
13 ❑ Feb 1970 Cover: 0.15 **NM** value: **10.00**
14 ❑ Apr 1970 Cover: 0.15 **NM** value: **10.00**
15 ❑ Jun 1970 Cover: 0.15 **NM** value: **10.00**
2 Wheeler Dealer; Surf's Up; No Littering; "Student Power"; Morning Review; Spaceman X-13; Buggy; Ivan Inventorsky the Inventor: Build Your Private Beach (text)
16 ❑ Aug 1970 Cover: 0.15 **NM** value: **10.00**
17 ❑ Oct 1970 Cover: 0.15 **NM** value: **10.00**
Timber Trouble!; Boom!; Don't Jus' Stand There...; Time On My Hands; Quiz #49 – ICU2; Supersnoot and the Fastest Gun in the West; Donut Nuts; Some Smiles (text) • Nutty daisy poster
18 ❑ Dec 1970 Cover: 0.15 **NM** value: **10.00**
19 ❑ Feb 1971 Cover: 0.15 **NM** value: **10.00**
20 ❑ Apr 1971 Cover: 0.15 **NM** value: **10.00**
21 ❑ Jun 1971 Cover: 0.15 **NM** value: **10.00**
22 ❑ Aug 1971 Cover: 0.20 **NM** value: **10.00**
final issue.

The CGC numbers printed in individual listings above represent the **number of copies examined** and given a **Universal** grade by CGC and the **best such copy** graded at press time. For current populations, watch for special ***Comics Buyer's Guide*** issues or check **www.cgccomics.com.**

ABBOTT AND COSTELLO (ST. JOHN) — St. John

"Who's on first, What's on second, I Don't Know's on third." If you've heard these words, you're probably familiar with Abbott and Costello, one of America's most popular movie comedy teams of the 1940s and early 1950s. During their heyday, Lou Costello's smallest facial tic was enough to convulse movie crowds to hysterics, and much of their fun-loving hilarity was translated intact to their comic-book series, thanks to the talented hand of artist Mort Drucker (later of Mad fame).

Abbott and Costello specialized in parodies of other genres, such as their classic horror send-up "Abbott and Costello Meet Frankenstein." The comics take off from this premise by putting the pair into familiar comics situations such as Buck Rogers, which were effective, thanks to Drucker's startling ability to mimic other artists' styles. Each issue featured two complete stories plus a two-page text section.

1 ❑ Feb 1948 Cover: 0.10 **NM** value: **375.00**
• **CGC:** 2 graded, best 5.5
2 ❑ Apr 1948 Cover: 0.10 **NM** value: **190.00**
• **CGC:** 1 graded, best 4.0
3 ❑ Jun 1948 Cover: 0.10 **NM** value: **120.00**
4 ❑ Sep 1948 Cover: 0.10 **NM** value: **120.00**
5 ❑ Dec 1948 Cover: 0.10 **NM** value: **120.00**
6 ❑ Feb 1949 Cover: 0.10 **NM** value: **120.00**
7 ❑ May 1949 Cover: 0.10 **NM** value: **120.00**
• **CGC:** 1 graded, best 3.0
8 ❑ Aug 1949 Cover: 0.10 **NM** value: **120.00**
9 ❑ Feb 1950 Cover: 0.10 **NM** value: **120.00**
10 ❑ Jun 1950 Cover: 0.10 **NM** value: **140.00**
Son of Sinbad **A:** Joe Kubert
11 ❑ Oct 1950 Cover: 0.10 **NM** value: **75.00**
12 ❑ Feb 1951 Cover: 0.10 **NM** value: **75.00**
13 ❑ Aug 1951 Cover: 0.10 **NM** value: **75.00**
14 ❑ Apr 1952 Cover: 0.10 **NM** value: **75.00**
15 ❑ Dec 1952 Cover: 0.10 **NM** value: **75.00**
16 ❑ 1953 Cover: 0.10 **NM** value: **75.00**
17 ❑ 1953 Cover: 0.10 **NM** value: **75.00**
18 ❑ 1953 Cover: 0.10 **NM** value: **75.00**
19 ❑ 1953 Cover: 0.10 **NM** value: **75.00**
20 ❑ 1953 Cover: 0.10 **NM** value: **75.00**
21 ❑ 1953 Cover: 0.10 **NM** value: **50.00**
About Space
22 ❑ Nov 1953 Cover: 0.10 **NM** value: **50.00**
23 ❑ Jan 1954 Cover: 0.10 **NM** value: **50.00**
Tropical Trappers; Teepee Town; Bent, but not Broke; Man in Uniform; Professor Birdbrain: Space Trip to Mars; Groan and Bear It!
24 ❑ Mar 1954 Cover: 0.10 **NM** value: **50.00**
25 ❑ May 1954 Cover: 0.10 **NM** value: **50.00**
26 ❑ Aug 1954 Cover: 0.10 **NM** value: **50.00**
27 ❑ Nov 1954 Cover: 0.10 **NM** value: **50.00**
28 ❑ Jan 1955 Cover: 0.10 **NM** value: **50.00**
29 ❑ Mar 1955 Cover: 0.10 **NM** value: **50.00**
30 ❑ May 1955 Cover: 0.10 **NM** value: **50.00**
31 ❑ Aug 1955 Cover: 0.10 **NM** value: **40.00**
32 ❑ Cover: 0.10 **NM** value: **40.00**
33 ❑ Cover: 0.10 **NM** value: **40.00**
34 ❑ Cover: 0.10 **NM** value: **40.00**
35 ❑ Cover: 0.10 **NM** value: **40.00**
36 ❑ 1956 Cover: 0.10 **NM** value: **40.00**
37 ❑ 1956 Cover: 0.10 **NM** value: **40.00**
38 ❑ 1956 Cover: 0.10 **NM** value: **40.00**
39 ❑ 1956 Cover: 0.10 **NM** value: **40.00**
40 ❑ Sep 1956 Cover: 0.10 **NM** value: **40.00**
3D 1 ❑ Nov 1953 Cover: 0.25 **NM** value: **280.00**
• 3-D issue with glasses

ABBOTT AND COSTELLO: THE CLASSIC COMICS — Eternity

Bk 1 ❑ b&w Cover: 14.95 **NM** value: **Cover or less**

A.B.C. WARRIORS — Fleetway-Quality

1 ❑ Cover: 1.95 **NM** value: **2.00**
ABC Warriors: The Tournament Of The Damned **A:** Brett Ewins **W:** Pat Mills
2 ❑ Cover: 1.95 **NM** value: **2.00**
W: Pat Mills
3 ❑ Cover: 1.95 **NM** value: **2.00**
4 ❑ Cover: 1.95 **NM** value: **2.00**
5 ❑ Cover: 1.95 **NM** value: **2.00**
6 ❑ Cover: 1.95 **NM** value: **2.00**
7 ❑ Cover: 1.95 **NM** value: **2.00**
8 ❑ Cover: 1.95 **NM** value: **2.00**
final issue.

ABC WARRIORS: KHRONICLES OF KHAOS — Fleetway-Quality

1 ❑ Cover: 2.95 **NM** value: **Cover or less**
2 ❑ Cover: 2.95 **NM** value: **Cover or less**
A: Kevin Walker **W:** Pat Mills; Tony Skinner
3 ❑ Cover: 2.95 **NM** value: **Cover or less**
W: Pat Mills; Tony Skinner
4 ❑ Cover: 2.95 **NM** value: **Cover or less**

ABE SAPIEN DRUMS OF THE DEAD — Dark Horse

1 ❑ Mar 1998 Cover: 2.95 **NM** value: **Cover or less**
Circ: Diamd. preorders: **16,111**

Other grades: Multiply prices above by **1.5 for Mint • 2/3 for Very Fine • 1/3 for Fine • 1/5 for Very Good • 1/8 for Good**

No issue number. One-shot. 📖 Drums of the Dead; Heads • Hellboy back-up **A:** Mike Mignola; Derek Thompson **W:** Mike Mignola; Brian McDonald ★ Appearance of Hellboy.

A. BIZARRO — DC

Bizarro has been one of Superman's most unusual and dangerous foes for more than 30 years, first appearing in Superboy #68. The chalky-skinned replica of The Man of Steel had all the powers but none of the intelligence. Recent continuity explains Bizarro as the result of a failed cloning experiment performed by Lex Luthor's scientists.

This four-part story reveals that Superman was not the only subject of those procedures. Albert Beezer, always looking for opportunities to move up the Lexcorp ladder, was more than willing to be used as a guinea pig. Little did he know that, more than two years later, an imperfect twin would wake from cryogenic sleep and end up knocking on his door.

The botched clone, Bizarro-Al, doesn't have Superman's strength but seems impervious to most harm. Unfortunately, he's confused as well as unintelligent. Keeping out of Lexcorp's hands is going to be pretty much impossible.

1 ❑ Jul 1999 Cover: 2.50 **NM** value: **Cover or less**
📖 Vivisimilitude **A:** Mark D. Bright **W:** Steve Gerber
2 ❑ Aug 1999 Cover: 2.50 **NM** value: **Cover or less**
📖 Silicon Dreamer **A:** Mark D. Bright **W:** Steve Gerber
3 ❑ Sep 1999 Cover: 2.50 **NM** value: **Cover or less**
📖 Nine-Inch Sonic Pumpkins **A:** Mark D. Bright **W:** Steve Gerber ★ Appearance of Granny Goodness.
4 ❑ Oct 1999 Cover: 2.50 **NM** value: **Cover or less**
📖 Viva Bizarro! **A:** Mark D. Bright **W:** Steve Gerber ★ Appearance of Superman.

A-BOMB — Antarctic / Venus

1 ❑ Dec 1993 Cover: 2.95 **NM** value: **Cover or less**
2 ❑ Mar 1994 Cover: 2.95 **NM** value: **Cover or less**
3 ❑ Jun 1994 Cover: 2.95 **NM** value: **Cover or less**
• Barr Girls story **A:** Donna Barr **W:** Donna Barr
4 ❑ Sep 1994 Cover: 2.95 **NM** value: **Cover or less**
• Barr Girls story **A:** Donna Barr **W:** Donna Barr
5 ❑ Dec 1994 Cover: 2.95 **NM** value: **Cover or less**
W: Donna Barr
6 ❑ Mar 1995 Cover: 2.95 **NM** value: **Cover or less**
📖 Strip F*cker; Knight after Knight; Merry Maria Melon **A:** Eddie Jackson; Shon Howell **W:** Lea Hernandez; The Wandering Kid; Tim Ely
7 ❑ Jun 1995 Cover: 2.95 **NM** value: **Cover or less**
📖 Merry Maria Melon; Tavern Tales; Drawings Based on the Mating Habits of Lines; Dix the Electric Cat; Inquisition **A:** Nebel Ungen; The Wandering Kid; Tim Ely; C.K. Penchant; Ann's 440 **W:** Lea Hernandez; Nebel Ungen; The Wandering Kid; Tim Ely; Ann's 440; Marc Jackson
8 ❑ Sep 1995 Cover: 2.95 **NM** value: **Cover or less**
W: Nebel Ungen; The Wandering Kid; Ann's 440; Marc Jackson
9 ❑ Nov 1995 Cover: 2.95 **NM** value: **Cover or less**
10 ❑ Jan 1996 Cover: 2.95 **NM** value: **Cover or less**
11 ❑ Mar 1996 Cover: 2.95 **NM** value: **Cover or less**
12 ❑ May 1996 Cover: 2.95 **NM** value: **Cover or less**
📖 Burma 1942, Part 2 **A:** Det Arumon **W:** Det Arumon
13 ❑ Jul 1996 Cover: 2.95 **NM** value: **Cover or less**
W: Det Arumon
14 ❑ Sep 1996 Cover: 2.95 **NM** value: **Cover or less**
Circ: Diamd. preorders: **2,940**
15 ❑ Nov 1996 Cover: 2.95 **NM** value: **Cover or less**
Circ: Diamd. preorders: **2,765**
📖 Passionate Immorality; Robin and Cindy: Kingdom Come
16 ❑ Jan 1997 Cover: 2.95 **NM** value: **Cover or less**
Circ: Direct Market orders: **2,699**
📖 Not Ninja High School; Burma 1942, Part 2; The Availability of Alice **A:** Fred Perry; Det Arumon; Azre **W:** Fred Perry; Det Arumon; Azre

ABOMINATIONS — Marvel

1 ❑ Dec 1996 Cover: 1.50 **NM** value: **Cover or less**
Circ: Direct Market orders: **53,500**
📖 Blood Rush • follows events in Hulk: Future Imperfect **A:** Angel Medina **W:** Ivan Velez Jr.
2 ❑ Jan 1997 Cover: 1.50 **NM** value: **Cover or less**
Circ: Direct Market orders: **44,250**
📖 The Fading Dead **A:** Angel Medina **W:** Ivan Velez Jr.
3 ❑ Feb 1997 Cover: 1.50 **NM** value: **Cover or less**
Circ: Direct Market orders: **35,000**
📖 Blur of Time final issue. **A:** Angel Medina **W:** Ivan Velez Jr.

ABRAHAM LINCOLN LIFE STORY — Dell

1 ❑ 1958 Cover: 0.25 **NM** value: **15.00**
• **CGC:** 1 graded, best 9.6
• Dell Giant

ABRAHAM STONE: COUNTRY MOUSE, CITY RAT — Platinum

Bk 1❑ Cover: 9.95 **NM** value: **Cover or less**
A: Joe Kubert
Bk 1/LE❑ Cover: 34.95 **NM** value: **Cover or less**
Limited hardcover. **A:** Joe Kubert

ABRAHAM STONE (EPIC) — Marvel / Epic

1 ❑ Jul 1995 Cover: 6.95 **NM** value: **Cover or less**
A: Joe Kubert **W:** Joe Kubert
2 ❑ Aug 1995 Cover: 6.95 **NM** value: **Cover or less**
A: Joe Kubert **W:** Joe Kubert

ABSLOM DAAK-DALEK KILLER — Marvel

Bk 1❑ Cover: 8.95 **NM** value: **Cover or less**

ABSOLUTE VERTIGO — DC / Vertigo

Absolute Vertigo was a one-shot that gave readers a preview of Vertigo's new offerings for 1995. Among them:

Vertigo Voices: The Eaters: a very, very black comedy by Peter Milligan about a family of suburban cannibals.

Jonah Hex: Riders of the Worm and Such: a darkly engaging tale of the old West by Joe Lansdale (Dead in the West).

Preacher: the story of Jesse Custer, a small-town preacher inhabited by an unholy spirit.

Ghostdancing: wherein Native American gods join with mankind to bring on a new age.

In addition, Absolute Vertigo features a new Invisibles story, artist "jam" pages, and a recap of Vertigo's line.

1 ❑ Win 1995 Cover: 0.99 **NM** value: **5.00**
• **CGC:** 2 graded, best 9.4

ABSOLUTE ZERO — Antarctic

1 ❑ Feb 1995 Cover: 3.50 **NM** value: **Cover or less**
📖 True Hero; Athena: Road Trip; To Beach…Or Not to Beach; The Jewel, Part 1; He Wanted to Grow a Beard; Hippy Exorcist **A:** Dean Hsieh; Ryan Kinnaird; David Hahn; Jim Conatser; S. Wasa; Studio Crispy Bug **W:** Dean Hsieh; Ryan Kinnaird; David Hahn; Jim Conatser; S. Wasa; Studio Crispy Bug ★ 1st Appearance of Athena.
2 ❑ May 1995 Cover: 2.95 **NM** value: **Cover or less**
📖 Mighty Tiny and the Mouse Marines; Like a Fisherman Needs a Bicycle; Athena: When in Athens…; The Jewel, Part 2; Rooftop; History of Anime Babes **A:** Dean Hsieh; Pat Kelley; Ryan Kinnaird; David Hahn(cover); Jim Novak; Mars Marshall; Mike DeWeese **W:** Dean Hsieh; Pat Kelley; Ryan Kinnaird; David Hahn; Jim Conatser; Mars Marshall; Mike DeWeese; S. Wasa; Studio Crispy Bug; Herb Mallette
3 ❑ Aug 1995 Cover: 2.95 **NM** value: **Cover or less**
W: Dean Hsieh; Pat Kelley; Ryan Kinnaird; Mars Marshall; Mike DeWeese; Herb Mallette

ABSURD ART OF J.J. GRANDVILLE, THE — Tome Press

1 ❑ b&w Cover: 2.50 **NM** value: **Cover or less**
• no date of publication

ABYSS, THE — Dark Horse

When an American nuclear submarine is lost at the edge of an undersea trench, the crew of the commercially owned Deepcore station is commandeered for rescue operations. Unfortunately for the crew, there's more to the submarine's wreck than accident can explain, and it turns out the Navy SEALs, who accompany the crew, are along for more than rescue duty.

Trapped beneath the sea, cut off from the surface by the hurricane, the people of Deepcore discover they are far from alone. Something has established a base in the depths of the three-mile canyon, something definitely not of this Earth. The already-tense situation escalates, when the SEALs' commander, suffering from the effects of deep pressure, decides to use the submarine's nuclear weapons.

This title was adapted from the Twentieth Century Fox motion picture.

1 ❑ Aug 1989 Cover: 2.25 **NM** value: **2.50**
Circ: CapCity orders: **8,950**
A: Michael W. Kaluta **W:** Randy Stradley
2 ❑ Sep 1989 Cover: 2.25 **NM** value: **2.50**
Circ: CapCity orders: **8,125**
A: Michael W. Kaluta **W:** Randy Stradley

AC ANNUAL — AC

1 ❑ Cover: 3.95 **NM** value: **Cover or less**
2 ❑ Cover: 5.00 **NM** value: **Cover or less**
3 ❑ Cover: 3.50 **NM** value: **Cover or less**
📖 Rocketman Returns!; Iron Jaw's Identity Crisis!; American Crusader: The Underwater World; American Crusader: Battle Inside the Sun! **A:** Rik Levins; Vic Bridges; Dan Reed **W:** Bill Black
4 ❑ Cover: 3.95 **NM** value: **Cover or less**

ACCELERATE — DC / Vertigo

1 ❑ Aug 2000 Cover: 2.95 **NM** value: **Cover or less**
Circ: Diamd. preorders: **10,510**
📖 (Untitled) **A:** Arnold Pander; Jacob Pander **C:** Arnold Pander; Jacob Pander **W:** Richard Kadrey
2 ❑ Sep 2000 Cover: 2.95 **NM** value: **Cover or less**
Circ: Diamd. preorders: **8,106**
📖 I Love Living in the City **A:** Arnold Pander; Jacob Pander **C:** Arnold Pander; Jacob Pander **W:** Richard Kadrey
3 ❑ Oct 2000 Cover: 2.95 **NM** value: **Cover or less**
Circ: Diamd. preorders: **7,527**
📖 Message from the Underground **A:** Arnold Pander; Jacob Pander **C:** Arnold Pander; Jacob Pander **W:** Richard Kadrey
4 ❑ Nov 2000 Cover: 2.95 **NM** value: **Cover or less**
Circ: Diamd. preorders: **6,672**
📖 Year One **A:** Arnold Pander; Jacob Pander **C:** Arnold Pander; Jacob Pander **W:** Richard Kadrey

ACCIDENTAL DEATH, AN — Fantagraphics

1 ❑ Dec 1993, b&w Cover: 3.50 **NM** value: **Cover or less**
No issue number. **A:** Eric Shanower **W:** Ed Brubaker

ACCIDENT MAN — Dark Horse

1 ❑ ca. 1993 Cover: 2.50 **NM** value: **Cover or less**
Circ: CapCity orders: **6,375**
A: Duke Mighten **W:** Pat Mills; Tony Skinner
2 ❑ ca. 1993 Cover: 2.50 **NM** value: **Cover or less**
Circ: CapCity orders: **4,300**
A: Duke Mighten **W:** Pat Mills; Tony Skinner
3 ❑ ca. 1993 Cover: 2.50 **NM** value: **Cover or less**
Circ: CapCity orders: **3,900**
A: Duke Mighten **W:** Pat Mills; Tony Skinner

ACCLAIM ADVENTURE ZONE — Acclaim

1 ❑ 1997 Cover: 4.50 **NM** value: **Cover or less**
No issue number. Ninjak on Cover. 📖 The Boss; While the Cat's Away; History, Herstory Whose Story is it?; Secrets; No Place Like Home Part2 **A:** Kevin West; James W. Fry III; Don Perlin; Steven Butler **W:** Bob Layton; Fabian Nicieza; Dan Slott; Robert L. Washington III
2 ❑ 1997 Cover: 4.50 **NM** value: **Cover or less**
No issue number. Turok on Cover. 📖 Extinction; Hero to the Fifth Power; How Gravity Works; Scorn on the Fourth of July; Window of Opportunity; No Place like Home **A:** Kevin West; Paul Pelletier; James W. Fry III; Don Perlin **W:** Bob Layton; Fabian Nicieza; Dan Slott; James PerhamBob Washington
3 ❑ 1997 Cover: 4.50 **NM** value: **Cover or less**
No issue number. Turok and Dinosaur on Cover. 📖 Dinosaur Rodeo; Reaction Time; How To Draw Superheros; Disguise and Doll; Nick of Time; No Place Like Home Part 3 **A:** Kevin West; James W. Fry III; Don Perlin; Steven Butler **W:** Bob Layton; Fabian Nicieza; Dan Slott; Michael Gallagher; Robert L. Washington III

ACE — Harrier

1 ❑ b&w Cover: 1.95 **NM** value: **Cover or less**
📖 In The Days of The Ace Rock'n'Roll Club; If Monkeys Fly; A Fine Romance • no indicia **A:** Eddie Campbell **W:** Eddie Campbell

ACE COMICS — McKay

1 ❑ Apr 1937 Cover: 0.10 **NM** value: **2250.00**
★ 1st Appearance of Jungle Jim (in comics).
2 ❑ May 1937 Cover: 0.10 **NM** value: **725.00**
3 ❑ Jun 1937 Cover: 0.10 **NM** value: **475.00**
4 ❑ Jul 1937 Cover: 0.10 **NM** value: **415.00**
5 ❑ Aug 1937 Cover: 0.10 **NM** value: **375.00**
6 ❑ Sep 1937 Cover: 0.10 **NM** value: **375.00**
7 ❑ Oct 1937 Cover: 0.10 **NM** value: **375.00**
8 ❑ Nov 1937 Cover: 0.10 **NM** value: **375.00**
9 ❑ Dec 1937 Cover: 0.10 **NM** value: **375.00**
10 ❑ Jan 1938 Cover: 0.10 **NM** value: **375.00**
11 ❑ Feb 1938 Cover: 0.10 **NM** value: **410.00**
• The Phantom begins
12 ❑ Mar 1938 Cover: 0.10 **NM** value: **240.00**
13 ❑ Apr 1938 Cover: 0.10 **NM** value: **240.00**
14 ❑ May 1938 Cover: 0.10 **NM** value: **240.00**
15 ❑ Jun 1938 Cover: 0.10 **NM** value: **200.00**
16 ❑ Jul 1938 Cover: 0.10 **NM** value: **200.00**
17 ❑ Aug 1938 Cover: 0.10 **NM** value: **200.00**
18 ❑ Sep 1938 Cover: 0.10 **NM** value: **200.00**
19 ❑ Oct 1938 Cover: 0.10 **NM** value: **200.00**
20 ❑ Nov 1938 Cover: 0.10 **NM** value: **200.00**
21 ❑ Dec 1938 Cover: 0.10 **NM** value: **175.00**
22 ❑ Jan 1939 Cover: 0.10 **NM** value: **175.00**
23 ❑ Feb 1939 Cover: 0.10 **NM** value: **175.00**
24 ❑ Mar 1939 Cover: 0.10 **NM** value: **175.00**
25 ❑ Apr 1939 Cover: 0.10 **NM** value: **175.00**
26 ❑ May 1939 Cover: 0.10 **NM** value: **650.00**
★ Origin of Prince Valiant. ★ 1st Appearance of Prince Valiant.
27 ❑ Jun 1939 Cover: 0.10 **NM** value: **175.00**
28 ❑ Jul 1939 Cover: 0.10 **NM** value: **175.00**
29 ❑ Aug 1939 Cover: 0.10 **NM** value: **175.00**
30 ❑ Sep 1939 Cover: 0.10 **NM** value: **175.00**
31 ❑ Oct 1939 Cover: 0.10 **NM** value: **150.00**
32 ❑ Nov 1939 Cover: 0.10 **NM** value: **150.00**
33 ❑ Dec 1939 Cover: 0.10 **NM** value: **150.00**
34 ❑ Jan 1940 Cover: 0.10 **NM** value: **150.00**
35 ❑ Feb 1940 Cover: 0.10 **NM** value: **150.00**
36 ❑ Mar 1940 Cover: 0.10 **NM** value: **150.00**
37 ❑ Apr 1940 Cover: 0.10 **NM** value: **135.00**
38 ❑ May 1940 Cover: 0.10 **NM** value: **135.00**
39 ❑ Jun 1940 Cover: 0.10 **NM** value: **135.00**
40 ❑ Jul 1940 Cover: 0.10 **NM** value: **135.00**
41 ❑ Aug 1940 Cover: 0.10 **NM** value: **105.00**
42 ❑ Sep 1940 Cover: 0.10 **NM** value: **105.00**
43 ❑ Oct 1940 Cover: 0.10 **NM** value: **105.00**
44 ❑ Nov 1940 Cover: 0.10 **NM** value: **105.00**
45 ❑ Dec 1940 Cover: 0.10 **NM** value: **105.00**
46 ❑ Jan 1941 Cover: 0.10 **NM** value: **105.00**
47 ❑ Feb 1941 Cover: 0.10 **NM** value: **105.00**
48 ❑ Mar 1941 Cover: 0.10 **NM** value: **105.00**
49 ❑ Apr 1941 Cover: 0.10 **NM** value: **105.00**
50 ❑ May 1941 Cover: 0.10 **NM** value: **105.00**
51 ❑ Jun 1941 Cover: 0.10 **NM** value: **105.00**
52 ❑ Jul 1941 Cover: 0.10 **NM** value: **105.00**
53 ❑ Aug 1941 Cover: 0.10 **NM** value: **105.00**
54 ❑ Sep 1941 Cover: 0.10 **NM** value: **105.00**
55 ❑ Oct 1941 Cover: 0.10 **NM** value: **105.00**
56 ❑ Nov 1941 Cover: 0.10 **NM** value: **105.00**
57 ❑ Dec 1941 Cover: 0.10 **NM** value: **105.00**
58 ❑ Jan 1942 Cover: 0.10 **NM** value: **105.00**
• **CGC:** 1 graded, best 6.5

CGC-graded: Multiply prices above by **33 for 9.9 M • 16 for 9.8 NM/M • 7 for 9.6 NM+ • 5 for 9.4 NM • 2.5 for 9.2 NM- • 1.5 for 9.0 VF/NM**

59 ❑ Feb 1942 Cover: 0.10 **NM** value: **105.00**
• **CGC:** 1 graded, best 5.5
60 ❑ Mar 1942 Cover: 0.10 **NM** value: **95.00**
• **CGC:** 1 graded, best 8.0
61 ❑ Apr 1942 Cover: 0.10 **NM** value: **95.00**
62 ❑ May 1942 Cover: 0.10 **NM** value: **95.00**
• **CGC:** 1 graded, best 9.2
63 ❑ Jun 1942 Cover: 0.10 **NM** value: **95.00**
64 ❑ Jul 1942 Cover: 0.10 **NM** value: **95.00**
65 ❑ Aug 1942 Cover: 0.10 **NM** value: **95.00**
66 ❑ Sep 1942 Cover: 0.10 **NM** value: **95.00**
67 ❑ Oct 1942 Cover: 0.10 **NM** value: **95.00**
68 ❑ Nov 1942 Cover: 0.10 **NM** value: **95.00**
69 ❑ Dec 1942 Cover: 0.10 **NM** value: **95.00**
70 ❑ Jan 1943 Cover: 0.10 **NM** value: **95.00**
71 ❑ Feb 1943 Cover: 0.10 **NM** value: **95.00**
72 ❑ Mar 1943 Cover: 0.10 **NM** value: **95.00**
73 ❑ Apr 1943 Cover: 0.10 **NM** value: **95.00**
74 ❑ May 1943 Cover: 0.10 **NM** value: **95.00**
75 ❑ Jun 1943 Cover: 0.10 **NM** value: **95.00**
76 ❑ Jul 1943 Cover: 0.10 **NM** value: **95.00**
77 ❑ Aug 1943 Cover: 0.10 **NM** value: **95.00**
78 ❑ Sep 1943 Cover: 0.10 **NM** value: **95.00**
📖 The Phantom; DaffyDoodles **A:** Chic Young; Alex Raymond; Jimmy Hatlo; A. Carter; Billy DeBeck; C.D. Russel; Doc Winner; Harold Foster; Harold Knerr; Joe Musial; Lyman Young; Norman Lynd; Russ Westover; Sgt. Dave Breger; Ray Moore **W:** Chic Young; Alex Raymond; Jimmy Hatlo; A. Carter; Billy DeBeck; C.D. Russel; Doc Winner; Harold Foster; Harold Knerr; Joe Musial; Lee Falk; Lyman Young; Norman Lynd; Russ Westover; Sgt. Dave Breger
79 ❑ Oct 1943 Cover: 0.10 **NM** value: **95.00**
80 ❑ Nov 1943 Cover: 0.10 **NM** value: **80.00**
81 ❑ Dec 1943 Cover: 0.10 **NM** value: **80.00**
82 ❑ Jan 1944 Cover: 0.10 **NM** value: **80.00**
83 ❑ Feb 1944 Cover: 0.10 **NM** value: **80.00**
84 ❑ Mar 1944 Cover: 0.10 **NM** value: **80.00**
85 ❑ Apr 1944 Cover: 0.10 **NM** value: **80.00**
86 ❑ May 1944 Cover: 0.10 **NM** value: **80.00**
87 ❑ Jun 1944 Cover: 0.10 **NM** value: **80.00**
88 ❑ Jul 1944 Cover: 0.10 **NM** value: **80.00**
89 ❑ Aug 1944 Cover: 0.10 **NM** value: **80.00**
90 ❑ Sep 1944 Cover: 0.10 **NM** value: **80.00**
91 ❑ Oct 1944 Cover: 0.10 **NM** value: **68.00**
92 ❑ Nov 1944 Cover: 0.10 **NM** value: **68.00**
93 ❑ Dec 1944 Cover: 0.10 **NM** value: **68.00**
94 ❑ Jan 1945 Cover: 0.10 **NM** value: **68.00**
95 ❑ Feb 1945 Cover: 0.10 **NM** value: **68.00**
96 ❑ Mar 1945 Cover: 0.10 **NM** value: **68.00**
97 ❑ Apr 1945 Cover: 0.10 **NM** value: **68.00**
98 ❑ May 1945 Cover: 0.10 **NM** value: **68.00**
99 ❑ Jun 1945 Cover: 0.10 **NM** value: **68.00**
100 ❑ Jul 1945 Cover: 0.10 **NM** value: **85.00**
• 100th anniversary issue.
101 ❑ Aug 1945 Cover: 0.10 **NM** value: **68.00**
102 ❑ Sep 1945 Cover: 0.10 **NM** value: **68.00**
103 ❑ Oct 1945 Cover: 0.10 **NM** value: **68.00**
104 ❑ Nov 1945 Cover: 0.10 **NM** value: **68.00**
105 ❑ Dec 1945 Cover: 0.10 **NM** value: **68.00**
106 ❑ Jan 1946 Cover: 0.10 **NM** value: **68.00**
107 ❑ Feb 1946 Cover: 0.10 **NM** value: **68.00**
108 ❑ Mar 1946 Cover: 0.10 **NM** value: **68.00**
109 ❑ Apr 1946 Cover: 0.10 **NM** value: **68.00**
110 ❑ May 1946 Cover: 0.10 **NM** value: **68.00**
111 ❑ Jun 1946 Cover: 0.10 **NM** value: **68.00**
112 ❑ Jul 1946 Cover: 0.10 **NM** value: **68.00**
113 ❑ Aug 1946 Cover: 0.10 **NM** value: **68.00**
114 ❑ Sep 1946 Cover: 0.10 **NM** value: **68.00**
115 ❑ Oct 1946 Cover: 0.10 **NM** value: **68.00**
116 ❑ Nov 1946 Cover: 0.10 **NM** value: **68.00**
117 ❑ Dec 1946 Cover: 0.10 **NM** value: **68.00**
118 ❑ Jan 1947 Cover: 0.10 **NM** value: **68.00**
119 ❑ Feb 1947 Cover: 0.10 **NM** value: **68.00**
120 ❑ Mar 1947 Cover: 0.10 **NM** value: **58.00**
121 ❑ Apr 1947 Cover: 0.10 **NM** value: **58.00**
122 ❑ May 1947 Cover: 0.10 **NM** value: **58.00**
123 ❑ Jun 1947 Cover: 0.10 **NM** value: **58.00**
124 ❑ Jul 1947 Cover: 0.10 **NM** value: **58.00**
125 ❑ Aug 1947 Cover: 0.10 **NM** value: **58.00**
126 ❑ Sep 1947 Cover: 0.10 **NM** value: **58.00**
127 ❑ Oct 1947 Cover: 0.10 **NM** value: **58.00**
128 ❑ Nov 1947 Cover: 0.10 **NM** value: **58.00**
129 ❑ Dec 1947 Cover: 0.10 **NM** value: **58.00**
130 ❑ Jan 1948 Cover: 0.10 **NM** value: **58.00**
131 ❑ Feb 1948 Cover: 0.10 **NM** value: **58.00**
132 ❑ Mar 1948 Cover: 0.10 **NM** value: **58.00**
133 ❑ Apr 1948 Cover: 0.10 **NM** value: **58.00**
134 ❑ May 1948 Cover: 0.10 **NM** value: **58.00**
135 ❑ Jun 1948 Cover: 0.10 **NM** value: **58.00**
136 ❑ Jul 1948 Cover: 0.10 **NM** value: **58.00**
137 ❑ Aug 1948 Cover: 0.10 **NM** value: **58.00**
138 ❑ Sep 1948 Cover: 0.10 **NM** value: **58.00**
139 ❑ Oct 1948 Cover: 0.10 **NM** value: **58.00**
140 ❑ Nov 1948 Cover: 0.10 **NM** value: **58.00**
141 ❑ Dec 1948 Cover: 0.10 **NM** value: **58.00**
142 ❑ Jan 1949 Cover: 0.10 **NM** value: **58.00**
143 ❑ Feb 1949 Cover: 0.10 **NM** value: **58.00**
144 ❑ Mar 1949 Cover: 0.10 **NM** value: **85.00**
Phantom cover.
145 ❑ Apr 1949 Cover: 0.10 **NM** value: **80.00**
Phantom cover.
146 ❑ May 1949 Cover: 0.10 **NM** value: **75.00**
Phantom cover.
147 ❑ Jun 1949 Cover: 0.10 **NM** value: **75.00**
Phantom cover.
148 ❑ Jul 1949 Cover: 0.10 **NM** value: **75.00**
Phantom cover.
149 ❑ Aug 1949 Cover: 0.10 **NM** value: **70.00**
Phantom cover.
150 ❑ Sep 1949 Cover: 0.10 **NM** value: **70.00**
Phantom cover.
151 ❑ Oct 1949 Cover: 0.10 **NM** value: **70.00**
final issue.

ACE COMICS PRESENTS — Ace

1 ❑ May 1987 Cover: 1.75 **NM** value: **2.00**
• Daredevil (Golden Age) vs. The Claw;Silver Streak **A:** Ralph Johns; Jack Cole; JC **W:** Ralph Johns; Jack Cole
2 ❑ Jul 1987 Cover: 1.75 **NM** value: **2.00**
• Jack Bradbury
3 ❑ Sep 1987 Cover: 1.75 **NM** value: **2.00**
📖 Bob and Swab; The Barker • The Golden Age of Klaus Nordling **A:** Klaus Nordling **W:** Klaus Nordling
4 ❑ Nov 1987 Cover: 1.75 **NM** value: **2.00**
• Lou Fine

ACE MCCOY — Avalon

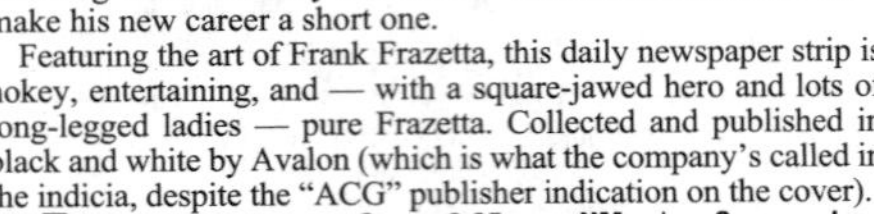

Johnny Comet is on the verge of a successful career as an action movie stuntman. There are only a couple of catches. First, he has to change his name to "Ace McCoy." Second, he'll have to cool his heels during a production break as a daring stunt performer at a traveling carnival. Neither requirement particularly bothers the hero — he's happy to use his skills to perform death-defying feats for carnival audiences — and he wears his new name well. Little does he suspect that his fellow stuntmen at the carny aren't too thrilled about new blood outdoing them and they intend to make his new career a short one.

Featuring the art of Frank Frazetta, this daily newspaper strip is hokey, entertaining, and — with a square-jawed hero and lots of long-legged ladies — pure Frazetta. Collected and published in black and white by Avalon (which is what the company's called in the indicia, despite the "ACG" publisher indication on the cover).

1 ❑ b&w Cover: 2.95 **NM** value: **Cover or less**
📖 From Comet to McCoy!; The Old Red Car **A:** Frank Frazetta; Jack Keller **C:** Frank Frazetta **W:** Jack Keller
2 ❑ b&w Cover: 2.95 **NM** value: **Cover or less**
📖 Circle of Fire; Moment of Truth **A:** Frank Frazetta; Nicholas Alascia; Don Perlin **C:** Frank Frazetta **W:** Joe Gill
3 ❑ b&w Cover: 2.95 **NM** value: **Cover or less**
📖 The Fastest Toy in Town **A:** Frank Frazetta **C:** Frank Frazetta **W:** Earl Baldwin

ACE OF SPADES — ZuZupetal

1 ❑ Cover: 2.50 **NM** value: **Cover or less**
📖 The Ace Is Drawn **A:** George Davis **W:** David Lathrap

ACES — Eclipse

Aces is a stylish black-and-white magazine produced by England's Acme Comics and distributed by Eclipse Comics' international branch. A serial anthology title, it specializes in Jazz Age genre fiction, filling its pages with the exploits of vicious gangsters and hard-boiled private investigators.

Among its features are "Hollywood Eye," a smart bit of Tinseltown detective intrigue by Francois Riviere, J.L. Bocquet, and artist Philippe Berthet; "Air Mail," a story by Attilio Micheluzi that mixes dashing pilots and nasty mobsters; and "Morgan" by Antonio Segura and Jose Ortiz, a bleak story of revenge which seems an early ancestor to Frank Miller's brilliant Sin City.

1 ❑ Apr 1988 Cover: 2.95 **NM** value: **3.00**
Circ: CapCity orders: **2,775**
📖 Airmail; Flying Down to Ohio; Hollywood Eye; Continental Update; Morgan **A:** Jose Ortiz; Attilio Micheluzzi; Francois Riviere; J.L. Bocquet; Phillipe Berthet; Antonio Segura **W:** Jose Ortiz; Attilio Micheluzzi; Francois Riviere; J.L. Bocquet; Phillipe Berthet; Antonio Segura
2 ❑ Cover: 2.95 **NM** value: **3.00**
3 ❑ Cover: 2.95 **NM** value: **3.00**
4 ❑ Cover: 2.95 **NM** value: **3.00**
5 ❑ Cover: 2.95 **NM** value: **3.00**
final issue.

To find the median price offered on eBay at press time for pre-1990 **CGC-graded comics**, multiply by:

9.9 (M): **32**	8.5 (VF+): **1.25**
9.8(NM/M): **16**	8.0 (VF): **0.85**
9.6 (NM+): **7**	7.5 (VF-): **0.6**
9.4 (NM): **5**	7.0 (F/VF): **0.5**
9.2 (NM-): **2.5**	6.5 (F+): **0.4**
9.0 (VF/NM): **1.5**	6.0 (F-): **0.33**

These are median prices of all CGC comics auctioned on eBay; prices for individual issues will vary.

ACES HIGH (E.C.) — E.C.

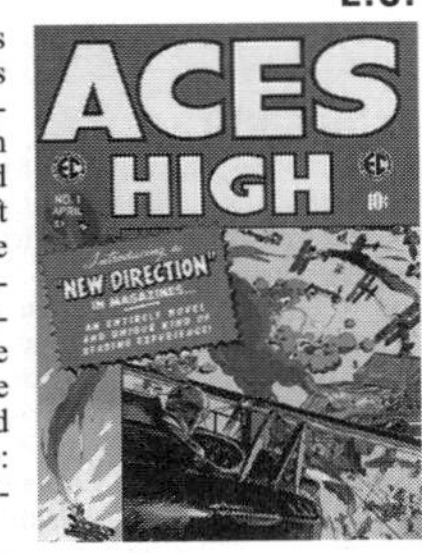

There were six E.C. titles in its "New Direction," cover-bannered as "an entirely novel and unique reading experience." The cover of each had a frame with the title on top and an identifying icon down the left side. The "New Direction" was one designed to accommodate the Comics Magazine Association of America's new Comics Code, though the first issue of each did not carry the Code stamp, and all but one lasted for five issues. The six titles were: Extra!, Impact, MD, Psychoanalysis, Valor — and Aces High.

The stories dealt with aviation combat, and four of the five covers by George Evans showed World War I biplane action. (The fifth featured the Flying Tigers.) — Maggie

1 ❑ Apr 1955 Cover: 0.10 **NM** value: **125.00**
• **CGC:** 4 graded, best 9.8
📖 The Way it was; The Stork with Talon (Text Story); The Outsider; The Mascot; The New C.O. **A:** George Evans; Wally Wood; Bernie Krigstein; Jack Davis **W:** George Evans; Wally Wood; Bernie Krigstein; Jack Davis
2 ❑ Jun 1955 Cover: 0.10 **NM** value: **100.00**
• **CGC:** 4 graded, best 9.4
📖 Chivalry!; The Ace of Aces (Text Story); Revenge, Locker 9; Footnote **A:** George Evans; Wally Wood; Bernie Krigstein; Jack Davis **W:** George Evans; Wally Wood; Bernie Krigstein; Jack Davis
3 ❑ Aug 1955 Cover: 0.10 **NM** value: **85.00**
• **CGC:** 4 graded, best 9.6
📖 The Rules; The Spy; Grease Monkey; The Acid Test (Text Story); The Case of Champagne **A:** George Evans; Wally Wood; Bernie Krigstein; Jack Davis **W:** George Evans; Wally Wood; Bernie Krigstein; Jack Davis
4 ❑ Oct 1955 Cover: 0.10 **NM** value: **85.00**
• **CGC:** 4 graded, best 9.2
📖 The Green Kids; The Good Luck Piece; The Novice Ace; The Last Laugh (Text Story); Home Again **A:** George Evans; Wally Wood; Bernie Krigstein; Jack Davis **W:** George Evans; Wally Wood; Bernie Krigstein; Jack Davis
5 ❑ Dec 1955 Cover: 0.10 **NM** value: **85.00**
• **CGC:** 2 graded, best 9.6
📖 C'est la Guerre!; Airman Unknown (Text Story); Iron Man!; Spade were Trump **A:** George Evans; Wally Wood; Bernie Krigstein; Jack Davis **W:** George Evans; Wally Wood; Bernie Krigstein; Jack Davis

ACES HIGH (RCP) — RCP

1 ❑ Apr 1999 Cover: 2.50 **NM** value: **Cover or less**
Circ: Diamd. preorders: **3,883**
📖 The Way it was; The Stork with Talon (Text Story); The Outsider; The Mascot; The New C.O. **A:** George Evans; Wally Wood; Bernie Krigstein; Jack Davis **W:** George Evans; Wally Wood; Bernie Krigstein; Jack Davis
2 ❑ May 1999 Cover: 2.50 **NM** value: **Cover or less**
Circ: Diamd. preorders: **3,616**
📖 Chivalry!; The Ace of Aces (Text Story); Revenge, Locker 9; Footnote **A:** George Evans; Wally Wood; Bernie Krigstein; Jack Davis **W:** George Evans; Wally Wood; Bernie Krigstein; Jack Davis
3 ❑ Jun 1999 Cover: 2.50 **NM** value: **Cover or less**
Circ: Diamd. preorders: **3,593**
📖 The Rules; The Spy; Grease Monkey; The Acid Test (Text Story); The Case of Champagne **A:** George Evans; Wally Wood; Bernie Krigstein; Jack Davis **W:** George Evans; Wally Wood; Bernie Krigstein; Jack Davis
4 ❑ Jul 1999 Cover: 2.50 **NM** value: **Cover or less**
Circ: Diamd. preorders: **3,534**
📖 The Green Kids; The Good Luck Piece; The Novice Ace; The Last Laugh (Text Story); Home Again **A:** George Evans; Wally Wood; Bernie Krigstein; Jack Davis **W:** George Evans; Wally Wood; Bernie Krigstein; Jack Davis
5 ❑ Aug 1999 Cover: 2.50 **NM** value: **Cover or less**
Circ: Diamd. preorders: **3,574**
📖 C'est la Guerre!; Airman Unknown (Text Story); Iron Man!; Spade were Trump **A:** George Evans; Wally Wood; Bernie Krigstein; Jack Davis **W:** George Evans; Wally Wood; Bernie Krigstein; Jack Davis
Anl 1 ❑ Cover: 13.50 **NM** value: **Cover or less**
• Collects Aces High #1-5 **A:** George Evans; Wally Wood; Bernie Krigstein; Jack Davis **W:** George Evans; Wally Wood; Bernie Krigstein; Jack Davis

ACG CHRISTMAS SPECIAL — Avalon

1 ❑ Cover: 2.95 **NM** value: **Cover or less**
Cover reads "Christmas Horror". 📖 Only A Toy; Terrible Teddy; The Things Some Kids Dream Up!; The Teddy Bear **A:** Pat Boyette; Mike Zeck; Jack Abel **W:** Joe Gill; Nicola Cutii; Joe Halloy

ACG'S CIVIL WAR — Avalon

1 ❑ 1995 Cover: 2.50 **NM** value: **Cover or less**

ACG'S HALLOWEEN SPECIAL — Avalon

1 ❑ Cover: 2.95 **NM** value: **Cover or less**
Cover reads "Halloween Horror". 📖 Bridal Night; The Flapping Head; Someone Else is Here; The Wrong Turn **A:** Sanho Kim

ACHILLES STORM: DARK SECRET — Brainstorm

1 ❑ Cover: 2.95 **NM** value: **Cover or less**
A: Sandra Chang **W:** Sandra Chang
2 ❑ Cover: 2.95 **NM** value: **Cover or less**
A: Sandra Chang **W:** Sandra Chang

ACHILLES STORM/RAZMATAZ — Aja Blu

1 ❑ Oct 1990 Cover: 2.25 **NM** value: **Cover or less**
2 ❑ Jan 1991 Cover: 2.25 **NM** value: **Cover or less**
3 ❑ May 1991 Cover: 2.25 **NM** value: **Cover or less**

Other grades: Multiply prices above by **1.5 for Mint • 2/3 for Very Fine • 1/3 for Fine • 1/5 for Very Good • 1/8 for Good**

ACID BATH CASE, THE — Kitchen Sink

1 ❑ Cover: 4.95 **NM** value: **Cover or less**
A: Kellie Strom **W:** Stephen Walsh

ACK THE BARBARIAN — Innovation

1 ❑ b&w Cover: 2.25 **NM** value: **Cover or less**
🕮 This Spell...This Monster!; Duck Soup **A:** Mario D. Macari **W:** Mario D. Macari

ACME — Fandom House

1 ❑ Cover: 3.00 **NM** value: **Cover or less**
2 ❑ Cover: 3.00 **NM** value: **Cover or less**
3 ❑ Cover: 3.00 **NM** value: **Cover or less**
4 ❑ Cover: 3.00 **NM** value: **Cover or less**
5 ❑ Cover: 3.00 **NM** value: **Cover or less**
6 ❑ Cover: 3.00 **NM** value: **Cover or less**
7 ❑ Cover: 3.00 **NM** value: **Cover or less**
8 ❑ Fal 1987 Cover: 2.00 **NM** value: **Cover or less**
9 ❑ Sum 1989 Cover: 3.00 **NM** value: **Cover or less**

ACME NOVELTY LIBRARY, THE — Fantagraphics

Regard Chris Ware, an American comics original. With humor that's sometimes subtle and sometimes bizarre, he follows his every flight of fancy in Acme Novelty Library, one of the true "alternative" comics hits during the late 1990s. Pathetic Jimmy Corrigan, "The Smartest Kid on Earth," stars in many issues, although there is a running cast of others.

Ware sets his own rules for panel layouts and issue design — and even the physcal size of his comics. Issues range in size from tiny pamphlets to giant tabloids, causing headaches for readers trying to store — or retailers trying to rack — this series. Fantagraphics responded in the late 1990s with a special display stand, designed by Ware, to hold his various issues. It's one of the best retail display pieces for a comic book, ever, and sure to become a prized collectible in its own right. — JJM

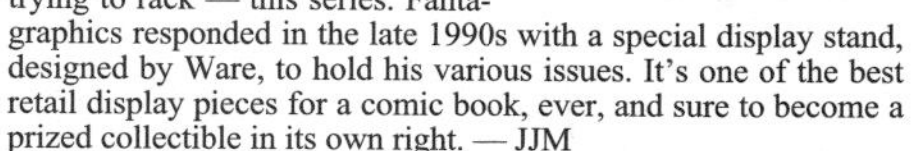

1 ❑ Win 1993 Cover: 3.50 **NM** value: **15.00**
Circ: CapCity orders: **2,320**
🕮 Jimmy Corrigan: A Souvenir Book Of Views; Jimmy Corrigan: Jimmy Gets Out of the House; Big Tex **A:** Chris Ware **W:** Chris Ware ★ 1st Appearance of Jimmy Corrigan.
1-2 ❑ Dec 1995 Cover: 3.50 **NM** value: **4.00**
2 ❑ Sum 1994 Cover: 4.95 **NM** value: **9.00**
• Quimby the Mouse **A:** Chris Ware **W:** Chris Ware
2-2 ❑ Sum 1995 Cover: 4.95 **NM** value: **5.00**
3 ❑ Aut 1994 Cover: 3.95 **NM** value: **7.00**
• digest-sized. 🕮 A Tour of Our Facilities; Mexican Reminiscences; Carolina Shout; Wish I Could Shimmy Like My Sister Kate; Chatanooga Choo Choo; Funny Picture Stories • Blind Man **A:** Chris Ware **W:** Chris Ware
4 ❑ Win 1994 Cover: 4.95 **NM** value: **6.00**
• Sparky's Best Comics and Stories **A:** Chris Ware **W:** Chris Ware
4-2 ❑ Cover: 4.95 **NM** value: **Cover or less**
A: Chris Ware **W:** Chris Ware
5 ❑ Cover: 3.95 **NM** value: **5.00**
• digest-sized. 🕮 Jimmy Corrigan • Jimmy Corrigan **A:** Chris Ware **W:** Chris Ware
6 ❑ Fal 1995 Cover: 3.95 **NM** value: **4.00**
• digest-sized. • Jimmy Corrigan **A:** Chris Ware **W:** Chris Ware
7 ❑ Cover: 6.95 **NM** value: **Cover or less**
• Oversized. • Book of Jokes **A:** Chris Ware **W:** Chris Ware
8 ❑ Win 1996 Cover: 4.75 **NM** value: **Cover or less**
Circ: Direct Market orders: **6,889**
• digest-sized. • Jimmy Corrigan **A:** Chris Ware **W:** Chris Ware
9 ❑ Win 1997 Cover: 4.50 **NM** value: **Cover or less**
Circ: Diamd. preorders: **6,553**
• digest-sized. • Jimmy Corrigan **A:** Chris Ware **W:** Chris Ware
10 ❑ Spr 1998 Cover: 4.95 **NM** value: **Cover or less**
Circ: Diamd. preorders: **6,615**
• digest-sized. • Jimmy Corrigan
11 ❑ Fal 1998 Cover: 4.50 **NM** value: **Cover or less**
Circ: Diamd. preorders: **6,594**
• digest-sized. • Jimmy Corrigan
12 ❑ Spr 1999 Cover: 4.50 **NM** value: **Cover or less**
Circ: Diamd. preorders: **6,758**
• digest-sized. • Jimmy Corrigan

ACOLYTE, THE — Mad Monkey

1 ❑ Cover: 3.95 **NM** value: **Cover or less**
A: Maria Cruz Garcia **W:** Andrew North

ACTION 21 — ITC

1 ❑ Jul 1988 Cover: 1.25 **NM** value: **3.50**
2 ❑ Cover: 1.25 **NM** value: **3.50**
3 ❑ **NM** value: **3.00**
4 ❑ **NM** value: **3.00**
5 ❑ **NM** value: **3.00**
6 ❑ **NM** value: **3.00**
7 ❑ **NM** value: **3.00**
8 ❑ **NM** value: **3.00**
9 ❑ **NM** value: **3.00**
10 ❑ **NM** value: **3.00**

Statement of Ownership figures are the average number of copies originally sold, as cited by the publisher to the U.S. Postal Service. These estimate **all** sales, in comics shops and on newsstands.

ACTION COMICS — DC

It all started back in 1938 with Action Comics #1. Though it began as an anthology title featuring a number of characters, it cover-featured the first appearance of a certain muscular guy from the planet Krypton — better known to the world as Superman. More than 50 years later, Superman is still going strong, appearing, not only here, but in several others comic titles, including Superman and Superman: The Man of Steel.

Action Comics is where the world first met Clark Kent, Lois Lane, and countless other of the most memorable characters in the world of comics. Over time, the comic book has updated itself somewhat, but the stories remain true to their classic form. Today, Superman still flies the skies over Metropolis, battling evildoers everywhere, fighting for truth, justice, and the American Way.

0 ❑ Oct 1994 Cover: 1.50 **NM** value: **2.50**
Circ: CapCity orders: **60,045**
🕮 The Yesterday Man • Peer Pressure, Part 4; ▲1994-40 **A:** Denis Rodier; Jackson Guice **W:** David Michelinie ★ 1st Appearance of Kenny Braverman.
1 ❑ Jun 1938 Cover: 0.10 **NM** value: **200000.00**
• **CGC:** 9 graded, best 8.5
🕮 Superman; "Chuck" Dawson; Zatara; South Sea Strategy; Sticky-Mitt Stimson; The Adventures of Marco Polo; Pep Morgan; Scoop Scanlon, Five Star Reporter; Tex Thompson; Stardust **A:** Joe Shuster; Bernard Baily; Bill Alger; Fred Guardineer; Hugh Fleming; Sven Elven; Will Ely **W:** Bernard Baily; Bill Alger; Fred Guardineer; Hugh Fleming; Jerry Siegel; Sven Elven; Will Ely ★ Origin of Superman. ★ 1st Appearance of Zatara, Superman, Tex Thomson, Lois Lane.
1-2 ❑ Cover: 0.50 **NM** value: **18.00**
• 2nd printing (giveaway, 1976?). 🕮 Superman; "Chuck" Dawson; Zatara; South Sea Strategy; Sticky-Mitt Stimson; The Adventures of Marco Polo; Pep Morgan; Scoop Scanlon, Five Star Reporter; Tex Thompson; Stardust **A:** Joe Shuster; Bernard Baily; Bill Alger; Fred Guardineer; Hugh Fleming; Sven Elven; Will Ely **W:** Bernard Baily; Bill Alger; Fred Guardineer; Hugh Fleming; Jerry Siegel; Sven Elven; Will Ely ★ Origin of Superman. ★ 1st Appearance of Zatara, Superman, Tex Thomson, Lois Lane.
1-3 ❑ Cover: 0.50 **NM** value: **14.00**
• **CGC:** 1 graded, best 9.4
• 3rd printing (giveaway, 1983?). 🕮 Superman; "Chuck" Dawson; Zatara; South Sea Strategy; Sticky-Mitt Stimson; The Adventures of Marco Polo; Pep Morgan; Scoop Scanlon, Five Star Reporter; Tex Thompson; Stardust **A:** Joe Shuster; Bernard Baily; Bill Alger; Fred Guardineer; Hugh Fleming; Sven Elven; Will Ely **W:** Bernard Baily; Bill Alger; Fred Guardineer; Hugh Fleming; Jerry Siegel; Sven Elven; Will Ely; David Michelinie ★ Origin of Superman. ★ 1st Appearance of Zatara, Superman, Tex Thomson, Lois Lane.
1-4 ❑ Cover: 0.50 **NM** value: **5.00**
• **CGC:** 2 graded, best 9.4
• 4th printing (Nestle Quik 16-page giveaway, 1988). 🕮 Superman **A:** Joe Shuster **W:** Jerry Siegel ★ Origin of Superman.
1-5 ❑ Cover: 1.00 **NM** value: **4.00**
• **CGC:** 1 graded, best 9.0
🕮 Superman; "Chuck" Dawson; Zatara; South Sea Strategy; Sticky-Mitt Stimson; The Adventures of Marco Polo; Pep Morgan; Scoop Scanlon, Five Star Reporter; Tex Thompson; Stardust • 5th printing (1992) **A:** Joe Shuster; Bernard Baily; Bill Alger; Fred Guardineer; Hugh Fleming; Sven Elven; Will Ely **W:** Bernard Baily; Bill Alger; Fred Guardineer; Hugh Fleming; Jerry Siegel; Sven Elven; Will Ely ★ Origin of Superman. ★ 1st Appearance of Zatara, Superman, Tex Thomson, Lois Lane.
1-6 ❑ **NM** value: **1.00**
• **CGC:** 5 graded, best 9.8
🕮 Superman • 6th printing (1998);U.S. Postal Service **A:** Joe Shuster **W:** Jerry Siegel ★ Origin of Superman. ★ 1st Appearance of Superman.
1-6 ❑ **NM** value: **1.00**
• **CGC:** 5 graded, best 9.8
🕮 Superman • 6th printing (1998);U.S. Postal Service **A:** Joe Shuster **W:** Jerry Siegel ★ Origin of Superman. ★ 1st Appearance of Superman.
2 ❑ Jul 1938 Cover: 0.10 **NM** value: **25500.00**
• **CGC:** 5 graded, best 7.0
🕮 War in San Monte, part 2 **A:** Joe Shuster **W:** Jerry Siegel
3 ❑ Aug 1938 Cover: 0.10 **NM** value: **16500.00**
• **CGC:** 5 graded, best 6.0
🕮 Superman Battles Death Underground
4 ❑ Sep 1938 Cover: 0.10 **NM** value: **8400.00**
• **CGC:** 7 graded, best 9.0
🕮 Superman, Gridiron Hero
5 ❑ Oct 1938 Cover: 0.10 **NM** value: **8400.00**
• **CGC:** 6 graded, best 6.5
🕮 The Big Scoop
6 ❑ Nov 1938 Cover: 0.10 **NM** value: **8700.00**
• **CGC:** 7 graded, best 7.0
🕮 The Man Who Sold Superman ★ 1st Appearance of Jimmy Olsen.
7 ❑ Dec 1938 Cover: 0.10 **NM** value: **13100.00**
• **CGC:** 3 graded, best 7.0
Superman cover. 🕮 Superman Joins the Circus
8 ❑ Jan 1939 Cover: 0.10 **NM** value: **6200.00**
• **CGC:** 1 graded, best 6.5
🕮 Superman in the Slums
9 ❑ Feb 1939 Cover: 0.10 **NM** value: **6200.00**
• **CGC:** 2 graded, best 3.5
🕮 Wanted: Superman!
10 ❑ Mar 1939 Cover: 0.10 **NM** value: **7800.00**
• **CGC:** 4 graded, best 7.0
Superman cover. 🕮 Superman Goes to Prison
11 ❑ Apr 1939 Cover: 0.10 **NM** value: **3850.00**
• **CGC:** 2 graded, best 5.5
🕮 Superman and the "Black Gold" Swindle
12 ❑ May 1939 Cover: 0.10 **NM** value: **3850.00**
• **CGC:** 1 graded, best 5.0
🕮 Superman Declares War on Reckless Drivers
13 ❑ Jun 1939 Cover: 0.10 **NM** value: **5800.00**
• **CGC:** 5 graded, best 7.0
Superman cover (stopping train). 🕮 Superman vs. the Cab Protective League
14 ❑ Jul 1939 Cover: 0.10 **NM** value: **3600.00**
• **CGC:** 3 graded, best 4.5
🕮 Superman Meets the Ultra-Humanite
15 ❑ Aug 1939 Cover: 0.10 **NM** value: **5000.00**
• **CGC:** 9 graded, best 7.0
Superman cover. 🕮 Superman on the High Seas
16 ❑ Sep 1939 Cover: 0.10 **NM** value: **2850.00**
• **CGC:** 2 graded, best 6.5
🕮 Superman and the Numbers Racket
17 ❑ Oct 1939 Cover: 0.10 **NM** value: **4100.00**
• **CGC:** 5 graded, best 7.0
Superman cover. 🕮 The Return of the Ultra-Humanite
18 ❑ Nov 1939 Cover: 0.10 **NM** value: **2750.00**
• **CGC:** 5 graded, best 9.0
🕮 Superman's Super-Campaign
19 ❑ Dec 1939 Cover: 0.10 **NM** value: **3800.00**
• **CGC:** 4 graded, best 9.0
Superman cover. 🕮 Superman and the Purple Plague
20 ❑ Jan 1940 Cover: 0.10 **NM** value: **3600.00**
• **CGC:** 4 graded, best 8.0
🕮 Superman and the Screen Sirens
21 ❑ Feb 1940 Cover: 0.10 **NM** value: **2350.00**
• **CGC:** 8 graded, best 8.5
🕮 Untitled Superman Story
22 ❑ Mar 1940 Cover: 0.10 **NM** value: **2350.00**
• **CGC:** 6 graded, best 9.2
🕮 Untitled Superman Story
23 ❑ Apr 1940 Cover: 0.10 **NM** value: **7000.00**
• **CGC:** 10 graded, best 7.5
🕮 Untitled Superman Story ★ 1st Appearance of Lex Luthor.
24 ❑ May 1940 Cover: 0.10 **NM** value: **2200.00**
• **CGC:** 4 graded, best 8.5
🕮 Untitled Superman Story
25 ❑ Jun 1940 Cover: 0.10 **NM** value: **2200.00**
• **CGC:** 4 graded, best 9.0
🕮 Untitled Superman Story
26 ❑ Jul 1940 Cover: 0.10 **NM** value: **1925.00**
• **CGC:** 8 graded, best 8.5
🕮 Untitled Superman Story
27 ❑ Aug 1940 Cover: 0.10 **NM** value: **1625.00**
• **CGC:** 8 graded, best 9.0
🕮 Untitled Superman Story
28 ❑ Sep 1940 Cover: 0.10 **NM** value: **1625.00**
• **CGC:** 7 graded, best 7.5
🕮 Untitled Superman Story
29 ❑ Oct 1940 Cover: 0.10 **NM** value: **1625.00**
• **CGC:** 5 graded, best 6.0
🕮 Untitled Superman Story
30 ❑ Nov 1940 Cover: 0.10 **NM** value: **1625.00**
• **CGC:** 8 graded, best 9.2
🕮 Untitled Superman Story
31 ❑ Dec 1940 Cover: 0.10 **NM** value: **1200.00**
• **CGC:** 3 graded, best 8.0
🕮 Untitled Superman Story
32 ❑ Jan 1941 Cover: 0.10 **NM** value: **1200.00**
• **CGC:** 5 graded, best 7.5
🕮 Untitled Superman Story ★ 1st Appearance of Krypto Ray Gun.
33 ❑ Feb 1941 Cover: 0.10 **NM** value: **1200.00**
• **CGC:** 5 graded, best 5.0
🕮 Untitled Superman Story ★ Origin of Mister America. ★ 1st Appearance of Mister America.
34 ❑ Mar 1941 Cover: 0.10 **NM** value: **1100.00**
• **CGC:** 7 graded, best 9.2
🕮 Untitled Superman Story
35 ❑ Apr 1941 Cover: 0.10 **NM** value: **1100.00**
• **CGC:** 7 graded, best 9.2
🕮 Untitled Superman Story
36 ❑ May 1941 Cover: 0.10 **NM** value: **1100.00**
• **CGC:** 5 graded, best 9.0
🕮 Untitled Superman Story
37 ❑ Jun 1941 Cover: 0.10 **NM** value: **1100.00**
• **CGC:** 4 graded, best 9.0
🕮 Untitled Superman Story ★ 1st Appearance of Congo Bill.
38 ❑ Jul 1941 Cover: 0.10 **NM** value: **1100.00**
• **CGC:** 3 graded, best 9.0
🕮 Untitled Superman Story
39 ❑ Aug 1941 Cover: 0.10 **NM** value: **1100.00**
• **CGC:** 3 graded, best 7.5
🕮 Untitled Superman Story
40 ❑ Sep 1941 Cover: 0.10 **NM** value: **1100.00**
• **CGC:** 4 graded, best 7.5
🕮 Untitled Superman Story
41 ❑ Oct 1941 Cover: 0.10 **NM** value: **1000.00**
• **CGC:** 4 graded, best 9.6
🕮 Untitled Superman Story
42 ❑ Nov 1941 Cover: 0.10 **NM** value: **1500.00**
• **CGC:** 5 graded, best 8.5
🕮 Untitled Superman Story ★ Origin of Vigilante I (Greg Saunders). ★ 1st Appearance of Vigilante I (Greg Saunders).
43 ❑ Dec 1941 Cover: 0.10 **NM** value: **925.00**
• **CGC:** 4 graded, best 9.0
🕮 Untitled Superman Story
44 ❑ Jan 1942 Cover: 0.10 **NM** value: **925.00**
• **CGC:** 5 graded, best 9.0
🕮 Untitled Superman Story

CGC-graded: Multiply prices above by **33 for 9.9 M • 16 for 9.8 NM/M • 7 for 9.6 NM+ • 5 for 9.4 NM • 2.5 for 9.2 NM- • 1.5 for 9.0 VF/NM**

45 ❑ Feb 1942 Cover: 0.10 **NM** value: **925.00**
• **CGC:** 4 graded, best 9.0
📖 Untitled Superman Story
46 ❑ Mar 1942 Cover: 0.10 **NM** value: **925.00**
• **CGC:** 4 graded, best 7.5
📖 Superman Does Battle with the Domino
47 ❑ Apr 1942 Cover: 0.10 **NM** value: **1250.00**
• **CGC:** 7 graded, best 9.0
1st Lex Luthor cover. 📖 The Startling Adventure of the "Power-stone" ★ Appearance of Lex Luthor.
48 ❑ May 1942 Cover: 0.10 **NM** value: **925.00**
• **CGC:** 3 graded, best 9.0
📖 Untitled Superman Story
49 ❑ Jun 1942 Cover: 0.10 **NM** value: **925.00**
• **CGC:** 4 graded, best 9.2
📖 The Wizard of Chance ★ 1st Appearance of Puzzler.
50 ❑ Jul 1942 Cover: 0.10 **NM** value: **925.00**
• **CGC:** 4 graded, best 9.2
📖 Untitled Superman Story
51 ❑ Aug 1942 Cover: 0.10 **NM** value: **925.00**
• **CGC:** 5 graded, best 9.2
📖 The Strange Story of the Prankster and the Foolproof Plot ★ 1st Appearance of Prankster.
52 ❑ Sep 1942 Cover: 0.10 **NM** value: **925.00**
• **CGC:** 2 graded, best 5.5
📖 Untitled Superman Story
53 ❑ Oct 1942 Cover: 0.10 **NM** value: **825.00**
• **CGC:** 3 graded, best 9.4
54 ❑ Nov 1942 Cover: 0.10 **NM** value: **690.00**
• **CGC:** 5 graded, best 9.6
55 ❑ Dec 1942 Cover: 0.10 **NM** value: **690.00**
• **CGC:** 5 graded, best 9.6
56 ❑ Jan 1943 Cover: 0.10 **NM** value: **690.00**
• **CGC:** 3 graded, best 8.0
57 ❑ Feb 1943 Cover: 0.10 **NM** value: **690.00**
• **CGC:** 3 graded, best 8.5
58 ❑ Mar 1943 Cover: 0.10 **NM** value: **690.00**
• **CGC:** 3 graded, best 9.4
59 ❑ Apr 1943 Cover: 0.10 **NM** value: **690.00**
• **CGC:** 5 graded, best 9.4
60 ❑ May 1943 Cover: 0.10 **NM** value: **690.00**
• **CGC:** 4 graded, best 8.0
61 ❑ Jun 1943 Cover: 0.10 **NM** value: **610.00**
• **CGC:** 2 graded, best 8.5
62 ❑ Jul 1943 Cover: 0.10 **NM** value: **610.00**
• **CGC:** 3 graded, best 9.0
63 ❑ Aug 1943 Cover: 0.10 **NM** value: **610.00**
• **CGC:** 4 graded, best 8.5
64 ❑ Sep 1943 Cover: 0.10 **NM** value: **750.00**
• **CGC:** 2 graded, best 9.4
★ 1st Appearance of Toyman.
65 ❑ Oct 1943 Cover: 0.10 **NM** value: **610.00**
• **CGC:** 2 graded, best 9.4
66 ❑ Nov 1943 Cover: 0.10 **NM** value: **610.00**
• **CGC:** 4 graded, best 9.2
67 ❑ Dec 1943 Cover: 0.10 **NM** value: **610.00**
• **CGC:** 3 graded, best 8.5
68 ❑ Jan 1944 Cover: 0.10 **NM** value: **610.00**
• **CGC:** 2 graded, best 9.4
69 ❑ Feb 1944 Cover: 0.10 **NM** value: **610.00**
• **CGC:** 1 graded, best 7.0
70 ❑ Mar 1944 Cover: 0.10 **NM** value: **610.00**
• **CGC:** 2 graded, best 9.6
71 ❑ Apr 1944 Cover: 0.10 **NM** value: **575.00**
• **CGC:** 4 graded, best 9.6
72 ❑ Apr 1944 Cover: 0.10 **NM** value: **575.00**
• **CGC:** 3 graded, best 9.0
73 ❑ Jun 1944 Cover: 0.10 **NM** value: **575.00**
• **CGC:** 5 graded, best 7.5
74 ❑ Jul 1944 Cover: 0.10 **NM** value: **575.00**
• **CGC:** 6 graded, best 9.6
75 ❑ Aug 1944 Cover: 0.10 **NM** value: **575.00**
• **CGC:** 3 graded, best 9.2
76 ❑ Sep 1944 Cover: 0.10 **NM** value: **575.00**
• **CGC:** 7 graded, best 9.6
77 ❑ Oct 1944 Cover: 0.10 **NM** value: **575.00**
• **CGC:** 3 graded, best 8.0
78 ❑ Nov 1944 Cover: 0.10 **NM** value: **575.00**
• **CGC:** 4 graded, best 9.6
79 ❑ Dec 1944 Cover: 0.10 **NM** value: **575.00**
• **CGC:** 6 graded, best 9.0
80 ❑ Jan 1945 Cover: 0.10 **NM** value: **925.00**
• **CGC:** 7 graded, best 9.4
★ 2nd Appearance of Mr. Mxyzptlk.
81 ❑ Feb 1945 Cover: 0.10 **NM** value: **575.00**
• **CGC:** 5 graded, best 9.6
82 ❑ Mar 1945 Cover: 0.10 **NM** value: **575.00**
• **CGC:** 3 graded, best 8.5
83 ❑ Mar 1945 Cover: 0.10 **NM** value: **575.00**
• **CGC:** 5 graded, best 8.5
★ 1st Appearance of Hocus & Pocus.
84 ❑ May 1945 Cover: 0.10 **NM** value: **575.00**
• **CGC:** 5 graded, best 9.2
85 ❑ Jun 1945 Cover: 0.10 **NM** value: **575.00**
• **CGC:** 4 graded, best 9.0
86 ❑ Jul 1945 Cover: 0.10 **NM** value: **575.00**
• **CGC:** 3 graded, best 7.0
87 ❑ Aug 1945 Cover: 0.10 **NM** value: **575.00**
• **CGC:** 5 graded, best 9.6
88 ❑ Sep 1945 Cover: 0.10 **NM** value: **575.00**
• **CGC:** 3 graded, best 9.4
89 ❑ Oct 1945 Cover: 0.10 **NM** value: **575.00**
• **CGC:** 4 graded, best 8.5
90 ❑ Nov 1945 Cover: 0.10 **NM** value: **575.00**
• **CGC:** 3 graded, best 5.5
91 ❑ Dec 1945 Cover: 0.10 **NM** value: **525.00**
• **CGC:** 4 graded, best 9.0
92 ❑ Jan 1946 Cover: 0.10 **NM** value: **525.00**
• **CGC:** 4 graded, best 9.4
93 ❑ Feb 1946 Cover: 0.10 **NM** value: **525.00**
• **CGC:** 3 graded, best 9.6
94 ❑ Mar 1946 Cover: 0.10 **NM** value: **525.00**
• **CGC:** 5 graded, best 9.6
95 ❑ Apr 1946 Cover: 0.10 **NM** value: **525.00**
• **CGC:** 8 graded, best 9.4
96 ❑ May 1946 Cover: 0.10 **NM** value: **525.00**
• **CGC:** 6 graded, best 9.4
97 ❑ Jun 1946 Cover: 0.10 **NM** value: **525.00**
• **CGC:** 2 graded, best 7.0
98 ❑ Jul 1946 Cover: 0.10 **NM** value: **525.00**
• **CGC:** 8 graded, best 9.8
99 ❑ Aug 1946 Cover: 0.10 **NM** value: **525.00**
• **CGC:** 9 graded, best 9.6
100 ❑ Sep 1946 Cover: 0.10 **NM** value: **1150.00**
• **CGC:** 6 graded, best 8.0
• 100th anniversary issue.
101 ❑ Oct 1946 Cover: 0.10 **NM** value: **700.00**
• **CGC:** 4 graded, best 9.0
Atom bomb cover.
102 ❑ Nov 1946 Cover: 0.10 **NM** value: **500.00**
• **CGC:** 2 graded, best 9.0
103 ❑ Dec 1946 Cover: 0.10 **NM** value: **500.00**
• **CGC:** 2 graded, best 7.5
104 ❑ Jan 1947 Cover: 0.10 **NM** value: **500.00**
• **CGC:** 3 graded, best 9.6
105 ❑ Feb 1947 Cover: 0.10 **NM** value: **500.00**
• **CGC:** 1 graded, best 2.5
106 ❑ Mar 1947 Cover: 0.10 **NM** value: **500.00**
• **CGC:** 3 graded, best 9.0
107 ❑ Apr 1947 Cover: 0.10 **NM** value: **500.00**
• **CGC:** 2 graded, best 7.5
108 ❑ May 1947 Cover: 0.10 **NM** value: **500.00**
• **CGC:** 4 graded, best 9.6
109 ❑ Jun 1947 Cover: 0.10 **NM** value: **500.00**
• **CGC:** 2 graded, best 9.6
110 ❑ Jul 1947 Cover: 0.10 **NM** value: **500.00**
• **CGC:** 3 graded, best 9.2
111 ❑ Aug 1947 Cover: 0.10 **NM** value: **500.00**
• **CGC:** 2 graded, best 9.4
112 ❑ Sep 1947 Cover: 0.10 **NM** value: **500.00**
• **CGC:** 8 graded, best 9.6
113 ❑ Oct 1947 Cover: 0.10 **NM** value: **500.00**
• **CGC:** 4 graded, best 9.4
114 ❑ Nov 1947 Cover: 0.10 **NM** value: **500.00**
• **CGC:** 1 graded, best 7.0
115 ❑ Dec 1947 Cover: 0.10 **NM** value: **500.00**
• **CGC:** 2 graded, best 9.8
116 ❑ Jan 1948 Cover: 0.10 **NM** value: **500.00**
• **CGC:** 4 graded, best 9.4
117 ❑ Feb 1948 Cover: 0.10 **NM** value: **500.00**
• **CGC:** 3 graded, best 8.0
118 ❑ Mar 1948 Cover: 0.10 **NM** value: **500.00**
• **CGC:** 4 graded, best 9.6
119 ❑ Apr 1948 Cover: 0.10 **NM** value: **500.00**
• **CGC:** 3 graded, best 9.4
120 ❑ May 1948 Cover: 0.10 **NM** value: **500.00**
• **CGC:** 4 graded, best 9.4
121 ❑ Jun 1948 Cover: 0.10 **NM** value: **500.00**
• **CGC:** 1 graded, best 3.5
122 ❑ Jul 1948 Cover: 0.10 **NM** value: **500.00**
• **CGC:** 2 graded, best 6.5
123 ❑ Aug 1948 Cover: 0.10 **NM** value: **500.00**
• **CGC:** 1 graded, best 4.5
124 ❑ Sep 1948 Cover: 0.10 **NM** value: **500.00**
• **CGC:** 2 graded, best 5.0
125 ❑ Oct 1948 Cover: 0.10 **NM** value: **500.00**
• **CGC:** 2 graded, best 4.5
126 ❑ Nov 1948 Cover: 0.10 **NM** value: **500.00**
• **CGC:** 2 graded, best 4.5
127 ❑ Dec 1948 Cover: 0.10 **NM** value: **600.00**
• **CGC:** 2 graded, best 3.5
• Superman on Truth or Consequences;Vigilante back-up;Tommy Tomorrow feature begins **A:** Joe Kubert
128 ❑ Jan 1949 Cover: 0.10 **NM** value: **500.00**
• **CGC:** 1 graded, best 5.0
129 ❑ Feb 1949 Cover: 0.10 **NM** value: **500.00**
• **CGC:** 1 graded, best 3.5
130 ❑ Mar 1949 Cover: 0.10 **NM** value: **500.00**
• **CGC:** 3 graded, best 9.6
131 ❑ Apr 1949 Cover: 0.10 **NM** value: **500.00**
• **CGC:** 2 graded, best 6.5
132 ❑ May 1949 Cover: 0.10 **NM** value: **500.00**
• **CGC:** 2 graded, best 5.5
133 ❑ Jun 1949 Cover: 0.10 **NM** value: **500.00**
• **CGC:** 2 graded, best 6.0
134 ❑ Jul 1949 Cover: 0.10 **NM** value: **500.00**
• **CGC:** 1 graded, best 7.5
135 ❑ Aug 1949 Cover: 0.10 **NM** value: **500.00**
• **CGC:** 2 graded, best 7.0
136 ❑ Sep 1949 Cover: 0.10 **NM** value: **500.00**
• **CGC:** 1 graded, best 4.5
137 ❑ Oct 1949 Cover: 0.10 **NM** value: **500.00**
• **CGC:** 1 graded, best 7.5
138 ❑ Nov 1949 Cover: 0.10 **NM** value: **500.00**
139 ❑ Dec 1949 Cover: 0.10 **NM** value: **500.00**
• **CGC:** 1 graded, best 5.0
140 ❑ Jan 1950 Cover: 0.10 **NM** value: **500.00**
• **CGC:** 2 graded, best 5.5
141 ❑ Feb 1950 Cover: 0.10 **NM** value: **500.00**
• **CGC:** 2 graded, best 5.0
142 ❑ Mar 1950 Cover: 0.10 **NM** value: **500.00**
• **CGC:** 1 graded, best 2.0
143 ❑ Apr 1950 Cover: 0.10 **NM** value: **500.00**
• **CGC:** 1 graded, best 5.5
144 ❑ May 1950 Cover: 0.10 **NM** value: **500.00**
• **CGC:** 1 graded, best 7.0
145 ❑ Jun 1950 Cover: 0.10 **NM** value: **500.00**
• **CGC:** 2 graded, best 7.5
146 ❑ Jul 1950 Cover: 0.10 **NM** value: **500.00**
• **CGC:** 1 graded, best 9.4
147 ❑ Aug 1950 Cover: 0.10 **NM** value: **500.00**
• **CGC:** 1 graded, best 4.0
148 ❑ Sep 1950 Cover: 0.10 **NM** value: **500.00**
• **CGC:** 1 graded, best 4.5
149 ❑ Oct 1950 Cover: 0.10 **NM** value: **500.00**
150 ❑ Nov 1950 Cover: 0.10 **NM** value: **500.00**
• **CGC:** 4 graded, best 9.2
151 ❑ Dec 1950 Cover: 0.10 **NM** value: **450.00**
• **CGC:** 3 graded, best 9.0
152 ❑ Jan 1951 Cover: 0.10 **NM** value: **450.00**
• **CGC:** 1 graded, best 7.0
153 ❑ Feb 1951 Cover: 0.10 **NM** value: **450.00**
• **CGC:** 2 graded, best 8.0
154 ❑ Mar 1951 Cover: 0.10 **NM** value: **450.00**
• **CGC:** 1 graded, best 2.5
155 ❑ Apr 1951 Cover: 0.10 **NM** value: **450.00**
• **CGC:** 1 graded, best 9.0
156 ❑ May 1951 Cover: 0.10 **NM** value: **450.00**
• **CGC:** 2 graded, best 8.0
157 ❑ Jun 1951 Cover: 0.10 **NM** value: **450.00**
• **CGC:** 1 graded, best 4.5
158 ❑ Jul 1951 Cover: 0.10 **NM** value: **750.00**
• **CGC:** 3 graded, best 8.5
★ Origin of Superman.
159 ❑ Aug 1951 Cover: 0.10 **NM** value: **450.00**
• **CGC:** 4 graded, best 8.0
160 ❑ Sep 1951 Cover: 0.10 **NM** value: **450.00**
161 ❑ Oct 1951 Cover: 0.10 **NM** value: **450.00**
162 ❑ Nov 1951 Cover: 0.10 **NM** value: **385.00**
• **CGC:** 2 graded, best 7.0
163 ❑ Dec 1951 Cover: 0.10 **NM** value: **385.00**
• **CGC:** 2 graded, best 8.0
164 ❑ Jan 1952 Cover: 0.10 **NM** value: **385.00**
• **CGC:** 1 graded, best 5.0
165 ❑ Feb 1952 Cover: 0.10 **NM** value: **385.00**
166 ❑ Mar 1952 Cover: 0.10 **NM** value: **385.00**
• **CGC:** 2 graded, best 7.0
167 ❑ Apr 1952 Cover: 0.10 **NM** value: **385.00**
• **CGC:** 1 graded, best 4.0
168 ❑ May 1952 Cover: 0.10 **NM** value: **385.00**
169 ❑ Jun 1952 Cover: 0.10 **NM** value: **385.00**
• **CGC:** 1 graded, best 3.5
170 ❑ Jul 1952 Cover: 0.10 **NM** value: **385.00**
171 ❑ Aug 1952 Cover: 0.10 **NM** value: **385.00**
172 ❑ Sep 1952 Cover: 0.10 **NM** value: **385.00**
• **CGC:** 2 graded, best 4.5
173 ❑ Oct 1952 Cover: 0.10 **NM** value: **385.00**
174 ❑ Nov 1952 Cover: 0.10 **NM** value: **385.00**
175 ❑ Dec 1952 Cover: 0.10 **NM** value: **385.00**
• **CGC:** 1 graded, best 7.5
176 ❑ Jan 1953 Cover: 0.10 **NM** value: **385.00**
• **CGC:** 1 graded, best 3.0
177 ❑ Feb 1953 Cover: 0.10 **NM** value: **385.00**
178 ❑ Mar 1953 Cover: 0.10 **NM** value: **385.00**
179 ❑ Apr 1953 Cover: 0.10 **NM** value: **385.00**
• **CGC:** 1 graded, best 2.5
180 ❑ May 1953 Cover: 0.10 **NM** value: **385.00**
• **CGC:** 1 graded, best 3.5
181 ❑ Jun 1953 Cover: 0.10 **NM** value: **340.00**
• **CGC:** 1 graded, best 2.5
182 ❑ Jul 1953 Cover: 0.10 **NM** value: **340.00**
• **CGC:** 2 graded, best 7.5
183 ❑ Aug 1953 Cover: 0.10 **NM** value: **340.00**
184 ❑ Sep 1953 Cover: 0.10 **NM** value: **340.00**
• **CGC:** 1 graded, best 4.5
185 ❑ Oct 1953 Cover: 0.10 **NM** value: **340.00**
• **CGC:** 1 graded, best 4.0
186 ❑ Nov 1953 Cover: 0.10 **NM** value: **340.00**
• **CGC:** 1 graded, best 2.5
187 ❑ Dec 1953 Cover: 0.10 **NM** value: **340.00**
• **CGC:** 1 graded, best 7.5
188 ❑ Jan 1954 Cover: 0.10 **NM** value: **340.00**
• **CGC:** 1 graded, best 5.0
189 ❑ Feb 1954 Cover: 0.10 **NM** value: **340.00**
• **CGC:** 1 graded, best 4.0
190 ❑ Mar 1954 Cover: 0.10 **NM** value: **340.00**
• **CGC:** 1 graded, best 4.0
191 ❑ Apr 1954 Cover: 0.10 **NM** value: **340.00**
192 ❑ May 1954 Cover: 0.10 **NM** value: **340.00**
• **CGC:** 1 graded, best 4.0
193 ❑ Jun 1954 Cover: 0.10 **NM** value: **340.00**
• **CGC:** 1 graded, best 4.5
194 ❑ Jul 1954 Cover: 0.10 **NM** value: **340.00**
• **CGC:** 1 graded, best 4.5
195 ❑ Aug 1954 Cover: 0.10 **NM** value: **340.00**
196 ❑ Sep 1954 Cover: 0.10 **NM** value: **340.00**
• **CGC:** 1 graded, best 7.5
197 ❑ Oct 1954 Cover: 0.10 **NM** value: **340.00**
• **CGC:** 2 graded, best 6.5
198 ❑ Nov 1954 Cover: 0.10 **NM** value: **340.00**
199 ❑ Dec 1954 Cover: 0.10 **NM** value: **340.00**
• **CGC:** 1 graded, best 7.5
200 ❑ Jan 1955 Cover: 0.10 **NM** value: **340.00**
• **CGC:** 2 graded, best 7.0
201 ❑ Feb 1955 Cover: 0.10 **NM** value: **340.00**
• **CGC:** 1 graded, best 8.0
202 ❑ Mar 1955 Cover: 0.10 **NM** value: **290.00**
• **CGC:** 1 graded, best 4.5
203 ❑ Apr 1955 Cover: 0.10 **NM** value: **290.00**
• **CGC:** 1 graded, best 4.0
204 ❑ May 1955 Cover: 0.10 **NM** value: **290.00**
205 ❑ Jun 1955 Cover: 0.10 **NM** value: **290.00**
• **CGC:** 1 graded, best 6.5
206 ❑ Jul 1955 Cover: 0.10 **NM** value: **290.00**
• **CGC:** 1 graded, best 7.0
207 ❑ Aug 1955 Cover: 0.10 **NM** value: **290.00**

Other grades: Multiply prices above by **1.5 for Mint • 2/3 for Very Fine • 1/3 for Fine • 1/5 for Very Good • 1/8 for Good**

208 ❑ Sep 1955 Cover: 0.10 **NM** value: **290.00**
• **CGC:** 1 graded, best 4.5
209 ❑ Oct 1955 Cover: 0.10 **NM** value: **290.00**
• **CGC:** 2 graded, best 7.5
210 ❑ Nov 1955 Cover: 0.10 **NM** value: **290.00**
211 ❑ Dec 1955 Cover: 0.10 **NM** value: **290.00**
212 ❑ Jan 1956 Cover: 0.10 **NM** value: **290.00**
• **CGC:** 1 graded, best 7.5
213 ❑ Feb 1956 Cover: 0.10 **NM** value: **290.00**
• **CGC:** 1 graded, best 5.5
214 ❑ Mar 1956 Cover: 0.10 **NM** value: **290.00**
• **CGC:** 3 graded, best 7.5
215 ❑ Apr 1956 Cover: 0.10 **NM** value: **290.00**
• **CGC:** 2 graded, best 8.0
216 ❑ May 1956 Cover: 0.10 **NM** value: **290.00**
217 ❑ Jun 1956 Cover: 0.10 **NM** value: **290.00**
• **CGC:** 1 graded, best 6.0
218 ❑ Jul 1956 Cover: 0.10 **NM** value: **290.00**
• **CGC:** 1 graded, best 8.0
219 ❑ Aug 1956 Cover: 0.10 **NM** value: **290.00**
• **CGC:** 2 graded, best 8.5
220 ❑ Sep 1956 Cover: 0.10 **NM** value: **290.00**
• **CGC:** 2 graded, best 8.0
221 ❑ Oct 1956 Cover: 0.10 **NM** value: **240.00**
222 ❑ Nov 1956 Cover: 0.10 **NM** value: **240.00**
• **CGC:** 1 graded, best 8.5
223 ❑ Dec 1956 Cover: 0.10 **NM** value: **240.00**
• **CGC:** 2 graded, best 5.5
224 ❑ Jan 1957 Cover: 0.10 **NM** value: **240.00**
• **CGC:** 1 graded, best 4.5
225 ❑ Feb 1957 Cover: 0.10 **NM** value: **240.00**
• **CGC:** 5 graded, best 7.5
226 ❑ Mar 1957 Cover: 0.10 **NM** value: **240.00**
• **CGC:** 3 graded, best 7.5
227 ❑ Apr 1957 Cover: 0.10 **NM** value: **240.00**
• **CGC:** 4 graded, best 8.5
228 ❑ May 1957 Cover: 0.10 **NM** value: **240.00**
• **CGC:** 2 graded, best 7.0
229 ❑ Jun 1957 Cover: 0.10 **NM** value: **240.00**
• **CGC:** 2 graded, best 7.5
230 ❑ Jul 1957 Cover: 0.10 **NM** value: **240.00**
• **CGC:** 1 graded, best 8.5
231 ❑ Aug 1957 Cover: 0.10 **NM** value: **240.00**
• **CGC:** 1 graded, best 5.5
232 ❑ Sep 1957 Cover: 0.10 **NM** value: **240.00**
• **CGC:** 3 graded, best 7.5
233 ❑ Oct 1957 Cover: 0.10 **NM** value: **240.00**
• **CGC:** 2 graded, best 6.5
234 ❑ Nov 1957 Cover: 0.10 **NM** value: **240.00**
• **CGC:** 1 graded, best 8.5
235 ❑ Dec 1957 Cover: 0.10 **NM** value: **240.00**
236 ❑ Jan 1958 Cover: 0.10 **NM** value: **240.00**
237 ❑ Feb 1958 Cover: 0.10 **NM** value: **240.00**
238 ❑ Mar 1958 Cover: 0.10 **NM** value: **240.00**
239 ❑ Apr 1958 Cover: 0.10 **NM** value: **240.00**
• **CGC:** 1 graded, best 4.0
240 ❑ May 1958 Cover: 0.10 **NM** value: **240.00**
• **CGC:** 2 graded, best 9.2
241 ❑ Jun 1958 Cover: 0.10 **NM** value: **250.00**
★ 1st Appearance of Fortress of Solitude.
242 ❑ Jul 1958 Cover: 0.10 **NM** value: **1250.00**
• **CGC:** 8 graded, best 5.0
★ Origin of Brainiac. ★ 1st Appearance of Kandor, Brainiac.
243 ❑ Aug 1958 Cover: 0.10 **NM** value: **185.00**
• **CGC:** 2 graded, best 8.0
244 ❑ Sep 1958 Cover: 0.10 **NM** value: **185.00**
• **CGC:** 2 graded, best 8.0
A: Curt Swan
245 ❑ Oct 1958 Cover: 0.10 **NM** value: **185.00**
• **CGC:** 1 graded, best 5.0
246 ❑ Nov 1958 Cover: 0.10 **NM** value: **185.00**
• **CGC:** 3 graded, best 7.5
247 ❑ Dec 1958 Cover: 0.10 **NM** value: **185.00**
• **CGC:** 1 graded, best 4.0
248 ❑ Jan 1959 Cover: 0.10 **NM** value: **185.00**
• **CGC:** 1 graded, best 3.0
★ 1st Appearance of Congorilla.
249 ❑ Feb 1959 Cover: 0.10 **NM** value: **185.00**
• **CGC:** 1 graded, best 5.0
250 ❑ Mar 1959 Cover: 0.10 **NM** value: **185.00**
• **CGC:** 2 graded, best 7.5
251 ❑ Apr 1959 Cover: 0.10 **NM** value: **185.00**
• **CGC:** 2 graded, best 7.5
• Tommy Tomorrow;Legion
252 ❑ May 1959 Cover: 0.10 **NM** value: **1200.00**
• **CGC:** 24 graded, best 9.0
📖 The Supergirl From Krypton! • Supergirl ★ Origin of Supergirl. ★ 1st Appearance of Anti-Kryptonite, Supergirl.
253 ❑ Jun 1959 Cover: 0.10 **NM** value: **375.00**
• **CGC:** 1 graded, best 7.0
📖 The Secret of the Super-Orphan! • Supergirl ★ 2nd Appearance of Supergirl.
254 ❑ Jul 1959 Cover: 0.10 **NM** value: **275.00**
• **CGC:** 4 graded, best 9.2
📖 Supergirl's Foster Parents! ★ Appearance of Bizarro.
255 ❑ Aug 1959 Cover: 0.10 **NM** value: **225.00**
• **CGC:** 4 graded, best 9.0
📖 Supergirl Visits the 21st Century! ★ 1st Appearance of Bizarro Lois Lane.
256 ❑ Sep 1959 Cover: 0.10 **NM** value: **100.00**
• **CGC:** 2 graded, best 7.5
📖 The Great Supergirl Mirage!
257 ❑ Oct 1959 Cover: 0.10 **NM** value: **100.00**
• **CGC:** 2 graded, best 9.0
📖 The Three Magic Wishes!
258 ❑ Nov 1959 Cover: 0.10 **NM** value: **100.00**
• **CGC:** 1 graded, best 5.0
📖 Supergirl's Farewell to Earth!
259 ❑ Dec 1959 Cover: 0.10 **NM** value: **100.00**
• **CGC:** 1 graded, best 4.0
📖 The Cave-Girl of Steel!
260 ❑ Jan 1960 Cover: 0.10 **NM** value: **100.00**
Circ: Statement: **458,000** • **CGC:** 2 graded, best 8.0
📖 Mighty Maid!
261 ❑ Feb 1960 Cover: 0.10 **NM** value: **100.00**
Circ: Statement: **458,000** • **CGC:** 2 graded, best 7.0
📖 Supergirl's Super-Pet! ★ Origin of Streaky the Supercat. ★ 1st Appearance of X-Kryptonite, Streaky the Supercat.
262 ❑ Mar 1960 Cover: 0.10 **NM** value: **90.00**
Circ: Statement: **458,000**
📖 Supergirl's Greatest Victory!
263 ❑ Apr 1960 Cover: 0.10 **NM** value: **100.00**
Circ: Statement: **458,000** • **CGC:** 2 graded, best 9.0
📖 Supergirl's Darkest Day! ★ Origin of Bizarro World.
264 ❑ May 1960 Cover: 0.10 **NM** value: **80.00**
Circ: Statement: **458,000** • **CGC:** 2 graded, best 4.5
📖 Supergirl Gets Adopted!
265 ❑ Jun 1960 Cover: 0.10 **NM** value: **80.00**
Circ: Statement: **458,000** • **CGC:** 1 graded, best 9.0
📖 The Day Supergirl Revealed Itself! **A:** Curt Swan
266 ❑ Jul 1960 Cover: 0.10 **NM** value: **80.00**
Circ: Statement: **458,000** • **CGC:** 3 graded, best 9.0
📖 The World's Mightiest Cat!
267 ❑ Aug 1960 Cover: 0.10 **NM** value: **240.00**
Circ: Statement: **458,000** • **CGC:** 7 graded, best 8.0
📖 The Three Super-Heroes! ★ 1st Appearance of Chameleon Boy, Colossal Boy, Invisible Kid I (Lyle Norg).
268 ❑ Sep 1960 Cover: 0.10 **NM** value: **80.00**
Circ: Statement: **458,000** • **CGC:** 3 graded, best 8.5
📖 The Mystery Supergirl!
269 ❑ Oct 1960 Cover: 0.10 **NM** value: **80.00**
Circ: Statement: **458,000** • **CGC:** 2 graded, best 7.5
270 ❑ Nov 1960 Cover: 0.10 **NM** value: **80.00**
Circ: Statement: **458,000** • **CGC:** 1 graded, best 9.2
271 ❑ Dec 1960 Cover: 0.10 **NM** value: **65.00**
Circ: Statement: **458,000** • **CGC:** 2 graded, best 9.4
272 ❑ Jan 1961 Cover: 0.10 **NM** value: **65.00**
Circ: Statement: **485,000** • **CGC:** 3 graded, best 9.2
273 ❑ Feb 1961 Cover: 0.10 **NM** value: **65.00**
Circ: Statement: **485,000** • **CGC:** 1 graded, best 9.4
📖 The World of Mr. Mxyzptlk!; Ollie; Little Pete; The Supergirl of Two Worlds!; Jerry the Jitterbug; Pick a New Hair Style for Linda (Supergirl) Lee!; Our American Heritage • Has 1960 Statement; avg total paid circ 458,000 ★ Versus Mxyzptlk.
274 ❑ Mar 1961 Cover: 0.10 **NM** value: **65.00**
Circ: Statement: **485,000** • **CGC:** 6 graded, best 9.0
275 ❑ Apr 1961 Cover: 0.10 **NM** value: **65.00**
Circ: Statement: **485,000** • **CGC:** 3 graded, best 9.2
276 ❑ May 1961 Cover: 0.10 **NM** value: **125.00**
Circ: Statement: **485,000** • **CGC:** 1 graded, best 7.5
📖 Supergirl's Three Super Girl Friends • Triplicate Girl, Phantom Girl, Brainiac 5, Shrinking Violet, Bouncing Boy joins team
277 ❑ Jun 1961 Cover: 0.10 **NM** value: **60.00**
Circ: Statement: **485,000** • **CGC:** 3 graded, best 9.2
278 ❑ Jul 1961 Cover: 0.10 **NM** value: **60.00**
Circ: Statement: **485,000** • **CGC:** 2 graded, best 9.2
279 ❑ Aug 1961 Cover: 0.10 **NM** value: **60.00**
Circ: Statement: **485,000** • **CGC:** 4 graded, best 8.5
280 ❑ Sep 1961 Cover: 0.10 **NM** value: **60.00**
Circ: Statement: **485,000** • **CGC:** 4 graded, best 9.2
281 ❑ Oct 1961 Cover: 0.10 **NM** value: **60.00**
Circ: Statement: **485,000** • **CGC:** 3 graded, best 9.4
282 ❑ Nov 1961 Cover: 0.10 **NM** value: **60.00**
Circ: Statement: **485,000** • **CGC:** 1 graded, best 4.0
283 ❑ Dec 1961 Cover: 0.12 **NM** value: **60.00**
Circ: Statement: **485,000** • **CGC:** 1 graded, best 9.2
• Legion of Super-Villains
284 ❑ Jan 1962 Cover: 0.12 **NM** value: **60.00**
Circ: Statement: **435,000** • **CGC:** 1 graded, best 9.4
• Mon-El
285 ❑ Feb 1962 Cover: 0.12 **NM** value: **100.00**
Circ: Statement: **435,000** • **CGC:** 5 graded, best 9.2
• Supergirl goes public **A:** Neal Adams ★ Appearance of Legion of Super-Heroes.
286 ❑ Mar 1962 Cover: 0.12 **NM** value: **55.00**
Circ: Statement: **435,000** • **CGC:** 2 graded, best 9.2
• Legion of Super-Villains; Has 1961 Statement; avg total paid circ 485,000
287 ❑ Apr 1962 Cover: 0.12 **NM** value: **55.00**
Circ: Statement: **435,000** • **CGC:** 2 graded, best 9.0
📖 Supergirl's Greatest Challenge! ★ Appearance of Legion of Super-Heroes.
288 ❑ May 1962 Cover: 0.12 **NM** value: **52.00**
Circ: Statement: **435,000** • **CGC:** 1 graded, best 9.4
• Mon-El
289 ❑ Jun 1962 Cover: 0.12 **NM** value: **52.00**
Circ: Statement: **435,000** • **CGC:** 3 graded, best 9.4
📖 Superman's Super-Courtship! ★ Appearance of Legion of Super-Heroes.
290 ❑ Jul 1962 Cover: 0.12 **NM** value: **52.00**
Circ: Statement: **435,000** • **CGC:** 1 graded, best 9.4
A: Curt Swan ★ Appearance of Legion of Super-Heroes.
291 ❑ Aug 1962 Cover: 0.12 **NM** value: **30.00**
Circ: Statement: **435,000** • **CGC:** 1 graded, best 8.5
A: Neal Adams
292 ❑ Sep 1962 Cover: 0.12 **NM** value: **30.00**
Circ: Statement: **435,000** • **CGC:** 3 graded, best 9.4
★ Appearance of Superhorse (Comet).
293 ❑ Oct 1962 Cover: 0.12 **NM** value: **35.00**
Circ: Statement: **435,000** • **CGC:** 6 graded, best 8.5
📖 The Feud Between Superman and Clark Kent!; The Secret Origin of Supergirl's Super-Horse! ★ Origin of Superhorse (Comet).
294 ❑ Nov 1962 Cover: 0.12 **NM** value: **30.00**
Circ: Statement: **435,000** • **CGC:** 2 graded, best 9.0
A: Curt Swan
295 ❑ Dec 1962 Cover: 0.12 **NM** value: **30.00**
Circ: Statement: **435,000**
296 ❑ Jan 1963 Cover: 0.12 **NM** value: **30.00**
• **CGC:** 2 graded, best 9.4
A: Curt Swan
297 ❑ Feb 1963 Cover: 0.12 **NM** value: **30.00**
• **CGC:** 1 graded, best 8.0
298 ❑ Mar 1963 Cover: 0.12 **NM** value: **30.00**
• **CGC:** 3 graded, best 9.0
A: Curt Swan
299 ❑ Apr 1963 Cover: 0.12 **NM** value: **30.00**
• **CGC:** 2 graded, best 9.0
300 ❑ May 1963 Cover: 0.12 **NM** value: **48.00**
• **CGC:** 3 graded, best 9.2
• 300th anniversary issue.
301 ❑ Jun 1963 Cover: 0.12 **NM** value: **25.00**
📖 The Trial of Superman
302 ❑ Jul 1963 Cover: 0.12 **NM** value: **25.00**
• **CGC:** 2 graded, best 9.4
A: Curt Swan
303 ❑ Aug 1963 Cover: 0.12 **NM** value: **25.00**
📖 The Monster from Krypton!; Supergirl's Big Brother! **A:** Curt Swan
304 ❑ Sep 1963 Cover: 0.12 **NM** value: **25.00**
📖 The Interplanetary Olympics!; The Maid of Menace! **A:** Curt Swan ★ 1st Appearance of Black Flame.
305 ❑ Oct 1963 Cover: 0.12 **NM** value: **18.00**
306 ❑ Nov 1963 Cover: 0.12 **NM** value: **18.00**
307 ❑ Dec 1963 Cover: 0.12 **NM** value: **18.00**
308 ❑ Jan 1964 Cover: 0.12 **NM** value: **18.00**
Circ: Statement: **518,026**
309 ❑ Feb 1964 Cover: 0.12 **NM** value: **18.00**
Circ: Statement: **518,026** • **CGC:** 1 graded, best 8.0
• Legion; Has 1963 Statement, filed 10/1/63; no circ figures published **A:** Neal Adams ★ Appearance of Supergirl's parents.
310 ❑ Mar 1964 Cover: 0.12 **NM** value: **24.00**
Circ: Statement: **518,026** • **CGC:** 1 graded, best 9.0
★ 1st Appearance of Jewel Kryptonite.
311 ❑ Apr 1964 Cover: 0.12 **NM** value: **16.00**
Circ: Statement: **518,026**
312 ❑ May 1964 Cover: 0.12 **NM** value: **16.00**
Circ: Statement: **518,026**
313 ❑ Jun 1964 Cover: 0.12 **NM** value: **16.00**
Circ: Statement: **518,026** • **CGC:** 1 graded, best 5.5
★ Appearance of Batman.
314 ❑ Jul 1964 Cover: 0.12 **NM** value: **16.00**
Circ: Statement: **518,026** • **CGC:** 2 graded, best 9.0
★ Appearance of Batman.
315 ❑ Aug 1964 Cover: 0.12 **NM** value: **16.00**
Circ: Statement: **518,026** • **CGC:** 2 graded, best 9.2
316 ❑ Sep 1964 Cover: 0.12 **NM** value: **16.00**
Circ: Statement: **518,026**
317 ❑ Oct 1964 Cover: 0.12 **NM** value: **16.00**
Circ: Statement: **518,026**
318 ❑ Nov 1964 Cover: 0.12 **NM** value: **16.00**
Circ: Statement: **518,026**
319 ❑ Dec 1964 Cover: 0.12 **NM** value: **16.00**
Circ: Statement: **518,026** • **CGC:** 2 graded, best 9.4
320 ❑ Jan 1965 Cover: 0.12 **NM** value: **16.00**
Circ: Statement: **525,254** • **CGC:** 2 graded, best 9.2
321 ❑ Feb 1965 Cover: 0.12 **NM** value: **16.00**
Circ: Statement: **525,254**
A: Curt Swan
322 ❑ Mar 1965 Cover: 0.12 **NM** value: **16.00**
Circ: Statement: **525,254**
323 ❑ Apr 1965 Cover: 0.12 **NM** value: **16.00**
Circ: Statement: **525,254** • **CGC:** 2 graded, best 9.0
324 ❑ May 1965 Cover: 0.12 **NM** value: **16.00**
Circ: Statement: **525,254** • **CGC:** 2 graded, best 9.2
325 ❑ Jun 1965 Cover: 0.12 **NM** value: **16.00**
Circ: Statement: **525,254** • **CGC:** 1 graded, best 9.0
326 ❑ Jul 1965 Cover: 0.12 **NM** value: **16.00**
Circ: Statement: **525,254** • **CGC:** 3 graded, best 9.4
327 ❑ Aug 1965 Cover: 0.12 **NM** value: **16.00**
Circ: Statement: **525,254** • **CGC:** 4 graded, best 9.0
📖 The Three Generations of Superman!; Supergirl... Fugitive From Justice!; How Superman Has Been Honored (text) • Imaginary Superman story; Has 1964 Statement, filed 10/1/64; avg print run 716,000; avg sales 513,000; avg subs 5,026; avg total paid 518,026; samples 387; max existent 518,413; 28% of run returned
328 ❑ Sep 1965 Cover: 0.12 **NM** value: **16.00**
Circ: Statement: **525,254** • **CGC:** 1 graded, best 9.4
📖 Superman's Hands of Doom!; The Ordeals of Dimension Z
329 ❑ Oct 1965 Cover: 0.12 **NM** value: **16.00**
Circ: Statement: **525,254** • **CGC:** 1 graded, best 9.2
330 ❑ Nov 1965 Cover: 0.12 **NM** value: **16.00**
Circ: Statement: **525,254** • **CGC:** 1 graded, best 9.4
331 ❑ Dec 1965 Cover: 0.12 **NM** value: **16.00**
Circ: Statement: **525,254** • **CGC:** 2 graded, best 9.2
332 ❑ Jan 1966 Cover: 0.12 **NM** value: **16.00**
Circ: Statement: **491,135** • **CGC:** 1 graded, best 9.2
📖 The Super-Vengeance of Lex Luthor!; How Superwoman Trained Superboy! • Imaginary Superwoman Story
333 ❑ Feb 1966 Cover: 0.12 **NM** value: **16.00**
Circ: Statement: **491,135**
📖 Superman's Super-Boo-Boos!; The Duel Between Superwoman and Superboy! • Imaginary Superwoman Story
334 ❑ Mar 1966 Cover: 0.25 **NM** value: **36.00**
Circ: Statement: **491,135**
• Giant-sized issue. ★ Origin of Supergirl.
335 ❑ Mar 1966 Cover: 0.12 **NM** value: **14.00**
Circ: Statement: **491,135** • **CGC:** 1 graded, best 9.6
336 ❑ Apr 1966 Cover: 0.12 **NM** value: **14.00**
Circ: Statement: **491,135** • **CGC:** 2 graded, best 9.2
★ Origin of Akvar.
337 ❑ May 1966 Cover: 0.12 **NM** value: **14.00**
Circ: Statement: **491,135** • **CGC:** 1 graded, best 8.5
338 ❑ Jun 1966 Cover: 0.12 **NM** value: **14.00**
Circ: Statement: **491,135**
A: Curt Swan

CGC-graded: Multiply prices above by **33 for 9.9 M** • **16 for 9.8 NM/M** • **7 for 9.6 NM+** • **5 for 9.4 NM** • **2.5 for 9.2 NM-** • **1.5 for 9.0 VF/NM**

339 ❑ Jul 1966 Cover: 0.12 **NM** value: **14.00**
Circ: Statement: **491,135**
A: Curt Swan

340 ❑ Aug 1966 Cover: 0.12 **NM** value: **14.00**
Circ: Statement: **491,135 • CGC:** 1 graded, best 8.5
★ 1st Appearance of Parasite.

341 ❑ Sep 1966 Cover: 0.12 **NM** value: **10.00**
Circ: Statement: **491,135**
★ Appearance of Batman.

342 ❑ Oct 1966 Cover: 0.12 **NM** value: **10.00**
Circ: Statement: **491,135 • CGC:** 2 graded, best 9.2
The Super-Human Bomb!; The Day Supergirl Became an Amazon!

343 ❑ Nov 1966 Cover: 0.12 **NM** value: **10.00**
Circ: Statement: **491,135 • CGC:** 1 graded, best 7.5
Eterno the Immortal!; Jimmy Olsen, Supergirl's Pal!

344 ❑ Dec 1966 Cover: 0.12 **NM** value: **10.00**
Circ: Statement: **491,135 • CGC:** 1 graded, best 9.0
★ Appearance of Batman.

345 ❑ Jan 1967 Cover: 0.12 **NM** value: **10.00**
Circ: Statement: **420,900 • CGC:** 5 graded, best 9.6
The Day Candid Camera Unmasked Clark Kent's Identity!; The Exile of Steel ★ Appearance of Allen Funt.

346 ❑ Feb 1967 Cover: 0.12 **NM** value: **10.00**
Circ: Statement: **420,900 • CGC:** 2 graded, best 9.2
• Has 1966 Statement, filed 10/1/66; avg print run 754,000; avg sales 485,000; avg subs 6,135; avg total paid 491,135; samples 330; max existent 491,465; 35% of run returned

347 ❑ Apr 1967 Cover: 0.25 **NM** value: **22.00**
Circ: Statement: **420,900 • CGC:** 4 graded, best 9.8
• Giant-sized issue. • Supergirl;reprints Superman #140 and Action #290 and #293

348 ❑ Mar 1967 Cover: 0.12 **NM** value: **9.00**
Circ: Statement: **420,900**

349 ❑ Apr 1967 Cover: 0.12 **NM** value: **9.00**
Circ: Statement: **420,900 • CGC:** 2 graded, best 9.4
The Face of Fear!; Supergirl's Black Deeds!

350 ❑ May 1967 Cover: 0.12 **NM** value: **9.00**
Circ: Statement: **420,900 • CGC:** 1 graded, best 9.4
The Secret of the Stone-Age Superman!; The Anti-Supergirl Plot!

351 ❑ Jun 1967 Cover: 0.12 **NM** value: **9.00**
Circ: Statement: **420,900**

352 ❑ Jul 1967 Cover: 0.12 **NM** value: **9.00**
Circ: Statement: **420,900 • CGC:** 1 graded, best 9.4

353 ❑ Aug 1967 Cover: 0.12 **NM** value: **9.00**
Circ: Statement: **420,900 • CGC:** 2 graded, best 9.2
The Battle of the Gods!; The Cosmic Collectors!

354 ❑ Sep 1967 Cover: 0.12 **NM** value: **9.00**
Circ: Statement: **420,900 • CGC:** 2 graded, best 9.0

355 ❑ Oct 1967 Cover: 0.12 **NM** value: **9.00**
Circ: Statement: **420,900 • CGC:** 1 graded, best 9.4
The Mighty Annihilator!; The Death of Luthor!

356 ❑ Nov 1967 Cover: 0.12 **NM** value: **9.00**
Circ: Statement: **420,900 • CGC:** 1 graded, best 9.4

357 ❑ Dec 1967 Cover: 0.12 **NM** value: **9.00**
Circ: Statement: **420,900 • CGC:** 2 graded, best 9.4
A: Curt Swan

358 ❑ Jan 1968 Cover: 0.12 **NM** value: **9.00**
Circ: Statement: **423,000 • CGC:** 2 graded, best 9.2
A: Curt Swan

359 ❑ Feb 1968 Cover: 0.12 **NM** value: **9.00**
Circ: Statement: **423,000 • CGC:** 1 graded, best 9.4
A: Curt Swan

360 ❑ Mar 1968 Cover: 0.25 **NM** value: **18.00**
Circ: Statement: **423,000 • CGC:** 3 graded, best 9.4
• Giant-sized issue. • Supergirl

361 ❑ Apr 1968 Cover: 0.12 **NM** value: **8.00**
Circ: Statement: **423,000 • CGC:** 2 graded, best 9.4

362 ❑ May 1968 Cover: 0.12 **NM** value: **8.00**
Circ: Statement: **423,000 • CGC:** 2 graded, best 9.4

363 ❑ Jun 1968 Cover: 0.12 **NM** value: **8.00**
Circ: Statement: **423,000**

364 ❑ Jul 1968 Cover: 0.12 **NM** value: **8.00**
Circ: Statement: **423,000 • CGC:** 2 graded, best 9.2
The Untouchable of Metropolis!; The Kiss of Death! ★ Death of Superman.

365 ❑ Aug 1968 Cover: 0.12 **NM** value: **8.00**
Circ: Statement: **423,000**
Superman's Funeral!; The Case of the Campus Crimes! ★ Death of Superman.

366 ❑ Sep 1968 Cover: 0.12 **NM** value: **8.00**
Circ: Statement: **423,000 • CGC:** 1 graded, best 9.0
The Substitute Superman!; Stanhope – Off Limits ★ Death of Superman.

367 ❑ Oct 1968 Cover: 0.12 **NM** value: **8.00**
Circ: Statement: **423,000 • CGC:** 2 graded, best 9.4
A: Curt Swan

368 ❑ Nov 1968 Cover: 0.12 **NM** value: **8.00**
Circ: Statement: **423,000**
The Unemployed Superman!; Supergirl's Stand to Save Stanhope!

369 ❑ Dec 1968 Cover: 0.12 **NM** value: **8.00**
Circ: Statement: **423,000 • CGC:** 1 graded, best 9.2

370 ❑ Jan 1969 Cover: 0.12 **NM** value: **8.00**
Circ: Statement: **377,535 • CGC:** 3 graded, best 9.4

371 ❑ Feb 1969 Cover: 0.12 **NM** value: **8.00**
Circ: Statement: **377,535 • CGC:** 1 graded, best 9.0

372 ❑ Mar 1969 Cover: 0.12 **NM** value: **8.00**
Circ: Statement: **377,535 • CGC:** 4 graded, best 9.4

373 ❑ Apr 1969 Cover: 0.25 **NM** value: **18.00**
Circ: Statement: **377,535 • CGC:** 4 graded, best 9.8
• Giant-sized issue. The Battle of the Super-Pets!; The Bride of Mr. Myxyzptlk!; Supergirl's Farewell to Earth!; The War Between Supergirl and the Supermen Emergency Squad!; Supergirl's Greatest Challenge! • Giant size; Supergirl stories **A:** Neal Adams ★ Appearance of Supergirl.

374 ❑ Mar 1969 Cover: 0.12 **NM** value: **7.00**
Circ: Statement: **377,535 • CGC:** 1 graded, best 8.0

375 ❑ Apr 1969 Cover: 0.12 **NM** value: **7.00**
Circ: Statement: **377,535 • CGC:** 1 graded, best 9.2

376 ❑ May 1969 Cover: 0.12 **NM** value: **7.00**
Circ: Statement: **377,535 • CGC:** 1 graded, best 9.2

377 ❑ Jun 1969 Cover: 0.15 **NM** value: **7.00**
Circ: Statement: **377,535**
The Cage of Doom; The Face Behind the Lead Mask • Legion; Reprint from Adventure Comics #300

378 ❑ Jul 1969 Cover: 0.15 **NM** value: **7.00**
Circ: Statement: **377,535**
The Forbidden Fruit • Legion **A:** Jim Shooter; Win Mortimer **W:** Jim Shooter

379 ❑ Aug 1969 Cover: 0.15 **NM** value: **7.00**
Circ: Statement: **377,535**
One of us is an Imposter • Legion **A:** Win Mortimer **W:** Jim Shooter; E. Nelson Bridwell

380 ❑ Sep 1969 Cover: 0.15 **NM** value: **7.00**
Circ: Statement: **377,535**
The Confessions of Superman!; Half a Legionaire? • Legion **A:** Jim Shooter; Win Mortimer **W:** Jim Shooter; E. Nelson Bridwell

381 ❑ Oct 1969 Cover: 0.15 **NM** value: **7.00**
Circ: Statement: **377,535 • CGC:** 1 graded, best 9.2
The Dictator of Earth!; The Hapless Hero • Legion **A:** Jim Shooter; Win Mortimer **W:** Jim Shooter

382 ❑ Nov 1969 Cover: 0.15 **NM** value: **7.00**
Circ: Statement: **377,535**
Clark Kent, Magician!; Kill a Friend to Save a World • Legion **A:** Jim Shooter; Win Mortimer **W:** Jim Shooter

383 ❑ Dec 1969 Cover: 0.15 **NM** value: **7.00**
Circ: Statement: **377,535 • CGC:** 1 graded, best 8.5
Chameleon Boy's Secret Identity • Legion **A:** Win Mortimer **W:** Jim Shooter; E. Nelson Bridwell

384 ❑ Jan 1970 Cover: 0.15 **NM** value: **7.00**
Circ: Statement: **329,925 • CGC:** 2 graded, best 9.2
The Forbidden Costume!; Lament for a Legionnaire • Legion **A:** Jim Shooter; Curt Swan **W:** Jim Shooter; E. Nelson Bridwell

385 ❑ Feb 1970 Cover: 0.15 **NM** value: **7.00**
Circ: Statement: **329,925**
The Immortal Superman!; The Fallen Star Boy • Legion **A:** Win Mortimer **W:** Jim Shooter; E. Nelson Bridwell

386 ❑ Mar 1970 Cover: 0.15 **NM** value: **7.00**
Circ: Statement: **329,925 • CGC:** 1 graded, best 9.4
The Home for Old Super-Heroes!; Zap Goes the Legion • Legion **A:** Win Mortimer **W:** E. Nelson Bridwell

387 ❑ Apr 1970 Cover: 0.15 **NM** value: **7.00**
Circ: Statement: **329,925**
Even a Superman Dies!; One Hero Too Many • Legion **A:** Win Mortimer **W:** E. Nelson Bridwell

388 ❑ May 1970 Cover: 0.15 **NM** value: **7.00**
Circ: Statement: **329,925**
Sun Boy's Lost Power • Legion;Reprints Legion story from Adventure Comics #302 **W:** E. Nelson Bridwell

389 ❑ Jun 1970 Cover: 0.15 **NM** value: **7.00**
Circ: Statement: **329,925**
The Kid Who Struck Out Superman!; The Mystery Legionnaire • Legion **A:** Win Mortimer **W:** Cary Bates

390 ❑ Jul 1970 Cover: 0.15 **NM** value: **7.00**
Circ: Statement: **329,925**
The Tyrant and the Traitor • Legion **A:** Win Mortimer **W:** Cary Bates; E. Nelson Bridwell

391 ❑ Aug 1970 Cover: 0.15 **NM** value: **7.00**
Circ: Statement: **329,925**
The Ordeal of Element Lad • Legion **A:** Win Mortimer **W:** E. Nelson Bridwell

392 ❑ Sep 1970 Cover: 0.15 **NM** value: **7.00**
Circ: Statement: **329,925**
The Shame of the Super-Son!; The Legionnaires Who Never Were • Super-Sons;Last Legion of Super-Heroes **W:** E. Nelson Bridwell

393 ❑ Oct 1970 Cover: 0.15 **NM** value: **7.00**
Circ: Statement: **329,925**

394 ❑ Nov 1970 Cover: 0.15 **NM** value: **7.00**
Circ: Statement: **329,925**

395 ❑ Dec 1970 Cover: 0.15 **NM** value: **7.00**
Circ: Statement: **329,925**

396 ❑ Jan 1971 Cover: 0.15 **NM** value: **5.50**
Circ: Statement: **325,618 • CGC:** 1 graded, best 7.0
The Super-Panhandler of Metropolis!; The Invaders from Nowhere! • Tales of the Fortress **A:** Murphy Anderson; Curt Swan **W:** Leo Dorfman

397 ❑ Feb 1971 Cover: 0.15 **NM** value: **5.50**
Circ: Statement: **325,618**
The Secret of the Wheel-Chair Superman!; The Super Captive of the Sea! • Tales of the Fortress

398 ❑ Mar 1971 Cover: 0.15 **NM** value: **5.50**
Circ: Statement: **325,618 • CGC:** 1 graded, best 9.2

399 ❑ Apr 1971 Cover: 0.15 **NM** value: **5.50**
Circ: Statement: **325,618 • CGC:** 3 graded, best 9.4

400 ❑ May 1971 Cover: 0.15 **NM** value: **5.50**
Circ: Statement: **325,618 • CGC:** 3 graded, best 9.4
My Son... Is He Man or Beast?; Duel of Doom!

401 ❑ Jun 1971 Cover: 0.15 **NM** value: **5.50**
Circ: Statement: **325,618 • CGC:** 1 graded, best 9.4

402 ❑ Jul 1971 Cover: 0.15 **NM** value: **5.50**
Circ: Statement: **325,618**
This Hostage Must Die!; Superman vs. Supergirl: The Feud of the Titans! • Tales of the Fortress

403 ❑ Aug 1971 Cover: 0.25 **NM** value: **5.50**
Circ: Statement: **325,618 • CGC:** 1 graded, best 6.5
Attack of the Micro-Murderer; The Man with the X-Ray Mind; Vigilante: The Impossible Legend; When Krypto was Superboy's Master! • Superboy and Vigilante reprint stories

404 ❑ Sep 1971 Cover: 0.25 **NM** value: **5.50**
Circ: Statement: **325,618 • CGC:** 1 graded, best 9.0

405 ❑ Oct 1971 Cover: 0.25 **NM** value: **5.50**
Circ: Statement: **325,618 • CGC:** 1 graded, best 9.0

406 ❑ Nov 1971 Cover: 0.25 **NM** value: **5.50**
Circ: Statement: **325,618**

407 ❑ Dec 1971 Cover: 0.25 **NM** value: **5.50**
Circ: Statement: **325,618**
The Fiend in the Fortress of Solitude; The Challenge of the Expanding World; The Planet of Prey! • Atom and Flash story

408 ❑ Jan 1972 Cover: 0.25 **NM** value: **5.50**
Circ: Statement: **252,317 • CGC:** 1 graded, best 9.2
• reprints The Atom #9 **A:** Gil Kane

409 ❑ Feb 1972 Cover: 0.25 **NM** value: **5.50**
Circ: Statement: **252,317**

410 ❑ Feb 1972 Cover: 0.25 **NM** value: **5.50**
Circ: Statement: **252,317 • CGC:** 4 graded, best 9.8

411 ❑ Apr 1972 Cover: 0.25 **NM** value: **6.00**
Circ: Statement: **252,317 • CGC:** 1 graded, best 9.4
★ Origin of Eclipso.

412 ❑ May 1972 Cover: 0.25 **NM** value: **4.50**
Circ: Statement: **252,317 • CGC:** 3 graded, best 9.4

413 ❑ Jun 1972 Cover: 0.25 **NM** value: **4.50**
Circ: Statement: **252,317 • CGC:** 2 graded, best 9.4
The Voodoo Doom of Superman; Super-Turtle; The Man Who Destroyed Eclipso; Super-Smiles; The 7 Sins of Simon Stagg • Metamorpho

414 ❑ Jul 1972 Cover: 0.20 **NM** value: **4.50**
Circ: Statement: **252,317 • CGC:** 2 graded, best 9.4

415 ❑ Aug 1972 Cover: 0.20 **NM** value: **4.50**
Circ: Statement: **252,317**

416 ❑ Sep 1972 Cover: 0.20 **NM** value: **4.50**
Circ: Statement: **252,317**

417 ❑ Oct 1972 Cover: 0.20 **NM** value: **4.50**
Circ: Statement: **252,317 • CGC:** 2 graded, best 9.4

418 ❑ Nov 1972 Cover: 0.20 **NM** value: **4.50**
Circ: Statement: **252,317**

419 ❑ Dec 1972 Cover: 0.20 **NM** value: **4.50**
Circ: Statement: **252,317 • CGC:** 1 graded, best 9.2
★ 1st Appearance of Human Target.

420 ❑ Jan 1973 Cover: 0.20 **NM** value: **4.50**
Circ: Statement: **240,558 • CGC:** 1 graded, best 9.2

421 ❑ Feb 1973 Cover: 0.20 **NM** value: **4.50**
Circ: Statement: **240,558 • CGC:** 1 graded, best 9.0
• Green Arrow begins

422 ❑ Mar 1973 Cover: 0.20 **NM** value: **4.50**
Circ: Statement: **240,558 • CGC:** 2 graded, best 9.2
• Has 1972 Statement; avg total paid circ 252,317

423 ❑ Apr 1973 Cover: 0.20 **NM** value: **4.50**
Circ: Statement: **240,558 • CGC:** 3 graded, best 9.2

424 ❑ Jun 1973 Cover: 0.20 **NM** value: **4.50**
Circ: Statement: **240,558 • CGC:** 2 graded, best 9.4
• Green Arrow **A:** Murphy Anderson; Dick Giordano; Curt Swan

425 ❑ Jul 1973 Cover: 0.20 **NM** value: **8.00**
Circ: Statement: **240,558 • CGC:** 1 graded, best 9.4
A: Murphy Anderson; Dick Giordano; Neal Adams; Curt Swan

426 ❑ Aug 1973 Cover: 0.20 **NM** value: **4.00**
Circ: Statement: **240,558**

427 ❑ Sep 1973 Cover: 0.20 **NM** value: **4.00**
Circ: Statement: **240,558**

428 ❑ Oct 1973 Cover: 0.20 **NM** value: **4.00**
Circ: Statement: **240,558**

429 ❑ Nov 1973 Cover: 0.20 **NM** value: **4.00**
Circ: Statement: **240,558**

430 ❑ Dec 1973 Cover: 0.20 **NM** value: **4.00**
Circ: Statement: **240,558 • CGC:** 1 graded, best 9.2
Bus-Ride to Nowhere!; Up Pops the Atom • Atom back-up

431 ❑ Jan 1974 Cover: 0.20 **NM** value: **4.00**
Circ: Statement: **237,166**
The Monster Who Unmasked Superman!; The Case of the Runaway Shoebox! • Green Arrow back-up

432 ❑ Feb 1974 Cover: 0.20 **NM** value: **4.00**
Circ: Statement: **237,166**

433 ❑ Mar 1974 Cover: 0.20 **NM** value: **4.00**
Circ: Statement: **237,166 • CGC:** 1 graded, best 9.6

434 ❑ Apr 1974 Cover: 0.20 **NM** value: **4.00**
Circ: Statement: **237,166 • CGC:** 1 graded, best 8.0
• Has 1973 Statement; avg total paid circ 240,558

435 ❑ May 1974 Cover: 0.20 **NM** value: **4.00**
Circ: Statement: **237,166**

436 ❑ Jun 1974 Cover: 0.20 **NM** value: **4.00**
Circ: Statement: **237,166 • CGC:** 1 graded, best 9.6

437 ❑ Jul 1974 Cover: 0.60 **NM** value: **9.00**
Circ: Statement: **237,166**
• Giant-sized issue (100 pages). • Green Arrow **A:** Carmine Infantino

438 ❑ Aug 1974 Cover: 0.20 **NM** value: **4.00**
Circ: Statement: **237,166 • CGC:** 1 graded, best 9.0
A: Curt Swan

439 ❑ Sep 1974 Cover: 0.20 **NM** value: **4.00**
Circ: Statement: **237,166 • CGC:** 1 graded, best 9.2
Too Big to Live!; Danger in Two Dimensions! • Atom back-up **A:** Curt Swan

440 ❑ Oct 1974 Cover: 0.20 **NM** value: **9.00**
Circ: Statement: **237,166**
• 1st Green Arrow by Mike Grell **A:** Mike Grell; Curt Swan

441 ❑ Nov 1974 Cover: 0.20 **NM** value: **6.00**
Circ: Statement: **237,166**
Weather War Over Metropolis!; The Mystery of the Wandering Dog • Green Arrow back-up **A:** Mike Grell; Curt Swan ★ Appearance of Flash.

442 ❑ Dec 1974 Cover: 0.20 **NM** value: **4.00**
Circ: Statement: **237,166**
A: Curt Swan

443 ❑ Jan 1975 Cover: 0.60 **NM** value: **9.00**
Circ: Statement: **231,000 • CGC:** 3 graded, best 9.4
• Giant-sized issue (100 pages). At Last! Clark Kent, Super-Hero!; 1 Threats in the 7 Seas!; The Ghost of the Deep!; Revolt in Painted Canyon!; The Super-Brain of Adam Strange!; Amazing Thefts of the I.Q. Gang!; Throne of Spain! • 100-Page Super Spectacular; JLA, Sea Devils, Matt Savage, Adam Strange, Hawkman and Black Pirate; reprints stories from Sea Devils #3, Western Comics #78, Mystery in Space #87 and Sensation Comics #4

444 ❑ Feb 1975 Cover: 0.25 **NM** value: **4.00**
Circ: Statement: **231,000**
Beware the Hero-Killers!; The Balck Canary Is Dead! • Green Arrow back-up ★ Appearance of Green Lantern.

Other grades: Multiply prices above by **1.5 for Mint • 2/3 for Very Fine • 1/3 for Fine • 1/5 for Very Good • 1/8 for Good**

445 ❑ Mar 1975 Cover: 0.25 **NM** value: **4.00**
Circ: Statement: **231,000**
446 ❑ Apr 1975 Cover: 0.25 **NM** value: **4.00**
Circ: Statement: **231,000**
447 ❑ May 1975 Cover: 0.25 **NM** value: **3.50**
Circ: Statement: **231,000**
• Has 1974 Statement; avg total paid circ 237,166
448 ❑ Jun 1975 Cover: 0.25 **NM** value: **3.50**
Circ: Statement: **231,000**
449 ❑ Jul 1975 Cover: 0.50 **NM** value: **3.50**
Circ: Statement: **231,000** • **CGC:** 1 graded, best 9.4
🕮 Mystery of the Giant Arrows; Prisoners of Dimension 0 • Green Arrow giant **A:** Jack Kirby
450 ❑ Aug 1975 Cover: 0.25 **NM** value: **3.50**
Circ: Statement: **231,000** • **CGC:** 2 graded, best 9.4
451 ❑ Sep 1975 Cover: 0.25 **NM** value: **3.50**
Circ: Statement: **231,000**
🕮 The Great Super-Hero Contest!; The Day the Dreaming Dies • Green Arrow back-up
452 ❑ Oct 1975 Cover: 0.25 **NM** value: **3.50**
Circ: Statement: **231,000**
453 ❑ Nov 1975 Cover: 0.25 **NM** value: **3.50**
Circ: Statement: **231,000**
🕮 Superman's Fantastic Face-Saving Feat!; Danger: Thoughts at Work! • Atom back-up
454 ❑ Dec 1975 Cover: 0.25 **NM** value: **3.50**
Circ: Statement: **231,000**
• last Atom back-up
455 ❑ Jan 1976 Cover: 0.25 **NM** value: **3.50**
Circ: Statement: **208,000**
456 ❑ Feb 1976 Cover: 0.25 **NM** value: **3.50**
Circ: Statement: **208,000**
🕮 Jaws of the Killer Shark!; Bail Out the Nutty Kid • Green Arrow/Black Canary back-up
457 ❑ Mar 1976 Cover: 0.30 **NM** value: **3.50**
Circ: Statement: **208,000** • **CGC:** 1 graded, best 8.5
🕮 Superman, You're NOT Clark Kent, and I Can Prove It!; Flight of the Nutty Kid • Green Arrow/Black Canary back-up;Superman reveals ID to Pete Ross' son
458 ❑ Apr 1976 Cover: 0.30 **NM** value: **3.50**
Circ: Statement: **208,000**
• Green Arrow **A:** Mike Grell; Curt Swan ★ 1st Appearance of Blackrock.
459 ❑ May 1976 Cover: 0.30 **NM** value: **3.50**
Circ: Statement: **208,000**
460 ❑ Jun 1976 Cover: 0.30 **NM** value: **3.50**
Circ: Statement: **208,000**
🕮 Superman, You'll Be the Death of Me Yet!; Welcome Home to Mxyzpolis! • Mxyzptlk back-up★ 1st Appearance of Karb-Brak.
461 ❑ Jul 1976 Cover: 0.30 **NM** value: **3.50**
Circ: Statement: **208,000** • **CGC:** 1 graded, best 9.2
• Superman in colonial America;Bicentennial #30★ Versus Karb-Brak.
462 ❑ Aug 1976 Cover: 0.30 **NM** value: **3.50**
Circ: Statement: **208,000**
463 ❑ Sep 1976 Cover: 0.30 **NM** value: **3.50**
Circ: Statement: **208,000**
🕮 Die Now, Live Later! • Bicentennial story
464 ❑ Oct 1976 Cover: 0.30 **NM** value: **3.50**
Circ: Statement: **208,000**
465 ❑ Nov 1976 Cover: 0.30 **NM** value: **3.50**
Circ: Statement: **208,000**
466 ❑ Dec 1976 Cover: 0.30 **NM** value: **3.50**
Circ: Statement: **208,000** • **CGC:** 1 graded, best 8.5
467 ❑ Jan 1977 Cover: 0.30 **NM** value: **3.50**
Circ: Statement: **179,714**
468 ❑ Feb 1977 Cover: 0.30 **NM** value: **3.50**
Circ: Statement: **179,714**
469 ❑ Mar 1977 Cover: 0.30 **NM** value: **3.50**
Circ: Statement: **179,714**
470 ❑ Apr 1977 Cover: 0.30 **NM** value: **3.50**
Circ: Statement: **179,714**
471 ❑ May 1977 Cover: 0.30 **NM** value: **3.50**
Circ: Statement: **179,714**
🕮 One of Our Phantoms Is Missing!; The Private Life of Clark Kent: The Long Weekend • Has 1976 Statement; avg total paid circ 208,000
472 ❑ Jun 1977 Cover: 0.30 **NM** value: **3.50**
Circ: Statement: **179,714**
🕮 The Phantom Touch Of Death; The Sporting Life of Steve Lombard: If I'm Over Here, What am I Doing Over There? **A:** Curt Swan; Tex Blaisdell **W:** Cary Bates ★ Versus Faora Hu-Ul.
473 ❑ Jul 1977 Cover: 0.35 **NM** value: **3.50**
Circ: Statement: **179,714**
W: Cary Bates
474 ❑ Aug 1977 Cover: 0.35 **NM** value: **3.50**
Circ: Statement: **179,714**
475 ❑ Sep 1977 Cover: 0.35 **NM** value: **3.50**
Circ: Statement: **179,714**
476 ❑ Oct 1977 Cover: 0.35 **NM** value: **3.50**
Circ: Statement: **179,714**
477 ❑ Nov 1977 Cover: 0.35 **NM** value: **3.50**
Circ: Statement: **179,714**
478 ❑ Dec 1977 Cover: 0.35 **NM** value: **3.50**
Circ: Statement: **179,714**
479 ❑ Jan 1978 Cover: 0.35 **NM** value: **3.50**
Circ: Statement: **183,601**
480 ❑ Feb 1978 Cover: 0.35 **NM** value: **3.50**
Circ: Statement: **183,601**
481 ❑ Mar 1978 Cover: 0.35 **NM** value: **3.50**
Circ: Statement: **183,601**
🕮 It's a Bird, It's a Plane, It's Supermobile! ★ 1st Appearance of Supermobile. ★ Versus Amazo.
482 ❑ Apr 1978 Cover: 0.35 **NM** value: **3.50**
Circ: Statement: **183,601**
🕮 This Is a Job for Supermobile!
483 ❑ May 1978 Cover: 0.35 **NM** value: **3.50**
Circ: Statement: **183,601**
🕮 Sleep No More! ★ Versus Amazo.
484 ❑ Jun 1978 Cover: 0.35 **NM** value: **3.50**
Circ: Statement: **183,601** • **CGC:** 4 graded, best 9.2
• 40th anniversary. 🕮 Superman Takes a Wife! • Wedding of E-2 Superman and Lois Lane
485 ❑ Jul 1978 Cover: 0.35 **NM** value: **3.50**
Circ: Statement: **183,601**
🕮 The Experiment That Backfired on Superman!
486 ❑ Aug 1978 Cover: 0.35 **NM** value: **3.50**
Circ: Statement: **183,601**
487 ❑ Sep 1978 Cover: 0.50 **NM** value: **3.50**
Circ: Statement: **183,601**
★ Origin of Atom.
488 ❑ Oct 1978 Cover: 0.50 **NM** value: **3.50**
Circ: Statement: **183,601**
489 ❑ Nov 1978 Cover: 0.50 **NM** value: **3.50**
Circ: Statement: **183,601**
🕮 Krypton Dies Again!; Where There's a Will, There's a Fray! • Atom back-up
490 ❑ Dec 1978 Cover: 0.40 **NM** value: **3.50**
Circ: Statement: **183,601**
491 ❑ Jan 1979 Cover: 0.40 **NM** value: **3.50**
Circ: Statement: **160,928**
492 ❑ Feb 1979 Cover: 0.40 **NM** value: **3.50**
Circ: Statement: **160,928**
493 ❑ Mar 1979 Cover: 0.40 **NM** value: **3.50**
Circ: Statement: **160,928**
494 ❑ Apr 1979 Cover: 0.40 **NM** value: **3.50**
Circ: Statement: **160,928**
495 ❑ May 1979 Cover: 0.40 **NM** value: **3.50**
Circ: Statement: **160,928**
★ 1st Appearance of Silver Banshee.
496 ❑ Jun 1979 Cover: 0.40 **NM** value: **3.50**
Circ: Statement: **160,928** • **CGC:** 1 graded, best 8.0
497 ❑ Jul 1979 Cover: 0.40 **NM** value: **3.50**
Circ: Statement: **160,928** • **CGC:** 1 graded, best 9.2
498 ❑ Aug 1979 Cover: 0.40 **NM** value: **3.50**
Circ: Statement: **160,928** • **CGC:** 1 graded, best 9.6
499 ❑ Sep 1979 Cover: 0.40 **NM** value: **3.50**
Circ: Statement: **160,928**
500 ❑ Oct 1979 Cover: 1.00 **NM** value: **4.00**
Circ: Statement: **160,928** • **CGC:** 7 graded, best 9.8
• Giant-sized. 🕮 The Life Story of Superman; Planet on the Edge of Oblivion!; A Legend Is Born!; Call Me Superman • Superman's life★ Origin of Superman.
501 ❑ Nov 1979 Cover: 0.40 **NM** value: **3.00**
Circ: Statement: **160,928**
502 ❑ Dec 1979 Cover: 0.40 **NM** value: **3.00**
Circ: Statement: **160,928**
503 ❑ Jan 1980 Cover: 0.40 **NM** value: **3.00**
Circ: Statement: **118,752**
504 ❑ Feb 1980 Cover: 0.40 **NM** value: **3.00**
Circ: Statement: **118,752**
505 ❑ Mar 1980 Cover: 0.40 **NM** value: **3.00**
Circ: Statement: **118,752**
506 ❑ Apr 1980 Cover: 0.40 **NM** value: **3.00**
Circ: Statement: **118,752**
• Has 1979 Statement, filed 10/1/79; avg print run 338,546; avg sales 159,885; avg subs 1,443; avg total paid 160,928; samples 0; office use 121; max existent 161,449; 52% of run returned
507 ❑ May 1980 Cover: 0.40 **NM** value: **3.00**
Circ: Statement: **118,752**
508 ❑ Jun 1980 Cover: 0.40 **NM** value: **3.00**
Circ: Statement: **118,752**
509 ❑ Jul 1980 Cover: 0.40 **NM** value: **3.00**
Circ: Statement: **118,752**
🕮 The Great Space-Travel Hoax!; The Computers That Saved Metropolis! • Radio Shack promo insert **A:** Jim Starlin; Joe Sinnott
510 ❑ Aug 1980 Cover: 0.40 **NM** value: **3.00**
Circ: Statement: **118,752**
511 ❑ Sep 1980 Cover: 0.50 **NM** value: **3.00**
Circ: Statement: **118,752**
512 ❑ Oct 1980 Cover: 0.50 **NM** value: **3.00**
Circ: Statement: **118,752**
🕮 Luthor's Day of Reckoning!; Sinister Spectacle of Sunspotter • Air Wave back-up
513 ❑ Nov 1980 Cover: 0.50 **NM** value: **3.00**
Circ: Statement: **118,752**
514 ❑ Dec 1980 Cover: 0.50 **NM** value: **3.00**
Circ: Statement: **118,752**
515 ❑ Jan 1981 Cover: 0.50 **NM** value: **3.00**
Circ: Statement: **111,729**
🕮 This Is My World, and You're Welcome To It!; Sorry, Wrong Powers! • Atom back-up★ Versus Vandal Savage.
516 ❑ Feb 1981 Cover: 0.50 **NM** value: **3.00**
Circ: Statement: **111,729**
🕮 Time and Time Again!; The Clueless Capers of Chronos! • Atom back-up★ Versus Vandal Savage.
517 ❑ Mar 1981 Cover: 0.50 **NM** value: **3.00**
Circ: Statement: **111,729**
518 ❑ Apr 1981 Cover: 0.50 **NM** value: **3.00**
Circ: Statement: **111,729**
🕮 Treasure Hunt on a Small Planet!; Beyond the Poseidon Adventure • Aquaman back-up
519 ❑ May 1981 Cover: 0.50 **NM** value: **3.00**
Circ: Statement: **111,729**
• Has 1980 Statement, filed 10/1/80; avg print run 324,114; avg sales 116,210; avg subs 2,542; avg total paid 118,752; samples 127; office use 3,315; max existent 122,194; 59% of run returned
520 ❑ Jun 1981 Cover: 0.50 **NM** value: **3.00**
Circ: Statement: **111,729**
521 ❑ Jul 1981 Cover: 0.50 **NM** value: **3.00**
Circ: Statement: **111,729**
🕮 The Deadly Rampage of the Lady Fox; Grow, Little Growfish! • Atom, Aquaman back-up★ 1st Appearance of Vixen.
522 ❑ Aug 1981 Cover: 0.50 **NM** value: **3.00**
Circ: Statement: **111,729**
🕮 The Time-Tornado of the Clockwork Man!; The Hurricane Harness Hijack! • Atom back-up
523 ❑ Sep 1981 Cover: 0.50 **NM** value: **3.00**
Circ: Statement: **111,729**
🕮 Steve Lombard's Double Life!; The Eye of the Storm! • Atom back-up
524 ❑ Oct 1981 Cover: 0.60 **NM** value: **3.00**
Circ: Statement: **111,729**
🕮 If I Can't Be Clark Kent, Nobody Can!; Catastrophe By Calculation! • Airwave and Atom back-up
525 ❑ Nov 1981 Cover: 0.60 **NM** value: **3.00**
Circ: Statement: **111,729**
★ 1st Appearance of Neutron.
526 ❑ Dec 1981 Cover: 0.60 **NM** value: **3.00**
Circ: Statement: **111,729**
527 ❑ Jan 1982 Cover: 0.60 **NM** value: **3.00**
Circ: Statement: **103,353**
🕮 Sorcery Over Stonehenge!; Air Wave Under the Waves! • Airwave, Aquaman back-up★ 1st Appearance of Lord Satanis.
528 ❑ Feb 1982 Cover: 0.60 **NM** value: **3.00**
Circ: Statement: **103,353**
🕮 Star-Kill!; Land-Masters of the Sea! • Aquaman back-up★ Appearance of Brainiac.
529 ❑ Mar 1982 Cover: 0.60 **NM** value: **3.00**
Circ: Statement: **103,353**
530 ❑ Apr 1982 Cover: 0.60 **NM** value: **3.00**
Circ: Statement: **103,353**
531 ❑ May 1982 Cover: 0.60 **NM** value: **3.00**
Circ: Statement: **103,353**
532 ❑ Jun 1982 Cover: 0.60 **NM** value: **3.00**
Circ: Statement: **103,353**
533 ❑ Jul 1982 Cover: 0.60 **NM** value: **3.00**
Circ: Statement: **103,353**
534 ❑ Aug 1982 Cover: 0.60 **NM** value: **3.00**
Circ: Statement: **103,353**
535 ❑ Sep 1982 Cover: 0.60 **NM** value: **3.00**
Circ: Statement: **103,353**
536 ❑ Oct 1982 Cover: 0.60 **NM** value: **3.00**
Circ: Statement: **103,353**
537 ❑ Nov 1982 Cover: 0.60 **NM** value: **3.00**
Circ: Statement: **103,353**
🕮 Half a Superman!; Fate Is the Killer; Something Fishy! • Aquaman back-up; Masters of the Universe preview
538 ❑ Dec 1982 Cover: 0.60 **NM** value: **3.00**
Circ: Statement: **103,353**
539 ❑ Jan 1983 Cover: 0.60 **NM** value: **3.00**
Circ: Statement: **105,394**
• Flash, Atom **A:** Gil Kane
540 ❑ Feb 1983 Cover: 0.60 **NM** value: **3.00**
Circ: Statement: **105,394**
🕮 World Enough and Time; Water-War One • Aquaman back-up **A:** Curt Swan
541 ❑ Mar 1983 Cover: 0.60 **NM** value: **3.00**
Circ: Statement: **105,394**
🕮 Once Again, Superman **A:** Curt Swan
542 ❑ Apr 1983 Cover: 0.60 **NM** value: **3.00**
Circ: Statement: **105,394**
🕮 Savage Awakening! **A:** Curt Swan ★ Versus Vandal Savage.
543 ❑ May 1983 Cover: 0.60 **NM** value: **3.00**
Circ: Statement: **105,394**
🕮 Within These Hands, Power! • Has 1982 Statement, filed 10/1/82; avg print run 284,046; avg sales 101,196; avg subs 2,157; avg total paid 103,353; samples 677; office use 2,403; max existent 106,433; 63% of run returned **A:** Curt Swan ★ Versus Neutron.
544 ❑ Jun 1983 Cover: 1.50 **NM** value: **3.00**
Circ: Statement: **105,394**
• 45th anniversary. 🕮 Luthor Unleashed!; Rebirth! • 45th Anniversay issue; New Luthor and Braniac; Joe Shuster pin-up **A:** Gil Kane; Curt Swan **C:** Dick Giordano; Gil Kane **W:** Cary Bates; Marv Wolfman ★ Origin of Brainiac (New), Lex Luthor (New). ★ 1st Appearance of Brainiac (New), Lex Luthor (New).
545 ❑ Jul 1983 Cover: 1.50 **NM** value: **3.00**
Circ: Statement: **105,394**
🕮 With But a Single Step! ★ Versus New Brainiac.
546 ❑ Aug 1983 Cover: 0.60 **NM** value: **3.00**
Circ: Statement: **105,394**
🕮 Showdown! • JLA, New Teen Titans★ Appearance of JLA, Titans.
547 ❑ Sep 1983 Cover: 1.50 **NM** value: **3.00**
Circ: Statement: **105,394**
548 ❑ Oct 1983 Cover: 1.50 **NM** value: **3.00**
Circ: Statement: **105,394**
549 ❑ Nov 1983 Cover: 1.50 **NM** value: **3.00**
Circ: Statement: **105,394**
550 ❑ Dec 1983 Cover: 0.75 **NM** value: **3.00**
Circ: Statement: **105,394**
551 ❑ Jan 1984 Cover: 0.75 **NM** value: **3.00**
Circ: Statement: **86,422**
🕮 Superman: Friend or Foe? ★ 1st Appearance of Red Star (Starfire).
552 ❑ Feb 1984 Cover: 0.75 **NM** value: **4.00**
Circ: Statement: **86,422**
🕮 Another Time! Another Death! • Cave Carson, Congorilla, Suicide Squad, Animal Man, Rip Hunter, Immortal Man, Sea Devils, Dolphin★ 1st Appearance of Legion of Forgotten Heroes. ★ Appearance of Animal Man.
553 ❑ Mar 1984 Cover: 0.75 **NM** value: **3.00**
Circ: Statement: **86,422**
🕮 The World at Time's End! • Cave Carson, Congorilla, Suicide Squad, Animal Man, Rip Hunter, Immortal Man, Sea Devils, Dolphin★ Appearance of Animal Man, Legion of Forgotten Heroes.
554 ❑ Apr 1984 Cover: 0.75 **NM** value: **2.00**
Circ: Statement: **86,422**
🕮 If Superman Didn't Exist... • Jerry and Joey create Superman
555 ❑ May 1984 Cover: 0.75 **NM** value: **2.00**
Circ: Statement: **86,422**
🕮 Reunion! • Anniversary of Supergirl's debut in Action Comics; Continues in Supergirl #20★ Appearance of Supergirl. ★ Versus Parasite.
556 ❑ Jun 1984 Cover: 0.75 **NM** value: **2.00**
Circ: Statement: **86,422**
🕮 Endings • Neutron★ Versus Vandal Savage.

CGC-graded: Multiply prices above by **33 for 9.9 M • 16 for 9.8 NM/M • 7 for 9.6 NM+ • 5 for 9.4 NM • 2.5 for 9.2 NM- • 1.5 for 9.0 VF/NM**

557 ❑ Jul 1984 Cover: 0.75 **NM** value: **2.00**
Circ: Statement: **86,422**
558 ❑ Aug 1984 Cover: 0.75 **NM** value: **2.00**
Circ: Statement: **86,422**
559 ❑ Sep 1984 Cover: 0.75 **NM** value: **2.00**
Circ: Statement: **86,422**
560 ❑ Oct 1984 Cover: 0.75 **NM** value: **2.00**
Circ: Statement: **86,422**
📖 Meet John Doe!; Ambush Bug • Ambush Bug back-up ★ Appearance of Ambush Bug.
561 ❑ Nov 1984 Cover: 0.75 **NM** value: **2.00**
Circ: Statement: **86,422**
562 ❑ Dec 1984 Cover: 0.75 **NM** value: **2.00**
Circ: Statement: **86,422**
563 ❑ Jan 1985 Cover: 0.75 **NM** value: **2.00**
Circ: Statement: **66,656**
📖 Black Beauty or "A Horse Is a Horse, of Course, of Course"; Mr. Mxyzptlk, Media Star!; Jimmy Olsen, Blob! • Ambush Bug vs. Mxyzptlk
564 ❑ Feb 1985 Cover: 0.75 **NM** value: **2.00**
Circ: Statement: **66,656**
565 ❑ Mar 1985 Cover: 0.75 **NM** value: **2.00**
Circ: Statement: **66,656**
📖 The Wizard City Warrior; $ellout or "Manna from Mando" • Ambush Bug back-up ★ Appearance of Ambush Bug.
566 ❑ Apr 1985 Cover: 0.75 **NM** value: **2.00**
Circ: Statement: **66,656**
★ Versus Captain Strong.
567 ❑ May 1985 Cover: 0.75 **NM** value: **2.00**
Circ: Statement: **66,656** CapCity orders: **4,450**
568 ❑ Jun 1985 Cover: 0.75 **NM** value: **2.00**
Circ: Statement: **66,656** CapCity orders: **4,450**
📖 Disappearing Act!; The Amazing Matchmaker of Metropolis!
569 ❑ Jul 1985 Cover: 0.75 **NM** value: **2.00**
Circ: Statement: **66,656** CapCity orders: **4,400**
📖 The Force of Revenge; Casting Call
570 ❑ Aug 1985 Cover: 0.75 **NM** value: **2.00**
Circ: Statement: **66,656** CapCity orders: **4,200**
📖 The Mystery of Jimmy Olsen's Alter Ego!; The Superman Who Came to Dinner
571 ❑ Sep 1985 Cover: 0.75 **NM** value: **2.00**
Circ: Statement: **66,656** CapCity orders: **5,250**
📖 Mission to Earth!
572 ❑ Oct 1985 Cover: 0.75 **NM** value: **2.00**
Circ: Statement: **66,656** CapCity orders: **4,500** • **CGC:** 2 graded, best 9.6
📖 The World of Superman Masqueraders!; SOS from Nowhere! The Puzzlw of the Purloined Fortress!
573 ❑ Nov 1985 Cover: 0.75 **NM** value: **2.00**
Circ: Statement: **66,656** CapCity orders: **4,050**
📖 The Sale of the Century!; Assault on Mount Mayhem; If I Were Superman... • MASK preview
574 ❑ Dec 1985 Cover: 0.75 **NM** value: **2.00**
Circ: Statement: **66,656** CapCity orders: **4,000**
📖 May the Best World Win!; Tomorrow Is Cancelled!
575 ❑ Jan 1986 Cover: 0.75 **NM** value: **2.00**
Circ: Statement: **61,157** CapCity orders: **3,950**
📖 The Great Brain Robbery!; Rodent on a Rampage!
576 ❑ Feb 1986 Cover: 0.75 **NM** value: **2.00**
Circ: Statement: **61,157** CapCity orders: **4,150**
📖 Earth's Sister Planet!; The 'Monumental' Menace of Metropolis!
577 ❑ Mar 1986 Cover: 0.75 **NM** value: **2.00**
Circ: Statement: **61,157** CapCity orders: **4,600**
📖 Caitiff: First of the Vampires!
578 ❑ Apr 1986 Cover: 0.75 **NM** value: **2.00**
Circ: Statement: **61,157** CapCity orders: **4,200**
579 ❑ May 1986 Cover: 0.75 **NM** value: **2.00**
Circ: Statement: **61,157** CapCity orders: **4,800**
580 ❑ Jun 1986 Cover: 0.75 **NM** value: **2.00**
Circ: Statement: **61,157** CapCity orders: **4,500**
📖 The Day Superman Couldn't Save!; The Most Dangerous Toy on Earth!; The Mystery of the Missing Moon!
581 ❑ Jul 1986 Cover: 0.75 **NM** value: **2.00**
Circ: Statement: **61,157** CapCity orders: **4,600**
📖 Superman for a Day!; Even a Superman Needs a Lawyer!
582 ❑ Aug 1986 Cover: 0.75 **NM** value: **2.00**
Circ: Statement: **61,157** CapCity orders: **4,550**
583 ❑ Sep 1986 Cover: 0.75 **NM** value: **5.00**
Circ: Statement: **61,157** CapCity orders: **14,600** • **CGC:** 3 graded, best 9.6
📖 Whatever Happened to the Man of Tomorrow, Part 2 • Continued from Superman #423; Last pre-Crisis on Infinite Earths Superman **W:** Alan Moore
584 ❑ Jan 1987 Cover: 0.75 **NM** value: **2.50**
Circ: Statement: **181,767** CapCity orders: **43,750**
📖 Squatter! • Teen Titans; Post-Crisis Superman begins **A:** John Byrne; Dick Giordano **W:** John Byrne
585 ❑ Feb 1987 Cover: 0.75 **NM** value: **2.00**
Circ: Statement: **181,767** CapCity orders: **35,150**
📖 And Graves Give Up Treir Dead... • Phantom Stranger **A:** John Byrne; Dick Giordano ★ Appearance of Phantom Stranger.
586 ❑ Mar 1987 Cover: 0.75 **NM** value: **2.00**
Circ: Statement: **181,767** CapCity orders: **34,550**
📖 The Champion! • New Gods; "Legends" Chapter 19 **A:** John Byrne; Dick Giordano ★ Appearance of Orion.
587 ❑ Apr 1987 Cover: 0.75 **NM** value: **2.00**
Circ: Statement: **181,767** CapCity orders: **28,500**
📖 Cityscape! • Demon; Has 1986 Statement, filed 10/1/86; avg print run 155,111; avg sales 59,827; avg subs 1,330; avg total paid 61,157; samples 163; office use 2,246; max existent 63,566; 59% of run returned **A:** John Byrne; Dick Giordano ★ Appearance of Demon.
588 ❑ May 1987 Cover: 0.75 **NM** value: **2.00**
Circ: Statement: **181,767** CapCity orders: **26,800**
📖 All Wars Must End, Part 2 • Hawkman; Shadow War; Continued from Hawkman #10, continues in Hawkman #11 and Action #589 **A:** John Byrne; Dick Giordano ★ Appearance of Hawkman.
589 ❑ Jun 1987 Cover: 0.75 **NM** value: **2.00**
Circ: Statement: **181,767** CapCity orders: **24,700**
📖 Green on Green • Green Lantern Corps **A:** John Byrne; Dick Giordano ★ Appearance of Green Lantern Corps.
590 ❑ Jul 1987 Cover: 0.75 **NM** value: **2.00**
Circ: Statement: **181,767** CapCity orders: **24,250**
📖 Better Dying Through Chemistry • Metal Men, new Chemo **A:** John Byrne; Dick Giordano ★ Appearance of Metal Men.
591 ❑ Aug 1987 Cover: 0.75 **NM** value: **2.00**
Circ: Statement: **181,767** CapCity orders: **26,100**
📖 Past Imperfect • Superboy **A:** John Byrne; Dick Giordano ★ Appearance of Superboy.
592 ❑ Sep 1987 Cover: 0.75 **NM** value: **2.00**
Circ: Statement: **181,767** CapCity orders: **26,850**
📖 A Walk on the Darkside! • Big Barda **A:** John Byrne; Dick Giordano ★ Appearance of Big Barda.
593 ❑ Oct 1987 Cover: 0.75 **NM** value: **2.00**
Circ: Statement: **181,767** CapCity orders: **24,800**
📖 The Suicide Snare • Mr. Miracle **A:** John Byrne; Dick Giordano ★ Appearance of Mr. Miracle.
594 ❑ Nov 1987 Cover: 0.75 **NM** value: **2.00**
Circ: Statement: **181,767** CapCity orders: **25,700**
📖 All That Glisters • Booster Gold, Batman and Robin; Continues in Booster Gold #23 **A:** John Byrne ★ Appearance of Batman.
595 ❑ Dec 1987 Cover: 0.75 **NM** value: **2.00**
Circ: Statement: **181,767** CapCity orders: **26,000**
📖 The Ghost of Superman • J'onn J'onzz **A:** John Byrne ★ Appearance of Batman.
596 ❑ Jan 1988 Cover: 0.75 **NM** value: **2.00**
Circ: Statement: **97,779** CapCity orders: **30,000**
📖 Hell Is Where the Heart Is... • Spectre; "Millennium" Week 4 **A:** John Byrne ★ Appearance of Spectre.
597 ❑ Feb 1988 Cover: 0.75 **NM** value: **2.00**
Circ: Statement: **97,779** CapCity orders: **25,850**
📖 Visitor • Lois Lane and Lana Lang **A:** John Byrne ★ Appearance of Lois Lane and Lana Lang.
598 ❑ Mar 1988 Cover: 0.75 **NM** value: **2.50**
Circ: Statement: **97,779** CapCity orders: **27,700**
📖 Checkmate! • Checkmate **A:** John Byrne ★ 1st Appearance of Checkmate.
599 ❑ Apr 1988 Cover: 0.75 **NM** value: **2.00**
Circ: Statement: **97,779** CapCity orders: **28,600**
📖 Element 126; The Karma Baggers • Metal Men; Bonus Book #1, Jimmy Olsen **A:** John Byrne; Ross Andru ★ Appearance of Metal Men.
600 ❑ May 1988 Cover: 2.50 **NM** value: **5.00**
Circ: Statement: **97,779** CapCity orders: **41,750** • **CGC:** 2 graded, best 9.6
• Giant-sized. 📖 Different Worlds; (Untitled Lois Lane story); Games People Play; A Friend in Need; The Dark Where Madness Lies • 50th Anniversary, 80-page Giant; Wonder Woman; pin-ups; "Genesis" prequel **A:** George Pérez; John Byrne
601 ❑ Aug 1988 Cover: 1.50 **NM** value: **2.00**
Circ: Statement: **97,779** CapCity orders: **41,700**
📖 And the Pain Shall Leave My Heart; Moral Stand: Point of Order; Listening to the Mockingbird; Faster Than a Speeding Bullet!; The Section Chief; Another Fine War • Superman, Blackhawk, Green Lantern, Deadman, Wild Dog, Secret Six;Action Comics begins weekly issues
602 ❑ Aug 1988 Cover: 1.50 **NM** value: **1.75**
Circ: Statement: **97,779** CapCity orders: **25,400**
📖 Requiem; Showdown; Moral Stand: Dog Gone; They Can Run, But They Can't Hide!; Look What Fell Out of the Sky Today; Another Fine War, Part 2 • Superman, Blackhawk, Green Lantern, Deadman, Wild Dog, Secret Six
603 ❑ Aug 1988 Cover: 1.50 **NM** value: **1.75**
Circ: Statement: **97,779** CapCity orders: **24,700**
📖 Retribution!; Spread Your Broken Wings and Learn to Fly; Talaoc's Tale!; More Powerful Than a Locomotive!; Moral Stand: Censored; Another Fine War, Part 3 • Superman, Blackhawk, Green Lantern, Deadman, Wild Dog, Secret Six
604 ❑ Aug 1988 Cover: 1.50 **NM** value: **1.75**
Circ: Statement: **97,779** CapCity orders: **23,700**
📖 I, the Jury; Moral Stand: Unleashed!; Haunts of the Very Rich; Final Escape?; Genie in a Bottle; Another Fine War, Part 4 • Superman, Blackhawk, Green Lantern, Deadman, Wild Dog, Secret Six
605 ❑ Aug 1988 Cover: 1.50 **NM** value: **1.75**
Circ: Statement: **97,779** CapCity orders: **23,000**
📖 Golgotha; Deadman Goes to Hell; Moral Stand: Sleeping Dogs Lie; Aftermath; If That Mockingbird Don't Sing; Enter... Red Dragon! (Another Fine War, Part 5) • Superman, Blackhawk, Green Lantern, Deadman, Wild Dog, Secret Six
606 ❑ Sep 1988 Cover: 1.50 **NM** value: **1.75**
Circ: Statement: **97,779** CapCity orders: **20,950**
📖 The List; The Sins of the Father; This Is Hell; The True Believer; Moral Stand: Stop the Presses!; Another Fine War, Part 6 • Superman, Blackhawk, Green Lantern, Deadman, Wild Dog, Secret Six
607 ❑ Sep 1988 Cover: 1.50 **NM** value: **1.75**
Circ: Statement: **97,779** CapCity orders: **20,800**
📖 Guilty!; Escape from Hell; Moral Stand: Legionnaire's Disease; Familiar Face?; Gino; Another Fine War, Part 7 • Superman, Blackhawk, Green Lantern, Deadman, Wild Dog, Secret Six
608 ❑ Sep 1988 Cover: 1.50 **NM** value: **1.75**
Circ: Statement: **97,779** CapCity orders: **20,700**
📖 Where the Heck Is Green Lantern?; Moral Stand: Winged Dog; Blind Impulse; Questions and Mysteries; Gala Reception; Another Fine War, Conclusion • Superman, Blackhawk, Green Lantern, Deadman, Wild Dog, Secret Six
609 ❑ Sep 1988 Cover: 1.50 **NM** value: **1.75**
Circ: Statement: **97,779** CapCity orders: **20,450**
📖 Bitter Fruit; Faux Pas; Canned in Boston; And There Will Be a Sign!; Moral Stand: Red Pencil; Cutting Remarks • Superman, Black Canary, Green Lantern, Deadman, Wild Dog, Secret Six **C:** Brian Bolland
610 ❑ Sep 1988 Cover: 1.50 **NM** value: **1.75**
Circ: Statement: **97,779** CapCity orders: **20,100**
📖 Risky Business; Kenny And the Demon!; Catfight; Show & Tell; Another Man's Poison; Bitter Fruit, Part 2 • Superman, Phantom Stranger, Black Canary, Green Lantern, Deadman, Secret Six **A:** Kyle Baker; Dan Jurgens; Curt Swan; Tod Smith **W:** Mike Baron; Roger Stern; Paul Kupperberg; Peter David
611 ❑ Oct 1988 Cover: 1.50 **NM** value: **1.75**
Circ: Statement: **97,779** CapCity orders: **19,150**
📖 Room Service; Will the Real Devil Please Stand Up?; Bringing Home the Bacon; Beyond Mortal Men!; The Tin Roof Club; Bitter Fruit, Part 3 • Superman, Catwoman, Black Canary, Green Lantern, Deadman, Secret Six **W:** Mike Baron; Roger Stern; Paul Kupperberg; Peter David
612 ❑ Oct 1988 Cover: 1.50 **NM** value: **1.75**
Circ: Statement: **97,779** CapCity orders: **19,000**
📖 Mind Over Matter; Out of the Frying Pan, Into the Fire; Take Us to Our Leader; Where Lurks the Evil?; The Tin Roof Club, Part 2; Bitter Fruit, Part 4 • Superman, Catwoman, Black Canary, Green Lantern, Deadman, Secret Six
613 ❑ Oct 1988 Cover: 1.50 **NM** value: **1.75**
Circ: Statement: **97,779** CapCity orders: **18,900**
📖 Head Trip; The Cheshire Contract; Can't Judge a Book; Wicked Business!; The Tin Roof Club, Part 3; Bitter Fruit, Part 5 • Superman, Nightwing/Speedy, Phantom Stranger, Catwoman, Black Canary, Green Lantern
614 ❑ Oct 1988 Cover: 1.50 **NM** value: **1.75**
Circ: Statement: **97,779** CapCity orders: **18,800**
📖 Bring Me a Man; Death God; The Cheshire Contract, Part 2: First Blood; Death Comes Calling; The Tin Roof Club, Part 4; Bitter Fruit, Part 6 • Superman, Nightwing/Speedy, Phantom Stranger, Catwoman, Black Canary, Green Lantern
615 ❑ Oct 1988 Cover: 1.50 **NM** value: **1.75**
Circ: Statement: **97,779** CapCity orders: **16,600**
📖 Freaks!; That Was No Lady; Fatal Distraction: Night Patrol; Fatal Flaw?; The Cheshire Contract, Part 3: Tracks of a Killer!; Bitter Fruit, Part 7 • Superman, Wild Dog, Blackhawk, Nightwing/Speedy, Black Canary, Green Lantern
616 ❑ Nov 1988 Cover: 1.50 **NM** value: **1.75**
Circ: Statement: **97,779** CapCity orders: **16,700**
📖 Safe at Home; Mission: Implausible; Fatal Distraction: Battle Gear; Dead Men Tell No Tales; The Cheshire Contract, Part 4: Counterpoint; Bitter Fruit, Conclusion • Superman, Wild Dog, Blackhawk, Nightwing/Speedy, Black Canary, Green Lantern
617 ❑ Nov 1988 Cover: 1.50 **NM** value: **1.75**
Circ: Statement: **97,779** CapCity orders: **16,600**
📖 Assault on a Green; Seems Like Old Times; Fatal Distraction: Puppy Dog Tale; Missing Person; Channel Switching; The Cheshire Contract, Part 5: Motives • Superman, Phantom Stranger, Wild Dog, Blackhawk, Nightwing/Speedy, Green Lantern
618 ❑ Nov 1988 Cover: 1.50 **NM** value: **1.75**
Circ: Statement: **97,779** CapCity orders: **16,450**
📖 First Encounter; Unhappy Landing; Fatal Distraction: Lucky Night; Out on the Town; Deadman, Part 1: Grave Doings; The Cheshire Contract, Conclusion • Superman, Deadman, Wild Dog, Blackhawk, Nightwing/Speedy, Green Lantern
619 ❑ Nov 1988 Cover: 1.50 **NM** value: **1.75**
Circ: Statement: **97,779** CapCity orders: **16,500**
📖 Veronica; Fatal Distraction: One Mass Murderer to Go; Deadman, Part 2; Protective Shield?; Once More Unto the Breach; What's a Nice Girl Like You...? • Superman, Secret Six, Deadman, Wild Dog, Blackhawk, Green Lantern
620 ❑ Dec 1988 Cover: 1.50 **NM** value: **1.75**
Circ: Statement: **97,779** CapCity orders: **15,400**
📖 Last Gasp!; Fatal Distraction: Tailed!; Just a Little Bug That's Going Around; Too Late, the Hero?; Deadman, Part 3; Most Guys Just Leave Her Hanging There • Superman, Secret Six, Deadman, Wild Dog, Blackhawk, Green Lantern
621 ❑ Dec 1988 Cover: 1.50 **NM** value: **1.75**
Circ: Statement: **97,779** CapCity orders: **15,000**
📖 Gremlins!; Fatal Distraction: Stab in the Dark; Guess What We Learned in School Today?; Let the Punishment Fit the Crime; Deadman, Part 4; It's Not the Heat, It's the Futility • Superman, Secret Six, Deadman, Wild Dog, Blackhawk, Green Lantern
622 ❑ Dec 1988 Cover: 1.50 **NM** value: **1.75**
Circ: Statement: **97,779** CapCity orders: **14,900**
📖 The Edge of Forever; Fatal Distraction: To Help a Child; Starman; Seeds of Doubt; Dead Man on Campus; The Big Blowoff • Superman, Starman, Secret Six, Wild Dog, Blackhawk, Green Lantern
623 ❑ Dec 1988 Cover: 1.50 **NM** value: **1.75**
Circ: Statement: **97,779** CapCity orders: **14,900**
📖 Priest; My Week in Valhalla; Seventeen; Revelations; Standard Allowable Abductions; The Devil Was a Baby • Superman, Deadman, Phantom Stranger, Shazam!, Secret Six, Green Lantern **A:** Brent Anderson(cover)
624 ❑ Dec 1988 Cover: 1.50 **NM** value: **1.75**
Circ: Statement: **97,779** CapCity orders: **14,000**
📖 Faith!; Shazam!, Chapter 2; The Sound of a Silent Heart; Pin the Tail; Wildwood; Knock 'em Dead, Part 1 • Superman, Black Canary, Deadman, Shazam!, Secret Six, Green Lantern
625 ❑ Dec 1988 Cover: 1.50 **NM** value: **1.75**
Circ: Statement: **97,779** CapCity orders: **15,400**
📖 The Law; Shazam!, Chapter 3; For Whom the Toll Builds; Out of the Frying Pan...; Tickle, Tickle; Knock 'em Dead, Part 2 • Superman, Black Canary, Deadman, Shazam!, Secret Six, Green Lantern
626 ❑ Dec 1988 Cover: 1.50 **NM** value: **1.75**
Circ: Statement: **97,779** CapCity orders: **13,900**
📖 Bethel; Shazam!, Chapter 4; Capitol Offenses; ...Into the Fire!; Deadman, Finale; Knock 'em Dead, Part 3 • Superman, Black Canary, Deadman, Shazam!, Secret Six, Green Lantern
627 ❑ Dec 1988 Cover: 1.50 **NM** value: **1.75**
Circ: Statement: **97,779** CapCity orders: **13,900**
📖 And Now, Captain Atom; A Bird in the Hand...; Knock 'em Dead, Part 4; Panic in the Sands!; Rocks and Hard Places, Part 1: Travels; Rocks and Hard Places, Part 2: Distractions • Superman, Nightwing/Speedy, Black Canary, Secret Six, Green Lantern
628 ❑ Jan 1989 Cover: 1.50 **NM** value: **1.75**
Circ: CapCity orders: **12,600**

Other grades: Multiply prices above by **1.5 for Mint • 2/3 for Very Fine • 1/3 for Fine • 1/5 for Very Good • 1/8 for Good**

Heroes; Knock 'em Dead, Part 5; Rocks and Hard Places, Part 3: Arrival; Wipeout!; Remains to Be Seen; And a Time to Gather Stones Together • Superman, Blackhawk, Nightwing/Speedy, Black Canary, Secret Six, Green Lantern

629 ❑ Jan 1989 Cover: 1.50 **NM** value: **1.75**
Circ: CapCity orders: **12,500**
So Long Ago the Garden; Knock 'em Dead, Part 6; Beginning of the End; Journey's End; Rocks and Hard Places, Part 4: New Friends, Old Enemies; Some Guys Can't Take "No" for an Answer • Superman, Blackhawk, Nightwing/Speedy, Black Canary, Secret Six, Green Lantern

630 ❑ Jan 1989 Cover: 1.50 **NM** value: **1.75**
Circ: CapCity orders: **12,500**
Will; Knock 'em Dead, Part 7; The Mockingbird Still Singing O'er Its Grave; The Power from Beyond!; Rocks and Hard Places, Part 5: Attacks; Mr. Blackhawk Goes to Washington • Superman, Blackhawk, Nightwing/Speedy, Black Canary, Secret Six, Green Lantern

631 ❑ Jan 1989 Cover: 1.50 **NM** value: **1.75**
Circ: CapCity orders: **12,400**
Détente; Knock 'em Dead, Part 8; Cat and Mouse, Chapter 1; Point Blank; Rocks and Hard Places, Part 6: Old Friends, New Enemies; Kissoff – That's a Russian Word, Isn't It? • Superman, Phantom Stranger, Blackhawk, Nightwing/Speedy, Black Canary, Green Lantern

632 ❑ Jan 1989 Cover: 1.50 **NM** value: **1.75**
Circ: CapCity orders: **11,300**
Beyond Phobus; Cat and Mouse, Chapter 2; Knock 'em Dead, Part 9; Holy War; Rocks and Hard Places, Part 7: A Time of Changes; Doing the Horizontal Goosestep • Superman, Phantom Stranger, Blackhawk, Nightwing/Speedy, Black Canary, Green Lantern

633 ❑ Jan 1989 Cover: 1.50 **NM** value: **1.75**
Circ: CapCity orders: **11,300**
Apocalypse; Knock 'em Dead, Part 10; Rocks and Hard Places, Part 8: Behind Closed Doors; Blood and Sand; Cat and Mouse, Chapter 3; Gremlins at Twelve O'Clock • Superman, Phantom Stranger, Blackhawk, Nightwing/Speedy, Black Canary, Green Lantern

634 ❑ Jan 1989 Cover: 1.50 **NM** value: **1.75**
Circ: CapCity orders: **11,200**
Total War; Cat and Mouse, Chapter 4; Knock 'em Dead, Part 11; Breathless!; Rocks and Hard Places, Part 9: The Circle Closes; Coming Down • Superman, Phantom Stranger, Blackhawk, Nightwing/Speedy, Black Canary, Green Lantern

635 ❑ Jan 1989 Cover: 1.50 **NM** value: **1.75**
Circ: CapCity orders: **11,450**
The Crash of '88; Power Failure!; The End • Superman, Blackhawk, Black Canary, Green Lantern; All characters in first story

636 ❑ Jan 1989 Cover: 1.50 **NM** value: **1.75**
Circ: CapCity orders: **11,150**
Exiles; The Demon; All That Jazz; The Face and the Voice!; Daddy's Girl; Crack Up: Wrong Turn • Superman, Phantom Lady, Wild Dog, Demon, Speedy, Phantom Stranger ★ 1st Appearance of new Phantom Lady.

637 ❑ Jan 1989 Cover: 1.50 **NM** value: **1.75**
Circ: CapCity orders: **11,150**
Exiles, Part 2; Never Trust a Demon!; Hero Hotline; The Power of Darkseid!; Luck Be a Lady; Crack Up: Easy M$ney • Superman, Hero Hotline, Phantom Lady, Wild Dog, Demon, Speedy ★ 1st Appearance of Hero Hotline.

638 ❑ Feb 1989 Cover: 1.50 **NM** value: **1.75**
Circ: CapCity orders: **11,100**
Exiles, Part 3; The Road to Hell; Hero Hotline; The Power Within; Toast of the Capitol; Crack Up: Burning Down the House • Superman, Hero Hotline, Phantom Lady, Wild Dog, Demon, Speedy **A:** Jack Kirby; Tony DeZuniga; Terry Austin ★ 2nd Appearance of Hero Hotline.

639 ❑ Feb 1989 Cover: 1.50 **NM** value: **1.75**
Circ: CapCity orders: **11,100**
Exiles, Part 4; Witches; Hero Hotline; An Eye for an Eye; Belle of the Ball; Crack Up: Rung by Rung! • Superman, Hero Hotline, Phantom Lady, Wild Dog, Demon, Speedy ★ Appearance of Hero Hotline.

640 ❑ Feb 1989 Cover: 1.50 **NM** value: **1.75**
Circ: CapCity orders: **11,050**
Exiles, Part 5; Abandon Hope; Hero Hotline; Where There's Smoke…; Lady of the House; Crack Up: 'Tween a Rock and a Hard Place • Superman, Hero Hotline, Phantom Lady, Wild Dog, Demon, Speedy ★ Appearance of Hero Hotline.

641 ❑ Feb 1989 Cover: 1.50 **NM** value: **1.75**
Circ: CapCity orders: **10,350**
Welcome to Hell; Lady Lost; The Pow! Zap! Wham! Contract; Justice for All; Tommy's Monster; Crack Up: Unfriendly Takeover! • Superman, Phantom Stranger, Human Target, Phantom Lady, Wild Dog, Demon; Has 1988 Statement, filed 10/31/88; avg print run 116,416; avg sales 97,261; avg subs 518; avg total paid 97,779; samples 327; office use 792; max existent 98,898; 15% of run returned

642 ❑ Mar 1989 Cover: 1.50 **NM** value: **1.75**
Circ: CapCity orders: **11,550**
Where There Is a Will! • Superman, Green Lantern, Nightwing, Deadman, Guy Gardner in one story; Last weekly issue

643 ❑ Jul 1989 Cover: 0.75 **NM** value: **1.75**
Circ: CapCity orders: **35,100**
Cover swipe from Superman #1. Superman on Earth • Title returns to Action Comics;Monthly issues begin again **A:** George Pérez

644 ❑ Aug 1989 Cover: 0.75 **NM** value: **1.75**
Circ: CapCity orders: **28,000**
Doppelganger **A:** George Pérez

645 ❑ Sep 1989 Cover: 0.75 **NM** value: **1.75**
Circ: CapCity orders: **25,850**
My Lady Maxima! • Starman **A:** George Pérez ★ 1st Appearance of Maxima. ★ Versus Maxima.

646 ❑ Oct 1989 Cover: 0.75 **NM** value: **1.75**
Circ: CapCity orders: **23,600**
Burial Ground **A:** George Pérez

647 ❑ Nov 1989 Cover: 0.75 **NM** value: **1.75**
Circ: CapCity orders: **23,600**
Brain Drain • Braniac Trilogy, Part 1 **A:** George Pérez ★ Origin of Brainiac.

648 ❑ Dec 1989 Cover: 0.75 **NM** value: **1.75**
Circ: CapCity orders: **22,100**
Body and Mind • Braniac Trilogy, Part 2 **A:** George Pérez

649 ❑ Jan 1990 Cover: 0.75 **NM** value: **1.75**
Circ: CapCity orders: **21,900**
Man and Machine • Braniac Trilogy, Part 3 **A:** George Pérez

650 ❑ Feb 1990 Cover: 1.50 **NM** value: **1.75**
Circ: CapCity orders: **22,750**
Reflections **A:** Joe Orlando; George Pérez

651 ❑ Mar 1990 Cover: 0.75 **NM** value: **1.75**
Circ: CapCity orders: **19,950**
Not of This Earth • Day of the Krypton Man, Part 3 ★ Versus Maxima.

652 ❑ Apr 1990 Cover: 0.75 **NM** value: **1.75**
Circ: CapCity orders: **19,300**
Wayward Son • Day of the Krypton Man, Part 6

653 ❑ May 1990 Cover: 0.75 **NM** value: **1.75**
Circ: CapCity orders: **19,500**
Love & Death

654 ❑ Jun 1990 Cover: 0.75 **NM** value: **1.75**
Circ: CapCity orders: **33,250**
Dark Knight Over Metropolis • Batman

655 ❑ Jul 1990 Cover: 0.75 **NM** value: **1.75**
Circ: CapCity orders: **21,200**
Survival!; Ma Kent's Photo Album

656 ❑ Aug 1990 Cover: 0.75 **NM** value: **1.75**
Circ: CapCity orders: **20,650**
Soul Search Part 1: Going to Blaze's

657 ❑ Sep 1990 Cover: 0.75 **NM** value: **1.75**
Circ: CapCity orders: **20,800**
There Is a Happy Land… Far, Far Away • Toyman

658 ❑ Oct 1990 Cover: 0.75 **NM** value: **1.75**
Circ: CapCity orders: **21,450**
The Sinbad Contract, Part 3 **A:** Curt Swan ★ Appearance of Sinbad.

659 ❑ Nov 1990 Cover: 0.75 **NM** value: **1.75**
Circ: CapCity orders: **20,550**
Breakout! • Krisis of the Krimson Kryptonite, Part 3

660 ❑ Dec 1990 Cover: 0.75 **NM** value: **2.50**
Circ: CapCity orders: **21,050**
Certain Death ★ Death of Lex Luthor (fake death).

661 ❑ Jan 1991 Cover: 1.00 **NM** value: **1.75**
Stretching a Point! • Plastic Man; ▲1991-3

662 ❑ Feb 1991 Cover: 1.00 **NM** value: **2.50**
Circ: CapCity orders: **18,050** • **CGC:** 5 graded, best 9.8
Secrets in the Night • Clark Kent reveals Superman identity to Lois Lane▲1991-6

662-2 ❑ Feb 1991 Cover: 1.00 **NM** value: **1.50**

663 ❑ Mar 1991 Cover: 1.00 **NM** value: **1.75**
Circ: CapCity orders: **21,800**
Time and Time Again, Part 2: In the '40s Tonight • Superman in 1940s; JSA; ▲1991-9

664 ❑ Apr 1991 Cover: 1.00 **NM** value: **1.75**
Circ: CapCity orders: **21,850**
Time and Time Again, Part 5: Many Long Years Ago… • Dinosaurs; ▲1991-12 ★ Appearance of Chronos.

665 ❑ May 1991 Cover: 1.00 **NM** value: **1.75**
Circ: CapCity orders: **21,050**
Wake the Dead! • ▲1991-15

666 ❑ Jun 1991 Cover: 1.00 **NM** value: **1.75**
Circ: CapCity orders: **24,100**
Red Glass, Part 3: Picking Up the Pieces • ▲1991-18

667 ❑ Jul 1991 Cover: 1.75 **NM** value: **2.00**
Circ: CapCity orders: **35,750**
The Final Chapter • ▲1991-22

668 ❑ Aug 1991 Cover: 1.00 **NM** value: **1.75**
Circ: CapCity orders: **25,950**
The Ghost of Luthor • ▲1991-26

669 ❑ Sep 1991 Cover: 1.00 **NM** value: **1.75**
Circ: CapCity orders: **26,350**
Paper Trail • Thorn; ▲1991-30 ★ Appearance of Thorn.

670 ❑ Oct 1991 Cover: 1.00 **NM** value: **1.75**
Circ: CapCity orders: **33,450**
Skullduggery • Armageddon; ▲1991-34 ★ 1st Appearance of Lex Luthor II.

671 ❑ Nov 1991 Cover: 1.00 **NM** value: **1.75**
Circ: CapCity orders: **24,750**
Missing in Action • Blackout, Part 2; ▲1991-38

672 ❑ Dec 1991 Cover: 1.00 **NM** value: **1.75**
Circ: CapCity orders: **24,200**
All This… And Lex Luthor II! • ▲1991-42

673 ❑ Jan 1992 Cover: 1.00 **NM** value: **1.75**
Circ: CapCity orders: **22,200**
Friends in Need • ▲1992-4 ★ Versus Hellgrammite.

674 ❑ Apr 1992 Cover: 1.00 **NM** value: **1.75**
Circ: CapCity orders: **23,050** • **CGC:** 2 graded, best 9.6
The Past Is Prologue • Pnic in the Sky, Prologue; Supergirl; ▲1992-8

675 ❑ Mar 1992 Cover: 1.00 **NM** value: **1.75**
Circ: CapCity orders: **22,350**
Divide and Conquer • Panic in the Sky, Part 4; ▲1992-12

676 ❑ Apr 1992 Cover: 1.00 **NM** value: **1.75**
Circ: CapCity orders: **19,850**
Man of the Hour • ▲1992-16

677 ❑ May 1992 Cover: 1.00 **NM** value: **1.75**
Circ: CapCity orders: **19,850**
In Love and War! • ▲1992-20

678 ❑ Jun 1992 Cover: 1.00 **NM** value: **2.00**
Circ: CapCity orders: **20,300**
Talking Heads! • ▲1992-24 ★ Origin of Luthor.

679 ❑ Jul 1992 Cover: 1.00 **NM** value: **1.75**
Circ: CapCity orders: **20,250**
Shellshocked • ▲1992-28

680 ❑ Aug 1992 Cover: 1.25 **NM** value: **1.75**
Circ: CapCity orders: **20,950**
Payment Due • Blaze/Satanus War; ▲1992-32

681 ❑ Sep 1992 Cover: 1.25 **NM** value: **1.75**
Circ: CapCity orders: **18,600**
Odds &… Endings • ▲1992-36 ★ Versus Rampage.

682 ❑ Oct 1992 Cover: 1.25 **NM** value: **1.75**
Circ: CapCity orders: **18,450**
Gauntlet! • ▲1992-40 ★ Versus Hi-Tech.

683 ❑ Nov 1992 Cover: 1.25 **NM** value: **2.50**
Circ: CapCity orders: **18,150** • **CGC:** 1 graded, best 9.4
The Trial of the Jackal • Doomsday; ▲1992-44

683-2 ❑ Nov 1992 Cover: 1.25 **NM** value: **1.50**

684 ❑ Dec 1992 Cover: 1.25 **NM** value: **2.50**
Circ: CapCity orders: **25,100** • **CGC:** 2 graded, best 9.8
Doomsday In Near! • Doomsday; ▲1992-48

684-2 ❑ Dec 1992 Cover: 1.25 **NM** value: **1.50**

685 ❑ Jan 1993 Cover: 1.25 **NM** value: **2.00**
Circ: CapCity orders: **74,250**
Re:Actions • Funeral For a Friend, Part 2; ▲1993-4 **A:** Denis Rodier; Jackson Guice **W:** Roger Stern

685-2 ❑ Jan 1993 Cover: 1.25 **NM** value: **Cover or less**
Re:Actions • Funeral For a Friend, Part 2; ▲1993-4, 2nd Printing **A:** Denis Rodier; Jackson Guice **W:** Roger Stern

685-3 ❑ Jan 1993 Cover: 1.25 **NM** value: **Cover or less**
Re:Actions • Funeral For a Friend, Part 2; ▲1993-4, 3rd Printing **A:** Denis Rodier; Jackson Guice **W:** Roger Stern

686 ❑ Feb 1993 Cover: 1.25 **NM** value: **2.00**
Circ: CapCity orders: **82,700**
Who's Buried in Superman's Tomb? • Funeral For a Friend, Part 6; ▲1993-8 **A:** Denis Rodier; Jackson Guice **W:** Roger Stern

687 ❑ Jun 1993 Cover: 1.50 **NM** value: **Cover or less**
Circ: CapCity orders: **110,600** • **CGC:** 1 graded, best 9.2
Born Again • Reign of the Supermen; ▲1993-12 **A:** Denis Rodier; Jackson Guice **W:** Roger Stern ★ 1st Appearance of alien Superman. ★ Appearance of ?1993-12, 1st.

687/CS ❑ Jun 1993 Cover: 1.95 **NM** value: **2.50**
Circ: CapCity orders: **403,900**
Die-cut cover. Born Again • Reign of the Supermen; Eradicator; ▲1993-12 **A:** Denis Rodier; Jackson Guice **W:** Roger Stern ★ 1st Appearance of alien Superman, die-cut cover, Last Son of Krypton.

688 ❑ Jul 1993 Cover: 1.50 **NM** value: **2.00**
Circ: CapCity orders: **119,650**
Eye For An Eye • Reign of the Supermen; Guy Gardner; ▲1993-16 **A:** Denis Rodier; Jackson Guice **W:** Roger Stern

689 ❑ Jul 1993 Cover: 1.50 **NM** value: **2.00**
Circ: CapCity orders: **120,350**
Who Is The Hero True? • Reign of the Supermen; ▲1993-20 **A:** Denis Rodier; Jackson Guice **W:** Roger Stern

690 ❑ Aug 1993 Cover: 1.50 **NM** value: **2.00**
Circ: CapCity orders: **108,600**
Lies & Revelations • Reign of the Supermen; ▲1993-24

691 ❑ Sep 1993 Cover: 1.50 **NM** value: **2.00**
Circ: CapCity orders: **88,600**
Secret Weapon • Reign of the Supermen; ▲1993-28 **A:** Denis Rodier; Jackson Guice **W:** Roger Stern

692 ❑ Oct 1993 Cover: 1.50 **NM** value: **2.00**
Circ: CapCity orders: **80,850**
And Who, Disguised as Clark Kent? • Clark Kent returns; ▲1993-32

693 ❑ Nov 1993 Cover: 1.50 **NM** value: **2.00**
Circ: CapCity orders: **79,750**
The Last Purge of Krypton! • ▲1993-36

694 ❑ Dec 1993 Cover: 1.50 **NM** value: **1.75**
Circ: CapCity orders: **80,500**
Spilled Blood, Part 2: Survival of the Fittest! • ▲1993-40 ★ Versus Hi-Tech.

695 ❑ Jan 1994 Cover: 1.50 **NM** value: **1.75**
Cauldron! • ▲1994-4 **A:** Denis Rodier; Jackson Guice **W:** Karl Kesel ★ Appearance of Lobo.

695/SC ❑ Jan 1994 Cover: 2.50 **NM** value: **Cover or less**
Circ: CapCity orders: **100,350**
enhanced cover. Cauldron! • ▲1994-4 **A:** Denis Rodier; Jackson Guice **W:** Karl Kesel ★ Appearance of Lobo.

696 ❑ Feb 1994 Cover: 1.50 **NM** value: **1.75**
Circ: CapCity orders: **74,900**
Champion • Return of Doomsday; ▲1994-8 **A:** Denis Rodier; Jackson Guice **W:** Roger Stern

697 ❑ Mar 1994 Cover: 1.50 **NM** value: **1.75**
Circ: CapCity orders: **69,050**
War of the Super-Powers • Bizarro's World, Part 3; ▲1994-12

698 ❑ Apr 1994 Cover: 1.50 **NM** value: **1.75**
Circ: CapCity orders: **57,400**
Losing It! • ▲1994-16

699 ❑ May 1994 Cover: 1.50 **NM** value: **1.75**
Circ: CapCity orders: **53,300**
Eye of the Hurricane • The Battle for Metropolis▲1994-20

700 ❑ Jun 1994 Cover: 2.95 **NM** value: **3.25**
Circ: CapCity orders: **77,750** • **CGC:** 3 graded, best 9.8
• Giant-size. Swan Song • The Fall Of Metropolis; Wedding of Pete Ross and Lana Lang;Destruction of the Daily Planet building;▲1994-24 **A:** Denis Rodier; Jackson Guice **W:** Roger Stern

700/PL ❑ Jun 1994 **NM** value: **5.00**
no cover price. • Giant-size. Swan Song • The Fall Of Metropolis; Wedding of Pete Ross and Lana Lang;Destruction of the Daily Planet building;▲1994-24

701 ❑ Jul 1994 Cover: 1.50 **NM** value: **1.75**
Circ: CapCity orders: **55,000**
Final Conflict • Fall of Metropolis; ▲1994-28

702 ❑ Aug 1994 Cover: 1.50 **NM** value: **1.75**
Circ: CapCity orders: **50,650**
Bad Sport! • ▲1994-32 ★ Versus Bloodsport.

703 ❑ Sep 1994 Cover: 1.50 **NM** value: **1.75**
Circ: CapCity orders: **53,100**
Chronocide! • Zero Hour; ▲1994-36

704 ❑ Nov 1994 Cover: 1.50 **NM** value: **1.75**
Circ: CapCity orders: **45,250**
Eradication Day! • Dead Again; ▲1994-44 ★ Versus Eradictor and The Outsiders.

705 ❑ Dec 1994 Cover: 1.50 **NM** value: **1.75**
Circ: CapCity orders: **44,050**
Bodies & Motion • Dead Again; ▲1994-48

706 ❑ Jan 1995 Cover: 1.50 **NM** value: **1.75**
Circ: CapCity orders: **41,150**
Saved By the Belle! • Supergirl; ▲1995-4

707 ❑ Feb 1995 Cover: 1.50 **NM** value: **1.75**
Circ: CapCity orders: **39,625**
Like Fire From the Dark • ▲1995-8 ★ Versus Shadowdragon.

CGC-graded: Multiply prices above by **33 for 9.9 M** • **16 for 9.8 NM/M** • **7 for 9.6 NM+** • **5 for 9.4 NM** • **2.5 for 9.2 NM-** • **1.5 for 9.0 VF/NM**

708 ❑ Mar 1995 Cover: 1.50 **NM** value: **1.75**
Circ: CapCity orders: **37,975**
🕮 Moving Miracle! • Mr. Miracle; ▲1995-12 ★ Appearance of Mister Miracle.

709 ❑ Apr 1995 Cover: 1.50 **NM** value: **1.75**
Circ: CapCity orders: **34,825**
🕮 Crime Tunnel! – or – When Warriors Strongly Disagree! • Guy Gardner; ▲1995-16 ★ Versus Guy Gardner.

710 ❑ Jun 1995 Cover: 1.95 **NM** value: **Cover or less**
Circ: CapCity orders: **40,000**
🕮 Men of Different Mettle • Death of Clark Kent; ▲1995-20

711 ❑ Jul 1995 Cover: 1.95 **NM** value: **Cover or less**
Circ: CapCity orders: **38,675**
🕮 Home and the Hollow Heart • Death of Clark Kent; ▲▲1995-24 ★ Death of Kenny Braverman (Conduit).

712 ❑ Aug 1995 Cover: 1.95 **NM** value: **Cover or less**
Circ: CapCity orders: **33,150**
🕮 The Jimmy Cage! • ▲1995-29

713 ❑ Sep 1995 Cover: 1.95 **NM** value: **Cover or less**
Circ: CapCity orders: **31,825**
🕮 Scarlet Salvation • ▲1995-33

714 ❑ Oct 1995 Cover: 1.95 **NM** value: **Cover or less**
Circ: CapCity orders: **26,800**
🕮 Crossing the [Punch] Line! • Joker; ▲1995-37 ★ Appearance of Joker.

715 ❑ Nov 1995 Cover: 1.95 **NM** value: **Cover or less**
🕮 Doc Parasite! • ▲1995-42 ★ Versus Parasite.

716 ❑ Dec 1995 Cover: 1.95 **NM** value: **Cover or less**
🕮 Fugitive Justice! • Trial of Superman; ▲1995-46

717 ❑ Jan 1996 Cover: 1.95 **NM** value: **Cover or less**
🕮 H'Tros City! • Trial of Superman; ▲1996-1

718 ❑ Feb 1996 Cover: 1.95 **NM** value: **Cover or less**
🕮 By Darker Reason • ▲1996-5 **A:** Denis Rodier; Kieron Dwyer **W:** David Michelinie ★ 1st Appearance of Demolitia.

719 ❑ Mar 1996 Cover: 1.95 **NM** value: **Cover or less**
🕮 Hazard's Choice • Batman; ▲1996-9 **A:** Denis Rodier; Kieron Dwyer **W:** David Michelinie ★ Appearance of Batman.

720 ❑ Apr 1996 Cover: 1.95 **NM** value: **2.00**
🕮 Love Breaks • Lois Lane breaks off engagement to Clark Kent; ▲1996-14 **A:** Denis Rodier; Kieron Dwyer **W:** David Michelinie

720-2 ❑ Apr 1996 Cover: 1.95 **NM** value: **Cover or less**

721 ❑ May 1996 Cover: 1.95 **NM** value: **Cover or less**
🕮 The Fortune Plague • ▲1996-18 ★ Appearance of Mxyzptlk.

722 ❑ Jun 1996 Cover: 1.95 **NM** value: **Cover or less**
🕮 Courageous Intent • ▲1996-22

723 ❑ Jul 1996 Cover: 1.95 **NM** value: **Cover or less**
🕮 Identity Crisis II: Keys • ▲1996-27

724 ❑ Aug 1996 Cover: 1.95 **NM** value: **Cover or less**
🕮 Losing Brawl! • ▲1996-31

725 ❑ Sep 1996 Cover: 1.95 **NM** value: **Cover or less**
🕮 Variations on a Scheme • The Bottle City, Part 1; ▲1996-35 ★ Versus Tolos.

726 ❑ Oct 1996 Cover: 1.95 **NM** value: **Cover or less**
🕮 Arms! • ▲1996-40 **A:** Tom Morgan **W:** David Michelinie ★ Versus Barrage.

727 ❑ Nov 1996 Cover: 1.95 **NM** value: **Cover or less**
Circ: Diamd. preorders: **63,599**
🕮 Cold Comfort! • Final Night; ▲1996-44 **A:** Denis Rodier **W:** David Michelinie

728 ❑ Dec 1996 Cover: 1.95 **NM** value: **Cover or less**
Circ: Diamd. preorders: **91,838**
🕮 I Killed Superman • Hawaiian Honeymoon; ▲1996-49 **A:** Denis Rodier; Tom Grummettt **W:** David Michelinie

729 ❑ Jan 1997 Cover: 1.95 **NM** value: **Cover or less**
Circ: Diamd. preorders: **60,552**
🕮 Generator X! • Power Struggle; ▲1997-3 **A:** Denis Rodier; Tom Grummettt **W:** David Michelinie ★ Appearance of Mr. Miracle, Big Barda.

730 ❑ Feb 1997 Cover: 1.95 **NM** value: **Cover or less**
Circ: Diamd. preorders: **55,842**
🕮 The President of the United Hates • Superman Revenge Squad; ▲1997-8 **A:** Denis Rodier; Tom Grummettt **W:** David Michelinie ★ Versus Superman Revenge Squad (Anomaly, Maxima, Misa, Barrage and Riot).

731 ❑ Mar 1997 Cover: 1.95 **NM** value: **Cover or less**
Circ: Diamd. preorders: **54,590**
🕮 ...Fire Burn and Cauldron Bubble! • ▲1997-12 **A:** Denis Rodier; Tom Grummettt **W:** David Michelinie ★ Versus Cauldron.

732 ❑ Apr 1997 Cover: 1.95 **NM** value: **Cover or less**
Circ: Diamd. preorders: **53,050**
🕮 The Saving Skull • more energy powers manifest; ▲1997-17 **A:** Denis Rodier; Tom Grummettt **W:** David Michelinie ★ Versus Atomic Skull.

733 ❑ May 1997 Cover: 1.95 **NM** value: **Cover or less**
Circ: Diamd. preorders: **96,928**
🕮 The Sins of Change • new uniform; Ray; ▲1997-21 ★ Appearance of Ray.

734 ❑ Jun 1997 Cover: 1.95 **NM** value: **Cover or less**
Circ: Diamd. preorders: **74,297**
🕮 Bottle Battle • Scorn vs. Rock; ▲1997-25

735 ❑ Jul 1997 Cover: 1.95 **NM** value: **Cover or less**
Circ: Diamd. preorders: **69,959**
🕮 Deadly Deliverance! • ▲1997-29 ★ Versus Saviour.

736 ❑ Aug 1997 Cover: 1.95 **NM** value: **Cover or less**
Circ: Diamd. preorders: **68,194**
🕮 Without and Within • ▲1997-33

737 ❑ Sep 1997 Cover: 1.95 **NM** value: **Cover or less**
Circ: Diamd. preorders: **66,144**
🕮 Burden of Proof • Jimmy pursued by Intergang; ▲1997-37

738 ❑ Oct 1997 Cover: 1.95 **NM** value: **Cover or less**
Circ: Diamd. preorders: **63,801**
🕮 Straight on 'Till Morning • ▲1997-42 ★ 1st Appearance of Inkling.

739 ❑ Nov 1997 Cover: 1.95 **NM** value: **Cover or less**
Circ: Diamd. preorders: **59,843**
🕮 Party Trappings • Lois captured by Naga; ▲1997-46 **A:** Jose Marzan Jr. **W:** Stuart Immonen ★ Appearance of Sam Lane. ★ Versus Locksmith.

740 ❑ Dec 1997 Cover: 1.95 **NM** value: **Cover or less**
Circ: Diamd. preorders: **58,163**
Face cover. 🕮 A Bag, a Bone, & a Hank of Hair • ▲1997-50 **A:** Stuart Immonen **W:** Stuart Immonen ★ Versus Ripper.

741 ❑ Jan 1998 Cover: 1.95 **NM** value: **Cover or less**
Circ: Diamd. preorders: **57,088**
🕮 A Cautionary Tale • Legion of Super-Heroes; ▲1998-4 ★ Appearance of Legion of Super-Heroes.

742 ❑ Mar 1998 Cover: 1.95 **NM** value: **Cover or less**
Circ: Diamd. preorders: **52,554**
🕮 Devil May Care • Cover forms diptych with Superman: Man of Steel #77; ▲1998-10

743 ❑ Apr 1998 Cover: 1.95 **NM** value: **Cover or less**
Circ: Diamd. preorders: **50,292**
🕮 Operation: Ink!; A Persistence of You • Orgin of Inkling; ▲1998-14 **A:** Jose Marzan Jr.; Greg Land **W:** Stuart Immonen

744 ❑ May 1998 Cover: 1.95 **NM** value: **Cover or less**
Circ: Diamd. preorders: **53,196**
🕮 Crossroads • Millennium Giants; ▲1998-18

745 ❑ Jun 1998 Cover: 1.95 **NM** value: **Cover or less**
Circ: Diamd. preorders: **59,414**
🕮 Polyester Year, Part 1: Ready, Fire, Aim • Toyman; ▲1998-23 ★ Versus Prankster.

746 ❑ Jul 1998 Cover: 1.95 **NM** value: **Cover or less**
Circ: Diamd. preorders: **53,157**
🕮 Polyester Year, Part 2: Love, Supervillain Style • Toyman; ▲1998-27 ★ Versus Prankster.

747 ❑ Aug 1998 Cover: 1.95 **NM** value: **Cover or less**
Circ: Diamd. preorders: **52,660**
🕮 Eye of the Storm • ▲1998-31 ★ Appearance of Dominus.

748 ❑ Sep 1998 Cover: 1.99 **NM** value: **Cover or less**
Circ: Diamd. preorders: **49,688**
🕮 Chasing the Ancient of Days • ▲1998-35 ★ Appearance of Waverider. ★ Versus Dominus.

749 ❑ Dec 1998 Cover: 1.99 **NM** value: **2.00**
Circ: Diamd. preorders: **46,756**
🕮 City of the Future • into Kandor; ▲1998-41

750 ❑ Jan 1999 Cover: 2.95 **NM** value: **Cover or less**
Circ: Diamd. preorders: **48,957**
• Giant-size. 🕮 Confidence Job • ▲1999-1 **A:** Jose Marzan Jr. **W:** Stuart Immonen ★ 1st Appearance of Crazytop.

751 ❑ Feb 1999 Cover: 1.99 **NM** value: **Cover or less**
Circ: Diamd. preorders: **43,424**
🕮 Sixes and Sevens • ▲1999-6 **A:** Stuart Immonen **W:** Stuart Immonen ★ Appearance of Lex Luthor, Geo-Force, DEO agents.

752 ❑ Mar 1999 Cover: 1.99 **NM** value: **Cover or less**
Circ: Diamd. preorders: **41,801**
🕮 Superman: Have You Forsaken Metropolis? • Superman of America; ▲1999-11 **A:** Stuart Immonen **W:** Stuart Immonen ★ Appearance of Supermen of America.

753 ❑ Apr 1999 Cover: 1.99 **NM** value: **Cover or less**
Circ: Diamd. preorders: **41,108**
🕮 A Law Unto Himself • JLA; ▲1999-15 **A:** Stuart Immonen **W:** Stuart Immonen; Mark Millar ★ Appearance of Justice League of America, JLA.

754 ❑ May 1999 Cover: 1.99 **NM** value: **Cover or less**
Circ: Diamd. preorders: **39,557**
🕮 The Aimless Blade of Science • ▲1999-20 **A:** Stuart Immonen **W:** Stuart Immonen; Mark Millar ★ Versus Dominus.

755 ❑ Jul 1999 Cover: 1.99 **NM** value: **Cover or less**
Circ: Diamd. preorders: **40,816**
🕮 Necropolis • ▲1999-25 **A:** Shawn Martinsbrough **W:** Stuart Immonen; Mark Millar

756 ❑ Aug 1999 Cover: 1.99 **NM** value: **Cover or less**
Circ: Diamd. preorders: **40,217**
🕮 Comeback **A:** Vince Giarrano **W:** John Rozum ★ Versus Doomslayers.

757 ❑ Sep 1999 Cover: 1.99 **NM** value: **Cover or less**
Circ: Diamd. preorders: **40,516**
🕮 One-Man JLA: Secret Origins, Part 3: Eyes of the Hawk • Superman as Hawkman; ▲1999-34 **A:** Tom Grindberg **W:** Tom Peyer

758 ❑ Oct 1999 Cover: 1.99 **NM** value: **Cover or less**
Circ: Diamd. preorders: **37,817**
🕮 (Untitled) • ▲1999-38 **A:** Stuart Immonen **W:** Stuart Immonen; Mark Millar ★ Versus Intergang.

759 ❑ Nov 1999 Cover: 1.99 **NM** value: **Cover or less**
Circ: Diamd. preorders: **37,577**
🕮 Who is Strange Visitor?, Part 3: Where? • ▲1999-42 **A:** Sal Buscema; Ron Frenz; Rand Frenz **W:** Ron Frenz; Ran Frenz ★ Appearance of Strange Visitor.

760 ❑ Dec 1999 Cover: 1.99 **NM** value: **Cover or less**
Circ: Diamd. preorders: **40,212**
🕮 ...Never-Ending Battle... • ▲1999-49 **A:** German Garcia **W:** Joe Kelly

761 ❑ Jan 2000 Cover: 1.99 **NM** value: **Cover or less**
Circ: Diamd. preorders: **37,785**
🕮 For a Thousand Years... • ▲2000-4 **A:** German Garcia **W:** Joe Kelly ★ Appearance of Wonder Woman.

762 ❑ Feb 2000 Cover: 1.99 **NM** value: **Cover or less**
Circ: Diamd. preorders: **39,578**
🕮 All I Want for Christmas • ▲2000-9

763 ❑ Mar 2000 Cover: 1.99 **NM** value: **Cover or less**
Circ: Diamd. preorders: **38,162**
🕮 Sacrifice for Tomorrow • ▲2000-13

764 ❑ Apr 2000 Cover: 1.99 **NM** value: **Cover or less**
Circ: Diamd. preorders: **37,083**
🕮 Quiet After the Storm • ▲2000-17 **A:** Kano **W:** Joe Kelly

765 ❑ May 2000 Cover: 1.99 **NM** value: **Cover or less**
Circ: Diamd. preorders: **40,251**
🕮 A Clown Comes to Metropolis • Joker, Harley Quinn; ▲2000-21 **A:** Kano **W:** Joe Kelly

766 ❑ Jun 2000 Cover: 1.99 **NM** value: **Cover or less**
Circ: Diamd. preorders: **40,052** • **CGC:** 1 graded, best 9.8
🕮 D.O.A. • ▲2000-25

767 ❑ Jul 2000 Cover: 1.99 **NM** value: **Cover or less**
Circ: Diamd. preorders: **39,222**
• ▲2000-29

768 ❑ Aug 2000 Cover: 2.25 **NM** value: **Cover or less**
Circ: Diamd. preorders: **40,669**
🕮 O, Captain, My Captain! • ▲2000-33 **A:** Duncan Rouleau **W:** Joe Kelly ★ Appearance of Captain Marvel Jr., Captain Marvel, Mary Marvel.

769 ❑ Sep 2000 Cover: 2.25 **NM** value: **Cover or less**
Circ: Diamd. preorders: **44,524**
🕮 Superman Arkham, Part 2: Supermanamrepus • ▲2000-37 **A:** Kano **W:** Joe Kelly

770 ❑ Oct 2000 Cover: 3.50 **NM** value: **Cover or less**
Circ: Diamd. preorders: **40,808**
• Giant-size. 🕮 The Reign of Emperor Joker, Part 5: He Who Laughs Last! • ▲2000-42 **A:** Kano **W:** Joe Kelly ★ Appearance of Joker.

771 ❑ Nov 2000 Cover: 2.25 **NM** value: **Cover or less**
Circ: Diamd. preorders: **40,324**
🕮 The Out of Towner • Nightwing; ▲2000-46 **A:** Pascual Ferry **W:** Chuck Dixon ★ Appearance of Nightwing.

772 ❑ Dec 2000 Cover: 2.25 **NM** value: **Cover or less**
Circ: Diamd. preorders: **39,936**
🕮 Kith & Kin, Part 1 • ▲2000-50 **A:** Kano **W:** Joe Kelly ★ Appearance of Encantadora, Talia.

773 ❑ Jan 2001 Cover: 2.25 **NM** value: **Cover or less**
Circ: Diamd. preorders: **39,749**
🕮 Kith & Kin, Part 2 • ▲2001-5 **A:** Aluir Amancio; Kano **W:** Joe Kelly

774 ❑ Feb 2001 Cover: 2.25 **NM** value: **Cover or less**
Circ: Diamd. preorders: **38,327**
🕮 Fireside Chat • ▲2001-9 **A:** Eric Canete **W:** Joe Kelly

775 ❑ Mar 2001 Cover: 3.75 **NM** value: **Cover or less**
Circ: Diamd. preorders: **37,076** • **CGC:** 11 graded, best 9.8
• Giant-size. 🕮 What's so Funny About Truth, Justice, & the American Way? • ▲2001-13 **A:** Lee Bermejo; Dough Mahnke **W:** Joe Kelly

776 ❑ Apr 2001 Cover: 2.25 **NM** value: **Cover or less**
Circ: Diamd. preorders: **38,512**
🕮 Escape from Krypton • ▲2001-17 **A:** Kano **W:** Joe Kelly

777 ❑ May 2001 Cover: 2.25 **NM** value: **Cover or less**
Circ: Diamd. preorders: **35,538**
🕮 Kancer • ▲2001-21 **A:** Kano **W:** Joe Kelly

778 ❑ Jun 2001 Cover: 2.25 **NM** value: **Cover or less**
Circ: Diamd. preorders: **37,858**

779 ❑ Jul 2001 Cover: 2.25 **NM** value: **Cover or less**
Circ: Diamd. preorders: **37,846**

780 ❑ Aug 2001 Cover: 2.25 **NM** value: **Cover or less**
Circ: Diamd. preorders: **45,692**

781 ❑ Sep 2001 Cover: 2.25 **NM** value: **Cover or less**
Circ: Diamd. preorders: **47,911**

1000000 ❑ Nov 1998 Cover: 1.99 **NM** value: **2.00**
Circ: Diamd. preorders: **57,212**
🕮 Brave New Hero **A:** Ron Lim **W:** Mark Schultz

Anl 1 ❑ Cover: 1.25 **NM** value: **4.00**
Circ: CapCity orders: **33,100** • **CGC:** 1 graded, best 9.8
🕮 Skeeter! • Batman, female vampire; 1987 Annual **A:** Arthur Adams; Dick Giordano

Anl 2 ❑ Cover: 1.75 **NM** value: **3.00**
Circ: CapCity orders: **26,150**
🕮 Memories of Krypton's Past; How I Spent My Super-Summer Vacation by George Perez (text); • Matrix and Cat Grant bios; pin-up; 1989 Annual **A:** Joe Orlando; George Pérez; Curt Swan ★ 1st Appearance of The Eradicator.

Anl 3 ❑ Cover: 2.00 **NM** value: **2.50**
Circ: CapCity orders: **42,200**
🕮 Executive Action • Armageddon 2001, Part 8; 1991 Annual

Anl 4 ❑ Cover: 2.50 **NM** value: **Cover or less**
Circ: CapCity orders: **25,250**
🕮 Living Daylights • Eclipso: The Darkness Within, Part 10; 1992 Annual **A:** Chris Wozniak **W:** Dan Vado

Anl 5 ❑ Cover: 2.50 **NM** value: **Cover or less**
Circ: CapCity orders: **41,450**
🕮 Loose Cannon! • Bloodlines: Earthplague; 1993 Annual **A:** Lee Moder **W:** Jeph Loeb ★ 1st Appearance of Loose Cannon.

Anl 6 ❑ ca. 1994 Cover: 2.95 **NM** value: **Cover or less**
Circ: CapCity orders: **36,750**
🕮 Legacy; Doomsday for the Fifth Dimension! • Elseworlds; 1994 Annual

Anl 7 ❑ ca. 1995 Cover: 3.95 **NM** value: **Cover or less**
🕮 Loss and Space! Superman: Year One • Year One; 1995 Annual

Anl 8 ❑ ca. 1996 Cover: 2.95 **NM** value: **Cover or less**
🕮 A World of Hurt • Bizarro; Legends of the Dead Earth; 1996 Annual **A:** Kieron Dwyer **W:** David Michelinie ★ Appearance of Bizarro.

Anl 9 ❑ ca. 1997 Cover: 3.95 **NM** value: **Cover or less**
Circ: Diamd. preorders: **45,672**
🕮 The Magnetic Medium • Pulp Heroes #9; 1997 Annual **A:** Brett Breeding; Vince Giarrano **W:** David Michelinie

A.C.T.I.O.N. FORCE (LIGHTNING) Lightning

1 ❑ Jan 1987 Cover: 1.75 **NM** value: **Cover or less**

ACTION GIRL COMICS Slave Labor

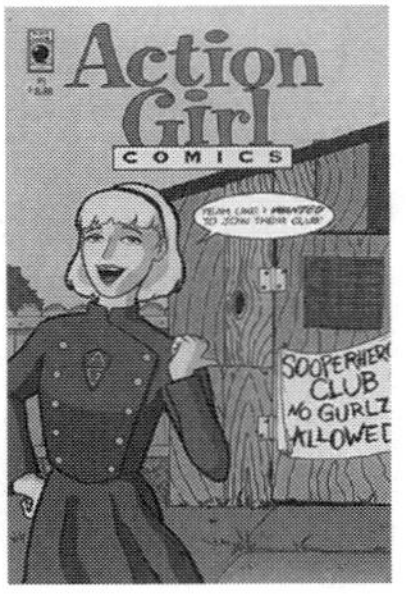

Sarah Dyer created Action Girl Comics as a sort of springboard for new women cartoonists to use to attract attention. Each issue features the work of numerous cartoonists, each of whom brings an individual style and sensibility to bear. Artistic styles can range from the anime-like characters of Elizabeth Watasin to the more darkly "alternative" work of Carolyn Ridsdale. For her part, Sarah Dyer both coordinates Action Girl and gives new installments of the adventures of the cheerful title character. Readers who are interested in the work of any of these artists can find further biographical and ordering information in the back of each issue.

Other grades: Multiply prices above by **1.5 for Mint • 2/3 for Very Fine • 1/3 for Fine • 1/5 for Very Good • 1/8 for Good**

Overall, Action Girl Comics is a pleasantly hip sampler of the world of women cartoonists. It's a perfect showcase, not only for their work, but for the very idea of artistic independence and self-publishing.

1 ❑ Oct 1994 Cover: 2.50 **NM** value: **3.50**
Soundtrack; Action Girl: Cakes & Dresses; River Baby Dream Child; All Girls Together; Damn Crow!; Reservoir; Hey, Amy! What do you Want to be When you Grow Up?; What's Been Going On; Fluffy: The Cat who Was a Rock Star!; A Poem; The Grunge **A:** Jennifer Sorensen; Rebecca Dart; Sarah Dyer; Amy Frushour; Carol Seatory; Elizabeth Watasin; Fallen Angel; Jessica Abel; Leanne Franson; Megan Kelso; Ms. Phink; She-Ra **W:** Jennifer Sorensen; Rebecca Dart; Sarah Dyer; Amy Frushour; Carol Seatory; Elizabeth Watasin; Fallen Angel; Jessica Abel; Leanne Franson; Megan Kelso; Ms. Phink; She-Ra
1-2 ❑ Feb 1996 Cover: 2.75 **NM** value: **Cover or less**
2 ❑ Jan 1995 Cover: 2.50 **NM** value: **3.00**
2-2 ❑ Oct 1995 Cover: 2.75 **NM** value: **Cover or less**
3 ❑ Apr 1995 Cover: 2.50 **NM** value: **3.00**
3-2 ❑ Feb 1996 Cover: 2.75 **NM** value: **Cover or less**
4 ❑ Jul 1995 Cover: 2.50 **NM** value: **3.00**
4-2 ❑ Jul 1996 Cover: 2.75 **NM** value: **3.00**
4-3 ❑ Cover: 2.75 **NM** value: **3.00**
5 ❑ Oct 1995 Cover: 2.50 **NM** value: **3.00**
6 ❑ Jan 1996 Cover: 2.50 **NM** value: **2.75**
6-2 ❑ Cover: 2.75 **NM** value: **Cover or less**
7 ❑ May 1996 Cover: 2.50 **NM** value: **2.75**
8 ❑ Jul 1996 Cover: 2.50 **NM** value: **2.75**
9 ❑ Cover: 2.50 **NM** value: **2.75**
10 ❑ Jan 1997 Cover: 2.75 **NM** value: **Cover or less**
Circ: Direct Market orders: **2,155**
Pivotal Scenes from My Life as a Stage Actress; MRE Blues: A True Army ROTC Story; The Adventures of Pezgal; Flip Flop; Bunnygrunt High; Hopster's Tracks: Sushi Lesson; My Reality; Life's Great Rewards
11 ❑ May 1997, b&w Cover: 2.75 **NM** value: **Cover or less**
Tobey's Holiday Dinner!; How I Became Beautiful; Going Dutch; Tiny Totz Comix in: Puberty Shmewberty!; Quitter; Pivotal Scenes from My Life as a Stage Actress; Fashion Is Silly;
12 ❑ Jul 1997 Cover: 2.75 **NM** value: **Cover or less**
Her Day Starring Ultra Girl; Pivotal Scenes from My Life as a Stage Actress; Captain Action Girl
13 ❑ Oct 1997 Cover: 2.75 **NM** value: **Cover or less**
14 ❑ Jul 1998 Cover: 2.75 **NM** value: **Cover or less**
The Spy Who Dug Me!; The Adventures of Armless Astrid; Bridezilla!; Blue Monday: The Ants Come Marching; Fielding Error

ACTION PLANET COMICS — Action Planet

1 ❑ b&w Cover: 3.95 **NM** value: **Cover or less**
Hero of the Beach; Nailz: the Fix; Scent of a Womyn; Uncle Slam & Fire Dog; Rumination on Ruination • Black and white **A:** John Heebink; Mike Manley; Ande Parks; Phil Hester; Aaron McClellan **W:** John Heebink; Mike Manley; Ande Parks; Phil Hester; Aaron McClellan
2 ❑ Sep 2000, b&w Cover: 3.95 **NM** value: **Cover or less**
3 ❑ Sep 1997, b&w Cover: 3.95 **NM** value: **Cover or less**
Ash 1❑b&w Cover: 2.00 **NM** value: **Cover or less**
• b&w preview of series;"Philly Ashcan Ed.";Black and white
GS 1❑Oct 1998 Cover: 5.95 **NM** value: **Cover or less**
• Giant size. Menace Before Midnight!; A Brannigan's Ghost Escapade; They Saved Reagan's Brain; Little Stiffy; An Atomic Moster Walks Among Us!; It's the Great Pumpkin, Uncle Slam; Black Angel; Hem -n- Haw **A:** William Wray; Bret Blevins; Jason Armstrong; Andy Kuhn; John Heebink; Mike Manley; Phil Hester; Colin Wales; Nick Bertozzi; Scott Cohn; Bill Curran; Marc Whelan **W:** William Wray; Bret Blevins; Jason Armstrong; John Heebink; Mike Manley; Ande Parks; Phil Hester; Scott Cohn ★ Appearance of Wretch, Brannigan's Ghost, Doc Thunder, Uncle Slam, Wrathbone, Fire Dog, Haw, Hem, Monsterman, Bitchula.

ACTIONS SPEAK (SERGIO ARAGONÉS...) — Dark Horse

1 ❑ Jan 2001 Cover: 2.99 **NM** value: **Cover or less**
A: Sergio Aragonés **W:** Sergio Aragonés
2 ❑ Feb 2001 Cover: 2.99 **NM** value: **Cover or less**
A: Sergio Aragonés **W:** Sergio Aragonés
3 ❑ Mar 2001 Cover: 2.99 **NM** value: **Cover or less**
A: Sergio Aragonés **W:** Sergio Aragonés
4 ❑ Apr 2001 Cover: 2.99 **NM** value: **Cover or less**
A: Sergio Aragonés **W:** Sergio Aragonés
5 ❑ May 2001 Cover: 2.99 **NM** value: **Cover or less**
A: Sergio Aragonés **W:** Sergio Aragonés
6 ❑ Jun 2001 Cover: 2.99 **NM** value: **Cover or less**
A: Sergio Aragonés **W:** Sergio Aragonés

A.D.A.M. — The Toy Man

1 ❑ Cover: 2.95 **NM** value: **Cover or less**
In the Beginning **A:** Joseph Grau **W:** Jonathan Clark
Ash 1❑ **NM** value: **1.00**
no cover price. • preview

ADAM-12 — Gold Key

"One Adam-12, One Adam-12!" Those memorable words from the police dispatcher in 1968 ushered in a TV cop show going behind the scenes to view the world of two uniformed policemen assigned to a patrol car. Jack Webb, whose Dragnet series about police detectives had been a major success on both radio and TV, saw to it that his new series (like Dragnet) featured a variety of cases. Some of the stories were played for laughs; some had tension-filled suspense moments. Gold Key delivered a solid comic-book version of the television show (with a little more mystery and action added for spice) and cool photo covers of the heroes, Pete Malloy and Jim Reed.

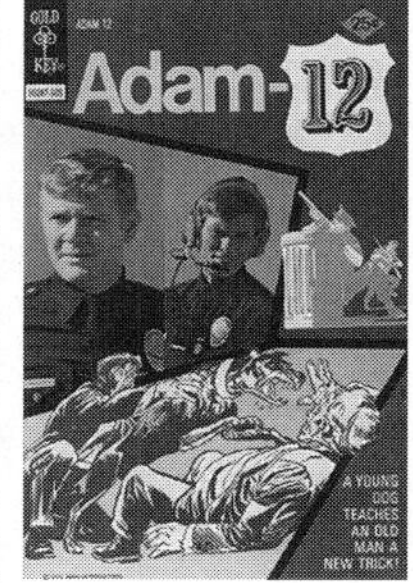

1 ❑ Dec 1973 Cover: 0.25 **NM** value: **30.00**
• **CGC:** 2 graded, best 8.5
2 ❑ Feb 1974 Cover: 0.25 **NM** value: **18.00**
3 ❑ Apr 1974 Cover: 0.25 **NM** value: **16.00**
4 ❑ Jun 1974 Cover: 0.25 **NM** value: **16.00**
5 ❑ Cover: 0.25 **NM** value: **16.00**
6 ❑ Mar 1975 Cover: 0.25 **NM** value: **14.00**
7 ❑ May 1975 Cover: 0.25 **NM** value: **14.00**
Photo cover. The Old Guard; Trouble in Tow
8 ❑ Cover: 0.25 **NM** value: **14.00**
9 ❑ 1975 Cover: 0.25 **NM** value: **14.00**
10 ❑ Feb 1976 Cover: 0.25 **NM** value: **14.00**
Photo cover. A Double Life; One Wild Night; They Get Their Man!

ADAM AND EVE A.D. — Bam

1 ❑ Sep 1985 Cover: 1.50 **NM** value: **Cover or less**
2 ❑ Nov 1985 Cover: 1.50 **NM** value: **Cover or less**
3 ❑ Jan 1986 Cover: 1.50 **NM** value: **Cover or less**
What Mortals These Fools Be
4 ❑ Mar 1986 Cover: 1.50 **NM** value: **Cover or less**
Arcane **A:** Shawn Sharp **W:** Shawn Sharp; Tim Zimmerman
5 ❑ May 1986 Cover: 1.50 **NM** value: **Cover or less**
6 ❑ Jul 1986 Cover: 1.50 **NM** value: **Cover or less**
7 ❑ Oct 1986 Cover: 1.50 **NM** value: **Cover or less**
With Friends Like These **A:** Shawn Sharp; Tim Zimmerman **W:** Shawn Sharp; Tim Zimmerman
8 ❑ Nov 1986 Cover: 1.50 **NM** value: **Cover or less**
9 ❑ Jan 1987 Cover: 1.50 **NM** value: **Cover or less**
10 ❑ Mar 1987 Cover: 1.50 **NM** value: **Cover or less**

ADAM BOMB COMICS — Blue Monkey

1 ❑ Sum 1999, b&w Cover: 2.00 **NM** value: **Cover or less**

ADAM STRANGE — DC

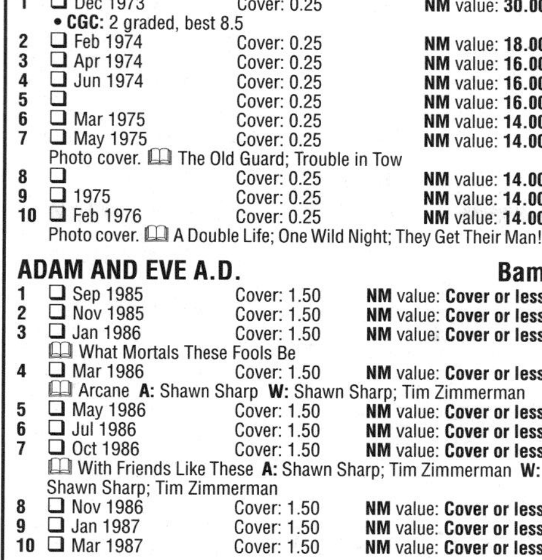

Adam Strange is an Earth-born space hero who was a regular star of DC's old Mystery in Space series. He got his start as a noted archaeologist who was excavating an ancient Inca city when he was struck by a "Zeta Beam" sent from the distant planet Rann. The beam had originally been sent by Rann's scientist Sardath as a way of contacting alien life forms, but, instead, it accidentally brought Strange back. While on Rann, he stopped an invasion and became a hero, but the beam's effects wore off and he was returned to Earth. Luckily, other beams had been sent, and, by catching them at the right place on Earth, he can travel back and forth.

In this three-issue series, Strange gets a 90s-style update, exposing more sinister sides of Sardath's plans and offering Strange one final chance to visit Earth before a "Mega-Zeta Beam" makes his transport to Rann permanent.

1 ❑ Mar 1990 Cover: 3.95 **NM** value: **Cover or less**
Circ: CapCity orders: **2,100**
Chapter 1 **A:** Andy Kubert **W:** Richard Bruning
2 ❑ May 1990 Cover: 3.95 **NM** value: **Cover or less**
Circ: CapCity orders: **16,600**
Chapter 2 **A:** Andy Kubert **W:** Richard Bruning
3 ❑ Jul 1990 Cover: 3.95 **NM** value: **Cover or less**
Circ: CapCity orders: **15,950**
Chapter 3 **A:** Andy Kubert **W:** Richard Bruning

ADDAM OMEGA — Antarctic

1 ❑ Jan 1997 Cover: 2.95 **NM** value: **Cover or less**
Circ: Direct Market orders: **2,217**
A: Bill Hughes **W:** Bill Hughes
2 ❑ Apr 1997 Cover: 2.95 **NM** value: **Cover or less**
A: Bill Hughes **W:** Bill Hughes
3 ❑ Jun 1997 Cover: 2.95 **NM** value: **Cover or less**
A: Bill Hughes **W:** Bill Hughes
4 ❑ Aug 1997 Cover: 2.95 **NM** value: **Cover or less**
A: Bill Hughes **W:** Bill Hughes

ADDAMS FAMILY EPISODE GUIDE — Comic Chronicles

1 ❑ b&w Cover: 5.95 **NM** value: **Cover or less**
No issue number. • illustrated episode guide to original TV series

ADELE & THE BEAST — NBM

1 ❑ 1990 Cover: 9.95 **NM** value: **Cover or less**
A: Jaques Tardi **W:** Jaques Tardi

ADOLESCENT RADIOACTIVE BLACK BELT HAMSTERS, THE — Eclipse

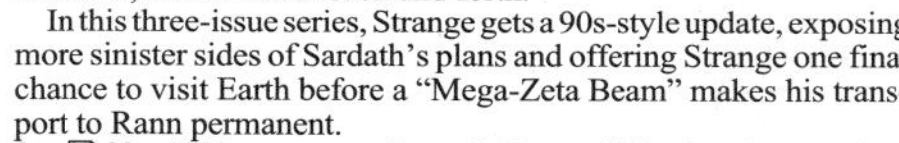

Bruce, Chuck, Jackie, and Clint are just four normal young rodents, selected to serve as guinea pigs (how humiliating for hamsters!) on the test launch of a new NASA rocket. Cosmic rays transform them into the Adolescent Radioactive Black Belt Hamsters, who, after years of martial arts schooling, turn their powers to the benefit of all mankind.

They say that imitation is the most sincere form of flattery. If that's true, then who could doubt the sincerity of writer Don Chin, artist Parsonavich, and Editor Cat Yronwode in their efforts to flatter (and capitalize on) the most surprising comics success story of the mid-1980s, Teenage Mutant Ninja Turtles?

1 ❑ b&w Cover: 1.50 **NM** value: **2.00**
A: Parsonavich **W:** Don Chin ★ Origin of The Adolescent Radioactive Black Belt Hamsters. ★ 1st Appearance of The Adolescent Radioactive Black Belt Hamsters.
1/GO❑ Cover: 2.95 **NM** value: **Cover or less**
• Gold edition. • Published by Parody
1-2 ❑ Cover: 1.50 **NM** value: **Cover or less**
2 ❑ Spr 1986 Cover: 1.50 **NM** value: **Cover or less**
3 ❑ Jul 1986 Cover: 1.50 **NM** value: **Cover or less**
4 ❑ Nov 1986 Cover: 1.50 **NM** value: **Cover or less**
5 ❑ Feb 1987 Cover: 1.50 **NM** value: **Cover or less**
6 ❑ May 1987 Cover: 1.50 **NM** value: **Cover or less**
7 ❑ Aug 1987 Cover: 1.50 **NM** value: **Cover or less**
Toe-Jam Monsters from Atlantis ★ Death of Bruce.
8 ❑ Oct 1987 Cover: 2.00 **NM** value: **Cover or less**
Secret Separation
9 ❑ Jan 1988 Cover: 2.00 **NM** value: **Cover or less**
Reminiscing final issue. **A:** Brent Anderson(cover)
Bk 1❑ Cover: 9.95 **NM** value: **Cover or less**
• America the Beautiful

ADOLESCENT RADIOACTIVE BLACK BELT HAMSTERS CLASSICS — Parody

1 ❑ Aug 1992, b&w Cover: 2.50 **NM** value: **Cover or less**
• Reprints ARBBH in 3-D #1 **A:** Ty Templeton **W:** Don Chin
2 ❑ b&w Cover: 2.50 **NM** value: **Cover or less**
• Reprints ARBBH in 3-D #2
3 ❑ Cover: 2.50 **NM** value: **Cover or less**
• Reprints ARBBH (Eclipse) #3
4 ❑ Cover: 2.50 **NM** value: **Cover or less**
• Reprints ARBBH: Massacre the Japanese Invasion
5 ❑ Cover: 2.50 **NM** value: **Cover or less**
holiday cover. • Reprints ARBBH in 3-D #4
Bk 1❑ Cover: 10.95 **NM** value: **Cover or less**
• The Death of Bruce
Bk 1/HC❑ Cover: 29.95 **NM** value: **Cover or less**

ADOLESCENT RADIOACTIVE BLACK BELT HAMSTERS IN 3-D — Eclipse

1 ❑ Jul 1986 Cover: 2.50 **NM** value: **Cover or less**
Circ: CapCity orders: **11,625**
2 ❑ Sep 1986 Cover: 2.50 **NM** value: **Cover or less**
Circ: CapCity orders: **11,025**
Hamsters Go Hollywood **A:** Gerald Forton; Marty C. **W:** Don Chin
3 ❑ Nov 1986 Cover: 2.50 **NM** value: **Cover or less**
Circ: CapCity orders: **6,650**
The Night of the Living Dolls • aka Eclipse 3-D #13 **A:** Tom Sutton **W:** Don Chin; Johnny Dooley; Mik Stengl
4 ❑ Dec 1986 Cover: 2.50 **NM** value: **Cover or less**
Circ: CapCity orders: **6,225**
• aka Eclipse 3-D #14

ADOLESCENT RADIOACTIVE BLACK BELT HAMSTERS: LOST AND ALONE IN NEW YORK — Parody Press

1 ❑ Cover: 2.95 **NM** value: **Cover or less**
Escape From New York **A:** Parsonavich **W:** Don Chin

ADOLESCENT RADIOACTIVE BLACK BELT HAMSTERS MASSACRE THE JAPANESE INVASION — Eclipse

1 ❑ Aug 1989, b&w Cover: 2.50 **NM** value: **Cover or less**

ADOLESCENT RADIOACTIVE BLACK BELT HAMSTERS: THE LOST TREASURES — Parody

1 ❑ b&w Cover: 2.95 **NM** value: **Cover or less**
cardstock cover. Big Name Artists Draw the Hamster!; Big Butt Hamhocks; The Night Light Zone; The Untold Story; • Reprints portions of ARBBH (Eclipse) #9 **A:** Parsonavich; Mark Lewis; Mark Martin; Bryan Robles **W:** Mark Lewis; Mark Martin; Don Chin; Ken Harville

ADOLF — Viz

Bk 1❑ Nov 1995 Cover: 16.95 **NM** value: **Cover or less**
• A Tale of the Twentieth Century
Bk 1/HC❑ Cover: 21.95 **NM** value: **Cover or less**
Bk 2❑ Cover: 16.95 **NM** value: **Cover or less**
• An Exile in Japan
Bk 2/HC❑ Cover: 21.95 **NM** value: **Cover or less**
Bk 3❑ Cover: 16.95 **NM** value: **Cover or less**
• The Half-Aryan
Bk 3/HC❑ Cover: 21.95 **NM** value: **Cover or less**
Bk 4❑ Cover: 16.95 **NM** value: **Cover or less**
• Days of Infamy
Bk 4/HC❑ Cover: 21.95 **NM** value: **Cover or less**
Bk 5❑ Cover: 16.95 **NM** value: **Cover or less**
• 1945 and All that Remains
Bk 5/HC❑ Cover: 21.95 **NM** value: **Cover or less**

AD POLICE — Viz

AD Police is a spinoff from the popular Bubblegum Crisis series. In 2025, Tokyo was utterly destroyed in the Kanto earthquake. Fortunately — or not — the Genom Corporation was all too ready to help rebuild. Within a few years, Genom had risen to become a great economic power in its own right, controlling nearly all of Tokyo.

Among the most popular of Genom's products were the "boomers" — increasingly sophisticated robots with brains modeled after those of humans. The boomers were designed for industry, for extraterrestrial use, and for battle. As a result, they were many times stronger than humans and nearly indestructible. And those electronic brains of theirs, held in check by several levels of blocks to prevent them from going renegade?

This graphic novel is about what happens when those blocks fail...

1 ❑ May 1994, b&w Cover: 14.95 **NM** value: **Cover or less**
A: Tony Takezaki **W:** Toshimichi Suzuki
1-2 ❑ Cover: 12.95 **NM** value: **Cover or less**
2nd printing with fold-out cover.

CGC-graded: Multiply prices above by **33 for 9.9 M • 16 for 9.8 NM/M • 7 for 9.6 NM+ • 5 for 9.4 NM • 2.5 for 9.2 NM- • 1.5 for 9.0 VF/NM**

ADRENALYNN — Image

1 ❑ Aug 1999 Cover: 2.50 **NM** value: **Cover or less**
Circ: Diamd. preorders: **25,966**
A: Marty Egeland **W:** Tony Daniel

2 ❑ Oct 1999 Cover: 2.50 **NM** value: **Cover or less**
Circ: Diamd. preorders: **20,785**
A: Marty Egeland **W:** Tony Daniel

3 ❑ Dec 1999 Cover: 2.50 **NM** value: **Cover or less**
Circ: Diamd. preorders: **20,477**
• Includes sketchbook pages **A:** Marty Egeland **W:** Tony Daniel

4 ❑ Feb 2000 Cover: 2.50 **NM** value: **Cover or less**
Circ: Diamd. preorders: **21,343** • **CGC:** 1 graded, best 9.6
• Pin-up page **A:** Marty Egeland **W:** Tony Daniel

ADULT ACTION FANTASY FEATURING: TAWNY'S TALES — Louisiana Leisure

All issues are adults only.

1 ❑ Cover: 2.50 **NM** value: **Cover or less**
2 ❑ Cover: 2.50 **NM** value: **Cover or less**

ADULTS ONLY! COMIC MAGAZINE — Inkwell

1 ❑ Aug 1979 Cover: 2.00 **NM** value: **2.50**
2 ❑ Fal 1985 Cover: 2.50 **NM** value: **Cover or less**
3 ❑ Cover: 2.50 **NM** value: **Cover or less**

ADVANCED DUNGEONS & DRAGONS — DC

1 ❑ Dec 1988 Cover: 1.25 **NM** value: **2.50**
Circ: CapCity orders: **18,350**

2 ❑ Jan 1989 Cover: 1.25 **NM** value: **1.50**
Circ: CapCity orders: **14,850**
The Bounty Seekers of Manshaka **A:** Jan Duursema **W:** Michael Fleisher

3 ❑ Feb 1989 Cover: 1.25 **NM** value: **1.50**
Circ: CapCity orders: **13,800**

4 ❑ Mar 1989 Cover: 1.50 **NM** value: **Cover or less**
Circ: CapCity orders: **15,250**

5 ❑ Apr 1989 Cover: 1.50 **NM** value: **Cover or less**
Circ: CapCity orders: **16,000**

6 ❑ May 1989 Cover: 1.50 **NM** value: **Cover or less**
Circ: CapCity orders: **17,200**

7 ❑ Jun 1989 Cover: 1.50 **NM** value: **Cover or less**
Circ: CapCity orders: **17,300**

8 ❑ Jul 1989 Cover: 1.50 **NM** value: **Cover or less**
Circ: CapCity orders: **16,550**
The Spirit Of Myrrth, Part 4 **A:** Jan Duursema; Ron Randall **W:** Dan Mishkin

9 ❑ Aug 1989 Cover: 1.50 **NM** value: **Cover or less**
Circ: CapCity orders: **15,850**

10 ❑ Sep 1989 Cover: 1.50 **NM** value: **Cover or less**
Circ: CapCity orders: **15,000**

11 ❑ Oct 1989 Cover: 1.50 **NM** value: **Cover or less**
Circ: CapCity orders: **14,500**

12 ❑ Nov 1989 Cover: 1.50 **NM** value: **Cover or less**
Circ: CapCity orders: **13,150**

13 ❑ Dec 1989 Cover: 1.50 **NM** value: **Cover or less**
Circ: CapCity orders: **12,600**

14 ❑ Jan 1990 Cover: 1.50 **NM** value: **Cover or less**
Circ: CapCity orders: **12,400**

15 ❑ Feb 1990 Cover: 1.50 **NM** value: **Cover or less**
Circ: CapCity orders: **12,250**

16 ❑ Mar 1990 Cover: 1.50 **NM** value: **Cover or less**
Circ: CapCity orders: **11,950**

17 ❑ Apr 1990 Cover: 1.50 **NM** value: **Cover or less**
Circ: CapCity orders: **11,650**

18 ❑ May 1990 Cover: 1.50 **NM** value: **Cover or less**
Circ: CapCity orders: **11,700**

19 ❑ Jun 1990 Cover: 1.50 **NM** value: **Cover or less**
Circ: CapCity orders: **11,500**

20 ❑ Jul 1990 Cover: 1.50 **NM** value: **Cover or less**
Circ: CapCity orders: **11,350**

21 ❑ Aug 1990 Cover: 1.50 **NM** value: **Cover or less**
Circ: CapCity orders: **11,250**

22 ❑ Sep 1990 Cover: 1.50 **NM** value: **Cover or less**
Circ: CapCity orders: **11,000**

23 ❑ Nov 1990 Cover: 1.50 **NM** value: **Cover or less**
Circ: CapCity orders: **11,150**

24 ❑ Dec 1990 Cover: 1.50 **NM** value: **Cover or less**
Circ: CapCity orders: **11,300**

25 ❑ Jan 1991 Cover: 1.75 **NM** value: **Cover or less**
Circ: CapCity orders: **11,000**

26 ❑ Feb 1991 Cover: 1.75 **NM** value: **Cover or less**
Circ: CapCity orders: **11,000**

27 ❑ Mar 1991 Cover: 1.75 **NM** value: **Cover or less**
Circ: CapCity orders: **10,850**

28 ❑ Apr 1991 Cover: 1.75 **NM** value: **Cover or less**
Circ: CapCity orders: **10,100**

29 ❑ May 1991 Cover: 1.75 **NM** value: **Cover or less**
Circ: CapCity orders: **10,050**

30 ❑ Jun 1991 Cover: 1.75 **NM** value: **Cover or less**
Circ: CapCity orders: **10,100**

31 ❑ Jul 1991 Cover: 1.75 **NM** value: **Cover or less**
Circ: CapCity orders: **10,150**

32 ❑ Aug 1991 Cover: 1.75 **NM** value: **Cover or less**
Circ: CapCity orders: **10,150**

33 ❑ Sep 1991 Cover: 1.75 **NM** value: **Cover or less**
Circ: CapCity orders: **9,800**

34 ❑ Oct 1991 Cover: 1.75 **NM** value: **Cover or less**
Circ: CapCity orders: **10,950**

35 ❑ Nov 1991 Cover: 1.75 **NM** value: **Cover or less**
Circ: CapCity orders: **9,450**

36 ❑ Dec 1991 Cover: 1.75 **NM** value: **Cover or less**
Circ: CapCity orders: **9,500**
final issue.

Anl 1 ❑ ca. 1990 Cover: 3.95 **NM** value: **Cover or less**
Circ: CapCity orders: **11,400**

ADVENTURE COMICS — DC

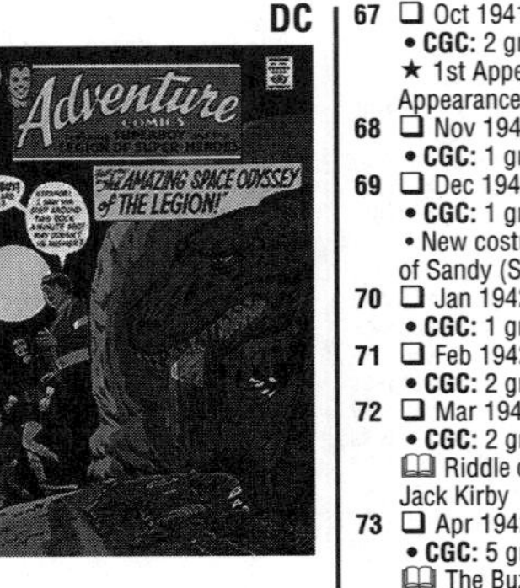

This classic series featured most of DC's favorite heroes and villains in its 45-year run. The Legion of Super-Heroes; Starman; Saturn Girl; the Sandman's sidekick, Sandy; Golden Boy; Hourman; Cosmic Boy; and others made their first appearances in this series. Superboy and Supergirl each starred in its pages for a time, and it was here that Superboy and Lois Lane first met (although Superboy would later encounter and date his mermaid girlfriend Lori Lemaris in this same series).

In December 1972, DC started featuring pure adventure without super-heroes, and in 1974 artist Mike Grell did his first comic-book work for this series. The change in format was short-lived, and, in 1975, DC switched back to the super-hero format, featuring Aquaman, Flash, Wonder Woman, Green Lantern, and many of the first adventures of the later Spectre.

32 ❑ Nov 1938 Cover: 0.10 **NM** value: **3000.00**
• Series continued from New Adventure #31

33 ❑ Dec 1938 Cover: 0.10 **NM** value: **1550.00**
• **CGC:** 1 graded, best 7.0

34 ❑ Jan 1939 Cover: 0.10 **NM** value: **1550.00**
35 ❑ Feb 1939 Cover: 0.10 **NM** value: **1550.00**
36 ❑ Mar 1939 Cover: 0.10 **NM** value: **1325.00**
37 ❑ Apr 1939 Cover: 0.10 **NM** value: **1325.00**
38 ❑ May 1939 Cover: 0.10 **NM** value: **1325.00**
39 ❑ Jun 1939 Cover: 0.10 **NM** value: **1550.00**
A: Jack Wood

40 ❑ Jul 1939 Cover: 0.10 **NM** value: **40000.00**
• **CGC:** 4 graded, best 7.0
★ 1st Appearance of Sandman I (Wesley Dodds).

41 ❑ Aug 1939 Cover: 0.10 **NM** value: **4850.00**
• **CGC:** 2 graded, best 6.5
Sandman cover. ★ Appearance of Sandman I (Wesley Dodds).

42 ❑ Sep 1939 Cover: 0.10 **NM** value: **5550.00**
• **CGC:** 3 graded, best 9.4
Sandman cover. ★ Appearance of Sandman I (Wesley Dodds).

43 ❑ Oct 1939 Cover: 0.10 **NM** value: **3250.00**
• **CGC:** 2 graded, best 9.6

44 ❑ Nov 1939 Cover: 0.10 **NM** value: **5600.00**
• **CGC:** 3 graded, best 7.5
Sandman cover. ★ Appearance of Sandman I (Wesley Dodds).

45 ❑ Dec 1939 Cover: 0.10 **NM** value: **2900.00**
• **CGC:** 3 graded, best 9.6

46 ❑ Jan 1940 Cover: 0.10 **NM** value: **4250.00**
• **CGC:** 1 graded, best 2.0
Sandman cover. ★ Appearance of Sandman I (Wesley Dodds).

47 ❑ Feb 1940 Cover: 0.10 **NM** value: **4250.00**
• **CGC:** 2 graded, best 5.0
Sandman cover. ★ Appearance of Sandman I (Wesley Dodds).

48 ❑ Mar 1940 Cover: 0.10 **NM** value: **22500.00**
• **CGC:** 2 graded, best 6.0
★ 1st Appearance of Hourman I (Rex Tyler).

49 ❑ Apr 1940 Cover: 0.10 **NM** value: **2000.00**
• **CGC:** 1 graded, best 6.5

50 ❑ May 1940 Cover: 0.10 **NM** value: **2000.00**
• **CGC:** 1 graded, best 8.0

51 ❑ Jun 1940 Cover: 0.10 **NM** value: **2700.00**
• **CGC:** 3 graded, best 9.2
Sandman cover. ★ Appearance of Sandman I (Wesley Dodds).

52 ❑ Jul 1940 Cover: 0.10 **NM** value: **1650.00**
• **CGC:** 3 graded, best 9.2

53 ❑ Aug 1940 Cover: 0.10 **NM** value: **1450.00**
• **CGC:** 1 graded, best 6.0
★ 1st Appearance of Minuteman.

54 ❑ Sep 1940 Cover: 0.10 **NM** value: **1450.00**
• **CGC:** 1 graded, best 1.0

55 ❑ Oct 1940 Cover: 0.10 **NM** value: **1450.00**
• **CGC:** 1 graded, best 3.5

56 ❑ Nov 1940 Cover: 0.10 **NM** value: **1450.00**
• **CGC:** 4 graded, best 9.2

57 ❑ Dec 1940 Cover: 0.10 **NM** value: **1450.00**
58 ❑ Jan 1941 Cover: 0.10 **NM** value: **1450.00**
• **CGC:** 3 graded, best 9.0

59 ❑ Feb 1941 Cover: 0.10 **NM** value: **1450.00**
• **CGC:** 1 graded, best 7.5

60 ❑ Mar 1941 Cover: 0.10 **NM** value: **2500.00**
• **CGC:** 4 graded, best 7.5
Sandman cover. ★ Appearance of Sandman I (Wesley Dodds).

61 ❑ Apr 1941 Cover: 0.10 **NM** value: **11500.00**
• **CGC:** 3 graded, best 5.5
Starman; Mark Lansing of Mikishawm; Facts; Federal Men; Steve Conrad, Adventurer; Peter and His Pup; The Quiz Page; Hourman; Paul Kirk, Manhunter; Cotton Carver, Defender of Barlunda; Case of the Black Cat; The Sandman **A:** Henry Boltinoff; Jack Burnley; Howard Purcell; Bernard Baily; Chad Grothkopf; Creig Flessel; Ed Moore; Jack Lehti; Ray McGirk; T.C. O'Neil **W:** Henry Boltinoff; Howard Purcell; Ed Moore; Jack Lehti; Jerry Siegel; Ray McGirk; Gardner Fox; Ken Fitch; T.C. O'Neil ★ 1st Appearance of Starman I (Ted Knight).

62 ❑ May 1941 Cover: 0.10 **NM** value: **1350.00**
• **CGC:** 5 graded, best 9.0

63 ❑ Jun 1941 Cover: 0.10 **NM** value: **1350.00**
• **CGC:** 2 graded, best 8.0

64 ❑ Jul 1941 Cover: 0.10 **NM** value: **1350.00**
• **CGC:** 2 graded, best 8.0

65 ❑ Aug 1941 Cover: 0.10 **NM** value: **1350.00**
• **CGC:** 1 graded, best 4.0

66 ❑ Sep 1941 Cover: 0.10 **NM** value: **1750.00**
• **CGC:** 2 graded, best 4.0
★ Origin of Shining Knight. ★ 1st Appearance of Shining Knight.

67 ❑ Oct 1941 Cover: 0.10 **NM** value: **1350.00**
• **CGC:** 2 graded, best 9.2
★ 1st Appearance of Nimbus. ★ 1st Appearance of the Mist. ★ Appearance of Adam Strange.

68 ❑ Nov 1941 Cover: 0.10 **NM** value: **1300.00**
• **CGC:** 1 graded, best 6.5

69 ❑ Dec 1941 Cover: 0.10 **NM** value: **1650.00**
• **CGC:** 1 graded, best 6.0
• New costume for Sandman I (Wesley Dodds) ★ 1st Appearance of Sandy (Sandman I's sidekick).

70 ❑ Jan 1942 Cover: 0.10 **NM** value: **1300.00**
• **CGC:** 1 graded, best 9.6

71 ❑ Feb 1942 Cover: 0.10 **NM** value: **1300.00**
• **CGC:** 2 graded, best 8.0

72 ❑ Mar 1942 Cover: 0.10 **NM** value: **10600.00**
• **CGC:** 2 graded, best 9.6
Riddle of the Slave Market • 1st Sandman by Simon & Kirby **A:** Jack Kirby **W:** Joe Simon

73 ❑ Apr 1942 Cover: 0.10 **NM** value: **11000.00**
• **CGC:** 5 graded, best 9.2
The Buzzard's Revenge; Bells of Madness • 1st Manhunter by Simon & Kirby; Sandman ★ Origin of Manhunter.

74 ❑ May 1942 Cover: 0.10 **NM** value: **1450.00**
• **CGC:** 2 graded, best 9.4
The Man Who Knew All the Answers; Scavenger Hunt • Sandman; Manhunter

75 ❑ Jun 1942 Cover: 0.10 **NM** value: **1450.00**
• **CGC:** 2 graded, best 9.4
Beware of Mr. Meek; The Villain from Valhalla • Manhunter; Sandman and a character named "Thor"

76 ❑ Jul 1942 Cover: 0.10 **NM** value: **1450.00**
• **CGC:** 2 graded, best 8.0
Mr. Noah Raids the Town; The Legend of the Silent Bear • Sandman; Manhunter

77 ❑ Aug 1942 Cover: 0.10 **NM** value: **1450.00**
Dreams of Doom; The Stone of Vengeance • Sandman; Manhunter

78 ❑ Sep 1942 Cover: 0.10 **NM** value: **1450.00**
• **CGC:** 1 graded, best 9.2
The Lady and the Tiger; The Miracle Maker • Manhunter; Sandman

79 ❑ Oct 1942 Cover: 0.10 **NM** value: **1450.00**
• **CGC:** 5 graded, best 8.0
Footprints in the Sands of Time; Cobras of the Deep • Sandman; Manhunter

80 ❑ Nov 1942 Cover: 0.10 **NM** value: **1450.00**
• **CGC:** 3 graded, best 8.0
The Man Who Couldn't Sleep; Man Trap Island • Sandman; Manhunter

81 ❑ Dec 1942 Cover: 0.10 **NM** value: **900.00**
• **CGC:** 2 graded, best 8.0
A Drama in Dreams • Sandman

82 ❑ Jan 1943 Cover: 0.10 **NM** value: **900.00**
• **CGC:** 4 graded, best 7.5
Santa Fronts for the Mob • Sandman

83 ❑ Jan 1943 Cover: 0.10 **NM** value: **900.00**
• **CGC:** 1 graded, best 8.5
The Lady and the Champ • Sandman

84 ❑ Mar 1943 Cover: 0.10 **NM** value: **900.00**
• **CGC:** 1 graded, best 6.5
Crime Carnival • Sandman

85 ❑ Apr 1943 Cover: 0.10 **NM** value: **900.00**
• **CGC:** 1 graded, best 7.0
The Unholy Dreams of Gentleman Jack • Sandman

86 ❑ Jun 1943 Cover: 0.10 **NM** value: **900.00**
• **CGC:** 1 graded, best 5.0
The Boy Who Was Too Big for His Breeches • Sandman

87 ❑ Aug 1943 Cover: 0.10 **NM** value: **900.00**
• **CGC:** 1 graded, best 6.5
I Hated the Sandman • Sandman

88 ❑ Oct 1943 Cover: 0.10 **NM** value: **900.00**
• **CGC:** 3 graded, best 9.2
The Cruise of the Crescent • Sandman

89 ❑ Jan 1944 Cover: 0.10 **NM** value: **900.00**
Prisoner of His Dreams • Sandman

90 ❑ Mar 1944 Cover: 0.10 **NM** value: **900.00**
• **CGC:** 1 graded, best 7.5
Sleepy Time Crimes • Sandman

91 ❑ May 1944 Cover: 0.10 **NM** value: **900.00**
Courage a la Carte • Sandman

92 ❑ Jun 1944 Cover: 0.10 **NM** value: **700.00**
• **CGC:** 2 graded, best 9.6

93 ❑ Sep 1944 Cover: 0.10 **NM** value: **700.00**
• **CGC:** 2 graded, best 9.4

94 ❑ Nov 1944 Cover: 0.10 **NM** value: **700.00**
• **CGC:** 2 graded, best 9.4

95 ❑ Jan 1945 Cover: 0.10 **NM** value: **700.00**
• **CGC:** 4 graded, best 9.2

96 ❑ Mar 1945 Cover: 0.10 **NM** value: **700.00**
• **CGC:** 3 graded, best 9.4

97 ❑ May 1945 Cover: 0.10 **NM** value: **700.00**
• **CGC:** 4 graded, best 9.0

98 ❑ Jul 1945 Cover: 0.10 **NM** value: **700.00**
• **CGC:** 4 graded, best 9.0

99 ❑ Sep 1945 Cover: 0.10 **NM** value: **700.00**
• **CGC:** 2 graded, best 9.0

100 ❑ Nov 1945 Cover: 0.10 **NM** value: **800.00**
• **CGC:** 7 graded, best 9.0
• 100th anniversary edition. Sweets for Swag • Sandman

101 ❑ Jan 1946 Cover: 0.10 **NM** value: **700.00**
• **CGC:** 2 graded, best 8.5

102 ❑ Mar 1946 Cover: 0.10 **NM** value: **700.00**
103 ❑ Apr 1946 Cover: 0.10 **NM** value: **2200.00**
• **CGC:** 5 graded, best 9.6
• Super-Heroes begin (Johnny Quick, Aquaman, Superboy & Green Arrow)

104 ❑ May 1946 Cover: 0.10 **NM** value: **800.00**
• **CGC:** 1 graded, best 3.0

Other grades: Multiply prices above by **1.5 for Mint • 2/3 for Very Fine • 1/3 for Fine • 1/5 for Very Good • 1/8 for Good**

105 ❑ Jun 1946 Cover: 0.10 **NM** value: **525.00**
• **CGC:** 3 graded, best 9.4
106 ❑ Jul 1946 Cover: 0.10 **NM** value: **525.00**
• **CGC:** 1 graded, best 5.0
107 ❑ Aug 1946 Cover: 0.10 **NM** value: **525.00**
• **CGC:** 1 graded, best 8.0
108 ❑ Sep 1946 Cover: 0.10 **NM** value: **525.00**
• **CGC:** 4 graded, best 9.2
109 ❑ Oct 1946 Cover: 0.10 **NM** value: **525.00**
• **CGC:** 10 graded, best 9.4
110 ❑ Nov 1946 Cover: 0.10 **NM** value: **525.00**
• **CGC:** 1 graded, best 6.5
111 ❑ Dec 1946 Cover: 0.10 **NM** value: **460.00**
112 ❑ Jan 1947 Cover: 0.10 **NM** value: **460.00**
• **CGC:** 3 graded, best 9.4
113 ❑ Feb 1947 Cover: 0.10 **NM** value: **460.00**
• **CGC:** 1 graded, best 4.5
114 ❑ Mar 1947 Cover: 0.10 **NM** value: **460.00**
• **CGC:** 1 graded, best 9.0
115 ❑ Apr 1947 Cover: 0.10 **NM** value: **460.00**
• **CGC:** 2 graded, best 8.0
116 ❑ May 1947 Cover: 0.10 **NM** value: **460.00**
• **CGC:** 2 graded, best 9.4
117 ❑ Jun 1947 Cover: 0.10 **NM** value: **460.00**
118 ❑ Jul 1947 Cover: 0.10 **NM** value: **460.00**
• **CGC:** 1 graded, best 9.0
119 ❑ Aug 1947 Cover: 0.10 **NM** value: **460.00**
120 ❑ Sep 1947 Cover: 0.10 **NM** value: **460.00**
• **CGC:** 2 graded, best 8.0
121 ❑ Oct 1947 Cover: 0.10 **NM** value: **400.00**
122 ❑ Nov 1947 Cover: 0.10 **NM** value: **400.00**
• **CGC:** 1 graded, best 9.4
123 ❑ Dec 1947 Cover: 0.10 **NM** value: **400.00**
124 ❑ Jan 1948 Cover: 0.10 **NM** value: **400.00**
• **CGC:** 1 graded, best 8.0
125 ❑ Feb 1948 Cover: 0.10 **NM** value: **400.00**
• **CGC:** 2 graded, best 9.2
126 ❑ Mar 1948 Cover: 0.10 **NM** value: **400.00**
• **CGC:** 1 graded, best 4.5
127 ❑ Apr 1948 Cover: 0.10 **NM** value: **450.00**
• **CGC:** 1 graded, best 6.0
★ Origin of Shining Knight.
128 ❑ May 1948 Cover: 0.10 **NM** value: **385.00**
• **CGC:** 1 graded, best 5.0
129 ❑ Jun 1948 Cover: 0.10 **NM** value: **385.00**
• **CGC:** 1 graded, best 3.5
130 ❑ Jul 1948 Cover: 0.10 **NM** value: **385.00**
• **CGC:** 2 graded, best 8.5
131 ❑ Aug 1948 Cover: 0.10 **NM** value: **350.00**
132 ❑ Sep 1948 Cover: 0.10 **NM** value: **350.00**
• **CGC:** 1 graded, best 7.0
133 ❑ Oct 1948 Cover: 0.10 **NM** value: **350.00**
• **CGC:** 2 graded, best 9.2
134 ❑ Nov 1948 Cover: 0.10 **NM** value: **350.00**
• **CGC:** 3 graded, best 9.2
135 ❑ Dec 1948 Cover: 0.10 **NM** value: **350.00**
• **CGC:** 1 graded, best 7.0
136 ❑ Jan 1949 Cover: 0.10 **NM** value: **350.00**
137 ❑ Feb 1949 Cover: 0.10 **NM** value: **350.00**
• **CGC:** 1 graded, best 8.5
138 ❑ Mar 1949 Cover: 0.10 **NM** value: **350.00**
139 ❑ Apr 1949 Cover: 0.10 **NM** value: **350.00**
• **CGC:** 1 graded, best 2.5
📖 (Untitled Superboy story); Reign of the Reptiles; The Man Who Owned the Sea!; Daffy Doodle; Knight Without Armor!; Peg; Varsity Vic; The Film of the Future?; Why Little Things Seem Big (text) • Green Arrow, Speedy, Aquaman; Shining Knight; Johnny Quick
140 ❑ May 1949 Cover: 0.10 **NM** value: **350.00**
• **CGC:** 1 graded, best 7.0
141 ❑ Jun 1949 Cover: 0.10 **NM** value: **350.00**
• **CGC:** 2 graded, best 9.4
142 ❑ Jul 1949 Cover: 0.10 **NM** value: **350.00**
143 ❑ Aug 1949 Cover: 0.10 **NM** value: **350.00**
144 ❑ Sep 1949 Cover: 0.10 **NM** value: **350.00**
• **CGC:** 1 graded, best 1.8
145 ❑ Oct 1949 Cover: 0.10 **NM** value: **350.00**
• **CGC:** 1 graded, best 5.0
146 ❑ Nov 1949 Cover: 0.10 **NM** value: **350.00**
• **CGC:** 2 graded, best 9.4
147 ❑ Dec 1949 Cover: 0.10 **NM** value: **350.00**
• **CGC:** 1 graded, best 9.6
148 ❑ Jan 1950 Cover: 0.10 **NM** value: **350.00**
• **CGC:** 1 graded, best 7.5
149 ❑ Feb 1950 Cover: 0.10 **NM** value: **350.00**
• **CGC:** 1 graded, best 7.5
150 ❑ Mar 1950 Cover: 0.10 **NM** value: **400.00**
• **CGC:** 1 graded, best 8.5
A: Frank Frazetta
151 ❑ Apr 1950 Cover: 0.10 **NM** value: **400.00**
• **CGC:** 1 graded, best 8.5
A: Frank Frazetta
152 ❑ May 1950 Cover: 0.10 **NM** value: **310.00**
• **CGC:** 1 graded, best 7.0
153 ❑ Jun 1950 Cover: 0.10 **NM** value: **400.00**
• **CGC:** 1 graded, best 5.0
A: Frank Frazetta
154 ❑ Jul 1950 Cover: 0.10 **NM** value: **310.00**
155 ❑ Aug 1950 Cover: 0.10 **NM** value: **400.00**
• **CGC:** 2 graded, best 8.5
A: Frank Frazetta
156 ❑ Sep 1950 Cover: 0.10 **NM** value: **310.00**
157 ❑ Oct 1950 Cover: 0.10 **NM** value: **400.00**
A: Frank Frazetta
158 ❑ Nov 1950 Cover: 0.10 **NM** value: **310.00**
159 ❑ Dec 1950 Cover: 0.10 **NM** value: **400.00**
• **CGC:** 1 graded, best 8.0
A: Frank Frazetta
160 ❑ Jan 1951 Cover: 0.10 **NM** value: **310.00**
• **CGC:** 2 graded, best 8.0
161 ❑ Feb 1951 Cover: 0.10 **NM** value: **400.00**
• **CGC:** 1 graded, best 9.4
A: Frank Frazetta
162 ❑ Mar 1951 Cover: 0.10 **NM** value: **310.00**
• **CGC:** 1 graded, best 6.0
163 ❑ Apr 1951 Cover: 0.10 **NM** value: **400.00**
A: Frank Frazetta
164 ❑ May 1951 Cover: 0.10 **NM** value: **310.00**
165 ❑ Jun 1951 Cover: 0.10 **NM** value: **310.00**
166 ❑ Jul 1951 Cover: 0.10 **NM** value: **310.00**
167 ❑ Aug 1951 Cover: 0.10 **NM** value: **310.00**
• **CGC:** 1 graded, best 8.0
168 ❑ Sep 1951 Cover: 0.10 **NM** value: **310.00**
• **CGC:** 1 graded, best 7.5
169 ❑ Oct 1951 Cover: 0.10 **NM** value: **310.00**
170 ❑ Nov 1951 Cover: 0.10 **NM** value: **260.00**
• **CGC:** 3 graded, best 7.5
171 ❑ Dec 1951 Cover: 0.10 **NM** value: **260.00**
• **CGC:** 1 graded, best 5.5
172 ❑ Jan 1952 Cover: 0.10 **NM** value: **260.00**
• **CGC:** 1 graded, best 1.8
173 ❑ Feb 1952 Cover: 0.10 **NM** value: **260.00**
174 ❑ Mar 1952 Cover: 0.10 **NM** value: **260.00**
175 ❑ Apr 1952 Cover: 0.10 **NM** value: **260.00**
176 ❑ May 1952 Cover: 0.10 **NM** value: **260.00**
177 ❑ Jun 1952 Cover: 0.10 **NM** value: **260.00**
• **CGC:** 1 graded, best 3.0
178 ❑ Jul 1952 Cover: 0.10 **NM** value: **260.00**
179 ❑ Aug 1952 Cover: 0.10 **NM** value: **260.00**
180 ❑ Sep 1952 Cover: 0.10 **NM** value: **260.00**
181 ❑ Oct 1952 Cover: 0.10 **NM** value: **250.00**
182 ❑ Nov 1952 Cover: 0.10 **NM** value: **250.00**
• **CGC:** 1 graded, best 4.0
183 ❑ Dec 1952 Cover: 0.10 **NM** value: **250.00**
• **CGC:** 1 graded, best 5.5
184 ❑ Jan 1953 Cover: 0.10 **NM** value: **250.00**
185 ❑ Feb 1953 Cover: 0.10 **NM** value: **250.00**
• **CGC:** 1 graded, best 3.0
186 ❑ Mar 1953 Cover: 0.10 **NM** value: **250.00**
• **CGC:** 2 graded, best 7.0
187 ❑ Apr 1953 Cover: 0.10 **NM** value: **250.00**
• **CGC:** 1 graded, best 1.8
188 ❑ May 1953 Cover: 0.10 **NM** value: **250.00**
189 ❑ Jun 1953 Cover: 0.10 **NM** value: **250.00**
190 ❑ Jul 1953 Cover: 0.10 **NM** value: **250.00**
• **CGC:** 1 graded, best .5
191 ❑ Aug 1953 Cover: 0.10 **NM** value: **250.00**
192 ❑ Sep 1953 Cover: 0.10 **NM** value: **250.00**
193 ❑ Oct 1953 Cover: 0.10 **NM** value: **250.00**
• **CGC:** 1 graded, best 4.0
194 ❑ Nov 1953 Cover: 0.10 **NM** value: **250.00**
• **CGC:** 2 graded, best 5.0
195 ❑ Dec 1953 Cover: 0.10 **NM** value: **250.00**
196 ❑ Jan 1954 Cover: 0.10 **NM** value: **250.00**
197 ❑ Feb 1954 Cover: 0.10 **NM** value: **250.00**
198 ❑ Mar 1954 Cover: 0.10 **NM** value: **250.00**
199 ❑ Apr 1954 Cover: 0.10 **NM** value: **250.00**
• **CGC:** 1 graded, best 7.0
200 ❑ May 1954 Cover: 0.10 **NM** value: **375.00**
• **CGC:** 1 graded, best 7.0
• 200th anniversary issue.
201 ❑ Jun 1954 Cover: 0.10 **NM** value: **275.00**
• **CGC:** 2 graded, best 7.5
202 ❑ Jul 1954 Cover: 0.10 **NM** value: **275.00**
• **CGC:** 1 graded, best 7.0
203 ❑ Aug 1954 Cover: 0.10 **NM** value: **275.00**
• **CGC:** 1 graded, best 4.5
204 ❑ Sep 1954 Cover: 0.10 **NM** value: **275.00**
• **CGC:** 1 graded, best 8.5
205 ❑ Oct 1954 Cover: 0.10 **NM** value: **275.00**
• **CGC:** 3 graded, best 7.5
206 ❑ Nov 1954 Cover: 0.10 **NM** value: **275.00**
• **CGC:** 2 graded, best 7.5
207 ❑ Dec 1954 Cover: 0.10 **NM** value: **275.00**
• **CGC:** 1 graded, best 5.0
208 ❑ Jan 1955 Cover: 0.10 **NM** value: **275.00**
• **CGC:** 4 graded, best 8.0
209 ❑ Feb 1955 Cover: 0.10 **NM** value: **275.00**
• **CGC:** 2 graded, best 7.0
210 ❑ Mar 1955 Cover: 0.10 **NM** value: **2500.00**
• **CGC:** 10 graded, best 9.0
★ 1st Appearance of Krypto.
211 ❑ Apr 1955 Cover: 0.10 **NM** value: **210.00**
212 ❑ May 1955 Cover: 0.10 **NM** value: **210.00**
• **CGC:** 2 graded, best 7.0
213 ❑ Jun 1955 Cover: 0.10 **NM** value: **210.00**
• **CGC:** 1 graded, best 8.0
214 ❑ Jul 1955 Cover: 0.10 **NM** value: **210.00**
• **CGC:** 3 graded, best 8.0
215 ❑ Aug 1955 Cover: 0.10 **NM** value: **210.00**
• **CGC:** 2 graded, best 6.5
216 ❑ Sep 1955 Cover: 0.10 **NM** value: **210.00**
• **CGC:** 1 graded, best 6.0
217 ❑ Oct 1955 Cover: 0.10 **NM** value: **210.00**
• **CGC:** 2 graded, best 7.5
218 ❑ Nov 1955 Cover: 0.10 **NM** value: **210.00**
219 ❑ Dec 1955 Cover: 0.10 **NM** value: **210.00**
220 ❑ Jan 1956 Cover: 0.10 **NM** value: **210.00**
• **CGC:** 3 graded, best 8.0
★ Appearance of Krypto.
221 ❑ Feb 1956 Cover: 0.10 **NM** value: **175.00**
222 ❑ Mar 1956 Cover: 0.10 **NM** value: **175.00**
• **CGC:** 2 graded, best 8.0
223 ❑ Apr 1956 Cover: 0.10 **NM** value: **175.00**
• **CGC:** 2 graded, best 7.5
224 ❑ May 1956 Cover: 0.10 **NM** value: **175.00**
225 ❑ Jun 1956 Cover: 0.10 **NM** value: **175.00**
226 ❑ Jul 1956 Cover: 0.10 **NM** value: **175.00**
• **CGC:** 1 graded, best 3.0
227 ❑ Aug 1956 Cover: 0.10 **NM** value: **175.00**
• **CGC:** 1 graded, best 7.5
228 ❑ Sep 1956 Cover: 0.10 **NM** value: **175.00**
• **CGC:** 4 graded, best 7.0
229 ❑ Oct 1956 Cover: 0.10 **NM** value: **175.00**
• **CGC:** 2 graded, best 7.5
230 ❑ Nov 1956 Cover: 0.10 **NM** value: **175.00**
• **CGC:** 1 graded, best 8.5
231 ❑ Dec 1956 Cover: 0.10 **NM** value: **175.00**
• **CGC:** 1 graded, best 4.0
232 ❑ Jan 1957 Cover: 0.10 **NM** value: **175.00**
• **CGC:** 2 graded, best 7.5
233 ❑ Feb 1957 Cover: 0.10 **NM** value: **175.00**
• **CGC:** 1 graded, best 6.5
234 ❑ Mar 1957 Cover: 0.10 **NM** value: **175.00**
• **CGC:** 1 graded, best 6.0
235 ❑ Apr 1957 Cover: 0.10 **NM** value: **175.00**
• **CGC:** 3 graded, best 8.5
236 ❑ May 1957 Cover: 0.10 **NM** value: **175.00**
• **CGC:** 2 graded, best 9.2
237 ❑ Jun 1957 Cover: 0.10 **NM** value: **175.00**
• **CGC:** 3 graded, best 9.0
238 ❑ Jul 1957 Cover: 0.10 **NM** value: **175.00**
• **CGC:** 2 graded, best 8.5
239 ❑ Aug 1957 Cover: 0.10 **NM** value: **175.00**
• **CGC:** 2 graded, best 8.5
240 ❑ Sep 1957 Cover: 0.10 **NM** value: **175.00**
• **CGC:** 2 graded, best 7.5
241 ❑ Oct 1957 Cover: 0.10 **NM** value: **175.00**
• **CGC:** 1 graded, best 6.5
242 ❑ Nov 1957 Cover: 0.10 **NM** value: **175.00**
• **CGC:** 2 graded, best 9.2
243 ❑ Dec 1957 Cover: 0.10 **NM** value: **175.00**
• **CGC:** 1 graded, best 8.5
244 ❑ Jan 1958 Cover: 0.10 **NM** value: **175.00**
245 ❑ Feb 1958 Cover: 0.10 **NM** value: **175.00**
• **CGC:** 1 graded, best 7.0
246 ❑ Mar 1958 Cover: 0.10 **NM** value: **175.00**
• **CGC:** 1 graded, best 8.5
247 ❑ Apr 1958 Cover: 0.10 **NM** value: **4700.00**
• **CGC:** 29 graded, best 9.4
📖 The Legion of Super-Heroes • Superboy joins team ★ Origin of Legion of Super-Heroes, Cosmic Boy, Saturn Girl, Lightning Lad. ★ 1st Appearance of Legion of Super-Heroes, Cosmic Boy, Saturn Girl, Lightning Lad.
248 ❑ May 1958 Cover: 0.10 **NM** value: **140.00**
• Green Arrow
249 ❑ Jun 1958 Cover: 0.10 **NM** value: **140.00**
• **CGC:** 1 graded, best 6.5
• Green Arrow
250 ❑ Jul 1958 Cover: 0.10 **NM** value: **140.00**
• **CGC:** 2 graded, best 7.0
📖 Green Arrows of the World • Green Arrow
251 ❑ Aug 1958 Cover: 0.10 **NM** value: **140.00**
📖 Case of the Super-Arrows • Green Arrow
252 ❑ Sep 1958 Cover: 0.10 **NM** value: **140.00**
• **CGC:** 1 graded, best 7.0
📖 Mystery of the Giant Arrows • Green Arrow
253 ❑ Oct 1958 Cover: 0.10 **NM** value: **190.00**
• **CGC:** 3 graded, best 8.5
📖 Prisoners of Dimension O • Green Arrow;Robin meets Superboy
254 ❑ Nov 1958 Cover: 0.10 **NM** value: **140.00**
• **CGC:** 1 graded, best 7.0
📖 Green Arrow's Last Stand • Green Arrow
255 ❑ Dec 1958 Cover: 0.10 **NM** value: **140.00**
• **CGC:** 3 graded, best 9.0
📖 The War That Never Ended • Green Arrow ★ 1st Appearance of Red Kryptonite.
256 ❑ Jan 1959 Cover: 0.10 **NM** value: **600.00**
• **CGC:** 3 graded, best 8.0
📖 The Green Arrow's First Case • Green Arrow **A:** Jack Kirby ★ Origin of Green Arrow.
257 ❑ Feb 1959 Cover: 0.10 **NM** value: **130.00**
258 ❑ Mar 1959 Cover: 0.10 **NM** value: **130.00**
• **CGC:** 1 graded, best 5.0
259 ❑ Apr 1959 Cover: 0.10 **NM** value: **130.00**
260 ❑ May 1959 Cover: 0.10 **NM** value: **600.00**
• **CGC:** 16 graded, best 9.2
★ Origin of Aquaman.
261 ❑ Jun 1959 Cover: 0.10 **NM** value: **80.00**
• **CGC:** 1 graded, best 7.5
• Lois Lane meets Superboy
262 ❑ Jul 1959 Cover: 0.10 **NM** value: **80.00**
• **CGC:** 1 graded, best 8.0
★ Origin of Speedy.
263 ❑ Aug 1959 Cover: 0.10 **NM** value: **80.00**
• **CGC:** 1 graded, best 9.0
264 ❑ Sep 1959 Cover: 0.10 **NM** value: **80.00**
• **CGC:** 2 graded, best 9.0
265 ❑ Oct 1959 Cover: 0.10 **NM** value: **80.00**
• **CGC:** 2 graded, best 8.5
★ Appearance of Superman.
266 ❑ Nov 1959 Cover: 0.10 **NM** value: **80.00**
• **CGC:** 2 graded, best 8.5
★ Appearance of Superman.
267 ❑ Dec 1959 Cover: 0.10 **NM** value: **785.00**
• **CGC:** 17 graded, best 9.0
📖 Prisoner of the Super-Heroes ★ 2nd Appearance of Legion of Super-Heroes.
268 ❑ Jan 1960 Cover: 0.10 **NM** value: **80.00**
Circ: Statement: **438,000**
269 ❑ Feb 1960 Cover: 0.10 **NM** value: **225.00**
Circ: Statement: **438,000** • **CGC:** 1 graded, best 9.0
★ 1st Appearance of Aqualad.
270 ❑ Mar 1960 Cover: 0.10 **NM** value: **80.00**
Circ: Statement: **438,000**
★ Appearance of Congorilla.

CGC-graded: Multiply prices above by **33 for 9.9 M • 16 for 9.8 NM/M • 7 for 9.6 NM+ • 5 for 9.4 NM • 2.5 for 9.2 NM- • 1.5 for 9.0 VF/NM**

271 ❑ Apr 1960 Cover: 0.10 **NM** value: **225.00**
Circ: Statement: **438,000** • **CGC:** 1 graded, best 3.0
★ Origin of Lex Luthor. ★ Appearance of Congorilla.

272 ❑ May 1960 Cover: 0.10 **NM** value: **65.00**
Circ: Statement: **438,000** • **CGC:** 2 graded, best 7.0
★ Appearance of Congorilla.

273 ❑ Jun 1960 Cover: 0.10 **NM** value: **65.00**
Circ: Statement: **438,000** • **CGC:** 1 graded, best 4.0
★ Appearance of Congorilla.

274 ❑ Jul 1960 Cover: 0.10 **NM** value: **65.00**
Circ: Statement: **438,000** • **CGC:** 1 graded, best 7.5
★ Appearance of Congorilla.

275 ❑ Aug 1960 Cover: 0.10 **NM** value: **150.00**
Circ: Statement: **438,000**
★ Origin of Superman/Batman Team-up. ★ Appearance of Congorilla.

276 ❑ Sep 1960 Cover: 0.10 **NM** value: **65.00**
Circ: Statement: **438,000** • **CGC:** 2 graded, best 8.0
★ 1st Appearance of Sun Boy. ★ Appearance of Congorilla.

277 ❑ Oct 1960 Cover: 0.10 **NM** value: **65.00**
Circ: Statement: **438,000**
★ Appearance of Congorilla.

278 ❑ Nov 1960 Cover: 0.10 **NM** value: **65.00**
Circ: Statement: **438,000**
★ Appearance of Supergirl. ★ Appearance of Congorilla.

279 ❑ Dec 1960 Cover: 0.10 **NM** value: **65.00**
Circ: Statement: **438,000** • **CGC:** 1 graded, best 8.0
A: Curt Swan ★ 1st Appearance of White Kryptonite. ★ Appearance of Congorilla.

280 ❑ Jan 1961 Cover: 0.10 **NM** value: **65.00**
Circ: Statement: **460,000** • **CGC:** 2 graded, best 9.0
🕮 Superboy and the Mermaid from Atlantis!; The Seven Faces of Congorilla!; The Lost Ocean!; • Superboy meets Lori Lemaris; Congo Bill, Aquaman/Aqualad ★ Appearance of Lori Lemaris, Congorilla.

281 ❑ Feb 1961 Cover: 0.10 **NM** value: **60.00**
Circ: Statement: **460,000** • **CGC:** 1 graded, best 9.0
🕮 Superboy's New Parents!; (Congo Bill story); Our American Heritage • Congo Bill; Has 1960 Statement; avg total paid circ 438,000 ★ Appearance of Congorilla.

282 ❑ Mar 1961 Cover: 0.10 **NM** value: **90.00**
Circ: Statement: **460,000** • **CGC:** 5 graded, best 8.5
🕮 Lana Lang and the Legion of Super-Heroes ★ Origin of Starboy. ★ 1st Appearance of Starboy. ★ Appearance of Congorilla.

283 ❑ Apr 1961 Cover: 0.10 **NM** value: **100.00**
Circ: Statement: **460,000** • **CGC:** 4 graded, best 8.5
★ 1st Appearance of Phantom Zone. ★ Appearance of Congorilla.

284 ❑ May 1961 Cover: 0.10 **NM** value: **60.00**
Circ: Statement: **460,000**
🕮 Clark Kent Goes to Reform School!; Shorty; How's Your Eye-Q?; The Charge of Aquaman's Sea Soldiers!; Little Pete

285 ❑ Jun 1961 Cover: 0.10 **NM** value: **115.00**
Circ: Statement: **460,000** • **CGC:** 2 graded, best 8.5
🕮 Gravity Girl of Smallville!; Ollie; The Shame of the Bizarro Family!; Parents Have Rights, Too!; Honey in Hollywood • Tales of the Bizarro World ★ 1st Appearance of Bizarro World.

286 ❑ Jul 1961 Cover: 0.10 **NM** value: **110.00**
Circ: Statement: **460,000** • **CGC:** 3 graded, best 8.0
🕮 The Witch of Smallville!; Homer; Shorty; Bizarro, Private Detective • Tales of the Bizarro World ★ 1st Appearance of Bizarro Mxyzptlk.

287 ❑ Aug 1961 Cover: 0.10 **NM** value: **60.00**
Circ: Statement: **460,000** • **CGC:** 1 graded, best 7.0
🕮 Tales of Bizarro World

288 ❑ Sep 1961 Cover: 0.10 **NM** value: **60.00**
Circ: Statement: **460,000** • **CGC:** 2 graded, best 7.0
🕮 Tales of Bizarro World ★ 1st Appearance of Dev-Em.

289 ❑ Oct 1961 Cover: 0.10 **NM** value: **60.00**
Circ: Statement: **460,000** • **CGC:** 2 graded, best 8.5
🕮 Tales of Bizarro World

290 ❑ Nov 1961 Cover: 0.10 **NM** value: **110.00**
Circ: Statement: **460,000** • **CGC:** 5 graded, best 9.0
🕮 The Secert of the Seventh Super-Hero; Tales of Bizarro World • Sun Boy joins Legion of Super-Heroes ★ Origin of Sun Boy. ★ Appearance of Legion of Super-Heroes.

291 ❑ Dec 1961 Cover: 0.12 **NM** value: **45.00**
Circ: Statement: **460,000** • **CGC:** 1 graded, best 8.0
🕮 Tales of Bizarro World • Superboy

292 ❑ Jan 1962 Cover: 0.12 **NM** value: **45.00**
Circ: Statement: **415,000** • **CGC:** 1 graded, best 9.4
🕮 Tales of Bizarro World • Superboy

293 ❑ Feb 1962 Cover: 0.12 **NM** value: **100.00**
Circ: Statement: **415,000** • **CGC:** 6 graded, best 8.5
🕮 The Legion of Super-Traitors; Tales of Bizarro World **A:** Curt Swan ★ Origin of Mon-El. ★ 1st Appearance of Mon-El in Legion, Legion of Super-Pets.

294 ❑ Mar 1962 Cover: 0.12 **NM** value: **95.00**
Circ: Statement: **415,000**
🕮 Tales of Bizarro World • Superboy; Has 1961 Statement; avg total paid circ 460,000 ★ 1st Appearance of Bizarro Marilyn Monroe.

295 ❑ Apr 1962 Cover: 0.12 **NM** value: **45.00**
Circ: Statement: **415,000**
🕮 Tales of Bizarro World • Superboy

296 ❑ May 1962 Cover: 0.12 **NM** value: **45.00**
Circ: Statement: **415,000** • **CGC:** 2 graded, best 9.4
🕮 Tales of Bizarro World • Superboy

297 ❑ Jun 1962 Cover: 0.12 **NM** value: **45.00**
Circ: Statement: **415,000**
🕮 Tales of Bizarro World • Superboy

298 ❑ Jul 1962 Cover: 0.12 **NM** value: **45.00**
Circ: Statement: **415,000** • **CGC:** 2 graded, best 9.0
🕮 Tales of Bizarro World • Superboy

299 ❑ Aug 1962 Cover: 0.10 **NM** value: **55.00**
Circ: Statement: **415,000** • **CGC:** 2 graded, best 9.2
• Superboy; Bizarro world story ★ 1st Appearance of Gold Kryptonite.

300 ❑ Sep 1962 Cover: 0.12 **NM** value: **325.00**
Circ: Statement: **415,000** • **CGC:** 16 graded, best 9.0
• 300th anniversary issue. 🕮 The Face Behind the Lead Mask • Legion; Mon-El joins team; Legion of Super-Heroes begins as a regular back-up feature

301 ❑ Oct 1962 Cover: 0.12 **NM** value: **80.00**
Circ: Statement: **415,000** • **CGC:** 3 graded, best 9.0
🕮 The Secret Origin of Bouncing Boy! ★ Origin of Bouncing Boy.

302 ❑ Nov 1962 Cover: 0.12 **NM** value: **65.00**
Circ: Statement: **415,000** • **CGC:** 1 graded, best 7.5
🕮 Sun Boy's Lost Power! • Legion

303 ❑ Dec 1962 Cover: 0.12 **NM** value: **70.00**
Circ: Statement: **415,000**
🕮 The Fantastic Spy! • Matter-Eater Lad joins team; Legion ★ 1st Appearance of Matter-Eater Lad.

304 ❑ Jan 1963 Cover: 0.12 **NM** value: **70.00**
• **CGC:** 1 graded, best 8.0
🕮 The Stolen Super Powers! • Legion ★ Death of Lightning Lad.

305 ❑ Feb 1963 Cover: 0.12 **NM** value: **65.00**
• **CGC:** 1 graded, best 8.5
🕮 The Secret of the Mystery Legionnaire • Legion; Has 1962 Statement, filed 10/1/62; avg total paid circ 415,000

306 ❑ Mar 1963 Cover: 0.12 **NM** value: **50.00**
• **CGC:** 2 graded, best 9.8
🕮 The 5th Dimensional High-School!; Casey the Cop; The Legion of Substitute Heroes • "Teen-age" Mxyzptlk ★ 1st Appearance of Legion of Substitute Heroes.

307 ❑ Apr 1963 Cover: 0.12 **NM** value: **55.00**
• **CGC:** 1 graded, best 9.6
🕮 The Secret Power of the Mystery Super-Hero • Element Lad joins team; Legion ★ 1st Appearance of Element Lad, Roxxas.

308 ❑ May 1963 Cover: 0.12 **NM** value: **55.00**
🕮 The Return of Lightning Lad • Legion; Lightning Lass joins team ★ 1st Appearance of Lightning Lass, Proty.

309 ❑ Jun 1963 Cover: 0.12 **NM** value: **50.00**
• **CGC:** 1 graded, best 8.0
🕮 Lthe Legion of Super Monsters • Legion

310 ❑ Jul 1963 Cover: 0.12 **NM** value: **50.00**
• **CGC:** 1 graded, best 8.5
🕮 The Doom of the Super-Heroes • Legion

311 ❑ Aug 1963 Cover: 0.12 **NM** value: **45.00**
🕮 The War Between the Substitute Heroes and the Legionnaires • Legion ★ 1st Appearance of Legion of Super-Heroes Headquarters. ★ Appearance of Legion of Substitute Heroes.

312 ❑ Sep 1963 Cover: 0.12 **NM** value: **45.00**
🕮 The Super-Sacrifice of the Legionnaires • Legion; Return of Lightning Lad ★ Death of Proty.

313 ❑ Oct 1963 Cover: 0.12 **NM** value: **35.00**
🕮 The Condemned Legionnaires • Legion **A:** Curt Swan

314 ❑ Nov 1963 Cover: 0.12 **NM** value: **35.00**
🕮 The Super-Villains of All Ages • Legion

315 ❑ Dec 1963 Cover: 0.12 **NM** value: **35.00**
• **CGC:** 1 graded, best 8.0
🕮 The Legionnaires' Super-Contest • Legion

316 ❑ Jan 1964 Cover: 0.12 **NM** value: **35.00**
🕮 The Renegade Super-Hero; The End of a Super-Traitor!; Super-Turtle; The Origin and Powers of the Legion of Super-Heroes • profile pages; Legion

317 ❑ Feb 1964 Cover: 0.12 **NM** value: **40.00**
• **CGC:** 1 graded, best 9.4
🕮 The Menace of Dream Girl • Dream Girl joins team; Legion; Has 1963 Statement, filed 10/1/63; no circ figures published ★ 1st Appearance of Dream Girl.

318 ❑ Mar 1964 Cover: 0.12 **NM** value: **35.00**
🕮 The Mutiny of Legionnaires • Legion

319 ❑ Apr 1964 Cover: 0.12 **NM** value: **35.00**
🕮 The Legion's Suicide Squad!; The Charge of the Substitute Heroes!; Superboy's Best Friend! • Legion

320 ❑ May 1964 Cover: 0.12 **NM** value: **35.00**
🕮 The Revenge of the Knave From Krypton • Legion

321 ❑ Jun 1964 Cover: 0.12 **NM** value: **45.00**
• **CGC:** 4 graded, best 9.2
🕮 The Code of the Legion • Legion ★ 1st Appearance of Time Trapper.

322 ❑ Jul 1964 Cover: 0.12 **NM** value: **30.00**
• **CGC:** 2 graded, best 9.4
🕮 The Super-Tests of the Super-Pets • Legion

323 ❑ Aug 1964 Cover: 0.12 **NM** value: **30.00**
🕮 The Eight Impossible Missions!; The Amazing Winner of the Great Proty Puzzle!; How Krypto Made History • Legion

324 ❑ Sep 1964 Cover: 0.12 **NM** value: **30.00**
• **CGC:** 1 graded, best 8.0
🕮 The Legion of Super-Outlaws • Legion ★ 1st Appearance of Duplicate Boy, Heroes of Lallor (later Wanderers).

325 ❑ Oct 1964 Cover: 0.12 **NM** value: **30.00**
• **CGC:** 2 graded, best 9.4
🕮 Lex Luthor Meets the Legion of Super-Heroes • Legion

326 ❑ Nov 1964 Cover: 0.12 **NM** value: **30.00**
• **CGC:** 2 graded, best 9.0
🕮 Revolt of the Girl Legionnaires • Legion

327 ❑ Dec 1964 Cover: 0.12 **NM** value: **30.00**
• **CGC:** 1 graded, best 8.5
🕮 The Lone Wolf Legionnaire • Timber Wolf joins team ★ 1st Appearance of Timber Wolf.

328 ❑ Jan 1965 Cover: 0.12 **NM** value: **30.00**
Circ: Statement: **520,440** • **CGC:** 2 graded, best 9.2
🕮 The Lad Who Wrecked the Legion • Legion

329 ❑ Feb 1965 Cover: 0.12 **NM** value: **30.00**
Circ: Statement: **520,440** • **CGC:** 2 graded, best 9.0
🕮 The Bizarro-Legion • Legion ★ 1st Appearance of Bizarro Legion of Super-Heroes.

330 ❑ Mar 1965 Cover: 0.12 **NM** value: **30.00**
Circ: Statement: **520,440** • **CGC:** 2 graded, best 9.4
🕮 The Secret of the Mystery Legionnaire!; The Victory of the Evil Legionnaire!; A Job for Super-Dog • Dynamo Boy joins team; Legion; Has 1964 Statement, filed 10/1/64; no circ figures published

331 ❑ Apr 1965 Cover: 0.12 **NM** value: **30.00**
Circ: Statement: **520,440** • **CGC:** 1 graded, best 9.2
🕮 The Triumpgh of the Legion of Super-Villains • Legion ★ 1st Appearance of Saturn Queen.

332 ❑ May 1965 Cover: 0.12 **NM** value: **30.00**
Circ: Statement: **520,440** • **CGC:** 2 graded, best 9.2
🕮 The Super-Moby Dick of Space • Legion

333 ❑ Jun 1965 Cover: 0.12 **NM** value: **30.00**
Circ: Statement: **520,440** • **CGC:** 3 graded, best 9.4
🕮 The War Between Krypton and Earth • Legion

334 ❑ Jul 1965 Cover: 0.12 **NM** value: **30.00**
Circ: Statement: **520,440** • **CGC:** 1 graded, best 9.2
🕮 The Unknown Legionnaire • Legion

335 ❑ Aug 1965 Cover: 0.12 **NM** value: **30.00**
Circ: Statement: **520,440** • **CGC:** 2 graded, best 9.4
🕮 Starfinger • Legion ★ 1st Appearance of Magnetic Kid, Starfinger.

336 ❑ Sep 1965 Cover: 0.12 **NM** value: **30.00**
Circ: Statement: **520,440** • **CGC:** 1 graded, best 9.4
🕮 The True Identity of Starfinger • Legion

337 ❑ Oct 1965 Cover: 0.12 **NM** value: **30.00**
Circ: Statement: **520,440** • **CGC:** 3 graded, best 9.4
🕮 The Weddings That Wrecked the Legion; The Legionnaire Drop-outs!; The Secret Lives of Superbaby! • Legion; Wedding of Lightning Lad and Saturn Girl, Mon-El and Phantom Girl (fake weddings)

338 ❑ Nov 1965 Cover: 0.12 **NM** value: **30.00**
Circ: Statement: **520,440** • **CGC:** 2 graded, best 9.6
🕮 The Menace of the Sinister Super-Babies ★ 1st Appearance of Glorith. ★ Versus Time-Trapper, Glorith.

339 ❑ Dec 1965 Cover: 0.12 **NM** value: **30.00**
Circ: Statement: **520,440** • **CGC:** 2 graded, best 9.0
🕮 Hunters of the Super-Beasts • Legion

340 ❑ Jan 1966 Cover: 0.12 **NM** value: **30.00**
Circ: Statement: **481,234** • **CGC:** 4 graded, best 9.2
🕮 Computo the Conqueror!; Mystery of the Space Trophies • Legion **A:** Curt Swan ★ 1st Appearance of Computo. ★ Death of one of Triplicate Girl's bodies.

341 ❑ Feb 1966 Cover: 0.12 **NM** value: **18.00**
Circ: Statement: **481,234** • **CGC:** 4 graded, best 9.6
🕮 The Weirdo Leagionnaire! • Legion **A:** Curt Swan

342 ❑ Mar 1966 Cover: 0.12 **NM** value: **16.00**
Circ: Statement: **481,234** • **CGC:** 1 graded, best 9.4
🕮 The Legionnaire Who Killed! • Legion **A:** Curt Swan ★ 1st Appearance of Color Kid.

343 ❑ Apr 1966 Cover: 0.12 **NM** value: **16.00**
Circ: Statement: **481,234**
🕮 The Evil Hands of the Luck Lords! • Legion **A:** Curt Swan

344 ❑ May 1966 Cover: 0.12 **NM** value: **16.00**
Circ: Statement: **481,234** • **CGC:** 2 graded, best 9.4
🕮 The Super-Stalag of Space!; The Test of Braniac 5!; The Millionaire Pupil! • Legion **A:** Curt Swan

345 ❑ Jun 1966 Cover: 0.12 **NM** value: **16.00**
Circ: Statement: **481,234** • **CGC:** 2 graded, best 9.4
🕮 The Execution of Matter-Eater Lad!; Duo Damsel's Double-Play!; Pa Kent's Dilemma! • Legion **A:** Curt Swan ★ 1st Appearance of Khunds. ★ Death of Blockade Boy, Weight Wizard.

346 ❑ Jul 1966 Cover: 0.12 **NM** value: **18.00**
Circ: Statement: **481,234** • **CGC:** 2 graded, best 9.4
🕮 One of Us Is a Traitor! • Karate Kid, Princess Projecta, Ferro Lad joins team; 1st a ★ 1st Appearance of Karate Kid, Princess Projectra, Ferro Lad.

347 ❑ Aug 1966 Cover: 0.12 **NM** value: **16.00**
Circ: Statement: **481,234** • **CGC:** 2 graded, best 9.0
🕮 The Traitor's Triumph!; The Legion and the Warlords! • Legion

348 ❑ Sep 1966 Cover: 0.12 **NM** value: **18.00**
Circ: Statement: **481,234** • **CGC:** 3 graded, best 9.2
🕮 Target – 21 Legionnaires!; And Then There Were None!; Birds in a Golden Cage • Legion ★ Origin of Sunboy. ★ 1st Appearance of Doctor Regulus. ★ Versus Doctor Regulus.

349 ❑ Oct 1966 Cover: 0.12 **NM** value: **16.00**
Circ: Statement: **481,234** • **CGC:** 1 graded, best 9.2
🕮 The Rogue Legionnaire! ★ 1st Appearance of Rond Vidar.

350 ❑ Nov 1966 Cover: 0.12 **NM** value: **16.00**
Circ: Statement: **481,234** • **CGC:** 3 graded, best 9.4
🕮 The Outcast Super-Heroes! • Legion **A:** Curt Swan ★ 1st Appearance of Mysa Nal, Prince Evillo.

351 ❑ Dec 1966 Cover: 0.12 **NM** value: **16.00**
Circ: Statement: **481,234** • **CGC:** 4 graded, best 9.4
🕮 The Forgotten Legion! **A:** Curt Swan ★ 1st Appearance of White Witch.

352 ❑ Jan 1967 Cover: 0.12 **NM** value: **13.00**
Circ: Statement: **412,800** • **CGC:** 7 graded, best 9.6
🕮 The Fatal Five! • Legion ★ 1st Appearance of The Fatal Five.

353 ❑ Feb 1967 Cover: 0.12 **NM** value: **18.00**
Circ: Statement: **412,800** • **CGC:** 1 graded, best 9.4
🕮 The Doomed Legionnaire!; Slain by the Sun-Eater! • Has 1966 Statement; avg print run 759,000; avg sales 472,000; avg subs 9,234; avg total paid 481,234; max existent 481,234; 37% of run returned ★ Death of Ferro Lad.

354 ❑ Mar 1967 Cover: 0.12 **NM** value: **12.00**
Circ: Statement: **412,800** • **CGC:** 2 graded, best 9.2
🕮 The Adult Legion! • Legion

355 ❑ Apr 1967 Cover: 0.12 **NM** value: **12.00**
Circ: Statement: **412,800** • **CGC:** 3 graded, best 9.4
🕮 The War of the Legions!; The Six-Legged Legionnaire! • Adult Legion story **A:** Curt Swan

356 ❑ May 1967 Cover: 0.12 **NM** value: **12.00**
Circ: Statement: **412,800** • **CGC:** 1 graded, best 6.5
🕮 The Five Legion Orphans!; Lana Lang and the Legion of Super-Heroes! • Legion

357 ❑ Jun 1967 Cover: 0.12 **NM** value: **12.00**
Circ: Statement: **412,800** • **CGC:** 2 graded, best 9.4
🕮 The Ghost of Ferro Lad! • Legion **A:** Curt Swan ★ 1st Appearance of Controllers.

358 ❑ Jul 1967 Cover: 0.12 **NM** value: **12.00**
Circ: Statement: **412,800** • **CGC:** 2 graded, best 9.2
🕮 The Hunter • Legion

359 ❑ Aug 1967 Cover: 0.12 **NM** value: **12.00**
Circ: Statement: **412,800**
🕮 The Outlawed Legionnaires! • Legion

360 ❑ Sep 1967 Cover: 0.12 **NM** value: **12.00**
Circ: Statement: **412,800** • **CGC:** 2 graded, best 9.2
🕮 The Legion Chain Gang! • Legion

361 ❑ Oct 1967 Cover: 0.12 **NM** value: **10.00**
Circ: Statement: **412,800** • **CGC:** 2 graded, best 9.0
🕮 The Unkillables! • Legion ★ Appearance of Dominators. ★ Versus Unkillables.

Other grades: Multiply prices above by **1.5 for Mint • 2/3 for Very Fine • 1/3 for Fine • 1/5 for Very Good • 1/8 for Good**

362 ❑ Nov 1967 Cover: 0.12 **NM** value: **10.00**
Circ: Statement: **412,800** • **CGC:** 2 graded, best 9.2
The Chemoids Are Coming!; Meet the Legionnaires! (text) • Legion★ Versus Mantis Morlo.

363 ❑ Dec 1967 Cover: 0.12 **NM** value: **10.00**
Circ: Statement: **412,800** • **CGC:** 2 graded, best 9.6
Black Day For the Legion! • Legion★ Versus Mantis Morlo.

364 ❑ Jan 1968 Cover: 0.12 **NM** value: **10.00**
Circ: Statement: **411,200** • **CGC:** 1 graded, best 9.6
The Revolt of the Super-Pets! • Legion **A:** Curt Swan

365 ❑ Feb 1968 Cover: 0.12 **NM** value: **10.00**
Circ: Statement: **411,200** • **CGC:** 2 graded, best 9.2
Escape of the Fatal Five!; The Origin and Powers of the Legion of Super-Heroes **A:** Neal Adams ★ 1st Appearance of Shadow Lass.

366 ❑ Mar 1968 Cover: 0.12 **NM** value: **10.00**
Circ: Statement: **411,200** • **CGC:** 3 graded, best 9.6
The Fight For the Championship of the Universe! • Legion; Shadow Lass joins Legion; Has 1967 Statement, filed 10/1/67; avg print run 707,000; avg sales 408,000; avg subs 4,800; avg total paid 412,800; samples 340; max existent 413,140; 42% of run returned **A:** Neal Adams ★ Versus Validus.

367 ❑ Apr 1968 Cover: 0.12 **NM** value: **10.00**
Circ: Statement: **411,200** • **CGC:** 2 graded, best 9.0
No Escape From the Circle of Death! • Legion★ 1st Appearance of The Dark Circle.

368 ❑ May 1968 Cover: 0.12 **NM** value: **10.00**
Circ: Statement: **411,200** • **CGC:** 2 graded, best 9.4
The Mutiny of the Super-Heroines; Ladies First! • Legion

369 ❑ Jun 1968 Cover: 0.12 **NM** value: **10.00**
Circ: Statement: **411,200** • **CGC:** 2 graded, best 9.4
Mordru the Merciless!; Mordru and the Mob! • Legion in Smallville★ 1st Appearance of Mordru.

370 ❑ Jul 1968 Cover: 0.12 **NM** value: **10.00**
Circ: Statement: **411,200** • **CGC:** 2 graded, best 9.0
The Devil's Jury • Legion

371 ❑ Aug 1968 Cover: 0.12 **NM** value: **10.00**
Circ: Statement: **411,200** • **CGC:** 4 graded, best 9.6
The Colossal Failure!; When Superboy Walked Out on the Legion! • Legion;Colossal Boy leaves team **A:** Neal Adams ★ 1st Appearance of Chemical King, Legion Academy.

372 ❑ Sep 1968 Cover: 0.12 **NM** value: **10.00**
Circ: Statement: **411,200** • **CGC:** 1 graded, best 9.4
School For Super-Villains • Legion;Chemical King joins Legion;Timber Wolf joins Legion **A:** Neal Adams

373 ❑ Oct 1968 Cover: 0.12 **NM** value: **9.00**
Circ: Statement: **411,200**
The Tornado Twins • Legion

374 ❑ Nov 1968 Cover: 0.12 **NM** value: **9.00**
Circ: Statement: **411,200** • **CGC:** 1 graded, best 9.4
Mission: Diabolical!; Infiltrate Taurus! • Legion

375 ❑ Dec 1968 Cover: 0.12 **NM** value: **9.00**
Circ: Statement: **411,200** • **CGC:** 3 graded, best 9.4
The King of the Legion!; Hero Against Hero! • Legion **A:** Neal Adams ★ 1st Appearance of Wanderers, Quantum Queen.

376 ❑ Jan 1969 Cover: 0.12 **NM** value: **9.00**
Circ: Statement: **354,123** • **CGC:** 1 graded, best 9.0
The Execution of Chameleon Boy; Cupid Clips Cham! • Legion

377 ❑ Feb 1969 Cover: 0.12 **NM** value: **9.00**
Circ: Statement: **354,123** • **CGC:** 3 graded, best 9.4
Heroes for Hire • Legion; Has 1968 Statement; avg print run 697,000; avg sales 406,000; avg subs 2,200; avg total paid 411,200; max existent 411,200; 41% of run returned **A:** Jim Shooter; Win Mortimer; Neal Adams(cover) **W:** Jim Shooter

378 ❑ Mar 1969 Cover: 0.12 **NM** value: **9.00**
Circ: Statement: **354,123** • **CGC:** 1 graded, best 8.5
Twelve Hours to Live!; In the Shadow of Death! • Legion **A:** Jim Shooter; Win Mortimer; Neal Adams(cover) **W:** Jim Shooter

379 ❑ Apr 1969 Cover: 0.12 **NM** value: **9.00**
Circ: Statement: **354,123** • **CGC:** 2 graded, best 9.4
Burial in Space!; Showdown on Seeris!; Help Comes… Too Late? • Legion **A:** Jim Shooter; Win Mortimer; Neal Adams(cover) **W:** Jim Shooter

380 ❑ Apr 1969 Cover: 0.12 **NM** value: **9.00**
Circ: Statement: **354,123** • **CGC:** 1 graded, best 8.0
The Legion's Space Odyssey!; The Building of the Ship!; No Welcome for the Wanderers!; Detective Comics #27 (May, 1939) Fact File #7 (text) • Legion;Legion of Super-Heroes stories end **A:** Jim Shooter; Win Mortimer; Curt Swan(cover); Mike Esposito(cover) **W:** Jim Shooter

381 ❑ Jun 1969 Cover: 0.15 **NM** value: **10.00**
Circ: Statement: **354,123** • **CGC:** 15 graded, best 9.4
• Supergirl stories begin

382 ❑ Jul 1969 Cover: 0.15 **NM** value: **8.00**
Circ: Statement: **354,123**

383 ❑ Aug 1969 Cover: 0.15 **NM** value: **8.00**
Circ: Statement: **354,123** • **CGC:** 1 graded, best 9.4

384 ❑ Sep 1969 Cover: 0.15 **NM** value: **8.00**
Circ: Statement: **354,123** • **CGC:** 1 graded, best 9.2

385 ❑ Oct 1969 Cover: 0.15 **NM** value: **8.00**
Circ: Statement: **354,123** • **CGC:** 2 graded, best 9.2

386 ❑ Nov 1969 Cover: 0.15 **NM** value: **8.00**
Circ: Statement: **354,123** • **CGC:** 1 graded, best 9.4
The Beast That Loved Supergirl!; The Brute Suitor with the Ape Shape!; Ollie; The Godmother of Steel!; Hy Wire • Supergirl★ Appearance of Mxyzptlk.

387 ❑ Dec 1969 Cover: 0.15 **NM** value: **8.00**
Circ: Statement: **354,123** • **CGC:** 2 graded, best 9.0
The Wolf-Girl of Stanhope!; The Linda Lee Hairstyle Poll; Lex Luthor's Outlaw Nephew! • Supergirl★ Versus Lex Luthor.

388 ❑ Jan 1970 Cover: 0.15 **NM** value: **8.00**
Circ: Statement: **310,123** • **CGC:** 1 graded, best 9.2
The Kindergarten Criminal!; The Romance Machine • Supergirl★ Versus Lex Luthor.

389 ❑ Feb 1970 Cover: 0.15 **NM** value: **8.00**
Circ: Statement: **310,123**

390 ❑ Apr 1970 Cover: 0.25 **NM** value: **8.00**
Circ: Statement: **310,123** • **CGC:** 6 graded, best 9.8
• Giant-size issue. When Supergirl Played Cupid!; The Secret Identity of Super-Horse!; Supergirl's Cowboy Hero!; The Great Supergirl Mirage!; Supergirl's Wedding Day! • 80-page Giant; All-Romance issue

391 ❑ Mar 1970 Cover: 0.15 **NM** value: **8.00**
Circ: Statement: **310,123**
• Has 1969 Statement; avg print run 664,000; avg sales 353,000; avg subs 1,123; avg total paid 354,123; max existent 354,123; 47% of run returned

392 ❑ Apr 1970 Cover: 0.15 **NM** value: **8.00**
Circ: Statement: **310,123**

393 ❑ May 1970 Cover: 0.15 **NM** value: **8.00**
Circ: Statement: **310,123**

394 ❑ Jun 1970 Cover: 0.15 **NM** value: **8.00**
Circ: Statement: **310,123**

395 ❑ Jul 1970 Cover: 0.15 **NM** value: **8.00**
Circ: Statement: **310,123**

396 ❑ Aug 1970 Cover: 0.15 **NM** value: **8.00**
Circ: Statement: **310,123** • **CGC:** 1 graded, best 9.4

397 ❑ Sep 1970 Cover: 0.15 **NM** value: **8.00**
Circ: Statement: **310,123**

398 ❑ Oct 1970 Cover: 0.15 **NM** value: **8.00**
Circ: Statement: **310,123**

399 ❑ Nov 1970 Cover: 0.15 **NM** value: **8.00**
Circ: Statement: **310,123**
Johnny Dee, Hero-Bum!; Television Told the Tale! • Black Canary

400 ❑ Dec 1970 Cover: 0.15 **NM** value: **12.00**
Circ: Statement: **310,123** • **CGC:** 2 graded, best 9.0
• 35th anniversary.

401 ❑ Jan 1971 Cover: 0.15 **NM** value: **6.00**
Circ: Statement: **288,941**

402 ❑ Feb 1971 Cover: 0.15 **NM** value: **6.00**
Circ: Statement: **288,941** • **CGC:** 1 graded, best 9.4
• Supergirl loses powers

403 ❑ Apr 1971 Cover: 0.25 **NM** value: **15.00**
Circ: Statement: **288,941** • **CGC:** 5 graded, best 9.4
• Giant-size. Fashion From Fans; Diagram of Legion Headquarters Complex

404 ❑ Mar 1971 Cover: 0.15 **NM** value: **5.00**
Circ: Statement: **288,941** • **CGC:** 1 graded, best 8.5
• Supergirl gets exo-skeleton; Has 1970 Statement; avg print run 591,190; avg sales 309,500; avg subs 613; avg total paid 310,123; max existent 310,113; 48% of run returned

405 ❑ Apr 1971 Cover: 0.15 **NM** value: **5.00**
Circ: Statement: **288,941**

406 ❑ May 1971 Cover: 0.15 **NM** value: **5.00**
Circ: Statement: **288,941** • **CGC:** 1 graded, best 8.0

407 ❑ Jun 1971 Cover: 0.15 **NM** value: **5.00**
Circ: Statement: **288,941**

408 ❑ Jul 1971 Cover: 0.15 **NM** value: **5.00**
Circ: Statement: **288,941** • **CGC:** 1 graded, best 8.5

409 ❑ Aug 1971 Cover: 0.25 **NM** value: **5.00**
Circ: Statement: **288,941** • **CGC:** 1 graded, best 9.4
• reprints Legion story from Adventure #313;Supergirl gets new costume

410 ❑ Sep 1971 Cover: 0.25 **NM** value: **5.00**
Circ: Statement: **288,941**

411 ❑ Oct 1971 Cover: 0.25 **NM** value: **5.00**
Circ: Statement: **288,941**

412 ❑ Nov 1971 Cover: 0.25 **NM** value: **4.50**
Circ: Statement: **288,941**
• Animal Man reprint;reprints Strange Adventures #180★ 1st Appearance of Animal Man.

413 ❑ Dec 1971 Cover: 0.25 **NM** value: **4.50**
Circ: Statement: **288,941** • **CGC:** 2 graded, best 9.2

414 ❑ Jan 1972 Cover: 0.25 **NM** value: **4.50**
Circ: Statement: **216,879**
★ Appearance of Animal Man.

415 ❑ Feb 1972 Cover: 0.25 **NM** value: **4.50**
Circ: Statement: **216,879** • **CGC:** 1 graded, best 9.4
• Animal Man reprint

416 ❑ Mar 1972 Cover: 0.50 **NM** value: **7.00**
Circ: Statement: **216,879** • **CGC:** 9 graded, best 9.6
wraparound cover. • Giant-size issue. • a.k.a. DC 100-Page Super Spectacular #DC-10;all-women issue

417 ❑ Mar 1972 Cover: 0.25 **NM** value: **4.50**
Circ: Statement: **216,879** • **CGC:** 4 graded, best 9.6
• Has 1971 Statement; avg print run 549,583; avg sales 288,783; avg subs 158; avg total paid 288,941; max existent 288,941; 47% of run returned **A:** Frank Frazetta

418 ❑ Apr 1972 Cover: 0.25 **NM** value: **4.50**
Circ: Statement: **216,879**
The Canary and the Cat!, part 1 • also contains previously unpublished Golden Age Doctor Mid-Nite story, Black Canary

419 ❑ May 1972 Cover: 0.25 **NM** value: **4.50**
Circ: Statement: **216,879** • **CGC:** 2 graded, best 9.4
The Canary and the Cat!, part 2 • Black Canary

420 ❑ Jun 1972 Cover: 0.25 **NM** value: **4.50**
Circ: Statement: **216,879** • **CGC:** 1 graded, best 9.4
• Animal Man reprint

421 ❑ Jul 1972 Cover: 0.20 **NM** value: **4.50**
Circ: Statement: **216,879**
• Animal Man reprint

422 ❑ Aug 1972 Cover: 0.20 **NM** value: **4.50**
Circ: Statement: **216,879**
Supergirl: Pawn of Peace; The Vigilante: Rodeo of Death **A:** Bob Oksner; Gray Morrow; Mike Sekowsky **W:** Steve Skeates; Bill Meredith

423 ❑ Sep 1972 Cover: 0.20 **NM** value: **4.50**
Circ: Statement: **216,879**

424 ❑ Oct 1972 Cover: 0.20 **NM** value: **4.50**
Circ: Statement: **216,879**

425 ❑ Jan 1973 Cover: 0.20 **NM** value: **4.50**
Circ: Statement: **168,379** • **CGC:** 4 graded, best 9.6
The Wings Of Jealous Gods; Sword Of The Dead **A:** Alex Toth ★ Origin of Captain Fear. ★ 1st Appearance of Captain Fear.

426 ❑ Mar 1973 Cover: 0.20 **NM** value: **4.50**
Circ: Statement: **168,379**

427 ❑ May 1973 Cover: 0.20 **NM** value: **4.50**
Circ: Statement: **168,379** • **CGC:** 1 graded, best 9.4
• Has 1972 Statement; avg total paid circ 216,879

428 ❑ Aug 1973 Cover: 0.20 **NM** value: **20.00**
Circ: Statement: **168,379** • **CGC:** 3 graded, best 9.4
★ 1st Appearance of Black Orchid.

429 ❑ Oct 1973 Cover: 0.20 **NM** value: **10.00**
Circ: Statement: **168,379** • **CGC:** 3 graded, best 9.4
★ Appearance of Black Orchid.

430 ❑ Dec 1973 Cover: 0.20 **NM** value: **9.00**
Circ: Statement: **168,379** • **CGC:** 1 graded, best 9.4
★ Appearance of Black Orchid.

431 ❑ Feb 1974 Cover: 0.20 **NM** value: **9.00**
Circ: Statement: **144,055** • **CGC:** 19 graded, best 9.8
The Wrath Of The Spectre; Is A Snerl Human? **A:** Alex Toth; Jim Aparo; Russell Carley **W:** Sheldon Mayer; Michael Fleisher ★ Appearance of Spectre.

432 ❑ Apr 1974 Cover: 0.20 **NM** value: **5.00**
Circ: Statement: **144,055** • **CGC:** 8 graded, best 9.6

433 ❑ Jun 1974 Cover: 0.20 **NM** value: **5.00**
Circ: Statement: **144,055** • **CGC:** 10 graded, best 9.6
• Has 1973 Statement; avg total paid circ 168,379 **A:** Jim Aparo ★ Appearance of Spectre.

434 ❑ Aug 1974 Cover: 0.20 **NM** value: **5.00**
Circ: Statement: **144,055** • **CGC:** 5 graded, best 9.4

435 ❑ Oct 1974 Cover: 0.20 **NM** value: **5.00**
Circ: Statement: **144,055** • **CGC:** 4 graded, best 9.4
• Aquaman back-up **A:** Jim Aparo ★ Appearance of Spectre.

436 ❑ Dec 1974 Cover: 0.20 **NM** value: **5.00**
Circ: Statement: **144,055** • **CGC:** 2 graded, best 9.6
• Aquaman back-up **A:** Jim Aparo ★ Appearance of Spectre.

437 ❑ Feb 1975 Cover: 0.25 **NM** value: **5.00**
Circ: Statement: **160,000** • **CGC:** 5 graded, best 9.8

438 ❑ Apr 1975 Cover: 0.25 **NM** value: **5.00**
Circ: Statement: **160,000** • **CGC:** 2 graded, best 9.8

439 ❑ Jun 1975 Cover: 0.25 **NM** value: **5.00**
Circ: Statement: **160,000** • **CGC:** 5 graded, best 9.6
• Has 1974 Statement; avg print run 379,251; avg sales 142,833; avg subs 1,222; avg total paid 144,055; samples 100; office use 929; max existent 144,984; 62% of run returned

440 ❑ Aug 1975 Cover: 0.25 **NM** value: **5.00**
Circ: Statement: **160,000** • **CGC:** 5 graded, best 9.8
★ Origin of Spectre-New.

441 ❑ Oct 1975 Cover: 0.25 **NM** value: **3.50**
Circ: Statement: **160,000** • **CGC:** 2 graded, best 9.6

442 ❑ Dec 1975 Cover: 0.25 **NM** value: **3.50**
Circ: Statement: **160,000** • **CGC:** 1 graded, best 9.6

443 ❑ Feb 1976 Cover: 0.25 **NM** value: **3.50**
Circ: Statement: **141,000** • **CGC:** 1 graded, best 9.6
• Seven Soldiers of Victory back-up;Aquaman

444 ❑ Apr 1976 Cover: 0.30 **NM** value: **3.50**
Circ: Statement: **141,000** • **CGC:** 1 graded, best 9.6
• Aquaman

445 ❑ Jun 1976 Cover: 0.30 **NM** value: **3.50**
Circ: Statement: **141,000** • **CGC:** 1 graded, best 9.6
• Has 1975 Statement; avg print run 371,000; avg sales 159,000; avg subs 1,000; avg total paid 160,000; samples 1,000; office use 1,000; max existent 161,000; 56% of run returned

446 ❑ Aug 1976 Cover: 0.30 **NM** value: **3.50**
Circ: Statement: **141,000** • **CGC:** 1 graded, best 9.8
• Bicentennial #31

447 ❑ Oct 1976 Cover: 0.30 **NM** value: **3.50**
Circ: Statement: **141,000** • **CGC:** 1 graded, best 9.6

448 ❑ Nov 1976 Cover: 0.30 **NM** value: **3.50**
Circ: Statement: **141,000** • **CGC:** 2 graded, best 9.6

449 ❑ Jan 1977 Cover: 0.30 **NM** value: **3.50**
Circ: Statement: **120,328** • **CGC:** 1 graded, best 9.8

450 ❑ Mar 1977 Cover: 0.30 **NM** value: **3.50**
Circ: Statement: **120,328** • **CGC:** 1 graded, best 9.6

451 ❑ May 1977 Cover: 0.30 **NM** value: **3.50**
Circ: Statement: **120,328**
• Has 1976 Statement; avg print run 343,000; avg sales 140,000; avg subs 1,000; avg total paid 141,000; samples 1,000; office use 4,000; max existent 145,000; 57% of run returned

452 ❑ Jul 1977 Cover: 0.35 **NM** value: **3.50**
Circ: Statement: **120,328**

453 ❑ Sep 1977 Cover: 0.35 **NM** value: **3.50**
Circ: Statement: **120,328** • **CGC:** 5 graded, best 9.8
• Superboy★ Appearance of Barbara Gordon.

454 ❑ Nov 1977 Cover: 0.35 **NM** value: **3.50**
Circ: Statement: **120,328**

455 ❑ Jan 1978 Cover: 0.35 **NM** value: **3.50**
Circ: Statement: **131,076**

456 ❑ Mar 1978 Cover: 0.35 **NM** value: **3.50**
Circ: Statement: **131,076**

457 ❑ May 1978 Cover: 0.35 **NM** value: **3.50**
Circ: Statement: **131,076**
• Has 1977 Statement; avg print run 329,143; avg sales 118,808; avg subs 1,520; avg total paid 120,328; samples 400; office use 2,422; max existent 122,750; 63% of run returned

458 ❑ Jul 1978 Cover: 0.35 **NM** value: **3.50**
Circ: Statement: **131,076**

459 ❑ Sep 1978 Cover: 1.00 **NM** value: **3.50**
Circ: Statement: **131,076**
• no ads;expands contents and raises price to $1 **A:** Don Newton; Joe Staton; Jim Aparo

460 ❑ Nov 1978 Cover: 1.00 **NM** value: **3.50**
Circ: Statement: **131,076** • **CGC:** 2 graded, best 9.6
A: Don Newton; Sergio Aragonés; Joe Staton

461 ❑ Jan 1979 Cover: 1.00 **NM** value: **6.00**
Circ: Statement: **83,642** • **CGC:** 1 graded, best 8.0
• Giant-size issue. • incorporates JSA story from unpublished All-Star Comics #75 **A:** Don Newton; Joe Staton; Jim Aparo

462 ❑ Mar 1979 Cover: 1.00 **NM** value: **6.00**
Circ: Statement: **83,642** • **CGC:** 2 graded, best 9.0
• Giant-size issue. **A:** Dick Giordano; Joe Staton; José Luis Garcia-Lopez ★ Death of E-2 Batman.

463 ❑ May 1979 Cover: 1.00 **NM** value: **3.50**
Circ: Statement: **83,642**

CGC-graded: Multiply prices above by **33 for 9.9 M • 16 for 9.8 NM/M • 7 for 9.6 NM+ • 5 for 9.4 NM • 2.5 for 9.2 NM- • 1.5 for 9.0 VF/NM**

• Has 1978 Statement; avg print run 367,889; avg sales 129,895; avg subs 1,181; avg total paid 131,076; samples 109; office use 3,933; max existent 135,009; 63% of run returned **A:** Frank McLaughlin; Don Heck; Joe Staton; José Luis Garcia-Lopez

464 ❑ Jul 1979 Cover: 1.00 **NM** value: **3.50**
Circ: Statement: **83,642**
• contains previously unpublished Deadman story from Showcase #105

465 ❑ Sep 1979 Cover: 1.00 **NM** value: **3.50**
Circ: Statement: **83,642**

466 ❑ Nov 1979 Cover: 1.00 **NM** value: **3.50**
Circ: Statement: **83,642**
• final JSA case before group retired in the '50s

467 ❑ Jan 1980 Cover: 0.40 **NM** value: **3.50**
Circ: Statement: **68,681**

468 ❑ Feb 1980 Cover: 0.40 **NM** value: **3.50**
Circ: Statement: **68,681**

469 ❑ Mar 1980 Cover: 0.40 **NM** value: **3.50**
Circ: Statement: **68,681**
★ Origin of Starman III (Prince Gavyn).

470 ❑ Apr 1980 Cover: 0.40 **NM** value: **3.50**
Circ: Statement: **68,681**
• Has 1979 Statement; avg print run 240,794; avg sales 82,665; avg subs 977; avg total paid 83,642; samples 0; office use 120; max existent 83,762; 65% of run returned ★ Origin of Starman III (Prince Gavyn).

471 ❑ May 1980 Cover: 0.40 **NM** value: **3.50**
Circ: Statement: **68,681**

472 ❑ Jun 1980 Cover: 0.40 **NM** value: **3.50**
Circ: Statement: **68,681**

473 ❑ Jul 1980 Cover: 0.40 **NM** value: **3.50**
Circ: Statement: **68,681**

474 ❑ Aug 1980 Cover: 0.40 **NM** value: **3.50**
Circ: Statement: **68,681**

475 ❑ Sep 1980 Cover: 0.50 **NM** value: **3.50**
Circ: Statement: **68,681**

476 ❑ Oct 1980 Cover: 0.50 **NM** value: **3.50**
Circ: Statement: **68,681**

477 ❑ Nov 1980 Cover: 0.50 **NM** value: **3.50**
Circ: Statement: **68,681**

478 ❑ Dec 1980 Cover: 0.50 **NM** value: **3.50**
Circ: Statement: **68,681**

479 ❑ Mar 1981 Cover: 0.50 **NM** value: **3.50**
🕮 Dial 'H' For Hero back-up ★ 1st Appearance of Victoria Grant, Christopher King.

480 ❑ Apr 1981 Cover: 0.50 **NM** value: **3.00**
🕮 Dial 'H' For Hero back-up

481 ❑ May 1981 Cover: 0.50 **NM** value: **3.00**
🕮 Dial 'H' For Hero back-up • Has 1980 Statement; avg print run 237,289; avg sales 67,829; avg subs 852; avg total paid 68,681; samples 127; office use 2,384; max existent 71,065; 70% of run returned

482 ❑ Jun 1981 Cover: 0.50 **NM** value: **3.00**
🕮 Dial 'H' For Hero back-up

483 ❑ Jul 1981 Cover: 0.50 **NM** value: **3.00**
🕮 Dial 'H' For Hero back-up • Dial H for Hero

484 ❑ Aug 1981 Cover: 0.50 **NM** value: **3.00**
🕮 Dial 'H' For Hero back-up

485 ❑ Sep 1981 Cover: 0.50 **NM** value: **3.00**
🕮 Dial 'H' For Hero back-up

486 ❑ Oct 1981 Cover: 0.60 **NM** value: **3.00**
🕮 Dial 'H' For Hero back-up

487 ❑ Nov 1981 Cover: 0.60 **NM** value: **3.00**
🕮 Dial 'H' For Hero back-up

488 ❑ Dec 1981 Cover: 0.60 **NM** value: **3.00**
🕮 Dial 'H' For Hero back-up

489 ❑ Jan 1982 Cover: 0.60 **NM** value: **3.00**
🕮 Dial 'H' For Hero back-up

490 ❑ Feb 1982 Cover: 0.60 **NM** value: **3.00**
🕮 Dial 'H' For Hero back-up

491 ❑ Sep 1982 Cover: 0.95 **NM** value: **3.00**
• digest size begins. 🕮 The Man Who Couldn't Sleep • Sandman

492 ❑ Oct 1982 Cover: 1.25 **NM** value: **3.00**
🕮 The Unholy Dreams of Gentleman Jack • Sandman

493 ❑ Nov 1982 Cover: 1.25 **NM** value: **3.00**
★ Appearance of Challengers of the Unknown.

494 ❑ Dec 1982 Cover: 1.25 **NM** value: **3.00**
★ Appearance of Challengers of the Unknown.

495 ❑ Jan 1983 Cover: 1.25 **NM** value: **3.00**
🕮 Crime Carnival • Sandman ★ Appearance of Challengers of the Unknown.

496 ❑ Feb 1983 Cover: 1.25 **NM** value: **3.00**
🕮 Dreams of Doom • Sandman ★ Appearance of Challengers of the Unknown.

497 ❑ Mar 1983 Cover: 1.25 **NM** value: **3.00**
★ Appearance of Challengers of the Unknown.

498 ❑ Apr 1983 Cover: 1.25 **NM** value: **3.00**
🕮 The Man Who Knew All the Answers • Sandman

499 ❑ May 1983 Cover: 1.25 **NM** value: **3.00**
🕮 The Villain from Valhalla • Sandman, "Thor"

500 ❑ Jun 1983 Cover: 1.25 **NM** value: **3.00**

501 ❑ Jul 1983 Cover: 1.25 **NM** value: **3.00**

502 ❑ Aug 1983 Cover: 1.25 **NM** value: **3.00**

503 ❑ Sep 1983 Cover: 1.25 **NM** value: **3.00**
🕮 Newsboy Legion final issue. • Newsboy Legion

Bk 1 ❑ Cover: 14.95 **NM** value: **Cover or less**
• Tales of the Bizarro World trade paperback;Collects Bizarro World series in Adventure Comics #285-299 **A:** Curt Swan; John Forte; Wayne Boring **W:** Jerry Siegel

ADVENTURE COMICS (2ND SERIES) DC

1 ❑ May 1999 Cover: 1.99 **NM** value: **Cover or less**
Circ: Diamd. preorders: **43,253**
🕮 Stars and Atoms **A:** Peter Snejbjerg **W:** James Robinson; David Goyer ★ Appearance of Atom, Starman.

GS 1 ❑ Oct 1998 Cover: 4.95 **NM** value: **Cover or less**
Circ: Diamd. preorders: **30,955**
• Giant size. 🕮 Wonder Woman: Darkness Fallen; Green Arrow: Longshot; Shazam!: The Great Divide; Superboy: Glug-Glug Ka-Pow; Legion of Super Heroes: Team Work; Supergirl: Child Labor; Tales of the Bizarro World: Bizarro Must Think • Wonder Woman, Captain Marvel, Superboy, Green Arrow, Legion, Supergirl, Bizarro **A:** Kevin West; Craig Rousseau; Rick Burchett; Phil Winslade; Steve Lightle; Louis Small Jr; Kevin O'Neill **W:** John Byrne; Chuck Dixon; Ivan Velez; Joan Weis; Pat McGreal; Tom McCraw; Tom Peyer

ADVENTURE INTO MYSTERY Atlas

1 ❑ May 1956 Cover: 0.10 **NM** value: **200.00**
2 ❑ Jul 1956 Cover: 0.10 **NM** value: **175.00**
3 ❑ Sep 1956 Cover: 0.10 **NM** value: **150.00**
• **CGC:** 1 graded, best 8.0
4 ❑ Nov 1956 Cover: 0.10 **NM** value: **150.00**
• **CGC:** 1 graded, best 6.5
5 ❑ Jan 1957 Cover: 0.10 **NM** value: **125.00**
6 ❑ Mar 1957 Cover: 0.10 **NM** value: **125.00**
• **CGC:** 2 graded, best 7.5
7 ❑ May 1957 Cover: 0.10 **NM** value: **100.00**
8 ❑ Jul 1957 Cover: 0.10 **NM** value: **100.00**
• **CGC:** 1 graded, best 8.0

ADVENTURE IS MY CAREER Street & Smith

1 ❑ ca. 1945 **NM** value: **100.00**

ADVENTURE OF THE NAVAL TREATY, THE Caliber / Tome

1 ❑ Cover: 3.50 **NM** value: **Cover or less**
No issue number. • illustrated story

ADVENTURERS, THE (AIRCEL) Aircel

1 ❑ Cover: 1.50 **NM** value: **2.00**
regular cover. 🕮 The Gate of Chaos **A:** Peter Hsu **W:** Scott Behnke
1/LE ❑ Cover: 1.50 **NM** value: **2.00**
skeleton cover. 🕮 The Gate of Chaos • Limited ed
2 ❑ Cover: 1.50 **NM** value: **2.00**
🕮 The Gate of Chaos

ADVENTURERS, THE (BOOK 1) Adventure

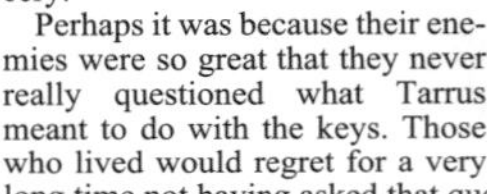
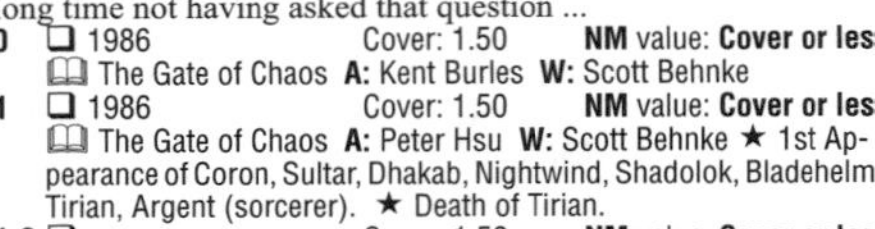

Following a brief introduction at Aircel, the Adventurers returned in this 1986 series at Adventure Publications, a division of Malibu. The title began by reprinting the first two Aircel issues. It then went on to complete the story "The Gate of Chaos," in which the heroes sought to retrieve the Keys of Telku for the evil lord Tarrus. In doing so, they had to overcome all manner of lethal traps, dread creatures, and dark sorcery.

Perhaps it was because their enemies were so great that they never really questioned what Tarrus meant to do with the keys. Those who lived would regret for a very long time not having asked that question ...

0 ❑ 1986 Cover: 1.50 **NM** value: **Cover or less**
🕮 The Gate of Chaos **A:** Kent Burles **W:** Scott Behnke
1 ❑ 1986 Cover: 1.50 **NM** value: **Cover or less**
🕮 The Gate of Chaos **A:** Peter Hsu **W:** Scott Behnke ★ 1st Appearance of Coron, Sultar, Dhakab, Nightwind, Shadolok, Bladehelm, Tirian, Argent (sorcerer). ★ Death of Tirian.
1-2 ❑ Cover: 1.50 **NM** value: **Cover or less**
2 ❑ Cover: 1.50 **NM** value: **Cover or less**
🕮 The Gate of Chaos **W:** Scott Behnke
3 ❑ 1986 Cover: 1.50 **NM** value: **Cover or less**
🕮 The Gate of Chaos • no indicia **W:** Scott Behnke
4 ❑ 1986 Cover: 1.50 **NM** value: **Cover or less**
🕮 The Gate of Chaos **A:** Kent Burles **W:** Scott Behnke
5 ❑ 1986 Cover: 1.50 **NM** value: **Cover or less**
🕮 The Gate of Chaos **A:** Kent Burles **W:** Scott Behnke
6 ❑ Jun 1987 Cover: 1.50 **NM** value: **Cover or less**
🕮 The Gate of Chaos **W:** Scott Behnke
7 ❑ Jul 1987 Cover: 1.50 **NM** value: **Cover or less**
🕮 The Gate of Chaos **W:** Scott Behnke
8 ❑ Sep 1987 Cover: 1.50 **NM** value: **Cover or less**
🕮 The Gate of Chaos **W:** Scott Behnke
9 ❑ 1986 Cover: 1.75 **NM** value: **Cover or less**
🕮 The Gate of Chaos **W:** Scott Behnke
10 ❑ 1986 Cover: 1.75 **NM** value: **Cover or less**
🕮 The Gate of Chaos **W:** Scott Behnke
Bk 1 ❑ Cover: 7.95 **NM** value: **Cover or less**
🕮 The Gate of Chaos • collects 1st series;The Chaos Gate

ADVENTURERS, THE (BOOK 2) Adventure

0 ❑ Jul 1988, b&w Cover: 1.95 **NM** value: **Cover or less**
1 ❑ Dec 1987 Cover: 1.95 **NM** value: **Cover or less**
regular cover. 🕮 The Grail Of Darkness **A:** Kent Burles **W:** Scott Behnke
1/LE ❑ Dec 1987 Cover: 1.95 **NM** value: **Cover or less**
• Limited edition cover.
2 ❑ Mar 1988 Cover: 1.95 **NM** value: **Cover or less**
W: Scott Behnke
3 ❑ Apr 1988 Cover: 1.95 **NM** value: **Cover or less**
W: Scott Behnke
4 ❑ Cover: 1.95 **NM** value: **Cover or less**
W: Scott Behnke
5 ❑ Cover: 1.95 **NM** value: **Cover or less**
W: Scott Behnke
6 ❑ Nov 1988 Cover: 1.95 **NM** value: **Cover or less**
W: Scott Behnke
7 ❑ Mar 1989, b&w Cover: 1.95 **NM** value: **Cover or less**
W: Scott Behnke
8 ❑ Cover: 1.95 **NM** value: **Cover or less**
W: Scott Behnke
9 ❑ Cover: 1.95 **NM** value: **Cover or less**
W: Scott Behnke
10 ❑ Cover: 1.95 **NM** value: **Cover or less**
W: Scott Behnke
Bk 1 ❑ Cover: 7.95 **NM** value: **Cover or less**
• The Halls Of Anubis

ADVENTURERS, THE (BOOK 3) Adventure

1 ❑ Oct 1989 Cover: 2.25 **NM** value: **Cover or less**
regular cover. **A:** Kent Burles **W:** Kent Burles
1/LE ❑ Oct 1989 Cover: 2.25 **NM** value: **Cover or less**
• Limited edition cover. **A:** Kent Burles; Mitch Foust(cover) **W:** Kent Burles
2 ❑ Nov 1989 Cover: 2.25 **NM** value: **Cover or less**
A: Kent Burles **W:** Kent Burles
3 ❑ Dec 1989 Cover: 2.25 **NM** value: **Cover or less**
A: Kent Burles **W:** Kent Burles
4 ❑ Jan 1990 Cover: 2.25 **NM** value: **Cover or less**
A: Kent Burles **W:** Kent Burles
5 ❑ Feb 1990 Cover: 2.25 **NM** value: **Cover or less**
A: Kent Burles **W:** Kent Burles
6 ❑ Mar 1990 Cover: 2.25 **NM** value: **Cover or less**
A: Kent Burles **W:** Kent Burles
Bk 1 ❑ Cover: 7.95 **NM** value: **Cover or less**
• Ways Of The Worm

ADVENTURES St. John

1 ❑ Nov 1949 Cover: 0.10 **NM** value: **150.00**
2 ❑ ca. 1950 Cover: 0.10 **NM** value: **150.00**

ADVENTURES FOR BOYS Bailey

1 ❑ ca. 1955 Cover: 0.10 **NM** value: **25.00**

ADVENTURES IN READING STARRING: THE AMAZING SPIDER-MAN Marvel

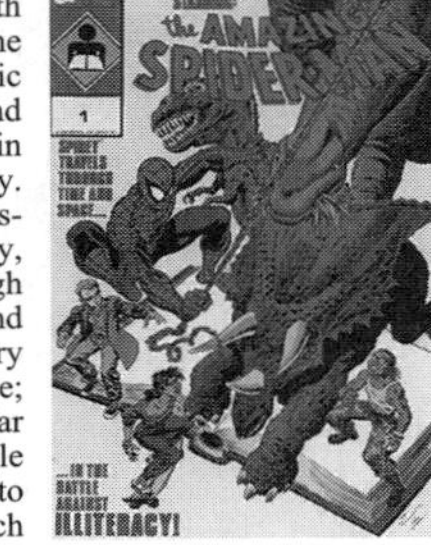

The Amazing Spider-Man was in the middle of a pitched battle with a heavy called The Troglodyte. The battle eventually spread to a public library, where Spider-Man and three nearby youths were caught in The Troglodyte's transporter ray. The transporter, affected by the assortment of books in the library, sent the group on a wild ride through time and space. The group found themselves caught up in the story "worlds" of such books as Ivanhoe; That Was Then, This Is Now; War of the Worlds; and The Jungle Book. It's a spectacular way to make literature come alive, which was exactly the point of this free comic book designed to promote books and libraries.

1 ❑ Sep 1990 **NM** value: **1.00**
• Giveaway to promote literacy.

ADVENTURES IN THE DC UNIVERSE DC

1 ❑ Apr 1997 Cover: 1.75 **NM** value: **2.50**
Circ: Diamd. preorders: **37,075** • **CGC:** 1 graded, best 9.6
• JLA
2 ❑ May 1997 Cover: 1.75 **NM** value: **2.00**
Circ: Diamd. preorders: **31,864**
🕮 The Flash: Bombs Away!; Catwoman: Catch as Cat Can **A:** John Delaney **W:** Steve Vance ★ Origin of The Flash III (Wally West).
3 ❑ Jun 1997 Cover: 1.75 **NM** value: **2.00**
Circ: Diamd. preorders: **31,123**
• Batman vs. Poison Ivy; Wonder Woman vs. Cheetah **A:** John Delaney **W:** Steve Vance
4 ❑ Jul 1997 Cover: 1.75 **NM** value: **2.00**
Circ: Diamd. preorders: **26,916**
• Mr. Miracle;Green Lantern **A:** John Delaney **W:** Steve Vance
5 ❑ Aug 1997 Cover: 1.75 **NM** value: **2.00**
Circ: Diamd. preorders: **24,410**
• Martian Manhunter **A:** John Delaney **W:** Steve Vance ★ Appearance of Ultra the Multi-Alien.
6 ❑ Sep 1997 Cover: 1.75 **NM** value: **2.00**
Circ: Diamd. preorders: **22,126**
• Power Girl;Aquaman **A:** John Delaney **W:** Steve Vance
7 ❑ Oct 1997 Cover: 1.75 **NM** value: **2.00**
Circ: Diamd. preorders: **20,152**
• Marvel Family: A: Lois Lane, Clark Kent **A:** John Delaney **W:** Steve Vance
8 ❑ Nov 1997 Cover: 1.75 **NM** value: **2.00**
Circ: Diamd. preorders: **18,747**
• Question;Blue Beetle, Booster Gold **A:** John Delaney **W:** Steve Vance
9 ❑ Dec 1997 Cover: 1.95 **NM** value: **2.00**
Circ: Diamd. preorders: **18,277**
• Flash vs. Gorilla Grodd **A:** John Delaney **W:** Steve Vance
10 ❑ Jan 1998 Cover: 1.95 **NM** value: **2.00**
Circ: Diamd. preorders: **18,698**
• Legion of Super-Heroes **A:** John Delaney **W:** Steve Vance
11 ❑ Feb 1998 Cover: 1.95 **NM** value: **2.00**
Circ: Diamd. preorders: **17,265**
• Wonder Woman, Green Lantern **A:** John Delaney **W:** Steve Vance
12 ❑ Mar 1998 Cover: 1.95 **NM** value: **2.00**
Circ: Diamd. preorders: **17,766**
🕮 Cipher Rules! • JLA vs. Cipher **A:** John Delaney **W:** Steve Vance
13 ❑ Apr 1998 Cover: 1.95 **NM** value: **Cover or less**
Circ: Diamd. preorders: **15,664**
• Green Arrow;Impulse, Martian Manhunter **A:** John Delaney **W:** Steve Vance
14 ❑ May 1998 Cover: 1.95 **NM** value: **Cover or less**
Circ: Diamd. preorders: **16,361**
• Nightwing;Superboy, Flash **A:** John Delaney **W:** Steve Vance

Other grades: Multiply prices above by **1.5 for Mint • 2/3 for Very Fine • 1/3 for Fine • 1/5 for Very Good • 1/8 for Good**

15 ❑ Jun 1998 Cover: 1.95 **NM** value: **Cover or less**
Circ: Diamd. preorders: **16,179**
• Aquaman;Captain Marvel **A:** John Delaney **W:** Steve Vance
16 ❑ Jul 1998 Cover: 1.95 **NM** value: **Cover or less**
Circ: Diamd. preorders: **15,423**
• Green Arrow;Green Lantern **A:** John Delaney **W:** Steve Vance
17 ❑ Aug 1998 Cover: 1.95 **NM** value: **Cover or less**
Circ: Diamd. preorders: **16,436**
• Creeper;Batman **A:** John Delaney **W:** Steve Vance
18 ❑ Sep 1998 Cover: 1.95 **NM** value: **Cover or less**
Circ: Diamd. preorders: **16,662**
• JLA vs. Amazo **A:** John Delaney **W:** Steve Vance
19 ❑ Oct 1998 Cover: 1.99 **NM** value: **Cover or less**
Circ: Diamd. preorders: **15,678**
final issue. • Wonder Woman, Catwoman **A:** John Delaney **W:** Steve Vance
Anl 1❑ Oct 1998 Cover: 3.95 **NM** value: **Cover or less**
Circ: Diamd. preorders: **17,020**
📖 Something Wicked This Way Comes! • Doctor Fate, Impulse, Superboy, Thorn, Mr. Miracle;events crossover with Superman Adventures Annual #1 and Batman & Robin Adventures Annual #2 **A:** John Delaney; Dick Giordano; Michael Avon Oeming; Andy Suriano; Mike Manley **W:** Hilary J. Bader

ADVENTURES IN THE MYSTWOOD Blackthorne

1 ❑ Aug 1986 Cover: 2.00 **NM** value: **Cover or less**
📖 Dreams...Sweet Dreams **A:** John Williams **W:** John Williams

ADVENTURES IN THE RIFLE BRIGADE DC / Vertigo

Many stories of World War II have been lost in the mists of time. Perhaps one such story is that of The Rifle Brigade, a bizarre collection of oddballs including a very proper British Captain Darcy, who brings his team behind Nazi lines and just may have found a way to get them out, and a wizened Scottish bloke whose bagpipes are not to be messed with. There's also the oafish Sargent Crumb, who smiles in the face of Death (and everything else). Together with the rest of their team, they are the Allies' best hope to steal a secret German formula that could win the War for the Nazis — which makes their capture by sadistic German killers a troubling occurrence.

Featuring action, adventure, and terribly inappropriate and unpleasant humor, the Vertigo mini-series is written by Garth Ennis and drawn by Carlos Ezquerra.

1 ❑ Oct 2000 Cover: 2.50 **NM** value: **Cover or less**
Circ: Diamd. preorders: **21,705**
📖 Once More into the Breach **A:** Carlos Ezquerra **W:** Garth Ennis
2 ❑ Nov 2000 Cover: 2.50 **NM** value: **Cover or less**
Circ: Diamd. preorders: **19,372**
📖 Definitely Not Cricket **A:** Carlos Ezquerra **W:** Garth Ennis
3 ❑ Dec 2000 Cover: 2.50 **NM** value: **Cover or less**
Circ: Diamd. preorders: **19,584**
📖 Up Yours, Fritz **A:** Carlos Ezquerra **W:** Garth Ennis

ADVENTURES IN 3-D Harvey

1 ❑ Nov 1953 Cover: 0.10 **NM** value: **100.00**
• **CGC:** 2 graded, best 9.6
📖 Breaking the Time Barrier!; Jungle Drum; Three-D Blinkey; The Hidden Depths; The Snowman; Sand
2 ❑ Jan 1954 Cover: 0.10 **NM** value: **90.00**
• **CGC:** 1 graded, best 9.2

ADVENTURES INTO DARKNESS Standard

5 ❑ ca. 1952 Cover: 0.10 **NM** value: **200.00**
6 ❑ ca. 1952 Cover: 0.10 **NM** value: **175.00**
7 ❑ ca. 1953 Cover: 0.10 **NM** value: **125.00**
8 ❑ ca. 1953 Cover: 0.10 **NM** value: **125.00**
9 ❑ ca. 1953 Cover: 0.10 **NM** value: **125.00**
10 ❑ ca. 1953 Cover: 0.10 **NM** value: **125.00**
• **CGC:** 1 graded, best 8.5
11 ❑ ca. 1953 Cover: 0.10 **NM** value: **100.00**
12 ❑ ca. 1953 Cover: 0.10 **NM** value: **100.00**
13 ❑ ca. 1954 Cover: 0.10 **NM** value: **100.00**
14 ❑ ca. 1954 Cover: 0.10 **NM** value: **100.00**

ADVENTURES INTO TERROR Atlas

1 ❑ Nov 1950 Cover: 0.10 **NM** value: **500.00**
• **CGC:** 2 graded, best 8.0
• continues numbering from previous series (#43)
2 ❑ Feb 1951 Cover: 0.10 **NM** value: **350.00**
• **CGC:** 1 graded, best 6.5
• continues numbering from previous series (#44)
3 ❑ Apr 1951 Cover: 0.10 **NM** value: **250.00**
4 ❑ Jun 1951 Cover: 0.10 **NM** value: **250.00**
• **CGC:** 2 graded, best 9.2
5 ❑ Aug 1951 Cover: 0.10 **NM** value: **250.00**
6 ❑ Oct 1951 Cover: 0.10 **NM** value: **250.00**
• **CGC:** 1 graded, best 5.5
7 ❑ Dec 1951 Cover: 0.10 **NM** value: **250.00**
• **CGC:** 1 graded, best 4.5
8 ❑ Feb 1952 Cover: 0.10 **NM** value: **250.00**
9 ❑ Apr 1952 Cover: 0.10 **NM** value: **200.00**
10 ❑ Jun 1952 Cover: 0.10 **NM** value: **200.00**
• **CGC:** 1 graded, best 8.0
11 ❑ Aug 1952 Cover: 0.10 **NM** value: **200.00**
12 ❑ Oct 1952 Cover: 0.10 **NM** value: **200.00**
13 ❑ Nov 1952 Cover: 0.10 **NM** value: **175.00**
14 ❑ Dec 1952 Cover: 0.10 **NM** value: **175.00**
15 ❑ Jan 1953 Cover: 0.10 **NM** value: **175.00**
• **CGC:** 1 graded, best 7.5
16 ❑ Feb 1963 Cover: 0.10 **NM** value: **175.00**
• **CGC:** 1 graded, best 6.0
17 ❑ Mar 1963 Cover: 0.10 **NM** value: **150.00**
18 ❑ Apr 1963 Cover: 0.10 **NM** value: **150.00**
19 ❑ May 1963 Cover: 0.10 **NM** value: **150.00**
20 ❑ Jun 1953 Cover: 0.10 **NM** value: **150.00**
• **CGC:** 1 graded, best 6.5
21 ❑ Jul 1953 Cover: 0.10 **NM** value: **150.00**
22 ❑ Aug 1953 Cover: 0.10 **NM** value: **125.00**
23 ❑ Sep 1953 Cover: 0.10 **NM** value: **125.00**
24 ❑ Oct 1953 Cover: 0.10 **NM** value: **125.00**
25 ❑ Nov 1953 Cover: 0.10 **NM** value: **125.00**
26 ❑ Dec 1953 Cover: 0.10 **NM** value: **125.00**
27 ❑ Jan 1954 Cover: 0.10 **NM** value: **125.00**
28 ❑ Feb 1954 Cover: 0.10 **NM** value: **125.00**
29 ❑ Mar 1954 Cover: 0.10 **NM** value: **125.00**
30 ❑ Apr 1954 Cover: 0.10 **NM** value: **125.00**
31 ❑ May 1954 Cover: 0.10 **NM** value: **125.00**
• **CGC:** 2 graded, best 6.5

ADVENTURES INTO THE UNKNOWN ACG

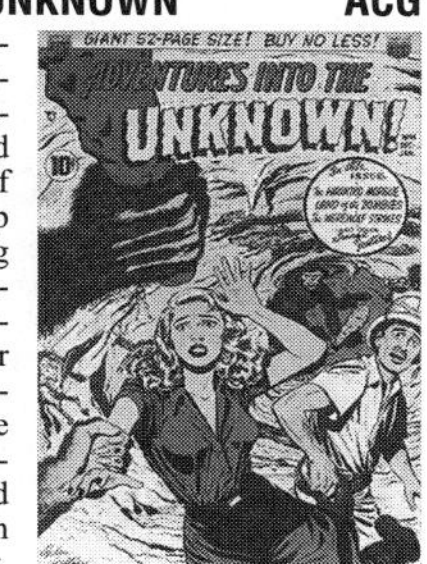

During the twilight of super-heroes in the early 1950s, science-fiction and horror comics were the hottest thing on the newsstands, and this title was one of the pioneers of the genre. Each issue served up three or four short stories featuring alien attacks, post-atomic nightmares, bug-eyed monsters, unexplained phenomena, and other meat-and-potatoes 1950s science-fantasy themes. Adventures into the Unknown was broad enough in format to allow straight mystery and suspense stories side by side with hardcore science fiction, horror, and monsters.

The ACG art and writing staff lacked the talent of such bigger publishers as E.C., Atlas (Marvel), and DC, but managed to produce clean, workmanlike art and entertaining stories.

1 ❑ Fal 1948 Cover: 0.10 **NM** value: **1350.00**
• **CGC:** 2 graded, best 7.5
2 ❑ Dec 1948 Cover: 0.10 **NM** value: **550.00**
3 ❑ Feb 1949 Cover: 0.10 **NM** value: **550.00**
A: Al Feldstein
4 ❑ Apr 1949 Cover: 0.10 **NM** value: **325.00**
5 ❑ Jun 1949 Cover: 0.10 **NM** value: **325.00**
6 ❑ Aug 1949 Cover: 0.10 **NM** value: **215.00**
7 ❑ Oct 1949 Cover: 0.10 **NM** value: **215.00**
8 ❑ Dec 1949 Cover: 0.10 **NM** value: **165.00**
9 ❑ Feb 1950 Cover: 0.10 **NM** value: **165.00**
10 ❑ Apr 1950 Cover: 0.10 **NM** value: **165.00**
11 ❑ Jun 1950 Cover: 0.10 **NM** value: **120.00**
12 ❑ Aug 1950 Cover: 0.10 **NM** value: **120.00**
13 ❑ Oct 1950 Cover: 0.10 **NM** value: **120.00**
14 ❑ Dec 1950 Cover: 0.10 **NM** value: **120.00**
15 ❑ Jan 1951 Cover: 0.10 **NM** value: **120.00**
• **CGC:** 1 graded, best 9.4
16 ❑ Feb 1951 Cover: 0.10 **NM** value: **100.00**
17 ❑ Mar 1951 Cover: 0.10 **NM** value: **100.00**
• **CGC:** 1 graded, best 9.2
18 ❑ Apr 1951 Cover: 0.10 **NM** value: **100.00**
• **CGC:** 2 graded, best 9.0
19 ❑ May 1951 Cover: 0.10 **NM** value: **100.00**
20 ❑ Jun 1951 Cover: 0.10 **NM** value: **100.00**
• **CGC:** 1 graded, best 8.5
21 ❑ Jul 1951 Cover: 0.10 **NM** value: **100.00**
22 ❑ Aug 1951 Cover: 0.10 **NM** value: **100.00**
• **CGC:** 1 graded, best 9.0
23 ❑ Sep 1951 Cover: 0.10 **NM** value: **100.00**
24 ❑ Oct 1951 Cover: 0.10 **NM** value: **100.00**
• **CGC:** 1 graded, best 9.4
25 ❑ Nov 1951 Cover: 0.10 **NM** value: **100.00**
26 ❑ Dec 1951 Cover: 0.10 **NM** value: **100.00**
• **CGC:** 1 graded, best 9.0
📖 The Phantom Seeker; The Ghost Train (text story); The Holland Haunt; Wizard of Evil; Nemesis of the Living Dead (text story); The Werewolf Burial; True Tales of Sorcery: The Saga of the Sorceress and the Stag; The Haunted Ghost
27 ❑ Jan 1952 Cover: 0.10 **NM** value: **150.00**
• **CGC:** 1 graded, best 7.5
A: Al Williamson
28 ❑ Feb 1952 Cover: 0.10 **NM** value: **100.00**
• **CGC:** 1 graded, best 9.0
29 ❑ Mar 1952 Cover: 0.10 **NM** value: **100.00**
• **CGC:** 1 graded, best 7.5
📖 Invasion of the Ghost Monsters; Corpse's Revenge (text story); Ship of Death; Mark of the Monster; Reunion (text story); The Hands of Darkness
30 ❑ Apr 1952 Cover: 0.10 **NM** value: **100.00**
• **CGC:** 1 graded, best 9.2
31 ❑ May 1952 Cover: 0.10 **NM** value: **90.00**
• **CGC:** 1 graded, best 9.2
32 ❑ Jun 1952 Cover: 0.10 **NM** value: **90.00**
33 ❑ Jul 1952 Cover: 0.10 **NM** value: **90.00**
34 ❑ Aug 1952 Cover: 0.10 **NM** value: **90.00**
• **CGC:** 2 graded, best 9.4
35 ❑ Sep 1952 Cover: 0.10 **NM** value: **90.00**
• **CGC:** 1 graded, best 9.0
36 ❑ Oct 1952 Cover: 0.10 **NM** value: **90.00**
• **CGC:** 1 graded, best 9.0
37 ❑ Nov 1952 Cover: 0.10 **NM** value: **90.00**
• **CGC:** 1 graded, best 8.0
38 ❑ Dec 1952 Cover: 0.10 **NM** value: **90.00**
• **CGC:** 1 graded, best 8.5
39 ❑ Jan 1953 Cover: 0.10 **NM** value: **90.00**
40 ❑ Feb 1953 Cover: 0.10 **NM** value: **90.00**
• **CGC:** 1 graded, best 7.5
41 ❑ Mar 1953 Cover: 0.10 **NM** value: **75.00**
42 ❑ Apr 1953 Cover: 0.10 **NM** value: **75.00**
• **CGC:** 1 graded, best 9.0
43 ❑ May 1953 Cover: 0.10 **NM** value: **75.00**
• **CGC:** 1 graded, best 9.2
44 ❑ Jun 1953 Cover: 0.10 **NM** value: **75.00**
45 ❑ Jul 1953 Cover: 0.10 **NM** value: **75.00**
• **CGC:** 1 graded, best 9.0
46 ❑ Aug 1953 Cover: 0.10 **NM** value: **75.00**
47 ❑ Sep 1953 Cover: 0.10 **NM** value: **75.00**
48 ❑ Oct 1953 Cover: 0.10 **NM** value: **75.00**
• **CGC:** 1 graded, best 7.5
49 ❑ Nov 1953 Cover: 0.10 **NM** value: **75.00**
50 ❑ Dec 1953 Cover: 0.10 **NM** value: **75.00**
51 ❑ Jan 1954 Cover: 0.10 **NM** value: **200.00**
3-D covers start.
52 ❑ Feb 1954 Cover: 0.10 **NM** value: **175.00**
• **CGC:** 2 graded, best 7.5
3-D cover, story.
53 ❑ Mar 1954 Cover: 0.10 **NM** value: **175.00**
• **CGC:** 1 graded, best 7.5
3-D cover, story.
54 ❑ Apr 1954 Cover: 0.10 **NM** value: **175.00**
3-D cover, story.
55 ❑ May 1954 Cover: 0.10 **NM** value: **175.00**
• **CGC:** 2 graded, best 7.0
3-D cover, story.
56 ❑ Jun 1954 Cover: 0.10 **NM** value: **175.00**
• **CGC:** 1 graded, best 6.5
3-D cover, story.
57 ❑ Jul 1954 Cover: 0.10 **NM** value: **175.00**
• **CGC:** 1 graded, best 7.5
3-D cover, story.
58 ❑ Aug 1954 Cover: 0.10 **NM** value: **175.00**
3-D cover, story.
59 ❑ Sep 1954 Cover: 0.10 **NM** value: **75.00**
• **CGC:** 1 graded, best 7.5
• 3-D story
60 ❑ Nov 1954 Cover: 0.10 **NM** value: **70.00**
61 ❑ Jan 1955 Cover: 0.10 **NM** value: **70.00**
62 ❑ Mar 1955 Cover: 0.10 **NM** value: **70.00**
63 ❑ May 1955 Cover: 0.10 **NM** value: **48.00**
64 ❑ Jul 1955 Cover: 0.10 **NM** value: **48.00**
65 ❑ Sep 1955 Cover: 0.10 **NM** value: **48.00**
66 ❑ Nov 1955 Cover: 0.10 **NM** value: **48.00**
67 ❑ Dec 1955 Cover: 0.10 **NM** value: **48.00**
68 ❑ Jan 1956 Cover: 0.10 **NM** value: **48.00**
69 ❑ Feb 1956 Cover: 0.10 **NM** value: **48.00**
70 ❑ Mar 1956 Cover: 0.10 **NM** value: **48.00**
71 ❑ Apr 1956 Cover: 0.10 **NM** value: **38.00**
72 ❑ May 1956 Cover: 0.10 **NM** value: **38.00**
73 ❑ Jun 1956 Cover: 0.10 **NM** value: **38.00**
74 ❑ Jul 1956 Cover: 0.10 **NM** value: **38.00**
75 ❑ Aug 1956 Cover: 0.10 **NM** value: **38.00**
76 ❑ Sep 1956 Cover: 0.10 **NM** value: **38.00**
77 ❑ Oct 1956 Cover: 0.10 **NM** value: **38.00**
78 ❑ Nov 1956 Cover: 0.10 **NM** value: **38.00**
79 ❑ Dec 1956 Cover: 0.10 **NM** value: **38.00**
80 ❑ Jan 1957 Cover: 0.10 **NM** value: **38.00**
81 ❑ Feb 1957 Cover: 0.10 **NM** value: **38.00**
82 ❑ Mar 1957 Cover: 0.10 **NM** value: **38.00**
83 ❑ Apr 1957 Cover: 0.10 **NM** value: **38.00**
84 ❑ May 1957 Cover: 0.10 **NM** value: **38.00**
85 ❑ Jun 1957 Cover: 0.10 **NM** value: **38.00**
86 ❑ Jul 1957 Cover: 0.10 **NM** value: **38.00**
87 ❑ Aug 1957 Cover: 0.10 **NM** value: **38.00**
88 ❑ Sep 1957 Cover: 0.10 **NM** value: **38.00**
89 ❑ Oct 1957 Cover: 0.10 **NM** value: **38.00**
90 ❑ Nov 1957 Cover: 0.10 **NM** value: **38.00**
91 ❑ Dec 1957 Cover: 0.10 **NM** value: **32.00**
92 ❑ Jan 1958 Cover: 0.10 **NM** value: **32.00**
93 ❑ Feb 1958 Cover: 0.10 **NM** value: **32.00**
94 ❑ Mar 1958 Cover: 0.10 **NM** value: **32.00**
95 ❑ Apr 1958 Cover: 0.10 **NM** value: **32.00**
96 ❑ May 1958 Cover: 0.10 **NM** value: **32.00**
97 ❑ Jun 1958 Cover: 0.10 **NM** value: **32.00**
98 ❑ Jul 1958 Cover: 0.10 **NM** value: **32.00**
99 ❑ Aug 1958 Cover: 0.10 **NM** value: **32.00**
100 ❑ Sep 1958 Cover: 0.10 **NM** value: **38.00**
📖 The Head Man!; Preliminary Hearing!; Phantom Submarine; Nothing Ever Happens to Halloran! **A:** Ogden Whitney; John Forte; Paul Feinman **W:** Ogden Whitney
101 ❑ Oct 1958 Cover: 0.10 **NM** value: **30.00**
102 ❑ Nov 1958 Cover: 0.10 **NM** value: **30.00**
103 ❑ Dec 1958 Cover: 0.10 **NM** value: **30.00**
104 ❑ Jan 1959 Cover: 0.10 **NM** value: **30.00**
• **CGC:** 1 graded, best 9.2
105 ❑ Feb 1959 Cover: 0.10 **NM** value: **30.00**
106 ❑ Mar 1959 Cover: 0.10 **NM** value: **30.00**
107 ❑ Apr 1959 Cover: 0.10 **NM** value: **30.00**
108 ❑ May 1959 Cover: 0.10 **NM** value: **30.00**
109 ❑ Jul 1959 Cover: 0.10 **NM** value: **30.00**
110 ❑ Aug 1959 Cover: 0.10 **NM** value: **30.00**
111 ❑ Oct 1959 Cover: 0.10 **NM** value: **30.00**
112 ❑ Dec 1959 Cover: 0.10 **NM** value: **30.00**
113 ❑ Jan 1960 Cover: 0.10 **NM** value: **30.00**
Circ: Statement: **192,500**
114 ❑ Feb 1960 Cover: 0.10 **NM** value: **30.00**
Circ: Statement: **192,500**
115 ❑ Mar 1960 Cover: 0.10 **NM** value: **30.00**
Circ: Statement: **192,500**
116 ❑ Apr 1960 Cover: 0.10 **NM** value: **30.00**
Circ: Statement: **192,500**
117 ❑ Jun 1960 Cover: 0.10 **NM** value: **30.00**
Circ: Statement: **192,500**

CGC-graded: Multiply prices above by **33 for 9.9 M • 16 for 9.8 NM/M • 7 for 9.6 NM+ • 5 for 9.4 NM • 2.5 for 9.2 NM- • 1.5 for 9.0 VF/NM**

118 ❑ Aug 1960 Cover: 0.10 **NM** value: **30.00**
Circ: Statement: **192,500**
119 ❑ Sep 1960 Cover: 0.10 **NM** value: **30.00**
Circ: Statement: **192,500**
120 ❑ Oct 1960 Cover: 0.10 **NM** value: **30.00**
Circ: Statement: **192,500**
121 ❑ Dec 1960 Cover: 0.10 **NM** value: **26.00**
Circ: Statement: **192,500**
🕮 The Maltese Cross; The Wanderers…; Egyptian Destiny; Below the Surface! **A:** Jack Sparling; Leo Morey; Ogden Whitney(cover); Tom Hickey **W:** Ace Aquila; Charles Lacoste; Shane O'Shea
122 ❑ Feb 1961 Cover: 0.10 **NM** value: **26.00**
Circ: Statement: **165,200**
123 ❑ Mar 1961 Cover: 0.10 **NM** value: **26.00**
Circ: Statement: **165,200**
124 ❑ Apr 1961 Cover: 0.10 **NM** value: **26.00**
Circ: Statement: **165,200**
125 ❑ Jun 1961 Cover: 0.10 **NM** value: **26.00**
Circ: Statement: **165,200**
126 ❑ Aug 1961 Cover: 0.10 **NM** value: **26.00**
Circ: Statement: **165,200**
127 ❑ Sep 1961 Cover: 0.10 **NM** value: **26.00**
Circ: Statement: **165,200**
128 ❑ Oct 1961 Cover: 0.10 **NM** value: **26.00**
Circ: Statement: **165,200**
129 ❑ Dec 1961 Cover: 0.12 **NM** value: **26.00**
Circ: Statement: **165,200** • **CGC:** 1 graded, best 9.2
130 ❑ Feb 1962 Cover: 0.12 **NM** value: **26.00**
Circ: Statement: **165,200**
🕮 For as Long as You Live!; White Streak; What's Behind the Superstition?: Throwing Your Hat on a Bed; The Boy With Second Sight **A:** Paul Reinman; Ogden Whitney; John Forte **W:** Greg Olivetti; Shane O'Shea
131 ❑ Mar 1962 Cover: 0.12 **NM** value: **26.00**
Circ: Statement: **165,200**
132 ❑ Apr 1962 Cover: 0.12 **NM** value: **26.00**
Circ: Statement: **165,200**
133 ❑ Jun 1962 Cover: 0.12 **NM** value: **26.00**
Circ: Statement: **165,200**
🕮 Robertson's Robots!; 321 Vista Avenue!; Race into the Unknown!; The Two Jeremy Fosters **A:** Chic Stone; Beck Hamilton; Ogden Whitney(cover) **W:** Greg Olivetti; Pierre Alonzo
134 ❑ Aug 1962 Cover: 0.12 **NM** value: **26.00**
Circ: Statement: **165,200**
🕮 Some Guys Have All the Luck; Visitors From Afar; On Wings of Fire!; The Reformation of Rudolf Rukeyster **A:** Pete Costanza; Rudi Palais; Tom Hickey **W:** Ace Aquila; Kurato Osaki; Shane O'Shea
135 ❑ Sep 1962 Cover: 0.12 **NM** value: **26.00**
Circ: Statement: **165,200**
136 ❑ Oct 1962 Cover: 0.12 **NM** value: **26.00**
Circ: Statement: **165,200**
137 ❑ Dec 1962 Cover: 0.12 **NM** value: **26.00**
Circ: Statement: **165,200**
138 ❑ Feb 1963 Cover: 0.12 **NM** value: **26.00**
Circ: Statement: **153,283**
🕮 The Machine Named Spotty!; The Flame Girl!; Mysterious Leader; Take Your Picture, Lady? **A:** Ogden Whitney; Beck Hamilton; John Forte; Tom Hickey **W:** John Forte; Ace Aquila; Greg Olivetti; Shane O'Shea
139 ❑ Mar 1963 Cover: 0.12 **NM** value: **26.00**
Circ: Statement: **153,283**
🕮 A House Can't Be Haunted!; Little Magic Man!; Missing Fireworks; The Girl on the Space-Screen! **A:** Chic Stone; Tom Hickey **W:** Bob Standish; Zev Zimmer
140 ❑ Apr 1963 Cover: 0.12 **NM** value: **26.00**
Circ: Statement: **153,283**
🕮 Look Out for the Little Men!; Bad Luck Omens; These Plants are Different!; You'll Sleep as if you were Dead!; 16th Century Space Probe **A:** Chic Stone; Edd Ashe **W:** Ace Aquila; Shane O'Shea; Zev Zimmer
141 ❑ Jun 1963 Cover: 0.12 **NM** value: **24.00**
Circ: Statement: **153,283**
142 ❑ Aug 1963 Cover: 0.12 **NM** value: **24.00**
Circ: Statement: **153,283**
143 ❑ Sep 1963 Cover: 0.12 **NM** value: **24.00**
Circ: Statement: **153,283**
144 ❑ Oct 1963 Cover: 0.12 **NM** value: **24.00**
Circ: Statement: **153,283**
145 ❑ Dec 1963 Cover: 0.12 **NM** value: **24.00**
Circ: Statement: **153,283**
146 ❑ Feb 1964 Cover: 0.12 **NM** value: **24.00**
Circ: Statement: **172,819**
147 ❑ Mar 1964 Cover: 0.12 **NM** value: **24.00**
Circ: Statement: **172,819**
148 ❑ Apr 1964 Cover: 0.12 **NM** value: **24.00**
Circ: Statement: **172,819**
149 ❑ Jun 1964 Cover: 0.12 **NM** value: **24.00**
Circ: Statement: **172,819**
150 ❑ Aug 1964 Cover: 0.12 **NM** value: **24.00**
Circ: Statement: **172,819** • **CGC:** 2 graded, best 9.4
151 ❑ Sep 1964 Cover: 0.12 **NM** value: **24.00**
Circ: Statement: **172,819**
152 ❑ Oct 1964 Cover: 0.12 **NM** value: **24.00**
Circ: Statement: **172,819**
153 ❑ Dec 1964 Cover: 0.12 **NM** value: **24.00**
Circ: Statement: **172,819**
154 ❑ Feb 1965 Cover: 0.12 **NM** value: **30.00**
Circ: Statement: **163,049**
★ Origin of Nemesis.
155 ❑ Mar 1965 Cover: 0.12 **NM** value: **24.00**
Circ: Statement: **163,049**
156 ❑ Apr 1965 Cover: 0.12 **NM** value: **24.00**
Circ: Statement: **163,049**
157 ❑ Jun 1965 Cover: 0.12 **NM** value: **24.00**
Circ: Statement: **163,049**
158 ❑ Aug 1965 Cover: 0.12 **NM** value: **24.00**
Circ: Statement: **163,049**
159 ❑ Sep 1965 Cover: 0.12 **NM** value: **24.00**
Circ: Statement: **163,049**
160 ❑ Oct 1965 Cover: 0.12 **NM** value: **24.00**
Circ: Statement: **163,049**
161 ❑ Dec 1965 Cover: 0.12 **NM** value: **20.00**
Circ: Statement: **163,049**
162 ❑ Feb 1966 Cover: 0.12 **NM** value: **20.00**
Circ: Statement: **155,102**
163 ❑ Mar 1966 Cover: 0.12 **NM** value: **20.00**
Circ: Statement: **155,102**
164 ❑ Apr 1966 Cover: 0.12 **NM** value: **20.00**
Circ: Statement: **155,102**
• Has 1965 Statement, filed 10/1/65; avg print run 334,375; avg sales 162,969; avg subs 80; avg total paid 163,049; max existent 163,049; 51% of run returned
165 ❑ Jun 1966 Cover: 0.12 **NM** value: **20.00**
Circ: Statement: **155,102**
166 ❑ Aug 1966 Cover: 0.12 **NM** value: **20.00**
Circ: Statement: **155,102**
167 ❑ Sep 1966 Cover: 0.12 **NM** value: **20.00**
Circ: Statement: **155,102**
168 ❑ Oct 1966 Cover: 0.12 **NM** value: **20.00**
Circ: Statement: **155,102**
A: Steve Ditko
169 ❑ Dec 1966 Cover: 0.12 **NM** value: **20.00**
Circ: Statement: **155,102**
170 ❑ Feb 1966 Cover: 0.12 **NM** value: **20.00**
171 ❑ Mar 1966 Cover: 0.12 **NM** value: **20.00**
172 ❑ Apr 1967 Cover: 0.12 **NM** value: **20.00**
173 ❑ Jun 1967 Cover: 0.12 **NM** value: **20.00**
174 ❑ Aug 1967 Cover: 0.12 **NM** value: **20.00**
• **CGC:** 1 graded, best 9.4
final issue.

ADVENTURES INTO THE UNKNOWN (A+) A-Plus

1 ❑ b&w Cover: 2.50 **NM** value: **Cover or less**
🕮 Dog Day; The Timeless Tribe!; Demon and Destruction; Dawn at Stonehence; The Strange Mr. Mique **A:** Al Williamson; Tom Sutton; Frank Frazetta; Ken Lan Dau; Nicola Cutii; Tom Himes **W:** Al Williamson; Tom Sutton; Frank Frazetta; Ken Lan Dau; Nicola Cutii; Tom Himes
2 ❑ Cover: 2.50 **NM** value: **Cover or less**
🕮 Hell House; To My Pal Joey…; Fuhrenbauer's Fake Folks!; Fatal Call!; Land of the Living Dead; Seekers of Evil **A:** Steve Ditko; Frank Frazetta; Sanho Kim; Kenneth Landau; PAIII **W:** Joe Gill; Kenneth Landau; Kurato Osaki; Roy Williams; Shane O'Shea
3 ❑ Cover: 2.50 **NM** value: **Cover or less**
🕮 Skull of the Sorcerer; Hades Universe; Bride of the Swamp; Snatcher; 1,000 Years Ago…in 1992; Unknown Rescuer; The Westphalian Werewolf **A:** Al Williamson; Ogden Whitney; Mike ZeckKenneth LandauRich Carson **W:** Tim Boxell; Al Williamson; Ogden Whitney; Kenneth Landau; Nicola Cutii
4 ❑ Cover: 2.50 **NM** value: **Cover or less**
🕮 Roll Me Down; To Die A Witch's Death; When The Bell Tolled; …A Spell of Misery; Lafferty's Widow; The Other Presence!; The Things in The Subway **A:** Sam Glanzman; Nicholas Alascia; Joe Staton; Dan Day; Rich Larson; F. Nieto **W:** Gordon Derry; Nicholas Alascia; Joe Gill; Nicola Cutii; L. Sabalys

ADVENTURES INTO WEIRD WORLDS Atlas

1 ❑ Jan 1952 Cover: 0.10 **NM** value: **400.00**
• **CGC:** 1 graded, best 4.0
2 ❑ Feb 1952 Cover: 0.10 **NM** value: **300.00**
• **CGC:** 3 graded, best 7.5
3 ❑ Mar 1952 Cover: 0.10 **NM** value: **200.00**
4 ❑ Mar 1952 Cover: 0.10 **NM** value: **200.00**
5 ❑ Apr 1952 Cover: 0.10 **NM** value: **200.00**
• **CGC:** 2 graded, best 7.0
6 ❑ May 1952 Cover: 0.10 **NM** value: **200.00**
7 ❑ Jun 1952 Cover: 0.10 **NM** value: **200.00**
• **CGC:** 1 graded, best 9.0
8 ❑ Jul 1952 Cover: 0.10 **NM** value: **200.00**
9 ❑ Aug 1952 Cover: 0.10 **NM** value: **200.00**
10 ❑ Sep 1952 Cover: 0.10 **NM** value: **200.00**
11 ❑ Oct 1952 Cover: 0.10 **NM** value: **150.00**
12 ❑ Nov 1952 Cover: 0.10 **NM** value: **150.00**
13 ❑ Dec 1952 Cover: 0.10 **NM** value: **150.00**
• **CGC:** 2 graded, best 8.0
14 ❑ Jan 1953 Cover: 0.10 **NM** value: **150.00**
15 ❑ Feb 1953 Cover: 0.10 **NM** value: **150.00**
• **CGC:** 1 graded, best 4.5
16 ❑ Mar 1953 Cover: 0.10 **NM** value: **150.00**
• **CGC:** 1 graded, best 9.0
17 ❑ Apr 1953 Cover: 0.10 **NM** value: **150.00**
18 ❑ May 1953 Cover: 0.10 **NM** value: **150.00**
19 ❑ Jun 1953 Cover: 0.10 **NM** value: **150.00**
20 ❑ Jul 1953 Cover: 0.10 **NM** value: **150.00**
21 ❑ Aug 1953 Cover: 0.10 **NM** value: **100.00**
22 ❑ Sep 1953 Cover: 0.10 **NM** value: **100.00**
23 ❑ Nov 1953 Cover: 0.10 **NM** value: **100.00**
• **CGC:** 1 graded, best 7.5
24 ❑ Dec 1953 Cover: 0.10 **NM** value: **100.00**
• **CGC:** 1 graded, best 8.5
25 ❑ Jan 1954 Cover: 0.10 **NM** value: **100.00**
26 ❑ Feb 1954 Cover: 0.10 **NM** value: **100.00**
27 ❑ Mar 1954 Cover: 0.10 **NM** value: **100.00**
28 ❑ Apr 1954 Cover: 0.10 **NM** value: **100.00**
29 ❑ May 1954 Cover: 0.10 **NM** value: **100.00**
30 ❑ Jun 1954 Cover: 0.10 **NM** value: **100.00**

ADVENTURES MADE IN AMERICA Rip Off

0 ❑ Cover: 2.75 **NM** value: **Cover or less**
• Preview
1 ❑ Cover: 2.75 **NM** value: **Cover or less**
A: Scott Rosema; Jack Snider **W:** Mark Hamlin; Roger McKenzie
2 ❑ Cover: 2.75 **NM** value: **Cover or less**
A: Scott Rosema; Jack Snider **W:** Mark Hamlin; Roger McKenzie
3 ❑ Cover: 2.75 **NM** value: **Cover or less**
A: Scott Rosema; Jack Snider **W:** Mark Hamlin; Roger McKenzie
4 ❑ Cover: 2.75 **NM** value: **Cover or less**
A: Scott Rosema; Jack Snider **W:** Mark Hamlin; Roger McKenzie
5 ❑ Cover: 2.75 **NM** value: **Cover or less**
A: Scott Rosema; Jack Snider **W:** Mark Hamlin; Roger McKenzie
6 ❑ Cover: 2.75 **NM** value: **Cover or less**
A: Scott Rosema; Jack Snider **W:** Mark Hamlin; Roger McKenzie

ADVENTURES OF AARON Chiasmus

1 ❑ Cover: 2.50 **NM** value: **Cover or less**
2 ❑ Jul 1995 Cover: 2.50 **NM** value: **Cover or less**
🕮 Babysitter Gone Bad, Part 1

ADVENTURES OF AARON (2ND SERIES) Image

1 ❑ Mar 1997 Cover: 2.95 **NM** value: **Cover or less**
Circ: Diamd. preorders: **9,674**
🕮 Babysitter Gone Bad, Part 1 **A:** Aaron Warner **W:** Aaron Warner; Michael Evans
2 ❑ May 1997 Cover: 2.95 **NM** value: **Cover or less**
Circ: Diamd. preorders: **7,879**
🕮 Babysitter Gone Bad, Part 2 **A:** Aaron Warner **W:** Aaron Warner
3 ❑ Sep 1997 Cover: 2.95 **NM** value: **Cover or less**
• "Adventures of Dad" back-up **A:** Aaron Warner **W:** Aaron Warner; Robert Brewer
100 ❑ Jul 1997 Cover: 2.95 **NM** value: **Cover or less**
Circ: Diamd. preorders: **5,601**
A: Aaron Warner; Gary Barker; Danny Watson; Linc Polderman; Mike Komarck; Robert Lewis **W:** Aaron Warner; Gary Barker; Danny Watson; Linc Polderman; Robert Lewis; Johnny Lauck

ADVENTURES OF ADAM & BYRON American Mule

1 ❑ May 1998 Cover: 2.50 **NM** value: **Cover or less**

ADVENTURES OF ALAN LADD DC

The title was one of several of its day featuring fictional adventures of real-life stars. Alan Ladd (1913-1964) starred in detective and Western films, among many others – usually as the tough romantic lead. Among his best-known films were This Gun for Hire (1942) and Shane (1953). Several of the comic-book issues had photo covers. — Maggie

1 ❑ Oct 1949 Cover: 0.10 **NM** value: **500.00**
• **CGC:** 2 graded, best 7.5
2 ❑ Dec 1949 Cover: 0.10 **NM** value: **300.00**
3 ❑ Feb 1950 Cover: 0.10 **NM** value: **300.00**
4 ❑ Apr 1950 Cover: 0.10 **NM** value: **300.00**
5 ❑ Jun 1950 Cover: 0.10 **NM** value: **300.00**
6 ❑ Aug 1950 Cover: 0.10 **NM** value: **250.00**
7 ❑ Oct 1950 Cover: 0.10 **NM** value: **250.00**
8 ❑ Dec 1950 Cover: 0.10 **NM** value: **250.00**
• **CGC:** 1 graded, best 9.0
9 ❑ Feb 1951 Cover: 0.10 **NM** value: **250.00**

ADVENTURES OF ALICE, THE Pentagon

1 ❑ ca. 1945 Cover: 0.10 **NM** value: **40.00**
2 ❑ ca. 1945 Cover: 0.10 **NM** value: **28.00**
3 ❑ Jan 1946 Cover: 0.10 **NM** value: **28.00**

ADVENTURES OF BARON MUNCHAUSEN, THE Now

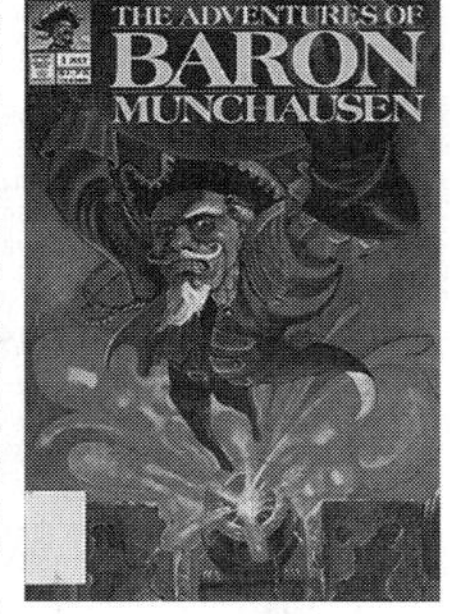

The Age of Enlightenment was not shaping up too well for the residents of a town besieged by the Turks. As cannons roared outside, a small theater company put on a production of the Adventures of Baron Munchausen to cheer the townspeople. In stark contrast to the cold realism of the intellectuals, Baron Munchausen was a man for whom nothing was impossible. He could fly to the moon, romance goddesses, and ride a cannonball into the heart of the enemy forces. With the aid of his four amazing friends, it seemed that there was nothing beyond his capabilities.

As the play began, fantasy and reality blurred for a girl, and soon she would join the great Baron Munchausen on his grandest adventure. His goals: to save the town and to restore everyone's faith in the fantastic.

This four-issue mini-series adapts the cult-favorite movie from Monty Python alumnus Terry Gilliam.

1 ❑ Jul 1989 Cover: 1.75 **NM** value: **2.00**
Circ: CapCity orders: **2,775**
🕮 Eighteenth Century Europe: The Age of Reason **A:** Ernie Guanlao; Mark Wheatley **W:** Mark Wheatley
2 ❑ Aug 1989 Cover: 1.75 **NM** value: **2.00**
Circ: CapCity orders: **2,500**
3 ❑ Sep 1989 Cover: 1.75 **NM** value: **2.00**
Circ: CapCity orders: **2,275**
A: Ernie Guanlao **W:** Mark Wheatley
4 ❑ Oct 1989 Cover: 1.75 **NM** value: **2.00**
Circ: CapCity orders: **2,275**
W: Mark Wheatley

The prices seen above do not represent the highest possible prices seen in online auctions, but rather the prices we have seen these issues reliably fetch in a variety of environments (storefront retail, mail order, auction and convention).

Other grades: Multiply prices above by **1.5 for Mint • 2/3 for Very Fine • 1/3 for Fine • 1/5 for Very Good • 1/8 for Good**

ADVENTURES OF BARRY WEEN, BOY GENIUS, THE — Image

Whoa! Einstein has nothing on little Barry! He had already figured out how to set the clock on the VCR before the doctor spanked his newborn butt. Unfortunately, his path to future greatness starts with an adolescence that's almost frighteningly normal.

Hampered in his research by less-than-brilliant parents, Barry performs most of his experiments in the mundane surroundings of his basement. But, like most great inventors, his projects often result in catastrophic accidents. Luckily, Barry does his best thinking under pressure, whether he has simply blown up the microwave or ripped a hole in the space-time continuum. The fate of the world, or even the universe, may be hanging by a thread, but somehow Barry always manages to put things right, often with the reluctant help of his best friend Jeremy. One can only imagine what things will be like when these two hit puberty.

1 ❑ Mar 1999 Cover: 2.95 **NM** value: **Cover or less**
Circ: Diamd. preorders: **3,245**
A: Judd Winick **W:** Judd Winick ★ Origin of Barry Ween.
2 ❑ Apr 1999 Cover: 2.95 **NM** value: **Cover or less**
Circ: Diamd. preorders: **2,591**
• Jeremy turned into dinosaur **A:** Judd Winick **W:** Judd Winick
3 ❑ May 1999 Cover: 2.95 **NM** value: **Cover or less**
Circ: Diamd. preorders: **2,916**
• at museum **A:** Judd Winick **W:** Judd Winick

ADVENTURES OF BARRY WEEN, BOY GENIUS 2.0, THE — Oni

1 ❑ Feb 2000, b&w Cover: 2.95 **NM** value: **Cover or less**
Circ: Diamd. preorders: **5,194**
📖 E.T. Go Home **A:** Judd Winick **C:** Judd Winick **W:** Judd Winick
2 ❑ Mar 2000, b&w Cover: 2.95 **NM** value: **Cover or less**
Circ: Diamd. preorders: **4,676**
• in the old West **A:** Judd Winick **C:** Judd Winick **W:** Judd Winick
3 ❑ Apr 2000, b&w Cover: 2.95 **NM** value: **Cover or less**
Circ: Diamd. preorders: **5,277**
A: Judd Winick **C:** Judd Winick **W:** Judd Winick

ADVENTURES OF BAYOU BILLY, THE — Archie

1 ❑ Sep 1989 Cover: 1.00 **NM** value: **Cover or less**
Archie, Jughead, Betty, and Veronica public service announcement inside back cover. 📖 Swamp Fire **A:** Amanda Conner **W:** R. P. M. ★ Origin of Bayou Billy.
2 ❑ Nov 1989 Cover: 1.00 **NM** value: **Cover or less**
3 ❑ Jan 1990 Cover: 1.00 **NM** value: **Cover or less**
4 ❑ Apr 1990 Cover: 1.00 **NM** value: **Cover or less**
📖 Billy's Night Out **A:** Amanda Conner; Mike Esposito **W:** Rich Margopoulos
5 ❑ Jun 1990 Cover: 1.00 **NM** value: **Cover or less**

ADVENTURES OF BOB HOPE, THE — DC

Entertainer Bob Hope was a star of stage, screen, radio, and television when the world was young and dinosaurs roamed the earth, so it's no surprise that he also enjoyed a successful comic-book series throughout the 1950s and '60s. With super-hero comics sales in the dumps, DC turned to humor, among other genres, to win readers in the 1950s and licensed the rights to produce comics about such famous film stars as Hope, Jerry Lewis, and Alan Ladd.

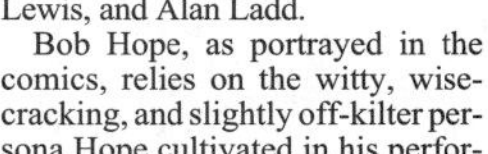

Bob Hope, as portrayed in the comics, relies on the witty, wisecracking, and slightly off-kilter persona Hope cultivated in his performances, combined with extravagant situations that only the comic book medium could provide. The Adventures of Bob Hope was clearly aimed at a young audience but provided work for some of DC's better artists of the time, including Gil Kane and Neal Adams.

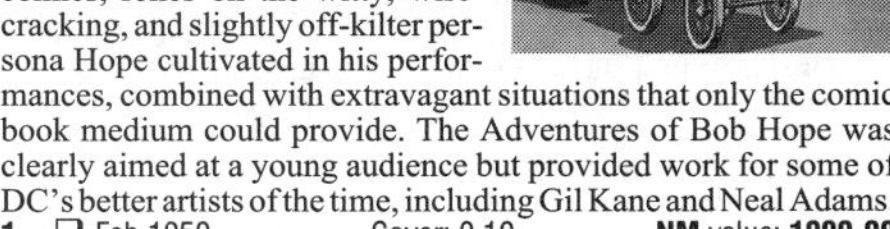

1 ❑ Feb 1950 Cover: 0.10 **NM** value: **1000.00**
• **CGC:** 1 graded, best 6.0
Photo cover.
2 ❑ Apr 1950 Cover: 0.10 **NM** value: **560.00**
Photo cover.
3 ❑ Jun 1950 Cover: 0.10 **NM** value: **500.00**
Photo cover.
4 ❑ Aug 1950 Cover: 0.10 **NM** value: **500.00**
Photo cover.
5 ❑ Oct 1950 Cover: 0.10 **NM** value: **275.00**
6 ❑ Dec 1950 Cover: 0.10 **NM** value: **275.00**
• **CGC:** 1 graded, best 9.2
7 ❑ Feb 1951 Cover: 0.10 **NM** value: **225.00**
• **CGC:** 2 graded, best 9.0
8 ❑ Apr 1951 Cover: 0.10 **NM** value: **225.00**
• **CGC:** 1 graded, best 7.5
9 ❑ Jun 1951 Cover: 0.10 **NM** value: **175.00**
• **CGC:** 2 graded, best 9.2
10 ❑ Aug 1951 Cover: 0.10 **NM** value: **175.00**
• **CGC:** 1 graded, best 8.5
11 ❑ Oct 1951 Cover: 0.10 **NM** value: **140.00**
• **CGC:** 1 graded, best 9.2
12 ❑ Dec 1951 Cover: 0.10 **NM** value: **140.00**
13 ❑ Feb 1952 Cover: 0.10 **NM** value: **140.00**
14 ❑ Apr 1952 Cover: 0.10 **NM** value: **140.00**
• **CGC:** 1 graded, best 6.5
15 ❑ Jun 1952 Cover: 0.10 **NM** value: **140.00**
• **CGC:** 1 graded, best 5.5
16 ❑ Aug 1952 Cover: 0.10 **NM** value: **100.00**
17 ❑ Oct 1952 Cover: 0.10 **NM** value: **100.00**
• **CGC:** 1 graded, best 5.5
18 ❑ Dec 1952 Cover: 0.10 **NM** value: **100.00**
19 ❑ Feb 1953 Cover: 0.10 **NM** value: **100.00**
20 ❑ Apr 1953 Cover: 0.10 **NM** value: **100.00**
21 ❑ Jun 1953 Cover: 0.10 **NM** value: **90.00**
22 ❑ Aug 1953 Cover: 0.10 **NM** value: **90.00**
23 ❑ Oct 1953 Cover: 0.10 **NM** value: **90.00**
24 ❑ Dec 1953 Cover: 0.10 **NM** value: **90.00**
25 ❑ Feb 1954 Cover: 0.10 **NM** value: **90.00**
26 ❑ Apr 1954 Cover: 0.10 **NM** value: **90.00**
27 ❑ Jun 1954 Cover: 0.10 **NM** value: **90.00**
28 ❑ Aug 1954 Cover: 0.10 **NM** value: **90.00**
29 ❑ Oct 1954 Cover: 0.10 **NM** value: **90.00**
30 ❑ Dec 1954 Cover: 0.10 **NM** value: **90.00**
31 ❑ Feb 1955 Cover: 0.10 **NM** value: **90.00**
• Last pre-Code issue
32 ❑ Apr 1955 Cover: 0.10 **NM** value: **75.00**
• 1st Code-approved issue
33 ❑ Jun 1955 Cover: 0.10 **NM** value: **60.00**
34 ❑ Aug 1955 Cover: 0.10 **NM** value: **60.00**
35 ❑ Oct 1955 Cover: 0.10 **NM** value: **60.00**
36 ❑ Dec 1955 Cover: 0.10 **NM** value: **60.00**
37 ❑ Feb 1956 Cover: 0.10 **NM** value: **60.00**
38 ❑ Apr 1956 Cover: 0.10 **NM** value: **60.00**
39 ❑ Jun 1956 Cover: 0.10 **NM** value: **60.00**
40 ❑ Aug 1956 Cover: 0.10 **NM** value: **60.00**
41 ❑ Oct 1956 Cover: 0.10 **NM** value: **60.00**
42 ❑ Dec 1956 Cover: 0.10 **NM** value: **60.00**
43 ❑ Feb 1957 Cover: 0.10 **NM** value: **60.00**
44 ❑ Apr 1957 Cover: 0.10 **NM** value: **60.00**
45 ❑ Jun 1957 Cover: 0.10 **NM** value: **60.00**
46 ❑ Aug 1957 Cover: 0.10 **NM** value: **60.00**
47 ❑ Oct 1957 Cover: 0.10 **NM** value: **60.00**
48 ❑ Dec 1957 Cover: 0.10 **NM** value: **60.00**
49 ❑ Feb 1958 Cover: 0.10 **NM** value: **60.00**
50 ❑ Apr 1958 Cover: 0.10 **NM** value: **60.00**
51 ❑ Jun 1958 Cover: 0.10 **NM** value: **45.00**
52 ❑ Aug 1958 Cover: 0.10 **NM** value: **45.00**
53 ❑ Oct 1958 Cover: 0.10 **NM** value: **45.00**
54 ❑ Dec 1958 Cover: 0.10 **NM** value: **45.00**
55 ❑ Feb 1959 Cover: 0.10 **NM** value: **45.00**
56 ❑ Apr 1959 Cover: 0.10 **NM** value: **45.00**
57 ❑ Jun 1959 Cover: 0.10 **NM** value: **45.00**
58 ❑ Aug 1959 Cover: 0.10 **NM** value: **45.00**
59 ❑ Oct 1959 Cover: 0.10 **NM** value: **45.00**
60 ❑ Dec 1959 Cover: 0.10 **NM** value: **45.00**
61 ❑ Feb 1960 Cover: 0.10 **NM** value: **40.00**
62 ❑ Apr 1960 Cover: 0.10 **NM** value: **40.00**
63 ❑ Jun 1960 Cover: 0.10 **NM** value: **40.00**
64 ❑ Aug 1960 Cover: 0.10 **NM** value: **40.00**
65 ❑ Oct 1960 Cover: 0.10 **NM** value: **40.00**
66 ❑ Dec 1960 Cover: 0.10 **NM** value: **40.00**
67 ❑ Feb 1961 Cover: 0.10 **NM** value: **40.00**
68 ❑ Apr 1961 Cover: 0.10 **NM** value: **40.00**
69 ❑ Jun 1961 Cover: 0.10 **NM** value: **40.00**
70 ❑ Aug 1961 Cover: 0.10 **NM** value: **40.00**
71 ❑ Oct 1961 Cover: 0.10 **NM** value: **32.00**
72 ❑ Dec 1961 Cover: 0.10 **NM** value: **32.00**
73 ❑ Feb 1962 Cover: 0.12 **NM** value: **32.00**
74 ❑ Apr 1962 Cover: 0.12 **NM** value: **32.00**
A: Mort Drucker
75 ❑ Jun 1962 Cover: 0.12 **NM** value: **32.00**
A: Mort Drucker
76 ❑ Aug 1962 Cover: 0.12 **NM** value: **32.00**
A: Mort Drucker
77 ❑ Oct 1962 Cover: 0.12 **NM** value: **32.00**
78 ❑ Dec 1962 Cover: 0.12 **NM** value: **32.00**
79 ❑ Feb 1963 Cover: 0.12 **NM** value: **32.00**
80 ❑ Apr 1963 Cover: 0.12 **NM** value: **32.00**
81 ❑ Jun 1963 Cover: 0.12 **NM** value: **26.00**
82 ❑ Aug 1963 Cover: 0.12 **NM** value: **26.00**
A: Mort Drucker
83 ❑ Oct 1963 Cover: 0.12 **NM** value: **26.00**
84 ❑ Dec 1963 Cover: 0.12 **NM** value: **26.00**
85 ❑ Feb 1964 Cover: 0.12 **NM** value: **26.00**
Circ: Statement: **163,346**
A: Mort Drucker
86 ❑ Apr 1964 Cover: 0.12 **NM** value: **26.00**
Circ: Statement: **163,346**
87 ❑ Jun 1964 Cover: 0.12 **NM** value: **26.00**
Circ: Statement: **163,346**
A: Mort Drucker
88 ❑ Aug 1964 Cover: 0.12 **NM** value: **26.00**
Circ: Statement: **163,346**
89 ❑ Oct 1964 Cover: 0.12 **NM** value: **26.00**
Circ: Statement: **163,346**
A: Mort Drucker
90 ❑ Dec 1964 Cover: 0.12 **NM** value: **26.00**
Circ: Statement: **163,346**
A: Mort Drucker
91 ❑ Feb 1965 Cover: 0.12 **NM** value: **20.00**
Circ: Statement: **191,656**
A: Mort Drucker
92 ❑ Apr 1965 Cover: 0.12 **NM** value: **20.00**
Circ: Statement: **191,656**
93 ❑ Jun 1965 Cover: 0.12 **NM** value: **20.00**
Circ: Statement: **191,656**
94 ❑ Aug 1965 Cover: 0.12 **NM** value: **20.00**
Circ: Statement: **191,656**
★ Appearance of Aquaman.
95 ❑ Oct 1965 Cover: 0.12 **NM** value: **20.00**
Circ: Statement: **191,656**
★ 1st Appearance of Super-Hip and monster faculty.
96 ❑ Dec 1965 Cover: 0.12 **NM** value: **20.00**
Circ: Statement: **191,656**
97 ❑ Feb 1966 Cover: 0.12 **NM** value: **20.00**
Circ: Statement: **194,004**
98 ❑ Apr 1966 Cover: 0.12 **NM** value: **20.00**
Circ: Statement: **194,004**
99 ❑ Jun 1966 Cover: 0.12 **NM** value: **20.00**
Circ: Statement: **194,004**
100 ❑ Aug 1966 Cover: 0.12 **NM** value: **20.00**
Circ: Statement: **194,004** • **CGC:** 1 graded, best 7.5
• Super-Hip as President
101 ❑ Oct 1966 Cover: 0.12 **NM** value: **20.00**
Circ: Statement: **194,004**
102 ❑ Dec 1966 Cover: 0.12 **NM** value: **20.00**
Circ: Statement: **194,004**
103 ❑ Feb 1967 Cover: 0.12 **NM** value: **20.00**
• Has 1966 Statement, filed 10/1/66; avg print run 351,000; avg sales 193,000; avg subs 1,004; avg total paid 194,004; samples 265; max existent 194,269; 45% of run returned ★ Appearance of Batman, Nancy, Ringo Starr, Frank Sinatra, Stanley and his Monster.
104 ❑ May 1967 Cover: 0.12 **NM** value: **20.00**
• **CGC:** 1 graded, best 8.0
105 ❑ Jun 1967 Cover: 0.12 **NM** value: **20.00**
★ Appearance of David Janssen, Dan Blocker, Ed Sullivan, Don Adams.
106 ❑ Aug 1967 Cover: 0.12 **NM** value: **40.00**
📖 Badger's Baby Brother Beastley **A:** Neal Adams(cover)
107 ❑ Oct 1967 Cover: 0.12 **NM** value: **40.00**
A: Neal Adams(cover)
108 ❑ Dec 1967 Cover: 0.12 **NM** value: **40.00**
• **CGC:** 1 graded, best 7.0
A: Neal Adams(cover)
109 ❑ Feb 1968 Cover: 0.12 **NM** value: **40.00**
final issue. **A:** Neal Adams; Neal Adams(cover)

ADVENTURES OF B.O.C., THE — Invasion

1 ❑ Nov 1986 Cover: 1.50 **NM** value: **Cover or less**
📖 Escape From Darkness **A:** James Pustorino **W:** James Pustorino; Paul Martin; Thomas Perry
2 ❑ Jan 1987 Cover: 1.50 **NM** value: **Cover or less**
3 ❑ Mar 1987 Cover: 1.50 **NM** value: **Cover or less**

ADVENTURES OF BROWSER & SEQUOIA, THE — SaberCat

1 ❑ Aug 1999 Cover: 2.95 **NM** value: **Cover or less**
📖 Sequoia's First Hunt **A:** Gene Gonzales **W:** Richard de Montebelle

ADVENTURES OF CAPTAIN AMERICA — Marvel

1 ❑ Sep 1991 Cover: 4.95 **NM** value: **Cover or less**
Circ: CapCity orders: **32,100**
2 ❑ Nov 1991 Cover: 4.95 **NM** value: **Cover or less**
Circ: CapCity orders: **22,900**
📖 Betrayed By Agent X **A:** Terry Austin **W:** Kevin Maguire; Fabian Nicieza ★ Origin of Bucky.
3 ❑ Dec 1991 Cover: 4.95 **NM** value: **Cover or less**
Circ: CapCity orders: **20,400**
4 ❑ Jan 1992 Cover: 4.95 **NM** value: **Cover or less**
Circ: CapCity orders: **20,500**

ADVENTURES OF CAPTAIN JACK, THE — Fantagraphics

Captain Jack is an intrepid feline traveling the universe in a funny-animal science-fictional search of action, adventure, and the intergalactic transportation of — fruits and vegetables? Mike Kazaleh (Ren & Stimpy) weaves hilarious, often bawdy tales in this series published by Fantagraphics Books. Joining Captain Jack are canine crewmembers Herman Feldman and his mischievous mini-sidekick Bub, as well as the robot Adam Fink who runs on batteries. Together, this motley crew navigates through all sorts of humorous situations including the always-popular farmer's daughter story. Animals have seldom been funnier or more risque.

1 ❑ Jun 1986 Cover: 2.00 **NM** value: **Cover or less**
2 ❑ Sep 1986 Cover: 2.00 **NM** value: **Cover or less**
3 ❑ Oct 1986 Cover: 2.00 **NM** value: **Cover or less**
4 ❑ Nov 1986 Cover: 2.00 **NM** value: **Cover or less**
5 ❑ Dec 1986 Cover: 2.00 **NM** value: **Cover or less**
📖 Farmer Fred, I'm in Love with your Daughter! • no indicia
6 ❑ Jan 1987 Cover: 2.00 **NM** value: **Cover or less**
7 ❑ Mar 1987 Cover: 2.00 **NM** value: **Cover or less**
8 ❑ Jul 1987 Cover: 2.00 **NM** value: **Cover or less**
9 ❑ Oct 1987 Cover: 2.00 **NM** value: **Cover or less**
10 ❑ May 1988 Cover: 2.00 **NM** value: **Cover or less**
11 ❑ Nov 1988 Cover: 2.00 **NM** value: **Cover or less**
12 ❑ Jan 1989 Cover: 2.00 **NM** value: **Cover or less**
Bk 1 ❑ Nov 1995, b&w Cover: 12.95 **NM** value: **Cover or less**
• collects stories from Critters #2 and Adventures of Captain Jack #1-3

ADVENTURES OF CAPTAIN NEMO, THE — Rip Off

1 ❑ b&w Cover: 2.50 **NM** value: **Cover or less**

ADVENTURES OF CHRISSIE CLAUS, THE — Hero

1 ❑ Spr 1991 Cover: 2.95 **NM** value: **Cover or less**
Circ: CapCity orders: **2,245**
📖 Trouble in Toyland; You'd Better Watch Out **A:** Mark Propst; Tim Burgard **W:** Shawn V. Wilson

CGC-graded: Multiply prices above by **33 for 9.9 M** • **16 for 9.8 NM/M** • **7 for 9.6 NM+** • **5 for 9.4 NM** • **2.5 for 9.2 NM-** • **1.5 for 9.0 VF/NM**

2 ❑ Jan 1994 Cover: 2.95 **NM** value: **Cover or less**
• w/ trading card **A:** Mark Propst; Tim Burgard **W:** Shawn V. Wilson

ADVENTURES OF CHUK THE BARBARIC — White Wolf

1 ❑ Jul 1987 Cover: 1.25 **NM** value: **1.50**
2 ❑ Aug 1987 Cover: 1.25 **NM** value: **1.50**
• becomes Chuk the Barbaric

ADVENTURES OF CYCLOPS AND PHOENIX, THE — Marvel

1 ❑ May 1994 Cover: 2.95 **NM** value: **Cover or less**
Circ: CapCity orders: **84,150** • **CGC:** 4 graded, best 9.8
📖 Wish You Were Here **A:** Gene Ha **W:** Scott Lobdell
2 ❑ Jun 1994 Cover: 2.95 **NM** value: **Cover or less**
Circ: CapCity orders: **66,750** • **CGC:** 1 graded, best 9.8
📖 Tenure **A:** Gene Ha **W:** Scott Lobdell
3 ❑ Jul 1994 Cover: 2.95 **NM** value: **Cover or less**
Circ: CapCity orders: **55,600** • **CGC:** 1 graded, best 9.8
4 ❑ Aug 1994 Cover: 2.95 **NM** value: **Cover or less**
Circ: CapCity orders: **49,800** • **CGC:** 1 graded, best 9.8
Bk 1❑ Cover: 14.95 **NM** value: **Cover or less**
• Collects The Adventures of Cyclops and Phoenix #1-4

ADVENTURES OF DEAN MARTIN & JERRY LEWIS, THE — DC

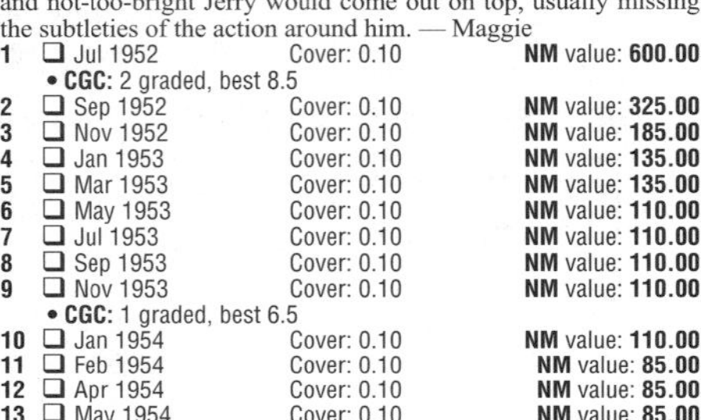

The series began using the film personas of Dean Martin (1917-1995) and Jerry Lewis (1926-), identified as foil and buffoon from their film debut in My Friend Irma (1949). They were one of the hottest comedy teams of their day. Their films could be counted on for long lines at the box office, and their break-up in 1956 led to a change in the DC title the following year.

DC, not surprisingly, went with the slapstack half of the team at that point, and the title became The Adventures of Jerry Lewis. His character typically would find himself in a situation in which the uninhibited and not-too-bright Jerry would come out on top, usually missing the subtleties of the action around him. — Maggie

1 ❑ Jul 1952 Cover: 0.10 **NM** value: **600.00**
• **CGC:** 2 graded, best 8.5
2 ❑ Sep 1952 Cover: 0.10 **NM** value: **325.00**
3 ❑ Nov 1952 Cover: 0.10 **NM** value: **185.00**
4 ❑ Jan 1953 Cover: 0.10 **NM** value: **135.00**
5 ❑ Mar 1953 Cover: 0.10 **NM** value: **135.00**
6 ❑ May 1953 Cover: 0.10 **NM** value: **110.00**
7 ❑ Jul 1953 Cover: 0.10 **NM** value: **110.00**
8 ❑ Sep 1953 Cover: 0.10 **NM** value: **110.00**
9 ❑ Nov 1953 Cover: 0.10 **NM** value: **110.00**
• **CGC:** 1 graded, best 6.5
10 ❑ Jan 1954 Cover: 0.10 **NM** value: **110.00**
11 ❑ Feb 1954 Cover: 0.10 **NM** value: **85.00**
12 ❑ Apr 1954 Cover: 0.10 **NM** value: **85.00**
13 ❑ May 1954 Cover: 0.10 **NM** value: **85.00**
• **CGC:** 1 graded, best 3.0
14 ❑ Jul 1954 Cover: 0.10 **NM** value: **85.00**
15 ❑ Aug 1954 Cover: 0.10 **NM** value: **85.00**
16 ❑ Oct 1954 Cover: 0.10 **NM** value: **65.00**
17 ❑ Nov 1954 Cover: 0.10 **NM** value: **65.00**
18 ❑ Jan 1955 Cover: 0.10 **NM** value: **65.00**
19 ❑ Feb 1955 Cover: 0.10 **NM** value: **65.00**
20 ❑ Apr 1955 Cover: 0.10 **NM** value: **65.00**
21 ❑ May 1955 Cover: 0.10 **NM** value: **45.00**
22 ❑ Jul 1955 Cover: 0.10 **NM** value: **45.00**
23 ❑ Aug 1955 Cover: 0.10 **NM** value: **45.00**
24 ❑ Oct 1955 Cover: 0.10 **NM** value: **45.00**
25 ❑ Nov 1955 Cover: 0.10 **NM** value: **45.00**
26 ❑ Jan 1956 Cover: 0.10 **NM** value: **45.00**
27 ❑ Feb 1956 Cover: 0.10 **NM** value: **45.00**
28 ❑ Apr 1956 Cover: 0.10 **NM** value: **45.00**
29 ❑ May 1956 Cover: 0.10 **NM** value: **45.00**
30 ❑ Jul 1956 Cover: 0.10 **NM** value: **45.00**
31 ❑ Aug 1956 Cover: 0.10 **NM** value: **36.00**
32 ❑ Oct 1956 Cover: 0.10 **NM** value: **36.00**
33 ❑ Nov 1956 Cover: 0.10 **NM** value: **36.00**
34 ❑ Jan 1957 Cover: 0.10 **NM** value: **36.00**
35 ❑ Feb 1957 Cover: 0.10 **NM** value: **36.00**
36 ❑ Apr 1957 Cover: 0.10 **NM** value: **36.00**
37 ❑ May 1957 Cover: 0.10 **NM** value: **36.00**
38 ❑ Jul 1957 Cover: 0.10 **NM** value: **36.00**
39 ❑ Aug 1957 Cover: 0.10 **NM** value: **36.00**
40 ❑ Oct 1957 Cover: 0.10 **NM** value: **36.00**
• Series continues as The Adventures of Jerry Lewis

ADVENTURES OF DR. GRAVES — A-Plus

1 ❑ b&w Cover: 2.50 **NM** value: **Cover or less**

ADVENTURES OF DOLO ROMY, THE — Dôlo Blue

1 ❑ Cover: 2.95 **NM** value: **Cover or less**
A: Karen Platt **W:** Karen Platt

ADVENTURES OF DORIS NELSON, ATOMIC HOUSEWIFE — Jake Comics

1 ❑ Aug 1996, b&w Cover: 2.95 **NM** value: **Cover or less**
• reprints Doris Nelson, Atomic Housewife

Creator Key
W = Writer • A = Artist • C = Cover Artist

ADVENTURES OF EDGAR MUDD AND ELAINE, THE — Wet Earth

1 ❑ Cover: 3.50 **NM** value: **Cover or less**

ADVENTURES OF EVIL & MALICE, THE — Image

Evelyn and Malinda are two somewhat ordinary teenage sisters — they do their homework, ride their bikes, and argue about everything.

Their father happens to be The Black Eye, the #1 criminal mastermind in Dooplis City, so they study at home (because they might otherwise wipe out their teachers), ride their bikes underneath the city in their father's underground secret tunnels, and design super-powered suits.

When the girls are forced to use some of their father's inventions to protect him from another group of super-villains, they suddenly find themselves labeled by the media as the new super-heroines Evil and Malice. In their spiffy pink and blue outfits, the girls will have to face such villains as the vicious Cold Heart, the sneering Chef, and the water-logged Drip — not to mention the embarassment of having become super-heroes in order to protect their super-villain dad!

1 ❑ Jun 1999 Cover: 3.50 **NM** value: **Cover or less**
A: Jimmie Robinson **W:** Jimmie Robinson
2 ❑ Aug 1999 Cover: 3.50 **NM** value: **Cover or less**
Circ: Diamd. preorders: **4,817**
A: Jimmie Robinson **W:** Jimmie Robinson
3 ❑ Nov 1999 Cover: 3.95 **NM** value: **Cover or less**
Circ: Diamd. preorders: **3,922**
cover says Oct, indicia says Nov. **A:** Jimmie Robinson **W:** Jimmie Robinson

ADVENTURES OF FELIX THE CAT — Harvey

1 ❑ Cover: 1.25 **NM** value: **1.50**

ADVENTURES OF FORD FAIRLANE, THE — DC

1 ❑ May 1990 Cover: 1.50 **NM** value: **Cover or less**
Circ: CapCity orders: **10,900**
📖 Stayin' Alive **A:** Don Heck(inks); Russell Braun; José Delbo **W:** Gerard Jones
2 ❑ Jun 1990 Cover: 1.50 **NM** value: **Cover or less**
Circ: CapCity orders: **9,250**
📖 I Write The Songs **A:** Don Heck(inks); Russell Braun; José Delbo **W:** Gerard Jones
3 ❑ Jul 1990 Cover: 1.50 **NM** value: **Cover or less**
Circ: CapCity orders: **7,850**
A: Don Heck(inks); Russell Braun; José Delbo **W:** Gerard Jones
4 ❑ Aug 1990 Cover: 1.50 **NM** value: **Cover or less**
Circ: CapCity orders: **6,700**
A: Don Heck(inks); Russell Braun; José Delbo **W:** Gerard Jones

ADVENTURES OF HOMER GHOST — Atlas

1 ❑ Jun 1957 Cover: 0.10 **NM** value: **35.00**
2 ❑ Aug 1957 Cover: 0.10 **NM** value: **35.00**

ADVENTURES OF HUCKLEBERRY FINN — Eternity

Bk 1❑ Cover: 12.95 **NM** value: **Cover or less**
• strips

ADVENTURES OF JERRY LEWIS, THE — DC

41 ❑ Nov 1957 Cover: 0.10 **NM** value: **40.00**
• Series continued from Adventures of Dean Martin & Jerry Lewis
42 ❑ Jan 1958 Cover: 0.10 **NM** value: **36.00**
43 ❑ Feb 1958 Cover: 0.10 **NM** value: **36.00**
44 ❑ Apr 1958 Cover: 0.10 **NM** value: **36.00**
45 ❑ May 1958 Cover: 0.10 **NM** value: **36.00**
46 ❑ Jul 1958 Cover: 0.10 **NM** value: **36.00**
47 ❑ Aug 1958 Cover: 0.10 **NM** value: **36.00**
48 ❑ Oct 1958 Cover: 0.10 **NM** value: **36.00**
49 ❑ Nov 1958 Cover: 0.10 **NM** value: **36.00**
50 ❑ Jan 1959 Cover: 0.10 **NM** value: **36.00**
51 ❑ Mar 1959 Cover: 0.10 **NM** value: **34.00**
52 ❑ May 1959 Cover: 0.10 **NM** value: **34.00**
53 ❑ Jul 1959 Cover: 0.10 **NM** value: **34.00**
54 ❑ Sep 1959 Cover: 0.10 **NM** value: **34.00**
55 ❑ Nov 1959 Cover: 0.10 **NM** value: **34.00**
56 ❑ Jan 1960 Cover: 0.10 **NM** value: **34.00**
57 ❑ Mar 1960 Cover: 0.10 **NM** value: **34.00**
58 ❑ May 1960 Cover: 0.10 **NM** value: **34.00**
59 ❑ Jul 1960 Cover: 0.10 **NM** value: **34.00**
60 ❑ Sep 1960 Cover: 0.10 **NM** value: **34.00**
61 ❑ Nov 1960 Cover: 0.10 **NM** value: **28.00**
62 ❑ Jan 1961 Cover: 0.10 **NM** value: **28.00**
63 ❑ Mar 1961 Cover: 0.10 **NM** value: **28.00**
64 ❑ May 1961 Cover: 0.10 **NM** value: **28.00**
65 ❑ Jul 1961 Cover: 0.10 **NM** value: **28.00**
66 ❑ Sep 1961 Cover: 0.10 **NM** value: **28.00**
67 ❑ Nov 1961 Cover: 0.10 **NM** value: **28.00**
68 ❑ Jan 1962 Cover: 0.12 **NM** value: **28.00**
Circ: Statement: **175,000** • **CGC:** 1 graded, best 9.2
69 ❑ Mar 1962 Cover: 0.12 **NM** value: **28.00**
Circ: Statement: **175,000**
70 ❑ May 1962 Cover: 0.12 **NM** value: **28.00**
Circ: Statement: **175,000**
71 ❑ Jul 1962 Cover: 0.12 **NM** value: **28.00**
Circ: Statement: **175,000**
72 ❑ Sep 1962 Cover: 0.12 **NM** value: **28.00**
Circ: Statement: **175,000**
A: Mort Drucker
73 ❑ Nov 1962 Cover: 0.12 **NM** value: **28.00**
Circ: Statement: **175,000**
74 ❑ Jan 1963 Cover: 0.12 **NM** value: **28.00**
Photo cover. • adapts It's Only Money
75 ❑ Mar 1963 Cover: 0.12 **NM** value: **28.00**
• Has 1962 Statement, filed 10/1/62; avg total paid circ 175,000
76 ❑ May 1963 Cover: 0.12 **NM** value: **28.00**
77 ❑ Jul 1963 Cover: 0.12 **NM** value: **28.00**
78 ❑ Sep 1963 Cover: 0.12 **NM** value: **28.00**
79 ❑ Nov 1963 Cover: 0.12 **NM** value: **28.00**
★ 1st Appearance of Mr. Yes.
80 ❑ Jan 1964 Cover: 0.12 **NM** value: **28.00**
Circ: Statement: **164,364**
81 ❑ Mar 1964 Cover: 0.12 **NM** value: **25.00**
Circ: Statement: **164,364**
82 ❑ May 1964 Cover: 0.12 **NM** value: **25.00**
Circ: Statement: **164,364**
83 ❑ Jul 1964 Cover: 0.12 **NM** value: **25.00**
Circ: Statement: **164,364**
84 ❑ Sep 1964 Cover: 0.12 **NM** value: **25.00**
Circ: Statement: **164,364**
• Jerry becomes The Fearless Tarantula
85 ❑ Nov 1964 Cover: 0.12 **NM** value: **25.00**
Circ: Statement: **164,364**
★ 1st Appearance of Renfrew.
86 ❑ Jan 1965 Cover: 0.12 **NM** value: **25.00**
Circ: Statement: **209,691**
📖 King Klonk The Killer Gorilla **A:** Bob Oksner **W:** Arnold Drake
87 ❑ Mar 1965 Cover: 0.12 **NM** value: **25.00**
Circ: Statement: **209,691**
• Has 1964 Statement, filed 10/1/64; avg print run 318,000; avg sales 164,000; avg subs 364; avg total paid 164,364; samples 387; max existent 164,751; 48% of run returned ★ Appearance of Renfrew.
88 ❑ May 1965 Cover: 0.12 **NM** value: **25.00**
Circ: Statement: **209,691**
★ 1st Appearance of Witch Kraft.
89 ❑ Jul 1965 Cover: 0.12 **NM** value: **25.00**
Circ: Statement: **209,691**
90 ❑ Sep 1965 Cover: 0.12 **NM** value: **25.00**
Circ: Statement: **209,691**
91 ❑ Nov 1965 Cover: 0.12 **NM** value: **25.00**
Circ: Statement: **209,691** • **CGC:** 1 graded, best 6.0
92 ❑ Jan 1966 Cover: 0.12 **NM** value: **30.00**
Circ: Statement: **211,934**
★ Appearance of Superman.
93 ❑ Mar 1966 Cover: 0.12 **NM** value: **25.00**
Circ: Statement: **211,934**
• Has 1965 Statement, filed 10/1/65; avg print run 351,000; avg sales 209,000; avg subs 691; avg total paid 209,691; samples 142; max existent 209,833; 40% of run returned
94 ❑ May 1966 Cover: 0.12 **NM** value: **25.00**
Circ: Statement: **211,934**
95 ❑ Jul 1966 Cover: 0.12 **NM** value: **25.00**
Circ: Statement: **211,934**
96 ❑ Sep 1966 Cover: 0.12 **NM** value: **25.00**
Circ: Statement: **211,934**
97 ❑ Nov 1966 Cover: 0.12 **NM** value: **35.00**
Circ: Statement: **211,934** • **CGC:** 3 graded, best 9.8
★ Appearance of Batman, Robin, Penguin, Riddler, Joker.
98 ❑ Jan 1967 Cover: 0.12 **NM** value: **25.00**
Circ: Statement: **180,800**
★ Appearance of Ringo Starr, Ilya Kurakin (on stamps).
99 ❑ Mar 1967 Cover: 0.12 **NM** value: **25.00**
Circ: Statement: **180,800**
• Has 1966 Statement, filed 10/1/66; avg print run 376,000; avg sales 211,000; avg subs 934; avg total paid 211,934; samples 265; max existent 212,199; 44% of run returned
100 ❑ May 1967 Cover: 0.12 **NM** value: **25.00**
Circ: Statement: **180,800**
★ 1st Appearance of Jerry Mess-terpiece pin-up.
101 ❑ Jul 1967 Cover: 0.12 **NM** value: **32.00**
Circ: Statement: **180,800**
A: Neal Adams(cover)
102 ❑ Sep 1967 Cover: 0.12 **NM** value: **55.00**
Circ: Statement: **180,800**
A: Neal Adams(cover) ★ Appearance of The Beatles.
103 ❑ Nov 1967 Cover: 0.12 **NM** value: **32.00**
Circ: Statement: **180,800**
A: Neal Adams(cover)
104 ❑ Jan 1968 Cover: 0.12 **NM** value: **32.00**
Circ: Statement: **197,250**
A: Neal Adams; Neal Adams(cover)
105 ❑ Mar 1968 Cover: 0.12 **NM** value: **32.00**
Circ: Statement: **197,250** • **CGC:** 1 graded, best 9.0
• Has 1967 Statement, filed 10/1/67; avg print run 341,000; avg sales 180,000; avg subs 800; avg total paid 180,800; samples 340; max existent 181,140; 47% of run returned ★ Appearance of Superman, Lex Luthor.
106 ❑ May 1968 Cover: 0.12 **NM** value: **14.00**
Circ: Statement: **197,250**
107 ❑ Jul 1968 Cover: 0.12 **NM** value: **14.00**
Circ: Statement: **197,250**
108 ❑ Sep 1968 Cover: 0.12 **NM** value: **14.00**
Circ: Statement: **197,250**
109 ❑ Nov 1968 Cover: 0.12 **NM** value: **14.00**
Circ: Statement: **197,250**
110 ❑ Jan 1969 Cover: 0.12 **NM** value: **14.00**
Circ: Statement: **174,125**
111 ❑ Mar 1969 Cover: 0.12 **NM** value: **14.00**
Circ: Statement: **174,125**
112 ❑ May 1969 Cover: 0.15 **NM** value: **14.00**
Circ: Statement: **174,125**
★ Appearance of Flash.
113 ❑ Jul 1969 Cover: 0.15 **NM** value: **14.00**
Circ: Statement: **174,125**
114 ❑ Sep 1969 Cover: 0.15 **NM** value: **14.00**
Circ: Statement: **174,125**
115 ❑ Nov 1969 Cover: 0.15 **NM** value: **14.00**
Circ: Statement: **174,125**
116 ❑ Jan 1970 Cover: 0.15 **NM** value: **14.00**
• **CGC:** 1 graded, best 9.4

Other grades: Multiply prices above by **1.5 for Mint • 2/3 for Very Fine • 1/3 for Fine • 1/5 for Very Good • 1/8 for Good**

117 ❑ Mar 1970 Cover: 0.15 **NM** value: **20.00**
• Has 1969 Statement, filed 10/1/69; avg print run 348,000; avg sales 174,000; avg subs 125; avg total paid 174,125; samples 346; max existent 174,471; 50% of run returned ★ Appearance of Wonder Woman.
118 ❑ May 1970 Cover: 0.15 **NM** value: **14.00**
119 ❑ Jul 1970 Cover: 0.15 **NM** value: **14.00**
120 ❑ Sep 1970 Cover: 0.15 **NM** value: **12.00**
121 ❑ Nov 1970 Cover: 0.15 **NM** value: **12.00**
122 ❑ Jan 1971 Cover: 0.15 **NM** value: **12.00**
123 ❑ Mar 1971 Cover: 0.15 **NM** value: **12.00**
124 ❑ May 1971 Cover: 0.15 **NM** value: **12.00**
final issue.

ADVENTURES OF KELLY BELLE: PERIL ON THE HIGH SEAS, THE — Atlantis
1 ❑ 1996b&w Cover: 2.95 **NM** value: **Cover or less**

ADVENTURES OF KOOL-AID MAN, THE — Marvel
1 ❑ Cover: 0.60 **NM** value: **1.00**
No issue number. 60Û value on cover. • giveaway.
5 ❑ Cover: 0.75 **NM** value: **1.00**

ADVENTURES OF LIBERAL MAN, THE — Political
Crushed by the Republicans' gaining control of both houses of Congress, a despondent Democrat decides to refocus his energies by chanting, "Liberals are good and caring ... Republicans must die ... Liberals are good and caring ... Republicans must die..." With his thoughts amplified by the pyramid he keeps over his bed, his chanting mystically transforms him into ... Liberal Man!

Determined to use his powers in the service of his party, Liberal Man immediately teams up with Media Man (a slick spin doctor), and his "equal-kick" ("sidekick" would be derogatory): a black, single mother and former crack baby with no other obvious qualifications. In #2, they stumble across 60s Man, a marijuana-smoking hippie with the super-power of emitting constant hemp fumes.

Often funny, if sometimes strident, Liberal Man is an interesting bit of political satire.

1 ❑ Cover: 2.95 **NM** value: **Cover or less**
A: Pete Garcia **W:** Marcus Pierce Jr. ★ Origin of Liberal Man. ★ 1st Appearance of Liberal Man, Media Man.
2 ❑ Cover: 2.95 **NM** value: **Cover or less**
📖 The Search for Equal Kick; Right Wing Radio Talk Show Hosts Must Die, Part 1 **A:** Pete Garcia **W:** Marcus Pierce Jr. ★ Origin of 60's Man. ★ 1st Appearance of 60's Man.
3 ❑ Cover: 2.95 **NM** value: **Cover or less**
📖 Right Wing Radio Talk Show Hosts Must Die, Part 2; Contract With America: Terminate With Extreme Prejudice, Part 1 **A:** Pete Garcia **W:** Marcus Pierce Jr.
4 ❑ Jul 1996 Cover: 2.95 **NM** value: **Cover or less**
📖 Contract with America: Termiante with Extreme Predjudice, Part 2 **A:** Pete Garcia **W:** Marcus Pierce Jr.
5 ❑ Sep 1996 Cover: 2.95 **NM** value: **Cover or less**
📖 Contract with America: Termiante with Extreme Predjudice, Part 3; The 1996 Campaign: A Nation on the Precipice, Part 1 **A:** Pete Garcia **W:** Marcus Pierce Jr.
6 ❑ Oct 1996 Cover: 2.95 **NM** value: **Cover or less**
📖 The 1996 Campaign: A Nation on the Precipice, Part 2; A Clinton Carol **A:** Pete Garcia **W:** Marcus Pierce Jr.

ADVENTURES OF LUTHER ARKWRIGHT, THE (DARK HORSE) — Dark Horse
1 ❑ 1990 Cover: 1.95 **NM** value: **2.50**
📖 The Disruption Spiral • Reprints Adventures of Luther Arkwright (Valkyrie) #1 **A:** Bryan Talbot **W:** Bryan Talbot
2 ❑ 1990 Cover: 1.95 **NM** value: **2.00**
• Reprints Adventures of Luther Arkwright (Valkyrie) #2 **A:** Bryan Talbot **W:** Bryan Talbot
3 ❑ May 1990 Cover: 1.95 **NM** value: **2.00**
• Reprints Adventures of Luther Arkwright (Valkyrie) #3 **A:** Bryan Talbot **W:** Bryan Talbot
4 ❑ 1990 Cover: 1.95 **NM** value: **2.00**
• Reprints Adventures of Luther Arkwright (Valkyrie) #4 **A:** Bryan Talbot **W:** Bryan Talbot
5 ❑ 1990 Cover: 1.95 **NM** value: **2.00**
• Reprints Adventures of Luther Arkwright (Valkyrie) #5 **A:** Bryan Talbot **W:** Bryan Talbot
6 ❑ 1990 Cover: 1.95 **NM** value: **2.00**
• Reprints Adventures of Luther Arkwright (Valkyrie) #6 **A:** Bryan Talbot **W:** Bryan Talbot
7 ❑ Nov 1990 Cover: 1.95 **NM** value: **2.00**
📖 Destiny's Angel • Reprints Adventures of Luther Arkwright (Valkyrie) #7 **A:** Bryan Talbot **W:** Bryan Talbot
8 ❑ Nov 1990 Cover: 1.95 **NM** value: **2.00**
• Reprints Adventures of Luther Arkwright (Valkyrie) #8 **A:** Bryan Talbot **W:** Bryan Talbot
9 ❑ 1990 Cover: 1.95 **NM** value: **2.00**
• trading cards;Reprints Adventures of Luther Arkwright (Valkyrie) #9 **A:** Bryan Talbot **W:** Bryan Talbot
Bk 1 ❑ Jul 1997, b&w Cover: 14.95 **NM** value: **Cover or less**
• collects Dark Horse series

ADVENTURES OF LUTHER ARKWRIGHT, THE (VALKYRIE) — Valkyrie
1 ❑ Oct 1987 Cover: 2.00 **NM** value: **2.50**
📖 The Disruption Spiral **A:** Bryan Talbot **W:** Bryan Talbot
2 ❑ Dec 1987 Cover: 2.00 **NM** value: **2.50**
A: Bryan Talbot **W:** Bryan Talbot
3 ❑ Feb 1988 Cover: 2.00 **NM** value: **2.50**
A: Bryan Talbot **W:** Bryan Talbot
4 ❑ Apr 1988 Cover: 2.00 **NM** value: **2.50**
A: Bryan Talbot **W:** Bryan Talbot
5 ❑ Jun 1988 Cover: 2.00 **NM** value: **2.50**
A: Bryan Talbot **W:** Bryan Talbot
6 ❑ Aug 1988 Cover: 2.00 **NM** value: **2.50**
A: Bryan Talbot **W:** Bryan Talbot
7 ❑ Oct 1988 Cover: 2.00 **NM** value: **2.50**
📖 Destiny's Angel **A:** Bryan Talbot **W:** Bryan Talbot
8 ❑ Dec 1988 Cover: 2.00 **NM** value: **2.50**
A: Bryan Talbot **W:** Bryan Talbot
9 ❑ Feb 1989 Cover: 2.00 **NM** value: **2.50**
A: Bryan Talbot **W:** Bryan Talbot
10 ❑ Apr 1989 Cover: 2.00 **NM** value: **2.50**
• Essays **A:** Bryan Talbot **W:** Bryan Talbot

ADVENTURES OF MARK TYME, THE — John Spencer & Co.
1 ❑ **NM** value: **2.00**
2 ❑ **NM** value: **2.00**
📖 Fight for Life; Planet of Fear; To Tame a Tyrant **A:** Michael Jay **W:** Michael Jay

ADVENTURES OF MIGHTY MOUSE (1ST SERIES) — St. John
The Terrytoons character of Mighty Mouse (released in 1942 in "The Mouse of Tomorrow") combined two trends of the early days of comics — super-hero fantasy and funny-animal humor — to produce a popular and long-lived concept that appeared in numerous film, television, and comic-book incarnations from the 1940s to the present day. During the early 1950s, Mighty Mouse was licensed to St. John Publishing, which began this series as Mighty Mouse Adventures, then changed the title to Adventures of Mighty Mouse with the second issue.

Each issue featured several short stories of the intrepid rodent in yellow tights and red cape, ranging from straight-out humor pieces to far-flung adventures on other planets. The series' open, colorful art kept things moving at a breezy, entertaining clip.

2 ❑ Jan 1952 Cover: 0.10 **NM** value: **120.00**
• Series continued from Mighty Mouse Adventures #1
3 ❑ Mar 1952 Cover: 0.10 **NM** value: **80.00**
4 ❑ May 1952 Cover: 0.10 **NM** value: **65.00**
5 ❑ Jul 1952 Cover: 0.10 **NM** value: **65.00**
6 ❑ Sep 1952 Cover: 0.10 **NM** value: **52.00**
7 ❑ Sep 1953 Cover: 0.10 **NM** value: **52.00**
8 ❑ Oct 1953 Cover: 0.10 **NM** value: **52.00**
9 ❑ Nov 1953 Cover: 0.10 **NM** value: **52.00**
10 ❑ Jan 1954 Cover: 0.10 **NM** value: **52.00**
11 ❑ Mar 1954 Cover: 0.10 **NM** value: **38.00**
12 ❑ May 1954 Cover: 0.10 **NM** value: **38.00**
📖 Mighty Mouse: The Freezing Terror; Chesty: Play Ball; Mighty Mouse: The Bank Robbers; Mighty Mouse: The Planet of Death
13 ❑ Jul 1954 Cover: 0.10 **NM** value: **38.00**
14 ❑ Sep 1954 Cover: 0.10 **NM** value: **38.00**
15 ❑ Nov 1954 Cover: 0.10 **NM** value: **38.00**
16 ❑ Jan 1955 Cover: 0.10 **NM** value: **38.00**
17 ❑ Mar 1955 Cover: 0.10 **NM** value: **38.00**
18 ❑ May 1955 Cover: 0.10 **NM** value: **38.00**

ADVENTURES OF MIGHTY MOUSE (2ND SERIES) — Literary Enterprises
126 ❑ Aug 1955 Cover: 0.10 **NM** value: **40.00**
• Series continued from Paul Terry's Comics #125
127 ❑ Oct 1955 Cover: 0.10 **NM** value: **34.00**
128 ❑ Nov 1955 Cover: 0.10 **NM** value: **34.00**
129 ❑ Apr 1956 Cover: 0.10 **NM** value: **34.00**
• Pines begins as publisher
130 ❑ Jul 1956 Cover: 0.10 **NM** value: **34.00**
131 ❑ Oct 1956 Cover: 0.10 **NM** value: **32.00**
132 ❑ Jan 1957 Cover: 0.10 **NM** value: **32.00**
133 ❑ Apr 1957 Cover: 0.10 **NM** value: **32.00**
134 ❑ Jul 1957 Cover: 0.10 **NM** value: **32.00**
135 ❑ Oct 1957 Cover: 0.10 **NM** value: **32.00**
136 ❑ Jan 1958 Cover: 0.10 **NM** value: **32.00**
137 ❑ Apr 1958 Cover: 0.10 **NM** value: **32.00**
138 ❑ Jul 1958 Cover: 0.10 **NM** value: **32.00**
139 ❑ Oct 1958 Cover: 0.10 **NM** value: **32.00**
140 ❑ Dec 1958 Cover: 0.10 **NM** value: **32.00**
141 ❑ Feb 1959 Cover: 0.10 **NM** value: **30.00**
142 ❑ Apr 1959 Cover: 0.10 **NM** value: **30.00**
143 ❑ Jun 1959 Cover: 0.10 **NM** value: **30.00**
144 ❑ Aug 1959 Cover: 0.10 **NM** value: **30.00**
• Dell begins publishing
145 ❑ Jan 1960 Cover: 0.10 **NM** value: **30.00**
146 ❑ Apr 1960 Cover: 0.10 **NM** value: **30.00**
147 ❑ Jul 1960 Cover: 0.10 **NM** value: **30.00**
148 ❑ Oct 1960 Cover: 0.10 **NM** value: **30.00**
149 ❑ Jan 1961 Cover: 0.10 **NM** value: **30.00**
150 ❑ Apr 1961 Cover: 0.10 **NM** value: **30.00**
151 ❑ Jul 1961 Cover: 0.10 **NM** value: **26.00**
152 ❑ Oct 1961 Cover: 0.10 **NM** value: **26.00**
153 ❑ Jan 1962 Cover: 0.10 **NM** value: **26.00**
154 ❑ Apr 1962 Cover: 0.10 **NM** value: **26.00**
155 ❑ Jul 1962 Cover: 0.10 **NM** value: **26.00**
156 ❑ Oct 1962 Cover: 0.10 **NM** value: **26.00**
• Gold Key begins as publisher
157 ❑ Jan 1963 Cover: 0.10 **NM** value: **26.00**
158 ❑ Apr 1963 Cover: 0.10 **NM** value: **26.00**
• Has 1962 Statement; only subscription figures published; avg subs 111
159 ❑ Jul 1963 Cover: 0.10 **NM** value: **26.00**
160 ❑ Oct 1963 Cover: 0.10 **NM** value: **26.00**
• Series continued as Mighty Mouse #161

ADVENTURES OF MR. PYRIDINE — Fantagraphics
1 ❑ b&w Cover: 2.50 **NM** value: **Cover or less**

ADVENTURES OF MISTY, THE — Forbidden Fruit
1 ❑ Apr 1991 Cover: 2.95 **NM** value: **Cover or less**
A: James McQuade **W:** James McQuade; Gil Porter
2 ❑ May 1991 Cover: 2.95 **NM** value: **Cover or less**
A: James McQuade **W:** James McQuade; Gil Porter
3 ❑ Jun 1991 Cover: 2.95 **NM** value: **Cover or less**
A: James McQuade **W:** James McQuade; Gil Porter
4 ❑ Jul 1991 Cover: 2.95 **NM** value: **Cover or less**
A: James McQuade **W:** James McQuade; Gil Porter
5 ❑ Aug 1991 Cover: 2.95 **NM** value: **Cover or less**
A: James McQuade **W:** James McQuade; Gil Porter
6 ❑ Oct 1991 Cover: 2.95 **NM** value: **Cover or less**
A: James McQuade **W:** James McQuade
7 ❑ Dec 1991 Cover: 2.95 **NM** value: **Cover or less**
A: James McQuade **W:** James McQuade
8 ❑ Feb 1992 Cover: 2.95 **NM** value: **Cover or less**
A: James McQuade **W:** James McQuade
9 ❑ Apr 1992 Cover: 2.95 **NM** value: **Cover or less**
A: James McQuade **W:** James McQuade
10 ❑ Jun 1992 Cover: 2.95 **NM** value: **Cover or less**
A: James McQuade **W:** James McQuade
11 ❑ Aug 1992 Cover: 3.50 **NM** value: **Cover or less**
A: James McQuade **W:** James McQuade
12 ❑ Oct 1992 Cover: 3.50 **NM** value: **Cover or less**
A: James McQuade **W:** James McQuade

ADVENTURES OF MONKEY, THE — Womp
1 ❑ Jul 1995 Cover: 1.50 **NM** value: **2.00**
2 ❑ Jun 1996 Cover: 1.50 **NM** value: **2.00**
3 ❑ Jun 1997 Cover: 2.00 **NM** value: **Cover or less**
4 ❑ Jun 1998 Cover: 2.00 **NM** value: **Cover or less**
• Freshmen back-up

ADVENTURES OF OAT WILLIE, THE — Austintatious Comics
1 ❑ Cover: 2.00 **NM** value: **3.00**
• Gilbert Shelton

ADVENTURES OF OZZIE AND HARRIET — DC
As with such series as The Adventures of Dean Martin & Jerry Lewis, this title focused on a comedy showbiz team, in this case the husband-and-wife duo of Ozzie (1906-1975) and Harriet (1909-1994) Nelson. While they ran for more than 20 years on radio and 15 years on TV (and their son Rick eventually became a pop star), their comic book lasted less than a year. — Maggie

1 ❑ Oct 1949 Cover: 0.10 **NM** value: **700.00**
2 ❑ Dec 1949 Cover: 0.10 **NM** value: **350.00**
3 ❑ Feb 1950 Cover: 0.10 **NM** value: **300.00**
4 ❑ Apr 1950 Cover: 0.10 **NM** value: **300.00**
• **CGC:** 1 graded, best 8.5
5 ❑ Jun 1950 Cover: 0.10 **NM** value: **300.00**
• **CGC:** 1 graded, best 8.5

ADVENTURES OF PETER RABBIT — Avon
1 ❑ Cover: 0.10 **NM** value: **200.00**
2 ❑ Cover: 0.10 **NM** value: **150.00**
3 ❑ 1948 Cover: 0.10 **NM** value: **150.00**
4 ❑ 1949 Cover: 0.10 **NM** value: **150.00**
5 ❑ 1949 Cover: 0.10 **NM** value: **150.00**
6 ❑ 1949 Cover: 0.10 **NM** value: **150.00**
7 ❑ 1950 Cover: 0.10 **NM** value: **100.00**
8 ❑ Cover: 0.10 **NM** value: **100.00**
9 ❑ Cover: 0.10 **NM** value: **100.00**
10 ❑ Cover: 0.10 **NM** value: **100.00**
11 ❑ Cover: 0.10 **NM** value: **100.00**
12 ❑ Cover: 0.10 **NM** value: **100.00**
13 ❑ Cover: 0.10 **NM** value: **100.00**
14 ❑ Cover: 0.10 **NM** value: **100.00**
15 ❑ Cover: 0.10 **NM** value: **100.00**
16 ❑ Cover: 0.10 **NM** value: **100.00**
17 ❑ 1953 Cover: 0.10 **NM** value: **100.00**
18 ❑ Cover: 0.10 **NM** value: **100.00**
19 ❑ Cover: 0.10 **NM** value: **100.00**
20 ❑ Cover: 0.10 **NM** value: **100.00**
21 ❑ Cover: 0.10 **NM** value: **75.00**
22 ❑ Cover: 0.10 **NM** value: **75.00**
23 ❑ Cover: 0.10 **NM** value: **75.00**
24 ❑ Cover: 0.10 **NM** value: **75.00**
25 ❑ Cover: 0.10 **NM** value: **75.00**
26 ❑ Cover: 0.10 **NM** value: **75.00**
27 ❑ Cover: 0.10 **NM** value: **75.00**
28 ❑ Cover: 0.10 **NM** value: **75.00**
29 ❑ Cover: 0.10 **NM** value: **75.00**
30 ❑ Cover: 0.10 **NM** value: **75.00**
31 ❑ Cover: 0.10 **NM** value: **75.00**
32 ❑ Cover: 0.10 **NM** value: **75.00**
33 ❑ Cover: 0.10 **NM** value: **75.00**
34 ❑ Cover: 0.10 **NM** value: **75.00**

ADVENTURES OF PINKY LEE — Atlas
Lee (1907-1993) was a burlesque comedian who had a short-lived prime-time TV career and went on to become star of an after-school kids' comedy show. Identified by his "checkered hat" and "checkered coat," he used his half-hour daily series to show his young audience such concepts as fast skits, wild puns, and blackout

CGC-graded: Multiply prices above by **33 for 9.9 M • 16 for 9.8 NM/M • 7 for 9.6 NM+ • 5 for 9.4 NM • 2.5 for 9.2 NM- • 1.5 for 9.0 VF/NM**

sketches long before the colorful, prime-time Laugh-In of more than a decade later.

His theme, which began, "Yoo hoo! It's me! My name is Pinky Lee! I skip and run with lots of fun for every he and she!" led into the show which served as a lead-in for NBC's Howdy Doody Show. Think today's fans couldn't connect? Pee Wee Herman's persona is doggone close. — Maggie

1 ❑ Jul 1955 Cover: 0.10 **NM** value: **175.00**
2 ❑ Aug 1955 Cover: 0.10 **NM** value: **100.00**

ADVENTURES OF PIONEER PETE Pioneer Chicken

1 ❑ **NM** value: **1.00**
• 1978 Giveaway. Adventures of Pioneer Pete and his Pals in Outer Space Take-Out

ADVENTURES OF QUIK BUNNY Marvel

1 ❑ **NM** value: **1.00**
No issue number. 60Û value on cover. • giveaway.

ADVENTURES OF REX THE WONDER DOG, THE DC

1 ❑ Jan 1952 Cover: 0.10 **NM** value: **660.00**
• **CGC:** 1 graded, best 4.5
2 ❑ Mar 1952 Cover: 0.10 **NM** value: **340.00**
3 ❑ May 1952 Cover: 0.10 **NM** value: **265.00**
• **CGC:** 1 graded, best 8.5
4 ❑ Jul 1952 Cover: 0.10 **NM** value: **220.00**
5 ❑ Sep 1952 Cover: 0.10 **NM** value: **220.00**
6 ❑ Nov 1952 Cover: 0.10 **NM** value: **165.00**
• **CGC:** 1 graded, best 6.0
7 ❑ Jan 1953 Cover: 0.10 **NM** value: **165.00**
8 ❑ Mar 1952 Cover: 0.10 **NM** value: **165.00**
9 ❑ May 1953 Cover: 0.10 **NM** value: **165.00**
• **CGC:** 1 graded, best 9.2
10 ❑ Jul 1953 Cover: 0.10 **NM** value: **165.00**
• **CGC:** 1 graded, best 8.5
11 ❑ Sep 1953 Cover: 0.10 **NM** value: **185.00**
Bomb cover.
12 ❑ Nov 1953 Cover: 0.10 **NM** value: **105.00**
13 ❑ Jan 1954 Cover: 0.10 **NM** value: **105.00**
14 ❑ Mar 1954 Cover: 0.10 **NM** value: **105.00**
15 ❑ May 1954 Cover: 0.10 **NM** value: **105.00**
16 ❑ Jul 1954 Cover: 0.10 **NM** value: **90.00**
17 ❑ Sep 1954 Cover: 0.10 **NM** value: **90.00**
18 ❑ Nov 1954 Cover: 0.10 **NM** value: **90.00**
• **CGC:** 1 graded, best 9.4
19 ❑ Jan 1955 Cover: 0.10 **NM** value: **90.00**
20 ❑ Mar 1955 Cover: 0.10 **NM** value: **90.00**
21 ❑ May 1955 Cover: 0.10 **NM** value: **65.00**
22 ❑ Jul 1955 Cover: 0.10 **NM** value: **65.00**
The Ship of Wanted Men!
23 ❑ Sep 1955 Cover: 0.10 **NM** value: **65.00**
24 ❑ Nov 1955 Cover: 0.10 **NM** value: **65.00**
25 ❑ Jan 1956 Cover: 0.10 **NM** value: **65.00**
26 ❑ Mar 1956 Cover: 0.10 **NM** value: **65.00**
27 ❑ May 1956 Cover: 0.10 **NM** value: **65.00**
28 ❑ Jul 1956 Cover: 0.10 **NM** value: **65.00**
29 ❑ Sep 1956 Cover: 0.10 **NM** value: **65.00**
30 ❑ Nov 1956 Cover: 0.10 **NM** value: **65.00**
31 ❑ Jan 1957 Cover: 0.10 **NM** value: **40.00**
32 ❑ Mar 1957 Cover: 0.10 **NM** value: **40.00**
33 ❑ May 1957 Cover: 0.10 **NM** value: **40.00**
34 ❑ Jul 1957 Cover: 0.10 **NM** value: **40.00**
35 ❑ Sep 1957 Cover: 0.10 **NM** value: **40.00**
36 ❑ Nov 1957 Cover: 0.10 **NM** value: **40.00**
37 ❑ Jan 1958 Cover: 0.10 **NM** value: **40.00**
38 ❑ Mar 1958 Cover: 0.10 **NM** value: **40.00**
39 ❑ May 1958 Cover: 0.10 **NM** value: **40.00**
40 ❑ Jul 1958 Cover: 0.10 **NM** value: **40.00**
41 ❑ Sep 1958 Cover: 0.10 **NM** value: **30.00**
42 ❑ Nov 1958 Cover: 0.10 **NM** value: **30.00**
43 ❑ Jan 1959 Cover: 0.10 **NM** value: **30.00**
44 ❑ Mar 1959 Cover: 0.10 **NM** value: **30.00**
45 ❑ May 1959 Cover: 0.10 **NM** value: **30.00**
46 ❑ Nov 1959 Cover: 0.10 **NM** value: **30.00**
final issue.

ADVENTURES OF RHEUMY PEEPERS & CHUNKY HIGHLIGHTS, THE Oni Press

1 ❑ Feb 1999 Cover: 2.95 **NM** value: **Cover or less**
Circ: Diamd. preorders: **4,935**
No issue number. **A:** Renée French **W:** Penn Jillette

ADVENTURES OF RICK RAYGUN, THE Stop Dragon

1 ❑ Sep 1986 Cover: 1.75 **NM** value: **2.00**
A: Rudy Holmes **W:** Rudy Holmes
2 ❑ Oct 1986 Cover: 1.75 **NM** value: **2.00**
A: Rudy Holmes **W:** Rudy Holmes
3 ❑ Fal 1986 Cover: 1.75 **NM** value: **2.00**
A: Rudy Holmes **W:** Rudy Holmes
4 ❑ Nov 1986 Cover: 1.75 **NM** value: **2.00**
A: Rudy Holmes **W:** Rudy Holmes
5 ❑ Jan 1987 Cover: 1.75 **NM** value: **2.00**
A: Rudy Holmes **W:** Rudy Holmes

ADVENTURES OF ROBIN HOOD, THE Gold Key

1 ❑ Mar 1974 Cover: 0.20 **NM** value: **8.00**
2 ❑ May 1974 Cover: 0.20 **NM** value: **5.00**
3 ❑ Jul 1974 Cover: 0.20 **NM** value: **4.00**
4 ❑ Aug 1974 Cover: 0.20 **NM** value: **4.00**
5 ❑ Sep 1974 Cover: 0.20 **NM** value: **4.00**
6 ❑ Nov 1974 Cover: 0.20 **NM** value: **4.00**
7 ❑ Jan 1975 Cover: 0.20 **NM** value: **4.00**

ADVENTURES OF ROMA Forbidden Fruit

All issues are adults only.
1 ❑ Jan 1993, b&w Cover: 3.50 **NM** value: **Cover or less**

ADVENTURES OF SNAKE PLISSKEN Marvel

1 ❑ Jan 1997 Cover: 2.50 **NM** value: **Cover or less**
Circ: Direct Market orders: **12,750**
Up and Running **A:** Rod Whigham; Dan Brereton(cover) **W:** Len Kaminski

ADVENTURES OF SPENCER SPOOK, THE Ace

1 ❑ Oct 1986 Cover: 1.95 **NM** value: **2.00**
The Comic Capercon; Spencer Spook • reprints stories from Giggle Comics #77 and Spencer Spook #102 **A:** Lynn Karp; Pat Boyette; Owen Fitzgerald **W:** Joe Gill; Richard E. Hughes
2 ❑ Dec 1986 Cover: 1.95 **NM** value: **2.00**
Wrassle Hassle!; Hector the Specter **A:** Ken Hultgren; Pat Boyette; Jack Bradbury **W:** Joe Gill; Richard E. Hughes
3 ❑ Jan 1987 Cover: 1.95 **NM** value: **2.00**
4 ❑ Mar 1987 Cover: 1.95 **NM** value: **2.00**
5 ❑ Cover: 1.95 **NM** value: **2.00**
6 ❑ Cover: 1.95 **NM** value: **2.00**

ADVENTURES OF SPIDER-MAN, THE Marvel

The Adventures of Spider-Man is the companion comic book to the animated television series. The title features a simpler art style and stories that are less dark and complicated than what will be found in the series aimed at older readers. Peter Parker is still living with Aunt May, instead of being married to Mary Jane, which made this title a non-continuity series when it was hitting newsstands. The lower price (only 99 cents at a time when the average comic price was climbing over $2) and concise storytelling made this an inviting series for readers who were familiar with the character only from his television appearances.

1 ❑ Apr 1996 Cover: 0.99 **NM** value: **1.50**
Shot In The Dark • animated series adaptations **A:** Alex Saviuk **W:** Nel Yomtov ★ Appearance of Punisher.
2 ❑ May 1996 Cover: 0.99 **NM** value: **1.25**
A: Alex Saviuk **W:** Nel Yomtov ★ Versus Hammerhead.
3 ❑ Jun 1996 Cover: 0.99 **NM** value: **1.25**
A: Alex Saviuk **W:** Nel Yomtov ★ Appearance of X-Men. ★ Versus Mr. Sinister.
4 ❑ Jul 1996 Cover: 0.99 **NM** value: **1.00**
A: Alex Saviuk **W:** Nel Yomtov
5 ❑ Aug 1996 Cover: 0.99 **NM** value: **1.00**
A: Alex Saviuk **W:** Nel Yomtov ★ Versus Rhino.
6 ❑ Sep 1996 Cover: 0.99 **NM** value: **1.00**
• Human Torch **A:** Alex Saviuk **W:** Nel Yomtov ★ Appearance of Thing.
7 ❑ Oct 1996 Cover: 0.99 **NM** value: **1.00**
A: Alex Saviuk **W:** Nel Yomtov ★ Versus Enforcers.
8 ❑ Nov 1996 Cover: 0.99 **NM** value: **1.00**
Circ: Direct Market orders: **19,500**
Where Demons Ride! **A:** Alex Saviuk **W:** Nel Yomtov ★ Versus Kingpin.
9 ❑ Dec 1996 Cover: 0.99 **NM** value: **1.00**
Circ: Direct Market orders: **18,500**
A: Alex Saviuk **W:** Nel Yomtov
10 ❑ Jan 1997 Cover: 0.99 **NM** value: **1.00**
Circ: Direct Market orders: **17,000**
To Catch a Spider **A:** Alex Saviuk **W:** Nel Yomtov ★ Versus Beetle.
11 ❑ Feb 1997 Cover: 0.99 **NM** value: **1.00**
Circ: Direct Market orders: **16,000**
Unions, Part 1 **A:** Alex Saviuk **W:** Glenn Greening ★ Appearance of Venom. ★ Versus Doctor Octopus and Venom.
12 ❑ Mar 1997 Cover: 0.99 **NM** value: **1.00**
Circ: Direct Market orders: **14,500**
Unions, Part 2 final issue. **A:** Alex Saviuk **W:** Glenn Greening ★ Appearance of Venom. ★ Versus Doctor Octopus and Venom.

ADVENTURES OF SUPERBOY, THE DC

19 ❑ Sep 1991 Cover: 1.25 **NM** value: **1.50**
Circ: CapCity orders: **6,200**
• Series continued from Superboy (2nd Series) #18
20 ❑ Oct 1991 Cover: 1.25 **NM** value: **1.50**
Circ: CapCity orders: **5,700**
The Secret (Until Now) Origin of Nicknack **A:** John Statema; Jim Mooney **W:** Scott Lobdell; Gilbert Gottfried ★ Origin of Knickknack.
21 ❑ Nov 1991 Cover: 1.25 **NM** value: **1.50**
Circ: CapCity orders: **5,650**
Fire and Ice
22 ❑ Dec 1991 Cover: 1.25 **NM** value: **1.50**
Circ: CapCity orders: **4,950**
Criminal Element final issue.

Capital City orders are the actual sales of comic books by Capital City Distribution, once one of the largest U.S. sellers of comics to comics shops. Capital City's share of comics shop sales, while not known exactly, increases from around 10-20% in the mid-1980s to 30-35% in the mid-1990s. Capital City's share of comic books sold on newsstands (most Marvels and DCs) will be less.

ADVENTURES OF SUPERMAN DC

It's a bird...it's a plane...it's...

Superman, of course, DC's greatest super-hero, and one of the world's best-known characters. With his super-strength, ability to fly, invulnerability, X-ray vision, and other super-powers, he's easily one of the mightiest characters ever created. The challenge is to make such a legendary character come across as fresh and believable to what is now its third or fourth generation of readers. As this title shows, DC is more than up to the job.

In 1987, Superman's character was modified, altering his origin and powers, as well as the backgrounds of his supporting cast. As part of that Superman rebirth, DC switched around its various Superman titles, renaming their old Superman series "The Adventures of Superman" and creating a new, second series of Superman.

0 ❑ Oct 1994 Cover: 1.50 **NM** value: **2.50**
Circ: CapCity orders: **61,800**
Peer Pressure, Part 3 • ▲1994-39 **A:** Barry Kitson **W:** Karl Kesel
424 ❑ Jan 1987 Cover: 0.75 **NM** value: **2.50**
Circ: CapCity orders: **32,200** • **CGC:** 2 graded, best 9.4
Man o' War! **A:** Jerry Ordway **W:** Marv Wolfman
425 ❑ Feb 1987 Cover: 0.75 **NM** value: **2.00**
Circ: CapCity orders: **24,200**
A: Jerry Ordway
426 ❑ Mar 1987 Cover: 0.75 **NM** value: **2.00**
Circ: CapCity orders: **32,000**
• Legends **A:** Jerry Ordway ★ 1st Appearance of Bibbo.
427 ❑ Apr 1987 Cover: 0.75 **NM** value: **2.00**
Circ: CapCity orders: **26,300**
A: Jerry Ordway
428 ❑ May 1987 Cover: 0.75 **NM** value: **2.00**
Circ: CapCity orders: **21,550**
A: Jerry Ordway
429 ❑ Jun 1987 Cover: 0.75 **NM** value: **2.00**
Circ: CapCity orders: **21,550**
A: Jerry Ordway
430 ❑ Jul 1987 Cover: 0.75 **NM** value: **2.00**
Circ: CapCity orders: **19,650**
A: Jerry Ordway
431 ❑ Aug 1987 Cover: 0.75 **NM** value: **2.00**
Circ: CapCity orders: **19,900**
A: Jerry Ordway
432 ❑ Sep 1987 Cover: 0.75 **NM** value: **2.00**
Circ: CapCity orders: **19,950**
A: Jerry Ordway ★ 1st Appearance of Jose Delgado (Gangbuster).
433 ❑ Oct 1987 Cover: 0.75 **NM** value: **2.00**
Circ: CapCity orders: **19,300**
A: Jerry Ordway
434 ❑ Nov 1987 Cover: 0.75 **NM** value: **2.00**
Circ: CapCity orders: **19,450**
A: Jerry Ordway ★ 1st Appearance of Gangbuster.
435 ❑ Dec 1987 Cover: 0.75 **NM** value: **2.00**
Circ: CapCity orders: **18,350**
A: Jerry Ordway
436 ❑ Jan 1988 Cover: 0.75 **NM** value: **2.00**
Circ: CapCity orders: **23,850**
Millennium • Millennium **A:** Jerry Ordway
437 ❑ Feb 1988 Cover: 0.75 **NM** value: **2.00**
Circ: CapCity orders: **24,100**
Millennium • Millennium **A:** Jerry Ordway ★ Versus Gangbuster.
438 ❑ Mar 1988 Cover: 0.75 **NM** value: **2.00**
Circ: CapCity orders: **19,950**
A: Jerry Ordway ★ Origin of Brainiac II (Milton Moses Fine). ★ 1st Appearance of Brainiac II (Milton Moses Fine).
439 ❑ Apr 1988 Cover: 0.75 **NM** value: **2.00**
Circ: CapCity orders: **19,950**
A: Jerry Ordway
440 ❑ May 1988 Cover: 0.75 **NM** value: **2.00**
Circ: CapCity orders: **23,400**
A: Jerry Ordway
441 ❑ Jun 1988 Cover: 0.75 **NM** value: **2.00**
Circ: CapCity orders: **18,600**
A: Jerry Ordway ★ Versus Mxyzptlk.
442 ❑ Jul 1988 Cover: 0.75 **NM** value: **2.00**
Circ: CapCity orders: **19,950**
A: Jerry Ordway; John Byrne
443 ❑ Aug 1988 Cover: 0.75 **NM** value: **2.00**
Circ: CapCity orders: **23,050**
A: Jerry Ordway
444 ❑ Sep 1988 Cover: 0.75 **NM** value: **2.00**
Circ: CapCity orders: **19,250**
• Supergirl **A:** Jerry Ordway
445 ❑ Oct 1988 Cover: 0.75 **NM** value: **2.00**
Circ: CapCity orders: **19,850**
A: Jerry Ordway
446 ❑ Nov 1988 Cover: 0.75 **NM** value: **2.00**
Circ: CapCity orders: **17,750**
A: Jerry Ordway ★ Appearance of Gangbuster.
447 ❑ Dec 1988 Cover: 0.75 **NM** value: **2.00**
Circ: CapCity orders: **17,950**
A: Jerry Ordway
448 ❑ Dec 1988 Cover: 0.75 **NM** value: **2.00**
Circ: CapCity orders: **17,000**
A: Jerry Ordway
449 ❑ Jan 1989 Cover: 0.75 **NM** value: **2.00**
Circ: CapCity orders: **18,950**
• Invasion!
450 ❑ Jan 1989 Cover: 0.75 **NM** value: **2.00**
Circ: CapCity orders: **18,000**
• Invasion!

Other grades: Multiply prices above by **1.5 for Mint • 2/3 for Very Fine • 1/3 for Fine • 1/5 for Very Good • 1/8 for Good**

451 ❑ Feb 1989 Cover: 0.75 **NM** value: **2.00**
Circ: CapCity orders: **15,850**

452 ❑ Mar 1989 Cover: 0.75 **NM** value: **2.00**
Circ: CapCity orders: **16,650**

453 ❑ Apr 1989 Cover: 0.75 **NM** value: **2.00**
Circ: CapCity orders: **16,800**

454 ❑ May 1989 Cover: 0.75 **NM** value: **2.00**
Circ: CapCity orders: **18,200**
★ 1st Appearance of Draaga.

455 ❑ Jun 1989 Cover: 0.75 **NM** value: **2.00**
Circ: CapCity orders: **19,300**

456 ❑ Jul 1989 Cover: 0.75 **NM** value: **2.00**
Circ: CapCity orders: **20,200**

457 ❑ Aug 1989 Cover: 0.75 **NM** value: **2.00**
Circ: CapCity orders: **20,550**

458 ❑ Sep 1989 Cover: 0.75 **NM** value: **2.00**
Circ: CapCity orders: **21,200**
• Jimmy as Elastic Lad

459 ❑ Oct 1989 Cover: 0.75 **NM** value: **2.00**
Circ: CapCity orders: **21,800**
• Eradicator buried in Antarctic

460 ❑ Nov 1989 Cover: 0.75 **NM** value: **2.00**
Circ: CapCity orders: **21,550**
★ 1st Appearance of Fortress of Solitude.

461 ❑ Dec 1989 Cover: 0.75 **NM** value: **2.00**
Circ: CapCity orders: **20,900**

462 ❑ Jan 1990 Cover: 0.75 **NM** value: **2.00**
Circ: CapCity orders: **20,300**

463 ❑ Feb 1990 Cover: 0.75 **NM** value: **3.00**
Circ: CapCity orders: **20,350**
• Superman/Flash race ★ Appearance of Flash.

464 ❑ Mar 1990 Cover: 0.75 **NM** value: **3.00**
Circ: CapCity orders: **20,300**
• Krypton Man ★ Versus Lobo.

465 ❑ Apr 1990 Cover: 0.75 **NM** value: **2.00**
Circ: CapCity orders: **19,000**
• Krypton Man

466 ❑ May 1990 Cover: 0.75 **NM** value: **3.00**
Circ: CapCity orders: **19,100**
★ 1st Appearance of Hank Henshaw (becomes cyborg Superman).

467 ❑ Jun 1990 Cover: 0.75 **NM** value: **2.00**
Circ: CapCity orders: **33,100**
• Batman

468 ❑ Jul 1990 Cover: 0.75 **NM** value: **2.00**
Circ: CapCity orders: **21,300**

469 ❑ Aug 1990 Cover: 0.75 **NM** value: **2.00**
Circ: CapCity orders: **20,600**
★ 1st Appearance of Blaze.

470 ❑ Sep 1990 Cover: 0.75 **NM** value: **2.00**
Circ: CapCity orders: **22,400**

471 ❑ Oct 1990 Cover: 0.75 **NM** value: **2.00**
Circ: CapCity orders: **21,350**
★ Appearance of Sinbad.

472 ❑ Nov 1990 Cover: 0.75 **NM** value: **2.00**
Circ: CapCity orders: **20,850**

473 ❑ Dec 1990 Cover: 0.75 **NM** value: **2.00**
Circ: CapCity orders: **21,150**
• Guy Gardner ★ Appearance of Green Lantern.

474 ❑ Jan 1991 Cover: 1.00 **NM** value: **2.00**
Circ: CapCity orders: **18,650**

475 ❑ Feb 1991 Cover: 1.00 **NM** value: **2.00**
Circ: CapCity orders: **18,550**
• Wonder Woman;Batman, Flash

476 ❑ Mar 1991 Cover: 1.00 **NM** value: **2.00**
Circ: CapCity orders: **21,600**
🕮 Time and Time Again, Part 1 ★ 1st Appearance of The Linear Men. ★ Versus Linear Man.

477 ❑ Apr 1991 Cover: 1.00 **NM** value: **2.00**
Circ: CapCity orders: **22,300**
🕮 Time and Time Again, Part 4 ★ Appearance of Legion.

478 ❑ May 1991 Cover: 1.00 **NM** value: **2.00**
Circ: CapCity orders: **24,650**
🕮 Time and Time Again, Part 7 ★ Versus Dev-Em.

479 ❑ Jun 1991 Cover: 1.00 **NM** value: **2.00**
Circ: CapCity orders: **24,250**

480 ❑ Jul 1991 Cover: 1.75 **NM** value: **2.25**
Circ: CapCity orders: **34,600**
• Giant-size.

481 ❑ Aug 1991 Cover: 1.00 **NM** value: **1.75**
Circ: CapCity orders: **26,450**

482 ❑ Sep 1991 Cover: 1.00 **NM** value: **1.75**
Circ: CapCity orders: **26,100**
★ Versus Parasite.

483 ❑ Oct 1991 Cover: 1.00 **NM** value: **1.75**
Circ: CapCity orders: **25,550**
★ 1st Appearance of Atomic Skull.

484 ❑ Nov 1991 Cover: 1.00 **NM** value: **1.75**
Circ: CapCity orders: **24,000**
• Blackout

485 ❑ Dec 1991 Cover: 1.00 **NM** value: **1.75**
Circ: CapCity orders: **23,150**
• Blackout

486 ❑ Jan 1992 Cover: 1.00 **NM** value: **1.75**
Circ: CapCity orders: **21,750**

487 ❑ Feb 1992 Cover: 1.00 **NM** value: **1.75**
Circ: CapCity orders: **20,100**

488 ❑ Mar 1992 Cover: 1.00 **NM** value: **1.75**
Circ: CapCity orders: **21,900**
🕮 Panic in Sky

489 ❑ Apr 1992 Cover: 1.00 **NM** value: **1.75**
Circ: CapCity orders: **20,600**
🕮 Panic in Sky

490 ❑ May 1992 Cover: 1.00 **NM** value: **1.75**
Circ: CapCity orders: **18,150**

491 ❑ Jun 1992 Cover: 1.00 **NM** value: **1.75**
Circ: CapCity orders: **19,350**
★ Versus Metallo.

492 ❑ Jul 1992 Cover: 1.00 **NM** value: **1.75**
Circ: CapCity orders: **20,700**
🕮 ...And Justice For All! • ▲1992-27 **A:** Peter Krause **W:** Jerry Ordway ★ Versus Agent Liberty.

493 ❑ Aug 1992 Cover: 1.25 **NM** value: **1.75**
Circ: CapCity orders: **20,800**
★ 1st Appearance of Lord Satanus. ★ Versus Blaze.

494 ❑ Sep 1992 Cover: 1.25 **NM** value: **1.75**
Circ: CapCity orders: **18,650**
★ 1st Appearance of Kismet.

495 ❑ Oct 1992 Cover: 1.25 **NM** value: **1.75**
Circ: CapCity orders: **18,600**
★ Appearance of Forever People.

496 ❑ Nov 1992 Cover: 1.25 **NM** value: **3.00**
Circ: CapCity orders: **17,700** • **CGC:** 1 graded, best 9.2
🕮 Doomsday • Mxyzptlk

496-2 ❑ Nov 1992 Cover: 1.25 **NM** value: **1.50**

497 ❑ Dec 1992 Cover: 1.25 **NM** value: **3.00**
Circ: CapCity orders: **25,450** • **CGC:** 2 graded, best 9.8
🕮 Doomsday, Under Fire • Doomsday;▲1992-47 **A:** Tom Grummettt **W:** Jerry Ordway

497-2 ❑ Dec 1992 Cover: 1.25 **NM** value: **2.00**
🕮 Doomsday, Under Fire • 2nd printing, ▲1992-47 **A:** Tom Grummettt **W:** Jerry Ordway

498 ❑ Jan 1993 Cover: 1.25 **NM** value: **3.00**
Circ: CapCity orders: **80,500**
🕮 Funeral for a Friend, Part 1 • ▲1993-3 **A:** Tom Grummettt **W:** Jerry Ordway

498-2 ❑ Jan 1993 Cover: 1.25 **NM** value: **2.00**

499 ❑ Feb 1993 Cover: 1.25 **NM** value: **2.50**
Circ: CapCity orders: **81,800**
🕮 Funeral for a Friend, Part 5 • ▲1993-7 **A:** Tom Grummettt **W:** Jerry Ordway

500 ❑ Jun 1993 Cover: 2.50 **NM** value: **3.00**
Circ: CapCity orders: **161,250** • **CGC:** 38 graded, best 9.9
🕮 Life After Death • begins return from dead **A:** Tom Grummettt **W:** Jerry Ordway

500/CS ❑ Jun 1993 Cover: 2.95 **NM** value: **3.50**
Circ: CapCity orders: **717,800** • **CGC:** 2 graded, best 9.4
translucent cover. 🕮 Life After Death • trading card;begins return from dead **A:** Tom Grummettt **W:** Jerry Ordway

500/SI ❑ Jun 1993 **NM** value: **10.00**
• **CGC:** 7 graded, best 9.4
• silver edition. 🕮 Life After Death **A:** Tom Grummettt **W:** Jerry Ordway

501 ❑ Jun 1993 Cover: 1.50 **NM** value: **2.00**
Circ: CapCity orders: **110,850**
🕮 Reign of the Supermen; ...When He Was a Boy • ▲1993-15 **A:** Tom Grummettt **W:** Karl Kesel ★ 1st Appearance of Superboy (clone).

501/SC ❑ Jun 1993 Cover: 1.95 **NM** value: **2.00**
Circ: CapCity orders: **403,350** • **CGC:** 1 graded, best 9.2
Die-cut cover.

502 ❑ Jul 1993 Cover: 1.50 **NM** value: **1.75**
Circ: CapCity orders: **121,950**
🕮 Boy Meets Girl • ▲1993-19 **A:** Tom Grummettt **W:** Karl Kesel ★ Appearance of Supergirl.

503 ❑ Aug 1993 Cover: 1.50 **NM** value: **1.75**
Circ: CapCity orders: **109,750**
• Superboy vs. Cyborg

504 ❑ Sep 1993 Cover: 1.50 **NM** value: **1.75**
Circ: CapCity orders: **89,050**

505 ❑ Oct 1993 Cover: 1.50 **NM** value: **1.75**
🕮 Reign Of The Superman • ▲1993-31 **A:** Tom Grummettt **W:** Karl Kesel

505/SC ❑ Oct 1993 Cover: 2.50 **NM** value: **Cover or less**
Circ: CapCity orders: **175,200** • **CGC:** 2 graded, best 9.2
🕮 Reign Of The Superman **A:** Tom Grummettt **W:** Karl Kesel

506 ❑ Nov 1993 Cover: 1.50 **NM** value: **Cover or less**
Circ: CapCity orders: **80,750**

507 ❑ Dec 1993 Cover: 1.50 **NM** value: **Cover or less**
Circ: CapCity orders: **82,650**
★ Versus Bloodsport.

508 ❑ Jan 1994 Cover: 1.50 **NM** value: **Cover or less**
Circ: CapCity orders: **79,300**
• Challengers

509 ❑ Feb 1994 Cover: 1.50 **NM** value: **Cover or less**
Circ: CapCity orders: **75,750**
★ Appearance of Auron.

510 ❑ Mar 1994 Cover: 1.50 **NM** value: **Cover or less**
Circ: CapCity orders: **64,900**
🕮 Bizarro's World, Part 2 • Bizarro

511 ❑ Apr 1994 Cover: 1.50 **NM** value: **Cover or less**
Circ: CapCity orders: **58,000**
★ Appearance of Guardian.

512 ❑ May 1994 Cover: 1.50 **NM** value: **Cover or less**
Circ: CapCity orders: **54,100**
★ Appearance of Guardian. ★ Versus Parasite.

513 ❑ Jun 1994 Cover: 1.50 **NM** value: **Cover or less**
Circ: CapCity orders: **56,350**
🕮 The Battle For Metropolis • ▲1994-23 **A:** Barry Kitson **W:** Karl Kesel; Barry Kitson

514 ❑ Jul 1994 Cover: 1.50 **NM** value: **Cover or less**
Circ: CapCity orders: **55,450**
🕮 Fall of Metropolis

515 ❑ Aug 1994 Cover: 1.50 **NM** value: **Cover or less**
Circ: CapCity orders: **51,300**
🕮 Massacre in Metropolis, Part 2 ★ Versus Massacre.

516 ❑ Sep 1994 Cover: 1.50 **NM** value: **Cover or less**
Circ: CapCity orders: **52,850**
• "Zero Hour" ★ Appearance of Alpha Centurion.

517 ❑ Nov 1994 Cover: 1.50 **NM** value: **Cover or less**
Circ: CapCity orders: **45,200**
🕮 Dead Again

518 ❑ Dec 1994 Cover: 1.50 **NM** value: **Cover or less**
Circ: CapCity orders: **44,150**
🕮 Dead Again ★ Appearance of Darkseid.

519 ❑ Jan 1995 Cover: 1.50 **NM** value: **Cover or less**
Circ: CapCity orders: **42,500**
🕮 Dead Again • Dead Again;▲1995-3 **A:** Barry Kitson **W:** Karl Kesel ★ Versus Brainiac.

520 ❑ Feb 1995 Cover: 1.50 **NM** value: **Cover or less**
Circ: CapCity orders: **39,925**
★ Appearance of Thorn.

521 ❑ Mar 1995 Cover: 1.50 **NM** value: **Cover or less**
Circ: CapCity orders: **37,475**
★ Appearance of Thorn.

522 ❑ Apr 1995 Cover: 1.50 **NM** value: **Cover or less**
Circ: CapCity orders: **35,425**
• Return of Metropolis

523 ❑ May 1995 Cover: 1.50 **NM** value: **Cover or less**
Circ: CapCity orders: **46,050**
🕮 Death of Clark Kent

524 ❑ Jun 1995 Cover: 1.95 **NM** value: **2.00**
Circ: CapCity orders: **40,500**
🕮 Where is Superman?

525 ❑ Jul 1995 Cover: 1.95 **NM** value: **2.00**
Circ: CapCity orders: **34,475**

526 ❑ Aug 1995 Cover: 1.95 **NM** value: **2.00**
Circ: CapCity orders: **33,375**
• Bloodsport vs. Bloodsport

527 ❑ Sep 1995 Cover: 1.95 **NM** value: **2.00**
Circ: CapCity orders: **31,925**
• Alpha-Centurion returns

528 ❑ Oct 1995 Cover: 1.95 **NM** value: **2.00**
Circ: CapCity orders: **26,725**

529 ❑ Nov 1995 Cover: 1.95 **NM** value: **2.00**
🕮 Trial of Superman

530 ❑ Dec 1995 Cover: 1.95 **NM** value: **2.00**
• SCU vs. Hellgrammite;"Trial of Superman/Underworld Unleashed"

531 ❑ Jan 1996 Cover: 1.95 **NM** value: **2.00**
🕮 Justice! • Cyborg Superman sentenced to a black hole;▲1996-4 **A:** Stuart Immonen **W:** Karl Kesel

532 ❑ Feb 1996 Cover: 1.95 **NM** value: **2.00**
🕮 Troubled Waters • Return of Lori Lemaris;▲1996-8 **A:** Stuart Immonen **W:** Karl Kesel

533 ❑ Mar 1996 Cover: 1.95 **NM** value: **2.00**
🕮 Scavenger Hunt • ▲1996-12 **A:** Stuart Immonen **W:** Karl Kesel ★ Appearance of Impulse.

534 ❑ May 1996 Cover: 1.95 **NM** value: **2.00**

535 ❑ Jun 1996 Cover: 1.95 **NM** value: **2.00**

536 ❑ Jul 1996 Cover: 1.95 **NM** value: **2.00**
• Brainiac takes over Superman's body

537 ❑ Aug 1996 Cover: 1.95 **NM** value: **2.00**

538 ❑ Sep 1996 Cover: 1.95 **NM** value: **2.00**
• Clark Kent named acting managing editor;Perry White has cancer

539 ❑ Oct 1996 Cover: 1.95 **NM** value: **2.00**
🕮 Doppelgangster **A:** Ron Lim **W:** Karl Kesel; Jerry Ordway ★ Origin of Anomaly. ★ 1st Appearance of Anomaly.

540 ❑ Nov 1996 Cover: 1.95 **NM** value: **2.00**
Circ: Diamd. preorders: **63,489**
🕮 Curtain Call • "Final Night";▲1996-43 **A:** Terry Dodson **W:** Karl Kesel; Jerry Ordway ★ 1st Appearance of Ferro.

541 ❑ Dec 1996 Cover: 1.95 **NM** value: **2.00**
Circ: Direct Market orders: **94,258**
🕮 Hawaiian Honeymoon; Happily Ever After • Clark shot by terrorists **A:** Stuart Immonen **W:** Karl Kesel ★ Appearance of Superboy.

542 ❑ Jan 1997 Cover: 1.95 **NM** value: **2.00**
Circ: Direct Market orders: **61,142**
🕮 Power Struggle; Power Trip! **A:** Denis Rodier; Paul Ryan **W:** Karl Kesel

543 ❑ Feb 1997 Cover: 1.95 **NM** value: **2.00**
Circ: Diamd. preorders: **56,135**
★ Versus Superman Revenge Squad.

544 ❑ Mar 1997 Cover: 1.95 **NM** value: **2.00**
Circ: Diamd. preorders: **54,236**
🕮 Dead Men Walking • return of Intergang;▲1997-11 **A:** Stuart Immonen **W:** Karl Kesel

545 ❑ Apr 1997 Cover: 1.95 **NM** value: **2.00**
Circ: Diamd. preorders: **52,774**
• energy powers begin ★ Versus Metallo.

546 ❑ May 1997 Cover: 1.95 **NM** value: **2.00**
Circ: Diamd. preorders: **100,614**
• new uniform ★ Versus Metallo.

547 ❑ Jun 1997 Cover: 1.95 **NM** value: **2.00**
Circ: Diamd. preorders: **73,951**
🕮 In Kandor ★ Appearance of Atom.

548 ❑ Jul 1997 Cover: 1.95 **NM** value: **2.00**
Circ: Diamd. preorders: **69,801**
★ Appearance of Phantom Stranger.

549 ❑ Aug 1997 Cover: 1.95 **NM** value: **2.00**
Circ: Diamd. preorders: **68,454**
★ Appearance of Newsboy Legion, Dingbats of Danger Street.

550 ❑ Sep 1997 Cover: 1.95 **NM** value: **3.50**
Circ: Diamd. preorders: **66,637**
• Jimmy's special airs

551 ❑ Oct 1997 Cover: 1.95 **NM** value: **Cover or less**
Circ: Diamd. preorders: **65,361**
★ Versus Cyborg Superman.

552 ❑ Nov 1997 Cover: 1.95 **NM** value: **Cover or less**
Circ: Diamd. preorders: **59,737**
🕮 Control of Power • ▲1997-45 **A:** Denis Rodier; Tom Grummett **W:** Karl Kesel ★ Versus Parasite.

553 ❑ Dec 1997 Cover: 1.95 **NM** value: **Cover or less**
Circ: Diamd. preorders: **58,039**
Face cover. 🕮 Energy Crisis **A:** Denis Rodier; Tom Grummett **W:** Karl Kesel

554 ❑ Dec 1997 Cover: 1.95 **NM** value: **Cover or less**
Circ: Diamd. preorders: **55,734**
★ Versus Ripper.

555 ❑ Feb 1998 Cover: 1.95 **NM** value: **Cover or less**
Circ: Diamd. preorders: **61,497**
• Superman Red vs. Superman Blue

556 ❑ Apr 1998 Cover: 1.95 **NM** value: **Cover or less**
Circ: Diamd. preorders: **50,059**

CGC-graded: Multiply prices above by **33 for 9.9 M • 16 for 9.8 NM/M • 7 for 9.6 NM+ • 5 for 9.4 NM • 2.5 for 9.2 NM- • 1.5 for 9.0 VF/NM**

🕮 Three to One!; I Was Alone Against Gargox, a Really Big Monster • ▲1998-13 **A:** Denis Rodier; Ron Frenz; Tom Grummett **W:** Karl Kesel ★ Versus Millennium Guard.
557 ❑ May 1998 Cover: 1.95 **NM** value: **Cover or less**
Circ: Diamd. preorders: **53,095**
• Millennium Giants
558 ❑ Jun 1998 Cover: 1.95 **NM** value: **Cover or less**
Circ: Diamd. preorders: **59,169**
• set in Silver Age
559 ❑ Jul 1998 Cover: 1.95 **NM** value: **Cover or less**
Circ: Diamd. preorders: **52,851**
• set in Silver Age
560 ❑ Aug 1998 Cover: 1.95 **NM** value: **Cover or less**
Circ: Diamd. preorders: **52,684**
• set in Silver Age ★ Appearance of Kismet.
561 ❑ Sep 1998 Cover: 1.99 **NM** value: **2.00**
Circ: Diamd. preorders: **49,631**
★ Versus Dominus.
562 ❑ Oct 1998 Cover: 1.99 **NM** value: **2.00**
Circ: Diamd. preorders: **47,463**
• Daily Planet closed ★ Death of "Machine" Gunn, Torcher.
563 ❑ Dec 1998 Cover: 1.99 **NM** value: **2.00**
Circ: Diamd. preorders: **46,738**
• in Kandor ★ Versus Cyborg.
564 ❑ Feb 1999 Cover: 1.99 **NM** value: **2.00**
Circ: Diamd. preorders: **43,077**
A: Tom Grummett **W:** Karl Kesel; Jerry Ordway ★ Appearance of Geo-Force.
565 ❑ Mar 1999 Cover: 1.99 **NM** value: **2.00**
Circ: Diamd. preorders: **42,497**
A: Tom Grummett **W:** Karl Kesel; Jerry Ordway ★ Appearance of D.E.O. agents, Justice League of America, Captain Boomerang, Metropolis Special Crimes Unit, Captain Cold.
566 ❑ Apr 1999 Cover: 1.99 **NM** value: **2.00**
Circ: Diamd. preorders: **39,836**
A: Tom Grummett **W:** Karl Kesel; Jerry Ordway ★ Appearance of Lex Luthor.
567 ❑ May 1999 Cover: 1.99 **NM** value: **2.00**
Circ: Diamd. preorders: **39,221**
🕮 The Pathway to Oblivion • Lois' robot guardian returns; ▲1999-19 **A:** Denis Rodier; Paul Ryan **W:** Karl Kesel; Jerry Ordway
568 ❑ Jun 1999 Cover: 1.99 **NM** value: **2.00**
Circ: Diamd. preorders: **40,535**
🕮 Lookin' Good • ▲1999-24 **A:** Denis Rodier; Tom Morgan **W:** Louise Simonson
569 ❑ Jul 1999 Cover: 1.99 **NM** value: **2.00**
Circ: Diamd. preorders: **40,161**
🕮 Power • SCU forms meta-unit; ▲1999-28 **A:** Tom Morgan **W:** Louise Simonson
570 ❑ Sep 1999 Cover: 1.99 **NM** value: **2.00**
Circ: Diamd. preorders: **40,473**
🕮 One-Man JLA; The Invader from Earth • Superman as protector of Rann **A:** Tom Grindberg **W:** Ron Marz; Tom Peyer
571 ❑ Oct 1999 Cover: 1.99 **NM** value: **2.00**
Circ: Diamd. preorders: **37,349**
🕮 Image is Everything **A:** Mike Collins **W:** Louise Simonson ★ Versus Atomic Skull.
572 ❑ Nov 1999 Cover: 1.99 **NM** value: **2.00**
Circ: Diamd. preorders: **37,577**
🕮 Who is Strange Visitor, Part 2 • ▲1999-41 **A:** Sal Buscema; Ron Frenz; Rand Frenz **W:** Ron Frenz; Rand Frenz ★ Appearance of Strange Visitor. ★ Versus War.
573 ❑ Dec 1999 Cover: 1.99 **NM** value: **2.00**
Circ: Diamd. preorders: **39,700**
🕮 Higher Ground • ▲1999-47 **A:** Steve Epting **W:** Stuart Immonen; Mark Millar
574 ❑ Jan 2000 Cover: 1.99 **NM** value: **2.00**
Circ: Diamd. preorders: **36,811**
🕮 Something Borrowed, Something Blue • ▲2000-2 **A:** Joe Phillips **W:** Stuart Immonen; Mark Millar
575 ❑ Feb 2000 Cover: 1.99 **NM** value: **2.00**
Circ: Diamd. preorders: **36,841**
🕮 A Night at the Opera • ▲2000-6 **A:** Yanick Paquette **W:** Stuart Immonen; Mark Millar
576 ❑ Mar 2000 Cover: 1.99 **NM** value: **2.00**
Circ: Diamd. preorders: **37,454**
577 ❑ Apr 2000 Cover: 1.99 **NM** value: **2.00**
Circ: Diamd. preorders: **35,895**
578 ❑ May 2000 Cover: 1.99 **NM** value: **2.00**
Circ: Diamd. preorders: **37,475**
🕮 Getting Away From it All • ▲2000-19 **A:** Pablo Raimondi **W:** J.M. DeMatteis
579 ❑ Jun 2000 Cover: 1.99 **NM** value: **2.00**
Circ: Diamd. preorders: **37,826**
🕮 Pranked! • ▲2000-23 **A:** Mike McKone **W:** J.M. DeMatteis
580 ❑ Jul 2000 Cover: 1.99 **NM** value: **2.00**
Circ: Diamd. preorders: **37,997**
• ▲2000-27
581 ❑ Aug 2000 Cover: 2.25 **NM** value: **Cover or less**
Circ: Diamd. preorders: **38,420**
🕮 Adversaries! • ▲2000-31; Lex Luthor announces candidacy for President **A:** Jose Marzan Jr.; Walden Wong; Mike Miller **W:** J.M. DeMatteis ★ Versus Adversary.
582 ❑ Sep 2000 Cover: 2.25 **NM** value: **Cover or less**
Circ: Diamd. preorders: **43,316**
🕮 Superman: Arkham, Part 2; Crazy About You • ▲2000-35 **A:** Mike Miller **W:** J.M. DeMatteis
583 ❑ Oct 2000 Cover: 2.25 **NM** value: **Cover or less**
Circ: Diamd. preorders: **39,605**
🕮 The Reign of Emperor Joker, Part 2; Life is But a (Very Bad) Dream • ▲2000-40 **A:** Mike Miller **W:** J.M. DeMatteis
584 ❑ Nov 2000 Cover: 2.25 **NM** value: **Cover or less**
Circ: Diamd. preorders: **38,048**
🕮 Bachelor Party • ▲2000-44 **A:** Patrick Zircher **W:** J.M. DeMatteis ★ 1st Appearance of Devouris the Conqueror. ★ Appearance of Lord Satanus.
585 ❑ Dec 2000 Cover: 2.25 **NM** value: **Cover or less**
Circ: Diamd. preorders: **38,733**
🕮 Doubles • ▲2000-48 **A:** Mike Miller; Mike McKone **W:** J.M. DeMatteis ★ Appearance of Rampage, Adversary, Thorn, Prankster.
586 ❑ Jan 2001 Cover: 2.25 **NM** value: **Cover or less**
Circ: Diamd. preorders: **37,510**
🕮 Soul of the City • ▲2000-52 **A:** Mike Miller **W:** J.M. DeMatteis
587 ❑ Feb 2001 Cover: 2.25 **NM** value: **Cover or less**
Circ: Diamd. preorders: **35,704**
🕮 Metropolis: Hell of a Town! • ▲2001-7 **A:** Mike Miller **W:** Joe Casey; J.M. DeMatteis
588 ❑ Mar 2001 Cover: 2.25 **NM** value: **Cover or less**
Circ: Diamd. preorders: **35,147**
🕮 Pillar of Earth • ▲2001-11 **A:** Mike Miller **W:** Joe Casey
589 ❑ Apr 2001 Cover: 2.25 **NM** value: **Cover or less**
Circ: Diamd. preorders: **37,251**
🕮 Return to Krypton, Part 2 • ▲2001-15 **A:** Joe Casey **W:** Second Honeymoon
590 ❑ May 2001 Cover: 2.25 **NM** value: **Cover or less**
Circ: Diamd. preorders: **34,278**
🕮 Don't Cry for me, Bialya • ▲2001-19 **A:** Derec Aucoin **W:** Joe Casey
591 ❑ Jun 2001 Cover: 2.25 **NM** value: **Cover or less**
Circ: Diamd. preorders: **36,990**
🕮 Infestation, Part 2 • ▲2001-23 **A:** Paco Medina **W:** Marv Wolfman
592 ❑ Jul 2001 Cover: 2.25 **NM** value: **Cover or less**
Circ: Diamd. preorders: **38,102**
593 ❑ Aug 2001 Cover: 2.25 **NM** value: **Cover or less**
Circ: Diamd. preorders: **45,864**
594 ❑ Sep 2001 Cover: 2.25 **NM** value: **Cover or less**
Circ: Diamd. preorders: **48,812** • **CGC:** 2 graded, best 9.8
1000000 ❑ Nov 1998 Cover: 1.99 **NM** value: **2.00**
Circ: Diamd. preorders: **55,724**
🕮 Keepers of Solitude **A:** Will Rosado **W:** Andy Lanning; Dan Abnett ★ Appearance of Resurrection Man.
Anl 1 ❑ Sep 1987 Cover: 1.25 **NM** value: **3.00**
Circ: CapCity orders: **22,250**
Anl 2 ❑ Aug 1990 Cover: 2.00 **NM** value: **3.00**
Circ: CapCity orders: **18,950**
• L.E.G.I.O.N. '90 **A:** John Byrne
Anl 3 ❑ Oct 1991 Cover: 2.00 **NM** value: **3.00**
Circ: CapCity orders: **43,500**
🕮 Armageddon 2001, Part 11 • Armageddon 2001
Anl 4 ❑ ca. 1992 Cover: 2.50 **NM** value: **3.00**
Circ: CapCity orders: **26,300**
🕮 Eclipso: The Darkness Within, Part 19 • Eclipso
Anl 5 ❑ ca. 1993 Cover: 2.50 **NM** value: **3.00**
Circ: CapCity orders: **42,100**
🕮 Bloodlines • Bloodlines ★ 1st Appearance of Sparx.
Anl 6 ❑ ca. 1994 Cover: 2.95 **NM** value: **Cover or less**
Circ: CapCity orders: **36,000**
🕮 The Super Seven • concludes in Superboy Annual #1 (1994); Elseworlds **A:** Brock L. Hor **W:** Karl Kesel
Anl 7 ❑ ca. 1995 Cover: 3.95 **NM** value: **Cover or less**
Circ: CapCity orders: **23,825**
• Year One ★ Versus Kalibak.
Anl 8 ❑ ca. 1996 Cover: 2.95 **NM** value: **Cover or less**
• Elseworlds; Legends of the Dead Earth **W:** John Rozum
Anl 9 ❑ Sep 1997 Cover: 3.95 **NM** value: **Cover or less**
Circ: Diamd. preorders: **48,369**
🕮 Terror of the Sierra Madre • Pulp Heroes **A:** Enrique Alcatena **W:** John Rozum

ADVENTURES OF TAD MARTIN, THE — Caliber

1 ❑ Cover: 2.50 **NM** value: **Cover or less**

ADVENTURES OF THE BIG BOY — WEBS Group

Created for the Elias Brothers chain of restaurants, Big Boy remains the most recognizable giveaway comics star of all time. Developed by advertising guru Manfred Bernhard, the early issues featuring the amiable (if a bit too well-fed) kid were farmed out to Timely, where Stan Lee and Bill Everett worked on them. Puzzles, games, and menus rounded out the offerings.

In the late 1970s, Bernhard's WEBS Advertising Group arranged for special issues featuring Superman, Battlestar Galactica, and other media favorites.

In 1996, the Elias chain dropped Bernhard's production company after 466 issues. Craig Yoe's Yoe Studios revamped the series, with slicker paper and even more media guests — and, surprisingly, an issue drawn by Steve Ditko.

Solidly part of Americana, many people collect all kinds of Big Boy merchandise, including the comics. Since different parts of the Elias chain had different names, the same issue may be found with many different regional variants. We have noticed no difference in price. A separate series with different content and numbering came from the Shoney's chain in the late 1970s and early 1980s following its separation from the Elias chain; it ran nearly 70 issues. — JJM

1 ❑ ca. 1956 Cover: 0.10 **NM** value: **750.00**
A: Bill Everett **W:** Stan Lee
2 ❑ ca. 1956 Cover: 0.10 **NM** value: **295.00**
3 ❑ **NM** value: **125.00**
4 ❑ **NM** value: **80.00**
5 ❑ **NM** value: **65.00**
6 ❑ **NM** value: **45.00**
7 ❑ **NM** value: **45.00**
8 ❑ **NM** value: **40.00**
9 ❑ **NM** value: **40.00**
10 ❑ **NM** value: **40.00**
11 ❑ **NM** value: **28.00**
12 ❑ **NM** value: **28.00**
13 ❑ **NM** value: **28.00**
14 ❑ **NM** value: **28.00**
15 ❑ **NM** value: **28.00**
16 ❑ **NM** value: **20.00**
17 ❑ **NM** value: **20.00**
18 ❑ **NM** value: **20.00**
19 ❑ **NM** value: **20.00**
20 ❑ **NM** value: **20.00**
21 ❑ **NM** value: **14.00**
22 ❑ **NM** value: **14.00**
23 ❑ **NM** value: **14.00**
24 ❑ **NM** value: **14.00**
25 ❑ **NM** value: **14.00**
26 ❑ **NM** value: **10.00**
27 ❑ **NM** value: **10.00**
28 ❑ **NM** value: **10.00**
29 ❑ **NM** value: **10.00**
30 ❑ **NM** value: **10.00**
31 ❑ **NM** value: **6.00**
32 ❑ **NM** value: **6.00**
33 ❑ **NM** value: **6.00**
34 ❑ ca. 1959 **NM** value: **6.00**
🕮 The Pleasant Secret; The Great Train Robbery; Invitation to the Dance • No creator credits listed
35 ❑ **NM** value: **6.00**
36 ❑ **NM** value: **6.00**
37 ❑ **NM** value: **6.00**
38 ❑ **NM** value: **6.00**
39 ❑ **NM** value: **6.00**
40 ❑ **NM** value: **6.00**
41 ❑ **NM** value: **4.00**
42 ❑ **NM** value: **4.00**
43 ❑ **NM** value: **4.00**
44 ❑ **NM** value: **4.00**
45 ❑ **NM** value: **4.00**
46 ❑ **NM** value: **4.00**
47 ❑ **NM** value: **4.00**
48 ❑ **NM** value: **4.00**
49 ❑ **NM** value: **4.00**
50 ❑ **NM** value: **4.00**
51 ❑ **NM** value: **3.00**
52 ❑ **NM** value: **3.00**
53 ❑ **NM** value: **3.00**
54 ❑ 1961 **NM** value: **3.00**
55 ❑ 1961 **NM** value: **3.00**
56 ❑ 1961 **NM** value: **3.00**
57 ❑ Jan 1962 **NM** value: **3.00**
58 ❑ Feb 1962 **NM** value: **3.00**
59 ❑ Mar 1962 **NM** value: **3.00**
60 ❑ Apr 1962 **NM** value: **3.00**
61 ❑ May 1962 **NM** value: **3.00**
62 ❑ Jun 1962 **NM** value: **3.00**
63 ❑ Jul 1962 **NM** value: **3.00**
64 ❑ Aug 1962 **NM** value: **3.00**
65 ❑ Sep 1962 **NM** value: **3.00**
66 ❑ Oct 1962 **NM** value: **3.00**
67 ❑ Nov 1962 **NM** value: **3.00**
68 ❑ Dec 1962 **NM** value: **3.00**
69 ❑ Jan 1963 **NM** value: **3.00**
70 ❑ Feb 1963 **NM** value: **3.00**
71 ❑ Mar 1963 **NM** value: **3.00**
72 ❑ Apr 1963 **NM** value: **3.00**
73 ❑ May 1963 **NM** value: **3.00**
74 ❑ Jun 1963 **NM** value: **3.00**
75 ❑ Jul 1963 **NM** value: **3.00**
76 ❑ Aug 1963 **NM** value: **3.00**
77 ❑ Sep 1963 **NM** value: **3.00**
78 ❑ Oct 1963 **NM** value: **3.00**
79 ❑ Nov 1963 **NM** value: **3.00**
80 ❑ Dec 1963 **NM** value: **3.00**
81 ❑ Jan 1964 **NM** value: **3.00**
82 ❑ Feb 1964 **NM** value: **3.00**
83 ❑ Mar 1964 **NM** value: **3.00**
84 ❑ Apr 1964 **NM** value: **3.00**
85 ❑ May 1964 **NM** value: **3.00**
86 ❑ Jun 1964 **NM** value: **3.00**
87 ❑ Jul 1964 **NM** value: **3.00**
88 ❑ Aug 1964 **NM** value: **3.00**
89 ❑ Sep 1964 **NM** value: **3.00**
90 ❑ Oct 1964 **NM** value: **3.00**
91 ❑ Nov 1964 **NM** value: **3.00**
92 ❑ Dec 1964 **NM** value: **3.00**
93 ❑ Jan 1965 **NM** value: **3.00**
94 ❑ Feb 1965 **NM** value: **3.00**
95 ❑ Mar 1965 **NM** value: **3.00**
96 ❑ Apr 1965 **NM** value: **3.00**
97 ❑ May 1965 **NM** value: **3.00**
98 ❑ Jun 1965 **NM** value: **3.00**
99 ❑ Jul 1965 **NM** value: **3.00**
100 ❑ Aug 1965 **NM** value: **3.00**
101 ❑ Sep 1965 **NM** value: **2.50**
102 ❑ Oct 1965 **NM** value: **2.50**
103 ❑ Nov 1965 **NM** value: **2.50**
104 ❑ Dec 1965 **NM** value: **2.50**
105 ❑ Jan 1966 **NM** value: **2.50**
106 ❑ Feb 1966 **NM** value: **2.50**
107 ❑ Mar 1966 **NM** value: **2.50**
108 ❑ Apr 1966 **NM** value: **2.50**
109 ❑ May 1966 **NM** value: **2.50**
110 ❑ Jun 1966 **NM** value: **2.50**
111 ❑ Jul 1966 **NM** value: **2.50**
112 ❑ Aug 1966 **NM** value: **2.50**
113 ❑ Sep 1966 **NM** value: **2.50**
114 ❑ Oct 1966 **NM** value: **2.50**
115 ❑ Nov 1966 **NM** value: **2.50**
116 ❑ Dec 1966 **NM** value: **2.50**
117 ❑ Jan 1967 **NM** value: **2.50**

Other grades: Multiply prices above by **1.5 for Mint • 2/3 for Very Fine • 1/3 for Fine • 1/5 for Very Good • 1/8 for Good**

118 ❑ Feb 1967 NM value: 2.50
119 ❑ Mar 1967 NM value: 2.50
120 ❑ Apr 1967 NM value: 2.50
121 ❑ May 1967 NM value: 2.50
122 ❑ Jun 1967 NM value: 2.50
123 ❑ Jul 1967 NM value: 2.50
124 ❑ Aug 1967 NM value: 2.50
125 ❑ Sep 1967 NM value: 2.50
126 ❑ Oct 1967 NM value: 2.50
127 ❑ Nov 1967 NM value: 2.50
128 ❑ Dec 1967 NM value: 2.50
129 ❑ Jan 1968 NM value: 2.50
130 ❑ Feb 1968 NM value: 2.50
131 ❑ Mar 1968 NM value: 2.50
132 ❑ Apr 1968 NM value: 2.50
133 ❑ May 1968 NM value: 2.50
134 ❑ Jun 1968 NM value: 2.50
135 ❑ Jul 1968 NM value: 2.50
136 ❑ Aug 1968 NM value: 2.50
137 ❑ Sep 1968 NM value: 2.50
The Case of the Kidnapped Kids, Part 1
138 ❑ Oct 1968 NM value: 2.50
The Case of the Kidnapped Kids, Part 2
139 ❑ Nov 1968 NM value: 2.50
140 ❑ Dec 1968 NM value: 2.50
The South Pole Mystery
141 ❑ Jan 1969 NM value: 2.50
142 ❑ Feb 1969 NM value: 2.50
143 ❑ Mar 1969 NM value: 2.50
144 ❑ Apr 1969 NM value: 2.50
145 ❑ May 1969 NM value: 2.50
146 ❑ Jun 1969 NM value: 2.50
147 ❑ Jul 1969 NM value: 2.50
148 ❑ Aug 1969 NM value: 2.50
149 ❑ Sep 1969 NM value: 2.50
150 ❑ Oct 1969 NM value: 2.50
151 ❑ Nov 1969 NM value: 2.50
152 ❑ Dec 1969 NM value: 2.50
153 ❑ Jan 1970 NM value: 2.50
154 ❑ Feb 1970 NM value: 2.50
155 ❑ Mar 1970 NM value: 2.50
156 ❑ Apr 1970 NM value: 2.50
157 ❑ May 1970 NM value: 2.50
158 ❑ Jun 1970 NM value: 2.50
159 ❑ Jul 1970 NM value: 2.50
160 ❑ Aug 1970 NM value: 2.50
161 ❑ Sep 1970 NM value: 2.50
162 ❑ Oct 1970 NM value: 2.50
163 ❑ Nov 1970 NM value: 2.50
164 ❑ Dec 1970 NM value: 2.50
165 ❑ Jan 1971 NM value: 2.50
166 ❑ Feb 1971 NM value: 2.50
167 ❑ Mar 1971 NM value: 2.50
168 ❑ Apr 1971 NM value: 2.50
169 ❑ May 1971 NM value: 2.50
170 ❑ Jun 1971 NM value: 2.50
171 ❑ Jul 1971 NM value: 2.50
172 ❑ Aug 1971 NM value: 2.50
173 ❑ Sep 1971 NM value: 2.50
174 ❑ Oct 1971 NM value: 2.50
• Has art contest
175 ❑ Nov 1971 NM value: 2.50
176 ❑ Dec 1971 NM value: 2.50
177 ❑ Jan 1972 NM value: 2.50
178 ❑ Feb 1972 NM value: 2.50
179 ❑ Mar 1972 NM value: 2.50
180 ❑ Apr 1972 NM value: 2.50
181 ❑ May 1972 NM value: 2.50
182 ❑ Jun 1972 NM value: 2.50
183 ❑ Jul 1972 NM value: 2.50
184 ❑ Aug 1972 NM value: 2.50
185 ❑ Sep 1972 NM value: 2.50
186 ❑ Oct 1972 NM value: 2.50
187 ❑ Nov 1972 NM value: 2.50
188 ❑ Dec 1972 NM value: 2.50
189 ❑ Jan 1973 NM value: 2.50
190 ❑ Feb 1973 NM value: 2.50
191 ❑ Mar 1973 NM value: 2.50
192 ❑ Apr 1973 NM value: 2.50
193 ❑ May 1973 NM value: 2.50
194 ❑ Jun 1973 NM value: 2.50
195 ❑ Jul 1973 NM value: 2.50
196 ❑ Aug 1973 NM value: 2.50
197 ❑ Sep 1973 NM value: 2.50
198 ❑ Oct 1973 NM value: 2.50
199 ❑ Nov 1973 NM value: 2.50
200 ❑ Dec 1973 NM value: 2.50
201 ❑ Jan 1974 NM value: 2.00
202 ❑ Feb 1974 NM value: 2.00
203 ❑ Mar 1974 NM value: 2.00
204 ❑ Apr 1974 NM value: 2.00
Trouble at Sea; Prepared for Everything Except...; So What's a Friend For? **A:** Uncred. **W:** Uncred.
205 ❑ May 1974 NM value: 2.00
206 ❑ Jun 1974 NM value: 2.00
207 ❑ Jul 1974 NM value: 2.00
208 ❑ Aug 1974 NM value: 2.00
209 ❑ Sep 1974 NM value: 2.00
210 ❑ Oct 1974 NM value: 2.00
211 ❑ Nov 1974 NM value: 2.00
The Phantom Thief; On the Front Page • Salute to Arizona; no creator credits listed
212 ❑ Dec 1974 NM value: 2.00
213 ❑ Jan 1975 NM value: 2.00
214 ❑ Feb 1975 NM value: 2.00
215 ❑ Mar 1975 NM value: 2.00
216 ❑ Apr 1975 NM value: 2.00
217 ❑ May 1975 NM value: 2.00
218 ❑ Jun 1975 NM value: 2.00
219 ❑ Jul 1975 NM value: 2.00
220 ❑ Aug 1975 NM value: 2.00
221 ❑ Sep 1975 NM value: 2.00
222 ❑ Oct 1975 NM value: 2.00
223 ❑ Nov 1975 NM value: 2.00
224 ❑ Dec 1975 NM value: 2.00
225 ❑ Jan 1976 NM value: 2.00
226 ❑ Feb 1976 NM value: 2.00
• Has special Bicentennial page
227 ❑ Mar 1976 NM value: 2.00
228 ❑ Apr 1976 NM value: 2.00
229 ❑ May 1976 NM value: 2.00
230 ❑ Jun 1976 NM value: 2.00
231 ❑ Jul 1976 NM value: 2.00
232 ❑ Aug 1976 NM value: 2.00
233 ❑ Sep 1976 NM value: 2.00
234 ❑ Oct 1976 NM value: 2.00
235 ❑ Jan 1976 NM value: 2.00
236 ❑ Dec 1976 NM value: 2.00
237 ❑ Jan 1977 NM value: 2.00
238 ❑ Feb 1977 NM value: 2.00
239 ❑ Mar 1977 NM value: 2.00
240 ❑ Apr 1977 NM value: 2.00
241 ❑ May 1977 NM value: 2.00
242 ❑ Jun 1977 NM value: 2.00
243 ❑ Jul 1977 NM value: 2.00
244 ❑ Aug 1977 NM value: 2.00
245 ❑ Sep 1977 NM value: 2.00
246 ❑ Oct 1977 NM value: 2.00
247 ❑ Nov 1977 NM value: 2.00
248 ❑ Dec 1977 NM value: 2.00
249 ❑ Jan 1978 NM value: 2.00
250 ❑ Feb 1978 NM value: 2.00
251 ❑ Mar 1978 NM value: 2.00
252 ❑ Apr 1978 NM value: 2.00
253 ❑ May 1978 NM value: 2.00
254 ❑ Jun 1978 NM value: 2.00
255 ❑ Jul 1978 NM value: 2.00
256 ❑ Aug 1978 NM value: 2.00
257 ❑ Sep 1978 NM value: 2.00
258 ❑ Oct 1978 NM value: 2.00
259 ❑ Nov 1978 NM value: 2.00
260 ❑ Dec 1978 NM value: 2.00
261 ❑ Jan 1979 NM value: 2.00
262 ❑ Feb 1979 NM value: 2.00
263 ❑ Mar 1979 NM value: 2.00
264 ❑ Apr 1979 NM value: 2.00
265 ❑ May 1979 NM value: 2.00
266 ❑ Jun 1979 NM value: 2.00
267 ❑ Jul 1979 NM value: 10.00
• Battlestar Galactica contest and story
268 ❑ Aug 1979 NM value: 2.00
269 ❑ Sep 1979 NM value: 2.00
270 ❑ Oct 1979 NM value: 2.00
271 ❑ Nov 1979 NM value: 2.00
272 ❑ Dec 1979 NM value: 2.00
273 ❑ Jan 1980 NM value: 2.00
274 ❑ Feb 1980 NM value: 2.00
275 ❑ Mar 1980 NM value: 2.00
276 ❑ Apr 1980 NM value: 2.00
277 ❑ May 1980 NM value: 2.00
278 ❑ Jun 1980 NM value: 2.00
279 ❑ Jul 1980 NM value: 2.00
280 ❑ Aug 1980 NM value: 2.00
281 ❑ Sep 1980 NM value: 2.00
282 ❑ Oct 1980 NM value: 2.00
283 ❑ Nov 1980 NM value: 2.00
284 ❑ Dec 1980 NM value: 2.00
285 ❑ Jan 1981 NM value: 2.00
286 ❑ Feb 1981 NM value: 2.00
287 ❑ Mar 1981 NM value: 2.00
288 ❑ Apr 1981 NM value: 2.00
289 ❑ May 1981 NM value: 2.00
290 ❑ Jun 1981 NM value: 2.00
291 ❑ Jul 1981 NM value: 2.00
292 ❑ Aug 1981 NM value: 2.00
293 ❑ Sep 1981 NM value: 2.00
294 ❑ Oct 1981 NM value: 2.00
295 ❑ Nov 1981 NM value: 2.00
296 ❑ Dec 1981 NM value: 2.00
297 ❑ Jan 1982 NM value: 2.00
298 ❑ Feb 1982 NM value: 2.00
299 ❑ Mar 1982 NM value: 2.00
300 ❑ Apr 1982 NM value: 2.00
301 ❑ May 1982 NM value: 1.50
302 ❑ Jun 1982 NM value: 1.50
303 ❑ Jul 1982 NM value: 1.50
304 ❑ Aug 1982 NM value: 1.50
305 ❑ Sep 1982 NM value: 1.50
306 ❑ Oct 1982 NM value: 1.50
307 ❑ Nov 1982 NM value: 1.50
308 ❑ Dec 1982 NM value: 1.50
309 ❑ Jan 1983 NM value: 1.50
310 ❑ Feb 1983 NM value: 1.50
311 ❑ Mar 1983 NM value: 1.50
312 ❑ Apr 1983 NM value: 1.50
313 ❑ May 1983 NM value: 1.50
314 ❑ Jun 1983 NM value: 1.50
315 ❑ Jul 1983 NM value: 1.50
316 ❑ Aug 1983 NM value: 1.50
317 ❑ Sep 1983 NM value: 1.50
318 ❑ Oct 1983 NM value: 1.50
319 ❑ Nov 1983 NM value: 1.50
320 ❑ Dec 1983 NM value: 1.50
321 ❑ Jan 1984 NM value: 1.50
322 ❑ Feb 1984 NM value: 1.50
323 ❑ Mar 1984 NM value: 1.50
324 ❑ Apr 1984 NM value: 1.50
325 ❑ May 1984 NM value: 1.50
326 ❑ Jun 1984 NM value: 1.50
327 ❑ Jul 1984 NM value: 1.50
328 ❑ Aug 1984 NM value: 1.50
329 ❑ Sep 1984 NM value: 1.50
330 ❑ Oct 1984 NM value: 1.50
Adventure of the Secret Tunnel • K. Bernhard story, Manny Stallman art credits
331 ❑ Nov 1984 NM value: 1.50
332 ❑ Dec 1984 NM value: 1.50
333 ❑ Jan 1985 NM value: 1.50
334 ❑ NM value: 1.50
335 ❑ NM value: 1.50
336 ❑ NM value: 1.50
337 ❑ NM value: 1.50
338 ❑ NM value: 1.50
339 ❑ NM value: 1.50
340 ❑ NM value: 1.50
341 ❑ NM value: 1.50
342 ❑ NM value: 1.50
343 ❑ NM value: 1.50
344 ❑ NM value: 1.50
345 ❑ NM value: 1.50
346 ❑ NM value: 1.50
347 ❑ NM value: 1.50
348 ❑ NM value: 1.50
349 ❑ NM value: 1.50
350 ❑ NM value: 1.50
351 ❑ NM value: 1.50
352 ❑ NM value: 1.50
353 ❑ NM value: 1.50
354 ❑ NM value: 1.50
355 ❑ NM value: 1.50
356 ❑ NM value: 1.50
357 ❑ NM value: 1.50
358 ❑ NM value: 1.50
359 ❑ NM value: 1.50
360 ❑ NM value: 1.50
361 ❑ NM value: 1.50
362 ❑ NM value: 1.50
363 ❑ NM value: 1.50
364 ❑ NM value: 1.50
365 ❑ NM value: 1.50
366 ❑ NM value: 1.50
367 ❑ NM value: 1.50
368 ❑ NM value: 1.50
369 ❑ NM value: 1.50
370 ❑ NM value: 1.50
371 ❑ NM value: 1.50
372 ❑ NM value: 1.50
373 ❑ NM value: 1.50
374 ❑ NM value: 1.50
375 ❑ NM value: 1.50
376 ❑ NM value: 1.50
377 ❑ NM value: 1.50
378 ❑ NM value: 1.50
379 ❑ NM value: 1.50
380 ❑ NM value: 1.50
381 ❑ NM value: 1.50
382 ❑ NM value: 1.50
383 ❑ NM value: 1.50
384 ❑ NM value: 1.50
385 ❑ NM value: 1.50
386 ❑ NM value: 1.50
387 ❑ NM value: 1.50
388 ❑ NM value: 1.50
389 ❑ NM value: 1.50
390 ❑ NM value: 1.50
391 ❑ NM value: 1.50
392 ❑ NM value: 1.50
393 ❑ NM value: 1.50
394 ❑ NM value: 1.50
395 ❑ NM value: 1.50
396 ❑ NM value: 1.50
397 ❑ NM value: 1.50
398 ❑ NM value: 1.50
399 ❑ NM value: 1.50
400 ❑ NM value: 1.50
401 ❑ NM value: 1.50
402 ❑ NM value: 1.50
403 ❑ NM value: 1.50
404 ❑ NM value: 1.50
405 ❑ NM value: 1.50
406 ❑ NM value: 1.50
407 ❑ NM value: 1.50
408 ❑ NM value: 1.50
409 ❑ NM value: 1.50
410 ❑ NM value: 1.50
411 ❑ NM value: 1.50
412 ❑ NM value: 1.50
413 ❑ NM value: 1.50
414 ❑ NM value: 1.50
415 ❑ NM value: 1.50
416 ❑ NM value: 1.50
417 ❑ NM value: 1.50
418 ❑ NM value: 1.50
419 ❑ NM value: 1.50
420 ❑ NM value: 1.50
421 ❑ NM value: 1.50
422 ❑ NM value: 1.50
423 ❑ NM value: 1.50
424 ❑ NM value: 1.50
425 ❑ NM value: 1.50
426 ❑ NM value: 1.50
427 ❑ NM value: 1.50
428 ❑ NM value: 1.50
429 ❑ NM value: 1.50

CGC-graded: Multiply prices above by **33 for 9.9 M • 16 for 9.8 NM/M • 7 for 9.6 NM+ • 5 for 9.4 NM • 2.5 for 9.2 NM- • 1.5 for 9.0 VF/NM**

430 ❑ NM value: 1.50
431 ❑ NM value: 1.50
432 ❑ NM value: 1.50
433 ❑ NM value: 1.50
434 ❑ NM value: 1.50
435 ❑ NM value: 1.50
436 ❑ NM value: 1.50
437 ❑ NM value: 1.50
438 ❑ NM value: 1.50
439 ❑ NM value: 1.50
440 ❑ NM value: 1.50
441 ❑ NM value: 1.50
442 ❑ NM value: 1.50
443 ❑ NM value: 1.50
444 ❑ NM value: 1.50
445 ❑ Nov 1994 NM value: 1.50
📖 Almost a Millionaire • No creator credits listed
446 ❑ Dec 1994 NM value: 1.50
447 ❑ Jan 1995 NM value: 1.50
448 ❑ Feb 1995 NM value: 1.50
449 ❑ Mar 1995 NM value: 1.50
450 ❑ Apr 1995 NM value: 1.50
451 ❑ May 1995 NM value: 1.50
452 ❑ Jun 1995 NM value: 1.50
453 ❑ Jul 1995 NM value: 1.50
454 ❑ Aug 1995 NM value: 1.50
455 ❑ Sep 1995 NM value: 1.50
456 ❑ Oct 1995 NM value: 1.50
📖 Happy Birthday, Comics • Bob Bindig, Buffalo credits; supports release of comics postage stamps; Yellow Kid, Katzenjammer Kids, Little Nemo, Buster Brown, Little Orphan Annie, Skeezix appearance
457 ❑ Nov 1995 NM value: 1.50
458 ❑ Dec 1995 NM value: 1.50
459 ❑ Jan 1996 NM value: 1.50
460 ❑ Feb 1996 NM value: 1.50
461 ❑ Mar 1996 NM value: 1.50
📖 A Lesson in Fairness • Lorina Mara credits
462 ❑ Apr 1996 NM value: 1.50
📖 The Bully's Secret • Lorina Mara credits
463 ❑ ca. 1996 NM value: 1.50
464 ❑ NM value: 1.50
465 ❑ NM value: 1.50
466 ❑ NM value: 1.00
• Last WEBS issue
467 ❑ NM value: 1.00
📖 Brush With Creepiness • First Yoe Studios issue; Weinerville
468 ❑ NM value: 1.00
469 ❑ NM value: 1.00
470 ❑ NM value: 1.00
📖 The Amazingly Incredibly Improbable Journey • Space Ghost interview
471 ❑ NM value: 1.00
472 ❑ NM value: 1.00
473 ❑ NM value: 1.00
474 ❑ NM value: 1.00
475 ❑ NM value: 1.00
476 ❑ NM value: 1.00
477 ❑ NM value: 1.00
478 ❑ NM value: 1.00
479 ❑ NM value: 1.00
📖 The Big Time Overflow! • Larisa Oleynik (Alex mack) photo cover
480 ❑ NM value: 1.00
481 ❑ NM value: 1.00
482 ❑ NM value: 1.00
483 ❑ NM value: 1.00
484 ❑ NM value: 1.00
485 ❑ NM value: 1.00
486 ❑ NM value: 1.00
487 ❑ NM value: 1.00
488 ❑ NM value: 1.00
1st printing.
489 ❑ NM value: 1.00
490 ❑ NM value: 1.00
491 ❑ NM value: 1.00
492 ❑ NM value: 1.00
493 ❑ NM value: 1.00
494 ❑ NM value: 1.00
495 ❑ NM value: 1.00
496 ❑ NM value: 1.00
497 ❑ NM value: 1.00
498 ❑ NM value: 1.00
499 ❑ NM value: 1.00
500 ❑ NM value: 1.00

ADVENTURES OF THE FLY — Archie / Radio

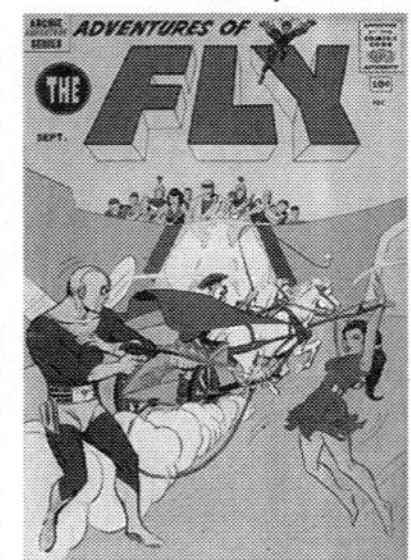

As super-heroes regained popularity in the late 1950s and early 1960s, the beginning of the Silver Age of Comics, the folks at Archie dusted off some of their Golden Age heroes from the 1940s and offered up new ones. One of those is the Fly, who first appeared in The Double Life of Private Strong #1 in 1959.

The Fly is secretly lawyer Thomas Troy; when the need arises, he touches his magic ring and transforms into his super-powered alter ego. Adventures of the Fly offers up standard super-hero fare, but the run is notable for the work of comics legends Joe Simon and Jack Kirby in early issues.

1 ❑ Aug 1959 Cover: 0.10 NM value: 350.00
• CGC: 2 graded, best 8.5
📖 The Strange New World of the Fly: The Fly Strikes; The Fly Discovers His Buzz Gun; Come into My Parlor; Sign of the Triangle A: Joe Simon; John Stanley; Jack Kirby ★ Origin of Fly.
2 ❑ Sep 1959 Cover: 0.10 NM value: 225.00
• CGC: 2 graded, best 9.2
📖 Tim O'Casey's Wrecking Crew; Sneak Atack; Marco's Eyes; The Master of Junk-ri-la • Private Strong A: Joe Simon; Al Williamson; John Stanley; Jack Kirby
3 ❑ Nov 1959 Cover: 0.10 NM value: 165.00
A: Jayson Disbrow; Jack Davis
4 ❑ Jan 1960 Cover: 0.10 NM value: 125.00
• CGC: 1 graded, best 7.5
📖 Muggsy's Masterpiece
5 ❑ Mar 1960 Cover: 0.10 NM value: 125.00
6 ❑ May 1960 Cover: 0.10 NM value: 90.00
7 ❑ Jul 1960 Cover: 0.10 NM value: 90.00
8 ❑ Sep 1960 Cover: 0.10 NM value: 75.00
📖 The Monster Gang; The Fly Versus Taxus the Tyrant; Apache (text story); The Puppet Fly
9 ❑ Nov 1960 Cover: 0.10 NM value: 75.00
10 ❑ Jan 1961 Cover: 0.10 NM value: 75.00
Circ: Statement: 240,452 • CGC: 1 graded, best 7.5
11 ❑ Mar 1961 Cover: 0.10 NM value: 60.00
Circ: Statement: 240,452
12 ❑ May 1961 Cover: 0.10 NM value: 60.00
Circ: Statement: 240,452 • CGC: 1 graded, best 8.0
13 ❑ Jul 1961 Cover: 0.10 NM value: 60.00
Circ: Statement: 240,452 • CGC: 1 graded, best 7.0
14 ❑ Sep 1961 Cover: 0.10 NM value: 60.00
Circ: Statement: 240,452
15 ❑ Oct 1961 Cover: 0.10 NM value: 60.00
Circ: Statement: 240,452
16 ❑ Nov 1961 Cover: 0.10 NM value: 45.00
Circ: Statement: 240,452
17 ❑ Jan 1962 Cover: 0.10 NM value: 45.00
18 ❑ Mar 1962 Cover: 0.10 NM value: 45.00
19 ❑ May 1962 Cover: 0.12 NM value: 45.00
• Has 1961 Statement, filed 10/1/61; avg total paid circ 240,452
20 ❑ Jul 1962 Cover: 0.12 NM value: 45.00
21 ❑ Sep 1962 Cover: 0.12 NM value: 34.00
22 ❑ Oct 1962 Cover: 0.12 NM value: 34.00
23 ❑ Nov 1962 Cover: 0.12 NM value: 34.00
24 ❑ Feb 1963 Cover: 0.12 NM value: 34.00
25 ❑ Apr 1963 Cover: 0.12 NM value: 34.00
26 ❑ Jun 1963 Cover: 0.12 NM value: 34.00
27 ❑ Aug 1963 Cover: 0.12 NM value: 34.00
28 ❑ Oct 1963 Cover: 0.12 NM value: 34.00
29 ❑ Jan 1964 Cover: 0.12 NM value: 34.00
Circ: Statement: 197,748
30 ❑ Oct 1964 Cover: 0.12 NM value: 34.00
Circ: Statement: 197,748
31 ❑ May 1965 Cover: 0.12 NM value: 34.00
final issue. • becomes Fly Man; Has 1964 Statement, filed 10/1/64; avg print run 332,516; avg sales 197,748; avg subs 0; avg total paid 197,748; samples 200; max existent 197,948; 41% of run returned

ADVENTURES OF THE JAGUAR — Archie / Radio

1 ❑ Sep 1961 Cover: 0.10 NM value: 90.00
• CGC: 1 graded, best 9.2
2 ❑ Oct 1961 Cover: 0.10 NM value: 55.00
• CGC: 1 graded, best 9.4
3 ❑ Nov 1961 Cover: 0.10 NM value: 45.00
• CGC: 1 graded, best 9.6
4 ❑ Jan 1962 Cover: 0.12 NM value: 35.00
5 ❑ Mar 1962 Cover: 0.12 NM value: 35.00
6 ❑ May 1962 Cover: 0.12 NM value: 25.00
7 ❑ Jul 1962 Cover: 0.12 NM value: 25.00
8 ❑ Aug 1962 Cover: 0.12 NM value: 25.00
9 ❑ Sep 1962 Cover: 0.12 NM value: 25.00
10 ❑ Nov 1962 Cover: 0.12 NM value: 25.00
11 ❑ Mar 1963 Cover: 0.12 NM value: 18.00
12 ❑ May 1963 Cover: 0.12 NM value: 18.00
13 ❑ Aug 1963 Cover: 0.12 NM value: 18.00
14 ❑ Oct 1963 Cover: 0.12 NM value: 18.00
📖 "Kick" of the Month Club; The Jaguar's Sinister Safari; The Black Hood Teaches Karate; The Teen-age Jaguard
15 ❑ Nov 1963 Cover: 0.12 NM value: 18.00
final issue.

ADVENTURES OF THE LITTLE GREEN DINOSAUR, THE — Last Gasp

1 ❑ b&w Cover: 0.50 NM value: 5.00
2 ❑ b&w Cover: 0.50 NM value: 5.00
📖 Blackratt's Gold; Thrill to Bloodlust Comics A: George Metzer; Johnny Chambers; Bob Inwood W: George Metzer; Johnny Chambers; Bob Inwood

ADVENTURES OF THE MAD HUNDA DAY DAY, THE — Thaumaturge

1 ❑ Win 1995, b&w Cover: 2.00 NM value: Cover or less
A: Tim Baer W: Tim Baer

ADVENTURES OF THE MASK — Dark Horse

1 ❑ Jan 1996 Cover: 2.50 NM value: Cover or less
📖 Who is that Masked Man? A: Neil Vokes W: Michael Eury
2 ❑ Feb 1996 Cover: 2.50 NM value: Cover or less
W: Michael Eury ★ Versus Walter.
3 ❑ Mar 1996 Cover: 2.50 NM value: Cover or less
W: Michael Eury
4 ❑ Apr 1996 Cover: 2.50 NM value: Cover or less
W: Michael Eury ★ 1st Appearance of Bombshell.
5 ❑ May 1996 Cover: 2.50 NM value: Cover or less
W: Michael Eury
6 ❑ Jun 1996 Cover: 2.50 NM value: Cover or less
W: Michael Eury
7 ❑ Jul 1996 Cover: 2.50 NM value: Cover or less
W: Michael Eury
8 ❑ Aug 1996 Cover: 2.50 NM value: Cover or less
📖 Dog Days • Milo dons the mask A: Neil Vokes W: Michael Eury
9 ❑ Sep 1996 Cover: 2.50 NM value: Cover or less
Circ: Diamd. preorders: 3,390
📖 Shaken and Stirred • James Bond parody A: Marc Campos W: Michael Eury
10 ❑ Oct 1996 Cover: 2.50 NM value: Cover or less
Circ: Diamd. preorders: 3,073
W: Michael Eury ★ Versus Walter.
11 ❑ Nov 1996 Cover: 2.50 NM value: Cover or less
Circ: Diamd. preorders: 2,921
• Mask as Santa W: Michael Eury
12 ❑ Dec 1996 Cover: 2.50 NM value: Cover or less
Circ: Direct Market orders: 2,668
📖 Trial of the Mask final issue. A: Marc Campos W: Michael Eury
SE 1 ❑ Oct 1996 NM value: 1.00
No issue number. newsprint cover. • Toys R Us Special Ed. Giveaway.

ADVENTURES OF THE OUTSIDERS, THE — DC

The Adventures of the Outsiders is the continuation of the series originally titled Batman and the Outsiders. No longer the inexperienced heroes that Batman once led, now The Outsiders are an effective team in their own right. Their number consists of Metamorpho, Black Lightning, Halo, swordswoman Katana, Looker, and new leader Geo-Force. Geo-Force's true identity is that of Prince Brion of Markovia, a position which allows him to fund The Outsiders' activities.

In addition to stories that stand out over many other "team" comics, The Outsiders are known for the offbeat foes that they face. These have included a family of robots ("the Nuclear Family"), who threaten to set off a nuclear explosion while spouting dialog straight out of "Leave It to Beaver."

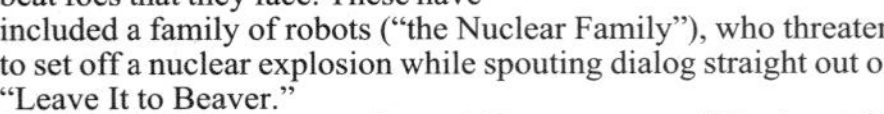

33 ❑ May 1986 Cover: 0.75 NM value: 1.00
Circ: CapCity orders: 9,450
• Continued from Batman and the Outsiders #32
34 ❑ Jun 1986 Cover: 0.75 NM value: 1.00
Circ: CapCity orders: 9,450
★ Versus Masters of Disaster.
35 ❑ Jul 1986 Cover: 0.75 NM value: 1.00
Circ: CapCity orders: 9,400
36 ❑ Aug 1986 Cover: 0.75 NM value: 1.00
Circ: CapCity orders: 9,450
37 ❑ Sep 1986 Cover: 0.75 NM value: 1.00
Circ: CapCity orders: 11,450
38 ❑ Oct 1986 Cover: 0.75 NM value: 1.00
Circ: CapCity orders: 9,200
39 ❑ Nov 1986 Cover: 0.75 NM value: 1.00
Circ: CapCity orders: 6,150
★ Versus Nuclear Family.
40 ❑ Dec 1986 Cover: 0.75 NM value: 1.00
Circ: CapCity orders: 5,700
📖 Family Ties A: Jim Aparo W: Mike W. Barr ★ Versus Nuclear Family.
41 ❑ Jan 1987 Cover: 0.75 NM value: 1.00
Circ: CapCity orders: 5,250
📖 Breaking The Bank A: Jim Aparo W: Mike W. Barr ★ Versus Force of July.
42 ❑ Feb 1987 Cover: 0.75 NM value: 1.00
Circ: CapCity orders: 4,900
43 ❑ Mar 1987 Cover: 0.75 NM value: 1.00
Circ: CapCity orders: 4,700
44 ❑ Apr 1987 Cover: 0.75 NM value: 1.00
Circ: CapCity orders: 4,400
★ Versus Duke of Oil.
45 ❑ May 1987 Cover: 0.75 NM value: 1.00
Circ: CapCity orders: 4,000
★ Versus Duke of Oil.
46 ❑ Jun 1987 Cover: 0.75 NM value: 1.00
Circ: CapCity orders: 3,850
final issue.

ADVENTURES OF THEOWN, THE — Pyramid

1 ❑ 1986 Cover: 1.70 NM value: 2.00
📖 Flight From Tomorrow A: Don Bryan; Kevin D. Duncan W: Kevin D. Duncan; Francine Mezo
2 ❑ 1986 Cover: 1.70 NM value: 2.00
3 ❑ 1986 Cover: 1.70 NM value: 2.00

ADVENTURES OF THE SCREAMER BROTHERS — Superstar

1 ❑ Dec 1990 Cover: 1.50 NM value: Cover or less
A: Gary McCluskey W: Kevin Juaire
2 ❑ Mar 1991 Cover: 1.50 NM value: Cover or less
3 ❑ Jun 1991 Cover: 1.50 NM value: Cover or less

Capital City orders are the actual sales of comic books by Capital City Distribution, once one of the largest U.S. sellers of comics to comics shops. Capital City's share of comics shop sales, while not known exactly, increases from around 10-20% in the mid-1980s to 30-35% in the mid-1990s. Capital City's share of comic books sold on newsstands (most Marvels and DCs) will be less.

Other grades: Multiply prices above by **1.5 for Mint • 2/3 for Very Fine • 1/3 for Fine • 1/5 for Very Good • 1/8 for Good**

ADVENTURES OF THE SCREAMER BROTHERS (VOL. 2) — Superstar

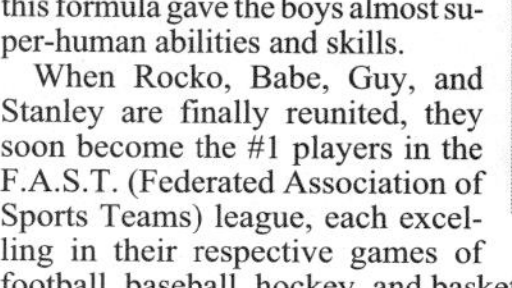

Orphaned during the eruption of Mt. St. Helens, these rambunctious quadruplets were separated for nine long years. During this time, their exploits in their chosen sports became legendary. The boys' father had been a genius in the field of sports medicine, and had developed a special nutritional formula. Along with a complete training and fitness program, this formula gave the boys almost super-human abilities and skills.

When Rocko, Babe, Guy, and Stanley are finally reunited, they soon become the #1 players in the F.A.S.T. (Federated Association of Sports Teams) league, each excelling in their respective games of football, baseball, hockey, and basketball.

Even off the playing field, the brothers are heroes, saving the day against wild bears, tornadoes, and molten steel.

1 ❑ Cover: 1.95 **NM** value: **Cover or less**
2 ❑ Cover: 1.95 **NM** value: **Cover or less**
3 ❑ Dec 1991 Cover: 1.95 **NM** value: **Cover or less**

ADVENTURES OF THE SUPER MARIO BROS. — Valiant

1 ❑ Feb 1991 Cover: 1.50 **NM** value: **2.50**
2 ❑ Mar 1991 Cover: 1.50 **NM** value: **2.50**
• swimsuit issue
3 ❑ Apr 1991 Cover: 1.50 **NM** value: **2.50**
4 ❑ May 1991 Cover: 1.50 **NM** value: **2.50**
5 ❑ Jun 1991 Cover: 1.50 **NM** value: **2.50**
6 ❑ Jul 1991 Cover: 1.50 **NM** value: **2.50**
7 ❑ Aug 1991 Cover: 1.50 **NM** value: **2.50**
8 ❑ Sep 1991 Cover: 1.50 **NM** value: **2.50**
9 ❑ Oct 1991 Cover: 1.50 **NM** value: **2.50**

ADVENTURES OF THE THING, THE — Marvel

1 ❑ Apr 1992 Cover: 1.25 **NM** value: **1.50**
Circ: CapCity orders: **13,700**
📖 Remembrance Of Things Past • Reprints Marvel Two-In-One #50;Thing vs. Thing **A:** John Byrne; Joe Sinnott **W:** John Byrne
2 ❑ May 1992 Cover: 1.25 **NM** value: **1.50**
Circ: CapCity orders: **12,600**
3 ❑ Jun 1992 Cover: 1.25 **NM** value: **1.50**
Circ: CapCity orders: **13,100**
4 ❑ Jul 1992 Cover: 1.25 **NM** value: **1.50**
Circ: CapCity orders: **11,600**
📖 Only The Swamp Survives • Reprints Marvel Two-In-One #77 **A:** Ron Wilson **W:** Tom DeFalco ★ Appearance of Man-Thing.

ADVENTURES OF THE VITAL-MAN — Budgie

1 ❑ Jun 1991, b&w Cover: 2.00 **NM** value: **Cover or less**
A: David Mack
2 ❑ Cover: 2.00 **NM** value: **Cover or less**
3 ❑ Cover: 2.00 **NM** value: **Cover or less**
4 ❑ Cover: 2.00 **NM** value: **Cover or less**

ADVENTURES OF THE X-MEN, THE — Marvel

1 ❑ Apr 1996 Cover: 0.99 **NM** value: **1.50**
📖 The Green Revolution, Part 1 • Wolverine vs. Hulk **A:** Ben Herrera **W:** Ralph Macchio
2 ❑ May 1996 Cover: 0.99 **NM** value: **1.25**
W: Ralph Macchio
3 ❑ Jun 1996 Cover: 0.99 **NM** value: **1.25**
W: Ralph Macchio ★ Appearance of Spider-Man. ★ Versus Mr. Sinister.
4 ❑ Jul 1996 Cover: 0.99 **NM** value: **1.25**
W: Ralph Macchio
5 ❑ Aug 1996 Cover: 0.99 **NM** value: **1.25**
W: Ralph Macchio ★ Versus Magneto.
6 ❑ Sep 1996 Cover: 0.99 **NM** value: **1.00**
• Magneto vs. Apocalypse **W:** Ralph Macchio
7 ❑ Oct 1996 Cover: 0.99 **NM** value: **1.00**
W: Ralph Macchio
8 ❑ Nov 1996 Cover: 0.99 **NM** value: **1.00**
Circ: Direct Market orders: **24,000**
📖 Vanished **A:** Derec Aucoin **W:** Ralph Macchio
9 ❑ Dec 1996 Cover: 0.99 **NM** value: **1.00**
Circ: Direct Market orders: **22,500**
W: Ralph Macchio ★ Versus Vanisher.
10 ❑ Jan 1997 Cover: 0.99 **NM** value: **1.00**
Circ: Direct Market orders: **21,500**
📖 Media Darlings **A:** Yancey Labat **W:** Ralph Macchio ★ Versus Mojo.
11 ❑ Feb 1997 Cover: 0.99 **NM** value: **1.00**
Circ: Direct Market orders: **18,500**
📖 Tower of Despair **A:** Yancey Labat **W:** Ralph Macchio ★ Appearance of Man-Thing.
12 ❑ Mar 1997 Cover: 0.99 **NM** value: **1.00**
Circ: Direct Market orders: **16,750**
📖 Better to Light A Small Candle... final issue. **A:** Yancey Labat **W:** Ralph Macchio

ADVENTURES OF TINTIN, THE — Mammoth

1 ❑ **NM** value: **10.00**
📖 The Blue Lotus **A:** Hergé **W:** Hergé
1-2 ❑ **NM** value: **8.50**
1-3 ❑ **NM** value: **8.50**
1-4 ❑ **NM** value: **8.50**
1-5 ❑ Cover: 4.99 **NM** value: **8.50**
2 ❑ Cover: 4.99 **NM** value: **8.50**
📖 The Making of Tintin in the World of the Inca **A:** Hergé **W:** Hergé
3 ❑ Cover: 4.99 **NM** value: **8.50**
📖 Tintin in America **A:** Hergé **W:** Hergé
4 ❑ Cover: 4.99 **NM** value: **8.50**
📖 Cigars of the Paraoh **A:** Hergé **W:** Hergé
5 ❑ Cover: 4.99 **NM** value: **8.50**
📖 Tintin and the Broken Ear **A:** Hergé **W:** Hergé
6 ❑ Cover: 4.99 **NM** value: **8.50**
📖 The Black Island **A:** Hergé **W:** Hergé
7 ❑ Cover: 4.99 **NM** value: **8.50**
📖 King Ottokar's Sceptre **A:** Hergé **W:** Hergé
8 ❑ Cover: 4.99 **NM** value: **8.50**
📖 The Crab with the Golden Claws **A:** Hergé **W:** Hergé
9 ❑ Cover: 4.99 **NM** value: **8.50**
📖 The Shooting Star **A:** Hergé **W:** Hergé
10 ❑ Cover: 4.99 **NM** value: **8.50**
📖 The Secret of the Unicorn **A:** Hergé **W:** Hergé
11 ❑ Cover: 4.99 **NM** value: **8.50**
📖 Red Rackham's Treasure **A:** Hergé **W:** Hergé
12 ❑ Cover: 4.99 **NM** value: **8.50**
📖 The Seven Crystal Balls **A:** Hergé **W:** Hergé
13 ❑ Cover: 4.99 **NM** value: **8.50**
📖 Prisoners of the sun **A:** Hergé **W:** Hergé
14 ❑ Cover: 4.99 **NM** value: **8.50**
📖 Land of Black Gold **A:** Hergé **W:** Hergé
15 ❑ Cover: 4.99 **NM** value: **8.50**
📖 Destination Moon **A:** Hergé **W:** Hergé
16 ❑ Cover: 4.99 **NM** value: **8.50**
📖 Explorers on the Moon **A:** Hergé **W:** Hergé
17 ❑ Cover: 4.99 **NM** value: **8.50**
📖 The Calculus Affair **A:** Hergé **W:** Hergé
18 ❑ Cover: 4.99 **NM** value: **8.50**
📖 The Red Sea Sharks **A:** Hergé **W:** Hergé
19 ❑ Cover: 4.99 **NM** value: **8.50**
📖 Tintin in Tibet **A:** Hergé **W:** Hergé
20 ❑ Cover: 4.99 **NM** value: **8.50**
📖 The Catafiore Emerald **A:** Hergé **W:** Hergé
21 ❑ Cover: 4.99 **NM** value: **8.50**
📖 Flight 714 **A:** Hergé **W:** Hergé
22 ❑ Cover: 4.99 **NM** value: **8.50**
📖 Tintin and the Picaros **A:** Hergé **W:** Hergé

ADVENTURES ON SPACE STATION FREEDOM — Tadcorps

1 ❑ **NM** value: **2.50**
No issue number. • educational giveaway on International Space Station.

ADVENTURES ON THE FRINGE — Fantagraphics

1 ❑ Mar 1992 Cover: 2.25 **NM** value: **Cover or less**
A: R.L. Crabb **W:** R.L. Crabb
2 ❑ May 1992 Cover: 2.25 **NM** value: **Cover or less**
A: R.L. Crabb **W:** R.L. Crabb
3 ❑ Jul 1992 Cover: 2.25 **NM** value: **Cover or less**
A: R.L. Crabb **W:** R.L. Crabb
4 ❑ Oct 1992 Cover: 2.25 **NM** value: **Cover or less**
Photo cover. **A:** R.L. Crabb **W:** R.L. Crabb
5 ❑ Feb 1993 Cover: 2.25 **NM** value: **Cover or less**
A: R.L. Crabb **W:** R.L. Crabb

ADVENTURES ON THE PLANET OF THE APES — Marvel

1 ❑ Oct 1975 Cover: 0.25 **NM** value: **6.00**
• **CGC:** 22 graded, best 9.6
• Adapts movie **A:** Jim Starlin(cover)
2 ❑ Nov 1975 Cover: 0.25 **NM** value: **4.00**
• **CGC:** 6 graded, best 9.6
📖 World of Captive Humans • Adapts movie
3 ❑ 1976 Cover: 0.25 **NM** value: **4.00**
• **CGC:** 4 graded, best 9.4
• Adapts movie
4 ❑ 1976 Cover: 0.25 **NM** value: **4.00**
• **CGC:** 4 graded, best 9.4
5 ❑ 1976 Cover: 0.25 **NM** value: **4.00**
• **CGC:** 5 graded, best 9.4
6 ❑ 1976 Cover: 0.25 **NM** value: **4.00**
• **CGC:** 3 graded, best 9.4
7 ❑ 1976 Cover: 0.25 **NM** value: **3.50**
• **CGC:** 2 graded, best 9.4
8 ❑ 1976 Cover: 0.25 **NM** value: **3.50**
• **CGC:** 2 graded, best 9.4
9 ❑ 1976 Cover: 0.25 **NM** value: **3.50**
• **CGC:** 3 graded, best 9.4
• Adapts Beneath the Planet of the Apes
10 ❑ Nov 1976 Cover: 0.25 **NM** value: **3.50**
• **CGC:** 1 graded, best 7.5
📖 Children of the Bomb • Adapts Beneath the Planet of the Apes **A:** Alfredo Alcala **W:** Doug Moench
11 ❑ Dec 1976 Cover: 0.25 **NM** value: **3.50**
• **CGC:** 1 graded, best 6.5
📖 The Hell of Holocaust final issue. • Adapts Beneath the Planet of the Apes;Destruction of Earth **A:** Alfredo Alcala **W:** Doug Moench

ADVENTURE STRIP DIGEST — WCG

1 ❑ Aug 1994 Cover: 2.00 **NM** value: **2.50**
A: Randy Reynaldo **W:** Randy Reynaldo
2 ❑ Apr 1995 Cover: 2.50 **NM** value: **Cover or less**
📖 The EC Express **A:** Randy Reynaldo **W:** Randy Reynaldo
3 ❑ Cover: 2.50 **NM** value: **Cover or less**
A: Randy Reynaldo **W:** Randy Reynaldo
4 ❑ Jun 1996 Cover: 2.50 **NM** value: **Cover or less**
📖 Hostile Takeover **A:** Randy Reynaldo **W:** Randy Reynaldo
Bk 1 ❑ Feb 1996 Cover: 13.95 **NM** value: **Cover or less**
• The Rob Hanes Archives

ADVENTUROUS UNCLE SCROOGE MCDUCK, THE (WALT DISNEY'S...) — Gladstone

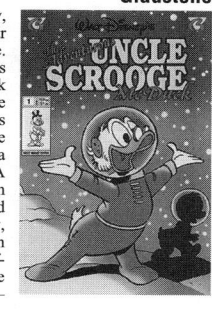

In honor of his 50th anniversary, Scrooge McDuck became the star of this new series from Gladstone. The series largely featured reprints from Scrooge's long comic-book history, kicking off with "The Twenty-Four Carat Moon." In this classic by Carl Barks, Uncle Scrooge hears of the discovery of a hidden moon made of solid gold. A space race against competitors soon commences, but Scrooge, Donald Duck, and Donald's nephews Huey, Dewey, and Louie manage to reach it first. There, the lone inhabitant offers to trade the rights to the entire planet for a mere handful of dirt — but, naturally, there's a catch.

1 ❑ Jan 1998 Cover: 1.95 **NM** value: **Cover or less**
Circ: Diamd. preorders: **8,114**
📖 The Twenty-Four Carat Moon; Time Bandits • reprints Barks' "The Twenty-Four Carat Moon" **A:** Carl Barks **W:** Carl Barks
2 ❑ Mar 1998 Cover: 1.95 **NM** value: **Cover or less**
Circ: Diamd. preorders: **6,237**
• 50th anniversary of Uncle Scrooge.

AEON FOCUS — Aeon

1 ❑ Mar 1994 Cover: 2.75 **NM** value: **2.95**
• Justin Hampton's Twitch **A:** Justin Hampton **W:** Justin Hampton
2 ❑ Jun 1994 Cover: 2.75 **NM** value: **2.95**
📖 Upton's Lives of the Saints: Saint Antony of Padua; I'm Not Angry, Anymore; Chris; Happy Shiny People; Nightmares • Colin Upton's Other Other Even Bigger Than Slightly Smaller That Got Bigger Big Thing **A:** Colin Upton **W:** Colin Upton
3 ❑ Oct 1994 Cover: 2.95 **NM** value: **Cover or less**
📖 El Sobrante • Filthy Habits **A:** Eric Jones **W:** Landry Walker
4 ❑ Nov 1994 Cover: 2.95 **NM** value: **Cover or less**
• Ward Sutton's Ink Blot
5 ❑ Cover: 2.50 **NM** value: **2.95**
📖 Slip **A:** Paul Sloboda **W:** Pia Guerra

AERTIMISAN: WAR OF SOULS — Almagest

1 ❑ Nov 1997 Cover: 2.75 **NM** value: **Cover or less**
2 ❑ Jan 1998 Cover: 2.75 **NM** value: **Cover or less**

AESOP'S DESECRATED MORALS — Magnecom

1 ❑ b&w Cover: 2.95 **NM** value: **Cover or less**

AESOP'S FABLES — Fantagraphics

Aesop's fables are a collection of stories and anecdotes that started in Ancient Greece as a satirical form of social and political commentary. A particular moral or lesson is often attached to the end of the fable, ensuring that the audience does not miss the subtleties of the tale. Charles Santino has adapted several of these short tales for graphic publication. Santino, however, does not belabor the moral, preferring to let readers decide for themselves the true meaning or value of each story.

Some lessons are much more obvious than others, of course, but none seem hard to grasp. Vanity proves to be the undoing of a majestic stag in "The Stag and the Lion," while greed and covetousness leaves "The Dog at the Bridge" with an empty stomach. Similar themes round out the rest of these anthropomorphic tales.

1 ❑ Spr 1991 Cover: 2.50 **NM** value: **Cover or less**
📖 The Wolf at the Cottage; The Ant and the Dove; The Stag and t **A:** Fred Hembeck; Val Semeiks; Rick Geary; Hilary Barta; Peter Kuper; John Caldwell; Shary Flenniken; George Trosley; Jay Rath; Randy Jones; Stanley Goldstein **W:** Fred Hembeck; Val Semeiks; Rick Geary; Hilary Barta; Peter Kuper; John Caldwell; Shary Flenniken; George Trosley; Jay Rath; Randy Jones; Stanley Goldstein
2 ❑ Fal 1991 Cover: 2.50 **NM** value: **Cover or less**
3 ❑ Win 1991 Cover: 2.50 **NM** value: **Cover or less**

AETERNUS — Brick

1 ❑ Jun 1997 Cover: 2.95 **NM** value: **Cover or less**

AETOS THE EAGLE — Orphan Underground

1 ❑ Sep 1994, b&w Cover: 2.50 **NM** value: **Cover or less**

AETOS THE EAGLE (VOL. 2) — Ground Zero

1 ❑ Aug 1997 Cover: 3.00 **NM** value: **Cover or less**
📖 Aetos the Eagle **A:** Dan Parsons **W:** Dan Parsons
2 ❑ Cover: 3.00 **NM** value: **Cover or less**
📖 The Children of the Graves! **A:** Dan Parsons **W:** Dan Parsons
3 ❑ Cover: 3.00 **NM** value: **Cover or less**
A: Dan Parsons **W:** Dan Parsons

AFFABLE TALES FOR YOUR IMAGINATON — Lee Roy Brown

1 ❑ Jan 1987, b&w Cover: 3.00 **NM** value: **Cover or less**

AFTER APOCALYPSE — Paragraphics

1 ❑ May 1987 Cover: 1.95 **NM** value: **Cover or less**
A: Mark Bagley **W:** Cliff Biggers

CGC-graded: Multiply prices above by **33 for 9.9 M • 16 for 9.8 NM/M • 7 for 9.6 NM+ • 5 for 9.4 NM • 2.5 for 9.2 NM- • 1.5 for 9.0 VF/NM**

AFTER DARK — Millennium

1 ❑ Cover: 2.95 **NM** value: **Cover or less**
Jack; Nico; The Seductress; Night's Children: Lost Soul; Vigil: Opposite Directions; Vampire's Requiem **A:** Wendy Snow-Lang; Louis Small Jr.; Arvin Loudermilk; Deodato Filho; Kim Elizabeth; Robert Suarez **W:** Wendy Snow-Lang; Mike Iverson; Charles Baudelaire; Chris Curtan; Faye Perozich; Julio Emilio Braz

AFTERMATH — Pinnacle

1 ❑ Cover: 1.50 **NM** value: **Cover or less**
• sequel to Messiah

AFTERMATH (CHAOS) — Chaos

1 ❑ ca. 2000 Cover: 2.95 **NM** value: **Cover or less**
Circ: Diamd. preorders: **17,740**

AFTER/SHOCK: BULLETINS FROM GROUND ZERO — Last Gasp

1 ❑ b&w Cover: 2.00 **NM** value: **Cover or less**

AFTER THE RAIN — NBM / ComicsLit

1 ❑ 1999 Cover: 12.95 **NM** value: **Cover or less**

AGAINST BLACKSHARD: 3-D-THE SAGA OF SKETCH, THE ROYAL ARTIST — Sirius

1 ❑ Cover: 2.25 **NM** value: **Cover or less**
Circ: CapCity orders: **3,850**
The Saga of Sketch, the Royal Artist **A:** Glen Johnson **W:** Peter Guinones

AGENCY, THE — Image

1 ❑ ca. 2001 Cover: 2.50 **NM** value: **Cover or less**
Circ: Diamd. preorders: **28,241** • **CGC:** 3 graded, best 9.6
2 ❑ ca. 2001 Cover: 2.50 **NM** value: **Cover or less**
Circ: Diamd. preorders: **20,126** • **CGC:** 1 graded, best 9.8
3 ❑ ca. 2001 Cover: 2.50 **NM** value: **Cover or less**
Circ: Diamd. preorders: **18,425**
4 ❑ ca. 2001 Cover: 2.95 **NM** value: **Cover or less**
Circ: Diamd. preorders: **15,557**

AGENT, THE — Marvel

1 ❑ Cover: 9.95 **NM** value: **Cover or less**

AGENT "00" SOUL — Twist Records

1 ❑ **NM** value: **2.00**
• no price

AGENT AMERICA — Awesome

Ash 1❑ **NM** value: **5.00**
• Preview edition. • Series preempted by Marvel lawsuit★ 1st Appearance of Coven.

AGENT LIBERTY SPECIAL — DC

Known best for his exploits in the pages of Superman, Agent Liberty explodes into action in this, his first solo adventure. It begins, when he encounters a strange paramilitary group trying to break into the Pentagon. Ben Lockewood, aka Agent Liberty, stops the group, but a second, lone agent manages to get inside the Pentagon undetected. Inside, the infiltrator steals two items: a cassette tape and a simple map of Iran.

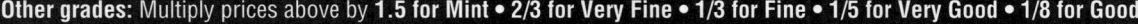

Working with his group, The Sons of Liberty, Lockewood connects this heist to a similar break-in in Iran. Before long, he will be called on to save our nation's capitol from nuclear devastation — and come face-to-face with a specter from his own past.

1 ❑ 1991 Cover: 2.00 **NM** value: **Cover or less**
Circ: CapCity orders: **22,050**
Disgrace **A:** Dusty Abell **W:** Dan Jurgens ★ Origin of Agent Liberty.

AGENTS OF LAW — Dark Horse

1 ❑ Mar 1995 Cover: 2.50 **NM** value: **Cover or less**
Circ: CapCity orders: **3,975**
What Price Utopia? **A:** Dan Lawlis; Lovern Kindzierski **W:** Keith Giffen; Lovern Kindzierski
2 ❑ 1995 Cover: 2.50 **NM** value: **Cover or less**
Circ: CapCity orders: **3,200**
3 ❑ 1995 Cover: 2.50 **NM** value: **Cover or less**
Circ: CapCity orders: **2,825**
4 ❑ 1995 Cover: 2.50 **NM** value: **Cover or less**
Circ: CapCity orders: **2,725**
5 ❑ 1995 Cover: 2.50 **NM** value: **Cover or less**
Circ: CapCity orders: **2,650**
6 ❑ Sep 1995 Cover: 2.50 **NM** value: **Cover or less**
Circ: CapCity orders: **3,875**
final issue.★ Versus Predators.

AGENT 13: THE MIDNIGHT AVENGER — TSR

1 ❑ Cover: 7.95 **NM** value: **Cover or less**
Circ: CapCity orders: **1,000**
No issue number. **A:** Dan Spiegle **W:** David Marconi; Flint Dille

AGENT THREE ZERO — Galaxinovels

1 ❑ Cover: 3.95 **NM** value: **Cover or less**
Circ: CapCity orders: **3,290**
Mirror Image • Galaxinovels w/ Trading Card and Poster **A:** Mark Bagley; Mark McKenna; Kevin Maguire; Jeff Johnson; Henry Martinez; Stephen Platt; Dan Panosian; John Estes; Darrick Robertson; Steve Darlington; Art Hogge; Tom Tomkin **W:** Mark Altamont

AGENT THREE ZERO: THE BLUE SULTAN'S QUEST/ BLUE SULTAN- GALAXI FACT FILES — Galaxinovels

1 ❑ Cover: 3.95 **NM** value: **Cover or less**
• Flip-book. The Blue Sultan's Quest • poster;trading card **A:** Terral Lawrence; Stephen Platt; Mark Poole; Steve Darlington **W:** John Christopher
1/PL❑ Cover: 2.95 **NM** value: **Cover or less**
• Platinum edition.
2 ❑ Cover: 2.95 **NM** value: **Cover or less**
3 ❑ Cover: 2.95 **NM** value: **Cover or less**
4 ❑ Cover: 2.95 **NM** value: **Cover or less**

AGENT UNKNOWN — Renegade

1 ❑ Oct 1987 Cover: 2.00 **NM** value: **Cover or less**
Raw Deal; Upwardly Mobil **A:** Dell Barras **W:** Robert Sodero
2 ❑ Jan 1988 Cover: 2.00 **NM** value: **Cover or less**
3 ❑ Apr 1988 Cover: 2.00 **NM** value: **Cover or less**

AGE OF APOCALYPSE: THE CHOSEN — Marvel

1 ❑ Cover: 2.50 **NM** value: **Cover or less**
• **CGC:** 1 graded, best 9.2
A: Scott Hanna; Ashley Underwood; Ian Churchill

AGE OF BRONZE — Image

Talk about your noble missions! This series from the talented Eric Shanower (The Enchanted Apples of Oz, The Elsewhere Prince) has as its goal retelling the complete story of the Trojan War, from young Paris' idyllic days on Mount Ida and his relationship with the beautiful Oenone to the heroes' departure for the homelands at the war's end. As is typical of Shanower's work, the art here is gorgeous — even in black and white — and the script is flawless. There is a sense of drama, as Oenone warns Paris of his death in her dreams, and readers know only too well what lies ahead, as Paris heads to Troy to win back a cow his family had intended as a sacrifice to the gods.

1 ❑ Nov 1998 Cover: 2.95 **NM** value: **Cover or less**
Circ: Diamd. preorders: **5,136**
A: Eric Shanower **W:** Eric Shanower
2 ❑ Jan 1999 Cover: 2.95 **NM** value: **Cover or less**
Circ: Diamd. preorders: **3,776**
A: Eric Shanower **W:** Eric Shanower
3 ❑ Mar 1999 Cover: 2.95 **NM** value: **Cover or less**
Circ: Diamd. preorders: **3,028**
A: Eric Shanower **W:** Eric Shanower
4 ❑ May 1999 Cover: 2.95 **NM** value: **Cover or less**
Circ: Diamd. preorders: **3,077**
A: Eric Shanower **W:** Eric Shanower
5 ❑ Oct 1999 Cover: 2.95 **NM** value: **Cover or less**
Circ: Diamd. preorders: **3,149**
A: Eric Shanower **W:** Eric Shanower
6 ❑ Jan 2000 Cover: 3.50 **NM** value: **Cover or less**
Circ: Diamd. preorders: **3,281**
cover says Dec, indicia says Jan. **A:** Eric Shanower **W:** Eric Shanower
7 ❑ Mar 2000 Cover: 3.50 **NM** value: **Cover or less**
Circ: Diamd. preorders: **3,009**
cover says Apr, indicia says Mar. **A:** Eric Shanower **W:** Eric Shanower
8 ❑ Aug 2000, b&w Cover: 3.50 **NM** value: **Cover or less**
Circ: Diamd. preorders: **3,128**
A: Eric Shanower **W:** Eric Shanower
9 ❑ Dec 2000 Cover: 3.50 **NM** value: **Cover or less**
Circ: Diamd. preorders: **3,282**
cover says Nov, indicia says Dec. **A:** Eric Shanower **W:** Eric Shanower
10 ❑ Feb 2001 Cover: 3.50 **NM** value: **Cover or less**
Circ: Diamd. preorders: **3,594**
Sacrifice, Part 1 **A:** Eric Shanower **W:** Eric Shanower
SE 1❑ Jul 1999 Cover: 2.95 **NM** value: **Cover or less**
Circ: Diamd. preorders: **3,288**
cover says Jun, indicia says Jul. House Of Horror **A:** Eric Shanower **W:** Eric Shanower

AGE OF HEROES, THE — Halloween

1 ❑ 1996b&w Cover: 2.95 **NM** value: **Cover or less**
Impressions **A:** John Ridgway **W:** James D. Hudnall
2 ❑ 1996b&w Cover: 2.95 **NM** value: **Cover or less**
A: John Ridgway **W:** James D. Hudnall
3 ❑ Mar 1997 Cover: 2.95 **NM** value: **Cover or less**
Circ: Diamd. preorders: **7,323**
A: John Ridgway **W:** James D. Hudnall
4 ❑ May 1997 Cover: 2.95 **NM** value: **Cover or less**
Circ: Diamd. preorders: **6,435**
A: John Ridgway **W:** James D. Hudnall
5 ❑ Sep 1998 Cover: 2.95 **NM** value: **Cover or less**
Circ: Diamd. preorders: **2,807**
A: John Ridgway **W:** James D. Hudnall
SE 1❑ Cover: 4.95 **NM** value: **Cover or less**
• reprints Age of Heroes #1 and 2 (Halloween)
SE 2❑ Cover: 6.95 **NM** value: **Cover or less**
A Day's Wages, a Hero's Burden **A:** John Ridgway **W:** James D. Hudnall

AGE OF HEROES, THE: WEX — Image

1 ❑ Nov 1998, b&w Cover: 2.95 **NM** value: **Cover or less**
Circ: Diamd. preorders: **3,224**
Wex **A:** Eric Shanower; Angel Fernandez **W:** James D. Hudnall

AGE OF INNOCENCE: THE REBIRTH OF IRON MAN — Marvel

Following the events of The Avengers: The Crossing and Avengers: Timeslide: Tony Stark, aka Iron Man, is dead. Yet he still lives. Paradox? Maybe. Iron Man had been corrupted by Kang and his cohorts and ultimately betrayed his teammates. In his final battle, he nearly killed himself, when he fought a younger version of Tony Stark brought forward through time.

Now, young Tony lies near death, and not even the mighty Avengers can help him. If he survives, will he follow in his own footsteps, once again becoming the armored Avenger?

As friends and foes gather to await Tony's fate, a series of flashbacks recall the life of the fallen Iron Man and the events that eventually led to his younger self's current predicament. Only time will tell whether Iron Man is really dead or whether he'll be reborn to redeem the honor of the fallen hero.

1 ❑ Cover: 2.50 **NM** value: **Cover or less**
A: Al Rio; Hector Collazo **W:** Terry Kavanagh ★ Origin of Iron Man, Pepper Potts, Happy Hogan.

AGE OF REPTILES — Dark Horse

1 ❑ Nov 1993 Cover: 2.50 **NM** value: **Cover or less**
Circ: CapCity orders: **6,100**
A: Ricardo Delgado **W:** Ricardo Delgado
2 ❑ Dec 1993 Cover: 2.50 **NM** value: **Cover or less**
A: Ricardo Delgado **W:** Ricardo Delgado
3 ❑ Jan 1994 Cover: 2.50 **NM** value: **Cover or less**
Circ: CapCity orders: **4,575**
A: Ricardo Delgado **W:** Ricardo Delgado
4 ❑ Feb 1994 Cover: 2.50 **NM** value: **Cover or less**
Circ: CapCity orders: **5,025**
A: Ricardo Delgado **W:** Ricardo Delgado
Bk 1❑ Feb 1996 Cover: 14.95 **NM** value: **Cover or less**
• "Tribal Warfare";Collects Age of Reptiles #1-4;Introductions by Ray Harryhausen & John Landis **A:** Ricardo Delgado **W:** Ricardo Delgado; John Landis; Ray Harryhausen

AGE OF REPTILES: THE HUNT — Dark Horse

1 ❑ May 1996 Cover: 2.95 **NM** value: **Cover or less**
A: Ricardo Delgado; John Landis; Ray Harryhausen **W:** Ricardo Delgado; John Landis; Ray Harryhausen
2 ❑ Jun 1996 Cover: 2.95 **NM** value: **Cover or less**
A: Ricardo Delgado; John Landis; Ray Harryhausen **W:** Ricardo Delgado; John Landis; Ray Harryhausen
3 ❑ Jul 1996 Cover: 2.95 **NM** value: **Cover or less**
A: Ricardo Delgado; John Landis; Ray Harryhausen **W:** Ricardo Delgado; John Landis; Ray Harryhausen
4 ❑ Aug 1996 Cover: 2.95 **NM** value: **Cover or less**
A: Ricardo Delgado; John Landis; Ray Harryhausen **W:** Ricardo Delgado; John Landis; Ray Harryhausen
5 ❑ Sep 1996 Cover: 2.95 **NM** value: **Cover or less**
Circ: Diamd. preorders: **12,021**
final issue. **A:** Ricardo Delgado; John Landis; Ray Harryhausen **W:** Ricardo Delgado; John Landis; Ray Harryhausen
Bk 1❑ Cover: 17.95 **NM** value: **Cover or less**
• collects series

AGGIE MACK — Superior

1 ❑ Jan 1948 Cover: 0.10 **NM** value: **200.00**
• **CGC:** 1 graded, best 7.0
2 ❑ Aug 1948 Cover: 0.10 **NM** value: **150.00**
3 ❑ Oct 1948 Cover: 0.10 **NM** value: **100.00**
4 ❑ Dec 1948 Cover: 0.10 **NM** value: **100.00**
• **CGC:** 1 graded, best 6.5
5 ❑ Feb 1949 Cover: 0.10 **NM** value: **100.00**
6 ❑ Apr 1949 Cover: 0.10 **NM** value: **100.00**
7 ❑ Jun 1949 Cover: 0.10 **NM** value: **100.00**
8 ❑ Aug 1949 Cover: 0.10 **NM** value: **100.00**

AGONY ACRES — AA 2 Entertainment

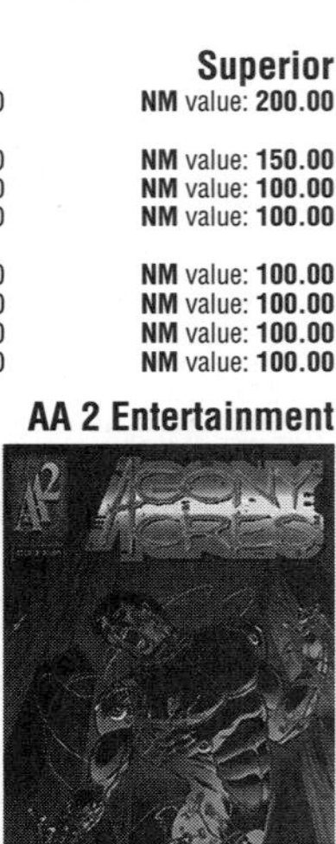

In the not-too-distant future, virtual-reality games become a big money spectator sport, complete with play-by-play commentary from a trio of sportscasters familiar to fans of Monday Night Football. And as is often the case, with big money comes corruption and murder. Agony Acres (the name of the series and the arena in which the gladiator-type virtual reality games are played) is a police-detective story with a science-fiction angle.

In a match with rookie Casey Longmaster, Scotch Stevens, aka the Skullcrusher, suffers sensory overload and dies. Can a rookie be that good, or is Mr. Wrathbone, the "owner" of the Skullcrusher, right in his accusation of murder? Detective Jack Calhoun and his partner, Lucky, are assigned to investigate the mysterious death. But Calhoun and his partner may not be allowed to solve the case, since Wrathbone seems to have his own agenda.

1 ❑ May 1995 Cover: 2.95 **NM** value: **Cover or less**
A: Ronn Stern **W:** Ronn Stern; Charles William Satterlee
1/Ash❑ 1996 **NM** value: **2.50**
A: Ronn Stern **W:** Ronn Stern; Charles William Satterlee

2 ❑ 1996 Cover: 2.95 **NM** value: **Cover or less**
A: Ronn Stern **W:** Ronn Stern; Charles William Satterlee
3 ❑ 1996b&w Cover: 2.95 **NM** value: **Cover or less**
4 ❑ 1996 Cover: 2.95 **NM** value: **Cover or less**
5 ❑ 1996 Cover: 2.95 **NM** value: **Cover or less**

AHLEA — Radio

1 ❑ Aug 1997 Cover: 2.95 **NM** value: **Cover or less**
A: Lazarus Berry **W:** Lazarus Berry
2 ❑ Oct 1997 Cover: 2.95 **NM** value: **Cover or less**
A: Lazarus Berry **W:** Lazarus Berry

AIDA-ZEE — Nate Butler

1 ❑ Cover: 1.50 **NM** value: **Cover or less**
Eterna-Teens; The Sons of Isaiah Glory; Alien Operation; Silent Night, Unholy Night; Bukki, Warrior of Ancient Israel; The Secret of the Salvation Saucer!; Do You Enjoy Reading Stories about Superheroes? **A:** Murphy Anderson; Nestor Redondo; Kerry Gammill; Jack Davis **W:** Gaylord DuBois; Irv Ziemann; Jose Ponce; Judi Ellingson; Nate Butler; Paul Thomas Hughes; Rob Bradford; Rudy Rankins; Vic Emert

AIR ACE — Street & Smith

1 ❑ Jul 1940 Cover: 0.10 **NM** value: **200.00**
2 ❑ ca. 1941 Cover: 0.10 **NM** value: **100.00**
3 ❑ Jun 1941 Cover: 0.10 **NM** value: **75.00**
4 ❑ Sep 1941 Cover: 0.10 **NM** value: **75.00**
5 ❑ Dec 1941 Cover: 0.10 **NM** value: **75.00**
6 ❑ Apr 1942 Cover: 0.10 **NM** value: **75.00**
7 ❑ Jul 1942 Cover: 0.10 **NM** value: **75.00**
8 ❑ Oct 1942 Cover: 0.10 **NM** value: **75.00**
9 ❑ Jan 1943 Cover: 0.10 **NM** value: **75.00**
• **CGC:** 1 graded, best 9.0
10 ❑ Apr 1943 Cover: 0.10 **NM** value: **75.00**
11 ❑ Jul 1943 Cover: 0.10 **NM** value: **50.00**
• **CGC:** 1 graded, best 6.0
12 ❑ Oct 1943 Cover: 0.10 **NM** value: **50.00**
13 ❑ Jan 1944 Cover: 0.10 **NM** value: **50.00**
• **CGC:** 2 graded, best 9.4
14 ❑ Mar 1944 Cover: 0.10 **NM** value: **50.00**
15 ❑ May 1944 Cover: 0.10 **NM** value: **50.00**
16 ❑ Jul 1944 Cover: 0.10 **NM** value: **50.00**
17 ❑ Sep 1944 Cover: 0.10 **NM** value: **50.00**
18 ❑ Nov 1944 Cover: 0.10 **NM** value: **50.00**
19 ❑ Jan 1945 Cover: 0.10 **NM** value: **50.00**
20 ❑ Mar 1945 Cover: 0.10 **NM** value: **50.00**

AIRBOY — Eclipse

1 ❑ Jul 1986 Cover: 0.50 **NM** value: **2.00**
Circ: CapCity orders: **14,775**
Chapter 1, On Wings Of Death; Part 2, Phoenix; The Wolf's Liar **A:** Tim Truman **W:** Chuck Dixon ★ Origin of Airboy II (modern). ★ 1st Appearance of Airboy II (modern). ★ Death of Airboy I (Golden Age).
2 ❑ Jul 1986 Cover: 0.50 **NM** value: **1.50**
Circ: CapCity orders: **12,475**
★ 1st Appearance of Skywolf (Golden Age, in modern era). ★ 1st Appearance of Marisa.
3 ❑ Aug 1986 Cover: 0.50 **NM** value: **1.50**
Circ: CapCity orders: **10,300**
★ Appearance of The Heap.
4 ❑ Aug 1986 Cover: 0.50 **NM** value: **1.50**
Circ: CapCity orders: **9,900**
Misery
5 ❑ Sep 1986 Cover: 0.50 **NM** value: **1.50**
Circ: CapCity orders: **10,400**
• Return of Valkyrie;Revival of Valkyrie **A:** Dave Stevens
6 ❑ Sep 1986 Cover: 0.50 **NM** value: **1.50**
Circ: CapCity orders: **9,550**
★ 1st Appearance of Iron Ace (in modern age).
7 ❑ Oct 1986 Cover: 0.50 **NM** value: **1.50**
Circ: CapCity orders: **11,300**
8 ❑ Oct 1986 Cover: 0.50 **NM** value: **1.50**
Circ: CapCity orders: **10,500**
9 ❑ Nov 1986 Cover: 1.25 **NM** value: **1.50**
Circ: CapCity orders: **8,875**
• Full-size issues begin. ★ Origin of Airboy (Golden Age). ★ 1st Appearance of Flying Fool (in modern age).
10 ❑ Nov 1986 Cover: 1.25 **NM** value: **Cover or less**
Circ: CapCity orders: **9,925**
★ 1st Appearance of Manic.
11 ❑ Dec 1986 Cover: 1.25 **NM** value: **Cover or less**
Circ: CapCity orders: **9,300**
• Skywolf back-up **A:** Ben Dunn ★ Origin of Airboy (Golden Age), Birdie. ★ 1st Appearance of Ito.
12 ❑ Dec 1986 Cover: 1.25 **NM** value: **Cover or less**
Circ: CapCity orders: **9,075**
• Iron Ace's identity revealed★ 1st Appearance of Kip Thorne.
13 ❑ Jan 1987 Cover: 1.25 **NM** value: **Cover or less**
Circ: CapCity orders: **8,075**
• Airfighters back-up★ 1st Appearance of Bald Eagle (in modern age).
14 ❑ Jan 1987 Cover: 1.25 **NM** value: **Cover or less**
Circ: CapCity orders: **7,975**
15 ❑ Feb 1987 Cover: 1.25 **NM** value: **Cover or less**
Circ: CapCity orders: **8,300**
16 ❑ Feb 1987 Cover: 1.25 **NM** value: **Cover or less**
Circ: CapCity orders: **7,950**
★ Death of Manic.
17 ❑ Mar 1987 Cover: 1.25 **NM** value: **Cover or less**
Circ: CapCity orders: **8,050**
★ 1st Appearance of Lacey Lyle. ★ Appearance of Harry Truman.
18 ❑ Mar 1987 Cover: 1.25 **NM** value: **Cover or less**
Circ: CapCity orders: **7,900**
W: Rick Veitch ★ 1st Appearance of Black Angel (in modern age).
19 ❑ Apr 1987 Cover: 1.25 **NM** value: **Cover or less**
Circ: CapCity orders: **8,050**
★ Versus Rats.
20 ❑ Apr 1987 Cover: 1.25 **NM** value: **Cover or less**
Circ: CapCity orders: **8,050**
★ 1st Appearance of The Rats (in modern age). ★ Versus Rats.
21 ❑ May 1987 Cover: 1.25 **NM** value: **Cover or less**
Circ: CapCity orders: **8,075**
A: George Evans ★ 1st Appearance of Rat Mother.
22 ❑ May 1987 Cover: 1.25 **NM** value: **Cover or less**
Circ: CapCity orders: **8,050**
Arctic Deathzone, Part 1 • Skywolf back-up story★ 1st Appearance of Lester Mansfield, El Lobo Alado (Skywolf's father).
23 ❑ Jun 1987 Cover: 1.25 **NM** value: **Cover or less**
Circ: CapCity orders: **7,600**
Arctic Deathzone, Part 2
24 ❑ Jun 1987 Cover: 1.25 **NM** value: **Cover or less**
Circ: CapCity orders: **7,575**
Arctic Deathzone, Part 3 ★ Appearance of Heap.
25 ❑ Jul 1987 Cover: 1.25 **NM** value: **Cover or less**
Circ: CapCity orders: **7,250**
★ Origin of Manure Man. ★ 1st Appearance of Manure Man. ★ Appearance of Heap.
26 ❑ Jul 1987 Cover: 1.25 **NM** value: **Cover or less**
Circ: CapCity orders: **7,250**
★ 1st Appearance of Flying Dutchman (in modern age), Road Rats.
27 ❑ Aug 1987 Cover: 1.25 **NM** value: **Cover or less**
Circ: CapCity orders: **6,900**
28 ❑ Aug 1987 Cover: 1.25 **NM** value: **Cover or less**
Circ: CapCity orders: **6,900**
★ 1st Appearance of Black Axis.
29 ❑ Sep 1987 Cover: 1.25 **NM** value: **Cover or less**
Circ: CapCity orders: **6,575**
30 ❑ Sep 1987 Cover: 1.25 **NM** value: **Cover or less**
Circ: CapCity orders: **6,575**
31 ❑ Oct 1987 Cover: 1.25 **NM** value: **Cover or less**
Circ: CapCity orders: **6,400**
32 ❑ Oct 1987 Cover: 1.25 **NM** value: **Cover or less**
Circ: CapCity orders: **6,425**
33 ❑ Nov 1987 Cover: 1.75 **NM** value: **Cover or less**
Circ: CapCity orders: **6,800**
34 ❑ Dec 1987 Cover: 1.75 **NM** value: **Cover or less**
Circ: CapCity orders: **6,375**
Barbed Wire Noose; Skywolf: Hot Potato **A:** Dan Spiegle; Stan Woch **W:** Chuck Dixon
35 ❑ Jan 1988 Cover: 1.75 **NM** value: **Cover or less**
Circ: CapCity orders: **6,025**
36 ❑ Feb 1988 Cover: 1.75 **NM** value: **Cover or less**
Circ: CapCity orders: **5,500**
37 ❑ Mar 1988 Cover: 1.75 **NM** value: **Cover or less**
Circ: CapCity orders: **5,650**
38 ❑ Apr 1988 Cover: 1.75 **NM** value: **Cover or less**
Circ: CapCity orders: **5,450**
39 ❑ May 1988 Cover: 1.75 **NM** value: **Cover or less**
Circ: CapCity orders: **5,175**
40 ❑ Jun 1988 Cover: 1.75 **NM** value: **Cover or less**
Circ: CapCity orders: **5,150**
41 ❑ Jul 1988 Cover: 1.75 **NM** value: **Cover or less**
Circ: CapCity orders: **4,900**
42 ❑ Aug 1988 Cover: 1.95 **NM** value: **Cover or less**
Circ: CapCity orders: **4,625**
43 ❑ Sep 1988 Cover: 1.95 **NM** value: **Cover or less**
Circ: CapCity orders: **4,400**
44 ❑ Oct 1988 Cover: 1.95 **NM** value: **Cover or less**
Circ: CapCity orders: **4,125**
45 ❑ Nov 1988 Cover: 1.95 **NM** value: **Cover or less**
Circ: CapCity orders: **4,200**
46 ❑ Jan 1989 Cover: 1.95 **NM** value: **Cover or less**
Circ: CapCity orders: **4,225**
• Airboy Diary
47 ❑ Mar 1989 Cover: 1.95 **NM** value: **Cover or less**
Circ: CapCity orders: **4,050**
• Airboy Diary
48 ❑ Apr 1989 Cover: 1.95 **NM** value: **Cover or less**
Circ: CapCity orders: **3,900**
• Airboy Diary
49 ❑ Jun 1989 Cover: 1.95 **NM** value: **Cover or less**
Circ: CapCity orders: **3,925**
• Airboy Diary
50 ❑ Oct 1989 Cover: 4.95 **NM** value: **Cover or less**
Circ: CapCity orders: **4,175**
• Giant-size. final issue. **A:** Joe Kubert

AIRBOY COMICS — Hillman

On the heels of the introduction of the Blackhawks in Military Comics #1, Hillman brought out Air Fighters #1. The first issue was filled with a variety of aviators who soloed for that single installment, but #2, a year later, brought such characters as Iron Ace, Black Angel, Flying Dutchman, and Sky Wolf, along with Airboy. That character was Davy Nelson, an orphaned teen (who grew older as time went on), who took to the skies in his own plane to oppose the Axis powers. That plane was nicknamed "Birdie," because it flew by flapping its wings like a bird. Airboy could call Birdie, much like a faithful pet, through a short-wave radio device. Within the first dozen issues, The Heap was introduced, initially as a villain, later as a force for good.

In 1986 Eclipse Comics published a new Airboy title, featuring a modern version of this Golden Age character.

Volume 2
11 ❑ Dec 1945 Cover: 0.10 **NM** value: **475.00**
• Series continued from Air Fighters Comics
12 ❑ Jan 1946 Cover: 0.10 **NM** value: **310.00**

Volume 3
1 ❑ Feb 1946 Cover: 0.10 **NM** value: **250.00**
2 ❑ Apr 1946 Cover: 0.10 **NM** value: **250.00**
4 ❑ May 1946 Cover: 0.10 **NM** value: **250.00**
5 ❑ Jun 1946 Cover: 0.10 **NM** value: **250.00**
6 ❑ Jul 1946 Cover: 0.10 **NM** value: **250.00**
7 ❑ Aug 1946 Cover: 0.10 **NM** value: **250.00**
8 ❑ Sep 1946 Cover: 0.10 **NM** value: **250.00**
9 ❑ Oct 1946 Cover: 0.10 **NM** value: **275.00**
★ Origin of The Heap.
10 ❑ Nov 1946 Cover: 0.10 **NM** value: **250.00**
11 ❑ Dec 1946 Cover: 0.10 **NM** value: **250.00**
12 ❑ Jan 1947 Cover: 0.10 **NM** value: **250.00**

Volume 4
1 ❑ Feb 1947 Cover: 0.10 **NM** value: **200.00**
2 ❑ Mar 1947 Cover: 0.10 **NM** value: **200.00**
3 ❑ Apr 1947 Cover: 0.10 **NM** value: **200.00**
4 ❑ May 1947 Cover: 0.10 **NM** value: **200.00**
A: Jack Kirby(cover) **W:** Joe Simon
5 ❑ Jun 1947 Cover: 0.10 **NM** value: **200.00**
A: Jack Kirby **W:** Joe Simon
6 ❑ Jul 1947 Cover: 0.10 **NM** value: **200.00**
Meets Riot O'Hara • Flyin' Fool **A:** Jack Kirby **W:** Joe Simon
7 ❑ Aug 1947 Cover: 0.10 **NM** value: **200.00**
Dynamite • Flyin' Fool **A:** Jack Kirby **W:** Joe Simon
8 ❑ Sep 1947 Cover: 0.10 **NM** value: **200.00**
You Can't Beat Cupid • Flyin' Fool **A:** Jack Kirby **W:** Joe Simon
9 ❑ Oct 1947 Cover: 0.10 **NM** value: **200.00**
His Brother's Keeper • Flyin' Fool **A:** Jack Kirby **W:** Joe Simon
10 ❑ Nov 1947 Cover: 0.10 **NM** value: **200.00**
Larceny in Old Lace • Flyin' Fool **A:** Jack Kirby **W:** Joe Simon
11 ❑ Dec 1947 Cover: 0.10 **NM** value: **200.00**
Face in the Storm • Flyin' Fool **A:** Jack Kirby **W:** Joe Simon
12 ❑ Jan 1948 Cover: 0.10 **NM** value: **185.00**
Peril Paradise • Flyin' Fool

Volume 5
1 ❑ Feb 1948 Cover: 0.10 **NM** value: **120.00**
2 ❑ Mar 1948 Cover: 0.10 **NM** value: **120.00**
3 ❑ Apr 1948 Cover: 0.10 **NM** value: **120.00**
4 ❑ May 1948 Cover: 0.10 **NM** value: **120.00**
5 ❑ Jun 1948 Cover: 0.10 **NM** value: **120.00**
6 ❑ Jul 1948 Cover: 0.10 **NM** value: **120.00**
7 ❑ Aug 1948 Cover: 0.10 **NM** value: **120.00**
8 ❑ Sep 1948 Cover: 0.10 **NM** value: **120.00**
9 ❑ Oct 1948 Cover: 0.10 **NM** value: **120.00**
10 ❑ Nov 1948 Cover: 0.10 **NM** value: **135.00**
★ Origin of The Heap.
11 ❑ Dec 1948 Cover: 0.10 **NM** value: **120.00**
12 ❑ Jan 1949 Cover: 0.10 **NM** value: **120.00**

Volume 6
1 ❑ Feb 1949 Cover: 0.10 **NM** value: **95.00**
2 ❑ Mar 1949 Cover: 0.10 **NM** value: **95.00**
3 ❑ Apr 1949 Cover: 0.10 **NM** value: **95.00**
4 ❑ May 1949 Cover: 0.10 **NM** value: **95.00**
5 ❑ Jun 1949 Cover: 0.10 **NM** value: **95.00**
6 ❑ Jul 1949 Cover: 0.10 **NM** value: **95.00**
7 ❑ Aug 1949 Cover: 0.10 **NM** value: **95.00**
8 ❑ Sep 1949 Cover: 0.10 **NM** value: **95.00**
★ Origin of The Heap.
9 ❑ Oct 1949 Cover: 0.10 **NM** value: **95.00**
10 ❑ Nov 1949 Cover: 0.10 **NM** value: **95.00**
11 ❑ Dec 1949 Cover: 0.10 **NM** value: **95.00**
12 ❑ Jan 1950 Cover: 0.10 **NM** value: **95.00**

Volume 7
1 ❑ Feb 1950 Cover: 0.10 **NM** value: **85.00**
2 ❑ Mar 1950 Cover: 0.10 **NM** value: **85.00**
3 ❑ Apr 1950 Cover: 0.10 **NM** value: **85.00**
4 ❑ May 1950 Cover: 0.10 **NM** value: **85.00**
5 ❑ Jun 1950 Cover: 0.10 **NM** value: **85.00**
6 ❑ Jul 1950 Cover: 0.10 **NM** value: **85.00**
7 ❑ Aug 1950 Cover: 0.10 **NM** value: **85.00**
8 ❑ Sep 1950 Cover: 0.10 **NM** value: **85.00**
9 ❑ Oct 1950 Cover: 0.10 **NM** value: **85.00**
10 ❑ Nov 1950 Cover: 0.10 **NM** value: **85.00**
11 ❑ Dec 1950 Cover: 0.10 **NM** value: **85.00**
12 ❑ Jan 1951 Cover: 0.10 **NM** value: **85.00**

Volume 8
1 ❑ Feb 1951 Cover: 0.10 **NM** value: **80.00**
2 ❑ Mar 1951 Cover: 0.10 **NM** value: **80.00**
3 ❑ Apr 1951 Cover: 0.10 **NM** value: **80.00**
4 ❑ May 1951 Cover: 0.10 **NM** value: **80.00**
5 ❑ Jun 1951 Cover: 0.10 **NM** value: **80.00**
6 ❑ Jul 1951 Cover: 0.10 **NM** value: **80.00**
7 ❑ Aug 1951 Cover: 0.10 **NM** value: **80.00**
8 ❑ Sep 1951 Cover: 0.10 **NM** value: **80.00**
The Best of Tiger Mountain; Grizzly; Land of Ice (text story); English Boy of Spain; Handlebar Hank; Dog of the Blue; The Heap
9 ❑ Oct 1951 Cover: 0.10 **NM** value: **80.00**
10 ❑ Nov 1951 Cover: 0.10 **NM** value: **80.00**
11 ❑ Dec 1951 Cover: 0.10 **NM** value: **80.00**
12 ❑ Jan 1952 Cover: 0.10 **NM** value: **80.00**

Volume 9
1 ❑ Feb 1952 Cover: 0.10 **NM** value: **75.00**
2 ❑ Mar 1952 Cover: 0.10 **NM** value: **75.00**
3 ❑ Apr 1952 Cover: 0.10 **NM** value: **75.00**
4 ❑ May 1952 Cover: 0.10 **NM** value: **75.00**
5 ❑ Jun 1952 Cover: 0.10 **NM** value: **75.00**
6 ❑ Jul 1952 Cover: 0.10 **NM** value: **75.00**
7 ❑ Aug 1952 Cover: 0.10 **NM** value: **75.00**
8 ❑ Sep 1952 Cover: 0.10 **NM** value: **75.00**
9 ❑ Oct 1952 Cover: 0.10 **NM** value: **75.00**
10 ❑ Nov 1952 Cover: 0.10 **NM** value: **75.00**
11 ❑ Dec 1952 Cover: 0.10 **NM** value: **75.00**
12 ❑ Jan 1953 Cover: 0.10 **NM** value: **75.00**

Volume 10
1 ❑ Feb 1953 Cover: 0.10 **NM** value: **75.00**
2 ❑ Mar 1953 Cover: 0.10 **NM** value: **75.00**
3 ❑ Apr 1953 Cover: 0.10 **NM** value: **75.00**

CGC-graded: Multiply prices above by **33 for 9.9 M • 16 for 9.8 NM/M • 7 for 9.6 NM+ • 5 for 9.4 NM • 2.5 for 9.2 NM- • 1.5 for 9.0 VF/NM**

4 ❑ May 1953 Cover: 0.10 **NM** value: **75.00**
final issue.

AIRBOY MEETS THE PROWLER — Eclipse

1 ❑ Dec 1987 Cover: 1.95 **NM** value: **Cover or less**
Circ: CapCity orders: **6,800**
A: John K. Snyder III **W:** Tim Truman; Chuck Dixon

AIRBOY-MR. MONSTER SPECIAL — Eclipse

1 ❑ Aug 1987 Cover: 1.75 **NM** value: **Cover or less**
Circ: CapCity orders: **6,975**
📖 The CafT at the Edge of the World **A:** Michael T. Gilbert; Mark Pacella **W:** Michael T. Gilbert

AIRBOY VERSUS THE AIRMAIDENS — Eclipse

1 ❑ Jul 1988 Cover: 1.95 **NM** value: **Cover or less**
Circ: CapCity orders: **5,300**

AIR FIGHTERS CLASSICS — Eclipse

1 ❑ Nov 1987 Cover: 3.95 **NM** value: **Cover or less**
cardstock cover. • squarebound;Reprints Air Fighters Comics#1
2 ❑ Jan 1988 Cover: 3.95 **NM** value: **Cover or less**
📖 Airboy; Skywolf; The Iron Ace; Warriors at Home; The Black Angel; Our Eagles; The Bald Eagle; Wun Wing Spin; The Flying Dutchman • Reprints Air Fighters Comics#2 **A:** Bob Fujitani; Harry Sahle **W:** Nathaniel Nitkin ★ Origin of Airboy.
3 ❑ Cover: 3.95 **NM** value: **Cover or less**
• Reprints Air Fighters Comics#3
4 ❑ Cover: 3.95 **NM** value: **Cover or less**
• Reprints Air Fighters Comics#4
5 ❑ 1989 Cover: 3.95 **NM** value: **Cover or less**
• Reprints Air Fighters Comics#5
6 ❑ Cover: 3.95 **NM** value: **Cover or less**
• Reprints Air Fighters Comics#6
7 ❑ Cover: 3.95 **NM** value: **Cover or less**
• Reprints Air Fighters Comics#7

AIR FIGHTERS COMICS — Hillman Periodicals

1 ❑ Nov 1941 Cover: 0.10 **NM** value: **1500.00**
• **CGC:** 6 graded, best 9.2
2 ❑ Nov 1942 Cover: 0.10 **NM** value: **2000.00**
• **CGC:** 6 graded, best 9.2
3 ❑ Dec 1942 Cover: 0.10 **NM** value: **1000.00**
• **CGC:** 2 graded, best 9.6
4 ❑ Jan 1943 Cover: 0.10 **NM** value: **750.00**
• **CGC:** 1 graded, best 9.4
5 ❑ Feb 1943 Cover: 0.10 **NM** value: **650.00**
• **CGC:** 1 graded, best 9.6
6 ❑ Mar 1943 Cover: 0.10 **NM** value: **650.00**
• **CGC:** 3 graded, best 9.6
7 ❑ Apr 1943 Cover: 0.10 **NM** value: **650.00**
• **CGC:** 1 graded, best 9.6
8 ❑ May 1943 Cover: 0.10 **NM** value: **650.00**
• **CGC:** 1 graded, best 9.6
9 ❑ Jun 1943 Cover: 0.10 **NM** value: **650.00**
• **CGC:** 2 graded, best 9.6
10 ❑ Jul 1943 Cover: 0.10 **NM** value: **650.00**
11 ❑ Aug 1943 Cover: 0.10 **NM** value: **500.00**
• **CGC:** 1 graded, best 9.0
12 ❑ Sep 1943 Cover: 0.10 **NM** value: **500.00**
13 ❑ Oct 1943 Cover: 0.10 **NM** value: **500.00**
• **CGC:** 1 graded, best 6.5
14 ❑ Nov 1943 Cover: 0.10 **NM** value: **500.00**
• **CGC:** 2 graded, best 9.4
15 ❑ Dec 1943 Cover: 0.10 **NM** value: **500.00**
• **CGC:** 3 graded, best 9.2
16 ❑ Jan 1944 Cover: 0.10 **NM** value: **400.00**
• **CGC:** 1 graded, best 9.2
17 ❑ Feb 1944 Cover: 0.10 **NM** value: **400.00**
• **CGC:** 1 graded, best 7.0
18 ❑ Mar 1944 Cover: 0.10 **NM** value: **400.00**
• **CGC:** 6 graded, best 9.2
19 ❑ Apr 1944 Cover: 0.10 **NM** value: **400.00**
• **CGC:** 1 graded, best 8.5
20 ❑ Fal 1944 Cover: 0.10 **NM** value: **300.00**
• **CGC:** 3 graded, best 9.4
21 ❑ Win 1945 Cover: 0.10 **NM** value: **300.00**
• **CGC:** 2 graded, best 9.4
22 ❑ Fal 1945 Cover: 0.10 **NM** value: **300.00**
• **CGC:** 1 graded, best 3.5
• Later issues published as Airboy Comics.

AIRFIGHTERS MEET SGT. STRIKE SPECIAL — Eclipse

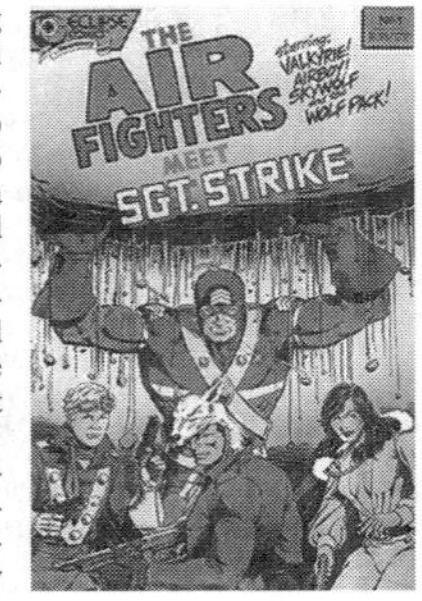

In an adventure set in the waning days of World War II, the original Airboy, gal-pal Valkyrie, SkyWolf, and the Airfighters meet up with super-soldier Sgt. Strike to prevent the Nazis from launching a fully functional space station called "Thor's Hammer." With action/adventure writer supreme Chuck Dixon (Birds of Prey, Nightwing) and artist extraordinaire Tom Lyle (The Amazing Spider-Man, Starman) at the creative helm, it's a wild ride.

Eclipse had picked up the characters from the 1940s and 1950s Hillman series that began as Air Fighters and changed its title to Airboy Comics. Eclipse then told new high-flying tales, including this one.

1 ❑ Jan 1988 Cover: 1.95 **NM** value: **Cover or less**
Circ: CapCity orders: **5,525**
📖 Tomorrow The Star **A:** Tom Lyle **W:** Chuck Dixon

AIRLOCK — Eclectus

1 ❑ Jun 1990, b&w Cover: 2.25 **NM** value: **2.50**
📖 Airlock; F-Mice: The Trouble with Flying; The Threat; Demon Birth; The Curse of the Gypsy; Have It Your Way!; Flip Gordon…Married to the Mob! **A:** Wayne Reid; Jorge Pacheco; Topper Helmers; Ed Quinby **W:** Wayne Reid; Jorge Pacheco; Ed Quinby; Rod Underhill
2 ❑ 1990 Cover: 2.50 **NM** value: **Cover or less**
3 ❑ 1990 Cover: 2.50 **NM** value: **Cover or less**

AIRMAIDENS SPECIAL — Eclipse

1 ❑ Aug 1987 Cover: 1.75 **NM** value: **Cover or less**
Circ: CapCity orders: **8,000**
📖 Three Day Weekend **A:** Larry Elmore **W:** Chuck Dixon ★ Origin of La Lupina.

AIRMAN — Malibu

1 ❑ Cover: 1.95 **NM** value: **Cover or less**
Circ: CapCity orders: **14,700**
📖 Shall The Sea Give Up Her Secrets? **A:** Matt Reynolds **W:** R.A. Jones ★ 1st Appearance of Thresher.

AIRMEN, THE — Mansion

1 ❑ Cover: 2.50 **NM** value: **Cover or less**
📖 Six Against Oblivion **A:** Clint Hilinski **W:** David Watkins

AIR RAIDERS — Marvel / Star

1 ❑ Nov 1987 Cover: 1.00 **NM** value: **Cover or less**
Circ: CapCity orders: **8,950**
📖 Sins Of The Father **A:** Kelley Jones **W:** Howard Mackie
2 ❑ Dec 1987 Cover: 1.00 **NM** value: **Cover or less**
Circ: CapCity orders: **3,950**
3 ❑ Jan 1988 Cover: 1.00 **NM** value: **Cover or less**
Circ: CapCity orders: **3,350**
4 ❑ Feb 1988 Cover: 1.00 **NM** value: **Cover or less**
Circ: CapCity orders: **3,100**
5 ❑ Mar 1988 Cover: 1.00 **NM** value: **Cover or less**
Circ: CapCity orders: **2,000**

AIRTIGHT GARAGE, THE — Marvel / Epic

The Airtight Garage is an asteroid built by a former Earthman who has since become a world-shaper. The man, Major Gruber, fell through a trans-time circle while fighting the war in Vietnam. This transported him to a technologically advanced spot called Randomearth SDX, where he met Lewis and Erik Carnellan. Eventually, these three would encounter Nagual, the Lord Creator of Worlds. They would become Nagual's servants in the fight against the Bakalites, who sought to uncreate the universe.

Eventually, Erik defected to the side of the Bakalites, and Major Gruber fled, stealing some of Nagual's technology. With it, he created the Airtight Garage, itself the home of several "pocket universes" or "levels." These levels ranged from the desert universe of the Third Level to the First Level, where the Major kept Nagual's technology. As this four-part story begins, the Bakalites are seeking to invade the First Level. If they succeed, the universe may perish!

1 ❑ Jul 1993 Cover: 2.50 **NM** value: **Cover or less**
Circ: CapCity orders: **4,500**
A: Moebius **W:** Moebius
2 ❑ Aug 1993 Cover: 2.50 **NM** value: **Cover or less**
Circ: CapCity orders: **3,700**
A: Moebius **W:** Moebius
3 ❑ Sep 1993 Cover: 2.50 **NM** value: **Cover or less**
Circ: CapCity orders: **3,700**
A: Moebius **W:** Moebius
4 ❑ Oct 1993 Cover: 2.50 **NM** value: **Cover or less**
Circ: CapCity orders: **3,200**
A: Moebius **W:** Moebius

AIR WARRIORS — Fantaco

Bk 1❑ Cover: 14.95 **NM** value: **Cover or less**
A: Derek Gray **W:** Noel K. Hannon

AIR WAR STORIES — Dell

1 ❑ Nov 1964 Cover: 0.12 **NM** value: **22.00**
2 ❑ Dec 1965 Cover: 0.12 **NM** value: **14.00**
📖 The Hurricane that Wasn't; Admiral's Country; The Crimson Coffin; Tag-Along Takes Over **A:** Sam Glanzman
3 ❑ 1966 Cover: 0.12 **NM** value: **14.00**
4 ❑ 1966 Cover: 0.12 **NM** value: **14.00**
5 ❑ 1966 Cover: 0.12 **NM** value: **14.00**
6 ❑ 1966 Cover: 0.12 **NM** value: **14.00**
7 ❑ 1966 Cover: 0.12 **NM** value: **14.00**
8 ❑ • Final issue? **NM** value: **14.00**

AIRWAVES — Caliber

1 ❑ Feb 1991 Cover: 2.50 **NM** value: **Cover or less**
📖 Chapter 1; Taken Under **A:** Michael Lark **W:** Michael Lark; Debra Rodia
2 ❑ 1991 Cover: 2.50 **NM** value: **Cover or less**
A: Michael Lark **W:** Michael Lark
3 ❑ 1991 Cover: 2.50 **NM** value: **Cover or less**
A: Michael Lark **W:** Michael Lark
4 ❑ 1991 Cover: 2.50 **NM** value: **Cover or less**
A: Michael Lark **W:** Michael Lark

Creator Key
W = Writer • A = Artist • C = Cover Artist

A.K.A. GOLDFISH — Caliber

Brian Michael Bendis wrote and drew the noir crime graphic novel, starting with a rough short version in 1988 and eventually developing the story into an attention-grabbing, award-winning dark adventure. The Image paperback collection (titled, simply, Goldfish) says, "Goldfish is the story of an enigmatic grifter with a heart of gold, who returns to his old haunts to find his old flame, Lauren, practically running the city's underbelly, and his oldest friend and ex-partner in crime, Izzy, a police detective. But Goldfish has come back for one reason, and one reason only, his son." — Maggie

1 ❑ Cover: 3.50 **NM** value: **Cover or less**
• Joker
2 ❑ Cover: 3.95 **NM** value: **Cover or less**
• Ace
3 ❑ Cover: 3.95 **NM** value: **Cover or less**
• Jack
4 ❑ Cover: 2.95 **NM** value: **Cover or less**
• Queen
5 ❑ Mar 1996 Cover: 3.95 **NM** value: **Cover or less**
cardstock cover. • King
Bk 1❑ Cover: 17.95 **NM** value: **Cover or less**
• collects mini-series
Bk 1-2❑ Cover: 16.95 **NM** value: **Cover or less**

AKIKO — Sirius

1 ❑ Mar 1996 Cover: 2.50 **NM** value: **6.00**
A: Mark Crilley **W:** Mark Crilley
2 ❑ Apr 1996 Cover: 2.50 **NM** value: **4.50**
A: Mark Crilley **W:** Mark Crilley
3 ❑ May 1996 Cover: 2.50 **NM** value: **4.00**
A: Mark Crilley **W:** Mark Crilley
4 ❑ Jun 1996 Cover: 2.50 **NM** value: **4.00**
A: Mark Crilley **W:** Mark Crilley
5 ❑ 1996 Cover: 2.50 **NM** value: **4.00**
• no indicia **A:** Mark Crilley **W:** Mark Crilley
6 ❑ Aug 1996 Cover: 2.50 **NM** value: **3.50**
A: Mark Crilley **W:** Mark Crilley
7 ❑ Sep 1996 Cover: 2.50 **NM** value: **3.50**
Circ: Diamd. preorders: **4,223**
A: Mark Crilley **W:** Mark Crilley
8 ❑ Oct 1996 Cover: 2.50 **NM** value: **3.50**
Circ: Diamd. preorders: **4,368**
A: Mark Crilley **W:** Mark Crilley
9 ❑ Dec 1996 Cover: 2.50 **NM** value: **3.50**
Circ: Direct Market orders: **4,059**
A: Mark Crilley **W:** Mark Crilley
10 ❑ Jan 1997 Cover: 2.50 **NM** value: **3.50**
Circ: Direct Market orders: **4,217**
A: Mark Crilley **W:** Mark Crilley
11 ❑ Feb 1997 Cover: 2.50 **NM** value: **Cover or less**
Circ: Diamd. preorders: **3,894**
A: Mark Crilley **W:** Mark Crilley
12 ❑ Mar 1997 Cover: 2.50 **NM** value: **Cover or less**
Circ: Diamd. preorders: **3,665**
A: Mark Crilley **W:** Mark Crilley
13 ❑ Apr 1997 Cover: 2.50 **NM** value: **Cover or less**
Circ: Diamd. preorders: **3,709**
A: Mark Crilley **W:** Mark Crilley
14 ❑ May 1997 Cover: 2.50 **NM** value: **Cover or less**
Circ: Diamd. preorders: **3,635**
A: Mark Crilley **W:** Mark Crilley
15 ❑ Jul 1997 Cover: 2.50 **NM** value: **Cover or less**
Circ: Diamd. preorders: **3,676**
A: Mark Crilley **W:** Mark Crilley
16 ❑ Aug 1997 Cover: 2.50 **NM** value: **Cover or less**
A: Mark Crilley **W:** Mark Crilley
17 ❑ Aug 1997 Cover: 2.50 **NM** value: **Cover or less**
• indicia says "Aug" **A:** Mark Crilley **W:** Mark Crilley
18 ❑ Sep 1997 Cover: 2.50 **NM** value: **Cover or less**
A: Mark Crilley **W:** Mark Crilley
19 ❑ Oct 1997 Cover: 2.50 **NM** value: **Cover or less**
📖 The Story Tree • Beeba's story **A:** Mark Crilley **W:** Mark Crilley
20 ❑ Nov 1997 Cover: 2.50 **NM** value: **Cover or less**
📖 The Story Tree • Beeba's story **A:** Mark Crilley **W:** Mark Crilley
21 ❑ Dec 1997 Cover: 2.50 **NM** value: **Cover or less**
📖 Spuckler's Story, Part 1 **A:** Mark Crilley **W:** Mark Crilley
22 ❑ Jan 1998 Cover: 2.50 **NM** value: **Cover or less**
Circ: Diamd. preorders: **3,464**
📖 Spuckler's Story, Part 2 **A:** Mark Crilley **W:** Mark Crilley
23 ❑ Feb 1998 Cover: 2.50 **NM** value: **Cover or less**
Circ: Diamd. preorders: **3,468**
📖 Gax's Story, Part 1 **A:** Mark Crilley **W:** Mark Crilley
24 ❑ Mar 1998 Cover: 2.50 **NM** value: **Cover or less**
Circ: Diamd. preorders: **3,438**
📖 Gax's Story, Part 2 **A:** Mark Crilley **W:** Mark Crilley
25 ❑ May 1998 Cover: 2.95 **NM** value: **Cover or less**
Circ: Diamd. preorders: **3,797**
A: Mark Crilley **W:** Mark Crilley
26 ❑ Jul 1998 Cover: 2.50 **NM** value: **Cover or less**
Circ: Diamd. preorders: **3,394**
A: Mark Crilley **W:** Mark Crilley
27 ❑ Aug 1998 Cover: 2.50 **NM** value: **Cover or less**
Circ: Diamd. preorders: **3,406**
A: Mark Crilley **W:** Mark Crilley
28 ❑ Oct 1998 Cover: 2.50 **NM** value: **Cover or less**
Circ: Diamd. preorders: **3,418**
A: Mark Crilley **W:** Mark Crilley
29 ❑ Nov 1998 Cover: 2.50 **NM** value: **Cover or less**
Circ: Diamd. preorders: **3,496**
A: Mark Crilley **W:** Mark Crilley

Do you have changes or corrections for the **Standard Catalog**? Send your original research to us at
allcomics@krause.com

Other grades: Multiply prices above by **1.5 for Mint • 2/3 for Very Fine • 1/3 for Fine • 1/5 for Very Good • 1/8 for Good**

30 ❑ Dec 1998 Cover: 2.50 **NM** value: **Cover or less**
Circ: Diamd. preorders: **3,549**
A: Mark Crilley **W:** Mark Crilley
31 ❑ Feb 1998 Cover: 2.50 **NM** value: **Cover or less**
Circ: Diamd. preorders: **3,495**
A: Mark Crilley **W:** Mark Crilley
32 ❑ Mar 1998 Cover: 2.50 **NM** value: **Cover or less**
Circ: Diamd. preorders: **3,448**
A: Mark Crilley **W:** Mark Crilley
33 ❑ May 1998 Cover: 2.50 **NM** value: **Cover or less**
Circ: Diamd. preorders: **3,355**
A: Mark Crilley **W:** Mark Crilley
34 ❑ Jun 1999 Cover: 2.50 **NM** value: **Cover or less**
Circ: Diamd. preorders: **3,263**
A: Mark Crilley **W:** Mark Crilley
35 ❑ Sep 1999, b&w Cover: 2.50 **NM** value: **Cover or less**
Circ: Diamd. preorders: **3,144**
Moonshopping, Part 1 **A:** Mark Crilley **W:** Mark Crilley
36 ❑ Oct 1999, b&w Cover: 2.50 **NM** value: **Cover or less**
Circ: Diamd. preorders: **3,137**
Moonshopping, Part 2 **A:** Mark Crilley **W:** Mark Crilley
37 ❑ Dec 1999, b&w Cover: 2.50 **NM** value: **Cover or less**
Moonshopping, Part 3 **A:** Mark Crilley **W:** Mark Crilley
38 ❑ Feb 2000, b&w Cover: 2.50 **NM** value: **Cover or less**
Circ: Diamd. preorders: **2,875**
Moonshopping, Part 4 **A:** Mark Crilley **W:** Mark Crilley
39 ❑ May 2000, b&w Cover: 2.50 **NM** value: **Cover or less**
Circ: Diamd. preorders: **2,803**
Spucky and Gax in Illegal Aliens; Akiko in Dream Sequence; Mr. Beeba's Alphabet Book (for the Verbally Precocious) **A:** Mark Crilley **W:** Mark Crilley
40 ❑ Aug 2000, b&w Cover: 2.95 **NM** value: **Cover or less**
Circ: Diamd. preorders: **2,915**
The Battle of Boach's Keep **A:** Mark Crilley **W:** Mark Crilley
41 ❑ Oct 2000, b&w Cover: 2.95 **NM** value: **Cover or less**
Circ: Diamd. preorders: **2,848**
The Battle of Boach's Keep **A:** Mark Crilley **W:** Mark Crilley
Bk 1❑ Jun 1998, b&w Cover: 11.95 **NM** value: **14.95**
A: Mark Crilley **W:** Mark Crilley
Bk 2❑ 1998b&w Cover: 11.95 **NM** value: **Cover or less**
• Collects Akiko #8-13 **A:** Mark Crilley **W:** Mark Crilley
Bk 3❑ Jan 1999, b&w Cover: 11.95 **NM** value: **Cover or less**
A: Mark Crilley **W:** Mark Crilley
Bk 4❑ Feb 2000, b&w Cover: 14.95 **NM** value: **Cover or less**
The Story Tree • collects Akiko #19-25

AKIKO ON THE PLANET SMOO — Sirius

Akiko, a 4th-grade girl, travels to the planet Smoo at the request of Smoo's leader, King Froptoppit. (Back on Earth, a robot duplicate of Akiko remains to take her school tests.) In this all-ages series, King Froptoppit charges Akiko with the task of finding his lost son. Akiko and four others, whom the king sends with her, set off to find the Prince. Along the way, the five travelers come across an old hermit who reluctantly agrees to help. The Prince's searchers have many marvelous adventures along the way. In one, they find themselves in a spaceship chase, riding gigantic bull-like creatures called Fubas and talking to living castles.

1 ❑ Dec 1995, b&w Cover: 3.95 **NM** value: **8.00**
Fold-out cover. **A:** Mark Crilley **W:** Mark Crilley
1/HC❑b&w Cover: 9.95 **NM** value: **19.95**
• Hardcover edition. **A:** Mark Crilley **W:** Mark Crilley
1-2 ❑ May 1998, b&w Cover: 3.50 **NM** value: **4.00**
FAN 1❑ **NM** value: **3.00**
• free promotional giveaway. **A:** Mark Crilley **W:** Mark Crilley

AKIKO ON THE PLANET SMOO: THE COLOR EDITION — Sirius

1 ❑ Feb 2000, full color Cover: 4.95 **NM** value: **Cover or less**
Circ: Diamd. preorders: **1,779**
cardstock cover.

AKIRA — Marvel / Epic

Akira — worshiped by some as a god, feared as a weapon of destruction more powerful than a nuclear bomb — is just a boy. After 38 years of cryogenic sleep, his name has passed into legend.

Tetsuo is the latest child captured by the secret government experiment that created Akira. He is the perfect test subject: an orphan and a member of a local gang. But the experiment unhinges his mind. When Tetsuo discovers that Akira may be more powerful, Tetsuo is enraged and goes in search of the sleeping boy, destroying everything in his path.

Kaneda is the leader of the gang from which Tetsuo was abducted. Searching for his missing friend, he becomes enamored of the girl Kay and follows her into a world of intrigue and rebels. The rebels, the government, Kaneda, and Tetsuo come together to witness the awakening of a legend. Nothing will ever be the same.

1 ❑ Sep 1988 Cover: 3.50 **NM** value: **9.00**
Circ: CapCity orders: **21,300** • **CGC:** 9 graded, best 9.8
1st printing. **A:** Katsuhiro Otomo **W:** Katsuhiro Otomo

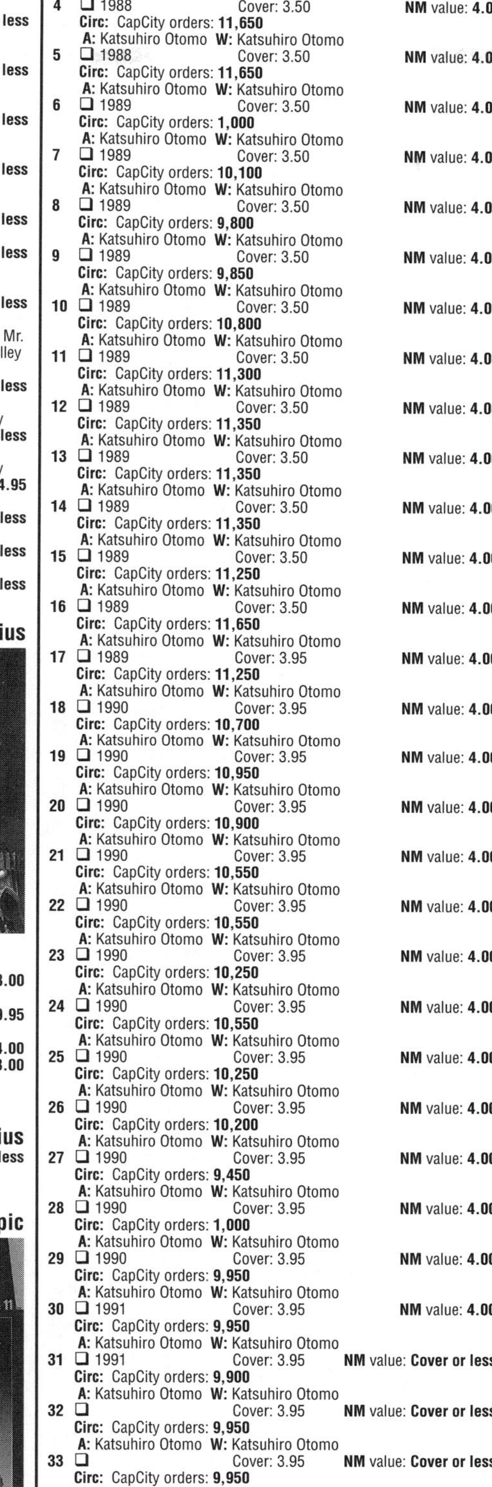

1-2 ❑ 1988 Cover: 3.95 **NM** value: **4.00**
2 ❑ 1988 Cover: 3.50 **NM** value: **5.00**
Circ: CapCity orders: **15,600** • **CGC:** 1 graded, best 9.8
1st printing. **A:** Katsuhiro Otomo **W:** Katsuhiro Otomo
2-2 ❑ 1988 Cover: 3.95 **NM** value: **4.00**
3 ❑ 1988 Cover: 3.50 **NM** value: **5.00**
Circ: CapCity orders: **14,100**
A: Katsuhiro Otomo **W:** Katsuhiro Otomo
4 ❑ 1988 Cover: 3.50 **NM** value: **4.00**
Circ: CapCity orders: **11,650**
A: Katsuhiro Otomo **W:** Katsuhiro Otomo
5 ❑ 1988 Cover: 3.50 **NM** value: **4.00**
Circ: CapCity orders: **11,650**
A: Katsuhiro Otomo **W:** Katsuhiro Otomo
6 ❑ 1989 Cover: 3.50 **NM** value: **4.00**
Circ: CapCity orders: **1,000**
A: Katsuhiro Otomo **W:** Katsuhiro Otomo
7 ❑ 1989 Cover: 3.50 **NM** value: **4.00**
Circ: CapCity orders: **10,100**
A: Katsuhiro Otomo **W:** Katsuhiro Otomo
8 ❑ 1989 Cover: 3.50 **NM** value: **4.00**
Circ: CapCity orders: **9,800**
A: Katsuhiro Otomo **W:** Katsuhiro Otomo
9 ❑ 1989 Cover: 3.50 **NM** value: **4.00**
Circ: CapCity orders: **9,850**
A: Katsuhiro Otomo **W:** Katsuhiro Otomo
10 ❑ 1989 Cover: 3.50 **NM** value: **4.00**
Circ: CapCity orders: **10,800**
A: Katsuhiro Otomo **W:** Katsuhiro Otomo
11 ❑ 1989 Cover: 3.50 **NM** value: **4.00**
Circ: CapCity orders: **11,300**
A: Katsuhiro Otomo **W:** Katsuhiro Otomo
12 ❑ 1989 Cover: 3.50 **NM** value: **4.00**
Circ: CapCity orders: **11,350**
A: Katsuhiro Otomo **W:** Katsuhiro Otomo
13 ❑ 1989 Cover: 3.50 **NM** value: **4.00**
Circ: CapCity orders: **11,350**
A: Katsuhiro Otomo **W:** Katsuhiro Otomo
14 ❑ 1989 Cover: 3.50 **NM** value: **4.00**
Circ: CapCity orders: **11,350**
A: Katsuhiro Otomo **W:** Katsuhiro Otomo
15 ❑ 1989 Cover: 3.50 **NM** value: **4.00**
Circ: CapCity orders: **11,250**
A: Katsuhiro Otomo **W:** Katsuhiro Otomo
16 ❑ 1989 Cover: 3.50 **NM** value: **4.00**
Circ: CapCity orders: **11,650**
A: Katsuhiro Otomo **W:** Katsuhiro Otomo
17 ❑ 1989 Cover: 3.95 **NM** value: **4.00**
Circ: CapCity orders: **11,250**
A: Katsuhiro Otomo **W:** Katsuhiro Otomo
18 ❑ 1990 Cover: 3.95 **NM** value: **4.00**
Circ: CapCity orders: **10,700**
A: Katsuhiro Otomo **W:** Katsuhiro Otomo
19 ❑ 1990 Cover: 3.95 **NM** value: **4.00**
Circ: CapCity orders: **10,950**
A: Katsuhiro Otomo **W:** Katsuhiro Otomo
20 ❑ 1990 Cover: 3.95 **NM** value: **4.00**
Circ: CapCity orders: **10,900**
A: Katsuhiro Otomo **W:** Katsuhiro Otomo
21 ❑ 1990 Cover: 3.95 **NM** value: **4.00**
Circ: CapCity orders: **10,550**
A: Katsuhiro Otomo **W:** Katsuhiro Otomo
22 ❑ 1990 Cover: 3.95 **NM** value: **4.00**
Circ: CapCity orders: **10,550**
A: Katsuhiro Otomo **W:** Katsuhiro Otomo
23 ❑ 1990 Cover: 3.95 **NM** value: **4.00**
Circ: CapCity orders: **10,250**
A: Katsuhiro Otomo **W:** Katsuhiro Otomo
24 ❑ 1990 Cover: 3.95 **NM** value: **4.00**
Circ: CapCity orders: **10,550**
A: Katsuhiro Otomo **W:** Katsuhiro Otomo
25 ❑ 1990 Cover: 3.95 **NM** value: **4.00**
Circ: CapCity orders: **10,250**
A: Katsuhiro Otomo **W:** Katsuhiro Otomo
26 ❑ 1990 Cover: 3.95 **NM** value: **4.00**
Circ: CapCity orders: **10,200**
A: Katsuhiro Otomo **W:** Katsuhiro Otomo
27 ❑ 1990 Cover: 3.95 **NM** value: **4.00**
Circ: CapCity orders: **9,450**
A: Katsuhiro Otomo **W:** Katsuhiro Otomo
28 ❑ 1990 Cover: 3.95 **NM** value: **4.00**
Circ: CapCity orders: **1,000**
A: Katsuhiro Otomo **W:** Katsuhiro Otomo
29 ❑ 1990 Cover: 3.95 **NM** value: **4.00**
Circ: CapCity orders: **9,950**
A: Katsuhiro Otomo **W:** Katsuhiro Otomo
30 ❑ 1991 Cover: 3.95 **NM** value: **4.00**
Circ: CapCity orders: **9,950**
A: Katsuhiro Otomo **W:** Katsuhiro Otomo
31 ❑ 1991 Cover: 3.95 **NM** value: **Cover or less**
Circ: CapCity orders: **9,900**
A: Katsuhiro Otomo **W:** Katsuhiro Otomo
32 ❑ Cover: 3.95 **NM** value: **Cover or less**
Circ: CapCity orders: **9,950**
A: Katsuhiro Otomo **W:** Katsuhiro Otomo
33 ❑ Cover: 3.95 **NM** value: **Cover or less**
Circ: CapCity orders: **9,950**
A: Katsuhiro Otomo **W:** Katsuhiro Otomo
34 ❑ Cover: 3.95 **NM** value: **Cover or less**
Circ: CapCity orders: **9,500**
A: Katsuhiro Otomo **W:** Katsuhiro Otomo
35 ❑ Cover: 3.95 **NM** value: **Cover or less**
Circ: CapCity orders: **8,950**
A: Katsuhiro Otomo **W:** Katsuhiro Otomo
36 ❑ 1995 Cover: 3.95 **NM** value: **Cover or less**
Circ: CapCity orders: **9,200**
A: Katsuhiro Otomo **W:** Katsuhiro Otomo ★ Appearance of Lady Miyako.
37 ❑ Cover: 3.95 **NM** value: **Cover or less**
A: Katsuhiro Otomo **W:** Katsuhiro Otomo
38 ❑ Cover: 3.95 **NM** value: **Cover or less**
final issue. **A:** Katsuhiro Otomo **W:** Katsuhiro Otomo
Bk 1❑ Cover: 13.95 **NM** value: **Cover or less**
Circ: CapCity orders: **1,950**
• Collects Akira #1-3 **A:** Katsuhiro Otomo **W:** Katsuhiro Otomo
Bk 2❑ Cover: 14.95 **NM** value: **Cover or less**
A: Katsuhiro Otomo **W:** Katsuhiro Otomo
Bk 3❑ Cover: 14.95 **NM** value: **Cover or less**
A: Katsuhiro Otomo **W:** Katsuhiro Otomo
Bk 4❑ Cover: 14.95 **NM** value: **Cover or less**
A: Katsuhiro Otomo **W:** Katsuhiro Otomo
Bk 5❑ Cover: 14.95 **NM** value: **Cover or less**
A: Katsuhiro Otomo **W:** Katsuhiro Otomo
Bk 6❑ Cover: 14.95 **NM** value: **Cover or less**
A: Katsuhiro Otomo **W:** Katsuhiro Otomo
Bk 7❑ Cover: 14.95 **NM** value: **16.95**
• Collects Akira #19-21 **A:** Katsuhiro Otomo **W:** Katsuhiro Otomo
Bk 8❑ Cover: 16.95 **NM** value: **Cover or less**
• Collects Akira #22-24 **A:** Katsuhiro Otomo **W:** Katsuhiro Otomo
Bk 9❑ Cover: 16.95 **NM** value: **Cover or less**
A: Katsuhiro Otomo **W:** Katsuhiro Otomo
Bk 10❑ Cover: 17.95 **NM** value: **Cover or less**
A: Katsuhiro Otomo **W:** Katsuhiro Otomo

A*K*Q*J — Fantagraphics

1 ❑ b&w Cover: 2.75 **NM** value: **Cover or less**
• Captain Jack

ALADDIN (DISNEY'S...) — Marvel

Picking up where the 1992 Disney hit animated film "Aladdin" left off, this short-lived series continues the adventures of Aladdin, his monkey-friend Abu, Princess Jasmine, and, of course, the Genie.

From time to time, new characters are introduced and familiar storylines are explored, but all in the great tradition of Disney comics, which means wholesome action, adventure, and all sorts of jokes that could never have been fit into the follow-up animated series or the home release video sequels. It's not quite the same without the voice of Robin Williams or award-winning songs, but still full of fun for young readers.

1 ❑ Oct 1994 Cover: 1.50 **NM** value: **Cover or less**
Circ: CapCity orders: **16,650**
Aladdin's Quest **A:** David Riguard **W:** Lee Nordling
2 ❑ Nov 1994 Cover: 1.50 **NM** value: **Cover or less**
Circ: CapCity orders: **9,950**
The Pharaoh's Curse **A:** David Riguard **W:** Dan Slott
3 ❑ Dec 1994 Cover: 1.50 **NM** value: **Cover or less**
Circ: CapCity orders: **8,200**
4 ❑ Jan 1995 Cover: 1.50 **NM** value: **Cover or less**
Circ: CapCity orders: **6,950**
5 ❑ Feb 1995 Cover: 1.50 **NM** value: **Cover or less**
Circ: CapCity orders: **6,025**
6 ❑ Mar 1995 Cover: 1.50 **NM** value: **Cover or less**
Circ: CapCity orders: **5,055**
7 ❑ Apr 1995 Cover: 1.50 **NM** value: **Cover or less**
Circ: CapCity orders: **4,450**
8 ❑ May 1995 Cover: 1.50 **NM** value: **Cover or less**
Circ: CapCity orders: **4,175**
9 ❑ Jun 1995 Cover: 1.50 **NM** value: **Cover or less**
Circ: CapCity orders: **3,975**
10 ❑ Jul 1995 Cover: 1.50 **NM** value: **Cover or less**
Circ: CapCity orders: **3,725**
11 ❑ Aug 1995 Cover: 1.50 **NM** value: **Cover or less**
Circ: CapCity orders: **3,650**
Bk 1❑ Cover: 4.95 **NM** value: **Cover or less**
• prestige format. **A:** Xavi **W:** Bobbi JG Weiss

ALARMING ADVENTURES — Harvey

1 ❑ Oct 1962 Cover: 0.12 **NM** value: **60.00**
The Lost Acre; The Night Visitor; The Aliens; Hermit; Paradise in Space (text); The Invaders (text); Silent Street
2 ❑ Dec 1962 Cover: 0.12 **NM** value: **40.00**
• **CGC:** 1 graded, best 4.0
3 ❑ Feb 1963 Cover: 0.12 **NM** value: **35.00**

ALARMING TALES — Harvey

1 ❑ Sep 1957 Cover: 0.10 **NM** value: **125.00**
• **CGC:** 3 graded, best 9.0
The Cadmus Seed; Logan's Next Life; The Fourth Dimension is a Many Splattered Thing; The Last Enemy; Donnegan's Daffy Chair
2 ❑ Nov 1957 Cover: 0.10 **NM** value: **100.00**
• **CGC:** 2 graded, best 5.0
Hole in the Wall; The Big Hunt; The Fireballs; I Want to Be a Man
3 ❑ Feb 1958 Cover: 0.10 **NM** value: **75.00**
This World is Ours
4 ❑ May 1958 Cover: 0.10 **NM** value: **75.00**
Forbidden Journey
5 ❑ Aug 1958 Cover: 0.10 **NM** value: **60.00**
6 ❑ Nov 1958 Cover: 0.10 **NM** value: **60.00**

ALBEDO (1ST SERIES) — Thoughts & Images

In this furry animal epic, Erma Felna and the EDF Corps fly around the galaxy, put down revolutions, discover new planets, and find the ancient remains of a spacecraft with a skeleton of an ape-like animal never seen before. It's sort of like "Planet of the Apes Goes to the Zoo — and Then to Outer Space."

CGC-graded: Multiply prices above by **33 for 9.9 M • 16 for 9.8 NM/M • 7 for 9.6 NM+ • 5 for 9.4 NM • 2.5 for 9.2 NM- • 1.5 for 9.0 VF/NM**

Steve Gallacci uses an unusual charcoal/pastel medium for his art that lends soft warmth and depth to his work. He is also a contributor to such other titles as Fusion and Command Review.

Early issues of this series were in very high demand during the black-and-white boom, but interest paled and the series' many starts and stops eventually killed interest in Gallacci's ongoing storyline. It's still fondly remembered in the "furry" community.

0 ❑ Cover: 2.00 **NM** value: **8.00**
Blue cover. 📖 Erma Felna; Bad Rubber • 500 printed **A:** Steven A. Gallacci **W:** Steven A. Gallacci

0/A ❑ Cover: 2.00 **NM** value: **30.00**
White cover (yellow table). • Only 50 copies printed **A:** Steven A. Gallacci **W:** Steven A. Gallacci

0/B ❑ Cover: 2.00 **NM** value: **15.00**
White cover (no yellow). • Less than 500 copies printed **A:** Steven A. Gallacci **W:** Steven A. Gallacci

0-2 ❑ Cover: 2.00 **NM** value: **5.00**

0-3 ❑ Cover: 0.50 **NM** value: **3.00**

0-4 ❑ Dec 1986 Cover: 1.00 **NM** value: **2.50**

1 ❑ Cover: 2.00 **NM** value: **14.00**
• **CGC:** 2 graded, best 9.2
Dark red cover. **A:** Steven A. Gallacci **W:** Steven A. Gallacci ★ 1st Appearance of Usagi Yojimbo.

1/A ❑ Cover: 2.00 **NM** value: **10.00**
Bright red cover.

1-2 ❑ Cover: 2.00 **NM** value: **10.00**

2 ❑ Nov 1984 Cover: 1.50 **NM** value: **8.00**
• **CGC:** 2 graded, best 9.4
A: Steven A. Gallacci **W:** Steven A. Gallacci ★ 2nd Appearance of Usagi Yojimbo.

3 ❑ Apr 1985 Cover: 2.00 **NM** value: **5.00**
• Usagi Yojimbo back-up **A:** Steven A. Gallacci **W:** Steven A. Gallacci

4 ❑ Jul 1985 Cover: 2.00 **NM** value: **4.00**
• **CGC:** 1 graded, best 9.6
• Usagi Yojimbo back-up **A:** Steven A. Gallacci **W:** Steven A. Gallacci

5 ❑ Oct 1985 Cover: 2.00 **NM** value: **4.00**
A: Steven A. Gallacci **W:** Steven A. Gallacci

6 ❑ Jan 1986 Cover: 2.00 **NM** value: **3.00**
A: Steven A. Gallacci **W:** Steven A. Gallacci

7 ❑ Mar 1986 Cover: 2.00 **NM** value: **3.00**
A: Steven A. Gallacci **W:** Steven A. Gallacci

8 ❑ Jul 1986 Cover: 2.00 **NM** value: **3.00**
A: Steven A. Gallacci **W:** Steven A. Gallacci

9 ❑ May 1987 Cover: 2.00 **NM** value: **Cover or less**
A: Steven A. Gallacci **W:** Steven A. Gallacci

10 ❑ Sep 1987 Cover: 2.00 **NM** value: **Cover or less**
cardstock cover. **A:** Steven A. Gallacci **W:** Steven A. Gallacci

11 ❑ Dec 1987 Cover: 2.00 **NM** value: **Cover or less**
A: Steven A. Gallacci **W:** Steven A. Gallacci

12 ❑ Mar 1988 Cover: 2.00 **NM** value: **Cover or less**
A: Steven A. Gallacci **W:** Steven A. Gallacci

13 ❑ Jun 1988 Cover: 2.00 **NM** value: **Cover or less**
A: Steven A. Gallacci **W:** Steven A. Gallacci

14 ❑ Spr 1989 Cover: 2.00 **NM** value: **Cover or less**
Photo cover. final issue. **A:** Steven A. Gallacci **W:** Steven A. Gallacci

ALBEDO (2ND SERIES) — Antarctic

1 ❑ Jun 1991 Cover: 2.50 **NM** value: **4.00**
2 ❑ Sep 1991 Cover: 2.50 **NM** value: **3.00**
3 ❑ Dec 1991 Cover: 2.50 **NM** value: **3.00**
4 ❑ Mar 1992 Cover: 2.50 **NM** value: **3.00**
5 ❑ Jun 1992 Cover: 2.50 **NM** value: **Cover or less**
6 ❑ Sep 1992 Cover: 2.50 **NM** value: **Cover or less**
7 ❑ Dec 1992 Cover: 2.50 **NM** value: **Cover or less**
8 ❑ Mar 1993 Cover: 2.50 **NM** value: **Cover or less**
9 ❑ Jun 1993 Cover: 2.50 **NM** value: **Cover or less**
10 ❑ Oct 1993 Cover: 2.75 **NM** value: **Cover or less**
SE 1 ❑ Jul 1993, full color Cover: 2.95 **NM** value: **Cover or less**
• Color special

ALBEDO (3RD SERIES) — Antarctic

1 ❑ Feb 1994 Cover: 2.95 **NM** value: **Cover or less**
A: Steven A. Gallacci **W:** Steven A. Gallacci

2 ❑ Oct 1994 Cover: 2.95 **NM** value: **Cover or less**
A: Steven A. Gallacci **W:** Steven A. Gallacci

3 ❑ Feb 1995 Cover: 2.95 **NM** value: **Cover or less**
A: Steven A. Gallacci **W:** Steven A. Gallacci

4 ❑ Jan 1996 Cover: 2.95 **NM** value: **Cover or less**

ALBEDO (4TH SERIES) — Antarctic

1 ❑ Dec 1996 Cover: 2.95 **NM** value: **Cover or less**
Circ: Direct Market orders: **2,922**
A: Steven A. Gallacci **W:** Steven A. Gallacci

2 ❑ Jan 1999 Cover: 2.95 **NM** value: **2.99**
Circ: Diamd. preorders: **1,604**
📖 Erma Felna, EDF **A:** Steven A. Gallacci **W:** Steven A. Gallacci

ALBEDO (5TH SERIES) — Antarctic

1 ❑ Cover: 2.99 **NM** value: **Cover or less**

ALBINO SPIDER OF DAJETTE — Verotik

1 ❑ ca. 1997 Cover: 2.95 **NM** value: **Cover or less**
Circ: Diamd. preorders: **8,073**

2 ❑ ca. 1997 Cover: 2.95 **NM** value: **Cover or less**
Circ: Diamd. preorders: **6,353**

0 ❑ ca. 1998 Cover: 2.95 **NM** value: **Cover or less**
Circ: Diamd. preorders: **4,003**

ALEC DEAR — Mediocre Concepts

1 ❑ 1996b&w **NM** value: **2.00**
no cover price. • magazine-sized comic book with cardstock cover.
📖 The Hospital

ALEC: LOVE AND BEERGLASSES — Escape

1 ❑ Cover: 1.95 **NM** value: **3.50**
A: Eddie Campbell **W:** Eddie Campbell

ALEX — Fantagraphics

1 ❑ Cover: 2.95 **NM** value: **Cover or less**
A: Mark Kalesniko **W:** Mark Kalesniko

2 ❑ Apr 1994 Cover: 2.95 **NM** value: **Cover or less**
A: Mark Kalesniko **W:** Mark Kalesniko

3 ❑ Jul 1994 Cover: 2.95 **NM** value: **Cover or less**
A: Mark Kalesniko **W:** Mark Kalesniko

4 ❑ Oct 1994 Cover: 2.95 **NM** value: **Cover or less**
A: Mark Kalesniko **W:** Mark Kalesniko

5 ❑ Nov 1994 Cover: 2.95 **NM** value: **Cover or less**
A: Mark Kalesniko **W:** Mark Kalesniko

ALEXIS (VOL. 2) — Eros

1 ❑ 1995 Cover: 2.95 **NM** value: **Cover or less**
A: Adam Kelly **W:** Adam Kelly

2 ❑ Jul 1995 Cover: 2.95 **NM** value: **Cover or less**
A: Adam Kelly **W:** Adam Kelly

3 ❑ 1995 Cover: 2.95 **NM** value: **Cover or less**
A: Adam Kelly **W:** Adam Kelly

4 ❑ 1995 Cover: 2.95 **NM** value: **Cover or less**
A: Adam Kelly **W:** Adam Kelly

5 ❑ Mar 1996 Cover: 2.95 **NM** value: **Cover or less**
A: Adam Kelly **W:** Adam Kelly

ALF — Marvel

ALF (Alien Life Form) is an alien from the planet Melmac. While traveling through space, his craft develops problems and he crashes on Earth, eventually winding up in the Tanner family's garage. Young Brian Tanner immediately takes a liking to ALF and introduces him to the others: sister Lynn and parents Kate and Willie. All of them eventually get used to having a wise-cracking alien who looks a bit like an ugly teddy bear. All of them, that is, except Lucky, the family cat. Cats, it seems, were something of a delicacy on Melmac, and ALF is continually chasing Lucky with dinner in mind.

A goofy, popular television show, which ran from 1986 to 1990, ALF also enjoyed a respectable run as a comic book. It ran 50 issues from 1988 to 1992, along with numerous special editions.

1 ❑ Mar 1988 Cover: 1.00 **NM** value: **2.00**
Circ: CapCity orders: **9,300** • **CGC:** 2 graded, best 9.6
📖 At Your Disposal; Snow Skin off My Nose; Play Misty for Me **A:** Dave Manak **W:** Michael Gallagher ★ 1st Appearance of Alf.

2 ❑ Apr 1988 Cover: 1.00 **NM** value: **1.25**
Circ: CapCity orders: **7,000**
📖 All's Fair; Jungle Love **A:** Dave Manak **W:** Michael Gallagher ★ 2nd Appearance of Alf.

3 ❑ May 1988 Cover: 1.00 **NM** value: **1.25**
Circ: CapCity orders: **6,250**
📖 Travels with Willie; One Tiny Mistake; Carrot Cards **A:** Dave Manak **W:** Michael Gallagher

4 ❑ Jun 1988 Cover: 1.00 **NM** value: **1.25**
Circ: CapCity orders: **7,800**

5 ❑ Jul 1988 Cover: 1.00 **NM** value: **1.25**
Circ: CapCity orders: **8,500**

6 ❑ Aug 1988 Cover: 1.00 **NM** value: **Cover or less**
Circ: CapCity orders: **8,900**

7 ❑ Sep 1988 Cover: 1.00 **NM** value: **Cover or less**
Circ: CapCity orders: **8,600**

8 ❑ Oct 1988 Cover: 1.00 **NM** value: **Cover or less**
Circ: CapCity orders: **8,800**

9 ❑ Nov 1988 Cover: 1.00 **NM** value: **Cover or less**
Circ: CapCity orders: **8,400**

10 ❑ Dec 1988 Cover: 1.00 **NM** value: **Cover or less**
Circ: CapCity orders: **8,000**

11 ❑ Jan 1989 Cover: 1.00 **NM** value: **Cover or less**
Circ: Statement: **108,600** CapCity orders: **7,600**

12 ❑ Feb 1989 Cover: 1.00 **NM** value: **Cover or less**
Circ: Statement: **108,600** CapCity orders: **7,300**

13 ❑ Mar 1989 Cover: 1.00 **NM** value: **Cover or less**
Circ: Statement: **108,600** CapCity orders: **7,350**

14 ❑ Apr 1989 Cover: 1.00 **NM** value: **Cover or less**
Circ: Statement: **108,600** CapCity orders: **7,200**

15 ❑ May 1989 Cover: 1.00 **NM** value: **Cover or less**
Circ: Statement: **108,600** CapCity orders: **6,800**

16 ❑ Jun 1989 Cover: 1.00 **NM** value: **Cover or less**
Circ: Statement: **108,600** CapCity orders: **6,500**

17 ❑ Jul 1989 Cover: 1.00 **NM** value: **Cover or less**
Circ: Statement: **108,600** CapCity orders: **6,600**

18 ❑ Aug 1989 Cover: 1.00 **NM** value: **Cover or less**
Circ: Statement: **108,600** CapCity orders: **7,450**

19 ❑ Sep 1989 Cover: 1.00 **NM** value: **Cover or less**
Circ: Statement: **108,600** CapCity orders: **6,350**

20 ❑ Oct 1989 Cover: 1.00 **NM** value: **Cover or less**
Circ: Statement: **108,600** CapCity orders: **6,000**
📖 Babe in the Woods, Part 1

21 ❑ Nov 1989 Cover: 1.00 **NM** value: **Cover or less**
Circ: Statement: **108,600** CapCity orders: **5,800**
📖 Babe in the Woods, Part 2 **A:** Dave Manak **W:** Michael Gallagher

22 ❑ Nov 1989 Cover: 1.00 **NM** value: **Cover or less**
Circ: Statement: **108,600** CapCity orders: **7,800**
• X-Men parody

23 ❑ Dec 1989 Cover: 1.00 **NM** value: **Cover or less**
Circ: Statement: **108,600** CapCity orders: **5,600**

24 ❑ Dec 1989 Cover: 1.00 **NM** value: **Cover or less**
Circ: Statement: **108,600** CapCity orders: **5,450**

25 ❑ Jan 1990 Cover: 1.00 **NM** value: **Cover or less**
Circ: Statement: **72,541** CapCity orders: **6,600**

26 ❑ Feb 1990 Cover: 1.00 **NM** value: **Cover or less**
Circ: Statement: **72,541** CapCity orders: **5,150**

27 ❑ Mar 1990 Cover: 1.00 **NM** value: **Cover or less**
Circ: Statement: **72,541** CapCity orders: **4,650**

28 ❑ Apr 1990 Cover: 1.00 **NM** value: **Cover or less**
Circ: Statement: **72,541** CapCity orders: **4,200**

29 ❑ May 1990 Cover: 1.00 **NM** value: **Cover or less**
Circ: Statement: **72,541**
"3-D" cover.

30 ❑ Jun 1990 Cover: 1.00 **NM** value: **Cover or less**
Circ: Statement: **72,541** CapCity orders: **4,200**

31 ❑ Jul 1990 Cover: 1.00 **NM** value: **Cover or less**
Circ: Statement: **72,541** CapCity orders: **4,050**

32 ❑ Aug 1990 Cover: 1.00 **NM** value: **Cover or less**
Circ: Statement: **72,541** CapCity orders: **3,700**

33 ❑ Sep 1990 Cover: 1.00 **NM** value: **Cover or less**
Circ: Statement: **72,541** CapCity orders: **3,750**

34 ❑ Oct 1990 Cover: 1.00 **NM** value: **Cover or less**
Circ: Statement: **72,541** CapCity orders: **3,300**

35 ❑ Nov 1990 Cover: 1.00 **NM** value: **Cover or less**
Circ: Statement: **72,541** CapCity orders: **3,250**

36 ❑ Dec 1990 Cover: 1.00 **NM** value: **Cover or less**
Circ: Statement: **72,541** CapCity orders: **3,100**

37 ❑ Jan 1991 Cover: 1.00 **NM** value: **Cover or less**
Circ: CapCity orders: **2,900**

38 ❑ Feb 1991 Cover: 1.00 **NM** value: **Cover or less**
Circ: CapCity orders: **2,800**

39 ❑ Mar 1991 Cover: 1.00 **NM** value: **Cover or less**
Circ: CapCity orders: **2,650**

40 ❑ Apr 1991 Cover: 1.00 **NM** value: **Cover or less**
Circ: CapCity orders: **2,550**

41 ❑ May 1991 Cover: 1.00 **NM** value: **Cover or less**
Circ: CapCity orders: **2,600**
📖 T.V.F.X.N.F.S! **A:** Dave Manak **W:** Michael Gallagher

42 ❑ Jun 1991 Cover: 1.00 **NM** value: **Cover or less**
Circ: CapCity orders: **2,600**
📖 Send in the Clones! **A:** Dave Manak **W:** Michael Gallagher

43 ❑ Jul 1991 Cover: 1.00 **NM** value: **Cover or less**
Circ: CapCity orders: **2,500**
📖 Secure From General Quarter Pounders **A:** Dave Manak **W:** Michael Gallagher

44 ❑ Aug 1991 Cover: 1.00 **NM** value: **Cover or less**
Circ: CapCity orders: **2,850**
• X-Men parody

45 ❑ Sep 1991 Cover: 1.00 **NM** value: **Cover or less**
Circ: CapCity orders: **2,500**

46 ❑ Oct 1991 Cover: 1.00 **NM** value: **Cover or less**
Circ: CapCity orders: **2,450**

47 ❑ Nov 1991 Cover: 1.00 **NM** value: **Cover or less**
Circ: CapCity orders: **2,450**

48 ❑ Dec 1991 Cover: 1.00 **NM** value: **Cover or less**
Circ: CapCity orders: **2,500**
📖 Th-Th-That's All, Folks!, Part 2 **A:** Dave Manak **W:** Michael Gallagher

49 ❑ Jan 1992 Cover: 1.00 **NM** value: **Cover or less**

50 ❑ Feb 1992 Cover: 1.75 **NM** value: **Cover or less**
Circ: CapCity orders: **2,750**
• Giant-size. final issue.

Anl 1 ❑ ca. 1988 Cover: 1.75 **NM** value: **Cover or less**
Circ: CapCity orders: **9,100**
• Dynamic Forces edition. 📖 The Return Of Rhonda; Back To Human Nature; Safe At Home; You Give Me Fever; A Campy Approach; **A:** Dave Manak **W:** Michael Gallagher

Anl 2 ❑ ca. 1989 Cover: 2.00 **NM** value: **Cover or less**
Circ: CapCity orders: **6,600**
A: Bill Sienkiewicz

Anl 3 ❑ ca. 1990 Cover: 2.00 **NM** value: **Cover or less**
Circ: CapCity orders: **4,650**
• TMNT parody

Bk 1 ❑ Cover: 4.95 **NM** value: **Cover or less**
• Alf Bookshelf Edition. 📖 At Your Disposal; Snow Skin off My Nose; Play Misty for Me; All's Fair; Jungle Love; Travels with Willie; One Tiny Mistake; Carrot Cards • Collects issues #1-3 **A:** Dave Manak **W:** Michael Gallagher

HS 1 ❑ Hol 1988 Cover: 1.75 **NM** value: **Cover or less**
• magazine-sized comic book with cardstock cover. • Holiday Special #1

HS 2 ❑ Hol 1989 Cover: 2.00 **NM** value: **Cover or less**
Circ: CapCity orders: **5,800**
• Dynamic Forces edition. • Holiday Special #2

ALF COMICS MAGAZINE — Marvel

1 ❑ Nov 1988 Cover: 1.50 **NM** value: **2.00**
Circ: CapCity orders: **1,900**
• digest.

2 ❑ Jan 1989 Cover: 1.50 **NM** value: **2.00**
Circ: CapCity orders: **900**
• digest.

ALIAS: — Now

1 ❑ Jul 1990 Cover: 1.75 **NM** value: **Cover or less**
A: Bill Sienkiewicz(cover) **W:** Chuck Dixon

2 ❑ Aug 1990 Cover: 1.75 **NM** value: **Cover or less**
W: Chuck Dixon

3 ❑ Sep 1990 Cover: 1.75 **NM** value: **Cover or less**
W: Chuck Dixon

4 ❑ Oct 1990 Cover: 1.75 **NM** value: **Cover or less**
W: Chuck Dixon

5 ❑ Nov 1990 Cover: 1.75 **NM** value: **Cover or less**
W: Chuck Dixon

The prices seen above do not represent the highest possible prices seen in online auctions, but rather the prices we have seen these issues reliably fetch in a variety of environments (storefront retail, mail order, auction and convention).

Other grades: Multiply prices above by **1.5 for Mint • 2/3 for Very Fine • 1/3 for Fine • 1/5 for Very Good • 1/8 for Good**

ALIAS (MARVEL) — Marvel / MAX

Private investigator Jessica Jones was once a member of The Avengers. After some mysterious circumstances she left the team and no longer uses her powers, choosing to work on more mundane cases.

Written by Brian Michael Bendis, the noir-ish series began with Jones being hired to follow a woman whose sister was concerned about her well-being. During the investigation, Jones came into some potential blackmail material against another super-hero and had to decide what, if anything, to do with it. Jones' wrestling with the ethics of using her powers and super-hero connections to aid her investigations are a good portion of what keeps the series going as are the occasional cameo by those self-same heroes, including Luke Cage, Captain America, and Warbird (the former Ms. Marvel). — Brent

1 ❑ ca. 2001 Cover: 2.99 **NM** value: **Cover or less**
Circ: Diamd. preorders: **52,379 • CGC:** 18 graded, best 9.8
2 ❑ ca. 2001 Cover: 2.99 **NM** value: **Cover or less**
Circ: Diamd. preorders: **43,112 • CGC:** 1 graded, best 9.8
3 ❑ ca. 2001 Cover: 2.99 **NM** value: **Cover or less**
Circ: Diamd. preorders: **43,750 • CGC:** 1 graded, best 9.8
4 ❑ ca. 2001 Cover: 2.99 **NM** value: **Cover or less**
Circ: Diamd. preorders: **41,099**
5 ❑ ca. 2002 Cover: 2.99 **NM** value: **Cover or less**
Circ: Diamd. preorders: **38,465**
6 ❑ ca. 2002 Cover: 2.99 **NM** value: **Cover or less**
Circ: Diamd. preorders: **36,946**

ALICE — Ziff-Davis

10 ❑ ca. 1951 Cover: 0.10 **NM** value: **125.00**
11 ❑ ca. 1951 Cover: 0.10 **NM** value: **75.00**

ALICE AND THE ENGINE — Straw Dog

1 ❑ Cover: 2.50 **NM** value: **Cover or less**
2 ❑ Cover: 2.50 **NM** value: **Cover or less**
3 ❑ Cover: 2.50 **NM** value: **Cover or less**

ALICE IN BLUNDERLAND — Industrial Services

1 ❑ **NM** value: **100.00**

ALICE IN LOST WORLD — Radio Comix

1 ❑ Cover: 2.95 **NM** value: **Cover or less**
Circ: Diamd. preorders: **1,912**
2 ❑ ca. 2001 Cover: 2.95 **NM** value: **Cover or less**
Circ: Diamd. preorders: **1,323**
3 ❑ ca. 2001 Cover: 2.95 **NM** value: **Cover or less**
Circ: Diamd. preorders: **1,106**
4 ❑ ca. 2001 Cover: 2.95 **NM** value: **Cover or less**
Circ: Diamd. preorders: **1,093**

ALIEN 3 — Dark Horse

1 ❑ 1992 Cover: 2.50 **NM** value: **Cover or less**
Circ: CapCity orders: **54,550**
A: Chris Taylor **W:** Steven Grant
2 ❑ 1992 Cover: 2.50 **NM** value: **Cover or less**
Circ: CapCity orders: **34,500**
A: Chris Taylor **W:** Steven Grant
3 ❑ 1992 Cover: 2.50 **NM** value: **Cover or less**
Circ: CapCity orders: **33,925**
A: Chris Taylor **W:** Steven Grant

ALIEN DUCKLINGS — Blackthorne

1 ❑ Oct 1986 Cover: 1.75 **NM** value: **2.00**
Clone Home **A:** Andy Ice **W:** Cliff MacGillivray
2 ❑ 1987 Cover: 1.75 **NM** value: **2.00**
3 ❑ 1987 Cover: 1.75 **NM** value: **2.00**
4 ❑ 1987 Cover: 1.75 **NM** value: **2.00**

ALIEN ENCOUNTERS (ECLIPSE) — Eclipse

To the great disappointment of many, Pacific Comics ceased publishing in 1984. Eclipse picked up a few of its more popular series, including Alien Worlds, continuing that title's run until #9, when its owners decided to cancel it. A year later, Eclipse decided to offer its own version of that series with Alien Encounters.

Running 14 issues in all, Alien Encounters offered respectable stories of science-fiction and the unexpected. For example: A two-page quickie by Marc Hempel shows a man with a bionic replacement hand worrying about fitting in — but, when he looks out the window, we see that the planet is populated by robots. More involved stories show people dreaming of families and children on the brink of doomsday, running from alien police, and going to outrageous (and deadly) extremes to remake bad robot movies from the 1950s.

1 ❑ Jun 1985 Cover: 1.75 **NM** value: **2.00**
Circ: CapCity orders: **8,500**
Pretending; Open Season; Gargonzo; Outcast **A:** Marc Hempel; Mike Hoffman; Mike Gustovich; Toren Smith **W:** Marc Hempel; Eric Dinehart; Ken Macklin; Buzz Dixon
2 ❑ Aug 1965 Cover: 1.75 **NM** value: **2.00**
Circ: CapCity orders: **5,625**
3 ❑ Oct 1985 Cover: 1.75 **NM** value: **2.00**
Circ: CapCity orders: **5,000**
The Heroine; M.O.T.H.E.R. Knows Best; Claustrophobia; Relativity **A:** Larry Elmore; Attilio Micheluzzi; Pedro Henry **W:** Jim Baikie; Buzz Dixon; Paul Alexander
4 ❑ Dec 1985 Cover: 1.75 **NM** value: **2.00**
Circ: CapCity orders: **4,175**
Luv's Story; Now Jr. Behave Yourself; Wish Upon a Jewel; Invasion! **A:** Larry Elmore; William Wray; Tim Truman; Tim Conrad **W:** Tim Truman; Tim Conrad; Charles Wagner; Gardner Fox
5 ❑ Feb 1986 Cover: 1.75 **NM** value: **2.00**
Circ: CapCity orders: **4,450**
6 ❑ Apr 1986 Cover: 1.75 **NM** value: **2.00**
Circ: CapCity orders: **4,350**
Standard Procedure; Freefall; Nada; For Want of a Nail... • Story "Nada" used as basis for movie "They Live" **A:** William Wray; Chuck Beckum; Lee Weeks; Ken Macklin **W:** William Wray; Bruce Jones; Toren Smith
7 ❑ Jun 1986 Cover: 1.75 **NM** value: **2.00**
Circ: CapCity orders: **4,700**
Under Tartuka; So You Want to Be in Pictures?; It Happened This Morning; Picture Me and You **A:** Bo Hampton; Richard Howell; Rick Geary; Chuck Beckum **W:** Rick Geary; Bruce Jones; Douglas M. Wheeler
8 ❑ Aug 1986 Cover: 1.75 **NM** value: **2.00**
Circ: CapCity orders: **4,850**
Take One Capsule Every Million Years; Joyriding; It's a Wonderful Day in Our Neighborhood!; Moving Violation **A:** Dan Day; Attilio Micheluzzi; Jim Sullivan; Ken Macklin **W:** Bruce Jones; Ken Macklin; Toren Smith; Buzz Dixon; Charles Wagner
9 ❑ Oct 1986 Cover: 1.75 **NM** value: **2.00**
Circ: CapCity orders: **4,225**
The Conquered; Strangers on a Subway; An Alien Encounter; Diseased! **A:** Larry Elmore; John Bolton; John K. Snyder III; Lee Weeks **W:** Bruce Jones; Douglas M. Wheeler; Howard Zimmerman; Tom Field
10 ❑ Dec 1986 Cover: 1.75 **NM** value: **2.00**
Circ: CapCity orders: **4,625**
The Exiles; Cracked Mirrors; Perfect Model; Arena **A:** Tom Sutton; Gray Morrow; Denis McFarling; Rafe Negrete **W:** Rafe Negrete; Ray Bradbury; Beppe Sabatini; Tim Smith
11 ❑ Feb 1987 Cover: 2.00 **NM** value: **Cover or less**
Circ: CapCity orders: **4,075**
A World A'Hurtin'; Dave's Dilemma; Old Soldiers Fade Away; Adrift **A:** Steve Oliff; Karl Waller; Scott Hampton; Peter Ledger **W:** Steve Oliff; Tim Truman; Scott Hampton; Chuck Dixon; Mark Kneece
12 ❑ Apr 1987 Cover: 2.00 **NM** value: **Cover or less**
Circ: CapCity orders: **4,375**
What a Relief!; Eyes of the Sibyl; The Great Outdoors; The Face of the Enemy! **A:** Karl Waller; Mark A. Nelson; Doug Medved **W:** Nicola Cutii; Buzz Dixon; Ruby
13 ❑ Jun 1987 Cover: 2.00 **NM** value: **Cover or less**
The Light at the End; Page One; The Midget and the Eyeball; The Ideal Solution **A:** Graham Nolan; Hilary Barta; Peter Ledger; Doug Medved **W:** Chuck Dixon; Douglas M. Wheeler; Ruby
14 ❑ Aug 1987 Cover: 2.00 **NM** value: **Cover or less**
Circ: CapCity orders: **3,875**
The Buster Crabbe Collector; In Other News, Aliens Landed Today!; J.D.'s; Stillborn final issue. **A:** John Ridgway; Graham Nolan; Tom Lyle; Thomas Wimbish **W:** Chuck Dixon; Eric Dinehart; Beppe Sabatini; Jack Butterworth

ALIEN ENCOUNTERS (FANTACO) — Fantaco

1 ❑ 1980 Cover: 1.25 **NM** value: **1.50**

ALIEN FIRE — Kitchen Sink

1 ❑ Jan 1987 Cover: 2.00 **NM** value: **Cover or less**
Distant Light, Distant Country **A:** Eric Vincent **W:** Anthony Smith
2 ❑ May 1987 Cover: 2.00 **NM** value: **Cover or less**
A: Eric Vincent **W:** Anthony Smith
3 ❑ May 1987 Cover: 2.00 **NM** value: **Cover or less**
A: Eric Vincent **W:** Anthony Smith

ALIEN FIRE: PASS IN THUNDER — Kitchen Sink

1 ❑ May 1995, b&w Cover: 6.95 **NM** value: **Cover or less**
No issue number. • squarebound

ALIEN HERO — Zen

1 ❑ Feb 1999 Cover: 8.95 **NM** value: **Cover or less**
• illustrated novella featuring Zen

ALIEN LEGION: A GREY DAY TO DIE — Marvel

1 ❑ Cover: 5.95 **NM** value: **Cover or less**

ALIEN LEGION: BINARY DEEP — Marvel / Epic

1 ❑ Sep 1993 Cover: 3.50 **NM** value: **Cover or less**
Circ: CapCity orders: **4,750**
No issue number. **A:** Enrique Alcatena **W:** Chuck Dixon

ALIEN LEGION: JUGGER GRIMROD — Marvel / Epic

1 ❑ Aug 1992 Cover: 5.95 **NM** value: **Cover or less**
Circ: CapCity orders: **5,200**
A: Mike McMahon **W:** Chuck Dixon

ALIEN LEGION: ONE PLANET AT A TIME — Marvel / Epic

1 ❑ ca. 1993 Cover: 4.95 **NM** value: **Cover or less**
Circ: CapCity orders: **6,750**
One Planet At A Time **A:** Hoang Nguyen **W:** Chuck Dixon
2 ❑ ca. 1993 Cover: 4.95 **NM** value: **Cover or less**
Circ: CapCity orders: **5,100**
Heavy Hitters **A:** Hoang Nguyen **W:** Chuck Dixon
3 ❑ ca. 1993 Cover: 4.95 **NM** value: **Cover or less**
Circ: CapCity orders: **4,400**
A: Hoang Nguyen **W:** Chuck Dixon

ALIEN LEGION: ON THE EDGE — Marvel / Epic

1 ❑ Nov 1990 Cover: 4.50 **NM** value: **Cover or less**
Circ: CapCity orders: **8,450**
A: Larry Stroman **W:** Chuck Dixon
2 ❑ Dec 1990 Cover: 4.50 **NM** value: **Cover or less**
Circ: CapCity orders: **7,700**
A: Larry Stroman **W:** Chuck Dixon
3 ❑ Jan 1991 Cover: 4.50 **NM** value: **Cover or less**
Circ: CapCity orders: **6,850**
A: Larry Stroman **W:** Chuck Dixon

ALIEN LEGION: TENANTS OF HELL — Marvel / Epic

1 ❑ ca. 1991 Cover: 4.50 **NM** value: **Cover or less**
Circ: CapCity orders: **9,300**
cardstock cover. Hell Is A Planet **A:** Larry Stroman **W:** Chuck Dixon
2 ❑ ca. 1991 Cover: 4.50 **NM** value: **Cover or less**
Circ: CapCity orders: **7,350**
A: Larry Stroman **W:** Chuck Dixon

ALIEN LEGION (VOL. 1) — Marvel / Epic

The Alien Legion is an interplanetary police force that could be likened to a mix between Star Trek's Starfleet Academy and DC's Green Lantern Corps.

The series focuses on a squad containing seven different life forms from planets that span the galaxy. Just a bit smarter (or luckier) than the rest, the squad's members are the only ones to survive a terrible massacre that killed hundreds of Legionnaires. The squad comprises Torie Montroc III, Sarigar, Jugger Grimrod, Durge, Meico, and Torqa Dun. As with most of the Alien Legion squads, this one must deal with underlying racial tensions in the squad as well as the expected enemies it is sent to battle.

Marvel Editor Carl Potts created the first Alien Legion series in 1984; Epic would later publish a second Alien Legion series in 1987.

1 ❑ Apr 1984 Cover: 2.00 **NM** value: **Cover or less**
• Giant-size. Survival of the Fittest **A:** Tony DeZuniga; Frank Cirocco; Terry Austin **W:** Alan Zelentz
2 ❑ Jun 1984 Cover: 1.50 **NM** value: **Cover or less**
Blind Trust
3 ❑ Aug 1984 Cover: 1.50 **NM** value: **Cover or less**
Last Gamble **A:** Frank Cirocco **W:** Alan Zelentz
4 ❑ Oct 1984 Cover: 1.50 **NM** value: **Cover or less**
5 ❑ Dec 1984 Cover: 1.50 **NM** value: **Cover or less**
6 ❑ Feb 1985 Cover: 1.50 **NM** value: **Cover or less**
7 ❑ Apr 1985 Cover: 1.50 **NM** value: **Cover or less**
Circ: CapCity orders: **9,700**
8 ❑ Jun 1985 Cover: 1.50 **NM** value: **Cover or less**
Circ: CapCity orders: **9,100**
9 ❑ Aug 1985 Cover: 1.50 **NM** value: **Cover or less**
Circ: CapCity orders: **8,000**
10 ❑ Oct 1985 Cover: 1.50 **NM** value: **Cover or less**
Circ: CapCity orders: **8,050**
11 ❑ Dec 1985 Cover: 1.50 **NM** value: **Cover or less**
Circ: CapCity orders: **7,600**
12 ❑ Feb 1986 Cover: 1.50 **NM** value: **Cover or less**
Circ: Statement: **40,007** CapCity orders: **7,250**
13 ❑ Apr 1986 Cover: 1.50 **NM** value: **Cover or less**
Circ: Statement: **40,007** CapCity orders: **7,250**
14 ❑ Jun 1986 Cover: 1.50 **NM** value: **Cover or less**
Circ: Statement: **40,007** CapCity orders: **7,200**
15 ❑ Aug 1986 Cover: 1.50 **NM** value: **Cover or less**
Circ: Statement: **40,007** CapCity orders: **7,400**
16 ❑ Oct 1986 Cover: 1.50 **NM** value: **Cover or less**
Circ: Statement: **40,007** CapCity orders: **7,200**
17 ❑ Dec 1986 Cover: 1.50 **NM** value: **Cover or less**
Circ: Statement: **40,007** CapCity orders: **7,200**
18 ❑ Feb 1987 Cover: 1.75 **NM** value: **Cover or less**
Circ: Statement: **36,700** CapCity orders: **7,400**
19 ❑ Apr 1987 Cover: 1.75 **NM** value: **Cover or less**
Circ: Statement: **36,700** CapCity orders: **7,200**
20 ❑ Jun 1987 Cover: 1.75 **NM** value: **Cover or less**
Circ: Statement: **36,700** CapCity orders: **7,550**
final issue.

ALIEN LEGION (VOL. 2) — Marvel / Epic

1 ❑ Oct 1987 Cover: 1.25 **NM** value: **1.50**
Circ: Statement: **36,700** CapCity orders: **12,700**
Dead And Buried **A:** Larry Stroman **W:** Chuck Dixon
2 ❑ Dec 1987 Cover: 1.25 **NM** value: **1.50**
Circ: Statement: **36,700** CapCity orders: **11,250**
3 ❑ Feb 1988 Cover: 1.25 **NM** value: **1.50**
Circ: CapCity orders: **12,200**
4 ❑ Apr 1988 Cover: 1.25 **NM** value: **1.50**
Circ: CapCity orders: **11,100**
5 ❑ Jun 1988 Cover: 1.25 **NM** value: **1.50**
Circ: CapCity orders: **10,550**
6 ❑ Aug 1988 Cover: 1.25 **NM** value: **1.50**
Circ: CapCity orders: **10,100**
7 ❑ Oct 1988 Cover: 1.25 **NM** value: **1.50**
Circ: CapCity orders: **10,100**
8 ❑ Dec 1988 Cover: 1.50 **NM** value: **Cover or less**
Circ: CapCity orders: **9,600**
9 ❑ Feb 1989 Cover: 1.50 **NM** value: **Cover or less**
Circ: CapCity orders: **9,800**
10 ❑ Apr 1989 Cover: 1.50 **NM** value: **Cover or less**
Circ: CapCity orders: **9,300**
11 ❑ Jun 1989 Cover: 1.50 **NM** value: **Cover or less**
Circ: CapCity orders: **9,300**

CGC-graded: Multiply prices above by **33 for 9.9 M • 16 for 9.8 NM/M • 7 for 9.6 NM+ • 5 for 9.4 NM • 2.5 for 9.2 NM- • 1.5 for 9.0 VF/NM**

12 ❑ Aug 1989 Cover: 1.50 **NM** value: **Cover or less**
Circ: CapCity orders: **8,950**
13 ❑ Oct 1989 Cover: 1.50 **NM** value: **Cover or less**
Circ: CapCity orders: **8,850**
14 ❑ Dec 1989 Cover: 1.50 **NM** value: **Cover or less**
Circ: CapCity orders: **8,600**
15 ❑ Feb 1990 Cover: 1.50 **NM** value: **Cover or less**
Circ: CapCity orders: **8,750**
16 ❑ Apr 1990 Cover: 1.50 **NM** value: **Cover or less**
Circ: CapCity orders: **8,350**
17 ❑ Jun 1990 Cover: 1.50 **NM** value: **Cover or less**
Circ: CapCity orders: **8,100**
18 ❑ Aug 1990 Cover: 1.50 **NM** value: **Cover or less**
Circ: CapCity orders: **7,950**
final issue.

ALIEN NATION — DC

DC's Alien Nation is based on the 1988 motion picture that helped spawn a successful television science fiction series (1989-1991). In it, a ship of alien "Newcomers" from the planet Tencton lands on Earth. The extraterrestrial immigrants soon find themselves a despised underclass in American society. One alien, George Francisco, decides to help his people by joining the police force, and is soon teamed with a hard-edged, embittered cop named Matthew Sikes. Together, the two root out the intrigues and secrecy that form around the edges where human and alien society meet.

The comic-book adaptation by Martin Pasko and Jerry Bingham closely followed Rockne S. O'Bannon's script for the movie and captured the characterizations and social commentary that helped lift the Alien Nation television show above the level of much comic-book science-fiction.

1 ❑ Dec 1988 Cover: 2.50 **NM** value: **3.00**
Circ: CapCity orders: **9,850**
A: Jerry Bingham **W:** Martin Pasko

ALIEN NATION: A BREED APART — Adventure

1 ❑ Nov 1990 Cover: 2.50 **NM** value: **Cover or less**
A: Stan Timmons **W:** Steve Jones
2 ❑ Dec 1990 Cover: 2.50 **NM** value: **Cover or less**
A: Stan Timmons **W:** Steve Jones
3 ❑ Jan 1991 Cover: 2.50 **NM** value: **Cover or less**
A: Stan Timmons **W:** Steve Jones
4 ❑ Mar 1991 Cover: 2.50 **NM** value: **Cover or less**
A: Stan Timmons **W:** Steve Jones

ALIEN NATION: THE FIRSTCOMERS — Adventure

1 ❑ May 1991 Cover: 2.50 **NM** value: **Cover or less**
📖 The Firstcomers, Part 1 **A:** Tim Eldred **W:** Martin Powell
2 ❑ Jun 1991 Cover: 2.50 **NM** value: **Cover or less**
📖 The Firstcomers, Part 2 **A:** Tim Eldred **W:** Martin Powell
3 ❑ Jul 1991 Cover: 2.50 **NM** value: **Cover or less**
📖 The Firstcomers, Part 3 **A:** Tim Eldred **W:** Martin Powell
4 ❑ Aug 1991 Cover: 2.50 **NM** value: **Cover or less**
📖 The Firstcomers, Part 4 **A:** Tim Eldred **W:** Martin Powell

ALIEN NATION: THE LOST EPISODE — Malibu

1 ❑ 1992b&w Cover: 4.95 **NM** value: **Cover or less**
No issue number. One-shot. • squarebound;adapts second season opener

ALIEN NATION: THE PUBLIC ENEMY — Adventure

1 ❑ Dec 1991 Cover: 2.50 **NM** value: **Cover or less**
📖 Gefore The Fall **A:** Sandy Carruthers **W:** Lowell Cunningham
2 ❑ Jan 1992 Cover: 2.50 **NM** value: **Cover or less**
📖 Fallen Angels! **A:** Sandy Carruthers **W:** Lowell Cunningham
3 ❑ Feb 1992 Cover: 2.50 **NM** value: **Cover or less**
A: Sandy Carruthers **W:** Lowell Cunningham
4 ❑ Mar 1992 Cover: 2.50 **NM** value: **Cover or less**
A: Sandy Carruthers **W:** Lowell Cunningham

ALIEN NATION: THE SKIN TRADE — Adventure

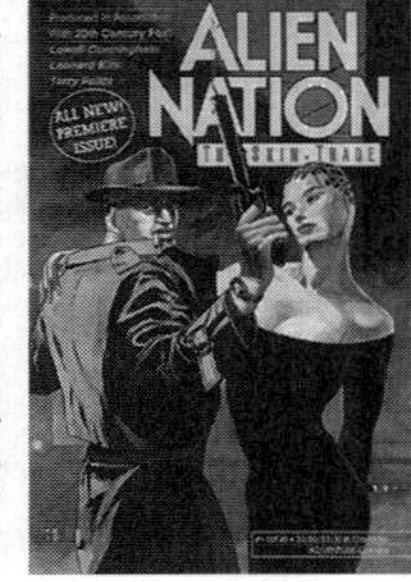

This black-and-white limited series from Men in Black creator Lowell Cunningham and Supergirl (3rd Series) artist Leonard Kirk spins out of the "Alien Nation" television show, which was based on the cult-favorite 1988 film. In the film, aliens — called "Newcomers" — have come to Earth and have tried to adapt to human society. The story chronicles "The Case of the Missing Milksop" and a trenchcoat-wearing alien private investigator named Mason Jar, a fellow who has seen "The Maltese Falcon" far too many times. This comic book lovingly captures the spirit of the television series and is definitely worth a look.

1 ❑ Mar 1991 Cover: 2.50 **NM** value: **Cover or less**
📖 The Case of The Missing Milksop **A:** Leonard Kirk **W:** Lowell Cunningham
2 ❑ Apr 1991 Cover: 2.50 **NM** value: **Cover or less**
A: Leonard Kirk **W:** Lowell Cunningham
3 ❑ May 1991 Cover: 2.50 **NM** value: **Cover or less**
A: Leonard Kirk **W:** Lowell Cunningham
4 ❑ Jun 1991 Cover: 2.50 **NM** value: **Cover or less**
📖 The Big Goodbye **A:** Leonard Kirk **W:** Lowell Cunningham

ALIEN NATION: THE SPARTANS — Adventure

1 ❑ Cover: 2.50 **NM** value: **Cover or less**
📖 Lost And Found • Yellow **A:** James Tucker **W:** Bill Spangler
1/A ❑ 1990 Cover: 2.50 **NM** value: **Cover or less**
📖 Lost And Found • Green **A:** James Tucker **W:** Bill Spangler
1/B ❑ 1990 Cover: 2.50 **NM** value: **Cover or less**
📖 Lost And Found • Blue **A:** James Tucker **W:** Bill Spangler
1/C ❑ 1990 Cover: 2.50 **NM** value: **Cover or less**
📖 Lost And Found • Red **A:** James Tucker **W:** Bill Spangler
1/LE❑ 1990 Cover: 2.50 **NM** value: **4.00**
📖 Lost And Found **A:** James Tucker **W:** Bill Spangler
2 ❑ 1990 Cover: 2.50 **NM** value: **Cover or less**
📖 Stone Walled **A:** James Tucker; Page Groh **W:** Bill Spangler
3 ❑ 1990 Cover: 2.50 **NM** value: **Cover or less**
📖 Take Back the Stars **A:** James Tucker **W:** Bill Spangler
4 ❑ 1990 Cover: 2.50 **NM** value: **Cover or less**
A: James Tucker **W:** Bill Spangler
Bk 1❑ Cover: 9.95 **NM** value: **Cover or less**

ALIEN RESURRECTION — Dark Horse

1 ❑ Oct 1997 Cover: 2.50 **NM** value: **Cover or less**
Circ: CapCity orders: **21,361**
A: Eduardo Risso **W:** James Vance
2 ❑ Nov 1997 Cover: 2.50 **NM** value: **Cover or less**
Circ: CapCity orders: **19,152**
A: Eduardo Risso **W:** James Vance

ALIENS, THE — Gold Key

It begins with a battle in deep space between an Earth ship and an equally matched craft from another world. Both ships were critically damaged by the fight, but neither would surrender, fearing that opposing forces would go on to make war on the other's homeworld. Thanks to the wisdom of Earth Captain Johner, however, a compromise was struck in which the two crews would intermingle, and each would travel home in the company of their new friends. What follows is a story of mistrust turned into mutual understanding and friendship.

The first issue of this title reprinted the "Captain Johner and the Aliens" backup story that had appeared in early issues of Gold Key's Magnus, Robot Fighter. Issue #2, which appeared 15 years later, reprinted issue #1, in turn. Finally, the series was recolored and released as Captain Johner & The Aliens in a new 1995 series from Valiant.

1 ❑ Cover: 0.12 **NM** value: **12.00**
📖 The Aliens; The Aliens: A Matter of Judgment; The Aliens: Suspense in Space; The Aliens: A Case of Nerves; The Aliens: The Dream Makers; The Aliens: An Alien Welcome; The Aliens: Talk-Down; The Aliens: Fear of the Unknown • 1982 reprint of #1;Reprints The Aliens stories from Magnus, Robot Fighter

ALIENS: ALCHEMY — Dark Horse

1 ❑ Oct 1997 Cover: 2.95 **NM** value: **Cover or less**
Circ: Diamd. preorders: **23,694**
A: Richard Corben **W:** John Arcudi
2 ❑ Nov 1997 Cover: 2.95 **NM** value: **Cover or less**
Circ: Diamd. preorders: **20,933**
A: Richard Corben **W:** John Arcudi
3 ❑ Nov 1997 Cover: 2.95 **NM** value: **Cover or less**
Circ: Diamd. preorders: **19,713**
A: Richard Corben **W:** John Arcudi

ALIENS: APOCALYPSE-THE DESTROYING ANGELS — Dark Horse

1 ❑ Jan 1999 Cover: 2.95 **NM** value: **Cover or less**
Circ: Diamd. preorders: **13,828**
A: Doug Wheatley **W:** Mark Schultz
2 ❑ Feb 1999 Cover: 2.95 **NM** value: **Cover or less**
Circ: Diamd. preorders: **12,107**
A: Doug Wheatley **W:** Mark Schultz
3 ❑ Mar 1999 Cover: 2.95 **NM** value: **Cover or less**
Circ: Diamd. preorders: **12,146**
A: Doug Wheatley **W:** Mark Schultz
4 ❑ Apr 1999 Cover: 2.95 **NM** value: **Cover or less**
Circ: Diamd. preorders: **12,807**
A: Doug Wheatley **W:** Mark Schultz

ALIENS: BERSERKER — Dark Horse

1 ❑ Jan 1995 Cover: 2.50 **NM** value: **Cover or less**
Circ: CapCity orders: **14,750**
A: Paul Mendoza; Kilian Plunkett(cover) **W:** John Wagner
2 ❑ Feb 1995 Cover: 2.50 **NM** value: **Cover or less**
Circ: CapCity orders: **12,600**
A: Paul Mendoza; Kilian Plunkett(cover) **W:** John Wagner
3 ❑ Mar 1995 Cover: 2.50 **NM** value: **Cover or less**
Circ: CapCity orders: **12,425**
A: Paul Mendoza; Kilian Plunkett(cover) **W:** John Wagner
4 ❑ Apr 1995 Cover: 2.50 **NM** value: **Cover or less**
Circ: CapCity orders: **12,125**
A: Paul Mendoza; Kilian Plunkett(cover) **W:** John Wagner

📖 indicates **Story Title** or **Storyline** information.
★ indicates **Character Appearance** information.

ALIENS: COLONIAL MARINES — Dark Horse

A research facility in outer space hasn't responded to signals, and the general feeling is that its inhabitants may have been destroyed by Aliens.

Armed with the latest weaponry and clad in special suits that resist the Aliens' acidic blood, the team seems ready for anything. But, in truth, the latest crew is far from the level of crack teams that have taken on Aliens in the past. This unit was abruptly thrown together from the dregs and misfits of the Colonial Marines, then sent on a suicide mission with a deadly alternate agenda. It has all the makings of a bloodbath. The only question remaining is: Whose blood will it be?

1 ❑ Jan 1993 Cover: 2.50 **NM** value: **Cover or less**
Circ: CapCity orders: **36,875**
A: Tony Akins **W:** Chris Warner
2 ❑ Feb 1993 Cover: 2.50 **NM** value: **Cover or less**
Circ: CapCity orders: **28,475**
A: Tony Akins **W:** Chris Warner
3 ❑ Mar 1993 Cover: 2.50 **NM** value: **Cover or less**
Circ: CapCity orders: **28,550**
A: Tony Akins **W:** Chris Warner
4 ❑ Apr 1993 Cover: 2.50 **NM** value: **Cover or less**
Circ: CapCity orders: **28,825**
A: Allen Nunis **W:** Kelley Puckett
5 ❑ May 1993 Cover: 2.50 **NM** value: **Cover or less**
Circ: CapCity orders: **26,975**
A: Allen Nunis **W:** Kelley Puckett
6 ❑ Jun 1993 Cover: 2.50 **NM** value: **Cover or less**
Circ: CapCity orders: **24,575**
A: Allen Nunis **W:** Kelley Puckett
7 ❑ Jul 1993 Cover: 2.50 **NM** value: **Cover or less**
Circ: CapCity orders: **21,525**
A: Tony Akins **W:** Chris Warner
8 ❑ Aug 1993 Cover: 2.50 **NM** value: **Cover or less**
Circ: CapCity orders: **17,650**
A: Tony Akins **W:** Paul Guinan
9 ❑ Sep 1993 Cover: 2.50 **NM** value: **Cover or less**
Circ: CapCity orders: **15,275**
A: John Nadeau **W:** Kelley Puckett
10 ❑ Oct 1993 Cover: 2.50 **NM** value: **Cover or less**
Circ: CapCity orders: **14,650**
final issue. **A:** John Nadeau **W:** Dan Jolley

ALIENS: EARTH ANGEL — Dark Horse

1 ❑ Aug 1994 Cover: 2.95 **NM** value: **Cover or less**
Circ: CapCity orders: **19,175**
No issue number. One-shot. **A:** John Byrne **W:** John Byrne

ALIENS: EARTH WAR — Dark Horse

1 ❑ Jun 1990 Cover: 2.50 **NM** value: **3.00**
Circ: CapCity orders: **50,225**
A: Sam Kieth **W:** Mark Verheiden
1-2 ❑ Cover: 2.50 **NM** value: **Cover or less**
2 ❑ Jul 1990 Cover: 2.50 **NM** value: **Cover or less**
Circ: CapCity orders: **40,975**
A: Sam Kieth **W:** Mark Verheiden
3 ❑ Sep 1990 Cover: 2.50 **NM** value: **Cover or less**
Circ: CapCity orders: **42,800** • **CGC:** 1 graded, best 8.5
A: Sam Kieth **W:** Mark Verheiden
4 ❑ Oct 1990 Cover: 2.50 **NM** value: **Cover or less**
Circ: CapCity orders: **44,675**
A: Sam Kieth **W:** Mark Verheiden
Bk 1❑ Cover: 13.95 **NM** value: **Cover or less**
• collection **A:** Sam Keith
Bk 1/LE❑ Cover: 59.95 **NM** value: **Cover or less**
• Limited edition hardcover. • Collects Aliens: Earth War #1-4 **A:** Sam Kieth **W:** Mark Verheiden
Bk 1-2❑Dec 1996 Cover: 16.95 **NM** value: **Cover or less**
• retitled Aliens: Female War **A:** Sam Kieth

ALIEN SEX/MONSTER LUST — Fantagraphics / Eros

All issues are adults only.

1 ❑ b&w Cover: 2.50 **NM** value: **Cover or less**

ALIENS: GENOCIDE — Dark Horse

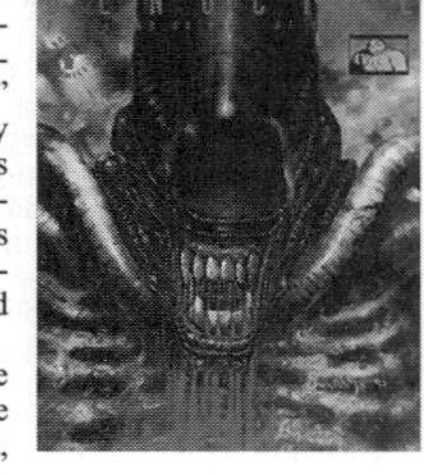

The parasitic Aliens have finally been annihilated on Earth, but, oddly enough, there are those who would like to have them back. The queen jelly from one of the Aliens is the essential ingredient in a super-speed and -endurance drug called "Xeno-Zip," created exclusively by a company called Neo-Pharm. When The Aliens are gone, Neo-Pharm creates synthetic substitutes which drive some users berserk, to the point of going on killing sprees or running into — and through — brick walls.

The U.S. Armed Forces loves the side effects, but other customers are not as pleased. The profit-oriented, unscrupulous president of Neo-Pharm, Daniel Grant, sponsors a trip to the Aliens' planet to bring back a queen mother — only to find the Aliens engaged in a genocidal war among themselves.

1 ❑ Nov 1991 Cover: 2.50 **NM** value: **Cover or less**
Circ: CapCity orders: **58,775**
A: Damon Willis **W:** Mike Richardson; John Arcudi

Other grades: Multiply prices above by **1.5 for Mint • 2/3 for Very Fine • 1/3 for Fine • 1/5 for Very Good • 1/8 for Good**

2 ❑ Dec 1991 Cover: 2.50 **NM** value: **Cover or less**
Circ: CapCity orders: **43,325**
A: Damon Willis **W:** Mike Richardson; John Arcudi
3 ❑ Jan 1992 Cover: 2.50 **NM** value: **Cover or less**
Circ: CapCity orders: **37,025**
A: Damon Willis **W:** Mike Richardson; John Arcudi
4 ❑ Feb 1992 Cover: 2.50 **NM** value: **Cover or less**
Circ: CapCity orders: **34,000**
A: Damon Willis **W:** Mike Richardson; John Arcudi
Bk 1❑ Feb 1997 Cover: 16.95 **NM** value: **Cover or less**
• collects mini-series;Collects Aliens: Genocide #1-4 **A:** Damon Willis **W:** Mike Richardson; John Arcudi
Bk 1-2❑ Cover: 14.95 **NM** value: **Cover or less**

ALIENS: GLASS CORRIDOR — Dark Horse

1 ❑ Jun 1998 Cover: 2.95 **NM** value: **Cover or less**
Circ: Diamd. preorders: **14,342**
No issue number. One-shot. **A:** David Lloyd **W:** David Lloyd

ALIENS: HAVOC — Dark Horse

1 ❑ Jun 1997 Cover: 2.95 **NM** value: **Cover or less**
Circ: Diamd. preorders: **23,235**
A: Leif Jones; Duncan Fegredo; John Stokes; John Totleben; D'Israeli **W:** Mark Schultz
2 ❑ Jul 1997 Cover: 2.95 **NM** value: **3.95**
Circ: Diamd. preorders: **19,586**
A: Leif Jones; Sergio Aragonés; Jon J. Muth; Frank Teran; David Lloyd; Rebecca Guay; Travis Charest; Sean Phillips; Mike Allred; P. Craig Russell; Kilian Plunkett; Moebius; Gene Ha; Derek Thompson; Tony Millionaire; John Stokes; Joel Napestek; Aidan Pots **W:** Mark Schultz

ALIENS: HIVE — Dark Horse

1 ❑ Feb 1992 Cover: 2.50 **NM** value: **Cover or less**
Circ: CapCity orders: **41,350**
A: Kelley Jones **W:** Jerry Prosser
2 ❑ Mar 1992 Cover: 2.50 **NM** value: **Cover or less**
Circ: CapCity orders: **36,800**
A: Kelley Jones **W:** Jerry Prosser
3 ❑ Apr 1992 Cover: 2.50 **NM** value: **Cover or less**
Circ: CapCity orders: **35,125**
A: Kelley Jones **W:** Jerry Prosser
4 ❑ May 1992 Cover: 2.50 **NM** value: **Cover or less**
Circ: CapCity orders: **35,450**
A: Kelley Jones **W:** Jerry Prosser
Bk 1❑ Feb 1998 Cover: 16.95 **NM** value: **Cover or less**
• Aliens: Harvest;collects Aliens: Hive **A:** Kelley Jones **W:** Jerry Prosser
Bk 1-2❑ Cover: 14.95 **NM** value: **Cover or less**

ALIENS: KIDNAPPED — Dark Horse

Apparently the risk of becoming an Aliens incubator, complete with the hatchling bursting forth from one's chest, is not sufficiently gruesome to inhibit smugglers from transporting Alien eggs as though they were just another illegal commodity.

This three-issue mini-series finds a salvage crew recovering the deadly embryos from a crash site for resale on the black market. After an initial confrontation with the Alien queen, which reduces the smugglers' ranks by a third, the remaining traffickers escape with 13 flash-frozen eggs for their trouble. Their buyer is suspicious of one, which seems a bit discolored, and refuses to take it, so the smugglers decide to sell it to a barkeeper in East Barbazon, a place where the niceties of civilization are only a rumor. Through all of this the reader anticipates the inevitable eruption and the horror that will follow.

1 ❑ Dec 1997 Cover: 2.50 **NM** value: **Cover or less**
Circ: Diamd. preorders: **17,154**
A: Francisco Solano Lopez **W:** Justin Green; Jim Woodring
2 ❑ Jan 1998 Cover: 2.50 **NM** value: **Cover or less**
Circ: Diamd. preorders: **15,819**
A: Francisco Solano Lopez **W:** Justin Green; Jim Woodring
3 ❑ Feb 1998 Cover: 2.50 **NM** value: **Cover or less**
Circ: Diamd. preorders: **14,686**
A: Francisco Solano Lopez **W:** Justin Green; Jim Woodring
Bk 1❑ Feb 1999 Cover: 9.95 **NM** value: **Cover or less**
• collects mini-series

ALIENS: LABYRINTH — Dark Horse

1 ❑ Sep 1993 Cover: 2.50 **NM** value: **Cover or less**
Circ: CapCity orders: **28,500**
2 ❑ Oct 1993 Cover: 2.50 **NM** value: **Cover or less**
Circ: CapCity orders: **21,975**
3 ❑ Nov 1993 Cover: 2.50 **NM** value: **Cover or less**
Circ: CapCity orders: **19,750**
4 ❑ Dec 1993 Cover: 2.50 **NM** value: **Cover or less**
Circ: CapCity orders: **16,500**
Bk 1❑ Aug 1995 Cover: 17.95 **NM** value: **Cover or less**
• collects Aliens: Labyrinth #1-4 and two-part Dark Horse Comics prequel "Aliens: Backsplash";collects series
Bk 1-2❑ Cover: 17.95 **NM** value: **Cover or less**
• collects Aliens: Labyrinth #1-4 and two-part Dark Horse Comics prequel "Aliens: Backsplash"

ALIENS: LOVESICK — Dark Horse

1 ❑ Dec 1996 Cover: 2.95 **NM** value: **Cover or less**
Circ: Direct Market orders: **24,377**
One-shot. **A:** Richard Fogues **W:** Richard Fogues; Thierry Gagnon

ALIENS (MAGAZINE) (VOL. 1) — Dark Horse

1 ❑ **NM** value: **3.50**
Aliens Vs. Predator, Part 1 **A:** Phil Norwood **W:** Randy Stradley
2 ❑ **NM** value: **3.25**
Aliens Vs. Predator, Part 2 **A:** Phil Norwood **W:** Randy Stradley
3 ❑ **NM** value: **3.25**
Aliens Vs. Predator, Part 3 **A:** Phil Norwood **W:** Randy Stradley
4 ❑ **NM** value: **3.25**
Aliens Vs. Predator, Part 4 **A:** Phil Norwood **W:** Randy Stradley
5 ❑ **NM** value: **3.25**
Aliens Vs. Predator, Part 5 **A:** Phil Norwood **W:** Randy Stradley
6 ❑ **NM** value: **3.00**
Aliens Vs. Predator, Part 6 **A:** Phil Norwood **W:** Randy Stradley
7 ❑ **NM** value: **3.00**
Aliens: Earth War, Part 1; Aliens Vs. Predator, Part 7 **A:** Phil Norwood **W:** Randy Stradley
8 ❑ Cover: 1.50 **NM** value: **3.00**
Aliens: Earth War, Part 2; Predator: Big Game, Part 1; Aliens Vs. Predator, Part 8 **A:** Phil Norwood **W:** Randy Stradley
9 ❑ Cover: 1.50 **NM** value: **3.00**
10 ❑ Cover: 1.50 **NM** value: **3.00**
11 ❑ Cover: 1.50 **NM** value: **3.00**
12 ❑ Cover: 1.50 **NM** value: **3.00**
13 ❑ Cover: 1.50 **NM** value: **3.00**
14 ❑ Cover: 1.50 **NM** value: **3.00**
15 ❑ Cover: 1.50 **NM** value: **3.00**
16 ❑ Cover: 1.50 **NM** value: **3.00**
17 ❑ Cover: 1.50 **NM** value: **3.00**

ALIENS (MAGAZINE) (VOL. 2) — Dark Horse

1 ❑ Cover: 1.50 **NM** value: **3.00**
Aliens: Hive, Part 1; Predator: Cold War, Part 1 • Also includes previously unpublished sequel to Give Me Liberty
2 ❑ Cover: 1.50 **NM** value: **3.00**
Aliens: Newt's Tale, Part 1; Aliens: Hive, Part 2; Predator: Cold War, Part 2
3 ❑ Cover: 1.50 **NM** value: **3.00**
Aliens: Newt's Tale, Part 2; Aliens: Hive, Part 3; Predator: Cold War, Part 3
4 ❑ Cover: 1.50 **NM** value: **3.00**
Aliens: Newt's Tale, Part 3; Aliens: Hive, Part 4; Predator: Cold War, Part 4
5 ❑ Cover: 1.50 **NM** value: **3.00**
Aliens: Newt's Tale, Part 4; Predator: Cold War, Part 5; Aliens: Hive, Part 5; Aliens vs. Predator, Part 6
6 ❑ Cover: 1.50 **NM** value: **3.00**
Aliens: Newt's Tale, Part 5; Predator: Cold War, Part 6; Aliens: Hive, Part 6; Aliens vs. Predator, Part 7
7 ❑ Cover: 1.50 **NM** value: **3.00**
Aliens: Newt's Tale, Part 6; Predator: Cold War, Part 7; Aliens: Hive, Part 7
8 ❑ Cover: 1.50 **NM** value: **3.00**
Predator: Cold War, Part 8; Aliens: Hive, Part 8
9 ❑ Cover: 1.50 **NM** value: **3.00**
Aliens: Sacrifice, Part 1; Aliens: Colonial Marines, Part 1; Aliens: Hive, Part 9
10 ❑ Cover: 1.50 **NM** value: **3.00**
Aliens: Sacrifice, Part 2; Aliens: Colonial Marines, Part 2; Aliens Vs. Predator, Part 11; Predator: Rite of Passage, Part 1; Aliens: Tribes, Part 1
11 ❑ Cover: 1.50 **NM** value: **3.00**
Aliens: Sacrifice, Part 3; Aliens: Colonial Marines, Part 3; Aliens Vs. Predator, Part 12; Predator: Rite of Passage, Part 2; Aliens: Tribes, Part 2
12 ❑ Cover: 1.50 **NM** value: **3.00**
Aliens: Tribes, Part 3; Aliens: Horror Show, Part 1
13 ❑ Cover: 1.50 **NM** value: **3.00**
Aliens: Tribes, Part 4; Aliens: Horror Show, Part 3
14 ❑ Cover: 1.50 **NM** value: **3.00**
Aliens: Tribes, Part 5; Aliens: Horror Show, Part 3
15 ❑ Cover: 1.50 **NM** value: **3.00**
Aliens: Tribes, Part 6
16 ❑ Cover: 1.50 **NM** value: **3.00**
Aliens: Tribes, Part 7; Aliens: Backsplash, Part 1
17 ❑ Cover: 1.50 **NM** value: **3.00**
Aliens: Backsplash, Part 2
18 ❑ Cover: 1.50 **NM** value: **3.00**
Aliens: Crusade, Part 6; Renegade, Part 1; Aliens: Cargo, Part 2; Aliens: Colonial Marines, Part 10
19 ❑ Cover: 1.50 **NM** value: **3.00**
20 ❑ Cover: 1.50 **NM** value: **3.00**
21 ❑ Cover: 1.50 **NM** value: **3.00**
22 ❑ Cover: 1.50 **NM** value: **3.00**

ALIENS: MONDO HEAT — Dark Horse

1 ❑ Feb 1996 Cover: 2.50 **NM** value: **Cover or less**
No issue number. One-shot. **A:** Ronnie del Carmen **W:** Henry Gilroy

ALIENS: MONDO PEST — Dark Horse

1 ❑ Cover: 2.95 **NM** value: **Cover or less**
Circ: CapCity orders: **10,125**

ALIENS: MUSIC OF THE SPEARS — Dark Horse

1 ❑ Jan 1994 Cover: 2.50 **NM** value: **Cover or less**
Circ: CapCity orders: **20,225**
A: Tim Hamilton **W:** Chet Williamson
2 ❑ Feb 1994 Cover: 2.50 **NM** value: **Cover or less**
Circ: CapCity orders: **16,150**
A: Tim Hamilton **W:** Chet Williamson
3 ❑ Mar 1994 Cover: 2.50 **NM** value: **Cover or less**
Circ: CapCity orders: **15,425**
A: Tim Hamilton **W:** Chet Williamson
4 ❑ Apr 1994 Cover: 2.50 **NM** value: **Cover or less**
Circ: CapCity orders: **15,175**
A: Tim Hamilton **W:** Chet Williamson

ALIENS: NEWT'S TALE — Dark Horse

1 ❑ Jun 1992 Cover: 4.95 **NM** value: **Cover or less**
Circ: CapCity orders: **31,850**
A: Jim Somerville; John Bolton(cover) **W:** Mike Richardson
2 ❑ Aug 1992 Cover: 4.95 **NM** value: **Cover or less**
Circ: CapCity orders: **29,200**
A: Jim Somerville; John Bolton(cover) **W:** Mike Richardson

ALIENS: PIG — Dark Horse

1 ❑ Mar 1997 Cover: 2.95 **NM** value: **Cover or less**
Circ: Diamd. preorders: **22,830**
A: Flint Henry **W:** Chuck Dixon

ALIENS/PREDATOR: THE DEADLIEST OF THE SPECIES — Dark Horse

Born and bred as a "trophy wife" for a rich businessman, Caryn Delacroix is almost genetically incapable of being unhappy. Now, Caryn is not just unhappy, she is terrified. She dreams each night of a strange creature who stalks her through the floating airship which has been her home. Cornered at last, she wakes up screaming.

In the wake of Aliens: Earth War, Montcalm Delacroix took to living in his floating city in the sky. That way, he felt he would at last be safe from the terrors of the Earth. But all too soon his sanctuary is invaded — not from below, but by a Predator from the stars. Now his — and Caryn's — worst fears are becoming reality.

The tag-team-sounding title of this series doesn't do justice to the gripping, well-developed story within. Written by Chris Claremont of X-Men fame, Aliens: The Deadliest of the Species is a first-rate thriller.

1 ❑ Jul 1993 Cover: 2.50 **NM** value: **Cover or less**
Circ: CapCity orders: **51,325**
W: Chris Claremont
1/LE❑ Jul 1993 no cover price. **NM** value: **4.00**
2 ❑ Sep 1993 Cover: 2.50 **NM** value: **Cover or less**
Circ: CapCity orders: **35,950**
The Hunt **A:** Jackson Guice **W:** Chris Claremont
3 ❑ Nov 1993 Cover: 2.50 **NM** value: **Cover or less**
Circ: CapCity orders: **30,275**
W: Chris Claremont
4 ❑ Jan 1994 Cover: 2.50 **NM** value: **Cover or less**
Circ: CapCity orders: **24,375**
W: Chris Claremont
5 ❑ Mar 1994 Cover: 2.50 **NM** value: **Cover or less**
Circ: CapCity orders: **22,825**
W: Chris Claremont
6 ❑ May 1994 Cover: 2.50 **NM** value: **Cover or less**
W: Chris Claremont
7 ❑ Aug 1994 Cover: 2.50 **NM** value: **Cover or less**
Circ: CapCity orders: **19,025**
W: Chris Claremont
8 ❑ Oct 1994 Cover: 2.50 **NM** value: **Cover or less**
Circ: CapCity orders: **19,325**
W: Chris Claremont
9 ❑ Dec 1994 Cover: 2.50 **NM** value: **Cover or less**
Circ: CapCity orders: **17,800**
W: Chris Claremont
10 ❑ Feb 1995 Cover: 2.50 **NM** value: **Cover or less**
Circ: CapCity orders: **16,375**
Queen's Gambit **A:** Eduardo Barreto **W:** Chris Claremont
11 ❑ May 1995 Cover: 2.50 **NM** value: **Cover or less**
Circ: CapCity orders: **16,100**
A: Eduardo Barreto **W:** Chris Claremont
12 ❑ Aug 1995 Cover: 2.50 **NM** value: **Cover or less**
Circ: CapCity orders: **17,150**
Renegade final issue. **A:** Eduardo Barreto **W:** Chris Claremont
Bk 1❑ Nov 1996 Cover: 29.95 **NM** value: **Cover or less**
• collects series **A:** Eduardo Barreto **W:** Chris Claremont
Bk 1/LE❑ Cover: 99.95 **NM** value: **Cover or less**
• Limited edition hardcover. **A:** Eduardo Barreto **W:** Chris Claremont

ALIENS: PURGE — Dark Horse

1 ❑ Aug 1997 Cover: 2.95 **NM** value: **Cover or less**
Circ: Diamd. preorders: **18,926**
No issue number. One-shot. **A:** Phil Hester **W:** Ian Edginton

ALIENS: ROGUE — Dark Horse

1 ❑ Apr 1993 Cover: 2.50 **NM** value: **Cover or less**
Circ: CapCity orders: **34,775**
A: William Simpson **W:** Ian Edginton
2 ❑ May 1993 Cover: 2.50 **NM** value: **Cover or less**
Circ: CapCity orders: **27,125**
A: William Simpson **W:** Ian Edginton
3 ❑ Jun 1993 Cover: 2.50 **NM** value: **Cover or less**
Circ: CapCity orders: **24,400**
A: William Simpson **W:** Ian Edginton
4 ❑ Jul 1993 Cover: 2.50 **NM** value: **Cover or less**
Circ: CapCity orders: **22,750**
A: William Simpson **W:** Ian Edginton
Bk 1❑ Aug 1997 Cover: 16.95 **NM** value: **Cover or less**
• Collects Aliens: Rogue #1-4 **A:** William Simpson **W:** Ian Edginton
Bk 1-2❑ Aug 1997 Cover: 16.95 **NM** value: **Cover or less**
• Collects Aliens: Rogue #1-4 **A:** William Simpson **W:** Ian Edginton

ALIENS: SACRIFICE — Dark Horse

1 ❑ ca. 1993 Cover: 4.95 **NM** value: **Cover or less**
Circ: CapCity orders: **21,925**
No issue number. **A:** Paul Johnson **W:** Peter Milligan

ALIENS: SALVATION — Dark Horse

1 ❑ ca. 1993 Cover: 4.95 **NM** value: **Cover or less**
Circ: CapCity orders: **19,050**
No issue number. **A:** Mike Mignola **W:** Dave Gibbons

CGC-graded: Multiply prices above by **33 for 9.9 M • 16 for 9.8 NM/M • 7 for 9.6 NM+ • 5 for 9.4 NM • 2.5 for 9.2 NM- • 1.5 for 9.0 VF/NM**

ALIENS: SALVATION AND SACRIFICE Dark Horse

1 ❑ Mar 2001 Cover: 12.95 **NM** value: **Cover or less**
A: Mike Mignola; Paul Johnson **W:** Dave Gibbons; Peter Milligan

ALIENS: SPECIAL Dark Horse

1 ❑ Jun 1997 Cover: 2.50 **NM** value: **Cover or less**
Circ: Diamd. preorders: **20,099**
No issue number. One-shot. 📖 45 Seconds; Elder Gods **A:** Leif Jones; Frank Teran **W:** Darko Macan; Nancy Collins

ALIENS: STALKER Dark Horse

1 ❑ Jun 1998 Cover: 2.50 **NM** value: **Cover or less**
Circ: Diamd. preorders: **15,604**
No issue number. One-shot. **A:** David Wenzel **W:** David Wenzel

ALIENS: STRONGHOLD Dark Horse

1 ❑ May 1994 Cover: 2.50 **NM** value: **Cover or less**
Circ: CapCity orders: **18,075**
A: Doug Mahnke **W:** John Arcudi
2 ❑ Jun 1994 Cover: 2.50 **NM** value: **Cover or less**
Circ: CapCity orders: **15,125**
A: Doug Mahnke **W:** John Arcudi
3 ❑ Jul 1994 Cover: 2.50 **NM** value: **Cover or less**
Circ: CapCity orders: **14,225**
A: Doug Mahnke **W:** John Arcudi
4 ❑ Sep 1994 Cover: 2.50 **NM** value: **Cover or less**
Circ: CapCity orders: **13,400**
A: Doug Mahnke **W:** John Arcudi
Bk 1❑ Jul 1997 Cover: 16.95 **NM** value: **Cover or less**
• collects mini-series **A:** Doug Mahnke **W:** John Arcudi
Bk 1-2❑ Cover: 16.95 **NM** value: **Cover or less**
• collects mini-series **A:** Doug Mahnke **W:** John Arcudi

ALIENS: SURVIVAL Dark Horse

1 ❑ Feb 1998 Cover: 2.95 **NM** value: **Cover or less**
Circ: Diamd. preorders: **15,743**
A: Guy Davis **W:** James Vance
2 ❑ Mar 1998 Cover: 2.95 **NM** value: **Cover or less**
Circ: Diamd. preorders: **14,320**
A: Guy Davis **W:** James Vance
3 ❑ Apr 1998 Cover: 2.95 **NM** value: **Cover or less**
Circ: Diamd. preorders: **14,262**
A: Guy Davis **W:** James Vance

ALIENS: TRIBES Dark Horse

1 ❑ Cover: 11.95 **NM** value: **Cover or less**
Circ: CapCity orders: **3,725**
1/HC❑ Cover: 24.95 **NM** value: **Cover or less**
No issue number. hardcover novel.
1/LE❑ Cover: 75.00 **NM** value: **Cover or less**
• Limited edition hardcover.

ALIENS VS. PREDATOR Dark Horse

It began on the remote world of Ryushi, where a small human settlement was engaged in raising the native Rhynth beasts on ranches. In that desert clime, a strange ship landed, depositing a cargo of Alien eggs. The eggs were eventually found by the Rhynths, and the Aliens incubated inside them. Meanwhile, a scientist investigating the larval Aliens stumbled across a party of Predators. Attempting to flee, he crashes his vehicle into the Predators' ship, exploding both.

This world of just over a hundred humans is now the host to a cargo load's worth of Rhynth-spawned Aliens — and several very angry Predators.

Drawing from a story which began in Dark Horse Presents #36, Aliens vs. Predator pits two legendary killers against each other — with mankind caught in the middle.

0 ❑ Jul 1990, b&w Cover: 1.95 **NM** value: **4.00**
• **CGC:** 5 graded, best 9.0
• reprints story from Dark Horse Presents #34-36 **A:** Phil Norwood **W:** Randy Stradley
1 ❑ Jun 1990, full color Cover: 2.50 **NM** value: **4.00**
Circ: CapCity orders: **94,600** • **CGC:** 8 graded, best 9.4
A: Phil Norwood **W:** Randy Stradley
1-2 ❑ Cover: 2.50 **NM** value: **Cover or less**
2 ❑ Aug 1990 Cover: 2.50 **NM** value: **3.50**
Circ: CapCity orders: **66,475**
A: Phil Norwood **W:** Randy Stradley
2-2 ❑ Cover: 2.50 **NM** value: **Cover or less**
3 ❑ Oct 1990 Cover: 2.50 **NM** value: **3.00**
Circ: CapCity orders: **57,275**
A: Phil Norwood **W:** Randy Stradley
3-2 ❑ Cover: 2.50 **NM** value: **Cover or less**
4 ❑ Dec 1990 Cover: 2.50 **NM** value: **3.00**
Circ: CapCity orders: **53,700**
A: Phil Norwood **W:** Randy Stradley
4-2 ❑ Cover: 2.50 **NM** value: **Cover or less**
Anl 1❑ Jul 1999 Cover: 4.95 **NM** value: **Cover or less**
📖 Hell-Bent; Lefty's Revenge; old Secrets; Pursuit; Chained to Life and Death **A:** Alex Maleev; Mel Rubi; Pop Mhan; Dave Ross; Tom Biondolillo **W:** Alex Maleev; Dave Ross; Mark Schultz; Brian McDonald; Ian Edginton
Bk 1❑ Cover: 19.95 **NM** value: **Cover or less**
Circ: CapCity orders: **2,728**
• collects mini-series;Collects Aliens vs. Predator #1-4 **A:** Phil Norwood **W:** Randy Stradley
Bk 1/LE❑ Cover: 79.95 **NM** value: **Cover or less**
• Limited edition hardcover. **A:** Phil Norwood **W:** Randy Stradley
Bk 1-2❑ Cover: 19.95 **NM** value: **Cover or less**

ALIENS VS. PREDATOR: BOOTY Dark Horse

1 ❑ Jan 1996 Cover: 2.50 **NM** value: **Cover or less**
No issue number. One-shot.

ALIENS VS. PREDATOR: DUEL Dark Horse

1 ❑ Mar 1995 Cover: 2.50 **NM** value: **Cover or less**
Circ: CapCity orders: **20,825**
A: Javier Saltares **W:** Randy Stradley
2 ❑ Cover: 2.50 **NM** value: **Cover or less**
Circ: CapCity orders: **17,200**
A: Javier Saltares **W:** Randy Stradley

ALIENS VS. PREDATOR: ETERNAL Dark Horse

1 ❑ Jun 1998 Cover: 2.50 **NM** value: **Cover or less**
Circ: Diamd. preorders: **20,084**
A: Alex Maleev **W:** Ian Edginton
2 ❑ Jul 1998 Cover: 2.50 **NM** value: **Cover or less**
Circ: Diamd. preorders: **17,462**
A: Alex Maleev **W:** Ian Edginton
3 ❑ Aug 1998 Cover: 2.50 **NM** value: **Cover or less**
Circ: Diamd. preorders: **16,581**
A: Alex Maleev **W:** Ian Edginton
4 ❑ Sep 1998 Cover: 2.50 **NM** value: **Cover or less**
Circ: Diamd. preorders: **15,678**
A: Alex Maleev **W:** Ian Edginton

ALIENS VS. PREDATOR VS. THE TERMINATOR Dark Horse

Foreseeing its defeat at the hands of the human resistance forces, Skynet went into hiding, leaving behind secret stealth Terminators. Centuries later, it awakened with their help. Now, Skynet's plan to conquer Earth rests with a deadly hybrid of robotic Terminators fused with killer Aliens. Even the deadly Predators understand this catastrophic threat to the universe. Humanity's only chance for survival is an ancient race of hunters and one lone human — Ripley.

The ultimate triple science fiction-horror motion picture tie-in combination has all the prerequisite gore and violence. Dark Horse excels at combining popular motion-picture series.

1 ❑ Apr 2000 Cover: 2.95 **NM** value: **Cover or less**
Circ: CapCity orders: **19,712**
A: Mel Rubi **W:** Mark Schultz ★ Appearance of Ripley.
2 ❑ May 2000 Cover: 2.95 **NM** value: **Cover or less**
Circ: CapCity orders: **17,142**
A: Mel Rubi **W:** Mark Schultz ★ Appearance of Ripley.
3 ❑ Jun 2000 Cover: 2.95 **NM** value: **Cover or less**
Circ: CapCity orders: **17,950**
A: Mel Rubi **W:** Mark Schultz ★ Appearance of Ripley.
4 ❑ Jul 2000 Cover: 2.95 **NM** value: **Cover or less**
Circ: CapCity orders: **18,900**
A: Mel Rubi **W:** Mark Schultz ★ Appearance of Ripley.

ALIENS VS. PREDATOR: WAR Dark Horse

0 ❑ 1995 Cover: 2.50 **NM** value: **Cover or less**
A: Chris Warner **W:** Randy Stradley
1 ❑ 1995 Cover: 2.50 **NM** value: **Cover or less**
Circ: CapCity orders: **20,000**
W: Randy Stradley
2 ❑ Jun 1995 Cover: 2.50 **NM** value: **Cover or less**
Circ: CapCity orders: **17,800**
W: Randy Stradley
3 ❑ Jul 1995 Cover: 2.50 **NM** value: **Cover or less**
Circ: CapCity orders: **17,900**
A: Jim Hall **W:** Randy Stradley
4 ❑ Aug 1995 Cover: 2.50 **NM** value: **Cover or less**
Circ: CapCity orders: **16,425**
W: Randy Stradley
Bk 1❑ May 1996 Cover: 19.95 **NM** value: **Cover or less**
• collects Aliens vs. Predator: Duel, Aliens vs. Predator: War and Dark Horse Comics #25

ALIENS VS. PREDATOR: XENOGENESIS Dark Horse

1 ❑ Dec 1999 Cover: 2.95 **NM** value: **Cover or less**
Circ: Diamd. preorders: **14,665**
A: Mel Rubi **W:** Andi Watson
2 ❑ Jan 2000 Cover: 2.95 **NM** value: **Cover or less**
Circ: Diamd. preorders: **11,969**
A: Mel Rubi **W:** Andi Watson
3 ❑ Feb 2000 Cover: 2.95 **NM** value: **Cover or less**
Circ: Diamd. preorders: **11,346**
A: Mel Rubi **W:** Andi Watson
4 ❑ Mar 2000 Cover: 2.95 **NM** value: **Cover or less**
Circ: Diamd. preorders: **10,964**
A: Mel Rubi **W:** Andi Watson

Statement of Ownership figures are the average number of copies originally sold, as cited by the publisher to the U.S. Postal Service. These estimate **all** sales, in comics shops and on newsstands.

ALIENS (VOL. 1) Dark Horse

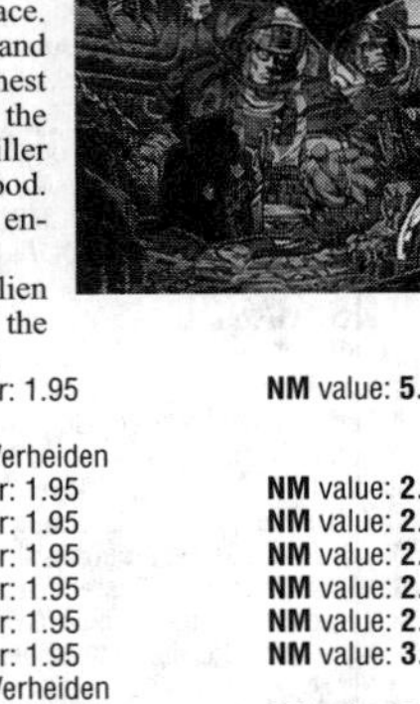

When the spacecraft Nostromo in the 1979 Alien feature film answers an emergency call and touches down on a desolate planet called Acheron, its crew encounters an Alien egg chamber. Without warning, a crab-like creature springs out of an egg, melts through a crewman's faceplate, and attaches itself to his face. It grows inside the crewman and eventually bursts through his chest in its second-stage form. Later, the Alien grows into a towering killer with twin jaws and acid for blood. That one Alien kills virtually the entire crew of the Nostromo.

Dark Horse acquired the Alien and Aliens license and provided the graphic-novel version of events.

1 ❑ May 1988 Cover: 1.95 **NM** value: **5.00**
• **CGC:** 5 graded, best 9.2
A: Mark A. Nelson **W:** Mark Verheiden
1-2 ❑ Cover: 1.95 **NM** value: **2.50**
1-3 ❑ Cover: 1.95 **NM** value: **2.00**
1-4 ❑ Cover: 1.95 **NM** value: **2.00**
1-5 ❑ Cover: 1.95 **NM** value: **2.00**
1-6 ❑ Cover: 1.95 **NM** value: **2.00**
2 ❑ Sep 1988 Cover: 1.95 **NM** value: **3.50**
A: Mark A. Nelson **W:** Mark Verheiden
2-2 ❑ Cover: 1.95 **NM** value: **2.50**
2-3 ❑ Cover: 1.95 **NM** value: **2.00**
2-4 ❑ Cover: 1.95 **NM** value: **2.00**
3 ❑ Jan 1989 Cover: 1.95 **NM** value: **2.50**
A: Mark A. Nelson **W:** Mark Verheiden
3-2 ❑ Cover: 1.95 **NM** value: **2.00**
4 ❑ Mar 1989 Cover: 1.95 **NM** value: **2.50**
A: Mark A. Nelson **W:** Mark Verheiden
4-2 ❑ Cover: 1.95 **NM** value: **2.00**
5 ❑ Jun 1989 Cover: 1.95 **NM** value: **2.50**
A: Mark A. Nelson **W:** Mark Verheiden
5-2 ❑ Cover: 1.95 **NM** value: **2.00**
6 ❑ Jul 1989 Cover: 1.95 **NM** value: **2.50**
A: Mark A. Nelson **W:** Mark Verheiden
6-2 ❑ Cover: 1.95 **NM** value: **2.00**
Bk 1❑ b&w Cover: 10.95 **NM** value: **11.95**
• collects mini-series **A:** Mark A. Nelson **W:** Mark Verheiden
Bk 1/HC❑ Cover: 24.95 **NM** value: **Cover or less**
• Hardcover edition. **A:** Mark A. Nelson **W:** Mark Verheiden
Bk 1-2❑ Jan 1996 Cover: 13.95 **NM** value: **Cover or less**
• 2nd Printing, b&w **A:** Mark A. Nelson
Bk 1-3❑ Aug 1996 Cover: 17.95 **NM** value: **Cover or less**

ALIENS (VOL. 2) Dark Horse

1 ❑ Aug 1989, full color Cover: 2.25 **NM** value: **3.00**
Circ: CapCity orders: **29,625** • **CGC:** 7 graded, best 9.0
A: Denis Beauvais **W:** Mark Verheiden
2 ❑ Dec 1989 Cover: 2.25 **NM** value: **2.50**
Circ: CapCity orders: **27,275**
A: Denis Beauvais **W:** Mark Verheiden
3 ❑ 1990 Cover: 2.25 **NM** value: **2.50**
Circ: CapCity orders: **26,875**
A: Denis Beauvais **W:** Mark Verheiden
4 ❑ May 1990 Cover: 2.25 **NM** value: **2.50**
Circ: CapCity orders: **26,125**
A: Denis Beauvais **W:** Mark Verheiden
Bk 1❑ Cover: 12.95 **NM** value: **Cover or less**
• Nightmare Asylum trade paperback **A:** Denis Beauvais **W:** Mark Verheiden
Bk 1/LE❑ Cover: 79.95 **NM** value: **Cover or less**
• Limited edition hardcover. **A:** Denis Beauvais **W:** Mark Verheiden
Bk 1-2❑ Oct 1996 Cover: 16.95 **NM** value: **Cover or less**
• Retitled: Nightmare Asylum trade paperback

ALIENS: WRAITH Dark Horse

1 ❑ Jul 1998 Cover: 2.95 **NM** value: **Cover or less**
Circ: Diamd. preorders: **13,511**
No issue number. One-shot. **A:** Eduardo Risso **W:** Jay Stephens

ALIENS: XENOGENESIS Dark Horse

1 ❑ Aug 1999 Cover: 2.95 **NM** value: **Cover or less**
Circ: Diamd. preorders: **13,862**
A: Dave Ross **W:** Mary Bierbaum; Tom Bierbaum
2 ❑ Sep 1999 Cover: 2.95 **NM** value: **Cover or less**
Circ: Diamd. preorders: **12,319**
A: Dave Ross **W:** Mary Bierbaum; Tom Bierbaum
3 ❑ Oct 1999 Cover: 2.95 **NM** value: **Cover or less**
Circ: Diamd. preorders: **11,904**
A: Dave Ross **W:** Mary Bierbaum; Tom Bierbaum
4 ❑ Nov 1999 Cover: 2.95 **NM** value: **Cover or less**
Circ: Diamd. preorders: **11,093**
A: Dave Ross **W:** Mary Bierbaum; Tom Bierbaum

ALIEN: THE ILLUSTRATED STORY HM Communications

1 ❑ Cover: 3.95 **NM** value: **4.00**
A: Walt Simonson **W:** Archie Goodwin

Other grades: Multiply prices above by **1.5 for Mint • 2/3 for Very Fine • 1/3 for Fine • 1/5 for Very Good • 1/8 for Good**

ALIEN WORLDS — Pacific

Alien Worlds is a collection of science-fiction stories by such famous authors as William F. Nolan and Richard Corben. In this series, readers will find post-nuclear worlds inhabited by a race of murderous children; playground hucksters who employ miniature aliens to help them scam their playmates; robots in love; and much, much more.

Following in the tradition of the pre-Code E.C. comics of the '50s, Alien Worlds is a must-read for fans of science-fiction. Sadly, this series ran only seven issues before publisher Pacific Comics went out of business. It then ran two final issues under the Eclipse Comics label before its cancellation.

1 ❑ Dec 1982 Cover: 1.50 **NM** value: **2.50**
• **CGC:** 3 graded, best 9.6
📖 The Few…The Far; Domain; Head of the Class; Talk to Tedi **A:** Al Williamson; Nestor Redondo; Val Mayerik; Tim Conrad **W:** Bruce Jones

2 ❑ May 1983 Cover: 1.50 **NM** value: **2.00**
• **CGC:** 6 graded, best 9.6
📖 Aurora; Vicious Circle; A Mind Of Her Own **A:** Bruce Jones; Dave Stevens **W:** Bruce Jones; Dave Stevens

3 ❑ Jul 1983 Cover: 1.50 **NM** value: **2.00**
• **CGC:** 4 graded, best 9.6
📖 The Inheritors; Pi in the Sky; Dark Passage **A:** Tom Yeates; Ken Steacy; Scott Hampton **W:** Bruce Jones

4 ❑ Sep 1983 Cover: 1.50 **NM** value: **2.00**
• **CGC:** 3 graded, best 9.8
📖 Princess Pam; Girl of my Schemes; One Day in Ohio; Deep Secrets; Land of the Fhre **A:** Al Williamson; Bo Hampton; Jeff Jones; Ken Steacy; Bruce Jones; Dave Stevens **W:** Bruce Jones

5 ❑ Cover: 1.50 **NM** value: **2.00**
• **CGC:** 2 graded, best 9.6
📖 Lip Service; Game Wars; Plastic; Wasteland **A:** John Bolton; Tom Yeates; Ken Steacy; Adolfo Buylla **W:** Bruce Jones

6 ❑ Cover: 1.50 **NM** value: **2.00**
• **CGC:** 1 graded, best 9.8
📖 Planet Perfict; The Test; Pride of the Fleet **A:** Frank Brunner; Roy G. Krenkel; Jim Sullivan **W:** Bruce Jones

7 ❑ Cover: 1.50 **NM** value: **2.00**
• **CGC:** 1 graded, best 9.6
📖 The Small World of Lewis Stillman; Small Change; It All Fits; Ride the Blue Bus **A:** Richard Corben; Gray Morrow; George Pérez; Brent Anderson **W:** Bruce Jones; William F. Nolan

8 ❑ Cover: 1.50 **NM** value: **2.00**
📖 …And Miles To Go Before I Sleep; Soft Boiled; Collector's Item; Stoney End • Eclipse Comics begins as publisher **A:** Al Williamson; Rand Holmes; Ken Steacy; Paul Rivoche **W:** Bruce Jones; Jan Strnad; William F. Nolan

9 ❑ Cover: 1.50 **NM** value: **2.00**
• **CGC:** 1 graded, best 9.2
final issue. **A:** Frank Brunner

3D 1❑ Cover: 3.00 **NM** value: **Cover or less**
• Full-size issues begin. 📖 Fair Play; Field Drill; Gifts; Away Off There Amid the Softly Winking Lights; Spaceman Go Home! **A:** William Wray; Arthur Adams; John Bolton; Dave Stevens; Jim Sullivan **W:** Bruce Jones

Bk 1❑ Cover: 4.95 **NM** value: **Cover or less**
Circ: CapCity orders: **4,625**
📖 Phony Express; Looking for Louie; Boots and Jackets; In the Meadow; Jupiter Rising; Worlds Apart • Eclipse trade paperback **A:** William Wray; Bob Fingerman; Eric Shanower; Ralph Reese; Thom Enriquez **W:** Bruce Jones

ALIEN WORLDS (BLACKTHORNE) — Blackthorne

1 ❑ b&w Cover: 5.95 **NM** value: **Cover or less**

ALISON DARE, LITTLE MISS ADVENTURES — Oni

1 ❑ Sep 2000, b&w Cover: 4.50 **NM** value: **Cover or less**
Circ: Diamd. preorders: **2,669**
📖 What I Did on My Summer Vacation or Tomb Raider, Too

ALISTER THE SLAYER — Midnight Press

1 ❑ Oct 1995 Cover: 2.50 **NM** value: **Cover or less**

ALIZARIN'S JOURNAL — Avatar

1 ❑ Mar 1999, b&w Cover: 3.50 **NM** value: **Cover or less**

ALLAGASH INCIDENT, THE — Tundra

1 ❑ Jul 1993 Cover: 2.95 **NM** value: **Cover or less**
A: Jack Weiner; Charles Rak **W:** Jack Weiner; Charles Rak; Joseph A. Citro

Diamond preorders are the estimated number of comics sold, prior to their release, to comics shops in North America by Diamond Comic Distributors, the largest distributor. These figures underreport the actual number of circulating copies by the amount of reorders Diamond took (usually 5-10% again of the preorders) and sales by publishers to newsstand and bookstore distributors. For many independent publishers, Diamond's preorders may be quite close to the actual number of copies in circulation.

ALL-AMERICAN COMICS — DC

Engineer Alan Scott was working on a railroad bridge, when it was blown up by a jealous competitor. When he managed to drag himself out of the wreckage, he came across a strange green lantern which began to speak to him. The lantern told Scott that it had originally been a meteor which had fallen to Earth. It had later been carved into, first a Chinese lamp, then into an engineer's lantern. Its purpose was to imbue its owner with power that would be used to fight against evil. Scott followed the lantern's instructions to create a ring from the lantern's material and to "recharge" the ring every day by touching it against the lantern.

With this ring, Scott became the Green Lantern, one of DC's first super-heroes and a founding member of The Justice Society of America. Among his powers were flight, the ability to walk through walls, and invulnerability to virtually any sort of attack. He had one weakness: Things that were wooden (including wooden bats, cudgels, etc.) could penetrate his shields. As a result, Green Lantern ended up getting bonked on the head perhaps more than any other hero.

This title, which originally featured strip reprints, humor pieces, and adventure stories, became famous, when it shifted to a primarily super-hero focus. Green Lantern made his debut in All-American Comics #16, followed shortly after by Doctor Mid-Nite. Green Lantern gained a comic-relief sidekick a year after his debut, with the introduction of Doiby Dickles, a taxi driver with a thick Brooklyn accent. Memorable villains also made their debut in this series, including Solomon Grundy and Harlequin, a femme fatale who would become something of an arch-nemesis (and romantic interest!) for Green Lantern.

As super-heroes faded following World War II, this series recast itself once more, becoming All-American Western with issue #103.

1 ❑ Apr 1939 Cover: 0.10 **NM** value: **6000.00**
• **CGC:** 3 graded, best 5.0
★ 1st Appearance of Hop Harrigan, Red, White and Blue.
2 ❑ May 1939 Cover: 0.10 **NM** value: **1950.00**
• Ripley's Believe It or Not! Features begin
3 ❑ Jun 1939 Cover: 0.10 **NM** value: **1300.00**
4 ❑ Jul 1939 Cover: 0.10 **NM** value: **1150.00**
5 ❑ Aug 1939 Cover: 0.10 **NM** value: **1150.00**
6 ❑ Sep 1939 Cover: 0.10 **NM** value: **900.00**
7 ❑ Oct 1939 Cover: 0.10 **NM** value: **900.00**
8 ❑ Nov 1939 Cover: 0.10 **NM** value: **1600.00**
• **CGC:** 1 graded, best 8.0
★ 1st Appearance of Ultra Man.
9 ❑ Dec 1939 Cover: 0.10 **NM** value: **900.00**
10 ❑ Jan 1940 Cover: 0.10 **NM** value: **900.00**
11 ❑ Feb 1940 Cover: 0.10 **NM** value: **975.00**
★ Appearance of Ultra Man.
12 ❑ Mar 1940 Cover: 0.10 **NM** value: **900.00**
13 ❑ Apr 1940 Cover: 0.10 **NM** value: **900.00**
14 ❑ May 1940 Cover: 0.10 **NM** value: **900.00**
15 ❑ Jun 1940 Cover: 0.10 **NM** value: **900.00**
★ Appearance of Ultra Man.
16 ❑ Jul 1940 Cover: 0.10 **NM** value: **67000.00**
• **CGC:** 6 graded, best 5.5
A: Martin Nodell; Shelly Moldoff(cover) **W:** Bill Finger ★ 1st Appearance of Green Lantern I (Alan Scott).
17 ❑ Aug 1940 Cover: 0.10 **NM** value: **15000.00**
• **CGC:** 3 graded, best 5.5
A: Martin Nodell; Shelly Moldoff(cover) **W:** Bill Finger ★ 2nd Appearance of Green Lanern I (Alan Scott).
18 ❑ Sep 1940 Cover: 0.10 **NM** value: **8500.00**
A: Martin Nodell; Shelly Moldoff(cover) **W:** Bill Finger
19 ❑ Oct 1940 Cover: 0.10 **NM** value: **13300.00**
• **CGC:** 1 graded, best 4.5
A: Martin Nodell; Shelly Moldoff(cover) **W:** Bill Finger ★ 1st Appearance of The Atom I (Al Pratt, without costume).
20 ❑ Nov 1940 Cover: 0.10 **NM** value: **4700.00**
• **CGC:** 2 graded, best 7.0
A: Martin Nodell; Shelly Moldoff(cover) **W:** Bill Finger ★ 1st Appearance of The Atom I (Al Pratt, with costume), The Red Tornado.
21 ❑ Dec 1940 Cover: 0.10 **NM** value: **1900.00**
• **CGC:** 1 graded, best 9.0
A: Martin Nodell; Shelly Moldoff(cover) **W:** Bill Finger
22 ❑ Jan 1941 Cover: 0.10 **NM** value: **1900.00**
• **CGC:** 1 graded, best 8.0
A: Martin Nodell; Shelly Moldoff(cover) **W:** Bill Finger
23 ❑ Feb 1941 Cover: 0.10 **NM** value: **1900.00**
A: E.E. Hibbard; Shelly Moldoff(cover) **W:** Bill Finger
24 ❑ Mar 1941 Cover: 0.10 **NM** value: **2400.00**
• **CGC:** 3 graded, best 7.5
• Preview of Doctor Mid-Nite **A:** Irwin Hasen(cover); Martin Nodell **W:** Bill Finger
25 ❑ Apr 1941 Cover: 0.10 **NM** value: **8300.00**
• **CGC:** 1 graded, best 6.0
A: Howard Purcell(cover); Martin Nodell **W:** Bill Finger ★ Origin of Doctor Mid-Nite. ★ 1st Appearance of Doctor Mid-Nite.
26 ❑ May 1941 Cover: 0.10 **NM** value: **2900.00**
• **CGC:** 1 graded, best 6.5
A: Howard Purcell(cover); Irwin Hasen **W:** Bill Finger ★ Origin of Sargon the Sorcerer. ★ 1st Appearance of Sargon the Sorcerer.
27 ❑ Jun 1941 Cover: 0.10 **NM** value: **3400.00**
• **CGC:** 2 graded, best 8.5
A: Howard Purcell(cover); Irwin Hasen **W:** Bill Finger ★ 1st Appearance of Doiby Dickles.
28 ❑ Jul 1941 Cover: 0.10 **NM** value: **1200.00**
• **CGC:** 2 graded, best 4.0
A: Howard Purcell(cover); Irwin Hasen **W:** Bill Finger
29 ❑ Aug 1941 Cover: 0.10 **NM** value: **1200.00**
• **CGC:** 2 graded, best 9.0
A: Howard Purcell(cover); Irwin Hasen **W:** Bill Finger
30 ❑ Sep 1941 Cover: 0.10 **NM** value: **1200.00**
• **CGC:** 3 graded, best 9.0
A: Howard Purcell(cover); Irwin Hasen **W:** Bill Finger
31 ❑ Oct 1941 Cover: 0.10 **NM** value: **1000.00**
• **CGC:** 1 graded, best 3.0
32 ❑ Nov 1941 Cover: 0.10 **NM** value: **1000.00**
• **CGC:** 1 graded, best 6.0
33 ❑ Dec 1941 Cover: 0.10 **NM** value: **1000.00**
• **CGC:** 1 graded, best 3.5
34 ❑ Jan 1942 Cover: 0.10 **NM** value: **1000.00**
• **CGC:** 1 graded, best 5.0
35 ❑ Feb 1942 Cover: 0.10 **NM** value: **1000.00**
36 ❑ Mar 1942 Cover: 0.10 **NM** value: **1000.00**
37 ❑ Apr 1942 Cover: 0.10 **NM** value: **1000.00**
• **CGC:** 2 graded, best 7.5
38 ❑ May 1942 Cover: 0.10 **NM** value: **1000.00**
• **CGC:** 1 graded, best 5.0
39 ❑ Jun 1942 Cover: 0.10 **NM** value: **1000.00**
40 ❑ Jul 1942 Cover: 0.10 **NM** value: **1000.00**
• **CGC:** 1 graded, best 2.0
41 ❑ Aug 1942 Cover: 0.10 **NM** value: **750.00**
42 ❑ Sep 1942 Cover: 0.10 **NM** value: **750.00**
43 ❑ Oct 1942 Cover: 0.10 **NM** value: **750.00**
• **CGC:** 1 graded, best 3.5
44 ❑ Nov 1942 Cover: 0.10 **NM** value: **750.00**
45 ❑ Dec 1942 Cover: 0.10 **NM** value: **750.00**
46 ❑ Jan 1943 Cover: 0.10 **NM** value: **750.00**
47 ❑ Feb 1943 Cover: 0.10 **NM** value: **750.00**
48 ❑ Mar 1943 Cover: 0.10 **NM** value: **750.00**
49 ❑ Apr 1943 Cover: 0.10 **NM** value: **750.00**
50 ❑ Jun 1943 Cover: 0.10 **NM** value: **750.00**
• **CGC:** 1 graded, best 5.0
51 ❑ Jul 1943 Cover: 0.10 **NM** value: **650.00**
52 ❑ Sep 1943 Cover: 0.10 **NM** value: **650.00**
• **CGC:** 3 graded, best 7.0
53 ❑ Oct 1943 Cover: 0.10 **NM** value: **650.00**
54 ❑ Dec 1943 Cover: 0.10 **NM** value: **650.00**
55 ❑ Jan 1944 Cover: 0.10 **NM** value: **650.00**
56 ❑ Mar 1944 Cover: 0.10 **NM** value: **650.00**
57 ❑ Apr 1944 Cover: 0.10 **NM** value: **650.00**
• **CGC:** 1 graded, best 5.5
58 ❑ Jun 1944 Cover: 0.10 **NM** value: **650.00**
• **CGC:** 1 graded, best 8.5
59 ❑ Jul 1944 Cover: 0.10 **NM** value: **650.00**
• **CGC:** 1 graded, best 7.5
60 ❑ Sep 1944 Cover: 0.10 **NM** value: **650.00**
• **CGC:** 2 graded, best 7.5
61 ❑ Oct 1944 Cover: 0.10 **NM** value: **4200.00**
• **CGC:** 3 graded, best 7.5
★ Origin of Solomon Grundy. ★ 1st Appearance of Solomon Grundy.
62 ❑ Dec 1944 Cover: 0.10 **NM** value: **575.00**
• **CGC:** 3 graded, best 9.0
63 ❑ Jan 1945 Cover: 0.10 **NM** value: **575.00**
• **CGC:** 5 graded, best 9.0
64 ❑ Mar 1945 Cover: 0.10 **NM** value: **575.00**
• **CGC:** 1 graded, best 7.0
65 ❑ Apr 1945 Cover: 0.10 **NM** value: **575.00**
• **CGC:** 1 graded, best 7.5
66 ❑ Jun 1945 Cover: 0.10 **NM** value: **575.00**
67 ❑ Aug 1945 Cover: 0.10 **NM** value: **575.00**
• **CGC:** 1 graded, best 6.0
68 ❑ Sep 1945 Cover: 0.10 **NM** value: **575.00**
• **CGC:** 2 graded, best 8.0
69 ❑ Nov 1945 Cover: 0.10 **NM** value: **575.00**
• **CGC:** 1 graded, best 8.5
70 ❑ Jan 1946 Cover: 0.10 **NM** value: **575.00**
• **CGC:** 4 graded, best 8.0
71 ❑ Mar 1946 Cover: 0.10 **NM** value: **525.00**
• **CGC:** 1 graded, best 7.0
72 ❑ Apr 1946 Cover: 0.10 **NM** value: **525.00**
• **CGC:** 2 graded, best 8.5
73 ❑ May 1946 Cover: 0.10 **NM** value: **525.00**
• **CGC:** 2 graded, best 7.0
74 ❑ Jun 1946 Cover: 0.10 **NM** value: **525.00**
75 ❑ Jul 1946 Cover: 0.10 **NM** value: **525.00**
• **CGC:** 2 graded, best 7.5
76 ❑ Aug 1946 Cover: 0.10 **NM** value: **525.00**
• **CGC:** 1 graded, best 8.5
77 ❑ Sep 1946 Cover: 0.10 **NM** value: **525.00**
78 ❑ Oct 1946 Cover: 0.10 **NM** value: **525.00**
• **CGC:** 1 graded, best 7.0
79 ❑ Nov 1946 Cover: 0.10 **NM** value: **525.00**
• **CGC:** 1 graded, best 5.0
80 ❑ Dec 1946 Cover: 0.10 **NM** value: **525.00**
• **CGC:** 1 graded, best 6.0
81 ❑ Jan 1947 Cover: 0.10 **NM** value: **525.00**
82 ❑ Feb 1947 Cover: 0.10 **NM** value: **525.00**
83 ❑ Mar 1947 Cover: 0.10 **NM** value: **525.00**
• **CGC:** 1 graded, best 6.0
84 ❑ Apr 1947 Cover: 0.10 **NM** value: **525.00**
85 ❑ May 1947 Cover: 0.10 **NM** value: **525.00**
• **CGC:** 2 graded, best 8.5
86 ❑ Jun 1947 Cover: 0.10 **NM** value: **525.00**
87 ❑ Jul 1947 Cover: 0.10 **NM** value: **525.00**
88 ❑ Aug 1947 Cover: 0.10 **NM** value: **525.00**
89 ❑ Sep 1947 Cover: 0.10 **NM** value: **900.00**
• **CGC:** 4 graded, best 9.2
★ 1st Appearance of Harlequin.
90 ❑ Oct 1947 Cover: 0.10 **NM** value: **700.00**
• **CGC:** 2 graded, best 7.0
★ 1st Appearance of Icicle.
91 ❑ Nov 1947 Cover: 0.10 **NM** value: **500.00**
• **CGC:** 2 graded, best 8.0

CGC-graded: Multiply prices above by **33 for 9.9 M • 16 for 9.8 NM/M • 7 for 9.6 NM+ • 5 for 9.4 NM • 2.5 for 9.2 NM- • 1.5 for 9.0 VF/NM**

92 ❑ Dec 1947 Cover: 0.12 **NM** value: **500.00**
• **CGC:** 1 graded, best 5.0
93 ❑ Jan 1948 Cover: 0.12 **NM** value: **500.00**
• **CGC:** 2 graded, best 7.5
94 ❑ Feb 1948 Cover: 0.12 **NM** value: **500.00**
• **CGC:** 1 graded, best 6.5
95 ❑ Mar 1948 Cover: 0.12 **NM** value: **500.00**
• **CGC:** 1 graded, best 8.0
96 ❑ Apr 1948 Cover: 0.12 **NM** value: **500.00**
97 ❑ May 1948 Cover: 0.12 **NM** value: **500.00**
• **CGC:** 2 graded, best 9.0
98 ❑ Jun 1948 Cover: 0.12 **NM** value: **500.00**
99 ❑ Jul 1948 Cover: 0.12 **NM** value: **500.00**
• **CGC:** 1 graded, best 7.0
100 ❑ Aug 1948 Cover: 0.12 **NM** value: **680.00**
• Westerns begin ★ Appearance of Johnny Thunder.
101 ❑ Sep 1948 Cover: 0.12 **NM** value: **680.00**
• **CGC:** 2 graded, best 8.0
• Scarce
102 ❑ Oct 1948 Cover: 0.12 **NM** value: **800.00**
• **CGC:** 6 graded, best 9.2
• Series continued in All-American Western #103;Scarce

ALL-AMERICAN COMICS (2ND SERIES) DC

1 ❑ May 1999 Cover: 1.99 **NM** value: **2.00**
Circ: Diamd. preorders: **43,555**
📖 Cold Heart **A:** Eduardo Barreto **W:** Ron Marz ★ Appearance of Johnny Thunder, Green Lantern.

ALL-AMERICAN MEN OF WAR DC

The title began as a general war comic book, with cover stories like "Lifenet to Beach Red!" and the cover description "Fighting actions on every front." Soon, cover copy evolved to showing a cover title and the words "and other stories of blazing action in hand-to-hand combat!" Nevertheless, some of the story titles indicated less than hand-to-hand action ("Diary of a Fighter Pilot"), and eventually the focus of the action was the sky.

Eventually, Johnny Cloud, the Navajo Ace, took the cover spot, and the stories involved fighter pilots, though some of the action could still take place on the ground. Stories shifted to covering "three wars," and finally in #112 (Dec 75) Lt. Steve Savage, "The Balloon Buster" appeared — which didn't mean Johnny Cloud was out of the action. In #115, readers found the issue was "Special: The scorching return of Navajo Ace Johnny Cloud! in the startling mission ... 'Killer Ace — Handle with Care!'" — Maggie

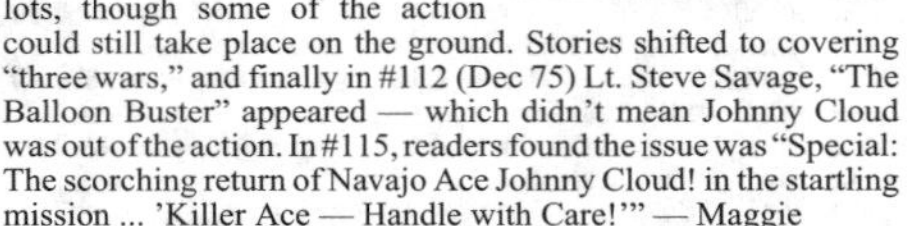

0 ❑ Aug 1952 Cover: 0.10 **NM** value: **850.00**
• Indicia reads #127;Series numbering continued from All-American Western
1 ❑ Oct 1952 Cover: 0.10 **NM** value: **475.00**
• Indicia reads #128;Series numbering continued from All-American Western
2 ❑ Dec 1952 Cover: 0.10 **NM** value: **350.00**
• **CGC:** 1 graded, best 7.0
3 ❑ Feb 1953 Cover: 0.10 **NM** value: **285.00**
4 ❑ Apr 1953 Cover: 0.10 **NM** value: **250.00**
5 ❑ Jun 1953 Cover: 0.10 **NM** value: **250.00**
6 ❑ Aug 1953 Cover: 0.10 **NM** value: **225.00**
7 ❑ Oct 1953 Cover: 0.10 **NM** value: **225.00**
8 ❑ Dec 1953 Cover: 0.10 **NM** value: **225.00**
• **CGC:** 1 graded, best 7.0
9 ❑ Feb 1954 Cover: 0.10 **NM** value: **225.00**
10 ❑ Apr 1954 Cover: 0.10 **NM** value: **225.00**
• **CGC:** 2 graded, best 8.0
11 ❑ Jun 1954 Cover: 0.10 **NM** value: **200.00**
12 ❑ Aug 1954 Cover: 0.10 **NM** value: **200.00**
• **CGC:** 2 graded, best 8.0
13 ❑ Sep 1954 Cover: 0.10 **NM** value: **200.00**
14 ❑ Oct 1954 Cover: 0.10 **NM** value: **200.00**
• **CGC:** 1 graded, best 7.0
15 ❑ Nov 1954 Cover: 0.10 **NM** value: **200.00**
16 ❑ Dec 1954 Cover: 0.10 **NM** value: **200.00**
17 ❑ Jan 1955 Cover: 0.10 **NM** value: **200.00**
• **CGC:** 1 graded, best 4.5
18 ❑ Feb 1955 Cover: 0.10 **NM** value: **200.00**
19 ❑ Mar 1955 Cover: 0.10 **NM** value: **160.00**
• Code-approved issues start
20 ❑ Apr 1955 Cover: 0.10 **NM** value: **160.00**
• **CGC:** 1 graded, best 9.0
21 ❑ May 1955 Cover: 0.10 **NM** value: **160.00**
22 ❑ Jun 1955 Cover: 0.10 **NM** value: **160.00**
23 ❑ Jul 1955 Cover: 0.10 **NM** value: **160.00**
24 ❑ Aug 1955 Cover: 0.10 **NM** value: **160.00**
25 ❑ Sep 1955 Cover: 0.10 **NM** value: **160.00**
26 ❑ Oct 1955 Cover: 0.10 **NM** value: **160.00**
27 ❑ Nov 1955 Cover: 0.10 **NM** value: **160.00**
28 ❑ Dec 1955 Cover: 0.10 **NM** value: **160.00**
29 ❑ Jan 1956 Cover: 0.10 **NM** value: **185.00**
30 ❑ Feb 1956 Cover: 0.10 **NM** value: **160.00**
31 ❑ Mar 1956 Cover: 0.10 **NM** value: **125.00**
32 ❑ Apr 1956 Cover: 0.10 **NM** value: **125.00**
33 ❑ May 1956 Cover: 0.10 **NM** value: **125.00**
34 ❑ Jun 1956 Cover: 0.10 **NM** value: **125.00**
35 ❑ Jul 1956 Cover: 0.10 **NM** value: **125.00**
36 ❑ Aug 1956 Cover: 0.10 **NM** value: **125.00**
37 ❑ Sep 1956 Cover: 0.10 **NM** value: **125.00**
38 ❑ Oct 1956 Cover: 0.10 **NM** value: **125.00**
39 ❑ Nov 1956 Cover: 0.10 **NM** value: **125.00**
40 ❑ Dec 1956 Cover: 0.10 **NM** value: **125.00**
• **CGC:** 1 graded, best 9.0
41 ❑ Jan 1957 Cover: 0.10 **NM** value: **100.00**
42 ❑ Feb 1957 Cover: 0.10 **NM** value: **100.00**
43 ❑ Mar 1957 Cover: 0.10 **NM** value: **100.00**
44 ❑ Apr 1957 Cover: 0.10 **NM** value: **100.00**
45 ❑ May 1957 Cover: 0.10 **NM** value: **100.00**
46 ❑ Jun 1957 Cover: 0.10 **NM** value: **100.00**
47 ❑ Jul 1957 Cover: 0.10 **NM** value: **100.00**
• **CGC:** 1 graded, best 8.0
48 ❑ Aug 1957 Cover: 0.10 **NM** value: **100.00**
49 ❑ Sep 1957 Cover: 0.10 **NM** value: **100.00**
50 ❑ Oct 1957 Cover: 0.10 **NM** value: **100.00**
51 ❑ Nov 1957 Cover: 0.10 **NM** value: **80.00**
52 ❑ Dec 1957 Cover: 0.10 **NM** value: **80.00**
53 ❑ Jan 1958 Cover: 0.10 **NM** value: **80.00**
54 ❑ Feb 1958 Cover: 0.10 **NM** value: **80.00**
55 ❑ Mar 1958 Cover: 0.10 **NM** value: **80.00**
56 ❑ Apr 1958 Cover: 0.10 **NM** value: **80.00**
57 ❑ May 1958 Cover: 0.10 **NM** value: **80.00**
58 ❑ Jun 1958 Cover: 0.10 **NM** value: **80.00**
59 ❑ Jul 1958 Cover: 0.10 **NM** value: **80.00**
60 ❑ Aug 1958 Cover: 0.10 **NM** value: **80.00**
61 ❑ Sep 1958 Cover: 0.10 **NM** value: **70.00**
62 ❑ Oct 1958 Cover: 0.10 **NM** value: **70.00**
63 ❑ Nov 1958 Cover: 0.10 **NM** value: **70.00**
64 ❑ Dec 1958 Cover: 0.10 **NM** value: **70.00**
65 ❑ Jan 1959 Cover: 0.10 **NM** value: **70.00**
66 ❑ Feb 1959 Cover: 0.10 **NM** value: **80.00**
★ 1st Appearance of Gunner & Sarge.
67 ❑ Mar 1959 Cover: 0.10 **NM** value: **130.00**
★ Appearance of Gunner & Sarge.
68 ❑ Apr 1959 Cover: 0.10 **NM** value: **70.00**
69 ❑ May 1959 Cover: 0.10 **NM** value: **70.00**
70 ❑ Jun 1959 Cover: 0.10 **NM** value: **70.00**
71 ❑ Jul 1959 Cover: 0.10 **NM** value: **65.00**
72 ❑ Aug 1959 Cover: 0.10 **NM** value: **65.00**
73 ❑ Sep 1959 Cover: 0.10 **NM** value: **65.00**
74 ❑ Oct 1959 Cover: 0.10 **NM** value: **65.00**
75 ❑ Nov 1959 Cover: 0.10 **NM** value: **65.00**
76 ❑ Dec 1959 Cover: 0.10 **NM** value: **65.00**
77 ❑ Feb 1960 Cover: 0.10 **NM** value: **65.00**
Circ: Statement: **176,000**
78 ❑ Apr 1960 Cover: 0.10 **NM** value: **65.00**
Circ: Statement: **176,000**
79 ❑ Jun 1960 Cover: 0.10 **NM** value: **65.00**
Circ: Statement: **176,000**
80 ❑ Aug 1960 Cover: 0.10 **NM** value: **65.00**
Circ: Statement: **176,000**
81 ❑ Oct 1960 Cover: 0.10 **NM** value: **48.00**
Circ: Statement: **176,000**
82 ❑ Dec 1960 Cover: 0.10 **NM** value: **125.00**
Circ: Statement: **176,000**
★ 1st Appearance of Johnny Cloud.
83 ❑ Feb 1961 Cover: 0.10 **NM** value: **48.00**
Circ: Statement: **180,000**
84 ❑ Apr 1961 Cover: 0.10 **NM** value: **48.00**
Circ: Statement: **180,000**
85 ❑ Jun 1961 Cover: 0.10 **NM** value: **48.00**
Circ: Statement: **180,000**
86 ❑ Aug 1961 Cover: 0.10 **NM** value: **48.00**
Circ: Statement: **180,000**
87 ❑ Oct 1961 Cover: 0.10 **NM** value: **48.00**
Circ: Statement: **180,000**
88 ❑ Dec 1961 Cover: 0.10 **NM** value: **48.00**
Circ: Statement: **180,000**
89 ❑ Feb 1962 Cover: 0.12 **NM** value: **48.00**
90 ❑ Apr 1962 Cover: 0.12 **NM** value: **48.00**
91 ❑ Jun 1962 Cover: 0.12 **NM** value: **32.00**
92 ❑ Aug 1962 Cover: 0.12 **NM** value: **32.00**
📖 The Battle Hawk!; Ace on a String!; Abundance of Strength...; Double Ace in Double Trouble!
93 ❑ Oct 1962 Cover: 0.12 **NM** value: **32.00**
94 ❑ Dec 1962 Cover: 0.12 **NM** value: **32.00**
95 ❑ Feb 1963 Cover: 0.12 **NM** value: **32.00**
96 ❑ Apr 1963 Cover: 0.12 **NM** value: **32.00**
97 ❑ Jun 1963 Cover: 0.12 **NM** value: **32.00**
98 ❑ Aug 1963 Cover: 0.12 **NM** value: **32.00**
99 ❑ Oct 1963 Cover: 0.12 **NM** value: **32.00**
100 ❑ Dec 1963 Cover: 0.12 **NM** value: **32.00**
101 ❑ Jan 1964 Cover: 0.12 **NM** value: **22.00**
102 ❑ Mar 1964 Cover: 0.12 **NM** value: **22.00**
103 ❑ May 1964 Cover: 0.12 **NM** value: **22.00**
104 ❑ Jul 1964 Cover: 0.12 **NM** value: **22.00**
• **CGC:** 1 graded, best 9.4
105 ❑ Sep 1964 Cover: 0.12 **NM** value: **22.00**
106 ❑ Nov 1964 Cover: 0.12 **NM** value: **22.00**
107 ❑ Jan 1965 Cover: 0.12 **NM** value: **22.00**
Circ: Statement: **247,717**
108 ❑ Mar 1965 Cover: 0.12 **NM** value: **22.00**
Circ: Statement: **247,717**
109 ❑ May 1965 Cover: 0.12 **NM** value: **22.00**
Circ: Statement: **247,717**
110 ❑ Jul 1965 Cover: 0.12 **NM** value: **22.00**
Circ: Statement: **247,717**
111 ❑ Sep 1965 Cover: 0.12 **NM** value: **18.00**
Circ: Statement: **247,717**
112 ❑ Nov 1965 Cover: 0.12 **NM** value: **18.00**
Circ: Statement: **247,717** • **CGC:** 1 graded, best 9.4
113 ❑ Jan 1966 Cover: 0.12 **NM** value: **18.00**
• **CGC:** 1 graded, best 9.6
114 ❑ Mar 1966 Cover: 0.12 **NM** value: **18.00**
• **CGC:** 1 graded, best 4.0
115 ❑ May 1966 Cover: 0.12 **NM** value: **18.00**
116 ❑ Jul 1966 Cover: 0.12 **NM** value: **18.00**
117 ❑ Sep 1966 Cover: 0.12 **NM** value: **18.00**
final issue.

ALL-AMERICAN WESTERN DC

103 ❑ Nov 1948 Cover: 0.10 **NM** value: **350.00**
• **CGC:** 2 graded, best 9.2
• continues numbering from All-American Comics #102
104 ❑ ca. 1949 Cover: 0.10 **NM** value: **250.00**
105 ❑ ca. 1949 Cover: 0.10 **NM** value: **200.00**
• **CGC:** 1 graded, best 9.0
106 ❑ ca. 1949 Cover: 0.10 **NM** value: **200.00**
• **CGC:** 1 graded, best 9.0
107 ❑ ca. 1949 Cover: 0.10 **NM** value: **200.00**
• **CGC:** 2 graded, best 9.8
108 ❑ ca. 1949 Cover: 0.10 **NM** value: **200.00**
• **CGC:** 2 graded, best 9.4
109 ❑ ca. 1949 Cover: 0.10 **NM** value: **200.00**
110 ❑ ca. 1949 Cover: 0.10 **NM** value: **200.00**
• **CGC:** 1 graded, best 7.5
111 ❑ ca. 1949 Cover: 0.10 **NM** value: **150.00**
• **CGC:** 1 graded, best 8.5
112 ❑ Feb 1950 Cover: 0.10 **NM** value: **150.00**
113 ❑ Apr 1950 Cover: 0.10 **NM** value: **150.00**
114 ❑ Jun 1950 Cover: 0.10 **NM** value: **150.00**
115 ❑ Aug 1950 Cover: 0.10 **NM** value: **150.00**
116 ❑ Oct 1950 Cover: 0.10 **NM** value: **150.00**
• Has 1965 Statement, filed 10/1/65; avg print run 418,000; avg sales 246,000; avg subs 1,717; avg total paid 247,717; samples 142; max existent 247,859; 41% of run returned
117 ❑ Dec 1950 Cover: 0.10 **NM** value: **150.00**
118 ❑ Feb 1951 Cover: 0.10 **NM** value: **150.00**
119 ❑ Apr 1951 Cover: 0.10 **NM** value: **150.00**
• **CGC:** 1 graded, best 8.5
120 ❑ Jun 1951 Cover: 0.10 **NM** value: **150.00**
• **CGC:** 1 graded, best 9.4
121 ❑ Aug 1951 Cover: 0.10 **NM** value: **100.00**
122 ❑ Oct 1951 Cover: 0.10 **NM** value: **100.00**
123 ❑ Dec 1951 Cover: 0.10 **NM** value: **100.00**
124 ❑ Feb 1952 Cover: 0.10 **NM** value: **100.00**
125 ❑ Apr 1952 Cover: 0.10 **NM** value: **100.00**
126 ❑ Jun 1952 Cover: 0.10 **NM** value: **100.00**

ALL DETECTIVE Avalon

Mystery, intrigue, death, and, of course, murder. Often these words are preceded by seemingly innocuous events. For example, the discovery of a fragment of paper with a note written on the back. Or, every so often, a detective in his smoking jacket sinking into a chair, filling his pipe, and saying, "It would be worth your while, Watson, to glance this over ..." In these instances, you know that the world's greatest detective, Sherlock Holmes, is on the case, and whoever is responsible for the aforementioned conditions won't go unpunished for long.

This collection (from Avalon, despite an "ACG" logo on the cover) reprints Sherlock Holmes strips from as far back as the 1930s, including the first comic strip featuring Sir Arthur Conan Doyle's character, not to mention his familiar associate, Dr. Watson. Printed in black and white.

1 ❑ b&w Cover: 2.95 **NM** value: **Cover or less**

ALLEGRA Image

1 ❑ Aug 1996 Cover: 2.50 **NM** value: **Cover or less**
A: Scott Clark; Patrick Lee **W:** Steven Seagle ★ 1st Appearance of Allegra.
1/SC ❑ Aug 1996 Cover: 2.50 **NM** value: **Cover or less**
foil cover. **A:** Scott Clark; Patrick Lee
2 ❑ Sep 1996 Cover: 2.50 **NM** value: **Cover or less**
A: Scott Clark; Patrick Lee **W:** Steven Seagle
3 ❑ Nov 1996 Cover: 2.50 **NM** value: **Cover or less**
Circ: Diamd. preorders: **25,996**
A: Scott Clark; Patrick Lee **W:** Steven Seagle
4 ❑ Dec 1996 Cover: 2.50 **NM** value: **Cover or less**
Circ: Direct Market orders: **22,800**
A: Scott Clark; Patrick Lee **W:** Steven Seagle

ALLEY CAT Image

1 ❑ Jul 1999 Cover: 2.50 **NM** value: **Cover or less**
Circ: Diamd. preorders: **36,173** • **CGC:** 1 graded, best 9.4
Photo cover. **A:** Bosco **W:** Bob Napton; Matt Hawkins
1/A ❑ Jul 1999 **NM** value: **4.25**
school girl cover. • Another Universe Edition.
1/B ❑ Jul 1999 **NM** value: **2.50**
• Wizard World Edition. • reclining with claws extended
2 ❑ Aug 1999 Cover: 2.50 **NM** value: **Cover or less**
Circ: Diamd. preorders: **22,878**
A: Bosco **W:** Bob Napton; Matt Hawkins
2/A ❑ Aug 1999 Cover: 3.00 **NM** value: **Cover or less**
• Monster Mart Edition. • in red dress with stake in hand **A:** Bosco **W:** Bob Napton; Matt Hawkins
3 ❑ Sep 1999 Cover: 2.50 **NM** value: **Cover or less**
Circ: Diamd. preorders: **21,757**
• in front of grave **A:** Bosco **W:** Bob Napton; Matt Hawkins
3/A ❑ Sep 1999 Cover: 2.50 **NM** value: **Cover or less**
Dorian cover. **A:** Bosco **W:** Bob Napton; Matt Hawkins
4 ❑ Oct 1999 Cover: 2.50 **NM** value: **Cover or less**
Circ: Diamd. preorders: **15,745**
📖 The Martyr, Part 1 **A:** Bosco **W:** Bob Napton; Matt Hawkins
5 ❑ Dec 1999 Cover: 2.50 **NM** value: **Cover or less**
Circ: Diamd. preorders: **15,408**
Photo cover. 📖 The Martyr, Part 2 **A:** Bosco **W:** Bob Napton; Matt Hawkins
6 ❑ Feb 2000 Cover: 2.95 **NM** value: **Cover or less**
Circ: Diamd. preorders: **13,958**
Photo cover. 📖 The Martyr, Part 3 • with headdress **A:** Bosco **W:** Bob Napton; Matt Hawkins
Ash 1 ❑ May 1999 **NM** value: **2.50**
Photo cover. • Limited Preview Edition on cover. • holding arms over head **A:** Bosco **W:** Bob Napton; Matt Hawkins

Other grades: Multiply prices above by **1.5 for Mint • 2/3 for Very Fine • 1/3 for Fine • 1/5 for Very Good • 1/8 for Good**

ASH 1/A ❑ May 1999 **NM** value: **5.00**
Photo cover. • Dynamic Forces edition.
ASH 1/B ❑ May 1999 **NM** value: **3.00**
Photo cover. • Dynamic Forces edition. • front shot;Wizard World logo at bottom right
ASH 1/C ❑ May 1999 **NM** value: **4.00**
sketch cover. • Dynamic Forces edition.
ASH 1/D ❑ May 1999 **NM** value: **4.00**
drawn color cover. • Dynamic Forces edition. • kneeling on rooftop

ALLEY CAT LINGERIE EDITION — Image

1 ❑ Oct 1999 Cover: 4.95 **NM** value: **Cover or less**
Circ: Diamd. preorders: **13,845**
cardstock cover. • photos and pin-ups **A:** Matt Busch; Michael Bair; Jason Johnson; Dan Fraga; Francis Manapul; Edwin Rosell; Greg Aronowitz; Marat Michaels; Bosco and Tie; Brett Evans; Bruce Brown; Dorian; Harvey Butts; Jennifer Janesco; Sean McCall

ALLEY CAT VS. LADY PENDRAGON — Image

1 ❑ 2000 **NM** value: **3.00**
1/A ❑ 2000 **NM** value: **3.00**
• Wizard Mall variant;flipbook with Alley Cat Con Exclusive Preview

ALLEY OOP ADVENTURES — Antarctic

Created in 1933 by V.T. Hamlin, America's oldest modern-day caveman made the transition from worldwide syndication into a comic book compiling his adventures. The comic strip revolves around the irrepressible caveman Alley Oop, who travels from prehistoric land of Moo all the way to the 21st century in his friend Doc Wonmug's time machine. This is an entertaining book for the entire family with many a good-natured humorous twist on historical events. Other regulars in the strip include King Guz and Queen Umpa of Moo, Doc Wonmug's assistants Oscar and Ava, and Oop's sensual girlfriend Ooola.

1 ❑ Aug 1998 Cover: 2.95 **NM** value: **Cover or less**
Circ: Diamd. preorders: **3,246**
2 ❑ Oct 1998 Cover: 2.95 **NM** value: **Cover or less**
Circ: Diamd. preorders: **2,409**
A: Jack Bender; Carole Bender **W:** Mike Chapman
3 ❑ Dec 1998 Cover: 2.95 **NM** value: **Cover or less**
Circ: Diamd. preorders: **1,758**
📖 Oop the Mighty!; Dinny and the Dinky Dino **A:** Jack Bender; Dan Davis **W:** Dan Davis

ALLEY OOP (ARGO) — Argo

1 ❑ Nov 1955 Cover: 0.10 **NM** value: **100.00**
2 ❑ Jan 1956 Cover: 0.10 **NM** value: **75.00**
3 ❑ Mar 1956 Cover: 0.10 **NM** value: **75.00**

ALLEY OOP (DELL) — Dell

1 ❑ Dec 1962 Cover: 0.10 **NM** value: **32.00**
• **CGC:** 1 graded, best 7.5
📖 Bronto Soreness; Foreign Entanglement; New Twist; Spain in the Neck; King for a Day; A Barbarous Act; Time-and-a-Hap **A:** Vincent Hamlin **W:** Vincent Hamlin
2 ❑ Cover: 0.10 **NM** value: **25.00**
A: Vincent Hamlin **W:** Vincent Hamlin

ALLEY OOP (DRAGON LADY) — Dragon Lady

1 ❑ Cover: 5.95 **NM** value: **Cover or less**
★ Origin of Oop, Dinny.
2 ❑ Cover: 6.95 **NM** value: **Cover or less**
• time machine
3 ❑ Cover: 7.95 **NM** value: **Cover or less**
• Hercules

ALLEY OOP QUARTERLY — Antarctic

1 ❑ Sep 1999 Cover: 2.50 **NM** value: **Cover or less**
📖 Alley Oop's Survival Guide **A:** Jack Bender **W:** Dan Davis
2 ❑ Dec 1999 Cover: 2.95 **NM** value: **Cover or less**
A: Jack Bender **W:** Dan Davis
3 ❑ Mar 2000 Cover: 2.95 **NM** value: **Cover or less**
A: Jack Bender **W:** Dan Davis

ALLEY OOP (STANDARD) — Standard

10 ❑ Oct 1947 Cover: 0.10 **NM** value: **150.00**
11 ❑ Dec 1947 Cover: 0.10 **NM** value: **125.00**
12 ❑ Mar 1948 Cover: 0.10 **NM** value: **125.00**
13 ❑ Jul 1948 Cover: 0.10 **NM** value: **125.00**
14 ❑ Oct 1948 Cover: 0.10 **NM** value: **125.00**
15 ❑ Dec 1948 Cover: 0.10 **NM** value: **125.00**
16 ❑ Mar 1949 Cover: 0.10 **NM** value: **125.00**
• **CGC:** 1 graded, best 8.0
17 ❑ Jul 1949 Cover: 0.10 **NM** value: **125.00**
18 ❑ Oct 1949 Cover: 0.10 **NM** value: **125.00**

ALLEY OOP (VISUAL EDITIONS) — Visual Editions

10 ❑ Cover: 0.10 **NM** value: **100.00**
📖 Crocodile Capers; Cleopatra's Clue; The Wrath of Wooluh!;
11 ❑ Cover: 0.10 **NM** value: **75.00**
12 ❑ Cover: 0.10 **NM** value: **75.00**
13 ❑ Cover: 0.10 **NM** value: **75.00**
14 ❑ Cover: 0.10 **NM** value: **75.00**
15 ❑ Cover: 0.10 **NM** value: **75.00**
16 ❑ Cover: 0.10 **NM** value: **75.00**
17 ❑ Cover: 0.10 **NM** value: **75.00**
18 ❑ Cover: 0.10 **NM** value: **75.00**

ALL-FAMOUS CRIME — Star Publications

4 ❑ Feb 1950 Cover: 0.10 **NM** value: **150.00**
5 ❑ May 1950 Cover: 0.10 **NM** value: **100.00**
8 ❑ May 1951 Cover: 0.10 **NM** value: **100.00**
• **CGC:** 1 graded, best 9.0
9 ❑ Aug 1951 Cover: 0.10 **NM** value: **100.00**
10 ❑ Nov 1951 Cover: 0.10 **NM** value: **100.00**

ALL FAMOUS CRIME STORIES — Fox

1 ❑ ca. 1949 Cover: 0.25 **NM** value: **300.00**
No issue number. • giant-size

ALL-FAMOUS POLICE CASES — Star Publications

6 ❑ Mar 1952 Cover: 0.10 **NM** value: **100.00**
• **CGC:** 1 graded, best 8.5
7 ❑ Sep 1952 Cover: 0.10 **NM** value: **75.00**
8 ❑ Dec 1952 Cover: 0.10 **NM** value: **75.00**
• **CGC:** 1 graded, best 8.5
9 ❑ Jan 1953 Cover: 0.10 **NM** value: **60.00**
10 ❑ Mar 1953 Cover: 0.10 **NM** value: **60.00**
11 ❑ Jun 1953 Cover: 0.10 **NM** value: **60.00**
12 ❑ Sep 1953 Cover: 0.10 **NM** value: **60.00**
13 ❑ Dec 1953 Cover: 0.10 **NM** value: **60.00**
14 ❑ Mar 1954 Cover: 0.10 **NM** value: **60.00**
• **CGC:** 1 graded, best 9.4
15 ❑ Jun 1954 Cover: 0.10 **NM** value: **60.00**
16 ❑ Sep 1954 Cover: 0.10 **NM** value: **60.00**

ALL-FLASH — DC

In part because of the size of Golden Age comics, it was common for characters that are icons today to begin their careers in anthology comics. So it was that, while The Flash was introduced in Flash Comics #1, that comic book also introduced Hawkman and Johnny Thunder in stories starring them.

It took more than a year to establish that Harry Lampert's character could carry his own title – but, since Flash Comics was still running as an anthology comic book, this different name was chosen for the solo series. The first issue began with a fast recap of the origin story and then filled the rest of the issue almost entirely with Flash episodes. (As with many comics of the era, the series contained occasional comedy fillers with other characters.) — Maggie

1 ❑ Sum 1941 Cover: 0.10 **NM** value: **12000.00**
• **CGC:** 12 graded, best 9.4
2 ❑ Fal 1941 Cover: 0.10 **NM** value: **2000.00**
• **CGC:** 5 graded, best 9.6
3 ❑ Win 1941 Cover: 0.10 **NM** value: **1500.00**
• **CGC:** 4 graded, best 9.6
4 ❑ Spr 1942 Cover: 0.10 **NM** value: **1500.00**
• **CGC:** 2 graded, best 4.0
5 ❑ Sum 1942 Cover: 0.10 **NM** value: **1000.00**
• **CGC:** 2 graded, best 8.5
6 ❑ Sep 1942 Cover: 0.10 **NM** value: **1000.00**
• **CGC:** 1 graded, best 4.5
7 ❑ Nov 1942 Cover: 0.10 **NM** value: **1000.00**
• **CGC:** 1 graded, best 8.0
8 ❑ Jan 1943 Cover: 0.10 **NM** value: **1000.00**
• **CGC:** 1 graded, best 2.0
9 ❑ Mar 1943 Cover: 0.10 **NM** value: **1000.00**
• **CGC:** 2 graded, best 5.5
10 ❑ May 1943 Cover: 0.10 **NM** value: **1000.00**
• **CGC:** 2 graded, best 9.4
11 ❑ Jul 1943 Cover: 0.10 **NM** value: **750.00**
• **CGC:** 1 graded, best 2.5
12 ❑ Fal 1943 Cover: 0.10 **NM** value: **750.00**
• **CGC:** 2 graded, best 9.4
13 ❑ Win 1943 Cover: 0.10 **NM** value: **750.00**
• **CGC:** 1 graded, best 7.5
14 ❑ Spr 1944 Cover: 0.10 **NM** value: **750.00**
• **CGC:** 3 graded, best 5.0
15 ❑ Sum 1944 Cover: 0.10 **NM** value: **750.00**
• **CGC:** 3 graded, best 8.5
16 ❑ Fal 1944 Cover: 0.10 **NM** value: **750.00**
17 ❑ Win 1944 Cover: 0.10 **NM** value: **750.00**
• **CGC:** 2 graded, best 9.0
18 ❑ Spr 1945 Cover: 0.10 **NM** value: **750.00**
• **CGC:** 4 graded, best 9.6
19 ❑ Sum 1945 Cover: 0.10 **NM** value: **750.00**
• **CGC:** 2 graded, best 9.4
20 ❑ Fal 1945 Cover: 0.10 **NM** value: **750.00**
• **CGC:** 2 graded, best 6.0
21 ❑ Win 1945 Cover: 0.10 **NM** value: **600.00**
• **CGC:** 3 graded, best 9.4
22 ❑ Apr 1946 Cover: 0.10 **NM** value: **600.00**
• **CGC:** 1 graded, best 9.6
23 ❑ Jun 1946 Cover: 0.10 **NM** value: **600.00**
• **CGC:** 1 graded, best 9.4
24 ❑ Aug 1946 Cover: 0.10 **NM** value: **600.00**
• **CGC:** 1 graded, best 9.2
25 ❑ Oct 1946 Cover: 0.10 **NM** value: **600.00**
• **CGC:** 2 graded, best 9.4
26 ❑ Dec 1946 Cover: 0.10 **NM** value: **600.00**
• **CGC:** 1 graded, best 9.6
27 ❑ Feb 1947 Cover: 0.10 **NM** value: **600.00**
• **CGC:** 3 graded, best 9.8
28 ❑ Apr 1947 Cover: 0.10 **NM** value: **600.00**
• **CGC:** 3 graded, best 8.5
29 ❑ Jun 1947 Cover: 0.10 **NM** value: **600.00**
• **CGC:** 1 graded, best 9.4
30 ❑ Aug 1947 Cover: 0.10 **NM** value: **600.00**
31 ❑ Oct 1947 Cover: 0.10 **NM** value: **600.00**
32 ❑ Dec 1947 Cover: 0.10 **NM** value: **600.00**
• **CGC:** 3 graded, best 9.0

ALL FOR LOVE — Prize

Volume 1
1 ❑ May 1957 Cover: 0.10 **NM** value: **50.00**
2 ❑ Jul 1957 Cover: 0.10 **NM** value: **35.00**
3 ❑ Sep 1957 Cover: 0.10 **NM** value: **35.00**
4 ❑ Nov 1957 Cover: 0.10 **NM** value: **35.00**
5 ❑ Jan 1958 Cover: 0.10 **NM** value: **35.00**
6 ❑ Mar 1958 Cover: 0.10 **NM** value: **35.00**

Volume 2
1 ❑ May 1958 Cover: 0.10 **NM** value: **20.00**
2 ❑ Jul 1958 Cover: 0.10 **NM** value: **20.00**
3 ❑ Sep 1958 Cover: 0.10 **NM** value: **20.00**
4 ❑ Nov 1958 Cover: 0.10 **NM** value: **20.00**
5 ❑ Jan 1959 Cover: 0.10 **NM** value: **15.00**
5/A ❑ Mar 1959 Cover: 0.10 **NM** value: **15.00**
• second #5 (probably a misprint)

Volume 3
1 ❑ May 1959 Cover: 0.10 **NM** value: **15.00**
1/A ❑ Jul 1959 Cover: 0.10 **NM** value: **15.00**
• second #1 (probably a misprint)
2 ❑ Sep 1959 Cover: 0.10 **NM** value: **15.00**
3 ❑ Nov 1959 Cover: 0.10 **NM** value: **15.00**
4 ❑ Jan 1960 Cover: 0.10 **NM** value: **15.00**

ALL FUNNY COMICS — DC

1 ❑ Win 1943 **NM** value: **350.00**
• **CGC:** 1 graded, best 9.6
2 ❑ Spr 1944 **NM** value: **175.00**
3 ❑ Sum 1944 **NM** value: **100.00**
4 ❑ Fal 1944 **NM** value: **100.00**
5 ❑ Win 1944 **NM** value: **100.00**
6 ❑ Spr 1945 **NM** value: **100.00**
7 ❑ Sum 1945 **NM** value: **100.00**
• **CGC:** 1 graded, best 9.4
8 ❑ Fal 1945 **NM** value: **100.00**
• **CGC:** 1 graded, best 9.2
9 ❑ Win 1945 **NM** value: **100.00**
• **CGC:** 1 graded, best 9.6
10 ❑ Mar 1946 **NM** value: **100.00**
11 ❑ May 1946 **NM** value: **75.00**
12 ❑ Jul 1946 **NM** value: **75.00**
13 ❑ Sep 1946 **NM** value: **75.00**
14 ❑ Nov 1946 **NM** value: **75.00**
• **CGC:** 1 graded, best 8.0
15 ❑ Jan 1947 **NM** value: **75.00**
16 ❑ Mar 1947 **NM** value: **75.00**
17 ❑ May 1947 **NM** value: **75.00**
18 ❑ Jul 1947 **NM** value: **75.00**
19 ❑ Sep 1947 **NM** value: **50.00**
20 ❑ Nov 1947 **NM** value: **50.00**
21 ❑ Jan 1948 **NM** value: **50.00**
• **CGC:** 1 graded, best 9.0
22 ❑ Mar 1948 **NM** value: **50.00**
23 ❑ May 1948 **NM** value: **50.00**

ALL GIRLS SCHOOL MEETS ALL BOYS SCHOOL — Angel / ACG

1 ❑ Cover: 3.00 **NM** value: **Cover or less**
📖 Dance of the Frustrated **A:** Mark Kuettner **W:** Monique

ALL GOOD COMICS — Fox

1 ❑ Spr 1946 **NM** value: **150.00**
• **CGC:** 3 graded, best 9.2

ALL GOOD (ST. JOHN) — St. John

1 ❑ ca. 1949 Cover: 0.50 **NM** value: **450.00**

ALL HALLOW'S EVE — Innovation

All Hallow's Eve is a deluxe format one-shot from Innovation Books. The story is set in Wicklow, Ireland, and features four children named Lauren, Trey, Ashley, and Rachael. Every Halloween, banshees and spooks roam the streets of Wicklow. The town's citizens lock their doors and stay inside their homes until morning. The four children are told to put a jack o'lantern in the window. Its purpose is to scare away the ghosts by giving them something more fearful than their own mugs. They are then told the story of Nesbitt's Abbey.

The abbey once was run by monks until they were driven away by the ghost of Sam O'hain (sic). Nobody has dared go near since. It is thought that other ghosts live in the abbey, too. The children take it upon themselves to rid the town of their "afterlife problem," teaming up with talking mice along the way.

1 ❑ Cover: 4.95 **NM** value: **Cover or less**
Circ: CapCity orders: **2,130**
A: John Lang **W:** Mitchell Perkins

ALL HERO COMICS — Fawcett

1 ❑ Mar 1943 **NM** value: **1000.00**
• **CGC:** 1 graded, best 5.0

ALL HITLER COMICS — Paragon

1 ❑ Cover: 4.95 **NM** value: **Cover or less**
📖 Holocaust 2001 **A:** Bill Black **W:** Bill Black

CGC-graded: Multiply prices above by **33 for 9.9 M • 16 for 9.8 NM/M • 7 for 9.6 NM+ • 5 for 9.4 NM • 2.5 for 9.2 NM- • 1.5 for 9.0 VF/NM**

ALL HUMOR COMICS — Quality

All Humor was a little-known funnybook put out by Quality Comics from 1946-1949. In addition to a slew of copycat animal characters (e.g. Nuttsy the squirrel, Giddy Goose), it was notable for two original characters: Kelly Poole and Atomictot.

Kelly was a comic Irishman and war vet whose adventures closely resembled those of the radio show Life of Riley, which had become a popular series starring William Bendix by that point. Atomictot, created by Gill Fox, was a character called Tommy Tot who changed into a loincloth-clad (!) super-hero using a combination of super-strength and brains to come out on top in a series of mild adventures.

1 ❑ Spr 1946 Cover: 0.10 **NM** value: **125.00**
2 ❑ Sum 1946 Cover: 0.10 **NM** value: **65.00**
3 ❑ Fal 1946 Cover: 0.10 **NM** value: **38.00**
4 ❑ Win 1946 Cover: 0.10 **NM** value: **32.00**
5 ❑ Spr 1947 Cover: 0.10 **NM** value: **32.00**
6 ❑ Sum 1947 Cover: 0.10 **NM** value: **25.00**
7 ❑ Fal 1947 Cover: 0.10 **NM** value: **25.00**
8 ❑ Win 1947 Cover: 0.10 **NM** value: **25.00**
9 ❑ Spr 1948 Cover: 0.10 **NM** value: **25.00**
10 ❑ Sum 1948 Cover: 0.10 **NM** value: **25.00**
11 ❑ Fal 1948 Cover: 0.10 **NM** value: **22.00**
12 ❑ Win 1948 Cover: 0.10 **NM** value: **22.00**
13 ❑ Spr 1949 Cover: 0.10 **NM** value: **22.00**
🕮 Kelly Poole; Giddy Goose; Pinky; Hickory; Atomictot; Kelly's Silent Partners (text story); Nutsy; Uncle Fuddly **A:** Gill Fox **W:** Gill Fox
14 ❑ Sum 1949 Cover: 0.10 **NM** value: **22.00**
15 ❑ Fal 1949 Cover: 0.10 **NM** value: **22.00**
16 ❑ Win 1949 Cover: 0.10 **NM** value: **22.00**
17 ❑ Dec 1949 Cover: 0.10 **NM** value: **22.00**
final issue.

ALLIANCE, THE — Image

1 ❑ Aug 1995 Cover: 2.50 **NM** value: **Cover or less**
Circ: CapCity orders: **16,550**
🕮 A Call to Arms **A:** Jim Valentino **W:** Jim Valentino
1/A ❑ Aug 1995 Cover: 2.50 **NM** value: **Cover or less**
variant cover. 🕮 A Call to Arms **A:** Jim Valentino **W:** Jim Valentino
2 ❑ Sep 1995 Cover: 2.50 **NM** value: **Cover or less**
Circ: CapCity orders: **9,575**
A: Jim Valentino **W:** Jim Valentino
2/A ❑ Sep 1995 Cover: 2.50 **NM** value: **Cover or less**
variant cover. **A:** Jim Valentino
3 ❑ Nov 1995 Cover: 2.50 **NM** value: **Cover or less**
A: Jim Valentino **W:** Jim Valentino
3/A ❑ Nov 1995 Cover: 2.50 **NM** value: **Cover or less**
variant cover. **A:** Jim Valentino

ALL I EVER NEEDED TO KNOW I LEARNED FROM MY GOLF-PLAYING CATS — NBM

1 ❑ Cover: 7.95 **NM** value: **Cover or less**
A: Ruben Bolling **W:** Ruben Bolling

ALL NEW ADVENTURES OF THE MIGHTY CRUSADERS — Archie / Red Circle

1 ❑ Mar 1983 Cover: 1.00 **NM** value: **Cover or less**
🕮 Atlantis Rising **A:** Rich Buckler **W:** Rich Buckler
2 ❑ May 1983 Cover: 1.00 **NM** value: **Cover or less**
A: Rich Buckler **W:** Rich Buckler
3 ❑ Jul 1983 Cover: 1.00 **NM** value: **Cover or less**
🕮 The Darkling Ingredient **A:** Rich Buckler **W:** Rich Buckler
4 ❑ Cover: 1.00 **NM** value: **Cover or less**
A: Rich Buckler **W:** Rich Buckler

ALL NEW COLLECTORS' EDITION — DC

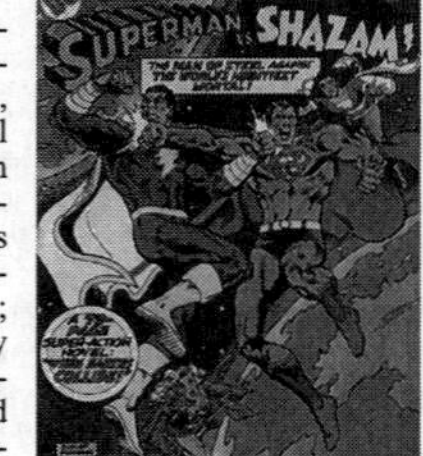

This series of treasury-size comics continued the inexplicable numbering system of DC's Limited Collectors' Editions (C-53, C-54, C-55, etc.) but presented all-new material — hence the name — rather than reprints. The content of the "collectors' editions" varied: Two issues featured collections of new Rudolph, the Red-Nosed Reindeer stories; the final issue was a photo-heavy magazine devoted to 1978's Superman: The Movie. A Superboy and the Legion of Super-Heroes installment took readers to the 30th-century wedding of founding Legionnaires Lightning Lad and Saturn Girl. The three remaining issues featured blockbuster battles between Superman and other heroes, namely Wonder Woman, Captain Marvel (aka Shazam!), and — are you ready for this? — real-life boxing champion Muhammad Ali!

53 ❑ Dec 1977 Cover: 2.00 **NM** value: **25.00**
• C-53
54 ❑ Jan 1978 Cover: 2.00 **NM** value: **10.00**
🕮 Superman vs. Wonder Woman • C-54
55 ❑ Feb 1978 Cover: 2.00 **NM** value: **15.00**
🕮 The Millennium Massacre • C-55;Legion;Wedding of Lightning Lad and Saturn Girl **A:** Mike Grell; Vince Colletta **W:** Paul Levitz
56 ❑ Apr 1978 Cover: 2.00 **NM** value: **20.00**
🕮 Superman vs. Muhammad Ali • C-56 **A:** Neal Adams **W:** Neal Adams; Denny O'Neil
57 ❑ May 1978 Cover: 2.00 **NM** value: **10.00**
• C-57
58 ❑ Jun 1978 Cover: 2.00 **NM** value: **10.00**
🕮 When Earths Collide • C-58;Superman vs. Shazam **A:** Rich Buckler; Dick Giordano **W:** Gerry Conway
60 ❑ ca. 1978 Cover: 2.00 **NM** value: **20.00**
🕮 Rudolph's Summer Fun • C-60
61 ❑ ca. 1979 Cover: 2.50 **NM** value: **10.00**
• C-61
62 ❑ Mar 1979 Cover: 2.50 **NM** value: **10.00**
• C-62

ALL-NEW COMICS — Harvey

1 ❑ Jan 1943 Cover: 0.10 **NM** value: **2000.00**
• **CGC:** 2 graded, best 7.0
2 ❑ ca. 1943 Cover: 0.10 **NM** value: **750.00**
3 ❑ ca. 1943 Cover: 0.10 **NM** value: **750.00**
4 ❑ ca. 1943 Cover: 0.10 **NM** value: **750.00**
5 ❑ ca. 1943 Cover: 0.10 **NM** value: **750.00**
6 ❑ Jan 1944 Cover: 0.10 **NM** value: **600.00**
7 ❑ Mar 1944 Cover: 0.10 **NM** value: **600.00**
• **CGC:** 1 graded, best 9.4
8 ❑ May 1944 Cover: 0.10 **NM** value: **600.00**
9 ❑ Jul 1944 Cover: 0.10 **NM** value: **600.00**
10 ❑ Sep 1944 Cover: 0.10 **NM** value: **500.00**
• **CGC:** 1 graded, best 9.0
11 ❑ Spr 1945 Cover: 0.10 **NM** value: **500.00**
• **CGC:** 1 graded, best 9.0
12 ❑ May 1946 Cover: 0.10 **NM** value: **500.00**
• **CGC:** 2 graded, best 9.0
13 ❑ Jul 1946 Cover: 0.10 **NM** value: **450.00**
🕮 Stuntman Battles the Diamond Curse • Stuntman
14 ❑ Nov 1946 Cover: 0.10 **NM** value: **450.00**
15 ❑ Mar 1947 Cover: 0.10 **NM** value: **450.00**

ALL NEW EXILES, THE — Malibu / Ultraverse

0 ❑ Sep 1995 Cover: 1.50 **NM** value: **Cover or less**
• "Black September";Number infinity
0/SC❑ Sep 1995 Cover: 1.50 **NM** value: **Cover or less**
alternate cover. • "Black September";Number infinity
1 ❑ Oct 1995 Cover: 1.50 **NM** value: **Cover or less**
• **CGC:** 1 graded, best 9.6
A: Ken Lashley **W:** Terry Kavanagh
2 ❑ Nov 1995 Cover: 1.50 **NM** value: **Cover or less**
3 ❑ Dec 1995 Cover: 1.50 **NM** value: **Cover or less**
4 ❑ Jan 1996 Cover: 1.50 **NM** value: **Cover or less**
★ Versus UltraForce.
5 ❑ Feb 1996 Cover: 2.50 **NM** value: **Cover or less**
6 ❑ Mar 1996 Cover: 1.50 **NM** value: **Cover or less**
7 ❑ Apr 1996 Cover: 1.50 **NM** value: **Cover or less**
8 ❑ May 1996 Cover: 1.50 **NM** value: **Cover or less**
10 ❑ Jul 1996 Cover: 1.50 **NM** value: **Cover or less**
★ Versus Aladdin.
11 ❑ Aug 1996 Cover: 1.50 **NM** value: **Cover or less**
final issue. • continues in UltraForce #12★ Versus Maxis.

ALL NEW UNDERGROUND COMIX — Last Gasp / Ultraverse

1 ❑ Cover: 0.50 **NM** value: **5.00**
2 ❑ Cover: 0.50 **NM** value: **3.00**
3 ❑ Cover: 0.50 **NM** value: **3.00**

ALL-OUT WAR — DC

1 ❑ Oct 1979 Cover: 1.00 **NM** value: **3.00**
🕮 The Viking Commando; Brother With Wings; Cardboard Marine; To Honor The Hero; Funeral March For a Guerrilla Fighter **A:** George Evans; Dick Ayers; E.R. Cruz; Jerry Grandienetti; Romeo Tanghal **W:** Evan Douglas; J.M. DeMatteis; Robert Kanigher ★ Origin of Viking Commando.
2 ❑ Dec 1979 Cover: 1.00 **NM** value: **2.50**
3 ❑ Feb 1980 Cover: 1.00 **NM** value: **2.50**
4 ❑ Apr 1980 Cover: 1.00 **NM** value: **2.50**
🕮 Execution on Demand; Death Comes in Threes; Road to Sunchon; The One-Minute War; 60-Second Vet
5 ❑ Jun 1980 Cover: 1.00 **NM** value: **2.50**
6 ❑ Aug 1980 Cover: 1.00 **NM** value: **2.50**
🕮 War Without a Name; Brothers on a Bulls-Eye; Hard-Hat Heroes; Double Death of Adolf Hitler; Zero Hour is 27 Years Long

ALLOY — Phenominal Chili

Ash 1❑ **NM** value: **0.50**
• White Ashcan edition. **A:** Joaquin Vigil; Peet Cooper **W:** Joaquin Vigil; Peet Cooper ★ 1st Appearance of Alloy.
ASH 1/A❑ **NM** value: **0.50**
• Green ashcan edition.

ALL PICTURE ADVENTURES — St. John

1 ❑ Oct 19552 Cover: 0.25 **NM** value: **175.00**
2 ❑ Nov 1952 Cover: 0.25 **NM** value: **250.00**
• **CGC:** 1 graded, best 4.0

ALL SELECT COMICS — Timely

1 ❑ Fal 1943 Cover: 0.10 **NM** value: **7500.00**
• **CGC:** 5 graded, best 9.2
2 ❑ ca. 1943 Cover: 0.10 **NM** value: **3000.00**
• **CGC:** 7 graded, best 9.4
3 ❑ ca. 1943 Cover: 0.10 **NM** value: **2000.00**
• **CGC:** 2 graded, best 8.0
4 ❑ Fal 1945 Cover: 0.10 **NM** value: **1500.00**
• **CGC:** 2 graded, best 7.5
5 ❑ Win 1944 Cover: 0.10 **NM** value: **1500.00**
• **CGC:** 1 graded, best 8.5
6 ❑ Mar 1945 Cover: 0.10 **NM** value: **1000.00**
• **CGC:** 3 graded, best 9.0
7 ❑ Spr 1945 Cover: 0.10 **NM** value: **1000.00**
• **CGC:** 1 graded, best 6.5
8 ❑ Sum 1945 Cover: 0.10 **NM** value: **1000.00**
• **CGC:** 2 graded, best 7.0
9 ❑ ca. 1945 Cover: 0.10 **NM** value: **1000.00**
• **CGC:** 3 graded, best 9.2
10 ❑ Sum 1946 Cover: 0.10 **NM** value: **850.00**
• **CGC:** 5 graded, best 9.4
11 ❑ Fal 1946 Cover: 0.10 **NM** value: **850.00**
• **CGC:** 6 graded, best 9.0

ALL SHOOK UP — Rip Off

1 ❑ Jun 1990, b&w Cover: 3.50 **NM** value: **Cover or less**
No issue number. • earthquake

ALL STAR ARCHIVES — DC

1 ❑ Cover: 49.95 **NM** value: **Cover or less**
• reprints All-Star Comics #3-6;Contains contents page
2 ❑ Cover: 49.95 **NM** value: **Cover or less**
• reprints All-Star Comics #7-10
3 ❑ Cover: 49.95 **NM** value: **Cover or less**
• reprints All-Star Comics #11-14
4 ❑ Cover: 49.95 **NM** value: **Cover or less**
• reprints All-Star Comics #15-18
6 ❑ Cover: 49.95 **NM** value: **Cover or less**
• Reprints All Star Comics #24-28 **A:** Joe Kubert; Joe Gallagher; Martin Naydel; Stan Aschmeier **W:** Gardner Fox; Jay Marr

ALL-STAR COMICS — DC

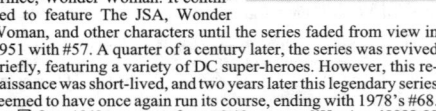

All-Star Comics was one of the key titles in DC history. Beginning with a collection of stories featuring such Golden Age heroes as the Flash, Green Lantern, and Hawkman, it moved on with #3 to introduce the world to its first super-hero group, The Justice Society of America. This historic team consisted of Batman, Green Lantern, Doctor Fate, the Atom, the Flash, Hawkman, The Spectre, Hourman, Superman, and The Sandman.

All-Star struck gold again with #8, with the introduction of Diana Prince, Wonder Woman. It continued to feature The JSA, Wonder Woman, and other characters until the series faded from view in 1951 with #57. A quarter of a century later, the series was revived briefly, featuring a variety of DC super-heroes. However, this renaissance was short-lived, and two years later this legendary series seemed to have once again run its course, ending with 1978's #68.

1 ❑ Sum 1940 Cover: 0.10 **NM** value: **12600.00**
• **CGC:** 9 graded, best 9.6
🕮 Stories untitled; Exile to Jupiter (text) • stories feature: Hawkman; Sandman; Ultra-Man; Flash; Spectre; Biff Bronson; Hourman; Red, White and Blue
2 ❑ Fal 1940 Cover: 0.10 **NM** value: **5000.00**
• **CGC:** 5 graded, best 9.2
🕮 Stories Untitled; The Invisible Star (text) • stories feature: Hawkman; Green Lantern; Spectre; Sandman; Red, White and Blue; Johnny Thunder; Hourman; Flash
3 ❑ Win 1940 Cover: 0.10 **NM** value: **32500.00**
• **CGC:** 7 graded, best 9.4
🕮 The First Meeting of the Justice Society of America; Guarding an Heiress (text) • membership includes Flash, Green Lantern, Hawkman, Atom, Sandman, Spectre, Dr. Fate and Hourman★ Origin of Justice Society of America. ★ 1st Appearance of Justice Society of America.
4 ❑ Mar 1941 Cover: 0.10 **NM** value: **4500.00**
• **CGC:** 10 graded, best 9.2
🕮 For America and Democracy; A Fortune Teller's Fortune (text)
5 ❑ Jun 1941 Cover: 0.10 **NM** value: **4000.00**
• **CGC:** 11 graded, best 9.4
🕮 The Mysterious Mister X; Johnny on the Spot (text) ★ 1st Appearance of Hawkgirl.
6 ❑ Aug 1941 Cover: 0.10 **NM** value: **2600.00**
• **CGC:** 5 graded, best 9.6
🕮 The Justice Society of America Initiates Johnny Thunder!; Dr. Mid-Nite Thinks Fast! (text) • Johnny Thunder joins team
7 ❑ Oct 1941 Cover: 0.10 **NM** value: **2600.00**
• **CGC:** 4 graded, best 9.2
🕮 $1,000,000 for War Orphans; "Secret Airport" (A Hop Harrigan Story) (text)
8 ❑ Jan 1942 Cover: 0.10 **NM** value: **24000.00**
• **CGC:** 12 graded, best 8.5
🕮 Two New Members Win Their Spurs; Introducing Wonder Woman; Sky Cutups (A Hop Harrigan Story) (text) **A:** Jack Burnley; Ben Flinton; Bernard Baily; Cliff Young; Everett E. Hibbard; Harry G. Peter; Sheldon Moldoff **W:** Gardner Fox; William Moulton Marston ★ Origin of Wonder Woman. ★ 1st Appearance of Wonder Woman.
9 ❑ Feb 1942 Cover: 0.10 **NM** value: **2450.00**
• **CGC:** 1 graded, best 9.2
🕮 Hemisphere Defense; Midnight Meeting (A Hop Harrigan Story) (text)
10 ❑ Apr 1942 Cover: 0.10 **NM** value: **2450.00**
• **CGC:** 3 graded, best 9.6
🕮 The Case of the Bomb Defense Formula; The Ghost Plane (A Hop Harrigan Story) (text)
11 ❑ Jun 1942 Cover: 0.10 **NM** value: **2000.00**
• **CGC:** 3 graded, best 9.6
🕮 The Justice Society Joins the War on Japan; "Outlaw Plane" (A Hop Harrigan Story) (text) • Wonder Woman stories begin
12 ❑ Aug 1942 Cover: 0.10 **NM** value: **2100.00**
• **CGC:** 4 graded, best 9.4
🕮 The Black Dragon Menace; "Mystery Island" (A Hop Harrigan Story) (text) • Wonder Woman joins team (as secretary!)
13 ❑ Oct 1942 Cover: 0.10 **NM** value: **1900.00**
• **CGC:** 4 graded, best 8.0
🕮 Shanghaied into Space!; "Turtles and T.N.T." (A Hop Harrigan Story) (text)

Other grades: Multiply prices above by **1.5 for Mint • 2/3 for Very Fine • 1/3 for Fine • 1/5 for Very Good • 1/8 for Good**

14 ❑ Dec 1942 Cover: 0.10 **NM** value: **1900.00**
• **CGC:** 4 graded, best 9.4
🕮 Food for Starving Patriots!; "The Statue of Buddha" (A Hop Harrigan Story) (text)

15 ❑ Feb 1943 Cover: 0.10 **NM** value: **1900.00**
• **CGC:** 5 graded, best 9.2
🕮 The Man Who Created Images ★ Origin of Brain Wave. ★ 1st Appearance of Brain Wave.

16 ❑ Apr 1943 Cover: 0.10 **NM** value: **1425.00**
• **CGC:** 1 graded, best 6.5
🕮 The Justice Society Fights for a United America

17 ❑ Jun 1943 Cover: 0.10 **NM** value: **1425.00**
• **CGC:** 3 graded, best 9.6
🕮 The Brain Wave Goes Berserk

18 ❑ Fal 1943 Cover: 0.10 **NM** value: **1425.00**
• **CGC:** 6 graded, best 8.5
🕮 Insects Turn to Crime

19 ❑ Win 1943 Cover: 0.10 **NM** value: **1425.00**
• **CGC:** 2 graded, best 5.5
🕮 The Crimes Set to Music; Hop Harrigan Over Torres Strait (text)

20 ❑ Spr 1944 Cover: 0.10 **NM** value: **1425.00**
• **CGC:** 5 graded, best 9.6
🕮 The Movie That Changed a Man's Life; Ghost Plane (A Hop Harrigan Story) (text)

21 ❑ Sum 1944 Cover: 0.10 **NM** value: **1225.00**
• **CGC:** 3 graded, best 9.4
🕮 The Man Who Relived His Life; Express to Berlin (A Hop Harrigan Story) (text)

22 ❑ Fal 1944 Cover: 0.10 **NM** value: **1225.00**
• **CGC:** 3 graded, best 9.6
🕮 A Cure for the World; Lend-Lease for China (A Hop Harrigan Story) (text)

23 ❑ Win 1944 Cover: 0.10 **NM** value: **1225.00**
• **CGC:** 3 graded, best 9.4
🕮 The Plunder of the Psycho-Pirate

24 ❑ Mar 1945 Cover: 0.10 **NM** value: **1225.00**
• **CGC:** 5 graded, best 9.6
🕮 This is Our Enemy!; Glider Plight (text) **A:** Joe Kubert; H.G. Peter; Joe Gallagher; Martin Naydel; Stan Aschmeier **W:** Gardner Fox; Jay Marr

25 ❑ Jun 1945 Cover: 0.10 **NM** value: **1225.00**
• **CGC:** 5 graded, best 8.0
🕮 The Mystery of the Forgotten Crime!; Lead in his Shoes (text) **A:** Joe Kubert; Martin Naydel; Stan Aschmeier **W:** Gardner Fox; Jay Marr

26 ❑ Sep 1945 Cover: 0.10 **NM** value: **1140.00**
• **CGC:** 2 graded, best 9.4
🕮 Vampires of the Void!; Hurricane Orders (text) **A:** Joe Gallagher; Martin Naydel; Stan Aschmeier **W:** Gardner Fox; Jim Robinson

27 ❑ Dec 1945 Cover: 0.10 **NM** value: **1140.00**
• **CGC:** 4 graded, best 8.0
🕮 A Place in the World; Money Trouble (text) **A:** Paul Reinman; Joe Kubert; Martin Naydel; Stan Aschmeier; Jon Cheste Kozlak **W:** Gardner Fox; Jim Robinson

28 ❑ Apr 1946 Cover: 0.10 **NM** value: **1140.00**
• **CGC:** 4 graded, best 9.4
🕮 The Paintings that Walked the Earth!; The Case of the Nifty Lifter (text) **A:** Joe Kubert; Joe Gallagher; Jon Chester Kozlak; Martin Naydel; Stan Aschmeier **W:** Gardner Fox; Jesse Merlan

29 ❑ Jun 1946 Cover: 0.10 **NM** value: **1140.00**
• **CGC:** 8 graded, best 9.6
🕮 The Man Who Knows Too Much

30 ❑ Aug 1946 Cover: 0.10 **NM** value: **1140.00**
• **CGC:** 5 graded, best 9.6
🕮 Dreams of Madness!

31 ❑ Oct 1946 Cover: 0.10 **NM** value: **1140.00**
• **CGC:** 15 graded, best 8.5
🕮 The Workshop of Willie Wonder

32 ❑ Dec 1946 Cover: 0.10 **NM** value: **1140.00**
• **CGC:** 7 graded, best 9.4
🕮 The Return of the Psycho-Pirate

33 ❑ Feb 1947 Cover: 0.10 **NM** value: **2550.00**
• **CGC:** 12 graded, best 9.4
🕮 The Revenge of Solomon Grundy ★ 1st Appearance of Solomon Grundy.

34 ❑ Apr 1947 Cover: 0.10 **NM** value: **925.00**
• **CGC:** 5 graded, best 8.0
🕮 The Wiles of the Wizard!

35 ❑ Jun 1947 Cover: 0.10 **NM** value: **925.00**
• **CGC:** 8 graded, best 9.6
🕮 The Day That Dropped Out of Time

36 ❑ Aug 1947 Cover: 0.10 **NM** value: **2150.00**
• **CGC:** 5 graded, best 9.6
🕮 5 Drowned Men! ★ Appearance of Batman.

37 ❑ Oct 1947 Cover: 0.10 **NM** value: **1250.00**
• **CGC:** 4 graded, best 9.0
🕮 The Injustice Society of the World! ★ 1st Appearance of The Injustice Society.

38 ❑ Dec 1947 Cover: 0.10 **NM** value: **1300.00**
• **CGC:** 7 graded, best 9.6
🕮 History's Crime Wave! ★ Appearance of Black Canary.

39 ❑ Feb 1948 Cover: 0.10 **NM** value: **850.00**
• **CGC:** 2 graded, best 8.0
🕮 The Invasion From Fairyland!

40 ❑ Mar 1948 Cover: 0.10 **NM** value: **850.00**
• **CGC:** 2 graded, best 9.2
🕮 The Plight of a Nation!

41 ❑ Jun 1948 Cover: 0.10 **NM** value: **850.00**
• **CGC:** 2 graded, best 7.0
🕮 The Case of the Patriotic Crimes!

42 ❑ Aug 1948 Cover: 0.10 **NM** value: **850.00**
• **CGC:** 1 graded, best 5.5
🕮 The Man Who Hated Science!

43 ❑ Oct 1948 Cover: 0.10 **NM** value: **850.00**
• **CGC:** 4 graded, best 9.4
🕮 The Secret of the Golden Universe!

44 ❑ Dec 1948 Cover: 0.10 **NM** value: **850.00**
• **CGC:** 2 graded, best 8.0
🕮 Evil Star Over Hollywood!

45 ❑ Feb 1949 Cover: 0.10 **NM** value: **850.00**
• **CGC:** 3 graded, best 9.2
🕮 The Case of the Cosmic Criminals!

46 ❑ Apr 1949 Cover: 0.10 **NM** value: **850.00**
• **CGC:** 3 graded, best 7.5
🕮 The Adventure of the Invisible Band!

47 ❑ Jun 1949 Cover: 0.10 **NM** value: **850.00**
• **CGC:** 3 graded, best 9.2
🕮 The Ghost of Billy the Kid!

48 ❑ Aug 1949 Cover: 0.10 **NM** value: **850.00**
• **CGC:** 1 graded, best 9.2
🕮 The Strange Lives of Edmund Blake!

49 ❑ Oct 1949 Cover: 0.10 **NM** value: **850.00**
• **CGC:** 2 graded, best 7.0
🕮 The Invasion of the Fire People!

50 ❑ Dec 1949 Cover: 0.10 **NM** value: **850.00**
• **CGC:** 3 graded, best 8.0
🕮 The Prophesy of Peril!

51 ❑ Feb 1950 Cover: 0.10 **NM** value: **850.00**
• **CGC:** 3 graded, best 7.5
🕮 Invaders from the World Below!

52 ❑ Apr 1950 Cover: 0.10 **NM** value: **850.00**
• **CGC:** 3 graded, best 9.0
🕮 The Secret Conquest of the Earth!

53 ❑ Jun 1950 Cover: 0.10 **NM** value: **850.00**
• **CGC:** 4 graded, best 8.5
🕮 The Gun That Dropped through Time!

54 ❑ Aug 1950 Cover: 0.10 **NM** value: **850.00**
• **CGC:** 2 graded, best 7.5
🕮 Circus of a Thousand Thrills

55 ❑ Oct 1950 Cover: 0.10 **NM** value: **850.00**
• **CGC:** 4 graded, best 8.5
🕮 The Man Who Conquered the Solar System!

56 ❑ Dec 1950 Cover: 0.10 **NM** value: **850.00**
• **CGC:** 3 graded, best 9.0
🕮 The Day the World Ended

57 ❑ Feb 1951 Cover: 0.10 **NM** value: **1100.00**
• **CGC:** 3 graded, best 7.5
🕮 The Mystery of the Vanishing Detectives! • Final issue of original run;Series continued in All-Star Western

58 ❑ Feb 1976 Cover: 0.25 **NM** value: **4.00**
• **CGC:** 5 graded, best 9.4
🕮 All Star Super Squad • Power Girl joins team;regrouping of JSA;Series begins again after hiatus (1976) **A:** Wally Wood; Ric Estrada **W:** Gerry Conway ★ 1st Appearance of Power Girl.

59 ❑ Apr 1976 Cover: 0.25 **NM** value: **3.00**
🕮 Brainwave Blows Up ★ Versus Brainwave, Per Degaton.

60 ❑ Jun 1976 Cover: 0.30 **NM** value: **3.00**
• **CGC:** 2 graded, best 9.6
🕮 Vulcan: Son of Fire **A:** Keith Giffen; Wally Wood ★ Versus Vulcan.

61 ❑ Aug 1976 Cover: 0.30 **NM** value: **3.00**
• **CGC:** 2 graded, best 9.6
🕮 Hellfire and Holocaust • Bicentennial #17 **A:** Keith Giffen; Wally Wood ★ Versus Vulcan.

62 ❑ Oct 1976 Cover: 0.30 **NM** value: **2.50**
• **CGC:** 1 graded, best 8.5
🕮 When Fall the Mighty **A:** Keith Giffen; Wally Wood; Keith Giffin **W:** Paul Levitz; Gerry Conway ★ Appearance of E-2 Superman. ★ Versus Zanadu.

63 ❑ Dec 1976 Cover: 0.30 **NM** value: **2.50**
🕮 The Death of Doctor Fate **A:** Keith Giffen; Wally Wood ★ Versus Injustice Gang, Solomon Grundy.

64 ❑ Feb 1977 Cover: 0.30 **NM** value: **2.50**
• **CGC:** 2 graded, best 9.4
🕮 Yesterday Begins Today! **A:** Wally Wood ★ Appearance of Shining Knight. ★ Versus Vandal Savage.

65 ❑ Apr 1977 Cover: 0.30 **NM** value: **2.50**
• **CGC:** 4 graded, best 9.8
🕮 The Master Plan of Vandal Savage **A:** Wally Wood ★ Versus Vandal Savage.

66 ❑ Jun 1977 Cover: 0.30 **NM** value: **2.50**
• **CGC:** 2 graded, best 9.6
🕮 Injustice Strikes Twice **A:** Bob Layton; Joe Staton ★ Versus Icicle, Wizard, Thinker.

67 ❑ Aug 1977 Cover: 0.35 **NM** value: **2.50**
🕮 The Attack of the Underlord **A:** Bob Layton; Joe Staton

68 ❑ Oct 1977 Cover: 0.35 **NM** value: **2.50**
🕮 Divided We Stand **A:** Bob Layton; Joe Staton ★ Versus Psycho Pirate.

69 ❑ Dec 1977 Cover: 0.35 **NM** value: **3.50**
🕮 United We Fall! • Original JSA vs. New JSA **A:** Bob Layton; Joe Staton ★ 1st Appearance of The Huntress II (Helena Wayne).

70 ❑ Feb 1978 Cover: 0.35 **NM** value: **2.50**
🕮 A Parting of the Ways! • Huntress **A:** Bob Layton; Joe Staton

71 ❑ Apr 1978 Cover: 0.35 **NM** value: **2.50**
🕮 The Deadliest Game in Town **A:** Bob Layton; Joe Staton

72 ❑ Jun 1978 Cover: 0.35 **NM** value: **2.50**
🕮 A Thorn By Any Other Name ★ Versus Thorn, Sportsmaster, original Huntress.

73 ❑ Aug 1978 Cover: 0.35 **NM** value: **2.50**
🕮 Be It Ever So Deadly **A:** Joe Staton ★ Versus Thorn, Sportsmaster, original Huntress.

74 ❑ Oct 1978 Cover: 0.50 **NM** value: **2.50**
🕮 World on the Edge of Ending final issue. **A:** Joe Staton ★ Versus Master Summoner.

ALL STAR COMICS (2ND SERIES) DC

1 ❑ May 1999 Cover: 2.95 **NM** value: **Cover or less**
Circ: Diamd. preorders: **50,571**
🕮 Justice Society Returns; Time's Keeper **A:** Michael Lark **W:** James Robinson; David Goyer

2 ❑ May 1999 Cover: 2.95 **NM** value: **Cover or less**
Circ: Diamd. preorders: **48,725**
🕮 Justice Society Returns; Time's Arrow **A:** William Rosado **W:** James Robinson; David Goyer

GS 1 ❑ Sep 1999 Cover: 4.95 **NM** value: **Cover or less**
Circ: Diamd. preorders: **27,689**
🕮 The Mighty Atom: Steam Engine; The Specture & Starman: **A:** Denys Cowan; Chris Jones; Duncan Rouleau; Dave Ross; Peter Pachoumis; Adam DeKraker; Kevin Sharpe **W:** James Robinson; Joe Kelly; David Goyer; Roy Thomas; Eric Luke; John Ostrander; Mark Waid

ALL-STAR INDEX, THE Eclipse / Independent

1 ❑ Feb 1987 Cover: 2.00 **NM** value: **Cover or less**
• background on members of the JSA and first four issues of All-Star Comics (1st series) and DC Special #29

ALL-STAR SQUADRON DC

For a new World War II-based series, writer Roy Thomas brought together all the heroes of DC's Golden Age, as well as the heroes from other companies that DC had acquired in the intervening years, such as Quality and Fawcett.

When the more powerful members of The Justice Society of America were unable to answer the President's call in the wake of the attack on Pearl Harbor, such heroes as Johnny Quick, Hawkman, Plastic Man, Dr. Mid-Nite, The Shining Knight, Liberty Belle, Robotman, and The Atom joined forces at the commander-in-chief's request and thwarted an attempt by time-traveling tyrant Per Degaton to take over the world.

As the series continued, more and more heroes joined the group (often for only one or two adventures or just a cameo appearance), and Thomas used the venue to explain what had happened to various heroes outside of their published adventures, going to such extremes as explaining why Doctor Fate's helmet switched from full-face to a half-mask and back again, and how the Quality heroes ended up on Earth-X, an event swiftly wiped out by the events of Crisis on Infinite Earths.

In addition to art by Jerry Ordway, the series also featured a Doctor Fate origin story by a young Todd McFarlane. — Brent

1 ❑ Sep 1981 Cover: 0.50 **NM** value: **2.50**
• **CGC:** 17 graded, best 9.6
🕮 The World on Fire! **A:** Rich Buckler **W:** Roy Thomas ★ 1st Appearance of Danette Reilly (later Firebrand II).

2 ❑ Oct 1981 Cover: 0.60 **NM** value: **2.00**
• **CGC:** 2 graded, best 9.8
🕮 The Tyrant Out of Time! **A:** Rich Buckler; Jerry Ordway **W:** Roy Thomas

3 ❑ Nov 1981 Cover: 0.60 **NM** value: **2.00**
• **CGC:** 1 graded, best 9.6
🕮 The Dooms of Dark December! **A:** Rich Buckler; Jerry Ordway **W:** Roy Thomas

4 ❑ Dec 1981 Cover: 0.60 **NM** value: **1.50**
• **CGC:** 1 graded, best 9.4
🕮 Day of the Dragon King **A:** Rich Buckler; Jerry Ordway **W:** Roy Thomas ★ 1st Appearance of Dragon King.

5 ❑ Jan 1982 Cover: 0.60 **NM** value: **1.50**
• **CGC:** 1 graded, best 9.0
🕮 Never Step on a Feathered Serpent! **A:** Rich Buckler; Jerry Ordway **W:** Roy Thomas ★ 1st Appearance of Firebrand II (Danette Reilly).

6 ❑ Feb 1982 Cover: 0.60 **NM** value: **1.50**
🕮 Mayhem in the Mile-High City!

7 ❑ Mar 1982 Cover: 0.60 **NM** value: **1.50**
🕮 Carnage for Christmas! **A:** Joe Kubert

8 ❑ Apr 1982 Cover: 0.60 **NM** value: **1.50**
🕮 Afternoon of the Assassins! ★ Origin of Steel. ★ Versus Kung.

9 ❑ May 1982 Cover: 0.60 **NM** value: **1.50**
🕮 Should Old Acquaintance Be Destroyed … **A:** Joe Kubert ★ Origin of Baron Blitzkrieg.

10 ❑ Jun 1982 Cover: 0.60 **NM** value: **1.50**
🕮 If An Eye Offend Thee … **A:** Joe Kubert

11 ❑ Jul 1982 Cover: 0.60 **NM** value: **1.25**
🕮 Star-Smasher's Secret! **A:** Joe Kubert

12 ❑ Aug 1982 Cover: 0.60 **NM** value: **1.25**
🕮 Doomsday Begins At Dawn! **A:** Joe Kubert ★ Versus Hastor.

13 ❑ Sep 1982 Cover: 0.60 **NM** value: **1.25**
🕮 One Day, During the War … **A:** Joe Kubert

14 ❑ Oct 1982 Cover: 0.60 **NM** value: **1.25**
🕮 Crisis on Earth-Prime!, Part 2; The Mystery Men of October! **A:** Joe Kubert

15 ❑ Nov 1982 Cover: 0.60 **NM** value: **1.25**
🕮 Crisis on Earth-Prime!, Part 4; Master of Worlds and Time! **A:** Joe Kubert

16 ❑ Dec 1982 Cover: 0.60 **NM** value: **1.25**
🕮 The Magnetic Marauder **A:** Joe Kubert ★ Versus Nuclear.

17 ❑ Jan 1983 Cover: 0.60 **NM** value: **1.25**
🕮 To Slay the Body Electric! • Trial of Robotman **A:** Joe Kubert

18 ❑ Feb 1983 Cover: 0.60 **NM** value: **1.25**
🕮 Vengeance from Valhalla **A:** Joe Kubert ★ Versus Villain from Valhalla.

19 ❑ Mar 1983 Cover: 0.60 **NM** value: **1.25**
🕮 Death, Considered as a State of Mind! ★ Versus Brainwave.

20 ❑ Apr 1983 Cover: 0.60 **NM** value: **1.25**
🕮 … For the Dark Things Cannot Stand the Light …! ★ Versus Brainwave.

21 ❑ May 1983 Cover: 0.60 **NM** value: **1.25**
🕮 A Tale of Three Citadels! ★ 1st Appearance of Deathbolt, Cyclotron. ★ Versus Cyclotron.

22 ❑ Jun 1983 Cover: 0.60 **NM** value: **1.25**
🕮 The Powerstone Corrupts – Absolutely!

23 ❑ Jul 1983 Cover: 0.60 **NM** value: **1.25**
🕮 When Fate Thy Measure Takes …! ★ 1st Appearance of Amazing Man.

24 ❑ Aug 1983 Cover: 0.60 **NM** value: **1.25**
🕮 The Man Who'll Know Too Much!; Mind Over Mystery-Man! ★ 1st Appearance of Infinity Inc., Brainwave Jr..

CGC-graded: Multiply prices above by **33 for 9.9 M • 16 for 9.8 NM/M • 7 for 9.6 NM+ • 5 for 9.4 NM • 2.5 for 9.2 NM- • 1.5 for 9.0 VF/NM**

25 ❑ Sep 1983 Cover: 0.60 **NM value: 1.25**
The Infinity Syndrome!

26 ❑ Oct 1983 Cover: 0.60 **NM value: 1.00**
Talons Across Time! ★ Origin of Infinity Inc.. ★ Appearance of Infinity Inc..

27 ❑ Nov 1983 Cover: 0.60 **NM value: 1.00**
A Spectre is Haunting the Multiverse! ★ Appearance of Spectre.

28 ❑ Dec 1983 Cover: 0.75 **NM value: 1.00**
By Hatred Possessed! ★ Appearance of Spectre.

29 ❑ Jan 1984 Cover: 0.75 **NM value: 1.00**
A Man Called Doome! ★ Appearance of Seven Soldiers of Victory.

30 ❑ Feb 1984 Cover: 0.75 **NM value: 1.00**
Day of the Black Dragon! ★ Versus Black Dragon Society.

31 ❑ Mar 1984 Cover: 0.75 **NM value: 1.00**
Uncle Sam Wants You! ★ Appearance of Uncle Sam.

32 ❑ Apr 1984 Cover: 0.75 **NM value: 1.00**
Crisis on Earth-X!, The Prequel

33 ❑ May 1984 Cover: 0.75 **NM value: 1.00**
The Battle of Santa Barbara – Times Two! ★ Origin of Freedom Fighters.

34 ❑ Jun 1984 Cover: 0.75 **NM value: 1.00**
The Wrath of Tsunami! ★ Versus Tsunami.

35 ❑ Jul 1984 Cover: 0.75 **NM value: 1.00**
… That Earths May Live! • Hourman vs. Baron Blitzkrieg ★ Death of Red Bee.

36 ❑ Aug 1984 Cover: 0.75 **NM value: 1.00**
• **CGC:** 1 graded, best 9.8
Thunder Over London! ★ Appearance of Captain Marvel.

37 ❑ Sep 1984 Cover: 0.75 **NM value: 1.00**
Lightning in Berlin! ★ Appearance of Marvel Family.

38 ❑ Oct 1984 Cover: 0.75 **NM value: 1.00**
Detroit is Dynamite ★ Appearance of Amazing Man.

39 ❑ Nov 1984 Cover: 0.75 **NM value: 1.00**
Nobody Gets Out of Paradise Valley Alive! • Junior JSA kit repro ★ Appearance of Amazing Man.

40 ❑ Dec 1984 Cover: 0.75 **NM value: 1.00**
The Rise and Fall of the Phantom Empire • Amazing Man vs. Real American ★ Appearance of Monitor.

41 ❑ Jan 1985 Cover: 0.75 **NM value: 1.00**
Circ: Statement: **69,398**
… Catch a Falling Starman! ★ Origin of Starman.

42 ❑ Feb 1985 Cover: 0.75 **NM value: 1.00**
Circ: Statement: **69,398**
Oh, Say, Can't You See…?

43 ❑ Mar 1985 Cover: 0.75 **NM value: 1.00**
Circ: Statement: **69,398**
Ultimate Victory!

44 ❑ Apr 1985 Cover: 0.75 **NM value: 1.00**
Circ: Statement: **69,398**
Night and Fog! ★ Versus Night and Fog.

45 ❑ May 1985 Cover: 0.75 **NM value: 1.00**
Circ: Statement: **69,398** CapCity orders: **5,900**
Give Me Liberty – Give Me Death! ★ 1st Appearance of Zyklon.

46 ❑ Jun 1985 Cover: 0.75 **NM value: 1.00**
Circ: Statement: **69,398** CapCity orders: **6,200**
Philadelphia – It Tolls for Thee! • Liberty Belle gets new powers

47 ❑ Jul 1985 Cover: 0.75 **NM value: 3.00**
Circ: Statement: **69,398** CapCity orders: **6,500**
The Secret Origin of Dr. Fate! **A:** Todd McFarlane ★ Origin of Doctor Fate.

48 ❑ Aug 1985 Cover: 0.75 **NM value: 1.00**
Circ: Statement: **69,398** CapCity orders: **6,100**
Camelot 1942! • Blackhawk ★ Appearance of Shining Knight.

49 ❑ Sep 1985 Cover: 0.75 **NM value: 1.00**
Circ: Statement: **69,398** CapCity orders: **6,200**
Death-Sword at Sunrise! ★ Appearance of Doctor Occult.

50 ❑ Oct 1985 Cover: 0.75 **NM value: 1.25**
Circ: Statement: **69,398** CapCity orders: **11,250**
• Double-size issue. Crisis on Infinite Earths; Crisis Point! • Mr. Mind to Earth-2;Crisis;Uncle Sam and others to Earth-X;Steel to Earth-1 ★ Appearance of Harbinger.

51 ❑ Nov 1985 Cover: 0.75 **NM value: 1.00**
Circ: Statement: **69,398** CapCity orders: **9,500**
Crisis on Infinite Earths; Monster Society of Evil! ★ Versus Monster Society of Evil (Oom, Mr. Who, Ramulus, Nyola, Mr. Mind).

52 ❑ Dec 1985 Cover: 0.75 **NM value: 1.00**
Circ: Statement: **69,398** CapCity orders: **9,700**
Crisis on Infinite Earths; From Fear to Eternity! • Crisis ★ Appearance of Captain Marvel.

53 ❑ Jan 1986 Cover: 0.75 **NM value: 1.00**
Circ: CapCity orders: **8,650**
Crisis on Infinite Earths; Worlds in Turmoil • Superman vs. Monster Society;Crisis

54 ❑ Feb 1986 Cover: 0.75 **NM value: 1.00**
Circ: CapCity orders: **9,250**
Crisis on Infinite Earths; The Crisis Comes to 1942! (And Vice Versa) • Crisis ★ Versus Monster Society.

55 ❑ Mar 1986 Cover: 0.75 **NM value: 1.00**
Circ: CapCity orders: **9,350**
Crisis on Infinite Earths; Crisis at Canaveral! • Crisis ★ Versus Ultra-Humanite in 1980s.

56 ❑ Apr 1986 Cover: 0.75 **NM value: 1.00**
Circ: CapCity orders: **7,700**
Crisis on Infinite Earths; The Sinister Secret of the Sixth Sense! • Crisis; Has 1985 Statement, filed 10/1/85; avg print run 195,291; avg sales 68,198; avg subs 1,200; avg total paid 69,398; samples 115; office use 1,367; max existent 70,880; 64% of run returned ★ Appearance of Seven Soldiers of Victory.

57 ❑ May 1986 Cover: 0.75 **NM value: 1.00**
Circ: CapCity orders: **7,750**
Kaleidoscope • Crisis

58 ❑ Jun 1986 Cover: 0.75 **NM value: 1.00**
Circ: CapCity orders: **7,500**
I Sing the Body Robotic! ★ Appearance of Mekanique.

59 ❑ Jul 1986 Cover: 0.75 **NM value: 1.00**
Circ: CapCity orders: **7,250**
Out of the Ashes … Mekanique! ★ 1st Appearance of Aquaman in All-Star Squadron.

60 ❑ Aug 1986 Cover: 0.75 **NM value: 1.00**
Circ: CapCity orders: **7,300**
The End of the Beginning! • events of Crisis catch up with All-Star Squadron **A:** Mike Clark; Arvell Jones **W:** Roy Thomas

61 ❑ Sep 1986 Cover: 0.75 **NM value: 1.00**
Circ: CapCity orders: **7,050**
The Origin of Liberty Belle ★ Origin of Liberty Belle.

62 ❑ Oct 1986 Cover: 0.75 **NM value: 1.00**
Circ: CapCity orders: **6,900**
The Origin of The Shining Knight ★ Origin of Shining Knight.

63 ❑ Nov 1986 Cover: 0.75 **NM value: 1.00**
Circ: CapCity orders: **6,950**
The Origin of the Golden Age Robotman ★ Origin of Robotman.

64 ❑ Dec 1986 Cover: 0.75 **NM value: 1.00**
Circ: CapCity orders: **6,900**
See You in the Funny Papers! • retells Golden Age Superman story post-Crisis

65 ❑ Jan 1987 Cover: 0.75 **NM value: 1.00**
Circ: CapCity orders: **6,850**
The Origin of Johnny Quick ★ Origin of Johnny Quick.

66 ❑ Feb 1987 Cover: 0.75 **NM value: 1.00**
Circ: CapCity orders: **6,950**
The Origin of Tarantula ★ Origin of Tarantula.

67 ❑ Mar 1987 Cover: 0.75 **NM value: 1.00**
Circ: CapCity orders: **7,650**
The First Case of the Justice Society of America final issue. • final issue: JSA's first case

Anl 1 ❑ Nov 1982 Cover: 1.00 **NM value: 1.25**
The Three Faces of Evil!; Secret Origins; Tragedy in Triplicate **A:** Jerry Ordway ★ Origin of Atom, Wildcat, Guardian.

Anl 2 ❑ Nov 1983 Cover: 1.00 **NM value: 1.25**
The Ultra War!; Divide For Conquest!; An Ending – And An Enigma! **A:** Jerry Ordway **W:** Roy Thomas ★ Appearance of Infinity Inc.. ★ Death of Cyclotron.

Anl 3 ❑ Sep 1984 Cover: 1.25 **NM value: Cover or less**
Untitled story **A:** Don Newton; Keith Giffen; Jerry Ordway; George Pérez; WB ★ Versus Ian Karkull.

ALL-STAR WESTERN (1ST SERIES) DC

Readers of DC's premier super-team series All-Star Comics must have been surprised, when, in April 1951, The Justice Society of America was unceremoniously ousted by a lineup of cowboys and outlaws, and the title of the series changed to All-Star Western. Though it must have taken getting used to, All-Star Western featured some of the best-told Western tales in comics, highlighted by the lead feature, Johnny Thunder, drawn with the stark and unforgiving clarity of a John Ford classic by Alex Toth. All-Star Western also featured early work of many DC Silver Age mainstays, including Gil Kane and Carmine Infantino. All-Star Western folded quietly in the early 1960s to make way for DC's newly popular super-hero comics.

58 ❑ Apr 1951 Cover: 0.10 **NM value: 300.00**
• **CGC:** 1 graded, best 8.0
• Series continued from All Star Comics #57

59 ❑ Jun 1951 Cover: 0.10 **NM value: 140.00**
• **CGC:** 1 graded, best 9.4

60 ❑ Aug 1951 Cover: 0.10 **NM value: 140.00**

61 ❑ Oct 1951 Cover: 0.10 **NM value: 150.00**
A: Alex Toth

62 ❑ Dec 1951 Cover: 0.10 **NM value: 150.00**
• **CGC:** 1 graded, best 9.4
A: Alex Toth

63 ❑ Feb 1952 Cover: 0.10 **NM value: 150.00**
A: Alex Toth

64 ❑ Apr 1952 Cover: 0.10 **NM value: 120.00**
• **CGC:** 1 graded, best 9.6

65 ❑ Jun 1952 Cover: 0.10 **NM value: 120.00**
66 ❑ Aug 1952 Cover: 0.10 **NM value: 120.00**
67 ❑ Oct 1952 Cover: 0.10 **NM value: 165.00**
• Johnny Thunder series starts **A:** Gil Kane

68 ❑ Dec 1952 Cover: 0.10 **NM value: 120.00**
69 ❑ Feb 1953 Cover: 0.10 **NM value: 120.00**
70 ❑ Apr 1953 Cover: 0.10 **NM value: 120.00**
71 ❑ Jun 1953 Cover: 0.10 **NM value: 85.00**
72 ❑ Aug 1953 Cover: 0.10 **NM value: 85.00**
73 ❑ Oct 1953 Cover: 0.10 **NM value: 85.00**
74 ❑ Dec 1953 Cover: 0.10 **NM value: 85.00**
75 ❑ Feb 1954 Cover: 0.10 **NM value: 85.00**
76 ❑ Apr 1954 Cover: 0.10 **NM value: 85.00**
77 ❑ Jun 1954 Cover: 0.10 **NM value: 85.00**
78 ❑ Aug 1954 Cover: 0.10 **NM value: 85.00**
79 ❑ Oct 1954 Cover: 0.10 **NM value: 85.00**
80 ❑ Dec 1954 Cover: 0.10 **NM value: 85.00**
81 ❑ Feb 1955 Cover: 0.10 **NM value: 60.00**
82 ❑ Apr 1955 Cover: 0.10 **NM value: 60.00**
83 ❑ Jun 1955 Cover: 0.10 **NM value: 60.00**
84 ❑ Aug 1955 Cover: 0.10 **NM value: 60.00**
85 ❑ Oct 1955 Cover: 0.10 **NM value: 60.00**
86 ❑ Dec 1955 Cover: 0.10 **NM value: 60.00**
87 ❑ Feb 1956 Cover: 0.10 **NM value: 60.00**
88 ❑ Apr 1956 Cover: 0.10 **NM value: 60.00**
89 ❑ Jul 1956 Cover: 0.10 **NM value: 60.00**
90 ❑ Sep 1956 Cover: 0.10 **NM value: 60.00**
91 ❑ Nov 1956 Cover: 0.10 **NM value: 60.00**
92 ❑ Jan 1957 Cover: 0.10 **NM value: 60.00**
93 ❑ Mar 1957 Cover: 0.10 **NM value: 60.00**
94 ❑ May 1957 Cover: 0.10 **NM value: 60.00**
95 ❑ Jul 1957 Cover: 0.10 **NM value: 60.00**
96 ❑ Sep 1957 Cover: 0.10 **NM value: 60.00**
97 ❑ Nov 1957 Cover: 0.10 **NM value: 60.00**
98 ❑ Jan 1958 Cover: 0.10 **NM value: 60.00**
99 ❑ Mar 1958 Cover: 0.10 **NM value: 65.00**
Ambush at Smoke Canyon **A:** Frank Frazetta

100 ❑ May 1958 Cover: 0.10 **NM value: 60.00**
101 ❑ Jul 1958 Cover: 0.10 **NM value: 50.00**
102 ❑ Sep 1958 Cover: 0.10 **NM value: 50.00**
103 ❑ Nov 1958 Cover: 0.10 **NM value: 50.00**
104 ❑ Jan 1959 Cover: 0.10 **NM value: 50.00**
105 ❑ Mar 1959 Cover: 0.10 **NM value: 50.00**
106 ❑ May 1959 Cover: 0.10 **NM value: 50.00**
107 ❑ Jul 1959 Cover: 0.10 **NM value: 50.00**
108 ❑ Sep 1959 Cover: 0.10 **NM value: 100.00**
★ Origin of Johnny Thunder.

109 ❑ Nov 1959 Cover: 0.10 **NM value: 50.00**
110 ❑ Jan 1960 Cover: 0.10 **NM value: 50.00**
111 ❑ Mar 1960 Cover: 0.10 **NM value: 50.00**
112 ❑ May 1960 Cover: 0.10 **NM value: 50.00**
113 ❑ Jul 1960 Cover: 0.10 **NM value: 50.00**
114 ❑ Sep 1960 Cover: 0.10 **NM value: 50.00**
115 ❑ Nov 1960 Cover: 0.10 **NM value: 50.00**
116 ❑ Jan 1961 Cover: 0.10 **NM value: 50.00**
117 ❑ Mar 1961 Cover: 0.10 **NM value: 50.00**
118 ❑ May 1961 Cover: 0.10 **NM value: 50.00**
119 ❑ Jul 1961 Cover: 0.10 **NM value: 50.00**
final issue.

ALL-STAR WESTERN (2ND SERIES) DC

1 ❑ Sep 1970 Cover: 0.15 **NM value: 25.00**
Gun Duel at Copper Creek!; The Return of the Fadeaway Outlaw! **A:** Carmine Infantino ★ Appearance of Pow-Wow Smith.

2 ❑ Nov 1970 Cover: 0.15 **NM value: 10.00**
3 ❑ Jan 1971 Cover: 0.15 **NM value: 10.00**
4 ❑ Mar 1971 Cover: 0.15 **NM value: 8.00**
5 ❑ May 1971 Cover: 0.15 **NM value: 8.00**
• **CGC:** 2 graded, best 9.4
Outlaw: Hangman Never Loses!; El Diablo: The Devil Rides for Vengeance! **A:** Dick Giordano; Jim Aparo **W:** Alan Weiss; Robert Kanigher

6 ❑ Jul 1971 Cover: 0.15 **NM value: 6.00**
• **CGC:** 1 graded, best 9.6

7 ❑ Sep 1971 Cover: 0.25 **NM value: 6.00**
8 ❑ Nov 1971 Cover: 0.25 **NM value: 6.00**
9 ❑ Jan 1972 Cover: 0.25 **NM value: 6.00**
10 ❑ Mar 1972 Cover: 0.25 **NM value: 135.00**
• **CGC:** 40 graded, best 9.6
Jonah Hex: Welcome to Paradise; El Diablo: The Devil's Secret; Bat Lash **A:** Gray Morrow; Tony DeZuniga; Nick Cardy; Tony DeZuñiga **W:** Sergio Aragonés; John Albano; Denny O'Neil; Robert Kanigher ★ 1st Appearance of Jonah Hex.

11 ❑ May 1972 Cover: 0.25 **NM value: 90.00**
• **CGC:** 15 graded, best 9.4
• Giant-size. Jonah Hex: The Hundred Dollar Deal!; El Diablo: Satan's Sanctuary; Pow-Wow Smith: The Buffalo-Hide Bandits; Bat Lash • Series continues as Weird Western Tales **A:** Gray Morrow; Nick Cardy; Tony De Zuniga ★ 2nd Appearance of Jonah Hex.

ALL SURPRISE Timely

1 ❑ Fal 1943 Cover: 0.10 **NM value: 150.00**
• **CGC:** 1 graded, best 3.0

2 ❑ ca. 1943 Cover: 0.10 **NM value: 75.00**
3 ❑ ca. 1944 Cover: 0.10 **NM value: 75.00**
4 ❑ ca. 1944 Cover: 0.10 **NM value: 75.00**
5 ❑ ca. 1944 Cover: 0.10 **NM value: 75.00**
6 ❑ ca. 1945 Cover: 0.10 **NM value: 50.00**
7 ❑ ca. 1945 Cover: 0.10 **NM value: 50.00**
8 ❑ ca. 1945 Cover: 0.10 **NM value: 50.00**
9 ❑ ca. 1945 Cover: 0.10 **NM value: 50.00**
10 ❑ ca. 1946 Cover: 0.10 **NM value: 50.00**
11 ❑ ca. 1946 Cover: 0.10 **NM value: 50.00**
12 ❑ ca. 1946 Cover: 0.10 **NM value: 50.00**

ALL SUSPENSE Avalon

1 ❑ 1998 b&w Cover: 2.95 **NM value: Cover or less**
The Ghost Who Loved a Girl!; Don't Let the Ghost Take Shape!; The Skeleton's Secret • reprints Nemesis and Mark Midnight stories **A:** Pete Costanza; Ditko Trapani **W:** Pierre Alonzo; Shane O'Shea

ALL THE RULES HAVE CHANGED Rip Off

1 ❑ Cover: 9.95 **NM value: Cover or less**
A: Ted Rall **W:** Ted Rall

ALL THE WRONG PLACES Laszlo

1 ❑ Cover: 2.95 **NM value: Cover or less**

ALL-THRILL COMICS Mansion

845 ❑ Cover: 2.95 **NM value: Cover or less**
• Actually #1 **A:** Wayne Reid **W:** David Watkins

ALL-TIME SPORTS COMICS Hillman Periodicals

4 ❑ Apr 1949 Cover: 0.10 **NM value: 125.00**
5 ❑ Jun 1949 Cover: 0.10 **NM value: 100.00**
6 ❑ Aug 1949 Cover: 0.10 **NM value: 100.00**
7 ❑ Oct 1949 Cover: 0.10 **NM value: 100.00**

ALL TOP COMICS Fox

1 ❑ Spr 1946 Cover: 0.10 **NM value: 125.00**
• **CGC:** 2 graded, best 5.0

2 ❑ Sum 1946 Cover: 0.10 **NM value: 75.00**
3 ❑ Fal 1946 Cover: 0.10 **NM value: 75.00**
4 ❑ Jan 1947 Cover: 0.10 **NM value: 75.00**
5 ❑ Mar 1947 Cover: 0.10 **NM value: 75.00**
6 ❑ May 1947 Cover: 0.10 **NM value: 75.00**
7 ❑ Jul 1947 Cover: 0.10 **NM value: 75.00**
8 ❑ Nov 1947 Cover: 0.10 **NM value: 1500.00**
• **CGC:** 3 graded, best 7.0

9 ❑ Jan 1948 Cover: 0.10 **NM value: 850.00**
• **CGC:** 4 graded, best 9.0

10 ❑ Mar 1948 Cover: 0.10 **NM value: 850.00**
• **CGC:** 5 graded, best 9.2

11 ❑ May 1948 Cover: 0.10 **NM value: 850.00**
• **CGC:** 3 graded, best 9.0

12 ❑ Jul 1948 Cover: 0.10 **NM value: 850.00**
• **CGC:** 2 graded, best 9.0

13 ❑ Sep 1948 Cover: 0.10 **NM value: 750.00**
• **CGC:** 1 graded, best 4.5

Other grades: Multiply prices above by **1.5 for Mint • 2/3 for Very Fine • 1/3 for Fine • 1/5 for Very Good • 1/8 for Good**

14 ❑ Nov 1948 Cover: 0.10 **NM** value: **750.00**
15 ❑ Jan 1949 Cover: 0.10 **NM** value: **750.00**
16 ❑ Mar 1949 Cover: 0.10 **NM** value: **750.00**
• **CGC:** 2 graded, best 7.5
17 ❑ May 1949 Cover: 0.10 **NM** value: **750.00**
18 ❑ Jul 1949 Cover: 0.10 **NM** value: **750.00**

ALL-TRUE CRIME — Leading

Formerly known as Official True Crime Cases, this series ran under the name All True Crime from 1948 until 1952. During its run, it turned out a respectable collection of crime stories claiming simultaneously to be "all true" yet carrying this disclaimer: "All names and places in these true-to-life stories are fictitious. Any similarity between actual persons or places and those used in these stories in purely coincidental." Which was a comic-book reader to believe?

Regardless of their basis in actual life, the stories were full of the sort of ruthless gangster action and criminal cunning that made crime comics such a hit in the early 1950s. Here, doctors swindle money from widows and murder the people who might expose them; gunmen engage in an endless series of double crosses; and nervous hoods continually outsmart themselves by pulling stunts such as hiding their loot in self-destructing places or unwittingly murdering the people meant to be their alibi.

26 ❑ Feb 1948 Cover: 0.10 **NM** value: **125.00**
• **CGC:** 1 graded, best 8.0
• Series continued from Official True Crime Cases #25
27 ❑ Apr 1958 Cover: 0.10 **NM** value: **85.00**
28 ❑ Jun 1948 Cover: 0.10 **NM** value: **85.00**
29 ❑ Sep 1948 Cover: 0.10 **NM** value: **85.00**
30 ❑ Nov 1948 Cover: 0.10 **NM** value: **60.00**
31 ❑ Jan 1949 Cover: 0.10 **NM** value: **60.00**
32 ❑ Mar 1949 Cover: 0.10 **NM** value: **60.00**
• **CGC:** 1 graded, best 6.5
33 ❑ May 1949 Cover: 0.10 **NM** value: **60.00**
34 ❑ Jul 1949 Cover: 0.10 **NM** value: **60.00**
35 ❑ Sep 1949 Cover: 0.10 **NM** value: **60.00**
36 ❑ Nov 1949 Cover: 0.10 **NM** value: **60.00**
37 ❑ Feb 1950 Cover: 0.10 **NM** value: **60.00**
38 ❑ May 1950 Cover: 0.10 **NM** value: **60.00**
39 ❑ Jul 1950 Cover: 0.10 **NM** value: **60.00**
40 ❑ Sep 1950 Cover: 0.10 **NM** value: **60.00**
41 ❑ Nov 1950 Cover: 0.10 **NM** value: **46.00**
42 ❑ Jan 1951 Cover: 0.10 **NM** value: **46.00**
43 ❑ Mar 1951 Cover: 0.10 **NM** value: **46.00**
44 ❑ May 1951 Cover: 0.10 **NM** value: **46.00**
45 ❑ Jul 1951 Cover: 0.10 **NM** value: **46.00**
46 ❑ Sep 1951 Cover: 0.10 **NM** value: **46.00**
🕮 Public Enemy; Death and Dr. Harlow; Double-Cross; The Black Robe; Gunman's Legacy; The Last Alibi! **A:** Robert Q. Sale; Gene Colan; Dan Loprino; Jay S. Pike; Sitton; Tony Di Preta
47 ❑ Nov 1951 Cover: 0.10 **NM** value: **46.00**
48 ❑ Jan 1952 Cover: 0.10 **NM** value: **46.00**
49 ❑ Mar 1952 Cover: 0.10 **NM** value: **46.00**
50 ❑ May 1952 Cover: 0.10 **NM** value: **46.00**
51 ❑ Jul 1952 Cover: 0.10 **NM** value: **40.00**
52 ❑ Sep 1952 Cover: 0.10 **NM** value: **40.00**
final issue.

ALL WESTERN WINNERS — Timely

2 ❑ Win 1948 Cover: 0.10 **NM** value: **600.00**
• **CGC:** 1 graded, best 8.5
3 ❑ Feb 1949 Cover: 0.10 **NM** value: **300.00**
4 ❑ Apr 1949 Cover: 0.10 **NM** value: **250.00**

ALL WINNERS COMICS — Timely

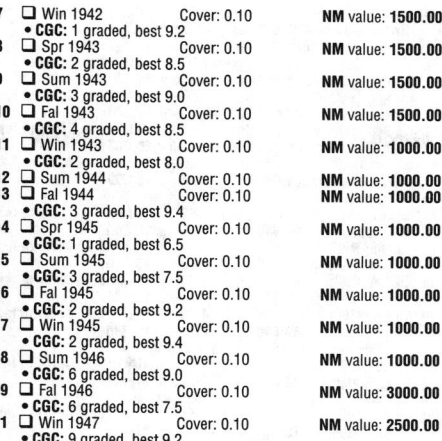

Beginning as just another Timely super-hero title, the stories quickly focused on fighting Axis enemies, as World War II progressed. Eventually (and for only two issues), it introduced the All Winners Squad, which comprised Captain America, Bucky, The Human Torch, Toro, The Sub-Mariner, The Whizzer, and Miss America (no relation to the Captain.

The concept was something of an imitation of the much more successful team of The Justice Society of America in DC's All-Star Comics, the problem being that Timely didn't have a roster that came close to matching the line-up boasted by All-Star. — Maggie

1 ❑ Sum 1941 Cover: 0.10 **NM** value: **12000.00**
• **CGC:** 7 graded, best 7.0
🕮 Case of the Hollow Men • Captain America
2 ❑ Fal 1941 Cover: 0.10 **NM** value: **6000.00**
• **CGC:** 3 graded, best 8.5
🕮 The Strange Case of the Malay Men • Captain America
3 ❑ Win 1941 Cover: 0.10 **NM** value: **3000.00**
4 ❑ Spr 1942 Cover: 0.10 **NM** value: **2500.00**
• **CGC:** 5 graded, best 5.0
5 ❑ Sum 1942 Cover: 0.10 **NM** value: **2000.00**
• **CGC:** 4 graded, best 7.0
6 ❑ Fal 1942 Cover: 0.10 **NM** value: **1500.00**
• **CGC:** 2 graded, best 7.5
7 ❑ Win 1942 Cover: 0.10 **NM** value: **1500.00**
• **CGC:** 1 graded, best 9.2
8 ❑ Spr 1943 Cover: 0.10 **NM** value: **1500.00**
• **CGC:** 2 graded, best 8.5
9 ❑ Sum 1943 Cover: 0.10 **NM** value: **1500.00**
• **CGC:** 3 graded, best 9.0
10 ❑ Fal 1943 Cover: 0.10 **NM** value: **1500.00**
• **CGC:** 4 graded, best 8.5
11 ❑ Win 1943 Cover: 0.10 **NM** value: **1000.00**
• **CGC:** 2 graded, best 8.0
12 ❑ Sum 1944 Cover: 0.10 **NM** value: **1000.00**
13 ❑ Fal 1944 Cover: 0.10 **NM** value: **1000.00**
• **CGC:** 3 graded, best 9.4
14 ❑ Spr 1945 Cover: 0.10 **NM** value: **1000.00**
• **CGC:** 1 graded, best 6.5
15 ❑ Sum 1945 Cover: 0.10 **NM** value: **1000.00**
• **CGC:** 3 graded, best 7.5
16 ❑ Fal 1945 Cover: 0.10 **NM** value: **1000.00**
• **CGC:** 2 graded, best 9.2
17 ❑ Win 1945 Cover: 0.10 **NM** value: **1000.00**
• **CGC:** 2 graded, best 9.4
18 ❑ Sum 1946 Cover: 0.10 **NM** value: **1000.00**
• **CGC:** 6 graded, best 9.0
19 ❑ Fal 1946 Cover: 0.10 **NM** value: **3000.00**
• **CGC:** 6 graded, best 7.5
21 ❑ Win 1947 Cover: 0.10 **NM** value: **2500.00**
• **CGC:** 9 graded, best 9.2
• No #20

ALLY — Ally-Winsor

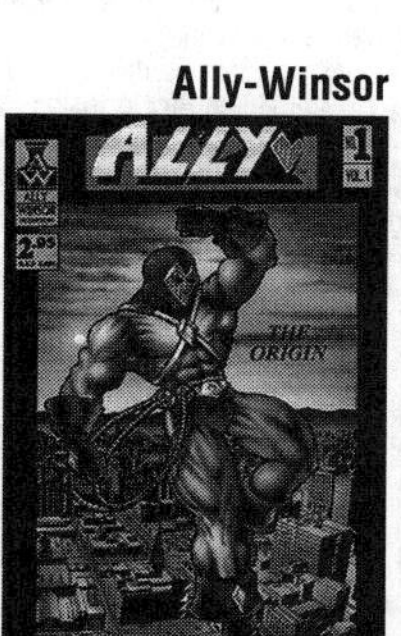

Ally is the name David Cruz uses when he wears a fantastic suit with built-in lasers, shields, and a holographic projector that enables him to go undercover by altering his appearance. From drive-by shootings and street-gang warfare to drug-running and fine art heists, Ally confronts whatever may come his way. The suit was developed by Cruz with his friend Jerry, whose death he is attempting to avenge. Cruz' girlfriend, Karina, was Jerry's sister, and David's activities are a constant reminder of her brother's tragic end.

The black-and-white art is stylized and employs unusual diamond-shaped word and thought balloons for Ally. This series has a decidedly Latin beat in portraying the gritty violence of the L.A. streets.

1 ❑ Fal 1995, b&w Cover: 2.95 **NM** value: **Cover or less**
A: Ruben Gerard **W:** Ruben Gerard ★ Origin of Ally. ★ 1st Appearance of Ally.
2 ❑ Cover: 2.95 **NM** value: **Cover or less**
A: Ruben Gerard **W:** Ruben Gerard; Max Espinoza
3 ❑ Cover: 2.95 **NM** value: **Cover or less**
• Flip-book. 🕮 Payback **A:** Michael Buntyn **W:** Max Espinoza

ALMURIC — Dark Horse

Written by Roy Thomas and drawn by Tim Conrad, the comic book adapts the Almuric story by Robert E. Howard (1906-1936): the tale of a warrior (Almuric) who lands on a planet with lots of gorgeous women and life-threatening dangers. — Maggie

1 ❑ Feb 1991 Cover: 10.95 **NM** value: **Cover or less**
No issue number. **A:** Tim Conrad **W:** Roy Thomas

ALONE IN THE SHADE SPECIAL — Alchemy

1 ❑ b&w Cover: 2.00 **NM** value: **Cover or less**
No issue number.

ALPHABET — Dark Visions

1 ❑ Dec 1993 Cover: 2.50 **NM** value: **Cover or less**
🕮 Eidolon: Unliving Hell, Part 1; The Enforcers **A:** B. Mullins; Kenneth Nelson Jr. **W:** Kenneth Nelson Jr.; C. Russell

ALPHA CENTURION SPECIAL — DC

1 ❑ Cover: 2.95 **NM** value: **Cover or less**
One-shot. 🕮 Protector of Earth? **A:** Stuart Immonen **W:** Stuart Immonen; Barbara Kesel ★ Origin of Alpha Centurion.

ALPHA FLIGHT — Marvel

Canada's answer to The Avengers — is it the X-Men? John Byrne created this super-team as a sometime foe, sometime friend for the X-Men, whose Wolverine was once a Canadian agent. Readers wanted to see more, and Byrne launched this series with the Alphans setting themselves up as independent from the Canadian government.

Puck and Marrina were introduced for the series, joining existing members Aurora, Northstar, Sasquatch, Shaman, Snowbird, and Guardian. Vintage Byrne soap opera ensued, with Aurora proving to have a split personality and Sasquatch having a problem with anger. (Team leader Guardian was just dull, and Byrne unceremoniously whacked him in #12.) Some subplots lingered long after Byrne left the series, with Northstar waiting until #106 to announce his sexual preference. Readers had known it for years, but Marvel made some public relations hay by announcing it suddenly had "the first gay superhero." — JJM

1 ❑ Aug 1983 Cover: 1.00 **NM** value: **2.50**
• **CGC:** 24 graded, best 9.6
🕮 Tundra! **A:** John Byrne **W:** John Byrne ★ 1st Appearance of Wildheart (not identified), Puck, Marina.
2 ❑ Sep 1983 Cover: 0.60 **NM** value: **1.75**
• **CGC:** 1 graded, best 9.6
🕮 Shadows Of The Past • Vindicator becomes Guardian I **A:** John Byrne **W:** John Byrne ★ Origin of Marina, Alpha Flight. ★ 1st Appearance of The Master, Guardian I (James Hudson).
3 ❑ Oct 1983 Cover: 0.60 **NM** value: **1.75**
• **CGC:** 1 graded, best 9.8
🕮 Yesterday Man **A:** John Byrne **W:** John Byrne ★ Origin of Marina, The Master, Alpha Flight.
4 ❑ Nov 1983 Cover: 0.60 **NM** value: **1.75**
• **CGC:** 1 graded, best 9.6
A: John Byrne **W:** John Byrne ★ Origin of Marina.
5 ❑ Dec 1983 Cover: 0.60 **NM** value: **1.75**
• **CGC:** 1 graded, best 9.6
🕮 What Fools These Mortals Be **A:** John Byrne **W:** John Byrne ★ Origin of Elizabeth Twoyoungmen. ★ 1st Appearance of Elizabeth Twoyoungmen.
6 ❑ Jan 1984 Cover: 0.60 **NM** value: **1.75**
🕮 Snowblind • all-white issue **A:** John Byrne **W:** John Byrne ★ Origin of Shaman.
7 ❑ Feb 1984 Cover: 0.60 **NM** value: **1.75**
🕮 The Importance Of Being Deadly **A:** John Byrne **W:** John Byrne ★ Origin of Snowbird.
8 ❑ Mar 1984 Cover: 0.60 **NM** value: **1.75**
🕮 Cold Hands Cold Heart **A:** John Byrne **W:** John Byrne
9 ❑ Apr 1984 Cover: 0.60 **NM** value: **1.75**
🕮 Things Aren't Always What They Seem **A:** John Byrne **W:** John Byrne ★ Origin of Aurora. ★ Appearance of Thing.
10 ❑ May 1984 Cover: 0.60 **NM** value: **1.75**
🕮 Blood Battle **A:** John Byrne **W:** John Byrne ★ Origin of Northstar, Sasquatch.
11 ❑ Jun 1984 Cover: 0.60 **NM** value: **1.75**
• **CGC:** 1 graded, best 9.4
🕮 Set-Up **A:** John Byrne **W:** John Byrne ★ Origin of Sasquatch. ★ 1st Appearance of Wild Child, Diamond Lil (identified).
12 ❑ Jul 1984 Cover: 0.60 **NM** value: **1.75**
• Double-size. 🕮 And One Shall Surely Die **A:** John Byrne **W:** John Byrne ★ Death of Guardian.
13 ❑ Aug 1984 Cover: 0.60 **NM** value: **2.50**
• **CGC:** 3 graded, best 9.4
🕮 Nightmare! **A:** John Byrne **W:** John Byrne ★ Appearance of Wolverine.
14 ❑ Sep 1984 Cover: 0.60 **NM** value: **1.50**
🕮 Biology Class **A:** John Byrne **W:** John Byrne
15 ❑ Oct 1984 Cover: 0.60 **NM** value: **1.50**
🕮 Blind Date **A:** John Byrne **W:** John Byrne ★ Appearance of Sub-Mariner.
16 ❑ Nov 1984 Cover: 0.60 **NM** value: **1.50**
🕮 ...And Forsaking All The Others • Wolverine cameo **A:** John Byrne **W:** John Byrne ★ Appearance of Sub-Mariner.
17 ❑ Dec 1984 Cover: 0.60 **NM** value: **2.00**
🕮 Dreams Die Hard... • X-Men crossover;Wolverine cameo **A:** John Byrne **W:** John Byrne
18 ❑ Jan 1985 Cover: 0.60 **NM** value: **1.50**
🕮 How Long Will A Man Lie In The Earth 'Ere He Rot? **A:** John Byrne **W:** John Byrne
19 ❑ Feb 1985 Cover: 0.60 **NM** value: **1.50**
🕮 Turn Again, Turn Again, Time In Thy Flight... **A:** John Byrne **W:** John Byrne ★ Origin of Talisman II (Elizabeth Twoyoungmen). ★ 1st Appearance of Talisman II (Elizabeth Twoyoungmen).
20 ❑ Mar 1985 Cover: 0.60 **NM** value: **1.50**
🕮 Gold And Love Affairs • New headquarters **A:** John Byrne **W:** John Byrne
21 ❑ Apr 1985 Cover: 0.65 **NM** value: **1.50**
🕮 Love Wrought New Alchemy... **A:** John Byrne **W:** John Byrne ★ Origin of Diablo. ★ Versus Diablo.
22 ❑ May 1985 Cover: 0.65 **NM** value: **1.50**
Circ: CapCity orders: **34,000**
🕮 Rub-Out **A:** John Byrne **W:** John Byrne
23 ❑ Jun 1985 Cover: 0.65 **NM** value: **1.50**
Circ: CapCity orders: **33,000**
🕮 Night Of The Beast **A:** John Byrne **W:** John Byrne
24 ❑ Jul 1985 Cover: 1.25 **NM** value: **1.50**
Circ: CapCity orders: **31,700**
• Double-size. 🕮 Final Conflict **A:** John Byrne **W:** John Byrne
25 ❑ Aug 1985 Cover: 0.65 **NM** value: **1.50**
Circ: CapCity orders: **32,400**
A: John Byrne **W:** John Byrne
26 ❑ Sep 1985 Cover: 0.65 **NM** value: **1.50**
Circ: CapCity orders: **31,100**
🕮 If At First You Don't Succeed... **A:** John Byrne **W:** John Byrne
27 ❑ Oct 1985 Cover: 0.65 **NM** value: **1.50**
Circ: CapCity orders: **30,700**
🕮 Betrayal **A:** John Byrne **W:** John Byrne
28 ❑ Nov 1985 Cover: 0.65 **NM** value: **1.50**
Circ: CapCity orders: **35,900**
🕮 Secret Wars II • Secret Wars II;Last Byrne issue **A:** John Byrne **W:** John Byrne
29 ❑ Dec 1985 Cover: 0.65 **NM** value: **1.50**
Circ: CapCity orders: **27,200**
★ Appearance of Hulk.
30 ❑ Jan 1986 Cover: 0.65 **NM** value: **1.50**
Circ: Statement: **239,584** CapCity orders: **25,300**
🕮 Enter...Scramble! **A:** Mike Mignola **W:** Bill Mantlo
31 ❑ Feb 1986 Cover: 0.75 **NM** value: **1.50**
Circ: Statement: **239,584** CapCity orders: **26,100**
🕮 The Grateful Dead! **A:** Mike Mignola **W:** Bill Mantlo
32 ❑ Mar 1986 Cover: 0.75 **NM** value: **1.50**
Circ: Statement: **239,584** CapCity orders: **26,900**
🕮 Short Story **A:** Jon Bogdanove **W:** Bill Mantlo
33 ❑ Apr 1986 Cover: 0.75 **NM** value: **2.00**
Circ: Statement: **239,584** CapCity orders: **34,300**
🕮 A Friend In Need • Wolverine **A:** Sal Buscema **W:** Bill Mantlo ★ Appearance of X-Men.

CGC-graded: Multiply prices above by **33 for 9.9 M • 16 for 9.8 NM/M • 7 for 9.6 NM+ • 5 for 9.4 NM • 2.5 for 9.2 NM- • 1.5 for 9.0 VF/NM**

34 ❑ May 1986 Cover: 0.75 **NM** value: **2.50**
Circ: Statement: **239,584** CapCity orders: **33,900**
Honor • Wolverine **A:** Sal Buscema **W:** Bill Mantlo ★ Origin of Wolverine.

35 ❑ Jun 1986 Cover: 0.75 **NM** value: **1.50**
Circ: Statement: **239,584** CapCity orders: **27,200**
• Wolverine **A:** Sal Buscema **W:** Bill Mantlo

36 ❑ Jul 1986 Cover: 0.75 **NM** value: **1.50**
Circ: Statement: **239,584** CapCity orders: **27,800**
• Wolverine **A:** Sal Buscema **W:** Bill Mantlo

37 ❑ Aug 1986 Cover: 0.75 **NM** value: **1.50**
Circ: Statement: **239,584** CapCity orders: **27,400**
Death Birth • Wolverine **A:** Dave Ross **W:** Bill Mantlo

38 ❑ Sep 1986 Cover: 0.75 **NM** value: **1.50**
Circ: Statement: **239,584** CapCity orders: **27,300**
• Wolverine

39 ❑ Oct 1986 Cover: 0.75 **NM** value: **1.50**
Circ: Statement: **239,584** CapCity orders: **27,400**
The Invasion Of Atlantis! • Wolverine **A:** Dave Ross **W:** Bill Mantlo

40 ❑ Nov 1986 Cover: 0.75 **NM** value: **1.50**
Circ: Statement: **239,584** CapCity orders: **27,300**
• Wolverine

41 ❑ Dec 1986 Cover: 0.75 **NM** value: **1.50**
Circ: Statement: **239,584** CapCity orders: **26,900**
• Wolverine

42 ❑ Jan 1987 Cover: 0.75 **NM** value: **1.50**
Circ: Statement: **201,692** CapCity orders: **25,400**
• Wolverine

43 ❑ Feb 1987 Cover: 0.75 **NM** value: **1.50**
Circ: Statement: **201,692** CapCity orders: **25,900**
• Wolverine

44 ❑ Mar 1987 Cover: 0.75 **NM** value: **1.50**
Circ: Statement: **201,692** CapCity orders: **25,800**
• Wolverine ★ Death of Snowbird.

45 ❑ Apr 1987 Cover: 0.75 **NM** value: **1.50**
Circ: Statement: **201,692** CapCity orders: **24,700**
• Wolverine

46 ❑ May 1987 Cover: 0.75 **NM** value: **1.50**
Circ: Statement: **201,692** CapCity orders: **23,800**
• Wolverine

47 ❑ Jun 1987 Cover: 0.75 **NM** value: **1.50**
Circ: Statement: **201,692** CapCity orders: **23,600**
• Wolverine

48 ❑ Jul 1987 Cover: 0.75 **NM** value: **1.50**
Circ: Statement: **201,692** CapCity orders: **23,400**
• Wolverine

49 ❑ Aug 1987 Cover: 0.75 **NM** value: **1.50**
Circ: Statement: **201,692** CapCity orders: **26,100**
• Wolverine

50 ❑ Sep 1987 Cover: 1.25 **NM** value: **1.50**
Circ: Statement: **201,692** CapCity orders: **28,700**

51 ❑ Oct 1987 Cover: 0.75 **NM** value: **2.50**
Circ: Statement: **201,692** CapCity orders: **26,500** • **CGC:** 2 graded, best 9.6
• 1st Jim Lee work at Marvel **A:** Jim Lee; José Luis Garcia-Lopez; José Luis Garcia-Lopezee ★ Appearance of Wolverine.

52 ❑ Nov 1987 Cover: 1.00 **NM** value: **2.00**
Circ: Statement: **201,692** CapCity orders: **30,800**
★ Appearance of Wolverine.

53 ❑ Dec 1987 Cover: 1.00 **NM** value: **2.00**
Circ: Statement: **201,692** CapCity orders: **29,200**
★ 1st Appearance of Laura Dean. ★ Appearance of Wolverine.

54 ❑ Jan 1988 Cover: 1.00 **NM** value: **1.50**
Circ: Statement: **129,540** CapCity orders: **25,900**
★ Origin of Laura Dean.

55 ❑ Feb 1988 Cover: 1.00 **NM** value: **1.50**
Circ: Statement: **129,540** CapCity orders: **26,600**
A: Jim Lee

56 ❑ Mar 1988 Cover: 1.00 **NM** value: **1.50**
Circ: Statement: **129,540** CapCity orders: **26,050**
A: Jim Lee ★ 1st Appearance of The Dreamqueen.

57 ❑ Apr 1988 Cover: 1.00 **NM** value: **1.50**
Circ: Statement: **129,540** CapCity orders: **26,600**
A: Jim Lee

58 ❑ May 1988 Cover: 1.00 **NM** value: **1.50**
Circ: Statement: **129,540** CapCity orders: **25,400**
A: Jim Lee

59 ❑ Jun 1988 Cover: 1.00 **NM** value: **1.50**
Circ: Statement: **129,540** CapCity orders: **24,000**
A: Jim Lee

60 ❑ Jul 1988 Cover: 1.25 **NM** value: **1.50**
Circ: Statement: **129,540** CapCity orders: **23,700**
A: Jim Lee

61 ❑ Aug 1988 Cover: 1.25 **NM** value: **1.50**
Circ: Statement: **129,540** CapCity orders: **23,900**
A: Jim Lee

62 ❑ Sep 1988 Cover: 1.25 **NM** value: **1.50**
Circ: Statement: **129,540** CapCity orders: **23,400**
A: Jim Lee

63 ❑ Oct 1988 Cover: 1.25 **NM** value: **Cover or less**
Circ: Statement: **129,540** CapCity orders: **22,900**

64 ❑ Nov 1988 Cover: 1.25 **NM** value: **Cover or less**
Circ: Statement: **129,540** CapCity orders: **21,500**

65 ❑ Dec 1988 Cover: 1.50 **NM** value: **Cover or less**
Circ: Statement: **129,540** CapCity orders: **21,200**

66 ❑ Jan 1989 Cover: 1.50 **NM** value: **Cover or less**
Circ: Statement: **89,640** CapCity orders: **20,100**

67 ❑ Feb 1989 Cover: 1.50 **NM** value: **Cover or less**
Circ: Statement: **89,640** CapCity orders: **19,300**
Wrath of the Dream Queen, Part 1 ★ Origin of The Dream Queen.

68 ❑ Mar 1989 Cover: 1.50 **NM** value: **Cover or less**
Circ: Statement: **89,640** CapCity orders: **19,800**
Wrath of the Dream Queen, Part 2

69 ❑ Apr 1989 Cover: 1.50 **NM** value: **Cover or less**
Circ: Statement: **89,640** CapCity orders: **19,800**
Wrath of the Dream Queen, Part 3

70 ❑ May 1989 Cover: 1.50 **NM** value: **Cover or less**
Circ: Statement: **89,640** CapCity orders: **19,900**
Wrath of the Dream Queen, Part 4

71 ❑ Jun 1989 Cover: 1.50 **NM** value: **Cover or less**
Circ: Statement: **89,640** CapCity orders: **20,250**
★ 1st Appearance of Llan the Sorcerer.

72 ❑ Jul 1989 Cover: 1.50 **NM** value: **Cover or less**
Circ: Statement: **89,640** CapCity orders: **20,200**

73 ❑ Aug 1989 Cover: 1.50 **NM** value: **Cover or less**
Circ: Statement: **89,640** CapCity orders: **20,100**

74 ❑ Sep 1989 Cover: 1.50 **NM** value: **Cover or less**
Circ: Statement: **89,640** CapCity orders: **20,300**

75 ❑ Oct 1989 Cover: 1.95 **NM** value: **2.25**
Circ: Statement: **89,640** CapCity orders: **19,600**
• Double-size.

76 ❑ Nov 1989 Cover: 1.50 **NM** value: **Cover or less**
Circ: Statement: **89,640** CapCity orders: **18,200**

77 ❑ Nov 1989 Cover: 1.95 **NM** value: **Cover or less**
Circ: Statement: **89,640** CapCity orders: **18,500**

78 ❑ Dec 1989 Cover: 1.50 **NM** value: **Cover or less**
Circ: Statement: **89,640** CapCity orders: **18,200**

79 ❑ Dec 1989 Cover: 1.50 **NM** value: **Cover or less**
Circ: Statement: **89,640** CapCity orders: **19,800**
Acts of Vengeance • Acts of Vengeance

80 ❑ Jan 1990 Cover: 1.50 **NM** value: **Cover or less**
Circ: Statement: **73,853** CapCity orders: **21,400**
Acts of Vengeance • Acts of Vengeance

81 ❑ Feb 1990 Cover: 1.50 **NM** value: **Cover or less**
Circ: Statement: **73,853** CapCity orders: **17,400**
Quest for Northstar, Part 1

82 ❑ Mar 1990 Cover: 1.50 **NM** value: **Cover or less**
Circ: Statement: **73,853** CapCity orders: **17,800**
Quest for Northstar, Part 2

83 ❑ Apr 1990 Cover: 1.50 **NM** value: **Cover or less**
Circ: Statement: **73,853** CapCity orders: **16,800**
★ Origin of Talisman II (Elizabeth Twoyoungmen).

84 ❑ May 1990 Cover: 1.50 **NM** value: **Cover or less**
Circ: Statement: **73,853** CapCity orders: **16,500**

85 ❑ Jun 1990 Cover: 1.50 **NM** value: **Cover or less**
Circ: Statement: **73,853** CapCity orders: **16,400**

86 ❑ Jul 1990 Cover: 1.50 **NM** value: **Cover or less**
Circ: Statement: **73,853** CapCity orders: **16,100**

87 ❑ Aug 1990 Cover: 1.50 **NM** value: **2.00**
Circ: Statement: **73,853** CapCity orders: **19,400**
• Wolverine **A:** Jim Lee(cover) ★ 1st Appearance of Windshear.

88 ❑ Sep 1990 Cover: 1.50 **NM** value: **2.00**
Circ: Statement: **73,853** CapCity orders: **20,500**
• Wolverine;Guardian I reappears as cyborg **A:** Jim Lee(cover)

89 ❑ Oct 1990 Cover: 1.50 **NM** value: **2.00**
Circ: Statement: **73,853** CapCity orders: **22,400**
• Wolverine;Guardian returns **A:** Jim Lee(cover)

90 ❑ Nov 1990 Cover: 1.50 **NM** value: **2.00**
Circ: Statement: **73,853** CapCity orders: **25,000**
A: Jim Lee(cover)

91 ❑ Dec 1990 Cover: 1.50 **NM** value: **1.75**
Circ: Statement: **73,853** CapCity orders: **20,100**
• Doctor Doom

92 ❑ Jan 1991 Cover: 1.50 **NM** value: **1.75**
Circ: CapCity orders: **21,200**
Compromising Positions

93 ❑ Feb 1991 Cover: 1.50 **NM** value: **1.75**
Circ: CapCity orders: **21,400**

94 ❑ Mar 1991 Cover: 1.50 **NM** value: **1.75**
Circ: CapCity orders: **21,400**
• Fantastic 4

95 ❑ Apr 1991 Cover: 1.50 **NM** value: **1.75**
Circ: CapCity orders: **19,900**

96 ❑ May 1991 Cover: 1.50 **NM** value: **1.75**
Circ: CapCity orders: **19,600**

97 ❑ Jun 1991 Cover: 1.50 **NM** value: **1.75**
Circ: CapCity orders: **21,800**
The Final Option, Part 1 **A:** Michael Bair **W:** Fabian Nicieza

98 ❑ Jul 1991 Cover: 1.50 **NM** value: **1.75**
Circ: CapCity orders: **19,400**
The Final Option, Part 2 **A:** Michael Bair **W:** Fabian Nicieza

99 ❑ Aug 1991 Cover: 1.50 **NM** value: **1.75**
Circ: CapCity orders: **19,400**
The Final Option, Part 3 **A:** Michael Bair **W:** Fabian Nicieza

100 ❑ Sep 1991 Cover: 2.00 **NM** value: **Cover or less**
Circ: CapCity orders: **25,600**
The Final Option, Part 4 **A:** Michael Bair **W:** Fabian Nicieza ★ Appearance of Galactus, Avengers.

101 ❑ Oct 1991 Cover: 1.50 **NM** value: **1.75**
Circ: CapCity orders: **19,700**

102 ❑ Nov 1991 Cover: 1.50 **NM** value: **1.75**
Circ: CapCity orders: **19,500**
★ 1st Appearance of Weapon Omega.

103 ❑ Dec 1991 Cover: 1.50 **NM** value: **1.75**
Circ: CapCity orders: **19,500**

104 ❑ Jan 1992 Cover: 1.50 **NM** value: **1.75**
Circ: CapCity orders: **19,500**

105 ❑ Feb 1992 Cover: 1.75 **NM** value: **Cover or less**
Circ: CapCity orders: **19,000**
The Bachelor Party

106 ❑ Mar 1992 Cover: 1.75 **NM** value: **2.00**
Circ: CapCity orders: **18,700** • **CGC:** 2 graded, best 9.6
1st printing. The Walking Wounded • Northstar admits he's gay

106-2 ❑ Mar 1992 Cover: 1.75 **NM** value: **Cover or less**

107 ❑ Apr 1992 Cover: 1.75 **NM** value: **Cover or less**
Circ: CapCity orders: **18,200**
★ Appearance of X-Factor.

108 ❑ May 1992 Cover: 1.75 **NM** value: **Cover or less**
Circ: CapCity orders: **17,200**
The Global Village **A:** Tom Morgan **W:** Scott Lobdell

109 ❑ Jun 1992 Cover: 1.75 **NM** value: **Cover or less**
Circ: CapCity orders: **19,600**
By Right Of Memory **A:** Craig Brasfield **W:** Sven Larsen

110 ❑ Jul 1992 Cover: 1.75 **NM** value: **Cover or less**
Circ: CapCity orders: **34,900**

111 ❑ Aug 1992 Cover: 1.75 **NM** value: **Cover or less**
Circ: CapCity orders: **33,300**

112 ❑ Sep 1992 Cover: 1.75 **NM** value: **Cover or less**
Circ: CapCity orders: **32,700**
Infinity War

113 ❑ Oct 1992 Cover: 1.75 **NM** value: **Cover or less**
Circ: CapCity orders: **21,600**
Speaking Of Experience **A:** Craig Brasfield **W:** Sven Larsen

114 ❑ Nov 1992 Cover: 1.75 **NM** value: **Cover or less**
Circ: CapCity orders: **21,700**

115 ❑ Dec 1992 Cover: 1.75 **NM** value: **Cover or less**
Circ: CapCity orders: **21,400**
Extreme Prejudice, Part 1 ★ 1st Appearance of Wyre.

116 ❑ Jan 1993 Cover: 1.75 **NM** value: **Cover or less**
Circ: CapCity orders: **19,000**
Extreme Prejudice, Part 2 **A:** Pat Broderick **W:** Simon Furman

117 ❑ Feb 1993 Cover: 1.75 **NM** value: **Cover or less**
Circ: CapCity orders: **18,600**
Extreme Prejudice, Part 3 **A:** Pat Broderick **W:** Simon Furman

118 ❑ Mar 1993 Cover: 1.75 **NM** value: **Cover or less**
Circ: CapCity orders: **17,450**
The Clampdown, Part 1 **A:** Pat Broderick **W:** Simon Furman ★ Origin of Wildheart. ★ 1st Appearance of Wildheart.

119 ❑ Apr 1993 Cover: 1.75 **NM** value: **Cover or less**
Circ: CapCity orders: **17,400**
The Clampdown, Part 2 **A:** Pat Broderick **W:** Simon Furman ★ Versus Wrecking Crew.

120 ❑ May 1993 Cover: 2.25 **NM** value: **Cover or less**
Circ: CapCity orders: **29,400**
The Clampdown, Part 3 • with poster **A:** Pat Broderick **W:** Simon Furman

121 ❑ Jun 1993 Cover: 1.75 **NM** value: **Cover or less**
Circ: CapCity orders: **20,800**
★ Appearance of Spider-Man.

122 ❑ Jul 1993 Cover: 1.75 **NM** value: **Cover or less**
Circ: CapCity orders: **22,000**
The Holy Terror, Part 1; Puck: Brothers in Arms, Part 1; Infinity Crusade **A:** Pat Broderick **W:** Simon Furman

123 ❑ Aug 1993 Cover: 1.75 **NM** value: **Cover or less**
Circ: CapCity orders: **23,200**
The Holy Terror, Part 2; Puck: Brothers in Arms, Part 2 **A:** Pat Broderick **W:** Simon Furman

124 ❑ Sep 1993 Cover: 1.75 **NM** value: **Cover or less**
Circ: CapCity orders: **19,100**
The Holy Terror, Part 3 • Infinity Crusade **A:** Pat Broderick **W:** Simon Furman

125 ❑ Oct 1993 Cover: 1.75 **NM** value: **Cover or less**
Circ: CapCity orders: **17,600**
W: Simon Furman

126 ❑ Nov 1993 Cover: 1.75 **NM** value: **Cover or less**
Circ: CapCity orders: **16,800**

127 ❑ Dec 1993 Cover: 1.75 **NM** value: **Cover or less**
Circ: CapCity orders: **15,700**

128 ❑ Jan 1994 Cover: 1.75 **NM** value: **Cover or less**
Circ: CapCity orders: **13,600**
No Future, Part 1

129 ❑ Feb 1994 Cover: 1.75 **NM** value: **Cover or less**
Circ: CapCity orders: **13,800**
No Future, Part 2

130 ❑ Mar 1994 Cover: 2.25 **NM** value: **Cover or less**
Circ: CapCity orders: **16,300**
No Future, Part 3 final issue.

Anl 1 ❑ Sep 1986 Cover: 1.25 **NM** value: **1.50**
Circ: CapCity orders: **27,400**

Anl 2 ❑ Dec 1987 Cover: 1.25 **NM** value: **Cover or less**
Circ: CapCity orders: **25,650**

SE 1 ❑ Jun 1992 Cover: 2.50 **NM** value: **2.95**
Circ: CapCity orders: **29,300**
No number on cover. Decisions Of Strength **A:** Michael Bair **W:** Fabian Nicieza ★ Appearance of Wolverine.

ALPHA FLIGHT: IN THE BEGINNING — Marvel

1 ❑ ca. 1997 Cover: 1.95 **NM** value: **Cover or less**
Circ: Diamd. preorders: **46,070**
No issue number. One-shot.

ALPHA FLIGHT SPECIAL — Marvel

This four-issue series reprints Alpha Flight #97-100, the "Final Option" storyline. In that story, Alpha Flight comes to the aid of an alien woman who was on the run from the Consortium, an intergalactic business conglomerate. The woman is J'Ridia Starduster, formerly the "Her" companion to Warlock, when he was simply known as "Him." (As What If Vol. 1 #34 postulates, their children would have been, "Them.") Anyway, she had offended the Consortium for helping a world in which it had business interests move from a "profitable" industrial state to a more placid agricultural economy. Now, the Consortium wants to punish her for the act, and will gladly destroy the city of Toronto if Alpha Flight insists on getting in its way.

1 ❑ Jul 1991 Cover: 1.50 **NM** value: **2.00**
Circ: CapCity orders: **9,100**
The Final Option; Decisions of Faith • Reprints Alpha Flight #97 **A:** Michael Bair **W:** Fabian Nicieza

2 ❑ Aug 1991 Cover: 1.50 **NM** value: **2.00**
Circ: CapCity orders: **6,000**
• Reprints Alpha Flight #98

3 ❑ Sep 1991 Cover: 1.50 **NM** value: **2.00**
Circ: CapCity orders: **5,900**
• Reprints Alpha Flight #99

4 ❑ Oct 1991 Cover: 2.00 **NM** value: **Cover or less**
Circ: CapCity orders: **5,500**
• Reprints Alpha Flight #100

Other grades: Multiply prices above by **1.5 for Mint • 2/3 for Very Fine • 1/3 for Fine • 1/5 for Very Good • 1/8 for Good**

ALPHA FLIGHT (VOL. 2) — Marvel

Alpha Flight, Canada's premier super-human strike force, was originally brought together under the auspices of a governmental organization, Department H, dedicated to the protection of the Canadian provinces and the planet Earth. Each member was recruited for the greater good of humanity, and to battle injustice and evil forces around the world.

In this late 1990s relaunch, something is amiss with the organization that founded them. Formerly plagued with insufficient funding which caused Alpha Flight to disband, Department H was now more stable and powerful, but it was harboring some deadly secrets. Would these secrets threaten the mission of Canada's greatest super-hero team?

Part of a spate of Marvel relaunches during its "bankruptcy period," this second series didn't get much chance to prove itself.

-1 ❑ Jul 1997 Cover: 1.99 **NM** value: **2.00**
• Wedding of James Hudson and Heather McNeil;"Flashback"

1 ❑ Aug 1997 Cover: 2.99 **NM** value: **3.00**
Circ: Diamd. preorders: **78,103** • **CGC:** 1 graded, best 9.0
wraparound cover. • gatefold summary. 🕮 Horoscope **A:** Scott Clark **W:** Steven Seagle

2 ❑ Sep 1997 Cover: 1.99 **NM** value: **2.00**
Circ: Diamd. preorders: **36,000**
"Presenting: The Master of Chaos" on cover. • gatefold summary. 🕮 The Fighting Masters **A:** Scott Clark **W:** Steven Seagle

2/A ❑ Sep 1997 Cover: 1.99 **NM** value: **2.00**
Circ: Diamd. preorders: **36,000**
alternate cover.

3 ❑ Oct 1997 Cover: 1.99 **NM** value: **2.00**
Circ: Diamd. preorders: **64,012**
• gatefold summary.

4 ❑ Nov 1997 Cover: 1.99 **NM** value: **2.00**
Circ: Diamd. preorders: **64,259**
• gatefold summary.

5 ❑ Dec 1997 Cover: 1.99 **NM** value: **2.00**
Circ: Diamd. preorders: **61,416**
• gatefold summary.

6 ❑ Jan 1998 Cover: 1.99 **NM** value: **Cover or less**
Circ: Diamd. preorders: **58,395**
• gatefold summary. ★ Origin of Sasquatch. ★ Appearance of Diamond Lil, Northstar.

7 ❑ Feb 1998 Cover: 1.99 **NM** value: **Cover or less**
Circ: Diamd. preorders: **52,485**
• gatefold summary.

8 ❑ Mar 1998 Cover: 1.99 **NM** value: **Cover or less**
Circ: Diamd. preorders: **49,314**
• gatefold summary.

9 ❑ Apr 1998 Cover: 1.99 **NM** value: **Cover or less**
Circ: Diamd. preorders: **55,150**
• gatefold summary. ★ Versus Wolverine.

10 ❑ May 1998 Cover: 1.99 **NM** value: **Cover or less**
Circ: Diamd. preorders: **44,625**
• gatefold summary.

11 ❑ Jun 1998 Cover: 1.99 **NM** value: **Cover or less**
Circ: Diamd. preorders: **45,099**
• gatefold summary.

12 ❑ Jul 1998 Cover: 2.99 **NM** value: **Cover or less**
Circ: Diamd. preorders: **44,137**
• gatefold summary. ★ Death of Sasquatch.

13 ❑ Aug 1998 Cover: 1.99 **NM** value: **Cover or less**
Circ: Diamd. preorders: **41,649**
• gatefold summary.

14 ❑ Sep 1998 Cover: 1.99 **NM** value: **Cover or less**
Circ: Diamd. preorders: **39,147**
• gatefold summary.

15 ❑ Oct 1998 Cover: 1.99 **NM** value: **Cover or less**
Circ: Diamd. preorders: **37,394**
• gatefold summary.

16 ❑ Nov 1998 Cover: 1.99 **NM** value: **Cover or less**
Circ: Diamd. preorders: **36,469**
• gatefold summary.

17 ❑ Dec 1998 Cover: 1.99 **NM** value: **Cover or less**
Circ: Diamd. preorders: **35,636**
• gatefold summary.

18 ❑ Jan 1999 Cover: 1.99 **NM** value: **Cover or less**
Circ: Diamd. preorders: **35,940**
• gatefold summary. 🕮 Alpha: Omega, Part 1 **A:** Rouleau **W:** Steven Seagle

19 ❑ Feb 1999 Cover: 1.99 **NM** value: **Cover or less**
Circ: Diamd. preorders: **33,506**
🕮 Alpha: Omega, Part 2 **A:** Rouleau **W:** Steven Seagle ★ Appearance of Old Alpha Flight team.

20 ❑ Mar 1999 Cover: 1.99 **NM** value: **Cover or less**
Circ: Diamd. preorders: **32,431**
🕮 Alpha: Omega, Part 3 final issue. **A:** Rouleau **W:** Steven Seagle ★ Appearance of Old Alpha Flight team, Weapon X.

Anl 1998❑ca. 1998 Cover: 3.50 **NM** value: **Cover or less**
Circ: Diamd. preorders: **29,164**
wraparound cover. • Alpha Flight/Inhumans '98

ALPHA ILLUSTRATED — Alpha Productions

0 ❑ Apr 1994, b&w **NM** value: **1.00**
• free; Preview

1 ❑ b&w Cover: 3.50 **NM** value: **Cover or less**

🕮 Time Travel Means Never Having to Say You're Sorry, Black Icon, Work in Progress, Arena, Only friends The Lone Star Tapes **A:** Scot Eaton; Dale Leroux; John Caponigro; Mark Usher; Milo & Otis; Rick Arthur; Johan Wanloo **W:** Dale Leroux; Milo & Otis; Rick Arthur; Chad Lewis; Pidde; Ron Fortier

ALPHA KORPS — Diversity

1 ❑ Sep 1996 Cover: 2.50 **NM** value: **Cover or less**

Ash 1❑ **NM** value: **1.00**
🕮 The Price of Freedom Part 1 • Preview issue **A:** Brent Evans **W:** Dave Chamberlain

ALPHA TEAM OMEGA — Fantasy Graphics

1 ❑ Cover: 1.25 **NM** value: **Cover or less**

ALPHA TRACK — Fantasy General

1 ❑ Feb 1985 Cover: 1.75 **NM** value: **Cover or less**

2 ❑ Cover: 1.75 **NM** value: **Cover or less**

ALPHA WAVE — Darkline

1 ❑ Cover: 1.75 **NM** value: **Cover or less**
Circ: CapCity orders: **2,075**

ALTERED IMAGE — Image

1 ❑ Apr 1998 Cover: 2.50 **NM** value: **Cover or less**
Circ: Diamd. preorders: **36,322**
🕮 The Day Reality Went Wild **A:** Jim Valentino **W:** Jim Valentino

2 ❑ Jun 1998 Cover: 2.50 **NM** value: **Cover or less**
Circ: Diamd. preorders: **24,451**
🕮 Everybody Smoosh **A:** Jim Valentino **W:** Jim Valentino

3 ❑ Oct 1998 Cover: 2.50 **NM** value: **Cover or less**
Circ: Diamd. preorders: **17,895**
cover says "Sep". 🕮 Middle Age Crisis • indicia says "Oct" **A:** Jim Valentino **W:** Jim Valentino

Bk 1❑ Cover: 9.95 **NM** value: **Cover or less**

ALTERED REALITIES — Altered Reality

1 ❑ Cover: 2.00 **NM** value: **Cover or less**
No issue number. 🕮 Funny Little Voices; Broken Donuts; Fat Boy Roy; Planet Hell; Existence X; Bruisa; Continuin' Ed; The Guy; American Hero **A:** Andy McDonald; Darrell Landa; Mike Mongello; Sal Cipriano; Brien Cordello **W:** Sal Cipriano; Anthony Collado; Darrel Landa

ALTER EGO — First

1 ❑ May 1986 Cover: 1.25 **NM** value: **1.50**
Circ: CapCity orders: **8,800**
🕮 Alter Ego Lives! **A:** Ron Harris **W:** Roy Thomas ★ 1st Appearance of Alter Ego.

2 ❑ Jul 1986 Cover: 1.25 **NM** value: **1.50**
Circ: CapCity orders: **6,675**

3 ❑ Sep 1986 Cover: 1.25 **NM** value: **1.50**
Circ: CapCity orders: **6,100**

4 ❑ Nov 1986 Cover: 1.25 **NM** value: **1.50**
Circ: CapCity orders: **5,300**

ALTERNATE HEROES — Prelude

1 ❑ Cover: 1.95 **NM** value: **Cover or less**
🕮 Initiations **A:** Hal Jones **W:** Hal Jones ★ 1st Appearance of The Equalizer, The Crimehater.

ALTERNATING CRIMES — Alternating Crimes Publishing

1 ❑ Fal 1996 Cover: 2.95 **NM** value: **Cover or less**

2 ❑ Fal 1997 Cover: 3.25 **NM** value: **Cover or less**

ALTERNATIVE COMICS — Revolutionary

1 ❑ Jan 1994 Cover: 2.50 **NM** value: **Cover or less**
• Pearl Jam/Cure/REM

ALTERNITY — Navigator

1 ❑ May 1992 Cover: 0.60 **NM** value: **2.50**

ALVAR MAYOR: DEATH AND SILVER — 4Winds

1 ❑ b&w Cover: 8.98 **NM** value: **Cover or less**

ALVIN — Dell

The stars of Alvin and the Chipmunks were the creation of Ross Bagdasarian (1919-1972, known as David Seville), who built one 1958 novelty record, "The Chipmunk Song," into an ongoing property, which included a 1961-62 prime-time TV series and eventual Saturday-morning cartoons. He had initially performed all the parts (three chipmunks and himself).

The comics and cartoon appearances were connected to the adventures of Seville and his attempts to cope with the lively Chipmunks, especially Alvin (who, on the initial record and those that followed) disrupted the smooth running of whatever project Seville had in mind. The comic-book version of their antics continued for several years. — Maggie

1 ❑ Oct 1962 Cover: 0.12 **NM** value: **35.00**
• 12-021-212

2 ❑ Jan 1963 Cover: 0.12 **NM** value: **25.00**
• 12-021-303

3 ❑ Apr 1963 Cover: 0.12 **NM** value: **18.00**
• 12-021-306

4 ❑ Jul 1963 Cover: 0.12 **NM** value: **18.00**
• 12-021-309

5 ❑ Oct 1963 Cover: 0.12 **NM** value: **18.00**
• 12-021-312

6 ❑ Jan 1964 Cover: 0.12 **NM** value: **18.00**
• 12-021-403

7 ❑ Apr 1964 Cover: 0.12 **NM** value: **18.00**
• 12-021-406

8 ❑ Jul 1964 Cover: 0.12 **NM** value: **18.00**
• **CGC:** 1 graded, best 9.0
• 12-021-409

9 ❑ Oct 1964 Cover: 0.12 **NM** value: **18.00**
• 12-021-412

10 ❑ Jan 1965 Cover: 0.12 **NM** value: **18.00**

11 ❑ Apr 1965 Cover: 0.12 **NM** value: **14.00**

12 ❑ Jul 1965 Cover: 0.12 **NM** value: **14.00**

13 ❑ 1965 Cover: 0.12 **NM** value: **14.00**

14 ❑ 1966 Cover: 0.12 **NM** value: **14.00**

15 ❑ 1966 Cover: 0.12 **NM** value: **14.00**

16 ❑ 1966 Cover: 0.12 **NM** value: **14.00**

17 ❑ 1966 Cover: 0.12 **NM** value: **14.00**

18 ❑ Mar 1967 Cover: 0.12 **NM** value: **14.00**

19 ❑ Cover: 0.12 **NM** value: **14.00**

20 ❑ Oct 1969 Cover: 0.15 **NM** value: **14.00**

21 ❑ Oct 1970 Cover: 0.15 **NM** value: **10.00**

22 ❑ 1971 Cover: 0.15 **NM** value: **10.00**

23 ❑ Jan 1972 Cover: 0.15 **NM** value: **10.00**
• 01-021-201

24 ❑ Apr 1972 Cover: 0.15 **NM** value: **10.00**
• 01-021-204

25 ❑ **NM** value: **10.00**

26 ❑ **NM** value: **10.00**

27 ❑ Jul 1973 Cover: 0.20 **NM** value: **10.00**
• **CGC:** 1 graded, best 9.6

28 ❑ Oct 1973 Cover: 0.20 **NM** value: **10.00**
• **CGC:** 1 graded, best 9.2

ALVIN AND THE CHIPMUNKS — Harvey

1 ❑ Cover: 1.25 **NM** value: **1.50**

2 ❑ Cover: 1.50 **NM** value: **Cover or less**

3 ❑ Cover: 1.50 **NM** value: **Cover or less**

4 ❑ Cover: 1.50 **NM** value: **Cover or less**

5 ❑ Cover: 1.50 **NM** value: **Cover or less**

AMALGAM AGE OF COMICS, THE: THE DC COMICS COLLECTION — Amalgam

1 ❑ Cover: 12.95 **NM** value: **Cover or less**
A: Dave Gibbons; John Byrne; Howard Porter; Jim Balent; Scott McDaniel; Jose Luis Garcia-Lopez **W:** Dave Gibbons; John Byrne; Larry Hama; D.G. Chichester; Gerard Jones; Mark Waid; Ron Marz

AMANDA AND GUNN — Image

1 ❑ Apr 1997, b&w Cover: 2.95 **NM** value: **Cover or less**
Circ: Diamd. preorders: **10,354**
A: Jimmie Robinson **W:** Jimmie Robinson

2 ❑ Jun 1997, b&w Cover: 2.95 **NM** value: **Cover or less**
Circ: Diamd. preorders: **6,582**
A: Jimmie Robinson **W:** Jimmie Robinson

3 ❑ Aug 1997, b&w Cover: 2.95 **NM** value: **Cover or less**
Circ: Diamd. preorders: **4,463**
A: Jimmie Robinson **W:** Jimmie Robinson

4 ❑ Oct 1997, b&w Cover: 2.95 **NM** value: **Cover or less**
A: Jimmie Robinson **W:** Jimmie Robinson

AMAZING ADULT FANTASY — Marvel

The series changed title twice and is best-remembered for its final issue under an evolved title. Under any name, it was introduced by Editor Stan Lee as an anthology series of fantasy stories. It began as Amazing Adventures. Then, it was Amazing Adult Fantasy, probably as an attempt to reach older consumers. But the last issue of Amazing Adult fantasy preceded a historic key comic book of the Silver Age.

Following Amazing Adult Fantasy #14, the series' final issue, #15, was retitled simply Amazing Fantasy. That was, of course, the comic book that introduced Stan Lee and Steve Ditko's Amazing Spider-Man to comics fans. — Maggie

7 ❑ Dec 1961 Cover: 0.12 **NM** value: **600.00**
• **CGC:** 4 graded, best 8.5
🕮 Why Won't They Believe Me?; The Last Man on Earth; Witch Hunt; Journey's End; The Icy Fingers Of Fear • Series continued from Amazing Adventures #6 **A:** Steve Ditko **W:** Stan Lee

8 ❑ Jan 1962 Cover: 0.12 **NM** value: **475.00**
• **CGC:** 2 graded, best 2.0
🕮 The Coming of the Krills; Everyone Likes a Ghost Story; The Eyes of Edward Morgo; The Yo-Yo; A Monster Among Us **A:** Steve Ditko **W:** Stan Lee

9 ❑ Feb 1962 Cover: 0.12 **NM** value: **425.00**
• **CGC:** 1 graded, best 8.0
🕮 The Terror of Tim Boo Ba; The Man Who Captured Death; I Came From the Black Void; The Spirit of Swami River; The Genie Lives **A:** Steve Ditko **W:** Stan Lee

10 ❑ Mar 1962 Cover: 0.12 **NM** value: **425.00**
• **CGC:** 2 graded, best 8.5
🕮 Those Who Change; The Mark of the Toad; No Sign of Life; Man on a Tightrope; Mister Universe **A:** Steve Ditko **W:** Stan Lee

11 ❑ Apr 1962 Cover: 0.12 **NM** value: **425.00**
• **CGC:** 3 graded, best 8.5
🕮 In Human Form; For The Rest Of Your Life; Secret Of The Universe; The Ice-Monster Cometh; Where Walks the Ghost **A:** Steve Ditko **W:** Stan Lee

CGC-graded: Multiply prices above by **33 for 9.9 M • 16 for 9.8 NM/M • 7 for 9.6 NM+ • 5 for 9.4 NM • 2.5 for 9.2 NM- • 1.5 for 9.0 VF/NM**

12 ❑ May 1962 Cover: 0.12 **NM** value: **425.00**
• **CGC:** 5 graded, best 8.0
📖 Melvin and the Martian; I, the Gargoyle; Something Fantastic?; The Plague; The Living Statues **A:** Steve Ditko **W:** Stan Lee

13 ❑ Jun 1962 Cover: 0.12 **NM** value: **425.00**
• **CGC:** 4 graded, best 9.0
📖 The Unsuspecting; Great Zeus; The Little Gypsy Tea Room; The Ultimate Weapon; At The Stroke of Midnight **A:** Steve Ditko **W:** Stan Lee

13-2❑ Cover: 0.12 **NM** value: **2.00**

14 ❑ Jul 1962 Cover: 0.12 **NM** value: **525.00**
• **CGC:** 1 graded, best 5.0
📖 Beware the Giants!; The Man in the Sky; What Happened in the Wax Museum; Footsteps at Midnight; Ozarr, the Mighty • series continues as Amazing Fantasy;Professor X prototype;Series continued in Amazing Fantasy #15 **A:** Steve Ditko

AMAZING ADVENTURE — Marvel

1 ❑ Jul 1988 Cover: 4.95 **NM** value: **Cover or less**
Circ: CapCity orders: **7,700**
📖 Solo; Men of Peace; Spies; Pogrom; The Turtle; In the Dark Ages; Ahhh…Christmas • squarebound **A:** John Ridgway; Michael Golden; Val Mayerik; Mike Vosburg; Rick Veitch; Larry Stroman; Huw Thomas **W:** Mike Vosburg; Mike Baron; Bill Mantlo; Chris Claremont; J.M. DeMatteis; Steve Perry

AMAZING ADVENTURE FUNNIES — Centaur

1 ❑ **NM** value: **1200.00**
• **CGC:** 1 graded, best 9.0

2 ❑ **NM** value: **750.00**

AMAZING ADVENTURES (1ST SERIES) — Ziff-Davis

1 ❑ Nov 1950 Cover: 0.10 **NM** value: **1000.00**
• **CGC:** 10 graded, best 8.5

2 ❑ Feb 1951 Cover: 0.10 **NM** value: **600.00**
• **CGC:** 3 graded, best 9.4

3 ❑ Apr 1951 Cover: 0.10 **NM** value: **450.00**

4 ❑ Jul 1951 Cover: 0.10 **NM** value: **450.00**
• **CGC:** 3 graded, best 9.2

5 ❑ Oct 1951 Cover: 0.10 **NM** value: **450.00**
• **CGC:** 1 graded, best 9.0

6 ❑ Fal 1952 Cover: 0.10 **NM** value: **450.00**
• **CGC:** 2 graded, best 9.0

AMAZING ADVENTURES (2ND SERIES) — Marvel

1 ❑ Jun 1961 Cover: 0.10 **NM** value: **850.00**
• **CGC:** 9 graded, best 8.0
📖 Torr; Midnight in the Wax Museum; I Am the Fantastic Doctor Droom • 1st appearance/origin Dr. Droom (first Marvel Silver Age superhero) **A:** Steve Ditko **W:** Stan Lee ★ Origin of Doctor Droom. ★ Appearance of Doctor Droom.

2 ❑ Jul 1961 Cover: 0.10 **NM** value: **500.00**
📖 I Led the Search for Manoo; The Secret of Manoo; The World Below; Rocky's Last Ride • Dr. Droom **A:** Steve Ditko **W:** Stan Lee ★ Appearance of Doctor Droom.

3 ❑ Aug 1961 Cover: 0.10 **NM** value: **400.00**
📖 We Were Trapped in the Twilight World; Trapped in the Twilight World; The Teddy Bear; Doctor Droom Meets Zemu • Dr. Droom **A:** Steve Ditko **W:** Stan Lee ★ Appearance of Doctor Droom.

4 ❑ Sep 1961 Cover: 0.10 **NM** value: **400.00**
• **CGC:** 1 graded, best 7.0
📖 I am Robot X; Who or What Was the Bootblack?; What Lurks Within? **A:** Steve Ditko **W:** Stan Lee ★ Appearance of Doctor Droom.

5 ❑ Oct 1961 Cover: 0.10 **NM** value: **400.00**
• **CGC:** 1 graded, best 9.2
📖 The Escape of Monsteroso!; Monsteroso; The Watchers; The Joker **A:** Steve Ditko **W:** Stan Lee ★ Appearance of Doctor Droom.

6 ❑ Nov 1961 Cover: 0.10 **NM** value: **400.00**
• **CGC:** 1 graded, best 4.0
📖 Sserpo, the Creature Who Crushed the Earth; The Fourth Man; Krogg • series continues as Amazing Adult Fantasy;Series continued in Amazing Adult Fantasy #7 **A:** Steve Ditko **W:** Stan Lee ★ Appearance of Doctor Droom.

AMAZING ADVENTURES (3RD SERIES) — Marvel

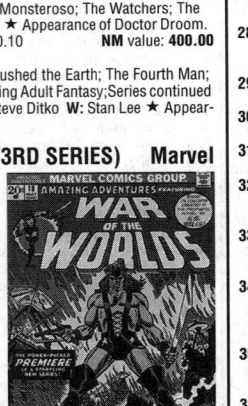

Amazing Adventures started as a double-feature starring The Inhumans and Black Widow. Later, the Beast and the X-Men were featured in their own monthly stories — having been out of circulation since their own series went reprints-only. The most famous issue of the series, #11, features the accident that turns Beast blue and furry. He's a lot more interesting this way.

Beginning with issue #18, Amazing Adventures switched formats, beginning a futuristic War of the Worlds storyline. The story takes place in a future where H.G. Wells' Martian invaders have taken over Earth and the remaining humans are kept as slaves, their society being driven back to a feudal state. Out of this wreckage, a new hero, Killraven, rises to lead humans in a war to reclaim their planet.

1 ❑ Aug 1970 Cover: 0.15 **NM** value: **22.00**
• **CGC:** 17 graded, best 9.6
📖 The Inhumans; Then Came…The Black Widow • Inhumans **A:** John Buscema; Jack Kirby **W:** Jack Kirby; Gary Friedrich

2 ❑ Sep 1970 Cover: 0.15 **NM** value: **12.00**
• **CGC:** 4 graded, best 9.4
📖 Friend Against Friend • Inhumans

3 ❑ Nov 1970 Cover: 0.15 **NM** value: **12.00**
• **CGC:** 3 graded, best 9.4
📖 Pawns of the Mandarin • Black Widow; Inhumans

4 ❑ Jan 1971 Cover: 0.15 **NM** value: **12.00**
• **CGC:** 5 graded, best 9.6
📖 With These Rings, I Thee Kill • Black Widow;Inhumans

5 ❑ Mar 1971 Cover: 0.15 **NM** value: **12.00**
• **CGC:** 10 graded, best 9.8
A: Neal Adams

6 ❑ May 1971 Cover: 0.15 **NM** value: **9.00**
• **CGC:** 5 graded, best 9.4
📖 Hell on Earth!; Blood Will Tell! • Inhumans, Black Widow **A:** Sal Buscema; Don Heck; Neal Adams **W:** Roy Thomas

7 ❑ Jul 1971 Cover: 0.15 **NM** value: **9.00**
• **CGC:** 7 graded, best 9.8
• Inhumans, Black Widow **A:** Neal Adams

8 ❑ Sep 1971 Cover: 0.15 **NM** value: **9.00**
• **CGC:** 4 graded, best 9.6
• Inhumans, Black Widow **A:** Neal Adams

9 ❑ Nov 1971 Cover: 0.20 **NM** value: **9.00**
★ Appearance of Black Bolt.

10 ❑ Jan 1972 Cover: 0.20 **NM** value: **9.00**
📖 The Origin of the Incomparable Inhumans • Inhumans; Reprinted from Thor #146

11 ❑ Mar 1972 Cover: 0.20 **NM** value: **35.00**
• **CGC:** 29 graded, best 9.8
★ Origin of Beast (in furry form). ★ 1st Appearance of Beast (in furry form).

12 ❑ May 1972 Cover: 0.20 **NM** value: **10.00**
• **CGC:** 5 graded, best 9.4
• Iron Man★ Appearance of Beast.

13 ❑ Jul 1972 Cover: 0.20 **NM** value: **10.00**
• **CGC:** 3 graded, best 9.4
★ 1st Appearance of Robert "Buzz" Baxter.

14 ❑ Sep 1972 Cover: 0.20 **NM** value: **9.00**
• **CGC:** 3 graded, best 9.6

15 ❑ Nov 1972 Cover: 0.20 **NM** value: **9.00**
• **CGC:** 1 graded, best 9.0
★ Origin of Griffin. ★ 1st Appearance of Griffin.

16 ❑ Jan 1973 Cover: 0.20 **NM** value: **9.00**
• **CGC:** 1 graded, best 9.2

17 ❑ Mar 1973 Cover: 0.20 **NM** value: **9.00**
• **CGC:** 2 graded, best 8.5

18 ❑ May 1973 Cover: 0.20 **NM** value: **8.00**
• **CGC:** 4 graded, best 9.0
📖 War of the Worlds **A:** Howard Chaykin; Neal Adams **W:** Gerry Conway ★ Origin of Killraven. ★ 1st Appearance of Killraven.

19 ❑ Jul 1973 Cover: 0.20 **NM** value: **3.00**
📖 War of the Worlds • Killraven

20 ❑ Sep 1973 Cover: 0.20 **NM** value: **3.00**
📖 War of the Worlds; The Warlord Strikes! • Killraven **A:** Herb Trimpe **W:** Marv Wolfman

21 ❑ Nov 1973 Cover: 0.20 **NM** value: **3.00**
📖 War of the Worlds • Killraven

22 ❑ Jan 1974 Cover: 0.20 **NM** value: **3.00**
📖 War of the Worlds • Killraven

23 ❑ Mar 1974 Cover: 0.20 **NM** value: **3.00**
📖 War of the Worlds • Killraven

24 ❑ May 1974 Cover: 0.25 **NM** value: **3.00**
📖 War of the Worlds; The Painting • Killraven;Marvel Value Stamp A/58 (The Mandarin) **A:** Herb Trimpe **W:** Don McGregor ★ Versus High Overlord.

25 ❑ Jul 1974 Cover: 0.25 **NM** value: **3.00**
📖 War of the Worlds • Killraven★ Versus Skar.

26 ❑ Sep 1974 Cover: 0.25 **NM** value: **3.00**
📖 War of the Worlds • Killraven **A:** Gene Colan

27 ❑ Nov 1974 Cover: 0.25 **NM** value: **3.00**
📖 War of the Worlds • Killraven **A:** Jim Starlin; P. Craig Russell; Joe Sinnott; PCR ★ Origin of Killraven.

28 ❑ Jan 1975 Cover: 0.25 **NM** value: **3.00**
📖 War of the Worlds • Killraven **A:** P. Craig Russell; PCR ★ Origin of Volcana.

29 ❑ Mar 1975 Cover: 0.25 **NM** value: **3.00**
📖 War of the Worlds • Killraven **A:** P. Craig Russell; PCR

30 ❑ May 1975 Cover: 0.25 **NM** value: **3.00**
📖 War of the Worlds • Killraven **A:** P. Craig Russell; PCR

31 ❑ Jul 1975 Cover: 0.25 **NM** value: **3.00**
📖 War of the Worlds • Killraven **A:** P. Craig Russell; PCR

32 ❑ Sep 1975 Cover: 0.25 **NM** value: **3.00**
📖 Only The Computer Shows Me Respect! • Killraven **A:** P. Craig Russell; PCR **W:** Don McGregor

33 ❑ Nov 1975 Cover: 0.25 **NM** value: **3.00**
📖 Sing Out Loudly…Death! • Killraven;Marvel Value Stamp A/52 (Quicksilver) **A:** Herb Trimpe; P. Craig Russell; PCR **W:** Bill Mantlo

34 ❑ Jan 1976 Cover: 0.25 **NM** value: **3.00**
📖 A Death In The Family • Killraven;Marvel Value Stamp B/10 **A:** P. Craig Russell; PCR **W:** Don McGregor ★ Death of Hawk. ★ Death of Grok.

35 ❑ Mar 1976 Cover: 0.25 **NM** value: **3.00**
📖 The 24-Hour Man • Killraven **A:** Keith Giffen; P. Craig Russell; Jack Abel; PCR **W:** Don McGregor

36 ❑ May 1976 Cover: 0.25 **NM** value: **3.00**
📖 Red Dust Legacy • Killraven **A:** P. Craig Russell; Sonny Trinidad; PCR **W:** Don McGregor

37 ❑ Jul 1976 Cover: 0.25 **NM** value: **3.00**
📖 Arena Kill! **A:** P. Craig Russell; PCR **W:** Don McGregor ★ Origin of Old Skull.

38 ❑ Sep 1976 Cover: 0.30 **NM** value: **3.00**
📖 Death's Dark Dreamer • Killraven **A:** Keith Giffen; P. Craig Russell; PCR **W:** Don McGregor

39 ❑ Nov 1976 Cover: 0.30 **NM** value: **3.00**
📖 Mourning Prey final issue. • Killraven **A:** P. Craig Russell; PCR **W:** Don McGregor

AMAZING ADVENTURES (4TH SERIES) — Marvel

1 ❑ Dec 1979 Cover: 0.40 **NM** value: **2.50**
• **CGC:** 1 graded, best 7.0
📖 X-Men; A Man Called X • Reprints first part of X-Men (1st Series) #1; 2nd story reprinted from X-Men 1st series) #38 **A:** Jack Kirby **W:** Stan Lee ★ 1st Appearance of the X-Men.

2 ❑ Jan 1980 Cover: 0.40 **NM** value: **1.75**
📖 When Mutants Clash; Lonely Are the Hunted • Reprints second half of X-Men (1st Series) #1; 2nd story reprinted from X-Men (1st Series) #39 **A:** Jack Kirby **W:** Stan Lee ★ Origin of Cyclops.

3 ❑ Feb 1980 Cover: 0.40 **NM** value: **1.75**
📖 No One Can Stop the Vanisher; The First Evil Mutant • Reprinted from X-Men (first series) #2; 2nd story reprinted from X-Men (1st Series) #40

4 ❑ Mar 1980 Cover: 0.40 **NM** value: **1.75**
📖 The Gentleman Vanishes; The Living Diamond • Reprinted from X-Men (first series) #2, retitled from "No One Can Stop the Vanisher"; 2nd story reprinted from X-Men (1st Series) #41

5 ❑ Apr 1980 Cover: 0.40 **NM** value: **1.75**
📖 Beware, the Blob; The End, or the Beginning? • Reprinted from X-Men (first series) #3; 2nd story reprinted from X-Men (1st Series) #42

6 ❑ May 1980 Cover: 0.40 **NM** value: **1.75**
📖 Carnival of Death; Call Him Cyclops • Reprinted from X-Men (first series) #3, retitled from "Beware, the Blob"; 2nd story reprinted from X-Men (1st Series) #43

7 ❑ Jun 1980 Cover: 0.40 **NM** value: **1.75**
📖 The Brotherhood of Evil Mutants; The Iceman Cometh • Reprinted from X-Men (first series) #4; 2nd story reprinted from X-Men (1st Series) #44

8 ❑ Jul 1980 Cover: 0.40 **NM** value: **1.75**
📖 Assault of Fortress Magneto; And the Mob Cried, Vengeance! • Reprinted from X-Men (first series) #4, retitled from "The Brotherhood of Evil Mutants"; 2nd story reprinted from X-Men (1st Series) #45

9 ❑ Aug 1980 Cover: 0.40 **NM** value: **1.75**
📖 To Fight Alone; And Then There Were Two • Reprinted from X-Men (first series) #5, retitled from "Trapped: One X-Man"; 2nd story reprinted from X-Men (1st Series) #46

10 ❑ Sep 1980 **NM** value: **1.75**
📖 Trapped: One X-Man; I, the Iceman • Reprinted from X-Men (first series) #5; 2nd story reprinted from X-Men (1st Series) #47

11 ❑ Oct 1980 Cover: 0.50 **NM** value: **1.75**
📖 Search for the Sub-Mariner; Yours Truly, the Beast • Reprinted from X-Men (first series) #6; 2nd story reprinted from X-Men (1st Series) #48

12 ❑ Nov 1980 Cover: 0.50 **NM** value: **1.75**
📖 To Join the Evil Mutants; Today Earth Died • Reprinted from X-Men (first series) #6, retitled from "Search for the Sub-Mariner"; 2nd story reprinted from Strange Tales #168

13 ❑ Dec 1980 Cover: 0.50 **NM** value: **1.75**
📖 The Return of the Blob • Reprinted from X-Men (first series) #7

14 ❑ Jan 1981 Cover: 0.50 **NM** value: **1.75**
📖 Unas, the Untouchable final issue. • Reprinted from X-Men (first series) #8

AMAZING ADVENTURES OF ACE INTERNATIONAL, THE — Starhead

1 ❑ Nov 1993, b&w Cover: 2.95 **NM** value: **Cover or less**

AMAZING ADVENTURES OF FRANK AND JOLLY (ALAN GROENING'S…) — Press This

1 ❑ Cover: 1.75 **NM** value: **Cover or less**
A: Alan Groening **W:** Alan Groening

2 ❑ Cover: 1.75 **NM** value: **Cover or less**
A: Alan Groening **W:** Alan Groening

3 ❑ Cover: 1.75 **NM** value: **Cover or less**
A: Alan Groening **W:** Alan Groening

4 ❑ Cover: 1.75 **NM** value: **Cover or less**
A: Alan Groening **W:** Alan Groening

5 ❑ Cover: 1.75 **NM** value: **Cover or less**
A: Alan Groening **W:** Alan Groening

6 ❑ Cover: 1.75 **NM** value: **Cover or less**
A: Alan Groening **W:** Alan Groening

7 ❑ Cover: 1.75 **NM** value: **Cover or less**
A: Alan Groening **W:** Alan Groening

8 ❑ Cover: 1.75 **NM** value: **Cover or less**
A: Alan Groening **W:** Alan Groening

9 ❑ Cover: 1.75 **NM** value: **Cover or less**
A: Alan Groening **W:** Alan Groening

AMAZING ADVENTURES OF PROFESSOR JONES, THE — Antarctic

1 ❑ Nov 1996 Cover: 2.95 **NM** value: **Cover or less**
A: Kazuaki Ishida **W:** Kazuaki Ishida

2 ❑ Dec 1996 Cover: 2.95 **NM** value: **Cover or less**
A: Kazuaki Ishida **W:** Kazuaki Ishida

3 ❑ Cover: 2.95 **NM** value: **Cover or less**
A: Kazuaki Ishida **W:** Kazuaki Ishida

4 ❑ Cover: 2.95 **NM** value: **Cover or less**
A: Kazuaki Ishida **W:** Kazuaki Ishida

AMAZING CHAN AND THE CHAN CLAN — Gold Key

Who would have taken the Chinese detective of Earl Derr Biggers (1884-1933) — who received no help from his children in those mystery novels, by the way — added 10 kids, and turned him into an animated show for kids? Hanna-Barbera, of course. What company would license the property? Western's Gold Key imprint, of course. The show started in 1972, and the comic book had four issues.

The animated series, like many of Hanna-Barbera's of the era, utilized such limited animation that the musical numbers simply had the kids in the band swaying back and forth in some sort of rhythm that wasn't even close to the beat of the song

Other grades: Multiply prices above by **1.5 for Mint • 2/3 for Very Fine • 1/3 for Fine • 1/5 for Very Good • 1/8 for Good**

they were performing. Even their super-intelligent father had trouble keeping the beat. In some ways, the comic book, even without the music and voices, was more animated since it wasn't limited to certain stock shots. — Maggie

1 ❑ May 1973 Cover: 0.20 **NM** value: **15.00**
• **CGC:** 1 graded, best 9.0
2 ❑ Aug 1973 Cover: 0.20 **NM** value: **10.00**
3 ❑ Nov 1973 Cover: 0.20 **NM** value: **10.00**
4 ❑ Feb 1974 Cover: 0.20 **NM** value: **10.00**

AMAZING COMICS — Timely

1 ❑ Fal 1944 Cover: 0.10 **NM** value: **1250.00**
• **CGC:** 6 graded, best 9.4

AMAZING COMICS — Avalon

1 ❑ b&w Cover: 2.95 **NM** value: **Cover or less**
• reprints Terry and the Pirates newspaper strips
2 ❑ b&w Cover: 2.95 **NM** value: **Cover or less**
Terry and the Pirates; No Bumbs or Bullets … Just a Prayer; No Bumbs of Bullets…Justa Prayer • reprints Terry and the Pirates newspaper strips **A:** Milton Caniff **W:** Milton Caniff
3 ❑ b&w Cover: 2.95 **NM** value: **Cover or less**
The Dragon Lady • reprints Terry and the Pirates newspaper strips **A:** Milton Caniff **W:** Milton Caniff

AMAZING COMICS PREMIERES — Amazing

1 ❑ 1987 Cover: 1.95 **NM** value: **Cover or less**
Ninja Bots **A:** Kevin Van Hook **W:** Roger McKenzie
2 ❑ 1987 Cover: 1.95 **NM** value: **Cover or less**
3 ❑ 1987 Cover: 1.95 **NM** value: **Cover or less**
Shadowalker **A:** Kevin Farrell **W:** Dennis J. Pimple
4 ❑ Jul 1987 Cover: 1.95 **NM** value: **Cover or less**
A: Sam Kieth
5 ❑ 1987 Cover: 1.95 **NM** value: **Cover or less**
• Stargrazers

AMAZING CYNICALMAN, THE — Eclipse

1 ❑ b&w Cover: 1.50 **NM** value: **2.50**
A: Matt Feazell **W:** Matt Feazell

AMAZING DETECTIVE CASES — Atlas

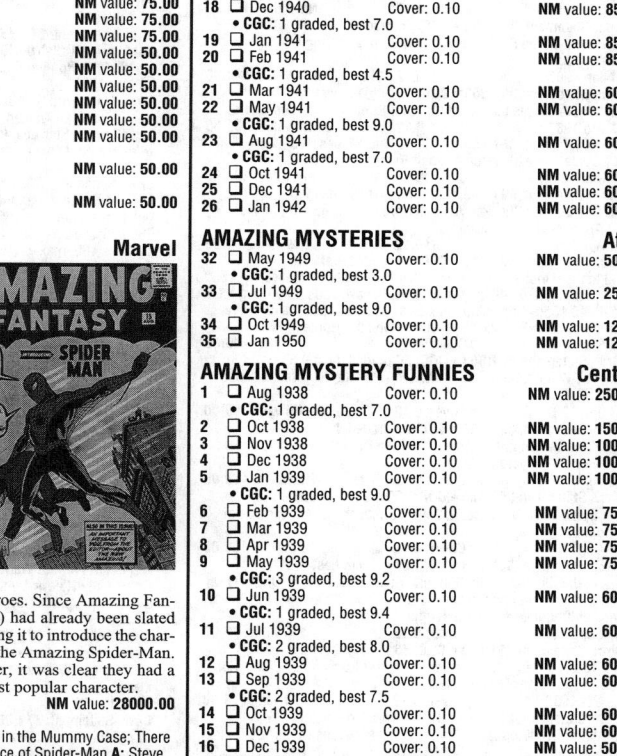

3 ❑ Nov 1950 Cover: 0.10 **NM** value: **150.00**
4 ❑ Jan 1951 Cover: 0.10 **NM** value: **75.00**
5 ❑ Mar 1951 Cover: 0.10 **NM** value: **75.00**
6 ❑ May 1951 Cover: 0.10 **NM** value: **75.00**
7 ❑ Jul 1951 Cover: 0.10 **NM** value: **50.00**
8 ❑ Sep 1951 Cover: 0.10 **NM** value: **50.00**
9 ❑ Nov 1951 Cover: 0.10 **NM** value: **50.00**
10 ❑ Jan 1951 Cover: 0.10 **NM** value: **50.00**
11 ❑ Mar 1952 Cover: 0.10 **NM** value: **50.00**
12 ❑ May 1952 Cover: 0.10 **NM** value: **50.00**
• **CGC:** 2 graded, best 8.5
13 ❑ Jul 1952 Cover: 0.10 **NM** value: **50.00**
• **CGC:** 2 graded, best 8.0
14 ❑ Sep 1952 Cover: 0.10 **NM** value: **50.00**
• **CGC:** 1 graded, best 8.5

AMAZING FANTASY — Marvel

During the '50s, Marvel was largely a publisher of monster and science-fiction stories. Super-heroes had largely been a phenomenon of World War II years and had since fallen into disuse. The early '60s saw them beginning to make a comeback. Companies began mass-producing gimmick super-heroes based on animals: apes, cheetahs, flies — whatever hadn't been done already.

In 1961, Stan Lee and Steve Ditko decided to make the company's next super-hero a shy teen who lived with his aunt and was targeted by bullies at school. They figured that readers would identify more with such a character than with stereotypically perfect heroes. Since Amazing Fantasy (formerly Amazing Adult Fantasy) had already been slated for cancellation, there was no risk in using it to introduce the character. That character was Peter Parker, the Amazing Spider-Man. When sales results came in months later, it was clear they had a hit. Today, Spider-Man is Marvel's most popular character.

15 ❑ Aug 1962 Cover: 0.12 **NM** value: **28000.00**
• **CGC:** 155 graded, best 9.6
Spider-Man!; The Bell-Ringer; Man in the Mummy Case; There are Martians Among Us • 1st appearance of Spider-Man **A:** Steve Ditko; Jack Kirby; Jack Kirby(cover) **W:** Steve Ditko; Stan Lee ★ Origin of Spider-Man. ★ 1st Appearance of Spider-Man.
16 ❑ Dec 1995 Cover: 3.95 **NM** value: **4.50**
• **CGC:** 2 graded, best 9.6
cardstock cover. An Amazing World • fills in gaps between Amazing Fantasy #15 and Amazing Spider-Man #1 **A:** Paul Lee **W:** Kurt Busiek
17 ❑ Jan 1996 Cover: 3.95 **NM** value: **4.00**
cardstock cover. Amazing Adventures **A:** Paul Lee; Alexi Taylor; Greg Loudon; Ken Myers Jr.; Terese Nielsen **W:** Kurt Busiek
18 ❑ Mar 1996 Cover: 3.95 **NM** value: **4.00**
cardstock cover. The Amazing Spider-Man final issue. **A:** Paul Lee; Richard Starkings **W:** Kurt Busiek

AMAZING HEROES SWIMSUIT SPECIAL — Fantagraphics

4 ❑ Mar 1993 Cover: 3.95 **NM** value: **Cover or less**
• published by Spoof Comics
5 ❑ Aug 1993 Cover: 4.95 **NM** value: **Cover or less**
• published by Spoof Comics **A:** Joseph Michael Linsner(cover)

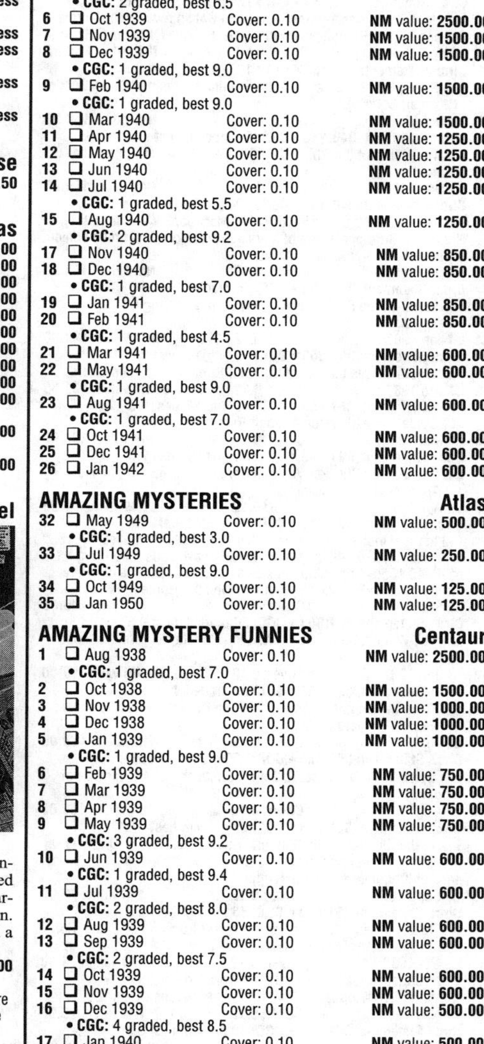

Anl 1990❑Jun 1990 Cover: 5.95 **NM** value: **7.00**
• **CGC:** 1 graded, best 9.4
Anl 1991❑Jun 1991 Cover: 6.95 **NM** value: **10.00**
Anl 1992❑Jun 1992 Cover: 7.95 **NM** value: **15.00**
A: Joseph Michael Linsner

AMAZING HIGH ADVENTURE — Marvel

1 ❑ Aug 1984 Cover: 2.00 **NM** value: **Cover or less**
The Pike!; Gold; Ambrose A. Abernathy's Amazing Adventure Apparatus; Death Stroke **A:** John Severin; Tony Salmons; Steve Leialoha **W:** Louise Simonson; Ann Nocenti; Steve Englehart
2 ❑ Sep 1985 Cover: 2.00 **NM** value: **Cover or less**
Circ: CapCity orders: **6,350**
A: Alan Weiss; Paul Smith; Gerry Talaoc; Topham Hayes **W:** Alan Weiss; Eliot Brown; Ann Nocenti; James Owsley; Steve Englehart
3 ❑ Oct 1986 Cover: 2.00 **NM** value: **Cover or less**
Circ: CapCity orders: **5,650**
4 ❑ Nov 1986 Cover: 2.00 **NM** value: **Cover or less**
Circ: CapCity orders: **5,550**
5 ❑ Dec 1986 Cover: 2.00 **NM** value: **Cover or less**
Circ: CapCity orders: **5,050**

AMAZING-MAN COMICS — Centaur

5 ❑ Sep 1939 Cover: 0.10 **NM** value: **12000.00**
• **CGC:** 1 graded, best 2.5
16 ❑ Oct 1940 Cover: 0.10 **NM** value: **850.00**
• **CGC:** 2 graded, best 6.5
6 ❑ Oct 1939 Cover: 0.10 **NM** value: **2500.00**
7 ❑ Nov 1939 Cover: 0.10 **NM** value: **1500.00**
8 ❑ Dec 1939 Cover: 0.10 **NM** value: **1500.00**
• **CGC:** 1 graded, best 9.0
9 ❑ Feb 1940 Cover: 0.10 **NM** value: **1500.00**
• **CGC:** 1 graded, best 9.0
10 ❑ Mar 1940 Cover: 0.10 **NM** value: **1500.00**
11 ❑ Apr 1940 Cover: 0.10 **NM** value: **1250.00**
12 ❑ May 1940 Cover: 0.10 **NM** value: **1250.00**
13 ❑ Jun 1940 Cover: 0.10 **NM** value: **1250.00**
14 ❑ Jul 1940 Cover: 0.10 **NM** value: **1250.00**
• **CGC:** 1 graded, best 5.5
15 ❑ Aug 1940 Cover: 0.10 **NM** value: **1250.00**
• **CGC:** 2 graded, best 9.2
17 ❑ Nov 1940 Cover: 0.10 **NM** value: **850.00**
18 ❑ Dec 1940 Cover: 0.10 **NM** value: **850.00**
• **CGC:** 1 graded, best 7.0
19 ❑ Jan 1941 Cover: 0.10 **NM** value: **850.00**
20 ❑ Feb 1941 Cover: 0.10 **NM** value: **850.00**
• **CGC:** 1 graded, best 4.5
21 ❑ Mar 1941 Cover: 0.10 **NM** value: **600.00**
22 ❑ May 1941 Cover: 0.10 **NM** value: **600.00**
• **CGC:** 1 graded, best 9.0
23 ❑ Aug 1941 Cover: 0.10 **NM** value: **600.00**
• **CGC:** 1 graded, best 7.0
24 ❑ Oct 1941 Cover: 0.10 **NM** value: **600.00**
25 ❑ Dec 1941 Cover: 0.10 **NM** value: **600.00**
26 ❑ Jan 1942 Cover: 0.10 **NM** value: **600.00**

AMAZING MYSTERIES — Atlas

32 ❑ May 1949 Cover: 0.10 **NM** value: **500.00**
• **CGC:** 1 graded, best 3.0
33 ❑ Jul 1949 Cover: 0.10 **NM** value: **250.00**
• **CGC:** 1 graded, best 9.0
34 ❑ Oct 1949 Cover: 0.10 **NM** value: **125.00**
35 ❑ Jan 1950 Cover: 0.10 **NM** value: **125.00**

AMAZING MYSTERY FUNNIES — Centaur

1 ❑ Aug 1938 Cover: 0.10 **NM** value: **2500.00**
• **CGC:** 1 graded, best 7.0
2 ❑ Oct 1938 Cover: 0.10 **NM** value: **1500.00**
3 ❑ Nov 1938 Cover: 0.10 **NM** value: **1000.00**
4 ❑ Dec 1938 Cover: 0.10 **NM** value: **1000.00**
5 ❑ Jan 1939 Cover: 0.10 **NM** value: **1000.00**
• **CGC:** 1 graded, best 9.0
6 ❑ Feb 1939 Cover: 0.10 **NM** value: **750.00**
7 ❑ Mar 1939 Cover: 0.10 **NM** value: **750.00**
8 ❑ Apr 1939 Cover: 0.10 **NM** value: **750.00**
9 ❑ May 1939 Cover: 0.10 **NM** value: **750.00**
• **CGC:** 3 graded, best 9.2
10 ❑ Jun 1939 Cover: 0.10 **NM** value: **600.00**
• **CGC:** 1 graded, best 9.4
11 ❑ Jul 1939 Cover: 0.10 **NM** value: **600.00**
• **CGC:** 2 graded, best 8.0
12 ❑ Aug 1939 Cover: 0.10 **NM** value: **600.00**
13 ❑ Sep 1939 Cover: 0.10 **NM** value: **600.00**
• **CGC:** 2 graded, best 7.5
14 ❑ Oct 1939 Cover: 0.10 **NM** value: **600.00**
15 ❑ Nov 1939 Cover: 0.10 **NM** value: **600.00**
16 ❑ Dec 1939 Cover: 0.10 **NM** value: **500.00**
• **CGC:** 4 graded, best 8.5
17 ❑ Jan 1940 Cover: 0.10 **NM** value: **500.00**
18 ❑ Feb 1940 Cover: 0.10 **NM** value: **500.00**
19 ❑ Mar 1940 Cover: 0.10 **NM** value: **500.00**
20 ❑ May 1940 Cover: 0.10 **NM** value: **500.00**
• **CGC:** 1 graded, best 7.5
21 ❑ Jun 1940 Cover: 0.10 **NM** value: **450.00**
22 ❑ Jul 1940 Cover: 0.10 **NM** value: **450.00**
23 ❑ Aug 1940 Cover: 0.10 **NM** value: **450.00**
24 ❑ Sep 1940 Cover: 0.10 **NM** value: **450.00**
• **CGC:** 2 graded, best 9.2

The prices seen above do not represent the highest possible prices seen in online auctions, but rather the prices we have seen these issues reliably fetch in a variety of environments (storefront retail, mail order, auction and convention).

AMAZING SCARLET SPIDER, THE — Marvel

In mid-1995, the Spider-Man "clone saga" was still dragging on. A storyline had disclosed that the clone Spider-Man thought killed in Amazing Spider-Man #149 was the genuine article, and Marvel sent the character people had known for years off into the sunset. Before adopting the mantle of Spider-Man, the clone (see how confusing this is?) became the Scarlet Spider.

In a summer stunt, Marvel retitled all its mainline Spider-Man titles for four issues each. Amazing Spider-Man became Amazing Scarlet Spider; Spectacular Spider-Man became Spectacular Scarlet Spider, etc.

The whole idea was to make Spider-Man young again, perhaps better appealing to readers who didn't identify with a married adult. It mostly only alienated longtime readers, however, and those who thought an unbroken monthly string of Amazing Spider-Man titles was a tradition worth preserving.

The original titles returned, except for Web of Spider-Man, which morphed into Sensational Spider-Man. The real Spider-Man returned, too, later than he should have. — JJM

1 ❑ Nov 1995 Cover: 1.95 **NM** value: **Cover or less**
Virtual Mortality, Part 2 **A:** Mark Bagley **W:** Tom DeFalco; Mike Lackey
2 ❑ Dec 1995 Cover: 1.50 **NM** value: **1.95**
Cyberwar, Part 2 **A:** Mark Bagley **W:** Tom DeFalco ★ Appearance of Joystick, Green Goblin IV.
2/DM❑Dec 1995 Cover: 1.95 **NM** value: **Cover or less**
• Direct Edition. Cyberwar, Part 2

AMAZING SPIDER-MAN, THE — Marvel

After being bitten by a radioactive spider, Peter Parker, a shy high school student, suddenly finds himself with the ability to sense danger, stick to walls, and possessed of the proportional strength of a spider. When his uncle is killed by a burglar, Peter resolves to use his new powers to fight crime. Thus is born the Amazing Spider-Man, Marvel's most popular character of all time.

The Amazing Spider-Man is the flagship of the Spider-Man titles — a list which has included Marvel Team-Up, Spectacular Spider-Man, Spidey Super Stories, Web of Spider-Man, and (just plain old) Spider-Man. Since its first issue in 1963, it has featured the wisecracking arachnid in many of his greatest adventures and has introduced such famous super-villains as the Green Goblin, Doctor Octopus, The Kingpin, The Vulture, and Venom.

Years later, Marvel restarted the series at #1, hungry for first-issue orders but irritating many long-time collectors.

-1 ❑ Jul 1997 Cover: 1.99 **NM** value: **2.50**
Circ: Diamd. preorders: **74,425**
• Flashback
1 ❑ Mar 1963 Cover: 0.12 **NM** value: **25000.00**
• **CGC:** 213 graded, best 9.8
Spider-Man; Spider-Man vs. the Chameleon; A Personal Message from Spider-Man **A:** Steve Ditko; Jack Kirby **W:** Steve Ditko; Stan Lee ★ Origin of Spider-Man. ★ 1st Appearance of John Jameson, J. Jonah Jameson, Chameleon. ★ Appearance of Fantastic Four.
1/GR❑ **NM** value: **250.00**
• **CGC:** 18 graded, best 9.8
• Golden Records reprint: No number or cover price.
2 ❑ May 1963 Cover: 0.12 **NM** value: **3200.00**
• **CGC:** 108 graded, best 9.4
Duel to the Death with the Vulture; The Uncanny Threat of the Terrible Tinkerer **A:** Steve Ditko **W:** Steve Ditko; Stan Lee ★ 1st Appearance of Mysterio (as "alien"), Tinkerer, Vulture.
3 ❑ Jul 1963 Cover: 0.12 **NM** value: **2500.00**
• **CGC:** 108 graded, best 9.6
Spider-Man Versus Doctor Octopus **A:** Steve Ditko **W:** Steve Ditko; Stan Lee ★ Origin of Doctor Octopus. ★ 1st Appearance of Doctor Octopus.
4 ❑ Sep 1963 Cover: 0.12 **NM** value: **1900.00**
• **CGC:** 107 graded, best 9.4
Nothing Can Stop the Sandman **A:** Steve Ditko **W:** Steve Ditko; Stan Lee ★ Origin of Sandman (Marvel). ★ 1st Appearance of Betty Brant, Sandman (Marvel).
5 ❑ Oct 1963 Cover: 0.12 **NM** value: **1600.00**
• **CGC:** 114 graded, best 9.6
Marked for Destruction by Dr. Doom **A:** Steve Ditko **W:** Steve Ditko; Stan Lee ★ Versus Doctor Doom.
6 ❑ Nov 1963 Cover: 0.12 **NM** value: **1250.00**
• **CGC:** 121 graded, best 9.8
Face-to-Face with the Lizard **A:** Steve Ditko **W:** Steve Ditko; Stan Lee ★ Origin of The Lizard. ★ 1st Appearance of The Lizard.
7 ❑ Dec 1963 Cover: 0.12 **NM** value: **900.00**
• **CGC:** 97 graded, best 9.4
Return of the Vulture **A:** Steve Ditko **W:** Steve Ditko; Stan Lee ★ 2nd Appearance of The Vulture. ★ Versus Vulture.
8 ❑ Jan 1964 Cover: 0.12 **NM** value: **900.00**
• **CGC:** 115 graded, best 9.8
The Terrible Threat of the Living Brain; Spider-Man Tackles the Torch **A:** Steve Ditko **W:** Steve Ditko; Stan Lee ★ Appearance of Human Torch. ★ Versus Flash Thompson. ★ Versus Living Brain.

CGC-graded: Multiply prices above by **33 for 9.9 M • 16 for 9.8 NM/M • 7 for 9.6 NM+ • 5 for 9.4 NM • 2.5 for 9.2 NM- • 1.5 for 9.0 VF/NM**

9 ❑ Feb 1964 Cover: 0.12 **NM** value: **1000.00**
• **CGC:** 115 graded, best 9.6
📖 The Man Called Electro **A:** Steve Ditko **W:** Steve Ditko; Stan Lee ★ Origin of Electro. ★ 1st Appearance of Doctor Bromwell, Electro.

10 ❑ Mar 1964 Cover: 0.12 **NM** value: **900.00**
• **CGC:** 126 graded, best 9.6
📖 The Enforcers **A:** Steve Ditko; Jack Kirby **W:** Steve Ditko; Stan Lee ★ 1st Appearance of Fancy Dan, Big Man, Montana, Enforcers, Ox.

11 ❑ Apr 1964 Cover: 0.12 **NM** value: **550.00**
• **CGC:** 56 graded, best 9.6
📖 Turning Point **A:** Steve Ditko **W:** Steve Ditko; Stan Lee ★ 2nd Appearance of Doctor Octopus. ★ Versus Doctor Octopus.

12 ❑ May 1964 Cover: 0.12 **NM** value: **550.00**
• **CGC:** 80 graded, best 9.6
📖 Unmasked by Dr. Octopus • Spider-Man unmasked **A:** Steve Ditko **W:** Steve Ditko; Stan Lee ★ Versus Doctor Octopus.

13 ❑ Jun 1964 Cover: 0.12 **NM** value: **700.00**
• **CGC:** 84 graded, best 9.6
📖 The Menace of Mysterio **A:** Steve Ditko **W:** Steve Ditko; Stan Lee ★ Origin of Mysterio. ★ 1st Appearance of Mysterio.

14 ❑ Jul 1964 Cover: 0.12 **NM** value: **1800.00**
• **CGC:** 246 graded, best 9.6
📖 The Grotesque Adventure of the Green Goblin **A:** Steve Ditko **W:** Steve Ditko; Stan Lee ★ 1st Appearance of Green Goblin I (Norman Osborn). ★ Appearance of Hulk, Enforcers.

15 ❑ Aug 1964 Cover: 0.12 **NM** value: **900.00**
• **CGC:** 83 graded, best 9.6
📖 Kraven the Hunter **A:** Steve Ditko **W:** Steve Ditko; Stan Lee ★ Origin of Kraven the Hunter. ★ 1st Appearance of Anna May Watson, Kraven the Hunter, Mary Jane Watson (name mentioned). ★ Appearance of Chameleon.

16 ❑ Sep 1964 Cover: 0.12 **NM** value: **425.00**
• **CGC:** 78 graded, best 9.8
📖 Duel with Daredevil **A:** Steve Ditko **W:** Steve Ditko; Stan Lee ★ 1st Appearance of The Great Gambonnos, Princess Python. ★ Appearance of Daredevil. ★ Versus Ringmaster and Circus of Crime.

17 ❑ Oct 1964 Cover: 0.12 **NM** value: **600.00**
• **CGC:** 129 graded, best 9.6
📖 The Return of the Green Goblin **A:** Steve Ditko **W:** Steve Ditko; Stan Lee ★ 2nd Appearance of Green Goblin I (Norman Osborn). ★ Appearance of Torch. ★ Versus Green Goblin I (Norman Osborn).

18 ❑ Nov 1964 Cover: 0.12 **NM** value: **385.00**
• **CGC:** 86 graded, best 9.6
📖 The End of Spider-Man **A:** Steve Ditko **W:** Steve Ditko; Stan Lee ★ Versus Sandman (Marvel).

19 ❑ Dec 1964 Cover: 0.12 **NM** value: **325.00**
• **CGC:** 141 graded, best 9.8
📖 Spidey Strikes Back **A:** Steve Ditko **W:** Steve Ditko; Stan Lee ★ 1st Appearance of Rock Gimpy, MacDonald "Mac" Gargan [later becomes the Scorpion]. ★ Versus Sandman (Marvel), Enforcers.

20 ❑ Jan 1965 Cover: 0.12 **NM** value: **425.00**
• **CGC:** 83 graded, best 9.6
📖 The Coming of the Scorpion **A:** Steve Ditko **W:** Steve Ditko; Stan Lee ★ Origin of The Scorpion. ★ 1st Appearance of The Scorpion.

21 ❑ Feb 1965 Cover: 0.12 **NM** value: **300.00**
• **CGC:** 64 graded, best 9.6
📖 Where Flies the Beetle **A:** Steve Ditko **W:** Steve Ditko; Stan Lee ★ 2nd Appearance of The Beetle. ★ Appearance of Torch. ★ Versus Beetle.

22 ❑ Mar 1965 Cover: 0.12 **NM** value: **250.00**
• **CGC:** 71 graded, best 9.6
📖 The Clown and His Masters of Menace **A:** Steve Ditko **W:** Steve Ditko; Stan Lee ★ Versus Ringmaster and Circus of Crime.

23 ❑ Apr 1965 Cover: 0.12 **NM** value: **400.00**
• **CGC:** 94 graded, best 9.6
📖 The Goblin and the Gangsters **A:** Steve Ditko **W:** Steve Ditko; Stan Lee ★ Appearance of Green Goblin I (Norman Osborn). ★ Versus Green Goblin I (Norman Osborn).

24 ❑ May 1965 Cover: 0.12 **NM** value: **200.00**
• **CGC:** 61 graded, best 9.4
📖 Spider-Man Goes Mad **A:** Steve Ditko **W:** Steve Ditko; Stan Lee ★ Versus Mysterio.

25 ❑ Jun 1965 Cover: 0.12 **NM** value: **220.00**
• **CGC:** 89 graded, best 9.6
📖 Captured by J. Jonah Jameson **A:** Steve Ditko **W:** Steve Ditko; Stan Lee ★ 1st Appearance of Spencer Smythe, Spider-Slayers, Mary Jane Watson (cameo-face not shown).

26 ❑ Jul 1965 Cover: 0.12 **NM** value: **300.00**
• **CGC:** 82 graded, best 9.6
📖 The Man in the Crime Master's Mask **A:** Steve Ditko **W:** Steve Ditko; Stan Lee ★ 1st Appearance of Crime-Master, Patch. ★ Appearance of Green Goblin I (Norman Osborn).

27 ❑ Aug 1965 Cover: 0.12 **NM** value: **275.00**
• **CGC:** 78 graded, best 9.6
📖 Bring Back My Goblin to Me **A:** Steve Ditko **W:** Steve Ditko; Stan Lee ★ Appearance of Green Goblin I (Norman Osborn). ★ Death of Crime-Master.

28 ❑ Sep 1965 Cover: 0.12 **NM** value: **350.00**
• **CGC:** 101 graded, best 9.6
📖 The Menace of the Molten Man • Peter Parker graduates from high school **A:** Steve Ditko **W:** Steve Ditko; Stan Lee ★ Origin of Molten Man, Molten Man. ★ 2nd Appearance of Spencer Smythe.

29 ❑ Oct 1965 Cover: 0.12 **NM** value: **175.00**
• **CGC:** 71 graded, best 9.6
📖 Never Step on a Scorpion **A:** Steve Ditko **W:** Steve Ditko; Stan Lee ★ 2nd Appearance of The Scorpion. ★ Versus The Scorpion.

30 ❑ Nov 1965 Cover: 0.12 **NM** value: **150.00**
• **CGC:** 81 graded, best 9.6
📖 The Claws of the Cat **A:** Steve Ditko ★ Versus Cat Burglar.

31 ❑ Dec 1965 Cover: 0.12 **NM** value: **175.00**
• **CGC:** 64 graded, best 9.6
📖 If This Be My Destiny ... • First Harry Osborn and Gwen Stacy **A:** Steve Ditko **W:** Stan Lee ★ 1st Appearance of Professor Warren, Gwen Stacy, Harry Osborn.

32 ❑ Jan 1966 Cover: 0.12 **NM** value: **150.00**
Circ: Statement: **340,155** • **CGC:** 66 graded, best 9.6
📖 Man on a Rampage • Master Planner revealed as Doctor Octopus **A:** Steve Ditko

33 ❑ Feb 1966 Cover: 0.12 **NM** value: **150.00**
Circ: Statement: **340,155** • **CGC:** 125 graded, best 9.8
📖 The Final Chapter **A:** Steve Ditko ★ Versus Doctor Octopus (as Master Planner).

34 ❑ Mar 1966 Cover: 0.12 **NM** value: **150.00**
Circ: Statement: **340,155** • **CGC:** 80 graded, best 9.8
📖 The Thrill of the Hunt **A:** Steve Ditko ★ Appearance of Green Goblin I (Norman Osborn). ★ Versus Kraven the Hunter.

35 ❑ Apr 1966 Cover: 0.12 **NM** value: **150.00**
Circ: Statement: **340,155** • **CGC:** 68 graded, best 9.6
📖 The Molten Man Regrets **A:** Steve Ditko ★ 1st Appearance of Spider Tracer. ★ Versus Molten Man.

36 ❑ May 1966 Cover: 0.12 **NM** value: **150.00**
Circ: Statement: **340,155** • **CGC:** 72 graded, best 9.6
📖 When Falls the Meteor **A:** Steve Ditko ★ 1st Appearance of Looter (later Meteor Man in Marvel Team-Up #33).

37 ❑ Jun 1966 Cover: 0.12 **NM** value: **140.00**
Circ: Statement: **340,155** • **CGC:** 71 graded, best 9.6
📖 Once Upon a Time, There Was a Robot **A:** Steve Ditko ★ 1st Appearance of Norman Osborn. ★ Appearance of Patch. ★ Versus Professor Mendel Stromm.

38 ❑ Jul 1966 Cover: 0.12 **NM** value: **140.00**
Circ: Statement: **340,155** • **CGC:** 85 graded, best 9.6
📖 Just a Guy Named Joe **A:** Steve Ditko ★ 2nd Appearance of Mary Jane Watson (cameo).

39 ❑ Aug 1966 Cover: 0.12 **NM** value: **275.00**
Circ: Statement: **340,155** • **CGC:** 137 graded, best 9.6
📖 How Green Was My Goblin • Green Goblin revealed as Norman Osborn **A:** John Romita ★ Versus Green Goblin I (Norman Osborn).

40 ❑ Sep 1966 Cover: 0.12 **NM** value: **350.00**
Circ: Statement: **340,155** • **CGC:** 162 graded, best 9.6
📖 Spidey Saves the Day **A:** John Romita ★ Origin of Green Goblin I (Norman Osborn).

41 ❑ Oct 1966 Cover: 0.12 **NM** value: **150.00**
Circ: Statement: **340,155** • **CGC:** 64 graded, best 9.8
📖 The Horns of the Rhino **A:** John Romita ★ 1st Appearance of Rhino.

42 ❑ Nov 1966 Cover: 0.12 **NM** value: **150.00**
Circ: Statement: **340,155** • **CGC:** 104 graded, best 9.6
📖 The Birth of a Super-Hero • First Mary Jane Watson **A:** John Romita ★ 3rd Appearance of Mary Jane Watson (first time her face is shown). ★ Appearance of 3rd.

43 ❑ Dec 1966 Cover: 0.12 **NM** value: **100.00**
Circ: Statement: **340,155** • **CGC:** 66 graded, best 9.8
📖 Rhino on the Rampage **A:** John Romita ★ Origin of Rhino. ★ Versus Rhino.

44 ❑ Jan 1967 Cover: 0.12 **NM** value: **100.00**
Circ: Statement: **361,663** • **CGC:** 49 graded, best 9.6
📖 Where Crawls the Lizard **A:** John Romita ★ Versus Lizard.

45 ❑ Feb 1967 Cover: 0.12 **NM** value: **100.00**
Circ: Statement: **361,663** • **CGC:** 97 graded, best 9.6
📖 Spidey Smashes Out **A:** John Romita ★ Versus Lizard.

46 ❑ Mar 1967 Cover: 0.12 **NM** value: **100.00**
Circ: Statement: **361,663** • **CGC:** 55 graded, best 9.6
📖 The Sinister Shocker **A:** John Romita ★ Origin of Shocker. ★ 1st Appearance of Shocker.

47 ❑ Apr 1967 Cover: 0.12 **NM** value: **95.00**
Circ: Statement: **361,663** • **CGC:** 91 graded, best 9.8
📖 In the Hands of the Hunter • Has 1966 Statement, filed 10/1/66; avg print run 516,748; avg sales 337,455; avg subs 2,700; avg total paid 340,155; samples 60; max existent 340,215; 34% of run returned **A:** John Romita ★ Versus Kraven the Hunter.

48 ❑ May 1967 Cover: 0.12 **NM** value: **95.00**
Circ: Statement: **361,663** • **CGC:** 50 graded, best 9.6
📖 The Wings of the Vulture **A:** John Romita ★ Versus second Vulture.

49 ❑ Jun 1967 Cover: 0.12 **NM** value: **95.00**
Circ: Statement: **361,663** • **CGC:** 53 graded, best 9.8
📖 From the Depths of Defeat **A:** John Romita ★ Versus Kraven the Hunter. ★ Versus Vulture.

50 ❑ Jul 1967 Cover: 0.12 **NM** value: **450.00**
Circ: Statement: **361,663** • **CGC:** 159 graded, best 9.6
📖 Spider-Man No More **A:** John Romita ★ 1st Appearance of Kingpin.

51 ❑ Aug 1967 Cover: 0.12 **NM** value: **150.00**
Circ: Statement: **361,663** • **CGC:** 62 graded, best 9.6
📖 In the Clutches of the Kingpin **A:** John Romita ★ Origin of Mysterio. ★ 1st Appearance of Robbie Robertson. ★ 2nd Appearance of Kingpin. ★ Versus Kingpin.

52 ❑ Sep 1967 Cover: 0.12 **NM** value: **70.00**
Circ: Statement: **361,663** • **CGC:** 38 graded, best 9.6
📖 To Die a Hero **A:** John Romita ★ 1st Appearance of Joe Robertson. ★ Death of Big Man (Frederick Foswell). ★ Versus Kingpin.

53 ❑ Oct 1967 Cover: 0.12 **NM** value: **70.00**
Circ: Statement: **361,663** • **CGC:** 42 graded, best 9.8
📖 Enter Dr. Octopus **A:** John Romita ★ Versus Doctor Octopus.

54 ❑ Nov 1967 Cover: 0.12 **NM** value: **70.00**
Circ: Statement: **361,663** • **CGC:** 60 graded, best 9.8
📖 The Tentacles and the Trap **A:** John Romita ★ Versus Doctor Octopus.

55 ❑ Dec 1967 Cover: 0.12 **NM** value: **70.00**
Circ: Statement: **361,663** • **CGC:** 36 graded, best 9.6
📖 Doc Ock Wins **A:** John Romita ★ Versus Doctor Octopus.

56 ❑ Jan 1968 Cover: 0.12 **NM** value: **70.00**
Circ: Statement: **373,303** • **CGC:** 59 graded, best 9.8
📖 Disaster **A:** John Romita ★ 1st Appearance of Captain Stacy. ★ Versus Doctor Octopus.

57 ❑ Feb 1968 Cover: 0.12 **NM** value: **70.00**
Circ: Statement: **373,303** • **CGC:** 56 graded, best 9.6
📖 The Comics of Ka-Zar • Ka-Zar, Zabu **A:** John Romita ★ Appearance of Ka-Zar and Zabu.

58 ❑ Mar 1968 Cover: 0.12 **NM** value: **60.00**
Circ: Statement: **373,303** • **CGC:** 48 graded, best 9.6
📖 To Kill a Spider-Man **A:** John Romita ★ Appearance of Ka-Zar and Zabu. ★ Versus Spencer Smythe. ★ Versus J. Jonah Jameson.

59 ❑ Apr 1968 Cover: 0.12 **NM** value: **65.00**
Circ: Statement: **373,303** • **CGC:** 79 graded, best 9.8
📖 The Brand of the Brainwasher • Has 1967 Statement, filed 10/1/67; avg print run 587,213; avg sales 359,363; avg subs 2,300; avg total paid 361,663; samples 95; max existent 361,758 %38 of run returned **A:** John Romita **W:** John Romita; Stan Lee ★ 1st Appearance of Doctor Winkler, Slade. ★ Versus Kingpin (as Brainwasher).

60 ❑ May 1968 Cover: 0.12 **NM** value: **65.00**
Circ: Statement: **373,303** • **CGC:** 39 graded, best 9.6
📖 O, Bitter Victory **A:** John Romita **W:** John Romita; Stan Lee ★ 2nd Appearance of Doctor Winkler. ★ 2nd Appearance of Slade. ★ Versus Kingpin.

61 ❑ Jun 1968 Cover: 0.12 **NM** value: **60.00**
Circ: Statement: **373,303** • **CGC:** 41 graded, best 9.6
📖 What a Tangled Web We Weave **A:** John Romita **W:** John Romita; Stan Lee ★ Versus Kingpin.

62 ❑ Jul 1968 Cover: 0.12 **NM** value: **60.00**
Circ: Statement: **373,303** • **CGC:** 87 graded, best 9.8
📖 Make Way for Medusa **A:** John Romita **W:** John Romita; Stan Lee ★ Appearance of Medusa.

63 ❑ Aug 1968 Cover: 0.12 **NM** value: **60.00**
Circ: Statement: **373,303** • **CGC:** 27 graded, best 9.4
📖 Wings in the Night **A:** John Romita **W:** John Romita; Stan Lee ★ Versus both Vultures.

64 ❑ Sep 1968 Cover: 0.12 **NM** value: **60.00**
Circ: Statement: **373,303** • **CGC:** 113 graded, best 9.8
📖 The Vulture's Prey **A:** John Romita **W:** John Romita; Stan Lee ★ Versus Vulture.

65 ❑ Oct 1968 Cover: 0.12 **NM** value: **60.00**
Circ: Statement: **373,303** • **CGC:** 58 graded, best 9.8
📖 The Impossible Escape **A:** John Romita **W:** John Romita; Stan Lee

66 ❑ Nov 1968 Cover: 0.12 **NM** value: **60.00**
Circ: Statement: **373,303** • **CGC:** 57 graded, best 9.8
📖 The Madness of Mysterio **A:** John Romita **W:** John Romita; Stan Lee ★ Appearance of Mysterio. ★ Versus Mysterio.

67 ❑ Dec 1968 Cover: 0.12 **NM** value: **60.00**
Circ: Statement: **373,303** • **CGC:** 80 graded, best 9.8
📖 To Squash a Spider **A:** John Romita **W:** John Romita; Stan Lee ★ 1st Appearance of Randy Robertson. ★ Versus Mysterio.

68 ❑ Jan 1969 Cover: 0.12 **NM** value: **60.00**
Circ: Statement: **372,352** • **CGC:** 55 graded, best 9.8
📖 Crisis on the Campus • Kingpin **A:** John Romita; Jim Mooney **W:** John Romita; Stan Lee ★ 1st Appearance of Louis Wilson. ★ Versus Kingpin.

69 ❑ Feb 1969 Cover: 0.12 **NM** value: **60.00**
Circ: Statement: **372,352** • **CGC:** 48 graded, best 9.8
📖 Mission: Crush the Kingpin • Kingpin **A:** John Romita; Jim Mooney **W:** John Romita; Stan Lee ★ Versus Kingpin.

70 ❑ Mar 1969 Cover: 0.12 **NM** value: **50.00**
Circ: Statement: **372,352** • **CGC:** 38 graded, best 9.6
📖 Spider-Man Wanted • Kingpin **A:** John Romita; Jim Mooney **W:** John Romita; Stan Lee ★ 1st Appearance of Vanessa Fisk (Kingpin's wife-face not shown). ★ Versus Kingpin.

71 ❑ Apr 1969 Cover: 0.12 **NM** value: **50.00**
Circ: Statement: **372,352** • **CGC:** 37 graded, best 9.8
📖 The Speedster and the Spider • Kingpin, Quicksilver, Scarlet Witch, the Toad; Has 1968 Statement, filed 10/1/68; avg print run 556,000; avg sales 369,431; avg subs 3,872; avg total paid 373,303; samples 400; max existent 373,703; 33% of run returned **A:** John Romita; Jim Mooney **W:** John Romita; Stan Lee ★ Appearance of Quicksilver.

72 ❑ May 1969 Cover: 0.12 **NM** value: **50.00**
Circ: Statement: **372,352** • **CGC:** 37 graded, best 9.6
📖 Rocked by the Shocker **A:** John Buscema; John Romita **W:** John Romita; Stan Lee ★ Versus Shocker.

73 ❑ Jun 1969 Cover: 0.12 **NM** value: **50.00**
Circ: Statement: **372,352** • **CGC:** 41 graded, best 9.8
📖 The Web Closes **A:** John Buscema; John Romita **W:** John Romita; Stan Lee ★ 1st Appearance of Man-Mountain Marko, Caesar Cicero, Silvermane.

74 ❑ Jul 1969 Cover: 0.12 **NM** value: **50.00**
Circ: Statement: **372,352** • **CGC:** 33 graded, best 9.8
📖 If This Be Bedlam **A:** John Romita; Jim Mooney **W:** John Romita; Stan Lee ★ Versus Man-Mountain Marko. ★ Versus Caesar Cicero. ★ Versus Silvermane.

75 ❑ Aug 1969 Cover: 0.15 **NM** value: **42.00**
Circ: Statement: **372,352** • **CGC:** 34 graded, best 9.8
📖 Death Without Warning **A:** John Romita; Jim Mooney **W:** John Romita; Stan Lee ★ Versus Man-Mountain Marko. ★ Versus Caesar Cicero. ★ Versus Silvermane.

76 ❑ Sep 1969 Cover: 0.15 **NM** value: **42.00**
Circ: Statement: **372,352** • **CGC:** 22 graded, best 9.6
📖 The Lizard Lives • Human Torch **A:** John Buscema; John Romita; Jim Mooney **W:** Stan Lee ★ Appearance of Human Torch. ★ Versus Lizard.

77 ❑ Oct 1969 Cover: 0.15 **NM** value: **42.00**
Circ: Statement: **372,352** • **CGC:** 36 graded, best 9.6
📖 In the Blaze of Battle • Human Torch **A:** John Buscema; John Romita; Jim Mooney **W:** John Romita; Stan Lee ★ Appearance of Human Torch. ★ Versus Lizard.

78 ❑ Nov 1969 Cover: 0.15 **NM** value: **48.00**
Circ: Statement: **372,352** • **CGC:** 29 graded, best 9.6
📖 The Night of the Prowler • The Prowler **A:** John Buscema; John Romita; Jim Mooney **W:** John Romita Jr.; Stan Lee ★ 1st Appearance of The Prowler.

79 ❑ Dec 1969 Cover: 0.15 **NM** value: **42.00**
Circ: Statement: **372,352** • **CGC:** 22 graded, best 9.4
📖 To Prowl No More **A:** John Buscema; John Romita; Jim Mooney **W:** Stan Lee ★ 2nd Appearance of The Prowler. ★ Versus The Prowler. ★ Versus Prowler.

80 ❑ Jan 1970 Cover: 0.15 **NM** value: **42.00**
Circ: Statement: **322,195** • **CGC:** 20 graded, best 9.6
📖 On the Trail of the Chameleon **A:** John Buscema; John Romita **W:** John Romita; Stan Lee ★ Versus Chameleon.

81 ❑ Feb 1970 Cover: 0.15 **NM** value: **42.00**
Circ: Statement: **322,195** • **CGC:** 37 graded, best 9.6
📖 The Coming of the Kangaroo **A:** John Buscema; John Romita **W:** John Romita; Stan Lee ★ Origin of The Kangaroo. ★ 1st Appearance of The Kangaroo.

Other grades: Multiply prices above by **1.5 for Mint • 2/3 for Very Fine • 1/3 for Fine • 1/5 for Very Good • 1/8 for Good**

82 ❑ Mar 1970 Cover: 0.15 **NM** value: **42.00**
Circ: Statement: **322,195 • CGC:** 30 graded, best 9.6
🕮 And Then Came Electro • Merv Griffin, Arthur Treacher **A:** John Buscema; John Romita **W:** John Romita; Stan Lee ★ Origin of Electro. ★ Versus Electro.

83 ❑ Apr 1970 Cover: 0.15 **NM** value: **42.00**
Circ: Statement: **322,195 • CGC:** 30 graded, best 9.8
🕮 The Schemer • Has 1969 Statement, filed 10/1/69; avg print run 574,910; avg sales X370,490 avg subs 1,862; avg total paid 372,352; samples 110; max existent 372,462; 35% of run returned **A:** John Romita **W:** John Romita; Stan Lee ★ 1st Appearance of Richard Fisk ("The Schemer"), Vanessa Fisk (Full-Kingpin's wife). ★ Versus Kingpin. ★ Versus Schemer.

84 ❑ May 1970 Cover: 0.15 **NM** value: **42.00**
Circ: Statement: **322,195 • CGC:** 29 graded, best 9.8
🕮 The Kingpin Strikes Back **A:** John Buscema; John Romita **W:** John Romita; Stan Lee ★ Versus Kingpin. ★ Versus Schemer.

85 ❑ Jun 1970 Cover: 0.15 **NM** value: **42.00**
Circ: Statement: **322,195 • CGC:** 25 graded, best 9.6
🕮 The Secret of the Schemer **A:** John Buscema; John Romita **W:** John Romita; Stan Lee ★ Versus Kingpin. ★ Versus Schemer.

86 ❑ Jul 1970 Cover: 0.15 **NM** value: **42.00**
Circ: Statement: **322,195 • CGC:** 25 graded, best 9.6
🕮 Beware the Black Widow **A:** John Romita; Jim Mooney **W:** John Romita; Stan Lee ★ Origin of Black Widow.

87 ❑ Aug 1970 Cover: 0.15 **NM** value: **42.00**
Circ: Statement: **322,195 • CGC:** 24 graded, best 9.6
🕮 Unmasked at Last • Peter reveals his secret identity **A:** John Romita; Jim Mooney • **W:** John Romita; Stan Lee

88 ❑ Sep 1970 Cover: 0.15 **NM** value: **42.00**
Circ: Statement: **322,195 • CGC:** 34 graded, best 9.8
🕮 The Arms of Dr. Octopus **A:** John Romita **W:** Stan Lee ★ Appearance of Doctor Octopus. ★ Versus Doctor Octopus.

89 ❑ Oct 1970 Cover: 0.15 **NM** value: **42.00**
Circ: Statement: **322,195 • CGC:** 19 graded, best 9.6
🕮 Doc Ock Lives **A:** Gil Kane; John Romita **W:** Stan Lee ★ Appearance of Doctor Octopus. ★ Versus Doctor Octopus.

90 ❑ Nov 1970 Cover: 0.15 **NM** value: **60.00**
Circ: Statement: **322,195 • CGC:** 36 graded, best 9.6
🕮 And Death Shall Come • Death of Captain Stacy **A:** Gil Kane **W:** Stan Lee ★ Appearance of Doctor Octopus. ★ Death of Captain Stacy.

91 ❑ Dec 1970 Cover: 0.15 **NM** value: **42.00**
Circ: Statement: **322,195 • CGC:** 64 graded, best 9.6
🕮 To Smash a Spider **A:** Gil Kane; John Romita **W:** Stan Lee ★ 1st Appearance of Sam Bullit.

92 ❑ Jan 1971 Cover: 0.15 **NM** value: **42.00**
Circ: Statement: **307,550 • CGC:** 26 graded, best 9.6
🕮 When Iceman Attacks • Iceman **A:** Gil Kane; John Romita **W:** Stan Lee ★ Appearance of Sam Bullit. ★ Appearance of Iceman.

93 ❑ Feb 1971 Cover: 0.15 **NM** value: **42.00**
Circ: Statement: **307,550 • CGC:** 25 graded, best 9.6
🕮 The Lady and the Prowler **A:** John Romita **W:** John Romita; Stan Lee ★ Appearance of Prowler.

94 ❑ Mar 1971 Cover: 0.15 **NM** value: **60.00**
Circ: Statement: **307,550 • CGC:** 44 graded, best 9.8
🕮 On Wings of Death • Spider-Man's Origin retold **A:** Sal Buscema; John Romita **W:** John Romita; Stan Lee ★ Origin of Spider-Man. ★ Appearance of Beetle.

95 ❑ Apr 1971 Cover: 0.15 **NM** value: **38.00**
Circ: Statement: **307,550 • CGC:** 40 graded, best 9.8
🕮 Trap for a Terrorist • Spider-Man goes to London; Has 1970 Statement, filed 10/1/70; avg print run 596,102; avg sales 319,664; avg subs 2,531; avg total paid 322,195; samples 0; office use 110; max existent 322,305; 46% of run returned **A:** Sal Buscema; John Romita **W:** John Romita; Stan Lee

96 ❑ May 1971 Cover: 0.15 **NM** value: **80.00**
Circ: Statement: **307,550 • CGC:** 46 graded, best 9.8
🕮 And Now, the Goblin • Drug topics not approved by CCA **A:** Gil Kane **W:** Stan Lee ★ Appearance of Green Goblin I (Norman Osborn).

97 ❑ Jun 1971 Cover: 0.15 **NM** value: **80.00**
Circ: Statement: **307,550 • CGC:** 90 graded, best 9.8
🕮 In the Grip of the Goblin • Drug topics not approved by CCA **A:** Gil Kane; John Romita **W:** John Romita; Stan Lee ★ Appearance of Green Goblin I (Norman Osborn).

98 ❑ Jul 1971 Cover: 0.15 **NM** value: **80.00**
Circ: Statement: **307,550 • CGC:** 98 graded, best 9.8
🕮 The Goblin's Last Gasp • Drug topics not approved by CCA **A:** Gil Kane **W:** Stan Lee ★ Appearance of Green Goblin I (Norman Osborn).

99 ❑ Aug 1971 Cover: 0.15 **NM** value: **42.00**
Circ: Statement: **307,550 • CGC:** 37 graded, best 9.6
🕮 A Day In The Life Of... • Johnny Carson, Ed McMahon **A:** Gil Kane **W:** Stan Lee ★ Appearance of Johnny Carson.

100 ❑ Sep 1971 Cover: 0.15 **NM** value: **165.00**
Circ: Statement: **307,550 • CGC:** 216 graded, best 9.8
• 100th anniversary issue. 🕮 The Spider or the Man? • Peter grows four extra arms **A:** Gil Kane; John Romita **W:** Stan Lee ★ Appearance of Green Goblin I (Norman Osborn).

101 ❑ Oct 1971 Cover: 0.15 **NM** value: **100.00**
Circ: Statement: **307,550 • CGC:** 79 graded, best 9.8
🕮 A Monster Called Morbius **A:** Gil Kane **W:** Gil Kane; Roy Thomas; Stan Lee ★ 1st Appearance of Morbius.

101-2 ❑ Cover: 1.75 **NM** value: **2.25**

102 ❑ Nov 1971 Cover: 0.25 **NM** value: **75.00**
Circ: Statement: **307,550 • CGC:** 88 graded, best 9.6
• Giant-sized. 🕮 Vampire at Large; The Way It Began; The Curse and the Cure **A:** Gil Kane **W:** Gil Kane; Roy Thomas; Stan Lee ★ Origin of Morbius. ★ Appearance of Lizard, Morbius.

103 ❑ Dec 1971 Cover: 0.20 **NM** value: **25.00**
Circ: Statement: **307,550 • CGC:** 22 graded, best 9.6
🕮 Walk The Savage Land; Gog • Ka-Zar, Zabu, Kraven the Hunter **A:** Gil Kane **W:** Gil Kane; Roy Thomas; Stan Lee ★ 1st Appearance of Gog. ★ Versus Kraven the Hunter.

104 ❑ Jan 1972 Cover: 0.20 **NM** value: **25.00**
Circ: Statement: **288,379 • CGC:** 17 graded, best 9.6
🕮 The Beauty and the Brute • Ka-Zar, Zabu, Gog, Kraven the Hunter **A:** Gil Kane **W:** Gil Kane; Roy Thomas ★ 2nd Appearance of Gog. ★ Versus Kraven the Hunter.

105 ❑ Feb 1972 Cover: 0.20 **NM** value: **25.00**
Circ: Statement: **288,379 • CGC:** 46 graded, best 9.8
🕮 The Spider Slayer **A:** Gil Kane **W:** Gil Kane; Stan Lee ★ Versus Spider Slayer. ★ Versus Spencer Smythe.

106 ❑ Mar 1972 Cover: 0.20 **NM** value: **25.00**
Circ: Statement: **288,379 • CGC:** 19 graded, best 9.8
🕮 Squash! Goes the Spider **A:** John Romita **W:** John Romita; Stan Lee ★ Versus Spider Slayer. ★ Versus Spencer Smythe.

107 ❑ Apr 1972 Cover: 0.20 **NM** value: **25.00**
Circ: Statement: **288,379 • CGC:** 29 graded, best 9.8
🕮 Spidey Smashes Thru **A:** John Romita **W:** John Romita; Stan Lee ★ Versus Spider Slayer. ★ Versus Spencer Smythe.

108 ❑ May 1972 Cover: 0.20 **NM** value: **25.00**
Circ: Statement: **288,379 • CGC:** 28 graded, best 9.8
🕮 Vengeance from Vietnam • Has 1971 Statement, filed 9/23/71; avg print run 520,862; avg sales 305,192; avg subs 2,358; avg total paid 307,550; samples 110; office use 2,305; max existent 309,965; 41% of run returned **A:** John Romita **W:** John Romita; Stan Lee ★ 1st Appearance of Sha Shan. ★ Appearance of Flash Thompson.

109 ❑ Jun 1972 Cover: 0.20 **NM** value: **25.00**
Circ: Statement: **288,379 • CGC:** 30 graded, best 9.8
🕮 Enter: Dr. Strange **A:** John Romita **W:** John Romita; Stan Lee ★ Appearance of Doctor Strange.

110 ❑ Jul 1972 Cover: 0.20 **NM** value: **25.00**
Circ: Statement: **288,379 • CGC:** 32 graded, best 9.6
🕮 The Birth of the Gibbon **A:** John Romita **W:** John Romita; Stan Lee ★ Origin of The Gibbon. ★ 1st Appearance of The Gibbon.

111 ❑ Aug 1972 Cover: 0.20 **NM** value: **25.00**
Circ: Statement: **288,379 • CGC:** 29 graded, best 9.8
🕮 To Stalk a Spider **A:** John Romita **W:** John Romita; Gerry Conway ★ Versus The Gibbon, Kraven the Hunter.

112 ❑ Sep 1972 Cover: 0.20 **NM** value: **25.00**
Circ: Statement: **288,379 • CGC:** 26 graded, best 9.6
🕮 Spidey Cops Out **A:** John Romita **W:** John Romita; Gerry Conway ★ Appearance of The Gibbon. ★ Versus Doctor Octopus.

113 ❑ Oct 1972 Cover: 0.20 **NM** value: **30.00**
Circ: Statement: **288,379 • CGC:** 41 graded, best 9.8
🕮 They Call the Doctor...Octopus **A:** Jim Starlin; John Romita; Joe Sinnott **W:** John Romita; Gerry Conway ★ 1st Appearance of Hammerhead. ★ Versus Doctor Octopus.

114 ❑ Nov 1972 Cover: 0.20 **NM** value: **25.00**
Circ: Statement: **288,379 • CGC:** 24 graded, best 9.6
🕮 Who the Heck is Hammerhead? **A:** Jim Starlin; John Romita; Joe Sinnott **W:** John Romita; Gerry Conway ★ Origin of Hammerhead. ★ 1st Appearance of Doctor Jonas Harrow.

115 ❑ Dec 1972 Cover: 0.20 **NM** value: **25.00**
Circ: Statement: **288,379 • CGC:** 26 graded, best 9.6
🕮 The Last Battle • Dr. Octopus, Hammerhead **A:** John Romita **W:** John Romita; Gerry Conway ★ Versus Hammerhead, Doctor Octopus.

116 ❑ Jan 1973 Cover: 0.20 **NM** value: **25.00**
Circ: Statement: **273,204 • CGC:** 35 graded, best 9.8
🕮 Suddenly, the Smasher • Reprints Spectacular Spider-Man #1 ("Lo, This Monster") with some new art and dialogue; Man Monster renamed Smasher **A:** John Romita **W:** John Romita; Stan Lee; Gerry Conway ★ 1st Appearance of Smasher (was Man Monster). ★ Versus Richard Raleigh.

117 ❑ Feb 1973 Cover: 0.20 **NM** value: **25.00**
Circ: Statement: **273,204 • CGC:** 36 graded, best 9.8
• reprints story from Spectacular Spider-Man (magazine) #1 with updates. 🕮 The Deadly Designs of the Disruptor • Reprints Spectacular Spider-Man #1 ("Lo, This Monster") with some new art and dialogue; Man Monster renamed Smasher **A:** Herb Trimpe; John Romita **W:** John Romita; Stan Lee; Gerry Conway ★ 1st Appearance of Disruptor.

118 ❑ Mar 1973 Cover: 0.20 **NM** value: **25.00**
Circ: Statement: **273,204 • CGC:** 22 graded, best 9.6
🕮 Countdown to Chaos • Reprints Spectacular Spider-Man #1 ("Lo, This Monster") with some new art and dialogue; Man Monster renamed Smasher; Has 1972 Statement, filed 9/21/72; avg print run 519,531; avg sales 285,623; avg subs 2,756; avg total paid 288,379; samples 110; office use 1,437; max existent 289,926; 44% of run returned **A:** John Romita **W:** John Romita; Stan Lee; Gerry Conway ★ Versus Disruptor, Smasher.

119 ❑ Apr 1973 Cover: 0.20 **NM** value: **38.00**
Circ: Statement: **273,204 • CGC:** 50 graded, best 9.6
🕮 The Gentleman's Name is Hulk • Incredible Hulk **A:** John Romita **W:** John Romita; Gerry Conway ★ Appearance of Incredible Hulk. ★ Versus Hulk in Canada.

120 ❑ May 1973 Cover: 0.20 **NM** value: **38.00**
Circ: Statement: **273,204 • CGC:** 29 graded, best 9.8
🕮 The Fight and the Fury • Incredible Hulk **A:** Paul Reinman; Gil Kane; John Romita **W:** Gil Kane; Gerry Conway ★ Appearance of Incredible Hulk. ★ Versus Hulk.

121 ❑ Jun 1973 Cover: 0.20 **NM** value: **175.00**
Circ: Statement: **273,204 • CGC:** 187 graded, best 9.8
🕮 The Night Gwen Stacy Died • Green Goblin; Death of Gwen Stacy **A:** Gil Kane; John Romita **W:** Gil Kane; Roy Thomas; Gerry Conway ★ Death of Gwen Stacy. ★ Versus Green Goblin I (Norman Osborn).

122 ❑ Jul 1973 Cover: 0.20 **NM** value: **200.00**
Circ: Statement: **273,204 • CGC:** 238 graded, best 9.8
🕮 The Goblin's Last Gasp • Death of Green Goblin (later revealed as false) **A:** Gil Kane; John Romita **W:** Gil Kane; Roy Thomas; Stan Lee; Gerry Conway ★ Death of Green Goblin I (Norman Osborn).

123 ❑ Aug 1973 Cover: 0.20 **NM** value: **20.00**
Circ: Statement: **273,204 • CGC:** 27 graded, best 9.6
🕮 Just a Man Called Cage **A:** Gil Kane; John Romita **W:** Gil Kane; Gerry Conway ★ Appearance of Luke Cage.

124 ❑ Sep 1973 Cover: 0.20 **NM** value: **20.00**
Circ: Statement: **273,204 • CGC:** 24 graded, best 9.6
🕮 The Mark of the Man-Wolf **A:** Gil Kane; John Romita **W:** Gil Kane; Gerry Conway ★ 1st Appearance of Man-Wolf.

125 ❑ Oct 1973 Cover: 0.20 **NM** value: **20.00**
Circ: Statement: **273,204 • CGC:** 26 graded, best 9.6
🕮 Wolfhunt **A:** John Romita; Ross Andru **W:** Gerry Conway ★ Origin of Man-Wolf.

126 ❑ Nov 1973 Cover: 0.20 **NM** value: **20.00**
Circ: Statement: **273,204 • CGC:** 50 graded, best 9.6
🕮 The Kangaroo Bounces Back • Human Torch; Harry Osborn becomes Green Goblin **A:** John Romita; Ross Andru **W:** Gerry Conway ★ Appearance of Doctor Jonas Harrow, Human Torch. ★ Death of Kangaroo.

127 ❑ Dec 1973 Cover: 0.20 **NM** value: **20.00**
Circ: Statement: **273,204 • CGC:** 37 graded, best 9.8
🕮 The Dark Wings of Death • Human Torch **A:** John Romita; Ross Andru **W:** Gerry Conway ★ Versus third Vulture.

128 ❑ Jan 1974 Cover: 0.20 **NM** value: **20.00**
Circ: Statement: **288,232 • CGC:** 46 graded, best 9.6
🕮 The Vulture Hangs High **A:** John Romita; Ross Andru **W:** Gerry Conway ★ Origin of third Vulture.

129 ❑ Feb 1974 Cover: 0.20 **NM** value: **175.00**
Circ: Statement: **288,232 • CGC:** 338 graded, best 9.6
🕮 The Punisher Strikes Twice • First Punisher **A:** Gil Kane; Ross Andru **W:** Gerry Conway ★ 1st Appearance of the Punisher, Jackal.

130 ❑ Mar 1974 Cover: 0.20 **NM** value: **15.00**
Circ: Statement: **288,232 • CGC:** 29 graded, best 9.8
🕮 Betrayed! • Human Torch **A:** John Romita; Ross Andru **W:** Gerry Conway ★ 1st Appearance of Spider-Mobile. ★ Versus Doctor Octopus. ★ Versus Hammerhead. ★ Versus Jackal.

131 ❑ Apr 1974 Cover: 0.20 **NM** value: **15.00**
Circ: Statement: **288,232 • CGC:** 14 graded, best 9.6
🕮 My Uncle...My Enemy? • Dr. Octopus, Hammerhead **A:** Gil Kane; Ross Andru **W:** Gerry Conway ★ Versus Doctor Octopus. ★ Versus Hammerhead.

132 ❑ May 1974 Cover: 0.25 **NM** value: **15.00**
Circ: Statement: **288,232 • CGC:** 20 graded, best 9.6
🕮 The Master Plan Of The Molten Man • Has 1973 Statement; avg sales 270,801; avg subs 2,403; avg total paid circ 273,204 **A:** Gil Kane; John Romita **W:** Gerry Conway ★ Versus Molten Man.

133 ❑ Jun 1974 Cover: 0.25 **NM** value: **15.00**
Circ: Statement: **288,232 • CGC:** 18 graded, best 9.6
🕮 The Molten Man Breaks Out • Molten Man's relationship to Liz Allan revealed **A:** John Romita; Ross Andru **W:** Gerry Conway ★ Versus Molten Man.

134 ❑ Jul 1974 Cover: 0.25 **NM** value: **30.00**
Circ: Statement: **288,232 • CGC:** 34 graded, best 9.8
🕮 Danger is a Man Name Tarantula **A:** John Romita; Ross Andru **W:** Gerry Conway ★ 1st Appearance of Tarantula I (Anton Rodriguez). ★ Appearance of Punisher.

135 ❑ Aug 1974 Cover: 0.25 **NM** value: **30.00**
Circ: Statement: **288,232 • CGC:** 46 graded, best 9.8
🕮 Shoot-Out in Central Park **A:** John Romita; Ross Andru **W:** Gerry Conway ★ Origin of Tarantula I (Anton Rodriguez). ★ Appearance of Punisher.

136 ❑ Sep 1974 Cover: 0.25 **NM** value: **35.00**
Circ: Statement: **288,232 • CGC:** 44 graded, best 9.8
🕮 The Green Goblin Lives Again **A:** John Romita; Ross Andru **W:** Gerry Conway ★ 1st Appearance of Green Goblin II (Harry Osborn).

137 ❑ Oct 1974 Cover: 0.25 **NM** value: **35.00**
Circ: Statement: **288,232 • CGC:** 43 graded, best 9.8
🕮 The Green Goblin Strikes; Death-Trap Times Three **A:** Gil Kane; Ross Andru **W:** Gerry Conway ★ 2nd Appearance of Green Goblin II (Harry Osborn). ★ Versus Green Goblin II (Harry Osborn).

138 ❑ Nov 1974 Cover: 0.25 **NM** value: **15.00**
Circ: Statement: **288,232 • CGC:** 27 graded, best 9.8
🕮 Madness Means...The Mindworm! • Peter moves in with Flash Thompson **A:** Gil Kane; Ross Andru **W:** Gerry Conway ★ Origin of The Mindworm. ★ 1st Appearance of The Mindworm.

139 ❑ Dec 1974 Cover: 0.25 **NM** value: **15.00**
Circ: Statement: **288,232 • CGC:** 20 graded, best 9.6
🕮 Day of the Grizzly **A:** Gil Kane; Ross Andru **W:** Gerry Conway ★ 1st Appearance of Grizzly. ★ Appearance of Jackal.

140 ❑ Jan 1975 Cover: 0.25 **NM** value: **15.00**
Circ: Statement: **273,773 • CGC:** 27 graded, best 9.6
🕮 And One Will Fall **A:** Gil Kane; Ross Andru **W:** Gerry Conway ★ Origin of Grizzly. ★ 1st Appearance of Gloria Grant. ★ Versus Jackal.

141 ❑ Feb 1975 Cover: 0.25 **NM** value: **15.00**
Circ: Statement: **273,773 • CGC:** 28 graded, best 9.6
🕮 The Man's Name Appears to be Mysterio • Spider-Mobile sinks in Hudson **A:** John Romita; Ross Andru **W:** Gerry Conway ★ Versus second Mysterio.

142 ❑ Mar 1975 Cover: 0.25 **NM** value: **15.00**
Circ: Statement: **273,773 • CGC:** 16 graded, best 9.6
🕮 Dead Man's Bluff **A:** John Romita; Ross Andru **W:** Gerry Conway ★ Versus second Mysterio.

143 ❑ Apr 1975 Cover: 0.25 **NM** value: **15.00**
Circ: Statement: **273,773 • CGC:** 26 graded, best 9.6
🕮 And The Wind Cries: Cyclone! **A:** Gil Kane; Ross Andru **W:** Gerry Conway ★ 1st Appearance of Cyclone.

144 ❑ May 1975 Cover: 0.25 **NM** value: **15.00**
Circ: Statement: **273,773 • CGC:** 24 graded, best 9.8
🕮 The Delusion Conspiracy • Has 1974 Statement; avg sales 285,431; avg subs 2,801; avg total paid circ 288,232 **A:** Gil Kane; Ross Andru **W:** Gerry Conway ★ Origin of Cyclone. ★ 1st Appearance of Gwen Stacy clone. ★ Versus Cyclone.

145 ❑ Jun 1975 Cover: 0.25 **NM** value: **15.00**
Circ: Statement: **273,773 • CGC:** 27 graded, best 9.6
🕮 Gwen Stacy is Alive...and, Well...?! **A:** Gil Kane; Ross Andru **W:** Gerry Conway ★ Appearance of Scorpion. ★ Versus Scorpion.

146 ❑ Jul 1975 Cover: 0.25 **NM** value: **15.00**
Circ: Statement: **273,773 • CGC:** 17 graded, best 9.8
🕮 Scorpion, Where is Thy Sting? • The Jackal **A:** John Romita; Ross Andru **W:** Gerry Conway ★ Appearance of Scorpion. ★ Versus Jackal, Scorpion.

147 ❑ Aug 1975 Cover: 0.25 **NM** value: **15.00**
Circ: Statement: **273,773 • CGC:** 28 graded, best 9.8
🕮 The Tarantula is a Very Deadly Beast **A:** John Romita; Ross Andru **W:** Gerry Conway ★ Versus Jackal, Tarantula.

148 ❑ Sep 1975 Cover: 0.25 **NM** value: **20.00**
Circ: Statement: **273,773 • CGC:** 24 graded, best 9.8
🕮 Jackal, Jackal, Who's Got the Jackal? • Professor Warren revealed as Jackal **A:** Gil Kane; Ross Andru **W:** Gerry Conway ★ Versus Jackal, Tarantula.

149 ❑ Oct 1975 Cover: 0.25 **NM** value: **40.00**
Circ: Statement: **273,773 • CGC:** 35 graded, best 9.6
🕮 Even if I Live, I Die! • First Spider-Man Clone **A:** Gil Kane; Ross Andru **W:** Gerry Conway ★ 1st Appearance of Ben Reilly. ★ Death of Jackal. ★ Death of Spider-clone (faked death).

150 ❑ Nov 1975 Cover: 0.25 **NM** value: **15.00**
Circ: Statement: **273,773 • CGC:** 30 graded, best 9.8

CGC-graded: Multiply prices above by **33 for 9.9 M • 16 for 9.8 NM/M • 7 for 9.6 NM+ • 5 for 9.4 NM • 2.5 for 9.2 NM- • 1.5 for 9.0 VF/NM**

📖 Spider-Man or Spider-Clone? • Spider-Man attempts to determine if he is the clone or the original **A:** Gil Kane **W:** Archie Goodwin ★ Appearance of Ben Reilly.

151 ❑ Dec 1975 Cover: 0.25 **NM** value: **15.00**
Circ: Statement: **273,773** • **CGC:** 11 graded, best 9.6
📖 Skirmish Beneath the Streets • Spider-Man disposes of clone's body (faked) **A:** John Romita; Ross Andru **W:** Len Wein ★ Appearance of Ben Reilly. ★ Versus Shocker.

152 ❑ Jan 1976 Cover: 0.25 **NM** value: **10.00**
Circ: Statement: **282,159** • **CGC:** 15 graded, best 9.6
📖 Shattered by the Shocker **A:** Gil Kane; Ross Andru **W:** Len Wein ★ Versus Shocker.

153 ❑ Feb 1976 Cover: 0.25 **NM** value: **10.00**
Circ: Statement: **282,159** • **CGC:** 25 graded, best 9.6
📖 The Longest Hundred Yards **A:** Gil Kane; Ross Andru **W:** Len Wein

154 ❑ Mar 1976 Cover: 0.25 **NM** value: **10.00**
Circ: Statement: **282,159** • **CGC:** 17 graded, best 9.6
📖 The Sandman Always Strikes Twice **A:** Sal Buscema; John Romita **W:** Len Wein ★ Versus Sandman (Marvel).

155 ❑ Apr 1976 Cover: 0.25 **NM** value: **10.00**
Circ: Statement: **282,159** • **CGC:** 31 graded, best 9.8
📖 Whodunit! • Has 1975 Statement; avg sales 269,167; avg subs 4,606; avg total paid circ 273,773 **A:** Sal Buscema; John Romita **W:** Len Wein

156 ❑ May 1976 Cover: 0.25 **NM** value: **10.00**
Circ: Statement: **282,159** • **CGC:** 11 graded, best 9.8
📖 On a Clear Day, You Can See the Mirage • Wedding of Betty Brant and Ned Leeds **A:** John Romita; Ross Andru **W:** Len Wein ★ Origin of Mirage I (Desmond Charne). ★ 1st Appearance of Mirage I (Desmond Charne).

157 ❑ Jun 1976 Cover: 0.25 **NM** value: **10.00**
Circ: Statement: **282,159** • **CGC:** 30 graded, best 9.6
📖 The Ghost That Haunted Octopus • return of Doctor Octopus **A:** John Romita; Ross Andru **W:** Len Wein

158 ❑ Jul 1976 Cover: 0.25 **NM** value: **10.00**
Circ: Statement: **282,159** • **CGC:** 50 graded, best 9.6
📖 Hammerhead Is Out • Hammerhead regains physical form **A:** Gil Kane; Ross Andru **W:** Len Wein ★ Versus Doctor Octopus.

159 ❑ Aug 1976 Cover: 0.25 **NM** value: **10.00**
Circ: Statement: **282,159** • **CGC:** 8 graded, best 9.6
📖 Arm-in-Arm-in-Arm-in-Arm-in-Arm-in-Arm with Doctor Octopus **A:** Gil Kane; Ross Andru **W:** Len Wein ★ 2nd Appearance of The Tinkerer. ★ Versus Doctor Octopus, Hammerhead.

160 ❑ Sep 1976 Cover: 0.30 **NM** value: **10.00**
Circ: Statement: **282,159** • **CGC:** 20 graded, best 9.6
📖 My Killer, the Car • return of Spider-Mobile **A:** Gil Kane; Ross Andru **W:** Len Wein ★ Versus Tinkerer.

161 ❑ Oct 1976 Cover: 0.30 **NM** value: **10.00**
Circ: Statement: **282,159** • **CGC:** 41 graded, best 9.8
📖 And the Nightcrawler Came Prowling, Prowling **A:** Gil Kane; Ross Andru **W:** Len Wein ★ Appearance of Punisher. ★ Appearance of Nightcrawler.

162 ❑ Nov 1976 Cover: 0.30 **NM** value: **10.00**
Circ: Statement: **282,159** • **CGC:** 27 graded, best 9.8
📖 Let the Punisher Fit the Crime **A:** Ross Andru **W:** Len Wein ★ Appearance of Punisher. ★ Appearance of Nightcrawler.

163 ❑ Dec 1976 Cover: 0.30 **NM** value: **6.00**
Circ: Statement: **282,159** • **CGC:** 17 graded, best 9.6
📖 All the Kingpin's Men **A:** Dave Cockrum; Ross Andru **W:** Len Wein ★ Versus Kingpin.

164 ❑ Jan 1977 Cover: 0.30 **NM** value: **6.00**
Circ: Statement: **281,860** • **CGC:** 11 graded, best 9.6
📖 Deadline! **A:** John Romita; Ross Andru **W:** Len Wein ★ Versus Kingpin.

165 ❑ Feb 1977 Cover: 0.30 **NM** value: **6.00**
Circ: Statement: **281,860** • **CGC:** 14 graded, best 9.6
📖 Stegron Stalks the City **A:** John Romita; Ross Andru **W:** Len Wein ★ Versus Stegron.

166 ❑ Mar 1977 Cover: 0.30 **NM** value: **6.00**
Circ: Statement: **281,860** • **CGC:** 25 graded, best 9.8
📖 War of the Reptile-Men **A:** John Romita; Ross Andru **W:** Len Wein ★ Versus Lizard. ★ Versus Stegron.

167 ❑ Apr 1977 Cover: 0.30 **NM** value: **6.00**
Circ: Statement: **281,860** • **CGC:** 19 graded, best 9.8
📖 Stalked by the Spider-Slayer • Has 1976 Statement; avg sales 278,909; avg subs 3,250; avg total paid circ 282,159 **A:** John Romita; Ross Andru **W:** Len Wein ★ 1st Appearance of Will o' the Wisp.

168 ❑ May 1977 Cover: 0.30 **NM** value: **6.00**
Circ: Statement: **281,860** • **CGC:** 35 graded, best 9.8
📖 Murder on the Wind **A:** Ross Andru **W:** Len Wein ★ Versus Will o' the Wisp.

169 ❑ Jun 1977 Cover: 0.30 **NM** value: **10.00**
Circ: Statement: **281,860** • **CGC:** 12 graded, best 9.6
📖 Confrontation • J. Jonah Jameson acquires photos showing Spider-Man disposing of clone's(?) body **A:** Al Milgrom; Ross Andru **W:** Len Wein

170 ❑ Jul 1977 Cover: 0.30 **NM** value: **6.00**
Circ: Statement: **281,860** • **CGC:** 19 graded, best 9.8
📖 Madness Is All In The Mind **A:** Ross Andru **W:** Len Wein ★ Versus Doctor Faustus.

171 ❑ Aug 1977 Cover: 0.30 **NM** value: **6.00**
Circ: Statement: **281,860** • **CGC:** 19 graded, best 9.8
📖 Photon Is Another Name For…? **A:** Ross Andru **W:** Len Wein ★ Appearance of Nova.

172 ❑ Sep 1977 Cover: 0.30 **NM** value: **6.00**
Circ: Statement: **281,860** • **CGC:** 11 graded, best 9.6
📖 The Fiend from the Fire **A:** Ross Andru **W:** Len Wein ★ 1st Appearance of Rocket Racer.

173 ❑ Oct 1977 Cover: 0.30 **NM** value: **6.00**
Circ: Statement: **281,860** • **CGC:** 8 graded, best 9.6
📖 If You Can't Stand the Heat **A:** Ross Andru **W:** Len Wein ★ Versus Molten Man.

174 ❑ Nov 1977 Cover: 0.35 **NM** value: **6.00**
Circ: Statement: **281,860** • **CGC:** 26 graded, best 9.6
📖 The Hitman's Back in Town **A:** Ross Andru **W:** Len Wein ★ Appearance of Punisher. ★ Versus Hitman.

175 ❑ Dec 1977 Cover: 0.35 **NM** value: **6.00**
Circ: Statement: **281,860** • **CGC:** 41 graded, best 9.8
📖 Big Apple Underground **A:** Ross Andru **W:** Len Wein ★ Appearance of Punisher. ★ Versus Hitman.

176 ❑ Jan 1978 Cover: 0.35 **NM** value: **6.00**
Circ: Statement: **258,156** • **CGC:** 15 graded, best 9.6
📖 He Who Laughs Last **A:** Ross Andru **W:** Len Wein ★ Origin of Green Goblin III (Doctor Barton Hamilton). ★ 1st Appearance of Green Goblin III (Doctor Barton Hamilton).

177 ❑ Feb 1978 Cover: 0.35 **NM** value: **6.00**
Circ: Statement: **258,156** • **CGC:** 33 graded, best 9.8
📖 Goblin in the Middle **A:** Ross Andru **W:** Len Wein ★ Appearance of Green Goblin III (Doctor Barton Hamilton). ★ Versus Silvermane.

178 ❑ Mar 1978 Cover: 0.35 **NM** value: **15.00**
Circ: Statement: **258,156** • **CGC:** 24 graded, best 9.6
📖 Green Grows the Goblin • Has 1977 Statement; avg sales 271,491; avg subs 10,369; avg total paid circ 281,860 **A:** Ross Andru **W:** Len Wein ★ Appearance of Green Goblin III (Doctor Barton Hamilton). ★ Versus Silvermane.

179 ❑ Apr 1978 Cover: 0.35 **NM** value: **15.00**
Circ: Statement: **258,156** • **CGC:** 45 graded, best 9.8
📖 The Goblin's Always Greener **A:** Ross Andru **W:** Len Wein ★ Appearance of Green Goblin III (Doctor Barton Hamilton). ★ Versus Silvermane.

180 ❑ May 1978 Cover: 0.35 **NM** value: **6.00**
Circ: Statement: **258,156** • **CGC:** 27 graded, best 9.8
📖 Who Was That Goblin I Saw You With? **A:** Ross Andru **W:** Len Wein ★ Appearance of Green Goblin III (Doctor Barton Hamilton). ★ Versus Silvermane.

181 ❑ Jun 1978 Cover: 0.35 **NM** value: **6.00**
Circ: Statement: **258,156** • **CGC:** 21 graded, best 9.6
📖 Flashback! **A:** Sal Buscema; Gil Kane **W:** Bill Mantlo ★ Origin of Spider-Man.

182 ❑ Jul 1978 Cover: 0.35 **NM** value: **6.00**
Circ: Statement: **258,156** • **CGC:** 15 graded, best 9.6
📖 The Rocket Racer's Back In Town! **A:** Ross Andru **W:** Marv Wolfman ★ Versus Rocket Racer.

183 ❑ Aug 1978 Cover: 0.35 **NM** value: **6.00**
Circ: Statement: **258,156** • **CGC:** 18 graded, best 9.8
📖 And Where the Big Wheel Stops, Nobody Knows **A:** Ross Andru **W:** Marv Wolfman ★ Origin of Big Wheel. ★ 1st Appearance of Big Wheel. ★ Death of Big Wheel. ★ Versus Tinkerer. ★ Versus Rocket Racer.

184 ❑ Sep 1978 Cover: 0.35 **NM** value: **6.00**
Circ: Statement: **258,156** • **CGC:** 8 graded, best 9.8
📖 White Dragon! Red Death! **A:** Ross Andru **W:** Marv Wolfman ★ 1st Appearance of White Dragon II.

185 ❑ Oct 1978 Cover: 0.35 **NM** value: **6.00**
Circ: Statement: **258,156** • **CGC:** 20 graded, best 9.6
📖 Spider, Spider, Burning Bright!; The Graduation of Peter Parker • Peter Parker graduates from college **A:** Ross Andru **W:** Marv Wolfman ★ Versus Dragon Gangs. ★ Versus White Dragon II.

186 ❑ Nov 1978 Cover: 0.35 **NM** value: **6.00**
Circ: Statement: **258,156** • **CGC:** 14 graded, best 9.6
📖 Chaos Is The Chameleon! **A:** Keith Pollard; Mike Esposito **W:** Marv Wolfman ★ Versus Chameleon.

187 ❑ Dec 1978 Cover: 0.35 **NM** value: **6.00**
Circ: Statement: **258,156** • **CGC:** 19 graded, best 9.8
📖 The Power of Electro **A:** Jim Starlin; Keith Pollard; Bob McLeod; Joe Sinnott **W:** Jim Starlin; Marv Wolfman ★ Appearance of Shield. ★ Appearance of Captain America. ★ Versus Electro.

188 ❑ Jan 1979 Cover: 0.35 **NM** value: **6.00**
• **CGC:** 14 graded, best 9.6
📖 The Jigsaw Is Up! **A:** Keith Pollard; Dave Cockrum; Mike Esposito **W:** Marv Wolfman ★ Origin of Jigsaw. ★ 1st Appearance of Jigsaw. ★ Versus Jigsaw.

189 ❑ Feb 1979 Cover: 0.35 **NM** value: **6.00**
• **CGC:** 29 graded, best 9.8
📖 Mayhem by Moonlight **A:** John Byrne **W:** Marv Wolfman ★ Appearance of Man-Wolf.

190 ❑ Mar 1979 Cover: 0.35 **NM** value: **6.00**
• **CGC:** 16 graded, best 9.8
📖 In Search of the Man-Wolf **A:** John Byrne; Keith Pollard; Jim Mooney **W:** Marv Wolfman ★ Appearance of Man-Wolf.

191 ❑ Apr 1979 Cover: 0.35 **NM** value: **5.00**
• **CGC:** 24 graded, best 9.8
📖 Wanted for Murder: Spider-Man • Has 1978 Statement; avg sales 230,208; avg subs 27,948; avg total paid circ 258,156 **A:** Al Milgrom; Keith Pollard; Mike Esposito **W:** Marv Wolfman ★ Versus Spider Slayer. ★ Versus Spencer Smythe.

192 ❑ May 1979 Cover: 0.40 **NM** value: **5.00**
• **CGC:** 19 graded, best 9.8
📖 24 Hours Till Doomsday! **A:** Keith Pollard; Mike Esposito **W:** Marv Wolfman ★ Death of Spencer Smythe. ★ Versus The Fly.

193 ❑ Jun 1979 Cover: 0.40 **NM** value: **5.00**
• **CGC:** 14 graded, best 9.8
📖 Wings Of The Fearsome Fly **A:** Keith Pollard; Jim Mooney **W:** Marv Wolfman ★ Versus The Fly.

194 ❑ Jul 1979 Cover: 0.40 **NM** value: **12.00**
• **CGC:** 46 graded, best 9.8
📖 Never Let the Black Cat Cross Your Path **A:** Al Milgrom; Keith Pollard **W:** Marv Wolfman ★ 1st Appearance of Black Cat.

195 ❑ Aug 1979 Cover: 0.40 **NM** value: **5.00**
• **CGC:** 22 graded, best 9.8
📖 Nine Lives Has the Black Cat • Peter Parker informed of Aunt May's death (faked death) **A:** Al Milgrom; Keith Pollard; Jim Mooney; Mike Esposito **W:** Marv Wolfman ★ Origin of Black Cat.

196 ❑ Sep 1979 Cover: 0.40 **NM** value: **5.00**
• **CGC:** 12 graded, best 9.8
📖 Requiem! **A:** Al Milgrom; Keith Pollard; Jim Mooney **W:** Marv Wolfman ★ Death of Aunt May (faked death). ★ Versus Kingpin. ★ Versus Mysterio.

197 ❑ Oct 1979 Cover: 0.40 **NM** value: **5.00**
• **CGC:** 13 graded, best 9.6
📖 The Kingpin's Midnight Massacre **A:** Keith Pollard; Jim Mooney **W:** Marv Wolfman ★ Versus Kingpin.

198 ❑ Nov 1979 Cover: 0.40 **NM** value: **5.00**
• **CGC:** 23 graded, best 9.6
📖 Mysterio Is Deadlier by the Dozen **A:** Sal Buscema; Keith Pollard; Jim Mooney **W:** Marv Wolfman ★ Versus Mysterio.

199 ❑ Dec 1979 Cover: 0.40 **NM** value: **5.00**
• **CGC:** 17 graded, best 9.6
📖 Now You See Me, Now You Die **A:** Sal Buscema; Keith Pollard; Jim Mooney **W:** Marv Wolfman ★ Versus Mysterio.

200 ❑ Jan 1980 Cover: 0.75 **NM** value: **14.00**
Circ: Statement: **296,712** • **CGC:** 133 graded, best 9.8
• Giant sized. 📖 The Spider And The Burglar…a Sequel; Less Spider Than Man; Let the Burglar Beware; Murder Most Foul; The Final Confrontation; Resolutions • Aunt May revealed to be alive **A:** Keith Pollard; John Romita; Jim Mooney **W:** Marv Wolfman ★ Origin of Spider-Man. ★ Death of unnamed burglar that shot Uncle Ben.

201 ❑ Feb 1980 Cover: 0.40 **NM** value: **8.00**
Circ: Statement: **296,712** • **CGC:** 12 graded, best 9.6
📖 Man-Hunt! **A:** Keith Pollard; John Romita; Jim Mooney **W:** Marv Wolfman ★ Appearance of Punisher.

202 ❑ Mar 1980 Cover: 0.40 **NM** value: **8.00**
Circ: Statement: **296,712** • **CGC:** 15 graded, best 9.6
📖 One for Those Long Gone **A:** Keith Pollard; John Romita; Jim Mooney **W:** Marv Wolfman ★ Appearance of Punisher.

203 ❑ Apr 1980 Cover: 0.40 **NM** value: **5.00**
Circ: Statement: **296,712** • **CGC:** 6 graded, best 9.6
📖 Bewitched, Bothered, And Be-Dazzled! **A:** Keith Pollard; John Romita; Frank Miller(cover) **W:** Marv Wolfman ★ 2nd Appearance of Dazzler. ★ Appearance of Dazzler.

204 ❑ May 1980 Cover: 0.40 **NM** value: **5.00**
Circ: Statement: **296,712** • **CGC:** 4 graded, best 9.6
📖 The Black Cat Always Lands on Her Feet **A:** Keith Pollard; John Romita Jr.; Pablo Marcos **W:** Marv Wolfman ★ Appearance of Black Cat.

205 ❑ Jun 1980 Cover: 0.40 **NM** value: **5.00**
Circ: Statement: **296,712** • **CGC:** 4 graded, best 9.6
📖 …In Love And War **A:** Al Milgrom; Keith Pollard **W:** David Michelinie ★ Appearance of Black Cat.

206 ❑ Jul 1980 Cover: 0.40 **NM** value: **5.00**
Circ: Statement: **296,712** • **CGC:** 1 graded, best 9.4
📖 A Method In His Madness! **A:** Al Milgrom; John Byrne **W:** Roger Stern

207 ❑ Aug 1980 Cover: 0.40 **NM** value: **5.00**
Circ: Statement: **296,712** • **CGC:** 2 graded, best 9.6
📖 Mesmero's Revenge **A:** Jim Mooney **W:** Denny O'Neil ★ Versus Mesmero.

208 ❑ Sep 1980 Cover: 0.50 **NM** value: **5.00**
Circ: Statement: **296,712** • **CGC:** 3 graded, best 9.6
📖 Fusion! **A:** Al Milgrom; John Romita Jr. **W:** Jim Shooter; Mark Gruenwald ★ Origin of Fusion. ★ 1st Appearance of Lance Bannon, Fusion.

209 ❑ Oct 1980 Cover: 0.50 **NM** value: **6.00**
Circ: Statement: **296,712** • **CGC:** 3 graded, best 9.6
📖 To Salvage My Honor! **A:** Alan Weiss **W:** Denny O'Neil ★ Origin of Calypso. ★ 1st Appearance of Calypso. ★ Versus Kraven the Hunter.

210 ❑ Nov 1980 Cover: 0.50 **NM** value: **5.00**
Circ: Statement: **296,712** • **CGC:** 7 graded, best 9.6
📖 The Prophecy Of Madame Web **A:** John Romita Jr. **W:** Denny O'Neil ★ Origin of Madame Web. ★ 1st Appearance of Madame Web.

211 ❑ Dec 1980 Cover: 0.50 **NM** value: **4.00**
Circ: Statement: **296,712** • **CGC:** 4 graded, best 9.8
📖 The Spider And The Sea-Scourge **A:** John Romita Jr.; Jim Mooney **W:** Denny O'Neil ★ Appearance of Sub-Mariner.

212 ❑ Jan 1981 Cover: 0.50 **NM** value: **4.00**
Circ: Statement: **242,781** • **CGC:** 5 graded, best 9.8
📖 The Coming of Hydroman **A:** John Romita Jr.; Jim Mooney **W:** Denny O'Neil ★ Origin of Sandman (Marvel), Hydro-Man. ★ 1st Appearance of Hydro-Man.

213 ❑ Feb 1981 Cover: 0.50 **NM** value: **4.00**
Circ: Statement: **242,781** • **CGC:** 7 graded, best 9.8
📖 All They Want To Do Is Kill You, Spider-Man **A:** John Romita Jr.; Jim Mooney **W:** Denny O'Neil ★ Versus Wizard.

214 ❑ Mar 1981 Cover: 0.50 **NM** value: **4.00**
Circ: Statement: **242,781** • **CGC:** 7 graded, best 9.6
📖 Then Shall We Both Be Betrayed **A:** John Romita Jr.; Jim Mooney **W:** Denny O'Neil ★ Appearance of Sub-Mariner. ★ Versus Frightful Four.

215 ❑ Apr 1981 Cover: 0.50 **NM** value: **4.00**
Circ: Statement: **242,781** • **CGC:** 4 graded, best 9.6
📖 By My Powers Shall I Be Vanquished! • Has 1980 Statement; avg sales 267,124; avg subs 29,588; avg total paid circ 296,712 **A:** John Romita Jr.; Jim Mooney **W:** Denny O'Neil

216 ❑ May 1981 Cover: 0.50 **NM** value: **4.00**
Circ: Statement: **242,781** • **CGC:** 3 graded, best 9.4
📖 Marathon **A:** John Romita Jr.; Jim Mooney **W:** Denny O'Neil

217 ❑ Jun 1981 Cover: 0.50 **NM** value: **4.00**
Circ: Statement: **242,781** • **CGC:** 11 graded, best 9.8
📖 Here's Mud In Your Eye! **A:** John Romita Jr.; Jim Mooney **W:** Denny O'Neil

218 ❑ Jul 1981 Cover: 0.50 **NM** value: **4.00**
Circ: Statement: **242,781** • **CGC:** 8 graded, best 9.8
📖 Eye Of The Beholder! **A:** John Romita Jr.; Frank Miller(cover) **W:** Denny O'Neil

219 ❑ Aug 1981 Cover: 0.50 **NM** value: **4.00**
Circ: Statement: **242,781** • **CGC:** 6 graded, best 9.6
📖 Peter Parker -Criminal! **A:** Jim Mooney; Frank Miller(cover) **W:** Denny O'Neil

220 ❑ Sep 1981 Cover: 0.50 **NM** value: **4.00**
Circ: Statement: **242,781** • **CGC:** 2 graded, best 9.4
📖 A Coffin For Spider-Man! **A:** Bob McLeod **W:** Michael Fleisher ★ Appearance of Moon Knight.

221 ❑ Oct 1981 Cover: 0.50 **NM** value: **4.00**
Circ: Statement: **242,781** • **CGC:** 4 graded, best 9.6
📖 Blues For Lonesome Pinky! **A:** Alan Kupperberg **W:** Denny O'Neil

222 ❑ Nov 1981 Cover: 0.50 **NM** value: **4.00**
Circ: Statement: **242,781** • **CGC:** 3 graded, best 9.6
📖 Faster Than The Eye **A:** Bob Hall **W:** Bill Mantlo

223 ❑ Dec 1981 Cover: 0.50 **NM** value: **4.00**
Circ: Statement: **242,781** • **CGC:** 3 graded, best 9.4
📖 Night Of The Ape **A:** John Romita Jr. **W:** J.M. DeMatteis

224 ❑ Jan 1982 Cover: 0.60 **NM** value: **4.00**
Circ: Statement: **240,683** • **CGC:** 4 graded, best 9.4

Other grades: Multiply prices above by **1.5 for Mint • 2/3 for Very Fine • 1/3 for Fine • 1/5 for Very Good • 1/8 for Good**

Let Fly These Aged Wings! **A:** John Romita Jr.; Pablo Marcos **W:** Roger Stern

225 ❑ Feb 1982 Cover: 0.60 **NM** value: **4.00**
Circ: Statement: **240,683** • **CGC:** 4 graded, best 9.6
Fools…Like Us! **A:** John Romita Jr.; Bob Wiacek **W:** Roger Stern ★ Appearance of Foolkiller II (Greg Salinger).

226 ❑ Mar 1982 Cover: 0.60 **NM** value: **4.00**
Circ: Statement: **240,683** • **CGC:** 3 graded, best 9.6
But the Cat Came Back! **A:** John Romita Jr. **W:** Roger Stern ★ Appearance of Black Cat.

227 ❑ Apr 1982 Cover: 0.60 **NM** value: **4.00**
Circ: Statement: **240,683** • **CGC:** 5 graded, best 9.6
Goin' Straight • Has 1981 Statement; avg sales 208,714; avg subs 34,057; avg total paid circ 242,781 **A:** John Romita Jr.; Jim Mooney **W:** Roger Stern ★ Appearance of Black Cat.

228 ❑ May 1982 Cover: 0.60 **NM** value: **4.00**
Circ: Statement: **240,683** • **CGC:** 8 graded, best 9.6
Murder By Spider **A:** Rick Leonardi; John Romita Jr. **W:** Jan Strnad

229 ❑ Jun 1982 Cover: 0.60 **NM** value: **4.00**
Circ: Statement: **240,683** • **CGC:** 2 graded, best 9.6
Nothing Can Stop the Juggernaut! **A:** John Romita Jr. **W:** Roger Stern

230 ❑ Jul 1982 Cover: 0.60 **NM** value: **4.00**
Circ: Statement: **240,683** • **CGC:** 6 graded, best 9.6
To Fight the Unbeatable Foe! **A:** John Romita Jr. **W:** Roger Stern

231 ❑ Aug 1982 Cover: 0.60 **NM** value: **4.00**
Circ: Statement: **240,683** • **CGC:** 6 graded, best 9.4
Caught In The Act… **A:** John Romita Jr.; Jim Mooney **W:** Roger Stern

232 ❑ Sep 1982 Cover: 0.60 **NM** value: **4.00**
Circ: Statement: **240,683** • **CGC:** 6 graded, best 9.8
Hyde…In Plain Sight **A:** John Romita Jr. **W:** Roger Stern

233 ❑ Oct 1982 Cover: 0.60 **NM** value: **4.00**
Circ: Statement: **240,683** • **CGC:** 8 graded, best 9.8
Where The @ó%# Is Nose Norton? **A:** John Romita Jr.; Jim Mooney **W:** Roger Stern

234 ❑ Nov 1982 Cover: 0.60 **NM** value: **4.00**
Circ: Statement: **240,683** • **CGC:** 4 graded, best 9.0
Now Shall Will-O'-The-Wisp Have His Revenge! • Free 16 page insert-Marvel Guide to Collecting Comics **A:** Dan Green; John Romita Jr. **W:** Roger Stern

235 ❑ Dec 1982 Cover: 0.60 **NM** value: **4.00**
Circ: Statement: **240,683** • **CGC:** 7 graded, best 9.8
Look Out, There's A Monster Coming! **A:** John Romita Jr.; Frank Giacoia **W:** Roger Stern ★ Origin of Will o' the Wisp.

236 ❑ Jan 1983 Cover: 0.60 **NM** value: **4.00**
Circ: Statement: **241,762** • **CGC:** 8 graded, best 9.6
Death Knell! **A:** John Romita Jr.; Frank Giacoia **W:** Roger Stern ★ Death of Tarantula I (Anton Rodriguez).

237 ❑ Feb 1983 Cover: 0.60 **NM** value: **4.00**
Circ: Statement: **241,762** • **CGC:** 5 graded, best 9.9
High And Mighty! **A:** Bob Hall **W:** Bill Mantlo

238 ❑ Mar 1983 Cover: 0.60 **NM** value: **40.00**
Circ: Statement: **241,762** • **CGC:** 241 graded, best 9.8
• Came with "Tattooz" temporary tattoo decal ★ 1st Appearance of Hobgoblin (Ned Leeds).

239 ❑ Apr 1983 Cover: 0.60 **NM** value: **20.00**
Circ: Statement: **241,762** • **CGC:** 106 graded, best 9.8
★ 2nd Appearance of Hobgoblin.

240 ❑ May 1983 Cover: 0.60 **NM** value: **5.00**
Circ: Statement: **241,762** • **CGC:** 9 graded, best 9.8
Wings Of Vengeance! • Has 1982 Statement; avg sales 203,475; avg subs 37,208; avg total paid circ 240,683 **A:** Bob Layton; John Romita Jr. **W:** Roger Stern

241 ❑ Jun 1983 Cover: 0.60 **NM** value: **5.00**
Circ: Statement: **241,762** • **CGC:** 6 graded, best 9.6
In The Beginning… **A:** John Romita Jr.; Frank Giacoia **W:** Roger Stern ★ Origin of Vulture.

242 ❑ Jul 1983 Cover: 0.60 **NM** value: **5.00**
Circ: Statement: **241,762** • **CGC:** 5 graded, best 9.8
Confrontations! **A:** John Romita Jr.; Kevin Dzuban **W:** Roger Stern

243 ❑ Aug 1983 Cover: 0.60 **NM** value: **5.00**
Circ: Statement: **241,762** • **CGC:** 6 graded, best 9.8

244 ❑ Sep 1983 Cover: 0.60 **NM** value: **6.00**
Circ: Statement: **241,762** • **CGC:** 17 graded, best 9.9
Ordeals! **A:** John Romita Jr.; Klaus Janson **W:** Roger Stern ★ Appearance of 3rd. ★ Versus Hobgoblin.

245 ❑ Oct 1983 Cover: 0.60 **NM** value: **8.00**
Circ: Statement: **241,762** • **CGC:** 21 graded, best 9.9
Sacrifice Play! • Lefty Donovan becomes Hobgoblin **A:** John Romita Jr.; Dave Simmons **W:** Roger Stern ★ Appearance of 4th.

246 ❑ Nov 1983 Cover: 0.60 **NM** value: **5.00**
Circ: Statement: **241,762** • **CGC:** 7 graded, best 9.8
The Daydreamers **A:** John Romita Jr. **W:** Roger Stern

247 ❑ Dec 1983 Cover: 0.60 **NM** value: **5.00**
Circ: Statement: **241,762** • **CGC:** 5 graded, best 9.6
Interruptions **A:** John Romita Jr. **W:** Roger Stern

248 ❑ Jan 1984 Cover: 0.60 **NM** value: **5.00**
Circ: Statement: **261,254** • **CGC:** 13 graded, best 9.8
And He Strikes Like A Thunderball! **W:** Roger Stern

249 ❑ Feb 1984 Cover: 0.60 **NM** value: **6.00**
Circ: Statement: **261,254** • **CGC:** 15 graded, best 9.6
★ Versus Hobgoblin.

250 ❑ Mar 1984 Cover: 0.60 **NM** value: **7.00**
Circ: Statement: **261,254** • **CGC:** 16 graded, best 9.6
Confessions! **A:** John Romita Jr.; Klaus Janson **W:** Roger Stern ★ Appearance of Hobgoblin.

251 ❑ Apr 1984 Cover: 0.60 **NM** value: **7.00**
Circ: Statement: **261,254** • **CGC:** 22 graded, best 9.8
Endings! • Last old costume **A:** Ron Frenz **W:** Tom DeFalco

252 ❑ May 1984 Cover: 0.60 **NM** value: **25.00**
Circ: Statement: **261,254** • **CGC:** 352 graded, best 9.8
• new costume; Has 1983 Statement, filed 10/4/83; avg print run 470,527; avg sales 202,633; avg subs 39,129; avg total paid 241,762; samples 843; office use 5,842; max existent 248,437; 47% of run returned

253 ❑ Jun 1984 Cover: 0.60 **NM** value: **5.00**
Circ: Statement: **261,254** • **CGC:** 17 graded, best 9.8
By Myself Betrayed! **A:** Rick Leonardi **W:** Tom DeFalco ★ 1st Appearance of The Rose.

254 ❑ Jul 1984 Cover: 0.60 **NM** value: **4.00**
Circ: Statement: **261,254** • **CGC:** 13 graded, best 9.8
With Great Power… **A:** Rick Leonardi **W:** Tom DeFalco

255 ❑ Aug 1984 Cover: 0.60 **NM** value: **4.00**
Circ: Statement: **261,254** • **CGC:** 12 graded, best 9.6
Even A Ghost Can Fear The Night! **A:** Ron Frenz **W:** Tom DeFalco ★ Versus Red Ghost.

256 ❑ Sep 1984 Cover: 0.60 **NM** value: **5.00**
Circ: Statement: **261,254** • **CGC:** 36 graded, best 9.8
★ Origin of Puma. ★ 1st Appearance of Puma. ★ Versus Puma.

257 ❑ Oct 1984 Cover: 0.60 **NM** value: **7.00**
Circ: Statement: **261,254** • **CGC:** 7 graded, best 9.6
Beware The Claws Of Puma! **A:** Ron Frenz **W:** Tom DeFalco ★ 2nd Appearance of Puma. ★ Appearance of Hobgoblin. ★ Versus Puma.

258 ❑ Nov 1984 Cover: 0.60 **NM** value: **8.00**
Circ: Statement: **261,254** • **CGC:** 27 graded, best 9.8
The Sinister Secret Of Spider-Man's New Costume! **A:** Ron Frenz **W:** Tom DeFalco ★ Appearance of Hobgoblin.

259 ❑ Dec 1984 Cover: 0.60 **NM** value: **8.00**
Circ: Statement: **261,254** • **CGC:** 27 graded, best 9.8
• Spider-Man back to old costume ★ Origin of Mary Jane Watson. ★ Appearance of Hobgoblin.

260 ❑ Jan 1985 Cover: 0.60 **NM** value: **7.00**
Circ: Statement: **326,695** • **CGC:** 10 graded, best 9.8
The Challenge Of Hobgoblin! **A:** Ron Frenz **W:** Tom DeFalco ★ Appearance of Hobgoblin. ★ Versus Hobgoblin.

261 ❑ Feb 1985 Cover: 0.60 **NM** value: **7.00**
Circ: Statement: **326,695** • **CGC:** 6 graded, best 9.6
The Sins Of My Father **A:** Ron Frenz **W:** Tom DeFalco ★ Appearance of Hobgoblin. ★ Versus Hobgoblin.

262 ❑ Mar 1985 Cover: 0.60 **NM** value: **5.00**
Circ: Statement: **326,695** • **CGC:** 5 graded, best 9.8
Photo cover. Trade Secret • Spider-man unmasked **A:** Bob Layton **W:** Bob Layton

263 ❑ Apr 1985 Cover: 0.65 **NM** value: **4.00**
Circ: Statement: **326,695** • **CGC:** 7 graded, best 9.8
The Spectacular Spider-Kid **A:** Ron Frenz **W:** Tom DeFalco ★ 1st Appearance of Spider-Kid.

264 ❑ May 1985 Cover: 0.65 **NM** value: **4.00**
Circ: Statement: **326,695** CapCity orders: **25,800** • **CGC:** 15 graded, best 9.8
Red 9 And Red Tape • Has 1984 Statement; avg sales 217,959; avg subs 43,295; avg total paid circ 261,254 **A:** Paty Cockrum **W:** Craig Anderson

265 ❑ Jun 1985 Cover: 0.65 **NM** value: **6.00**
Circ: Statement: **326,695** CapCity orders: **24,500** • **CGC:** 13 graded, best 9.8
★ 1st Appearance of Silver Sable.

265-2 ❑ Cover: 1.25 **NM** value: **2.00**

266 ❑ Jul 1985 Cover: 0.65 **NM** value: **3.00**
Circ: Statement: **326,695** CapCity orders: **24,300** • **CGC:** 6 graded, best 9.6
Jump For My Love or Spring Is In The Air **A:** Sal Buscema **W:** Peter David

267 ❑ Aug 1985 Cover: 0.65 **NM** value: **3.00**
Circ: Statement: **326,695** CapCity orders: **23,700** • **CGC:** 5 graded, best 9.8

268 ❑ Sep 1985 Cover: 0.65 **NM** value: **3.00**
Circ: Statement: **326,695** CapCity orders: **31,800** • **CGC:** 29 graded, best 9.8
• Secret Wars II **A:** Ron Frenz **W:** Tom DeFalco ★ Appearance of Kingpin. ★ Appearance of Beyonder.

269 ❑ Oct 1985 Cover: 0.65 **NM** value: **3.00**
Circ: Statement: **326,695** CapCity orders: **23,100** • **CGC:** 4 graded, best 9.6
Burn, Spider, Burn! **A:** Ron Frenz **W:** Tom DeFalco ★ Versus Firelord.

270 ❑ Nov 1985 Cover: 0.65 **NM** value: **3.00**
Circ: Statement: **326,695** CapCity orders: **22,800** • **CGC:** 3 graded, best 9.8
The Hero And The Holocaust! **A:** Ron Frenz **W:** Tom DeFalco ★ 1st Appearance of Kate Cushing (Peter Parker's supervisor at the Bugle). ★ Appearance of Avengers. ★ Versus Firelord.

271 ❑ Dec 1985 Cover: 0.65 **NM** value: **3.00**
Circ: Statement: **326,695** CapCity orders: **23,000** • **CGC:** 3 graded, best 9.4
Whatever Happened To Crusher Hogan? **A:** Ron Frenz **W:** Tom DeFalco

272 ❑ Jan 1986 Cover: 0.65 **NM** value: **3.00**
Circ: Statement: **276,064** CapCity orders: **22,600** • **CGC:** 6 graded, best 9.9
Make Way For Slyde! **A:** Sal Buscema **W:** Tom DeFalco ★ Versus Slyde.

273 ❑ Feb 1986 Cover: 0.75 **NM** value: **3.00**
Circ: Statement: **276,064** CapCity orders: **29,300** • **CGC:** 5 graded, best 9.8
Secret Wars II; To Challenge To Beyonder • Secret Wars II **A:** Ron Frenz **W:** Tom DeFalco ★ Appearance of Puma.

274 ❑ Mar 1986 Cover: 0.75 **NM** value: **3.00**
Circ: Statement: **276,064** CapCity orders: **27,800** • **CGC:** 8 graded, best 9.8
Secret Wars II • Secret Wars II ★ Appearance of Zarathos (the spirit of vengeance).

275 ❑ Apr 1986 Cover: 1.25 **NM** value: **7.00**
Circ: Statement: **276,064** CapCity orders: **27,700** • **CGC:** 20 graded, best 9.8
• double-sized. The Choice And The Challenge • Hobgoblin story; E6221 **A:** Ron Frenz **W:** Tom DeFalco ★ Origin of Spider-Man.

276 ❑ May 1986 Cover: 0.75 **NM** value: **6.00**
Circ: Statement: **276,064** CapCity orders: **28,200** • **CGC:** 14 graded, best 9.8
Unmasked! **A:** Ron Frenz **W:** Tom DeFalco ★ Appearance of Hobgoblin. ★ Death of Fly.

277 ❑ Jun 1986 Cover: 0.75 **NM** value: **3.00**
Circ: Statement: **276,064** CapCity orders: **26,500** • **CGC:** 6 graded, best 9.8
The Rules Of The Game **A:** Ron Frenz **W:** Tom DeFalco

278 ❑ Jul 1986 Cover: 0.75 **NM** value: **3.00**
Circ: Statement: **276,064** CapCity orders: **25,100** • **CGC:** 5 graded, best 9.8
★ Death of Wraith.

279 ❑ Aug 1986 Cover: 0.75 **NM** value: **4.00**
Circ: Statement: **276,064** CapCity orders: **26,200** • **CGC:** 7 graded, best 9.6
Jack O' Lantern cover/story. Savage Is The Sable • Jack O' Lantern versus Silver Sable **A:** Rick Leonardi **W:** Tom DeFalco

280 ❑ Sep 1986 Cover: 0.75 **NM** value: **3.00**
Circ: Statement: **276,064** CapCity orders: **26,200** • **CGC:** 4 graded, best 9.8

281 ❑ Oct 1986 Cover: 0.75 **NM** value: **8.00**
Circ: Statement: **276,064** CapCity orders: **26,400** • **CGC:** 7 graded, best 9.6
Jack O' Lantern cover/story. ★ Versus Sinister Syndicate.

282 ❑ Nov 1986 Cover: 0.75 **NM** value: **3.00**
Circ: Statement: **276,064** CapCity orders: **30,900** • **CGC:** 11 graded, best 9.8
The Fury Of X-Factor **A:** Rick Leonardi **W:** Tom DeFalco

283 ❑ Dec 1986 Cover: 0.75 **NM** value: **3.00**
Circ: Statement: **276,064** CapCity orders: **27,600** • **CGC:** 8 graded, best 9.6
With Foes Like These… **A:** Ron Frenz **W:** Tom DeFalco

284 ❑ Jan 1987 Cover: 0.75 **NM** value: **7.00**
Circ: Statement: **284,692** CapCity orders: **28,500** • **CGC:** 5 graded, best 9.6
Gang War; Gang War, Part 1; And Who Shall Stand Against Them? **A:** Brett Breeding **W:** Ron Frenz; Tom DeFalco ★ Appearance of Punisher.

285 ❑ Feb 1987 Cover: 0.75 **NM** value: **7.00**
Circ: Statement: **284,692** CapCity orders: **29,100** • **CGC:** 18 graded, best 9.8
Gang War; Gang War, Part 2 ★ Appearance of Punisher, Hobgoblin.

286 ❑ Mar 1986 Cover: 0.75 **NM** value: **5.00**
Circ: Statement: **284,692** CapCity orders: **29,000** • **CGC:** 3 graded, best 9.8
Gang War; Gang War, Part 3; Thy Father's Son **A:** Alan Kupperberg **W:** James Owsley

287 ❑ Apr 1987 Cover: 0.75 **NM** value: **5.00**
Circ: Statement: **284,692** CapCity orders: **29,900** • **CGC:** 4 graded, best 9.6
Gang War; Gang War, Part 4; …And There Shall Be A Reckoning • Has 1986 Statement; avg sales 253,273; avg subs 22,791; avg total paid circ 276,064 **A:** Erik Larsen **W:** James Owsley ★ Appearance of Hobgoblin. ★ Appearance of Daredevil.

288 ❑ May 1987 Cover: 0.75 **NM** value: **5.00**
Circ: Statement: **284,692** CapCity orders: **28,300** • **CGC:** 3 graded, best 9.6
Gang War; Gang War, Part 5 **A:** Alan Kupperberg **W:** James Owsley ★ Appearance of Hobgoblin.

289 ❑ Jun 1987 Cover: 1.25 **NM** value: **10.00**
Circ: Statement: **284,692** CapCity orders: **31,800** • **CGC:** 50 graded, best 9.9
• double-sized issue. • Hobgoblin unmasked;Hobgoblin's identity revealed;Jack O' Lantern becomes Hobgoblin ★ 1st Appearance of Hobgoblin II (Jason Macendale).

290 ❑ Jul 1987 Cover: 0.75 **NM** value: **3.00**
Circ: Statement: **284,692** CapCity orders: **29,800** • **CGC:** 6 graded, best 9.6
The Big Question • Peter Parker proposes to Mary Jane **A:** John Romita Jr. **W:** David Michelinie

291 ❑ Aug 1987 Cover: 0.75 **NM** value: **3.00**
Circ: Statement: **284,692** CapCity orders: **31,100** • **CGC:** 5 graded, best 9.6
Dark Journey! **A:** John Romita Jr. **W:** David Michelinie ★ Versus Spider-Slayer.

292 ❑ Sep 1987 Cover: 0.75 **NM** value: **3.00**
Circ: Statement: **284,692** CapCity orders: **36,600** • **CGC:** 5 graded, best 9.8
Growing Pains! **A:** Alex Saviuk **W:** David Michelinie

293 ❑ Oct 1987 Cover: 0.75 **NM** value: **6.00**
Circ: Statement: **284,692** CapCity orders: **34,900** • **CGC:** 9 graded, best 9.8
Kraven's Last Hunt, Part 2; Crawling **A:** Mike Zeck **W:** J.M. DeMatteis ★ Versus Kraven the Hunter.

294 ❑ Nov 1987 Cover: 0.75 **NM** value: **6.00**
Circ: Statement: **284,692** CapCity orders: **36,500** • **CGC:** 5 graded, best 9.4
Kraven's Last Hunt, Part 5; Thunder **A:** Mike Zeck; Bob McLeod **W:** J.M. DeMatteis ★ Death of Kraven. ★ Versus Kraven the Hunter.

295 ❑ Dec 1987 Cover: 0.75 **NM** value: **4.00**
Circ: Statement: **284,692** CapCity orders: **33,500** • **CGC:** 10 graded, best 9.6
Mad Dogs **A:** Bill Sienkiewicz; Cynthia Martin **W:** Ann Nocenti

296 ❑ Jan 1988 Cover: 0.75 **NM** value: **4.00**
Circ: Statement: **271,100** CapCity orders: **34,100** • **CGC:** 5 graded, best 9.6
Force Of Arms **A:** Alex Saviuk **W:** David Michelinie ★ Versus Doctor Octopus.

297 ❑ Feb 1988 Cover: 0.75 **NM** value: **4.00**
Circ: Statement: **271,100** CapCity orders: **35,200** • **CGC:** 15 graded, best 9.9
I'll Take Manhattan! **A:** Alex Saviuk **W:** David Michelinie ★ Versus Doctor Octopus.

298 ❑ Mar 1988 Cover: 0.75 **NM** value: **15.00**
Circ: Statement: **271,100** CapCity orders: **36,300** • **CGC:** 249 graded, best 9.8
• w/o costume **A:** Todd McFarlane ★ 1st Appearance of Venom (cameo).

299 ❑ Apr 1988 Cover: 0.75 **NM** value: **10.00**
Circ: Statement: **271,100** CapCity orders: **36,300** • **CGC:** 125 graded, best 9.8
A: Todd McFarlane ★ 1st Appearance of Venom (cameo).

CGC-graded: Multiply prices above by **33 for 9.9 M** • **16 for 9.8 NM/M** • **7 for 9.6 NM+** • **5 for 9.4 NM** • **2.5 for 9.2 NM-** • **1.5 for 9.0 VF/NM**

300 ❑ May 1988 Cover: 1.50 **NM** value: **35.00**
Circ: Statement: **271,100** • **CGC**: 483 graded, best 9.9
• 25th anniversary. • Last black costume for Spider-Man **A**: Todd McFarlane ★ Origin of Venom. ★ 1st Appearance of Venom (Full).

300/A ❑ May 1988 **NM** value: **14.00**
Circ: Statement: **271,100** CapCity orders: **42,900**
chromium cover. • 25th anniversary. • Last black costume for Spider-Man **A**: Todd McFarlane ★ Origin of Venom. ★ 1st Appearance of Venom (Full).

300/B ❑ May 1988 **NM** value: **18.00**
chromium cover. • 25th anniversary. • Last black costume for Spider-Man **A**: Todd McFarlane ★ Origin of Venom. ★ 1st Appearance of Venom (Full).

301 ❑ Jun 1988 Cover: 1.00 **NM** value: **8.00**
Circ: Statement: **271,100** CapCity orders: **33,100** • **CGC**: 37 graded, best 9.6
• Has 1987 Statement; avg sales 267,567; avg subs 17,125; avg total paid circ 284,692 **A**: Todd McFarlane

302 ❑ Jul 1988 Cover: 1.00 **NM** value: **8.00**
Circ: Statement: **271,100** CapCity orders: **33,700** • **CGC**: 22 graded, best 9.8
A: Todd McFarlane

303 ❑ Aug 1988 Cover: 1.00 **NM** value: **8.00**
Circ: Statement: **271,100** CapCity orders: **35,200** • **CGC**: 25 graded, best 9.8
A: Todd McFarlane

304 ❑ Sep 1988 Cover: 1.00 **NM** value: **6.00**
Circ: Statement: **271,100** CapCity orders: **35,700** • **CGC**: 20 graded, best 9.8
A: Todd McFarlane

305 ❑ Sep 1988 Cover: 1.00 **NM** value: **6.00**
Circ: Statement: **271,100** CapCity orders: **35,000** • **CGC**: 20 graded, best 9.8
A: Todd McFarlane

306 ❑ Oct 1988 Cover: 1.00 **NM** value: **6.00**
Circ: Statement: **271,100** CapCity orders: **36,400** • **CGC**: 28 graded, best 9.9
A: Todd McFarlane

307 ❑ Oct 1988 Cover: 1.00 **NM** value: **6.00**
Circ: Statement: **271,100** CapCity orders: **36,200** • **CGC**: 30 graded, best 9.9
A: Todd McFarlane ★ Origin of Chameleon.

308 ❑ Nov 1988 Cover: 1.00 **NM** value: **6.00**
Circ: Statement: **271,100** CapCity orders: **35,200** • **CGC**: 17 graded, best 9.8
📖 Dread **A**: Todd McFarlane **W**: David Michelinie

309 ❑ Nov 1988 Cover: 1.00 **NM** value: **6.00**
Circ: Statement: **271,100** CapCity orders: **35,000** • **CGC**: 27 graded, best 9.8
📖 Styx And Stone **A**: Todd McFarlane **W**: David Michelinie

310 ❑ Dec 1988 Cover: 1.00 **NM** value: **6.00**
Circ: Statement: **271,100** CapCity orders: **36,200** • **CGC**: 21 graded, best 9.8
📖 Shrike Force! **A**: Todd McFarlane **W**: David Michelinie

311 ❑ Jan 1989 Cover: 1.00 **NM** value: **6.00**
Circ: Statement: **266,100** CapCity orders: **40,600** • **CGC**: 30 graded, best 9.8
• Inferno **A**: Todd McFarlane

312 ❑ Feb 1989 Cover: 1.00 **NM** value: **9.00**
Circ: Statement: **266,100** CapCity orders: **42,400** • **CGC**: 112 graded, best 9.9
• Inferno;Hobgoblin vs. Green Goblin II (Harry Osborn) **A**: Todd McFarlane

313 ❑ Mar 1989 Cover: 1.00 **NM** value: **5.00**
Circ: Statement: **266,100** CapCity orders: **45,900** • **CGC**: 34 graded, best 9.9
• Inferno **A**: Todd McFarlane

314 ❑ Apr 1989 Cover: 1.00 **NM** value: **5.00**
Circ: Statement: **266,100** CapCity orders: **42,200** • **CGC**: 26 graded, best 9.9
📖 Down And Out In Forest Hills **A**: Todd McFarlane

315 ❑ May 1989 Cover: 1.00 **NM** value: **8.00**
Circ: Statement: **266,100** CapCity orders: **41,400** • **CGC**: 37 graded, best 9.8
• Has 1988 Statement; avg sales 256,500; avg subs 14,600; avg total paid circ 271,100 **A**: Todd McFarlane ★ Appearance of Venom.

316 ❑ Jun 1989 Cover: 1.00 **NM** value: **8.00**
Circ: Statement: **266,100** CapCity orders: **44,100** • **CGC**: 41 graded, best 9.9
A: Todd McFarlane ★ Appearance of Venom.

317 ❑ Jul 1989 Cover: 1.00 **NM** value: **8.00**
Circ: Statement: **266,100** CapCity orders: **44,700** • **CGC**: 47 graded, best 9.8
A: Todd McFarlane ★ Appearance of Venom.

318 ❑ Aug 1989 Cover: 1.00 **NM** value: **6.00**
Circ: Statement: **266,100** CapCity orders: **45,900** • **CGC**: 25 graded, best 9.9
📖 Sting Your Partner! **A**: Todd McFarlane **W**: David Michelinie ★ Appearance of Venom.

319 ❑ Sep 1989 Cover: 1.00 **NM** value: **6.00**
Circ: Statement: **266,100** CapCity orders: **48,800** • **CGC**: 17 graded, best 9.9
📖 The Scorpions Tale Of Woe! **A**: Todd McFarlane **W**: David Michelinie

320 ❑ Sep 1989 Cover: 1.00 **NM** value: **6.00**
Circ: Statement: **266,100** CapCity orders: **48,600** • **CGC**: 33 graded, best 9.8
📖 Assassin Nation Plot, Part 1 **A**: Todd McFarlane ★ Appearance of Silver Sable.

321 ❑ Oct 1989 Cover: 1.00 **NM** value: **4.00**
Circ: Statement: **266,100** CapCity orders: **49,800** • **CGC**: 36 graded, best 10.0
📖 Assassin Nation Plot, Part 2 **A**: Todd McFarlane ★ Appearance of Silver Sable.

322 ❑ Oct 1989 Cover: 1.00 **NM** value: **4.00**
Circ: Statement: **266,100** CapCity orders: **49,200** • **CGC**: 52 graded, best 9.8
📖 Assassin Nation Plot, Part 3; Ceremony **A**: Todd McFarlane ★ Appearance of Silver Sable.

323 ❑ Nov 1989 Cover: 1.00 **NM** value: **4.00**
Circ: Statement: **266,100** CapCity orders: **51,900** • **CGC**: 31 graded, best 9.8
📖 Assassin Nation Plot, Part 4 **A**: Todd McFarlane ★ Appearance of Silver Sable.

324 ❑ Nov 1989 Cover: 1.00 **NM** value: **5.00**
Circ: Statement: **266,100** CapCity orders: **51,600** • **CGC**: 41 graded, best 9.8
A: Todd McFarlane; Todd McFarlane(cover) ★ Appearance of Sabretooth.

325 ❑ Nov 1989 Cover: 1.00 **NM** value: **4.00**
Circ: Statement: **266,100** CapCity orders: **56,400** • **CGC**: 16 graded, best 9.6
A: Todd McFarlane

326 ❑ Dec 1989 Cover: 1.00 **NM** value: **3.00**
Circ: Statement: **266,100** CapCity orders: **60,300** • **CGC**: 13 graded, best 9.8
📖 Acts of Vengeance • Acts of Vengeance

327 ❑ Dec 1989 Cover: 1.00 **NM** value: **3.00**
Circ: Statement: **266,100** CapCity orders: **55,100** • **CGC**: 13 graded, best 9.8
📖 Acts of Vengeance • cosmic Spider-Man;Acts of Vengeance

328 ❑ Jan 1990 Cover: 1.00 **NM** value: **4.50**
Circ: Statement: **334,893** CapCity orders: **73,300** • **CGC**: 82 graded, best 9.9
📖 Acts of Vengeance; Shaw's Gambit • Hulk;Acts of Vengeance;Last McFarlane Issue **A**: Todd McFarlane **W**: David Michelinie

329 ❑ Feb 1990 Cover: 1.00 **NM** value: **3.00**
Circ: Statement: **334,893** CapCity orders: **58,200** • **CGC**: 7 graded, best 9.6
• Acts of Vengeance

330 ❑ Mar 1990 Cover: 1.00 **NM** value: **3.00**
Circ: Statement: **334,893** CapCity orders: **72,000** • **CGC**: 5 graded, best 9.6
★ Appearance of Punisher.

331 ❑ Apr 1990 Cover: 1.00 **NM** value: **3.00**
Circ: Statement: **334,893** CapCity orders: **67,500** • **CGC**: 5 graded, best 9.6
A: Erik Larsen ★ Appearance of Punisher.

332 ❑ May 1990 Cover: 1.00 **NM** value: **3.00**
Circ: Statement: **334,893** CapCity orders: **58,500** • **CGC**: 4 graded, best 9.4
• Has 1989 Statement; avg sales 255,350; avg subs 10,750; avg total paid circ 266,100 **A**: Erik Larsen ★ Appearance of Venom.

333 ❑ Jun 1990 Cover: 1.00 **NM** value: **3.00**
Circ: Statement: **334,893** CapCity orders: **59,400** • **CGC**: 2 graded, best 9.6
★ Appearance of Venom.

334 ❑ Jul 1990 Cover: 1.00 **NM** value: **2.50**
Circ: Statement: **334,893** CapCity orders: **63,300** • **CGC**: 1 graded, best 9.2
📖 The Return Of The Sinister Six, Part 1 • Sinister Six **A**: Erik Larsen **W**: David Michelinie

335 ❑ Jul 1990 Cover: 1.00 **NM** value: **2.50**
Circ: Statement: **334,893** CapCity orders: **61,800** • **CGC**: 1 graded, best 9.4
📖 The Return Of The Sinister Six, Part 2; Shocks! • Sinister Six **A**: Erik Larsen **W**: David Michelinie

336 ❑ Aug 1990 Cover: 1.00 **NM** value: **2.50**
Circ: Statement: **334,893** CapCity orders: **59,400** • **CGC**: 1 graded, best 9.2
📖 The Return Of The Sinister Six, Part 3; The Wagers Of Sin • Sinister Six **A**: Erik Larsen **W**: David Michelinie

337 ❑ Aug 1990 Cover: 1.00 **NM** value: **2.50**
Circ: Statement: **334,893** CapCity orders: **58,800** • **CGC**: 2 graded, best 9.2
📖 The Return Of The Sinister Six, Part 4 • Sinister Six **A**: Erik Larsen **W**: David Michelinie

338 ❑ Sep 1990 Cover: 1.00 **NM** value: **2.50**
Circ: Statement: **334,893** CapCity orders: **60,000**
📖 The Return Of The Sinister Six, Part 5; Death From Above • Sinister Six **A**: Erik Larsen **W**: David Michelinie

339 ❑ Sep 1990 Cover: 1.00 **NM** value: **2.50**
Circ: Statement: **334,893** CapCity orders: **59,700**
📖 The Return Of The Sinister Six, Part 6; The Killing Cure • Sinister Six **A**: Erik Larsen **W**: David Michelinie

340 ❑ Oct 1990 Cover: 1.00 **NM** value: **2.50**
Circ: Statement: **334,893** CapCity orders: **57,300** • **CGC**: 1 graded, best 9.6

341 ❑ Nov 1990 Cover: 1.00 **NM** value: **2.50**
Circ: Statement: **334,893** CapCity orders: **56,100** • **CGC**: 1 graded, best 9.6
• Powerless;Spider-Man loses powers

342 ❑ Dec 1990 Cover: 1.00 **NM** value: **2.50**
Circ: Statement: **334,893** CapCity orders: **57,900**
• Powerless

343 ❑ Jan 1991 Cover: 1.00 **NM** value: **2.50**
Circ: Statement: **340,977** CapCity orders: **58,500**
• Spider-Man gets his powers back

344 ❑ Feb 1991 Cover: 1.00 **NM** value: **5.00**
Circ: Statement: **340,977** CapCity orders: **61,500** • **CGC**: 14 graded, best 9.9
★ 1st Appearance of Cardiac, Cletus Kassidy (later becomes Carnage)-cameo.

345 ❑ Mar 1991 Cover: 1.00 **NM** value: **6.00**
Circ: Statement: **340,977** CapCity orders: **60,000** • **CGC**: 10 graded, best 9.8
• Has 1990 Statement; avg sales 324,060; avg subs 10,833; avg total paid circ 334,893 ★ Origin of Cletus Kasady. ★ Appearance of Cletus Kassidy (later becomes Carnage)-full.

346 ❑ Apr 1991 Cover: 1.00 **NM** value: **4.00**
Circ: Statement: **340,977** CapCity orders: **64,800** • **CGC**: 2 graded, best 9.6
★ Appearance of Venom.

347 ❑ May 1991 Cover: 1.00 **NM** value: **4.00**
Circ: Statement: **340,977** CapCity orders: **63,000** • **CGC**: 3 graded, best 9.6
★ Appearance of Venom.

348 ❑ Jun 1991 Cover: 1.00 **NM** value: **2.00**
Circ: Statement: **340,977** CapCity orders: **59,100**
📖 Righteous Sand **A**: Erik Larsen **W**: David Michelinie ★ Appearance of Avengers.

349 ❑ Jul 1991 Cover: 1.00 **NM** value: **2.00**
Circ: Statement: **340,977** CapCity orders: **65,100** • **CGC**: 1 graded, best 9.8
📖 Man Of Steal **A**: Erik Larsen **W**: David Michelinie

350 ❑ Aug 1991 Cover: 1.50 **NM** value: **2.00**
Circ: Statement: **340,977** CapCity orders: **75,600** • **CGC**: 2 graded, best 9.8
📖 Doom Service! **A**: Erik Larsen **W**: David Michelinie ★ Versus Doctor Doom.

351 ❑ Sep 1991 Cover: 1.00 **NM** value: **2.00**
Circ: Statement: **340,977** • **CGC**: 2 graded, best 9.6
📖 The Three Faces Of Evil **A**: Mark Bagley **W**: David Michelinie ★ Appearance of Nova. ★ Versus Tri-Sentinel.

352 ❑ Oct 1991 Cover: 1.00 **NM** value: **2.00**
Circ: Statement: **340,977** CapCity orders: **65,400**
📖 Death Walk! **A**: Mark Bagley **W**: David Michelinie ★ Appearance of Nova. ★ Versus Tri-Sentinel.

353 ❑ Nov 1991 Cover: 1.00 **NM** value: **2.00**
Circ: Statement: **340,977** CapCity orders: **79,200** • **CGC**: 1 graded, best 9.4
📖 Round Robin: The Sidekick's Revenge, Part 1; When Midnight Strikes! **A**: Mark Bagley **W**: Al Milgrom ★ Appearance of Punisher, Moon Knight.

354 ❑ Nov 1991 Cover: 1.00 **NM** value: **2.00**
Circ: Statement: **340,977** CapCity orders: **76,800** • **CGC**: 1 graded, best 9.8
📖 Round Robin: The Sidekick's Revenge, Part 2; Wilde At Heart! **A**: Mark Bagley **W**: Al Milgrom ★ Appearance of Punisher, Moon Knight.

355 ❑ Dec 1991 Cover: 1.00 **NM** value: **2.00**
Circ: Statement: **340,977** CapCity orders: **78,300** • **CGC**: 1 graded, best 9.6
📖 Round Robin: The Sidekick's Revenge, Part 3; Total Eclipse Of The Moon…Knight! **A**: Mark Bagley **W**: Al Milgrom ★ Appearance of Punisher, Moon Knight.

356 ❑ Dec 1991 Cover: 1.00 **NM** value: **2.00**
Circ: Statement: **340,977** CapCity orders: **79,500** • **CGC**: 2 graded, best 9.8
📖 Round Robin: The Sidekick's Revenge, Part 4; After Midnight! **A**: Mark Bagley **W**: Al Milgrom ★ Appearance of Punisher, Moon Knight.

357 ❑ Jan 1992 Cover: 1.00 **NM** value: **2.00**
Circ: Statement: **544,900** CapCity orders: **76,500** • **CGC**: 1 graded, best 9.6
📖 Round Robin: The Sidekick's Revenge, Part 5; A Bagel With Nova! **A**: Mark Bagley **W**: Al Milgrom ★ Appearance of Punisher, Moon Knight.

358 ❑ Jan 1992 Cover: 1.00 **NM** value: **2.00**
Circ: Statement: **544,900** CapCity orders: **98,400**
📖 Round Robin: The Sidekick's Revenge, Part 6 **A**: Mark Bagley **W**: Al Milgrom ★ Appearance of Punisher, Moon Knight.

359 ❑ Feb 1992 Cover: 1.25 **NM** value: **2.00**
Circ: Statement: **544,900** CapCity orders: **60,600** • **CGC**: 1 graded, best 9.8
📖 Toy Death! **A**: Chris Marrinan **W**: David Michelinie

360 ❑ Mar 1992 Cover: 1.25 **NM** value: **3.00**
Circ: Statement: **544,900** CapCity orders: **57,300** • **CGC**: 3 graded, best 9.4
📖 Death Toy! • Has 1991 Statement; avg sales 328,881; avg subs 12,096; avg total paid circ 340,977 **A**: Chris Marrinan **W**: David Michelinie ★ Origin of Cardiac. ★ 1st Appearance of Carnage (cameo).

361 ❑ Apr 1992 Cover: 1.25 **NM** value: **6.00**
Circ: Statement: **544,900** CapCity orders: **68,700** • **CGC**: 79 graded, best 9.8
📖 Carnage, Part 1 **A**: Mark Bagley **W**: David Michelinie ★ 1st Appearance of Carnage (full appearance).

361-2 ❑ Cover: 1.25 **NM** value: **1.50**

362 ❑ May 1992 Cover: 1.25 **NM** value: **4.00**
Circ: Statement: **544,900** CapCity orders: **76,800** • **CGC**: 55 graded, best 9.9
📖 Carnage, Part 2; Savage Alliance **A**: Mark Bagley **W**: David Michelinie ★ Appearance of Carnage, Venom.

362-2 ❑ Cover: 1.25 **NM** value: **1.50**

363 ❑ Jun 1992 Cover: 1.25 **NM** value: **3.00**
Circ: Statement: **544,900** CapCity orders: **102,600** • **CGC**: 18 graded, best 9.8
📖 Carnage, Part 3 **A**: Mark Bagley **W**: David Michelinie ★ Appearance of Carnage, Venom.

364 ❑ Jul 1992 Cover: 1.25 **NM** value: **2.00**
Circ: Statement: **544,900** CapCity orders: **72,000**
📖 The Pain Of Fast Air • Peter Parker's parents (false parents) appear **A**: Mark Bagley **W**: David Michelinie ★ Versus Shocker.

365 ❑ Aug 1992 Cover: 3.95 **NM** value: **Cover or less**
Circ: Statement: **544,900** CapCity orders: **221,700** • **CGC**: 17 graded, best 9.8
Hologram cover. 📖 Fathers And Sins; The Saga Of Spidey's Parents; How I created Spider-Man; I Remember Gwen; A Friend In Need • Peter Parker meets his (false) parents;Gatefold poster with Venom and Carnage;Lizard back-up story **A**: Aaron Lopresti; Mark Bagley; Rick Leonardi **W**: David Michelinie; Peter David ★ 1st Appearance of Spider-Man 2099.

366 ❑ Sep 1992 Cover: 1.25 **NM** value: **2.00**
Circ: Statement: **544,900** CapCity orders: **89,100**
📖 Skullwork! **A**: Jerry Bingham **W**: David Michelinie ★ Appearance of Red Skull. ★ Versus Red Skull.

367 ❑ Oct 1992 Cover: 1.25 **NM** value: **2.00**
Circ: Statement: **544,900** CapCity orders: **77,700**
📖 Skullduggery **A**: Jerry Bingham **W**: David Michelinie

368 ❑ Nov 1992 Cover: 1.25 **NM** value: **2.00**
Circ: Statement: **544,900** CapCity orders: **71,700**
📖 Invasion of the Spider-Slayers, Part 1; On Razored Wings **A**: Mark Bagley **W**: David Michelinie ★ Versus Spider-Slayers.

369 ❑ Nov 1992 Cover: 1.25 **NM** value: **2.00**
Circ: Statement: **544,900** CapCity orders: **71,100**
📖 Invasion of the Spider-Slayers, Part 2; Electric Doom **A**: Mark Bagley **W**: David Michelinie ★ Versus Spider-Slayers.

Other grades: Multiply prices above by **1.5 for Mint • 2/3 for Very Fine • 1/3 for Fine • 1/5 for Very Good • 1/8 for Good**

370 ❑ Dec 1992 Cover: 1.25 **NM** value: **2.00**
Circ: Statement: **544,900** CapCity orders: **67,000**
Invasion of the Spider-Slayers, Part 3 **A:** Mark Bagley **W:** David Michelinie ★ Versus Spider-Slayers.

371 ❑ Dec 1992 Cover: 1.25 **NM** value: **2.00**
Circ: Statement: **544,900** CapCity orders: **66,400**
Invasion of the Spider-Slayers, Part 4; One Flew Over The Cuckoo's Nest **A:** Mark Bagley **W:** David Michelinie ★ Appearance of Black Cat. ★ Versus Spider-Slayers.

372 ❑ Jan 1993 Cover: 1.25 **NM** value: **2.00**
Circ: Statement: **592,442** CapCity orders: **63,100**
Invasion of the Spider-Slayers, Part 5; Arachnophobia Too! **A:** Mark Bagley **W:** David Michelinie ★ Versus Spider-Slayers.

373 ❑ Jan 1993 Cover: 1.25 **NM** value: **2.00**
Circ: Statement: **592,442** CapCity orders: **64,200** • **CGC:** 1 graded, best 9.2
Invasion of the Spider-Slayers, Part 6; The Bedlam Perspective **A:** Mark Bagley **W:** David Michelinie ★ Versus Spider-Slayers.

374 ❑ Feb 1993 Cover: 1.25 **NM** value: **2.00**
Circ: Statement: **592,442** CapCity orders: **95,400** • **CGC:** 1 graded, best 9.4
Murder on Parade **A:** Aaron Lopresti; Mark Bagley; Patrick Olliffe; Dan Panosian **W:** David Michelinie ★ Versus Venom.

375 ❑ Mar 1993 Cover: 3.95 **NM** value: **5.00**
Circ: Statement: **592,442** CapCity orders: **208,200** • **CGC:** 23 graded, best 9.8
Metallic ink cover. • 30th anniversary special. The Bride Of Venom; True Friends; The Monster Within; Echoes • Sets stage for Venom #1; E6320 ★ Appearance of Venom.

376 ❑ Apr 1993 Cover: 1.25 **NM** value: **2.00**
Circ: Statement: **592,442** CapCity orders: **67,400**
★ Origin of Cardiac. ★ Versus Cardiac, Styx and Stone.

377 ❑ May 1993 Cover: 1.25 **NM** value: **2.00**
Circ: Statement: **592,442** CapCity orders: **66,600**
Dust to Dust **A:** Jeff Johnson **W:** Steven Grant ★ Versus Cardiac.

378 ❑ Jun 1993 Cover: 1.25 **NM** value: **2.00**
Circ: Statement: **592,442** CapCity orders: **146,700**
Maximum Carnage; Maximum Carnage, Part 3; Demons On Broadway **A:** Mark Bagley **W:** David Michelinie ★ Appearance of Carnage, Venom.

379 ❑ Jul 1993 Cover: 1.25 **NM** value: **2.00**
Circ: Statement: **592,442** CapCity orders: **121,800**
Maximum Carnage; Maximum Carnage, Part 7; The Gathering Storm **A:** Mark Bagley **W:** David Michelinie ★ Appearance of Carnage, Venom.

380 ❑ Aug 1993 Cover: 1.25 **NM** value: **2.00**
Circ: Statement: **592,442** CapCity orders: **119,400**
Maximum Carnage, Part 11

381 ❑ Sep 1993 Cover: 1.25 **NM** value: **2.00**
Circ: Statement: **592,442** CapCity orders: **72,000**
Samson Unleashed **A:** Mark Bagley **W:** David Michelinie ★ Appearance of Hulk. ★ Versus Hulk.

382 ❑ Oct 1993 Cover: 1.25 **NM** value: **2.00**
Circ: Statement: **592,442** CapCity orders: **96,400**
Emerald Rage! **A:** Mark Bagley **W:** David Michelinie ★ Appearance of Hulk. ★ Versus Hulk.

383 ❑ Nov 1993 Cover: 1.25 **NM** value: **2.00**
Circ: Statement: **592,442** CapCity orders: **71,100**
Trial by Jury; Trial By Jury, Part 1; Judgment Night **A:** Mark Bagley **W:** David Michelinie

384 ❑ Dec 1993 Cover: 1.25 **NM** value: **2.00**
Circ: Statement: **592,442** CapCity orders: **66,700**
Trial by Jury; Trial By Jury, Part 2; Dreams Of Innocence **A:** Mark Bagley **W:** David Michelinie

385 ❑ Jan 1994 Cover: 1.25 **NM** value: **2.00**
Circ: Statement: **353,025** CapCity orders: **60,500**
Trial by Jury

386 ❑ Feb 1994 Cover: 1.25 **NM** value: **2.00**
Circ: Statement: **353,025** CapCity orders: **61,800**
Lifetheft; Lifetheft, Part 1, The Wings Of Age • Has 1993 Statement; avg sales 561,683; avg subs 30,759; avg total paid circ 592,442 **A:** Mark Bagley **W:** David Michelinie ★ Versus Vulture.

387 ❑ Mar 1994 Cover: 1.25 **NM** value: **2.00**
Circ: Statement: **353,025** CapCity orders: **53,250**
Lifetheft; Lifetheft, Part 2 ★ Versus Vulture.

388 ❑ Apr 1994 Cover: 2.25 **NM** value: **3.25**
• Double-size. Lifetheft; Lifetheft, Part 3 ★ Death of Peter Parker's parents (false parents). ★ Versus Vulture.

388/SC ❑ Apr 1994 Cover: 2.95 **NM** value: **Cover or less**
Circ: Statement: **353,025** CapCity orders: **82,750**
foil cover. • Double-size. Lifetheft; Lifetheft, Part 3; The Sadness Of Truth **A:** Mark Bagley **W:** David Michelinie ★ Death of Peter Parker's parents (false parents). ★ Versus Vulture.

389 ❑ May 1994 Cover: 1.50 **NM** value: **Cover or less**
Circ: Statement: **353,025** CapCity orders: **51,700** • **CGC:** 1 graded, best 9.0
Pursuit

390 ❑ Jun 1994 Cover: 1.50 **NM** value: **Cover or less**
Shrieking, Part 1; Behind The Walls **A:** Mark Bagley **W:** J.M. DeMatteis

390/CS ❑ Jun 1994 Cover: 2.95 **NM** value: **3.00**
Circ: Statement: **353,025** CapCity orders: **67,850**
Shrieking, Part 1; Behind The Walls • print;poster **A:** Mark Bagley **W:** J.M. DeMatteis

391 ❑ Jul 1994 Cover: 1.50 **NM** value: **Cover or less**
Circ: Statement: **353,025** CapCity orders: **48,050**
Shrieking, Part 2; The Burning Fuse! • Aunt May suffers stroke **A:** Mark Bagley **W:** J.M. DeMatteis ★ Versus Shriek.

392 ❑ Aug 1994 Cover: 1.50 **NM** value: **Cover or less**
Circ: Statement: **353,025** CapCity orders: **46,300**

393 ❑ Sep 1994 Cover: 1.50 **NM** value: **Cover or less**
Circ: Statement: **353,025** CapCity orders: **43,850**
• Carrion ★ Versus Shriek.

394 ❑ Oct 1994 Cover: 1.50 **NM** value: **2.00**
• **CGC:** 1 graded, best 9.6
Power & Responsibility, Part 2 ★ Origin of Ben Reilly. ★ Appearance of Ben Reilly.

394/SC ❑ Oct 1994 Cover: 2.95 **NM** value: **3.50**
Circ: Statement: **353,025** CapCity orders: **46,750**
enhanced cover. • Giant-size. Power and Responsibility, Part 2; The Double, Part 2 ★ Origin of Ben Reilly. ★ Appearance of Ben Reilly.

395 ❑ Nov 1994 Cover: 1.50 **NM** value: **Cover or less**
Circ: Statement: **353,025** CapCity orders: **47,600**
Back from the Edge, Part 1; Outcasts! • continues in Spectacular Spider-Man #218 **A:** Mark Bagley **W:** J.M. DeMatteis ★ Versus Puma.

396 ❑ Dec 1994 Cover: 1.50 **NM** value: **Cover or less**
Circ: Statement: **353,025** CapCity orders: **43,500**
Back from the Edge, Part 3; Deadmen • continues in Spectacular Spider-Man #219 ★ Appearance of Daredevil.

397 ❑ Jan 1995 Cover: 2.25 **NM** value: **Cover or less**
Circ: Statement: **234,290** CapCity orders: **42,425**
• Double-size. Web of Death, Part 1; Tentacles • flip book with illustrated story from The Ultimate Spider-Man back-up; continues in Spectacular Spider-Man #220 ★ Versus Lizard. ★ Versus Doctor Octopus.

398 ❑ Feb 1995 Cover: 1.50 **NM** value: **Cover or less**
Circ: Statement: **234,290** CapCity orders: **41,475**
Web of Death, Part 3; Before I Wake • continues in Spectacular Spider-Man #221 ★ Versus Doctor Octopus.

399 ❑ Mar 1995 Cover: 1.50 **NM** value: **Cover or less**
Circ: Statement: **234,290** CapCity orders: **39,250**
Smoke & Mirrors, Part 2; Resurrection • continues in Spider-Man #56 ★ Appearance of Jackal.

400 ❑ Apr 1995 Cover: 2.95 **NM** value: **4.00**
Circ: Statement: **234,290** • **CGC:** 13 graded, best 9.6
The Parker Legacy, Part 1; The Gift; The Morning After • Has 1994 Statement; avg sales 319,575; avg subs 33,450; avg total paid circ 353,025 **A:** Mark Bagley; John Romita Jr.; Tom Grummettt **W:** Stan Lee; J.M. DeMatteis ★ Death of Aunt May (fake death).

400/A ❑ Apr 1995 Cover: 3.95 **NM** value: **5.00**
Circ: CapCity orders: **62,975** • **CGC:** 8 graded, best 9.6
White cover. • white cover edition (no ads, back-up story). The Parker Legacy, Part 1; The Gift; The Morning After **A:** Mark Bagley; John Romita Jr.; Tom Grummettt **W:** Stan Lee; J.M. DeMatteis ★ Death of Aunt May (fake death).

400/B ❑ Apr 1995 Cover: 3.95 **NM** value: **5.00**
enhanced second cover. The Parker Legacy, Part 1; The Gift; The Morning After **A:** Mark Bagley; John Romita Jr.; Tom Grummettt **W:** Stan Lee; J.M. DeMatteis ★ Death of Aunt May (fake death).

401 ❑ May 1995 Cover: 1.50 **NM** value: **Cover or less**
Circ: Statement: **234,290** CapCity orders: **39,750**
Mark of Kaine, Part 2; The Mark of Kaine, Part 2

402 ❑ Jun 1995 Cover: 1.50 **NM** value: **Cover or less**
Circ: Statement: **234,290** CapCity orders: **38,875**

403 ❑ Jul 1995 Cover: 1.50 **NM** value: **Cover or less**
Circ: Statement: **234,290** CapCity orders: **38,375**
Trial of Peter Parker, Part 2 ★ Appearance of Carnage.

404 ❑ Aug 1995 Cover: 1.50 **NM** value: **Cover or less**
Circ: Statement: **234,290** CapCity orders: **41,375**
Maximum Clonage, Part 3

405 ❑ Sep 1995 Cover: 1.50 **NM** value: **Cover or less**
Circ: Statement: **234,290**
Exiled, Part 2

406 ❑ Oct 1995 Cover: 1.50 **NM** value: **Cover or less**
Circ: Statement: **216,779**
• OverPower cards inserted;(continues in Amazing Scarlet Spider);(continues in Amazing Scarlet Spider) ★ 1st Appearance of Doctor Octopus II.

407 ❑ Jan 1996 Cover: 1.50 **NM** value: **Cover or less**
Circ: Statement: **216,779**
• Has 1995 Statement, filed 10/1/95; avg print run 395,486; avg sales 208,090; avg subs 26,200; avg total paid 234,290; samples 750; office use 500; max existent 235,540; 40% of run returned ★ Appearance of Silver Sable, Human Torch, Sandman.

408 ❑ Feb 1996 Cover: 1.50 **NM** value: **Cover or less**
Circ: Statement: **216,779** • **CGC:** 1 graded, best 9.4
Media Blizzard, Part 2

409 ❑ Mar 1996 Cover: 1.50 **NM** value: **Cover or less**
Circ: Statement: **216,779**
Return of Kaine, Part 3; The Return of Kaine, Part 3; Of Wagers And Wars **A:** Mark Bagley **W:** Tom DeFalco

410 ❑ Apr 1996 Cover: 1.50 **NM** value: **Cover or less**
Circ: Statement: **216,779**
Web of Carnage, Part 2; And Now, Spider-Carnage **A:** Mark Bagley **W:** Tom DeFalco

411 ❑ May 1996 Cover: 1.50 **NM** value: **Cover or less**
Circ: Statement: **216,779**
Blood Brothers, Part 2

412 ❑ Jun 1996 Cover: 1.50 **NM** value: **Cover or less**
Circ: Statement: **216,779**
Blood Brothers, Part 6

413 ❑ Jul 1996 Cover: 1.50 **NM** value: **Cover or less**
Circ: Statement: **216,779**

414 ❑ Aug 1996 Cover: 1.50 **NM** value: **Cover or less**
Circ: Statement: **216,779**
★ Appearance of Delilah.

415 ❑ Sep 1996 Cover: 1.50 **NM** value: **Cover or less**
Circ: Statement: **159,950**
Onslaught • "Onslaught: Impact 2" ★ Versus Sentinel.

416 ❑ Oct 1996 Cover: 1.50 **NM** value: **Cover or less**
Circ: Statement: **159,950**
Heroes' Farewell; Onslaught • post-Onslaught memories

417 ❑ Nov 1996 Cover: 1.50 **NM** value: **Cover or less**
Circ: Statement: **159,950** Direct Market orders: **88,000**
• Has 1996 Statement, filed 10/1/96; avg print run 318,992; avg sales 203,454; avg subs 13,325; avg total paid 216,779; samples 600; office use 125; max existent 217,504; 32% of run returned

418 ❑ Dec 1996 Cover: 1.50 **NM** value: **2.00**
Circ: Statement: **159,950** Direct Market orders: **112,250**
Revelations, Part 3; Torment • birth of Peter and Mary Jane's baby;Return of Norman Osborn (face shown) **A:** Steve Skroce **W:** Tom DeFalco

419 ❑ Jan 1997 Cover: 1.50 **NM** value: **Cover or less**
Circ: Statement: **159,950** Direct Market orders: **87,750**
Beware Of The Black Tarantula! **A:** Steve Skroce **W:** Tom DeFalco ★ Versus Black Tarantula.

420 ❑ Feb 1997 Cover: 1.50 **NM** value: **Cover or less**
Circ: Statement: **159,950** Direct Market orders: **92,250**
Twas the Night Before Christmas... **A:** Steve Skroce **W:** Tom DeFalco ★ Appearance of X-Man. ★ Death of El Uno.

421 ❑ Mar 1997 Cover: 1.99 **NM** value: **2.00**
Circ: Statement: **159,950** Direct Market orders: **81,250**
And Death Shall Fly Like a Dragon **A:** Steve Skroce **W:** Tom DeFalco ★ Origin of The Dragonfly. ★ 1st Appearance of The Dragonfly.

422 ❑ Apr 1997 Cover: 1.99 **NM** value: **2.00**
Circ: Statement: **159,950** Direct Market orders: **79,500**
Exposed Wiring **A:** Joe Bennett **W:** Tom DeFalco ★ Origin of Electro.

423 ❑ May 1997 Cover: 1.99 **NM** value: **2.00**
Circ: Statement: **159,950** Diamd. preorders: **79,818**
Choices **A:** Joe Bennett **W:** Tom DeFalco ★ Versus Electro.

424 ❑ Jun 1997 Cover: 1.99 **NM** value: **2.00**
Circ: Statement: **159,950** Diamd. preorders: **79,143**
Then Came...Elektra **A:** Joe Bennett **W:** Tom DeFalco ★ Appearance of Elektra. ★ Versus Elektra.

425 ❑ Aug 1997 Cover: 1.99 **NM** value: **2.00**
Circ: Statement: **159,950** Diamd. preorders: **79,803**

426 ❑ Sep 1997 Cover: 1.99 **NM** value: **2.00**
Circ: Statement: **159,950** Diamd. preorders: **71,807**
• gatefold summary.

427 ❑ Oct 1997 Cover: 1.99 **NM** value: **2.00**
Circ: Statement: **119,547** Diamd. preorders: **72,364**
• gatefold summary. • return of Doctor Octopus

428 ❑ Nov 1997 Cover: 1.99 **NM** value: **2.00**
Circ: Statement: **119,547** Diamd. preorders: **69,905**
• gatefold summary. ★ Versus Doctor Octopus.

429 ❑ Dec 1997 Cover: 1.99 **NM** value: **2.00**
Circ: Statement: **119,547** Diamd. preorders: **69,182**
• gatefold summary. • Has 1997 Statement, filed 10/1/97; avg print run 274,400; avg sales 149,453; avg subs 10,497; avg total paid 159,950; samples 600; office use 125; max existent 160,675; 41% of run returned ★ Versus Absorbing Man.

430 ❑ Jan 1998 Cover: 1.99 **NM** value: **2.00**
Circ: Statement: **119,547** Diamd. preorders: **69,277**
• gatefold summary. ★ Appearance of Silver Surfer. ★ Versus Carnage.

431 ❑ Feb 1998 Cover: 1.99 **NM** value: **2.00**
Circ: Statement: **119,547** Diamd. preorders: **66,218**
• gatefold summary. Spider-Hunt, Part 2 ★ Appearance of Silver Surfer. ★ Versus Carnage.

432 ❑ Mar 1998 Cover: 1.99 **NM** value: **2.00**
Circ: Statement: **119,547** Diamd. preorders: **68,174**
• gatefold summary.

433 ❑ Apr 1998 Cover: 1.99 **NM** value: **2.00**
Circ: Statement: **119,547** Diamd. preorders: **63,604**
• gatefold summary. Identity Crisis

434 ❑ May 1998 Cover: 1.99 **NM** value: **2.00**
Circ: Statement: **119,547** Diamd. preorders: **70,493**
• gatefold summary. Identity Crisis

435 ❑ Jun 1998 Cover: 1.99 **NM** value: **2.00**
Circ: Statement: **119,547** Diamd. preorders: **70,009**
• gatefold summary. Identity Crisis **A:** Joe Bennett **W:** Tom DeFalco ★ Appearance of Ricochet.

436 ❑ Jul 1998 Cover: 1.99 **NM** value: **2.00**
Circ: Statement: **119,547** Diamd. preorders: **66,041**
• gatefold summary.

437 ❑ Aug 1998 Cover: 1.99 **NM** value: **2.00**
Circ: Statement: **119,547** Diamd. preorders: **66,566**
• gatefold summary. ★ Appearance of Synch.

438 ❑ Sep 1998 Cover: 1.99 **NM** value: **2.00**
Circ: Statement: **119,547** Diamd. preorders: **63,689**
• gatefold summary. ★ Appearance of Daredevil.

439 ❑ Sep 1998 Cover: 1.99 **NM** value: **2.00**
Circ: Statement: **127,915** Diamd. preorders: **63,480**
• gatefold summary. ★ Appearance of Zack and Lana.

440 ❑ Oct 1998 Cover: 1.99 **NM** value: **2.00**
Circ: Statement: **127,915** Diamd. preorders: **64,496**
• gatefold summary. The Gathering of Five, Part 2 ★ Versus Molten Man.

441 ❑ Nov 1998 Cover: 1.99 **NM** value: **2.00**
Circ: Statement: **127,915** Diamd. preorders: **69,052**
• gatefold summary. The Final Chapter, Part 1 final issue. • Has 1998 Statement, filed 10/1/98; avg print run 219,917; avg sales 112,670; avg subs 6,877; avg total paid 119,547; samples 600; office use 125; max existent 120,272; 45% of run returned ★ Appearance of Molten Man. ★ Death of Madame Web.

AIM 1 ❑ ca. 1980 **NM** value: **2.00**
No issue number. • Giveaway from Aim Toothpaste. • Spider-Man vs. Doctor Octopus ★ Appearance of Doctor Octopus.

AIM 2 ❑ **NM** value: **2.00**
• **CGC:** 3 graded, best 9.8
No issue number. • Aim toothpaste giveaway. Crisis at Cape Canaveral ★ Appearance of Green Goblin.

Anl 1 ❑ Cover: 0.25 **NM** value: **575.00**
• **CGC:** 70 graded, best 9.6
The Sinister Six; The Secrets of Spider-Man; How Stan Lee and Steve Ditko Create Spider-Man (text) **A:** Steve Ditko **W:** Steve Ditko; Stan Lee ★ 1st Appearance of Sinister Six (Doctor Octopus, Vulture, Electro, Sandman, Mysterio, Kraven the Hunter).

Anl 2 ❑ Cover: 0.25 **NM** value: **250.00**
• **CGC:** 48 graded, best 9.4
• Cover reads "King-Size Special". The Wondrous World of Dr. Strange; Spider-Man; The Uncanny Threat of the Terrible Tinkerer; A Gallery of Spider-Man's Most Famous Foes; Marked for Destruction by Dr. Doom • reprints Amazing Spider-Man #1, 2, and 5, plus a new story **A:** Steve Ditko **W:** Steve Ditko; Stan Lee ★ 1st Appearance of Xandu. ★ Appearance of Doctor Strange.

Anl 3 ❑ Nov 1966 Cover: 0.25 **NM** value: **90.00**
• **CGC:** 26 graded, best 9.8
• Cover reads "King-Size Special". To Become an Avenger; Turning Point; Unmasked by Dr. Octopus • New story; reprints Amazing Spider-Man #11 and 12 **A:** Don Heck; John Romita ★ Appearance of Daredevil. ★ Appearance of Avengers. ★ Versus Hulk.

CGC-graded: Multiply prices above by **33 for 9.9 M • 16 for 9.8 NM/M • 7 for 9.6 NM+ • 5 for 9.4 NM • 2.5 for 9.2 NM- • 1.5 for 9.0 VF/NM**

Anl 4❑Nov 1967 Cover: 0.25 **NM** value: **90.00**
• **CGC:** 35 graded, best 9.6
• Cover reads "King-Size Special". 📖 The Web and the Flame; The Coffee Bean Barn • Human Torch ★ Appearance of Torch. ★ Versus Mysterio. ★ Versus Wizard.

Anl 5❑Nov 1968 Cover: 0.25 **NM** value: **90.00**
• **CGC:** 31 graded, best 9.6
• Cover reads "King-Size Special". 📖 The Parents of Peter Parker!; A Day at the Daily Bugle; Peter Parker, the Super Sports Star; Where It's At; This Is Spidey as We Know Him, But…; Here We Go A-Plotting • fate of Peter Parker's parents revealed **A:** John Romita; Marie Severin; Larry Lieber; Mickey Demeo **W:** John Romita; Stan Lee ★ 1st Appearance of Peter Parker's parents. ★ Appearance of Red Skull.

Anl 5-2❑ Cover: 0.25 **NM** value: **1.50**

Anl 6❑Nov 1969 Cover: 0.25 **NM** value: **26.00**
• **CGC:** 7 graded, best 9.4
• Cover reads "King-Size Special". 📖 The Sinister Six; The Fabulous Fantastic Four Meet Spider-Man; Spider-Man Tackles the Torch • reprints stories from Amazing Spider-Man #8, Annual #1 and Fantastic Four Annual #1 **A:** Steve Ditko **W:** Steve Ditko; Stan Lee

Anl 7❑Dec 1970 Cover: 0.25 **NM** value: **26.00**
• **CGC:** 15 graded, best 9.6
• Cover reads "King-Size Special". 📖 Spider-Man vs. the Chameleon; Duel to the Death with the Vulture; Just a Guy Named Joe • reprints stories from Amazing Spider-Man #1, 2, and 38 **A:** Steve Ditko; John Romita **C:** John Romita **W:** Steve Ditko; Stan Lee

Anl 8❑Dec 1971 Cover: 0.25 **NM** value: **26.00**
• **CGC:** 8 graded, best 9.8
• Cover reads "King-Size Special". 📖 The Sinister Shocker; On the Trail of Spider-Man; Spider-Man No More • reprints stories from Amazing Spider-Man #46 and 50 and Tales to Astonish #57 **W:** Stan Lee

Anl 9❑ca. 1973 Cover: 0.35 **NM** value: **26.00**
• **CGC:** 6 graded, best 9.6
• reprints Spectacular Spider-Man (magazine) #2. 📖 The Goblin Lives • reprinted with changes from Spectacular Spider-Man #2 **A:** John Romita; Jim Mooney **W:** John Romita; Stan Lee ★ Appearance of Hobgoblin.

Anl 10❑Sep 1976 Cover: 0.50 **NM** value: **10.00**
• **CGC:** 5 graded, best 9.4
📖 Step into My Parlor; Said the Spider to the Fly **A:** Gil Kane **W:** Bill Mantlo ★ Origin of Human Fly. ★ 1st Appearance of Human Fly.

Anl 11❑Sep 1977 Cover: 0.50 **NM** value: **10.00**
• **CGC:** 6 graded, best 9.8
📖 Spawn of the Spider; Chaos at the Coffee Bean **A:** John Romita Jr.; Gil Kane; Don Perlin **W:** Archie Goodwin; Bill Mantlo; Scott Edelman

Anl 12❑Aug 1978 Cover: 0.60 **NM** value: **10.00**
• **CGC:** 10 graded, best 9.6
📖 The Gentleman's Name Is Hulk; The Fight and the Fury • Reprints Hulk story from Amazing Spider-Man #119-120 **A:** Paul Reinman; John Byrne; Gil Kane; John Romita **W:** Gil Kane; John Romita; Gerry Conway

Anl 13❑Nov 1979 Cover: 0.75 **NM** value: **10.00**
• **CGC:** 7 graded, best 9.8
📖 The Arms of Doctor Octopus; Spider-Man! I Know Who You R **A:** John Byrne; Keith Pollard; Ed Hannigan; Tony DeZuniga; Jim Mooney; Terry Austin **W:** Marv Wolfman ★ Versus Doctor Octopus.

Anl 14❑Dec 1980 Cover: 0.75 **NM** value: **10.00**
• **CGC:** 15 graded, best 9.8
📖 Bend Sinister **A:** Frank Miller **W:** Frank Miller; Denny O'Neil ★ Appearance of Doctor Strange. ★ Versus Doctor Doom.

Anl 15❑ca. 1981 Cover: 0.75 **NM** value: **6.00**
• **CGC:** 21 graded, best 9.8
A: Frank Miller ★ Appearance of Punisher.

Anl 16❑ca. 1982 Cover: 1.00 **NM** value: **7.00**
• **CGC:** 3 graded, best 9.6
★ Origin of Captain Marvel II (Monica Rambeau). ★ 1st Appearance of Captain Marvel II (Monica Rambeau).

Anl 17❑ca. 1983 Cover: 1.00 **NM** value: **6.00**
• **CGC:** 1 graded, best 8.0

Anl 18❑ca. 1984 Cover: 1.00 **NM** value: **6.00**
• Wedding of J. Jonah Jameson

Anl 19❑ca. 1985 Cover: 1.25 **NM** value: **6.00**
Circ: CapCity orders: **19,800**

Anl 20❑ca. 1986 Cover: 1.25 **NM** value: **6.00**
★ Death of Blizzard.

Anl 21❑ca. 1987 Cover: 1.25 **NM** value: **6.00**
Circ: CapCity orders: **32,000** • **CGC:** 20 graded, best 9.8
• newsstand edition. 📖 The Wedding • Wedding of Peter Parker and Mary Jane Watson

Anl 21/DM❑ca. 1987 Cover: 1.25 **NM** value: **6.00**
Circ: CapCity orders: **32,000** • **CGC:** 1 graded, best 9.6
• Direct Market edition. 📖 The Wedding • Wedding of Peter Parker and Mary Jane Watson

Anl 22❑ca. 1988 Cover: 1.75 **NM** value: **4.00**
Circ: CapCity orders: **36,200**
📖 Evolutionary War, Part 5 **A:** Mark Bagley **W:** Tom DeFalco; David Michelinie ★ Origin of High Evolutionary. ★ 1st Appearance of Speedball. ★ Appearance of Daredevil.

Anl 23❑ca. 1989 Cover: 2.00 **NM** value: **3.00**
📖 Atlantis Attacks, Part 4; Abominations; My Science Project; Standards Of Behavior; Saga Of The Serpent Crown: Cataclysm • Atlantis Attacks **A:** Mark Bagley; Keith Williams **W:** David Michelinie; Gerry Conway; Peter Sanderson ★ Origin of Spider-Man.

Anl 24❑ca. 1990 Cover: 2.00 **NM** value: **3.00**
Circ: CapCity orders: **54,600**
📖 The Mercy Bomb; Quark Enterprises, or Honey, I Shrunk The Non-Mutant Super Hero; A Time To Choose; Amazing Fantasy **A:** Steve Ditko; Gil Kane; Mike Zeck; Eliot Brown **W:** Tom DeFalco; Dan Cuddy; David Michelinie; J.M. DeMatteis; Tony Isabella ★ Appearance of Ant-Man.

Anl 25❑ca. 1991 Cover: 2.00 **NM** value: **4.00**
• **CGC:** 2 graded, best 9.8
📖 The Vibranium Vendetta, Part 1; The Origin Of The Amazing Spider-Man; Outlaw Justice, Part 1; Second Chance; Truck Stop To Doom • Vibranium Vendetta;1st solo Venom story **A:** Alan Kupperberg; Guang Yap; Paris Cullins **W:** David Michelinie ★ Origin of Spider-Man.

Anl 26❑ca. 1998 Cover: 2.25 **NM** value: **3.00**
Circ: CapCity orders: **71,000** • **CGC:** 2 graded, best 9.8
📖 Hero Killers, Part 1 ★ 1st Appearance of Dreadnought 2000.

Anl 27❑ca. 1993 Cover: 2.95 **NM** value: **3.00**
Circ: CapCity orders: **65,600** • **CGC:** 1 graded, best 9.4
• trading card ★ 1st Appearance of Annex.

Anl 28❑ca. 1994 Cover: 2.95 **NM** value: **3.00**
Circ: CapCity orders: **36,450**
• Carnage

Anl 1996❑ca. 1995 Cover: 2.99 **NM** value: **Cover or less**

Anl 1997❑ca. 1996 Cover: 2.99 **NM** value: **Cover or less**
Circ: Direct Market orders: **53,250**
wraparound cover. ★ Versus Sundown.

Ash 1❑b&w Cover: 0.75 **NM** value: **Cover or less**
No issue number. • ashcan edition. • ashcan ★ Origin of Spider-Man.

Bk 1❑ Cover: 12.95 **NM** value: **Cover or less**
Circ: CapCity orders: **5,925**
📖 Spider-Man Masterworks • Collects Amazing Fantasy #15, and Amazing Spider-Man #1-5 **A:** Steve Ditko **W:** Stan Lee

Bk 2❑ Sep 1988 Cover: 9.95 **NM** value: **12.95**
Circ: CapCity orders: **4,850**
📖 Saga of the Alien Costume • Saga Of The Alien Costume;Collects Amazing Spider-Man #252-259 **A:** Rick Leonardi; Ron Frenz **W:** Roger Stern; Tom DeFalco

Bk 3❑ Cover: 12.95 **NM** value: **Cover or less**
Circ: CapCity orders: **4,500**
📖 Torment **A:** Todd McFarlane **W:** Todd McFarlane

Bk 4❑ Cover: 9.95 **NM** value: **12.95**
Circ: CapCity orders: **3,875**
📖 Spider-Man vs. Venom • Spider-Man Vs. Venom;Collects Amazing Spider-Man #300,315-317 **A:** Todd McFarlane **W:** David Michelinie

Bk 5❑ Cover: 14.95 **NM** value: **Cover or less**
• The Assassin Nation Plot **A:** Todd McFarlane

Bk 6❑ Jun 1989 Cover: 15.95 **NM** value: **Cover or less**
• Fearful Symmetry: Kraven's Last Hunt

Bk 7❑ Jan 1991 Cover: 10.95 **NM** value: **Cover or less**
• The Death Of Jean De Wolff

Bk 8❑ Nov 1991 Cover: 15.95 **NM** value: **Cover or less**
• The Wedding

Bk 9❑ Cover: 14.95 **NM** value: **Cover or less**
• The Origin Of The Hobgoblin

Bk 10❑ Cover: 8.95 **NM** value: **Cover or less**
• Parallel Lives

Bk 11❑ Cover: 18.95 **NM** value: **Cover or less**
• Spirits of the Dead

Bk 12❑ Cover: 6.95 **NM** value: **Cover or less**
• Carnage

Bk 13❑Jul 1994 Cover: 15.95 **NM** value: **Cover or less**
• Round Robin The Sidekick's Revenge;collects Amazing Spider-Man #353-358

Bk 14❑Apr 1995 Cover: 15.95 **NM** value: **Cover or less**
• Invasion Of The Spider-Slayers;collects Amazing Spider-Man #368-373

GS 1❑ Cover: 0.50 **NM** value: **18.00**
📖 Ship of Fiends; The Masque of the Black Death; The Human Torch On the Trail of the Amazing Spider-Man • Human Torch, Count Dracula; E6437 Third story reprinted from Strange Tales Annual #2 **A:** Ross Andru **W:** Len Wein ★ Appearance of Dracula.

GS 2❑ Cover: 0.50 **NM** value: **10.00**
📖 Masterstroke; Cross and Double-Cross; Pinnacle of Doom; To Become an Avenger • Master of Kung Fu; Last story reprinted from Amazing Spider-Man Annual #3 **A:** Ross Andru **W:** Len Wein

GS 3❑ Cover: 0.50 **NM** value: **10.00**
📖 The Yesterday Connection; The Secret Out of Time; Tomorrow Is Too Late; Other People, Other Times; The Future is Now; Duel with Daredevil • Doc Savage; Last story reprinted with changes from Amazing Spider-Man #16 **A:** Ross Andru **W:** Gerry Conway

GS 4❑ Cover: 0.50 **NM** value: **20.00**
📖 To Sow the Seeds of Death's Day; Attack of the War Machine; Death-Camp at the Edge of the World; The Wondrous World of Dr. Strange • Punisher; Last story reprinted from Amazing Spider-Man Annual #2 **A:** Ross Andru **W:** Gerry Conway ★ 1st Appearance of Moses Magnum (Magnum Force). ★ Appearance of Punisher.

GS 5❑ Cover: 0.50 **NM** value: **7.00**
📖 Beware the Path of the Monster; The Lurker in the Swamp; Bring Back My Man-Thing to Me; Where Flies the Beetle • Man-Thing; Last story reprinted with changes from Amazing Spider-Man #21 **A:** Ross Andru **W:** Gerry Conway

GS 6❑ Cover: 0.50 **NM** value: **7.00**
📖 The Web and the Flame • reprints Amazing Spider-Man Annual #4

AMAZING SPIDER-MAN 30TH ANNIVERSARY POSTER MAGAZINE — Marvel

1 ❑ Cover: 3.95 **NM** value: **Cover or less**
No issue number.

AMAZING SPIDER-MAN (FIRESIDE BOOK) — Marvel

1 ❑ Cover: 3.95 **NM** value: **Cover or less**
• (Simon & Schuster Fireside tpb)

AMAZING SPIDER-MAN GIVEAWAYS — Marvel

1 ❑ **NM** value: **1.00**
• (two different, both #1)

2 ❑ **NM** value: **1.00**
No issue number. • Managing Materials

3 ❑ Feb 1977 **NM** value: **1.00**
• Planned Parenthood giveaway. • miniature;... vs. The Prodigy!

5 ❑ **NM** value: **1.00**
No issue number. • child abuse;with New Mutants

AMAZING SPIDER-MAN GOLDEN ALL-STAR BOOK — Western Publishing

1 ❑ 1977 Cover: 0.59 **NM** value: **5.00**
No issue number.

AMAZING SPIDER-MAN: HOOKY — Marvel

1 ❑ Cover: 6.95 **NM** value: **Cover or less**
No issue number. **A:** Berni Wrightson **W:** Susan Putney

AMAZING SPIDER-MAN, THE (POCKET BOOKS) — Marvel

1 ❑ Apr 1980 Cover: 2.50 **NM** value: **Cover or less**
• (Pocket Books) **A:** John Romita **W:** Stan Lee

2 ❑ Cover: 1.95 **NM** value: **Cover or less**
• (Pocket Books)

3 ❑ Cover: 2.25 **NM** value: **Cover or less**
• (Pocket Books)

4 ❑ Cover: 2.50 **NM** value: **Cover or less**
• (Pocket Books strip reprints)

AMAZING SPIDER-MAN, THE (PUBLIC SERVICE SERIES) — Marvel

Originally distributed only in Canada, this public-service series took Spider-Man north of the border. Spider-Man thwarts Electro's efforts to smuggle drugs into Winnipeg, foils The Chameleon's plans to swipe a valuable scientific secret, brings a drunk driver to justice, and defeats The Frightful Four, a set of super-villains who want to kidnap a Nobel prize-winning scientist.

Even with all that, there's a serious side to this four-part series, yet another instance (as with Spidery Super Stories) of using Marvel's most popular character to educate. Interspersed with the action are lessons about drug abuse, bicycle safety, and honesty.

1 ❑ Cover: 1.25 **NM** value: **2.50**
• **CGC:** 1 graded, best 9.2
• Skating on Thin Ice! **A:** Todd McFarlane

1-2 ❑ Cover: 1.50 **NM** value: **2.00**
• US Edition. • Skating on Thin Ice **A:** Todd McFarlane

2 ❑ Cover: 1.50 **NM** value: **2.50**
• **CGC:** 1 graded, best 9.4
• Double Trouble! **A:** Todd McFarlane

2-2 ❑ Cover: 1.50 **NM** value: **2.00**
• US Edition. • Double Trouble **A:** Todd McFarlane

3 ❑ Cover: 1.50 **NM** value: **2.50**
• **CGC:** 1 graded, best 9.4
• Hit and Run! **A:** Todd McFarlane

3-2 ❑ Cover: 1.50 **NM** value: **2.00**
• US Edition. • Hit and Run **A:** Todd McFarlane ★ Appearance of Ghost Rider.

4 ❑ Feb 1993 Cover: 1.50 **NM** value: **2.50**
• Chaos in Calgary **A:** Todd McFarlane ★ 1st Appearance of Turbine.

4-2 ❑ Cover: 1.50 **NM** value: **2.00**
• US Edition. • Chaos in Calgary

AMAZING SPIDER-MAN, THE: SOUL OF THE HUNTER — Marvel

1 ❑ Aug 1992 Cover: 5.95 **NM** value: **Cover or less**
No issue number. **A:** Mike Zeck **W:** J.M. DeMatteis

AMAZING SPIDER-MAN SUPER SPECIAL, THE — Marvel

1 ❑ Cover: 3.95 **NM** value: **Cover or less**
Circ: CapCity orders: **24,675**
• Flip-book. 📖 The Far Cry • two of the stories continue in Spider-Man Super Special #1;Amazing Scarlet Spider on other side **A:** Dave Hoover; Phil Gosier **W:** Terry Kavanagh; David Michelinie

AMAZING SPIDER-MAN, THE: THE BIRTH OF A SUPER HERO! — Marvel

1 ❑ **NM** value: **1.00**
• was attached to Eye magazine. • small reprint

AMAZING SPIDER-MAN, THE (VOL. 2) — Marvel

Peter Parker lives in a luxurious midtown penthouse with his beautiful super-model wife, Mary Jane Watson. Living with them is Aunt May. Peter also lands the dream job of his life with the Tri Corp Research Foundation. And he has given up being Spider-Man. So, even though the rest of the super-hero community wonders about Spider-Man's absence, life is good.

Such are the circumstances of the reboot of one of Marvel's flagship characters. The convoluted state of affairs that the Spider-Man continuity had become in 1998 led Marvel to simplify the series by making drastic alterations, undoing a few missteps, and restarting the numbering. Since Spider-Man's distinctive role in comics history has always been as the down-on-his-luck, isolated, everyman-type character, such complacency is in direct contrast to the approach that made Spider-Man popular. Already, events in the first issue do not bode well for Parker's continued tranquillity.

1 ❑ Jan 1999 Cover: 2.99 **NM** value: **3.00**
Circ: Statement: **127,915** • **CGC:** 19 graded, best 9.8
wraparound cover. **A:** John Byrne **W:** Howard Mackie

1/A ❑ Jan 1999 **NM** value: **15.00**
C: John Romita Jr.

1/B ❑ Jan 1999 **NM** value: **45.00**

1/C ❑ Jan 1999 **NM** value: **5.00**
• **CGC:** 7 graded, best 9.6
DFE alternate cover

Other grades: Multiply prices above by **1.5 for Mint • 2/3 for Very Fine • 1/3 for Fine • 1/5 for Very Good • 1/8 for Good**

1/D ❑ Jan 1999 NM value: **15.00**
1/E ❑ Jan 1999 NM value: **10.00**
• Marvel Authentix edition.
2/A ❑ Feb 1999 Cover: 1.99 NM value: **Cover or less**
Circ: Statement: **127,915** Diamd. preorders: **102,000** • **CGC:** 1 graded, best 9.6
Cover A. • gatefold summary. • new Spider-Man's identity revealed;Skeleton grabbing Spider-Man **A:** John Byrne **W:** Howard Mackie ★ Versus Shadrac.
2/B ❑ Feb 1999 Cover: 1.99 NM value: **Cover or less**
Cover B. • gatefold summary. • new Spider-Man's identity revealed **A:** John Byrne **W:** Howard Mackie ★ Versus Shadrac.
3 ❑ Mar 1999 Cover: 1.99 NM value: **Cover or less**
Circ: Statement: **127,915** Diamd. preorders: **83,890**
A: John Byrne **W:** Howard Mackie ★ Origin of Shadrac.
4 ❑ Apr 1999 Cover: 1.99 NM value: **Cover or less**
Circ: Statement: **127,915** Diamd. preorders: **78,781**
📖 Betrayals **A:** John Byrne **W:** Howard Mackie ★ Appearance of Fantastic Four. ★ Versus Trapster. ★ Versus Sandman.
5 ❑ May 1999 Cover: 1.99 NM value: **Cover or less**
Circ: Statement: **127,915** Diamd. preorders: **76,829**
★ Appearance of new Spider-Woman.
6 ❑ Jun 1999 Cover: 1.99 NM value: **Cover or less**
Circ: Statement: **127,915** Diamd. preorders: **74,475**
★ Versus Spider-Woman.
7 ❑ Jul 1999 Cover: 1.99 NM value: **Cover or less**
Circ: Statement: **127,915** Diamd. preorders: **71,579**
• Flash Thompson's fantasy
8 ❑ Aug 1999 Cover: 1.99 NM value: **Cover or less**
Circ: Statement: **127,915** Diamd. preorders: **70,032**
★ Versus Mysterio.
9 ❑ Sep 1999 Cover: 1.99 NM value: **Cover or less**
Circ: Statement: **113,685** Diamd. preorders: **67,264**
★ Appearance of Doctor Octopus.
10 ❑ Oct 1999 Cover: 1.99 NM value: **Cover or less**
Circ: Statement: **113,685** Diamd. preorders: **64,059**
★ Appearance of Doctor Octopus. ★ Versus Captain Power.
11 ❑ Nov 1999 Cover: 1.99 NM value: **Cover or less**
Circ: Statement: **113,685** Diamd. preorders: **61,134**
• Has 1999 Statement, filed 10/1/99; avg print run 206,591; avg sales 120,569; avg subs 7,346; avg total paid 127,915; samples 5,653; office use 125; max existent 133,693; 38% of run returned ★ Versus Blob.
12 ❑ Dec 1999 Cover: 2.99 NM value: **Cover or less**
Circ: Statement: **113,685** Diamd. preorders: **62,018**
• Giant-size.
13 ❑ Jan 2000 Cover: 1.99 NM value: **Cover or less**
Circ: Statement: **113,685** Diamd. preorders: **58,883** • **CGC:** 1 graded, best 9.4
14 ❑ Feb 2000 Cover: 1.99 NM value: **Cover or less**
Circ: Statement: **113,685** Diamd. preorders: **61,917**
📖 A Surfeit of Spiders **A:** John Byrne; Dan Green **W:** John Byrne
15 ❑ Mar 2000 Cover: 1.99 NM value: **Cover or less**
Circ: Statement: **113,685** Diamd. preorders: **56,413**
📖 We're All Doomed...Again! **A:** John Byrne; Howard Mackie **W:** John Byrne; Howard Mackie
16 ❑ Apr 2000 Cover: 1.99 NM value: **Cover or less**
Circ: Statement: **113,685** Diamd. preorders: **53,222**
17 ❑ May 2000 Cover: 1.99 NM value: **Cover or less**
Circ: Statement: **113,685** Diamd. preorders: **54,096**
18 ❑ Jun 2000 Cover: 2.25 NM value: **Cover or less**
Circ: Statement: **113,685** Diamd. preorders: **53,218**
19 ❑ Jul 2000 Cover: 2.25 NM value: **Cover or less**
Circ: Statement: **113,685** Diamd. preorders: **52,994**
📖 Mirror Mirror **A:** Erik Larsen **W:** Howard Mackie ★ Appearance of Venom.
20 ❑ Aug 2000 Cover: 2.99 NM value: **3.99**
Circ: Statement: **113,685** Diamd. preorders: **53,514**
📖 Setup!; Captured by J. Jonah Jameson; To Kill a Spider-Man!; 24 Hours Till Doomsday! **A:** Steve Ditko; Keith Pollard; John Romita; Jim Mooney; Erik Larsen **C:** Erik Larsen **W:** Howard Mackie; Stan Lee; Marv Wolfman
21 ❑ Sep 2000 Cover: 2.25 NM value: **Cover or less**
Circ: Statement: **113,685** Diamd. preorders: **51,902**
📖 Slayers to the Left of Me ... **A:** Erik Larsen; John Beatty **C:** Erik Larsen **W:** Howard Mackie ★ Versus Spider-Slayers.
22 ❑ Oct 2000 Cover: 2.25 NM value: **Cover or less**
Circ: Statement: **113,557** Diamd. preorders: **49,890**
23 ❑ Nov 2000 Cover: 2.25 NM value: **Cover or less**
Circ: Statement: **113,557** Diamd. preorders: **49,291**
📖 The Distinguished Gentleman from New York, Part 2 **A:** John Romita Jr. **W:** Howard Mackie
24 ❑ Dec 2000 Cover: 2.25 NM value: **Cover or less**
Circ: Statement: **113,557** Diamd. preorders: **50,182**
📖 Maximum Security; The Distinguished Gentleman from New York, Part 3: Failure is Not an Option • Has 2000 Statement, filed 10/1/2000; avg print run 173,967; avg sales 106,488; avg subs 7,197; avg total paid 113,685; samples 600; office use 125; max existent 114,410; 34% of run returned **A:** John Romita Jr. **W:** Howard Mackie
25 ❑ Jan 2001 Cover: 3.99 NM value: **Cover or less**
Circ: Statement: **113,557** Diamd. preorders: **45,390** • **CGC:** 2 graded, best 9.8
26 ❑ Feb 2001 Cover: 2.25 NM value: **Cover or less**
Circ: Statement: **113,557** Diamd. preorders: **49,547**
27 ❑ Mar 2001 Cover: 2.25 NM value: **Cover or less**
Circ: Statement: **113,557** Diamd. preorders: **49,189**
📖 The Stray **A:** John Romita Jr. **W:** Howard Mackie ★ Appearance of Mr. Q, Mr. P.
28 ❑ Apr 2001 Cover: 2.25 NM value: **Cover or less**
Circ: Statement: **113,557** Diamd. preorders: **48,558** • **CGC:** 1 graded, best 9.4
📖 Distractions **A:** Joe Bennett **W:** Howard Mackie
29 ❑ May 2001 Cover: 2.25 NM value: **Cover or less**
Circ: Statement: **113,557** Diamd. preorders: **48,804**
📖 Mary Jane • Return of Mary Jane **A:** Lee Weeks **W:** Howard Mackie
30 ❑ Jun 2001 Cover: 2.25 NM value: **Cover or less**
Circ: Statement: **113,557** Diamd. preorders: **77,314** • **CGC:** 142 graded, best 9.9
31 ❑ Jul 2001 Cover: 2.25 NM value: **Cover or less**
Circ: Statement: **113,557** Diamd. preorders: **73,743** • **CGC:** 13 graded, best 9.8
32 ❑ Aug 2001 Cover: 2.25 NM value: **Cover or less**
Circ: Statement: **113,557** Diamd. preorders: **82,328** • **CGC:** 10 graded, best 9.8
33 ❑ Sep 2001 Cover: 2.25 NM value: **Cover or less**
Circ: Statement: **113,557** Diamd. preorders: **89,812** • **CGC:** 5 graded, best 9.6
34 ❑ Oct 2001 Cover: 2.25 NM value: **Cover or less**
Circ: Diamd. preorders: **90,496** • **CGC:** 6 graded, best 10.0
35 ❑ Nov 2001 Cover: 2.25 NM value: **Cover or less**
Circ: Diamd. preorders: **89,993** • **CGC:** 3 graded, best 9.8
36 ❑ Dec 2001 Cover: 2.25 NM value: **Cover or less**
Circ: Diamd. preorders: **92,765** • **CGC:** 85 graded, best 9.9
1st printing.
37 ❑ Jan 2002 Cover: 2.25 NM value: **Cover or less**
Circ: Diamd. preorders: **93,495**
• Has 2001 Statement, filed 10/1/2001; avg print run 131,367; avg sales 106,566; avg subs 6,991; avg total paid 113,557; samples 600; office use 0; max existent 114,157; 13% of run returned
38 ❑ Feb 2002 Cover: 2.25 NM value: **Cover or less**
Circ: Diamd. preorders: **95,296**
Anl 1999 ❑ Jun 1999 Cover: 3.50 NM value: **Cover or less**
Circ: Diamd. preorders: **49,296**
• 1999 Annual ★ Versus Trapster. ★ Versus Wizard.
Anl 2001 ❑ ca. 2001 Cover: 2.99 NM value: **Cover or less**
Circ: Diamd. preorders: **38,330**
📖 Passages
Anl 2000 ❑ ca. 2000 Cover: 3.50 NM value: **Cover or less**
Circ: Diamd. preorders: **39,177**

AMAZING STRIP — Antarctic

1 ❑ Feb 1994 Cover: 2.95 NM value: **Cover or less**
2 ❑ Mar 1994 Cover: 2.95 NM value: **Cover or less**
3 ❑ Apr 1994 Cover: 2.95 NM value: **Cover or less**
4 ❑ May 1994 Cover: 2.95 NM value: **Cover or less**
5 ❑ Jun 1994 Cover: 2.95 NM value: **Cover or less**
6 ❑ Jul 1994 Cover: 2.95 NM value: **Cover or less**
7 ❑ Aug 1994 Cover: 2.95 NM value: **Cover or less**
8 ❑ Sep 1994 Cover: 2.95 NM value: **Cover or less**
9 ❑ Nov 1994 Cover: 2.95 NM value: **Cover or less**
10 ❑ Dec 1994 Cover: 2.95 NM value: **Cover or less**
Bk 1 ❑ Cover: 10.95 NM value: **Cover or less**
• Collects Amazing Strip #1-5
Bk 2 ❑ Cover: 10.95 NM value: **Cover or less**
• Collects Amazing Strip #6-10

AMAZING WAHZOO — Solson

Richard W. Buckler, son of comics veteran Rich Buckler, made his debut with this short-lived indie series from 1986. Buckler, who was 14 at the time, showed a remarkable grasp of the comics medium, as well as an ability to get a story across without the gratuitous posing and grimacing that mar so many freshman efforts.

The Amazing Wahzoo is a strange, over-the-top super-hero whom a couple of kids are working on (much like their real-life creators), but who comes to life, due to a computer glitch in the writer's computer. The problem then becomes how to hide the diminutive super-hero and keep their parents from finding out about him.

In contrast to young Richard Buckler's surprisingly mature work, the backup feature, "Star King" by 32-year-old Rich Sawyer, is amateurish space and super-hero fiction.

1 ❑ 1986 Cover: 1.75 NM value: **Cover or less**
📖 Howard!; ...When Clouds Gather! **A:** Rich Buckler; Rich Sawyer; R.W. Buckler **W:** Rich Sawyer; John Holiwski; R.W. Buckler ★ Origin of Amazing Wahzoo. ★ 1st Appearance of Howard Wasnuski, Amazing Wahzoo.

AMAZING WILLIE MAYS — Famous Funnies

1 ❑ Sep 1954 Cover: 0.10 NM value: **500.00**
• **CGC:** 3 graded, best 9.4

AMAZING WORLD OF SUPERMAN — DC

1 ❑ 1973 Cover: 2.00 NM value: **3.00**

AMAZING X-MEN — Marvel

1 ❑ Mar 1995 Cover: 1.95 NM value: **Cover or less**
Circ: CapCity orders: **92,650** • **CGC:** 1 graded, best 9.0
📖 The Crossing Guards **A:** Andy Kubert **W:** Fabian Nicieza
2 ❑ Apr 1995 Cover: 1.95 NM value: **Cover or less**
Circ: CapCity orders: **89,775**
A: Andy Kubert **W:** Fabian Nicieza
3 ❑ May 1995 Cover: 1.95 NM value: **Cover or less**
Circ: CapCity orders: **104,300**
A: Andy Kubert **W:** Fabian Nicieza
4 ❑ Jun 1995 Cover: 1.95 NM value: **Cover or less**
Circ: CapCity orders: **108,050**
A: Andy Kubert **W:** Fabian Nicieza
Bk 1 ❑ May 1995 Cover: 8.95 NM value: **Cover or less**
Gold foil cover. • Ultimate Amazing X-Men;collects four-issue series **A:** Andy Kubert **W:** Fabian Nicieza

Do you have changes or corrections for the **Standard Catalog**? Send your original research to us at **allcomics@krause.com**

AMAZON — DC / Amalgam

Amazon is one of 12 one-shot titles created by Marvel and DC when their universes "merged" in Marvel versus DC/DC versus Marvel #3. The new Amalgam titles combine features of characters from both universes.

This title was created by Wonder Woman veteran John Byrne, who managed to endow it with a sense of history despite its one-shot nature. The title character is a mix of Storm (from Marvel's X-Men) and DC's Amazon princess Wonder Woman. In this rendition, she is Princess Ororo of Themyscira, a woman who was taken in by Amazons as a girl, when the god Poseidon destroyed the ship upon which her family had been traveling. Later, she grows to become the Amazons' protector, in addition to discovering her own mutant ability to control the weather. This one-shot relates her origin, as well as taking her once again to confront the sea god Poseidon.

1 ❑ Apr 1996 Cover: 1.95 NM value: **Cover or less**
Circ: Diamd. preorders: **4,134** • **CGC:** 1 graded, best 9.4
📖 Family History **A:** John Byrne **W:** John Byrne ★ Origin of Wonder Woman (Amalgam).

AMAZON ATTACK 3-D — 3-D Zone

1 ❑ Cover: 3.95 NM value: **Cover or less**
No issue number.

AMAZONS — Fantagraphics

1 ❑ b&w Cover: 2.95 NM value: **Cover or less**

AMAZON TALES — Fantaco

1 ❑ Cover: 2.95 NM value: **Cover or less**
📖 Texoma Red **A:** Tom Simonton **W:** Tom Simonton
2 ❑ Cover: 2.95 NM value: **Cover or less**
3 ❑ Cover: 2.95 NM value: **Cover or less**

AMAZON, THE — Comico

1 ❑ Mar 1989 Cover: 1.95 NM value: **Cover or less**
Circ: CapCity orders: **4,100**
📖 Spirit Of The Amazon **A:** Tim Sale **W:** Steven Seagle
2 ❑ Apr 1989 Cover: 1.95 NM value: **Cover or less**
Circ: CapCity orders: **3,450**
3 ❑ May 1989 Cover: 1.95 NM value: **Cover or less**
Circ: CapCity orders: **3,200**

AMAZON WARRIORS — AC

1 ❑ 1989 Cover: 2.50 NM value: **Cover or less**
• b&w Reprint

AMAZON WOMAN (1ST SERIES) — Fantaco

1 ❑ Cover: 2.95 NM value: **Cover or less**
A: Tom Simonton **W:** Tom Simonton
2 ❑ Cover: 2.95 NM value: **Cover or less**
A: Tom Simonton **W:** Tom Simonton

AMAZON WOMAN (2ND SERIES) — Fantaco

1 ❑ Cover: 2.95 NM value: **Cover or less**
📖 Curse Of The Amazon **A:** Tom Simonton **W:** Tom Simonton
2 ❑ Cover: 2.95 NM value: **Cover or less**
A: Tom Simonton **W:** Tom Simonton
3 ❑ Cover: 2.95 NM value: **Cover or less**
A: Tom Simonton **W:** Tom Simonton
4 ❑ Cover: 2.95 NM value: **Cover or less**
A: Tom Simonton **W:** Tom Simonton

AMBER: NINE PRINCES IN AMBER (ROGER ZELAZNY'S...) — DC

1 ❑ ca. 1996 Cover: 6.95 NM value: **Cover or less**
• prestige format. • adapts Zelazny story
2 ❑ ca. 1996 Cover: 6.95 NM value: **Cover or less**
• prestige format. • adapts Zelazny story
3 ❑ ca. 1996 Cover: 6.95 NM value: **Cover or less**
• prestige format. • adapts Zelazny story

AMBER: THE GUNS OF AVALON (ROGER ZELAZNY'S...) — DC

1 ❑ ca. 1996 Cover: 6.95 NM value: **Cover or less**
• prestige format. **A:** Andrew Pepoy; Christopher Schenck **W:** Roger Zelazny; Terry Bisson
2 ❑ ca. 1996 Cover: 6.95 NM value: **Cover or less**
• prestige format. **A:** Andrew Pepoy; Christopher Schenck **W:** Roger Zelazny; Terry Bisson
3 ❑ ca. 1996 Cover: 6.95 NM value: **Cover or less**
• prestige format. final issue. **A:** Andrew Pepoy; Christopher Schenck **W:** Roger Zelazny; Terry Bisson

There are two different pricing tiers in the modern comic-book hobby. **The prices seen above** are the prices we have seen **loose copies** of these issues reliably fetch in a variety of environments. Condition alters the price by the fractions seen on the bar on the bottom of left-hand pages of this book. **Comics graded by CGC** usually sell for more. Use the guide on the bottom of right-hand pages of this book to estimate what copies have brought on eBay.

CGC-graded: Multiply prices above by **33 for 9.9 M • 16 for 9.8 NM/M • 7 for 9.6 NM+ • 5 for 9.4 NM • 2.5 for 9.2 NM- • 1.5 for 9.0 VF/NM**

AMBUSH BUG — DC

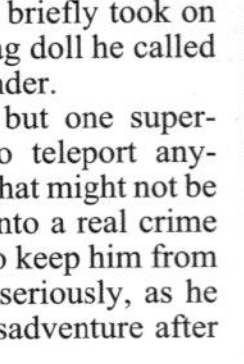

This corny character started out as a villain but now has his own series as a wanna-be super-hero. Some characters consider him insane; others simply realize that Ambush Bug has trouble thinking logically. He once fantasized he was Superman's partner, but in this series briefly took on his own sidekick, a rag doll he called Cheeks, the Toy Wonder.

Ambush Bug has but one superpower: the ability to teleport anywhere at will. While that might not be enough to turn him into a real crime fighter, it does help to keep him from injuring himself too seriously, as he stumbles through misadventure after misadventure.

1 ❑ Jun 1985 Cover: 0.75 **NM** value: **1.00**
🕮 Wipe Out **A:** Keith Giffen **W:** Keith Giffen

2 ❑ Jul 1985 Cover: 0.75 **NM** value: **1.00**
🕮 Ambush Bug vs The koala Who Wlkas Like a Man!! (Awwwww, Cute) **A:** Keith Giffen **W:** Keith Giffen

3 ❑ Aug 1985 Cover: 0.75 **NM** value: **1.00**
🕮 The Ambush Bug History of the DC Universe **A:** Keith Giffen **W:** Keith Giffen

4 ❑ Sep 1985 Cover: 0.75 **NM** value: **1.00**
🕮 Coincidence; Professor Schwab's Mystery Picture; The Death of Ambush Bug; Hard Socks; Ambush Bug Family Tree **A:** Keith Giffen **W:** Keith Giffen

AMBUSH BUG NOTHING SPECIAL — DC

1 ❑ Sep 1992 Cover: 2.50 **NM** value: **Cover or less**
Circ: CapCity orders: **12,450**
🕮 The Book Of Jobs **A:** Keith Giffen **W:** Keith Giffen

AMBUSH BUG STOCKING STUFFER — DC

1 ❑ Mar 1986 Cover: 1.25 **NM** value: **Cover or less**
Circ: CapCity orders: **12,150**
🕮 I Knew I Should Have Taken That Left Toyn Back In Albakoyky **A:** Keith Giffen **W:** Keith Giffen

AMELIA RULES — Renaissance

1 ❑ ca. 2001 Cover: 2.95 **NM** value: **Cover or less**
Circ: Diamd. preorders: **2,821**

2 ❑ ca. 2001 Cover: 2.95 **NM** value: **Cover or less**
Circ: Diamd. preorders: **2,651**

3 ❑ ca. 2001 Cover: 2.95 **NM** value: **Cover or less**
Circ: Diamd. preorders: **2,074**

4 ❑ ca. 2001 Cover: 2.95 **NM** value: **Cover or less**
Circ: Diamd. preorders: **2,258**

AMERICA IN ACTION — Dell

1 ❑ ca. 1945 Cover: 0.10 **NM** value: **100.00**
2 ❑ ca. 1942 Cover: 0.10 **NM** value: **75.00**

AMERICA MENACED! — Vital Publications

1 ❑ ca. 1950 **NM** value: **175.00**

AMERICAN, THE — Dark Horse

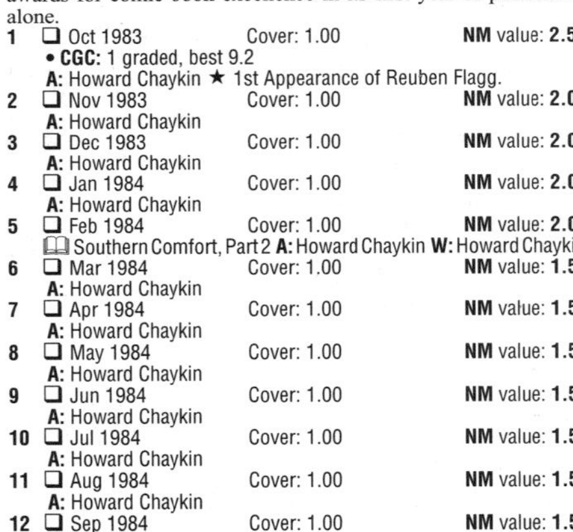

The American was a black-and-white series from Dark Horse that made its debut in 1987. Created and written by Mark Verheiden, it was inspired by an all-but-unknown title of the same name published by Watchfob Comics Group in the early 1960s.

Verheiden's remake is an intriguing tale of "official super-heroes" and the abuse of power. The American has supposedly been protecting American beliefs of life, liberty, and the pursuit of happiness for nearly 50 years. However, a news program finds footage and documentation which suggests that The American is a fake and that his fights were all staged. The report states that The American was simply a propaganda tool used to keep up United States citizens' morale in hard times. Rumors fly, as the U.S. government scrambles to save face and restore faith in The American. One thing is certain: There is much more to this "hero" than the public has been led to believe ...

1 ❑ Aug 1987, b&w Cover: 1.50 **NM** value: **Cover or less**
Circ: CapCity orders: **6,000**
🕮 Dead Wrong **A:** Grant Miehm **W:** Mark Verheiden ★ 1st Appearance of The American (modern).

2 ❑ Oct 1987 Cover: 1.75 **NM** value: **Cover or less**
A: Grant Miehm **W:** Mark Verheiden

3 ❑ Dec 1987 Cover: 1.75 **NM** value: **Cover or less**
🕮 America's Team **A:** Grant Miehm **W:** Mark Verheiden

4 ❑ Apr 1988 Cover: 1.75 **NM** value: **Cover or less**
A: Grant Miehm **W:** Mark Verheiden

5 ❑ Jul 1988 Cover: 1.75 **NM** value: **Cover or less**
🕮 Bearing Witness **A:** Grant Miehm **W:** Mark Verheiden

6 ❑ Sep 1988 Cover: 1.75 **NM** value: **Cover or less**
A: Grant Miehm **W:** Mark Verheiden

7 ❑ Oct 1988 Cover: 1.75 **NM** value: **Cover or less**
🕮 The Reality, Part 1 **A:** Grant Miehm **W:** Mark Verheiden

8 ❑ Feb 1989 Cover: 1.75 **NM** value: **Cover or less**
🕮 The Reality, Part 2 **A:** Grant Miehm **W:** Mark Verheiden

Bk 1❑ Cover: 5.95 **NM** value: **Cover or less**
• The American Collection;Collects The American #1-8 **A:** Grant Miehm **W:** Mark Verheiden

SE 1❑ b&w Cover: 2.25 **NM** value: **Cover or less**
Circ: CapCity orders: **3,575**
• Special edition.

AMERICAN AIR FORCES — Wise Publications

1 ❑ Sep 1944 Cover: 0.10 **NM** value: **75.00**
2 ❑ Nov 1944 Cover: 0.10 **NM** value: **45.00**
• **CGC:** 1 graded, best 8.0
3 ❑ ca. 1945 Cover: 0.10 **NM** value: **45.00**
4 ❑ ca. 1945 Cover: 0.10 **NM** value: **45.00**

AMERICAN ARTISTS W.O.W. THE WORLD OF WARD — Allied

1 ❑ Cover: 3.95 **NM** value: **Cover or less**
A: Bill Ward; Jack Cole

AMERICAN BOOK, THE — Dark Horse

1 ❑ Oct 1988, b&w Cover: 5.95 **NM** value: **Cover or less**
A: Chris Warner **W:** Mark Verheiden ★ Origin of American.

AMERICAN CENTURY — Vertigo

1 ❑ May 2001 Cover: 2.50 **NM** value: **Cover or less**
Circ: Diamd. preorders: **19,408**
🕮 Borrowed Time: Interest Computed Daily **A:** Marc Laming **W:** Howard Chaykin; David Tischman

2 ❑ Jun 2001 Cover: 2.50 **NM** value: **Cover or less**
Circ: Diamd. preorders: **15,969**
A: Marc Laming **W:** Howard Chaykin; David Tischman

3 ❑ Jul 2001 Cover: 2.50 **NM** value: **Cover or less**
Circ: Diamd. preorders: **15,976**
A: Marc Laming **W:** Howard Chaykin; David Tischman

4 ❑ Aug 2001 Cover: 2.50 **NM** value: **Cover or less**
Circ: Diamd. preorders: **17,111**
A: Marc Laming **W:** Howard Chaykin; David Tischman

5 ❑ Aug 2001 Cover: 2.50 **NM** value: **Cover or less**
Circ: Diamd. preorders: **17,600**
A: Marc Laming **W:** Howard Chaykin; David Tischman

AMERICAN FLAGG — First

It's 2076, and the world is falling apart. America has become a mass-media ghetto where the very idea of morality seems charmingly old-fashioned. Daily, the great television networks broadcast a steady diet of sex and violence to a nation of depraved viewers. Someone's got to put it back together, and that someone seems to be Reuben Flagg.

Told in a style which mimics the quick edits of a music video, American Flagg! was hailed as a revolutionary series which brought the world of comics up to the level of adults. Created by Howard Chaykin (Black Kiss, Midnight Men), this extraordinary series won seven Eagle awards for comic-book excellence in its first year of publication alone.

1 ❑ Oct 1983 Cover: 1.00 **NM** value: **2.50**
• **CGC:** 1 graded, best 9.2
A: Howard Chaykin ★ 1st Appearance of Reuben Flagg.

2 ❑ Nov 1983 Cover: 1.00 **NM** value: **2.00**
A: Howard Chaykin

3 ❑ Dec 1983 Cover: 1.00 **NM** value: **2.00**
A: Howard Chaykin

4 ❑ Jan 1984 Cover: 1.00 **NM** value: **2.00**
A: Howard Chaykin

5 ❑ Feb 1984 Cover: 1.00 **NM** value: **2.00**
🕮 Southern Comfort, Part 2 **A:** Howard Chaykin **W:** Howard Chaykin

6 ❑ Mar 1984 Cover: 1.00 **NM** value: **1.50**
A: Howard Chaykin

7 ❑ Apr 1984 Cover: 1.00 **NM** value: **1.50**
A: Howard Chaykin

8 ❑ May 1984 Cover: 1.00 **NM** value: **1.50**
A: Howard Chaykin

9 ❑ Jun 1984 Cover: 1.00 **NM** value: **1.50**
A: Howard Chaykin

10 ❑ Jul 1984 Cover: 1.00 **NM** value: **1.50**
A: Howard Chaykin

11 ❑ Aug 1984 Cover: 1.00 **NM** value: **1.50**
A: Howard Chaykin

12 ❑ Sep 1984 Cover: 1.00 **NM** value: **1.50**
A: Howard Chaykin

13 ❑ Oct 1984 Cover: 1.00 **NM** value: **1.50**
A: Howard Chaykin

14 ❑ Nov 1984 Cover: 1.25 **NM** value: **Cover or less**
A: Pat Broderick

15 ❑ Dec 1984 Cover: 1.25 **NM** value: **Cover or less**
A: Howard Chaykin

16 ❑ Jan 1985 Cover: 1.25 **NM** value: **Cover or less**
Circ: Statement: **43,624**
A: Howard Chaykin

17 ❑ Feb 1985 Cover: 1.25 **NM** value: **Cover or less**
Circ: Statement: **43,624**
A: Howard Chaykin

18 ❑ Mar 1985 Cover: 1.25 **NM** value: **Cover or less**
Circ: Statement: **43,624**
A: Howard Chaykin

19 ❑ Apr 1985 Cover: 1.25 **NM** value: **Cover or less**
Circ: Statement: **43,624**
A: Howard Chaykin

20 ❑ May 1985 Cover: 1.25 **NM** value: **Cover or less**
Circ: Statement: **43,624** CapCity orders: **10,000**
A: Howard Chaykin

21 ❑ Jun 1985 Cover: 1.25 **NM** value: **Cover or less**
Circ: Statement: **43,624** CapCity orders: **9,975**
W: Alan Moore

22 ❑ Jul 1985 Cover: 1.25 **NM** value: **Cover or less**
Circ: Statement: **43,624** CapCity orders: **10,325**
C: Howard Chaykin **W:** Alan Moore

23 ❑ Aug 1985 Cover: 1.25 **NM** value: **Cover or less**
Circ: Statement: **43,624** CapCity orders: **9,850**
C: Howard Chaykin **W:** Alan Moore

24 ❑ Sep 1985 Cover: 1.25 **NM** value: **Cover or less**
Circ: Statement: **43,624** CapCity orders: **9,925**
C: Howard Chaykin **W:** Alan Moore

25 ❑ Oct 1985 Cover: 1.25 **NM** value: **Cover or less**
Circ: Statement: **43,624** CapCity orders: **9,625**
C: Howard Chaykin **W:** Alan Moore

26 ❑ Nov 1985 Cover: 1.25 **NM** value: **Cover or less**
Circ: Statement: **43,624** CapCity orders: **9,025**
C: Howard Chaykin **W:** Alan Moore

27 ❑ Dec 1985 Cover: 1.25 **NM** value: **Cover or less**
Circ: Statement: **43,624** CapCity orders: **8,925**
A: Howard Chaykin **W:** Alan Moore

28 ❑ Apr 1986 Cover: 1.25 **NM** value: **Cover or less**
Circ: CapCity orders: **8,200**
• Has 1985 Statement; avg print run 44,766; avg sales 43,445; avg subs 179; avg total paid 43,624; samples 140; office use 1,002; max existent 44,766; 0% of run returned **A:** Howard Chaykin; Joe Staton

29 ❑ May 1986 Cover: 1.25 **NM** value: **Cover or less**
Circ: CapCity orders: **8,200**
🕮 The Fire Next Time, Part Two **A:** Howard Chaykin; Joe Staton

30 ❑ Jun 1986 Cover: 1.25 **NM** value: **Cover or less**
Circ: CapCity orders: **8,150**
A: Howard Chaykin; Joe Staton

31 ❑ Jul 1986 Cover: 1.25 **NM** value: **Cover or less**
Circ: CapCity orders: **7,800**
A: Howard Chaykin ★ Origin of Bob Violence.

32 ❑ Aug 1986 Cover: 1.25 **NM** value: **Cover or less**
Circ: CapCity orders: **7,575**
A: Howard Chaykin

33 ❑ Sep 1986 Cover: 1.25 **NM** value: **Cover or less**
Circ: CapCity orders: **7,600**

34 ❑ Nov 1986 Cover: 1.25 **NM** value: **Cover or less**
Circ: CapCity orders: **7,525**

35 ❑ Dec 1986 Cover: 1.25 **NM** value: **Cover or less**
Circ: CapCity orders: **7,175**

36 ❑ Jan 1987 Cover: 1.25 **NM** value: **Cover or less**
Circ: CapCity orders: **6,225**

37 ❑ Feb 1987 Cover: 1.25 **NM** value: **Cover or less**
Circ: CapCity orders: **6,125**

38 ❑ Mar 1987 Cover: 1.25 **NM** value: **Cover or less**
Circ: CapCity orders: **6,025**
A: Howard Chaykin

39 ❑ Apr 1987 Cover: 1.25 **NM** value: **Cover or less**
Circ: CapCity orders: **5,550**
A: Howard Chaykin

40 ❑ May 1987 Cover: 1.25 **NM** value: **Cover or less**
Circ: CapCity orders: **5,125**
A: Howard Chaykin

41 ❑ Jun 1987 Cover: 1.25 **NM** value: **Cover or less**
Circ: CapCity orders: **5,025**
A: Howard Chaykin

42 ❑ Jul 1987 Cover: 1.25 **NM** value: **Cover or less**
Circ: CapCity orders: **4,875**
A: Howard Chaykin

43 ❑ Aug 1987 Cover: 1.25 **NM** value: **Cover or less**
Circ: CapCity orders: **4,750**
A: Howard Chaykin

44 ❑ Sep 1987 Cover: 1.25 **NM** value: **Cover or less**
Circ: CapCity orders: **4,925**
🕮 Reuben Redux? **A:** Mark Badger; Howard Chaykin **W:** J.M. DeMatteis

45 ❑ Oct 1987 Cover: 1.25 **NM** value: **Cover or less**
Circ: CapCity orders: **4,725**

46 ❑ Nov 1987 Cover: 1.25 **NM** value: **1.75**
Circ: CapCity orders: **5,100**
• apology **C:** Howard Chaykin

47 ❑ Dec 1987 Cover: 1.75 **NM** value: **Cover or less**
Circ: CapCity orders: **5,100**
A: Howard Chaykin

48 ❑ Jan 1988 Cover: 1.75 **NM** value: **Cover or less**
Circ: CapCity orders: **5,675**
A: Howard Chaykin

49 ❑ Feb 1988 Cover: 1.75 **NM** value: **Cover or less**
Circ: CapCity orders: **6,175**
A: Howard Chaykin

50 ❑ Mar 1988 Cover: 1.75 **NM** value: **Cover or less**
Circ: CapCity orders: **7,625**
A: Howard Chaykin

SE 1❑ Nov 1986 Cover: 1.75 **NM** value: **Cover or less**
Circ: CapCity orders: **12,725**
🕮 Back on the Track for '76 • Special #1 **A:** Howard Chaykin **W:** Howard Chaykin

AMERICAN FLAGG (HOWARD CHAYKIN'S...) — First

1 ❑ May 1988 Cover: 1.75 **NM** value: **Cover or less**
Circ: CapCity orders: **12,825**

2 ❑ Jun 1988 Cover: 1.75 **NM** value: **Cover or less**
Circ: CapCity orders: **8,475**

3 ❑ Jul 1988 Cover: 1.75 **NM** value: **Cover or less**
Circ: CapCity orders: **7,925**

4 ❑ Aug 1988 Cover: 1.75 **NM** value: **Cover or less**
Circ: CapCity orders: **7,275**

5 ❑ Sep 1988 Cover: 1.75 **NM** value: **Cover or less**
Circ: CapCity orders: **7,000**

6 ❑ Oct 1988 Cover: 1.75 **NM** value: **1.95**
Circ: CapCity orders: **6,900**

7 ❑ Nov 1988 Cover: 1.75 **NM** value: **1.95**
Circ: CapCity orders: **6,450**

8 ❑ Dec 1988 Cover: 1.75 **NM** value: **1.95**
Circ: CapCity orders: **6,450**

Other grades: Multiply prices above by **1.5 for Mint • 2/3 for Very Fine • 1/3 for Fine • 1/5 for Very Good • 1/8 for Good**

9 ❑ Jan 1989 Cover: 1.95 **NM** value: **Cover or less**
Circ: CapCity orders: **6,125**
10 ❑ Feb 1989 Cover: 1.95 **NM** value: **Cover or less**
Circ: CapCity orders: **5,900**
11 ❑ Mar 1989 Cover: 1.95 **NM** value: **Cover or less**
Circ: CapCity orders: **5,850**
12 ❑ Apr 1989 Cover: 1.95 **NM** value: **Cover or less**
Circ: CapCity orders: **5,725**

AMERICAN FLYER — Last Gasp

1 ❑ Cover: 0.50 **NM** value: **3.00**
2 ❑ Cover: 0.50 **NM** value: **3.00**
📖 The Wizard's Challenge; Star Wench on Mars; Right On Squad; Let's Make a Buck the Hardway; 52nd Century **A:** Larry Welz; Larry Sutherland; Larry Todd **W:** Larry Welz; Larry Sutherland; Larry Todd

AMERICAN FREAK: A TALE OF THE UN-MEN — DC / Vertigo

1 ❑ Feb 1994 Cover: 1.95 **NM** value: **2.00**
Circ: CapCity orders: **13,200**
📖 The Nature Of The Beast **A:** Vincent Locke **W:** Dave Louapre
2 ❑ Mar 1994 Cover: 1.95 **NM** value: **2.00**
Circ: CapCity orders: **9,500**
📖 The Covenant of Freaks **A:** Vincent Locke **W:** Dave Louapre
3 ❑ Apr 1994 Cover: 1.95 **NM** value: **2.00**
Circ: CapCity orders: **8,250**
📖 Blue Skies of Purgatory **A:** Vincent Locke **W:** Dave Louapre
4 ❑ May 1994 Cover: 1.95 **NM** value: **2.00**
Circ: CapCity orders: **7,900**
A: Vincent Locke **W:** Dave Louapre
5 ❑ Jun 1994 Cover: 1.95 **NM** value: **2.00**
Circ: CapCity orders: **7,150**
📖 The Dark Family **A:** Vincent Locke **W:** Dave Louapre

AMERICAN HEROES — Personality

1 ❑ b&w Cover: 2.95 **NM** value: **Cover or less**

AMERICAN LIBRARY — David McKay

1 ❑ ca. 1944 Cover: 0.15 **NM** value: **200.00**
No issue number. 📖 Thirty Seconds Over Tokyo • adapts Capt. Ted Lawson's book
2 ❑ ca. 1945 Cover: 0.10 **NM** value: **150.00**
• **CGC:** 1 graded, best 7.5
No issue number. 📖 Guadalcanal Diary • adapts Richard Tregaskis book
3 ❑ ca. 1945 Cover: 0.15 **NM** value: **100.00**
📖 Look to the Mountain • adapts Le Grand Cannon Jr.'s book
4 ❑ ca. 1945 Cover: 0.15 **NM** value: **100.00**
📖 The Case of the Crooked Candle • adapts Perry Mason story
5 ❑ ca. 1945 Cover: 0.15 **NM** value: **100.00**
📖 Duel in the Sun • adapts Niven Busch's book
6 ❑ ca. 1945 Cover: 0.15 **NM** value: **100.00**
📖 Wingate's Raiders • adapts Charles Rolo's book

AMERICAN, THE: LOST IN AMERICA — Dark Horse

1 ❑ Jul 1992 Cover: 2.50 **NM** value: **Cover or less**
Circ: CapCity orders: **8,100**
A: Chris Marrinan **W:** Mark Verheiden
2 ❑ Aug 1992 Cover: 2.50 **NM** value: **Cover or less**
Circ: CapCity orders: **5,850**
A: Chris Marrinan **W:** Mark Verheiden
3 ❑ Sep 1992 Cover: 2.50 **NM** value: **Cover or less**
Circ: CapCity orders: **5,200**
A: Chris Marrinan **W:** Mark Verheiden
4 ❑ Oct 1992 Cover: 2.50 **NM** value: **Cover or less**
Circ: CapCity orders: **5,225**
A: Chris Marrinan **W:** Mark Verheiden

AMERICAN PRIMITIVE — 3-D Zone

1 ❑ b&w Cover: 2.50 **NM** value: **Cover or less**
• not 3-D

AMERICAN SPLENDOR — Pekar

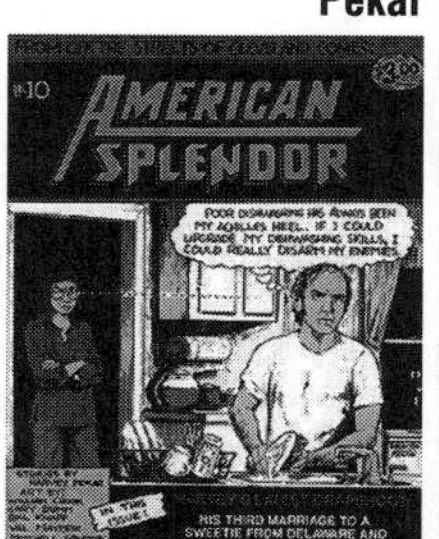

The spirit of independent publishing is alive and well, deep within the pages of American Splendor. Written by Cleveland-based author Harvey Pekar, American Splendor turns the "simple" complexities of everyday life into highly addictive, hard-to-put-down short stories.

Ethical issues such as social prejudice, personal insecurities, and street violence are at the core of every self-contained story — each reading more like a "day in the life" journal entry rather than standard comic-book fare. But perhaps the most personal tales, the ones most likely to have caught the attention of comic-book publisher Dark Horse Comics, are the ones relating to Pekar's bout with cancer. So touching are these stories, in fact, that they act as the precursor to the writer's graphic non-novel, co-written with Joyce Brabner, Our Cancer Year.

1 ❑ **W:** Harvey Pekar **NM** value: **10.00**
2 ❑ **W:** Harvey Pekar **NM** value: **6.00**
3 ❑ **W:** Harvey Pekar **NM** value: **5.00**
4 ❑ **W:** Harvey Pekar **NM** value: **5.00**
5 ❑ **W:** Harvey Pekar **NM** value: **5.00**
6 ❑ **W:** Harvey Pekar **NM** value: **4.00**
7 ❑ **W:** Harvey Pekar **NM** value: **4.00**
8 ❑ **W:** Harvey Pekar **NM** value: **4.00**
9 ❑ **W:** Harvey Pekar **NM** value: **4.00**
10 ❑ **W:** Harvey Pekar **NM** value: **4.00**
11 ❑ **W:** Harvey Pekar **NM** value: **3.00**
12 ❑ **W:** Harvey Pekar **NM** value: **3.00**
13 ❑ **W:** Harvey Pekar **NM** value: **3.00**
14 ❑ **W:** Harvey Pekar **NM** value: **3.00**
15 ❑ **W:** Harvey Pekar **NM** value: **3.00**
17 ❑ **W:** Harvey Pekar Cover: 4.95 **NM** value: **Cover or less**
Bk 1❑ **NM** value: **14.50**
• Collection published by Doubleday **W:** Harvey Pekar

AMERICAN SPLENDOR: BEDTIME STORIES — Dark Horse

1 ❑ Jun 2000 Cover: 3.95 **NM** value: **Cover or less**
Circ: Diamd. preorders: **4,283**
📖 Interviewing the Interviewer; "Pop's" Little Friend; Bo Diddley The Good Times Are Gone **A:** Joe Sacco; Frank Stack; David Collier; Dean Haspiel; Spain Rodriguez **W:** Harvey Pekar

AMERICAN SPLENDOR: COMIC-CON COMICS — Dark Horse

1 ❑ Aug 1996, b&w Cover: 2.95 **NM** value: **Cover or less**
No issue number. 📖 An Invitation; Huckster **A:** Gary Dumm; Joe Zabel; Scott Gilbert **W:** Harvey Pekar

AMERICAN SPLENDOR: MUSIC COMICS — Dark Horse

1 ❑ Nov 1997, b&w Cover: 2.95 **NM** value: **Cover or less**
Circ: Diamd. preorders: **4,085**
No issue number. • collects Pekar's stories about music **A:** Joe Sacco **W:** Harvey Pekar

AMERICAN SPLENDOR: ODDS & ENDS — Dark Horse

1 ❑ Dec 1997, b&w Cover: 2.95 **NM** value: **Cover or less**
Circ: Diamd. preorders: **4,268**
No issue number. • collects short pieces **W:** Harvey Pekar

AMERICAN SPLENDOR: ON THE JOB — Dark Horse

1 ❑ May 1997, b&w Cover: 2.95 **NM** value: **Cover or less**
Circ: Diamd. preorders: **5,482**
No issue number. One-shot. **W:** Harvey Pekar

AMERICAN SPLENDOR: PORTRAIT OF THE AUTHOR IN HIS DECLINING YEARS — Dark Horse

1 ❑ Apr 2001 Cover: 3.99 **NM** value: **Cover or less**
Circ: Diamd. preorders: **3,957**
📖 Payback; Dennis McGee; Sidney Bechet; Why I Haven't Visited the Rock 'n' Roll Hall of Fame; Ameritech; Danielle; Reduction; Scenes from the Market **A:** Gary Dumm; Frank Stack; David Collier; Dennis Haspiel; Josh Neufield **W:** Harvey Pekar

AMERICAN SPLENDOR SPECIAL: A STEP OUT OF THE NEST — Dark Horse

1 ❑ Aug 1994, b&w Cover: 2.95 **NM** value: **Cover or less**
W: Harvey Pekar

AMERICAN SPLENDOR: TERMINAL — Dark Horse

1 ❑ Sep 1999 Cover: 2.95 **NM** value: **Cover or less**
Circ: Diamd. preorders: **4,752**
📖 The Terminal Years **A:** Gary Dumm **W:** Harvey Pekar

AMERICAN SPLENDOR: TRANSATLANTIC COMICS — Dark Horse

1 ❑ Jul 1998 Cover: 2.95 **NM** value: **Cover or less**
Circ: Diamd. preorders: **3,899**
No issue number. **A:** Joe Sacco; Frank Stack; Colin Warneford **W:** Harvey Pekar

AMERICAN SPLENDOR: WINDFALL — Dark Horse

1 ❑ 1995b&w Cover: 3.95 **NM** value: **Cover or less**
Circ: CapCity orders: **2,450**
📖 Flight to Chicago; Ethnicity; Windfall Gained; A Decision; Bloodletting **A:** Gary Dumm; Joe Zabel; Frank Stack; Josh **W:** Harvey Pekar
2 ❑ Oct 1995, b&w Cover: 3.95 **NM** value: **Cover or less**
W: Harvey Pekar

AMERICAN TAIL, AN: FIEVEL GOES WEST — Marvel

In the animated 1991 movie An American Tail, young Fievel Mousekewitz and his family won the hearts of millions. Like real immigrants in the late 1800s and early 1900s, these mice sacrificed everything to travel to America, the so-called Land of Opportunity. In this sequel, they once again head out in search of a better life, this time facing the dangers of America's Wild West.

This three-issue series is adapted from Flint Dille's screenplay and a story by Charles Swenson and features art by George Wildman. All the favorite characters are back, along with a few new faces. It's a good thing, too, because Fievel will need all the help he can get to foil the plans of the villainous Cat R. Waul.

1 ❑ Cover: 1.00 **NM** value: **1.25**
Circ: CapCity orders: **6,500**
📖 Go West, Young Mousekewitz **A:** George Wildman **W:** Charles Swenson; D.G. Chichester; Flint Dillie
2 ❑ Cover: 1.00 **NM** value: **1.25**
Circ: CapCity orders: **5,600**
A: George Wildman **W:** Charles Swenson; D.G. Chichester; Flint Dillie
3 ❑ Cover: 1.00 **NM** value: **1.25**
Circ: CapCity orders: **4,300**
A: George Wildman **W:** Charles Swenson; D.G. Chichester; Flint Dillie

AMERICAN WOMAN — Antarctic

1 ❑ Jun 1998 Cover: 2.95 **NM** value: **Cover or less**
Circ: Diamd. preorders: **13,515**
A: Brian Denham **W:** Richard Stockton ★ 1st Appearance of American Woman.
2 ❑ Oct 1998 Cover: 2.95 **NM** value: **Cover or less**
Circ: Diamd. preorders: **5,495**
A: Brian Denham **W:** Richard Stockton

AMERICA'S BEST COMICS — America's Best

SE 1❑ Cover: 6.95 **NM** value: **Cover or less**
Circ: Diamd. preorders: **25,693**
📖 Tom Strong: Skull **A:** Humberto Ramos; Rick Veitch; Kevin Nowlan; Zander Cannon; Eric Shanower; John Cassaday; Alex Ross(cover); Dame Darcy; Gene Ha(cover) **W:** Alan Moore

AMERICA'S BEST COMICS (NEDOR) — Nedor

1 ❑ Feb 1942 Cover: 0.10 **NM** value: **1500.00**
2 ❑ Sep 1942 Cover: 0.10 **NM** value: **750.00**
• **CGC:** 2 graded, best 8.5
3 ❑ Nov 1942 Cover: 0.10 **NM** value: **750.00**
4 ❑ Jan 1943 Cover: 0.10 **NM** value: **500.00**
5 ❑ Apr 1943 Cover: 0.10 **NM** value: **500.00**
6 ❑ Jul 1943 Cover: 0.10 **NM** value: **500.00**
• **CGC:** 2 graded, best 9.6
7 ❑ Oct 1943 Cover: 0.10 **NM** value: **450.00**
8 ❑ Jan 1944 Cover: 0.10 **NM** value: **450.00**
• **CGC:** 1 graded, best 9.0
9 ❑ Apr 1944 Cover: 0.10 **NM** value: **450.00**
• **CGC:** 1 graded, best 9.6
10 ❑ Jul 1944 Cover: 0.10 **NM** value: **450.00**
• **CGC:** 2 graded, best 9.2
11 ❑ Oct 1944 Cover: 0.10 **NM** value: **350.00**
12 ❑ Jan 1945 Cover: 0.10 **NM** value: **350.00**
13 ❑ Apr 1945 Cover: 0.10 **NM** value: **350.00**
• **CGC:** 1 graded, best 8.0
14 ❑ Jun 1945 Cover: 0.10 **NM** value: **350.00**
• **CGC:** 1 graded, best 9.8
15 ❑ Oct 1945 Cover: 0.10 **NM** value: **350.00**
• **CGC:** 2 graded, best 9.2
16 ❑ Jan 1946 Cover: 0.10 **NM** value: **350.00**
• **CGC:** 2 graded, best 9.0
17 ❑ Mar 1946 Cover: 0.10 **NM** value: **350.00**
• **CGC:** 1 graded, best 9.2
18 ❑ Jun 1946 Cover: 0.10 **NM** value: **350.00**
• **CGC:** 2 graded, best 8.5
19 ❑ Sep 1946 Cover: 0.10 **NM** value: **350.00**
• **CGC:** 1 graded, best 7.0
20 ❑ Dec 1946 Cover: 0.10 **NM** value: **350.00**
21 ❑ Mar 1947 Cover: 0.10 **NM** value: **300.00**
• **CGC:** 2 graded, best 9.2
22 ❑ Jun 1947 Cover: 0.10 **NM** value: **300.00**
23 ❑ Sep 1947 Cover: 0.10 **NM** value: **300.00**
• **CGC:** 1 graded, best 4.5
24 ❑ Dec 1947 Cover: 0.10 **NM** value: **300.00**
25 ❑ Mar 1948 Cover: 0.10 **NM** value: **300.00**
• **CGC:** 2 graded, best 6.5
26 ❑ Jun 1948 Cover: 0.10 **NM** value: **300.00**
• **CGC:** 1 graded, best 9.0
27 ❑ Aug 1948 Cover: 0.10 **NM** value: **300.00**
• **CGC:** 1 graded, best 8.0
28 ❑ Nov 1948 Cover: 0.10 **NM** value: **300.00**
29 ❑ Feb 1949 Cover: 0.10 **NM** value: **300.00**
• **CGC:** 1 graded, best 9.2
30 ❑ May 1949 Cover: 0.10 **NM** value: **300.00**
31 ❑ Jul 1949 Cover: 0.10 **NM** value: **300.00**

AMERICA'S BEST COMICS PREVIEW — America's Best

1 ❑ **NM** value: **1.50**
📖 Preview and Sketchbook • Included in Wizard #91 **A:** Chris Sprouse; J.H. Williams; Rick Veitch; Kevin Nowlan; Jim Baikie; Gene Ha; Melinda Gebbie **W:** Alan Moore

AMERICA'S BEST TV COMICS — ABC

To promote its fall Saturday morning TV lineup in 1967, ABC issued the one-shot "America's Best TV Comics," with stories featuring each of the animated shows. The lineup includes Casper the Friendly Ghost (with Wendy the Good Little Witch), an animated version of King Kong, the Jay Ward Tarzan spoof George of the Jungle ("watch out for that tree!"), and Journey to the Center of the Earth. In addition to these TV-originated stories, two represented shows are based on Marvel comics characters — the Amazing Spider-Man and Fantastic Four — which are featured with reprints from their regular comic books.

1 ❑ ca. 1967 Cover: 0.25 **NM** value: **55.00**
• **CGC:** 13 graded, best 9.8
No issue number. • Giant-size. 📖 Casper the Friendly Ghost: The Flying Horse; The Fantastic Four: Prisoners of the Pharaoh; The Birth of a Super-Hero; Journey to the Center of the Earth; King Kong; George of the Jungle • promotional comic published by Marvel for ABC to promote Saturday morning cartoons **A:** Jack Kirby; John Romita **W:** Stan Lee

AMERICA'S BIGGEST COMICS BOOK — Wise Publications

1 ❑ ca. 1944 Cover: 0.50 **NM** value: **250.00**

CGC-graded: Multiply prices above by **33 for 9.9 M • 16 for 9.8 NM/M • 7 for 9.6 NM+ • 5 for 9.4 NM • 2.5 for 9.2 NM- • 1.5 for 9.0 VF/NM**

AMERICA'S GREATEST COMICS — Fawcett

1 ❑ Fal 1941 Cover: 0.15 **NM** value: **2000.00**
• **CGC:** 3 graded, best 6.0
2 ❑ Feb 1942 Cover: 0.15 **NM** value: **1500.00**
• **CGC:** 1 graded, best 8.0
3 ❑ Jun 1942 Cover: 0.15 **NM** value: **750.00**
4 ❑ Sep 1942 Cover: 0.15 **NM** value: **750.00**
5 ❑ Dec 1942 Cover: 0.15 **NM** value: **750.00**
6 ❑ Feb 1943 Cover: 0.15 **NM** value: **500.00**
7 ❑ May 1943 Cover: 0.15 **NM** value: **500.00**
• **CGC:** 2 graded, best 7.0
8 ❑ Sum 1943 Cover: 0.15 **NM** value: **500.00**
• **CGC:** 1 graded, best 9.6

AMERICA VS. THE JUSTICE SOCIETY — DC

Earth Two's Batman has died, and his diary makes a shocking accusation: that The Justice Society of America is guilty of treason. It claims that The JSA was persuaded by Hitler in 1940 to become agents of Nazi Germany and that it sabotaged the work on an anti-bomb project that could have stopped the Japanese attack on Pearl Harbor.

These are serious accusations, indeed, and cause for The JSA to be called in front of a joint session of Congress for a special tribunal. But fear not: The real reason for this four-issue mini-series is to give fans a chance to relive the great JSA adventures of the Golden Age. Included are checklists and annotations covering the first appearances of The Atom, the original Black Canary, Doctor Fate, Doctor Mid-Nite, the original Flash, Green Arrow, and the other members of that legendary organization.

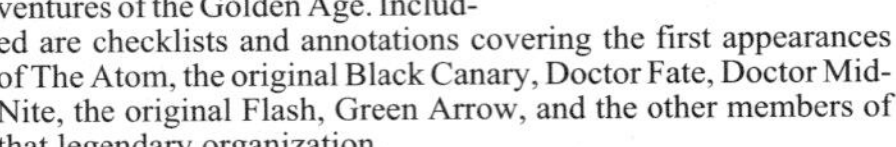

1 ❑ Jan 1985 Cover: 1.50 **NM** value: **Cover or less**
• Giant-size. Chapter 1, I Accuse; Chapter 2; Witness For The Persecution **A:** Rafael Kayanan **W:** Roy Thomas ★ Origin of JSA.
2 ❑ Feb 1985 Cover: 1.00 **NM** value: **Cover or less**
A: Alfredo Alcala; Mike Hernandez **W:** Roy Thomas ★ Origin of All-Star Squadron.
3 ❑ Mar 1985 Cover: 1.00 **NM** value: **Cover or less**
• Wizard **W:** Roy Thomas ★ Origin of Freedom Fighters.
4 ❑ Apr 1985 Cover: 1.00 **NM** value: **Cover or less**
• multiverse (Flash of Two Worlds) **W:** Roy Thomas ★ Origin of JSA revival.

AMERICOMICS — AC

1 ❑ Apr 1983 Cover: 3.00 **NM** value: **Cover or less**
★ Origin of the Shade (Americomics). ★ 1st Appearance of the Shade (Americomics).
2 ❑ Jun 1983 Cover: 2.00 **NM** value: **Cover or less**
3 ❑ Aug 1983 Cover: 2.00 **NM** value: **Cover or less**
4 ❑ Oct 1983 Cover: 2.00 **NM** value: **Cover or less**
★ Origin of Dragonfly.
5 ❑ Dec 1983 Cover: 1.75 **NM** value: **2.00**
6 ❑ Mar 1984 Cover: 1.75 **NM** value: **2.00**
SE 1 ❑ Jan 1983 Cover: 2.00 **NM** value: **Cover or less**
Sentinels of Justice • Special **A:** Greg Guler; Matt Feazell **W:** Greg Guler; Dan St. John ★ Appearance of The Question, Nightshade, Blue Beetle, Captain Atom.

AMETHYST — DC

1 ❑ Jan 1985 Cover: 0.75 **NM** value: **1.00**
The Long Way Home **A:** Ernie Colon; Ric Estrada **W:** Dan Mishkin; Gary Cohn ★ 1st Appearance of Fire Jade.
2 ❑ Feb 1985 Cover: 0.75 **NM** value: **1.00**
3 ❑ Mar 1985 Cover: 0.75 **NM** value: **1.00**
4 ❑ Apr 1985 Cover: 0.75 **NM** value: **1.00**
5 ❑ May 1985 Cover: 0.75 **NM** value: **1.00**
Circ: CapCity orders: **6,700**
6 ❑ Jun 1985 Cover: 0.75 **NM** value: **1.00**
Circ: CapCity orders: **6,400**
7 ❑ Jul 1985 Cover: 0.75 **NM** value: **1.00**
Circ: CapCity orders: **6,000**
8 ❑ Aug 1985 Cover: 0.75 **NM** value: **1.00**
Circ: CapCity orders: **5,600**
9 ❑ Sep 1985 Cover: 0.75 **NM** value: **1.00**
Circ: CapCity orders: **5,550**
10 ❑ Oct 1985 Cover: 0.75 **NM** value: **1.00**
Circ: CapCity orders: **5,600**
11 ❑ Nov 1985 Cover: 0.75 **NM** value: **1.00**
Circ: CapCity orders: **5,050**
12 ❑ Dec 1985 Cover: 0.75 **NM** value: **1.00**
Circ: CapCity orders: **4,775**
13 ❑ Feb 1986 Cover: 0.75 **NM** value: **1.00**
Circ: CapCity orders: **7,050**
Crisis on Infinite Earths ★ Appearance of Doctor Fate.
14 ❑ Apr 1986 Cover: 0.75 **NM** value: **1.00**
Circ: CapCity orders: **5,100**
15 ❑ Jun 1986 Cover: 0.75 **NM** value: **1.00**
Circ: CapCity orders: **5,250**
★ 1st Appearance of Child, Flaw.
16 ❑ Aug 1986 Cover: 0.75 **NM** value: **1.00**
Circ: CapCity orders: **5,050**
final issue.
SE 1 ❑ Oct 1986 Cover: 1.25 **NM** value: **Cover or less**
Circ: CapCity orders: **6,150**
• Special

AMETHYST (MINI-SERIES) — DC

1 ❑ Nov 1987 Cover: 1.25 **NM** value: **Cover or less**
Circ: CapCity orders: **13,300**
...And Wait The Pointed Hour **A:** Esteban Maroto **W:** Mindy Newell
2 ❑ Dec 1987 Cover: 1.25 **NM** value: **Cover or less**
Circ: CapCity orders: **11,250**
3 ❑ Jan 1988 Cover: 1.25 **NM** value: **Cover or less**
Circ: CapCity orders: **11,450**
4 ❑ Feb 1988 Cover: 1.25 **NM** value: **Cover or less**
Circ: CapCity orders: **11,450**

AMETHYST, PRINCESS OF GEMWORLD — DC

1 ❑ May 1983 Cover: 0.60 **NM** value: **1.00**
• **CGC:** 2 graded, best 9.8
The Birthright **A:** Ernie Colon **W:** Dan Mishkin; Gary Cohn ★ Origin of Amethyst.
2 ❑ Jun 1983 Cover: 0.60 **NM** value: **1.00**
3 ❑ Jul 1983 Cover: 0.60 **NM** value: **1.00**
4 ❑ Aug 1983 Cover: 0.60 **NM** value: **1.00**
5 ❑ Sep 1983 Cover: 0.60 **NM** value: **1.00**
6 ❑ Oct 1983 Cover: 0.60 **NM** value: **1.00**
7 ❑ Nov 1983 Cover: 0.60 **NM** value: **1.00**
8 ❑ Dec 1983 Cover: 0.60 **NM** value: **1.00**
9 ❑ Jan 1984 Cover: 0.75 **NM** value: **1.00**
Dreams of Glory, Dreams of Death! **A:** Ernie Colon **W:** Gary Cohn
10 ❑ Feb 1984 Cover: 0.75 **NM** value: **1.00**
Blackout **A:** Ernie Chan; Karl Kesel; Ernie Colon; Ernie Colon **W:** Gary Cohn
11 ❑ Mar 1984 Cover: 0.75 **NM** value: **1.00**
A: Ernie Chan; Ernie Colon
12 ❑ Apr 1984 Cover: 0.75 **NM** value: **1.00**
A: Ernie Chan; Ernie Colon
Anl 1 ❑ Cover: 1.25 **NM** value: **Cover or less**

AMMO ARMAGEDDON — Atomeka

1 ❑ Cover: 4.95 **NM** value: **Cover or less**
Kicking The Monolithic Habit; Mechonismechs; Sergeant Kirby; Harlequin Bones: Kil 4/11/44 **A:** Dean Ormston; Phil Winslade; Henry Flint; Jerry Paris; Jon Beeston **W:** Warren Ellis; Jerry Paris; Jon Beeston; John Tomlinson; Ian Edginton

AMORA (GRAY MORROW'S...) — Fantagraphics / Eros

All issues are adults only.
1 ❑ b&w Cover: 2.95 **NM** value: **Cover or less**
Blazing Stewardess; Panache Gordon: Sexual Lierator of the Universe; The Tournaments of Schlongo; Dream Girl of the Starways; Introducing...Amora; Ms. Minx; Sexpot of the Airlines; Sex Suzerain of the Starlanes; the Journey; Sprite **A:** Gray Morrow **W:** Gray Morrow

AMUSING STORIES — Renegade

1 ❑ b&w Cover: 2.00 **NM** value: **Cover or less**
Success Formula; It's Time to Meet...Urban Gorilla **A:** Don Dougherty; Scott Shaw **W:** Don Dougherty; Scott Shaw ★ Appearance of Gail Aardvark, Ol' Doc Murphy, Prof Hackle, Thub, Blast, Voyd.

AMY PAPUDA — Northstar

1 ❑ Cover: 2.50 **NM** value: **Cover or less**
A: Michael Pearlstein **W:** Michael Pearlstein
2 ❑ Cover: 2.50 **NM** value: **Cover or less**
Hard Times Papuda **A:** Michael Pearlstein **W:** Michael Pearlstein

AMY RACECAR COLOR SPECIAL — El Capitan

1 ❑ ca. 1997 Cover: 2.95 **NM** value: **Cover or less**
Circ: Diamd. preorders: **12,072**
2 ❑ ca. 1999 Cover: 3.50 **NM** value: **Cover or less**
Circ: Diamd. preorders: **7,193**

ANARCHY COMICS — Last Gasp

1 ❑ Cover: 2.50 **NM** value: **Cover or less**
2 ❑ Cover: 2.50 **NM** value: **Cover or less**
3 ❑ Cover: 2.50 **NM** value: **Cover or less**
4 ❑ Cover: 2.50 **NM** value: **Cover or less**
Armageddon Outtahere!; You rule the World!; 1871; Public Enemy; Mister Helpful; Anrchy=Panarchy **A:** Robert Williams; Paul Mavrides; Harry S. Robins; Jay Kinney; Jimmy Heather-Hayes; Norman Dog **W:** Robert Williams; Paul Mavrides; Harry S. Robins; Jay Kinney; Jimmy Heather-Hayes; Norman Dog

ANARKY — DC

1 ❑ May 1999 Cover: 2.50 **NM** value: **Cover or less**
Circ: Diamd. preorders: **28,187**
Aberration, Part 1 **A:** Norm Breyfogle **W:** Alan Grant ★ Appearance of JLA.
2 ❑ Jun 1999 Cover: 2.50 **NM** value: **Cover or less**
Circ: Diamd. preorders: **22,789**
Aberration, Part 2 **A:** Norm Breyfogle **W:** Alan Grant ★ Appearance of Green Lantern.
3 ❑ Jul 1999 Cover: 2.50 **NM** value: **Cover or less**
Circ: Diamd. preorders: **20,283**
Aberration, Part 3 **A:** Norm Breyfogle **W:** Alan Grant ★ Appearance of Green Lantern. ★ Versus Green Lantern.
4 ❑ Aug 1999 Cover: 2.50 **NM** value: **Cover or less**
Circ: Diamd. preorders: **18,316**
War and Peace Part 1 **A:** Norm Breyfogle **W:** Alan Grant ★ Appearance of Ra's Al Ghul.
5 ❑ Sep 1999 Cover: 2.50 **NM** value: **Cover or less**
Circ: Diamd. preorders: **17,505**
War and Peace Part 2 **A:** Norm Breyfogle **W:** Alan Grant ★ Appearance of Ra's Al Ghul.
6 ❑ Oct 1999 Cover: 2.50 **NM** value: **Cover or less**
Circ: Diamd. preorders: **16,009**
War and Peace Part 3 **A:** Norm Breyfogle **W:** Alan Grant ★ Appearance of Ra's Al Ghul.
7 ❑ Nov 1999 Cover: 2.50 **NM** value: **Cover or less**
Circ: Diamd. preorders: **17,444**
When Johnny Comes Marching Home • Day of Judgment **A:** Norm Breyfogle **W:** Alan Grant ★ Appearance of Haunted Tank.
8 ❑ Dec 1999 Cover: 2.50 **NM** value: **Cover or less**
Circ: Diamd. preorders: **14,008**
final issue.

ANARKY (MINI-SERIES) — DC

1 ❑ May 1997 Cover: 2.50 **NM** value: **Cover or less**
Circ: Diamd. preorders: **30,817**
Metamorphosis, Part 1 **A:** Norm Breyfogle **W:** Alan Grant ★ Appearance of Demon.
2 ❑ Jun 1997 Cover: 2.50 **NM** value: **Cover or less**
Circ: Diamd. preorders: **26,028**
Metamorphosis, Part 2 **A:** Norm Breyfogle **W:** Alan Grant ★ Appearance of Darkseid.
3 ❑ Jul 1997 Cover: 2.50 **NM** value: **Cover or less**
Circ: Diamd. preorders: **22,456**
A: Norm Breyfogle **W:** Alan Grant ★ Appearance of Batman.
4 ❑ Aug 1997 Cover: 2.50 **NM** value: **Cover or less**
Circ: Diamd. preorders: **20,641**
A: Norm Breyfogle **W:** Alan Grant

ANCHORS ANDREWS — St. John

1 ❑ Jan 1953 Cover: 0.10 **NM** value: **100.00**
• becomes Anchors the Salt Water Daffy
2 ❑ Mar 1953 Cover: 0.10 **NM** value: **40.00**
3 ❑ May 1953 Cover: 0.10 **NM** value: **40.00**
4 ❑ Jul 1953 Cover: 0.10 **NM** value: **40.00**

ANCIENT JOE — Dark Horse

1 ❑ ca. 2001 Cover: 3.50 **NM** value: **Cover or less**
Circ: Diamd. preorders: **4,903**
2 ❑ ca. 2001 Cover: 3.50 **NM** value: **Cover or less**
Circ: Diamd. preorders: **4,191**
3 ❑ ca. 2002 Cover: 3.50 **NM** value: **Cover or less**
Circ: Diamd. preorders: **4,126**

ANDROMEDA (ANDROMEDA) — Andromeda

1 ❑ Mar 1995 Cover: 2.50 **NM** value: **Cover or less**
A: Lionel Torres

ANDROMEDA (SILVER SNAIL) — Silver Snail

1 ❑ Cover: 2.00 **NM** value: **Cover or less**
2 ❑ Cover: 2.00 **NM** value: **Cover or less**
3 ❑ Cover: 2.00 **NM** value: **Cover or less**
4 ❑ Cover: 2.00 **NM** value: **Cover or less**
5 ❑ Cover: 2.00 **NM** value: **Cover or less**
6 ❑ Cover: 2.00 **NM** value: **Cover or less**

ANDY DEVINE WESTERN — Fawcett

Fawcett's line of Western comic books was apparently so successful it even spun off titles featuring comedy relief characters. This brief run featured Andy Devine (1905-1977), best known for his heft and distinctive rasping voice, which took him through such films as Stagecoach (1939, he drove the team himself, no small feat) and TV shows Adventures of Wild Bill Hickok (1951-8), Andy's Gang (1957-8), and Flipper (1964-5). — Maggie

1 ❑ Dec 1950 Cover: 0.10 **NM** value: **400.00**
• **CGC:** 1 graded, best 6.5
2 ❑ ca. 1951 Cover: 0.10 **NM** value: **300.00**

ANDY PANDA (GOLD KEY) — Gold Key / Whitman

1 ❑ Aug 1973 Cover: 0.20 **NM** value: **3.00**
2 ❑ Nov 1973 Cover: 0.20 **NM** value: **2.00**
3 ❑ Feb 1974 Cover: 0.20 **NM** value: **2.00**
4 ❑ May 1974 Cover: 0.20 **NM** value: **2.00**
5 ❑ Aug 1974 Cover: 0.25 **NM** value: **1.50**
6 ❑ Nov 1974 Cover: 0.25 **NM** value: **1.50**
7 ❑ Feb 1975 Cover: 0.25 **NM** value: **1.50**
8 ❑ May 1975 Cover: 0.25 **NM** value: **1.50**
9 ❑ 1975 Cover: 0.25 **NM** value: **1.50**
10 ❑ 1975 Cover: 0.25 **NM** value: **1.50**
11 ❑ 1976 Cover: 0.25 **NM** value: **1.50**
12 ❑ 1976 Cover: 0.25 **NM** value: **1.50**
13 ❑ 1976 Cover: 0.25 **NM** value: **1.50**
14 ❑ Jul 1976 Cover: 0.25 **NM** value: **1.50**
15 ❑ Sep 1976 Cover: 0.30 **NM** value: **1.50**
16 ❑ Nov 1976 Cover: 0.30 **NM** value: **1.50**
17 ❑ Jan 1977 Cover: 0.30 **NM** value: **1.50**
18 ❑ Mar 1977 Cover: 0.30 **NM** value: **1.50**
19 ❑ May 1977 Cover: 0.30 **NM** value: **1.50**
20 ❑ Jul 1977 Cover: 0.30 **NM** value: **1.50**
21 ❑ Sep 1977 Cover: 0.30 **NM** value: **1.50**
22 ❑ Nov 1977 Cover: 0.30 **NM** value: **1.50**
23 ❑ Jan 1978 Cover: 0.35 **NM** value: **1.50**

ANDY PANDA (WALTER LANTZ...) — Dell

16 ❑ Nov 1952 Cover: 0.10 **NM** value: **12.00**
17 ❑ Jan 1953 Cover: 0.10 **NM** value: **12.00**
18 ❑ Mar 1953 Cover: 0.10 **NM** value: **12.00**
19 ❑ May 1953 Cover: 0.10 **NM** value: **12.00**
20 ❑ Jul 1953 Cover: 0.10 **NM** value: **12.00**
21 ❑ Sep 1953 Cover: 0.10 **NM** value: **10.00**
22 ❑ Nov 1953 Cover: 0.10 **NM** value: **10.00**
23 ❑ Jan 1954 Cover: 0.10 **NM** value: **10.00**
24 ❑ Mar 1954 Cover: 0.10 **NM** value: **10.00**
25 ❑ May 1954 Cover: 0.10 **NM** value: **10.00**
26 ❑ Jul 1954 Cover: 0.10 **NM** value: **10.00**
27 ❑ Sep 1954 Cover: 0.10 **NM** value: **10.00**
28 ❑ Nov 1954 Cover: 0.10 **NM** value: **10.00**
29 ❑ 1955 Cover: 0.10 **NM** value: **10.00**
30 ❑ Apr 1955 Cover: 0.10 **NM** value: **10.00**
31 ❑ 1955 Cover: 0.10 **NM** value: **9.00**
32 ❑ Jan 1956 Cover: 0.10 **NM** value: **9.00**
33 ❑ Cover: 0.10 **NM** value: **9.00**
34 ❑ Cover: 0.10 **NM** value: **9.00**
35 ❑ Cover: 0.10 **NM** value: **9.00**
36 ❑ Cover: 0.10 **NM** value: **9.00**

Other grades: Multiply prices above by **1.5 for Mint • 2/3 for Very Fine • 1/3 for Fine • 1/5 for Very Good • 1/8 for Good**

37 ❑ Feb 1957 Cover: 0.10 **NM** value: **9.00**
38 ❑ May 1957 Cover: 0.10 **NM** value: **9.00**
39 ❑ Aug 1957 Cover: 0.10 **NM** value: **9.00**
40 ❑ Nov 1957 Cover: 0.10 **NM** value: **9.00**
41 ❑ Feb 1958 Cover: 0.10 **NM** value: **9.00**
42 ❑ May 1958 Cover: 0.10 **NM** value: **9.00**
43 ❑ Aug 1958 Cover: 0.10 **NM** value: **9.00**
44 ❑ Nov 1958 Cover: 0.10 **NM** value: **9.00**
45 ❑ Feb 1959 Cover: 0.10 **NM** value: **9.00**
46 ❑ May 1959 Cover: 0.10 **NM** value: **9.00**
47 ❑ Aug 1959 Cover: 0.10 **NM** value: **9.00**
48 ❑ Nov 1959 Cover: 0.10 **NM** value: **9.00**
49 ❑ Feb 1960 Cover: 0.10 **NM** value: **9.00**
50 ❑ May 1960 Cover: 0.10 **NM** value: **9.00**
51 ❑ Aug 1960 Cover: 0.10 **NM** value: **8.00**
52 ❑ Nov 1960 Cover: 0.10 **NM** value: **8.00**
53 ❑ Feb 1961 Cover: 0.10 **NM** value: **8.00**
54 ❑ May 1961 Cover: 0.10 **NM** value: **8.00**
55 ❑ Aug 1961 Cover: 0.10 **NM** value: **8.00**
56 ❑ Nov 1961 Cover: 0.10 **NM** value: **8.00**
final issue.

A-NEXT — Marvel

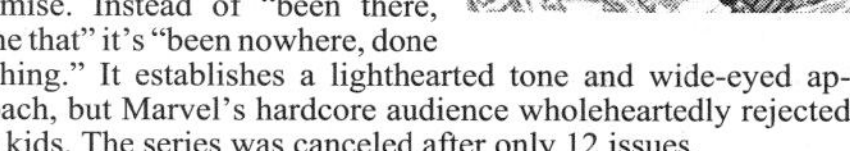

This is another entry from the Marvel Comics 2 universe, aka MC-2. The current universe of characters has been saving mankind from various menaces for almost 40 years. The entire concept had been derived from the original characters' getting older and slower. As a result, it was decided that the originals' progeny should replace the originals. In fact, this new team nearly resembles the original Avengers' abilities of a man — or woman. Imagine the level of brainstorming and the amount of coffee consumed fleshing out that premise. Instead of "been there, done that" it's "been nowhere, done nothing." It establishes a lighthearted tone and wide-eyed approach, but Marvel's hardcore audience wholeheartedly rejected the kids. The series was canceled after only 12 issues.

1 ❑ Oct 1998 Cover: 1.99 **NM** value: **Cover or less**
Circ: Diamd. preorders: **51,942**
🕮 Second Coming • next generation of Avengers **A:** Ron Frenz; Tom DeFalco **W:** Ron Frenz; Tom DeFalco ★ Appearance of Tyrus, the Terrible, Mainframe, Thunderstryke, Jubilee, Speedball, Juggernaut 2, Stinger, Jolt.
2/A ❑ Nov 1998 Cover: 1.99 **NM** value: **Cover or less**
Circ: Diamd. preorders: **24,000**
🕮 Suddenly … The Sentry! **A:** Ron Frenz **W:** Tom DeFalco ★ 1st Appearance of Earth Sentry.
2/B ❑ Nov 1998 Cover: 1.99 **NM** value: **Cover or less**
Circ: Diamd. preorders: **23,000**
3 ❑ Dec 1998 Cover: 1.99 **NM** value: **Cover or less**
Circ: Diamd. preorders: **42,965**
★ 1st Appearance of Doc Magus. ★ Versus Defenders.
4 ❑ Jan 1999 Cover: 1.99 **NM** value: **Cover or less**
Circ: Diamd. preorders: **42,935**
A: Ron Frenz **W:** Tom DeFalco ★ 1st Appearance of Freebooter, Coal Tiger, Crimson Curse, Bluestreak, American Dream.
5 ❑ Feb 1999 Cover: 1.99 **NM** value: **Cover or less**
Circ: Diamd. preorders: **39,794**
🕮 Ghosts of the Past **A:** Ron Frenz **W:** Tom DeFalco ★ Appearance of Doctor Doom.
6 ❑ Mar 1999 Cover: 1.99 **NM** value: **Cover or less**
Circ: Diamd. preorders: **36,429**
🕮 Majority Rules! **A:** Ron Frenz **W:** Tom DeFalco ★ Appearance of Argos.
7 ❑ Apr 1999 Cover: 1.99 **NM** value: **Cover or less**
Circ: Diamd. preorders: **33,881**
🕮 The Last Days of the Avengers **A:** Ron Frenz **W:** Tom DeFalco ★ 1st Appearance of Iron Man (villain).
8 ❑ May 1999 Cover: 1.99 **NM** value: **Cover or less**
Circ: Diamd. preorders: **32,259**
9 ❑ Jun 1999 Cover: 1.99 **NM** value: **Cover or less**
Circ: Diamd. preorders: **31,592**
10 ❑ Jul 1999 Cover: 1.99 **NM** value: **Cover or less**
Circ: Diamd. preorders: **30,617**
★ Versus Thunder Guard.
11 ❑ Aug 1999 Cover: 1.99 **NM** value: **Cover or less**
Circ: Diamd. preorders: **29,908**
★ Appearance of Captain America.

ANGEL (1ST SERIES) — Dell

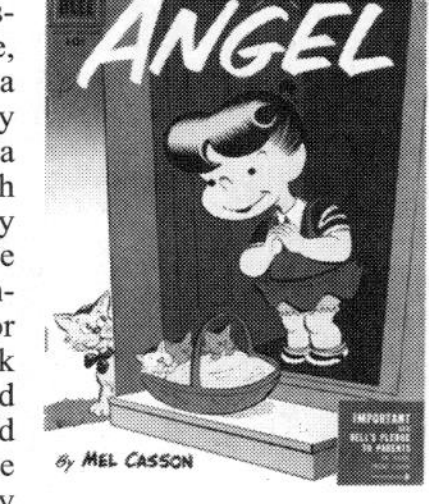

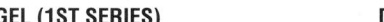

Angel was a simple and good-humored kid strip drawn by Mel Casson. Casson has drawn such newspaper strips as Boomer and Redeye, in addition. Angel appeared in a comic-book version published by Dell during the 1950s. Angel is a little girl of 6 or 7 and she and such pals as Henry and Milton find funny ways to get in and out of trouble with their peers, parents, and teachers in breezy, fast-moving four-or eight-page stories. The comic-book series was produced with a tone and style reminiscent of such other kid strips popular around the same time as Dennis the Menace and Nancy and Sluggo and such comic books as Marge's Little Lulu (a magazine cartoon adapted to comic-book formats by John Stanley).

2 ❑ May 1955 Cover: 0.10 **NM** value: **8.00**
A: Mel Casson **W:** Mel Casson ★ Appearance of Series continued from.
3 ❑ Aug 1955 Cover: 0.10 **NM** value: **8.00**
A: Mel Casson **W:** Mel Casson
4 ❑ Nov 1955 Cover: 0.10 **NM** value: **8.00**
🕮 The Escape; The Report Cards; The Party; Wild Animal Tamer (text story); Stanley Gets his Man **A:** Mel Casson **W:** Mel Casson
5 ❑ Feb 1956 Cover: 0.10 **NM** value: **8.00**
A: Mel Casson **W:** Mel Casson
6 ❑ May 1956 Cover: 0.10 **NM** value: **8.00**
A: Mel Casson **W:** Mel Casson
7 ❑ Aug 1956 Cover: 0.10 **NM** value: **8.00**
A: Mel Casson **W:** Mel Casson
8 ❑ Nov 1956 Cover: 0.10 **NM** value: **8.00**
A: Mel Casson **W:** Mel Casson
9 ❑ Feb 1957 Cover: 0.10 **NM** value: **8.00**
A: Mel Casson **W:** Mel Casson
10 ❑ May 1957 Cover: 0.10 **NM** value: **8.00**
A: Mel Casson **W:** Mel Casson
11 ❑ Aug 1957 Cover: 0.10 **NM** value: **8.00**
A: Mel Casson **W:** Mel Casson
12 ❑ Nov 1957 Cover: 0.10 **NM** value: **8.00**
A: Mel Casson **W:** Mel Casson
13 ❑ Feb 1958 Cover: 0.10 **NM** value: **8.00**
A: Mel Casson **W:** Mel Casson
14 ❑ May 1958 Cover: 0.10 **NM** value: **8.00**
A: Mel Casson **W:** Mel Casson
15 ❑ Aug 1958 Cover: 0.10 **NM** value: **8.00**
A: Mel Casson **W:** Mel Casson
16 ❑ Nov 1959 Cover: 0.10 **NM** value: **8.00**
final issue. **A:** Mel Casson **W:** Mel Casson

ANGEL (2ND SERIES) — Dark Horse

1 ❑ Nov 1999 Cover: 2.95 **NM** value: **Cover or less**
Circ: Diamd. preorders: **29,951** • **CGC:** 1 graded, best 9.8
🕮 Surrogates, Part 1; Surrogates, Part 2 **A:** Christian Zanier; Jeff Matsuda(cover); Marvin Mariano **W:** Christopher Golden
1/A ❑ Nov 1999 **NM** value: **3.00**
• Dynamic Forces gold logo variant **C:** Dave Stewart
1/SC❑Nov 1999 Cover: 2.95 **NM** value: **Cover or less**
Photo cover.
2 ❑ Dec 1999 Cover: 2.95 **NM** value: **Cover or less**
Circ: Diamd. preorders: **29,158**
W: Christopher Golden
2/SC❑Dec 1999 Cover: 2.95 **NM** value: **Cover or less**
Photo cover. **W:** Christopher Golden
3 ❑ Jan 2000 Cover: 2.95 **NM** value: **Cover or less**
Circ: Diamd. preorders: **22,216**
W: Christopher Golden
3/A ❑ Jan 2000 **NM** value: **3.00**
Dynamic Forces purple foil variant (white cover). • Valentine's Day Edition. **W:** Christopher Golden
3/SC❑Jan 2000 Cover: 2.95 **NM** value: **Cover or less**
Photo cover. **W:** Christopher Golden
4 ❑ Feb 2000 Cover: 2.95 **NM** value: **Cover or less**
Circ: Diamd. preorders: **20,063**
W: Christopher Golden
4/SC❑Feb 2000 Cover: 2.95 **NM** value: **Cover or less**
Photo cover. **W:** Christopher Golden
5 ❑ Mar 2000 Cover: 2.95 **NM** value: **Cover or less**
Circ: Diamd. preorders: **19,760**
W: Christopher Golden
5/SC❑Mar 2000 Cover: 2.95 **NM** value: **Cover or less**
Photo cover. **W:** Christopher Golden
6 ❑ Apr 2000 Cover: 2.95 **NM** value: **Cover or less**
Circ: Diamd. preorders: **18,822**
W: Christopher Golden
6/SC❑Apr 2000 Cover: 2.95 **NM** value: **Cover or less**
Photo cover. **W:** Christopher Golden
7 ❑ May 2000 Cover: 2.95 **NM** value: **Cover or less**
Circ: Diamd. preorders: **18,669**
A: Christian Zanier; Marvin Mariano **W:** Christopher Golden; Tom Sniegoski
7/A ❑ May 2000 **NM** value: **3.00**
• Dynamic Forces Lucky 7 foil variant (limited to 1500 copies)
7/SC❑May 2000 Cover: 2.95 **NM** value: **Cover or less**
Photo cover.
8 ❑ Jun 2000 Cover: 2.95 **NM** value: **Cover or less**
Circ: Diamd. preorders: **18,205**
🕮 Beneath the Surface **A:** Eric Powell **W:** Christopher Golden; Tom Sniegoski
8/SC❑Jun 2000 Cover: 2.95 **NM** value: **Cover or less**
Photo cover.
9 ❑ Jul 2000 Cover: 2.95 **NM** value: **Cover or less**
Circ: Diamd. preorders: **17,575**
🕮 Beneath the Surface **A:** Eric Powell **W:** Christopher Golden; Tom Sniegoski
9/SC❑Jul 2000 Cover: 2.95 **NM** value: **Cover or less**
Photo cover.
10 ❑ Aug 2000 Cover: 2.95 **NM** value: **Cover or less**
Circ: Diamd. preorders: **16,532**
🕮 Strange Bedfellows; Strange Bedfellows, Part 1 **A:** Christian Zanier **W:** Christopher Golden; Tom Sniegoski
10/SC❑Aug 2000 Cover: 2.95 **NM** value: **Cover or less**
Photo cover. 🕮 Strange Bedfellows; Strange Bedfellows, Part 1 **A:** Christian Zanier **W:** Christopher Golden; Tom Sniegoski
11 ❑ Sep 2000 Cover: 2.95 **NM** value: **Cover or less**
Circ: Diamd. preorders: **16,161**
🕮 Strange Bedfellows; Strange Bedfellows, Part 2 **A:** Christian Zanier; Marvin Mariano **W:** Christopher Golden; Tom Sniegoski
11/SC❑Sep 2000 Cover: 2.95 **NM** value: **Cover or less**
Photo cover.
12 ❑ Oct 2000 Cover: 2.95 **NM** value: **2.99**
Circ: Diamd. preorders: **15,884**
🕮 Vermin; Vermin, Part 1 **A:** Christian Zanier; Marvin Mariano **C:** Mike Mignola **W:** Christopher Golden; Tom Sniegoski
12/SC❑Oct 2000 Cover: 2.95 **NM** value: **2.99**
Photo cover.
13 ❑ Nov 2000 Cover: 2.99 **NM** value: **Cover or less**
Circ: Diamd. preorders: **15,512**
🕮 Vermin, Part 2 **A:** Christian Zanier; Marvin Mariano **W:** Christopher Golden; Tom Sniegoski
13/SC❑Nov 2000 Cover: 2.99 **NM** value: **Cover or less**
Photo cover.
14 ❑ Dec 2000 Cover: 2.99 **NM** value: **Cover or less**
Circ: Diamd. preorders: **15,027**
🕮 Little Girl Lost **A:** Eric Powell **W:** Christopher Golden; Tom Sniegoski
14/SC❑Dec 2000 Cover: 2.99 **NM** value: **Cover or less**
Photo cover.
15 ❑ Feb 2001 Cover: 2.99 **NM** value: **Cover or less**
Circ: Diamd. preorders: **14,504**
🕮 Past Lives, Part 1 **A:** Christian Zanier **W:** Christopher Golden; Tom Sniegoski
15/SC❑Feb 2001 Cover: 2.99 **NM** value: **Cover or less**
Photo cover.
16 ❑ Mar 2001 Cover: 2.99 **NM** value: **Cover or less**
Circ: Diamd. preorders: **14,254**
🕮 Past Lives, Part 3 **A:** Christian Zanier **W:** Christopher Golden; Tom Sniegoski
16/SC❑Mar 2001 Cover: 2.99 **NM** value: **Cover or less**
Photo cover.
17 ❑ Apr 2001 Cover: 2.99 **NM** value: **Cover or less**
🕮 Cordelia **A:** Eric Powell **W:** Christopher Golden; Tom Sniegoski
17/SC❑Apr 2001 Cover: 2.99 **NM** value: **Cover or less**
Photo cover.

ANGELA — Image

1 ❑ Dec 1994 Cover: 2.25 **NM** value: **4.00**
Circ: CapCity orders: **79,250** • **CGC:** 14 graded, best 9.8
A: Greg Capullo **W:** Neil Gaiman ★ Appearance of Spawn.
1/A ❑ Dec 1994 Cover: 2.25 **NM** value: **4.00**
• **CGC:** 7 graded, best 9.8
Pirate Spawn cover.
2 ❑ Jan 1995 Cover: 2.25 **NM** value: **3.00**
Circ: CapCity orders: **58,450** • **CGC:** 1 graded, best 9.8
A: Greg Capullo **W:** Neil Gaiman ★ Appearance of Spawn.
3 ❑ Feb 1995 Cover: 2.25 **NM** value: **3.00**
Circ: CapCity orders: **53,100** • **CGC:** 1 graded, best 9.4
A: Greg Capullo **W:** Neil Gaiman
Bk 1❑ Cover: 9.95 **NM** value: **Cover or less**
• collects mini-series and special

ANGELA/GLORY: RAGE OF ANGELS — Image

1/A ❑ Mar 1996 Cover: 2.50 **NM** value: **Cover or less**
1/B ❑ Mar 1996 Cover: 2.50 **NM** value: **Cover or less**

ANGEL AND THE APE — DC

1 ❑ Nov 1968 **NM** value: **30.00**
• **CGC:** 4 graded, best 9.4
2 ❑ Jan 1969 **NM** value: **22.00**
3 ❑ Mar 1969 **NM** value: **18.00**
4 ❑ May 1969 **NM** value: **18.00**
• **CGC:** 2 graded, best 9.2
5 ❑ Jul 1969 **NM** value: **18.00**
6 ❑ Sep 1969 **NM** value: **18.00**
7 ❑ Nov 1969 **NM** value: **18.00**

ANGEL & THE APE — DC / Vertigo

1 ❑ ca. 2001 Cover: 2.95 **NM** value: **Cover or less**
Circ: Diamd. preorders: **18,187**
2 ❑ ca. 2001 Cover: 2.95 **NM** value: **Cover or less**
Circ: Diamd. preorders: **14,238**
3 ❑ ca. 2001 Cover: 2.95 **NM** value: **Cover or less**
Circ: Diamd. preorders: **13,352**
4 ❑ ca. 2001 Cover: 2.95 **NM** value: **Cover or less**
Circ: Diamd. preorders: **13,352**

ANGEL AND THE APE (MINI-SERIES) — DC

It was way back in 1968 that this comical duo last had their own series. But this four-issue 1991 mini-series shows that Angel O'Day and Sam Simeon haven't lost their talent to amuse and delight readers.

Angel (whose sister, Athena, was "Dumb Bunny" of The Inferior Five) first met the talking gorilla when she was a girl traveling in Africa. Now they're the best of friends and have opened their own detective agency. Together they've investigated countless mysteries, but their latest is the strangest of all: For a split second, all the humans in the world became apes, and Sam became human. Is the world going ape? Count on Angel and Sam to get to the bottom of things in this amusing series.

1 ❑ Mar 1991 Cover: 1.00 **NM** value: **1.25**
Circ: CapCity orders: **21,700**
🕮 Shaking The Family Tree **A:** Phil Foglio **W:** Phil Foglio
2 ❑ Apr 1991 Cover: 1.00 **NM** value: **1.25**
Circ: CapCity orders: **14,150**
A: Phil Foglio
3 ❑ May 1991 Cover: 1.00 **NM** value: **1.25**
Circ: CapCity orders: **12,450**
A: Phil Foglio
4 ❑ Jun 1991 Cover: 1.00 **NM** value: **1.25**
Circ: CapCity orders: **10,500**
A: Phil Foglio

CGC-graded: Multiply prices above by **33 for 9.9 M • 16 for 9.8 NM/M • 7 for 9.6 NM+ • 5 for 9.4 NM • 2.5 for 9.2 NM- • 1.5 for 9.0 VF/NM**

ANGEL FIRE — Crusade

1/A ❑ Jun 1997 Cover: 2.95 **NM value: Cover or less**
Circ: Diamd. preorders: **21,987**
wraparound photo cover. **A:** Roberto Flores **W:** Dan Mishkin
1/B ❑ Jun 1997 Cover: 2.95 **NM value: Cover or less**
black background cover. **A:** Roberto Flores **W:** Dan Mishkin
1/C ❑ Jun 1997 Cover: 2.95 **NM value: Cover or less**
white background cover. **A:** Roberto Flores **W:** Dan Mishkin
2 ❑ Aug 1997 Cover: 2.95 **NM value: Cover or less**
Circ: Diamd. preorders: **14,127**
A: Roberto Flores **W:** Dan Mishkin ★ Appearance of Shi.
3 ❑ Oct 1997, b&w Cover: 2.95 **NM value: Cover or less**
Circ: Diamd. preorders: **11,490**
A: Roberto Flores **W:** Dan Mishkin

ANGEL GIRL — Angel

0 ❑ Cover: 2.95 **NM value: Cover or less**
Circ: Diamd. preorders: **2,408**
0/Nude❑ Cover: 5.00 **NM value: Cover or less**
Nude cover.

ANGEL GIRL: BEFORE THE WINGS — Angel

1 ❑ Aug 1997 Cover: 2.95 **NM value: Cover or less**
A: Mark Kuettner **W:** Ellis Bell

ANGEL GIRL VS. VAMPIRE GIRLS — Angel

1 ❑ Cover: 2.95 **NM value: Cover or less**
Circ: Diamd. preorders: **1,808**
A: Reynaldo Batista **W:** Lloyd Chasseur
1/Nude❑ Cover: 9.95 **NM value: Cover or less**
• Nude edition. **A:** Reynaldo Batista **W:** Lloyd Chasseur

ANGEL LOVE — DC

1 ❑ Aug 1986 Cover: 0.75 **NM value: 1.00**
• **CGC:** 3 graded, best 9.8
A: Barbara Slate **W:** Barbara Slate
2 ❑ Sep 1986 Cover: 0.75 **NM value: 1.00**
A: Barbara Slate **W:** Barbara Slate
3 ❑ Oct 1986 Cover: 0.75 **NM value: 1.00**
A: Barbara Slate **W:** Barbara Slate
4 ❑ Nov 1986 Cover: 0.75 **NM value: 1.00**
A: Barbara Slate **W:** Barbara Slate
5 ❑ Dec 1986 Cover: 0.75 **NM value: 1.00**
📖 The Search for Mary Beth, Part 1 **A:** Barbara Slate **W:** Barbara Slate
6 ❑ Jan 1987 Cover: 0.75 **NM value: 1.00**
📖 The Search for Mary Beth, Part 2 **A:** Barbara Slate **W:** Barbara Slate
7 ❑ Feb 1987 Cover: 0.75 **NM value: 1.00**
📖 The Search for Mary Beth, Part 3 **A:** Barbara Slate **W:** Barbara Slate
8 ❑ Mar 1987 Cover: 0.75 **NM value: 1.00**
📖 The Search for Mary Beth, Part 4 **A:** Barbara Slate **W:** Barbara Slate
Anl 1❑ Cover: 1.25 **NM value: Cover or less**
A: Barbara Slate **W:** Barbara Slate
SE 1❑ Cover: 1.25 **NM value: Cover or less**
Circ: CapCity orders: **3,000**
• Special **A:** Barbara Slate

ANGEL OF DEATH — Innovation

1 ❑ Cover: 2.25 **NM value: Cover or less**
📖 Do Dead Men Dream, Part 1 **A:** Mike Roberts **W:** Michael Lail
2 ❑ Cover: 2.25 **NM value: Cover or less**
📖 Do Dead Men Dream, Part 2 **A:** Mike Roberts **W:** Michael Lail
3 ❑ Cover: 2.25 **NM value: Cover or less**
📖 Do Dead Men Dream, Part 3 **A:** Mike Roberts **W:** Michael Lail
4 ❑ Cover: 2.25 **NM value: Cover or less**
A: Mike Roberts **W:** Michael Lail

ANGELS OF DESTRUCTION — Malibu

1 ❑ Oct 1996 Cover: 2.50 **NM value: Cover or less**
Circ: Diamd. preorders: **38,208**
One-shot. **A:** Vinton Heuck; Leonard Kirk; Shannon Gallant; David Mowry; Jim Amash; Robert DeCastro **W:** Brian Michael Bendis

ANGRY CHRIST COMICS — Sirius

Bk 1❑ Sep 1994, b&w Cover: 12.95 **NM value: Cover or less**
Circ: CapCity orders: **8,640**
• collects Linsner stories from Cry for Dawn plus one new story

ANGRYMAN — Caliber

1 ❑ Cover: 2.50 **NM value: Cover or less**
2 ❑ Cover: 2.50 **NM value: Cover or less**
3 ❑ Cover: 2.50 **NM value: Cover or less**

ANGRYMAN (2ND SERIES) — Iconografix

1 ❑ Cover: 2.50 **NM value: Cover or less**
2 ❑ Cover: 2.50 **NM value: Cover or less**
3 ❑ Cover: 2.50 **NM value: Cover or less**

ANGRY SHADOWS — Innovation

1 ❑ b&w Cover: 4.95 **NM value: Cover or less**

ANIMA — DC

0 ❑ Oct 1994 Cover: 1.75 **NM value: Cover or less**
Circ: CapCity orders: **10,900**
📖 Zero Summer • Series continued in Anima #8 **A:** Will Blyberg **W:** Elizabeth Hand; Paul Witcover
1 ❑ Mar 1994 Cover: 1.75 **NM value: Cover or less**
Circ: CapCity orders: **18,450**
📖 Snap Shots **A:** Malcolm Davis **W:** Elizabeth Hand; Paul Witcover
2 ❑ Apr 1994 Cover: 1.75 **NM value: Cover or less**
Circ: CapCity orders: **9,500**
📖 False Dawn **A:** Malcolm Davis **W:** Elizabeth Hand; Paul Witcover
3 ❑ May 1994 Cover: 1.75 **NM value: Cover or less**
Circ: CapCity orders: **8,150**
📖 Running With The Wolf **A:** Steve Crespo **W:** Elizabeth Hand; Paul Witcover
4 ❑ Jun 1994 Cover: 1.75 **NM value: Cover or less**
Circ: CapCity orders: **6,700**
A: Steve Crespo **W:** Elizabeth Hand; Paul Witcover
5 ❑ Jul 1994 Cover: 1.75 **NM value: Cover or less**
Circ: CapCity orders: **6,150**
📖 Wheel of Fortune **A:** Steve Crespo **W:** Elizabeth Hand; Paul Witcover
6 ❑ Aug 1994 Cover: 1.95 **NM value: Cover or less**
Circ: CapCity orders: **4,900**
7 ❑ Sep 1994 Cover: 1.95 **NM value: Cover or less**
Circ: CapCity orders: **6,200**
📖 Suddenly, Johnny Gets a Feeling... • Zero Hour **A:** Brent Anderson
8 ❑ Nov 1994 Cover: 1.95 **NM value: Cover or less**
Circ: CapCity orders: **4,450**
• Series continued from Anima #0
9 ❑ Dec 1994 Cover: 1.95 **NM value: Cover or less**
Circ: CapCity orders: **4,900**
📖 N.O. Future **A:** Steve Crespo **W:** Elizabeth Hand; Paul Witcover
10 ❑ Jan 1995 Cover: 1.95 **NM value: Cover or less**
Circ: CapCity orders: **4,850**
11 ❑ Feb 1995 Cover: 1.95 **NM value: Cover or less**
Circ: CapCity orders: **3,800**
★ Appearance of Conan O'Brien.
12 ❑ Mar 1995 Cover: 1.95 **NM value: Cover or less**
Circ: CapCity orders: **3,475**
13 ❑ Apr 1995 Cover: 1.95 **NM value: Cover or less**
Circ: CapCity orders: **3,075**
14 ❑ Jun 1995 Cover: 2.25 **NM value: Cover or less**
Circ: CapCity orders: **2,625**
15 ❑ Jul 1995 Cover: 2.25 **NM value: Cover or less**
Circ: CapCity orders: **2,475**
final issue.

ANIMAL ANTICS (MOVIETOWN'S...) — DC

Animal Antics was a so-called "funny-animal" title from action-oriented publisher DC during the mid-1940s to mid-1950s lull in interest in its usual line of super-hero titles. The goofy Raccoon Kids anchored the Animal Antics lineup, with two stories per issue. The remainder of the pages were filled with the antics of the Tortoise and the Hare and the furry chipmunk team of Nip and Chip.

Cute, harmless, and slavish in their imitation of such major-league funny animal stars as Porky Pig, Woody Woodpecker, and Bugs Bunny, the stories in Animal Antics occasionally rose to a higher level, thanks to the inspired slapstick humor of writer-artist-editor Sheldon Meyer.

1 ❑ Mar 1946 Cover: 0.10 **NM value: 340.00**
• **CGC:** 1 graded, best 7.0
2 ❑ May 1946 Cover: 0.10 **NM value: 170.00**
3 ❑ Jul 1946 Cover: 0.10 **NM value: 115.00**
4 ❑ Sep 1946 Cover: 0.10 **NM value: 115.00**
5 ❑ Nov 1946 Cover: 0.10 **NM value: 95.00**
6 ❑ Jan 1947 Cover: 0.10 **NM value: 95.00**
7 ❑ Mar 1947 Cover: 0.10 **NM value: 95.00**
8 ❑ May 1947 Cover: 0.10 **NM value: 95.00**
9 ❑ Jul 1947 Cover: 0.10 **NM value: 95.00**
10 ❑ Sep 1947 Cover: 0.10 **NM value: 95.00**
11 ❑ Nov 1947 Cover: 0.10 **NM value: 75.00**
12 ❑ Jan 1948 Cover: 0.10 **NM value: 75.00**
13 ❑ Mar 1948 Cover: 0.10 **NM value: 75.00**
14 ❑ May 1948 Cover: 0.10 **NM value: 75.00**
15 ❑ Jul 1948 Cover: 0.10 **NM value: 75.00**
16 ❑ Sep 1948 Cover: 0.10 **NM value: 75.00**
17 ❑ Nov 1948 Cover: 0.10 **NM value: 75.00**
18 ❑ Jan 1949 Cover: 0.10 **NM value: 75.00**
19 ❑ Mar 1949 Cover: 0.10 **NM value: 75.00**
20 ❑ May 1949 Cover: 0.10 **NM value: 75.00**
21 ❑ Jul 1949 Cover: 0.10 **NM value: 55.00**
22 ❑ Sep 1949 Cover: 0.10 **NM value: 55.00**
23 ❑ Nov 1949 Cover: 0.10 **NM value: 55.00**
24 ❑ Jan 1950 Cover: 0.10 **NM value: 55.00**
25 ❑ Mar 1950 Cover: 0.10 **NM value: 55.00**
26 ❑ May 1950 Cover: 0.10 **NM value: 55.00**
27 ❑ Jul 1950 Cover: 0.10 **NM value: 55.00**
28 ❑ Sep 1950 Cover: 0.10 **NM value: 55.00**
29 ❑ Nov 1950 Cover: 0.10 **NM value: 55.00**
📖 Rover: The Reunion; Jigg and Mooch; Albert and Pogo; Nibble and Nubble; Uncle Wiggily **A:** Walt Kelly; Dan Noonan **W:** Walt Kelly; Dan Noonan
30 ❑ Jan 1951 Cover: 0.10 **NM value: 55.00**
31 ❑ Mar 1951 Cover: 0.10 **NM value: 45.00**
32 ❑ May 1951 Cover: 0.10 **NM value: 45.00**
33 ❑ Jul 1951 Cover: 0.10 **NM value: 45.00**
34 ❑ Sep 1951 Cover: 0.10 **NM value: 45.00**
35 ❑ Nov 1951 Cover: 0.10 **NM value: 45.00**
36 ❑ Jan 1952 Cover: 0.10 **NM value: 45.00**
37 ❑ Mar 1952 Cover: 0.10 **NM value: 45.00**
38 ❑ May 1952 Cover: 0.10 **NM value: 45.00**
39 ❑ Jul 1952 Cover: 0.10 **NM value: 45.00**
40 ❑ Sep 1952 Cover: 0.10 **NM value: 45.00**
41 ❑ Nov 1952 Cover: 0.10 **NM value: 38.00**
42 ❑ Jan 1953 Cover: 0.10 **NM value: 38.00**
43 ❑ Mar 1953 Cover: 0.10 **NM value: 38.00**
44 ❑ May 1953 Cover: 0.10 **NM value: 38.00**
45 ❑ Jul 1953 Cover: 0.10 **NM value: 38.00**
46 ❑ Sep 1953 Cover: 0.10 **NM value: 38.00**
47 ❑ Nov 1953 Cover: 0.10 **NM value: 38.00**
48 ❑ Jan 1954 Cover: 0.10 **NM value: 38.00**
49 ❑ Mar 1954 Cover: 0.10 **NM value: 38.00**
📖 The Raccoon Kids: It's a Knockout; The Tortoise and the Hare: Treasure Pleasure!; Nip and Chip; Bo Bunny; Scared Stiff (text story); The Raccoon Kids: Boom!
50 ❑ May 1954 Cover: 0.10 **NM value: 38.00**
51 ❑ Jul 1954 Cover: 0.10 **NM value: 38.00**
• Series continued in Raccoon Kids

ANIMAL COMICS — Dell

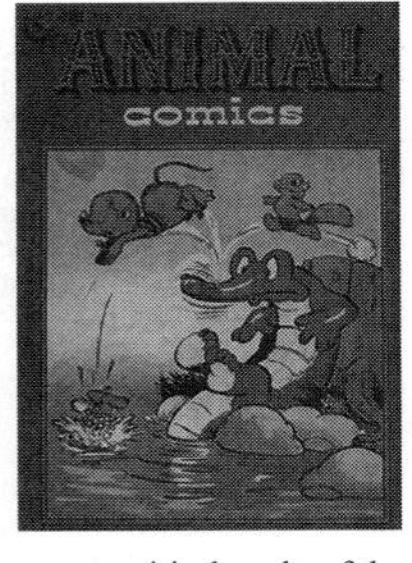

Animal Comics, one of the many "funny-books" for young readers in the 1940s, introduced one of the endearing classics of the funny animal world, Walt Kelly's Pogo the Possum. Pogo and his pals Albert the Alligator, Howland Owl, and turtle Churchy LaFemme, inhabit the world of the Okeefenokee Swamp and speak in a Southern accent. Kelly played Pogo strictly for laughs during the few years Animal Comics ran, but, when the strip was picked up for syndication in newspaper-strip form, Pogo took on an epic allegorical and sociological dimension and is considered one of the great satirical works of the century.

Kelly's characters were not the only notable tenants of Animal Comics. The outstanding Dan Noonan adventure stories of the dog Rover and a comic-book version of the rabbit Uncle Wiggily were only two of the other features that ran in the title.

1 ❑ Dec 1942 Cover: 0.10 **NM value: 875.00**
A: Walt Kelly **W:** Walt Kelly ★ 1st Appearance of Pogo.
2 ❑ Feb 1943 Cover: 0.10 **NM value: 440.00**
A: Walt Kelly **W:** Walt Kelly
3 ❑ Jun 1943 Cover: 0.10 **NM value: 325.00**
A: Walt Kelly **W:** Walt Kelly
4 ❑ Aug 1943 Cover: 0.10 **NM value: 150.00**
• No Pogo
5 ❑ Oct 1943 Cover: 0.10 **NM value: 290.00**
A: Walt Kelly **W:** Walt Kelly
6 ❑ Dec 1943 Cover: 0.10 **NM value: 135.00**
• No Pogo
7 ❑ Feb 1944 Cover: 0.10 **NM value: 135.00**
• No Pogo
8 ❑ Apr 1944 Cover: 0.10 **NM value: 220.00**
• **CGC:** 1 graded, best 9.2
A: Walt Kelly **W:** Walt Kelly
9 ❑ Jun 1944 Cover: 0.10 **NM value: 220.00**
A: Walt Kelly **W:** Walt Kelly
10 ❑ Aug 1944 Cover: 0.10 **NM value: 220.00**
A: Walt Kelly **W:** Walt Kelly
11 ❑ Oct 1944 Cover: 0.10 **NM value: 165.00**
A: Walt Kelly **W:** Walt Kelly
12 ❑ Dec 1944 Cover: 0.10 **NM value: 165.00**
A: Walt Kelly **W:** Walt Kelly
13 ❑ Feb 1945 Cover: 0.10 **NM value: 165.00**
A: Walt Kelly **W:** Walt Kelly
14 ❑ Apr 1945 Cover: 0.10 **NM value: 165.00**
A: Walt Kelly **W:** Walt Kelly
15 ❑ Jun 1945 Cover: 0.10 **NM value: 165.00**
A: Walt Kelly **W:** Walt Kelly
16 ❑ Aug 1945 Cover: 0.10 **NM value: 125.00**
A: Walt Kelly **W:** Walt Kelly
17 ❑ Oct 1945 Cover: 0.10 **NM value: 125.00**
A: Walt Kelly **W:** Walt Kelly
18 ❑ Dec 1945 Cover: 0.10 **NM value: 125.00**
A: Walt Kelly **W:** Walt Kelly
19 ❑ Feb 1946 Cover: 0.10 **NM value: 125.00**
A: Walt Kelly **W:** Walt Kelly
20 ❑ Apr 1946 Cover: 0.10 **NM value: 125.00**
A: Walt Kelly **W:** Walt Kelly
21 ❑ Jun 1946 Cover: 0.10 **NM value: 100.00**
📖 Uncle Wiggily; Albert and Pogo and the Fountain of Youth; Rover; Prehysteria; Rusty and Rowdy; Bucky Beaver to the Rescue (text story) **A:** Walt Kelly; Howard R. Garis **W:** Walt Kelly; Howard R. Garis
22 ❑ Aug 1946 Cover: 0.10 **NM value: 100.00**
• **CGC:** 1 graded, best 8.5
📖 Bobby Robin Sees the Snow (text story); Uncle Wiggily; Albert and Pogo; Rover; Royal Predicament; Sitara; Elephunnies; Peter Pigeon (text story) **A:** Walt Kelly; Howard R. Garis **W:** Walt Kelly; Howard R. Garis
23 ❑ Oct 1946 Cover: 0.10 **NM value: 100.00**
A: Walt Kelly **W:** Walt Kelly
24 ❑ Dec 1946 Cover: 0.10 **NM value: 100.00**
A: Walt Kelly **W:** Walt Kelly
25 ❑ Feb 1947 Cover: 0.10 **NM value: 100.00**
• **CGC:** 1 graded, best 9.0
A: Walt Kelly **W:** Walt Kelly
26 ❑ Apr 1947 Cover: 0.10 **NM value: 75.00**
A: Walt Kelly **W:** Walt Kelly
27 ❑ Jun 1947 Cover: 0.10 **NM value: 75.00**
• **CGC:** 1 graded, best 8.5
A: Walt Kelly **W:** Walt Kelly
28 ❑ Aug 1947 Cover: 0.10 **NM value: 75.00**
A: Walt Kelly **W:** Walt Kelly
29 ❑ Oct 1947 Cover: 0.10 **NM value: 75.00**
A: Walt Kelly **W:** Walt Kelly
30 ❑ Dec 1947 Cover: 0.10 **NM value: 75.00**
📖 Rover; Jigg and Mooch; Albert and Pogo; Chuckwagon Charley's Tales; Putnam's Cave (text story); Nibble; Uncle Wiggily final issue. **A:** Moe Gollub; Walt Kelly; Biff; Dan Noonan; Howard R. Garis **W:** Walt Kelly; Biff; Dan Noonan; Howard R. Garis; Gaylord DuBois; Harriet Smith Hawley

Other grades: Multiply prices above by **1.5 for Mint • 2/3 for Very Fine • 1/3 for Fine • 1/5 for Very Good • 1/8 for Good**

ANIMAL CONFIDENTIAL — Dark Horse

1 ❑ May 1992, b&w Cover: 2.25 **NM** value: **Cover or less**
No issue number. One-shot. 🕮 The Spy; Horseshoes Ain't Lucky; Advertisement; Authentic Pet Miracles; I Was a Teenage Hairball; Mary the Elephant; My True Story **A:** Eric Vincent; Mark Martin; Rick Geary; Nina Paley; Jack Pollock **W:** Mark Martin; Rick Geary; Nina Paley; Jack Pollock; Francis Shoemaker; Randy Stradley

ANIMAL FABLES — E.C.

Face it, fans who think of E.C. do not initially conjure up an image of funny animal titles. But, as the publisher sought to find its niche in its earliest days, it tried a number of genres before striking the successful field of fantastic horror, striking art, and satire.

The series' primary continuing character was Human Torch imitation Freddy Firefly; other characters included Hector the Inspector and Korky Kangaroo. In addition, several of the stories were modernizations of the anthropomorphic stories of Aesop. Two issues carried work by Minute Movies creator Ed Wheelan, and the final issue promoted Moon Girl and the Prince, a title that seemed to be aimed at a more mature audience. — Maggie

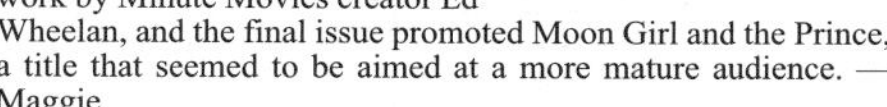

1 ❑ Jul 1946 Cover: 0.10 **NM** value: **250.00**
• **CGC:** 3 graded, best 9.0
🕮 Freddy Firefly; Korky Kangroo; Petey Pig; Little Danny Demon; Hector the Inspector; Willie the Weasel; Bozo the Bowlegged Bull

2 ❑ Fal 1946 Cover: 0.10 **NM** value: **175.00**
• **CGC:** 1 graded, best 7.0
🕮 Freddy the Firefly; The Lion and the Mouse; Bozo the Bowlegged Bull; Fox and the Grapes; Porky Possum Goes A' Hunting; From Ocean to Ocean; Hector the Inspector; Young George Washington

3 ❑ Spr 1947 Cover: 0.10 **NM** value: **150.00**
• **CGC:** 4 graded, best 7.0
🕮 Freddy Firefly; The Hare and the Tortoise; Korky Kangroo; The Frog and the Ox; Spots before His eyes; The Ant and the Grasshopper; Hector the Inspector

4 ❑ Sum 1947 Cover: 0.10 **NM** value: **150.00**
• **CGC:** 1 graded, best 8.5
🕮 Freddy Firefly meets Professor Mantis; Korky Kangroo; The Goose with the Golden Eggs; Jimmy Dugan's Magic Harp; The Fox and the Crow; Little Danny Demon

5 ❑ Jul 1947 Cover: 0.10 **NM** value: **150.00**
• **CGC:** 1 graded, best 6.0
🕮 Freddy Firefly; The Dog and the Bone; Little Danny Demon; Fat and Slat; The Wind and the Sun; Hector the Inspector

6 ❑ Sep 1947 Cover: 0.10 **NM** value: **150.00**
• **CGC:** 1 graded, best 7.5
🕮 Freddy Firefly; Hector the Inspector; Fat and Slat; Korky Kangroo; The Circus Parade; Danny Demon

7 ❑ Nov 1947 Cover: 0.10 **NM** value: **150.00**
🕮 Freddy Firefly versus Atomic Bug!; Rusty the Lonesome Train; Danny Demon; Introducing Moon Girl and the Prince; The Ugly Caterpillar; Hector the Inspector

ANIMAL MAN — DC

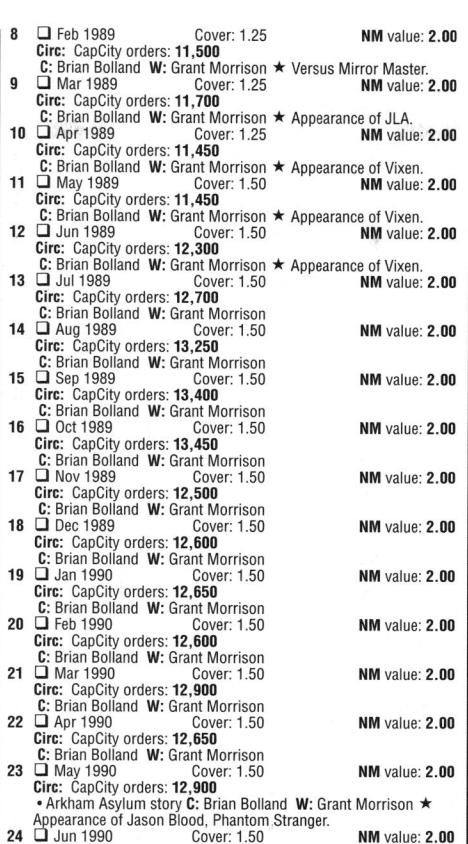

Buddy Baker gets a bit more than he bargains for, when he decides to use his powers to become a superhero again. Originally a stunt man, he finds that radiation from an alien spaceship allows him to assume any nearby animal's powers. He can pick up the grace of a cat, the flight of an eagle, the speed of a cheetah — usually for only a limited time, but long enough to make him a hero. He retires but, against the wishes of his wife, decides to go public once again for fame and glory.

Under the scripting hand of Grant Morrison, this series has taken on a darker aspect. Rather than just adopting the animals' powers, Animal Man can now prowl around in their bodies like a second consciousness, traveling from body to body. This title evolves into dealing with adult themes, such as alcoholism and death and takes a philosophical look at the relationship between man and animal.

1 ❑ Sep 1988 Cover: 1.25 **NM** value: **5.00**
Circ: CapCity orders: **16,200** • **CGC:** 6 graded, best 9.6
C: Brian Bolland **W:** Grant Morrison

2 ❑ Oct 1988 Cover: 1.25 **NM** value: **3.00**
Circ: CapCity orders: **12,450**
C: Brian Bolland **W:** Grant Morrison

3 ❑ Nov 1988 Cover: 1.25 **NM** value: **2.50**
Circ: CapCity orders: **11,650**
C: Brian Bolland **W:** Grant Morrison

4 ❑ Dec 1988 Cover: 1.25 **NM** value: **2.50**
Circ: CapCity orders: **11,800**
C: Brian Bolland **W:** Grant Morrison ★ Appearance of B'wana Beast.

5 ❑ Dec 1988 Cover: 1.25 **NM** value: **2.50**
Circ: CapCity orders: **11,550**
• Road Runner-Coyote **C:** Brian Bolland **W:** Grant Morrison

6 ❑ Jan 1989 Cover: 1.25 **NM** value: **2.00**
Circ: CapCity orders: **13,600**
• Invasion! **C:** Brian Bolland **W:** Grant Morrison

7 ❑ Jan 1989 Cover: 1.25 **NM** value: **2.00**
Circ: CapCity orders: **11,550**
C: Brian Bolland **W:** Grant Morrison

8 ❑ Feb 1989 Cover: 1.25 **NM** value: **2.00**
Circ: CapCity orders: **11,500**
C: Brian Bolland **W:** Grant Morrison ★ Versus Mirror Master.

9 ❑ Mar 1989 Cover: 1.25 **NM** value: **2.00**
Circ: CapCity orders: **11,700**
C: Brian Bolland **W:** Grant Morrison ★ Appearance of JLA.

10 ❑ Apr 1989 Cover: 1.25 **NM** value: **2.00**
Circ: CapCity orders: **11,450**
C: Brian Bolland **W:** Grant Morrison ★ Appearance of Vixen.

11 ❑ May 1989 Cover: 1.50 **NM** value: **2.00**
Circ: CapCity orders: **11,450**
C: Brian Bolland **W:** Grant Morrison ★ Appearance of Vixen.

12 ❑ Jun 1989 Cover: 1.50 **NM** value: **2.00**
Circ: CapCity orders: **12,300**
C: Brian Bolland **W:** Grant Morrison ★ Appearance of Vixen.

13 ❑ Jul 1989 Cover: 1.50 **NM** value: **2.00**
Circ: CapCity orders: **12,700**
C: Brian Bolland **W:** Grant Morrison

14 ❑ Aug 1989 Cover: 1.50 **NM** value: **2.00**
Circ: CapCity orders: **13,250**
C: Brian Bolland **W:** Grant Morrison

15 ❑ Sep 1989 Cover: 1.50 **NM** value: **2.00**
Circ: CapCity orders: **13,400**
C: Brian Bolland **W:** Grant Morrison

16 ❑ Oct 1989 Cover: 1.50 **NM** value: **2.00**
Circ: CapCity orders: **13,450**
C: Brian Bolland **W:** Grant Morrison

17 ❑ Nov 1989 Cover: 1.50 **NM** value: **2.00**
Circ: CapCity orders: **12,500**
C: Brian Bolland **W:** Grant Morrison

18 ❑ Dec 1989 Cover: 1.50 **NM** value: **2.00**
Circ: CapCity orders: **12,600**
C: Brian Bolland **W:** Grant Morrison

19 ❑ Jan 1990 Cover: 1.50 **NM** value: **2.00**
Circ: CapCity orders: **12,650**
C: Brian Bolland **W:** Grant Morrison

20 ❑ Feb 1990 Cover: 1.50 **NM** value: **2.00**
Circ: CapCity orders: **12,600**
C: Brian Bolland **W:** Grant Morrison

21 ❑ Mar 1990 Cover: 1.50 **NM** value: **2.00**
Circ: CapCity orders: **12,900**
C: Brian Bolland **W:** Grant Morrison

22 ❑ Apr 1990 Cover: 1.50 **NM** value: **2.00**
Circ: CapCity orders: **12,650**
C: Brian Bolland **W:** Grant Morrison

23 ❑ May 1990 Cover: 1.50 **NM** value: **2.00**
Circ: CapCity orders: **12,900**
• Arkham Asylum story **C:** Brian Bolland **W:** Grant Morrison ★ Appearance of Jason Blood, Phantom Stranger.

24 ❑ Jun 1990 Cover: 1.50 **NM** value: **2.00**
Circ: CapCity orders: **13,700**
C: Brian Bolland **W:** Grant Morrison ★ Appearance of Inferior Five.

25 ❑ Jul 1990 Cover: 1.50 **NM** value: **2.00**
Circ: CapCity orders: **13,950**
C: Brian Bolland **W:** Grant Morrison

26 ❑ Aug 1990 Cover: 1.50 **NM** value: **2.00**
Circ: CapCity orders: **14,650**
• Morrison puts himself in story **C:** Brian Bolland **W:** Grant Morrison

27 ❑ Sep 2000 Cover: 1.50 **NM** value: **2.00**
Circ: CapCity orders: **14,550**
C: Brian Bolland **W:** Peter Milligan

28 ❑ Oct 1990 Cover: 1.50 **NM** value: **2.00**
Circ: CapCity orders: **14,250**
C: Brian Bolland **W:** Peter Milligan

29 ❑ Nov 1990 Cover: 1.50 **NM** value: **2.00**
Circ: CapCity orders: **14,250**
C: Brian Bolland **W:** Peter Milligan ★ Death of The Notional Man.

30 ❑ Dec 1990 Cover: 1.50 **NM** value: **2.00**
Circ: CapCity orders: **14,250**
C: Brian Bolland **W:** Peter Milligan

31 ❑ Jan 1991 Cover: 1.50 **NM** value: **2.00**
Circ: CapCity orders: **14,600**
C: Brian Bolland **W:** Peter Milligan

32 ❑ Feb 1991 Cover: 1.50 **NM** value: **2.00**
Circ: CapCity orders: **14,350**
C: Brian Bolland **W:** Peter Milligan

33 ❑ Mar 1991 Cover: 1.50 **NM** value: **2.00**
Circ: CapCity orders: **14,100**
C: Brian Bolland **W:** Rick Veitch

34 ❑ Apr 1991 Cover: 1.50 **NM** value: **2.00**
Circ: CapCity orders: **12,850**
C: Brian Bolland **W:** Rick Veitch

35 ❑ May 1991 Cover: 1.50 **NM** value: **2.00**
Circ: CapCity orders: **12,200**
C: Brian Bolland **W:** Rick Veitch

36 ❑ Jun 1991 Cover: 1.50 **NM** value: **2.00**
Circ: CapCity orders: **11,800**
C: Brian Bolland **W:** Rick Veitch

37 ❑ Jul 1991 Cover: 1.50 **NM** value: **2.00**
Circ: CapCity orders: **11,900**
C: Brian Bolland **W:** Rick Veitch

38 ❑ Aug 2000 Cover: 1.50 **NM** value: **2.00**
Circ: CapCity orders: **11,850**
• Punisher parody **C:** Brian Bolland

39 ❑ Sep 1991 Cover: 1.50 **NM** value: **2.00**
Circ: CapCity orders: **11,400**

40 ❑ Oct 1991 Cover: 1.50 **NM** value: **2.00**
Circ: CapCity orders: **15,350**
🕮 War of the Gods, Part 15

41 ❑ Nov 1991 Cover: 1.75 **NM** value: **2.00**
Circ: CapCity orders: **11,250**

42 ❑ Dec 1991 Cover: 1.50 **NM** value: **2.00**
Circ: CapCity orders: **11,400**

43 ❑ Jan 1992 Cover: 1.75 **NM** value: **2.00**
Circ: CapCity orders: **11,050**

44 ❑ Feb 1992 Cover: 1.75 **NM** value: **2.00**
Circ: CapCity orders: **10,850**

45 ❑ Mar 1992 Cover: 1.75 **NM** value: **2.00**
Circ: CapCity orders: **10,300**

46 ❑ Apr 1992 Cover: 1.75 **NM** value: **2.00**
Circ: CapCity orders: **9,550**

47 ❑ May 1992 Cover: 1.75 **NM** value: **2.00**
Circ: CapCity orders: **9,300**

48 ❑ Jun 1992 Cover: 1.75 **NM** value: **2.00**
Circ: CapCity orders: **9,250**

49 ❑ Jul 1992 Cover: 1.75 **NM** value: **2.00**
Circ: CapCity orders: **8,950**

50 ❑ Aug 1992 Cover: 2.95 **NM** value: **3.00**
Circ: CapCity orders: **10,450**
• Giant-size.

51 ❑ Sep 1992 Cover: 1.75 **NM** value: **2.00**
Circ: CapCity orders: **9,400**
🕮 Flesh & Blood; Flesh and Blood, Part 1

52 ❑ Oct 1992 Cover: 1.75 **NM** value: **2.00**
Circ: CapCity orders: **9,000**
🕮 Flesh & Blood; Flesh and Blood, Part 2

53 ❑ Nov 1992 Cover: 1.75 **NM** value: **2.00**
Circ: CapCity orders: **8,750**
🕮 Flesh & Blood; Flesh and Blood, Part 3

54 ❑ Dec 1992 Cover: 1.75 **NM** value: **2.00**
Circ: CapCity orders: **8,950**
🕮 Flesh & Blood; Flesh and Blood, Part 4

55 ❑ Jan 1993 Cover: 1.75 **NM** value: **2.00**
Circ: CapCity orders: **9,200**
🕮 Flesh & Blood; Flesh and Blood, Part 5

56 ❑ Feb 1993 Cover: 3.50 **NM** value: **Cover or less**
Circ: CapCity orders: **9,900**
• Giant-size. 🕮 Flesh & Blood; Flesh and Blood, Part 6; Flesh and Blood, Part 7

57 ❑ Mar 1993 Cover: 1.75 **NM** value: **2.00**
Circ: CapCity orders: **24,150**
• Begin Vertigo line

58 ❑ Apr 1993 Cover: 1.75 **NM** value: **2.00**
Circ: CapCity orders: **13,650**

59 ❑ May 1993 Cover: 1.75 **NM** value: **2.00**
Circ: CapCity orders: **13,950**

60 ❑ Jun 1993 Cover: 1.95 **NM** value: **2.00**
Circ: CapCity orders: **13,700**
C: Brian Bolland

61 ❑ Jul 1993 Cover: 1.95 **NM** value: **2.00**
Circ: CapCity orders: **12,850**
🕮 Tooth and Claw, Part 1 **A:** Steve Pugh **W:** Jamie Delano

62 ❑ Aug 1993 Cover: 1.95 **NM** value: **2.00**
Circ: CapCity orders: **12,900**
🕮 Tooth and Claw, Part 2 **A:** Steve Pugh **W:** Jamie Delano

63 ❑ Sep 1993 Cover: 1.95 **NM** value: **2.00**
Circ: CapCity orders: **11,450**
🕮 Tooth and Claw, Part 3 **A:** Steve Pugh **W:** Jamie Delano

64 ❑ Oct 1993 Cover: 1.95 **NM** value: **2.00**
Circ: CapCity orders: **10,950**

65 ❑ Nov 1993 Cover: 1.95 **NM** value: **2.00**
Circ: CapCity orders: **10,200**

66 ❑ Dec 1993 Cover: 1.95 **NM** value: **2.00**
Circ: CapCity orders: **9,950**

67 ❑ Jan 1994 Cover: 1.95 **NM** value: **2.00**
Circ: CapCity orders: **9,400**
🕮 Mysterious Ways, Part 1

68 ❑ Feb 1994 Cover: 1.95 **NM** value: **2.00**
Circ: CapCity orders: **9,000**
🕮 Mysterious Ways, Part 2

69 ❑ Mar 1994 Cover: 1.95 **NM** value: **2.00**
Circ: CapCity orders: **8,600**

70 ❑ Apr 1994 Cover: 1.95 **NM** value: **2.00**
Circ: CapCity orders: **8,250**

71 ❑ May 1994 Cover: 1.95 **NM** value: **Cover or less**
Circ: CapCity orders: **8,100**

72 ❑ Jun 1994 Cover: 1.95 **NM** value: **Cover or less**
Circ: CapCity orders: **7,950**

73 ❑ Jul 1994 Cover: 1.95 **NM** value: **Cover or less**
Circ: CapCity orders: **7,950**

74 ❑ Aug 1994 Cover: 1.95 **NM** value: **Cover or less**
Circ: CapCity orders: **7,850**

75 ❑ Sep 1994 Cover: 1.95 **NM** value: **Cover or less**
Circ: CapCity orders: **7,750**

76 ❑ Oct 1994 Cover: 1.95 **NM** value: **Cover or less**
Circ: CapCity orders: **7,400**

77 ❑ Nov 1994 Cover: 1.95 **NM** value: **Cover or less**
Circ: CapCity orders: **7,000**

78 ❑ Dec 1994 Cover: 1.95 **NM** value: **Cover or less**
Circ: CapCity orders: **6,950**

79 ❑ Jan 1995 Cover: 1.95 **NM** value: **Cover or less**
Circ: CapCity orders: **6,500**

80 ❑ Feb 1995 Cover: 1.95 **NM** value: **Cover or less**
Circ: CapCity orders: **6,075**

81 ❑ Mar 1995 Cover: 1.95 **NM** value: **Cover or less**
Circ: CapCity orders: **5,650**
🕮 Wild Type, Part 1

82 ❑ Apr 1995 Cover: 1.95 **NM** value: **Cover or less**
Circ: CapCity orders: **5,375**
🕮 Wild Type, Part 2

83 ❑ May 1995 Cover: 2.25 **NM** value: **Cover or less**
Circ: CapCity orders: **5,300**
🕮 Wild Type, Part 3

84 ❑ Jun 1995 Cover: 2.25 **NM** value: **Cover or less**
Circ: CapCity orders: **5,075**

85 ❑ Jul 1995 Cover: 2.25 **NM** value: **Cover or less**
Circ: CapCity orders: **4,950**

86 ❑ Aug 1995 Cover: 2.25 **NM** value: **Cover or less**
Circ: CapCity orders: **4,925**

87 ❑ Sep 1995 Cover: 2.25 **NM** value: **Cover or less**
Circ: CapCity orders: **4,525**

88 ❑ Oct 1995 Cover: 2.25 **NM** value: **Cover or less**
Circ: CapCity orders: **3,875**

89 ❑ Nov 1995 Cover: 2.25 **NM** value: **Cover or less**
final issue.

Anl 1 ❑ Cover: 3.95 **NM** value: **4.00**
Circ: CapCity orders: **13,300**
🕮 The Children's Crusade, Part 3 • "Children's Crusade"

Bk 1 ❑ Sep 1991 Cover: 19.95 **NM** value: **Cover or less**
• Trade Paperback. • collection;Reprints Animal Man #1-9

CGC-graded: Multiply prices above by **33 for 9.9 M • 16 for 9.8 NM/M • 7 for 9.6 NM+ • 5 for 9.4 NM • 2.5 for 9.2 NM- • 1.5 for 9.0 VF/NM**

ANIMAL MYSTIC — Cry for Dawn

Animal Mystic is a fantasy-oriented adventure strip which relates how Nikki Ranoakke, a voluptuous young woman from Southern California, is awakened to her role as a goddess on a far-off planet called Praktill. There, after hooking up with a cute dragon and a no-nonsense centaur, she assumes the identity of Queen Jatarri and aids the local population against the hordes of Spigmodites.

Someone referring to himself as The Dark One is credited as the writer and artist, even though the book is copyrighted by someone named Greg Williams. The lush inkwash art, reminiscent of Vaughn Bode's underground strip Cheech Wizard, is the real attraction, since the kindling of a young novice's potential in the heat of battle with the aid of mysterious mentors is standard fantasy fare.

1 ❑ Cover: 3.50 **NM** value: **18.00**
Circ: CapCity orders: **3,035** • **CGC:** 5 graded, best 9.6
A: Dark One **W:** Dark One; Robb Horan

1/LE❑ Cover: 3.50 **NM** value: **25.00**
• **CGC:** 1 graded, best 8.5
• limited edition with alternate cover and eight additional pages

1-2 ❑ Cover: 3.50 **NM** value: **4.00**

2 ❑ Jun 1994 Cover: 2.50 **NM** value: **12.00**
Circ: CapCity orders: **3,365** • **CGC:** 2 graded, best 9.2
A: Dark One **W:** Dark One; Robb Horan

2-2 ❑ May 1995 Cover: 2.50 **NM** value: **4.00**

3 ❑ Oct 1994 Cover: 2.50 **NM** value: **8.00**
Circ: CapCity orders: **4,685** • **CGC:** 1 graded, best 8.5
A: Dark One **W:** Dark One; Robb Horan

3-2 ❑ Cover: 2.50 **NM** value: **4.00**

4 ❑ Cover: 3.50 **NM** value: **5.00**
Circ: CapCity orders: **6,305** • **CGC:** 1 graded, best 9.2
A: Dark One **W:** Dark One; Robb Horan

4-2 ❑ Cover: 3.50 **NM** value: **4.00**

Bk 1❑ Cover: 14.95 **NM** value: **Cover or less**
• Collects Animal Mystic #1-4 **A:** Dark One **W:** Dark One; Robb Horan

Bk 1-2❑ Cover: 14.95 **NM** value: **Cover or less**

ANIMAL MYSTIC WATER WARS — Sirius

1 ❑ ca. 1996 Cover: 2.95 **NM** value: **Cover or less**
A: Dark One **W:** Dark One

2 ❑ Sep 1996 Cover: 2.95 **NM** value: **Cover or less**
Circ: Diamd. preorders: **20,814**
A: Dark One **W:** Dark One

3 ❑ Jan 1997 Cover: 2.95 **NM** value: **Cover or less**
Circ: Direct Market orders: **16,835**
A: Dark One **W:** Dark One

4 ❑ Aug 1997 Cover: 2.95 **NM** value: **Cover or less**
Circ: Diamd. preorders: **14,240**

5 ❑ May 1998 Cover: 2.95 **NM** value: **Cover or less**
Circ: Diamd. preorders: **12,355**

6 ❑ Oct 1998 Cover: 2.95 **NM** value: **Cover or less**
Circ: Diamd. preorders: **10,607**

Ash 1❑ **NM** value: **2.50**
• Preview edition. **A:** Dark One **W:** Dark One

Bk 1❑ Jun 1999 Cover: 19.95 **NM** value: **Cover or less**

ANIMAL RIGHTS COMICS — Stabur

1 ❑ **NM** value: **2.50**
The Silver Spring Monkeys, Part 1, Just Their Faces are Different • Benefit comic for PETA **A:** Mark Badger; Joyce Brabner **W:** Mark Badger; Joyce Brabner

ANIMAL WEIRDNESS — Cozmic

1 ❑ Cover: 0.75 **NM** value: **3.00**
Eddie Trunker's: The Daily Grind; Tales of Heavy Cheddar; Quatermouse; Last hedhog in Liverpool; Jiveass Jackal; The Tea Party; The Dumb Bun', Rats' Tails; The Right On RabbitHumpty Dumpty and The Movement, Snook; Rats; Foxy Lady **A:** Chris Tyler; Geoff Rowley; John Seven; Malcolm Poynter; Rowley & Prodes; William Rankin; Brian Hawcroft **W:** Chris Tyler; John Seven; Malcolm Poynter; Rowley & Prodes; William Rankin; Brian Hawcroft; Jules

ANIMANIACS — DC

Warner Bros., best known for cartoon characters like Bugs Bunny and Porky Pig, introduced this series in 1995 in conjunction with a popular afternoon television show. Its stars are — you guessed it — the Warner Brothers (and a Warner sister), also known as The Animaniacs. This trio of cartoon troublemakers is known for their zany, over-the-top antics which never fail to reel in the laughs.

Although Animaniacs are aimed squarely at the pre-teen crowd, their occasional co-stars Pinky and the Brain have a more devilishly adult sensibility. Pinky is a punked-out goofball of a mouse, but his partner, the Brain, has a definite goal for life: to take over the world. To that end, he puts his incredible brain power to work to launch scheme after scheme. He's a megalomaniac, but endearing in his own way.

1 ❑ May 1995 Cover: 1.50 **NM** value: **2.25**
Circ: CapCity orders: **9,825**

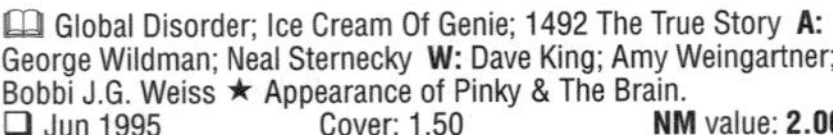

Global Disorder; Ice Cream Of Genie; 1492 The True Story **A:** George Wildman; Neal Sternecky **W:** Dave King; Amy Weingartner; Bobbi J.G. Weiss ★ Appearance of Pinky & The Brain.

2 ❑ Jun 1995 Cover: 1.50 **NM** value: **2.00**
Circ: CapCity orders: **6,750**

3 ❑ Jul 1995 Cover: 1.50 **NM** value: **2.00**
Circ: CapCity orders: **6,100**

4 ❑ Aug 1995 Cover: 1.50 **NM** value: **2.00**
Circ: CapCity orders: **6,075**

5 ❑ Sep 1995 Cover: 1.50 **NM** value: **2.00**
Circ: CapCity orders: **5,575**

6 ❑ Oct 1995 Cover: 1.50 **NM** value: **1.75**
Circ: CapCity orders: **4,275**

7 ❑ Nov 1995 Cover: 1.50 **NM** value: **1.75**

8 ❑ Dec 1995 Cover: 1.50 **NM** value: **1.75**

9 ❑ Jan 1996 Cover: 1.50 **NM** value: **1.75**
Pulp Fiction parody cover.

10 ❑ Feb 1996 Cover: 1.50 **NM** value: **1.75**
gratuitous pin-up cover. A Comic Book is Born; The Ice Cream Man Cometh **A:** Leo Batic; Neal Sternecky **W:** Dana Kurtin; Jesse McCann

11 ❑ Mar 1996 Cover: 1.50 **NM** value: **1.75**
Brain for Brain; Frankly Frankenstein • Brain duplicates himself **A:** Cosme Quartieri; Walter Carzon **W:** Dave King; Bobbi JG Weiss

12 ❑ Apr 1996 Cover: 1.50 **NM** value: **1.75**
A Blast from Hipsville; The Mod Couple **A:** Walter Carzon **W:** Charles Howell; Dana Kurtin; Gordon Bressack

13 ❑ May 1996 Cover: 1.75 **NM** value: **Cover or less**

14 ❑ Jun 1996 Cover: 1.75 **NM** value: **Cover or less**

15 ❑ Jul 1996 Cover: 1.75 **NM** value: **Cover or less**

16 ❑ Aug 1996 Cover: 1.75 **NM** value: **Cover or less**
• Wrestling issue

17 ❑ Sep 1996 Cover: 1.75 **NM** value: **Cover or less**
• Animaniacs judge a beauty contest

18 ❑ Oct 1996 Cover: 1.75 **NM** value: **Cover or less**
Dupe Du Jour; Good Idea/French Idea; Slappytime in Paris • All France issue **A:** Leo Batic; Omar Aranda **W:** Dan Slott; Dana Kurtin

19 ❑ Nov 1996 Cover: 1.75 **NM** value: **Cover or less**
Circ: Diamd. preorders: **10,311**
The Y Files; Sheep!; Little Green Mice **A:** Charles Adlard; Walter Carzon; Omar Aranda; Scott McRae **W:** Dave King

20 ❑ Dec 1996 Cover: 1.75 **NM** value: **Cover or less**
Circ: Direct Market orders: **9,367**
Rebels Just Cause!; East of Burbank; Grande! • James Dean tribute **A:** Leo Batic; Omar Aranda; Scott McRae **W:** Jennifer Moore; Sean Carolan

21 ❑ Jan 1997 Cover: 1.75 **NM** value: **Cover or less**
Circ: Direct Market orders: **9,271**
Radio Dazed; ER: Emergency Roomies • Christmas issue **A:** Omar Aranda; Scott McRae **W:** Gary Glasberg

22 ❑ Feb 1997 Cover: 1.75 **NM** value: **Cover or less**
Circ: Diamd. preorders: **8,663**

23 ❑ Mar 1997 Cover: 1.75 **NM** value: **Cover or less**
Circ: Diamd. preorders: **8,206**
Hello Nurse, Agent of H.U.B.B.A.; Useless Facts; Warro for President **A:** Leo Batic; Omar Aranda **W:** Jenifer Moore; Mark McKain; Sean Carolan

24 ❑ Apr 1997 Cover: 1.75 **NM** value: **Cover or less**
Circ: Diamd. preorders: **7,745**

25 ❑ May 1997 Cover: 1.75 **NM** value: **Cover or less**
Circ: Diamd. preorders: **7,927**
• Anniversary issue.

26 ❑ Jun 1997 Cover: 1.75 **NM** value: **Cover or less**
Circ: Diamd. preorders: **7,861**
Tales from the Crypt cover parody. Pancake House of Horor!; Randy Beaman's Tales of Terror: Bubble Doom; A Paw Worth Fihting For!; Good Things Come in Buckets; Tickle-Me Evil!; Randy Beaman's Tales of Terror: Claw Deal **A:** Leo Batic; Omar Aranda **W:** Jennifer Moore; Sean Carolan

27 ❑ Jul 1997 Cover: 1.75 **NM** value: **Cover or less**
Circ: Diamd. preorders: **7,312**
• Slappy's plane is hijacked

28 ❑ Aug 1997 Cover: 1.75 **NM** value: **Cover or less**
Circ: Diamd. preorders: **7,424**
• Star Trek parody;Science issue

29 ❑ Sep 1997 Cover: 1.75 **NM** value: **Cover or less**
Circ: Diamd. preorders: **7,110**
The Return of Hello Nurse, Agent of H.U.B.B.A.

30 ❑ Oct 1997 Cover: 1.75 **NM** value: **Cover or less**
Circ: Diamd. preorders: **7,161**
• "Electra Woman and Dyna Girl" parody

31 ❑ Nov 1997 Cover: 1.75 **NM** value: **Cover or less**
Circ: Diamd. preorders: **6,791**
101 Darnations; The Usual Boo! • 101 Dalmations parody **A:** Leo Batic; Omar Aranda **W:** Bill Matheny

32 ❑ Dec 1997 Cover: 1.95 **NM** value: **Cover or less**
Circ: Diamd. preorders: **6,685**
• Dot hosts a slumber party

33 ❑ Jan 1998 Cover: 1.95 **NM** value: **Cover or less**
Circ: Diamd. preorders: **6,356**
Lost World cover. ★ 1st Appearance of Sakko Warner.

34 ❑ Feb 1998 Cover: 1.95 **NM** value: **Cover or less**
Circ: Diamd. preorders: **6,206**

35 ❑ Mar 1998 Cover: 1.95 **NM** value: **Cover or less**
Circ: Diamd. preorders: **5,860**
★ Appearance of Freakazoid.

36 ❑ Apr 1998 Cover: 1.95 **NM** value: **Cover or less**
Circ: Diamd. preorders: **5,498**

37 ❑ May 1998 Cover: 1.95 **NM** value: **Cover or less**
Circ: Diamd. preorders: **5,707**

38 ❑ Jun 1998 Cover: 1.95 **NM** value: **Cover or less**
Circ: Diamd. preorders: **5,672**
manga-style cover.

39 ❑ Jul 1998 Cover: 1.95 **NM** value: **Cover or less**
Circ: Diamd. preorders: **5,430**
★ Appearance of Alfred Nobel.

40 ❑ Sep 1998 Cover: 1.99 **NM** value: **Cover or less**
Circ: Diamd. preorders: **5,198**
• Spice Girls parody

41 ❑ Oct 1998 Cover: 1.99 **NM** value: **Cover or less**
Circ: Diamd. preorders: **5,002**
• Little Nemo and Little Mermaid parodies

42 ❑ Nov 1998 Cover: 1.99 **NM** value: **Cover or less**
Circ: Diamd. preorders: **4,906**
• Love Boat parody

43 ❑ Dec 1998 Cover: 1.99 **NM** value: **Cover or less**
Circ: Diamd. preorders: **4,982**
• Pinky & the Brain

44 ❑ Jan 1999 Cover: 1.99 **NM** value: **Cover or less**
Circ: Diamd. preorders: **4,834**
• Pinky & the Brain

45 ❑ Feb 1999 Cover: 1.99 **NM** value: **Cover or less**
Circ: Diamd. preorders: **4,898**
Brain Loses His Mind; The Warner Twins • The Warner Twins;Featuring Pinky and the Brain

46 ❑ Mar 1999 Cover: 1.99 **NM** value: **Cover or less**
Circ: Diamd. preorders: **5,107**
• Dot the Vampire Slayer;Featuring Pinky and the Brain

47 ❑ Apr 1999 Cover: 1.99 **NM** value: **Cover or less**
Circ: Diamd. preorders: **4,876**
Brainita • Evita parody;Featuring Pinky and the Brain

48 ❑ May 1999 Cover: 1.99 **NM** value: **Cover or less**
Circ: Diamd. preorders: **4,754**

49 ❑ Jun 1999 Cover: 1.99 **NM** value: **Cover or less**
Circ: Diamd. preorders: **4,772**
The Lit-Wit Issue; MacBoo; Brainwulf; Pride and Pigeon-ness (aka Coo-less); Romeo and Juliet (translated by Yakko Warner) • literature issue;Featuring Pinky and the Brain;It's the Animaniacal Guide to the Classics!! **A:** Walter Carzon; Leo Batic **W:** Jeff Suess

50 ❑ Jul 1999 Cover: 1.99 **NM** value: **Cover or less**
Circ: Diamd. preorders: **4,803**
Mime Time; Hello Nurse and the Animaniacs: Riki-Tiki Terror! • Hello Nurse as super-hero;Featuring Pinky and the Brain **A:** Walter Carzon; Leo Batic **W:** Jennifer Moore; Sean Carolan

51 ❑ Aug 1999 Cover: 1.99 **NM** value: **Cover or less**
Circ: Diamd. preorders: **4,510**
Away With Wurds!; Crossed Signals; Monster of the Bride • Featuring Pinky and the Brain **A:** Walter Carzon; B. Jennifer Moore; Leo Batic **W:** Frank Strom; Joe Edkin; Sean Carolan

52 ❑ Sep 1999 Cover: 1.99 **NM** value: **Cover or less**
Circ: Diamd. preorders: **4,467**
Baby Bowl; Fear and Loathing on Mars!; I Never Promised You a Kindergarten • football;Featuring Pinky and the Brain **A:** Walter Carzon; Leo Batic; Vince DeFortier **W:** Frank Strom; Jesse Leon McCann; Joe Edkin

53 ❑ Oct 1999 Cover: 1.99 **NM** value: **Cover or less**
Circ: Diamd. preorders: **4,378**
Future Stock; The Contest • Featuring Pinky and the Brain **A:** Walter Carzon; Leo Batic **W:** Frank Strom; Matt Wayne

54 ❑ Nov 1999 Cover: 1.99 **NM** value: **Cover or less**
Circ: Diamd. preorders: **4,318**

55 ❑ Dec 1999 Cover: 1.99 **NM** value: **Cover or less**
Circ: Diamd. preorders: **4,149**
Theme Park Buttons; Waiting for Godot; Operation: Slumberland • Featuring Pinky and the Brain **A:** Walter Carzon; Leo Batic; Rusty Haller **W:** Jennifer Moore; Jesse Leon McCann; Joe Edkin; Sean Carolan

56 ❑ Jan 2000 Cover: 1.99 **NM** value: **Cover or less**
Circ: Diamd. preorders: **4,076**
Te Britches of Madison County; This Year's Model; Thanksgiving Boo; Animaniacs: Things that go Bonk in the Night! • Featuring Pinky and the Brain **A:** Walter Carzon; Leo Batic **W:** Jennifer Moore; Chuck Kim; Joe Edkin; Sean Carolan

57 ❑ Feb 2000 Cover: 1.99 **NM** value: **Cover or less**
Circ: Diamd. preorders: **4,197**

58 ❑ Mar 2000 Cover: 1.99 **NM** value: **Cover or less**
Circ: Diamd. preorders: **3,726**
From Bad to Nurse • Hello Nurse, Agent of H.U.B.B.A. **A:** Walter Carzon **W:** Jennifer Moore; Sean Carolan

59 ❑ Apr 2000 Cover: 1.99 **NM** value: **Cover or less**
Circ: Diamd. preorders: **3,550**
Far Lap • Featuring Pinky and the Brain **A:** Walter Carzon; Leo Batic **W:** Jennifer Moore; Sean Carolan

HS 1❑Dec 1994 Cover: 1.50 **NM** value: **2.00**
Circ: CapCity orders: **15,550**
• double-sized. 'Twas the Day Before Christmas; The Taming of the Screwy **A:** George Wildman; Neal Sternecky **W:** Bobbi JG Weiss; Paul Rugg

ANIMATED COMICS — E.C.

1 ❑ Win 1947 Cover: 0.10 **NM** value: **500.00**
• **CGC:** 5 graded, best 7.0
Bouncy Bunny in the Friendly Forest; Kangy Roo; Animated Movies; Flitty Flicker; Fergy Frog; Carrot Chops

ANIMATED FUNNY COMIC TUNES — U.S.A.

16 ❑ Sum 1944 Cover: 0.10 **NM** value: **75.00**
17 ❑ Fal 1944 Cover: 0.10 **NM** value: **60.00**
18 ❑ Win 1944 Cover: 0.10 **NM** value: **60.00**
19 ❑ Jul 1945 Cover: 0.10 **NM** value: **60.00**
20 ❑ Fal 1945 Cover: 0.10 **NM** value: **60.00**
21 ❑ Apr 1946 Cover: 0.10 **NM** value: **50.00**
22 ❑ Sum 1946 Cover: 0.10 **NM** value: **50.00**
23 ❑ Fal 1946 Cover: 0.10 **NM** value: **50.00**

ANIMATED MOVIE-TUNES — Margood

1 ❑ Fal 1945 Cover: 0.10 **NM** value: **125.00**
2 ❑ Sum 1946 Cover: 0.10 **NM** value: **125.00**

ANIMAX — Marvel / Star

1 ❑ Dec 1986 Cover: 0.75 **NM** value: **1.00**
Circ: CapCity orders: **8,300**

2 ❑ Jan 1987 Cover: 0.75 **NM** value: **1.00**
Circ: CapCity orders: **4,950**

3 ❑ Feb 1987 Cover: 0.75 **NM** value: **1.00**
Circ: CapCity orders: **3,500**
The Retread Plot **A:** Steve Purcell **W:** Walt Simonson

4 ❑ Mar 1987 Cover: 0.75 **NM** value: **1.00**
Circ: CapCity orders: **2,150**

Other grades: Multiply prices above by **1.5 for Mint • 2/3 for Very Fine • 1/3 for Fine • 1/5 for Very Good • 1/8 for Good**

ANIMERICA EXTRA — Viz

1 ❑ ca. 1998 Cover: 4.95 NM value: **Cover or less**
2 ❑ ca. 1998 Cover: 4.95 NM value: **Cover or less**

ANIMERICA EXTRA (VOL. 2) — Viz

1 ❑ ca. 1998 Cover: 4.95 NM value: **Cover or less**
2 ❑ ca. 1999 Cover: 4.95 NM value: **Cover or less**
3 ❑ ca. 1999 Cover: 4.95 NM value: **Cover or less**
4 ❑ ca. 1999 Cover: 4.95 NM value: **Cover or less**
5 ❑ ca. 1999 Cover: 4.95 NM value: **Cover or less**
6 ❑ ca. 1999 Cover: 4.95 NM value: **Cover or less**
7 ❑ ca. 1999 Cover: 4.95 NM value: **Cover or less**

ANIMERICA EXTRA (VOL. 3) — Viz

1 ❑ ca. 2000 Cover: 4.95 NM value: **Cover or less**
2 ❑ ca. 2000 Cover: 4.95 NM value: **Cover or less**
3 ❑ ca. 2000 Cover: 4.95 NM value: **Cover or less**
4 ❑ ca. 2000 Cover: 4.95 NM value: **Cover or less**
5 ❑ ca. 2000 Cover: 4.95 NM value: **Cover or less**
6 ❑ ca. 2000 Cover: 4.95 NM value: **Cover or less**
• contains poster
7 ❑ ca. 2000 Cover: 4.95 NM value: **Cover or less**
8 ❑ ca. 2000 Cover: 4.95 NM value: **Cover or less**
9 ❑ ca. 2000 Cover: 4.95 NM value: **Cover or less**
10 ❑ ca. 2000 Cover: 4.95 NM value: **Cover or less**

ANIMISM — Centurion

1 ❑ Jan 1987 NM value: **1.50**
A: Ed Decker **W:** Ed Decker

ANIVERSE, THE — Weebee

1 ❑ NM value: **1.95**
2 ❑ NM value: **1.95**

ANNEX — Marvel

1 ❑ Aug 1994 Cover: 1.75 NM value: **Cover or less**
Circ: CapCity orders: **18,350**
📖 Crucible Of Power **A:** Walter McDaniel **W:** Jack Harris ★ Origin of Annex.
2 ❑ Sep 1994 Cover: 1.75 NM value: **Cover or less**
Circ: CapCity orders: **12,050**
📖 Crucible Of Power, Part 2 **W:** Jack Harris
3 ❑ Oct 1994 Cover: 1.75 NM value: **Cover or less**
Circ: CapCity orders: **8,950**
📖 Crucible Of Power, Part 3 **W:** Jack Harris
4 ❑ Nov 1994 Cover: 1.75 NM value: **Cover or less**
Circ: CapCity orders: **7,450**
📖 Crucible Of Power, Part 4 **W:** Jack Harris

ANNIE — Marvel

This is the comic-book adaptation of the 1982 movie adaptation of a Broadway musical that was, itself, an adaptation of the popular Little Orphan Annie comic strip of Harold Gray (1894-1968). This story follows the adventures of a spunky orphan in 1930s New York. The clever little redhead escapes from the harsh orphanage, but her freedom is short-lived, and the authorities soon return her to the wicked administrator, Miss Hannigan. Destiny seems to be smiling on young Annie, as the tyke, along with her newfound dog, Sandy, soon finds herself living in luxury in a magnificent mansion. It's all part of a public relations stunt to enhance the humanitarian image of billionaire Oliver Warbucks. Her good fortune, however, will only last a week and then Annie will be back in the vindictive clutches of Miss Hannigan, and Sandy will be on the way to a sausage factory. Unless, of course, the spirited child can melt the heart of the imperturbable Warbucks.

1 ❑ Oct 1982 Cover: 0.60 NM value: **1.00**
• Official movie adaptation **A:** Win Mortimer **W:** Tom DeFalco; Carol Sobieski
1/SE❑ Cover: 2.00 NM value: **5.00**
• Tabloid size. **A:** Win Mortimer **W:** Tom DeFalco; Carol Sobieski
2 ❑ Nov 1982 Cover: 0.60 NM value: **1.00**
• Official movie adaptation **A:** Win Mortimer **W:** Tom DeFalco; Carol Sobieski

ANNIE OAKLEY — Timely

1 ❑ Spr 1948 Cover: 0.10 NM value: **300.00**
• **CGC:** 2 graded, best 9.0
2 ❑ Jul 1948 Cover: 0.10 NM value: **175.00**
3 ❑ Sep 1948 Cover: 0.10 NM value: **150.00**
4 ❑ Nov 1948 Cover: 0.10 NM value: **150.00**
5 ❑ Jun 1955 Cover: 0.10 NM value: **100.00**
6 ❑ Aug 1955 Cover: 0.10 NM value: **100.00**
7 ❑ Oct 1955 Cover: 0.10 NM value: **100.00**
8 ❑ Dec 1955 Cover: 0.10 NM value: **100.00**
9 ❑ Feb 1956 Cover: 0.10 NM value: **100.00**
10 ❑ Apr 1956 Cover: 0.10 NM value: **100.00**
11 ❑ Jun 1956 Cover: 0.10 NM value: **100.00**

The prices seen above do not represent the highest possible prices seen in online auctions, but rather the prices we have seen these issues reliably fetch in a variety of environments (storefront retail, mail order, auction and convention).

ANNIE OAKLEY AND TAGG — Dell

Annie Oakley (1860-1926) was, of course, a real person, called by many the greatest sharpshooter of all time. She joined Buffalo Bill's Wild West Show in 1885; while there, Sioux Chief Sitting Bull adopted her as his daughter into the Sioux nation and gave her the name "Little Sureshot."

In one of her fictional incarnations (never forgetting that she was the female lead in the Broadway show and film Annie Get Your Gun), she shared the title with her kid brother, Tagg. That incarnation was a daytime syndicated TV show that was broadcast from 1954 to 1956 (and in reruns later) and starred trick shot artist Gail Davis as Annie. The era of the show's stories preceded Annie's Wild West Show adventures, and the comic-book version was based on the TV show, photo covers and all. — Maggie

4 ❑ Jul 1955 Cover: 0.10 NM value: **75.00**
5 ❑ Oct 1955 Cover: 0.10 NM value: **75.00**
6 ❑ Jan 1956 Cover: 0.10 NM value: **75.00**
7 ❑ Apr 1956 Cover: 0.10 NM value: **75.00**
8 ❑ Jul 1956 Cover: 0.10 NM value: **75.00**
• **CGC:** 1 graded, best 9.4
9 ❑ Oct 1956 Cover: 0.10 NM value: **75.00**
10 ❑ Jan 1957 Cover: 0.10 NM value: **75.00**
11 ❑ Apr 1957 Cover: 0.10 NM value: **60.00**
• **CGC:** 1 graded, best 9.4
12 ❑ Jul 1957 Cover: 0.10 NM value: **60.00**
13 ❑ Oct 1957 Cover: 0.10 NM value: **60.00**
14 ❑ Jan 1958 Cover: 0.10 NM value: **60.00**
15 ❑ Apr 1958 Cover: 0.10 NM value: **60.00**
16 ❑ Jul 1958 Cover: 0.10 NM value: **60.00**
• **CGC:** 1 graded, best 9.4
17 ❑ Oct 1959 Cover: 0.10 NM value: **60.00**
18 ❑ Jan 1959 Cover: 0.10 NM value: **60.00**

ANNIE SPRINKLE IS MISS TIMED — Rip Off

1 ❑ Sep 1991 Cover: 2.50 NM value: **Cover or less**
2 ❑ Oct 1991 Cover: 2.50 NM value: **Cover or less**
3 ❑ Nov 1991 Cover: 2.50 NM value: **Cover or less**
4 ❑ Dec 1991 Cover: 2.50 NM value: **Cover or less**

ANOMALIES, THE — Abnormal Fun

1 ❑ Oct 2000 Cover: 2.95 NM value: **Cover or less**
A: Sam Gaffin **W:** Sam Gaffin

ANOMALY — Bud Plant

1 ❑ Cover: 0.50 NM value: **8.00**
2 ❑ Cover: 0.50 NM value: **5.00**
3 ❑ Cover: 0.50 NM value: **5.00**
4 ❑ Cover: 0.50 NM value: **5.00**
📖 Alice in Wonderlust; Leander and the Fat Queen; Encounter at War **A:** Richard Corben; Bob Kline **W:** Richard Corben; Jan Strnad

ANOMALY (BRASS RING) — Brass Ring

1 ❑ NM value: **3.95**
2 ❑ Jun 2000 Cover: 3.95 NM value: **Cover or less**
📖 Sting of the Scorpion; The Sincerest Form of Flattery; Best Friends; Are You Ready to Rumble?; HERO is a Four-Letter Word; The Hitch; The Big Score; Upgrade; A Christmas Story: Page One **A:** Dan Hoagland; Dennis Shumate; Ellen Topkiss; Johnny Lowe; Raymond E. Brown; Caleb Gerard **W:** Dan Hoagland; Dennis Shumate; Ellen Topkiss; Johnny Lowe; Raymond E. Brown; Caleb Gerard

ANOTHER CHANCE TO GET IT RIGHT — Dark Horse

1 ❑ Cover: 9.95 NM value: **Cover or less**
W: Andrew Vachss
1-2 ❑ Mar 1995 Cover: 9.95 NM value: **Cover or less**

ANOTHER DAY — Raised Brow

1 ❑ Oct 1995, b&w Cover: 2.75 NM value: **Cover or less**

ANTABUSE — High Drive

1 ❑ Cover: 2.50 NM value: **Cover or less**
2 ❑ Cover: 2.50 NM value: **Cover or less**

ANTARCTIC PRESS JAM 1996 — Antarctic

1 ❑ Dec 1996 Cover: 2.95 NM value: **Cover or less**
Circ: Direct Market orders: **3,209**
📖 Ninja High School; Twilight X; Tigerhawk II; Movie Night **A:** Ben Dunn **W:** Kyle Davies ★ Appearance of Ninja High School, Gold Digger, Twilight X, Tigers of Terra.

ANTARES CIRCLE — Antarctic

1 ❑ Cover: 1.95 NM value: **Cover or less**
2 ❑ Cover: 1.95 NM value: **Cover or less**

ANT BOY — Steeldragon

1 ❑ Cover: 1.75 NM value: **Cover or less**
2 ❑ Oct 1988 Cover: 1.75 NM value: **Cover or less**

ANT FARM — Gallant

1 ❑ Jun 1998 Cover: 2.50 NM value: **Cover or less**
📖 Legacy of Gray **A:** Alberto Melendez **W:** Alberto Melendez; Tony Melendez
2 ❑ Cover: 2.50 NM value: **Cover or less**

For up-to-the-week CGC ratios, consult the current issue of **Comics Buyer's Guide**.

ANTHRO — DC

Anthro lives at the dawn of human history. His father is chief of the bear people, and his destiny is one day to become a chief himself. In the meanwhile, his abilities as a hunter makes him well-loved by his people.

In this prehistoric adventure series, Anthro battles for survival in a hostile world. Using brains, brawn, and skill he takes on all manner of huge beasts and engages in the ages-old battle of the heart, as he attempts to win a beautiful woman from another tribe as his wife.

Following a debut in Showcase #74, Anthro was featured in this 1968 solo series. Although it lasted only six issues, the character survived far longer as DC's "oldest," including an appearance in DC's Crisis on Infinite Earths.

1 ❑ Aug 1968 Cover: 0.12 NM value: **35.00**
• **CGC:** 5 graded, best 9.4
📖 It Could Be You **A:** Howie Post

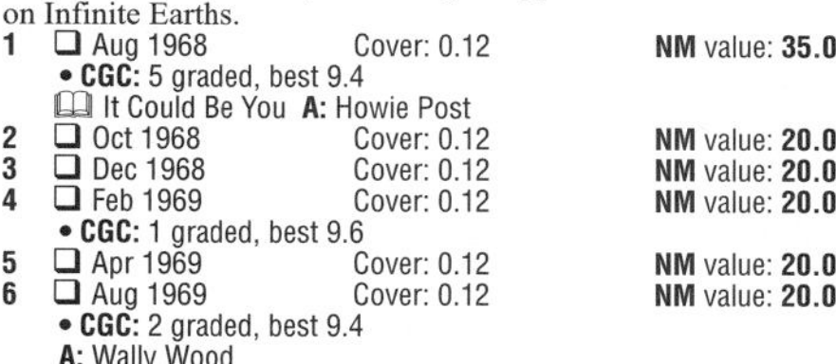

2 ❑ Oct 1968 Cover: 0.12 NM value: **20.00**
3 ❑ Dec 1968 Cover: 0.12 NM value: **20.00**
4 ❑ Feb 1969 Cover: 0.12 NM value: **20.00**
• **CGC:** 1 graded, best 9.6
5 ❑ Apr 1969 Cover: 0.12 NM value: **20.00**
6 ❑ Aug 1969 Cover: 0.12 NM value: **20.00**
• **CGC:** 2 graded, best 9.4
A: Wally Wood

ANTIETAM: THE FIERY TRAIL — Heritage Collection

1 ❑ 1997 Cover: 3.50 NM value: **Cover or less**
No issue number.

ANTI-HITLER COMICS — New England

1 ❑ Cover: 2.75 NM value: **Cover or less**
2 ❑ Cover: 2.75 NM value: **Cover or less**

ANTI-SOCIAL — Helpless Anger

1 ❑ b&w Cover: 2.00 NM value: **Cover or less**
2 ❑ Cover: 2.50 NM value: **Cover or less**
3 ❑ Cover: 2.50 NM value: **Cover or less**
4 ❑ Cover: 2.75 NM value: **Cover or less**

ANTI SOCIAL FOR THE DISABLED — Helpless Anger

1 ❑ b&w Cover: 5.00 NM value: **Cover or less**

ANTI SOCIAL JR. — Helpless Anger

1 ❑ b&w Cover: 1.75 NM value: **Cover or less**
No issue number.

ANT-MAN'S BIG CHRISTMAS — Marvel

1 ❑ Feb 2000 Cover: 5.95 NM value: **Cover or less**
Circ: Diamd. preorders: **15,518**
• prestige format. **A:** Phil Winslade **W:** Bob Gale

ANTON'S DREKBOOK — Fantagraphics / Eros

All issues are adults only.
1 ❑ b&w Cover: 2.50 NM value: **Cover or less**

ANUBIS — Super Crew

1 ❑ Cover: 2.50 NM value: **Cover or less**
A: Scott Berwanger **W:** Scott Berwanger

ANUBIS (2ND SERIES) — Super Crew

1 ❑ Cover: 2.95 NM value: **Cover or less**

ANYTHING BUT MONDAY — Anything But Monday Productions

1 ❑ Dec 1988 Cover: 1.75 NM value: **2.00**
2 ❑ Cover: 1.75 NM value: **2.00**
📖 Reindeer Games; Sappy Days Are Here Again!; The Best Way to Damage Certain Objects; Corporate Cocks; Nomads; Big Nuclear!; World War Waifs **A:** Frank Panucci; Cullen Cavallaro; Dave Kopperman; Mike Knobbe; Ralf Schulze **W:** Frank Nora; Mike Massotto

ANYTHING GOES! — Fantagraphics

1 ❑ Oct 1986, full color Cover: 2.00 NM value: **Cover or less**
Circ: CapCity orders: **6,600**
📖 Savage!; Who"s Stronger…?; Heroes; Come to Papa; Mr. Monster; Man…the Automotive Machine; I, Carrot; Cartoon Man **A:** Marc Hempel; Alex Toth; Bob Burden; Gil Kane; Gilbert Hernandez; Michael T. Gilbert; Dave Garcia **C:** Gil Kane **W:** Marc Hempel; Alex Toth; Bob Burden; Gil Kane; Michael T. Gilbert; Jan Strnad; Mike Baron; Scott Deschaine
2 ❑ Dec 1986, full color Cover: 2.00 NM value: **Cover or less**
Circ: CapCity orders: **6,350**
📖 In Pictopia; Those Wild and Mixed Up Locas; And Speaking of Those Abstract Pretentious Stories That Make You Feel Stupid If You Don't Get Them; Chrysalis; Walt Disney Lives **A:** Sam Kieth; Jack Kirby; Art Spiegelman; Jaime Hernandez; Joe Sinnott; Dennis Fujitake; Don Simpson **C:** Frank Miller **W:** Sam Kieth; Art Spiegelman; Jaime Hernandez; Alan Moore
3 ❑ Mar 1987, full color Cover: 2.00 NM value: **Cover or less**
Circ: CapCity orders: **7,375**
📖 Cerebus in Breaking Up is Hard to Do (illustrated text piece); Last Blood; They Call It the Purchaser's Clearing House; Captain Jack in The Laundromat at the Edge of Everything; For Losers Only; Ultimate Potential; A Prediction! **A:** Dave Sim; Pat Boyette; Gary Kwapisz; Daniel Clowes; Mark Wheatley; Howard Cruse **C:** Neal Adams **W:** Dave Sim; Pat Boyette; Mike Kazaleh; Daniel Clowes; Mark Wheatley; Howard Cruse; Marty Lyles; Marv Wolfman
4 ❑ May 1987, full color Cover: 2.00 NM value: **Cover or less**
Circ: CapCity orders: **5,025**

CGC-graded: Multiply prices above by **33 for 9.9 M • 16 for 9.8 NM/M • 7 for 9.6 NM+ • 5 for 9.4 NM • 2.5 for 9.2 NM- • 1.5 for 9.0 VF/NM**

📖 Heartbreak Soup: Space Case; Dance Class; The White Ship; The Divisible Man; Enigma Funnies; Girly Girl; Popeye **A:** Peter Bagge; Gilbert Hernandez; Trina Robbins; Gary Fields; Alec Stevens; E.C. Segar; Mort Todd **C:** George Perez **W:** Peter Bagge; Gilbert Hernandez; Gary Fields; Alec Stevens; Arn Saba; E.C. Segar; Mort Todd

5 ❑ Oct 1987 Cover: 2.00 **NM** value: **Cover or less**
Circ: CapCity orders: **7,675**
• TMNT

6 ❑ Oct 1987, b&w Cover: 2.00 **NM** value: **Cover or less**

A-OK — Antarctic

1 ❑ Sep 1992 Cover: 2.50 **NM** value: **Cover or less**
Circ: Diamd. preorders: **28,507**
📖 The Mission **A:** Edward Pun **W:** Edward Pun

2 ❑ Nov 1992 Cover: 2.50 **NM** value: **Cover or less**
A: Edward Pun **W:** Edward Pun

3 ❑ Jan 1993 Cover: 2.50 **NM** value: **Cover or less**
A: Edward Pun **W:** Edward Pun

4 ❑ Feb 1993 Cover: 2.50 **NM** value: **Cover or less**
📖 War! **A:** Edward Pun **W:** Edward Pun

APACHE DICK — Eternity

1 ❑ Cover: 2.25 **NM** value: **Cover or less**
📖 The Dick And The Doll, Part 1 **A:** Darick Robertson **W:** Will Jacobs

2 ❑ Cover: 2.25 **NM** value: **Cover or less**
3 ❑ Cover: 2.25 **NM** value: **Cover or less**
4 ❑ Cover: 2.25 **NM** value: **Cover or less**
Bk 1❑ Cover: 9.95 **NM** value: **Cover or less**

APACHE KID — Atlas

1 ❑ Dec 1950 Cover: 0.10 **NM** value: **200.00**
2 ❑ Feb 1951 Cover: 0.10 **NM** value: **150.00**
3 ❑ Mar 1951 Cover: 0.10 **NM** value: **150.00**
• **CGC:** 1 graded, best 9.0
4 ❑ May 1951 Cover: 0.10 **NM** value: **150.00**
5 ❑ Jun 1951 Cover: 0.10 **NM** value: **150.00**
6 ❑ Jul 1951 Cover: 0.10 **NM** value: **125.00**
7 ❑ Sep 1951 Cover: 0.10 **NM** value: **125.00**
8 ❑ Oct 1951 Cover: 0.10 **NM** value: **125.00**
9 ❑ Nov 1951 Cover: 0.10 **NM** value: **125.00**
10 ❑ Cover: 0.10 **NM** value: **125.00**
11 ❑ Dec 1954 Cover: 0.10 **NM** value: **100.00**
C: Russ Heath
12 ❑ Feb 1955 Cover: 0.10 **NM** value: **100.00**
13 ❑ Apr 1955 Cover: 0.10 **NM** value: **100.00**
14 ❑ Jun 1955 Cover: 0.10 **NM** value: **100.00**
15 ❑ Aug 1955 Cover: 0.10 **NM** value: **100.00**
16 ❑ Oct 1955 Cover: 0.10 **NM** value: **100.00**
17 ❑ Dec 1955 Cover: 0.10 **NM** value: **100.00**
18 ❑ Feb 1956 Cover: 0.10 **NM** value: **100.00**
19 ❑ Apr 1956 Cover: 0.10 **NM** value: **100.00**
• Becomes Western Gunfighters (1st series)

APACHE TRAIL — Steinway

1 ❑ Sep 1957 Cover: 0.10 **NM** value: **55.00**
📖 Apache Attack!; The Sheriff's Return!; Take My Word for It... (text story); Triple Twist!; A Tribe Betrayed!
2 ❑ Nov 1957 Cover: 0.10 **NM** value: **40.00**
3 ❑ Feb 1958 Cover: 0.10 **NM** value: **40.00**
4 ❑ Jun 1958 Cover: 0.10 **NM** value: **40.00**

APATHY KAT — Express / Entity

1 ❑ ca. 1995, b&w Cover: 2.50 **NM** value: **Cover or less**
A: Harold Buchholz **C:** Harold Buchholz **W:** Harold Buchholz
2 ❑ ca. 1996 Cover: 2.75 **NM** value: **Cover or less**
3 ❑ ca. 1996 Cover: 2.75 **NM** value: **Cover or less**
4 ❑ ca. 1996 Cover: 2.75 **NM** value: **Cover or less**
Bk 1❑ Cover: 7.95 **NM** value: **Cover or less**
• Kartoon Kollection;collects first three issues

APE, THE — Catalan

1 ❑ Cover: 10.95 **NM** value: **Cover or less**
A: Milo Manara **W:** Silverio Pisu

APE CITY — Adventure

1 ❑ Cover: 2.50 **NM** value: **Cover or less**
📖 Monkey Business • Planet of the Apes story **A:** M.C. Wyman **W:** Charles Marshall
2 ❑ Cover: 2.50 **NM** value: **Cover or less**
Circ: CapCity orders: **3,080**
• Planet of the Apes story **A:** M.C. Wyman **W:** Charles Marshall
3 ❑ Cover: 2.50 **NM** value: **Cover or less**
• Planet of the Apes story **A:** M.C. Wyman **W:** Charles Marshall
4 ❑ Cover: 2.50 **NM** value: **Cover or less**
• Planet of the Apes story **A:** M.C. Wyman **W:** Charles Marshall

APE NATION — Adventure

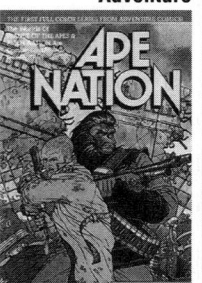

This series unites two of the most popular science-fiction "worlds" together in Adventure Comics' first color series. It begins when a Tenctonese (the aliens of Alien Nation) ship lands on the Planet of the Apes-a world where apes have become intelligent and have overthrown the humans as rulers of the world. Once there, the alien leader, a tyrant called Denada the Destroyer forms an alliance between General Ollo of the apes, and Simon, of the surviving humans. Their goal: to take this world as their own.

Against them are arrayed an earnest, but motley collection of aliens, apes, and humans. Still, this band seems to stand little chance of stopping the Denada's well-organized troops from marching on Ape City.

1 ❑ Feb 1991, full color Cover: 2.50 **NM** value: **Cover or less**
Circ: CapCity orders: **5,540**
📖 Plans • Alien Nation/Planet of Apes crossover;Alien Nation/Planet of the Apes crossover **A:** M.C. Wyman; Peter Hsu **W:** Charles Marshall
1/LE❑ full color Cover: 5.95 **NM** value: **Cover or less**
• limited edition. • Alien Nation/Planet of the Apes crossover **A:** Peter Hsu
2 ❑ Apr 1991 Cover: 2.50 **NM** value: **Cover or less**
• Alien Nation/Planet of the Apes crossover **A:** M.C. Wyman **W:** Charles Marshall
3 ❑ May 1991 Cover: 2.50 **NM** value: **Cover or less**
Circ: CapCity orders: **3,120**
• Alien Nation/Planet of the Apes crossover **A:** M.C. Wyman **W:** Charles Marshall
4 ❑ Jun 1991 Cover: 2.50 **NM** value: **Cover or less**
Circ: CapCity orders: **3,350**
• Alien Nation/Planet of the Apes crossover **A:** M.C. Wyman **W:** Charles Marshall

APEX — Aztec

1 ❑ b&w Cover: 2.00 **NM** value: **Cover or less**
📖 Dimensions; Tale of Two Cities; Paths; Captain Beyond; Zena; Dirty Dwarf; Kill Man **A:** Robb Phipps; Patrick Blaine; Jason Wiebe; John Waite; Mike Lane; Tom Hall; John Austin **W:** Robb Phipps; Patrick Blaine; Jason Wiebe; Mike Lane; John Austin

APEX PROJECT, THE — Stellar

1 ❑ Cover: 1.00 **NM** value: **Cover or less**
2 ❑ Cover: 1.00 **NM** value: **Cover or less**

APHRODISIA — Eros

1 ❑ Cover: 2.95 **NM** value: **Cover or less**
A: Nicolas Lajeunesse **W:** Nicolas Lajeunesse
2 ❑ Mar 1995 Cover: 2.95 **NM** value: **Cover or less**
A: Nicolas Lajeunesse **W:** Nicolas Lajeunesse

APHRODITE IX — Image

She is a beautiful woman with green hair. She is also Aphrodite IX, a purely synthetic being created in a lab and trained to be a killer. Too bad no one told her. Now she is beginning to question her existence, but it's difficult for someone to remember her past when her memory is erased 15 minutes after every mission. Her only hope is a mysterious man named Burch who may be able to provide her with answers. In a futuristic world in which humans have begun to alter their bodies with synthetics, Aphrodite IX must follow orders, relentlessly carrying out her duties as a trained assassin, yet unable to recall her past. Top Cow adds another buxom beauty to its line-up in this series written by Dave Finch (Batman/Darkness) and illustrated by David Wohl (Witchblade).

0/A ❑ May 2001 **NM** value: **10.00**
Circ: Diamd. preorders: **28,538** • **CGC:** 1 graded, best 9.6
• Wizard Gold Foil Edition. **A:** Dave Finch **W:** David Wohl
0/B ❑ May 2001 **NM** value: **10.00**
• **CGC:** 1 graded, best 9.8
• Wizard Blue Foil Edition. **A:** Dave Finch **W:** David Wohl
1/A ❑ Sep 2000 Cover: 2.50 **NM** value: **Cover or less**
Circ: Diamd. preorders: **103,129**
Aphrodite reclining against left edge of cover, gun up. **A:** Dave Finch **W:** David Wohl
1/B ❑ Sep 2000 Cover: 2.50 **NM** value: **Cover or less**
• Aphrodite walking on metallic planks **A:** Dave Finch **W:** David Wohl
1/C ❑ Sep 2000 Cover: 2.50 **NM** value: **Cover or less**
Red background, Aphrodite shooting on cover. **A:** Dave Finch **W:** David Wohl
1/D ❑ Sep 2000 Cover: 2.50 **NM** value: **Cover or less**
• Green background, standing with guns up **A:** Dave Finch **W:** David Wohl
1/E ❑ Sep 2000 **NM** value: **5.00**
• Tower records exclusive **A:** Dave Finch **W:** David Wohl
1/F ❑ Sep 2000 **NM** value: **5.00**
• Tower records exclusive w/foil **A:** Dave Finch **W:** David Wohl
1/G ❑ Sep 2000 **NM** value: **5.00**
• **CGC:** 12 graded, best 9.8
• Wizard World exclusive **A:** Dave Finch **W:** David Wohl
1/H ❑ Sep 2000 **NM** value: **5.00**
• **CGC:** 3 graded, best 9.6
• Wizard World exclusive w/foil **A:** Dave Finch **W:** David Wohl
1/I ❑ Sep 2000 **NM** value: **5.00**
• **CGC:** 6 graded, best 9.8
• Dynamic Forces exclusive **A:** Dave Finch **W:** David Wohl
2 ❑ Mar 2001 Cover: 2.50 **NM** value: **Cover or less**
Circ: Diamd. preorders: **46,406**
A: Dave Finch **W:** David Wohl
Ash 1❑ Dec 2000 Cover: 3.00 **NM** value: **5.00**
Circ: Diamd. preorders: **7,228**
• Convention Preview **A:** Dave Finch **W:** David Wohl

APOCALYPSE — Apocalypse

1 ❑ Cover: 3.95 **NM** value: **Cover or less**
2 ❑ Cover: 3.95 **NM** value: **Cover or less**
3 ❑ Cover: 3.95 **NM** value: **Cover or less**
4 ❑ Cover: 3.95 **NM** value: **Cover or less**
5 ❑ Cover: 3.95 **NM** value: **Cover or less**
6 ❑ Cover: 3.95 **NM** value: **Cover or less**
7 ❑ Cover: 3.95 **NM** value: **Cover or less**
• Makabre

APOLLO SMILE — Mixx

1 ❑ Jul 1998 Cover: 2.95 **NM** value: **4.00**
Circ: Diamd. preorders: **3,575**
2 ❑ Sep 1998 Cover: 2.95 **NM** value: **3.00**
Circ: Diamd. preorders: **1,913**

APPARITION, THE — Caliber

1 ❑ 1996 Cover: 2.95 **NM** value: **Cover or less**
📖 Whispered Promises, Part 1 **A:** Gene Gonzales **W:** James Pruett
2 ❑ 1996 Cover: 2.95 **NM** value: **Cover or less**
3 ❑ 1996 Cover: 2.95 **NM** value: **Cover or less**
4 ❑ 1996 Cover: 2.95 **NM** value: **Cover or less**
5 ❑ 1996 Cover: 2.95 **NM** value: **Cover or less**

APPARITION, THE: ABANDONED — Caliber

1 ❑ 1995 Cover: 3.95 **NM** value: **Cover or less**
One-shot. • prestige format.

APPARITION, THE: VISITATIONS — Caliber

1 ❑ Aug 1995 Cover: 3.95 **NM** value: **Cover or less**
One-shot. 📖 Alone Like Me; Salt of My Tears; An Ordinary Man; Seven Deadly Sins; An Apparition and the Airy Sailor Who Caused Faith

APPLE, P.I. — Parrot Communications

1 ❑ Sep 1996 Cover: 1.95 **NM** value: **Cover or less**
• pronounced "Apple Pie" **A:** Muntasir Ali; Patrick Morgan **W:** Kenneth Kolb; Tim Pyle

APPLESEED BOOK 1 — Eclipse

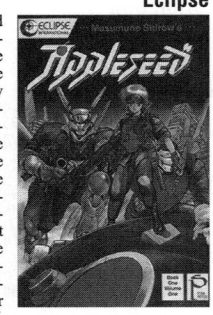

Masamune Shirow's Appleseed is an influential Japanese manga series, as well as a series of anime films. The futuristic tale takes place after World War III, when society looks for new ideas, as it begins rebuilding its cities. The city of Olympus is meant to be the perfect place to live, a shining example to the world around it. In Olympus, there is almost no crime, no homelessness, and the residents lack for nothing. In order to create the perfect city, however, perfect citizens are required. Olympus' builders supplied these, using genetic engineering to create a population suited for life in paradise. In total, some 80% of Olympus' population have been bio-engineered for life there.

Among the few that were not are Deunan Knute, a hard-fighting leader of the city's S.W.A.T. unit. Her job is to keep the peace, even as paradise began showing signs of cracking under the strain of perfection.

1 ❑ Sep 1988 Cover: 2.50 **NM** value: **10.00**
A: Masamune Shirow **W:** Masamune Shirow
2 ❑ Oct 1988 Cover: 2.50 **NM** value: **6.00**
A: Masamune Shirow **W:** Masamune Shirow
3 ❑ Nov 1988 Cover: 2.50 **NM** value: **5.00**
📖 Even Bets; Hospitality; Hot Potato • Squarebound **A:** Masamune Shirow **W:** Masamune Shirow
4 ❑ Jan 1989 Cover: 2.75 **NM** value: **4.00**
A: Masamune Shirow **W:** Masamune Shirow
5 ❑ Feb 1989 Cover: 2.75 **NM** value: **4.00**
A: Masamune Shirow **W:** Masamune Shirow
Bk 1❑ Cover: 12.95 **NM** value: **Cover or less**
📖 Promethean Challenge • Book One: The Promethean Challenge;Collects Appleseed Book 1 #1-5 **A:** Masamune Shirow **W:** Masamune Shirow
Bk 1-2❑ Cover: 14.95 **NM** value: **Cover or less**

APPLESEED BOOK 2 — Eclipse

1 ❑ Feb 1989 Cover: 2.75 **NM** value: **6.00**
A: Masamune Shirow; Arthur Adams(cover) **W:** Masamune Shirow
2 ❑ Mar 1989 Cover: 2.75 **NM** value: **4.00**
A: Masamune Shirow **W:** Masamune Shirow
3 ❑ Apr 1989 Cover: 2.75 **NM** value: **3.50**
A: Masamune Shirow **W:** Masamune Shirow
4 ❑ May 1989 Cover: 2.75 **NM** value: **3.50**
A: Masamune Shirow **W:** Masamune Shirow
5 ❑ Jun 1989 Cover: 2.75 **NM** value: **3.50**
A: Masamune Shirow **W:** Masamune Shirow
Bk 2❑ Cover: 14.95 **NM** value: **Cover or less**
📖 Prometheus Unbound • Collects Appleseed Book 2 #1-5 **A:** Masamune Shirow **W:** Masamune Shirow

APPLESEED BOOK 3 — Eclipse

1 ❑ Aug 1989 Cover: 2.75 **NM** value: **5.00**
• Squarebound **A:** Masamune Shirow; Arthur Adams(cover) **W:** Masamune Shirow
2 ❑ Cover: 2.75 **NM** value: **4.00**
A: Masamune Shirow **W:** Masamune Shirow
3 ❑ Cover: 2.75 **NM** value: **3.50**
A: Masamune Shirow **W:** Masamune Shirow
4 ❑ Cover: 2.75 **NM** value: **3.50**
A: Masamune Shirow **W:** Masamune Shirow
5 ❑ Cover: 3.50 **NM** value: **Cover or less**
A: Masamune Shirow **W:** Masamune Shirow
Bk 3❑ Cover: 14.95 **NM** value: **Cover or less**
📖 Scales of Prometheus • Collects Appleseed Book 3 #1-5 **A:** Masamune Shirow **W:** Masamune Shirow

APPLESEED BOOK 4 — Eclipse

1 ❑ Jan 1991 Cover: 3.50 **NM** value: **Cover or less**
A: Masamune Shirow **W:** Masamune Shirow
2 ❑ Cover: 3.50 **NM** value: **Cover or less**
A: Masamune Shirow **W:** Masamune Shirow

Other grades: Multiply prices above by **1.5 for Mint • 2/3 for Very Fine • 1/3 for Fine • 1/5 for Very Good • 1/8 for Good**

3 ❑ Cover: 3.50 **NM** value: **Cover or less**
A: Masamune Shirow **W:** Masamune Shirow
4 ❑ Cover: 3.50 **NM** value: **Cover or less**
A: Masamune Shirow **W:** Masamune Shirow

APPLESEED DATABOOK — Dark Horse

1 ❑ Apr 1994 Cover: 3.50 **NM** value: **Cover or less**
Circ: CapCity orders: **4,850**
A: Masamune Shirow **W:** Masamune Shirow
2 ❑ May 1994 Cover: 3.50 **NM** value: **Cover or less**
Circ: CapCity orders: **4,375**
• Flip-book. • Squarebound **A:** Masamune Shirow **W:** Masamune Shirow
Bk 1❑ Sep 1995, b&w Cover: 12.95 **NM** value: **Cover or less**
• collects the two-issue series **A:** Masamune Shirow **W:** Masamune Shirow

APPROVED COMICS — St. John

1 ❑ Mar 1954 Cover: 0.10 **NM** value: **75.00**
2 ❑ Mar 1954 Cover: 0.10 **NM** value: **75.00**
3 ❑ Apr 1954 Cover: 0.10 **NM** value: **75.00**
4 ❑ Apr 1954 Cover: 0.10 **NM** value: **75.00**
5 ❑ Apr 1954 Cover: 0.10 **NM** value: **75.00**
6 ❑ Apr 1954 Cover: 0.10 **NM** value: **75.00**
7 ❑ Apr 1954 Cover: 0.10 **NM** value: **75.00**
8 ❑ May 1954 Cover: 0.10 **NM** value: **75.00**
9 ❑ Jun 1954 Cover: 0.10 **NM** value: **75.00**
10 ❑ Jun 1954 Cover: 0.10 **NM** value: **75.00**
11 ❑ Jul 1954 Cover: 0.10 **NM** value: **75.00**
12 ❑ Aug 1954 Cover: 0.10 **NM** value: **75.00**

APRIL HORRORS — Rip Off

1 ❑ Sep 1993, b&w Cover: 2.95 **NM** value: **Cover or less**

AQUABLUE — Dark Horse

1 ❑ Nov 1989 Cover: 6.95 **NM** value: **Cover or less**
A: Olivier Vatine **W:** Thierry Cailleteau

AQUABLUE: THE BLUE PLANET — Dark Horse

1 ❑ Aug 1990 Cover: 8.95 **NM** value: **Cover or less**
A: Olivier Vatine **W:** Thierry Cailleteau

AQUA KNIGHT — Viz

1 ❑ ca. 2000 Cover: 3.50 **NM** value: **Cover or less**
Circ: Diamd. preorders: **6,744**
2 ❑ ca. 2000 Cover: 3.50 **NM** value: **Cover or less**
Circ: Diamd. preorders: **5,022**
3 ❑ ca. 2000 Cover: 3.50 **NM** value: **Cover or less**
Circ: Diamd. preorders: **4,809**
4 ❑ ca. 2000 Cover: 3.50 **NM** value: **Cover or less**
Circ: Diamd. preorders: **4,341**
5 ❑ ca. 2000 Cover: 3.50 **NM** value: **Cover or less**
Circ: Diamd. preorders: **3,919**
6 ❑ ca. 2000 Cover: 2.95 **NM** value: **Cover or less**
Circ: Diamd. preorders: **3,865**

AQUA KNIGHT PART 2 — Viz

1 ❑ Oct 2000 Cover: 3.50 **NM** value: **Cover or less**
Circ: Diamd. preorders: **3,919**
📖 The Bitter Trials of Desire **A:** Yukito Kishiro **W:** Yukito Kishiro
2 ❑ Nov 2000 Cover: 3.50 **NM** value: **Cover or less**
Circ: Diamd. preorders: **3,522**
A: Yukito Kishiro **W:** Yukito Kishiro
3 ❑ Dec 2000 Cover: 3.50 **NM** value: **Cover or less**
Circ: Diamd. preorders: **3,305**
A: Yukito Kishiro **W:** Yukito Kishiro
4 ❑ Jan 2001 Cover: 3.50 **NM** value: **Cover or less**
Circ: Diamd. preorders: **3,079**
A: Yukito Kishiro **W:** Yukito Kishiro
5 ❑ Feb 2001 Cover: 3.50 **NM** value: **Cover or less**
Circ: Diamd. preorders: **2,998**
A: Yukito Kishiro **W:** Yukito Kishiro

AQUA KNIGHT PART 3 — Viz

1 ❑ ca. 2001 Cover: 3.50 **NM** value: **Cover or less**
Circ: Diamd. preorders: **2,903**
2 ❑ ca. 2001 Cover: 3.50 **NM** value: **Cover or less**
Circ: Diamd. preorders: **2,812**
3 ❑ ca. 2001 Cover: 3.50 **NM** value: **Cover or less**
Circ: Diamd. preorders: **2,686**
4 ❑ ca. 2001 Cover: 3.50 **NM** value: **Cover or less**
Circ: Diamd. preorders: **2,645**
5 ❑ ca. 2001 Cover: 3.50 **NM** value: **Cover or less**
Circ: Diamd. preorders: **2,782**

AQUAMAN (1ST SERIES) — DC

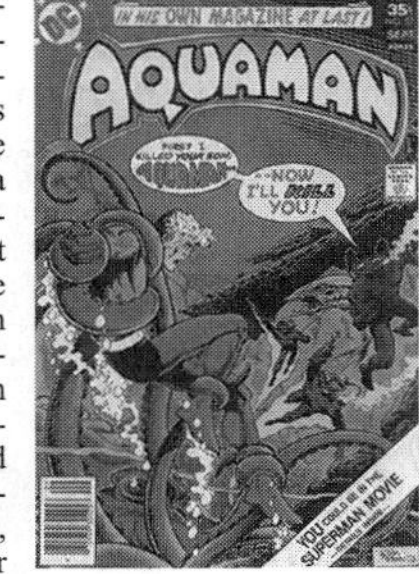

Aquaman, half-human, half-Atlantean, can communicate telepathically with sea animals and, to a limited extent, with humans. He has physically evolved to manage the greater pressures of the sea, has a strength far beyond that of Earth-bound humans, and can swim at more than 100 miles an hour. These super-powers, however, give him no advantage whatsoever in his personal life, which weaves through the series, giving the character motivation and personality. By the end of the series, Aquaman has discovered his Atlantean heritage, loved, wed, and suffered the brutal murder of his beloved son. He has also matched wits and might with some of the cleverest arch-villains in comics.

Long a guest-star in various DC titles, in 1962 Aquaman finally got this, his first solo series. Successful at first, its popularity faded, and the series went on hiatus in 1971. It was brought back for a few final issues in 1977.

1 ❑ Feb 1962 Cover: 0.12 **NM** value: **600.00**
• **CGC:** 43 graded, best 9.4
★ 1st Appearance of Quisp.
2 ❑ Apr 1962 Cover: 0.12 **NM** value: **275.00**
• **CGC:** 5 graded, best 9.2
3 ❑ Jun 1962 Cover: 0.12 **NM** value: **150.00**
• **CGC:** 13 graded, best 9.6
4 ❑ Aug 1962 Cover: 0.12 **NM** value: **150.00**
• **CGC:** 6 graded, best 9.4
5 ❑ Oct 1962 Cover: 0.12 **NM** value: **150.00**
• **CGC:** 7 graded, best 9.2
6 ❑ Dec 1962 Cover: 0.12 **NM** value: **90.00**
• **CGC:** 3 graded, best 9.4
7 ❑ Feb 1963 Cover: 0.12 **NM** value: **90.00**
• **CGC:** 3 graded, best 9.4
8 ❑ Apr 1963 Cover: 0.12 **NM** value: **90.00**
• **CGC:** 1 graded, best 8.0
9 ❑ Jun 1963 Cover: 0.12 **NM** value: **90.00**
• **CGC:** 3 graded, best 9.0
10 ❑ Aug 1963 Cover: 0.12 **NM** value: **90.00**
• **CGC:** 2 graded, best 9.0
11 ❑ Oct 1963 Cover: 0.12 **NM** value: **75.00**
• **CGC:** 1 graded, best 9.2
★ 1st Appearance of Mera.
12 ❑ Dec 1963 Cover: 0.12 **NM** value: **65.00**
• **CGC:** 2 graded, best 8.5
13 ❑ Feb 1964 Cover: 0.12 **NM** value: **65.00**
Circ: Statement: **226,578** • **CGC:** 1 graded, best 9.2
14 ❑ Apr 1964 Cover: 0.12 **NM** value: **65.00**
Circ: Statement: **226,578** • **CGC:** 1 graded, best 7.5
• Has 1963 Statement, filed 10/1/63; no circ figures published
15 ❑ Jun 1964 Cover: 0.12 **NM** value: **65.00**
Circ: Statement: **226,578** • **CGC:** 3 graded, best 9.2
16 ❑ Aug 1964 Cover: 0.12 **NM** value: **65.00**
Circ: Statement: **226,578**
17 ❑ Oct 1964 Cover: 0.12 **NM** value: **65.00**
Circ: Statement: **226,578** • **CGC:** 2 graded, best 9.2
18 ❑ Dec 1964 Cover: 0.12 **NM** value: **65.00**
Circ: Statement: **226,578** • **CGC:** 2 graded, best 8.5
• Aquaman marries Mera ★ Appearance of Justice League of America.
19 ❑ Feb 1965 Cover: 0.12 **NM** value: **65.00**
Circ: Statement: **247,140** • **CGC:** 5 graded, best 9.2
20 ❑ Apr 1965 Cover: 0.12 **NM** value: **65.00**
Circ: Statement: **247,140** • **CGC:** 2 graded, best 9.0
• Has 1964 Statement, filed 10/1/64; avg print run 337,000; avg sales 226,000; avg subs 578; avg total paid 226,578; samples 387; max existent 226,965; 33% of run returned
21 ❑ Jun 1965 Cover: 0.12 **NM** value: **45.00**
Circ: Statement: **247,140** • **CGC:** 2 graded, best 9.2
★ 1st Appearance of Fisherman.
22 ❑ Aug 1965 Cover: 0.12 **NM** value: **45.00**
Circ: Statement: **247,140** • **CGC:** 2 graded, best 9.4
23 ❑ Oct 1965 Cover: 0.12 **NM** value: **45.00**
Circ: Statement: **247,140** • **CGC:** 2 graded, best 9.0
• Birth of Aquababy
24 ❑ Dec 1965 Cover: 0.12 **NM** value: **45.00**
Circ: Statement: **247,140** • **CGC:** 1 graded, best 8.5
25 ❑ Feb 1966 Cover: 0.12 **NM** value: **45.00**
Circ: Statement: **228,403** • **CGC:** 1 graded, best 9.2
26 ❑ Apr 1966 Cover: 0.12 **NM** value: **45.00**
Circ: Statement: **228,403** • **CGC:** 2 graded, best 9.2
• Has 1965 Statement, filed 10/1/65; avg print run 372,000; avg sales 246,000; avg subs 1,140; avg total paid 247,140; samples 142; max existent 247,282; 34% of run returned
27 ❑ Jun 1966 Cover: 0.12 **NM** value: **45.00**
Circ: Statement: **228,403** • **CGC:** 2 graded, best 7.5
28 ❑ Aug 1966 Cover: 0.12 **NM** value: **45.00**
Circ: Statement: **228,403** • **CGC:** 3 graded, best 9.2
29 ❑ Oct 1966 Cover: 0.12 **NM** value: **45.00**
Circ: Statement: **228,403** • **CGC:** 4 graded, best 9.4
★ 1st Appearance of Ocean Master.
30 ❑ Dec 1966 Cover: 0.12 **NM** value: **45.00**
Circ: Statement: **228,403** • **CGC:** 4 graded, best 9.4
31 ❑ Feb 1967 Cover: 0.12 **NM** value: **35.00**
Circ: Statement: **234,200** • **CGC:** 3 graded, best 9.6
32 ❑ Apr 1967 Cover: 0.12 **NM** value: **35.00**
Circ: Statement: **234,200** • **CGC:** 1 graded, best 6.5
• Has 1966 Statement, filed 10/1/66; avg print run 376,000; avg sales 227,000; avg subs 1,403; avg total paid 228,403; max existent 228,403; 0% of run returned
33 ❑ Jun 1967 Cover: 0.12 **NM** value: **60.00**
Circ: Statement: **234,200** • **CGC:** 1 graded, best 9.2
★ 1st Appearance of Aqua-Girl.
34 ❑ Aug 1967 Cover: 0.12 **NM** value: **30.00**
Circ: Statement: **234,200** • **CGC:** 2 graded, best 9.2
35 ❑ Oct 1967 Cover: 0.12 **NM** value: **30.00**
Circ: Statement: **234,200**
★ 1st Appearance of Black Manta.
36 ❑ Dec 1967 Cover: 0.12 **NM** value: **30.00**
Circ: Statement: **234,200**
37 ❑ Feb 1968 Cover: 0.12 **NM** value: **30.00**
Circ: Statement: **184,650** • **CGC:** 4 graded, best 9.6
38 ❑ Apr 1968 Cover: 0.12 **NM** value: **30.00**
Circ: Statement: **184,650** • **CGC:** 3 graded, best 9.2
39 ❑ Jun 1968 Cover: 0.12 **NM** value: **30.00**
Circ: Statement: **184,650** • **CGC:** 3 graded, best 9.4
40 ❑ Aug 1968 Cover: 0.12 **NM** value: **30.00**
Circ: Statement: **184,650** • **CGC:** 4 graded, best 9.6
41 ❑ Oct 1968 Cover: 0.12 **NM** value: **20.00**
Circ: Statement: **184,650** • **CGC:** 2 graded, best 9.4
42 ❑ Dec 1968 Cover: 0.12 **NM** value: **20.00**
Circ: Statement: **184,650** • **CGC:** 5 graded, best 9.0
43 ❑ Feb 1969 Cover: 0.12 **NM** value: **20.00**
Circ: Statement: **156,307** • **CGC:** 3 graded, best 9.2
44 ❑ Apr 1969 Cover: 0.12 **NM** value: **20.00**
Circ: Statement: **156,307** • **CGC:** 2 graded, best 9.6
45 ❑ Jun 1969 Cover: 0.12 **NM** value: **20.00**
Circ: Statement: **156,307** • **CGC:** 5 graded, best 9.4
46 ❑ Aug 1969 Cover: 0.15 **NM** value: **20.00**
Circ: Statement: **156,307** • **CGC:** 3 graded, best 9.6
47 ❑ Oct 1969 Cover: 0.15 **NM** value: **20.00**
Circ: Statement: **156,307** • **CGC:** 2 graded, best 7.5
48 ❑ Dec 1969 Cover: 0.15 **NM** value: **25.00**
Circ: Statement: **156,307** • **CGC:** 1 graded, best 9.0
A: Jim Aparo ★ Origin of Aquaman.
49 ❑ Feb 1970 Cover: 0.15 **NM** value: **12.00**
Circ: Statement: **141,210** • **CGC:** 2 graded, best 9.2
A: Jim Aparo
50 ❑ Apr 1970 Cover: 0.15 **NM** value: **30.00**
Circ: Statement: **141,210** • **CGC:** 4 graded, best 9.4
• Has 1969 Statement, filed 10/1/69; avg print run 298,000; avg sales 156,000; avg subs 307; avg total paid 156,307; samples 346; max existent 156,653; 47% of run returned **A:** Neal Adams ★ Appearance of Deadman.
51 ❑ Jun 1970 Cover: 0.15 **NM** value: **30.00**
Circ: Statement: **141,210** • **CGC:** 2 graded, best 9.4
A: Neal Adams ★ Appearance of Deadman.
52 ❑ Aug 1970 Cover: 0.15 **NM** value: **30.00**
Circ: Statement: **141,210** • **CGC:** 4 graded, best 9.4
A: Neal Adams ★ Appearance of Deadman.
53 ❑ Oct 1970 Cover: 0.15 **NM** value: **7.00**
Circ: Statement: **141,210**
A: Jim Aparo
54 ❑ Dec 1970 Cover: 0.15 **NM** value: **7.00**
Circ: Statement: **141,210** • **CGC:** 1 graded, best 9.2
A: Jim Aparo
55 ❑ Feb 1971 Cover: 0.15 **NM** value: **7.00**
A: Jim Aparo
56 ❑ Apr 1971 Cover: 0.15 **NM** value: **7.00**
• **CGC:** 1 graded, best 6.5
📖 A Life For A Life **A:** Jim Aparo **W:** David Michelinie ★ Origin of Crusader. ★ 1st Appearance of Crusader.
57 ❑ Aug 1977 Cover: 0.35 **NM** value: **5.00**
A: Jim Aparo
58 ❑ Oct 1977 Cover: 0.35 **NM** value: **5.00**
A: Jim Aparo ★ Origin of Aquaman.
59 ❑ Dec 1977 Cover: 0.35 **NM** value: **5.00**
60 ❑ Feb 1978 Cover: 0.35 **NM** value: **5.00**
61 ❑ Apr 1978 Cover: 0.35 **NM** value: **5.00**
• **CGC:** 1 graded, best 9.4
62 ❑ Jun 1978 Cover: 0.35 **NM** value: **5.00**
63 ❑ Sep 1978 Cover: 0.35 **NM** value: **5.00**
• **CGC:** 1 graded, best 9.2
final issue.

AQUAMAN (2ND SERIES) — DC

Some nine years after the conclusion of the first Aquaman solo series, the Atlantean returned in 1986 for this four-issue mini-series. This title finds Aquaman busy on all fronts: trying to defend his adopted home of Venice, Fla., against the villains who attack it simply to get at Aquaman; battling Ocean Master, Aquaman's half-brother and mortal enemy; preventing war between the peoples of Atlantis and the surface world; and reclaiming the seal of Atlantis from a rebellious faction in Thierna Na Oge.

To accomplish his Atlantean missions, it becomes necessary for Aquaman to move unnoticed among the Atlanteans. To this end, he abandons his traditional costume in #1 for a camouflage dark blue outfit which does not mark him as a super-hero. (The sight of a man swimming underwater at high speed is nothing extraordinary to the Atlanteans.) This series, although not wildly successful, probably helped pave the way for later Aquaman revivals.

1 ❑ Feb 1986 Cover: 0.75 **NM** value: **4.00**
Circ: CapCity orders: **13,300**
• New costume **A:** Craig Hamilton **W:** Neal Pozner
2 ❑ Mar 1986 Cover: 0.75 **NM** value: **3.00**
Circ: CapCity orders: **11,450**
3 ❑ Apr 1986 Cover: 0.75 **NM** value: **3.00**
Circ: CapCity orders: **11,950**
4 ❑ May 1986 Cover: 0.75 **NM** value: **3.00**
Circ: CapCity orders: **14,400**
SE 1❑ Jun 1988 Cover: 1.50 **NM** value: **3.00**

AQUAMAN (3RD SERIES) — DC

1 ❑ Jun 1989 Cover: 1.00 **NM** value: **Cover or less**
Circ: CapCity orders: **25,100** • **CGC:** 5 graded, best 9.8
📖 Aquarium **A:** Keith Giffen; Curt Swan **W:** Robert Loren Flemming
2 ❑ Jul 1989 Cover: 1.00 **NM** value: **Cover or less**
Circ: CapCity orders: **19,450**
W: Robert Loren Flemming
3 ❑ Aug 1989 Cover: 1.00 **NM** value: **Cover or less**
Circ: CapCity orders: **18,350**
W: Robert Loren Flemming
4 ❑ Sep 1989 Cover: 1.00 **NM** value: **Cover or less**
Circ: CapCity orders: **18,050**
📖 The Tide Of Battle **A:** Curt Swan **W:** Robert Loren Flemming
5 ❑ Oct 1989 Cover: 1.00 **NM** value: **Cover or less**
Circ: CapCity orders: **17,450**
W: Robert Loren Flemming
SE 1❑ Apr 1989 Cover: 2.00 **NM** value: **Cover or less**
Circ: CapCity orders: **18,850**
• Legend of Aquaman **A:** Curt Swan

CGC-graded: Multiply prices above by **33 for 9.9 M • 16 for 9.8 NM/M • 7 for 9.6 NM+ • 5 for 9.4 NM • 2.5 for 9.2 NM- • 1.5 for 9.0 VF/NM**

AQUAMAN (4TH SERIES) DC

1 ❑ Dec 1991 Cover: 1.00 **NM** value: **Cover or less**
Circ: CapCity orders: **65,800**
🕮 A Small World Incident **A:** Ken Hooper **W:** Shaun McLaughlin

2 ❑ Jan 1992 Cover: 1.00 **NM** value: **Cover or less**
Circ: CapCity orders: **35,800**

3 ❑ Feb 1992 Cover: 1.00 **NM** value: **Cover or less**
Circ: CapCity orders: **28,000**

4 ❑ Mar 1992 Cover: 1.00 **NM** value: **Cover or less**
Circ: CapCity orders: **23,400**

5 ❑ Apr 1992 Cover: 1.00 **NM** value: **Cover or less**
Circ: CapCity orders: **20,400**

6 ❑ May 1992 Cover: 1.25 **NM** value: **Cover or less**
Circ: CapCity orders: **18,850**

7 ❑ Jun 1992 Cover: 1.25 **NM** value: **Cover or less**
Circ: CapCity orders: **18,700**
🕮 What Matters Most **A:** Ken Hooper **W:** Shaun McLaughlin

8 ❑ Jul 1992 Cover: 1.25 **NM** value: **Cover or less**
🕮 Demons in Thought & Deed ★ Appearance of Batman. ★ Versus Nicodemus.

9 ❑ Aug 1992 Cover: 1.25 **NM** value: **Cover or less**
Circ: CapCity orders: **17,600**

10 ❑ Sep 1992 Cover: 1.25 **NM** value: **Cover or less**
Circ: CapCity orders: **15,550**

11 ❑ Oct 1992 Cover: 1.25 **NM** value: **Cover or less**
Circ: CapCity orders: **15,050**

12 ❑ Nov 1992 Cover: 1.25 **NM** value: **Cover or less**
Circ: CapCity orders: **13,950**

13 ❑ Dec 1992 Cover: 1.25 **NM** value: **Cover or less**
Circ: CapCity orders: **12,750**
final issue. **A:** Christopher Schenck **W:** Shaun McLaughlin ★ Appearance of Scavanger.

AQUAMAN (5TH SERIES) DC

Aquaman is one of DC's oldest and most famous super-heroes. Nevertheless, his solo titles have had notoriously little success. This 1994 series hoped to change all that, following, as it did, on the heels of the acclaimed Aquaman: Time and Tide mini-series.

Writer Peter David makes big changes to Aquaman in this new series. The most evident is the loss of Aquaman's left arm in a battle against arch-villain Black Manta. Still feverish from the resulting sickness, Aquaman replaces it with a harpoon. His thinking is that he needs a symbol — something to both tell of his watery heritage and to show surface dwellers how their own weapons can be used against them. David also revitalized Aquaman by dispensing with much of his previous angst and indecisiveness. The result is an interesting — but very different — Aquaman.

0 ❑ Oct 1994 Cover: 1.50 **NM** value: **3.50**
Circ: CapCity orders: **23,525 • CGC:** 2 graded, best 9.6
• Aquaman gets harpoon for arm **W:** Peter David

1 ❑ Aug 1994 Cover: 1.50 **NM** value: **3.50**
Circ: CapCity orders: **26,650 • CGC:** 2 graded, best 9.4
W: Peter David

2 ❑ Sep 1994 Cover: 1.50 **NM** value: **3.50**
Circ: CapCity orders: **18,000 • CGC:** 3 graded, best 9.2
🕮 Single Wet Female • Aquaman loses hand **W:** Peter David ★ Versus Charybdis.

3 ❑ Nov 1994 Cover: 1.50 **NM** value: **2.00**
Circ: CapCity orders: **18,450**
🕮 Arthur Goes Hawaiian **W:** Peter David ★ Versus Superboy.

4 ❑ Dec 1994 Cover: 1.50 **NM** value: **2.00**
Circ: CapCity orders: **19,350**
🕮 A Porpoise in Life **A:** Marty Egeland **W:** Peter David ★ Appearance of Lobo. ★ Versus Lobo.

5 ❑ Jan 1995 Cover: 1.50 **NM** value: **2.00**
Circ: CapCity orders: **20,000**
W: Peter David

6 ❑ Feb 1995 Cover: 1.50 **NM** value: **2.00**
Circ: CapCity orders: **19,700**
W: Peter David

7 ❑ Mar 1995 Cover: 1.50 **NM** value: **2.00**
Circ: CapCity orders: **19,700**
W: Peter David

8 ❑ Apr 1995 Cover: 1.50 **NM** value: **2.00**
Circ: CapCity orders: **17,650**
W: Peter David

9 ❑ Jun 1995 Cover: 1.75 **NM** value: **Cover or less**
Circ: CapCity orders: **15,775**
W: Peter David

10 ❑ Jul 1995 Cover: 1.75 **NM** value: **Cover or less**
Circ: CapCity orders: **16,125**
W: Peter David

11 ❑ Aug 1995 Cover: 1.75 **NM** value: **Cover or less**
Circ: CapCity orders: **16,150**
W: Peter David

12 ❑ Sep 1995 Cover: 1.75 **NM** value: **Cover or less**
Circ: CapCity orders: **14,850**
• Mera returns **W:** Peter David

13 ❑ Oct 1995 Cover: 1.75 **NM** value: **Cover or less**
Circ: CapCity orders: **12,675**
W: Peter David

14 ❑ Nov 1995 Cover: 1.75 **NM** value: **Cover or less**
🕮 Underworld Unleashed • "Underworld Unleashed" **W:** Peter David

15 ❑ Dec 1995 Cover: 1.75 **NM** value: **Cover or less**
W: Peter David

16 ❑ Jan 1996 Cover: 1.75 **NM** value: **Cover or less**
W: Peter David ★ Versus Justice League.

17 ❑ Feb 1996 Cover: 1.75 **NM** value: **Cover or less**
🕮 Numbers **A:** Jim Calafiore **W:** Peter David

18 ❑ Mar 1996 Cover: 1.75 **NM** value: **Cover or less**
🕮 Biblical Sense **A:** Marty Egeland **W:** Peter David ★ Origin of Dolphin.

19 ❑ Apr 1996 Cover: 1.75 **NM** value: **Cover or less**
🕮 Brother's Keeper • Aqualad returns **A:** Marty Egeland **W:** Peter David

20 ❑ May 1996 Cover: 1.75 **NM** value: **Cover or less**
W: Peter David

21 ❑ Jun 1996 Cover: 1.75 **NM** value: **Cover or less**
W: Peter David

22 ❑ Jul 1996 Cover: 1.75 **NM** value: **Cover or less**
W: Peter David

23 ❑ Aug 1996 Cover: 1.75 **NM** value: **Cover or less**
W: Peter David ★ Appearance of Sea Devils, Power Girl, Tsunami, Arion.

24 ❑ Sep 1996 Cover: 1.75 **NM** value: **Cover or less**
W: Peter David

25 ❑ Oct 1996 Cover: 1.75 **NM** value: **Cover or less**
🕮 Betwixt and Between **A:** Marty Egeland **W:** Peter David

26 ❑ Nov 1996 Cover: 1.75 **NM** value: **Cover or less**
Circ: Diamd. preorders: **39,351**
🕮 Twilight • "Final Night" **A:** Jim Calafiore **W:** Peter David

27 ❑ Dec 1996 Cover: 1.75 **NM** value: **Cover or less**
Circ: Direct Market orders: **34,153**
🕮 The Rising Sun • Aquaman declares war on Japan **A:** Marty Egeland **W:** Peter David

28 ❑ Jan 1997 Cover: 1.75 **NM** value: **Cover or less**
Circ: Direct Market orders: **33,929**
🕮 Setting Sun **A:** Jim Calafiore **W:** Peter David ★ Appearance of Martian Manhunter.

29 ❑ Feb 1997 Cover: 1.75 **NM** value: **Cover or less**
Circ: Diamd. preorders: **32,565**
W: Peter David ★ Versus Black Manta.

30 ❑ Mar 1997 Cover: 1.75 **NM** value: **Cover or less**
Circ: Diamd. preorders: **31,515**
🕮 In Darkness He Waits **A:** Marty Egeland **W:** Peter David

31 ❑ Apr 1997 Cover: 1.75 **NM** value: **Cover or less**
Circ: Diamd. preorders: **30,386**
W: Peter David

32 ❑ May 1997 Cover: 1.75 **NM** value: **Cover or less**
Circ: Diamd. preorders: **30,303**
W: Peter David ★ Appearance of Swamp Thing.

33 ❑ Jun 1997 Cover: 1.75 **NM** value: **Cover or less**
Circ: Diamd. preorders: **30,995**
W: Peter David

34 ❑ Jul 1997 Cover: 1.75 **NM** value: **Cover or less**
Circ: Diamd. preorders: **30,733**
W: Peter David ★ Versus Triton.

35 ❑ Aug 1997 Cover: 1.75 **NM** value: **Cover or less**
Circ: Diamd. preorders: **30,670**
• Aquaman blind **W:** Peter David ★ Appearance of Animal Man. ★ Versus Gamesman.

36 ❑ Sep 1997 Cover: 1.75 **NM** value: **Cover or less**
Circ: Diamd. preorders: **30,066**
W: Peter David

37 ❑ Oct 1997 Cover: 1.75 **NM** value: **Cover or less**
Circ: Diamd. preorders: **32,745**
• "Genesis" **W:** Peter David ★ Versus Parademons.

38 ❑ Nov 1997 Cover: 1.75 **NM** value: **Cover or less**
Circ: Diamd. preorders: **30,028**
🕮 Open for Business • Poseidonis becomes a tourist attraction **A:** Jim Calafiore **W:** Peter David

39 ❑ Dec 1997 Cover: 1.95 **NM** value: **2.00**
Circ: Diamd. preorders: **30,269**
Face cover. 🕮 Bad Relations **A:** Jim Calafiore **W:** Peter David ★ Appearance of Neptune Perkins.

40 ❑ Jan 1998 Cover: 1.95 **NM** value: **2.00**
Circ: Diamd. preorders: **29,892**
W: Peter David ★ Versus Doctor Polaris.

41 ❑ Feb 1998 Cover: 1.95 **NM** value: **2.00**
Circ: Diamd. preorders: **38,835**
W: Peter David ★ Appearance of Maxima.

42 ❑ Mar 1998 Cover: 1.95 **NM** value: **2.00**
Circ: Diamd. preorders: **28,144**
🕮 Necessary Poisons **A:** Jim Calafiore **W:** Jim Calafiore; Peter David ★ Versus Sea Wolf.

43 ❑ Apr 1998 Cover: 1.95 **NM** value: **2.00**
Circ: Diamd. preorders: **31,165**
• "Millennium Giants"

44 ❑ May 1998 Cover: 1.95 **NM** value: **2.00**
Circ: Diamd. preorders: **27,902**
★ Appearance of Golden Age Flash, Sentinel.

45 ❑ Jun 1998 Cover: 1.95 **NM** value: **2.00**
Circ: Diamd. preorders: **28,186**
• Destruction of Poseidonis

46 ❑ Jul 1998 Cover: 1.95 **NM** value: **2.00**
Circ: Diamd. preorders: **27,409**

47 ❑ Aug 1998 Cover: 1.95 **NM** value: **2.00**
Circ: Diamd. preorders: **26,896**

48 ❑ Sep 1998 Cover: 1.99 **NM** value: **2.00**
Circ: Diamd. preorders: **25,641**

49 ❑ Oct 1998 Cover: 1.99 **NM** value: **2.00**
Circ: Diamd. preorders: **25,004**

50 ❑ Dec 1998 Cover: 1.99 **NM** value: **2.00**
Circ: Diamd. preorders: **30,201**
A: Erik Larsen

51 ❑ Jan 1999 Cover: 1.99 **NM** value: **2.00**
Circ: Diamd. preorders: **26,524**
A: Eric Battle; Erik Larsen **W:** Erik Larsen ★ Appearance of King Noble.

52 ❑ Feb 1999 Cover: 1.99 **NM** value: **2.00**
Circ: Diamd. preorders: **25,503**
A: Eric Battle; Erik Larsen; Jim Aparo; Bill Sienkiewicz(inks) **W:** Erik Larsen ★ Appearance of Fire Trolls, Mera, Lava Lord, Noble.

53 ❑ Mar 1999 Cover: 1.99 **NM** value: **2.00**
Circ: Diamd. preorders: **26,229**
A: Eric Battle; Erik Larsen **W:** Erik Larsen ★ Appearance of Superman, Shrapnel.

54 ❑ Apr 1999 Cover: 1.99 **NM** value: **2.00**
Circ: Diamd. preorders: **23,474**
A: Eric Battle; Erik Larsen **W:** Erik Larsen ★ Appearance of Shiva the Mermaid, Landlovers, Blubber, Lagoon Boy.

55 ❑ May 1999 Cover: 1.99 **NM** value: **2.00**
Circ: Diamd. preorders: **22,858**
🕮 Desperate Times **A:** Mike Miller; Erik Larsen **W:** Chris Eliopoulos; Erik Larsen

56 ❑ Jun 1999 Cover: 1.99 **NM** value: **2.00**
Circ: Diamd. preorders: **23,147**
🕮 Madman Across the Water **A:** Eric Battle; Erik Larsen **W:** Chris Eliopoulos; Erik Larsen

57 ❑ Jul 1999 Cover: 1.99 **NM** value: **2.00**
Circ: Diamd. preorders: **21,952**
🕮 Piranhaman Bites! **A:** Eric Battle; Erik Larsen **W:** Chris Eliopoulos; Erik Larsen

58 ❑ Aug 1999 Cover: 1.99 **NM** value: **2.00**
Circ: Diamd. preorders: **21,290**
🕮 Watery Crave **A:** Erik Larsen; Andy Smith **W:** Erik Larsen; Gary Carlson

59 ❑ Sep 1999 Cover: 1.99 **NM** value: **2.00**
Circ: Diamd. preorders: **20,794**
🕮 Drugs of Choice **A:** Eric Battle; Erik Larsen **W:** Erik Larsen; Gary Carlson

60 ❑ Oct 1999 Cover: 1.99 **NM** value: **2.00**
Circ: Diamd. preorders: **20,630**
🕮 Marriage Vows • Wedding of Tempest and Dolphin **A:** Eric Battle; Erik Larsen **W:** Erik Larsen; Gary Carlson

61 ❑ Nov 1999 Cover: 1.99 **NM** value: **2.00**
Circ: Diamd. preorders: **22,403**

62 ❑ Dec 1999 Cover: 1.99 **NM** value: **2.00**
Circ: Diamd. preorders: **19,792**
🕮 Resolutions **A:** Eric Battle **W:** Erik Larsen; Gary Carlson

63 ❑ Jan 2000 Cover: 1.99 **NM** value: **2.00**
Circ: Diamd. preorders: **20,831**
🕮 King Arthur **A:** Steve Epting **W:** Dan Jurgens

64 ❑ Feb 2000 Cover: 1.99 **NM** value: **2.00**
Circ: Diamd. preorders: **20,051**

65 ❑ Mar 2000 Cover: 1.99 **NM** value: **2.00**
Circ: Diamd. preorders: **18,607**

66 ❑ Apr 2000 Cover: 1.99 **NM** value: **2.00**
Circ: Diamd. preorders: **18,103**
🕮 Common Battleground **A:** Paul Ryan **W:** Dan Jurgens

67 ❑ May 2000 Cover: 1.99 **NM** value: **2.00**
Circ: Diamd. preorders: **18,013**
🕮 Clash of Kings **A:** Steve Epting **W:** Dan Jurgens

68 ❑ Jun 2000 Cover: 1.99 **NM** value: **2.00**
Circ: Diamd. preorders: **17,896**
A: Steve Epting **W:** Dan Jurgens

69 ❑ Jul 2000 Cover: 1.99 **NM** value: **2.00**
Circ: Diamd. preorders: **18,029**
A: Steve Epting **W:** Dan Jurgens

70 ❑ Aug 2000 Cover: 1.99 **NM** value: **2.00**
Circ: Diamd. preorders: **18,105**
🕮 Unifaction by Division **A:** Steve Epting **W:** Dan Jurgens

71 ❑ Sep 2000 Cover: 2.50 **NM** value: **Cover or less**
Circ: Diamd. preorders: **18,148**
🕮 To Enter the Lost World… **A:** Steve Epting **W:** Dan Jurgens ★ Appearance of Warlord.

72 ❑ Oct 2000 Cover: 2.50 **NM** value: **Cover or less**
Circ: Diamd. preorders: **16,875**
🕮 World's Apart **A:** Steve Epting; Norm Rapmund **W:** Dan Jurgens

73 ❑ Nov 2000 Cover: 2.50 **NM** value: **Cover or less**
Circ: Diamd. preorders: **16,793**
🕮 Power Game **A:** Steve Epting **W:** Dan Jurgens

74 ❑ Dec 2000 Cover: 2.50 **NM** value: **Cover or less**
Circ: Diamd. preorders: **16,392**
🕮 From the Core **A:** Steve Epting **W:** Dan Jurgens

75 ❑ Jan 2001 Cover: 2.50 **NM** value: **Cover or less**
Circ: Diamd. preorders: **16,871**
🕮 No Future **A:** Steve Epting; Norm Rapmund **W:** Dan Jurgens

1000000❑Nov 1998 Cover: 1.99 **NM** value: **2.00**
Circ: Diamd. preorders: **33,689**
🕮 The Banks and Shoals of Time **A:** Andy Lanning **W:** Dan Abnett

Anl 1❑ca. 1995 Cover: 3.50 **NM** value: **Cover or less**
Circ: CapCity orders: **14,000**
★ Appearance of Wonder Woman, Superman,.

Anl 2❑ca. 1996 Cover: 2.95 **NM** value: **Cover or less**
• Legends of the Dead Earth

Anl 3❑Jul 1997 Cover: 3.95 **NM** value: **Cover or less**
Circ: Diamd. preorders: **27,799**
• Pulp Heroes

Anl 4❑Sep 1998 Cover: 2.95 **NM** value: **Cover or less**
Circ: Diamd. preorders: **22,713**
• Ghosts**Anl 5**❑Sep 1999Cover: 2.95**NM** value: **Cover or less**
Circ: Diamd. preorders: **24,960**
🕮 20,000 Apes under the Sea • JLApe **A:** Mark D. Bright **W:** John Ostrander

AQUAMAN SECRET FILES DC

1 ❑ Dec 1998 Cover: 4.95 **NM** value: **Cover or less**
Circ: Diamd. preorders: **20,400**
🕮 Left for Dead; Aquacave Schematic; The Myth of Aquaman; Map of Poseidonis; Tempest Interview; Timeline; Aquaman; Mera; Tempest; Black Manta; Ocean Master; Noble; The Landlovers; Supporting Cast; Molten Man King **A:** Erik Larsen **W:** Erik Larsen; Steve Vance; Scott Beatty ★ Origin of Aquaman. ★ Appearance of Charybdis.

Other grades: Multiply prices above by **1.5 for Mint • 2/3 for Very Fine • 1/3 for Fine • 1/5 for Very Good • 1/8 for Good**

AQUAMAN: TIME AND TIDE — DC

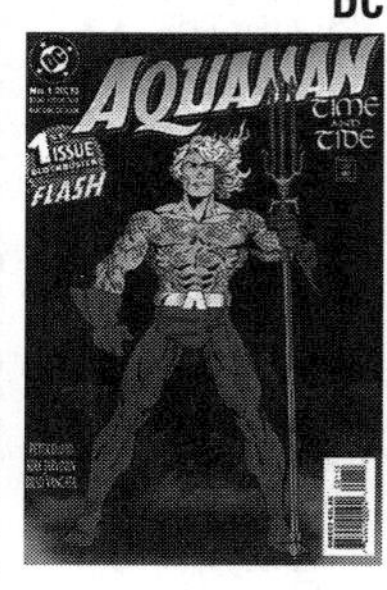

The four-issue mini-series recounts the highlights of Aquaman's life, including his hazy Atlantean origins and his first encounter with the air-breathing super-heroes.

Writer Peter David is at his humorous best here, keeping the story lively while peppering it with funny in-jokes and comedic episodes.

For example, everyone knows that Aquaman can talk to fish — but did anyone ever think about how dull the conversation could get? Even readers who have minimal interest in stories set beneath the waves will find a variety of entertainment in Aquaman: Time and Tide.

1 ❑ Dec 1993 Cover: 1.50 **NM** value: **2.50**
Circ: CapCity orders: **27,700** • **CGC:** 1 graded, best 9.4
🕮 Flash Back **A:** Kirk Jarvinen **W:** Peter David ★ Origin of Aquaman.

2 ❑ Jan 1994 Cover: 1.50 **NM** value: **2.50**
Circ: CapCity orders: **19,250**
A: Kirk Jarvinen **W:** Peter David

3 ❑ Feb 1994 Cover: 1.50 **NM** value: **2.50**
Circ: CapCity orders: **17,000**
🕮 Snowball In Hell **A:** Kirk Jarvinen **W:** Peter David

4 ❑ Mar 1994 Cover: 1.50 **NM** value: **2.50**
Circ: CapCity orders: **16,250**
🕮 King Of The Sea **A:** Kirk Jarvinen **W:** Peter David ★ Origin of Ocean Master.

Bk 1❑ Cover: 9.95 **NM** value: **Cover or less**
• Collects Aquaman: Time and Tide #1-4 **A:** Kirk Jarvinen **W:** Peter David

AQUARIUM — CPM Manga

1/A ❑ Apr 2000, b&w Cover: 2.95 **NM** value: **Cover or less**
Circ: Diamd. preorders: **3,066**
wraparound cover. **A:** Tomoko Taniguchi **C:** Tomoko Taniguchi **W:** Tomoko Taniguchi

1/B ❑ Apr 2000, b&w Cover: 2.95 **NM** value: **Cover or less**
alternate wraparound cover.

2 ❑ ca. 2000 Cover: 2.95 **NM** value: **Cover or less**
Circ: Diamd. preorders: **2,513**

3 ❑ ca. 2000 Cover: 2.95 **NM** value: **Cover or less**
Circ: Diamd. preorders: **2,254**

4 ❑ ca. 2000 Cover: 2.95 **NM** value: **Cover or less**
Circ: Diamd. preorders: **2,115**

ARABIAN NIGHTS ON THE WORLD OF MAGIC: THE GATHERING — Acclaim / Armada

1 ❑ Dec 1995 Cover: 2.50 **NM** value: **Cover or less**
Circ: CapCity orders: **13,300**
🕮 A Time to Gather **A:** Alex Maleev **W:** Jeof Vita; Susan Wright

2 ❑ Cover: 2.50 **NM** value: **Cover or less**
Circ: CapCity orders: **8,400**
A: Alex Maleev **W:** Jeof Vita; Susan Wright

ARAGONÉS 3-D — 3-D Zone

1 ❑ Cover: 4.95 **NM** value: **Cover or less**
• paperback **A:** Sergio Aragonés **W:** Sergio Aragonés

ARAKNIS — Mushroom

1 ❑ 1995 Cover: 2.50 **NM** value: **Cover or less**
Circ: CapCity orders: **2,535**

2 ❑ ca. 1996 Cover: 2.50 **NM** value: **Cover or less**

3 ❑ ca. 1996 Cover: 2.50 **NM** value: **Cover or less**

4 ❑ ca. 1996 Cover: 2.50 **NM** value: **Cover or less**

5 ❑ ca. 1996 Cover: 2.50 **NM** value: **Cover or less**
Circ: Diamd. preorders: **5,762**

6 ❑ ca. 1996 Cover: 2.50 **NM** value: **Cover or less**
Circ: Diamd. preorders: **5,530**

ARAK SON OF THUNDER — DC

On a Viking expedition in ages past, Norsemen come across a sinking boat. The sole passenger turns out to be a boy with skin the color of fire. Taken in by the Vikings, the boy is called "Eric," which he interprets as "Arak." He soon grows into a man and proves a naturally skilled warrior.

Years later, Arak accompanies the Vikings on a raid in which the party is destroyed by mystical forces. Arak is the sole survivor. He then sets out on a path of adventure in an age of swords and sorcery, becoming a legend in an age of legends.

First appearing in Warlord #48, Arak is one of a number of epic fantasy titles tied into the Warlord world, including Arion, Lord of Atlantis, and Conqueror of the Barren Earth.

1 ❑ Sep 1981 Cover: 0.60 **NM** value: **1.00**
• **CGC:** 2 graded, best 9.8
🕮 The Sword And The Serpent **A:** Ernie Chan; Ernie Colon; Ernie Colon **W:** Roy Thomas ★ Origin of Arak. ★ 1st Appearance of Angelica.

2 ❑ Oct 1981 Cover: 0.60 **NM** value: **1.00**
A: Ernie Chan; Ernie Colon ★ 1st Appearance of Malagigi.

3 ❑ Nov 1981 Cover: 0.60 **NM** value: **1.00**
A: Ernie Chan; Ernie Colon ★ 1st Appearance of Valda.

4 ❑ Dec 1981 Cover: 0.60 **NM** value: **1.00**
A: Ernie Chan; Ernie Colon

5 ❑ Jan 1982 Cover: 0.60 **NM** value: **1.00**
A: Ernie Chan; Ernie Colon

6 ❑ Feb 1982 Cover: 0.60 **NM** value: **1.00**
A: Ernie Chan; Ernie Colon

7 ❑ Mar 1982 Cover: 0.60 **NM** value: **1.00**
8 ❑ Apr 1982 Cover: 0.60 **NM** value: **1.00**
9 ❑ May 1982 Cover: 0.60 **NM** value: **1.00**
10 ❑ Jun 1982 Cover: 0.60 **NM** value: **1.00**
11 ❑ Jul 1982 Cover: 0.60 **NM** value: **1.00**
12 ❑ Aug 1982 Cover: 0.60 **NM** value: **1.00**
13 ❑ Sep 1982 Cover: 0.60 **NM** value: **1.00**
14 ❑ Oct 1982 Cover: 0.60 **NM** value: **1.00**
15 ❑ Nov 1982 Cover: 0.60 **NM** value: **1.00**
16 ❑ Dec 1982 Cover: 0.60 **NM** value: **1.00**
17 ❑ Jan 1983 Cover: 0.60 **NM** value: **1.00**
18 ❑ Feb 1983 Cover: 0.60 **NM** value: **1.00**
19 ❑ Mar 1983 Cover: 0.60 **NM** value: **1.00**
20 ❑ Apr 1983 Cover: 0.60 **NM** value: **1.00**
★ Origin of Angelica.
21 ❑ May 1983 Cover: 0.60 **NM** value: **1.00**
22 ❑ Jun 1983 Cover: 0.60 **NM** value: **1.00**
23 ❑ Jul 1983 Cover: 0.60 **NM** value: **1.00**
24 ❑ Aug 1983 Cover: 1.00 **NM** value: **Cover or less**
25 ❑ Sep 1983 Cover: 0.60 **NM** value: **1.00**
26 ❑ Oct 1983 Cover: 0.60 **NM** value: **1.00**
27 ❑ Nov 1983 Cover: 0.60 **NM** value: **1.00**
28 ❑ Dec 1983 Cover: 0.75 **NM** value: **1.00**
29 ❑ Jan 1984 Cover: 0.75 **NM** value: **1.00**
30 ❑ Feb 1984 Cover: 0.75 **NM** value: **1.00**
31 ❑ Mar 1984 Cover: 0.75 **NM** value: **1.00**
32 ❑ Apr 1984 Cover: 0.75 **NM** value: **1.00**
33 ❑ May 1984 Cover: 0.75 **NM** value: **1.00**
34 ❑ Jun 1984 Cover: 0.75 **NM** value: **1.00**
35 ❑ Jul 1984 Cover: 0.75 **NM** value: **1.00**
36 ❑ Aug 1984 Cover: 0.75 **NM** value: **1.00**
37 ❑ Sep 1984 Cover: 0.75 **NM** value: **1.00**
38 ❑ Nov 1984 Cover: 0.75 **NM** value: **1.00**
39 ❑ Dec 1984 Cover: 0.75 **NM** value: **1.00**
40 ❑ Jan 1985 Cover: 0.75 **NM** value: **1.00**
41 ❑ Feb 1985 Cover: 0.75 **NM** value: **1.00**
42 ❑ Mar 1985 Cover: 0.75 **NM** value: **1.00**
43 ❑ Apr 1985 Cover: 0.75 **NM** value: **1.00**
44 ❑ May 1985 Cover: 0.75 **NM** value: **1.00**
Circ: CapCity orders: **3,650**
45 ❑ Jun 1985 Cover: 0.75 **NM** value: **1.00**
Circ: CapCity orders: **3,650**
46 ❑ Jul 1985 Cover: 0.75 **NM** value: **1.00**
Circ: CapCity orders: **3,700**
47 ❑ Aug 1985 Cover: 0.75 **NM** value: **1.00**
Circ: CapCity orders: **3,650**
48 ❑ Sep 1985 Cover: 0.75 **NM** value: **1.00**
Circ: CapCity orders: **3,650**
49 ❑ Oct 1985 Cover: 0.75 **NM** value: **1.00**
Circ: CapCity orders: **3,600**
50 ❑ Nov 1985 Cover: 1.25 **NM** value: **Cover or less**
Circ: CapCity orders: **4,250**
• Giant-size.
Anl 1❑ Cover: 1.25 **NM** value: **Cover or less**

ARAMIS — Comics Interview

1 ❑ Cover: 1.95 **NM** value: **Cover or less**
2 ❑ Cover: 1.95 **NM** value: **Cover or less**
3 ❑ Cover: 1.95 **NM** value: **Cover or less**

ARCADE — Print Mint

1 ❑ Mar 1975 Cover: 1.25 **NM** value: **10.00**
🕮 Cracking Jokes **A:** Justin Green; Gilbert Shelton; Art Spiegelman; Jay Lynch; Harrison Cady; Diane Noomin; Bill Griffith; George Kuchar; Jay Kinney; Kim Deitch; Michael McMillan; R. Crumb; S. Clay Wilson; Willy Murphy; Aldo Bobbo; Aline Kominsky **W:** Justin Green; Gilbert Shelton; Art Spiegelman; Jay Lynch; Harrison Cady; Diane Noomin; Bill Griffith; George Kuchar; Jay Kinney; Kim Deitch; Michael McMillan; R. Crumb; Willy Murphy; Aldo Bobbo; Aline Kominsky; Will Fowler

2 ❑ Jun 1975 Cover: 1.25 **NM** value: **8.00**

3 ❑ Sep 1975 Cover: 1.25 **NM** value: **8.00**
🕮 That's Life; New York Journal; In Xanadu; Mickey Rat; A Fool's **A:** R. Cru **W:** R. Crumb; Spain; Art Spi

4 ❑ **NM** value: **8.00**
5 ❑ **NM** value: **7.00**

6 ❑ Jun 1976 Cover: 1.50 **NM** value: **6.00**
A: Art Spiegelman; Bill Griffith; R. Crumb **W:** Art Spiegelman; Bill Griffith; R. Crumb

7 ❑ Cover: 1.50 **NM** value: **5.00**

ARCANA — DC / Vertigo

Anl 1❑ Cover: 3.95 **NM** value: **4.00**
Circ: CapCity orders: **13,100**
🕮 The Children's Crusade, Part 6 • "Children's Crusade" **A:** Peter Gross **W:** John Ney Rieber

ARCANA (WELLS & CLARK) — Wells & Clark

1 ❑ Cover: 3.00 **NM** value: **Cover or less**
A: Rob Clark **W:** T.S. Wells

2 ❑ Mar 1995 Cover: 2.25 **NM** value: **3.00**
A: Rob Clark **W:** T.S. Wells

3 ❑ May 1995 Cover: 2.25 **NM** value: **3.00**
A: Rob Clark **W:** T.S. Wells

4 ❑ Jul 1995 Cover: 2.25 **NM** value: **Cover or less**
A: Rob Clark **W:** T.S. Wells

5 ❑ Sep 1995 Cover: 2.25 **NM** value: **Cover or less**
A: Rob Clark **W:** T.S. Wells

6 ❑ Cover: 2.25 **NM** value: **Cover or less**
A: Rob Clark **W:** T.S. Wells

7 ❑ Cover: 2.25 **NM** value: **Cover or less**
A: Rob Clark **W:** T.S. Wells

8 ❑ Jul 1996 Cover: 2.25 **NM** value: **Cover or less**
9 ❑ Sep 1996 Cover: 2.25 **NM** value: **Cover or less**
10 ❑ Cover: 2.25 **NM** value: **Cover or less**

ARCANE — Arcane

1 ❑ Cover: 2.00 **NM** value: **Cover or less**
2 ❑ Cover: 9.95 **NM** value: **Cover or less**
• Fly in My Eye

ARCANE (2ND SERIES) — Graphik

1 ❑ b&w Cover: 1.25 **NM** value: **Cover or less**

ARCANUM — Image

0.5 ❑ Dec 1997 **NM** value: **5.00**
A: Brandon Peterson **W:** Brandon Peterson

0.5/GO❑Dec 1997 **NM** value: **6.00**

1 ❑ Apr 1997 Cover: 2.50 **NM** value: **Cover or less**
Circ: Diamd. preorders: **33,867**

1/A ❑ Apr 1997 Cover: 2.50 **NM** value: **Cover or less**
variant cover. **A:** Marc Silvestri(cover)

2 ❑ May 1997 Cover: 2.50 **NM** value: **Cover or less**
Circ: Diamd. preorders: **46,347**

2/A ❑ May 1997 Cover: 2.50 **NM** value: **Cover or less**
variant cover.

3 ❑ Jun 1997 Cover: 2.50 **NM** value: **Cover or less**
Circ: Diamd. preorders: **44,416**

3/A ❑ Jun 1997 Cover: 2.50 **NM** value: **Cover or less**
variant cover.

4 ❑ Jul 1997 Cover: 2.50 **NM** value: **Cover or less**
Circ: Diamd. preorders: **40,146**

4/A ❑ Jul 1997 Cover: 2.50 **NM** value: **Cover or less**
Circ: Diamd. preorders: **5,389**
variant cover. **A:** Michael Turner(cover)

5 ❑ Sep 1997 Cover: 2.50 **NM** value: **2.95**
Circ: Diamd. preorders: **34,974**
A: Brandon Peterson **W:** Brandon Peterson

6 ❑ Nov 1997 Cover: 2.50 **NM** value: **2.95**
Circ: Diamd. preorders: **33,662**
A: Brandon Peterson **W:** Brandon Peterson

7 ❑ Jan 1998 Cover: 2.50 **NM** value: **2.95**
Circ: Diamd. preorders: **31,172**
A: Brandon Peterson **W:** Brandon Peterson

8 ❑ Feb 1998 Cover: 2.50 **NM** value: **2.95**
Circ: Diamd. preorders: **29,100**
final issue. **A:** Brandon Peterson **W:** Brandon Peterson

ARCHANGEL — Marvel

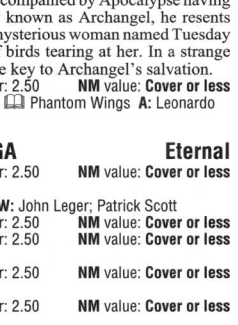

This one is an oddity — a super-hero comic book from Marvel printed in glossy black-and-white. Published in February 1996 and written by Peter Milligan, Archangel has an alternative-comics feel to it, accentuated by Leonardo Manco's slightly eerie art.

The one-shot title focuses on the former X-Men and X-Factor member Archangel coming to terms with his alien wings. The wings were made for him to replace his old wings, stolen from him by Apocalypse in the pages of X-Factor. The old wings were beautiful, giving him his original nickname of Angel. The new ones are mechanical and weaponlike, a transformation accompanied by Apocalypse having turned Angel's skin blue. Now known as Archangel, he resents his new form. Then he meets a mysterious woman named Tuesday who is tormented by visions of birds tearing at her. In a strange way, aiding Tuesday may be the key to Archangel's salvation.

1 ❑ Feb 1996, b&w Cover: 2.50 **NM** value: **Cover or less**
One-shot. wraparound cover. 🕮 Phantom Wings **A:** Leonardo Manco **W:** Peter Milligan

ARCHANGELS: THE SAGA — Eternal

1 ❑ Cover: 2.50 **NM** value: **Cover or less**
Circ: CapCity orders: **3,950**
A: Andy Orjuela; John Leger **W:** John Leger; Patrick Scott

1-2 ❑ Cover: 2.50 **NM** value: **Cover or less**

2 ❑ Cover: 2.50 **NM** value: **Cover or less**
Circ: CapCity orders: **2,810**

3 ❑ Cover: 2.50 **NM** value: **Cover or less**
Circ: CapCity orders: **3,878**

4 ❑ Cover: 2.50 **NM** value: **Cover or less**
Circ: CapCity orders: **3,920**

5 ❑ Cover: 2.50 **NM** value: **Cover or less**
6 ❑ Cover: 2.50 **NM** value: **Cover or less**
7 ❑ Cover: 2.50 **NM** value: **Cover or less**
8 ❑ Cover: 2.50 **NM** value: **Cover or less**

ARCHER & ARMSTRONG — Valiant

Archer was the son of a twisted fundamentalist minister and his equally twisted wife. Unbeknownst to their flock, the couple would conduct special "prayer sessions" in which young members were tortured and killed for the sick thrill of it all. When young Obie Archer discovers his parents' secret life, they try to have him killed. He escapes, stowed away on a boat to Hong Kong, and eventually enters a monastery, where he will train for his eventual revenge.

Armstrong meets Archer while hiding out as a down-and-out bum. In actuality, "Armstrong" is really Aram, the Eternal Warrior Gilly's

CGC-graded: Multiply prices above by **33 for 9.9 M** • **16 for 9.8 NM/M** • **7 for 9.6 NM+** • **5 for 9.4 NM** • **2.5 for 9.2 NM-** • **1.5 for 9.0 VF/NM**

brother. When the two meet, the near-immortal Armstrong is on the run from a group of assassins who believe him to be Satan. Archer comes to his defense, and the two began a life of adventure together ...

0 ❑ Jul 1992 Cover: 2.50 **NM** value: **Cover or less**
Circ: CapCity orders: **21,500**
A: Barry Windsor-Smith ★ Origin of Archer & Armstrong.

0/GO❑ Cover: 2.50 **NM** value: **Cover or less**
• Gold edition. **A:** Barry Windsor-Smith ★ Origin of Archer & Armstrong.

1 ❑ Aug 1992 Cover: 2.50 **NM** value: **Cover or less**
Circ: CapCity orders: **33,600**
📖 Unity, Part 3 • Unity **A:** Barry Windsor-Smith; Frank Miller(cover) **C:** Frank Miller **W:** Jim Shooter; Barry Windsor-Smith

2 ❑ Sep 1992 Cover: 2.50 **NM** value: **Cover or less**
Circ: CapCity orders: **31,900**
📖 Unity, Part 11 • Unity **A:** Barry Windsor-Smith; Walt Simonson **W:** Jim Shooter; Barry Windsor-Smith

3 ❑ Oct 1992 Cover: 2.50 **NM** value: **Cover or less**
Circ: CapCity orders: **22,800**

4 ❑ Nov 1992 Cover: 2.50 **NM** value: **Cover or less**
Circ: CapCity orders: **21,300**

5 ❑ Dec 1992 Cover: 2.50 **NM** value: **Cover or less**
Circ: CapCity orders: **21,600**

6 ❑ Jan 1993 Cover: 2.50 **NM** value: **Cover or less**

7 ❑ Feb 1993 Cover: 2.50 **NM** value: **Cover or less**
Circ: CapCity orders: **23,200**

8 ❑ Mar 1993 Cover: 4.50 **NM** value: **Cover or less**
• Double-sized: is also "Eternal Warrior #8". • Flip-book with Eternal Warrior #8 ★ 1st Appearance of Timewalker (Ivar).

9 ❑ Apr 1993 Cover: 2.50 **NM** value: **Cover or less**
Circ: CapCity orders: **35,000**
📖 Darque Daze **A:** Bernard Chang **W:** Bob Layton ★ 1st Appearance of Mademoiselle Noir.

10 ❑ May 1993 Cover: 2.50 **NM** value: **Cover or less**
Circ: CapCity orders: **47,500**

11 ❑ Jun 1993 Cover: 2.50 **NM** value: **Cover or less**
Circ: CapCity orders: **59,600**
📖 A Snatch in Time **A:** Barry Windsor-Smith **W:** Barry Windsor-Smith ★ Appearance of Solar.

12 ❑ Jul 1993 Cover: 2.50 **NM** value: **Cover or less**
Circ: CapCity orders: **79,800**
A: Barry Windsor-Smith **W:** Barry Windsor-Smith

13 ❑ Jul 1993 Cover: 2.50 **NM** value: **Cover or less**
Circ: CapCity orders: **63,200**

14 ❑ Jul 1993 Cover: 2.50 **NM** value: **Cover or less**
Circ: CapCity orders: **58,700**

15 ❑ Jul 1993 Cover: 2.50 **NM** value: **Cover or less**
Circ: CapCity orders: **46,000**

16 ❑ Jul 1993 Cover: 2.50 **NM** value: **Cover or less**
Circ: CapCity orders: **39,025**

17 ❑ Jul 1993 Cover: 2.50 **NM** value: **Cover or less**
Circ: CapCity orders: **35,775**

18 ❑ Jul 1993 Cover: 2.50 **NM** value: **Cover or less**
Circ: CapCity orders: **30,625**

19 ❑ Jan 1994 Cover: 2.50 **NM** value: **Cover or less**
Circ: CapCity orders: **26,550**

20 ❑ Mar 1994 Cover: 2.50 **NM** value: **Cover or less**
Circ: CapCity orders: **21,975**

21 ❑ Apr 1994 Cover: 2.50 **NM** value: **Cover or less**
Circ: CapCity orders: **21,375**
★ Appearance of Shadowman.

22 ❑ May 1994 Cover: 2.50 **NM** value: **Cover or less**
Circ: CapCity orders: **24,975**
• trading card

23 ❑ Jun 1994 Cover: 2.50 **NM** value: **Cover or less**
Circ: CapCity orders: **16,150**

24 ❑ Aug 1994 Cover: 2.50 **NM** value: **Cover or less**
Circ: CapCity orders: **15,700**

25 ❑ Sep 1994 Cover: 2.50 **NM** value: **Cover or less**
Circ: CapCity orders: **14,950**
★ Appearance of Eternal Warrior.

26 ❑ Oct 1994 Cover: 2.75 **NM** value: **Cover or less**
📖 The Chaos Effect: Gamma, Part 4 final issue. • Flip-book with Eternal Warrior #26;indicia says August

ARCHIE — Archie

Archie Andrews is an American icon. For more than 50 years, he and his perpetually teen-aged supporting cast have been entertaining children of all ages. Created by Bob Montana on assignment, Archie was introduced in Pep #22 in 1941. He received his own series shortly after. After more than 400 issues, Archie, blonde Betty, rich Veronica, dense-but-lovable Jughead, ox-like Moose, and the crafty Reggie are still getting into trouble and having laughs at Riverdale High School.

Naturally, a series with this sort of long-term appeal was bound to result in numerous spinoff titles. Among them are Betty and Veronica, Archie and Me, Archie Digest Magazine, Archie's Date Book, Reggie, and even The Punisher Meets Archie. All feature the Riverdale teens in adventures suitable for young readers.

2002 marked Archie's 60th year in comics.

1 ❑ Win 1942 Cover: 0.10 **NM** value: **10600.00**
• **CGC:** 3 graded, best 5.0
★ 1st Appearance of Mrs. Andrews.

2 ❑ Spr 1943 Cover: 0.10 **NM** value: **2700.00**
• **CGC:** 2 graded, best 3.0

3 ❑ Jul 1943 Cover: 0.10 **NM** value: **1725.00**
4 ❑ Sep 1943 Cover: 0.10 **NM** value: **980.00**
5 ❑ Nov 1943 Cover: 0.10 **NM** value: **900.00**
6 ❑ Jan 1944 Cover: 0.10 **NM** value: **675.00**
7 ❑ Mar 1944 Cover: 0.10 **NM** value: **600.00**
8 ❑ May 1944 Cover: 0.10 **NM** value: **600.00**
9 ❑ Jul 1944 Cover: 0.10 **NM** value: **600.00**
10 ❑ Sep 1944 Cover: 0.10 **NM** value: **525.00**
11 ❑ Dec 1944 Cover: 0.10 **NM** value: **440.00**
12 ❑ Jan 1945 Cover: 0.10 **NM** value: **440.00**
13 ❑ Mar 1945 Cover: 0.10 **NM** value: **440.00**
14 ❑ May 1945 Cover: 0.10 **NM** value: **440.00**
• **CGC:** 2 graded, best 7.5
15 ❑ Jul 1945 Cover: 0.10 **NM** value: **440.00**
16 ❑ Sep 1945 Cover: 0.10 **NM** value: **375.00**
17 ❑ Nov 1945 Cover: 0.10 **NM** value: **375.00**
18 ❑ Jan 1946 Cover: 0.10 **NM** value: **375.00**
19 ❑ Mar 1946 Cover: 0.10 **NM** value: **375.00**
20 ❑ May 1946 Cover: 0.10 **NM** value: **375.00**
21 ❑ Jul 1946 Cover: 0.10 **NM** value: **310.00**
22 ❑ Sep 1946 Cover: 0.10 **NM** value: **310.00**
• **CGC:** 2 graded, best 6.5
23 ❑ Nov 1946 Cover: 0.10 **NM** value: **310.00**
24 ❑ Jan 1947 Cover: 0.10 **NM** value: **310.00**
• **CGC:** 1 graded, best 8.0
25 ❑ Mar 1947 Cover: 0.10 **NM** value: **250.00**
26 ❑ May 1947 Cover: 0.10 **NM** value: **250.00**
27 ❑ Jul 1947 Cover: 0.10 **NM** value: **250.00**
28 ❑ Sep 1947 Cover: 0.10 **NM** value: **250.00**
29 ❑ Nov 1947 Cover: 0.10 **NM** value: **250.00**
30 ❑ Jan 1948 Cover: 0.10 **NM** value: **250.00**
• **CGC:** 1 graded, best 9.2
31 ❑ Mar 1948 Cover: 0.10 **NM** value: **195.00**
32 ❑ May 1948 Cover: 0.10 **NM** value: **195.00**
33 ❑ Jul 1948 Cover: 0.10 **NM** value: **195.00**
34 ❑ Sep 1948 Cover: 0.10 **NM** value: **195.00**
35 ❑ Nov 1948 Cover: 0.10 **NM** value: **195.00**
36 ❑ Jan 1949 Cover: 0.10 **NM** value: **155.00**
• **CGC:** 1 graded, best 6.5
37 ❑ Mar 1949 Cover: 0.10 **NM** value: **155.00**
38 ❑ May 1949 Cover: 0.10 **NM** value: **155.00**
39 ❑ Jul 1949 Cover: 0.10 **NM** value: **155.00**
40 ❑ Sep 1949 Cover: 0.10 **NM** value: **155.00**
41 ❑ Nov 1949 Cover: 0.10 **NM** value: **110.00**
42 ❑ Jan 1950 Cover: 0.10 **NM** value: **110.00**
43 ❑ Mar 1950 Cover: 0.10 **NM** value: **110.00**
44 ❑ May 1950 Cover: 0.10 **NM** value: **110.00**
45 ❑ Jul 1950 Cover: 0.10 **NM** value: **110.00**
46 ❑ Sep 1950 Cover: 0.10 **NM** value: **110.00**
47 ❑ Nov 1950 Cover: 0.10 **NM** value: **110.00**
48 ❑ Jan 1951 Cover: 0.10 **NM** value: **110.00**
49 ❑ Mar 1951 Cover: 0.10 **NM** value: **110.00**
50 ❑ May 1951 Cover: 0.10 **NM** value: **110.00**
51 ❑ Jul 1951 Cover: 0.10 **NM** value: **95.00**
52 ❑ Sep 1951 Cover: 0.10 **NM** value: **95.00**
53 ❑ Nov 1951 Cover: 0.10 **NM** value: **95.00**
• **CGC:** 1 graded, best 8.5
54 ❑ Jan 1952 Cover: 0.10 **NM** value: **95.00**
• **CGC:** 1 graded, best 9.4
55 ❑ Mar 1952 Cover: 0.10 **NM** value: **95.00**
56 ❑ May 1952 Cover: 0.10 **NM** value: **95.00**
57 ❑ Jul 1952 Cover: 0.10 **NM** value: **95.00**
58 ❑ Sep 1952 Cover: 0.10 **NM** value: **95.00**
59 ❑ Nov 1952 Cover: 0.10 **NM** value: **95.00**
60 ❑ Jan 1953 Cover: 0.10 **NM** value: **95.00**
61 ❑ Mar 1953 Cover: 0.10 **NM** value: **60.00**
62 ❑ May 1953 Cover: 0.10 **NM** value: **60.00**
63 ❑ Jul 1953 Cover: 0.10 **NM** value: **60.00**
64 ❑ Sep 1953 Cover: 0.10 **NM** value: **60.00**
65 ❑ Nov 1953 Cover: 0.10 **NM** value: **60.00**
66 ❑ Jan 1954 Cover: 0.10 **NM** value: **60.00**
67 ❑ Mar 1954 Cover: 0.10 **NM** value: **60.00**
68 ❑ May 1954 Cover: 0.10 **NM** value: **60.00**
69 ❑ Jul 1954 Cover: 0.10 **NM** value: **60.00**
70 ❑ Sep 1954 Cover: 0.10 **NM** value: **60.00**
71 ❑ Nov 1954 Cover: 0.10 **NM** value: **50.00**
72 ❑ Jan 1955 Cover: 0.10 **NM** value: **50.00**
73 ❑ Mar 1955 Cover: 0.10 **NM** value: **50.00**
74 ❑ May 1955 Cover: 0.10 **NM** value: **50.00**
75 ❑ Jul 1955 Cover: 0.10 **NM** value: **50.00**
76 ❑ Sep 1955 Cover: 0.10 **NM** value: **50.00**
77 ❑ Nov 1955 Cover: 0.10 **NM** value: **50.00**
78 ❑ Jan 1956 Cover: 0.10 **NM** value: **50.00**
79 ❑ Mar 1956 Cover: 0.10 **NM** value: **50.00**
80 ❑ May 1956 Cover: 0.10 **NM** value: **50.00**
81 ❑ Jul 1956 Cover: 0.10 **NM** value: **38.00**
82 ❑ Sep 1956 Cover: 0.10 **NM** value: **38.00**
83 ❑ Nov 1956 Cover: 0.10 **NM** value: **38.00**
84 ❑ Jan 1957 Cover: 0.10 **NM** value: **38.00**
85 ❑ Mar 1957 Cover: 0.10 **NM** value: **38.00**
86 ❑ May 1957 Cover: 0.10 **NM** value: **38.00**
87 ❑ Jul 1957 Cover: 0.10 **NM** value: **38.00**
88 ❑ Sep 1957 Cover: 0.10 **NM** value: **38.00**
89 ❑ Nov 1957 Cover: 0.10 **NM** value: **38.00**
90 ❑ Jan 1958 Cover: 0.10 **NM** value: **38.00**
91 ❑ Mar 1958 Cover: 0.10 **NM** value: **27.00**
92 ❑ May 1958 Cover: 0.10 **NM** value: **27.00**
93 ❑ Jul 1958 Cover: 0.10 **NM** value: **27.00**
94 ❑ Sep 1958 Cover: 0.10 **NM** value: **27.00**
95 ❑ Oct 1958 Cover: 0.10 **NM** value: **27.00**
96 ❑ Nov 1958 Cover: 0.10 **NM** value: **27.00**
97 ❑ Dec 1958 Cover: 0.10 **NM** value: **27.00**
98 ❑ Feb 1959 Cover: 0.10 **NM** value: **27.00**
99 ❑ Mar 1959 Cover: 0.10 **NM** value: **27.00**
100 ❑ Apr 1959 Cover: 0.10 **NM** value: **40.00**
101 ❑ Jun 1959 Cover: 0.10 **NM** value: **18.00**
102 ❑ Jul 1959 Cover: 0.10 **NM** value: **18.00**
103 ❑ Aug 1959 Cover: 0.10 **NM** value: **18.00**
104 ❑ Sep 1959 Cover: 0.10 **NM** value: **18.00**
105 ❑ Nov 1959 Cover: 0.10 **NM** value: **18.00**
106 ❑ Dec 1959 Cover: 0.10 **NM** value: **18.00**
107 ❑ Feb 1960 Cover: 0.10 **NM** value: **18.00**
108 ❑ Mar 1960 Cover: 0.10 **NM** value: **18.00**
109 ❑ Apr 1960 Cover: 0.10 **NM** value: **18.00**
110 ❑ Jun 1960 Cover: 0.10 **NM** value: **18.00**
111 ❑ Jul 1960 Cover: 0.10 **NM** value: **18.00**
112 ❑ Aug 1960 Cover: 0.10 **NM** value: **18.00**
113 ❑ Sep 1960 Cover: 0.10 **NM** value: **18.00**
114 ❑ Nov 1960 Cover: 0.10 **NM** value: **18.00**
115 ❑ Dec 1960 Cover: 0.10 **NM** value: **18.00**
116 ❑ Feb 1961 Cover: 0.10 **NM** value: **18.00**
117 ❑ Mar 1961 Cover: 0.10 **NM** value: **18.00**
118 ❑ Apr 1961 Cover: 0.10 **NM** value: **18.00**
119 ❑ Jun 1961 Cover: 0.10 **NM** value: **18.00**
120 ❑ Jul 1961 Cover: 0.10 **NM** value: **18.00**
121 ❑ Aug 1961 Cover: 0.10 **NM** value: **15.00**
122 ❑ Sep 1961 Cover: 0.10 **NM** value: **15.00**
123 ❑ Nov 1961 Cover: 0.10 **NM** value: **15.00**
124 ❑ Dec 1961 Cover: 0.10 **NM** value: **15.00**
125 ❑ Feb 1962, four-color Cover: 0.12 **NM** value: **15.00**
Circ: Statement: **457,689**
126 ❑ Mar 1962, four-color Cover: 0.12 **NM** value: **15.00**
Circ: Statement: **457,689**
127 ❑ Apr 1962, four-color Cover: 0.12 **NM** value: **15.00**
Circ: Statement: **457,689**
📖 The Cure, The Unwanted, Leave it to Grundy, One of Those Days
128 ❑ Jun 1962, four-color Cover: 0.12 **NM** value: **15.00**
Circ: Statement: **457,689**
129 ❑ Jul 1962, four-color Cover: 0.12 **NM** value: **15.00**
Circ: Statement: **457,689**
130 ❑ Aug 1962, four-color Cover: 0.12 **NM** value: **15.00**
Circ: Statement: **457,689**
131 ❑ Sep 1962, four-color Cover: 0.12 **NM** value: **15.00**
Circ: Statement: **457,689**
132 ❑ Nov 1962, four-color Cover: 0.12 **NM** value: **15.00**
Circ: Statement: **457,689**
133 ❑ Dec 1962, four-color Cover: 0.12 **NM** value: **15.00**
Circ: Statement: **457,689**
134 ❑ Feb 1963, four-color Cover: 0.12 **NM** value: **15.00**
Circ: Statement: **471,166**
135 ❑ Mar 1963, four-color Cover: 0.12 **NM** value: **15.00**
Circ: Statement: **471,166**
• Has 1962 Statement; avg total paid circ 457,689
136 ❑ Apr 1963, four-color Cover: 0.12 **NM** value: **15.00**
Circ: Statement: **471,166**
137 ❑ Jun 1963, four-color Cover: 0.12 **NM** value: **15.00**
Circ: Statement: **471,166**
138 ❑ Jul 1963, four-color Cover: 0.12 **NM** value: **15.00**
Circ: Statement: **471,166**
139 ❑ Aug 1963, four-color Cover: 0.12 **NM** value: **15.00**
Circ: Statement: **471,166**
140 ❑ Sep 1963, four-color Cover: 0.12 **NM** value: **15.00**
Circ: Statement: **471,166**
141 ❑ Nov 1963, four-color Cover: 0.12 **NM** value: **12.00**
Circ: Statement: **471,166**
142 ❑ Dec 1963, four-color Cover: 0.12 **NM** value: **12.00**
Circ: Statement: **471,166**
143 ❑ Feb 1964, four-color Cover: 0.12 **NM** value: **12.00**
Circ: Statement: **484,704**
144 ❑ Mar 1964, four-color Cover: 0.12 **NM** value: **12.00**
Circ: Statement: **484,704**
145 ❑ Apr 1964, four-color Cover: 0.12 **NM** value: **12.00**
Circ: Statement: **484,704**
146 ❑ Jun 1964, four-color Cover: 0.12 **NM** value: **12.00**
Circ: Statement: **484,704**
147 ❑ Jul 1964, four-color Cover: 0.12 **NM** value: **12.00**
Circ: Statement: **484,704**
148 ❑ Aug 1964, four-color Cover: 0.12 **NM** value: **12.00**
Circ: Statement: **484,704**
149 ❑ Sep 1964, four-color Cover: 0.12 **NM** value: **12.00**
Circ: Statement: **484,704**
150 ❑ Nov 1964, four-color Cover: 0.12 **NM** value: **12.00**
Circ: Statement: **484,704**
151 ❑ Dec 1964, four-color Cover: 0.12 **NM** value: **8.00**
Circ: Statement: **484,704**
152 ❑ Feb 1965, four-color Cover: 0.12 **NM** value: **8.00**
Circ: Statement: **467,552**
153 ❑ Mar 1965 Cover: 0.12 **NM** value: **8.00**
Circ: Statement: **467,552**
154 ❑ Apr 1965 Cover: 0.12 **NM** value: **8.00**
Circ: Statement: **467,552**
155 ❑ Jun 1965 Cover: 0.12 **NM** value: **8.00**
Circ: Statement: **467,552**
156 ❑ Jul 1965 Cover: 0.12 **NM** value: **8.00**
Circ: Statement: **467,552**
157 ❑ Aug 1965 Cover: 0.12 **NM** value: **8.00**
Circ: Statement: **467,552**
158 ❑ Sep 1965 Cover: 0.12 **NM** value: **8.00**
Circ: Statement: **467,552**
159 ❑ Nov 1965 Cover: 0.12 **NM** value: **8.00**
Circ: Statement: **467,552**
160 ❑ Dec 1965 Cover: 0.12 **NM** value: **8.00**
Circ: Statement: **467,552**
161 ❑ Feb 1966 Cover: 0.12 **NM** value: **8.00**
Circ: Statement: **491,691**
162 ❑ Mar 1966 Cover: 0.12 **NM** value: **8.00**
Circ: Statement: **491,691**
163 ❑ Apr 1966 Cover: 0.12 **NM** value: **8.00**
Circ: Statement: **491,691**
164 ❑ Jun 1966 Cover: 0.12 **NM** value: **8.00**
Circ: Statement: **491,691**
• Has 1965 Statement, filed 10/1/65; avg print run 850,115; avg sales 465,552; avg subs 2,000; avg total paid 467,552; samples 0; office use 0; max existent 467,552; 45% of run returned
165 ❑ Jul 1966 Cover: 0.12 **NM** value: **8.00**
Circ: Statement: **491,691**

Other grades: Multiply prices above by **1.5 for Mint • 2/3 for Very Fine • 1/3 for Fine • 1/5 for Very Good • 1/8 for Good**

166 ☐ Aug 1966 Cover: 0.12 **NM** value: **8.00**
Circ: Statement: **491,691**
167 ☐ Sep 1966 Cover: 0.12 **NM** value: **8.00**
Circ: Statement: **491,691**
168 ☐ Nov 1966 Cover: 0.12 **NM** value: **8.00**
Circ: Statement: **491,691**
169 ☐ Dec 1966 Cover: 0.12 **NM** value: **8.00**
Circ: Statement: **491,691**
170 ☐ Feb 1967 Cover: 0.12 **NM** value: **8.00**
Circ: Statement: **484,648**
171 ☐ Mar 1967 Cover: 0.12 **NM** value: **8.00**
Circ: Statement: **484,648**
172 ☐ Apr 1967 Cover: 0.12 **NM** value: **8.00**
Circ: Statement: **484,648**
173 ☐ Jun 1967 Cover: 0.12 **NM** value: **8.00**
Circ: Statement: **484,648**
• Has 1966 Statement; avg total paid circ 491,691
174 ☐ Jul 1967 Cover: 0.12 **NM** value: **8.00**
Circ: Statement: **484,648**
175 ☐ Aug 1967 Cover: 0.12 **NM** value: **8.00**
Circ: Statement: **484,648**
176 ☐ Sep 1967 Cover: 0.12 **NM** value: **8.00**
Circ: Statement: **484,648**
177 ☐ Nov 1967 Cover: 0.12 **NM** value: **8.00**
Circ: Statement: **484,648**
178 ☐ Dec 1967 Cover: 0.12 **NM** value: **8.00**
Circ: Statement: **484,648**
179 ☐ Feb 1968 Cover: 0.12 **NM** value: **8.00**
Circ: Statement: **566,587**
180 ☐ Mar 1968 Cover: 0.12 **NM** value: **8.00**
Circ: Statement: **566,587**
181 ☐ Apr 1968 Cover: 0.12 **NM** value: **5.00**
Circ: Statement: **566,587**
182 ☐ Jun 1968 Cover: 0.12 **NM** value: **5.00**
Circ: Statement: **566,587**
• Has 1967 Statement; avg total paid circ 484,648
183 ☐ Jul 1968 Cover: 0.12 **NM** value: **5.00**
Circ: Statement: **566,587**
184 ☐ Aug 1968 Cover: 0.12 **NM** value: **5.00**
Circ: Statement: **566,587**
185 ☐ Sep 1968 Cover: 0.12 **NM** value: **5.00**
Circ: Statement: **566,587**
186 ☐ Nov 1968 Cover: 0.12 **NM** value: **5.00**
Circ: Statement: **566,587**
187 ☐ Dec 1968 Cover: 0.12 **NM** value: **5.00**
Circ: Statement: **566,587**
188 ☐ Feb 1969 Cover: 0.12 **NM** value: **5.00**
Circ: Statement: **515,356**
189 ☐ Mar 1969 Cover: 0.12 **NM** value: **5.00**
Circ: Statement: **515,356**
190 ☐ Apr 1969 Cover: 0.12 **NM** value: **5.00**
Circ: Statement: **515,356**
191 ☐ Jun 1969 Cover: 0.12 **NM** value: **5.00**
Circ: Statement: **515,356**
• Has 1968 Statement, filed 11/1/68; avg print run 910,307; avg sales 563,187; avg subs 3,400; avg total paid 566,587; samples 0; office use 0; max existent 566,587; 38% of run returned
192 ☐ Jul 1969 Cover: 0.15 **NM** value: **5.00**
Circ: Statement: **515,356**
193 ☐ Aug 1969 Cover: 0.15 **NM** value: **5.00**
Circ: Statement: **515,356**
194 ☐ Sep 1969 Cover: 0.15 **NM** value: **5.00**
Circ: Statement: **515,356**
195 ☐ Nov 1969 Cover: 0.15 **NM** value: **5.00**
Circ: Statement: **515,356**
196 ☐ Dec 1969 Cover: 0.15 **NM** value: **5.00**
Circ: Statement: **515,356**
197 ☐ Feb 1970 Cover: 0.15 **NM** value: **5.00**
Circ: Statement: **482,945**
198 ☐ Mar 1970 Cover: 0.15 **NM** value: **5.00**
Circ: Statement: **482,945**
199 ☐ Apr 1970 Cover: 0.15 **NM** value: **5.00**
Circ: Statement: **482,945**
• Has 1969 Statement, filed 10/1/69; avg print run 886,643; avg sales 513,506; avg subs 1,850; avg total paid 515,356; samples 0; office use 0; max existent 515,356; 42% of run returned
200 ☐ Jun 1970 Cover: 0.15 **NM** value: **5.00**
Circ: Statement: **482,945**
201 ☐ Jul 1970 Cover: 0.15 **NM** value: **3.00**
Circ: Statement: **482,945**
202 ☐ Aug 1970 Cover: 0.15 **NM** value: **3.00**
Circ: Statement: **482,945**
203 ☐ Sep 1970 Cover: 0.15 **NM** value: **3.00**
Circ: Statement: **482,945**
204 ☐ Nov 1970 Cover: 0.15 **NM** value: **3.00**
Circ: Statement: **482,945**
205 ☐ Dec 1970 Cover: 0.15 **NM** value: **3.00**
Circ: Statement: **482,945**
206 ☐ Feb 1971 Cover: 0.15 **NM** value: **3.00**
207 ☐ Mar 1971 Cover: 0.15 **NM** value: **3.00**
208 ☐ May 1971 Cover: 0.15 **NM** value: **3.00**
• Has 1970 Statement, filed 10/1/70; avg print run 853,590; avg sales 480,773; avg subs 2,172; avg total paid 482,945; samples 0; office use 0; max existent 482,945; 43% of run returned
209 ☐ Jun 1971 Cover: 0.15 **NM** value: **3.00**
210 ☐ Jul 1971 Cover: 0.15 **NM** value: **3.00**
211 ☐ Aug 1971 Cover: 0.15 **NM** value: **3.00**
212 ☐ Sep 1971 Cover: 0.15 **NM** value: **3.00**
213 ☐ Nov 1971 Cover: 0.15 **NM** value: **3.00**
214 ☐ Dec 1971 Cover: 0.15 **NM** value: **3.00**
215 ☐ Feb 1972 Cover: 0.15 **NM** value: **3.00**
Circ: Statement: **390,408**
216 ☐ Mar 1972 Cover: 0.15 **NM** value: **3.00**
Circ: Statement: **390,408**
217 ☐ Apr 1972 Cover: 0.15 **NM** value: **3.00**
Circ: Statement: **390,408**
218 ☐ Jun 1972 Cover: 0.20 **NM** value: **3.00**
Circ: Statement: **390,408**
219 ☐ Jul 1972 Cover: 0.20 **NM** value: **3.00**
Circ: Statement: **390,408**
220 ☐ Aug 1972 Cover: 0.20 **NM** value: **3.00**
Circ: Statement: **390,408**
221 ☐ Sep 1972 Cover: 0.20 **NM** value: **3.00**
Circ: Statement: **390,408**
222 ☐ Nov 1972 Cover: 0.20 **NM** value: **3.00**
Circ: Statement: **390,408**
223 ☐ Dec 1972 Cover: 0.20 **NM** value: **3.00**
Circ: Statement: **390,408**
224 ☐ Feb 1973 Cover: 0.20 **NM** value: **3.00**
Circ: Statement: **345,087**
225 ☐ Apr 1973 Cover: 0.20 **NM** value: **3.00**
Circ: Statement: **345,087**
226 ☐ Jun 1973 Cover: 0.20 **NM** value: **3.00**
Circ: Statement: **345,087**
• Has 1972 Statement, filed 10/1/72; avg print run 810,400; avg sales 388,245; avg subs 2,163; avg total paid 390,408; samples 0; office use 0; max existent 390,408; 52% of run returned
227 ☐ Jul 1973 Cover: 0.20 **NM** value: **3.00**
Circ: Statement: **345,087**
228 ☐ Aug 1973 Cover: 0.20 **NM** value: **3.00**
Circ: Statement: **345,087**
229 ☐ Sep 1973 Cover: 0.20 **NM** value: **3.00**
Circ: Statement: **345,087**
230 ☐ Nov 1973 Cover: 0.20 **NM** value: **3.00**
Circ: Statement: **345,087**
231 ☐ Dec 1973 Cover: 0.20 **NM** value: **3.00**
Circ: Statement: **345,087**
232 ☐ Feb 1974 Cover: 0.20 **NM** value: **3.00**
Circ: Statement: **272,272**
233 ☐ Mar 1974 Cover: 0.20 **NM** value: **3.00**
Circ: Statement: **272,272**
234 ☐ Apr 1974 Cover: 0.25 **NM** value: **3.00**
Circ: Statement: **272,272**
• Has 1973 Statement; avg total paid circ 345,087
235 ☐ Jun 1974 Cover: 0.25 **NM** value: **3.00**
Circ: Statement: **272,272**
236 ☐ Jul 1974 Cover: 0.25 **NM** value: **3.00**
Circ: Statement: **272,272**
237 ☐ Aug 1974 Cover: 0.25 **NM** value: **3.00**
Circ: Statement: **272,272**
238 ☐ Sep 1974 Cover: 0.25 **NM** value: **3.00**
Circ: Statement: **272,272**
239 ☐ Nov 1974 Cover: 0.25 **NM** value: **3.00**
Circ: Statement: **272,272**
240 ☐ Dec 1974 Cover: 0.25 **NM** value: **3.00**
Circ: Statement: **272,272**
241 ☐ Feb 1975 Cover: 0.25 **NM** value: **3.00**
Circ: Statement: **199,918**
242 ☐ Mar 1975 Cover: 0.25 **NM** value: **3.00**
Circ: Statement: **199,918**
243 ☐ Apr 1975 Cover: 0.25 **NM** value: **3.00**
Circ: Statement: **199,918**
• Has 1974 Statement; avg total paid circ 272,272
244 ☐ Jun 1975 Cover: 0.25 **NM** value: **3.00**
Circ: Statement: **199,918**
245 ☐ Jul 1975 Cover: 0.25 **NM** value: **3.00**
Circ: Statement: **199,918**
246 ☐ Aug 1975 Cover: 0.25 **NM** value: **3.00**
Circ: Statement: **199,918**
247 ☐ Sep 1975 Cover: 0.25 **NM** value: **3.00**
Circ: Statement: **199,918**
248 ☐ Nov 1975 Cover: 0.25 **NM** value: **3.00**
Circ: Statement: **199,918**
249 ☐ Dec 1975 Cover: 0.25 **NM** value: **3.00**
Circ: Statement: **199,918**
250 ☐ Feb 1976 Cover: 0.30 **NM** value: **3.00**
Circ: Statement: **181,827**
251 ☐ Mar 1976 Cover: 0.30 **NM** value: **2.00**
Circ: Statement: **181,827**
252 ☐ Apr 1976 Cover: 0.30 **NM** value: **2.00**
Circ: Statement: **181,827**
• Has 1975 Statement; avg total paid circ 199,918
253 ☐ Jun 1976 Cover: 0.30 **NM** value: **2.00**
Circ: Statement: **181,827**
254 ☐ Jul 1976 Cover: 0.30 **NM** value: **2.00**
Circ: Statement: **181,827**
255 ☐ Aug 1976 Cover: 0.30 **NM** value: **2.00**
Circ: Statement: **181,827**
256 ☐ Sep 1976 Cover: 0.30 **NM** value: **2.00**
Circ: Statement: **181,827**
257 ☐ Nov 1976 Cover: 0.30 **NM** value: **2.00**
Circ: Statement: **181,827**
258 ☐ Dec 1976 Cover: 0.30 **NM** value: **2.00**
Circ: Statement: **181,827**
259 ☐ Feb 1977 Cover: 0.30 **NM** value: **2.00**
Circ: Statement: **155,252**
260 ☐ Mar 1977 Cover: 0.30 **NM** value: **2.00**
Circ: Statement: **155,252**
261 ☐ Apr 1977 Cover: 0.30 **NM** value: **2.00**
Circ: Statement: **155,252**
• Has 1976 Statement, filed 10/1/76; avg print run 423,959; avg sales 181,436; avg subs 391; avg total paid 181,827; samples 0; office use 300; max existent 182,127; 57% of run returned
262 ☐ Jun 1977 Cover: 0.30 **NM** value: **2.00**
Circ: Statement: **155,252**
263 ☐ Jul 1977 Cover: 0.35 **NM** value: **2.00**
Circ: Statement: **155,252**
264 ☐ Aug 1977 Cover: 0.35 **NM** value: **2.00**
Circ: Statement: **155,252**
265 ☐ Sep 1977 Cover: 0.35 **NM** value: **2.00**
Circ: Statement: **155,252**
266 ☐ Nov 1977 Cover: 0.35 **NM** value: **2.00**
Circ: Statement: **155,252**
267 ☐ Dec 1977 Cover: 0.35 **NM** value: **2.00**
Circ: Statement: **155,252**
268 ☐ Feb 1978 Cover: 0.35 **NM** value: **2.00**
269 ☐ Mar 1978 Cover: 0.35 **NM** value: **2.00**
270 ☐ Apr 1978 Cover: 0.35 **NM** value: **2.00**
• Has 1977 Statement, filed 10/1/77; avg print run 360,831; avg sales 154,887; avg subs 365; avg total paid 155,252; samples 0; office use 300; max existent 155,552; 57% of run returned
271 ☐ Jun 1978 Cover: 0.35 **NM** value: **2.00**
272 ☐ Jul 1978 Cover: 0.35 **NM** value: **2.00**
273 ☐ Aug 1978 Cover: 0.35 **NM** value: **2.00**
274 ☐ Sep 1978 Cover: 0.35 **NM** value: **2.00**
275 ☐ Nov 1978 Cover: 0.35 **NM** value: **2.00**
276 ☐ Dec 1978 Cover: 0.35 **NM** value: **2.00**
277 ☐ Feb 1979 Cover: 0.35 **NM** value: **2.00**
278 ☐ Mar 1979 Cover: 0.35 **NM** value: **2.00**
279 ☐ Apr 1979 Cover: 0.40 **NM** value: **2.00**
280 ☐ May 1979 Cover: 0.40 **NM** value: **2.00**
281 ☐ Jun 1979 Cover: 0.40 **NM** value: **2.00**
282 ☐ Jul 1979 Cover: 0.40 **NM** value: **2.00**
283 ☐ Aug 1979 Cover: 0.40 **NM** value: **2.00**
284 ☐ Sep 1979 Cover: 0.40 **NM** value: **2.00**
285 ☐ Oct 1979 Cover: 0.40 **NM** value: **2.00**
286 ☐ Nov 1979 Cover: 0.40 **NM** value: **2.00**
287 ☐ Dec 1979 Cover: 0.40 **NM** value: **2.00**
288 ☐ Jan 1980 Cover: 0.40 **NM** value: **2.00**
289 ☐ Feb 1980 Cover: 0.40 **NM** value: **2.00**
290 ☐ Mar 1980 Cover: 0.40 **NM** value: **2.00**
291 ☐ Apr 1980 Cover: 0.40 **NM** value: **2.00**
292 ☐ May 1980 Cover: 0.40 **NM** value: **2.00**
293 ☐ Jun 1980 Cover: 0.40 **NM** value: **2.00**
294 ☐ Jul 1980 Cover: 0.40 **NM** value: **2.00**
295 ☐ Aug 1980 Cover: 0.50 **NM** value: **2.00**
296 ☐ Sep 1980 Cover: 0.50 **NM** value: **2.00**
297 ☐ Oct 1980 Cover: 0.50 **NM** value: **2.00**
298 ☐ Nov 1980 Cover: 0.50 **NM** value: **2.00**
299 ☐ Dec 1980 Cover: 0.50 **NM** value: **2.00**
300 ☐ Jan 1981 Cover: 0.50 **NM** value: **2.00**
301 ☐ Feb 1981 Cover: 0.50 **NM** value: **1.50**
302 ☐ Mar 1981 Cover: 0.50 **NM** value: **1.50**
303 ☐ Apr 1981 Cover: 0.50 **NM** value: **1.50**
304 ☐ May 1981 Cover: 0.50 **NM** value: **1.50**
305 ☐ Jun 1981 Cover: 0.50 **NM** value: **1.50**
306 ☐ Jul 1981 Cover: 0.50 **NM** value: **1.50**
307 ☐ Aug 1981 Cover: 0.50 **NM** value: **1.50**
308 ☐ Sep 1981 Cover: 0.50 **NM** value: **1.50**
309 ☐ Oct 1981 Cover: 0.50 **NM** value: **1.50**
310 ☐ Nov 1981 Cover: 0.50 **NM** value: **1.50**
311 ☐ Dec 1981 Cover: 0.60 **NM** value: **1.50**
312 ☐ Jan 1982 Cover: 0.60 **NM** value: **1.50**
313 ☐ Feb 1982 Cover: 0.60 **NM** value: **1.50**
314 ☐ Mar 1982 Cover: 0.60 **NM** value: **1.50**
315 ☐ Apr 1982 Cover: 0.60 **NM** value: **1.50**
316 ☐ May 1982 Cover: 0.60 **NM** value: **1.50**
317 ☐ Jun 1982 Cover: 0.60 **NM** value: **1.50**
318 ☐ Jul 1982 Cover: 0.60 **NM** value: **1.50**
319 ☐ Sep 1982 Cover: 0.60 **NM** value: **1.50**
320 ☐ Nov 1982 Cover: 0.60 **NM** value: **1.50**
321 ☐ Jan 1983 Cover: 0.60 **NM** value: **1.50**
Circ: Statement: **69,697**
322 ☐ Mar 1983 Cover: 0.60 **NM** value: **1.50**
Circ: Statement: **69,697**
323 ☐ May 1983 Cover: 0.60 **NM** value: **1.50**
Circ: Statement: **69,697**
324 ☐ Jul 1983 Cover: 0.60 **NM** value: **1.50**
Circ: Statement: **69,697**
325 ☐ Sep 1983 Cover: 0.60 **NM** value: **1.50**
Circ: Statement: **69,697**
326 ☐ Nov 1983 Cover: 0.60 **NM** value: **1.50**
Circ: Statement: **69,697**
327 ☐ Jan 1984 Cover: 0.60 **NM** value: **1.50**
Circ: Statement: **64,781**
328 ☐ Mar 1984 Cover: 0.60 **NM** value: **1.50**
Circ: Statement: **64,781**
329 ☐ May 1984 Cover: 0.60 **NM** value: **1.50**
Circ: Statement: **64,781**
330 ☐ Jul 1984 Cover: 0.60 **NM** value: **1.50**
Circ: Statement: **64,781**
331 ☐ Sep 1984 Cover: 0.60 **NM** value: **1.50**
Circ: Statement: **64,781**
332 ☐ Nov 1984 Cover: 0.60 **NM** value: **1.50**
Circ: Statement: **64,781**
333 ☐ Jan 1985 Cover: 0.65 **NM** value: **1.50**
Circ: Statement: **63,143**
334 ☐ Mar 1985 Cover: 0.65 **NM** value: **1.50**
Circ: Statement: **63,143**
335 ☐ May 1985 Cover: 0.65 **NM** value: **1.50**
Circ: Statement: **63,143**
336 ☐ Jul 1985 Cover: 0.65 **NM** value: **1.50**
Circ: Statement: **63,143**
337 ☐ Sep 1985 Cover: 0.65 **NM** value: **1.50**
Circ: Statement: **63,143**
338 ☐ Nov 1985 Cover: 0.65 **NM** value: **1.50**
Circ: Statement: **63,143**
339 ☐ Jan 1986 Cover: 0.65 **NM** value: **1.50**
Circ: Statement: **67,059**
340 ☐ Mar 1986 Cover: 0.65 **NM** value: **1.50**
Circ: Statement: **67,059**
341 ☐ May 1986 Cover: 0.65 **NM** value: **1.50**
Circ: Statement: **67,059**
342 ☐ Jul 1986 Cover: 0.75 **NM** value: **1.50**
Circ: Statement: **67,059**
343 ☐ Sep 1986 Cover: 0.75 **NM** value: **1.50**
Circ: Statement: **67,059**
344 ☐ Nov 1986 Cover: 0.75 **NM** value: **1.50**
Circ: Statement: **67,059**
345 ☐ Jan 1987 Cover: 0.75 **NM** value: **1.50**
Circ: Statement: **66,176**
346 ☐ Mar 1987 Cover: 0.75 **NM** value: **1.50**
Circ: Statement: **66,176**
347 ☐ May 1987 Cover: 0.75 **NM** value: **1.50**
Circ: Statement: **66,176**

CGC-graded: Multiply prices above by **33 for 9.9 M • 16 for 9.8 NM/M • 7 for 9.6 NM+ • 5 for 9.4 NM • 2.5 for 9.2 NM- • 1.5 for 9.0 VF/NM**

348 ❑ Jun 1987 Cover: 0.75 **NM** value: **1.50**
Circ: Statement: **66,176**
349 ❑ Jul 1987 Cover: 0.75 **NM** value: **1.50**
Circ: Statement: **66,176**
350 ❑ Aug 1987 Cover: 0.75 **NM** value: **1.50**
Circ: Statement: **66,176**
351 ❑ Sep 1987 Cover: 0.75 **NM** value: **1.50**
Circ: Statement: **66,176**
352 ❑ Oct 1987 Cover: 0.75 **NM** value: **1.50**
Circ: Statement: **66,176**
353 ❑ Nov 1987 Cover: 0.75 **NM** value: **1.50**
Circ: Statement: **66,176**
354 ❑ Jan 1988 Cover: 0.75 **NM** value: **1.50**
Circ: Statement: **74,223**
355 ❑ Mar 1988 Cover: 0.75 **NM** value: **1.50**
Circ: Statement: **74,223**
356 ❑ May 1988 Cover: 0.75 **NM** value: **1.50**
Circ: Statement: **74,223**
357 ❑ Jun 1988 Cover: 0.75 **NM** value: **1.50**
Circ: Statement: **74,223**
358 ❑ Jul 1988 Cover: 0.75 **NM** value: **1.50**
Circ: Statement: **74,223**
359 ❑ Aug 1988 Cover: 0.75 **NM** value: **1.50**
Circ: Statement: **74,223**
360 ❑ Sep 1988 Cover: 0.75 **NM** value: **1.50**
Circ: Statement: **74,223**
361 ❑ Oct 1988 Cover: 0.75 **NM** value: **1.50**
Circ: Statement: **74,223**
362 ❑ Nov 1988 Cover: 0.75 **NM** value: **1.50**
Circ: Statement: **74,223**
363 ❑ Jan 1989 Cover: 0.75 **NM** value: **1.50**
Circ: Statement: **67,423**
364 ❑ Feb 1989 Cover: 0.75 **NM** value: **1.50**
Circ: Statement: **67,423**
365 ❑ Mar 1989 Cover: 0.75 **NM** value: **1.50**
Circ: Statement: **67,423**
366 ❑ Apr 1989 Cover: 0.75 **NM** value: **1.50**
Circ: Statement: **67,423**
367 ❑ May 1989 Cover: 0.75 **NM** value: **1.50**
Circ: Statement: **67,423**
368 ❑ Jul 1989 Cover: 0.95 **NM** value: **1.50**
Circ: Statement: **67,423**
369 ❑ Aug 1993 Cover: 0.95 **NM** value: **1.50**
Circ: Statement: **67,423**
370 ❑ Sep 1989 Cover: 0.95 **NM** value: **1.50**
Circ: Statement: **67,423**
371 ❑ Oct 1989 Cover: 0.95 **NM** value: **1.50**
Circ: Statement: **67,423**
372 ❑ Nov 1989 Cover: 0.95 **NM** value: **1.50**
Circ: Statement: **67,423**
373 ❑ Jan 1990 Cover: 1.00 **NM** value: **1.50**
Circ: Statement: **56,855**
374 ❑ Feb 1990 Cover: 1.00 **NM** value: **1.50**
Circ: Statement: **56,855**
375 ❑ Mar 1990 Cover: 1.00 **NM** value: **1.50**
Circ: Statement: **56,855**
376 ❑ Apr 1990 Cover: 1.00 **NM** value: **1.50**
Circ: Statement: **56,855**
377 ❑ May 1990 Cover: 1.00 **NM** value: **1.50**
Circ: Statement: **56,855**
378 ❑ Jul 1990 Cover: 1.00 **NM** value: **1.50**
Circ: Statement: **56,855**
379 ❑ Aug 1990 Cover: 1.00 **NM** value: **1.50**
Circ: Statement: **56,855**
380 ❑ Sep 1990 Cover: 1.00 **NM** value: **1.50**
Circ: Statement: **56,855**
381 ❑ Oct 1990 Cover: 1.00 **NM** value: **1.50**
Circ: Statement: **56,855**
382 ❑ Nov 1990 Cover: 1.00 **NM** value: **1.50**
Circ: Statement: **56,855**
383 ❑ Dec 1990 Cover: 1.00 **NM** value: **1.50**
Circ: Statement: **56,855**
384 ❑ Feb 1991 Cover: 1.00 **NM** value: **1.50**
Circ: Statement: **45,960**
385 ❑ Mar 1991 Cover: 1.00 **NM** value: **1.50**
Circ: Statement: **45,960**
386 ❑ Apr 1991 Cover: 1.00 **NM** value: **1.50**
Circ: Statement: **45,960**
387 ❑ May 1991 Cover: 1.00 **NM** value: **1.50**
Circ: Statement: **45,960**
388 ❑ Jun 1991 Cover: 1.00 **NM** value: **1.50**
Circ: Statement: **45,960**
389 ❑ Jul 1991 Cover: 1.00 **NM** value: **1.50**
Circ: Statement: **45,960**
390 ❑ Aug 1991 Cover: 1.00 **NM** value: **1.50**
Circ: Statement: **45,960**
391 ❑ Sep 1991 Cover: 1.00 **NM** value: **1.50**
Circ: Statement: **45,960**
392 ❑ Oct 1991 Cover: 1.00 **NM** value: **1.50**
Circ: Statement: **45,960**
393 ❑ Nov 1991 Cover: 1.00 **NM** value: **1.50**
Circ: Statement: **45,960**
394 ❑ Dec 1991 Cover: 1.00 **NM** value: **1.50**
Circ: Statement: **45,960**
395 ❑ Jan 1992 Cover: 1.00 **NM** value: **1.50**
Circ: Statement: **47,530**
396 ❑ Feb 1992 Cover: 1.00 **NM** value: **1.50**
Circ: Statement: **47,530**
397 ❑ Mar 1992 Cover: 1.00 **NM** value: **1.50**
Circ: Statement: **47,530**
398 ❑ Apr 1992 Cover: 1.00 **NM** value: **1.50**
Circ: Statement: **47,530**
399 ❑ May 1992 Cover: 1.25 **NM** value: **1.50**
Circ: Statement: **47,530**
400 ❑ Jun 1992 Cover: 1.25 **NM** value: **1.50**
Circ: Statement: **47,530**
401 ❑ Jul 1992 Cover: 1.25 **NM** value: **1.50**
Circ: Statement: **47,530**
402 ❑ Aug 1992 Cover: 1.25 **NM** value: **1.50**
Circ: Statement: **47,530**
403 ❑ Sep 1992 Cover: 1.25 **NM** value: **1.50**
Circ: Statement: **47,530**
404 ❑ Oct 1992 Cover: 1.25 **NM** value: **1.50**
Circ: Statement: **47,530**
405 ❑ Nov 1992 Cover: 1.25 **NM** value: **1.50**
Circ: Statement: **47,530**
406 ❑ Dec 1992 Cover: 1.25 **NM** value: **1.50**
Circ: Statement: **47,530**
407 ❑ Jan 1993 Cover: 1.25 **NM** value: **1.50**
Circ: Statement: **44,547**
408 ❑ Feb 1993 Cover: 1.25 **NM** value: **1.50**
Circ: Statement: **44,547**
409 ❑ Mar 1993 Cover: 1.25 **NM** value: **1.50**
Circ: Statement: **44,547**
410 ❑ Apr 1993 Cover: 1.25 **NM** value: **1.50**
Circ: Statement: **44,547**
• Has 1992 Statement, filed 10/1/92; avg print run 167,245; avg sales 46,044; avg subs 1,486; avg total paid 47,530; samples 2,187; office use 5,535; max existent 55,252; 67% of run returned
411 ❑ May 1993 Cover: 1.25 **NM** value: **1.50**
Circ: Statement: **44,547**
412 ❑ Jun 1993 Cover: 1.25 **NM** value: **1.50**
Circ: Statement: **44,547**
413 ❑ Jul 1993 Cover: 1.25 **NM** value: **1.50**
Circ: Statement: **44,547**
📖 Archie: Food Choice; Archie: Quiz Biz!; Archie: Diamond Demon; Archie: Blow the Man Down **A:** Stan Goldberg **W:** Frank Doyle; Joe Edwards; Mike Pellowski
414 ❑ Aug 1993 Cover: 1.25 **NM** value: **1.50**
Circ: Statement: **44,547**
• prom poster
415 ❑ Sep 1993 Cover: 1.25 **NM** value: **1.50**
Circ: Statement: **44,547**
416 ❑ Oct 1993 Cover: 1.25 **NM** value: **1.50**
Circ: Statement: **44,547**
417 ❑ Nov 1993 Cover: 1.25 **NM** value: **1.50**
Circ: Statement: **44,547**
418 ❑ Dec 1993 Cover: 1.25 **NM** value: **1.50**
Circ: Statement: **44,547**
419 ❑ Jan 1994 Cover: 1.25 **NM** value: **1.50**
420 ❑ Feb 1994 Cover: 1.25 **NM** value: **1.50**
421 ❑ Mar 1994 Cover: 1.25 **NM** value: **1.50**
422 ❑ Apr 1994 Cover: 1.25 **NM** value: **1.50**
• Has 1993 Statement, filed 10/1/93; avg print run 152,085; avg sales 43,230; avg subs 1,317; avg total paid 44,547; samples 609; office use 3,888; max existent 49,044; 68% of run returned
423 ❑ May 1994 Cover: 1.25 **NM** value: **1.50**
424 ❑ Jun 1994 Cover: 1.25 **NM** value: **1.50**
425 ❑ Jul 1994 Cover: 1.25 **NM** value: **1.50**
426 ❑ Aug 1994 Cover: 1.50 **NM** value: **Cover or less**
427 ❑ Sep 1994 Cover: 1.50 **NM** value: **Cover or less**
428 ❑ Oct 1994 Cover: 1.50 **NM** value: **Cover or less**
429 ❑ Nov 1994 Cover: 1.50 **NM** value: **Cover or less**
📖 Love Showdown, Part 1
430 ❑ Dec 1994 Cover: 1.50 **NM** value: **Cover or less**
431 ❑ Jan 1995 Cover: 1.50 **NM** value: **Cover or less**
Circ: Statement: **43,885**
432 ❑ Feb 1995 Cover: 1.50 **NM** value: **Cover or less**
Circ: Statement: **43,885**
📖 Technical Advisor; Snow Brawling, Treasure In The Attic **A:** Stan Goldberg **W:** Hal Smith; Mike Pellowski
433 ❑ Mar 1995 Cover: 1.50 **NM** value: **Cover or less**
Circ: Statement: **43,885**
434 ❑ Apr 1995 Cover: 1.50 **NM** value: **Cover or less**
Circ: Statement: **43,885**
• Has 1994 Statement, filed 10/1/94; avg print run 153,534; avg sales 44,474; avg subs 1,559; avg total paid 46,033; samples 427; office use 3,304; max existent 49,764; 68% of run returned
435 ❑ May 1995 Cover: 1.50 **NM** value: **Cover or less**
Circ: Statement: **43,885**
436 ❑ Jun 1995 Cover: 1.50 **NM** value: **Cover or less**
Circ: Statement: **43,885**
437 ❑ Jul 1995 Cover: 1.50 **NM** value: **Cover or less**
Circ: Statement: **43,885**
438 ❑ Aug 1995 Cover: 1.50 **NM** value: **Cover or less**
Circ: Statement: **43,885**
439 ❑ Sep 1995 Cover: 1.50 **NM** value: **Cover or less**
Circ: Statement: **43,885**
440 ❑ Oct 1995 Cover: 1.50 **NM** value: **Cover or less**
Circ: Statement: **43,885**
441 ❑ Nov 1995 Cover: 1.50 **NM** value: **Cover or less**
Circ: Statement: **43,885**
442 ❑ Dec 1995 Cover: 1.50 **NM** value: **Cover or less**
Circ: Statement: **43,885**
📖 House of Riverdale, Part 1 • continues in Betty & Veronica #95
443 ❑ Jan 1996 Cover: 1.50 **NM** value: **Cover or less**
Circ: Statement: **45,067**
Photo cover.
444 ❑ Feb 1996 Cover: 1.50 **NM** value: **Cover or less**
Circ: Statement: **45,067**
445 ❑ Mar 1996 Cover: 1.50 **NM** value: **Cover or less**
Circ: Statement: **45,067**
446 ❑ Apr 1996 Cover: 1.50 **NM** value: **Cover or less**
Circ: Statement: **45,067**
• Has 446 Statement; avg total paid circ 43,885
447 ❑ May 1996 Cover: 1.50 **NM** value: **Cover or less**
Circ: Statement: **45,067**
448 ❑ Jun 1996 Cover: 1.50 **NM** value: **Cover or less**
Circ: Statement: **45,067**
449 ❑ Jul 1996 Cover: 1.50 **NM** value: **Cover or less**
Circ: Statement: **45,067**
450 ❑ Aug 1996 Cover: 1.50 **NM** value: **Cover or less**
Circ: Statement: **45,067**
451 ❑ Sep 1996 Cover: 1.50 **NM** value: **Cover or less**
Circ: Statement: **45,067**
452 ❑ Oct 1996 Cover: 1.50 **NM** value: **Cover or less**
Circ: Statement: **45,067**
453 ❑ Nov 1996 Cover: 1.50 **NM** value: **Cover or less**
Circ: Statement: **45,067**
454 ❑ Dec 1996 Cover: 1.50 **NM** value: **Cover or less**
Circ: Statement: **45,067** Direct Market orders: **5,144**
455 ❑ Jan 1997 Cover: 1.50 **NM** value: **Cover or less**
Circ: Statement: **41,134** Direct Market orders: **5,370**
456 ❑ Feb 1997 Cover: 1.50 **NM** value: **Cover or less**
Circ: Statement: **41,134** Diamd. preorders: **5,489**
457 ❑ Mar 1997 Cover: 1.50 **NM** value: **Cover or less**
Circ: Statement: **41,134** Diamd. preorders: **5,305**
458 ❑ Apr 1997 Cover: 1.50 **NM** value: **Cover or less**
Circ: Statement: **41,134** Diamd. preorders: **4,905**
• Has 1996 Statement, filed 9/27/96; avg print run 129,795; avg sales 43,298; avg subs 1,139; avg total paid 45,067; samples 434; office use 1,591; max existent 46,462; 64% of run returned
459 ❑ May 1997 Cover: 1.50 **NM** value: **Cover or less**
Circ: Statement: **41,134** Diamd. preorders: **4,770**
460 ❑ Jun 1997 Cover: 1.50 **NM** value: **Cover or less**
Circ: Statement: **41,134** Diamd. preorders: **4,834**
461 ❑ Jul 1997 Cover: 1.50 **NM** value: **Cover or less**
Circ: Statement: **41,134** Diamd. preorders: **4,979**
462 ❑ Aug 1997 Cover: 1.50 **NM** value: **Cover or less**
Circ: Statement: **41,134** Diamd. preorders: **4,863**
463 ❑ Sep 1997 Cover: 1.50 **NM** value: **Cover or less**
Circ: Statement: **41,134** Diamd. preorders: **5,441**
464 ❑ Oct 1997 Cover: 1.50 **NM** value: **Cover or less**
Circ: Statement: **41,134** Diamd. preorders: **5,192**
465 ❑ Nov 1997 Cover: 1.50 **NM** value: **Cover or less**
Circ: Statement: **41,134** Diamd. preorders: **5,366**
466 ❑ Dec 1997 Cover: 1.50 **NM** value: **Cover or less**
Circ: Statement: **41,134** Diamd. preorders: **5,382**
467 ❑ Jan 1998 Cover: 1.75 **NM** value: **Cover or less**
Circ: Statement: **35,801** Diamd. preorders: **6,201**
468 ❑ Feb 1998 Cover: 1.75 **NM** value: **Cover or less**
Circ: Statement: **35,801** Diamd. preorders: **6,853**
469 ❑ Mar 1998 Cover: 1.75 **NM** value: **Cover or less**
Circ: Statement: **35,801** Diamd. preorders: **5,400**
470 ❑ Apr 1998 Cover: 1.75 **NM** value: **Cover or less**
Circ: Statement: **35,801** Diamd. preorders: **5,227**
• Has 1997 Statement, filed 11/1/97; avg print run 130,481; avg sales 39,544; avg subs 1,590; avg total paid 41,134; samples 426; office use 1,810; max existent 43,370; 67% of run returned
471 ❑ May 1998 Cover: 1.75 **NM** value: **Cover or less**
Circ: Statement: **35,801** Diamd. preorders: **4,705**
472 ❑ Jun 1998 Cover: 1.75 **NM** value: **Cover or less**
Circ: Statement: **35,801** Diamd. preorders: **4,814**
473 ❑ Jul 1998 Cover: 1.75 **NM** value: **Cover or less**
Circ: Statement: **35,801** Diamd. preorders: **4,807**
474 ❑ Aug 1998 Cover: 1.75 **NM** value: **Cover or less**
Circ: Statement: **35,801** Diamd. preorders: **4,818**
475 ❑ Sep 1998 Cover: 1.75 **NM** value: **Cover or less**
Circ: Statement: **35,801** Diamd. preorders: **4,965**
📖 The Warning; Circus Atmosphere; The Catch; Current Events; Surf Turf; Laptop Lament **A:** Stan Goldberg **W:** Angelo Decesare; George Gladir; Mike Pellowski
476 ❑ Oct 1998 Cover: 1.75 **NM** value: **Cover or less**
Circ: Statement: **35,801** Diamd. preorders: **4,651**
477 ❑ Nov 1998 Cover: 1.75 **NM** value: **Cover or less**
Circ: Statement: **35,801** Diamd. preorders: **4,377**
📖 Tuba or not Tuba; Hocus-Focus **A:** Stan Goldberg **W:** Angelo Decesare
478 ❑ Dec 1998 Cover: 1.75 **NM** value: **Cover or less**
Circ: Statement: **35,801** Diamd. preorders: **4,431**
479 ❑ Jan 1999 Cover: 1.75 **NM** value: **Cover or less**
Circ: Diamd. preorders: **4,538**
480 ❑ Feb 1999 Cover: 1.75 **NM** value: **Cover or less**
Circ: Diamd. preorders: **4,447**
481 ❑ Mar 1999 Cover: 1.75 **NM** value: **Cover or less**
Circ: Diamd. preorders: **4,294**
📖 Axe of Friendship **A:** Stan Goldberg **W:** Angelo Decesare
482 ❑ Apr 1999 Cover: 1.79 **NM** value: **Cover or less**
Circ: Diamd. preorders: **4,016**
📖 Losers Can Be Winners • Has 1998 Statement, filed 11/1/98; avg print run 112,065; avg sales 34,230; avg subs 1,571; avg total paid 35,801; samples 421; office use 3,208; max existent 39,430; 69% of run returned **A:** Stan Goldberg **W:** George Gladir
483 ❑ May 1999 Cover: 1.79 **NM** value: **Cover or less**
Circ: Diamd. preorders: **3,824**
📖 Pup-ularity Contest **A:** Stan Goldberg **W:** Angelo Decesare
484 ❑ Jun 1999 Cover: 1.79 **NM** value: **Cover or less**
Circ: Diamd. preorders: **3,770**
485 ❑ Jul 1999 Cover: 1.79 **NM** value: **Cover or less**
Circ: Diamd. preorders: **3,962**
486 ❑ Aug 1999 Cover: 1.79 **NM** value: **Cover or less**
Circ: Diamd. preorders: **3,976**
487 ❑ Sep 1999 Cover: 1.79 **NM** value: **Cover or less**
Circ: Diamd. preorders: **4,200**
488 ❑ Oct 1999 Cover: 1.79 **NM** value: **Cover or less**
Circ: Diamd. preorders: **3,956**
489 ❑ Nov 1999 Cover: 1.79 **NM** value: **Cover or less**
Circ: Diamd. preorders: **3,623**
490 ❑ Dec 1999 Cover: 1.79 **NM** value: **Cover or less**
Circ: Diamd. preorders: **3,713**
491 ❑ Jan 2000 Cover: 1.79 **NM** value: **Cover or less**
Circ: Diamd. preorders: **3,917**
492 ❑ Feb 2000 Cover: 1.79 **NM** value: **Cover or less**
Circ: Diamd. preorders: **3,950**
493 ❑ Mar 2000 Cover: 1.99 **NM** value: **Cover or less**
Circ: Diamd. preorders: **4,030**
494 ❑ Apr 2000 Cover: 1.99 **NM** value: **Cover or less**
Circ: Diamd. preorders: **3,522**
495 ❑ May 2000 Cover: 1.99 **NM** value: **Cover or less**
Circ: Diamd. preorders: **3,488**
496 ❑ Jun 2000 Cover: 1.99 **NM** value: **Cover or less**
Circ: Diamd. preorders: **3,512**
497 ❑ Jul 2000 Cover: 1.99 **NM** value: **Cover or less**
Circ: Diamd. preorders: **3,481**
498 ❑ Aug 2000 Cover: 1.99 **NM** value: **Cover or less**

Other grades: Multiply prices above by **1.5 for Mint • 2/3 for Very Fine • 1/3 for Fine • 1/5 for Very Good • 1/8 for Good**

Circ: Diamd. preorders: **3,576**
499 ❑ Sep 2000 Cover: 1.99 **NM** value: **Cover or less**
Circ: Diamd. preorders: **8,242**
500 ❑ Oct 2000 Cover: 1.99 **NM** value: **Cover or less**
Circ: Diamd. preorders: **3,580**
501 ❑ Nov 2000 Cover: 1.99 **NM** value: **Cover or less**
Circ: Diamd. preorders: **3,718**
502 ❑ Dec 2000 Cover: 1.99 **NM** value: **Cover or less**
Circ: Diamd. preorders: **3,690**
503 ❑ Jan 2001 Cover: 1.99 **NM** value: **Cover or less**
Circ: Statement: **24,285** Diamd. preorders: **3,558**
504 ❑ Feb 2001 Cover: 1.99 **NM** value: **Cover or less**
Circ: Statement: **24,285** Diamd. preorders: **3,518**
505 ❑ Mar 2001 Cover: 1.99 **NM** value: **Cover or less**
Circ: Statement: **24,285** Diamd. preorders: **3,267**
506 ❑ Apr 2001 Cover: 1.99 **NM** value: **Cover or less**
Circ: Statement: **24,285** Diamd. preorders: **3,358**
507 ❑ May 2001 Cover: 1.99 **NM** value: **Cover or less**
Circ: Statement: **24,285** Diamd. preorders: **3,230**
508 ❑ Jun 2001 Cover: 1.99 **NM** value: **Cover or less**
Circ: Statement: **24,285** Diamd. preorders: **3,502**
509 ❑ Jul 2001 Cover: 1.99 **NM** value: **Cover or less**
Circ: Statement: **24,285** Diamd. preorders: **3,518**
510 ❑ Aug 2001 Cover: 1.99 **NM** value: **Cover or less**
Circ: Statement: **24,285** Diamd. preorders: **3,919**
511 ❑ Sep 2001 Cover: 1.99 **NM** value: **Cover or less**
Circ: Statement: **24,285** Diamd. preorders: **3,835**
512 ❑ Oct 2001 Cover: 1.99 **NM** value: **Cover or less**
Circ: Statement: **24,285** Diamd. preorders: **3,613**
513 ❑ Nov 2001 Cover: 1.99 **NM** value: **Cover or less**
Circ: Statement: **24,285** Diamd. preorders: **3,861**
Anl 1 ❑ ca. 1950 Cover: 0.25 **NM** value: **1225.00**
Anl 2 ❑ ca. 1951 Cover: 0.25 **NM** value: **600.00**
Anl 3 ❑ ca. 1952 Cover: 0.25 **NM** value: **450.00**
Anl 4 ❑ ca. 1953 Cover: 0.25 **NM** value: **325.00**
Anl 5 ❑ ca. 1954 Cover: 0.25 **NM** value: **275.00**
Anl 6 ❑ ca. 1955 Cover: 0.25 **NM** value: **170.00**
Anl 7 ❑ ca. 1956 Cover: 0.25 **NM** value: **150.00**
Anl 8 ❑ ca. 1957 Cover: 0.25 **NM** value: **130.00**
Anl 9 ❑ ca. 1958 Cover: 0.25 **NM** value: **115.00**
Anl 10 ❑ ca. 1959 Cover: 0.25 **NM** value: **100.00**
Anl 11 ❑ ca. 1960 Cover: 0.25 **NM** value: **65.00**
Anl 12 ❑ ca. 1961 Cover: 0.25 **NM** value: **55.00**
Anl 13 ❑ ca. 1962 Cover: 0.25 **NM** value: **55.00**
Anl 14 ❑ ca. 1963 Cover: 0.25 **NM** value: **45.00**
Anl 15 ❑ ca. 1964 Cover: 0.25 **NM** value: **45.00**
Anl 16 ❑ ca. 1965 Cover: 0.25 **NM** value: **25.00**
Anl 17 ❑ ca. 1966 Cover: 0.25 **NM** value: **25.00**
Anl 18 ❑ ca. 1967 Cover: 0.25 **NM** value: **20.00**
Anl 19 ❑ ca. 1968 Cover: 0.25 **NM** value: **20.00**
Anl 20 ❑ ca. 1969 Cover: 0.25 **NM** value: **13.00**
Anl 21 ❑ ca. 1970 Cover: 0.25 **NM** value: **8.00**
Anl 22 ❑ ca. 1971 Cover: 0.25 **NM** value: **8.00**
Anl 23 ❑ ca. 1972 Cover: 0.25 **NM** value: **8.00**
Anl 24 ❑ ca. 1973 Cover: 0.25 **NM** value: **8.00**
Anl 25 ❑ ca. 1974 Cover: 0.35 **NM** value: **8.00**
Anl 26 ❑ ca. 1975 Cover: 0.35 **NM** value: **8.00**

ARCHIE ALL CANADIAN DIGEST — Archie

1 ❑ Aug 1996 Cover: 1.75 **NM** value: **2.00**
• digest. • reprints Archie stories set in Canada

ARCHIE AMERICANA SERIES — Archie

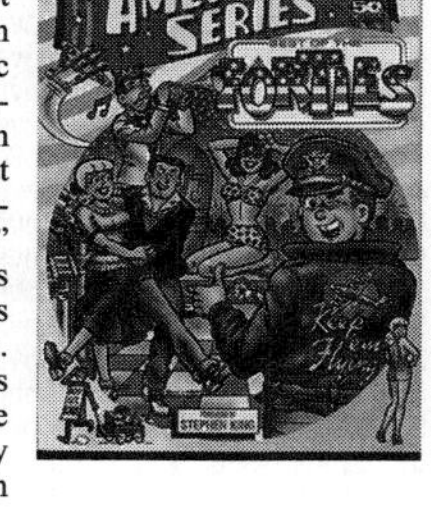

The eternal teen from Riverdale has been read and revered since his introduction in 1941. The highest popularity of the series occurred in the 1950s, when some of the classic characterizations were firmly established. This issue is a collection of some of the best stories from that era featuring "good, clean, wholesome, family oriented comics," which is probably why the series survived the seductive comics "trash" witch-hunts of the 1950s. Archie had become one of the titles (or series of titles) that embodied the heart of the Comics Code Authority before it was even established in 1954.

1 ❑ Cover: 8.95 **NM** value: **Cover or less**
• Best of the Forties
2 ❑ Cover: 8.95 **NM** value: **9.95**
• Best of the Fifties **W:** Dan Decarlo
2-2 ❑ Cover: 9.95 **NM** value: **Cover or less**
3 ❑ Cover: 9.95 **NM** value: **Cover or less**
• Best of the Sixties
4 ❑ Cover: 9.95 **NM** value: **Cover or less**
• Best of the Seventies **A:** Stan Goldberg

ARCHIE AND FRIENDS — Archie

1 ❑ Dec 1992 Cover: 1.25 **NM** value: **2.50**
📖 The Diary, Part 1; The Diary, Part 2; The Diary, Part 3; The Diary, Part 4 **A:** Stan Goldberg **W:** George Gladir ★ Appearance of Great Rondo, Hiram Lodge.
2 ❑ Feb 1992 Cover: 1.25 **NM** value: **2.00**
3 ❑ Apr 1992 Cover: 1.25 **NM** value: **2.00**
4 ❑ Jun 1992 Cover: 1.25 **NM** value: **1.50**
5 ❑ Aug 1992 Cover: 1.25 **NM** value: **1.50**
6 ❑ Oct 1992 Cover: 1.25 **NM** value: **1.50**
★ Appearance of Sabrina.
7 ❑ Mar 1993 Cover: 1.25 **NM** value: **1.50**
8 ❑ Cover: 1.25 **NM** value: **1.50**
9 ❑ Jun 1994 Cover: 1.25 **NM** value: **1.50**
10 ❑ Aug 1994 Cover: 1.50 **NM** value: **Cover or less**
11 ❑ Oct 1994 Cover: 1.50 **NM** value: **Cover or less**
12 ❑ Dec 1994 Cover: 1.50 **NM** value: **Cover or less**
13 ❑ Feb 1995 Cover: 1.50 **NM** value: **Cover or less**
14 ❑ May 1995 Cover: 1.50 **NM** value: **Cover or less**
15 ❑ Aug 1995 Cover: 1.50 **NM** value: **Cover or less**
16 ❑ Nov 1995 Cover: 1.50 **NM** value: **Cover or less**
17 ❑ Feb 1996 Cover: 1.50 **NM** value: **Cover or less**
Circ: Statement: **32,639**
18 ❑ May 1996 Cover: 1.50 **NM** value: **Cover or less**
Circ: Statement: **32,639**
19 ❑ Aug 1996 Cover: 1.50 **NM** value: **Cover or less**
Circ: Statement: **32,639**
• X-Men and E.R. parodies
20 ❑ Nov 1996 Cover: 1.50 **NM** value: **Cover or less**
Circ: Statement: **32,639**
21 ❑ Feb 1997 Cover: 1.50 **NM** value: **Cover or less**
Circ: Statement: **28,324**
• The class puts on Romeo and Juliet
22 ❑ Apr 1997 Cover: 1.50 **NM** value: **Cover or less**
Circ: Statement: **28,324** Diamd. preorders: **3,375**
• Friends parody; Has 1996 Statement, filed 9/27/96; avg print run 88,083; avg sales 31,221; avg subs 1,418; avg total paid 32,639; samples 396; office use 1,504; max existent 34,539; 61% of run returned
23 ❑ Jun 1997 Cover: 1.50 **NM** value: **Cover or less**
Circ: Statement: **28,324** Diamd. preorders: **3,709**
24 ❑ Aug 1997 Cover: 1.50 **NM** value: **Cover or less**
Circ: Statement: **28,324** Diamd. preorders: **4,173**
25 ❑ Oct 1997 Cover: 1.50 **NM** value: **Cover or less**
Circ: Statement: **28,324** Diamd. preorders: **3,975**
26 ❑ Dec 1997 Cover: 1.50 **NM** value: **Cover or less**
Circ: Statement: **28,324** Diamd. preorders: **4,035**
27 ❑ Feb 1998 Cover: 1.75 **NM** value: **Cover or less**
Circ: Statement: **26,453** Diamd. preorders: **4,163**
28 ❑ Apr 1998 Cover: 1.75 **NM** value: **Cover or less**
Circ: Statement: **26,453** Diamd. preorders: **3,653**
• Has 1997 Statement, filed 11/1/97; avg print run 80,986; avg sales 27,263; avg subs 1,060; avg total paid 28,324; samples 422; office use 1,922; max existent 30,667; 62% of run returned
29 ❑ Jun 1998 Cover: 1.75 **NM** value: **Cover or less**
Circ: Statement: **26,453** Diamd. preorders: **3,464**
• Pops opens a cyber-cafe
30 ❑ Aug 1998 Cover: 1.75 **NM** value: **Cover or less**
Circ: Statement: **26,453**
31 ❑ Oct 1998 Cover: 1.75 **NM** value: **Cover or less**
Circ: Statement: **26,453** Diamd. preorders: **3,418**
32 ❑ Dec 1998 Cover: 1.75 **NM** value: **Cover or less**
Circ: Statement: **26,453** Diamd. preorders: **3,341**
33 ❑ Feb 1999 Cover: 1.75 **NM** value: **Cover or less**
Circ: Diamd. preorders: **3,322**
34 ❑ Apr 1999 Cover: 1.79 **NM** value: **Cover or less**
Circ: Diamd. preorders: **2,930**
📖 That's Snow Business • Has 1998 Statement, filed 11/1/98; avg print run 73,139; avg sales 25,619; avg subs 834; avg total paid 26,453; samples 420; office use 1,730; max existent 28,603; 61% of run returned
35 ❑ Jun 1999 Cover: 1.79 **NM** value: **Cover or less**
Circ: Diamd. preorders: **2,854**
36 ❑ Aug 1999 Cover: 1.79 **NM** value: **Cover or less**
Circ: Diamd. preorders: **3,025**
37 ❑ Oct 1999 Cover: 1.79 **NM** value: **Cover or less**
Circ: Diamd. preorders: **2,944**
38 ❑ Dec 1999 Cover: 1.79 **NM** value: **Cover or less**
Circ: Diamd. preorders: **2,772**
39 ❑ Feb 2000 Cover: 1.99 **NM** value: **Cover or less**
Circ: Diamd. preorders: **2,841**
40 ❑ Apr 2000 Cover: 1.99 **NM** value: **Cover or less**
Circ: Diamd. preorders: **2,635**
41 ❑ Jun 2000 Cover: 1.99 **NM** value: **Cover or less**
Circ: Diamd. preorders: **2,537**
42 ❑ Aug 2000 Cover: 1.99 **NM** value: **Cover or less**
Circ: Diamd. preorders: **2,962**
43 ❑ Oct 2000 Cover: 1.99 **NM** value: **Cover or less**
Circ: Diamd. preorders: **2,852**
44 ❑ Dec 2000 Cover: 1.99 **NM** value: **Cover or less**
Circ: Diamd. preorders: **2,637**
45 ❑ Feb 2001 Cover: 1.99 **NM** value: **Cover or less**
Circ: Diamd. preorders: **2,612**
46 ❑ Apr 2001 Cover: 1.99 **NM** value: **Cover or less**
Circ: Diamd. preorders: **2,607**
📖 Riverdale High Exposed!
47 ❑ Jun 2001 Cover: 1.99 **NM** value: **Cover or less**
Circ: Diamd. preorders: **2,443**
48 ❑ Sep 2001 Cover: 1.99 **NM** value: **Cover or less**
Circ: Diamd. preorders: **2,608**
49 ❑ Oct 2001 Cover: 1.99 **NM** value: **Cover or less**
Circ: Diamd. preorders: **3,612**
50 ❑ Nov 2001 Cover: 1.99 **NM** value: **Cover or less**
Circ: Diamd. preorders: **3,804**

ARCHIE AND ME — Archie

Within a few years of the time this series was launched in 1964, forces as diverse as feminism and the war in Vietnam would call into question many of the traditional values of American life.

Archie, however, lived in a world of his own. Indeed, a great deal of his appeal lies in the very timelessness of Archie's good-natured high-school antics. The "Me" of the title is Mr. Weatherbee, and the stories in this series feature the fluctuating relationship between principal and student. The environment is the high school, and in some stories, the two are antagonists, pursuing different ends; in others, they work together to solve problems.

1 ❑ Oct 1964 Cover: 0.12 **NM** value: **125.00**
• **CGC:** 2 graded, best 8.5
📖 Archie: Muscle Bound!; Mr. Weatherbee: Wish You Were Here; Archie: Teacher's Pest; Archie: Desk Jockey's; Archie: Counselor at Lore
2 ❑ Cover: 0.12 **NM** value: **75.00**
3 ❑ Cover: 0.12 **NM** value: **45.00**
4 ❑ Cover: 0.12 **NM** value: **34.00**
5 ❑ Cover: 0.12 **NM** value: **34.00**
6 ❑ Cover: 0.12 **NM** value: **20.00**
7 ❑ Cover: 0.12 **NM** value: **20.00**
8 ❑ Cover: 0.12 **NM** value: **20.00**
9 ❑ Cover: 0.12 **NM** value: **20.00**
10 ❑ Cover: 0.12 **NM** value: **20.00**
11 ❑ Cover: 0.12 **NM** value: **12.00**
12 ❑ Cover: 0.12 **NM** value: **12.00**
13 ❑ Cover: 0.12 **NM** value: **12.00**
14 ❑ Apr 1967 Cover: 0.12 **NM** value: **12.00**
15 ❑ Jun 1967 Cover: 0.12 **NM** value: **12.00**
16 ❑ Aug 1967 Cover: 0.12 **NM** value: **12.00**
17 ❑ Oct 1967 Cover: 0.12 **NM** value: **12.00**
18 ❑ Dec 1967 Cover: 0.12 **NM** value: **12.00**
19 ❑ Feb 1968 Cover: 0.12 **NM** value: **12.00**
Circ: Statement: **333,212**
20 ❑ Apr 1968 Cover: 0.12 **NM** value: **12.00**
Circ: Statement: **333,212**
21 ❑ Jun 1968 Cover: 0.12 **NM** value: **8.00**
Circ: Statement: **333,212**
22 ❑ 1968 **NM** value: **8.00**
Circ: Statement: **333,212**
23 ❑ 1968 **NM** value: **8.00**
Circ: Statement: **333,212**
24 ❑ **NM** value: **8.00**
25 ❑ **NM** value: **8.00**
26 ❑ **NM** value: **8.00**
27 ❑ **NM** value: **8.00**
28 ❑ Jun 1969 **NM** value: **8.00**
Circ: Statement: **345,869**
29 ❑ 1969 **NM** value: **8.00**
Circ: Statement: **345,869**
30 ❑ 1969 **NM** value: **8.00**
Circ: Statement: **345,869**
31 ❑ **NM** value: **6.00**
32 ❑ **NM** value: **6.00**
33 ❑ **NM** value: **6.00**
34 ❑ Apr 1970 **NM** value: **6.00**
Circ: Statement: **297,739**
35 ❑ Jun 1970 **NM** value: **6.00**
Circ: Statement: **297,739**
36 ❑ 1970 **NM** value: **6.00**
Circ: Statement: **297,739**
37 ❑ 1970 **NM** value: **6.00**
Circ: Statement: **297,739**
38 ❑ **NM** value: **6.00**
39 ❑ **NM** value: **6.00**
40 ❑ **NM** value: **6.00**
41 ❑ Apr 1971 **NM** value: **4.00**
Circ: Statement: **271,635**
42 ❑ Jun 1971 **NM** value: **4.00**
Circ: Statement: **271,635**
43 ❑ 1971 **NM** value: **4.00**
Circ: Statement: **271,635**
44 ❑ 1971 **NM** value: **4.00**
Circ: Statement: **271,635**
45 ❑ **NM** value: **4.00**
46 ❑ **NM** value: **4.00**
47 ❑ **NM** value: **4.00**
48 ❑ Apr 1972 **NM** value: **4.00**
Circ: Statement: **208,328**
49 ❑ Jun 1972 **NM** value: **4.00**
Circ: Statement: **208,328**
50 ❑ **NM** value: **4.00**
51 ❑ **NM** value: **2.50**
52 ❑ **NM** value: **2.50**
53 ❑ **NM** value: **2.50**
54 ❑ Feb 1973 Cover: 0.25 **NM** value: **2.50**
Circ: Statement: **190,982**
55 ❑ Apr 1973 **NM** value: **2.50**
Circ: Statement: **190,982**
56 ❑ Jun 1973 **NM** value: **2.50**
Circ: Statement: **190,982**
57 ❑ Jul 1973 **NM** value: **2.50**
Circ: Statement: **190,982**
58 ❑ Aug 1973 **NM** value: **2.50**
Circ: Statement: **190,982**
59 ❑ Sep 1973 **NM** value: **2.50**
Circ: Statement: **190,982**
60 ❑ Oct 1973 **NM** value: **2.50**
Circ: Statement: **190,982**
61 ❑ Dec 1973 **NM** value: **2.50**
Circ: Statement: **190,982**
62 ❑ Jan 1974 **NM** value: **2.50**
Circ: Statement: **189,334**
63 ❑ Feb 1974 **NM** value: **2.50**
Circ: Statement: **189,334**
64 ❑ Apr 1974 **NM** value: **2.50**
Circ: Statement: **189,334**
65 ❑ Jun 1974 **NM** value: **2.50**
Circ: Statement: **189,334**
66 ❑ Jul 1974 **NM** value: **2.50**
Circ: Statement: **189,334**
67 ❑ Aug 1974 **NM** value: **2.50**
Circ: Statement: **189,334**
68 ❑ Sep 1974 **NM** value: **2.50**
Circ: Statement: **189,334**
69 ❑ Oct 1974 **NM** value: **2.50**
Circ: Statement: **189,334**
70 ❑ Dec 1974 **NM** value: **2.50**
Circ: Statement: **189,334**

CGC-graded: Multiply prices above by **33 for 9.9 M • 16 for 9.8 NM/M • 7 for 9.6 NM+ • 5 for 9.4 NM • 2.5 for 9.2 NM- • 1.5 for 9.0 VF/NM**

71 ❑ Jan 1975 **NM** value: **2.50**
Circ: Statement: **151,741**
72 ❑ Feb 1975 **NM** value: **2.50**
Circ: Statement: **151,741**
73 ❑ Apr 1975 **NM** value: **2.50**
Circ: Statement: **151,741**
74 ❑ Jun 1975 **NM** value: **2.50**
Circ: Statement: **151,741**
• Has 1974 Statement; avg print run 371,933; avg sales 189,063; avg subs 271; avg total paid 189,334; max existent 189,334; 49% of run returned
75 ❑ Jul 1975 **NM** value: **2.50**
Circ: Statement: **151,741**
76 ❑ Aug 1975 **NM** value: **2.50**
Circ: Statement: **151,741**
77 ❑ Sep 1975 **NM** value: **2.50**
Circ: Statement: **151,741**
78 ❑ Oct 1975 **NM** value: **2.50**
Circ: Statement: **151,741**
79 ❑ Dec 1975 **NM** value: **2.50**
Circ: Statement: **151,741**
80 ❑ Jan 1976 **NM** value: **2.50**
Circ: Statement: **141,825**
81 ❑ Feb 1976 **NM** value: **1.50**
Circ: Statement: **141,825**
82 ❑ Apr 1976 **NM** value: **1.50**
Circ: Statement: **141,825**
• Has 1975 Statement; avg print run 341,911; avg sales 151,541; avg subs 200; avg total paid 151,741; office use 300; max existent 152,041; 56% of run returned
83 ❑ Jun 1976 **NM** value: **1.50**
Circ: Statement: **141,825**
84 ❑ Jul 1976 **NM** value: **1.50**
Circ: Statement: **141,825**
85 ❑ Aug 1976 **NM** value: **1.50**
Circ: Statement: **141,825**
86 ❑ Sep 1976 **NM** value: **1.50**
Circ: Statement: **141,825**
87 ❑ Oct 1976 **NM** value: **1.50**
Circ: Statement: **141,825**
88 ❑ Dec 1976 **NM** value: **1.50**
Circ: Statement: **141,825**
89 ❑ Jan 1977 **NM** value: **1.50**
Circ: Statement: **122,736**
90 ❑ Feb 1977 **NM** value: **1.50**
Circ: Statement: **122,736**
91 ❑ Apr 1977 **NM** value: **1.50**
Circ: Statement: **122,736**
• Has 1976 Statement; avg print run 327,589; avg sales 141,768; avg subs 57; avg total paid 141,825; office use 300; max existent 142,125; 57% of run returned
92 ❑ Jun 1977 **NM** value: **1.50**
Circ: Statement: **122,736**
93 ❑ Jul 1977 **NM** value: **1.50**
Circ: Statement: **122,736**
94 ❑ Aug 1977 **NM** value: **1.50**
Circ: Statement: **122,736**
95 ❑ Sep 1977 Cover: 0.35 **NM** value: **1.50**
Circ: Statement: **122,736**
96 ❑ Oct 1977 Cover: 0.35 **NM** value: **1.50**
Circ: Statement: **122,736**
97 ❑ Dec 1977 Cover: 0.35 **NM** value: **1.50**
Circ: Statement: **122,736**
98 ❑ Jan 1978 Cover: 0.35 **NM** value: **1.50**
Circ: Statement: **110,245**
99 ❑ Feb 1978 **NM** value: **1.50**
Circ: Statement: **110,245**
100 ❑ Apr 1978 **NM** value: **1.50**
Circ: Statement: **110,245**
• Has 1977 Statement; avg print run 300,080; avg sales 122,593; avg subs 143; avg total paid 122,736; office use 300; max existent 123,036; 59% of run returned
101 ❑ Jun 1978 **NM** value: **1.00**
Circ: Statement: **110,245**
102 ❑ Jul 1978 **NM** value: **1.00**
Circ: Statement: **110,245**
103 ❑ Aug 1978 **NM** value: **1.00**
Circ: Statement: **110,245**
104 ❑ Sep 1978 **NM** value: **1.00**
Circ: Statement: **110,245**
105 ❑ Oct 1978 **NM** value: **1.00**
Circ: Statement: **110,245**
106 ❑ Dec 1978 **NM** value: **1.00**
Circ: Statement: **110,245**
107 ❑ Jan 1979 **NM** value: **1.00**
Circ: Statement: **102,191**
108 ❑ Feb 1979 **NM** value: **1.00**
Circ: Statement: **102,191**
109 ❑ Apr 1979 **NM** value: **1.00**
Circ: Statement: **102,191**
• Has 1978 Statement; avg print run 289,621; avg sales 110,221; avg subs 24; avg total paid 110,245; office use 300; max existent 110,545; 62% of run returned
110 ❑ Jun 1979 **NM** value: **1.00**
Circ: Statement: **102,191**
111 ❑ Jul 1979 **NM** value: **1.00**
Circ: Statement: **102,191**
112 ❑ Aug 1979 **NM** value: **1.00**
Circ: Statement: **102,191**
113 ❑ Sep 1979 **NM** value: **1.00**
Circ: Statement: **102,191**
114 ❑ Oct 1979 **NM** value: **1.00**
Circ: Statement: **102,191**
115 ❑ Dec 1979 **NM** value: **1.00**
Circ: Statement: **102,191**
116 ❑ Jan 1980 **NM** value: **1.00**
Circ: Statement: **86,928**
117 ❑ Feb 1980 **NM** value: **1.00**
Circ: Statement: **86,928**
118 ❑ Apr 1980 **NM** value: **1.00**
Circ: Statement: **86,928**
• Has 1979 Statement; avg print run 272,896; avg sales 102,107; avg subs 84; avg total paid 102,191; office use 300; max existent 102,491; 62% of run returned
119 ❑ Jun 1980 **NM** value: **1.00**
Circ: Statement: **86,928**
120 ❑ Jul 1980 **NM** value: **1.00**
Circ: Statement: **86,928**
121 ❑ Aug 1980 **NM** value: **1.00**
Circ: Statement: **86,928**
122 ❑ Sep 1980 **NM** value: **1.00**
Circ: Statement: **86,928**
123 ❑ Oct 1980 **NM** value: **1.00**
Circ: Statement: **86,928**
124 ❑ Dec 1980 **NM** value: **1.00**
Circ: Statement: **86,928**
125 ❑ Feb 1981 **NM** value: **1.00**
Circ: Statement: **79,639**
126 ❑ Apr 1981 **NM** value: **1.00**
Circ: Statement: **79,639**
• Has 1980 Statement; avg print run 255,620; avg sales 86,818; avg subs 118; avg total paid 86,928; office use 300; max existent 87,236; 66% of run returned
127 ❑ 1981 **NM** value: **1.00**
Circ: Statement: **79,639**
128 ❑ 1981 **NM** value: **1.00**
Circ: Statement: **79,639**
129 ❑ 1981 **NM** value: **1.00**
Circ: Statement: **79,639**
130 ❑ 1981 **NM** value: **1.00**
Circ: Statement: **79,639**
131 ❑ 1981 **NM** value: **1.00**
Circ: Statement: **79,639**
132 ❑ Feb 1982 **NM** value: **1.00**
Circ: Statement: **63,824**
133 ❑ Apr 1982 **NM** value: **1.00**
Circ: Statement: **63,824**
• Has 1981 Statement; avg print run 266,688; avg sales 79,569; avg subs 70; avg total paid 79,639; office use 300; max existent 79,939; 55% of run returned
134 ❑ Jun 1982 **NM** value: **1.00**
Circ: Statement: **63,824**
135 ❑ Aug 1982 **NM** value: **1.00**
Circ: Statement: **63,824**
136 ❑ Oct 1982 **NM** value: **1.00**
Circ: Statement: **63,824**
137 ❑ Dec 1982 **NM** value: **1.00**
Circ: Statement: **63,824**
138 ❑ Feb 1983 **NM** value: **1.00**
Circ: Statement: **65,139**
139 ❑ May 1983 **NM** value: **1.00**
Circ: Statement: **65,139**
• Has 1982 Statement; avg print run 199,805; avg sales 63,699; avg subs 125; avg total paid 63,824; office use 300; max existent 64,124; 68% of run returned
140 ❑ 1983 **NM** value: **1.00**
Circ: Statement: **65,139**
141 ❑ 1983 **NM** value: **1.00**
Circ: Statement: **65,139**
142 ❑ 1983 **NM** value: **1.00**
Circ: Statement: **65,139**
143 ❑ Feb 1984 **NM** value: **1.00**
Circ: Statement: **59,836**
144 ❑ Apr 1984 **NM** value: **1.00**
Circ: Statement: **59,836**
145 ❑ Jun 1984 **NM** value: **1.00**
Circ: Statement: **59,836**
• Has 1983 Statement; avg print run 163,177; avg sales 64,991; avg subs 148; avg total paid 65,139; office use 300; max existent 65,439; 60% of run returned
146 ❑ Aug 1984 **NM** value: **1.00**
Circ: Statement: **59,836**
147 ❑ Oct 1984 **NM** value: **1.00**
Circ: Statement: **59,836**
148 ❑ Dec 1984 **NM** value: **1.00**
Circ: Statement: **59,836**
149 ❑ Feb 1985 **NM** value: **1.00**
Circ: Statement: **58,571**
150 ❑ Apr 1985 **NM** value: **1.00**
Circ: Statement: **58,571**
• Has 1984 Statement; avg print run 152,116; avg sales 59,670; avg subs 166; avg total paid 59,836; office use 300; max existent 60,136; 61% of run returned
151 ❑ Jun 1985 **NM** value: **1.00**
Circ: Statement: **58,571**
152 ❑ Aug 1985 **NM** value: **1.00**
Circ: Statement: **58,571**
153 ❑ Oct 1985 **NM** value: **1.00**
Circ: Statement: **58,571**
154 ❑ Dec 1985 **NM** value: **1.00**
Circ: Statement: **58,571**
155 ❑ Feb 1986 **NM** value: **1.00**
156 ❑ Apr 1986 **NM** value: **1.00**
• Has 1985 Statement; avg print run 148,270; avg sales 58,401; avg subs 170; avg total paid 58,571; office use 300; max existent 58,871; 60% of run returned
157 ❑ Jun 1986 **NM** value: **1.00**
158 ❑ Aug 1986 **NM** value: **1.00**
159 ❑ Oct 1986 **NM** value: **1.00**
160 ❑ Dec 1986 **NM** value: **1.00**
161 ❑ Feb 1987 **NM** value: **1.00**
final issue.

ARCHIE ANNUAL DIGEST MAGAZINE — Archie

66	❑ Jun 1995	Cover: 1.75	**NM** value: **Cover or less**
67	❑ Oct 1995	Cover: 1.75	**NM** value: **Cover or less**
68	❑ Apr 1997	Cover: 1.79	**NM** value: **Cover or less**

ARCHIE...ARCHIE ANDREWS, WHERE ARE YOU? DIGEST MAGAZINE — Archie

Archie Comics introduced a number of digests, which offered several advantages to young purchasers: The issues contained many more pages than regular-size comics; they were small enough to fit in many pockets; and they were racked by store checkouts for impulse buying. As a result, the digests tended to have larger circulations than even the best-known of the regular-size Archie comics.

Among the several Archie digests, this title contained more modern stories (and fewer reprints of the classic material of earlier years), and many of the covers were focused on Archie and his mom and dad. — Maggie

1	❑ Feb 1977	Cover: 0.75	**NM** value: **15.00**
2	❑ May 1977	Cover: 0.75	**NM** value: **10.00**
3	❑ Aug 1977	Cover: 0.75	**NM** value: **10.00**
4	❑ Nov 1977	Cover: 0.75	**NM** value: **10.00**
5	❑ Feb 1978	Cover: 0.75	**NM** value: **10.00**
6	❑ May 1978	Cover: 0.75	**NM** value: **10.00**
7	❑ Aug 1978	Cover: 0.75	**NM** value: **10.00**
8	❑ Nov 1978	Cover: 0.75	**NM** value: **10.00**
	📖 The Strange New World of the Fly • reprints story from Adventures of the Fly #1 **A:** Jack Kirby		
9	❑ Feb 1979	Cover: 0.75	**NM** value: **10.00**
10	❑ May 1979	Cover: 0.75	**NM** value: **10.00**
11	❑ Aug 1979	Cover: 0.75	**NM** value: **7.50**
12	❑ Nov 1979	Cover: 0.75	**NM** value: **7.50**
13	❑ Feb 1980	Cover: 0.75	**NM** value: **7.50**
14	❑ May 1980	Cover: 0.75	**NM** value: **7.50**
15	❑ Aug 1980	Cover: 0.75	**NM** value: **7.50**
16	❑ Nov 1980	Cover: 0.75	**NM** value: **7.50**
17	❑ Feb 1981	Cover: 0.95	**NM** value: **7.50**
18	❑ May 1981	Cover: 0.95	**NM** value: **7.50**
19	❑ Aug 1981	Cover: 0.95	**NM** value: **7.50**
20	❑ Nov 1981	Cover: 0.95	**NM** value: **7.50**
21	❑ Feb 1982	Cover: 0.95	**NM** value: **5.00**
22	❑ May 1982	Cover: 0.95	**NM** value: **5.00**
23	❑ Aug 1982	Cover: 0.95	**NM** value: **5.00**
24	❑ Nov 1982	Cover: 1.00	**NM** value: **5.00**
25	❑ Feb 1983	Cover: 1.00	**NM** value: **5.00**
26	❑ May 1983	Cover: 1.00	**NM** value: **5.00**
27	❑ Aug 1983	Cover: 1.00	**NM** value: **5.00**
28	❑ Oct 1983	Cover: 1.00	**NM** value: **5.00**
29	❑ Dec 1983	Cover: 1.00	**NM** value: **5.00**
30	❑ Feb 1984	Cover: 1.00	**NM** value: **5.00**
31	❑ Apr 1984	Cover: 1.00	**NM** value: **5.00**
32	❑ Jun 1984	Cover: 1.00	**NM** value: **5.00**
33	❑ Aug 1984	Cover: 1.00	**NM** value: **5.00**
34	❑ Oct 1984	Cover: 1.00	**NM** value: **5.00**
35	❑ Dec 1984	Cover: 1.00	**NM** value: **5.00**
36	❑ Feb 1985	Cover: 1.25	**NM** value: **5.00**
37	❑ Apr 1985	Cover: 1.25	**NM** value: **5.00**
38	❑ Jun 1985	Cover: 1.25	**NM** value: **5.00**
39	❑ Aug 1985	Cover: 1.25	**NM** value: **5.00**
40	❑ Oct 1985	Cover: 1.25	**NM** value: **5.00**
41	❑ Dec 1985	Cover: 1.25	**NM** value: **5.00**
42	❑ Feb 1986	Cover: 1.25	**NM** value: **5.00**
43	❑ Apr 1986	Cover: 1.25	**NM** value: **5.00**
44	❑ Jun 1986	Cover: 1.25	**NM** value: **5.00**
45	❑ Aug 1986	Cover: 1.25	**NM** value: **5.00**
46	❑ Oct 1986	Cover: 1.25	**NM** value: **5.00**
47	❑ Dec 1986	Cover: 1.25	**NM** value: **5.00**
48	❑ Feb 1987	Cover: 1.25	**NM** value: **5.00**
49	❑ Apr 1987	Cover: 1.25	**NM** value: **5.00**
50	❑ Jun 1987	Cover: 1.25	**NM** value: **5.00**
51	❑ Aug 1987	Cover: 1.35	**NM** value: **5.00**
52	❑ Oct 1987	Cover: 1.35	**NM** value: **5.00**
53	❑ Dec 1987	Cover: 1.35	**NM** value: **5.00**
54	❑ Feb 1988	Cover: 1.35	**NM** value: **5.00**
55	❑ Apr 1988	Cover: 1.35	**NM** value: **5.00**
56	❑ Jun 1988	Cover: 1.35	**NM** value: **5.00**
57	❑ Aug 1988	Cover: 1.35	**NM** value: **5.00**
58	❑ Oct 1988	Cover: 1.35	**NM** value: **5.00**
59	❑ Dec 1988	Cover: 1.35	**NM** value: **5.00**
60	❑ Feb 1989	Cover: 1.35	**NM** value: **5.00**
61	❑ Apr 1989	Cover: 1.35	**NM** value: **5.00**
62	❑ Jun 1989	Cover: 1.35	**NM** value: **5.00**
63	❑ Aug 1989	Cover: 1.35	**NM** value: **5.00**
64	❑ Oct 1989	Cover: 1.35	**NM** value: **5.00**
65	❑ Dec 1989	Cover: 1.35	**NM** value: **5.00**
66	❑ Feb 1990	Cover: 1.50	**NM** value: **5.00**
67	❑ Apr 1990	Cover: 1.50	**NM** value: **5.00**
68	❑ Jun 1990	Cover: 1.50	**NM** value: **5.00**
69	❑ Aug 1990	Cover: 1.50	**NM** value: **5.00**
70	❑ Oct 1990	Cover: 1.50	**NM** value: **5.00**
71	❑ Dec 1990	Cover: 1.50	**NM** value: **5.00**
72	❑ Feb 1991	Cover: 1.50	**NM** value: **3.00**
73	❑ Apr 1991	Cover: 1.50	**NM** value: **3.00**
74	❑ Jun 1991	Cover: 1.50	**NM** value: **3.00**
75	❑ Aug 1991	Cover: 1.50	**NM** value: **3.00**
76	❑ Oct 1991	Cover: 1.50	**NM** value: **3.00**
77	❑ Dec 1991	Cover: 1.50	**NM** value: **3.00**
78	❑ Feb 1992	Cover: 1.50	**NM** value: **3.00**
79	❑ Apr 1992	Cover: 1.50	**NM** value: **3.00**
80	❑ Jun 1992	Cover: 1.50	**NM** value: **3.00**
81	❑ Aug 1992	Cover: 1.50	**NM** value: **3.00**
82	❑ Oct 1992	Cover: 1.50	**NM** value: **3.00**
83	❑ Dec 1992	Cover: 1.50	**NM** value: **3.00**
84	❑ Jan 1993	Cover: 1.50	**NM** value: **3.00**

Other grades: Multiply prices above by **1.5 for Mint • 2/3 for Very Fine • 1/3 for Fine • 1/5 for Very Good • 1/8 for Good**

85 ❑ Feb 1993 Cover: 1.50 **NM** value: **3.00**
86 ❑ Apr 1993 Cover: 1.50 **NM** value: **2.00**
87 ❑ Jun 1993 Cover: 1.50 **NM** value: **2.00**
88 ❑ Aug 1993 Cover: 1.50 **NM** value: **2.00**
89 ❑ Oct 1993 Cover: 1.50 **NM** value: **2.00**
90 ❑ Dec 1993 Cover: 1.50 **NM** value: **2.00**
91 ❑ Feb 1994 Cover: 1.75 **NM** value: **2.00**
92 ❑ Mar 1994 Cover: 1.75 **NM** value: **2.00**
93 ❑ May 1994 Cover: 1.75 **NM** value: **2.00**
94 ❑ Jul 1994 Cover: 1.75 **NM** value: **2.00**
95 ❑ Sep 1994 Cover: 1.75 **NM** value: **2.00**
96 ❑ Nov 1994 Cover: 1.75 **NM** value: **2.00**
97 ❑ Jan 1995 Cover: 1.75 **NM** value: **Cover or less**
Circ: Statement: **98,516**
98 ❑ Feb 1995 Cover: 1.75 **NM** value: **Cover or less**
Circ: Statement: **98,516**
99 ❑ Apr 1995 Cover: 1.75 **NM** value: **Cover or less**
Circ: Statement: **98,516**
100 ❑ Jun 1995 Cover: 1.75 **NM** value: **Cover or less**
Circ: Statement: **98,516**
101 ❑ Aug 1995 Cover: 1.75 **NM** value: **Cover or less**
Circ: Statement: **98,516**
102 ❑ Oct 1995 Cover: 1.75 **NM** value: **Cover or less**
Circ: Statement: **98,516**
103 ❑ Dec 1995 Cover: 1.75 **NM** value: **Cover or less**
Circ: Statement: **98,516**
104 ❑ Jan 1996 Cover: 1.75 **NM** value: **Cover or less**
Circ: Statement: **96,996**
105 ❑ Mar 1996 Cover: 1.75 **NM** value: **Cover or less**
Circ: Statement: **96,996**
106 ❑ May 1996 Cover: 1.75 **NM** value: **Cover or less**
Circ: Statement: **96,996**
107 ❑ Aug 1996 Cover: 1.75 **NM** value: **Cover or less**
Circ: Statement: **96,996**
108 ❑ Nov 1996 Cover: 1.79 **NM** value: **Cover or less**
Circ: Statement: **96,996**
109 ❑ Feb 1997 Cover: 1.79 **NM** value: **Cover or less**
110 ❑ May 1997 Cover: 1.79 **NM** value: **Cover or less**
111 ❑ Sep 1997 Cover: 1.79 **NM** value: **Cover or less**
112 ❑ Nov 1997 Cover: 1.79 **NM** value: **Cover or less**
113 ❑ Feb 1998 Cover: 1.95 **NM** value: **Cover or less**
114 ❑ May 1998 Cover: 1.95 **NM** value: **Cover or less**
Circ: Diamd. preorders: **2,986**
115 ❑ Sep 1998 Cover: 1.95 **NM** value: **Cover or less**
116 ❑ Nov 1998 Cover: 1.95 **NM** value: **Cover or less**
117 ❑ Feb 1999 Cover: 1.95 **NM** value: **Cover or less**

ARCHIE AS PUREHEART THE POWERFUL Archie

1 ❑ Sep 1966 Cover: 0.15 **NM** value: **50.00**
• **CGC:** 1 graded, best 3.5
2 ❑ Cover: 0.15 **NM** value: **35.00**
3 ❑ Cover: 0.15 **NM** value: **25.00**
4 ❑ Cover: 0.15 **NM** value: **25.00**
5 ❑ Cover: 0.15 **NM** value: **25.00**
6 ❑ Nov 1967 Cover: 0.15 **NM** value: **25.00**

ARCHIE AT RIVERDALE HIGH Archie

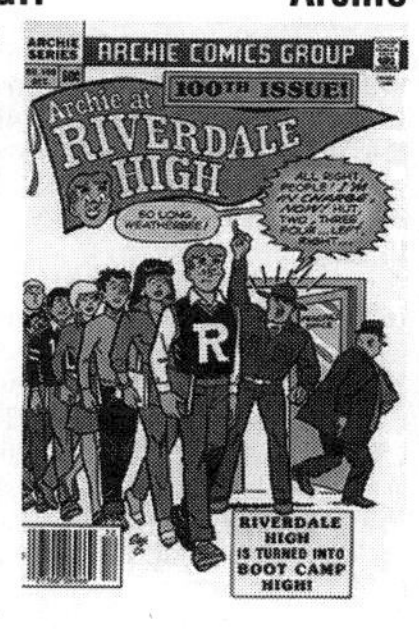

Teen humor is an eternal constant in the comics universe, and Archie, of course, features it as the ongoing focus. Archie at Riverdale High is another in the endless line of Archie titles pumped out to satisfy America's nearly inexhaustible appetite for the lovably bumbling redheaded teenager. This title features the adventures of Archie, Jughead, Moose, Reggie, Betty, Veronica, and the rest of the gang at their alma mater, Riverdale High. Mr. Weatherbee, Riverdale's long-suffering principal, also takes center stage, along with the various teachers, coaches, secretaries, lunchroom ladies, and other familiar denizens of the high-school world.

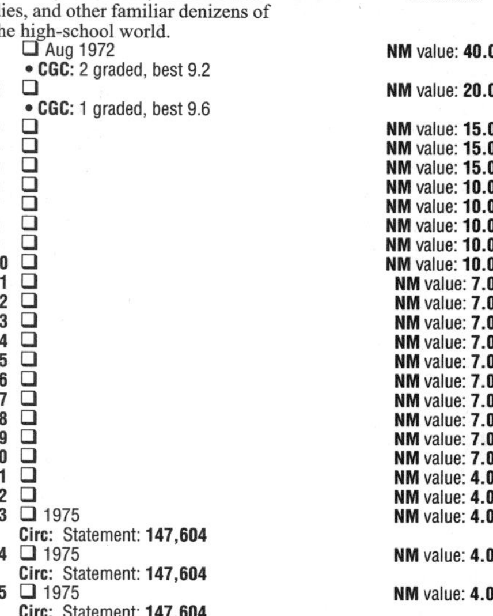

1 ❑ Aug 1972 **NM** value: **40.00**
• **CGC:** 2 graded, best 9.2
2 ❑ **NM** value: **20.00**
• **CGC:** 1 graded, best 9.6
3 ❑ **NM** value: **15.00**
4 ❑ **NM** value: **15.00**
5 ❑ **NM** value: **15.00**
6 ❑ **NM** value: **10.00**
7 ❑ **NM** value: **10.00**
8 ❑ **NM** value: **10.00**
9 ❑ **NM** value: **10.00**
10 ❑ **NM** value: **10.00**
11 ❑ **NM** value: **7.00**
12 ❑ **NM** value: **7.00**
13 ❑ **NM** value: **7.00**
14 ❑ **NM** value: **7.00**
15 ❑ **NM** value: **7.00**
16 ❑ **NM** value: **7.00**
17 ❑ **NM** value: **7.00**
18 ❑ **NM** value: **7.00**
19 ❑ **NM** value: **7.00**
20 ❑ **NM** value: **7.00**
21 ❑ **NM** value: **4.00**
22 ❑ **NM** value: **4.00**
23 ❑ 1975 **NM** value: **4.00**
Circ: Statement: **147,604**
24 ❑ 1975 **NM** value: **4.00**
Circ: Statement: **147,604**
25 ❑ 1975 **NM** value: **4.00**
Circ: Statement: **147,604**
26 ❑ 1975 **NM** value: **4.00**
Circ: Statement: **147,604**
27 ❑ 1975 **NM** value: **4.00**
Circ: Statement: **147,604**
28 ❑ 1975 **NM** value: **4.00**
Circ: Statement: **147,604**
29 ❑ 1975 **NM** value: **4.00**
Circ: Statement: **147,604**
30 ❑ 1975 **NM** value: **4.00**
Circ: Statement: **147,604**
31 ❑ Dec 1975 **NM** value: **4.00**
Circ: Statement: **147,604**
32 ❑ 1976 **NM** value: **4.00**
Circ: Statement: **134,374**
33 ❑ 1976 **NM** value: **4.00**
Circ: Statement: **134,374**
34 ❑ 1976 **NM** value: **4.00**
Circ: Statement: **134,374**
35 ❑ May 1976 **NM** value: **4.00**
Circ: Statement: **134,374**
• Has 1975 Statement, avg print run 329,858; avg sales 147,461; avg subs 143; avg total paid 147,604; office use 300; max existent 147,904; 55% of run returned
36 ❑ 1976 **NM** value: **4.00**
Circ: Statement: **134,374**
37 ❑ 1976 **NM** value: **4.00**
Circ: Statement: **134,374**
38 ❑ 1976 **NM** value: **4.00**
Circ: Statement: **134,374**
39 ❑ 1976 **NM** value: **4.00**
Circ: Statement: **134,374**
40 ❑ 1976 **NM** value: **4.00**
Circ: Statement: **134,374**
41 ❑ Dec 1976 **NM** value: **3.00**
Circ: Statement: **134,374**
42 ❑ 1977 **NM** value: **3.00**
Circ: Statement: **119,017**
43 ❑ 1977 **NM** value: **3.00**
Circ: Statement: **119,017**
44 ❑ May 1977 **NM** value: **3.00**
Circ: Statement: **119,017**
• Has 1976 Statement, filed 10/1/1976; avg print run 310,499; avg sales 134,227; avg subs 147; avg total paid 134,374; office use 300; max existent 134,674; 57% of run returned
45 ❑ 1977 **NM** value: **3.00**
Circ: Statement: **119,017**
46 ❑ 1977 **NM** value: **3.00**
Circ: Statement: **119,017**
47 ❑ 1977 **NM** value: **3.00**
Circ: Statement: **119,017**
48 ❑ 1977 **NM** value: **3.00**
Circ: Statement: **119,017**
49 ❑ 1977 **NM** value: **3.00**
Circ: Statement: **119,017**
50 ❑ Dec 1977 **NM** value: **3.00**
Circ: Statement: **119,017**
51 ❑ 1978 **NM** value: **3.00**
Circ: Statement: **104,076**
52 ❑ 1978 **NM** value: **3.00**
Circ: Statement: **104,076**
53 ❑ May 1978 **NM** value: **3.00**
Circ: Statement: **104,076**
• Has1977 Statement; avg print run 287,593; avg sales 118,829; avg subs 188; avg total paid 119,017; office use 300; max existent 119,317; 59% of run returned
54 ❑ 1978 **NM** value: **3.00**
Circ: Statement: **104,076**
55 ❑ 1978 **NM** value: **3.00**
Circ: Statement: **104,076**
56 ❑ 1978 **NM** value: **3.00**
Circ: Statement: **104,076**
57 ❑ 1978 **NM** value: **3.00**
Circ: Statement: **104,076**
58 ❑ 1978 **NM** value: **3.00**
Circ: Statement: **104,076**
59 ❑ Dec 1978 **NM** value: **3.00**
Circ: Statement: **104,076**
60 ❑ 1979 **NM** value: **3.00**
Circ: Statement: **100,047**
61 ❑ 1979 **NM** value: **2.00**
Circ: Statement: **100,047**
62 ❑ May 1979 **NM** value: **2.00**
Circ: Statement: **100,047**
• Has1978 Statement; avg print run 288,157; avg sales 104,052; avg subs 24; avg total paid 104,076; office use 300; max existent 104,376; 64% of run returned
63 ❑ 1979 **NM** value: **2.00**
Circ: Statement: **100,047**
64 ❑ 1979 **NM** value: **2.00**
Circ: Statement: **100,047**
65 ❑ 1979 **NM** value: **2.00**
Circ: Statement: **100,047**
66 ❑ 1979 **NM** value: **2.00**
Circ: Statement: **100,047**
67 ❑ 1979 **NM** value: **2.00**
Circ: Statement: **100,047**
68 ❑ Dec 1979 **NM** value: **2.00**
Circ: Statement: **100,047**
69 ❑ 1980 **NM** value: **2.00**
Circ: Statement: **84,200**
70 ❑ 1980 **NM** value: **2.00**
Circ: Statement: **84,200**
71 ❑ May 1980 **NM** value: **2.00**
Circ: Statement: **84,200**
• Has1979 Statement; avg print run 268,472; avg sales 99,936; avg subs 111; avg total paid 100,047; office use 300; max existent 100,347; 63% of run returned
72 ❑ 1980 **NM** value: **2.00**
Circ: Statement: **84,200**
73 ❑ 1980 **NM** value: **2.00**
Circ: Statement: **84,200**
74 ❑ 1980 **NM** value: **2.00**
Circ: Statement: **84,200**
75 ❑ 1980 **NM** value: **2.00**
Circ: Statement: **84,200**
76 ❑ 1980 **NM** value: **2.00**
Circ: Statement: **84,200**
77 ❑ 1980 **NM** value: **2.00**
Circ: Statement: **84,200**
78 ❑ Feb 1981 **NM** value: **2.00**
Circ: Statement: **77,714**
79 ❑ Apr 1981 **NM** value: **2.00**
Circ: Statement: **77,714**
• Has 1980 Statement, filed 10/1/1980; avg print run 242,025; avg sales 84,159; avg subs 41; avg total paid 84,200; office use 300; max existent 84,500; 65% of run returned
80 ❑ Jun 1981 **NM** value: **2.00**
Circ: Statement: **77,714**
81 ❑ Aug 1981 **NM** value: **2.00**
Circ: Statement: **77,714**
82 ❑ Oct 1981 **NM** value: **2.00**
Circ: Statement: **77,714**
83 ❑ Dec 1981 **NM** value: **2.00**
Circ: Statement: **77,714**
84 ❑ Feb 1982 **NM** value: **2.00**
85 ❑ Apr 1982 **NM** value: **2.00**
• Has 1981 Statement; avg print run 225,184; avg sales 77,650; avg subs 64; avg total paid 77,714; office use 300; max existent 78,014; 65% of run returned
86 ❑ 1982 **NM** value: **2.00**
87 ❑ **NM** value: **2.00**
88 ❑ **NM** value: **2.00**
89 ❑ **NM** value: **2.00**
90 ❑ **NM** value: **2.00**
91 ❑ May 1983 **NM** value: **2.00**
Circ: Statement: **65,789**
• Has 1982 Statement; avg print run 225,184; avg sales 77,650; avg subs 64; avg total paid 77,714; office use 300; max existent 78,014; 65% of run returned
92 ❑ **NM** value: **2.00**
93 ❑ **NM** value: **2.00**
94 ❑ **NM** value: **2.00**
95 ❑ **NM** value: **2.00**
96 ❑ **NM** value: **2.00**
97 ❑ Jun 1984 **NM** value: **2.00**
Circ: Statement: **57,357**
• Has 1983 Statement; avg print run 164,808; avg sales 65,624; avg subs 165; avg total paid 65,789; office use 300; max existent 66,089; 60% of run returned
98 ❑ Aug 1984 **NM** value: **2.00**
Circ: Statement: **57,357**
99 ❑ Oct 1984 **NM** value: **2.00**
Circ: Statement: **57,357**
100 ❑ Dec 1984 Cover: 0.60 **NM** value: **2.00**
Circ: Statement: **57,357**
• 100th anniversary issue. 📖 Boot Camp High; Glenn Scarpelli in Hollywood **A:** Stan Goldberg **W:** Rich Margopoulos
101 ❑ Feb 1985 **NM** value: **1.00**
Circ: Statement: **54,243**
102 ❑ Apr 1985 **NM** value: **1.00**
Circ: Statement: **54,243**
• Has1984 Statement; avg print run 147,647; avg sales 57,170; avg subs 187; avg total paid 57,357; office use 300; max existent 57,657; 61% of run returned
103 ❑ Jun 1985 **NM** value: **1.00**
Circ: Statement: **54,243**
104 ❑ Aug 1985 **NM** value: **1.00**
Circ: Statement: **54,243**
105 ❑ Oct 1985 **NM** value: **1.00**
Circ: Statement: **54,243**
106 ❑ Dec 1985 **NM** value: **1.00**
Circ: Statement: **54,243**
107 ❑ Feb 1986 **NM** value: **1.00**
108 ❑ Apr 1986 **NM** value: **1.00**
• Has 1985 Statement; avg print run 143,409; avg sales 54,076; avg subs 167; avg total paid 54,243; office use 300; max existent 54,543; 62% of run returned
109 ❑ 1986 **NM** value: **1.00**
110 ❑ 1986 **NM** value: **1.00**
111 ❑ 1986 **NM** value: **1.00**
112 ❑ 1986 **NM** value: **1.00**
113 ❑ 1986 **NM** value: **1.00**
114 ❑ 1987 **NM** value: **1.00**
final issue.

ARCHIE COMICS PRESENTS THE LOVE SHOWDOWN COLLECTION Archie

1 ❑ 1994 Cover: 4.95 **NM** value: **Cover or less**
No issue number. • prestige format one-shot;collects multi-part storyline

ARCHIE DIGEST MAGAZINE Archie

Published seven times a year, this magazine is one of the oldest Archie digest series. Like the others, it's a compendium of previously published Archie stories, with panels expanded to fill more pages of this diminutive (albeit thick) publication.

Oddly enough, most Archie material is not aimed at the beginning reader, with much of the content focusing on dating and which teen is cutest. But the ongoing romantic tensions attract pre-teens looking for entertaining material based on what will be coming up in their teen-age

CGC-graded: Multiply prices above by **33 for 9.9 M • 16 for 9.8 NM/M • 7 for 9.6 NM+ • 5 for 9.4 NM • 2.5 for 9.2 NM- • 1.5 for 9.0 VF/NM**

years. This digest series also contained occasional stories of significance to collectors, and featuring the appearance of such characters as Bill Woggon's Katy Keene and The Fly by Joe Simon and Jack Kirby.

1 ❑ Aug 1973 **NM** value: **26.00**
• **CGC:** 1 graded, best 9.6
2 ❑ Oct 1973 **NM** value: **10.00**
3 ❑ Dec 1973 **NM** value: **6.00**
4 ❑ Feb 1974 **NM** value: **6.00**
Circ: Statement: **137,857**
5 ❑ Apr 1974 **NM** value: **6.00**
Circ: Statement: **137,857**
6 ❑ Jun 1974 **NM** value: **4.00**
Circ: Statement: **137,857**
7 ❑ Aug 1974 **NM** value: **4.00**
Circ: Statement: **137,857**
8 ❑ Oct 1974 **NM** value: **4.00**
Circ: Statement: **137,857**
9 ❑ Dec 1974 **NM** value: **4.00**
Circ: Statement: **137,857**
10 ❑ Feb 1975 **NM** value: **4.00**
Circ: Statement: **145,459**
11 ❑ Apr 1975 **NM** value: **2.50**
Circ: Statement: **145,459**
• Has 1974 Statement, filed 10/1/74; avg print run 260,001; avg sales 137,740; avg subs 117; avg total paid 137,857; samples 0; office use 0; max existent 137,857; 47% of run returned
12 ❑ Jun 1975 **NM** value: **2.50**
Circ: Statement: **145,459**
13 ❑ Aug 1975 **NM** value: **2.50**
Circ: Statement: **145,459**
14 ❑ Oct 1975 **NM** value: **2.50**
Circ: Statement: **145,459**
15 ❑ Dec 1975 **NM** value: **2.50**
Circ: Statement: **145,459**
16 ❑ Feb 1976 **NM** value: **2.50**
Circ: Statement: **153,406**
17 ❑ Apr 1976 **NM** value: **2.50**
Circ: Statement: **153,406**
• Has 1975 Statement, filed 10/1/75; avg print run 258,452; avg sales 145,189; avg subs 270; avg total paid 145,459; samples 0; office use 300; max existent 145,759; 44% of run returned
18 ❑ Jun 1976 **NM** value: **2.50**
Circ: Statement: **153,406**
19 ❑ Aug 1976 **NM** value: **2.50**
Circ: Statement: **153,406**
20 ❑ Oct 1976 **NM** value: **2.50**
Circ: Statement: **153,406**
21 ❑ Dec 1976 **NM** value: **2.00**
Circ: Statement: **153,406**
22 ❑ Feb 1977 **NM** value: **2.00**
Circ: Statement: **158,668**
23 ❑ Apr 1977 **NM** value: **2.00**
Circ: Statement: **158,668**
• Has 1976 Statement; avg total paid circ 153,406
24 ❑ Jun 1977 **NM** value: **2.00**
Circ: Statement: **158,668**
25 ❑ Aug 1977 Cover: 0.75 **NM** value: **2.00**
Circ: Statement: **158,668**
26 ❑ Oct 1977 Cover: 0.75 **NM** value: **2.00**
Circ: Statement: **158,668**
27 ❑ Dec 1977 Cover: 0.75 **NM** value: **2.00**
Circ: Statement: **158,668**
28 ❑ Feb 1978 Cover: 0.75 **NM** value: **2.00**
29 ❑ Apr 1978 Cover: 0.75 **NM** value: **2.00**
• Has 1977 Statement; avg total paid circ 158,668
30 ❑ Jun 1978 Cover: 0.75 **NM** value: **2.00**
31 ❑ Aug 1978 Cover: 0.75 **NM** value: **2.00**
32 ❑ Oct 1978 Cover: 0.75 **NM** value: **2.00**
33 ❑ Dec 1978 Cover: 0.75 **NM** value: **2.00**
34 ❑ Feb 1979 Cover: 0.75 **NM** value: **2.00**
Circ: Statement: **144,962**
35 ❑ Apr 1979 Cover: 0.75 **NM** value: **2.00**
Circ: Statement: **144,962**
36 ❑ Jun 1979 Cover: 0.75 **NM** value: **2.00**
Circ: Statement: **144,962**
37 ❑ Aug 1979 Cover: 0.75 **NM** value: **2.00**
Circ: Statement: **144,962**
38 ❑ Oct 1979 Cover: 0.75 **NM** value: **2.00**
Circ: Statement: **144,962**
📖 The Thing; Room for Improvement; The Collector; The Sport of Danger; The All-Time Champ; The Case In Brief; Pool Fool; Home-Made; Li'l Jinx: Comic Books • Reprints Li'l Jinx story featuring comic-book collector paying $1,000 for old Red Circle comics
39 ❑ Dec 1979 **NM** value: **2.00**
Circ: Statement: **144,962**
40 ❑ Feb 1980 **NM** value: **2.00**
41 ❑ Apr 1980 **NM** value: **2.00**
• Has 1979 Statement, filed 10/1/79; avg print run 258,288; avg sales 144,855; avg subs 107; avg total paid 144,962; samples 0; office use 300; max existent 145,262; 44% of run returned
42 ❑ **NM** value: **2.00**
43 ❑ **NM** value: **2.00**
44 ❑ **NM** value: **2.00**
45 ❑ **NM** value: **2.00**
46 ❑ 1981 **NM** value: **2.00**
Circ: Statement: **141,739**
47 ❑ 1981 **NM** value: **2.00**
Circ: Statement: **141,739**
48 ❑ 1981 **NM** value: **2.00**
Circ: Statement: **141,739**
49 ❑ 1981 **NM** value: **2.00**
Circ: Statement: **141,739**
50 ❑ **NM** value: **2.00**
51 ❑ **NM** value: **1.50**
52 ❑ Apr 1982 **NM** value: **1.50**
• Has 1981 Statement, filed 10/1/81; avg print run 257,413; avg sales 141,659; avg subs 75; avg total paid 141,739; samples 0; office use 300; max existent 142,034; 45% of run returned
53 ❑ **NM** value: **1.50**
54 ❑ **NM** value: **1.50**
55 ❑ **NM** value: **1.50**
56 ❑ **NM** value: **1.50**
57 ❑ **NM** value: **1.50**
58 ❑ 1983 **NM** value: **1.50**
Circ: Statement: **142,278**
59 ❑ 1983 **NM** value: **1.50**
Circ: Statement: **142,278**
60 ❑ 1983 **NM** value: **1.50**
Circ: Statement: **142,278**
61 ❑ 1983 **NM** value: **1.50**
Circ: Statement: **142,278**
62 ❑ **NM** value: **1.50**
63 ❑ **NM** value: **1.50**
64 ❑ **NM** value: **1.50**
65 ❑ **NM** value: **1.50**
66 ❑ Jun 1984 **NM** value: **1.50**
Circ: Statement: **161,561**
• Has 1983 Statement, filed 10/1/83; avg print run 257,058; avg sales 142,105; avg subs 173; avg total paid 142,278; samples 0; office use 300; max existent 142,578; 45% of run returned
67 ❑ 1984 **NM** value: **1.50**
Circ: Statement: **161,561**
68 ❑ **NM** value: **1.50**
69 ❑ **NM** value: **1.50**
70 ❑ **NM** value: **1.50**
71 ❑ **NM** value: **1.50**
72 ❑ 1985 **NM** value: **1.50**
Circ: Statement: **165,193**
73 ❑ **NM** value: **1.50**
74 ❑ **NM** value: **1.50**
75 ❑ **NM** value: **1.50**
76 ❑ **NM** value: **1.50**
77 ❑ 1986 **NM** value: **1.50**
Circ: Statement: **178,150**
78 ❑ **NM** value: **1.50**
79 ❑ **NM** value: **1.50**
80 ❑ **NM** value: **1.50**
81 ❑ **NM** value: **1.50**
82 ❑ 1987 **NM** value: **1.50**
Circ: Statement: **181,160**
83 ❑ 1987 **NM** value: **1.50**
Circ: Statement: **181,160**
84 ❑ 1987 **NM** value: **1.50**
Circ: Statement: **181,160**
85 ❑ **NM** value: **1.50**
86 ❑ **NM** value: **1.50**
87 ❑ **NM** value: **1.50**
88 ❑ Apr 1988 **NM** value: **1.50**
Circ: Statement: **196,698**
• Has 1987 Statement, filed 10/1/87; avg print run 361,589; avg sales 180,927; avg subs 233; avg total paid 181,160; samples 0; office use 300; max existent 181,460; 50% of run returned
89 ❑ 1988 **NM** value: **1.50**
Circ: Statement: **196,698**
90 ❑ 1988 **NM** value: **1.50**
Circ: Statement: **196,698**
91 ❑ 1988 **NM** value: **1.50**
Circ: Statement: **196,698**
92 ❑ **NM** value: **1.50**
93 ❑ **NM** value: **1.50**
94 ❑ **NM** value: **1.50**
95 ❑ Apr 1989 **NM** value: **1.50**
Circ: Statement: **209,630**
• Has 1988 Statement, filed 10/1/88; avg print run 378,781; avg sales 194,288; avg subs 2,410; avg total paid 196,698; samples 614; office use 3,656; max existent 200,968; 47% of run returned
96 ❑ **NM** value: **1.50**
97 ❑ **NM** value: **1.50**
98 ❑ **NM** value: **1.50**
99 ❑ **NM** value: **1.50**
100 ❑ **NM** value: **1.50**
101 ❑ **NM** value: **1.79**
102 ❑ **NM** value: **1.79**
103 ❑ 1990 **NM** value: **1.79**
Circ: Statement: **198,720**
104 ❑ **NM** value: **1.79**
105 ❑ **NM** value: **1.79**
106 ❑ **NM** value: **1.79**
107 ❑ **NM** value: **1.79**
108 ❑ **NM** value: **1.79**
109 ❑ **NM** value: **1.79**
110 ❑ **NM** value: **1.79**
111 ❑ **NM** value: **1.79**
112 ❑ **NM** value: **1.79**
113 ❑ **NM** value: **1.79**
114 ❑ **NM** value: **1.79**
115 ❑ **NM** value: **1.79**
116 ❑ **NM** value: **1.79**
117 ❑ **NM** value: **1.79**
118 ❑ 1992 **NM** value: **1.79**
Circ: Statement: **177,579**
119 ❑ **NM** value: **1.79**
120 ❑ **NM** value: **1.79**
121 ❑ **NM** value: **1.79**
122 ❑ **NM** value: **1.79**
• Has 1992 Statement, filed 10/1/92; avg print run 430,287; avg sales 175,938; avg subs 1,641; avg total paid 177,579; samples 501; office use 8,536; max existent 186,616; 57% of run returned
123 ❑ **NM** value: **1.79**
124 ❑ 1993 **NM** value: **1.79**
Circ: Statement: **173,222**
125 ❑ **NM** value: **1.79**
126 ❑ **NM** value: **1.79**
127 ❑ **NM** value: **1.79**
128 ❑ **NM** value: **1.79**
• Has 1993 Statement, filed 10/1/93; avg print run 410,808; avg sales 171,723; avg subs 1,499; avg total paid 173,222; samples 431; office use 6,954; max existent 180,607; 56% of run returned
129 ❑ **NM** value: **1.79**
130 ❑ **NM** value: **1.79**
Circ: Statement: **155,157**
131 ❑ Dec 1994 Cover: 1.75 **NM** value: **1.79**
Circ: Statement: **155,157**
132 ❑ 1995 Cover: 1.75 **NM** value: **1.79**
Circ: Statement: **139,634**
133 ❑ Apr 1995 Cover: 1.75 **NM** value: **1.79**
Circ: Statement: **139,634**
134 ❑ May 1995 Cover: 1.75 **NM** value: **1.79**
Circ: Statement: **139,634**
• Has 1994 Statement, filed 10/1/94; avg print run 401,968; avg sales 153,446; avg subs 1,711; avg total paid 155,157; samples 351; office use 7,019; max existent 16+E88992,527; 60% of run returned
135 ❑ Jul 1995 Cover: 1.75 **NM** value: **1.79**
Circ: Statement: **139,634**
136 ❑ Sep 1995 Cover: 1.75 **NM** value: **1.79**
Circ: Statement: **139,634**
137 ❑ Nov 1995 Cover: 1.75 **NM** value: **1.79**
Circ: Statement: **139,634**
138 ❑ Jan 1996 Cover: 1.75 **NM** value: **1.79**
Circ: Statement: **136,502**
139 ❑ Mar 1996 Cover: 1.75 **NM** value: **1.79**
Circ: Statement: **136,502**
140 ❑ Apr 1996 Cover: 1.75 **NM** value: **1.79**
Circ: Statement: **136,502**
• Has 1995 Statement, filed 10/1/95; avg print run 379,079; avg sales 138,495; avg subs 1,139; avg total paid 139,634; samples 376; office use 8,265; max existent 148,275; 61% of run returned
141 ❑ 1996 **NM** value: **1.79**
Circ: Statement: **136,502**
142 ❑ 1996 **NM** value: **1.79**
Circ: Statement: **136,502**
143 ❑ 1996 **NM** value: **1.79**
Circ: Statement: **136,502**
144 ❑ Dec 1996 Cover: 1.79 **NM** value: **Cover or less**
Circ: Statement: **136,502** Direct Market orders: **3,220**
📖 Archie: Name Exclaim!; L'il Jinx: Look of Knowledge; Archie: Face Case; Archie: A Change of Vending; Archie: Kid Stuff; Archie: Serf Turf; Prof. Flootsnoot: The Weatherbee Balloon; Archie: Exam Cram!; Archie: Hide and Shriek **A:** Fernando Ruiz **W:** Hal Smith; Mike Pellowski
145 ❑ Jan 1997 Cover: 1.79 **NM** value: **Cover or less**
Circ: Direct Market orders: **3,612**
146 ❑ Mar 1997 Cover: 1.79 **NM** value: **Cover or less**
Circ: Diamd. preorders: **3,293**
147 ❑ Apr 1997 Cover: 1.79 **NM** value: **Cover or less**
Circ: Diamd. preorders: **3,230**
• Has 1996 Statement, filed 9/27/96; avg print run 353,699; avg sales 135,626; avg subs 877; avg total paid 136,502; samples 386; office use 4,060; max existent 140,949; 60% of run returned
148 ❑ Jun 1997 Cover: 1.79 **NM** value: **Cover or less**
Circ: Diamd. preorders: **3,488**
149 ❑ Aug 1997 Cover: 1.79 **NM** value: **Cover or less**
Circ: Diamd. preorders: **3,466**
150 ❑ Sep 1997 Cover: 1.79 **NM** value: **Cover or less**
Circ: Diamd. preorders: **3,884**
151 ❑ Nov 1997 Cover: 1.79 **NM** value: **Cover or less**
152 ❑ Jan 1998 Cover: 1.95 **NM** value: **Cover or less**
Circ: Statement: **120,543**
153 ❑ Mar 1998 Cover: 1.95 **NM** value: **Cover or less**
Circ: Statement: **120,543**
154 ❑ Apr 1998 Cover: 1.95 **NM** value: **Cover or less**
Circ: Statement: **120,543** Diamd. preorders: **3,592**
155 ❑ Jun 1998 Cover: 1.95 **NM** value: **Cover or less**
Circ: Statement: **120,543** Diamd. preorders: **3,087**
156 ❑ Jul 1998 Cover: 1.95 **NM** value: **Cover or less**
Circ: Statement: **120,543** Diamd. preorders: **3,375**
157 ❑ Sep 1998 Cover: 1.95 **NM** value: **Cover or less**
Circ: Statement: **120,543** Diamd. preorders: **3,158**
158 ❑ Oct 1998 Cover: 1.95 **NM** value: **Cover or less**
Circ: Statement: **120,543** Diamd. preorders: **3,070**
159 ❑ Dec 1998 Cover: 1.95 **NM** value: **Cover or less**
Circ: Statement: **120,543** Diamd. preorders: **3,101**
160 ❑ Jan 1999 Cover: 1.95 **NM** value: **Cover or less**
Circ: Diamd. preorders: **3,315**
161 ❑ Mar 1999 Cover: 1.95 **NM** value: **Cover or less**
Circ: Diamd. preorders: **3,087**
162 ❑ Apr 1999 Cover: 1.99 **NM** value: **Cover or less**
Circ: Diamd. preorders: **2,743**
• Has 1998 Statement, filed 11/1/98; avg print run 320,045; avg sales 119,636; avg subs 907; avg total paid 120,543; samples 421; office use 7,095; max existent 128,059; 60% of run returned
163 ❑ Jun 1999 Cover: 1.99 **NM** value: **Cover or less**
Circ: Diamd. preorders: **2,840**
164 ❑ Jul 1999 Cover: 1.99 **NM** value: **Cover or less**
Circ: Diamd. preorders: **2,923**
165 ❑ Sep 1999 Cover: 1.99 **NM** value: **Cover or less**
Circ: Diamd. preorders: **2,922**
166 ❑ Oct 1999 Cover: 1.99 **NM** value: **Cover or less**
Circ: Diamd. preorders: **2,879**
167 ❑ Nov 1999 Cover: 1.99 **NM** value: **Cover or less**
Circ: Diamd. preorders: **2,975**
168 ❑ Jan 2000 Cover: 1.99 **NM** value: **Cover or less**
Circ: Diamd. preorders: **2,662**
169 ❑ Feb 2000 Cover: 1.99 **NM** value: **Cover or less**
Circ: Diamd. preorders: **2,684**
170 ❑ Apr 2000 Cover: 1.99 **NM** value: **Cover or less**
Circ: Diamd. preorders: **2,865**
171 ❑ Jun 2000 Cover: 2.19 **NM** value: **Cover or less**
Circ: Diamd. preorders: **2,681**
172 ❑ Jul 2000 Cover: 2.19 **NM** value: **Cover or less**
Circ: Diamd. preorders: **2,433**

Other grades: Multiply prices above by **1.5 for Mint • 2/3 for Very Fine • 1/3 for Fine • 1/5 for Very Good • 1/8 for Good**

173 ❑ Aug 2000 Cover: 2.19 **NM** value: **Cover or less**
Circ: Diamd. preorders: **2,664**
174 ❑ Oct 2000 Cover: 2.19 **NM** value: **Cover or less**
Circ: Diamd. preorders: **3,007**
175 ❑ Nov 2000 Cover: 2.19 **NM** value: **Cover or less**
Circ: Diamd. preorders: **2,524**
176 ❑ Jan 2001 Cover: 2.19 **NM** value: **Cover or less**
Circ: Statement: **160,994** Diamd. preorders: **2,604**
177 ❑ Feb 2001 Cover: 2.19 **NM** value: **Cover or less**
Circ: Statement: **160,994** Diamd. preorders: **2,492**
178 ❑ Mar 2001 Cover: 2.19 **NM** value: **Cover or less**
Circ: Statement: **160,994** Diamd. preorders: **2,334**
179 ❑ Apr 2001 Cover: 2.19 **NM** value: **Cover or less**
Circ: Statement: **160,994** Diamd. preorders: **2,337**
180 ❑ May 2001 Cover: 2.19 **NM** value: **Cover or less**
Circ: Statement: **160,994** Diamd. preorders: **2,408**
181 ❑ Jul 2001 Cover: 2.19 **NM** value: **Cover or less**
Circ: Statement: **160,994** Diamd. preorders: **2,721**
182 ❑ Aug 2001 Cover: 2.19 **NM** value: **Cover or less**
Circ: Statement: **160,994** Diamd. preorders: **3,058**
183 ❑ Sep 2001 Cover: 2.19 **NM** value: **Cover or less**
Circ: Statement: **160,994** Diamd. preorders: **2,895**

ARCHIE GIANT SERIES MAGAZINE — Archie

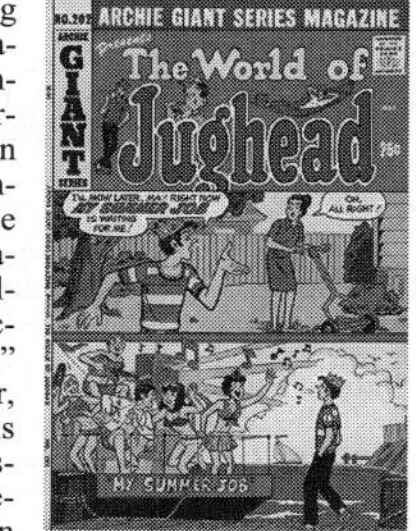

Perhaps the most remarkable thing about the Archie Giant Series Magazine is its weird penchant for discontiguous issue numbering and alternate names. Basically, it's an umbrella title for various Archie family stories, virtually indistinguishable from numerous other Archie magazines. Each issue, however, nominally features a different Archie character, calling itself "World of Jughead," "World of Archie," etc. on the cover, in rotating fashion. Adding to this complication are strange gaps in issue numbering: The issue immediately following #35 was #136. Later, an even bigger chasm opened in the issue numbering sequence, when issue #251 was followed by #452. Whether these gaps were meant to make the series seem more long-lived or whether they were merely the case of typographical errors gone uncorrected is anyone's guess.

1 ❑ Win 1954 Cover: 0.25 **NM** value: **875.00**
• Archie's Christmas Stocking (1954)
2 ❑ Win 1955 Cover: 0.25 **NM** value: **525.00**
• Archie's Christmas Stocking (1955)
3 ❑ Win 1956 Cover: 0.25 **NM** value: **350.00**
• **CGC:** 1 graded, best 9.0
• Archie's Christmas Stocking (1956)
4 ❑ Win 1957 Cover: 0.25 **NM** value: **350.00**
• **CGC:** 1 graded, best 7.5
• Archie's Christmas Stocking (1957)
5 ❑ Win 1958 Cover: 0.25 **NM** value: **350.00**
• **CGC:** 1 graded, best 6.0
• Archie's Christmas Stocking (1958)
6 ❑ Win 1959 Cover: 0.25 **NM** value: **350.00**
• **CGC:** 1 graded, best 7.5
• Archie's Christmas Stocking (1959)
7 ❑ Sep 1960 Cover: 0.25 **NM** value: **225.00**
• Katy Keene Holiday Fun
8 ❑ Oct 1960 Cover: 0.25 **NM** value: **225.00**
9 ❑ Dec 1960 Cover: 0.25 **NM** value: **225.00**
10 ❑ Jan 1961 Cover: 0.25 **NM** value: **225.00**
Circ: Statement: **257,460**
11 ❑ Jun 1961 Cover: 0.25 **NM** value: **175.00**
Circ: Statement: **257,460**
12 ❑ ca. 1961 Cover: 0.25 **NM** value: **125.00**
Circ: Statement: **257,460**
13 ❑ ca. 1961 Cover: 0.25 **NM** value: **175.00**
Circ: Statement: **257,460**
14 ❑ Dec 1961 Cover: 0.25 **NM** value: **125.00**
Circ: Statement: **257,460**
15 ❑ Mar 1962 Cover: 0.25 **NM** value: **125.00**
Circ: Statement: **246,299**
16 ❑ Jun 1962 Cover: 0.25 **NM** value: **175.00**
Circ: Statement: **246,299**
• Has 1961 Statement, filed 6/11/60; avg total paid circ 257,460
17 ❑ Sep 1962 Cover: 0.25 **NM** value: **125.00**
Circ: Statement: **246,299**
18 ❑ ca. 1962 Cover: 0.25 **NM** value: **175.00**
Circ: Statement: **246,299**
19 ❑ ca. 1962 Cover: 0.25 **NM** value: **125.00**
Circ: Statement: **246,299**
20 ❑ Jan 1963 Cover: 0.25 **NM** value: **125.00**
Circ: Statement: **246,857**
21 ❑ ca. 1963 Cover: 0.25 **NM** value: **100.00**
Circ: Statement: **246,857**
22 ❑ ca. 1963 Cover: 0.25 **NM** value: **60.00**
Circ: Statement: **246,857**
23 ❑ ca. 1963 Cover: 0.25 **NM** value: **90.00**
Circ: Statement: **246,857**
24 ❑ ca. 1963 Cover: 0.25 **NM** value: **60.00**
Circ: Statement: **246,857**
25 ❑ ca. 1964 Cover: 0.25 **NM** value: **60.00**
Circ: Statement: **238,137**
26 ❑ ca. 1964 Cover: 0.25 **NM** value: **90.00**
Circ: Statement: **238,137**
27 ❑ Jun 1964 Cover: 0.25 **NM** value: **60.00**
Circ: Statement: **238,137**
28 ❑ Sep 1964 Cover: 0.25 **NM** value: **90.00**
Circ: Statement: **238,137**
29 ❑ ca. 1964 Cover: 0.25 **NM** value: **60.00**
Circ: Statement: **238,137**
30 ❑ ca. 1964 Cover: 0.25 **NM** value: **60.00**
Circ: Statement: **238,137**
31 ❑ ca. 1965 Cover: 0.25 **NM** value: **40.00**
Circ: Statement: **256,516**
32 ❑ ca. 1965 Cover: 0.25 **NM** value: **40.00**
Circ: Statement: **256,516**
33 ❑ ca. 1965 Cover: 0.25 **NM** value: **40.00**
Circ: Statement: **256,516**
34 ❑ ca. 1965 Cover: 0.25 **NM** value: **40.00**
Circ: Statement: **256,516**
35 ❑ ca. 1965 Cover: 0.25 **NM** value: **40.00**
Circ: Statement: **256,516**
• Series continued in #136
136 ❑ ca. 1965 Cover: 0.25 **NM** value: **40.00**
Circ: Statement: **256,516**
137 ❑ ca. 1966 Cover: 0.25 **NM** value: **40.00**
Circ: Statement: **252,427**
138 ❑ ca. 1966 Cover: 0.25 **NM** value: **40.00**
Circ: Statement: **252,427**
139 ❑ ca. 1966 Cover: 0.25 **NM** value: **40.00**
Circ: Statement: **252,427**
140 ❑ ca. 1966 Cover: 0.25 **NM** value: **40.00**
Circ: Statement: **252,427**
141 ❑ ca. 1966 Cover: 0.25 **NM** value: **40.00**
Circ: Statement: **252,427**
142 ❑ ca. 1966 Cover: 0.25 **NM** value: **42.00**
Circ: Statement: **252,427**
★ Origin of Captain Pureheart.
143 ❑ ca. 1967 Cover: 0.25 **NM** value: **20.00**
Circ: Statement: **248,241**
144 ❑ ca. 1967 Cover: 0.25 **NM** value: **20.00**
Circ: Statement: **248,241**
145 ❑ ca. 1967 Cover: 0.25 **NM** value: **20.00**
Circ: Statement: **248,241**
146 ❑ ca. 1967 Cover: 0.25 **NM** value: **20.00**
Circ: Statement: **248,241**
147 ❑ ca. 1967 Cover: 0.25 **NM** value: **20.00**
Circ: Statement: **248,241**
148 ❑ ca. 1967 Cover: 0.25 **NM** value: **20.00**
Circ: Statement: **248,241**
149 ❑ ca. 1967 Cover: 0.25 **NM** value: **20.00**
Circ: Statement: **248,241**
150 ❑ ca. 1967 Cover: 0.25 **NM** value: **20.00**
Circ: Statement: **248,241**
151 ❑ ca. 1967 Cover: 0.25 **NM** value: **20.00**
Circ: Statement: **248,241**
152 ❑ Feb 1968 Cover: 0.25 **NM** value: **20.00**
153 ❑ ca. 1968 Cover: 0.25 **NM** value: **20.00**
154 ❑ ca. 1968 Cover: 0.25 **NM** value: **20.00**
155 ❑ ca. 1968 Cover: 0.25 **NM** value: **20.00**
156 ❑ ca. 1968 Cover: 0.25 **NM** value: **20.00**
157 ❑ ca. 1968 Cover: 0.25 **NM** value: **20.00**
158 ❑ ca. 1969 Cover: 0.25 **NM** value: **20.00**
Circ: Statement: **271,699**
159 ❑ ca. 1969 Cover: 0.25 **NM** value: **20.00**
Circ: Statement: **271,699**
160 ❑ ca. 1969 Cover: 0.25 **NM** value: **20.00**
Circ: Statement: **271,699**
161 ❑ ca. 1969 Cover: 0.25 **NM** value: **12.00**
Circ: Statement: **271,699**
162 ❑ ca. 1969 Cover: 0.25 **NM** value: **12.00**
Circ: Statement: **271,699**
163 ❑ ca. 1969 Cover: 0.25 **NM** value: **12.00**
Circ: Statement: **271,699**
164 ❑ ca. 1969 Cover: 0.25 **NM** value: **12.00**
Circ: Statement: **271,699**
165 ❑ ca. 1969 Cover: 0.25 **NM** value: **12.00**
Circ: Statement: **271,699**
166 ❑ ca. 1969 Cover: 0.25 **NM** value: **12.00**
Circ: Statement: **271,699**
167 ❑ ca. 1970 Cover: 0.25 **NM** value: **12.00**
168 ❑ ca. 1970 Cover: 0.25 **NM** value: **12.00**
169 ❑ ca. 1970 Cover: 0.25 **NM** value: **12.00**
170 ❑ ca. 1970 Cover: 0.25 **NM** value: **12.00**
171 ❑ ca. 1970 Cover: 0.25 **NM** value: **12.00**
172 ❑ ca. 1970 Cover: 0.25 **NM** value: **12.00**
173 ❑ ca. 1970 Cover: 0.25 **NM** value: **12.00**
174 ❑ ca. 1970 Cover: 0.25 **NM** value: **12.00**
175 ❑ ca. 1970 Cover: 0.25 **NM** value: **12.00**
176 ❑ ca. 1970 Cover: 0.25 **NM** value: **12.00**
177 ❑ ca. 1970 Cover: 0.25 **NM** value: **12.00**
178 ❑ ca. 1970 Cover: 0.25 **NM** value: **12.00**
179 ❑ ca. 1971 Cover: 0.25 **NM** value: **12.00**
Circ: Statement: **197,765**
180 ❑ ca. 1971 Cover: 0.25 **NM** value: **12.00**
Circ: Statement: **197,765**
181 ❑ ca. 1971 Cover: 0.25 **NM** value: **10.00**
Circ: Statement: **197,765**
182 ❑ ca. 1971 Cover: 0.25 **NM** value: **10.00**
Circ: Statement: **197,765**
183 ❑ ca. 1971 Cover: 0.25 **NM** value: **10.00**
Circ: Statement: **197,765**
184 ❑ ca. 1971 Cover: 0.25 **NM** value: **10.00**
Circ: Statement: **197,765**
185 ❑ ca. 1971 Cover: 0.25 **NM** value: **10.00**
Circ: Statement: **197,765**
186 ❑ ca. 1971 Cover: 0.25 **NM** value: **10.00**
Circ: Statement: **197,765**
187 ❑ ca. 1971 Cover: 0.25 **NM** value: **10.00**
Circ: Statement: **197,765**
188 ❑ ca. 1971 **NM** value: **10.00**
Circ: Statement: **197,765**
189 ❑ ca. 1971 **NM** value: **10.00**
Circ: Statement: **197,765**
190 ❑ ca. 1971 **NM** value: **10.00**
Circ: Statement: **197,765**
191 ❑ ca. 1972 **NM** value: **10.00**
Circ: Statement: **202,944**
192 ❑ ca. 1972 **NM** value: **10.00**
Circ: Statement: **202,944**
193 ❑ ca. 1972 **NM** value: **10.00**
Circ: Statement: **202,944**
194 ❑ ca. 1972 **NM** value: **10.00**
Circ: Statement: **202,944**
195 ❑ ca. 1972 **NM** value: **10.00**
Circ: Statement: **202,944**
196 ❑ ca. 1972 **NM** value: **10.00**
Circ: Statement: **202,944**
197 ❑ Jun 1972 **NM** value: **10.00**
Circ: Statement: **202,944**
• Has 1971 Statement, filed 10/1/71; avg print run 420,531; avg sales 192,885; avg subs 4,880; avg total paid 197,765; samples 0; max existent 197,765; 53% of run returned
198 ❑ ca. 1972 **NM** value: **10.00**
Circ: Statement: **202,944**
199 ❑ ca. 1972 **NM** value: **10.00**
Circ: Statement: **202,944**
200 ❑ ca. 1972 **NM** value: **10.00**
Circ: Statement: **202,944**
201 ❑ ca. 1972 **NM** value: **8.00**
Circ: Statement: **202,944**
202 ❑ ca. 1972 **NM** value: **8.00**
Circ: Statement: **202,944**
203 ❑ ca. 1972 **NM** value: **8.00**
Circ: Statement: **202,944**
204 ❑ ca. 1973 **NM** value: **8.00**
205 ❑ ca. 1973 **NM** value: **8.00**
206 ❑ ca. 1973 **NM** value: **8.00**
207 ❑ ca. 1973 **NM** value: **8.00**
208 ❑ ca. 1973 **NM** value: **8.00**
209 ❑ ca. 1973 **NM** value: **8.00**
210 ❑ Jun 1973 **NM** value: **8.00**
• Has 1972 Statement; avg total paid circ 202,944
211 ❑ Jul 1973 **NM** value: **8.00**
212 ❑ Aug 1973 **NM** value: **8.00**
213 ❑ Sep 1973 **NM** value: **8.00**
214 ❑ Oct 1973 **NM** value: **8.00**
215 ❑ Nov 1973 **NM** value: **8.00**
216 ❑ Dec 1973 **NM** value: **8.00**
217 ❑ Jan 1974 **NM** value: **8.00**
Circ: Statement: **173,179**
218 ❑ Feb 1974 **NM** value: **8.00**
Circ: Statement: **173,179**
219 ❑ Mar 1974 **NM** value: **8.00**
Circ: Statement: **173,179**
220 ❑ Apr 1974 **NM** value: **8.00**
Circ: Statement: **173,179**
221 ❑ May 1974 **NM** value: **6.00**
Circ: Statement: **173,179**
222 ❑ Jun 1974 **NM** value: **6.00**
Circ: Statement: **173,179**
223 ❑ Jul 1974 **NM** value: **6.00**
Circ: Statement: **173,179**
224 ❑ Aug 1974 **NM** value: **6.00**
Circ: Statement: **173,179**
225 ❑ Sep 1974 **NM** value: **6.00**
Circ: Statement: **173,179**
226 ❑ Oct 1974 **NM** value: **6.00**
Circ: Statement: **173,179**
227 ❑ Nov 1974 **NM** value: **6.00**
Circ: Statement: **173,179**
228 ❑ Dec 1974 **NM** value: **6.00**
Circ: Statement: **173,179**
229 ❑ Jan 1975 **NM** value: **6.00**
Circ: Statement: **156,002**
230 ❑ Feb 1975 **NM** value: **6.00**
Circ: Statement: **156,002**
231 ❑ Mar 1975 **NM** value: **6.00**
Circ: Statement: **156,002**
232 ❑ Apr 1975 **NM** value: **6.00**
Circ: Statement: **156,002**
233 ❑ May 1975 **NM** value: **6.00**
Circ: Statement: **156,002**
234 ❑ Jun 1975 **NM** value: **6.00**
Circ: Statement: **156,002**
• Has 1974 Statement; avg total paid circ 173,179
235 ❑ ca. 1975 **NM** value: **6.00**
Circ: Statement: **156,002**
236 ❑ ca. 1975 **NM** value: **6.00**
Circ: Statement: **156,002**
237 ❑ ca. 1975 **NM** value: **6.00**
Circ: Statement: **156,002**
238 ❑ ca. 1975 **NM** value: **6.00**
Circ: Statement: **156,002**
239 ❑ ca. 1975 **NM** value: **6.00**
Circ: Statement: **156,002**
240 ❑ ca. 1975 **NM** value: **6.00**
Circ: Statement: **156,002**
241 ❑ ca. 1975 **NM** value: **6.00**
Circ: Statement: **156,002**
242 ❑ ca. 1976 **NM** value: **6.00**
Circ: Statement: **148,964**
243 ❑ ca. 1976 **NM** value: **6.00**
Circ: Statement: **148,964**
244 ❑ ca. 1976 **NM** value: **6.00**
Circ: Statement: **148,964**
245 ❑ ca. 1976 **NM** value: **6.00**
Circ: Statement: **148,964**
246 ❑ ca. 1976 **NM** value: **6.00**
Circ: Statement: **148,964**
247 ❑ ca. 1976 **NM** value: **6.00**
Circ: Statement: **148,964**
248 ❑ ca. 1976 **NM** value: **6.00**
Circ: Statement: **148,964**
249 ❑ ca. 1976 **NM** value: **6.00**
Circ: Statement: **148,964**
250 ❑ ca. 1976 **NM** value: **6.00**
Circ: Statement: **148,964**
251 ❑ ca. 1976 **NM** value: **4.00**
Circ: Statement: **148,964**
• Series continued in #452
452 ❑ ca. 1976 **NM** value: **3.00**
Circ: Statement: **148,964**

CGC-graded: Multiply prices above by **33 for 9.9 M • 16 for 9.8 NM/M • 7 for 9.6 NM+ • 5 for 9.4 NM • 2.5 for 9.2 NM- • 1.5 for 9.0 VF/NM**

453 ❑ ca. 1976 **NM** value: **3.00**
Circ: Statement: **148,964**
454 ❑ ca. 1976 Cover: 0.30 **NM** value: **3.00**
Circ: Statement: **148,964**
455 ❑ Jan 1977 Cover: 0.30 **NM** value: **3.00**
Circ: Statement: **138,506**
456 ❑ ca. 1977 **NM** value: **3.00**
Circ: Statement: **138,506**
457 ❑ ca. 1977 **NM** value: **3.00**
Circ: Statement: **138,506**
458 ❑ Jun 1977 **NM** value: **3.00**
Circ: Statement: **138,506**
• Has 1976 Statement; avg total paid circ 148,964
459 ❑ ca. 1977 **NM** value: **3.00**
Circ: Statement: **138,506**
460 ❑ ca. 1977 **NM** value: **3.00**
Circ: Statement: **138,506**
461 ❑ ca. 1977 **NM** value: **3.00**
Circ: Statement: **138,506**
462 ❑ ca. 1977 **NM** value: **3.00**
Circ: Statement: **138,506**
463 ❑ ca. 1977 **NM** value: **3.00**
Circ: Statement: **138,506**
464 ❑ ca. 1977 **NM** value: **3.00**
Circ: Statement: **138,506**
465 ❑ ca. 1978 **NM** value: **3.00**
Circ: Statement: **121,479**
466 ❑ ca. 1978 **NM** value: **3.00**
Circ: Statement: **121,479**
467 ❑ ca. 1978 **NM** value: **3.00**
Circ: Statement: **121,479**
468 ❑ ca. 1978 **NM** value: **3.00**
Circ: Statement: **121,479**
469 ❑ ca. 1978 **NM** value: **3.00**
Circ: Statement: **121,479**
470 ❑ Jun 1978 **NM** value: **3.00**
Circ: Statement: **121,479**
• Has 1977 Statement; avg total paid circ 138,506
471 ❑ Jul 1978 **NM** value: **3.00**
Circ: Statement: **121,479**
472 ❑ Aug 1978 **NM** value: **3.00**
Circ: Statement: **121,479**
473 ❑ Sep 1978 **NM** value: **3.00**
Circ: Statement: **121,479**
474 ❑ Oct 1978 **NM** value: **3.00**
Circ: Statement: **121,479**
475 ❑ Nov 1978 **NM** value: **3.00**
Circ: Statement: **121,479**
476 ❑ Dec 1978 **NM** value: **3.00**
Circ: Statement: **121,479**
477 ❑ Jan 1979 **NM** value: **3.00**
478 ❑ Feb 1979 **NM** value: **3.00**
479 ❑ Mar 1979 **NM** value: **3.00**
480 ❑ Apr 1979 **NM** value: **3.00**
481 ❑ May 1979 **NM** value: **3.00**
482 ❑ Jun 1979 **NM** value: **3.00**
• Has 1978 Statement, filed 10/1/78; avg print run 299,699; avg sales 120,879; avg subs 600; avg total paid 121,479; samples 0; office use 300; max existent 121,779; 59% of run returned
483 ❑ ca. 1979 **NM** value: **3.00**
484 ❑ ca. 1979 **NM** value: **3.00**
485 ❑ ca. 1979 **NM** value: **3.00**
486 ❑ ca. 1979 **NM** value: **3.00**
487 ❑ ca. 1979 **NM** value: **3.00**
488 ❑ ca. 1979 **NM** value: **3.00**
489 ❑ ca. 1980 **NM** value: **3.00**
490 ❑ ca. 1980 **NM** value: **3.00**
491 ❑ ca. 1980 **NM** value: **3.00**
492 ❑ ca. 1980 **NM** value: **3.00**
493 ❑ ca. 1980 Cover: 0.40 **NM** value: **3.00**
📖 Jughead: Woe Blow; Greg: Cleaning Up; Jughead: Power Man; Fruit Salad ala Jughead; Jughead: The Quiet Man • World of Jughead
494 ❑ ca. 1980 **NM** value: **3.00**
495 ❑ ca. 1980 **NM** value: **3.00**
496 ❑ ca. 1980 **NM** value: **3.00**
497 ❑ ca. 1980 **NM** value: **3.00**
498 ❑ ca. 1980 **NM** value: **3.00**
499 ❑ ca. 1980 **NM** value: **3.00**
500 ❑ ca. 1980 **NM** value: **2.50**
501 ❑ ca. 1981 **NM** value: **2.50**
502 ❑ ca. 1981 **NM** value: **2.50**
503 ❑ ca. 1981 **NM** value: **2.50**
504 ❑ ca. 1981 **NM** value: **2.50**
505 ❑ ca. 1981 **NM** value: **2.50**
506 ❑ ca. 1981 **NM** value: **2.50**
507 ❑ ca. 1981 **NM** value: **2.50**
508 ❑ ca. 1981 **NM** value: **2.50**
509 ❑ ca. 1981 **NM** value: **2.50**
510 ❑ ca. 1981 **NM** value: **2.50**
511 ❑ ca. 1981 **NM** value: **2.50**
512 ❑ ca. 1981 **NM** value: **2.50**
513 ❑ ca. 1981 **NM** value: **2.50**
514 ❑ ca. 1982 **NM** value: **2.50**
515 ❑ ca. 1982 **NM** value: **2.50**
516 ❑ ca. 1982 **NM** value: **2.50**
517 ❑ ca. 1982 **NM** value: **2.50**
518 ❑ ca. 1982 **NM** value: **2.50**
519 ❑ ca. 1982 **NM** value: **2.50**
520 ❑ ca. 1982 **NM** value: **2.50**
521 ❑ ca. 1982 **NM** value: **2.50**
522 ❑ ca. 1982 **NM** value: **2.50**
523 ❑ ca. 1983 **NM** value: **2.50**
Circ: Statement: **76,375**
524 ❑ ca. 1983 **NM** value: **2.50**
Circ: Statement: **76,375**
525 ❑ ca. 1983 **NM** value: **2.50**
Circ: Statement: **76,375**
526 ❑ ca. 1983 **NM** value: **2.50**
Circ: Statement: **76,375**
527 ❑ ca. 1983 **NM** value: **2.50**
Circ: Statement: **76,375**
528 ❑ ca. 1983 **NM** value: **2.50**
Circ: Statement: **76,375**
529 ❑ ca. 1983 **NM** value: **2.50**
Circ: Statement: **76,375**
530 ❑ ca. 1983 **NM** value: **2.50**
Circ: Statement: **76,375**
531 ❑ ca. 1983 **NM** value: **2.50**
Circ: Statement: **76,375**
532 ❑ ca. 1983 **NM** value: **2.50**
Circ: Statement: **76,375**
533 ❑ ca. 1983 **NM** value: **2.50**
Circ: Statement: **76,375**
534 ❑ ca. 1984 **NM** value: **2.50**
Circ: Statement: **69,013**
535 ❑ ca. 1984 **NM** value: **2.50**
Circ: Statement: **69,013**
536 ❑ ca. 1984 **NM** value: **2.50**
Circ: Statement: **69,013**
537 ❑ ca. 1984 **NM** value: **2.50**
Circ: Statement: **69,013**
538 ❑ ca. 1984 **NM** value: **2.50**
Circ: Statement: **69,013**
539 ❑ ca. 1984 **NM** value: **2.50**
Circ: Statement: **69,013**
540 ❑ ca. 1984 **NM** value: **2.50**
Circ: Statement: **69,013**
541 ❑ ca. 1984 **NM** value: **2.50**
Circ: Statement: **69,013**
542 ❑ ca. 1984 **NM** value: **2.50**
Circ: Statement: **69,013**
543 ❑ ca. 1984 **NM** value: **2.50**
Circ: Statement: **69,013**
544 ❑ ca. 1984 **NM** value: **2.50**
Circ: Statement: **69,013**
545 ❑ ca. 1984 **NM** value: **2.50**
Circ: Statement: **69,013**
546 ❑ ca. 1984 **NM** value: **2.50**
Circ: Statement: **69,013**
547 ❑ ca. 1984 **NM** value: **2.50**
Circ: Statement: **69,013**
548 ❑ ca. 1984 **NM** value: **2.50**
Circ: Statement: **69,013**
549 ❑ ca. 1985 **NM** value: **2.50**
Circ: Statement: **64,444**
550 ❑ ca. 1985 **NM** value: **2.50**
Circ: Statement: **64,444**
551 ❑ ca. 1985 **NM** value: **2.00**
Circ: Statement: **64,444**
552 ❑ ca. 1985 **NM** value: **2.00**
Circ: Statement: **64,444**
553 ❑ ca. 1985 **NM** value: **2.00**
Circ: Statement: **64,444**
554 ❑ ca. 1985 **NM** value: **2.00**
Circ: Statement: **64,444**
555 ❑ ca. 1985 **NM** value: **2.00**
Circ: Statement: **64,444**
556 ❑ ca. 1986 **NM** value: **2.00**
Circ: Statement: **62,768**
557 ❑ ca. 1986 **NM** value: **2.00**
Circ: Statement: **62,768**
558 ❑ ca. 1986 **NM** value: **2.00**
Circ: Statement: **62,768**
559 ❑ ca. 1986 **NM** value: **2.00**
Circ: Statement: **62,768**
560 ❑ ca. 1986 **NM** value: **2.00**
Circ: Statement: **62,768**
561 ❑ ca. 1986 **NM** value: **2.00**
Circ: Statement: **62,768**
562 ❑ ca. 1986 **NM** value: **2.00**
Circ: Statement: **62,768**
563 ❑ ca. 1986 **NM** value: **2.00**
Circ: Statement: **62,768**
564 ❑ ca. 1986 **NM** value: **2.00**
Circ: Statement: **62,768**
565 ❑ ca. 1986 **NM** value: **2.00**
Circ: Statement: **62,768**
566 ❑ ca. 1986 **NM** value: **2.00**
Circ: Statement: **62,768**
567 ❑ ca. 1986 **NM** value: **2.00**
Circ: Statement: **62,768**
568 ❑ ca. 1986 **NM** value: **2.00**
Circ: Statement: **62,768**
569 ❑ ca. 1987 **NM** value: **2.00**
Circ: Statement: **57,250**
570 ❑ ca. 1987 **NM** value: **2.00**
Circ: Statement: **57,250**
571 ❑ ca. 1987 **NM** value: **2.00**
Circ: Statement: **57,250**
572 ❑ ca. 1987 **NM** value: **2.00**
Circ: Statement: **57,250**
573 ❑ ca. 1987 **NM** value: **2.00**
Circ: Statement: **57,250**
574 ❑ ca. 1987 **NM** value: **2.00**
Circ: Statement: **57,250**
575 ❑ ca. 1987 **NM** value: **2.00**
Circ: Statement: **57,250**
576 ❑ ca. 1987 **NM** value: **2.00**
Circ: Statement: **57,250**
577 ❑ ca. 1987 **NM** value: **2.00**
Circ: Statement: **57,250**
578 ❑ ca. 1987 **NM** value: **2.00**
Circ: Statement: **57,250**
579 ❑ ca. 1987 **NM** value: **2.00**
Circ: Statement: **57,250**
580 ❑ ca. 1988 **NM** value: **2.00**
581 ❑ ca. 1988 **NM** value: **2.00**
582 ❑ ca. 1988 **NM** value: **2.00**
583 ❑ ca. 1988 **NM** value: **2.00**
584 ❑ ca. 1988 **NM** value: **2.00**
585 ❑ ca. 1988 **NM** value: **2.00**
586 ❑ ca. 1988 **NM** value: **2.00**
587 ❑ ca. 1988 **NM** value: **2.00**
588 ❑ ca. 1988 **NM** value: **2.00**
589 ❑ ca. 1988 **NM** value: **2.00**
590 ❑ ca. 1988 **NM** value: **2.00**
591 ❑ ca. 1988 **NM** value: **2.00**
592 ❑ ca. 1989 **NM** value: **2.00**
593 ❑ ca. 1989 **NM** value: **2.00**
594 ❑ ca. 1989 **NM** value: **2.00**
595 ❑ ca. 1989 **NM** value: **2.00**
596 ❑ ca. 1989 **NM** value: **2.00**
597 ❑ ca. 1989 **NM** value: **2.00**
598 ❑ ca. 1989 **NM** value: **2.00**
599 ❑ ca. 1989 **NM** value: **2.00**
600 ❑ ca. 1989 **NM** value: **2.00**
601 ❑ ca. 1989 **NM** value: **1.50**
602 ❑ ca. 1989 **NM** value: **1.50**
603 ❑ ca. 1990 **NM** value: **1.50**
604 ❑ ca. 1990 **NM** value: **1.50**
605 ❑ ca. 1990 **NM** value: **1.50**
606 ❑ ca. 1990 **NM** value: **1.50**
607 ❑ ca. 1990 Cover: 1.00 **NM** value: **1.50**
• Archie Giant Series Magazine Presents Little Archie. 📖 Shine a Little Light; Little Sabrina: Night before Christmas; Target for Tonight, Chapter 1; Target for Tonight, Chapter 2; Snow Use; Mr. Weatherbee; Miss Grundy **A:** Bob Bolling **W:** Bob Bolling ★ Appearance of Little Sabrina, Chester Punkett, South-Side Serpents, Mad Doctor Doom, Sue Stringly.
608 ❑ ca. 1990 Cover: 1.00 **NM** value: **1.50**
609 ❑ ca. 1990 Cover: 1.00 **NM** value: **1.50**
610 ❑ ca. 1990 Cover: 1.00 **NM** value: **1.50**
611 ❑ ca. 1990 Cover: 1.00 **NM** value: **1.50**
612 ❑ ca. 1990 Cover: 1.00 **NM** value: **1.50**
613 ❑ ca. 1990 Cover: 1.00 **NM** value: **1.50**
614 ❑ Oct 1990 Cover: 1.00 **NM** value: **1.50**
• Pep Comics;Archie characters meet Archie Comics staff
615 ❑ ca. 1990 **NM** value: **1.50**
616 ❑ ca. 1990 **NM** value: **1.50**
617 ❑ ca. 1991 **NM** value: **1.50**
618 ❑ ca. 1991 **NM** value: **1.50**
619 ❑ ca. 1991 **NM** value: **1.50**
620 ❑ ca. 1991 **NM** value: **1.50**
621 ❑ ca. 1991 **NM** value: **1.50**
622 ❑ ca. 1991 **NM** value: **1.50**
623 ❑ ca. 1991 **NM** value: **1.50**
624 ❑ ca. 1991 **NM** value: **1.50**
625 ❑ ca. 1991 **NM** value: **1.50**
626 ❑ ca. 1992 **NM** value: **1.50**
627 ❑ ca. 1992 **NM** value: **1.50**
628 ❑ ca. 1992 **NM** value: **1.50**
629 ❑ ca. 1992 **NM** value: **1.50**
630 ❑ ca. 1992 **NM** value: **1.50**
631 ❑ Jun 1992 Cover: 1.25 **NM** value: **1.50**
632 ❑ Jul 1992 Cover: 1.25 **NM** value: **1.50**
final issue.

ARCHIE MEETS THE PUNISHER — Marvel

It's the crossover they said could never happen. The Punisher, Marvel's grim 'n' gritty vigilante, is on the track of a villain who has escaped to Riverdale, all-American town and home to Archie Andrews. The villain, a two-bit mobster named "Red" Fever, is a virtual double for Archie, causing no end of trouble for all involved. Eventually, the Punisher gets his man, Archie gets out of trouble, and Riverdale reverts to its old self. Next stop for the Punisher: Gotham City (for the Batman/Punisher: Lake of Fire crossover).

This improbable crossover is a remarkable piece of work, largely because of the talents of writer Batton Lash (Wolff & Byrd, Counselors of the Macabre). All the characters stay true to themselves and to their genres while at the same time joining up to tell what from The Punisher's perspective is a gritty manhunt, and what from the Archie side is another wacky adventure.

This special was published both as "Archie Meets the Punisher" and a die-cut "The Punisher Meets Archie" with identical contents.

1 ❑ Aug 1994 Cover: 2.95 **NM** value: **3.25**
Archie cover. **W:** Batton Lash

ARCHIE'S CHRISTMAS STOCKING (2ND SERIES) — Archie

This is a continuing seasonal classic begun originally in 1954 as part of the Archie Giant Series Magazine put out by Archie Publications.

Archie, Jughead, Veronica, Betty and the entire supporting cast from Riverdale run their usual teen jokes and adventures in Christmas-themed stories. Many of the shorts are new, although sprinkled throughout are classic reprints from earlier Yuletide adventures of the '50s and beyond. Each issue includes a one-page calendar/poster for the coming year.

Early issues are highly sought after, because they're nice giants and because the nostalgia factor is high: Many parents did, indeed, use them as stocking stuffers, so many of today's adults have fond memories of the first time they read the stories.

Other grades: Multiply prices above by **1.5 for Mint • 2/3 for Very Fine • 1/3 for Fine • 1/5 for Very Good • 1/8 for Good**

1 ❑ Jan 1994 Cover: 2.00 **NM** value: **Cover or less**
📖 A Jingle for Justice; Fresh Idea!; Dis-Missile; Too Many Clauses; Picture Frame; Christmas Cheer Up; Close Shave • For 1993 holiday season **A:** Dan Decarlo; Stan Goldberg **W:** Frank Doyle; Mike Pellowski
2 ❑ Cover: 2.00 **NM** value: **Cover or less**
• For 1994 holiday season
3 ❑ Cover: 2.00 **NM** value: **Cover or less**
• For 1995 holiday season
4 ❑ Cover: 2.00 **NM** value: **Cover or less**
• For 1996 holiday season
5 ❑ Cover: 2.25 **NM** value: **Cover or less**
• For 1997 holiday season
6 ❑ Cover: 2.25 **NM** value: **Cover or less**
• For 1998 holiday season
7 ❑ Cover: 2.29 **NM** value: **Cover or less**
• For 1999 holiday season

ARCHIE'S DATE BOOK — Spire

1 ❑ Cover: 0.69 **NM** value: **3.00**
No issue number. • religious

ARCHIE'S DOUBLE DIGEST MAGAZINE — Archie

1 ❑ ca. 1981 Cover: 1.95 **NM** value: **6.00**
2 ❑ ca. 1981 **NM** value: **3.50**
3 ❑ **NM** value: **3.50**
4 ❑ **NM** value: **3.50**
5 ❑ **NM** value: **3.50**
6 ❑ **NM** value: **3.50**
7 ❑ **NM** value: **3.50**
8 ❑ **NM** value: **3.50**
9 ❑ **NM** value: **3.50**
10 ❑ **NM** value: **3.50**
11 ❑ **NM** value: **3.00**
12 ❑ **NM** value: **3.00**
13 ❑ **NM** value: **3.00**
14 ❑ **NM** value: **3.00**
15 ❑ **NM** value: **3.00**
16 ❑ **NM** value: **3.00**
17 ❑ **NM** value: **3.00**
18 ❑ **NM** value: **3.00**
19 ❑ **NM** value: **3.00**
20 ❑ **NM** value: **3.00**
21 ❑ **NM** value: **3.00**
22 ❑ **NM** value: **3.00**
23 ❑ **NM** value: **3.00**
24 ❑ **NM** value: **3.00**
25 ❑ **NM** value: **3.00**
26 ❑ **NM** value: **3.00**
27 ❑ **NM** value: **3.00**
28 ❑ **NM** value: **3.00**
29 ❑ **NM** value: **3.00**
30 ❑ **NM** value: **3.00**
31 ❑ **NM** value: **3.00**
32 ❑ **NM** value: **3.00**
33 ❑ **NM** value: **3.00**
34 ❑ **NM** value: **3.00**
35 ❑ **NM** value: **3.00**
36 ❑ **NM** value: **3.00**
37 ❑ **NM** value: **3.00**
38 ❑ **NM** value: **3.00**
39 ❑ **NM** value: **3.00**
40 ❑ **NM** value: **3.00**
41 ❑ **NM** value: **3.00**
42 ❑ **NM** value: **3.00**
43 ❑ **NM** value: **3.00**
44 ❑ **NM** value: **3.00**
45 ❑ **NM** value: **3.00**
46 ❑ **NM** value: **3.00**
47 ❑ **NM** value: **3.00**
48 ❑ **NM** value: **3.00**
49 ❑ 1987 **NM** value: **3.00**
Circ: Statement: **138,413**
50 ❑ **NM** value: **3.00**
51 ❑ **NM** value: **3.00**
52 ❑ **NM** value: **3.00**
53 ❑ **NM** value: **3.00**
54 ❑ **NM** value: **3.00**
55 ❑ **NM** value: **3.00**
56 ❑ **NM** value: **3.00**
57 ❑ **NM** value: **3.00**
58 ❑ **NM** value: **3.00**
59 ❑ **NM** value: **3.00**
60 ❑ **NM** value: **3.00**
61 ❑ **NM** value: **3.00**
62 ❑ **NM** value: **3.00**
63 ❑ **NM** value: **3.00**
64 ❑ Jan 1993 **NM** value: **3.00**
Circ: Statement: **167,502**
65 ❑ Mar 1993 **NM** value: **3.00**
Circ: Statement: **167,502**
66 ❑ May 1993 **NM** value: **3.00**
Circ: Statement: **167,502**
67 ❑ Jul 1993 **NM** value: **3.00**
Circ: Statement: **167,502**
68 ❑ Sep 1993 **NM** value: **3.00**
Circ: Statement: **167,502**
69 ❑ Nov 1993 **NM** value: **3.00**
Circ: Statement: **167,502**
70 ❑ Jan 1994 **NM** value: **3.00**
Circ: Statement: **164,202**
71 ❑ Mar 1994 **NM** value: **3.00**
Circ: Statement: **164,202**
72 ❑ May 1994 **NM** value: **3.00**
Circ: Statement: **164,202**
• Has 1993 Statement, filed 10/1/93; avg print run 353,794; avg sales 165,358; avg subs 2,144; avg total paid 167,502; samples 429; office use 7,169; max existent 175,100; 51% of run returned
73 ❑ Jul 1994 **NM** value: **3.00**
Circ: Statement: **164,202**
74 ❑ Sep 1994 **NM** value: **3.00**
Circ: Statement: **164,202**
75 ❑ Nov 1994 Cover: 2.75 **NM** value: **3.00**
Circ: Statement: **164,202**
76 ❑ Jan 1995 Cover: 2.75 **NM** value: **3.00**
Circ: Statement: **143,681**
77 ❑ Mar 1995 Cover: 2.75 **NM** value: **3.00**
Circ: Statement: **143,681**
78 ❑ May 1995 Cover: 2.75 **NM** value: **3.00**
Circ: Statement: **143,681**
• Has 1994 Statement, filed 10/1/94; avg print run 364,260; avg sales 162,072; avg subs 2,130; avg total paid 164,202; samples 357; office use 6,916; max existent 171,475; 53% of run returned
79 ❑ Jul 1995 Cover: 2.75 **NM** value: **3.00**
Circ: Statement: **143,681**
80 ❑ Aug 1995 Cover: 2.75 **NM** value: **Cover or less**
Circ: Statement: **143,681**
81 ❑ Oct 1995 Cover: 2.75 **NM** value: **Cover or less**
Circ: Statement: **143,681**
82 ❑ Dec 1995 Cover: 2.75 **NM** value: **Cover or less**
Circ: Statement: **143,681**
83 ❑ Feb 1996 Cover: 2.75 **NM** value: **Cover or less**
Circ: Statement: **153,385**
84 ❑ Apr 1996 Cover: 2.75 **NM** value: **Cover or less**
Circ: Statement: **153,385**
• Has 1995 Statement, filed 10/1/95; avg print run 363,222; avg sales 141,957; avg subs 1,724; avg total paid 143,681; samples 377; office use 7,714; max existent 151,772; 49% of run returned
85 ❑ May 1996 Cover: 2.75 **NM** value: **Cover or less**
Circ: Statement: **153,385**
86 ❑ Jul 1996 Cover: 2.75 **NM** value: **Cover or less**
Circ: Statement: **153,385**
87 ❑ Sep 1996 Cover: 2.75 **NM** value: **Cover or less**
Circ: Statement: **153,385**
88 ❑ Oct 1996 Cover: 2.75 **NM** value: **Cover or less**
Circ: Statement: **153,385**
89 ❑ Dec 1996 Cover: 2.75 **NM** value: **Cover or less**
Circ: Statement: **153,385** Direct Market orders: **3,427**
📖 Leaf It To Reggie; Practice Makes Perfect; Reggie's Cam-Pain; Ego buster; The Signature; The Outcasts, Part 1; The Outcasts, Part 2; Dress Up Day; Wish You Were Here; Father And S; Father And Son Stuff; The **A:** Fernando Ruiz **W:** Barbara Slate; George Gladir
90 ❑ Feb 1997 Cover: 2.75 **NM** value: **Cover or less**
Circ: Diamd. preorders: **3,639**
91 ❑ Mar 1997 Cover: 2.75 **NM** value: **Cover or less**
Circ: Diamd. preorders: **3,554**
92 ❑ May 1997 Cover: 2.75 **NM** value: **Cover or less**
Circ: Diamd. preorders: **3,028**
• Has 1996 Statement, filed 9/27/1996; avg print run 356,798; avg sales 151,907; avg subs 1,478; avg total paid 153,385; samples 386; office use 3,831; max existent 157,602; 56% of run returned
93 ❑ Jul 1997 Cover: 2.75 **NM** value: **Cover or less**
Circ: Diamd. preorders: **3,927**
94 ❑ Aug 1997 Cover: 2.75 **NM** value: **Cover or less**
Circ: Diamd. preorders: **4,331**
95 ❑ Oct 1997 Cover: 2.79 **NM** value: **Cover or less**
Circ: Diamd. preorders: **4,289**
96 ❑ Dec 1997 Cover: 2.79 **NM** value: **Cover or less**
Circ: Diamd. preorders: **4,175**
97 ❑ Feb 1998 Cover: 2.95 **NM** value: **Cover or less**
Circ: Statement: **141,445** Diamd. preorders: **4,451**
98 ❑ Mar 1998 Cover: 2.95 **NM** value: **Cover or less**
Circ: Statement: **141,445**
99 ❑ May 1998 Cover: 2.95 **NM** value: **Cover or less**
Circ: Statement: **141,445**
100 ❑ Jul 1998 Cover: 2.95 **NM** value: **Cover or less**
Circ: Statement: **141,445** Diamd. preorders: **3,852**
101 ❑ Aug 1998 Cover: 2.95 **NM** value: **Cover or less**
Circ: Statement: **141,445** Diamd. preorders: **3,824**
102 ❑ Sep 1998 Cover: 2.95 **NM** value: **Cover or less**
Circ: Statement: **141,445** Diamd. preorders: **3,559**
103 ❑ Nov 1998 Cover: 2.95 **NM** value: **Cover or less**
Circ: Statement: **141,445** Diamd. preorders: **3,424**
A: Stan Goldberg **W:** Dan Decarlo
104 ❑ Dec 1998 Cover: 2.95 **NM** value: **Cover or less**
Circ: Statement: **141,445** Diamd. preorders: **3,756**
105 ❑ Feb 1999 Cover: 2.95 **NM** value: **Cover or less**
Circ: Diamd. preorders: **3,820**
106 ❑ Apr 1999 Cover: 2.95 **NM** value: **Cover or less**
Circ: Diamd. preorders: **3,686**
107 ❑ May 1999 Cover: 2.99 **NM** value: **Cover or less**
Circ: Diamd. preorders: **3,302**
• Has 1998 Statement, filed 11/1/1998; avg print run 323,240; avg sales 139,765; avg subs 1,680; avg total paid 141,445; samples 421; office use 6,177; max existent 148,043; 54% of run returned
108 ❑ Jun 1999 Cover: 2.99 **NM** value: **Cover or less**
Circ: Diamd. preorders: **3,374**
109 ❑ Aug 1999 Cover: 2.99 **NM** value: **Cover or less**
Circ: Diamd. preorders: **3,394**
110 ❑ Sep 1999 Cover: 2.99 **NM** value: **Cover or less**
Circ: Diamd. preorders: **3,496**
111 ❑ Nov 1999 Cover: 2.99 **NM** value: **Cover or less**
Circ: Diamd. preorders: **3,612**
112 ❑ Dec 1999 Cover: 2.99 **NM** value: **Cover or less**
Circ: Diamd. preorders: **2,968**
113 ❑ Feb 2000 Cover: 2.99 **NM** value: **Cover or less**
Circ: Diamd. preorders: **3,176**
114 ❑ Mar 2000 Cover: 2.99 **NM** value: **Cover or less**
Circ: Diamd. preorders: **3,559**
115 ❑ May 2000 Cover: 2.99 **NM** value: **Cover or less**
Circ: Diamd. preorders: **3,392**
116 ❑ Jul 2000 Cover: 3.19 **NM** value: **Cover or less**
Circ: Diamd. preorders: **2,878**
117 ❑ Aug 2000 Cover: 3.19 **NM** value: **Cover or less**
Circ: Diamd. preorders: **3,304**
118 ❑ Sep 2000 Cover: 3.19 **NM** value: **Cover or less**
Circ: Diamd. preorders: **3,727**
119 ❑ Nov 2000 Cover: 3.19 **NM** value: **Cover or less**
Circ: Diamd. preorders: **3,027**
120 ❑ Dec 2000 Cover: 3.19 **NM** value: **Cover or less**
Circ: Diamd. preorders: **3,114**
121 ❑ Jan 2001 Cover: 3.19 **NM** value: **Cover or less**
Circ: Diamd. preorders: **3,192**
122 ❑ Mar 2001 Cover: 3.19 **NM** value: **Cover or less**
Circ: Diamd. preorders: **3,128**
123 ❑ Apr 2001 Cover: 3.29 **NM** value: **Cover or less**
Circ: Diamd. preorders: **2,763**
124 ❑ 2001 Cover: 3.29 **NM** value: **Cover or less**
Circ: Diamd. preorders: **2,903**
125 ❑ 2001 Cover: 3.29 **NM** value: **Cover or less**
Circ: Diamd. preorders: **3,124**
126 ❑ 2001 Cover: 3.29 **NM** value: **Cover or less**
Circ: Diamd. preorders: **3,288**
127 ❑ 2001 Cover: 3.29 **NM** value: **Cover or less**
Circ: Diamd. preorders: **3,528**

ARCHIE'S FAMILY ALBUM — Spire

1 ❑ Cover: 0.49 **NM** value: **2.50**
A: Al Hartley **W:** Al Hartley

ARCHIE'S GIRLS BETTY & VERONICA — Archie

Archie, Jughead, and Betty were introduced in Pep #22 (Dec 41), and Veronica didn't come along until #26 (Apr 42). When she showed up, she set off the ongoing triangle of Archie, Betty, and Veronica that fueled constant stories to the present day. It was almost a decade later that Archie Comics tried providing the girls with their own title, and it soon became popular enough to sustain a long run. The earliest issues focused on the triangle; as time went on, the character designs smoothed out, with Veronica losing the "Dragon Lady" look and taking on more of a "Veronica Lake" appearance.

As the series progressed, the duo evolved a growing friendship and an attention to fashions of the day. The '70s saw them in cutoffs and tie-dyed shirts and joining protest groups. Focus of the stories tended to be on them or their gang, less on the teachers and school environment. — Maggie

1 ❑ ca. 1950 Cover: 0.10 **NM** value: **925.00**
• **CGC:** 2 graded, best 6.0
2 ❑ ca. 1951 Cover: 0.10 **NM** value: **485.00**
3 ❑ ca. 1951 Cover: 0.10 **NM** value: **375.00**
4 ❑ ca. 1951 Cover: 0.10 **NM** value: **300.00**
• **CGC:** 2 graded, best 9.2
5 ❑ Sum 1952 Cover: 0.10 **NM** value: **300.00**
6 ❑ Cover: 0.10 **NM** value: **240.00**
• **CGC:** 1 graded, best 7.5
7 ❑ Cover: 0.10 **NM** value: **240.00**
8 ❑ Cover: 0.10 **NM** value: **240.00**
9 ❑ Cover: 0.10 **NM** value: **240.00**
10 ❑ Fal 1953 Cover: 0.10 **NM** value: **240.00**
• **CGC:** 1 graded, best 6.5
11 ❑ Feb 1954 Cover: 0.10 **NM** value: **185.00**
12 ❑ Apr 1954 Cover: 0.10 **NM** value: **185.00**
13 ❑ Jun 1954 Cover: 0.10 **NM** value: **185.00**
14 ❑ Aug 1954 Cover: 0.10 **NM** value: **185.00**
15 ❑ Nov 1954 Cover: 0.10 **NM** value: **185.00**
16 ❑ Jan 1955 Cover: 0.10 **NM** value: **185.00**
17 ❑ Mar 1955 Cover: 0.10 **NM** value: **185.00**
18 ❑ May 1955 Cover: 0.10 **NM** value: **185.00**
19 ❑ Jul 1955 Cover: 0.10 **NM** value: **185.00**
20 ❑ Sep 1955 Cover: 0.10 **NM** value: **135.00**
21 ❑ Nov 1955 Cover: 0.10 **NM** value: **135.00**
22 ❑ Jan 1956 Cover: 0.10 **NM** value: **135.00**
23 ❑ Mar 1956 Cover: 0.10 **NM** value: **135.00**
24 ❑ May 1956 Cover: 0.10 **NM** value: **135.00**
25 ❑ Jul 1956 Cover: 0.10 **NM** value: **135.00**
26 ❑ Sep 1956 Cover: 0.10 **NM** value: **135.00**
27 ❑ Nov 1956 Cover: 0.10 **NM** value: **135.00**
• **CGC:** 1 graded, best 8.0
28 ❑ Jan 1957 Cover: 0.10 **NM** value: **135.00**
29 ❑ Mar 1957 Cover: 0.10 **NM** value: **135.00**
30 ❑ May 1957 Cover: 0.10 **NM** value: **90.00**
31 ❑ Jul 1957 Cover: 0.10 **NM** value: **90.00**
32 ❑ Sep 1957 Cover: 0.10 **NM** value: **90.00**
33 ❑ Nov 1957 Cover: 0.10 **NM** value: **90.00**
34 ❑ Jan 1958 Cover: 0.10 **NM** value: **90.00**
35 ❑ Mar 1958 Cover: 0.10 **NM** value: **90.00**
36 ❑ May 1958 Cover: 0.10 **NM** value: **90.00**
• Has 1957 Statement; no circ figures published
37 ❑ Jul 1958 Cover: 0.10 **NM** value: **90.00**
38 ❑ Sep 1958 Cover: 0.10 **NM** value: **90.00**
39 ❑ Nov 1958 Cover: 0.10 **NM** value: **90.00**
40 ❑ Jan 1959 Cover: 0.10 **NM** value: **70.00**
41 ❑ Mar 1959 Cover: 0.10 **NM** value: **70.00**
42 ❑ May 1959 Cover: 0.10 **NM** value: **70.00**
• Has 1958 Statement; no circ figures published
43 ❑ Jul 1959 Cover: 0.10 **NM** value: **70.00**
44 ❑ Aug 1959 Cover: 0.10 **NM** value: **70.00**
45 ❑ Sep 1959 Cover: 0.10 **NM** value: **70.00**
46 ❑ Oct 1959 Cover: 0.10 **NM** value: **70.00**
47 ❑ Nov 1959 Cover: 0.10 **NM** value: **70.00**
48 ❑ Dec 1959 Cover: 0.10 **NM** value: **70.00**
49 ❑ Jan 1960 Cover: 0.10 **NM** value: **70.00**
50 ❑ Feb 1960 Cover: 0.10 **NM** value: **70.00**

CGC-graded: Multiply prices above by **33 for 9.9 M • 16 for 9.8 NM/M • 7 for 9.6 NM+ • 5 for 9.4 NM • 2.5 for 9.2 NM- • 1.5 for 9.0 VF/NM**

51 ❑ Mar 1960 Cover: 0.10 **NM** value: **48.00**
52 ❑ Apr 1960 Cover: 0.10 **NM** value: **48.00**
53 ❑ May 1960 Cover: 0.10 **NM** value: **48.00**
54 ❑ Jun 1960 Cover: 0.10 **NM** value: **48.00**
55 ❑ Jul 1960 Cover: 0.10 **NM** value: **48.00**
56 ❑ Aug 1960 Cover: 0.10 **NM** value: **48.00**
57 ❑ Sep 1960 Cover: 0.10 **NM** value: **48.00**
58 ❑ Oct 1960 Cover: 0.10 **NM** value: **48.00**
59 ❑ Nov 1960 Cover: 0.10 **NM** value: **48.00**
60 ❑ Dec 1960 Cover: 0.10 **NM** value: **48.00**
61 ❑ Jan 1961 Cover: 0.10 **NM** value: **40.00**
Circ: Statement: **308,227**
62 ❑ Feb 1961 Cover: 0.10 **NM** value: **40.00**
Circ: Statement: **308,227**
63 ❑ Mar 1961 Cover: 0.10 **NM** value: **40.00**
Circ: Statement: **308,227**
64 ❑ Apr 1961 Cover: 0.10 **NM** value: **40.00**
Circ: Statement: **308,227**
65 ❑ May 1961 Cover: 0.10 **NM** value: **40.00**
Circ: Statement: **308,227**
66 ❑ Jun 1961 Cover: 0.10 **NM** value: **40.00**
Circ: Statement: **308,227**
67 ❑ Jul 1961 Cover: 0.10 **NM** value: **40.00**
Circ: Statement: **308,227**
68 ❑ Aug 1961 Cover: 0.10 **NM** value: **40.00**
Circ: Statement: **308,227**
69 ❑ Sep 1961 Cover: 0.10 **NM** value: **40.00**
Circ: Statement: **308,227**
70 ❑ Oct 1961 Cover: 0.10 **NM** value: **40.00**
Circ: Statement: **308,227**
71 ❑ Nov 1961 Cover: 0.10 **NM** value: **28.00**
Circ: Statement: **308,227**
72 ❑ Dec 1961 Cover: 0.10 **NM** value: **28.00**
Circ: Statement: **308,227**
73 ❑ Jan 1962 Cover: 0.12 **NM** value: **28.00**
Circ: Statement: **302,820**
74 ❑ Feb 1962 Cover: 0.12 **NM** value: **28.00**
Circ: Statement: **302,820**
75 ❑ Mar 1962 Cover: 0.12 **NM** value: **28.00**
Circ: Statement: **302,820**
76 ❑ Apr 1962 Cover: 0.12 **NM** value: **28.00**
Circ: Statement: **302,820**
• Has 1961 Statement; avg total paid circ 308,227
77 ❑ May 1962 Cover: 0.12 **NM** value: **28.00**
Circ: Statement: **302,820**
78 ❑ Jun 1962 Cover: 0.12 **NM** value: **28.00**
Circ: Statement: **302,820**
79 ❑ Jul 1962 Cover: 0.12 **NM** value: **28.00**
Circ: Statement: **302,820**
80 ❑ Aug 1962 Cover: 0.12 **NM** value: **28.00**
Circ: Statement: **302,820**
81 ❑ Sep 1962 Cover: 0.12 **NM** value: **28.00**
Circ: Statement: **302,820**
82 ❑ Oct 1962 Cover: 0.12 **NM** value: **28.00**
Circ: Statement: **302,820**
83 ❑ Nov 1962 Cover: 0.12 **NM** value: **28.00**
Circ: Statement: **302,820**
84 ❑ Dec 1962 Cover: 0.12 **NM** value: **28.00**
Circ: Statement: **302,820**
85 ❑ Jan 1963 Cover: 0.12 **NM** value: **28.00**
Circ: Statement: **320,605**
86 ❑ Feb 1963 Cover: 0.12 **NM** value: **28.00**
Circ: Statement: **320,605**
87 ❑ Mar 1963 Cover: 0.12 **NM** value: **28.00**
Circ: Statement: **320,605**
88 ❑ Apr 1963 Cover: 0.12 **NM** value: **28.00**
Circ: Statement: **320,605**
89 ❑ May 1963 Cover: 0.12 **NM** value: **28.00**
Circ: Statement: **320,605**
90 ❑ Jun 1963 Cover: 0.12 **NM** value: **28.00**
Circ: Statement: **320,605**
91 ❑ Jul 1963 Cover: 0.12 **NM** value: **20.00**
Circ: Statement: **320,605**
92 ❑ Aug 1963 Cover: 0.12 **NM** value: **20.00**
Circ: Statement: **320,605**
93 ❑ Sep 1963 Cover: 0.12 **NM** value: **20.00**
Circ: Statement: **320,605**
94 ❑ Oct 1963 Cover: 0.12 **NM** value: **20.00**
Circ: Statement: **320,605**
95 ❑ Nov 1963 Cover: 0.12 **NM** value: **20.00**
Circ: Statement: **320,605**
96 ❑ Dec 1963 Cover: 0.12 **NM** value: **20.00**
Circ: Statement: **320,605**
97 ❑ Jan 1964 Cover: 0.12 **NM** value: **20.00**
Circ: Statement: **333,833**
98 ❑ Feb 1964 Cover: 0.12 **NM** value: **20.00**
Circ: Statement: **333,833**
99 ❑ Mar 1964 Cover: 0.12 **NM** value: **20.00**
Circ: Statement: **333,833**
100 ❑ Apr 1964 Cover: 0.12 **NM** value: **20.00**
Circ: Statement: **333,833**
101 ❑ May 1964 Cover: 0.12 **NM** value: **20.00**
Circ: Statement: **333,833**
102 ❑ Jun 1964 Cover: 0.12 **NM** value: **20.00**
Circ: Statement: **333,833**
103 ❑ Jul 1964 Cover: 0.12 **NM** value: **20.00**
Circ: Statement: **333,833**
104 ❑ Aug 1964 Cover: 0.12 **NM** value: **20.00**
Circ: Statement: **333,833**
105 ❑ Sep 1964 Cover: 0.12 **NM** value: **20.00**
Circ: Statement: **333,833**
106 ❑ Oct 1964 Cover: 0.12 **NM** value: **20.00**
Circ: Statement: **333,833**
107 ❑ Nov 1964 Cover: 0.12 **NM** value: **20.00**
Circ: Statement: **333,833**
108 ❑ Dec 1964 Cover: 0.12 **NM** value: **20.00**
Circ: Statement: **333,833**
109 ❑ Jan 1965 Cover: 0.12 **NM** value: **20.00**
Circ: Statement: **328,969**
110 ❑ Feb 1965 Cover: 0.12 **NM** value: **20.00**
Circ: Statement: **328,969**
111 ❑ Mar 1965 Cover: 0.12 **NM** value: **14.00**
Circ: Statement: **328,969**
112 ❑ Apr 1965 Cover: 0.12 **NM** value: **14.00**
Circ: Statement: **328,969**
113 ❑ May 1965 Cover: 0.12 **NM** value: **14.00**
Circ: Statement: **328,969**
114 ❑ Jun 1965 Cover: 0.12 **NM** value: **14.00**
Circ: Statement: **328,969**
115 ❑ Jul 1965 Cover: 0.12 **NM** value: **14.00**
Circ: Statement: **328,969**
116 ❑ Aug 1965 Cover: 0.12 **NM** value: **14.00**
Circ: Statement: **328,969**
117 ❑ Sep 1965 Cover: 0.12 **NM** value: **14.00**
Circ: Statement: **328,969**
118 ❑ Oct 1965 Cover: 0.12 **NM** value: **14.00**
Circ: Statement: **328,969**
119 ❑ Nov 1965 Cover: 0.12 **NM** value: **14.00**
Circ: Statement: **328,969**
120 ❑ Dec 1965 Cover: 0.12 **NM** value: **14.00**
Circ: Statement: **328,969**
121 ❑ Jan 1966 Cover: 0.12 **NM** value: **14.00**
Circ: Statement: **342,295**
122 ❑ Feb 1966 Cover: 0.12 **NM** value: **14.00**
Circ: Statement: **342,295**
123 ❑ Mar 1966 Cover: 0.12 **NM** value: **14.00**
Circ: Statement: **342,295**
124 ❑ Apr 1966 Cover: 0.12 **NM** value: **14.00**
Circ: Statement: **342,295**
125 ❑ May 1966 Cover: 0.12 **NM** value: **14.00**
Circ: Statement: **342,295**
126 ❑ Jun 1966 Cover: 0.12 **NM** value: **14.00**
Circ: Statement: **342,295**
127 ❑ Jul 1966 Cover: 0.12 **NM** value: **14.00**
Circ: Statement: **342,295**
128 ❑ Aug 1966 Cover: 0.12 **NM** value: **14.00**
Circ: Statement: **342,295**
129 ❑ Sep 1966 Cover: 0.12 **NM** value: **14.00**
Circ: Statement: **342,295**
130 ❑ Oct 1966 Cover: 0.12 **NM** value: **14.00**
Circ: Statement: **342,295**
131 ❑ Nov 1966 Cover: 0.12 **NM** value: **14.00**
Circ: Statement: **342,295**
132 ❑ Dec 1966 Cover: 0.12 **NM** value: **14.00**
Circ: Statement: **342,295**
133 ❑ Jan 1967 Cover: 0.12 **NM** value: **14.00**
Circ: Statement: **349,632**
134 ❑ Feb 1967 Cover: 0.12 **NM** value: **14.00**
Circ: Statement: **349,632**
135 ❑ Mar 1967 Cover: 0.12 **NM** value: **14.00**
Circ: Statement: **349,632**
136 ❑ Apr 1967 Cover: 0.12 **NM** value: **14.00**
Circ: Statement: **349,632**
137 ❑ May 1967 Cover: 0.12 **NM** value: **14.00**
Circ: Statement: **349,632**
138 ❑ Jun 1967 Cover: 0.12 **NM** value: **14.00**
Circ: Statement: **349,632**
139 ❑ Jul 1967 Cover: 0.12 **NM** value: **14.00**
Circ: Statement: **349,632**
140 ❑ Aug 1967 Cover: 0.12 **NM** value: **14.00**
Circ: Statement: **349,632**
141 ❑ Sep 1967 Cover: 0.12 **NM** value: **10.00**
Circ: Statement: **349,632**
142 ❑ Oct 1967 Cover: 0.12 **NM** value: **10.00**
Circ: Statement: **349,632**
143 ❑ Nov 1967 Cover: 0.12 **NM** value: **10.00**
Circ: Statement: **349,632**
144 ❑ Dec 1967 Cover: 0.12 **NM** value: **10.00**
Circ: Statement: **349,632**
145 ❑ Jan 1968 Cover: 0.12 **NM** value: **10.00**
Circ: Statement: **419,544**
146 ❑ Feb 1968 Cover: 0.12 **NM** value: **10.00**
Circ: Statement: **419,544**
147 ❑ Mar 1968 Cover: 0.12 **NM** value: **10.00**
Circ: Statement: **419,544**
148 ❑ Apr 1968 Cover: 0.12 **NM** value: **10.00**
Circ: Statement: **419,544**
149 ❑ May 1968 Cover: 0.12 **NM** value: **10.00**
Circ: Statement: **419,544**
150 ❑ Jun 1968 Cover: 0.12 **NM** value: **10.00**
Circ: Statement: **419,544**
151 ❑ Jul 1968 Cover: 0.12 **NM** value: **10.00**
Circ: Statement: **419,544**
152 ❑ Aug 1968 Cover: 0.12 **NM** value: **10.00**
Circ: Statement: **419,544**
153 ❑ Sep 1968 Cover: 0.12 **NM** value: **10.00**
Circ: Statement: **419,544**
154 ❑ Oct 1968 Cover: 0.12 **NM** value: **10.00**
Circ: Statement: **419,544**
155 ❑ Nov 1968 Cover: 0.12 **NM** value: **10.00**
Circ: Statement: **419,544**
156 ❑ Dec 1968 Cover: 0.12 **NM** value: **10.00**
Circ: Statement: **419,544**
157 ❑ Jan 1969 Cover: 0.12 **NM** value: **10.00**
Circ: Statement: **384,789**
158 ❑ Feb 1969 Cover: 0.12 **NM** value: **10.00**
Circ: Statement: **384,789**
159 ❑ Mar 1969 Cover: 0.12 **NM** value: **10.00**
Circ: Statement: **384,789**
160 ❑ Apr 1969 Cover: 0.12 **NM** value: **10.00**
Circ: Statement: **384,789**
161 ❑ May 1969 Cover: 0.12 **NM** value: **8.00**
Circ: Statement: **384,789**
• Has 1968 Statement, filed 11/1/68; avg print run 627,162; avg sales 417,344; avg subs 2,200; avg total paid 419,544; samples 0; max existent 419,544; 33% of run returned
162 ❑ Jun 1969 Cover: 0.12 **NM** value: **8.00**
Circ: Statement: **384,789**
163 ❑ Jul 1969 Cover: 0.15 **NM** value: **8.00**
Circ: Statement: **384,789**
164 ❑ Aug 1969 Cover: 0.15 **NM** value: **8.00**
Circ: Statement: **384,789**
165 ❑ Sep 1969 Cover: 0.15 **NM** value: **8.00**
Circ: Statement: **384,789**
166 ❑ Oct 1969 Cover: 0.15 **NM** value: **8.00**
Circ: Statement: **384,789**
167 ❑ Nov 1969 Cover: 0.15 **NM** value: **8.00**
Circ: Statement: **384,789**
168 ❑ Dec 1969 Cover: 0.15 **NM** value: **8.00**
Circ: Statement: **384,789**
169 ❑ Jan 1970 Cover: 0.15 **NM** value: **8.00**
Circ: Statement: **344,478**
170 ❑ Feb 1970 Cover: 0.15 **NM** value: **8.00**
Circ: Statement: **344,478**
171 ❑ Mar 1970 Cover: 0.15 **NM** value: **8.00**
Circ: Statement: **344,478**
172 ❑ Apr 1970 Cover: 0.15 **NM** value: **8.00**
Circ: Statement: **344,478**
• Has 1969 Statement, filed 10/1/69; avg print run 624,942; avg sales 383,646; avg subs 1,143; avg total paid 384,789; samples 0; max existent 384,789; 38% of run returned
173 ❑ May 1970 Cover: 0.15 **NM** value: **8.00**
Circ: Statement: **344,478**
174 ❑ Jun 1970 Cover: 0.15 **NM** value: **8.00**
Circ: Statement: **344,478**
175 ❑ Jul 1970 Cover: 0.15 **NM** value: **8.00**
Circ: Statement: **344,478**
176 ❑ Aug 1970 Cover: 0.15 **NM** value: **8.00**
Circ: Statement: **344,478**
177 ❑ Sep 1970 Cover: 0.15 **NM** value: **8.00**
Circ: Statement: **344,478**
178 ❑ Oct 1970 Cover: 0.15 **NM** value: **8.00**
Circ: Statement: **344,478**
179 ❑ Nov 1970 Cover: 0.15 **NM** value: **8.00**
Circ: Statement: **344,478**
180 ❑ Dec 1970 Cover: 0.15 **NM** value: **8.00**
Circ: Statement: **344,478**
181 ❑ Jan 1971 Cover: 0.15 **NM** value: **6.00**
182 ❑ Feb 1971 Cover: 0.15 **NM** value: **6.00**
183 ❑ Mar 1971 Cover: 0.15 **NM** value: **6.00**
184 ❑ Apr 1971 Cover: 0.15 **NM** value: **6.00**
185 ❑ May 1971 Cover: 0.15 **NM** value: **6.00**
• Has 1970 Statement, filed 10/1/70; avg print run 568,656; avg sales 343,318; avg subs 1,160; avg total paid 344,478; samples 0; max existent 344,478; 39% of run returned
186 ❑ Jun 1971 Cover: 0.15 **NM** value: **6.00**
187 ❑ Jul 1971 Cover: 0.15 **NM** value: **6.00**
188 ❑ Aug 1971 Cover: 0.15 **NM** value: **6.00**
189 ❑ Sep 1971 Cover: 0.15 **NM** value: **6.00**
190 ❑ Oct 1971 Cover: 0.15 **NM** value: **6.00**
191 ❑ Nov 1971 Cover: 0.15 **NM** value: **6.00**
192 ❑ Dec 1971 Cover: 0.15 **NM** value: **6.00**
193 ❑ Jan 1972 Cover: 0.15 **NM** value: **6.00**
Circ: Statement: **293,297**
194 ❑ Feb 1972 Cover: 0.15 **NM** value: **6.00**
Circ: Statement: **293,297**
195 ❑ Mar 1972 Cover: 0.15 **NM** value: **6.00**
Circ: Statement: **293,297**
196 ❑ Apr 1972 Cover: 0.15 **NM** value: **6.00**
Circ: Statement: **293,297**
197 ❑ May 1972 Cover: 0.20 **NM** value: **6.00**
Circ: Statement: **293,297**
198 ❑ Jun 1972 Cover: 0.20 **NM** value: **6.00**
Circ: Statement: **293,297**
199 ❑ Jul 1972 Cover: 0.20 **NM** value: **6.00**
Circ: Statement: **293,297**
200 ❑ Aug 1972 Cover: 0.20 **NM** value: **6.00**
Circ: Statement: **293,297**
201 ❑ Sep 1972 Cover: 0.20 **NM** value: **4.00**
Circ: Statement: **293,297**
202 ❑ Oct 1972 Cover: 0.20 **NM** value: **4.00**
Circ: Statement: **293,297**
203 ❑ Nov 1972 Cover: 0.20 **NM** value: **4.00**
Circ: Statement: **293,297**
204 ❑ Dec 1972 Cover: 0.20 **NM** value: **4.00**
Circ: Statement: **293,297**
205 ❑ Jan 1973 Cover: 0.20 **NM** value: **4.00**
Circ: Statement: **249,541**
206 ❑ Feb 1973 Cover: 0.20 **NM** value: **4.00**
Circ: Statement: **249,541**
207 ❑ Mar 1973 Cover: 0.20 **NM** value: **4.00**
Circ: Statement: **249,541**
208 ❑ Apr 1973 Cover: 0.20 **NM** value: **4.00**
Circ: Statement: **249,541**
• Has 1972 Statement; avg total paid circ 293,297
209 ❑ May 1973 Cover: 0.20 **NM** value: **4.00**
Circ: Statement: **249,541**
210 ❑ Jun 1973 Cover: 0.20 **NM** value: **4.00**
Circ: Statement: **249,541**
211 ❑ Jul 1973 Cover: 0.20 **NM** value: **4.00**
Circ: Statement: **249,541**
212 ❑ Aug 1973 Cover: 0.20 **NM** value: **4.00**
Circ: Statement: **249,541**
213 ❑ Sep 1973 Cover: 0.20 **NM** value: **4.00**
Circ: Statement: **249,541**
214 ❑ Oct 1973 Cover: 0.20 **NM** value: **4.00**
Circ: Statement: **249,541**
215 ❑ Nov 1973 Cover: 0.20 **NM** value: **4.00**
Circ: Statement: **249,541**
216 ❑ Dec 1973 Cover: 0.20 **NM** value: **4.00**
Circ: Statement: **249,541**
217 ❑ Jan 1974 Cover: 0.20 **NM** value: **4.00**
Circ: Statement: **220,566**
218 ❑ Feb 1974 Cover: 0.20 **NM** value: **4.00**
Circ: Statement: **220,566**
219 ❑ Mar 1974 Cover: 0.20 **NM** value: **4.00**
Circ: Statement: **220,566**

Other grades: Multiply prices above by **1.5 for Mint • 2/3 for Very Fine • 1/3 for Fine • 1/5 for Very Good • 1/8 for Good**

220 ❑ Apr 1974 Cover: 0.25 **NM** value: **4.00**
Circ: Statement: **220,566** • **CGC:** 11 graded, best 9.4
• Has 1973 Statement; avg total paid circ 249,541
221 ❑ May 1974 Cover: 0.25 **NM** value: **4.00**
Circ: Statement: **220,566**
222 ❑ Jun 1974 Cover: 0.25 **NM** value: **4.00**
Circ: Statement: **220,566**
223 ❑ Jul 1974 Cover: 0.25 **NM** value: **4.00**
Circ: Statement: **220,566**
224 ❑ Aug 1974 Cover: 0.25 **NM** value: **4.00**
Circ: Statement: **220,566**
225 ❑ Sep 1974 Cover: 0.25 **NM** value: **4.00**
Circ: Statement: **220,566**
226 ❑ Oct 1974 Cover: 0.25 **NM** value: **4.00**
Circ: Statement: **220,566**
227 ❑ Nov 1974 Cover: 0.25 **NM** value: **4.00**
Circ: Statement: **220,566**
228 ❑ Dec 1974 Cover: 0.25 **NM** value: **4.00**
Circ: Statement: **220,566**
229 ❑ Jan 1975 Cover: 0.25 **NM** value: **4.00**
Circ: Statement: **161,275**
230 ❑ Feb 1975 Cover: 0.25 **NM** value: **4.00**
Circ: Statement: **161,275**
231 ❑ Mar 1975 Cover: 0.25 **NM** value: **4.00**
Circ: Statement: **161,275**
232 ❑ Apr 1975 Cover: 0.25 **NM** value: **4.00**
Circ: Statement: **161,275**
• Has 1974 Statement; avg total paid circ 220,566
233 ❑ May 1975 Cover: 0.25 **NM** value: **4.00**
Circ: Statement: **161,275**
234 ❑ Jun 1975 Cover: 0.25 **NM** value: **4.00**
Circ: Statement: **161,275**
235 ❑ Jul 1975 Cover: 0.25 **NM** value: **4.00**
Circ: Statement: **161,275**
236 ❑ Aug 1975 Cover: 0.25 **NM** value: **4.00**
Circ: Statement: **161,275**
237 ❑ Sep 1975 Cover: 0.25 **NM** value: **4.00**
Circ: Statement: **161,275**
238 ❑ Oct 1975 Cover: 0.25 **NM** value: **4.00**
Circ: Statement: **161,275**
239 ❑ Nov 1975 Cover: 0.25 **NM** value: **4.00**
Circ: Statement: **161,275**
240 ❑ Dec 1975 Cover: 0.25 **NM** value: **Cover or less**
Circ: Statement: **161,275**
241 ❑ Jan 1976 Cover: 0.30 **NM** value: **4.00**
Circ: Statement: **155,349**
242 ❑ Feb 1976 Cover: 0.30 **NM** value: **4.00**
Circ: Statement: **155,349**
243 ❑ Mar 1976 Cover: 0.30 **NM** value: **4.00**
Circ: Statement: **155,349**
244 ❑ Apr 1976 Cover: 0.30 **NM** value: **4.00**
Circ: Statement: **155,349**
245 ❑ May 1976 Cover: 0.30 **NM** value: **4.00**
Circ: Statement: **155,349**
246 ❑ Jun 1976 Cover: 0.30 **NM** value: **4.00**
Circ: Statement: **155,349**
247 ❑ Jul 1976 Cover: 0.30 **NM** value: **4.00**
Circ: Statement: **155,349**
248 ❑ Aug 1976 Cover: 0.30 **NM** value: **4.00**
Circ: Statement: **155,349**
249 ❑ Sep 1976 Cover: 0.30 **NM** value: **4.00**
Circ: Statement: **155,349**
250 ❑ Oct 1976 Cover: 0.30 **NM** value: **4.00**
Circ: Statement: **155,349**
251 ❑ Nov 1976 Cover: 0.30 **NM** value: **3.00**
Circ: Statement: **155,349**
252 ❑ Dec 1976 Cover: 0.30 **NM** value: **3.00**
Circ: Statement: **155,349**
253 ❑ Jan 1977 Cover: 0.30 **NM** value: **3.00**
Circ: Statement: **138,474**
254 ❑ Feb 1977 Cover: 0.30 **NM** value: **3.00**
Circ: Statement: **138,474**
255 ❑ Mar 1977 Cover: 0.30 **NM** value: **3.00**
Circ: Statement: **138,474**
256 ❑ Apr 1977 Cover: 0.30 **NM** value: **3.00**
Circ: Statement: **138,474**
• Has 1976 Statement, filed 10/1/76; avg print run 343,513; avg sales 155,032; avg subs 317; avg total paid 155,349; samples 0; office use 300; max existent 155,649; 55% of run returned
257 ❑ May 1977 Cover: 0.30 **NM** value: **3.00**
Circ: Statement: **138,474**
258 ❑ Jun 1977 Cover: 0.30 **NM** value: **3.00**
Circ: Statement: **138,474**
259 ❑ Jul 1977 Cover: 0.30 **NM** value: **3.00**
Circ: Statement: **138,474**
260 ❑ Aug 1977 Cover: 0.30 **NM** value: **3.00**
Circ: Statement: **138,474**
261 ❑ Sep 1977 Cover: 0.30 **NM** value: **3.00**
Circ: Statement: **138,474**
262 ❑ Oct 1977 Cover: 0.30 **NM** value: **3.00**
Circ: Statement: **138,474**
263 ❑ Nov 1977 Cover: 0.30 **NM** value: **3.00**
Circ: Statement: **138,474**
264 ❑ Dec 1977 Cover: 0.30 **NM** value: **3.00**
Circ: Statement: **138,474**
265 ❑ Jan 1978 Cover: 0.30 **NM** value: **3.00**
Circ: Statement: **112,215**
266 ❑ Feb 1978 Cover: 0.30 **NM** value: **3.00**
Circ: Statement: **112,215**
267 ❑ Mar 1978 Cover: 0.30 **NM** value: **3.00**
Circ: Statement: **112,215**
268 ❑ Apr 1978 Cover: 0.30 **NM** value: **3.00**
Circ: Statement: **112,215**
• Has 1977 Statement; avg total paid circ 138,474
269 ❑ May 1978 Cover: 0.30 **NM** value: **3.00**
Circ: Statement: **112,215**
270 ❑ Jun 1978 Cover: 0.30 **NM** value: **3.00**
Circ: Statement: **112,215**
271 ❑ Jul 1978 Cover: 0.35 **NM** value: **3.00**
Circ: Statement: **112,215**
272 ❑ Aug 1978 Cover: 0.35 **NM** value: **3.00**
Circ: Statement: **112,215**
273 ❑ Sep 1978 Cover: 0.35 **NM** value: **3.00**
Circ: Statement: **112,215**
274 ❑ Oct 1978 Cover: 0.35 **NM** value: **3.00**
Circ: Statement: **112,215**
275 ❑ Nov 1978 Cover: 0.35 **NM** value: **3.00**
Circ: Statement: **112,215**
276 ❑ Dec 1978 Cover: 0.35 **NM** value: **3.00**
Circ: Statement: **112,215**
277 ❑ Jan 1979 Cover: 0.35 **NM** value: **3.00**
278 ❑ Feb 1979 Cover: 0.35 **NM** value: **3.00**
279 ❑ Mar 1979 Cover: 0.35 **NM** value: **3.00**
280 ❑ Apr 1979 Cover: 0.40 **NM** value: **3.00**
281 ❑ May 1979 Cover: 0.40 **NM** value: **3.00**
282 ❑ Jun 1979 Cover: 0.40 **NM** value: **3.00**
283 ❑ Jul 1979 Cover: 0.40 **NM** value: **3.00**
284 ❑ Aug 1979 Cover: 0.40 **NM** value: **3.00**
285 ❑ Sep 1979 Cover: 0.40 **NM** value: **3.00**
286 ❑ Oct 1979 Cover: 0.40 **NM** value: **3.00**
287 ❑ Nov 1979 Cover: 0.40 **NM** value: **3.00**
288 ❑ Dec 1979 Cover: 0.40 **NM** value: **3.00**
289 ❑ Jan 1980 Cover: 0.40 **NM** value: **3.00**
290 ❑ Feb 1980 Cover: 0.40 **NM** value: **3.00**
291 ❑ Mar 1980 Cover: 0.40 **NM** value: **3.00**
292 ❑ Apr 1980 Cover: 0.40 **NM** value: **3.00**
• Has 1979 Statement, filed 10/1/79; avg print run 284,300; avg sales 112,056; avg subs 159; avg total paid 112,215; samples 0; office use 300; max existent 112,515; 60% of run returned
293 ❑ May 1980 Cover: 0.40 **NM** value: **3.00**
294 ❑ Jun 1980 Cover: 0.40 **NM** value: **3.00**
295 ❑ Jul 1980 Cover: 0.40 **NM** value: **3.00**
296 ❑ Aug 1980 Cover: 0.50 **NM** value: **3.00**
297 ❑ Sep 1980 Cover: 0.50 **NM** value: **3.00**
298 ❑ Oct 1980 Cover: 0.50 **NM** value: **3.00**
299 ❑ Nov 1980 Cover: 0.50 **NM** value: **3.00**
300 ❑ Dec 1980 Cover: 0.50 **NM** value: **3.00**
301 ❑ Jan 1981 Cover: 0.50 **NM** value: **2.50**
302 ❑ Feb 1981 Cover: 0.50 **NM** value: **2.50**
303 ❑ Mar 1981 Cover: 0.50 **NM** value: **2.50**
304 ❑ Apr 1981 Cover: 0.50 **NM** value: **2.50**
305 ❑ May 1981 Cover: 0.50 **NM** value: **2.50**
306 ❑ Jun 1981 Cover: 0.50 **NM** value: **2.50**
307 ❑ Jul 1981 Cover: 0.50 **NM** value: **2.50**
308 ❑ Aug 1981 Cover: 0.50 **NM** value: **2.50**
309 ❑ Sep 1981 Cover: 0.50 **NM** value: **2.50**
310 ❑ Oct 1981 Cover: 0.50 **NM** value: **2.50**
311 ❑ Nov 1981 Cover: 0.50 **NM** value: **2.50**
312 ❑ Dec 1981 Cover: 0.60 **NM** value: **2.50**
313 ❑ Jan 1982 Cover: 0.60 **NM** value: **2.50**
314 ❑ Feb 1982 Cover: 0.60 **NM** value: **2.50**
315 ❑ Mar 1982 Cover: 0.60 **NM** value: **2.50**
316 ❑ Apr 1982 Cover: 0.60 **NM** value: **2.50**
317 ❑ May 1982 Cover: 0.60 **NM** value: **2.50**
318 ❑ Jun 1982 Cover: 0.60 **NM** value: **2.50**
319 ❑ Aug 1982 Cover: 0.60 **NM** value: **2.50**
320 ❑ Oct 1982 Cover: 0.60 **NM** value: **8.00**
★ 1st Appearance of Cheryl Blossom.
321 ❑ Dec 1982 Cover: 0.60 **NM** value: **4.00**
322 ❑ Feb 1983 Cover: 0.60 **NM** value: **3.00**
Circ: Statement: **68,532**
323 ❑ Apr 1983 Cover: 0.60 **NM** value: **3.00**
Circ: Statement: **68,532**
324 ❑ Jun 1983 Cover: 0.60 **NM** value: **2.50**
Circ: Statement: **68,532**
325 ❑ Aug 1983 Cover: 0.60 **NM** value: **2.50**
Circ: Statement: **68,532**
326 ❑ Oct 1983 Cover: 0.60 **NM** value: **2.50**
Circ: Statement: **68,532**
327 ❑ Dec 1983 Cover: 0.60 **NM** value: **2.50**
Circ: Statement: **68,532**
328 ❑ Feb 1984 Cover: 0.60 **NM** value: **2.50**
Circ: Statement: **64,516**
329 ❑ Apr 1984 Cover: 0.60 **NM** value: **2.50**
Circ: Statement: **64,516**
330 ❑ Jun 1984 Cover: 0.60 **NM** value: **2.50**
Circ: Statement: **64,516**
331 ❑ Aug 1984 Cover: 0.60 **NM** value: **2.50**
Circ: Statement: **64,516**
332 ❑ Oct 1984 Cover: 0.60 **NM** value: **2.50**
Circ: Statement: **64,516**
333 ❑ Dec 1984 Cover: 0.60 **NM** value: **2.50**
Circ: Statement: **64,516**
334 ❑ Feb 1985 Cover: 0.60 **NM** value: **2.50**
Circ: Statement: **64,908**
335 ❑ Apr 1985 Cover: 0.65 **NM** value: **2.50**
Circ: Statement: **64,908**
336 ❑ Jun 1985 Cover: 0.65 **NM** value: **2.50**
Circ: Statement: **64,908**
337 ❑ Aug 1985 Cover: 0.65 **NM** value: **2.50**
Circ: Statement: **64,908**
338 ❑ Oct 1985 Cover: 0.65 **NM** value: **2.50**
Circ: Statement: **64,908**
339 ❑ Dec 1985 Cover: 0.65 **NM** value: **2.50**
Circ: Statement: **64,908**
340 ❑ Feb 1986 Cover: 0.65 **NM** value: **2.50**
Circ: Statement: **69,111**
341 ❑ Apr 1986 Cover: 0.65 **NM** value: **2.50**
Circ: Statement: **69,111**
342 ❑ Jun 1986 Cover: 0.65 **NM** value: **2.50**
Circ: Statement: **69,111**
343 ❑ Aug 1986 Cover: 0.75 **NM** value: **2.50**
Circ: Statement: **69,111**
344 ❑ Oct 1986 Cover: 0.75 **NM** value: **2.50**
Circ: Statement: **69,111**
345 ❑ Dec 1986 Cover: 0.75 **NM** value: **2.50**
Circ: Statement: **69,111**
346 ❑ Feb 1987 Cover: 0.75 **NM** value: **2.50**
Circ: Statement: **66,179**
347 ❑ Apr 1987 Cover: 0.75 **NM** value: **2.50**
Circ: Statement: **66,179**
Anl 1 ❑ ca. 1953 Cover: 0.25 **NM** value: **600.00**
• **CGC:** 1 graded, best 6.0
Anl 2 ❑ ca. 1954 Cover: 0.25 **NM** value: **550.00**
📖 Ladies Man!; Flash in the Pan!; Fur, Fur Away; The Lid's Off; Heartburn!; Ladies of the Lake; Who's Hula?; Ballet Whoopee!; Star Glazed!; Phoney Surprise; Duel Pigeons; Plots to You!; No Eggs-Cuse; Fright Night; Dark Doings; Watch Out!; Knight Must Fall; Fur Crying Out Loud!; A Fight at the Opera; It's a Darned Shamus; Poison Girls Together; It's in the Brag; All Schemed Up; The Nose Knows (text)
Anl 3 ❑ ca. 1955 Cover: 0.25 **NM** value: **500.00**
Anl 4 ❑ ca. 1956 Cover: 0.25 **NM** value: **500.00**
Anl 5 ❑ ca. 1957 Cover: 0.25 **NM** value: **475.00**
Anl 6 ❑ ca. 1958 Cover: 0.25 **NM** value: **450.00**
Anl 7 ❑ ca. 1959 Cover: 0.25 **NM** value: **450.00**
• **CGC:** 1 graded, best 7.0

ARCHIE'S HOLIDAY FUN DIGEST MAGAZINE

Archie

1 ❑ Feb 1997 Cover: 1.79 **NM** value: **1.95**
2 ❑ Feb 1998 Cover: 1.95 **NM** value: **Cover or less**
3 ❑ Feb 1999 Cover: 1.95 **NM** value: **Cover or less**
4 ❑ Feb 2000 Cover: 1.99 **NM** value: **Cover or less**
5 ❑ Jan 2001 Cover: 2.19 **NM** value: **Cover or less**

ARCHIE'S JOKEBOOK MAGAZINE

Archie

There's little to distinguish Archie's Jokebook from any of the other long-running Archie titles — except that the stories tend to be shorter. It's essentially another series of one-page gag strips featuring Archie, Jughead, and rest of the Riverdale gang.

Of note, however, is that #41 features art from major artist-to-be Neal Adams, getting his first break in professional comics. Those humble first panels, however, show little of the trademark style that would eventually place him in the ranks of the comics greats. Then, it was harmless gags, done in as near to Archie house style as always.

1 ❑ ca. 1953 Cover: 0.10 **NM** value: **600.00**
• **CGC:** 2 graded, best 8.0
• No #
2 ❑ ca. 1954 Cover: 0.10 **NM** value: **375.00**
3 ❑ Sum 1954 Cover: 0.10 **NM** value: **275.00**
15 ❑ Fal 1954 Cover: 0.10 **NM** value: **165.00**
16 ❑ Win 1954 Cover: 0.10 **NM** value: **135.00**
17 ❑ Spr 1955 Cover: 0.10 **NM** value: **135.00**
18 ❑ Sum 1955 Cover: 0.10 **NM** value: **135.00**
19 ❑ Aut 1955 Cover: 0.10 **NM** value: **135.00**
20 ❑ Jan 1956 Cover: 0.10 **NM** value: **135.00**
21 ❑ Mar 1956 Cover: 0.10 **NM** value: **100.00**
22 ❑ May 1956 Cover: 0.10 **NM** value: **100.00**
23 ❑ Jul 1956 Cover: 0.10 **NM** value: **100.00**
• **CGC:** 1 graded, best 9.4
24 ❑ Sep 1956 Cover: 0.10 **NM** value: **100.00**
25 ❑ Nov 1956 Cover: 0.10 **NM** value: **100.00**
26 ❑ Jan 1957 Cover: 0.10 **NM** value: **100.00**
27 ❑ Mar 1957 Cover: 0.10 **NM** value: **100.00**
28 ❑ May 1957 Cover: 0.10 **NM** value: **100.00**
29 ❑ Jul 1957 Cover: 0.10 **NM** value: **100.00**
30 ❑ Sep 1957 Cover: 0.10 **NM** value: **100.00**
31 ❑ Nov 1957 Cover: 0.10 **NM** value: **75.00**
32 ❑ Jan 1958 Cover: 0.10 **NM** value: **75.00**
33 ❑ Mar 1958 Cover: 0.10 **NM** value: **75.00**
34 ❑ May 1958 Cover: 0.10 **NM** value: **75.00**
35 ❑ Jul 1958 Cover: 0.10 **NM** value: **75.00**
36 ❑ Sep 1958 Cover: 0.10 **NM** value: **75.00**
37 ❑ Nov 1958 Cover: 0.10 **NM** value: **75.00**
38 ❑ Jan 1959 Cover: 0.10 **NM** value: **75.00**
39 ❑ Mar 1959 Cover: 0.10 **NM** value: **75.00**
40 ❑ May 1959 Cover: 0.10 **NM** value: **75.00**
41 ❑ Jul 1959 Cover: 0.10 **NM** value: **135.00**
• First pro work by Neal Adams **A:** Neal Adams
42 ❑ Sep 1959 Cover: 0.10 **NM** value: **65.00**
43 ❑ Nov 1959 Cover: 0.10 **NM** value: **65.00**
44 ❑ Jan 1960 Cover: 0.10 **NM** value: **70.00**
A: Neal Adams
45 ❑ Mar 1960 Cover: 0.10 **NM** value: **70.00**
A: Neal Adams
46 ❑ May 1960 Cover: 0.10 **NM** value: **70.00**
A: Neal Adams
47 ❑ Jul 1960 Cover: 0.10 **NM** value: **70.00**
A: Neal Adams
48 ❑ Sep 1960 Cover: 0.10 **NM** value: **70.00**
A: Neal Adams
49 ❑ Nov 1960 Cover: 0.10 **NM** value: **35.00**

The CGC numbers printed in individual listings above represent the **number of copies examined** and given a **Universal** grade by CGC and the **best such copy** graded at press time. For current populations, watch for special ***Comics Buyer's Guide*** issues or check **www.cgccomics.com.**

CGC-graded: Multiply prices above by **33 for 9.9 M • 16 for 9.8 NM/M • 7 for 9.6 NM+ • 5 for 9.4 NM • 2.5 for 9.2 NM- • 1.5 for 9.0 VF/NM**

50 ❑ Dec 1960 Cover: 0.10 **NM** value: **35.00**
51 ❑ Feb 1961 Cover: 0.10 **NM** value: **35.00**
52 ❑ Apr 1961 Cover: 0.10 **NM** value: **35.00**
53 ❑ May 1961 Cover: 0.10 **NM** value: **35.00**
54 ❑ Jun 1961 Cover: 0.10 **NM** value: **35.00**
55 ❑ Jul 1961 Cover: 0.10 **NM** value: **35.00**
56 ❑ Aug 1961 Cover: 0.10 **NM** value: **35.00**
57 ❑ Sep 1961 Cover: 0.10 **NM** value: **35.00**
58 ❑ Oct 1961 Cover: 0.10 **NM** value: **35.00**
59 ❑ Dec 1961 Cover: 0.12 **NM** value: **35.00**
60 ❑ Feb 1962 Cover: 0.12 **NM** value: **35.00**
61 ❑ Apr 1962 Cover: 0.12 **NM** value: **24.00**
62 ❑ Jun 1962 Cover: 0.12 **NM** value: **24.00**
• **CGC:** 1 graded, best 7.5
63 ❑ Jul 1962 Cover: 0.12 **NM** value: **24.00**
64 ❑ Aug 1962 Cover: 0.12 **NM** value: **24.00**
65 ❑ Sep 1962 Cover: 0.12 **NM** value: **24.00**
66 ❑ Oct 1962 Cover: 0.12 **NM** value: **24.00**
67 ❑ Dec 1962 Cover: 0.12 **NM** value: **24.00**
68 ❑ Feb 1963 Cover: 0.12 **NM** value: **24.00**
69 ❑ Apr 1963 Cover: 0.12 **NM** value: **24.00**
70 ❑ Jun 1963 Cover: 0.12 **NM** value: **24.00**
71 ❑ Jul 1963 Cover: 0.12 **NM** value: **16.00**
72 ❑ Aug 1963 Cover: 0.12 **NM** value: **16.00**
73 ❑ Sep 1963 Cover: 0.12 **NM** value: **16.00**
74 ❑ Oct 1963 Cover: 0.12 **NM** value: **16.00**
75 ❑ Dec 1963 Cover: 0.12 **NM** value: **16.00**
76 ❑ Feb 1964 Cover: 0.12 **NM** value: **16.00**
Circ: Statement: **295,946**
77 ❑ Apr 1964 Cover: 0.12 **NM** value: **16.00**
Circ: Statement: **295,946**
78 ❑ Jun 1964 Cover: 0.12 **NM** value: **16.00**
Circ: Statement: **295,946**
79 ❑ Jul 1964 Cover: 0.12 **NM** value: **16.00**
Circ: Statement: **295,946**
80 ❑ Aug 1964 Cover: 0.12 **NM** value: **16.00**
Circ: Statement: **295,946**
81 ❑ Sep 1964 Cover: 0.12 **NM** value: **12.00**
Circ: Statement: **295,946**
82 ❑ Oct 1964 Cover: 0.12 **NM** value: **12.00**
Circ: Statement: **295,946**
83 ❑ Dec 1964 Cover: 0.12 **NM** value: **12.00**
Circ: Statement: **295,946**
84 ❑ Jan 1965 Cover: 0.12 **NM** value: **12.00**
Circ: Statement: **273,679**
85 ❑ Feb 1965 Cover: 0.12 **NM** value: **12.00**
Circ: Statement: **273,679**
86 ❑ Mar 1965 Cover: 0.12 **NM** value: **12.00**
Circ: Statement: **273,679**
87 ❑ Apr 1965 Cover: 0.12 **NM** value: **12.00**
Circ: Statement: **273,679**
88 ❑ May 1965 Cover: 0.12 **NM** value: **12.00**
Circ: Statement: **273,679**
89 ❑ Jun 1965 Cover: 0.12 **NM** value: **12.00**
Circ: Statement: **273,679**
• Has 1964 Statement, filed 10/1/64; avg print run 489,768; avg sales 295,946; avg subs 0; avg total paid 295,946; samples 200; max existent 296,146; 40% of run returned
90 ❑ Jul 1965 Cover: 0.12 **NM** value: **12.00**
Circ: Statement: **273,679**
91 ❑ Aug 1965 Cover: 0.12 **NM** value: **8.00**
Circ: Statement: **273,679**
Veronica: The Wet Set; Archie: Stamp Champ; Betty: Scintillating Scent
92 ❑ Sep 1965 Cover: 0.12 **NM** value: **8.00**
Circ: Statement: **273,679**
93 ❑ Oct 1965 Cover: 0.12 **NM** value: **8.00**
Circ: Statement: **273,679**
94 ❑ Nov 1965 Cover: 0.12 **NM** value: **8.00**
Circ: Statement: **273,679**
95 ❑ Dec 1965 Cover: 0.12 **NM** value: **8.00**
Circ: Statement: **273,679**
96 ❑ Jan 1966 Cover: 0.12 **NM** value: **8.00**
97 ❑ Feb 1966 Cover: 0.12 **NM** value: **8.00**
98 ❑ Mar 1966 Cover: 0.12 **NM** value: **8.00**
99 ❑ Apr 1966 Cover: 0.12 **NM** value: **8.00**
100 ❑ May 1966 Cover: 0.12 **NM** value: **8.00**
101 ❑ Jun 1966 Cover: 0.12 **NM** value: **5.00**
102 ❑ Jul 1966 Cover: 0.12 **NM** value: **5.00**
103 ❑ Aug 1966 Cover: 0.12 **NM** value: **5.00**
104 ❑ Sep 1966 Cover: 0.12 **NM** value: **5.00**
105 ❑ Oct 1966 Cover: 0.12 **NM** value: **5.00**
106 ❑ Nov 1966 Cover: 0.12 **NM** value: **5.00**
107 ❑ Dec 1966 Cover: 0.12 **NM** value: **5.00**
108 ❑ Jan 1967 Cover: 0.12 **NM** value: **5.00**
Circ: Statement: **282,199**
109 ❑ Feb 1967 Cover: 0.12 **NM** value: **5.00**
Circ: Statement: **282,199**
110 ❑ Mar 1967 Cover: 0.12 **NM** value: **5.00**
Circ: Statement: **282,199**
111 ❑ Apr 1967 Cover: 0.12 **NM** value: **5.00**
Circ: Statement: **282,199**
112 ❑ May 1967 Cover: 0.12 **NM** value: **5.00**
Circ: Statement: **282,199**
113 ❑ Jun 1967 Cover: 0.12 **NM** value: **5.00**
Circ: Statement: **282,199**
114 ❑ Jul 1967 Cover: 0.12 **NM** value: **5.00**
Circ: Statement: **282,199**
115 ❑ Aug 1967 Cover: 0.12 **NM** value: **5.00**
Circ: Statement: **282,199**
116 ❑ Aug 1967 Cover: 0.12 **NM** value: **5.00**
Circ: Statement: **282,199**
117 ❑ Oct 1967 Cover: 0.12 **NM** value: **5.00**
Circ: Statement: **282,199**
118 ❑ Nov 1967 Cover: 0.12 **NM** value: **5.00**
Circ: Statement: **282,199**
119 ❑ Dec 1967 Cover: 0.12 **NM** value: **5.00**
Circ: Statement: **282,199**
120 ❑ Jan 1968 Cover: 0.12 **NM** value: **5.00**
Circ: Statement: **339,066**
121 ❑ Feb 1968 Cover: 0.12 **NM** value: **3.00**
Circ: Statement: **339,066**
122 ❑ Mar 1968 Cover: 0.12 **NM** value: **3.00**
Circ: Statement: **339,066**
123 ❑ Apr 1968 Cover: 0.12 **NM** value: **3.00**
Circ: Statement: **339,066**
• Has 1967 Statement, filed 10/1/67; avg print run 483,198; avg sales 282,199; avg subs 0; avg total paid 282,199; samples 0; max existent 282,199; 42% of run returned
124 ❑ May 1968 Cover: 0.12 **NM** value: **3.00**
Circ: Statement: **339,066**
125 ❑ Jun 1968 Cover: 0.12 **NM** value: **3.00**
Circ: Statement: **339,066**
126 ❑ Jul 1968 Cover: 0.12 **NM** value: **3.00**
Circ: Statement: **339,066**
127 ❑ Aug 1968 Cover: 0.12 **NM** value: **3.00**
Circ: Statement: **339,066**
128 ❑ Sep 1968 Cover: 0.12 **NM** value: **3.00**
Circ: Statement: **339,066**
129 ❑ Oct 1968 Cover: 0.12 **NM** value: **3.00**
Circ: Statement: **339,066**
130 ❑ Nov 1968 Cover: 0.12 **NM** value: **3.00**
Circ: Statement: **339,066**
131 ❑ Dec 1968 Cover: 0.12 **NM** value: **3.00**
Circ: Statement: **339,066**
132 ❑ Jan 1969 Cover: 0.12 **NM** value: **3.00**
133 ❑ Feb 1969 Cover: 0.12 **NM** value: **3.00**
134 ❑ Mar 1969 Cover: 0.12 **NM** value: **3.00**
135 ❑ Apr 1969 Cover: 0.12 **NM** value: **3.00**
136 ❑ May 1969 Cover: 0.12 **NM** value: **3.00**
• Has 1968 Statement, filed 11/1/68; avg print run 510,606; avg sales 337,062; avg subs 2,004; avg total paid 339,066; samples 0; max existent 339,066; 34% of run returned
137 ❑ Jun 1969 Cover: 0.12 **NM** value: **3.00**
138 ❑ Jul 1969 Cover: 0.15 **NM** value: **3.00**
139 ❑ Aug 1969 Cover: 0.15 **NM** value: **3.00**
140 ❑ Sep 1969 Cover: 0.15 **NM** value: **3.00**
141 ❑ Oct 1969 Cover: 0.15 **NM** value: **3.00**
142 ❑ Nov 1969 Cover: 0.15 **NM** value: **3.00**
143 ❑ Dec 1969 Cover: 0.15 **NM** value: **3.00**
144 ❑ Jan 1970 Cover: 0.15 **NM** value: **3.00**
Circ: Statement: **290,795**
145 ❑ Feb 1970 Cover: 0.15 **NM** value: **3.00**
Circ: Statement: **290,795**
146 ❑ Mar 1970 Cover: 0.15 **NM** value: **3.00**
Circ: Statement: **290,795**
147 ❑ Apr 1970 Cover: 0.15 **NM** value: **3.00**
Circ: Statement: **290,795**
148 ❑ May 1970 Cover: 0.15 **NM** value: **3.00**
Circ: Statement: **290,795**
149 ❑ Jun 1970 Cover: 0.15 **NM** value: **3.00**
Circ: Statement: **290,795**
150 ❑ Jul 1970 Cover: 0.15 **NM** value: **3.00**
Circ: Statement: **290,795**
151 ❑ Aug 1970 Cover: 0.15 **NM** value: **2.00**
Circ: Statement: **290,795**
152 ❑ Sep 1970 Cover: 0.15 **NM** value: **2.00**
Circ: Statement: **290,795**
153 ❑ Oct 1970 Cover: 0.15 **NM** value: **2.00**
Circ: Statement: **290,795**
154 ❑ Nov 1970 Cover: 0.15 **NM** value: **2.00**
Circ: Statement: **290,795**
155 ❑ Dec 1970 Cover: 0.15 **NM** value: **2.00**
Circ: Statement: **290,795**
156 ❑ Jan 1971 Cover: 0.15 **NM** value: **2.00**
Circ: Statement: **261,593**
157 ❑ Feb 1971 Cover: 0.15 **NM** value: **2.00**
Circ: Statement: **261,593**
158 ❑ Mar 1971 Cover: 0.15 **NM** value: **2.00**
Circ: Statement: **261,593**
159 ❑ Apr 1971 Cover: 0.15 **NM** value: **2.00**
Circ: Statement: **261,593**
160 ❑ May 1971 Cover: 0.15 **NM** value: **2.00**
Circ: Statement: **261,593**
161 ❑ Jun 1971 Cover: 0.15 **NM** value: **2.00**
Circ: Statement: **261,593**
162 ❑ Jul 1971 Cover: 0.15 **NM** value: **2.00**
Circ: Statement: **261,593**
163 ❑ Aug 1971 Cover: 0.15 **NM** value: **2.00**
Circ: Statement: **261,593**
164 ❑ Sep 1971 Cover: 0.15 **NM** value: **2.00**
Circ: Statement: **261,593**
165 ❑ Oct 1971 Cover: 0.15 **NM** value: **2.00**
Circ: Statement: **261,593**
166 ❑ Nov 1971 Cover: 0.15 **NM** value: **2.00**
Circ: Statement: **261,593**
167 ❑ Dec 1971 Cover: 0.15 **NM** value: **2.00**
Circ: Statement: **261,593**
168 ❑ Jan 1972 Cover: 0.15 **NM** value: **2.00**
Circ: Statement: **244,956**
169 ❑ Feb 1972 Cover: 0.15 **NM** value: **2.00**
Circ: Statement: **244,956**
170 ❑ Mar 1972 Cover: 0.15 **NM** value: **2.00**
Circ: Statement: **244,956**
171 ❑ Apr 1972 Cover: 0.15 **NM** value: **2.00**
Circ: Statement: **244,956**
172 ❑ May 1972 Cover: 0.20 **NM** value: **2.00**
Circ: Statement: **244,956**
173 ❑ Jun 1972 Cover: 0.20 **NM** value: **2.00**
Circ: Statement: **244,956**
174 ❑ Jul 1972 Cover: 0.20 **NM** value: **2.00**
Circ: Statement: **244,956**
175 ❑ Aug 1972 Cover: 0.20 **NM** value: **2.00**
Circ: Statement: **244,956**
176 ❑ Sep 1972 Cover: 0.20 **NM** value: **2.00**
Circ: Statement: **244,956**
177 ❑ Oct 1972 Cover: 0.20 **NM** value: **2.00**
Circ: Statement: **244,956**
178 ❑ Nov 1972 Cover: 0.20 **NM** value: **2.00**
Circ: Statement: **244,956**
179 ❑ Dec 1972 Cover: 0.20 **NM** value: **2.00**
Circ: Statement: **244,956**
180 ❑ Jan 1973 Cover: 0.20 **NM** value: **2.00**
Circ: Statement: **200,838**
181 ❑ Feb 1973 Cover: 0.20 **NM** value: **1.50**
Circ: Statement: **200,838**
182 ❑ Mar 1973 Cover: 0.20 **NM** value: **1.50**
Circ: Statement: **200,838**
183 ❑ Apr 1973 Cover: 0.20 **NM** value: **1.50**
Circ: Statement: **200,838**
• Has 1972 Statement; avg total paid circ 244,956
184 ❑ May 1973 Cover: 0.20 **NM** value: **1.50**
Circ: Statement: **200,838**
185 ❑ Jun 1973 Cover: 0.20 **NM** value: **1.50**
Circ: Statement: **200,838** • **CGC:** 1 graded, best 9.2
186 ❑ Jul 1973 Cover: 0.20 **NM** value: **1.50**
Circ: Statement: **200,838**
187 ❑ Aug 1973 Cover: 0.20 **NM** value: **1.50**
Circ: Statement: **200,838**
188 ❑ Sep 1973 Cover: 0.20 **NM** value: **1.50**
Circ: Statement: **200,838**
189 ❑ Oct 1973 Cover: 0.20 **NM** value: **1.50**
Circ: Statement: **200,838**
190 ❑ Nov 1973 Cover: 0.20 **NM** value: **1.50**
Circ: Statement: **200,838**
191 ❑ Dec 1973 Cover: 0.20 **NM** value: **1.50**
Circ: Statement: **200,838**
192 ❑ Jan 1974 Cover: 0.20 **NM** value: **1.50**
Circ: Statement: **187,099**
193 ❑ Feb 1974 Cover: 0.20 **NM** value: **1.50**
Circ: Statement: **187,099**
194 ❑ Mar 1974 Cover: 0.20 **NM** value: **1.50**
Circ: Statement: **187,099**
195 ❑ Apr 1974 Cover: 0.25 **NM** value: **1.50**
Circ: Statement: **187,099**
• Has 1973 Statement, filed 10/1/73; avg print run 427,800; avg sales 200,496; avg subs 342; avg total paid 200,838; samples 0; max existent 200,838; 53% of run returned
196 ❑ May 1974 Cover: 0.25 **NM** value: **1.50**
Circ: Statement: **187,099**
197 ❑ Jun 1974 Cover: 0.25 **NM** value: **1.50**
Circ: Statement: **187,099**
198 ❑ Jul 1974 Cover: 0.25 **NM** value: **1.50**
Circ: Statement: **187,099**
199 ❑ Aug 1974 Cover: 0.25 **NM** value: **1.50**
Circ: Statement: **187,099**
200 ❑ Sep 1974 Cover: 0.25 **NM** value: **1.50**
Circ: Statement: **187,099**
201 ❑ Oct 1974 Cover: 0.25 **NM** value: **1.00**
Circ: Statement: **187,099**
202 ❑ Nov 1974 Cover: 0.25 **NM** value: **1.00**
Circ: Statement: **187,099**
203 ❑ Dec 1974 Cover: 0.25 **NM** value: **1.00**
Circ: Statement: **187,099**
204 ❑ Jan 1975 Cover: 0.25 **NM** value: **1.00**
Circ: Statement: **139,205**
205 ❑ Feb 1975 Cover: 0.25 **NM** value: **1.00**
Circ: Statement: **139,205**
206 ❑ Mar 1975 Cover: 0.25 **NM** value: **1.00**
Circ: Statement: **139,205**
207 ❑ Apr 1975 Cover: 0.25 **NM** value: **1.00**
Circ: Statement: **139,205**
• Has 1974 Statement; avg total paid circ 187,099
208 ❑ May 1975 Cover: 0.25 **NM** value: **1.00**
Circ: Statement: **139,205**
209 ❑ Jun 1975 Cover: 0.25 **NM** value: **1.00**
Circ: Statement: **139,205**
210 ❑ Jul 1975 Cover: 0.25 **NM** value: **1.00**
Circ: Statement: **139,205**
211 ❑ Aug 1975 Cover: 0.25 **NM** value: **1.00**
Circ: Statement: **139,205**
212 ❑ Sep 1975 Cover: 0.25 **NM** value: **1.00**
Circ: Statement: **139,205**
213 ❑ Oct 1975 Cover: 0.25 **NM** value: **1.00**
Circ: Statement: **139,205**
214 ❑ Nov 1975 Cover: 0.25 **NM** value: **1.00**
Circ: Statement: **139,205**
215 ❑ Dec 1975 Cover: 0.25 **NM** value: **1.00**
Circ: Statement: **139,205**
216 ❑ Jan 1976 Cover: 0.30 **NM** value: **1.00**
Circ: Statement: **129,941**
217 ❑ Feb 1976 Cover: 0.30 **NM** value: **1.00**
Circ: Statement: **129,941**
218 ❑ Mar 1976 Cover: 0.30 **NM** value: **1.00**
Circ: Statement: **129,941**
219 ❑ Apr 1976 Cover: 0.30 **NM** value: **1.00**
Circ: Statement: **129,941**
220 ❑ May 1976 Cover: 0.30 **NM** value: **1.00**
Circ: Statement: **129,941**
221 ❑ Jun 1976 Cover: 0.30 **NM** value: **1.00**
Circ: Statement: **129,941**
222 ❑ Jul 1976 Cover: 0.30 **NM** value: **1.00**
Circ: Statement: **129,941**
223 ❑ Aug 1976 Cover: 0.30 **NM** value: **1.00**
Circ: Statement: **129,941**
224 ❑ Sep 1976 Cover: 0.30 **NM** value: **1.00**
Circ: Statement: **129,941**
225 ❑ Oct 1976 Cover: 0.30 **NM** value: **1.00**
Circ: Statement: **129,941**
226 ❑ Nov 1976 Cover: 0.30 **NM** value: **1.00**
Circ: Statement: **129,941**
227 ❑ Dec 1976 Cover: 0.30 **NM** value: **1.00**
Circ: Statement: **129,941**
228 ❑ Jan 1977 Cover: 0.30 **NM** value: **1.00**
Circ: Statement: **124,215**

Other grades: Multiply prices above by **1.5 for Mint • 2/3 for Very Fine • 1/3 for Fine • 1/5 for Very Good • 1/8 for Good**

229 ❑ Feb 1977 Cover: 0.30 **NM** value: **1.00**
Circ: Statement: **124,215**
230 ❑ Mar 1977 Cover: 0.30 **NM** value: **1.00**
Circ: Statement: **124,215**
231 ❑ Apr 1977 Cover: 0.30 **NM** value: **1.00**
Circ: Statement: **124,215**
• Has 1976 Statement; avg total paid circ 129,941
232 ❑ May 1977 Cover: 0.30 **NM** value: **1.00**
Circ: Statement: **124,215**
233 ❑ Jun 1977 Cover: 0.30 **NM** value: **1.00**
Circ: Statement: **124,215**
234 ❑ Jul 1977 Cover: 0.35 **NM** value: **1.00**
Circ: Statement: **124,215**
235 ❑ Aug 1977 Cover: 0.35 **NM** value: **1.00**
Circ: Statement: **124,215**
236 ❑ Sep 1977 Cover: 0.35 **NM** value: **1.00**
Circ: Statement: **124,215**
237 ❑ Oct 1977 Cover: 0.35 **NM** value: **1.00**
Circ: Statement: **124,215**
238 ❑ Nov 1977 Cover: 0.35 **NM** value: **1.00**
Circ: Statement: **124,215**
239 ❑ Dec 1977 Cover: 0.35 **NM** value: **1.00**
Circ: Statement: **124,215**
240 ❑ Jan 1978 Cover: 0.35 **NM** value: **1.00**
241 ❑ Feb 1978 Cover: 0.35 **NM** value: **1.00**
242 ❑ Mar 1978 Cover: 0.35 **NM** value: **1.00**
243 ❑ Apr 1978 Cover: 0.35 **NM** value: **1.00**
• Has 1977 Statement; avg total paid circ 124,215
244 ❑ May 1978 Cover: 0.35 **NM** value: **1.00**
245 ❑ Jun 1978 Cover: 0.35 **NM** value: **1.00**
246 ❑ Jul 1978 Cover: 0.35 **NM** value: **1.00**
247 ❑ Aug 1978 Cover: 0.35 **NM** value: **1.00**
248 ❑ Sep 1978 Cover: 0.35 **NM** value: **1.00**
249 ❑ Oct 1978 Cover: 0.35 **NM** value: **1.00**
250 ❑ Nov 1978 Cover: 0.35 **NM** value: **1.00**
251 ❑ Dec 1978 Cover: 0.35 **NM** value: **1.00**
252 ❑ Jan 1979 Cover: 0.35 **NM** value: **1.00**
Circ: Statement: **98,042**
253 ❑ Feb 1979 Cover: 0.35 **NM** value: **1.00**
Circ: Statement: **98,042**
254 ❑ Mar 1979 Cover: 0.35 **NM** value: **1.00**
Circ: Statement: **98,042**
255 ❑ Apr 1979 Cover: 0.40 **NM** value: **1.00**
Circ: Statement: **98,042**
256 ❑ May 1979 Cover: 0.40 **NM** value: **1.00**
Circ: Statement: **98,042**
257 ❑ Jun 1979 Cover: 0.40 **NM** value: **1.00**
Circ: Statement: **98,042**
258 ❑ Jul 1979 Cover: 0.40 **NM** value: **1.00**
Circ: Statement: **98,042**
259 ❑ Aug 1979 Cover: 0.40 **NM** value: **1.00**
Circ: Statement: **98,042**
260 ❑ Sep 1979 Cover: 0.40 **NM** value: **1.00**
Circ: Statement: **98,042**
261 ❑ Oct 1979 Cover: 0.40 **NM** value: **1.00**
Circ: Statement: **98,042**
262 ❑ Nov 1979 Cover: 0.40 **NM** value: **1.00**
Circ: Statement: **98,042**
263 ❑ Dec 1979 Cover: 0.40 **NM** value: **1.00**
Circ: Statement: **98,042**
264 ❑ Jan 1980 Cover: 0.40 **NM** value: **1.00**
265 ❑ Feb 1980 Cover: 0.40 **NM** value: **1.00**
266 ❑ Mar 1980 Cover: 0.40 **NM** value: **1.00**
267 ❑ Apr 1980 Cover: 0.40 **NM** value: **1.00**
• Has 1979 Statement, filed 10/1/79; avg print run 271,022; avg sales 97,920; avg subs 122; avg total paid 98,042; samples 0; office use 300; max existent 98,342; 64% of run returned
268 ❑ May 1980 Cover: 0.40 **NM** value: **1.00**
269 ❑ Jun 1980 Cover: 0.40 **NM** value: **1.00**
270 ❑ Jul 1980 Cover: 0.40 **NM** value: **1.00**
271 ❑ Aug 1980 Cover: 0.50 **NM** value: **1.00**
272 ❑ Sep 1980 Cover: 0.50 **NM** value: **1.00**
273 ❑ Nov 1980 Cover: 0.50 **NM** value: **1.00**
274 ❑ Jan 1981 Cover: 0.50 **NM** value: **1.00**
Circ: Statement: **77,340**
275 ❑ Mar 1981 Cover: 0.50 **NM** value: **1.00**
Circ: Statement: **77,340**
276 ❑ May 1981 Cover: 0.50 **NM** value: **1.00**
Circ: Statement: **77,340**
277 ❑ Jun 1981 Cover: 0.50 **NM** value: **1.00**
Circ: Statement: **77,340**
278 ❑ Jul 1981 Cover: 0.50 **NM** value: **1.00**
Circ: Statement: **77,340**
279 ❑ Aug 1981 Cover: 0.50 **NM** value: **1.00**
Circ: Statement: **77,340**
280 ❑ Sep 1981 Cover: 0.50 **NM** value: **1.00**
Circ: Statement: **77,340**
281 ❑ Oct 1981 Cover: 0.50 **NM** value: **1.00**
Circ: Statement: **77,340**
282 ❑ Nov 1981 Cover: 0.50 **NM** value: **1.00**
Circ: Statement: **77,340**
283 ❑ Jan 1982 Cover: 0.60 **NM** value: **1.00**
284 ❑ Mar 1982 Cover: 0.60 **NM** value: **1.00**
285 ❑ May 1982 Cover: 0.60 **NM** value: **1.00**
• Has 1981 Statement, filed 10/1/81; avg print run 228,498; avg sales 77,229; avg subs 111; avg total paid 77,340; samples 0; office use 300; max existent 77,640; 66% of run returned
286 ❑ Jul 1982 Cover: 0.60 **NM** value: **1.00**
287 ❑ Sep 1982 Cover: 0.60 **NM** value: **1.00**
288 ❑ Nov 1982 Cover: 0.60 **NM** value: **1.00**
final issue.

ARCHIE'S MADHOUSE — Archie

Archie himself was sometimes hard to find in this spinoff series, although the covers occassionally had appearances by the Archie gang. Archie's Madhouse instead featured various backup characters, as well as a stable of unrelated humor and adventure characters such as Professor Transistor and Captain Sprocket.

The super-hero parodies were sometimes corny, sometimes clever, but certainly a step above the Pureheart the Powerful stories featuring Archie as a super-hero.

The highlight of the series was undoubtedly issue #22's introduction of Sabrina, the Teen-Age Witch. This likable character would later cross over into the core Archie titles, as well as making numerous cartoon and live-action TV appearances.

1 ❑ Sep 1959 Cover: 0.10 **NM** value: **175.00**
2 ❑ Nov 1959 Cover: 0.10 **NM** value: **95.00**
3 ❑ Jan 1960 Cover: 0.10 **NM** value: **68.00**
4 ❑ Mar 1960 Cover: 0.10 **NM** value: **50.00**
5 ❑ Jun 1960 Cover: 0.10 **NM** value: **50.00**
6 ❑ Aug 1960 Cover: 0.10 **NM** value: **38.00**
7 ❑ Sep 1960 Cover: 0.10 **NM** value: **38.00**
8 ❑ Oct 1960 Cover: 0.10 **NM** value: **38.00**
9 ❑ Dec 1960 Cover: 0.10 **NM** value: **38.00**
10 ❑ Feb 1961 Cover: 0.10 **NM** value: **38.00**
11 ❑ Apr 1961 Cover: 0.10 **NM** value: **26.00**
12 ❑ Jun 1961 Cover: 0.10 **NM** value: **26.00**
13 ❑ Aug 1961 Cover: 0.10 **NM** value: **26.00**
14 ❑ Sep 1961 Cover: 0.10 **NM** value: **26.00**
15 ❑ Oct 1961 Cover: 0.10 **NM** value: **26.00**
16 ❑ Dec 1961 Cover: 0.10 **NM** value: **23.00**
📖 Madhouse Musicians; Monster Institute of Transylvania; Why is It?; Double Take; Guess Who Said; His Secret Shame; I Got My Job Through the Mad House Want Ads!; The Discovery of Ears
17 ❑ Feb 1962 Cover: 0.12 **NM** value: **23.00**
18 ❑ Apr 1962 Cover: 0.12 **NM** value: **23.00**
19 ❑ Jun 1962 Cover: 0.12 **NM** value: **23.00**
20 ❑ Aug 1962 Cover: 0.12 **NM** value: **23.00**
21 ❑ Sep 1962 Cover: 0.12 **NM** value: **18.00**
22 ❑ Oct 1962 Cover: 0.12 **NM** value: **100.00**
• **CGC:** 2 graded, best 9.0
★ 1st Appearance of Sabrina the Teen-age Witch.
23 ❑ Dec 1962 Cover: 0.12 **NM** value: **18.00**
📖 I Was an Exiled Monster!; Professor Transistor; King Kingo Lets His Hair Down; Video Wonderland; Have Typewriter, Will Travel; The Gabooza
24 ❑ Feb 1963 Cover: 0.12 **NM** value: **18.00**
25 ❑ Apr 1963 Cover: 0.12 **NM** value: **18.00**
26 ❑ Jun 1963 Cover: 0.12 **NM** value: **14.00**
27 ❑ Aug 1963 Cover: 0.12 **NM** value: **14.00**
28 ❑ Sep 1963 Cover: 0.12 **NM** value: **14.00**
29 ❑ Oct 1963 Cover: 0.12 **NM** value: **14.00**
30 ❑ Dec 1963 Cover: 0.12 **NM** value: **14.00**
31 ❑ Feb 1963 Cover: 0.12 **NM** value: **9.00**
32 ❑ Apr 1964 Cover: 0.12 **NM** value: **9.00**
33 ❑ Jun 1964 Cover: 0.12 **NM** value: **9.00**
34 ❑ Aug 1964 Cover: 0.12 **NM** value: **9.00**
35 ❑ Sep 1964 Cover: 0.12 **NM** value: **9.00**
36 ❑ Oct 1964 Cover: 0.12 **NM** value: **9.00**
37 ❑ Dec 1964 Cover: 0.12 **NM** value: **9.00**
38 ❑ Feb 1965 Cover: 0.12 **NM** value: **9.00**
39 ❑ Apr 1965 Cover: 0.12 **NM** value: **9.00**
40 ❑ Jun 1965 Cover: 0.12 **NM** value: **9.00**
• Has 1964 Statement, filed 11/1/64; avg print run 424,831; avg sales 252,261; avg subs 0; avg total paid 252,261; samples 200; max existent 252,261; 41% of run returned
41 ❑ Aug 1965 Cover: 0.12 **NM** value: **6.00**
42 ❑ Sep 1965 Cover: 0.12 **NM** value: **6.00**
43 ❑ Oct 1965 Cover: 0.12 **NM** value: **6.00**
44 ❑ Dec 1965 Cover: 0.12 **NM** value: **6.00**
45 ❑ Feb 1966 Cover: 0.12 **NM** value: **6.00**
46 ❑ Apr 1966 Cover: 0.12 **NM** value: **6.00**
📖 Spy Spoof; Professor Transistor: Mission Mish-Mash; The Mad House Race for Space; The Diamond Demon; Hold that Tiger; The Mad House Race for Space; The Diamond Demon; Hold that Tiger
47 ❑ Jun 1966 Cover: 0.12 **NM** value: **6.00**
48 ❑ Aug 1966 Cover: 0.12 **NM** value: **6.00**
49 ❑ Sep 1966 Cover: 0.12 **NM** value: **6.00**
50 ❑ Oct 1966 Cover: 0.12 **NM** value: **6.00**
51 ❑ Dec 1966 Cover: 0.12 **NM** value: **3.50**
52 ❑ Feb 1967 Cover: 0.12 **NM** value: **3.50**
53 ❑ Apr 1967 Cover: 0.12 **NM** value: **3.50**
54 ❑ Jun 1967 Cover: 0.12 **NM** value: **3.50**
55 ❑ Aug 1967 Cover: 0.12 **NM** value: **3.50**
56 ❑ Sep 1967 Cover: 0.12 **NM** value: **3.50**
57 ❑ Oct 1967 Cover: 0.12 **NM** value: **3.50**
58 ❑ Dec 1967 Cover: 0.12 **NM** value: **3.50**
59 ❑ Feb 1968 Cover: 0.12 **NM** value: **3.50**
60 ❑ Apr 1968 Cover: 0.12 **NM** value: **3.50**
61 ❑ Jun 1968 Cover: 0.12 **NM** value: **3.50**
62 ❑ Aug 1968 Cover: 0.12 **NM** value: **3.50**
63 ❑ Sep 1968 Cover: 0.12 **NM** value: **3.50**
64 ❑ Oct 1968 Cover: 0.12 **NM** value: **3.50**
65 ❑ Dec 1968 Cover: 0.12 **NM** value: **3.50**
• Series continues as Madhouse Ma-ad Jokes
66 ❑ Feb 1969 Cover: 0.12 **NM** value: **3.50**
final issue.
Anl 1 ❑ ca. 1962 **NM** value: **65.00**
Anl 2 ❑ ca. 1964 **NM** value: **25.00**
Anl 3 ❑ ca. 1965 **NM** value: **15.00**
Anl 4 ❑ ca. 1966 **NM** value: **10.00**
Anl 5 ❑ ca. 1968 **NM** value: **10.00**
Anl 6 ❑ ca. 1969 **NM** value: **10.00**

ARCHIE'S PAL, JUGHEAD — Archie

1 ❑ ca. 1949 Cover: 0.10 **NM** value: **1000.00**
2 ❑ ca. 1950 Cover: 0.10 **NM** value: **500.00**
3 ❑ Dec 1950 Cover: 0.10 **NM** value: **350.00**
4 ❑ Feb 1951 Cover: 0.10 **NM** value: **300.00**
5 ❑ Apr 1951 Cover: 0.10 **NM** value: **275.00**
6 ❑ Jun 1951 Cover: 0.10 **NM** value: **250.00**
7 ❑ Aug 1951 Cover: 0.10 **NM** value: **250.00**
8 ❑ Oct 1951 Cover: 0.10 **NM** value: **150.00**
9 ❑ Dec 1951 Cover: 0.10 **NM** value: **150.00**
10 ❑ Feb 1952 Cover: 0.10 **NM** value: **150.00**
11 ❑ Apr 1952 Cover: 0.10 **NM** value: **150.00**
12 ❑ Jun 1952 Cover: 0.10 **NM** value: **150.00**
13 ❑ Aug 1952 Cover: 0.10 **NM** value: **150.00**
14 ❑ Oct 1952 Cover: 0.10 **NM** value: **150.00**
15 ❑ Dec 1952 Cover: 0.10 **NM** value: **150.00**
16 ❑ Feb 1953 Cover: 0.10 **NM** value: **150.00**
17 ❑ Apr 1953 Cover: 0.10 **NM** value: **150.00**
18 ❑ Jun 1953 Cover: 0.10 **NM** value: **150.00**
19 ❑ Aug 1953 Cover: 0.10 **NM** value: **150.00**
20 ❑ Oct 1953 Cover: 0.10 **NM** value: **75.00**
21 ❑ Dec 1953 Cover: 0.10 **NM** value: **75.00**
22 ❑ Feb 1954 Cover: 0.10 **NM** value: **75.00**
23 ❑ Apr 1954 Cover: 0.10 **NM** value: **75.00**
24 ❑ Jun 1954 Cover: 0.10 **NM** value: **75.00**
25 ❑ Aug 1954 Cover: 0.10 **NM** value: **75.00**
26 ❑ Oct 1954 Cover: 0.10 **NM** value: **75.00**
27 ❑ Dec 1954 Cover: 0.10 **NM** value: **75.00**
28 ❑ Feb 1955 Cover: 0.10 **NM** value: **75.00**
29 ❑ Apr 1955 Cover: 0.10 **NM** value: **50.00**
30 ❑ Jun 1955 Cover: 0.10 **NM** value: **50.00**
31 ❑ Aug 1955 Cover: 0.10 **NM** value: **50.00**
32 ❑ Oct 1955 Cover: 0.10 **NM** value: **50.00**
33 ❑ Dec 1955 Cover: 0.10 **NM** value: **50.00**
34 ❑ Feb 1956 Cover: 0.10 **NM** value: **50.00**
35 ❑ Apr 1956 Cover: 0.10 **NM** value: **50.00**
36 ❑ Jun 1956 Cover: 0.10 **NM** value: **35.00**
37 ❑ Aug 1956 Cover: 0.10 **NM** value: **35.00**
38 ❑ Oct 1956 Cover: 0.10 **NM** value: **35.00**
39 ❑ Dec 1956 Cover: 0.10 **NM** value: **35.00**
40 ❑ Feb 1957 Cover: 0.10 **NM** value: **35.00**
41 ❑ Apr 1957 Cover: 0.10 **NM** value: **35.00**
42 ❑ Jun 1957 Cover: 0.10 **NM** value: **35.00**
43 ❑ Aug 1957 Cover: 0.10 **NM** value: **35.00**
44 ❑ Oct 1957 Cover: 0.10 **NM** value: **35.00**
45 ❑ Dec 1957 Cover: 0.10 **NM** value: **35.00**
46 ❑ Feb 1958 Cover: 0.10 **NM** value: **35.00**
47 ❑ Apr 1958 Cover: 0.10 **NM** value: **35.00**
48 ❑ Jun 1958 Cover: 0.10 **NM** value: **35.00**
49 ❑ Aug 1958 Cover: 0.10 **NM** value: **35.00**
50 ❑ Cover: 0.10 **NM** value: **35.00**
51 ❑ Cover: 0.10 **NM** value: **35.00**
52 ❑ Cover: 0.10 **NM** value: **35.00**
53 ❑ Cover: 0.10 **NM** value: **35.00**
54 ❑ Jul 1959 Cover: 0.10 **NM** value: **35.00**
55 ❑ 1959 Cover: 0.10 **NM** value: **35.00**
56 ❑ Cover: 0.10 **NM** value: **35.00**
57 ❑ Cover: 0.10 **NM** value: **35.00**
58 ❑ Cover: 0.10 **NM** value: **35.00**
59 ❑ Cover: 0.10 **NM** value: **35.00**
60 ❑ 1960 Cover: 0.10 **NM** value: **20.00**
61 ❑ 1960 Cover: 0.10 **NM** value: **20.00**
62 ❑ 1960 Cover: 0.10 **NM** value: **20.00**
63 ❑ Aug 1960 Cover: 0.10 **NM** value: **20.00**
64 ❑ Sep 1960 Cover: 0.10 **NM** value: **20.00**
65 ❑ Oct 1960 Cover: 0.10 **NM** value: **20.00**
66 ❑ Nov 1960 Cover: 0.10 **NM** value: **20.00**
67 ❑ Dec 1960 Cover: 0.10 **NM** value: **20.00**
68 ❑ Jan 1961 Cover: 0.10 **NM** value: **20.00**
69 ❑ Feb 1961 Cover: 0.10 **NM** value: **20.00**
70 ❑ Mar 1961 Cover: 0.10 **NM** value: **20.00**
71 ❑ Apr 1961 Cover: 0.10 **NM** value: **20.00**
72 ❑ May 1961 Cover: 0.10 **NM** value: **20.00**
73 ❑ Jun 1961 Cover: 0.10 **NM** value: **20.00**
74 ❑ Jul 1961 Cover: 0.10 **NM** value: **20.00**
75 ❑ Aug 1961 Cover: 0.10 **NM** value: **20.00**
76 ❑ Sep 1961 Cover: 0.10 **NM** value: **20.00**
77 ❑ Oct 1961 Cover: 0.10 **NM** value: **20.00**
78 ❑ Nov 1961 **NM** value: **20.00**
79 ❑ Dec 1961 **NM** value: **20.00**
80 ❑ Jan 1962 Cover: 0.12 **NM** value: **20.00**
81 ❑ Feb 1962 Cover: 0.12 **NM** value: **20.00**
82 ❑ Mar 1962 Cover: 0.12 **NM** value: **20.00**
83 ❑ Apr 1962 Cover: 0.12 **NM** value: **20.00**
84 ❑ May 1962 Cover: 0.12 **NM** value: **20.00**
85 ❑ Jun 1962 Cover: 0.12 **NM** value: **20.00**
86 ❑ Jul 1962 Cover: 0.12 **NM** value: **17.00**
87 ❑ Aug 1962 Cover: 0.12 **NM** value: **17.00**
88 ❑ Sep 1962 Cover: 0.12 **NM** value: **17.00**
89 ❑ Oct 1962 Cover: 0.12 **NM** value: **17.00**
90 ❑ Nov 1962 Cover: 0.12 **NM** value: **17.00**
91 ❑ Dec 1962 **NM** value: **17.00**
92 ❑ Jan 1963 Cover: 0.15 **NM** value: **17.00**
93 ❑ Feb 1963 **NM** value: **17.00**
94 ❑ Mar 1963 **NM** value: **17.00**
95 ❑ Apr 1963 **NM** value: **17.00**
96 ❑ May 1963 Cover: 0.12 **NM** value: **17.00**
97 ❑ Jun 1963 Cover: 0.12 **NM** value: **17.00**
98 ❑ Jul 1963 Cover: 0.12 **NM** value: **17.00**
99 ❑ Aug 1963 Cover: 0.12 **NM** value: **17.00**
100 ❑ Sep 1963 Cover: 0.12 **NM** value: **20.00**
101 ❑ Oct 1963 Cover: 0.12 **NM** value: **15.00**
102 ❑ Nov 1963 Cover: 0.12 **NM** value: **15.00**

CGC-graded: Multiply prices above by **33 for 9.9 M • 16 for 9.8 NM/M • 7 for 9.6 NM+ • 5 for 9.4 NM • 2.5 for 9.2 NM- • 1.5 for 9.0 VF/NM**

103 ❑ Dec 1963 Cover: 0.12 **NM** value: **15.00**
104 ❑ Jan 1964 Cover: 0.12 **NM** value: **15.00**
105 ❑ Feb 1964 Cover: 0.12 **NM** value: **15.00**
106 ❑ Mar 1964 Cover: 0.12 **NM** value: **15.00**
107 ❑ Apr 1964 Cover: 0.12 **NM** value: **15.00**
108 ❑ May 1964 Cover: 0.12 **NM** value: **15.00**
109 ❑ Jun 1964 Cover: 0.12 **NM** value: **15.00**
110 ❑ Jul 1964 Cover: 0.12 **NM** value: **15.00**
111 ❑ Aug 1964 Cover: 0.12 **NM** value: **15.00**
112 ❑ Sep 1964 Cover: 0.12 **NM** value: **15.00**
113 ❑ Oct 1964 Cover: 0.12 **NM** value: **15.00**
114 ❑ Nov 1964 Cover: 0.12 **NM** value: **15.00**
115 ❑ Dec 1964 Cover: 0.12 **NM** value: **15.00**
116 ❑ Jan 1965 Cover: 0.12 **NM** value: **15.00**
117 ❑ Feb 1965 Cover: 0.12 **NM** value: **15.00**
118 ❑ Mar 1965 Cover: 0.12 **NM** value: **15.00**
119 ❑ Apr 1965 Cover: 0.12 **NM** value: **15.00**
120 ❑ May 1965 Cover: 0.12 **NM** value: **15.00**
121 ❑ Jun 1965 Cover: 0.12 **NM** value: **15.00**
122 ❑ Jul 1965 Cover: 0.12 **NM** value: **15.00**
123 ❑ Aug 1965 Cover: 0.12 **NM** value: **15.00**
124 ❑ Sep 1965 Cover: 0.12 **NM** value: **15.00**
125 ❑ Oct 1965 Cover: 0.12 **NM** value: **15.00**
126 ❑ Nov 1965 Cover: 0.12 **NM** value: **15.00**
• Series continues as Jughead, Vol. 1
Anl 1 ❑ ca. 1953 Cover: 0.25 **NM** value: **350.00**
Anl 2 ❑ ca. 1954 Cover: 0.25 **NM** value: **200.00**
Anl 3 ❑ ca. 1955 Cover: 0.25 **NM** value: **100.00**
Anl 4 ❑ ca. 1956 Cover: 0.25 **NM** value: **100.00**
Anl 5 ❑ ca. 1957 Cover: 0.25 **NM** value: **100.00**
Anl 6 ❑ ca. 1958 Cover: 0.25 **NM** value: **100.00**
Anl 7 ❑ ca. 1959 Cover: 0.25 **NM** value: **100.00**
Anl 8 ❑ ca. 1960 Cover: 0.25 **NM** value: **100.00**

ARCHIE'S PAL JUGHEAD COMICS — Archie

The goofy hat-wearing Jughead made his appearance right along with Archie in Pep #22, at a time when decorated beanies cut from men's hats were a teen fad. In 1987, Archie Comics released a new Jughead series, and, 45 issues later, it changed names to Archie's Pal Jughead Comics.

No matter what the name, this good-natured series continues to serve up the gags starring one of the world's hungriest teen-agers. Jughead Forsythe is the teen-age version of Popeye's pal Wimpy. He's always short of money and looking for a free meal. Luckily, his dad runs the local soda shoppe and is always willing to extend his ravenous son enough credit for a triple-fudge sundae. Although Jughead's not the cleverest of the Riverdale bunch, he's a good friend to Archie, Betty, Veronica, and all the rest.

46 ❑ Jun 1993 Cover: 1.25 **NM** value: **1.50**
Circ: Statement: **28,015**
• Series continued from Jughead #45
47 ❑ Jul 1993 Cover: 1.25 **NM** value: **1.50**
Circ: Statement: **28,015**
48 ❑ Aug 1993 Cover: 1.25 **NM** value: **1.50**
Circ: Statement: **28,015**
49 ❑ Sep 1993 Cover: 1.25 **NM** value: **1.50**
Circ: Statement: **28,015**
50 ❑ Nov 1993 Cover: 1.25 **NM** value: **1.50**
Circ: Statement: **28,015**
51 ❑ Dec 1993 Cover: 1.25 **NM** value: **1.50**
Circ: Statement: **28,015**
52 ❑ Jan 1994 Cover: 1.25 **NM** value: **1.50**
Circ: Statement: **34,905**
53 ❑ Feb 1994 Cover: 1.25 **NM** value: **1.50**
Circ: Statement: **34,905**
54 ❑ Mar 1994 Cover: 1.25 **NM** value: **1.50**
Circ: Statement: **34,905**
55 ❑ Apr 1994 Cover: 1.25 **NM** value: **1.50**
Circ: Statement: **34,905**
56 ❑ May 1994 Cover: 1.25 **NM** value: **1.50**
Circ: Statement: **34,905**
57 ❑ Jun 1994 Cover: 1.25 **NM** value: **1.50**
Circ: Statement: **34,905**
58 ❑ Jul 1994 Cover: 1.25 **NM** value: **1.50**
Circ: Statement: **34,905**
59 ❑ Aug 1994 Cover: 1.50 **NM** value: **Cover or less**
Circ: Statement: **34,905**
60 ❑ Sep 1994 Cover: 1.50 **NM** value: **Cover or less**
Circ: Statement: **34,905**
61 ❑ Oct 1994 Cover: 1.50 **NM** value: **Cover or less**
Circ: Statement: **34,905**
62 ❑ Nov 1994 Cover: 1.50 **NM** value: **Cover or less**
Circ: Statement: **34,905**
63 ❑ Dec 1994 Cover: 1.50 **NM** value: **Cover or less**
Circ: Statement: **34,905**
64 ❑ Jan 1995 Cover: 1.50 **NM** value: **Cover or less**
Circ: Statement: **28,478**
65 ❑ Feb 1995 Cover: 1.50 **NM** value: **Cover or less**
Circ: Statement: **28,478**
66 ❑ Mar 1995 Cover: 1.50 **NM** value: **Cover or less**
Circ: Statement: **28,478**
67 ❑ Apr 1995 Cover: 1.50 **NM** value: **Cover or less**
Circ: Statement: **28,478**
68 ❑ May 1995 Cover: 1.50 **NM** value: **Cover or less**
Circ: Statement: **28,478**
69 ❑ Jun 1995 Cover: 1.50 **NM** value: **Cover or less**
Circ: Statement: **28,478**
70 ❑ Jul 1995 Cover: 1.50 **NM** value: **Cover or less**
Circ: Statement: **28,478**
71 ❑ Aug 1995 Cover: 1.50 **NM** value: **Cover or less**
Circ: Statement: **28,478**
72 ❑ Sep 1995 Cover: 1.50 **NM** value: **Cover or less**
Circ: Statement: **28,478**
• Jellybean's real name revealed
73 ❑ Oct 1995 Cover: 1.50 **NM** value: **Cover or less**
Circ: Statement: **28,478**
74 ❑ Nov 1995 Cover: 1.50 **NM** value: **Cover or less**
Circ: Statement: **28,478**
75 ❑ Dec 1995 Cover: 1.50 **NM** value: **Cover or less**
Circ: Statement: **28,478**
76 ❑ Jan 1996 Cover: 1.50 **NM** value: **Cover or less**
Circ: Statement: **28,649**
📖 House of Riverdale, Part 3
77 ❑ Feb 1996 Cover: 1.50 **NM** value: **Cover or less**
Circ: Statement: **28,649**
78 ❑ Mar 1996 Cover: 1.50 **NM** value: **Cover or less**
Circ: Statement: **28,649**
79 ❑ Apr 1996 Cover: 1.50 **NM** value: **Cover or less**
Circ: Statement: **28,649**
80 ❑ May 1996 Cover: 1.50 **NM** value: **Cover or less**
Circ: Statement: **28,649**
81 ❑ Jun 1996 Cover: 1.50 **NM** value: **Cover or less**
Circ: Statement: **28,649**
82 ❑ Jul 1996 Cover: 1.50 **NM** value: **Cover or less**
Circ: Statement: **28,649**
83 ❑ Aug 1996 Cover: 1.50 **NM** value: **Cover or less**
Circ: Statement: **28,649**
84 ❑ Sep 1996 Cover: 1.50 **NM** value: **Cover or less**
Circ: Statement: **28,649**
85 ❑ Oct 1996 Cover: 1.50 **NM** value: **Cover or less**
Circ: Statement: **28,649**
86 ❑ Nov 1996 Cover: 1.50 **NM** value: **Cover or less**
Circ: Statement: **28,649**
87 ❑ Dec 1996 Cover: 1.50 **NM** value: **Cover or less**
Circ: Statement: **28,649** Direct Market orders: **3,383**
📖 Fangs for the Memory; The Cash Flow Problem; The Old Ball Game; TV Programmed; Similar Tastes **A:** Fernando Ruiz; Stan Goldberg **W:** Craig Boldman; George Gladir
88 ❑ Jan 1997 Cover: 1.50 **NM** value: **Cover or less**
Circ: Statement: **26,493**
89 ❑ Feb 1997 Cover: 1.50 **NM** value: **Cover or less**
Circ: Statement: **26,493** Diamd. preorders: **3,924**
★ 1st Appearance of Trula Twist and J.U.S.T..
90 ❑ Mar 1997 Cover: 1.50 **NM** value: **Cover or less**
Circ: Statement: **26,493**
• Jughead asks Trula out
91 ❑ Apr 1997 Cover: 1.50 **NM** value: **Cover or less**
Circ: Statement: **26,493**
• Trula Twyst's true plan revealed
92 ❑ May 1997 Cover: 1.50 **NM** value: **Cover or less**
Circ: Statement: **26,493**
93 ❑ Jun 1997 Cover: 1.50 **NM** value: **Cover or less**
Circ: Statement: **26,493** Diamd. preorders: **3,386**
★ Appearance of Trula Twyst.
94 ❑ Jul 1997 Cover: 1.50 **NM** value: **Cover or less**
Circ: Statement: **26,493** Diamd. preorders: **3,562**
★ Appearance of Trula Twyst.
95 ❑ Aug 1997 Cover: 1.50 **NM** value: **Cover or less**
Circ: Statement: **26,493**
96 ❑ Sep 1997 Cover: 1.50 **NM** value: **Cover or less**
Circ: Statement: **26,493**
97 ❑ Oct 1997 Cover: 1.50 **NM** value: **Cover or less**
Circ: Statement: **26,493**
★ Appearance of Trula Twyst.
98 ❑ Nov 1997 Cover: 1.50 **NM** value: **Cover or less**
Circ: Statement: **26,493**
99 ❑ Dec 1997 Cover: 1.50 **NM** value: **Cover or less**
Circ: Statement: **26,493**
★ Appearance of Trula Twyst.
100 ❑ Jan 1998 Cover: 1.75 **NM** value: **Cover or less**
Circ: Statement: **23,886**
📖 A Storm Over Uniforms, Part 1 • continues in Archie #467
101 ❑ Feb 1998 Cover: 1.75 **NM** value: **Cover or less**
Circ: Statement: **23,886**
★ 1st Appearance of Googie Gilmore.
102 ❑ Mar 1998 Cover: 1.75 **NM** value: **Cover or less**
Circ: Statement: **23,886**
103 ❑ Apr 1998 Cover: 1.75 **NM** value: **Cover or less**
Circ: Statement: **23,886**
104 ❑ May 1998 Cover: 1.75 **NM** value: **Cover or less**
Circ: Statement: **23,886**
105 ❑ Jun 1998 Cover: 1.75 **NM** value: **Cover or less**
Circ: Statement: **23,886**
106 ❑ Jul 1998 Cover: 1.75 **NM** value: **Cover or less**
Circ: Statement: **23,886**
★ Appearance of Googie Gilmore.
107 ❑ Aug 1998 Cover: 1.75 **NM** value: **Cover or less**
Circ: Statement: **23,886**
108 ❑ Sep 1998 Cover: 1.75 **NM** value: **Cover or less**
Circ: Statement: **23,886**
📖 Crown Town; Beach Bummed; Kook-Out! **A:** Rex Lindsey **W:** Craig Boldman
109 ❑ Oct 1998 Cover: 1.75 **NM** value: **Cover or less**
Circ: Statement: **23,886**
110 ❑ Nov 1998 Cover: 1.75 **NM** value: **Cover or less**
Circ: Statement: **23,886**
A: Stan Goldberg **W:** Craig Boldman
111 ❑ Dec 1998 Cover: 1.75 **NM** value: **Cover or less**
Circ: Statement: **23,886**
112 ❑ Jan 1999 Cover: 1.75 **NM** value: **Cover or less**
★ Appearance of Trula Twyst.
113 ❑ Feb 1999 Cover: 1.75 **NM** value: **Cover or less**
114 ❑ Mar 1999 Cover: 1.75 **NM** value: **Cover or less**
A: Stan Goldberg **W:** Craig Boldman ★ Appearance of Trula Twyst.
115 ❑ Apr 1999 Cover: 1.79 **NM** value: **Cover or less**
A: Stan Goldberg **W:** Craig Boldman
116 ❑ May 1999 Cover: 1.79 **NM** value: **Cover or less**
📖 Meals on Wheels **A:** Stan Goldberg **W:** Craig Boldman
117 ❑ Jun 1999 Cover: 1.79 **NM** value: **Cover or less**
★ Appearance of Trula Twyst.
118 ❑ Jul 1999 Cover: 1.79 **NM** value: **Cover or less**
★ Appearance of Trula Twyst.
119 ❑ Aug 1999 Cover: 1.79 **NM** value: **Cover or less**
• Ethel gets Jughead's baby pictures
120 ❑ Sep 1999 Cover: 1.79 **NM** value: **Cover or less**
★ Appearance of Trula Twyst.
121 ❑ Oct 1999 Cover: 1.79 **NM** value: **Cover or less**
122 ❑ Nov 1999 Cover: 1.79 **NM** value: **Cover or less**
123 ❑ Dec 1999 Cover: 1.79 **NM** value: **Cover or less**
124 ❑ Jan 2000 Cover: 1.79 **NM** value: **Cover or less**
125 ❑ Feb 2000 Cover: 1.79 **NM** value: **Cover or less**
126 ❑ Apr 2000 Cover: 1.79 **NM** value: **Cover or less**
127 ❑ May 2000 Cover: 1.79 **NM** value: **Cover or less**
128 ❑ Jul 2000 Cover: 1.99 **NM** value: **Cover or less**
129 ❑ Aug 2000 Cover: 1.99 **NM** value: **Cover or less**
130 ❑ Sep 2000 Cover: 1.99 **NM** value: **Cover or less**
131 ❑ Oct 2000 Cover: 1.99 **NM** value: **Cover or less**
132 ❑ Dec 2000 Cover: 1.99 **NM** value: **Cover or less**
133 ❑ Jan 2001 Cover: 1.99 **NM** value: **Cover or less**
134 ❑ Feb 2001 Cover: 1.99 **NM** value: **Cover or less**
135 ❑ Apr 2001 Cover: 1.99 **NM** value: **Cover or less**
136 ❑ May 2001 Cover: 1.99 **NM** value: **Cover or less**
137 ❑ Jul 2001 Cover: 1.99 **NM** value: **Cover or less**
138 ❑ Aug 2001 Cover: 1.99 **NM** value: **Cover or less**
139 ❑ Sep 2001 Cover: 1.99 **NM** value: **Cover or less**

ARCHIE'S PALS 'N GALS — Archie

Archie's Pals 'n Gals began as an annual special during the early 1950s, a time of great expansion for the Archie Comics line. After a number of giant-sized issues, it settled on a more standard size and a more frequent publishing schedule. In this form, it ran for almost 40 years before it fell victim to a general housecleaning of the Archie line in 1991.

In early issues, focus was often on Archie and Betty or Veronica sharing a soda with Jughead smirking in the background, as the plot evolved to reveal such quandaries as Archie's having made a date with both girls for the same night. Later in the series' run, the focus broadened to include Moose, Midge, and other cast members. Moreover, many of the later plots focused on Betty and Veronica and their trouble with the guys.

1 ❑ ca. 1952 Cover: 0.25 **NM** value: **550.00**
• **CGC:** 1 graded, best 9.2
2 ❑ ca. 1954 Cover: 0.25 **NM** value: **275.00**
3 ❑ ca. 1955 Cover: 0.25 **NM** value: **200.00**
4 ❑ ca. 1956 Cover: 0.25 **NM** value: **175.00**
• **CGC:** 1 graded, best 8.5
5 ❑ ca. 1957 Cover: 0.25 **NM** value: **175.00**
• **CGC:** 1 graded, best 7.5
6 ❑ ca. 1958 Cover: 0.25 **NM** value: **125.00**
7 ❑ ca. 1958 Cover: 0.25 **NM** value: **125.00**
8 ❑ Spr 1959 Cover: 0.25 **NM** value: **75.00**
9 ❑ Sum 1959 Cover: 0.25 **NM** value: **75.00**
10 ❑ Fal 1959 Cover: 0.25 **NM** value: **75.00**
11 ❑ Win 1959 Cover: 0.25 **NM** value: **40.00**
12 ❑ Spr 1960 Cover: 0.25 **NM** value: **40.00**
13 ❑ Sum 1960 Cover: 0.25 **NM** value: **40.00**
14 ❑ Fal 1960 Cover: 0.25 **NM** value: **40.00**
15 ❑ Win 1960 Cover: 0.25 **NM** value: **40.00**
16 ❑ Spr 1961 Cover: 0.25 **NM** value: **40.00**
Circ: Statement: **244,897**
17 ❑ Sum 1961 Cover: 0.25 **NM** value: **40.00**
Circ: Statement: **244,897**
18 ❑ Fal 1961 Cover: 0.25 **NM** value: **40.00**
Circ: Statement: **244,897** • **CGC:** 1 graded, best 8.0
19 ❑ Win 1961 Cover: 0.25 **NM** value: **40.00**
Circ: Statement: **244,897**
20 ❑ Spr 1962 Cover: 0.25 **NM** value: **40.00**
Circ: Statement: **250,851**
21 ❑ Sum 1962 Cover: 0.25 **NM** value: **20.00**
Circ: Statement: **250,851**
22 ❑ Fal 1962 Cover: 0.25 **NM** value: **20.00**
Circ: Statement: **250,851**
23 ❑ Win 1962 Cover: 0.25 **NM** value: **20.00**
Circ: Statement: **250,851**
24 ❑ Spr 1963 Cover: 0.25 **NM** value: **20.00**
Circ: Statement: **243,652**
25 ❑ Sum 1963 Cover: 0.25 **NM** value: **20.00**
Circ: Statement: **243,652**
26 ❑ Fal 1963 Cover: 0.25 **NM** value: **20.00**
Circ: Statement: **243,652**
27 ❑ Win 1963 Cover: 0.25 **NM** value: **20.00**
Circ: Statement: **243,652**
📖 Open and Shut Case;Sound Your "A";Dyeing to Live;Leave It to Dad;Jughead: Cyrano the Second;Li'l Jinx: Sound Proof;Betty and Veronica: Mask me no Questions!;Archie: Sing Along With Arch!;Archie: Sculpture Vulture!;Archie: Dedication Frustration
28 ❑ Spr 1964 Cover: 0.25 **NM** value: **20.00**
Circ: Statement: **239,171**
29 ❑ Sum 1964 Cover: 0.25 **NM** value: **40.00**
Circ: Statement: **239,171**
★ Appearance of The Beatles.
30 ❑ Fal 1964 Cover: 0.25 **NM** value: **20.00**
Circ: Statement: **239,171**
31 ❑ Win 1964 Cover: 0.25 **NM** value: **12.00**
Circ: Statement: **239,171**

Other grades: Multiply prices above by **1.5 for Mint • 2/3 for Very Fine • 1/3 for Fine • 1/5 for Very Good • 1/8 for Good**

32 ❑ Spr 1965 Cover: 0.25 **NM** value: **12.00**
Circ: Statement: **253,860**
33 ❑ Sum 1965 Cover: 0.25 **NM** value: **12.00**
Circ: Statement: **253,860**
34 ❑ Fal 1965 Cover: 0.25 **NM** value: **12.00**
Circ: Statement: **253,860**
35 ❑ Win 1965 Cover: 0.25 **NM** value: **12.00**
Circ: Statement: **253,860**
36 ❑ Spr 1966 Cover: 0.25 **NM** value: **12.00**
Circ: Statement: **265,476**
37 ❑ Sum 1966 Cover: 0.25 **NM** value: **12.00**
Circ: Statement: **265,476**
38 ❑ Fal 1966 Cover: 0.25 **NM** value: **12.00**
Circ: Statement: **265,476**
39 ❑ Win 1966 Cover: 0.25 **NM** value: **12.00**
Circ: Statement: **265,476**
40 ❑ Spr 1967 Cover: 0.25 **NM** value: **12.00**
Circ: Statement: **240,407**
41 ❑ Aug 1967 Cover: 0.25 **NM** value: **8.00**
Circ: Statement: **240,407**
42 ❑ Oct 1967 Cover: 0.25 **NM** value: **8.00**
Circ: Statement: **240,407**
43 ❑ Dec 1967 Cover: 0.25 **NM** value: **8.00**
Circ: Statement: **240,407**
44 ❑ Feb 1968 Cover: 0.25 **NM** value: **8.00**
Circ: Statement: **265,514**
45 ❑ Apr 1968 Cover: 0.25 **NM** value: **8.00**
Circ: Statement: **265,514**
46 ❑ Jun 1968 Cover: 0.25 **NM** value: **8.00**
Circ: Statement: **265,514**
47 ❑ Aug 1968 Cover: 0.25 **NM** value: **8.00**
Circ: Statement: **265,514**
48 ❑ Oct 1968 Cover: 0.25 **NM** value: **8.00**
Circ: Statement: **265,514**
49 ❑ Dec 1968 Cover: 0.25 **NM** value: **8.00**
Circ: Statement: **265,514**
50 ❑ Feb 1969 Cover: 0.25 **NM** value: **8.00**
Circ: Statement: **253,206**
51 ❑ Apr 1969 Cover: 0.25 **NM** value: **6.00**
Circ: Statement: **253,206**
52 ❑ Jun 1969 Cover: 0.25 **NM** value: **6.00**
Circ: Statement: **253,206**
• Has 1968 Statement, filed 11/1/68; avg print run 440,949; avg sales 265,303; avg subs 4,211; avg total paid 265,514; samples 0; max existent 269,514; 39% of run returned
53 ❑ Aug 1969 Cover: 0.25 **NM** value: **6.00**
Circ: Statement: **253,206**
54 ❑ Oct 1969 Cover: 0.25 **NM** value: **6.00**
Circ: Statement: **253,206**
55 ❑ Dec 1969 Cover: 0.25 **NM** value: **6.00**
Circ: Statement: **253,206**
56 ❑ Feb 1970 Cover: 0.25 **NM** value: **6.00**
57 ❑ Apr 1970 Cover: 0.25 **NM** value: **6.00**
• Has 1969 Statement, filed 10/1/69; avg print run 446,155; avg sales 247,024; avg subs 6,182; avg total paid 253,206; samples 0; office use 0; max existent 253,206; 43% of run returned
58 ❑ Jun 1970 Cover: 0.25 **NM** value: **6.00**
59 ❑ Aug 1970 Cover: 0.25 **NM** value: **6.00**
60 ❑ Oct 1970 Cover: 0.25 **NM** value: **6.00**
61 ❑ Dec 1970 Cover: 0.25 **NM** value: **6.00**
62 ❑ Feb 1971 Cover: 0.25 **NM** value: **6.00**
Circ: Statement: **224,425**
63 ❑ Apr 1971 Cover: 0.25 **NM** value: **6.00**
Circ: Statement: **224,425**
64 ❑ Jun 1971 Cover: 0.25 **NM** value: **6.00**
Circ: Statement: **224,425**
65 ❑ Aug 1971 Cover: 0.25 **NM** value: **6.00**
Circ: Statement: **224,425**
66 ❑ Oct 1971 Cover: 0.25 **NM** value: **6.00**
Circ: Statement: **224,425**
67 ❑ Dec 1971 Cover: 0.25 **NM** value: **6.00**
Circ: Statement: **224,425**
68 ❑ Feb 1972 Cover: 0.25 **NM** value: **6.00**
Circ: Statement: **222,929**
69 ❑ Apr 1972 Cover: 0.25 **NM** value: **6.00**
Circ: Statement: **222,929**
• Has 1971 Statement, filed 10/1/71; avg print run 434,714; avg sales 221,273; avg subs 3,152; avg total paid 224,425; samples 0; max existent 224,425; 48% of run returned
70 ❑ Jun 1972 Cover: 0.25 **NM** value: **6.00**
Circ: Statement: **222,929**
71 ❑ Aug 1972 Cover: 0.25 **NM** value: **4.00**
Circ: Statement: **222,929**
72 ❑ Sep 1972 Cover: 0.25 **NM** value: **4.00**
Circ: Statement: **222,929**
73 ❑ Oct 1972 Cover: 0.25 **NM** value: **4.00**
Circ: Statement: **222,929**
74 ❑ Dec 1972 Cover: 0.25 **NM** value: **4.00**
Circ: Statement: **222,929**
75 ❑ Feb 1973 Cover: 0.25 **NM** value: **4.00**
Circ: Statement: **201,791**
76 ❑ Apr 1973 Cover: 0.25 **NM** value: **4.00**
Circ: Statement: **201,791**
• Has 1972 Statement; avg total paid circ 222,929
77 ❑ Jun 1973 Cover: 0.25 **NM** value: **4.00**
Circ: Statement: **201,791**
78 ❑ Jul 1973 Cover: 0.25 **NM** value: **4.00**
Circ: Statement: **201,791**
79 ❑ Aug 1973 Cover: 0.25 **NM** value: **4.00**
Circ: Statement: **201,791**
80 ❑ Sep 1973 Cover: 0.25 **NM** value: **4.00**
Circ: Statement: **201,791**
81 ❑ Nov 1973 Cover: 0.25 **NM** value: **4.00**
Circ: Statement: **201,791**
82 ❑ Dec 1973 Cover: 0.25 **NM** value: **3.00**
Circ: Statement: **201,791**
83 ❑ Jan 1974 Cover: 0.25 **NM** value: **3.00**
Circ: Statement: **199,448**
84 ❑ Apr 1974 Cover: 0.25 **NM** value: **3.00**
Circ: Statement: **199,448** • **CGC:** 11 graded, best 9.6
• Has 1973 Statement; avg total paid circ 201,791
85 ❑ Jun 1974 Cover: 0.25 **NM** value: **3.00**
Circ: Statement: **199,448**
86 ❑ Jul 1974 Cover: 0.25 **NM** value: **3.00**
Circ: Statement: **199,448**
87 ❑ Aug 1974 Cover: 0.25 **NM** value: **3.00**
Circ: Statement: **199,448**
88 ❑ Sep 1974 Cover: 0.25 **NM** value: **3.00**
Circ: Statement: **199,448**
89 ❑ Oct 1974 Cover: 0.25 **NM** value: **3.00**
Circ: Statement: **199,448**
90 ❑ Nov 1974 Cover: 0.25 **NM** value: **3.00**
Circ: Statement: **199,448**
91 ❑ Dec 1974 Cover: 0.25 **NM** value: **3.00**
Circ: Statement: **199,448**
92 ❑ Mar 1975 Cover: 0.25 **NM** value: **3.00**
Circ: Statement: **154,110**
93 ❑ Apr 1975 Cover: 0.25 **NM** value: **3.00**
Circ: Statement: **154,110**
• Has 1974 Statement; avg total paid circ 199,448
94 ❑ Jun 1975 Cover: 0.25 **NM** value: **3.00**
Circ: Statement: **154,110**
95 ❑ Jul 1975 Cover: 0.25 **NM** value: **3.00**
Circ: Statement: **154,110**
96 ❑ Aug 1975 Cover: 0.25 **NM** value: **3.00**
Circ: Statement: **154,110**
97 ❑ Sep 1975 Cover: 0.25 **NM** value: **3.00**
Circ: Statement: **154,110**
98 ❑ Oct 1975 Cover: 0.25 **NM** value: **3.00**
Circ: Statement: **154,110**
99 ❑ Nov 1975 Cover: 0.25 **NM** value: **3.00**
Circ: Statement: **154,110**
100 ❑ Dec 1975 Cover: 0.25 **NM** value: **3.00**
Circ: Statement: **154,110**
101 ❑ Jan 1976 Cover: 0.25 **NM** value: **2.00**
Circ: Statement: **139,943**
102 ❑ Feb 1976 Cover: 0.30 **NM** value: **2.00**
Circ: Statement: **139,943**
103 ❑ Mar 1976 Cover: 0.30 **NM** value: **2.00**
Circ: Statement: **139,943**
104 ❑ May 1976 Cover: 0.30 **NM** value: **2.00**
Circ: Statement: **139,943**
• Has 1975 Statement, filed 10/1/75; avg print run 339,463; avg sales 153,283; avg subs 827; avg total paid 154,110; samples 0; office use 300; max existent 154,410; 55% of run returned
105 ❑ Jun 1976 Cover: 0.30 **NM** value: **2.00**
Circ: Statement: **139,943**
106 ❑ Jul 1976 Cover: 0.30 **NM** value: **2.00**
Circ: Statement: **139,943**
107 ❑ Aug 1976 Cover: 0.30 **NM** value: **2.00**
Circ: Statement: **139,943**
108 ❑ Sep 1976 Cover: 0.30 **NM** value: **2.00**
Circ: Statement: **139,943**
109 ❑ Oct 1976 Cover: 0.30 **NM** value: **2.00**
Circ: Statement: **139,943**
110 ❑ Dec 1976 Cover: 0.30 **NM** value: **2.00**
Circ: Statement: **139,943**
111 ❑ Jan 1977 Cover: 0.30 **NM** value: **2.00**
Circ: Statement: **131,395**
112 ❑ Mar 1977 Cover: 0.30 **NM** value: **2.00**
Circ: Statement: **131,395**
113 ❑ May 1977 Cover: 0.30 **NM** value: **2.00**
Circ: Statement: **131,395**
• Has 1976 Statement, filed 10/1/76; avg print run 325,386; avg sales 139,663; avg subs 280; avg total paid 139,943; samples 0; office use 300; max existent 140,243; 56% of run returned
114 ❑ Jun 1977 Cover: 0.30 **NM** value: **2.00**
Circ: Statement: **131,395**
115 ❑ Jul 1977 Cover: 0.35 **NM** value: **2.00**
Circ: Statement: **131,395**
116 ❑ Aug 1977 Cover: 0.35 **NM** value: **2.00**
Circ: Statement: **131,395**
117 ❑ Sep 1977 Cover: 0.35 **NM** value: **2.00**
Circ: Statement: **131,395**
118 ❑ Oct 1977 Cover: 0.35 **NM** value: **2.00**
Circ: Statement: **131,395**
119 ❑ Dec 1977 Cover: 0.35 **NM** value: **2.00**
Circ: Statement: **131,395**
120 ❑ Jan 1978 Cover: 0.35 **NM** value: **2.00**
Circ: Statement: **109,891**
121 ❑ Mar 1978 Cover: 0.35 **NM** value: **2.00**
Circ: Statement: **109,891**
122 ❑ May 1978 Cover: 0.35 **NM** value: **2.00**
Circ: Statement: **109,891**
• Has 1977 Statement; avg total paid circ 131,395
123 ❑ Jun 1978 Cover: 0.35 **NM** value: **2.00**
Circ: Statement: **109,891**
124 ❑ Jul 1978 Cover: 0.35 **NM** value: **2.00**
Circ: Statement: **109,891**
125 ❑ Aug 1978 Cover: 0.35 **NM** value: **2.00**
Circ: Statement: **109,891**
126 ❑ Sep 1978 Cover: 0.35 **NM** value: **2.00**
Circ: Statement: **109,891**
127 ❑ Oct 1978 Cover: 0.35 **NM** value: **2.00**
Circ: Statement: **109,891**
128 ❑ Dec 1978 Cover: 0.35 **NM** value: **2.00**
Circ: Statement: **109,891**
129 ❑ Jan 1979 Cover: 0.35 **NM** value: **2.00**
Circ: Statement: **106,101**
130 ❑ Mar 1979 Cover: 0.35 **NM** value: **2.00**
Circ: Statement: **106,101**
131 ❑ May 1979 Cover: 0.40 **NM** value: **2.00**
Circ: Statement: **106,101**
• Has 1978 Statement, filed 10/1/78; avg print run 292,829; avg sales 109,808; avg subs 83; avg total paid 109,891; samples 0; office use 300; max existent 110,191; 62% of run returned
132 ❑ Jun 1979 Cover: 0.40 **NM** value: **2.00**
Circ: Statement: **106,101**
133 ❑ Jul 1979 Cover: 0.40 **NM** value: **2.00**
Circ: Statement: **106,101**
134 ❑ Aug 1979 Cover: 0.40 **NM** value: **2.00**
Circ: Statement: **106,101**
135 ❑ Sep 1979 Cover: 0.40 **NM** value: **2.00**
Circ: Statement: **106,101**
136 ❑ Oct 1979 Cover: 0.40 **NM** value: **2.00**
Circ: Statement: **106,101**
137 ❑ Dec 1979 Cover: 0.40 **NM** value: **2.00**
Circ: Statement: **106,101**
138 ❑ Jan 1980 Cover: 0.40 **NM** value: **2.00**
139 ❑ Mar 1980 Cover: 0.40 **NM** value: **2.00**
140 ❑ May 1980 Cover: 0.40 **NM** value: **2.00**
• Has 1979 Statement, filed 10/1/79; avg print run 270,631; avg sales 105,944; avg subs 157; avg total paid 106,101; samples 0; office use 300; max existent 106,401; 61% of run returned
141 ❑ Jun 1980 Cover: 0.40 **NM** value: **2.00**
142 ❑ Jul 1980 Cover: 0.40 **NM** value: **2.00**
143 ❑ Aug 1980 Cover: 0.50 **NM** value: **2.00**
144 ❑ Sep 1980 Cover: 0.50 **NM** value: **2.00**
145 ❑ Oct 1980 Cover: 0.50 **NM** value: **2.00**
146 ❑ Dec 1980 Cover: 0.50 **NM** value: **2.00**
147 ❑ Jan 1981 Cover: 0.50 **NM** value: **2.00**
Circ: Statement: **82,747**
148 ❑ Mar 1981 Cover: 0.50 **NM** value: **2.00**
Circ: Statement: **82,747**
149 ❑ May 1981 Cover: 0.50 **NM** value: **2.00**
Circ: Statement: **82,747**
150 ❑ Jun 1981 Cover: 0.50 **NM** value: **2.00**
Circ: Statement: **82,747**
151 ❑ Jul 1981 Cover: 0.50 **NM** value: **2.00**
Circ: Statement: **82,747**
152 ❑ Aug 1981 Cover: 0.50 **NM** value: **2.00**
Circ: Statement: **82,747**
153 ❑ Sep 1981 Cover: 0.50 **NM** value: **2.00**
Circ: Statement: **82,747**
154 ❑ Oct 1981 Cover: 0.50 **NM** value: **2.00**
Circ: Statement: **82,747**
155 ❑ Dec 1981 Cover: 0.60 **NM** value: **2.00**
Circ: Statement: **82,747**
156 ❑ Jan 1982 Cover: 0.60 **NM** value: **2.00**
157 ❑ Mar 1982 Cover: 0.60 **NM** value: **2.00**
158 ❑ May 1982 Cover: 0.60 **NM** value: **2.00**
• Has 1981 Statement, filed 10/1/81; avg print run 237,151; avg sales 82,654; avg subs 93; avg total paid 82,747; samples 0; office use 300; max existent 83,047; 65% of run returned
159 ❑ Jul 1982 Cover: 0.60 **NM** value: **2.00**
160 ❑ Sep 1982 Cover: 0.60 **NM** value: **2.00**
161 ❑ Nov 1982 Cover: 0.60 **NM** value: **2.00**
162 ❑ Jan 1983 Cover: 0.60 **NM** value: **2.00**
Circ: Statement: **61,713**
163 ❑ May 1983 Cover: 0.60 **NM** value: **2.00**
Circ: Statement: **61,713**
164 ❑ Jul 1983 Cover: 0.60 **NM** value: **2.00**
Circ: Statement: **61,713**
165 ❑ Sep 1983 Cover: 0.60 **NM** value: **2.00**
Circ: Statement: **61,713**
166 ❑ Nov 1983 Cover: 0.60 **NM** value: **2.00**
Circ: Statement: **61,713**
167 ❑ Jan 1984 Cover: 0.60 **NM** value: **2.00**
Circ: Statement: **59,442**
168 ❑ Mar 1984 Cover: 0.60 **NM** value: **2.00**
Circ: Statement: **59,442**
169 ❑ May 1984 Cover: 0.60 **NM** value: **2.00**
Circ: Statement: **59,442**
170 ❑ Jul 1984 Cover: 0.60 **NM** value: **2.00**
Circ: Statement: **59,442**
171 ❑ Sep 1984 Cover: 0.60 **NM** value: **2.00**
Circ: Statement: **59,442**
172 ❑ Nov 1984 Cover: 0.60 **NM** value: **2.00**
Circ: Statement: **59,442**
173 ❑ Jan 1985 Cover: 0.60 **NM** value: **2.00**
Circ: Statement: **59,787**
174 ❑ Mar 1985 Cover: 0.65 **NM** value: **2.00**
Circ: Statement: **59,787**
175 ❑ May 1985 Cover: 0.65 **NM** value: **2.00**
Circ: Statement: **59,787**
• Has 1984 Statement, filed 10/1/84; avg print run 151,233; avg sales 59,260; avg subs 182; avg total paid 59,442; samples 0; office use 300; max existent 59,742; 61% of run returned
176 ❑ Jul 1985 Cover: 0.65 **NM** value: **2.00**
Circ: Statement: **59,787**
177 ❑ Sep 1985 Cover: 0.65 **NM** value: **2.00**
Circ: Statement: **59,787**
178 ❑ Nov 1985 Cover: 0.65 **NM** value: **2.00**
Circ: Statement: **59,787**
179 ❑ Jan 1986 Cover: 0.65 **NM** value: **2.00**
Circ: Statement: **60,774**
180 ❑ Mar 1986 Cover: 0.65 **NM** value: **2.00**
Circ: Statement: **60,774**
181 ❑ May 1986 Cover: 0.65 **NM** value: **2.00**
Circ: Statement: **60,774**
182 ❑ Jul 1986 Cover: 0.75 **NM** value: **2.00**
Circ: Statement: **60,774**
183 ❑ Sep 1986 Cover: 0.75 **NM** value: **2.00**
Circ: Statement: **60,774**
184 ❑ Nov 1986 Cover: 0.75 **NM** value: **2.00**
Circ: Statement: **60,774**
185 ❑ Jan 1987 Cover: 0.75 **NM** value: **2.00**
Circ: Statement: **57,937**
186 ❑ Mar 1987 Cover: 0.75 **NM** value: **2.00**
Circ: Statement: **57,937**
187 ❑ May 1987 Cover: 0.75 **NM** value: **2.00**
Circ: Statement: **57,937**
188 ❑ Jun 1987 Cover: 0.75 **NM** value: **2.00**
Circ: Statement: **57,937**
189 ❑ Jul 1987 Cover: 0.75 **NM** value: **2.00**

CGC-graded: Multiply prices above by **33 for 9.9 M • 16 for 9.8 NM/M • 7 for 9.6 NM+ • 5 for 9.4 NM • 2.5 for 9.2 NM- • 1.5 for 9.0 VF/NM**

Circ: Statement: **57,937**
190 ❑ Aug 1987 Cover: 0.75 **NM** value: **2.00**
Circ: Statement: **57,937**
191 ❑ Sep 1987 Cover: 0.75 **NM** value: **2.00**
Circ: Statement: **57,937**
192 ❑ Oct 1987 Cover: 0.75 **NM** value: **2.00**
Circ: Statement: **57,937**
193 ❑ Nov 1987 Cover: 0.75 **NM** value: **2.00**
Circ: Statement: **57,937**
194 ❑ Jan 1988 Cover: 0.75 **NM** value: **2.00**
Circ: Statement: **61,181**
195 ❑ Mar 1988 Cover: 0.75 **NM** value: **2.00**
Circ: Statement: **61,181**
196 ❑ May 1988 Cover: 0.75 **NM** value: **2.00**
Circ: Statement: **61,181**
197 ❑ Jun 1988 Cover: 0.75 **NM** value: **2.00**
Circ: Statement: **61,181**
198 ❑ Jul 1988 Cover: 0.75 **NM** value: **2.00**
Circ: Statement: **61,181**
199 ❑ Aug 1988 Cover: 0.75 **NM** value: **2.00**
Circ: Statement: **61,181**
200 ❑ Sep 1988 Cover: 0.75 **NM** value: **2.00**
Circ: Statement: **61,181**
201 ❑ Oct 1988 Cover: 0.75 **NM** value: **1.00**
Circ: Statement: **61,181**
202 ❑ Nov 1988 Cover: 0.75 **NM** value: **1.00**
Circ: Statement: **61,181**
203 ❑ Jan 1989 Cover: 0.75 **NM** value: **1.00**
Circ: Statement: **59,255**
204 ❑ Mar 1989 Cover: 0.75 **NM** value: **1.00**
Circ: Statement: **59,255**
205 ❑ May 1989 Cover: 0.75 **NM** value: **1.00**
Circ: Statement: **59,255**
206 ❑ Jun 1989 Cover: 0.75 **NM** value: **1.00**
Circ: Statement: **59,255**
207 ❑ Jul 1989 Cover: 0.95 **NM** value: **1.00**
Circ: Statement: **59,255**
208 ❑ Aug 1989 Cover: 0.95 **NM** value: **1.00**
Circ: Statement: **59,255**
209 ❑ Sep 1989 Cover: 0.95 **NM** value: **1.00**
Circ: Statement: **59,255**
210 ❑ Oct 1989 Cover: 0.95 **NM** value: **1.00**
Circ: Statement: **59,255**
211 ❑ Nov 1989 Cover: 0.95 **NM** value: **1.00**
Circ: Statement: **59,255**
212 ❑ Jan 1990 Cover: 1.00 **NM** value: **Cover or less**
Circ: Statement: **48,898**
213 ❑ Mar 1990 Cover: 1.00 **NM** value: **Cover or less**
Circ: Statement: **48,898**
214 ❑ May 1990 Cover: 1.00 **NM** value: **Cover or less**
Circ: Statement: **48,898**
215 ❑ Jun 1990 Cover: 1.00 **NM** value: **Cover or less**
Circ: Statement: **48,898**
216 ❑ Jul 1990 Cover: 1.00 **NM** value: **Cover or less**
Circ: Statement: **48,898**
217 ❑ Aug 1990 Cover: 1.00 **NM** value: **Cover or less**
Circ: Statement: **48,898**
218 ❑ Sep 1990 Cover: 1.00 **NM** value: **Cover or less**
Circ: Statement: **48,898**
219 ❑ Nov 1990 Cover: 1.00 **NM** value: **Cover or less**
Circ: Statement: **48,898**
220 ❑ Jan 1991 Cover: 1.00 **NM** value: **Cover or less**
221 ❑ Mar 1991 Cover: 1.00 **NM** value: **Cover or less**
222 ❑ May 1991 Cover: 1.00 **NM** value: **Cover or less**
223 ❑ Jul 1991 Cover: 1.00 **NM** value: **Cover or less**
224 ❑ Sep 1991 Cover: 1.00 **NM** value: **Cover or less**

ARCHIE'S PALS 'N' GALS DOUBLE DIGEST
Archie

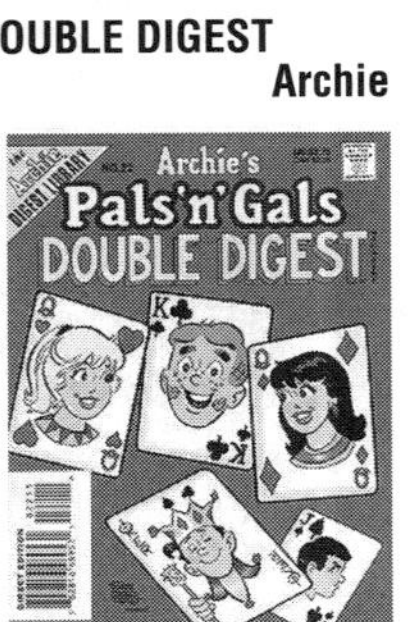

As the title suggests, this is a collection of stories about the perpetual teen Archie and all of his friends. Whether your favorite character is the redhead himself, his best buddy Jughead, or his favorite girls Betty and Veronica, you'll be sure to find a story (or more) to entertain you.

Gathering stories both old and recent, the Digest series provides a look at the kids from Riverdale from the perspective of a variety of writers and artists. Although the gang has had more than their fair share of dangerous, exciting adventures, these stories tend to focus on the lighter side of their lives. Whether they're on a date, at a football game, or just trying to outwit their principal, Mr. Weatherbee, these kids always manage to have fun. And the Double Digest series, obviously, have more pages than the mere Digest series.

1 ❑ Cover: 2.50 **NM** value: **4.00**
2 ❑ Cover: 2.50 **NM** value: **3.00**
3 ❑ Cover: 2.50 **NM** value: **3.00**
4 ❑ Cover: 2.75 **NM** value: **3.00**
5 ❑ Cover: 2.75 **NM** value: **3.00**
6 ❑ Cover: 2.75 **NM** value: **Cover or less**
7 ❑ Cover: 2.75 **NM** value: **Cover or less**
8 ❑ Cover: 2.75 **NM** value: **Cover or less**
9 ❑ Jan 1995 Cover: 2.75 **NM** value: **Cover or less**
10 ❑ Feb 1995 Cover: 2.75 **NM** value: **Cover or less**
11 ❑ Apr 1995 Cover: 2.75 **NM** value: **Cover or less**
12 ❑ Jun 1995 Cover: 2.75 **NM** value: **Cover or less**
13 ❑ Aug 1995 Cover: 2.75 **NM** value: **Cover or less**
14 ❑ Oct 1995 Cover: 2.75 **NM** value: **Cover or less**
15 ❑ Dec 1995 Cover: 2.75 **NM** value: **Cover or less**
16 ❑ Jan 1996 Cover: 2.75 **NM** value: **Cover or less**
17 ❑ Mar 1996 Cover: 2.75 **NM** value: **Cover or less**
18 ❑ May 1996 Cover: 2.75 **NM** value: **Cover or less**
19 ❑ Jul 1996 Cover: 2.75 **NM** value: **Cover or less**
20 ❑ Aug 1996 Cover: 2.75 **NM** value: **Cover or less**
21 ❑ Oct 1996 Cover: 2.75 **NM** value: **Cover or less**
22 ❑ Dec 1996 Cover: 2.75 **NM** value: **Cover or less**
Circ: Direct Market orders: **3,073**
📖 Now You Tell Me!; Leap Of Faith; First In Line; Helping Hand; Writer's Cramp; Chemistry Class; Uncouth Youth; The French Connection; The Comeback Trail, Part 1; The Comeback Trail, Part 2; Make That **A:** Jeff Schultz; Sean Murphy **W:** Dan Parent; Hal Smith
23 ❑ Jan 1997 Cover: 2.75 **NM** value: **Cover or less**
24 ❑ Mar 1997 Cover: 2.75 **NM** value: **Cover or less**
Circ: Diamd. preorders: **3,143**
25 ❑ May 1997 Cover: 2.75 **NM** value: **Cover or less**
26 ❑ Jul 1997 Cover: 2.75 **NM** value: **Cover or less**
27 ❑ Aug 1997 Cover: 2.79 **NM** value: **Cover or less**
Circ: Diamd. preorders: **3,699**
28 ❑ Oct 1997 Cover: 2.79 **NM** value: **Cover or less**
29 ❑ Dec 1997 Cover: 2.79 **NM** value: **Cover or less**
30 ❑ Jan 1998 Cover: 2.95 **NM** value: **Cover or less**
Circ: Statement: **107,428**
31 ❑ Mar 1998 Cover: 2.95 **NM** value: **Cover or less**
Circ: Statement: **107,428**
32 ❑ May 1998 Cover: 2.95 **NM** value: **Cover or less**
Circ: Statement: **107,428**
33 ❑ Jun 1998 Cover: 2.95 **NM** value: **Cover or less**
Circ: Statement: **107,428**
34 ❑ Aug 1998 Cover: 2.95 **NM** value: **Cover or less**
Circ: Statement: **107,428** Diamd. preorders: **3,397**
35 ❑ Sep 1998 Cover: 2.95 **NM** value: **Cover or less**
Circ: Statement: **107,428**
36 ❑ Oct 1998 Cover: 2.95 **NM** value: **Cover or less**
Circ: Statement: **107,428**
37 ❑ Dec 1998 Cover: 2.95 **NM** value: **Cover or less**
Circ: Statement: **107,428**
38 ❑ Feb 1999 Cover: 2.95 **NM** value: **Cover or less**
39 ❑ Apr 1999 Cover: 2.95 **NM** value: **Cover or less**
40 ❑ May 1999 Cover: 2.99 **NM** value: **Cover or less**
• Has 1998 Statement, filed 11/1/98; avg print run 244,129; avg sales 106,319; avg subs 1,108; avg total paid 107,428; samples 419; office use 5,735; max existent 113,581; 54% of run returned
41 ❑ Jun 1999 Cover: 2.99 **NM** value: **Cover or less**
42 ❑ Aug 1999 Cover: 2.99 **NM** value: **Cover or less**
43 ❑ Sep 1999 Cover: 2.99 **NM** value: **Cover or less**
44 ❑ Oct 1999 Cover: 2.99 **NM** value: **Cover or less**
45 ❑ Dec 1999 Cover: 2.99 **NM** value: **Cover or less**
46 ❑ Feb 2000 Cover: 2.99 **NM** value: **Cover or less**
47 ❑ Mar 2000 Cover: 2.99 **NM** value: **Cover or less**
48 ❑ May 2000 Cover: 2.99 **NM** value: **Cover or less**
49 ❑ Jun 2000 Cover: 3.19 **NM** value: **Cover or less**
50 ❑ Aug 2000 Cover: 3.19 **NM** value: **Cover or less**
51 ❑ Sep 2000 Cover: 3.19 **NM** value: **Cover or less**
52 ❑ Oct 2000 Cover: 3.19 **NM** value: **Cover or less**
53 ❑ Dec 2000 Cover: 3.19 **NM** value: **Cover or less**
54 ❑ Feb 2001 Cover: 3.19 **NM** value: **Cover or less**
55 ❑ Mar 2001 Cover: 3.19 **NM** value: **Cover or less**
56 ❑ May 2001 Cover: 3.19 **NM** value: **3.29**
57 ❑ Jun 2001 Cover: 3.19 **NM** value: **3.29**
58 ❑ Aug 2001 Cover: 3.19 **NM** value: **3.29**
59 ❑ Sep 2001 Cover: 3.19 **NM** value: **3.29**
60 ❑ Oct 2001 Cover: 3.19 **NM** value: **3.29**

ARCHIE'S R/C RACERS
Archie

When Archie and Reggie aren't bickering over who gets to date Betty and Veronica, they find other things to fuel their rivalry — like racing radio control cars. When a small race on a closed course results in Archie once again walking away with the prize, Reggie comes up with the ultimate challenge for his longtime rival: a cross-country R/C rally to finally settle who's the better racer. With corporate sponsorship and handpicked support teams for each car, the kids from Riverdale set off on their nationwide jaunt, equipped with customized recreational vehicles trailing their model cars in the race of the century.

1 ❑ Cover: 0.95 **NM** value: **1.00**
📖 On Your Mark; ...Get Ready...; ...Get Set...; ...Go! • Reggie appearanc **A:** Bill Golliher; Rex Lindsey **W:** Bill Golliher
2 ❑ **NM** value: **1.00**
3 ❑ **NM** value: **1.00**
4 ❑ **NM** value: **1.00**
5 ❑ **NM** value: **1.00**
6 ❑ **NM** value: **1.00**
7 ❑ **NM** value: **1.00**
8 ❑ **NM** value: **1.00**
9 ❑ **NM** value: **1.00**
10 ❑ **NM** value: **1.00**

ARCHIE'S RIVAL REGGIE
Archie

1 ❑ ca. 1950 Cover: 0.10 **NM** value: **500.00**
2 ❑ ca. 1950 Cover: 0.10 **NM** value: **225.00**
3 ❑ ca. 1950 Cover: 0.10 **NM** value: **150.00**
4 ❑ ca. 1951 Cover: 0.10 **NM** value: **150.00**
• **CGC:** 1 graded, best 9.4
5 ❑ ca. 1951 Cover: 0.10 **NM** value: **150.00**
• **CGC:** 2 graded, best 9.0
6 ❑ ca. 1952 Cover: 0.10 **NM** value: **100.00**
7 ❑ ca. 1952 Cover: 0.10 **NM** value: **100.00**
8 ❑ ca. 1952 Cover: 0.10 **NM** value: **100.00**
9 ❑ Jun 1953 Cover: 0.10 **NM** value: **100.00**
10 ❑ Dec 1953 Cover: 0.10 **NM** value: **100.00**
11 ❑ Feb 1954 Cover: 0.10 **NM** value: **75.00**
12 ❑ Apr 1954 Cover: 0.10 **NM** value: **75.00**
13 ❑ Jun 1954 Cover: 0.10 **NM** value: **75.00**
14 ❑ Aug 1954 Cover: 0.10 **NM** value: **75.00**

ARCHIE'S SPRING BREAK
Archie

1 ❑ 1996 Cover: 2.00 **NM** value: **Cover or less**
2 ❑ 1997 Cover: 2.00 **NM** value: **Cover or less**
3 ❑ 1998 Cover: 2.25 **NM** value: **Cover or less**
Circ: Diamd. preorders: **3,427**
4 ❑ 1999 Cover: 2.29 **NM** value: **Cover or less**
Circ: Diamd. preorders: **2,864**
5 ❑ 2000 Cover: 2.49 **NM** value: **Cover or less**
Circ: Diamd. preorders: **2,477**

ARCHIE'S STORY & GAME DIGEST MAGAZINE
Archie

32 ❑ Jul 1995 Cover: 1.75 **NM** value: **Cover or less**
33 ❑ Sep 1995 Cover: 1.75 **NM** value: **Cover or less**
34 ❑ Mar 1996 Cover: 1.75 **NM** value: **Cover or less**
35 ❑ May 1996 Cover: 1.75 **NM** value: **Cover or less**
36 ❑ Cover: 1.75 **NM** value: **Cover or less**
37 ❑ Jan 1997 Cover: 1.79 **NM** value: **Cover or less**
Circ: Direct Market orders: **2,478**
38 ❑ Aug 1997 Cover: 1.79 **NM** value: **Cover or less**
39 ❑ Jan 1998 Cover: 1.95 **NM** value: **Cover or less**

ARCHIE'S SUPER-HERO SPECIAL
Archie / Red Circle

1 ❑ Jan 1979 Cover: 0.95 **NM** value: **10.00**
📖 Marco's Eyes; The Double Life of Private Strong; Spawn of the X-World; Mystery of the Vanished Wreckage • reprints Adventures of the Fly #2; reprints Double Life of Private Strong #1 **A:** Jack Kirby
2 ❑ Aug 1979 Cover: 0.95 **NM** value: **10.00**
📖 The Menace of the Micro-Men; The Ultra-Sonic Spies • reprints Double Life of Private Strong #1; reprints Double Life of Private Strong #2 **A:** Jack Kirby

ARCHIE'S SUPER TEENS
Archie

1 ❑ 1994 Cover: 2.00 **NM** value: **Cover or less**
• poster
2 ❑ 1995 Cover: 2.00 **NM** value: **Cover or less**
3 ❑ 1995 Cover: 2.00 **NM** value: **Cover or less**
4 ❑ 1996 Cover: 2.00 **NM** value: **Cover or less**

ARCHIE'S TEN ISSUE COLLECTOR'S SET
Archie

1 ❑ Jun 1997 Cover: 1.50 **NM** value: **Cover or less**
📖 Food Choice; Diamond Demon; Blow the Man Down **A:** Stan Goldberg **W:** Frank Doyle; Joe Edwards
2 ❑ Jun 1997 Cover: 1.50 **NM** value: **Cover or less**
3 ❑ Jun 1997 Cover: 1.50 **NM** value: **Cover or less**
4 ❑ Jun 1997 Cover: 1.50 **NM** value: **Cover or less**
5 ❑ Jun 1997 Cover: 1.50 **NM** value: **Cover or less**
6 ❑ Jun 1997 Cover: 1.50 **NM** value: **Cover or less**
📖 I Told You So!, Chapter 1, I Told You So!, Chapter 2; Plain Jane **A:** Rex Lindsey **W:** Bob Bolling
7 ❑ Jun 1997 Cover: 1.50 **NM** value: **Cover or less**
8 ❑ Jun 1997 Cover: 1.50 **NM** value: **Cover or less**
9 ❑ Jun 1997 Cover: 1.50 **NM** value: **Cover or less**
10 ❑ Jun 1997 Cover: 1.50 **NM** value: **Cover or less**

ARCHIE'S TV LAUGH-OUT
Archie

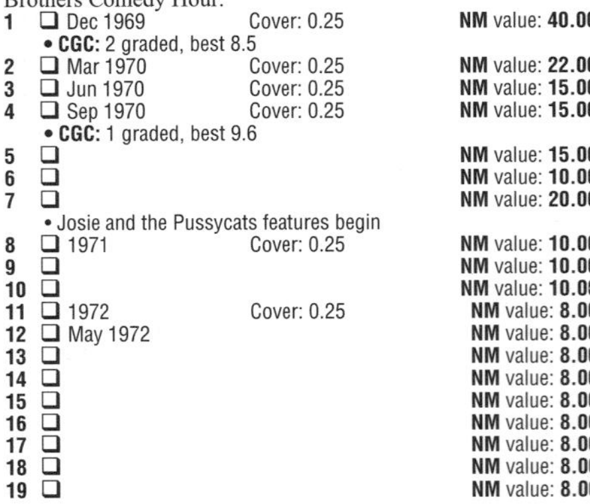

Rowan & Martin's Laugh-In was first broadcast in January 1968; Archie's TV Laugh-Out took almost two years to hit the newsstand, but when it did it introduced such properties as "Sabrina the Teenage Witch" — which ran through issue #105 — and "Josie and the Pussycats" — which ran through issue #106. And, of course, Archie and the gang were around, too, often getting caught up in the pop culture of the day.

As the stories focused on popular culture, it spoofed such fads as disco, Michael Jackson, and The A-Team. And it was peppered with the sort of fast stand-alone gags that evoked the type of comedy to be found in Laugh-In, The Flip Wilson Show, and The Smothers Brothers Comedy Hour.

1 ❑ Dec 1969 Cover: 0.25 **NM** value: **40.00**
• **CGC:** 2 graded, best 8.5
2 ❑ Mar 1970 Cover: 0.25 **NM** value: **22.00**
3 ❑ Jun 1970 Cover: 0.25 **NM** value: **15.00**
4 ❑ Sep 1970 Cover: 0.25 **NM** value: **15.00**
• **CGC:** 1 graded, best 9.6
5 ❑ **NM** value: **15.00**
6 ❑ **NM** value: **10.00**
7 ❑ **NM** value: **20.00**
• Josie and the Pussycats features begin
8 ❑ 1971 Cover: 0.25 **NM** value: **10.00**
9 ❑ **NM** value: **10.00**
10 ❑ **NM** value: **10.00**
11 ❑ 1972 Cover: 0.25 **NM** value: **8.00**
12 ❑ May 1972 **NM** value: **8.00**
13 ❑ **NM** value: **8.00**
14 ❑ **NM** value: **8.00**
15 ❑ **NM** value: **8.00**
16 ❑ **NM** value: **8.00**
17 ❑ **NM** value: **8.00**
18 ❑ **NM** value: **8.00**
19 ❑ **NM** value: **8.00**

Other grades: Multiply prices above by **1.5 for Mint • 2/3 for Very Fine • 1/3 for Fine • 1/5 for Very Good • 1/8 for Good**

20 ❑ NM value: 8.00
21 ❑ NM value: 6.00
22 ❑ NM value: 6.00
23 ❑ NM value: 6.00
24 ❑ NM value: 6.00
25 ❑ NM value: 6.00
Circ: Statement: 156,261
26 ❑ NM value: 6.00
Circ: Statement: 156,261
27 ❑ NM value: 6.00
Circ: Statement: 156,261
28 ❑ Oct 1974 Cover: 0.25 NM value: 6.00
Circ: Statement: 156,261
29 ❑ NM value: 6.00
30 ❑ NM value: 6.00
31 ❑ May 1975 NM value: 6.00
Circ: Statement: 125,786
• Has 1974 Statement; avg total paid circ 156,261
32 ❑ 1975 NM value: 6.00
Circ: Statement: 125,786
33 ❑ 1975 NM value: 6.00
Circ: Statement: 125,786
34 ❑ 1975 NM value: 6.00
Circ: Statement: 125,786
35 ❑ NM value: 6.00
36 ❑ NM value: 6.00
37 ❑ Feb 1976 NM value: 6.00
Circ: Statement: 129,338
38 ❑ Mar 1976 NM value: 6.00
Circ: Statement: 129,338
39 ❑ Apr 1976 NM value: 6.00
Circ: Statement: 129,338
40 ❑ Jun 1976 NM value: 6.00
Circ: Statement: 129,338
41 ❑ Jul 1976 NM value: 4.00
Circ: Statement: 129,338
42 ❑ Aug 1976 NM value: 4.00
Circ: Statement: 129,338
43 ❑ Sep 1976 NM value: 4.00
Circ: Statement: 129,338
44 ❑ Nov 1976 NM value: 4.00
Circ: Statement: 129,338
45 ❑ Dec 1976 NM value: 4.00
Circ: Statement: 129,338
46 ❑ Feb 1977 NM value: 4.00
Circ: Statement: 130,586
47 ❑ Mar 1977 NM value: 4.00
Circ: Statement: 130,586
48 ❑ Apr 1977 NM value: 4.00
Circ: Statement: 130,586
• Has 1976 Statement; avg total paid circ 129,338
49 ❑ Jun 1977 NM value: 4.00
Circ: Statement: 130,586
50 ❑ Jul 1977 NM value: 4.00
Circ: Statement: 130,586
51 ❑ Aug 1977 NM value: 4.00
Circ: Statement: 130,586
52 ❑ Sep 1977 NM value: 4.00
Circ: Statement: 130,586
53 ❑ Nov 1977 NM value: 4.00
Circ: Statement: 130,586
54 ❑ Dec 1977 Cover: 0.35 NM value: 4.00
Circ: Statement: 130,586
55 ❑ Feb 1978 Cover: 0.35 NM value: 4.00
Circ: Statement: 109,526
56 ❑ Mar 1978 NM value: 4.00
Circ: Statement: 109,526
57 ❑ Apr 1978 NM value: 4.00
Circ: Statement: 109,526
• Has 1977 Statement, filed 10/1/77; avg print run 309,374; avg sales 130,311; avg subs 275; avg total paid 130,586; samples 0; office use 300; max existent 130,886; 58% of run returned
58 ❑ Jun 1978 NM value: 4.00
Circ: Statement: 109,526
59 ❑ Jul 1978 NM value: 4.00
Circ: Statement: 109,526
60 ❑ Aug 1978 NM value: 4.00
Circ: Statement: 109,526
61 ❑ Sep 1978 NM value: 3.00
Circ: Statement: 109,526
62 ❑ Nov 1978 NM value: 3.00
Circ: Statement: 109,526
63 ❑ Dec 1978 NM value: 3.00
Circ: Statement: 109,526
64 ❑ Feb 1979 NM value: 3.00
65 ❑ Mar 1979 NM value: 3.00
66 ❑ Apr 1979 NM value: 3.00
• Has 1978 Statement, filed 10/1/78; avg print run 288,785; avg sales 109,507; avg subs 19; avg total paid 109,526; samples 0; office use 300; max existent 109,826; 62% of run returned
67 ❑ NM value: 3.00
68 ❑ NM value: 3.00
69 ❑ NM value: 3.00
70 ❑ NM value: 3.00
71 ❑ NM value: 3.00
72 ❑ NM value: 3.00
73 ❑ NM value: 3.00
74 ❑ NM value: 3.00
75 ❑ NM value: 3.00
76 ❑ NM value: 3.00
77 ❑ NM value: 3.00
78 ❑ NM value: 3.00
79 ❑ NM value: 3.00
80 ❑ NM value: 3.00
81 ❑ NM value: 2.50
82 ❑ NM value: 2.50
83 ❑ NM value: 2.50
84 ❑ NM value: 2.50
85 ❑ NM value: 2.50
86 ❑ 1982 NM value: 2.50
87 ❑ Feb 1983 NM value: 2.50
Circ: Statement: 63,297
88 ❑ Apr 1983 NM value: 2.50
Circ: Statement: 63,297
89 ❑ Jun 1983 NM value: 2.50
Circ: Statement: 63,297
90 ❑ Aug 1983 NM value: 2.50
Circ: Statement: 63,297
91 ❑ Oct 1983 NM value: 2.50
Circ: Statement: 63,297
92 ❑ Dec 1983 NM value: 2.50
Circ: Statement: 63,297
93 ❑ Feb 1984 Cover: 0.60 NM value: 2.50
Circ: Statement: 57,857
94 ❑ Apr 1984 Cover: 0.60 NM value: 2.50
Circ: Statement: 57,857
95 ❑ Jun 1984 Cover: 0.60 NM value: 2.50
Circ: Statement: 57,857
• Has 1983 Statement, filed 10/1/83; avg print run 163,444; avg sales 63,170; avg subs 127; avg total paid 63,297; samples 0; office use 300; max existent 63,597; 61% of run returned
96 ❑ Aug 1984 Cover: 0.60 NM value: 2.50
Circ: Statement: 57,857
97 ❑ Oct 1984 Cover: 0.60 NM value: 2.50
Circ: Statement: 57,857
98 ❑ Dec 1984 Cover: 0.60 NM value: 2.50
Circ: Statement: 57,857
99 ❑ Feb 1985 Cover: 0.65 NM value: 2.50
100 ❑ Apr 1985 Cover: 0.65 NM value: 2.50
📖 The Archies…The Book; Glenn Scarpelli in Hollywood…Nightmare; Josie and the Pussycats…Have an Ice Day A: Dan Decarlo; Henry Scarpelli; Stan G. W: Henry Scarpelli; Frank Doyle; George Gladir ★ Appearance of Jackie Maxon.
101 ❑ Jun 1985 Cover: 0.65 NM value: 2.50
102 ❑ Aug 1985 Cover: 0.65 NM value: 2.50
103 ❑ Oct 1985 Cover: 0.65 NM value: 2.50
104 ❑ Dec 1985 Cover: 0.65 NM value: 2.50
105 ❑ Feb 1986 Cover: 0.65 NM value: 2.50
106 ❑ Apr 1986 Cover: 0.65 NM value: 2.50

ARCHIE'S VACATION SPECIAL — Archie

Since the debut of Archie and the gang in the 1940s, there have been few more consistently successful formulas in the history of American comics. Archie, the teen ne'er-do-well; his dueling girlfriends Betty and Veronica; and his pals: big, dumb, lovable Moose; spoiled rich brat Reggie; and hamburger-chomping Jughead, together with various buffoonish adults are an almost inexhaustible mine of gags, situation comedy, and physical humor for the adolescent and adolescent-at-heart.

Archie's Vacation Special serves up 48 pages of goofy laughs in the tried-and-true Archie tradition. The deluxe format and better-than-average color reproduction make the Vacation Special a double-sized treat for fans.

1 ❑ Sum 1994 Cover: 2.00 NM value: Cover or less
📖 Have A Nice Trip, Part 1; Have A Nice Trip, Part 2; Making Waves; A Dog Day Afternoon; What's So Funny; The Personal Touch; Defense Zone; Slang Harangue; Sand Castle Captive; A: Doug Crane; Dan Decarlo; Stan Goldberg; Dan Parent; Tim Kennedy W: Dan Parent; Frank Doyle; George Gladir; Joe Edwards; Mike Pellowski
2 ❑ Win 1995 Cover: 2.00 NM value: Cover or less
3 ❑ Sum 1995 Cover: 2.00 NM value: Cover or less
4 ❑ Sum 1996 Cover: 2.00 NM value: Cover or less
5 ❑ Sum 1997 Cover: 2.00 NM value: Cover or less
Circ: Diamd. preorders: 3,466
6 ❑ Sum 1998 Cover: 2.25 NM value: Cover or less
Circ: Diamd. preorders: 3,367
7 ❑ Sum 1999 Cover: 2.29 NM value: Cover or less
Circ: Diamd. preorders: 2,786
8 ❑ Sum 2000 Cover: 2.49 NM value: Cover or less
Circ: Diamd. preorders: 2,881

ARCHIE'S WEIRD MYSTERIES — Archie

1 ❑ Feb 2000 Cover: 1.79 NM value: Cover or less
2 ❑ Mar 2000 Cover: 1.79 NM value: Cover or less
3 ❑ Apr 2000 Cover: 1.79 NM value: Cover or less
4 ❑ May 2000 Cover: 1.99 NM value: Cover or less
Circ: Diamd. preorders: 2,927
5 ❑ Jun 2000 Cover: 1.99 NM value: Cover or less
Circ: Diamd. preorders: 2,875
6 ❑ Jul 2000 Cover: 1.99 NM value: Cover or less
Circ: Diamd. preorders: 2,833
7 ❑ Aug 2000 Cover: 1.99 NM value: Cover or less
Circ: Diamd. preorders: 2,896
8 ❑ Sep 2000 Cover: 1.99 NM value: Cover or less
Circ: Diamd. preorders: 3,045
9 ❑ Oct 2000 Cover: 1.99 NM value: Cover or less
Circ: Diamd. preorders: 2,964
10 ❑ Dec 2000 Cover: 1.99 NM value: Cover or less
Circ: Diamd. preorders: 2,643
11 ❑ Feb 2001 Cover: 1.99 NM value: Cover or less
Circ: Diamd. preorders: 2,692
12 ❑ Apr 2001 Cover: 1.99 NM value: Cover or less
Circ: Diamd. preorders: 2,675
13 ❑ 2001 Cover: 1.99 NM value: Cover or less
Circ: Diamd. preorders: 2,086
14 ❑ 2001 Cover: 1.99 NM value: Cover or less
Circ: Diamd. preorders: 2,721
15 ❑ 2001 Cover: 1.99 NM value: Cover or less
Circ: Diamd. preorders: 2,469
16 ❑ 2001 Cover: 1.99 NM value: Cover or less
Circ: Diamd. preorders: 2,513
Ash 1 ❑ NM value: 1.00
• Giveaway from Diamond. 📖 The Case of the Haunted Comic Shop A: Bill Golliher W: Paul Castiglia

ARCHIE 3000 — Archie

1 ❑ May 1989 Cover: 0.75 NM value: 3.00
2 ❑ Jul 1989 Cover: 0.75 NM value: 2.00
3 ❑ Aug 1989 Cover: 0.95 NM value: 2.00
4 ❑ Oct 1989 Cover: 0.95 NM value: 2.00
5 ❑ Nov 1989 Cover: 0.95 NM value: 2.00
6 ❑ Jan 1990 Cover: 1.00 NM value: Cover or less
7 ❑ Mar 1990 Cover: 1.00 NM value: Cover or less
8 ❑ May 1990 Cover: 1.00 NM value: Cover or less
9 ❑ Jul 1990 Cover: 1.00 NM value: Cover or less
10 ❑ Aug 1990 Cover: 1.00 NM value: Cover or less
11 ❑ Oct 1990 Cover: 1.00 NM value: Cover or less
12 ❑ Nov 1990 Cover: 1.00 NM value: Cover or less
13 ❑ Jan 1991 Cover: 1.00 NM value: Cover or less
14 ❑ Mar 1991 Cover: 1.00 NM value: Cover or less
15 ❑ May 1991 Cover: 1.00 NM value: Cover or less

ARCOMICS PREMIERE — Arcomics

1 ❑ Jul 1993, b&w Cover: 2.95 NM value: Cover or less
Circ: CapCity orders: 5,270
lenticular animation cover.

ARCTIC COMICS — Nick Burns

1 ❑ Cover: 1.00 NM value: Cover or less
Circ: CapCity orders: 3,850
📖 Spring; Glossary; My Northern Summer Vacation; Inui Language Inuktitut; Stragglers • souvenir A: Nick Burns W: Nick Burns

AREA 52 — Image

1 ❑ Jan 2001 Cover: 2.95 NM value: Cover or less
Circ: Diamd. preorders: 18,479 • CGC: 1 graded, best 9.8
📖 Here Nothing Can Go Wrong A: Clayton Henry W: Brian Haberlin
2 ❑ Mar 2001 Cover: 2.95 NM value: Cover or less
Circ: Diamd. preorders: 13,270
A: Clayton Henry W: Brian Haberlin
3 ❑ Apr 2001 Cover: 2.95 NM value: Cover or less
Circ: Diamd. preorders: 13,057
A: Clayton Henry W: Brian Haberlin
4 ❑ ca. 2001 Cover: 2.95 NM value: Cover or less
Circ: Diamd. preorders: 12,878

AREA 88 — Eclipse / Viz

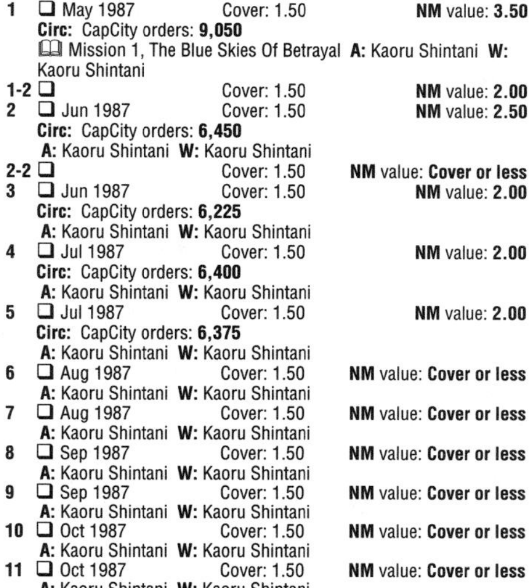

Comics in Japan run from science-fiction to adult fiction, and are read by millions of Japanese. According to its editors, Area 88 was the first large scale attempt to bring Japanese comics ("manga") to the U.S. in a traditional comic book form. In doing so, it helped open the U.S. comic marketplace to the amazing variety of Japanese comic storytelling.

The Area 88 of this series is a battleground in North Africa, right at the front lines of the war between Asran and its enemy. Asran employs a force of mercenaries to do their dirty work, running their air force much like a taxi company. The pilots provide their own planes, pay for their own ammunition and fuel, then receive payment for the kills they make. To survive at this game takes both skill and cunning, a combination which is best found in Shin Kazama, a blonde, Japanese mercenary, and the hero of the series.

1 ❑ May 1987 Cover: 1.50 NM value: 3.50
Circ: CapCity orders: 9,050
📖 Mission 1, The Blue Skies Of Betrayal A: Kaoru Shintani W: Kaoru Shintani
1-2 ❑ Cover: 1.50 NM value: 2.00
2 ❑ Jun 1987 Cover: 1.50 NM value: 2.50
Circ: CapCity orders: 6,450
A: Kaoru Shintani W: Kaoru Shintani
2-2 ❑ Cover: 1.50 NM value: Cover or less
3 ❑ Jun 1987 Cover: 1.50 NM value: 2.00
Circ: CapCity orders: 6,225
A: Kaoru Shintani W: Kaoru Shintani
4 ❑ Jul 1987 Cover: 1.50 NM value: 2.00
Circ: CapCity orders: 6,400
A: Kaoru Shintani W: Kaoru Shintani
5 ❑ Jul 1987 Cover: 1.50 NM value: 2.00
Circ: CapCity orders: 6,375
A: Kaoru Shintani W: Kaoru Shintani
6 ❑ Aug 1987 Cover: 1.50 NM value: Cover or less
A: Kaoru Shintani W: Kaoru Shintani
7 ❑ Aug 1987 Cover: 1.50 NM value: Cover or less
A: Kaoru Shintani W: Kaoru Shintani
8 ❑ Sep 1987 Cover: 1.50 NM value: Cover or less
A: Kaoru Shintani W: Kaoru Shintani
9 ❑ Sep 1987 Cover: 1.50 NM value: Cover or less
A: Kaoru Shintani W: Kaoru Shintani
10 ❑ Oct 1987 Cover: 1.50 NM value: Cover or less
A: Kaoru Shintani W: Kaoru Shintani
11 ❑ Oct 1987 Cover: 1.50 NM value: Cover or less
A: Kaoru Shintani W: Kaoru Shintani
12 ❑ Nov 1987 Cover: 1.50 NM value: Cover or less
A: Kaoru Shintani W: Kaoru Shintani

CGC-graded: Multiply prices above by **33 for 9.9 M • 16 for 9.8 NM/M • 7 for 9.6 NM+ • 5 for 9.4 NM • 2.5 for 9.2 NM- • 1.5 for 9.0 VF/NM**

13 ❑ Nov 1987 Cover: 1.50 **NM** value: **Cover or less**
A: Kaoru Shintani **W:** Kaoru Shintani
14 ❑ Dec 1987 Cover: 1.50 **NM** value: **Cover or less**
A: Kaoru Shintani **W:** Kaoru Shintani
15 ❑ Dec 1987 Cover: 1.50 **NM** value: **Cover or less**
A: Kaoru Shintani **W:** Kaoru Shintani
16 ❑ Jan 1988 Cover: 1.50 **NM** value: **Cover or less**
A: Kaoru Shintani **W:** Kaoru Shintani
17 ❑ Jan 1988 Cover: 1.50 **NM** value: **Cover or less**
A: Kaoru Shintani **W:** Kaoru Shintani
18 ❑ Feb 1988 Cover: 1.50 **NM** value: **Cover or less**
A: Kaoru Shintani **W:** Kaoru Shintani
19 ❑ Feb 1988 Cover: 1.50 **NM** value: **Cover or less**
A: Kaoru Shintani **W:** Kaoru Shintani
20 ❑ Mar 1988 Cover: 1.50 **NM** value: **Cover or less**
A: Kaoru Shintani **W:** Kaoru Shintani
21 ❑ Mar 1988 Cover: 1.50 **NM** value: **Cover or less**
A: Kaoru Shintani **W:** Kaoru Shintani
22 ❑ Apr 1988 Cover: 1.50 **NM** value: **Cover or less**
A: Kaoru Shintani **W:** Kaoru Shintani
23 ❑ Apr 1988 Cover: 1.50 **NM** value: **Cover or less**
A: Kaoru Shintani **W:** Kaoru Shintani
24 ❑ May 1988 Cover: 1.50 **NM** value: **Cover or less**
A: Kaoru Shintani **W:** Kaoru Shintani
25 ❑ May 1988 Cover: 1.50 **NM** value: **Cover or less**
A: Kaoru Shintani **W:** Kaoru Shintani
26 ❑ Jun 1988 Cover: 1.50 **NM** value: **Cover or less**
A: Kaoru Shintani **W:** Kaoru Shintani
27 ❑ Jun 1988 Cover: 1.50 **NM** value: **Cover or less**
A: Kaoru Shintani **W:** Kaoru Shintani
28 ❑ Jul 1988 Cover: 1.50 **NM** value: **Cover or less**
A: Kaoru Shintani **W:** Kaoru Shintani
29 ❑ Jul 1988 Cover: 1.50 **NM** value: **Cover or less**
A: Kaoru Shintani **W:** Kaoru Shintani
30 ❑ Aug 1988 Cover: 1.50 **NM** value: **Cover or less**
A: Kaoru Shintani **W:** Kaoru Shintani
31 ❑ Aug 1988 Cover: 1.50 **NM** value: **Cover or less**
A: Kaoru Shintani **W:** Kaoru Shintani
32 ❑ Sep 1988 Cover: 1.50 **NM** value: **Cover or less**
A: Kaoru Shintani **W:** Kaoru Shintani
33 ❑ Sep 1988 Cover: 1.50 **NM** value: **Cover or less**
A: Kaoru Shintani **W:** Kaoru Shintani
34 ❑ Oct 1988 Cover: 1.50 **NM** value: **Cover or less**
A: Kaoru Shintani **W:** Kaoru Shintani
35 ❑ Oct 1988 Cover: 1.50 **NM** value: **Cover or less**
A: Kaoru Shintani **W:** Kaoru Shintani
36 ❑ Nov 1988 Cover: 1.50 **NM** value: **Cover or less**
A: Kaoru Shintani **W:** Kaoru Shintani
37 ❑ Nov 1988 Cover: 1.75 **NM** value: **Cover or less**
A: Kaoru Shintani **W:** Kaoru Shintani
38 ❑ Dec 1988 Cover: 1.75 **NM** value: **Cover or less**
A: Kaoru Shintani **W:** Kaoru Shintani
39 ❑ Dec 1988 Cover: 1.75 **NM** value: **Cover or less**
A: Kaoru Shintani **W:** Kaoru Shintani
40 ❑ Jan 1989 Cover: 1.75 **NM** value: **Cover or less**
A: Kaoru Shintani **W:** Kaoru Shintani
41 ❑ Jan 1989 Cover: 1.75 **NM** value: **Cover or less**
A: Kaoru Shintani **W:** Kaoru Shintani
42 ❑ Feb 1989 Cover: 2.00 **NM** value: **Cover or less**
final issue. **A:** Kaoru Shintani **W:** Kaoru Shintani
Bk 1❑ Cover: 12.95 **NM** value: **Cover or less**
• b&w, reprint

AREALA: ANGEL OF WAR — Antarctic

1 ❑ Sep 1998 Cover: 2.95 **NM** value: **Cover or less**
Circ: Diamd. preorders: **6,111**
A: Craig Babiar **W:** Jim Gelvin ★ Origin of Auria.
2 ❑ Nov 1998 Cover: 2.95 **NM** value: **Cover or less**
Circ: Diamd. preorders: **4,380**
A: Craig Babiar **W:** Jim Gelvin
3 ❑ Feb 1999 Cover: 2.95 **NM** value: **Cover or less**
Circ: Diamd. preorders: **3,874**
A: Craig Babiar **W:** Jim Gelvin
4 ❑ ca. 1999 Cover: 2.99 **NM** value: **Cover or less**
Circ: Diamd. preorders: **3,372**

ARENA — Alchemy

1 ❑ b&w Cover: 1.50 **NM** value: **Cover or less**
Circ: CapCity orders: **2,400**

ARGONAUTS, THE (ETERNITY) — Eternity

1 ❑ Cover: 1.95 **NM** value: **Cover or less**
A: Patrick Olliffe **W:** Bill Spangler
2 ❑ Cover: 1.95 **NM** value: **Cover or less**
A Touch of Doomsday **A:** Patrick Olliffe **W:** Bill Spangler
3 ❑ Cover: 1.95 **NM** value: **Cover or less**
A: Patrick Olliffe **W:** Bill Spangler
4 ❑ Cover: 1.95 **NM** value: **Cover or less**
A: Patrick Olliffe **W:** Bill Spangler

ARGONAUTS, THE: SYSTEM CRASH — Alpha Productions

1 ❑ Cover: 2.50 **NM** value: **Cover or less**
System Crash, Part 1 **A:** John Ross **W:** Bill Spangler
2 ❑ Cover: 2.50 **NM** value: **Cover or less**
System Crash, Part 2 **A:** John Ross **W:** Bill Spangler

ARGON ZARK! — Arclight Publishing

1 ❑ 1997 Cover: 6.95 **NM** value: **Cover or less**
• based on on-line comics series

ARGUS — DC

Nicky Kovak grew up under the wing of mob boss D'Angelo. To Kovak, D'Angelo was more like a father than his real father was, and the mob became his family. That relationship culminated in high school when Nicky Kovak would kill his real father before dropping out of sight. Many years later, Nicky Kovak would become Nick Kelly, an undercover operative working as a federal agent. In his identity of Argus, he wears a high-tech suit of weaponry, and "eyes" that give him tactical readouts on the enemies he faces.

Nick's various identities clash when he is assigned to infiltrate D'Angelo's organization. This Argus will be taking arms against the man he considered a father just as the Argus of legend fought against father Zeus to disastrous results. To make matters worse, D'Angelo's super-powered enforcers Shiv and Hartley join together to give the "returning son" a very deadly homecoming.

1 ❑ Apr 1995 Cover: 1.50 **NM** value: **Cover or less**
Circ: CapCity orders: **10,375**
Light In Dark, Part 1, God Of Vengeance **A:** Phil Hester **W:** Mark Wheatley; Allan Gross
2 ❑ Jun 1995 Cover: 1.75 **NM** value: **Cover or less**
Circ: CapCity orders: **5,725**
A: Phil Hester **W:** Mark Wheatley; Allan Gross
3 ❑ Jul 1995 Cover: 1.75 **NM** value: **Cover or less**
Circ: CapCity orders: **4,650**
A: Phil Hester **W:** Mark Wheatley; Allan Gross
4 ❑ Aug 1995 Cover: 1.75 **NM** value: **Cover or less**
Circ: CapCity orders: **3,925**
A: Phil Hester **W:** Mark Wheatley; Allan Gross
5 ❑ Sep 1995 Cover: 1.75 **NM** value: **Cover or less**
Circ: CapCity orders: **3,325**
A: Phil Hester **W:** Mark Wheatley; Allan Gross
6 ❑ Oct 1995 Cover: 1.75 **NM** value: **Cover or less**
Circ: CapCity orders: **2,550**
final issue. **A:** Phil Hester **W:** Mark Wheatley; Allan Gross

ARIA — Image

1 ❑ Jan 1999 Cover: 2.50 **NM** value: **3.00**
Circ: Diamd. preorders: **81,425**
Fairy Tale Endings **A:** Erren Jay Anacleto **W:** Brian Holguin
1/A ❑ Jan 1999 Cover: 2.50 **NM** value: **4.00**
white background cover.
1/B ❑ Jan 1999 Cover: 2.50 **NM** value: **4.00**
Woman looking from balcony on cover.
2 ❑ Apr 1999 Cover: 2.50 **NM** value: **Cover or less**
Circ: Diamd. preorders: **56,066**
The Shores of Sorrow **A:** Erren Jay Anacleto; Roy Allen Martinez **W:** Brian Holguin
3 ❑ May 1999 Cover: 2.50 **NM** value: **Cover or less**
Circ: Diamd. preorders: **48,614**
A: Erren Jay Anacleto **W:** Brian Holguin
4/A ❑ Nov 1999 Cover: 2.50 **NM** value: **Cover or less**
Circ: Diamd. preorders: **49,515**
Textured cover stock. Among Ruins • Close-up shot of woman in green pointing at chest **A:** Erren Jay Anacleto **W:** Brian Holguin
4/B ❑ Nov 1999 Cover: 2.50 **NM** value: **Cover or less**
Variant cover with Angela.
5 ❑ ca. 1999 Cover: 2.50 **NM** value: **Cover or less**
Circ: Diamd. preorders: **53,073**
Ash 1❑Nov 1998, b&w Cover: 2.95 **NM** value: **3.50**
Circ: Diamd. preorders: **21,837**
The World of Aria • preview issue **A:** Erren Jay Anacleto **W:** Brian Holguin
Bk 1❑ Jul 2000 Cover: 13.95 **NM** value: **Cover or less**
• The Magic of Aria;Collects Aria #1-4 **A:** Erren Jay Anacleto **W:** Brian Holguin
6 ❑ ca. 1999 Cover: 2.50 **NM** value: **Cover or less**
Circ: Diamd. preorders: **47,169**
7 ❑ ca. 1999 Cover: 2.50 **NM** value: **Cover or less**
Circ: Diamd. preorders: **38,736**

ARIA ANGELA — Image

1/A ❑ Feb 2000 Cover: 2.95 **NM** value: **Cover or less**
Circ: Diamd. preorders: **80,190**
Aria and Angela in profile on cover. Heavenly Creatures, Part 1 **A:** Erren Jay Anacleto **W:** Brian Holguin
1/B ❑ Feb 2000 Cover: 2.95 **NM** value: **Cover or less**
Aria sitting on stairs on cover. Heavenly Creatures, Part 1 • Angela smiling, front **A:** Erren Jay Anacleto **W:** Brian Holguin
1/C ❑ Feb 2000 Cover: 2.95 **NM** value: **Cover or less**
Close-up on Aria (right half of 1/H cover in close-up). Heavenly Creatures, Part 1 **A:** Erren Jay Anacleto **W:** Brian Holguin
1/D ❑ Feb 2000 Cover: 2.95 **NM** value: **Cover or less**
Woman walking through astral plane on cover. Heavenly Creatures, Part 1 **A:** Erren Jay Anacleto **W:** Brian Holguin
1/E ❑ Feb 2000 Cover: 2.95 **NM** value: **Cover or less**
Woman walking through astral plane on cover. Heavenly Creatures, Part 1 **A:** Erren Jay Anacleto **W:** Brian Holguin
1/F ❑ Feb 2000 Cover: 2.95 **NM** value: **Cover or less**
Two women, hawk on cover. Heavenly Creatures, Part 1 **A:** Erren Jay Anacleto **W:** Brian Holguin
1/G ❑ Feb 2000 Cover: 2.95 **NM** value: **Cover or less**
Woman with sword (between legs) on cover. Heavenly Creatures, Part 1 • Tower records variant **A:** Erren Jay Anacleto **W:** Brian Holguin
1/H ❑ Feb 2000 Cover: 2.95 **NM** value: **Cover or less**
Heavenly Creatures, Part 1 **A:** Erren Jay Anacleto **W:** Brian Holguin
1/I ❑ Feb 2000 **NM** value: **2.95**
chromium cover. Heavenly Creatures, Part 1 **A:** Erren Jay Anacleto **W:** Brian Holguin
2 ❑ Oct 2000 Cover: 2.95 **NM** value: **Cover or less**
Circ: Diamd. preorders: **49,585**
Heavenly Creatures, Part 2 **A:** Erren Jay Anacleto **W:** Brian Holguin

ARIA ANGELA BLANC & NOIR — Image

1 ❑ Apr 2000 Cover: 2.95 **NM** value: **Cover or less**
Heavenly Creatures, Part 1 • Reprints Aria Angela #1 in black & white **A:** Erren Jay Anacleto **W:** Brian Holguin

ARIA BLANC & NOIR — Image

Brian Holguin's story and Jay Anacleto's art combine to weave the ever-expanding story of Aria. The art was so good that reader demand begged for the original pencil art to be published and Image agreed.

In modern New York City, Kildare leads a fairly normal life with her shop of bizarre and mysterious odds and ends. People of all sorts come to her for help. What they don't realize is that she has been around for a very long time-since the earth was young. Through Lady Kildare we learn that magic does still exist. As an entity, it gets together for a party now and then with various other entities who happen to be passing by. And sometimes, in the past as well as the present, evil projects its ugly fangs.

1 ❑ Mar 1999 Cover: 2.50 **NM** value: **Cover or less**
Circ: Diamd. preorders: **29,652**
wraparound cover. • b&w reprint of Aria #1
2 ❑ Mar 1999 Cover: 2.50 **NM** value: **Cover or less**
Circ: Diamd. preorders: **16,658**
Fairy Tale Endings **A:** Erren Jay Anacleto **W:** Brian Holguin

ARIANE & BLUEBEARD — Eclipse

1 ❑ Cover: 3.95 **NM** value: **Cover or less**
Circ: CapCity orders: **2,625**
A: P. Craig Russell **W:** P. Craig Russell

ARIANNE — Slave Labor

1 ❑ May 1991 Cover: 2.50 **NM** value: **4.95**
A: Noel Tuazon **W:** Rafael Nieves
2 ❑ Oct 1991 Cover: 2.95 **NM** value: **Cover or less**

ARIANNE (MOONSTONE) — Moonstone

1 ❑ Dec 1995, b&w Cover: 4.95 **NM** value: **Cover or less**

ARIA: THE SOUL MARKET — Image

1 ❑ Mar 2001 Cover: 2.95 **NM** value: **Cover or less**
Circ: Diamd. preorders: **25,172** • **CGC:** 1 graded, best 9.6
A: David Yardin **W:** Brian Holguin
2 ❑ Apr 2001 Cover: 2.95 **NM** value: **Cover or less**
Circ: Diamd. preorders: **22,791**
A: David Yardin **W:** Brian Holguin

ARIK KHAN (A+) — A-Plus

1 ❑ Cover: 2.50 **NM** value: **Cover or less**
Arik Kha: Crusade; Captain Crossbones; To the Shores of Tripoli • b&w, reprint **A:** Franc Reyes; Ogden Whitney **W:** Franc Reyes; Ogden Whitney
2 ❑ Cover: 2.50 **NM** value: **Cover or less**
A: Franc Reyes **W:** Franc Reyes

ARIK KHAN (ANDROMEDA) — Andromeda

1 ❑ Cover: 1.95 **NM** value: **Cover or less**
A: Franc Reyes; Ogden Whitney **W:** Franc Reyes; Ogden Whitney
2 ❑ Cover: 1.95 **NM** value: **Cover or less**
A: Franc Reyes **W:** Franc Reyes
3 ❑ Cover: 1.95 **NM** value: **Cover or less**
A: Franc Reyes **W:** Franc Reyes

ARION, LORD OF ATLANTIS — DC

Like Arak, Son of Thunder, and Conqueror of the Barren Earth, Arion has its origins in the pages of Warlord. First appearing in Warlord #55, Arion is a young mage, created out of cosmic forces. He is part human, part cosmic matter, and a force to be contended with by any reckoning.

Arion owes his allegiance to Atlantis, which he must save from the mortal and mystical forces that imperil it. 45,000 years before the birth of Christ, Atlantis was a world of magic and marvel, swords and sorcery. Aided by his friends Wyynde, Chian, and Mara, Arion battles everything from cyborg jackal-warriors to cosmic witches to save Atlantis.

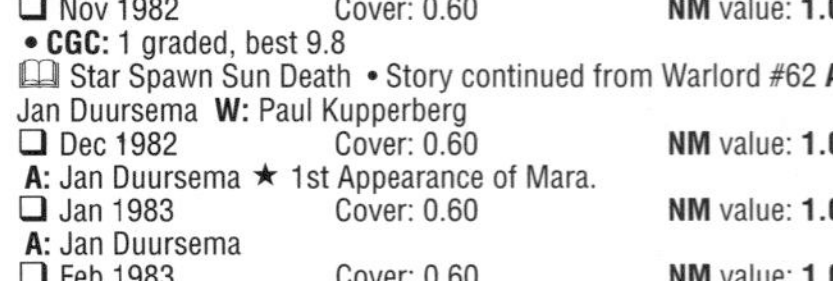

1 ❑ Nov 1982 Cover: 0.60 **NM** value: **1.00**
• **CGC:** 1 graded, best 9.8
Star Spawn Sun Death • Story continued from Warlord #62 **A:** Jan Duursema **W:** Paul Kupperberg
2 ❑ Dec 1982 Cover: 0.60 **NM** value: **1.00**
A: Jan Duursema ★ 1st Appearance of Mara.
3 ❑ Jan 1983 Cover: 0.60 **NM** value: **1.00**
A: Jan Duursema
4 ❑ Feb 1983 Cover: 0.60 **NM** value: **1.00**
A: Jan Duursema

Other grades: Multiply prices above by **1.5 for Mint • 2/3 for Very Fine • 1/3 for Fine • 1/5 for Very Good • 1/8 for Good**

5 ❑ Mar 1983 Cover: 0.60 **NM** value: **1.00**
A: Jan Duursema
6 ❑ Apr 1983 Cover: 0.60 **NM** value: **1.00**
A: Jan Duursema
7 ❑ May 1983 Cover: 0.60 **NM** value: **1.00**
A: Jan Duursema
8 ❑ Jun 1983 Cover: 0.60 **NM** value: **1.00**
9 ❑ Jul 1983 Cover: 0.60 **NM** value: **1.00**
10 ❑ Aug 1983 Cover: 0.60 **NM** value: **1.00**
11 ❑ Sep 1983 Cover: 0.60 **NM** value: **1.00**
12 ❑ Oct 1983 Cover: 0.60 **NM** value: **1.00**
🕮 Sanctuary Of Sorcery **A:** Jan Duursema **W:** Paul Kupperberg
13 ❑ Nov 1983 Cover: 0.60 **NM** value: **1.00**
14 ❑ Dec 1983 Cover: 0.75 **NM** value: **1.00**
15 ❑ Jan 1984 Cover: 0.75 **NM** value: **1.00**
16 ❑ Feb 1984 Cover: 0.75 **NM** value: **1.00**
17 ❑ Mar 1984 Cover: 0.75 **NM** value: **1.00**
18 ❑ Apr 1984 Cover: 0.75 **NM** value: **1.00**
19 ❑ May 1984 Cover: 0.75 **NM** value: **1.00**
20 ❑ Jun 1984 Cover: 0.75 **NM** value: **1.00**
21 ❑ Jul 1984 Cover: 0.75 **NM** value: **1.00**
22 ❑ Aug 1984 Cover: 0.75 **NM** value: **1.00**
23 ❑ Sep 1984 Cover: 0.75 **NM** value: **1.00**
24 ❑ Oct 1984 Cover: 0.75 **NM** value: **1.00**
25 ❑ Nov 1984 Cover: 0.75 **NM** value: **1.00**
26 ❑ Dec 1984 Cover: 0.75 **NM** value: **1.00**
27 ❑ Jan 1985 Cover: 0.75 **NM** value: **1.00**
28 ❑ Feb 1985 Cover: 0.75 **NM** value: **1.00**
29 ❑ Mar 1985 Cover: 0.75 **NM** value: **1.00**
30 ❑ Apr 1985 Cover: 0.75 **NM** value: **1.00**
31 ❑ May 1985 Cover: 0.75 **NM** value: **1.00**
Circ: CapCity orders: **4,250**
32 ❑ Jun 1985 Cover: 0.75 **NM** value: **1.00**
Circ: CapCity orders: **4,300**
33 ❑ Jul 1985 Cover: 0.75 **NM** value: **1.00**
Circ: CapCity orders: **4,350**
34 ❑ Aug 1985 Cover: 0.75 **NM** value: **1.00**
Circ: CapCity orders: **4,450**
35 ❑ Sep 1985 Cover: 0.75 **NM** value: **1.00**
Circ: CapCity orders: **4,450**
final issue.
SE 1❑ Cover: 1.25 **NM** value: **Cover or less**
Circ: CapCity orders: **5,700**
• Special

ARION THE IMMORTAL — DC

1 ❑ Jul 1992 Cover: 1.50 **NM** value: **Cover or less**
Circ: CapCity orders: **15,650**
🕮 Excuse Me, Sir, How Do I Get To Carney Hall? **A:** Ron Wilson **W:** Paul Kupperberg
2 ❑ Aug 1992 Cover: 1.50 **NM** value: **Cover or less**
Circ: CapCity orders: **11,200**
🕮 Shoot The Dog **A:** Ron Wilson **W:** Paul Kupperberg
3 ❑ Sep 1992 Cover: 1.50 **NM** value: **Cover or less**
Circ: CapCity orders: **9,150**
4 ❑ Oct 1992 Cover: 1.50 **NM** value: **Cover or less**
Circ: CapCity orders: **8,450**
5 ❑ Nov 1992 Cover: 1.50 **NM** value: **Cover or less**
Circ: CapCity orders: **7,500**
6 ❑ Dec 1992 Cover: 1.50 **NM** value: **Cover or less**
Circ: CapCity orders: **6,600**
final issue. ★ Appearance of Power Girl.

ARISTOCATS, THE — Gold Key

1 ❑ Mar 1971 Cover: 0.25 **NM** value: **3.00**
• 30045-103;poster

ARISTOCRATIC X-TRATERRESTRIAL TIME-TRAVELING THIEVES — Comics Interview

Produced during the height of the black-and-white boom in the mid-1980s, this series, published by Comics Interview, never took itself too seriously with the adventures of Fred and Bianca, a pair of felons-for-hire. In their first adventure in the ongoing series (the concept was introduced in a one-shot "micro-series"), the pair tangled with Comics Interview's super-team The Southern Knights during a mission to recover the formula for Coca-Cola.

Later issues dealt with censorship, smart cars, and, eventually, romance, as the duo was engaged to be married. Unfortunately, as their nuptials approached, the series was canceled, leaving readers to wonder if the marriage ever came to be. — Brent

1 ❑ Feb 1987 Cover: 1.75 **NM** value: **2.00**
2 ❑ Apr 1987 Cover: 1.75 **NM** value: **2.00**
3 ❑ Jun 1987 Cover: 1.75 **NM** value: **2.00**
4 ❑ Aug 1987 Cover: 1.75 **NM** value: **2.00**
5 ❑ Oct 1987 Cover: 1.75 **NM** value: **2.00**
6 ❑ Dec 1987 Cover: 1.75 **NM** value: **2.00**
7 ❑ Feb 1988 Cover: 1.75 **NM** value: **2.00**
8 ❑ Apr 1988 Cover: 1.75 **NM** value: **2.00**
9 ❑ Jun 1988 Cover: 1.75 **NM** value: **2.00**
10 ❑ Aug 1988 Cover: 1.95 **NM** value: **2.00**
11 ❑ Oct 1988 Cover: 1.95 **NM** value: **2.00**
12 ❑ Dec 1988 Cover: 1.95 **NM** value: **2.00**
Bk 1❑ b&w Cover: 6.50 **NM** value: **Cover or less**
• X-Thieves
Bk 2❑ b&w Cover: 6.50 **NM** value: **Cover or less**
• X-Thieves
Bk 3❑ b&w Cover: 6.95 **NM** value: **Cover or less**
• X-Thieves
Bk 4❑ b&w Cover: 6.95 **NM** value: **Cover or less**
• X-Thieves

ARISTOCRATIC X-TRATERRESTRIAL TIME-TRAVELING THIEVES MICRO-SERIES — Comics Interview

1 ❑ Aug 1986 Cover: 1.75 **NM** value: **2.00**
One-shot.
1-2 ❑ Cover: 1.75 **NM** value: **2.00**

ARISTOKITTENS, THE — Gold Key

1 ❑ **NM** value: **10.00**
2 ❑ **NM** value: **7.00**
3 ❑ **NM** value: **5.00**
4 ❑ **NM** value: **5.00**
5 ❑ **NM** value: **5.00**
6 ❑ **NM** value: **3.00**
7 ❑ **NM** value: **3.00**
8 ❑ **NM** value: **3.00**
9 ❑ **NM** value: **3.00**

ARIZONA: A SIMPLE HORROR — London Night

1 ❑ Cover: 3.00 **NM** value: **Cover or less**
A: Jerry Beck **W:** Jerry Kennedy

ARIZONA KID — Atlas

1 ❑ Mar 1951 Cover: 0.10 **NM** value: **125.00**
2 ❑ May 1951 Cover: 0.10 **NM** value: **75.00**
3 ❑ Jul 1951 Cover: 0.10 **NM** value: **75.00**
4 ❑ Sep 1951 Cover: 0.10 **NM** value: **50.00**
5 ❑ Nov 1951 Cover: 0.10 **NM** value: **50.00**
6 ❑ Jan 1952 Cover: 0.10 **NM** value: **50.00**

ARKAGA — Image

1 ❑ Sep 1997 Cover: 2.95 **NM** value: **Cover or less**
Circ: Diamd. preorders: **10,737**
A: Arnie Jorgensen **W:** Arnie Jorgensen; David Meikis
2 ❑ Nov 1997 Cover: 2.95 **NM** value: **Cover or less**
Circ: Diamd. preorders: **6,096**
A: Arnie Jorgensen **W:** Arnie Jorgensen; David Meikis

ARKEOLOGY — Valkyrie

1 ❑ Apr 1989 Cover: 2.00 **NM** value: **Cover or less**
No issue number. • companion one-shot for The Adventures of Luther Arkwright

ARLINGTON HAMMER IN: "GET ME TO THE CHURCH ON TIME" — One Shot

1 ❑ Cover: 2.50 **NM** value: **Cover or less**
No issue number. • comic for sale at conventions only

A.R.M. — Adventure

1 ❑ Cover: 2.50 **NM** value: **Cover or less**
🕮 Death by Ecstasy! • Introduction by Larry Niven **A:** Steve Stiles; Terry Tidwell **W:** Bill Spangler; Larry Niven
2 ❑ Cover: 2.50 **NM** value: **Cover or less**
A: Steve Stiles; Terry Tidwell **W:** Bill Spangler; Larry Niven
3 ❑ Cover: 2.50 **NM** value: **Cover or less**
A: Steve Stiles; Terry Tidwell **W:** Bill Spangler; Larry Niven

ARMADILLO COMICS — Rip Off

1 ❑ Cover: 0.50 **NM** value: **2.50**
A: Jim Franklin **W:** Jim Franklin
2 ❑ Cover: 0.50 **NM** value: **2.50**
A: Jim Franklin **W:** Jim Franklin

ARMAGEDDON — Last Gasp

1 ❑ Cover: 0.50 **NM** value: **2.50**
A: Barney Steel **W:** Barney Steel
2 ❑ Cover: 0.50 **NM** value: **2.50**
A: Barney Steel **W:** Barney Steel

ARMAGEDDON (CHAOS) — Chaos

1 ❑ Oct 1999 Cover: 2.95 **NM** value: **Cover or less**
Circ: Diamd. preorders: **24,327**
🕮 The Beginning of the End **A:** Len Kaminski **W:** Brian Pulido
2 ❑ Nov 1999 Cover: 2.95 **NM** value: **Cover or less**
Circ: Diamd. preorders: **19,275**
🕮 Not of This Earth **A:** Len Kaminski **W:** Brian Pulido
3 ❑ Dec 1999 Cover: 2.95 **NM** value: **Cover or less**
Circ: Diamd. preorders: **19,209**
🕮 It Conquered the Earth **A:** Len Kaminski **W:** Brian Pulido
4 ❑ Jan 2000 Cover: 2.95 **NM** value: **Cover or less**
Circ: Diamd. preorders: **18,852**
A: Len Kaminski **W:** Brian Pulido

ARMAGEDDON FACTOR, THE — AC

1 ❑ Jun 1987 Cover: 1.95 **NM** value: **Cover or less**
2 ❑ Aug 1987 Cover: 1.95 **NM** value: **Cover or less**
Circ: CapCity orders: **2,100**
3 ❑ Cover: 1.95 **NM** value: **Cover or less**

ARMAGEDDON FACTOR, THE: THE CONCLUSION — AC

1 ❑ 1990b&w Cover: 3.95 **NM** value: **Cover or less**
No issue number. 🕮 The Last Days of Man on Earth **A:** Frank Turner; Darren Goodhart; Bill Marimon **W:** Rik Levins

ARMAGEDDON: INFERNO — DC

1 ❑ Apr 1992 Cover: 1.00 **NM** value: **Cover or less**
Circ: CapCity orders: **32,600**
🕮 Seeds Of Doom **A:** Tom Mandrake; Arthur Adams; Michael Netzer; Luke McDonnell; Walter Simpson **W:** John Ostrander
2 ❑ May 1992 Cover: 1.00 **NM** value: **Cover or less**
Circ: CapCity orders: **24,150**
3 ❑ Jun 1992 Cover: 1.00 **NM** value: **Cover or less**
4 ❑ Jul 1992 Cover: 1.00 **NM** value: **Cover or less**
Circ: CapCity orders: **24,850**
• JSA returns from limbo

ARMAGEDDON PATROL: THE SHOT — Alchemy Texts

1 ❑ 1998b&w Cover: 2.95 **NM** value: **Cover or less**

ARMAGEDDONQUEST — Starhead

All issues are adults only.

Tazio has a tail, cat-like eyes, no gender, and the ability to heal. He is also the "Beast" prophesied in the last book of the Bible. But Tazio refuses to believe that prophecy cannot be changed and has no intention of turning to evil. He rejects the destiny laid out for him and chooses to help people instead. Yet even his rejections soon weave their own tapestries as events carry him to affect the lives of those around him.

Ronald Russel Roach created a 20-chapter novel filled with numerous subplots and intrigue. The reader is taken on a journey which is the life of a being who has no desire to destroy the world, despite what others say he will do. For mature audiences, this series stretches many biblical concepts beyond what some may consider accurate, but is nevertheless an excellent story.

1 ❑ 1994 Cover: 3.95 **NM** value: **Cover or less**
🕮 Tazio **A:** Ronald Russel Roach **W:** Ronald Russel Roach
2 ❑ 1994 Cover: 3.95 **NM** value: **Cover or less**
Bk 1❑ May 1997, b&w Cover: 13.00 **NM** value: **Cover or less**
• collects series
Bk 2❑ Jun 1997, b&w Cover: 13.00 **NM** value: **Cover or less**
• collects series

ARMAGEDDON RISING — Millennium

1 ❑ 1997b&w Cover: 4.95 **NM** value: **Cover or less**
No issue number. • special foil edition. • features characters from Song of the Sirens

ARMAGEDDON SQUAD, THE — Haze Studios

1 ❑ b&w Cover: 1.50 **NM** value: **Cover or less**

ARMAGEDDON: THE ALIEN AGENDA — DC

1 ❑ Nov 1991 Cover: 1.00 **NM** value: **Cover or less**
Circ: CapCity orders: **61,200**
🕮 Days Of Thunder Lizards **A:** Dan Jurgens **W:** Jonathan Peterson
2 ❑ Dec 1991 Cover: 1.00 **NM** value: **Cover or less**
Circ: CapCity orders: **48,100**
3 ❑ Jan 1992 Cover: 1.00 **NM** value: **Cover or less**
Circ: CapCity orders: **42,800**
4 ❑ Feb 1992 Cover: 1.00 **NM** value: **Cover or less**
Circ: CapCity orders: **38,350**

ARMAGEDDON 2001 — DC

In the dark future of 2001, a tyrant called Monarch had built up a society of immense cruelty and callousness. Innocents are gunned down by legalized gangs; the police, high on drugs, act with incredible indifference. And the bodies of victims are casually thrown into landfills for disposal. Who is this tyrant called Monarch? By all accounts, he was once one of Earth's heroes.

A being called Waverider travels back from that future into the present day in an attempt to stop the future from happening. Waverider is able to sense the timelines around anyone he touches, and hopes to find and stop the hero that will become Monarch. One by one, Waverider eliminates the possibilities...only to discover that the mere act of interfering with today's heroes may have brought about Monarch's creation!

This saga is continued in Armageddon: The Alien Agenda.

1 ❑ May 1991 Cover: 2.00 **NM** value: **Cover or less**
Circ: CapCity orders: **56,350**
1st printing. 🕮 Armageddon 2001, Part 1 **A:** Dan Jurgens **W:** Archie Goodwin ★ 1st Appearance of Monarch, Waverider.
1-2 ❑ May 1991 Cover: 2.00 **NM** value: **Cover or less**
1-3 ❑ May 1991 Cover: 2.00 **NM** value: **Cover or less**
3rd printing (silver ink on cover). 🕮 Armageddon 2001, Part 1 **A:** Dan Jurgens **W:** Archie Goodwin ★ 1st Appearance of Monarch, Waverider.
2 ❑ Oct 1991 Cover: 2.00 **NM** value: **Cover or less**
Circ: CapCity orders: **67,650**
🕮 Armageddon 2001, Part 14 • Monarch's ID revealed **A:** Dan Jurgens **W:** Denny O'Neil

ARMATURE — Olyoptics

1 ❑ Nov 1996 Cover: 2.95 **NM** value: **Cover or less**
Circ: Diamd. preorders: **11,589**
🕮 Ghostarama **A:** Steve Oliff **W:** Steve Oliff
2 ❑ Dec 1996 Cover: 2.95 **NM** value: **Cover or less**
Circ: Direct Market orders: **8,924**
A: Steve Oliff **W:** Steve Oliff

CGC-graded: Multiply prices above by **33 for 9.9 M** • **16 for 9.8 NM/M** • **7 for 9.6 NM+** • **5 for 9.4 NM** • **2.5 for 9.2 NM-** • **1.5 for 9.0 VF/NM**

ARMED AND DANGEROUS (ACCLAIM)
Acclaim / Armada

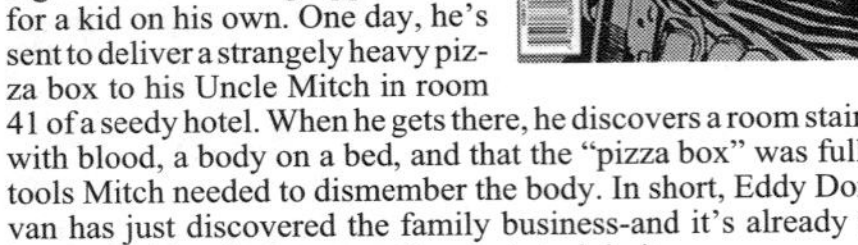

Comics noir doesn't come much darker than this. Bob Hall's Armed and Dangerous draws on influences from Mickey Spillane to Quentin Tarantino movies to give us the comics equivalent of Pulp Fiction. It's harsh and visceral, but hard to put down.

Armed & Dangerous focuses on Eddy Donovan, a 15-year-old kid who's been raised in a boarding school after his parents died. He's been called down to New York City by his Uncle Mitch and is discovering that life in the Big Apple is hard for a kid on his own. One day, he's sent to deliver a strangely heavy pizza box to his Uncle Mitch in room 41 of a seedy hotel. When he gets there, he discovers a room stained with blood, a body on a bed, and that the "pizza box" was full of tools Mitch needed to dismember the body. In short, Eddy Donovan has just discovered the family business-and it's already too late to decide whether or not he wants to join it.

1 ❑ Apr 1996, b&w Cover: 2.95 **NM** value: **Cover or less**
📖 Picking Up The Pieces **A:** Bob Hall **W:** Bob Hall
2 ❑ May 1996, b&w Cover: 2.95 **NM** value: **Cover or less**
📖 Dire Street **A:** Bob Hall **W:** Bob Hall
3 ❑ Jun 1996, b&w Cover: 2.95 **NM** value: **Cover or less**
A: Bob Hall **W:** Bob Hall
4 ❑ Jul 1996, b&w Cover: 2.95 **NM** value: **Cover or less**
Circ: Diamd. preorders: **5,247**
A: Bob Hall **W:** Bob Hall
Bk 1❑ Cover: 9.95 **NM** value: **Cover or less**
• Collects Armed & Dangerous #1-4 **A:** Bob Hall **W:** Bob Hall
SE 1❑ Aug 1996, b&w Cover: 2.95 **NM** value: **Cover or less**
• one-shot special;later indicias show this is really issue #5 of series

ARMED & DANGEROUS: HELL'S SLAUGHTERHOUSE
Acclaim

1 ❑ Cover: 2.95 **NM** value: **Cover or less**
📖 Terminal bar **A:** Bob Hall **W:** Bob Hall
2 ❑ Cover: 2.95 **NM** value: **Cover or less**
📖 Whiskey Dreams **A:** Bob Hall **W:** Bob Hall
3 ❑ Cover: 2.95 **NM** value: **Cover or less**
📖 The Brotherhood Of Cain **A:** Bob Hall **W:** Bob Hall
4 ❑ Cover: 2.95 **NM** value: **Cover or less**
A: Bob Hall **W:** Bob Hall

ARMED & DANGEROUS (KITCHEN SINK)
Kitchen Sink

1 ❑ Jul 1995 Cover: 9.95 **NM** value: **Cover or less**
• magazine-sized graphic novel.

ARMEN DEEP & BUG BOY
Dilemma

2 ❑ 1995b&w Cover: 2.50 **NM** value: **Cover or less**
cardstock cover.

ARMITAGE
Fleetway-Quality

1 ❑ Cover: 2.95 **NM** value: **Cover or less**
cardstock cover.
2 ❑ Cover: 2.95 **NM** value: **Cover or less**
cardstock cover. 📖 Armitage; Future Shock **A:** Mick Austin **W:** John Tomlinson

ARMOR
Continuity

1 ❑ Cover: 2.00 **NM** value: **Cover or less**
Circ: CapCity orders: **5,575**
A: Brian Apthorp **W:** Neal Adams
2 ❑ Cover: 2.00 **NM** value: **Cover or less**
Circ: CapCity orders: **5,225**
3 ❑ Cover: 2.00 **NM** value: **Cover or less**
Circ: CapCity orders: **5,125**
4 ❑ Jul 1988 Cover: 2.00 **NM** value: **Cover or less**
Circ: CapCity orders: **4,100**
5 ❑ Dec 1988 Cover: 2.00 **NM** value: **Cover or less**
Circ: CapCity orders: **3,975**
6 ❑ Apr 1989 Cover: 2.00 **NM** value: **Cover or less**
7 ❑ Jan 1990 Cover: 2.00 **NM** value: **Cover or less**
Circ: CapCity orders: **3,900**
A: Brian Apthorp **W:** Neal Adams ★ Origin of Armor.
8 ❑ Apr 1990 Cover: 2.00 **NM** value: **Cover or less**
Circ: CapCity orders: **3,175**
9 ❑ Apr 1991 Cover: 2.00 **NM** value: **Cover or less**
Circ: CapCity orders: **3,225**
10 ❑ Aug 1991 Cover: 2.00 **NM** value: **Cover or less**
Circ: CapCity orders: **2,575**
11 ❑ Nov 1991 Cover: 2.00 **NM** value: **Cover or less**
Circ: CapCity orders: **1,775**
12 ❑ Mar 1992 Cover: 2.00 **NM** value: **Cover or less**
Circ: CapCity orders: **2,550**
13 ❑ Apr 1992 Cover: 2.00 **NM** value: **Cover or less**
Circ: CapCity orders: **2,475**

ARMOR (2ND SERIES)
Continuity

1 ❑ Apr 1993 Cover: 2.50 **NM** value: **Cover or less**
wraparound foil cardstock cover. 📖 Deathwatch 2000, Part 3 • 2 trading cards
2 ❑ May 1993 Cover: 2.50 **NM** value: **Cover or less**
diecut outer cover. 📖 Deathwatch 2000, Part 9 • trading card
3 ❑ Aug 1993 Cover: 2.50 **NM** value: **Cover or less**
📖 Deathwatch 2000, Part 15 **A:** Brian Apthorp **W:** Peter Stone
4 ❑ Oct 1993 Cover: 2.50 **NM** value: **Cover or less**
5 ❑ Nov 1993 Cover: 2.50 **NM** value: **Cover or less**
6 ❑ Nov 1993 Cover: 2.50 **NM** value: **Cover or less**
📖 Rise of Magic **A:** Brian Apthorp **W:** Peter Stone

ARMORED TROOPER VOTOMS
CPM

1 ❑ Jul 1996 Cover: 2.95 **NM** value: **Cover or less**

ARMORINES
Valiant

0 ❑ Feb 1993 **NM** value: **2.00**
no cover price. • "Fall Fling Preview Edition".
1 ❑ Jun 1994 Cover: 2.25 **NM** value: **Cover or less**
📖 Fathoms Below, Part 1, Fathoms Below **A:** Jim Calafiore **W:** Jorge Gonzçlez; Jorge Gonzßlez
2 ❑ Aug 1994 Cover: 2.25 **NM** value: **Cover or less**
📖 Fathoms Below, Part 2 **A:** Jim Calafiore **W:** Jorge Gonzçlez; Jorge Gonzßlez
3 ❑ Sep 1994 Cover: 2.25 **NM** value: **Cover or less**
📖 Fathoms Below, Part 3 **A:** Jim Calafiore **W:** Jorge Gonzçlez; Jorge Gonzßlez
4 ❑ Oct 1994 Cover: 2.25 **NM** value: **Cover or less**
📖 The Chaos Effect prelude **A:** Jim Calafiore **W:** Jorge Gonzçlez; Jorge Gonzßlez
5 ❑ Nov 1994 Cover: 2.25 **NM** value: **Cover or less**
📖 The Chaos Effect: Delta, Part 2, The Gathering • Continues from Harbinger #34 **A:** Jim Calafiore **W:** Jorge Gonzçlez; Jorge Gonzßlez
6 ❑ Dec 1994 Cover: 2.25 **NM** value: **Cover or less**
★ Appearance of X-O.
7 ❑ Jan 1995 Cover: 2.25 **NM** value: **Cover or less**
wraparound cover. 📖 The Chaos Effect aftermath
8 ❑ Feb 1995 Cover: 2.25 **NM** value: **Cover or less**
9 ❑ Mar 1995 Cover: 2.25 **NM** value: **Cover or less**
10 ❑ Apr 1995 Cover: 2.25 **NM** value: **Cover or less**
11 ❑ May 1995 Cover: 2.25 **NM** value: **Cover or less**
Circ: CapCity orders: **6,350**
12 ❑ Jun 1995 Cover: 2.25 **NM** value: **Cover or less**
Circ: CapCity orders: **5,575**
final issue.

ARMORINES (VOL. 2)
Acclaim

1 ❑ Oct 1999 Cover: 3.95 **NM** value: **Cover or less**
Circ: Diamd. preorders: **5,114**
📖 Return to Sender **A:** Jim Calafiore **W:** Michael Marts; Omar Banmally
2 ❑ Nov 1999 Cover: 3.95 **NM** value: **Cover or less**
Circ: Diamd. preorders: **4,505**
A: Jim Calafiore **W:** Michael Marts; Omar Banmally
3 ❑ Dec 1999 Cover: 2.50 **NM** value: **3.95**
Circ: Diamd. preorders: **4,396**
📖 Return to Sender **A:** Jim Calafiore **W:** Michael Marts; Omar Banmally
4 ❑ Jan 2000 Cover: 2.50 **NM** value: **3.95**
Circ: Diamd. preorders: **4,103**
📖 Bugs Must Die **A:** Jim Calafiore **W:** Michael Marts; Omar Banmally ★ Appearance of X-O Manowar.

ARM'S LENGTH
Third Wind Press

1 ❑ Jul 2000, b&w Cover: 3.95 **NM** value: **Cover or less**
📖 My Favorite Roadshow; The Artist at Sixty; Beat the System!

ARMY AND NAVY COMICS
Street & Smith

1 ❑ May 1941 Cover: 0.10 **NM** value: **350.00**
• **CGC:** 1 graded, best 9.0
2 ❑ Oct 1941 Cover: 0.10 **NM** value: **200.00**
3 ❑ Jan 1942 Cover: 0.10 **NM** value: **150.00**
4 ❑ Apr 1942 Cover: 0.10 **NM** value: **150.00**
5 ❑ Jul 1942 Cover: 0.10 **NM** value: **150.00**

ARMY ANTS (MICHAEL T. DESING'S...)
Michael T. Desing

8 ❑ b&w Cover: 2.50 **NM** value: **Cover or less**

ARMY OF DARKNESS
Dark Horse

Army of Darkness was the big-budget sequel to cult video releases Evil Dead and Evil Dead II. Its story begins when a man named Ash finds the Necronomicon at a remote cabin he had rented with his wife Linda. The book, a leftover from Evil Dead was an unspeakably evil artifact bound in human flesh and written in blood. When Ash began reading it, a demonic force was unleashed that stole his wife. Then it got into Ash's body through his hand. To stop it, he had to lop the hand off. Ash tried reading a different passage of the book which was meant to open a hole in time that would send the evil back. Unfortunately, it ended up sending Ash back into a dark age of sorcery in approximately 1130 A.D.

This three-issue movie adaptation features dark painted art by John Bolton (Black Dragon).

1 ❑ Cover: 2.50 **NM** value: **6.00**
Circ: CapCity orders: **14,675** • **CGC:** 1 graded, best 9.9
A: John Bolton **W:** Ivan Raimi; Sam Raimi
2 ❑ Cover: 2.50 **NM** value: **5.00**
Circ: CapCity orders: **8,675**
A: John Bolton **W:** Ivan Raimi; Sam Raimi
3 ❑ Oct 1993 Cover: 2.50 **NM** value: **5.00**
Circ: CapCity orders: **7,950**
A: John Bolton **W:** Ivan Raimi; Sam Raimi

ARMY SURPLUS KOMIKZ FEATURING: CUTEY BUNNY
Quagmire

1 ❑ Cover: 1.50 **NM** value: **3.00**
• Quagmire publishes **A:** Joshua Quagmire **W:** Joshua Quagmire
2 ❑ Cover: 1.50 **NM** value: **2.00**
A: Joshua Quagmire **W:** Joshua Quagmire
3 ❑ Cover: 1.50 **NM** value: **2.00**
A: Joshua Quagmire **W:** Joshua Quagmire
4 ❑ Cover: 1.50 **NM** value: **2.00**
A: Joshua Quagmire **W:** Joshua Quagmire
5 ❑ 1985b&w Cover: 1.50 **NM** value: **2.00**
final issue. • X-Men parody;Eclipse publishes **A:** Joshua Quagmire **W:** Joshua Quagmire

ARMY WAR HEROES
Charlton

1 ❑ 1963 Cover: 0.12 **NM** value: **15.00**
2 ❑ 1964 Cover: 0.12 **NM** value: **7.00**
3 ❑ Cover: 0.12 **NM** value: **6.00**
4 ❑ Cover: 0.12 **NM** value: **6.00**
5 ❑ Cover: 0.12 **NM** value: **6.00**
6 ❑ Cover: 0.12 **NM** value: **5.00**
7 ❑ Cover: 0.12 **NM** value: **5.00**
📖 Doom Squad; Hidden Enemy; The Steel Coffin; Night Raider; Fast Armor;
8 ❑ Cover: 0.12 **NM** value: **5.00**
9 ❑ Cover: 0.12 **NM** value: **5.00**
10 ❑ Cover: 0.12 **NM** value: **5.00**
11 ❑ Cover: 0.12 **NM** value: **5.00**
12 ❑ Cover: 0.12 **NM** value: **5.00**
13 ❑ 1966 Cover: 0.12 **NM** value: **5.00**
Circ: Statement: **133,205**
14 ❑ 1966 Cover: 0.12 **NM** value: **5.00**
Circ: Statement: **133,205**
15 ❑ 1966 Cover: 0.12 **NM** value: **5.00**
Circ: Statement: **133,205**
16 ❑ 1966 Cover: 0.12 **NM** value: **5.00**
Circ: Statement: **133,205**
17 ❑ Cover: 0.12 **NM** value: **5.00**
18 ❑ 1967 Cover: 0.12 **NM** value: **5.00**
Circ: Statement: **140,005**
19 ❑ 1967 Cover: 0.12 **NM** value: **5.00**
Circ: Statement: **140,005**
20 ❑ Jul 1967 Cover: 0.12 **NM** value: **3.50**
Circ: Statement: **140,005**
• Has 1966 Statement, filed 9/30/66; avg print run 236,400; avg sales 133,200; avg subs 5; avg total paid 133,205; samples 25; max existent 133,230; 44% of run returned
21 ❑ Sep 1967 Cover: 0.12 **NM** value: **3.50**
Circ: Statement: **140,005**
22 ❑ Nov 1967 Cover: 0.12 **NM** value: **5.00**
Circ: Statement: **140,005**
★ Origin of Iron Corporal. ★ 1st Appearance of Iron Corporal.
23 ❑ Jan 1968 Cover: 0.12 **NM** value: **3.50**
Circ: Statement: **135,020**
24 ❑ Mar 1968 Cover: 0.12 **NM** value: **3.50**
Circ: Statement: **135,020**
25 ❑ 1968 Cover: 0.12 **NM** value: **3.50**
Circ: Statement: **135,020**
26 ❑ 1968 Cover: 0.12 **NM** value: **3.50**
Circ: Statement: **135,020**
27 ❑ 1968 Cover: 0.12 **NM** value: **3.50**
Circ: Statement: **135,020**
28 ❑ **NM** value: **3.50**
29 ❑ 1969 **NM** value: **3.50**
30 ❑ 1969 **NM** value: **3.50**
31 ❑ 1969 **NM** value: **3.50**
32 ❑ Jun 1969 **NM** value: **3.50**
• Has 1968 Statement, filed 9/30/68; avg print run 225,000; avg sales 135,000; avg subs 20; avg total paid 135,020; samples 125; max existent 135,145; 40% of run returned
33 ❑ Aug 1969 **NM** value: **3.50**
34 ❑ Oct 1969 Cover: 0.15 **NM** value: **3.50**
35 ❑ Dec 1969 Cover: 0.15 **NM** value: **3.50**
36 ❑ Feb 1970 Cover: 0.15 **NM** value: **3.50**
📖 Life and Death on the Forward Perimeter; Hitler's Scourge; The Rice Soldiers (text story); A Course in Murder; This Modern War; The Brave Go First **A:** Sam Glanzman **C:** Sam Glanzman **W:** Willi Franz ★ Appearance of Iron Corporal.
37 ❑ Apr 1970 Cover: 0.15 **NM** value: **3.50**
38 ❑ Jun 1970 Cover: 0.15 **NM** value: **3.50**
📖 Something for EverybodyWhere Can You Hide a 40 Ton Tank?; Always Alert (text story); One Night in Normandy **A:** Nicholas Alascia **W:** Nicholas Alascia

AROUND THE WORLD UNDER THE SEA
Dell

1 ❑ Dec 1966 **NM** value: **25.00**
• **CGC:** 1 graded, best 9.4
No issue number.

ARRGH!
Marvel

Over the years, Marvel has created a huge number of gag magazines such as Not Brand Echh, Spoof, and Crazy, to name just a few. This series took a slightly different approach and specialized in the forgotten art of "genre spoofing." Instead of making fun of a particular story or film, Arrgh! took aim at the entire field of horror. Its tales were filled with monsters, vampires, and werewolves and usually ended on an ironic note. On the way, however, they were filled with humor, gags, and ridiculous situations.

Other grades: Multiply prices above by **1.5 for Mint • 2/3 for Very Fine • 1/3 for Fine • 1/5 for Very Good • 1/8 for Good**

1 ❑ Dec 1974 Cover: 0.25 **NM** value: **5.00**
• **CGC:** 2 graded, best 9.6
📖 Fangs For The Memory!; Whacks' Museum **A:** Tom Sutton; Mike Sekowsky **W:** Roy Thomas; Jack Younger
2 ❑ Feb 1975 Cover: 0.25 **NM** value: **4.00**
A: Tom Sutton **W:** Roy Thomas; RTh
3 ❑ May 1975 Cover: 0.25 **NM** value: **3.00**
A: Alfredo Alcala **W:** Roy Thomas; RTh
4 ❑ Jul 1975 Cover: 0.25 **NM** value: **3.00**
W: Roy Thomas; RTh
5 ❑ Sep 1975 Cover: 0.25 **NM** value: **3.00**
📖 The Invisible Mr. Mann; Count Varicose; The Some-Thing; Der Spider und der Fly **A:** Ross Andru; Mike Esposito **W:** Mike Esposito

ARROW — Malibu
1 ❑ Cover: 1.95 **NM** value: **Cover or less**
Circ: CapCity orders: **10,775**
📖 Shaft of Steel, Heart of Stone **A:** Lee Moder **W:** Roland Mann

ARROW ANTHOLOGY — Arrow
1 ❑ Nov 1997 Cover: 3.95 **NM** value: **Cover or less**
• The Fool, Jabberwocky, Great Scott, Night Streets, Battle Bot
2 ❑ Jan 1998 Cover: 3.95 **NM** value: **Cover or less**
• Simone & Ajax, Battle Bot, Night Streets, Miss Chevious, Dark Oz
3 ❑ Mar 1998 Cover: 3.95 **NM** value: **Cover or less**
• The Fool, Dragon Storm, Great Scott, Ninja Duck, Simone & Ajax, Samantha
4 ❑ Sep 1998 Cover: 3.95 **NM** value: **Cover or less**
📖 August; Mr. Nightmare: Right Place, Wrong Time; Corhawk the Assassin: Politically Corrected; The Adventures of Simone & Ajax, Part 2 • August, Land of Oz, Corhawk, Mr. Nightmare, Simone & Ajax **A:** Andrew Pepoy; Randy Zimmerman; Dave Ulanski; Mike Montgomery; Brian Douglas Ahern **W:** Scott Rosema; Andrew Pepoy; Randy Zimmerman; Dave Ulanski
5 ❑ Cover: 3.95 **NM** value: **Cover or less**

ARROW (CENTAUR) — Centaur
1 ❑ Oct 1940 Cover: 0.10 **NM** value: **2000.00**
• **CGC:** 1 graded, best 5.0
2 ❑ Nov 1940 Cover: 0.10 **NM** value: **1000.00**
• **CGC:** 2 graded, best 6.5
3 ❑ Dec 1940 Cover: 0.10 **NM** value: **1000.00**

ARROWHEAD — Atlas
1 ❑ Apr 1954 Cover: 0.10 **NM** value: **100.00**
2 ❑ Jun 1954 Cover: 0.10 **NM** value: **50.00**
3 ❑ Aug 1954 Cover: 0.10 **NM** value: **50.00**

ARROWMAN — Parody
1 ❑ b&w Cover: 2.50 **NM** value: **Cover or less**

ARROW SPOTLIGHT — Arrow
Simone is a pretty, young woman with the naivete of a child, which is an advantage for associating with Ajax, a miniature brontosaurus who appears to be a collection of geometric shapes. Together they engage in grave and solemn exploits such as saving Christmas by beating up a comics publisher or helping to quell an uprising of angry cherubs at an art museum. Andrew Pepoy's whimsical creation is the lead-off strip in Arrow Comics anthology title, Arrow Spotlight, which also features Talonback, a hapless adventurer who succeeds in spite of himself.

Other issues included Allison Chains, from editor-in-chief Randy Zimmerman, and Max Velocity by Jack Snider.

1 ❑ 1998b&w Cover: 2.95 **NM** value: **Cover or less**
📖 A Christmas Calamity; What's Going On?; The Origin; Talonback; A Fool for Christmas • Simone & Ajax **A:** Andrew Pepoy; Randy Zimmerman; Tyler Walpole **W:** Andrew Pepoy; Randy Zimmerman; Tyler Walpole; Tony Hatzigiannakis

ARSENAL — DC
1 ❑ Oct 1998 Cover: 2.50 **NM** value: **Cover or less**
Circ: Diamd. preorders: **23,362**
★ Appearance of Black Canary.
2 ❑ Nov 1998 Cover: 2.50 **NM** value: **Cover or less**
Circ: Diamd. preorders: **18,654**
★ Appearance of Green Arrow.
3 ❑ Dec 1998 Cover: 2.50 **NM** value: **Cover or less**
Circ: Diamd. preorders: **17,555**
★ Versus Vandal Savage.
4 ❑ Jan 1999 Cover: 2.50 **NM** value: **Cover or less**
Circ: Diamd. preorders: **17,354**
A: Rick Mays **W:** Devin Grayson ★ Appearance of Vandal Savage. ★ Versus Vandal Savage.

ARSENAL SPECIAL — DC
1 ❑ 1996 Cover: 2.95 **NM** value: **Cover or less**
One-shot. 📖 The Readiness to Die **A:** Will Rosado **W:** C.J. Henderson

ARSENIC LULLABY — A. Silent
1 ❑ Dec 1998 Cover: 2.50 **NM** value: **Cover or less**
📖 This Is the Enemy; Slow Boat to China, Part 1; The Devil and Keesler Foods; Slow Boat to China, Part 2; Employee of the Month; Dotti and Liquid Sam; Chef's Surprise **A:** Douglas Paszkiewicz **W:** Douglas Paszkiewicz
1 ❑ Dec 1998 Cover: 2.50 **NM** value: **Cover or less**
📖 This Is the Enemy; Slow Boat to China, Part 1; The Devil and Keesler Foods; Slow Boat to China, Part 2; Employee of the Month; Dotti and Liquid Sam; Chef's Surprise **A:** Douglas Paszkiewicz **W:** Douglas Paszkiewicz
2 ❑ 1999 Cover: 2.50 **NM** value: **Cover or less**
3 ❑ 1999 Cover: 2.50 **NM** value: **Cover or less**
4 ❑ 1999 Cover: 2.50 **NM** value: **Cover or less**
5 ❑ 1999 Cover: 2.50 **NM** value: **Cover or less**
6 ❑ 2000 Cover: 2.50 **NM** value: **Cover or less**
7 ❑ 2000 Cover: 2.50 **NM** value: **Cover or less**
8 ❑ 2000 Cover: 2.50 **NM** value: **Cover or less**
9 ❑ 2000 Cover: 2.50 **NM** value: **Cover or less**
10 ❑ May 2001 Cover: 2.50 **NM** value: **Cover or less**

ART & BEAUTY MAGAZINE — Kitchen Sink
All issues are adults only.
1 ❑ b&w Cover: 4.95 **NM** value: **Cover or less**
No issue number. cardstock cover. • over-sized. **A:** Robert Crumb

ARTBABE (VOL. 2) — Fantagraphics
1 ❑ May 1997 Cover: 2.95 **NM** value: **Cover or less**
2 ❑ Nov 1997 Cover: 2.95 **NM** value: **Cover or less**
3 ❑ Aug 1998 Cover: 2.95 **NM** value: **Cover or less**
4 ❑ Apr 1999 Cover: 2.95 **NM** value: **Cover or less**

ART D'ECCO — Fantagraphics
1 ❑ b&w Cover: 2.50 **NM** value: **Cover or less**
2 ❑ b&w Cover: 2.50 **NM** value: **Cover or less**
3 ❑ Cover: 2.75 **NM** value: **Cover or less**

ARTEMIS: REQUIEM — DC
1 ❑ Jun 1996 Cover: 1.75 **NM** value: **Cover or less**
📖 Into the Pit **A:** Ed Benés **W:** William Messner-Loebs
2 ❑ Jul 1996 Cover: 1.75 **NM** value: **Cover or less**
📖 Tribes **A:** Ed Benés **W:** William Messner-Loebs
3 ❑ Aug 1996 Cover: 1.75 **NM** value: **Cover or less**
A: Ed Benés **W:** William Messner-Loebs
4 ❑ Sep 1996 Cover: 1.75 **NM** value: **Cover or less**
A: Ed Benés **W:** William Messner-Loebs
5 ❑ Oct 1996 Cover: 1.75 **NM** value: **Cover or less**
A: Ed Benés **W:** William Messner-Loebs
6 ❑ Nov 1996 Cover: 1.75 **NM** value: **Cover or less**
Circ: Diamd. preorders: **34,162**
📖 Ev'ry Little Imp and Demon **A:** Ed Benés **W:** William Messner-Loebs

ARTESIA — Sirius
Artesia is not a place. It is a woman. A beautiful woman. A woman who is at once warrior, priestess, concubine, and spiritwalker. The goddesses smile upon her.

The story begins in battle. Artesia leads her lord's troops into battle against a rival noble house. Though the field is hers, something is not quite right. In religious ecstasy, she witnesses spirits guiding the dead to the underworld. Though Geniche, Dark Queen of the Underworld, assures Artesia that they do not come for her, the Dark Queen kisses Artesia, and that cannot be an omen of peace and contentment. The portents warn also that Geniche will walk the Earth again and Artesia's lord plans to betray her to the witch hunters. If Artesia is to survive, the goddesses must indeed be with her.

1 ❑ Jan 1999 Cover: 2.95 **NM** value: **Cover or less**
Circ: Diamd. preorders: **8,586**
A: Mark Smylie **W:** Mark Smylie
2 ❑ Feb 1999 Cover: 2.95 **NM** value: **Cover or less**
Circ: Diamd. preorders: **6,092**
A: Mark Smylie **W:** Mark Smylie
3 ❑ Mar 1999 Cover: 2.95 **NM** value: **Cover or less**
Circ: Diamd. preorders: **5,477**
A: Mark Smylie **W:** Mark Smylie
4 ❑ Apr 1999 Cover: 2.95 **NM** value: **Cover or less**
Circ: Diamd. preorders: **5,323**
A: Mark Smylie **W:** Mark Smylie
5 ❑ May 1999 Cover: 2.95 **NM** value: **Cover or less**
Circ: Diamd. preorders: **5,089**
A: Mark Smylie **W:** Mark Smylie
6 ❑ Jun 1999 Cover: 2.95 **NM** value: **Cover or less**
Circ: Diamd. preorders: **5,136**
A: Mark Smylie **W:** Mark Smylie

ARTESIA AFIELD — Sirius
1 ❑ Jul 2000 Cover: 2.95 **NM** value: **Cover or less**
Circ: Diamd. preorders: **5,569**
wraparound cover. 📖 Who Kills a King **A:** Mark Smylie **W:** Mark Smylie
2 ❑ Aug 2000 Cover: 2.95 **NM** value: **Cover or less**
Circ: Diamd. preorders: **4,056**
wraparound cover. 📖 Becomes a Worm **A:** Mark Smylie **W:** Mark Smylie
3 ❑ Sep 2000 Cover: 2.95 **NM** value: **Cover or less**
Circ: Diamd. preorders: **4,140**
wraparound cover. 📖 Becomes a Raven **A:** Mark Smylie **W:** Mark Smylie
4 ❑ Oct 2000 Cover: 2.95 **NM** value: **Cover or less**
Circ: Diamd. preorders: **3,843**
wraparound cover. 📖 Becomes a Ghost **A:** Mark Smylie **W:** Mark Smylie

ARTHUR KING OF BRITAIN — Tome
1 ❑ Cover: 2.95 **NM** value: **Cover or less**
A: Michael Fraley **W:** Michael Fraley
2 ❑ Cover: 2.95 **NM** value: **Cover or less**
A: Michael Fraley **W:** Michael Fraley
3 ❑ Cover: 2.95 **NM** value: **Cover or less**
A: Michael Fraley **W:** Michael Fraley
4 ❑ Cover: 2.95 **NM** value: **Cover or less**
📖 The Monster of the Mont-Saint-Michel **A:** Michael Fraley **W:** Michael Fraley
5 ❑ Cover: 3.95 **NM** value: **Cover or less**
A: Michael Fraley **W:** Michael Fraley

ARTHUR SEX — Aircel
All issues are adults only.
1 ❑ b&w Cover: 2.50 **NM** value: **Cover or less**
2 ❑ b&w Cover: 2.50 **NM** value: **Cover or less**
3 ❑ b&w Cover: 2.50 **NM** value: **Cover or less**
4 ❑ b&w Cover: 2.50 **NM** value: **Cover or less**
5 ❑ b&w Cover: 2.50 **NM** value: **Cover or less**
6 ❑ b&w Cover: 2.50 **NM** value: **Cover or less**
7 ❑ Nov 1991, b&w Cover: 2.50 **NM** value: **Cover or less**
📖 Castle of Ill Repute, Part 1
8 ❑ b&w Cover: 2.50 **NM** value: **Cover or less**

ARTILLERY ONE-SHOT — Red Bullet
1 ❑ 1995b&w Cover: 2.50 **NM** value: **Cover or less**

ART IN SHAMBLES — Max Hopper
1 ❑ b&w Cover: 2.50 **NM** value: **Cover or less**

ARTISTIC COMICS — Kitchen Sink
1 ❑ Aug 1995, b&w Cover: 4.95 **NM** value: **Cover or less**
No issue number. • adults only;new printing;squarebound **A:** Robert Crumb **W:** Robert Crumb
1-2 ❑ Cover: 2.50 **NM** value: **Cover or less**

ARTISTIC LICENTIOUSNESS — Starhead
All issues are adults only.
1 ❑ b&w Cover: 2.50 **NM** value: **Cover or less**
A: Roberta Gregory **W:** Roberta Gregory
2 ❑ Cover: 2.95 **NM** value: **Cover or less**
A: Roberta Gregory **W:** Roberta Gregory

ART OF ABRAMS, THE — Lightning
1 ❑ Dec 1996 Cover: 3.50 **NM** value: **Cover or less**
• b&w pin-ups

ART OF AUBREY BEARDSLEY, THE — Tome Press
1 ❑ b&w Cover: 2.95 **NM** value: **Cover or less**

ART OF CHIODO — Wildstorm Productions
1 ❑ Cover: 19.95 **NM** value: **Cover or less**
• collects Joe Chiodo work
1/HC❑ Cover: 29.95 **NM** value: **Cover or less**
hardcover. • collects Joe Chiodo work

ART OF HEATH ROBINSON — Tome Press
1 ❑ b&w Cover: 2.95 **NM** value: **Cover or less**

ART OF HOMAGE STUDIOS, THE — Image
1 ❑ 1993 Cover: 4.95 **NM** value: **5.50**
A: J. Scott Campbell; Joe Chiodo; Whilce Portacio; Ryan Benjamin; Brett Booth; Joe Benitez; Jim Lee; Brandon Peterson; Marc Silvestri; Aron Wiesenfeld; Scott Williams; Jeff Mariotte; Alex Garner ★ 1st Appearance of Gen13 (pin-ups, sketches).

ART OF MOEBIUS, THE — Marvel / Epic
1 ❑ Cover: 14.95 **NM** value: **Cover or less**

ART OF MUCHA — Tome Press
1 ❑ 1992 Cover: 2.95 **NM** value: **Cover or less**

ART OF USAGI YOJIMBO, THE — Radio
1 ❑ Apr 1997 Cover: 3.95 **NM** value: **Cover or less**
2 ❑ Jan 1998 Cover: 3.95 **NM** value: **Cover or less**

ART OF WALTER SIMONSON — DC
1 ❑ Cover: 19.95 **NM** value: **Cover or less**
Circ: CapCity orders: **2,150**

ART OF WRIGHTSON, THE — Side Show
1 ❑ Cover: 9.98 **NM** value: **Cover or less**
A: Bernie Wrightson

ART SCHOOL SUPERSTARS — Fantagraphics
1 ❑ **NM** value: **2.50**

ASCENSION — Image
Two thousand years ago two tribes-the Mineans, a race of angelic, winged people, and the Dayaks, blue skinned and demonic—existed as one. To the Dayaks a child named Viovodul was born. So strong was his evil that scientists from both sides imprisoned him in a realm between their world and ours.

The pages containing the full formula to free him were scattered to both realms, coming into the possession of Lucien and Andromeda, who have been given fantastic powers and whose destiny it is to stop Viovodul from being released.

Originally a tale of heaven and hell, centering on the war between the tribes, the series spun into a new direction after Batt, one of the co-creators and owners, departed after issue #7 due to creative differences.

0 ❑ **NM** value: **4.00**
• **CGC:** 1 graded, best 9.8
• Included with Wizard Top Cow Special **A:** David Finch **W:** David Finch
0/GO❑ **NM** value: **5.00**
• Gold edition. **A:** David Finch **W:** David Finch
0/LE❑ **NM** value: **9.00**
Gold cover. • Wizard "Certified Authentic" **A:** David Finch **W:** David Finch

CGC-graded: Multiply prices above by **33 for 9.9 M • 16 for 9.8 NM/M • 7 for 9.6 NM+ • 5 for 9.4 NM • 2.5 for 9.2 NM- • 1.5 for 9.0 VF/NM**

0.5 ❑ NM value: 5.00
A: David Finch W: David Finch
1 ❑ Oct 1997 Cover: 2.50 NM value: 3.00
Circ: Diamd. preorders: 107,825
1/A ❑ Oct 1997 Cover: 2.50 NM value: 4.00
Variant cover: Lucien holding head. A: Batt(cover); David Finch(cover)
1/B ❑ Oct 1997 Cover: 2.50 NM value: 5.00
• Fan club edition. • Top Cow Fan Club exclusive
1/C ❑ Oct 1997 Cover: 2.50 NM value: 5.00
• American Entertainment exclusive
1/D ❑ Oct 1997 Cover: 2.50 NM value: 3.00
• Sendaway edition. • angels on pile of bodies
2 ❑ Nov 1997 Cover: 2.50 NM value: Cover or less
Circ: Diamd. preorders: 74,364
2/A ❑ Nov 1997 Cover: 2.50 NM value: 5.00
• American Entertainment exclusive
2/GO❑Nov 1997 NM value: 4.00
• Gold edition.
3 ❑ Dec 1997 Cover: 2.50 NM value: Cover or less
Circ: Diamd. preorders: 74,987
A: David Finch W: David Finch; Batt
4 ❑ Feb 1998 Cover: 2.50 NM value: Cover or less
Circ: Diamd. preorders: 67,239
A: David Finch W: David Finch; Batt
5 ❑ Mar 1998 Cover: 2.50 NM value: Cover or less
Circ: Diamd. preorders: 61,737
A: David Finch W: David Finch; Batt
6 ❑ May 1998 Cover: 2.50 NM value: Cover or less
Circ: Diamd. preorders: 61,581
A: David Finch; Brian Ching; Randy Green; Billy Tan W: David Finch
7 ❑ Jul 1998 Cover: 2.50 NM value: Cover or less
Circ: Diamd. preorders: 56,499
A: David Finch; Brian Ching; Clarence Lansang; Randy Green W: David Finch
8 ❑ Aug 1998 Cover: 2.50 NM value: Cover or less
Circ: Diamd. preorders: 56,620
A: David Finch; Brian Ching; Mark Pajarillo; Dan Fraga W: David Finch; David Wohl
9 ❑ Oct 1998 Cover: 2.50 NM value: Cover or less
Circ: Diamd. preorders: 50,920
A: David Finch; Brian Ching; Clarence Lansang W: David Finch
10 ❑ Nov 1998 Cover: 2.50 NM value: Cover or less
Circ: Diamd. preorders: 48,550
A: David Finch; Brian Ching; Clarence Lansang W: David Finch
11 ❑ Feb 1999 Cover: 2.50 NM value: Cover or less
Circ: Diamd. preorders: 44,704
A: David Finch; Clarence Lansang W: David Finch; David Quinn
12 ❑ Apr 1999 Cover: 2.50 NM value: Cover or less
Circ: Diamd. preorders: 39,689
A: Brian Ching W: David Finch; David Quinn
13 ❑ May 1999 Cover: 2.50 NM value: Cover or less
Circ: Diamd. preorders: 37,481
A: Brian Ching; Roger Cruz; Andy Park W: David Finch; David Quinn
14 ❑ Jun 1999 Cover: 2.50 NM value: Cover or less
Circ: Diamd. preorders: 34,521
A: Brian Ching W: David Quinn
15 ❑ Jul 1999 Cover: 2.50 NM value: Cover or less
Circ: Diamd. preorders: 34,238
A: Brian Ching; David Boller; Ken Lashley W: David Quinn
16 ❑ Jul 1999 Cover: 2.50 NM value: Cover or less
Circ: Diamd. preorders: 31,917
A: Ken Lashley W: David Quinn
17 ❑ Aug 1999 Cover: 2.50 NM value: Cover or less
Circ: Diamd. preorders: 31,232
A: Brian Ching W: David Quinn
18 ❑ Sep 1999 Cover: 2.50 NM value: Cover or less
Circ: Diamd. preorders: 29,815
A: Brian Ching W: David Quinn
19 ❑ Oct 1999 Cover: 2.50 NM value: Cover or less
Circ: Diamd. preorders: 26,329
A: Brian Ching W: David Quinn
20 ❑ Nov 1999 Cover: 2.50 NM value: Cover or less
Circ: Diamd. preorders: 26,388
A: Brian Ching W: Maria Chen
21 ❑ Dec 1999 Cover: 2.95 NM value: Cover or less
Circ: Diamd. preorders: 23,908
cover says Nov, indicia says Dec. A: Brian Ching W: Marcia Chen
22 ❑ Mar 2000 Cover: 2.95 NM value: Cover or less
Circ: Diamd. preorders: 21,987
A: Brian Ching; David Boller W: Marcia Chen
Ash 1❑Jun 1997 NM value: 4.00
• Preview edition. A: David Finch W: David Finch; Batt
Bk 1❑ May 1998 Cover: 4.95 NM value: Cover or less
Circ: Diamd. preorders: 11,423
• prestige format. • collects issues #1 and 2;Collects Ascension #1-2 A: David Finch W: David Finch
Bk 2❑ Oct 1998 Cover: 4.95 NM value: Cover or less
• prestige format. • collects issues #3 and 4;Collects Ascension #3-4 A: David Finch W: David Finch

Diamond preorders are the estimated number of comics sold, prior to their release, to comics shops in North America by Diamond Comic Distributors, the largest distributor. These figures underreport the actual number of circulating copies by the amount of reorders Diamond took (usually 5-10% again of the preorders) and sales by publishers to newsstand and bookstore distributors. For many independent publishers, Diamond's preorders may be quite close to the actual number of copies in circulation.

ASH — Event

Joe Quesada and Jimmy Palmiotti's Ash has one of the more complicated origin stories in comics. The title character is Ashley Quinn, a fireman who "probably died" while saving a child from a burning building. He was revived, however, by the unexpected intervention of a futuristic warrior named Gunther Del-Sandiago.

Gunther ("Gun") had been leader of the few human survivors in the Devolutionary War. Their enemy was Adam-an alien who arrived on Earth in Quinn's time, and had been conducting genetic experiments on the populace that would eventually result in the creation of a new race. A century later, this race would enslave and annihilate mankind. Gun's final plan was to stop this by changing the past. Accordingly, he sent a regenerative unit back into the past to heal Ashley, giving him power over fire, and endowing him with a mission to save the future from Adam.

0 ❑ May 1996 Cover: 3.50 NM value: Cover or less
enhanced wraparound cover. • "Present" edition. A: Joe Quesada W: Joe Quesada; Jimmy Palmiotti ★ Origin of Ash.
0/A ❑ May 1996 Cover: 3.50 NM value: Cover or less
alternate enhanced wraparound cover. • "Future" edition. A: Joe Quesada W: Joe Quesada; Jimmy Palmiotti ★ Origin of Ash.
0/B ❑ May 1996 NM value: 4.00
• Red foil logo-Present edition. A: Joe Quesada W: Joe Quesada; Jimmy Palmiotti
0/C ❑ May 1996 NM value: 4.00
• Red foil logo-Future edition. A: Joe Quesada W: Joe Quesada; Jimmy Palmiotti
0.5 ❑ NM value: 2.50
A: Joe Quesada W: Joe Quesada; Jimmy Palmiotti
0.5/LE❑ NM value: 4.00
• Wizard authentic edition.
0.5/PI❑ NM value: 4.00
• Platinum edition.
1 ❑ Nov 1994 Cover: 2.50 NM value: 3.00
Circ: CapCity orders: 24,800 • CGC: 5 graded, best 9.9
Burn, Baby, Burn A: Joe Quesada W: Joe Quesada; Jimmy Palmiotti ★ 1st Appearance of Ash.
1/A ❑ Nov 1994 NM value: 4.00
Commemorative Omnichrome cover.
1/B ❑ Nov 1994 NM value: 3.00
Dynamic Forces exclusive (DF on cover).
2 ❑ Cover: 2.50 NM value: 3.00
Circ: CapCity orders: 19,600 • CGC: 1 graded, best 9.8
A: Joe Quesada W: Joe Quesada; Jimmy Palmiotti
3 ❑ May 1995 Cover: 2.50 NM value: 3.00
Circ: CapCity orders: 17,275 • CGC: 1 graded, best 9.8
A: Joe Quesada W: Joe Quesada; Jimmy Palmiotti
4 ❑ Jul 1995 Cover: 2.50 NM value: 3.00
Circ: CapCity orders: 18,000
A: Joe Quesada W: Joe Quesada; Jimmy Palmiotti
4/A ❑ NM value: 3.00
• Red Edition. A: Joe Quesada W: Joe Quesada; Jimmy Palmiotti
4/B ❑ NM value: 3.00
• White edition. A: Joe Quesada W: Joe Quesada; Jimmy Palmiotti
4/GO❑ NM value: 3.00
• Gold edition. A: Joe Quesada W: Joe Quesada; Jimmy Palmiotti
5 ❑ Sep 1995 Cover: 2.50 NM value: 3.00
Circ: CapCity orders: 17,325
A: Joe Quesada C: Greg Hildebrandt; Tim Hildebrandt W: Joe Quesada; Jimmy Palmiotti
6 ❑ Dec 1995 Cover: 2.50 NM value: Cover or less
A: Joe Quesada W: Joe Quesada; Jimmy Palmiotti
6/A ❑ Dec 1995 Cover: 2.50 NM value: Cover or less
alternate cover by Mark Texeira.
Bk 1❑ Cover: 14.95 NM value: Cover or less
•Collects Ash #1-5 A: Joe Quesada W: Joe Quesada; Jimmy Palmiotti

ASH/22 BRIDES — Event

1 ❑ Dec 1996 Cover: 2.95 NM value: Cover or less
Circ: Direct Market orders: 33,475
Something Butt-Ugly This Way Comes! A: Humberto Ramos W: Fabian Nicieza
2 ❑ Apr 1997 Cover: 2.95 NM value: Cover or less
Circ: Diamd. preorders: 27,416

ASH: CINDER & SMOKE — Event

1 ❑ May 1997 Cover: 2.95 NM value: Cover or less
Circ: Diamd. preorders: 26,174
House Afire A: Humberto Ramos W: Brian Augustyn; Mark Waid
2 ❑ Jun 1997 Cover: 2.95 NM value: Cover or less
Circ: Diamd. preorders: 14,513
A: Humberto Ramos W: Brian Augustyn; Mark Waid
2/A ❑ Jun 1997 Cover: 2.95 NM value: Cover or less
Circ: Diamd. preorders: 12,686
variant cover. A: Joe Quesada(cover)
3 ❑ Jul 1997 Cover: 2.95 NM value: Cover or less
Circ: Diamd. preorders: 13,928
A: Humberto Ramos W: Brian Augustyn; Mark Waid
3/A ❑ Jul 1997 Cover: 2.95 NM value: Cover or less
Circ: Diamd. preorders: 10,816
variant cover. A: Humberto Ramos; Joe Quesada(cover) W: Brian Augustyn; Mark Waid
4 ❑ Aug 1997 Cover: 2.95 NM value: Cover or less
Circ: Diamd. preorders: 9,923
A: Humberto Ramos W: Brian Augustyn; Mark Waid
4/A ❑ Aug 1997 Cover: 2.95 NM value: Cover or less
Circ: Diamd. preorders: 13,225
variant cover. A: Joe Quesada(cover)
5 ❑ Sep 1997 Cover: 2.95 NM value: Cover or less
Circ: Diamd. preorders: 12,610
A: Humberto Ramos W: Brian Augustyn; Mark Waid
5/A ❑ Sep 1997 Cover: 2.95 NM value: Cover or less
variant cover. A: Joe Quesada(cover)
6 ❑ Oct 1997 Cover: 2.95 NM value: Cover or less
A: Humberto Ramos W: Brian Augustyn; Mark Waid
6/A ❑ Oct 1997 Cover: 2.95 NM value: Cover or less
variant cover. A: Joe Quesada(cover)

ASHEN VICTOR — Viz

Originally published in Japan as Haisha, Yukito Kishiro has adopted a minimalist style for this four-part story that seems as dark as anything Frank Miller ever conceived.

Ashen Victor is a Motorball sports-drama set in the depressing world of the Scrapyard. There, people give up their humanity to become super-powerful cyborgs engaged in the racing and fighting of the deadly sport. Snev is a cyborg warrior who starts off his first race with a bang when a member of the audience runs out in front of him and is cut to shreds. Now Snev is not only trying to find out who's attempting to kill him before more of his friends are murdered, but what is the mysterious drug "Adam" that's being experimented on within him?

For more of the Scrapyard's universe of sudden death and dismemberment, check out the Battle Angel Alita saga.

1 ❑ 1997 Cover: 2.95 NM value: Cover or less
Circ: Diamd. preorders: 6,714
A: Yukito Kishiro W: Yukito Kishiro
2 ❑ 1997 Cover: 3.25 NM value: Cover or less
Circ: Diamd. preorders: 5,410
A: Yukito Kishiro W: Yukito Kishiro
3 ❑ 1997 Cover: 2.95 NM value: Cover or less
Circ: Diamd. preorders: 4,698
Pain and Anger A: Yukito Kishiro W: Yukito Kishiro
4 ❑ 1997 Cover: 2.95 NM value: Cover or less
Circ: Diamd. preorders: 4,179
A: Yukito Kishiro W: Yukito Kishiro
Bk 1❑ Cover: 14.95 NM value: Cover or less
No issue number. • digest-sized tpb. • collects series A: Yukito Kishiro W: Yukito Kishiro

ASHES — Caliber

1 ❑ Cover: 2.50 NM value: Cover or less
2 ❑ Cover: 2.50 NM value: Cover or less
3 ❑ Cover: 2.50 NM value: Cover or less
4 ❑ Cover: 2.50 NM value: Cover or less
5 ❑ Cover: 2.50 NM value: Cover or less

ASH FILES, THE — Event

1 ❑ Mar 1997 Cover: 2.95 NM value: Cover or less
Circ: Diamd. preorders: 17,130
• background on series A: Humberto Ramos; Scott Lee; Jimmy Palmiotti; Joe Queseda W: Kim Johnson

ASH: FIRE AND CROSSFIRE — Event

1 ❑ Jan 1999 Cover: 2.95 NM value: Cover or less
Circ: Diamd. preorders: 17,213
Fire and Crossfire, Part 1 A: Joe Quesada W: James Robinson
1/A ❑ Jan 1999 NM value: 8.00
2 ❑ 1999 Cover: 2.95 NM value: Cover or less
Circ: Diamd. preorders: 11,151
A: Joe Quesada W: James Robinson

ASHLEY DUST — Knight Press

1 ❑ Cover: 2.95 NM value: Cover or less
Wurms A: Rick McCollum W: Rick McCollum
2 ❑ Dec 1994 Cover: 2.95 NM value: Cover or less
3 ❑ Mar 1995 Cover: 2.95 NM value: Cover or less

ASHPILE — Side Show

1 ❑ Cover: 8.95 NM value: Cover or less
A: Jim Ridings W: Jim Ridings

ASH: THE FIRE WITHIN — Event

1 ❑ Sep 1996 Cover: 2.95 NM value: Cover or less
God's Never Been to Brooklyn A: Joe Quesada W: Joe Quesada; Jimmy Palmiotti
2 ❑ Cover: 2.95 NM value: Cover or less
A: Joe Quesada W: Joe Quesada; Jimmy Palmiotti

ASKANI'SON — Marvel

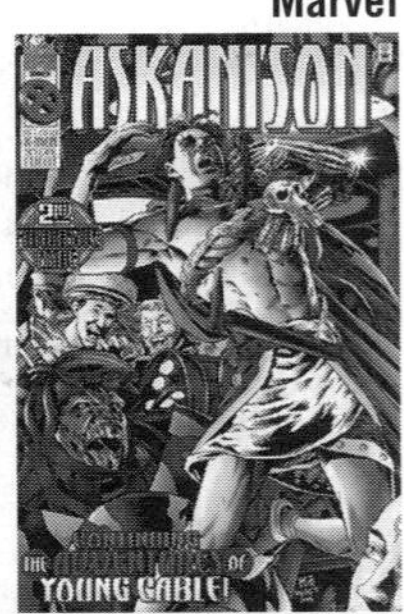

Cable, the enigmatic former-leader of X-Force acquires a past in Askani'Son. Subtitled, "The Adventures of Young Cable," the history manufactured for Nathan Christopher Dayspring finds him two thousand years in the future where he was transported to save his life, after being infected with a techno-organic virus by Apocalypse. He was raised by a mythic clan of women identified as the Askani, having been born of familiar, yet unspecified lineage. His adopted parents were Redd and Slym, two names that are phonetically familiar to X-Men readers.

Other grades: Multiply prices above by **1.5 for Mint • 2/3 for Very Fine • 1/3 for Fine • 1/5 for Very Good • 1/8 for Good**

Askani'Son has many Star Wars-like elements. Young Cable has a disembodied voice called Professor advising him a la Obi Wan Kenobi, and a Yoda-like cryptic advisor identified as Blaquesmith. Then there is Stryfe, cloned by Apocalypse from Cable, thus making the villain a more immediate relative than even Darth Vader.

1 ❑ Jan 1996 Cover: 2.95 **NM** value: **Cover or less**
cover says "Feb," indicia says "Jan". A Tiny Spark **A:** Gene Ha **W:** Scott Lobdell
2 ❑ Apr 1996 Cover: 2.95 **NM** value: **Cover or less**
cover says "Mar", indicia says "Apr".
3 ❑ Apr 1996 Cover: 2.95 **NM** value: **Cover or less**
cardstock wraparound cover.
4 ❑ May 1996 Cover: 2.95 **NM** value: **Cover or less**
cardstock wraparound cover. final issue.

ASRIAL VS. CHEETAH — Antarctic

1 ❑ Mar 1996 Cover: 2.95 **NM** value: **Cover or less**
2 ❑ Apr 1996 Cover: 2.95 **NM** value: **Cover or less**
Bk 1❑ Nov 1998, b&w Cover: 4.95 **NM** value: **Cover or less**
• "Special Compilation";collects mini-series **A:** Fred Perry **W:** Fred Perry

ASSASSINATION OF MALCOLM X, THE — Zone

The Assassination of Malcolm X presents a detailed account of the murder of the famous Black Nationalist leader in 1965. But don't expect a conventional comic-book approach. The text-based presentation is politically charged and accompanied by full-page black-and-white illustrations in stark, high-contrast woodcut style. Many of the images, which appear to be based on photographs or video clips, make a powerful and disturbing impression.

The story discusses the mysterious circumstances surrounding the murder of Malcolm X and the possibility of conspiracies and plots against him by former associates in the Nation of Islam, as well as by government agencies who kept close tabs on many radical leaders during the 1960s. Rather than suggest a clear answer, The Assassination of Malcolm X leaves conclusions to the reader, but furnishes much more information and evidence than is generally presented in mainstream sources.

1 ❑ Cover: 2.95 **NM** value: **Cover or less**
A: Michael Avon Oeming **W:** Jack Herman; Karen Herman

ASSASSINETTE — Pocket Change

1 ❑ 1994 Cover: 2.50 **NM** value: **Cover or less**
silver foil cover. **A:** Ed Ball **W:** Bob Dixon
2 ❑ Cover: 2.50 **NM** value: **Cover or less**
3 ❑ Cover: 2.50 **NM** value: **Cover or less**
4 ❑ Cover: 2.50 **NM** value: **Cover or less**
5 ❑ Cover: 2.50 **NM** value: **Cover or less**
6 ❑ Cover: 2.50 **NM** value: **Cover or less**
7 ❑ Cover: 2.50 **NM** value: **Cover or less**

ASSASSINS — DC / Amalgam

1 ❑ Apr 1996 Cover: 1.95 **NM** value: **Cover or less**
Political Suicide **A:** Scott McDaniel **W:** D.G. Chichester

ASSASSINS INC. — Silverline

1 ❑ Cover: 1.95 **NM** value: **Cover or less**
2 ❑ Cover: 1.95 **NM** value: **Cover or less**

ASTER — Express / Entity

0 ❑ Oct 1994 Cover: 2.95 **NM** value: **Cover or less**
Circ: CapCity orders: **5,495**
1 ❑ Oct 1994, b&w Cover: 2.95 **NM** value: **Cover or less**
Circ: CapCity orders: **9,745**
A: Jae Lee(cover); Oliver Isabedra; Ronaldo; Roxas **W:** Narcisco Roxas Jr.; Ronaldo Roxas
1/GO❑Oct 1994, b&w Cover: 10.00 **NM** value: **Cover or less**
• Gold edition.
2 ❑ Nov 1994 Cover: 2.95 **NM** value: **Cover or less**
Circ: CapCity orders: **6,345**
enhanced cardstock cover.
3 ❑ Jan 1995 Cover: 2.95 **NM** value: **Cover or less**
Circ: CapCity orders: **5,085**
3/A ❑ Jan 1995 Cover: 2.95 **NM** value: **Cover or less**
alternate cover.
3/B ❑ Jan 1995 Cover: 2.95 **NM** value: **Cover or less**
enhanced cover.
Ash 1❑ **NM** value: **1.00**
no cover price. • b&w preview
Bk 1❑ Cover: 12.95 **NM** value: **Cover or less**
• collects issues #1-4

ASTER: THE LAST CELESTIAL KNIGHT — Express / Entity

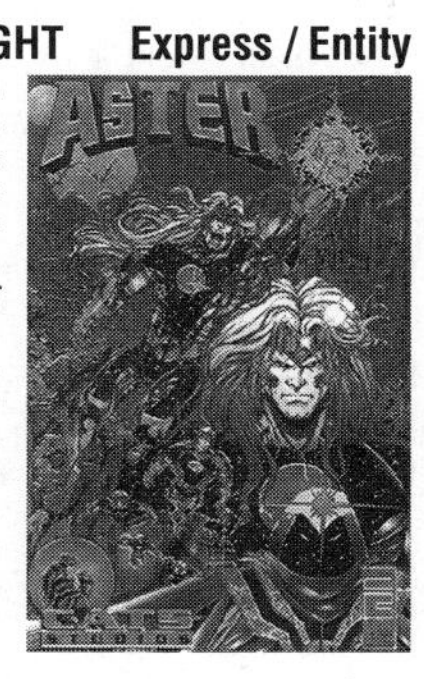

As his fellow Celestial Knights fell, Lord Aster rebelled against his masters and saved an entire planet from an evil god called Dessa, but in the process, he lost someone near and dear to him. Now, Aster is hailed as a hero, but he finds himself uncomfortable in the role, restless, and longing for his lost love Shaiana. Will he find a reason to continue in his role as an all-powerful guardian? Will he fall before the might of Dhumat, one of Dessa's loyal servants, before he resolves his issues? Find out in this chromium-covered, beautifully colored series from Entity Comics.

1 ❑ 1995 Cover: 3.75**NM** value: **Cover or less**
Circ: CapCity orders: **5,950**
Chronium Cover. **W:** Narcisco Roxas; Ronaldo Roxas

ASTONISH! — Wehner

1 ❑ b&w Cover: 2.00 **NM** value: **Cover or less**

ASTONISHING — Atlas

3 ❑ Cover: 0.10 **NM** value: **600.00**
Mister Death; The Runaway Planet; Fright; Time-Bomb Terror; The Invisible Horror (text) • was Marvel Boy
4 ❑ Jun 1951 Cover: 0.10 **NM** value: **450.00**
Screaming Tomb; When a Planet Dies; The Nightmare; Marvel Boy and the Walking Ghost; The Man Who Vanished (text)
5 ❑ Aug 1951 Cover: 0.10 **NM** value: **450.00**
Caves of Doom; The Serpent Strikes; Death from the Sky; Menace from the Moon; The Deadly Decision; The Walking Ghost (text)
6 ❑ Oct 1951 Cover: 0.10 **NM** value: **450.00**
Murder By Magic; The Phantom Pen; The Coffin; Unseen Terror; The Hills of Venus (text)
7 ❑ Dec 1951 Cover: 0.10 **NM** value: **250.00**
• **CGC:** 1 graded, best 7.5
8 ❑ Jan 1952 Cover: 0.10 **NM** value: **250.00**
• **CGC:** 1 graded, best 6.5
9 ❑ Feb 1952 Cover: 0.10 **NM** value: **250.00**
• **CGC:** 1 graded, best 6.0
10 ❑ Mar 1952 Cover: 0.10 **NM** value: **250.00**
• **CGC:** 1 graded, best 6.0
11 ❑ Mar 1952 Cover: 0.10 **NM** value: **200.00**
12 ❑ Apr 1952 Cover: 0.10 **NM** value: **200.00**
13 ❑ May 1952 Cover: 0.10 **NM** value: **200.00**
14 ❑ Jun 1952 Cover: 0.10 **NM** value: **200.00**
• **CGC:** 3 graded, best 9.0
15 ❑ Jul 1952 Cover: 0.10 **NM** value: **200.00**
• **CGC:** 1 graded, best 7.0
16 ❑ Aug 1952 Cover: 0.10 **NM** value: **200.00**
• **CGC:** 1 graded, best 7.0
17 ❑ Sep 1952 Cover: 0.10 **NM** value: **200.00**
• **CGC:** 1 graded, best 8.5
18 ❑ Oct 1952 Cover: 0.10 **NM** value: **200.00**
19 ❑ Nov 1952 Cover: 0.10 **NM** value: **200.00**
• **CGC:** 2 graded, best 9.0
20 ❑ Dec 1952 Cover: 0.10 **NM** value: **200.00**
21 ❑ Jan 1953 Cover: 0.10 **NM** value: **150.00**
22 ❑ Feb 1953 Cover: 0.10 **NM** value: **150.00**
• **CGC:** 1 graded, best 7.0
23 ❑ Mar 1953 Cover: 0.10 **NM** value: **150.00**
• **CGC:** 1 graded, best 5.5
24 ❑ Apr 1953 Cover: 0.10 **NM** value: **150.00**
25 ❑ Jun 1953 Cover: 0.10 **NM** value: **150.00**
• **CGC:** 2 graded, best 7.5
26 ❑ Aug 1953 Cover: 0.10 **NM** value: **150.00**
27 ❑ Oct 1953 Cover: 0.10 **NM** value: **150.00**
• **CGC:** 2 graded, best 7.5
28 ❑ Dec 1953 Cover: 0.10 **NM** value: **150.00**
29 ❑ Jan 1954 Cover: 0.10 **NM** value: **150.00**
30 ❑ Feb 1954 Cover: 0.10 **NM** value: **150.00**
• **CGC:** 1 graded, best 9.2
31 ❑ Mar 1954 Cover: 0.10 **NM** value: **125.00**
32 ❑ Apr 1954 Cover: 0.10 **NM** value: **125.00**
33 ❑ Jun 1954 Cover: 0.10 **NM** value: **125.00**
34 ❑ Aug 1954 Cover: 0.10 **NM** value: **125.00**
35 ❑ Oct 1954 Cover: 0.10 **NM** value: **125.00**
36 ❑ Dec 1954 Cover: 0.10 **NM** value: **125.00**
37 ❑ Feb 1955 Cover: 0.10 **NM** value: **125.00**
38 ❑ Apr 1955 Cover: 0.10 **NM** value: **125.00**
39 ❑ Jun 1955 Cover: 0.10 **NM** value: **125.00**
• **CGC:** 1 graded, best 9.2
40 ❑ Aug 1955 Cover: 0.10 **NM** value: **125.00**
41 ❑ Sep 1955 Cover: 0.10 **NM** value: **100.00**
42 ❑ Oct 1955 Cover: 0.10 **NM** value: **100.00**
43 ❑ Nov 1955 Cover: 0.10 **NM** value: **100.00**
44 ❑ Dec 1955 Cover: 0.10 **NM** value: **100.00**
• **CGC:** 1 graded, best 7.5
45 ❑ Jan 1956 Cover: 0.10 **NM** value: **100.00**
46 ❑ Feb 1956 Cover: 0.10 **NM** value: **100.00**
47 ❑ Mar 1956 Cover: 0.10 **NM** value: **100.00**
48 ❑ Apr 1956 Cover: 0.10 **NM** value: **100.00**
49 ❑ May 1956 Cover: 0.10 **NM** value: **100.00**
50 ❑ Jun 1956 Cover: 0.10 **NM** value: **100.00**
51 ❑ Jul 1956 Cover: 0.10 **NM** value: **75.00**
52 ❑ Aug 1956 Cover: 0.10 **NM** value: **75.00**
53 ❑ Sep 1956 Cover: 0.10 **NM** value: **75.00**
54 ❑ Oct 1956 Cover: 0.10 **NM** value: **75.00**
55 ❑ Nov 1956 Cover: 0.10 **NM** value: **75.00**
56 ❑ Dec 1956 Cover: 0.10 **NM** value: **75.00**
• **CGC:** 1 graded, best 7.5
Afraid to Dream
57 ❑ Jan 1957 Cover: 0.10 **NM** value: **75.00**
58 ❑ Feb 1957 Cover: 0.10 **NM** value: **75.00**
59 ❑ Mar 1957 Cover: 0.10 **NM** value: **75.00**
• **CGC:** 2 graded, best 8.5
60 ❑ 1957 Cover: 0.10 **NM** value: **75.00**
61 ❑ 1957 Cover: 0.10 **NM** value: **75.00**
• **CGC:** 1 graded, best 5.0
62 ❑ 1957 Cover: 0.10 **NM** value: **75.00**
• **CGC:** 1 graded, best 7.5
63 ❑ Aug 1957 Cover: 0.10 **NM** value: **75.00**

ASTONISHING EXCITEMENT — All-Jonh

503❑ Cover: 3.50 **NM** value: **Cover or less**
Tricky & Nuby; Sanwich High; El Destinos; Captain Soft **A:** Anonymous; Dennis C. Miller; Jarrod Poon **W:** Anonymous; Dennis C. Miller; Jarrod Poon; "King" Jonh Stevens; Josh Gemmell

ASTONISHING TALES — Marvel

1 ❑ Aug 1970 Cover: 0.15 **NM** value: **25.00**
• **CGC:** 13 graded, best 9.2
The Power of Ka-Zar!; Unto You is Born: The Doomsman! • Ka-Zar, Doctor Doom **A:** Jack Kirby; Wally Wood **W:** Roy Thomas; Stan Lee ★ Appearance of Kraven the Hunter.
2 ❑ Oct 1970 Cover: 0.15 **NM** value: **12.00**
• **CGC:** 10 graded, best 9.4
Frenzy on the Fortieth Floor; Revolution • Ka-Zar, Doctor Doom **A:** Jack Kirby; Wally Wood ★ Appearance of Kraven the Hunter.
3 ❑ Dec 1970 Cover: 0.15 **NM** value: **15.00**
• **CGC:** 10 graded, best 9.6
Back to the Savage Land; Doom Must Die • Ka-Zar, Doctor Doom **A:** Wally Wood ★ 1st Appearance of Zaladane.
4 ❑ Feb 1971 Cover: 0.15 **NM** value: **15.00**
• **CGC:** 5 graded, best 9.4
The Sun God; The Invaders • Ka-Zar, Doctor Doom **A:** Wally Wood
5 ❑ Apr 1971 Cover: 0.15 **NM** value: **15.00**
• **CGC:** 4 graded, best 9.6
Rampage; A Land Enslaved • Ka-Zar, Doctor Doom★ Appearance of Red Skull.
6 ❑ Jun 1971 Cover: 0.15 **NM** value: **15.00**
• **CGC:** 2 graded, best 9.6
Ware the Winds of Death; The Tentacles of the Tyrant • Ka-Zar, Doctor Doom★ 1st Appearance of Mockingbird (as Bobbi Morse).
7 ❑ Aug 1971 Cover: 0.15 **NM** value: **10.00**
• **CGC:** 3 graded, best 9.6
Deluge; And If I Be Called Traitor • Ka-Zar, Doctor Doom
8 ❑ Oct 1971 Cover: 0.25 **NM** value: **10.00**
• **CGC:** 3 graded, best 9.8
The Battle of New Britannia; This Badge Bedeviled; Though Some Call It Magic • Ka-Zar, Doctor Doom
9 ❑ Dec 1971 Cover: 0.20 **NM** value: **4.00**
• **CGC:** 1 graded, best 9.4
The Legend of the Lizard Men; Lorna, the Jungle Girl • Ka-Zar
10 ❑ Feb 1972 Cover: 0.20 **NM** value: **7.00**
• **CGC:** 3 graded, best 9.6
To End in Flame • Ka-Zar **A:** Sal Buscema; Barry Windsor-Smith
11 ❑ Apr 1972 Cover: 0.20 **NM** value: **7.00**
• **CGC:** 2 graded, best 9.4
A Day of Tigers • Ka-Zar★ Origin of Ka-Zar.
12 ❑ Jun 1972 Cover: 0.20 **NM** value: **8.00**
• **CGC:** 2 graded, best 9.4
Terror Stalks the Everglades!; Man-Thing • Ka-Zar **A:** John Buscema; Neal Adams **W:** Len Wein; Roy Thomas ★ Appearance of Man-Thing.
13 ❑ Aug 1972 Cover: 0.20 **NM** value: **3.00**
• **CGC:** 1 graded, best 7.0
Man-Thing! • Ka-Zar **A:** Rich Buckler; John Buscema; Dan Adkins **W:** Roy Thomas ★ Appearance of Man-Thing.
14 ❑ Oct 1972 Cover: 0.20 **NM** value: **3.00**
The Night of the Looter; Jungle Fever • Ka-Zar; reprinted from Savage Tales #1 and Jungle Tales #2
15 ❑ Dec 1972 Cover: 0.20 **NM** value: **3.00**
And Who Will Call Him Savage? • Ka-Zar
16 ❑ Feb 1973 Cover: 0.20 **NM** value: **3.00**
To Stalk a City • Ka-Zar
17 ❑ Apr 1973 Cover: 0.20 **NM** value: **3.00**
Target: Ka-Zar • Ka-Zar
18 ❑ Jun 1973 Cover: 0.20 **NM** value: **3.00**
Gog Cometh • Ka-Zar
19 ❑ Aug 1973 Cover: 0.20 **NM** value: **3.00**
• **CGC:** 1 graded, best 9.0
And Men Shall Name Him Victorius • Ka-Zar
20 ❑ Oct 1973 Cover: 0.20 **NM** value: **3.00**
The Final Battle • Ka-Zar
21 ❑ Dec 1973 Cover: 0.25 **NM** value: **3.00**
• **CGC:** 1 graded, best 9.4
It!; The Man Who Captured Death • Reprinted from Amazing Adult Fantasy #9
22 ❑ Feb 1974 Cover: 0.25 **NM** value: **3.00**
We, the Gargoyles; Gorgolla • Reprinted from Strange Tales #74
23 ❑ Apr 1974 Cover: 0.25 **NM** value: **3.00**
Conquerors Three; Fin Fang Foom • Reprinted from Strange Tales #89
24 ❑ Jun 1974 Cover: 0.25 **NM** value: **3.00**
Five Claws of Death
25 ❑ Aug 1974 Cover: 0.25 **NM** value: **20.00**
• **CGC:** 26 graded, best 9.6
A Cold Knight's Frenzy; Mindlock x 3 • 1st Perez work in comics **A:** Rich Buckler ★ Origin of Deathlok I (Luther Manning). ★ 1st Appearance of Deathlok I (Luther Manning).
26 ❑ Oct 1974 Cover: 0.25 **NM** value: **7.00**
• **CGC:** 1 graded, best 9.4
The Enemy: Us ★ Appearance of Deathlok.
27 ❑ Dec 1974 Cover: 0.25 **NM** value: **5.00**
Dead Reckoning ★ Appearance of Deathlok.
28 ❑ Feb 1975 Cover: 0.25 **NM** value: **5.00**
Five to One, Deathlok, One in Five- D11395; -No One Here Gets Out Alive; Deathman, Follow Me No More ★ Appearance of Deathlok.
29 ❑ Apr 1975 Cover: 0.25 **NM** value: **5.00**
• **CGC:** 1 graded, best 9.4
Earth Shall Overcome • Reprinted from Marvel Super-Heroes #18★ Origin of Guardians of the Galaxy. ★ 1st Appearance of Guardians of Galaxy.
30 ❑ Jun 2000 Cover: 0.25 **NM** value: **5.00**
The Soft Parade of Slow, Sliding Death; Shootout at the Flesh Factory **A:** Rich Buckler; Keith Pollard ★ Appearance of Deathlok.
31 ❑ Aug 1975 Cover: 0.25 **NM** value: **5.00**
Twice Removed From Yesterday…; Tales of the Watcher: Why Won't They Believe Me? • Reprinted from Silver Surfer #3 **A:** Rich Buckler; Gene Colan; Keith Pollard **W:** Stan Lee; Doug Moench ★ Appearance of Deathlok.
32 ❑ Nov 1976 Cover: 0.25 **NM** value: **5.00**
The Man Who Sold the World ★ Appearance of Deathlok.
33 ❑ Jan 1976 Cover: 0.25 **NM** value: **5.00**
Reflections in a Crimson Eye; Some of Us Are Programmed to Die ★ Appearance of Deathlok.
34 ❑ Mar 1976 Cover: 0.25 **NM** value: **5.00**
• **CGC:** 2 graded, best 9.4
And All the King's Madmen Couldn't Put Deathlok Together Again – Or Could They? ★ Appearance of Deathlok.
35 ❑ May 1976 Cover: 0.25 **NM** value: **5.00**
• **CGC:** 1 graded, best 9.4

CGC-graded: Multiply prices above by **33 for 9.9 M • 16 for 9.8 NM/M • 7 for 9.6 NM+ • 5 for 9.4 NM • 2.5 for 9.2 NM- • 1.5 for 9.0 VF/NM**

📖 And Once Removed from Never; The Resurrection and the Death ★ Appearance of Deathlok.

36 ❑ Jul 1976 Cover: 0.25 **NM** value: **5.00**
• **CGC:** 2 graded, best 9.4
📖 Confessions of a Demolished Man; What to Do After the Apocalypse final issue. ★ Appearance of Deathlok.

ASTONISHING X-MEN **Marvel**

The Age of Apocalypse began when Professor Xavier was murdered in Israel-years before he otherwise would have founded his school for mutants. The only good result of his death was that Eric Lehnsherr (Magneto) was forced to lead tomorrow's mutants in his place, rather than becoming Professor X's arch-enemy.

The downside was that the villain Apocalypse managed to conquer North America, ushering in a reign of terror unlike any humanity had ever seen before. In this alternate-reality title, Magneto's tiny group of X-Men must challenge all odds in order to stand against Apocalypse and his mutant armies.

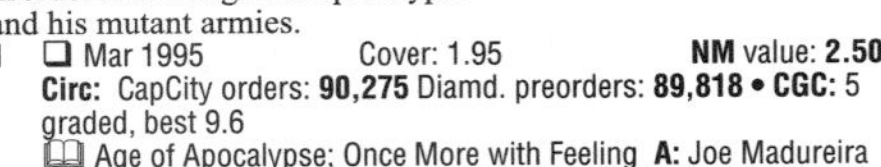

1 ❑ Mar 1995 Cover: 1.95 **NM** value: **2.50**
Circ: CapCity orders: **90,275** Diamd. preorders: **89,818** • **CGC:** 5 graded, best 9.6
📖 Age of Apocalypse; Once More with Feeling **A:** Joe Madureira **C:** Joe Madureira **W:** Scott Lobdell

2 ❑ Apr 1995 Cover: 1.95 **NM** value: **2.00**
Circ: CapCity orders: **87,425** Diamd. preorders: **75,775**

3 ❑ May 1995 Cover: 1.95 **NM** value: **2.00**
Circ: CapCity orders: **101,700** Diamd. preorders: **71,638**

4 ❑ Jun 1995 Cover: 1.95 **NM** value: **2.00**
Circ: CapCity orders: **106,350**

Bk 1❑ Aug 1995 Cover: 8.95 **NM** value: **Cover or less**
Gold foil cover. • Ultimate Astonishing X-Men;collects four-issue series

ASTONISHING X-MEN (2ND SERIES) **Marvel**

1 ❑ Sep 1999 Cover: 2.50 **NM** value: **Cover or less**
• **CGC:** 4 graded, best 9.8
📖 Call to Arms! **A:** Brandon Peterson; Dan Panosian; Howard Mackie; Tim Townsend **W:** Brandon Peterson; Dan Panosian; Howard Mackie; Tim Townsend

ASTOUNDING SPACE THRILLS **Day 1**

1 ❑ May 1998, b&w Cover: 2.95 **NM** value: **Cover or less**
A: Steve Conley **W:** Steve Conley

2 ❑ Jul 1998, b&w Cover: 2.95 **NM** value: **Cover or less**
A: Steve Conley **C:** Greg Hildebrandt; Tim Hildebrandt **W:** Steve Conley

3 ❑ Jan 1999, b&w Cover: 2.95 **NM** value: **Cover or less**
A: Steve Conley **W:** Steve Conley

ASTOUNDING SPACE THRILLS: THE COMIC BOOK **Image**

Savvy collectors knew it would be a matter of time before the Internet and the world of comics came crashing together. The result: no, not ComicBase! It's Astounding Space Thrills from Image Comics. With benefits for both the publisher and strip creators, the World Wide Web offers a unique form of marketing and yet another means by which to attract more readers.

Starting with the book's title story, Steve Conley has adapted his popular cyber-strip for the printed page, continuing the 21st century adventures of Argosy Smith and crew as they fight evil capitalists after the time and space altering "Shift." The book's backup story, The Crater Kid, is another popular Internet comic that tells the story of a 1950s retro-futuristic boy hero, protecting the universe from robots, aliens, and every other form of space bad guy imaginable.

Weaving self-contained stories independent of their cyber brethren, both features manage to refer back to their corresponding websites as a resource for story elaboration, marrying both the virtual and printed worlds.

1 ❑ Apr 2000 Cover: 2.95 **NM** value: **Cover or less**
Circ: Diamd. preorders: **6,410**
📖 The Cydonian Contract; The Crater Kid: The Fear Chip **A:** Steve Conley; Martin Bauman **C:** Ken Kelly **W:** Steve Conley; Martin Bauman

2 ❑ Jul 2000 Cover: 2.95 **NM** value: **Cover or less**
Circ: Diamd. preorders: **4,458**
📖 The Criminal Code; The Crater Kid: The Replacements **A:** Steve Conley; Martin Bauman **W:** Steve Conley; Martin Bauman

3 ❑ Sep 2000 Cover: 2.95 **NM** value: **Cover or less**
Circ: Diamd. preorders: **3,878**
📖 Gordo: Earthling Prime; The Crater Kid: The Holein Heaven **A:** Steve Conley; Martin Bauman **W:** Steve Conley; Martin Bauman

4 ❑ Dec 2000 Cover: 2.95 **NM** value: **Cover or less**
Circ: Diamd. preorders: **3,509**
📖 Hostile Takeover; The Crate Kid: The Blue Skull **A:** Steve Conley; Martin Bauman **W:** Steve Conley; Martin Bauman

ASTRIDER HUGO **Radio Comix**

1 ❑ Jul 2000, b&w Cover: 3.95 **NM** value: **Cover or less**

ASTRO BOY (GOLD KEY) **Gold Key**

1 ❑ Aug 1965 Cover: 0.12 **NM** value: **350.00**
Circ: Diamd. preorders: **2,595** • **CGC:** 6 graded, best 9.4

ASTRO CITY (VOL. 1) (KURT BUSIEK'S...) **Image**

Kurt Busiek rocketed to fame for his writing on the critically acclaimed Marvels limited series. In 1995, Busiek set up camp at Image Comics and released the six-issue Astro City, a series that was about an entire city of heroes, rather than just one hero.

The genius of the series is that the characters seem real. Through their eyes we can see what it would really be like to live in a city alongside superhumans with miraculous powers. In addition, it lets us see the real, human conflicts that the heroes face. For example, The Samaritan, Astro City's answer to Superman, leads a joyless life where he actually times how long he gets to enjoy flying between rescues. For him, the only moral way to live is to save as many people as possible with his powers. This, of course, leaves him no time at all for his own life. And even then, he can't save everyone.

1 ❑ Aug 1995 Cover: 2.25 **NM** value: **7.00**
Circ: CapCity orders: **27,000** • **CGC:** 24 graded, best 9.8
📖 In Dreams **A:** Brent Anderson; Alex Ross(cover) **C:** Alex Ross **W:** Kurt Busiek ★ 1st Appearance of The Honor Guard, The Menagerie Gang, Doctor Saturday, The Samaritan, Samaritan.

2 ❑ Sep 1995 Cover: 2.25 **NM** value: **5.00**
Circ: CapCity orders: **16,700** • **CGC:** 6 graded, best 9.6
📖 The Scoop **A:** Brent Anderson; Alex Ross(cover) **C:** Alex Ross **W:** Kurt Busiek ★ Appearance of Silver Agent, Honor Guard.

3 ❑ Oct 1995 Cover: 2.25 **NM** value: **4.00**
Circ: CapCity orders: **9,900** • **CGC:** 3 graded, best 9.8
📖 Dinner At Eight **A:** Brent Anderson; Alex Ross(cover) **C:** Alex Ross **W:** Kurt Busiek ★ Appearance of Jack in the Box.

4 ❑ Nov 1995 Cover: 2.25 **NM** value: **4.00**
• **CGC:** 3 graded, best 9.6
A: Brent Anderson; Alex Ross(cover) **C:** Alex Ross **W:** Kurt Busiek ★ 1st Appearance of The Hanged Man. ★ Appearance of First Family, Winged Victory.

5 ❑ Dec 1995 Cover: 2.25 **NM** value: **4.00**
• **CGC:** 3 graded, best 9.6
A: Brent Anderson; Alex Ross(cover) **C:** Alex Ross **W:** Kurt Busiek ★ Appearance of Crackerjack, Astro City Irregulars.

6 ❑ Jan 1996 Cover: 2.25 **NM** value: **4.00**
• **CGC:** 3 graded, best 9.6
A: Brent Anderson; Alex Ross(cover) **C:** Alex Ross **W:** Kurt Busiek ★ Origin of The Samaritan.

Bk 1❑ Cover: 19.95 **NM** value: **Cover or less**
📖 Life in the Big City • Life in the Big City **A:** Brent Anderson; Alex Ross(cover) **C:** Alex Ross **W:** Kurt Busiek

Bk 1/HC❑ Cover: 49.95 **NM** value: **Cover or less**
• Limited edition hardcover.

ASTRO CITY (VOL. 2) (KURT BUSIEK'S...) **Image**

Kurt Busiek's Astro City can almost be called an anthology title. Created by Kurt Busiek, (Marvels, Untold Tales of Spider-Man), Astro City features a day-in-the-life style of storytelling that discloses the exploits of The Samaritan, The Hanged Man, The Old Soldier, Jack-in-the-Box, First Family, and Winged Victory, as well as the hopes and dreams of the average citizen.

Although Astro City is home to an assortment of new and fascinating individuals, those characters are simply a tapestry on which Busiek shows the reader that life in a place as wondrous as this has much in common with ours. The title has a rich backstory of the Astro City universe already established, and the course of each story reveals intriguing clues about its history. Kurt Busiek's Astro City evokes a time when super-heroes were idealistic and approachable, instead of cynical and grim.

0.5 ❑ Jan 2000 Cover: 2.50 **NM** value: **4.00**
• **CGC:** 2 graded, best 9.6
📖 The Nearness of You • Wizard promotional item **A:** Brent Anderson; Alex Ross(cover) **C:** Alex Ross **W:** Kurt Busiek

0.5/DM❑ Jan 1998 Cover: 2.50 **NM** value: **3.00**
• **CGC:** 10 graded, best 9.8
• Direct Market edition. 📖 The Nearness of You; Clash of Titans (A New York Romance) • reprints "The Nearness of You" and "Clash of Titans" **A:** Brent Anderson; Alex Ross(cover) **C:** Alex Ross **W:** Kurt Busiek

1 ❑ Sep 1996 Cover: 2.50 **NM** value: **6.00**
• **CGC:** 4 graded, best 9.6
📖 Welcome to Astro City **A:** Brent Anderson; Alex Ross(cover) **C:** Alex Ross **W:** Kurt Busiek

1/3D❑ Dec 1997 Cover: 4.95 **NM** value: **5.00**
Circ: Diamd. preorders: **12,417**
• Signed hardcover edition. **A:** Brent Anderson; Alex Ross(cover) **C:** Alex Ross **W:** Kurt Busiek

2 ❑ Oct 1996 Cover: 2.50 **NM** value: **4.00**
Circ: Diamd. preorders: **40,685** • **CGC:** 2 graded, best 9.6
📖 Everyday Life **A:** Brent Anderson; Alex Ross(cover) **C:** Alex Ross **W:** Kurt Busiek ★ Appearance of First Family.

3 ❑ Nov 1996 Cover: 2.50 **NM** value: **4.00**
Circ: Diamd. preorders: **39,194** • **CGC:** 2 graded, best 9.4
A: Brent Anderson; Alex Ross(cover) **C:** Alex Ross **W:** Kurt Busiek ★ Appearance of Astra, First Family.

4 ❑ Dec 1996 Cover: 2.50 **NM** value: **4.00**
Circ: Direct Market orders: **40,903** • **CGC:** 2 graded, best 9.8
📖 New Kid in Town **A:** Brent Anderson; Alex Ross(cover) **C:** Alex Ross **W:** Kurt Busiek ★ 1st Appearance of Brian Kinney (The Altar Boy) (out of costume).

5 ❑ Jan 1997 Cover: 2.50 **NM** value: **4.00**
Circ: Direct Market orders: **42,785** • **CGC:** 2 graded, best 9.6
📖 Learning the Game **A:** Brent Anderson; Alex Ross(cover) **C:** Alex Ross **W:** Kurt Busiek ★ Origin of The Altar Boy. ★ 1st Appearance of The Altar Boy (Brian Kinney in costume).

6 ❑ Feb 1997 Cover: 2.50 **NM** value: **4.00**
Circ: Diamd. preorders: **44,905** • **CGC:** 2 graded, best 9.6
📖 The Gathering Dark • The Confessor revealed as vampire **A:** Brent Anderson; Alex Ross(cover) **C:** Alex Ross **W:** Kurt Busiek ★ 1st Appearance of The Gunslinger.

7 ❑ Mar 1997 Cover: 2.50 **NM** value: **3.50**
Circ: Diamd. preorders: **43,833** • **CGC:** 1 graded, best 9.4
📖 Eye of the Storm **A:** Brent Anderson; Alex Ross(cover) **C:** Alex Ross **W:** Kurt Busiek ★ Origin of The Confessor I.

8 ❑ Apr 1997 Cover: 2.50 **NM** value: **3.50**
Circ: Diamd. preorders: **44,207** • **CGC:** 1 graded, best 9.6
📖 Patterns **A:** Brent Anderson; Alex Ross(cover) **C:** Alex Ross **W:** Kurt Busiek ★ Death of The Confessor I.

9 ❑ May 1997 Cover: 2.50 **NM** value: **3.50**
Circ: Diamd. preorders: **45,101** • **CGC:** 1 graded, best 9.2
📖 My Father's Son **A:** Brent Anderson; Alex Ross(cover) **C:** Alex Ross **W:** Kurt Busiek ★ 1st Appearance of The Confessor II.

10 ❑ Oct 1997 Cover: 2.50 **NM** value: **3.50**
Circ: Diamd. preorders: **44,758**
📖 Shoe 'em All **A:** Brent Anderson; Alex Ross(cover) **C:** Alex Ross **W:** Kurt Busiek ★ Origin of Junkman.

11 ❑ Nov 1997 Cover: 2.50 **NM** value: **Cover or less**
Circ: Diamd. preorders: **44,567** • **CGC:** 1 graded, best 5.0
📖 Serpent's Teeth • Jack-in-the-Box vs. alternate versions **A:** Brent Anderson; Alex Ross(cover) **C:** Alex Ross **W:** Kurt Busiek ★ 1st Appearance of The Box, The Jackson.

12 ❑ Dec 1997 Cover: 2.50 **NM** value: **Cover or less**
Circ: Diamd. preorders: **46,953** • **CGC:** 1 graded, best 9.0
📖 Father's Day **A:** Brent Anderson; Alex Ross(cover) **C:** Alex Ross **W:** Kurt Busiek ★ 1st Appearance of Jack-in-the-Box II (Roscoe James).

13 ❑ Feb 1998 Cover: 2.50 **NM** value: **Cover or less**
Circ: Diamd. preorders: **45,846** • **CGC:** 1 graded, best 7.5
📖 In the Spotlight **A:** Brent Anderson; Alex Ross(cover) **C:** Alex Ross **W:** Kurt Busiek ★ Origin of Loony Leo. ★ 1st Appearance of Loony Leo.

14 ❑ Apr 1998 Cover: 2.50 **NM** value: **Cover or less**
Circ: Diamd. preorders: **49,293**
A: Brent Anderson; Alex Ross(cover) **C:** Alex Ross **W:** Kurt Busiek ★ Origin of Steeljack. ★ 1st Appearance of Steeljack.

15 ❑ Dec 1998 Cover: 2.50 **NM** value: **Cover or less**
Circ: Diamd. preorders: **47,616**
📖 The Long Treadmill **A:** Brent Anderson; Alex Ross(cover) **C:** Alex Ross **W:** Kurt Busiek ★ 1st Appearance of new Goldenglove. ★ 2nd Appearance of Steeljack. ★ Appearance of Steeljack.

16 ❑ Mar 1999 Cover: 2.50 **NM** value: **Cover or less**
Circ: Diamd. preorders: **46,663**
📖 The Tarnished Angel **A:** Brent Anderson; Alex Ross(cover) **C:** Alex Ross **W:** Kurt Busiek ★ Origin of El Hombre.

17 ❑ May 1999 Cover: 2.50 **NM** value: **Cover or less**
Circ: Diamd. preorders: **45,529**
📖 The Voice of the Turtle **A:** Brent Anderson; Alex Ross(cover) **C:** Alex Ross **W:** Kurt Busiek ★ Origin of The Mock Turtle.

18 ❑ Aug 1999 Cover: 2.50 **NM** value: **Cover or less**
Circ: Diamd. preorders: **45,333**
📖 The Empty Shell **A:** Brent Anderson; Alex Ross(cover) **C:** Alex Ross **W:** Kurt Busiek

19 ❑ Nov 1999 Cover: 2.50 **NM** value: **Cover or less**
Circ: Diamd. preorders: **43,825**
📖 The Only Chance **A:** Brent Anderson; Alex Ross(cover) **C:** Alex Ross **W:** Kurt Busiek

20 ❑ Jan 2000 Cover: 2.50 **NM** value: **Cover or less**
Circ: Diamd. preorders: **42,044**
📖 The Wow Finish **A:** Brent Anderson; Alex Ross(cover) **C:** Alex Ross **W:** Kurt Busiek

21 ❑ Mar 2000 Cover: 2.50 **NM** value: **Cover or less**
Circ: Diamd. preorders: **40,645**
📖 Where the Action Is **A:** Brent Anderson; Alex Ross(cover) **C:** Alex Ross **W:** Kurt Busiek

22 ❑ Aug 2000 Cover: 2.50 **NM** value: **Cover or less**
Circ: Diamd. preorders: **39,672**
📖 Great Expectations **A:** Brent Anderson **C:** Alex Ross **W:** Kurt Busiek ★ Origin of Crimson Cougar. ★ 1st Appearance of Crimson Cougar.

Bk 1❑ Cover: 19.95 **NM** value: **Cover or less**
• Confession Graphic Novel **A:** Brent Anderson; Alex Ross(cover) **C:** Alex Ross **W:** Kurt Busiek; Neil Gaiman

Bk 1/HC❑ Cover: 29.95 **NM** value: **49.95**
• Confession Graphic Novel **A:** Brent Anderson; Alex Ross(cover) **C:** Alex Ross **W:** Kurt Busiek; Neil Gaiman

Bk 2❑ Cover: 19.95 **NM** value: **Cover or less**
📖 Family Album • Family Album;collects #1-3 and #10-13 **A:** Brent Anderson; Alex Ross(cover) **C:** Alex Ross **W:** Kurt Busiek; Neil Gaiman

Bk 2/HC❑ Cover: 49.95 **NM** value: **Cover or less**
Family Album, hardcover. 📖 Family Album **A:** Brent Anderson; Alex Ross(cover) **C:** Alex Ross **W:** Kurt Busiek; Neil Gaiman

Bk 3/HC❑ Cover: 29.95 **NM** value: **Cover or less**
• The Tarnished Angel **A:** Brent Anderson; Alex Ross(cover) **W:** Kurt Busiek

ASTROCOMICS — Harvey

Plane trips can often be long and boring, especially for kids. So American Airlines joined forces with Harvey Comics to develop a comic book for distribution on American's flights. It's a great idea, giving the kids something fun and familiar to occupy their time. And, if the kids are happy, then of course so are their parents. As American Airlines is aware, happy customers are return customers.

Some of Harvey's most popular and famous characters are featured, including the friendly ghost Casper; Richie Rich, the richest kid in the world; and even Little Audrey. All the stories, however, are reprints and were originally presented in Harvey's regular line of titles.

1 ❑ **NM** value: **2.00**
• Giveaway from American Airlines. 📖 Flight Through the Ages; Richie Rich...Achooo!; Playful Little Audrey; Richie Rich and Casper...The Midas Touch; Richie Rich; Little Audrey and Melvin; Richie Rich and Casper...The Wizard of Wealth; All About Your Flight Crew (text); The Story of your • Reprints Harvey Comics stories

ASTRONAUTS IN TROUBLE: SPACE 1959 — AiT

1 ❑ **NM** value: **2.50**

ASTROTHRILL — Cheeky Press

1 ❑ May 1999 Cover: 12.95 **NM** value: **Cover or less**
No issue number. cardstock cover. • new material and reprints from Nemesister;CD

ASYLUM (MAXIMUM) — Maximum

1 ❑ Dec 1995 Cover: 2.95 **NM** value: **Cover or less**
Beanworld/Avengelyne flip covers. • Flip-book. 📖 Beanworld, Part 1; Avengelyne, Warchild, Doubletap **A:** John Fang; Arthur Adams; Rob Liefeld; Stephen Platt; Pop Mhan; Larry Marder **W:** Rob Liefeld; Robert Napton; Stephen Platt; Larry Marder
1/A ❑ Dec 1995 Cover: 2.95 **NM** value: **Cover or less**
Warchild/Doubletake flip covers.
2 ❑ Jan 1996 Cover: 2.95 **NM** value: **Cover or less**
• Flip-book. 📖 Beanworld, Part 2; Cybrid: Chrysalis, Part 1 **A:** Larry Marder **W:** Larry Marder
3 ❑ Apr 1996 Cover: 2.95 **NM** value: **Cover or less**
• Flip-book. 📖 Beanworld, Part 3; Cybrid: Chrysalis, Part 2 **A:** Larry Marder **W:** Larry Marder ★ Appearance of Cybrid.
4 ❑ 1996 Cover: 2.95 **NM** value: **Cover or less**
• Flip-book. 📖 Beanworld, Part 4; Christian: Heads I Win, Tails You Lose; Cybrid: Chrysalis, Part 3; Battlestar Galactica **A:** Sam Liu; Chris Scalf; Pop Mhan; Larry Marder **W:** Chris Scalf; Rob Liefeld; Robert Napton; Larry Marder; Garrett Omata; Robert Loren Flemming
5 ❑ 1996 Cover: 2.95 **NM** value: **Cover or less**
6 ❑ 1996 Cover: 2.95 **NM** value: **Cover or less**
7 ❑ 1996 Cover: 2.95 **NM** value: **Cover or less**
8 ❑ Oct 1996 Cover: 2.95 **NM** value: **Cover or less**
Circ: Diamd. preorders: **11,951**
📖 Megaton Man, Part 2 **A:** Donald Simpson **W:** Donald Simpson
9 ❑ Nov 1996 Cover: 2.95 **NM** value: **Cover or less**
Circ: Diamd. preorders: **10,532**
10 ❑ Dec 1996 Cover: 2.95 **NM** value: **Cover or less**
Circ: Direct Market orders: **9,757**
11 ❑ Jan 1997 Cover: 2.99 **NM** value: **Cover or less**
Circ: Direct Market orders: **8,952**
📖 Blindside: Look Up Look Down; Megaton Man, Part 3; Lethal: Killing Time **A:** Donald Simpson; Marat Mychaels **W:** Donald Simpson; Marat Mychaels; Robert Loren Flemming
12 ❑ Feb 1997 Cover: 2.99 **NM** value: **Cover or less**
Circ: Diamd. preorders: **8,081**
13 ❑ Mar 1997 Cover: 2.99 **NM** value: **Cover or less**
Circ: Diamd. preorders: **7,161**

ASYLUM (MILLENNIUM) — Millennium

1 ❑ Cover: 2.50 **NM** value: **Cover or less**
Circ: CapCity orders: **5,925**
📖 The Wishing Hour; The Latchkey Fiend; One Evening on a Small Planet; The Conqueror Worm; Blood Brothers **A:** John Bolton; Matt Howarth; P. Craig Russell; Al Williams; Duncan Eagleson **W:** Matt Howarth; Edgar Allan Poe; Steven Seagle
2 ❑ Cover: 2.50 **NM** value: **Cover or less**
Circ: CapCity orders: **7,755**
A: Mark Buckingham **W:** Neil Gaiman
3 ❑ Cover: 4.95 **NM** value: **Cover or less**
A: Howard Chaykin

ASYLUM (NCG) — New Comics

1 ❑ b&w Cover: 1.95 **NM** value: **Cover or less**
📖 The Call; Spurs; The Ninth Skeleton **A:** Bernie Wrightson; Christopher Schenck; Alex Nino; Valarie Jones; John B. Bright; Alex Nino **W:** Stephen R. Bissette; Clark Aston Smith; James Robert Wrightson
2 ❑ Cover: 2.25 **NM** value: **Cover or less**

Capital City orders are the actual sales of comic books by Capital City Distribution, once one of the largest U.S. sellers of comics to comics shops. Capital City's share of comics shop sales, while not known exactly, increases from around 10-20% in the mid-1980s to 30-35% in the mid-1990s. Capital City's share of comic books sold on newsstands (most Marvels and DCs) will be less.

ATARI FORCE — DC

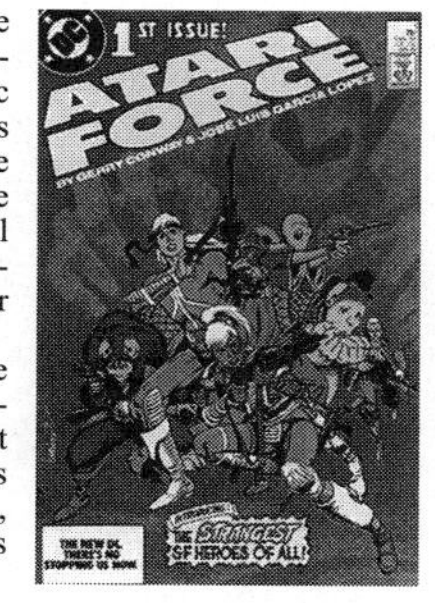

Officially it's an acronym for the Advanced Technology And Research Institute, but this comic book, focusing on a team of rebels and renegades, originated from the comics shipped with Atari home computer games. Don't let that fool you. The characters have personality and motivation that belies their arcade game origins.

The first five adventures of the Atari force were included as mini-comics in several of Atari's most popular home videogames, such as Defender and Phoenix. This series, written by Gerry Conway, marks their debut in mainstream comics.

1 ❑ Jan 1984 Cover: 0.75 **NM** value: **1.00**
• **CGC:** 1 graded, best 9.8
📖 First Blood **A:** José Luis Garcia-Lopez **W:** Roy Thomas; Gerry Conway ★ 1st Appearance of Dark Destroyer, Babe, Atari Force (in standard comics), Dart, Blackjak.
2 ❑ Feb 1984 Cover: 0.75 **NM** value: **1.00**
★ 1st Appearance of Martin Champion.
3 ❑ Mar 1984 Cover: 0.75 **NM** value: **1.00**
4 ❑ Apr 1984 Cover: 0.75 **NM** value: **1.00**
5 ❑ May 1984 Cover: 0.75 **NM** value: **1.00**
6 ❑ Jun 1984 Cover: 0.75 **NM** value: **1.00**
7 ❑ Jul 1984 Cover: 0.75 **NM** value: **1.00**
8 ❑ Aug 1984 Cover: 0.75 **NM** value: **1.00**
9 ❑ Sep 1984 Cover: 0.75 **NM** value: **1.00**
10 ❑ Oct 1984 Cover: 0.75 **NM** value: **1.00**
11 ❑ Nov 1984 Cover: 0.75 **NM** value: **1.00**
12 ❑ Dec 1984 Cover: 0.75 **NM** value: **1.00**
13 ❑ Jan 1985 Cover: 0.75 **NM** value: **1.00**
14 ❑ Feb 1985 Cover: 0.75 **NM** value: **1.00**
15 ❑ Mar 1985 Cover: 0.75 **NM** value: **1.00**
16 ❑ Apr 1985 Cover: 0.75 **NM** value: **1.00**
17 ❑ May 1985 Cover: 0.75 **NM** value: **1.00**
Circ: CapCity orders: **6,350**
18 ❑ Jun 1985 Cover: 0.75 **NM** value: **1.00**
Circ: CapCity orders: **6,950**
19 ❑ Jul 1985 Cover: 0.75 **NM** value: **1.00**
Circ: CapCity orders: **7,350**
20 ❑ Aug 1985 Cover: 0.75 **NM** value: **1.00**
Circ: CapCity orders: **6,750**
final issue.
SE 1❑ 1986 Cover: 2.00 **NM** value: **Cover or less**
Circ: CapCity orders: **8,100**
• Giant-size. 📖 Codename: Dart: A Mercenary's Story; The Adventures of the Hukka!; Second Skin! **A:** James W. Fry III; Tristan Shane; Marshall Rogers **W:** Andy Helfer; Dwight Jon Zimmerman; Paul Kupperberg

A-TEAM, THE — Marvel

1 ❑ Mar 1984 Cover: 0.60 **NM** value: **2.00**
• **CGC:** 1 graded, best 9.6
• based on TV series
2 ❑ Apr 1984 Cover: 0.60 **NM** value: **2.00**
📖 Who Kidnapped Kuramoto? **A:** Jim Mooney; Joe Giella **W:** Jim Salicrup
3 ❑ May 1984 Cover: 0.60 **NM** value: **2.00**

ATHENA — Antarctic

0 ❑ Cover: 2.95 **NM** value: **Cover or less**
📖 Zero • Antarctic publishes **A:** Dean Hsieh **W:** Dean Hsieh
1 ❑ Cover: 2.95 **NM** value: **Cover or less**
• A.M. Press publishes **A:** Dean Hsieh **W:** Dean Hsieh
2 ❑ Cover: 2.95 **NM** value: **Cover or less**
A: Dean Hsieh **W:** Dean Hsieh
3 ❑ Cover: 2.95 **NM** value: **Cover or less**
A: Dean Hsieh **W:** Dean Hsieh
4 ❑ Cover: 2.95 **NM** value: **Cover or less**
A: Dean Hsieh **W:** Dean Hsieh
5 ❑ Cover: 2.95 **NM** value: **Cover or less**
A: Dean Hsieh **W:** Dean Hsieh
6 ❑ Cover: 2.95 **NM** value: **Cover or less**
A: Dean Hsieh **W:** Dean Hsieh

ATLANTIS CHRONICLES, THE — DC

1 ❑ Mar 1990 Cover: 2.95 **NM** value: **3.00**
Circ: CapCity orders: **16,950** • **CGC:** 1 graded, best 9.4
📖 The Deluge **A:** Estebán Maroto **W:** Peter David
2 ❑ Apr 1990 Cover: 2.95 **NM** value: **3.00**
Circ: CapCity orders: **13,250**
A: Estebán Maroto **W:** Peter David
3 ❑ May 1990 Cover: 2.95 **NM** value: **3.00**
Circ: CapCity orders: **12,550**
A: Estebán Maroto **W:** Peter David
4 ❑ Jun 1990 Cover: 2.95 **NM** value: **3.00**
Circ: CapCity orders: **12,100**
A: Estebán Maroto **W:** Peter David
5 ❑ Jul 1990 Cover: 2.95 **NM** value: **3.00**
Circ: CapCity orders: **11,500**
A: Estebán Maroto **W:** Peter David
6 ❑ Aug 1990 Cover: 2.95 **NM** value: **3.00**
Circ: CapCity orders: **11,300**
A: Estebán Maroto **W:** Peter David
7 ❑ Sep 1990 Cover: 2.95 **NM** value: **3.00**
Circ: CapCity orders: **10,900** • **CGC:** 1 graded, best 9.0
final issue. **A:** Estebán Maroto **W:** Peter David ★ Origin of Aquaman.

ATLAS — Dark Horse

1 ❑ Feb 1994 Cover: 2.50 **NM** value: **Cover or less**
Circ: CapCity orders: **3,575**
A: Bruce Zick **W:** Bruce Zick
2 ❑ Apr 1994 Cover: 2.50 **NM** value: **Cover or less**
Circ: CapCity orders: **2,350**
A: Bruce Zick **W:** Bruce Zick
3 ❑ Jun 1994 Cover: 2.50 **NM** value: **Cover or less**
A: Bruce Zick **W:** Bruce Zick
4 ❑ Aug 1994 Cover: 2.50 **NM** value: **Cover or less**
A: Bruce Zick **W:** Bruce Zick

ATOM, THE — DC

Ray Palmer, a professor at the prestigious Ivy University, developed a portable shrinking device which he used to shrink himself down to six inches and smaller — as well as to adjust his weight from feather-light to the 180 pounds he weighs at his natural size. Unfortunately for the bad guys, Palmer, instead of publishing his great discovery, used it to fight crime as The Atom, the world's smallest superhero.

This delightful science-fiction title also touched on history and art without ever being overbearing, preachy or surreal. After the Atom became a full-time member of the Justice League of America, he shared this series with fellow League member Hawkman.

1 ❑ Jul 1962 Cover: 0.12 **NM** value: **750.00**
• **CGC:** 37 graded, best 9.4
📖 Master of the Plant World! **A:** Murphy Anderson; Gil Kane ★ 1st Appearance of Plant Master.
2 ❑ Sep 1962 Cover: 0.12 **NM** value: **280.00**
• **CGC:** 8 graded, best 9.2
📖 The Oddest Man on Earth!; The Prisoner Who Vanished! **A:** Murphy Anderson; Gil Kane
3 ❑ Nov 1962 Cover: 0.12 **NM** value: **200.00**
• **CGC:** 5 graded, best 9.2
📖 The Time Trap!; The Secret of "Al Atom's" Lamp! **A:** Murphy Anderson; Gil Kane ★ 1st Appearance of Chronos.
4 ❑ Jan 1963 Cover: 0.12 **NM** value: **140.00**
• **CGC:** 11 graded, best 9.6
📖 The Machine That Made "Miracles"!; The Case of the Innocent Thief! **A:** Murphy Anderson; Gil Kane
5 ❑ Mar 1963 Cover: 0.12 **NM** value: **140.00**
• **CGC:** 9 graded, best 9.4
📖 The Diamond of Deadly Dooms!; The Spectre of 3000-Moons Lake! **A:** Murphy Anderson; Gil Kane
6 ❑ May 1963 Cover: 0.12 **NM** value: **105.00**
• **CGC:** 4 graded, best 8.5
A: Murphy Anderson; Gil Kane
7 ❑ Jul 1963 Cover: 0.12 **NM** value: **250.00**
• **CGC:** 18 graded, best 9.4
A: Murphy Anderson; Gil Kane ★ Appearance of Hawkman.
8 ❑ Sep 1963 Cover: 0.12 **NM** value: **105.00**
• **CGC:** 5 graded, best 9.2
A: Murphy Anderson; Gil Kane ★ Appearance of Justice League of America.
9 ❑ Nov 1963 Cover: 0.12 **NM** value: **105.00**
• **CGC:** 4 graded, best 8.5
A: Murphy Anderson; Gil Kane
10 ❑ Jan 1964 Cover: 0.12 **NM** value: **105.00**
Circ: Statement: **265,304** • **CGC:** 5 graded, best 9.2
A: Murphy Anderson; Gil Kane
11 ❑ Mar 1964 Cover: 0.12 **NM** value: **80.00**
Circ: Statement: **265,304** • **CGC:** 1 graded, best 8.0
• Has 1963 Statement, filed 10/1/63; no circ figures published **A:** Murphy Anderson; Gil Kane
12 ❑ May 1964 Cover: 0.12 **NM** value: **80.00**
Circ: Statement: **265,304** • **CGC:** 3 graded, best 9.2
A: Murphy Anderson; Gil Kane
13 ❑ Jul 1964 Cover: 0.12 **NM** value: **80.00**
Circ: Statement: **265,304** • **CGC:** 5 graded, best 9.6
14 ❑ Sep 1964 Cover: 0.12 **NM** value: **80.00**
Circ: Statement: **265,304** • **CGC:** 4 graded, best 9.4
15 ❑ Nov 1964 Cover: 0.12 **NM** value: **80.00**
Circ: Statement: **265,304**
16 ❑ Jan 1965 Cover: 0.12 **NM** value: **50.00**
Circ: Statement: **255,254** • **CGC:** 7 graded, best 9.6
A: Murphy Anderson; Gil Kane
17 ❑ Mar 1965 Cover: 0.12 **NM** value: **50.00**
Circ: Statement: **255,254** • **CGC:** 2 graded, best 9.2
A: Murphy Anderson; Gil Kane
18 ❑ May 1965 Cover: 0.12 **NM** value: **50.00**
Circ: Statement: **255,254** • **CGC:** 2 graded, best 9.4
• Has 1964 Statement, filed 10/1/64; avg print run 382,000; avg sales 263,000; avg subs 2,304; avg total paid 265,304; samples 387;max existent 265,691; 30% of run returned **A:** Murphy Anderson; Gil Kane
19 ❑ Jul 1965 Cover: 0.12 **NM** value: **50.00**
Circ: Statement: **255,254**
A: Murphy Anderson; Gil Kane
20 ❑ Sep 1965 Cover: 0.12 **NM** value: **50.00**
Circ: Statement: **255,254** • **CGC:** 1 graded, best 8.0
A: Murphy Anderson; Gil Kane
21 ❑ Nov 1965 Cover: 0.12 **NM** value: **38.00**
Circ: Statement: **255,254** • **CGC:** 2 graded, best 9.6
22 ❑ Jan 1966 Cover: 0.12 **NM** value: **38.00**
Circ: Statement: **232,850** • **CGC:** 1 graded, best 9.2
23 ❑ Mar 1966 Cover: 0.12 **NM** value: **38.00**
Circ: Statement: **232,850** • **CGC:** 2 graded, best 9.4
24 ❑ May 1966 Cover: 0.12 **NM** value: **38.00**
Circ: Statement: **232,850** • **CGC:** 1 graded, best 9.4
• Has 1965 Statement, filed 10/1/65; avg print run 408,000; avg sales 252,000; avg subs 3,245; avg total paid 255,254; samples 142; max existent 255,387; 3% of run returned
25 ❑ Jul 1966 Cover: 0.12 **NM** value: **38.00**
Circ: Statement: **232,850** • **CGC:** 1 graded, best 9.2

CGC-graded: Multiply prices above by **33 for 9.9 M • 16 for 9.8 NM/M • 7 for 9.6 NM+ • 5 for 9.4 NM • 2.5 for 9.2 NM- • 1.5 for 9.0 VF/NM**

26 ❑ Sep 1966 Cover: 0.12 **NM** value: **38.00**
Circ: Statement: **232,850** • **CGC:** 2 graded, best 9.2
★ 1st Appearance of Bug-Eyed Bandit.
27 ❑ Nov 1966 Cover: 0.12 **NM** value: **38.00**
Circ: Statement: **232,850** • **CGC:** 2 graded, best 9.2
★ Versus Panther.
28 ❑ Jan 1967 Cover: 0.12 **NM** value: **38.00**
Circ: Statement: **184,100**
29 ❑ Mar 1967 Cover: 0.12 **NM** value: **140.00**
Circ: Statement: **184,100** • **CGC:** 13 graded, best 9.4
★ Appearance of Atom I (Al Pratt).
30 ❑ May 1967 Cover: 0.12 **NM** value: **38.00**
Circ: Statement: **184,100** • **CGC:** 2 graded, best 9.2
31 ❑ Jul 1967 Cover: 0.12 **NM** value: **38.00**
Circ: Statement: **184,100** • **CGC:** 2 graded, best 9.2
★ Appearance of Hawkman.
32 ❑ Sep 1967 Cover: 0.12 **NM** value: **38.00**
Circ: Statement: **184,100** • **CGC:** 3 graded, best 9.4
33 ❑ Nov 1967 Cover: 0.12 **NM** value: **38.00**
Circ: Statement: **184,100** • **CGC:** 3 graded, best 9.4
34 ❑ Jan 1968 Cover: 0.12 **NM** value: **38.00**
• **CGC:** 4 graded, best 9.6
35 ❑ Mar 1968 Cover: 0.12 **NM** value: **38.00**
• **CGC:** 2 graded, best 9.2
📖 Plight Of the Pin-Up Atom! **A:** Gil Kane; Sid Greene **W:** Gardner Fox
36 ❑ May 1968 Cover: 0.12 **NM** value: **50.00**
• **CGC:** 4 graded, best 9.4
★ Appearance of Atom I (Al Pratt).
37 ❑ Jul 1968 Cover: 0.12 **NM** value: **38.00**
• **CGC:** 3 graded, best 9.6
★ Appearance of Hawkman.
38 ❑ Sep 1968 Cover: 0.12 **NM** value: **38.00**
• **CGC:** 3 graded, best 9.2
• Series continued in Atom and Hawkman #39
SE 1❑ ca. 1993 Cover: 2.50 **NM** value: **Cover or less**
Circ: CapCity orders: **21,650**
SE 2❑ ca. 1995 Cover: 2.50 **NM** value: **Cover or less**
Circ: CapCity orders: **10,400**
📖 Critical Mass • 1995 **A:** Luke McDonnell **W:** Tennessee Peyer

ATOM-AGE COMBAT (1ST SERIES) — St. John

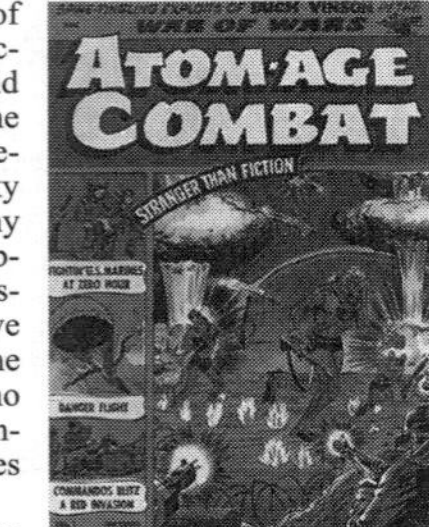

This series lived up to its claim of being "stranger than [most] fiction." In the first issue, the intrepid Captain Buck Vinson leads the charge of flipper-wearing, bare-chested sea commandos up a rocky beach into the face of terrible enemy fire. Looking behind him, he observes, "This is rough! Guided missiles with atomic warheads have struck our sub!" Nevertheless, the half-naked commandos have no trouble routing the goggle-and antenna-wearing Communist hordes that threatened them.

There was no subtlety at play here, and lest you have trouble telling the good guys from the bad, the Communists were the ones with the exaggerated Mongoloid features who were so yellow that it looked as if each had late-stage jaundice. Even the Communist fighter pilots who are covered head-to-toe in flight gear have blazing yellow eyes underneath their goggles. Atom-Age Combat is not a great series, but it stands as a real curiosity piece of Cold War fantasy.

1 ❑ Jun 1952 Cover: 0.10 **NM** value: **250.00**
• **CGC:** 1 graded, best 9.0
📖 Operation Wolverine (text story); Commandos Blitz a Red Invasion; Underground Action; Zero Hour Ahead; Private Thistlewait: Perfect Fit; Dangerous Flight
2 ❑ Sep 1952 Cover: 0.10 **NM** value: **150.00**
3 ❑ Nov 1952 Cover: 0.10 **NM** value: **110.00**
• **CGC:** 1 graded, best 3.5
4 ❑ Jan 1953 Cover: 0.10 **NM** value: **150.00**
• **CGC:** 1 graded, best 7.0
5 ❑ Apr 1953 Cover: 0.10 **NM** value: **110.00**
• **CGC:** 1 graded, best 9.0

ATOM-AGE COMBAT (2ND SERIES) — St. John

1 ❑ Feb 1958 Cover: 0.10 **NM** value: **100.00**
• changes publisher to Fago
2 ❑ Jan 1959 Cover: 0.10 **NM** value: **150.00**
• Fago begins publication
3 ❑ Mar 1959 Cover: 0.10 **NM** value: **100.00**

ATOMAN — Spark Publications

1 ❑ Feb 1946 Cover: 0.10 **NM** value: **400.00**
• **CGC:** 2 graded, best 9.4
2 ❑ Apr 1946 Cover: 0.10 **NM** value: **300.00**

ATOM AND HAWKMAN — DC

39 ❑ Oct 1968 Cover: 0.12 **NM** value: **32.00**
• **CGC:** 1 graded, best 9.2
• Series continued from Atom #38 **A:** Joe Kubert **W:** Gardner Fox
40 ❑ Dec 1968 Cover: 0.12 **NM** value: **32.00**
• **CGC:** 4 graded, best 9.0
📖 The Explosive Exploit of the Split-Atom **A:** Dick Dillin; Sid Greene
41 ❑ Feb 1969 Cover: 0.12 **NM** value: **32.00**
• **CGC:** 3 graded, best 9.0
42 ❑ Apr 1969 Cover: 0.12 **NM** value: **32.00**
• **CGC:** 5 graded, best 9.6
43 ❑ Jun 1969 Cover: 0.12 **NM** value: **32.00**
• **CGC:** 1 graded, best 9.2
A: Joe Kubert
44 ❑ Aug 1969 Cover: 0.12 **NM** value: **32.00**
• **CGC:** 2 graded, best 9.4
45 ❑ Oct 1969 **NM** value: **32.00**
• **CGC:** 3 graded, best 9.6
final issue.

ATOM ANT — Gold Key

1 ❑ Jan 1966 Cover: 0.12 **NM** value: **150.00**
• **CGC:** 2 graded, best 9.4

ATOMIC AGE — Epic

1 ❑ Nov 1990 Cover: 4.50 **NM** value: **Cover or less**
Circ: CapCity orders: **6,050**
📖 Broken Silence **A:** Michael Okamoto; Al Williamson(inks) **W:** Frank Lovece
2 ❑ Dec 1990 Cover: 4.50 **NM** value: **Cover or less**
Circ: CapCity orders: **4,950**
A: Michael Okamoto; Al Williamson(inks) **W:** Frank Lovece
3 ❑ Jan 1991 Cover: 4.50 **NM** value: **Cover or less**
Circ: CapCity orders: **3,850**
A: Michael Okamoto; Al Williamson(inks) **W:** Frank Lovece
4 ❑ Feb 1991 Cover: 4.50 **NM** value: **Cover or less**
Circ: CapCity orders: **2,950**
📖 Everybody Mambo **A:** Michael Okamoto; Al Williamson(inks) **W:** Frank Lovece

ATOMIC AGE TRUCKSTOP WAITRESS — Fantagraphics / Eros

All issues are adults only.
1 ❑ b&w Cover: 2.25 **NM** value: **Cover or less**

ATOMIC BOMB — Jay Burtis

1 ❑ ca. 1945 Cover: 0.10 **NM** value: **350.00**
• **CGC:** 7 graded, best 9.4

ATOMIC CITY TALES — Kitchen Sink

1 ❑ 1996 Cover: 2.95 **NM** value: **Cover or less**
📖 Night Of The Monkey, Part 1, Consumer Pangs; Night Of The Monkey, Part 2, Rat Race Blues; Night Of The Monkey, Part 3, Organ Grinder
2 ❑ 1996 Cover: 2.95 **NM** value: **Cover or less**
3 ❑ Sep 1996 Cover: 2.95 **NM** value: **Cover or less**
Circ: Diamd. preorders: **2,837**
Bk 1❑ Jan 1997 Cover: 12.95 **NM** value: **Cover or less**
• Go Power!
SE 1❑ Cover: 2.95 **NM** value: **Cover or less**

ATOMIC COMICS — Green Publications

1 ❑ Jan 1946 Cover: 0.10 **NM** value: **1000.00**
• **CGC:** 13 graded, best 9.4
2 ❑ Mar 1946 Cover: 0.10 **NM** value: **500.00**
• **CGC:** 2 graded, best 8.5
3 ❑ May 1946 Cover: 0.10 **NM** value: **350.00**
4 ❑ Jul 1946 Cover: 0.10 **NM** value: **350.00**
• **CGC:** 2 graded, best 8.5

ATOMIC MAN — Blackthorne

1 ❑ Cover: 1.75 **NM** value: **Cover or less**
A: Jeff Bonivert **W:** Jeff Bonivert
2 ❑ Cover: 1.75 **NM** value: **Cover or less**
A: Jeff Bonivert **W:** Jeff Bonivert
3 ❑ Cover: 1.75 **NM** value: **Cover or less**
A: Jeff Bonivert **W:** Jeff Bonivert

ATOMIC MOUSE — Charlton

Atomic Mouse, a funny animal super-hero, enjoyed a 10-year run as a comic book, television, and movie character during the 1950s and 1960s. Atomic Mouse helps keep the world safe from fiendish (and generally feline) menaces to the funny animal community, using his atomically-enhanced powers, which include super strength and flight, to foil their schemes.

Illustrated with insane energy by Al Fago, one of the true masters of the funny animal style, Atomic Mouse provided fun, entertaining, and "wholesome" reading (it even says so on the cover!) for younger fans. Atomic Mouse made an encore appearance in the 1980s, courtesy of Charlton Comics.

1 ❑ Mar 1953 Cover: 1.00 **NM** value: **150.00**
(#3 on cover)b&w. **A:** Al Fago **W:** Al Fago ★ 1st Appearance of Atomic Mouse.
2 ❑ Cover: 0.10 **NM** value: **75.00**
A: Al Fago **W:** Al Fago
3 ❑ Cover: 0.10 **NM** value: **50.00**
A: Al Fago **W:** Al Fago
4 ❑ Cover: 0.10 **NM** value: **50.00**
A: Al Fago **W:** Al Fago
5 ❑ Cover: 0.10 **NM** value: **50.00**
A: Al Fago **W:** Al Fago
6 ❑ Cover: 0.10 **NM** value: **35.00**
A: Al Fago **W:** Al Fago
7 ❑ Cover: 0.10 **NM** value: **35.00**
A: Al Fago **W:** Al Fago
8 ❑ Cover: 0.10 **NM** value: **35.00**
A: Al Fago **W:** Al Fago
9 ❑ Cover: 0.10 **NM** value: **35.00**
📖 Bank Night in Mouseville; Rodney's Road Race (text story); Count Gatto; Food for Thought; Professor Invento: Mending the Ending **A:** Al Fago **W:** Al Fago
10 ❑ Oct 1954 Cover: 0.10 **NM** value: **35.00**
A: Al Fago **W:** Al Fago
11 ❑ Cover: 0.10 **NM** value: **25.00**
A: Al Fago **W:** Al Fago
12 ❑ Cover: 0.10 **NM** value: **25.00**
A: Al Fago **W:** Al Fago
13 ❑ Cover: 0.10 **NM** value: **25.00**
A: Al Fago **W:** Al Fago
14 ❑ Cover: 0.10 **NM** value: **25.00**
A: Al Fago **W:** Al Fago
15 ❑ 1955 Cover: 0.10 **NM** value: **25.00**
A: Al Fago **W:** Al Fago
16 ❑ Dec 1955 Cover: 0.10 **NM** value: **25.00**
A: Al Fago **W:** Al Fago
17 ❑ Cover: 0.10 **NM** value: **25.00**
A: Al Fago **W:** Al Fago
18 ❑ Cover: 0.10 **NM** value: **25.00**
A: Al Fago **W:** Al Fago
19 ❑ Cover: 0.10 **NM** value: **25.00**
A: Al Fago **W:** Al Fago
20 ❑ Cover: 0.10 **NM** value: **25.00**
A: Al Fago **W:** Al Fago
21 ❑ Cover: 0.10 **NM** value: **18.00**
A: Al Fago **W:** Al Fago
22 ❑ Cover: 0.10 **NM** value: **18.00**
A: Al Fago **W:** Al Fago
23 ❑ Cover: 0.10 **NM** value: **18.00**
A: Al Fago **W:** Al Fago
24 ❑ Cover: 0.10 **NM** value: **18.00**
A: Al Fago **W:** Al Fago
25 ❑ Feb 1958 Cover: 0.10 **NM** value: **18.00**
A: Al Fago **W:** Al Fago
26 ❑ May 1958 Cover: 0.15 **NM** value: **45.00**
• **CGC:** 1 graded, best 8.0
• Double-size. **A:** Al Fago **W:** Al Fago
27 ❑ Sep 1958 Cover: 0.10 **NM** value: **18.00**
A: Al Fago **W:** Al Fago
28 ❑ Nov 1958 Cover: 0.10 **NM** value: **18.00**
A: Al Fago **W:** Al Fago
29 ❑ Cover: 0.10 **NM** value: **18.00**
A: Al Fago **W:** Al Fago
30 ❑ Apr 1959 Cover: 0.10 **NM** value: **15.00**
A: Al Fago **W:** Al Fago
31 ❑ Jun 1959 Cover: 0.10 **NM** value: **15.00**
A: Al Fago **W:** Al Fago
32 ❑ Cover: 0.10 **NM** value: **15.00**
A: Al Fago **W:** Al Fago
33 ❑ Cover: 0.10 **NM** value: **15.00**
A: Al Fago **W:** Al Fago
34 ❑ Cover: 0.10 **NM** value: **15.00**
A: Al Fago **W:** Al Fago
35 ❑ Cover: 0.10 **NM** value: **15.00**
A: Al Fago **W:** Al Fago
36 ❑ Cover: 0.10 **NM** value: **15.00**
A: Al Fago **W:** Al Fago
37 ❑ Jul 1960 Cover: 0.10 **NM** value: **15.00**
A: Al Fago **W:** Al Fago
38 ❑ Cover: 0.10 **NM** value: **15.00**
A: Al Fago **W:** Al Fago
39 ❑ Cover: 0.10 **NM** value: **15.00**
A: Al Fago **W:** Al Fago
40 ❑ Cover: 0.10 **NM** value: **15.00**
A: Al Fago **W:** Al Fago
41 ❑ Cover: 0.10 **NM** value: **13.00**
A: Al Fago **W:** Al Fago
42 ❑ Cover: 0.10 **NM** value: **13.00**
A: Al Fago **W:** Al Fago
43 ❑ Cover: 0.10 **NM** value: **13.00**
A: Al Fago **W:** Al Fago
44 ❑ Cover: 0.10 **NM** value: **13.00**
A: Al Fago **W:** Al Fago
45 ❑ Cover: 0.10 **NM** value: **13.00**
A: Al Fago **W:** Al Fago
46 ❑ Cover: 0.10 **NM** value: **13.00**
A: Al Fago **W:** Al Fago
47 ❑ Apr 1962 Cover: 0.10 **NM** value: **13.00**
• **CGC:** 1 graded, best 8.5
A: Al Fago **W:** Al Fago
48 ❑ Jun 1962 Cover: 0.10 **NM** value: **13.00**
A: Al Fago **W:** Al Fago
49 ❑ Aug 1962 Cover: 0.10 **NM** value: **13.00**
A: Al Fago **W:** Al Fago
50 ❑ Oct 1962 Cover: 0.12 **NM** value: **13.00**
A: Al Fago **W:** Al Fago
51 ❑ Dec 1962 Cover: 0.12 **NM** value: **12.00**
A: Al Fago **W:** Al Fago
52 ❑ Feb 1963 Cover: 0.12 **NM** value: **12.00**
A: Al Fago **W:** Al Fago
53 ❑ Apr 1963 Cover: 0.12 **NM** value: **12.00**
A: Al Fago **W:** Al Fago
54 ❑ Jun 1963 Cover: 0.12 **NM** value: **12.00**
final issue. **A:** Al Fago **W:** Al Fago

ATOMIC MOUSE (A+) — A+

1 ❑ Cover: 2.50 **NM** value: **Cover or less**
2 ❑ Cover: 2.50 **NM** value: **Cover or less**
3 ❑ Cover: 2.50 **NM** value: **Cover or less**

ATOMICOW — Vision

1 ❑ Aug 1990 Cover: 2.50 **NM** value: **Cover or less**
A: Rodney Dunn **W:** Kelly Strong; Mark Petlock

ATOMIC RABBIT & FRIENDS — Avalon

1 ❑ b&w Cover: 2.50 **NM** value: **Cover or less**
• reprints Charlton stories

Other grades: Multiply prices above by **1.5 for Mint** • **2/3 for Very Fine** • **1/3 for Fine** • **1/5 for Very Good** • **1/8 for Good**

ATOMICS, THE — AAA Pop

In Snap City, a group of young street beatniks, mutated and disfigured by alien spores, have become outcasts of society. But several of them have tired of their self-imposed exile, and struggle to overcome the hardships of their mutations. Inspired by their friend Jack, now called Mr. Gum, and aided by former nemesis Frank Einstein, (aka the zany Madman), they learn the spores have given them the potential for great power. Along with an alien teen using the moniker Zapman, the street beatniks form their own super-hero team.

The Atomics, and the publishing company AAA Pop Comics, are the work of Madman creator Mike Allred and his wife Laura.

16 ❑ **NM** value: **Cover or less**
1 ❑ Jan 2000 Cover: 2.95 **NM** value: **Cover or less**
Circ: Diamd. preorders: **12,805**
2 ❑ Feb 2000 Cover: 2.95 **NM** value: **Cover or less**
Circ: Diamd. preorders: **9,382**
3 ❑ Mar 2000 Cover: 2.95 **NM** value: **Cover or less**
Circ: Diamd. preorders: **9,954**
4 ❑ Apr 2000 Cover: 2.95 **NM** value: **Cover or less**
Circ: Diamd. preorders: **10,498**
5 ❑ May 2000 Cover: 2.95 **NM** value: **Cover or less**
Circ: Diamd. preorders: **10,472**
6 ❑ Jun 2000 Cover: 2.95 **NM** value: **Cover or less**
Circ: Diamd. preorders: **10,515**
7 ❑ Jul 2000 Cover: 2.95 **NM** value: **Cover or less**
Circ: Diamd. preorders: **10,400**
8 ❑ Aug 2000 Cover: 2.95 **NM** value: **Cover or less**
Circ: Diamd. preorders: **9,567**
9 ❑ Sep 2000 Cover: 2.95 **NM** value: **Cover or less**
Circ: Diamd. preorders: **9,457**
10 ❑ Oct 2000 Cover: 2.95 **NM** value: **Cover or less**
Circ: Diamd. preorders: **9,222**
11 ❑ Nov 2000 Cover: 2.95 **NM** value: **Cover or less**
Circ: Diamd. preorders: **8,928**
12 ❑ Dec 2000 Cover: 3.50 **NM** value: **Cover or less**
Circ: Diamd. preorders: **8,760**
13 ❑ Jan 2001 Cover: 3.50 **NM** value: **Cover or less**
Circ: Diamd. preorders: **8,935**
14 ❑ Feb 2001 Cover: 3.50 **NM** value: **Cover or less**
Circ: Diamd. preorders: **8,879**
15 ❑ Mar 2001 Cover: 3.50 **NM** value: **Cover or less**
Circ: Diamd. preorders: **8,620**

ATOMIC SPY CASES — Avon

1 ❑ Mar 1950 Cover: 0.10 **NM** value: **200.00**

ATOMIC THUNDERBOLT — Regor

1 ❑ Feb 1946 Cover: 0.10 **NM** value: **400.00**
• **CGC:** 1 graded, best 7.5
2 ❑ **NM** value: **Cover or less**

ATOMIC TOYBOX — Image

1 ❑ Nov 1999 Cover: 2.95 **NM** value: **Cover or less**
Circ: Diamd. preorders: **13,683**
cover says Dec, indicia says Nov. 📖 Cruel Times **A:** Aaron Lopresti; Steve Ellis **W:** Aaron Lopresti; Peter Gutierrez
1/A ❑ Nov 1999 Cover: 2.95 **NM** value: **Cover or less**
A: Steve Ellis **W:** Peter Gutierrez
1/B ❑ Nov 1999 Cover: 2.95 **NM** value: **Cover or less**
A: Steve Ellis **W:** Peter Gutierrez

ATOMIC WAR! — Ace

1 ❑ Nov 1952 Cover: 0.10 **NM** value: **650.00**
• **CGC:** 1 graded, best 8.0
2 ❑ Dec 1952 Cover: 0.10 **NM** value: **400.00**
• **CGC:** 2 graded, best 9.2
3 ❑ Feb 1953 Cover: 0.10 **NM** value: **400.00**
• **CGC:** 2 graded, best 9.2
4 ❑ Apr 1953 Cover: 0.10 **NM** value: **400.00**
• **CGC:** 2 graded, best 8.0

ATOMIK ANGELS (WILLIAM TUCCI'S...) — Crusade

1 ❑ May 1996 Cover: 2.95 **NM** value: **Cover or less**
A: Steve Ellis **W:** Peter Gutierrez ★ Appearance of Freefall.
1/SC ❑ May 1996 Cover: 2.95 **NM** value: **3.50**
variant cover.
2 ❑ Jul 1996 Cover: 2.95 **NM** value: **Cover or less**
A: Steve Ellis **W:** Peter Gutierrez
3 ❑ Sep 1996 Cover: 2.95 **NM** value: **Cover or less**
A: Steve Ellis **W:** Peter Gutierrez
3/SC ❑ Sep 1996 Cover: 2.95 **NM** value: **3.50**
alternate cover (orange background with Statue of Liberty).
4 ❑ Nov 1996 Cover: 2.95 **NM** value: **Cover or less**
Circ: Diamd. preorders: **18,853**
• flipbook with Manga Shi 2000 preview **A:** Steve Ellis **W:** Peter Gutierrez
SE 1 ❑ Feb 1996, b&w **NM** value: **3.00**
No issue number. • "The Intrep-edition". • promotional comic for U.S.S. Intrepid

ATOM THE ATOMIC CAT — Avalon

1 ❑ Cover: 2.95 **NM** value: **Cover or less**
📖 Two Little Prizes; House Moving; Conversation Piece; I Was Mary's Little Lamb (text); Li'l Lumberjack...A Trip to the City; Commissioner of Fish ★ Appearance of Yin, Aunt Tessie., Chappy, Doctor Mole, Li'l Lumberjack.

ATOMZ MAN AND SUPER SEEKER — Atomz

1 ❑ **NM** value: **0.25**
• Promotional giveaway form Atomz.com. **A:** Peter McDonald

ATTACK (1ST SERIES) — Youthful

1 ❑ May 1952 Cover: 0.10 **NM** value: **200.00**
2 ❑ Jul 1952 Cover: 0.10 **NM** value: **100.00**
3 ❑ Sep 1952 Cover: 0.10 **NM** value: **100.00**
4 ❑ Nov 1952 Cover: 0.10 **NM** value: **100.00**
5 ❑ Jan 1953 Cover: 0.10 **NM** value: **75.00**
• Trojan begins publishing
6 ❑ Mar 1953 Cover: 0.10 **NM** value: **50.00**
7 ❑ May 1953 Cover: 0.10 **NM** value: **50.00**
8 ❑ Jul 1953 Cover: 0.10 **NM** value: **50.00**

ATTACK (2ND SERIES) — Trojan

1 ❑ Jan 1953 Cover: 0.10 **NM** value: **Cover or less**
2 ❑ Mar 1953 Cover: 0.10 **NM** value: **Cover or less**
3 ❑ May 1953 Cover: 0.10 **NM** value: **Cover or less**
4 ❑ Jul 1953 Cover: 0.10 **NM** value: **Cover or less**
5 ❑ Sep 1953 Cover: 0.10 **NM** value: **50.00**
• fifth issue published by Trojan after four issues of 1st series

ATTACK (3RD SERIES) — Charlton

War comics held on long after their heyday. Some had high profile stars like Sgt. Rock and Sgt. Fury to act as a catalyst for the story. Others were anthology titles featuring the "everyman soldier." Attack, which existed in several incarnations, was one of these.

Rather than glorify the idea of war, the stories in Attack portrayed the deadly situations and grim circumstances that were part of the loyal soldier's duty. Locales were as divergent as the Congo, on a rescue mission for the U.N., to Nazi-occupied France during World War II.

1 ❑ 1962 Cover: 0.12 **NM** value: **25.00**
No number in indicia or cover. 📖 Katanga Crisis; Operation Rat-Hunt; Colini Conquers (text); The Fighting Machine; The Run To the Beach! **A:** Nicholas Alascia **W:** Nicholas Alascia
2 ❑ 1963 Cover: 0.12 **NM** value: **15.00**
3 ❑ 1964 Cover: 0.12 **NM** value: **12.00**
4 ❑ 1964 Cover: 0.12 **NM** value: **12.00**

ATTACK (4TH SERIES) — Charlton

1 ❑ Sep 1971 Cover: 0.20 **NM** value: **6.00**
• **CGC:** 1 graded, best 9.0
2 ❑ Nov 1971 Cover: 0.20 **NM** value: **3.00**
3 ❑ Jan 1972 Cover: 0.20 **NM** value: **3.00**
4 ❑ Mar 1972 Cover: 0.20 **NM** value: **2.50**
5 ❑ May 1972 Cover: 0.20 **NM** value: **2.50**
6 ❑ Jul 1972 Cover: 0.20 **NM** value: **2.00**
7 ❑ Sep 1972 Cover: 0.20 **NM** value: **2.00**
8 ❑ Nov 1972 Cover: 0.20 **NM** value: **2.00**
9 ❑ Dec 1972 Cover: 0.20 **NM** value: **2.00**
10 ❑ Feb 1973 Cover: 0.20 **NM** value: **2.00**
11 ❑ May 1973 Cover: 0.20 **NM** value: **2.00**
12 ❑ Jul 1973 Cover: 0.20 **NM** value: **2.00**
13 ❑ Sep 1973 Cover: 0.20 **NM** value: **2.00**
14 ❑ Nov 1973 Cover: 0.20 **NM** value: **2.00**
15 ❑ Mar 1975 Cover: 0.25 **NM** value: **2.00**
16 ❑ **NM** value: **2.00**
17 ❑ Sep 1979 Cover: 0.40 **NM** value: **2.00**
18 ❑ Nov 1979 Cover: 0.40 **NM** value: **2.00**
19 ❑ Jan 1980 Cover: 0.40 **NM** value: **2.00**
20 ❑ Mar 1980 Cover: 0.40 **NM** value: **2.00**
21 ❑ May 1980 Cover: 0.40 **NM** value: **2.00**
22 ❑ 1980 **NM** value: **2.00**
23 ❑ 1980 **NM** value: **2.00**
24 ❑ 1980 **NM** value: **2.00**
25 ❑ Dec 1980 Cover: 0.50 **NM** value: **2.00**
26 ❑ Feb 1981 Cover: 0.50 **NM** value: **2.00**
27 ❑ Apr 1981 Cover: 0.50 **NM** value: **2.00**
28 ❑ May 1981 Cover: 0.50 **NM** value: **2.00**
29 ❑ Jul 1981 Cover: 0.50 **NM** value: **2.00**
30 ❑ Sep 1981 Cover: 0.50 **NM** value: **2.00**
31 ❑ Nov 1981 Cover: 0.50 **NM** value: **1.50**
32 ❑ Jan 1982 Cover: 0.60 **NM** value: **1.50**
33 ❑ Mar 1982 Cover: 0.60 **NM** value: **1.50**
34 ❑ May 1982 Cover: 0.60 **NM** value: **1.50**
35 ❑ Jul 1982 Cover: 0.60 **NM** value: **1.50**
36 ❑ Sep 1982 Cover: 0.60 **NM** value: **1.50**
📖 Iron Corporal: And One Bomb; One Night in Normandy; The Soft-Hearted Conqueror
37 ❑ Nov 1982 Cover: 0.60 **NM** value: **1.50**
38 ❑ Jan 1983 Cover: 0.60 **NM** value: **1.50**
39 ❑ Mar 1983 Cover: 0.60 **NM** value: **1.50**
40 ❑ May 1983 Cover: 0.60 **NM** value: **1.50**
41 ❑ Jul 1983 Cover: 0.60 **NM** value: **1.50**
42 ❑ Sep 1983 Cover: 0.60 **NM** value: **1.50**
43 ❑ 1983 Cover: 0.60 **NM** value: **1.50**
44 ❑ 1984 Cover: 0.60 **NM** value: **1.50**
45 ❑ 1984 Cover: 0.60 **NM** value: **1.50**
46 ❑ 1984 Cover: 0.60 **NM** value: **1.50**
47 ❑ 1984 Cover: 0.60 **NM** value: **1.50**
48 ❑ Oct 1984 Cover: 0.60 **NM** value: **1.50**
final issue.

ATTACK OF THE AMAZON GIRLS — Fantaco

1 ❑ Cover: 4.95 **NM** value: **Cover or less**
No issue number. 📖 Amazon, Mara, Sirens **A:** Tom Simonton **W:** Tom Simonton

ATTACK OF THE MUTANT MONSTERS — A-Plus

1 ❑ b&w Cover: 2.50 **NM** value: **Cover or less**
A: Steve Ditko

ATTACK ON PLANET MARS — Avon

1 ❑ ca. 1951 Cover: 0.10 **NM** value: **500.00**
• **CGC:** 5 graded, best 9.0
No issue number.

AT THE SEAMS — Alternative

1 ❑ Jun 1997, b&w Cover: 2.95 **NM** value: **Cover or less**
No issue number.

ATTITUDE LAD — Slave Labor

Paul Tobin and Phil Hester's Attitude Lad is a cartoon id gone wild. He's the horny devil at the bar who has no problems proposing indecent liaisons to any female in the room. He's the guy who answers his door with a gun when a salesman comes to call. And he's the babysitter from hell who loves nothing better than messing with the minds of his young charges. In short, he's loud, obnoxious, and funny as heck.

Formerly at Iconographix, this 1994 title moved Attitude Lad to Campbell, California's Slave Labor Graphics. He's joined by the equally colorful Attitude Lass, hardened bartender-on-wheels Chesterfield, and the bodily function-obsessed Poodh & Boodw. A lot of the humor here is well beyond the bounds of good taste, but like the popular British magazine Viz, Attitude Lad manages to successfully mix the hilarious with the utterly appalling.

1 ❑ Cover: 2.95 **NM** value: **Cover or less**
📖 Little Conversations

ATTRACTIVE FORCES — NBM / Amerotica

1 ❑ Cover: 9.95 **NM** value: **Cover or less**
No issue number. • adults, graphic novel

ATTU — 4Winds

1 ❑ b&w Cover: 9.95 **NM** value: **Cover or less**
2 ❑ b&w Cover: 9.95 **NM** value: **Cover or less**

AUGIE DOGGIE — Gold Key

1 ❑ Dec 1963 Cover: 0.12 **NM** value: **90.00**
• **CGC:** 1 graded, best 9.2

AUGUST — Arrow

1 ❑ Cover: 2.95 **NM** value: **Cover or less**
2 ❑ Cover: 2.95 **NM** value: **Cover or less**
3 ❑ Cover: 2.95 **NM** value: **Cover or less**

AURORA COMIC SCENES — Aurora

1 ❑ ca. 1974 **NM** value: **25.00**
• really 181-140; small comic included in Aurora model kits
2 ❑ ca. 1974 **NM** value: **25.00**
• really 182-140; small comic included in Aurora model kits
3 ❑ ca. 1974 **NM** value: **25.00**
• really 183-140; small comic included in Aurora model kits
4 ❑ ca. 1974 **NM** value: **25.00**
• really 184-140; small comic included in Aurora model kits
5 ❑ ca. 1974 **NM** value: **25.00**
• really 185-140; small comic included in Aurora model kits
6 ❑ ca. 1974 **NM** value: **25.00**
• really 186-140; small comic included in Aurora model kits
7 ❑ ca. 1974 **NM** value: **25.00**
• really 187-140; small comic included in Aurora model kits
8 ❑ ca. 1974 **NM** value: **25.00**
• really 188-140; small comic included in Aurora model kits
9 ❑ ca. 1974 **NM** value: **25.00**
• really 192-140; small comic included in Aurora model kits
10 ❑ ca. 1974 **NM** value: **25.00**
• really 193-140; small comic included in Aurora model kits

AUTHENTIC POLICE CASES — St. John

1 ❑ Feb 1948 Cover: 0.10 **NM** value: **250.00**
• **CGC:** 1 graded, best 7.5
2 ❑ Apr 1948 Cover: 0.10 **NM** value: **175.00**
3 ❑ Jun 1948 Cover: 0.10 **NM** value: **150.00**
4 ❑ Aug 1948 Cover: 0.10 **NM** value: **150.00**
5 ❑ Oct 1948 Cover: 0.10 **NM** value: **150.00**
6 ❑ Nov 1948 Cover: 0.10 **NM** value: **150.00**
7 ❑ Apr 1949 Cover: 0.10 **NM** value: **150.00**
8 ❑ Aug 1949 Cover: 0.10 **NM** value: **150.00**
9 ❑ Oct 1949 Cover: 0.10 **NM** value: **150.00**
10 ❑ Dec 1949 Cover: 0.10 **NM** value: **150.00**
11 ❑ Feb 1950 Cover: 0.10 **NM** value: **125.00**
12 ❑ Apr 1950 Cover: 0.10 **NM** value: **125.00**
13 ❑ Jun 1950 Cover: 0.10 **NM** value: **125.00**
14 ❑ Aug 1950 Cover: 0.10 **NM** value: **125.00**
15 ❑ Oct 1950 Cover: 0.10 **NM** value: **125.00**
16 ❑ Dec 1950 Cover: 0.10 **NM** value: **125.00**
17 ❑ Feb 1951 Cover: 0.10 **NM** value: **125.00**
18 ❑ Apr 1951 Cover: 0.10 **NM** value: **125.00**
• **CGC:** 2 graded, best 7.0
19 ❑ Jun 1951 Cover: 0.10 **NM** value: **125.00**
20 ❑ Aug 1951 Cover: 0.10 **NM** value: **125.00**
21 ❑ Oct 1951 Cover: 0.10 **NM** value: **100.00**
22 ❑ Dec 1951 Cover: 0.10 **NM** value: **100.00**
23 ❑ Jan 1952 Cover: 0.10 **NM** value: **100.00**
24 ❑ Mar 1952 Cover: 0.10 **NM** value: **100.00**

CGC-graded: Multiply prices above by **33 for 9.9 M • 16 for 9.8 NM/M • 7 for 9.6 NM+ • 5 for 9.4 NM • 2.5 for 9.2 NM- • 1.5 for 9.0 VF/NM**

25 ❑ Cover: 0.25 **NM** value: **100.00**
26 ❑ Cover: 0.25 **NM** value: **100.00**
27 ❑ Cover: 0.25 **NM** value: **100.00**
28 ❑ 1953 Cover: 0.25 **NM** value: **100.00**
29 ❑ Cover: 0.10 **NM** value: **100.00**
30 ❑ Cover: 0.10 **NM** value: **100.00**
31 ❑ Cover: 0.10 **NM** value: **75.00**
32 ❑ Cover: 0.10 **NM** value: **75.00**
33 ❑ 1954 Cover: 0.10 **NM** value: **75.00**
34 ❑ 1954 Cover: 0.10 **NM** value: **75.00**
35 ❑ 1954 Cover: 0.10 **NM** value: **75.00**
36 ❑ 1954 Cover: 0.10 **NM** value: **75.00**
37 ❑ Jan 1955 Cover: 0.10 **NM** value: **75.00**
38 ❑ Mar 1955 Cover: 0.10 **NM** value: **75.00**

AUTHORITY, THE — DC / Wildstorm

The Authority, from WildStorm, picks up where StormWatch (Vol. 2) left off. With the international Stormwatch group now scattered to the winds, there is no one to defend Earth's population against a super-powered menace. Now, such an enemy exists. His army of super-villians at first savage Moscow, and next plan to cut a swath across civilization as we know it. Kaizen Gamorra, evil ruler of the island nation of Parousia will make the world his own, that is, unless the members of the Authority can stop him.

Writer Warren Ellis (Hellblazer, Transmetropolitan) and artist Bryan Hitch, the team behind the second StormWatch series, team up again to continue the adventures of the surviving members of that series in a new arena.

1 ❑ May 1999 Cover: 2.50 **NM** value: **5.00**
Circ: Diamd. preorders: **40,086** • **CGC:** 56 graded, best 9.8
wraparound cover. The Circle, Part 1 **A:** Bryan Hitch **W:** Warren Ellis

2 ❑ Jun 1999 Cover: 2.50 **NM** value: **4.00**
Circ: Diamd. preorders: **33,493** • **CGC:** 13 graded, best 9.8
The Circle, Part 2 **A:** Bryan Hitch **W:** Warren Ellis

3 ❑ Jul 1999 Cover: 2.50 **NM** value: **4.00**
Circ: Diamd. preorders: **32,878** • **CGC:** 5 graded, best 9.8
The Circle, Part 3 **A:** Bryan Hitch **W:** Warren Ellis

4 ❑ Aug 1999 Cover: 2.50 **NM** value: **3.00**
Circ: Diamd. preorders: **32,980** • **CGC:** 2 graded, best 9.6
The Circle, Part 4 **A:** Bryan Hitch **W:** Warren Ellis

5 ❑ Oct 1999 Cover: 2.50 **NM** value: **3.00**
Circ: Diamd. preorders: **32,668** • **CGC:** 3 graded, best 9.8
cover says "Sep", indicia says "Oct". Shiftships Part 1 **A:** Bryan Hitch **W:** Warren Ellis

6 ❑ Oct 1999 Cover: 2.50 **NM** value: **3.00**
Circ: Diamd. preorders: **31,702** • **CGC:** 4 graded, best 9.6
Shiftships Part 2 **A:** Bryan Hitch **W:** Warren Ellis

7 ❑ Nov 1999 Cover: 2.50 **NM** value: **3.00**
Circ: Diamd. preorders: **30,823** • **CGC:** 1 graded, best 9.0
Shiftships Part 3 **A:** Bryan Hitch **W:** Warren Ellis

8 ❑ Dec 1999 Cover: 2.50 **NM** value: **3.00**
Circ: Diamd. preorders: **31,802** • **CGC:** 3 graded, best 9.6
Shiftships Part 4 **A:** Bryan Hitch **W:** Warren Ellis

9 ❑ Jan 2000 Cover: 2.50 **NM** value: **3.00**
Circ: Diamd. preorders: **31,270** • **CGC:** 2 graded, best 9.2
Outer Dark, Part 1 **A:** Bryan Hitch **W:** Warren Ellis

10 ❑ Feb 2000 Cover: 2.50 **NM** value: **3.00**
Circ: Diamd. preorders: **31,131** • **CGC:** 1 graded, best 8.0
Outer Dark, Part 2 **A:** Bryan Hitch **W:** Warren Ellis

11 ❑ Mar 2000 Cover: 2.50 **NM** value: **Cover or less**
Circ: Diamd. preorders: **31,137** • **CGC:** 2 graded, best 9.4
Outer Dark, Part 3 **A:** Bryan Hitch **W:** Warren Ellis

12 ❑ Apr 2000 Cover: 2.50 **NM** value: **Cover or less**
Circ: Diamd. preorders: **30,202** • **CGC:** 1 graded, best 8.5
Outer Dark, Part 4 **A:** Bryan Hitch **W:** Warren Ellis

13 ❑ May 2000 Cover: 2.50 **NM** value: **Cover or less**
Circ: Diamd. preorders: **30,809** • **CGC:** 9 graded, best 9.8
The Nativity, Part 1 **A:** Frank Quitely **W:** Mark Millar

14 ❑ Jun 2000 Cover: 2.50 **NM** value: **Cover or less**
Circ: Diamd. preorders: **30,166** • **CGC:** 1 graded, best 9.6
The Nativity, Part 2 **A:** Frank Quitely **W:** Mark Millar

15 ❑ Jul 2000 Cover: 2.50 **NM** value: **Cover or less**
Circ: Diamd. preorders: **30,154**
The Nativity, Part 3 **A:** Frank Quitely **W:** Mark Millar

16 ❑ Aug 2000 Cover: 2.50 **NM** value: **Cover or less**
Circ: Diamd. preorders: **32,137**
The Nativity, Part 4 **A:** Frank Quitely **W:** Mark Millar

17 ❑ Sep 2000 Cover: 2.50 **NM** value: **Cover or less**
Circ: Diamd. preorders: **33,080**
Earth Inferno, Part 1 **A:** Chris Weston **W:** Mark Millar

18 ❑ Sep 2000 Cover: 2.50 **NM** value: **Cover or less**
Circ: Diamd. preorders: **32,722**
Earth Inferno, Part 2 **A:** Chris Weston **W:** Mark Millar

19 ❑ Nov 2000 Cover: 2.50 **NM** value: **Cover or less**
Circ: Diamd. preorders: **35,437**
Earth Inferno, Part 3 **A:** Frank Quitely **W:** Mark Millar

20 ❑ Jan 2001 Cover: 2.50 **NM** value: **Cover or less**
Circ: Diamd. preorders: **36,156** • **CGC:** 1 graded, best 9.8
Earth Inferno, Part 4 **A:** Frank Quitely **W:** Mark Millar

21 ❑ Feb 2001 Cover: 2.50 **NM** value: **Cover or less**
Circ: Diamd. preorders: **37,492** • **CGC:** 1 graded, best 9.6
Once Upon a Time… **A:** John McCrea **W:** Doselle Young

22 ❑ Mar 2001 Cover: 2.50 **NM** value: **Cover or less**
Circ: Diamd. preorders: **37,668** • **CGC:** 4 graded, best 9.8
Brave New World, Part 1 **A:** Frank Quitely **W:** Mark Millar

23 ❑ Apr 2001 Cover: 2.50 **NM** value: **Cover or less**
Circ: Diamd. preorders: **44,699** • **CGC:** 4 graded, best 9.6
Brave New World, Part 2 **A:** Frank Quitely **W:** Mark Millar

24 ❑ May 2001 Cover: 2.50 **NM** value: **Cover or less**
Circ: Diamd. preorders: **46,975** • **CGC:** 1 graded, best 9.8
Brave New World, Part 3 **A:** Frank Quitely **W:** Mark Millar

25 ❑ Jun 2001 Cover: 2.50 **NM** value: **Cover or less**
Circ: Diamd. preorders: **46,672** • **CGC:** 1 graded, best 9.8
Brave New World, Part 4 **A:** Frank Quitely **W:** Mark Millar

Anl 2000❑ Dec 2000 Cover: 3.50 **NM** value: **Cover or less**
Circ: Diamd. preorders: **26,341** • **CGC:** 1 graded, best 9.4
The Breaks **A:** Cully Hamner **W:** Joe Casey

Bk 2❑ Cover: 17.95 **NM** value: **Cover or less**
Outer Dark; The Nativity • Under New Management; Collects The Authority #9-16 **A:** Bryan Hitch; Frank Quitely **W:** Warren Ellis; Mark Millar

AUTOMATON — Image

1 ❑ Sep 1998 Cover: 2.95 **NM** value: **Cover or less**
Circ: Diamd. preorders: **10,799**
The Measure of Life, Part 1 **A:** Peter Vale **W:** A.A. Jones

2 ❑ Oct 1998 Cover: 2.95 **NM** value: **Cover or less**
Circ: Diamd. preorders: **7,636**
To Never See Home Again, Part 2 • no month of publication **A:** Peter Vale **W:** A.A. Jones

3 ❑ Nov 1998 Cover: 2.95 **NM** value: **Cover or less**
Circ: Diamd. preorders: **7,049**
Dawn's Last Light! • no month of publication **A:** Peter Vale **W:** A.A. Jones

AUTUMN — Caliber

1 ❑ 1995 Cover: 2.95 **NM** value: **Cover or less**
Lammas **A:** Horus **W:** Chris Dows; Colin Clayton
2 ❑ 1995 Cover: 2.95 **NM** value: **Cover or less**
3 ❑ Cover: 2.95 **NM** value: **Cover or less**

AUTUMN ADVENTURES (WALT DISNEY'S) — Disney

1 ❑ Cover: 2.95 **NM** value: **Cover or less**
Circ: CapCity orders: **6,200**

AVALON — Harrier

Avalon is an anthology series published by Britain's Harrier Comics. It served as a tryout book for new artists, so quality varies, although some is quite good.

Leading off the first issue was "Diana is...The Power" by Ron Sharp and Staz Johnson. This is a rather dark story of a woman with multiple personality disorder. One half of Diana's personality is a shy and conservative police officer. The other, more dominant side is "Janet," a sexy seductress with little regard for the law. When Janet takes over control of the mind, she does everything she can to screw up Diana's life. Other stories in the debut issue included "Mutant Love," a surrealistic story of doomed love by Dave Thorpe & Phil Elliott; "Grun," a lighthearted look at terrorism; and "The Alchemist" by Howard Stangroom and Peter Martin. Most of the stories in this series are of an adult nature and should be read by mature audiences only.

1 ❑ Oct 1986 Cover: 1.95 **NM** value: **Cover or less**
Diana is…The Power; Mutant Love; The Alchemist; Aces; Grunin Bombay **A:** Art Wetherell; Phil Elliott; Staz Johnson; Howard Stangroom; Paul Marshall; Pete Martin **W:** Howard Stangroom; Paul Marshall; Pete Martin; Dave Thorpe; Rob Sharp; Simon Bradshaw; Steen Agreo ★ Origin of Diana.

2 ❑ Cover: 1.95 **NM** value: **Cover or less**
Sparky's Dream; The Real Thing; Frozen Beef; Grun in Lacostêtoska, Part 1; The Unicorn: Sky Writing-Castle in the Air; Grun in Lacostatoska, Part 1

3 ❑ Cover: 1.95 **NM** value: **Cover or less**
4 ❑ Cover: 1.95 **NM** value: **Cover or less**
5 ❑ Cover: 1.95 **NM** value: **Cover or less**
6 ❑ Cover: 1.95 **NM** value: **Cover or less**
7 ❑ Cover: 1.95 **NM** value: **Cover or less**
8 ❑ Cover: 1.95 **NM** value: **Cover or less**
9 ❑ Cover: 1.95 **NM** value: **Cover or less**
10 ❑ Cover: 1.95 **NM** value: **Cover or less**
Diana is…The Power: Self Analysis; For Better…; Three Way Split, Part 3; City Lights, Part 3 **A:** Nigel Dobbyn; Dean Willette; Jon Howard; Pete Martin **W:** Nigel Dobbyn; Gary Orchard; Rob Sharp
11 ❑ Cover: 1.95 **NM** value: **Cover or less**
12 ❑ Cover: 1.95 **NM** value: **Cover or less**
13 ❑ Cover: 1.95 **NM** value: **Cover or less**
14 ❑ Cover: 1.95 **NM** value: **Cover or less**

AVANT GUARD: HEROES AT THE FUTURE'S EDGE — Day One

1 ❑ Mar 1994, b&w Cover: 2.50 **NM** value: **Cover or less**

AVATAARS: COVENANT OF THE SHIELD — Marvel

1 ❑ Cover: 2.99 **NM** value: **Cover or less**
A: Javier Saltares **W:** Len Kaminski
2 ❑ Cover: 2.99 **NM** value: **Cover or less**
A: Javier Saltares **W:** Len Kaminski
3 ❑ Nov 2000 Cover: 2.99 **NM** value: **Cover or less**
The Siege of Dreadkeep **A:** Javier Saltares **W:** Len Kaminski

AVATAR — DC

1 ❑ Cover: 5.95 **NM** value: **Cover or less**
Circ: CapCity orders: **8,750**
Forgotten Realms: Shadowdale **A:** Dameon Willich **W:** Barbara Kesel

2 ❑ Cover: 5.95 **NM** value: **Cover or less**
Circ: CapCity orders: **5,900**
Forgotten Realms: Tantras **A:** Dameon Willich **W:** Barbara Kesel

3 ❑ Cover: 5.95 **NM** value: **Cover or less**
Circ: CapCity orders: **5,150**

AVELON — Drawbridge

1 ❑ 1997 Cover: 2.95 **NM** value: **Cover or less**
The Scrolls of Dyom
2 ❑ Cover: 2.95 **NM** value: **Cover or less**
3 ❑ Cover: 2.95 **NM** value: **Cover or less**
4 ❑ Cover: 2.95 **NM** value: **Cover or less**
5 ❑ Cover: 2.95 **NM** value: **Cover or less**
6 ❑ Cover: 2.95 **NM** value: **Cover or less**
7 ❑ Cover: 2.95 **NM** value: **Cover or less**
The Legacy of Thrain **A:** Manny Vega **W:** Blaine Loyd
8 ❑ Cover: 2.95 **NM** value: **Cover or less**
9 ❑ Cover: 2.95 **NM** value: **Cover or less**

AVENGEBLADE — Maximum

1 ❑ Cover: 2.95 **NM** value: **Cover or less**
W: Rob Liefeld; Robert Napton
2 ❑ Cover: 2.95 **NM** value: **Cover or less**
A: Ching Lau; Mark Pajarillo; Dan Fraga; Michael Chang; Andy Park; Patrick Lee **W:** Rob Liefeld; Robert Napton

AVENGELYNE ARMAGEDDON — Maximum

1 ❑ Dec 1996 Cover: 2.99 **NM** value: **Cover or less**
Circ: Direct Market orders: **30,378**
2 ❑ Jan 1997 Cover: 2.99 **NM** value: **Cover or less**
Circ: Direct Market orders: **27,279**
3 ❑ Feb 1997 Cover: 2.99 **NM** value: **Cover or less**
Circ: Diamd. preorders: **24,942**
A: Scott Clark **W:** Rob Liefeld; Robert Napton

AVENGELYNE BIBLE — Maximum

1 ❑ Oct 1996 Cover: 3.50 **NM** value: **Cover or less**
A: Ching Lau; John Stinsman; Andy Park; Randy Queen; Ed Benés **W:** Robert Napton

AVENGELYNE: DEADLY SINS — Maximum

1 ❑ Feb 1996 Cover: 2.95 **NM** value: **Cover or less**
A: John Stinsman **W:** Robert Napton
1/SC❑ Feb 1996 Cover: 2.95 **NM** value: **3.50**
• **CGC:** 1 graded, best 9.4
alternate cover (photo).
2 ❑ Mar 1996 Cover: 2.95 **NM** value: **Cover or less**
A: John Stinsman

AVENGELYNE/GLORY — Maximum

This one-shot story marks the first teaming of Image Comic's co-founder Rob Liefeld's two femme fatales, Glory and Avengelyne.

The two women became smitten with a man named Devlin, an art lover and genuine Casanova. Devlin shuffled his schedule around in an effort to date both of the heroines, but the women's not-inconsiderable charms were not his true object. Devlin is a thief, and his selected prize is the Scepter of Amazonia, a powerful weapon that represents the Amazon way of life. Avengelyne ties into the story because Devlin is half-human and half-angel. His mother fell from grace, much like Avengelyne herself. Devlin's plan was to trick Glory and Avengelyne into fighting each other and ignoring him while he steals the staff.

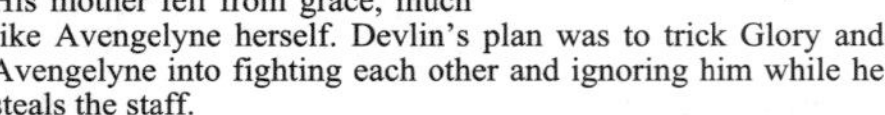

1 ❑ Sep 1995 Cover: 3.95 **NM** value: **Cover or less**
Circ: CapCity orders: **32,200** • **CGC:** 2 graded, best 9.8
wraparound chromium cover. **A:** John Stinsman **W:** Robert Napton
1/SC❑ Sep 1995 Cover: 3.95 **NM** value: **Cover or less**
variant cover. **A:** John Stinsman **W:** Robert Napton

AVENGELYNE/GLORY: THE GODYSSEY — Maximum

1 ❑ Cover: 2.99 **NM** value: **Cover or less**
A: Michael Chang; Ed Benés **W:** Rob Liefeld; Robert Napton
1/SC❑ Cover: 2.99 **NM** value: **Cover or less**
Photo cover.

AVENGELYNE (MINI-SERIES) — Maximum

1 ❑ May 1995 Cover: 2.50 **NM** value: **4.00**
Circ: CapCity orders: **29,600**
Photo cover. **A:** Rob Liefeld; John Stinsman **W:** Rob Liefeld; Robert Napton ★ Origin of Avengelyne. ★ 1st Appearance of Avengelyne.
1/A ❑ May 1995 Cover: 2.50 **NM** value: **4.00**
Photo cover. **A:** John Stinsman **W:** Rob Liefeld; Robert Napton ★ Origin of Avengelyne. ★ 1st Appearance of Avengelyne.
1/GO❑ May 1995 **NM** value: **8.00**
• Gold edition. **A:** John Stinsman **W:** Rob Liefeld; Robert Napton ★ Origin of Avengelyne. ★ 1st Appearance of Avengelyne.
1/SC❑ May 1995 Cover: 3.50 **NM** value: **4.00**
• **CGC:** 6 graded, best 9.9
chromium cover. **A:** John Stinsman **W:** Rob Liefeld; Robert Napton ★ Origin of Avengelyne. ★ 1st Appearance of Avengelyne.
2 ❑ Jun 1995 Cover: 2.50 **NM** value: **3.00**
Circ: CapCity orders: **22,925**
• polybagged with card **A:** John Stinsman **W:** Rob Liefeld; Robert Napton
3/A ❑ Jul 1995 Cover: 2.50 **NM** value: **3.00**
Circ: CapCity orders: **22,900**
Avengelyne striking with sword on cover. **A:** John Stinsman **W:** Rob Liefeld; Robert Napton

Other grades: Multiply prices above by **1.5 for Mint • 2/3 for Very Fine • 1/3 for Fine • 1/5 for Very Good • 1/8 for Good**

3/B ❑ Jul 1995 Cover: 2.50 **NM** value: **3.00**
Avengelyne standing with demons prominent on cover. **A:** John Stinsman; Arthur Adams(cover) **W:** Rob Liefeld; Robert Napton

Ash 1❑ **NM** value: **6.00**
A: John Stinsman; Arthur Adams (cover) **W:** Rob Liefeld; Robert Napton

Bk 1❑ Cover: 9.95 **NM** value: **Cover or less**
• Collects Avengelyne (Mini-Series) #1-3 **A:** John Stinsman; Arthur Adams(cover) **W:** Rob Liefeld; Robert Napton

AVENGELYNE: POWER — Maximum

1/A ❑ Nov 1995 Cover: 2.50 **NM** value: **Cover or less**
Red background on cover. **A:** John Stinsman **W:** Rob Liefeld; Robert Napton

1/B ❑ Nov 1995 Cover: 2.50 **NM** value: **Cover or less**
Blue background on cover. **A:** John Stinsman **W:** Rob Liefeld; Robert Napton

2 ❑ Dec 1995 Cover: 2.50 **NM** value: **Cover or less**

3 ❑ Jan 1996 Cover: 2.50 **NM** value: **Cover or less**

AVENGELYNE • PROPHET — Maximum

1 ❑ May 1996 Cover: 2.95 **NM** value: **Cover or less**

AVENGELYNE SWIMSUIT — Maximum

1 ❑ Aug 1995 Cover: 2.95 **NM** value: **Cover or less**
Circ: CapCity orders: **22,125** • **CGC:** 1 graded, best 9.2
• both drawn and photographed;pin-ups

1/SC❑Aug 1995 Cover: 2.95 **NM** value: **3.50**
alternate cover. • pin-ups, both drawn and photographed

AVENGELYNE (VOL. 2) — Maximum

After numerous mini-series and one-shots, Avengelyne got her first ongoing series in 1996. Avengelyne is "a fallen angel who was sent to earth as a punishment for her sins. Once a fearsome member of God's Warhost, Avengelyne must now live as a mortal, albeit with extraordinary physical strength." She also has a big sword, and disarmingly skimpy clothes. With these, she takes on a demonic conspiracy headed by B'liale, assorted businessmen, and their supernatural allies.

Avengelyne is based on the likeness of Cathy Christian, a very pretty model who made her mark posing on the convention circuit as Vampirella. She and Harris Comics parted ways in the early 1990s, only to reemerge the next year wearing a leather outfit and sword. She announced that a new comics character had been created especially for her by Rob Liefeld. That character, of course, was Avengelyne.

0 ❑ Oct 1996 Cover: 2.99 **NM** value: **3.00**
Circ: Diamd. preorders: **40,867**

0.5 ❑ **NM** value: **3.00**
• **CGC:** 3 graded, best 9.6
• Wizard promotional mail-in edition. **A:** Andy Park **W:** Rob Liefeld; Robert Napton

0.5/PI❑ **NM** value: **6.00**
• Platinum edition with certificate of authenticity (Wizard promo). **A:** Andy Park **W:** Rob Liefeld; Robert Napton

1 ❑ Apr 1996 Cover: 2.50 **NM** value: **3.00**
Circ: Diamd. preorders: **32,555**

1/SC❑Apr 1996 Cover: 2.95 **NM** value: **3.50**
alternate cover (photo wraparound).

2 ❑ May 1996 Cover: 2.50 **NM** value: **4.00**
Circ: Diamd. preorders: **21,345** • **CGC:** 2 graded, best 9.8
★ 1st Appearance of Darkchylde.

2/A ❑ May 1996 Cover: 2.50 **NM** value: **8.00**
• **CGC:** 2 graded, best 9.6
Photo cover. ★ 1st Appearance of Darkchylde.

2/B ❑ May 1996 Cover: 2.50 **NM** value: **15.00**
• **CGC:** 1 graded, best 9.0
Nude cover. ★ 1st Appearance of Darkchylde.

3 ❑ Jun 1996 Cover: 2.50 **NM** value: **Cover or less**
Circ: Diamd. preorders: **19,621**

4 ❑ Jul 1996 Cover: 2.50 **NM** value: **Cover or less**
A: Andy Park **W:** Tom Sniegoski ★ Appearance of Cybrid.

5 ❑ Aug 1996 Cover: 2.99 **NM** value: **Cover or less**
Circ: Diamd. preorders: **37,287**
• flipbook with Blindside preview **A:** Andy Park **W:** Rob Liefeld; Tom Sniegoski ★ Appearance of Cybrid.

6 ❑ Sep 1996 Cover: 2.99 **NM** value: **Cover or less**
Circ: Diamd. preorders: **31,991**
A: John Stinsman **W:** Rob Liefeld; Robert Napton

7 ❑ Nov 1996 Cover: 2.99 **NM** value: **Cover or less**
Circ: Diamd. preorders: **30,105**

8 ❑ Dec 1996 Cover: 2.99 **NM** value: **Cover or less**
Circ: Direct Market orders: **27,621**
A: John Stinsman **W:** Rob Liefeld; Robert Napton

9 ❑ Jan 1997 Cover: 2.99 **NM** value: **Cover or less**
Circ: Direct Market orders: **27,345**

10 ❑ Feb 1997 Cover: 2.99 **NM** value: **Cover or less**
Circ: Diamd. preorders: **27,297**
The Possession, Part 1 **A:** John Stinsman **W:** Rob Liefeld; Robert Napton

11 ❑ Mar 1997 Cover: 2.99 **NM** value: **Cover or less**
Circ: Diamd. preorders: **27,297**
The Possession, Part 2

11/SC❑Mar 1997 Cover: 2.99 **NM** value: **Cover or less**
alternate cover (multiple characters behind Avengelyne). The Possession, Part 2

12 ❑ Cover: 2.99 **NM** value: **Cover or less**

13 ❑ Cover: 2.99 **NM** value: **Cover or less**

14 ❑ Cover: 2.99 **NM** value: **Cover or less**

15 ❑ Cover: 2.99 **NM** value: **Cover or less**
final issue.

AVENGELYNE (VOL. 3) — Awesome

1 ❑ Mar 1999 Cover: 2.50 **NM** value: **Cover or less**
A: Dan Fraga **W:** Rob Liefeld; Robert Napton

AVENGELYNE/WARRIOR NUN AREALA — Maximum

1/A ❑ Nov 1996 Cover: 2.99 **NM** value: **Cover or less**
Avengelynein front on cover. **A:** Dan Fraga; Michael Chang **W:** Rob Liefeld; Robert Napton

1/B ❑ Nov 1996 Cover: 2.99 **NM** value: **Cover or less**
Two women back-to-back on cover. **A:** Dan Fraga; Michael Chang **W:** Rob Liefeld; Robert Napton

AVENGER, THE — AC

Ash 0❑ Cover: 5.95 **NM** value: **Cover or less**

AVENGERS, THE — Marvel

September 1963 gave birth to two of Marvel's greatest super-groups: The Uncanny X-Men and the Avengers, "Earth's Mightiest Heroes." Originally consisting of Thor, Iron Man, Ant-Man, Wasp, and The Incredible Hulk, the team was soon joined by Captain America (in issue #4). Since then, it seems that virtually every Marvel super-hero has served as a one-time Avenger. Even such famous loners as Spider-Man have briefly served with this legendary fighting team.

Like a large corporation, The Avengers have even divisionalized, giving birth to the Great Lakes Avengers and the more famous West Coast Avengers. These teams operated independently, although they occasionally combined forces, as in the Infinity Gauntlet series, to fight a great enemy.

-1 ❑ Cover: 1.99 **NM** value: **2.00**
• Flashback

0 ❑ **NM** value: **3.00**
• Wizard promotional edition.

1 ❑ Sep 1963 Cover: 0.12 **NM** value: **2300.00**
• **CGC:** 140 graded, best 9.6
The Coming of the Avengers • 1st appearance/origin of the Avengers; Team consists of Thor, Ant-Man, Wasp, Hulk, and Iron Man **A:** Jack Kirby **W:** Jack Kirby; Stan Lee ★ Origin of Avengers.

1.5 ❑ Dec 1999 Cover: 2.50 **NM** value: **Cover or less**
The Death-Trap of Doctor Doom! • Issue #1-1/2 **A:** Bruce Timm **W:** Roger Stern

2 ❑ Nov 1963 Cover: 0.12 **NM** value: **600.00**
• **CGC:** 88 graded, best 9.6
The Avengers Battle the Space Phantom • Hulk leaves Avengers;Ant-Man becomes Giant-Man **A:** Jack Kirby **W:** Jack Kirby; Stan Lee ★ 1st Appearance of Space Phantom.

3 ❑ Jan 1964 Cover: 0.12 **NM** value: **400.00**
• **CGC:** 44 graded, best 9.6
The Avengers Meet Sub-Mariner • Avengers vs. Sub-Mariner and Hulk **A:** Jack Kirby **W:** Jack Kirby; Stan Lee

4 ❑ Mar 1964 Cover: 0.12 **NM** value: **1525.00**
• **CGC:** 193 graded, best 9.6
Captain America Joins the Avengers • Captain America returns;Capt. America returns **A:** Jack Kirby **W:** Jack Kirby; Stan Lee ★ 1st Appearance of Baron Zemo.

5 ❑ May 1964 Cover: 0.12 **NM** value: **225.00**
• **CGC:** 37 graded, best 9.6
The Invasion of the Lava Man • Hulk leaves team **A:** Jack Kirby **W:** Jack Kirby; Stan Lee

6 ❑ Jul 1964 Cover: 0.12 **NM** value: **175.00**
• **CGC:** 32 graded, best 9.8
Masters of Evil **A:** Jack Kirby **W:** Jack Kirby; Stan Lee ★ 1st Appearance of Masters of Evil.

7 ❑ Aug 1964 Cover: 0.12 **NM** value: **175.00**
• **CGC:** 32 graded, best 9.4
Their Darkest Hour **A:** Jack Kirby **W:** Jack Kirby; Stan Lee

8 ❑ Sep 1964 Cover: 0.12 **NM** value: **175.00**
• **CGC:** 31 graded, best 9.6
Kang, the Conqueror **A:** Jack Kirby **W:** Jack Kirby; Stan Lee ★ Origin of Kang. ★ 1st Appearance of Kang.

9 ❑ Oct 1964 Cover: 0.12 **NM** value: **185.00**
• **CGC:** 25 graded, best 9.6
The Coming of the Wonder Man **A:** Don Heck; Jack Kirby **W:** Stan Lee ★ Origin of Wonder Man. ★ 1st Appearance of Wonder Man. ★ Death of Wonder Man.

10 ❑ Nov 1964 Cover: 0.12 **NM** value: **160.00**
• **CGC:** 38 graded, best 9.8
The Avengers Break Up **A:** Don Heck; Jack Kirby **W:** Stan Lee ★ 1st Appearance of Hercules, Immortus.

11 ❑ Dec 1964 Cover: 0.12 **NM** value: **140.00**
• **CGC:** 67 graded, best 9.6
The Mighty Avengers Meet Spider-Man • Spider-Man **A:** Don Heck; Jack Kirby **W:** Stan Lee ★ Appearance of Spider-Man.

12 ❑ Jan 1965 Cover: 0.12 **NM** value: **90.00**
• **CGC:** 24 graded, best 9.6
This Hostage Earth **A:** Don Heck; Jack Kirby **W:** Stan Lee ★ 1st Appearance of Monk Keefer (later becomes Ape-Man I). ★ Versus Mole Man.

13 ❑ Feb 1965 Cover: 0.12 **NM** value: **90.00**
• **CGC:** 22 graded, best 9.6
The Castle of Count Nefaria **A:** Don Heck; Jack Kirby **W:** Stan Lee ★ 1st Appearance of Count Nefaria.

14 ❑ Mar 1965 Cover: 0.12 **NM** value: **90.00**
• **CGC:** 38 graded, best 9.8
Even Avengers Can Die • The Watcher **A:** Jack Kirby **W:** Jack Kirby; Stan Lee; Paul Laiken ★ 1st Appearance of Ogor and Kallusians.

15 ❑ Apr 1965 Cover: 0.12 **NM** value: **90.00**
• **CGC:** 36 graded, best 9.8
Now, By My Hand, Shall Die a Villain • Death of Baron Zemo **A:** Jack Kirby **W:** Jack Kirby; Stan Lee ★ Death of Baron Zemo I (Heinrich Zemo).

16 ❑ May 1965 Cover: 0.12 **NM** value: **90.00**
• **CGC:** 32 graded, best 9.6
The Old Order Changeth • Cap assembles new team of Hawkeye, Quicksilver, Scarlet Witch;New team begins: Captain America, Hawkeye, Quicksilver, and Scarlet Witch **A:** Jack Kirby **W:** Jack Kirby; Stan Lee

17 ❑ Jun 1965 Cover: 0.12 **NM** value: **70.00**
• **CGC:** 25 graded, best 9.6
Four Against the Minotaur **A:** Jack Kirby **W:** Stan Lee

18 ❑ Jul 1965 Cover: 0.12 **NM** value: **70.00**
• **CGC:** 31 graded, best 9.6
When the Commissar Commands **A:** Don Heck; Jack Kirby **W:** Stan Lee

19 ❑ Aug 1965 Cover: 0.12 **NM** value: **75.00**
• **CGC:** 22 graded, best 9.6
The Coming of the Swordsman • origin of Hawkeye **A:** Don Heck; Jack Kirby **W:** Stan Lee ★ Origin of Hawkeye. ★ 1st Appearance of Swordsman.

20 ❑ Sep 1965 Cover: 0.12 **NM** value: **40.00**
• **CGC:** 20 graded, best 9.8
Vengeance is Ours **A:** Don Heck; Wally Wood **W:** Stan Lee ★ Versus Swordsman.

21 ❑ Oct 1965 Cover: 0.12 **NM** value: **40.00**
• **CGC:** 8 graded, best 9.8
The Bitter Taste of Defeat • Power Man **A:** Don Heck; Jack Kirby **W:** Stan Lee ★ Origin of Power Man I (Erik Josten). ★ 1st Appearance of Power Man I (Erik Josten).

22 ❑ Nov 1965 Cover: 0.12 **NM** value: **40.00**
• **CGC:** 28 graded, best 9.6
The Road Back **A:** Don Heck; Jack Kirby **W:** Stan Lee

23 ❑ Dec 1965 Cover: 0.12 **NM** value: **40.00**
• **CGC:** 12 graded, best 9.6
Once an Avenger **A:** Don Heck; Jack Kirby **W:** Stan Lee ★ 1st Appearance of Ravonna.

24 ❑ Jan 1966 Cover: 0.12 **NM** value: **40.00**
Circ: Statement: **269,994** • **CGC:** 47 graded, best 9.8
From the Ashes of Defeat **A:** Don Heck; Jack Kirby **W:** Stan Lee ★ Appearance of Kang, Doctor Doom, Princess Ravonna.

25 ❑ Feb 1966 Cover: 0.12 **NM** value: **40.00**
Circ: Statement: **269,994** • **CGC:** 13 graded, best 9.6
Enter Dr. Doom **A:** Don Heck; Jack Kirby **W:** Stan Lee ★ Appearance of Mr. Fantastic, Invisible Girl, Thing, Human Torch, Doctor Doom.

26 ❑ Mar 1966 Cover: 0.12 **NM** value: **40.00**
Circ: Statement: **269,994** • **CGC:** 13 graded, best 9.4
The Voice of the Wasp **A:** Don Heck; Jack Kirby **W:** Stan Lee ★ Appearance of Henry Pym, Puppet Master, Beetle, Tony Stark, Attuma, Sub-Mariner, The Wasp.

27 ❑ Apr 1966 Cover: 0.12 **NM** value: **40.00**
Circ: Statement: **269,994** • **CGC:** 20 graded, best 9.6
Four Against the Floodtide **A:** Don Heck; Jack Kirby **W:** Stan Lee ★ Appearance of Mr. Fantastic, Invisible Girl, Collector, Henry Pym, Beetle, Attuma.

28 ❑ May 1966 Cover: 0.12 **NM** value: **40.00**
Circ: Statement: **269,994** • **CGC:** 7 graded, best 9.4
Among Us Walks a Goliath • Giant-Man becomes Goliath;Goliath rejoins Avengers;Wasp rejoins Avengers **A:** Don Heck; Jack Kirby **W:** Stan Lee ★ 1st Appearance of The Collector, Goliath. ★ Appearance of Beetle.

29 ❑ Jun 1966 Cover: 0.12 **NM** value: **40.00**
Circ: Statement: **269,994** • **CGC:** 8 graded, best 9.4
This Power Unleashed • Power Man I; Black Widow **A:** Don Heck; Jack Kirby **W:** Stan Lee ★ 1st Appearance of Hu Chen, Doctor Yen. ★ Appearance of Black Widow, S.H.I.E.L.D., Swordsman.

30 ❑ Jul 1966 Cover: 0.12 **NM** value: **40.00**
Circ: Statement: **269,994** • **CGC:** 8 graded, best 9.6
Frenzy in a Far-Off Land • Quicksilver & Scarlet Witch leave Avengers **A:** Don Heck; Jack Kirby **W:** Stan Lee ★ 1st Appearance of Doctor Frantz Anton, Keeper of the Flame, Prince Rey. ★ Appearance of Black Widow, Power Man I, Hu Chen, Swordsman.

31 ❑ Aug 1966 Cover: 0.12 **NM** value: **26.00**
Circ: Statement: **269,994** • **CGC:** 10 graded, best 9.6
Never Bug a Giant **A:** Don Heck; Jack Kirby **W:** Stan Lee

32 ❑ Sep 1966 Cover: 0.12 **NM** value: **26.00**
Circ: Statement: **269,994** • **CGC:** 21 graded, best 9.6
The Sign of the Serpent • Black Widow **A:** Don Heck **W:** Stan Lee ★ 1st Appearance of Sons of the Serpent, Supreme Serpent I, Bill Foster (Giant-Man II). ★ Appearance of Black Widow, Scarlet Witch, Quicksilver, Nick Fury, Tony Stark.

33 ❑ Oct 1966 Cover: 0.12 **NM** value: **26.00**
Circ: Statement: **269,994** • **CGC:** 11 graded, best 9.6
To Smash a Serpent • Black Widow **A:** Don Heck **W:** Stan Lee ★ Appearance of Black Widow.

34 ❑ Nov 1966 Cover: 0.12 **NM** value: **26.00**
Circ: Statement: **269,994** • **CGC:** 10 graded, best 9.4
The Living Laser **A:** Don Heck **W:** Stan Lee ★ Origin of Living Laser. ★ 1st Appearance of Living Laser, Lucy Barton.

35 ❑ Dec 1966 Cover: 0.12 **NM** value: **26.00**
Circ: Statement: **269,994** • **CGC:** 11 graded, best 9.6
The Light that Failed **A:** Don Heck **W:** Roy Thomas; Stan Lee ★ 1st Appearance of Ultrana (off page). ★ 2nd Appearance of Living Laser, Lucy Barton. ★ Appearance of Black Widow, Bill Foster.

36 ❑ Jan 1967 Cover: 0.12 **NM** value: **26.00**
Circ: Statement: **269,139** • **CGC:** 13 graded, best 9.6
The Ultroids Attack • Quicksilver & Scarlet Witch rejoin Avengers **A:** Don Heck **W:** Roy Thomas ★ 1st Appearance of Ultroids, Ultrana (full), Ixar. ★ Appearance of Black Widow.

37 ❑ Feb 1967 Cover: 0.12 **NM** value: **26.00**
Circ: Statement: **269,139** • **CGC:** 15 graded, best 9.4

CGC-graded: Multiply prices above by **33 for 9.9 M** • **16 for 9.8 NM/M** • **7 for 9.6 NM+** • **5 for 9.4 NM** • **2.5 for 9.2 NM-** • **1.5 for 9.0 VF/NM**

To Conquer a Colossus • Black Widow; Ultroids consolidate into giant robot Ultroid **A:** Don Heck **W:** Roy Thomas ★ 2nd Appearance of Ultroids, Ultrana, Ixar. ★ Appearance of Black Widow.

38 ❑ Mar 1967 Cover: 0.12 **NM** value: **26.00**
Circ: Statement: **269,139 • CGC:** 11 graded, best 9.6
In Our Midst, an Immortal • Hercules; Captain America leaves Avengers; Has 1966 Statement, filed 10/1/66; avg print run 423,601; avg sales 267,994X; avg subs 2,000; avg total paid 269,994; samples 60; max existent 270,054; 36% of run returned **A:** Don Heck **W:** Roy Thomas ★ Appearance of Hercules, Black Widow.

39 ❑ Apr 1967 Cover: 0.12 **NM** value: **26.00**
Circ: Statement: **269,139 • CGC:** 12 graded, best 9.6
The Torment and the Triumph • Hercules **A:** Don Heck **W:** Roy Thomas ★ Appearance of Hercules, Black Widow, S.H.I.E.L.D., Jasper Sitwell, Dum Dum Dugan, Nick Fury, Mad Thinker.

40 ❑ May 1967 Cover: 0.12 **NM** value: **26.00**
Circ: Statement: **269,139 • CGC:** 17 graded, best 9.6
Suddenly, the Sub-Mariner **A:** Don Heck **W:** Roy Thomas ★ Appearance of Hercules, Black Widow, Sub-Mariner. ★ Versus Sub-Mariner.

41 ❑ Jun 1967 Cover: 0.12 **NM** value: **20.00**
Circ: Statement: **269,139 • CGC:** 10 graded, best 9.6
Let Sleeping Dragons Lie • Mr. Fantastic cameo;Human Torch cameo **A:** John Buscema **W:** Roy Thomas ★ 1st Appearance of Colonel Ling. ★ 2nd Appearance of Doctor Yen. ★ Appearance of Hercules, Black Widow, Dragon Man, Bill Foster, Diablo.

42 ❑ Jul 1967 Cover: 0.12 **NM** value: **20.00**
Circ: Statement: **269,139 • CGC:** 11 graded, best 9.8
The Plan and the Power • Captain America rejoins the Avengers **A:** John Buscema **W:** Roy Thomas ★ Versus Diablo, Dragon Man.

43 ❑ Aug 1967 Cover: 0.12 **NM** value: **20.00**
Circ: Statement: **269,139 • CGC:** 10 graded, best 9.4
Color Him the Red Guardian **A:** John Buscema **W:** Roy Thomas ★ 1st Appearance of General Yuri Brushov, Red Guardian I (Alexi Shostakov). ★ Appearance of Hercules, Black Widow, Edwin Jarvis, Colonel Ling.

44 ❑ Sep 1967 Cover: 0.12 **NM** value: **20.00**
Circ: Statement: **269,139 • CGC:** 13 graded, best 9.6
The Valiant also Die **A:** John Buscema **W:** Roy Thomas ★ Origin of Red Guardian I (Alexi Shostakov), Black Widow (part). ★ 2nd Appearance of Red Guardian I (Alexi Shostakov). ★ Appearance of Hercules, Black Widow, Colonel Ling. ★ Death of Red Guardian I (Alexi Shostakov).

45 ❑ Oct 1967 Cover: 0.12 **NM** value: **20.00**
Circ: Statement: **269,139 • CGC:** 8 graded, best 9.6
Blitzkrieg in Central Park • Hercules joins team; Hercules joins Avengers; Black Widow retires **A:** Don Heck **W:** Don Heck; Roy Thomas ★ Appearance of Super-Adaptoid, Iron Man I, Thor. ★ Versus Super-Adaptoid.

46 ❑ Nov 1967 Cover: 0.12 **NM** value: **20.00**
Circ: Statement: **269,139 • CGC:** 11 graded, best 9.6
The Agony and the Ant-Hill! • Goliath regains Ant-Man powers **W:** Roy Thomas ★ 1st Appearance of Whirlwind.

47 ❑ Dec 1967 Cover: 0.12 **NM** value: **20.00**
Circ: Statement: **269,139 • CGC:** 14 graded, best 9.6
Magneto Walks the Earth! • New Black Knight (Dr. Dane Whitman) origin part 1 **W:** Roy Thomas ★ Death of Black Knight II (Nathan Garrett).

48 ❑ Jan 1968 Cover: 0.12 **NM** value: **20.00**
Circ: Statement: **276,951 • CGC:** 16 graded, best 9.6
The Black Knight Lives Again! • New Black Knight (Dr. Dane Whitman) origin part 2 **W:** Roy Thomas ★ Origin of Aragorn. ★ 1st Appearance of Black Knight III (Dane Whitman), Aragorn.

49 ❑ Feb 1968 Cover: 0.12 **NM** value: **20.00**
Circ: Statement: **276,951 • CGC:** 13 graded, best 9.6
Mine Is The Power! • Quicksilver & Scarlet Witch leave Avengers; Goliath loses powers **A:** John Buscema **W:** Roy Thomas ★ Appearance of Magneto.

50 ❑ Mar 1968 Cover: 0.12 **NM** value: **20.00**
Circ: Statement: **276,951 • CGC:** 22 graded, best 9.6
To Tame A Titan! • Herculese leaves the Avengers; Has 1967 Statement, filed 10/1/67; avg print run 454,498; avg sales 267,639; avg subs 1,500; avg total paid 269,139; samples 95; max existent 269,234; 41% of run returned **A:** John Buscema **W:** Roy Thomas

51 ❑ Apr 1968 Cover: 0.12 **NM** value: **20.00**
Circ: Statement: **276,951 • CGC:** 9 graded, best 9.4
In The Clutches Of The Collector! • Thor, Iron Man; Goliath regains powers, new costume **A:** John Buscema **W:** Roy Thomas

52 ❑ May 1968 Cover: 0.12 **NM** value: **24.00**
Circ: Statement: **276,951 • CGC:** 16 graded, best 9.8
Death Calls for the Arch-Heroes! • Black Panther joins★ Origin of Grim Reaper. ★ 1st Appearance of Grim Reaper.

53 ❑ Jun 1968 Cover: 0.12 **NM** value: **35.00**
Circ: Statement: **276,951 • CGC:** 23 graded, best 9.6
In Battle Joined! **A:** John Buscema ★ Appearance of X-Men.

54 ❑ Jul 1968 Cover: 0.12 **NM** value: **18.00**
Circ: Statement: **276,951 • CGC:** 8 graded, best 9.4
And Deliver Us From the Masters of Evil! **A:** John Buscema ★ 1st Appearance of Crimson Cowl.

55 ❑ Aug 1968 Cover: 0.12 **NM** value: **18.00**
Circ: Statement: **276,951 • CGC:** 13 graded, best 9.8
Mayhem Over Manhattan! **A:** John Buscema ★ 1st Appearance of Ultron-5.

56 ❑ Sep 1968 Cover: 0.12 **NM** value: **18.00**
Circ: Statement: **276,951 • CGC:** 7 graded, best 9.4
Death Be Not Proud **A:** John Buscema

57 ❑ Oct 1968 Cover: 0.12 **NM** value: **65.00**
Circ: Statement: **276,951 • CGC:** 49 graded, best 9.6
Behold, the Vision! • First Vision **A:** John Buscema ★ 1st Appearance of The Vision II (android).

58 ❑ Nov 1968 Cover: 0.12 **NM** value: **45.00**
Circ: Statement: **276,951 • CGC:** 19 graded, best 9.6
Even An Android Can Cry • Origin of the Vision; The Vision joins the Avengers; Thor, Captain America, Iron Man **A:** John Buscema ★ Origin of The Vision II (android).

59 ❑ Dec 1968 Cover: 0.12 **NM** value: **22.00**
Circ: Statement: **276,951 • CGC:** 6 graded, best 9.4
The Name Is Yellowjacket! • Goliath becomes Yellowjacket **A:** John Buscema ★ 1st Appearance of Yellowjacket.

60 ❑ Jan 1969 Cover: 0.12 **NM** value: **22.00**
Circ: Statement: **239,986 • CGC:** 5 graded, best 9.4
'Till Death Do Us Part! • Yellowjacket marries Wasp; Captain America **A:** John Buscema

61 ❑ Feb 1969 Cover: 0.12 **NM** value: **18.00**
Circ: Statement: **239,986 • CGC:** 5 graded, best 9.4
Some Say the World Will End in Fire, Some Say in Ice • Doctor Strange **A:** John Buscema **W:** Roy Thomas

62 ❑ Mar 1969 Cover: 0.12 **NM** value: **18.00**
Circ: Statement: **239,986 • CGC:** 3 graded, best 9.6
The Monarch and the Man-Ape • Has 1968 Statement, filed 10/1/68; avg print run 428,600; avg sales 275,421; avg subs 1,530; avg total paid 276,951; samples 400; max existent 277,351; 35% of run returned **A:** John Buscema **W:** Roy Thomas ★ 1st Appearance of W'Kabi, The Man-Ape.

63 ❑ Apr 1969 Cover: 0.12 **NM** value: **18.00**
Circ: Statement: **239,986 • CGC:** 2 graded, best 9.4
And in This Corner, Goliath **A:** Gene Colan **W:** Roy Thomas ★ Origin of Goliath-New (Hawkeye). ★ 1st Appearance of Goliath-New (Hawkeye).

64 ❑ May 1969 Cover: 0.12 **NM** value: **18.00**
Circ: Statement: **239,986 • CGC:** 7 graded, best 9.6
Like a Death Ray From the Sky • Black Widow; Hawkeye's identity revealed **A:** Gene Colan **W:** Roy Thomas

65 ❑ Jun 1969 Cover: 0.12 **NM** value: **18.00**
Circ: Statement: **239,986 • CGC:** 5 graded, best 9.6
Mightier Than the Sword? **A:** Gene Colan **W:** Roy Thomas ★ Origin of Hawkeye.

66 ❑ Jul 1969 Cover: 0.15 **NM** value: **18.00**
Circ: Statement: **239,986 • CGC:** 7 graded, best 9.6
Betrayal! **A:** Barry Windsor-Smith **W:** Roy Thomas

67 ❑ Aug 1969 Cover: 0.15 **NM** value: **18.00**
Circ: Statement: **239,986 • CGC:** 6 graded, best 9.6
We Stand at Armageddon **A:** Barry Windsor-Smith **W:** Roy Thomas

68 ❑ Sep 1969 Cover: 0.15 **NM** value: **15.00**
Circ: Statement: **239,986 • CGC:** 5 graded, best 9.4
And We Battle for the Earth **A:** Sal Buscema **W:** Roy Thomas

69 ❑ Oct 1969 Cover: 0.15 **NM** value: **15.00**
Circ: Statement: **239,986 • CGC:** 5 graded, best 9.4
Let the Game Begin • First Nighthawk; Captain America and Black Panther rejoin **A:** Sal Buscema **W:** Roy Thomas ★ 1st Appearance of Grandmaster, Nighthawk II (Kyle Richmond)-Full.

70 ❑ Nov 1969 Cover: 0.15 **NM** value: **15.00**
Circ: Statement: **239,986 • CGC:** 1 graded, best 9.2
When Strikes the Squadron Sinister **A:** Sal Buscema **W:** Roy Thomas

71 ❑ Dec 1969 Cover: 0.15 **NM** value: **20.00**
Circ: Statement: **239,986 • CGC:** 9 graded, best 9.4
Endgame • Human Torch, Golden Age Captain America and Sub-Mariner; Black Knight joins Avengers **A:** Sal Buscema **W:** Roy Thomas ★ 1st Appearance of Invaders (prototype).

72 ❑ Jan 1970 Cover: 0.15 **NM** value: **12.00**
Circ: Statement: **217,394**
Did You Hear the One About Scorpio? **A:** Sal Buscema **W:** Roy Thomas ★ 1st Appearance of Zodiac I, Taurus, Pisces I.

73 ❑ Feb 1970 Cover: 0.15 **NM** value: **12.00**
Circ: Statement: **217,394 • CGC:** 3 graded, best 9.8
The Sting of the Serpent • Quicksilver, Scarlet Witch return; Yellowjacket and Wasp leave **A:** Herb Trimpe; Frank Giacoia **W:** Roy Thomas

74 ❑ Mar 1970 Cover: 0.15 **NM** value: **12.00**
Circ: Statement: **217,394 • CGC:** 6 graded, best 9.8
Pursue the Panther • Has 1969 Statement, filed 10/1/69; avg print run 411,541; avg sales 238,606; avg subs 1,380; avg total paid ,239,986; samples 110; max existent 240,096; 42% of run returned **A:** John Buscema **W:** Roy Thomas

75 ❑ Apr 1970 Cover: 0.15 **NM** value: **14.00**
Circ: Statement: **217,394 • CGC:** 2 graded, best 9.4
The Warlord and the Witch **A:** John Buscema **W:** Roy Thomas ★ 1st Appearance of Arkon.

76 ❑ May 1970 Cover: 0.15 **NM** value: **12.00**
Circ: Statement: **217,394 • CGC:** 2 graded, best 9.4
The Blaze of Battle, the Flames of Love **A:** John Buscema **W:** Roy Thomas

77 ❑ Jun 1970 Cover: 0.15 **NM** value: **12.00**
Circ: Statement: **217,394 • CGC:** 2 graded, best 9.6
Heroes for Hire **A:** John Buscema **W:** Roy Thomas ★ 1st Appearance of the Split-Second Squad.

78 ❑ Jul 1970 Cover: 0.15 **NM** value: **12.00**
Circ: Statement: **217,394 • CGC:** 2 graded, best 9.4
The Man-Ape Always Strikes Twice **A:** John Buscema **W:** Roy Thomas

79 ❑ Aug 1970 Cover: 0.15 **NM** value: **12.00**
Circ: Statement: **217,394 • CGC:** 3 graded, best 9.4
Lo, the Lethal Legion **A:** John Buscema **W:** Roy Thomas

80 ❑ Sep 1970 Cover: 0.15 **NM** value: **12.00**
Circ: Statement: **217,394 • CGC:** 4 graded, best 9.4
The Coming of Red Wolf **A:** John Buscema **W:** Roy Thomas ★ Origin of Red Wolf. ★ 1st Appearance of Red Wolf.

81 ❑ Oct 1970 Cover: 0.15 **NM** value: **12.00**
Circ: Statement: **217,394 • CGC:** 1 graded, best 9.8
When Dies a Legend **A:** John Buscema **W:** Roy Thomas

82 ❑ Nov 1970 Cover: 0.15 **NM** value: **12.00**
Circ: Statement: **217,394 • CGC:** 1 graded, best 9.2
Hostage • Daredevil **A:** John Buscema **W:** Roy Thomas

83 ❑ Dec 1970 Cover: 0.15 **NM** value: **13.00**
Circ: Statement: **217,394 • CGC:** 2 graded, best 9.6
Come On In, the Revolution's Fine • First Valkyrie **A:** John Buscema **W:** Roy Thomas ★ 1st Appearance of Valkyrie.

84 ❑ Jan 1971 Cover: 0.15 **NM** value: **12.00**
Circ: Statement: **206,478 • CGC:** 1 graded, best 9.2
The Sword and the Sorceress • Black Knight's sword destroyed **A:** John Buscema **W:** Roy Thomas

85 ❑ Feb 1971 Cover: 0.15 **NM** value: **12.00**
Circ: Statement: **206,478 • CGC:** 2 graded, best 9.6
The World Is Not For Burning **A:** John Buscema **W:** Roy Thomas ★ 1st Appearance of Whizzer II (Stanley Stewart), Hawkeye II (Wyatt McDonald), American Eagle II (James Dore Jr.), Tom Thumb, Doctor Spectrum I (Joe Ledger).

86 ❑ Mar 1971 Cover: 0.15 **NM** value: **12.00**
Circ: Statement: **206,478 • CGC:** 2 graded, best 9.0
Brain-Child to the Dark Tower Came • Has 1970 Statement, filed 10/1/70; avg print run 385,239; avg sales 216,059; avg subs 1,335; avg total paid 217,394; samples 0; office use 110; max existent 217,504; 44% of run returned **A:** John Buscema; Sal Buscema **W:** Roy Thomas ★ 1st Appearance of Brain-Child.

87 ❑ Apr 1971 Cover: 0.15 **NM** value: **25.00**
Circ: Statement: **206,478 • CGC:** 5 graded, best 9.4
Look Homeward, Avenger • Black Panther origin retold **A:** Frank Giacoia **W:** Roy Thomas ★ Origin of Black Panther.

88 ❑ May 1971 Cover: 0.15 **NM** value: **12.00**
Circ: Statement: **206,478 • CGC:** 1 graded, best 9.4
The Summons of Psyklop **A:** Sal Buscema **W:** Roy Thomas; Harlan Ellison ★ 1st Appearance of Psyklop.

88-2 ❑ Cover: 0.15 **NM** value: **1.50**

89 ❑ Jun 1971 Cover: 0.15 **NM** value: **12.00**
Circ: Statement: **206,478 • CGC:** 1 graded, best 8.5
The Only Good Alien • Kree/Skrull War part 1; Captain Marvel **A:** Sal Buscema **W:** Roy Thomas

90 ❑ Jul 1971 Cover: 0.15 **NM** value: **12.00**
Circ: Statement: **206,478 • CGC:** 1 graded, best 9.4
Judgment Day • Kree/Skrull War part 2; Captain Marvel origin retold **A:** Sal Buscema **W:** Roy Thomas

91 ❑ Aug 1971 Cover: 0.15 **NM** value: **12.00**
Circ: Statement: **206,478**
Take One Giant Step-Backward • Kree/Skrull War part 3; Captain Marvel **A:** Sal Buscema **W:** Roy Thomas

92 ❑ Sep 1971 Cover: 0.15 **NM** value: **12.00**
Circ: Statement: **206,478 • CGC:** 5 graded, best 9.8
All Things Must End • Kree/Skrull War part 4; Captain Marvel **A:** Sal Buscema; Neal Adams; Neal Adams(cover) **W:** Roy Thomas

93 ❑ Nov 1971 Cover: 0.25 **NM** value: **45.00**
Circ: Statement: **206,478 • CGC:** 12 graded, best 9.6
• Double-size. This Beachhead Earth; A Journey to the Center of the Android; War of the Weirds • Kree/Skrull War part 5; Captain Marvel **A:** Neal Adams **W:** Roy Thomas

94 ❑ Dec 1971 Cover: 0.20 **NM** value: **32.00**
Circ: Statement: **206,478 • CGC:** 10 graded, best 9.8
More Than Inhuman; 1971: A Space Odyssey; Behold the Mandroids • Kree/Skrull War part 6; Captain Marvel **A:** John Buscema; Neal Adams **W:** Roy Thomas ★ 1st Appearance of Mandroid armor.

95 ❑ Jan 1972 Cover: 0.20 **NM** value: **32.00**
Circ: Statement: **189,961 • CGC:** 12 graded, best 9.6
Something Inhuman This Way Comes • Kree/Skrull War part 7; Inhumans crosover with Amazing Adventures #5-8 **A:** Neal Adams **W:** Roy Thomas ★ Origin of Black Bolt.

96 ❑ Feb 1972 Cover: 0.20 **NM** value: **32.00**
Circ: Statement: **189,961 • CGC:** 16 graded, best 9.8
The Andromeda Swarm • Kree/Skrull War part 8; Captain Marvel **A:** Neal Adams **W:** Roy Thomas

97 ❑ Mar 1972 Cover: 0.20 **NM** value: **18.00**
Circ: Statement: **189,961 • CGC:** 6 graded, best 9.4
Godhood's End • Kree/Skrull War part 9; Captain Marvel **A:** John Buscema; Bill Everett; Sal Buscema; Gil Kane **W:** Neal Adams; Roy Thomas

98 ❑ Apr 1972 Cover: 0.20 **NM** value: **24.00**
Circ: Statement: **189,961 • CGC:** 18 graded, best 9.8
Let Slip the Dogs of War • Goliath becomes Hawkeye again **A:** Barry Windsor-Smith **W:** Roy Thomas ★ 1st Appearance of The Warhawks.

99 ❑ May 1972 Cover: 0.20 **NM** value: **24.00**
Circ: Statement: **189,961 • CGC:** 6 graded, best 9.4
They First Make Mad • Has 1971 Statement, filed 9/23/71; avg print run 342,236; avg sales 205,169; avg subs 1,309; avg total paid 206,478; samples 110; office use 1,125; max existent 207,713; 39% of run returned **A:** Barry Windsor-Smith **W:** Roy Thomas

100 ❑ Jun 1972 Cover: 0.20 **NM** value: **60.00**
Circ: Statement: **189,961 • CGC:** 47 graded, best 9.8
• 100th anniversary issue. Whatever Gods There Be • Black Knight regains magic sword **A:** Barry Windsor-Smith **W:** Roy Thomas

101 ❑ Jul 1972 Cover: 0.20 **NM** value: **10.00**
Circ: Statement: **189,961 • CGC:** 3 graded, best 9.8
Five Dooms to Save Tomorrow • The Watcher **A:** Rich Buckler **W:** Roy Thomas; Harlan Ellison

102 ❑ Aug 1972 Cover: 0.20 **NM** value: **10.00**
Circ: Statement: **189,961 • CGC:** 2 graded, best 9.6
What to Do Till the Sentinels Come **A:** Rich Buckler **W:** Roy Thomas; Chris Claremont

103 ❑ Sep 1972 Cover: 0.20 **NM** value: **10.00**
Circ: Statement: **189,961**
The Sentinels Are Alive and Well **A:** Rich Buckler **W:** Roy Thomas

104 ❑ Oct 1972 Cover: 0.20 **NM** value: **10.00**
Circ: Statement: **189,961 • CGC:** 1 graded, best 9.4
With a Bang and a Whimper **A:** Rich Buckler **W:** Roy Thomas

105 ❑ Nov 1972 Cover: 0.20 **NM** value: **10.00**
Circ: Statement: **189,961**
In the Beginning Was the World Within **A:** John Buscema **W:** Steve Englehart

106 ❑ Dec 1972 Cover: 0.20 **NM** value: **10.00**
Circ: Statement: **189,961 • CGC:** 1 graded, best 9.6
A Traitor Stalks Among Us **A:** Rich Buckler; George Tuska **W:** Steve Englehart

107 ❑ Jan 1973 Cover: 0.20 **NM** value: **10.00**
Circ: Statement: **185,039 • CGC:** 1 graded, best 9.4
The Master Plan of the Space Phantom **A:** Jim Starlin; George Tuska; Dave Cockrum **W:** Steve Englehart

108 ❑ Feb 1973 Cover: 0.20 **NM** value: **10.00**
Circ: Statement: **185,039**
Check and Mate **A:** Don Heck **W:** Steve Englehart

109 ❑ Mar 1973 Cover: 0.20 **NM** value: **10.00**
Circ: Statement: **185,039 • CGC:** 1 graded, best 9.6

Other grades: Multiply prices above by **1.5 for Mint • 2/3 for Very Fine • 1/3 for Fine • 1/5 for Very Good • 1/8 for Good**

📖 The Measure of a Man • Hawkeye leaves Avengers; Has 1972 Statement, filed 9/21/72; avg print run 349,793; avg sales 188,579; avg subs 1,382; avg total paid 189,961; samples 110; office use 1,458X; max existent 191,529; 45% of run returned **A:** Don Heck **W:** Steve Englehart ★ 1st Appearance of Imus Champion.

110 ❑ Apr 1973 Cover: 0.20 **NM** value: **18.00**
Circ: Statement: **185,039** • **CGC:** 9 graded, best 9.8
📖 And Now, Magneto • X-Men; crossover with Fantastic Four #132 **A:** Don Heck **W:** Steve Englehart ★ Appearance of X-Men.

111 ❑ May 1973 Cover: 0.20 **NM** value: **18.00**
Circ: Statement: **185,039** • **CGC:** 1 graded, best 9.2
📖 With Two Beside Them • Daredevil **A:** Don Heck **W:** Steve Englehart ★ Appearance of X-Men.

112 ❑ Jun 1973 Cover: 0.20 **NM** value: **10.00**
Circ: Statement: **185,039** • **CGC:** 1 graded, best 9.4
📖 The Lion God Lives • Black Widow leaves **A:** Don Heck **W:** Steve Englehart ★ 1st Appearance of Mantis.

113 ❑ Jul 1973 Cover: 0.20 **NM** value: **8.00**
Circ: Statement: **185,039**
📖 Your Young Men Shall Slay Visions • Silver Surfer **A:** Bob Brown **W:** Steve Englehart ★ 1st Appearance of The Living Bombs. ★ Death of The Living Bombs.

114 ❑ Aug 1973 Cover: 0.20 **NM** value: **8.00**
Circ: Statement: **185,039** • **CGC:** 1 graded, best 9.2
📖 Night of the Swordsman • Silver Surfer **A:** Bob Brown **W:** Steve Englehart

115 ❑ Sep 1973 Cover: 0.20 **NM** value: **8.00**
Circ: Statement: **185,039**
📖 Below Us the Battle; Alliance Most Foul • Silver Surfer; Avengers and Defenders vs. Loki and Dormammu, part 1 – continues in Defenders #8 **A:** Bob Brown **W:** Steve Englehart

116 ❑ Oct 1973 Cover: 0.20 **NM** value: **8.00**
Circ: Statement: **185,039** • **CGC:** 5 graded, best 9.6
📖 Betrayal; The Silver Surfer vs. The Vision and the Scarlet Witch • Silver Surfer; Avengers and Defenders vs. Loki and Dormammu, part 3 – continues in Defenders #9 **A:** Bob Brown **W:** Steve Englehart

117 ❑ Nov 1973 Cover: 0.20 **NM** value: **8.00**
Circ: Statement: **185,039** • **CGC:** 6 graded, best 9.6
📖 Holocaust; Swordsman vs. the Valkyrie; Captain America vs. the Submariner • Silver Surfer; Avengers and Defenders vs. Loki and Dormammu, part 5 – continues in Defenders #10 **A:** Bob Brown **W:** Steve Englehart

118 ❑ Dec 1973 Cover: 0.20 **NM** value: **8.00**
Circ: Statement: **185,039** • **CGC:** 2 graded, best 9.2
📖 To the Death • Silver Surfer; Avengers and Defenders vs. Loki and Dormammu, part 7 – continues in Defenders #11 **A:** Bob Brown **W:** Steve Englehart

119 ❑ Jan 1974 Cover: 0.20 **NM** value: **8.00**
Circ: Statement: **188,084**
📖 Night of the Collector • Silver Surfer **A:** Bob Brown **W:** Steve Englehart

120 ❑ Feb 1974 Cover: 0.20 **NM** value: **8.00**
Circ: Statement: **188,084** • **CGC:** 2 graded, best 9.2
📖 Death-Stars of the Zodiac **A:** Jim Starlin; Don Heck; Joe Sinnott; Bob Brown **W:** Steve Englehart

121 ❑ Mar 1974 Cover: 0.20 **NM** value: **8.00**
Circ: Statement: **188,084** • **CGC:** 2 graded, best 9.4
📖 Houses Divided Cannot Stand **A:** John Buscema **W:** Steve Englehart

122 ❑ Apr 1974 Cover: 0.20 **NM** value: **8.00**
Circ: Statement: **188,084** • **CGC:** 3 graded, best 9.6
📖 Trapped in Outer Space **A:** Bob Brown **W:** Steve Englehart

123 ❑ May 1974 Cover: 0.25 **NM** value: **8.00**
Circ: Statement: **188,084** • **CGC:** 1 graded, best 8.5
📖 Vengeance in Viet Nam! • Origin of Mantis, part 1; Has 1973 Statement, filed 9/25/73; avg print run 360,675; avg sales 183,702; avg subs 1,337; avg total paid 185,039; samples 150X; office use 161; max existent 185,350; 49% of run returned ★ Origin of Mantis.

124 ❑ Jun 1974 Cover: 0.25 **NM** value: **8.00**
Circ: Statement: **188,084** • **CGC:** 1 graded, best 9.4
📖 Beware the Star-Stalker! • Origin of Mantis, part 2

125 ❑ Jul 1974 Cover: 0.25 **NM** value: **8.00**
Circ: Statement: **188,084** • **CGC:** 1 graded, best 9.4
📖 The Power of Babel! • Thanos; Crossover with Captain Marvel #32 and 33 ★ Appearance of Thanos.

126 ❑ Aug 1974 Cover: 0.25 **NM** value: **8.00**
Circ: Statement: **188,084** • **CGC:** 1 graded, best 9.4
📖 All the Sights and Sounds of Death!

127 ❑ Sep 1974 Cover: 0.25 **NM** value: **8.00**
Circ: Statement: **188,084** • **CGC:** 1 graded, best 9.6
📖 Bride and Doom • continues in Fantastic Four #150 (wedding of Crystal and Quicksilver) **A:** Sal Buscema; Frank Frazetta **W:** Steve Englehart ★ 1st Appearance of Ultron-7. ★ Appearance of Fantastic Four, Inhumans.

128 ❑ Oct 1974 Cover: 0.25 **NM** value: **8.00**
Circ: Statement: **188,084**
📖 Bewitched, Bothered, and Dead **A:** Sal Buscema **W:** Steve Englehart

129 ❑ Nov 1974 Cover: 0.25 **NM** value: **8.00**
Circ: Statement: **188,084** • **CGC:** 3 graded, best 9.2
📖 Bid Tomorrow Goodbye **A:** Sal Buscema **W:** Steve Englehart

130 ❑ Dec 1974 Cover: 0.25 **NM** value: **8.00**
Circ: Statement: **188,084** • **CGC:** 1 graded, best 9.2
📖 The Reality Problem **A:** Sal Buscema **W:** Steve Englehart ★ 1st Appearance of The Slasher. ★ Versus Titanium Man, Radioactive Man, Crimson Dynamo, Slasher.

131 ❑ Jan 1975 Cover: 0.25 **NM** value: **6.50**
• **CGC:** 1 graded, best 9.4
📖 A Quiet Half-Hour in Saigon • Immortus **A:** Sal Buscema **W:** Steve Englehart

132 ❑ Feb 1975 Cover: 0.25 **NM** value: **6.50**
• **CGC:** 3 graded, best 9.4
📖 Kang War II • Iron Man dies (resurrected in Giant-Size Avengers #3) **A:** Sal Buscema **W:** Steve Englehart

133 ❑ Mar 1975 Cover: 0.25 **NM** value: **6.50**
• **CGC:** 2 graded, best 9.4
📖 Yesterday and Beyond • origin of the Vision and Golden Age Human Torch, part 1 **A:** Sal Buscema **W:** Steve Englehart

134 ❑ Apr 1975 Cover: 0.25 **NM** value: **6.50**
• **CGC:** 3 graded, best 9.4
📖 The Times That Bind • origin of the Vision and Golden Age Human Torch, part 2 **A:** Sal Buscema **W:** Steve Englehart ★ Origin of Vision II (android).

135 ❑ May 1975 Cover: 0.25 **NM** value: **6.50**
• **CGC:** 3 graded, best 9.4
📖 The Torch is Passed • origin of the Vision and Golden Age Human Torch, part 3; Has 1974 Statement, filed 9/13/74; avg print run 342,917X; avg sales 186,814; avg subs 1,270; avg total paid 188,084; samples 0; office use 3,228; max existent 191,312; 44% of run returned **A:** George Tuska **W:** Steve Englehart ★ Origin of Moondragon, Vision II (android)-real origin.

136 ❑ Jun 1975 Cover: 0.25 **NM** value: **6.50**
• **CGC:** 3 graded, best 9.6
📖 Iron Man: D.O.A. • reprints with changes Amazing Adventures #12

137 ❑ Jul 1975 Cover: 0.25 **NM** value: **6.50**
• **CGC:** 2 graded, best 9.4
📖 We Do Seek Out New Avengers • membership becomes Beast, Iron Man, Moondragon, Thor, Wasp and Yellowjacket **A:** George Tuska **W:** Steve Englehart

138 ❑ Aug 1975 Cover: 0.25 **NM** value: **6.50**
• **CGC:** 1 graded, best 9.6
📖 Stranger in a Strange Man **A:** George Tuska **W:** Steve Englehart

139 ❑ Sep 1975 Cover: 0.25 **NM** value: **6.50**
📖 Prescription: Violence **A:** George Tuska **W:** Steve Englehart

140 ❑ Oct 1975 Cover: 0.25 **NM** value: **6.50**
📖 A Journey to the Center of the Ant • Vision and Scarlet Witch return **A:** George Tuska **W:** Steve Englehart

141 ❑ Nov 1975 Cover: 0.25 **NM** value: **5.50**
• **CGC:** 1 graded, best 9.4
📖 The Phantom Empire • Squadron Sinister **A:** George Pérez **W:** Steve Englehart ★ 1st Appearance of Golden Archer II (Wyatt McDonald).

142 ❑ Dec 1975 Cover: 0.25 **NM** value: **5.50**
📖 Go West, Young Gods • Rawhide Kid, Two-Gun Kid, Kid Colt, Night Rider **A:** George Pérez **W:** Steve Englehart

143 ❑ Jan 1976 Cover: 0.25 **NM** value: **5.50**
Circ: Statement: **172,813**
📖 Right Between the Eons **A:** George Pérez **W:** Steve Englehart

144 ❑ Feb 1976 Cover: 0.25 **NM** value: **5.50**
Circ: Statement: **172,813** • **CGC:** 2 graded, best 9.4
📖 Claws • Hellcat **A:** George Pérez **W:** Steve Englehart ★ Origin of Hellcat. ★ 1st Appearance of Hellcat.

145 ❑ Mar 1976 Cover: 0.25 **NM** value: **5.50**
Circ: Statement: **172,813**
📖 The Taking of the Avengers; Target: Captain America; The Small Hours **A:** Don Heck **W:** Scott Edelman; Tony Isabella

146 ❑ Apr 1976 Cover: 0.25 **NM** value: **5.50**
Circ: Statement: **172,813** • **CGC:** 1 graded, best 9.6
📖 The Assassin Never Fails!; The Better to Kill Them With!; Nothing But Our Own Death • Falcon; 25¢ and 30¢ versions exist **A:** Keith Pollard; Don Heck **W:** Tony Isabella

147 ❑ May 1976 Cover: 0.25 **NM** value: **5.50**
Circ: Statement: **172,813** • **CGC:** 2 graded, best 9.8
📖 Crisis on Other-Earth! • Hellcat

148 ❑ Jun 1976 Cover: 0.25 **NM** value: **5.50**
Circ: Statement: **172,813** • **CGC:** 1 graded, best 9.8
📖 20,000 Leagues Under Justice!; Cap'n Hawk, Tom Thumb and Amphibion vs. the Beast and Hellcat; Doctor Spectrum and the Whizzer vs. Captain America and Iron Man • Hellcat ★ 1st Appearance of Cap'n Hawk.

149 ❑ Jun 1976 Cover: 0.25 **NM** value: **5.50**
Circ: Statement: **172,813** • **CGC:** 2 graded, best 9.4
📖 The Gods and the Gang!

150 ❑ Aug 1976 Cover: 0.25 **NM** value: **5.50**
Circ: Statement: **172,813** • **CGC:** 2 graded, best 9.4
📖 Avengers Assemble • New team: Captain America, Iron Man, Yellowjacket, Wasp, Beast, Vision II (android), and Scarlet Witch; Partial Reprint from Avengers #16, retitled from "The Old Order Changeth" **A:** George Pérez

151 ❑ Sep 1976 Cover: 0.30 **NM** value: **5.50**
Circ: Statement: **172,813**
📖 At Last: The Decision! • New Avengers lineup: Beast, Captain America, Iron Man, Scarlet Witch, Vision, Wasp, Yellowjacket; Wonder Man comes back from dead, new costume **A:** George Pérez **W:** Jim Shooter; Gerry Conway; Steve Englehart

152 ❑ Oct 1976 Cover: 0.30 **NM** value: **5.50**
Circ: Statement: **172,813** • **CGC:** 1 graded, best 9.6
📖 Nightmare in New Orleans! ★ 1st Appearance of Black Talon II.

153 ❑ Nov 1976 Cover: 0.30 **NM** value: **5.50**
Circ: Statement: **172,813**
📖 Home is the Hero

154 ❑ Dec 1976 Cover: 0.30 **NM** value: **5.50**
Circ: Statement: **172,813**
📖 When Strikes Attuma!

155 ❑ Jan 1977 Cover: 0.30 **NM** value: **5.50**
Circ: Statement: **168,164** • **CGC:** 1 graded, best 9.4
📖 To Stand Alone!

156 ❑ Feb 1977 Cover: 0.30 **NM** value: **5.50**
Circ: Statement: **168,164**
📖 The Private War of Dr. Doom! ★ 1st Appearance of Tyrack.

157 ❑ Mar 1977 Cover: 0.30 **NM** value: **5.50**
Circ: Statement: **168,164**
📖 A Ghost of Stone • Has 1976 Statement, filed 9/20/76; avg print run 368,200; avg sales 171,100; avg subs 1,713; avg total paid 172,813; samples 0; office use 485; max existent 173,298; 53% of run returned

158 ❑ Apr 1977 Cover: 0.30 **NM** value: **5.50**
Circ: Statement: **168,164** • **CGC:** 1 graded, best 9.4
📖 When Avengers Clash

159 ❑ May 1977 Cover: 0.30 **NM** value: **5.50**
Circ: Statement: **168,164** • **CGC:** 1 graded, best 9.4
📖 Siege By Stealth And Storm **A:** Sal Buscema; Pablo Marcos **W:** Jim Shooter

160 ❑ Jun 1977 Cover: 0.30 **NM** value: **5.50**
Circ: Statement: **168,164** • **CGC:** 1 graded, best 3.5
📖 The Trail!

161 ❑ Jul 1977 Cover: 0.30 **NM** value: **5.50**
Circ: Statement: **168,164** • **CGC:** 2 graded, best 9.6
📖 Beware the Ant-Man **A:** George Pérez; John Byrne; Pablo Marcos **W:** Jim Shooter

162 ❑ Aug 1977 Cover: 0.30 **NM** value: **5.50**
Circ: Statement: **168,164** • **CGC:** 1 graded, best 9.4
📖 The Bride Of Ultron! **A:** George Pérez; John Byrne **W:** Jim Shooter ★ Origin of Jocasta. ★ 1st Appearance of Jocasta.

163 ❑ Sep 1977 Cover: 0.30 **NM** value: **5.50**
Circ: Statement: **168,164**
📖 The Demi-god Must Die! **A:** George Pérez; John Byrne

164 ❑ Oct 1977 Cover: 0.30 **NM** value: **5.50**
Circ: Statement: **168,164**
📖 To Fall By Treachery! **A:** George Pérez; John Byrne

165 ❑ Nov 1977 Cover: 0.35 **NM** value: **5.50**
Circ: Statement: **168,164**
📖 Hammer Of Vengeance **A:** John Byrne **W:** Jim Shooter

166 ❑ Dec 1977 Cover: 0.35 **NM** value: **5.50**
Circ: Statement: **168,164** • **CGC:** 1 graded, best 9.4
📖 Day of the Godslayer **A:** John Byrne

167 ❑ Jan 1978 Cover: 0.35 **NM** value: **3.50**
Circ: Statement: **162,996** • **CGC:** 2 graded, best 9.4
📖 Tomorrow Dies Today! **A:** John Byrne

168 ❑ Feb 1978 Cover: 0.35 **NM** value: **3.50**
Circ: Statement: **162,996** • **CGC:** 3 graded, best 9.6
📖 First Blood! **A:** John Byrne

169 ❑ Mar 1978 Cover: 0.35 **NM** value: **3.50**
Circ: Statement: **162,996** • **CGC:** 1 graded, best 9.4
📖 If We Should Fail, The World Dies Tonight! **A:** John Byrne

170 ❑ Apr 1978 Cover: 0.35 **NM** value: **3.50**
Circ: Statement: **162,996** • **CGC:** 1 graded, best 9.4
📖 Though Hell Should Bar the Way! • Has 1977 Statement, filed 9/20/77; avg print run 366,970; avg sales 163,597; avg subs 4,567; avg total paid 168,164; samples 175; office use 1,760; max existent 170,099; 54% of run returned **A:** John Byrne

171 ❑ May 1978 Cover: 0.35 **NM** value: **3.50**
Circ: Statement: **162,996**
📖 Where Angels Fear to Tread! **A:** John Byrne

172 ❑ Jun 1978 Cover: 0.35 **NM** value: **3.50**
Circ: Statement: **162,996** • **CGC:** 2 graded, best 9.6
📖 Holocaust in New York Harbor!

173 ❑ Jul 1978 Cover: 0.35 **NM** value: **3.50**
Circ: Statement: **162,996** • **CGC:** 1 graded, best 9.6
📖 Threshold of Oblivion

174 ❑ Aug 1978 Cover: 0.35 **NM** value: **3.50**
Circ: Statement: **162,996** • **CGC:** 1 graded, best 8.0
📖 Captives of the Collector!

175 ❑ Sep 1978 Cover: 0.35 **NM** value: **3.50**
Circ: Statement: **162,996** • **CGC:** 1 graded, best 9.6
📖 The End and the Beginning!

176 ❑ Oct 1978 Cover: 0.35 **NM** value: **3.50**
Circ: Statement: **162,996** • **CGC:** 1 graded, best 9.2
📖 Destiny Hunt

177 ❑ Nov 1978 Cover: 0.35 **NM** value: **3.50**
Circ: Statement: **162,996** • **CGC:** 2 graded, best 9.6
📖 The Hope...and the Slaughter **A:** David Wenzel **W:** Jim Shooter

178 ❑ Dec 1978 Cover: 0.35 **NM** value: **3.50**
Circ: Statement: **162,996** • **CGC:** 2 graded, best 9.6
📖 The Martyr Perplex **A:** Carmine Infantino; John Byrne **W:** Steve Gerber

179 ❑ Jan 1979 Cover: 0.35 **NM** value: **3.50**
Circ: Statement: **229,690** • **CGC:** 2 graded, best 9.6
📖 Slowly Slays the Stinger **A:** Jim Mooney **W:** Tom DeFalco ★ 1st Appearance of The Monolith, The Stinger II.

180 ❑ Feb 1979 Cover: 0.35 **NM** value: **3.50**
Circ: Statement: **229,690** • **CGC:** 1 graded, best 9.2
📖 Berserker's Holiday **A:** Jim Mooney **W:** Tom DeFalco

181 ❑ Mar 1979 Cover: 0.35 **NM** value: **4.50**
Circ: Statement: **229,690** • **CGC:** 2 graded, best 9.6
📖 On the Matter of Heroes • New team: Captain America, Falcon, Iron Man, Beast, Vision II (android), and Scarlet Witch **A:** George Pérez; John Byrne; Tony DeZuniga; Terry Austin **W:** David Michelinie

182 ❑ Apr 1979 Cover: 0.35 **NM** value: **4.00**
Circ: Statement: **229,690** • **CGC:** 1 graded, best 9.6
📖 Honor Thy Father • Has 1978 Statement, filed 9/25/78; avg print run 370,012; avg sales 154,156; avg subs 8,840; avg total paid 162,996; samples 250; office use 1,450; max existent 164,696; 56% of run returned **A:** John Byrne **W:** David Michelinie

183 ❑ May 1979 Cover: 0.40 **NM** value: **4.00**
Circ: Statement: **229,690**
📖 The Redoubtable Return of Crusher Creel **A:** John Byrne **W:** David Michelinie

184 ❑ Jun 1979 Cover: 0.40 **NM** value: **4.00**
Circ: Statement: **229,690**
📖 Death on the Hudson **A:** John Byrne **W:** David Michelinie

185 ❑ Jul 1979 Cover: 0.40 **NM** value: **4.00**
Circ: Statement: **229,690** • **CGC:** 3 graded, best 9.6
📖 The Yesterday Quest! **A:** John Byrne **W:** David Michelinie ★ Origin of Scarlet Witch, Quicksilver. ★ 1st Appearance of Chthon (in human body).

186 ❑ Aug 1979 Cover: 0.40 **NM** value: **4.00**
Circ: Statement: **229,690**
📖 Nights Of Wundagore! **A:** John Byrne **W:** David Michelinie

187 ❑ Sep 1979 Cover: 0.40 **NM** value: **4.00**
Circ: Statement: **229,690**
📖 The Call Of Mountain Thing **A:** John Byrne **W:** David Michelinie ★ 1st Appearance of Chthon (in real human form).

188 ❑ Oct 1979 Cover: 0.40 **NM** value: **4.00**
Circ: Statement: **229,690**
📖 Elementary, Dear Avengers **A:** John Byrne; Dan Green; Frank Springer **W:** Bill Mantlo

189 ❑ Nov 1979 Cover: 0.40 **NM** value: **4.00**
Circ: Statement: **229,690** • **CGC:** 1 graded, best 9.6
📖 Wings and Arrows **A:** John Byrne **W:** Roger Stern; David Michelinie; Mark Gruenwald

190 ❑ Dec 1979 Cover: 0.40 **NM** value: **4.00**
Circ: Statement: **229,690** • **CGC:** 1 graded, best 9.4

CGC-graded: Multiply prices above by **33 for 9.9 M • 16 for 9.8 NM/M • 7 for 9.6 NM+ • 5 for 9.4 NM • 2.5 for 9.2 NM- • 1.5 for 9.0 VF/NM**

Heart of Stone • Daredevil **A:** John Byrne **W:** Roger Stern; Steven Grant

191 ❑ Jan 1980 Cover: 0.40 **NM** value: **4.00**
Circ: Statement: **235,791** • **CGC:** 2 graded, best 9.4
Back to the Stone Age **A:** George Pérez; John Byrne **W:** Roger Stern; Steven Grant

192 ❑ Feb 1980 Cover: 0.40 **NM** value: **2.50**
Circ: Statement: **235,791**
Steel City Nightmare **A:** Ricardo Villamonte; Arvell Jones **W:** David Michelinie

193 ❑ Mar 1980 Cover: 0.40 **NM** value: **2.50**
Circ: Statement: **235,791**
Battleground: Pittsburgh • Has 1979 Statement; avg print run 428,935; avg sales 218,440; avg subs 11,250; avg total paid 229,690; samples 0; office use 1,000; max existent 230,690; 46% of run returned **A:** Sal Buscema; Dan Green; Frank Miller(cover) **W:** David Michelinie; Pittsburgh Comix Club

194 ❑ Apr 1980 Cover: 0.40 **NM** value: **2.50**
Circ: Statement: **235,791**
Interlude **A:** George Pérez **W:** David Michelinie

195 ❑ May 1980 Cover: 0.40 **NM** value: **3.00**
Circ: Statement: **235,791**
Assault on a Mind Cage **A:** George Pérez **W:** David Michelinie ★ 1st Appearance of Taskmaster.

196 ❑ Jun 1980 Cover: 0.40 **NM** value: **3.00**
Circ: Statement: **235,791** • **CGC:** 1 graded, best 9.6
The Terrible Toll of the Taskmaster **A:** George Pérez **W:** David Michelinie ★ Origin of Taskmaster.

197 ❑ Jul 1980 Cover: 0.40 **NM** value: **2.50**
Circ: Statement: **235,791**
Prelude Of The War-Devil! **A:** Carmine Infantino **W:** David Michelinie

198 ❑ Aug 1980 Cover: 0.40 **NM** value: **2.50**
Circ: Statement: **235,791**
Better Red than Ronin **A:** George Pérez **W:** David Michelinie

199 ❑ Sep 1980 Cover: 0.50 **NM** value: **2.50**
Circ: Statement: **235,791**
Last Stand on Long Island **A:** George Pérez **W:** David Michelinie

200 ❑ Oct 1980 Cover: 0.75 **NM** value: **2.50**
Circ: Statement: **235,791** • **CGC:** 9 graded, best 9.8
• double-sized. The Child Is Father To...? • Ms. Marvel leaves team **A:** George Pérez; Dan Green(inks) **W:** David Michelinie

201 ❑ Nov 1980 Cover: 0.50 **NM** value: **2.50**
Circ: Statement: **235,791**
The Evil Reborn **A:** George Pérez **W:** David Michelinie

202 ❑ Dec 1980 Cover: 0.50 **NM** value: **2.50**
Circ: Statement: **235,791**
This Evil Undying **A:** George Pérez **W:** David Michelinie ★ Versus Ultron.

203 ❑ Jan 1981 Cover: 0.50 **NM** value: **2.50**
Circ: Statement: **221,394**
Night Of The Crawler **A:** Carmine Infantino **W:** David Michelinie

204 ❑ Feb 1981 Cover: 0.50 **NM** value: **2.50**
Circ: Statement: **221,394**
Claws Across The Water **A:** Don Newton **W:** David Michelinie ★ Appearance of Yellow Claw.

205 ❑ Mar 1981 Cover: 0.50 **NM** value: **2.50**
Circ: Statement: **221,394**
Shadow Of The Claw **A:** Alan Kupperberg **W:** David Michelinie ★ Appearance of Yellow Claw.

206 ❑ Apr 1981 Cover: 0.50 **NM** value: **2.50**
Circ: Statement: **221,394**
Fire In The Streets • Has 1980 Statement; avg total paid circ 235,791 **A:** Gene Colan **W:** Bill Mantlo

207 ❑ May 1981 Cover: 0.50 **NM** value: **2.50**
Circ: Statement: **221,394**
Beyond A Shadow **A:** Gene Colan **W:** Bob Budiansky; Danny Fingeroth

208 ❑ Jun 1981 Cover: 0.50 **NM** value: **2.50**
Circ: Statement: **221,394**
Eve Of Destruction **A:** Gene Colan **W:** Bob Budiansky; Danny Fingeroth

209 ❑ Jul 1981 Cover: 0.50 **NM** value: **2.50**
Circ: Statement: **221,394**
The Resurrection Stone **A:** Alan Kupperberg **W:** J.M. DeMatteis

210 ❑ Aug 1981 Cover: 0.50 **NM** value: **2.50**
Circ: Statement: **221,394**
You Don't Need The Weathermen To Know Which Way The Wind Blows! **A:** Gene Colan; Dick Giordano **W:** Bill Mantlo

211 ❑ Sep 1981 Cover: 0.50 **NM** value: **2.50**
Circ: Statement: **221,394**
By Force Of Mind! • Moon Knight, Dazzler;New team begins **A:** Gene Colan; Dick Giordano **W:** Jim Shooter

212 ❑ Oct 1981 Cover: 0.50 **NM** value: **2.50**
Circ: Statement: **221,394**
Men Of Deadly Pride **A:** Alan Kupperberg **W:** Jim Shooter

213 ❑ Nov 1981 Cover: 0.50 **NM** value: **2.50**
Circ: Statement: **221,394**
Court-Martial • Yellowjacket's court martial;Yellowjacket leaves **A:** Bob Hall **W:** Jim Shooter

214 ❑ Dec 1981 Cover: 0.50 **NM** value: **3.00**
Circ: Statement: **221,394**
Three Angels Have Fallen! **A:** Bob Hall **W:** Jim Shooter ★ Appearance of Ghost Rider.

215 ❑ Jan 1982 Cover: 0.60 **NM** value: **2.50**
Circ: Statement: **223,335**
All the Ways of Power **A:** Alan Weiss **W:** Jim Shooter ★ Appearance of Silver Surfer.

216 ❑ Feb 1982 Cover: 0.60 **NM** value: **2.50**
Circ: Statement: **223,335**
To Avenge The Avengers! **A:** Alan Weiss **W:** Jim Shooter ★ Appearance of Silver Surfer.

217 ❑ Mar 1982 Cover: 0.60 **NM** value: **2.00**
Circ: Statement: **223,335** • **CGC:** 1 graded, best 6.0
Double-Cross • Yellowjacket jailed;Yellowjacket & Wasp return **A:** Bob Hall **W:** Jim Shooter

218 ❑ Apr 1982 Cover: 0.60 **NM** value: **2.00**
Circ: Statement: **223,335**
Born Again(And Again And Again...) **A:** Don Perlin **W:** J.M. DeMatteis

219 ❑ May 1982 Cover: 0.60 **NM** value: **2.00**
Circ: Statement: **223,335**
...By Divine Right **A:** Bob Hall **W:** Jim Shooter ★ Appearance of Drax.

220 ❑ Jun 1982 Cover: 0.60 **NM** value: **2.00**
Circ: Statement: **223,335**
War Against The Gods! **A:** Bob Hall **W:** Jim Shooter ★ Appearance of Drax. ★ Death of Drax the Destroyer.

221 ❑ Jul 1982 Cover: 0.60 **NM** value: **2.00**
Circ: Statement: **223,335**
Wolverine on cover only. ...New Blood! • Hawkeye rejoins;She-Hulk joins **A:** Bob Hall **W:** Jim Shooter; David Michelinie

222 ❑ Aug 1982 Cover: 0.60 **NM** value: **2.00**
Circ: Statement: **223,335**
A Gathering Of Evil **A:** Greg LaRocque **W:** Jim Shooter; Steven Grant ★ Versus Masters of Evil.

223 ❑ Sep 1982 Cover: 0.60 **NM** value: **2.00**
Circ: Statement: **223,335**
Of Robin Hoods and Roustabouts **A:** Greg LaRocque **W:** David Michelinie ★ Appearance of Ant-Man.

224 ❑ Oct 1982 Cover: 0.60 **NM** value: **2.00**
Circ: Statement: **223,335**
Two from the Heart • Tony Stark/Wasp romance **A:** Mark D. Bright **W:** Jim Shooter; Alan Zelentz

225 ❑ Nov 1982 Cover: 0.60 **NM** value: **2.00**
Circ: Statement: **223,335**
The Fall Of Avalon **A:** Greg LaRocque **W:** Steven Grant ★ 1st Appearance of Balor. ★ Appearance of Black Knight.

226 ❑ Dec 1982 Cover: 0.60 **NM** value: **2.00**
Circ: Statement: **223,335**
An Eye For An Eye **A:** Greg LaRocque **W:** Steven Grant ★ 1st Appearance of Valinor. ★ Appearance of Black Knight.

227 ❑ Jan 1983 Cover: 0.60 **NM** value: **2.00**
Circ: Statement: **229,645**
Testing...1...2...3! • Captain Marvel II joins team;Captain Marvel II (female) joins team **A:** Sal Buscema **W:** Roger Stern ★ Origin of Yellowjacket, Ant-Man, Goliath, Wasp, Giant-Man, Avengers.

228 ❑ Feb 1983 Cover: 0.60 **NM** value: **2.00**
Circ: Statement: **229,645**
Trial of Yellowjacket; Trial And Error! **A:** Al Milgrom **W:** Roger Stern

229 ❑ Mar 1983 Cover: 0.60 **NM** value: **2.00**
Circ: Statement: **229,645**
Final Curtain! **A:** Al Milgrom **W:** Roger Stern ★ Versus Egghead.

230 ❑ Apr 1983 Cover: 0.60 **NM** value: **2.00**
Circ: Statement: **229,645**
The Last Farewell • Yellowjacket leaves **A:** Al Milgrom **W:** Roger Stern ★ Death of Egghead.

231 ❑ May 1983 Cover: 0.60 **NM** value: **2.00**
Circ: Statement: **229,645**
Up From The Depths! • Iron Man leaves **A:** Al Milgrom **W:** Roger Stern

232 ❑ Jun 1983 Cover: 0.60 **NM** value: **2.00**
Circ: Statement: **229,645**
Starfox! • Starfox (Eros) joins **A:** Al Milgrom **W:** Roger Stern ★ Appearance of Starfox.

233 ❑ Jul 1983 Cover: 0.60 **NM** value: **2.00**
Circ: Statement: **229,645**
The Annihilation Gambit **A:** John Byrne; Joe Sinnott **W:** John Byrne; Roger Stern

234 ❑ Aug 1983 Cover: 0.60 **NM** value: **2.00**
Circ: Statement: **229,645**
The Witch's Tale! **A:** Al Milgrom **W:** Roger Stern ★ Origin of Scarlet Witch, Quicksilver.

235 ❑ Sep 1983 Cover: 0.60 **NM** value: **2.00**
Circ: Statement: **229,645**
Havoc On The Home front **A:** Bob Budiansky **W:** Roger Stern ★ Versus Wizard.

236 ❑ Oct 1983 Cover: 0.60 **NM** value: **2.00**
Circ: Statement: **229,645**
I Want To be An Avenger • Spider-Man;New logo **A:** Al Milgrom **W:** Roger Stern

237 ❑ Nov 1983 Cover: 0.60 **NM** value: **2.00**
Circ: Statement: **229,645**
Meltdowns And Mayhem • Spider-Man **A:** Al Milgrom **W:** Roger Stern

238 ❑ Dec 1983 Cover: 0.60 **NM** value: **2.00**
Circ: Statement: **229,645**
Unlimited Vision **A:** Al Milgrom **W:** Roger Stern ★ Origin of Blackout I (Marcus Daniels).

239 ❑ Jan 1984 Cover: 0.60 **NM** value: **2.00**
Circ: Statement: **241,463**
Late Night Of The Super-Stars! **A:** Al Milgrom **W:** Roger Stern ★ Appearance of David Letterman. ★ Death of Blackout I (Marcus Daniels).

240 ❑ Feb 1984 Cover: 0.60 **NM** value: **2.00**
Circ: Statement: **241,463**
The Ghost Of Jessica Drew! • Spider-Woman revived **A:** Al Milgrom **W:** Roger Stern ★ Appearance of Spider-Woman.

241 ❑ Mar 1984 Cover: 0.60 **NM** value: **2.00**
Circ: Statement: **241,463**
Dark Angel! **A:** Al Milgrom **W:** Roger Stern ★ Appearance of Spider-Woman.

242 ❑ Apr 1984 Cover: 0.60 **NM** value: **2.00**
Circ: Statement: **241,463**
Easy Come...East Go! **A:** Al Milgrom **W:** Roger Stern

243 ❑ May 1984 Cover: 0.60 **NM** value: **2.00**
Circ: Statement: **241,463**
Chain Of Command! **A:** Al Milgrom **W:** Roger Stern

244 ❑ Jun 1984 Cover: 0.60 **NM** value: **2.00**
Circ: Statement: **241,463**
And The Rocket's Red Glare! **A:** Al Milgrom **W:** Roger Stern ★ Versus Dire Wraiths.

245 ❑ Jul 1984 Cover: 0.60 **NM** value: **2.00**
Circ: Statement: **241,463**
Bombshells **A:** Al Milgrom **W:** Roger Stern ★ Versus Dire Wraiths.

246 ❑ Aug 1984 Cover: 0.60 **NM** value: **2.00**
Circ: Statement: **241,463**
Gatherings **A:** Al Milgrom **W:** Roger Stern ★ Appearance of Sersi.

247 ❑ Sep 1984 Cover: 0.60 **NM** value: **2.00**
Circ: Statement: **241,463**
The Ties That Bind! **A:** Al Milgrom **W:** Roger Stern ★ Appearance of Uni-Mind.

248 ❑ Oct 1984 Cover: 0.60 **NM** value: **2.00**
Circ: Statement: **241,463**
To Save The Eternals! **A:** Al Milgrom **W:** Roger Stern ★ Appearance of Eternals.

249 ❑ Nov 1984 Cover: 0.60 **NM** value: **2.00**
Circ: Statement: **241,463**
The Snows Of Summer **A:** Al Milgrom **W:** Roger Stern ★ Appearance of Fantastic Four.

250 ❑ Dec 1984 Cover: 1.00 **NM** value: **2.50**
Circ: Statement: **241,463**
World Power • Maelstrom **A:** Al Milgrom **W:** Roger Stern

251 ❑ Jan 1985 Cover: 0.60 **NM** value: **1.75**
Circ: Statement: **241,966**
Deceptions! **A:** Bob Hall **W:** Roger Stern

252 ❑ Feb 1985 Cover: 0.60 **NM** value: **1.75**
Circ: Statement: **241,966**
Deciding Factor! **A:** Bob Hall **W:** Roger Stern

253 ❑ Mar 1985 Cover: 0.60 **NM** value: **1.75**
Circ: Statement: **241,966**
Conquering Vision **W:** Roger Stern

254 ❑ Apr 1985 Cover: 0.65 **NM** value: **1.75**
Circ: Statement: **241,966**
Absolute Vision **W:** Roger Stern

255 ❑ May 1985 Cover: 0.65 **NM** value: **1.75**
Circ: Statement: **241,966** CapCity orders: **19,700**
The Legacy Of Thanos! • Has 1984 Statement, filed 9/28/84; avg print run 406,623; avg sales 224,647; avg subs 16,816; avg total paid 241,463; samples 132; office use 1,352; max existent 242,947; 40% of run returned **A:** John Buscema **W:** Roger Stern

256 ❑ Jun 1985 Cover: 0.65 **NM** value: **1.75**
Circ: Statement: **241,966** CapCity orders: **19,700**
This Power Unleashed! • Savage Land **A:** John Buscema **W:** Roger Stern

257 ❑ Jul 1985 Cover: 0.65 **NM** value: **1.75**
Circ: Statement: **241,966** CapCity orders: **19,400**
Holocaust in a Hidden Land **A:** John Buscema **W:** Roger Stern ★ 1st Appearance of Nebula.

258 ❑ Aug 1985 Cover: 0.65 **NM** value: **1.75**
Circ: Statement: **241,966** CapCity orders: **20,000**
Pyrrhic Victory! • Spider-Man vs. Firelord

259 ❑ Sep 1985 Cover: 0.65 **NM** value: **1.75**
Circ: Statement: **241,966** CapCity orders: **20,400**
Duty Over All ★ Versus Skrulls.

260 ❑ Oct 1985 Cover: 0.65 **NM** value: **1.75**
Circ: Statement: **241,966** CapCity orders: **29,000**
Assault On Sanctuary II • Secret Wars II **A:** John Buscema **W:** Roger Stern ★ Appearance of Nebula.

261 ❑ Nov 1985 Cover: 0.65 **NM** value: **1.75**
Circ: Statement: **241,966** CapCity orders: **28,000**
Earth And Beyond • Secret Wars II **A:** John Buscema **W:** Roger Stern

262 ❑ Dec 1985 Cover: 0.65 **NM** value: **1.75**
Circ: Statement: **241,966** CapCity orders: **21,400**
Many Brave Hearts! **A:** John Buscema **W:** Roger Stern ★ Appearance of Sub-Mariner.

263 ❑ Jan 1986 Cover: 0.65 **NM** value: **3.50**
Circ: Statement: **237,241** CapCity orders: **21,500** • **CGC:** 2 graded, best 9.8
What Lurks Below? ★ 1st Appearance of X-Factor. ★ Death of Melter.

264 ❑ Feb 1986 Cover: 0.75 **NM** value: **1.75**
Circ: Statement: **237,241** CapCity orders: **22,900**
Stings and Sorrows

265 ❑ Mar 1986 Cover: 0.75 **NM** value: **1.75**
Circ: Statement: **237,241** CapCity orders: **27,800**
Eve Of Destruction • Secret Wars II **A:** John Buscema **W:** Roger Stern

266 ❑ Apr 1986 Cover: 0.75 **NM** value: **1.50**
Circ: Statement: **237,241** CapCity orders: **30,500**
...And The War's Desolation • Secret Wars II Epilogue **A:** John Buscema **W:** Roger Stern

267 ❑ May 1986 Cover: 0.75 **NM** value: **1.50**
Circ: Statement: **237,241** CapCity orders: **24,200**
Time-And Time Again **A:** John Buscema **W:** Roger Stern ★ Versus Kang.

268 ❑ Jun 1986 Cover: 0.75 **NM** value: **1.50**
Circ: Statement: **237,241** CapCity orders: **24,000**
The Kang Dynasty **A:** John Buscema **W:** Roger Stern ★ Versus Kang.

269 ❑ Jul 1986 Cover: 0.75 **NM** value: **1.50**
Circ: Statement: **237,241** CapCity orders: **24,200**
The Once and Future King **A:** John Buscema **W:** Roger Stern ★ Origin of Rama-Tut. ★ Versus Kang.

270 ❑ Aug 1986 Cover: 0.75 **NM** value: **1.50**
Circ: Statement: **237,241** CapCity orders: **24,300**
Wild In The Streets **A:** John Buscema **W:** Roger Stern ★ Appearance of Namor.

271 ❑ Sep 1986 Cover: 0.75 **NM** value: **1.50**
Circ: Statement: **237,241** CapCity orders: **23,500**
Breakaway! **A:** John Buscema **W:** Roger Stern

272 ❑ Oct 1986 Cover: 0.75 **NM** value: **1.50**
Circ: Statement: **237,241** CapCity orders: **24,600**
Assault on Atlantis **A:** John Buscema **W:** Roger Stern ★ Appearance of Alpha Flight.

273 ❑ Nov 1986 Cover: 0.75 **NM** value: **1.50**
Circ: Statement: **237,241** CapCity orders: **24,500**
Rites Of Conquest! **A:** John Buscema **W:** Roger Stern

274 ❑ Dec 1986 Cover: 0.75 **NM** value: **1.50**
Circ: Statement: **237,241** CapCity orders: **23,300**

Other grades: Multiply prices above by **1.5 for Mint • 2/3 for Very Fine • 1/3 for Fine • 1/5 for Very Good • 1/8 for Good**

📖 Divided...We Fall! **A:** John Buscema **W:** Roger Stern
275 ❑ Jan 1987 Cover: 0.75 **NM** value: **1.50**
Circ: Statement: **216,841** CapCity orders: **23,500**
📖 Even a God Can Die **A:** John Buscema **W:** Roger Stern
276 ❑ Feb 1987 Cover: 0.75 **NM** value: **1.50**
Circ: Statement: **216,841** CapCity orders: **24,900**
📖 Revenge **A:** John Buscema **W:** Roger Stern
277 ❑ Mar 1987 Cover: 0.75 **NM** value: **1.50**
Circ: Statement: **216,841** CapCity orders: **23,900**
📖 The Price of Victory **A:** John Buscema **W:** Roger Stern ★ Death of Blackout.
278 ❑ Apr 1987 Cover: 0.75 **NM** value: **1.50**
Circ: Statement: **216,841** CapCity orders: **25,200**
📖 Pressure **A:** John Buscema **W:** Roger Stern
279 ❑ May 1987 Cover: 0.75 **NM** value: **1.50**
Circ: Statement: **216,841** CapCity orders: **23,800**
📖 Command Decision
280 ❑ Jun 1987 Cover: 0.75 **NM** value: **1.50**
Circ: Statement: **216,841** CapCity orders: **24,500**
📖 Faithful Servant
281 ❑ Jul 1987 Cover: 0.75 **NM** value: **1.50**
Circ: Statement: **216,841** CapCity orders: **24,800**
📖 By Gods Betrayed
282 ❑ Aug 1987 Cover: 0.75 **NM** value: **1.50**
Circ: Statement: **216,841** CapCity orders: **25,800**
📖 Captives ★ Versus Neptune.
283 ❑ Sep 1987 Cover: 0.75 **NM** value: **1.50**
Circ: Statement: **216,841**
📖 Whom the Gods Would Destroy
284 ❑ Oct 1987 Cover: 0.75 **NM** value: **1.50**
Circ: Statement: **216,841**
📖 Battleground: Olympus • on Olympus
285 ❑ Nov 1987 Cover: 0.75 **NM** value: **1.50**
Circ: Statement: **216,841**
📖 Twilight of the Gods ★ Versus Zeus.
286 ❑ Dec 1987 Cover: 0.75 **NM** value: **1.50**
Circ: Statement: **216,841**
📖 The Fix Is On! **A:** John Buscema **W:** Ralph Macchio ★ Versus Super Adaptoid.
287 ❑ Jan 1988 Cover: 0.75 **NM** value: **1.50**
📖 Invasion! **A:** John Buscema **W:** Ralph Macchio ★ Versus Fixer.
288 ❑ Feb 1988 Cover: 0.75 **NM** value: **1.50**
📖 Heavy Metal **A:** John Buscema **W:** Ralph Macchio ★ Versus Sentry Sinister.
289 ❑ Mar 1988 Cover: 0.75 **NM** value: **1.50**
📖 Attack! **A:** John Buscema **W:** Ralph Macchio ★ Versus Super Adaptoid, Sentry Sinister, Machine Man, Tess-One, Fixer.
290 ❑ Apr 1988 Cover: 0.75 **NM** value: **1.50**
📖 The World According to the Adaptoid **A:** John Buscema **W:** Ralph Macchio; Mark Gruenwald
291 ❑ May 1988 Cover: 1.00 **NM** value: **1.50**
Circ: CapCity orders: **31,800**
📖 Shadows of the Future Past **A:** John Buscema **W:** Walt Simonson
292 ❑ Jun 1988 Cover: 1.00 **NM** value: **1.50**
Circ: CapCity orders: **28,300**
📖 The Dragon in the Sea **A:** John Buscema **W:** Walt Simonson ★ 1st Appearance of Leviathan III (Marina). ★ Death of Leviathan III (Marina).
293 ❑ Jul 1988 Cover: 1.00 **NM** value: **1.50**
Circ: CapCity orders: **29,800**
📖 And Flights Of Angels! **A:** John Buscema **W:** Walt Simonson ★ 1st Appearance of Nebula. ★ Death of Marina, Marrina.
294 ❑ Aug 1988 Cover: 1.00 **NM** value: **1.50**
Circ: CapCity orders: **29,100**
📖 If Wishes Were Horses... • Captain Marvel leaves team;Capt. Marvel leaves team **A:** John Buscema **W:** Walt Simonson
295 ❑ Sep 1988 Cover: 1.00 **NM** value: **1.50**
Circ: CapCity orders: **28,900**
📖 ...Beggars Would Ride! **A:** John Buscema **W:** Walt Simonson
296 ❑ Oct 1988 Cover: 1.00 **NM** value: **1.50**
Circ: CapCity orders: **29,600**
📖 Hearts Of Oak...And Heads To Match! **A:** John Buscema **W:** Walt Simonson
297 ❑ Nov 1988 Cover: 1.00 **NM** value: **1.50**
Circ: CapCity orders: **28,900**
📖 Futures Imperfect • Thor, Black Knight, She-Hulk leaves team;She-Hulk, Thor, and Black Knight leave **A:** John Buscema **W:** Walt Simonson ★ Death of Doctor Druid.
298 ❑ Dec 1988 Cover: 1.00 **NM** value: **1.50**
Circ: CapCity orders: **32,600**
📖 Disaster! • Inferno **A:** John Buscema **W:** Walt Simonson
299 ❑ Jan 1989 Cover: 1.00 **NM** value: **1.50**
Circ: Statement: **201,600** CapCity orders: **30,400**
📖 I Love NY • Inferno **A:** John Buscema **W:** Walt Simonson
300 ❑ Feb 1989 Cover: 1.75 **NM** value: **2.50**
Circ: Statement: **201,600** CapCity orders: **41,200**
• 300th anniversary issue. 📖 Inferno • Inferno;new team;Thor Joins **A:** John Buscema **W:** Walt Simonson
301 ❑ Mar 1989 Cover: 1.00 **NM** value: **1.50**
Circ: Statement: **201,600** CapCity orders: **31,500**
📖 Super-Nova Saga, Part 1; Super-Nova Unbound **A:** Bob Hall **W:** Ralph Macchio
302 ❑ Apr 1989 Cover: 1.00 **NM** value: **1.50**
Circ: Statement: **201,600** CapCity orders: **31,700**
📖 Super-Nova Saga, Part 2; Earth Rocks! **A:** Rich Buckler **W:** Ralph Macchio
303 ❑ May 1989 Cover: 1.00 **NM** value: **1.50**
Circ: Statement: **201,600** CapCity orders: **31,300**
📖 Super-Nova Saga, Part 3; Reckoning **A:** Rich Buckler **W:** Ralph Macchio
304 ❑ Jun 1989 Cover: 1.00 **NM** value: **1.50**
Circ: Statement: **201,600** CapCity orders: **30,700**
📖 ...Yearning To Breathe Free **A:** Rich Buckler **W:** Danny Fingeroth ★ 1st Appearance of Portal. ★ Appearance of Puma. ★ Versus U-Foes.
305 ❑ Jul 1989 Cover: 1.00 **NM** value: **1.50**
Circ: Statement: **201,600** CapCity orders: **34,500**
📖 Attack Of The Lava Men! **A:** John Byrne; Paul Ryan **W:** John Byrne
306 ❑ Aug 1989 Cover: 1.00 **NM** value: **1.50**
Circ: Statement: **201,600** CapCity orders: **35,700**
📖 There Is A Fire Down Below **A:** Paul Ryan **W:** John Byrne
307 ❑ Sep 1989 Cover: 1.00 **NM** value: **1.50**
Circ: Statement: **201,600** CapCity orders: **35,100**
📖 To Crush An Eternal! **A:** Paul Ryan **W:** John Byrne
308 ❑ Oct 1989 Cover: 1.00 **NM** value: **1.50**
Circ: Statement: **201,600** CapCity orders: **35,300**
📖 Journey **A:** Paul Ryan **W:** John Byrne
309 ❑ Nov 1989 Cover: 1.00 **NM** value: **1.50**
Circ: Statement: **201,600** CapCity orders: **34,200**
📖 To Find Olympia! **A:** Paul Ryan; Tom Palmer **W:** John Byrne
310 ❑ Nov 1989 Cover: 1.00 **NM** value: **1.50**
Circ: Statement: **201,600** CapCity orders: **34,500**
📖 Death in Olympia **A:** Paul Ryan **W:** John Byrne
311 ❑ Dec 1989 Cover: 1.00 **NM** value: **1.50**
Circ: Statement: **201,600** CapCity orders: **37,500**
📖 Acts of Vengeance, Part 2, The Weakest Point • "Acts of Vengeance" **A:** Paul Ryan; Tom Palmer **W:** John Byrne
312 ❑ Dec 1989 Cover: 1.00 **NM** value: **1.50**
Circ: Statement: **201,600** CapCity orders: **37,300**
📖 Acts of Vengeance, Part 11, Has The Whole World Gone Mad?!? • "Acts of Vengeance" **A:** Paul Ryan; Tom Palmer **W:** John Byrne
313 ❑ Jan 1990 Cover: 1.00 **NM** value: **1.50**
Circ: Statement: **207,516** CapCity orders: **39,000**
📖 Acts of Vengeance, Part 20; Thieves' Honor • "Acts of Vengeance" **A:** Paul Ryan **W:** John Byrne
314 ❑ Feb 1990 Cover: 1.00 **NM** value: **1.50**
Circ: Statement: **207,516** CapCity orders: **34,800**
📖 Along Came a Spider... • Spider-Man **A:** Paul Ryan **W:** John Byrne
315 ❑ Mar 1990 Cover: 1.00 **NM** value: **1.50**
Circ: Statement: **207,516** CapCity orders: **42,600**
📖 Doomsday Plus One! • Spider-Man;Spider-Man x-over **A:** Paul Ryan; Tom Palmer **W:** John Byrne
316 ❑ Apr 1990 Cover: 1.00 **NM** value: **1.50**
Circ: Statement: **207,516** CapCity orders: **39,600**
📖 Spiders and Stars • Spider-Man **A:** Paul Ryan **W:** John Byrne
317 ❑ May 1990 Cover: 1.00 **NM** value: **1.50**
Circ: Statement: **207,516** CapCity orders: **39,600**
📖 Business as Usual • Spider-Man **A:** Paul Ryan **W:** John Byrne; Fabian Nicieza
318 ❑ Jun 1990 Cover: 1.00 **NM** value: **1.50**
Circ: Statement: **207,516** CapCity orders: **38,400**
📖 A Vengeful God • Spider-Man **A:** Paul Ryan; Tom Morgan **W:** Fabian Nicieza
319 ❑ Jul 1990 Cover: 1.00 **NM** value: **1.50**
Circ: Statement: **207,516** CapCity orders: **37,500**
📖 The Crossing Line!; The Crossing Line!, Part 1 **A:** Rik Levins **W:** Fabian Nicieza
320 ❑ Aug 1990 Cover: 1.00 **NM** value: **1.50**
Circ: Statement: **207,516** CapCity orders: **35,400**
📖 The Crossing Line!; The Crossing Line!, Part 2, Underlying Currents **A:** Paul Ryan **W:** Fabian Nicieza ★ Appearance of Alpha Flight.
321 ❑ Aug 1990 Cover: 1.00 **NM** value: **1.50**
Circ: Statement: **207,516** CapCity orders: **35,400**
📖 The Crossing Line!; The Crossing Line!, Part 3, Missing Links **A:** Rik Levins **W:** Fabian Nicieza
322 ❑ Sep 1990 Cover: 1.00 **NM** value: **1.50**
Circ: Statement: **207,516** CapCity orders: **36,600**
📖 The Crossing Line!; The Crossing Line!, Part 4, Bombs Away! **A:** Paul Ryan **W:** Fabian Nicieza ★ Appearance of Alpha Flight.
323 ❑ Sep 1990 Cover: 1.00 **NM** value: **1.50**
Circ: Statement: **207,516** CapCity orders: **34,500**
📖 The Crossing Line!; The Crossing Line!, Part 5, One World's Not Enough For All Of Us **A:** Rik Levins **W:** Fabian Nicieza ★ Appearance of Alpha Flight.
324 ❑ Oct 1990 Cover: 1.00 **NM** value: **1.50**
Circ: Statement: **207,516** CapCity orders: **32,400**
📖 The Crossing Line!; The Crossing Line!, Part 6 **A:** Paul Ryan **W:** Fabian Nicieza
325 ❑ Oct 1990 Cover: 1.00 **NM** value: **1.50**
Circ: Statement: **207,516** CapCity orders: **32,400**
📖 Party Games **A:** Rik Levins **W:** Mark Gruenwald
326 ❑ Nov 1990 Cover: 1.00 **NM** value: **1.50**
Circ: Statement: **207,516** CapCity orders: **31,200**
📖 Wind From the East **A:** Paul Ryan **W:** Larry Hama ★ 1st Appearance of Rage.
327 ❑ Dec 1990 Cover: 1.00 **NM** value: **1.50**
Circ: Statement: **207,516** CapCity orders: **30,300**
📖 Into a Darkling Plain **A:** Paul Ryan **W:** Larry Hama
328 ❑ Jan 1991 Cover: 1.00 **NM** value: **1.50**
Circ: Statement: **172,679** CapCity orders: **35,100**
📖 Powers That Be **A:** Paul Ryan **W:** Larry Hama ★ Origin of Rage, Turbo.
329 ❑ Feb 1991 Cover: 1.00 **NM** value: **1.50**
Circ: Statement: **172,679** CapCity orders: **30,000**
📖 Starting Line-Up **A:** Paul Ryan **W:** Larry Hama
330 ❑ Mar 1991 Cover: 1.00 **NM** value: **1.50**
Circ: Statement: **172,679** CapCity orders: **31,800**
📖 In A Strange Land **A:** Paul Ryan **W:** Larry Hama
331 ❑ Apr 1991 Cover: 1.00 **NM** value: **1.50**
Circ: Statement: **172,679** CapCity orders: **29,050**
📖 Pediments of Clay **A:** Paul Ryan **W:** Larry Hama
332 ❑ May 1991 Cover: 1.00 **NM** value: **1.50**
Circ: Statement: **172,679** CapCity orders: **30,300**
📖 The Many Faces Of Doom **A:** Paul Ryan **W:** Larry Hama
333 ❑ Jun 1991 Cover: 1.00 **NM** value: **1.50**
Circ: Statement: **172,679** CapCity orders: **30,600**
📖 Life Of The Party! **A:** Herb Trimpe **W:** Larry Hama
334 ❑ Jul 1991 Cover: 1.00 **NM** value: **1.50**
Circ: Statement: **172,679** CapCity orders: **30,300**
📖 The Collection Obsession, Part 1, First Encounter **A:** Andy Kubert **W:** Bob Harras
335 ❑ Aug 1991 Cover: 1.00 **NM** value: **1.50**
Circ: Statement: **172,679** CapCity orders: **31,200**
📖 The Collection Obsession, Part 2, Bloody Encounter **A:** Steve Epting **W:** Bob Harras
336 ❑ Aug 1991 Cover: 1.00 **NM** value: **1.50**
Circ: Statement: **172,679** CapCity orders: **31,500**
📖 The Collection Obsession, Part 3, For Here We Make Your Stand **A:** Steve Epting **W:** Bob Harras
337 ❑ Sep 1991 Cover: 1.00 **NM** value: **1.50**
Circ: Statement: **172,679** CapCity orders: **30,900**
📖 The Collection Obsession, Part 4, Mud And Glory? **A:** Steve Epting **W:** Bob Harras
338 ❑ Sep 1991 Cover: 1.00 **NM** value: **1.50**
Circ: Statement: **172,679** CapCity orders: **31,200**
📖 Collection Obsession, Part 4; The Collection Obsession, Part 5, Infectious Compulses **A:** Steve Epting **W:** Bob Harras
339 ❑ Oct 1991 Cover: 1.00 **NM** value: **1.50**
Circ: Statement: **172,679** CapCity orders: **30,900**
📖 The Collection Obsession, Part 6, Final Redemption **A:** Steve Epting **W:** Bob Harras
340 ❑ Oct 1991 Cover: 1.00 **NM** value: **1.50**
Circ: Statement: **172,679** CapCity orders: **34,800**
📖 Clay Soldiers **A:** Paul Abrams **W:** Scott Lobdell
341 ❑ Nov 1991 Cover: 1.00 **NM** value: **1.50**
Circ: Statement: **172,679** CapCity orders: **29,700**
342 ❑ Dec 1991 Cover: 1.00 **NM** value: **1.50**
Circ: Statement: **172,679** CapCity orders: **29,700**
📖 By Reason Of Insanity? **A:** Steve Epting **W:** Fabian Nicieza ★ Appearance of New Warriors.
343 ❑ Jan 1992 Cover: 1.00 **NM** value: **1.50**
Circ: Statement: **175,025** CapCity orders: **28,900**
344 ❑ Feb 1992 Cover: 1.25 **NM** value: **1.50**
Circ: Statement: **175,025** CapCity orders: **28,600**
345 ❑ Mar 1992 Cover: 1.25 **NM** value: **1.50**
Circ: Statement: **175,025** CapCity orders: **35,100**
📖 Storm Gatherings • Operation: Galactic Storm, Part 5; Has 1991 Statement, filed 10/1/91; avg print run 280,254; avg sales 167,871; avg subs 4,808; avg total paid 172,679; samples 250; office use 500; max existent 173,429; 38% of run returned **A:** Steve Epting **W:** Bob Harras
346 ❑ Apr 1992 Cover: 1.25 **NM** value: **1.50**
Circ: Statement: **175,025** CapCity orders: **33,000**
📖 Assassination • Operation: Galactic Storm, Part 12 **A:** Steve Epting **W:** Bob Harras
347 ❑ May 1992 Cover: 1.75 **NM** value: **2.00**
Circ: Statement: **175,025** CapCity orders: **34,500**
📖 Empire's End • Operation: Galactic Storm, Part 19;Conclusion to Operation: Galactic Storm **A:** Steve Epting **W:** Bob Harras ★ Death of Supreme Intelligence (apparent death).
348 ❑ Jun 1992 Cover: 1.25 **NM** value: **1.50**
Circ: Statement: **175,025** CapCity orders: **28,200**
📖 Familiar Connections **A:** Kirk Jarvinen **W:** Bob Harras
349 ❑ Jul 1992 Cover: 1.25 **NM** value: **1.50**
Circ: Statement: **175,025** CapCity orders: **29,000**
350 ❑ Aug 1992 Cover: 2.50 **NM** value: **Cover or less**
Circ: Statement: **175,025** CapCity orders: **45,300**
Gatefold covers. • Dbl. Size. 📖 Repercussions **A:** Steve Epting **W:** Bob Harras
351 ❑ Aug 1992 Cover: 1.25 **NM** value: **Cover or less**
Circ: Statement: **175,025** CapCity orders: **31,900**
📖 Retribution! **A:** Kevin West **W:** Bob Harras
352 ❑ Sep 1992 Cover: 1.25 **NM** value: **Cover or less**
Circ: Statement: **175,025** CapCity orders: **26,800**
📖 Fear the Reaper, Part 1, Son Of Darkness **A:** M.C. Wyman **W:** Len Kaminski ★ Versus Grim Reaper.
353 ❑ Sep 1992 Cover: 1.25 **NM** value: **Cover or less**
Circ: Statement: **175,025** CapCity orders: **26,700**
📖 Fear the Reaper, Part 2, To Wake The Dead **A:** M.C. Wyman **W:** Len Kaminski ★ Versus Grim Reaper.
354 ❑ Oct 1992 Cover: 1.25 **NM** value: **Cover or less**
Circ: Statement: **175,025** CapCity orders: **26,300**
📖 Fear the Reaper, Part 3, The Conqueror Worm **A:** M.C. Wyman **W:** Len Kaminski ★ Versus Grim Reaper.
355 ❑ Oct 1992 Cover: 1.25 **NM** value: **Cover or less**
Circ: Statement: **175,025** CapCity orders: **26,400**
📖 When Come The Gatherers! **A:** Steve Epting **W:** Bob Harras
356 ❑ Nov 1992 Cover: 1.25 **NM** value: **Cover or less**
Circ: Statement: **175,025** CapCity orders: **26,000**
📖 Death In A Gathering Place **A:** Steve Epting **W:** Bob Harras
357 ❑ Dec 1992 Cover: 1.25 **NM** value: **Cover or less**
Circ: Statement: **175,025** CapCity orders: **23,600**
358 ❑ Jan 1993 Cover: 1.25 **NM** value: **Cover or less**
Circ: Statement: **188,688** CapCity orders: **22,900**
📖 Arkon's Asylum **A:** Steve Epting **W:** Bob Harras
359 ❑ Feb 1993 Cover: 1.25 **NM** value: **Cover or less**
Circ: Statement: **188,688** CapCity orders: **22,300**
📖 Gift Of The Gods **A:** Steve Epting **W:** Bob Harras
360 ❑ Mar 1993 Cover: 2.95 **NM** value: **Cover or less**
Circ: Statement: **188,688** CapCity orders: **61,800** • **CGC:** 1 graded, best 9.2
foil cover. 📖 Alternate Visions • Has 1992 Statement, filed 10/1/92; avg print run 267,483; avg sales 170,800; avg subs 4,225; avg total paid 175,025; samples 250; office use 500; max existent 175,775; 34% of run returned **A:** Steve Epting **W:** Bob Harras
361 ❑ Apr 1993 Cover: 1.25 **NM** value: **Cover or less**
Circ: Statement: **188,688** CapCity orders: **25,400**
362 ❑ May 1993 Cover: 1.25 **NM** value: **Cover or less**
Circ: Statement: **188,688** CapCity orders: **23,500**
363 ❑ Jun 1993 Cover: 2.95 **NM** value: **Cover or less**
Circ: Statement: **188,688** CapCity orders: **88,200**
Silver embossed cover. 📖 A Gathering Of Hate **A:** Steve Epting **W:** Bob Harras
364 ❑ Jul 1993 Cover: 1.25 **NM** value: **Cover or less**
Circ: Statement: **188,688** CapCity orders: **26,000**
365 ❑ Aug 1993 Cover: 1.25 **NM** value: **Cover or less**
Circ: Statement: **188,688** CapCity orders: **38,700**
366 ❑ Sep 1993 Cover: 3.95 **NM** value: **Cover or less**
Circ: Statement: **188,688** CapCity orders: **60,400** • **CGC:** 1 graded, best 9.6
sculpted foil cover.
367 ❑ Oct 1993 Cover: 1.25 **NM** value: **Cover or less**
Circ: Statement: **188,688** CapCity orders: **28,300**
A: Steve Epting **W:** Bob Harras ★ Appearance of Sersi, Black Knight.

CGC-graded: Multiply prices above by **33 for 9.9 M** • **16 for 9.8 NM/M** • **7 for 9.6 NM+** • **5 for 9.4 NM** • **2.5 for 9.2 NM-** • **1.5 for 9.0 VF/NM**

368 ❑ Nov 1993 Cover: 1.25 **NM value: Cover or less**
Circ: Statement: **188,688** CapCity orders: **103,900**
📖 Bloodties, Part 1

369 ❑ Dec 1993 Cover: 2.95 **NM value: Cover or less**
Circ: Statement: **188,688** CapCity orders: **89,100**
sculpted foil cover.

370 ❑ Jan 1994 Cover: 1.25 **NM value: Cover or less**
Circ: Statement: **165,408** CapCity orders: **30,400**

371 ❑ Feb 1994 Cover: 1.25 **NM value: Cover or less**
Circ: Statement: **165,408** CapCity orders: **27,200**

372 ❑ Mar 1994 Cover: 1.25 **NM value: Cover or less**
Circ: Statement: **165,408** CapCity orders: **27,850**

373 ❑ Apr 1994 Cover: 1.25 **NM value: Cover or less**
Circ: Statement: **165,408** CapCity orders: **26,500**

374 ❑ May 1994 Cover: 1.50 **NM value: Cover or less**
Circ: Statement: **165,408** CapCity orders: **25,200**
• cards

375 ❑ Jun 1994 Cover: 2.50 **NM value: Cover or less**
• Giant-size. 📖 The Last Gathering • poster;Dane Whitman and Sersi leave the Avengers **A:** Steve Epting **W:** Bob Harras ★ Death of Proctor.

375/CS❑Jun 1994 Cover: 2.50 **NM value: Cover or less**
Circ: Statement: **165,408** CapCity orders: **30,100**
• Giant-size. 📖 The Last Gathering • Dane Whitman and Sersi leave the Avengers **A:** Steve Epting **W:** Bob Harras ★ Death of Proctor.

376 ❑ Jul 1994 Cover: 1.50 **NM value: Cover or less**
Circ: Statement: **165,408** CapCity orders: **25,250**

377 ❑ Aug 1994 Cover: 1.50 **NM value: Cover or less**
Circ: Statement: **165,408** CapCity orders: **23,700**

378 ❑ Sep 1994 Cover: 1.50 **NM value: Cover or less**
Circ: Statement: **165,408** CapCity orders: **24,650**

379 ❑ Oct 1994 Cover: 1.50 **NM value: Cover or less**
Circ: CapCity orders: **18,150**

379/A❑Oct 1994 Cover: 2.50 **NM value: Cover or less**
Circ: Statement: **165,408** CapCity orders: **16,450**
• Double-feature with Giant-Man

380 ❑ Nov 1994 Cover: 1.50 **NM value: Cover or less**
Circ: CapCity orders: **17,000**
★ Versus High Evolutionary.

380/A❑Nov 1994 Cover: 2.50 **NM value: Cover or less**
Circ: Statement: **165,408** CapCity orders: **11,050**
• second indicia gives name as "Marvel Double Feature ... The Avengers/Giant Man"

381 ❑ Dec 1994 Cover: 1.50 **NM value: Cover or less**
Circ: CapCity orders: **17,300**

381/A❑Dec 1994 Cover: 2.50 **NM value: Cover or less**
Circ: Statement: **165,408** CapCity orders: **9,700**
• second indicia gives name as "Marvel Double Feature ... The Avengers/Giant Man"

382 ❑ Jan 1995 Cover: 1.50 **NM value: Cover or less**
Circ: CapCity orders: **14,650**

382/A❑Jan 1995 Cover: 2.50 **NM value: Cover or less**
Circ: Statement: **85,165** CapCity orders: **8,650**
• second indicia gives name as "Marvel Double Feature ... The Avengers/Giant Man"

383 ❑ Feb 1995 Cover: 1.50 **NM value: Cover or less**
Circ: Statement: **85,165** CapCity orders: **17,525**

384 ❑ Mar 1995 Cover: 1.50 **NM value: Cover or less**
Circ: Statement: **85,165** CapCity orders: **17,675**
• Has 1994 Statement, filed 10/1/94; avg print run 253,950X; avg sales 162,217; avg subs 3,191; avg total paid 165,408; samples 125; office use 500; max existent 166,033; 35% of run returned

385 ❑ Apr 1995 Cover: 1.50 **NM value: Cover or less**
Circ: Statement: **85,165** CapCity orders: **17,625**

386 ❑ May 1995 Cover: 1.50 **NM value: Cover or less**
Circ: Statement: **85,165** CapCity orders: **16,500**

387 ❑ Jun 1995 Cover: 1.50 **NM value: Cover or less**
Circ: Statement: **85,165** CapCity orders: **16,675**
📖 Taking A.I.M., Part 2

388 ❑ Jul 1995 Cover: 1.50 **NM value: Cover or less**
Circ: Statement: **85,165** CapCity orders: **16,350**
📖 Taking A.I.M., Part 4

389 ❑ Aug 1995 Cover: 1.50 **NM value: Cover or less**
Circ: Statement: **85,165** CapCity orders: **16,275**

390 ❑ Sep 1995 Cover: 1.50 **NM value: Cover or less**
Circ: Statement: **85,165**

391 ❑ Oct 1995 Cover: 1.50 **NM value: Cover or less**
Circ: Statement: **85,165**

392 ❑ Nov 1995 Cover: 1.50 **NM value: Cover or less**
Circ: Statement: **123,581**
• Mantis returns

393 ❑ Dec 1995 Cover: 1.50 **NM value: Cover or less**
Circ: Statement: **123,581**
• "The Crossing";Wasp critically injured **A:** Mike Deodato **W:** Bob Harras ★ Appearance of Tony Stark.

394 ❑ Jan 1996 Cover: 1.50 **NM value: Cover or less**
Circ: Statement: **123,581**
• "The Crossing"; Has 1995 Statement, filed 10/1/95; avg print run 339,865; avg sales 81,899; avg subs 3,266; avg total paid 85,165; samples 750; office use 500; max existent 86,415; 75% of run returned★ 1st Appearance of New Wasp.

395 ❑ Feb 1996 Cover: 1.50 **NM value: Cover or less**
Circ: Statement: **123,581**
📖 Avengers: Timeslide ★ Death of Tony Stark.

396 ❑ Mar 1996 Cover: 1.50 **NM value: Cover or less**
Circ: Statement: **123,581**
📖 First Sign, Part 4, Balance Of Power **A:** John Statema **W:** Terry Kavanagh

397 ❑ Apr 1996 Cover: 1.50 **NM value: Cover or less**
Circ: Statement: **123,581**
📖 Crawling From the Wreckage **A:** Mike Deodato Jr. **W:** Howard Mackie; Terry Kavanagh

398 ❑ May 1996 Cover: 1.50 **NM value: Cover or less**
Circ: Statement: **123,581**

399 ❑ Jun 1996 Cover: 1.50 **NM value: Cover or less**
Circ: Statement: **123,581**

400 ❑ Jul 1996 Cover: 2.50 **NM value: 4.00**
Circ: Statement: **123,581**
wraparound cover. **W:** Mark Waid

401 ❑ Aug 1996 Cover: 1.50 **NM value: 2.50**
Circ: Statement: **123,581**
W: Mark Waid ★ Appearance of Magneto, Rogue.

402 ❑ Sep 1996 Cover: 1.50 **NM value: 2.50**
Circ: Statement: **123,581**
final issue. • "Onslaught: Impact 2";story continues in X-Men #56 and Onslaught: Marvel **W:** Mark Waid

Anl 1❑Sep 1967 Cover: 0.25 **NM value: 50.00**
• **CGC:** 12 graded, best 9.4
• Cover reads "King-Size Special". 📖 The Monstrous Master Plan of the Mandarin; To Perish by the Sword; Struggle in a Strange Land; And a Monster Shall Stalk the Land; Showdown in Space **A:** Don Heck **W:** Roy Thomas ★ Appearance of Hercules, Iron Man I, Mandarin, Black Widow, Edwin Jarvis, Power Man I, Living Laser, Thor.

Anl 2❑Sep 1968 Cover: 0.25 **NM value: 25.00**
• **CGC:** 12 graded, best 9.4
• Cover reads "King-Size Special". 📖 And Time, the Rushing River; The Avengers Must Die

Anl 3❑Sep 1969 Cover: 0.25 **NM value: 25.00**
• **CGC:** 7 graded, best 9.4
• Cover reads "King-Size Special". 📖 Captain America Joins the Avengers; The Fantastic Origin of the Red Skull; Lest Tyranny Triumph; The Sentinel and the Spy • Reprinted from Avengers #4 and Tales of Suspense #66, #67, and #68 respectively

Anl 4❑Jan 1971 Cover: 0.25 **NM value: 9.00**
• **CGC:** 5 graded, best 9.4
• Cover reads "King-Size Special". 📖 Invasion of the Lava Men; Masters of Evil • Reprinted from Avengers #5 & #6 respectively★ Origin of Moondragon.

Anl 5❑Jan 1972 Cover: 0.25 **NM value: 9.00**
• **CGC:** 1 graded, best 8.5
• Cover reads "King-Size Special". 📖 Kang, the Conquerer; The Mighty Avengers Meet Spider-Man • Reprinted from Avengers #8 and 11

Anl 6❑ca. 1976 Cover: 0.50 **NM value: 6.00**
• **CGC:** 1 graded, best 4.5
📖 No Final Victory; Interlude; Confrontation; Climax; Night Vision **A:** George Pérez ★ Versus Nuklo.

Anl 7❑ca. 1977 Cover: 0.60 **NM value: 12.50**
• **CGC:** 12 graded, best 9.6
📖 The Final Threat • Warlock **A:** Jim Starlin; Joe Sinnott ★ Death of Gamora. ★ Death of Warlock.

Anl 8❑ca. 1978 Cover: 0.60 **NM value: 5.00**
📖 Spectrums of Deceit **A:** George Pérez **W:** Roger Slifer ★ Appearance of Ms. Marvel.

Anl 9❑ca. 1979 Cover: 0.60 **NM value: 4.00**
• **CGC:** 1 graded, best 9.4
📖 ...Today the Avengers Die! **A:** Don Newton **W:** Bill Mantlo

Anl 10❑ca. 1981 Cover: 0.75 **NM value: 20.00**
• **CGC:** 150 graded, best 9.8
📖 By Friends-Betrayed! • X-Men **A:** Michael Golden **W:** Chris Claremont ★ 1st Appearance of Rogue, Destiny.

Anl 11❑ca. 1982 Cover: 1.00 **NM value: 3.50**
📖 In Honor's Name **A:** Al Milgrom **W:** J.M. DeMatteis

Anl 12❑ca. 1983 Cover: 1.00 **NM value: 3.50**
📖 Moonrise **A:** Jackson Guice **W:** Bill Mantlo ★ Appearance of Inhumans.

Anl 13❑ca. 1984 Cover: 1.00 **NM value: 3.50**
📖 In Memory Yet Green! **A:** Steve Ditko; John Byrne **W:** Roger Stern ★ Death of Nebulon.

Anl 14❑ca. 1985 Cover: 1.25 **NM value: 3.50**
Circ: CapCity orders: **21,200**
📖 Fifth Column **A:** John Byrne

Anl 15❑ca. 1986 Cover: 1.25 **NM value: 3.50**
Circ: CapCity orders: **23,300**
📖 Betrayal! **A:** Steve Ditko **W:** Danny Fingeroth

Anl 16❑ca. 1987 Cover: 1.25 **NM value: 3.50**
Circ: CapCity orders: **29,700**
📖 The Day Death Died

Anl 17❑ca. 1988 Cover: 1.75 **NM value: 3.00**
Circ: CapCity orders: **36,500**
📖 Evolutionary War, Part 11, Prometheus Mutants! **A:** Mark D. Bright **W:** Walt Simonson

Anl 18❑ca. 1989 Cover: 2.00 **NM value: 2.50**
Circ: CapCity orders: **42,000**
📖 Atlantis Attacks, Part 8; Avengers Assembled; The Initiation Of Quasar; Avengerability; Saga Of The Serpent Crown: Manifest Destiny • Atlantis Attacks **A:** Mark Bagley; Ron Wilson; Paul Ryan **W:** Fabian Nicieza; Mark Gruenwald; Michael Higgins; Peter Sanderson

Anl 19❑ca. 1990 Cover: 2.00 **NM value: 2.50**
📖 The Terminus Factor, Part 5; Beat Me In St. Louis!; Acts Of Vengeance Epilogue; Media Watch; Day The Strangers Came; Clowning Around • Terminus **A:** Vince Mielcarek; Richard Howell; Herb Trimpe; Steve Buccellato; Jim Reddington **W:** Kurt Busiek; Dwayne McDuffie; Roy Thomas; Dann Thomas; Gary Barnum; Mark Gruenwald

Anl 20❑ca. 1991 Cover: 2.00 **NM value: 2.50**
Circ: CapCity orders: **38,900**
📖 Subterranean Odyssey, Part 1; Of Moles And Mutates; A History Of Subterranea; Burning Vision; A Wind And A Prayer • Subterranean Wars **A:** Kevin West; Michael Bair; Jeff Moore; Ed Murr **W:** Roy Thomas; Dann Thomas; Eric Fein; Michael Higgins; Peter Sanderson

Anl 21❑ca. 1992 Cover: 2.25 **NM value: 2.50**
Circ: CapCity orders: **26,200**
📖 Citizen Kang, Part 4, Kang's World; Chronopolis; The Avengers Top Ten Villains; Secrets Of The Avengers Communicard; Boys' Night Out; The Puzzle • Citizen Kang **A:** Ron Lim; Herb Trimpe; Rich Yanizeski; Eliot Brown; Karl Altstaetter **W:** George Caragonne; Mark Gruenwald; Peter Sanderson; Scott Benson ★ Origin of Terminatrix. ★ 1st Appearance of Terminatrix.

Anl 22❑ca. 1993 Cover: 2.95 **NM value: Cover or less**
Circ: CapCity orders: **34,500**
• trading card;Polybagged with trading card★ 1st Appearance of Bloodwraith.

Anl 23❑ca. 1994 Cover: 2.95 **NM value: Cover or less**
Circ: CapCity orders: **18,000**

Bk 1❑ Cover: 1.75 **NM value: 14.95**
Circ: CapCity orders: **8,000**
📖 Essential Avengers • (Lancer);Collects issues #1-24

Bk 2❑ Oct 1994 Cover: 6.95 **NM value: 16.95**
📖 Under Siege • collects Avengers #181-2, 185-7;Collects issues #54-59?

Bk 3❑ Jan 1991 Cover: 12.95 **NM value: Cover or less**
• reprints #167, 168, 170-177

GS 1❑Aug 1974 Cover: 0.50 **NM value: 12.00**
📖 Nuklo, The Invader that Time Forgot; The Child is Father to the Fiend; What Hell Hath Joined Together; The Ray of Madness; The Magician and the Maiden • Quicksilver and Scarlet Witch children of Whizzer (Bob Frank) and Miss America; also, reprints Human Torch #33, Tales To Astonish #58★ 1st Appearance of Whizzer I (Robert Frank). ★ Death of Miss America.

GS 2❑Nov 1974 Cover: 0.50 **NM value: 6.00**
📖 A Blast From the Past; Prisoners of the Pharoh • "Prisoners..." reprinted from Fantastic Four #19 **A:** Dave Cockrum **W:** Steve Englehart ★ Origin of Rama-Tut. ★ Death of Swordsman.

GS 3❑Feb 1975 Cover: 0.50 **NM value: 6.00**
📖 What Time Hath Put Asunder; The Avengers Battle the Space Phantom • Iron Man resurrected; Vision is reconstruction of Golden Age Human Torch; "...Space Phantom" reprinted from Avengers #2 **A:** Dave Cockrum **W:** Roy Thomas ★ Origin of Immortus, Kang.

GS 4❑Jun 1975 Cover: 0.50 **NM value: 6.00**
📖 Let All Men Bring Together; Betrayed By the Ants • Vision and Scarlet Witch marry; Swordsman marries Mantis/Celestial Madonna; "Betrayed..." reprinted from Tales to Astonish #38 (Antman) **A:** Don Heck **W:** Steve Englehart

GS 5❑Dec 1975 Cover: 0.50 **NM value: 5.00**
📖 The Monstrous Master Plan of the Mandarin • reprinted from Avengers Annual #1

AVENGERS CASEBOOK — Marvel

1999❑ca. 1999 Cover: 2.99 **NM value: Cover or less**
Circ: Diamd. preorders: **16,565**

AVENGERS: CELESTIAL QUEST — Marvel

1 ❑ Sep 2001 Cover: 2.50 **NM value: Cover or less**
Circ: Diamd. preorders: **46,582**

2 ❑ Oct 2001 Cover: 2.99 **NM value: Cover or less**
Circ: Diamd. preorders: **40,789**

3 ❑ Nov 2001 Cover: 2.99 **NM value: Cover or less**
Circ: Diamd. preorders: **37,113**

4 ❑ Dec 2001 Cover: 2.99 **NM value: Cover or less**
Circ: Diamd. preorders: **34,479**

5 ❑ Jan 2002 Cover: 2.50 **NM value: Cover or less**
Circ: Diamd. preorders: **31,959**

6 ❑ Feb 2002 Cover: 2.50 **NM value: Cover or less**
Circ: Diamd. preorders: **29,938**

AVENGERS: DEATH TRAP, THE VAULT — Marvel

1 ❑ Sep 1991 Cover: 9.95 **NM value: Cover or less**
Circ: CapCity orders: **6,850**
• also published as Venom: Deathtrap – The Vault

AVENGERS FOREVER — Marvel

In this 12-issue mini-series, Avengers from the past, present, and future were drawn together for a universe-shattering confrontation with the classic Avengers' villain Immortus.

The Avengers pulled from the timestream were: the archer Hawkeye and a super-strong but disillusioned Captain America from the mid-1970s; the Wasp and Giant-Man from the Busiek-Perez present-day (1990s) Avengers; Captain Marvel and Songbird from the near future; and another Hank Pym, the deranged Yellowjacket, immediately prior to his wedding to the Wasp.

Now this mishmash of Avengers had to unite to save the life of Rick Jones, and their ally in this endeavor appeared to be none other than an earlier incarnation of Immortus, Kang the Conqueror!

Written and co-plotted by Kurt Busiek (Marvels, Astro City), Avengers Forever weaved a time-traveling story through the web of Avengers continuity that took into account everything from the origin of the Space Phantom to the Kree-Skrull War and the Celestial Madonna saga.

1 ❑ Dec 1998 Cover: 2.99 **NM value: Cover or less**
Circ: Diamd. preorders: **91,755** • **CGC:** 1 graded, best 9.6
📖 Destiny Made Manifest **A:** Carlos Pacheco **W:** Kurt Busiek

1/WF❑Dec 1998 Cover: 4.95 **NM value: Cover or less**
• **CGC:** 4 graded, best 9.8
Westfield alternate cover. 📖 Destiny Made Manifest **A:** Carlos Pacheco **W:** Kurt Busiek

2 ❑ Jan 1999 Cover: 2.99 **NM value: Cover or less**
Circ: Diamd. preorders: **74,295** • **CGC:** 3 graded, best 9.6
📖 Now is the Time for All Good Men... **A:** Carlos Pacheco **W:** Kurt Busiek

3 ❑ Feb 1999 Cover: 2.99 **NM value: Cover or less**
Circ: Diamd. preorders: **70,113**
📖 City at the Heart of Forever **A:** Carlos Pacheco **W:** Kurt Busiek; Roger Stern

4/A ❑ Mar 1999 Cover: 2.99 **NM value: Cover or less**
Circ: Diamd. preorders: **71,009**
Avengers of Tomorrow cover. 📖 Running Out of Time **A:** Carlos Pacheco; George Pérez(cover) **W:** Kurt Busiek; Roger Stern ★ Appearance of 1950s Avengers.

4/B ❑ Mar 1999 Cover: 2.99 **NM value: Cover or less**
Kang in the Old West cover. 📖 Running Out of Time **A:** Carlos Pacheco; John Buscema(cover) **W:** Kurt Busiek; Roger Stern

4/C ❑ Mar 1999 Cover: 2.99 **NM value: Cover or less**
Avengers throughout time cover. 📖 Running Out of Time **A:** Carlos Pacheco; Jeff Smith(cover) **W:** Kurt Busiek; Roger Stern

Other grades: Multiply prices above by **1.5 for Mint • 2/3 for Very Fine • 1/3 for Fine • 1/5 for Very Good • 1/8 for Good**

4/D ❑ Mar 1999 Cover: 2.99 **NM** value: **Cover or less**
Avengers of the '50s cover. 📖 Running Out of Time **A:** Carlos Pacheco; Frank Quitely(cover) **W:** Kurt Busiek; Roger Stern

5 ❑ Apr 1999 Cover: 2.99 **NM** value: **Cover or less**
Circ: Diamd. preorders: **62,584**
📖 Past Imperfect...Future Tense! **A:** Carlos Pacheco **W:** Kurt Busiek; Roger Stern ★ Appearance of Rawhide Kid, 1950s Avengers, Avengers of Tomorrow, Kid Colt, Two-Gun Kid.

6 ❑ May 1999 Cover: 2.99 **NM** value: **Cover or less**
Circ: Diamd. preorders: **62,846**
A: Carlos Pacheco **W:** Kurt Busiek; Roger Stern

7 ❑ Jun 1999 Cover: 2.99 **NM** value: **Cover or less**
Circ: Diamd. preorders: **64,804**
📖 Into a Limbo Large and Broad ... **A:** Carlos Pacheco **W:** Kurt Busiek; Roger Stern

8 ❑ Jul 1999 Cover: 2.99 **NM** value: **Cover or less**
Circ: Diamd. preorders: **62,799**
📖 The Secret History of the Avengers **A:** Carlos Pacheco **W:** Kurt Busiek; Roger Stern ★ Appearance of Human Torch.

9 ❑ Aug 1999 Cover: 2.99 **NM** value: **Cover or less**
Circ: Diamd. preorders: **61,937**
📖 Break: Reflections of the Conqueror **A:** Carlos Pacheco **W:** Kurt Busiek; Roger Stern

10 ❑ Oct 1999 Cover: 2.99 **NM** value: **Cover or less**
Circ: Diamd. preorders: **61,068**
📖 Tomorrow and Tomorrow and Tomorrow ... **A:** Carlos Pacheco **W:** Kurt Busiek; Roger Stern

11 ❑ Jan 2000 Cover: 2.99 **NM** value: **Cover or less**
Circ: Diamd. preorders: **58,993**
A: Carlos Pacheco **W:** Kurt Busiek; Roger Stern

12 ❑ Feb 2000 Cover: 2.99 **NM** value: **Cover or less**
Circ: Diamd. preorders: **57,615**
final issue. **A:** Carlos Pacheco **W:** Kurt Busiek; Roger Stern

AVENGERS (GOLD KEY) Gold Key

1 ❑ Cover: 0.10 **NM** value: **145.00**
• **CGC:** 7 graded, best 9.4
• based on TV series

AVENGERS INFINITY Marvel

1 ❑ Sep 2000 Cover: 2.99 **NM** value: **Cover or less**
Circ: Diamd. preorders: **45,610**

2 ❑ Oct 2000 Cover: 2.99 **NM** value: **Cover or less**
Circ: Diamd. preorders: **38,795**

3 ❑ Nov 2000 Cover: 2.99 **NM** value: **Cover or less**
Circ: Diamd. preorders: **37,301**
📖 They Walk Among the Stars! **A:** Sean Chen **W:** Roger Stern

4 ❑ Dec 2000 Cover: 2.99 **NM** value: **Cover or less**
Circ: Diamd. preorders: **35,900**
📖 The Hand of the Infinites **A:** Sean Chen **W:** Roger Stern

AVENGERS LOG Marvel

1 ❑ Feb 1994 Cover: 1.95 **NM** value: **Cover or less**
Circ: CapCity orders: **18,050**
A: George Pérez **W:** Peter Sanderson

AVENGERS MASTERWORKS Marvel

Bk 1 ❑ Cover: 15.95 **NM** value: **Cover or less**

AVENGERS SPOTLIGHT Marvel

Whereas Solo Avengers brought readers the exploits of individual Avengers, the title's change to Avengers Spotlight meant a metamorphosis to stories featuring subgroups of The Avengers working in teams.

Over the years, the ranks of active and reserve Avengers have swelled to include a huge number of characters. With two storylines running in each issue, Avengers Spotlight had the opportunity to give such lesser-known Marvel characters as Starfox, Swordsman, and Vision a chance to grab the spotlight, with a team-up focus on The Avengers' member Hawkeye, the archer.

21 ❑ Aug 1989 Cover: 0.75 **NM** value: **1.00**
Circ: CapCity orders: **16,300**
• Starfox; Series continued from Solo Avengers #20

22 ❑ Sep 1989 Cover: 1.00 **NM** value: **Cover or less**
Circ: CapCity orders: **18,100**
• Swordsman

23 ❑ Oct 1989 Cover: 1.00 **NM** value: **Cover or less**
Circ: CapCity orders: **17,800**
• Vision

24 ❑ Nov 1989 Cover: 1.00 **NM** value: **Cover or less**
Circ: CapCity orders: **16,200**
📖 A Show of Hands ★ Appearance of Trickshot.

25 ❑ Nov 1989 Cover: 1.00 **NM** value: **Cover or less**
Circ: CapCity orders: **15,900**
📖 Forewarned is Disarmed ★ Appearance of Crossfire, Mockingbird, Trickshot.

26 ❑ Dec 1989 Cover: 1.00 **NM** value: **Cover or less**
Circ: CapCity orders: **19,300**
📖 Acts of Vengeance, Part 1 • "Acts of Vengeance"

27 ❑ Dec 1989 Cover: 1.00 **NM** value: **Cover or less**
Circ: CapCity orders: **19,000**
📖 Acts of Vengeance, Part 9, Hurting Inside • "Acts of Vengeance" **A:** Al Milgrom **W:** Howard Mackie

28 ❑ Jan 1990 Cover: 1.00 **NM** value: **Cover or less**
Circ: CapCity orders: **21,200**
📖 Acts of Vengeance, Part 18 • "Acts of Vengeance"

29 ❑ Feb 1990 Cover: 1.00 **NM** value: **Cover or less**
Circ: CapCity orders: **21,800**
📖 Acts of Vengeance, Part 27 • "Acts of Vengeance"

30 ❑ Mar 1990 Cover: 1.00 **NM** value: **Cover or less**
Circ: CapCity orders: **18,200**
• new Hawkeye costume

31 ❑ Apr 1990 Cover: 1.00 **NM** value: **Cover or less**
Circ: CapCity orders: **17,800**

32 ❑ May 1990 Cover: 1.00 **NM** value: **Cover or less**
Circ: CapCity orders: **17,400**

33 ❑ Jun 1990 Cover: 1.00 **NM** value: **Cover or less**
Circ: CapCity orders: **17,200**

34 ❑ Jul 1990 Cover: 1.00 **NM** value: **Cover or less**
Circ: CapCity orders: **17,200**

35 ❑ Aug 1990 Cover: 1.00 **NM** value: **Cover or less**
Circ: CapCity orders: **15,900**
📖 Call Me Whatshisname ★ Appearance of Gilgamesh.

36 ❑ Sep 1990 Cover: 1.00 **NM** value: **Cover or less**
Circ: CapCity orders: **15,800**

37 ❑ Oct 1990 Cover: 1.00 **NM** value: **Cover or less**
Circ: CapCity orders: **15,100**

38 ❑ Nov 1990 Cover: 1.00 **NM** value: **Cover or less**
Circ: CapCity orders: **14,800**

39 ❑ Dec 1990 Cover: 1.00 **NM** value: **Cover or less**
Circ: CapCity orders: **14,600**

40 ❑ Jan 1991 Cover: 1.00 **NM** value: **Cover or less**
Circ: CapCity orders: **14,400**
final issue.

AVENGERS STRIKE FILE Marvel

1 ❑ Jan 1994 Cover: 1.75 **NM** value: **Cover or less**
Circ: CapCity orders: **26,300**
A: Jeff Moore **W:** Bob Harras

AVENGERS: THE CROSSING Marvel

1 ❑ Sep 1995 Cover: 4.95 **NM** value: **Cover or less**
• **CGC:** 1 graded, best 9.9
Chronium Cover. **A:** Mike Deodato and Studio **W:** Terry Kavanagh; Bob Harras

AVENGERS: THE TERMINATRIX OBJECTIVE Marvel

1 ❑ Sep 1993 Cover: 2.50 **NM** value: **Cover or less**
Circ: CapCity orders: **41,800**
Holo-grafix cover. **A:** Mike Gustovich **W:** Mark Gruenwald

2 ❑ Oct 1993 Cover: 1.25 **NM** value: **Cover or less**
Circ: CapCity orders: **24,700**
• New Avengers vs. Old Avengers **A:** Mike Gustovich **W:** Mark Gruenwald ★ Appearance of Terminatrix.

3 ❑ Nov 1993 Cover: 1.25 **NM** value: **Cover or less**
Circ: CapCity orders: **23,700**
A: Mike Gustovich **W:** Mark Gruenwald

4 ❑ Dec 1993 Cover: 1.25 **NM** value: **Cover or less**
Circ: CapCity orders: **22,900**
A: Mike Gustovich **W:** Mark Gruenwald

AVENGERS: THE ULTRON IMPERATIVE Marvel

1 ❑ Oct 2001 Cover: 5.99 **NM** value: **Cover or less**
Circ: Diamd. preorders: **30,437**

AVENGERS: TIMESLIDE Marvel

This one-shot comic is the pivotal chapter in the Avengers storyline "The Crossing." In it, Tony Stark, aka Iron Man, sent the Avengers back in time to recruit the help of a younger version of himself in battling Kang the Conqueror and his Anachronauts. At the conclusion of this storyline, it would be the younger, less jaded Tony Stark who assumed the mantle of today's Iron Man.

The fun part to this book was that the Avengers had traveled to a time just preceding the start of the Marvel universe. As a result, readers got to see some of the more popular characters before their lives were changed and they took up hero identities. A young Peter Parker was shown as he walked with his Uncle Ben and Aunt May. Sue Richards and Ben Grimm were shown as they made their way to the fateful meeting that gave birth to Reed's experimental rocket. Matt Murdock came into contact with The Vision and Tony Stark was only 19 years old.

1 ❑ Feb 1996 Cover: 4.95 **NM** value: **Cover or less**
No issue number. One-shot. enhanced wraparound cardstock cover. 📖 The Crossing **A:** Roger Cruz; Luke Ross; Fabio Laguna **W:** Terry Kavanagh; Bob Harras ★ Appearance of early.

AVENGERS TWO: WONDER MAN & BEAST Marvel

1 ❑ May 2000 Cover: 2.99 **NM** value: **Cover or less**
Circ: Diamd. preorders: **36,923**
📖 Second Chances **A:** Mark Bagley **W:** Roger Stern

2 ❑ Jun 2000 Cover: 2.99 **NM** value: **Cover or less**
Circ: Diamd. preorders: **31,795**
A: Mark Bagley **W:** Roger Stern

3 ❑ Jul 2000 Cover: 2.99 **NM** value: **Cover or less**
Circ: Diamd. preorders: **31,524**
📖 It's Alive! **A:** Mark Bagley **W:** Roger Stern

Statement of Ownership figures are the average number of copies originally sold, as cited by the publisher to the U.S. Postal Service. These estimate **all** sales, in comics shops and on newsstands.

AVENGERS/ULTRAFORCE Marvel

The powerful Infinity Gems have been the catalyst for a number of cosmically oriented series from Marvel such as Infinity Watch and Infinity Gauntlet, as well as an important part of the Adam Warlock and Silver Surfer series. Now the ubiquitous role of cosmic bait falls to the Gems again, as Loki, the Norse God of Mischief, and an Elder of the universe, the Grandmaster, engage in a cosmic Dungeons & Dragons-type of role-playing game which they call Worlds and Warriors.

With Loki manipulating the Malibu group, UltraForce, and the Grandmaster employing The Avengers, various members square off against one another as pawns in a drama that holds a few surprises for everyone involved.

1 ❑ Oct 1995 Cover: 3.95 **NM** value: **Cover or less**
• **CGC:** 1 graded, best 9.6
• continues in UltraForce/Avengers #1;Foil logo **A:** Angel Medina; M.C. Wyman **W:** Glenn Herdling

AVENGERS: ULTRON UNLEASHED Marvel

1 ❑ Aug 1999 Cover: 3.50 **NM** value: **Cover or less**
No issue number. • collects Avengers (1st series) #57-58 and #170-171

AVENGERS: UNITED THEY STAND Marvel

1 ❑ Nov 1999 Cover: 1.99 **NM** value: **2.99**
Circ: Diamd. preorders: **30,947**
📖 The Ultimate Creation **A:** Derec Aucoin **W:** Ty Templeton

2 ❑ Dec 1999 Cover: 1.99 **NM** value: **Cover or less**
Circ: Diamd. preorders: **27,047**
📖 Hail and Farewell **A:** Jason Armstrong **W:** Ty Templeton

3 ❑ Jan 2000 Cover: 1.99 **NM** value: **Cover or less**
Circ: Diamd. preorders: **20,627**

4 ❑ Feb 2000 Cover: 1.99 **NM** value: **Cover or less**
Circ: Diamd. preorders: **17,465**

5 ❑ Mar 2000 Cover: 1.99 **NM** value: **Cover or less**
Circ: Diamd. preorders: **13,509**

6 ❑ Apr 2000 Cover: 1.99 **NM** value: **Cover or less**
Circ: Diamd. preorders: **10,695**

7 ❑ May 2000 Cover: 1.99 **NM** value: **Cover or less**
Circ: Diamd. preorders: **9,269**

AVENGERS UNIVERSE Marvel

1 ❑ Aug 2000 Cover: 2.99 **NM** value: **Cover or less**
Circ: Diamd. preorders: **3,937**

2 ❑ Sep 2000 Cover: 2.99 **NM** value: **Cover or less**
Circ: Diamd. preorders: **2,910**

3 ❑ Oct 2000 Cover: 2.99 **NM** value: **Cover or less**
Circ: Diamd. preorders: **2,679**

4 ❑ Nov 2000 Cover: 2.99 **NM** value: **Cover or less**
Circ: Diamd. preorders: **2,482**
• reprints Iron Fist: Wolverine #1;indicia is for Iron Fist: Wolverine #1 **A:** Jamal Igle **W:** Jay Faerber

5 ❑ Dec 2000 Cover: 2.99 **NM** value: **Cover or less**
Circ: Diamd. preorders: **2,235**
📖 A Gathering of Forces • reprints Iron Fist: Wolverine #2;indicia is for Iron Fist: Wolverine #2 **A:** Jamal Igle **W:** Jay Faerber

6 ❑ Jan 2001 Cover: 2.99 **NM** value: **Cover or less**
📖 Against the Wall • reprints Iron Fist: Wolverine #3;indicia is for Iron Fist: Wolverine #3 **A:** Jamal Igle **W:** Jay Faerber

AVENGERS UNPLUGGED Marvel

1 ❑ Oct 1995 Cover: 0.99 **NM** value: **1.00**
📖 Unchain my Heart **A:** M.C. Wyman **W:** Glenn Herdling

2 ❑ Dec 1995 Cover: 0.99 **NM** value: **1.00**
A: M.C. Wyman **W:** Glenn Herdling ★ Appearance of Gravitron.

3 ❑ Dec 1996 Cover: 0.99 **NM** value: **1.00**
📖 Ladies Nite • Luna;Black Widow **A:** M.C. Wyman **W:** Mike Lackey

4 ❑ Feb 1996 Cover: 0.99 **NM** value: **1.00**
📖 The Old Ball and Chain • Wedding of Thunderball and Titania;Peter David appears as reverend in story **A:** John Statema **W:** Glenn Herdling

5 ❑ Jun 1996 Cover: 0.99 **NM** value: **1.00**
★ Appearance of Captain Marvel.

6 ❑ Aug 1996 Cover: 0.99 **NM** value: **1.00**
final issue.

AVENGERS (VOL. 2) Marvel

Under the guidance of Rob Liefeld as writer, artist, and editor, this venerable title got a new start as part of the Jim Lee-Rob Liefeld universe, which resulted from dwindling market share as much as the Onslaught crossover in the Marvel line in 1996.

The Avengers, this time, were a government-funded organization overseen by S.H.I.E.L.D., comprised of Captain America, Hawkeye, The Swordsman, The Scarlet Witch, Hellcat, and The Vision.

An archeological expedition in Norway discovered an impressive figure frozen in ice, believed to be the Norse god of thunder, Thor. Captain America and his team of heroes were dispatched to investigate. These were the circumstances that Loki, the god of lies, and brother of Thor, attempted to turn to his own nefarious ends in the relaunch of Earth's Mightiest Heroes.

CGC-graded: Multiply prices above by **33 for 9.9 M • 16 for 9.8 NM/M • 7 for 9.6 NM+ • 5 for 9.4 NM • 2.5 for 9.2 NM- • 1.5 for 9.0 VF/NM**

1 ❑ Nov 1996 Cover: 2.95 **NM** value: **3.00**
Circ: Statement: **166,046** Direct Market orders: **276,750** • **CGC:** 3 graded, best 9.6
📖 Awaken The Thunder • Thor revived **A:** Rob Liefeld; Chap Yaep; Rob Liefeld(cover) **W:** Jim Valentino

1/A ❑ Nov 1996 Cover: 2.95 **NM** value: **3.00**
• **CGC:** 1 graded, best 9.6
Alternate cover (Chap Yaep). 📖 Awaken The Thunder • Thor revived **A:** Rob Liefeld; Chap Yaep **W:** Jim Valentino

2 ❑ Dec 1996 Cover: 1.95 **NM** value: **2.00**
Circ: Statement: **166,046** Direct Market orders: **131,000**
📖 First Blood • Has 1996 Statement, filed 10/1/96; avg print run 126,858; avg sales 115,857; avg subs 1,931; avg total paid 123,581; samples 600; office use 125; max existent 118,513; 2% of run returned **A:** Chap Yaep **W:** Jeph Loeb; Jim Valentino; Rob Liefeld ★ Appearance of Mantis. ★ Versus Kang.

3 ❑ Jan 1997 Cover: 1.95 **NM** value: **2.00**
Circ: Statement: **166,046** Direct Market orders: **125,250**
📖 In Love & War **A:** Chap Yaep **W:** Jeph Loeb; Jim Valentino; Rob Liefeld ★ Appearance of Mantis, Nick Fury.

4 ❑ Feb 1997 Cover: 1.95 **NM** value: **2.00**
Circ: Statement: **166,046** Direct Market orders: **118,750**
📖 That Which Gods Have Joined Together… **A:** Ian Churchill; Chap Yaep **W:** Jeph Loeb; Rob Liefeld ★ Versus Hulk.

5 ❑ Mar 1997 Cover: 1.95 **NM** value: **2.00**
Circ: Statement: **166,046** Direct Market orders: **114,000**
📖 …Let No Man Tear Asunder • Thor vs. Hulk **A:** Ian Churchill; Rob Liefeld **W:** Jeph Loeb; Scott Lobdell

5/A ❑ Mar 1997 Cover: 1.95 **NM** value: **2.00**
White cover. 📖 …Let No Man Tear Asunder • Thor vs. Hulk **A:** Ian Churchill; Rob Liefeld **W:** Jeph Loeb; Scott Lobdell

6 ❑ Apr 1997 Cover: 1.95 **NM** value: **Cover or less**
Circ: Statement: **166,046** Direct Market orders: **120,250**
📖 Industrial Revolution, Part 1 • continues in Iron Man #6 **A:** Ian Churchill **W:** Jeph Loeb; Rob Liefeld

7 ❑ May 1997 Cover: 1.95 **NM** value: **Cover or less**
Circ: Statement: **166,046** Diamd. preorders: **118,560**
📖 Help! **A:** Ian Churchill **W:** Jeph Loeb; Rob Liefeld ★ Versus Lethal Legion (Enchantress, Wonder Man, Ultron 5, Executioner, Scarlet Witch).

8 ❑ Jun 1997 Cover: 1.95 **NM** value: **Cover or less**
Circ: Statement: **166,046** Diamd. preorders: **120,937**
📖 Shadowplay **A:** Michael Ryan **W:** Walt Simonson

9 ❑ Jul 1997 Cover: 1.95 **NM** value: **Cover or less**
Circ: Statement: **166,046** Diamd. preorders: **114,895**
★ Versus Masters of Evil.

10 ❑ Aug 1997 Cover: 1.99 **NM** value: **Cover or less**
Circ: Statement: **166,046** Diamd. preorders: **104,388**
• gatefold summary. ★ Versus doppleganger s.

11 ❑ Sep 1997 Cover: 1.99 **NM** value: **Cover or less**
Circ: Statement: **166,046** Diamd. preorders: **110,083**
• gatefold summary. ★ Death of Thor. ★ Versus Loki.

12 ❑ Oct 1997 Cover: 1.99 **NM** value: **2.99**
Circ: Statement: **166,903** Diamd. preorders: **114,787**
cover forms quadtych with Fantastic Four #12, Iron Man #12, and Captain America #12.

13 ❑ Nov 1997 Cover: 1.99 **NM** value: **Cover or less**
Circ: Statement: **166,903** Diamd. preorders: **109,463**
cover forms quadtych with Fantastic Four #13, Iron Man #13, and Captain America #13. final issue.

AVENGERS (VOL. 3) — Marvel

The third volume of The Avengers ("Heroes Return") puts back in place what was torn apart to form Avengers (Vol. 2) ("Heroes Reborn"). In that volume, Marvel turned control of the core Avengers characters to Image artists. The result was an alternate reality filled with versions of the Avenger characters which were similar — but not the same — as the ones comics readers had followed for decades.

Now, with Vol. 3, the "real" Avengers returned to the mainstream Marvel universe. Curiously enough, the return took them through yet another alternate universe, this one created by sorceress Morgan LeFay. LeFay used the reality-warping Twilight Sword to create a medieval world where The Avengers had alternate identities and all served her. But even the most powerful spell could not hope to control the minds of the World's Mightiest Mortals.

0 ❑ **NM** value: **1.00**
• Promotional edition included with Wizard. 📖 Our Top Story Tonight **A:** Stuart Immonen **W:** Kurt Busiek

1 ❑ Feb 1998 Cover: 2.99 **NM** value: **4.00**
Circ: Statement: **166,903** Diamd. preorders: **194,439**
• gatefold summary. 📖 Once an Avenger…, Part 1 • Has 1997 Statement, filed 10/1/97; avg print run 209,391; avg sales 163,342; avg subs 2,704; avg total paid 166,046; samples 270; office use 125; max existent 166,441; 21% of run returned **A:** George Pérez **W:** Kurt Busiek

1/A ❑ **NM** value: **6.00**
chromium cover. 📖 Once an Avenger…, Part 1 **A:** George Pérez **W:** Kurt Busiek

1/B ❑ Jul 1998 Cover: 2.99 **NM** value: **4.00**
cardstock cover. 📖 Once an Avenger…, Part 1 • Avengers Rough Cut **A:** George Pérez **W:** Kurt Busiek

1/C ❑ Feb 1998 Cover: 2.99 **NM** value: **4.00**
alternate cover. • gatefold summary. **W:** Kurt Busiek

1/SC❑ Cover: 2.99 **NM** value: **5.00**
variant cover. 📖 Once an Avenger…, Part 1 **A:** George Pérez **W:** Kurt Busiek

2 ❑ Mar 1998 Cover: 1.99 **NM** value: **3.00**
Circ: Statement: **166,903** • **CGC:** 1 graded, best 9.4
• gatefold summary. 📖 Once an Avenger…, Part 2; The Call **A:** George Pérez **W:** Kurt Busiek

2/SC❑Mar 1998 Cover: 1.99 **NM** value: **3.00**
Circ: Statement: **166,903** • **CGC:** 3 graded, best 9.8
alternate cover. • gatefold summary. 📖 Once an Avenger…, Part 2; The Call **A:** George Pérez; Ray Lago(cover) **W:** Kurt Busiek

3 ❑ Apr 1998 Cover: 1.99 **NM** value: **2.00**
Circ: Statement: **166,903** Diamd. preorders: **111,036**
📖 Once an Avenger …, Part 3; Fata Morgana **W:** Kurt Busiek ★ Appearance of Wonder Man gatefold summary.

4 ❑ May 1998 Cover: 1.99 **NM** value: **2.00**
Circ: Statement: **166,903**
📖 Too Many Avengers! • New team announced gatefold summary;New team begins **W:** Kurt Busiek

5 ❑ Jun 1998 Cover: 1.99 **NM** value: **2.00**
Circ: Statement: **166,903** Diamd. preorders: **116,640**
• gatefold summary. 📖 Accusation Most Foul **W:** Kurt Busiek ★ Versus Squadron Supreme.

6 ❑ Jul 1998 Cover: 1.99 **NM** value: **2.00**
Circ: Statement: **166,903** Diamd. preorders: **112,322**
• gatefold summary. 📖 Earth's Mightiest Frauds? **A:** George Pérez **W:** Kurt Busiek ★ Versus Squadron Supreme.

7 ❑ Aug 1998 Cover: 1.99 **NM** value: **Cover or less**
Circ: Statement: **166,903** Diamd. preorders: **114,805**
• gatefold summary. 📖 Live Kree or Die, Part 4; The Court Martial of Carol Danvers • Warbird leaves **W:** Kurt Busiek ★ Appearance of Supreme Intelligence.

8 ❑ Sep 1998 Cover: 1.99 **NM** value: **Cover or less**
Circ: Statement: **123,078** Diamd. preorders: **108,860**
• gatefold summary. 📖 Turbulence! **W:** Kurt Busiek ★ 1st Appearance of Silverclaw, Triathlon.

9 ❑ Oct 1998 Cover: 1.99 **NM** value: **Cover or less**
Circ: Statement: **123,078** Diamd. preorders: **105,835**
• gatefold summary. 📖 The Villain Who Fell from Grace with the Earth **W:** Kurt Busiek ★ Versus Moses Magnum.

10 ❑ Nov 1998 Cover: 1.99 **NM** value: **Cover or less**
Circ: Statement: **123,078**
• Anniversary issue. 📖 Pomp & Pageantry • Has 1998 Statement, filed 10/1/98; avg print run 236,730; avg sales 163,775; avg subs 3,148; avg total paid 166,903; samples 270; office use 125; max existent 167,318; 29% of run returned **W:** Kurt Busiek ★ Versus Grim Reaper.

11 ❑ Dec 1998 Cover: 1.99 **NM** value: **Cover or less**
Circ: Statement: **123,078** Diamd. preorders: **102,299**
• gatefold summary. 📖 … Always an Avenger! **W:** Kurt Busiek ★ Appearance of Wonder Man, Mockingbird, Doctor Druid, Captain Marvel, Hellcat, Swordsman. ★ Versus Grim Reaper.

12 ❑ Jan 1999 Cover: 2.99 **NM** value: **Cover or less**
Circ: Statement: **123,078** Diamd. preorders: **100,068** • **CGC:** 6 graded, best 9.8
wraparound cover. • double-sized. 📖 Old Entanglements • Continued from Thunderbolts #22 **A:** George Pérez **W:** Kurt Busiek ★ Versus Thunderbolts.

12/A❑Jan 1999 Cover: 29.95 **NM** value: **Cover or less**
DFE alternate cover. 📖 Old Entanglements • Continued from Thunderbolts #22 **A:** George Pérez **W:** Kurt Busiek

12/SC❑Jan 1999 Cover: 6.95 **NM** value: **Cover or less**
• **CGC:** 1 graded, best 9.8
DFE alternate cover. 📖 Old Entanglements • Continued from Thunderbolts #22 **A:** George Pérez **W:** Kurt Busiek

13 ❑ Feb 1999 Cover: 1.99 **NM** value: **Cover or less**
Circ: Statement: **123,078** Diamd. preorders: **94,752**
📖 Lords & Leaders **A:** George Pérez **W:** Kurt Busiek ★ Appearance of New Warriors.

14 ❑ Mar 1999 Cover: 1.99 **NM** value: **Cover or less**
Circ: Statement: **123,078** Diamd. preorders: **93,836**
📖 Hi Honey … I'm Home! • Return of Beast to team **A:** George Pérez **W:** Kurt Busiek ★ Appearance of Lord Templar, George P…rez, Beast, Kurt Busiek.

15 ❑ Apr 1999 Cover: 1.99 **NM** value: **Cover or less**
Circ: Statement: **123,078** Diamd. preorders: **90,047**
📖 The Three Fold Path **A:** George Pérez **W:** Kurt Busiek ★ Appearance of Lord Templar, Triathalon.

16 ❑ May 1999 Cover: 1.99 **NM** value: **Cover or less**
Circ: Statement: **123,078** Diamd. preorders: **93,265**
📖 Mistaken Identity ★ Versus Wrecking Crew.

17 ❑ Jun 1999 Cover: 1.99 **NM** value: **Cover or less**
Circ: Statement: **123,078** Diamd. preorders: **89,105**
📖 Cage of Freedom ★ Versus Doomsday Man.

18 ❑ Jul 1999 Cover: 1.99 **NM** value: **Cover or less**
Circ: Statement: **123,078** Diamd. preorders: **85,864**
📖 The Battle for Imperion City ★ Versus Wrecking Crew.

19 ❑ Aug 1999 Cover: 1.99 **NM** value: **Cover or less**
Circ: Statement: **97,835** Diamd. preorders: **87,811**
📖 This Evil Renewed ★ Appearance of Black Panther. ★ Versus Ultron.

20 ❑ Sep 1999 Cover: 1.99 **NM** value: **Cover or less**
Circ: Statement: **97,835** Diamd. preorders: **85,830**
📖 This Evil Unfolding ★ Versus Ultron.

21 ❑ Oct 1999 Cover: 1.99 **NM** value: **Cover or less**
Circ: Statement: **97,835** Diamd. preorders: **82,869**
📖 This Evil Unveiled ★ Versus Ultron.

22 ❑ Oct 1999 Cover: 1.99 **NM** value: **Cover or less**
Circ: Statement: **97,835** Diamd. preorders: **81,082**
📖 This Evil Triumphant! • Has 1999 Statement, filed 10/1/99; avg print run 175,250; avg sales 119,525; avg subs 3,553; avg total paid 123,078; samples 2,513; office use 125; max existent 125,716; 29% of run returned★ Versus Ultron.

23 ❑ Dec 1999 Cover: 1.99 **NM** value: **Cover or less**
Circ: Statement: **97,835** Diamd. preorders: **82,153**
📖 Showdown • Wonder Man versus Vision

24 ❑ Jan 2000 Cover: 1.99 **NM** value: **Cover or less**
Circ: Statement: **97,835** Diamd. preorders: **79,877**
📖 Harsh Judgments

25 ❑ Feb 2000 Cover: 2.99 **NM** value: **Cover or less**
Circ: Statement: **97,835** Diamd. preorders: **85,867**
• Giant-size. 📖 The Ninth Day ★ Appearance of Juggernaut.

26 ❑ Mar 2000 Cover: 1.99 **NM** value: **Cover or less**
Circ: Statement: **97,835** Diamd. preorders: **76,534**

27 ❑ Apr 2000 Cover: 1.99 **NM** value: **Cover or less**
Circ: Statement: **97,835** Diamd. preorders: **75,576**

28 ❑ May 2000 Cover: 1.99 **NM** value: **Cover or less**
Circ: Statement: **97,835** Diamd. preorders: **76,125**

29 ❑ Jun 2000 Cover: 2.25 **NM** value: **Cover or less**
Circ: Statement: **97,835** Diamd. preorders: **75,010**
📖 The Death-Song of Kulan Gath, Part 2; A Dream of Bitter Ash

30 ❑ Jul 2000 Cover: 2.25 **NM** value: **Cover or less**
Circ: Statement: **97,835** Diamd. preorders: **74,731**

31 ❑ Aug 2000 Cover: 2.25 **NM** value: **Cover or less**
Circ: Statement: **97,835** Diamd. preorders: **75,347**
📖 And So It Begins … ★ Appearance of Madame Masque, Grim Reaper.

32 ❑ Sep 2000 Cover: 2.25 **NM** value: **Cover or less**
Circ: Statement: **97,835** Diamd. preorders: **74,160**
📖 Behind the Masque! ★ Appearance of Madame Masque.

33 ❑ Oct 2000 Cover: 2.25 **NM** value: **Cover or less**
Circ: Statement: **82,849** Diamd. preorders: **69,789**
📖 Tainted Love ★ Appearance of Madame Masque, Thunderbolts. ★ Versus Count Nefaria.

34 ❑ Nov 2000 Cover: 2.99 **NM** value: **Cover or less**
Circ: Statement: **82,849** Diamd. preorders: **70,403**
• double-sized issue. 📖 The Nefaria Protocols ★ Appearance of Madame Masque, Thunderbolts. ★ Versus Count Nefaria.

35 ❑ Dec 2000 Cover: 2.25 **NM** value: **Cover or less**
Circ: Statement: **82,849** Diamd. preorders: **69,497**
📖 Maximum Security • Has 2000 Statement, filed 10/1/2000; avg print run 132,917; avg sales 94,496; avg subs 3,339; avg total paid 97,835; samples 600; office use 125; max existent 98,560; 26% of run returned

36 ❑ Jan 2001 Cover: 2.25 **NM** value: **Cover or less**
Circ: Statement: **82,849** Diamd. preorders: **67,575**
📖 No Rest for the Weary **A:** Steve Epting **W:** Kurt Busiek ★ Appearance of Ten-Thirtifor.

37 ❑ Feb 2001 Cover: 2.25 **NM** value: **Cover or less**
Circ: Statement: **82,849** Diamd. preorders: **66,367**
📖 Scorched Earth **A:** Steve Epting **W:** Kurt Busiek ★ Appearance of Bloodwraith.

38 ❑ Mar 2001 Cover: 1.99 **NM** value: **Cover or less**
Circ: Statement: **82,849** Diamd. preorders: **67,598**
📖 Above and Beyond • Slashback issue;price reduced **A:** Alan Davis **W:** Kurt Busiek

39 ❑ Apr 2001 Cover: 2.25 **NM** value: **Cover or less**
Circ: Statement: **82,849** Diamd. preorders: **65,558**
📖 Condition: Green **A:** Alan Davis **W:** Kurt Busiek

40 ❑ May 2001 Cover: 2.25 **NM** value: **Cover or less**
Circ: Statement: **82,849** Diamd. preorders: **64,853**

41 ❑ Jun 2001 Cover: 2.25 **NM** value: **Cover or less**
Circ: Statement: **82,849** Diamd. preorders: **67,719**

42 ❑ Jul 2001 Cover: 2.25 **NM** value: **Cover or less**
Circ: Statement: **82,849** Diamd. preorders: **67,741**

43 ❑ Aug 2001 Cover: 2.25 **NM** value: **Cover or less**
Circ: Statement: **82,849** Diamd. preorders: **69,127**

44 ❑ Sep 2001 Cover: 2.25 **NM** value: **Cover or less**
Circ: Statement: **82,849** Diamd. preorders: **70,669**

45 ❑ Oct 2001 Cover: 2.25 **NM** value: **Cover or less**
Circ: Diamd. preorders: **70,011**

46 ❑ Nov 2001 Cover: 2.25 **NM** value: **Cover or less**
Circ: Diamd. preorders: **65,398**

47 ❑ Dec 2001 Cover: 2.25 **NM** value: **Cover or less**
Circ: Diamd. preorders: **63,060**

48 ❑ Jan 2002 Cover: 3.50 **NM** value: **Cover or less**
Circ: Diamd. preorders: **63,346**

49 ❑ Feb 2002 Cover: 2.25 **NM** value: **Cover or less**
Circ: Diamd. preorders: **62,031**
• Has 2001 Statement, filed 10/1/2001; avg print run 107,992; avg sales 79,763; avg subs 3,086; avg total paid 82,849; samples 600; office use 0; max existent 83,449; 24% of run returned

50 ❑ Mar 2002 Cover: 3.50 **NM** value: **Cover or less**
Circ: Diamd. preorders: **60,119**

Anl 1998❑ca. 1998 Cover: 2.99 **NM** value: **Cover or less**
Circ: Diamd. preorders: **61,505**
wraparound cover. • gatefold summary. • Avengers/Squadron Supreme '98

Anl 1999❑Jul 1999 Cover: 3.50 **NM** value: **Cover or less**
Circ: Diamd. preorders: **52,873**
• Jarvis' story

Anl 2001❑ca. 2001 Cover: 2.99 **NM** value: **Cover or less**
Circ: Diamd. preorders: **51,543**
• 2001 Annual

AVENGERS WEST COAST — Marvel

Within the space of a year, Marvel took a look at the sales figures for two of its titles — West Coast Avengers and Classic X-Men — and decided that they'd be better off if retailers who sorted comics alphabetically racked them with their "parent" titles. As such, West Coast Avengers became Avengers West Coast, significant in that it's something no character would likely say. One can visualize the conversation: "Hi! We're the Avengers West Coast!" "Glad to meet you! We're the Cheerleaders Dallas Cowboy!"

Ahem. Well, anyway, this series continued the adventures of the Californian offshoot of Earth's Mightiest Heroes. It was cancelled just as the bubble market of the early 1990s burst, levelling many of the Marvel spinoffs. — JJM

47 ❑ Aug 1989 Cover: 0.75 **NM** value: **1.50**
Circ: Statement: **181,165** CapCity orders: **39,300**

48 ❑ Sep 1989 Cover: 1.00 **NM** value: **1.50**
Circ: Statement: **181,165** CapCity orders: **40,800**

Other grades: Multiply prices above by **1.5 for Mint • 2/3 for Very Fine • 1/3 for Fine • 1/5 for Very Good • 1/8 for Good**

49 ❑ Oct 1989 Cover: 1.00 **NM** value: **1.50**
Circ: Statement: **181,165** CapCity orders: **39,600**
📖 Baptism of Fire ★ Appearance of Great Lakes Avengers.

50 ❑ Nov 1989 Cover: 1.00 **NM** value: **1.50**
Circ: Statement: **181,165** CapCity orders: **41,500**
• Golden Age Human Torch returns ★ Appearance of 1st Silver Age.

51 ❑ Nov 1989 Cover: 1.00 **NM** value: **1.50**
Circ: Statement: **181,165** CapCity orders: **39,300**
📖 I Sing of Arms and Heroes ... ★ Appearance of Iron Man.

52 ❑ Dec 1989 Cover: 1.00 **NM** value: **1.50**
Circ: Statement: **181,165** CapCity orders: **39,300**

53 ❑ Dec 1989 Cover: 1.00 **NM** value: **1.50**
Circ: Statement: **181,165**
📖 Acts of Vengeance, Part 7; The Plan Proceeds • "Acts of Vengeance" ★ Versus U-Foes.

54 ❑ Jan 1990 Cover: 1.00 **NM** value: **1.50**
Circ: Statement: **206,933** CapCity orders: **42,300**
Fantastic Four #1 cover homage. 📖 Acts of Vengeance, Part 16; The Troubled Earth • "Acts of Vengeance" ★ Versus Mole Man.

55 ❑ Feb 1990 Cover: 1.00 **NM** value: **1.50**
Circ: Statement: **206,933** CapCity orders: **42,600**
📖 Acts of Vengeance, Part 24; The Breaking Strain • "Acts of Vengeance" ★ Versus Loki.

56 ❑ Mar 1990 Cover: 1.00 **NM** value: **1.50**
Circ: Statement: **206,933** CapCity orders: **39,600**
📖 Darker Than Scarlet **A:** John Byrne

57 ❑ Apr 1990 Cover: 1.00 **NM** value: **1.50**
Circ: Statement: **206,933** CapCity orders: **39,300**
📖 Family Reunion **A:** John Byrne ★ Appearance of Magneto, Quicksilver.

58 ❑ May 1990 Cover: 1.00 **NM** value: **1.50**
Circ: Statement: **206,933** CapCity orders: **39,600**
• Has 1989 Statement, filed 11/1/89; avg print run 289,150; avg sales 176,030; avg subs 5,135; avg total paid 181,165; samples 125; office use 600; max existent 181,890; 37% of run returned

59 ❑ Jun 1990 Cover: 1.00 **NM** value: **1.50**
Circ: Statement: **206,933** CapCity orders: **35,700**

60 ❑ Jul 1990 Cover: 1.00 **NM** value: **1.50**
Circ: Statement: **206,933** CapCity orders: **35,400**

61 ❑ Aug 1990 Cover: 1.00 **NM** value: **1.25**
Circ: Statement: **206,933** CapCity orders: **32,700**

62 ❑ Sep 1990 Cover: 1.00 **NM** value: **1.25**
Circ: Statement: **206,933** CapCity orders: **31,800**

63 ❑ Oct 1990 Cover: 1.00 **NM** value: **1.25**
Circ: Statement: **206,933** CapCity orders: **30,600**
★ Origin of Living Lightning. ★ 1st Appearance of Living Lightning.

64 ❑ Nov 1990 Cover: 1.00 **NM** value: **1.25**
Circ: Statement: **206,933** CapCity orders: **30,300**
★ Appearance of Captain America.

65 ❑ Dec 1990 Cover: 1.00 **NM** value: **1.25**
Circ: Statement: **206,933** CapCity orders: **30,000**

66 ❑ Jan 1991 Cover: 1.00 **NM** value: **1.25**
Circ: Statement: **152,442** CapCity orders: **29,100**
★ Versus Ultron.

67 ❑ Feb 1991 Cover: 1.00 **NM** value: **1.25**
Circ: Statement: **152,442** CapCity orders: **28,500**

68 ❑ Mar 1991 Cover: 1.00 **NM** value: **1.25**
Circ: Statement: **152,442** CapCity orders: **27,300**
• Has 1990 Statement, filed 10/1/90; avg print run 316,550; avg sales 202,100; avg subs 4,833; avg total paid 206,933; samples 100; office use 600; max existent 207,633; 34% of run returned

69 ❑ Apr 1991 Cover: 1.00 **NM** value: **1.25**
Circ: Statement: **152,442** CapCity orders: **26,700**

70 ❑ May 1991 Cover: 1.00 **NM** value: **1.25**
Circ: Statement: **152,442** CapCity orders: **27,300**

71 ❑ Jun 1991 Cover: 1.00 **NM** value: **1.25**
Circ: Statement: **152,442** CapCity orders: **27,300**

72 ❑ Jul 1991 Cover: 1.00 **NM** value: **1.25**
Circ: Statement: **152,442** CapCity orders: **27,900**

73 ❑ Aug 1991 Cover: 1.00 **NM** value: **1.25**
Circ: Statement: **152,442** CapCity orders: **28,200**

74 ❑ Sep 1991 Cover: 1.00 **NM** value: **1.25**
Circ: Statement: **152,442** CapCity orders: **27,600**

75 ❑ Oct 1991 Cover: 1.50 **NM** value: **Cover or less**
Circ: Statement: **152,442** CapCity orders: **29,100**
• Double-size issue. ★ Appearance of Fantastic Four, Thundra.

76 ❑ Nov 1991 Cover: 1.00 **NM** value: **1.25**
Circ: Statement: **152,442** CapCity orders: **26,700**

77 ❑ Dec 1991 Cover: 1.00 **NM** value: **1.25**
Circ: Statement: **152,442** CapCity orders: **26,200**

78 ❑ Jan 1992 Cover: 1.00 **NM** value: **1.25**
Circ: CapCity orders: **25,700**

79 ❑ Feb 1992 Cover: 1.25 **NM** value: **Cover or less**
Circ: CapCity orders: **24,100**

80 ❑ Mar 1992 Cover: 1.25 **NM** value: **Cover or less**
Circ: CapCity orders: **33,900**
📖 Operation: Galactic Storm, Part 2; Turn of the Sentry • Galactic Storm; Has 1991 Statement, filed 10/1/91; avg print run 243,158; avg sales 148,550; avg subs 3,892; avg total paid 152,442; samples 125; office use 250; max existent 152,817; 37% of run returned

81 ❑ Apr 1992 Cover: 1.25 **NM** value: **Cover or less**
Circ: CapCity orders: **30,700**
📖 Operation: Galactic Storm, Part 9; They Also Serve ... • Galactic Storm

82 ❑ May 1992 Cover: 1.25 **NM** value: **Cover or less**
Circ: CapCity orders: **31,500**
📖 Operation: Galactic Storm, Part 16; Shi'ar Hatred • Galactic Storm

83 ❑ Jun 1992 Cover: 1.25 **NM** value: **Cover or less**
Circ: CapCity orders: **24,900**

84 ❑ Jul 1992 Cover: 1.25 **NM** value: **Cover or less**
Circ: CapCity orders: **30,800**
★ Origin of Spider Woman.

85 ❑ Aug 1992 Cover: 1.25 **NM** value: **Cover or less**
Circ: CapCity orders: **30,100**

86 ❑ Sep 1992 Cover: 1.25 **NM** value: **Cover or less**
Circ: CapCity orders: **24,500**

87 ❑ Oct 1992 Cover: 1.25 **NM** value: **Cover or less**
Circ: CapCity orders: **28,900**

88 ❑ Nov 1992 Cover: 1.25 **NM** value: **Cover or less**
Circ: CapCity orders: **27,600**

89 ❑ Dec 1992 Cover: 1.25 **NM** value: **Cover or less**
Circ: CapCity orders: **21,900**

90 ❑ Jan 1993 Cover: 1.25 **NM** value: **Cover or less**
Circ: CapCity orders: **20,700**

91 ❑ Feb 1993 Cover: 1.25 **NM** value: **Cover or less**
Circ: CapCity orders: **20,900**

92 ❑ Mar 1993 Cover: 1.25 **NM** value: **Cover or less**
Circ: CapCity orders: **19,500**

93 ❑ Apr 1993 Cover: 1.25 **NM** value: **Cover or less**
Circ: CapCity orders: **21,100**

94 ❑ May 1993 Cover: 1.25 **NM** value: **Cover or less**
Circ: CapCity orders: **21,100**

95 ❑ Jun 1993 Cover: 1.25 **NM** value: **Cover or less**
Circ: CapCity orders: **20,800**

96 ❑ Jul 1993 Cover: 1.25 **NM** value: **Cover or less**
Circ: CapCity orders: **25,000**
📖 Infinity Crusade

97 ❑ Aug 1993 Cover: 1.25 **NM** value: **Cover or less**
Circ: CapCity orders: **26,200**
📖 Infinity Crusade

98 ❑ Sep 1993 Cover: 1.25 **NM** value: **Cover or less**
Circ: CapCity orders: **21,200**

99 ❑ Oct 1993 Cover: 1.25 **NM** value: **Cover or less**
Circ: CapCity orders: **21,000**
A: Dave Ross **W:** Roy Thomas ★ Appearance of Lethal Legion, Hangman.

100 ❑ Nov 1993 Cover: 3.95 **NM** value: **Cover or less**
Circ: CapCity orders: **44,100**
sculpted foil cover.

101 ❑ Dec 1993 Cover: 1.25 **NM** value: **Cover or less**
Circ: CapCity orders: **58,100**
📖 Bloodties, Part 3

102 ❑ Jan 1994 Cover: 1.25 **NM** value: **Cover or less**
Circ: CapCity orders: **25,700**
final issue.

Anl 4 ❑ ca. 1989 Cover: 2.00 **NM** value: **2.50**
Circ: CapCity orders: **47,600**
📖 Atlantis Attacks, Part 12 • see West Coast Avengers for previous Annuals;"Atlantis Attacks"

Anl 5 ❑ ca. 1990 Cover: 2.00 **NM** value: **2.50**
Circ: CapCity orders: **35,200**
📖 The Terminus Factor, Part 4; When Titan Trash!; Media Watch; Tanks for Nothing; Don't You Daaare Miss It!; Honey, I Shrunk the Hyperatomic Anti-Proton Cannon • "Terminus Factor" **A:** James W. Fry III; Grant Miehm; Brad Vancata; Jim Reddington **W:** Dwayne McDuffie; Roy Thomas; Bob Tokar; Carrie Barre; Dann Thomas; Gary Barnum

Anl 6 ❑ Cover: 2.00 **NM** value: **2.50**
Circ: CapCity orders: **32,100**
📖 Subterranean Wars, Part 5; West Side Story!; A Wasp in Hollywood!; Justice, Like Lightning

Anl 7 ❑ ca. 1992 Cover: 2.25 **NM** value: **Cover or less**
Circ: CapCity orders: **29,400**
📖 Assault on Armor City, Part 2

Anl 8 ❑ Cover: 2.95 **NM** value: **Cover or less**
Circ: CapCity orders: **22,500**
📖 If Volcanic Winter Comes • Polybagged with trading card ★ 1st Appearance of Raptor.

AVENGERS/X-MEN: BLOODTIES — Marvel

1 ❑ Jan 1995 Cover: 15.95 **NM** value: **Cover or less**
• Trade Paperback. • collects Avengers #368 and 369, Avengers West Coast #101, Uncanny X-Men #307, and X-Men #26

AVENUE D — Fantagraphics

All issues are adults only.

1 ❑ b&w Cover: 3.50 **NM** value: **Cover or less**

AVENUE X — Purple Spiral Productions

1 ❑ Cover: 3.00 **NM** value: **Cover or less**

AVIATION CADETS — Street & Smith

1 ❑ **NM** value: **100.00**

AVIGON — Image

1 ❑ Oct 2000 Cover: 5.95 **NM** value: **Cover or less**
Circ: Diamd. preorders: **6,025**
A: Jimmie Robinson **W:** Ché Gilson

A-V IN 3-D — Aardvark-Vanaheim

A-V in 3-D was a one-shot special designed to introduce new readers to Aardvark Vanaheim's 1984 lineup. Aardvark-Vanaheim's founder, Dave Sim, is the creator of the highly successful comic book series Cerebus the Aardvark. Among A-V's other offerings were such worthwhile titles as Ms. Tree from Max Collins, Bob Burden's Flaming Carrot, Valentino's Normalman, Bill Messner-Loebs' Journey, and Arn Saba's Neil the Horse.

This special is an oddity for Aardvark-Vanaheim, which is known for their straightforward "no gimmicks" approach to comics publishing. In an attempt to boost sales and bring more readers into the Aardvark-Vanaheim stable, Publishers Deni Loubert and Sim made an exception and printed this special with a 3-D process. The effect (which was used in a similar line of books by Pacific Comics) can be quite striking at times, such as when illustrating the dream sequence found in the issue's Cerebus story.

1 ❑ Dec 1984 Cover: 2.00 **NM** value: **5.00**
📖 Mist-Tree Tale In Tree-D • glasses **A:** Gary Kato; Zone **W:** Terry Beatty; Max Allan Collins

AWAKENING, THE — Image

1 ❑ Oct 1997 Cover: 2.95 **NM** value: **Cover or less**
Circ: Diamd. preorders: **6,983**
📖 To Sleep Perchance to Dream! **A:** Stephen Blue **W:** Stephen Blue

2 ❑ Dec 1997 Cover: 2.95 **NM** value: **Cover or less**
Circ: Diamd. preorders: **1,926**
A: Stephen Blue **W:** Stephen Blue

3 ❑ Feb 1998 Cover: 2.95 **NM** value: **Cover or less**
Circ: Diamd. preorders: **3,552**
A: Stephen Blue **W:** Stephen Blue

4 ❑ Apr 1998 Cover: 2.95 **NM** value: **Cover or less**
Circ: Diamd. preorders: **3,245**
A: Stephen Blue **W:** Stephen Blue

Bk 1 ❑ b&w Cover: 9.95 **NM** value: **Cover or less**
• collects mini-series **A:** Stephen Blue **W:** Stephen Blue

AWAKENING COMICS — Awakening Comics

1 ❑ Cover: 3.50 **NM** value: **Cover or less**

2 ❑ Nov 1997 Cover: 3.50 **NM** value: **Cover or less**
📖 Reminiscing; Karma Komix: Back to Bardo; Crumb on the Street; Hangin' With Joe; Monster in a Box; Circus of Heaven; Rabbit Hell vs. Cerebus; Rabbit Hell: In the Beginning **A:** Dave Sim; Steve Peters; Nowell ★ Appearance of Cerebus the Aardvark, Cerebus.

3 ❑ Aug 1998 Cover: 2.95 **NM** value: **Cover or less**
wraparound cover. • "The Everwinds Awakening War"

4 ❑ **NM** value: **2.95**
A: Jeff Peters **W:** Jeff Peters ★ 1st Appearance of Melvin G. Moose, Private Eye.

AWAKENING COMICS 1999 — Awakening Comics

1 ❑ 1999b&w Cover: 3.50 **NM** value: **Cover or less**

AWESOME ADVENTURES — Awesome

1/A ❑ Aug 1999 Cover: 2.50 **NM** value: **Cover or less**
Circ: Diamd. preorders: **13,000**
Woman standing (full length) on cover. 📖 Youngblood: Dandy in the Underworld **A:** Steve Skroce **W:** Alan Moore

1/B ❑ Aug 1999 Cover: 2.50 **NM** value: **Cover or less**
Circ: Diamd. preorders: **12,000**
Woman standing (3/4 length) on cover. 📖 Youngblood: Dandy in the Underworld **A:** Steve Skroce **W:** Alan Moore

AWESOME HOLIDAY SPECIAL — Awesome

1 ❑ Dec 1997 Cover: 2.50 **NM** value: **Cover or less**
Circ: Diamd. preorders: **22,623**
Flip cover. 📖 Fighting America; Shaft; Coven; Kaboom • Youngblood side has gold foil logo **A:** Ian Churchill; Rob Liefeld; Jeff Matsuda; Steve Skroce **W:** Jeph Loeb; Alan Moore

AWESOME PREVIEW — Awesome

1 ❑ 1997 **NM** value: **1.00**
No issue number. • b&w and color previews of upcoming Awesome series given out at Comic-Con International: San Diego '97 **A:** Alex Ross(cover)

AWFUL OSCAR — Marvel

11 ❑ Jun 1949 Cover: 0.10 **NM** value: **50.00**
12 ❑ Dec 1949 Cover: 0.10 **NM** value: **50.00**

AWKWARD — Slave Labor

1 ❑ Cover: 4.95 **NM** value: **Cover or less**
A: Ariel Schrag **W:** Ariel Schrag

AWKWARD UNIVERSE — Slave Labor

1 ❑ Dec 1995 Cover: 9.95 **NM** value: **Cover or less**
No issue number. One-shot.

AXA (KEN PIERCE) — Ken Pierce

1 ❑ Cover: 5.95 **NM** value: **Cover or less**
Circ: CapCity orders: **6,625**
📖 The Beginning; The Chosen **A:** Enrique Romero **W:** Donne Avenell; Maggie Thgompson

2 ❑ Cover: 5.95 **NM** value: **Cover or less**
Circ: CapCity orders: **5,175**
📖 The Desired **A:** Enrique Romero **W:** Donne Avenell

3 ❑ Cover: 5.95 **NM** value: **Cover or less**
📖 The Brave; The Gambler **A:** Enrique Romero **W:** C.C. Beck; Donne Avenell

4 ❑ Cover: 5.95 **NM** value: **Cover or less**
📖 The Earthbound; The Tempted **A:** Enrique Romero **W:** Donne Avenell

5 ❑ Cover: 5.95 **NM** value: **Cover or less**
📖 The Eager; The Carefree **A:** Enrique Romero **W:** Donne Avenell

6 ❑ Cover: 5.95 **NM** value: **Cover or less**
📖 The Dwarfed; The Untamed **A:** Enrique Romero **W:** Donne Avenell

7 ❑ Cover: 5.95 **NM** value: **Cover or less**
📖 The Mobile; The Unmasked **A:** Enrique Romero **W:** Donne Avenell

8 ❑ Cover: 5.95 **NM** value: **Cover or less**
A: Enrique Romero **W:** Donne Avenell

GN 1 ❑ Cover: 5.95 **NM** value: **Cover or less**
A: Enrique Romero **W:** Donne Avenell

AXED FILES — Express / Parody

1 ❑ 1995b&w Cover: 2.50 **NM** value: **Cover or less**
Circ: CapCity orders: **2,670**

AXEL PRESSBUTTON — Eclipse

1 ❑ Nov 1984 Cover: 1.50 **NM** value: **2.00**
📖 Laser Eraser and Pressbutton; Zirk: Silver Sweater of the Spaceways **A:** Steve Dillon **W:** Pedro Henry

2 ❑ Jan 1985 Cover: 1.50 **NM** value: **2.00**
3 ❑ Mar 1985 Cover: 1.50 **NM** value: **2.00**
Circ: CapCity orders: **4,300**

CGC-graded: Multiply prices above by **33 for 9.9 M • 16 for 9.8 NM/M • 7 for 9.6 NM+ • 5 for 9.4 NM • 2.5 for 9.2 NM- • 1.5 for 9.0 VF/NM**

4 ❑ May 1985 Cover: 1.50 **NM** value: **2.00**
Circ: CapCity orders: **4,525**

5 ❑ Jul 1985 Cover: 1.75 **NM** value: **2.00**
Circ: CapCity orders: **4,325**
• Continues as Pressbutton

6 ❑ Sep 1985 Cover: 1.75 **NM** value: **2.00**
Circ: CapCity orders: **3,725**

AXIS ALPHA — Axis

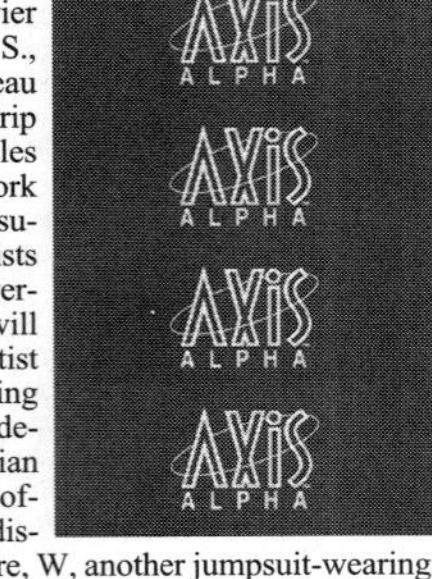

Axis Alpha was a sampler of titles from Axis Comics, circa 1994. Javier Saltares delivered B.E.A.S.T.I.E.S., an X-flavored supergroup. Beau Smith and Jim Callahan's DethGrip featured a freelancer with big muscles and firearms. Gene Ha's fine artwork graced Todd Johnson's Shelter, a supersecret agency of superspecialists laced with conspiracy-theory overtones. Fans of artist Neal Adams will have fun identifying panels that artist Larry Stroman swiped in illustrating Johnson's Tribe, about an outside-the-law armored mercenary. Brian McDonald and Brian O'Connell offered credible storytelling and distinctive artwork for the final feature, W, another jumpsuit-wearing, gun-toting private security expert.

1 ❑ Feb 1994 Cover: 2.50 **NM** value: **Cover or less**
B.E.A.S.T.I.E.S.; Dethgrip; Shelter; Tribe; W **A:** Jim Callahan; Gene Ha; Javier Saltares; Brian O'Connell; Larry Stroman **W:** Javier Saltares; Beau Smith; Brian McDonald; Todd Johnson

AXIS MUNDI — Amaze Ink

2 ❑ b&w Cover: 2.95 **NM** value: **Cover or less**
wraparound cover. • no indicia

AZ — Comico

1 ❑ b&w Cover: 1.50 **NM** value: **Cover or less**
• **CGC:** 1 graded, best 8.5
Comes Death

2 ❑ b&w Cover: 1.50 **NM** value: **Cover or less**
• **CGC:** 1 graded, best 8.5
A: Phil Lasorda **W:** Phil Lasorda

AZRAEL — DC

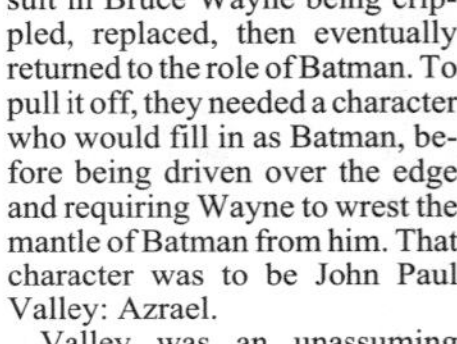

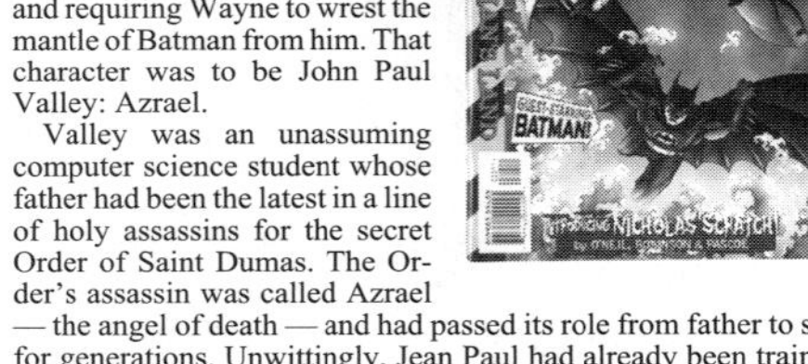

In 1992, the editors of DC were already planning the 71-part Knightfall saga which would result in Bruce Wayne being crippled, replaced, then eventually returned to the role of Batman. To pull it off, they needed a character who would fill in as Batman, before being driven over the edge and requiring Wayne to wrest the mantle of Batman from him. That character was to be John Paul Valley: Azrael.

Valley was an unassuming computer science student whose father had been the latest in a line of holy assassins for the secret Order of Saint Dumas. The Order's assassin was called Azrael — the angel of death — and had passed its role from father to son for generations. Unwittingly, Jean Paul had already been trained to assume the role through a subconscious sort of training called "The System." When his father died, the shy computer scientist suddenly discovered within himself a knowledge of advanced martial techniques — and a violent destiny as the new Azrael.

1 ❑ Feb 1995 Cover: 1.95 **NM** value: **3.00**
Circ: CapCity orders: **57,975** • **CGC:** 5 graded, best 9.6
★ Appearance of Batman.

2 ❑ Mar 1995 Cover: 1.95 **NM** value: **2.00**
Circ: CapCity orders: **37,400**
Some Say In Ice **A:** Barry Kitson **W:** Denny O'Neil ★ Appearance of Batman.

3 ❑ Apr 1995 Cover: 1.95 **NM** value: **2.00**
Circ: CapCity orders: **33,075**

4 ❑ May 1995 Cover: 1.95 **NM** value: **2.00**
Circ: CapCity orders: **30,350**

5 ❑ Jun 1995 Cover: 1.95 **NM** value: **2.00**
Circ: CapCity orders: **28,225**

6 ❑ Jul 1995 Cover: 1.95 **NM** value: **2.00**
Circ: CapCity orders: **26,500**

7 ❑ Aug 1995 Cover: 1.95 **NM** value: **2.00**
Circ: CapCity orders: **25,400**

8 ❑ Sep 1995 Cover: 1.95 **NM** value: **2.00**
Circ: CapCity orders: **23,600**

9 ❑ Oct 1995 Cover: 1.95 **NM** value: **2.00**
Circ: CapCity orders: **19,950**

10 ❑ Nov 1995 Cover: 1.95 **NM** value: **2.00**
Underworld Unleashed • "Underworld Unleashed"

11 ❑ Dec 1995 Cover: 1.95 **NM** value: **2.00**

12 ❑ Jan 1996 Cover: 1.95 **NM** value: **2.00**

13 ❑ Feb 1996 Cover: 1.95 **NM** value: **2.00**
Demon Time, Part 1 **A:** Barry Kitson **W:** Denny O'Neil

14 ❑ Mar 1996 Cover: 1.95 **NM** value: **2.00**
Demon Time, Part 2 **A:** Barry Kitson **W:** Denny O'Neil

15 ❑ Mar 1996 Cover: 1.95 **NM** value: **2.00**
Marked as Contagion, Part 4 on cover. Contagion, Part 4; Contagion, Part 5 **A:** Barry Kitson **W:** Denny O'Neil

16 ❑ Apr 1996 Cover: 1.95 **NM** value: **2.00**
Contagion, Part 10 **A:** Barry Kitson **W:** Denny O'Neil

17 ❑ May 1996 Cover: 1.95 **NM** value: **2.00**

18 ❑ Jun 1996 Cover: 1.95 **NM** value: **2.00**

19 ❑ Jul 1996 Cover: 1.95 **NM** value: **2.00**

20 ❑ Aug 1996 Cover: 1.95 **NM** value: **2.00**

21 ❑ Sep 1996 Cover: 1.95 **NM** value: **2.00**
Angel in Waiting, Part 1 **A:** Barry Kitson **W:** Denny O'Neil

22 ❑ Oct 1996 Cover: 1.95 **NM** value: **2.00**
Angel in Hiding, Part 2 **A:** Barry Kitson **W:** Denny O'Neil

23 ❑ Oct 1996 Cover: 1.95 **NM** value: **2.00**
Circ: Diamd. preorders: **41,377**
Angel in Hiding, Part 3 **A:** Barry Kitson **W:** Denny O'Neil

24 ❑ Dec 1996 Cover: 1.95 **NM** value: **2.00**
Circ: Direct Market orders: **40,678**
The Fall of Saint Dumas, Part 1 **A:** Barry Kitson **W:** Denny O'Neil

25 ❑ Jan 1997 Cover: 1.95 **NM** value: **2.00**
Circ: Direct Market orders: **38,985**
The Fall of Saint Dumas, Part 2 **A:** Barry Kitson **W:** Denny O'Neil

26 ❑ Feb 1997 Cover: 1.95 **NM** value: **2.00**
Circ: Diamd. preorders: **37,135**
The Fall of Saint Dumas, Part 3 **A:** Barry Kitson **W:** Denny O'Neil

27 ❑ Mar 1997 Cover: 1.95 **NM** value: **2.00**
Angel Insane, Part 1 **A:** Barry Kitson **W:** Denny O'Neil

28 ❑ Apr 1997 Cover: 1.95 **NM** value: **2.00**
Circ: Diamd. preorders: **34,892**
Angel Insane, Part 2 **A:** Barry Kitson **W:** Denny O'Neil

29 ❑ May 1997 Cover: 1.95 **NM** value: **2.00**
Circ: Diamd. preorders: **34,090**

30 ❑ Jun 1997 Cover: 1.95 **NM** value: **2.00**
Circ: Diamd. preorders: **34,473**
★ Appearance of Ra's Al Ghul.

31 ❑ Jul 1997 Cover: 1.95 **NM** value: **2.00**
Circ: Diamd. preorders: **32,580**

32 ❑ Aug 1997 Cover: 1.95 **NM** value: **2.00**
Circ: Diamd. preorders: **31,690**

33 ❑ Sep 1997 Cover: 1.99 **NM** value: **2.00**
Circ: Diamd. preorders: **30,560**

34 ❑ Oct 1997 Cover: 1.95 **NM** value: **2.00**
Circ: Diamd. preorders: **32,563**
• "Genesis" ★ Versus Parademons.

35 ❑ Nov 1997 Cover: 1.95 **NM** value: **2.00**
Circ: Diamd. preorders: **29,905**
The Angel and the Hitman **A:** Roger Robinson **W:** Denny O'Neil ★ Appearance of Hitman.

36 ❑ Dec 1997 Cover: 1.95 **NM** value: **2.00**
Circ: Diamd. preorders: **30,499**
Face cover. Azrael and Bane **A:** Roger Robinson **W:** Denny O'Neil ★ Appearance of Batman. ★ Versus Bane.

37 ❑ Jan 1998 Cover: 1.95 **NM** value: **2.00**
Circ: Diamd. preorders: **28,910**
★ Versus Bane.

38 ❑ Feb 1998 Cover: 1.95 **NM** value: **2.00**
Circ: Diamd. preorders: **28,224**
★ Versus Bane.

39 ❑ Mar 1998 Cover: 1.95 **NM** value: **2.00**
Circ: Diamd. preorders: **27,991**
★ Versus Bane.

40 ❑ Apr 1998 Cover: 1.95 **NM** value: **2.00**
Circ: Diamd. preorders: **35,013**
Cataclysm, Part 4 • continues in Detective Comics #720 **A:** Roger Robinson **W:** Denny O'Neil ★ Versus Bane.

41 ❑ May 1998 Cover: 1.99 **NM** value: **2.00**
Circ: Diamd. preorders: **28,173**

42 ❑ Jun 1998 Cover: 1.99 **NM** value: **2.00**
Circ: Diamd. preorders: **28,774**

43 ❑ Jul 1998 Cover: 1.99 **NM** value: **2.00**
Circ: Diamd. preorders: **26,987**

44 ❑ Aug 1998 Cover: 1.99 **NM** value: **2.00**
Circ: Diamd. preorders: **25,896**

45 ❑ Sep 1998 Cover: 2.25 **NM** value: **Cover or less**
Circ: Diamd. preorders: **24,408**
★ Versus Deathstroke.

46 ❑ Oct 1998 Cover: 1.99 **NM** value: **2.00**
Circ: Diamd. preorders: **23,184**

47 ❑ Dec 1998 Cover: 3.95 **NM** value: **4.00**
• Title changes to "Azrael: Agent of the Bat";"Road to No Man's Land";flipbook with Batman: Shadow of the Bat #80 (true title) ★ 1st Appearance of Nicholas Scratch. ★ Death of Senator Halivan.

47/LE ❑ Dec 1998 Cover: 15.95 **NM** value: **Cover or less**
• Series name changes to "Azrael: Agent of the Bat"

48 ❑ Jan 1999 Cover: 2.25 **NM** value: **Cover or less**
Circ: Diamd. preorders: **23,776**
Road to No Man's Land • "Road to No Man's Land";Batman cameo **A:** Roger Robinson **W:** Denny O'Neil ★ Appearance of Nicholas Scratch. ★ Versus Nicholas Scratch.

49 ❑ Feb 1999 Cover: 2.25 **NM** value: **Cover or less**
Circ: Diamd. preorders: **23,136**
• "Road to No Man's Land" **A:** Roger Robinson **W:** Denny O'Neil ★ Appearance of Batman, Nicholas Scratch.

50 ❑ Mar 1999 Cover: 2.25 **NM** value: **Cover or less**
Circ: Diamd. preorders: **26,190**
• "No Man's Land" **A:** Roger Robinson **W:** Denny O'Neil ★ Appearance of Batman.

51 ❑ Apr 1999 Cover: 2.25 **NM** value: **Cover or less**
Circ: Diamd. preorders: **23,177**
• "No Man's Land";new costume **A:** Roger Robinson **W:** Denny O'Neil ★ Appearance of Nicholas Scratch.

52 ❑ May 1999 Cover: 2.25 **NM** value: **Cover or less**
Circ: Diamd. preorders: **24,857**
• "No Man's Land"

53 ❑ Jun 1999 Cover: 2.25 **NM** value: **Cover or less**
Circ: Diamd. preorders: **28,761**
Jellybean Deathtrap • "No Man's Land" **A:** Roger Robinson **W:** Denny O'Neil ★ Appearance of Joker. ★ Versus Joker.

54 ❑ Jul 1999 Cover: 2.25 **NM** value: **Cover or less**
Circ: Diamd. preorders: **26,895**
Step into the Light • "No Man's Land" **A:** Roger Robinson **W:** Denny O'Neil ★ Appearance of Oracle.

55 ❑ Aug 1999 Cover: 2.25 **NM** value: **Cover or less**
Circ: Diamd. preorders: **27,053**
Misery Dance • "No Man's Land" **A:** Roger Robinson **W:** Denny O'Neil

56 ❑ Sep 1999 Cover: 2.25 **NM** value: **Cover or less**
Circ: Diamd. preorders: **29,137**
The Night Foretold! • "No Man's Land" **A:** Roger Robinson **W:** Denny O'Neil ★ Appearance of Batgirl.

57 ❑ Oct 1999 Cover: 2.25 **NM** value: **Cover or less**
Circ: Diamd. preorders: **28,569**
Scratched Out! • "No Man's Land" **A:** Roger Robinson **W:** Denny O'Neil ★ Appearance of Batgirl.

58 ❑ Nov 1999 Cover: 2.25 **NM** value: **Cover or less**
Circ: Diamd. preorders: **28,511**
Ghosts • "No Man's Land";Day of Judgment **A:** Roger Robinson **W:** Denny O'Neil ★ Appearance of Saint Dumas.

59 ❑ Dec 1999 Cover: 2.25 **NM** value: **Cover or less**
Circ: Diamd. preorders: **28,322**
Pilgrim's Return • No Man's Land **A:** Roger Robinson **W:** Denny O'Neil

60 ❑ Jan 2000 Cover: 2.25 **NM** value: **Cover or less**
Circ: Diamd. preorders: **27,968**
Evacuation • No Man's Land **A:** Roger Robinson **W:** Denny O'Neil

61 ❑ Feb 2000 Cover: 2.25 **NM** value: **Cover or less**
Circ: Diamd. preorders: **29,765**
A: Roger Robinson **W:** Denny O'Neil

62 ❑ Mar 2000 Cover: 2.25 **NM** value: **Cover or less**
Circ: Diamd. preorders: **24,235**
A: Roger Robinson **W:** Denny O'Neil

63 ❑ Apr 2000 Cover: 2.25 **NM** value: **Cover or less**
Circ: Diamd. preorders: **23,249**
A: Roger Robinson **W:** Denny O'Neil

64 ❑ May 2000 Cover: 2.25 **NM** value: **Cover or less**
Circ: Diamd. preorders: **23,018**
Fugitive **A:** Roger Robinson **W:** Denny O'Neil

65 ❑ Jun 2000 Cover: 2.25 **NM** value: **Cover or less**
Circ: Diamd. preorders: **22,197**
The Witness **A:** Roger Robinson **W:** Denny O'Neil

66 ❑ Jul 2000 Cover: 2.25 **NM** value: **Cover or less**
Circ: Diamd. preorders: **22,099**
New Order **A:** Roger Robinson **W:** Denny O'Neil

67 ❑ Aug 2000 Cover: 2.25 **NM** value: **Cover or less**
Circ: Diamd. preorders: **21,817**
Maternal Instinct **A:** Roger Robinson **W:** Denny O'Neil

68 ❑ Sep 2000 Cover: 2.25 **NM** value: **Cover or less**
Circ: Diamd. preorders: **21,461**
Mirage **A:** Roger Robinson **W:** Denny O'Neil

69 ❑ Oct 2000 Cover: 2.50 **NM** value: **Cover or less**
Circ: Diamd. preorders: **19,784**
The Pursuit **A:** Sergio Carielo **W:** Denny O'Neil

70 ❑ Nov 2000 Cover: 2.50 **NM** value: **Cover or less**
Circ: Diamd. preorders: **19,436**
Cry for Atonement **A:** Sergio Carielo **W:** Denny O'Neil

71 ❑ Dec 2000 Cover: 2.50 **NM** value: **Cover or less**
Circ: Diamd. preorders: **18,964**
Brothers **A:** Sergio Carielo **W:** Denny O'Neil

72 ❑ Jan 2001 Cover: 2.50 **NM** value: **Cover or less**
Circ: Diamd. preorders: **18,466**
Hell & Back **A:** Sergio Carielo **W:** Denny O'Neil

73 ❑ Feb 2001 Cover: 2.50 **NM** value: **Cover or less**
Circ: Diamd. preorders: **18,309**
Losses, Part 1 **A:** Sergio Carielo **W:** Denny O'Neil

74 ❑ Mar 2001 Cover: 2.50 **NM** value: **Cover or less**
Circ: Diamd. preorders: **17,526**
Losses, Part 2 **A:** Sergio Carielo **W:** Denny O'Neil

75 ❑ Apr 2001 Cover: 3.95 **NM** value: **Cover or less**
Circ: Diamd. preorders: **18,320**
• Giant-size. Losses, Part 3 **A:** Sergio Carielo **W:** Denny O'Neil

76 ❑ May 2001 Cover: 2.50 **NM** value: **Cover or less**
Circ: Diamd. preorders: **17,025**
There Shall Be a Beginning **A:** Sergio Carielo **W:** Denny O'Neil

77 ❑ Jun 2001 Cover: 2.50 **NM** value: **Cover or less**
Circ: Diamd. preorders: **17,024**
Poison Road **A:** Sergio Carielo **W:** Denny O'Neil

78 ❑ Jul 2001 Cover: 2.50 **NM** value: **Cover or less**
Circ: Diamd. preorders: **16,678**

79 ❑ Aug 2001 Cover: 2.50 **NM** value: **Cover or less**
Circ: Diamd. preorders: **16,672**

80 ❑ Sep 2001 Cover: 2.50 **NM** value: **Cover or less**
Circ: Diamd. preorders: **17,046**

1000000 ❑ Nov 1998 Cover: 2.25 **NM** value: **Cover or less**
Circ: Diamd. preorders: **31,661**
Angel Wings • becomes Azrael: Agent of the Bat **A:** Vince Giarrano **W:** Denny O'Neil

Anl 1 ❑ ca. 1995 Cover: 3.95 **NM** value: **Cover or less**
Circ: CapCity orders: **16,178**
Year One; Requiem • Year One;1995 Annual **A:** David Zimmerman; Barry Kitson **W:** Denny O'Neil

Anl 2 ❑ ca. 1996 Cover: 2.95 **NM** value: **Cover or less**
• Legends of the Dead Earth

Anl 3 ❑ ca. 1997 Cover: 3.95 **NM** value: **Cover or less**
Circ: Diamd. preorders: **27,010**
• Pulp Heroes

AZRAEL/ASH — DC

1 ❑ ca. 1997 Cover: 4.95 **NM** value: **Cover or less**
Circ: Diamd. preorders: **45,553**
A: Joe Quesada; Jimmy Palmiotti **W:** Denny O'Neil

AZRAEL PLUS — DC

1 ❑ Dec 1996 Cover: 2.95 **NM** value: **Cover or less**
Circ: Direct Market orders: **38,556**
★ Appearance of The Question.

Other grades: Multiply prices above by **1.5 for Mint • 2/3 for Very Fine • 1/3 for Fine • 1/5 for Very Good • 1/8 for Good**

AZTEC ACE — Eclipse

Aztec Ace is a defender of time itself. Hailing from a time 400 years in our future, he uses advanced technology to allow him to slip in and out of the timestream, making small but vital changes along the way.

As it turns out, he is not alone in his ability to alter history. A group known as the Ebonites have made it their business to disrupt history for their own ends. Merely by preventing Ben Franklin from flying his kite that fateful day, or by disrupting the events of a German beer hall in 1923, they could profoundly change the course of world events.

Ace's job is to stop them, but it's a lot more complicated than it might seem. For even the slightest misstep could cause an anomaly which could destroy history as we know it.

1 ❑ Mar 1984 Cover: 2.25 **NM** value: **2.50**
• Giant-size. ★ 1st Appearance of Aztec Ace.
2 ❑ 1984 Cover: 1.50 **NM** value: **2.00**
3 ❑ 1984 Cover: 1.50 **NM** value: **2.00**
4 ❑ 1984 Cover: 1.75 **NM** value: **2.00**
5 ❑ 1984 Cover: 1.75 **NM** value: **2.00**
6 ❑ 1984 Cover: 1.75 **NM** value: **2.00**
7 ❑ 1984 Cover: 1.75 **NM** value: **2.00**
8 ❑ 1984 Cover: 1.75 **NM** value: **2.00**
9 ❑ Jan 1985 Cover: 1.75 **NM** value: **2.00**
10 ❑ 1985 Cover: 1.75 **NM** value: **2.00**
Circ: CapCity orders: **4,000**
11 ❑ 1985 Cover: 1.75 **NM** value: **2.00**
Circ: CapCity orders: **3,850**
12 ❑ 1985 Cover: 1.75 **NM** value: **2.00**
Circ: CapCity orders: **3,750**
13 ❑ 1985 Cover: 1.75 **NM** value: **2.00**
Circ: CapCity orders: **3,775**
14 ❑ 1985 Cover: 1.75 **NM** value: **2.00**
Circ: CapCity orders: **3,600**
15 ❑ Sep 1985 Cover: 1.75 **NM** value: **2.00**
Circ: CapCity orders: **3,350**

AZTEC ANTHROPOMORPHIC AMAZONS — Antarctic

1 ❑ Mar 1994, b&w Cover: 2.75 **NM** value: **Cover or less**

AZTEC OF THE CITY — El Salto

1 ❑ May 1993 Cover: 2.25 **NM** value: **Cover or less**
Nacimiento **A:** Luis Rodriguez **W:** Fernando Rodriguez ★ Origin of Aztec. ★ 1st Appearance of Aztec.

AZTEC OF THE CITY (VOL. 2) — El Salto

1 ❑ Cover: 2.50 **NM** value: **Cover or less**
A: Kasey Quevedo **W:** Fernando Rodriguez
2 ❑ May 1996 Cover: 2.50 **NM** value: **Cover or less**
Enter: La Llorna **W:** Fernando Rodriguez

AZTEK: THE ULTIMATE MAN — DC

1 ❑ Aug 1996 Cover: 1.75 **NM** value: **Cover or less**
A town called Vanity **A:** N. Steven Harris **W:** Grant Morrison; Mark Millar
2 ❑ Sep 1996 Cover: 1.75 **NM** value: **Cover or less**
A: N. Steven Harris **W:** Grant Morrison; Mark Millar ★ Appearance of Green Lantern. ★ Versus Major Force.
3 ❑ Oct 1996 Cover: 1.75 **NM** value: **Cover or less**
The Girl Who Was Death **A:** N. Steven Harris **W:** Grant Morrison; Mark Millar
4 ❑ Nov 1996 Cover: 1.75 **NM** value: **Cover or less**
Circ: Diamd. preorders: **20,747**
The Lizard King **A:** N. Steven Harris **W:** Grant Morrison; Mark Millar
5 ❑ Dec 1996 Cover: 1.75 **NM** value: **Cover or less**
Circ: Direct Market orders: **19,078**
Deathtrap **A:** N. Steven Harris **W:** Grant Morrison; Mark Millar
6 ❑ Jan 1997 Cover: 1.75 **NM** value: **Cover or less**
Circ: Direct Market orders: **17,046**
A Child's Garden of Sinister Capers? **A:** N. Steven Harris **W:** Grant Morrison; Mark Millar ★ Versus Joker.
7 ❑ Feb 1997 Cover: 1.75 **NM** value: **Cover or less**
Circ: Diamd. preorders: **16,273**
A: N. Steven Harris **W:** Grant Morrison; Mark Millar ★ Appearance of Batman.
8 ❑ Mar 1997 Cover: 1.75 **NM** value: **Cover or less**
Circ: Diamd. preorders: **14,787**
Invisible Hand **A:** N. Steven Harris **W:** Grant Morrison; Mark Millar
9 ❑ Apr 1997 Cover: 1.75 **NM** value: **Cover or less**
Circ: Diamd. preorders: **15,202**
A: N. Steven Harris **W:** Grant Morrison; Mark Millar ★ Versus Parasite.
10 ❑ May 1997 Cover: 1.75 **NM** value: **Cover or less**
Circ: Diamd. preorders: **15,058**
A: N. Steven Harris **W:** Grant Morrison; Mark Millar ★ Appearance of JLA.

BABE — Dark Horse / Legend

1 ❑ Jul 1994 Cover: 2.50 **NM** value: **Cover or less**
Circ: CapCity orders: **16,775**
It Was a Dark and Stormy Night… **A:** John Byrne **W:** John Byrne
2 ❑ Aug 1994 Cover: 2.50 **NM** value: **Cover or less**
Circ: CapCity orders: **14,375**
A: John Byrne **W:** John Byrne
3 ❑ Sep 1994 Cover: 2.50 **NM** value: **Cover or less**
Circ: CapCity orders: **13,575**
Mr. Longshadow Regrets…; Prototykes: Into the Web **A:** John Byrne **W:** John Byrne ★ 1st Appearance of The Prototykes.
4 ❑ Oct 1994 Cover: 2.50 **NM** value: **Cover or less**
Circ: CapCity orders: **13,900**
Meeting Adjourned **A:** John Byrne **W:** John Byrne

BABE 2 — Dark Horse / Legend

1 ❑ Mar 1995 Cover: 2.50 **NM** value: **Cover or less**
Circ: CapCity orders: **11,825**
Pipe Schemes **A:** John Byrne **W:** John Byrne
2 ❑ Apr 1995 Cover: 2.50 **NM** value: **Cover or less**
Circ: CapCity orders: **10,450**
A: John Byrne **W:** John Byrne

BABE, DARLING OF THE HILLS — Feature Publications

Enjoy homespun humor with Babe, Darling of the Hills, as the Appalachian Apollonia discovers new friends and new fun. A certified country girl, Babe finds mirth and mischief around every corner of the globe. Often her down-home country cousins join Babe on her wacky travels, as the beautiful Southern supergal takes on every adventure that comes her way.

The book is similar to Li'l Abner with its cartoonish stories and barefoot, backwoods characters. The book is light in tone and features a variety of events and world calamities to challenge the enthusiastic Babe. But no matter how big the situation, Babe never forgets her rural roots in this funny, entertaining title by Sparky Watts artist-writer Boody Rogers.

1 ❑ Jun 1948 Cover: 0.10 **NM** value: **85.00**
A: Boody Rogers **W:** Boody Rogers
2 ❑ Aug 1948 Cover: 0.10 **NM** value: **60.00**
A: Boody Rogers **W:** Boody Rogers
3 ❑ Oct 1948 Cover: 0.10 **NM** value: **50.00**
A: Boody Rogers **W:** Boody Rogers
4 ❑ Dec 1948 Cover: 0.10 **NM** value: **50.00**
A: Boody Rogers **W:** Boody Rogers
5 ❑ Feb 1949 Cover: 0.10 **NM** value: **50.00**
• **CGC:** 1 graded, best 7.5
A: Boody Rogers **W:** Boody Rogers
6 ❑ May 1949 Cover: 0.10 **NM** value: **50.00**
A: Boody Rogers **W:** Boody Rogers
7 ❑ Aug 1949 Cover: 0.10 **NM** value: **50.00**
• **CGC:** 1 graded, best 8.5
A: Boody Rogers **W:** Boody Rogers
8 ❑ Oct 1949 Cover: 0.10 **NM** value: **50.00**
A: Boody Rogers **W:** Boody Rogers
9 ❑ Dec 1949 Cover: 0.10 **NM** value: **50.00**
A: Boody Rogers **W:** Boody Rogers
10 ❑ Feb 1950 Cover: 0.10 **NM** value: **50.00**
A: Boody Rogers **W:** Boody Rogers
11 ❑ Apr 1950 Cover: 0.10 **NM** value: **50.00**
• **CGC:** 1 graded, best 8.5
final issue. **A:** Boody Rogers **W:** Boody Rogers

BABE RUTH SPORTS COMICS — Harvey

1 ❑ Apr 1949 Cover: 0.10 **NM** value: **250.00**
2 ❑ Jun 1949 Cover: 0.10 **NM** value: **175.00**
3 ❑ Aug 1949 Cover: 0.10 **NM** value: **150.00**
4 ❑ Oct 1949 Cover: 0.10 **NM** value: **150.00**
5 ❑ Dec 1949 Cover: 0.10 **NM** value: **150.00**
• **CGC:** 1 graded, best 6.5
6 ❑ Feb 1950 Cover: 0.10 **NM** value: **150.00**
7 ❑ ca. 1950 Cover: 0.10 **NM** value: **150.00**
8 ❑ ca. 1950 Cover: 0.10 **NM** value: **150.00**
9 ❑ ca. 1950 Cover: 0.10 **NM** value: **150.00**
10 ❑ ca. 1950 Cover: 0.10 **NM** value: **150.00**

BABES OF BROADWAY — Broadway

1 ❑ May 1996 Cover: 2.95 **NM** value: **Cover or less**
• pin-ups and previews of upcoming Broadway series

BABEWATCH — Express / Parody

1 ❑ 1995b&w Cover: 2.50 **NM** value: **Cover or less**
1/A ❑ 1995 Cover: 2.95 **NM** value: **Cover or less**
1/SC❑ 1995 Cover: 2.95 **NM** value: **Cover or less**

BABY ANGEL X — Brainstorm

All issues are adults only.

1 ❑ b&w Cover: 2.95 **NM** value: **Cover or less**
A: Scott Harrison **W:** Scott Harrison

BABY HUEY DIGEST — Harvey

1 ❑ Cover: 1.75 **NM** value: **Cover or less**

BABY HUEY IN 3-D — Blackthorne

1 ❑ Cover: 2.50 **NM** value: **Cover or less**

> **Capital City** orders are the actual sales of comic books by Capital City Distribution, once one of the largest U.S. sellers of comics to comics shops. Capital City's share of comics shop sales, while not known exactly, increases from around 10-20% in the mid-1980s to 30-35% in the mid-1990s. Capital City's share of comic books sold on newsstands (most Marvels and DCs) will be less.

BABY HUEY THE BABY GIANT — Harvey

Big Baby Huey, a huge yellow duck clad in a giant diaper and baby bonnet, is a loveable but dim-witted and super-powerful toddler. His stories usually involve his amiable attempts to be friends with a bunch of nasty kid ducks, whom he later saves, or "helping" his parents with disastrous results.

He has a long history, beginning with his first appearance in Casper the Friendly Ghost #1, in 1949. He was a regular feature in Paramount Animated Comics, starting with "Quack a Doodle Do" in 1950, before getting his own regular title in 1956, which ran until 1972. There was a weak attempt at a revival in 1980, but it only lasted one issue. Harvey Comics tried again in 1990, with both this title and a new Baby Huey, which also began with #100. The second title outlasted this one by six issues, running until June 1994.

Huey has also appeared in Harvey Hits, Harvey Comics Hits, and a few digests and quarterly comics bearing his name.

1 ❑ Sep 1956 Cover: 0.10 **NM** value: **150.00**
• **CGC:** 1 graded, best 6.5
2 ❑ Nov 1956 Cover: 0.10 **NM** value: **85.00**
3 ❑ Jan 1957 Cover: 0.10 **NM** value: **48.00**
4 ❑ Mar 1957 Cover: 0.10 **NM** value: **36.00**
5 ❑ May 1957 Cover: 0.10 **NM** value: **36.00**
6 ❑ Jul 1957 Cover: 0.10 **NM** value: **20.00**
7 ❑ Sep 1957 Cover: 0.10 **NM** value: **20.00**
8 ❑ Nov 1957 Cover: 0.10 **NM** value: **20.00**
9 ❑ Jan 1958 Cover: 0.10 **NM** value: **20.00**
10 ❑ Mar 1958 Cover: 0.10 **NM** value: **20.00**
11 ❑ 1958 Cover: 0.10 **NM** value: **15.00**
12 ❑ 1958 Cover: 0.10 **NM** value: **15.00**
13 ❑ 1958 Cover: 0.10 **NM** value: **15.00**
14 ❑ 1958 Cover: 0.10 **NM** value: **15.00**
15 ❑ 1958 Cover: 0.10 **NM** value: **15.00**
16 ❑ 1958 Cover: 0.10 **NM** value: **15.00**
17 ❑ 1958 Cover: 0.10 **NM** value: **15.00**
18 ❑ 1958 Cover: 0.10 **NM** value: **15.00**
19 ❑ 1959 Cover: 0.10 **NM** value: **15.00**
20 ❑ 1959 Cover: 0.10 **NM** value: **15.00**
21 ❑ 1959 Cover: 0.10 **NM** value: **12.00**
22 ❑ Jul 1959 Cover: 0.10 **NM** value: **12.00**
23 ❑ Apr 1960 Cover: 0.10 **NM** value: **12.00**
24 ❑ 1960 Cover: 0.10 **NM** value: **12.00**
25 ❑ 1960 Cover: 0.10 **NM** value: **12.00**
26 ❑ 1960 Cover: 0.10 **NM** value: **12.00**
27 ❑ 1960 Cover: 0.10 **NM** value: **12.00**
28 ❑ Nov 1960 Cover: 0.10 **NM** value: **12.00**
29 ❑ Dec 1960 Cover: 0.10 **NM** value: **12.00**
30 ❑ Jan 1961 Cover: 0.10 **NM** value: **12.00**
31 ❑ 1961 Cover: 0.10 **NM** value: **9.00**
32 ❑ 1961 Cover: 0.10 **NM** value: **9.00**
33 ❑ 1961 Cover: 0.10 **NM** value: **9.00**
34 ❑ 1961 Cover: 0.10 **NM** value: **9.00**
35 ❑ 1961 Cover: 0.10 **NM** value: **9.00**
36 ❑ 1961 Cover: 0.10 **NM** value: **9.00**
37 ❑ 1961 Cover: 0.10 **NM** value: **9.00**
38 ❑ 1961 Cover: 0.10 **NM** value: **9.00**
39 ❑ 1961 Cover: 0.10 **NM** value: **9.00**
40 ❑ 1961 Cover: 0.10 **NM** value: **9.00**
41 ❑ Dec 1961 Cover: 0.10 **NM** value: **6.00**
• **CGC:** 1 graded, best 9.2
42 ❑ Jan 1962 Cover: 0.10 **NM** value: **6.00**
• **CGC:** 1 graded, best 9.2
43 ❑ Feb 1962 Cover: 0.10 **NM** value: **6.00**
• **CGC:** 1 graded, best 9.0
44 ❑ Mar 1962 Cover: 0.10 **NM** value: **6.00**
• **CGC:** 1 graded, best 9.4
45 ❑ Apr 1962 Cover: 0.10 **NM** value: **6.00**
• **CGC:** 1 graded, best 9.0
46 ❑ Jun 1962 Cover: 0.12 **NM** value: **6.00**
47 ❑ Aug 1962 Cover: 0.12 **NM** value: **6.00**
48 ❑ Oct 1962 Cover: 0.12 **NM** value: **6.00**
49 ❑ Dec 1962 Cover: 0.12 **NM** value: **6.00**
50 ❑ Feb 1963 Cover: 0.12 **NM** value: **6.00**
• **CGC:** 1 graded, best 9.0
51 ❑ Apr 1963 Cover: 0.12 **NM** value: **4.00**
52 ❑ Jun 1963 Cover: 0.12 **NM** value: **4.00**
53 ❑ Aug 1963 Cover: 0.12 **NM** value: **4.00**
54 ❑ Oct 1963 Cover: 0.12 **NM** value: **4.00**
55 ❑ Dec 1963 Cover: 0.12 **NM** value: **4.00**
56 ❑ Feb 1964 Cover: 0.12 **NM** value: **4.00**
57 ❑ Apr 1964 Cover: 0.12 **NM** value: **4.00**
58 ❑ Jun 1964 Cover: 0.12 **NM** value: **4.00**
• Has 1963 Statement, filed 10/1/63; no circ figures published
59 ❑ Aug 1964 Cover: 0.12 **NM** value: **4.00**
60 ❑ Oct 1964 Cover: 0.12 **NM** value: **4.00**
61 ❑ Dec 1964 Cover: 0.12 **NM** value: **4.00**
62 ❑ Feb 1965 Cover: 0.12 **NM** value: **4.00**
63 ❑ Apr 1965 Cover: 0.12 **NM** value: **4.00**
64 ❑ Jun 1965 Cover: 0.12 **NM** value: **4.00**
65 ❑ Aug 1965 Cover: 0.12 **NM** value: **4.00**
66 ❑ Oct 1965 Cover: 0.12 **NM** value: **4.00**
67 ❑ Dec 1965 Cover: 0.12 **NM** value: **4.00**
68 ❑ Feb 1966 Cover: 0.12 **NM** value: **4.00**
69 ❑ Apr 1966 Cover: 0.12 **NM** value: **4.00**
70 ❑ Jun 1966 Cover: 0.12 **NM** value: **4.00**
71 ❑ Aug 1966 Cover: 0.12 **NM** value: **2.50**
72 ❑ Oct 1966 Cover: 0.12 **NM** value: **2.50**
73 ❑ Dec 1966 Cover: 0.12 **NM** value: **2.50**

CGC-graded: Multiply prices above by **33 for 9.9 M • 16 for 9.8 NM/M • 7 for 9.6 NM+ • 5 for 9.4 NM • 2.5 for 9.2 NM- • 1.5 for 9.0 VF/NM**

74 ❑ Feb 1967 Cover: 0.12 **NM** value: **2.50**
75 ❑ Apr 1967 Cover: 0.12 **NM** value: **2.50**
• Has 1965 Statement, filed 10/1/65; no circ figures published
76 ❑ Jun 1967 Cover: 0.12 **NM** value: **2.50**
77 ❑ Aug 1967 Cover: 0.12 **NM** value: **2.50**
78 ❑ Oct 1967 Cover: 0.12 **NM** value: **2.50**
79 ❑ Dec 1967 Cover: 0.12 **NM** value: **2.50**
80 ❑ Dec 1967 Cover: 0.25 **NM** value: **2.50**
81 ❑ Feb 1968 Cover: 0.25 **NM** value: **2.50**
82 ❑ Apr 1968 Cover: 0.25 **NM** value: **2.50**
83 ❑ Jun 1968 Cover: 0.25 **NM** value: **2.50**
84 ❑ Aug 1968 Cover: 0.25 **NM** value: **2.50**
85 ❑ Oct 1968 Cover: 0.25 **NM** value: **2.50**
86 ❑ Dec 1968 Cover: 0.25 **NM** value: **2.50**
87 ❑ Feb 1969 Cover: 0.25 **NM** value: **2.50**
88 ❑ Apr 1969 Cover: 0.25 **NM** value: **2.50**
89 ❑ Jun 1969 Cover: 0.25 **NM** value: **2.50**
90 ❑ Aug 1969 Cover: 0.25 **NM** value: **2.50**
91 ❑ Oct 1969 Cover: 0.25 **NM** value: **2.50**
92 ❑ Dec 1969 Cover: 0.25 **NM** value: **2.50**
93 ❑ Feb 1970 Cover: 0.25 **NM** value: **2.50**
94 ❑ 1971 **NM** value: **2.50**
95 ❑ **NM** value: **2.50**
96 ❑ **NM** value: **2.50**
97 ❑ **NM** value: **2.50**
98 ❑ Cover: 0.20 **NM** value: **2.50**
99 ❑ **NM** value: **2.50**
100 ❑ Oct 1990 Cover: 1.00 **NM** value: **Cover or less**
📖 Some Bull; Tin Can Buddy; Buzzy the Funny Crow; The Mewzeem; A Peck of Trouble; Soap Box Derby • Series begins again after hiatus
101 ❑ **NM** value: **1.00**
102 ❑ **NM** value: **1.00**

BABY HUEY (VOL. 2) — Harvey

1 ❑ 1991 Cover: 1.00 **NM** value: **1.25**
Circ: CapCity orders: **1,875**
2 ❑ Jan 1992 Cover: 1.00 **NM** value: **1.25**
3 ❑ Apr 1992 Cover: 1.25 **NM** value: **Cover or less**
4 ❑ Aug 1992 Cover: 1.25 **NM** value: **Cover or less**
5 ❑ Nov 1992 Cover: 1.25 **NM** value: **Cover or less**
📖 The Baby Sitter; Stumbo the Giant Baby; What Makes 'em Move?; The Ice Cream Caper; It's Magic; **A:** Marty Taras
6 ❑ Mar 1993 Cover: 1.25 **NM** value: **Cover or less**
7 ❑ Jun 1993 Cover: 1.25 **NM** value: **Cover or less**
8 ❑ Cover: 1.50 **NM** value: **Cover or less**
9 ❑ Cover: 1.50 **NM** value: **Cover or less**

BABYLON 5 — DC

1 ❑ Jan 1995 Cover: 1.95 **NM** value: **10.00**
Circ: CapCity orders: **15,100 • CGC:** 8 graded, best 9.8
2 ❑ Feb 1995 Cover: 1.95 **NM** value: **8.00**
Circ: CapCity orders: **9,850**
3 ❑ Mar 1995 Cover: 1.95 **NM** value: **6.00**
Circ: CapCity orders: **8,650**
4 ❑ Apr 1995 Cover: 1.95 **NM** value: **6.00**
Circ: CapCity orders: **8,625**
5 ❑ Jun 1995 Cover: 2.50 **NM** value: **4.00**
Circ: CapCity orders: **8,925**
📖 Shadows Past and Present, Part 1
6 ❑ Jul 1995 Cover: 2.50 **NM** value: **4.00**
Circ: CapCity orders: **8,775**
📖 Shadows Past and Present, Part 2 **A:** John Ridgway **W:** J. Michael Straczynski; Tim DeHaas
7 ❑ Aug 1995 Cover: 2.50 **NM** value: **4.00**
Circ: CapCity orders: **9,100**
8 ❑ Sep 1995 Cover: 2.50 **NM** value: **3.50**
Circ: CapCity orders: **8,250**
9 ❑ Oct 1995 Cover: 2.50 **NM** value: **3.50**
Circ: CapCity orders: **7,100**
10 ❑ Nov 1995 Cover: 2.50 **NM** value: **3.50**
11 ❑ Dec 1995 Cover: 2.50 **NM** value: **3.50**
final issue.
Bk 1 ❑ Cover: 9.95 **NM** value: **Cover or less**
• The Price of Peace, collects #1-4;Collects Babylon 5 #1-4
Bk 1/LE ❑ Cover: 24.95 **NM** value: **Cover or less**

BABYLON 5: IN VALEN'S NAME — DC

A popular and well-crafted, science-fiction series, Babylon 5 is unusual because it was created with a definite conclusion in mind. Babylon 5 is an immense space station, built to be a neutral zone for warring planets. Its numerical designation is determined by the four space stations that preceded it. Three were sabotaged and the fourth was mysteriously sent back in time. In this three-issue mini-series, Babylon 4 makes an enigmatic reappearance, prompting Commander Sheridan and the rest of the prominent characters to investigate.

This title contains stunning art by Michael Collins and David Roach (who successfully capture the actors' likenesses), and was written by the series creator, J. Michael Straczynski. It may be considered unusual for a television dramatist to involve himself in a comic book spinoff of his work, but Babylon 5 is Straczynski's personal creation, and he maintains strict and loving control over the franchise. He would go on, in fact, to write Marvel's Amazing Spider-Man.

1 ❑ Mar 1998 Cover: 2.50 **NM** value: **4.00**
Circ: Diamd. preorders: **33,739 • CGC:** 1 graded, best 9.4
A: Mike Collins **W:** J. Michael Straczynski; J. Michael Straczynski
2 ❑ Apr 1998 Cover: 2.50 **NM** value: **3.00**
Circ: Diamd. preorders: **27,395**
A: Mike Collins **W:** J. Michael Straczynski; J. Michael Straczynski
3 ❑ May 1998 Cover: 2.50 **NM** value: **3.00**
Circ: Diamd. preorders: **27,546**
A: Mike Collins **W:** J. Michael Straczynski; J. Michael Straczynski

BABYLON CRUSH — Boneyard

1 ❑ May 1995 Cover: 2.95 **NM** value: **Cover or less**
Circ: CapCity orders: **4,625**
cardstock cover, b&w.
2 ❑ Jul 1995 Cover: 2.95 **NM** value: **Cover or less**
Circ: CapCity orders: **3,510**
cardstock cover, b&w. 📖 Epitaphs **A:** Thomas Derenick **W:** Hart Fisher
3 ❑ Oct 1995, b&w Cover: 2.95 **NM** value: **Cover or less**
4 ❑ Cover: 2.95 **NM** value: **Cover or less**
Xmas 1 ❑ Jan 1998 Cover: 2.95 **NM** value: **Cover or less**
📖 A Present for Santa; Palm Leaf Christmas; Mite Xmas **A:** Dan plegel; Jay Bruce Bogle; Rich Fuscia **W:** Hart Fisher; Jay Bruce Bogle; Rich Fuscia

BABY'S FIRST DEADPOOL BOOK — Marvel

1 ❑ Dec 1998 Cover: 2.99 **NM** value: **Cover or less**
📖 Dresspool (activity); Make Way for Deadpool! (text); The Etiquette Lesson; Friends Share because Friends Care; The Alphadead; Pool-by-Numbers (activity) • children's-book style stories **A:** Joe Cooper; Pond Scum; Scott Koblish; Walden Wang; Brian Smith **W:** Pete Woods; Joe Kelly

BABY SURPRISE IN MY POCKET MAGAZINE — Burghley

1 ❑ Cover: 1.99 **NM** value: **3.00**
2 ❑ Cover: 1.99 **NM** value: **3.00**
📖 Mud Pies; Happy Birthday, Little Tiger; The Biggest Coconut **A:** David Brian; Paul Green **W:** Karen King

BABY, YOU'RE REALLY SOMETHING! — Fantagraphics / Eros

1 ❑ b&w Cover: 2.50 **NM** value: **Cover or less**
A: Frank Frazetta

BACCHUS COLOR SPECIAL — Dark Horse

1 ❑ Apr 1995 Cover: 2.95 **NM** value: **3.25**
Circ: CapCity orders: **4,025**
No issue number. One-shot. **A:** Eddie Campbell **W:** Eddie Campbell

BACCHUS (EDDIE CAMPBELL'S...) — Eddie Campbell

1 ❑ May 1999 Cover: 2.95 **NM** value: **5.00**
Circ: CapCity orders: **2,740**
📖 The Face on the Bar-Room Floor **A:** Eddie Campbell **W:** Eddie Campbell
1-2 ❑ Cover: 2.95 **NM** value: **3.00**
A: Eddie Campbell **W:** Eddie Campbell
2 ❑ Cover: 2.95 **NM** value: **4.00**
Circ: CapCity orders: **2,465**
A: Eddie Campbell **W:** Eddie Campbell
3 ❑ Cover: 2.95 **NM** value: **4.00**
Circ: CapCity orders: **2,510**
A: Eddie Campbell **W:** Eddie Campbell
4 ❑ Cover: 2.95 **NM** value: **3.50**
Circ: CapCity orders: **2,495**
A: Eddie Campbell **W:** Eddie Campbell
5 ❑ Cover: 2.95 **NM** value: **3.50**
Circ: CapCity orders: **2,415**
A: Eddie Campbell **W:** Eddie Campbell
6 ❑ Cover: 2.95 **NM** value: **3.00**
A: Eddie Campbell **W:** Eddie Campbell
7 ❑ Cover: 2.95 **NM** value: **3.00**
A: Eddie Campbell **W:** Eddie Campbell
8 ❑ Cover: 2.95 **NM** value: **3.00**
A: Eddie Campbell **W:** Eddie Campbell
9 ❑ Jan 2000 Cover: 2.95 **NM** value: **3.00**
📖 The Landscape of Sex **A:** Eddie Campbell **W:** Eddie Campbell
10 ❑ Cover: 2.95 **NM** value: **3.00**
A: Eddie Campbell **W:** Eddie Campbell
11 ❑ Cover: 2.95 **NM** value: **3.00**
A: Eddie Campbell **W:** Eddie Campbell
12 ❑ Cover: 2.95 **NM** value: **3.00**
A: Eddie Campbell **W:** Eddie Campbell
13 ❑ Cover: 2.95 **NM** value: **3.00**
A: Eddie Campbell **W:** Eddie Campbell
14 ❑ Cover: 2.95 **NM** value: **3.00**
A: Eddie Campbell **W:** Eddie Campbell
15 ❑ Cover: 2.95 **NM** value: **3.00**
A: Eddie Campbell **W:** Eddie Campbell
16 ❑ Cover: 2.95 **NM** value: **3.00**
A: Eddie Campbell **W:** Eddie Campbell
17 ❑ Sep 1996 Cover: 2.95 **NM** value: **3.00**
Circ: Diamd. preorders: **4,400**
A: Eddie Campbell **W:** Eddie Campbell
18 ❑ Oct 1996, b&w Cover: 2.95 **NM** value: **3.00**
Circ: Diamd. preorders: **4,382**
A: Eddie Campbell **W:** Eddie Campbell
19 ❑ Nov 1996 Cover: 2.95 **NM** value: **3.00**
Circ: Diamd. preorders: **4,168**
A: Eddie Campbell **W:** Eddie Campbell
20 ❑ Dec 1996 Cover: 2.95 **NM** value: **3.00**
Circ: Direct Market orders: **4,165**
A: Eddie Campbell **W:** Eddie Campbell
21 ❑ Jan 1997 Cover: 2.95 **NM** value: **Cover or less**
Circ: Direct Market orders: **3,856**
A: Eddie Campbell **W:** Eddie Campbell
22 ❑ Feb 1997 Cover: 2.95 **NM** value: **Cover or less**
Circ: Diamd. preorders: **3,659**
A: Eddie Campbell **W:** Eddie Campbell
23 ❑ Mar 1997 Cover: 2.95 **NM** value: **Cover or less**
Circ: Diamd. preorders: **3,619**
A: Eddie Campbell **W:** Eddie Campbell
24 ❑ 1997 Cover: 2.95 **NM** value: **Cover or less**
A: Eddie Campbell **W:** Eddie Campbell
25 ❑ 1997 Cover: 2.95 **NM** value: **Cover or less**
A: Eddie Campbell **W:** Eddie Campbell
26 ❑ 1997 Cover: 2.95 **NM** value: **Cover or less**
A: Eddie Campbell **W:** Eddie Campbell
27 ❑ 1997 Cover: 2.95 **NM** value: **Cover or less**
A: Eddie Campbell **W:** Eddie Campbell
28 ❑ 1997 Cover: 2.95 **NM** value: **Cover or less**
A: Eddie Campbell **W:** Eddie Campbell
29 ❑ 1997 Cover: 2.95 **NM** value: **Cover or less**
A: Eddie Campbell **W:** Eddie Campbell
30 ❑ 1997 Cover: 2.95 **NM** value: **Cover or less**
A: Eddie Campbell **W:** Eddie Campbell
31 ❑ 1997 Cover: 2.95 **NM** value: **Cover or less**
A: Eddie Campbell **W:** Eddie Campbell
32 ❑ 1998 Cover: 2.95 **NM** value: **Cover or less**
A: Eddie Campbell **W:** Eddie Campbell
33 ❑ 1998 Cover: 2.95 **NM** value: **Cover or less**
A: Eddie Campbell **W:** Eddie Campbell
34 ❑ Apr 1998 Cover: 2.95 **NM** value: **Cover or less**
Circ: Diamd. preorders: **2,557**
A: Eddie Campbell **W:** Eddie Campbell
35 ❑ 1998 Cover: 2.95 **NM** value: **Cover or less**
A: Eddie Campbell **W:** Eddie Campbell
36 ❑ 1998 Cover: 2.95 **NM** value: **Cover or less**
A: Eddie Campbell **W:** Eddie Campbell
37 ❑ 1998 Cover: 2.95 **NM** value: **Cover or less**
A: Eddie Campbell **W:** Eddie Campbell
38 ❑ Sep 1998 Cover: 2.95 **NM** value: **Cover or less**
Circ: Diamd. preorders: **2,235**
A: Eddie Campbell **W:** Eddie Campbell
39 ❑ Oct 1998 Cover: 2.95 **NM** value: **Cover or less**
Circ: Diamd. preorders: **2,142**
A: Eddie Campbell **W:** Eddie Campbell
40 ❑ Dec 1998 Cover: 2.95 **NM** value: **Cover or less**
Circ: Diamd. preorders: **2,075**
A: Eddie Campbell **W:** Eddie Campbell
41 ❑ Jan 1999 Cover: 2.95 **NM** value: **Cover or less**
Circ: Diamd. preorders: **2,017**
A: Eddie Campbell **W:** Eddie Campbell
42 ❑ Feb 1999 Cover: 2.95 **NM** value: **Cover or less**
Circ: Diamd. preorders: **1,930**
A: Eddie Campbell **W:** Eddie Campbell
Bk 1 ❑ Cover: 9.95 **NM** value: **Cover or less**
• Immortality Isn't Forever;Collects Eddie Campbell's Bacchus #1-4 **A:** Eddie Campbell **W:** Eddie Campbell
Bk 2 ❑ Cover: 9.95 **NM** value: **Cover or less**
• The Gods of Business;Collects Eddie Campbell's Bacchus #5-8 **A:** Eddie Campbell **W:** Eddie Campbell
Bk 3 ❑ Cover: 9.95 **NM** value: **Cover or less**
A: Eddie Campbell **W:** Eddie Campbell
Bk 4 ❑ Cover: 17.95 **NM** value: **Cover or less**
• Doing the Islands with Bacchus;Collects old stories from Bacchus #9-19 **A:** Eddie Campbell **W:** Eddie Campbell
Bk 5 ❑ Cover: 9.95 **NM** value: **Cover or less**
• Earth, Air, Water & Fire **A:** Eddie Campbell **W:** Eddie Campbell
Bk 9 ❑ Cover: 12.95 **NM** value: **Cover or less**
• King Bacchus;Collects Eddie Campbell's Bacchus #1-15 **A:** Eddie Campbell **W:** Eddie Campbell

BACCHUS (HARRIER) — Harrier

1 ❑ Cover: 1.95 **NM** value: **5.00**
📖 The Crazy Bastard **A:** Eddie Campbell **W:** Eddie Campbell
2 ❑ Cover: 1.95 **NM** value: **4.00**
A: Eddie Campbell **W:** Eddie Campbell

BACK DOWN THE LINE — Eclipse

1 ❑ Cover: 8.95 **NM** value: **Cover or less**
No issue number. **A:** John Bolton

BACKLASH — Image

Backlash is Marc Slayton, one of the core members of the U.N. troubleshooting team StormWatch. Slayton is a skilled fighter armed with an energy whip and with the ability to turn incorporeal.

As this solo series begins, he'll need all his abilities to save the life of his lady love Diane LaSalle. LaSalle has been possessed by a Daemonite, one of the dread elder beings which the WildC.A.T.s were founded to stop. Under Daemonite control, LaSalle is about to destroy StormWatch's orbital station, when Backlash is forced to battle her. He succeeds in forcing the Daemonite out of LaSalle's body, but, in leaving, the Daemonite rips away part of her mind. Backlash will do anything to save her — even if that means breaking into an ultra-security prison to enlist a dangerous super-villain's help.

1 ❑ Nov 1994 Cover: 1.95 **NM** value: **2.50**
Circ: CapCity orders: **45,700**
Double cover. **A:** Brett Booth; Alex Garner(cover); Sal Regla(cover) **W:** Brett Booth; Jeff Mariotte; Sean Ruffner ★ 1st Appearance of Taboo.
2 ❑ Dec 1994 Cover: 1.95 **NM** value: **2.50**
Circ: CapCity orders: **31,950**
3 ❑ Jan 1995 Cover: 2.50 **NM** value: **Cover or less**
Circ: CapCity orders: **27,925**
4 ❑ Feb 1995 Cover: 2.50 **NM** value: **Cover or less**
Circ: CapCity orders: **27,425**
5 ❑ Feb 1995 Cover: 2.50 **NM** value: **Cover or less**
Circ: CapCity orders: **24,400**

Other grades: Multiply prices above by **1.5 for Mint • 2/3 for Very Fine • 1/3 for Fine • 1/5 for Very Good • 1/8 for Good**

6 ❑ Mar 1995 Cover: 2.50 **NM** value: **Cover or less**
Circ: CapCity orders: **24,100**
7 ❑ Apr 1995 Cover: 2.50 **NM** value: **Cover or less**
Circ: CapCity orders: **24,075**
★ 1st Appearance of Crimson.
8 ❑ May 1995 Cover: 2.50 **NM** value: **Cover or less**
Circ: CapCity orders: **31,300**
📖 WildStorm Rising, Part 8 • bound-in trading cards **A:** Brett Booth **W:** Ron Marz
9 ❑ Jun 1995 Cover: 2.50 **NM** value: **Cover or less**
Circ: CapCity orders: **24,425**
10 ❑ Jul 1995 Cover: 2.50 **NM** value: **Cover or less**
Circ: CapCity orders: **22,525**
indicia says Jul, cover says Aug.
11 ❑ Aug 1995 Cover: 2.50 **NM** value: **Cover or less**
Circ: CapCity orders: **21,675**
12 ❑ Sep 1995 Cover: 2.95 **NM** value: **Cover or less**
Circ: CapCity orders: **17,775**
indicia says Sep, cover says Oct. ★ 1st Appearance of Serge, Mahkinot.
13 ❑ Nov 1995 Cover: 2.50 **NM** value: **Cover or less**
Circ: CapCity orders: **11,675**
14 ❑ Nov 1995 Cover: 2.50 **NM** value: **Cover or less**
indicia says Nov, cover says Dec.
15 ❑ Dec 1995 Cover: 2.50 **NM** value: **Cover or less**
indicia says Dec, cover says Jan.
16 ❑ Jan 1996 Cover: 2.50 **NM** value: **Cover or less**
indicia says Jan, cover says Feb.
17 ❑ Feb 1996 Cover: 2.50 **NM** value: **Cover or less**
18 ❑ Mar 1996 Cover: 2.50 **NM** value: **Cover or less**
19 ❑ Apr 1996 Cover: 2.50 **NM** value: **Cover or less**
📖 Fire from Heaven, Part 2
20 ❑ May 1996 Cover: 2.50 **NM** value: **Cover or less**
📖 Fire from Heaven, Part 10
21 ❑ Jun 1996 Cover: 2.50 **NM** value: **Cover or less**
22 ❑ Jul 1996 Cover: 2.50 **NM** value: **Cover or less**
23 ❑ Aug 1996 Cover: 2.50 **NM** value: **Cover or less**
24 ❑ Sep 1996 Cover: 2.50 **NM** value: **Cover or less**
Circ: Diamd. preorders: **35,319**
★ 1st Appearance of Omni.
25 ❑ Nov 1996 Cover: 3.95 **NM** value: **Cover or less**
Circ: Diamd. preorders: **35,175**
• Giant-size. ★ 1st Appearance of Gramalkin.
26 ❑ Nov 1996 Cover: 2.50 **NM** value: **Cover or less**
Circ: Diamd. preorders: **30,777**
A: Juvaun Kirby **W:** Brett Booth; Sean Ruffner
27 ❑ Dec 1996 Cover: 2.50 **NM** value: **Cover or less**
Circ: Direct Market orders: **28,497**
A: Michael Ryan **W:** Brett Booth; Sean Ruffner
28 ❑ Jan 1997 Cover: 2.50 **NM** value: **Cover or less**
Circ: Direct Market orders: **28,202**
A: Pete Woods; Juvaun Kirby **W:** Brett Booth; Sean Ruffner
29 ❑ Feb 1997 Cover: 2.50 **NM** value: **Cover or less**
Circ: Diamd. preorders: **26,738**
A: Pete Woods **W:** Brett Booth; Sean Ruffner
30 ❑ Mar 1997 Cover: 2.50 **NM** value: **Cover or less**
Circ: Diamd. preorders: **26,809**
31 ❑ Apr 1997 Cover: 2.50 **NM** value: **Cover or less**
Circ: Diamd. preorders: **25,584**
32 ❑ May 1997 Cover: 2.50 **NM** value: **Cover or less**
Circ: Diamd. preorders: **25,110**
final issue.

BACKLASH & TABOO'S AFRICAN HOLIDAY — DC / Wildstorm

1 ❑ Sep 1999 Cover: 5.95 **NM** value: **Cover or less**
Circ: Diamd. preorders: **13,694**
A: Brett Booth **W:** Brett Booth

BACKLASH/SPIDER-MAN — Image

1 ❑ Aug 1996 Cover: 2.50 **NM** value: **Cover or less**
A: Brett Booth **W:** Brett Booth; Sean Ruffner
1/A ❑ Aug 1996 Cover: 2.50 **NM** value: **Cover or less**
crossover with Marvel, cover says Jul, indicia says Aug.
1/B ❑ Aug 1996 Cover: 2.50 **NM** value: **Cover or less**
alternate cover, crossover with Marvel, cover says Jul, indicia says Aug.
2 ❑ Oct 1996 Cover: 2.50 **NM** value: **Cover or less**
• crossover with Marvel
Bk 1❑ Jun 1997 Cover: 4.95 **NM** value: **Cover or less**
• collects crossover with Marvel

BACKPACK MARVELS: AVENGERS — Marvel

1 ❑ Jan 2001 Cover: 6.95 **NM** value: **Cover or less**
📖 On the Matter of Heroes; Honor Thy Father...; The Redoubtable Return of Crusher Creel; Death on the Hudson; The Yesterday Quest!; Nights of Wundagore!; The Call of the Mountain Thing!; Elementary, Dear Avengers; Wings and Arrows **A:** John Byrne; Gene Day **W:** David Michelinie

BACKPACK MARVELS: X-MEN — Marvel

1 ❑ Cover: 6.95 **NM** value: **Cover or less**
2 ❑ Nov 2000 Cover: 6.95 **NM** value: **Cover or less**
📖 Romances; 'Til Death; Decisions; Sanction; Hell Hath No Fury; What Happened to Kitty?; First Friends • Reprints Uncanny X-Men #167-173 **A:** Paul Smith **W:** Chris Claremont

BACK-TO-BACK HORROR SPECIAL — Timbuktu Graphix

1 ❑ 1989 Cover: 1.50 **NM** value: **Cover or less**
No issue number. • flipbook with Zombie Boy's Hoodoo Tales #1 and Joe Dinosaur-Head #3

BACK TO THE FUTURE — Harvey

This Harvey Comics series is based on the animated TV series, which is, in turn, based on the popular trilogy of Michael J. Fox films from Universal. Here, the premise is that Marty McFly and his pal, Doc Emmett Brown, travel to different points in time via their time machine — a truly snazzed-up DeLorean automobile — righting wrongs and correcting inconsistencies in the space-time continuum. The art is reminiscent in that of some of Harvey's other titles, particularly Richie Rich and Casper, and the stories by Dwayne McDuffie (Damage Control, Deathlok, Hardware) are action-filled and fun.

1 ❑ Nov 1991 Cover: 1.25 **NM** value: **1.50**
Circ: CapCity orders: **6,350**
📖 The Gang's All Here **A:** Nelson Dewey; Gil Kane(cover) **W:** Dwayne McDuffie
2 ❑ Nov 1991 Cover: 1.50 **NM** value: **Cover or less**
Circ: CapCity orders: **3,300**
3 ❑ Jan 1992 Cover: 1.50 **NM** value: **Cover or less**
4 ❑ Jun 1992 Cover: 1.25 **NM** value: **1.50**
SE 1❑ **NM** value: **1.00**
• Universal Studios-Florida giveaway.

BACK TO THE FUTURE:FORWARD TO THE FUTURE — Harvey

1 ❑ Oct 1992 Cover: 1.50 **NM** value: **Cover or less**
A: Nelson Dewey **W:** Dwayne McDuffie
2 ❑ Nov 1992 Cover: 1.50 **NM** value: **Cover or less**
A: Nelson Dewey **W:** Dwayne McDuffie
3 ❑ Jan 1993 Cover: 1.50 **NM** value: **Cover or less**
A: Nelson Dewey **W:** Dwayne McDuffie

BAD APPLES — High Impact

1 ❑ Jan 1997 Cover: 2.95 **NM** value: **Cover or less**
Circ: Direct Market orders: **4,248**
2 ❑ ca. 1997 Cover: 2.95 **NM** value: **Cover or less**
Circ: Diamd. preorders: **2,710**

BAD ART COLLECTION, THE — Slave Labor

1 ❑ Apr 1996 Cover: 1.95 **NM** value: **Cover or less**
No issue number. • Oversized.

BADAXE — Adventure

1 ❑ Cover: 2.25 **NM** value: **Cover or less**
2 ❑ Cover: 2.25 **NM** value: **Cover or less**
3 ❑ Cover: 2.25 **NM** value: **Cover or less**

BAD BOY — Oni Press

1 ❑ Dec 1997 Cover: 4.95 **NM** value: **Cover or less**
Circ: Diamd. preorders: **24,050**
No issue number. • oversized one-shot.

BAD COMICS — Cat-Head

1 ❑ b&w Cover: 2.75 **NM** value: **Cover or less**

BAD COMPANY — Fleetway-Quality

1 ❑ Cover: 1.50 **NM** value: **Cover or less**
Circ: CapCity orders: **2,875**
📖 War Zombies **A:** Brett Ewins; James McCarthy **W:** Peter Milligan ★ Origin of Bad Company.
2 ❑ Cover: 1.50 **NM** value: **Cover or less**
Circ: CapCity orders: **1,725**
3 ❑ Cover: 1.50 **NM** value: **Cover or less**
Circ: CapCity orders: **1,675**
4 ❑ Cover: 1.50 **NM** value: **Cover or less**
Circ: CapCity orders: **1,500**
5 ❑ Cover: 1.50 **NM** value: **Cover or less**
Circ: CapCity orders: **1,550**
6 ❑ Cover: 1.50 **NM** value: **Cover or less**
Circ: CapCity orders: **1,525**
7 ❑ Cover: 1.50 **NM** value: **Cover or less**
Circ: CapCity orders: **1,625**
8 ❑ Cover: 1.50 **NM** value: **Cover or less**
Circ: CapCity orders: **1,750**
9 ❑ Cover: 1.50 **NM** value: **Cover or less**
Circ: CapCity orders: **1,575**
10 ❑ Cover: 1.50 **NM** value: **Cover or less**
Circ: CapCity orders: **1,500**
11 ❑ Cover: 1.50 **NM** value: **Cover or less**
Circ: CapCity orders: **1,500**
12 ❑ Cover: 1.50 **NM** value: **Cover or less**
Circ: CapCity orders: **1,475**
13 ❑ Cover: 1.50 **NM** value: **Cover or less**
Circ: CapCity orders: **1,400**
14 ❑ Cover: 1.50 **NM** value: **Cover or less**
Circ: CapCity orders: **1,375**
15 ❑ Cover: 1.50 **NM** value: **Cover or less**
Circ: CapCity orders: **1,375**
16 ❑ Cover: 1.75 **NM** value: **Cover or less**
Circ: CapCity orders: **1,275**
17 ❑ Cover: 1.75 **NM** value: **Cover or less**
Circ: CapCity orders: **1,200**
18 ❑ Cover: 1.75 **NM** value: **Cover or less**
Circ: CapCity orders: **1,125**
19 ❑ Cover: 1.75 **NM** value: **Cover or less**
Circ: CapCity orders: **1,075**
📖 The Mean Area; Tharg's Future Shocks: The Perfect Wife? final issue. **A:** Brett Ewins; James McCarthy **W:** Peter Milligan

BADE BIKER & ORSON — Mirage

1 ❑ Nov 1986 Cover: 1.50 **NM** value: **Cover or less**
A: Jim Lawson **W:** Jim Lawson
2 ❑ Jan 1987 Cover: 1.50 **NM** value: **Cover or less**
A: Jim Lawson **W:** Jim Lawson
3 ❑ Mar 1987 Cover: 1.50 **NM** value: **Cover or less**
A: Jim Lawson **W:** Jim Lawson
4 ❑ Jun 1987 Cover: 1.50 **NM** value: **Cover or less**
A: Jim Lawson **W:** Jim Lawson
Bk 1❑ Cover: 9.95 **NM** value: **Cover or less**
• Collected Bade Biker And Orson

BAD EGGS, THE — Acclaim / Armada

This series follows the anachronistic adventures of raptor brothers Claude and Ript, as told by writer Bob Layton and artist Don Perlin.

Claude, the bespectacled intellectual dinosaur, worries about future extinction and abstains from raptor reproductive activity which generally involves disembowelment. Ript, the only raptor who regularly wears a backwards baseball cap, is regularly disemboweled. If only the female raptors didn't have to play so rough!

The boys avoid T-Rexs, argue about the size of Brontosaurus "equipment," and try to find creatures to eat that don't wallow in their own waste. If they have to feed some psychedelic Wingo Weed to a few predators to escape death, it's all in a day's work. As Claude says, "Sex, drugs, and dookie-wallowing...the harbingers of a decaying culture." Can extinction be far behind?

1 ❑ Jun 1996 Cover: 2.95 **NM** value: **Cover or less**
📖 Sex, Lie and Vertebrates **A:** Don Perlin **W:** Bob Layton
2 ❑ Jul 1996 Cover: 2.95 **NM** value: **Cover or less**
3 ❑ Aug 1996 Cover: 2.95 **NM** value: **Cover or less**
4 ❑ Sep 1996 Cover: 2.95 **NM** value: **Cover or less**
Circ: Diamd. preorders: **3,523**
5 ❑ Sep 1996 Cover: 2.95 **NM** value: **Cover or less**
cover says Oct, indicia says Sep. 📖 That Dirty Yellow Mustard, Part 1
6 ❑ Nov 1996 Cover: 2.95 **NM** value: **Cover or less**
shoplifting instructions on cover. 📖 That Dirty Yellow Mustard, Part 2
7 ❑ Dec 1996 Cover: 2.95 **NM** value: **Cover or less**
📖 That Dirty Yellow Mustard, Part 3
8 ❑ Jan 1997 Cover: 2.95 **NM** value: **Cover or less**
📖 That Dirty Yellow Mustard, Part 4; Much Do-Do About Nothing **A:** Don Perlin; Gonzalo Mayo **W:** Bob Layton ★ Appearance of Fabian Nicieza, Ivar, Turok.

BADGE — Vanguard

1 ❑ 1981 Cover: 2.95 **NM** value: **Cover or less**

BADGER (VOL. 1) — Capital

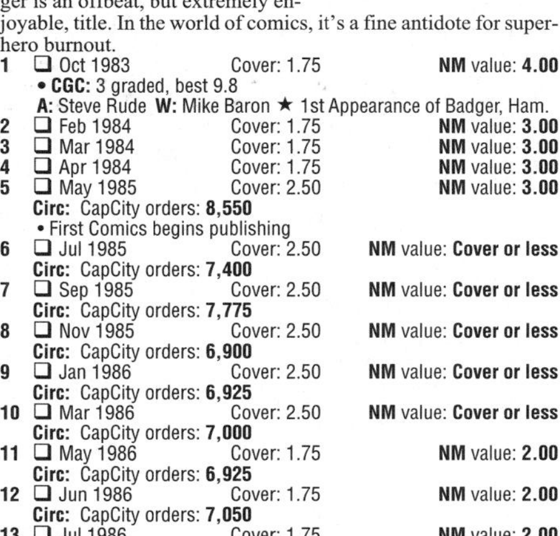

Badger gives Madison, Wis., a super-hero to call its own. OK, so this particular super-hero is a little unhinged, suffers from multiple personality disorder, and sometimes lets murderers get away so he can devote his energies to brutalizing litterbugs. He may not be the ideal super-hero, but, heck, Madison's gotta start somewhere. By the way, Badger is hooked up with a powerful druid-wizard named Ham, making for a dangerous combination, indeed.

Brought to you by writer Mike Baron (the same writer who co-created Nexus with Steve Rude), Badger is an offbeat, but extremely enjoyable, title. In the world of comics, it's a fine antidote for super-hero burnout.

1 ❑ Oct 1983 Cover: 1.75 **NM** value: **4.00**
• **CGC:** 3 graded, best 9.8
A: Steve Rude **W:** Mike Baron ★ 1st Appearance of Badger, Ham.
2 ❑ Feb 1984 Cover: 1.75 **NM** value: **3.00**
3 ❑ Mar 1984 Cover: 1.75 **NM** value: **3.00**
4 ❑ Apr 1984 Cover: 1.75 **NM** value: **3.00**
5 ❑ May 1985 Cover: 2.50 **NM** value: **3.00**
Circ: CapCity orders: **8,550**
• First Comics begins publishing
6 ❑ Jul 1985 Cover: 2.50 **NM** value: **Cover or less**
Circ: CapCity orders: **7,400**
7 ❑ Sep 1985 Cover: 2.50 **NM** value: **Cover or less**
Circ: CapCity orders: **7,775**
8 ❑ Nov 1985 Cover: 2.50 **NM** value: **Cover or less**
Circ: CapCity orders: **6,900**
9 ❑ Jan 1986 Cover: 2.50 **NM** value: **Cover or less**
Circ: CapCity orders: **6,925**
10 ❑ Mar 1986 Cover: 2.50 **NM** value: **Cover or less**
Circ: CapCity orders: **7,000**
11 ❑ May 1986 Cover: 1.75 **NM** value: **2.00**
Circ: CapCity orders: **6,925**
12 ❑ Jun 1986 Cover: 1.75 **NM** value: **2.00**
Circ: CapCity orders: **7,050**
13 ❑ Jul 1986 Cover: 1.75 **NM** value: **2.00**
Circ: CapCity orders: **7,250**
14 ❑ Aug 1986 Cover: 1.75 **NM** value: **2.00**
Circ: CapCity orders: **7,825**
15 ❑ Sep 1986 Cover: 1.75 **NM** value: **2.00**
Circ: CapCity orders: **7,575**

CGC-graded: Multiply prices above by **33 for 9.9 M • 16 for 9.8 NM/M • 7 for 9.6 NM+ • 5 for 9.4 NM • 2.5 for 9.2 NM- • 1.5 for 9.0 VF/NM**

16 ❑ Oct 1986 Cover: 1.75 **NM** value: **2.00**
Circ: CapCity orders: **8,125**

17 ❑ Nov 1986 Cover: 1.75 **NM** value: **2.00**
Circ: CapCity orders: **7,900**

18 ❑ Dec 1986 Cover: 1.75 **NM** value: **2.00**
Circ: CapCity orders: **8,050**

19 ❑ Jan 1987 Cover: 1.75 **NM** value: **2.00**
Circ: CapCity orders: **7,225**

20 ❑ Feb 1987 Cover: 1.75 **NM** value: **2.00**
Circ: CapCity orders: **7,600**

21 ❑ Mar 1987 Cover: 1.75 **NM** value: **2.00**
Circ: CapCity orders: **7,475**

22 ❑ Apr 1987 Cover: 1.75 **NM** value: **2.00**
Circ: CapCity orders: **7,350**

23 ❑ May 1987 Cover: 1.75 **NM** value: **2.00**
Circ: CapCity orders: **6,875**

24 ❑ Jun 1987 Cover: 1.75 **NM** value: **2.00**
Circ: CapCity orders: **7,200**

25 ❑ Jul 1987 Cover: 1.75 **NM** value: **2.00**
Circ: CapCity orders: **6,850**

26 ❑ Aug 1987 Cover: 1.75 **NM** value: **2.00**
Circ: CapCity orders: **7,100**
• Roach Wrangler

27 ❑ Sep 1987 Cover: 1.75 **NM** value: **2.00**
Circ: CapCity orders: **7,600**
• Roach Wrangler

28 ❑ Oct 1987 Cover: 1.75 **NM** value: **2.00**
Circ: CapCity orders: **7,400**

29 ❑ Nov 1987 Cover: 1.75 **NM** value: **2.00**
Circ: CapCity orders: **7,375**

30 ❑ Dec 1987 Cover: 1.75 **NM** value: **2.00**
Circ: CapCity orders: **7,025**

31 ❑ Jan 1988 Cover: 1.75 **NM** value: **2.00**
Circ: CapCity orders: **6,925**

32 ❑ Feb 1988 Cover: 1.75 **NM** value: **2.00**
Circ: CapCity orders: **7,125**

33 ❑ Mar 1988 Cover: 1.75 **NM** value: **2.00**
Circ: CapCity orders: **7,175**
A: Ron Lim

34 ❑ Apr 1988 Cover: 1.75 **NM** value: **2.00**
Circ: CapCity orders: **6,925**
A: Ron Lim

35 ❑ May 1988 Cover: 1.75 **NM** value: **2.00**
Circ: CapCity orders: **6,950**
A: Ron Lim

36 ❑ Jun 1988 Cover: 1.75 **NM** value: **2.00**
Circ: CapCity orders: **6,625**
A: Ron Lim

37 ❑ Jul 1988 Cover: 1.75 **NM** value: **2.00**
Circ: CapCity orders: **6,825**

38 ❑ Aug 1988 Cover: 1.75 **NM** value: **2.00**
Circ: CapCity orders: **7,050**

39 ❑ Sep 1988 Cover: 1.75 **NM** value: **2.00**
Circ: CapCity orders: **6,675**

40 ❑ Oct 1988 Cover: 1.75 **NM** value: **2.00**
Circ: CapCity orders: **6,850**
A: Ron Lim

41 ❑ Nov 1988 Cover: 1.95 **NM** value: **2.00**
Circ: CapCity orders: **6,750**
A: Ron Lim

42 ❑ Dec 1988 Cover: 1.95 **NM** value: **2.00**
Circ: CapCity orders: **6,925**
A: Ron Lim

43 ❑ Jan 1989 Cover: 1.95 **NM** value: **2.00**
Circ: CapCity orders: **6,675**
A: Ron Lim

44 ❑ Feb 1989 Cover: 1.95 **NM** value: **2.00**
Circ: CapCity orders: **6,525**
A: Ron Lim ★ 1st Appearance of Steve Marmel ("The Hiraliator"-in comics).

45 ❑ Mar 1989 Cover: 1.95 **NM** value: **2.00**
Circ: CapCity orders: **6,500**
A: Ron Lim

46 ❑ Apr 1989 Cover: 1.95 **NM** value: **2.00**
Circ: CapCity orders: **6,800**
A: Ron Lim

47 ❑ May 1989 Cover: 1.95 **NM** value: **2.00**
Circ: CapCity orders: **6,650**
A: Ron Lim

48 ❑ Jun 1989 Cover: 1.95 **NM** value: **2.00**
Circ: CapCity orders: **6,450**
A: Ron Lim

49 ❑ Jul 1989 Cover: 1.95 **NM** value: **2.00**
Circ: CapCity orders: **6,575**
A: Ron Lim

50 ❑ Aug 1989 Cover: 3.95 **NM** value: **Cover or less**
Circ: CapCity orders: **7,550**
• Double-size. **A:** Ron Lim

51 ❑ Sep 1989 Cover: 1.95 **NM** value: **2.00**
Circ: CapCity orders: **6,550**

52 ❑ Oct 1989 Cover: 1.95 **NM** value: **3.00**
Circ: CapCity orders: **7,325**
A: Tim Vigil; Tim Vigil(cover)

53 ❑ Nov 1989 Cover: 1.95 **NM** value: **3.00**
Circ: CapCity orders: **7,525**
A: Tim Vigil; Tim Vigil(cover)

54 ❑ Dec 1989 Cover: 1.95 **NM** value: **3.00**
Circ: CapCity orders: **7,525**
A: Tim Vigil; Tim Vigil(cover)

55 ❑ Jan 1990 Cover: 1.95 **NM** value: **2.00**
Circ: CapCity orders: **7,425**

56 ❑ Feb 1990 Cover: 1.95 **NM** value: **2.00**
Circ: CapCity orders: **6,900**

57 ❑ Mar 1990 Cover: 1.95 **NM** value: **2.00**
Circ: CapCity orders: **7,125**

58 ❑ Apr 1990 Cover: 1.95 **NM** value: **2.00**
Circ: CapCity orders: **6,875**

59 ❑ May 1990 Cover: 1.95 **NM** value: **2.00**
Circ: CapCity orders: **6,400**

60 ❑ Jun 1990 Cover: 1.95 **NM** value: **2.00**
Circ: CapCity orders: **6,375**

61 ❑ Jul 1990 Cover: 1.95 **NM** value: **2.00**
Circ: CapCity orders: **6,250**

62 ❑ Aug 1990 Cover: 1.95 **NM** value: **2.00**
Circ: CapCity orders: **6,075**

63 ❑ Sep 1990 Cover: 1.95 **NM** value: **2.00**
Circ: CapCity orders: **6,425**

64 ❑ Oct 1990 Cover: 2.25 **NM** value: **Cover or less**
Circ: CapCity orders: **5,975**

65 ❑ Nov 1990 Cover: 2.25 **NM** value: **Cover or less**
Circ: CapCity orders: **6,050**

66 ❑ Dec 1990 Cover: 2.25 **NM** value: **Cover or less**
Circ: CapCity orders: **5,975**

67 ❑ Jan 1991 Cover: 2.25 **NM** value: **Cover or less**
Circ: CapCity orders: **5,775**

68 ❑ Feb 1991 Cover: 2.25 **NM** value: **Cover or less**
Circ: CapCity orders: **5,650**

69 ❑ Mar 1991 Cover: 2.25 **NM** value: **Cover or less**
Circ: CapCity orders: **6,575**

70 ❑ Apr 1991 Cover: 2.25 **NM** value: **Cover or less**
Circ: CapCity orders: **5,525**
final issue.

BADGER (VOL. 2) First

1 ❑ May 1991 Cover: 4.95 **NM** value: **Cover or less**
Circ: CapCity orders: **4,650**
🕮 Badger Bedlam • Badger Bedlam **A:** Steven Butler **W:** Mike Baron
★ Origin of Badger.

BADGER (VOL. 3) Image

1 ❑ May 1997, b&w Cover: 2.95 **NM** value: **Cover or less**
Circ: Diamd. preorders: **14,513**
• indicia says #78 in series **A:** Joe Comstock **W:** Mike Baron

2 ❑ Jun 1997, b&w Cover: 2.95 **NM** value: **Cover or less**
Circ: Diamd. preorders: **11,084**
• indicia says #79 in series **A:** Joe Comstock **W:** Mike Baron

3 ❑ Jul 1997, b&w Cover: 2.95 **NM** value: **Cover or less**
Circ: Diamd. preorders: **9,835**
• indicia says #80 in series **A:** Joe Comstock **W:** Mike Baron

4 ❑ Aug 1997, b&w Cover: 2.95 **NM** value: **Cover or less**
Circ: Diamd. preorders: **8,281**
• indicia says #81 in series **A:** Joe Comstock **W:** Mike Baron

5 ❑ Sep 1997, b&w Cover: 2.95 **NM** value: **Cover or less**
Circ: Diamd. preorders: **7,216**
• indicia says #82 in series **A:** Joe Comstock **W:** Mike Baron

6 ❑ Oct 1997, b&w Cover: 2.95 **NM** value: **Cover or less**
Circ: Diamd. preorders: **6,370**
🕮 The Prime Minister of Klactoveedesteen • indicia says #83 in series **A:** Joe Comstock **W:** Mike Baron

7 ❑ Nov 1997, b&w Cover: 2.95 **NM** value: **Cover or less**
Circ: Diamd. preorders: **6,084**
• indicia says #84 in series **A:** Joe Comstock **W:** Mike Baron

8 ❑ Dec 1997, b&w Cover: 2.95 **NM** value: **Cover or less**
Circ: Diamd. preorders: **5,511**
🕮 The Root of All Evil • indicia says #85 in series **A:** Joe Comstock **W:** Mike Baron

9 ❑ Jan 1998, b&w Cover: 2.95 **NM** value: **Cover or less**
Circ: Diamd. preorders: **4,997**
🕮 Vapor Trail • indicia says #86 in series **A:** Joe Comstock **W:** Mike Baron

10 ❑ Feb 1998, b&w Cover: 2.95 **NM** value: **Cover or less**
Circ: Diamd. preorders: **4,504**
🕮 Tuesday Ruby • indicia says #87 in series **A:** Joe Comstock **W:** Mike Baron

11 ❑ Apr 1998, b&w Cover: 2.95 **NM** value: **Cover or less**
Circ: Diamd. preorders: **4,309**
🕮 The Crowded Skies • indicia says #88 in series **A:** Joe Comstock **W:** Mike Baron

BADGER GOES BERSERK First

Norbert Sykes is The Badger, a mentally unbalanced super-hero who trounces jaywalkers, litterbugs, and those who are unkind to animals. In Badger Goes Berserk readers go back in time to explore the roots of Norbert's psychosis, following a trail of child abuse and general weirdness that turned him into the signature super-hero of Madison, Wis. It also pits Norbert against his adoptive father and a mad plot to spark a nationwide race war.

Badger had started its life with Capital Comics before transferring to become one of First's first titles. First published this four-issue mini-series to celebrate Badger's 50th issue. To make it happen, it enlisted the help of a creative cast of 16 people, including Badger creator Mike Baron, along with Denys Cowan, Jill Thompson, Rob Liefeld, and other notables. Even Kitchen Sink publisher Denis Kitchen lent a hand to letter several pages.

1 ❑ Sep 1989 Cover: 1.95 **NM** value: **2.00**
Circ: CapCity orders: **8,950**
A: Denis Kitchen; Denys Cowan; Steve Epting; Jill Thompson; Jay Geldhof; Malcolm Jones III **W:** Mike Baron

2 ❑ Oct 1989 Cover: 1.95 **NM** value: **2.00**
Circ: CapCity orders: **8,000**

3 ❑ Nov 1989 Cover: 1.95 **NM** value: **2.00**
Circ: CapCity orders: **7,775**

4 ❑ Dec 1989 Cover: 1.95 **NM** value: **2.00**
Circ: CapCity orders: **8,100**

BADGER: SHATTERED MIRROR Dark Horse

1 ❑ Jul 1994 Cover: 2.50 **NM** value: **Cover or less**
Circ: CapCity orders: **12,075**
A: Jill Thompson **W:** Mike Baron

2 ❑ Aug 1994 Cover: 2.50 **NM** value: **Cover or less**
Circ: CapCity orders: **8,325**
A: Jill Thompson **W:** Mike Baron

3 ❑ Sep 1994 Cover: 2.50 **NM** value: **Cover or less**
Circ: CapCity orders: **7,475**
A: Jill Thompson **W:** Mike Baron

4 ❑ Oct 1994 Cover: 2.50 **NM** value: **Cover or less**
Circ: CapCity orders: **6,700**
A: Jill Thompson **W:** Mike Baron

BADGER: ZEN POP FUNNY-ANIMAL VERSION Dark Horse

1 ❑ Jul 1994 Cover: 2.50 **NM** value: **Cover or less**
Circ: CapCity orders: **10,825**
A: Steven Butler **W:** Mike Baron

2 ❑ Aug 1994 Cover: 2.50 **NM** value: **Cover or less**
Circ: CapCity orders: **7,650**

BAD GIRLS (BILL WARD'S...) Forbidden Fruit

1 ❑ Cover: 1.50 **NM** value: **Cover or less**

BAD GIRLS OF BLACKOUT Blackout

1994 and 1995 continued the emergence of a "Bad Girl" trend in comics. With such comics characters as Lady Death, Razor, and Avengelyne, it seemed as if suddenly every female character came equipped with a sword, a skimpy costume, and a bad attitude.

Blackout Comics was no stranger to this phenomenon. Its Bad Girls of Blackout title served as a sampler to the adventures of its own stable of "Bad Girl" beauties. The "Zero issue" preview, for instance, unites age-old vampire Lady Vampre with the invulnerable Violet (from Extremes of Violet) and vigilantes Ms. Cyanide & Ice against a magic-endowed Jack the Ripper. Later issues added the female Ninja Hari Kari ("Her art is death!") to the mix.

0 ❑ 1995 Cover: 3.50 **NM** value: **Cover or less**
Circ: CapCity orders: **5,315**
🕮 Lady Vampire; Extremes Of Violet; Ms. Cyanide & Ice; The Battle Of The Centuries **A:** Guy Dorian; Jake Jacobsen; Rick Buckler Jr. **W:** John Platt

1 ❑ 1995 Cover: 3.50 **NM** value: **Cover or less**
Circ: CapCity orders: **5,360**
A: Guy Dorian; Jesse Chen; Scott Cohn **W:** John Platt

Anl 1❑ Cover: 3.50 **NM** value: **Cover or less**

BAD HAIR DAY Slab-O-Concrete

1 ❑ **NM** value: **1.00**
• Postcard Comic **A:** Craig Conlan **W:** Craig Conlan

BAD KITTY Chaos

1 ❑ Feb 2001 Cover: 2.99 **NM** value: **Cover or less**
Circ: Diamd. preorders: **17,286** • **CGC:** 2 graded, best 9.8
A: Adriano Batista **W:** Steven Grant; Brian Pulido

2 ❑ Mar 2001 Cover: 2.99 **NM** value: **Cover or less**
Circ: Diamd. preorders: **12,371**
A: Adriano Batista **W:** Steven Grant; Brian Pulido

3 ❑ Apr 2001 Cover: 2.99 **NM** value: **Cover or less**
Circ: Diamd. preorders: **12,259**
A: Adriano Batista **W:** Steven Grant; Brian Pulido

BADLANDS Dark Horse

1 ❑ Jul 1991 Cover: 2.25 **NM** value: **2.50**
A: Vince Giarrano **W:** Steven Grant

2 ❑ Cover: 2.25 **NM** value: **2.50**
A: Vince Giarrano **W:** Steven Grant

3 ❑ Cover: 2.25 **NM** value: **2.50**
A: Vince Giarrano **W:** Steven Grant

4 ❑ Cover: 2.25 **NM** value: **2.50**
Circ: CapCity orders: **1,635**
A: Vince Giarrano **W:** Steven Grant

5 ❑ Cover: 2.25 **NM** value: **2.50**
Circ: CapCity orders: **1,960**
A: Vince Giarrano **W:** Steven Grant

6 ❑ Cover: 2.25 **NM** value: **2.50**
Circ: CapCity orders: **1,780**
A: Vince Giarrano **W:** Steven Grant

BAD LUCK Hero

1 ❑ Cover: 3.50 **NM** value: **Cover or less**

BAD MEAT Fantagraphics / Eros

All issues are adults only.

1 ❑ Jul 1991, b&w Cover: 2.25 **NM** value: **Cover or less**
W: Jim Blanchard; Arthur C. Kegel

2 ❑ Cover: 2.75 **NM** value: **Cover or less**
W: Jim Blanchard; Arthur C. Kegel

BAD NEWS Fantagraphics

3 ❑ b&w Cover: 3.50 **NM** value: **Cover or less**

BADROCK Image

1/A ❑ Mar 1995 Cover: 1.75 **NM** value: **Cover or less**
Circ: CapCity orders: **14,325**

Todd McFarlane inks on cover. **A:** Bob Layton; Rob Liefeld **W:** Eric Stephenson
1/B ❑ Mar 1995 Cover: 1.75 **NM** value: **Cover or less**
Stephen Platt inks on cover. **A:** Rob Liefeld **W:** Eric Stephenson
1/C ❑ Mar 1995 Cover: 1.75 **NM** value: **Cover or less**
Dan Fraga inks on cover. **A:** Bob Layton; Rob Liefeld **W:** Eric Stephenson
2 ❑ Cover: 1.75 **NM** value: **Cover or less**
Circ: CapCity orders: **13,800**
3 ❑ Cover: 1.75 **NM** value: **Cover or less**
Circ: CapCity orders: **12,250**
Anl 1 ❑ Jul 1995 Cover: 2.95 **NM** value: **Cover or less**
Circ: CapCity orders: **10,525**

BADROCK & COMPANY — Image
1 ❑ Sep 1994 Cover: 2.50 **NM** value: **Cover or less**
Circ: CapCity orders: **29,050**
A: Todd Nauck **W:** Keith Giffen
2 ❑ Oct 1994 Cover: 2.50 **NM** value: **Cover or less**
Circ: CapCity orders: **24,100**
A: Todd Nauck **W:** Keith Giffen
3 ❑ Nov 1994 Cover: 2.50 **NM** value: **Cover or less**
Circ: CapCity orders: **19,400**
A: Todd Nauck **W:** Keith Giffen
4 ❑ Dec 1994 Cover: 2.50 **NM** value: **Cover or less**
Circ: CapCity orders: **15,650**
A: Todd Nauck **W:** Keith Giffen
5 ❑ Jan 1995 Cover: 2.50 **NM** value: **Cover or less**
Circ: CapCity orders: **12,725**
A: Todd Nauck **W:** Keith Giffen
6 ❑ Oct 1995 Cover: 2.50 **NM** value: **Cover or less**
Circ: CapCity orders: **10,900**
cover says Feb 95, indicia says Oct 94. **A:** Todd Nauck **W:** Keith Giffen
SE 1 ❑ Sep 1994 Cover: 2.50 **NM** value: **Cover or less**
• San Diego Comic-Con edition.

BADROCK/WOLVERINE — Image
1/A ❑ Jun 1996 Cover: 4.95 **NM** value: **Cover or less**
Savage **A:** Chap Yaep **W:** Jim Valentino
1/B ❑ Jun 1996 Cover: 4.95 **NM** value: **Cover or less**
Savage **A:** Chap Yaep **W:** Jim Valentino
1/C ❑ Jun 1996 Cover: 4.95 **NM** value: **Cover or less**
Savage **A:** Chap Yaep **W:** Jim Valentino
1/D ❑ Jun 1996 Cover: 4.95 **NM** value: **Cover or less**
Savage **A:** Chap Yaep **W:** Jim Valentino

BAFFLING MYSTERIES — Ace
5 ❑ Nov 1951 Cover: 0.10 **NM** value: **200.00**
6 ❑ Jan 1952 Cover: 0.10 **NM** value: **125.00**
7 ❑ Mar 1952 Cover: 0.10 **NM** value: **125.00**
• **CGC:** 1 graded, best 7.0
8 ❑ May 1952 Cover: 0.10 **NM** value: **125.00**
9 ❑ Jul 1952 Cover: 0.10 **NM** value: **125.00**
10 ❑ Sep 1952 Cover: 0.10 **NM** value: **125.00**
11 ❑ Nov 1952 Cover: 0.10 **NM** value: **125.00**
• **CGC:** 1 graded, best 9.6
12 ❑ Dec 1952 Cover: 0.10 **NM** value: **125.00**
13 ❑ Jan 1953 Cover: 0.10 **NM** value: **125.00**
• **CGC:** 1 graded, best 7.5
14 ❑ Mar 1953 Cover: 0.10 **NM** value: **125.00**
• **CGC:** 2 graded, best 8.5
15 ❑ May 1953 Cover: 0.10 **NM** value: **125.00**
16 ❑ Jul 1953 Cover: 0.10 **NM** value: **100.00**
17 ❑ Sep 1953 Cover: 0.10 **NM** value: **100.00**
18 ❑ Nov 1953 Cover: 0.10 **NM** value: **100.00**
• **CGC:** 1 graded, best 8.5
19 ❑ Jan 1954 Cover: 0.10 **NM** value: **100.00**
• **CGC:** 1 graded, best 6.5
20 ❑ Apr 1954 Cover: 0.10 **NM** value: **100.00**
• **CGC:** 4 graded, best 9.2
21 ❑ Jul 1954 Cover: 0.10 **NM** value: **100.00**
22 ❑ Sep 1954 Cover: 0.10 **NM** value: **100.00**
• **CGC:** 1 graded, best 5.5
23 ❑ Nov 1954 Cover: 0.10 **NM** value: **100.00**
• **CGC:** 1 graded, best 9.2
24 ❑ Jan 1955 Cover: 0.10 **NM** value: **Cover or less**
• **CGC:** 1 graded, best 4.0
25 ❑ Jul 1955 Cover: 0.10 **NM** value: **100.00**

BAKERSFIELD KOUNTRY COMICS — Last Gasp
1 ❑ Cover: 0.50 **NM** value: **Cover or less**
Clear Jammer; Bakersfield Blues; Tumbleweeds **A:** Larry Welz; Larry Sutherland **W:** Larry Welz; Larry Sutherland

BAKER STREET — Caliber
1 ❑ Mar 1989 Cover: 1.95 **NM** value: **2.50**
Circ: CapCity orders: **2,375**
2 ❑ Cover: 1.95 **NM** value: **2.50**
Circ: CapCity orders: **1,850**
3 ❑ Cover: 1.95 **NM** value: **2.50**
4 ❑ Cover: 1.95 **NM** value: **2.50**
5 ❑ Cover: 2.50 **NM** value: **Cover or less**
6 ❑ Cover: 2.50 **NM** value: **Cover or less**
7 ❑ Cover: 2.50 **NM** value: **Cover or less**
8 ❑ Cover: 2.50 **NM** value: **Cover or less**
9 ❑ Cover: 2.50 **NM** value: **Cover or less**
10 ❑ Cover: 2.50 **NM** value: **Cover or less**
Bk 1 ❑ Cover: 14.95 **NM** value: **Cover or less**
• Honour Among Punks, collects issues #1-5
Bk 2 ❑ Cover: 14.95 **NM** value: **Cover or less**
• Children of the Night, collects issues #6-10

BAKER STREET GRAFFITI — Caliber
1 ❑ b&w Cover: 2.50 **NM** value: **Cover or less**

BAKER STREET SKETCHBOOK — Caliber
1 ❑ Cover: 3.95 **NM** value: **Cover or less**

BALANCE OF POWER — Mu Press
1 ❑ b&w Cover: 2.00 **NM** value: **2.50**
2 ❑ Cover: 2.25 **NM** value: **2.50**
3 ❑ Mar 1991 Cover: 2.50 **NM** value: **Cover or less**
4 ❑ Jul 1991 Cover: 2.50 **NM** value: **Cover or less**

BALDER THE BRAVE — Marvel
With Thor returning to popularity under the guidance of Walter Simonson, Marvel launched this spinoff limited series to further explore Thor's world.

Thor's friend, Balder, was the bravest of warriors, a skilled fighter that could be touched by no weapon unless he allowed it. He had only two weaknesses: Mistletoe, and his love for Karnilla, the Norn Queen. The first of these had caused his death once, but in the world of Asgard, death is not always forever. Balder returned from Hela's realm, and lives with Karnilla in Nornkeep as the series begins.

When a rider comes to ask Balder to join Thor's quest to save mortal souls unjustly trapped in Hela's realm, the proud and jealous Karnilla has the rider imprisoned before his message can be delivered. In time, however, Balder discovered her deception, and resolved to take up Thor's quest. Balder, who knew its terrors firsthand, was about to venture back into Hel...

1 ❑ Nov 1985 Cover: 0.75 **NM** value: **1.00**
Circ: CapCity orders: **20,200**
The Sword Of Prey **A:** Sal Buscema **W:** Walt Simonson
2 ❑ Jan 1986 Cover: 0.75 **NM** value: **1.00**
Circ: CapCity orders: **16,600**
3 ❑ Mar 1986 Cover: 0.75 **NM** value: **1.00**
Circ: CapCity orders: **17,300**
4 ❑ May 1986 Cover: 0.75 **NM** value: **1.00**
Circ: CapCity orders: **16,600**

BALLAD OF HALO JONES, THE — Fleetway-Quality
1 ❑ Sep 1987 Cover: 1.25 **NM** value: **1.50**
Circ: CapCity orders: **5,525**
Tharg's Future Shocks: Sunburn • Reprints The Ballad of Halo Jones from 2000 A.D. **A:** Ian Gibson; Jesus Redondo **W:** Alan Moore ★ 1st Appearance of Halo Jones.
2 ❑ Oct 1987 Cover: 1.25 **NM** value: **1.50**
Circ: CapCity orders: **4,025**
Fleurs Du Mall **A:** Ian Gibson **W:** Alan Moore
3 ❑ Cover: 1.25 **NM** value: **1.50**
Circ: CapCity orders: **3,825**
A Postcard From Pluto **A:** Ian Gibson **W:** Alan Moore
4 ❑ Cover: 1.25 **NM** value: **1.50**
Circ: CapCity orders: **3,450**
W: Alan Moore
5 ❑ Cover: 1.25 **NM** value: **1.50**
Circ: CapCity orders: **2,875**
W: Alan Moore
6 ❑ Cover: 1.25 **NM** value: **1.50**
Circ: CapCity orders: **2,600**
W: Alan Moore
7 ❑ Cover: 1.25 **NM** value: **1.50**
Circ: CapCity orders: **2,525**
The Last Dance; Anderson Division; The Double Decker-Dome **A:** Barry Kitson; Ian Gibson **W:** Alan Moore; T.B. Grover
8 ❑ Cover: 1.25 **NM** value: **1.50**
Circ: CapCity orders: **2,250**
Tarantula Rising; Halfway to Paradise; The Multi-Storey Mind Mellows Out! **A:** Paul Neary; John Cooper **W:** Alan Moore
9 ❑ Cover: 1.25 **NM** value: **1.50**
Circ: CapCity orders: **2,175**
W: Alan Moore
10 ❑ Cover: 1.25 **NM** value: **1.50**
Circ: CapCity orders: **2,150**
Armies of the Night; Sooner or Later **A:** Ian Gibson; Brendan McCarthy **W:** Alan Moore
11 ❑ Cover: 1.50 **NM** value: **Cover or less**
Circ: CapCity orders: **2,075**
W: Alan Moore
12 ❑ Cover: 1.50 **NM** value: **Cover or less**
Circ: CapCity orders: **1,975**
final issue. **W:** Alan Moore

BALLAD OF UTOPIA, THE — Black Daze
1 ❑ Aug 1998 Cover: 2.95 **NM** value: **Cover or less**
A: Barry Buchanan **W:** Barry Buchanan
2 ❑ Sep 1999 Cover: 2.95 **NM** value: **Cover or less**
3 ❑ Nov 1999 Cover: 2.95 **NM** value: **Cover or less**

Diamond preorders are the estimated number of comics sold, prior to their release, to comics shops in North America by Diamond Comic Distributors, the largest distributor. These figures underreport the actual number of circulating copies by the amount of reorders Diamond took (usually 5-10% again of the preorders) and sales by publishers to newsstand and bookstore distributors. For many independent publishers, Diamond's preorders may be quite close to the actual number of copies in circulation.

BALL AND CHAIN — DC / Homage
Slaughter was one of the most brilliant yet unethical scientists on his world. He escaped to Earth to await the completion of a perfect neuro-schematic communications system, which needed only one key component. Edgar and Mallory were once a happy couple now on the verge of divorce when they happened to absorb that key component which gave them tremendous super powers, but only whenever they were near each other. Their mission: stop Slaughter without killing each other first.

Written and created by Scott Lobdell with art by Ale Garza and Richard Bennett, the series bounced from romantic comedy to super-heroics and back again through all four issues.

1 ❑ Nov 1999 Cover: 2.50 **NM** value: **Cover or less**
Circ: Diamd. preorders: **16,389**
A: Ale Garza; Richard Bennett **W:** Scott Lobdell
2 ❑ Dec 1999 Cover: 2.50 **NM** value: **Cover or less**
Circ: Diamd. preorders: **12,347**
Marital Law **A:** Ale Garza; Richard Bennett **W:** Scott Lobdell
3 ❑ Jan 2000 Cover: 2.50 **NM** value: **Cover or less**
Circ: Diamd. preorders: **10,753**
Love, Honore, and-Say What?! **A:** Ale Garza; Richard Bennett **W:** Scott Lobdell
4 ❑ Feb 2000 Cover: 2.50 **NM** value: **Cover or less**
Circ: Diamd. preorders: **10,221**
A: Ale Garza; Richard Bennett **W:** Scott Lobdell

BALLISTIC — Image
1 ❑ Sep 1995 Cover: 2.50 **NM** value: **Cover or less**
Circ: CapCity orders: **33,025**
A: Michael Turner **W:** Brian Haberlin ★ Appearance of Wetworks.
2 ❑ Oct 1995 Cover: 2.50 **NM** value: **Cover or less**
Circ: CapCity orders: **23,625**
3 ❑ Nov 1995 Cover: 2.50 **NM** value: **Cover or less**
Circ: CapCity orders: **20,375**

BALLISTIC ACTION — Image
1 ❑ May 1996 Cover: 2.95 **NM** value: **Cover or less**
• pin-ups

BALLISTIC IMAGERY — Image
1 ❑ Jan 1996 Cover: 2.50 **NM** value: **Cover or less**
Hellcop; True Stories of Cyberforce: Heatwave; Heavy Space **A:** Adam McDaniel; Marc Silvestri; Brian Haberlin; Dean White; Ian Graham; Richard Isanove **W:** Brian Holguin; Brian Haberlin; Kirk Dilbeck
2 ❑ Cover: 2.50 **NM** value: **Cover or less**

BALLISTIC STUDIOS SWIMSUIT SPECIAL — Image
1 ❑ May 1995 Cover: 2.95 **NM** value: **Cover or less**
• pin-ups **A:** Anthony Chun; Joe Benitez; Billy Tan; Michael Turner; Randy Queen; Anthony Winn

BALLISTIC/WOLVERINE — Top Cow
1 ❑ Feb 1997 Cover: 2.95 **NM** value: **3.50**
Circ: Diamd. preorders: **69,778**
Devil's Reign, Part 4 • crossover with Marvel, continues in Wolverine/Witchblade

BALLOONATIKS, THE — Best
1 ❑ Cover: 2.50 **NM** value: **Cover or less**

BALLOON VENDOR COMIX — Rip Off
1 ❑ Cover: 0.50 **NM** value: **4.00**

BAMBI AND HER FRIENDS — Friendly
1 ❑ Jan 1991 Cover: 2.50 **NM** value: **Cover or less**
2 ❑ Feb 1991 Cover: 2.50 **NM** value: **Cover or less**
3 ❑ Mar 1991 Cover: 2.50 **NM** value: **Cover or less**
4 ❑ Apr 1991 Cover: 2.50 **NM** value: **Cover or less**
5 ❑ May 1991 Cover: 2.50 **NM** value: **Cover or less**
6 ❑ Jun 1991 Cover: 2.95 **NM** value: **Cover or less**
7 ❑ Jul 1991 Cover: 2.95 **NM** value: **Cover or less**
8 ❑ Aug 1991 Cover: 2.95 **NM** value: **Cover or less**
9 ❑ Sep 1991 Cover: 2.95 **NM** value: **Cover or less**

BAMBI IN HEAT — Friendly
1 ❑ Cover: 2.95 **NM** value: **Cover or less**
2 ❑ Cover: 2.95 **NM** value: **Cover or less**
3 ❑ Cover: 2.95 **NM** value: **Cover or less**
Bambi be Good!; When Larry Met Betty **A:** Art Hacker; Kira; Mike Gibbs **W:** Buddy Perot

BAMBI THE HUNTER — Friendly
1 ❑ Cover: 2.95 **NM** value: **Cover or less**
2 ❑ Cover: 2.95 **NM** value: **Cover or less**
3 ❑ Cover: 2.95 **NM** value: **Cover or less**
4 ❑ Cover: 2.95 **NM** value: **Cover or less**
5 ❑ Cover: 2.95 **NM** value: **Cover or less**

BAMBI (WALT DISNEY...) — Whitman
1 ❑ Cover: 0.60 **NM** value: **2.50**
• Reprint of 1942 story

BAMM-BAMM AND PEBBLES FLINTSTONE — Gold Key
1 ❑ ca. 1964 Cover: 0.12 **NM** value: **75.00**
• **CGC:** 1 graded, best 9.4

CGC-graded: Multiply prices above by **33 for 9.9 M • 16 for 9.8 NM/M • 7 for 9.6 NM+ • 5 for 9.4 NM • 2.5 for 9.2 NM- • 1.5 for 9.0 VF/NM**

BANANA SPLITS, THE (HANNA BARBERA...) Gold Key

In 1968, The Banana Splits Adventure Hour featured as hosts the (live-action performers in animal costumes) team consisting of gorilla Bingo, lion Drooper, dog Fleegle, and elephant Snorky: The Banana Splits. They were a "funny animal" rock and roll quartet who presided over an anthology show featuring their own adventures, a live-action adventure story, and cartoon segments. They were Hanna-Barbera's first live-action show.

Gold Key provides the standard kiddie-comics adaptation, with colorful art and fast-moving stories featuring the crazy Splits in the Old West, on a riverboat, and in an assortment of other wild adventures.

1 ❑ Jun 1969 Cover: 0.15 **NM** value: **30.00**
• **CGC:** 1 graded, best 9.2
📖 The Loan Rangers; River Rock; Parcel Post Panic ★ 1st Appearance of Snorky (in comics), Fleegle (in comics), Drooper (in comics), Bingo (in comics).
2 ❑ Apr 1970 Cover: 0.15 **NM** value: **15.00**
• **CGC:** 1 graded, best 6.5
3 ❑ Jul 1970 Cover: 0.15 **NM** value: **12.00**
4 ❑ Oct 1970 Cover: 0.15 **NM** value: **12.00**
5 ❑ Jan 1971 Cover: 0.15 **NM** value: **12.00**
6 ❑ Apr 1971 Cover: 0.15 **NM** value: **10.00**
7 ❑ Jul 1971 Cover: 0.15 **NM** value: **10.00**
8 ❑ Oct 1971 Cover: 0.15 **NM** value: **10.00**

BANDY MAN, THE Caliber

1 ❑ Cover: 2.95 **NM** value: **3.50**
A: Miran Kim **W:** Stefan Petrucha
2 ❑ Nov 1996 Cover: 2.95 **NM** value: **3.25**
Circ: Diamd. preorders: **3,531**
📖 Includes notes by Lee Schlessinger, preview of Level X; Origin of Bandy Man **A:** Miran Kim **W:** Stefan Petrucha
3 ❑ ca. 1997 Cover: 2.95 **NM** value: **Cover or less**
Circ: Diamd. preorders: **2,604**

BANG GANG Fantagraphics / Eros

All issues are adults only.
1 ❑ b&w Cover: 2.50 **NM** value: **Cover or less**

BANGS AND THE GANG Shhwing

All issues are adults only.
1 ❑ Feb 1994, b&w Cover: 2.95 **NM** value: **Cover or less**
Circ: CapCity orders: **2,845**

BAOH Viz

1 ❑ Cover: 2.95 **NM** value: **4.00**
📖 The Ultimate Weapons **A:** Hirohiko Araki **W:** Hirohiko Araki
2 ❑ Cover: 2.95 **NM** value: **3.50**
3 ❑ Cover: 2.95 **NM** value: **3.50**
4 ❑ Cover: 2.95 **NM** value: **3.25**
5 ❑ Cover: 2.95 **NM** value: **3.25**
6 ❑ Cover: 2.95 **NM** value: **3.25**
7 ❑ Cover: 2.95 **NM** value: **3.25**
8 ❑ Cover: 2.95 **NM** value: **3.25**
Bk 1 ❑ May 1995 Cover: 14.95 **NM** value: **Cover or less**
Bk 2 ❑ Cover: 14.95 **NM** value: **Cover or less**

BARABBAS Slave Labor

1 ❑ Aug 1986 Cover: 1.50 **NM** value: **Cover or less**
📖 Tempting Fate and Chasing Ghosts **A:** Gino Attanasio **W:** Gino Attanasio; Dan Vado
2 ❑ Nov 1985 Cover: 1.50 **NM** value: **Cover or less**
A: Gino Attanasio **W:** Gino Attanasio; Dan Vado

BARBARIAN COMICS California

1 ❑ ca. 1972 Cover: 0.50 **NM** value: **3.00**
2 ❑ ca. 1973 Cover: 0.50 **NM** value: **2.50**
📖 Hall of Kings; Hameka; Starsmith; Fast'n'Nuff; Crom; **A:** John Williams; Ron Harris; Hale Han; Tom Bird; W.A. Meugniot **W:** John Williams; Ron Harris; Hale Han; Tom Bird; W.A. Meugniot

BARBARIANS Atlas-Seaboard

1 ❑ Jun 1975 Cover: 0.25 **NM** value: **1.50**
• **CGC:** 3 graded, best 9.4
📖 The Mountain Of Mutants **A:** Pablo Marcos **W:** Gary Friedrich ★ Origin of Andrax. ★ 1st Appearance of Ironjaw.

BARBARIANS AND BEAUTIES AC

1 ❑ 1990 Cover: 2.75 **NM** value: **Cover or less**

BARBARIANS (AVALON) Avalon

1 ❑ Cover: 2.95 **NM** value: **Cover or less**
📖 The Guardian Spiders!; The Great Battles of History: Shiraz!; Who; Oberyll; Ambia! **A:** Joe Staton; Wayne Howard **W:** Nicola Cutii; Wayne Howard
2 ❑ Cover: 2.95 **NM** value: **Cover or less**

BARBARIC TALES Pyramid

1 ❑ Cover: 1.50 **NM** value: **1.70**
📖 The Warriors Three; Damlog; The Last Laugh **A:** Mark Paniccia; Ragne Naess; Bill Cavalier **W:** Mark Paniccia; Ragne Naess; Bill Cavalier
2 ❑ Cover: 1.50 **NM** value: **1.70**

BARBARIENNE (FANTAGRAPHICS) Fantagraphics / Eros

All issues are adults only.
2 ❑ b&w Cover: 2.50 **NM** value: **Cover or less**
3 ❑ b&w Cover: 2.50 **NM** value: **Cover or less**

BARBARIENNE (HARRIER) Harrier

1 ❑ Mar 1987 Cover: 1.95 **NM** value: **2.00**
📖 Memree: The Girl in the Iron Gag **A:** Nick Neocleous **W:** Martin Lock
2 ❑ Cover: 1.95 **NM** value: **2.00**
3 ❑ Cover: 1.95 **NM** value: **2.00**
4 ❑ Cover: 1.95 **NM** value: **2.00**
5 ❑ Cover: 1.95 **NM** value: **2.00**
6 ❑ Cover: 1.95 **NM** value: **2.00**
★ Versus Cuirass.
7 ❑ Cover: 1.95 **NM** value: **2.00**
★ Versus Cuirass.
8 ❑ Cover: 1.95 **NM** value: **2.00**
★ Versus Cuirass.

BARBIE Marvel

Mattel's Barbie remains one of the most recognizable toy properties, and it was only natural that Marvel, during its "mini-Disney" stage (in which it sought to become a broad "youth entertainment company")would seek out the venerable-yet-always-young Barbie's fans.

One of the few comic books aimed at girls by Marvel in the 1990s, Barbie (and its sister title, Barbie Fashion), delivered lighthearted adventures with Barbie participating in various sports and school events.

The Barbie titles were unusual in the portion of their sales that came from subscriptions — far, far above what's typical for comics. That's, in part, due to the marketing of then-Marvel exec Jerry Calabrese, who built huge mailing lists of children for the company and worked subscription promotions involving many other properties, including Barbie. That's why there seem to be more Barbie copies around that one would have guessed from the small numbers ordered by retailers at the time; they went by mail.(Calabrese would, in 1994, get in trouble with comics retailers for trying to launch Marvel Mart, a mail-order service for Marvel.) — JJM

1 ❑ Jan 1991 Cover: 1.00 **NM** value: **5.00**
Circ: CapCity orders: **15,550** • **CGC:** 1 graded, best 9.2
📖 The Fashion Show Must Go On; Dirty Dancing; Prize Pet; Looking Good, Feeling Great; Funny Fashions; Speaking of Dancing; Career Quest **A:** Mary Wilshire **W:** Lisa Trusiani
1/A ❑ Jan 1991 Cover: 1.00 **NM** value: **5.00**
1/B ❑ Jan 1991 Cover: 1.00 **NM** value: **5.00**
📖 The Fashion Show Must Go On; Dirty Dancing; Prize Pet; Looking Good, Feeling Great; Funny Fashions; Speaking of Dancing; Career Quest **A:** Mary Wilshire
2 ❑ Feb 1991 Cover: 1.00 **NM** value: **3.00**
Circ: CapCity orders: **7,000**
📖 Surf 'n' Turf; The Co-Star; Birthday Beat; You Can Paint a Rainbow **A:** Amanda Conner; June Brigman **W:** Barbara Slate; Lisa Trusiani
3 ❑ Mar 1991 Cover: 1.00 **NM** value: **2.50**
Circ: CapCity orders: **6,050**
📖 Ice Capades; Starry, Starry Night; Snakes Alive! **A:** Anna-Maria Cool; Amanda Conner; June Brigman **W:** Lisa Trusiani
4 ❑ Apr 1991 Cover: 1.00 **NM** value: **2.50**
Circ: CapCity orders: **5,660**
5 ❑ May 1991 Cover: 1.00 **NM** value: **2.50**
Circ: CapCity orders: **5,300**
📖 Pleasure Cruise; Safety First; Packing Lightly; Saved by the North Star **A:** Anna-Maria Cool; Barb Rausch; Amanda Conner; Gavin Curtis **W:** Barbara Slate
6 ❑ Jun 1991 Cover: 1.00 **NM** value: **2.00**
Circ: CapCity orders: **5,200**
📖 Horse Cents; Craft Shop; Girls Can Do Anything; The Big Fall **A:** Anna-Maria Cool; Amanda Conner; Mary Wilshire; James Brock **W:** Barbara Slate; Lisa Trusiani
7 ❑ Jul 1991 Cover: 1.00 **NM** value: **2.00**
Circ: CapCity orders: **4,700**
📖 Oui, Oui, C'est Paris!; Bon Voyage; Grand Entrance; Paris Style; Scrapbook; Parlez-Vous Francais?; Craft Shop **A:** Amanda Conner; Gavin Curtis **W:** Barbara Slate; Lisa Trusiani
8 ❑ Aug 1991 Cover: 1.00 **NM** value: **2.00**
Circ: CapCity orders: **4,700**
9 ❑ Sep 1991 Cover: 1.00 **NM** value: **2.00**
Circ: CapCity orders: **4,500**
10 ❑ Oct 1991 Cover: 1.00 **NM** value: **2.00**
Circ: CapCity orders: **4,100**
11 ❑ Nov 1991 Cover: 1.00 **NM** value: **2.00**
Circ: CapCity orders: **4,100**
12 ❑ Dec 1991 Cover: 1.00 **NM** value: **2.00**
Circ: CapCity orders: **4,000**
13 ❑ Jan 1992 Cover: 1.00 **NM** value: **2.00**
Circ: CapCity orders: **4,200**
14 ❑ Feb 1992 Cover: 1.25 **NM** value: **2.00**
Circ: CapCity orders: **3,700**
15 ❑ Mar 1992 Cover: 1.25 **NM** value: **2.00**
Circ: CapCity orders: **3,500**
16 ❑ Apr 1992 Cover: 1.25 **NM** value: **2.00**
Circ: CapCity orders: **3,200**
17 ❑ May 1992 Cover: 1.25 **NM** value: **2.00**
Circ: CapCity orders: **3,400**
18 ❑ Jun 1992 Cover: 1.25 **NM** value: **2.00**
Circ: CapCity orders: **3,400**
19 ❑ Jul 1992 Cover: 1.25 **NM** value: **2.00**
Circ: CapCity orders: **3,300**
20 ❑ Aug 1992 Cover: 1.25 **NM** value: **2.00**
Circ: CapCity orders: **3,400**
21 ❑ Sep 1992 Cover: 1.25 **NM** value: **2.00**
22 ❑ Oct 1992 Cover: 1.25 **NM** value: **2.00**
Circ: CapCity orders: **3,000**
23 ❑ Nov 1992 Cover: 1.25 **NM** value: **2.00**
Circ: CapCity orders: **3,000**
24 ❑ Dec 1992 Cover: 1.25 **NM** value: **2.00**
Circ: CapCity orders: **2,800**
25 ❑ Jan 1993 Cover: 1.25 **NM** value: **2.00**
Circ: CapCity orders: **2,800**
26 ❑ Feb 1993 Cover: 1.25 **NM** value: **2.00**
Circ: CapCity orders: **2,800**
27 ❑ Mar 1993 Cover: 1.25 **NM** value: **2.00**
Circ: CapCity orders: **3,000**
28 ❑ Apr 1993 Cover: 1.25 **NM** value: **2.00**
Circ: CapCity orders: **3,600**
29 ❑ May 1993 Cover: 1.25 **NM** value: **2.00**
Circ: CapCity orders: **3,700**
30 ❑ Jun 1993 Cover: 1.25 **NM** value: **2.00**
Circ: CapCity orders: **4,300**
31 ❑ Jul 1993 Cover: 1.25 **NM** value: **2.00**
Circ: CapCity orders: **4,000**
32 ❑ Aug 1993 Cover: 1.25 **NM** value: **2.00**
Circ: CapCity orders: **5,100**
33 ❑ Sep 1993 Cover: 1.25 **NM** value: **2.00**
Circ: CapCity orders: **3,900**
34 ❑ Oct 1993 Cover: 1.25 **NM** value: **2.00**
Circ: CapCity orders: **4,000**
A: Jose Delbo **W:** Lisa Trusiani ★ Appearance of Teresa.
35 ❑ Nov 1993 Cover: 1.25 **NM** value: **2.00**
Circ: CapCity orders: **4,100**
36 ❑ Dec 1993 Cover: 1.25 **NM** value: **2.00**
Circ: CapCity orders: **4,200**
37 ❑ Jan 1994 Cover: 1.25 **NM** value: **2.00**
Circ: Statement: **70,375** CapCity orders: **3,950**
38 ❑ Feb 1994 Cover: 1.25 **NM** value: **2.00**
Circ: Statement: **70,375** CapCity orders: **4,050**
39 ❑ Mar 1994 Cover: 1.25 **NM** value: **2.00**
Circ: Statement: **70,375** CapCity orders: **3,900**
40 ❑ Apr 1994 Cover: 1.25 **NM** value: **2.00**
Circ: Statement: **70,375** CapCity orders: **3,600**
41 ❑ May 1994 Cover: 1.25 **NM** value: **2.00**
Circ: Statement: **70,375** CapCity orders: **3,550**
42 ❑ Jun 1994 Cover: 1.50 **NM** value: **2.00**
Circ: Statement: **70,375** CapCity orders: **3,850**
43 ❑ Jul 1994 Cover: 1.50 **NM** value: **2.00**
Circ: Statement: **70,375** CapCity orders: **3,700**
44 ❑ Aug 1994 Cover: 1.50 **NM** value: **2.00**
Circ: Statement: **70,375** CapCity orders: **3,800**
45 ❑ Sep 1994 Cover: 1.50 **NM** value: **2.00**
Circ: Statement: **70,375** CapCity orders: **3,500**
46 ❑ Oct 1994 Cover: 1.50 **NM** value: **2.00**
Circ: Statement: **70,375** CapCity orders: **3,300**
47 ❑ Nov 1994 Cover: 1.50 **NM** value: **2.00**
Circ: Statement: **70,375** CapCity orders: **3,350**
48 ❑ Dec 1994 Cover: 1.50 **NM** value: **2.00**
Circ: Statement: **55,037** CapCity orders: **3,300**
49 ❑ Jan 1995 Cover: 1.50 **NM** value: **2.00**
Circ: Statement: **55,037** CapCity orders: **2,975**
50 ❑ Feb 1995 Cover: 2.25 **NM** value: **Cover or less**
Circ: Statement: **55,037** CapCity orders: **3,475**
51 ❑ Mar 1995 Cover: 1.50 **NM** value: **2.00**
Circ: Statement: **55,037** CapCity orders: **2,525**
• Has 1994 Statement, filed 10/1/94; avg print run 119,867; avg sales 50,733; avg subs 19,642; avg total paid 70,375; samples 125; office use 500; max existent 71,000; 41% of run returned
52 ❑ Apr 1995 Cover: 1.50 **NM** value: **2.00**
Circ: Statement: **55,037** CapCity orders: **2,350**
53 ❑ May 1995 Cover: 1.50 **NM** value: **2.00**
Circ: Statement: **55,037** CapCity orders: **2,375**
54 ❑ Jun 1995 Cover: 1.50 **NM** value: **2.00**
Circ: Statement: **55,037** CapCity orders: **2,400**
55 ❑ Jul 1995 Cover: 1.50 **NM** value: **2.00**
Circ: Statement: **55,037** CapCity orders: **2,300**
56 ❑ Aug 1995 Cover: 1.50 **NM** value: **2.00**
Circ: Statement: **55,037** CapCity orders: **2,350**
57 ❑ Sep 1995 Cover: 1.50 **NM** value: **2.00**
Circ: Statement: **55,037**
58 ❑ Oct 1995 Cover: 1.50 **NM** value: **2.00**
59 ❑ Nov 1995 Cover: 1.50 **NM** value: **2.00**
60 ❑ Dec 1995 Cover: 1.50 **NM** value: **2.00**
📖 Halloween Hero **A:** Barb Rausch **W:** Lisa Trusiani
61 ❑ Jan 1996 Cover: 1.50 **NM** value: **2.00**
• Has 1995 Statement, filed 10/1/95; avg print run 97,970; avg sales 38,621; avg subs 16,416; avg total paid 55,037; samples 750; office use 500; max existent 56,287; 43% of run returned
62 ❑ Feb 1996 Cover: 1.50 **NM** value: **2.00**
• Nutcracker Suite references
63 ❑ Mar 1996 Cover: 1.50 **NM** value: **2.00**
📖 Catch The Courage; Raging River final issue. **A:** Mary Wilshire **W:** Lisa Trusiani

BARBIE AND KEN Dell

1 ❑ May 1962 Cover: 0.12 **NM** value: **350.00**
• **CGC:** 2 graded, best 9.2
2 ❑ Aug 1962 Cover: 0.12 **NM** value: **250.00**
• **CGC:** 3 graded, best 9.6
3 ❑ May 1963 Cover: 0.12 **NM** value: **250.00**
• **CGC:** 3 graded, best 9.4
4 ❑ Aug 1963 Cover: 0.12 **NM** value: **250.00**
• **CGC:** 3 graded, best 9.4
5 ❑ Nov 1963 Cover: 0.12 **NM** value: **250.00**
• **CGC:** 2 graded, best 9.6

Other grades: Multiply prices above by **1.5 for Mint • 2/3 for Very Fine • 1/3 for Fine • 1/5 for Very Good • 1/8 for Good**

BARBIE FASHION — Marvel

America's fashion dress-up doll of 1959 had her coming-out party in a comic-book format in the short-lived Dell comic book in the 1960s. When Marvel Comics obtained the license, it introduced two comics in 1991: Barbie and Barbie Fashion. The first issue of each was bagged with a premium: In the case of Barbie Fashion, it was a doorknob-hanging notice.

In the series, Barbie and her buddies were living in San Francisco. Barbie's not just a fashion plate (though she does have a fair pick of cute outfits); she's also a good friend. In addition to the charming adventures featuring Barbie, Ken, and Skipper, the series also features a page for readers' fashion designs for Barbie.

1 ❑ Jan 1991 Cover: 1.00 **NM** value: **5.00**
Circ: CapCity orders: **13,750**
Fall Fashion Issue; Be a Barbie Jewelry Designer; Barbie Craft Shop; White Wash; Career Quest with Marilyn the Fashion Buyer **A:** Anna-Maria Cool **W:** Lisa Trusiani

1/A ❑ Jan 1991 Cover: 1.00 **NM** value: **5.00**
Fall Fashion Issue; Be a Barbie Jewelry Designer; Barbie Craft Shop; White Wash; Career Quest with Marilyn the Fashion Buyer **A:** Anna-Maria Cool

2 ❑ Feb 1991 Cover: 1.00 **NM** value: **3.00**
Circ: CapCity orders: **6,300**

3 ❑ Mar 1991 Cover: 1.00 **NM** value: **2.50**
Circ: CapCity orders: **5,350**

4 ❑ Apr 1991 Cover: 1.00 **NM** value: **2.50**
Circ: CapCity orders: **5,100**

5 ❑ May 1991 Cover: 1.00 **NM** value: **2.50**
Circ: CapCity orders: **4,800**
Picture Perfect; Beauty Sleep; The Latest Fashion; This Old Chair **A:** Anna-Maria Cool; June Brigman **W:** Barbara Slate

6 ❑ Jun 1991 Cover: 1.00 **NM** value: **2.00**
Circ: CapCity orders: **4,600**
Ability; Be a Sport; Craft Shop; Culture Cat **A:** James Brock **W:** Lisa Trusiani

7 ❑ Jul 1991 Cover: 1.00 **NM** value: **2.00**
Circ: CapCity orders: **4,200**

8 ❑ Aug 1991 Cover: 1.00 **NM** value: **2.00**
Circ: CapCity orders: **4,200**

9 ❑ Sep 1991 Cover: 1.00 **NM** value: **2.00**
Circ: CapCity orders: **3,900**

10 ❑ Oct 1991 Cover: 1.00 **NM** value: **2.00**
Circ: CapCity orders: **3,700**

11 ❑ Nov 1991 Cover: 1.00 **NM** value: **2.00**
Circ: CapCity orders: **3,500**

12 ❑ Dec 1991 Cover: 1.00 **NM** value: **2.00**
Circ: CapCity orders: **3,800**

13 ❑ Jan 1992 Cover: 1.00 **NM** value: **2.00**
Circ: CapCity orders: **3,800**

14 ❑ Feb 1992 Cover: 1.00 **NM** value: **2.00**
Circ: CapCity orders: **3,300**

15 ❑ Mar 1992 Cover: 1.00 **NM** value: **2.00**
Circ: CapCity orders: **3,100**

16 ❑ Apr 1992 Cover: 1.00 **NM** value: **2.00**
Circ: CapCity orders: **2,900**

17 ❑ May 1992 Cover: 1.00 **NM** value: **2.00**
Circ: CapCity orders: **3,000**

18 ❑ Jun 1992 Cover: 1.00 **NM** value: **2.00**
Circ: CapCity orders: **3,100**

19 ❑ Jul 1992 Cover: 1.00 **NM** value: **2.00**
Circ: CapCity orders: **3,000**

20 ❑ Aug 1992 Cover: 1.00 **NM** value: **2.00**
Circ: CapCity orders: **2,900**

21 ❑ Sep 1992 Cover: 1.00 **NM** value: **2.00**

22 ❑ Oct 1992 Cover: 1.00 **NM** value: **2.00**
Circ: CapCity orders: **2,700**

23 ❑ Nov 1992 Cover: 1.00 **NM** value: **2.00**
Circ: CapCity orders: **2,600**

24 ❑ Dec 1992 Cover: 1.00 **NM** value: **2.00**
Circ: CapCity orders: **2,500**

25 ❑ Jan 1993 Cover: 1.00 **NM** value: **2.00**
Circ: CapCity orders: **2,500**

26 ❑ Feb 1993 Cover: 1.00 **NM** value: **2.00**
Circ: CapCity orders: **2,500**

27 ❑ Mar 1993 Cover: 1.00 **NM** value: **2.00**
Circ: CapCity orders: **2,600**

28 ❑ Apr 1993 Cover: 1.00 **NM** value: **2.00**
Circ: CapCity orders: **3,400**

29 ❑ May 1993 Cover: 1.00 **NM** value: **2.00**
Circ: CapCity orders: **3,300**

30 ❑ Jun 1993 Cover: 1.00 **NM** value: **2.00**
Circ: CapCity orders: **3,800**

31 ❑ Jul 1993 Cover: 1.25 **NM** value: **2.00**
Circ: CapCity orders: **3,400**

32 ❑ Aug 1993 Cover: 1.25 **NM** value: **2.00**
Circ: CapCity orders: **4,200**

33 ❑ Sep 1993 Cover: 1.25 **NM** value: **2.00**
Circ: CapCity orders: **3,300**

34 ❑ Oct 1993 Cover: 1.25 **NM** value: **2.00**
Circ: CapCity orders: **3,550**
A: Kathleen Webb **W:** Barbara Slate

35 ❑ Nov 1993 Cover: 1.25 **NM** value: **2.00**
Circ: CapCity orders: **3,600**

36 ❑ Dec 1993 Cover: 1.25 **NM** value: **2.00**
Circ: CapCity orders: **3,600**

37 ❑ Jan 1994 Cover: 1.25 **NM** value: **2.00**
Circ: Statement: **50,083** CapCity orders: **3,500**

38 ❑ Feb 1994 Cover: 1.25 **NM** value: **2.00**
Circ: Statement: **50,083** CapCity orders: **3,400**

39 ❑ Mar 1994 Cover: 1.25 **NM** value: **2.00**
Circ: Statement: **50,083** CapCity orders: **3,200**

40 ❑ Apr 1994 Cover: 1.25 **NM** value: **2.00**
Circ: Statement: **50,083** CapCity orders: **3,350**

41 ❑ May 1994 Cover: 1.25 **NM** value: **2.00**
Circ: Statement: **50,083** CapCity orders: **3,100**

42 ❑ Jun 1994 Cover: 1.50 **NM** value: **2.00**
Circ: Statement: **50,083** CapCity orders: **3,150**

43 ❑ Jul 1994 Cover: 1.50 **NM** value: **2.00**
Circ: Statement: **50,083** CapCity orders: **3,100**

44 ❑ Aug 1994 Cover: 1.50 **NM** value: **2.00**
Circ: Statement: **50,083** CapCity orders: **3,200**

45 ❑ Sep 1994 Cover: 1.50 **NM** value: **2.00**
Circ: Statement: **50,083**

46 ❑ Oct 1994 Cover: 1.50 **NM** value: **2.00**
Circ: Statement: **50,083**

47 ❑ Nov 1994 Cover: 1.50 **NM** value: **2.00**
Circ: Statement: **50,083** CapCity orders: **2,800**

48 ❑ Dec 1994 Cover: 1.50 **NM** value: **2.00**
Circ: Statement: **50,083** CapCity orders: **2,600**

49 ❑ Jan 1995 Cover: 1.50 **NM** value: **2.00**
Circ: CapCity orders: **2,900**

50 ❑ Feb 1995 Cover: 2.25 **NM** value: **Cover or less**
Circ: CapCity orders: **2,925**

51 ❑ Mar 1995 Cover: 1.50 **NM** value: **2.00**
Circ: CapCity orders: **2,050**
• Has 1994 Statement, filed 10/1/94; avg print run 103,933; avg sales 38,250; avg subs 11,833; avg total paid 50,083; samples 125; office use 500; max existent 50,708; 51% of run returned

52 ❑ Apr 1995 Cover: 1.50 **NM** value: **2.00**
Circ: CapCity orders: **1,875**

53 ❑ May 1995 Cover: 1.50 **NM** value: **2.00**
Circ: CapCity orders: **1,950**
final issue.

54 ❑ Cover: 1.50 **NM** value: **2.00**
Circ: CapCity orders: **1,925**

55 ❑ Cover: 1.50 **NM** value: **2.00**

BARBI TWINS ADVENTURES, THE — Topps

Once upon a time, two matching blondes made a minor splash posing for Playboy and eventually starred in a comic book based on them.

The one-issue series contains two stories — which is one more than it has jokes. Twins Sia and Shane are cast as secret agents who seem to be continually too busy doing their makeup to actually go out and stop bad guys. When they actually do battle, it's with cutesy compacts that turn into guns and other such Barbarella-style hokiness.

Although Peter Hsu (The Adventurers), Steve Fastner, and Rich Larson do their usual great job of art on the flip-side story ("The Barbi Twins & Razor Versus the Queen City Mob"), the story ends up no better. Making matters worse is the guest appearance of the similarly character-deprived "heroine" Razor.

1 ❑ Jul 1995 Cover: 2.50 **NM** value: **Cover or less**
Circ: CapCity orders: **9,200**
• Flip-book. Prelude to a Mission; Virtual Phony; The Barbi Twins and Razor Versus The Queen City Mob **A:** Matt Haley; Peter Hsu; Rich Larson; Steve Fastner **W:** Robert Conte

BARB WIRE — Dark Horse

1 ❑ Apr 1994 Cover: 2.00 **NM** value: **2.50**
Circ: CapCity orders: **13,025**
Devil in the Dark **A:** Lee Moder **W:** John Arcudi

2 ❑ May 1994 Cover: 2.00 **NM** value: **2.50**
Circ: CapCity orders: **9,025**
The Wild, The Beautiful, & The Damned **A:** Dan Lawlis **W:** John Arcudi

3 ❑ Jun 1994 Cover: 2.00 **NM** value: **2.50**
Circ: CapCity orders: **7,550**
W: John Arcudi

4 ❑ Aug 1994 Cover: 2.00 **NM** value: **2.50**
Circ: CapCity orders: **6,450**
Ghost in the Machine, Part 1 **W:** John Arcudi

5 ❑ Sep 1994 Cover: 2.50 **NM** value: **Cover or less**
Circ: CapCity orders: **5,850**
Ghost in the Machine, Part 2 **A:** Dan Lawlis **W:** John Arcudi

6 ❑ Oct 1994 Cover: 2.50 **NM** value: **Cover or less**
Circ: CapCity orders: **5,525**

7 ❑ Nov 1994 Cover: 2.50 **NM** value: **Cover or less**
Circ: CapCity orders: **4,825**

8 ❑ Jan 1995 Cover: 2.50 **NM** value: **Cover or less**
Circ: CapCity orders: **4,100**

9 ❑ Feb 1995 Cover: 2.50 **NM** value: **Cover or less**
Circ: CapCity orders: **3,650**

Bk 1 ❑ Cover: 8.95 **NM** value: **Cover or less**
• collects #2, 5, and 6

BARB WIRE: ACE OF SPADES — Dark Horse

1 ❑ May 1996 Cover: 2.95 **NM** value: **Cover or less**
2 ❑ Jun 1996 Cover: 2.95 **NM** value: **Cover or less**
3 ❑ Jul 1996 Cover: 2.95 **NM** value: **Cover or less**
A: Chris Warner **W:** Chris Warner
4 ❑ Sep 1996 Cover: 2.95 **NM** value: **Cover or less**
A: Chris Warner **W:** Chris Warner

Creator Key
W = Writer • A = Artist • C = Cover Artist

BARB WIRE COMICS MAGAZINE SPECIAL — Dark Horse

1 ❑ May 1996 Cover: 3.50 **NM** value: **Cover or less**
No issue number. • magazine-sized adaptation of movie, b&w, poster. **A:** Gordon Purcell **W:** Sarah Byam

BARB WIRE MOVIE SPECIAL — Dark Horse

1 ❑ May 1996 Cover: 3.95 **NM** value: **Cover or less**
No issue number. • adapts movie **A:** Gordon Purcell **W:** Sarah Byam

BAR CRAWL OF THE DAMNED — Mortco

1 ❑ 1997b&w Cover: 2.50 **NM** value: **Cover or less**

BAREFOOTZ FUNNIES — Kitchen Sink

All issues are adults only.

1 ❑ b&w Cover: 1.00 **NM** value: **3.00**
The Eclipse; Hint & Run; It All Fits **A:** Howard Cruse **W:** Howard Cruse

2 ❑ b&w Cover: 0.75 **NM** value: **2.00**
A: Howard Cruse **W:** Howard Cruse

3 ❑ b&w Cover: 1.25 **NM** value: **2.00**
A: Howard Cruse **W:** Howard Cruse

BAREFOOTZ THE COMIX BOOK STORIES (HOWARD CRUSE'S...) — Renegade

1 ❑ Cover: 1.70 **NM** value: **2.50**
The Boss Bug; Mamasoyboy Vumulukrishkrosh and a Pox on Your Panty Hose; Water's in His Quarters; Dolly Gets a Faith Lift; Glory Frogs Again **A:** Howard Cruse **W:** Howard Cruse ★ Appearance of Dolly, Barefootz, Headrack.

BARF — Revolutionary

1 ❑ Apr 1990, b&w Cover: 1.95 **NM** value: **Cover or less**
2 ❑ Jun 1990, b&w Cover: 2.50 **NM** value: **Cover or less**
3 ❑ Sep 1990, b&w Cover: 2.50 **NM** value: **Cover or less**

BARNEY AND BETTY RUBBLE — Charlton

1 ❑ Jan 1973 Cover: 0.20 **NM** value: **14.00**
2 ❑ Jan 1973 Cover: 0.20 **NM** value: **9.00**
3 ❑ Mar 1973 Cover: 0.20 **NM** value: **6.00**
4 ❑ May 1973 Cover: 0.20 **NM** value: **6.00**
5 ❑ Jul 1973 Cover: 0.20 **NM** value: **6.00**
6 ❑ Sep 1973 Cover: 0.20 **NM** value: **5.00**
7 ❑ May 1974 Cover: 0.25 **NM** value: **5.00**
8 ❑ Jul 1974 Cover: 0.25 **NM** value: **5.00**
9 ❑ Sep 1974 Cover: 0.25 **NM** value: **5.00**
10 ❑ Nov 1974 Cover: 0.25 **NM** value: **5.00**
11 ❑ Feb 1975 Cover: 0.25 **NM** value: **5.00**
12 ❑ Mar 1975 Cover: 0.25 **NM** value: **4.00**
13 ❑ May 1975 Cover: 0.25 **NM** value: **4.00**
14 ❑ Jun 1975 Cover: 0.25 **NM** value: **4.00**
15 ❑ Aug 1975 Cover: 0.25 **NM** value: **4.00**
16 ❑ Oct 1975 Cover: 0.25 **NM** value: **4.00**
17 ❑ Dec 1975 **NM** value: **4.00**
18 ❑ Feb 1976 **NM** value: **4.00**
19 ❑ Apr 1976 Cover: 0.30 **NM** value: **4.00**
20 ❑ Jun 1976 Cover: 0.30 **NM** value: **4.00**
21 ❑ Aug 1976 Cover: 0.30 **NM** value: **4.00**
Boredom Blues; Garbage Can Caper; Present Problems; Fight Delight; Fuel Fool; Hapless Hero; Machine Master; The Man of the House (text)
22 ❑ Oct 1976 Cover: 0.30 **NM** value: **4.00**
23 ❑ Dec 1976 Cover: 0.30 **NM** value: **4.00**

BARNEY BEAR HOME PLATE — Barbour

1 ❑ Cover: 0.49 **NM** value: **2.00**
A: Al Hartley **W:** Al Hartley

BARNEY BEAR LOST AND FOUND — Spire

1 ❑ **NM** value: **2.00**
A: Al Hartley **W:** Al Hartley

BARNEY THE INVISIBLE TURTLE — Amazing

1 ❑ Cover: 1.95 **NM** value: **Cover or less**
The Cold Clint of Death **A:** Rick Rodolfo **W:** Rick Rodolfo

BARNYARD COMICS — Animated

If Barney Rooster, Snooze the dog, Hucky Duck, Professor Bacon, Robin Hood Robin, and Francois Feline aren't the household names that some of the other funny animals of the comics and movies have become, it isn't for lack of wacky mishaps, goofy humor, and zany merriment produced in the pages of their series, Barnyard Comics, during the 1940s.

Issues featured each of the characters in their own eight-page adventure, often with a guest appearance from one or more of the others. And readers could enjoy a couple of text stories between comics sections. Some of the spot illustrations for these stories were provided by a young Frank Frazetta, who went on to become a hugely successful fantasy illustrator and painter. Barnyard Comics was also specifically cited as an influence by underground comics pioneer Robert Crumb.

1 ❑ Jun 1944 Cover: 0.10 **NM** value: **120.00**
2 ❑ Cover: 0.10 **NM** value: **60.00**
3 ❑ Cover: 0.10 **NM** value: **40.00**
4 ❑ Cover: 0.10 **NM** value: **40.00**
5 ❑ Cover: 0.10 **NM** value: **40.00**
6 ❑ Cover: 0.10 **NM** value: **30.00**

CGC-graded: Multiply prices above by **33 for 9.9 M • 16 for 9.8 NM/M • 7 for 9.6 NM+ • 5 for 9.4 NM • 2.5 for 9.2 NM- • 1.5 for 9.0 VF/NM**

7 ❑ Cover: 0.10 **NM** value: **30.00**
8 ❑ Cover: 0.10 **NM** value: **30.00**
9 ❑ Cover: 0.10 **NM** value: **30.00**
10 ❑ Feb 1947 Cover: 0.10 **NM** value: **30.00**
11 ❑ Apr 1947 Cover: 0.10 **NM** value: **22.00**
12 ❑ Jun 1947 Cover: 0.10 **NM** value: **22.00**
13 ❑ Aug 1947 Cover: 0.10 **NM** value: **40.00**
A: Frank Frazetta(text illustrations)
14 ❑ Oct 1947 Cover: 0.10 **NM** value: **40.00**
A: Frank Frazetta(text illustrations)
15 ❑ Dec 1947 Cover: 0.10 **NM** value: **40.00**
A: Frank Frazetta(text illustrations)
16 ❑ Feb 1948 Cover: 0.10 **NM** value: **22.00**
17 ❑ Apr 1948 Cover: 0.10 **NM** value: **40.00**
A: Frank Frazetta(text illustrations)
18 ❑ Jun 1948 Cover: 0.10 **NM** value: **75.00**
A: Frank Frazetta
19 ❑ Aug 1948 Cover: 0.10 **NM** value: **75.00**
A: Frank Frazetta
20 ❑ Oct 1948 Cover: 0.10 **NM** value: **75.00**
A: Frank Frazetta
21 ❑ Dec 1948 Cover: 0.10 **NM** value: **40.00**
A: Frank Frazetta(text illustrations)
22 ❑ Feb 1949 Cover: 0.10 **NM** value: **75.00**
A: Frank Frazetta
23 ❑ Apr 1949 Cover: 0.10 **NM** value: **40.00**
📖 One Man Show; Vanishing Garden; What, No Music?; History Repeats Itself; Robin Hood Robin; Francois Feline; Adam **A:** Frank Frazetta(text illustrations)
24 ❑ Jun 1949 Cover: 0.10 **NM** value: **75.00**
A: Frank Frazetta
25 ❑ Aug 1949 Cover: 0.10 **NM** value: **75.00**
A: Frank Frazetta
26 ❑ Oct 1949 Cover: 0.10 **NM** value: **40.00**
A: Frank Frazetta(text illustrations)
27 ❑ Dec 1949 Cover: 0.10 **NM** value: **40.00**
A: Frank Frazetta(text illustrations)
28 ❑ Feb 1950 Cover: 0.10 **NM** value: **22.00**
29 ❑ Cover: 0.10 **NM** value: **40.00**
A: Frank Frazetta(text illustrations)
30 ❑ Cover: 0.10 **NM** value: **20.00**
31 ❑ Cover: 0.10 **NM** value: **20.00**
• Series Continued in Dizzy Duck #32

BARR GIRLS, THE — Antarctic / Venus

All issues are adults only.
1 ❑ b&w Cover: 2.95 **NM** value: **Cover or less**
Circ: Diamd. preorders: **2,582**
A: Donna Barr **W:** Donna Barr

BARRON STOREY'S WATCH ANNUAL (VOL. 2) — Vanguard

1 ❑ Cover: 5.95 **NM** value: **Cover or less**
• b&w anthology, squarebound

BARRY WINDSOR-SMITH: STORYTELLER — Dark Horse

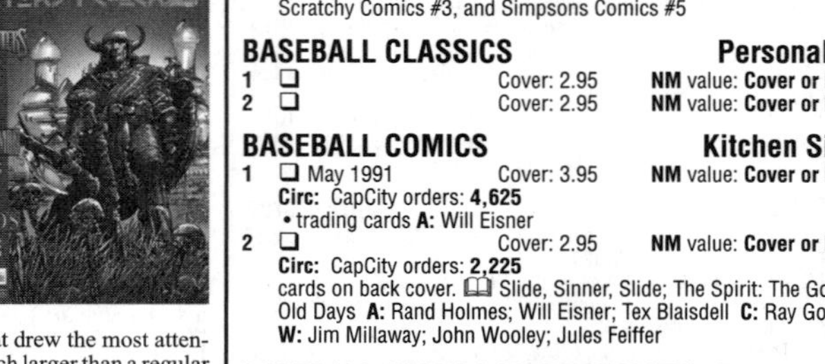

Barry Windsor-Smith spun three separate serials in this short-lived oversized anthology series published in 1996 and 1997 by Dark Horse.

The Freebooters featured the drunken barbarian Axus the Great and his misadventures; The Paradoxman starred a time-traveler whose main mode of transportation was a motorcycle that could break the time barrier; and Young Gods was a tribute to Jack Kirby's New Gods.

While the stories were engaging and, as with all of Windsor-Smith's work, well-drawn, it was the packaging that drew the most attention to the series. The oversized comics, much larger than a regular comic book or magazine, although smaller than the mid-1970 treasury-sized comics, proved difficult to store and display and retailers and fans let their displeasure be known. A slipcase was produced and marked to hold the first 12 issues, but only nine were ever produced.

Adastra, the heroine of Young Gods, did reappear in the Fantagraphics hardcover Adastra in Africa, which recycled an unused X-Men story. — Brent

1 ❑ Oct 1996 Cover: 4.95 **NM** value: **Cover or less**
Circ: Diamd. preorders: **31,037**
1/SC❑ Oct 1996 Cover: 4.95 **NM** value: **Cover or less**
alternate cover (logoless), cover with logos appears as back cover.
2 ❑ Nov 1996 Cover: 4.95 **NM** value: **Cover or less**
Circ: Diamd. preorders: **23,681**
3 ❑ Dec 1996 Cover: 4.95 **NM** value: **Cover or less**
Circ: Direct Market orders: **19,755**
4 ❑ Jan 1997 Cover: 4.95 **NM** value: **Cover or less**
Circ: Direct Market orders: **18,030**
5 ❑ Feb 1997 Cover: 4.95 **NM** value: **Cover or less**
Circ: Diamd. preorders: **17,299**
6 ❑ Mar 1997 Cover: 4.95 **NM** value: **Cover or less**
Circ: Diamd. preorders: **16,506**
7 ❑ May 1997 Cover: 4.95 **NM** value: **Cover or less**
Circ: Diamd. preorders: **14,951**
8 ❑ Jun 1997 Cover: 4.95 **NM** value: **Cover or less**
Circ: Diamd. preorders: **14,185**
9 ❑ Jul 1997 Cover: 4.95 **NM** value: **Cover or less**
Circ: Diamd. preorders: **13,524**

📖 indicates **Story Title** or **Storyline** information.

BAR SINISTER — Windjammer / Acclaim

1 ❑ Jun 1995 Cover: 2.50 **NM** value: **Cover or less**
Circ: CapCity orders: **9,325**
A: Rick Hoberg; Mike Grell **W:** Mike Grell ★ 1st Appearance of Bar Sinister.
2 ❑ Jul 1995 Cover: 2.50 **NM** value: **Cover or less**
Circ: CapCity orders: **6,550**
A: Rick Hoberg; Mike Grell **W:** Mike Grell
3 ❑ Aug 1995 Cover: 2.50 **NM** value: **Cover or less**
Circ: CapCity orders: **5,600**
A: Rick Hoberg; Mike Grell **W:** Mike Grell
4 ❑ Sep 1995 Cover: 2.50 **NM** value: **Cover or less**
Circ: CapCity orders: **4,950**
A: Mike Grell

BARTMAN — Bongo

The Simpsons' son Bart has a rich fantasy life, along with a propensity for getting into trouble. All that made him the perfect candidate to become "Bartman, Arch-enemy of Evil!" Of course, Bartman is really nothing more than Bart in a superhero outfit with no super-powers to match. That doesn't stop him from taking on all manner of evildoers, not the least of which are the school bullies who have taken jobs at the local comic book printing plant. These villains are running scams by stealing comics before they can be appropriately "cover-enhanced" (with silver foil or whatnot), then selling them through local comic stores as "error copies." Who can stand up for the rights of comics collectors when such villains strike?

That's right: Bartman!

1 ❑ 1993 Cover: 2.95 **NM** value: **4.00**
Circ: CapCity orders: **41,700** • **CGC:** 2 graded, best 9.6
Silver ink cover. 📖 The Comic Cover Caper **A:** Phil Ortiz **W:** Steve Vance
2 ❑ 1994 Cover: 1.95 **NM** value: **2.50**
Circ: CapCity orders: **32,375**
📖 Where Stalks The Penalizer **A:** Steve Vance **W:** Jan Strnad
3 ❑ 1994 Cover: 2.25 **NM** value: **2.50**
Circ: CapCity orders: **22,325**
📖 The Final Collision • trading card **A:** Steve Vance **W:** Jan Strnad
4 ❑ 1995 Cover: 2.25 **NM** value: **2.50**
Circ: CapCity orders: **14,725**
5 ❑ 1995 Cover: 2.25 **NM** value: **2.50**
Circ: CapCity orders: **13,400**
★ 1st Appearance of Lisa the Conjuror, The Great Maggeena.
6 ❑ 1995 Cover: 2.25 **NM** value: **2.50**
Circ: CapCity orders: **10,650**
📖 The Great Purple Hope **A:** Luis Escobar; Chris Clements; Tim Bavington **W:** Bill Morrison; Gary Glasberg ★ Origin of Bart Dog. ★ 1st Appearance of Bart Dog.
Bk 1❑ Cover: 10.00 **NM** value: **Cover or less**
• The Best of the Best, collects stories from Bartman #1-3, Itchy & Scratchy Comics #3, and Simpsons Comics #5

BASEBALL CLASSICS — Personality

1 ❑ Cover: 2.95 **NM** value: **Cover or less**
2 ❑ Cover: 2.95 **NM** value: **Cover or less**

BASEBALL COMICS — Kitchen Sink

1 ❑ May 1991 Cover: 3.95 **NM** value: **Cover or less**
Circ: CapCity orders: **4,625**
• trading cards **A:** Will Eisner
2 ❑ Cover: 2.95 **NM** value: **Cover or less**
Circ: CapCity orders: **2,225**
cards on back cover. 📖 Slide, Sinner, Slide; The Spirit: The Good Old Days **A:** Rand Holmes; Will Eisner; Tex Blaisdell **C:** Ray Gotto **W:** Jim Millaway; John Wooley; Jules Feiffer

BASEBALL COMICS (PERSONALITY) — Personality

1 ❑ Cover: 2.95 **NM** value: **Cover or less**
2 ❑ Cover: 2.95 **NM** value: **Cover or less**

BASEBALL GREATS — Dark Horse

1 ❑ Oct 1992 Cover: 2.95 **NM** value: **Cover or less**
📖 The Jimmy Piersall Story • Jimmy Piersall, with cards **A:** Norm Dwyer **W:** Paul Guinan; John Arcudi
2 ❑ Cover: 2.95 **NM** value: **Cover or less**
• Bob Gibson
3 ❑ Cover: 2.95 **NM** value: **Cover or less**
• 2 trading cards

BASEBALL HALL OF SHAME IN 3-D — Blackthorne

1 ❑ Cover: 2.50 **NM** value: **Cover or less**

BASEBALL HEROES — Fawcett

1 ❑ ca. 1952 Cover: 0.10 **NM** value: **500.00**
• **CGC:** 6 graded, best 9.0

BASEBALL LEGENDS — Revolutionary

1 ❑ Mar 1992, b&w Cover: 2.50 **NM** value: **Cover or less**
• Babe Ruth
2 ❑ Apr 1992, b&w Cover: 2.50 **NM** value: **Cover or less**
• Ty Cobb
3 ❑ May 1992, b&w Cover: 2.50 **NM** value: **Cover or less**
• Ted Williams
4 ❑ Jun 1992, b&w Cover: 2.50 **NM** value: **Cover or less**
• Mickey Mantle
5 ❑ Jul 1992, b&w Cover: 2.50 **NM** value: **Cover or less**
• Joe DiMaggio
6 ❑ Aug 1992, b&w Cover: 2.50 **NM** value: **Cover or less**
• Jackie Robinson
7 ❑ Sep 1992, b&w Cover: 2.50 **NM** value: **Cover or less**
• Sandy Koufax
8 ❑ Oct 1992, b&w Cover: 2.50 **NM** value: **Cover or less**
• Willie Mays
9 ❑ Nov 1992, b&w Cover: 2.50 **NM** value: **Cover or less**
• Honus Wagner
10 ❑ Dec 1992, full color Cover: 2.75 **NM** value: **Cover or less**
• Roberto Clemente
11 ❑ Jan 1993, full color Cover: 2.75 **NM** value: **Cover or less**
• Yogi Berra
12 ❑ Feb 1993, full color Cover: 2.75 **NM** value: **Cover or less**
• Billy Martin
13 ❑ Mar 1993, full color Cover: 2.95 **NM** value: **Cover or less**
• Hank Aaron
14 ❑ Apr 1993, b&w Cover: 2.95 **NM** value: **Cover or less**
• Carl Yastrzemski
15 ❑ May 1993, b&w Cover: 2.95 **NM** value: **Cover or less**
• Satchel Paige
16 ❑ Jun 1993, b&w Cover: 2.95 **NM** value: **Cover or less**
• Johnny Bench
17 ❑ Jul 1993, b&w Cover: 2.95 **NM** value: **Cover or less**
• Shoeless Joe Jackson
18 ❑ Aug 1993, b&w Cover: 2.95 **NM** value: **Cover or less**
• Lou Gehrig
19 ❑ Sep 1993, b&w Cover: 2.95 **NM** value: **Cover or less**
• Casey Stengel

BASEBALL'S GREATEST HEROES — Magnum

1 ❑ **NM** value: **2.50**
• **CGC:** 1 graded, best 8.5
• Mickey Mantle
2 ❑ **NM** value: **2.50**
Circ: CapCity orders: **3,050**

BASEBALL SLUGGERS — Personality

1 ❑ Cover: 2.95 **NM** value: **Cover or less**
2 ❑ Cover: 2.95 **NM** value: **Cover or less**
3 ❑ Cover: 2.95 **NM** value: **Cover or less**
4 ❑ Cover: 2.95 **NM** value: **Cover or less**

BASEBALL SUPERSTARS COMICS — Revolutionary

1 ❑ Nov 1991 Cover: 2.50 **NM** value: **Cover or less**
• Nolan Ryan
2 ❑ Feb 1992 Cover: 2.50 **NM** value: **Cover or less**
• Bo Jackson
3 ❑ Mar 1992 Cover: 2.50 **NM** value: **Cover or less**
• Ken Griffey Jr.
4 ❑ Apr 1992 Cover: 2.50 **NM** value: **Cover or less**
• Pete Rose
5 ❑ May 1992 Cover: 2.50 **NM** value: **Cover or less**
• Rickey Henderson **A:** Jim McWeeney **W:** Mitsuko Herrera
6 ❑ Jun 1992 Cover: 2.50 **NM** value: **Cover or less**
• Jose Canseco
7 ❑ Jul 1992 Cover: 2.50 **NM** value: **Cover or less**
• Cal Ripkin Jr.
8 ❑ Aug 1992 Cover: 2.50 **NM** value: **Cover or less**
• Carlton Fisk
9 ❑ Sep 1992 Cover: 2.50 **NM** value: **Cover or less**
• George Brett
10 ❑ Oct 1992 Cover: 2.50 **NM** value: **Cover or less**
• Darryl Strawberry
11 ❑ Nov 1992 Cover: 2.50 **NM** value: **Cover or less**
• Frank Thomas
12 ❑ Dec 1992, full color Cover: 2.75 **NM** value: **Cover or less**
• Ryne Sandberg
13 ❑ Jan 1993, full color Cover: 2.75 **NM** value: **Cover or less**
• Kirby Puckett
14 ❑ Feb 1993, full color Cover: 2.75 **NM** value: **Cover or less**
• Roberto and Sandi Alomar
15 ❑ Mar 1993, full color Cover: 2.95 **NM** value: **Cover or less**
• Roger Clemens
16 ❑ Apr 1993, b&w Cover: 2.95 **NM** value: **Cover or less**
• Mark McGuire
17 ❑ May 1993, b&w Cover: 2.95 **NM** value: **Cover or less**
• Avery/Glavine
18 ❑ Jun 1993, b&w Cover: 2.95 **NM** value: **Cover or less**
• Dennis Eckersley
19 ❑ Jul 1993, b&w Cover: 2.95 **NM** value: **Cover or less**
• Dave Winfield
20 ❑ Aug 1993, b&w Cover: 2.95 **NM** value: **Cover or less**
• Jim Abbott

BASEBALL THRILLS 3-D — 3-D Zone

1 ❑ Cover: 2.95 **NM** value: **Cover or less**
No issue number. 📖 Wolrd Series; The Splendid Splinter; Classic Baseball Cartons **A:** Willard Mullin

BASICALLY STRANGE — John C.

1 ❑ Nov 1982 Cover: 1.95 **NM** value: **5.00**
📖 Bladerunner; To Kill Death; Tetragrammaton; Earth Invader; Swamp Thing; Benefactor; The Power; Death is My Love's Name; The Creator **A:** Vincente Alcazar; Alex Toth; Frank Thorne; Wally Wood; Bruce Jones; Rick Bryant **W:** Wally Wood; Bruce Jones; Marvin Channing; T. Casey Brennan; Tim Ryan

BASTARD TALES — Baboon Books

1 ❑ 1998b&w Cover: 2.95 **NM** value: **Cover or less**

BAT, THE (APPLE) — Apple

1 ❑ Mar 1994, b&w Cover: 2.25 **NM** value: **2.50**
📖 The Bat **A:** Neil Vokes

BATBABE — Spoof

2 ❑ Cover: 2.50 **NM** value: **Cover or less**

Other grades: Multiply prices above by **1.5 for Mint** • **2/3 for Very Fine** • **1/3 for Fine** • **1/5 for Very Good** • **1/8 for Good**

BATCH — Caliber

1 ❑ b&w Cover: 2.95 **NM** value: **Cover or less**

BATGIRL — DC

Since the crippling of Barbara Gordon in Batman: The Killing Joke, fans had been clamoring for a new Batgirl — or for the miraculous return of the Commissioner's daughter to the cape-and-cowl business. But with Barbara firmly established as Oracle — the DC universe's hacker supreme and an integral part of the Birds of Prey — a new Batgirl arose from the ashes of the Bat-titles' No Man's Land storyline. She is the non-speaking daughter of Cain, the world's deadliest assassin, and she has been trained by her father to be a living weapon. Now, under the tutelage of both Batman and Oracle, she is learning to use her skills in the war against crime as one of Gotham City's many costumed protectors. This ain't your daddy's Batgirl by any stretch of the imagination, but she's definitely worth a look.

1 ❑ Apr 2000 Cover: 2.50 **NM** value: **3.00**
Circ: Diamd. preorders: **64,296** • **CGC:** 108 graded, best 10.0
A: Damion Scott **W:** Kelley Puckett; Scott Peterson

1-2 ❑ Apr 2000 Cover: 2.50 **NM** value: **Cover or less**
Circ: Diamd. preorders: **2,175** • **CGC:** 2 graded, best 9.8

2 ❑ May 2000 Cover: 2.50 **NM** value: **Cover or less**
Circ: Diamd. preorders: **49,465** • **CGC:** 43 graded, best 9.8
A: Damion Scott **W:** Kelley Puckett; Scott Peterson

3 ❑ Jun 2000 Cover: 2.50 **NM** value: **Cover or less**
Circ: Diamd. preorders: **49,231**
A: Damion Scott **W:** Kelley Puckett; Scott Peterson

4 ❑ Jul 2000 Cover: 2.50 **NM** value: **Cover or less**
Circ: Diamd. preorders: **47,740**
A: Damion Scott

5 ❑ Aug 2000 Cover: 2.50 **NM** value: **Cover or less**
Circ: Diamd. preorders: **46,400**
A: Damion Scott

6 ❑ Sep 2000 Cover: 2.50 **NM** value: **Cover or less**
Circ: Diamd. preorders: **45,145**
A: Damion Scott

7 ❑ Oct 2000 Cover: 2.50 **NM** value: **Cover or less**
Circ: Diamd. preorders: **42,696**
A: Damion Scott **W:** Kelley Puckett

8 ❑ Nov 2000 Cover: 2.50 **NM** value: **Cover or less**
Circ: Diamd. preorders: **42,705**
A: Damion Scott **W:** Kelley Puckett

9 ❑ Dec 2000 Cover: 2.50 **NM** value: **Cover or less**
Circ: Diamd. preorders: **41,867**
A: Damion Scott **W:** Kelley Puckett

10 ❑ Jan 2001 Cover: 2.50 **NM** value: **Cover or less**
Circ: Diamd. preorders: **41,503**
A: Damion Scott **W:** Kelley Puckett

11 ❑ Feb 2001 Cover: 2.50 **NM** value: **Cover or less**
Circ: Diamd. preorders: **43,317**
A: Damion Scott; Coy Turnbull **W:** Kelley Puckett

12 ❑ Mar 2001 Cover: 2.50 **NM** value: **Cover or less**
Circ: Diamd. preorders: **42,522**
📖 Mute Witness • Officer Down **A:** Dale Eaglesham **W:** Chuck Dixon

13 ❑ Apr 2001 Cover: 2.50 **NM** value: **Cover or less**
Circ: Diamd. preorders: **39,503**
A: Damion Scott **W:** Kelley Puckett

14 ❑ May 2001 Cover: 2.50 **NM** value: **Cover or less**
Circ: Diamd. preorders: **39,212**
A: Damion Scott **W:** Kelley Puckett

15 ❑ Jun 2001 Cover: 2.50 **NM** value: **Cover or less**
Circ: Diamd. preorders: **39,529**
A: Damion Scott **W:** Kelley Puckett

16 ❑ Jul 2001 Cover: 2.50 **NM** value: **Cover or less**
Circ: Diamd. preorders: **38,457**

17 ❑ Aug 2001 Cover: 2.50 **NM** value: **Cover or less**
Circ: Diamd. preorders: **39,439**

18 ❑ Sep 2001 Cover: 2.50 **NM** value: **Cover or less**
Circ: Diamd. preorders: **40,622**

Bk 1❑ Cover: 12.95 **NM** value: **Cover or less**
• Silent Running;Collects Batgirl #1-6 **A:** Damion Scott **W:** Kelley Puckett; Scott Peterson

BATGIRL ADVENTURES, THE — DC

1 ❑ Feb 1998 Cover: 2.95 **NM** value: **3.25**
Circ: Diamd. preorders: **28,440** • **CGC:** 3 graded, best 9.6
★ Versus Harley Quinn, Poison Ivy.

BATGIRL SPECIAL — DC

1 ❑ Jul 1988 Cover: 1.50 **NM** value: **2.50**
Circ: CapCity orders: **28,250** • **CGC:** 8 graded, best 9.6

BATHING MACHINE — C&T

1 ❑ b&w Cover: 2.50 **NM** value: **Cover or less**
2 ❑ Cover: 1.50 **NM** value: **Cover or less**
3 ❑ Cover: 1.50 **NM** value: **Cover or less**

BATHROOM GIRLS — Modern

1 ❑ 1997 b&w Cover: 2.95 **NM** value: **Cover or less**
2 ❑ 1998 b&w Cover: 2.95 **NM** value: **Cover or less**

Do you have changes or corrections for the **Standard Catalog**? Send your original research to us at
allcomics@krause.com

BAT LASH — DC

Introduced in Showcase #76 (Aug 68), Bat Lash soon moved into this short-lived solo series in 1969. It was that rarest of all genres, a humorous Western adventure series — and was clearly inspired by 1967's comedy Western film Waterhole #3 starring James Coburn.

The comic-book star, Batton A. "Bat" Lash, is a no-good drifter, gambler, and gunslinger. He is also quite the dandy, noted for the goofy-looking daisy he wears in his cowboy hat. He travels from town to town, inevitably finding himself up to his neck in trouble. It is only though his quick wit (and the help of his many lady friends) that he escapes whatever disaster he brings on himself.

1 ❑ Nov 1968 Cover: 0.12 **NM** value: **20.00**
• **CGC:** 2 graded, best 9.0

2 ❑ Jan 1969 Cover: 0.12 **NM** value: **10.00**
• **CGC:** 1 graded, best 9.0

3 ❑ Mar 1969 Cover: 0.12 **NM** value: **10.00**
• **CGC:** 2 graded, best 9.4

4 ❑ May 1969 Cover: 0.12 **NM** value: **10.00**
• **CGC:** 1 graded, best 9.4

5 ❑ Jul 1969 Cover: 0.12 **NM** value: **10.00**
• **CGC:** 1 graded, best 9.2

6 ❑ Sep 1969 Cover: 0.12 **NM** value: **10.00**
• **CGC:** 1 graded, best 9.4

7 ❑ Nov 1969 Cover: 0.12 **NM** value: **10.00**
• **CGC:** 1 graded, best 9.0
final issue. **A:** Nick Cardy **W:** Sergio Aragonés; Denny O'Neil

BATMAN — DC

Since his debut in Detective Comics #27 (May 39), Batman has become one of the best-known comics heroes of all time. Created by the legendary Bob Kane, Batman is one of the rare characters that have transcended comics to become cultural icons.

Batman (aka Bruce Wayne) protects the citizens of Gotham City from a never-ending array of criminals. Over the years, his foes have included such famous villains as The Joker, The Penguin, and Catwoman.

Where once he was a fairly straightforward super-hero (complete with Robin, the boy sidekick), Batman has been transformed over time into an increasingly complex character. Now he is The Dark Knight, an avenger of evil who also must face up to the darkness within his own soul.

0 ❑ Oct 1994 Cover: 1.50 **NM** value: **2.50**
Circ: CapCity orders: **64,200** • **CGC:** 2 graded, best 9.6
★ Origin of Batman.

1 ❑ Apr 1940 Cover: 0.10 **NM** value: **64000.00**
• **CGC:** 21 graded, best 8.5
📖 The Legend of the Batman-Who He Is and How He Came to Be!; The Joker; Professor Hugo Strange and the Monsters; The Cat; The Joker Returns; The Legend of the Batman-Who He Is and **A:** Bob Kane; George Papp; Paul Gustavson; Ted Raye **W:** Bill Finger; George Papp; Paul Gustavson; Ted Raye; Gardner Fox; George Shute; Guy Monroe ★ Origin of Batman. ★ 1st Appearance of Joker, Catwoman ("The Cat").

2 ❑ Jun 1940 Cover: 0.10 **NM** value: **11000.00**
• **CGC:** 11 graded, best 8.5
📖 Joker Meets Cat-Woman; Wolf, the Crime Master; The Case of the Clubfoot Murderers; The Case of the Missing Link • Joker/Catwoman team-up **A:** Bob Kane **W:** Bill Finger ★ 2nd Appearance of Catwoman, Joker.

3 ❑ Sep 1940 Cover: 0.10 **NM** value: **8000.00**
• **CGC:** 16 graded, best 9.2
📖 The Strange Case of the Diabolical Puppet Master; The Ugliest Man in the World; The Crime School for Boys!!; The Batman vs. The Cat-Woman!; The Bayman Says **A:** Bob Kane **W:** Bill Finger ★ 1st Appearance of Catwoman (in costume).

4 ❑ Jan 1941 Cover: 0.10 **NM** value: **6000.00**
• **CGC:** 20 graded, best 9.2
📖 The Case of the Joker's Crime Circus!; Blackbeard's Crew and the Yacht Society; Public Enemy No. 1; Victory for the Dynamic Duo! **A:** Bob Kane **W:** Bill Finger ★ Appearance of Joker.

5 ❑ Spr 1941 Cover: 0.10 **NM** value: **4600.00**
• **CGC:** 17 graded, best 8.5
★ 1st Appearance of Batmobile, Joker.

6 ❑ Aug 1941 Cover: 0.10 **NM** value: **3600.00**
• **CGC:** 17 graded, best 9.6

7 ❑ Oct 1941 Cover: 0.10 **NM** value: **3500.00**
• **CGC:** 15 graded, best 9.0
★ Appearance of Joker.

8 ❑ Dec 1941 Cover: 0.10 **NM** value: **3500.00**
• **CGC:** 10 graded, best 8.0

9 ❑ Feb 1942 Cover: 0.10 **NM** value: **3500.00**
• **CGC:** 10 graded, best 9.2
📖 The Four Fates; The White Whale!; The Case of the Lucky Law-Breakers!; Christmas **A:** Bob Kane **W:** Bill Finger ★ Appearance of Joker.

10 ❑ Apr 1942 Cover: 0.10 **NM** value: **3500.00**
• **CGC:** 14 graded, best 8.0
📖 The Isle that Time Forgot!; Report Card Blues!; The Princess of Plunder!; The Sheriff of Ghost Town! **A:** Bob Kane; Bill Finger; Jerry Robinson **W:** Jack Schiff; Joseph Greene

11 ❑ Jun 1942 Cover: 0.10 **NM** value: **4200.00**
• **CGC:** 20 graded, best 9.0
Joker cover. 📖 The Joker's Advertising Campaign; Payment in Full; Bandits in Toyland!; Four Birds of a Feather! **A:** Bob Kane **W:** Bill Finger

12 ❑ Sep 1942 Cover: 0.10 **NM** value: **2450.00**
• **CGC:** 10 graded, best 9.2
📖 Brothers in Crime!; The Wizard of Worlds!; They Thrill to Conquer!; Around the Clock with the Batman! **A:** Bob Kane; Jack Burnley **W:** Don Cameron; Bill Finger ★ 1st Appearance of Batcave.

13 ❑ Oct 1942 Cover: 0.10 **NM** value: **2300.00**
• **CGC:** 9 graded, best 9.2

14 ❑ Dec 1942 Cover: 0.10 **NM** value: **2300.00**
• **CGC:** 14 graded, best 9.2
★ Appearance of Penguin.

15 ❑ Feb 1943 Cover: 0.10 **NM** value: **2300.00**
• **CGC:** 15 graded, best 8.5

16 ❑ Apr 1943 Cover: 0.10 **NM** value: **4600.00**
• **CGC:** 12 graded, best 9.0
★ Origin of Alfred. ★ 1st Appearance of Alfred.

17 ❑ Jun 1943 Cover: 0.10 **NM** value: **1550.00**
• **CGC:** 14 graded, best 9.4

18 ❑ Aug 1943 Cover: 0.10 **NM** value: **1550.00**
• **CGC:** 7 graded, best 8.0
"Buy War Bonds" propaganda-style cover.

19 ❑ Oct 1943 Cover: 0.10 **NM** value: **1550.00**
• **CGC:** 19 graded, best 9.2

20 ❑ Dec 1943 Cover: 0.10 **NM** value: **1550.00**
• **CGC:** 14 graded, best 9.2

21 ❑ Feb 1944 Cover: 0.10 **NM** value: **1125.00**
• **CGC:** 13 graded, best 9.2

22 ❑ Apr 1944 Cover: 0.10 **NM** value: **1125.00**
• **CGC:** 14 graded, best 9.2

23 ❑ Jun 1944 Cover: 0.10 **NM** value: **1675.00**
• **CGC:** 25 graded, best 9.6
★ Appearance of Joker.

24 ❑ Aug 1944 Cover: 0.10 **NM** value: **1125.00**
• **CGC:** 22 graded, best 9.4

25 ❑ Oct 1944 Cover: 0.10 **NM** value: **1750.00**
• **CGC:** 12 graded, best 9.0
• Penguin and Joker team up against Batman

26 ❑ Dec 1945 Cover: 0.10 **NM** value: **1125.00**
• **CGC:** 19 graded, best 9.2

27 ❑ Feb 1945 Cover: 0.10 **NM** value: **1125.00**
• **CGC:** 17 graded, best 9.4
Santa cover.

28 ❑ Apr 1945 Cover: 0.10 **NM** value: **1125.00**
• **CGC:** 11 graded, best 9.2

29 ❑ Jun 1945 Cover: 0.10 **NM** value: **1125.00**
• **CGC:** 9 graded, best 9.0

30 ❑ Aug 1945 Cover: 0.10 **NM** value: **1125.00**
• **CGC:** 15 graded, best 9.4

31 ❑ Oct 1945 Cover: 0.10 **NM** value: **850.00**
• **CGC:** 9 graded, best 9.4

32 ❑ Dec 1945 Cover: 0.10 **NM** value: **850.00**
• **CGC:** 10 graded, best 9.0
★ Appearance of Joker.

33 ❑ Feb 1946 Cover: 0.10 **NM** value: **900.00**
• **CGC:** 9 graded, best 9.2
Christmas cover.

34 ❑ Apr 1946 Cover: 0.10 **NM** value: **850.00**
• **CGC:** 17 graded, best 9.6

35 ❑ Jun 1946 Cover: 0.10 **NM** value: **850.00**
• **CGC:** 11 graded, best 9.0

36 ❑ Aug 1946 Cover: 0.10 **NM** value: **850.00**
• **CGC:** 17 graded, best 9.4

37 ❑ Oct 1946 Cover: 0.10 **NM** value: **1100.00**
• **CGC:** 6 graded, best 9.0
★ Appearance of Joker.

38 ❑ Dec 1947 Cover: 0.10 **NM** value: **925.00**
• **CGC:** 11 graded, best 9.2
★ Appearance of Penguin.

39 ❑ Feb 1947 Cover: 0.10 **NM** value: **850.00**
• **CGC:** 13 graded, best 9.4

40 ❑ Apr 1947 Cover: 0.10 **NM** value: **1050.00**
• **CGC:** 18 graded, best 9.4
★ Appearance of Joker.

41 ❑ Jun 1947 Cover: 0.10 **NM** value: **700.00**
• **CGC:** 16 graded, best 9.6

42 ❑ Aug 1947 Cover: 0.10 **NM** value: **700.00**
• **CGC:** 11 graded, best 9.0

43 ❑ Oct 1947 Cover: 0.10 **NM** value: **700.00**
• **CGC:** 12 graded, best 9.0

44 ❑ Dec 1947 Cover: 0.10 **NM** value: **1000.00**
• **CGC:** 8 graded, best 8.5
★ Appearance of Joker.

45 ❑ Feb 1948 Cover: 0.10 **NM** value: **700.00**
• **CGC:** 7 graded, best 8.5

46 ❑ Apr 1948 Cover: 0.10 **NM** value: **700.00**
• **CGC:** 8 graded, best 8.0

47 ❑ Jun 1948 Cover: 0.10 **NM** value: **2800.00**
• **CGC:** 20 graded, best 8.5
★ Origin of Batman.

48 ❑ Aug 1948 Cover: 0.10 **NM** value: **875.00**
• **CGC:** 9 graded, best 8.5
• Batcave secrets explained

49 ❑ Oct 1948 Cover: 0.10 **NM** value: **1250.00**
• **CGC:** 12 graded, best 9.4
★ 1st Appearance of Vicki Vale, Mad Hatter I (Jervis Tetch). ★ Appearance of Joker.

50 ❑ Dec 1948 Cover: 0.10 **NM** value: **640.00**
• **CGC:** 6 graded, best 9.4

51 ❑ Feb 1949 Cover: 0.10 **NM** value: **640.00**
• **CGC:** 3 graded, best 8.5

52 ❑ Apr 1949 Cover: 0.10 **NM** value: **800.00**
• **CGC:** 4 graded, best 7.0
★ Appearance of Joker.

CGC-graded: Multiply prices above by **33 for 9.9 M** • **16 for 9.8 NM/M** • **7 for 9.6 NM+** • **5 for 9.4 NM** • **2.5 for 9.2 NM-** • **1.5 for 9.0 VF/NM**

53 ❑ Jun 1949 Cover: 0.10 **NM** value: **640.00**
• **CGC:** 3 graded, best 9.0
54 ❑ Aug 1949 Cover: 0.10 **NM** value: **640.00**
• **CGC:** 5 graded, best 7.0
55 ❑ Oct 1949 Cover: 0.10 **NM** value: **800.00**
• **CGC:** 5 graded, best 8.0
★ Appearance of Joker.
56 ❑ Dec 1949 Cover: 0.10 **NM** value: **640.00**
• **CGC:** 5 graded, best 9.6
57 ❑ Feb 1950 Cover: 0.10 **NM** value: **640.00**
• **CGC:** 2 graded, best 5.0
58 ❑ Apr 1950 Cover: 0.10 **NM** value: **685.00**
• **CGC:** 4 graded, best 7.5
★ Appearance of Penguin.
59 ❑ Jun 1950 Cover: 0.10 **NM** value: **640.00**
• **CGC:** 8 graded, best 9.0
★ 1st Appearance of Deadshot.
60 ❑ Aug 1950 Cover: 0.10 **NM** value: **640.00**
• **CGC:** 6 graded, best 8.0
61 ❑ Oct 1950 Cover: 0.10 **NM** value: **640.00**
• **CGC:** 1 graded, best 7.5
62 ❑ Dec 1950 Cover: 0.10 **NM** value: **865.00**
• **CGC:** 6 graded, best 9.2
★ Origin of Catwoman.
63 ❑ Feb 1951 Cover: 0.10 **NM** value: **525.00**
• **CGC:** 1 graded, best 7.0
★ Origin of Killer Moth. ★ 1st Appearance of Killer Moth. ★ Appearance of Joker.
64 ❑ Apr 1951 Cover: 0.10 **NM** value: **465.00**
• **CGC:** 7 graded, best 9.2
65 ❑ Jun 1951 Cover: 0.10 **NM** value: **525.00**
• **CGC:** 1 graded, best 7.0
★ Appearance of Catwoman.
66 ❑ Cover: 0.10 **NM** value: **610.00**
• **CGC:** 8 graded, best 9.2
★ Appearance of Joker.
67 ❑ Oct 1951 Cover: 0.10 **NM** value: **465.00**
• **CGC:** 4 graded, best 8.5
68 ❑ Jan 1952 Cover: 0.10 **NM** value: **465.00**
• **CGC:** 3 graded, best 9.6
69 ❑ Feb 1952 Cover: 0.10 **NM** value: **525.00**
• **CGC:** 3 graded, best 7.5
★ Appearance of Catwoman.
70 ❑ Apr 1952 Cover: 0.10 **NM** value: **465.00**
• **CGC:** 4 graded, best 7.5
71 ❑ Jun 1952 Cover: 0.10 **NM** value: **465.00**
72 ❑ Aug 1952 Cover: 0.10 **NM** value: **465.00**
• **CGC:** 3 graded, best 7.0
73 ❑ Oct 1952 Cover: 0.10 **NM** value: **610.00**
• **CGC:** 4 graded, best 8.0
★ Appearance of Joker.
74 ❑ Dec 1952 Cover: 0.10 **NM** value: **475.00**
• **CGC:** 4 graded, best 6.5
★ Appearance of Joker.
75 ❑ Feb 1953 Cover: 0.10 **NM** value: **460.00**
• **CGC:** 3 graded, best 9.0
76 ❑ Apr 1953 Cover: 0.10 **NM** value: **460.00**
• **CGC:** 4 graded, best 7.0
77 ❑ Jun 1953 Cover: 0.10 **NM** value: **460.00**
• **CGC:** 1 graded, best 7.0
78 ❑ Aug 1953 Cover: 0.10 **NM** value: **575.00**
• **CGC:** 1 graded, best 6.0
★ 1st Appearance of Manhunter from Mars.
79 ❑ Oct 1953 Cover: 0.10 **NM** value: **460.00**
• **CGC:** 5 graded, best 8.0
80 ❑ Jan 1954 Cover: 0.10 **NM** value: **460.00**
• **CGC:** 1 graded, best 4.5
81 ❑ Feb 1954 Cover: 0.10 **NM** value: **450.00**
• **CGC:** 3 graded, best 9.2
★ Appearance of Two-Face.
82 ❑ Mar 1954 Cover: 0.10 **NM** value: **410.00**
• **CGC:** 1 graded, best 7.0
83 ❑ Apr 1954 Cover: 0.10 **NM** value: **410.00**
• **CGC:** 2 graded, best 8.0
84 ❑ Jun 1954 Cover: 0.10 **NM** value: **450.00**
• **CGC:** 5 graded, best 8.5
★ Appearance of Catwoman.
85 ❑ Aug 1954 Cover: 0.10 **NM** value: **410.00**
• **CGC:** 2 graded, best 8.0
86 ❑ Sep 1954 Cover: 0.10 **NM** value: **410.00**
• **CGC:** 2 graded, best 7.5
87 ❑ Oct 1954 Cover: 0.10 **NM** value: **410.00**
• **CGC:** 2 graded, best 4.5
88 ❑ Dec 1954 Cover: 0.10 **NM** value: **410.00**
• **CGC:** 2 graded, best 3.5
89 ❑ Feb 1955 Cover: 0.10 **NM** value: **410.00**
• **CGC:** 2 graded, best 8.0
90 ❑ Mar 1955 Cover: 0.10 **NM** value: **410.00**
• **CGC:** 1 graded, best 3.0
91 ❑ Apr 1955 Cover: 0.10 **NM** value: **370.00**
92 ❑ Jun 1955 Cover: 0.10 **NM** value: **370.00**
• **CGC:** 4 graded, best 8.0
★ 1st Appearance of Bat-Hound ("Ace").
93 ❑ Aug 1955 Cover: 0.10 **NM** value: **370.00**
• **CGC:** 2 graded, best 6.0
94 ❑ Sep 1955 Cover: 0.10 **NM** value: **370.00**
• **CGC:** 4 graded, best 9.2
95 ❑ Oct 1955 Cover: 0.10 **NM** value: **370.00**
• **CGC:** 2 graded, best 4.5
96 ❑ Dec 1955 Cover: 0.10 **NM** value: **370.00**
97 ❑ Feb 1956 Cover: 0.10 **NM** value: **370.00**
• **CGC:** 4 graded, best 8.5
98 ❑ Mar 1956 Cover: 0.10 **NM** value: **370.00**
• **CGC:** 3 graded, best 8.5
99 ❑ Apr 1956 Cover: 0.10 **NM** value: **370.00**
• **CGC:** 1 graded, best 6.5
100 ❑ Jun 1956 Cover: 0.10 **NM** value: **1850.00**
• **CGC:** 25 graded, best 8.5
• 100th anniversary issue.
101 ❑ Aug 1956 Cover: 0.10 **NM** value: **340.00**
• **CGC:** 2 graded, best 3.5
102 ❑ Sep 1956 Cover: 0.10 **NM** value: **340.00**
• **CGC:** 5 graded, best 9.2
103 ❑ Oct 1956 Cover: 0.10 **NM** value: **340.00**
• **CGC:** 6 graded, best 9.0
104 ❑ Dec 1956 Cover: 0.10 **NM** value: **340.00**
• **CGC:** 7 graded, best 8.0
105 ❑ Feb 1957 Cover: 0.10 **NM** value: **450.00**
• **CGC:** 1 graded, best 3.5
★ 2nd Appearance of Batwoman. ★ Appearance of Batwoman.
106 ❑ Mar 1957 Cover: 0.10 **NM** value: **340.00**
• **CGC:** 2 graded, best 8.0
107 ❑ Apr 1957 Cover: 0.10 **NM** value: **340.00**
• **CGC:** 2 graded, best 7.5
108 ❑ Jun 1957 Cover: 0.10 **NM** value: **340.00**
• **CGC:** 8 graded, best 9.0
109 ❑ Jul 1957 Cover: 0.10 **NM** value: **340.00**
• **CGC:** 1 graded, best 8.5
110 ❑ Sep 1957 Cover: 0.10 **NM** value: **360.00**
• **CGC:** 6 graded, best 9.0
★ Appearance of Joker. ★ Versus Joker.
111 ❑ Oct 1957 Cover: 0.10 **NM** value: **250.00**
• **CGC:** 1 graded, best 8.5
112 ❑ Dec 1957 Cover: 0.10 **NM** value: **250.00**
• **CGC:** 3 graded, best 9.0
★ 1st Appearance of The Signalman.
113 ❑ Feb 1958 Cover: 0.10 **NM** value: **250.00**
• **CGC:** 2 graded, best 9.2
★ 1st Appearance of Fatman.
114 ❑ Mar 1958 Cover: 0.10 **NM** value: **250.00**
• **CGC:** 4 graded, best 9.0
115 ❑ Apr 1958 Cover: 0.10 **NM** value: **250.00**
• **CGC:** 4 graded, best 9.2
116 ❑ Jun 1958 Cover: 0.10 **NM** value: **250.00**
• **CGC:** 3 graded, best 9.0
117 ❑ Jul 1958 Cover: 0.10 **NM** value: **250.00**
• **CGC:** 3 graded, best 7.0
118 ❑ Sep 1958 Cover: 0.10 **NM** value: **250.00**
• **CGC:** 1 graded, best 7.0
119 ❑ Oct 1958 Cover: 0.10 **NM** value: **250.00**
• **CGC:** 1 graded, best 5.0
120 ❑ Dec 1958 Cover: 0.10 **NM** value: **250.00**
• **CGC:** 5 graded, best 9.2
121 ❑ Feb 1959 Cover: 0.10 **NM** value: **340.00**
• **CGC:** 6 graded, best 6.5
★ Origin of Mr. Zero (later Mr. Freeze). ★ 1st Appearance of Mr. Zero (later Mr. Freeze).
122 ❑ Mar 1959 Cover: 0.10 **NM** value: **185.00**
• **CGC:** 4 graded, best 9.4
123 ❑ Apr 1959 Cover: 0.10 **NM** value: **210.00**
• **CGC:** 1 graded, best 4.5
★ Appearance of Joker.
124 ❑ Jun 1959 Cover: 0.10 **NM** value: **185.00**
• **CGC:** 4 graded, best 9.2
125 ❑ Aug 1959 Cover: 0.10 **NM** value: **185.00**
126 ❑ Sep 1959 Cover: 0.10 **NM** value: **185.00**
• **CGC:** 3 graded, best 8.5
127 ❑ Oct 1959 Cover: 0.10 **NM** value: **225.00**
• **CGC:** 3 graded, best 8.0
★ Appearance of Joker, Superman.
128 ❑ Dec 1959 Cover: 0.10 **NM** value: **185.00**
• **CGC:** 4 graded, best 9.2
129 ❑ Feb 1960 Cover: 0.10 **NM** value: **240.00**
Circ: Statement: **502,000** • **CGC:** 3 graded, best 8.0
★ Origin of Robin I (Dick Grayson).
130 ❑ Mar 1960 Cover: 0.10 **NM** value: **185.00**
Circ: Statement: **502,000** • **CGC:** 2 graded, best 6.5
★ Appearance of Lex Luthor.
131 ❑ Apr 1960 Cover: 0.10 **NM** value: **135.00**
Circ: Statement: **502,000** • **CGC:** 2 graded, best 7.0
★ 1st Appearance of 2nd Batman.
132 ❑ Jun 1960 Cover: 0.10 **NM** value: **125.00**
Circ: Statement: **502,000** • **CGC:** 2 graded, best 9.0
133 ❑ Aug 1960 Cover: 0.10 **NM** value: **125.00**
Circ: Statement: **502,000** • **CGC:** 2 graded, best 7.5
134 ❑ Sep 1960 Cover: 0.10 **NM** value: **125.00**
Circ: Statement: **502,000** • **CGC:** 3 graded, best 8.0
135 ❑ Oct 1960 Cover: 0.10 **NM** value: **125.00**
Circ: Statement: **502,000** • **CGC:** 6 graded, best 8.5
136 ❑ Dec 1960 Cover: 0.10 **NM** value: **200.00**
Circ: Statement: **502,000** • **CGC:** 12 graded, best 9.2
★ Appearance of Joker. ★ Versus Joker.
137 ❑ Feb 1961 Cover: 0.10 **NM** value: **135.00**
Circ: Statement: **485,000** • **CGC:** 3 graded, best 7.5
• Has 1960 Statement, filed 9/20/60; avg total paid circ 502,000★ Appearance of Mr. Marvel.
138 ❑ Mar 1961 Cover: 0.10 **NM** value: **135.00**
Circ: Statement: **485,000** • **CGC:** 5 graded, best 9.0
139 ❑ Apr 1961 Cover: 0.10 **NM** value: **135.00**
Circ: Statement: **485,000** • **CGC:** 5 graded, best 7.0
★ 1st Appearance of Batgirl (Golden Age).
140 ❑ Jun 1961 Cover: 0.10 **NM** value: **135.00**
Circ: Statement: **485,000** • **CGC:** 3 graded, best 8.0
★ Appearance of Joker.
141 ❑ Aug 1961 Cover: 0.10 **NM** value: **135.00**
Circ: Statement: **485,000** • **CGC:** 2 graded, best 7.5
142 ❑ Sep 1961 Cover: 0.10 **NM** value: **135.00**
Circ: Statement: **485,000** • **CGC:** 3 graded, best 9.2
143 ❑ Oct 1961 Cover: 0.10 **NM** value: **135.00**
Circ: Statement: **485,000** • **CGC:** 9 graded, best 9.0
144 ❑ Dec 1961 Cover: 0.12 **NM** value: **135.00**
Circ: Statement: **485,000** • **CGC:** 3 graded, best 7.0
★ Appearance of Joker.
145 ❑ Feb 1962 Cover: 0.12 **NM** value: **135.00**
Circ: Statement: **410,000** • **CGC:** 9 graded, best 9.4
• Has 1961 Statement, filed 10/1/61; avg total paid circ 485,000★ Appearance of Joker.
146 ❑ Mar 1962 Cover: 0.12 **NM** value: **105.00**
Circ: Statement: **410,000** • **CGC:** 3 graded, best 8.0
147 ❑ May 1962 Cover: 0.12 **NM** value: **105.00**
Circ: Statement: **410,000** • **CGC:** 3 graded, best 9.0
148 ❑ Jul 1962 Cover: 0.12 **NM** value: **135.00**
Circ: Statement: **410,000** • **CGC:** 7 graded, best 9.4
★ Appearance of Joker.
149 ❑ Aug 1962 Cover: 0.12 **NM** value: **105.00**
Circ: Statement: **410,000** • **CGC:** 1 graded, best 9.4
150 ❑ Oct 1962 Cover: 0.12 **NM** value: **105.00**
Circ: Statement: **410,000** • **CGC:** 1 graded, best 7.5
151 ❑ Nov 1962 Cover: 0.12 **NM** value: **80.00**
Circ: Statement: **410,000** • **CGC:** 4 graded, best 9.2
152 ❑ Dec 1962 Cover: 0.12 **NM** value: **90.00**
Circ: Statement: **410,000** • **CGC:** 2 graded, best 9.2
★ Appearance of Joker.
153 ❑ Feb 1963 Cover: 0.12 **NM** value: **70.00**
• **CGC:** 5 graded, best 9.4
• Has 1962 Statement, filed 10/1/62; avg total paid circ 410,000
154 ❑ Mar 1963 Cover: 0.12 **NM** value: **70.00**
• **CGC:** 4 graded, best 9.2
155 ❑ Apr 1963 Cover: 0.12 **NM** value: **325.00**
• **CGC:** 24 graded, best 9.2
★ 1st Appearance of Penguin (in Silver Age).
156 ❑ Jun 1963 Cover: 0.12 **NM** value: **70.00**
• **CGC:** 4 graded, best 9.2
157 ❑ Aug 1963 Cover: 0.12 **NM** value: **70.00**
• **CGC:** 3 graded, best 9.4
158 ❑ Sep 1963 Cover: 0.12 **NM** value: **70.00**
• **CGC:** 5 graded, best 9.0
159 ❑ Nov 1963 Cover: 0.12 **NM** value: **85.00**
• **CGC:** 5 graded, best 9.2
★ Appearance of Joker.
160 ❑ Dec 1963 Cover: 0.12 **NM** value: **70.00**
• **CGC:** 2 graded, best 8.0
161 ❑ Feb 1964 Cover: 0.12 **NM** value: **70.00**
• **CGC:** 1 graded, best 5.5
• Has 1963 Statement, filed 10/1/63; no circ figures published
162 ❑ Mar 1964 Cover: 0.12 **NM** value: **70.00**
• **CGC:** 3 graded, best 8.0
163 ❑ May 1964 Cover: 0.12 **NM** value: **85.00**
• **CGC:** 7 graded, best 9.2
★ Appearance of Joker.
164 ❑ Jun 1964 Cover: 0.12 **NM** value: **70.00**
165 ❑ Aug 1964 Cover: 0.12 **NM** value: **70.00**
• **CGC:** 7 graded, best 9.0
166 ❑ Sep 1964 Cover: 0.12 **NM** value: **70.00**
• **CGC:** 4 graded, best 9.0
167 ❑ Nov 1964 Cover: 0.12 **NM** value: **70.00**
• **CGC:** 4 graded, best 9.4
168 ❑ Dec 1964 Cover: 0.12 **NM** value: **70.00**
• **CGC:** 2 graded, best 9.0
169 ❑ Feb 1965 Cover: 0.12 **NM** value: **80.00**
Circ: Statement: **453,745** • **CGC:** 14 graded, best 9.4
★ Appearance of Penguin.
170 ❑ Mar 1965 Cover: 0.12 **NM** value: **70.00**
Circ: Statement: **453,745** • **CGC:** 6 graded, best 9.2
• Has 1964 Statement, filed 10/1/64; no circ figures published
171 ❑ May 1965 Cover: 0.12 **NM** value: **425.00**
Circ: Statement: **453,745** • **CGC:** 22 graded, best 9.4
A: Carmine Infantino ★ Appearance of 1s.
172 ❑ Jun 1965 Cover: 0.12 **NM** value: **48.00**
Circ: Statement: **453,745** • **CGC:** 2 graded, best 8.0
173 ❑ Aug 1965 Cover: 0.12 **NM** value: **48.00**
Circ: Statement: **453,745** • **CGC:** 5 graded, best 9.0
174 ❑ Sep 1965 Cover: 0.12 **NM** value: **48.00**
Circ: Statement: **453,745** • **CGC:** 4 graded, best 9.4
175 ❑ Nov 1965 Cover: 0.12 **NM** value: **48.00**
Circ: Statement: **453,745** • **CGC:** 7 graded, best 9.4
176 ❑ Dec 1965 Cover: 0.25 **NM** value: **70.00**
Circ: Statement: **453,745** • **CGC:** 7 graded, best 9.8
★ Appearance of Joker.
177 ❑ Dec 1965 Cover: 0.12 **NM** value: **48.00**
Circ: Statement: **453,745** • **CGC:** 7 graded, best 9.4
178 ❑ Feb 1966 Cover: 0.12 **NM** value: **48.00**
Circ: Statement: **898,470** • **CGC:** 6 graded, best 9.2
179 ❑ Mar 1966 Cover: 0.12 **NM** value: **105.00**
Circ: Statement: **898,470** • **CGC:** 4 graded, best 9.0
★ Appearance of Riddler.
180 ❑ May 1966 Cover: 0.12 **NM** value: **48.00**
Circ: Statement: **898,470** • **CGC:** 10 graded, best 9.6
181 ❑ Jun 1966 Cover: 0.12 **NM** value: **125.00**
Circ: Statement: **898,470** • **CGC:** 12 graded, best 9.4
★ 1st Appearance of Poison Ivy.
182 ❑ Aug 1966 Cover: 0.25 **NM** value: **48.00**
Circ: Statement: **898,470** • **CGC:** 7 graded, best 9.6
★ Appearance of Joker.
183 ❑ Aug 1966 Cover: 0.12 **NM** value: **48.00**
Circ: Statement: **898,470** • **CGC:** 11 graded, best 9.6
• TV show reference
184 ❑ Sep 1966 Cover: 0.12 **NM** value: **48.00**
Circ: Statement: **898,470** • **CGC:** 1 graded, best 5.0
📖 Mystery of the Missing Manhunters; The Boy Wonder's Boo-boo Patrol! • Has 1965 Statement, filed 10/1/65; avg print run 694,000; avg sales 448,000; avg subs 5,745; avg total paid 453,745; samples 142; max existent 453,887; 35% of run returned
185 ❑ Nov 1966 Cover: 0.25 **NM** value: **48.00**
Circ: Statement: **898,470** • **CGC:** 4 graded, best 9.6
186 ❑ Nov 1966 Cover: 0.12 **NM** value: **48.00**
Circ: Statement: **898,470** • **CGC:** 9 graded, best 9.6
★ Appearance of Joker.
187 ❑ Dec 1966 Cover: 0.25 **NM** value: **60.00**
Circ: Statement: **898,470** • **CGC:** 7 graded, best 9.6
★ Appearance of Joker.
188 ❑ Jan 1967 Cover: 0.12 **NM** value: **28.00**
Circ: Statement: **805,700** • **CGC:** 5 graded, best 9.6
189 ❑ Feb 1967 Cover: 0.12 **NM** value: **60.00**
Circ: Statement: **805,700** • **CGC:** 29 graded, best 9.6
★ 1st Appearance of The Scarecrow (in Silver Age).

Other grades: Multiply prices above by **1.5 for Mint • 2/3 for Very Fine • 1/3 for Fine • 1/5 for Very Good • 1/8 for Good**

190 ❑ Mar 1967 Cover: 0.12 **NM** value: **35.00**
Circ: Statement: **805,700** • **CGC:** 8 graded, best 9.4
★ Appearance of Penguin.

191 ❑ May 1967 Cover: 0.12 **NM** value: **28.00**
Circ: Statement: **805,700** • **CGC:** 7 graded, best 9.6

192 ❑ Jun 1967 Cover: 0.12 **NM** value: **28.00**
Circ: Statement: **805,700** • **CGC:** 6 graded, best 9.6

193 ❑ Aug 1967 Cover: 0.25 **NM** value: **40.00**
Circ: Statement: **805,700** • **CGC:** 6 graded, best 9.6

194 ❑ Aug 1967 Cover: 0.12 **NM** value: **28.00**
Circ: Statement: **805,700** • **CGC:** 5 graded, best 9.4

195 ❑ Sep 1967 Cover: 0.12 **NM** value: **28.00**
Circ: Statement: **805,700** • **CGC:** 5 graded, best 9.4

196 ❑ Nov 1967 Cover: 0.12 **NM** value: **28.00**
Circ: Statement: **805,700** • **CGC:** 1 graded, best 9.0

197 ❑ Dec 1967 Cover: 0.12 **NM** value: **55.00**
Circ: Statement: **805,700** • **CGC:** 7 graded, best 9.6
★ Appearance of Catwoman.

198 ❑ Jan 1968 Cover: 0.25 **NM** value: **70.00**
Circ: Statement: **533,450** • **CGC:** 8 graded, best 9.6
★ Origin of Batman. ★ Appearance of Joker.

199 ❑ Feb 1968 Cover: 0.12 **NM** value: **28.00**
Circ: Statement: **533,450** • **CGC:** 10 graded, best 9.4

200 ❑ Mar 1968 Cover: 0.12 **NM** value: **140.00**
Circ: Statement: **533,450** • **CGC:** 61 graded, best 9.8
A: Neal Adams ★ Origin of Robin I (Dick Grayson), Batman. ★ Appearance of Joker.

201 ❑ May 1968 Cover: 0.12 **NM** value: **35.00**
Circ: Statement: **533,450** • **CGC:** 5 graded, best 9.6
★ Appearance of Joker.

202 ❑ Jun 1968 Cover: 0.12 **NM** value: **20.00**
Circ: Statement: **533,450** • **CGC:** 5 graded, best 9.8

203 ❑ Aug 1968 Cover: 0.25 **NM** value: **20.00**
Circ: Statement: **533,450** • **CGC:** 8 graded, best 9.4
• Giant-size.

204 ❑ Aug 1968 Cover: 0.12 **NM** value: **18.00**
Circ: Statement: **533,450** • **CGC:** 5 graded, best 9.2

205 ❑ Sep 1968 Cover: 0.12 **NM** value: **18.00**
Circ: Statement: **533,450** • **CGC:** 2 graded, best 9.4

206 ❑ Nov 1968 Cover: 0.12 **NM** value: **18.00**
Circ: Statement: **533,450** • **CGC:** 2 graded, best 9.4

207 ❑ Dec 1968 Cover: 0.12 **NM** value: **18.00**
Circ: Statement: **533,450** • **CGC:** 5 graded, best 9.4

208 ❑ Jan 1969 Cover: 0.25 **NM** value: **35.00**
Circ: Statement: **355,782** • **CGC:** 4 graded, best 9.6
★ Origin of Batman (new origin).

209 ❑ Jan 1969 Cover: 0.12 **NM** value: **18.00**
Circ: Statement: **355,782** • **CGC:** 3 graded, best 9.2

210 ❑ Mar 1969 Cover: 0.12 **NM** value: **18.00**
Circ: Statement: **355,782** • **CGC:** 2 graded, best 9.4
• Has 1968 Statement, filed 10/1/68; avg print run 941,000; avg sales 531,000; avg subs 2,450; avg total paid 533,450; samples 386; max existent 533,836; 43% of run returned

211 ❑ May 1969 Cover: 0.12 **NM** value: **18.00**
Circ: Statement: **355,782** • **CGC:** 3 graded, best 9.4

212 ❑ Jun 1969 Cover: 0.12 **NM** value: **16.00**
Circ: Statement: **355,782** • **CGC:** 3 graded, best 9.6

213 ❑ Aug 1969 Cover: 0.25 **NM** value: **52.00**
Circ: Statement: **355,782** • **CGC:** 12 graded, best 9.8
• Giant-size. • Joker reprint ★ Origin of Robin I (Dick Grayson-new origin). ★ Appearance of Joker.

214 ❑ Aug 1969 Cover: 0.15 **NM** value: **16.00**
Circ: Statement: **355,782** • **CGC:** 1 graded, best 9.2

215 ❑ Sep 1969 Cover: 0.15 **NM** value: **16.00**
Circ: Statement: **355,782**

216 ❑ Nov 1969 Cover: 0.15 **NM** value: **16.00**
Circ: Statement: **355,782**

217 ❑ Dec 1969 Cover: 0.15 **NM** value: **16.00**
Circ: Statement: **355,782** • **CGC:** 1 graded, best 9.0

218 ❑ Feb 1970 Cover: 0.25 **NM** value: **30.00**
Circ: Statement: **293,897** • **CGC:** 6 graded, best 9.6
• Giant-size.

219 ❑ Feb 1970 Cover: 0.15 **NM** value: **30.00**
Circ: Statement: **293,897** • **CGC:** 4 graded, best 9.6
A: Neal Adams

220 ❑ Mar 1970 Cover: 0.15 **NM** value: **14.00**
Circ: Statement: **293,897** • **CGC:** 4 graded, best 9.4
A: Neal Adams

221 ❑ May 1970 Cover: 0.15 **NM** value: **14.00**
Circ: Statement: **293,897** • **CGC:** 3 graded, best 9.4
A: Neal Adams

222 ❑ Jun 1970 Cover: 0.15 **NM** value: **32.00**
Circ: Statement: **293,897** • **CGC:** 2 graded, best 9.0
A: Neal Adams ★ Appearance of The Beatles.

223 ❑ Aug 1970 Cover: 0.25 **NM** value: **30.00**
Circ: Statement: **293,897** • **CGC:** 6 graded, best 9.6
• Giant-size. **A:** Murphy Anderson

224 ❑ Aug 1970 Cover: 0.15 **NM** value: **14.00**
Circ: Statement: **293,897** • **CGC:** 1 graded, best 9.0
A: Neal Adams

225 ❑ Sep 1970 Cover: 0.15 **NM** value: **14.00**
Circ: Statement: **293,897**
A: Neal Adams

226 ❑ Nov 1970 Cover: 0.15 **NM** value: **14.00**
Circ: Statement: **293,897** • **CGC:** 3 graded, best 9.4
A: Neal Adams

227 ❑ Dec 1970 Cover: 0.15 **NM** value: **14.00**
Circ: Statement: **293,897** • **CGC:** 8 graded, best 9.4
• Robin back-up **A:** Neal Adams

228 ❑ Feb 1971 Cover: 0.25 **NM** value: **24.00**
Circ: Statement: **244,488** • **CGC:** 6 graded, best 9.6
• Giant-size. • giant **A:** Murphy Anderson

229 ❑ Feb 1971 Cover: 0.15 **NM** value: **14.00**
Circ: Statement: **244,488** • **CGC:** 3 graded, best 9.6

230 ❑ Mar 1971 Cover: 0.15 **NM** value: **14.00**
Circ: Statement: **244,488** • **CGC:** 2 graded, best 9.6

231 ❑ May 1971 Cover: 0.15 **NM** value: **14.00**
Circ: Statement: **244,488** • **CGC:** 3 graded, best 9.6

232 ❑ Jun 1971 Cover: 0.15 **NM** value: **85.00**
Circ: Statement: **244,488** • **CGC:** 80 graded, best 9.6
A: Dick Giordano; Neal Adams ★ Origin of Batman. ★ 1st Appearance of Ra's Al Ghul.

233 ❑ Aug 1971 Cover: 0.25 **NM** value: **24.00**
Circ: Statement: **244,488** • **CGC:** 6 graded, best 9.4
• Giant-size. • giant

234 ❑ Aug 1971 Cover: 0.25 **NM** value: **115.00**
Circ: Statement: **244,488** • **CGC:** 55 graded, best 9.6
A: Carmine Infantino; Neal Adams ★ 1st Appearance of Two-Face (in Silver Age).

235 ❑ Sep 1971 Cover: 0.25 **NM** value: **13.00**
Circ: Statement: **244,488** • **CGC:** 8 graded, best 9.4
A: Carmine Infantino

236 ❑ Nov 1971 Cover: 0.25 **NM** value: **13.00**
Circ: Statement: **244,488** • **CGC:** 7 graded, best 9.4
A: Neal Adams

237 ❑ Dec 1971 Cover: 0.25 **NM** value: **40.00**
Circ: Statement: **244,488** • **CGC:** 14 graded, best 9.4
A: Neal Adams ★ 1st Appearance of The Reaper.

238 ❑ Jan 1972 Cover: 0.50 **NM** value: **24.00**
Circ: Statement: **185,283** • **CGC:** 5 graded, best 9.0
a.k.a. DC 100-Page Super Spectacular #DC-8, wraparound cover. • Giant-size. **A:** Joe Kubert; Neal Adams; Jack Cole

239 ❑ Feb 1972 Cover: 0.25 **NM** value: **13.00**
Circ: Statement: **185,283** • **CGC:** 4 graded, best 9.0
A: Rich Buckler; Neal Adams

240 ❑ Mar 1972 Cover: 0.25 **NM** value: **13.00**
Circ: Statement: **185,283** • **CGC:** 20 graded, best 9.6
A: Rich Buckler; Neal Adams

241 ❑ May 1972 Cover: 0.25 **NM** value: **13.00**
Circ: Statement: **185,283** • **CGC:** 5 graded, best 9.6
A: Rich Buckler; Neal Adams

242 ❑ Jun 1972 Cover: 0.25 **NM** value: **13.00**
Circ: Statement: **185,283** • **CGC:** 6 graded, best 9.4
A: Rich Buckler; Michael W. Kaluta

243 ❑ Aug 1972 Cover: 0.20 **NM** value: **28.00**
Circ: Statement: **185,283** • **CGC:** 6 graded, best 9.4
• Ra's al Ghul **A:** Dick Giordano; Neal Adams

244 ❑ Sep 1972 Cover: 0.20 **NM** value: **28.00**
Circ: Statement: **185,283** • **CGC:** 19 graded, best 9.6
The Demon Lives Again! • Ra's al Ghul **A:** Dick Giordano; Neal Adams **W:** Denny O'Neil

245 ❑ Oct 1972 Cover: 0.20 **NM** value: **28.00**
Circ: Statement: **185,283** • **CGC:** 2 graded, best 9.6
A: Dick Giordano; Neal Adams; Irv Novick **C:** Frank Miller

246 ❑ Dec 1972 Cover: 0.20 **NM** value: **13.00**
Circ: Statement: **185,283** • **CGC:** 3 graded, best 9.2

247 ❑ Feb 1973 Cover: 0.20 **NM** value: **13.00**
Circ: Statement: **200,574** • **CGC:** 4 graded, best 9.6

248 ❑ Apr 1973 Cover: 0.20 **NM** value: **13.00**
Circ: Statement: **200,574** • **CGC:** 4 graded, best 9.6
• Has 1972 Statement; avg total paid circ 185,283

249 ❑ Jun 1973 Cover: 0.20 **NM** value: **13.00**
Circ: Statement: **200,574** • **CGC:** 3 graded, best 9.6

250 ❑ Jul 1973 Cover: 0.20 **NM** value: **13.00**
Circ: Statement: **200,574** • **CGC:** 2 graded, best 9.0

251 ❑ Sep 1973 Cover: 0.20 **NM** value: **45.00**
Circ: Statement: **200,574** • **CGC:** 35 graded, best 9.6
A: Neal Adams ★ Appearance of Joker.

252 ❑ Sep 1973 Cover: 0.20 **NM** value: **12.00**
Circ: Statement: **200,574** • **CGC:** 3 graded, best 9.6

253 ❑ Nov 1973 Cover: 0.20 **NM** value: **12.00**
Circ: Statement: **200,574** • **CGC:** 1 graded, best 9.0

254 ❑ Feb 1974 Cover: 0.50 **NM** value: **20.00**
Circ: Statement: **193,223** • **CGC:** 4 graded, best 9.4
A: Neal Adams; Gil Kane

255 ❑ Apr 1974 Cover: 0.50 **NM** value: **20.00**
Circ: Statement: **193,223** • **CGC:** 6 graded, best 9.4
A: Carmine Infantino; Dick Giordano; Neal Adams; Gil Kane

256 ❑ Jun 1974 Cover: 0.60 **NM** value: **20.00**
Circ: Statement: **193,223** • **CGC:** 3 graded, best 9.6
• Has 1973 Statement; avg total paid circ 200,574

257 ❑ Aug 1974 Cover: 0.60 **NM** value: **20.00**
Circ: Statement: **193,223** • **CGC:** 4 graded, best 9.6

258 ❑ Oct 1974 Cover: 0.60 **NM** value: **20.00**
Circ: Statement: **193,223** • **CGC:** 6 graded, best 9.4

259 ❑ Dec 1974 Cover: 0.60 **NM** value: **20.00**
Circ: Statement: **193,223** • **CGC:** 4 graded, best 9.4

260 ❑ Feb 1975 Cover: 0.60 **NM** value: **28.00**
Circ: Statement: **154,000** • **CGC:** 7 graded, best 9.6
★ Appearance of Joker.

261 ❑ Mar 1975 Cover: 0.60 **NM** value: **20.00**
Circ: Statement: **154,000** • **CGC:** 5 graded, best 9.4

262 ❑ Apr 1975 Cover: 0.50 **NM** value: **13.00**
Circ: Statement: **154,000** • **CGC:** 7 graded, best 9.6
• Giant-size.

263 ❑ May 1975 Cover: 0.25 **NM** value: **9.00**
Circ: Statement: **154,000**
• Has 1974 Statement; avg total paid circ 193,223

264 ❑ Jun 1975 Cover: 0.25 **NM** value: **9.00**
Circ: Statement: **154,000** • **CGC:** 1 graded, best 8.5
Death of a Daredevil **A:** Ernie Chua; Dick Giordano **W:** Denny O'Neil ★ Versus Devil Dayre.

265 ❑ Jul 1975 Cover: 0.25 **NM** value: **9.00**
Circ: Statement: **154,000** • **CGC:** 1 graded, best 7.0

266 ❑ Aug 1975 Cover: 0.25 **NM** value: **9.00**
Circ: Statement: **154,000** • **CGC:** 1 graded, best 8.0
• Catwoman goes back to old costume ★ Appearance of Catwoman.

267 ❑ Sep 1975 Cover: 0.25 **NM** value: **9.00**
Circ: Statement: **154,000** • **CGC:** 4 graded, best 9.4

268 ❑ Oct 1975 Cover: 0.25 **NM** value: **9.00**
Circ: Statement: **154,000** • **CGC:** 1 graded, best 8.0

269 ❑ Nov 1975 Cover: 0.25 **NM** value: **9.00**
Circ: Statement: **154,000**

270 ❑ Dec 1975 Cover: 0.25 **NM** value: **9.00**
Circ: Statement: **154,000** • **CGC:** 1 graded, best 9.2

271 ❑ Jan 1976 Cover: 0.25 **NM** value: **9.00**
Circ: Statement: **178,000** • **CGC:** 1 graded, best 9.4

272 ❑ Feb 1976 Cover: 0.25 **NM** value: **9.00**
Circ: Statement: **178,000**

273 ❑ Mar 1976 Cover: 0.25 **NM** value: **9.00**
Circ: Statement: **178,000**

274 ❑ Apr 1976 Cover: 0.30 **NM** value: **9.00**
Circ: Statement: **178,000**

275 ❑ May 1976 Cover: 0.30 **NM** value: **9.00**
Circ: Statement: **178,000** • **CGC:** 1 graded, best 9.4

276 ❑ Jun 1976 Cover: 0.30 **NM** value: **9.00**
Circ: Statement: **178,000** • **CGC:** 1 graded, best 9.6

277 ❑ Jul 1976 Cover: 0.30 **NM** value: **9.00**
Circ: Statement: **178,000** • **CGC:** 2 graded, best 9.4
• Bicentennial #11

278 ❑ Aug 1976 Cover: 0.30 **NM** value: **9.00**
Circ: Statement: **178,000** • **CGC:** 1 graded, best 9.4

279 ❑ Sep 1976 Cover: 0.30 **NM** value: **9.00**
Circ: Statement: **178,000**

280 ❑ Oct 1976 Cover: 0.30 **NM** value: **9.00**
Circ: Statement: **178,000**

281 ❑ Nov 1976 Cover: 0.30 **NM** value: **9.00**
Circ: Statement: **178,000** • **CGC:** 1 graded, best 8.0

282 ❑ Dec 1976 Cover: 0.30 **NM** value: **9.00**
Circ: Statement: **178,000** • **CGC:** 1 graded, best 9.0

283 ❑ Jan 1977 Cover: 0.30 **NM** value: **9.00**
Circ: Statement: **168,164** • **CGC:** 2 graded, best 9.6
Omega Bomb Target: Gotham City **A:** Ernie Chua **W:** David Reed ★ Versus Omega.

284 ❑ Feb 1977 Cover: 0.30 **NM** value: **9.00**
Circ: Statement: **168,164**

285 ❑ Mar 1977 Cover: 0.30 **NM** value: **9.00**
Circ: Statement: **168,164** • **CGC:** 2 graded, best 9.4

286 ❑ Apr 1977 Cover: 0.30 **NM** value: **12.00**
Circ: Statement: **168,164** • **CGC:** 4 graded, best 9.8
★ Appearance of Joker.

287 ❑ May 1977 Cover: 0.30 **NM** value: **9.00**
Circ: Statement: **168,164** • **CGC:** 3 graded, best 9.4
• Has 1976 Statement; avg total paid circ 178,000

288 ❑ Jun 1977 Cover: 0.35 **NM** value: **9.00**
Circ: Statement: **168,164** • **CGC:** 1 graded, best 9.4

289 ❑ Jul 1977 Cover: 0.35 **NM** value: **9.00**
Circ: Statement: **168,164** • **CGC:** 4 graded, best 9.6

290 ❑ Aug 1977 Cover: 0.35 **NM** value: **9.00**
Circ: Statement: **168,164**

291 ❑ Sep 1977 Cover: 0.35 **NM** value: **9.00**
Circ: Statement: **168,164** • **CGC:** 3 graded, best 9.4
Underworld Olympics, Part 1 ★ Appearance of Joker.

292 ❑ Oct 1977 Cover: 0.35 **NM** value: **9.00**
Circ: Statement: **168,164**
Underworld Olympics, Part 2

293 ❑ Nov 1977 Cover: 0.35 **NM** value: **9.00**
Circ: Statement: **168,164**
Underworld Olympics, Part 3 ★ Appearance of Lex Luthor, Superman.

294 ❑ Dec 1977 Cover: 0.35 **NM** value: **9.00**
Circ: Statement: **168,164** • **CGC:** 1 graded, best 9.6
Underworld Olympics, Part 4 ★ Appearance of Joker.

295 ❑ Jan 1978 Cover: 0.35 **NM** value: **8.00**
Circ: Statement: **125,421**

296 ❑ Feb 1978 Cover: 0.35 **NM** value: **8.00**
Circ: Statement: **125,421**
The Sinister Straws of the Scarecrow **A:** Sal Amendola **W:** David Reed ★ Versus Scarecrow.

297 ❑ Mar 1978 Cover: 0.35 **NM** value: **8.00**
Circ: Statement: **125,421** • **CGC:** 1 graded, best 9.4

298 ❑ Apr 1978 Cover: 0.35 **NM** value: **8.00**
Circ: Statement: **125,421**

299 ❑ May 1978 Cover: 0.35 **NM** value: **8.00**
Circ: Statement: **125,421** • **CGC:** 1 graded, best 9.4
• Has 1977 Statement; avg total paid circ 168,164

300 ❑ Jun 1978 Cover: 0.60 **NM** value: **15.00**
Circ: Statement: **125,421** • **CGC:** 9 graded, best 9.4
• Double-size.

301 ❑ Jul 1978 Cover: 0.35 **NM** value: **8.00**
Circ: Statement: **125,421** • **CGC:** 1 graded, best 9.6

302 ❑ Aug 1978 Cover: 0.35 **NM** value: **8.00**
Circ: Statement: **125,421** • **CGC:** 1 graded, best 9.6

303 ❑ Sep 1978 Cover: 0.50 **NM** value: **8.00**
Circ: Statement: **125,421** • **CGC:** 1 graded, best 9.0

304 ❑ Oct 1978 Cover: 0.50 **NM** value: **8.00**
Circ: Statement: **125,421** • **CGC:** 1 graded, best 9.4

305 ❑ Nov 1978 Cover: 0.50 **NM** value: **8.00**
Circ: Statement: **125,421** • **CGC:** 1 graded, best 9.4

306 ❑ Dec 1978 Cover: 0.40 **NM** value: **8.00**
Circ: Statement: **125,421**

307 ❑ Jan 1979 Cover: 0.40 **NM** value: **8.00**
Circ: Statement: **166,640**

308 ❑ Feb 1979 Cover: 0.40 **NM** value: **8.00**
Circ: Statement: **166,640** • **CGC:** 2 graded, best 9.4

309 ❑ Mar 1979 Cover: 0.40 **NM** value: **8.00**
Circ: Statement: **166,640**

310 ❑ Apr 1979 Cover: 0.40 **NM** value: **8.00**
Circ: Statement: **166,640**

311 ❑ May 1979 Cover: 0.40 **NM** value: **8.00**
Circ: Statement: **166,640** • **CGC:** 1 graded, best 9.2

312 ❑ Jun 1979 Cover: 0.40 **NM** value: **8.00**
Circ: Statement: **166,640**

313 ❑ Jul 1979 Cover: 0.40 **NM** value: **8.00**
Circ: Statement: **166,640** • **CGC:** 2 graded, best 9.4

314 ❑ Aug 1979 Cover: 0.40 **NM** value: **8.00**
Circ: Statement: **166,640** • **CGC:** 1 graded, best 9.4

315 ❑ Sep 1979 Cover: 0.40 **NM** value: **8.00**
Circ: Statement: **166,640**

316 ❑ Oct 1979 Cover: 0.40 **NM** value: **8.00**
Circ: Statement: **166,640**

317 ❑ Nov 1979 Cover: 0.40 **NM** value: **8.00**
Circ: Statement: **166,640**

318 ❑ Dec 1979 Cover: 0.40 **NM** value: **8.00**
Circ: Statement: **166,640** • **CGC:** 1 graded, best 9.6
★ 1st Appearance of Firebug.

CGC-graded: Multiply prices above by **33 for 9.9 M** • **16 for 9.8 NM/M** • **7 for 9.6 NM+** • **5 for 9.4 NM** • **2.5 for 9.2 NM-** • **1.5 for 9.0 VF/NM**

319 ❑ Jan 1980 Cover: 0.40 **NM** value: **8.00**
Circ: Statement: **129,299 • CGC:** 1 graded, best 9.6

320 ❑ Feb 1980 Cover: 0.40 **NM** value: **8.00**
Circ: Statement: **129,299**

321 ❑ Mar 1980 Cover: 0.40 **NM** value: **9.00**
Circ: Statement: **129,299 • CGC:** 2 graded, best 9.6
★ Appearance of Catwoman, Joker.

322 ❑ Apr 1980 Cover: 0.40 **NM** value: **7.00**
Circ: Statement: **129,299**
• Has 1979 Statement, filed 10/1/79; avg print run 333,231; avg sales 165,623; avg subs 1,017; avg total paid 166,640; office use 122; max existent 166,762; 50% of run returned

323 ❑ May 1980 Cover: 0.40 **NM** value: **7.00**
Circ: Statement: **129,299 • CGC:** 1 graded, best 9.4

324 ❑ Jun 1980 Cover: 0.40 **NM** value: **7.00**
Circ: Statement: **129,299**

325 ❑ Jul 1980 Cover: 0.40 **NM** value: **7.00**
Circ: Statement: **129,299**

326 ❑ Aug 1980 Cover: 0.40 **NM** value: **7.00**
Circ: Statement: **129,299**
★ 1st Appearance of Arkham Asylum.

327 ❑ Sep 1980 Cover: 0.50 **NM** value: **7.00**
Circ: Statement: **129,299**

328 ❑ Oct 1980 Cover: 0.50 **NM** value: **7.00**
Circ: Statement: **129,299**

329 ❑ Nov 1980 Cover: 0.50 **NM** value: **7.00**
Circ: Statement: **129,299**

330 ❑ Dec 1980 Cover: 0.50 **NM** value: **7.00**
Circ: Statement: **129,299**

331 ❑ Jan 1981 Cover: 0.50 **NM** value: **7.00**
Circ: Statement: **110,997**
★ 1st Appearance of Electrocutioner.

332 ❑ Feb 1981 Cover: 0.50 **NM** value: **8.00**
Circ: Statement: **110,997 • CGC:** 1 graded, best 9.6
• 1st solo Catwoman story

333 ❑ Mar 1981 Cover: 0.50 **NM** value: **7.00**
Circ: Statement: **110,997**

334 ❑ Apr 1981 Cover: 0.50 **NM** value: **7.00**
Circ: Statement: **110,997**

335 ❑ May 1981 Cover: 0.50 **NM** value: **7.00**
Circ: Statement: **110,997**
• Has 1980 Statement, filed 10/1/80; avg print run 301,102; avg sales 127,274; avg subs 2,025; avg total paid 129,299; samples 127; office use 3,608; max existent 133,034; 56% of run returned

336 ❑ Jun 1981 Cover: 0.50 **NM** value: **7.00**
Circ: Statement: **110,997**

337 ❑ Jul 1981 Cover: 0.50 **NM** value: **7.00**
Circ: Statement: **110,997**

338 ❑ Aug 1981 Cover: 0.50 **NM** value: **7.00**
Circ: Statement: **110,997 • CGC:** 1 graded, best 9.6

339 ❑ Sep 1981 Cover: 0.50 **NM** value: **7.00**
Circ: Statement: **110,997**

340 ❑ Oct 1981 Cover: 0.60 **NM** value: **7.00**
Circ: Statement: **110,997**

341 ❑ Nov 1981 Cover: 0.60 **NM** value: **7.00**
Circ: Statement: **110,997 • CGC:** 1 graded, best 9.4

342 ❑ Dec 1981 Cover: 0.60 **NM** value: **7.00**
Circ: Statement: **110,997 • CGC:** 1 graded, best 9.4

343 ❑ Jan 1982 Cover: 0.60 **NM** value: **7.00**
Circ: Statement: **108,234 • CGC:** 2 graded, best 9.6

344 ❑ Feb 1982 Cover: 0.60 **NM** value: **7.00**
Circ: Statement: **108,234 • CGC:** 2 graded, best 9.6

345 ❑ Mar 1982 Cover: 0.60 **NM** value: **7.00**
Circ: Statement: **108,234 • CGC:** 1 graded, best 9.6

346 ❑ Apr 1982 Cover: 0.60 **NM** value: **7.00**
Circ: Statement: **108,234 • CGC:** 1 graded, best 9.2
★ Versus Two-Face.

347 ❑ May 1982 Cover: 0.60 **NM** value: **7.00**
Circ: Statement: **108,234**

348 ❑ Jun 1982 Cover: 0.60 **NM** value: **7.00**
Circ: Statement: **108,234**

349 ❑ Jul 1982 Cover: 0.60 **NM** value: **7.00**
Circ: Statement: **108,234**

350 ❑ Aug 1982 Cover: 0.60 **NM** value: **7.00**
Circ: Statement: **108,234 • CGC:** 1 graded, best 9.6

351 ❑ Sep 1982 Cover: 0.60 **NM** value: **7.00**
Circ: Statement: **108,234 • CGC:** 1 graded, best 9.2

352 ❑ Oct 1982 Cover: 0.60 **NM** value: **7.00**
Circ: Statement: **108,234**

353 ❑ Nov 1982 Cover: 0.60 **NM** value: **9.50**
Circ: Statement: **108,234 • CGC:** 3 graded, best 9.4
★ Appearance of Joker.

354 ❑ Dec 1982 Cover: 0.60 **NM** value: **7.00**
Circ: Statement: **108,234**

355 ❑ Jan 1983 Cover: 0.60 **NM** value: **7.00**
Circ: Statement: **97,741**

356 ❑ Feb 1983 Cover: 0.60 **NM** value: **7.00**
Circ: Statement: **97,741**

357 ❑ Mar 1983 Cover: 0.60 **NM** value: **9.00**
Circ: Statement: **97,741 • CGC:** 3 graded, best 9.6
★ 1st Appearance of Killer Croc, Jason Todd.

358 ❑ Apr 1983 Cover: 0.60 **NM** value: **7.00**
Circ: Statement: **97,741**

359 ❑ May 1983 Cover: 0.60 **NM** value: **9.00**
Circ: Statement: **97,741 • CGC:** 2 graded, best 9.6
• Has 1982 Statement, filed 10/1/82; avg print run 275,830; avg sales 105,895; avg subs 2,339; avg total paid 108,234; samples 677; office use 2,703; max existent 111,614; 60% of run returned ★ Appearance of Joker.

360 ❑ Jun 1983 Cover: 0.60 **NM** value: **7.00**
Circ: Statement: **97,741**

361 ❑ Jul 1983 Cover: 0.60 **NM** value: **7.00**
Circ: Statement: **97,741**
★ 1st Appearance of Harvey Bullock.

362 ❑ Aug 1983 Cover: 0.60 **NM** value: **7.00**
Circ: Statement: **97,741**

363 ❑ Sep 1983 Cover: 0.60 **NM** value: **7.00**
Circ: Statement: **97,741**

364 ❑ Oct 1983 Cover: 0.60 **NM** value: **7.00**
Circ: Statement: **97,741**

365 ❑ Nov 1983 Cover: 0.60 **NM** value: **7.00**
Circ: Statement: **97,741**

366 ❑ Dec 1983 Cover: 0.75 **NM** value: **10.00**
Circ: Statement: **97,741 • CGC:** 12 graded, best 9.6
★ 1st Appearance of Jason Todd in Robin costume. ★ Appearance of Joker.

367 ❑ Jan 1984 Cover: 0.75 **NM** value: **7.00**
Circ: Statement: **89,217**

368 ❑ Feb 1984 Cover: 0.75 **NM** value: **8.00**
Circ: Statement: **89,217 • CGC:** 16 graded, best 9.8
A: Don Newton; Alfredo Alcala ★ 1st Appearance of Robin II (Jason Todd).

369 ❑ Mar 1984 Cover: 0.75 **NM** value: **6.00**
Circ: Statement: **89,217**
★ Versus Deadshot.

370 ❑ Apr 1984 Cover: 0.75 **NM** value: **6.00**
Circ: Statement: **89,217**

371 ❑ May 1984 Cover: 0.75 **NM** value: **5.00**
Circ: Statement: **89,217**
★ Versus Catman.

372 ❑ Jun 1984 Cover: 0.75 **NM** value: **5.00**
Circ: Statement: **89,217**
🕮 What Price, the Prize?

373 ❑ Jul 1984 Cover: 0.75 **NM** value: **5.00**
Circ: Statement: **89,217**
★ Versus Scarecrow.

374 ❑ Aug 1984 Cover: 0.75 **NM** value: **5.00**
Circ: Statement: **89,217**
★ Versus Penguin.

375 ❑ Sep 1984 Cover: 0.75 **NM** value: **5.00**
Circ: Statement: **89,217**
★ Versus Mr. Freeze.

376 ❑ Oct 1984 Cover: 0.75 **NM** value: **5.00**
Circ: Statement: **89,217**

377 ❑ Nov 1984 Cover: 0.75 **NM** value: **5.00**
Circ: Statement: **89,217**

378 ❑ Dec 1984 Cover: 0.75 **NM** value: **5.00**
Circ: Statement: **89,217**
★ Versus Mad Hatter.

379 ❑ Jan 1985 Cover: 0.75 **NM** value: **5.00**
Circ: Statement: **75,303**
★ Versus Mad Hatter.

380 ❑ Feb 1985 Cover: 0.75 **NM** value: **5.00**
Circ: Statement: **75,303**

381 ❑ Mar 1985 Cover: 0.75 **NM** value: **5.00**
Circ: Statement: **75,303**

382 ❑ Apr 1985 Cover: 0.75 **NM** value: **5.00**
Circ: Statement: **75,303 • CGC:** 1 graded, best 9.4
C: Gil Kane ★ Appearance of Catwoman.

383 ❑ May 1985 Cover: 0.75 **NM** value: **5.00**
Circ: Statement: **75,303** CapCity orders: **6,500**

384 ❑ Jun 1985 Cover: 0.75 **NM** value: **5.00**
Circ: Statement: **75,303** CapCity orders: **6,250**
★ Versus Calendar Man.

385 ❑ Jul 1985 Cover: 0.75 **NM** value: **5.00**
Circ: Statement: **75,303** CapCity orders: **6,350 • CGC:** 1 graded, best 9.4

386 ❑ Aug 1985 Cover: 0.75 **NM** value: **5.00**
Circ: Statement: **75,303** CapCity orders: **6,400**
★ 1st Appearance of Black Mask.

387 ❑ Sep 1985 Cover: 0.75 **NM** value: **5.00**
Circ: Statement: **75,303** CapCity orders: **6,500**
★ Versus Black Mask.

388 ❑ Oct 1985 Cover: 0.75 **NM** value: **5.00**
Circ: Statement: **75,303** CapCity orders: **6,500**
★ Versus Mirror Master. ★ Versus Capt. Boomerang. ★ Versus Captain Boomerang.

389 ❑ Nov 1985 Cover: 0.75 **NM** value: **5.00**
Circ: Statement: **75,303** CapCity orders: **6,600**
★ Appearance of Catwoman.

390 ❑ Dec 1985 Cover: 0.75 **NM** value: **5.00**
Circ: Statement: **75,303** CapCity orders: **6,650**
★ Appearance of Catwoman.

391 ❑ Jan 1986 Cover: 0.75 **NM** value: **5.00**
Circ: Statement: **89,747** CapCity orders: **6,600**
★ Appearance of Catwoman.

392 ❑ Feb 1986 Cover: 0.75 **NM** value: **5.00**
Circ: Statement: **89,747** CapCity orders: **6,850**

393 ❑ Mar 1986 Cover: 0.75 **NM** value: **5.00**
Circ: Statement: **89,747** CapCity orders: **8,150**

394 ❑ Apr 1986 Cover: 0.75 **NM** value: **5.00**
Circ: Statement: **89,747** CapCity orders: **8,200**

395 ❑ May 1986 Cover: 0.75 **NM** value: **5.00**
Circ: Statement: **89,747** CapCity orders: **7,100**

396 ❑ Jun 1986 Cover: 0.75 **NM** value: **5.00**
Circ: Statement: **89,747** CapCity orders: **7,800**

397 ❑ Jul 1986 Cover: 0.75 **NM** value: **5.00**
Circ: Statement: **89,747** CapCity orders: **7,950**
★ Versus Two-Face.

398 ❑ Aug 1986 Cover: 0.75 **NM** value: **5.00**
Circ: Statement: **89,747** CapCity orders: **8,150**
★ Appearance of Catwoman. ★ Versus Two-Face, Two-Face, A: Catwoman.

399 ❑ Sep 1986 Cover: 0.75 **NM** value: **5.00**
Circ: Statement: **89,747** CapCity orders: **8,750**

400 ❑ Oct 1986 Cover: 1.50 **NM** value: **14.00**
Circ: Statement: **89,747** CapCity orders: **27,650 • CGC:** 17 graded, best 9.6
• Anniversary edition.

401 ❑ Nov 1986 Cover: 0.75 **NM** value: **4.00**
Circ: Statement: **89,747** CapCity orders: **15,800 • CGC:** 1 graded, best 9.0
🕮 Legends, Part 1 • Legends ★ Versus Magpie.

402 ❑ Dec 1986 Cover: 0.75 **NM** value: **4.00**
Circ: Statement: **89,747** CapCity orders: **15,400 • CGC:** 1 graded, best 7.5

403 ❑ Jan 1987 Cover: 0.75 **NM** value: **4.00**
Circ: Statement: **193,000** CapCity orders: **15,500**

404 ❑ Feb 1987 Cover: 0.75 **NM** value: **6.00**
Circ: Statement: **193,000** CapCity orders: **51,050 • CGC:** 74 graded, best 9.8
🕮 Year One; Batman: Year 1, Part 1 **A:** David Mazzucchelli **W:** Frank Miller ★ Origin of Batman. ★ 1st Appearance of Catwoman (new).

405 ❑ Mar 1987 Cover: 0.75 **NM** value: **5.00**
Circ: Statement: **193,000** CapCity orders: **46,450 • CGC:** 22 graded, best 9.8
🕮 Batman: Year 1, Part 2 • Year One **A:** David Mazzucchelli **W:** Frank Miller

406 ❑ Apr 1987 Cover: 0.75 **NM** value: **5.00**
Circ: Statement: **193,000** CapCity orders: **45,300 • CGC:** 26 graded, best 9.8
🕮 Batman: Year 1, Part 3 • Year One **A:** David Mazzucchelli **W:** Frank Miller

407 ❑ May 1987 Cover: 0.75 **NM** value: **5.00**
Circ: Statement: **193,000** CapCity orders: **45,500 • CGC:** 24 graded, best 9.8
🕮 Batman: Year 1, Part 4 • Year One **A:** David Mazzucchelli **W:** Frank Miller

408 ❑ Jun 1987 Cover: 0.75 **NM** value: **4.00**
Circ: Statement: **193,000** CapCity orders: **20,585 • CGC:** 1 graded, best 9.6
★ Origin of Jason Todd (new origin).

409 ❑ Jul 1987 Cover: 0.75 **NM** value: **3.00**
Circ: Statement: **193,000** CapCity orders: **19,150**

410 ❑ Aug 1987 Cover: 0.75 **NM** value: **3.00**
Circ: Statement: **193,000** CapCity orders: **21,400**
★ Versus Two-Face.

411 ❑ Sep 1987 Cover: 0.75 **NM** value: **3.00**
Circ: Statement: **193,000** CapCity orders: **24,400**

412 ❑ Oct 1987 Cover: 0.75 **NM** value: **3.00**
Circ: Statement: **193,000** CapCity orders: **24,650**
★ Origin of Mime. ★ 1st Appearance of Mime.

413 ❑ Nov 1987 Cover: 0.75 **NM** value: **3.00**
Circ: Statement: **193,000** CapCity orders: **25,600**

414 ❑ Dec 1987 Cover: 0.75 **NM** value: **3.00**
Circ: Statement: **193,000** CapCity orders: **23,100**
🕮 Victims! • Millennium **A:** Jim Aparo **W:** Jim Starlin

415 ❑ Jan 1988 Cover: 0.75 **NM** value: **3.00**
Circ: CapCity orders: **28,050**
🕮 Millennium • Millennium

416 ❑ Feb 1988 Cover: 0.75 **NM** value: **3.00**
Circ: CapCity orders: **23,150**
A: Jim Aparo ★ Appearance of Nightwing.

417 ❑ Mar 1988 Cover: 0.75 **NM** value: **5.00**
Circ: CapCity orders: **23,050 • CGC:** 7 graded, best 9.8
🕮 Ten Nights of the Beast **C:** Mike Zeck ★ 1st Appearance of KGBeast. ★ Versus KGBeast.

418 ❑ Apr 1988 Cover: 0.75 **NM** value: **4.00**
Circ: CapCity orders: **23,350 • CGC:** 3 graded, best 9.6
🕮 Ten Nights of the Beast **C:** Mike Zeck ★ Versus KGBeast.

419 ❑ May 1988 Cover: 0.75 **NM** value: **4.00**
Circ: CapCity orders: **24,900 • CGC:** 3 graded, best 9.6
🕮 Ten Nights of the Beast **C:** Mike Zeck ★ Versus KGBeast.

420 ❑ Jun 1988 Cover: 0.75 **NM** value: **4.00**
Circ: CapCity orders: **26,100 • CGC:** 3 graded, best 9.6
🕮 Ten Nights of the Beast **C:** Mike Zeck ★ Versus KGBeast.

421 ❑ Jul 1988 Cover: 0.75 **NM** value: **3.00**
Circ: CapCity orders: **24,200**

422 ❑ Aug 1988 Cover: 0.75 **NM** value: **3.00**
Circ: CapCity orders: **24,650**

423 ❑ Sep 1988 Cover: 0.75 **NM** value: **3.00**
Circ: CapCity orders: **24,800 • CGC:** 2 graded, best 9.2
🕮 You Shoulda Seen Him…

424 ❑ Oct 1988 Cover: 0.75 **NM** value: **3.00**
Circ: CapCity orders: **24,650**

425 ❑ Nov 1988 Cover: 0.75 **NM** value: **3.00**
Circ: CapCity orders: **22,950 • CGC:** 1 graded, best 9.2

426 ❑ Dec 1988 Cover: 1.50 **NM** value: **7.00**
Circ: CapCity orders: **32,550 • CGC:** 25 graded, best 9.8
🕮 Death in Family; A Death in the Family, Part 1

427 ❑ Dec 1988 Cover: 1.50 **NM** value: **7.00**
🕮 A Death in the Family, Part 2 ★ Death of Robin, newsstand.

427/DM ❑ Dec 1988 Cover: 1.50 **NM** value: **7.00**
Circ: CapCity orders: **31,250 • CGC:** 18 graded, best 9.8
★ Death of Robin, direct sale.

428 ❑ Jan 1989 Cover: 0.75 **NM** value: **7.00**
Circ: CapCity orders: **32,450 • CGC:** 34 graded, best 9.6
🕮 A Death in the Family, Part 3 • Robin declared dead ★ Death of Robin II (Jason Todd).

429 ❑ Jan 1989 Cover: 0.75 **NM** value: **5.00**
Circ: CapCity orders: **38,250 • CGC:** 18 graded, best 9.8
🕮 A Death in the Family, Part 4 **A:** Jim Aparo **W:** Jim Starlin

430 ❑ Feb 1989 Cover: 0.75 **NM** value: **5.00**
Circ: CapCity orders: **26,200 • CGC:** 1 graded, best 9.2

431 ❑ Mar 1989 Cover: 0.75 **NM** value: **2.00**
Circ: CapCity orders: **31,500**

432 ❑ Apr 1989 Cover: 0.75 **NM** value: **2.00**
Circ: CapCity orders: **33,950**

433 ❑ May 1989 Cover: 0.75 **NM** value: **2.00**
Circ: CapCity orders: **75,650 • CGC:** 1 graded, best 9.6
🕮 Many Deaths of the Batman; The Many Deaths of Batman, Part 1 **A:** John Byrne **W:** John Byrne

434 ❑ Jun 1989 Cover: 0.75 **NM** value: **2.00**
Circ: CapCity orders: **72,250 • CGC:** 1 graded, best 9.8
🕮 Many Deaths of the Batman; The Many Deaths of Batman, Part 2 **A:** John Byrne **W:** John Byrne

435 ❑ Jul 1989 Cover: 0.75 **NM** value: **2.00**
Circ: CapCity orders: **82,000**
🕮 Many Deaths of the Batman; The Many Deaths of Batman, Part 3 **A:** John Byrne; Jim Aparo **W:** John Byrne

436 ❑ Aug 1989 Cover: 0.75 **NM** value: **3.00**
Circ: CapCity orders: **118,650 • CGC:** 2 graded, best 9.4
🕮 Batman: Year 3, Part 1

Other grades: Multiply prices above by **1.5 for Mint • 2/3 for Very Fine • 1/3 for Fine • 1/5 for Very Good • 1/8 for Good**

436-2❑ Cover: 0.75 **NM** value: **1.25**
437 ❑ Aug 1989 Cover: 0.75 **NM** value: **2.00**
Circ: CapCity orders: **111,250**
📖 Batman: Year 3, Part 2
438 ❑ Sep 1989 Cover: 1.00 **NM** value: **2.00**
Circ: CapCity orders: **107,400**
📖 Batman: Year 3, Part 3
439 ❑ Sep 1989 Cover: 1.00 **NM** value: **2.00**
Circ: CapCity orders: **108,800** • **CGC:** 1 graded, best 9.6
📖 Batman: Year 3, Part 4
440 ❑ Oct 1989 Cover: 1.00 **NM** value: **2.00**
Circ: CapCity orders: **122,550**
📖 A Lonely Place of Dying, Part 1 **A:** Jim Aparo; Mike DeCarlo **W:** Marv Wolfman ★ 1st Appearance of Timothy Drake.
441 ❑ Nov 1989 Cover: 1.00 **NM** value: **2.00**
Circ: CapCity orders: **123,850**
📖 A Lonely Place of Dying, Part 3
442 ❑ Dec 1989 Cover: 1.00 **NM** value: **3.00**
Circ: CapCity orders: **152,450** • **CGC:** 3 graded, best 9.6
📖 A Lonely Place of Dying ★ 1st Appearance of Robin III (Timothy Drake).
443 ❑ Jan 1990 Cover: 1.00 **NM** value: **1.50**
Circ: CapCity orders: **98,600**
444 ❑ Feb 1990 Cover: 1.00 **NM** value: **1.50**
Circ: CapCity orders: **91,650** • **CGC:** 2 graded, best 8.5
📖 Crimesmith And Punishment **A:** Jim Aparo **W:** Marv Wolfman ★ Versus Crimesmith.
445 ❑ Mar 1990 Cover: 1.00 **NM** value: **1.50**
Circ: CapCity orders: **95,550** • **CGC:** 1 graded, best 9.2
📖 When the Earth Dies, Part 1 **A:** Jim Aparo **W:** Marv Wolfman ★ 1st Appearance of NKVDemon. ★ Versus NKVDemon.
446 ❑ Apr 1990 Cover: 1.00 **NM** value: **1.50**
Circ: CapCity orders: **84,350**
★ Versus NKVDemon.
447 ❑ May 1990 Cover: 1.00 **NM** value: **1.50**
Circ: CapCity orders: **79,250**
★ Versus NKVDemon.
448 ❑ Jun 1990 Cover: 1.00 **NM** value: **1.50**
Circ: CapCity orders: **82,250**
★ Versus Penguin.
449 ❑ Jun 1990 Cover: 1.00 **NM** value: **1.50**
Circ: CapCity orders: **80,750**
★ Versus Penguin.
450 ❑ Jul 1990 Cover: 1.00 **NM** value: **1.50**
Circ: CapCity orders: **82,950** • **CGC:** 3 graded, best 9.6
★ Versus Joker.
451 ❑ Jul 1990 Cover: 1.00 **NM** value: **1.50**
Circ: CapCity orders: **83,350** • **CGC:** 1 graded, best 9.4
★ Versus Joker.
452 ❑ Aug 1990 Cover: 1.00 **NM** value: **1.50**
Circ: CapCity orders: **72,050** • **CGC:** 1 graded, best 9.6
📖 Dark Knight, Dark City, Part 1 **A:** Kieron Dwyer **W:** Peter Milligan ★ Versus Riddler.
453 ❑ Aug 1990 Cover: 1.00 **NM** value: **1.50**
Circ: CapCity orders: **71,050**
📖 Dark Knight, Dark City, Part 2 ★ Versus Riddler.
454 ❑ Sep 1990 Cover: 1.00 **NM** value: **1.50**
Circ: CapCity orders: **65,800**
📖 Dark Knight, Dark City, Part 3 ★ Versus Riddler.
455 ❑ Oct 1990 Cover: 1.00 **NM** value: **1.50**
Circ: CapCity orders: **62,500**
📖 Identity Crisis, Part 1 **A:** Norm Breyfogle **W:** Alan Grant
456 ❑ Nov 1990 Cover: 1.00 **NM** value: **1.50**
Circ: CapCity orders: **58,750**
📖 Identity Crisis, Part 2
457 ❑ Dec 1990 Cover: 1.00 **NM** value: **3.00**
📖 A Master of Fear • Timothy Drake as Robin **A:** Norm Breyfogle **W:** Alan Grant ★ 1st Appearance of new Robin costume.
457/DM❑Dec 1990 Cover: 1.00 **NM** value: **3.00**
Circ: CapCity orders: **66,700** • **CGC:** 3 graded, best 9.4
• with #000 on indicia
457-2❑Dec 1990 Cover: 1.00 **NM** value: **2.00**
458 ❑ Jan 1991 Cover: 1.00 **NM** value: **1.50**
Circ: CapCity orders: **56,350**
★ 1st Appearance of Harold.
459 ❑ Feb 1991 Cover: 1.00 **NM** value: **1.50**
Circ: CapCity orders: **54,500**
460 ❑ Mar 1991 Cover: 1.00 **NM** value: **1.50**
Circ: CapCity orders: **60,300**
📖 Sisters in Arms, Part 1 • Catwoman
461 ❑ Apr 1991 Cover: 1.00 **NM** value: **1.50**
Circ: CapCity orders: **54,300**
📖 Sisters in Arms, Part 2 • Catwoman
462 ❑ May 1991 Cover: 1.00 **NM** value: **1.50**
Circ: CapCity orders: **56,500**
📖 Spirit of the Beast, Part 1
463 ❑ Jun 1991 Cover: 1.00 **NM** value: **1.50**
Circ: CapCity orders: **50,700**
📖 Spirit of the Beast, Part 2
464 ❑ Jul 1991 Cover: 1.00 **NM** value: **1.50**
Circ: CapCity orders: **51,900**
📖 Spirit of the Beast, Part 3 **A:** Norm Breyfogle **W:** Alan Grant
465 ❑ Jul 1991 Cover: 1.00 **NM** value: **1.50**
Circ: CapCity orders: **59,550**
• Robin
466 ❑ Aug 1991 Cover: 1.00 **NM** value: **1.50**
Circ: CapCity orders: **52,100**
• Robin
467 ❑ Aug 1991 Cover: 1.00 **NM** value: **1.50**
Circ: CapCity orders: **58,700**
Robin, covers form triptych.
468 ❑ Sep 1991 Cover: 1.00 **NM** value: **1.50**
Circ: CapCity orders: **55,350**
Robin, covers form triptych.
469 ❑ Sep 1991 Cover: 1.00 **NM** value: **1.50**
Circ: CapCity orders: **55,100**
Robin, covers form triptych.
470 ❑ Oct 1991 Cover: 1.00 **NM** value: **1.50**
Circ: CapCity orders: **55,700**
📖 War of the Gods, Part 13 • War of the Gods
471 ❑ Nov 1991 Cover: 1.00 **NM** value: **1.50**
Circ: CapCity orders: **47,900**
472 ❑ Dec 1991 Cover: 1.00 **NM** value: **1.50**
Circ: CapCity orders: **47,750**
473 ❑ Jan 1992 Cover: 1.00 **NM** value: **1.50**
Circ: CapCity orders: **46,050**
474 ❑ Feb 1992 Cover: 1.00 **NM** value: **1.50**
Circ: CapCity orders: **44,200**
📖 Destroyer, Part 1 • Anton Furst's Gotham City
475 ❑ Mar 1992 Cover: 1.00 **NM** value: **1.50**
Circ: CapCity orders: **40,750**
★ Versus Ventriloquist, Two-Face.
476 ❑ Apr 1992 Cover: 1.00 **NM** value: **1.50**
Circ: CapCity orders: **44,300**
477 ❑ May 1992 Cover: 1.25 **NM** value: **1.50**
Circ: CapCity orders: **39,100**
Photo cover. 📖 A Gotham Tale
478 ❑ May 1992 Cover: 1.25 **NM** value: **1.50**
Photo cover. 📖 A Gotham Tale
479 ❑ Jun 1992 Cover: 1.25 **NM** value: **1.50**
Circ: CapCity orders: **38,150**
480 ❑ Jun 1992 Cover: 1.25 **NM** value: **1.50**
Circ: CapCity orders: **38,150**
481 ❑ Jul 1992 Cover: 1.25 **NM** value: **1.50**
Circ: CapCity orders: **40,350**
482 ❑ Jul 1992 Cover: 1.25 **NM** value: **1.50**
Circ: CapCity orders: **40,000**
483 ❑ Aug 1992 Cover: 1.25 **NM** value: **1.50**
Circ: CapCity orders: **41,650**
📖 Crash & Burn: A Love Story **A:** Jim Aparo **W:** Doug Moench
484 ❑ Sep 1992 Cover: 1.25 **NM** value: **1.50**
Circ: CapCity orders: **37,100**
485 ❑ Oct 1992 Cover: 1.25 **NM** value: **1.50**
Circ: CapCity orders: **35,600**
486 ❑ Nov 1992 Cover: 1.25 **NM** value: **1.50**
Circ: CapCity orders: **32,400**
★ Versus Metalhead.
487 ❑ Dec 1992 Cover: 1.25 **NM** value: **Cover or less**
Circ: CapCity orders: **30,500**
488 ❑ Jan 1993 Cover: 1.25 **NM** value: **4.00**
Circ: CapCity orders: **30,350** • **CGC:** 1 graded, best 9.8
• Robin trains Azrael
489 ❑ Feb 1993 Cover: 1.25 **NM** value: **4.00**
Circ: CapCity orders: **30,150**
★ 1st Appearance of Azrael (as Batman). ★ Appearance of Bane.
490 ❑ Mar 1993 Cover: 1.25 **NM** value: **3.00**
Circ: CapCity orders: **29,550** • **CGC:** 1 graded, best 9.4
• Riddler on Venom
491 ❑ Apr 1993 Cover: 1.25 **NM** value: **3.00**
Circ: CapCity orders: **34,400** • **CGC:** 1 graded, best 9.4
• Knightfall prequel **A:** Jim Aparo **W:** Doug Moench
492 ❑ May 1993 Cover: 1.25 **NM** value: **3.00**
Circ: CapCity orders: **36,750**
📖 Knightfall, Part 1 **A:** Norm Breyfogle **W:** Doug Moench
492/SI❑ **NM** value: **6.00**
• **CGC:** 4 graded, best 9.6
• Silver edition printing. 📖 Knightfall, Part 1 **A:** Norm Breyfogle **W:** Doug Moench
492-2❑ Cover: 1.25 **NM** value: **2.00**
493 ❑ May 1993 Cover: 1.25 **NM** value: **2.00**
Circ: CapCity orders: **36,650**
📖 Knightfall, Part 3 **A:** Norm Breyfogle **W:** Doug Moench ★ Versus Mr. Zsasz.
494 ❑ Jun 1993 Cover: 1.25 **NM** value: **2.00**
Circ: CapCity orders: **46,200**
📖 Knightfall, Part 5 **A:** Jim Aparo **W:** Doug Moench ★ Versus Scarecrow.
495 ❑ Jun 1993 Cover: 1.25 **NM** value: **2.00**
Circ: CapCity orders: **46,150**
📖 Knightfall, Part 7 **A:** Jim Aparo **W:** Doug Moench ★ Versus Poison Ivy.
496 ❑ Jul 1993 Cover: 1.25 **NM** value: **2.00**
Circ: CapCity orders: **87,500**
📖 Knightfall, Part 9 **A:** Jim Aparo **W:** Doug Moench ★ Versus Joker.
497 ❑ Jul 1993 Cover: 1.25 **NM** value: **3.50**
Circ: CapCity orders: **110,350** • **CGC:** 25 graded, best 9.8
partial overlay outer cover. 📖 Knightfall, Part 11 • Bane cripples Batman **A:** Jim Aparo **W:** Doug Moench
497-2❑Jul 1993 Cover: 1.25 **NM** value: **2.00**
📖 Knightfall, Part 11 • 2nd Printing, also has partial overlay; Bane cripples Batman **A:** Jim Aparo **W:** Doug Moench
498 ❑ Aug 1993 Cover: 1.25 **NM** value: **2.00**
Circ: CapCity orders: **133,200**
📖 Knightfall, Part 13; Knightfall, Part 15 • Azrael takes on role of Batman **A:** Jim Aparo **W:** Doug Moench
499 ❑ Sep 1993 Cover: 1.25 **NM** value: **2.00**
Circ: CapCity orders: **121,725**
📖 Knightfall, Part 15; Knightfall, Part 17 **A:** Jim Aparo **W:** Doug Moench
500 ❑ Oct 1993 Cover: 2.50 **NM** value: **3.00**
• **CGC:** 2 graded, best 9.6
• Giant-size. 📖 Knightfall, Part 19 • Azrael vs. Bane, with poster **A:** Jim Aparo **W:** Doug Moench
500/CS❑Oct 1993 Cover: 3.95 **NM** value: **4.50**
Circ: CapCity orders: **318,450** • **CGC:** 9 graded, best 9.8
two-level cover. • Giant-size. 📖 Knightfall, Part 19 • diecut; Azrael vs. Bane;Collector's set **A:** Jim Aparo **W:** Doug Moench
501 ❑ Nov 1993 Cover: 1.50 **NM** value: **2.00**
Circ: CapCity orders: **101,100**
📖 Knightquest: The Crusade; Knightquest: The Crusade, Code Name: Mekros **A:** Mike Manley **W:** Doug Moench
502 ❑ Dec 1993 Cover: 1.50 **NM** value: **2.00**
Circ: CapCity orders: **91,800**
📖 Knightquest: The Crusade; Knightquest: The Crusade, Phoenix In Chaos **A:** Mike Manley **W:** Doug Moench
503 ❑ Jan 1994 Cover: 1.50 **NM** value: **2.00**
Circ: CapCity orders: **82,850** • **CGC:** 1 graded, best 9.4
📖 Knightquest: The Crusade; Knightquest: The Crusade, Night Becomes Woman **A:** Mike Manley **W:** Doug Moench ★ Appearance of Catwoman.
504 ❑ Feb 1994 Cover: 1.50 **NM** value: **2.00**
Circ: CapCity orders: **76,400**
📖 Knightquest: The Crusade **A:** Mike Manley **W:** Doug Moench ★ Appearance of Catwoman.
505 ❑ Mar 1994 Cover: 1.50 **NM** value: **2.00**
Circ: CapCity orders: **65,500**
📖 Knightquest: The Crusade **A:** Mike Manley **W:** Doug Moench
506 ❑ Apr 1994 Cover: 1.50 **NM** value: **2.00**
Circ: CapCity orders: **57,500** • **CGC:** 1 graded, best 9.2
📖 Knightquest: The Crusade **W:** Doug Moench
507 ❑ May 1994 Cover: 1.50 **NM** value: **2.00**
Circ: CapCity orders: **54,850**
📖 Knightquest: The Crusade; Knightquest: The Crusade, Ballistic **A:** Jim Balent **W:** Doug Moench
508 ❑ Jun 1994 Cover: 1.50 **NM** value: **2.00**
Circ: CapCity orders: **54,750**
📖 Knightquest: The Crusade; Knightquest: The Crusade, Mortal Remains **A:** Mike Manley **W:** Doug Moench ★ Death of Abattoir.
509 ❑ Jul 1994 Cover: 1.50 **NM** value: **2.00**
Circ: CapCity orders: **58,650**
📖 KnightsEnd, Part 1 **W:** Doug Moench
510 ❑ Aug 1994 Cover: 1.50 **NM** value: **2.00**
Circ: CapCity orders: **57,550**
📖 KnightsEnd, Part 7 **A:** Mike Manley **W:** Doug Moench
511 ❑ Sep 1994 Cover: 1.50 **NM** value: **2.00**
Circ: CapCity orders: **49,350**
• Zero Hour, A: Batgirl **W:** Doug Moench
512 ❑ Nov 1994 Cover: 1.50 **NM** value: **2.00**
Circ: CapCity orders: **49,650**
📖 Prodigal, Part 1; Prodigal, Part 1, Robin And Batman **A:** Mike Gustovich; Romeo Tanghal **W:** Doug Moench
513 ❑ Dec 1994 Cover: 1.50 **NM** value: **2.00**
Circ: CapCity orders: **47,350**
📖 Prodigal, Part 5
514 ❑ Jan 1995 Cover: 1.50 **NM** value: **2.00**
Circ: CapCity orders: **44,750**
📖 Prodigal, Part 9 **A:** Ron Wagner; Joe Rubinstein **W:** Doug Moench
515 ❑ Feb 1995 Cover: 1.50 **NM** value: **2.00**
📖 Troika, Part 1 • Return of Bruce Wayne as Batman
515/SC❑Feb 1995 Cover: 2.50 **NM** value: **Cover or less**
Circ: CapCity orders: **51,900** • **CGC:** 4 graded, best 9.8
Embossed cover. 📖 Troika, Part 1 • Return of Bruce Wayne as Batman
516 ❑ Mar 1995 Cover: 1.50 **NM** value: **2.00**
Circ: CapCity orders: **41,000**
517 ❑ Apr 1995 Cover: 1.50 **NM** value: **2.00**
Circ: CapCity orders: **39,050**
518 ❑ May 1995 Cover: 1.50 **NM** value: **2.00**
Circ: CapCity orders: **38,525**
★ Versus Black Mask.
519 ❑ Jun 1995 Cover: 1.95 **NM** value: **2.00**
Circ: CapCity orders: **36,500**
📖 Black Spider: Web of Scars
520 ❑ Jul 1995 Cover: 1.95 **NM** value: **2.00**
Circ: CapCity orders: **34,825**
521 ❑ Aug 1995 Cover: 1.95 **NM** value: **2.00**
Circ: CapCity orders: **34,900**
★ Versus Killer Croc.
522 ❑ Sep 1995 Cover: 1.95 **NM** value: **2.00**
Circ: CapCity orders: **32,900**
★ Versus Killer Croc, Swamp Thing.
523 ❑ Oct 1995 Cover: 1.95 **NM** value: **2.00**
Circ: CapCity orders: **27,800**
★ Versus Scarecrow.
524 ❑ Nov 1995 Cover: 1.95 **NM** value: **2.00**
★ Versus Scarecrow.
525 ❑ Dec 1995 Cover: 1.95 **NM** value: **2.00**
• Underworld Unleashed, V: Mr. Freeze
526 ❑ Jan 1996 Cover: 1.95 **NM** value: **2.00**
527 ❑ Feb 1996 Cover: 1.95 **NM** value: **2.00**
📖 The Face Schism **A:** Kelley Jones **W:** Doug Moench ★ Versus Two-Face.
528 ❑ Mar 1996 Cover: 1.95 **NM** value: **2.00**
📖 Rtwo-Face, Part 2 **A:** Kelley Jones **W:** Doug Moench
529 ❑ Apr 1996 Cover: 1.95 **NM** value: **2.00**
📖 Contagion, Part 6 **A:** Kelley Jones **W:** Doug Moench
530 ❑ May 1996 Cover: 1.95 **NM** value: **Cover or less**
Glow-in-the-dark cover. 📖 The Deadman Connection
530/SC❑May 1996 Cover: 2.50 **NM** value: **Cover or less**
• **CGC:** 1 graded, best 9.6
glow-in-the-darkcover. 📖 The Deadman Connection
531 ❑ Jun 1996 Cover: 1.95 **NM** value: **Cover or less**
Glow-in-the-dark cover. 📖 The Deadman Connection
531/SC❑Jun 1996 Cover: 2.50 **NM** value: **Cover or less**
glow-in-the-darkcover. 📖 The Deadman Connection
532 ❑ Jul 1996 Cover: 1.95 **NM** value: **Cover or less**
Glow-in-the-dark cover. 📖 The Deadman Connection
532/SC❑Jul 1996 Cover: 2.50 **NM** value: **Cover or less**
• **CGC:** 1 graded, best 9.6
glow-in-the-dark cardstock cover. 📖 The Deadman Connection
533 ❑ Aug 1996 Cover: 1.95 **NM** value: **2.00**
📖 Legacy Prelude
534 ❑ Sep 1996 Cover: 1.95 **NM** value: **2.00**
📖 Legacy, Part 5
535 ❑ Oct 1996 Cover: 2.95 **NM** value: **Cover or less**
📖 The Ogre and the Ape • self-contained story, V: The Ogre and The Ape **A:** Kelley Jones **W:** Doug Moench
535/SC❑Oct 1996 Cover: 3.95 **NM** value: **4.00**
Die-cut cover. 📖 The Ogre and the Ape • self-contained story **A:** Kelley Jones **W:** Doug Moench ★ Versus The Ogre and The Ape. ★ Versus The Ogre and The Ape.
536 ❑ Nov 1996 Cover: 1.95 **NM** value: **2.00**
Circ: Diamd. preorders: **73,704** • **CGC:** 1 graded, best 9.6
📖 Darkest Night of the Man-Bat, Part 1 • Final Night **A:** Kelley Jones **W:** Doug Moench

CGC-graded: Multiply prices above by **33 for 9.9 M** • **16 for 9.8 NM/M** • **7 for 9.6 NM+** • **5 for 9.4 NM** • **2.5 for 9.2 NM-** • **1.5 for 9.0 VF/NM**

537 ❑ Dec 1996 Cover: 1.95 **NM** value: **2.00**
Circ: Direct Market orders: **70,014**
📖 Darkest Night of the Man-Bat, Part 2 **A:** Kelley Jones **W:** Doug Moench ★ Versus Man-Bat.

538 ❑ Jan 1997 Cover: 1.95 **NM** value: **2.00**
Circ: Direct Market orders: **67,777**
📖 Darkest Night of the Man-Bat, Part 3 **A:** Kelley Jones **W:** Doug Moench ★ Appearance of Man-Bat.

539 ❑ Feb 1997 Cover: 1.95 **NM** value: **2.00**
Circ: Diamd. preorders: **65,092**
📖 Boneyard Blues **A:** Kelley Jones **W:** Doug Moench

540 ❑ Mar 1997 Cover: 1.95 **NM** value: **2.00**
Circ: Diamd. preorders: **63,220**
📖 The Spectre of Vengeance, Part 1 **A:** Kelley Jones **W:** Doug Moench ★ Appearance of Spectre.

541 ❑ Apr 1997 Cover: 1.95 **NM** value: **2.00**
Circ: Diamd. preorders: **60,087**

542 ❑ May 1997 Cover: 1.95 **NM** value: **2.00**
Circ: Diamd. preorders: **59,828**
📖 Faceless, Part 1

543 ❑ Jun 1997 Cover: 1.95 **NM** value: **2.00**
Circ: Diamd. preorders: **59,705**

544 ❑ Jul 1997 Cover: 1.95 **NM** value: **2.00**
Circ: Diamd. preorders: **58,450**
★ Appearance of Demon.

545 ❑ Aug 1997 Cover: 1.95 **NM** value: **2.00**
Circ: Diamd. preorders: **57,640**
★ Appearance of Demon.

546 ❑ Sep 1997 Cover: 1.95 **NM** value: **2.00**
Circ: Diamd. preorders: **56,073**
★ Appearance of Demon.

547 ❑ Oct 1997 Cover: 1.95 **NM** value: **2.00**
Circ: Diamd. preorders: **58,651**
• Genesis

548 ❑ Nov 1997 Cover: 1.95 **NM** value: **2.00**
Circ: Diamd. preorders: **55,897**
📖 The Penguin Returns, Part 1 **A:** Kelley Jones **W:** Doug Moench ★ Versus Penguin.

549 ❑ Dec 1997 Cover: 1.95 **NM** value: **2.00**
Circ: Diamd. preorders: **56,273**
Face cover. 📖 The Penguin Returns, Part 2 **A:** Kelley Jones **W:** Doug Moench ★ Versus Penguin.

550 ❑ Jan 1998 Cover: 2.95 **NM** value: **3.00**
Circ: Diamd. preorders: **57,777**
★ 2nd Appearance of Chase.

550/SC❑Jan 1998 Cover: 3.50 **NM** value: **Cover or less**
★ 2nd Appearance of Chase.

551 ❑ Feb 1998 Cover: 1.95 **NM** value: **2.00**
Circ: Diamd. preorders: **52,638**
★ Appearance of Ragman.

552 ❑ Mar 1998 Cover: 1.95 **NM** value: **4.00**
Circ: Diamd. preorders: **51,097**
📖 The Greatest Evil **A:** Kelley Jones **W:** Doug Moench ★ Appearance of Ragman.

553 ❑ Apr 1998 Cover: 1.95 **NM** value: **3.00**
Circ: Diamd. preorders: **52,866**
📖 Cataclysm, Part 3 • continues in Azrael #40

554 ❑ May 1998 Cover: 1.95 **NM** value: **2.00**
Circ: Diamd. preorders: **53,138**
📖 Cataclysm, Part 12; Cataclysm ★ Versus Quakemaster, continues in Batman: Huntress Spoiler – Blunt Trauma #1.

555 ❑ Jun 1998 Cover: 1.95 **NM** value: **2.00**
Circ: Diamd. preorders: **52,090**
• Aftershock, V: Ratcatcher

556 ❑ Jul 1998 Cover: 1.95 **NM** value: **2.00**
Circ: Diamd. preorders: **50,190**
• Aftershock

557 ❑ Aug 1998 Cover: 1.95 **NM** value: **2.00**
Circ: Diamd. preorders: **49,506**
• Aftershock, A: Ballistic

558 ❑ Sep 1998 Cover: 1.99 **NM** value: **2.00**
Circ: Diamd. preorders: **47,607**
• Aftershock

559 ❑ Oct 1998 Cover: 1.99 **NM** value: **2.00**
Circ: Diamd. preorders: **45,603**
• Aftershock

560 ❑ Dec 1998 Cover: 1.99 **NM** value: **2.00**
Circ: Diamd. preorders: **45,293**
• Road to No Man's Land, Bruce Wayne testifies

561 ❑ Jan 1999 Cover: 1.99 **NM** value: **2.00**
Circ: Diamd. preorders: **44,474**
📖 Road to No Man's Land • Road to No Man's Land, Bruce Wayne testifies **A:** Jim Aparo **W:** Chuck Dixon

562 ❑ Feb 1999 Cover: 1.99 **NM** value: **2.00**
Circ: Diamd. preorders: **43,424**
📖 Mr. Wayne Goes to Washington • Road to No Man's Land, Gotham City is cut off **A:** Jim Aparo **W:** Chuck Dixon ★ Appearance of Mayor Grange.

563 ❑ Mar 1999 Cover: 1.99 **NM** value: **3.00**
Circ: Diamd. preorders: **48,047**
📖 No Law and a New Order, Part 3; No Law & a New Order • No Man's Land, V: Joker **A:** Alex Maleev ★ Appearance of Oracle.

564 ❑ Apr 1999 Cover: 1.99 **NM** value: **2.50**
Circ: Diamd. preorders: **45,741**
📖 Fear of Faith, Part 3 • No Man's Land, A: Scarecrow/Huntress

565 ❑ May 1999 Cover: 1.99 **NM** value: **2.00**
Circ: Diamd. preorders: **49,477 • CGC:** 1 graded, best 9.6
📖 Mosaic, Part 1 • No Man's Land **A:** Frank Teran **W:** Greg Rucka

566 ❑ Jun 1999 Cover: 1.99 **NM** value: **2.00**
Circ: Diamd. preorders: **51,935**
📖 The Visitor • No Man's Land, A: Superman;No Man's Land **A:** Jon Bogdanove **W:** Kelley Puckett

567 ❑ Jul 1999 Cover: 1.99 **NM** value: **2.00**
Circ: Diamd. preorders: **51,982 • CGC:** 4 graded, best 9.8
📖 Mark of Cain, Part 1 • No Man's Land **A:** Todd Klein **W:** John Floyd

568 ❑ Aug 1999 Cover: 1.99 **NM** value: **2.00**
Circ: Diamd. preorders: **51,726**
📖 Fruit of the Earth, Part 2 • No Man's Land, A: Poison Ivy, V: Clayface;No Man's Land **A:** Bill Sienkiewicz **W:** Dan Jurgens; Greg Rucka

569 ❑ Sep 1999 Cover: 1.99 **NM** value: **Cover or less**
Circ: Diamd. preorders: **53,828**
📖 I Cover the Waterfront • No Man's Land **A:** Sergio Cariello **W:** Janet Harvey

570 ❑ Oct 1999 Cover: 1.99 **NM** value: **Cover or less**
Circ: Diamd. preorders: **56,350**
📖 The Code, Part 1 • No Man's Land, V: Joker;No Man's Land **A:** Mike Deodato **W:** Brownwyn Carlton

571 ❑ Nov 1999 Cover: 1.99 **NM** value: **Cover or less**
Circ: Diamd. preorders: **51,717**
📖 Goin' Downtown, Part 1 • No Man's Land, V: Bane;No Man's Land

572 ❑ Dec 1999 Cover: 1.99 **NM** value: **Cover or less**
Circ: Diamd. preorders: **52,723**
📖 Jurisprudence, Part 1 • No Man's Land **A:** Damian Scott **W:** Greg Rucka

573 ❑ Jan 2000 Cover: 1.99 **NM** value: **Cover or less**
Circ: Diamd. preorders: **52,326**
📖 Shellgame, Part 1 • No Man's Land **A:** Sergio Cariello **W:** Greg Rucka

574 ❑ Feb 2000 Cover: 1.99 **NM** value: **Cover or less**
Circ: Diamd. preorders: **52,339**
📖 Endame, Part 2 • No Man's Land **A:** Dale Eaglesham **W:** Greg Rucka

575 ❑ Mar 2000 Cover: 1.99 **NM** value: **Cover or less**
Circ: Diamd. preorders: **50,978**

576 ❑ Apr 2000 Cover: 1.99 **NM** value: **Cover or less**
Circ: Diamd. preorders: **47,917**
📖 In the Dark Places **A:** Scott McDaniel **W:** Larry Hama

577 ❑ May 2000 Cover: 1.99 **NM** value: **Cover or less**
Circ: Diamd. preorders: **49,748**

578 ❑ Jun 2000 Cover: 1.99 **NM** value: **Cover or less**
Circ: Diamd. preorders: **50,597**
📖 Mike and Allie **A:** Scott McDaniel **W:** Larry Hama

579 ❑ Jul 2000 Cover: 1.99 **NM** value: **Cover or less**
Circ: Diamd. preorders: **50,375**
📖 Orca, Part 1 **A:** Scott McDaniel **W:** Larry Hama; Scott McDaniel

580 ❑ Aug 2000 Cover: 2.25 **NM** value: **Cover or less**
Circ: Diamd. preorders: **50,098**
📖 Orca, Part 2; Going Under **A:** Scott McDaniel **W:** Larry Hama; Scott McDaniel ★ Versus Orca.

581 ❑ Sep 2000 Cover: 2.25 **NM** value: **Cover or less**
Circ: Diamd. preorders: **48,511**
📖 Orca, Part 3; Diver Down **A:** Scott McDaniel **W:** Larry Hama; Scott McDaniel ★ Versus Orca.

582 ❑ Oct 2000 Cover: 2.25 **NM** value: **Cover or less**
Circ: Diamd. preorders: **45,733**
📖 Fearless, Part 1 **A:** Scott McDaniel **W:** Ed Brubaker

583 ❑ Nov 2000 Cover: 2.25 **NM** value: **Cover or less**
Circ: Diamd. preorders: **45,796**
📖 Fearless, Part 2 **A:** Scott McDaniel **W:** Ed Brubaker

584 ❑ Dec 2000 Cover: 2.25 **NM** value: **Cover or less**
Circ: Diamd. preorders: **44,898**
📖 The Dark Knight Project **A:** Scott McDaniel **W:** Ed Brubaker

585 ❑ Jan 2001 Cover: 2.25 **NM** value: **Cover or less**
Circ: Diamd. preorders: **44,422**
📖 Measure for Measure **A:** Scott McDaniel **W:** Ed Brubaker

586 ❑ Feb 2001 Cover: 2.25 **NM** value: **Cover or less**
Circ: Diamd. preorders: **46,423**
📖 Penguin Dreams **A:** Scott McDaniel **W:** Ed Brubaker

587 ❑ Mar 2001 Cover: 2.25 **NM** value: **Cover or less**
Circ: Diamd. preorders: **47,152 • CGC:** 1 graded, best 9.8
📖 Officer Down, Part 1 **A:** Rick Burchett **W:** Greg Rucka

588 ❑ Apr 2001 Cover: 2.25 **NM** value: **Cover or less**
Circ: Diamd. preorders: **42,896**
📖 Close Before Striking, Part 1 **A:** Scott McDaniel **W:** Brian K. Vaughan

589 ❑ May 2001 Cover: 2.25 **NM** value: **Cover or less**
Circ: Diamd. preorders: **43,014**
📖 Close Before Striking, Part 2 **A:** Scott McDaniel **W:** Brian K. Vaughan

590 ❑ Jun 2001 Cover: 2.25 **NM** value: **Cover or less**
Circ: Diamd. preorders: **43,395**
📖 Close Before Striking, Part 3 **A:** Scott McDaniel **W:** Brian K. Vaughan

591 ❑ Jul 2001 Cover: 2.25 **NM** value: **Cover or less**
Circ: Diamd. preorders: **43,332**

592 ❑ Aug 2001 Cover: 2.25 **NM** value: **Cover or less**
Circ: Diamd. preorders: **43,943**

593 ❑ Sep 2001 Cover: 2.25 **NM** value: **Cover or less**
Circ: Diamd. preorders: **49,277**

1000000❑Nov 1998 Cover: 1.99 **NM** value: **Cover or less**
Circ: Diamd. preorders: **54,513**
📖 Peril Within the Prison Planet **A:** Yvel Guichet; Sal Buscema **W:** Doug Moench

Anl 1❑ca. 1961 Cover: 0.25 **NM** value: **450.00**
• **CGC:** 8 graded, best 9.4
📖 How to be the Batman!; The Strange Costumes of Batman!; Untold Tales of the Bat-Signal!; The Origin of the Bat-Cave!; Batman's Electronic Crime-File!; Thrilling Escapes of Batman and Robin!; The Amazing Adventures of Batman **A:** Bob Kane; Curt Swan **W:** Bob Kane ★ Origin of The Batcave.

Anl 1-2❑ Cover: 4.95 **NM** value: **5.00**
Circ: Diamd. preorders: **23,427 • CGC:** 1 graded, best 9.8
cardstock cover. 📖 How to be the Batman!; The Strange Costumes of Batman!; Untold Tales of the Bat-Signal!; The Origin of the Bat-Cave!; Batman's Electronic Crime-File!; Thrilling Escapes of Batman and Robin!; The Amazing Adventures of Batman • Reprint (1999) **A:** Bob Kane **W:** Bob Kane ★ Origin of The Batcave.

Anl 2❑ca. 1961 Cover: 0.25 **NM** value: **260.00**
• **CGC:** 5 graded, best 8.5

Anl 3❑Sum 1962 Cover: 0.25 **NM** value: **200.00**
• **CGC:** 4 graded, best 9.4

Anl 4❑Win 1963 Cover: 0.25 **NM** value: **100.00**
• **CGC:** 4 graded, best 9.2

Anl 5❑Sum 1963 Cover: 0.25 **NM** value: **100.00**
• **CGC:** 4 graded, best 9.2

Anl 6❑Win 1964 Cover: 0.25 **NM** value: **75.00**
• **CGC:** 3 graded, best 9.0

Anl 7❑Sum 1964 **NM** value: **75.00**
• **CGC:** 4 graded, best 9.4

Anl 8❑1982 Cover: 1.00 **NM** value: **7.00**
★ Appearance of Ra's Al Ghul.

Anl 9❑1985 Cover: 1.25 **NM** value: **6.00**
Circ: CapCity orders: **80,400**
A: Jerry Ordway; Paul Smith; Alex Nino; Alex Nino

Anl 10❑1986 Cover: 1.25 **NM** value: **6.00**
Circ: CapCity orders: **9,100**

Anl 11❑1987 Cover: 1.25 **NM** value: **6.00**
Circ: CapCity orders: **22,850**
W: Alan Moore

Anl 12❑1988 Cover: 1.50 **NM** value: **5.00**
Circ: CapCity orders: **24,850**
C: Michael W. Kaluta

Anl 13❑1989 Cover: 1.75 **NM** value: **5.00**
Circ: CapCity orders: **49,200**
• Who's Who entries

Anl 14❑1990 Cover: 2.00 **NM** value: **3.00**
Circ: CapCity orders: **68,150**
★ Origin of Two-Face.

Anl 15❑1991 Cover: 2.00 **NM** value: **3.00**
📖 Armageddon 2001, Part 3 • 1st printing, Armageddon 2001 ★ Appearance of Joker.

Anl 15-2❑ Cover: 2.00 **NM** value: **Cover or less**

Anl 15-2❑ Cover: 2.00 **NM** value: **Cover or less**

Anl 17❑1993 Cover: 2.50 **NM** value: **3.00**
Circ: CapCity orders: **37,450**
📖 Bloodlines • Bloodlines ★ 1st Appearance of Ballistic.

Anl 18❑1994 Cover: 2.95 **NM** value: **3.00**
Circ: CapCity orders: **31,900**
📖 Black Masterpiece • Elseworlds **A:** Frederico Cueva **W:** Doug Moench

Anl 19❑1995 Cover: 3.95 **NM** value: **Cover or less**
Circ: CapCity orders: **24,800**
• Year One ★ Origin of Scarecrow.

Anl 20❑1996 Cover: 2.95 **NM** value: **Cover or less**
• Legends of the Dead Earth

Anl 21❑1997 Cover: 3.95 **NM** value: **Cover or less**
Circ: Diamd. preorders: **47,596**
• Pulp Heroes

Anl 22❑1998 Cover: 2.95 **NM** value: **Cover or less**
Circ: Diamd. preorders: **38,300**
• Ghosts

Anl 23❑Sep 1999 Cover: 2.95 **NM** value: **Cover or less**
Circ: Diamd. preorders: **41,012**
📖 Jungle Rules • JLApe **A:** Graham Nolan **W:** Chuck Dixon

Anl 24❑Oct 2000 Cover: 3.50 **NM** value: **Cover or less**
Circ: Diamd. preorders: **33,074**
📖 Planet DC; Lost Boys **A:** Jim Aparo **W:** John Ostrander ★ 1st Appearance of The Boggart.

Bk 1❑ Cover: 5.95 **NM** value: **Cover or less**
• Ten Nights of the Beast, collects Batman #417-420

Bk 2❑ Cover: 3.95 **NM** value: **Cover or less**
📖 A Death in the Family • collects Batman #426-429 **A:** Jim Aparo

GS 1❑Aug 1998 Cover: 4.95 **NM** value: **Cover or less**
Circ: Diamd. preorders: **36,966**
📖 Batman: Maintaining Appearances; Penguin: Possessions; Harvey Bullock: The Last Bite; Huntress: Banished from the Pack; Batman: Big Mouth Strikes Again; Ventriloquist and Scarface: The Rhino's Tale; The Heroes of Gotham City: Desires **A:** Brian Stelfreeze; Flint Henry; Tommy Castillo; Frank Teran; Rick Burchett; Klaus Janson; Rodolfo DaMaggio; Dylan Teague **W:** Frank Teran; Rick Burchett; Klaus Janson; Chuck Dixon; Alan Grant; Devin Grayson; Doug Moench; Ron Marz

GS 2❑Oct 1999 Cover: 4.95 **NM** value: **Cover or less**
Circ: Diamd. preorders: **30,328**
📖 Gotham Roulette; Hunting for Answers; Lucky Break; Footsteps; In Clover; Lucky's Seven; A Run of Bad Luck **A:** N. Steven Harris; Steve Pugh; Karl Waller; Sal Buscema; Jim Balent; William Rosado; Jordan Raskin **W:** Jim Alexander; Scott Beatty; Peter Hogan; Ben Raab; D.G. Chichester; Ian Edginton; Janet Harvey

GS 3❑Jul 2000 Cover: 5.95 **NM** value: **Cover or less**
Circ: Diamd. preorders: **27,373**
📖 All the Deadly Days; A Month of Sundays; Harsh Monday; The Terrible Tuesdays; Wednesday's Stepchild; Bloodthirsty Thursday; God Forbid, It's Friday!; Shatterday **A:** Bill Sienkiewicz; Mike Deodato; Dale Eaglesham; Graham Nolan; Joe Staton; David Roach; Louis Small Jr.; Caesar; John Floyd; Manuel Gutierrez; Mark Pennington; Bud Larosa **C:** Dale Eaglesham; John Floyd **W:** Chuck Dixon

BATMAN 3-D — DC

1 ❑ ca. 1990 Cover: 9.95 **NM** value: **Cover or less**
Circ: CapCity orders: **14,950**
No issue number. **A:** John Byrne

BATMAN ADVENTURES, THE — DC

The Fox network cartoon featuring The Dark Knight has already garnered a great deal of critical acclaim. In The Batman Adventures, DC emulates the fast-pacing and streamlined art of the animated series so well put together by such creators as Bruce Timm and Paul Dini. The result is an unusual series that will delight old and new readers alike.

The art, in particular, emulates the simpler lines of the cartoon, which is a refreshing change from the more realistic style of art used in contemporary titles. The stories are original but capture the pacing and dialogue of the television show. Best of all, the favorite fantastic foes, including Penguin, Catwoman, and The Riddler, appear frequently in their ongoing efforts to outwit Batman.

1 ❑ Oct 1992 Cover: 1.25 **NM** value: **4.00**
Circ: CapCity orders: **45,350 • CGC:** 8 graded, best 9.6

Other grades: Multiply prices above by **1.5 for Mint • 2/3 for Very Fine • 1/3 for Fine • 1/5 for Very Good • 1/8 for Good**

📖 Penguin's Big Score, Act One: Charm School • based on animated series, V: Penguin **A:** Ty Templeton **W:** Kelley Puckett ★ Appearance of Penguin.

1/SI ❑ 1992 Cover: 1.95 **NM value: Cover or less**
• silver edition. 📖 Penguin's Big Score, Act One: Charm School **A:** Ty Templeton **W:** Kelley Puckett

2 ❑ Nov 1992 Cover: 1.25 **NM** value: **2.50**
Circ: CapCity orders: **35,350**
★ Appearance of Catwoman. ★ Versus Catwoman.

3 ❑ Dec 1992 Cover: 1.25 **NM** value: **2.50**
Circ: CapCity orders: **26,900**
★ Appearance of Joker. ★ Versus Joker.

4 ❑ Jan 1993 Cover: 1.25 **NM** value: **2.50**
Circ: CapCity orders: **23,300**
📖 Riot Act, Part 1 • Robin

5 ❑ Feb 1993 Cover: 1.25 **NM** value: **2.50**
Circ: CapCity orders: **21,500**
📖 Riot Act, Part 2 **A:** Brad Rader **W:** Kelley Puckett ★ Appearance of Scarecrow. ★ Versus Scarecrow.

6 ❑ Mar 1993 Cover: 1.25 **NM** value: **2.00**
Circ: CapCity orders: **19,500**

7 ❑ Apr 1993 Cover: 1.25 **NM** value: **4.00**
★ Versus Killer Croc.

7/CS ❑ Apr 1993 Cover: 1.25 **NM** value: **4.00**
Circ: CapCity orders: **22,350** • **CGC:** 1 graded, best 7.5
• trading card, V: Killer Croc

8 ❑ May 1993 Cover: 1.25 **NM** value: **2.00**
Circ: CapCity orders: **21,100**
📖 Larceny, My Sweet **A:** Mike Parobeck **W:** Kelley Puckett

9 ❑ Jun 1993 Cover: 1.25 **NM** value: **2.00**
Circ: CapCity orders: **19,650**
A: Mike Parobeck **W:** Kelley Puckett

10 ❑ Jul 1993 Cover: 1.25 **NM** value: **2.00**
Circ: CapCity orders: **21,300**
A: Mike Parobeck **W:** Kelley Puckett ★ Versus Riddler.

11 ❑ Aug 1993 Cover: 1.25 **NM** value: **1.50**
Circ: CapCity orders: **25,500**
A: Mike Parobeck **W:** Kelley Puckett ★ Versus Man-Bat.

12 ❑ Sep 1993 Cover: 1.25 **NM** value: **1.50**
Circ: CapCity orders: **19,200** • **CGC:** 1 graded, best 9.4
📖 Batgirl: Day One • Batgirl **A:** Mike Parobeck **W:** Kelley Puckett

13 ❑ Oct 1993 Cover: 1.25 **NM** value: **1.50**
Circ: CapCity orders: **19,050**

14 ❑ Nov 1993 Cover: 1.25 **NM** value: **1.50**
Circ: CapCity orders: **19,600**
• Robin

15 ❑ Dec 1993 Cover: 1.25 **NM** value: **1.50**
Circ: CapCity orders: **19,200**

16 ❑ Jan 1994 Cover: 1.50 **NM value: Cover or less**
Circ: CapCity orders: **18,350**
📖 The Killing Book **A:** Mike Parobeck **W:** Kelley Puckett ★ Appearance of Joker. ★ Versus Joker.

17 ❑ Feb 1994 Cover: 1.50 **NM value: Cover or less**
Circ: CapCity orders: **17,700**
📖 The Tangled Web **A:** Mike Parobeck **W:** Kelley Puckett

18 ❑ Mar 1994 Cover: 1.50 **NM value: Cover or less**
Circ: CapCity orders: **16,350**
• Batgirl-Robin

19 ❑ Apr 1994 Cover: 1.50 **NM value: Cover or less**
Circ: CapCity orders: **15,550**
★ Versus Scarecrow.

20 ❑ May 1994 Cover: 1.50 **NM value: Cover or less**
Circ: CapCity orders: **15,100**

21 ❑ Jun 1994 Cover: 1.50 **NM value: Cover or less**
Circ: CapCity orders: **14,900**
★ Appearance of Catwoman. ★ Versus Man-Bat.

22 ❑ Jul 1994 Cover: 1.50 **NM value: Cover or less**
Circ: CapCity orders: **14,850**
★ Versus Two-Face.

23 ❑ Aug 1994 Cover: 1.50 **NM value: Cover or less**
Circ: CapCity orders: **14,450**
★ Versus Poison Ivy.

24 ❑ Sep 1994 Cover: 1.50 **NM value: Cover or less**
Circ: CapCity orders: **13,700**

25 ❑ Oct 1994 Cover: 2.50 **NM value: Cover or less**
Circ: CapCity orders: **17,000**
• Giant-size. ★ Appearance of Lex Luthor. ★ Appearance of Superman.

26 ❑ Nov 1994 Cover: 1.50 **NM value: Cover or less**
Circ: CapCity orders: **15,250**
★ Appearance of Batgirl.

27 ❑ Dec 1994 Cover: 1.50 **NM value: Cover or less**
Circ: CapCity orders: **13,850**

28 ❑ Jan 1995 Cover: 1.50 **NM value: Cover or less**
Circ: CapCity orders: **14,100**
★ Appearance of Harley Quinn.

29 ❑ Feb 1995 Cover: 1.50 **NM value: Cover or less**
Circ: CapCity orders: **13,525**
★ Versus Ra's Al Ghul.

30 ❑ Mar 1995 Cover: 1.50 **NM value: Cover or less**
Circ: CapCity orders: **12,675**
★ Origin of The Perfesser, Mister Nice, Mastermind (DC).

31 ❑ Apr 1995 Cover: 1.50 **NM value: Cover or less**
Circ: CapCity orders: **12,150**

32 ❑ Jun 1995 Cover: 1.50 **NM value: Cover or less**
Circ: CapCity orders: **11,525**

33 ❑ Jul 1995 Cover: 1.75 **NM value: Cover or less**
Circ: CapCity orders: **11,600**

34 ❑ Aug 1995 Cover: 1.75 **NM value: Cover or less**
Circ: CapCity orders: **11,425**
★ Versus Hugo Strange, A: Catwoman.

35 ❑ Sep 1995 Cover: 1.75 **NM value: Cover or less**
Circ: CapCity orders: **10,850**
★ Versus Hugo Strange, A: Catwoman.

36 ❑ Oct 1995 Cover: 1.75 **NM value: Cover or less**
Circ: CapCity orders: **9,550**
final issue. ★ Versus Hugo Strange, A: Catwoman.

Anl 1 ❑ 1994 Cover: 2.95 **NM value: Cover or less**
Circ: CapCity orders: **16,150** • **CGC:** 3 graded, best 9.8

Anl 2 ❑ 1995 Cover: 3.50 **NM value: Cover or less**
Circ: CapCity orders: **11,250**
★ Appearance of The Demon.

Bk 1 ❑ Cover: 7.95 **NM value: Cover or less**
• Collects issues #1-6 **A:** Ty Templeton; Brad Rader **W:** Kelley Puckett; Martin Pasko

Bk 1-2 ❑ Cover: 7.95 **NM value: Cover or less**

Bk 2 ❑ Cover: 5.95 **NM** value: **7.95**
📖 The Dark Knight Adventures • collects The Batman Adventures #7-12 **A:** Mike Parobeck **W:** Kelley Puckett

HS 1 ❑ Jan 1995 Cover: 2.95 **NM value: Cover or less**
Circ: CapCity orders: **13,675**
• gatefold summary. ★ Versus Mr. Freeze.

BATMAN ADVENTURES, THE: MAD LOVE — DC

The Joker plays a winning hand at Arkham Asylum, when he tricks his new psychologist, Harleen ("Harley") Quinzel, into feeling sympathy for him. Quinzel, a would-be pop psychologist with a flawed past of her own, falls madly in love with The Clown Price of Crime. After the object of her affections escapes the asylum and Batman returns him — badly scathed — she springs him herself, having donned a clown costume herself, calling herself Harley Quinn ("Harlequin").

The character was introduced in the Batman Adventures TV series as a goofy, infatuated sidekick; this prequel takes a darker, inspired look at how she became what she is. It's one of the top Done in One comics stories of the last decade, alternating comedy with a grim look at an insane relationship usually played for laughs.

1 ❑ Feb 1994 Cover: 3.95 **NM** value: **15.00**
Circ: CapCity orders: **14,550** • **CGC:** 19 graded, best 9.6
No issue number. **A:** Bruce Timm **W:** Paul Dini ★ Origin of Harley Quinn. ★ Appearance of Joker.

1-2 ❑ 1994 Cover: 4.95 **NM** value: **5.50**
No issue number. • prestige format. **A:** Bruce Timm **W:** Paul Dini ★ Origin of Harley Quinn. ★ Appearance of Joker.

BATMAN ADVENTURES, THE: THE LOST YEARS — DC

1 ❑ Jan 1998 Cover: 1.95 **NM value: Cover or less**
• fills in time between first and second Batman animated series **A:** Bo Hampton **W:** Hilary Bader

2 ❑ Feb 1998 Cover: 1.95 **NM value: Cover or less**
A: Bo Hampton **W:** Hilary Bader ★ Appearance of Robin II.

3 ❑ Mar 1998 Cover: 1.95 **NM value: Cover or less**
📖 How You See 'em **A:** Bo Hampton **W:** Hilary Bader ★ Versus Two-Face.

4 ❑ Apr 1998 Cover: 1.95 **NM value: Cover or less**
A: Bo Hampton **W:** Hilary Bader

5 ❑ May 1998 Cover: 1.95 **NM value: Cover or less**
A: Bo Hampton **W:** Hilary Bader ★ Appearance of Nightwing.

Bk 1 ❑ Cover: 9.95 **NM value: Cover or less**
No issue number. • Trade Paperback. • collects and corrects mini-series **A:** Bo Hampton **W:** Hilary Bader

BATMAN/ALIENS — Dark Horse

1 ❑ Mar 1997 Cover: 4.95 **NM value: Cover or less**
Circ: Diamd. preorders: **73,763**
• prestige format. • crossover with DC **A:** Bernie Wrightson **W:** Ron Marz

2 ❑ Apr 1997 Cover: 4.95 **NM value: Cover or less**
Circ: Diamd. preorders: **64,934**
• prestige format. • crossover with DC **A:** Bernie Wrightson **W:** Ron Marz

Bk 1 ❑ Cover: 14.95 **NM value: Cover or less**
• collects mini-series with material from Dark Horse Presents #101 and 102

BATMAN: A LONELY PLACE OF DYING — DC

Bk 1 ❑ Sep 1990 Cover: 3.95 **NM value: Cover or less**
Circ: CapCity orders: **13,250**
• tpb, reprint

BATMAN AND DRACULA: RED RAIN — DC

Bk 1 ❑ Cover: 9.95 **NM value: Cover or less**
• Trade Paperback. 📖 Red Rain • Elseworlds;Part 1, followed by Bloodstorm and Crimson Mist **A:** Kelley Jones **W:** Doug Moench

Bk 1/HC ❑ ca. 1992 Cover: 24.95 **NM value: Cover or less**
Circ: CapCity orders: **8,600**
hardcover. **A:** Kelley Jones

BATMAN & ME — Eclipse

Bk 1 ❑ Cover: 14.95 **NM value: Cover or less**
• Bob Kane bio **A:** Pat Broderick

BATMAN AND OTHER DC CLASSICS — DC

1 ❑ ca. 1989 **NM** value: **1.00**
• **CGC:** 1 graded, best 9.2
📖 Reprints from Batman #47, Camelot 3000, Justice League (87), New Teen Titans **A:** George Pérez; Brian Bolland; Frank Miller; David Mazzucchelli; Al Gordon; Lou Schwartz **W:** Bob Kane; Keith Giffen; J.M. DeMatteis; Don & Maggie Thompson (text piece); Marv Wolfman; Mike W. Barr ★ Origin of Batman.

BATMAN AND ROBIN ADVENTURES, THE — DC

1 ❑ Nov 1995 Cover: 1.75 **NM** value: **3.00**

2 ❑ Dec 1995 Cover: 1.75 **NM** value: **2.00**
★ Versus Two-Face.

3 ❑ Jan 1996 Cover: 1.75 **NM** value: **2.00**
📖 Christmas Riddle **A:** Ty Templeton **W:** Paul Dini ★ Versus Riddler.

4 ❑ Feb 1996 Cover: 1.75 **NM** value: **2.00**
📖 Birdcage **A:** Rick Burchett **W:** Ty Templeton ★ Versus Penguin.

5 ❑ Mar 1996 Cover: 1.75 **NM** value: **2.00**
📖 Second Banana **A:** Tim Harkins **W:** Ty Templeton ★ Versus Joker.

6 ❑ May 1996 Cover: 1.75 **NM value: Cover or less**

7 ❑ Jun 1996 Cover: 1.75 **NM value: Cover or less**
★ Versus Scarface.

8 ❑ Jul 1996 Cover: 1.75 **NM value: Cover or less**
• Robin is enslaved by Poison Ivy

9 ❑ Aug 1996 Cover: 1.75 **NM value: Cover or less**
• Batgirl versus Talia

10 ❑ Sep 1996 Cover: 1.75 **NM value: Cover or less**
★ Versus Ra's Al Ghul.

11 ❑ Oct 1996 Cover: 1.75 **NM value: Cover or less**
📖 Windows to the Soul **A:** Rick Burchett; Dev Madan **W:** Ty Templeton

12 ❑ Nov 1996 Cover: 1.75 **NM value: Cover or less**
Circ: Diamd. preorders: **26,902**
📖 To Live and Die in Gotham City! **A:** Brandon Kruse **W:** Ty Templeton ★ Versus Bane.

13 ❑ Dec 1996 Cover: 1.75 **NM value: Cover or less**
Circ: Direct Market orders: **27,158**
📖 Knightmare **A:** Brandon Kruse **W:** Ty Templeton ★ Versus Scarecrow.

14 ❑ Jan 1997 Cover: 1.75 **NM value: Cover or less**
Circ: Direct Market orders: **26,284**
📖 Dagger's Tale **A:** Brandon Kruse **W:** Ty Templeton

15 ❑ Feb 1997 Cover: 1.75 **NM value: Cover or less**
Circ: Diamd. preorders: **25,483**
A: Brandon Kruse **W:** Ty Templeton ★ Appearance of Deadman.

16 ❑ Mar 1997 Cover: 1.75 **NM value: Cover or less**
Circ: Diamd. preorders: **24,700**
📖 It Takes a Cat **A:** Brandon Kruse **W:** Ty Templeton ★ Appearance of Catwoman.

17 ❑ Apr 1997 Cover: 1.75 **NM value: Cover or less**
Circ: Diamd. preorders: **23,710**
A: Brandon Kruse **W:** Ty Templeton

18 ❑ May 1997 Cover: 1.75 **NM value: Cover or less**
Circ: Diamd. preorders: **24,021**
A: Brandon Kruse **W:** Ty Templeton ★ Versus Joker.

19 ❑ Jun 1997 Cover: 1.75 **NM value: Cover or less**
Circ: Diamd. preorders: **24,678**
📖 Duty of the Huntress **A:** Brandon Kruse **W:** Ty Templeton

20 ❑ Jul 1997 Cover: 1.75 **NM value: Cover or less**
Circ: Diamd. preorders: **23,140**

21 ❑ Aug 1997 Cover: 1.75 **NM value: Cover or less**
Circ: Diamd. preorders: **23,016**
• Batgirl vs. Riddler

22 ❑ Sep 1997 Cover: 1.75 **NM value: Cover or less**
Circ: Diamd. preorders: **22,491**
★ Versus Two-Face.

23 ❑ Oct 1997 Cover: 1.75 **NM value: Cover or less**
Circ: Diamd. preorders: **21,941**
★ Versus Killer Croc.

24 ❑ Nov 1997 Cover: 1.75 **NM value: Cover or less**
Circ: Diamd. preorders: **21,973**
📖 Touch of Death **A:** Bo Hampton **W:** Kelley Puckett ★ Versus Poison Ivy.

25 ❑ Dec 1997 Cover: 2.95 **NM value: Cover or less**
Circ: Diamd. preorders: **22,813**
Face cover. • Giant-size. 📖 Demon in the Sky final issue. **A:** Bo Hampton **W:** Ty Templeton ★ Versus Ra's Al Ghul.

Anl 1 ❑ Nov 1996 Cover: 2.95 **NM value: Cover or less**
Circ: Diamd. preorders: **26,858**
📖 Shadow of the Phantasm • sequel to Batman: Mask of the Phantasm **A:** Ty Templeton **W:** Paul Dini

Anl 2 ❑ Nov 1997 Cover: 3.95 **NM value: Cover or less**
Circ: Diamd. preorders: **21,308**
📖 Token of Faith • ties in with Adventures in the DC Universe Annual #1 and Superman Adventures Annual #1 **A:** Joe Staton **W:** Hilary J. Bader ★ Appearance of Zatara. ★ Appearance of Zatanna.

BATMAN AND ROBIN ADVENTURES, THE: SUB-ZERO — DC

1 ❑ 1998 Cover: 3.95 **NM value: Cover or less**
Circ: Diamd. preorders: **20,931**
No issue number. cover says 98. • adapts direct-to-video movie;indicia says 97 ★ Versus Mr. Freeze.

BATMAN AND ROBIN: THE OFFICIAL ADAPTATION OF THE WARNER BROS. MOTION PICTURE — DC

1 ❑ ca. 1997 Cover: 5.95 **NM value: Cover or less**
Circ: Diamd. preorders: **14,104**
No issue number. • prestige format. **A:** Rodolfo DaMaggio; Bill Sienkiewicz(inks) **W:** Denny O'Neil

BATMAN & SUPERMAN ADVENTURES: WORLD'S FINEST — DC

1 ❑ 1997 Cover: 6.95 **NM value: Cover or less**
No issue number. • prestige format. • adapts 90-minute special **A:** Joe Staton **W:** Paul Dini

There are two different pricing tiers in the modern comic-book hobby. **The prices seen above** are the prices we have seen **loose copies** of these issues reliably fetch in a variety of environments. Condition alters the price by the fractions seen on the bar on the bottom of left-hand pages of this book. **Comics graded by CGC** usually sell for more. Use the guide on the bottom of right-hand pages of this book to estimate what copies have brought on eBay.

CGC-graded: Multiply prices above by **33 for 9.9 M** • **16 for 9.8 NM/M** • **7 for 9.6 NM+** • **5 for 9.4 NM** • **2.5 for 9.2 NM-** • **1.5 for 9.0 VF/NM**

BATMAN AND SUPERMAN: WORLD'S FINEST DC

Batman and Superman have teamed up many times over the years. The two heroes are opposites in many ways. Batman rules in dark Gotham and cultivates fear, while Superman builds trust in clean, bright Metropolis. Batman believes he could clean up Gotham in one day with Superman's powers. But Superman thinks Batman couldn't handle super-villains, aliens, and scientific experiments gone awry. Unfortunately, their lack of teamwork during an early mission causes a terrible tragedy.

Now, each year on the anniversary of the event, the two heroes are drawn together once more. As they patrol each other's cities together, a begrudging respect grows. This series chronicles how their relationship and this respect develop year-by-year and adventure-by-adventure.

1 ❑ Apr 1999 Cover: 4.95 **NM value: Cover or less**
Circ: Diamd. preorders: **39,246**
• prestige format. **A:** David Taylor **W:** Karl Kesel
1/Aut❑ **NM value: 18.95**
A: David Taylor **W:** Karl Kesel
2 ❑ May 1999 Cover: 1.99 **NM value: 2.00**
Circ: Diamd. preorders: **38,261**
🕮 A Tale of Two Cities **A:** David Taylor **W:** Karl Kesel
3 ❑ Jun 1999 Cover: 1.99 **NM value: 2.00**
Circ: Diamd. preorders: **39,257**
🕮 Light in the Darkness **A:** David Taylor **W:** Karl Kesel ★ Versus Joker.
4 ❑ Jul 1999 Cover: 1.99 **NM value: Cover or less**
Circ: Diamd. preorders: **40,177**
🕮 Underworlds **A:** David Taylor **W:** Karl Kesel
5 ❑ Aug 1999 Cover: 1.99 **NM value: Cover or less**
Circ: Diamd. preorders: **40,212**
🕮 A Woman's Work **A:** Tom Morgan; David Taylor **W:** Karl Kesel ★ Appearance of Batgirl.
6 ❑ Sep 1999 Cover: 1.99 **NM value: Cover or less**
Circ: Diamd. preorders: **40,317**
🕮 The Imp-Possible Dream **A:** Peter Doherty **W:** Karl Kesel ★ Appearance of Bat-Mite. ★ Appearance of Mr. Mxyzptlk.
7 ❑ Oct 1999 Cover: 1.99 **NM value: Cover or less**
Circ: Diamd. preorders: **38,994**
🕮 A Better World **A:** Peter Doherty **W:** Karl Kesel
8 ❑ Nov 1999 Cover: 1.99 **NM value: Cover or less**
Circ: Diamd. preorders: **37,769**
W: Karl Kesel
9 ❑ Dec 1999 Cover: 1.99 **NM value: Cover or less**
Circ: Diamd. preorders: **37,322**
🕮 When it Reigns…It Pours! **A:** Graham Nolan **W:** Karl Kesel
10 ❑ Jan 2000 Cover: 4.95 **NM value: Cover or less**
Circ: Diamd. preorders: **36,032**
🕮 War of the Worlds! **A:** Tom Morgan; David Taylor **W:** Karl Kesel

BATMAN AND THE OUTSIDERS DC

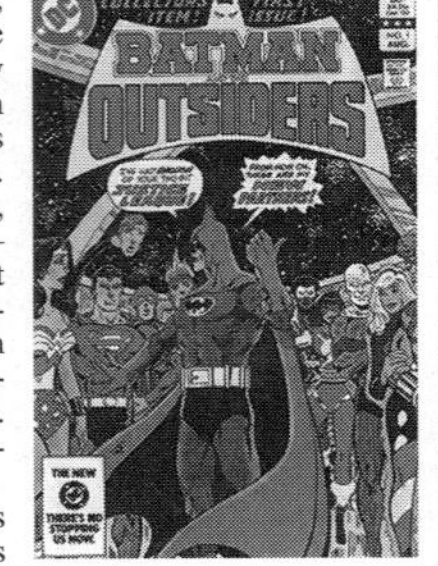

The Outsiders unite against evil, even though, individually, they are puzzling out who they are and how to use their powers. It takes Batman to bring them together as a team; as a team, they're formidable, indeed. Three of the Outsiders — Halo, Black Lightning, and Geo-Force — can throw powerful blasts against enemies. Katana is a master swordswoman. And Metamorpho can transform himself, or parts of himself, into anything, including gas. Batman, of course, needs no introduction.

With issue #33, Batman goes his own way, and the title changes its name to The Adventures of the Outsiders.

1 ❑ Aug 1983 Cover: 0.60 **NM value: 3.00**
• **CGC:** 6 graded, best 9.6
★ Origin of Geo-Force. ★ 1st Appearance of Baron Bedlam.
2 ❑ Sep 1983 Cover: 0.60 **NM value: 2.00**
🕮 Markovia's Last Stand! **A:** Jim Aparo **W:** Mike W. Barr ★ Versus Baron Bedlam.
3 ❑ Oct 1983 Cover: 0.60 **NM value: 2.00**
A: Jim Aparo ★ Versus Agent Orange.
4 ❑ Nov 1983 Cover: 0.60 **NM value: 2.00**
A: Jim Aparo
5 ❑ Dec 1983 Cover: 0.75 **NM value: 2.00**
A: Jim Aparo ★ Appearance of New Teen Titans.
6 ❑ Jan 1984 Cover: 0.75 **NM value: 1.50**
7 ❑ Feb 1984 Cover: 0.75 **NM value: 1.50**
8 ❑ Mar 1984 Cover: 0.75 **NM value: 1.50**
9 ❑ Apr 1984 Cover: 0.75 **NM value: 1.50**
★ 1st Appearance of Masters of Disaster.
10 ❑ May 1984 Cover: 0.75 **NM value: 1.50**
★ Versus Masters of Disaster.
11 ❑ Jun 1984 Cover: 0.75 **NM value: 1.25**
★ Origin of Katana.
12 ❑ Jul 1984 Cover: 0.75 **NM value: 1.25**
★ Origin of Katana.
13 ❑ Aug 1984 Cover: 0.75 **NM value: 1.25**
14 ❑ Oct 1984 Cover: 0.75 **NM value: 1.25**
★ Versus Maxie Zeus.
15 ❑ Nov 1984 Cover: 0.75 **NM value: 1.25**
★ Versus Maxie Zeus.
16 ❑ Dec 1984 Cover: 0.75 **NM value: 1.25**
🕮 The Truth About Halo, Part 1
17 ❑ Jan 1985 Cover: 0.75 **NM value: 1.25**
18 ❑ Feb 1985 Cover: 0.75 **NM value: 1.25**
19 ❑ Mar 1985 Cover: 0.75 **NM value: 1.25**
20 ❑ Apr 1985 Cover: 0.75 **NM value: 1.25**
🕮 The Truth About Halo, Part 2 ★ 1st Appearance of Syonide II.
21 ❑ May 1985 Cover: 0.75 **NM value: 1.25**
Circ: CapCity orders: **9,700**
22 ❑ Jun 1985 Cover: 0.75 **NM value: 1.25**
Circ: CapCity orders: **9,950**
🕮 The Truth About Halo, Part 3
23 ❑ Jul 1985 Cover: 0.75 **NM value: 1.25**
Circ: CapCity orders: **9,750**
🕮 The Truth About Halo, Part 4
24 ❑ Aug 1985 Cover: 0.75 **NM value: 1.25**
Circ: CapCity orders: **9,900**
25 ❑ Sep 1985 Cover: 0.75 **NM value: 1.25**
Circ: CapCity orders: **9,950**
26 ❑ Oct 1985 Cover: 0.75 **NM value: 1.25**
Circ: CapCity orders: **9,750**
★ Versus Kobra.
27 ❑ Nov 1985 Cover: 0.75 **NM value: 1.25**
Circ: CapCity orders: **9,600**
28 ❑ Dec 1985 Cover: 0.75 **NM value: 1.25**
Circ: CapCity orders: **9,550**
🕮 The Truth About Looker, Part 1
29 ❑ Jan 1986 Cover: 0.75 **NM value: 1.25**
Circ: CapCity orders: **9,500**
🕮 The Truth About Looker, Part 2
30 ❑ Feb 1986 Cover: 0.75 **NM value: 1.25**
Circ: CapCity orders: **10,950**
🕮 The Truth About Looker, Part 3
31 ❑ Mar 1986 Cover: 0.75 **NM value: 1.25**
Circ: CapCity orders: **9,800**
🕮 The Truth About Looker, Part 4
32 ❑ Apr 1986 Cover: 0.75 **NM value: 1.25**
Circ: CapCity orders: **10,450**
🕮 A New War's Winning • Series continues as Adventures of the Outsiders;Batman leaves
Anl 1❑ca. 1984 Cover: 1.25 **NM value: 1.50**
A: Frank Miller(cover) **C:** Frank Miller ★ 1st Appearance of Force of July. ★ 1st Appearance of Major Victory.
Anl 2❑ca. 1985 Cover: 1.25 **NM value: Cover or less**
Circ: CapCity orders: **10,350**
• Wedding of Metamorpho and Sapphire Stag **A:** Jim Aparo

BATMAN ARCHIVES DC

1 ❑ Cover: 39.95 **NM value: Cover or less**
Circ: CapCity orders: **7,650**
hardcover, reprint. ★ Appearance of Collects Batman.
2 ❑ Cover: 39.95 **NM value: Cover or less**
Circ: CapCity orders: **3,650**
hardcover, reprint. ★ Appearance of Collects Batman.
3 ❑ Cover: 39.95 **NM value: Cover or less**
hardcover, reprint. ★ Appearance of Collects Batman.
4 ❑ Cover: 49.95 **NM value: Cover or less**
hardcover, reprints Detective Comics #87-102.
5 ❑ Cover: 49.95 **NM value: Cover or less**
hardcover, reprints Detective Comics #103-119. 🕮 Denny O'Neil, Alvin Schwartz, Don Cameron, Bill Finger **W:** Jack Burnley; Dick Sprang; Win Mortimer

BATMAN: ARKHAM ASYLUM DC

1 ❑ Cover: 14.95 **NM value: Cover or less**
Circ: CapCity orders: **9,800**
Softcover book. • paperback **A:** Dave McKean **W:** Grant Morrison ★ Appearance of Joker.
1/HC❑ Cover: 24.95 **NM value: 25.00**
Circ: CapCity orders: **27,900**
Hardcover book. **A:** Dave McKean **W:** Grant Morrison ★ Appearance of Joker.

BATMAN: ARKHAM ASYLUM – TALES OF MADNESS DC

1 ❑ May 1998 Cover: 2.95 **NM value: Cover or less**
Circ: Diamd. preorders: **39,965**
One-shot. 🕮 Cataclysm, Part 16

BATMAN: A WORD TO THE WISE DC

1 ❑ Cover: 1.25 **NM value: Cover or less**
• **CGC:** 1 graded, best 9.6
No issue number. • (DC giveaway).

BATMAN: BANE DC

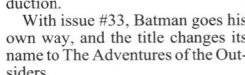

Bane, the man who broke Batman's back, stars in this one-shot special, in which he is once again planning to destroy Gotham City and Batman. After his humiliating defeat to Batman at the end of the Legacy storyline, Bane drifts in and out of consciousness while lost on the ocean. While reliving events of the past, Bane comes upon a floating nuclear power plant, which he intends to use to destroy Gotham once and for all.

Will Gotham be destroyed in a ball of nuclear fire? Not if Batman, Robin, and Nightwing have anything to say about it!

1 ❑ Jul 1997 Cover: 4.95 **NM value: Cover or less**
Circ: Diamd. preorders: **41,856**
No issue number. prestige format one-shot, cover is part of quadtych.
A: Rick Burchett **W:** Chuck Dixon

BATMAN: BANE OF THE DEMON DC

1 ❑ Mar 1998 Cover: 1.95 **NM value: Cover or less**
Circ: Diamd. preorders: **43,606**
A: Graham Nolan **W:** Chuck Dixon ★ Origin of Bane.
2 ❑ Apr 1998 Cover: 1.95 **NM value: Cover or less**
Circ: Diamd. preorders: **37,535**
A: Graham Nolan **W:** Chuck Dixon
3 ❑ May 1998 Cover: 1.95 **NM value: Cover or less**
Circ: Diamd. preorders: **35,618**
A: Graham Nolan **W:** Chuck Dixon
4 ❑ Jun 1998 Cover: 1.95 **NM value: Cover or less**
Circ: Diamd. preorders: **35,098**
A: Graham Nolan **W:** Chuck Dixon

BATMAN: BATGIRL DC

1 ❑ Jul 1997 Cover: 4.95 **NM value: Cover or less**
Circ: Diamd. preorders: **43,913**
No issue number. cover is part of quadtych. • prestige format one-shot **A:** Matt Haley **W:** Kelley Puckett

BATMAN: BATGIRL (GIRLFRENZY) DC

1 ❑ Jun 1998 Cover: 1.95 **NM value: Cover or less**
Circ: Diamd. preorders: **46,762**
One-shot. 🕮 Scars • Girlfrenzy;one-shot, V: Mr. Zsasz **A:** Rick Burchett; Jim Balent **W:** Kelley Puckett ★ Versus Mr. Zsasz.

BATMAN BEYOND DC

1 ❑ Nov 1999 Cover: 1.99 **NM value: 2.50**
Circ: Diamd. preorders: **27,984** • **CGC:** 2 graded, best 9.6
• adapts first episode
2 ❑ Dec 1999 Cover: 1.99 **NM value: 2.00**
Circ: Diamd. preorders: **22,444**
🕮 Ebony Tears • adapts first episode **A:** Craig Rousseau **W:** Hilary J. Bader
3 ❑ Jan 2000 Cover: 1.99 **NM value: 2.00**
Circ: Diamd. preorders: **20,559**
🕮 Zoologically Speaking **A:** Craig Rousseau **W:** Hilary J. Bader ★ Versus Blight.
4 ❑ Feb 2000 Cover: 1.99 **NM value: Cover or less**
Circ: Diamd. preorders: **20,904**
A: Craig Rousseau **W:** Hilary J. Bader ★ Appearance of Demon.
5 ❑ Mar 2000 Cover: 1.99 **NM value: Cover or less**
Circ: Diamd. preorders: **17,883**
A: Craig Rousseau **W:** Hilary J. Bader
6 ❑ Apr 2000 Cover: 1.99 **NM value: Cover or less**
Circ: Diamd. preorders: **16,244**
🕮 Most Dangerous Island **A:** Craig Rousseau **W:** Hilary J. Bader
7 ❑ May 2000 Cover: 1.99 **NM value: Cover or less**
Circ: Diamd. preorders: **16,063**
🕮 McGinnis' Secret **A:** Min Ku **W:** Hilary J. Bader
8 ❑ Jun 2000 Cover: 1.99 **NM value: Cover or less**
Circ: Diamd. preorders: **15,401**
W: Hilary J. Bader
9 ❑ Jul 2000 Cover: 1.99 **NM value: Cover or less**
Circ: Diamd. preorders: **14,850**
🕮 The Last of Her Kind **A:** Craig Rousseau **W:** Hilary J. Bader; Rich Fogel
10 ❑ Aug 2000 Cover: 1.99 **NM value: Cover or less**
Circ: Diamd. preorders: **14,768**
🕮 Toy Wonder **A:** Craig Rousseau **W:** Hilary J. Bader ★ Versus Golem.
11 ❑ Sep 2000 Cover: 1.99 **NM value: Cover or less**
Circ: Diamd. preorders: **14,121**
🕮 The Perfect You **A:** Craig Rousseau **W:** Hilary J. Bader
12 ❑ Oct 2000 Cover: 1.99 **NM value: Cover or less**
Circ: Diamd. preorders: **13,372**
🕮 Terminal Velocity **A:** Craig Rousseau; Hilary J. Bader **W:** Hilary J. Bader ★ Versus Terminal.
13 ❑ Nov 2000 Cover: 1.99 **NM value: Cover or less**
Circ: Diamd. preorders: **12,978**
🕮 Commissioner of Fear **A:** Min S. Ku **W:** Hilary J. Bader ★ Appearance of Scarecrow. ★ Appearance of Batgirl.
14 ❑ Dec 2000 Cover: 1.99 **NM value: Cover or less**
Circ: Diamd. preorders: **12,751**
🕮 May Flights of Demons Sing Thee to Thy Rest **A:** Min S. Ku **W:** Hilary J. Bader ★ Appearance of Demon.
15 ❑ Jan 2001 Cover: 1.99 **NM value: Cover or less**
Circ: Diamd. preorders: **12,416**
🕮 Lightning and Rain **A:** Craig Rousseau **W:** Jason Hernandez-Rosenblatt
16 ❑ Feb 2001 Cover: 1.99 **NM value: Cover or less**
Circ: Diamd. preorders: **12,172**
🕮 Snake Food **A:** Craig Rousseau **W:** Hilary J. Bader
17 ❑ Mar 2001 Cover: 1.99 **NM value: Cover or less**
Circ: Diamd. preorders: **11,957**
🕮 A Sinking Ship **A:** Craig Rousseau **W:** Hilary J. Bader
18 ❑ Apr 2001 Cover: 1.99 **NM value: Cover or less**
Circ: Diamd. preorders: **11,860**
🕮 Prey or Hunter, Hunter or Prey **A:** Craig Rousseau **W:** Hilary J. Bader
19 ❑ May 2001 Cover: 1.99 **NM value: Cover or less**
Circ: Diamd. preorders: **11,596**
🕮 Royal Mayhem **A:** Craig Rousseau **W:** Hilary J. Bader
20 ❑ Jun 2001 Cover: 1.99 **NM value: Cover or less**
Circ: Diamd. preorders: **11,773**
21 ❑ Jul 2001 Cover: 1.99 **NM value: Cover or less**
Circ: Diamd. preorders: **13,745**
22 ❑ Aug 2001 Cover: 1.99 **NM value: Cover or less**
Circ: Diamd. preorders: **13,644**
23 ❑ Sep 2001 Cover: 1.99 **NM value: Cover or less**
Circ: Diamd. preorders: **12,322**

Other grades: Multiply prices above by **1.5 for Mint • 2/3 for Very Fine • 1/3 for Fine • 1/5 for Very Good • 1/8 for Good**

BATMAN BEYOND (MINI-SERIES) DC

In the near-future, Barbara Gordon is Gotham City's tough-as-nails police commissioner, millionaire Bruce Wayne is a bitter old man of 70, and Batman is a wise-cracking teen-ager named Terry McGinnis. This six-issue mini-series brings Batman Beyond, the Kids' WB animated series, to comics and, like its source material, provides good, old-fashioned Bat-fun — no matter who's behind the mask. Sure, Terry McGinnis has a different style from that of his mentor and predecessor Bruce Wayne, but things in Gotham haven't changed much: The criminals are still a superstitious, cowardly lot, and Batman is there to scare the bejeezus out of them and bring them to justice.

1 ❑ Mar 1999 Cover: 1.99 **NM** value: **2.50**
Circ: Diamd. preorders: **27,920**
Not On My Watch! • adapts first episode **A:** Rick Burchett **W:** Hilary J. Bader ★ Origin of Batman II (Terry McGuiness).

2 ❑ Apr 1999 Cover: 1.99 **NM** value: **2.00**
Circ: Diamd. preorders: **24,741**
Rebirth, part 2 • adapts first episode **A:** Rick Burchett **W:** Hilary J. Bader ★ Origin of Batman II (Terry McGuiness). ★ Appearance of Derek Powers.

3 ❑ May 1999 Cover: 1.99 **NM** value: **2.00**
Circ: Diamd. preorders: **24,293**
Never Mix , Never Worry **A:** Rick Burchett **W:** Hilary J. Bader ★ Versus Blight.

4 ❑ Jun 1999 Cover: 1.99 **NM** value: **2.00**
Circ: Diamd. preorders: **25,053**
Magic Is Everywhere! **A:** Joe Staton **W:** Hilary J. Bader ★ Appearance of Demon.

5 ❑ Jul 1999 Cover: 1.99 **NM** value: **2.00**
Circ: Diamd. preorders: **23,501**
Mummy, Oh! And Juliet **A:** Rick Burchett **W:** Hilary J. Bader

6 ❑ Aug 1999 Cover: 1.99 **NM** value: **2.00**
Circ: Diamd. preorders: **23,028**
Permanent Inque Stains **A:** Joe Staton **W:** Hilary J. Bader

Bk 1❑ Cover: 9.95 **NM** value: **Cover or less**
A: Joe Staton **W:** Hilary J. Bader

BATMAN BEYOND: RETURN OF THE JOKER DC

1 ❑ Feb 2001 Cover: 2.95 **NM** value: **Cover or less**
Circ: Diamd. preorders: **15,409** • **CGC:** 1 graded, best 9.8
A: Craig Rousseau **W:** Darren Vincenzo

BATMAN BEYOND SPECIAL ORIGIN ISSUE DC

1 ❑ Jun 1999 **NM** value: **0.50**
Rebirth • Free **A:** Rick Burchett **W:** Hilary J. Bader

BATMAN: BIRTH OF THE DEMON DC

1 ❑ Cover: 12.95 **NM** value: **Cover or less**
Embossed cover. **A:** Norm Breyfogle **W:** Denny O'Neil ★ Origin of Ra's Al Ghul.

1/HC❑ Cover: 24.95 **NM** value: **Cover or less**
hardcover. • Hardcover edition. **A:** Norm Breyfogle **W:** Denny O'Neil ★ Origin of Ra's Al Ghul.

BATMAN BLACK AND WHITE DC

This anthology was designed to get attention and to provide a showcase for writers and (especially) artists who would find storytelling without color a challenge. Some of the contributions to the unusual (for a major publisher) project are outstanding and compelling.

Writers involved in the four-issue mini-series included Neil Gaiman, Brian Bolland, Howard Chaykin, Archie Goodwin, Joe Kubert, Ted McKeever, Bill Sienkiewicz, Walter Simonson, and Bruce Timm, while artists included Jim Lee, Simon Bisley, Bolland, Chaykin, Gary Gianni, Sienkiewicz, Simonson, Brian Stelfreeze, and Kent Williams. Covers were by Jim Lee and Scott Williams, Frank Miller, Barry Windsor-Smith, and Alex Toth. — Maggie

1 ❑ Jun 1996, b&w Cover: 2.95 **NM** value: **4.00**
• **CGC:** 12 graded, best 9.6
C: Jim Lee

2 ❑ Jul 1996, b&w Cover: 2.95 **NM** value: **3.50**
• **CGC:** 3 graded, best 9.2
C: Frank Miller

3 ❑ Aug 1996, b&w Cover: 2.95 **NM** value: **3.50**
• **CGC:** 1 graded, best 9.6
C: Barry Windsor-Smith

4 ❑ Sep 1996, b&w Cover: 2.95 **NM** value: **3.50**
• **CGC:** 1 graded, best 9.2
final issue. **C:** Alex Toth

Bk 1❑ Cover: 19.95 **NM** value: **Cover or less**
• Collects mini-series **A:** Richard Corben; Ted McKeever; Barry Windsor-Smith; Howard Chaykin; Joe Kubert; Simon Bisley; Frank Miller; Jim Lee; Walt Simonson; Klaus Janson; Kent Williams; Bruce Timm; Jorge Zaffino; José Muñoz **W:** Ted McKeever; Howard Chaykin; Joe Kubert; Frank Miller; Walt Simonson; Kent Williams; Bruce Timm; Chuck Dixon; Jan Strnad; Archie Goodwin; Neil Gaiman

Bk 1/HC❑ Cover: 29.95 **NM** value: **39.95**
hardcover. • collects mini-series with Steranko tip-in plate **A:** Barry Windsor-Smith; Jim Lee **W:** Frank Miller; Neil Gaiman

BATMAN: BLACKGATE DC

1 ❑ Jan 1997 Cover: 3.95 **NM** value: **Cover or less**
Circ: Direct Market orders: **49,687**
One-shot. Hatred's Home **A:** Joe Staton **W:** Chuck Dixon

BATMAN: BLACKGATE-ISLE OF MEN DC

1 ❑ Apr 1998 Cover: 2.95 **NM** value: **Cover or less**
Circ: Diamd. preorders: **39,893**
Cataclysm, Part 8 • one-shot, continues in Batman: Shadow of the Bat #74 **A:** Jim Aparo **W:** Doug Moench

BATMAN: BLIND JUSTICE DC

Bk 1❑ Cover: 7.50 **NM** value: **Cover or less**
Circ: CapCity orders: **3,200**
A: Pat Broderick

BATMAN: BLOODSTORM DC

1 ❑ Cover: 12.95 **NM** value: **Cover or less**
• Trade Paperback. Bloodstorm • Elseworlds story;Preceded by Batman and Dracula: Red Rain, and followed by Crimson Mist **A:** Kelley Jones **W:** Doug Moench

1/HC❑ Cover: 24.95 **NM** value: **Cover or less**
hardcover. **A:** Kelley Jones **W:** Doug Moench

BATMAN: BOOK OF THE DEAD DC

1 ❑ Jun 1999 Cover: 4.95 **NM** value: **Cover or less**
Circ: Diamd. preorders: **28,496**
A: Barry Kitson **W:** Doug Moench

2 ❑ Jul 1999 Cover: 4.95 **NM** value: **Cover or less**
Circ: Diamd. preorders: **26,188**
A: Barry Kitson **W:** Doug Moench

BATMAN: BRIDE OF THE DEMON DC

A glow of lost romance, a touch of environmental fervor, and lots of good old-fashioned action blend in this taut story by writer Mike W. Barr with art by Tom Grindberg.

When an ancient enemy of Batman decides to save the world by destroying everyone on the planet — leaving it pure for the emergence of himself and his wife as the new Adam and Eve — The Caped Crusader must find a way to stop a cataclysmic release of ozone into the atmosphere. But to succeed, he must come to grips with his feelings for the madman's daughter, save a hapless scientist and his child, beat back an invasion of the Bat Cave, and keep Tim Drake from feeling useless.

Published by DC in 1990, the handsome hard and softbound versions of this work found its way into mainstream bookstores across the country, helping prove it could be done.

1 ❑ Cover: 19.95 **NM** value: **Cover or less**
Circ: CapCity orders: **12,550**
hardcover. Bride of the Demon **A:** Tom Grindberg

Bk 1/HC❑ Cover: 19.95 **NM** value: **Cover or less**
Painted cover. • Hardcover edition. Bride of the Demon **A:** Tom Grindberg **W:** Mike W. Barr

BATMAN: BULLOCK'S LAW DC

1 ❑ Aug 1999 Cover: 4.95 **NM** value: **Cover or less**
Circ: Diamd. preorders: **21,932**
One-shot. Bullock's Law **A:** Flint Henry **W:** Chuck Dixon

BATMAN/CAPTAIN AMERICA DC

1 ❑ 1996 Cover: 5.95 **NM** value: **Cover or less**
• prestige format crossover with Marvel, Elseworlds;prestige format crossover with Marvel;Elseworlds **A:** John Byrne **W:** John Byrne

BATMAN: CASTLE OF THE BAT DC

1 ❑ 1994 Cover: 5.95 **NM** value: **Cover or less**
• prestige format. • Elseworlds **A:** Bo Hampton **W:** Jack Harris

BATMAN: CATACLYSM DC

1 ❑ Cover: 17.95 **NM** value: **Cover or less**
• Collects Cataclysm storyline from Batman #553-554, Detective Comics #719-721, Batman: Shadow of the Bat #73-74, etc. **A:** Stewart Johnson; Alex Maleev; Mark Buckingham; Graham Nolan; Rick Burchett; Jim Balent; Scott McDaniel; Eduardo Barreto; Klaus Janson; Chris Renaud; Jim Aparo **W:** Rick Burchett; Klaus Janson; Chris Renaud; Chuck Dixon; Kelley Puckett; Alan Grant; Devin Grayson; Doug Moench

BATMAN: CATWOMAN DEFIANT DC

Catwoman's not evil, but she is bad. Very bad. She's been a thorn in Batman's side since Detective Comics #122 (Apr 46). In Catwoman Defiant, she appears for the first time in her own graphic novel.

An obsessed gangster named Johnny Handsome has made it his business to seek out and destroy great objects of beauty. Eventually, his sights become fixed on Catwoman, whom he considers the epitome of feline grace. Torn apart by a dark secret of his own, Handsome spins a web of intrigue that encircles Batman, Catwoman, and himself. When the circle closes, it threatens to destroy them all.

1 ❑ Cover: 4.95 **NM** value: **5.00**
Circ: CapCity orders: **37,100**
No issue number. cover forms diptych with Batman: Penguin Triumphant. • prestige format. **A:** Tom Grindberg **W:** Peter Milligan

BATMAN CHRONICLES, THE DC

1 ❑ Jun 1995 Cover: 2.95 **NM** value: **4.00**
Circ: CapCity orders: **36,650** • **CGC:** 1 graded, best 9.6
• Giant-size. Midnight Train; Anarky: Tomorrow Belongs to Us; Death Mask **A:** Stewart Johnson; Brian Apthorp; Lee Weeks; Bill Sienkiewicz(inks); Terry Austin(inks) **W:** Chuck Dixon; Alan Grant; Doug Moench

2 ❑ Sep 1995 Cover: 2.95 **NM** value: **3.50**
Circ: CapCity orders: **21,125**

3 ❑ Dec 1995 Cover: 2.95 **NM** value: **3.50**
The Riddle of the Jinxed Sphinx; The First Cut is Deepest; Killer Croc: Workin' My Way Back to You **A:** Brian Stelfreeze; Bill Sienkiewicz; Jennifer Graves; Gabriel Gecko **C:** Brian Bolland **W:** Chuck Dixon; Alan Grant; Doug Moench ★ Origin of Mr. Zsasz, A: Riddler, Killer Croc.

4 ❑ Mar 1996 Cover: 2.95 **NM** value: **8.00**
• **CGC:** 6 graded, best 9.6
Contagion; Hitman; The Huntress: Exposure; Beggar's Banquet **A:** Matt Haley; John McCrea; Frank Fosco **W:** Chuck Dixon; Christopher Priest; Garth Ennis ★ Appearance of Hitman.

5 ❑ Jun 1996 Cover: 2.95 **NM** value: **3.50**
C: Howard Chaykin

6 ❑ Sep 1996 Cover: 2.95 **NM** value: **3.50**
Choices; Shadow Job; Cityscape **A:** Curt Swan; Enrique Alcatena; Dave D'Antiquis; Jesse Delperdang; Ray McCarthy **C:** Michael W. Kaluta **W:** Brian Augustyn; Denny O'Neil; Mark Nevins

7 ❑ Dec 1996 Cover: 2.95 **NM** value: **3.50**
Circ: Direct Market orders: **42,516**
C: Joe Orlando ★ Appearance of Superman.

8 ❑ Mar 1997 Cover: 2.95 **NM** value: **3.50**
Circ: Diamd. preorders: **38,389**
A: Sal Buscema **C:** Walt Simonson ★ Versus Ra's Al Ghul.

9 ❑ Jun 1997 Cover: 2.95 **NM** value: **3.50**
Circ: Diamd. preorders: **36,327**
Movie poster cover.

10 ❑ Sep 1997 Cover: 2.95 **NM** value: **3.50**
Circ: Diamd. preorders: **35,883**
A: Bill Sienkiewicz

11 ❑ Dec 1997 Cover: 2.95 **NM** value: **3.50**
Circ: Diamd. preorders: **34,418**
A: Paul Pope

12 ❑ Mar 1998 Cover: 2.95 **NM** value: **3.50**
Circ: Diamd. preorders: **36,585**
Cataclysm, Part 10

13 ❑ Jun 1998 Cover: 2.95 **NM** value: **Cover or less**
Circ: Diamd. preorders: **29,989**

14 ❑ Sep 1998 Cover: 2.95 **NM** value: **Cover or less**
Circ: Diamd. preorders: **27,763**
• Aftershock

15 ❑ Dec 1998 Cover: 2.95 **NM** value: **Cover or less**
Circ: Diamd. preorders: **28,250**
Road to No Man's Land • team-up issue ★ Appearance of Man-Bat. ★ Appearance of Green Lantern. ★ Appearance of Question. ★ Appearance of Oracle.

16 ❑ Mar 1999 Cover: 2.95 **NM** value: **Cover or less**
Circ: Diamd. preorders: **28,716**
Two Down • No Man's Land **A:** Damian Scott; Jason Pearson **W:** Scott Beatty; Greg Rucka ★ Appearance of Renee Montoya. ★ Appearance of Batgirl. ★ Appearance of Two Face.

17 ❑ Jun 1999 Cover: 2.95 **NM** value: **Cover or less**
Circ: Diamd. preorders: **32,743**
Little Bat Lost; Turn On, Tune In, Freak Out; Identity Crisis • No Man's Land;Man-Bat's child **A:** Bill Sienkiewicz; Graham Nolan; Pascal Alixe; Eduardo Barreto **W:** Scott Beatty; Chris Renaud; Dafydd Wyn

18 ❑ Sep 1999 Cover: 2.95 **NM** value: **Cover or less**
Circ: Diamd. preorders: **34,086**
Spiritual Currency • No Man's Land **A:** Dale Eaglesham **W:** Devin Grayson

19 ❑ Dec 1999 Cover: 2.95 **NM** value: **Cover or less**
Circ: Diamd. preorders: **29,810**
Got a Date with an Angel; Rapscallions; The Penny Plunderers **A:** Eric Battle; Graham Nolan; Javier Pulido **W:** Graham Nolan; Joseph Harris; Steve Englehart

20 ❑ Mar 2000 Cover: 2.95 **NM** value: **Cover or less**
Circ: Diamd. preorders: **27,322**
Whippersnappers of Mass Destruction; Photo Finish; The Rage of Angels **A:** Yvel Guichet; Dean Zachary; Mshindo **W:** Scott Beatty; Devin Grayson; Ian Edginton

21 ❑ Jun 2000 Cover: 2.95 **NM** value: **Cover or less**
Circ: Diamd. preorders: **28,557**

22 ❑ Sep 2000 Cover: 2.95 **NM** value: **Cover or less**
Circ: Diamd. preorders: **25,601**
Pay the Ferryman; Cry, Uncle; Daughter of the Demon **A:** Jordan Raskin; Rodolfo DaMaggio; Gordon Purchell **W:** Chuck Dixon; Christopher Gordon; Darren Vincenzo; Tom Sniegoski

23 ❑ Dec 2000 Cover: 2.95 **NM** value: **Cover or less**
Circ: Diamd. preorders: **24,814**
The Bomb, the Bull, the Butler & the Bat; Automotive; The Mimic; The Many Foes of Batman Pinup **A:** Bo Hampton; Paul Ryan; Kevin Nowlan; Cam Smith **W:** Michael Jan Friedman; Kevin Nowlan; Doug Moench; Jay Faerber

BATMAN CHRONICLES GALLERY, THE DC

1 ❑ May 1997 Cover: 3.50 **NM** value: **Cover or less**
Circ: Diamd. preorders: **18,744**
• pin-ups

BATMAN CHRONICLES: THE GAUNTLET DC

1 ❑ 1997 Cover: 4.95 **NM** value: **Cover or less**
Circ: Diamd. preorders: **36,716**
No issue number. • prestige format. • 1st Robin solo adventure

BATMAN: COLLECTED LEGENDS OF THE DARK KNIGHT DC

Bk 1❑ Cover: 12.95 **NM** value: **Cover or less**

BATMAN: CONTAGION DC

Bk 1❑ Cover: 12.95 **NM** value: **Cover or less**
• collects Batman titles crossover

CGC-graded: Multiply prices above by **33 for 9.9 M** • **16 for 9.8 NM/M** • **7 for 9.6 NM+** • **5 for 9.4 NM** • **2.5 for 9.2 NM-** • **1.5 for 9.0 VF/NM**

BATMAN: CRIMSON MIST — DC

1 ❑ Cover: 24.95 **NM value: Cover or less**
Crimson Mist • Elseworlds story;Preceded by Batman and Dracula: Red Rain and Bloodstorm **A:** Kelley Jones **W:** Doug Moench

1/LE❑ Cover: 39.95 **NM value: Cover or less**
hardcover. Crimson Mist • Elseworlds story;Preceded by Batman and Dracula: Red Rain and Bloodstorm **A:** Kelley Jones **W:** Doug Moench

BATMAN/DAREDEVIL — DC

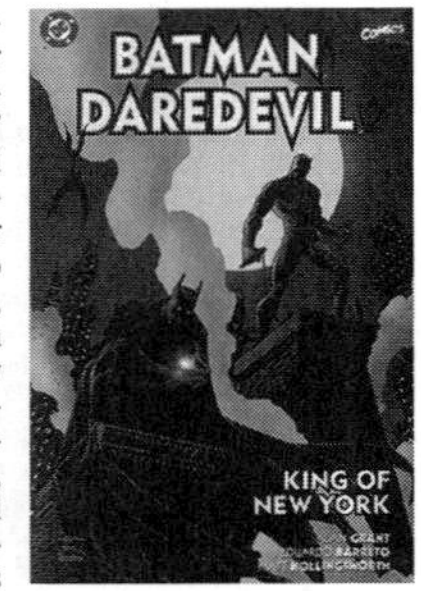

This joint publishing venture reteams two heroes first seen together in 1997's Daredevil/Batman one-shot. Marvel's "Man without Fear" journeys to Gotham City on the trail of Catwoman, who has stolen a detailed file on New York's premier crime-lord, the Kingpin. Hoping to track the thief back to her employer, DD has an inevitable confrontation with Gotham's Dark Knight. They reluctantly find themselves working together against one of Batman's most bizarre and deadly foes, The Scarecrow, whose powerful fear gas renders most people completely helpless and sometimes even causes death.

The Scarecrow has set his sights on the Kingpin's criminal empire and he'll do anything it takes to get it. Starting a massive gangland war is just the first step in The Scarecrow's plan to make himself the King of New York. Unleashing his gas on the city's millions of unsuspecting citizens is his ultimate, terrifying goal.

1 ❑ Jan 2000 Cover: 5.95 **NM value: Cover or less**
Circ: Diamd. preorders: **38,925**
King of New York **A:** Eduardo Barreto **W:** Alan Grant

BATMAN: DARK ALLEGIANCES — DC

1 ❑ 1996 Cover: 5.95 **NM value: Cover or less**
A: Howard Chaykin **W:** Howard Chaykin

BATMAN: DARK JOKER-THE WILD — DC

Bk 1❑ Cover: 9.95 **NM value: Cover or less**
Circ: CapCity orders: **4,450**
• Elseworlds story

Bk 1/HC❑ Cover: 24.95 **NM value: Cover or less**
hardcover.

BATMAN: DARK KNIGHT ADVENTURES — DC

1 ❑ Cover: 7.95 **NM value: Cover or less**

BATMAN: DARK KNIGHT DYNASTY — DC

1 ❑ Cover: 14.95 **NM value: Cover or less**
Dark Past; Dark Present; Dark Future • nn, Elseworlds story **A:** Bill Sienkiewicz; Gary Frank; Scott McDaniel; Cam Smith; Scott Hampton **W:** Mike W. Barr

1/HC❑ Cover: 24.95 **NM value: Cover or less**
No issue number. nn, Hardcover. Dark Past; Dark Present; Dark Future • Elseworlds story **A:** Bill Sienkiewicz; Gary Frank; Scott McDaniel; Cam Smith; Scott Hampton **W:** Mike W. Barr

1/SC❑ Cover: 24.95 **NM value: Cover or less**
hardcover.

BATMAN: DARK KNIGHT GALLERY — DC

1 ❑ Jan 1996 Cover: 3.50 **NM value: Cover or less**
Circ: CapCity orders: **15,975**
• pin-ups **A:** Scott Hanna; Kieron Dwyer; Kelley Jones; Bill Sienkiewicz; Gary Frank; Mike Parobeck; Jim Balent; Mark Farmer; Ray McCarthy; Wayne Faucher; Grham Nolan

BATMAN: DARK KNIGHT OF THE ROUND TABLE — DC

1 ❑ ca. 1999 Cover: 4.95 **NM value: Cover or less**
Circ: Diamd. preorders: **28,240**
• prestige format. • Elseworlds story

2 ❑ ca. 1999 Cover: 4.95 **NM value: Cover or less**
Circ: Diamd. preorders: **25,808**
• prestige format. • Elseworlds story **A:** Dick Giordano **W:** Bob Layton

BATMAN: DARK VICTORY — DC

0 ❑ ca. 1999 **NM value: 1.00**
• **CGC:** 2 graded, best 8.5
• Wizard giveaway. **A:** Tim Sale **W:** Jeph Loeb

1 ❑ Dec 1999 Cover: 4.95 **NM value: Cover or less**
Circ: Diamd. preorders: **57,115 • CGC:** 5 graded, best 9.8
• prestige format. War **A:** Tim Sale **W:** Jeph Loeb

2 ❑ Jan 2000 Cover: 2.95 **NM value: Cover or less**
Circ: Diamd. preorders: **50,689 • CGC:** 1 graded, best 9.4
cardstock cover. **A:** Tim Sale **W:** Jeph Loeb

3 ❑ Feb 2000 Cover: 2.95 **NM value: Cover or less**
Circ: Diamd. preorders: **55,427**
cardstock cover. **A:** Tim Sale **W:** Jeph Loeb

4 ❑ Mar 2000 Cover: 2.95 **NM value: Cover or less**
Circ: Diamd. preorders: **50,795**
cardstock cover. **A:** Tim Sale **W:** Jeph Loeb

5 ❑ Apr 2000 Cover: 2.95 **NM value: Cover or less**
Circ: Diamd. preorders: **48,564**
cardstock cover. Love **A:** Tim Sale **W:** Jeph Loeb

6 ❑ May 2000 Cover: 2.95 **NM value: Cover or less**
Circ: Diamd. preorders: **49,723**
cardstock cover. Hate **A:** Tim Sale **W:** Jeph Loeb

7 ❑ Jun 2000 Cover: 2.95 **NM value: Cover or less**
Circ: Diamd. preorders: **49,656**
cardstock cover. **A:** Tim Sale **W:** Jeph Loeb

8 ❑ Jul 2000 Cover: 2.95 **NM value: Cover or less**
Circ: Diamd. preorders: **50,032**
cardstock cover. Battle **A:** Tim Sale **W:** Jeph Loeb

9 ❑ Aug 2000 Cover: 2.95 **NM value: Cover or less**
Circ: Diamd. preorders: **50,719**
cardstock cover. **A:** Tim Sale **W:** Jeph Loeb

10 ❑ Sep 2000 Cover: 2.95 **NM value: Cover or less**
Circ: Diamd. preorders: **50,020**
cardstock cover. Justice **A:** Tim Sale **W:** Jeph Loeb

11 ❑ Oct 2000 Cover: 2.95 **NM value: Cover or less**
Circ: Diamd. preorders: **46,927**
cardstock cover. Passion **A:** Tim Sale **W:** Jeph Loeb

12 ❑ Nov 2000 Cover: 2.95 **NM value: Cover or less**
Circ: Diamd. preorders: **47,560**
cardstock cover. Revenge **A:** Tim Sale **W:** Jeph Loeb

13 ❑ Dec 2000 Cover: 4.95 **NM value: Cover or less**
Circ: Diamd. preorders: **47,161 • CGC:** 3 graded, best 9.8
• prestige format. Peace **A:** Tim Sale **W:** Jeph Loeb

BATMAN: DAY OF JUDGMENT — DC

1 ❑ Nov 1999 Cover: 3.95 **NM value: Cover or less**
Circ: Diamd. preorders: **40,789**
Original Gangsters **A:** Dean Zachary **W:** Scott Beatty

BATMAN/DEADMAN: DEATH AND GLORY — DC

1 ❑ Cover: 12.95 **NM value: Cover or less**
A: John Estes **W:** James Robinson

BATMAN: DEATH OF INNOCENTS — DC

IBatman faces enemies that even he may be powerless to defeat. These enemies kill indiscriminately. It makes no difference whether the victims are adults or children, men or women. These enemies can't be seen until it is too late. The enemies are land mines.

Bruce Wayne travels to Kravia, a war-torn country in Europe, to find the missing daughter of one of his employees. Her father was killed when his vehicle ran over a land mine, and, although she escaped injury, she became lost afterward. Batman must face the danger of being in the middle of a civil war and the possibility that any step he takes could be his last.

This one-shot special was created to draw attention to the hazard of land mines, which can maim and kill innocents long after any war is over.

1 ❑ Dec 1996 Cover: 3.95 **NM value: Cover or less**
Circ: Direct Market orders: **49,241**
• one-shot about the dangers of landmines and unexploded ordnance **A:** Joe Staton; Bill Sienkiewicz(inks) **W:** Denny O'Neil

BATMAN/DEMON — DC

1 ❑ 1996 Cover: 4.95 **NM value: Cover or less**
No issue number. • prestige format one-shot **A:** David Roach; Brian Stelfreeze(cover) **W:** Alan Grant

BATMAN/DEMON: A TRAGEDY — DC

1 ❑ Cover: 5.95 **NM value: Cover or less**
A: Jim Murray **W:** Alan Grant

BATMAN: DIGITAL JUSTICE — DC

1990's Digital Justice was a tour de force for computer-generated comics. Drawing from Mike Saenz' earlier work on First Comics' Shatter, artist Pepe Moreno spent more than a year creating one of the first graphic novels to be completely developed on a computer.

Digital Justice's storyline matches the series' high-tech origins and style. Many years in the future, Gotham will have become a sprawling metropolis, watched over by a vast network of computers, which will control everything from ATM machines to the police force. It was meant to be a techno-utopia, but someone has thrown a monkey wrench into the works. Police robots are committing murder. Corruption is ruining the system. Behind it all is The Joker, who now lives on in the form of a devilish computer virus. To stop him, a descendent of James Gordon will have to revive the role of a legend — and Batman will live again!

1 ❑ Cover: 24.95 **NM value: Cover or less**
Circ: CapCity orders: **32,450**
hardcover.

BATMAN: DOA — DC

1 ❑ Jan 2000 Cover: 6.95 **NM value: Cover or less**
Circ: Diamd. preorders: **24,347**
A: Bob Hall **W:** Bob Hall

BATMAN: DREAMLAND — DC

1 ❑ Jul 2000 Cover: 5.95 **NM value: Cover or less**
Circ: Diamd. preorders: **23,112**
A: Norm Breyfogle **W:** Norm Breyfogle; Alan Grant

BATMAN: EGO — DC

1 ❑ Oct 2000 Cover: 6.95 **NM value: Cover or less**
Circ: Diamd. preorders: **20,379**
A: Darwyn Cooke **W:** Darwyn Cooke

BATMAN FAMILY, THE — DC

This anthology series showcased two of Batman's partners, Batgirl and Robin, dubbing them The Dynamite Duo in team-up stories. In addition, each issue reprints several stories involving other characters in the family. These ranged from copycat versions of The Caped Crusader, such as Batwoman, to major characters that got their start in the Batman titles, such as Elongated Man and Hawkman. Later issues featured solo stories of The Huntress.

In their team-ups, the "Boy Wonder" and the "Dominoed Daredoll" were portrayed as adult heroes, not young sidekicks. Barbara Gordon is a congresswoman, while Dick Grayson pursues his college education. These stories take place before his adventures in The New Titans and as Nightwing.

Although the series only lasted for 20 issues, the digest concept was continued for a while in Detective Comics beginning with #481 (Dec 78). DC put out several other similar titles during the late 70s, including Superman Family and Super-Team Family.

1 ❑ Oct 1975 Cover: 0.50 **NM value: 14.00**
• **CGC:** 14 graded, best 9.4

2 ❑ Dec 1975 Cover: 0.50 **NM value: 10.00**
• **CGC:** 2 graded, best 9.8

3 ❑ Feb 1976 Cover: 0.50 **NM value: 7.00**
• **CGC:** 3 graded, best 9.0

4 ❑ Apr 1976 Cover: 0.50 **NM value: 7.00**
• **CGC:** 4 graded, best 9.4
Batgirl: Cage Me or Kill Me!; Robin: Robin's Very White Christmas!; Batman: Batman Meets Fatman; Batman: The Secret War of the Phantom General **A:** Janet L. Hetherington; Carmine Infantino; Pablo Marcos; Jose Delbo; Joe Giella; Vince Colletta **W:** Bob Kane; Bob Rozakis; Elliott S! Maggin; John Broome ★ Appearance of Fatman.

5 ❑ Jun 1976 Cover: 0.50 **NM value: 7.00**
• **CGC:** 7 graded, best 9.4

6 ❑ Aug 1976 Cover: 0.50 **NM value: 7.00**
• **CGC:** 1 graded, best 8.5

7 ❑ Sep 1976 Cover: 0.50 **NM value: 6.00**
• **CGC:** 1 graded, best 8.5

8 ❑ Nov 1976 Cover: 0.50 **NM value: 6.00**
• **CGC:** 1 graded, best 7.0

9 ❑ Jan 1977 Cover: 0.50 **NM value: 7.00**
• **CGC:** 1 graded, best 9.4
★ Appearance of Duela Dent.

10 ❑ Mar 1977 Cover: 0.50 **NM value: 7.00**
• **CGC:** 1 graded, best 9.4

11 ❑ May 1977 Cover: 0.50 **NM value: 5.00**

12 ❑ Jul 1977 Cover: 0.60 **NM value: 5.00**

13 ❑ Sep 1977 Cover: 0.60 **NM value: 5.00**
★ Versus Outsider, A: Man-Bat.

14 ❑ Oct 1977 Cover: 0.60 **NM value: 5.00**

15 ❑ Dec 1977 Cover: 0.60 **NM value: 5.00**

16 ❑ Feb 1978 Cover: 0.60 **NM value: 5.00**

17 ❑ Apr 1978 Cover: 1.00 **NM value: 6.00**

18 ❑ Jun 1978 Cover: 1.00 **NM value: 6.00**

19 ❑ Aug 1978 Cover: 1.00 **NM value: 6.00**

20 ❑ Oct 1978 Cover: 1.00 **NM value: 6.00**
• **CGC:** 1 graded, best 9.4
final issue.

BATMAN: FEATURING TWO-FACE AND THE RIDDLER — DC

Bk 1❑ Cover: 12.95 **NM value: Cover or less**
• Trade Paperback. • collects Batman #179, Annual #14, Detective Comics #66, 68, 140, 377, Secret Origins Special #1

BATMAN FOREVER: THE OFFICIAL COMIC ADAPTATION OF THE WARNER BROS. MOTION PICTURE — DC

1 ❑ 1995 Cover: 3.95 **NM value: Cover or less**
Circ: CapCity orders: **11,475**
No issue number.

1/PR❑ Cover: 5.95 **NM value: Cover or less**
Circ: CapCity orders: **21,350**
No issue number. • movie adaptation, prestige format

BATMAN: FORTUNATE SON — DC

1 ❑ Cover: 24.95 **NM value: Cover or less**
A: Gene Ha **W:** Gerard Jones

BATMAN: FOUR OF A KIND — DC

Bk 1❑ Cover: 14.95 **NM value: Cover or less**
No issue number. • Trade Paperback. • collects Batman Annual #19, Batman: Legends of the Dark Knight Annual #5, Batman: Shadow of the Bat Annual #3, and Detective Comics Annual #8 **A:** Kieron Dwyer; Brian Apthorp; Bret Blevins; Stan Woch; Mike Manley; Quique Alcatena **W:** Chuck Dixon; Alan Grant; Doug Moench ★ Origin of Scarecrow, Riddler, Man-Bat, Poison Ivy.

BATMAN: FULL CIRCLE — DC

1 ❑ Cover: 5.95 **NM value: 6.00**
Circ: CapCity orders: **42,700 • CGC:** 1 graded, best 9.4
No issue number. • prestige format. **A:** Alan Davis **W:** Mike W. Barr

BATMAN GALLERY, THE — DC

1 ❑ Cover: 2.95 **NM value: Cover or less**
Circ: CapCity orders: **36,950**

Other grades: Multiply prices above by **1.5 for Mint • 2/3 for Very Fine • 1/3 for Fine • 1/5 for Very Good • 1/8 for Good**

A: Murphy Anderson; Todd McFarlane; George Pérez; Dick Giordano; Joe Kubert; Brian Bolland; Frank Miller; Neal Adams; Walt Simonson; Car; Carmine Infantion

BATMAN: GCPD DC

1 ❑ Aug 1996 Cover: 2.25 **NM** value: **Cover or less**
Model Citizens **A:** Jim Aparo; Bill Sienkiewicz(inks) **W:** Chuck Dixon

2 ❑ Sep 1996 Cover: 2.25 **NM** value: **Cover or less**
A: Jim Aparo; Bill Sienkiewicz(inks) **W:** Chuck Dixon

3 ❑ Oct 1996 Cover: 2.25 **NM** value: **Cover or less**
This Year's Murder **A:** Jim Aparo; Bill Sienkiewicz(inks) **W:** Chuck Dixon

4 ❑ Nov 1996 Cover: 2.25 **NM** value: **Cover or less**
Circ: Diamd. preorders: **31,648**
Mortl Remains **A:** Jim Aparo; Bill Sienkiewicz(inks) **W:** Chuck Dixon

BATMAN: GHOSTS DC

1 ❑ 1995 Cover: 4.95 **NM** value: **Cover or less**
No issue number. A Tale Of Halloween In Gotham City • prestige format one-shot **A:** Greg Wright **W:** Jeph Loeb; Tim Sale

BATMAN: GORDON OF GOTHAM DC

Denny O'Neil has had a long, prolific career in comics. Although he has scripted countless adventures of Batman, his work really shines when he explores the more human characters of Gotham.

Batman: Gordon of Gotham is a nicely executed cop story, following a young patrolman named James Gordon (later Commissioner Gordon), as he tries to do his best in a police department racked by corruption. It begins when his partner, Sgt. Davidson, tries to bust the head of a local hippie. Gordon stops him, then makes the mistake of "making waves" by reporting the abusive conduct.

Gordon knows Davidson is a bad cop, but he doesn't know how bad. Davidson — and many others in the department — are on the take. And when Gordon began to uncover their scheme, the bad cops decide to set Gordon up — for murder!

1 ❑ Jun 1998 Cover: 1.95 **NM** value: **Cover or less**
Circ: Diamd. preorders: **29,696**
Dumb as a Rock **A:** Dick Giordano; Klaus Janson **W:** Denny O'Neil

2 ❑ Jul 1998 Cover: 1.95 **NM** value: **Cover or less**
Circ: Diamd. preorders: **25,522**
A: Dick Giordano; Klaus Janson **W:** Denny O'Neil

3 ❑ Aug 1998 Cover: 1.95 **NM** value: **Cover or less**
Circ: Diamd. preorders: **24,515**
To Al Capone... **A:** Dick Giordano; Klaus Janson **W:** Denny O'Neil

4 ❑ Sep 1998 Cover: 1.95 **NM** value: **Cover or less**
Circ: Diamd. preorders: **21,418**
A: Dick Giordano; Klaus Janson **W:** Denny O'Neil

BATMAN: GORDON'S LAW DC

1 ❑ Dec 1996 Cover: 1.95 **NM** value: **Cover or less**
Circ: Direct Market orders: **41,000**
Dirty Deal **A:** Klaus Janson **W:** Chuck Dixon

2 ❑ Jan 1997 Cover: 1.95 **NM** value: **Cover or less**
Circ: Direct Market orders: **33,875**
Suspicious Minds **A:** Klaus Janson **W:** Chuck Dixon

3 ❑ Feb 1997 Cover: 1.95 **NM** value: **Cover or less**
Circ: Diamd. preorders: **29,434**
A: Klaus Janson **W:** Chuck Dixon

4 ❑ Mar 1997 Cover: 1.95 **NM** value: **Cover or less**
Circ: Diamd. preorders: **27,526**
A: Klaus Janson **W:** Chuck Dixon

BATMAN: GOTHAM ADVENTURES DC

1 ❑ Jun 1998 Cover: 2.95 **NM** value: **3.00**
Circ: Diamd. preorders: **28,373 • CGC:** 1 graded, best 9.6
• based on animated series, Joker has a price on his head

2 ❑ Jul 1998 Cover: 1.95 **NM** value: **2.50**
A: Rick Burchett **W:** Ty Templeton ★ Versus Two-Face.

3 ❑ Aug 1998 Cover: 1.95 **NM** value: **2.50**
Circ: Diamd. preorders: **24,312**
cover is toy package mock-up. Just Another Day **A:** Rick Burchett **W:** Ty Templeton

4 ❑ Sep 1998 Cover: 1.99 **NM** value: **2.50**
Circ: Diamd. preorders: **22,880**
A: Rick Burchett **W:** Ty Templeton ★ Versus Catwoman.

5 ❑ Oct 1998 Cover: 1.99 **NM** value: **2.50**
Circ: Diamd. preorders: **22,559**
A: Rick Burchett **W:** Ty Templeton

6 ❑ Nov 1998 Cover: 1.99 **NM** value: **2.50**
Circ: Diamd. preorders: **21,761**
A: Rick Burchett **W:** Ty Templeton ★ Appearance of Deadman.

7 ❑ Dec 1998 Cover: 1.99 **NM** value: **2.50**
Circ: Diamd. preorders: **20,776**
Dagger's Secret **A:** Rick Burchett **W:** Ty Templeton

8 ❑ Jan 1999 Cover: 1.99 **NM** value: **2.50**
Circ: Diamd. preorders: **20,298**
A: Rick Burchett **W:** Ty Templeton ★ 1st Appearance of Hunchback. ★ Appearance of Batgirl.

9 ❑ Feb 1999 Cover: 1.99 **NM** value: **2.50**
Circ: Diamd. preorders: **19,532**
A: Rick Burchett **W:** Ty Templeton ★ Appearance of League of Assassins, Batgirl. ★ Versus Sensei.

10 ❑ Mar 1999 Cover: 1.99 **NM** value: **2.50**
Circ: Diamd. preorders: **19,579 • CGC:** 1 graded, best 8.0
A: Rick Burchett **W:** Ty Templeton ★ Appearance of Joker, Nightwing, Harley Quinn, Robin III (Timothy Drake).

11 ❑ Apr 1999 Cover: 1.99 **NM** value: **2.00**
Circ: Diamd. preorders: **18,388**
A: Rick Burchett **W:** Ty Templeton ★ Appearance of Riddler. ★ Versus Riddler.

12 ❑ May 1999 Cover: 1.99 **NM** value: **2.00**
Circ: Diamd. preorders: **18,697**
★ Versus Two-Face.

13 ❑ Jun 1999 Cover: 1.99 **NM** value: **2.00**
Circ: Diamd. preorders: **19,735**
The End **A:** Rick Burchett **W:** Kelley Puckett ★ Appearance of final.

14 ❑ Jul 1999 Cover: 1.99 **NM** value: **2.00**
Circ: Diamd. preorders: **19,758**
Masks of Love **A:** Craig Rousseau **W:** Ty Templeton ★ Versus Harley Quinn.

15 ❑ Aug 1999 Cover: 1.99 **NM** value: **2.00**
Circ: Diamd. preorders: **18,957**
Cash 'n the Hood! **A:** Tim Levins **W:** Scott Peterson ★ Appearance of Bane. ★ Versus Venom.

16 ❑ Sep 1999 Cover: 1.99 **NM** value: **2.00**
Circ: Diamd. preorders: **18,845**
Captive Audience • Alfred is kidnapped **A:** Craig Rousseau **W:** Scott Peterson

17 ❑ Oct 1999 Cover: 1.99 **NM** value: **2.00**
Circ: Diamd. preorders: **18,319**
Daddy Dearest **A:** Tim Levins **W:** Scott Peterson

18 ❑ Nov 1999 Cover: 1.99 **NM** value: **2.00**
Circ: Diamd. preorders: **17,635**
Like a Bat Outta Gotham **A:** Craig Rousseau **W:** Scott Peterson ★ Appearance of Man-Bat.

19 ❑ Dec 1999 Cover: 1.99 **NM** value: **2.00**
Circ: Diamd. preorders: **17,514**
W: Scott Peterson

20 ❑ Jan 2000 Cover: 1.99 **NM** value: **2.00**
Circ: Diamd. preorders: **16,514**
...And Oh So Delicious! **A:** Tim Levins **W:** Scott Peterson

21 ❑ Feb 2000 Cover: 1.99 **NM** value: **2.00**
Circ: Diamd. preorders: **16,235**
How the World Goes! **A:** Tim Levins **W:** Scott Peterson

22 ❑ Mar 2000 Cover: 1.99 **NM** value: **2.00**
Circ: Diamd. preorders: **16,007**
W: Scott Peterson

23 ❑ Apr 2000 Cover: 1.99 **NM** value: **2.00**
Circ: Diamd. preorders: **15,151**
W: Scott Peterson

24 ❑ May 2000 Cover: 1.99 **NM** value: **2.00**
Circ: Diamd. preorders: **15,397**
Missed Connections **A:** Tim Levins **W:** Scott Peterson

25 ❑ Jun 2000 Cover: 1.99 **NM** value: **2.00**
Circ: Diamd. preorders: **16,003**
...Recognized, in Flashes, and With Glory... **A:** Tim Levins **W:** Scott Peterson

26 ❑ Jul 2000 Cover: 1.99 **NM** value: **2.00**
Circ: Diamd. preorders: **15,485**

27 ❑ Aug 2000 Cover: 1.99 **NM** value: **2.00**
Circ: Diamd. preorders: **15,941**

28 ❑ Sep 2000 Cover: 1.99 **NM** value: **Cover or less**
Circ: Diamd. preorders: **15,586**

29 ❑ Oct 2000 Cover: 1.99 **NM** value: **Cover or less**
Circ: Diamd. preorders: **15,275**
Six Hours to Kill **A:** Joe Staton **W:** Chuck Dixon

30 ❑ Nov 2000 Cover: 1.99 **NM** value: **Cover or less**
Circ: Diamd. preorders: **14,389**
Deals **A:** Tim Levins **W:** Scott Peterson

31 ❑ Dec 2000 Cover: 1.99 **NM** value: **Cover or less**
Circ: Diamd. preorders: **14,282**
A: Terry Beatty **W:** Ty Templeton ★ Appearance of Joker.

32 ❑ Jan 2001 Cover: 1.99 **NM** value: **Cover or less**
Circ: Diamd. preorders: **13,868**
The Remote Controller **A:** Tim Levins **W:** Scott Peterson

33 ❑ Feb 2001 Cover: 1.99 **NM** value: **Cover or less**
Circ: Diamd. preorders: **13,889**
World Without Batman **A:** Brad Rader **W:** Scott Peterson

34 ❑ Mar 2001 Cover: 1.99 **NM** value: **Cover or less**
Circ: Diamd. preorders: **13,320**
When in Rome **A:** Tim Levins **W:** Scott Peterson

35 ❑ Apr 2001 Cover: 1.99 **NM** value: **Cover or less**
Circ: Diamd. preorders: **13,383**
Stepping Forward **A:** Tim Levins **W:** Scott Peterson

36 ❑ May 2001 Cover: 1.99 **NM** value: **Cover or less**
Circ: Diamd. preorders: **13,485**
A: Tim Levins **W:** Scott Peterson

37 ❑ Jun 2001 Cover: 1.99 **NM** value: **Cover or less**
Circ: Diamd. preorders: **13,561**
Images **A:** Tim Levins **W:** Scott Peterson ★ Appearance of Joker.

38 ❑ Jul 2001 Cover: 1.99 **NM** value: **Cover or less**
Circ: Diamd. preorders: **13,537**

39 ❑ Aug 2001 Cover: 1.99 **NM** value: **Cover or less**
Circ: Diamd. preorders: **13,481**

40 ❑ Sep 2001 Cover: 1.99 **NM** value: **Cover or less**
Circ: Diamd. preorders: **13,993**

There are two different pricing tiers in the modern comic-book hobby. **The prices seen above** are the prices we have seen **loose copies** of these issues reliably fetch in a variety of environments. Condition alters the price by the fractions seen on the bar on the bottom of left-hand pages of this book. **Comics graded by CGC** usually sell for more. Use the guide on the bottom of right-hand pages of this book to estimate what copies have brought on eBay.

BATMAN: GOTHAM BY GASLIGHT DC

What if Batman had been active in the late 19th Century? That's the question asked by Gotham by Gaslight, the first installation in DC's Elseworlds line.

An arch-criminal, broadly suggested to be Jack the Ripper, travels to Gotham City from London. Unfortunately for him (and fortunately for Gotham's residents), there's a crazy millionaire in town who's been dressing up as a bat at night.

This is an interesting and stylish interpretation, but its success is to blame for what followed: what, to some, seemed an interminable number of unimaginative historical Elseworlds one-shots, with Superman fighting in the Civil War, etc. — JJM

1 ❑ Cover: 3.95 **NM** value: **4.00**
Circ: CapCity orders: **99,650 • CGC:** 3 graded, best 9.6
No issue number. One-shot. • prestige format. • first Elseworlds story;Victorian-era Batman;Prelude by Robert Bloch **A:** Mike Mignola; P. Craig Russell

BATMAN GOTHAM CITY SECRET FILES DC

1 ❑ Apr 2000 Cover: 4.95 **NM** value: **Cover or less**

BATMAN: GOTHAM KNIGHTS DC

1 ❑ Mar 2000 Cover: 2.50 **NM** value: **Cover or less**
Circ: Diamd. preorders: **51,264 • CGC:** 8 graded, best 9.8

2 ❑ Apr 2000 Cover: 2.50 **NM** value: **Cover or less**
Circ: Diamd. preorders: **41,084**
Down with the Ship **A:** Dale Eaglesham **W:** Devin Grayson

3 ❑ May 2000 Cover: 2.50 **NM** value: **Cover or less**
Circ: Diamd. preorders: **41,709**
Samsara, Part 1; Broken Nose **A:** Paul Pope; Paul Ryan **W:** Paul Pope; Devin Grayson

4 ❑ Jun 2000 Cover: 2.50 **NM** value: **Cover or less**
Circ: Diamd. preorders: **42,638**

5 ❑ Jul 2000 Cover: 2.50 **NM** value: **Cover or less**
Circ: Diamd. preorders: **42,511**

6 ❑ Aug 2000 Cover: 2.50 **NM** value: **Cover or less**
Circ: Diamd. preorders: **41,847**

7 ❑ Sep 2000 Cover: 2.50 **NM** value: **Cover or less**
Circ: Diamd. preorders: **40,677**
Oblation **A:** Paul Ryan **W:** Devin Grayson

8 ❑ Oct 2000 Cover: 2.50 **NM** value: **Cover or less**
Circ: Diamd. preorders: **38,032**
Transference, Part 1 **A:** Roger Robinson **W:** Devin Grayson

9 ❑ Nov 2000 Cover: 2.50 **NM** value: **Cover or less**
Circ: Diamd. preorders: **37,480**
Transference, Part 2 **A:** Roger Robinson **W:** Devin Grayson

10 ❑ Dec 2000 Cover: 2.50 **NM** value: **Cover or less**
Circ: Diamd. preorders: **36,618**
Transference, Part 3 **A:** Roger Robinson **W:** Devin Grayson

11 ❑ Jan 2001 Cover: 2.50 **NM** value: **Cover or less**
Circ: Diamd. preorders: **35,928**
Transference, Part 4 **A:** Roger Robinson **W:** Devin Grayson

12 ❑ Feb 2001 Cover: 2.50 **NM** value: **Cover or less**
Circ: Diamd. preorders: **37,640**
Damages **A:** Coy Turnbull **W:** Jen Van Meter

13 ❑ Mar 2001 Cover: 2.50 **NM** value: **Cover or less**
Circ: Diamd. preorders: **40,070**
Officer Down, Part 7 **A:** Rick Burchett **W:** Greg Rucka

14 ❑ Apr 2001 Cover: 2.50 **NM** value: **Cover or less**
Circ: Diamd. preorders: **35,492**
Sibling Rivalry **A:** Roger Robinson **W:** Devin Grayson

15 ❑ May 2001 Cover: 2.50 **NM** value: **Cover or less**
Circ: Diamd. preorders: **34,437**
Far From the Tree **A:** Roger Robinson **W:** Devin Grayson

16 ❑ Cover: 2.50 **NM** value: **Cover or less**
Circ: Diamd. preorders: **35,072**

17 ❑ Cover: 2.50 **NM** value: **Cover or less**
Circ: Diamd. preorders: **34,566 • CGC:** 1 graded, best 9.4

18 ❑ Cover: 2.50 **NM** value: **Cover or less**
Circ: Diamd. preorders: **35,335**

19 ❑ Cover: 2.50 **NM** value: **Cover or less**
Circ: Diamd. preorders: **35,876**

BATMAN: GOTHAM NOIR DC

1 ❑ May 2001 Cover: 6.95 **NM** value: **Cover or less**
Circ: Diamd. preorders: **19,016**
• Elseworlds **A:** Sean Phillips **W:** Ed Brubaker

BATMAN/GREEN ARROW: THE POISON TOMORROW DC

1 ❑ Cover: 5.95 **NM** value: **6.00**
Circ: CapCity orders: **21,700**
No issue number. • prestige format. **A:** Michael Netzer **W:** Denny O'Neil

Capital City orders are the actual sales of comic books by Capital City Distribution, once one of the largest U.S. sellers of comics to comics shops. Capital City's share of comics shop sales, while not known exactly, increases from around 10-20% in the mid-1980s to 30-35% in the mid-1990s. Capital City's share of comic books sold on newsstands (most Marvels and DCs) will be less.

CGC-graded: Multiply prices above by **33 for 9.9 M • 16 for 9.8 NM/M • 7 for 9.6 NM+ • 5 for 9.4 NM • 2.5 for 9.2 NM- • 1.5 for 9.0 VF/NM**

BATMAN/GRENDEL (1ST SERIES) DC / Comico

Things have been much too quiet for Grendel lately, so he goes to Gotham City in search of a challenge. Intrigued by that city's protector, Batman, he launches an involved plot to draw out The Caped Crusader.

Grendel's plot runs true to his cunning nature. Posing as The Riddler, he seeks to interfere with Bruce Wayne's shipment of the ancient Sphinx head. But, while Batman is not fooled by Grendel's Riddler impersonation, he has no idea what a deadly foe Grendel truly is.

Devil's Riddle brings Grendel into the DC universe for the first time. As expected, it's an exciting showdown, when the dark assassin meets the Dark Knight.

Note: the second issue of this series reversed titles, becoming "Grendel/Batman: Devil's Masque."

1 ❑ Cover: 4.95 **NM** value: **6.00**
Circ: CapCity orders: **51,900**
• prestige format. Devil's Riddle **A:** Matt Wagner

2 ❑ Cover: 4.95 **NM** value: **6.00**
Circ: CapCity orders: **46,700**
prestige format, cover indicates Grendel/Batman. Devil's Riddle • Index title: Grendel/Batman: Devil's Masque **A:** Matt Wagner

BATMAN/GRENDEL (2ND SERIES) DC / Dark Horse

1 ❑ Jun 1996 Cover: 4.95 **NM** value: **5.00**
• Batman/Grendel: Devil's Bones;prestige format crossover with Dark Horse;concludes in Grendel/Batman: Devil's Dance

2 ❑ Jul 1996 Cover: 4.95 **NM** value: **5.00**
• prestige format. • Grendel/Batman: Devil's Dance;continued from Batman/Grendel: Devil's Bones **A:** Matt Wagner **W:** Matt Wagner

BATMAN: HARLEY QUINN DC

1 ❑ ca. 1999 Cover: 5.95 **NM** value: **6.50**
Circ: Diamd. preorders: **55,173 • CGC:** 26 graded, best 9.9
No issue number. • prestige format. **A:** Yvel Guichet; Alex Ross(cover) **W:** Paul Dini

1-2 ❑ Cover: 5.95 **NM** value: **Cover or less**

BATMAN: HARVEST BREED DC

Bk 1/HC❑ Cover: 24.95 **NM** value: **Cover or less**
hardcover. **A:** George Pratt **W:** George Pratt

BATMAN: HAUNTED GOTHAM DC

1 ❑ Feb 2000 Cover: 4.95 **NM** value: **Cover or less**
Circ: Diamd. preorders: **32,319**
• prestige format. Hell's Hunting Ground • Elseworlds **A:** Kelley Jones **W:** Doug Moench

2 ❑ Mar 2000 Cover: 4.95 **NM** value: **Cover or less**
Circ: Diamd. preorders: **25,484**
• prestige format. • Elseworlds **A:** Kelley Jones **W:** Doug Moench

3 ❑ Apr 2000 Cover: 4.95 **NM** value: **Cover or less**
Circ: Diamd. preorders: **23,618**
• prestige format. Shattered Serpent • Elseworlds **A:** Kelley Jones **W:** Doug Moench

4 ❑ May 2000 Cover: 4.95 **NM** value: **Cover or less**
Circ: Diamd. preorders: **23,153**
• prestige format. • Elseworlds **A:** Kelley Jones **W:** Doug Moench

BATMAN: HAUNTED KNIGHT DC

1 ❑ Cover: 12.95 **NM** value: **Cover or less**
• Double-size. Fears; Madness; Ghosts • Collects Batman: Legends of the Dark Knight Halloween Special #1-3 **A:** Tim Sale **W:** Jeph Loeb

BATMAN/HELLBOY/STARMAN DC / Dark Horse

1 ❑ Jan 1999 Cover: 2.50 **NM** value: **Cover or less**
Gotham Gray Evil **A:** Mike Mignola **W:** James Robinson

1/Aut❑ Cover: 24.99 **NM** value: **Cover or less**
A: Mike Mignola **W:** James Robinson

2 ❑ Feb 1999 Cover: 2.50 **NM** value: **Cover or less**
A: Mike Mignola **W:** James Robinson ★ Appearance of Golden-Age Starman.

BATMAN: HOLLYWOOD KNIGHT DC

1 ❑ Apr 2001 Cover: 2.50 **NM** value: **Cover or less**
Circ: Diamd. preorders: **25,295**
Tinseltown Terror • Elseworlds **A:** Dick Giordano **W:** Bob Layton

2 ❑ May 2001 Cover: 2.50 **NM** value: **Cover or less**
Circ: Diamd. preorders: **22,711**
A Devil in the City of Angels • Elseworlds **A:** Dick Giordano **W:** Bob Layton

3 ❑ Jun 2001 Cover: 2.50 **NM** value: **Cover or less**
Circ: Diamd. preorders: **21,945**
• Elseworlds **A:** Dick Giordano **W:** Bob Layton

CGC price ratios appearing on the bottom of right-hand pages are for pre-1990 comic books "slabbed" by Comics Guaranty Corp.

They represent the median price offered on eBay above our printed prices for comics in each grade. These are only a guide; individual prices vary by interest in the issue and the number of CGC-graded copies on the market.

BATMAN: HOLY TERROR DC

This alternate-reality Batman story takes place in a world where Oliver Cromwell never lost his grip on power. As a result, Church and State were never separated in England, or later in the Americas. A totalitarian state arose in which homosexuals were murdered by the millions and sexual deviation was dealt with using brutal "medical treatments."

Bruce Wayne's parents were elite officials in the religious hierarchy, but they secretly helped regime's opposition. When they were discovered, a secret "Star Chamber" arranged for a murderer named Joe Chill to kill them in what was meant to look like a random act of street crime. Bruce Wayne would later discover the shocking truth behind his parents' death, vowing to fight the regime as a dark crusader, even while he served it as a religious minister.

A nice alternate history skillfully making use of the DC universe, and much fresher than many Elseworlds stories to follow.

1 ❑ Oct 1991 Cover: 4.95 **NM** value: **5.00**
Circ: CapCity orders: **42,600**
No issue number. One-shot. • prestige format. • Elseworlds **A:** Norm Breyfogle

BATMAN/HOUDINI: THE DEVIL'S WORKSHOP DC

1 ❑ Cover: 3.95 **NM** value: **4.50**
Circ: CapCity orders: **24,450**
No issue number. • prestige format. • Elseworlds

BATMAN/HUNTRESS: CRY FOR BLOOD DC

1 ❑ Jun 2000 Cover: 2.50 **NM** value: **Cover or less**
Circ: Diamd. preorders: **35,205**
A: Rick Burchett **W:** Greg Rucka

2 ❑ Jul 2000 Cover: 2.50 **NM** value: **Cover or less**
Circ: Diamd. preorders: **30,663**
A: Rick Burchett **W:** Greg Rucka

3 ❑ Aug 2000 Cover: 2.50 **NM** value: **Cover or less**
Circ: Diamd. preorders: **30,093**
A: Rick Burchett **W:** Greg Rucka ★ Appearance of Question.

4 ❑ Sep 2000 Cover: 2.50 **NM** value: **Cover or less**
Circ: Diamd. preorders: **29,568**
A: Rick Burchett **W:** Greg Rucka ★ Origin of The Huntress.

5 ❑ Oct 2000 Cover: 2.50 **NM** value: **Cover or less**
Circ: Diamd. preorders: **27,883**
A: Rick Burchett **W:** Greg Rucka

6 ❑ Nov 2000 Cover: 2.50 **NM** value: **Cover or less**
Circ: Diamd. preorders: **28,055**
A: Rick Burchett **W:** Greg Rucka

BATMAN: I, JOKER DC

1 ❑ Oct 1998 Cover: 4.95 **NM** value: **Cover or less**
Circ: Diamd. preorders: **32,104**
No issue number. One-shot. • prestige format. • Elseworlds **A:** Bob Hall **W:** Bob Hall

BATMAN: IN DARKEST KNIGHT DC

1 ❑ Cover: 4.95 **NM** value: **Cover or less**
No issue number. One-shot. • prestige format. • Elseworlds;Bruce Wayne as Green Lantern **A:** Jerry Bingham **W:** Mike W. Barr

BATMAN IN THE SEVENTIES DC

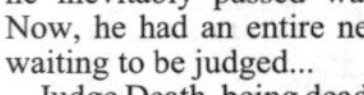

This too-cool trade paperback features tales from what many consider to be the Batman's second Golden Age, the 1970s. Having shed the camp trappings of the 1960s television series, The World's Greatest Detective returned to his darker roots, operating in the shadows of Gotham City and fighting an all-out war against crime in an effort to avenge the murder of his parents.

Here, readers will find exemplary work from such stalwarts as Denny O'Neil, Neal Adams, Frank Robbins, Irv Novick, Elliot S! Maggin, Mike Grell, Archie Goodwin, Alex Toth, Paul Levitz, Joe Staton, Dick Giordano, and Marshall Rogers — a virtual who's who of comic-book creators. And the stories? Well, there's the first appearance of the Batgirl-Robin team from Batman Family #1; the origin of the Huntress, the daughter of the Golden Age Batman and Catwoman; and the coming of Ra's al Ghul, one of The Dark Knight's most sinister foes. This is an incredible package, definitely worth the price of admission.

1 ❑ **NM** value: **19.95**

BATMAN IN THE SIXTIES DC

1 ❑ Cover: 19.95 **NM** value: **Cover or less**
• Batgirl appearnce;Introduction by Adam West★ Appearance of Bat-Mite, Joker, Clayface, Robin, Blockbuster, Poison Ivy.

BATMAN: JOKER'S APPRENTICE DC

1 ❑ May 1999 Cover: 3.95 **NM** value: **Cover or less**
Circ: Diamd. preorders: **28,410**
Joker's Apprentice **A:** Trevor Von Eeden; Trevor Von Eden **W:** C.J. Henderson

BATMAN: JOKER TIME DC

1 ❑ Cover: 4.95 **NM** value: **Cover or less**
Circ: Diamd. preorders: **27,303 • CGC:** 1 graded, best 9.8
• prestige format. **A:** Bob Hall **W:** Bob Hall

2 ❑ Cover: 4.95 **NM** value: **Cover or less**
Circ: Diamd. preorders: **25,855**
• prestige format. **A:** Bob Hall **W:** Bob Hall

3 ❑ Cover: 4.95 **NM** value: **Cover or less**
Circ: Diamd. preorders: **24,770 • CGC:** 1 graded, best 9.6
• prestige format. **A:** Bob Hall **W:** Bob Hall

BATMAN/JUDGE DREDD: DIE LAUGHING DC

1 ❑ Cover: 4.95 **NM** value: **Cover or less**
• prestige format. • Joker in Mega-City One **A:** Glenn Fabry **W:** Alan Grant; John Wagner

2 ❑ Cover: 4.95 **NM** value: **Cover or less**
• prestige format. • Joker in Mega-City One

BATMAN/JUDGE DREDD: JUDGMENT ON GOTHAM DC

In the first of the Batman/Judge Dredd crossovers, Judge Death has somehow found a way across the dimensions into Gotham City. For Judge Death, life itself was the source of all crime, and the sentence he inevitably passed was Death. Now, he had an entire new world waiting to be judged...

Judge Death, being dead himself, could not be killed. But luckily, Batman managed to force Death's spirit from its host body, temporarily ending the conflict. While investigating the body, however, Batman inadvertently triggered the dimensional transport device Death had used, flinging him into Judge Dredd's reality. Although the two tough crimefighters were bound to knock heads, especially since vigilantism is illegal in Mega-City One, they were forced to eventually join forces in order to stop Judge Death's latest rampage.

1 ❑ Cover: 5.95 **NM** value: **Cover or less**
Circ: CapCity orders: **45,650 • CGC:** 1 graded, best 9.8
No issue number. **A:** Simon Bisley **W:** Alan Grant

BATMAN/JUDGE DREDD: THE ULTIMATE RIDDLE DC

1 ❑ Cover: 4.95 **NM** value: **5.00**
No issue number. • prestige format. **A:** Dermot Power; Carl Critchlow **W:** Alan Grant; John Wagner

BATMAN/JUDGE DREDD: VENDETTA IN GOTHAM DC

1 ❑ Cover: 5.95 **NM** value: **6.00**
Circ: CapCity orders: **31,600**
No issue number. **A:** Cam Kennedy **W:** Alan Grant; John Wagner

BATMAN: KNIGHTSEND DC

Bk 1❑ Cover: 14.95 **NM** value: **Cover or less**
• Trade Paperback.

BATMAN: LEAGUE OF BATMEN DC

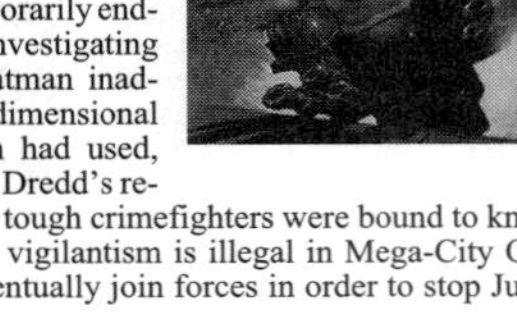
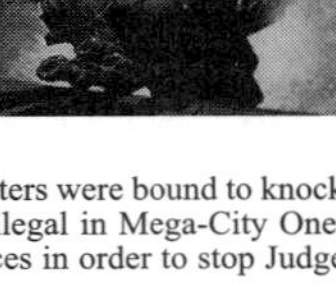

1 ❑ Cover: 5.95 **NM** value: **Cover or less**
Circ: Diamd. preorders: **22,626**
A: Mark D. Bright **W:** Doug Moench

2 ❑ Cover: 5.95 **NM** value: **Cover or less**
Circ: Diamd. preorders: **20,353 • CGC:** 1 graded, best 9.8
A: Mark D. Bright **W:** Doug Moench

BATMAN: LEGACY DC

Bk 1❑ Cover: 17.95 **NM** value: **Cover or less**
• Legacy storyline from the Batman titles **A:** Graham Nolan; Jim Balent; Staz Johnson; Mike Wieringo; Jim Aparo; Dave Taylor **W:** Chuck Dixon; Doug Moench

BATMAN: LEGEND OF THE DARK KNIGHT DC

1 ❑ Cover: 4.95 **NM** value: **Cover or less**
2 ❑ Cover: 4.95 **NM** value: **Cover or less**
3 ❑ Cover: 4.95 **NM** value: **Cover or less**
4 ❑ Cover: 4.95 **NM** value: **Cover or less**

BATMAN: LEGENDS OF THE DARK KNIGHT DC

Although it eventually became just another of the many Batman titles, Legends of the Dark Knight began by telling stories of Batman's earliest adventures, reinventing the legend in the process. With dark, impressionistic art and multi-issue storylines by such greats as Matt Wagner and Grant Morrison, Legends of the Dark Knight raises Batman from a costumed crime fighter to a mythic figure. He's the lone savior of Gotham, a city whose heart seems as dark as a cave; and, when he battles a villain such as Two-Face, he seems to be fighting, not just another bad-guy, but a symptom of the disease that has infected the city.

0 ❑ Oct 1994 Cover: 1.95 **NM** value: **2.50**

Other grades: Multiply prices above by **1.5 for Mint • 2/3 for Very Fine • 1/3 for Fine • 1/5 for Very Good • 1/8 for Good**

Circ: CapCity orders: **49,800** • **CGC:** 1 graded, best 9.6
Viewpoint **A:** Vince Giarrano

1 ❑ Nov 1989 Cover: 1.50 **NM** value: **4.00**
Circ: CapCity orders: **216,050** • **CGC:** 12 graded, best 9.6
Outer cover comes in four different colors (yellow, blue, orange, pink). The Shaman of Gotham, Part 1 • poster **A:** Ed Hannigan **W:** Denny O'Neil

2 ❑ Dec 1989 Cover: 1.50 **NM** value: **3.00**
Circ: CapCity orders: **155,650** • **CGC:** 2 graded, best 9.8
The Shaman of Gotham, Part 2 **A:** Ed Hannigan **W:** Denny O'Neil

3 ❑ Jan 1990 Cover: 1.00 **NM** value: **3.00**
Circ: CapCity orders: **126,900** • **CGC:** 2 graded, best 9.8
The Shaman of Gotham, Part 3 **A:** Ed Hannigan **W:** Denny O'Neil

4 ❑ Feb 1990 Cover: 1.50 **NM** value: **3.00**
Circ: CapCity orders: **125,550** • **CGC:** 1 graded, best 9.6
The Shaman of Gotham, Part 4 **A:** Ed Hannigan **W:** Denny O'Neil

5 ❑ Mar 1990 Cover: 1.50 **NM** value: **3.00**
Circ: CapCity orders: **126,200**
The Shaman of Gotham, Part 5 **A:** Ed Hannigan **W:** Denny O'Neil

6 ❑ Apr 1990 Cover: 1.50 **NM** value: **2.50**
Circ: CapCity orders: **106,650** • **CGC:** 1 graded, best 9.6
Gothic, Part 1 **A:** Klaus Janson **W:** Grant Morrison

7 ❑ May 1990 Cover: 1.50 **NM** value: **2.50**
Circ: CapCity orders: **95,750**
Gothic, Part 2 **A:** Klaus Janson **W:** Grant Morrison

8 ❑ Jun 1990 Cover: 1.50 **NM** value: **2.50**
Circ: CapCity orders: **84,950**
Gothic, Part 3 **A:** Klaus Janson **W:** Grant Morrison

9 ❑ Jul 1990 Cover: 1.50 **NM** value: **2.50**
Circ: CapCity orders: **81,000**
Gothic, Part 4 **A:** Klaus Janson **W:** Grant Morrison

10 ❑ Aug 1990 Cover: 1.50 **NM** value: **2.50**
Circ: CapCity orders: **74,850**
Gothic, Part 5 **A:** Klaus Janson **W:** Grant Morrison

11 ❑ Sep 1990 Cover: 1.50 **NM** value: **2.50**
Circ: CapCity orders: **72,450**
Prey, Part 1 **A:** Paul Gulacy; Tony DeZuniga

12 ❑ Oct 1990 Cover: 1.50 **NM** value: **2.50**
Circ: CapCity orders: **65,800** • **CGC:** 1 graded, best 9.6
Prey, Part 2 **A:** Paul Gulacy; Tony DeZuniga **W:** Doug Moench

13 ❑ Nov 1990 Cover: 1.50 **NM** value: **2.50**
Circ: CapCity orders: **61,250**
Prey, Part 3 **A:** Paul Gulacy; Tony DeZuniga

14 ❑ Dec 1990 Cover: 1.50 **NM** value: **2.50**
Circ: CapCity orders: **60,750**
Prey, Part 4 **A:** Paul Gulacy; Tony DeZuniga

15 ❑ Feb 1991 Cover: 1.50 **NM** value: **2.50**
Circ: CapCity orders: **59,350**
Prey, Part 5 **A:** Paul Gulacy; Tony DeZuniga **W:** Doug Moench

16 ❑ Mar 1991 Cover: 1.50 **NM** value: **3.50**
Circ: CapCity orders: **59,500**
Venom, Part 1 • Tie-in to Bane/KnightsEnd

17 ❑ Apr 1991 Cover: 1.50 **NM** value: **2.50**
Circ: CapCity orders: **55,650**
Venom, Part 2 • Tie-in to Bane/KnightsEnd

18 ❑ May 1991 Cover: 1.50 **NM** value: **2.50**
Circ: CapCity orders: **55,200**
Venom, Part 3 • Tie-in to Bane/KnightsEnd

19 ❑ Jun 1991 Cover: 1.50 **NM** value: **2.50**
Circ: CapCity orders: **55,250**
Venom, Part 4 • Tie-in to Bane/KnightsEnd

20 ❑ Jul 1991 Cover: 1.75 **NM** value: **2.50**
Circ: CapCity orders: **57,150**
Venom, Part 5 • Tie-in to Bane/KnightsEnd

21 ❑ Aug 1991 Cover: 1.75 **NM** value: **2.00**
Circ: CapCity orders: **59,250**
Faith, Part 1

22 ❑ Sep 1991 Cover: 1.75 **NM** value: **2.00**
Circ: CapCity orders: **57,900**
Faith, Part 2

23 ❑ Oct 1991 Cover: 1.75 **NM** value: **2.00**
Circ: CapCity orders: **57,250**
Faith, Part 3

24 ❑ Nov 1991 Cover: 1.75 **NM** value: **2.00**
Circ: CapCity orders: **55,400**
Flyer, Part 1 **A:** Gil Kane

25 ❑ Dec 1991 Cover: 1.75 **NM** value: **2.00**
Circ: CapCity orders: **53,500**
Flyer, Part 2 **A:** Gil Kane

26 ❑ Jan 1992 Cover: 1.75 **NM** value: **2.00**
Circ: CapCity orders: **51,600**
Flyer, Part 3 **A:** Gil Kane

27 ❑ Feb 1992 Cover: 1.75 **NM** value: **2.50**
Circ: CapCity orders: **46,850**
Destroyer, Part 2 • Gotham City Visions by Anton Furst feature

28 ❑ Mar 1992 Cover: 1.75 **NM** value: **2.00**
Circ: CapCity orders: **51,500**
Faces, Part 1 • Two-Face **A:** Matt Wagner

29 ❑ Apr 1992 Cover: 1.75 **NM** value: **2.00**
Circ: CapCity orders: **44,750**
Faces, Part 2 • Two-Face **A:** Matt Wagner

30 ❑ May 1992 Cover: 1.75 **NM** value: **2.00**
Circ: CapCity orders: **43,150**
Faces, Part 3 • Two-Face **A:** Matt Wagner

31 ❑ Jun 1992 Cover: 1.75 **NM** value: **2.00**
Circ: CapCity orders: **42,350**
Family **A:** Brent Anderson **W:** James D. Hudnall

32 ❑ Jun 1992 Cover: 1.75 **NM** value: **2.00**
Circ: CapCity orders: **42,150**
Blades; Blades, Part 1 **W:** James Robinson

33 ❑ Jul 1992 Cover: 1.75 **NM** value: **2.00**
Circ: CapCity orders: **42,200**
Blades; Blades, Part 2 **A:** Tim Sale **W:** James Robinson

34 ❑ Jul 1992 Cover: 1.75 **NM** value: **2.00**
Circ: CapCity orders: **42,100**
Blades; Blades, Part 3 **A:** Tim Sale **W:** James Robinson

35 ❑ Aug 1992 Cover: 1.75 **NM** value: **2.00**
Circ: CapCity orders: **44,200**
Destiny, Part 1 **A:** Bo Hampton **W:** Mark Kneece

36 ❑ Aug 1992 Cover: 1.75 **NM** value: **2.00**
Circ: CapCity orders: **44,200**
Destiny, Part 2 **A:** Bo Hampton **W:** Mark Kneece

37 ❑ Aug 1992 Cover: 1.75 **NM** value: **2.00**
Circ: CapCity orders: **38,500**
Mercy • Series continues as Batman: Legends of the Dark Knight **A:** Colin MacNeil **W:** Andy Lanning; Dan Abnett

38 ❑ Oct 1992 Cover: 1.75 **NM** value: **2.00**
Circ: CapCity orders: **41,450**
Legends of the Dark Mite **A:** Kevin O'Neill **W:** Alan Grant ★ Appearance of Bat-Mite.

39 ❑ Nov 1992 Cover: 1.75 **NM** value: **2.00**
Circ: CapCity orders: **36,900**
Mask, Part 1 **A:** Bryan Talbot

40 ❑ Dec 1992 Cover: 1.75 **NM** value: **2.00**
Circ: CapCity orders: **34,650**
Mask, Part 2 **A:** Bryan Talbot **W:** Bryan Talbot

41 ❑ Jan 1993 Cover: 1.75 **NM** value: **2.00**
Circ: CapCity orders: **33,250**
Sunset **A:** Jim Fern **W:** Keith Wilson; Tom Joyner

42 ❑ Feb 1993 Cover: 1.75 **NM** value: **2.00**
Circ: CapCity orders: **35,100**
Hothouse, Part 1 **A:** P. Craig Russell **W:** John Francis Moore

43 ❑ Mar 1993 Cover: 1.75 **NM** value: **2.00**
Circ: CapCity orders: **34,450**
Hothouse, Part 2 **A:** P. Craig Russell **W:** John Francis Moore

44 ❑ Apr 1993 Cover: 1.75 **NM** value: **2.00**
Circ: CapCity orders: **35,800**
Turf, Part 1 **A:** Shawn McManus **W:** Steven Grant

45 ❑ May 1993 Cover: 1.75 **NM** value: **2.00**
Circ: CapCity orders: **36,100**
Turf, Part 2 **A:** Shawn McManus **W:** Steven Grant

46 ❑ Jun 1993 Cover: 1.75 **NM** value: **2.00**
Circ: CapCity orders: **37,950**
Heat, Part 1 **A:** Russ Heath **W:** Doug Moench ★ Appearance of Catwoman. ★ Versus Catman.

47 ❑ Jul 1993 Cover: 1.75 **NM** value: **2.00**
Circ: CapCity orders: **35,200**
Heat, Part 2 **A:** Russ Heath **W:** Doug Moench ★ Appearance of Catwoman. ★ Versus Catman.

48 ❑ Aug 1993 Cover: 1.75 **NM** value: **2.00**
Circ: CapCity orders: **35,000**
Heat, Part 3 ★ Appearance of Catwoman. ★ Versus Catman.

49 ❑ Aug 1993 Cover: 1.75 **NM** value: **2.00**
Circ: CapCity orders: **35,000**
Heat, Part 4 ★ Appearance of Catwoman. ★ Versus Catman.

50 ❑ Sep 1993 Cover: 3.95 **NM** value: **4.50**
Circ: CapCity orders: **54,950** • **CGC:** 2 graded, best 9.4
foil cover. • Giant-size. ★ Appearance of Joker.

51 ❑ Sep 1993 Cover: 1.75 **NM** value: **2.00**
Circ: CapCity orders: **34,550**
Snitch **A:** David Klein **C:** Joe Kubert **W:** Robert Loren Flemming

52 ❑ Oct 1993 Cover: 1.75 **NM** value: **2.00**
Circ: CapCity orders: **34,650**
Tao, Part 1 **A:** Arthur Ranson **W:** Alan Grant

53 ❑ Oct 1993 Cover: 1.75 **NM** value: **2.00**
Circ: CapCity orders: **34,550**
Tao; Tao, Part 2 **A:** Arthur Ranson **W:** Alan Grant

54 ❑ Nov 1993 Cover: 1.75 **NM** value: **2.00**
Circ: CapCity orders: **36,900**

55 ❑ Dec 1993 Cover: 1.75 **NM** value: **2.00**
Circ: CapCity orders: **39,600**
Watchtower, Part 1 **A:** Mike McMahon **W:** Chuck Dixon

56 ❑ Jan 1994 Cover: 1.75 **NM** value: **2.00**
Circ: CapCity orders: **35,250**
Watchtower, Part 2 **A:** Mike McMahon **W:** Chuck Dixon

57 ❑ Feb 1994 Cover: 1.75 **NM** value: **2.00**
Circ: CapCity orders: **33,100**
Watchtower, Part 3 **A:** Mike McMahon **W:** Chuck Dixon

58 ❑ Mar 1994 Cover: 1.75 **NM** value: **2.00**
Circ: CapCity orders: **31,450**
Storm **A:** John Higgins **W:** Andrew Donkin; Graham Brand

59 ❑ Apr 1994 Cover: 1.75 **NM** value: **2.00**
Circ: CapCity orders: **38,600**
Knightquest: The Search; Quarry, Part 1

60 ❑ May 1994 Cover: 1.75 **NM** value: **2.00**
Circ: CapCity orders: **37,300**
Knightquest: The Search; Quarry, Part 2

61 ❑ Jun 1994 Cover: 1.75 **NM** value: **2.00**
Circ: CapCity orders: **39,850**
Knightquest: The Search; Quarry, Part 3 **A:** Eduardo Barreto **W:** Denny O'Neil

62 ❑ Jul 1994 Cover: 1.75 **NM** value: **2.00**
Circ: CapCity orders: **42,400**
KnightsEnd, Part 4

63 ❑ Aug 1994 Cover: 1.75 **NM** value: **2.00**
Circ: CapCity orders: **54,350**
KnightsEnd, Part 10

64 ❑ Sep 1994 Cover: 1.95 **NM** value: **2.00**
Circ: CapCity orders: **36,650**

65 ❑ Nov 1994 Cover: 1.95 **NM** value: **2.00**
Circ: CapCity orders: **37,550**
Going Sane, Part 1 **A:** Joe Staton **W:** J.M. DeMatteis ★ Appearance of Joker. ★ Versus Joker.

66 ❑ Dec 1994 Cover: 1.95 **NM** value: **2.00**
Circ: CapCity orders: **35,750**
Going Sane; Going Sane, Part 2 **A:** Joe Staton **W:** J.M. DeMatteis ★ Appearance of Joker. ★ Versus Joker.

67 ❑ Jan 1995 Cover: 1.95 **NM** value: **2.00**
Circ: CapCity orders: **34,750**
Going Sane; Going Sane, Part 3 **A:** Joe Staton **W:** J.M. DeMatteis ★ Appearance of Joker. ★ Versus Joker.

68 ❑ Feb 1995 Cover: 1.95 **NM** value: **2.00**
Circ: CapCity orders: **33,950**
Going Sane ★ Versus Joker.

69 ❑ Mar 1995 Cover: 1.95 **NM** value: **2.00**
Circ: CapCity orders: **31,775**
Criminals; Criminals, Part 1

70 ❑ Apr 1995 Cover: 1.95 **NM** value: **2.00**
Circ: CapCity orders: **32,225**
Criminals; Criminals, Part 2

71 ❑ May 1995 Cover: 1.95 **NM** value: **2.00**
Circ: CapCity orders: **30,200**
Werewolf, Part 1 of 3

72 ❑ Jun 1995 Cover: 1.95 **NM** value: **2.00**
Circ: CapCity orders: **29,425**
Werewolf, Part 2 of 3

73 ❑ Jul 1995 Cover: 1.95 **NM** value: **2.00**
Circ: CapCity orders: **28,425**
Werewolf, Part 3 of 3

74 ❑ Aug 1995 Cover: 1.95 **NM** value: **2.00**
Circ: CapCity orders: **28,350**
Engines, Part 1 of 2

75 ❑ Sep 1995 Cover: 1.95 **NM** value: **2.00**
Circ: CapCity orders: **27,175**
Engines, Part 2 of 2

76 ❑ Oct 1995 Cover: 1.95 **NM** value: **2.00**
Circ: CapCity orders: **22,875**
The Sleeping, Part 1 of 3

77 ❑ Nov 1995 Cover: 1.95 **NM** value: **2.00**
The Sleeping, Part 2 of 3

78 ❑ Dec 1995 Cover: 1.95 **NM** value: **2.00**
The Sleeping, Part 3 of 3

79 ❑ Jan 1996 Cover: 1.95 **NM** value: **2.00**
Favorite Things **A:** Steve Yeowell **W:** Mark Millar

80 ❑ Feb 1996 Cover: 1.95 **NM** value: **2.00**
Idols, Part 1 **A:** Dougie Braithwaite **W:** James Vance

81 ❑ Mar 1996 Cover: 1.95 **NM** value: **2.00**
Idols, Part 2 **A:** Dougie Braithwaite **W:** James Vance

82 ❑ May 1996 Cover: 1.95 **NM** value: **2.00**
Idols, Part 3 **A:** Dougie Braithwaite **W:** James Vance

83 ❑ Jun 1996 Cover: 1.95 **NM** value: **2.00**
Infected, Part 1 of 2

84 ❑ Jul 1996 Cover: 1.95 **NM** value: **2.00**
Infected, Part 2 of 2

85 ❑ Aug 1996 Cover: 1.95 **NM** value: **2.00**
Citadel

86 ❑ Sep 1996 Cover: 1.95 **NM** value: **2.00**
Conspiracy, Part 1 of 3 **A:** J.H. Williams III **W:** Doug Moench

87 ❑ Oct 1996 Cover: 1.95 **NM** value: **2.00**
Conspiracy, Part 2 of 3 **A:** J.H. Williams III **W:** Doug Moench

88 ❑ Nov 1996 Cover: 1.95 **NM** value: **2.00**
Circ: Diamd. preorders: **52,205**
Conspiracy, Part 3 of 3 **A:** J.H. Williams III **W:** Doug Moench

89 ❑ Dec 1996 Cover: 1.95 **NM** value: **2.00**
Circ: Direct Market orders: **51,579**
Clay, Part 1 of 2 **A:** Quique Alcatena **W:** Alan Grant ★ Origin of Clayface (Matt Hagen).

90 ❑ Jan 1997 Cover: 1.95 **NM** value: **2.00**
Circ: Direct Market orders: **51,239**
Clay, Part 2 of 2 **A:** Quique Alcatena **W:** Alan Grant

91 ❑ Feb 1997 Cover: 1.95 **NM** value: **2.00**
Circ: Diamd. preorders: **51,930**
Freakout, Part 1 of 3 **A:** William Simpson **W:** Garth Ennis

92 ❑ Mar 1997 Cover: 1.95 **NM** value: **2.00**
Circ: Diamd. preorders: **50,917**
Freakout, Part 2 of 3 **A:** William Simpson **W:** Garth Ennis

93 ❑ Apr 1997 Cover: 1.95 **NM** value: **2.00**
Circ: Diamd. preorders: **49,006**
Freakout, Part 3 of 3 **A:** William Simpson **W:** Garth Ennis

94 ❑ May 1997 Cover: 1.95 **NM** value: **2.00**
Circ: Diamd. preorders: **46,690**
Stories • three eras of Batman

95 ❑ Jun 1997 Cover: 1.95 **NM** value: **2.00**
Circ: Diamd. preorders: **46,803**
Dirty Tricks, Part 1 of 3

96 ❑ Jul 1997 Cover: 1.95 **NM** value: **2.00**
Circ: Diamd. preorders: **43,948**
Dirty Tricks, Part 2 of 3

97 ❑ Aug 1997 Cover: 1.95 **NM** value: **2.00**
Circ: Diamd. preorders: **43,697**
Dirty Tricks, Part 3 of 3

98 ❑ Sep 1997 Cover: 1.95 **NM** value: **2.00**
Circ: Diamd. preorders: **42,582**
Steps, Part 1 of 2

99 ❑ Oct 1997 Cover: 1.95 **NM** value: **2.00**
Circ: Diamd. preorders: **42,375**
Steps, Part 2 of 2

100 ❑ Nov 1997 Cover: 3.95 **NM** value: **4.50**
Circ: Diamd. preorders: **56,970**
• Double-size. The Choice; A Great Day for Everyone • pin-up gallery **A:** Mike Mignola; Frank Miller; Curt Swan; George Pratt; Walt Simonson; Klaus Janson; Gene Ha; J.H. Williams III; Joe Quesada; John Estes; Dusty Abell; Lee Weeks; Alex Ross(cover); Dave Taylor; Drew Geraci; Jimmy Palmiotti; Mick Gray **W:** James Robinson; Denny O'Neil ★ Origin of Robin I and Robin II, pin-up gallery, Robin I and Robin II. ★ Appearance of Joker.

101 ❑ Dec 1997 Cover: 1.95 **NM** value: **2.00**
Circ: Diamd. preorders: **43,307**
Face cover. The Incredible Adventures of Batman • 100 years in the future **A:** Carlos Ezquerra **W:** John Wagner

102 ❑ Jan 1998 Cover: 1.95 **NM** value: **2.00**
Circ: Diamd. preorders: **42,297**
Spook, Part 1 of 3 **A:** Paul Johnson **W:** James Robinson

103 ❑ Feb 1998 Cover: 1.95 **NM** value: **2.00**
Circ: Diamd. preorders: **41,526**
Spook, Part 2 of 3 **A:** Paul Johnson **W:** James Robinson

104 ❑ Mar 1998 Cover: 1.95 **NM** value: **2.00**
Circ: Diamd. preorders: **40,551**
Spook, Part 3 of 3 **A:** Paul Johnson **W:** James Robinson

CGC-graded: Multiply prices above by **33 for 9.9 M • 16 for 9.8 NM/M • 7 for 9.6 NM+ • 5 for 9.4 NM • 2.5 for 9.2 NM- • 1.5 for 9.0 VF/NM**

105 ❑ Apr 1998 Cover: 1.95 **NM** value: **2.00**
Circ: Diamd. preorders: **38,455**
Duty, Part 1 of 2
106 ❑ May 1998 Cover: 1.95 **NM** value: **2.00**
Circ: Diamd. preorders: **38,078**
Duty, Part 2 of 2 • Gordon vs. Joker
107 ❑ Jun 1998 Cover: 1.95 **NM** value: **2.00**
Circ: Diamd. preorders: **38,609**
Stalking, Part 1 of 2
108 ❑ Jul 1998 Cover: 1.95 **NM** value: **2.00**
Circ: Diamd. preorders: **36,644**
Stalking, Part 2 of 2
109 ❑ Aug 1998 Cover: 1.95 **NM** value: **2.00**
Circ: Diamd. preorders: **37,144**
The Primal Riddle, Part 1 ★ Versus Riddler.
110 ❑ Sep 1998 Cover: 1.99 **NM** value: **2.00**
Circ: Diamd. preorders: **35,282**
The Primal Riddle, Part 2 ★ Versus Riddler.
111 ❑ Oct 1998 Cover: 1.99 **NM** value: **2.00**
Circ: Diamd. preorders: **34,343**
The Primal Riddle, Part 3 ★ Versus Riddler.
112 ❑ Nov 1998 Cover: 1.99 **NM** value: **2.00**
Circ: Diamd. preorders: **33,575**
Shipwreck, Part 1
113 ❑ Dec 1998 Cover: 1.99 **NM** value: **2.00**
Circ: Diamd. preorders: **33,073**
Shipwreck, Part 2
114 ❑ Jan 1999 Cover: 1.99 **NM** value: **2.00**
Circ: Diamd. preorders: **34,930**
Playground
115 ❑ Feb 1999 Cover: 1.99 **NM** value: **2.00**
Circ: Diamd. preorders: **32,546**
• The Darkness **A:** Luke McDonnell **W:** Darren Vincenzo
116 ❑ Apr 1999 Cover: 1.99 **NM** value: **2.00**
Circ: Diamd. preorders: **34,782**
Fear of Faith, Part 1 • No Man's Land ★ Appearance of Scarecrow. ★ Appearance of Huntress.
117 ❑ May 1999 Cover: 1.99 **NM** value: **2.00**
Circ: Diamd. preorders: **38,182**
Bread and Circuses, Part 1 • No Man's Land ★ Versus Penguin.
118 ❑ Jun 1999 Cover: 1.99 **NM** value: **2.00**
Circ: Diamd. preorders: **42,036**
Balance • No Man's Land **A:** Jason Pearson **W:** Greg Rucka
119 ❑ Jul 1999 Cover: 1.99 **NM** value: **2.00**
Circ: Diamd. preorders: **43,670**
Claim Jumping, Part 1 • No Man's Land **A:** Mike Deodato **W:** Greg Rucka ★ Appearance of Two-Face.
120 ❑ Aug 1999 Cover: 1.99 **NM** value: **3.00**
Circ: Diamd. preorders: **47,728** • **CGC:** 14 graded, best 9.8
Assembly • No Man's Land **A:** Mike Deodato **W:** Greg Rucka ★ 1st Appearance of Batgirl III (in costume), Huntress, Nightwing, Robin.
121 ❑ Sep 1999 Cover: 1.99 **NM** value: **Cover or less**
Circ: Diamd. preorders: **45,081**
Power Play • No Man's Land **A:** Rick Burchett **W:** Larry Hama ★ Versus Mr. Freeze.
122 ❑ Oct 1999 Cover: 1.99 **NM** value: **Cover or less**
Circ: Diamd. preorders: **46,359**
Low Road to Golden Mountain, Part 1; ...Where the Lights are Burning Low • No Man's Land **A:** Paul Gulacy **W:** Larry Hama ★ Appearance of Lynx.
123 ❑ Nov 1999 Cover: 1.99 **NM** value: **Cover or less**
Circ: Diamd. preorders: **44,849**
Underground Railroad, Part 1 • No Man's Land **A:** Paul Ryan **W:** Steven Barnes
124 ❑ Dec 1999 Cover: 1.99 **NM** value: **Cover or less**
Circ: Diamd. preorders: **46,449**
• No Man's Land
125 ❑ Jan 2000 Cover: 1.99 **NM** value: **Cover or less**
Circ: Diamd. preorders: **47,282**
Falling Back • No Man's Land;Batman attempts to reveal identity to Commissioner Gordon **A:** Rick Burchett **W:** Greg Rucka
126 ❑ Feb 2000 Cover: 1.99 **NM** value: **Cover or less**
Circ: Diamd. preorders: **47,523**
Endgame, Part 1 • No Man's Land **A:** Damian Scott; Dale Eaglesham **W:** Devin Grayson; Greg Rucka
127 ❑ Mar 2000 Cover: 1.99 **NM** value: **Cover or less**
Circ: Diamd. preorders: **41,675**
The Arrow and the Bat, Part 1 **A:** Sergio Cariello **W:** Denny O'Neil
128 ❑ Apr 2000 Cover: 1.99 **NM** value: **Cover or less**
Circ: Diamd. preorders: **40,073**
The Arrow and the Bat, Part 2 **A:** Sergio Cariello **W:** Denny O'Neil
129 ❑ May 2000 Cover: 1.99 **NM** value: **Cover or less**
Circ: Diamd. preorders: **40,390**
The Arrow and the Bat, Part 3 **A:** Sergio Cariello **W:** Denny O'Neil
130 ❑ Jun 2000 Cover: 1.99 **NM** value: **Cover or less**
Circ: Diamd. preorders: **40,184**
The Arrow and the Bat, Part 4 **A:** Sergio Cariello **W:** Denny O'Neil
131 ❑ Jul 2000 Cover: 1.99 **NM** value: **Cover or less**
Circ: Diamd. preorders: **40,038**
132 ❑ Aug 2000 Cover: 2.25 **NM** value: **Cover or less**
Circ: Diamd. preorders: **41,511**
Siege, Part 1; Assembly **A:** James Robinson **W:** Archie Goodwin ★ Appearance of Silver St. Cloud.
133 ❑ Sep 2000 Cover: 2.25 **NM** value: **Cover or less**
Circ: Diamd. preorders: **40,201**
Siege, Part 2; Assault **A:** James Robinson **W:** Archie Goodwin ★ Appearance of Silver St. Cloud.
134 ❑ Oct 2000 Cover: 2.25 **NM** value: **Cover or less**
Circ: Diamd. preorders: **37,231**
Siege, Part 3; Breach **A:** James Robinson **W:** Archie Goodwin ★ Appearance of Silver St. Cloud.
135 ❑ Nov 2000 Cover: 2.25 **NM** value: **Cover or less**
Circ: Diamd. preorders: **36,921**
Siege, Part 4 **A:** James Robinson **W:** Archie Goodwin
136 ❑ Dec 2000 Cover: 2.25 **NM** value: **Cover or less**
Circ: Diamd. preorders: **36,205**
Siege, Part 5 **A:** James Robinson **W:** Archie Goodwin
137 ❑ Jan 2001 Cover: 2.25 **NM** value: **Cover or less**
Circ: Diamd. preorders: **35,662**
Terror, Part 1 **A:** Paul Gulacy **W:** Doug Moench
138 ❑ Feb 2001 Cover: 2.25 **NM** value: **Cover or less**
Circ: Diamd. preorders: **34,441**
Terror, Part 2 **A:** Paul Gulacy **W:** Doug Moench
139 ❑ Mar 2001 Cover: 2.25 **NM** value: **Cover or less**
Circ: Diamd. preorders: **33,950**
Terror, Part 3 **A:** Paul Gulacy **W:** Doug Moench
140 ❑ Apr 2001 Cover: 2.25 **NM** value: **Cover or less**
Circ: Diamd. preorders: **34,214**
Terror, Part 4 **A:** Paul Gulacy **W:** Doug Moench
141 ❑ May 2001 Cover: 2.25 **NM** value: **Cover or less**
Circ: Diamd. preorders: **33,822**
Terror, Part 5 **A:** Paul Gulacy **W:** Doug Moench
142 ❑ Jun 2001 Cover: 2.25 **NM** value: **Cover or less**
Circ: Diamd. preorders: **34,582**
The Demon Laughs, Part 1 **A:** Jim Aparo **W:** Chuck Dixon
143 ❑ Jul 2001 Cover: 2.25 **NM** value: **Cover or less**
Circ: Diamd. preorders: **34,497**
144 ❑ Aug 2001 Cover: 2.25 **NM** value: **Cover or less**
Circ: Diamd. preorders: **35,212**
145 ❑ Sep 2001 Cover: 2.25 **NM** value: **Cover or less**
Circ: Diamd. preorders: **37,459** • **CGC:** 1 graded, best 9.8
Anl 1 ❑ Dec 1991 Cover: 3.95 **NM** value: **4.50**
Duel **A:** Don Spiegle; Michael Golden; Keith Giffen; Jim Aparo **W:** Denny O'Neil
Anl 2 ❑ ca. 1992 Cover: 3.50 **NM** value: **Cover or less**
Circ: CapCity orders: **31,400**
Vows • Wedding of James Gordon **A:** Michael Netzer **W:** Denny O'Neil
Anl 3 ❑ ca. 1993 Cover: 3.50 **NM** value: **Cover or less**
Circ: CapCity orders: **37,100**
Bloodlines ★ 1st Appearance of Cardinal Sin.
Anl 4 ❑ ca. 1994 Cover: 3.50 **NM** value: **Cover or less**
Elseworlds: Citizen Wayne **A:** Joe Staton **W:** Brian Augustyn; Mark Waid
Anl 5 ❑ ca. 1995 Cover: 3.95 **NM** value: **Cover or less**
Circ: CapCity orders: **24,300**
Wings • Year One ★ Origin of Man-Bat.
Anl 6 ❑ ca. 1996 Cover: 2.95 **NM** value: **Cover or less**
• Legends of the Dead Earth
Anl 7 ❑ ca. 1997 Cover: 3.95 **NM** value: **Cover or less**
Circ: Diamd. preorders: **38,099**
• Pulp Heroes ★ Appearance of Balloon Buster.
Bk 1 ❑ Cover: 9.95 **NM** value: **Cover or less**
• Faces;collects Batman: Legends of the Dark Knight #28-30
SE 1 ❑ ca. 1993 Cover: 6.95 **NM** value: **Cover or less**
• prestige format.

BATMAN: LEGENDS OF THE DARK KNIGHT: JAZZ — DC

1 ❑ Apr 1995 Cover: 2.50 **NM** value: **Cover or less**
Circ: CapCity orders: **22,250**
A: Mark Badger **W:** Gerard Jones
2 ❑ May 1995 Cover: 2.50 **NM** value: **Cover or less**
Circ: CapCity orders: **19,850**
A: Mark Badger **W:** Gerard Jones
3 ❑ Jun 1995 Cover: 2.50 **NM** value: **Cover or less**
Circ: CapCity orders: **17,825**
A: Mark Badger **W:** Gerard Jones

BATMAN: MADNESS A LEGENDS OF THE DARK KNIGHT HALLOWEEN SPECIAL — DC

Jervis Tetch, aka The Mad Hatter, has never been nearly as murderous or as effective a foe for Batman as The Joker or Ra's Al Ghul. Yet, in this one-shot special by the superb team of Jeph Loeb and Tim Sale, Tetch's Alice in Wonderland fetish is warped into something chilling. A young Barbara Gordon finds herself in the clutches of the demented Hatter, sparking a psychological battle of wills that not only tests her policeman father, but The Batman, as well. As often as extraneous details are grafted onto the night Bruce Wayne lost his parents, Loeb's addition is a moving footnote about Wayne's mother and the time they spent reading Alice together just before that fateful evening in Gotham City. Everyone faces their demons by story's end, and Wayne comes to terms with his loss in a novel way.

1 ❑ Cover: 4.95 **NM** value: **Cover or less**
Circ: CapCity orders: **24,500**
One-shot. • prestige format. **A:** Tim Sale **W:** Jeph Loeb

BATMAN: MANBAT — DC

1 ❑ Cover: 4.95 **NM** value: **5.00**
Circ: CapCity orders: **24,275**
• prestige format. The Subterraneans, Part 1 • Elseworlds **A:** John Bolton **W:** Jamie Delano
2 ❑ Cover: 4.95 **NM** value: **5.00**
• prestige format. The Subterraneans, Part 2 • Elseworlds **A:** John Bolton **W:** Jamie Delano
3 ❑ Cover: 4.95 **NM** value: **5.00**
• prestige format. The Subterraneans, Part 3 • Elseworlds **A:** John Bolton **W:** Jamie Delano
Bk 1 ❑ Cover: 14.95 **NM** value: **Cover or less**
• collects mini-series

For up-to-the-week CGC ratios, consult the current issue of **Comics Buyer's Guide**.

BATMAN: MASK OF THE PHANTASM-THE ANIMATED MOVIE — DC

When a scythe-wielding vigilante is blamed for the violent deaths of several reputed mobsters, suspicion arises that Batman may have become too aggressive in his crusade. Then, the return of long-lost love Andrea Beaumont, a woman of uncommon spirit and beauty, stirs Batman's memories of his beginnings (shown in a series of flashbacks). Combined with an ambitious power-hungry politician and the maniacal machinations of The Joker, excitement and passion radiate from this plot-intensive epic.

This adaptation of the 1993 animated movie (which was produced by the same crew as the acclaimed television series) is a poignant narrative which reveals the heretofore-untold story of a love so intense that Bruce Wayne considered foregoing his graveside vow because he "didn't count on being happy."

1 ❑ Cover: 2.95 **NM** value: **Cover or less**
• **CGC:** 1 graded, best 9.4
No issue number. Shady Lady • newstand **A:** Mike Parobeck **W:** Kelley Puckett
1/PR ❑ Cover: 4.95 **NM** value: **Cover or less**
No issue number. Shady Lady • slick paper **A:** Mike Parobeck **W:** Kelley Puckett

BATMAN: MASQUE — DC

1 ❑ Jan 1997 Cover: 6.95 **NM** value: **Cover or less**
Circ: Direct Market orders: **40,941**
No issue number. • prestige format. • Elseworlds;Phantom of the Opera theme;prestige format, Elseworlds, Phantom of the Opera theme **A:** Mike Grell **W:** Mike Grell

BATMAN: MASTER OF THE FUTURE — DC

1 ❑ Cover: 5.95 **NM** value: **Cover or less**
Circ: CapCity orders: **35,750**
No issue number.

BATMAN MASTERPIECES — DC

1 ❑ Cover: 40.00 **NM** value: **Cover or less**
• **CGC:** 1 graded, best 9.4

BATMAN: MR. FREEZE — DC

1 ❑ May 1997 Cover: 4.95 **NM** value: **Cover or less**
Circ: Diamd. preorders: **41,277**
No issue number. One-shot. cover is part of quadtych. • prestige format. **A:** Mark Buckingham **W:** Paul Dini ★ Origin of Mr. Freeze.

BATMAN: MITEFALL — DC

1 ❑ Cover: 4.95 **NM** value: **Cover or less**
Circ: CapCity orders: **13,375**
One-shot. • prestige format. • prestige format one-shot **A:** Kevin O'Neill **W:** Alan Grant ★ Death of Bob Overdog.

BATMAN: NIGHT CRIES — DC

Bk 1 ❑ Cover: 12.95 **NM** value: **Cover or less**
Circ: CapCity orders: **7,545**
A: Scott Hampton **W:** Archie Goodwin
Bk 1/HC ❑ Cover: 24.95 **NM** value: **Cover or less**
A: Scott Hampton **W:** Archie Goodwin

BATMAN: NO LAW AND A NEW ORDER — DC

1 ❑ Cover: 5.95 **NM** value: **Cover or less**
No issue number. • collects Batman: No Man's Land #1, Batman #563, Batman: Shadow of the Bat #83, and Detective Comics #730

BATMAN: NO MAN'S LAND — DC

After the massive earthquake that leveled Gotham City, the United States government declared the ruins "no man's land" — off-limits to any citizen — and told the survivors to leave. Many didn't. Some were too poor, some too stubborn, and some saw it as an opportunity to rule. Guns are useless without a supply of ammunition to feed them, and apples are worth more than diamonds to those who remaine. Many sector lords come from Arkham Asylum, which opened its gates and let the criminals back on the streets. The Gotham City Police Department becomes a territory depending on the strong-arm tactics it once fought. Overnight, stately Wayne Manor becomes an ugly pile of stone and wood.

And for three months, many have wondered where The Batman has gone...

0 ❑ Dec 1999 Cover: 4.95 **NM** value: **Cover or less**
Circ: Diamd. preorders: **49,707** • **CGC:** 2 graded, best 9.6
Ground Zero **A:** Greg Land **W:** Greg Rucka; Jordon B. Gorfinkel
1 ❑ Mar 1999 Cover: 3.95 **NM** value: **Cover or less**
Circ: Diamd. preorders: **54,336**
No Law and a New Order, Part 1 **A:** Alex Maleev; Alex Ross(cover) **W:** Bob Gale
1/Aut ❑ Mar 1999 Cover: 3.95 **NM** value: **17.95**

Other grades: Multiply prices above by **1.5 for Mint • 2/3 for Very Fine • 1/3 for Fine • 1/5 for Very Good • 1/8 for Good**

📖 No Law and a New Order, part 1 **A:** Alex Maleev; Alex Ross(cover) **W:** Bob Gale

1/SC❑Mar 1999 Cover: 2.95 **NM value: 3.95**
Circ: Diamd. preorders: **13,328 • CGC:** 7 graded, best 9.8
lenticular animation cover. 📖 No Law and a New Order, part 1 **A:** Alex Maleev; Alex Ross(cover) **C:** Alex Ross **W:** Bob Gale

2 ❑ Cover: 2.95 **NM value: Cover or less**
📖 No Law and a New Order, part 2 **W:** Bob Gale

3 ❑ Cover: 2.95 **NM value: Cover or less**
📖 No Law and a New Order, part 3 **W:** Bob Gale

4 ❑ Cover: 2.95 **NM value: Cover or less**
📖 No Law and a New Order, part 4 **W:** Bob Gale

Bk 1❑ Cover: 5.95 **NM value: Cover or less**
• Collects Batman: No Man's Land #1, Batman #563, Batman: Shadow of the Bat #83, Detective Comics #730 **A:** Alex Maleev; Alex Ross(cover) **W:** Bob Gale

Bk 3❑ Cover: 12.95 **NM value: Cover or less**
• Collects Batman #566-569, Batman: Legends of the Dark Knight #120-121, Batman: Shadow of the Bat #88, Detective Comics #734-735 **A:** Damion Scott; Mike Deodato; Dan Jurgens; Rick Burchett; Sergio Cariello; Jon Bogdanove **W:** Larry Hama; Kelley Puckett; Greg Rucka; Janet Harvey

Bk 4❑ Cover: 12.95 **NM value: Cover or less**
• Collects Batman #571-572, Batman Chronicles #18, Batman: Legends of the Dark Knight #125, Batman Shadow of the Bat #92-93, Detective Comics #736, 738, 739 **A:** Damion Scott; Matt Broome; Paul Ryan; Mike Deodato; Dale Eaglesham; Rick Burchett **W:** Larry Hama; Chuck Dixon; Devin Grayson; Greg Rucka

Bk 5❑ Cover: 12.95 **NM value: Cover or less**
• Collects Batman #573-574, Batman: Legends of the Dark Knight #126, Batman: No Man's Land #0, Batman: Shadow of the Bat #94, Detective Comics #740-741 **A:** Damion Scott; Dale Eaglesham; Sergio Cariello; Greg Land; Pablo Raimondi **W:** Devin Grayson; Greg Rucka; Jordan B. Gorfinkel

BATMAN: NO MAN'S LAND GALLERY — DC

1 ❑ Jul 1999 Cover: 3.95 **NM value: Cover or less**
Circ: Diamd. preorders: **19,347**
• pin-ups **A:** Norm Breyfogle; Terry Dodson; Dale Eaglesham; William Rosado; Shawn Martinbrough; John Cassaday; Dam J; Rachel Dodson; Sean Parsons

BATMAN: NO MAN'S LAND SECRET FILES — DC

1 ❑ Dec 1999 Cover: 4.95 **NM value: Cover or less**
Circ: Diamd. preorders: **36,199**
📖 The Message; Batcaves; Day in the Life; No Man's Land: the Animated Series; Top 10 Reasons to Stay in Gotham; Senate NML Notes **A:** Craig Rousseau; Sal Velluto; Michael Zulli; Stan Woch **W:** Scott Beatty; Chuck Dixon; Alisa Kwitney; Jordan Gorfinkel; Scott Peterson

BATMAN: NOSFERATU — DC

1 ❑ May 1999 Cover: 5.95 **NM value: Cover or less**
Circ: Diamd. preorders: **24,679**
No issue number. One-shot. • prestige format. • Elseworlds **A:** Ted McKeever **W:** Randy & Jean-Marc Lofficier

BATMAN: OTHER REALMS — DC

Bk 1❑ Cover: 12.95 **NM value: Cover or less**
• collects Hampton stories

BATMAN: OUTLAWS — DC

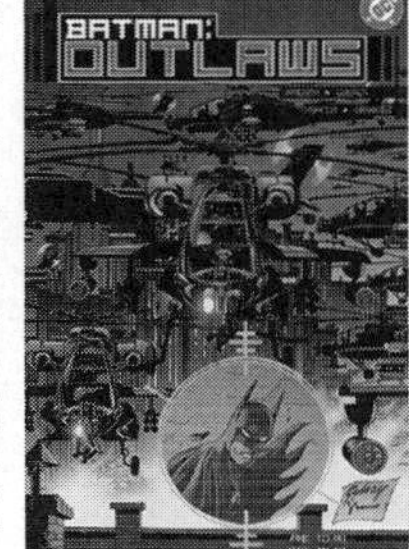

Writer Doug Moench (Moon Knight) and artist Paul Gulacy (Star Wars: Crimson Empire) are known for their run on Marvel Comics' Master of Kung Fu, as well as their occasional collaborations involving DC's Batman. This three-issue prestige format limited series is another jewel in the Moench-Gulacy crown and finds The Caped Crusader and his cadre of agents — Robin, Nightwing, Batgirl, the Huntress, Oracle, and even Catwoman — the targets of a federal task force called The Bloodhawks. Under the command of the mysterious David Atlee Redmun, the Bloodhawks have a single mission: ridding Gotham City of the vigilantes who often work hand-in-hand with Police Commissioner James Gordon and his department. As an agent of the Justice Department, Redmun overrides Gordon's authority, and the Gotham Knights are cut off from the GCPD and on the run. Just how dependent on their relationship with the Gotham City Police Department are Batman and his partners? Can they survive without the law on their side? And is there more to Redmun's mission that meets the eye? The information is in this excellent Bat-series from two comics industry legends.

1 ❑ Sep 2000 Cover: 4.95 **NM value: Cover or less**
Circ: Diamd. preorders: **28,791**
A: Paul Gulacy **W:** Doug Moench

2 ❑ Oct 2000 Cover: 4.95 **NM value: Cover or less**
Circ: Diamd. preorders: **23,790**
A: Paul Gulacy **W:** Doug Moench

3 ❑ Nov 2000 Cover: 4.95 **NM value: Cover or less**
Circ: Diamd. preorders: **23,090**
A: Paul Gulacy **W:** Doug Moench

BATMAN: PENGUIN TRIUMPHANT — DC

1 ❑ Cover: 4.95 **NM value: 5.00**
Circ: CapCity orders: **35,850**
No issue number. cover forms diptych with Batman: Catwoman Defiant. • prestige format. **A:** Joe Staton **W:** John Ostrander

BATMAN/PHANTOM STRANGER — DC

1 ❑ Dec 1997 Cover: 4.95 **NM value: Cover or less**
Circ: Diamd. preorders: **34,787**
No issue number. • prestige format. **A:** Arthur Ranson **W:** Alan Grant

BATMAN PLUS — DC

1 ❑ Feb 1997 Cover: 2.95 **NM value: Cover or less**
Circ: Diamd. preorders: **49,847**
📖 Beauty and the Beast **A:** Rodolfo DaMaggio **W:** Devin Grayson
★ Appearance of Arsenal.

BATMAN: POISON IVY — DC

Poison Ivy, whose horticultural expertise is enhanced by her supernatural control of pheromones and all things photosynthetic, has established a piece of paradise on a Caribbean island. Her idyllic existence is short-lived, however, when black-market gunrunners use her island to test a new incendiary device and leave it a smoldering wasteland. Poison Ivy's thirst for retribution brings her back to Gotham City — to the ex-KGB operatives who have allied themselves with a perfume magnate and associate of Bruce Wayne.

In anticipation of the fourth live-action Batman movie, "Batman and Robin," DC published four prestige-format titles highlighting the characters introduced in the film: Mr. Freeze, Poison Ivy, Bane, and Batgirl. Other than the name recognition of the characters, these titles had no direct connection to the movie.

1 ❑ Jul 1997 Cover: 4.95 **NM value: Cover or less**
Circ: Diamd. preorders: **41,610**
No issue number. One-shot. cover is part of quadtych. • prestige format. **A:** Brian Apthorp **W:** John Francis Moore ★ Origin of Poison Ivy. ★ Appearance of Croc, Batman, Poison Ivy.

BATMAN/PREDATOR III — DC

1 ❑ Nov 1997 Cover: 1.95 **NM value: Cover or less**
Circ: Diamd. preorders: **55,891**
A: Rodolfo DaMaggio **W:** Chuck Dixon

2 ❑ Dec 1997 Cover: 1.95 **NM value: Cover or less**
Circ: Diamd. preorders: **48,614**
A: Rodolfo DaMaggio **W:** Chuck Dixon

3 ❑ Jan 1998 Cover: 1.95 **NM value: Cover or less**
Circ: Diamd. preorders: **45,062**
A: Rodolfo DaMaggio **W:** Chuck Dixon

4 ❑ Feb 1998 Cover: 1.95 **NM value: Cover or less**
Circ: Diamd. preorders: **43,389**
A: Rodolfo DaMaggio **W:** Chuck Dixon

BATMAN: PREY — DC

Bk 1❑ Cover: 12.95 **NM value: Cover or less**
No issue number.

BATMAN: PRODIGAL — DC

1 ❑ Cover: 14.95 **NM value: Cover or less**
📖 Prodigal • collects Batman #512-514, Batman: Shadow of the Bat #32-34, Detective Comics #679-681, and Robin #11-13 **A:** Mark D. Bright; Ron Wagner; Phil Jimenez; Graham Nolan; Mike Gustovich; Bret Blevins; John Cleary; Lee Weeks **W:** Chuck Dixon; Alan Grant; Doug Moench

BATMAN/PUNISHER: LAKE OF FIRE — DC / Marvel

1 ❑ 1994 Cover: 4.95 **NM value: 5.00**
Circ: CapCity orders: **57,100 • CGC:** 1 graded, best 9.0
A: Barry Kitson; James Pascoe **W:** Denny O'Neil

BATMAN: REIGN OF TERROR — DC

1 ❑ Feb 1999 Cover: 4.95 **NM value: Cover or less**
Circ: Diamd. preorders: **24,469**
No issue number. • prestige format. • Elseworlds **A:** José Luis Garcia-Lopez **W:** Mike W. Barr

BATMAN RETURNS: THE OFFICIAL COMIC ADAPTATION OF THE WARNER BROS. MOTION PICTURE — DC

In Gotham's shrouded past, the wealthy Cobblepot family gave birth to a hideously deformed child. For a while, this unfortunate babe was kept out of sight in a caged crib, but one day the parents were driven to do the unthinkable. They threw the baby, stroller and all, into the chill waters that led to Gotham's sewers. Miraculously, the stroller floated and the baby survived, growing up underneath the Gotham City Zoo. Then one day, he emerged from the sewers to bring terror to the people of Gotham.

Batman Returns was the sequel to Warner Brothers' 1989 blockbuster Batman. The only way they could hope to match Jack Nicholson's incredible Joker from the first movie was to have the sequel feature two of Batman's greatest enemies: the Penguin (played by Danny Devito) and Catwoman (slinkily portrayed by Michelle Pfeiffer). These two alternately team up and square off with Batman and Gotham in the middle.

1 ❑ Cover: 3.95 **NM value: 4.00**
Circ: CapCity orders: **30,150**
No issue number. • Comic adaptation of Warner Bros. Movie **A:** Steve Erwin **W:** Denny O'Neil

1/PR❑ Cover: 5.95 **NM value: 6.00**
Circ: CapCity orders: **23,500**
No issue number. • prestige format. • Comic adaptation of Warner Bros. Movie **A:** Steve Erwin **W:** Denny O'Neil

BATMAN: RIDDLER-THE RIDDLE FACTORY — DC

1 ❑ Cover: 4.95 **NM value: Cover or less**
Circ: CapCity orders: **19,475**
No issue number. cover forms diptych with Batman: Two-Face – Crime and Punishment. • prestige format. **A:** David Taylor **W:** Matt Wagner

BATMAN: RUN, RIDDLER, RUN — DC

1 ❑ Cover: 4.95 **NM value: 5.00**
Circ: CapCity orders: **36,050**
• prestige format. 📖 The Road To Hell **A:** Mark Badger **W:** Mark Badger; Gerard Jones

2 ❑ Cover: 4.95 **NM value: 5.00**
Circ: CapCity orders: **29,800**
• prestige format. **A:** Mark Badger **W:** Mark Badger; Gerard Jones

3 ❑ Cover: 4.95 **NM value: 5.00**
Circ: CapCity orders: **28,600**
• prestige format. 📖 ...With Good Intentions **A:** Mark Badger **W:** Mark Badger; Gerard Jones

BATMAN/SCARECROW 3-D — DC

1 ❑ Dec 1998 Cover: 3.95 **NM value: Cover or less**
Circ: Diamd. preorders: **27,311**
📖 Concert of Fear • with glasses **A:** Carl Critchlow **W:** John Francis Moore

1/SC❑Dec 1998 Cover: 16.95 **NM value: Cover or less**
📖 Concert of Fear **A:** Carl Critchlow **W:** John Francis Moore

BATMAN/SCARFACE: A PSYCHODRAMA — DC

1 ❑ Mar 2001 Cover: 5.95 **NM value: Cover or less**
Circ: Diamd. preorders: **19,738 • CGC:** 1 graded, best 9.6
A: Charles Adlard **W:** Alan Grant

BATMAN: SCAR OF THE BAT — DC

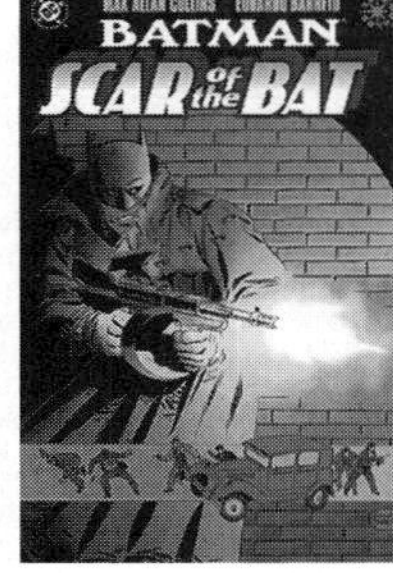

When "Scarface" Al Capone ruled the Chicago underworld, he was alleged to have once killed two untrustworthy associates with a baseball bat. In this Elseworlds story, another man takes up a bat and takes on Capone's mob. He becomes a "Batman" of sorts, but a very different one than the one known to readers of DC comics.

Writer Max Allan Collins spins a tale which deftly mixes super-hero adventure with historical fiction. In it, he gives his take on how Elliott Ness and his "Capone Squad" managed to bring down the most infamous gangster of all time. In a city where the mob ran everything from illegal booze to crooked cops, federal agent Ness was forced to recruit carefully to form a squad of cops who couldn't be bought. As a result, his squad was known as "The Untouchables" and became part of popular legend. In this tale, however, the legend is expanded to include a masked man who set out to strike fear into the hearts of criminals.

1 ❑ Cover: 4.95 **NM value: Cover or less**
No issue number. • prestige format. • Elseworlds **A:** Eduardo Barreto **W:** Max Allan Collins

BATMAN: SCOTTISH CONNECTION — DC

1 ❑ Cover: 5.95 **NM value: Cover or less**
No issue number. One-shot. • prestige format. 📖 Isle of Mists **A:** Frank Quitely **W:** Alan Grant

BATMAN SECRET FILES — DC

1 ❑ Oct 1997 Cover: 4.95 **NM value: Cover or less**
Circ: Diamd. preorders: **33,660**
📖 Gazing • background information **A:** Roger Robinson; Brian Apthorp; Gary Frank; Mark Buckingham; Graham Nolan; Jim Balent; Scott McDaniel; Stefano Raffaele; Staz Johnson; Jim Aparo; Lee Weeks; James A. Hodgkins **W:** Graham Nolan; Scott Beatty; Chuck Dixon; Kelley Puckett; Devin Grayson; Doug Moench

BATMAN: SEDUCTION OF THE GUN — DC

1 ❑ Feb 1993 Cover: 2.50 **NM value: 3.50**
Circ: CapCity orders: **33,600**
• Special edition on gun control. • dedicated to John Reisenbach (Son of DC editor slain in gun killing) **A:** Vince Giarrano **W:** John Ostrander

To find the median price offered on eBay at press time for pre-1990 **CGC-graded comics**, multiply by:

9.9 (M): **32**	8.5 (VF+): **1.25**
9.8(NM/M): **16**	8.0 (VF): **0.85**
9.6 (NM+): **7**	7.5 (VF-): **0.6**
9.4 (NM): **5**	7.0 (F/VF): **0.5**
9.2 (NM-): **2.5**	6.5 (F+): **0.4**
9.0 (VF/NM): **1.5**	6.0 (F-): **0.33**

These are median prices of all CGC comics auctioned on eBay; prices for individual issues will vary.

CGC-graded: Multiply prices above by **33 for 9.9 M • 16 for 9.8 NM/M • 7 for 9.6 NM+ • 5 for 9.4 NM • 2.5 for 9.2 NM- • 1.5 for 9.0 VF/NM**

BATMAN: SHADOW OF THE BAT DC

This brilliant series begins with a bang. Arkham Asylum, that home of lunatics, paranoids, and the murderously insane, is being torn down and rebuilt. The son of the original architect, Jeremiah Arkham, is the new chief administrator, and he's ripping out the old and bringing in the new. Now, instead of the dark Victorian corridors and dank cells, there are shiny new fluorescent lights illuminating a floor plan laid out like a labyrinth — all of this, of course, in the name of progress.

But in the new asylum are the same old inmates: Cornelius Stirk, the murderously insane night-dweller; Scarecrow, whose greatest joy is to bring fear to others; and Mr. Zsasz, the serial killer who has laid waste to more than 100 lives — as well as one other, very special guest of Arkham Asylum: Batman.

0 ❑ Cover: 1.95 **NM** value: **2.50**
Circ: CapCity orders: **50,000**
The Beginning Of Tomorrow • falls between issues #31 and 32 **A:** Bret Blevins **W:** Alan Grant ★ Origin of Batman.

1 ❑ Cover: 1.50 **NM** value: **4.00**
Circ: CapCity orders: **71,950** • **CGC:** 2 graded, best 9.4
The Last Arkham, Part 1 • Last Arkham **A:** Norm Breyfogle **W:** Alan Grant

1/CS ❑ Jun 1992 Cover: 2.00 **NM** value: **5.50**
Circ: CapCity orders: **97,550**
The Last Arkham, Part 1 • collector's set **A:** Norm Breyfogle **W:** Alan Grant

2 ❑ Cover: 1.50 **NM** value: **3.00**
Circ: CapCity orders: **73,500**
The Last Arkham, Part 2 • Last Arkham **A:** Norm Breyfogle **W:** Alan Grant

3 ❑ Cover: 1.50 **NM** value: **3.00**
Circ: CapCity orders: **63,850**
The Last Arkham, Part 3 • Last Arkham **A:** Norm Breyfogle **W:** Alan Grant

4 ❑ Cover: 1.50 **NM** value: **3.00**
Circ: CapCity orders: **61,100**
The Last Arkham, Part 4 • Last Arkham **A:** Norm Breyfogle **W:** Alan Grant

5 ❑ Oct 1992 Cover: 1.50 **NM** value: **3.00**
Circ: CapCity orders: **49,650**
The Black Spider **A:** Norm Breyfogle **W:** Alan Grant

6 ❑ Nov 1992 Cover: 1.50 **NM** value: **2.50**
Circ: CapCity orders: **43,400**
The Ugly American **A:** Dan Jurgens **W:** Alan Grant

7 ❑ Dec 1992 Cover: 1.50 **NM** value: **2.50**
Circ: CapCity orders: **40,600**
The Misfits, Part 1 **A:** Tim Sale **W:** Alan Grant

8 ❑ Jan 1993 Cover: 1.75 **NM** value: **2.50**
Circ: CapCity orders: **35,950**
The Misfits, Part 2 • Misfits **A:** Tim Sale **W:** Alan Grant

9 ❑ Feb 1993 Cover: 1.75 **NM** value: **2.50**
Circ: CapCity orders: **35,400**
The Misfits, Part 3 **A:** Tim Sale **W:** Alan Grant

10 ❑ Mar 1993 Cover: 1.75 **NM** value: **2.50**
Circ: CapCity orders: **33,800**
The Thane of Gotham **A:** Mike Collins **W:** Alan Grant

11 ❑ Apr 1993 Cover: 1.75 **NM** value: **2.50**
Circ: CapCity orders: **33,600**
The Human Flea, Part 1 **A:** Vince Giarrano **W:** Alan Grant

12 ❑ May 1993 Cover: 1.75 **NM** value: **2.50**
Circ: CapCity orders: **33,050**
The Human Flea, Part 2 **A:** Vince Giarrano **W:** Alan Grant

13 ❑ Jun 1993 Cover: 1.75 **NM** value: **2.50**
Circ: CapCity orders: **32,400**
The Nobody **A:** Norm Breyfogle **W:** Alan Grant

14 ❑ Jul 1993 Cover: 1.75 **NM** value: **2.50**
Circ: CapCity orders: **31,500**
Gotham Freaks, Part 1 **A:** Joe Staton **W:** Alan Grant

15 ❑ Aug 1993 Cover: 1.75 **NM** value: **2.50**
Circ: CapCity orders: **30,750**
Gotham Freaks, Part 2 **A:** Joe Staton **W:** Alan Grant

16 ❑ Sep 1993 Cover: 1.75 **NM** value: **2.50**
Circ: CapCity orders: **66,850**
The God of Fear, Part 1 **A:** Bret Blevins **W:** Alan Grant ★ Versus Scarecrow.

17 ❑ Sep 1993 Cover: 1.75 **NM** value: **2.50**
Circ: CapCity orders: **67,700**
The God of Fear, Part 2 **A:** Bret Blevins **W:** Alan Grant ★ Versus Scarecrow.

18 ❑ Oct 1993 Cover: 1.75 **NM** value: **2.50**
Circ: CapCity orders: **82,600**
Knightfall; The God of Fear, Part 3 **A:** Bret Blevins **W:** Alan Grant ★ Versus Scarecrow.

19 ❑ Oct 1993 Cover: 1.75 **NM** value: **2.50**
Circ: CapCity orders: **60,350**
Knightquest: The Crusade; The Tally Man, Part 1 **A:** Vince Giarrano **W:** Alan Grant ★ Versus Tally Man.

20 ❑ Nov 1993 Cover: 1.75 **NM** value: **2.50**
Circ: CapCity orders: **65,100**
Knightquest: The Crusade; The Tally Man, Part 2 **A:** Vince Giarrano **W:** Alan Grant ★ Versus Tally Man.

21 ❑ Nov 1993 Cover: 1.75 **NM** value: **2.50**
Circ: CapCity orders: **64,050**
Knightquest: The Search; Bruce Wayne, Part 1 **A:** Bret Blevins **W:** Alan Grant

22 ❑ Dec 1993 Cover: 1.75 **NM** value: **2.50**
Circ: CapCity orders: **59,500**
Knightquest: The Search; Bruce Wayne, Part 2 **A:** Bret Blevins **W:** Alan Grant

23 ❑ Jan 1994 Cover: 1.75 **NM** value: **2.50**
Circ: CapCity orders: **58,350**
Knightquest: The Crusade; Bruce Wayne, Part 3; Knightquest: The Search **A:** Bret Blevins **W:** Alan Grant

24 ❑ Feb 1994 Cover: 1.75 **NM** value: **2.50**
Circ: CapCity orders: **51,650**
Knightquest: The Crusade; The Immigrant **A:** Vince Giarrano **W:** Alan Grant

25 ❑ Mar 1994 Cover: 1.75 **NM** value: **2.50**
Circ: CapCity orders: **46,100**
Knightquest: The Crusade **A:** Bret Blevins **W:** Alan Grant ★ Appearance of Joe Public.

26 ❑ Apr 1994 Cover: 1.75 **NM** value: **2.50**
Circ: CapCity orders: **42,500**
Knightquest: The Crusade **W:** Alan Grant ★ Versus Clayface.

27 ❑ May 1994 Cover: 1.75 **NM** value: **2.50**
Circ: CapCity orders: **40,650**
Knightquest: The Crusade **W:** Alan Grant

28 ❑ Jun 1994 Cover: 1.75 **NM** value: **2.50**
Circ: CapCity orders: **42,550**
Knightquest: The Crusade **A:** Bret Blevins **W:** Alan Grant

29 ❑ Jul 1994 Cover: 2.95 **NM** value: **Cover or less**
Circ: CapCity orders: **43,250**
• Giant-size. KnightsEnd, Part 2 **A:** Bret Blevins **W:** Alan Grant

30 ❑ Aug 1994 Cover: 1.95 **NM** value: **2.50**
Circ: CapCity orders: **46,050**
KnightsEnd, Part 8 **A:** Bret Blevins **W:** Alan Grant

31 ❑ Sep 1994 Cover: 1.95 **NM** value: **2.50**
Circ: CapCity orders: **36,450**
• Zero Hour, R: Alfred as detective **W:** Alan Grant

32 ❑ Nov 1994 Cover: 1.95 **NM** value: **2.50**
Circ: CapCity orders: **36,800**
Prodigal, Part 2 **W:** Alan Grant

33 ❑ Dec 1994 Cover: 1.95 **NM** value: **2.50**
Circ: CapCity orders: **35,200**
Prodigal, Part 6 **A:** Bret Blevins **W:** Alan Grant

34 ❑ Jan 1995 Cover: 1.95 **NM** value: **2.50**
Circ: CapCity orders: **34,000**
Prodigal, Part 10 **A:** M.D. Bright **W:** Alan Grant

35 ❑ Feb 1995 Cover: 1.95 **NM** value: **2.50**
W: Alan Grant

35/SC ❑ Feb 1995 Cover: 2.95 **NM** value: **Cover or less**
Circ: CapCity orders: **41,875** • **CGC:** 2 graded, best 9.4
enhanced cover. **W:** Alan Grant

36 ❑ Mar 1995 Cover: 1.95 **NM** value: **2.00**
Circ: CapCity orders: **32,700**
Black Canary: In the Name of the Father; Black Canary II (Dinah Lance) appearance; Origin of Black Canary II (Dinah Lance) **A:** Barry Kitson **W:** Alan Grant ★ Appearance of Black Canary.

37 ❑ Apr 1995 Cover: 1.95 **NM** value: **2.00**
Circ: CapCity orders: **31,125**

38 ❑ May 1995 Cover: 1.95 **NM** value: **2.00**
Circ: CapCity orders: **31,450**

39 ❑ Jun 1995 Cover: 1.95 **NM** value: **2.00**
Circ: CapCity orders: **29,450**
★ Versus Anarky.

40 ❑ Jul 1995 Cover: 1.95 **NM** value: **2.00**
Circ: CapCity orders: **27,725**
★ Versus Anarky.

41 ❑ Aug 1995 Cover: 1.95 **NM** value: **2.00**
Circ: CapCity orders: **28,400**

42 ❑ Sep 1995 Cover: 1.95 **NM** value: **2.00**
Circ: CapCity orders: **26,200**
Feedback: The Day the Music Died

43 ❑ Oct 1995 Cover: 1.95 **NM** value: **2.00**
Circ: CapCity orders: **22,025**
Ratcatcher: The Secret of the Universe, Part 1

44 ❑ Nov 1995 Cover: 1.95 **NM** value: **2.00**

45 ❑ Dec 1995 Cover: 1.95 **NM** value: **2.00**
• Wayne Manor history

46 ❑ Jan 1996 Cover: 1.95 **NM** value: **2.00**
Cornelius Stirk, Part 1 of 2 **A:** Tommy Lee Edwards **W:** Alan Grant

47 ❑ Feb 1996 Cover: 1.95 **NM** value: **2.00**
Cornelius Stirk, Part 2 of 2 **A:** Tommy Lee Edwards **W:** Alan Grant

48 ❑ Mar 1996 Cover: 1.95 **NM** value: **2.00**
Contagion, Part 1 • trading card bound in **A:** Vince Giarrano **W:** Alan Grant

49 ❑ Apr 1996 Cover: 1.95 **NM** value: **2.00**
Contagion, Part 7 **A:** Vince Giarrano **W:** Alan Grant

50 ❑ May 1996 Cover: 1.95 **NM** value: **2.00**

51 ❑ Jun 1996 Cover: 1.95 **NM** value: **Cover or less**

52 ❑ Jul 1996 Cover: 1.95 **NM** value: **Cover or less**

53 ❑ Aug 1996 Cover: 1.95 **NM** value: **Cover or less**
Legacy Prelude **A:** David Taylor **W:** Alan Grant ★ Appearance of Huntress.

54 ❑ Sep 1996 Cover: 1.95 **NM** value: **Cover or less**
Legacy, Part 4

55 ❑ Oct 1996 Cover: 1.95 **NM** value: **Cover or less**
Stamdard Operating Procedure **A:** Rick Burchett; Klaus Janson **W:** Alan Grant

56 ❑ Nov 1996 Cover: 1.95 **NM** value: **Cover or less**
Circ: Diamd. preorders: **54,018**
Leaves of Grass, Part 1 **A:** David Taylor **W:** Alan Grant ★ Versus Poison Ivy.

57 ❑ Dec 1996 Cover: 1.95 **NM** value: **Cover or less**
Circ: Direct Market orders: **53,960**
Leaves of Grass, Part 2 **A:** David Taylor **W:** Alan Grant ★ Versus Poison Ivy.

58 ❑ Jan 1997 Cover: 1.95 **NM** value: **Cover or less**
Circ: Direct Market orders: **51,287**
Leaves of Grass, Part 3 **A:** David Taylor **W:** Alan Grant ★ Versus Floronic Man.

59 ❑ Feb 1997 Cover: 1.95 **NM** value: **Cover or less**
Circ: Diamd. preorders: **49,085**
Killer Killer, Part 1 **A:** David Taylor **W:** Alan Grant ★ Versus Scarface.

60 ❑ Mar 1997 Cover: 1.95 **NM** value: **Cover or less**
Circ: Diamd. preorders: **47,282**
Killer Killer, Part 2 **A:** David Taylor **W:** Alan Grant ★ Versus Scarface.

61 ❑ Apr 1997 Cover: 1.95 **NM** value: **Cover or less**
Circ: Diamd. preorders: **45,521**

62 ❑ May 1997 Cover: 1.95 **NM** value: **Cover or less**
Circ: Diamd. preorders: **44,608**
Janus, Part 1 ★ Versus Two-Face.

63 ❑ Jun 1997 Cover: 1.95 **NM** value: **Cover or less**
Circ: Diamd. preorders: **45,818**
Janus, Part 2 ★ Versus Two-Face.

64 ❑ Jul 1997 Cover: 1.95 **NM** value: **Cover or less**
Circ: Diamd. preorders: **42,961**
The Wedding Present **A:** David Taylor **W:** Alan Grant

65 ❑ Aug 1997 Cover: 1.95 **NM** value: **Cover or less**
Circ: Diamd. preorders: **42,354**

66 ❑ Sep 1997 Cover: 1.95 **NM** value: **Cover or less**
Circ: Diamd. preorders: **41,124**

67 ❑ Oct 1997 Cover: 1.95 **NM** value: **Cover or less**
Circ: Diamd. preorders: **41,208**

68 ❑ Nov 1997 Cover: 1.95 **NM** value: **Cover or less**
Circ: Diamd. preorders: **40,754**

69 ❑ Dec 1997 Cover: 1.95 **NM** value: **Cover or less**
Circ: Diamd. preorders: **41,675**
The Spirit of 2000, Part 1 **A:** Mark Buckingham **W:** Alan Grant ★ Appearance of Fate.

70 ❑ Jan 1998 Cover: 1.95 **NM** value: **Cover or less**
Circ: Diamd. preorders: **40,158**
The Spirit of 2000, Part 2 **A:** Mark Buckingham **W:** Alan Grant ★ Appearance of Fate.

71 ❑ Feb 1998 Cover: 1.95 **NM** value: **Cover or less**
Circ: Diamd. preorders: **39,236**

72 ❑ Mar 1998 Cover: 1.95 **NM** value: **Cover or less**
Circ: Diamd. preorders: **38,011**
★ 1st Appearance of Drakken.

73 ❑ Apr 1998 Cover: 1.95 **NM** value: **Cover or less**
Circ: Diamd. preorders: **44,027**
Cataclysm, Part 1 • continues in Nightwing #19 **A:** Mark Buckingham **W:** Alan Grant

74 ❑ May 1998 Cover: 1.95 **NM** value: **Cover or less**
Circ: Diamd. preorders: **42,680**
Cataclysm, Part 9 • continues in Batman Chronicles #12

75 ❑ Jun 1998 Cover: 2.95 **NM** value: **Cover or less**
Circ: Diamd. preorders: **43,427**
• Aftershock ★ Versus Clayface. ★ Versus Mr. Freeze.

76 ❑ Jul 1998 Cover: 1.95 **NM** value: **Cover or less**
Circ: Diamd. preorders: **39,414**
• Aftershock

77 ❑ Aug 1998 Cover: 1.95 **NM** value: **Cover or less**
Circ: Diamd. preorders: **39,085**
• Aftershock

78 ❑ Sep 1998 Cover: 1.99 **NM** value: **Cover or less**
Circ: Diamd. preorders: **37,167**
• Aftershock

79 ❑ Oct 1998 Cover: 1.99 **NM** value: **Cover or less**
Circ: Diamd. preorders: **35,907**
• Aftershock

80 ❑ Dec 1998 Cover: 3.95 **NM** value: **Cover or less**
Circ: Diamd. preorders: **42,675**
Waxman and the Clown, Part 1 • Road to No Man's Land;flipbook with Azrael: Agent of the Bat #47;Road to No Man's Land, flipbook with Azrael: Agent of the Bat #47

80/LE ❑ Dec 1998 Cover: 3.95 **NM** value: **Cover or less**
• Extra-sized flip-book.

81 ❑ Jan 1999 Cover: 1.99 **NM** value: **Cover or less**
Circ: Diamd. preorders: **35,610**
Waxman and the Clown, Part 2; Road to No Man's Land • Road to No Man's Land **A:** Mark Buckingham **W:** Alan Grant ★ Appearance of Jeremiah Arkham.

82 ❑ Feb 1999 Cover: 1.99 **NM** value: **Cover or less**
Circ: Diamd. preorders: **35,443**
Waxman and the Clown, Part 3; Road to No Man's Land • Road to No Man's Land **A:** Mark Buckingham **W:** Alan Grant

83 ❑ Mar 1999 Cover: 1.99 **NM** value: **9.00**
Circ: Diamd. preorders: **42,108** • **CGC:** 27 graded, best 9.8
No Law and a New Order, Part 2 • No Man's Land **A:** Alex Maleev ★ 1st Appearance of new Batgirl.

84 ❑ Apr 1999 Cover: 1.99 **NM** value: **Cover or less**
Circ: Diamd. preorders: **36,419**
Fear of Faith, Part 2 • No Man's Land ★ Appearance of Scarecrow, Huntress, Batgirl.

85 ❑ May 1999 Cover: 1.99 **NM** value: **Cover or less**
Circ: Diamd. preorders: **39,567**
Bread and Circuses, Part 2 • No Man's Land ★ Appearance of Batgirl. ★ Versus Penguin.

86 ❑ Jun 1999 Cover: 1.99 **NM** value: **Cover or less**
Circ: Diamd. preorders: **42,841**
Home Sweet Home; No Man's Land: Home Sweet Home • No Man's Land **A:** Guy Davis **W:** Lisa Klink

87 ❑ Jul 1999 Cover: 1.99 **NM** value: **Cover or less**
Circ: Diamd. preorders: **44,153**
Claim Jumping, Part 2 • No Man's Land **A:** Mike Deodato **W:** Greg Rucka ★ Appearance of Two-Face.

88 ❑ Aug 1999 Cover: 1.99 **NM** value: **Cover or less**
Circ: Diamd. preorders: **45,333**
Fruit of the Earth, Part 1 • No Man's Land;continues in Batman #568 **A:** Bill Sienkiewicz; Dan Jurgens **W:** Greg Rucka ★ Appearance of Poison Ivy. ★ Versus Clayface.

89 ❑ Sep 1999 Cover: 1.99 **NM** value: **Cover or less**
Circ: Diamd. preorders: **44,850**
The King • No Man's Land **A:** Jason Minor **W:** Ian Edginton ★ Versus Killer Croc.

90 ❑ Oct 1999 Cover: 1.99 **NM** value: **Cover or less**
Circ: Diamd. preorders: **45,835**
Low Road to Golden Mountain, Part 2; Positive Role Model • No Man's Land **A:** Paul Gulacy **W:** Larry Hama ★ Appearance of Lynx.

91 ❑ Nov 1999 Cover: 1.99 **NM** value: **Cover or less**
Circ: Diamd. preorders: **44,311**

Other grades: Multiply prices above by **1.5 for Mint • 2/3 for Very Fine • 1/3 for Fine • 1/5 for Very Good • 1/8 for Good**

92 ❑ Dec 1999 Cover: 1.99 **NM** value: **Cover or less**
Circ: Diamd. preorders: **46,950**
Stormy Weather • No Man's Land **A:** Dale Eaglesham **W:** Devin Grayson

93 ❑ Jan 2000 Cover: 1.99 **NM** value: **Cover or less**
Circ: Diamd. preorders: **45,236**
Assembly Redux • No Man's Land **A:** Bill Sienkiewicz; Paul Ryan **W:** Greg Rucka

94 ❑ Feb 2000 Cover: 1.99 **NM** value: **Cover or less**
Circ: Diamd. preorders: **49,301**
final issue.

1000000❑Nov 1998 Cover: 1.99 **NM** value: **Cover or less**
Circ: Diamd. preorders: **45,279**
• Aftershock

Anl 1❑ca. 1993 Cover: 3.50 **NM** value: **4.00**
Circ: CapCity orders: **44,650**
Bloodlines • Bloodlines★ 1st Appearance of Joe Public.

Anl 2❑ca. 1994 Cover: 3.95 **NM** value: **Cover or less**
Circ: CapCity orders: **26,850**
• Elseworlds

Anl 3❑ca. 1995 Cover: 3.95 **NM** value: **Cover or less**
Circ: CapCity orders: **17,675**
• Year One★ Origin of Poison Ivy.

Anl 4❑Nov 1996 Cover: 2.95 **NM** value: **Cover or less**
Circ: Diamd. preorders: **44,414**
King Batman • Legends of the Dead Earth;1996 Annual **A:** Brian Apthorp **W:** Alan Grant

Anl 5❑Oct 1997 Cover: 3.95 **NM** value: **Cover or less**
Circ: Diamd. preorders: **34,487**
• 1997 Annual;Pulp Heroes★ Versus Poison Ivy.

Bk 1❑ Cover: 12.95 **NM** value: **Cover or less**
• Trade Paperback. I was the Love Slave of a Plant-Based Killer! • The Last Arkham;collects Batman: Shadow of the Bat #1-4 **A:** Stefano Raffaele **W:** Alan Grant

BATMAN: SHAMAN — DC

Bk 1❑ Cover: 12.95 **NM** value: **Cover or less**

BATMAN: SON OF THE DEMON — DC

Bk 1❑ Dec 1987 Cover: 8.95 **NM** value: **Cover or less**
Circ: CapCity orders: **8,850**

Bk 1/HC❑ Cover: 50.00 **NM** value: **Cover or less**
Circ: CapCity orders: **10,700**
hardcover.

Bk 1-2❑ Cover: 9.95 **NM** value: **Cover or less**
Circ: CapCity orders: **5,100**

BATMAN-SPAWN: WAR DEVIL — DC

1 ❑ Cover: 4.95 **NM** value: **Cover or less**
Circ: CapCity orders: **104,800** • **CGC:** 9 graded, best 9.8
No issue number. • prestige format. • crossover with Image **A:** Klaus Janson **W:** Chuck Dixon; Alan Grant; Doug Moench

BATMAN SPECIAL — DC

1 ❑ Cover: 1.25 **NM** value: **2.00**
...The Player on the Other Side **A:** Michael Golden

BATMAN/SPIDER-MAN — DC

This was yet another DC-Marvel crossover — in this case, by J.M. DeMatteis, Graham Nolan, and Karl Kesel.

Batman and Spider-Man join forces to combat the schemes of Bat-villain Ra's al Ghul and Spider-villain The Kingpin.

The Kingpin's wife, Vanessa, is dying of a disease to which al Ghul has the cure. The story spends quite a bit of time with negotiation between the two rival camps and little on action. There's very little chemistry between Batman and Spider-Man, making the reader wonder why the two were ever teamed in the first place. — Brent

1 ❑ Oct 1997 Cover: 4.95 **NM** value: **Cover or less**
Circ: Diamd. preorders: **63,883**
No issue number. • prestige format. • crossover with Marvel★ Versus Kingpin. ★ Versus Ra's Al Ghul.

BATMAN: SPOILER/HUNTRESS - BLUNT TRAUMA — DC

1 ❑ Cover: 2.95 **NM** value: **Cover or less**
A: Eduardo Barreto **W:** Chuck Dixon

2 ❑ Cover: 2.95 **NM** value: **Cover or less**
A: Eduardo Barreto **W:** Chuck Dixon

3 ❑ Cover: 2.95 **NM** value: **Cover or less**
A: Eduardo Barreto **W:** Chuck Dixon

4 ❑ Cover: 2.95 **NM** value: **Cover or less**
A: Eduardo Barreto **W:** Chuck Dixon

There are two different pricing tiers in the modern comic-book hobby. **The prices seen above** are the prices we have seen **loose copies** of these issues reliably fetch in a variety of environments. Condition alters the price by the fractions seen on the bar on the bottom of left-hand pages of this book. **Comics graded by CGC** usually sell for more. Use the guide on the bottom of right-hand pages of this book to estimate what copies have brought on eBay.

BATMAN: SWORD OF AZRAEL — DC

For centuries, the secret order of St. Dumas has chosen one of its members to become Azrael, the angel of death. Azrael's purpose: to exact deadly vengeance on those who spread the evils of crime and corruption. When the current Azrael encounters arms merchant Carlton LeHah, however, he finds that his armor is no match for the arms dealer's Teflon bullets. Azrael falls, mortally wounded, into the midst of a parade in Gotham City, escaping only to die at the house of his young son.

The son, discovering that he is heir to a terrible legacy, travels to Switzerland to assume the role of the new Azrael. Meanwhile, Batman's investigation of the strange disturbance at the parade leads him to uncover Azrael's secret. He follows the boy to Switzerland, only to find himself in the midst of a war of vengeance.

1 ❑ Oct 1992 Cover: 1.75 **NM** value: **6.00**
• **CGC:** 15 graded, best 9.8
Wraparound, gatefold cover. **A:** Joe Quesada **W:** Denny O'Neil ★ 1st Appearance of Azrael.

1/SI❑ Oct 1992 Cover: 1.95 **NM** value: **Cover or less**
Circ: CapCity orders: **59,100**
• silver edition. **A:** Joe Quesada **W:** Denny O'Neil

2 ❑ Nov 1992 Cover: 1.75 **NM** value: **4.00**
• **CGC:** 2 graded, best 9.6
A: Joe Quesada **W:** Denny O'Neil

2/SI❑ Nov 1992 Cover: 1.95 **NM** value: **Cover or less**
Circ: CapCity orders: **38,100**
• silver edition. **A:** Joe Quesada **W:** Denny O'Neil

3 ❑ Dec 1992 Cover: 1.75 **NM** value: **3.00**
• **CGC:** 3 graded, best 9.8
A: Joe Quesada **W:** Denny O'Neil

3/SI❑ Dec 1992 Cover: 1.95 **NM** value: **Cover or less**
Circ: CapCity orders: **34,500**
• silver edition. **A:** Joe Quesada **W:** Denny O'Neil

4 ❑ Jan 1993 Cover: 1.75 **NM** value: **3.00**
• **CGC:** 3 graded, best 9.6
A: Joe Quesada **W:** Denny O'Neil

4/SI❑ Jan 1993 Cover: 1.95 **NM** value: **Cover or less**
Circ: CapCity orders: **31,400**
• silver edition. **A:** Joe Quesada **W:** Denny O'Neil

Bk 1❑ Cover: 9.95 **NM** value: **Cover or less**
• Collects Sword of Azrael 1-4 **A:** Joe Quesada **W:** Denny O'Neil

Bk 1/GO❑ **NM** value: **12.00**
• **CGC:** 2 graded, best 9.8
• Gold logo limited edition. • Collects Sword of Azrael 1-4 **A:** Joe Quesada **W:** Denny O'Neil

Bk 1/PL❑ **NM** value: **25.00**
• Platinum limited edition. • Collects Sword of Azrael 1-4 **A:** Joe Quesada

BATMAN: TALES OF THE DEMON — DC

Bk 1❑ Cover: 17.95 **NM** value: **Cover or less**
• reprints Ra's Al Ghul stories

BATMAN/TARZAN: CLAWS OF THE CAT-WOMAN — Dark Horse

1 ❑ Sep 1999 Cover: 2.95 **NM** value: **Cover or less**
Circ: Diamd. preorders: **33,745**
A: Igor Kordey; Dave Dorman(cover) **W:** Ron Marz

2 ❑ Oct 1999 Cover: 2.95 **NM** value: **Cover or less**
Circ: Diamd. preorders: **30,974**
A: Igor Kordey; Dave Dorman(cover) **W:** Ron Marz

3 ❑ Nov 1999 Cover: 2.95 **NM** value: **Cover or less**
Circ: Diamd. preorders: **27,748**
A: Igor Kordey; Dave Dorman(cover) **W:** Ron Marz

4 ❑ Dec 1999 Cover: 2.95 **NM** value: **Cover or less**
Circ: Diamd. preorders: **25,441**
A: Igor Kordey; Dave Dorman(cover) **W:** Ron Marz

BATMAN: THE ABDUCTION — DC

1 ❑ Jun 1998 Cover: 5.95 **NM** value: **Cover or less**
Circ: Diamd. preorders: **31,691**
No issue number. One-shot. • prestige format. • Batman kidnapped by aliens

BATMAN: THE BLUE, THE GREY, AND THE BAT — DC

1 ❑ 1992 Cover: 5.95 **NM** value: **Cover or less**
Circ: CapCity orders: **23,500**
No issue number. • prestige format. • Elseworlds

BATMAN: THE BOOK OF SHADOWS — DC

1 ❑ Cover: 5.95 **NM** value: **Cover or less**
No issue number. • prestige format. **A:** Duke Mighten **W:** Debbie Gallagher; Pat Mills

BATMAN: THE CHALICE — DC

1 ❑ Jan 2000 Cover: 14.95 **NM** value: **Cover or less**
A: John Van Fleet **W:** Chuck Dixon

1/HC❑ Cover: 24.95 **NM** value: **Cover or less**
hardcover. **A:** John Van Fleet **W:** Chuck Dixon

BATMAN: THE CULT — DC

1 ❑ Aug 1988 Cover: 3.50 **NM** value: **5.00**
Circ: CapCity orders: **52,400** • **CGC:** 18 graded, best 9.9
A: Jim Starlin; Bernie Wrightson **W:** Jim Starlin

2 ❑ Sep 1988 Cover: 3.50 **NM** value: **4.00**
Circ: CapCity orders: **43,450** • **CGC:** 5 graded, best 9.9
A: Jim Starlin; Bernie Wrightson **W:** Jim Starlin

3 ❑ Oct 1988 Cover: 3.50 **NM** value: **4.00**
Circ: CapCity orders: **47,050** • **CGC:** 3 graded, best 9.8
Escape **A:** Jim Starlin; Bernie Wrightson **W:** Jim Starlin

4 ❑ Nov 1988 Cover: 3.50 **NM** value: **4.00**
Circ: CapCity orders: **49,300** • **CGC:** 4 graded, best 9.8
Combat **A:** Jim Starlin; Bernie Wrightson **W:** Jim Starlin

Bk 1❑ Mar 1991 Cover: 14.95 **NM** value: **Cover or less**
Circ: CapCity orders: **5,750**
• Collects Batman: The Cult #1-4 **A:** Bernie Wrightson **W:** Jim Starlin

BATMAN: THE DAILIES — DC / Kitchen Sink

1 ❑ Nov 1990 Cover: 12.95 **NM** value: **Cover or less**
Circ: CapCity orders: **6,200**
• strip reprints

2 ❑ Dec 1990 Cover: 12.95 **NM** value: **Cover or less**
Circ: CapCity orders: **4,750**
• strip reprints

3 ❑ Jan 1991 Cover: 12.95 **NM** value: **Cover or less**
Circ: CapCity orders: **4,150**
• strip reprints

BATMAN: THE DARK KNIGHT — DC

The super-heroes have been persecuted, then regulated. Wonder Woman has gone back to her people; Green Lantern has left for the stars; and Superman is an agent for the government, quietly fighting its dirty little wars for it. Only Batman — that aging legend — dares laugh in their faces.

The world is poised on the brink of nuclear war; Batman has been declared an outlaw; and Commissioner Gordon has been replaced by a woman whose dearest desire is to see Batman dead or behind bars.

And The Joker is guest-starring on late-night TV.

This four-issue series by Frank Miller changed the legend of the Batman forever and introduced a new format for comics. Before, he was just a crimefighter. When it's over, he'll have truly become The Dark Knight.

1 ❑ Mar 1986 Cover: 2.95 **NM** value: **35.00**
Circ: CapCity orders: **24,100** • **CGC:** 141 graded, best 9.8
The Dark Knight Returns • Squarebound **A:** Frank Miller **W:** Frank Miller

1-2 ❑ Cover: 2.95 **NM** value: **9.00**

1-3 ❑ Cover: 2.95 **NM** value: **7.50**

2 ❑ Mar 1986 Cover: 2.95 **NM** value: **12.00**
Circ: CapCity orders: **21,950** • **CGC:** 70 graded, best 9.8
A: Frank Miller **W:** Frank Miller

2-2 ❑ Cover: 2.95 **NM** value: **4.00**
• **CGC:** 4 graded, best 9.6

2-3 ❑ Cover: 2.95 **NM** value: **3.00**

3 ❑ Cover: 2.95 **NM** value: **8.00**
Circ: CapCity orders: **26,300** • **CGC:** 82 graded, best 9.8
Hunt The Dark Knight **A:** Frank Miller **W:** Frank Miller ★ Death of Joker (future).

3-2 ❑ Cover: 2.95 **NM** value: **3.00**

4 ❑ Cover: 2.95 **NM** value: **6.00**
Circ: CapCity orders: **43,950** • **CGC:** 73 graded, best 9.8
The Dark Knight Falls **A:** Frank Miller **W:** Frank Miller ★ Death of Alfred (future).

Bk 1/HC❑ **NM** value: **100.00**
Circ: CapCity orders: **24,162**
A: Frank Miller **W:** Frank Miller

BATMAN: THE DARK KNIGHT ARCHIVES — DC

1 ❑ Cover: 39.95 **NM** value: **Cover or less**
The Legend of the Batman- • Reprints Batman #1-4 **A:** Bob Kane **W:** Bob Kane; Bill Finger; Gardner Fox ★ 1st Appearance of Joker.

2 ❑ **NM** value: **49.95**
• Reprints Batman #5-8

3 ❑ Cover: 49.95 **NM** value: **Cover or less**
The Four Fates!; The The White Whale!; The Case of the Lucky Law-Breakers!; The Isle that Time Forgot!; Report Card Blues • Reprints Batman #9-12 **A:** Bob Kane; Jerry Robinson **W:** Don Cameron; Bill Finger; Edmond Hamilton; Jack Schiff; Joseph Greene; Mike W. Barr

BATMAN: THE DOOM THAT CAME TO GOTHAM — DC

1 ❑ Nov 2000 Cover: 4.95 **NM** value: **Cover or less**
Circ: Diamd. preorders: **23,992**
A: Troy Nixey **W:** Mike Mignola

2 ❑ Dec 2000 Cover: 4.95 **NM** value: **Cover or less**
Circ: Diamd. preorders: **21,955**
A: Troy Nixey **W:** Mike Mignola

3 ❑ Jan 2001 Cover: 4.95 **NM** value: **Cover or less**
Circ: Diamd. preorders: **21,775**
A: Troy Nixey **W:** Mike Mignola

BATMAN: THE HILL — DC

1 ❑ May 2000 Cover: 2.95 **NM** value: **Cover or less**
Circ: Diamd. preorders: **27,491**
Heretic **A:** Shawn Martinbrough **W:** Christopher Priest

Looking for further information about a specific comic book or line of comics? Write a letter to ***Comics Buyer's Guide*** at ohso@krause.com — if we don't know, one of our readers always does!

CGC-graded: Multiply prices above by **33 for 9.9 M** • **16 for 9.8 NM/M** • **7 for 9.6 NM+** • **5 for 9.4 NM** • **2.5 for 9.2 NM-** • **1.5 for 9.0 VF/NM**

BATMAN: THE KILLING JOKE DC

The story begins with a visit to Arkham Asylum. There, in a cell which belongs to The Joker, a psychotic killer and Batman's greatest enemy, it seems that a switch has taken place. Another has taken The Joker's place, allowing The Joker to escape. Soon, Gotham City will once again face the terror the green-haired madman brings.

Scripted by Alan Moore, this is one of the best Joker stories ever told. It's a mad tale of terror that ushers in a new level of fear to the dark world of Batman, while simultaneously updating The Joker's origin, showing why Batman and The Joker need each other and providing a turning point in Barbara Gordon's life.

1 ❑ Jul 1988 Cover: 3.50 **NM** value: **11.00**
Circ: CapCity orders: **661,510** • **CGC:** 134 graded, best 10.0
• prestige format. • first printing **A:** Brian Bolland; Brian Bolland(cover) **W:** Alan Moore ★ Origin of Joker. ★ Versus Joker.
1-2 ❑ Cover: 3.50 **NM** value: **5.00**
1-3 ❑ Cover: 4.95 **NM** value: **5.00**
1-4 ❑ Cover: 4.95 **NM** value: **5.00**
1-5 ❑ Cover: 4.95 **NM** value: **5.00**
1-6 ❑ Cover: 4.95 **NM** value: **5.00**
1-7 ❑ Cover: 4.95 **NM** value: **5.00**
1-8 ❑ Cover: 4.95 **NM** value: **5.00**

BATMAN: THE LAST ANGEL DC

Bk 1❑ Cover: 12.95 **NM** value: **Cover or less**
Circ: CapCity orders: **7,550**
• prestige format.

BATMAN: THE LONG HALLOWEEN DC

Halloween can be a scary night for many people. For Batman, it's even worse. This Halloween promises to last for a year. A killer, dubbed "Holiday" by the media, goes on a killing spree, bumping off victims on holidays throughout the year, and the law is powerless to stop it. So Captain James Gordon and District Attorney Harvey Dent strike an alliance with Batman to bring down the killer before more people die.

This series also features an all-star cast of Gotham's villains: Catwoman, Solomon Grundy, The Joker, Poison Ivy, and The Riddler, to name a few.

This unusual "holiday special" is actually a 13-part mini-series, written by Jeph Loeb and featuring art by Tim Sale.

1 ❑ Dec 1996 Cover: 4.95 **NM** value: **12.00**
Circ: Direct Market orders: **63,230** • **CGC:** 8 graded, best 9.6
• prestige format. 📖 Crime **A:** Tim Sale **W:** Jeph Loeb
2 ❑ Jan 1997 Cover: 2.95 **NM** value: **9.00**
Circ: Direct Market orders: **56,770** • **CGC:** 2 graded, best 9.4
cardstock cover. 📖 Thanksgiving **A:** Tim Sale **W:** Jeph Loeb ★ Versus Solomon Grundy.
3 ❑ Feb 1997 Cover: 2.95 **NM** value: **8.00**
Circ: Diamd. preorders: **53,453** • **CGC:** 1 graded, best 9.6
cardstock cover. **A:** Tim Sale **W:** Jeph Loeb ★ Versus Joker.
4 ❑ Mar 1997 Cover: 2.95 **NM** value: **7.00**
Circ: Diamd. preorders: **52,744** • **CGC:** 1 graded, best 9.2
cardstock cover. 📖 New Year's Eve **A:** Tim Sale **W:** Jeph Loeb ★ Versus Joker.
5 ❑ Apr 1997 Cover: 2.95 **NM** value: **5.00**
Circ: Diamd. preorders: **51,392** • **CGC:** 1 graded, best 9.2
cardstock cover. **A:** Tim Sale **W:** Jeph Loeb ★ Appearance of Catwoman, Poison Ivy.
6 ❑ May 1997 Cover: 2.95 **NM** value: **5.00**
Circ: Diamd. preorders: **52,697** • **CGC:** 1 graded, best 9.4
cardstock cover. 📖 St. Patrick's Day **A:** Tim Sale **W:** Jeph Loeb ★ Versus Poison Ivy.
7 ❑ Jun 1997 Cover: 2.95 **NM** value: **4.00**
Circ: Diamd. preorders: **53,686** • **CGC:** 1 graded, best 9.4
cardstock cover. **A:** Tim Sale **W:** Jeph Loeb ★ Versus Riddler.
8 ❑ Jul 1997 Cover: 2.95 **NM** value: **4.00**
Circ: Diamd. preorders: **51,921** • **CGC:** 1 graded, best 9.2
cardstock cover. **A:** Tim Sale **W:** Jeph Loeb ★ Versus Scarecrow.
9 ❑ Aug 1997 Cover: 2.95 **NM** value: **4.00**
Circ: Diamd. preorders: **51,444** • **CGC:** 1 graded, best 9.4
cardstock cover. **A:** Tim Sale **W:** Jeph Loeb
10 ❑ Sep 1997 Cover: 2.95 **NM** value: **4.00**
Circ: Diamd. preorders: **50,146** • **CGC:** 1 graded, best 9.2
cardstock cover. **A:** Tim Sale **W:** Jeph Loeb ★ Appearance of Catwoman. ★ Versus Scarecrow, Mad Hatter.
11 ❑ Oct 1997 Cover: 2.95 **NM** value: **3.50**
Circ: Diamd. preorders: **50,663** • **CGC:** 1 graded, best 9.4
cardstock cover. **A:** Tim Sale **W:** Jeph Loeb ★ Origin of Two-Face.
12 ❑ Nov 1997 Cover: 2.95 **NM** value: **3.50**
Circ: Diamd. preorders: **51,157** • **CGC:** 1 graded, best 9.6
cardstock cover. 📖 Labor Day • identity of Holiday revealed **A:** Tim Sale **W:** Jeph Loeb ★ Death of Maroni.
13 ❑ Dec 1997 Cover: 4.95 **NM** value: **6.00**
Circ: Diamd. preorders: **52,176** • **CGC:** 1 graded, best 9.4
• prestige format. **A:** Tim Sale **W:** Jeph Loeb ★ 1st Appearance of Holiday. ★ Versus Arkham inmates.

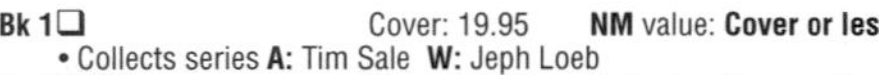

Bk 1❑ Cover: 19.95 **NM** value: **Cover or less**
• Collects series **A:** Tim Sale **W:** Jeph Loeb
Bk 1/HC❑ Cover: 29.95 **NM** value: **Cover or less**
• Hardcover edition. **A:** Tim Sale **W:** Jeph Loeb
Bk 1/LE❑ Cover: 59.95 **NM** value: **Cover or less**
A: Tim Sale **W:** Jeph Loeb

BATMAN: THE MOVIES DC

Bk 1❑ Cover: 19.95 **NM** value: **Cover or less**
• collects adaptations of first four Batman movies

BATMAN: THE OFFICIAL COMIC ADAPTATION OF THE WARNER BROS. MOTION PICTURE DC

1 ❑ Cover: 2.50 **NM** value: **3.00**
Circ: CapCity orders: **39,750**
• regular edition. • newsstand format;Comic adaptation of Warner Bros. Movie **A:** Jerry Ordway **W:** Denny O'Neil
1/PR❑ Cover: 4.95 **NM** value: **5.00**
Circ: CapCity orders: **20,900** • **CGC:** 3 graded, best 9.9
• prestige format. • Comic adaptation of Warner Bros. Movie

BATMAN: THE SUNDAY CLASSICS 1943-46 DC / Kitchen Sink

1 ❑ Cover: 19.95 **NM** value: **Cover or less**
Circ: CapCity orders: **3,800**
1/HC❑ Cover: 75.00 **NM** value: **Cover or less**
hardcover slipcased.

BATMAN: THE ULTIMATE EVIL DC

1 ❑ Cover: 5.95 **NM** value: **6.00**
• prestige format. • adapts Andrew Vachss novel **A:** Denys Cowan **W:** Andrew Vachss; Neal Barrett Jr.
2 ❑ Cover: 5.95 **NM** value: **6.00**
• prestige format. • adapts Andrew Vachss novel **A:** Denys Cowan **W:** Andrew Vachss; Neal Barrett Jr.

BATMAN: THRILLKILLER DC

1 ❑ Cover: 12.95 **NM** value: **Cover or less**
• collects Thrillkiller #1-3 and Thrillkiller '62

BATMAN: TOYMAN DC

1 ❑ Nov 1998 Cover: 2.25 **NM** value: **Cover or less**
Circ: Diamd. preorders: **28,914**
📖 Incident Report: The Cops' Story **A:** Anthony Williams **W:** Larry Hama
2 ❑ Dec 1998 Cover: 2.25 **NM** value: **Cover or less**
Circ: Diamd. preorders: **26,080**
A: Anthony Williams **W:** Larry Hama
3 ❑ Jan 1999 Cover: 2.25 **NM** value: **Cover or less**
Circ: Diamd. preorders: **24,172**
• Wordless issue **A:** Anthony Williams **W:** Larry Hama
4 ❑ Feb 1999 Cover: 2.25 **NM** value: **Cover or less**
Circ: Diamd. preorders: **21,334**
A: Anthony Williams **W:** Larry Hama

BATMAN: TURNING POINTS DC

This series looks at pivotal moments in the lives of Batman and James Gordon, Gotham Police Commissioner and one of Batman's staunchest supporters. It concentrates on the great tragedies that have shaped both men over the years, such as the crippling of Gordon's daughter (aka Batgirl/Oracle) and the death of Jason Todd, the second Robin. Often, these "turning points" in their lives might have led them in vastly different directions, even causing them to abandon their role as heroes. The extent of despair they have faced over the years might even have driven lesser men to suicide. But both have been forged into better and stronger heroes by the anguish in their lives, usually emerging not only victorious but also rededicated to their battle against crime. Often, it was their enduring alliance and increasing friendship that made the difference in trying times.

1 ❑ Jan 2001 Cover: 2.50 **NM** value: **Cover or less**
Circ: Diamd. preorders: **35,795**
📖 'Til Death Do Us Part **A:** Steve Lieber **W:** Greg Rucka
2 ❑ Jan 2001 Cover: 2.50 **NM** value: **Cover or less**
Circ: Diamd. preorders: **34,547**
📖 From Generation to Generation like Cancer **A:** Steve Lieber; Joe Giella **W:** Ed Brubaker; Greg Rucka
3 ❑ Jan 2001 Cover: 2.50 **NM** value: **Cover or less**
Circ: Diamd. preorders: **34,476**
📖 Haunted **A:** Steve Lieber; Dick Giordano **W:** Ed Brubaker; Greg Rucka
4 ❑ Jan 2001 Cover: 2.50 **NM** value: **Cover or less**
Circ: Diamd. preorders: **34,187**
A: Steve Lieber **W:** Greg Rucka
5 ❑ Jan 2001 Cover: 2.50 **NM** value: **Cover or less**
Circ: Diamd. preorders: **34,400**
📖 Old as the Stars **A:** Steve Lieber; Paul Pope **W:** Greg Rucka

BATMAN: TWO-FACE-CRIME AND PUNISHMENT DC

1 ❑ Cover: 4.95 **NM** value: **Cover or less**
Circ: CapCity orders: **19,225**
No issue number. One-shot. cover forms diptych with Batman: Riddler – The Riddle Factory. • prestige format. **A:** Scott McDaniel **W:** J.M. DeMatteis

BATMAN: TWO FACES DC

1 ❑ Nov 1998 Cover: 4.95 **NM** value: **Cover or less**
Circ: Diamd. preorders: **26,117**
No issue number. • Elseworlds **A:** Anthony Williams **W:** Andy Lanning; Dan Abnett
1/LE❑ Nov 1998 Cover: 17.95 **NM** value: **Cover or less**
A: Anthony Williams **W:** Andy Lanning; Dan Abnett

BATMAN: TWO-FACE STRIKES TWICE DC

Harvey Dent was a rising young district attorney, until "Boss" Moron threw acid in his face during a trial. Dent, who had been handsome, was suddenly cursed by a face whose entire left side was greenish and twisted. The shock of this drove him over the edge of sanity, and he became the criminal Two-Face, obsessed with the number 2 and habitually flipping a two-headed coin to decide his next action. One side of the coin is "scarred" by marks etched into it. If that side comes up, his next act will be evil. If the other side came up, he will act for the cause of goodness.

Two-Face Strikes Back epitomizes this Batman villain's character in its very format. It's a set of two graphic novels, published as a flip-book. One side gives a classic Two-Face story drawn in the style of the Golden Age. The other is a more contemporary tale featuring modern, painted art.

1 ❑ Cover: 4.95 **NM** value: **5.00**
Circ: CapCity orders: **27,750**
📖 The Two Faces Of Janus **A:** Joe Staton **W:** Mike W. Barr
2 ❑ Cover: 4.95 **NM** value: **5.00**
Circ: CapCity orders: **26,250**
A: Daerick Gröss Jr. **W:** Mike W. Barr

BATMAN: VENGEANCE OF BANE II DC

1 ❑ Cover: 3.95 **NM** value: **4.00**
Circ: CapCity orders: **27,450**
No issue number. One-shot. **A:** Graham Nolan **W:** Chuck Dixon

BATMAN: VENGEANCE OF BANE SPECIAL DC

1 ❑ Jan 1993 Cover: 2.50 **NM** value: **6.00**
Circ: CapCity orders: **33,300** • **CGC:** 25 graded, best 9.8
A: Graham Nolan; Glenn Fabry(cover) **W:** Chuck Dixon ★ Origin of Bane. ★ 1st Appearance of Bane.

BATMAN VERSUS PREDATOR DC / Dark Horse

1 ❑ Cover: 1.95 **NM** value: **2.50**
• **CGC:** 3 graded, best 9.4
• newsstand **A:** Andy Kubert **W:** Dave Gibbons
1/A ❑ Cover: 4.95 **NM** value: **5.00**
• **CGC:** 7 graded, best 9.8
Batman on front cover. • prestige format. • trading cards **A:** Andy Kubert
1/B ❑ Cover: 4.95 **NM** value: **5.00**
Batman on back cover. • prestige format. • trading cards; Predator on front **A:** Andy Kubert
2 ❑ Cover: 1.95 **NM** value: **2.50**
Circ: CapCity orders: **40,750**
• newsstand **A:** Andy Kubert **W:** Dave Gibbons
2/PR❑ Cover: 4.95 **NM** value: **5.00**
Circ: CapCity orders: **66,050** • **CGC:** 2 graded, best 9.6
• prestige format. • pin-ups **A:** Andy Kubert **W:** Dave Gibbons
3 ❑ Cover: 1.95 **NM** value: **2.50**
Circ: CapCity orders: **34,850**
• newsstand **A:** Andy Kubert **W:** Dave Gibbons
3/PR❑ Cover: 4.95 **NM** value: **5.00**
Circ: CapCity orders: **61,200**
• prestige format. **A:** Andy Kubert **W:** Dave Gibbons
Bk 1❑ Cover: 5.95 **NM** value: **6.00**
Circ: CapCity orders: **91,900**
• Collects Batman Versus Predator #1-3 **A:** Andy Kubert **W:** Dave Gibbons

BATMAN VERSUS PREDATOR II: BLOODMATCH DC / Dark Horse

1 ❑ Cover: 2.50 **NM** value: **Cover or less**
Circ: CapCity orders: **57,000**
📖 Bloodmatch, Part 1 • Crossover, no year in indicia **A:** Paul Gulacy **W:** Doug Moench
2 ❑ Cover: 2.50 **NM** value: **Cover or less**
Circ: CapCity orders: **45,650**
📖 Bloodmatch, Part 2 • Crossover **A:** Paul Gulacy **W:** Doug Moench
3 ❑ Cover: 2.50 **NM** value: **Cover or less**
Circ: CapCity orders: **42,475**
📖 Bloodmatch, Part 3 • Crossover **A:** Paul Gulacy **W:** Doug Moench
4 ❑ Cover: 2.50 **NM** value: **Cover or less**
Circ: CapCity orders: **39,875**
📖 Bloodmatch, Part 4 • Crossover **A:** Paul Gulacy **W:** Doug Moench
Bk 1❑ Cover: 6.95 **NM** value: **Cover or less**
• collects mini-series

BATMAN VS. THE INCREDIBLE HULK DC

1 ❑ Fal 1981 Cover: 2.50 **NM** value: **Cover or less**
• oversized, (DC Special Series #27).
1-2 ❑ Cover: 3.95 **NM** value: **Cover or less**
• 2nd Printing, comics-sized.

BATMAN VILLAINS SECRET FILES DC

1 ❑ Oct 1998 Cover: 4.95 **NM** value: **Cover or less**
Circ: Diamd. preorders: **30,891**

Other grades: Multiply prices above by **1.5 for Mint • 2/3 for Very Fine • 1/3 for Fine • 1/5 for Very Good • 1/8 for Good**

BATMAN: WAR ON CRIME — DC

1 ❑ Nov 1999 Cover: 9.95 **NM** value: **Cover or less**
A: Alex Ross **W:** Paul Dini

BATMAN/WILDCAT — DC

The sweet science of professional boxing, constrained by rules and the constructs of civilization, is considered too tame for a few select, decadent individuals who have the money and stomach for something far more brutal. This circumstance gives rise to "The Secret Ring," a clandestine organization that arranges incredibly gruesome fights to the death. When both Bruce Wayne and Ted Grant see a video of Killer Croc beating the new Wildcat (Grant's protege) to death, these champions of justice, masters of pugilism themselves, take separate paths to end this savagery. Those paths lead them to face each other unknowingly in the most highly anticipated match of this barbarous business.

This three-issue mini-series presents a powerful pairing of Batman with Wildcat, the veteran crimefighter, who (in retroactive continuity adjustment) schooled the novice Bruce Wayne in the art of boxing during Batman's rookie days.

1 ❑ Apr 1997 Cover: 2.25 **NM** value: **Cover or less**
Circ: Diamd. preorders: **49,956**
📖 Lights, Cameras, Death **A:** Sergio Cariello **W:** Chuck Dixon; Beau Smith

2 ❑ May 1997 Cover: 2.25 **NM** value: **Cover or less**
Circ: Diamd. preorders: **44,377**

3 ❑ Jun 1997 Cover: 2.25 **NM** value: **Cover or less**
Circ: Diamd. preorders: **43,579**

BATMAN: YEAR ONE — DC

Bk 1❑ Cover: 9.95 **NM** value: **Cover or less**
Circ: CapCity orders: **3,900**
• paperback

Bk 1/HC❑ Cover: 30.00 **NM** value: **Cover or less**
Circ: CapCity orders: **8,200**
hardcover.

BATMAN YEAR TWO — DC

Bk 1❑ Cover: 9.95 **NM** value: **Cover or less**
Circ: CapCity orders: **17,100**
• paperback

BAT, THE (MARY ROBERTS RINEHART'S) — Adventure

1 ❑ Aug 1992, b&w Cover: 2.50 **NM** value: **Cover or less**
📖 Another Angry Young Bastard Adventure; True-Life Stories that Make Me Laugh; Wet Dream; The Man with One Arm; Bob's Life; Signs **A:** Neil Vokes **W:** Mark Wheatley; Rick Shanklin

BAT MASTERSON — Dell

Masterson was a real person (1853-1921), but this series was based on the Gene Barry TV series (1959-61) and featured photo covers of Barry. The real Masterson served as a Dodge City sheriff, and his appearance was set off by a derby and cane – which Barry's costuming echoed. The comic book's run did not continue long beyond the airing of the TV show. — Maggie

2 ❑ Feb 1960 Cover: 0.10 **NM** value: **30.00**
• **CGC:** 1 graded, best 9.2
3 ❑ May 1960 Cover: 0.10 **NM** value: **30.00**
• **CGC:** 2 graded, best 9.4
4 ❑ Aug 1960 Cover: 0.10 **NM** value: **30.00**
5 ❑ Nov 1960 Cover: 0.10 **NM** value: **30.00**
6 ❑ Feb 1961 Cover: 0.15 **NM** value: **30.00**
• **CGC:** 1 graded, best 7.0
7 ❑ May 1961 Cover: 0.15 **NM** value: **30.00**
8 ❑ Aug 1961 Cover: 0.15 **NM** value: **30.00**
9 ❑ Nov 1961 Cover: 0.15 **NM** value: **30.00**

BAT MEN — Avalon

1 ❑ Cover: 2.95 **NM** value: **Cover or less**
📖 Babe Ruth: The Sultan of Swat; Hero Gallery **A:** Joe Sinnott **W:** Joe Sinnott

BATS, CATS & CADILLACS — Now

1 ❑ Oct 1990 Cover: 1.75 **NM** value: **2.00**
Circ: CapCity orders: **2,925**
2 ❑ Nov 1990 Cover: 1.75 **NM** value: **2.00**
Circ: CapCity orders: **1,975**

To find prices for other grades for comic books not graded by CGC, multiply the above prices by:

Mint: 150%	VF-: 55%	VG-: 17%
NM/M:125%	F/VF: 48%	G+: 14%
NM+: 110%	F+: 40%	**Good: 12.5%**
NM-: 90%	**Fine: 33.3%**	G-: 11%
VF/NM: 83%	F-: 30%	FR/G: 10%
VF+: 75%	VG/F: 25%	**Fair: 8%**
Very Fine: 66.6%	VG+: 23%	**Poor: 2%**
	Very Good: 20%	

BAT-THING — DC / Amalgam

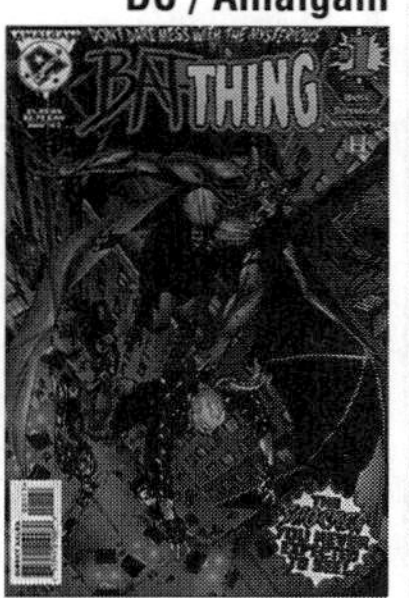

Dr. Kirk Sallis uses himself as a guinea pig for his genetic experiments, thinking a gene splice might cure him of a terminal illness. Instead, the gene splice — along with an unfortunate encounter with toxic sludge — turns him into a swamp creature that is part man, part bat. Enter Bat-Thing!

This character was one of several introduced in the second round of Amalgam comics in mid-1997. A combination of Marvel's Man-Thing and DC's Man-Bat, this hideously mutated monster lurks in the shadows while trying to protect the lives of his wife and daughter from a mobster and a crazed motorcycle gang.

1 ❑ Jun 1997 Cover: 1.95 **NM** value: **Cover or less**
Circ: Diamd. preorders: **123,338**
📖 Someone to Watch Over Me **A:** Rodolfo DaMaggio **W:** Larry Hama

BATTLE — Atlas

1 ❑ Mar 1951 Cover: 0.10 **NM** value: **150.00**
1 ❑ Mar 1951 Cover: 0.10 **NM** value: **150.00**
2 ❑ May 1951 Cover: 0.10 **NM** value: **100.00**
3 ❑ Jul 1951 Cover: 0.10 **NM** value: **75.00**
4 ❑ Sep 1951 Cover: 0.10 **NM** value: **50.00**
5 ❑ Nov 1951 Cover: 0.10 **NM** value: **50.00**
6 ❑ Jan 1952 Cover: 0.10 **NM** value: **50.00**
7 ❑ Mar 1952 Cover: 0.10 **NM** value: **50.00**
8 ❑ May 1952 Cover: 0.10 **NM** value: **50.00**
9 ❑ Jun 1952 Cover: 0.10 **NM** value: **50.00**
10 ❑ Jul 1952 Cover: 0.10 **NM** value: **50.00**
11 ❑ Aug 1952 Cover: 0.10 **NM** value: **42.00**
12 ❑ Sep 1952 Cover: 0.10 **NM** value: **42.00**
13 ❑ Oct 1952 Cover: 0.10 **NM** value: **42.00**
14 ❑ Nov 1952 Cover: 0.10 **NM** value: **42.00**
15 ❑ Dec 1952 Cover: 0.10 **NM** value: **42.00**
16 ❑ Jan 1953 Cover: 0.10 **NM** value: **42.00**
17 ❑ Feb 1953 Cover: 0.10 **NM** value: **42.00**
18 ❑ Mar 1953 Cover: 0.10 **NM** value: **42.00**
19 ❑ Apr 1953 Cover: 0.10 **NM** value: **42.00**
20 ❑ May 1953 Cover: 0.10 **NM** value: **42.00**
21 ❑ 1953 Cover: 0.10 **NM** value: **55.00**
A: Bernie Krigstein
22 ❑ 1953 Cover: 0.10 **NM** value: **40.00**
23 ❑ 1953 Cover: 0.10 **NM** value: **55.00**
A: Bernie Krigstein
24 ❑ 1953 Cover: 0.10 **NM** value: **40.00**
25 ❑ Cover: 0.10 **NM** value: **40.00**
26 ❑ Cover: 0.10 **NM** value: **40.00**
27 ❑ Mar 1954 Cover: 0.10 **NM** value: **40.00**
28 ❑ 1954 Cover: 0.10 **NM** value: **40.00**
29 ❑ 1954 Cover: 0.10 **NM** value: **40.00**
30 ❑ 1954 Cover: 0.10 **NM** value: **40.00**
31 ❑ 1954 Cover: 0.10 **NM** value: **30.00**
32 ❑ 1954 Cover: 0.10 **NM** value: **30.00**
33 ❑ 1954 Cover: 0.10 **NM** value: **30.00**
34 ❑ Nov 1954 Cover: 0.10 **NM** value: **30.00**
35 ❑ Dec 1954 Cover: 0.10 **NM** value: **30.00**
36 ❑ Jan 1955 Cover: 0.10 **NM** value: **30.00**
37 ❑ Feb 1955 Cover: 0.10 **NM** value: **30.00**
A: Joe Kubert
38 ❑ 1955 Cover: 0.10 **NM** value: **30.00**
39 ❑ 1955 Cover: 0.10 **NM** value: **30.00**
40 ❑ 1955 Cover: 0.10 **NM** value: **30.00**
41 ❑ 1955 Cover: 0.10 **NM** value: **30.00**
42 ❑ Sep 1955 Cover: 0.10 **NM** value: **30.00**
📖 The Flaming Field of Battle; Night Patrol; Top Man (text story); The Tattered Troops; Platoon Leader!
43 ❑ Cover: 0.10 **NM** value: **30.00**
44 ❑ Cover: 0.10 **NM** value: **30.00**
45 ❑ Cover: 0.10 **NM** value: **30.00**
46 ❑ Cover: 0.10 **NM** value: **30.00**
47 ❑ Cover: 0.10 **NM** value: **30.00**
48 ❑ Cover: 0.10 **NM** value: **30.00**
49 ❑ Cover: 0.10 **NM** value: **30.00**
50 ❑ Cover: 0.10 **NM** value: **30.00**
📖 Reds All Around Us!; We Attack at Dawn!; I Was Captured by the Enemy!; Face to Face!; When the Enemy Comes! **A:** Paul Reinman; Don Heck; Mac Pakula
51 ❑ Cover: 0.10 **NM** value: **25.00**
52 ❑ May 1957 Cover: 0.10 **NM** value: **25.00**
53 ❑ 1957 Cover: 0.10 **NM** value: **25.00**
54 ❑ 1957 Cover: 0.10 **NM** value: **25.00**
55 ❑ Cover: 0.10 **NM** value: **50.00**
A: Al Williamson
56 ❑ 1958 Cover: 0.10 **NM** value: **25.00**
57 ❑ 1958 Cover: 0.10 **NM** value: **25.00**
58 ❑ 1958 Cover: 0.10 **NM** value: **25.00**
59 ❑ Cover: 0.10 **NM** value: **25.00**
60 ❑ Cover: 0.10 **NM** value: **25.00**
61 ❑ Cover: 0.10 **NM** value: **25.00**
62 ❑ Cover: 0.10 **NM** value: **25.00**
63 ❑ Cover: 0.10 **NM** value: **25.00**
64 ❑ Jun 1959 Cover: 0.10 **NM** value: **45.00**
📖 Action on Quemoy **A:** Jack Kirby
65 ❑ Aug 1959 Cover: 0.10 **NM** value: **45.00**
📖 Find 'em, Chase 'em, Blast 'em; Ring of Steel **A:** Jack Kirby
66 ❑ Oct 1959 Cover: 0.10 **NM** value: **45.00**
• **CGC:** 1 graded, best 7.5
📖 Submarine **A:** Jack Kirby
67 ❑ Dec 1959 Cover: 0.10 **NM** value: **55.00**
📖 The Invincible Enemy **A:** Al Williamson
68 ❑ Feb 1960 Cover: 0.10 **NM** value: **55.00**
📖 Sitting Duck; Guard Duty **A:** Al Williamson
69 ❑ Apr 1960 Cover: 0.10 **NM** value: **45.00**
📖 Doom Under the Deep **A:** Al Williamson
70 ❑ Jun 1960 Cover: 0.10 **NM** value: **45.00**
📖 A Tank Knows No Mercy; The Thick of the Battle final issue. **A:** Al Williamson

BATTLE ACTION — Atlas

1 ❑ Feb 1952 Cover: 0.10 **NM** value: **150.00**
• **CGC:** 3 graded, best 8.5
2 ❑ Apr 1952 Cover: 0.10 **NM** value: **75.00**
3 ❑ Jun 1952 Cover: 0.10 **NM** value: **50.00**
4 ❑ Aug 1952 Cover: 0.10 **NM** value: **50.00**
5 ❑ Oct 1952 Cover: 0.10 **NM** value: **50.00**
6 ❑ Nov 1952 Cover: 0.10 **NM** value: **50.00**
7 ❑ Dec 1952 Cover: 0.10 **NM** value: **50.00**
8 ❑ Jan 1953 Cover: 0.10 **NM** value: **50.00**
9 ❑ Feb 1953 Cover: 0.10 **NM** value: **50.00**
10 ❑ Mar 1953 Cover: 0.10 **NM** value: **50.00**
11 ❑ Cover: 0.10 **NM** value: **40.00**
12 ❑ Cover: 0.10 **NM** value: **40.00**
13 ❑ Cover: 0.10 **NM** value: **40.00**
14 ❑ Dec 1954 Cover: 0.10 **NM** value: **40.00**
15 ❑ Feb 1955 Cover: 0.10 **NM** value: **40.00**
16 ❑ Apr 1955 Cover: 0.10 **NM** value: **40.00**
17 ❑ Jun 1955 Cover: 0.10 **NM** value: **40.00**
18 ❑ Aug 1955 Cover: 0.10 **NM** value: **40.00**
19 ❑ Oct 1955 Cover: 0.10 **NM** value: **40.00**
20 ❑ Dec 1955 Cover: 0.10 **NM** value: **40.00**
21 ❑ Feb 1956 Cover: 0.10 **NM** value: **35.00**
22 ❑ Apr 1956 Cover: 0.10 **NM** value: **35.00**
23 ❑ Jun 1956 Cover: 0.10 **NM** value: **35.00**
24 ❑ Aug 1956 Cover: 0.10 **NM** value: **35.00**
25 ❑ Oct 1956 Cover: 0.10 **NM** value: **35.00**
26 ❑ Dec 1956 Cover: 0.10 **NM** value: **35.00**
27 ❑ Feb 1957 Cover: 0.10 **NM** value: **35.00**
28 ❑ Apr 1957 Cover: 0.10 **NM** value: **35.00**
29 ❑ Jun 1957 Cover: 0.10 **NM** value: **35.00**
30 ❑ Aug 1957 Cover: 0.10 **NM** value: **35.00**

BATTLE ANGEL ALITA PART 1 — Viz

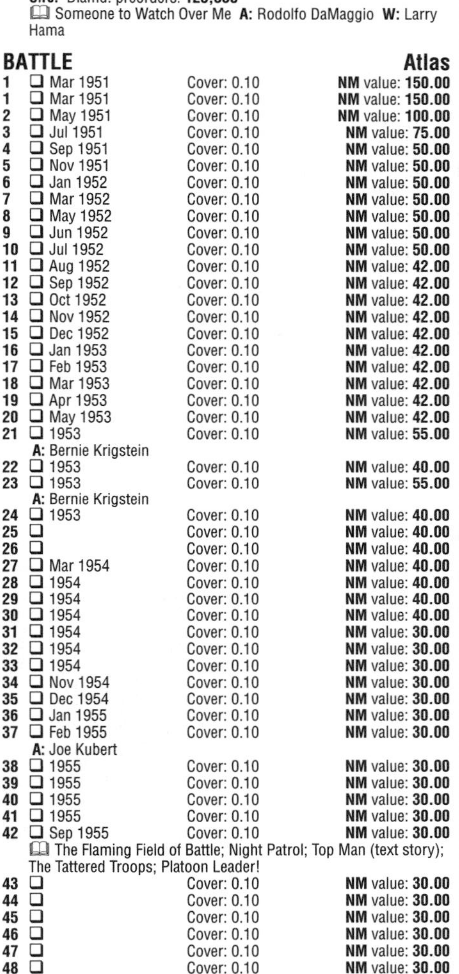

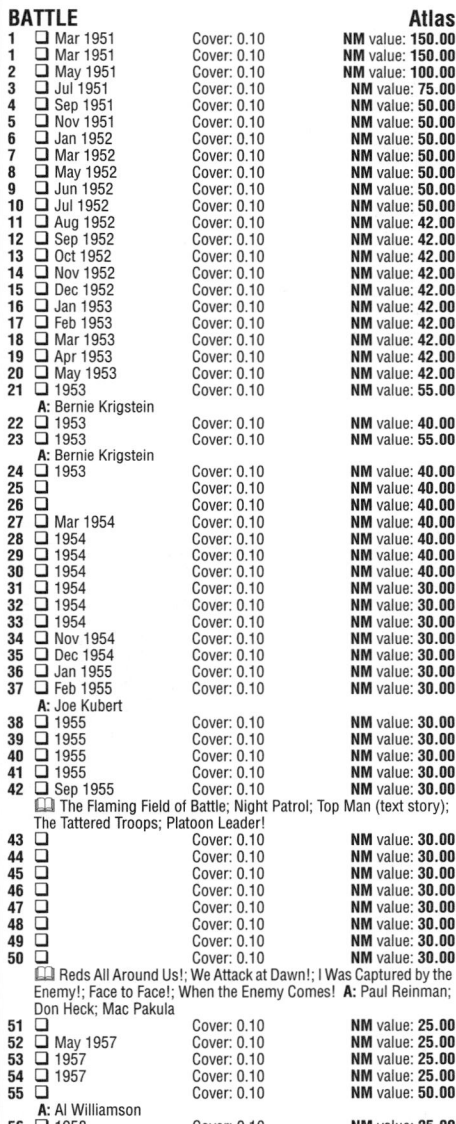

Scavenging in the junkyard, Doctor Daisuke discovers the head of a cyborg girl. She has lost her memory, so he names her Alita. As he tries to find parts to rebuild her, he discovers that she may not be the angel he had sought to create. His dreams of tranquility are replaced by his recognition of the incredible martial skills she instinctively possesses, and they are drawn into the consequences that having such power can bring.

Creator Yukito Kishiro was inspired to create Alita by the toys he'd played with when young. The world is one in which the garbage of a beautiful floating island provides the source of material for the poor — and in which cyborg gladiators compete.

1 ❑ Jul 1992 Cover: 2.75 **NM** value: **4.00**
A: Yukito Kishiro **W:** Yukito Kishiro ★ 1st Appearance of Alita.
2 ❑ Aug 1992 Cover: 2.75 **NM** value: **3.50**
Circ: CapCity orders: **3,500**
A: Yukito Kishiro **W:** Yukito Kishiro
3 ❑ Sep 1992 Cover: 2.75 **NM** value: **3.50**
Circ: CapCity orders: **3,200**
A: Yukito Kishiro **W:** Yukito Kishiro
4 ❑ Oct 1992 Cover: 2.75 **NM** value: **3.00**
Circ: CapCity orders: **3,275**
📖 Resurgence **A:** Yukito Kishiro **W:** Yukito Kishiro
5 ❑ Nov 1992 Cover: 2.75 **NM** value: **3.00**
Circ: CapCity orders: **3,450**
A: Yukito Kishiro **W:** Yukito Kishiro
6 ❑ Dec 1992 Cover: 2.75 **NM** value: **3.00**
Circ: CapCity orders: **3,650**
A: Yukito Kishiro **W:** Yukito Kishiro
7 ❑ Jan 1993 Cover: 2.75 **NM** value: **3.00**
Circ: CapCity orders: **3,550**
A: Yukito Kishiro **W:** Yukito Kishiro
8 ❑ Feb 1993 Cover: 2.75 **NM** value: **3.00**
Circ: CapCity orders: **4,175**
A: Yukito Kishiro **W:** Yukito Kishiro
9 ❑ Mar 1993 Cover: 2.75 **NM** value: **3.00**
Circ: CapCity orders: **3,825**
A: Yukito Kishiro **W:** Yukito Kishiro
Bk 1❑ Cover: 16.95 **NM** value: **Cover or less**
A: Yukito Kishiro **W:** Yukito Kishiro
Bk 2❑ Cover: 15.95 **NM** value: **Cover or less**
📖 Tears of an Angel **A:** Yukito Kishiro **W:** Yukito Kishiro

BATTLE ANGEL ALITA PART 2 — Viz

1 ❑ Apr 1993 Cover: 2.75 **NM** value: **3.00**
Circ: CapCity orders: **3,750**
A: Yukito Kishiro **W:** Yukito Kishiro
2 ❑ May 1993 Cover: 2.75 **NM** value: **Cover or less**
Circ: CapCity orders: **3,625**
A: Yukito Kishiro **W:** Yukito Kishiro
3 ❑ Jun 1993 Cover: 2.75 **NM** value: **Cover or less**
Circ: CapCity orders: **3,600**
A: Yukito Kishiro **W:** Yukito Kishiro
4 ❑ Jul 1993 Cover: 2.75 **NM** value: **Cover or less**
Circ: CapCity orders: **3,400**
A: Yukito Kishiro **W:** Yukito Kishiro

CGC-graded: Multiply prices above by **33 for 9.9 M • 16 for 9.8 NM/M • 7 for 9.6 NM+ • 5 for 9.4 NM • 2.5 for 9.2 NM- • 1.5 for 9.0 VF/NM**

5 ❑ Aug 1993 Cover: 2.75 **NM** value: **Cover or less**
Circ: CapCity orders: **3,400**
A: Yukito Kishiro **W:** Yukito Kishiro

6 ❑ Sep 1993 Cover: 2.75 **NM** value: **Cover or less**
Circ: CapCity orders: **3,525**
A: Yukito Kishiro **W:** Yukito Kishiro

7 ❑ Oct 1993 Cover: 2.75 **NM** value: **Cover or less**
Circ: CapCity orders: **3,450**
A: Yukito Kishiro **W:** Yukito Kishiro

BATTLE ANGEL ALITA PART 3 — Viz

1 ❑ Nov 1993 Cover: 2.75 **NM** value: **Cover or less**
Circ: CapCity orders: **3,825**
A: Yukito Kishiro **W:** Yukito Kishiro

2 ❑ Dec 1993 Cover: 2.75 **NM** value: **Cover or less**
Circ: CapCity orders: **3,500**
A: Yukito Kishiro **W:** Yukito Kishiro

3 ❑ Jan 1994 Cover: 2.75 **NM** value: **Cover or less**
Circ: CapCity orders: **3,350**
📖 The Skull Challenge **A:** Yukito Kishiro **W:** Yukito Kishiro

4 ❑ Feb 1994 Cover: 2.75 **NM** value: **Cover or less**
Circ: CapCity orders: **3,300**
A: Yukito Kishiro **W:** Yukito Kishiro

5 ❑ Mar 1994 Cover: 2.75 **NM** value: **Cover or less**
Circ: CapCity orders: **3,450**
A: Yukito Kishiro **W:** Yukito Kishiro

6 ❑ Apr 1994 Cover: 2.75 **NM** value: **Cover or less**
Circ: CapCity orders: **3,725**
A: Yukito Kishiro **W:** Yukito Kishiro

7 ❑ May 1994 Cover: 2.75 **NM** value: **Cover or less**
Circ: CapCity orders: **4,000**
A: Yukito Kishiro **W:** Yukito Kishiro

8 ❑ Jun 1994 Cover: 2.75 **NM** value: **Cover or less**
A: Yukito Kishiro **W:** Yukito Kishiro

9 ❑ Jul 1994 Cover: 2.75 **NM** value: **Cover or less**
Circ: CapCity orders: **4,125**
A: Yukito Kishiro **W:** Yukito Kishiro

10 ❑ Aug 1994 Cover: 2.75 **NM** value: **Cover or less**
Circ: CapCity orders: **4,225**
A: Yukito Kishiro **W:** Yukito Kishiro

11 ❑ Sep 1994 Cover: 2.75 **NM** value: **Cover or less**
Circ: CapCity orders: **4,100**
A: Yukito Kishiro **W:** Yukito Kishiro

12 ❑ Oct 1994 Cover: 2.75 **NM** value: **Cover or less**
Circ: CapCity orders: **4,100**
A: Yukito Kishiro **W:** Yukito Kishiro

13 ❑ Nov 1994 Cover: 2.75 **NM** value: **Cover or less**
Circ: CapCity orders: **4,050**
A: Yukito Kishiro **W:** Yukito Kishiro

Bk 3❑ Cover: 15.95 **NM** value: **Cover or less**
A: Yukito Kishiro **W:** Yukito Kishiro

Bk 4❑ Cover: 15.95 **NM** value: **Cover or less**
A: Yukito Kishiro **W:** Yukito Kishiro

BATTLE ANGEL ALITA PART 4 — Viz

1 ❑ Dec 1994 Cover: 2.75 **NM** value: **Cover or less**
Circ: CapCity orders: **4,200**
A: Yukito Kishiro **W:** Yukito Kishiro

2 ❑ Jan 1995 Cover: 2.75 **NM** value: **Cover or less**
Circ: CapCity orders: **3,925**
📖 Dog Master Cycle 2: Melody of Redemption **A:** Yukito Kishiro **W:** Yukito Kishiro

3 ❑ Feb 1995 Cover: 2.75 **NM** value: **Cover or less**
Circ: CapCity orders: **3,875**
A: Yukito Kishiro **W:** Yukito Kishiro

4 ❑ Mar 1995 Cover: 2.75 **NM** value: **Cover or less**
Circ: CapCity orders: **3,925**
A: Yukito Kishiro **W:** Yukito Kishiro

5 ❑ Apr 1995 Cover: 2.75 **NM** value: **Cover or less**
Circ: CapCity orders: **3,800**
A: Yukito Kishiro **W:** Yukito Kishiro

6 ❑ May 1995 Cover: 2.75 **NM** value: **Cover or less**
Circ: CapCity orders: **3,875**
A: Yukito Kishiro **W:** Yukito Kishiro

7 ❑ Jun 1995 Cover: 2.75 **NM** value: **Cover or less**
Circ: CapCity orders: **3,875**
A: Yukito Kishiro **W:** Yukito Kishiro

Bk 5❑ Cover: 15.95 **NM** value: **Cover or less**
A: Yukito Kishiro **W:** Yukito Kishiro

BATTLE ANGEL ALITA PART 5 — Viz

1 ❑ Jul 1995 Cover: 2.75 **NM** value: **Cover or less**
Circ: CapCity orders: **4,625**
📖 Beyond the Yellow Door **A:** Yukito Kishiro **W:** Yukito Kishiro

2 ❑ Aug 1995 Cover: 2.75 **NM** value: **Cover or less**
Circ: CapCity orders: **3,975**
A: Yukito Kishiro **W:** Yukito Kishiro

3 ❑ Sep 1995 Cover: 2.75 **NM** value: **Cover or less**
Circ: CapCity orders: **3,725**
A: Yukito Kishiro **W:** Yukito Kishiro

4 ❑ Oct 1995 Cover: 2.75 **NM** value: **Cover or less**
A: Yukito Kishiro **W:** Yukito Kishiro

5 ❑ Nov 1995 Cover: 2.75 **NM** value: **Cover or less**
A: Yukito Kishiro **W:** Yukito Kishiro

6 ❑ Dec 1995 Cover: 2.75 **NM** value: **Cover or less**
A: Yukito Kishiro **W:** Yukito Kishiro

7 ❑ Jan 1996 Cover: 2.95 **NM** value: **Cover or less**
A: Yukito Kishiro **W:** Yukito Kishiro

Bk 6❑ Cover: 15.95 **NM** value: **Cover or less**
A: Yukito Kishiro **W:** Yukito Kishiro

BATTLE ANGEL ALITA PART 6 — Viz

1 ❑ Feb 1996 Cover: 2.95 **NM** value: **Cover or less**
2 ❑ Mar 1996 Cover: 2.95 **NM** value: **Cover or less**
3 ❑ Apr 1996 Cover: 2.95 **NM** value: **Cover or less**
4 ❑ May 1996 Cover: 2.95 **NM** value: **Cover or less**
5 ❑ Jun 1996 Cover: 2.95 **NM** value: **Cover or less**
6 ❑ Jul 1996 Cover: 2.95 **NM** value: **Cover or less**
7 ❑ Aug 1996 Cover: 2.95 **NM** value: **Cover or less**
8 ❑ Sep 1996 Cover: 2.95 **NM** value: **Cover or less**
Circ: Diamd. preorders: **8,991**

Bk 7❑ Cover: 15.95 **NM** value: **Cover or less**

BATTLE ANGEL ALITA PART 7 — Viz

1 ❑ Oct 1996 Cover: 2.95 **NM** value: **Cover or less**
Circ: Diamd. preorders: **9,711**

2 ❑ Nov 1996 Cover: 2.95 **NM** value: **Cover or less**
Circ: Diamd. preorders: **9,041**

3 ❑ Dec 1996 Cover: 2.95 **NM** value: **Cover or less**
Circ: Direct Market orders: **8,819**

4 ❑ Jan 1997 Cover: 2.95 **NM** value: **Cover or less**
Circ: Direct Market orders: **8,591**

5 ❑ Feb 1997 Cover: 2.95 **NM** value: **Cover or less**
Circ: Diamd. preorders: **8,292**

6 ❑ Mar 1997 Cover: 2.95 **NM** value: **Cover or less**
Circ: Diamd. preorders: **7,933**

7 ❑ Apr 1997 Cover: 2.95 **NM** value: **Cover or less**
Circ: Diamd. preorders: **8,128**

8 ❑ May 1997 Cover: 2.95 **NM** value: **Cover or less**
Circ: Diamd. preorders: **7,493**

Bk 8❑ Nov 1997 Cover: 15.95 **NM** value: **Cover or less**

BATTLE ANGEL ALITA PART 8 — Viz

1 ❑ Jun 1997 Cover: 2.95 **NM** value: **Cover or less**
Circ: Diamd. preorders: **8,917**

2 ❑ Jul 1997 Cover: 2.95 **NM** value: **Cover or less**
Circ: Diamd. preorders: **7,996**

3 ❑ Aug 1997 Cover: 2.95 **NM** value: **Cover or less**
Circ: Diamd. preorders: **7,917**

4 ❑ Sep 1997 Cover: 2.95 **NM** value: **Cover or less**
Circ: Diamd. preorders: **8,060**

5 ❑ Oct 1997 Cover: 2.95 **NM** value: **Cover or less**
Circ: Diamd. preorders: **9,774**

6 ❑ Nov 1997 Cover: 2.95 **NM** value: **Cover or less**
Circ: Diamd. preorders: **8,188**

7 ❑ Dec 1997 Cover: 2.95 **NM** value: **Cover or less**
Circ: Diamd. preorders: **7,895**

8 ❑ Jan 1998 Cover: 2.95 **NM** value: **Cover or less**
Circ: Diamd. preorders: **7,802**

9 ❑ Feb 1998 Cover: 2.95 **NM** value: **Cover or less**
Circ: Diamd. preorders: **7,491**

Bk 9❑ Jul 1998 Cover: 16.95 **NM** value: **Cover or less**

BATTLE ARMOR — Eternity

1 ❑ Oct 1988 Cover: 1.95 **NM** value: **Cover or less**
A: Frank Turner **W:** Chris Ulm; Paul O'Connor

2 ❑ Cover: 1.95 **NM** value: **Cover or less**
A: Frank Turner **W:** Chris Ulm; Paul O'Connor

3 ❑ Cover: 1.95 **NM** value: **Cover or less**
A: Frank Turner **W:** Chris Ulm; Paul O'Connor

BATTLE AXE — Comics Interview

1 ❑ b&w Cover: 2.50 **NM** value: **Cover or less**

BATTLEAXES — Vertigo

In this innovative limited series, writer Terry LaBan (The Dreaming) and artist Alex Horley turn the notion of a traditional blood-and-guts Norse saga on its ear, not just by making the main characters women, but by making them funny, savage, quasi-Lesbian women. Carving out an unusual narrative niche, somewhere between Strangers in Paradise and Conan in a skirt, this four-issue limited series revolves around the mother-daughter team of Hrotha and Freya, ultra-butch warriors Sigga and Bruna, and the mystical Skold. On one side of the story, LaBan pits the Battleaxes against a bloodthirsty Khan and his Tengut horde. On the other side, there is an extra-dimensional, shape-changing, man-eating slug who first tries to woo one of the women, then decides to destroy them all. When the two collide — and they collide in a big, messy way — it's in a battle royal guaranteed to awe even the most battle-hardened sword-and-sorcery devotee.

1 ❑ May 2000 Cover: 2.50 **NM** value: **Cover or less**
Circ: Diamd. preorders: **12,974**
📖 Medereus No More **A:** Alex Horley **W:** Terry Laban

2 ❑ Jun 2000 Cover: 2.50 **NM** value: **Cover or less**
Circ: Diamd. preorders: **10,514**
📖 How the Other Half Lives **A:** Alex Horley **W:** Terry Laban

3 ❑ Jul 2000 Cover: 2.50 **NM** value: **Cover or less**
Circ: Diamd. preorders: **8,578**
A: Alex Horley **W:** Terry Laban

4 ❑ Aug 2000 Cover: 2.50 **NM** value: **Cover or less**
Circ: Diamd. preorders: **8,150**
📖 The Fiery Finish! **A:** Alex Horley **W:** Terry Laban

BATTLE BEASTS — Blackthorne

1 ❑ Cover: 1.50 **NM** value: **1.75**
Circ: CapCity orders: **2,575**

2 ❑ Cover: 1.50 **NM** value: **Cover or less**
Circ: CapCity orders: **1,275**

3 ❑ Cover: 1.50 **NM** value: **Cover or less**
Circ: CapCity orders: **1,100**

4 ❑ Cover: 1.75 **NM** value: **Cover or less**

BATTLE BINDER PLUS — Antarctic / Venus

1 ❑ Nov 1994 Cover: 3.50 **NM** value: **Cover or less**
A: Rulia 046 **W:** Rulia 046

2 ❑ Dec 1994 Cover: 2.95 **NM** value: **Cover or less**
A: Rulia 046 **W:** Rulia 046

3 ❑ Jan 1995 Cover: 2.95 **NM** value: **Cover or less**
📖 Act 4 • Key Word **A:** Rulia 046 **W:** Rulia 046

4 ❑ Feb 1995 Cover: 2.95 **NM** value: **Cover or less**
A: Rulia 046 **W:** Rulia 046

5 ❑ Mar 1995 Cover: 2.95 **NM** value: **Cover or less**
A: Rulia 046 **W:** Rulia 046

6 ❑ Apr 1995 Cover: 2.95 **NM** value: **Cover or less**
final issue. **A:** Rulia 046 **W:** Rulia 046

BATTLE CHASERS — Image / Cliffhanger

1 ❑ Apr 1998 Cover: 2.50 **NM** value: **10.00**
Circ: Diamd. preorders: **78,479** • **CGC:** 14 graded, best 9.8
A: Joe Madureira **W:** Joe Madureira; Munier Sharrieff

1/A ❑ Apr 1998 Cover: 2.50 **NM** value: **12.00**
• **CGC:** 2 graded, best 9.8
alternate cover, logo on back side of wraparound cover. **A:** Joe Madureira **W:** Joe Madureira; Munier Sharrieff

1/B ❑ Apr 1998 Cover: 2.50 **NM** value: **30.00**
Limited holochrome cover (limited to 5,000 copies). • Wrap-around **A:** Joe Madureira **W:** Joe Madureira; Munier Sharrieff

1/C ❑ Apr 1998 Cover: 4.50 **NM** value: **25.00**
Circ: Diamd. preorders: **32,243**
Gold "Come onÓtake a peek" cover (Monika). **A:** Joe Madureira **W:** Joe Madureira; Munier Sharrieff

1-2 ❑ Apr 1998 Cover: 2.50 **NM** value: **4.00**

2 ❑ May 1998 Cover: 2.50 **NM** value: **5.00**
Circ: Diamd. preorders: **63,049** • **CGC:** 7 graded, best 9.8
A: Joe Madureira **W:** Joe Madureira; Munier Sharrieff

2/A ❑ **NM** value: **10.00**
Special "omnichrome" cover from Dynamic Forces. **A:** Joe Madureira **W:** Joe Madureira; Munier Sharrieff

2/B ❑ **NM** value: **15.00**
• Battlechrome edition. **A:** Joe Madureira **W:** Joe Madureira; Munier Sharrieff

3 ❑ Jul 1998 Cover: 2.50 **NM** value: **4.00**
Circ: Diamd. preorders: **80,230**
📖 Divine Intervention **A:** Joe Madureira **W:** Joe Madureira; Munier Sharrieff

4/A ❑ Cover: 2.50 **NM** value: **3.00**
Circ: Diamd. preorders: **143,545**
four alternate back covers form quadtych. **A:** Joe Madureira **W:** Joe Madureira; Munier Sharrieff

4/B ❑ Cover: 2.50 **NM** value: **3.00**
Old man on cover. **A:** Joe Madureira **W:** Joe Madureira; Munier Sharrieff

4/C ❑ Cover: 2.50 **NM** value: **3.00**
four alternate back covers form quadtych. **A:** Joe Madureira **W:** Joe Madureira; Munier Sharrieff

4/D ❑ Oct 1998 Cover: 2.50 **NM** value: **3.00**
four alternate back covers form quadtych. **A:** Joe Madureira **W:** Joe Madureira

5 ❑ May 1999 Cover: 2.50 **NM** value: **Cover or less**
Circ: Diamd. preorders: **107,359**
A: Joe Madureira **W:** Joe Madureira; Munier Sharrieff

6 ❑ Aug 1999 Cover: 2.50 **NM** value: **Cover or less**
Circ: Diamd. preorders: **122,401**
A: Joe Madureira **W:** Joe Madureira; Munier Sharrieff

7 ❑ Jan 2001 Cover: 2.50 **NM** value: **Cover or less**
Circ: Diamd. preorders: **86,708**
A: Joe Madureira **W:** Joe Madureira; Munier Sharrieff

8 ❑ May 2001 Cover: 2.50 **NM** value: **Cover or less**
Circ: Diamd. preorders: **86,873** • **CGC:** 1 graded, best 9.8
A: Joe Madureira **W:** Joe Madureira; Munier Sharrieff

Ash 1❑Aug 1998 **NM** value: **5.00**
• Preview edition. **A:** Joe Madureira **W:** Joe Madureira; Munier Sharrieff ★ 1st Appearance of Battle Chasers.

Ash 1/GO❑Aug 1998 Cover: 10.00 **NM** value: **Cover or less**
Circ: Diamd. preorders: **20,489**
• Preview edition. • Gold logo **A:** Joe Madureira **W:** Joe Madureira; Munier Sharrieff ★ 1st Appearance of Battle Chasers.

Bk 1❑ Nov 1998 Cover: 5.95 **NM** value: **Cover or less**
Circ: Diamd. preorders: **31,924**
• Collected Edition #1. • Collects Battle Chasers #1-2 **A:** Joe Madureira **W:** Joe Madureira; Munier Sharrieff

Bk 2❑ May 1999 Cover: 5.95 **NM** value: **Cover or less**
Circ: Diamd. preorders: **22,047**
• Collected Edition #2. • Collects Battle Chasers #3-4 **A:** Joe Madureira **W:** Joe Madureira; Munier Sharrieff

Dlx 1❑Dec 1999 Cover: 24.95 **NM** value: **Cover or less**
hardcover. • A Gathering of Heroes **A:** Joe Madureira **W:** Joe Madureira; Munier Sharrieff

BATTLE CLASSICS — DC

1 ❑ Oct 1978 Cover: 0.50 **NM** value: **5.00**
• **CGC:** 1 graded, best 9.6

BATTLEFIELD — Atlas

1 ❑ Apr 1952 Cover: 0.10 **NM** value: **125.00**
• **CGC:** 1 graded, best 9.2

2 ❑ Jun 1952 Cover: 0.10 **NM** value: **60.00**
3 ❑ Aug 1952 Cover: 0.10 **NM** value: **60.00**
4 ❑ Oct 1952 Cover: 0.10 **NM** value: **60.00**
5 ❑ Nov 1952 Cover: 0.10 **NM** value: **60.00**
6 ❑ Dec 1952 Cover: 0.10 **NM** value: **50.00**
7 ❑ Jan 1953 Cover: 0.10 **NM** value: **50.00**
8 ❑ Feb 1953 Cover: 0.10 **NM** value: **50.00**
9 ❑ Mar 1953 Cover: 0.10 **NM** value: **50.00**
10 ❑ Apr 1953 Cover: 0.10 **NM** value: **50.00**
11 ❑ May 1953 Cover: 0.10 **NM** value: **50.00**

BATTLEFIELD ACTION — Charlton

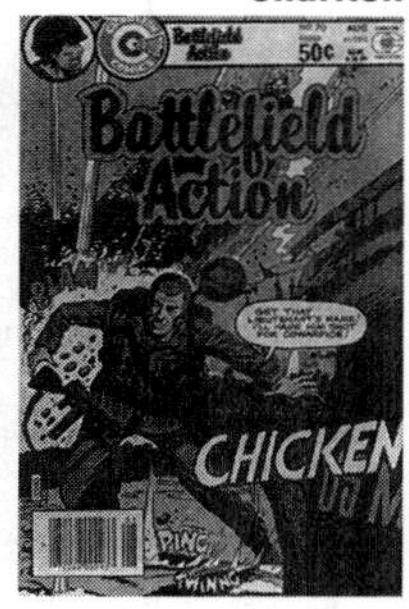

Known as "Foreign Intrigues" for its first 15 issues, this title ran on and off for almost 30 years. During the best of those times, it presented unusual tales of battle and bravery, from the beaches of Tarawa Atoll to the jungles of Vietnam.

Started in the late 1950s, this series went on hiatus in 1966. Unfortunately, when it reappeared, it was during a time when Charlton was relying solely on reprint material. Its latter run included good stories, but nothing readers hadn't (literally) seen before. The series eventually concluded with #89 in 1984.

16 ☐ Cover: 0.10 **NM** value: **28.00**
• Continued From Foreign Intrigues #15
17 ☐ Cover: 0.10 **NM** value: **13.00**
18 ☐ Mar 1958 Cover: 0.10 **NM** value: **10.00**
19 ☐ May 1958 Cover: 0.10 **NM** value: **10.00**
20 ☐ Jul 1958 Cover: 0.10 **NM** value: **10.00**
21 ☐ Sep 1958 Cover: 0.10 **NM** value: **9.00**
22 ☐ Dec 1958 Cover: 0.10 **NM** value: **9.00**
23 ☐ 1959 Cover: 0.10 **NM** value: **9.00**
24 ☐ 1959 Cover: 0.10 **NM** value: **9.00**
25 ☐ Jul 1959 Cover: 0.10 **NM** value: **9.00**
26 ☐ Sep 1959 Cover: 0.10 **NM** value: **9.00**
27 ☐ 1959 Cover: 0.10 **NM** value: **9.00**
28 ☐ Jan 1960 Cover: 0.10 **NM** value: **9.00**
29 ☐ 1960 Cover: 0.10 **NM** value: **9.00**
30 ☐ Jun 1960 Cover: 0.10 **NM** value: **9.00**
31 ☐ Cover: 0.10 **NM** value: **7.00**
32 ☐ Cover: 0.10 **NM** value: **7.00**
33 ☐ Cover: 0.10 **NM** value: **7.00**
34 ☐ Cover: 0.10 **NM** value: **7.00**
35 ☐ 1961 Cover: 0.10 **NM** value: **7.00**
36 ☐ 1961 Cover: 0.10 **NM** value: **7.00**
37 ☐ 1961 Cover: 0.10 **NM** value: **7.00**
38 ☐ Nov 1961 Cover: 0.10 **NM** value: **7.00**
39 ☐ Dec 1961 Cover: 0.10 **NM** value: **7.00**
• **CGC:** 1 graded, best 9.6
40 ☐ Feb 1962 Cover: 0.10 **NM** value: **7.00**
41 ☐ May 1962 Cover: 0.12 **NM** value: **6.00**
42 ☐ ca. 1962 Cover: 0.12 **NM** value: **6.00**
43 ☐ ca. 1962 Cover: 0.12 **NM** value: **6.00**
44 ☐ ca. 1962 Cover: 0.12 **NM** value: **6.00**
45 ☐ Jan 1963 Cover: 0.12 **NM** value: **6.00**
46 ☐ ca. 1963 **NM** value: **6.00**
47 ☐ ca. 1963 **NM** value: **6.00**
48 ☐ ca. 1963 **NM** value: **6.00**
49 ☐ ca. 1963 **NM** value: **6.00**
50 ☐ ca. 1963 **NM** value: **6.00**
51 ☐ ca. 1963 **NM** value: **5.00**
52 ☐ Sep 1963 Cover: 0.10 **NM** value: **5.00**
53 ☐ Jun 1964 Cover: 0.12 **NM** value: **5.00**
54 ☐ ca. 1964 Cover: 0.12 **NM** value: **5.00**
55 ☐ Nov 1964 Cover: 0.12 **NM** value: **5.00**
56 ☐ Jan 1965 Cover: 0.12 **NM** value: **5.00**
57 ☐ ca. 1965 Cover: 0.12 **NM** value: **5.00**
58 ☐ Jul 1965 Cover: 0.12 **NM** value: **5.00**
59 ☐ ca. 1965 Cover: 0.12 **NM** value: **5.00**
60 ☐ Oct 1965 Cover: 0.12 **NM** value: **5.00**
61 ☐ Cover: 0.12 **NM** value: **5.00**
62 ☐ Feb 1966 Cover: 0.12 **NM** value: **5.00**
• Last issue of 1960s run
63 ☐ Jul 1980 Cover: 0.40 **NM** value: **2.00**
• Series begins again, 1980
64 ☐ Sep 1980 **NM** value: **2.00**
65 ☐ Nov 1980 Cover: 0.50 **NM** value: **2.00**
66 ☐ Jan 1981 Cover: 0.50 **NM** value: **2.00**
67 ☐ Mar 1981 Cover: 0.50 **NM** value: **2.00**
68 ☐ Apr 1981 Cover: 0.50 **NM** value: **2.00**
69 ☐ Jun 1981 Cover: 0.50 **NM** value: **2.00**
70 ☐ Aug 1981 Cover: 0.50 **NM** value: **2.00**
71 ☐ Oct 1981 Cover: 0.50 **NM** value: **2.00**
72 ☐ Dec 1981 Cover: 0.50 **NM** value: **2.00**
73 ☐ Feb 1982 Cover: 0.60 **NM** value: **2.00**
74 ☐ Apr 1982 Cover: 0.60 **NM** value: **2.00**
75 ☐ Jun 1982 Cover: 0.60 **NM** value: **2.00**
76 ☐ Aug 1982 Cover: 0.60 **NM** value: **2.00**
77 ☐ Oct 1982 Cover: 0.60 **NM** value: **2.00**
78 ☐ Dec 1982 Cover: 0.60 **NM** value: **2.00**
79 ☐ Feb 1983 Cover: 0.60 **NM** value: **2.00**
80 ☐ Apr 1983 Cover: 0.60 **NM** value: **2.00**
81 ☐ Jun 1983 Cover: 0.60 **NM** value: **2.00**
82 ☐ Aug 1983 Cover: 0.60 **NM** value: **2.00**
83 ☐ Oct 1983 Cover: 0.60 **NM** value: **2.00**
84 ☐ Dec 1983 Cover: 0.60 **NM** value: **2.00**
📖 Listen to the Boidie; Even Steven; Lucky Stiff • Reprints from Foxhole #6 ("Boidie" & "Steven"), and #5 ("Stiff")
85 ☐ 1984 Cover: 0.60 **NM** value: **2.00**
86 ☐ 1984 Cover: 0.60 **NM** value: **2.00**
87 ☐ 1984 Cover: 0.60 **NM** value: **2.00**
88 ☐ Sep 1984 Cover: 0.60 **NM** value: **2.00**
89 ☐ Nov 1984 Cover: 0.75 **NM** value: **2.00**
final issue.

BATTLE FOR A THREE DIMENSIONAL WORLD — 3-D Cosmic

1 ☐ **NM** value: **2.50**
no cover price. 📖 Battle for a Three Dimensional World **A:** Jack Kirby **W:** Ray Zone

BATTLEFORCE — Blackthorne

1 ☐ full color Cover: 1.75 **NM** value: **Cover or less**
Circ: CapCity orders: **3,800**
2 ☐ b&w Cover: 1.75 **NM** value: **Cover or less**
Circ: CapCity orders: **3,275**

BATTLEFRONT — Marvel

Pack up your mess kit and join the patrol with the soldiers of Battlefront! This war series ran from 1952 to 1957 and covered most of the wars in which Americans have fought. In both text stories and regular comic-book tales, the heroism of American forces is extolled, while readers are repeatedly told just why the Communist menace is something worth fighting. Typical stories might include the saga of a soldier escaping from an enemy prison or the difficulties encountered by a young man assigned to a unit commanded by his father. Battlefront isn't just an entertaining collection of war stories; it's also a glimpse into the way the world was perceived during many of the early years of the Cold War era.

1 ☐ Jun 1952 Cover: 0.10 **NM** value: **130.00**
• **CGC:** 1 graded, best 7.0
2 ☐ Jul 1952 Cover: 0.10 **NM** value: **75.00**
3 ☐ Aug 1952 Cover: 0.10 **NM** value: **55.00**
4 ☐ Sep 1952 Cover: 0.10 **NM** value: **55.00**
5 ☐ Oct 1952 Cover: 0.10 **NM** value: **55.00**
6 ☐ Nov 1952 Cover: 0.10 **NM** value: **40.00**
7 ☐ Dec 1952 Cover: 0.10 **NM** value: **40.00**
8 ☐ Jan 1953 Cover: 0.10 **NM** value: **40.00**
9 ☐ ca. 1953 Cover: 0.10 **NM** value: **40.00**
10 ☐ ca. 1953 Cover: 0.10 **NM** value: **40.00**
11 ☐ ca. 1953 Cover: 0.10 **NM** value: **32.00**
12 ☐ ca. 1953 Cover: 0.10 **NM** value: **32.00**
13 ☐ ca. 1953 Cover: 0.10 **NM** value: **32.00**
14 ☐ ca. 1953 Cover: 0.10 **NM** value: **32.00**
15 ☐ Cover: 0.10 **NM** value: **32.00**
16 ☐ Cover: 0.10 **NM** value: **32.00**
17 ☐ Cover: 0.10 **NM** value: **32.00**
18 ☐ Apr 1954 Cover: 0.10 **NM** value: **32.00**
19 ☐ May 1954 Cover: 0.10 **NM** value: **32.00**
20 ☐ Jun 1954 Cover: 0.10 **NM** value: **32.00**
21 ☐ Jul 1954 Cover: 0.10 **NM** value: **26.00**
22 ☐ Aug 1954 Cover: 0.10 **NM** value: **26.00**
23 ☐ Sep 1954 Cover: 0.10 **NM** value: **26.00**
24 ☐ Oct 1954 Cover: 0.10 **NM** value: **26.00**
25 ☐ Nov 1954 Cover: 0.10 **NM** value: **26.00**
26 ☐ Dec 1954 Cover: 0.10 **NM** value: **26.00**
27 ☐ Jan 1955 Cover: 0.10 **NM** value: **26.00**
28 ☐ Feb 1955 Cover: 0.10 **NM** value: **26.00**
29 ☐ Mar 1955 Cover: 0.10 **NM** value: **26.00**
30 ☐ Apr 1955 Cover: 0.10 **NM** value: **26.00**
31 ☐ May 1955 Cover: 0.10 **NM** value: **20.00**
32 ☐ Jun 1955 Cover: 0.10 **NM** value: **20.00**
33 ☐ Jul 1955 Cover: 0.10 **NM** value: **20.00**
34 ☐ Aug 1955 Cover: 0.10 **NM** value: **20.00**
35 ☐ Sep 1955 Cover: 0.10 **NM** value: **20.00**
36 ☐ Oct 1955 Cover: 0.10 **NM** value: **20.00**
• **CGC:** 1 graded, best 8.0
37 ☐ Cover: 0.10 **NM** value: **20.00**
38 ☐ Cover: 0.10 **NM** value: **20.00**
39 ☐ 1956 Cover: 0.10 **NM** value: **20.00**
40 ☐ 1956 Cover: 0.10 **NM** value: **20.00**
41 ☐ 1956 Cover: 0.10 **NM** value: **20.00**
42 ☐ 1956 Cover: 0.10 **NM** value: **20.00**
43 ☐ Nov 1956 Cover: 0.10 **NM** value: **20.00**
• **CGC:** 1 graded, best 7.0
📖 Missing in Action!; Hungry Victory (text story); Survival!; The Last Man!; The Fighting Man!; Thirty Seconds! **A:** Paul Reinman
44 ☐ Cover: 0.10 **NM** value: **20.00**
45 ☐ Cover: 0.10 **NM** value: **20.00**
46 ☐ Cover: 0.10 **NM** value: **20.00**
47 ☐ Cover: 0.10 **NM** value: **20.00**
48 ☐ Aug 1957 Cover: 0.10 **NM** value: **20.00**
final issue.

BATTLE GIRLZ — Antarctic

1 ☐ ca. 2002, b&w Cover: 2.99 **NM** value: **Cover or less**
Circ: Diamd. preorders: **2,992**

BATTLE GODS: WARRIORS OF THE CHAAK — Dark Horse

1 ☐ Apr 2000 Cover: 2.95 **NM** value: **Cover or less**
Circ: Diamd. preorders: **10,640**
A: Francisco Ruiz Velasco **W:** Francisco Ruiz Velasco
2 ☐ May 2000 Cover: 2.95 **NM** value: **Cover or less**
Circ: Diamd. preorders: **7,858**
A: Francisco Ruiz Velasco **W:** Francisco Ruiz Velasco
3 ☐ Jun 2000 Cover: 2.95 **NM** value: **Cover or less**
Circ: Diamd. preorders: **8,150**
A: Francisco Ruiz Velasco **W:** Francisco Ruiz Velasco

BATTLEGROUND — Marvel

1 ☐ Sep 1954 Cover: 0.10 **NM** value: **90.00**
2 ☐ Nov 1954 Cover: 0.10 **NM** value: **48.00**
3 ☐ Jan 1955 Cover: 0.10 **NM** value: **30.00**
• **CGC:** 1 graded, best 7.0
4 ☐ Mar 1955 Cover: 0.10 **NM** value: **30.00**
5 ☐ May 1955 Cover: 0.10 **NM** value: **30.00**
6 ☐ Jul 1955 Cover: 0.10 **NM** value: **22.00**
7 ☐ Sep 1955 Cover: 0.10 **NM** value: **22.00**
8 ☐ Nov 1955 Cover: 0.10 **NM** value: **22.00**
9 ☐ Jan 1956 Cover: 0.10 **NM** value: **30.00**
A: Bernie Krigstein
10 ☐ Mar 1956 Cover: 0.10 **NM** value: **22.00**
11 ☐ May 1956 Cover: 0.10 **NM** value: **18.00**
12 ☐ Jul 1956 Cover: 0.10 **NM** value: **18.00**
13 ☐ Sep 1956 Cover: 0.10 **NM** value: **30.00**
A: Al Williamson
14 ☐ Nov 1956 Cover: 0.10 **NM** value: **35.00**
📖 Mine Field **A:** Jack Kirby
15 ☐ 1957 Cover: 0.10 **NM** value: **18.00**
16 ☐ 1957 Cover: 0.10 **NM** value: **18.00**
17 ☐ 1957 Cover: 0.10 **NM** value: **18.00**
18 ☐ 1957 Cover: 0.10 **NM** value: **30.00**
A: Al Williamson
19 ☐ 1957 Cover: 0.10 **NM** value: **18.00**
📖 Get that Tank!; Hopeful Defeat (text story); Bombardment!; Escape!; Battle Banner!; At Gun Point! **A:** Jack Keller; Joe Maneely(cover)
20 ☐ 1957 Cover: 0.10 **NM** value: **18.00**
final issue.

BATTLEGROUND EARTH — Best

1 ☐ b&w Cover: 2.50 **NM** value: **Cover or less**
2 ☐ b&w Cover: 2.50 **NM** value: **Cover or less**

BATTLE GROUP PEIPER — Tome Press

1 ☐ b&w Cover: 2.95 **NM** value: **Cover or less**

BATTLE OF THE PLANETS — Gold Key / Whitman

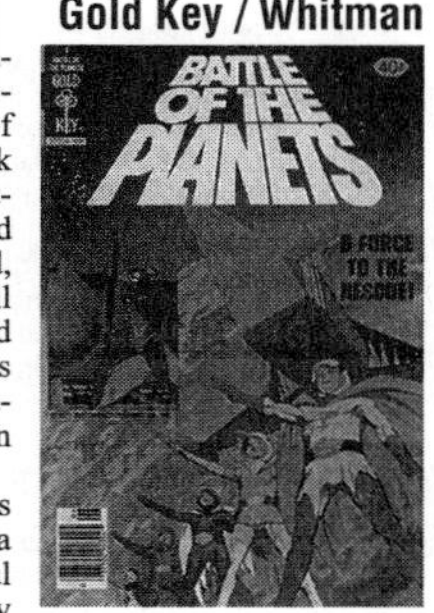

One of the better early anime adaptations, Battle of the Planets follows the adventures of a group of children known, in the Sandy Frank U.S. version, as G-Force. (It's Gatchaman in Japan.) The kids defend Earth against alien aggressors and, when put to great challenge, call upon a fiery bird effect to surround their ship. (It may call Marvel's Phoenix to mind, but the Gatchaman series premiered in Japan in 1972.)

Costume coloring helps readers tell the G-Force characters apart, a trick that would later prove helpful to readers of the various Mighty Morphin Power Rangers comics series.

Notable for being among the earlier comics adaptations of a Japanese comics series — if only via its U.S. syndicated version — Battle of the Planets enjoyed a revival in 2002, with a new Image series in the works. — JJM

1 ☐ Jun 1979 Cover: 0.40 **NM** value: **6.00**
• **CGC:** 12 graded, best 9.6
📖 Operation: Decoy; Undersea Threat
2 ☐ Aug 1979 Cover: 0.40 **NM** value: **4.00**
📖 Ice Creature; The Flaming Menace
3 ☐ Oct 1979 Cover: 0.40 **NM** value: **4.00**
📖 Solar Blockade; The Lake Monster
4 ☐ Dec 1979 Cover: 0.40 **NM** value: **4.00**
5 ☐ Feb 1980 Cover: 0.40 **NM** value: **4.00**
6 ☐ Apr 1980 Cover: 0.40 **NM** value: **4.00**
📖 Ghost Ship
7 ☐ **NM** value: **4.00**
8 ☐ **NM** value: **4.00**
9 ☐ **NM** value: **4.00**
10 ☐ Cover: 0.50 **NM** value: **4.00**

BATTLE OF THE ULTRA-BROTHERS — Viz

1 ☐ Cover: 4.95 **NM** value: **Cover or less**
2 ☐ Cover: 4.95 **NM** value: **Cover or less**
3 ☐ Cover: 4.95 **NM** value: **Cover or less**
4 ☐ Cover: 4.95 **NM** value: **Cover or less**
5 ☐ Cover: 4.95 **NM** value: **Cover or less**

BATTLE POPE — Funk-O-Tron

77 ☐ Jul 2001, b&w Cover: 2.95 **NM** value: **Cover or less**
• A.K.A. Battle Pope: Mayhem #2
1 ☐ Jun 2000, b&w Cover: 2.95 **NM** value: **Cover or less**
Circ: Diamd. preorders: **2,399**
2 ☐ Jul 2000, b&w Cover: 2.95 **NM** value: **Cover or less**
Circ: Diamd. preorders: **2,275**
3 ☐ Aug 2000, b&w Cover: 2.95 **NM** value: **Cover or less**
4 ☐ Sep 2000, b&w Cover: 2.95 **NM** value: **Cover or less**
Circ: Diamd. preorders: **2,126**
5 ☐ Mar 2001, b&w Cover: 4.95 **NM** value: **Cover or less**
Circ: Diamd. preorders: **1,849**
• A.K.A. Battle Pope Shorts #1
6 ☐ Jun 2001, b&w Cover: 2.95 **NM** value: **Cover or less**
Circ: Diamd. preorders: **2,312**
• A.K.A. Battle Pope: Mayhem #1
7 ☐ Jul 2001, b&w Cover: 2.95 **NM** value: **Cover or less**
Circ: Diamd. preorders: **2,052**
• A.K.A. Battle Pope: Mayhem #2

BATTLE REPORT — Farrell

1 ☐ Aug 1952 Cover: 0.10 **NM** value: **50.00**
• **CGC:** 1 graded, best 7.0

BATTLESTAR GALACTICA 1999 TOUR BOOK — Realm

1/A ☐ May 1999 Cover: 2.99 **NM** value: **Cover or less**
Circ: Diamd. preorders: **3,378**
1/B ☐ May 1999 **NM** value: **3.00**
• Dynamic Forces Edition, no cover price.

CGC-graded: Multiply prices above by **33 for 9.9 M • 16 for 9.8 NM/M • 7 for 9.6 NM+ • 5 for 9.4 NM • 2.5 for 9.2 NM- • 1.5 for 9.0 VF/NM**

1/C ❑ May 1999 Cover: 6.99 **NM** value: **Cover or less**
white background cover.

BATTLESTAR GALACTICA: APOLLO'S JOURNEY — Maximum

1 ❑ Apr 1995 Cover: 2.95 **NM** value: **Cover or less**
A: Hector Gomez **W:** Richard Hatch

BATTLESTAR GALACTICA EVE OF DESTRUCTION PRELUDE — Realm

1 ❑ ca. 2000 Cover: 3.99 **NM** value: **Cover or less**
Circ: Diamd. preorders: **5,071**
A: Matt Busch **W:** Matt Busch

BATTLESTAR GALACTICA: JOURNEY'S END — Maximum

1 ❑ Aug 1996 Cover: 2.99 **NM** value: **Cover or less**
A: Hector Gomez **W:** Robert Napton
2 ❑ Sep 1996 Cover: 2.99 **NM** value: **Cover or less**
3 ❑ Oct 1996 Cover: 2.99 **NM** value: **Cover or less**
Circ: Diamd. preorders: **16,318**
4 ❑ Nov 1996 Cover: 2.99 **NM** value: **Cover or less**
Circ: Diamd. preorders: **16,180**

BATTLESTAR GALACTICA (MARVEL) — Marvel

Star Wars was at least a partial inspiration for Glen Larsen's expensive TV space epic, so it shouldn't surprise that Marvel would also snag the rights to the Battlestar Galactica comic book. (Actually, the TV series shares a lot more with such series television as Baa Baa Black Sheep, but that's neither here nor there.)

The first three issues adapt the TV movie, with #4 and #5 tackling the first series episode, "The Lost Gods of Kobol." But as with Marvel's Star Wars series, most issues are original stories. Issues from #6 on deal with Adama trying to remember what he'd seen of Earth's location in the Kobol temple, so early issues find him stuck in a "Memory Machine." He finally remembers in the last issue of the series.

Roger Mackenzie and Will Simonson even get to do a couple of stories playing with major elements of the character's pasts, including a story from Adama's youth and a story of what happened to his wife after the Cylon invasion. Excepting some issues with a red Hulk clone, the series is better than it probably had to be — and better than the Maximum Press adaptations to follow. — JJM

1 ❑ Mar 1979 Cover: 0.35 **NM** value: **5.00**
• **CGC:** 42 graded, best 9.9
📖 Annihilation! • Pilot movie adaptation; reformatted from Marvel Super Special #8 **A:** Ernie Colon **W:** Roger McKenzie
1-2 ❑ Cover: 4.99 **NM** value: **Cover or less**
• 20 Yahren reunion edition. 📖 Annihilation! • reprint
2 ❑ Apr 1979 Cover: 0.35 **NM** value: **3.00**
• **CGC:** 8 graded, best 9.8
📖 Exodus • Pilot movie adaptation; reformatted from Marvel Super Special #8 **A:** Ernie Colon **W:** Roger McKenzie
3 ❑ May 1979 Cover: 0.40 **NM** value: **3.00**
• **CGC:** 3 graded, best 9.8
📖 Deathtrap! • Pilot movie adaptation; reformatted from Marvel Super Special #8
4 ❑ Jun 1979 Cover: 0.40 **NM** value: **3.00**
• **CGC:** 3 graded, best 9.8
📖 The Lost Gods of Kobol – Part One • Adapts first hour-long episode of TV series
5 ❑ Jul 1979 Cover: 0.40 **NM** value: **3.00**
• **CGC:** 2 graded, best 10.0
📖 The Lost Gods of Kobol – Part Two: A Death in the Family • Adapts second hour-long episode of TV series
6 ❑ Aug 1979 Cover: 0.40 **NM** value: **3.00**
• **CGC:** 2 graded, best 9.6
📖 The Memory Machine • First original comics story
7 ❑ Sep 1979 Cover: 0.40 **NM** value: **3.00**
📖 All Things Past and Present • Adama trapped in Memory Machine
8 ❑ Oct 1979 Cover: 0.40 **NM** value: **3.00**
• **CGC:** 1 graded, best 9.6
📖 Shuttle-Diplomacy • Young Adama on Scorpia; fill-in issue
9 ❑ Nov 1979 Cover: 0.40 **NM** value: **3.00**
• **CGC:** 1 graded, best 9.8
📖 Space-Mimic
10 ❑ Dec 1979 Cover: 0.40 **NM** value: **3.00**
• **CGC:** 1 graded, best 9.6
📖 This Planet Hungers • Flashback story **A:** Pat Broderick **W:** Tom DeFalco
11 ❑ Jan 1980 Cover: 0.40 **NM** value: **2.00**
📖 Scavenge World **A:** Walt Simonson; Klaus Janson **W:** Roger McKenzie
12 ❑ Feb 1980 Cover: 0.40 **NM** value: **2.00**
📖 The Trap! • Adama leaves Memory Machine **A:** Walt Simonson **W:** Roger McKenzie
13 ❑ Mar 1980 Cover: 0.40 **NM** value: **2.00**
📖 Collision Course!
14 ❑ Apr 1980 Cover: 0.40 **NM** value: **2.00**
📖 Trial and Error • Muffit Two is melted
15 ❑ May 1980 Cover: 0.40 **NM** value: **2.00**
📖 Derelict! • Boomer discovers Adama's wife alive **A:** Walt Simonson; Klaus Janson **W:** Roger McKenzie
16 ❑ Jun 1980 Cover: 0.40 **NM** value: **2.00**
📖 Berserker
17 ❑ Jul 1980 Cover: 0.40 **NM** value: **2.00**
📖 Ape and Essence • Red "Hulks"
18 ❑ Aug 1980 Cover: 0.40 **NM** value: **2.00**
📖 Forbidden Fruit • Red "Hulks"
19 ❑ Sep 1980 Cover: 0.50 **NM** value: **2.00**
📖 The Daring Escape of the Space Cowboy • Starbuck returns
20 ❑ Oct 1980 Cover: 0.50 **NM** value: **2.00**
📖 Hell Hath No Fury
21 ❑ Nov 1980 Cover: 0.50 **NM** value: **2.00**
📖 A World for the Killing **A:** Brent Anderson
22 ❑ Dec 1980 Cover: 0.50 **NM** value: **2.00**
📖 Black is the Color of My True Love's Hair
23 ❑ Jan 1981 Cover: 0.50 **NM** value: **2.00**
📖 The Last Hiding Place final issue. • Last issue
Bk 1 ❑ Cover: 1.95 **NM** value: **Cover or less**
• Ace Paperback; reprints #1-3
Bk 2 ❑ Cover: 2.25 **NM** value: **Cover or less**
• Ace Paperback; reprints #4-6

BATTLESTAR GALACTICA (MAXIMUM) — Maximum

1 ❑ Jul 1995 Cover: 2.50 **NM** value: **Cover or less**
Circ: CapCity orders: **14,725** • **CGC:** 2 graded, best 9.6
📖 War of Eden **A:** Hector Gomez; Karl Altstaetter **W:** Rob Liefeld; Robert Napton
2 ❑ Aug 1995 Cover: 2.50 **NM** value: **Cover or less**
Circ: CapCity orders: **10,175**
3 ❑ Sep 1995 Cover: 2.50 **NM** value: **Cover or less**
Circ: CapCity orders: **8,125**
4 ❑ Nov 1995 Cover: 2.50 **NM** value: **Cover or less**
Circ: CapCity orders: **6,900**
Bk 1 ❑ Cover: 12.95 **NM** value: **Cover or less**
• Collects series

BATTLESTAR GALACTICA (REALM) — Realm

1/A ❑ Dec 1997 Cover: 2.99 **NM** value: **Cover or less**
Circ: Diamd. preorders: **11,948**
Spaceships cover. 📖 The Law of Volahd
1/B ❑ Dec 1997 Cover: 2.99 **NM** value: **Cover or less**
Cylons cover. 📖 The Law of Volahd
2 ❑ Jan 1998 Cover: 2.99 **NM** value: **Cover or less**
Circ: Diamd. preorders: **9,484**
📖 The Law of Volahd
3 ❑ Mar 1998 Cover: 2.99 **NM** value: **Cover or less**
Circ: Diamd. preorders: **10,744**
📖 Prison of Souls
3/SC ❑ Mar 1998 Cover: 2.99 **NM** value: **Cover or less**
alternate cover (eyes in background). 📖 Prison of Souls
4 ❑ ca. 1998 Cover: 2.99 **NM** value: **Cover or less**
Circ: Diamd. preorders: **10,688**
5 ❑ ca. 1998 Cover: 2.99 **NM** value: **Cover or less**
Circ: Diamd. preorders: **9,867**

BATTLESTAR GALACTICA: SEARCH FOR SANCTUARY — Realm

1 ❑ Sep 1998 Cover: 2.99 **NM** value: **Cover or less**
Circ: Diamd. preorders: **8,460**

BATTLESTAR GALACTICA: SEASON III — Realm

1 ❑ Jun 1999 Cover: 2.99 **NM** value: **Cover or less**
Circ: Diamd. preorders: **7,340**
📖 No Place Like Home **A:** Chris Scalf; Robert Scott **W:** James A. Kuhoric
1/A ❑ Jun 1999 Cover: 5.00 **NM** value: **Cover or less**
• Special Convention Edition. 📖 No Place Like Home **A:** Chris Scalf; Robert Scott **W:** James A. Kuhoric
1/B ❑ Jun 1999 Cover: 4.99 **NM** value: **Cover or less**
📖 No Place Like Home **A:** Chris Scalf; Robert Scott **W:** James A. Kuhoric
2 ❑ Jul 1999 Cover: 4.99 **NM** value: **Cover or less**
Circ: Diamd. preorders: **6,475**

BATTLESTAR GALACTICA: STARBUCK — Maximum

Battlestar Galactica was a prime-time television space opera (1978-1980) with vaguely Star Wars-like special effects. The series followed the adventures of the crew of a giant interstellar aircraft carrier, Galactica, leading a "ragtag fugitive fleet" of survivors from an alien ambush toward the legendary home of the 13th tribe of humans, the planet called Earth. Galactica's firepower was provided by its fighter craft, piloted by hot-shot top guns like brash, headstrong, ladies' man Starbuck (played by Dirk Benedict), here featured in his own spinoff title, courtesy of Rob Liefeld's Maximum Press.

The comics series, like the television show, provides lots of space-faring drama for people who want stuff "just like Star Wars but different," This title, like the Star Wars comics empire, combines big science-fiction art with intricate, slow-moving plots to keep readers coming back for more, month after month.

1 ❑ Cover: 2.95 **NM** value: **Cover or less**
A: Hector Gomez **W:** Rob Liefeld; Robert Napton
2 ❑ Cover: 2.95 **NM** value: **Cover or less**
A: Hector Gomez **W:** Rob Liefeld; Robert Napton
3 ❑ Mar 1996 Cover: 2.95 **NM** value: **Cover or less**
A: Hector Gomez **W:** Rob Liefeld; Robert Napton

BATTLESTAR GALACTICA: THE COMPENDIUM — Maximum

1 ❑ ca. 1997 Cover: 2.95 **NM** value: **Cover or less**
Circ: Diamd. preorders: **11,602**

BATTLESTAR GALACTICA: THE ENEMY WITHIN — Maximum

1 ❑ Nov 1995 Cover: 2.50 **NM** value: **Cover or less**
2 ❑ Cover: 2.50 **NM** value: **Cover or less**
3 ❑ Feb 1996 Cover: 2.95 **NM** value: **Cover or less**
3/SC ❑ Feb 1996 Cover: 2.95 **NM** value: **Cover or less**
alternate cover.

BATTLESTONE — Image

1 ❑ Cover: 2.50 **NM** value: **Cover or less**
Circ: CapCity orders: **26,700**
A: Marat Mychaels; Al Vey(inks) **W:** Rob Liefeld; Eric Stephenson
1/A ❑ Nov 1994 Cover: 2.50 **NM** value: **Cover or less**
A: Marat Mychaels; Al Vey(inks)
1/B ❑ Nov 1994 Cover: 2.50 **NM** value: **Cover or less**
alternate cover.
2 ❑ Dec 1994 Cover: 2.50 **NM** value: **Cover or less**
Circ: CapCity orders: **17,750**
A: Marat Mychaels; Al Vey(inks) **W:** Rob Liefeld; Eric Stephenson

BATTLE STORIES — Fawcett

Battle Stories was a K-ration-quality war series set in Korea, published in the early 1950s by Fawcett, which was clearly running out of creative steam by that point. Stories like "You'll Never Be Twenty," "Platoon Forward" and "Land-Lubber" offer war combat action in all its violence and gritty detail, with stock characters falling on grenades to save the rest of the squadron, grizzled veterans warning the fresh-faced recruits about the dangers ahead, and courageous soldiers overmatched by scores of enemy troops finding a way back home against all odds. The ugly stories are matched with ugly, claustrophobic art and a generally malevolent editorial tone.

1 ❑ Jan 1952 Cover: 0.10 **NM** value: **70.00**
2 ❑ Mar 1952 Cover: 0.10 **NM** value: **40.00**
3 ❑ May 1952 Cover: 0.10 **NM** value: **22.00**
4 ❑ Jul 1952 Cover: 0.10 **NM** value: **22.00**
5 ❑ Sep 1952 Cover: 0.10 **NM** value: **22.00**
6 ❑ Nov 1952 Cover: 0.10 **NM** value: **22.00**
7 ❑ Jan 1953 Cover: 0.10 **NM** value: **22.00**
📖 You'll Never Be Twenty!; ...And Then the Bugle Blew!; Decoy (text story); Platoon Forward!; Landlubber! **W:** John Martin
8 ❑ Mar 1953 Cover: 0.10 **NM** value: **22.00**
9 ❑ May 1953 Cover: 0.10 **NM** value: **22.00**
10 ❑ Jul 1953 Cover: 0.10 **NM** value: **22.00**
11 ❑ Sep 1953 Cover: 0.10 **NM** value: **22.00**
final issue.

BATTLETECH — Malibu

0 ❑ Cover: 2.95 **NM** value: **Cover or less**
Circ: CapCity orders: **5,950**
📖 BattleTech: Overture **A:** Tim Eldred **W:** Roland Mann

BATTLETECH (BLACKTHORNE) — Blackthorne

1 ❑ Oct 1997, full color Cover: 1.75 **NM** value: **2.00**
Circ: CapCity orders: **7,800**
A: Palmer Worley **W:** Joe Judt
2 ❑ b&w Cover: 1.75 **NM** value: **2.00**
Circ: CapCity orders: **4,875**
3 ❑ b&w Cover: 1.75 **NM** value: **2.00**
Circ: CapCity orders: **4,175**
4 ❑ b&w Cover: 1.75 **NM** value: **2.00**
Circ: CapCity orders: **3,025**
5 ❑ b&w Cover: 1.75 **NM** value: **2.00**
Circ: CapCity orders: **2,375**
6 ❑ b&w Cover: 1.75 **NM** value: **2.00**
Circ: CapCity orders: **2,300**

BATTLETECH: FALLOUT — Malibu

1 ❑ Cover: 2.50 **NM** value: **Cover or less**
Circ: CapCity orders: **8,900**
2 ❑ Cover: 2.50 **NM** value: **Cover or less**
Circ: CapCity orders: **5,675**
3 ❑ Cover: 2.50 **NM** value: **Cover or less**
4 ❑ Cover: 2.50 **NM** value: **Cover or less**
Circ: CapCity orders: **4,550**

BATTLETECH IN 3-D — Blackthorne

1 ❑ Cover: 2.50 **NM** value: **Cover or less**
Circ: CapCity orders: **1,650**

CGC price ratios appearing on the bottom of right-hand pages are for pre-1990 comic books "slabbed" by Comics Guaranty Corp.

They represent the median price offered on eBay above our printed prices for comics in each grade. These are only a guide; individual prices vary by interest in the issue and the number of CGC-graded copies on the market.

For up-to-the-week CGC ratios, consult the current issue of **Comics Buyer's Guide**.

Other grades: Multiply prices above by **1.5 for Mint • 2/3 for Very Fine • 1/3 for Fine • 1/5 for Very Good • 1/8 for Good**

BATTLETIDE — Marvel

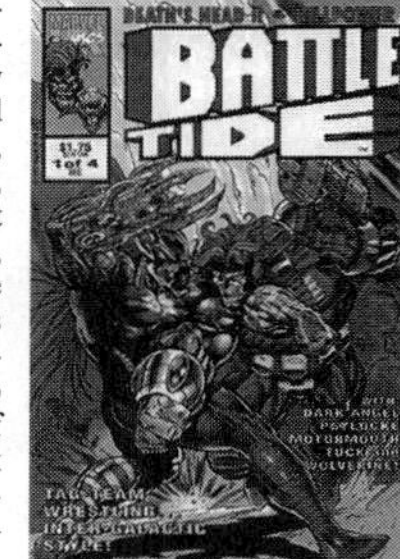

Merging characters from the successful Death's Head II and Motormouth (Motormouth is Harley Davis, able to phase across myriad dimensions of the universe) titles, BattleTide pits the over-brawned, under-brained Killpower against the schizoid killing machine, Death's Head II. The two are brought together by the inhabitants of Colosseum, a planetoid dedicated to bloody gladiatorial battle. To complicate things, several more of Earth's heroes — including Dark Angel, Motormouth, and the X-Men's Wolverine and Psylocke — are also captured.

Colosseum's goal is to use these heroes as competitors in an intergalactic battle royal.

1 ❑ Dec 1992 Cover: 1.75 **NM** value: **Cover or less**
Circ: CapCity orders: **33,900**
A: Geoff Senior **W:** Andy Lanning; Dan Abnett

2 ❑ Jan 1993 Cover: 1.75 **NM** value: **Cover or less**
Circ: CapCity orders: **16,500**
A: Geoff Senior **W:** Andy Lanning; Dan Abnett

3 ❑ Feb 1993 Cover: 1.75 **NM** value: **Cover or less**
Circ: CapCity orders: **12,300**
A: Geoff Senior **W:** Andy Lanning; Dan Abnett

4 ❑ Mar 1993 Cover: 1.75 **NM** value: **Cover or less**
Circ: CapCity orders: **10,450**
A: Geoff Senior **W:** Andy Lanning; Dan Abnett

BATTLETIDE II — Marvel

1 ❑ Aug 1993 Cover: 2.95 **NM** value: **Cover or less**
Circ: CapCity orders: **5,950**
Embossed cover.

2 ❑ Sep 1993 Cover: 1.75 **NM** value: **Cover or less**
Circ: CapCity orders: **4,050**
★ Appearance of Hulk.

3 ❑ Oct 1993 Cover: 1.75 **NM** value: **Cover or less**
Circ: CapCity orders: **3,850**
📖 Pecs, Lies and Videoscapes **A:** Geoff Senior **W:** Andy Lanning; Dan Abnett

4 ❑ Nov 1993 Cover: 1.75 **NM** value: **Cover or less**
Circ: CapCity orders: **3,450**

BATTLE TO THE DEATH — Imperial

1 ❑ b&w Cover: 1.80 **NM** value: **Cover or less**
2 ❑ Cover: 1.95 **NM** value: **Cover or less**
3 ❑ Cover: 1.95 **NM** value: **Cover or less**

BATTLEZONES: DREAM TEAM 2 — Malibu

1 ❑ Mar 1996 Cover: 3.95 **NM** value: **Cover or less**
• pin-ups of battles between Malibu and Marvel characters **A:** Sam Liu; Kyle Hotz; Chris Warner; Mike Wieringo; Art Thibert; Carlos Pacheco; Gary Martin; Mike Christian

BATTRON — NEC

1 ❑ b&w Cover: 2.75 **NM** value: **Cover or less**
2 ❑ b&w Cover: 2.75 **NM** value: **Cover or less**

BATTRON'S 4 QUEENS: GUNS, BABES & INTRIGUE — Commode

1 ❑ Cover: 3.50 **NM** value: **Cover or less**

BAY CITY JIVE — DC / Wildstorm

1 ❑ Jul 2001 Cover: 2.95 **NM** value: **Cover or less**
Circ: Diamd. preorders: **10,521**

1/A ❑ Jul 2001 Cover: 2.95 **NM** value: **Cover or less**
alternate cover.

2 ❑ Aug 2001 Cover: 2.95 **NM** value: **Cover or less**
Circ: Diamd. preorders: **7,843**

3 ❑ Sep 2001 Cover: 2.95 **NM** value: **Cover or less**
Circ: Diamd. preorders: **7,390**

BAYWATCH COMIC STORIES — Acclaim / Armada

1 ❑ Cover: 4.95 **NM** value: **Cover or less**
2 ❑ Cover: 4.95 **NM** value: **Cover or less**
3 ❑ Cover: 4.95 **NM** value: **Cover or less**
4 ❑ Cover: 4.95 **NM** value: **Cover or less**

BAZOOKA JULES — Com.x

1 ❑ ca. 2001 Cover: 2.99 **NM** value: **Cover or less**
Circ: Diamd. preorders: **3,256** • **CGC:** 2 graded, best 9.6

2 ❑ ca. 2001 Cover: 2.95 **NM** value: **Cover or less**
Circ: Diamd. preorders: **2,768**

B-BAR-B RIDERS — AC

1 ❑ **NM** value: **2.00**
A: Frank Frazetta

BEACH HIGH — Big

1 ❑ Feb 1997 Cover: 3.25 **NM** value: **Cover or less**
Circ: Diamd. preorders: **6,418**
• illustrated text story, one-shot

BEACH PARTY — Eternity

1 ❑ Cover: 2.50 **NM** value: **Cover or less**
• b&w pin-ups **A:** Scott Benefiel; Barry Blair; Jimmy Palmiotti

📖 indicates **Story Title** or **Storyline** information.
★ indicates **Character Appearance** information.
W = Writer • A = Artist • C = Cover Artist

BEAGLE BOYS, THE — Gold Key

Here's something unique in a comic-book series: You can read it and you can like it, but you'll never really know any of the characters' names — or care.

Carl Barks invented The Beagle Boys as foils for Uncle Scrooge, and this title features their failed get-rich attempts (usually, but not always, involving robbing Scrooge).

With the exception of some "specialty" beagles, all the characters were ideniftified by their prisoner numbers, like 176-176. And most were some permutation of 1, 7, and 6, so keeping characters straight was nearly impossible. Fortunately, that's not really necessary. It's the Beagle's schemes that are the real stars in this title. — JJM

1 ❑ Nov 1964 Cover: 0.12 **NM** value: **20.00**
2 ❑ Nov 1965 Cover: 0.12 **NM** value: **15.00**
3 ❑ Aug 1966 Cover: 0.12 **NM** value: **15.00**
4 ❑ Nov 1966 Cover: 0.12 **NM** value: **15.00**
5 ❑ Feb 1967 Cover: 0.12 **NM** value: **12.00**
6 ❑ May 1967 Cover: 0.12 **NM** value: **12.00**
7 ❑ Cover: 0.12 **NM** value: **12.00**
8 ❑ Oct 1968 Cover: 0.15 **NM** value: **12.00**
9 ❑ Apr 1970 Cover: 0.15 **NM** value: **12.00**
10 ❑ Cover: 0.15 **NM** value: **12.00**
11 ❑ Cover: 0.15 **NM** value: **8.00**
12 ❑ Sep 1971 Cover: 0.15 **NM** value: **8.00**
13 ❑ Cover: 0.15 **NM** value: **8.00**
14 ❑ Sep 1972 Cover: 0.15 **NM** value: **8.00**
15 ❑ Cover: 0.15 **NM** value: **8.00**
16 ❑ Apr 1973 Cover: 0.15 **NM** value: **8.00**
📖 Scientific Deduction; The Whistling Teakettle ★ Appearance of Uncle Scrooge.
17 ❑ Jul 1973 **NM** value: **8.00**
18 ❑ Oct 1973 Cover: 0.20 **NM** value: **8.00**
19 ❑ Jan 1974 Cover: 0.20 **NM** value: **8.00**
20 ❑ Apr 1974 Cover: 0.20 **NM** value: **8.00**
📖 Beagle Bloopers; Fakery in the Bakery
21 ❑ Jul 1974 Cover: 0.20 **NM** value: **5.00**
22 ❑ Oct 1974 Cover: 0.25 **NM** value: **5.00**
23 ❑ Jan 1975 Cover: 0.25 **NM** value: **5.00**
24 ❑ Apr 1975 Cover: 0.25 **NM** value: **5.00**
25 ❑ Jul 1975 Cover: 0.25 **NM** value: **5.00**
26 ❑ Oct 1975 Cover: 0.25 **NM** value: **5.00**
27 ❑ Jan 1976 Cover: 0.25 **NM** value: **5.00**
28 ❑ Mar 1976 Cover: 0.25 **NM** value: **5.00**
29 ❑ May 1976 Cover: 0.25 **NM** value: **5.00**
30 ❑ Jul 1976 **NM** value: **5.00**
31 ❑ Sep 1976 Cover: 0.30 **NM** value: **3.00**
📖 Crime, Sweet Crime; Bah! Bah! Black Sheep; Over-Wanted; Ye Olde Rip-Off
32 ❑ Nov 1976 Cover: 0.30 **NM** value: **3.00**
33 ❑ Jan 1977 Cover: 0.30 **NM** value: **3.00**
34 ❑ Apr 1977 Cover: 0.30 **NM** value: **3.00**
35 ❑ Jun 1977 Cover: 0.30 **NM** value: **3.00**
36 ❑ Aug 1977 Cover: 0.30 **NM** value: **3.00**
37 ❑ Sep 1977 Cover: 0.30 **NM** value: **3.00**
38 ❑ Oct 1977 Cover: 0.30 **NM** value: **3.00**
39 ❑ Dec 1977 **NM** value: **3.00**
40 ❑ Jan 1978 **NM** value: **3.00**
41 ❑ Apr 1978 Cover: 0.35 **NM** value: **2.00**
42 ❑ Jun 1978 Cover: 0.35 **NM** value: **2.00**
43 ❑ Aug 1978 Cover: 0.35 **NM** value: **2.00**
📖 The Mush Quest; A Bad Day with Buttinski; Visionary Harry; Old Time Crime
44 ❑ Sep 1978 Cover: 0.35 **NM** value: **2.00**
📖 A Very Special Cat; Stolen Luck; Ratty's Reward; Back to Nature
45 ❑ Oct 1978 Cover: 0.35 **NM** value: **2.00**
46 ❑ Dec 1978 Cover: 0.35 **NM** value: **2.00**
📖 Mascot Woes; The Tunnel Muddle; The Hocus-Pocus Plot; Cousin Catnip's Caper
47 ❑ Cover: 0.35 **NM** value: **2.00**

BEAGLE BOYS VERSUS UNCLE SCROOGE, THE — Gold Key / Whitman

1 ❑ Mar 1979 Cover: 0.35 **NM** value: **5.00**
• **CGC:** 1 graded, best 9.2
2 ❑ Apr 1979 Cover: 0.40 **NM** value: **5.00**
3 ❑ May 1979 Cover: 0.40 **NM** value: **3.00**
📖 The Armored Car Caper; The Guardian Sword
4 ❑ Jun 1979 Cover: 0.40 **NM** value: **3.00**
📖 The Great Gift Grab; The Rare Stamp Episode
5 ❑ Jul 1979 Cover: 0.40 **NM** value: **3.00**
6 ❑ Aug 1979 Cover: 0.40 **NM** value: **3.00**
7 ❑ Sep 1979 Cover: 0.40 **NM** value: **3.00**
8 ❑ Oct 1979 Cover: 0.40 **NM** value: **2.00**
9 ❑ Nov 1979 Cover: 0.40 **NM** value: **2.00**
10 ❑ Dec 1979 Cover: 0.40 **NM** value: **2.00**
11 ❑ Jan 1980 Cover: 0.40 **NM** value: **2.00**
12 ❑ Feb 1980 Cover: 0.40 **NM** value: **2.00**

BEANY AND CECIL — Dell

1 ❑ Jul 1962 Cover: 0.15 **NM** value: **75.00**
• **CGC:** 1 graded, best 7.0
2 ❑ Oct 1962 Cover: 0.10 **NM** value: **60.00**
3 ❑ Jan 1963 Cover: 0.10 **NM** value: **60.00**
4 ❑ Apr 1963 Cover: 0.10 **NM** value: **60.00**
5 ❑ Jul 1963 Cover: 0.10 **NM** value: **60.00**
• **CGC:** 1 graded, best 9.6

BEARFAX FUNNIES — Treasure

1 ❑ Cover: 2.75 **NM** value: **Cover or less**

BEARSKIN: A GRIMM TALE — Thecomic.Com

1 ❑ b&w **NM** value: **1.50**
No issue number. One-shot. no cover price.

BEAST, THE — Marvel

1 ❑ May 1997 Cover: 2.50 **NM** value: **Cover or less**
Circ: Diamd. preorders: **75,703**
📖 Bad Karma **A:** Cedric Nocon **W:** Keith Giffen ★ Appearance of Karma, Cannonball, Viper, Spiral, Gateway.

2 ❑ Jun 1997 Cover: 2.50 **NM** value: **Cover or less**
Circ: Diamd. preorders: **60,800**

3 ❑ Jul 1997 Cover: 2.50 **NM** value: **Cover or less**
Circ: Diamd. preorders: **53,797**

BEAST BOY — DC

1 ❑ Jan 2000 Cover: 2.95 **NM** value: **Cover or less**
Circ: Diamd. preorders: **19,837**
A: Justiniano **W:** Ben Raab; Geof Johns

2 ❑ Feb 2000 Cover: 2.95 **NM** value: **Cover or less**
Circ: Diamd. preorders: **17,088**
📖 Nobody's Hero **A:** Justiniano **W:** Ben Raab; Geof Johns

3 ❑ Mar 2000 Cover: 2.95 **NM** value: **Cover or less**
Circ: Diamd. preorders: **14,768**
A: Justiniano **W:** Ben Raab; Geof Johns

4 ❑ Apr 2000 Cover: 2.95 **NM** value: **Cover or less**
Circ: Diamd. preorders: **13,148**
📖 Beast War! **A:** Justiniano **W:** Ben Raab; Geof Johns

B.E.A.S.T.I.E.S. — Axis

1 ❑ Apr 1994 Cover: 1.95 **NM** value: **Cover or less**
Circ: CapCity orders: **5,860**
📖 Induction **A:** Javier Saltares **W:** Javier Saltares

BEAST WARRIORS OF SHAOLIN — Pied Piper

1 ❑ Jul 1987 Cover: 1.95 **NM** value: **Cover or less**
A: Glen Johnson; Peter Quinones **W:** Glen Johnson; Peter Quinones
2 ❑ Cover: 1.95 **NM** value: **Cover or less**
3 ❑ Cover: 1.95 **NM** value: **Cover or less**

BEATLES — Dell

1 ❑ Sep 1964 Cover: 0.35 **NM** value: **300.00**
• **CGC:** 5 graded, best 9.0

BEATLES, THE — Personality

1 ❑ b&w Cover: 2.95 **NM** value: **5.00**
• **CGC:** 1 graded, best 9.0
1/LE ❑ Cover: 5.95 **NM** value: **8.00**
• limited edition, b&w.
2 ❑ b&w Cover: 2.95 **NM** value: **4.00**

BEATLES EXPERIENCE, THE — Revolutionary

1 ❑ Mar 1991 Cover: 2.50 **NM** value: **Cover or less**
A: Mike Sagara **W:** Todd Loren
2 ❑ May 1991 Cover: 2.50 **NM** value: **Cover or less**
A: Mike Sagara **W:** Todd Loren
3 ❑ Jul 1991 Cover: 2.50 **NM** value: **Cover or less**
Circ: CapCity orders: **3,450**
A: Mike Sagara **W:** Todd Loren
4 ❑ Sep 1991 Cover: 2.50 **NM** value: **Cover or less**
A: Mike Sagara **W:** Todd Loren
5 ❑ Nov 1991 Cover: 2.50 **NM** value: **Cover or less**
A: Mike Sagara **W:** Todd Loren
6 ❑ Jan 1992 Cover: 2.50 **NM** value: **Cover or less**
A: Mike Sagara **W:** Todd Loren
7 ❑ Mar 1992 Cover: 2.50 **NM** value: **Cover or less**
A: Mike Sagara **W:** Todd Loren
8 ❑ May 1992 Cover: 2.50 **NM** value: **Cover or less**
A: Mike Sagara **W:** Todd Loren

BEATLES VS. THE ROLLING STONES, THE — Celebrity

1 ❑ May 1992 Cover: 2.95 **NM** value: **Cover or less**
A: Neil Feigeles **W:** Kevin Dwyer

BEATRIX — Vision

1 ❑ Cover: 2.95 **NM** value: **Cover or less**
2 ❑ Mar 1997 Cover: 2.95 **NM** value: **Cover or less**
A: Taral Wayne **W:** One of those Days; Duty Calls

BEAUTIES & BARBARIANS — AC

1 ❑ Cover: 1.25 **NM** value: **1.50**
A: Wally Wood

BEAUTIFUL PEOPLE — Slave Labor

1 ❑ Apr 1994 Cover: 4.50 **NM** value: **Cover or less**
No issue number. • Oversized.

There are two different pricing tiers in the modern comic-book hobby. **The prices seen above** are the prices we have seen **loose copies** of these issues reliably fetch in a variety of environments. Condition alters the price by the fractions seen on the bar on the bottom of left-hand pages of this book. **Comics graded by CGC** usually sell for more. Use the guide on the bottom of right-hand pages of this book to estimate what copies have brought on eBay.

CGC-graded: Multiply prices above by **33 for 9.9 M** • **16 for 9.8 NM/M** • **7 for 9.6 NM+** • **5 for 9.4 NM** • **2.5 for 9.2 NM-** • **1.5 for 9.0 VF/NM**

BEAUTIFUL STORIES FOR UGLY CHILDREN
DC / Piranha

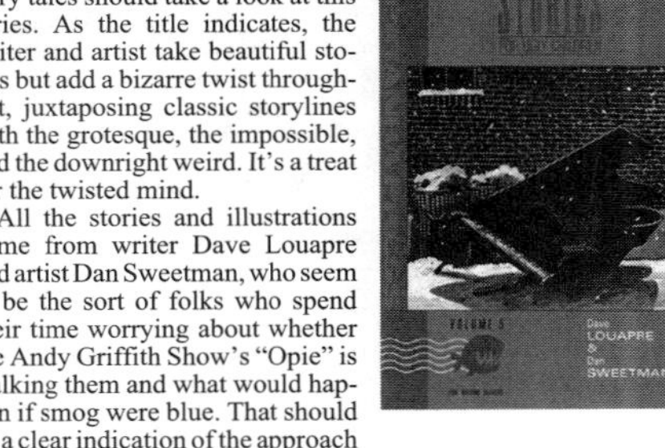

Those who like slightly off-kilter fairy tales should take a look at this series. As the title indicates, the writer and artist take beautiful stories but add a bizarre twist throughout, juxtaposing classic storylines with the grotesque, the impossible, and the downright weird. It's a treat for the twisted mind.

All the stories and illustrations come from writer Dave Louapre and artist Dan Sweetman, who seem to be the sort of folks who spend their time worrying about whether the Andy Griffith Show's "Opie" is stalking them and what would happen if smog were blue. That should be a clear indication of the approach of this series.

1 ❑ Cover: 2.00 **NM** value: **2.50**
Circ: CapCity orders: **10,200**
A: Dan Sweetman **W:** Dave Louapre
2 ❑ Cover: 2.00 **NM** value: **2.50**
Circ: CapCity orders: **7,450**
A: Dan Sweetman **W:** Dave Louapre
3 ❑ Cover: 2.00 **NM** value: **2.50**
A: Dan Sweetman **W:** Dave Louapre
4 ❑ Cover: 2.00 **NM** value: **2.50**
A: Dan Sweetman **W:** Dave Louapre
5 ❑ Cover: 2.00 **NM** value: **2.50**
A: Dan Sweetman **W:** Dave Louapre
6 ❑ Cover: 2.50 **NM** value: **Cover or less**
📖 Happy Birthday to Hell **A:** Dan Sweetman **W:** Dave Louapre
7 ❑ Cover: 2.00 **NM** value: **2.50**
A: Dan Sweetman **W:** Dave Louapre
8 ❑ Cover: 2.00 **NM** value: **2.50**
A: Dan Sweetman **W:** Dave Louapre
9 ❑ Cover: 2.00 **NM** value: **2.50**
A: Dan Sweetman **W:** Dave Louapre
10 ❑ Cover: 2.00 **NM** value: **2.50**
A: Dan Sweetman **W:** Dave Louapre
11 ❑ Cover: 2.00 **NM** value: **2.50**
A: Dan Sweetman **W:** Dave Louapre
12 ❑ Cover: 2.50 **NM** value: **Cover or less**
A: Dan Sweetman **W:** Dave Louapre
13 ❑ Cover: 2.50 **NM** value: **Cover or less**
A: Dan Sweetman **W:** Dave Louapre
14 ❑ Cover: 2.50 **NM** value: **Cover or less**
A: Dan Sweetman **W:** Dave Louapre
15 ❑ Cover: 2.50 **NM** value: **Cover or less**
A: Dan Sweetman **W:** Dave Louapre
16 ❑ Cover: 2.50 **NM** value: **Cover or less**
A: Dan Sweetman **W:** Dave Louapre
17 ❑ Cover: 2.50 **NM** value: **Cover or less**
A: Dan Sweetman **W:** Dave Louapre
18 ❑ Cover: 2.50 **NM** value: **Cover or less**
A: Dan Sweetman **W:** Dave Louapre
19 ❑ Cover: 2.50 **NM** value: **Cover or less**
📖 Nice Girls Don't Massacre Ants **A:** Dan Sweetman **W:** Dave Louapre
20 ❑ Cover: 2.50 **NM** value: **Cover or less**
A: Dan Sweetman **W:** Dave Louapre
21 ❑ Cover: 2.50 **NM** value: **Cover or less**
A: Dan Sweetman **W:** Dave Louapre
22 ❑ Cover: 2.50 **NM** value: **Cover or less**
A: Dan Sweetman **W:** Dave Louapre
23 ❑ Cover: 2.50 **NM** value: **Cover or less**
A: Dan Sweetman **W:** Dave Louapre
24 ❑ Cover: 2.50 **NM** value: **Cover or less**
Circ: CapCity orders: **2,650**
A: Dan Sweetman **W:** Dave Louapre
25 ❑ Cover: 2.50 **NM** value: **Cover or less**
A: Dan Sweetman **W:** Dave Louapre
26 ❑ Cover: 2.50 **NM** value: **Cover or less**
A: Dan Sweetman **W:** Dave Louapre
27 ❑ Cover: 2.50 **NM** value: **Cover or less**
Circ: CapCity orders: **2,300**
A: Dan Sweetman **W:** Dave Louapre
28 ❑ Cover: 2.50 **NM** value: **Cover or less**
📖 The Guilty Orphan **A:** Dan Sweetman **W:** Dave Louapre
29 ❑ Cover: 2.50 **NM** value: **Cover or less**
📖 Gravity Sucks **A:** Dan Sweetman **W:** Dave Louapre
30 ❑ Cover: 2.50 **NM** value: **Cover or less**
A: Dan Sweetman **W:** Dave Louapre

BEAUTY AND THE BEAST
Disney

1 ❑ Cover: 2.50 **NM** value: **Cover or less**
No issue number.
1/DM❑ Cover: 4.95 **NM** value: **Cover or less**
Circ: CapCity orders: **4,350**
No issue number. • squarebound

BEAUTY AND THE BEAST (DISNEY'S...)
Disney

1 ❑ Sep 1994 Cover: 1.50 **NM** value: **Cover or less**
Circ: CapCity orders: **14,450**
2 ❑ Oct 1994 Cover: 1.50 **NM** value: **Cover or less**
Circ: CapCity orders: **10,000**
3 ❑ Nov 1994 Cover: 1.50 **NM** value: **Cover or less**
Circ: CapCity orders: **8,500**
4 ❑ Dec 1994 Cover: 1.50 **NM** value: **Cover or less**
Circ: CapCity orders: **7,200**
5 ❑ Jan 1995 Cover: 1.50 **NM** value: **Cover or less**
Circ: CapCity orders: **6,300**
6 ❑ Feb 1995 Cover: 1.50 **NM** value: **Cover or less**
Circ: CapCity orders: **5,550**
7 ❑ Mar 1995 Cover: 1.50 **NM** value: **Cover or less**
Circ: CapCity orders: **4,775**
8 ❑ Apr 1995 Cover: 1.50 **NM** value: **Cover or less**
Circ: CapCity orders: **4,200**
9 ❑ May 1995 Cover: 1.50 **NM** value: **Cover or less**
Circ: CapCity orders: **4,025**
10 ❑ Jun 1995 Cover: 1.50 **NM** value: **Cover or less**
Circ: CapCity orders: **3,825**
11 ❑ Jul 1995 Cover: 1.50 **NM** value: **Cover or less**
Circ: CapCity orders: **3,550**
12 ❑ Aug 1995 Cover: 1.50 **NM** value: **Cover or less**
Circ: CapCity orders: **3,675**
13 ❑ Sep 1995 Cover: 1.50 **NM** value: **Cover or less**
HS 1❑ Cover: 4.50 **NM** value: **Cover or less**
• digest. • based on direct-to-video feature

BEAUTY AND THE BEAST (INNOVATION)
Innovation

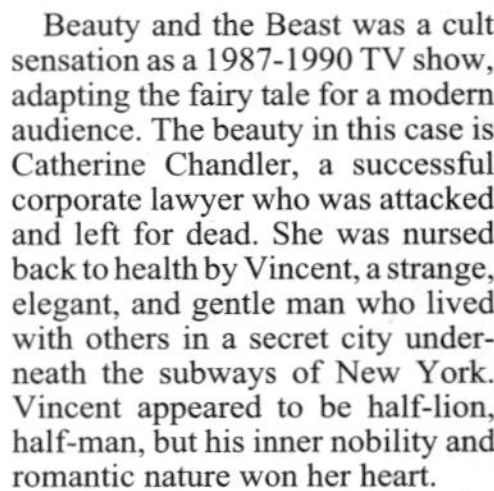

Beauty and the Beast was a cult sensation as a 1987-1990 TV show, adapting the fairy tale for a modern audience. The beauty in this case is Catherine Chandler, a successful corporate lawyer who was attacked and left for dead. She was nursed back to health by Vincent, a strange, elegant, and gentle man who lived with others in a secret city underneath the subways of New York. Vincent appeared to be half-lion, half-man, but his inner nobility and romantic nature won her heart.

This six-issue series adapts the television pilot starring Linda Hamilton ("Sarah Connor" in The Terminator) and Ron Perlman as Vincent. The series was adapted for comics by David Campiti and Cynthy J. Wood, with airbrushed art by Mike Deodato.

1 ❑ May 1993 Cover: 2.50 **NM** value: **Cover or less**
A: Mike Deodato **W:** David Campiti; Cynthy J. Wood; Ron Koslow
1/CS❑ Cover: 3.95 **NM** value: **Cover or less**
Circ: CapCity orders: **9,875**
A: Mike Deodato **W:** David Campiti; Cynthy J. Wood; Ron Koslow
2 ❑ Jun 1993 Cover: 2.50 **NM** value: **Cover or less**
Circ: CapCity orders: **8,030**
A: Mike Deodato **W:** David Campiti; Cynthy J. Wood; Ron Koslow
3 ❑ Jul 1993 Cover: 2.50 **NM** value: **Cover or less**
Circ: CapCity orders: **6,815**
A: Mike Deodato **W:** David Campiti; Cynthy J. Wood; Ron Koslow
4 ❑ Aug 1993 Cover: 2.50 **NM** value: **Cover or less**
Circ: CapCity orders: **5,685**
A: Mike Deodato **W:** David Campiti; Cynthy J. Wood; Ron Koslow
5 ❑ Sep 1993 Cover: 2.50 **NM** value: **Cover or less**
Circ: CapCity orders: **5,635**
A: Mike Deodato **W:** David Campiti; Cynthy J. Wood; Ron Koslow
6 ❑ Oct 1993 Cover: 2.50 **NM** value: **Cover or less**
Circ: CapCity orders: **5,045**
• indicia says Jul, should be Oct **A:** Mike Deodato **W:** David Campiti; Cynthy J. Wood; Ron Koslow

BEAUTY AND THE BEAST (MARVEL)
Marvel

1 ❑ Cover: 0.75 **NM** value: **2.00**
Circ: CapCity orders: **13,350** • **CGC:** 1 graded, best 9.6
A: Don Perlin
2 ❑ Cover: 0.75 **NM** value: **2.00**
Circ: CapCity orders: **9,350**
A: Don Perlin
3 ❑ Cover: 0.75 **NM** value: **2.00**
A: Don Perlin
4 ❑ Cover: 0.75 **NM** value: **2.00**
A: Don Perlin

BEAUTY AND THE BEAST (STAN SHAW'S...)
Dark Horse

1 ❑ Cover: 4.95 **NM** value: **Cover or less**
Circ: CapCity orders: **2,925**
No issue number.

BEAUTY OF THE BEASTS
Mu Press

1 ❑ Nov 1991, b&w Cover: 2.50 **NM** value: **Cover or less**
2 ❑ Jul 1993, b&w Cover: 2.50 **NM** value: **Cover or less**

BEAVIS & BUTT-HEAD
Marvel

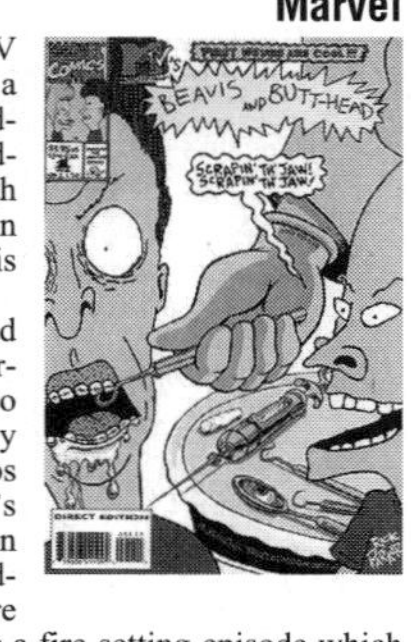

In addition to music videos, MTV has had a big role in popularizing a new wave of cartoon features, including Ren & Stimpy and Rocko's Modern Life. They also came up with something of a national sensation in the early 1990s with their own Beavis & Butt-Head.

Beavis (the blond) and Butt-Head (the brunet) are two losers in their early teens. Too young to drive and too stupid to have actual hobbies, they spend their time watching rock videos and getting into trouble. (In Marvel's adaptation, they read and comment on comic books instead of watching videos.) Their infamy in popular culture lies partly in their antics, including a fire-setting episode which was blamed for inspiring a real-life trailer fire. The pair is even more famous for the way they talk and laugh ("huh ... huh-huh-huh!"). Unfortunately, this quality is hard to capture in print. As a result, the lowbrow humor sometimes comes across as more cruel than funny.

1 ❑ Mar 1994 Cover: 1.95 **NM** value: **3.00**
Circ: Statement: **172,744** CapCity orders: **110,550** • **CGC:** 7 graded, best 9.8
📖 Dental Hygiene Dilemma; How to Sneak Home After School and Not Get Beat Up!; Be Cool to Your School! **A:** Rick Parker **W:** Mike Lackey ★ 1st Appearance of Beavis & Butt-Head (in comics). ★ Appearance of Punisher.
1-2 ❑ Cover: 1.95 **NM** value: **Cover or less**
2 ❑ Apr 1994 Cover: 1.95 **NM** value: **2.50**
Circ: Statement: **172,744** CapCity orders: **56,850** • **CGC:** 1 graded, best 6.5
A: Rick Parker
3 ❑ May 1994 Cover: 1.95 **NM** value: **2.50**
Circ: Statement: **172,744** CapCity orders: **52,450**
A: Rick Parker
4 ❑ Jun 1994 Cover: 1.95 **NM** value: **2.50**
Circ: Statement: **172,744** CapCity orders: **53,100**
A: Rick Parker
5 ❑ Jul 1994 Cover: 1.95 **NM** value: **2.50**
Circ: Statement: **172,744** CapCity orders: **49,550**
A: Rick Parker
6 ❑ Aug 1994 Cover: 1.95 **NM** value: **2.00**
Circ: Statement: **172,744** CapCity orders: **45,750**
A: Rick Parker
7 ❑ Sep 1994 Cover: 1.95 **NM** value: **2.00**
Circ: Statement: **172,744** CapCity orders: **40,700**
A: Rick Parker
8 ❑ Oct 1994 Cover: 1.95 **NM** value: **2.00**
Circ: Statement: **172,744** CapCity orders: **35,800**
A: Rick Parker
9 ❑ Nov 1994 Cover: 1.95 **NM** value: **2.00**
Circ: Statement: **172,744** CapCity orders: **31,650**
A: Rick Parker
10 ❑ Dec 1994 Cover: 1.95 **NM** value: **2.00**
Circ: Statement: **172,744** CapCity orders: **30,700**
A: Rick Parker
11 ❑ Jan 1995 Cover: 1.95 **NM** value: **2.00**
Circ: Statement: **82,360** CapCity orders: **26,825**
A: Rick Parker
12 ❑ Feb 1995 Cover: 1.95 **NM** value: **2.00**
Circ: Statement: **82,360** CapCity orders: **23,175**
A: Rick Parker
13 ❑ Mar 1995 Cover: 1.95 **NM** value: **2.00**
Circ: Statement: **82,360** CapCity orders: **21,225**
A: Rick Parker
14 ❑ Apr 1995 Cover: 1.95 **NM** value: **2.00**
Circ: Statement: **82,360** CapCity orders: **19,450**
A: Rick Parker
15 ❑ May 1995 Cover: 1.95 **NM** value: **2.00**
Circ: Statement: **82,360** CapCity orders: **19,575**
A: Rick Parker
16 ❑ Jun 1995 Cover: 1.95 **NM** value: **2.00**
Circ: Statement: **82,360** CapCity orders: **18,550**
A: Rick Parker
17 ❑ Jul 1995 Cover: 1.95 **NM** value: **2.00**
Circ: Statement: **82,360** CapCity orders: **16,825**
A: Rick Parker
18 ❑ Aug 1995 Cover: 1.95 **NM** value: **2.00**
Circ: Statement: **82,360** CapCity orders: **15,325**
A: Rick Parker
19 ❑ Sep 1995 Cover: 1.95 **NM** value: **2.00**
Circ: Statement: **82,360**
A: Rick Parker
20 ❑ Oct 1995 Cover: 1.95 **NM** value: **2.00**
📖 Printing for Dollar$ **A:** Rick Parker **W:** Glenn Herdling
21 ❑ Nov 1995 Cover: 1.95 **NM** value: **2.00**
22 ❑ Dec 1995 Cover: 1.95 **NM** value: **2.00**
A: Rick Parker **W:** Guy Maxtone-Graham
23 ❑ Jan 1996 Cover: 1.50 **NM** value: **2.00**
• Has 1995 Statement, filed 10/1/95; avg print run 146,854; avg sales 81,027; avg subs 1,333; avg total paid 82,360; samples 750; office use 500; max existent 83,610; 43% of run returned
24 ❑ Feb 1996 Cover: 1.95 **NM** value: **2.00**
25 ❑ Mar 1996 Cover: 1.95 **NM** value: **2.00**
26 ❑ Apr 1996 Cover: 1.95 **NM** value: **2.00**
27 ❑ May 1996 Cover: 1.95 **NM** value: **2.00**
28 ❑ Cover: 1.95 **NM** value: **2.00**
final issue.
Bk 1❑ Jun 1994 Cover: 12.95 **NM** value: **Cover or less**
• Greatest Hits, collects Beavis & Butt-Head #1-4
Bk 2❑ Cover: 12.95 **NM** value: **Cover or less**
• Trashcan Edition. • collects Beavis & Butt-Head #5-8
Bk 3❑ Cover: 12.95 **NM** value: **Cover or less**
• Holidazed and Confused

BECK & CAUL INVESTIGATIONS
Caliber

1 ❑ Jan 1994 Cover: 2.95 **NM** value: **Cover or less**
★ Origin of Caul (Mercedes Guillane).
2 ❑ Mar 1994 Cover: 2.95 **NM** value: **Cover or less**
3 ❑ May 1994 Cover: 2.95 **NM** value: **Cover or less**
4 ❑ Aug 1994 Cover: 2.95 **NM** value: **Cover or less**
5 ❑ Cover: 2.95 **NM** value: **Cover or less**
Anl 1❑May 1995 Cover: 3.50 **NM** value: **Cover or less**

BEDLAM!
Eclipse

1 ❑ Aug 1985 Cover: 1.75 **NM** value: **Cover or less**
📖 Lo; Sneaky Pete; The Day After Tomorrow; Cell Food **A:** Rick Veitch; Stephen R. Bissette **W:** Rick Veitch; Stephen R. Bissette
2 ❑ Sep 1985 Cover: 1.75 **NM** value: **Cover or less**
📖 Conquest of the Banana Planet; Scraps; Game Over; Arena; Nutpeas **A:** Rick Veitch; Stephen R. Bissette **W:** Rick Veitch; Stephen R. Bissette

BEDLAM (CHAOS)
Chaos

1 ❑ Sep 2000 Cover: 2.95 **NM** value: **Cover or less**
Circ: CapCity orders: **4,750** Diamd. preorders: **10,866**
A: David Brewer **W:** Steven Grant

Other grades: Multiply prices above by **1.5 for Mint • 2/3 for Very Fine • 1/3 for Fine • 1/5 for Very Good • 1/8 for Good**

1/SC❑Sep 2000 Cover: 2.95 **NM** value: **Cover or less**
Circ: CapCity orders: **4,400**
Premium cover by David Michael Beck. **A:** David Brewer **W:** Steven Grant

BEELZELVIS — Slave Labor

1 ❑ Feb 1994 Cover: 2.95 **NM** value: **Cover or less**
A: Andy Garcia **W:** Andy Garcia

BEEP BEEP, THE ROAD RUNNER (DELL) — Dell

4 ❑ Feb 1960 Cover: 0.10 **NM** value: **20.00**
5 ❑ May 1960 Cover: 0.10 **NM** value: **20.00**
6 ❑ Aug 1960 Cover: 0.10 **NM** value: **20.00**
7 ❑ Nov 1960 Cover: 0.10 **NM** value: **20.00**
8 ❑ Feb 1961 Cover: 0.15 **NM** value: **20.00**
9 ❑ May 1961 Cover: 0.15 **NM** value: **20.00**
10 ❑ Aug 1961 Cover: 0.15 **NM** value: **15.00**
11 ❑ Nov 1961 Cover: 0.15 **NM** value: **15.00**
12 ❑ Feb 1962 Cover: 0.15 **NM** value: **15.00**
13 ❑ May 1962 Cover: 0.15 **NM** value: **15.00**
14 ❑ Aug 1962 Cover: 0.12 **NM** value: **15.00**

BEEP BEEP, THE ROAD RUNNER (GOLD KEY) — Gold Key

1 ❑ Oct 1966 Cover: 0.12 **NM** value: **25.00**
2 ❑ Jan 1967 Cover: 0.12 **NM** value: **25.00**
3 ❑ Apr 1967 Cover: 0.12 **NM** value: **20.00**
4 ❑ Jul 1967 Cover: 0.12 **NM** value: **20.00**
📖 Lunch on the Run; Cheated by a Cheetah; The Big Getaway
5 ❑ Oct 1967 Cover: 0.12 **NM** value: **20.00**
6 ❑ Jan 1968 Cover: 0.12 **NM** value: **15.00**
7 ❑ Apr 1968 Cover: 0.12 **NM** value: **15.00**
8 ❑ Jul 1968 Cover: 0.12 **NM** value: **15.00**
9 ❑ Oct 1968 Cover: 0.15 **NM** value: **15.00**
10 ❑ Feb 1969 Cover: 0.15 **NM** value: **15.00**
11 ❑ Apr 1969 Cover: 0.15 **NM** value: **15.00**
12 ❑ Jun 1969 Cover: 0.15 **NM** value: **15.00**
13 ❑ Aug 1969 Cover: 0.15 **NM** value: **15.00**
14 ❑ Oct 1969 Cover: 0.15 **NM** value: **15.00**
15 ❑ Dec 1969 Cover: 0.15 **NM** value: **15.00**
16 ❑ Feb 1970 Cover: 0.15 **NM** value: **10.00**
17 ❑ Apr 1970 Cover: 0.15 **NM** value: **10.00**
18 ❑ Jun 1970 Cover: 0.15 **NM** value: **10.00**
19 ❑ Aug 1970 Cover: 0.25 **NM** value: **10.00**
20 ❑ Oct 1970 Cover: 0.15 **NM** value: **10.00**
21 ❑ Dec 1970 Cover: 0.15 **NM** value: **10.00**
Circ: Statement: **206,918**
22 ❑ Feb 1971 Cover: 0.15 **NM** value: **10.00**
Circ: Statement: **206,918**
23 ❑ Apr 1971 Cover: 0.15 **NM** value: **10.00**
Circ: Statement: **206,918**
24 ❑ Jun 1971 Cover: 0.15 **NM** value: **10.00**
Circ: Statement: **206,918**
25 ❑ Aug 1971 Cover: 0.15 **NM** value: **10.00**
Circ: Statement: **206,918**
26 ❑ Oct 1971 Cover: 0.15 **NM** value: **10.00**
Circ: Statement: **206,918**
27 ❑ Dec 1971 Cover: 0.15 **NM** value: **10.00**
28 ❑ Feb 1972 Cover: 0.15 **NM** value: **10.00**
• Has 1971 Statement; avg print run 325,937; avg total paid circ 206,918
29 ❑ Apr 1972 Cover: 0.15 **NM** value: **10.00**
30 ❑ Jun 1972 Cover: 0.15 **NM** value: **10.00**
31 ❑ Aug 1972 Cover: 0.15 **NM** value: **10.00**
32 ❑ Oct 1972 Cover: 0.15 **NM** value: **10.00**
33 ❑ Dec 1972 Cover: 0.15 **NM** value: **10.00**
34 ❑ Feb 1973 Cover: 0.15 **NM** value: **10.00**
35 ❑ Apr 1973 Cover: 0.15 **NM** value: **10.00**
36 ❑ Jun 1973 Cover: 0.20 **NM** value: **10.00**
37 ❑ Aug 1973 Cover: 0.20 **NM** value: **10.00**
38 ❑ Sep 1973 Cover: 0.20 **NM** value: **10.00**
39 ❑ Oct 1973 Cover: 0.20 **NM** value: **10.00**
40 ❑ Dec 1973 Cover: 0.20 **NM** value: **10.00**
41 ❑ Feb 1974 Cover: 0.20 **NM** value: **8.00**
42 ❑ Apr 1974 Cover: 0.20 **NM** value: **8.00**
43 ❑ Jun 1974 Cover: 0.20 **NM** value: **8.00**
44 ❑ Aug 1974 Cover: 0.25 **NM** value: **8.00**
45 ❑ Sep 1974 Cover: 0.25 **NM** value: **8.00**
46 ❑ Oct 1974 Cover: 0.25 **NM** value: **8.00**
47 ❑ Dec 1974 Cover: 0.25 **NM** value: **8.00**
48 ❑ Feb 1975 Cover: 0.25 **NM** value: **8.00**
49 ❑ Apr 1975 Cover: 0.25 **NM** value: **8.00**
50 ❑ Jun 1975 Cover: 0.25 **NM** value: **8.00**
51 ❑ Jul 1975 Cover: 0.25 **NM** value: **8.00**
52 ❑ Aug 1975 Cover: 0.25 **NM** value: **8.00**
53 ❑ Oct 1975 Cover: 0.25 **NM** value: **8.00**
54 ❑ Dec 1975 Cover: 0.25 **NM** value: **8.00**
55 ❑ Jan 1976 Cover: 0.25 **NM** value: **8.00**
56 ❑ Mar 1976 Cover: 0.25 **NM** value: **8.00**
57 ❑ May 1976 Cover: 0.25 **NM** value: **8.00**
58 ❑ Jul 1976 Cover: 0.25 **NM** value: **8.00**
59 ❑ Sep 1976 Cover: 0.30 **NM** value: **8.00**
60 ❑ Oct 1976 Cover: 0.30 **NM** value: **6.00**
61 ❑ Nov 1976 Cover: 0.30 **NM** value: **6.00**
62 ❑ Jan 1977 Cover: 0.30 **NM** value: **6.00**
63 ❑ Mar 1977 Cover: 0.30 **NM** value: **6.00**
64 ❑ May 1977 Cover: 0.30 **NM** value: **6.00**
65 ❑ Jul 1977 Cover: 0.30 **NM** value: **6.00**
66 ❑ Sep 1977 Cover: 0.30 **NM** value: **6.00**
67 ❑ Oct 1977 Cover: 0.30 **NM** value: **6.00**
68 ❑ Nov 1977 Cover: 0.30 **NM** value: **6.00**
69 ❑ Jan 1978 Cover: 0.35 **NM** value: **6.00**
70 ❑ Mar 1978 Cover: 0.35 **NM** value: **6.00**
71 ❑ May 1978 Cover: 0.35 **NM** value: **6.00**
72 ❑ Jul 1978 Cover: 0.35 **NM** value: **6.00**
73 ❑ Sep 1978 Cover: 0.35 **NM** value: **6.00**
74 ❑ Oct 1978 Cover: 0.35 **NM** value: **6.00**
75 ❑ Nov 1978 Cover: 0.35 **NM** value: **6.00**
76 ❑ Jan 1979 Cover: 0.35 **NM** value: **6.00**
77 ❑ Mar 1979 Cover: 0.40 **NM** value: **6.00**
78 ❑ Apr 1979 Cover: 0.40 **NM** value: **6.00**
79 ❑ May 1979 Cover: 0.40 **NM** value: **6.00**
80 ❑ Jun 1979 Cover: 0.40 **NM** value: **3.00**
81 ❑ Jul 1979 Cover: 0.40 **NM** value: **3.00**
82 ❑ Aug 1979 Cover: 0.40 **NM** value: **3.00**
83 ❑ Sep 1979 Cover: 0.40 **NM** value: **3.00**
84 ❑ Oct 1979 Cover: 0.40 **NM** value: **3.00**
85 ❑ Nov 1979 Cover: 0.40 **NM** value: **3.00**
86 ❑ Dec 1979 Cover: 0.40 **NM** value: **3.00**
87 ❑ Jan 1980 Cover: 0.40 **NM** value: **3.00**
88 ❑ Feb 1980 Cover: 0.40 **NM** value: **3.00**
89 ❑ Apr 1980 Cover: 0.40 **NM** value: **3.00**
90 ❑ Jul 1980 Cover: 0.40 **NM** value: **3.00**
91 ❑ Aug 1980 Cover: 0.40 **NM** value: **3.00**
92 ❑ Sep 1980 Cover: 0.40 **NM** value: **3.00**
93 ❑ Oct 1980 Cover: 0.40 **NM** value: **3.00**
94 ❑ Feb 1981 Cover: 0.50 **NM** value: **3.00**
95 ❑ 1981 Cover: 0.50 **NM** value: **3.00**
96 ❑ 1981 Cover: 0.50 **NM** value: **3.00**
97 ❑ Sep 1981 Cover: 0.50 **NM** value: **3.00**
98 ❑ 1981 Cover: 0.50 **NM** value: **3.00**
99 ❑ 1981 Cover: 0.50 **NM** value: **3.00**
100 ❑ 1982 Cover: 0.60 **NM** value: **3.00**
101 ❑ Apr 1982 Cover: 0.60 **NM** value: **3.00**
102 ❑ 1982 Cover: 0.60 **NM** value: **3.00**
103 ❑ 1982 Cover: 0.60 **NM** value: **3.00**
104 ❑ 1982 Cover: 0.60 **NM** value: **3.00**
105 ❑ ca. 1983 Cover: 0.60 **NM** value: **3.00**

BEER & ROAMING IN LAS VEGAS — Slave Labor

A thief who falls in with a bad crowd of Elvis impersonators must reclaim a stolen tape and convince a cop he's really a good guy at heart in this rambling tale with too many digressions and not enough core story. Still, the Done in One story does have the flow of real-life randomness, so it's the pacing is deliberate. And, while too many of the characters wear the same faces but different clothes, the art isn't bad.

F. Andrew Taylor's other works include Camping with Bigfoot and On The Bus, also available from Slave Labor Graphics.

1 ❑ b&w Cover: 12.95**NM** value: **Cover or less**
📖 The Elvis Masters **A:** F. Andrew Taylor **W:** F. Andrew Taylor
Ash 1❑ **NM** value: **1.00**
A: F. Andrew Taylor **W:** F. Andrew Taylor

BEER NUTZ — Tundra

1 ❑ Cover: 2.95 **NM** value: **Cover or less**
2 ❑ Cover: 2.00 **NM** value: **Cover or less**
3 ❑ b&w Cover: 2.25 **NM** value: **Cover or less**

BEETHOVEN — Harvey

1 ❑ Mar 1994 Cover: 1.50 **NM** value: **Cover or less**
📖 Beethoven's 2nd **A:** Howard Bender **W:** Angelo Decesare; Len Blum
2 ❑ Cover: 1.50 **NM** value: **Cover or less**
3 ❑ Jul 1994 Cover: 1.50 **NM** value: **Cover or less**

BEETLE BAILEY BIG BOOK — Harvey

2 ❑ Cover: 1.95 **NM** value: **Cover or less**

BEETLE BAILEY FEATURING SARGE SNORKEL — Charlton

1 ❑ Oct 1973 **NM** value: **3.00**
• **CGC:** 1 graded, best 9.2
2 ❑ **NM** value: **2.00**
3 ❑ Jun 1974 Cover: 0.25 **NM** value: **1.50**
4 ❑ **NM** value: **1.50**
5 ❑ **NM** value: **1.50**
6 ❑ **NM** value: **1.50**
7 ❑ **NM** value: **1.50**
8 ❑ May 1975 Cover: 0.25 **NM** value: **1.50**
9 ❑ **NM** value: **1.50**
10 ❑ **NM** value: **1.50**
11 ❑ **NM** value: **1.50**
12 ❑ **NM** value: **1.50**
13 ❑ **NM** value: **1.50**
14 ❑ **NM** value: **1.50**
15 ❑ Aug 1976 Cover: 0.30 **NM** value: **1.50**
📖 Placing the Blame; Look Alike; Efficiency Report; Sneak-a-Snack; Tone of Voice; Service with a Smile; Well-Earned Rest; Dream On (text); Messed-Up Message; The Power of Suggestion; Defeat Switch; Dinner Decision; Pep Talk
16 ❑ Oct 1976 **NM** value: **1.50**
17 ❑ Dec 1976 **NM** value: **1.50**

The CGC numbers printed in individual listings above represent the **number of copies examined** and given a **Universal** grade by CGC and the **best such copy** graded at press time. For current populations, watch for special ***Comics Buyer's Guide*** issues or check **www.cgccomics.com.**

BEETLE BAILEY (VOL. 1) — Dell

Mort Walker's bumbling G.I. Beetle Bailey was long a favorite of the newspaper comics pages. After making several appearances in Dell's Four Color Comics, he received this, his first self-titled comic-book series, in 1962. The title then ran through several publishers during its 18-year run, finally concluding in 1980.

Beetle Bailey is one of the most enduring (and lighthearted) strips to base its humor on the foibles of Army life. Beetle, a layabout private, is constantly running into trouble and getting called on the carpet by blowhard Sergeant Snorkel. The hijinks continue up the chain of command, culminating with General Halftrack, a lecherous Army lifer whose ogling of his nubile assistant was taken as good fun for the 1960s but drew complaints from some readers in later years, though Miss Buxley was clearly shown as competent and unthreatened by the general, who was the butt of many gags.

1 ❑ May 1953 Cover: 0.10 **NM** value: **100.00**
• FC 469
2 ❑ Cover: 0.10 **NM** value: **50.00**
• FC 521
3 ❑ Cover: 0.10 **NM** value: **45.00**
• FC 552
4 ❑ Cover: 0.10 **NM** value: **35.00**
• FC 622
5 ❑ Apr 1956 Cover: 0.10 **NM** value: **22.00**
A: Mort Walker **W:** Mort Walker ★ Appearance of Series continued from.
6 ❑ 1956 Cover: 0.10 **NM** value: **22.00**
A: Mort Walker **W:** Mort Walker
7 ❑ Aug 1956 Cover: 0.10 **NM** value: **22.00**
A: Mort Walker **W:** Mort Walker
8 ❑ Nov 1956 Cover: 0.10 **NM** value: **22.00**
A: Mort Walker **W:** Mort Walker
9 ❑ Feb 1957 Cover: 0.10 **NM** value: **22.00**
A: Mort Walker **W:** Mort Walker
10 ❑ May 1957 Cover: 0.10 **NM** value: **22.00**
A: Mort Walker **W:** Mort Walker
11 ❑ Aug 1957 Cover: 0.10 **NM** value: **16.00**
A: Mort Walker **W:** Mort Walker
12 ❑ Nov 1957 Cover: 0.10 **NM** value: **16.00**
A: Mort Walker **W:** Mort Walker
13 ❑ Feb 1958 Cover: 0.10 **NM** value: **16.00**
A: Mort Walker **W:** Mort Walker
14 ❑ Apr 1958 Cover: 0.10 **NM** value: **16.00**
A: Mort Walker **W:** Mort Walker
15 ❑ Jun 1958 Cover: 0.10 **NM** value: **16.00**
A: Mort Walker **W:** Mort Walker
16 ❑ Aug 1958 Cover: 0.10 **NM** value: **16.00**
A: Mort Walker **W:** Mort Walker
17 ❑ Oct 1958 Cover: 0.10 **NM** value: **16.00**
A: Mort Walker **W:** Mort Walker
18 ❑ Dec 1958 Cover: 0.10 **NM** value: **16.00**
A: Mort Walker **W:** Mort Walker
19 ❑ Feb 1959 Cover: 0.10 **NM** value: **16.00**
A: Mort Walker **W:** Mort Walker
20 ❑ Apr 1959 Cover: 0.10 **NM** value: **16.00**
A: Mort Walker **W:** Mort Walker
21 ❑ Jun 1959 Cover: 0.10 **NM** value: **12.00**
A: Mort Walker **W:** Mort Walker
22 ❑ Aug 1959 Cover: 0.10 **NM** value: **12.00**
A: Mort Walker **W:** Mort Walker
23 ❑ Oct 1959 Cover: 0.10 **NM** value: **12.00**
A: Mort Walker **W:** Mort Walker
24 ❑ Dec 1959 Cover: 0.10 **NM** value: **12.00**
A: Mort Walker **W:** Mort Walker
25 ❑ Feb 1960 Cover: 0.10 **NM** value: **12.00**
A: Mort Walker **W:** Mort Walker
26 ❑ Apr 1960 Cover: 0.10 **NM** value: **12.00**
A: Mort Walker **W:** Mort Walker
27 ❑ Jun 1960 Cover: 0.10 **NM** value: **12.00**
A: Mort Walker **W:** Mort Walker
28 ❑ 1960 Cover: 0.10 **NM** value: **12.00**
A: Mort Walker **W:** Mort Walker
29 ❑ 1960 Cover: 0.10 **NM** value: **12.00**
A: Mort Walker **W:** Mort Walker
30 ❑ 1960 Cover: 0.10 **NM** value: **12.00**
A: Mort Walker **W:** Mort Walker
31 ❑ Mar 1961 Cover: 0.15 **NM** value: **9.00**
A: Mort Walker **W:** Mort Walker
32 ❑ May 1961 Cover: 0.15 **NM** value: **9.00**
A: Mort Walker **W:** Mort Walker
33 ❑ Jul 1961 Cover: 0.15 **NM** value: **9.00**
A: Mort Walker **W:** Mort Walker
34 ❑ Sep 1961 Cover: 0.15 **NM** value: **9.00**
A: Mort Walker **W:** Mort Walker
35 ❑ Nov 1961 Cover: 0.15 **NM** value: **9.00**
A: Mort Walker **W:** Mort Walker
36 ❑ Jan 1962 Cover: 0.15 **NM** value: **9.00**
A: Mort Walker **W:** Mort Walker
37 ❑ Mar 1962 Cover: 0.15 **NM** value: **9.00**
A: Mort Walker **W:** Mort Walker
38 ❑ May 1962 Cover: 0.15 **NM** value: **9.00**
A: Mort Walker **W:** Mort Walker
39 ❑ Nov 1962 Cover: 0.12 **NM** value: **9.00**
A: Mort Walker **W:** Mort Walker
40 ❑ Feb 1963 Cover: 0.12 **NM** value: **9.00**
A: Mort Walker **W:** Mort Walker
41 ❑ May 1963 Cover: 0.12 **NM** value: **7.00**
A: Mort Walker **W:** Mort Walker

CGC-graded: Multiply prices above by **33 for 9.9 M • 16 for 9.8 NM/M • 7 for 9.6 NM+ • 5 for 9.4 NM • 2.5 for 9.2 NM- • 1.5 for 9.0 VF/NM**

42 ❑ Aug 1963 Cover: 0.12 **NM** value: **7.00**
A: Mort Walker **W:** Mort Walker
43 ❑ Nov 1963 Cover: 0.12 **NM** value: **7.00**
A: Mort Walker **W:** Mort Walker
44 ❑ Feb 1964 Cover: 0.12 **NM** value: **7.00**
A: Mort Walker **W:** Mort Walker
45 ❑ May 1964 Cover: 0.12 **NM** value: **7.00**
A: Mort Walker **W:** Mort Walker
46 ❑ Aug 1964 Cover: 0.12 **NM** value: **7.00**
A: Mort Walker **W:** Mort Walker
47 ❑ Nov 1964 Cover: 0.12 **NM** value: **7.00**
A: Mort Walker **W:** Mort Walker
48 ❑ Feb 1965 Cover: 0.12 **NM** value: **7.00**
Circ: Statement: **237,700**
A: Mort Walker **W:** Mort Walker
49 ❑ May 1965 Cover: 0.12 **NM** value: **7.00**
Circ: Statement: **237,700**
A: Mort Walker **W:** Mort Walker
50 ❑ Aug 1965 Cover: 0.12 **NM** value: **7.00**
Circ: Statement: **237,700**
A: Mort Walker **W:** Mort Walker
51 ❑ Nov 1965 Cover: 0.12 **NM** value: **6.00**
Circ: Statement: **237,700**
A: Mort Walker **W:** Mort Walker
52 ❑ Feb 1966 Cover: 0.12 **NM** value: **6.00**
A: Mort Walker **W:** Mort Walker
53 ❑ May 1966 Cover: 0.12 **NM** value: **6.00**
• Has 1965 Statement; avg total paid circ 237,700 **A:** Mort Walker **W:** Mort Walker
54 ❑ Aug 1966 Cover: 0.12 **NM** value: **6.00**
A: Mort Walker **W:** Mort Walker
55 ❑ Oct 1966 Cover: 0.12 **NM** value: **6.00**
A: Mort Walker **W:** Mort Walker
56 ❑ Dec 1966 Cover: 0.12 **NM** value: **6.00**
A: Mort Walker **W:** Mort Walker
57 ❑ Feb 1967 Cover: 0.12 **NM** value: **6.00**
A: Mort Walker **W:** Mort Walker
58 ❑ Apr 1967 Cover: 0.12 **NM** value: **6.00**
A: Mort Walker **W:** Mort Walker
59 ❑ Jun 1967 Cover: 0.12 **NM** value: **6.00**
A: Mort Walker **W:** Mort Walker
60 ❑ Jul 1967 Cover: 0.12 **NM** value: **6.00**
A: Mort Walker **W:** Mort Walker
61 ❑ Aug 1967 Cover: 0.12 **NM** value: **5.00**
A: Mort Walker **W:** Mort Walker
62 ❑ Sep 1967 Cover: 0.12 **NM** value: **5.00**
A: Mort Walker **W:** Mort Walker
63 ❑ 1968 Cover: 0.12 **NM** value: **5.00**
A: Mort Walker **W:** Mort Walker
64 ❑ 1968 Cover: 0.12 **NM** value: **5.00**
A: Mort Walker **W:** Mort Walker
65 ❑ 1968 Cover: 0.15 **NM** value: **5.00**
A: Mort Walker **W:** Mort Walker
66 ❑ 1968 Cover: 0.12 **NM** value: **5.00**
A: Mort Walker **W:** Mort Walker
67 ❑ Feb 1969 Cover: 0.12 **NM** value: **5.00**
Circ: Statement: **198,020**
A: Mort Walker **W:** Mort Walker
68 ❑ Apr 1969 Cover: 0.12 **NM** value: **5.00**
Circ: Statement: **198,020**
A: Mort Walker **W:** Mort Walker
69 ❑ Jun 1969 Cover: 0.12 **NM** value: **5.00**
Circ: Statement: **198,020**
A: Mort Walker **W:** Mort Walker
70 ❑ ca. 1969 **NM** value: **5.00**
Circ: Statement: **198,020**
A: Mort Walker **W:** Mort Walker
71 ❑ Oct 1969 Cover: 0.15 **NM** value: **3.00**
Circ: Statement: **198,020**
A: Mort Walker **W:** Mort Walker
72 ❑ Nov 1969 Cover: 0.15 **NM** value: **3.00**
Circ: Statement: **198,020**
A: Mort Walker **W:** Mort Walker
73 ❑ Jan 1970 Cover: 0.15 **NM** value: **3.00**
A: Mort Walker **W:** Mort Walker
74 ❑ Mar 1970 Cover: 0.15 **NM** value: **3.00**
A: Mort Walker **W:** Mort Walker
75 ❑ May 1970 Cover: 0.15 **NM** value: **3.00**
• Has 1969 Statement, filed 9/30/1969; avg print run 300,000; avg sales 198,000; avg subs 20; avg total paid 198,020; samples 200; max existent 198,220; 34% of run returned **A:** Mort Walker **W:** Mort Walker
76 ❑ Jul 1970 Cover: 0.15 **NM** value: **3.00**
A: Mort Walker **W:** Mort Walker
77 ❑ Sep 1970 Cover: 0.15 **NM** value: **3.00**
A: Mort Walker **W:** Mort Walker
78 ❑ Nov 1970 Cover: 0.15 **NM** value: **3.00**
A: Mort Walker **W:** Mort Walker
79 ❑ Jan 1971 Cover: 0.15 **NM** value: **3.00**
Circ: Statement: **180,090**
A: Mort Walker **W:** Mort Walker
80 ❑ Mar 1971 Cover: 0.15 **NM** value: **3.00**
Circ: Statement: **180,090**
A: Mort Walker **W:** Mort Walker
81 ❑ May 1971 Cover: 0.15 **NM** value: **3.00**
Circ: Statement: **180,090**
A: Mort Walker **W:** Mort Walker
82 ❑ Jul 1971 Cover: 0.15 **NM** value: **3.00**
Circ: Statement: **180,090**
A: Mort Walker **W:** Mort Walker
83 ❑ Sep 1971 Cover: 0.15 **NM** value: **3.00**
Circ: Statement: **180,090**
A: Mort Walker **W:** Mort Walker
84 ❑ Oct 1971 Cover: 0.20 **NM** value: **3.00**
Circ: Statement: **180,090**
A: Mort Walker **W:** Mort Walker
85 ❑ Nov 1971 Cover: 0.20 **NM** value: **3.00**
Circ: Statement: **180,090**
A: Mort Walker **W:** Mort Walker
86 ❑ Dec 1971 Cover: 0.20 **NM** value: **3.00**
Circ: Statement: **180,090**
A: Mort Walker **W:** Mort Walker
87 ❑ Jan 1972 Cover: 0.20 **NM** value: **3.00**
Circ: Statement: **137,200**
Sarge Gets Shot!; Sergeant of the Apes; Ladies' Escort; Killer Gets His Kicks; Sarge: Double Orders; Boner's Ark; The Anniversary Present; Bugs Vs. Beetle **A:** Mort Walker **W:** Mort Walker
88 ❑ Mar 1972 Cover: 0.20 **NM** value: **3.00**
Circ: Statement: **137,200**
A: Mort Walker **W:** Mort Walker
89 ❑ Apr 1972 Cover: 0.20 **NM** value: **3.00**
Circ: Statement: **137,200**
• Has 1971 Statement, filed 9/30/1971; avg print run 260,000; avg sales 180,000; avg subs 90; avg total paid 180,090; samples 200; office use 100; max existent 180,390; 30% of run returned **A:** Mort Walker **W:** Mort Walker
90 ❑ Jun 1972 Cover: 0.20 **NM** value: **3.00**
Circ: Statement: **137,200**
A: Mort Walker **W:** Mort Walker
91 ❑ Jul 1972 Cover: 0.20 **NM** value: **3.00**
Circ: Statement: **137,200**
A: Mort Walker **W:** Mort Walker
92 ❑ Aug 1972 Cover: 0.20 **NM** value: **3.00**
Circ: Statement: **137,200**
A: Mort Walker **W:** Mort Walker
93 ❑ Oct 1972 Cover: 0.20 **NM** value: **3.00**
Circ: Statement: **137,200**
A: Mort Walker **W:** Mort Walker
94 ❑ Nov 1972 Cover: 0.20 **NM** value: **3.00**
Circ: Statement: **137,200**
A: Mort Walker **W:** Mort Walker
95 ❑ Dec 1972 Cover: 0.20 **NM** value: **3.00**
Circ: Statement: **137,200**
A: Mort Walker **W:** Mort Walker
96 ❑ Jan 1973 Cover: 0.20 **NM** value: **3.00**
Circ: Statement: **130,292**
A: Mort Walker **W:** Mort Walker
97 ❑ Mar 1973 Cover: 0.20 **NM** value: **3.00**
Circ: Statement: **130,292**
A: Mort Walker **W:** Mort Walker
98 ❑ Apr 1973 Cover: 0.20 **NM** value: **3.00**
Circ: Statement: **130,292**
• Has1972 Statement; avg total paid circ 137,200 **A:** Mort Walker **W:** Mort Walker
99 ❑ Jun 1973 Cover: 0.20 **NM** value: **3.00**
Circ: Statement: **130,292**
A: Mort Walker **W:** Mort Walker
100 ❑ Jul 1973 Cover: 0.20 **NM** value: **3.00**
Circ: Statement: **130,292**
A: Mort Walker **W:** Mort Walker
101 ❑ Aug 1973 Cover: 0.20 **NM** value: **2.00**
Circ: Statement: **130,292**
A: Mort Walker **W:** Mort Walker
102 ❑ Oct 1973 Cover: 0.20 **NM** value: **2.00**
Circ: Statement: **130,292**
A: Mort Walker **W:** Mort Walker
103 ❑ Nov 1973 Cover: 0.20 **NM** value: **2.00**
Circ: Statement: **130,292**
A: Mort Walker **W:** Mort Walker
104 ❑ 1974 **NM** value: **2.00**
Circ: Statement: **140,150**
A: Mort Walker **W:** Mort Walker
105 ❑ May 1974 **NM** value: **2.00**
Circ: Statement: **140,150**
• Has 1973 Statement; avg total paid circ 130,292 **A:** Mort Walker **W:** Mort Walker
106 ❑ Jul 1974 Cover: 0.25 **NM** value: **2.00**
Circ: Statement: **140,150**
A: Mort Walker **W:** Mort Walker
107 ❑ Oct 1974 Cover: 0.25 **NM** value: **2.00**
Circ: Statement: **140,150**
A: Mort Walker **W:** Mort Walker
108 ❑ 1974 Cover: 0.25 **NM** value: **2.00**
Circ: Statement: **140,150**
A: Mort Walker **W:** Mort Walker
109 ❑ 1975 Cover: 0.25 **NM** value: **2.00**
Circ: Statement: **106,230**
A: Mort Walker **W:** Mort Walker
110 ❑ Apr 1975 Cover: 0.25 **NM** value: **2.00**
Circ: Statement: **106,230**
• Has 1974 Statement; avg total paid circ 140,150 **A:** Mort Walker **W:** Mort Walker
111 ❑ Jun 1975 Cover: 0.25 **NM** value: **2.00**
Circ: Statement: **106,230**
A: Mort Walker **W:** Mort Walker
112 ❑ Sep 1975 Cover: 0.25 **NM** value: **2.00**
Circ: Statement: **106,230**
A: Mort Walker **W:** Mort Walker
113 ❑ 1975 Cover: 0.25 **NM** value: **2.00**
Circ: Statement: **106,230**
A: Mort Walker **W:** Mort Walker
114 ❑ 1976 Cover: 0.25 **NM** value: **2.00**
A: Mort Walker **W:** Mort Walker
115 ❑ Mar 1976 Cover: 0.25 **NM** value: **2.00**
A: Mort Walker **W:** Mort Walker
116 ❑ May 1976 Cover: 0.30 **NM** value: **2.00**
• Has1975 Statement, filed 9/30/1975; avg print run 230,000; avg sales 105,900; avg subs 330; avg total paid 106,230; samples 200; office use 15,000; max existent 121,430; 47% of run returned **A:** Mort Walker **W:** Mort Walker
117 ❑ Jul 1976 Cover: 0.30 **NM** value: **2.00**
Sarge's Daily Dozen; Sarge's Big Day; Zero: Giggle Fits; Beetle's Message; The Thinkers; Beetle Bailey: Judo Class; Rain Hike; The General: Letting Go **A:** Mort Walker **W:** Mort Walker
118 ❑ Sep 1976 Cover: 0.30 **NM** value: **2.00**
Rabbit Ears; Beauty Call; The Nut Dr.; Dance Time; Zero's Idea; Turkey Run; Rocky's Pass; General for a Day (text) **A:** Mort Walker **W:** Mort Walker
119 ❑ **NM** value: **2.00**
A: Mort Walker **W:** Mort Walker
120 ❑ Apr 1978 Cover: 0.35 **NM** value: **2.00**
A: Mort Walker **W:** Mort Walker
121 ❑ Jun 1978 Cover: 0.35 **NM** value: **2.00**
A: Mort Walker **W:** Mort Walker
122 ❑ Aug 1978 Cover: 0.35 **NM** value: **2.00**
A: Mort Walker **W:** Mort Walker
123 ❑ Oct 1978 Cover: 0.35 **NM** value: **2.00**
A: Mort Walker **W:** Mort Walker
124 ❑ Dec 1978 Cover: 0.35 **NM** value: **2.00**
A: Mort Walker **W:** Mort Walker
125 ❑ Feb 1979 Cover: 0.35 **NM** value: **2.00**
A: Mort Walker **W:** Mort Walker
126 ❑ Apr 1979 **NM** value: **2.00**
A: Mort Walker **W:** Mort Walker
127 ❑ Jun 1979 Cover: 0.40 **NM** value: **2.00**
A: Mort Walker **W:** Mort Walker
128 ❑ Aug 1979 Cover: 0.40 **NM** value: **2.00**
A: Mort Walker **W:** Mort Walker
129 ❑ Oct 1979 Cover: 0.40 **NM** value: **2.00**
A: Mort Walker **W:** Mort Walker
130 ❑ Dec 1979 Cover: 0.40 **NM** value: **2.00**
A: Mort Walker **W:** Mort Walker
131 ❑ Feb 1980 Cover: 0.40 **NM** value: **2.00**
A: Mort Walker **W:** Mort Walker
132 ❑ Apr 1980 **NM** value: **2.00**
final issue. **A:** Mort Walker **W:** Mort Walker

BEETLE BAILEY (VOL. 2) Harvey

1 ❑ Sep 1992 Cover: 1.25 **NM** value: **2.00**
Typing Orders!; The General's Shower; Beetle Strikes Out!; Strife of the Party; Bang-Up Chef; The Water Scout!; Nature Boy; Beetle the Bold; High Flyers; Starch Raving Mad!; Puncture Proof
2 ❑ Jan 1993 Cover: 1.25 **NM** value: **1.50**
The General's Bridge; Taxi Service; Sarge and Otto: Sir Meets Cur; Screw Loose; General Alert; Mister Clean; Color Blind; Sound Advice; Hi and Lois **A:** Mort Walker; Dick Browne **W:** Mort Walker; Dick Browne
3 ❑ Apr 1993 Cover: 1.25 **NM** value: **1.50**
4 ❑ Jul 1993 Cover: 1.25 **NM** value: **1.50**
5 ❑ Oct 1993 Cover: 1.50 **NM** value: **Cover or less**
6 ❑ Jan 1994 Cover: 1.50 **NM** value: **Cover or less**
7 ❑ Apr 1994 Cover: 1.50 **NM** value: **Cover or less**
8 ❑ Jun 1994 Cover: 1.50 **NM** value: **Cover or less**
9 ❑ Aug 1994 Cover: 1.50 **NM** value: **Cover or less**
final issue.
GS 1 ❑ Cover: 2.25 **NM** value: **Cover or less**
• Giant-size. Beetle Gets Shot!; Patch-Work Package; The Letter!; The Truth Hurts!; Mister Breger: Horse Costume!; Double Duty!; Schnooks Beware!; Shy Sarge; The Drop-Out!; Dog Talk; Not at Home on the Range!; Mister Breger: Shorty Image! **A:** Jorge Pacheco
GS 2 ❑ Cover: 2.25 **NM** value: **Cover or less**
• Giant-size.

BEETLEJUICE Harvey

1 ❑ Cover: 1.25 **NM** value: **1.50**
Circ: CapCity orders: **5,150**
2 ❑ Cover: 1.50 **NM** value: **Cover or less**
Circ: CapCity orders: **3,225**

BEETLEJUICE: CRIMEBUSTERS ON THE HAUNT Harvey

1 ❑ Cover: 1.50 **NM** value: **Cover or less**

BEETLEJUICE: ELLIOT MESS AND THE UNWASHABLES Harvey

The normally deadbeat Beetlejuice, having stopped the evil Clean-Up gang, is hailed as a hero, while his goody-two-shoes brother Donny seems to be the mastermind behind the gang's scrubspree. Beetle doesn't much like being a good guy and recruits the help of his living friend, Lydia, to try to figure out what's really happening. Together they discover that Donny has been framed. But in their attempt to save Beetle's brother from being banished to the horrible Sandworm Land, all three are sentenced to life imprisonment (make that death imprisonment) at escape-proof Oilcatraz Island! Even if Beetlejuice can get them out of this nasty predicament, they still have to expose the real Mr. Big and prove Donny's innocence.

This comic book is based on the popular Beetlejuice cartoon, which was based on the 1988 movie of the same name. Michael Keaton had the starring role, and Winona Ryder played Lydia.

1 ❑ Cover: 1.50 **NM** value: **Cover or less**
2 ❑ Oct 1992 Cover: 1.50 **NM** value: **Cover or less**
Oilcatraz Island **A:** Dave Manak **W:** Angelo Decesare
3 ❑ Nov 1992 Cover: 1.50 **NM** value: **Cover or less**
The Violence on the Lam **A:** Dave Manak **W:** Angelo Decesare

BEETLEJUICE HOLIDAY SPECIAL Harvey

1 ❑ Feb 1992 Cover: 1.25 **NM** value: **1.50**

BEETLEJUICE IN THE NEITHERWORLD Harvey

1 ❑ Cover: 1.50 **NM** value: **Cover or less**
The Neitherworld Beauty (You've Gotta be Kidding!) Pageant; Where the Ghouls Are **A:** Ernie Colon; Dave Manak **W:** Michael Gallagher
2 ❑ Cover: 1.50 **NM** value: **Cover or less**

Other grades: Multiply prices above by **1.5 for Mint • 2/3 for Very Fine • 1/3 for Fine • 1/5 for Very Good • 1/8 for Good**

BEFORE THE FANTASTIC FOUR: BEN GRIMM AND LOGAN — Marvel

1 ❑ Jul 2000 Cover: 2.99 **NM value: Cover or less**
Circ: Diamd. preorders: **38,149**
📖 Mission to Nowhere **A:** Kaare Andrews **W:** Larry Hama
2 ❑ Aug 2000 Cover: 2.99 **NM value: Cover or less**
Circ: Diamd. preorders: **31,391**
A: Kaare Andrews **W:** Larry Hama
3 ❑ Sep 2000 Cover: 2.99 **NM value: Cover or less**
Circ: Diamd. preorders: **29,364**
A: Kaare Andrews **W:** Larry Hama
4 ❑ Oct 2000 Cover: 2.99 **NM value: Cover or less**
A: Kaare Andrews **W:** Larry Hama

BEFORE THE FF: REED RICHARDS — Marvel

Move over, Indiana Jones, because you've got competition in the form of — Reed Richards? That's right. Before Mr. Fantastic, before that historic space flight which forever changed his life, this "average" man led a life that was far from ordinary. According to the background provided in this mini-series, the world's smartest man was actually involved in several globetrotting adventures — the likes of which are the focus of this story.

When Franklin Richards finds a box of mysterious artifacts hidden inside his father's closet, the boy is subjected to a "back in my day" type of story by his "old man." Its focus: the search for the Claw of Bast — an ancient Egyptian artifact said to give life to the dead or the dying. Richards, who was apparently quite the ladies' man in his day, was inadvertently thrust into the search for this object to aid his dying physics professor. But the stakes were raised when Victor Von Doom (in his pre-Doctor Doom days) also set out in search of the talisman. What ensued was a good old-fashioned romp — without super-powers — the type that was found in the Saturday afternoon serials of old.

1 ❑ Sep 2000 Cover: 2.99 **NM value: Cover or less**
Circ: Diamd. preorders: **25,827**
📖 Reed Richards & the Riddle of Bast, Part 1 **A:** Duncan Fegredo **C:** Duncan Fegredo **W:** Peter David
2 ❑ Oct 2000 Cover: 2.99 **NM value: Cover or less**
Circ: Diamd. preorders: **21,952**
📖 Reed Richards & the Riddle of Bast, Part 2 **A:** Duncan Fegredo **C:** Duncan Fegredo **W:** Peter David
3 ❑ Dec 2000 Cover: 2.99 **NM value: Cover or less**
Circ: Diamd. preorders: **19,972**
📖 Reed Richards & the Riddle of Bast, Part 3 **A:** Duncan Fegredo **C:** Duncan Fegredo **W:** Peter David
4 ❑ Dec 2000 Cover: 2.99 **NM value: Cover or less**
A: Duncan Fegredo **W:** Peter David

BEFORE THE FF: THE STORMS — Marvel

1 ❑ Dec 2000 Cover: 2.99 **NM value: Cover or less**
Circ: Diamd. preorders: **18,547**
📖 Burn Victims **A:** Charles Adlard **C:** Charles Adlard **W:** Terry Kavanagh
2 ❑ Jan 2001 Cover: 2.99 **NM value: Cover or less**
Circ: Diamd. preorders: **16,405**
📖 Into the Fire **A:** Charles Adlard **C:** Charles Adlard **W:** Terry Kavanagh
3 ❑ Feb 2001 Cover: 2.99 **NM value: Cover or less**
Circ: Diamd. preorders: **15,301**
📖 Firepower **A:** Charles Adlard **C:** Charles Adlard **W:** Terry Kavanagh

BEHOLD 3-D — Edge Group

1 ❑ Cover: 3.95 **NM value: Cover or less**
📖 Sunship G'hide-E1; Apollyon!; Sir Rafeem Knight for the Light; Chariots of the Bible **A:** Nestor Redondo; Pat Boyette; Bill Webb Jr.; Farel Dalrymple; Jeff Anderson **W:** Curt Fischer; Garzon; Garz-n; Irv Ziemaan; Nate Butler

BELIEVE IN YOURSELF PRODUCTIONS — Believe in Yourself Productions

1/Ash❑ Cover: 3.50 **NM value: Cover or less**
• Ashcan Edition. Cardstock cover. Includes 6 page story only available in Ashcan format with 14 pin-u.
1/B ❑ Cover: 25.00 **NM value: Cover or less**
• Sapphire Edition. Only 25 made.
1/LE❑ Cover: 8.00 **NM value: Cover or less**

BELLA DONNA — Pinnacle

1 ❑ b&w Cover: 1.75 **NM value: Cover or less**

BEN CASEY FILM STORIES — Gold Key

1 ❑ ca. 1962 Cover: 0.25 **NM value: 50.00**
• **CGC:** 1 graded, best 7.5

BENEATH THE PLANET OF THE APES — Gold Key

1 ❑ Dec 1970 Cover: 0.25 **NM value: 35.00**
• **CGC:** 5 graded, best 9.4
Photo cover. 📖 Beneath the Planet of the Apes **W:** Mort Abrahams; Paul Dehn

BENZANGO OBSCURO — Starhead

1 ❑ Cover: 2.75 **NM value: Cover or less**

BENZINE — Antarctic

1 ❑ Oct 2000 Cover: 4.95 **NM value: Cover or less**
📖 Asrial Salusian Armored Corps; Tiger-X; Tomorrow Man **A:** Ben Dunn; Terry Pallot; Holly Daugherty **W:** Ben Dunn; Holly Daugherty; Kevin Gunstone
2 ❑ Nov 2000 Cover: 4.95 **NM value: Cover or less**
Circ: Diamd. preorders: **1,488**
3 ❑ Dec 2000 Cover: 4.95 **NM value: Cover or less**
Circ: Diamd. preorders: **1,290**
4 ❑ Jan 2001 Cover: 4.95 **NM value: Cover or less**
Circ: Diamd. preorders: **1,188**
5 ❑ Feb 2001 Cover: 4.95 **NM value: Cover or less**
Circ: Diamd. preorders: **1,231**
6 ❑ Mar 2001 Cover: 4.95 **NM value: Cover or less**
Circ: Diamd. preorders: **1,083**
7 ❑ May 2001 Cover: 4.95 **NM value: Cover or less**
Circ: Diamd. preorders: **1,065**

BEOWULF — DC

1 ❑ May 1975 Cover: 0.25 **NM value: 1.50**
• **CGC:** 4 graded, best 9.6
📖 The Curse of Castle Hrothgar **A:** Ricardo Villamonte **W:** Michael Uslan ★ 1st Appearance of Grendel (monster), Beowulf.
2 ❑ Jul 1975 Cover: 0.25 **NM value: 1.00**
3 ❑ Sep 1975 Cover: 0.25 **NM value: 1.00**
4 ❑ Nov 1975 Cover: 0.25 **NM value: 1.00**
5 ❑ Jan 1976 Cover: 0.25 **NM value: 1.00**
6 ❑ Mar 1976 Cover: 0.25 **NM value: 1.00**
final issue.

BEOWULF (COMIC.COM) — Comic.Com

1 ❑ ca. 1999 Cover: 4.95 **NM value: Cover or less**
Circ: Diamd. preorders: **2,591**
2 ❑ 1999 Cover: 4.95 **NM value: Cover or less**
3 ❑ 1999 Cover: 4.95 **NM value: Cover or less**

BERLIN — Black Eye

1 ❑ Apr 1996 Cover: 2.50 **NM value: Cover or less**
2 ❑ Jul 1996 Cover: 2.50 **NM value: Cover or less**
3 ❑ Feb 1997 Cover: 2.50 **NM value: Cover or less**
Circ: Diamd. preorders: **5,615**
4 ❑ Feb 1998 Cover: 2.50 **NM value: Cover or less**
Circ: Diamd. preorders: **5,177**

BERLIN (DRAWN & QUARTERLY) — Drawn & Quarterly

5 ❑ ca. 1998 Cover: 2.95 **NM value: Cover or less**
Circ: Diamd. preorders: **3,990**
7 ❑ Apr 2000, b&w Cover: 2.95 **NM value: Cover or less**
Circ: Diamd. preorders: **3,374**
• smaller than normal comic book **A:** Jason Lutes **W:** Jason Lutes
6 ❑ ca. 1999 Cover: 2.95 **NM value: Cover or less**
Circ: Diamd. preorders: **3,768**
8 ❑ Cover: 2.95 **NM value: Cover or less**

BERNIE WRIGHTSON, MASTER OF THE MACABRE — Pacific

Turn your mind back to the 1950s: Eisenhower was in the White House, the Cold War was under way, and E.C. comics terrified children with its brilliantly gruesome horror comics. Before the Comics Code Authority dictated what could and could not be shown in comic books, the genre was filled with ax murderers, alien monsters, and some of the best horror and science-fiction stories ever in comics.

Unfortunately, most of today's comics buffs were born too late to catch the original E.C. comics. Luckily, Pacific Comics brought out some of the work of Bernie Wrightson, one of the great masters of horror, in this fantastic series. So read, if you dare, but make sure you leave a light on.

Note: Although Wrightson's first name is spelled "Berni" for this title, it is listed here (and elsewhere in ComicBase) as "Bernie" for consistency with the spelling he used on his later work.

1 ❑ Cover: 1.50 **NM value: 2.50**
• **CGC:** 2 graded, best 9.6
📖 The Muck Monster; The Pepper Lake Monster; The Black Cat • Edgar Allen Poe adaptation ("The Black Cat") **A:** Bernie Wrightson **W:** Bernie Wrightson
2 ❑ Cover: 1.50 **NM value: 2.00**
• **CGC:** 2 graded, best 9.2
📖 Jennifer; Cool Air; Four Classic Martians; The Laughing Man; Clarice **A:** Bernie Wrightson **W:** Bernie Wrightson
3 ❑ Cover: 1.50 **NM value: 2.00**
• **CGC:** 1 graded, best 9.8
📖 King of the Mountain, Man; A Martian Saga; Nightfall; The Last Hunters **A:** Bernie Wrightson **W:** Bernie Wrightson
4 ❑ Cover: 1.50 **NM value: 2.00**
• **CGC:** 1 graded, best 9.2
📖 The Task; The Legend of Sleepy Hollow **A:** Bernie Wrightson **W:** Bernie Wrightson
5 ❑ Cover: 1.50 **NM value: 2.00**
• **CGC:** 1 graded, best 9.6
📖 Feed It!; Mother Load; Limpstrel; Ain't She Sweet?; Uncle Bill's Barrel final issue. **A:** Bernie Wrightson **W:** Bernie Wrightson

BERZERKER — Gauntlet

1 ❑ Feb 1993 Cover: 2.95 **NM value: Cover or less**
Circ: CapCity orders: **11,125**
• Medina **A:** Rob Liefeld; Erik Larsen
2 ❑ Cover: 2.95 **NM value: Cover or less**
3 ❑ Cover: 2.95 **NM value: Cover or less**
4 ❑ Cover: 2.95 **NM value: Cover or less**
5 ❑ Cover: 2.95 **NM value: Cover or less**

BERZERKERS — Image

1 ❑ Aug 1995 Cover: 2.50 **NM value: Cover or less**
Circ: CapCity orders: **17,800**
📖 Berzerkers **A:** Dan Fraga **W:** Beau Smith
1/SC❑ Aug 1995 Cover: 2.50 **NM value: Cover or less**
alternate cover.
2 ❑ Sep 1995 Cover: 2.50 **NM value: Cover or less**
Circ: CapCity orders: **11,000**
📖 Into The Darklands **A:** Dan Fraga **W:** Beau Smith
3 ❑ Oct 1995 Cover: 2.50 **NM value: Cover or less**
Circ: CapCity orders: **6,250**

BEST CELLARS — Out of the Cellar

1 ❑ Cover: 2.50 **NM value: Cover or less**
📖 Monster Boy; Krystal Kalisto; Umbrus; Navaho Moon; Crimewraith; The commited **A:** Chuck Angell; Larry Underwood; Mike Lynch; Rebecca Baerman **W:** Eric Powell; Charles B. Rhoades; Duncan Milner; James Reed; Jesse Dean Wright

BEST FROM BOYS' LIFE COMICS, THE — Gilberton

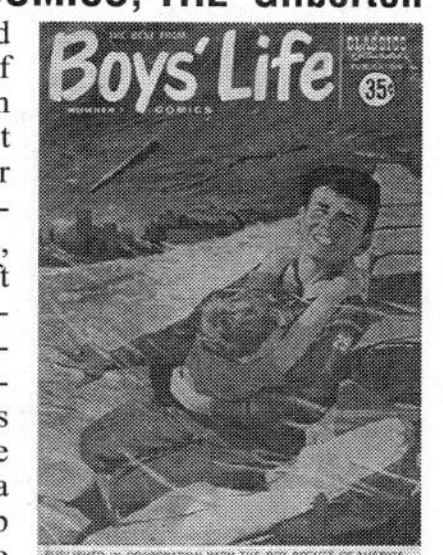

In 1957, Classics Illustrated teamed with the Boy Scouts of America to publish a selection from what was once arguably the most popular American magazine for boys. In addition to Western, science-fiction, and adventure strips, the book includes how-to craft projects, articles on fishing, breaking codes, and how to dribble a basketball, and a cautionary fiction story about a doomed hiking trip. It's a well-rounded book — where else can you learn both how to make a charcoal grill and how to develop film? — it was a handy reference book for the 1950s American boy.

1 ❑ Oct 1957 Cover: 0.35 **NM value: 45.00**
📖 Pee Wee Harris **A:** Irv Novick; Al Stenzel; Alsten; John Sink; Mal Eaton; Percy K. Fitzhugh; Stan Pashko **W:** Irv Novick; Al Stenzel; Alsten; John Sink; Mal Eaton; Percy K. Fitzhugh; Stan Pashko; Ernest Dickinson; Frank Giles; Howard G. McEntee; Jack W. Hankins; James W. English; John Taylor; Ted Collins
2 ❑ Jan 1958 Cover: 0.35 **NM value: 30.00**
3 ❑ Apr 1958 Cover: 0.35 **NM value: 24.00**
4 ❑ Jul 1958 Cover: 0.35 **NM value: 35.00**
5 ❑ Oct 1958 Cover: 0.35 **NM value: 24.00**
6 ❑ Cover: 0.35 **NM value: 24.00**

BEST OF BARRON STOREY'S W.A.T.C.H. MAGAZINE — Vanguard

1 ❑ Dec 1993 Cover: 2.95 **NM value: Cover or less**

BEST OF DARK HORSE PRESENTS, THE — Dark Horse

1 ❑ b&w Cover: 5.95 **NM value: Cover or less**
📖 The Gray Embrace; Cortege; The Sack Murder of 1954; Fossil; Paleolove; Black Cross; Forgotten; Dinosaur Tales; Concrete/Sky of Heads; His World; The Visit; Bob the Alien; Mindwalk; Masque; Message from Earth; Sead; Brighter! **A:** Doug Potter; Mark Badger; Rick Geary; Michael T. Gilbert; Chris Warner; Mark A. Nelson; Gary Davis; Paul Chadwick; Randy Emberlin; Geaf Darrow; Rich Rice; Tom Salmons; Tony Salmon; Carel Moiseiwitsch **W:** Doug Potter; Mark Badger; Rick Geary; Michael T. Gilbert; Chris Warner; Mark A. Nelson; Gary Davis; Paul Chadwick; Geaf Darrow; Randy Stradley; Rich Rice; Ross Evan West; Tom Salmons; Tony Salmon
2 ❑ b&w Cover: 8.95 **NM value: Cover or less**

BEST OF DC, THE — DC

The day-to-day life of folks working for everyone's favorite great metropolitan newspaper is chronicled in this digest-sized collection of some of DC's most memorable stories involving Superman and his day job. Remember the time Clark Kent had to pose as Superman for a Planet-sponsored publicity stunt? How about the tale of "How Lois Lane Got Her Job"? Regardless of how readers may stand on the question of Super-continuity, these pre-Crisis stories give everyone a chance to brush up on DC history and permit long-time fans to revisit a variety of adventures.

1 ❑ Sep 1979 Cover: 0.95 **NM value: 3.00**
2 ❑ Nov 1979 Cover: 0.95 **NM value: 3.00**
3 ❑ Jan 1980 Cover: 0.95 **NM value: 3.00**
4 ❑ Mar 1980 Cover: 0.95 **NM value: 3.00**
5 ❑ May 1980 Cover: 0.95 **NM value: 3.00**
6 ❑ Jul 1980 Cover: 0.95 **NM value: 3.00**
7 ❑ Sep 1980 Cover: 0.95 **NM value: 3.00**
• Superboy
8 ❑ Nov 1980 Cover: 0.95 **NM value: 3.00**
• Superman, Other Identities
9 ❑ Jan 1981 Cover: 0.95 **NM value: 3.00**
10 ❑ Mar 1981 Cover: 0.95 **NM value: 3.00**
11 ❑ Apr 1981 Cover: 0.95 **NM value: 3.00**
12 ❑ May 1981 Cover: 0.95 **NM value: 3.00**
13 ❑ Jun 1981 Cover: 0.95 **NM value: 3.00**
14 ❑ Jul 1981 Cover: 0.95 **NM value: 3.00**
15 ❑ Aug 1981 Cover: 0.95 **NM value: 3.00**
• Superboy
16 ❑ Sep 1981 Cover: 0.95 **NM value: 3.00**
• Superman Anniversaries
17 ❑ Oct 1981 Cover: 0.95 **NM value: 3.00**

CGC-graded: Multiply prices above by **33 for 9.9 M • 16 for 9.8 NM/M • 7 for 9.6 NM+ • 5 for 9.4 NM • 2.5 for 9.2 NM- • 1.5 for 9.0 VF/NM**

18 ❑ Nov 1981 Cover: 0.95 **NM value: 3.00**
19 ❑ Dec 1981 Cover: 0.95 **NM value: 3.00**
• Superman, Imaginary Stories
20 ❑ Jan 1982 Cover: 0.95 **NM value: 3.00**
21 ❑ Feb 1982 Cover: 0.95 **NM value: 3.00**
• Justice Society
22 ❑ Mar 1982 Cover: 0.95 **NM value: 3.00**
The Seal-Men's War on Santa Claus • Sandman
23 ❑ Apr 1982 Cover: 1.25 **NM value: 3.00**
24 ❑ May 1982 Cover: 0.95 **NM value: 3.00**
• Legion
25 ❑ Jun 1982 Cover: 0.95 **NM value: 3.00**
26 ❑ Jul 1982 Cover: 0.95 **NM value: 3.00**
• Brave and the Bold
27 ❑ Aug 1982 Cover: 0.95 **NM value: 3.00**
• Superman vs. Luthor
28 ❑ Sep 1982 Cover: 0.95 **NM value: 3.00**
29 ❑ Oct 1982 Cover: 1.25 **NM value: 3.00**
30 ❑ Nov 1982 Cover: 1.25 **NM value: 3.00**
• Batman
31 ❑ Dec 1982 Cover: 1.25 **NM value: 3.00**
• Justice League
32 ❑ Jan 1983 Cover: 1.25 **NM value: 3.00**
• Superman
33 ❑ Feb 1983 Cover: 1.25 **NM value: 3.00**
34 ❑ Mar 1983 Cover: 1.25 **NM value: 3.00**
• Metal Men
35 ❑ Apr 1983 Cover: 1.75 **NM value: 3.00**
• Year's Best 82
36 ❑ May 1983 Cover: 1.25 **NM value: 3.00**
• Superman vs. Kryptonite
37 ❑ Jun 1983 Cover: 1.25 **NM value: 3.00**
38 ❑ Jul 1983 Cover: 1.25 **NM value: 3.00**
39 ❑ Aug 1983 Cover: 1.25 **NM value: 3.00**
40 ❑ Sep 1983 Cover: 1.25 **NM value: 3.00**
• Superman, Krypton
41 ❑ Oct 1983 Cover: 1.25 **NM value: 3.00**
42 ❑ Nov 1983 Cover: 1.25 **NM value: 3.00**
43 ❑ Dec 1983 Cover: 1.25 **NM value: 3.00**
44 ❑ Jan 1984 Cover: 1.25 **NM value: 3.00**
• Legion
45 ❑ Feb 1984 Cover: 1.25 **NM value: 3.00**
• Binky
46 ❑ Mar 1984 Cover: 1.25 **NM value: 3.00**
• Jimmy Olsen
47 ❑ Apr 1984 Cover: 1.25 **NM value: 3.00**
48 ❑ May 1984 Cover: 1.25 **NM value: 3.00**
49 ❑ Jun 1984 Cover: 1.25 **NM value: 3.00**
50 ❑ Jul 1984 Cover: 1.25 **NM value: 3.00**
• Superman
51 ❑ Aug 1984 **NM value: 3.00**
52 ❑ Sep 1984 Cover: 1.75 **NM value: 3.00**
• Year's Best 83
53 ❑ Oct 1984 **NM value: 3.00**
54 ❑ Nov 1984 **NM value: 3.00**
55 ❑ Dec 1984 **NM value: 3.00**
56 ❑ Jan 1985 Cover: 1.50 **NM value: 3.00**
• Superman
57 ❑ Feb 1985 Cover: 1.50 **NM value: 3.00**
• Legion
58 ❑ Mar 1985 Cover: 1.50 **NM value: 3.00**
• Superman Jrs.
59 ❑ Apr 1985 Cover: 1.50 **NM value: 3.00**
• Superman
60 ❑ May 1985 Cover: 1.50 **NM value: 3.00**
Circ: CapCity orders: **1,300**
61 ❑ Jun 1985 Cover: 1.50 **NM value: 3.00**
Circ: CapCity orders: **1,250**
62 ❑ Jul 1985 Cover: 1.50 **NM value: 3.00**
Circ: CapCity orders: **1,150**
• Batman
63 ❑ Aug 1985 Cover: 1.50 **NM value: 3.00**
Circ: CapCity orders: **1,050**
64 ❑ Sep 1985 Cover: 1.50 **NM value: 3.00**
Circ: CapCity orders: **1,350**
• Legion
65 ❑ Oct 1985 Cover: 1.50 **NM value: 3.00**
Circ: CapCity orders: **1,100**
• Sugar & Spike
66 ❑ Nov 1985 Cover: 1.50 **NM value: 3.00**
Circ: CapCity orders: **1,100**
• Superman
67 ❑ Dec 1985 Cover: 1.50 **NM value: 3.00**
Circ: CapCity orders: **1,250**
68 ❑ Jan 1986 Cover: 1.50 **NM value: 3.00**
Circ: CapCity orders: **900**
• Sugar & Spike
69 ❑ Feb 1986 Cover: 1.50 **NM value: 3.00**
Circ: CapCity orders: **1,350**
• Year's Best 85
70 ❑ Mar 1986 Cover: 1.50 **NM value: 3.00**
Circ: CapCity orders: **800**
• Binky's Buddies

BEST OF DONALD DUCK AND UNCLE SCROOGE, THE — Gold Key

1 ❑ Nov 1964 Cover: 0.25 **NM value: 50.00**
The Old Castle's Secret; The Golden Helmet • Reprints stories from Four Color Comics #189 and 408 (Donald Duck)
2 ❑ Sep 1967 Cover: 0.25 **NM value: 50.00**
Luck of the North; Seven Cities of Cibola; Uncle Scrooge (Untitled) • Reprints stories from Four Color Comics #256 (Donald Duck) and Uncle Scrooge #7 and 8 **A:** Carl Barks

BEST OF DORK TOWER — Dork Storm Press

1 ❑ ca. 2001, b&w Cover: 1.95 **NM value: Cover or less**
Circ: Diamd. preorders: **2,582**

BEST OF FURRLOUGH — Antarctic

1 ❑ Jan 1995, b&w Cover: 3.95 **NM value: Cover or less**
Romanics; Hairlift; Under Realm; The Last Step **A:** Fred Perry; Joe Rosales; Noel Tominack; Toivo Rovainen; L'amazing Productions **W:** Fred Perry; Joe Rosales; Noel Tominack; Toivo Rovainen; L'amazing Productions
2 ❑ Cover: 3.95 **NM value: Cover or less**
Stosstrupp; Dog Star; Colonel Bogie; The Prototype; Rainy Season **A:** Brian Sutton; Mel White; Pat Dolan; Ted Sheppard **W:** Brian Sutton; Mel White; Pat Dolan; Ted Sheppard

BEST OF GOLD DIGGER — Antarctic

Anl 1❑May 1999, b&w Cover: 2.99 **NM value: Cover or less**
Circ: Diamd. preorders: **2,178**
Proving Ground; Fish Tale; Amulets of Doom; GD -18; Showdown in Aisle Seven **A:** Jim Schumaker; Dave McKechnie; Diana X. Sprinkle; Jerzy Drozd; Mike Kelly **W:** Jim Schumaker; Dave McKechnie; Diana X. Sprinkle; Mike Kelly; Tom Root

BEST OF HORROR AND SCIENCE FICTION — Webster

1 ❑ Cover: 2.00 **NM value: Cover or less**
The Brain-Bats of Venus; Colorama; Gave Life to Save Life; Library of Horror; Chicken Little; Mother's Advice **A:** Steve Ditko; Basil Wolverton; Frank Frazetta; Bob Powell; Mortellaro; Richard Doxsee

BEST OF MARVEL COMICS, THE — Marvel

1 ❑ ca. 1987 **NM value: 25.00**
Circ: CapCity orders: **3,200**
hardcover, padded covers, no price listed. The Black Panther; The Way It Began; The Answer at Last; The Wrath of the Wrecker • Reprinted from Fantastic Four #52 ("Panther") and #53 ("Way"), and Thor #159 ("Answer") and #171 ("Wrath")

BEST OF NEGATIVE BURN: YEAR ONE — Caliber

Bk 1❑ Cover: 9.95 **NM value: Cover or less**

BEST OF NORTHSTAR, THE — Northstar

1 ❑ b&w Cover: 1.95 **NM value: Cover or less**

BEST OF RATED-X — Aircel

All issues are adults only.
Bk 1❑ b&w Cover: 9.95 **NM value: Cover or less**

BEST OF SPICY TALES — Eternity

Bk 1❑ Cover: 9.95 **NM value: Cover or less**
• reprints, b&w

BEST OF SPIDER-MAN — Marvel

Bk 1❑ Cover: 9.95 **NM value: Cover or less**
• (newspaper strips, Ballantine Books TPB)

BEST OF STAR TREK — DC

Bk 1❑ Cover: 19.95 **NM value: Cover or less**
Circ: CapCity orders: **2,500**

BEST OF THE BRAVE AND THE BOLD, THE — DC

The Brave and the Bold began its 28-year career with adventure stories featuring The Viking Prince, later moving on to super-heroes, most notably a string of super-hero team-ups between Batman and other characters in the DC universe.

This six-issue series brings back some of the most memorable stories from that extended run, including rare material. Stories illustrated by Neal Adams and Joe Kubert are part of the package, released four years after the last issue of The Brave and the Bold was published. This series offered the material for new readers and old, providing new covers and re-colored art.

1 ❑ Oct 1988 Cover: 2.50 **NM value: Cover or less**
Circ: CapCity orders: **13,900**
• Batman, Green Arrow **A:** Joe Kubert; Neal Adams
2 ❑ Nov 1988 Cover: 2.50 **NM value: Cover or less**
Circ: CapCity orders: **10,500**
• Batman, Flash **A:** Joe Kubert; Neal Adams
3 ❑ Dec 1988 Cover: 2.50 **NM value: Cover or less**
Circ: CapCity orders: **10,400**
• Batman, Aquaman **A:** Joe Kubert; Neal Adams
4 ❑ Dec 1988 Cover: 2.50 **NM value: Cover or less**
Circ: CapCity orders: **10,000**
• Batman, Creeper **A:** Joe Kubert; Neal Adams
5 ❑ Jan 1989 Cover: 2.50 **NM value: Cover or less**
Circ: CapCity orders: **9,400**
• Batman, House of Mystery **A:** Joe Kubert; Neal Adams
6 ❑ Jan 1989 Cover: 2.50 **NM value: Cover or less**
Circ: CapCity orders: **9,300**
• Batman, Teen Titans **A:** Joe Kubert; Neal Adams

BEST OF THE BRITISH INVASION — Revolutionary

1 ❑ Sep 1993, b&w Cover: 2.50 **NM value: Cover or less**
2 ❑ Jan 1994, b&w Cover: 2.50 **NM value: Cover or less**

BEST OF THE WEST — Magazine Enterprises

1 ❑ ca. 1951 Cover: 0.10 **NM value: 200.00**
2 ❑ ca. 1951 Cover: 0.10 **NM value: 150.00**
3 ❑ ca. 1952 Cover: 0.10 **NM value: 150.00**
4 ❑ ca. 1952 Cover: 0.10 **NM value: 150.00**
5 ❑ Oct 1952 Cover: 0.10 **NM value: 150.00**
• **CGC:** 1 graded, best 8.0
6 ❑ ca. 1953 Cover: 0.10 **NM value: 125.00**
7 ❑ ca. 1953 Cover: 0.10 **NM value: 125.00**
8 ❑ ca. 1953 Cover: 0.10 **NM value: 125.00**
9 ❑ ca. 1953 Cover: 0.10 **NM value: 125.00**
10 ❑ ca. 1953 Cover: 0.10 **NM value: 125.00**
11 ❑ ca. 1954 Cover: 0.10 **NM value: 125.00**
12 ❑ ca. 1954 Cover: 0.10 **NM value: 125.00**

BEST OF TRIBUNE CO., THE — Dragon Lady

1 ❑ Cover: 2.95 **NM value: Cover or less**
2 ❑ Cover: 2.95 **NM value: Cover or less**
3 ❑ Cover: 2.95 **NM value: Cover or less**
4 ❑ Cover: 2.95 **NM value: Cover or less**
• (becomes Thrilling Adventure Strips)

BEST OF WALT DISNEY COMICS, THE — Western

1 ❑ ca. 1974 Cover: 1.50 **NM value: 18.00**
Frozen in Gold; Mystery of the Swamp • 96170; Reprints stories from Four Color Comics #62 (Donald Duck)
2 ❑ ca. 1974 Cover: 1.50 **NM value: 12.00**
Mickey Mouse and the Bat Bandit of Inferno Gulch • 96171
3 ❑ ca. 1974 Cover: 1.50 **NM value: 12.00**
Only a Poor Man; Uncle Scrooge (Untitled); Uncle Scrooge (Untitled) • 96172; Reprints stories from Four Color Comics #386 and 495 (Uncle Scrooge) and Uncle Scrooge #7
4 ❑ ca. 1974 Cover: 1.50 **NM value: 12.00**
Donald Duck in the Ghost of the Grotto; Donald Duck: Christmas on Bear Mountain • 96173; Reprints stories from Four Color Comics #159 and 178 (Donald Duck)

BETA SEXUS — Fantagraphics / Eros

All issues are adults only.
1 ❑ b&w Cover: 2.75 **NM value: Cover or less**
2 ❑ Jul 1994, b&w Cover: 2.75 **NM value: Cover or less**

BETTA: TIME WARRIOR — Immortal / Eros

1 ❑ Cover: 2.95 **NM value: Cover or less**
The Beginning's End, Part 1 **A:** Eric C. Smith **W:** Patrick Burnett
2 ❑ Cover: 2.95 **NM value: Cover or less**
The Beginning's End, Part 2 **A:** Eric C. Smith **W:** Patrick Burnett
3 ❑ Cover: 2.95 **NM value: Cover or less**
The Beginning's End, Part 3 **A:** Eric C. Smith **W:** Patrick Burnett

BETTI COZMO — Antarctic

1 ❑ Apr 1999 Cover: 2.99 **NM value: Cover or less**
Circ: Diamd. preorders: **1,817**
A: John Fang **W:** John Fang
2 ❑ Jun 1999 Cover: 2.99 **NM value: Cover or less**
A: John Fang **W:** John Fang

BETTIE PAGE COMICS — Dark Horse

1 ❑ Mar 1996 Cover: 3.95 **NM value: Cover or less**
one-shot, cardstock cover. Sandbar Skirmish; Mars Wants Bettie; Jumpin' Jungle Jive **A:** Dave Stevens(cover)

BETTIE PAGE COMICS: SPICY ADVENTURE — Dark Horse

1 ❑ Jan 1997 Cover: 2.95 **NM value: Cover or less**
Circ: Direct Market orders: **23,676**
No issue number. One-shot. **A:** Jim Silke **W:** Jim Silke

BETTIE PAGE: QUEEN OF THE NILE — Dark Horse

There's nothing wrong with a little bit of silly cheesecake. This latest tribute to a woman who is arguably the most beloved and rendered pinup girl in history is just that.

Bettie finds herself abducted from New York City and taken to a planet in the far future, where she is more valuable than gold. Here, a crazy computer has created a world based on the pulp adventures of the 1920s and 1930s, with Bettie its principal goddess: the sort of goddess tribes tie up and sell to the highest bidder.

There are white slavers, Egyptian priests, a randy mummy, and many more annoyances Bettie handles, all the while posing in her underwear and tossing off saucy comments. All she really wants to do is get back home, where a modeling contract awaits.

This limited series was created by Jim Silke and has the bonus of some cover art from Dave Stevens, creator of The Rocketeer.

1 ❑ Dec 1999 Cover: 2.95 **NM value: Cover or less**
Circ: Diamd. preorders: **18,229** • **CGC:** 1 graded, best 9.6
A: Jim Silke **W:** Jim Silke
2 ❑ Feb 2000 Cover: 2.95 **NM value: Cover or less**
Circ: Diamd. preorders: **15,146**
A: Jim Silke **W:** Jim Silke
3 ❑ Apr 2000 Cover: 2.95 **NM value: Cover or less**
Circ: Diamd. preorders: **14,971**
A: Jim Silke **W:** Jim Silke

The CGC numbers printed in individual listings above represent the **number of copies examined** and given a **Universal** grade by CGC and the **best such copy** graded at press time. For current populations, watch for special ***Comics Buyer's Guide*** issues or check **www.cgccomics.com.**

Other grades: Multiply prices above by **1.5 for Mint • 2/3 for Very Fine • 1/3 for Fine • 1/5 for Very Good • 1/8 for Good**

BETTY **Archie**

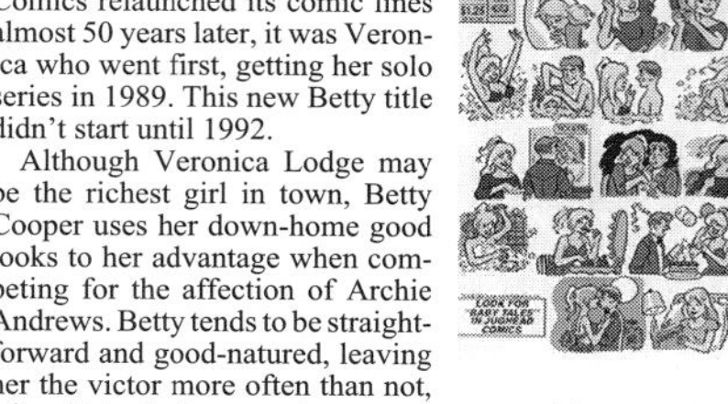

The blonde, all-American girl Betty Cooper got the jump on rival Veronica Lodge, appearing with Archie right from the beginning, in Pep #22 (Dec 41). When Archie Comics relaunched its comic lines almost 50 years later, it was Veronica who went first, getting her solo series in 1989. This new Betty title didn't start until 1992.

Although Veronica Lodge may be the richest girl in town, Betty Cooper uses her down-home good looks to her advantage when competing for the affection of Archie Andrews. Betty tends to be straightforward and good-natured, leaving her the victor more often than not, when Veronica's own schemes to attract Archie's attention backfire. However, when the notoriously undecided Archie finally was forced to choose in the well-publicized "Love Showdown," the winner was the little-known Cheryl Blossom. As could be expected, Betty and Veronica were not long in returning to the picture.

1 ❑ Sep 1992 Cover: 1.25 **NM** value: **4.00**
Circ: Statement: **40,512**

2 ❑ Oct 1992 Cover: 1.25 **NM** value: **2.00**
Circ: Statement: **40,512**

3 ❑ Dec 1992 Cover: 1.25 **NM** value: **2.00**
Circ: Statement: **40,512**

4 ❑ Feb 1993 Cover: 1.25 **NM** value: **2.00**
Circ: Statement: **41,753**

5 ❑ Apr 1993 Cover: 1.25 **NM** value: **2.00**
Circ: Statement: **41,753**
• Has 1992 Statement, filed 10/1/1992; avg print run 128,624; avg sales 38,877; avg subs 1,635; avg total paid 40,512; samples 544; office use 4,437; max existent 45,493; 65% of run returned

6 ❑ Jun 1993 Cover: 1.25 **NM** value: **1.50**
Circ: Statement: **41,753**
📖 Gym Dandy; The Alternative Whirl; I've Tumbled for You!; Just Ducky **A:** Doug Crane **W:** Bob Bolling

7 ❑ Aug 1993 Cover: 1.25 **NM** value: **1.50**
Circ: Statement: **41,753**

8 ❑ Sep 1993 Cover: 1.25 **NM** value: **1.50**
Circ: Statement: **41,753**

9 ❑ Oct 1993 Cover: 1.25 **NM** value: **1.50**
Circ: Statement: **41,753**

10 ❑ Nov 1993 Cover: 1.25 **NM** value: **1.50**
Circ: Statement: **41,753**

11 ❑ Dec 1993 Cover: 1.25 **NM** value: **1.50**
Circ: Statement: **41,753**

12 ❑ Feb 1994 Cover: 1.25 **NM** value: **1.50**
Circ: Statement: **40,371**

13 ❑ Apr 1994 Cover: 1.25 **NM** value: **1.50**
Circ: Statement: **40,371**
• Has 1993 Statement, filed 10/1/93; avg print run 120,198; avg sales 40,050; avg subs 1,703; avg total paid 41,753; samples 600; office use 3,416; max existent 45,769; 62% of run returned

14 ❑ Jun 1994 Cover: 1.25 **NM** value: **1.50**
Circ: Statement: **40,371**

15 ❑ Jul 1994 Cover: 1.25 **NM** value: **1.50**
Circ: Statement: **40,371**

16 ❑ Aug 1994 Cover: 1.25 **NM** value: **1.50**
Circ: Statement: **40,371**

17 ❑ Sep 1994 Cover: 1.50 **NM** value: **Cover or less**
Circ: Statement: **40,371**

18 ❑ Oct 1994 Cover: 1.50 **NM** value: **Cover or less**
Circ: Statement: **40,371**

19 ❑ Nov 1994 Cover: 1.50 **NM** value: **Cover or less**
Circ: Statement: **40,371**
📖 Love Showdown, Part 2

20 ❑ Dec 1994 Cover: 1.50 **NM** value: **Cover or less**
Circ: Statement: **40,371**

21 ❑ Jan 1995 Cover: 1.50 **NM** value: **Cover or less**
Circ: Statement: **36,867**

22 ❑ Feb 1995 Cover: 1.50 **NM** value: **Cover or less**
Circ: Statement: **36,867**

23 ❑ Mar 1995 Cover: 1.50 **NM** value: **Cover or less**
Circ: Statement: **36,867**

24 ❑ Apr 1995 Cover: 1.50 **NM** value: **Cover or less**
Circ: Statement: **36,867**

25 ❑ May 1995 Cover: 1.50 **NM** value: **Cover or less**
Circ: Statement: **36,867**

26 ❑ Jun 1995 Cover: 1.50 **NM** value: **Cover or less**
Circ: Statement: **36,867**

27 ❑ Jul 1995 Cover: 1.50 **NM** value: **Cover or less**
Circ: Statement: **36,867**

28 ❑ Aug 1995 Cover: 1.50 **NM** value: **Cover or less**
Circ: Statement: **36,867**

29 ❑ Sep 1995 Cover: 1.50 **NM** value: **Cover or less**
Circ: Statement: **36,867**

30 ❑ Oct 1995 Cover: 1.50 **NM** value: **Cover or less**
Circ: Statement: **36,867**

31 ❑ Nov 1995 Cover: 1.50 **NM** value: **Cover or less**
Circ: Statement: **36,867**

32 ❑ Dec 1995 Cover: 1.50 **NM** value: **Cover or less**
Circ: Statement: **36,867**

33 ❑ Jan 1996 Cover: 1.50 **NM** value: **Cover or less**
Circ: Statement: **34,455**

34 ❑ Feb 1996 Cover: 1.50 **NM** value: **Cover or less**
Circ: Statement: **34,455**

35 ❑ Mar 1996 Cover: 1.50 **NM** value: **Cover or less**
Circ: Statement: **34,455**

36 ❑ Apr 1996 Cover: 1.50 **NM** value: **Cover or less**
Circ: Statement: **34,455**

37 ❑ May 1996 Cover: 1.50 **NM** value: **Cover or less**
Circ: Statement: **34,455**

38 ❑ Jun 1996 Cover: 1.50 **NM** value: **Cover or less**
Circ: Statement: **34,455**

39 ❑ Jul 1996 Cover: 1.50 **NM** value: **Cover or less**
Circ: Statement: **34,455**

40 ❑ Aug 1996 Cover: 1.50 **NM** value: **Cover or less**
Circ: Statement: **34,455**

41 ❑ Sep 1996 Cover: 1.50 **NM** value: **Cover or less**
Circ: Statement: **34,455**

42 ❑ Oct 1996 Cover: 1.50 **NM** value: **Cover or less**
Circ: Statement: **34,455**
cover has reader sketches of Betty.

43 ❑ Nov 1996 Cover: 1.50 **NM** value: **Cover or less**
Circ: Statement: **34,455**

44 ❑ Dec 1996 Cover: 1.50 **NM** value: **Cover or less**
Circ: Statement: **34,455** Direct Market orders: **4,510**
📖 The Nation's Most Wanted; Dream Catalog; Cowgirl Blues

45 ❑ Jan 1997 Cover: 1.50 **NM** value: **Cover or less**
Circ: Statement: **32,595** Direct Market orders: **4,697**

46 ❑ Feb 1997 Cover: 1.50 **NM** value: **Cover or less**
Circ: Statement: **32,595** Diamd. preorders: **4,798**

47 ❑ Mar 1997 Cover: 1.50 **NM** value: **Cover or less**
Circ: Statement: **32,595** Diamd. preorders: **4,549**

48 ❑ Apr 1997 Cover: 1.50 **NM** value: **Cover or less**
Circ: Statement: **32,595** Diamd. preorders: **4,235**
• Has 1996 Statement, filed 9/27/1996; avg print run 104,714; avg sales 33,769; avg subs 686; avg total paid 34,455; samples 518; office use 1,915; max existent 36,888; 65% of run returned

49 ❑ May 1997 Cover: 1.50 **NM** value: **Cover or less**
Circ: Statement: **32,595** Diamd. preorders: **4,097**

50 ❑ Jun 1997 Cover: 1.50 **NM** value: **Cover or less**
Circ: Statement: **32,595** Diamd. preorders: **4,265**

51 ❑ Jul 1997 Cover: 1.50 **NM** value: **Cover or less**
Circ: Statement: **32,595** Diamd. preorders: **4,328**

52 ❑ Aug 1997 Cover: 1.50 **NM** value: **Cover or less**
Circ: Statement: **32,595** Diamd. preorders: **4,442**

53 ❑ Sep 1997 Cover: 1.50 **NM** value: **Cover or less**
Circ: Statement: **32,595** Diamd. preorders: **4,703**

54 ❑ Oct 1997 Cover: 1.50 **NM** value: **Cover or less**
Circ: Statement: **32,595** Diamd. preorders: **4,665**
📖 The Zine Machine, Parts 3 and 4

55 ❑ Nov 1997 Cover: 1.50 **NM** value: **Cover or less**
Circ: Statement: **32,595** Diamd. preorders: **4,698**

56 ❑ Dec 1997 Cover: 1.50 **NM** value: **Cover or less**
Circ: Statement: **32,595** Diamd. preorders: **4,818**
• return of Polly Cooper

57 ❑ Jan 1998 Cover: 1.75 **NM** value: **Cover or less**
Circ: Statement: **28,691** Diamd. preorders: **5,514**

58 ❑ Feb 1998 Cover: 1.75 **NM** value: **Cover or less**
Circ: Statement: **28,691** Diamd. preorders: **5,177**
• Virtual Pets

59 ❑ Mar 1998 Cover: 1.75 **NM** value: **Cover or less**
Circ: Statement: **28,691** Diamd. preorders: **4,721**

60 ❑ Apr 1998 Cover: 1.75 **NM** value: **Cover or less**
Circ: Statement: **28,691** Diamd. preorders: **4,496**
• Has 1997 Statement, filed 11/1/1997; avg print run 107,701; avg sales 31,897; avg subs 698; avg total paid 32,595; samples 426; office use 2,031; max existent 35,052; 68% of run returned

61 ❑ May 1998 Cover: 1.75 **NM** value: **Cover or less**
Circ: Statement: **28,691** Diamd. preorders: **4,213**

62 ❑ Jun 1998 Cover: 1.75 **NM** value: **Cover or less**
Circ: Statement: **28,691** Diamd. preorders: **4,229**

63 ❑ Jul 1998 Cover: 1.75 **NM** value: **Cover or less**
Circ: Statement: **28,691** Diamd. preorders: **4,245**

64 ❑ Aug 1998 Cover: 1.75 **NM** value: **Cover or less**
Circ: Statement: **28,691** Diamd. preorders: **4,231**

65 ❑ Sep 1998 Cover: 1.75 **NM** value: **Cover or less**
Circ: Statement: **28,691** Diamd. preorders: **4,361**
📖 A Day to Remember; Heel, Rover; Sabrina: Dandy Detour; Watered Down; He Loves Me, He Loves Me Not...! **A:** Stan Goldberg **W:** Kathleen Webb; George Gladir; Mike Pellowski

66 ❑ Oct 1998 Cover: 1.75 **NM** value: **Cover or less**
Circ: Statement: **28,691** Diamd. preorders: **4,132**

67 ❑ Nov 1998 Cover: 1.75 **NM** value: **Cover or less**
Circ: Statement: **28,691** Diamd. preorders: **3,807**
📖 The Good Sport! **A:** Stan Goldberg **W:** Barbara Slate

68 ❑ Dec 1998 Cover: 1.75 **NM** value: **Cover or less**
Circ: Statement: **28,691** Diamd. preorders: **3,935**

69 ❑ Jan 1999 Cover: 1.75 **NM** value: **Cover or less**
Circ: Diamd. preorders: **4,053**

70 ❑ Feb 1999 Cover: 1.75 **NM** value: **Cover or less**
Circ: Diamd. preorders: **3,927**

71 ❑ Mar 1999 Cover: 1.75 **NM** value: **Cover or less**
Circ: Diamd. preorders: **3,843**
📖 A Day to Remember **W:** George Gladir

72 ❑ Apr 1999 Cover: 1.79 **NM** value: **Cover or less**
Circ: Diamd. preorders: **3,565**
📖 Special Delivery • Has 1998 Statement, filed 11/1/1998; avg print run 91,196; avg sales 27,857; avg subs 834; avg total paid 28,691; samples 421; office use 2,478; max existent 31,590; 65% of run returned **A:** Stan Goldberg **W:** Kathleen Webb

73 ❑ May 1999 Cover: 1.79 **NM** value: **Cover or less**
Circ: Diamd. preorders: **3,416**
📖 Pet Set Session **A:** Stan Goldberg **W:** George Gladir

74 ❑ Jun 1999 Cover: 1.79 **NM** value: **Cover or less**
Circ: Diamd. preorders: **3,324**

75 ❑ Jul 1999 Cover: 1.79 **NM** value: **Cover or less**
Circ: Diamd. preorders: **3,417**

76 ❑ Aug 1999 Cover: 1.79 **NM** value: **Cover or less**
Circ: Diamd. preorders: **3,488**

77 ❑ Sep 1999 Cover: 1.79 **NM** value: **Cover or less**
Circ: Diamd. preorders: **3,703**

78 ❑ Oct 1999 Cover: 1.79 **NM** value: **Cover or less**
Circ: Diamd. preorders: **3,418**

79 ❑ Nov 1999 Cover: 1.79 **NM** value: **Cover or less**
Circ: Diamd. preorders: **3,313**

80 ❑ Dec 1999 Cover: 1.79 **NM** value: **Cover or less**
Circ: Diamd. preorders: **3,242**

81 ❑ Jan 2000 Cover: 1.79 **NM** value: **Cover or less**
Circ: Diamd. preorders: **3,506**

82 ❑ Feb 2000 Cover: 1.79 **NM** value: **Cover or less**
Circ: Diamd. preorders: **3,348**

83 ❑ Mar 2000 Cover: 1.79 **NM** value: **Cover or less**
Circ: Diamd. preorders: **3,302**

84 ❑ Apr 2000 Cover: 1.79 **NM** value: **Cover or less**
Circ: Diamd. preorders: **3,099**

85 ❑ May 2000 Cover: 1.79 **NM** value: **Cover or less**
Circ: Diamd. preorders: **3,090**

86 ❑ Jun 2000 Cover: 1.79 **NM** value: **Cover or less**
Circ: Diamd. preorders: **3,099**

87 ❑ Jul 2000 Cover: 1.99 **NM** value: **Cover or less**
Circ: Diamd. preorders: **3,076**

88 ❑ Aug 2000 Cover: 1.99 **NM** value: **Cover or less**
Circ: Diamd. preorders: **3,239**

89 ❑ Sep 2000 Cover: 1.99 **NM** value: **Cover or less**
Circ: Diamd. preorders: **3,506**

90 ❑ Oct 2000 Cover: 1.99 **NM** value: **Cover or less**
Circ: Diamd. preorders: **3,308**

91 ❑ Nov 2000 Cover: 1.99 **NM** value: **Cover or less**
Circ: Diamd. preorders: **3,146**

92 ❑ Dec 2000 Cover: 1.99 **NM** value: **Cover or less**
Circ: Diamd. preorders: **3,123**

93 ❑ Jan 2001 Cover: 1.99 **NM** value: **Cover or less**
Circ: Diamd. preorders: **3,201**

94 ❑ Feb 2001 Cover: 1.99 **NM** value: **Cover or less**
Circ: Diamd. preorders: **3,162**

95 ❑ Mar 2001 Cover: 1.99 **NM** value: **Cover or less**
Circ: Diamd. preorders: **2,985**

96 ❑ Apr 2001 Cover: 1.99 **NM** value: **Cover or less**
Circ: Diamd. preorders: **2,862**

97 ❑ May 2001 Cover: 1.99 **NM** value: **Cover or less**
Circ: Diamd. preorders: **2,856**

98 ❑ Jun 2001 Cover: 1.99 **NM** value: **Cover or less**
Circ: Diamd. preorders: **2,813**

99 ❑ Jul 2001 Cover: 1.99 **NM** value: **Cover or less**
Circ: Diamd. preorders: **3,358**

100 ❑ Aug 2001 Cover: 1.99 **NM** value: **Cover or less**
Circ: Diamd. preorders: **3,882**

101 ❑ Sep 2001 Cover: 1.99 **NM** value: **Cover or less**
Circ: Diamd. preorders: **3,475**

102 ❑ Oct 2001 Cover: 1.99 **NM** value: **Cover or less**
Circ: Diamd. preorders: **3,389**

BETTY & ME **Archie**

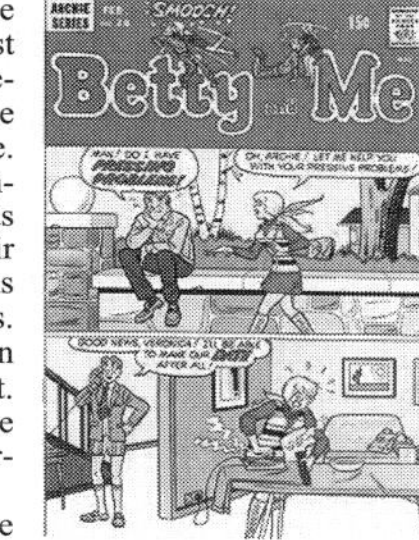

Betty Cooper has been Archie Andrew's girlfriend since their first appearance in 1941, but she sometimes finds herself outshone by the rich and exciting Veronica Lodge. Although Betty and Veronica eventually became the best of friends over the ensuing decades, their competition for Archie's affections has reached legendary proportions. And of course, the redheaded teen vacillates about whom he likes best. Archie is apparently the "Me" of the title and almost invariably is cover-featured.

Betty represents the idea of the all-American girl-next-door, and she and Archie have a lot of special moments together. These are the times this series focuses on. And every once in a while, Betty even gets the best of Veronica.

Betty & Me ran for 200 issues, from 1965 through August 1992, when it was replaced by Betty.

1 ❑ Aug 1965 Cover: 0.15 **NM** value: **60.00**
2 ❑ Nov 1965 Cover: 0.12 **NM** value: **38.00**
3 ❑ Aug 1966 Cover: 0.12 **NM** value: **22.00**
4 ❑ Oct 1966 Cover: 0.12 **NM** value: **22.00**
5 ❑ Dec 1966 Cover: 0.12 **NM** value: **22.00**
6 ❑ Feb 1967 Cover: 0.12 **NM** value: **13.00**
7 ❑ Apr 1967 Cover: 0.12 **NM** value: **13.00**
8 ❑ Jun 1967 Cover: 0.12 **NM** value: **13.00**
9 ❑ Aug 1967 Cover: 0.12 **NM** value: **13.00**
10 ❑ Oct 1967 Cover: 0.12 **NM** value: **13.00**
11 ❑ Dec 1967 Cover: 0.12 **NM** value: **9.00**
12 ❑ Feb 1968 Cover: 0.12 **NM** value: **9.00**
13 ❑ Apr 1968 Cover: 0.12 **NM** value: **9.00**
14 ❑ Jun 1968 Cover: 0.12 **NM** value: **9.00**
15 ❑ Aug 1968 Cover: 0.12 **NM** value: **9.00**
16 ❑ Sep 1968 Cover: 0.12 **NM** value: **9.00**
17 ❑ Oct 1968 Cover: 0.12 **NM** value: **9.00**
18 ❑ Dec 1968 Cover: 0.12 **NM** value: **9.00**
19 ❑ Feb 1969 Cover: 0.12 **NM** value: **9.00**
20 ❑ Apr 1969 Cover: 0.12 **NM** value: **9.00**
21 ❑ Jun 1969 **NM** value: **6.00**
22 ❑ Aug 1969 **NM** value: **6.00**
23 ❑ Sep 1969 Cover: 0.15 **NM** value: **6.00**
24 ❑ Oct 1969 Cover: 0.15 **NM** value: **6.00**
25 ❑ Dec 1969 Cover: 0.15 **NM** value: **6.00**
26 ❑ Feb 1970 Cover: 0.15 **NM** value: **6.00**
Circ: Statement: **302,591**

27 ❑ Apr 1970 Cover: 0.15 **NM** value: **6.00**
Circ: Statement: **302,591**

28 ❑ Jun 1970 Cover: 0.15 **NM** value: **6.00**
Circ: Statement: **302,591**

29 ❑ Aug 1970 Cover: 0.15 **NM** value: **6.00**
Circ: Statement: **302,591**

30 ❑ Sep 1970 Cover: 0.15 **NM** value: **6.00**
Circ: Statement: **302,591**

31 ❑ Oct 1970 Cover: 0.15 **NM** value: **5.00**
Circ: Statement: **302,591**

32 ❑ Dec 1970 Cover: 0.15 **NM** value: **5.00**
Circ: Statement: **302,591**

33 ❑ Feb 1971 Cover: 0.15 **NM** value: **5.00**
Circ: Statement: **257,368**

CGC-graded: Multiply prices above by **33 for 9.9 M • 16 for 9.8 NM/M • 7 for 9.6 NM+ • 5 for 9.4 NM • 2.5 for 9.2 NM- • 1.5 for 9.0 VF/NM**

34 ❑ Apr 1971 Cover: 0.15 **NM** value: **5.00**
Circ: Statement: **257,368**
35 ❑ Jun 1971 Cover: 0.15 **NM** value: **5.00**
Circ: Statement: **257,368**
• Has1970 Statement, filed 10/1/1970; avg print run 501,647; avg sales 302,591; avg total paid 302,591; max existent 302,591; 40% of run returned
36 ❑ Aug 1971 Cover: 0.25 **NM** value: **5.00**
Circ: Statement: **257,368**
37 ❑ Sep 1971 Cover: 0.25 **NM** value: **5.00**
Circ: Statement: **257,368**
38 ❑ Oct 1971 Cover: 0.25 **NM** value: **5.00**
Circ: Statement: **257,368**
39 ❑ Dec 1971 Cover: 0.25 **NM** value: **5.00**
Circ: Statement: **257,368**
40 ❑ Feb 1972 Cover: 0.25 **NM** value: **5.00**
Circ: Statement: **198,831**
41 ❑ Apr 1972 Cover: 0.25 **NM** value: **4.00**
Circ: Statement: **198,831**
42 ❑ Jun 1972 Cover: 0.25 **NM** value: **4.00**
Circ: Statement: **198,831**
43 ❑ Aug 1972 Cover: 0.25 **NM** value: **4.00**
Circ: Statement: **198,831**
44 ❑ Sep 1972 Cover: 0.25 **NM** value: **4.00**
Circ: Statement: **198,831**
45 ❑ Oct 1972 Cover: 0.25 **NM** value: **4.00**
Circ: Statement: **198,831**
46 ❑ Dec 1972 Cover: 0.25 **NM** value: **4.00**
Circ: Statement: **198,831**
47 ❑ Feb 1973 Cover: 0.25 **NM** value: **4.00**
Circ: Statement: **198,142**
48 ❑ Apr 1973 Cover: 0.25 **NM** value: **4.00**
Circ: Statement: **198,142**
• Has1972 Statement; avg total paid circ 198,831
49 ❑ Jun 1973 Cover: 0.25 **NM** value: **4.00**
Circ: Statement: **198,142**
50 ❑ Jul 1973 Cover: 0.25 **NM** value: **4.00**
Circ: Statement: **198,142**
51 ❑ Aug 1973 Cover: 0.25 **NM** value: **4.00**
Circ: Statement: **198,142**
52 ❑ Sep 1973 Cover: 0.25 **NM** value: **4.00**
Circ: Statement: **198,142**
53 ❑ Oct 1973 Cover: 0.25 **NM** value: **4.00**
Circ: Statement: **198,142**
54 ❑ Dec 1973 Cover: 0.25 **NM** value: **4.00**
Circ: Statement: **198,142**
55 ❑ Feb 1974 Cover: 0.25 **NM** value: **4.00**
Circ: Statement: **193,240**
56 ❑ Apr 1974 Cover: 0.25 **NM** value: **4.00**
Circ: Statement: **193,240**
• Has 1973 Statement; avg total paid circ 198,142
57 ❑ Jun 1974 Cover: 0.25 **NM** value: **4.00**
Circ: Statement: **193,240**
58 ❑ Jul 1974 Cover: 0.25 **NM** value: **4.00**
Circ: Statement: **193,240**
59 ❑ Aug 1974 Cover: 0.25 **NM** value: **4.00**
Circ: Statement: **193,240**
60 ❑ Sep 1974 Cover: 0.25 **NM** value: **4.00**
Circ: Statement: **193,240**
61 ❑ Oct 1974 Cover: 0.25 **NM** value: **3.00**
Circ: Statement: **193,240**
62 ❑ Dec 1974 Cover: 0.25 **NM** value: **3.00**
Circ: Statement: **193,240**
63 ❑ Feb 1975 Cover: 0.25 **NM** value: **3.00**
Circ: Statement: **162,788**
64 ❑ Mar 1975 Cover: 0.25 **NM** value: **3.00**
Circ: Statement: **162,788**
65 ❑ Apr 1975 Cover: 0.25 **NM** value: **3.00**
Circ: Statement: **162,788**
• Has 1974 Statement; avg total paid circ 193,240
66 ❑ May 1975 Cover: 0.25 **NM** value: **3.00**
Circ: Statement: **162,788**
67 ❑ Jul 1975 Cover: 0.25 **NM** value: **3.00**
Circ: Statement: **162,788**
68 ❑ Aug 1975 Cover: 0.25 **NM** value: **3.00**
Circ: Statement: **162,788**
69 ❑ Sep 1975 Cover: 0.25 **NM** value: **3.00**
Circ: Statement: **162,788**
70 ❑ Oct 1975 Cover: 0.25 **NM** value: **3.00**
Circ: Statement: **162,788**
71 ❑ Dec 1975 Cover: 0.25 **NM** value: **2.00**
Circ: Statement: **162,788**
72 ❑ Feb 1976 **NM** value: **2.00**
Circ: Statement: **145,873**
73 ❑ Mar 1976 Cover: 0.30 **NM** value: **2.00**
Circ: Statement: **145,873**
74 ❑ Apr 1976 Cover: 0.30 **NM** value: **2.00**
Circ: Statement: **145,873**
75 ❑ May 1976 Cover: 0.30 **NM** value: **2.00**
Circ: Statement: **145,873**
76 ❑ Jul 1976 Cover: 0.30 **NM** value: **2.00**
Circ: Statement: **145,873**
77 ❑ Aug 1976 Cover: 0.30 **NM** value: **2.00**
Circ: Statement: **145,873**
78 ❑ Sep 1976 Cover: 0.30 **NM** value: **2.00**
Circ: Statement: **145,873**
79 ❑ Oct 1976 Cover: 0.30 **NM** value: **2.00**
Circ: Statement: **145,873**
80 ❑ Dec 1976 Cover: 0.30 **NM** value: **2.00**
Circ: Statement: **145,873**
81 ❑ Feb 1977 Cover: 0.30 **NM** value: **2.00**
Circ: Statement: **116,456**
82 ❑ Mar 1977 Cover: 0.30 **NM** value: **2.00**
Circ: Statement: **116,456**
83 ❑ Apr 1977 Cover: 0.30 **NM** value: **2.00**
Circ: Statement: **116,456**
• Has1976 Statement; avg total paid circ 145,873
84 ❑ May 1977 Cover: 0.30 **NM** value: **2.00**
Circ: Statement: **116,456**
85 ❑ Jul 1977 Cover: 0.35 **NM** value: **2.00**
Circ: Statement: **116,456**
86 ❑ Aug 1977 Cover: 0.35 **NM** value: **2.00**
Circ: Statement: **116,456**
87 ❑ Sep 1977 Cover: 0.35 **NM** value: **2.00**
Circ: Statement: **116,456**
88 ❑ Oct 1977 Cover: 0.35 **NM** value: **2.00**
Circ: Statement: **116,456**
89 ❑ Dec 1977 Cover: 0.35 **NM** value: **2.00**
Circ: Statement: **116,456**
90 ❑ Feb 1978 Cover: 0.35 **NM** value: **2.00**
Circ: Statement: **116,456**
91 ❑ Mar 1978 Cover: 0.35 **NM** value: **2.00**
Circ: Statement: **116,456**
92 ❑ Apr 1978 Cover: 0.35 **NM** value: **2.00**
Circ: Statement: **116,456**
• Has 1977 Statement, filed 10/1/1977; avg print run 309,002; avg sales 127,328; avg subs 170; avg total paid 127,498; office use 300; max existent 127,798; 55% of run returned
93 ❑ May 1978 Cover: 0.35 **NM** value: **2.00**
Circ: Statement: **116,456**
94 ❑ Jul 1978 Cover: 0.35 **NM** value: **2.00**
Circ: Statement: **116,456**
95 ❑ Aug 1978 Cover: 0.35 **NM** value: **2.00**
Circ: Statement: **116,456**
96 ❑ Sep 1978 Cover: 0.35 **NM** value: **2.00**
Circ: Statement: **116,456**
97 ❑ Oct 1978 Cover: 0.35 **NM** value: **2.00**
Circ: Statement: **116,456**
98 ❑ Dec 1978 Cover: 0.35 **NM** value: **2.00**
Circ: Statement: **116,456**
99 ❑ Feb 1979 Cover: 0.35 **NM** value: **2.00**
100 ❑ Mar 1979 **NM** value: **2.00**
101 ❑ Apr 1979 **NM** value: **1.50**
102 ❑ May 1979 Cover: 0.40 **NM** value: **1.50**
103 ❑ Jul 1979 Cover: 0.40 **NM** value: **1.50**
104 ❑ Aug 1979 Cover: 0.40 **NM** value: **1.50**
105 ❑ Sep 1979 Cover: 0.40 **NM** value: **1.50**
106 ❑ Oct 1979 Cover: 0.40 **NM** value: **1.50**
107 ❑ Dec 1979 Cover: 0.40 **NM** value: **1.50**
108 ❑ Feb 1980 Cover: 0.40 **NM** value: **1.50**
109 ❑ Mar 1980 Cover: 0.40 **NM** value: **1.50**
110 ❑ 1980 Cover: 0.40 **NM** value: **1.50**
111 ❑ 1980 Cover: 0.40 **NM** value: **1.50**
112 ❑ 1980 Cover: 0.40 **NM** value: **1.50**
113 ❑ 1980 Cover: 0.50 **NM** value: **1.50**
114 ❑ Cover: 0.50 **NM** value: **1.50**
115 ❑ Cover: 0.50 **NM** value: **1.50**
116 ❑ Cover: 0.50 **NM** value: **1.50**
117 ❑ Cover: 0.50 **NM** value: **1.50**
118 ❑ Cover: 0.50 **NM** value: **1.50**
119 ❑ Cover: 0.50 **NM** value: **1.50**
120 ❑ Cover: 0.50 **NM** value: **1.50**
121 ❑ Cover: 0.50 **NM** value: **1.50**
122 ❑ Cover: 0.50 **NM** value: **1.50**
123 ❑ Cover: 0.50 **NM** value: **1.50**
124 ❑ Cover: 0.50 **NM** value: **1.50**
125 ❑ Cover: 0.60 **NM** value: **1.50**
126 ❑ 1982 Cover: 0.60 **NM** value: **1.50**
Circ: Statement: **68,581**
127 ❑ 1982 Cover: 0.60 **NM** value: **1.50**
Circ: Statement: **68,581**
128 ❑ 1982 Cover: 0.60 **NM** value: **1.50**
Circ: Statement: **68,581**
129 ❑ 1982 Cover: 0.60 **NM** value: **1.50**
Circ: Statement: **68,581**
130 ❑ 1982 Cover: 0.60 **NM** value: **1.50**
Circ: Statement: **68,581**
131 ❑ 1982 Cover: 0.60 **NM** value: **1.50**
Circ: Statement: **68,581**
132 ❑ Jan 1983 Cover: 0.60 **NM** value: **1.50**
Circ: Statement: **64,909**
133 ❑ 1983 Cover: 0.60 **NM** value: **1.50**
Circ: Statement: **64,909**
134 ❑ 1983 Cover: 0.60 **NM** value: **1.50**
Circ: Statement: **64,909**
135 ❑ 1983 Cover: 0.60 **NM** value: **1.50**
Circ: Statement: **64,909**
136 ❑ 1983 Cover: 0.60 **NM** value: **1.50**
Circ: Statement: **64,909**
137 ❑ Jan 1984 Cover: 0.60 **NM** value: **1.50**
Circ: Statement: **61,328**
138 ❑ Mar 1984 Cover: 0.60 **NM** value: **1.50**
Circ: Statement: **61,328**
139 ❑ May 1984 Cover: 0.60 **NM** value: **1.50**
Circ: Statement: **61,328**
140 ❑ Jul 1984 Cover: 0.60 **NM** value: **1.50**
Circ: Statement: **61,328**
141 ❑ Sep 1984 Cover: 0.60 **NM** value: **1.50**
Circ: Statement: **61,328**
142 ❑ Nov 1984 Cover: 0.60 **NM** value: **1.50**
Circ: Statement: **61,328**
143 ❑ Jan 1985 Cover: 0.60 **NM** value: **1.50**
Circ: Statement: **58,023**
144 ❑ Mar 1985 Cover: 0.65 **NM** value: **1.50**
Circ: Statement: **58,023**
145 ❑ May 1985 Cover: 0.65 **NM** value: **1.50**
Circ: Statement: **58,023**
146 ❑ Jul 1985 Cover: 0.65 **NM** value: **1.50**
Circ: Statement: **58,023**
147 ❑ Sep 1985 Cover: 0.65 **NM** value: **1.50**
Circ: Statement: **58,023**
148 ❑ Nov 1985 Cover: 0.65 **NM** value: **1.50**
Circ: Statement: **58,023**
149 ❑ Jan 1986 Cover: 0.65 **NM** value: **1.50**
Circ: Statement: **56,551**
150 ❑ Mar 1986 Cover: 0.65 **NM** value: **1.50**
Circ: Statement: **56,551**
151 ❑ May 1986 Cover: 0.65 **NM** value: **1.00**
Circ: Statement: **56,551**
152 ❑ Jul 1986 Cover: 0.75 **NM** value: **1.00**
Circ: Statement: **56,551**
153 ❑ Sep 1986 Cover: 0.75 **NM** value: **1.00**
Circ: Statement: **56,551**
154 ❑ Nov 1986 Cover: 0.75 **NM** value: **1.00**
Circ: Statement: **56,551**
155 ❑ Jan 1987 Cover: 0.75 **NM** value: **1.00**
Circ: Statement: **52,082**
156 ❑ Mar 1987 Cover: 0.75 **NM** value: **1.00**
Circ: Statement: **52,082**
157 ❑ May 1987 Cover: 0.75 **NM** value: **1.00**
Circ: Statement: **52,082**
158 ❑ Jun 1987 Cover: 0.75 **NM** value: **1.00**
Circ: Statement: **52,082**
159 ❑ Jul 1987 Cover: 0.75 **NM** value: **1.00**
Circ: Statement: **52,082**
160 ❑ Aug 1987 Cover: 0.75 **NM** value: **1.00**
Circ: Statement: **52,082**
161 ❑ Sep 1987 Cover: 0.75 **NM** value: **1.00**
Circ: Statement: **52,082**
162 ❑ Oct 1987 Cover: 0.75 **NM** value: **1.00**
Circ: Statement: **52,082**
163 ❑ Dec 1987 Cover: 0.75 **NM** value: **1.00**
Circ: Statement: **52,082**
164 ❑ Jan 1988 Cover: 0.75 **NM** value: **1.00**
Circ: Statement: **54,661**
165 ❑ Mar 1988 Cover: 0.75 **NM** value: **1.00**
Circ: Statement: **54,661**
166 ❑ May 1988 Cover: 0.75 **NM** value: **1.00**
Circ: Statement: **54,661**
167 ❑ Jun 1988 Cover: 0.75 **NM** value: **1.00**
Circ: Statement: **54,661**
168 ❑ Jul 1988 Cover: 0.75 **NM** value: **1.00**
Circ: Statement: **54,661**
169 ❑ Aug 1988 Cover: 0.75 **NM** value: **1.00**
Circ: Statement: **54,661**
170 ❑ Sep 1988 Cover: 0.75 **NM** value: **1.00**
Circ: Statement: **54,661**
171 ❑ Oct 1988 Cover: 0.75 **NM** value: **1.00**
Circ: Statement: **54,661**
172 ❑ Jan 1989 Cover: 0.75 **NM** value: **1.00**
Circ: Statement: **58,484**
173 ❑ Mar 1989 Cover: 0.75 **NM** value: **1.00**
Circ: Statement: **58,484**
174 ❑ May 1989 Cover: 0.75 **NM** value: **1.00**
Circ: Statement: **58,484**
175 ❑ Jun 1989 Cover: 0.95 **NM** value: **1.00**
Circ: Statement: **58,484**
176 ❑ Jul 1989 Cover: 0.95 **NM** value: **1.00**
Circ: Statement: **58,484**
177 ❑ Aug 1989 Cover: 0.95 **NM** value: **1.00**
Circ: Statement: **58,484**
178 ❑ Sep 1989 Cover: 0.95 **NM** value: **1.00**
Circ: Statement: **58,484**
📖 Shy Guy; Betty: Soda (activity); Betty and Veronica...A Jarring Note; The Flapper; She's a Card; Dear Betty; Betty's Mixed Bag Fashion; Laffs 'n' Gaffs **A:** Stan Goldman **W:** Frank Doyle; George Gladir
★ Appearance of Veronica Lodge.
179 ❑ Oct 1989 Cover: 0.95 **NM** value: **1.00**
Circ: Statement: **58,484**
180 ❑ Jan 1990 Cover: 1.00 **NM** value: **Cover or less**
Circ: Statement: **49,134**
181 ❑ Mar 1990 Cover: 1.00 **NM** value: **Cover or less**
Circ: Statement: **49,134**
182 ❑ May 1990 Cover: 1.00 **NM** value: **Cover or less**
Circ: Statement: **49,134**
183 ❑ Jun 1990 Cover: 1.00 **NM** value: **Cover or less**
Circ: Statement: **49,134**
184 ❑ Jul 1990 Cover: 1.00 **NM** value: **Cover or less**
Circ: Statement: **49,134**
185 ❑ Aug 1990 Cover: 1.00 **NM** value: **Cover or less**
Circ: Statement: **49,134**
186 ❑ Sep 1990 Cover: 1.00 **NM** value: **Cover or less**
Circ: Statement: **49,134**
187 ❑ Oct 1990 Cover: 1.00 **NM** value: **Cover or less**
Circ: Statement: **49,134**
188 ❑ Jan 1991 Cover: 1.00 **NM** value: **Cover or less**
189 ❑ Mar 1991 Cover: 1.00 **NM** value: **Cover or less**
190 ❑ May 1991 Cover: 1.00 **NM** value: **Cover or less**
191 ❑ Jul 1991 Cover: 1.00 **NM** value: **Cover or less**
192 ❑ Aug 1991 Cover: 1.00 **NM** value: **Cover or less**
193 ❑ Sep 1991 Cover: 1.00 **NM** value: **Cover or less**
194 ❑ Oct 1991 Cover: 1.00 **NM** value: **Cover or less**
195 ❑ Nov 1991 Cover: 1.00 **NM** value: **Cover or less**
196 ❑ Jan 1992 Cover: 1.00 **NM** value: **Cover or less**
197 ❑ Mar 1992 Cover: 1.00 **NM** value: **Cover or less**
198 ❑ May 1992 Cover: 1.25 **NM** value: **Cover or less**
199 ❑ Jul 1992 Cover: 1.25 **NM** value: **Cover or less**
200 ❑ Aug 1992 Cover: 1.25 **NM** value: **Cover or less**

Diamond preorders are the estimated number of comics sold, prior to their release, to comics shops in North America by Diamond Comic Distributors, the largest distributor. These figures underreport the actual number of circulating copies by the amount of reorders Diamond took (usually 5-10% again of the preorders) and sales by publishers to newsstand and bookstore distributors. For many independent publishers, Diamond's preorders may be quite close to the actual number of copies in circulation.

Other grades: Multiply prices above by **1.5 for Mint • 2/3 for Very Fine • 1/3 for Fine • 1/5 for Very Good • 1/8 for Good**

BETTY AND VERONICA — Archie

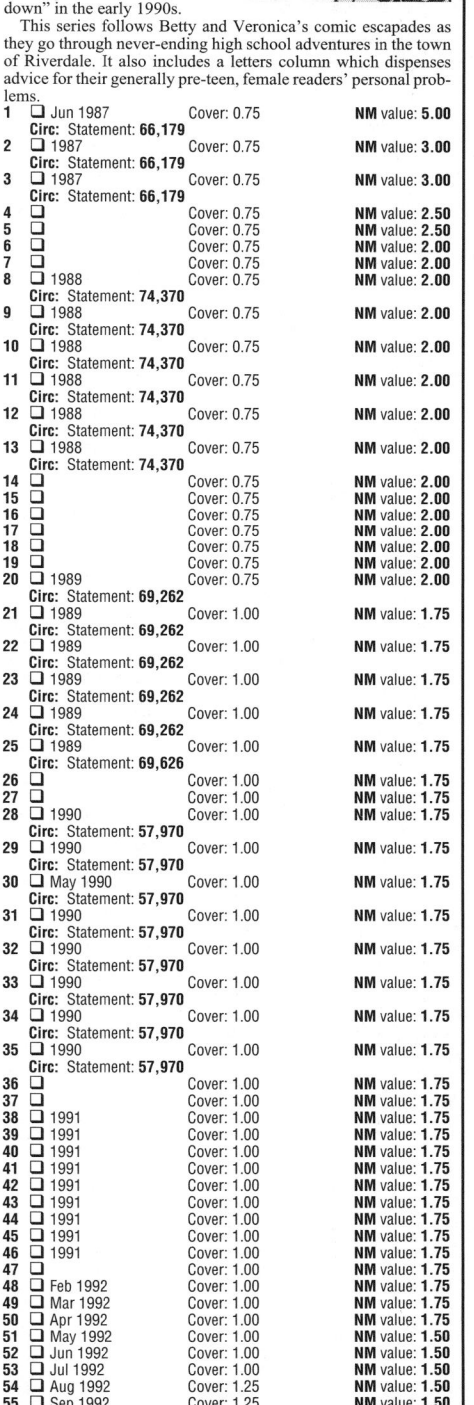

The main women in Archie's life, Betty Cooper and Veronica Lodge, return to the spotlight in this series. Veronica, the brunette, is the more worldly of the two, having been born into the rich Lodge family. Betty, on the other hand, combines a cheerful personality with blonde good looks. The two have grown closer together as friends over the years since their introduction in Pep Comics, as well as acting as occasional rivals for Archie Andrews' affections. Ironically, it was newcomer Cheryl Blossom who appeared to steal his heart in a well-publicized "Love Showdown" in the early 1990s.

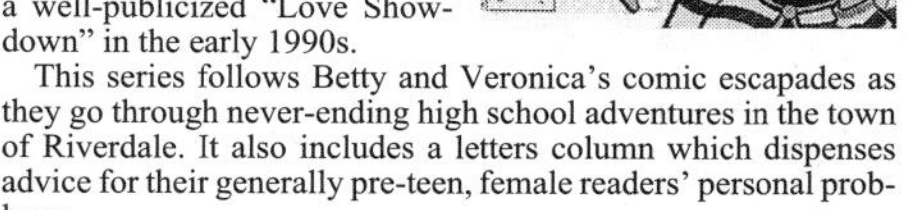

This series follows Betty and Veronica's comic escapades as they go through never-ending high school adventures in the town of Riverdale. It also includes a letters column which dispenses advice for their generally pre-teen, female readers' personal problems.

1 ❑ Jun 1987 Cover: 0.75 **NM** value: **5.00**
Circ: Statement: **66,179**
2 ❑ 1987 Cover: 0.75 **NM** value: **3.00**
Circ: Statement: **66,179**
3 ❑ 1987 Cover: 0.75 **NM** value: **3.00**
Circ: Statement: **66,179**
4 ❑ Cover: 0.75 **NM** value: **2.50**
5 ❑ Cover: 0.75 **NM** value: **2.50**
6 ❑ Cover: 0.75 **NM** value: **2.00**
7 ❑ Cover: 0.75 **NM** value: **2.00**
8 ❑ 1988 Cover: 0.75 **NM** value: **2.00**
Circ: Statement: **74,370**
9 ❑ 1988 Cover: 0.75 **NM** value: **2.00**
Circ: Statement: **74,370**
10 ❑ 1988 Cover: 0.75 **NM** value: **2.00**
Circ: Statement: **74,370**
11 ❑ 1988 Cover: 0.75 **NM** value: **2.00**
Circ: Statement: **74,370**
12 ❑ 1988 Cover: 0.75 **NM** value: **2.00**
Circ: Statement: **74,370**
13 ❑ 1988 Cover: 0.75 **NM** value: **2.00**
Circ: Statement: **74,370**
14 ❑ Cover: 0.75 **NM** value: **2.00**
15 ❑ Cover: 0.75 **NM** value: **2.00**
16 ❑ Cover: 0.75 **NM** value: **2.00**
17 ❑ Cover: 0.75 **NM** value: **2.00**
18 ❑ Cover: 0.75 **NM** value: **2.00**
19 ❑ Cover: 0.75 **NM** value: **2.00**
20 ❑ 1989 Cover: 0.75 **NM** value: **2.00**
Circ: Statement: **69,262**
21 ❑ 1989 Cover: 1.00 **NM** value: **1.75**
Circ: Statement: **69,262**
22 ❑ 1989 Cover: 1.00 **NM** value: **1.75**
Circ: Statement: **69,262**
23 ❑ 1989 Cover: 1.00 **NM** value: **1.75**
Circ: Statement: **69,262**
24 ❑ 1989 Cover: 1.00 **NM** value: **1.75**
Circ: Statement: **69,262**
25 ❑ 1989 Cover: 1.00 **NM** value: **1.75**
Circ: Statement: **69,626**
26 ❑ Cover: 1.00 **NM** value: **1.75**
27 ❑ Cover: 1.00 **NM** value: **1.75**
28 ❑ 1990 Cover: 1.00 **NM** value: **1.75**
Circ: Statement: **57,970**
29 ❑ 1990 Cover: 1.00 **NM** value: **1.75**
Circ: Statement: **57,970**
30 ❑ May 1990 Cover: 1.00 **NM** value: **1.75**
Circ: Statement: **57,970**
31 ❑ 1990 Cover: 1.00 **NM** value: **1.75**
Circ: Statement: **57,970**
32 ❑ 1990 Cover: 1.00 **NM** value: **1.75**
Circ: Statement: **57,970**
33 ❑ 1990 Cover: 1.00 **NM** value: **1.75**
Circ: Statement: **57,970**
34 ❑ 1990 Cover: 1.00 **NM** value: **1.75**
Circ: Statement: **57,970**
35 ❑ 1990 Cover: 1.00 **NM** value: **1.75**
Circ: Statement: **57,970**
36 ❑ Cover: 1.00 **NM** value: **1.75**
37 ❑ Cover: 1.00 **NM** value: **1.75**
38 ❑ 1991 Cover: 1.00 **NM** value: **1.75**
39 ❑ 1991 Cover: 1.00 **NM** value: **1.75**
40 ❑ 1991 Cover: 1.00 **NM** value: **1.75**
41 ❑ 1991 Cover: 1.00 **NM** value: **1.75**
42 ❑ 1991 Cover: 1.00 **NM** value: **1.75**
43 ❑ 1991 Cover: 1.00 **NM** value: **1.75**
44 ❑ 1991 Cover: 1.00 **NM** value: **1.75**
45 ❑ 1991 Cover: 1.00 **NM** value: **1.75**
46 ❑ 1991 Cover: 1.00 **NM** value: **1.75**
47 ❑ Cover: 1.00 **NM** value: **1.75**
48 ❑ Feb 1992 Cover: 1.00 **NM** value: **1.75**
49 ❑ Mar 1992 Cover: 1.00 **NM** value: **1.75**
50 ❑ Apr 1992 Cover: 1.00 **NM** value: **1.75**
51 ❑ May 1992 Cover: 1.00 **NM** value: **1.50**
52 ❑ Jun 1992 Cover: 1.00 **NM** value: **1.50**
53 ❑ Jul 1992 Cover: 1.00 **NM** value: **1.50**
54 ❑ Aug 1992 Cover: 1.25 **NM** value: **1.50**
55 ❑ Sep 1992 Cover: 1.25 **NM** value: **1.50**
56 ❑ Oct 1992 Cover: 1.25 **NM** value: **1.50**
57 ❑ Nov 1992 Cover: 1.25 **NM** value: **1.50**
58 ❑ Dec 1992 Cover: 1.25 **NM** value: **1.50**
59 ❑ Jan 1993 Cover: 1.25 **NM** value: **1.50**
60 ❑ Feb 1993 Cover: 1.25 **NM** value: **1.50**
61 ❑ Mar 1993 Cover: 1.25 **NM** value: **1.50**
62 ❑ Apr 1993 Cover: 1.25 **NM** value: **1.50**
63 ❑ May 1993 Cover: 1.25 **NM** value: **1.50**
64 ❑ Jun 1993 Cover: 1.25 **NM** value: **1.50**
65 ❑ Jul 1993 Cover: 1.25 **NM** value: **1.50**
66 ❑ Aug 1993 Cover: 1.25 **NM** value: **1.50**
📖 Hold the Phone; Fab Job; Sweater Girl; The Big Switch **A:** Dan Decarlo **W:** Frank Doyle; George Gladir
67 ❑ Sep 1993 Cover: 1.25 **NM** value: **1.50**
68 ❑ Oct 1993 Cover: 1.25 **NM** value: **1.50**
69 ❑ Nov 1993 Cover: 1.25 **NM** value: **1.50**
70 ❑ Dec 1993 Cover: 1.25 **NM** value: **1.50**
71 ❑ Jan 1994 Cover: 1.25 **NM** value: **1.50**
72 ❑ Feb 1994 Cover: 1.25 **NM** value: **1.50**
73 ❑ Mar 1994 Cover: 1.25 **NM** value: **1.50**
74 ❑ Apr 1994 Cover: 1.25 **NM** value: **1.50**
75 ❑ May 1994 Cover: 1.25 **NM** value: **1.50**
76 ❑ Jun 1994 Cover: 1.25 **NM** value: **1.50**
77 ❑ Jul 1994 Cover: 1.25 **NM** value: **1.50**
78 ❑ Aug 1994 Cover: 1.50 **NM** value: **Cover or less**
79 ❑ Sep 1994 Cover: 1.50 **NM** value: **Cover or less**
80 ❑ Oct 1994 Cover: 1.50 **NM** value: **Cover or less**
81 ❑ Nov 1994 Cover: 1.50 **NM** value: **Cover or less**
82 ❑ Dec 1994 Cover: 1.50 **NM** value: **Cover or less**
📖 Love Showdown, Part 3
83 ❑ Jan 1995 Cover: 1.50 **NM** value: **Cover or less**
Circ: Statement: **45,587**
84 ❑ Feb 1995 Cover: 1.50 **NM** value: **Cover or less**
Circ: Statement: **45,587**
85 ❑ Mar 1995 Cover: 1.50 **NM** value: **Cover or less**
Circ: Statement: **45,587**
86 ❑ Apr 1995 Cover: 1.50 **NM** value: **Cover or less**
Circ: Statement: **45,587**
87 ❑ May 1995 Cover: 1.50 **NM** value: **Cover or less**
Circ: Statement: **45,587**
88 ❑ Jun 1995 Cover: 1.50 **NM** value: **Cover or less**
Circ: Statement: **45,587**
89 ❑ Jul 1995 Cover: 1.50 **NM** value: **Cover or less**
Circ: Statement: **45,587**
90 ❑ Aug 1995 Cover: 1.50 **NM** value: **Cover or less**
Circ: Statement: **45,587**
91 ❑ Sep 1995 Cover: 1.50 **NM** value: **Cover or less**
Circ: Statement: **45,587**
92 ❑ Oct 1995 Cover: 1.50 **NM** value: **Cover or less**
Circ: Statement: **45,587**
93 ❑ Nov 1995 Cover: 1.50 **NM** value: **Cover or less**
Circ: Statement: **45,587**
94 ❑ Dec 1995 Cover: 1.50 **NM** value: **Cover or less**
Circ: Statement: **45,587**
95 ❑ Jan 1996 Cover: 1.50 **NM** value: **Cover or less**
Circ: Statement: **47,010**
📖 House of Riverdale, Part 2 • concludes in Archie's Pal Jughead #76
96 ❑ Feb 1996 Cover: 1.50 **NM** value: **Cover or less**
Circ: Statement: **47,010**
97 ❑ Mar 1996 Cover: 1.50 **NM** value: **Cover or less**
Circ: Statement: **47,010**
98 ❑ Apr 1996 Cover: 1.50 **NM** value: **Cover or less**
Circ: Statement: **47,010**
99 ❑ May 1996 Cover: 1.50 **NM** value: **Cover or less**
Circ: Statement: **47,010**
100 ❑ Jun 1996 Cover: 1.50 **NM** value: **Cover or less**
Circ: Statement: **47,010**
101 ❑ Jul 1996 Cover: 1.50 **NM** value: **Cover or less**
Circ: Statement: **47,010**
102 ❑ Aug 1996 Cover: 1.50 **NM** value: **Cover or less**
Circ: Statement: **47,010**
103 ❑ Sep 1996 Cover: 1.50 **NM** value: **Cover or less**
Circ: Statement: **47,010**
104 ❑ Oct 1996 Cover: 1.50 **NM** value: **Cover or less**
Circ: Statement: **47,010**
105 ❑ Nov 1996 Cover: 1.50 **NM** value: **Cover or less**
Circ: Statement: **47,010**
106 ❑ Dec 1996 Cover: 1.50 **NM** value: **Cover or less**
Circ: Statement: **47,010** Direct Market orders: **4,739**
📖 Hearing Aided; Style No-Show; A Fishy License; Fair Exchange
107 ❑ Jan 1997 Cover: 1.50 **NM** value: **Cover or less**
Circ: Statement: **44,658** Direct Market orders: **5,006**
108 ❑ Feb 1997 Cover: 1.50 **NM** value: **Cover or less**
Circ: Statement: **44,658** Diamd. preorders: **5,029**
109 ❑ Mar 1997 Cover: 1.50 **NM** value: **Cover or less**
Circ: Statement: **44,658** Diamd. preorders: **4,875**
110 ❑ Apr 1997 Cover: 1.50 **NM** value: **Cover or less**
Circ: Statement: **44,658** Diamd. preorders: **4,507**
• Has 1996 Statement, filed 9/27/96; avg print run 130,063; avg sales 45,615; avg subs 1,395; avg total paid 47,010; samples 430; office use 1,964; max existent 49,404; 62% of run returned
111 ❑ May 1997 Cover: 1.50 **NM** value: **Cover or less**
Circ: Statement: **44,658** Diamd. preorders: **4,398**
112 ❑ Jun 1997 Cover: 1.50 **NM** value: **Cover or less**
Circ: Statement: **44,658** Diamd. preorders: **4,493**
113 ❑ Jul 1997 Cover: 1.50 **NM** value: **Cover or less**
Circ: Statement: **44,658** Diamd. preorders: **4,797**
114 ❑ Aug 1997 Cover: 1.50 **NM** value: **Cover or less**
Circ: Statement: **44,658** Diamd. preorders: **4,804**
115 ❑ Sep 1997 Cover: 1.50 **NM** value: **Cover or less**
Circ: Statement: **44,658** Diamd. preorders: **5,112**
116 ❑ Oct 1997 Cover: 1.50 **NM** value: **Cover or less**
Circ: Statement: **44,658** Diamd. preorders: **5,085**
117 ❑ Nov 1997 Cover: 1.50 **NM** value: **Cover or less**
Circ: Statement: **44,658** Diamd. preorders: **5,049**
118 ❑ Dec 1997 Cover: 1.50 **NM** value: **Cover or less**
Circ: Statement: **44,658** Diamd. preorders: **5,053**
119 ❑ Jan 1998 Cover: 1.75 **NM** value: **Cover or less**
Circ: Statement: **38,714** Diamd. preorders: **5,711**
120 ❑ Feb 1998 Cover: 1.75 **NM** value: **Cover or less**
Circ: Statement: **38,714** Diamd. preorders: **5,332**
121 ❑ Mar 1998 Cover: 1.75 **NM** value: **Cover or less**
Circ: Statement: **38,714** Diamd. preorders: **5,032**
122 ❑ Apr 1998 Cover: 1.75 **NM** value: **Cover or less**
Circ: Statement: **38,714** Diamd. preorders: **4,782**
• Has 1997 Statement, filed 11/1/97; avg print run 133,769; avg sales 42,823; avg subs 1,835; avg total paid 44,658; samples 426; office use 1,657; max existent 46,741; 65% of run returned
123 ❑ May 1998 Cover: 1.75 **NM** value: **Cover or less**
Circ: Statement: **38,714** Diamd. preorders: **4,398**
124 ❑ Jun 1998 Cover: 1.75 **NM** value: **Cover or less**
Circ: Statement: **38,714** Diamd. preorders: **4,479**
125 ❑ Jul 1998 Cover: 1.75 **NM** value: **Cover or less**
Circ: Statement: **38,714** Diamd. preorders: **4,537**
126 ❑ Aug 1998 Cover: 1.75 **NM** value: **Cover or less**
Circ: Statement: **38,714** Diamd. preorders: **4,492**
127 ❑ Sep 1998 Cover: 1.75 **NM** value: **Cover or less**
Circ: Statement: **38,714** Diamd. preorders: **4,683**
📖 Home Alone Comfort Zone; Faithfully Yours; Beachy Keen; Beach Nuts **A:** Dan Decarlo **W:** Kathleen Webb; Dan Parent; Mike Pellowski
128 ❑ Oct 1998 Cover: 1.75 **NM** value: **Cover or less**
Circ: Statement: **38,714** Diamd. preorders: **4,451**
129 ❑ Nov 1998 Cover: 1.75 **NM** value: **Cover or less**
Circ: Statement: **38,714** Diamd. preorders: **4,250**
📖 Express Yourself; The Big Obsession **A:** Dan Decarlo **W:** Barbara Slate; George Gladir
130 ❑ Dec 1998 Cover: 1.75 **NM** value: **Cover or less**
Circ: Statement: **38,714** Diamd. preorders: **4,203**
131 ❑ Jan 1999 Cover: 1.75 **NM** value: **Cover or less**
Circ: Diamd. preorders: **4,293**
132 ❑ Feb 1999 Cover: 1.75 **NM** value: **Cover or less**
Circ: Diamd. preorders: **4,327**
• Has 1998 Statement, filed 11/1/98; avg print run 116,847; avg sales 36,899; avg subs 1,815; avg total paid 38,714; samples 421; office use 1,518; max existent 40,653; 65% of run returned
133 ❑ Mar 1999 Cover: 1.75 **NM** value: **Cover or less**
Circ: Diamd. preorders: **4,242**
📖 Fashion Fling **A:** Dan Decarlo **W:** Barbara Slate
134 ❑ Apr 1999 Cover: 1.79 **NM** value: **Cover or less**
Circ: Diamd. preorders: **3,786**
135 ❑ May 1999 Cover: 1.79 **NM** value: **Cover or less**
Circ: Diamd. preorders: **3,663**
📖 Media Manipulation **A:** Dan Decarlo
136 ❑ Jun 1999 Cover: 1.79 **NM** value: **Cover or less**
Circ: Diamd. preorders: **3,597**
137 ❑ Jul 1999 Cover: 1.79 **NM** value: **Cover or less**
Circ: Diamd. preorders: **3,765**
138 ❑ Aug 1999 Cover: 1.79 **NM** value: **Cover or less**
Circ: Diamd. preorders: **3,732**
139 ❑ Sep 1999 Cover: 1.79 **NM** value: **Cover or less**
Circ: Diamd. preorders: **3,972**
140 ❑ Oct 1999 Cover: 1.79 **NM** value: **Cover or less**
Circ: Diamd. preorders: **3,751**
141 ❑ Nov 1999 Cover: 1.79 **NM** value: **Cover or less**
Circ: Diamd. preorders: **3,623**
142 ❑ Dec 1999 Cover: 1.79 **NM** value: **Cover or less**
Circ: Diamd. preorders: **3,547**
143 ❑ Jan 2000 Cover: 1.79 **NM** value: **Cover or less**
Circ: Diamd. preorders: **3,664**
144 ❑ Feb 2000 Cover: 1.79 **NM** value: **Cover or less**
Circ: Diamd. preorders: **3,600**
145 ❑ Mar 2000 Cover: 1.79 **NM** value: **Cover or less**
Circ: Diamd. preorders: **3,595**
146 ❑ Apr 2000 Cover: 1.79 **NM** value: **Cover or less**
Circ: Diamd. preorders: **3,328**
147 ❑ May 2000 Cover: 1.79 **NM** value: **Cover or less**
Circ: Diamd. preorders: **3,229**
148 ❑ Jun 2000 Cover: 1.79 **NM** value: **Cover or less**
Circ: Diamd. preorders: **3,263**
149 ❑ Jul 2000 Cover: 1.99 **NM** value: **Cover or less**
Circ: Diamd. preorders: **3,339**
150 ❑ Aug 2000 Cover: 1.99 **NM** value: **Cover or less**
Circ: Diamd. preorders: **3,647**
151 ❑ Sep 2000 Cover: 1.99 **NM** value: **Cover or less**
Circ: Diamd. preorders: **3,647**
152 ❑ Oct 2000 Cover: 1.99 **NM** value: **Cover or less**
Circ: Diamd. preorders: **3,667**
153 ❑ Nov 2000 Cover: 1.99 **NM** value: **Cover or less**
Circ: Diamd. preorders: **3,274**
154 ❑ Dec 2000 Cover: 1.99 **NM** value: **Cover or less**
Circ: Diamd. preorders: **3,407**
155 ❑ Jan 2001 Cover: 1.99 **NM** value: **Cover or less**
Circ: Statement: **22,531** Diamd. preorders: **3,448**
156 ❑ Feb 2001 Cover: 1.99 **NM** value: **Cover or less**
Circ: Statement: **22,531** Diamd. preorders: **3,371**
157 ❑ Mar 2001 Cover: 1.99 **NM** value: **Cover or less**
Circ: Statement: **22,531** Diamd. preorders: **3,198**
158 ❑ Apr 2001 Cover: 1.99 **NM** value: **Cover or less**
Circ: Statement: **22,531** Diamd. preorders: **3,074**
159 ❑ May 2001 Cover: 1.99 **NM** value: **Cover or less**
Circ: Statement: **22,531** Diamd. preorders: **3,140**
160 ❑ Jun 2001 Cover: 1.99 **NM** value: **Cover or less**
Circ: Statement: **22,531** Diamd. preorders: **2,972**
161 ❑ Jul 2001 Cover: 1.99 **NM** value: **Cover or less**
Circ: Statement: **22,531** Diamd. preorders: **3,167**
162 ❑ Aug 2001 Cover: 1.99 **NM** value: **Cover or less**
Circ: Statement: **22,531** Diamd. preorders: **3,171**
163 ❑ Sep 2001 Cover: 1.99 **NM** value: **Cover or less**
Circ: Statement: **22,531** Diamd. preorders: **3,002**
164 ❑ Oct 2001 Cover: 1.99 **NM** value: **Cover or less**
Circ: Statement: **22,531** Diamd. preorders: **3,634**
165 ❑ Nov 2001 Cover: 1.99 **NM** value: **Cover or less**
Circ: Statement: **22,531** Diamd. preorders: **3,519**

CGC-graded: Multiply prices above by **33 for 9.9 M • 16 for 9.8 NM/M • 7 for 9.6 NM+ • 5 for 9.4 NM • 2.5 for 9.2 NM- • 1.5 for 9.0 VF/NM**

BETTY & VERONICA ANNUAL DIGEST MAGAZINE — Archie

12 ☐ Jan 1995 Cover: 1.75 **NM** value: **Cover or less**
13 ☐ Sep 1995 Cover: 1.75 **NM** value: **Cover or less**
14 ☐ Feb 1996 Cover: 1.75 **NM** value: **Cover or less**
15 ☐ Jul 1996 Cover: 1.75 **NM** value: **Cover or less**
16 ☐ Aug 1997 Cover: 1.79 **NM** value: **Cover or less**

BETTY AND VERONICA COMICS DIGEST — Archie

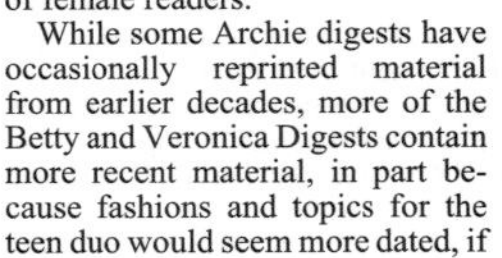

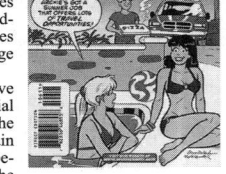

Archie Comics digests have had the highest circulations of the company's line traditionally, because of the advantages of placement near grocery-store checkouts and the like. While many of the Archie titles were aimed at a fairly general readership, the Betty and Veronica titles tended to have a larger percentage of female readers.

While some Archie digests have occasionally reprinted material from earlier decades, more of the Betty and Veronica Digests contain more recent material, in part because fashions and topics for the teen duo would seem more dated, if they came from earlier years. Betty and Veronica, of course, are the two principal love interests in the world of Archie Andrews. But everyone knows that, right?

— Maggie

1 ☐ **NM** value: **8.00**
2 ☐ **NM** value: **4.50**
3 ☐ **NM** value: **4.00**
4 ☐ **NM** value: **4.00**
5 ☐ **NM** value: **4.00**
6 ☐ **NM** value: **3.00**
7 ☐ **NM** value: **3.00**
8 ☐ **NM** value: **3.00**
9 ☐ **NM** value: **3.00**
10 ☐ Cover: 1.00 **NM** value: **3.00**
11 ☐ **NM** value: **3.00**
12 ☐ **NM** value: **3.00**
13 ☐ **NM** value: **3.00**
14 ☐ **NM** value: **3.00**
15 ☐ **NM** value: **3.00**
16 ☐ **NM** value: **3.00**
17 ☐ **NM** value: **3.00**
18 ☐ **NM** value: **3.00**
19 ☐ **NM** value: **3.00**
20 ☐ **NM** value: **3.00**
21 ☐ 1986 **NM** value: **2.50**
Circ: Statement: **131,134**
22 ☐ 1986 **NM** value: **2.50**
Circ: Statement: **131,134**
23 ☐ **NM** value: **2.50**
24 ☐ **NM** value: **2.50**
25 ☐ **NM** value: **2.50**
26 ☐ 1987 **NM** value: **2.50**
Circ: Statement: **130,002**
27 ☐ 1987 **NM** value: **2.50**
Circ: Statement: **130,002**
28 ☐ **NM** value: **2.50**
29 ☐ **NM** value: **2.50**
30 ☐ 1988 **NM** value: **2.50**
Circ: Statement: **143,348**
31 ☐ 1988 **NM** value: **2.50**
Circ: Statement: **143,348**
32 ☐ **NM** value: **2.50**
33 ☐ **NM** value: **2.50**
34 ☐ 1989 **NM** value: **2.50**
Circ: Statement: **148,694**
35 ☐ 1989 **NM** value: **2.50**
Circ: Statement: **148,694**
36 ☐ 1989 **NM** value: **2.50**
Circ: Statement: **148,694**
37 ☐ **NM** value: **2.50**
38 ☐ **NM** value: **2.50**
39 ☐ **NM** value: **2.50**
40 ☐ 1990 **NM** value: **2.50**
Circ: Statement: **142,357**
41 ☐ 1990 **NM** value: **2.50**
Circ: Statement: **142,357**
42 ☐ 1990 **NM** value: **2.50**
Circ: Statement: **142,357**
43 ☐ 1990 **NM** value: **2.50**
Circ: Statement: **142,357**
44 ☐ 1990 **NM** value: **2.50**
Circ: Statement: **142,357**
45 ☐ **NM** value: **2.50**
46 ☐ 1991 **NM** value: **2.50**
47 ☐ 1991 **NM** value: **2.50**
48 ☐ 1991 **NM** value: **2.50**
49 ☐ 1991 **NM** value: **2.50**
50 ☐ Sep 1991 **NM** value: **2.50**
51 ☐ **NM** value: **2.00**
52 ☐ **NM** value: **2.00**
53 ☐ **NM** value: **2.00**
54 ☐ **NM** value: **2.00**
55 ☐ **NM** value: **2.00**
56 ☐ **NM** value: **2.00**
57 ☐ **NM** value: **2.00**
58 ☐ **NM** value: **2.00**
59 ☐ **NM** value: **2.00**
60 ☐ **NM** value: **2.00**
61 ☐ **NM** value: **2.00**
62 ☐ **NM** value: **2.00**
63 ☐ **NM** value: **2.00**
64 ☐ **NM** value: **2.00**
65 ☐ **NM** value: **2.00**
66 ☐ **NM** value: **2.00**
67 ☐ 1994 **NM** value: **2.00**
Circ: Statement: **130,337**
68 ☐ 1994 **NM** value: **2.00**
Circ: Statement: **130,337**
69 ☐ 1994 **NM** value: **2.00**
Circ: Statement: **130,337**
70 ☐ 1994 **NM** value: **2.00**
Circ: Statement: **130,337**
71 ☐ 1994 **NM** value: **2.00**
Circ: Statement: **130,337**
72 ☐ **NM** value: **2.00**
73 ☐ 1995 **NM** value: **2.00**
Circ: Statement: **116,917**
74 ☐ 1995 **NM** value: **2.00**
Circ: Statement: **116,917**
75 ☐ 1995 **NM** value: **2.00**
Circ: Statement: **116,917**
76 ☐ 1995 **NM** value: **2.00**
Circ: Statement: **116,917**
77 ☐ 1995 **NM** value: **2.00**
Circ: Statement: **116,917**
78 ☐ **NM** value: **2.00**
79 ☐ 1996 **NM** value: **2.00**
Circ: Statement: **115,789**
80 ☐ Apr 1996 **NM** value: **2.00**
Circ: Statement: **115,789**
• Has 1995 Statement, filed 10/1/1995; avg print run 300,120; avg sales 115,377; avg subs 1,540; avg total paid 116,917; samples 370; office use 6,922; max existent 124,209; 59% of run returned
81 ☐ 1996 **NM** value: **1.95**
Circ: Statement: **115,789**
82 ☐ 1996 **NM** value: **1.95**
Circ: Statement: **115,789**
83 ☐ 1996 **NM** value: **1.95**
Circ: Statement: **115,789**
84 ☐ 1996 **NM** value: **1.95**
Circ: Statement: **115,789**
85 ☐ Jan 1997 Cover: 1.79 **NM** value: **1.95**
Circ: Statement: **109,186**
86 ☐ Feb 1997 Cover: 1.79 **NM** value: **1.95**
Circ: Statement: **109,186**
87 ☐ Apr 1997 Cover: 1.79 **NM** value: **1.95**
Circ: Statement: **109,186**
• Has 1996 Statement, filed 9/27/1996; avg print run 291,533; avg sales 114,609; avg subs 1,180; avg total paid 115,789; samples 384; office use 3,301; max existent 119,474; 58% of run returned
88 ☐ Jun 1997 Cover: 1.79 **NM** value: **1.95**
Circ: Statement: **109,186**
89 ☐ Jul 1997 Cover: 1.79 **NM** value: **1.95**
Circ: Statement: **109,186**
90 ☐ Sep 1997 Cover: 1.79 **NM** value: **1.95**
Circ: Statement: **109,186**
91 ☐ Oct 1997 Cover: 1.79 **NM** value: **1.95**
Circ: Statement: **109,186**
92 ☐ Dec 1997 Cover: 1.79 **NM** value: **1.95**
Circ: Statement: **109,186**
93 ☐ Feb 1998 Cover: 1.95 **NM** value: **Cover or less**
Circ: Statement: **107,732**
94 ☐ Apr 1998 Cover: 1.95 **NM** value: **Cover or less**
Circ: Statement: **107,732**
95 ☐ Jun 1998 Cover: 1.95 **NM** value: **Cover or less**
Circ: Statement: **107,732**
• Has 1997 Statement, filed 11/1/1997; avg print run 280,471; avg sales 108,083; avg subs 1,103; avg total paid 109,186; samples 460; office use 6,269; max existent 115,915; 59% of run returned
96 ☐ Jul 1998 Cover: 1.95 **NM** value: **Cover or less**
Circ: Statement: **107,732**
97 ☐ Aug 1998 Cover: 1.95 **NM** value: **Cover or less**
Circ: Statement: **107,732**
98 ☐ Sep 1998 Cover: 1.95 **NM** value: **Cover or less**
Circ: Statement: **107,732**
99 ☐ Nov 1998 Cover: 1.95 **NM** value: **Cover or less**
Circ: Statement: **107,732**
A: Dan Decarlo
100 ☐ Dec 1998 Cover: 1.95 **NM** value: **Cover or less**
Circ: Statement: **107,732**
101 ☐ Feb 1999 Cover: 1.95 **NM** value: **Cover or less**
102 ☐ Apr 1999 Cover: 1.95 **NM** value: **Cover or less**
• Has 1998 Statement, filed 11/1/1998; avg print run 261,498; avg sales 106,656; avg subs 1,076; avg total paid 107,732; samples 418; office use 6,771; max existent 114,921; 56% of run returned
103 ☐ May 1999 Cover: 1.95 **NM** value: **Cover or less**
104 ☐ Jul 1999 Cover: 1.95 **NM** value: **Cover or less**
105 ☐ Aug 1999 Cover: 1.95 **NM** value: **Cover or less**
106 ☐ Sep 1999 Cover: 1.95 **NM** value: **Cover or less**
107 ☐ Nov 1999 Cover: 1.95 **NM** value: **Cover or less**
108 ☐ Jan 2000 Cover: 1.95 **NM** value: **Cover or less**
109 ☐ Feb 2000 Cover: 1.95 **NM** value: **Cover or less**
110 ☐ Apr 2000 Cover: 2.19 **NM** value: **Cover or less**
111 ☐ May 2000 Cover: 2.19 **NM** value: **Cover or less**
112 ☐ Jul 2000 Cover: 2.19 **NM** value: **Cover or less**

BETTY AND VERONICA DIGEST MAGAZINE — Archie

72 ☐ Jan 1995 Cover: 1.75 **NM** value: **Cover or less**
73 ☐ Mar 1995 Cover: 1.75 **NM** value: **Cover or less**
74 ☐ Apr 1995 Cover: 1.75 **NM** value: **Cover or less**
75 ☐ Jun 1995 Cover: 1.75 **NM** value: **Cover or less**
76 ☐ Aug 1995 Cover: 1.75 **NM** value: **Cover or less**
77 ☐ Oct 1995 Cover: 1.75 **NM** value: **Cover or less**
78 ☐ Dec 1995 Cover: 1.75 **NM** value: **Cover or less**
79 ☐ Feb 1996 Cover: 1.75 **NM** value: **Cover or less**
80 ☐ Apr 1996 Cover: 1.75 **NM** value: **Cover or less**
81 ☐ Jun 1996 Cover: 1.75 **NM** value: **Cover or less**
82 ☐ Jul 1996 Cover: 1.75 **NM** value: **Cover or less**
83 ☐ Sep 1996 Cover: 1.75 **NM** value: **Cover or less**
84 ☐ Nov 1996 Cover: 1.79 **NM** value: **Cover or less**
85 ☐ Jan 1997 Cover: 1.79 **NM** value: **Cover or less**
Circ: Direct Market orders: **3,472**
86 ☐ Feb 1997 Cover: 1.79 **NM** value: **Cover or less**
Circ: Diamd. preorders: **3,476**
87 ☐ Apr 1997 Cover: 1.79 **NM** value: **Cover or less**
Circ: Diamd. preorders: **3,255**
88 ☐ Jun 1997 Cover: 1.79 **NM** value: **Cover or less**
Circ: Diamd. preorders: **3,494**
89 ☐ Jul 1997 Cover: 1.79 **NM** value: **Cover or less**
90 ☐ Sep 1997 Cover: 1.79 **NM** value: **Cover or less**
Circ: Diamd. preorders: **3,873**
91 ☐ Oct 1997 Cover: 1.79 **NM** value: **Cover or less**
Circ: Diamd. preorders: **3,941**
92 ☐ Dec 1997 Cover: 1.79 **NM** value: **Cover or less**
Circ: Diamd. preorders: **3,694**
93 ☐ Feb 1998 Cover: 1.95 **NM** value: **Cover or less**
Circ: Diamd. preorders: **3,844**
94 ☐ Apr 1998 Cover: 1.95 **NM** value: **Cover or less**
Circ: Diamd. preorders: **3,576**
95 ☐ May 1998 Cover: 1.95 **NM** value: **Cover or less**
96 ☐ Jul 1998 Cover: 1.95 **NM** value: **Cover or less**
Circ: Diamd. preorders: **3,411**
97 ☐ Aug 1998 Cover: 1.95 **NM** value: **Cover or less**
Circ: Diamd. preorders: **3,473**
98 ☐ Sep 1998 Cover: 1.95 **NM** value: **Cover or less**
Circ: Diamd. preorders: **3,133**
99 ☐ Nov 1998 Cover: 1.95 **NM** value: **Cover or less**
Circ: Diamd. preorders: **3,046**
100 ☐ Dec 1998 Cover: 1.95 **NM** value: **Cover or less**
Circ: Diamd. preorders: **3,461**
101 ☐ Feb 1999 Cover: 1.95 **NM** value: **Cover or less**
Circ: Diamd. preorders: **3,171**
102 ☐ Apr 1999 Cover: 1.99 **NM** value: **Cover or less**
Circ: Diamd. preorders: **2,810**
103 ☐ May 1999 Cover: 1.99 **NM** value: **Cover or less**
Circ: Diamd. preorders: **2,730**
104 ☐ Jul 1999 Cover: 1.99 **NM** value: **Cover or less**
Circ: Diamd. preorders: **2,814**
105 ☐ Aug 1999 Cover: 1.99 **NM** value: **Cover or less**
Circ: Diamd. preorders: **3,030**
106 ☐ Sep 1999 Cover: 1.99 **NM** value: **Cover or less**
Circ: Diamd. preorders: **2,943**
107 ☐ Nov 1999 Cover: 1.99 **NM** value: **Cover or less**
Circ: Diamd. preorders: **2,969**
108 ☐ Sep 1999 Cover: 1.99 **NM** value: **Cover or less**
Circ: Diamd. preorders: **2,668**
109 ☐ Feb 2000 Cover: 1.99 **NM** value: **Cover or less**
Circ: Diamd. preorders: **2,862**
110 ☐ Apr 2000 Cover: 1.99 **NM** value: **Cover or less**
Circ: Diamd. preorders: **2,865**
111 ☐ May 2000 Cover: 1.99 **NM** value: **Cover or less**
Circ: Diamd. preorders: **2,740**
112 ☐ Jul 2000 Cover: 2.19 **NM** value: **Cover or less**
Circ: Diamd. preorders: **2,555**
113 ☐ Aug 2000 Cover: 2.19 **NM** value: **Cover or less**
Circ: Diamd. preorders: **2,836**
114 ☐ Oct 2000 Cover: 2.19 **NM** value: **Cover or less**
Circ: Diamd. preorders: **3,065**
115 ☐ Nov 2000 Cover: 2.19 **NM** value: **Cover or less**
Circ: Diamd. preorders: **2,611**
116 ☐ Dec 2000 Cover: 2.19 **NM** value: **Cover or less**
Circ: Diamd. preorders: **2,564**
117 ☐ Feb 2001 Cover: 2.19 **NM** value: **Cover or less**
Circ: Diamd. preorders: **2,532**
118 ☐ Apr 2001 Cover: 2.19 **NM** value: **Cover or less**
Circ: Diamd. preorders: **2,516**
119 ☐ May 2001 Cover: 2.19 **NM** value: **Cover or less**
Circ: Diamd. preorders: **2,316**
120 ☐ Jun 2001 Cover: 2.19 **NM** value: **Cover or less**
Circ: Diamd. preorders: **2,451**
121 ☐ Aug 2001 Cover: 2.19 **NM** value: **Cover or less**
Circ: Diamd. preorders: **2,764**
122 ☐ Sep 2001 Cover: 2.19 **NM** value: **Cover or less**
Circ: Diamd. preorders: **3,049**
123 ☐ Oct 2001 Cover: 2.19 **NM** value: **Cover or less**
Circ: Diamd. preorders: **3,028**

BETTY AND VERONICA DOUBLE DIGEST — Archie

1 ☐ 1987 Cover: 2.75 **NM** value: **7.00**
2 ☐ 1987 Cover: 2.75 **NM** value: **4.00**
3 ☐ 1987 Cover: 2.75 **NM** value: **4.00**
4 ☐ Dec 1987 Cover: 2.75 **NM** value: **4.00**
5 ☐ 1988 Cover: 2.75 **NM** value: **4.00**
6 ☐ Cover: 2.75 **NM** value: **4.00**
7 ☐ Cover: 2.75 **NM** value: **4.00**
8 ☐ Cover: 2.75 **NM** value: **4.00**
9 ☐ Cover: 2.75 **NM** value: **4.00**
10 ☐ Cover: 2.75 **NM** value: **4.00**
11 ☐ Cover: 2.75 **NM** value: **3.00**
12 ☐ Cover: 2.75 **NM** value: **3.00**
13 ☐ Cover: 2.75 **NM** value: **3.00**
14 ☐ Cover: 2.75 **NM** value: **3.00**
15 ☐ Cover: 2.75 **NM** value: **3.00**
16 ☐ Cover: 2.75 **NM** value: **3.00**
17 ☐ Cover: 2.75 **NM** value: **3.00**
18 ☐ Cover: 2.75 **NM** value: **3.00**
19 ☐ Cover: 2.75 **NM** value: **3.00**
20 ☐ Cover: 2.75 **NM** value: **3.00**
21 ☐ Cover: 2.75 **NM** value: **3.00**
22 ☐ Cover: 2.75 **NM** value: **3.00**
23 ☐ Cover: 2.75 **NM** value: **3.00**
24 ☐ Cover: 2.75 **NM** value: **3.00**
25 ☐ Cover: 2.75 **NM** value: **3.00**

Other grades: Multiply prices above by **1.5 for Mint • 2/3 for Very Fine • 1/3 for Fine • 1/5 for Very Good • 1/8 for Good**

26 ❑ Cover: 2.75 **NM** value: **3.00**
27 ❑ Cover: 2.75 **NM** value: **3.00**
28 ❑ Cover: 2.75 **NM** value: **3.00**
29 ❑ Cover: 2.75 **NM** value: **3.00**
30 ❑ Cover: 2.75 **NM** value: **3.00**
31 ❑ Cover: 2.75 **NM** value: **3.00**
32 ❑ Jul 1992 Cover: 2.75 **NM** value: **3.00**
33 ❑ Sep 1992 Cover: 2.75 **NM** value: **3.00**
34 ❑ Cover: 2.75 **NM** value: **3.00**
35 ❑ Cover: 2.75 **NM** value: **3.00**
36 ❑ Cover: 2.75 **NM** value: **3.00**
37 ❑ 1993 Cover: 2.75 **NM** value: **3.00**
Circ: Statement: **161,725**
38 ❑ 1993 Cover: 2.75 **NM** value: **3.00**
Circ: Statement: **161,725**
39 ❑ 1993 Cover: 2.75 **NM** value: **3.00**
Circ: Statement: **161,725**
40 ❑ 1993 Cover: 2.75 **NM** value: **3.00**
Circ: Statement: **161,725**
📖 Summer Squall; Josie: Language Barrier; Li'l Jinx: Happy Mirthday; and more
41 ❑ 1993 Cover: 2.75 **NM** value: **3.00**
Circ: Statement: **161,725**
42 ❑ Cover: 2.75 **NM** value: **3.00**
43 ❑ Cover: 2.75 **NM** value: **3.00**
Circ: Statement: **150,607**
44 ❑ Cover: 2.75 **NM** value: **3.00**
Circ: Statement: **150,607**
45 ❑ Cover: 2.75 **NM** value: **3.00**
Circ: Statement: **150,607**
46 ❑ Cover: 2.75 **NM** value: **3.00**
Circ: Statement: **150,607**
47 ❑ 1994 Cover: 2.75 **NM** value: **3.00**
Circ: Statement: **150,607**
48 ❑ Dec 1994 Cover: 2.75 **NM** value: **3.00**
Circ: Statement: **150,607**
49 ❑ 1995 Cover: 2.75 **NM** value: **3.00**
Circ: Statement: **141,256**
50 ❑ Apr 1995 Cover: 2.75 **NM** value: **3.00**
Circ: Statement: **141,256**
51 ❑ Jun 1995 Cover: 2.75 **NM** value: **3.00**
Circ: Statement: **141,256**
52 ❑ Aug 1995 Cover: 2.75 **NM** value: **3.00**
Circ: Statement: **141,256**
53 ❑ Sep 1995 Cover: 2.75 **NM** value: **3.00**
Circ: Statement: **141,256**
54 ❑ 1995 Cover: 2.75 **NM** value: **3.00**
Circ: Statement: **141,256**
55 ❑ Jan 1996 Cover: 2.75 **NM** value: **3.00**
Circ: Statement: **140,086**
56 ❑ Mar 1996 Cover: 2.75 **NM** value: **3.00**
Circ: Statement: **140,086**
57 ❑ Apr 1996 Cover: 2.75 **NM** value: **3.00**
Circ: Statement: **140,086**
• Has 1995 Statement, filed 10/1/1995; avg print run 341,440; avg sales 139,124; avg subs 2,132; avg total paid 141,256; samples 376; office use 6,433; max existent 148,065; 57% of run returned
58 ❑ 1996 Cover: 2.75 **NM** value: **3.00**
Circ: Statement: **140,086**
59 ❑ Aug 1996 Cover: 2.75 **NM** value: **3.00**
Circ: Statement: **140,086**
60 ❑ Oct 1996 Cover: 2.75 **NM** value: **3.00**
Circ: Statement: **140,086**
61 ❑ Nov 1996 Cover: 2.75 **NM** value: **3.00**
Circ: Statement: **140,086**
62 ❑ Jan 1997 Cover: 2.75 **NM** value: **3.00**
Circ: Statement: **138,331** Direct Market orders: **4,053**
63 ❑ Mar 1997 Cover: 2.75 **NM** value: **3.00**
Circ: Statement: **138,331** Diamd. preorders: **3,599**
64 ❑ Apr 1997 Cover: 2.75 **NM** value: **3.00**
Circ: Statement: **138,331** Diamd. preorders: **3,824**
• Has1996 Statement, filed 9/27/1996; avg print run 331,530; avg sales 138,304; avg subs 1,782; avg total paid 140,086; samples 381; office use 3,546; max existent 144,013; 57% of run returned
65 ❑ Jun 1997 Cover: 2.75 **NM** value: **3.00**
Circ: Statement: **138,331** Diamd. preorders: **4,176**
66 ❑ Aug 1997 Cover: 2.79 **NM** value: **3.00**
Circ: Statement: **138,331** Diamd. preorders: **4,494**
67 ❑ Sep 1997 Cover: 2.79 **NM** value: **3.00**
Circ: Statement: **138,331** Diamd. preorders: **4,582**
68 ❑ Nov 1997 Cover: 2.79 **NM** value: **3.00**
Circ: Statement: **138,331**
69 ❑ Jan 1998 Cover: 2.95 **NM** value: **3.00**
Circ: Statement: **133,972** Diamd. preorders: **4,434**
70 ❑ Mar 1998 Cover: 2.95 **NM** value: **3.00**
Circ: Statement: **133,972**
71 ❑ Apr 1998 Cover: 2.95 **NM** value: **3.00**
Circ: Statement: **133,972** Diamd. preorders: **4,276**
• Has 1997 Statement, filed 11/1/1997; avg print run 327,032; avg sales 136,622; avg subs 1,709; avg total paid 138,331; samples 459; office use 4,882; max existent 143,672; 56% of run returned
72 ❑ Jun 1998 Cover: 2.95 **NM** value: **3.00**
Circ: Statement: **133,972** Diamd. preorders: **3,655**
73 ❑ Jul 1998 Cover: 2.95 **NM** value: **3.00**
Circ: Statement: **133,972** Diamd. preorders: **4,307**
74 ❑ Sep 1998 Cover: 2.95 **NM** value: **3.00**
Circ: Statement: **133,972** Diamd. preorders: **3,638**
75 ❑ Oct 1998 Cover: 2.95 **NM** value: **3.00**
Circ: Statement: **133,972** Diamd. preorders: **3,370**
76 ❑ Dec 1998 Cover: 2.95 **NM** value: **3.00**
Circ: Statement: **133,972** Diamd. preorders: **3,832**
77 ❑ Jan 1999 Cover: 2.95 **NM** value: **3.00**
Circ: Diamd. preorders: **4,094**
78 ❑ Mar 1999 Cover: 2.95 **NM** value: **3.00**
Circ: Diamd. preorders: **3,916**
79 ❑ Apr 1999 Cover: 2.99 **NM** value: **3.00**
Circ: Diamd. preorders: **3,420**
• Has 1998 Statement, filed 11/1/1998; avg print run 312,592; avg sales 131,978; avg subs 1,994; avg total paid 133,972; samples 421; office use 6,184; max existent 140,577;100 % of run returned
80 ❑ Jun 1999 Cover: 2.99 **NM** value: **3.00**
Circ: Diamd. preorders: **3,354**
81 ❑ Jul 1999 Cover: 2.99 **NM** value: **3.00**
Circ: Diamd. preorders: **3,479**
82 ❑ Sep 1999 Cover: 2.99 **NM** value: **3.00**
Circ: Diamd. preorders: **3,558**
83 ❑ Oct 1999 Cover: 2.99 **NM** value: **3.00**
Circ: Diamd. preorders: **3,714**
84 ❑ Dec 1999 Cover: 2.99 **NM** value: **3.00**
Circ: Diamd. preorders: **3,061**
85 ❑ Jan 2000 Cover: 2.99 **NM** value: **3.00**
Circ: Diamd. preorders: **3,147**
86 ❑ Mar 2000 Cover: 2.99 **NM** value: **3.00**
Circ: Diamd. preorders: **3,621**
87 ❑ Apr 2000 Cover: 2.99 **NM** value: **3.00**
Circ: Diamd. preorders: **3,502**
88 ❑ Jun 2000 Cover: 3.19 **NM** value: **Cover or less**
Circ: Diamd. preorders: **3,338**
89 ❑ Jul 2000 Cover: 3.19 **NM** value: **Cover or less**
Circ: Diamd. preorders: **2,853**
90 ❑ Sep 2000 Cover: 3.19 **NM** value: **Cover or less**
Circ: Diamd. preorders: **3,877**
91 ❑ Oct 2000 Cover: 3.19 **NM** value: **Cover or less**
Circ: Diamd. preorders: **3,686**
92 ❑ Nov 2000 Cover: 3.19 **NM** value: **Cover or less**
Circ: Diamd. preorders: **3,091**
93 ❑ Jan 2001 Cover: 3.19 **NM** value: **Cover or less**
Circ: Diamd. preorders: **3,228**
94 ❑ Feb 2001 Cover: 3.19 **NM** value: **Cover or less**
Circ: Diamd. preorders: **3,078**
95 ❑ Apr 2001 Cover: 3.29 **NM** value: **Cover or less**
Circ: Diamd. preorders: **2,782**

BETTY AND VERONICA SPECTACULAR Archie

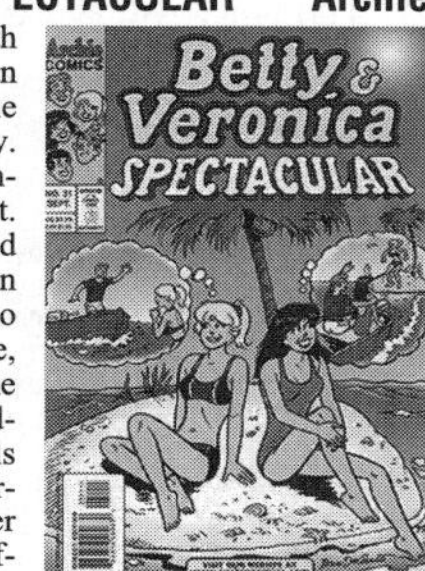

Blonde, perky, and beautiful with a personality that's sweeter than honey, Betty Cooper has a smile that will brighten the darkest day. She's kind, generous to a fault, considerate, and a tomboy at heart. Sexy, gorgeous, sophisticated, and rich to the hilt, Veronica Lodge can literally bring traffic screeching to a halt. She's glamour, style, culture, and class, all wrapped up in one stunning package. There is a good-natured rivalry between the girls over the usual items: boys, popularity, and intelligence. But neither will compromise on their mutual affection for one lucky guy, Archie Andrews. When Cheryl Blossom comes back with #14 and begins attracting Archie's attention as well, the girls join forces against their new competition. But for most of the run, the duo's competition is each other, and their friendship is, too.

1 ❑ Oct 1992 Cover: 1.25 **NM** value: **3.00**
2 ❑ Cover: 1.25 **NM** value: **2.50**
3 ❑ May 1993 Cover: 1.25 **NM** value: **2.50**
4 ❑ 1993 Cover: 1.25 **NM** value: **2.00**
5 ❑ Oct 1993 Cover: 1.25 **NM** value: **2.00**
6 ❑ Feb 1994 Cover: 1.25 **NM** value: **2.00**
7 ❑ Apr 1994 Cover: 1.25 **NM** value: **2.00**
8 ❑ May 1994 Cover: 1.25 **NM** value: **2.00**
9 ❑ Jul 1994 Cover: 1.25 **NM** value: **1.75**
10 ❑ Sep 1994 Cover: 1.50 **NM** value: **1.75**
11 ❑ Nov 1994 Cover: 1.50 **NM** value: **1.75**
12 ❑ Jan 1995 Cover: 1.50 **NM** value: **1.75**
13 ❑ Feb 1995 Cover: 1.50 **NM** value: **1.75**
14 ❑ Apr 1995 Cover: 1.50 **NM** value: **1.75**
15 ❑ Jul 1995 Cover: 1.50 **NM** value: **1.75**
16 ❑ Oct 1995 Cover: 1.50 **NM** value: **1.75**
17 ❑ Jan 1996 Cover: 1.50 **NM** value: **1.75**
Circ: Statement: **32,017**
18 ❑ Apr 1996 Cover: 1.50 **NM** value: **1.75**
Circ: Statement: **32,017**
19 ❑ Jul 1996 Cover: 1.50 **NM** value: **1.75**
Circ: Statement: **32,017**
20 ❑ Oct 1996 Cover: 1.50 **NM** value: **1.75**
Circ: Statement: **32,017**
21 ❑ Jan 1997 Cover: 1.50 **NM** value: **1.75**
Circ: Statement: **28,375** Direct Market orders: **4,193**
• Betty becomes a fashion model
22 ❑ Mar 1997 Cover: 1.50 **NM** value: **1.75**
Circ: Statement: **28,375** Diamd. preorders: **3,944**
23 ❑ May 1997 Cover: 1.50 **NM** value: **1.75**
Circ: Statement: **28,375** Diamd. preorders: **3,599**
• Has 1996 Statement, filed 9/27/96; avg print run 91,735; avg sales 30,559; avg subs 1,418; avg total paid 32,017; samples 417; office use 1,633; max existent 34,027; 63% of run returned
24 ❑ Jul 1997 Cover: 1.50 **NM** value: **1.75**
Circ: Statement: **28,375** Diamd. preorders: **3,745**
• Betty and Veronica set up web pages
25 ❑ Sep 1997 Cover: 1.50 **NM** value: **1.75**
Circ: Statement: **28,375** Diamd. preorders: **4,230**
26 ❑ Nov 1997 Cover: 1.50 **NM** value: **1.75**
Circ: Statement: **28,375** Diamd. preorders: **4,217**
27 ❑ Feb 1998 Cover: 1.75 **NM** value: **Cover or less**
Circ: Diamd. preorders: **4,484**
28 ❑ Mar 1998 Cover: 1.75 **NM** value: **Cover or less**
29 ❑ May 1998 Cover: 1.75 **NM** value: **Cover or less**
Circ: Diamd. preorders: **3,642**
• Has 1997 Statement, filed 11/1/97; avg print run 84,318; avg sales 27,272; avg subs 1,103; avg total paid 28,375; samples 427; office use 3,208; max existent 32,010; 62% of run returned
30 ❑ Jul 1998 Cover: 1.75 **NM** value: **Cover or less**
Circ: Diamd. preorders: **3,984**
31 ❑ Sep 1998 Cover: 1.75 **NM** value: **Cover or less**
Circ: Diamd. preorders: **3,811**
📖 Lost At Sea; How Refreshing; Burned Up **A:** Fernando Ruiz **W:** Dan Parent
32 ❑ Nov 1998 Cover: 1.75 **NM** value: **Cover or less**
Circ: Diamd. preorders: **3,420**
📖 Maid for Each Other • Betty and Veronica are maids for each other **A:** Fernando Ruiz **W:** Kathleen Webb
33 ❑ Jan 1999 Cover: 1.75 **NM** value: **Cover or less**
Circ: Diamd. preorders: **3,464**
• talent competition
34 ❑ Mar 1999 Cover: 1.75 **NM** value: **Cover or less**
Circ: Diamd. preorders: **3,191**
📖 Give Me the Simple Life **A:** Fernando Ruiz **W:** George Gladir
35 ❑ May 1999 Cover: 1.79 **NM** value: **Cover or less**
Circ: Diamd. preorders: **2,936**
📖 Swing Time • Swing issue **W:** Dan Parent
36 ❑ Jul 1999 Cover: 1.79 **NM** value: **Cover or less**
Circ: Diamd. preorders: **3,116**
37 ❑ Sep 1999 Cover: 1.79 **NM** value: **Cover or less**
Circ: Diamd. preorders: **3,217**
38 ❑ Nov 1999 Cover: 1.79 **NM** value: **Cover or less**
Circ: Diamd. preorders: **2,913**
39 ❑ Jan 2000 Cover: 1.79 **NM** value: **Cover or less**
Circ: Diamd. preorders: **2,973**
40 ❑ Mar 2000 Cover: 1.79 **NM** value: **Cover or less**
41 ❑ May 2000 Cover: 1.79 **NM** value: **Cover or less**
Circ: Diamd. preorders: **2,558**
42 ❑ Jul 2000 Cover: 1.99 **NM** value: **Cover or less**
Circ: Diamd. preorders: **2,691**
43 ❑ Sep 2000 Cover: 1.99 **NM** value: **Cover or less**
Circ: Diamd. preorders: **3,171**
44 ❑ Nov 2000 Cover: 1.99 **NM** value: **Cover or less**
Circ: Diamd. preorders: **2,922**
45 ❑ Jan 2001 Cover: 1.99 **NM** value: **Cover or less**
Circ: Diamd. preorders: **2,833**

BETTY & VERONICA SUMMER FUN Archie

1 ❑ Sum 1994 Cover: 2.00 **NM** value: **2.50**
2 ❑ Sum 1995 Cover: 2.00 **NM** value: **2.50**
3 ❑ Sum 1996 Cover: 2.00 **NM** value: **2.50**
4 ❑ Sum 1997 Cover: 2.00 **NM** value: **2.50**
5 ❑ Sum 1998 Cover: 2.25 **NM** value: **Cover or less**
📖 Surf on Turf; Dizzy Tizzy; Paper Caper; Animal E. R.; Razor Razzer; Peace & Chaos; Hold This; The New Thrill; Wave Waver; What's in a Name?; The Edge; Free as a Bird **A:** Fernando Ruiz; Stan Goldberg; Dan Parent; Adal Maldonado; Kate Worley **W:** Barbara Slate; Dan Parent; George Gladir; Smith
6 ❑ Sum 1999 Cover: 2.29 **NM** value: **Cover or less**

BETTY BOOP 3-D Blackthorne

1 ❑ Nov 1986 Cover: 2.50 **NM** value: **Cover or less**
Circ: CapCity orders: **3,300**
📖 The Contract **A:** Bud Counihan **W:** Bud Counihan

BETTY BOOP'S BIG BREAK First

1 ❑ Cover: 5.95 **NM** value: **Cover or less**
No issue number.

BETTY IN BONDAGE: BETTY MAE Shunga

1 ❑ Cover: 6.95 **NM** value: **Cover or less**
A: Teo Jonelli **W:** Teo Jonelli

BETTY IN BONDAGE (TEO JONELLI'S...) Shunga

All issues are adults only.

1 ❑ b&w Cover: 3.00 **NM** value: **Cover or less**
A: Teo Jonelli
2 ❑ b&w Cover: 3.00 **NM** value: **Cover or less**
A: Teo Jonelli
3 ❑ b&w Cover: 3.00 **NM** value: **Cover or less**
A: Teo Jonelli
4 ❑ b&w Cover: 3.00 **NM** value: **Cover or less**
A: Teo Jonelli
5 ❑ Cover: 3.00 **NM** value: **Cover or less**
A: Teo Jonelli
6 ❑ Cover: 3.00 **NM** value: **Cover or less**
A: Teo Jonelli
7 ❑ Cover: 3.00 **NM** value: **Cover or less**
A: Teo Jonelli
8 ❑ Cover: 3.00 **NM** value: **Cover or less**
A: Teo Jonelli
Anl 1❑ Cover: 5.95 **NM** value: **Cover or less**
• 1993 Annual **A:** Teo Jonelli
Anl 2❑ Cover: 5.95 **NM** value: **Cover or less**
• 1994 Annual **A:** Teo Jonelli
Anl 3❑ Cover: 5.95 **NM** value: **Cover or less**
• 1995 Annual **A:** Teo Jonelli

BETTY PAGE 3-D COMICS 3-D Zone

1 ❑ Cover: 3.95 **NM** value: **Cover or less**
Circ: CapCity orders: **2,550**

BETTY PAGE 3-D PICTURE BOOK, THE 3-D Zone

1 ❑ Cover: 3.95 **NM** value: **Cover or less**
• photos, adult

BETTY PAGE CAPTURED JUNGLE GIRL 3-D 3-D Zone

1 ❑ Cover: 3.95 **NM** value: **Cover or less**
• photos

CGC-graded: Multiply prices above by **33 for 9.9 M • 16 for 9.8 NM/M • 7 for 9.6 NM+ • 5 for 9.4 NM • 2.5 for 9.2 NM- • 1.5 for 9.0 VF/NM**

BETTY PAGES, THE — Pure Imagination

1 ❑ Cover: 5.00 **NM** value: **6.00**
• Ward, photos **A:** Dave Stevens
1-2 ❑ Cover: 5.00 **NM** value: **Cover or less**
2 ❑ Cover: 5.00 **NM** value: **Cover or less**
2-2 ❑ Cover: 5.00 **NM** value: **Cover or less**
3 ❑ Cover: 5.00 **NM** value: **Cover or less**
4 ❑ Cover: 5.00 **NM** value: **Cover or less**
5 ❑ Win 1989 Cover: 4.50 **NM** value: **Cover or less**
6 ❑ Cover: 4.50 **NM** value: **Cover or less**
7 ❑ Cover: 4.50 **NM** value: **Cover or less**
8 ❑ Cover: 4.50 **NM** value: **Cover or less**
9 ❑ Cover: 5.00 **NM** value: **Cover or less**

BETTY PAGE: THE 50'S RAGE — Illustration

Betty [aka Bettie Mae] Page (1923-) was one of the most popular pinup girls of the 20th century. Her ability to project the image of exuberance, youth, eagerness, and sheer delight while maintaining an unquenchable beauty made the magazines and other spots where her photos appeared true collectors' items. Her poses ran the gamut from simple attractive poses to unabashed full nudity.

Don Paresi has put together a pinup portfolio of his Betty drawings that capture the feel of her classic poses. Along with material and help from Steve Woron, this set is as inviting and playful as Betty herself. Like many of the photographs of the model, it's for adults only.

1/A ❑ Jan 1993 Cover: 3.25 **NM** value: **Cover or less**
tame cover. **A:** Don Paresi; Steve Woron
1/B ❑ Jan 1993 Cover: 3.25 **NM** value: **Cover or less**
Adult cover. **A:** Don Paresi; Steve Woron
2/A ❑ Cover: 3.25 **NM** value: **Cover or less**
tame cover. **A:** Don Paresi; Steve Woron
2/B ❑ Cover: 3.25 **NM** value: **Cover or less**
Adult cover. **A:** Don Paresi; Steve Woron

BETTY'S DIARY — Archie

1 ❑ 1986 Cover: 0.75 **NM** value: **3.00**
2 ❑ 1986 Cover: 0.75 **NM** value: **2.00**
3 ❑ 1986 Cover: 0.75 **NM** value: **2.00**
4 ❑ 1986 Cover: 0.75 **NM** value: **2.00**
5 ❑ 1986 Cover: 0.75 **NM** value: **2.00**
6 ❑ 1986 Cover: 0.75 **NM** value: **1.50**
7 ❑ 1987 Cover: 0.75 **NM** value: **1.50**
Circ: Statement: **58,797**
8 ❑ 1987 Cover: 0.75 **NM** value: **1.50**
Circ: Statement: **58,797**
9 ❑ 1987 Cover: 0.75 **NM** value: **1.50**
Circ: Statement: **58,797**
10 ❑ 1987 Cover: 0.75 **NM** value: **1.50**
Circ: Statement: **58,797**
11 ❑ 1987 Cover: 0.75 **NM** value: **1.50**
Circ: Statement: **58,797**
12 ❑ 1987 Cover: 0.75 **NM** value: **1.50**
Circ: Statement: **58,797**
13 ❑ 1987 Cover: 0.75 **NM** value: **1.50**
Circ: Statement: **58,797**
14 ❑ 1987 Cover: 0.75 **NM** value: **1.50**
Circ: Statement: **58,797**
15 ❑ 1988 Cover: 0.75 **NM** value: **1.50**
Circ: Statement: **56,950**
16 ❑ 1988 Cover: 0.75 **NM** value: **1.50**
Circ: Statement: **56,950**
17 ❑ 1988 Cover: 0.75 **NM** value: **1.50**
Circ: Statement: **56,950**
18 ❑ 1988 Cover: 0.75 **NM** value: **1.50**
Circ: Statement: **56,950**
19 ❑ 1988 Cover: 0.75 **NM** value: **1.50**
Circ: Statement: **56,950**
20 ❑ 1988 Cover: 0.75 **NM** value: **1.50**
Circ: Statement: **56,950**
21 ❑ 1988 Cover: 0.75 **NM** value: **1.00**
Circ: Statement: **56,950**
22 ❑ 1988 Cover: 0.75 **NM** value: **1.00**
Circ: Statement: **56,950**
23 ❑ 1989 Cover: 0.75 **NM** value: **1.00**
Circ: Statement: **56,808**
24 ❑ 1989 Cover: 0.75 **NM** value: **1.00**
Circ: Statement: **56,808**
25 ❑ 1989 Cover: 0.75 **NM** value: **1.00**
Circ: Statement: **56,808**
26 ❑ 1989 Cover: 0.75 **NM** value: **1.00**
Circ: Statement: **56,808**
27 ❑ 1989 Cover: 0.75 **NM** value: **1.00**
Circ: Statement: **56,808**
28 ❑ 1989 Cover: 0.75 **NM** value: **1.00**
Circ: Statement: **56,808**
29 ❑ 1989 Cover: 0.75 **NM** value: **1.00**
Circ: Statement: **56,808**
30 ❑ 1989 Cover: 0.75 **NM** value: **1.00**
Circ: Statement: **56,808**
31 ❑ 1990 Cover: 0.75 **NM** value: **1.00**
Circ: Statement: **49,751**
32 ❑ 1990 Cover: 0.75 **NM** value: **1.00**
Circ: Statement: **49,751**
33 ❑ 1990 Cover: 0.75 **NM** value: **1.00**
Circ: Statement: **49,751**
34 ❑ 1990 Cover: 0.75 **NM** value: **1.00**
Circ: Statement: **49,751**
35 ❑ 1990 Cover: 0.75 **NM** value: **1.00**
Circ: Statement: **49,751**
36 ❑ 1990 Cover: 0.75 **NM** value: **1.00**
Circ: Statement: **49,751**
37 ❑ 1990 Cover: 0.75 **NM** value: **1.00**
Circ: Statement: **49,751**
38 ❑ 1990 Cover: 0.75 **NM** value: **1.00**
Circ: Statement: **49,751**
39 ❑ 1991 Cover: 0.75 **NM** value: **1.00**
40 ❑ 1991 Cover: 0.75 **NM** value: **1.00**

BETTY'S DIGEST MAGAZINE — Archie

1 ❑ Nov 1996 Cover: 1.79 **NM** value: **2.00**
2 ❑ Nov 1997 Cover: 1.79 **NM** value: **2.00**

BEVERLY HILLBILLIES, THE — Dell

1 ❑ Apr 1963 Cover: 0.12 **NM** value: **60.00**
Photo cover.
2 ❑ Jul 1963 Cover: 0.12 **NM** value: **35.00**
• **CGC:** 1 graded, best 9.4
3 ❑ Oct 1963 Cover: 0.12 **NM** value: **25.00**
• **CGC:** 2 graded, best 9.2
4 ❑ Jan 1964 Cover: 0.12 **NM** value: **20.00**
• **CGC:** 6 graded, best 9.6
5 ❑ Apr 1964 Cover: 0.12 **NM** value: **20.00**
• **CGC:** 2 graded, best 9.6
6 ❑ Jul 1964 Cover: 0.12 **NM** value: **15.00**
• **CGC:** 1 graded, best 9.4
7 ❑ Oct 1964 Cover: 0.12 **NM** value: **15.00**
• **CGC:** 1 graded, best 9.2
8 ❑ Jan 1965 Cover: 0.12 **NM** value: **15.00**
• **CGC:** 1 graded, best 8.0
9 ❑ Apr 1965 Cover: 0.12 **NM** value: **15.00**
• **CGC:** 1 graded, best 9.4
10 ❑ ca. 1965 Cover: 0.12 **NM** value: **15.00**
11 ❑ Dec 1965 Cover: 0.12 **NM** value: **12.00**
• **CGC:** 1 graded, best 9.4
12 ❑ Mar 1966 Cover: 0.12 **NM** value: **12.00**
13 ❑ Jun 1966 Cover: 0.12 **NM** value: **12.00**
14 ❑ Sep 1966 Cover: 0.12 **NM** value: **12.00**
• **CGC:** 1 graded, best 9.0
15 ❑ Dec 1966 Cover: 0.12 **NM** value: **12.00**
16 ❑ Mar 1967 Cover: 0.12 **NM** value: **12.00**
17 ❑ May 1967 Cover: 0.12 **NM** value: **12.00**
18 ❑ Aug 1967 Cover: 0.12 **NM** value: **10.00**
19 ❑ Oct 1969 Cover: 0.15 **NM** value: **10.00**
Same cover as #1.
20 ❑ Oct 1970 Cover: 0.15 **NM** value: **10.00**
• **CGC:** 1 graded, best 9.0
21 ❑ Oct 1971 Cover: 0.15 **NM** value: **10.00**

BEWARE — Trojan

1 ❑ Jan 1953 Cover: 0.10 **NM** value: **350.00**
• **CGC:** 2 graded, best 7.5
2 ❑ Mar 1953 Cover: 0.10 **NM** value: **250.00**
3 ❑ May 1953 Cover: 0.10 **NM** value: **200.00**
4 ❑ Jul 1953 Cover: 0.10 **NM** value: **200.00**
• **CGC:** 1 graded, best 7.5
5 ❑ Sep 1953 Cover: 0.10 **NM** value: **150.00**
6 ❑ Nov 1953 Cover: 0.10 **NM** value: **150.00**
• **CGC:** 1 graded, best 8.0
7 ❑ Jan 1954 Cover: 0.10 **NM** value: **150.00**
8 ❑ Mar 1954 Cover: 0.10 **NM** value: **150.00**
• **CGC:** 1 graded, best 7.5
9 ❑ May 1954 Cover: 0.10 **NM** value: **150.00**
• **CGC:** 1 graded, best 7.5
10 ❑ Jul 1954 Cover: 0.10 **NM** value: **150.00**
• **CGC:** 4 graded, best 9.0
11 ❑ Sep 1954 Cover: 0.10 **NM** value: **125.00**
• **CGC:** 1 graded, best 7.5
12 ❑ Nov 1954 Cover: 0.10 **NM** value: **125.00**
13 ❑ Jan 1955 Cover: 0.10 **NM** value: **125.00**
• **CGC:** 1 graded, best 6.5
14 ❑ Mar 1955 Cover: 0.10 **NM** value: **125.00**
15 ❑ May 1955 Cover: 0.10 **NM** value: **125.00**

BEWARE (MARVEL) — Marvel

When the Comics Code was originally devised in 1954, it specifically prohibited "scenes dealing with, or instruments associated with walking dead, torture, vampires, and vampirism, ghouls, cannibalism, and werewolfism." Other parts of the Code prohibited "scenes of horror, excessive bloodshed, gory or gruesome crimes" as well as "all lurid, unsavory, gruesome illustrations." Almost overnight, horror comics that had been so popular in the '50s began to die off, having been stripped of both their favorite monsters and the essence of the genre. Countless stories, ready for publication, were destined for the file drawer, instead.

The Code was relaxed a bit in 1971, ushering in a blitz of such monster and werewolf titles as Frankenstein (The Monster of...), Werewolf by Night, and catalog titles like Crypt of Shadows. Beware was another such Marvel effort, reprinting forgotten (and generally average) monster stories from the 1950s.

1 ❑ Mar 1973 Cover: 0.20 **NM** value: **6.00**
• **CGC:** 5 graded, best 9.4
📖 The Werewolf Was Afraid; On the Trail of the Witch; Behind the Door • "Witch" reprinted from Tales of Suspense #27
2 ❑ May 1973 Cover: 0.20 **NM** value: **4.00**
• **CGC:** 1 graded, best 9.0
3 ❑ Jul 1973 Cover: 0.20 **NM** value: **4.00**
• **CGC:** 1 graded, best 9.4
4 ❑ Sep 1973 Cover: 0.20 **NM** value: **4.00**
5 ❑ Nov 1973 Cover: 0.20 **NM** value: **4.00**
6 ❑ Jan 1974 Cover: 0.20 **NM** value: **4.00**
7 ❑ Mar 1974 Cover: 0.20 **NM** value: **4.00**
8 ❑ May 1974 Cover: 0.25 **NM** value: **4.00**
• Series continued in Tomb of Darkness #9

BEWARE TERROR TALES — Fawcett

1 ❑ May 1952 Cover: 0.10 **NM** value: **300.00**
• **CGC:** 5 graded, best 9.2
2 ❑ Jul 1952 Cover: 0.10 **NM** value: **200.00**
• **CGC:** 2 graded, best 9.0
3 ❑ Sep 1952 Cover: 0.10 **NM** value: **150.00**
4 ❑ Nov 1952 Cover: 0.10 **NM** value: **150.00**
• **CGC:** 1 graded, best 8.5
5 ❑ Jan 1953 Cover: 0.10 **NM** value: **150.00**
• **CGC:** 1 graded, best 4.5
6 ❑ Mar 1953 Cover: 0.10 **NM** value: **150.00**
• **CGC:** 2 graded, best 8.0
7 ❑ May 1953 Cover: 0.10 **NM** value: **150.00**
• **CGC:** 2 graded, best 9.0
8 ❑ Jul 1953 Cover: 0.10 **NM** value: **150.00**
• **CGC:** 1 graded, best 8.5

BEWARE THE CREEPER — DC

First appearing in Showcase #73 (Apr 68), The Creeper soon moved into this solo series. The Creeper's true identity was Jack Ryder, a security agent. While searching for a kidnapped scientist, he was forced to don an impromptu costume and infiltrate a costume party. Once there, he located the scientist but was stabbed by the kidnappers in the process. The scientist gave Ryder an injection which gave him superstrength and implanted a "molecular rearranger" in his body. This device, when triggered by an activator attached to his wristwatch, makes The Creeper's costume appear and disappear.

These new abilities, of course, make The Creeper a natural super-hero. Looking a bit demented in his costume, Ryder also cultivates a maniacal laugh which makes him all the more terrifying to criminals. However, it also leads many to consider him a criminal.

1 ❑ Jun 1968 Cover: 0.12 **NM** value: **40.00**
• **CGC:** 53 graded, best 9.8
A: Steve Ditko
2 ❑ Aug 1968 Cover: 0.12 **NM** value: **25.00**
• **CGC:** 2 graded, best 9.4
A: Steve Ditko
3 ❑ Oct 1968 Cover: 0.12 **NM** value: **25.00**
• **CGC:** 2 graded, best 9.6
A: Steve Ditko
4 ❑ Dec 1968 Cover: 0.12 **NM** value: **25.00**
• **CGC:** 1 graded, best 8.0
A: Steve Ditko
5 ❑ Feb 1969 Cover: 0.12 **NM** value: **20.00**
• **CGC:** 1 graded, best 8.0
A: Steve Ditko
6 ❑ Apr 1969 Cover: 0.12 **NM** value: **20.00**
• **CGC:** 1 graded, best 7.5
final issue. **A:** Steve Ditko

BEWITCHED — Dell

1 ❑ Apr 1965 Cover: 0.12 **NM** value: **125.00**
• **CGC:** 2 graded, best 9.0
2 ❑ Jul 1965 Cover: 0.12 **NM** value: **75.00**
3 ❑ Oct 1965 Cover: 0.12 **NM** value: **50.00**
4 ❑ Mar 1966 Cover: 0.12 **NM** value: **50.00**
5 ❑ Jun 1966 Cover: 0.12 **NM** value: **50.00**
6 ❑ Sep 1966 Cover: 0.12 **NM** value: **50.00**
7 ❑ Dec 1966 Cover: 0.12 **NM** value: **50.00**
• **CGC:** 1 graded, best 7.5
8 ❑ Mar 1967 Cover: 0.12 **NM** value: **50.00**
• **CGC:** 2 graded, best 9.4
9 ❑ Apr 1967 Cover: 0.12 **NM** value: **50.00**
• **CGC:** 1 graded, best 7.5
10 ❑ Jul 1967 Cover: 0.12 **NM** value: **50.00**
📖 Witch Pretty Baby?; Beach Boy Darrin; Noisy Neighbors
11 ❑ Oct 1967 Cover: 0.12 **NM** value: **45.00**
12 ❑ Oct 1968 Cover: 0.12 **NM** value: **45.00**
• **CGC:** 1 graded, best 9.4
13 ❑ Jan 1969 Cover: 0.12 **NM** value: **45.00**
14 ❑ Oct 1969 Cover: 0.12 **NM** value: **45.00**

BEYOND — Blue

1 ❑ Jun 1996 Cover: 2.95 **NM** value: **Cover or less**

BEYOND — Ace

1 ❑ Nov 1950 Cover: 0.10 **NM** value: **Cover or less**
• **CGC:** 3 graded, best 8.0
2 ❑ Jan 1951 Cover: 0.10 **NM** value: **250.00**
• **CGC:** 2 graded, best 9.2
3 ❑ Mar 1951 Cover: 0.10 **NM** value: **175.00**
• **CGC:** 2 graded, best 7.0
4 ❑ May 1951 Cover: 0.10 **NM** value: **100.00**
• **CGC:** 1 graded, best 7.5
5 ❑ Jul 1951 Cover: 0.10 **NM** value: **100.00**
6 ❑ Sep 1951 Cover: 0.10 **NM** value: **100.00**
• **CGC:** 1 graded, best 4.5
7 ❑ Nov 1951 Cover: 0.10 **NM** value: **100.00**
• **CGC:** 1 graded, best 5.0
8 ❑ Jan 1952 Cover: 0.10 **NM** value: **100.00**
• **CGC:** 1 graded, best 7.5
9 ❑ Mar 1952 Cover: 0.10 **NM** value: **100.00**
10 ❑ Apr 1952 Cover: 0.10 **NM** value: **100.00**
11 ❑ May 1952 Cover: 0.10 **NM** value: **75.00**
• **CGC:** 1 graded, best 7.0
12 ❑ Jun 1952 Cover: 0.10 **NM** value: **75.00**
• **CGC:** 2 graded, best 8.0
13 ❑ Jul 1952 Cover: 0.10 **NM** value: **75.00**
• **CGC:** 1 graded, best 5.0

Other grades: Multiply prices above by **1.5 for Mint • 2/3 for Very Fine • 1/3 for Fine • 1/5 for Very Good • 1/8 for Good**

14 ❑ Aug 1952 Cover: 0.10 **NM** value: **75.00**
15 ❑ Sep 1952 Cover: 0.10 **NM** value: **75.00**
16 ❑ Oct 1952 Cover: 0.10 **NM** value: **75.00**
• **CGC:** 1 graded, best 7.5
17 ❑ Nov 1952 Cover: 0.10 **NM** value: **75.00**
18 ❑ Jan 1953 Cover: 0.10 **NM** value: **75.00**
• **CGC:** 2 graded, best 7.5
19 ❑ Mar 1953 Cover: 0.10 **NM** value: **75.00**
20 ❑ May 1953 Cover: 0.10 **NM** value: **75.00**
• **CGC:** 1 graded, best 7.0
21 ❑ Jul 1953 Cover: 0.10 **NM** value: **60.00**
22 ❑ Sep 1953 Cover: 0.10 **NM** value: **60.00**
23 ❑ Nov 1953 Cover: 0.10 **NM** value: **60.00**
24 ❑ Jan 1954 Cover: 0.10 **NM** value: **60.00**
25 ❑ Mar 1954 Cover: 0.10 **NM** value: **60.00**
26 ❑ May 1954 Cover: 0.10 **NM** value: **60.00**
27 ❑ Jul 1954 Cover: 0.10 **NM** value: **60.00**
28 ❑ Sep 1954 Cover: 0.10 **NM** value: **60.00**
29 ❑ Nov 1954 Cover: 0.10 **NM** value: **60.00**
30 ❑ Jan 1955 Cover: 0.10 **NM** value: **60.00**

BEYOND COMMUNION — Caliber

1 ❑ Cover: 2.95 **NM** value: **Cover or less**
A: Shane White **W:** Martin Powell; Whitley Strieber

BEYOND MARS — Blackthorne

0 ❑ Cover: 2.00 **NM** value: **Cover or less**
• book 1-3
1 ❑ Cover: 6.95 **NM** value: **Cover or less**
2 ❑ Cover: 6.95 **NM** value: **Cover or less**

BEYOND THE GRAVE — Charlton

1 ❑ Jul 1975 Cover: 0.25 **NM** value: **6.00**
• **CGC:** 1 graded, best 9.0
2 ❑ Oct 1975 Cover: 0.25 **NM** value: **4.00**
3 ❑ Dec 1975 Cover: 0.25 **NM** value: **4.00**
4 ❑ Feb 1976 Cover: 0.25 **NM** value: **3.00**
5 ❑ Cover: 0.25 **NM** value: **3.00**
6 ❑ Jun 1976 Cover: 0.25 **NM** value: **2.50**
The Stones of Brytagalon; Three Went Forth; Creatures (Text Story); They Got Away **A:** Rich Larson; C. Nicholas **W:** Tim Boxell; Joe Gill
7 ❑ Cover: 0.25 **NM** value: **2.50**
8 ❑ Cover: 0.25 **NM** value: **2.50**
9 ❑ Cover: 0.25 **NM** value: **2.50**
10 ❑ Aug 1983 Cover: 0.60 **NM** value: **2.50**
11 ❑ 1983 Cover: 0.60 **NM** value: **2.50**
12 ❑ 1983 Cover: 0.60 **NM** value: **2.50**
13 ❑ Feb 1984 Cover: 0.60 **NM** value: **2.50**
14 ❑ Apr 1984 Cover: 0.60 **NM** value: **2.50**
15 ❑ Jun 1984 Cover: 0.60 **NM** value: **2.50**
16 ❑ Aug 1984 Cover: 0.60 **NM** value: **2.50**
17 ❑ Cover: 0.60 **NM** value: **2.50**
final issue.

BIG — Dark Horse

1 ❑ Mar 1989 Cover: 2.00 **NM** value: **2.50**
• adaptation

BIG ALL-AMERICAN COMIC BOOK — DC

1 ❑ ca. 1944 Cover: 0.25 **NM** value: **11000.00**
• **CGC:** 6 graded, best 8.5

BIG BAD BLOOD OF DRACULA — Apple

1 ❑ Cover: 2.75 **NM** value: **Cover or less**
• reprints, b&w **A:** Bernie Wrightson
2 ❑ Cover: 2.95 **NM** value: **Cover or less**

BIG BANG COMICS (VOL. 1) — Caliber / Big Bang

Go back in time to the dark days of 1994. Everywhere, countless super-heroes clutter the comics landscape, all either part of some government "Black Ops" team or engaged in endless battles with legions of indistinguishable super-villains. The comics world is cynical, jaded, and tired of cookie-cutter characters who seem to lack characterization beyond lined grimaces.

Enter Big Bang Comics. This series, launched by Gary S. Carlson with art by Chris Ecker, Ed DeGeorge, and others, takes modern readers back in time into an alternate comics world. In this original series, they create such new super-heroes as The Knight Watchman and Dr. Weird, then feature them in Golden Age, Silver Age, and Modern stories. The result is both nostalgic and refreshingly new. It's a bit like reading through a cache of long-forgotten comics you've found in your attic — only these comics come from a past that never really existed.

0 ❑ May 1995, b&w and colorCover: 2.95 **NM** value: **3.50**
Knight Watchman: The Time Crimes of Grandfather Clock!; Thunder Girl: The Robber Robot; Doctor Weird: The Curse of the Mummy!! **A:** Tom King; Bill Fugate; Alex Ross(cover); Chris Woods **C:** Alex Ross **W:** Ed DeGeorge; Gary Carlson
1 ❑ Spr 1994, b&w Cover: 1.95 **NM** value: **2.50**
Circ: CapCity orders: **2,480**
Knight Watchman: The Man Called Mr. Mask; The Badge: The Shrine of Crime; The Beacon: The Razor's Edge; Venus: The Baby-Napping Plot of Madame X **A:** Mark Lewis; Tom King; Randy Zimmerman **W:** Tom King; Bud Hanzel; Ed DeGeorge; Gary Carlson
2 ❑ Sum 1994, b&w Cover: 1.95 **NM** value: **2.50**
Ultiman vs. The Sub-oteurs; The Blitz: Night of 1000 Stars and Stripes; The Human Sub: Meet the Human Sub **A:** Stan Timmons; Jon Schuler; Mike Obre **W:** Stan Timmons; Chris Ecker; Gary Carlson

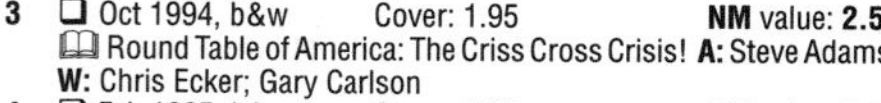

3 ❑ Oct 1994, b&w Cover: 1.95 **NM** value: **2.50**
Round Table of America: The Criss Cross Crisis! **A:** Steve Adams **W:** Chris Ecker; Gary Carlson
4 ❑ Feb 1995, b&w Cover: 1.95 **NM** value: **2.50**
A: Bart Schmitz **W:** Chris Ecker; Gary Carlson

BIG BANG COMICS (VOL. 2) — Image

1 ❑ May 1996 Cover: 1.95 **NM** value: **3.00**
Mighty Man and the Critter Crime Wave; Knight Watchman; Master of Ghosts (text story) • Mighty Man, Knight Watchman, Doctor Weird **A:** Bill Fugate; Chris Ecker; Stephanie Sanderson **W:** Chris Ecker; Ed DeGeorge; Gary Carlson
2 ❑ Jun 1996 Cover: 2.50 **NM** value: **2.75**
• Silver Age Shadowhawk, Knight Watchman, The Badge
3 ❑ Jul 1996 Cover: 2.50 **NM** value: **2.75**
Ultiman: The Crimes of Ultiman!; Thunder Girl Meets Her Evil Imitator • Knight Watchman, Ultiman, Thunder Girl **A:** Jeff Weigel; Mark Lewis; Bill Fugate; Jim Valentino **W:** Bill Fugate; Gary Carlson
4 ❑ Sep 1996 Cover: 2.50 **NM** value: **2.75**
Circ: Diamd. preorders: **7,569**
Knights of Justice
5 ❑ Oct 1996 Cover: 2.95 **NM** value: **Cover or less**
Circ: Diamd. preorders: **7,274**
• origins issue
6 ❑ Nov 1996 Cover: 2.95 **NM** value: **Cover or less**
Circ: Diamd. preorders: **6,804**
Criss-Cross Crisis; Round Table of America: Criss Cross Crisis! **A:** Steve Adams; Curt Swan(cover) **W:** Chris Ecker; Gary Carlson
7 ❑ Dec 1996 Cover: 2.95 **NM** value: **Cover or less**
Circ: Direct Market orders: **6,476**
Mighty Man: Ominous Reprieve; Shanghai Breeze: Assassination Run; I Met Oogur from Outer Space; Knight Watchman: The Ghost Robbers of the Wax Museum • Mighty Man vs. Mighty Man **A:** Stan Timmons; Chris Ecker; Darren Goodhart; Frank Fosco **W:** Stan Timmons; Chris Ecker; Carl Gafford; Terrance Griep Jr. Jr.
8 ❑ Jan 1997 Cover: 2.95 **NM** value: **Cover or less**
Circ: Direct Market orders: **6,201**
Mister U.S.: Birth of a Legend; A Hero Bestowed; By Any Other Name... **A:** Mark Lewis **W:** Nat Gertler ★ 1st Appearance of Mister U.S..
9 ❑ Mar 1997 Cover: 2.95 **NM** value: **Cover or less**
Circ: Diamd. preorders: **6,066**
• Showplace★ Appearance of Sphinx, Blitz.
10 ❑ May 1997 Cover: 2.95 **NM** value: **Cover or less**
Circ: Diamd. preorders: **5,806**
11 ❑ Jul 1997 Cover: 2.95 **NM** value: **Cover or less**
Circ: Diamd. preorders: **5,418**
• Knight Watchman vs. Faulty Towers
12 ❑ Sep 1997 Cover: 2.95 **NM** value: **Cover or less**
Circ: Diamd. preorders: **6,156**
★ Appearance of Savage Dragon.
13 ❑ Aug 1997 Cover: 2.95 **NM** value: **Cover or less**
Circ: Diamd. preorders: **5,108**
cover says Jul, indicia says Aug. The Sphinx
14 ❑ Oct 1997 Cover: 2.95 **NM** value: **Cover or less**
Circ: Diamd. preorders: **5,125**
A: Mark Lewis; David Zimmerman; Bill Fugate; Dan Preece; Joe Cooper; John Thompson; Ken Lester; Joe Zierman **W:** Gary Carlson ★ Appearance of Savage Dragon.
15 ❑ Oct 1997 Cover: 2.95 **NM** value: **Cover or less**
Circ: Diamd. preorders: **4,591**
Doctor Weird vs. Bog Swamp Demon, cover says Dec, indicia says Oct/Nov. Dr. Weird: Terror in the Swamp; Blitz: Clickety Split; Dr. Weird: Sorcerer's Death Wish; Knight Watchman: There Was an Old Lady (text story) **A:** Ed Quinby; Shawn Van Briesen **W:** Tom King; Ed Quinby; Ed DeGeorge; Howard Keltner
16 ❑ Jan 1998 Cover: 2.95 **NM** value: **Cover or less**
Circ: Diamd. preorders: **4,311**
Thunder Girl: The Clock That Turned Back Time!; Shadow Lady; The Absolute; Johnny Ruckus and the Monster Patrol • Thunder Girl **A:** Jeff Weigel; Frank Kurtz; Darren Goodhart; Ship of Fools Design Group; Time Stiles; Jerry Acerno **W:** Jeff Weigel; Frank Kurtz; Ryan Brown; Jerry Acerno; Daniel Wilson; Gary Carlson
17 ❑ Feb 1998 Cover: 2.95 **NM** value: **Cover or less**
Circ: Diamd. preorders: **4,522**
Murder by Microphone, Part 1; Shadow Lady: Murder by Microphone; Zhantika: Princess of the Jungle; Venus: Eye of the Gorgon • Shadow Lady **A:** Mark Lewis; Tony Mangineli; Jerry Acerno **W:** Jerry Acerno; Ed DeGeorge; Lyle Dodd
18 ❑ Apr 1998 Cover: 2.95 **NM** value: **Cover or less**
Circ: Diamd. preorders: **4,134**
End of Time! **A:** Jeff Weigel; Darren Goodhart; Dave Cockrum(cover); Hason Millet; Jason Howard; Joe Cooper; Steve Collins; Joe Zierman **W:** Gary Carlson ★ Appearance of Savage Dragon, Pantheon of Heroes.
19 ❑ Jun 1998 Cover: 2.95 **NM** value: **Cover or less**
Circ: Diamd. preorders: **3,719**
cover says Apr, indicia says Jun. The Golden Age Beacon; The Hummingbird; The Silver Age Beacon **A:** Jeff Weigel; Chris Ecker; Carl Taylor **W:** Chris Ecker; Bud Hanzel; Terrance Griep Jr. Jr. ★ Origin of The Beacon II (Doctor Julia Gardner), The Hummingbird, The Beacon I (Scott Martin).
20 ❑ Jul 1998 Cover: 2.95 **NM** value: **Cover or less**
Circ: Diamd. preorders: **3,658**
photo back cover. D Is for Daughter, Deceit and Death!; Little Girl Lost...; Local Hero Lost; Knight Errant; The Twain Shall Meet; The sphinx on the Trail of the Doom Sayer; Two Against the Terrible Titan!; The Outrageous Animator! **A:** Jeff Weigel; Dan Reed; Chris Khalaf **W:** Jeff Weigel; Dan Reed; Chris Khalaf ★ Appearance of Dimensioneer, Knight Watchman, The Blitz, The Sphinx.
21 ❑ Aug 1998 Cover: 2.95 **NM** value: **Cover or less**
Circ: Diamd. preorders: **3,732**
Murder by Microphone, Part 2; Shadow Lady: Murder by Microphone, Part 2; Masker: Plunder of the Air Pirates; Dimensioneer: The Better Half!; Ladybug: Miss the Beatles! • Shadow Lady **A:** Dan Reed; Carl Gafford; Ed Quinby; Jerry Acerno **W:** Dan Reed; Carl Gafford; Jerry Acerno; Gary Carlson
22 ❑ Sep 1998 Cover: 2.95 **NM** value: **Cover or less**
Circ: Diamd. preorders: **3,479**
Knight Watchman: Crime From the Skies!; The Dimensioneer: Dr. Insect and his Ant Men!; Agents of Badge; Pantheon of Heroes • Knight Watchman **A:** Dan Reed; Chris Ecker; Darren Goodhart; Dan Preece **W:** Dan Reed; Gary Carlson; Mark Schirmer
23 ❑ Nov 1998 Cover: 2.95 **NM** value: **3.95**
Circ: Diamd. preorders: **3,351**
The Sphinx; Who Do You Think You Are? • Tales of the Sphinx, Book 2 **A:** Jeff Weigel **W:** Jeff Weigel
24 ❑ Apr 1999 Cover: 3.95 **NM** value: **Cover or less**
Circ: Diamd. preorders: **3,209**
History of Big Bang Comics, Part 1 • The Big Bang History of Comics **A:** Chris Ecker **W:** Gary Carlson
25 ❑ Jun 1999 Cover: 3.95 **NM** value: **Cover or less**
Circ: Diamd. preorders: **2,988**
Father Flamingo and the Boys of Bad Town; The Shattering Show-down with The Super-Science Sprite! **A:** Mike Worley; Chris Ecker; Tim Stiles **W:** Chris Ecker; Doug Mabry; Terrance Griep Jr. Jr.
26 ❑ Jul 1999 Cover: 2.95 **NM** value: **Cover or less**
Circ: Diamd. preorders: **2,987**
Shadow Lady: Murder by Miicrophone, Part 3; Blue Bird: South of the Border **A:** Terry Pavlet; Jerry Acerno **W:** Jerry Acerno; Brian Peterson
27 ❑ Oct 1999 Cover: 3.95 **NM** value: **Cover or less**
Circ: Diamd. preorders: **2,880**
• The Big Bang History of Comics, Part 2 **W:** Gary Carlson
28 ❑ Dec 1999 Cover: 3.95 **NM** value: **Cover or less**
Circ: Diamd. preorders: **2,715**
Knight Watchman: Knight of the Living Dead!; The Pink Flamingo's Bubble Trouble • Knight Watchman **A:** Chris Ecker; Stuart Sayger **W:** Chris Ecker; Stuart Sayger; Gary Carlson
29 ❑ Feb 2000 Cover: 3.95 **NM** value: **Cover or less**
Circ: Diamd. preorders: **2,487**
Knight of the Living Dead; The Pink Feather Mystery; Spaceman From the Dead; Remembering...The Spook **A:** Jeff Weigel; Mark Lewis; Chris Ecker; Andrew Sheppard; Glenn Whitmore; Jeff Wood; John Thompson; Tim Stiles **W:** Chris Ecker; Gary Carlson; Kirk Uhlman
30 ❑ Mar 2000 Cover: 3.99 **NM** value: **Cover or less**
Circ: Diamd. preorders: **2,515**
31 ❑ Apr 2000 Cover: 3.95 **NM** value: **Cover or less**
Circ: Diamd. preorders: **2,459**
32 ❑ Jun 2000 Cover: 3.95 **NM** value: **Cover or less**
Circ: Diamd. preorders: **2,369**
The Knight Watchman: The Pink Flamingo's Real Gone Rebop Roost; The Knight Watchman: Knight of the Living Dead, Part 3 **A:** Mike Worley; Chris Ecker; Tim Stiles **W:** Chris Ecker; Terrance Griep Jr.
33 ❑ Jul 2000 Cover: 3.95 **NM** value: **Cover or less**
Circ: Diamd. preorders: **2,396**
The Round Table of America: Peril on Parallel Planets!; Gil Kane Tribute; Savage & Dragon & The Whiz Kids: Out of Time: The Missing Chapter **A:** Anthony Borderlon; Darren Hoodhart **W:** James Chambers; Chris Mills; Gary Carlson
34 ❑ Aug 2000 Cover: 3.95 **NM** value: **Cover or less**
Circ: Diamd. preorders: **2,291**
Venus: Odyssey to Save the Gods; Renegade & Ladybug: Along Came the Ladybug **A:** Sterling Clark; Chad Sergesketter; Joe Zierman **W:** Chris Ecker; Sterling Clark; Gary Carlson
35 ❑ Jan 2001 Cover: 3.95 **NM** value: **Cover or less**
Circ: Diamd. preorders: **2,739**
Big Bang vs. 1963; Mighty Man:Wicked Worm's Circus of Evil; Mighty Man Battles the Conqueror Worm **A:** Bill Fugate; Jim Valentino; John Thompson **W:** Jim Valentino; Gary Carlson

BIG BANG (RED CALLOWAY'S...) — Zoo Arsonist

1 ❑ Cover: 2.95 **NM** value: **Cover or less**

BIG BLACK KISS — Vortex

1 ❑ Sep 1989 Cover: 3.75 **NM** value: **3.95**
Circ: CapCity orders: **6,150**
A: Howard Chaykin **W:** Howard Chaykin
2 ❑ Oct 1989 Cover: 3.75 **NM** value: **3.95**
Circ: CapCity orders: **5,225**
A: Howard Chaykin **W:** Howard Chaykin
3 ❑ Nov 1989 Cover: 3.75 **NM** value: **3.95**
Circ: CapCity orders: **5,400**
A: Howard Chaykin **W:** Howard Chaykin
Bk 1❑ Cover: 8.95 **NM** value: **Cover or less**
• Thick Black Kiss;Collects series **A:** Howard Chaykin **W:** Howard Chaykin

BIG BLACK THING (COLIN UPTON'S...) — Upton

All issues are adults only.
1 ❑ b&w Cover: 3.25 **NM** value: **Cover or less**

BIG BLOWN BABY — Dark Horse

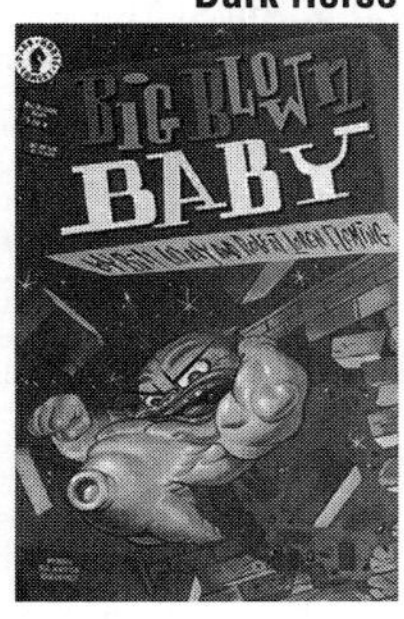

Bill Wray and Robert Loren Fleming's Big Blown Baby mini-series is aimed at hardcore comics fans. From Stan Lee's prose stylings to Jack Kirby's gleaming towers of godlike machinery, everything about the famous Marvel Silver Age style is subjected to good-natured, raunchy parody by a couple of guys who clearly know their material inside and out.

BBB features a divine tot, sent to Earth by his omnipotent (though perpetually constipated) father, and adopted by a working-class family. The backup stories offer "Tales from the Voyeur," "Procreation of the Gods," and "The Men behind

CGC-graded: Multiply prices above by **33 for 9.9 M • 16 for 9.8 NM/M • 7 for 9.6 NM+ • 5 for 9.4 NM • 2.5 for 9.2 NM- • 1.5 for 9.0 VF/NM**

Big Blown Baby," wherein Wray and Fleming explain their method in a dead-on spoof of Marvel's own self-promoting features.

1 ❑ Aug 1996 Cover: 2.95 **NM** value: **Cover or less**
📖 Tales of Fetusdom; Procreation of the Gods; The Men Behind the Baby **A:** William Wray; Stephen DeStefano **W:** William Wray; Robert Loren Flemming

2 ❑ Sep 1996 Cover: 2.95 **NM** value: **Cover or less**
Circ: Diamd. preorders: **5,992**
A: William Wray **W:** William Wray; Robert Loren Flemming

3 ❑ Oct 1996 Cover: 2.95 **NM** value: **Cover or less**
Circ: Diamd. preorders: **5,489**
A: William Wray **W:** William Wray; Robert Loren Flemming

4 ❑ Nov 1996 Cover: 2.95 **NM** value: **Cover or less**
Circ: Diamd. preorders: **4,459**
A: William Wray **W:** William Wray; Robert Loren Flemming

BIG BLUE COUCH COMIX — Couch Press

1 ❑ b&w Cover: 1.50 **NM** value: **2.00**

BIG BOOB BONDAGE — Antarctic / Venus

1 ❑ Jan 1997 Cover: 2.95 **NM** value: **Cover or less**
Circ: Direct Market orders: **3,268**
• b&w pin-ups, adult **A:** Dementia **W:** Dementia

BIG BOOK OF BAD, THE — DC / Paradox

1 ❑ b&w Cover: 14.95 **NM** value: **Cover or less**
A: Roger Langridge; George Freeman; Steve Leialoha; Eddie Newell; Lennie Mace **W:** Anina Bennett; Jonathan Vankin; Poaul Kirchner

BIG BOOK OF CONSPIRACIES, THE — DC / Paradox

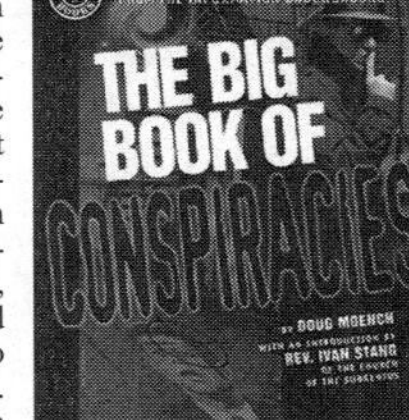

The fourth of Paradox Press's Big Books takes a look at the shadowy world of conspiracy theories. With rumored plots and cover-ups like Watergate, Silkwood, and the Iran-Contra scandal, it's easy for some to become a little bit nervous about the establishment. Add in the assassinations of John F. Kennedy (with its magic bullets, grassy knolls, Mafia figures, and CIA connections), Malcolm X, Robert Kennedy, and Martin Luther King, it's enough to turn almost anyone into a paranoid.

Well, not anyone. But this edition explores all these schemes and more in comics form, using a stream of real and imagined "facts" to explain how shadowy forces including the CIA, the Freemasons, the Vatican, the Trilateral Commission, and even aliens from outer space may be conspiring to shape world events. It also covers some plots even the authors admit are far-fetched.

1 ❑ Cover: 12.95 **NM** value: **Cover or less**
W: Doug Moench

BIG BOOK OF DEATH, THE — DC / Paradox

1 ❑ Cover: 12.95 **NM** value: **Cover or less**

BIG BOOK OF FREAKS, THE — DC / Paradox

1 ❑ Cover: 14.95 **NM** value: **Cover or less**
• Introduction by Ricky Jay **A:** Art Wetherell; Gahan Wilson; Tom Sutton; Rafael Kayanan; Richard Piers Rayner; Randy DuBurke; Frank Quitely; Mike McMahon; Mary Wilshire; Russ Heath; Eric Shanower; Jim Fern; Lennie Mace; D'Israeli; Donald David; Graham Higgins **W:** Gahan Wilson

BIG BOOK OF GRIMM, THE — DC / Paradox

1 ❑ Cover: 14.95 **NM** value: **Cover or less**
A: Roger Langridge; Charles Adlard; Randy DuBurke; George Freeman; Charles Vess; Shepherd Hendrix; Adam DeKraker; Christopher Schenck; Nick Bertozzi; Chris Jordan; Bob; Wm. Marshall Rogers **W:** Jonathan Vankin

BIG BOOK OF HOAXES, THE — DC / Paradox

1 ❑ Cover: 14.95 **NM** value: **Cover or less**

BIG BOOK OF LETHARGIC LAD — Destination Entertainment

1 ❑ Aug 1998 Cover: 15.95 **NM** value: **Cover or less**
No issue number. • Trade Paperback. • collects Lethargic Lad stories from Lethargic Comics Weakly #1-12, Lethargic Comics #1-14, and Lethargic Lad #1-3

BIG BOOK OF LITTLE CRIMINALS, THE — DC / Paradox

Paradox Press' Big Books series gives readers a comics tour of the weird side of life (and death!), and it was probably inevitable that it would eventually cover the stories of the world's greatest-and strangest-criminals.

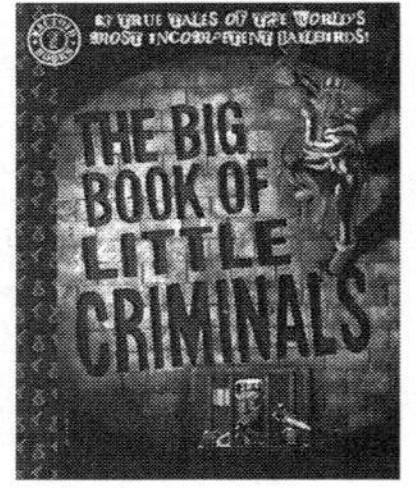

The Big Book of Little Criminals recounts the tales of such legendary felons as Shanghai Kelly, who made his living "recruiting" crews for ships by knocking wayfarers unconscious, selling them in their stupors, and letting them discover they'd begun new careers as sailors when they awoke. This is followed by U.S. Senators caning their colleagues, colonial counterfeiters, Hitler's diaries, and a crook who nearly succeeded in buying Portugal. All of this, of course, is illustrated by a collection of comics greats, adding up to a criminally delightful book.

1 ❑ Cover: 14.95 **NM** value: **Cover or less**
A: Brent Anderson

BIG BOOK OF LOSERS, THE — DC / Paradox

1 ❑ Cover: 14.95 **NM** value: **Cover or less**
A: Jason Lutes; Tom Sutton; Bryan Talbot; Gray Morrow; Tayyar Ozkan; Gordon Purcell; Ty Templeton; Bob Fingerman; Shepherd Hendrix; Andrew Wendel; Steve Vance; Glenn Barr; Peter Kuper; Shannon Wheeler; Bruce Patterson; Robbie Busch; Scott Shaw; Alex Waid **W:** Paul Kirchner

BIG BOOK OF MARTYRS, THE — DC / Paradox

1 ❑ b&w Cover: 14.95 **NM** value: **Cover or less**
A: Michael Dubisch; Steve Carr; Gregory Benton; Randy DuBurke; Dan Burr; Bob Fingerman; Michael Cherkas; Brian Buniak; Colleen Doran; Jim Fern; Kirk Etienne; Shary Flenniken; Dave DeVries; D'Israeli; Charles Drost; Donald David **W:** John Wagner

BIG BOOK OF SCANDAL, THE — DC / Paradox

The twelfth Big Book from Paradox Press wallows in the lurid world of tabloid news. Here readers will find showbiz greats such as Fatty Arbuckle and Charlie Chaplin, whose legends were soiled by personal indiscretions

Of course, political figures, such as Richard Nixon and Oliver North, also figure prominently in this book of scandal. The most interesting piece, however, is probably the savage dissecting of O.J. Simpson's murder defense, and the circus-like trial(s!) that followed.

This Big Book was written by Jonathan Vankin, and illustrated by a host of comic artists including Paul Gulacy, Rick Geary, David Lloyd, and Sergio Aragones.

1 ❑ b&w Cover: 14.95 **NM** value: **Cover or less**
A: Alan Weiss; Anthony Castrillo; David Lloyd; Steve Pugh; Gregory Benton; Paul Gulacy; Rick Geary; Ty Templeton; Marie Severin; Hilary Barta; Craig Hamilton; Brian Buniak; Colleen Doran; Arnold Pander; Michael Perkins; D'Israeli; Alex Wald **W:** Jonathan Vankin

BIG BOOK OF THE '70S, THE — DC / Paradox

1 ❑ Cover: 14.95 **NM** value: **Cover or less**
A: Seth Fisher; Eric Shanower; Langdon Foss; Danny Hellm; Jen Sorensen; Nick Bertozzi **W:** Jonathan Vankin

BIG BOOK OF THE UNEXPLAINED, THE — DC / Paradox

1 ❑ b&w Cover: 14.95 **NM** value: **Cover or less**
A: Rick Parker; Robin Smith; Steve Mannion; Gahan Wilson; Steve Lieber; Sergio Aragonés; Jeff Parker; Joe Orlando; Randy DuBurke; Paul Gulacy; Ted Slampyak; Rick Geary; Brent Anderson; Russ Heath; Gary Fields; Steve Leialoha; Eric Shanower; Ward Sutton **W:** Doug Moench

BIG BOOK OF THUGS, THE — DC / Paradox

1 ❑ b&w Cover: 14.95 **NM** value: **Cover or less**
A: Karen Platt; Robin Smith; Roger Langridge; Kieron Dwyer; Rafael Kayanan; Gray Morrow; Randy DuBurke; Rick Geary; Joe Staton; Fred Harper; Gordon Purcell; Chris Mcloughlin; James Romberger; Batton Lash; Bill Alger; David BlueStein; Kim Deitch; D'Israeli **W:** Joel Rose

BIG BOOK OF URBAN LEGENDS, THE — DC / Paradox

1 ❑ b&w Cover: 12.95 **NM** value: **Cover or less**
A: Brent Anderson

BIG BOOK OF VICE, THE — DC / Paradox

1 ❑ Cover: 14.95 **NM** value: **Cover or less**
A: Alan Kupperberg; Tom Sutton; Rick Geary; Dan Spiegle; Bob Fingerman; Deryl Skelton; Alwyn Talbot; Ivan Brunetti; Lennie **W:** Steve Vance; Dave Stern

BIG BOOK OF WEIRDOS, THE — DC / Paradox

The Big Book of Weirdos is the amusing follow-up to Paradox Press's The Big Book of Urban Legends. This giant-sized book collects the biographies of sixty-seven of the world's greatest eccentrics in comic form. Among the characters covered are the mad emperor Caligula of ancient Rome, Henrietta Howland Robinson ("The Witch of Wall Street"), escape artist Harry Houdini, and the depraved Marquis de Sade.

The collection was assembled by Carl Posey, and the individual biographies are illustrated by a long list of talented comic artists.

Readers may not agree with the inclusion of some historical figures here, but that simply makes the volume even better fodder for discussion.

1 ❑ Cover: 12.95 **NM** value: **Cover or less**
W: Gahan Wilson

BIG BRUISERS — Image

1 ❑ Jul 1996 Cover: 3.50 **NM** value: **Cover or less**
A: Jeff Rebner **W:** Tom Harrington

BIG CHIEF WAHOO — Eastern Color

This series stemmed from one of the most-metamorphosed newspaper strips in the field. It began in 1936 with The Great Gusto by Elmer Woggon. The medicine-show windbag had Big Chief Wahoo as a sidekick — and Wahoo took over the strip and its title, by now written by Allen Saunders. While seemingly packed with stereotypes, the strip's title character is far from typical: He's rich and kind, and the usual plot consists of crooks who think they can put one over on him. Other characters include Wahoo's sweetheart Minnie Ha Cha (who, by the way, has entertained in night clubs). Of note is the fact that a character introduced to the strip's continuity in 1940 was Steve Roper, who took over the strip from Wahoo in the late 1940s — only to be replaced in turn by Mike Nomad. This Wahoo-focused comic-book series ran seven issues from 1942 until 1944 and featured gag continuity.

1 ❑ Win 1941 Cover: 0.10 **NM** value: **300.00**
• **CGC:** 1 graded, best 8.5

2 ❑ Spr 1942 Cover: 0.10 **NM** value: **85.00**

3 ❑ Sum 1942 Cover: 0.10 **NM** value: **70.00**
📖 Minmie-Ha-Cha; Pigtails; Gusto; Mooseface; Princess; Butterball's Papooses **A:** Saunders & Woggon **W:** Saunders & Woggon

4 ❑ ca. 1942 Cover: 0.10 **NM** value: **70.00**
A: Saunders & Woggon **W:** Saunders & Woggon

5 ❑ Sum 1943 Cover: 0.10 **NM** value: **70.00**

6 ❑ Cover: 0.10 **NM** value: **50.00**

7 ❑ Cover: 0.10 **NM** value: **50.00**

BIG CITY: COMPLETE OBLIVION CITY SAGA — Slave Labor

Bk 1❑ Cover: 19.95 **NM** value: **Cover or less**
• digest-sized collection of Oblivion City #1-9.

BIG CRAP SCARE — Fireman

1 ❑ Cover: 2.95 **NM** value: **Cover or less**
📖 Bill Marvell; Dr. Grave; Zombie Kid; Crazy Train • A Celebration of Hell's Christmas **A:** Edvis; Jim Mahfood; Ruben Martinez; Tony Elwood **W:** Edvis; Jim Mahfood; Rob Schrab; Mondy Carter

BIG DOG FUNNIES — Rip Off

1 ❑ Jun 1992 Cover: 2.50 **NM** value: **Cover or less**
No issue number.

BIG EDSEL BAND — Ace

1 ❑ Cover: 1.75 **NM** value: **Cover or less**
📖 Wrestle-Maniacs **A:** Frank McLaughlin; Win Mortimer **W:** Frank McLaughlin; Win Mortimer ★ 1st Appearance of Billy Dee, Big Edsel Band, Tom "Gonzo" Seesberg, Artie Ebert, Allan "Flash" Wallace.

BIG FUNNIES — Radio

1 ❑ ca. 2001 Cover: 3.95 **NM** value: **Cover or less**
Circ: Diamd. preorders: **1,442**

2 ❑ ca. 2001 Cover: 3.99 **NM** value: **Cover or less**
Circ: Diamd. preorders: **1,224**

3 ❑ ca. 2001 Cover: 3.99 **NM** value: **Cover or less**

BIGGER: WILL RISON & THE DEVIL'S CONCUBINE — Free Lunch

1 ❑ Dec 1998 Cover: 2.95 **NM** value: **Cover or less**
📖 Black and Blues **A:** Matt C. Ryan **W:** Matt C. Ryan; G. Allan Holcomb

BIG GUY AND RUSTY THE BOY ROBOT, THE — Dark Horse / Legend

1 ❑ Jul 1995 Cover: 4.95 **NM** value: **6.00**
Circ: CapCity orders: **13,825**
A: Geof Darrow **W:** Frank Miller

2 ❑ Aug 1995 Cover: 4.95 **NM** value: **6.00**
Circ: CapCity orders: **10,750**
A: Geof Darrow **W:** Frank Miller

Bk 1❑ Cover: 14.95 **NM** value: **Cover or less**
collection, cover gallery and pin-ups in back.

BIG HAIR PRODUCTIONS — Image / Legend

1 ❑ Feb 2000 Cover: 3.50 **NM** value: **Cover or less**
Circ: Diamd. preorders: **2,635**
A: Andy Suriano **W:** Andy Suriano

BIG LOU — Side Show / Legend

1 ❑ Cover: 2.95 **NM** value: **Cover or less**
A: Jim Ridings **W:** Jim Ridings

BIG MONSTER FIGHT — Kidgang Comics

Those who love Godzilla movies will love — or at least recognize — Big Monster Fight. Published in 1995 by Minneapolis-based Kidgang Comics, the title is basically an excuse to draw lots of different monsters wreaking havoc and destroying cities. Just as in old Japanese monster movies, these menaces crush houses, knock over buildings, and generally make a nuisance of themselves.

It's pointless, violent, and funny stuff, with stories like "It's a Big Monster World" and "Horror of the Jabberwock." No artist

Other grades: Multiply prices above by **1.5 for Mint • 2/3 for Very Fine • 1/3 for Fine • 1/5 for Very Good • 1/8 for Good**

credits appear in the issue, but Mark Stegbauer and Carl Gafford are thanked for their "valuable technical advice."
0 ❑ Cover: 2.50 NM value: Cover or less

BIG MOUTH — Starhead

1 ❑ b&w Cover: 2.95 NM value: Cover or less
A: Donna Barr W: Pat Moriarty
2 ❑ b&w Cover: 2.95 NM value: Cover or less
A: Donna Barr W: Pat Moriarty
3 ❑ Cover: 2.95 NM value: Cover or less
A: Donna Barr W: Pat Moriarty
4 ❑ Cover: 2.95 NM value: Cover or less
A: Donna Barr W: Pat Moriarty
5 ❑ Cover: 2.95 NM value: Cover or less
• no indicia, b&w A: Donna Barr W: Pat Moriarty
6 ❑ Dec 1996 Cover: 2.95 NM value: Cover or less
7 ❑ Jan 1998 Cover: 2.95 NM value: Cover or less

BIG NUMBERS — Mad Love

1 ❑ Cover: 5.50 NM value: Cover or less
Circ: CapCity orders: 13,050
A: Bill Sienkiewicz W: Alan Moore
2 ❑ Cover: 5.50 NM value: Cover or less
Circ: CapCity orders: 10,425
• Final published issue A: Bill Sienkiewicz W: Alan Moore

BIG PRIZE, THE — Eternity

1 ❑ May 1988, b&w Cover: 1.95 NM value: Cover or less
The Time Drifter's Odyssey A: Mike Roberts; Bryon Carson W: Gerard Jones
2 ❑ Aug 1985, b&w Cover: 1.95 NM value: Cover or less
A: Mike Roberts; Bryon Carson W: Gerard Jones

BIG SHOT — Columbia

Started in 1940, Big Shot Comics was a wide-ranging compendium of humor and adventure strips, many in reprint form.

Newspaper-strip reprints of such features as J.P. McEvoy and John H. Striebel's Dixie Dugan, Ham Fisher's Joe Palooka, Lank Leonard's Mickey Finn, and Harry Tuthill's The Bungle Family appeared alongside such characters as Ogden Whitney's heroic Skyman, Captain Devildog of the U.S. Marines, Boody Rogers' Sparky Watts, and the startling character The Face (aka Tony Trent). A solid middle player in the comics scene, Big Shot ran until 1949.

1 ❑ May 1940 Cover: 0.10 NM value: 975.00
2 ❑ Jun 1940 Cover: 0.10 NM value: 450.00
3 ❑ Jul 1940 Cover: 0.10 NM value: 350.00
• CGC: 1 graded, best 8.5
4 ❑ Aug 1940 Cover: 0.10 NM value: 300.00
5 ❑ Sep 1940 Cover: 0.10 NM value: 300.00
• CGC: 1 graded, best 8.0
6 ❑ Oct 1940 Cover: 0.10 NM value: 250.00
• CGC: 1 graded, best 7.0
7 ❑ Nov 1940 Cover: 0.10 NM value: 250.00
8 ❑ Dec 1940 Cover: 0.10 NM value: 250.00
9 ❑ Jan 1941 Cover: 0.10 NM value: 250.00
10 ❑ Feb 1941 Cover: 0.10 NM value: 250.00
11 ❑ Mar 1941 Cover: 0.10 NM value: 210.00
12 ❑ Apr 1941 Cover: 0.10 NM value: 210.00
13 ❑ May 1941 Cover: 0.10 NM value: 210.00
14 ❑ Jun 1941 Cover: 0.10 NM value: 285.00
★ Origin of Sparky Watts. ★ 1st Appearance of Sparky Watts.
15 ❑ Jul 1941 Cover: 0.10 NM value: 325.00
★ Origin of The Cloak.
16 ❑ Aug 1941 Cover: 0.10 NM value: 150.00
17 ❑ Sep 1941 Cover: 0.10 NM value: 150.00
18 ❑ Oct 1941 Cover: 0.10 NM value: 150.00
• CGC: 1 graded, best 8.0
19 ❑ Nov 1941 Cover: 0.10 NM value: 150.00
20 ❑ Dec 1941 Cover: 0.10 NM value: 150.00
21 ❑ Jan 1942 Cover: 0.10 NM value: 125.00
22 ❑ Feb 1942 Cover: 0.10 NM value: 125.00
23 ❑ Apr 1942 Cover: 0.10 NM value: 125.00
24 ❑ Jun 1942 Cover: 0.10 NM value: 125.00
25 ❑ Jul 1942 Cover: 0.10 NM value: 125.00
26 ❑ Aug 1942 Cover: 0.10 NM value: 125.00
27 ❑ Sep 1942 Cover: 0.10 NM value: 125.00
28 ❑ Oct 1942 Cover: 0.10 NM value: 170.00
• CGC: 1 graded, best 5.0
29 ❑ Nov 1942 Cover: 0.10 NM value: 125.00
30 ❑ Dec 1942 Cover: 0.10 NM value: 125.00
• CGC: 1 graded, best 9.2
31 ❑ Jan 1943 Cover: 0.10 NM value: 105.00
32 ❑ Feb 1943 Cover: 0.10 NM value: 105.00
33 ❑ Mar 1943 Cover: 0.10 NM value: 105.00
• CGC: 1 graded, best 9.0
34 ❑ Apr 1943 Cover: 0.10 NM value: 105.00
35 ❑ May 1943 Cover: 0.10 NM value: 105.00
36 ❑ Jun 1943 Cover: 0.10 NM value: 105.00
37 ❑ Jul 1943 Cover: 0.10 NM value: 105.00
38 ❑ Aug 1943 Cover: 0.10 NM value: 105.00
39 ❑ Sep 1943 Cover: 0.10 NM value: 105.00
40 ❑ Oct 1943 Cover: 0.10 NM value: 105.00
41 ❑ Dec 1943 Cover: 0.10 NM value: 90.00
42 ❑ Jan 1944 Cover: 0.10 NM value: 90.00
43 ❑ Feb 1944 Cover: 0.10 NM value: 90.00
44 ❑ Mar 1944 Cover: 0.10 NM value: 90.00
45 ❑ Apr 1944 Cover: 0.10 NM value: 90.00
46 ❑ Jun 1944 Cover: 0.10 NM value: 90.00
• CGC: 2 graded, best 9.6
47 ❑ Jul 1944 Cover: 0.10 NM value: 90.00
48 ❑ Aug 1944 Cover: 0.10 NM value: 90.00
49 ❑ Oct 1944 Cover: 0.10 NM value: 90.00
50 ❑ Nov 1944 Cover: 0.10 NM value: 80.00
51 ❑ Dec 1944 Cover: 0.10 NM value: 80.00
52 ❑ Jan 1945 Cover: 0.10 NM value: 80.00
53 ❑ Feb 1945 Cover: 0.10 NM value: 80.00
54 ❑ Mar 1945 Cover: 0.10 NM value: 80.00
• CGC: 1 graded, best 8.5
55 ❑ Apr 1945 Cover: 0.10 NM value: 80.00
56 ❑ Jun 1945 Cover: 0.10 NM value: 80.00
57 ❑ Jul 1945 Cover: 0.10 NM value: 80.00
• CGC: 1 graded, best 9.2
58 ❑ Aug 1945 Cover: 0.10 NM value: 80.00
59 ❑ Sep 1945 Cover: 0.10 NM value: 80.00
Joe Palooka; Skyman; Sparky Watts; Capt Yank!; Brass Knuckles; The Man Who Stole the Sixth Avenue L (text story); Charlie Chan; Bo; Dixie Dugan; The Face A: Alfred Andriola; Frank Beck; Frank Tinsley; Mart Bailey; Marty; McVoy; Streibel W: Alfred Andriola; Frank Beck; Frank Tinsley; Mart Bailey; Marty; McVoy; Streibel
60 ❑ Oct 1945 Cover: 0.10 NM value: 80.00
61 ❑ Nov 1945 Cover: 0.10 NM value: 60.00
62 ❑ Jan 1946 Cover: 0.10 NM value: 60.00
63 ❑ Feb 1946 Cover: 0.10 NM value: 60.00
64 ❑ Mar 1946 Cover: 0.10 NM value: 60.00
65 ❑ Apr 1946 Cover: 0.10 NM value: 60.00
66 ❑ May 1946 Cover: 0.10 NM value: 60.00
67 ❑ Jun 1946 Cover: 0.10 NM value: 60.00
68 ❑ Aug 1946 Cover: 0.10 NM value: 60.00
69 ❑ Sep 1946 Cover: 0.10 NM value: 60.00
• CGC: 1 graded, best 8.0
70 ❑ Oct 1946 Cover: 0.10 NM value: 60.00
71 ❑ Nov 1946 Cover: 0.10 NM value: 50.00
• CGC: 1 graded, best 6.5
72 ❑ Dec 1946 Cover: 0.10 NM value: 50.00
• CGC: 1 graded, best 7.5
73 ❑ Jan 1947 Cover: 0.10 NM value: 50.00
74 ❑ Feb 1947 Cover: 0.10 NM value: 50.00
75 ❑ Mar 1947 Cover: 0.10 NM value: 50.00
• CGC: 1 graded, best 8.5
All in a Lifetime; Mickey Finn; Dixie Dugan; The Skyman; Sparky Watts; Brass Knuckles; Good Old Bumpy (text); Cranberry Boggs; Charlie Chan; Bo; Tony Trent; Hollywood Husband…His Wife's in Pictures! A: Ogden Whitney; Lank Leonard; Don Dean; Frank Beck; Jeff Machamer; Mart Bailey W: Ogden Whitney; Lank Leonard; Don Dean; Frank Beck; Jeff Machamer; Mart Bailey
76 ❑ Apr 1947 Cover: 0.10 NM value: 50.00
77 ❑ May 1947 Cover: 0.10 NM value: 50.00
• CGC: 1 graded, best 8.0
78 ❑ Jun 1947 Cover: 0.10 NM value: 50.00
79 ❑ Jul 1947 Cover: 0.10 NM value: 50.00
80 ❑ Aug 1947 Cover: 0.10 NM value: 50.00
Sparky Watts; Dixie Dugan; Mickey Finn; Cranberry Boggs; Trouble for Everyone (text story); Brass Knuckles; Skyman; Bo; Hollywood Johnnie; June Bride; Tony Trent A: Boody Rogers; Ogden Whitney; Frank Beck; Jim Fabian; Mart Bailey; Marty Marion; Striebel W: Boody Rogers; Ogden Whitney; Lank Leonard; Frank Beck; Mart Bailey; Marty Marion; Benny McEvoy
81 ❑ Sep 1947 Cover: 0.10 NM value: 45.00
82 ❑ Oct 1947 Cover: 0.10 NM value: 45.00
83 ❑ Nov 1947 Cover: 0.10 NM value: 45.00
84 ❑ Dec 1947 Cover: 0.10 NM value: 45.00
• CGC: 1 graded, best 5.5
85 ❑ Jan 1948 Cover: 0.10 NM value: 45.00
• CGC: 1 graded, best 7.5
86 ❑ Feb 1948 Cover: 0.10 NM value: 45.00
87 ❑ Mar 1948 Cover: 0.10 NM value: 45.00
88 ❑ Apr 1948 Cover: 0.10 NM value: 45.00
89 ❑ May 1948 Cover: 0.10 NM value: 45.00
90 ❑ Jun 1948 Cover: 0.10 NM value: 45.00
91 ❑ Jul 1948 Cover: 0.10 NM value: 45.00
92 ❑ Aug 1948 Cover: 0.10 NM value: 45.00
93 ❑ Sep 1948 Cover: 0.10 NM value: 45.00
94 ❑ Oct 1948 Cover: 0.10 NM value: 45.00
95 ❑ Nov 1948 Cover: 0.10 NM value: 45.00
96 ❑ Dec 1948 Cover: 0.10 NM value: 45.00
97 ❑ Jan 1949 Cover: 0.10 NM value: 45.00
98 ❑ Feb 1949 Cover: 0.10 NM value: 45.00
99 ❑ Mar 1949 Cover: 0.10 NM value: 45.00
100 ❑ Apr 1949 Cover: 0.10 NM value: 45.00
101 ❑ May 1949 Cover: 0.10 NM value: 45.00
102 ❑ Jun 1949 Cover: 0.10 NM value: 45.00
103 ❑ Jul 1949 Cover: 0.10 NM value: 45.00
104 ❑ Aug 1949 Cover: 0.10 NM value: 45.00
final issue.

BIG 3 — Fox

1 ❑ Fal 1940 Cover: 0.10 NM value: 1250.00
• CGC: 2 graded, best 9.4
2 ❑ Spr 1941 Cover: 0.10 NM value: 650.00
3 ❑ May 1941 Cover: 0.10 NM value: 450.00
4 ❑ Jul 1941 Cover: 0.10 NM value: 450.00
5 ❑ Sep 1941 Cover: 0.10 NM value: 450.00
6 ❑ Nov 1941 Cover: 0.10 NM value: 400.00
7 ❑ Jan 1942 Cover: 0.10 NM value: 400.00

BIG TIME — Delta

1 ❑ Mar 1996 Cover: 1.95 NM value: Cover or less
A: Jeff Salisbury W: Shawn Svacha

BIG TOP, THE — Toby

1 ❑ ca. 1951 Cover: 0.10 NM value: 48.00
2 ❑ Apr 1951 Cover: 0.10 NM value: 35.00
The Sad Circus; The Space Ship; The "Gooflesnoof"; True Tales From the Big Top; Battling Bingo

BIG TOP BONDAGE — Fantagraphics / Eros

All issues are adults only.
1 ❑ b&w Cover: 2.50 NM value: Cover or less

BIG TOWN — DC

1 ❑ Jan 1951 Cover: 0.10 NM value: 475.00
• CGC: 3 graded, best 9.6
2 ❑ Feb 1951 Cover: 0.10 NM value: 240.00
3 ❑ Mar 1951 Cover: 0.10 NM value: 175.00
• CGC: 1 graded, best 5.0
4 ❑ Apr 1951 Cover: 0.10 NM value: 130.00
5 ❑ May 1951 Cover: 0.10 NM value: 130.00
6 ❑ Jun 1951 Cover: 0.10 NM value: 100.00
7 ❑ Jul 1951 Cover: 0.10 NM value: 100.00
8 ❑ Aug 1951 Cover: 0.10 NM value: 100.00
• CGC: 1 graded, best 9.6
9 ❑ Sep 1951 Cover: 0.10 NM value: 100.00
• CGC: 1 graded, best 8.5
10 ❑ Oct 1951 Cover: 0.10 NM value: 100.00
• CGC: 1 graded, best 9.6
11 ❑ Nov 1951 Cover: 0.10 NM value: 70.00
12 ❑ Dec 1951 Cover: 0.10 NM value: 70.00
13 ❑ Jan 1952 Cover: 0.10 NM value: 70.00
Superboy Public Service Announcement inside back cover. The Hermit of Big Town!; Stand-In for Murder!; Johnny Law, Headquarters Detective in… The Big House Express; Old Newsmen Never Die!; Famous "Newspaper" Duels!; Superboy says "Share with Others!"
14 ❑ Mar 1952 Cover: 0.10 NM value: 70.00
• CGC: 1 graded, best 9.4
15 ❑ May 1952 Cover: 0.10 NM value: 70.00
16 ❑ Jul 1952 Cover: 0.10 NM value: 70.00
• CGC: 1 graded, best 9.0
17 ❑ Sep 1952 Cover: 0.10 NM value: 70.00
18 ❑ Nov 1952 Cover: 0.10 NM value: 70.00
19 ❑ Jan 1953 Cover: 0.10 NM value: 70.00
20 ❑ Mar 1953 Cover: 0.10 NM value: 70.00
21 ❑ May 1953 Cover: 0.10 NM value: 60.00
22 ❑ Jul 1953 Cover: 0.10 NM value: 60.00
23 ❑ Sep 1953 Cover: 0.10 NM value: 60.00
24 ❑ Nov 1953 Cover: 0.10 NM value: 60.00
• CGC: 1 graded, best 7.0
25 ❑ Jan 1954 Cover: 0.10 NM value: 60.00
26 ❑ Mar 1954 Cover: 0.10 NM value: 60.00
27 ❑ May 1954 Cover: 0.10 NM value: 60.00
28 ❑ Jul 1954 Cover: 0.10 NM value: 60.00
• CGC: 1 graded, best 7.5
29 ❑ Sep 1954 Cover: 0.10 NM value: 60.00
30 ❑ Nov 1954 Cover: 0.10 NM value: 60.00
31 ❑ Jan 1955 Cover: 0.10 NM value: 48.00
32 ❑ Mar 1955 Cover: 0.10 NM value: 48.00
33 ❑ May 1955 Cover: 0.10 NM value: 48.00
34 ❑ Jul 1955 Cover: 0.10 NM value: 48.00
35 ❑ Sep 1955 Cover: 0.10 NM value: 48.00
36 ❑ Nov 1955 Cover: 0.10 NM value: 48.00
37 ❑ Jan 1956 Cover: 0.10 NM value: 48.00
38 ❑ Mar 1956 Cover: 0.10 NM value: 48.00
39 ❑ May 1956 Cover: 0.10 NM value: 48.00
40 ❑ Jul 1956 Cover: 0.10 NM value: 48.00
41 ❑ Sep 1956 Cover: 0.10 NM value: 48.00
42 ❑ Nov 1956 Cover: 0.10 NM value: 48.00
43 ❑ Jan 1957 Cover: 0.10 NM value: 48.00
44 ❑ Mar 1957 Cover: 0.10 NM value: 48.00
45 ❑ May 1957 Cover: 0.10 NM value: 48.00
46 ❑ Jul 1957 Cover: 0.10 NM value: 48.00
47 ❑ Sep 1957 Cover: 0.10 NM value: 48.00
48 ❑ Nov 1957 Cover: 0.10 NM value: 48.00
49 ❑ Jan 1958 Cover: 0.10 NM value: 48.00
50 ❑ Mar 1958 Cover: 0.10 NM value: 48.00
final issue.

BIG TOWN (MARVEL) — Marvel

1 ❑ Jan 2001 Cover: 3.50 NM value: Cover or less
says Fantastic Four Big Town on cover. • alternate Marvel history A: Mike McKone W: Steve Englehart ★ Appearance of X-Men, Avengers.
2 ❑ Feb 2001 Cover: 2.99 NM value: 3.50
A: Mike McKone W: Steve Englehart ★ Appearance of Hulk, Avengers., Sub-Mariner.
3 ❑ Mar 2001 Cover: 2.99 NM value: Cover or less
A: Mike McKone W: Steve Englehart ★ Appearance of Hulk, Avengers, Sub-Mariner.
4 ❑ Mar 2001 Cover: 2.99 NM value: 3.50
A: Mike McKone W: Steve Englehart ★ Appearance of Hulk, Avengers, Sub-Mariner.

BIG VALLEY — Dell

1 ❑ ca. 1966 Cover: 0.12 NM value: 40.00
• CGC: 2 graded, best 9.4
2 ❑ ca. 1966 Cover: 0.12 NM value: 25.00
3 ❑ ca. 1967 Cover: 0.12 NM value: 25.00
4 ❑ ca. 1967 Cover: 0.12 NM value: 25.00
5 ❑ ca. 1967 Cover: 0.12 NM value: 25.00
6 ❑ ca. 1967 Cover: 0.12 NM value: 25.00

There are two different pricing tiers in the modern comic-book hobby. **The prices seen above** are the prices we have seen **loose copies** of these issues reliably fetch in a variety of environments. Condition alters the price by the fractions seen on the bar on the bottom of left-hand pages of this book. **Comics graded by CGC** usually sell for more. Use the guide on the bottom of right-hand pages of this book to estimate what copies have brought on eBay.

CGC-graded: Multiply prices above by **33 for 9.9 M • 16 for 9.8 NM/M • 7 for 9.6 NM+ • 5 for 9.4 NM • 2.5 for 9.2 NM- • 1.5 for 9.0 VF/NM**

BIJOU FUNNIES — Kitchen Sink

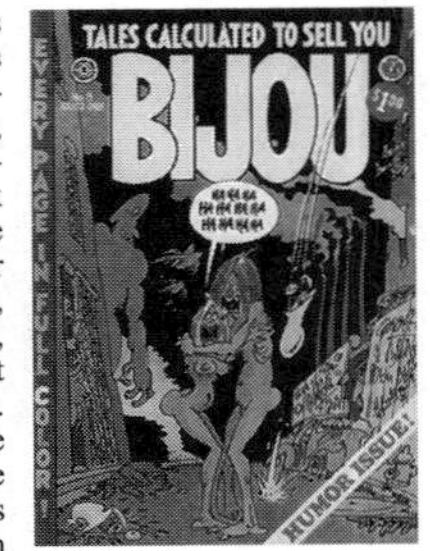

The anthology series Bijou offers many of the most notable examples of talent and stories that the underground comix genre has to offer, and full-color #8 featured its creators providing spoofs of the comix genre. Among the creators whose work appear in Bijou are Roger Brand, Robert Crumb, Justin green, Kim Deitch, (Editor) Jay Lynch, Jim Osborne, Gilbert Shelton, Art Spiegelman, and Skip Williamson. Each issue running from the late 1960s to the mid-1970s had more than one printing, and the press runs on those printings could be as high as 10,000 — or more. Such characters as Nard n' Pat were featured.

1 ❑ Cover: 0.50 **NM** value: **175.00**
1-2 ❑ **NM** value: **40.00**
2 ❑ 1970 Cover: 0.50 **NM** value: **50.00**
3 ❑ Cover: 0.50 **NM** value: **35.00**
3-2 ❑ **NM** value: **15.00**
3-3 ❑ **NM** value: **10.00**
4 ❑ 1972 Cover: 0.50 **NM** value: **25.00**
5 ❑ Cover: 0.50 **NM** value: **25.00**
6 ❑ Cover: 0.50 **NM** value: **20.00**
7 ❑ Cover: 0.50 **NM** value: **20.00**
8 ❑ 1973 Cover: 0.50 **NM** value: **20.00**
📖 Geek Brothers!; Snazzy Melvin Snoot!; Melvin Natural!; Hungry Irving Biscuits!; Melvin Wizard!; Pard 'n' Nat; Inside Dopes; Bufo Boffo; Checkered Cherub!; The Wuper of Skeetee Grunt: A Case of Outlined Lettering; Mashman Meets Spleen Queen **A:** Denis Kitchen **W:** Denis Kitchen
8-2 ❑ Cover: 1.00 **NM** value: **4.00**

BIKER MICE FROM MARS — Marvel

1 ❑ Nov 1993 Cover: 1.50 **NM** value: **2.00**
Circ: CapCity orders: **9,100**
2 ❑ Dec 1993 Cover: 1.50 **NM** value: **2.00**
Circ: CapCity orders: **5,100**
3 ❑ Jan 1994 Cover: 1.50 **NM** value: **2.00**
Circ: CapCity orders: **4,000**

BIKINI ASSASSIN TEAM, THE — Catfish

1 ❑ Cover: 2.50 **NM** value: **Cover or less**

BIKINI BATTLE 3-D — 3-D Zone

All issues are adults only.
1 ❑ Cover: 3.95 **NM** value: **Cover or less**
No issue number. **A:** Robert Crumb

BILL & TED'S BOGUS JOURNEY — Marvel

1 ❑ Sep 1991 Cover: 2.95 **NM** value: **Cover or less**
A: Evan Dorkin **W:** Evan Dorkin

BILL & TED'S EXCELLENT ADVENTURE MOVIE ADAPTATION — DC

1 ❑ **NM** value: **1.50**
No issue number. adapts movie, wraparound cover, no cover price.

BILL & TED'S EXCELLENT COMIC BOOK — Marvel

1 ❑ Dec 1991 Cover: 1.00 **NM** value: **1.50**
Circ: CapCity orders: **13,900**
A: Evan Dorkin **W:** Evan Dorkin
2 ❑ Jan 1992 Cover: 1.00 **NM** value: **1.25**
Circ: CapCity orders: **7,700**
A: Evan Dorkin **W:** Evan Dorkin
3 ❑ Feb 1992 Cover: 1.25 **NM** value: **Cover or less**
Circ: CapCity orders: **5,700**
A: Evan Dorkin **W:** Evan Dorkin
4 ❑ Mar 1992 Cover: 1.25 **NM** value: **Cover or less**
Circ: CapCity orders: **4,100**
A: Evan Dorkin **W:** Evan Dorkin
5 ❑ Apr 1992 Cover: 1.25 **NM** value: **Cover or less**
Circ: CapCity orders: **3,300**
A: Evan Dorkin **W:** Evan Dorkin
6 ❑ May 1992 Cover: 1.25 **NM** value: **Cover or less**
Circ: CapCity orders: **3,000**
A: Evan Dorkin **W:** Evan Dorkin
7 ❑ Jun 1992 Cover: 1.25 **NM** value: **Cover or less**
A: Evan Dorkin **W:** Evan Dorkin
8 ❑ Jul 1992 Cover: 1.25 **NM** value: **Cover or less**
A: Evan Dorkin **W:** Evan Dorkin
9 ❑ Aug 1992 Cover: 1.25 **NM** value: **Cover or less**
A: Evan Dorkin **W:** Evan Dorkin
10 ❑ Sep 1992 Cover: 1.25 **NM** value: **Cover or less**
📖 Don't Believe the Hype **A:** Evan Dorkin **W:** Evan Dorkin
11 ❑ Oct 1992 Cover: 1.25 **NM** value: **Cover or less**
A: Evan Dorkin
12 ❑ Nov 1992 Cover: 1.25 **NM** value: **Cover or less**
A: Evan Dorkin

BILL BARNES COMICS — Street & Smith

1 ❑ ca. 1940 Cover: 0.10 **NM** value: **500.00**
• **CGC:** 1 graded, best 6.5
2 ❑ ca. 1941 Cover: 0.10 **NM** value: **300.00**
3 ❑ ca. 1941 Cover: 0.10 **NM** value: **250.00**
4 ❑ ca. 1941 Cover: 0.10 **NM** value: **250.00**
5 ❑ ca. 1941 Cover: 0.10 **NM** value: **250.00**
6 ❑ ca. 1942 Cover: 0.10 **NM** value: **200.00**
7 ❑ ca. 1942 Cover: 0.10 **NM** value: **200.00**
8 ❑ ca. 1942 Cover: 0.10 **NM** value: **200.00**
9 ❑ ca. 1942 Cover: 0.10 **NM** value: **200.00**
10 ❑ ca. 1943 Cover: 0.10 **NM** value: **200.00**
11 ❑ ca. 1943 Cover: 0.10 **NM** value: **200.00**
12 ❑ ca. 1943 Cover: 0.10 **NM** value: **200.00**

BILL, THE GALACTIC HERO — Topps

Lowly fuse tender Bill becomes a hero when he helps save his spaceship, The Christine Keeler, when it falls under attack. In doing so, however, he loses his left arm. The ship's doctors then make a bad situation worse, when they replace his lost left arm with a spare right one. And this, unfortunately, is only the beginning of Bill's problems, as he finds himself "rewarded" with another seven-year tour of duty. His only hope of surviving his term is to keep in mind the all-important rules of military life: (1) Keep your mouth shut, and (2) Don't volunteer for anything.

In 1994, Topps released the three-issue mini-series, taken from the series of books by science-fiction writer Harry Harrison. Art is by Mike Gustovich and Randy Dunn.

1 ❑ Jul 1994 Cover: 4.95 **NM** value: **Cover or less**
Circ: CapCity orders: **4,350**
• prestige format, based on Harry Harrison novel series **A:** Rodney Dunn; Mike Gustovich; Rich Larson(cover); Steve Fastner(cover) **W:** Ken Grobe
2 ❑ Cover: 4.95 **NM** value: **Cover or less**
Circ: CapCity orders: **3,275**
A: Rodney Dunn; Mike Gustovich; Rich Larson(cover); Steve Fastner(cover) **W:** Ken Grobe
3 ❑ Cover: 4.95 **NM** value: **Cover or less**
Circ: CapCity orders: **2,600**
A: Rodney Dunn; Mike Gustovich; Rich Larson(cover); Steve Fastner(cover) **W:** Ken Grobe

BILLI 99 — Dark Horse

1 ❑ Cover: 3.50 **NM** value: **Cover or less**
A: Tim Sale **W:** Sarah Byam
2 ❑ Cover: 3.50 **NM** value: **Cover or less**
📖 Trespasses **A:** Tim Sale **W:** Sarah Byam
3 ❑ Cover: 3.50 **NM** value: **Cover or less**
A: Tim Sale **W:** Sarah Byam
4 ❑ Cover: 3.95 **NM** value: **Cover or less**
A: Tim Sale **W:** Sarah Byam

BILL THE BULL: BURNT CAIN — Boneyard

Bill Parchem and Nicholas Stone go back a long way — back to when Nick worked for the Chicago Police Department and Bill wasn't a seven-foot tall behemoth with horns. Nowadays, they run The Blackmoon Agency, a private investigation firm. They live on the fringes, busting up creeps and investigating weirdos. But their latest case is to prove the weirdest of all.

They are employed by Mrs. Cain, a rich resident of Chicago's affluent Winnetka suburb, to find her missing husband. Mr. Cain, it seems, has a bit of a drinking problem. Still, he hasn't been seen in days, and Mrs. Cain is worried.

And with good cause. No sooner do Bill and Nick take the case, than bodies start piling up around them. The trail leads them from flop houses to a rich psychologist's office, then down to a dark basement with a terrible secret.

1 ❑ Jul 1992 Cover: 2.50 **NM** value: **4.95**
A: Duncan Rouleau **W:** Hart D. Fisher
2 ❑ Cover: 2.50 **NM** value: **4.95**
A: Duncan Rouleau **W:** Hart D. Fisher
3 ❑ Cover: 4.95 **NM** value: **Cover or less**
A: Duncan Rouleau **W:** Hart D. Fisher

BILL THE BULL: ONE SHOT, ONE BOURBON, ONE BEER — Boneyard

1 ❑ Dec 1994 Cover: 2.95 **NM** value: **Cover or less**
📖 Whore **A:** Matt Roach **W:** Hart Fisher
2 ❑ Cover: 2.95 **NM** value: **Cover or less**
• indicia says Mar 94, a misprint

BILL THE CLOWN — Slave Labor

1 ❑ Feb 1992, b&w Cover: 2.50 **NM** value: **Cover or less**
• 2nd Printing, b&w
1-2 ❑ Cover: 2.95 **NM** value: **Cover or less**
• 2nd Printing, b&w

BILL THE CLOWN: COMEDY ISN'T PRETTY — Slave Labor

1 ❑ Nov 1992, b&w Cover: 2.50 **NM** value: **Cover or less**

BILL THE CLOWN: DEATH & CLOWN WHITE — Slave Labor

1 ❑ Sep 1993, b&w Cover: 2.95 **NM** value: **Cover or less**

BILLY BOY THE SICK LITTLE FAT KID — Asylum

1 ❑ ca. 2001 Cover: 2.95 **NM** value: **Cover or less**
Circ: Diamd. preorders: **1,140**

BILLY BUCKSKIN — Atlas

1 ❑ Nov 1955 Cover: 0.10 **NM** value: **75.00**
• **CGC:** 1 graded, best 9.2
2 ❑ Jan 1956 Cover: 0.10 **NM** value: **60.00**
3 ❑ Mar 1956 Cover: 0.10 **NM** value: **60.00**

BILLY COLE — Cult

1 ❑ Jun 1994, b&w Cover: 2.75 **NM** value: **Cover or less**
A: Billy Cole; Ted Seko **W:** Billy Cole; Ted Seko
2 ❑ Cover: 2.75 **NM** value: **Cover or less**
A: Billy Cole; Ted Seko **W:** Billy Cole; Ted Seko
3 ❑ Cover: 2.75 **NM** value: **Cover or less**
A: Billy Cole; Ted Seko **W:** Billy Cole; Ted Seko
4 ❑ Cover: 2.75 **NM** value: **Cover or less**
A: Billy Cole; Ted Seko **W:** Billy Cole; Ted Seko

BILLY DOGMA — Modern

1 ❑ Apr 1997 Cover: 2.95 **NM** value: **Cover or less**
2 ❑ Aug 1997 Cover: 2.95 **NM** value: **Cover or less**
3 ❑ Dec 1997 Cover: 2.95 **NM** value: **Cover or less**

BILLY JOE VAN HELSING: REDNECK VAMPIRE HUNTER — Alpha

1 ❑ Cover: 2.50 **NM** value: **Cover or less**
📖 Her Comes Billy Joe Van Helsing; The Devil and David Duke; Billy Joe Buys a Round; The Horror of the South; Li'l Billy Joe & Li'l Maxi; Southern Discomfort; The Crypt-Kicker **A:** Joe Paradise; Donna Franklin; Tad Ghostal **W:** Bill Kieffer; John Migliore

BILLY NGUYEN, PRIVATE EYE — Attitude

1 ❑ Mar 1988 Cover: 2.00 **NM** value: **Cover or less**
📖 Powers What Am **A:** Stanley Shaw **W:** John Hartman
2 ❑ Cover: 2.00 **NM** value: **Cover or less**
3 ❑ Cover: 2.00 **NM** value: **Cover or less**

BILLY NGUYEN, PRIVATE EYE (VOL. 2) — Caliber

1 ❑ b&w Cover: 2.50 **NM** value: **Cover or less**
Circ: CapCity orders: **1,400**

BILLY RAY CYRUS — Marvel Music

1 ❑ Cover: 5.95 **NM** value: **Cover or less**
No issue number. • prestige format.

BILLY THE KID — Charlton

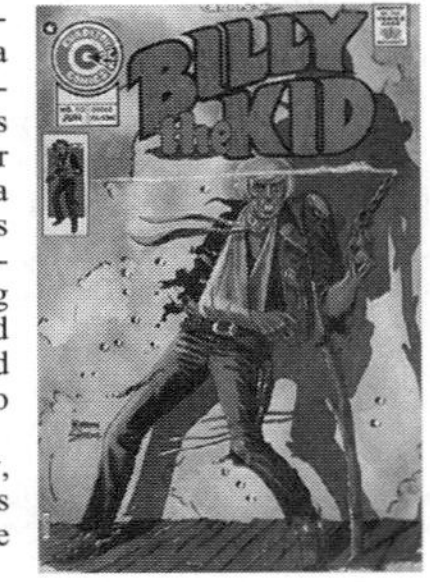

A villain in real life, this legendary figure of the old West gets a facelift in this Charlton series. William Bonney, aka Billy the Kid, was actually a hot-tempered gunslinger who once was said to have killed a man for snoring too loudly. In this title, however, he becomes a dashing and heroic figure, helping homesteaders defend their land from greedy cattle ranchers and forcing con men and gamblers to hightail it out of town.

And in a final contrast to reality, any money that falls into The Kid's hands is usually turned over to the less fortunate or the local church.

9 ❑ Nov 1957 Cover: 0.10 **NM** value: **55.00**
• Series continued from Masked Raider #8
10 ❑ Dec 1957 Cover: 0.10 **NM** value: **32.00**
11 ❑ 1958 Cover: 0.10 **NM** value: **35.00**
• Double-size.
12 ❑ 1958 Cover: 0.10 **NM** value: **28.00**
13 ❑ 1958 Cover: 0.10 **NM** value: **40.00**
A: Al Williamson
14 ❑ 1958 Cover: 0.10 **NM** value: **28.00**
15 ❑ 1958 Cover: 0.10 **NM** value: **40.00**
★ Origin of Billy the Kid.
16 ❑ Cover: 0.10 **NM** value: **40.00**
17 ❑ 1959 Cover: 0.10 **NM** value: **28.00**
18 ❑ 1959 Cover: 0.10 **NM** value: **28.00**
19 ❑ 1959 Cover: 0.10 **NM** value: **28.00**
20 ❑ 1959 Cover: 0.10 **NM** value: **35.00**
21 ❑ 1959 Cover: 0.10 **NM** value: **35.00**
22 ❑ Cover: 0.10 **NM** value: **35.00**
23 ❑ 1960 Cover: 0.10 **NM** value: **20.00**
24 ❑ 1960 Cover: 0.10 **NM** value: **35.00**
25 ❑ 1960 Cover: 0.10 **NM** value: **35.00**
26 ❑ 1960 Cover: 0.10 **NM** value: **35.00**
27 ❑ **NM** value: **20.00**
28 ❑ 1961 **NM** value: **20.00**
29 ❑ 1961 **NM** value: **20.00**
30 ❑ 1961 **NM** value: **20.00**
31 ❑ 1961 **NM** value: **14.00**
32 ❑ **NM** value: **14.00**
33 ❑ Apr 1962 Cover: 0.12 **NM** value: **14.00**
34 ❑ 1962 Cover: 0.12 **NM** value: **14.00**
35 ❑ 1962 Cover: 0.12 **NM** value: **14.00**
36 ❑ Cover: 0.12 **NM** value: **14.00**
37 ❑ 1963 Cover: 0.12 **NM** value: **14.00**
38 ❑ 1963 Cover: 0.12 **NM** value: **14.00**
• **CGC:** 1 graded, best 7.0
39 ❑ 1963 Cover: 0.12 **NM** value: **14.00**
40 ❑ 1963 Cover: 0.12 **NM** value: **14.00**
41 ❑ Cover: 0.12 **NM** value: **8.00**
42 ❑ Cover: 0.12 **NM** value: **8.00**
43 ❑ 1964 Cover: 0.12 **NM** value: **8.00**
44 ❑ 1964 Cover: 0.12 **NM** value: **8.00**
45 ❑ 1964 Cover: 0.12 **NM** value: **8.00**
46 ❑ 1964 Cover: 0.12 **NM** value: **8.00**

Other grades: Multiply prices above by **1.5 for Mint • 2/3 for Very Fine • 1/3 for Fine • 1/5 for Very Good • 1/8 for Good**

47 ❑ Cover: 0.12 **NM** value: **8.00**
48 ❑ Cover: 0.12 **NM** value: **8.00**
49 ❑ 1965 Cover: 0.12 **NM** value: **8.00**
Circ: Statement: **140,635**
50 ❑ 1965 Cover: 0.12 **NM** value: **8.00**
Circ: Statement: **140,635**
51 ❑ 1965 Cover: 0.12 **NM** value: **7.00**
Circ: Statement: **140,635**
52 ❑ 1965 Cover: 0.12 **NM** value: **7.00**
Circ: Statement: **140,635**
53 ❑ 1965 Cover: 0.12 **NM** value: **7.00**
Circ: Statement: **140,635**
54 ❑ 1966 Cover: 0.12 **NM** value: **7.00**
55 ❑ 1966 Cover: 0.12 **NM** value: **7.00**
56 ❑ 1966 Cover: 0.12 **NM** value: **7.00**
• **CGC:** 1 graded, best 8.0
57 ❑ 1966 Cover: 0.12 **NM** value: **7.00**
58 ❑ Nov 1966 Cover: 0.12 **NM** value: **7.00**
59 ❑ Jan 1967 Cover: 0.12 **NM** value: **7.00**
Circ: Statement: **136,615**
60 ❑ Mar 1967 Cover: 0.12 **NM** value: **7.00**
Circ: Statement: **136,615**
61 ❑ 1967 Cover: 0.12 **NM** value: **5.00**
Circ: Statement: **136,615**
62 ❑ Cover: 0.12 **NM** value: **5.00**
Circ: Statement: **136,615**
63 ❑ Cover: 0.12 **NM** value: **5.00**
Circ: Statement: **136,615**
64 ❑ Cover: 0.12 **NM** value: **5.00**
65 ❑ Cover: 0.12 **NM** value: **5.00**
66 ❑ Cover: 0.12 **NM** value: **5.00**
67 ❑ Cover: 0.12 **NM** value: **5.00**
68 ❑ Cover: 0.12 **NM** value: **5.00**
69 ❑ Nov 1968 Cover: 0.12 **NM** value: **5.00**
70 ❑ Jan 1969 **NM** value: **5.00**
71 ❑ Mar 1969 **NM** value: **4.00**
72 ❑ May 1969 **NM** value: **4.00**
73 ❑ Jul 1969 **NM** value: **4.00**
74 ❑ Sep 1969 Cover: 0.15 **NM** value: **4.00**
75 ❑ Nov 1969 Cover: 0.15 **NM** value: **4.00**
76 ❑ Jan 1970 Cover: 0.15 **NM** value: **4.00**
77 ❑ Mar 1970 Cover: 0.15 **NM** value: **4.00**
78 ❑ May 1970 Cover: 0.15 **NM** value: **4.00**
79 ❑ Jul 1970 Cover: 0.15 **NM** value: **4.00**
80 ❑ Sep 1970 Cover: 0.15 **NM** value: **4.00**
81 ❑ Nov 1970 Cover: 0.15 **NM** value: **3.50**
82 ❑ Jan 1971 Cover: 0.15 **NM** value: **3.50**
Circ: Statement: **142,050**
83 ❑ Mar 1971 Cover: 0.15 **NM** value: **3.50**
Circ: Statement: **142,050**
84 ❑ May 1971 Cover: 0.15 **NM** value: **3.50**
Circ: Statement: **142,050**
85 ❑ Jul 1971 Cover: 0.15 **NM** value: **3.50**
Circ: Statement: **142,050**
86 ❑ Sep 1971 Cover: 0.15 **NM** value: **3.50**
Circ: Statement: **142,050**
87 ❑ Nov 1971 **NM** value: **3.50**
Circ: Statement: **142,050**
88 ❑ 1971 **NM** value: **3.50**
Circ: Statement: **142,050**
89 ❑ 1972 **NM** value: **3.50**
Circ: Statement: **152,035**
90 ❑ Mar 1972 Cover: 0.20 **NM** value: **3.50**
Circ: Statement: **152,035**
91 ❑ Apr 1972 Cover: 0.20 **NM** value: **3.50**
Circ: Statement: **152,035**
• Has 1971 Statement, filed 9/30/1971; avg print run 215,000; avg sales 142,000; avg subs 50; avg total paid 142,050; samples 200; office use 100; max existent 142,350; 34% of run returned
92 ❑ 1972 Cover: 0.20 **NM** value: **3.50**
Circ: Statement: **152,035**
93 ❑ 1972 Cover: 0.20 **NM** value: **3.50**
Circ: Statement: **152,035**
94 ❑ Aug 1972 Cover: 0.20 **NM** value: **3.50**
Circ: Statement: **152,035**
95 ❑ Oct 1972 Cover: 0.20 **NM** value: **3.50**
Circ: Statement: **152,035**
96 ❑ Nov 1972 Cover: 0.20 **NM** value: **3.50**
Circ: Statement: **152,035**
97 ❑ Dec 1972 Cover: 0.20 **NM** value: **3.50**
Circ: Statement: **152,035**
98 ❑ Jan 1973 Cover: 0.20 **NM** value: **3.50**
Circ: Statement: **110,360**
99 ❑ Feb 1973 Cover: 0.20 **NM** value: **3.50**
Circ: Statement: **110,360**
100 ❑ Mar 1973 Cover: 0.20 **NM** value: **3.50**
Circ: Statement: **110,360**
• Has 1972 Statement; avg total paid circ 152,035
101 ❑ 1973 Cover: 0.20 **NM** value: **3.00**
Circ: Statement: **110,360**
102 ❑ 1973 Cover: 0.20 **NM** value: **3.00**
Circ: Statement: **110,360**
103 ❑ Aug 1973 Cover: 0.20 **NM** value: **3.00**
Circ: Statement: **110,360**
📖 Mr. Young: Last Round; The Vultures are Waiting • Spanish lesson text piece; no credits listed
104 ❑ 1973 **NM** value: **3.00**
Circ: Statement: **110,360**
105 ❑ 1973 **NM** value: **3.00**
Circ: Statement: **110,360**
106 ❑ 1974 **NM** value: **3.00**
Circ: Statement: **116,120**
107 ❑ May 1974 **NM** value: **3.00**
Circ: Statement: **116,120**
• Has 1973 Statement; avg total paid circ 110,360
108 ❑ 1974 **NM** value: **3.00**
Circ: Statement: **116,120**
109 ❑ 1974 **NM** value: **3.00**
Circ: Statement: **116,120**
110 ❑ 1974 **NM** value: **3.00**
Circ: Statement: **116,120**
111 ❑ Feb 1975 Cover: 0.25 **NM** value: **3.00**
Circ: Statement: **97,700**
112 ❑ Apr 1975 Cover: 0.25 **NM** value: **3.00**
Circ: Statement: **97,700**
• Has 1974 Statement; avg total paid circ 116,120
113 ❑ 1975 Cover: 0.25 **NM** value: **3.00**
Circ: Statement: **97,700**
114 ❑ Oct 1975 Cover: 0.25 **NM** value: **3.00**
Circ: Statement: **97,700**
115 ❑ Dec 1975 Cover: 0.25 **NM** value: **3.00**
Circ: Statement: **97,700**
116 ❑ 1976 **NM** value: **3.00**
117 ❑ 1976 **NM** value: **3.00**
118 ❑ 1976 **NM** value: **3.00**
119 ❑ 1976 **NM** value: **3.00**
120 ❑ Oct 1976 Cover: 0.30 **NM** value: **3.00**
121 ❑ **NM** value: **2.50**
122 ❑ **NM** value: **2.50**
123 ❑ Cover: 0.35 **NM** value: **2.50**
124 ❑ Cover: 0.35 **NM** value: **2.50**
125 ❑ Cover: 0.35 **NM** value: **2.50**
126 ❑ Jan 1979 Cover: 0.35 **NM** value: **2.50**
127 ❑ 1979 **NM** value: **2.50**
128 ❑ 1979 **NM** value: **2.50**
129 ❑ 1979 **NM** value: **2.50**
130 ❑ Aug 1979 Cover: 0.40 **NM** value: **2.50**
131 ❑ Sep 1979 Cover: 0.40 **NM** value: **2.50**
132 ❑ Oct 1979 Cover: 0.40 **NM** value: **2.50**
133 ❑ Dec 1979 Cover: 0.40 **NM** value: **2.50**
📖 Thre for the Money; Apache Red: The Invaders; Turkey Shoot (text); • Joe Gill story, Warren Sattler art credits
134 ❑ Feb 1980 Cover: 0.40 **NM** value: **2.50**
135 ❑ **NM** value: **2.50**
136 ❑ **NM** value: **2.50**
137 ❑ **NM** value: **2.50**
138 ❑ **NM** value: **2.50**
139 ❑ **NM** value: **2.50**
140 ❑ **NM** value: **2.50**
141 ❑ **NM** value: **2.50**
142 ❑ **NM** value: **2.50**
143 ❑ **NM** value: **2.50**
144 ❑ Oct 1981 Cover: 0.50 **NM** value: **2.50**
145 ❑ **NM** value: **2.50**
146 ❑ **NM** value: **2.50**
147 ❑ **NM** value: **2.50**
148 ❑ **NM** value: **2.50**
149 ❑ **NM** value: **2.50**
150 ❑ **NM** value: **2.50**
151 ❑ **NM** value: **2.50**
152 ❑ **NM** value: **2.50**
153 ❑ **NM** value: **2.50**
final issue.

BILLY THE KID (FAWCETT) — Fawcett

1 ❑ Cover: 0.10 **NM** value: **50.00**
2 ❑ Cover: 0.10 **NM** value: **40.00**
3 ❑ Sep 1946 Cover: 0.10 **NM** value: **40.00**
📖 Stagecoach Shenanigans; Dagger of Danger

BILLY WEST — Standard

1 ❑ ca. 1949 Cover: 0.10 **NM** value: **75.00**
2 ❑ Jul 1949 Cover: 0.10 **NM** value: **45.00**
• **CGC:** 1 graded, best 9.4
3 ❑ Sep 1949 Cover: 0.10 **NM** value: **35.00**
4 ❑ Nov 1949 Cover: 0.10 **NM** value: **35.00**
• **CGC:** 1 graded, best 9.0
5 ❑ Feb 1950 Cover: 0.10 **NM** value: **35.00**
• **CGC:** 1 graded, best 9.4
6 ❑ May 1950 Cover: 0.10 **NM** value: **35.00**
• **CGC:** 1 graded, best 8.0
7 ❑ Aug 1950 Cover: 0.10 **NM** value: **35.00**
8 ❑ Nov 1950 Cover: 0.10 **NM** value: **35.00**
9 ❑ Feb 1951 Cover: 0.10 **NM** value: **35.00**

BINKY — DC

Binky is a lovable, but unlucky teen-ager whose efforts to impress girls, act chivalrous, or lend a helping hand almost always end in disaster. Binky is joined in his misadventures by his girlfriend, Peggy, and a collection of their teen pals.

This series bears an uncanny resemblance to the Archie comics. Note that the title is a continuation of Leave It to Binky, and by this time in the series, Binky is making an obvious, and often clumsy, effort to be "hip." In Binky, the "chicks" are really "groovy," and the "cats" are "terrif!" The gags are often based on this generational lingo: "Someone stole my old bag!" — "You mean someone stole your mother?!" — "No, my purse!" However the funniest aspect of the series comes when DC's editors try to use the same "with it" language to explain how they need to "rap" with their fans about needing to raise the price of their comics, etc.

72 ❑ Cover: 0.25 **NM** value: **6.00**
• Series continued from "Leave it to Binky #71"
73 ❑ Cover: 0.25 **NM** value: **6.00**
74 ❑ Cover: 0.25 **NM** value: **6.00**
75 ❑ Cover: 0.25 **NM** value: **6.00**
76 ❑ Cover: 0.25 **NM** value: **5.00**
77 ❑ Cover: 0.25 **NM** value: **5.00**
78 ❑ Cover: 0.25 **NM** value: **5.00**
79 ❑ Cover: 0.25 **NM** value: **5.00**
80 ❑ Cover: 0.25 **NM** value: **5.00**
81 ❑ Cover: 0.25 **NM** value: **5.00**
• Final issue of original series
82 ❑ **NM** value: **2.50**
• 1977 one-shot revival

BINKY BROWN SAMPLER — Last Gasp

Bk 1 ❑ b&w Cover: 16.95 **NM** value: **Cover or less**
• collects stories **A:** Justin Green

BINKY'S BUDDIES — DC

1 ❑ Jan 1969 Cover: 0.12 **NM** value: **25.00**
• **CGC:** 1 graded, best 8.0
2 ❑ Mar 1969 Cover: 0.12 **NM** value: **15.00**
3 ❑ May 1969 Cover: 0.12 **NM** value: **12.00**
4 ❑ Jul 1969 Cover: 0.12 **NM** value: **10.00**
5 ❑ Sep 1969 Cover: 0.12 **NM** value: **10.00**
• **CGC:** 1 graded, best 9.2
6 ❑ Nov 1969 Cover: 0.12 **NM** value: **10.00**
7 ❑ Jan 1970 Cover: 0.12 **NM** value: **10.00**
8 ❑ Mar 1970 Cover: 0.12 **NM** value: **10.00**
9 ❑ May 1970 Cover: 0.12 **NM** value: **10.00**
10 ❑ Jul 1970 Cover: 0.12 **NM** value: **10.00**
11 ❑ Sep 1970 Cover: 0.12 **NM** value: **10.00**
12 ❑ Nov 1970 Cover: 0.12 **NM** value: **10.00**

BIO 90 — Bullet

1 ❑ b&w Cover: 2.50 **NM** value: **Cover or less**

BIO-BOOSTER ARMOR GUYVER — Viz

1 ❑ Cover: 2.75 **NM** value: **4.00**
Circ: CapCity orders: **5,700**
📖 Awesome! **A:** Yoshiki Takaya **W:** Yoshiki Takaya
2 ❑ Cover: 2.75 **NM** value: **3.50**
Circ: CapCity orders: **3,900**
A: Yoshiki Takaya **W:** Yoshiki Takaya
3 ❑ Cover: 2.75 **NM** value: **3.50**
Circ: CapCity orders: **3,650**
A: Yoshiki Takaya **W:** Yoshiki Takaya
4 ❑ Cover: 2.75 **NM** value: **3.50**
Circ: CapCity orders: **3,225**
A: Yoshiki Takaya **W:** Yoshiki Takaya
5 ❑ Cover: 2.75 **NM** value: **3.50**
Circ: CapCity orders: **2,950**
A: Yoshiki Takaya **W:** Yoshiki Takaya
6 ❑ Cover: 2.75 **NM** value: **3.00**
Circ: CapCity orders: **3,025**
A: Yoshiki Takaya **W:** Yoshiki Takaya
7 ❑ Cover: 2.75 **NM** value: **3.00**
Circ: CapCity orders: **2,975**
A: Yoshiki Takaya **W:** Yoshiki Takaya
8 ❑ Cover: 2.75 **NM** value: **3.00**
Circ: CapCity orders: **3,150**
📖 Explosive **A:** Yoshiki Takaya **W:** Yoshiki Takaya
9 ❑ Cover: 2.75 **NM** value: **3.00**
Circ: CapCity orders: **3,200**
A: Yoshiki Takaya **W:** Yoshiki Takaya
10 ❑ Cover: 2.75 **NM** value: **3.00**
📖 Adversarial **A:** Yoshiki Takaya **W:** Yoshiki Takaya
11 ❑ Cover: 2.75 **NM** value: **3.00**
Circ: CapCity orders: **3,100**
A: Yoshiki Takaya **W:** Yoshiki Takaya
12 ❑ Cover: 2.75 **NM** value: **3.00**
Circ: CapCity orders: **2,950**
A: Yoshiki Takaya **W:** Yoshiki Takaya
Bk 1 ❑ Apr 1995 Cover: 15.95 **NM** value: **Cover or less**
• collects first six issues
Bk 2 ❑ Cover: 15.95 **NM** value: **Cover or less**
• Revenge of Chronos

BIO-BOOSTER ARMOR GUYVER PART 2 — Viz

1 ❑ Oct 1994 Cover: 2.75 **NM** value: **3.00**
Circ: CapCity orders: **3,500**
📖 Betrayed! **A:** Yoshiki Takaya **W:** Yoshiki Takaya
2 ❑ Nov 1994 Cover: 2.75 **NM** value: **3.00**
Circ: CapCity orders: **2,950**
A: Yoshiki Takaya **W:** Yoshiki Takaya
3 ❑ Dec 1994 Cover: 2.75 **NM** value: **3.00**
Circ: CapCity orders: **2,875**
A: Yoshiki Takaya **W:** Yoshiki Takaya
4 ❑ Jan 1995 Cover: 2.75 **NM** value: **3.00**
Circ: CapCity orders: **2,625**
A: Yoshiki Takaya **W:** Yoshiki Takaya
5 ❑ Feb 1995 Cover: 2.75 **NM** value: **3.00**
Circ: CapCity orders: **2,450**
A: Yoshiki Takaya **W:** Yoshiki Takaya
6 ❑ Mar 1995 Cover: 2.75 **NM** value: **3.00**
Circ: CapCity orders: **2,525**
A: Yoshiki Takaya **W:** Yoshiki Takaya
Bk 3 ❑ Cover: 15.95 **NM** value: **Cover or less**
• Dark Masters

BIO-BOOSTER ARMOR GUYVER PART 3 — Viz

1 ❑ Apr 1995 Cover: 2.75 **NM** value: **Cover or less**
Circ: CapCity orders: **2,625**
2 ❑ May 1995 Cover: 2.75 **NM** value: **Cover or less**
Circ: CapCity orders: **2,450**
3 ❑ Jun 1995 Cover: 2.75 **NM** value: **Cover or less**
Circ: CapCity orders: **2,500**
4 ❑ Jul 1995 Cover: 2.75 **NM** value: **Cover or less**
Circ: CapCity orders: **2,525**
5 ❑ Aug 1995 Cover: 2.75 **NM** value: **Cover or less**
Circ: CapCity orders: **2,225**
6 ❑ Sep 1995 Cover: 2.75 **NM** value: **Cover or less**
Circ: CapCity orders: **2,100**

CGC-graded: Multiply prices above by **33 for 9.9 M • 16 for 9.8 NM/M • 7 for 9.6 NM+ • 5 for 9.4 NM • 2.5 for 9.2 NM- • 1.5 for 9.0 VF/NM**

7 ☐ Oct 1995 Cover: 2.75 **NM** value: **Cover or less**
Bk 4☐ Cover: 15.95 **NM** value: **Cover or less**
• Escape from Chronos

BIO-BOOSTER ARMOR GUYVER PART 4 — Viz

1 ☐ Nov 1995 Cover: 2.75 **NM** value: **Cover or less**
2 ☐ Dec 1995 Cover: 2.75 **NM** value: **Cover or less**
3 ☐ Jan 1996 Cover: 2.95 **NM** value: **Cover or less**
4 ☐ Feb 1996 Cover: 2.95 **NM** value: **Cover or less**
5 ☐ Mar 1996 Cover: 2.95 **NM** value: **Cover or less**
6 ☐ Apr 1996 Cover: 2.95 **NM** value: **Cover or less**
Bk 5☐ Cover: 15.95 **NM** value: **Cover or less**
• Guyver Reborn!

BIO-BOOSTER ARMOR GUYVER PART 5 — Viz

1 ☐ May 1996 Cover: 2.95 **NM** value: **Cover or less**
2 ☐ Jun 1996 Cover: 2.95 **NM** value: **Cover or less**
3 ☐ Jul 1996 Cover: 2.95 **NM** value: **Cover or less**
4 ☐ Aug 1996 Cover: 2.95 **NM** value: **Cover or less**
5 ☐ Sep 1996 Cover: 2.95 **NM** value: **Cover or less**
Circ: Diamd. preorders: **4,709**
6 ☐ Oct 1996 Cover: 2.95 **NM** value: **Cover or less**
Circ: Diamd. preorders: **4,648**
7 ☐ Nov 1996 Cover: 2.95 **NM** value: **Cover or less**
Circ: Diamd. preorders: **4,486**
Bk 6☐ Cover: 15.95 **NM** value: **Cover or less**
• Heart of Chronos

BIO-BOOSTER ARMOR GUYVER PART 6 — Viz

1 ☐ Dec 1996 Cover: 2.95 **NM** value: **Cover or less**
Circ: Direct Market orders: **4,986**
2 ☐ Jan 1997 Cover: 2.95 **NM** value: **Cover or less**
Circ: Direct Market orders: **4,444**
3 ☐ Feb 1997 Cover: 2.95 **NM** value: **Cover or less**
Circ: Diamd. preorders: **4,103**
4 ☐ Mar 1997 Cover: 2.95 **NM** value: **Cover or less**
Circ: Diamd. preorders: **3,912**
5 ☐ Apr 1997 Cover: 2.95 **NM** value: **Cover or less**
Circ: Diamd. preorders: **3,958**
6 ☐ May 1997 Cover: 2.95 **NM** value: **Cover or less**
Circ: Diamd. preorders: **3,594**
Bk 7☐ Cover: 15.95 **NM** value: **Cover or less**
• Armageddon

BIOLOGIC SHOW, THE — Fantagraphics

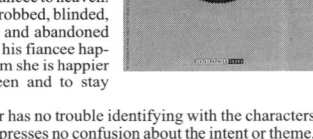

Fantagraphics has a longstanding position as a publisher of esoteric and bizarre work, and, here, the symbolic, expressionistic offerings are heavily slanted toward sexual, oral, and cerebral mutilation.

For example in the title piece, Mr. Lucy is persuaded by a police detective to commit suicide in order to follow his dead fiancee to heaven. After he does, he is robbed, blinded, crippled, castrated, and abandoned on the street. When his fiancee happens by, she tells him she is happier than she's ever been and to stay away from her.

Even if the reader has no trouble identifying with the characters and situations or expresses no confusion about the intent or theme, there is still the matter of the grotesque art and difficult-to-read lettering to contend with.

Some of these visions by artist-writer Al Columbia were first published in Deadline UK.

0 ☐ Oct 1994, b&w Cover: 2.95 **NM** value: **Cover or less**
cardstock cover. • magazine.
1 ☐ Jan 1995, b&w Cover: 2.75 **NM** value: **Cover or less**

BIONEERS — Mirage

1 ☐ Aug 1994 Cover: 2.75 **NM** value: **Cover or less**
Circ: CapCity orders: **6,125**
★ 1st Appearance of Bioneers.
2 ☐ Cover: 2.75 **NM** value: **Cover or less**
3 ☐ Cover: 2.75 **NM** value: **Cover or less**

BIONIC WOMAN, THE — Charlton

The Bionic Woman (1976-1978) was the television spinoff from The Six Million Dollar Man (1974-1978). The Bionic Woman is Jaime Sommers, a tennis player whose body was damaged in a skydiving accident. Using the same bionics technology that had saved Steve Austin, Jaime's body was rebuilt, giving her mechanically enhanced legs, an incredibly powerful arm, and super-sensitive hearing.

She uses these abilities as an agent for O.S.I., reporting to Oscar Goldman. Her missions send her across the world, where she uses her unique gifts to stop bombers, save people from fires, and more. The comic-book run didn't outlast the television series.

1 ☐ Oct 1977 Cover: 0.35 **NM** value: **6.00**
• **CGC:** 3 graded, best 9.2
2 ☐ Feb 1978 Cover: 0.35 **NM** value: **4.00**
3 ☐ Mar 1978 Cover: 0.35 **NM** value: **4.00**
4 ☐ May 1978 Cover: 0.35 **NM** value: **4.00**
5 ☐ Jun 1978 Cover: 0.35 **NM** value: **4.00**
25 ☐ Mar 1981 **NM** value: **2.00**
26 ☐ May 1981 **NM** value: **2.00**
27 ☐ Jul 1981 **NM** value: **2.00**
28 ☐ Oct 1981 **NM** value: **2.00**

BIONIX — Maximum

1 ☐ ca. 1996 Cover: 2.99 **NM** value: **Cover or less**
Circ: Diamd. preorders: **17,587**

BIRD, THE — Entertainment

1 ☐ Cover: 1.50 **NM** value: **Cover or less**
★ Origin of Bird.

BIRDLAND — Fantagraphics / Eros

All issues are adults only.

1 ☐ b&w Cover: 1.95 **NM** value: **Cover or less**
A: Gilbert Hernandez **W:** Gilbert Hernandez
2 ☐ Cover: 2.25 **NM** value: **Cover or less**
A: Gilbert Hernandez **W:** Gilbert Hernandez
3 ☐ Cover: 2.25 **NM** value: **Cover or less**
A: Gilbert Hernandez **W:** Gilbert Hernandez

BIRDLAND (VOL. 2) — Fantagraphics / Eros

1 ☐ Jun 1994, b&w Cover: 2.95 **NM** value: **Cover or less**
A: Gilbert Hernandez **W:** Gilbert Hernandez

BIRDS OF PREY — DC

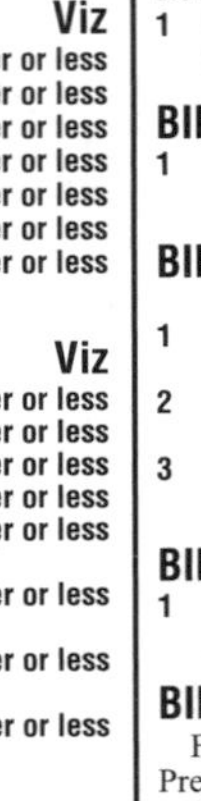

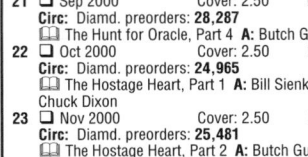

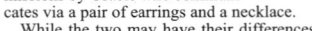

Following a series of Birds of Prey mini-series and one-shots, writer Chuck Dixon and artists Greg Land and Drew Geraci put the duo of Oracle and Black Canary into their own ongoing series.

Oracle is Barbara Gordon, the former Batgirl, now a wheelchair-bound paraplegic computer whiz who provides information to many heroes in the DC universe. Black Canary is an independent woman who works with Oracle to put the kibosh to various nefarious schemes around the globe. Using her natural beauty and crimefighting skills, The Canary is aided in her missions by Oracle who communicates via a pair of earrings and a necklace.

While the two may have their differences from time to time, they do make an effective team. — Brent

1 ☐ Jan 1999 Cover: 1.99 **NM** value: **3.00**
Circ: Diamd. preorders: **33,934** • **CGC:** 2 graded, best 9.6
📖 Long Time Gone **A:** Greg Land **W:** Chuck Dixon ★ Appearance of Hellhound, Oracle.
1/Aut☐ Jan 1999 Cover: 14.99 **NM** value: **Cover or less**
📖 Long Time Gone **A:** Greg Land **W:** Chuck Dixon ★ Appearance of Hellhound, Oracle.
2 ☐ Feb 1999 Cover: 1.99 **NM** value: **2.00**
Circ: Diamd. preorders: **28,551** • **CGC:** 1 graded, best 9.6
A: Greg Land **W:** Chuck Dixon ★ Appearance of Hellhound, Black Canary, Jackie Pajamas.
3 ☐ Mar 1999 Cover: 1.99 **NM** value: **2.00**
Circ: Diamd. preorders: **27,305** • **CGC:** 1 graded, best 9.8
A: Greg Land **W:** Chuck Dixon ★ Appearance of Hellhound, Black Canary.
4 ☐ Apr 1999 Cover: 1.99 **NM** value: **2.00**
Circ: Diamd. preorders: **25,368** • **CGC:** 1 graded, best 9.8
A: Greg Land **W:** Chuck Dixon ★ Appearance of Ravens, Kobra.
5 ☐ May 1999 Cover: 1.99 **NM** value: **2.00**
Circ: Diamd. preorders: **25,743** • **CGC:** 1 graded, best 9.4
A: Greg Land **W:** Chuck Dixon ★ Appearance of Ravens.
6 ☐ Jun 1999 Cover: 1.99 **NM** value: **Cover or less**
Circ: Diamd. preorders: **26,424** • **CGC:** 1 graded, best 9.4
📖 That's Rainbow **A:** Greg Land **W:** Chuck Dixon
7 ☐ Jul 1999 Cover: 1.99 **NM** value: **Cover or less**
Circ: Diamd. preorders: **26,095**
📖 The Villain **A:** Greg Land **W:** Chuck Dixon
8 ☐ Aug 1999 Cover: 1.99 **NM** value: **Cover or less**
Circ: Diamd. preorders: **26,556** • **CGC:** 20 graded, best 9.6
📖 On Wings **A:** Greg Land **W:** Chuck Dixon ★ Appearance of Nightwing.
9 ☐ Sep 1999 Cover: 1.99 **NM** value: **Cover or less**
Circ: Diamd. preorders: **25,714**
📖 Girls Rules **A:** Greg Land **W:** Chuck Dixon
10 ☐ Oct 1999 Cover: 1.99 **NM** value: **Cover or less**
Circ: Diamd. preorders: **25,915**
📖 The Wrong Guy **A:** Greg Land **W:** Chuck Dixon
11 ☐ Nov 1999 Cover: 1.99 **NM** value: **Cover or less**
Circ: Diamd. preorders: **25,294**
📖 State of War **A:** Dick Giordano **W:** Chuck Dixon
12 ☐ Dec 1999 Cover: 1.99 **NM** value: **Cover or less**
Circ: Diamd. preorders: **25,839**
W: Chuck Dixon
13 ☐ Jan 2000 Cover: 1.99 **NM** value: **Cover or less**
Circ: Diamd. preorders: **24,661**
📖 Apokolips Express, Part 1 **A:** Patrick Zircher; Greg Land; Drew Geraci **W:** Chuck Dixon
14 ☐ Feb 2000 Cover: 1.99 **NM** value: **Cover or less**
Circ: Diamd. preorders: **23,897**
📖 Apokolips Express, Part 2 **A:** Patrick Zircher; Greg Land; Drew Geraci **W:** Chuck Dixon
15 ☐ Mar 2000 Cover: 1.99 **NM** value: **Cover or less**
Circ: Diamd. preorders: **23,740**
W: Chuck Dixon
16 ☐ Apr 2000 Cover: 1.99 **NM** value: **Cover or less**
Circ: Diamd. preorders: **23,144**
📖 The Joker's Tale **A:** Butch Guice **W:** Chuck Dixon ★ Appearance of Joker.
17 ☐ May 2000 Cover: 1.99 **NM** value: **Cover or less**
Circ: Diamd. preorders: **23,287**
📖 Nuclear Roulette **A:** Butch Guice **W:** Chuck Dixon
18 ☐ Jun 2000 Cover: 1.99 **NM** value: **Cover or less**
Circ: Diamd. preorders: **23,512**
A: Butch Guice **W:** Chuck Dixon
19 ☐ Jul 2000 Cover: 1.99 **NM** value: **Cover or less**
Circ: Diamd. preorders: **27,524**
A: Butch Guice **W:** Chuck Dixon
20 ☐ Aug 2000 Cover: 2.50 **NM** value: **Cover or less**
Circ: Diamd. preorders: **28,545**
📖 The Hunt for Oracle, Part 2 **A:** Butch Guice **W:** Chuck Dixon
21 ☐ Sep 2000 Cover: 2.50 **NM** value: **Cover or less**
Circ: Diamd. preorders: **28,287**
📖 The Hunt for Oracle, Part 4 **A:** Butch Guice **W:** Chuck Dixon
22 ☐ Oct 2000 Cover: 2.50 **NM** value: **Cover or less**
Circ: Diamd. preorders: **24,965**
📖 The Hostage Heart, Part 1 **A:** Bill Sienkiewicz; Butch Guice **W:** Chuck Dixon
23 ☐ Nov 2000 Cover: 2.50 **NM** value: **Cover or less**
Circ: Diamd. preorders: **25,481**
📖 The Hostage Heart, Part 2 **A:** Butch Guice **W:** Chuck Dixon
24 ☐ Dec 2000 Cover: 2.50 **NM** value: **Cover or less**
Circ: Diamd. preorders: **25,587**
📖 The Hostage Heart, Part 3 **A:** Butch Guice **W:** Chuck Dixon
25 ☐ Jan 2001 Cover: 2.50 **NM** value: **Cover or less**
Circ: Diamd. preorders: **25,613**
📖 Old Habits **A:** Butch Guice **W:** Chuck Dixon
26 ☐ Feb 2001 Cover: 2.50 **NM** value: **Cover or less**
Circ: Diamd. preorders: **28,736**
📖 The Suitor! **A:** Butch Guice **W:** Chuck Dixon
27 ☐ Mar 2001 Cover: 2.50 **NM** value: **Cover or less**
Circ: Diamd. preorders: **31,460**
📖 Officer Down, Part 3 **A:** D. Steven Harris **W:** Chuck Dixon
28 ☐ Apr 2001 Cover: 2.50 **NM** value: **Cover or less**
Circ: Diamd. preorders: **25,403**
📖 History Lesson, Part 1 **A:** Butch Guice **W:** Chuck Dixon
29 ☐ May 2001 Cover: 2.50 **NM** value: **Cover or less**
Circ: Diamd. preorders: **25,752**
📖 History Lesson, Part 2 **A:** Butch Guice **W:** Chuck Dixon
30 ☐ Jun 2001 Cover: 2.50 **NM** value: **Cover or less**
Circ: Diamd. preorders: **26,185**
31 ☐ Jul 2001 Cover: 2.50 **NM** value: **Cover or less**
Circ: Diamd. preorders: **25,648**
32 ☐ Aug 2001 Cover: 2.50 **NM** value: **Cover or less**
Circ: Diamd. preorders: **25,478**
33 ☐ Sep 2001 Cover: 2.50 **NM** value: **Cover or less**
Circ: Diamd. preorders: **26,495**
Bk 1☐ Cover: 17.95 **NM** value: **Cover or less**
• collects Black Canary/Oracle: Birds of Prey, Birds of Prey: Revolution, Showcase '96 #3, and Birds of Prey: Manhunt #1-4 **A:** Matt Haley; Gary Frank; Stefano Raffaele; Jennifer Graves **W:** Chuck Dixon; Jordan Gorfinkel

BIRDS OF PREY: BATGIRL — DC

1 ☐ Feb 1998 Cover: 2.95 **NM** value: **Cover or less**
Circ: Diamd. preorders: **35,588**

BIRDS OF PREY: MANHUNT — DC

1 ☐ Sep 1996 Cover: 1.95 **NM** value: **2.25**
• **CGC:** 1 graded, best 9.8
A: Matt Haley **W:** Chuck Dixon
2 ☐ Oct 1996 Cover: 1.95 **NM** value: **2.00**
• **CGC:** 1 graded, best 9.2
📖 Girl Crazy **A:** Matt Haley **W:** Chuck Dixon
3 ☐ Nov 1996 Cover: 1.95 **NM** value: **2.00**
Circ: Diamd. preorders: **32,636** • **CGC:** 1 graded, best 9.8
📖 The Man that got Away **A:** Matt Haley **W:** Chuck Dixon
4 ☐ Dec 1996 Cover: 1.95 **NM** value: **2.00**
Circ: Direct Market orders: **33,620** • **CGC:** 1 graded, best 9.8
📖 Ladies' Choice final issue. **A:** Matt Haley; Sal Buscema **W:** Chuck Dixon

BIRDS OF PREY: REVOLUTION — DC

1 ☐ Apr 1997 Cover: 2.95 **NM** value: **Cover or less**
Circ: Diamd. preorders: **31,016** • **CGC:** 1 graded, best 9.6
One-shot. **A:** Stefano Raffaele **W:** Chuck Dixon

BIRDS OF PREY: THE RAVENS — DC

1 ☐ Jun 1998 Cover: 1.95 **NM** value: **Cover or less**
Circ: Diamd. preorders: **34,350**
One-shot. 📖 S.I.M.O.N. Says Armageddon • Girlfrenzy **A:** Nelson DeCastro **W:** Chuck Dixon ★ Appearance of Vicious, Termina, Pistolera, Cheshire.

BIRDS OF PREY: WOLVES — DC

1 ☐ Oct 1997 Cover: 2.95 **NM** value: **Cover or less**
Circ: Diamd. preorders: **28,164**
One-shot.

BIRTH CAUL — Eddie Campbell

1 ☐ ca. 1999 Cover: 5.95 **NM** value: **Cover or less**
Circ: Diamd. preorders: **7,329**
No issue number. **W:** Alan Moore

BIRTHDAY BOY, THE — Beetlebomb

1 ☐ Cover: 2.95 **NM** value: **Cover or less**
📖 The Birthday Boy **A:** Jason Lethcoe **W:** Jason Lethcoe
2 ☐ Cover: 2.95 **NM** value: **Cover or less**
📖 Moonstuck! **A:** Jason Lethcoe **W:** Jason Lethcoe
3 ☐ Cover: 2.95 **NM** value: **Cover or less**
📖 Hugo's Test **A:** Jason Lethcoe **W:** Jason Lethcoe
4 ☐ Cover: 2.95 **NM** value: **Cover or less**
📖 The Showdown! **A:** Jason Lethcoe **W:** Jason Lethcoe
Bk 1☐ Cover: 7.95 **NM** value: **Cover or less**
📖 The Birthday Boy; Moonstuck!; Hugo's Test; The Showdown! • Collects issues #1-4 **A:** Jason Lethcoe **W:** Jason Lethcoe

BIRTHDAY BOY, THE (VOL. 2) — Beetlebomb

1 ☐ Cover: 2.95 **NM** value: **Cover or less**
A: Jason Lethcoe **W:** Jason Lethcoe

Other grades: Multiply prices above by **1.5 for Mint • 2/3 for Very Fine • 1/3 for Fine • 1/5 for Very Good • 1/8 for Good**

BIRTHRIGHT — Fantagraphics

1 ☐ Cover: 2.00 **NM** value: **2.50**
A: Monika Livingston **W:** Steven A. Gallacci
2 ☐ Cover: 2.00 **NM** value: **2.50**
A: Monika Livingston **W:** Steven A. Gallacci
3 ☐ Cover: 2.00 **NM** value: **2.50**
A: Monika Livingston **W:** Steven A. Gallacci

BIRTHRIGHT (TSR) — TSR

1 ☐ **NM** value: **1.50**
Serpent's Eye **A:** Dave Gross **W:** Ed Stark

BIRTH RITE — Congress

1 ☐ Cover: 2.50 **NM** value: **Cover or less**
2 ☐ Cover: 2.50 **NM** value: **Cover or less**
3 ☐ Cover: 2.50 **NM** value: **Cover or less**
4 ☐ Cover: 2.50 **NM** value: **Cover or less**

BISHOP — Marvel

Bishop is a mutant from the future who crossed over into our time in Uncanny X-Men #282. In his own time, he was a member of the XSE, a police force charged with hunting down mutant criminals using any amount of force necessary. Bishop's own power is the ability to absorb and rechannel energy, making any energy attack against him futile. He remains vulnerable, however, to projectiles.

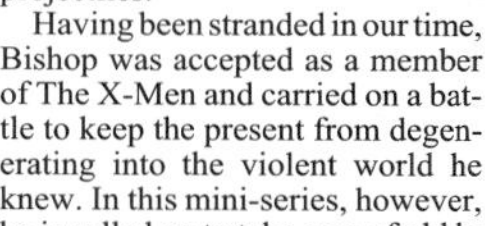

Having been stranded in our time, Bishop was accepted as a member of The X-Men and carried on a battle to keep the present from degenerating into the violent world he knew. In this mini-series, however, he is called on to take care of old business in the form of a mutant criminal who escaped in the time rift in which Bishop had crossed over. The mutant is called Mountjoy and he has the ability to usurp the bodies and wills of others. Unless Bishop can stop him, Mountjoy intends to use this time period as his own sick playground.

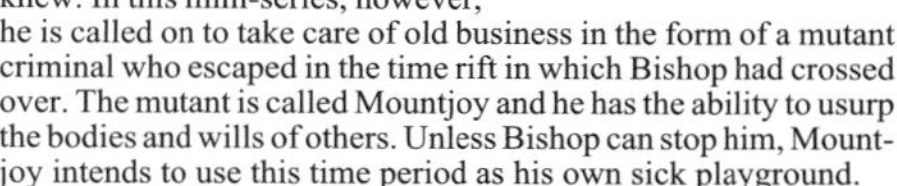

1 ☐ Dec 1994 Cover: 2.95 **NM** value: **Cover or less**
Circ: CapCity orders: **76,150** • **CGC:** 1 graded, best 9.8
foil cover. ★ 1st Appearance of Mountjoy.
2 ☐ Jan 1995 Cover: 2.95 **NM** value: **Cover or less**
Circ: CapCity orders: **57,325**
3 ☐ Feb 1995 Cover: 2.95 **NM** value: **Cover or less**
Circ: CapCity orders: **51,075**
4 ☐ Mar 1995 Cover: 2.95 **NM** value: **Cover or less**
Circ: CapCity orders: **47,075**

BISHOP THE LAST X-MAN — Marvel

1 ☐ Oct 1999 Cover: 2.99 **NM** value: **Cover or less**
Circ: Diamd. preorders: **54,130**
2 ☐ Nov 1999 Cover: 2.99 **NM** value: **Cover or less**
Circ: Diamd. preorders: **46,204**
3 ☐ Dec 1999 Cover: 2.99 **NM** value: **Cover or less**
Circ: Diamd. preorders: **41,234**
4 ☐ Jan 2000 Cover: 2.99 **NM** value: **Cover or less**
Circ: Diamd. preorders: **38,073**
5 ☐ Feb 2000 Cover: 2.99 **NM** value: **Cover or less**
Circ: Diamd. preorders: **38,997**
6 ☐ Mar 2000 Cover: 2.99 **NM** value: **Cover or less**
Circ: Diamd. preorders: **32,708**
7 ☐ Apr 2000 Cover: 2.99 **NM** value: **Cover or less**
Circ: Diamd. preorders: **29,948**
8 ☐ May 2000 Cover: 2.99 **NM** value: **Cover or less**
Circ: Diamd. preorders: **29,306**
9 ☐ Jun 2000 Cover: 2.99 **NM** value: **Cover or less**
Circ: Diamd. preorders: **27,777**
10 ☐ Jul 2000 Cover: 2.99 **NM** value: **Cover or less**
Circ: Diamd. preorders: **27,746**
11 ☐ Aug 2000 Cover: 2.99 **NM** value: **Cover or less**
Circ: Diamd. preorders: **27,754**
12 ☐ Sep 2000 Cover: 2.99 **NM** value: **Cover or less**
Circ: Diamd. preorders: **27,123**
• double-sized. The Chronowar, Act 1: Helter Skelter **A:** Georges Jeanty **W:** Joseph Harris
13 ☐ Oct 2000 Cover: 2.25 **NM** value: **Cover or less**
Circ: Diamd. preorders: **24,956**
14 ☐ Nov 2000 Cover: 2.25 **NM** value: **Cover or less**
Circ: Diamd. preorders: **24,753**
The Chronowar, Act 3: Remain in Light **A:** Georges Jeanty **W:** Joseph Harris
15 ☐ Dec 2000 Cover: 2.25 **NM** value: **Cover or less**
Circ: Diamd. preorders: **27,643**
Maximum Security; ... Been a Long Lonely, Lonely, Lonely, Lonely, Lonely Time! **A:** Georges Jeanty **W:** Joseph Harris
16 ☐ Jan 2001 Cover: 2.25 **NM** value: **Cover or less**
Circ: Diamd. preorders: **31,850** • **CGC:** 2 graded, best 9.6
Dream's End, Part 3 final issue. **A:** Thomas Derenick **W:** Scott Lobdell; Joe Pruett

BISHOP: XSE — Marvel

1 ☐ Jan 1998 Cover: 2.50 **NM** value: **Cover or less**
Circ: Diamd. preorders: **56,896**
• gatefold summary. Rook Takes Pawn **A:** Steve Epting **W:** John Ostrander
2 ☐ Feb 1998 Cover: 2.50 **NM** value: **Cover or less**
Circ: Diamd. preorders: **47,826**
• gatefold summary. **A:** Steve Epting **W:** John Ostrander
3 ☐ Mar 1998 Cover: 2.50 **NM** value: **Cover or less**
Circ: Diamd. preorders: **43,264**
A: Steve Epting **W:** John Ostrander

BISLEY'S SCRAPBOOK — Atomeka

Three shorts and several pinups make up this one-shot by a creator whose realistic paintings and fearless use of gore has attracted fans from both sides of the Atlantic.

In the first, a woman and child on the run deal with wolves, a cyborg, and cannibals in a vicious story with an unpleasant end. Next, a barbarian warrior hacks his way to the throne he wishes to conquer, only to have things work out to his disadvantage. Finally, to lighten it up, an Old West zombie and his dead horse ride into town seeking revenge — but he's got the wrong town.

Simon Bisley's vast collection of other works include contributions to Heavy Metal, several issues of Lobo, and Judge Dredd.

1 ☐ Cover: 2.50 **NM** value: **Cover or less**
No issue number. Max Carnage; Kyrn; Once Upon a Time in the West **A:** Simon Bisley **W:** Simon Bisley; Dave Elliott

BITCH IN HEAT — Eros

1 ☐ Mar 1997 Cover: 2.95 **NM** value: **Cover or less**
Circ: Diamd. preorders: **2,632**
A: Giovanna Casotto **W:** Giovanna Casotto
2 ☐ Cover: 2.95 **NM** value: **Cover or less**
A: Giovanna Casotto **W:** Giovanna Casotto
3 ☐ Cover: 2.95 **NM** value: **Cover or less**
A: Giovanna Casotto **W:** Giovanna Casotto
4 ☐ Cover: 2.95 **NM** value: **Cover or less**
A: Giovanna Casotto **W:** Giovanna Casotto
5 ☐ Jul 1998 Cover: 2.95 **NM** value: **Cover or less**
Circ: Diamd. preorders: **2,218**
A: Giovanna Casotto **W:** Giovanna Casotto
6 ☐ Sep 1998 Cover: 2.95 **NM** value: **Cover or less**
Circ: Diamd. preorders: **2,393**
A: Giovanna Casotto **W:** Giovanna Casotto
7 ☐ Jan 1999 Cover: 2.95 **NM** value: **Cover or less**
Circ: Diamd. preorders: **2,541**
A: Giovanna Casotto **W:** Giovanna Casotto
8 ☐ Apr 1999 Cover: 2.95 **NM** value: **Cover or less**
Circ: Diamd. preorders: **2,456**
A: Giovanna Casotto **W:** Giovanna Casotto
9 ☐ ca. 1999 Cover: 2.95 **NM** value: **Cover or less**
10 ☐ ca. 2000 Cover: 2.95 **NM** value: **Cover or less**
Circ: Diamd. preorders: **2,176**

BITCHY BUTCH WORLD'S ANGRIEST DYKE! — Fantagraphics

Bk 1☐ May 1999 Cover: 9.95 **NM** value: **Cover or less**

BITTER CAKE — Tin Cup

1 ☐ b&w Cover: 2.00 **NM** value: **Cover or less**

BIZARRE 3-D ZONE — Blackthorne

1 ☐ Jul 1986 Cover: 2.25 **NM** value: **Cover or less**
Circ: CapCity orders: **4,725**
2 ☐ Cover: 2.25 **NM** value: **Cover or less**
3 ☐ Cover: 2.25 **NM** value: **Cover or less**
4 ☐ Cover: 2.25 **NM** value: **Cover or less**
5 ☐ Jul 1986 Cover: 2.25 **NM** value: **Cover or less**
Dark Follower; July 4, 1976; Zone One; The Wrath of Romborr!; Zone Two; Zone Three; G; Zone Four; Space Waif; Zone Five; Zone Six **A:** Jack C. Harris; John Pound; Mike Sekowski; Rob William; Terry Stroud; William Tout **W:** John Pound; Mike Sekowski; Rob William; Spain Rodriguez; Terry Stroud; William Tout

BIZARRE ADVENTURES — Marvel

25 ☐ Mar 1981 Cover: 1.25 **NM** value: **2.00**
Circ: Statement: **59,000**
• Lethal Ladies;Was Marvel Preview ★ Appearance of Black Widow.
26 ☐ May 1981 Cover: 1.25 **NM** value: **2.00**
Circ: Statement: **59,000**
• King Kull
27 ☐ Jul 1981 Cover: 1.25 **NM** value: **4.00**
Circ: Statement: **59,000**
• X-Men
28 ☐ Oct 1981 Cover: 1.50 **NM** value: **3.00**
Circ: Statement: **59,000**
• Unlikely Heroes **A:** Frank Miller **W:** Frank Miller ★ Appearance of Elektra.
29 ☐ Dec 1981 Cover: 1.50 **NM** value: **2.00**
Circ: Statement: **59,000**
• Stephen King;Horror
30 ☐ Cover: 1.50 **NM** value: **2.00**
• Paradox;Tomorrow
31 ☐ Cover: 1.50 **NM** value: **2.00**
• After the Violence Stops **A:** Frank Miller
32 ☐ Aug 1982 Cover: 1.50 **NM** value: **2.00**
• Thor and other Gods **A:** Joe Jusko(cover)
33 ☐ Cover: 1.50 **NM** value: **2.00**
Photo cover. • Dracula;Zombie;Horror ★ 1st Appearance of Varnae.
34 ☐ Feb 1983 Cover: 2.00 **NM** value: **Cover or less**
• gatefold summary. Son of Santa!; Howard The Duck's Christmas; Slay Bells; Santa Bites the Big Apple!; Bucky Bizarre • Format changes to comic book **A:** Alan Kupperberg; Al Milgrom; Paul Smith; Joe Jusko(cover); Mike Carlin **W:** Al Milgrom; Mike Carlin; Steven Grant; Mark Gruenwald ★ Appearance of Howard the Duck.

BIZARRE FANTASY — Flashback

0 ☐ Cover: 2.50 **NM** value: **Cover or less**
A: Steve Busti **W:** Steve Busti
0/AUT☐ Cover: 9.95 **NM** value: **Cover or less**
• 1500 copies printed **A:** Steve Busti **W:** Steve Busti
1 ☐ Cover: 2.50 **NM** value: **Cover or less**
Crisis at the Dawn of Time; Cowboys & Aliens; Waiting for the Aliens **A:** Steve Busti **W:** Steve Busti ★ 1st Appearance of Morguu, The Evolver.
2 ☐ Cover: 2.50 **NM** value: **Cover or less**
A: Steve Busti; Dick Ayers(cover) **W:** Steve Busti

BIZARRE HEROES — Kitchen Sink

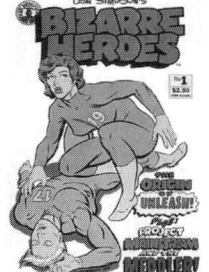

A group of clones with enhanced abilities battle another set of clones out to destroy them and the lesser humans the bad clones intend to replace. It's "Project Mainstream," and only a newspaper columnist, who was cloned against his will by a mad scientist, knows the full secret. Can he find a way to tell the world and help the four clone outcasts without being laughed out of town — let alone killed? And what's with the guy who almost, but not quite, looks like a mummy?

Created by Don Simpson, this series became a repository for his current series as well as old ideas from high school. First released as a 1990 one-shot, which was later reprinted as #0, the full series launched in 1994. It snagged two Eisner and one Harvey nominations before ending at #15. Simpson's other works include Megaton Man.

1 ☐ May 1990 Cover: 2.50 **NM** value: **Cover or less**
• parody, b&w

BIZARRE HEROES (DON SIMPSON'S...) — Fiasco

0 ☐ Dec 1994 Cover: 2.95 **NM** value: **Cover or less**
1 ☐ May 1994 Cover: 2.95 **NM** value: **3.25**
The Apocalypse Affiliation; Clone But Not Forgotten; Meanwhile...The Meddler; X-Ray Boy; **A:** Donald Simpson **W:** Donald Simpson
2 ☐ Jun 1994 Cover: 2.95 **NM** value: **Cover or less**
A: Donald Simpson **W:** Donald Simpson
3 ☐ Jul 1994 Cover: 2.95 **NM** value: **Cover or less**
A: Donald Simpson **W:** Donald Simpson
4 ☐ Aug 1994 Cover: 2.95 **NM** value: **Cover or less**
A: Donald Simpson **W:** Donald Simpson
5 ☐ Sep 1994 Cover: 2.95 **NM** value: **Cover or less**
A: Donald Simpson **W:** Donald Simpson
6 ☐ Oct 1994 Cover: 2.95 **NM** value: **Cover or less**
A: Donald Simpson **W:** Donald Simpson
7 ☐ Nov 1994 Cover: 2.95 **NM** value: **Cover or less**
A: Donald Simpson **W:** Donald Simpson
8 ☐ Dec 1994 Cover: 2.95 **NM** value: **Cover or less**
A: Donald Simpson **W:** Donald Simpson
9 ☐ Cover: 2.95 **NM** value: **Cover or less**
A: Donald Simpson **W:** Donald Simpson
10 ☐ Cover: 2.95 **NM** value: **Cover or less**
A: Donald Simpson **W:** Donald Simpson
11 ☐ Cover: 2.95 **NM** value: **Cover or less**
A: Donald Simpson **W:** Donald Simpson
12 ☐ Cover: 2.95 **NM** value: **Cover or less**
A: Donald Simpson **W:** Donald Simpson
13 ☐ Cover: 2.95 **NM** value: **Cover or less**
A: Donald Simpson **W:** Donald Simpson
14 ☐ Oct 1995 Cover: 2.95 **NM** value: **Cover or less**
• Title changes to Bizarre Heroes **A:** Donald Simpson **W:** Donald Simpson
15 ☐ Jan 1996 Cover: 2.95 **NM** value: **Cover or less**
A: Donald Simpson **W:** Donald Simpson ★ Origin of The Slick.

BIZARRE SEX — Kitchen Sink

All issues are adults only.

1 ☐ **NM** value: **18.00**
2 ☐ **NM** value: **10.00**
3 ☐ **NM** value: **8.00**
White "remove this outer cover at your own risk" cover.
4 ☐ **NM** value: **5.00**
4-2 ☐ **NM** value: **4.00**
4-3 ☐ **NM** value: **6.00**
5 ☐ **NM** value: **6.00**
6 ☐ **NM** value: **6.00**
7 ☐ **NM** value: **6.00**
8 ☐ **NM** value: **6.00**
9 ☐ Aug 1981, b&w Cover: 2.00 **NM** value: **20.00**
★ 1st Appearance of Omaha.

BIZZARIAN — Ironcat

1 ☐ ca. 2000 Cover: 2.95 **NM** value: **Cover or less**
2 ☐ ca. 2000 Cover: 2.95 **NM** value: **Cover or less**
3 ☐ ca. 2000 Cover: 2.95 **NM** value: **Cover or less**
4 ☐ ca. 2000 Cover: 2.95 **NM** value: **Cover or less**
Circ: Diamd. preorders: **1,290**
5 ☐ ca. 2001 Cover: 2.95 **NM** value: **Cover or less**
Circ: Diamd. preorders: **1,362**
6 ☐ ca. 2001 Cover: 2.95 **NM** value: **Cover or less**
Circ: Diamd. preorders: **1,312**
7 ☐ ca. 2001 Cover: 2.95 **NM** value: **Cover or less**
Circ: Diamd. preorders: **1,260**
8 ☐ ca. 2001 Cover: 2.95 **NM** value: **Cover or less**
Circ: Diamd. preorders: **1,206**

B. KRIGSTEIN SAMPLER, A — Independent

1 ☐ **NM** value: **2.50**
The Man Who Shrunk; The Hypnotist; The Man Who Went Black; Someone is Calling; They Wait Below; Dinosaur; The Sinister Suit; The Last Look; Out of This World; Phantom of the Farm **A:** Bernard Krigstein **W:** Bernard Krigstein

BLAB! — Kitchen Sink

8 ☐ Sum 1995 Cover: 16.95 **NM** value: **Cover or less**
• odd-sized anthology. **C:** Chris Ware
9 ☐ Fal 1997 Cover: 18.95 **NM** value: **Cover or less**
• odd-sized anthology.
10 ☐ Fal 1998 Cover: 19.95 **NM** value: **Cover or less**
• odd-sized anthology.

CGC-graded: Multiply prices above by **33 for 9.9 M • 16 for 9.8 NM/M • 7 for 9.6 NM+ • 5 for 9.4 NM • 2.5 for 9.2 NM- • 1.5 for 9.0 VF/NM**

BLACK & WHITE — Image

1 ❑ Feb 1996 Cover: 2.50 **NM** value: **Cover or less**
Beginnings **A:** Art Thibert **W:** Art Thibert; Pamela Thibert
Ash 1❑ **NM** value: **1.00**
No issue number. no cover price. • ashcan preview of series

BLACK AND WHITE COMICS — Apex Novelties

1 ❑ Cover: 0.75 **NM** value: **4.00**
Squirrely the Squirrel; Namby Pamby and Her friends; Patricia Goes Shopping; Bill the Pill; Big Fine Legs; Robert Crumb vs. The Sisterhood; Those Goddamn Blues **A:** Robert Crumb **W:** Robert Crumb

BLACK & WHITE (MINI-SERIES) — Image

1 ❑ Oct 1994 Cover: 1.95 **NM** value: **Cover or less**
Circ: CapCity orders: **46,050**
#1 Black **A:** Art Thibert **W:** Art Thibert; Pamela Thibert
2 ❑ Nov 1994 Cover: 1.95 **NM** value: **Cover or less**
Circ: CapCity orders: **29,650**
A: Art Thibert **W:** Art Thibert; Pamela Thibert
3 ❑ Jan 1995 Cover: 1.95 **NM** value: **Cover or less**
Circ: CapCity orders: **24,500**
A: Art Thibert **W:** Art Thibert; Pamela Thibert

BLACK AND WHITE THEATER — Double M

1 ❑ Jun 1996, b&w Cover: 2.95 **NM** value: **Cover or less**
2 ❑ b&w Cover: 2.95 **NM** value: **Cover or less**

BLACK & WHITE (VIZ) — Viz

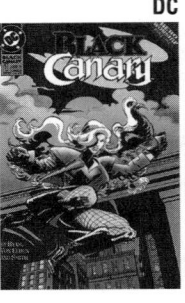

Made popular in the pages of Pulp Magazine, Viz Comics retells the story of Black and White in its own —you guessed it— black and white series. Originally presented as a serialized story (the way comics are read in Japan), the comic-book rendition packs two chapters of the story's overall tale within the pages of each title.

Mean kids practice random acts of violence and senseless ugliness on the streets of Treasure Town. Black (a streetwise sinner) and White (a dimwitted innocent) have always been inseparable, as they rampage their way through the city's surreal streets. But when the police take White into protective custody, Black is left to run amok — no calming influence to temper his violent tendencies.

Moreover, a strange alien cult is out to exterminate the anti-heroes? Welcome to the violently adult manga world of Black and White.

1 ❑ Aug 1999 Cover: 3.25 **NM** value: **Cover or less**
Circ: Diamd. preorders: **1,791**
A: Taiyo Matsumoto **W:** Taiyo Matsumoto
2 ❑ 1999 Cover: 3.25 **NM** value: **Cover or less**
The Color of Black **A:** Taiyo Matsumoto **W:** Taiyo Matsumoto
3 ❑ 1999 Cover: 3.25 **NM** value: **Cover or less**
A: Taiyo Matsumoto **W:** Taiyo Matsumoto
Bk 1❑ b&w Cover: 15.95 **NM** value: **Cover or less**
• collects story serialized in Pulp **A:** Taiyo Matsumoto **W:** Taiyo Matsumoto

BLACK ANGEL — Verotik

1 ❑ Sep 1996 Cover: 9.95 **NM** value: **Cover or less**
No issue number. • prestige format. • reprints Golden Age stories

BLACK AXE — Marvel

1 ❑ Apr 1993 Cover: 1.75 **NM** value: **Cover or less**
Circ: CapCity orders: **59,100**
★ 1st Appearance of Black Axe. ★ Appearance of Death's Head II.
2 ❑ May 1993 Cover: 1.75 **NM** value: **Cover or less**
Circ: CapCity orders: **24,900**
The Spirit of the Sword **A:** Ed Perryman **W:** Simon Jowett
3 ❑ Jun 1993 Cover: 1.75 **NM** value: **Cover or less**
Circ: CapCity orders: **20,600**
4 ❑ Jul 1993 Cover: 1.75 **NM** value: **Cover or less**
Circ: CapCity orders: **15,700**
5 ❑ Aug 1993 Cover: 1.75 **NM** value: **Cover or less**
Circ: CapCity orders: **11,400**
6 ❑ Sep 1993 Cover: 1.75 **NM** value: **Cover or less**
Circ: CapCity orders: **8,000**
7 ❑ Oct 1993 Cover: 1.75 **NM** value: **Cover or less**
Circ: CapCity orders: **6,800**
final issue. **A:** Ed Perryman **W:** Simon Jowett ★ Appearance of Afrikka, Black Panther, She.

BLACKBALL COMICS — Blackball

1 ❑ Mar 1994 Cover: 3.00 **NM** value: **Cover or less**
Circ: CapCity orders: **4,830**
Folklaw; The Seuling Legacy; Radical Dreamer **A:** Keith Giffen; Simon Bisley; Mark Wheatley; Kevin O'neil **W:** Keith Giffen; Simon Bisley; Mark Wheatley; Kevin O'neil

BLACK BOOK (BRIAN BOLLAND'S...) — Eclipse

1 ❑ Cover: 1.75 **NM** value: **2.00**
Circ: CapCity orders: **6,000**
Vampire Carnival; Plague of the Undead **A:** Brian Bolland; Trevor Goring **W:** Steve Parkhouse; Steve Moore

Do you have changes or corrections for the **Standard Catalog**? Send your original research to us at
allcomics@krause.com

BLACK CANARY — DC

Known to readers of the Green Arrow series as the Arrow's love interest, Black Canary gets a chance to strike out on her own in this new series.

The Canary's sole super-power was her sonic scream (a la the Uncanny X-Men's Banshee), a power she lost for good in Green Arrow: The Longbow Hunters. Luckily, she learned early on never to rely upon her super-power as her only weapon, and she trains hard to become an accomplished martial artist. She uses these talents to fight crime on an up-close and personal level.

The Black Canary has garnered praise for its portrayal of a strong female character, and she went on to more adventures in later stories.

1 ❑ Jan 1993 Cover: 1.75 **NM** value: **2.00**
Circ: CapCity orders: **19,300**
Hero Worship, Part 1
2 ❑ Feb 1993 Cover: 1.75 **NM** value: **2.00**
Circ: CapCity orders: **11,950**
Hero Worship, Part 2
3 ❑ Mar 1993 Cover: 1.75 **NM** value: **2.00**
Circ: CapCity orders: **11,050**
Hero Worship, Part 3
4 ❑ Apr 1993 Cover: 1.75 **NM** value: **2.00**
Circ: CapCity orders: **10,400**
5 ❑ May 1993 Cover: 1.75 **NM** value: **2.00**
Circ: CapCity orders: **9,100**
6 ❑ Jun 1993 Cover: 1.75 **NM** value: **Cover or less**
Circ: CapCity orders: **9,250**
7 ❑ Jul 1993 Cover: 1.75 **NM** value: **Cover or less**
Circ: CapCity orders: **8,150**
8 ❑ Aug 1993 Cover: 1.75 **NM** value: **Cover or less**
Circ: CapCity orders: **7,750**
★ Appearance of The Ray.
9 ❑ Sep 1993 Cover: 1.75 **NM** value: **Cover or less**
Circ: CapCity orders: **7,300**
10 ❑ Oct 1993 Cover: 1.75 **NM** value: **Cover or less**
Circ: CapCity orders: **7,100**
11 ❑ Nov 1993 Cover: 1.75 **NM** value: **Cover or less**
Circ: CapCity orders: **6,400**
Weaker Weasels **A:** Trevor Von Eeden **W:** Sarah E. Byam
12 ❑ Dec 1993 Cover: 1.75 **NM** value: **Cover or less**
Circ: CapCity orders: **5,950**
final issue.

BLACK CANARY ARCHIVES — DC

1 ❑ Cover: 49.95 **NM** value: **Cover or less**
• Collects Black Canary stories from Flash Comics #86-104, DC Special #3, Adventure Comics #399, 418, 419, and Brave and the Bold #61-62 **A:** Carmine Infantino **W:** Carmine Infantino; Robert Kanigher

BLACK CANARY (MINI-SERIES) — DC

1 ❑ Nov 1991 Cover: 1.75 **NM** value: **2.50**
Circ: CapCity orders: **30,000**
New Wings, Part 1
2 ❑ Dec 1991 Cover: 1.75 **NM** value: **2.00**
Circ: CapCity orders: **21,600**
New Wings, Part 2
3 ❑ Jan 1992 Cover: 1.75 **NM** value: **2.00**
Circ: CapCity orders: **18,650**
New Wings, Part 3
4 ❑ Feb 1992 Cover: 1.75 **NM** value: **2.00**
Circ: CapCity orders: **16,000**
New Wings, Part 4

BLACK CANARY/ORACLE: BIRDS OF PREY — DC

1 ❑ Cover: 3.95 **NM** value: **Cover or less**
One-shot. **A:** Gary Frank **W:** Chuck Dixon

BLACK CAT COMICS — Harvey

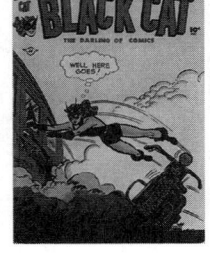

Imagine it's the late 1940s. Imagine Elizabeth Taylor is not only one of the most gorgeous young women in Hollywood, but in her spare time she dons a disguise (complete with fishnet stockings) and careens around town on her motorcycle, fighting crime. That's pretty much the premise of Black Cat Comics. The Black Cat is gorgeous movie star Linda Turner: not only a popular actress but a woman trained in the martial arts.

She had starred in short comics stories in Speed Comics but finally got her own title. Artist Lee Elias drew her with verve, including illustrations for several how-to judo features. — Maggie

1 ❑ Jun 1946 Cover: 0.10 **NM** value: **400.00**
• **CGC:** 2 graded, best 9.4
2 ❑ Aug 1946 Cover: 0.10 **NM** value: **265.00**
3 ❑ Dec 1946 Cover: 0.10 **NM** value: **200.00**
• **CGC:** 3 graded, best 9.0
4 ❑ Feb 1947 Cover: 0.10 **NM** value: **200.00**
5 ❑ Apr 1947 Cover: 0.10 **NM** value: **200.00**
• **CGC:** 1 graded, best 5.0
My City Is No More • Duke of Broadway
6 ❑ Jul 1947 Cover: 0.10 **NM** value: **165.00**
• **CGC:** 1 graded, best 7.5
Story of a Guilty Conscience • Duke of Broadway
7 ❑ Sep 1947 Cover: 0.10 **NM** value: **165.00**
Death Trap Deluxe; Topsy Turvy Tavern • Vagabond Prince
8 ❑ Nov 1947 Cover: 0.10 **NM** value: **175.00**
• **CGC:** 1 graded, best 8.5
The Madness of Doctor Altu
9 ❑ Jan 1948 Cover: 0.10 **NM** value: **225.00**
• **CGC:** 1 graded, best 8.5
Killer in the Big Top • Reprinted from Stuntman Comics #1
10 ❑ Mar 1948 Cover: 0.10 **NM** value: **125.00**
11 ❑ May 1948 Cover: 0.10 **NM** value: **125.00**
12 ❑ Jul 1948 Cover: 0.10 **NM** value: **125.00**
13 ❑ Sep 1948 Cover: 0.10 **NM** value: **125.00**
14 ❑ Nov 1948 Cover: 0.10 **NM** value: **125.00**
15 ❑ Jan 1949 Cover: 0.10 **NM** value: **125.00**
• **CGC:** 1 graded, best 8.5
16 ❑ Mar 1949 Cover: 0.10 **NM** value: **125.00**
17 ❑ May 1949 Cover: 0.10 **NM** value: **125.00**
• **CGC:** 1 graded, best 6.5
18 ❑ Jul 1949 Cover: 0.10 **NM** value: **125.00**
19 ❑ Sep 1949 Cover: 0.10 **NM** value: **125.00**
• **CGC:** 1 graded, best 5.0
20 ❑ Nov 1949 Cover: 0.10 **NM** value: **125.00**
• **CGC:** 1 graded, best 8.0
21 ❑ Feb 1950 Cover: 0.10 **NM** value: **85.00**
• **CGC:** 2 graded, best 9.2
22 ❑ Apr 1950 Cover: 0.10 **NM** value: **85.00**
23 ❑ Jun 1950 Cover: 0.10 **NM** value: **85.00**
24 ❑ Aug 1950 Cover: 0.10 **NM** value: **85.00**
• **CGC:** 2 graded, best 9.4
25 ❑ Oct 1950 Cover: 0.10 **NM** value: **85.00**
26 ❑ Dec 1950 Cover: 0.10 **NM** value: **85.00**
• **CGC:** 2 graded, best 9.2
27 ❑ Feb 1951 Cover: 0.10 **NM** value: **85.00**
28 ❑ Apr 1951 Cover: 0.10 **NM** value: **85.00**
• **CGC:** 3 graded, best 9.2
29 ❑ Jun 1951 Cover: 0.10 **NM** value: **85.00**
• **CGC:** 2 graded, best 9.0
30 ❑ Aug 1951 Cover: 0.10 **NM** value: **85.00**
• **CGC:** 5 graded, best 9.2
• Title switches to Black Cat Mystery
31 ❑ Oct 1951 Cover: 0.10 **NM** value: **100.00**
• **CGC:** 3 graded, best 9.0
32 ❑ Dec 1951 Cover: 0.10 **NM** value: **80.00**
• **CGC:** 5 graded, best 9.4
33 ❑ Feb 1952 Cover: 0.10 **NM** value: **80.00**
• **CGC:** 3 graded, best 9.0
34 ❑ Apr 1952 Cover: 0.10 **NM** value: **80.00**
• **CGC:** 4 graded, best 9.2
35 ❑ May 1952 Cover: 0.10 **NM** value: **80.00**
• **CGC:** 2 graded, best 8.0
36 ❑ Jun 1952 Cover: 0.10 **NM** value: **80.00**
• **CGC:** 4 graded, best 9.2
37 ❑ Jul 1952 Cover: 0.10 **NM** value: **80.00**
• **CGC:** 3 graded, best 9.0
38 ❑ Aug 1952 Cover: 0.10 **NM** value: **80.00**
• **CGC:** 1 graded, best 8.5
39 ❑ Sep 1952 Cover: 0.10 **NM** value: **80.00**
40 ❑ Oct 1952 Cover: 0.10 **NM** value: **80.00**
41 ❑ Dec 1952 Cover: 0.10 **NM** value: **70.00**
• **CGC:** 3 graded, best 9.2
42 ❑ Feb 1953 Cover: 0.10 **NM** value: **70.00**
• **CGC:** 3 graded, best 8.5
43 ❑ Apr 1953 Cover: 0.10 **NM** value: **70.00**
• **CGC:** 3 graded, best 9.0
44 ❑ Jun 1953 Cover: 0.10 **NM** value: **70.00**
• **CGC:** 2 graded, best 9.2
45 ❑ Aug 1953 Cover: 0.10 **NM** value: **70.00**
• **CGC:** 5 graded, best 9.0
46 ❑ Oct 1953 Cover: 0.10 **NM** value: **70.00**
• **CGC:** 2 graded, best 9.2
47 ❑ Dec 1953 Cover: 0.10 **NM** value: **70.00**
• **CGC:** 3 graded, best 9.2
48 ❑ Feb 1954 Cover: 0.10 **NM** value: **70.00**
• **CGC:** 4 graded, best 9.4
49 ❑ Apr 1954 Cover: 0.10 **NM** value: **70.00**
• **CGC:** 1 graded, best 7.5
50 ❑ Jun 1954 Cover: 0.10 **NM** value: **150.00**
• **CGC:** 6 graded, best 9.4
graphic cover.
51 ❑ Aug 1954 Cover: 0.10 **NM** value: **50.00**
• **CGC:** 5 graded, best 9.4
52 ❑ Oct 1954 Cover: 0.10 **NM** value: **50.00**
• **CGC:** 4 graded, best 9.4
53 ❑ Dec 1954 Cover: 0.10 **NM** value: **50.00**
54 ❑ Feb 1955 Cover: 0.10 **NM** value: **50.00**
The Golden Guns; Lost (text piece); Room of the Past! (text piece); A Day With Linda Turner: Double Trouble; Winnie the Waitress; Mountain Terror (text piece) • really Black Cat Western Mystery **A:** Lee Elias
55 ❑ Apr 1955 Cover: 0.10 **NM** value: **50.00**
• **CGC:** 1 graded, best 9.0
56 ❑ Oct 1955 Cover: 0.10 **NM** value: **50.00**
57 ❑ Jan 1956 Cover: 0.10 **NM** value: **50.00**
58 ❑ Sep 1956 Cover: 0.10 **NM** value: **50.00**
Read to Us, Mr. Zimmer; Mystery Vision; Gizmo; Help
59 ❑ Sep 1956 Cover: 0.10 **NM** value: **50.00**
Today I am A? A Weemer is the Best of All; The Great Stone Face; Take Off, Mr. Zimmer
60 ❑ Nov 1956 Cover: 0.10 **NM** value: **50.00**
A Snap of the Fingers; The Woman Who Discovered America; A Town Full of Babies; The Ant Extract; Shadow Brother
61 ❑ Jan 1958 Cover: 0.10 **NM** value: **50.00**
62 ❑ Mar 1958 Cover: 0.10 **NM** value: **50.00**
• **CGC:** 1 graded, best 7.5
63 ❑ Oct 1962 Cover: 0.10 **NM** value: **70.00**
• **CGC:** 1 graded, best 9.0
• Giant-size. ★ Origin of the Black Kitten.
64 ❑ Jan 1963 Cover: 0.10 **NM** value: **70.00**
• **CGC:** 1 graded, best 9.4
• Giant-size.

Other grades: Multiply prices above by **1.5 for Mint • 2/3 for Very Fine • 1/3 for Fine • 1/5 for Very Good • 1/8 for Good**

65 ❑ Apr 1963 Cover: 0.10 **NM** value: **70.00**
• **CGC:** 1 graded, best 9.4
• Giant-size.

BLACK CAT (THE ORIGINS) — Lorne-Harvey

1 ❑ Cover: 3.50 **NM** value: **Cover or less**
Circ: CapCity orders: **4,180**
• color and b&w;reprints Black Cat and Sad Sack strips;text feature on Alfred Harvey **A:** Murphy Anderson **W:** Mark Evanier ★ Origin of The Black Cat.

BLACK CAT THE WAR YEARS — Recollections

1 ❑ Cover: 1.00 **NM** value: **Cover or less**
Circ: CapCity orders: **1,725**
• Golden Age reprints, b&w

BLACK CAULDRON, THE — Scholastic

1 ❑ Cover: 2.95 **NM** value: **4.00**

BLACK COBRA — Ajax

1 ❑ Oct 1954 Cover: 0.10 **NM** value: **175.00**
• **CGC:** 1 graded, best 8.5
2 ❑ Dec 1954 Cover: 0.10 **NM** value: **125.00**
3 ❑ Feb 1955 Cover: 0.10 **NM** value: **100.00**

BLACK CONDOR — DC

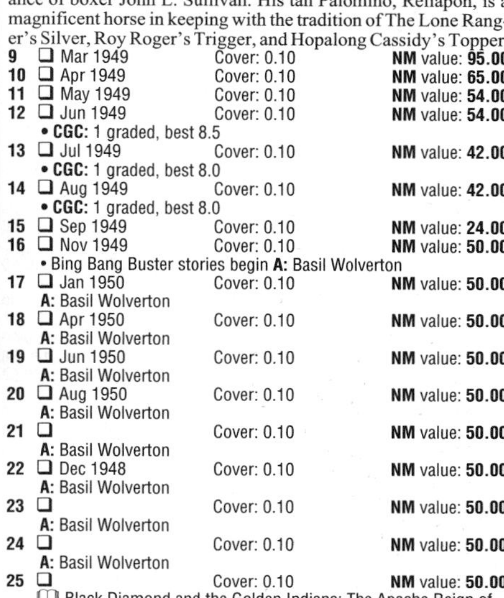

A secret organization that wanted its own super-being used the grandson of its leader for the purpose. After augmenting the boy to become "Golden Eagle," the group was dismayed to learn that the boy, Ryan, wanted no part of them or their plans. All he wanted to do was fly. He found that in addition to flight, he also had limited mental powers.

Other than the character's name, the series had little, if any connection to the original Quality character, who had been raised by birds and assumed the identity of a dead senator during the 1940s. However, a number of other Quality-based characters, including The Sky Pirate and The Ray did make appearances in the series.

Unfortunately, even a Batman appearance couldn't save the series and it was canceled after just 12 issues. — Brent

1 ❑ Jun 1992 Cover: 1.25 **NM** value: **1.50**
Circ: CapCity orders: **25,000**
📖 A Dream of Flying **A:** Rags Morales **W:** Brian Augustyn ★ Origin of Black Condor II. ★ 1st Appearance of The Black Condor II.
2 ❑ Jul 1992 Cover: 1.25 **NM** value: **Cover or less**
Circ: CapCity orders: **14,000**
3 ❑ Aug 1992 Cover: 1.25 **NM** value: **Cover or less**
Circ: CapCity orders: **12,400**
4 ❑ Sep 1992 Cover: 1.25 **NM** value: **Cover or less**
Circ: CapCity orders: **11,750**
5 ❑ Oct 1992 Cover: 1.25 **NM** value: **Cover or less**
Circ: CapCity orders: **9,350**
6 ❑ Nov 1992 Cover: 1.25 **NM** value: **Cover or less**
Circ: CapCity orders: **8,250**
7 ❑ Dec 1992 Cover: 1.25 **NM** value: **Cover or less**
Circ: CapCity orders: **7,200**
📖 Scorched Earth
8 ❑ Jan 1993 Cover: 1.25 **NM** value: **Cover or less**
Circ: CapCity orders: **6,750**
📖 Deadly Verdict
9 ❑ Feb 1993 Cover: 1.25 **NM** value: **Cover or less**
Circ: CapCity orders: **6,850**
10 ❑ Mar 1993 Cover: 1.25 **NM** value: **Cover or less**
Circ: CapCity orders: **6,600**
★ Appearance of The Ray.
11 ❑ Apr 1993 Cover: 1.25 **NM** value: **Cover or less**
Circ: CapCity orders: **6,350**
12 ❑ May 1993 Cover: 1.25 **NM** value: **Cover or less**
Circ: CapCity orders: **6,850**
final issue.★ Appearance of Batman.

BLACK CROSS: DIRTY WORK — Dark Horse

1 ❑ Apr 1997 Cover: 2.95 **NM** value: **Cover or less**
Circ: Diamd. preorders: **7,849**
No issue number. **A:** Chris Warner **W:** Chris Warner

BLACK CROSS SPECIAL — Dark Horse

1 ❑ Jan 1988, b&w Cover: 1.75 **NM** value: **3.50**
1-2 ❑ Cover: 1.75 **NM** value: **Cover or less**

BLACK DIAMOND — AC

1 ❑ May 1983 Cover: 2.00 **NM** value: **Cover or less**
A: Mark Beachum; Rick Burchett; Don Secrease; Bill Black; Paul Gulacy(frontispiece) **W:** Don Secrease; Bill Black ★ 1st Appearance of Colt, Darkfire, Black Diamond.
2 ❑ Jul 1983 Cover: 2.00 **NM** value: **Cover or less**
3 ❑ Dec 1983 Cover: 2.00 **NM** value: **Cover or less**
4 ❑ Feb 1984 Cover: 2.00 **NM** value: **Cover or less**
5 ❑ May 1984 Cover: 2.00 **NM** value: **Cover or less**

BLACK DIAMOND EFFECT, THE — Black Diamond Effect

1 ❑ Cover: 3.10 **NM** value: **Cover or less**
2 ❑ Cover: 3.10 **NM** value: **Cover or less**
3 ❑ Cover: 3.10 **NM** value: **Cover or less**
4 ❑ Cover: 3.10 **NM** value: **Cover or less**
5 ❑ Cover: 3.10 **NM** value: **Cover or less**
6 ❑ Dec 1992 Cover: 2.75 **NM** value: **3.00**
7 ❑ Cover: 3.10 **NM** value: **Cover or less**

BLACK DIAMOND WESTERN — Lev Gleason

In the mold of The Lone Ranger or Zorro, The Black Diamond is a masked Western character. Clad in a red shirt, black hat, and mask which wraps around his head like Zorro's, Black Diamond roams the West securing justice for settlers and thwarting the schemes of outlaws. But, unlike the vigilante Lone Ranger, Black Diamond has legal standing as a badge-carrying Federal marshal. His territory is uncommonly vast, as he is involved locales as widespread as Montana and Arizona.

In place of Tonto, The Black Diamond's companion is a man named Bumper, whose handlebar mustache gives him the appearance of boxer John L. Sullivan. His tan Palomino, Reliapon, is a magnificent horse in keeping with the tradition of The Lone Ranger's Silver, Roy Roger's Trigger, and Hopalong Cassidy's Topper.

9 ❑ Mar 1949 Cover: 0.10 **NM** value: **95.00**
10 ❑ Apr 1949 Cover: 0.10 **NM** value: **65.00**
11 ❑ May 1949 Cover: 0.10 **NM** value: **54.00**
12 ❑ Jun 1949 Cover: 0.10 **NM** value: **54.00**
• **CGC:** 1 graded, best 8.5
13 ❑ Jul 1949 Cover: 0.10 **NM** value: **42.00**
• **CGC:** 1 graded, best 8.0
14 ❑ Aug 1949 Cover: 0.10 **NM** value: **42.00**
• **CGC:** 1 graded, best 8.0
15 ❑ Sep 1949 Cover: 0.10 **NM** value: **24.00**
16 ❑ Nov 1949 Cover: 0.10 **NM** value: **50.00**
• Bing Bang Buster stories begin **A:** Basil Wolverton
17 ❑ Jan 1950 Cover: 0.10 **NM** value: **50.00**
A: Basil Wolverton
18 ❑ Apr 1950 Cover: 0.10 **NM** value: **50.00**
A: Basil Wolverton
19 ❑ Jun 1950 Cover: 0.10 **NM** value: **50.00**
A: Basil Wolverton
20 ❑ Aug 1950 Cover: 0.10 **NM** value: **50.00**
A: Basil Wolverton
21 ❑ Cover: 0.10 **NM** value: **50.00**
A: Basil Wolverton
22 ❑ Dec 1948 Cover: 0.10 **NM** value: **50.00**
A: Basil Wolverton
23 ❑ Cover: 0.10 **NM** value: **50.00**
A: Basil Wolverton
24 ❑ Cover: 0.10 **NM** value: **50.00**
A: Basil Wolverton
25 ❑ Cover: 0.10 **NM** value: **50.00**
📖 Black Diamond and the Golden Indians; The Apache Reign of Terror; Black Diamond Meets Reliapon's Double **A:** Basil Wolverton
26 ❑ Cover: 0.10 **NM** value: **50.00**
A: Basil Wolverton
27 ❑ 1951 Cover: 0.10 **NM** value: **50.00**
A: Basil Wolverton
28 ❑ Nov 1951 Cover: 0.10 **NM** value: **50.00**
A: Basil Wolverton
29 ❑ Dec 1951 Cover: 0.10 **NM** value: **28.00**
30 ❑ Jan 1952 Cover: 0.10 **NM** value: **28.00**
31 ❑ Feb 1952 Cover: 0.10 **NM** value: **28.00**
32 ❑ Mar 1952 Cover: 0.10 **NM** value: **28.00**
33 ❑ Apr 1952 Cover: 0.10 **NM** value: **28.00**
34 ❑ May 1952 Cover: 0.10 **NM** value: **28.00**
35 ❑ Jun 1952 Cover: 0.10 **NM** value: **28.00**
36 ❑ Jul 1952 Cover: 0.10 **NM** value: **28.00**
37 ❑ Aug 1952 Cover: 0.10 **NM** value: **28.00**
38 ❑ Sep 1952 Cover: 0.10 **NM** value: **28.00**
39 ❑ Oct 1952 Cover: 0.10 **NM** value: **28.00**
40 ❑ 1952 Cover: 0.10 **NM** value: **28.00**
41 ❑ Cover: 0.10 **NM** value: **28.00**
42 ❑ Cover: 0.10 **NM** value: **28.00**
43 ❑ Mar 1953 Cover: 0.10 **NM** value: **28.00**
44 ❑ Apr 1953 Cover: 0.10 **NM** value: **28.00**
45 ❑ Cover: 0.10 **NM** value: **28.00**
46 ❑ Cover: 0.10 **NM** value: **28.00**
47 ❑ Cover: 0.10 **NM** value: **28.00**
48 ❑ Cover: 0.10 **NM** value: **28.00**
49 ❑ Cover: 0.10 **NM** value: **28.00**
50 ❑ Cover: 0.10 **NM** value: **28.00**
51 ❑ Jun 1954 Cover: 0.10 **NM** value: **65.00**
• 3-D.
52 ❑ Cover: 0.10 **NM** value: **65.00**
• 3-D.
53 ❑ Cover: 0.10 **NM** value: **22.00**
54 ❑ Cover: 0.10 **NM** value: **22.00**
55 ❑ Apr 1955 Cover: 0.10 **NM** value: **22.00**
56 ❑ 1955 Cover: 0.10 **NM** value: **22.00**
57 ❑ 1955 Cover: 0.10 **NM** value: **22.00**
58 ❑ 1955 Cover: 0.10 **NM** value: **22.00**
59 ❑ Cover: 0.10 **NM** value: **22.00**
60 ❑ Feb 1956 Cover: 0.10 **NM** value: **22.00**
final issue.

BLACK DRAGON, THE — Marvel / Epic

1 ❑ May 1985 Cover: 1.50 **NM** value: **3.00**
Circ: CapCity orders: **14,100**
A: John Bolton **W:** Chris Claremont
2 ❑ Jun 1985 Cover: 1.50 **NM** value: **2.50**
Circ: CapCity orders: **10,350**
A: John Bolton **W:** Chris Claremont
3 ❑ Jul 1985 Cover: 1.50 **NM** value: **2.50**
Circ: CapCity orders: **10,900**
A: John Bolton **W:** Chris Claremont
4 ❑ Aug 1985 Cover: 1.50 **NM** value: **2.50**
Circ: CapCity orders: **11,100**
A: John Bolton **W:** Chris Claremont
5 ❑ Sep 1985 Cover: 1.50 **NM** value: **2.00**
Circ: CapCity orders: **11,450**
A: John Bolton **W:** Chris Claremont
6 ❑ Oct 1985 Cover: 1.50 **NM** value: **2.00**
Circ: CapCity orders: **12,050**
A: John Bolton **W:** Chris Claremont
Bk 1❑ b&w Cover: 17.95 **NM** value: **Cover or less**
• collects Epic mini-series **A:** John Bolton **W:** Chris Claremont

BLACK FLAG (IMAGE) — Image

1 ❑ Jun 1994, b&w Cover: 1.95 **NM** value: **Cover or less**
Fold-out cover. 📖 Once Upon A Time **A:** Dan Fraga **W:** Dan Fraga; Eric Stephenson ★ 1st Appearance of Black Rain, Geisha, Sniper.
Ash 1❑ Cover: 1.95 **NM** value: **Cover or less**
Circ: CapCity orders: **22,825**
• Preview edition. 📖 Guerrilla In The Midst! ★ 1st Appearance of Black Rain, Geisha, Sniper.

BLACK FLAG (MAXIMUM) — Maximum Press

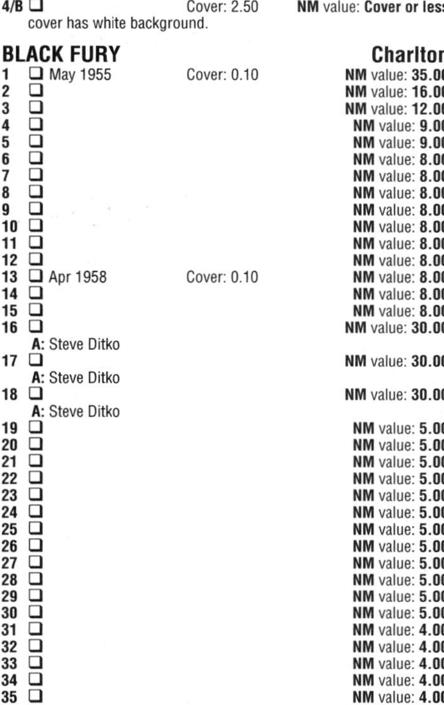

The title appeared only once from Image before changing its publisher's imprint to Maximum. It featured a couple of kids who imagine themselves as interdimensional adventurers; a covert operations veteran called Sniper, who faces a bestial version of himself named Black Rain; the requisite scantily clad mercenary-babe who goes by the name Geisha, although she appears to be a brassy American; and a seven-foot tall, intelligent gorilla with weapons training. Although the book was created, plotted, and drawn by Dan Fraga, Black Flag shows heavy influence from the style and sensibilities of publisher Rob Liefeld. From the shell-casing-strewn cover to the heavily armed men and lightly attired women making up the Black Flag team, this is a comic book that could have come from Liefeld's pen.

Fraga's art is striking and dynamic, although the story sometimes neglects a discernable plot in favor of opportunities for full page, heroically posed pinup shots. In any case, it wasn't around for long.

0 ❑ Jul 1995 Cover: 2.50 **NM** value: **Cover or less**
Circ: CapCity orders: **9,650**
A: Shelby Robertson; Dan Fraga; Logan Lubera; Karl Altstaetter; Patrick Lee; Rob Liefeld(cover) **W:** Dan Fraga
1 ❑ Jan 1995 Cover: 2.50 **NM** value: **Cover or less**
Circ: CapCity orders: **11,300**
2/A ❑ Feb 1995 Cover: 2.50 **NM** value: **Cover or less**
Circ: CapCity orders: **8,275**
Woman on cover.
2/B ❑ Cover: 2.50 **NM** value: **Cover or less**
Variant cover with man.
3 ❑ Mar 1995 Cover: 2.50 **NM** value: **Cover or less**
Circ: CapCity orders: **7,200**
4/A ❑ Cover: 2.50 **NM** value: **Cover or less**
Circ: CapCity orders: **7,475**
cover has black background.
4/B ❑ Cover: 2.50 **NM** value: **Cover or less**
cover has white background.

BLACK FURY — Charlton

1 ❑ May 1955 Cover: 0.10 **NM** value: **35.00**
2 ❑ **NM** value: **16.00**
3 ❑ **NM** value: **12.00**
4 ❑ **NM** value: **9.00**
5 ❑ **NM** value: **9.00**
6 ❑ **NM** value: **8.00**
7 ❑ **NM** value: **8.00**
8 ❑ **NM** value: **8.00**
9 ❑ **NM** value: **8.00**
10 ❑ **NM** value: **8.00**
11 ❑ **NM** value: **8.00**
12 ❑ **NM** value: **8.00**
13 ❑ Apr 1958 Cover: 0.10 **NM** value: **8.00**
14 ❑ **NM** value: **8.00**
15 ❑ **NM** value: **8.00**
16 ❑ **NM** value: **30.00**
A: Steve Ditko
17 ❑ **NM** value: **30.00**
A: Steve Ditko
18 ❑ **NM** value: **30.00**
A: Steve Ditko
19 ❑ **NM** value: **5.00**
20 ❑ **NM** value: **5.00**
21 ❑ **NM** value: **5.00**
22 ❑ **NM** value: **5.00**
23 ❑ **NM** value: **5.00**
24 ❑ **NM** value: **5.00**
25 ❑ **NM** value: **5.00**
26 ❑ **NM** value: **5.00**
27 ❑ **NM** value: **5.00**
28 ❑ **NM** value: **5.00**
29 ❑ **NM** value: **5.00**
30 ❑ **NM** value: **5.00**
31 ❑ **NM** value: **4.00**
32 ❑ **NM** value: **4.00**
33 ❑ **NM** value: **4.00**
34 ❑ **NM** value: **4.00**
35 ❑ **NM** value: **4.00**
36 ❑ **NM** value: **4.00**
37 ❑ **NM** value: **4.00**
38 ❑ **NM** value: **4.00**
39 ❑ **NM** value: **4.00**

CGC-graded: Multiply prices above by **33 for 9.9 M • 16 for 9.8 NM/M • 7 for 9.6 NM+ • 5 for 9.4 NM • 2.5 for 9.2 NM- • 1.5 for 9.0 VF/NM**

40 ❑ NM value: 4.00
41 ❑ NM value: 4.00
42 ❑ NM value: 4.00
43 ❑ NM value: 4.00
44 ❑ NM value: 4.00
45 ❑ NM value: 4.00
46 ❑ NM value: 4.00
47 ❑ Cover: 0.12 NM value: 4.00
48 ❑ Cover: 0.12 NM value: 4.00
49 ❑ Cover: 0.12 NM value: 4.00
🕮 Death Legend
50 ❑ Cover: 0.12 NM value: 4.00
51 ❑ Cover: 0.12 NM value: 4.00
52 ❑ Cover: 0.12 NM value: 4.00
53 ❑ Cover: 0.12 NM value: 4.00
54 ❑ 1965 Cover: 0.12 NM value: 4.00
55 ❑ Cover: 0.12 NM value: 4.00
56 ❑ Cover: 0.12 NM value: 4.00
57 ❑ Mar 1966 Cover: 0.12 NM value: 4.00
• Series continued in Wild West #58

BLACK GOLIATH — Marvel

1 ❑ Feb 1976 Cover: 0.25 NM value: 5.00
• CGC: 13 graded, best 9.6
🕮 Black Goliath A: George Tuska W: Tony Isabella ★ Origin of Black Goliath.
2 ❑ Apr 1976 Cover: 0.25 NM value: 3.50
🕮 White Fire, Atomic Death
3 ❑ Jun 1976 Cover: 0.25 NM value: 3.00
• CGC: 1 graded, best 8.0
🕮 Dance to the Murder
4 ❑ Aug 1976 Cover: 0.25 NM value: 3.00
🕮 Enter Stilt-Man, Exit Black Goliath
5 ❑ Nov 1976 Cover: 0.30 NM value: 3.00
🕮 Survival final issue.

BLACKHAWK (1ST SERIES) — DC

The Blackhawks are Allied ace fighter pilots, who, when they're not fighting Axis intrigue, share their stories about their wartime adventures and lessons about human nature with the reader. The team contained such members as Blackhawk himself, Olaf, Andre, Hendrickson, and comic relief Chop Chop.

The Blackhawk Squadron had its origin in 1941's Military Comics (created by The Spirit's Will Eisner), later spinning off into Modern Comics and Uncle Sam Quarterly. That latter series changed its name with #4 to Blackhawk and ran under that name until 1957. DC revived the series for brief runs, in 1976-1977 and in 1982-1984. It also inspired two later series in 1988 and 1989.

9 ❑ Win 1944, four-color Cover: 0.10 NM value: 2250.00
• CGC: 7 graded, best 9.6
• Series continued from Uncle Sam Quarterly #8
10 ❑ Spr 1946 Cover: 0.10 NM value: 850.00
• CGC: 3 graded, best 9.0
11 ❑ Sum 1946 Cover: 0.10 NM value: 560.00
• CGC: 4 graded, best 9.4
12 ❑ Fal 1946 Cover: 0.10 NM value: 500.00
• CGC: 2 graded, best 9.6
13 ❑ Win 1946 Cover: 0.10 NM value: 500.00
• CGC: 3 graded, best 9.4
14 ❑ Spr 1947 Cover: 0.10 NM value: 500.00
• CGC: 4 graded, best 9.6
15 ❑ Sum 1947 Cover: 0.10 NM value: 500.00
• CGC: 2 graded, best 9.4
16 ❑ Fal 1947 Cover: 0.10 NM value: 400.00
• CGC: 4 graded, best 9.2
17 ❑ Win 1947 Cover: 0.10 NM value: 400.00
• CGC: 2 graded, best 9.2
18 ❑ Spr 1948 Cover: 0.10 NM value: 400.00
• CGC: 2 graded, best 9.4
19 ❑ Jun 1948 Cover: 0.10 NM value: 400.00
• CGC: 2 graded, best 9.2
20 ❑ Aug 1948 Cover: 0.10 NM value: 400.00
• CGC: 2 graded, best 9.0
A: Bill Ward
21 ❑ Oct 1948 Cover: 0.10 NM value: 335.00
• CGC: 2 graded, best 7.0
22 ❑ Dec 1948 Cover: 0.10 NM value: 335.00
23 ❑ Feb 1949 Cover: 0.10 NM value: 335.00
24 ❑ Apr 1949 Cover: 0.10 NM value: 335.00
• CGC: 1 graded, best 5.5
25 ❑ Jun 1949 Cover: 0.10 NM value: 335.00
26 ❑ Aug 1949 Cover: 0.10 NM value: 285.00
27 ❑ Oct 1949 Cover: 0.10 NM value: 285.00
28 ❑ Dec 1949 Cover: 0.10 NM value: 285.00
29 ❑ Feb 1950 Cover: 0.10 NM value: 285.00
• CGC: 1 graded, best 1.5
30 ❑ Apr 1950, four-color Cover: 0.10 NM value: 285.00
• CGC: 1 graded, best 4.0
31 ❑ Jun 1950 Cover: 0.10 NM value: 260.00
• CGC: 1 graded, best 4.5
A: Jack Cole
32 ❑ Aug 1950 Cover: 0.10 NM value: 260.00
• CGC: 2 graded, best 9.0
33 ❑ Oct 1950 Cover: 0.10 NM value: 260.00
• CGC: 1 graded, best 4.0
34 ❑ Nov 1950 Cover: 0.10 NM value: 260.00
• CGC: 1 graded, best 6.0
35 ❑ Dec 1950 Cover: 0.10 NM value: 260.00
• CGC: 1 graded, best 2.5
36 ❑ Jan 1951 Cover: 0.10 NM value: 200.00
• CGC: 2 graded, best 8.5
37 ❑ Feb 1951 Cover: 0.10 NM value: 200.00
• CGC: 1 graded, best 5.5
38 ❑ Mar 1951 Cover: 0.10 NM value: 200.00
39 ❑ Apr 1951 Cover: 0.10 NM value: 200.00
40 ❑ May 1951 Cover: 0.10 NM value: 200.00
• CGC: 1 graded, best 7.0
41 ❑ Jun 1951 Cover: 0.10 NM value: 165.00
42 ❑ Jul 1951 Cover: 0.10 NM value: 165.00
43 ❑ Aug 1951 Cover: 0.10 NM value: 165.00
44 ❑ Sep 1951 Cover: 0.10 NM value: 165.00
45 ❑ Oct 1951 Cover: 0.10 NM value: 165.00
46 ❑ Nov 1951 Cover: 0.10 NM value: 165.00
47 ❑ Dec 1951 Cover: 0.10 NM value: 165.00
48 ❑ Jan 1952 Cover: 0.10 NM value: 165.00
49 ❑ Feb 1952 Cover: 0.10 NM value: 165.00
• CGC: 1 graded, best 7.5
50 ❑ Mar 1952 Cover: 0.10 NM value: 185.00
• CGC: 1 graded, best 7.5
★ 1st Appearance of Killer Shark II.
51 ❑ Apr 1952 Cover: 0.10 NM value: 160.00
• CGC: 1 graded, best 6.5
52 ❑ May 1952 Cover: 0.10 NM value: 160.00
• CGC: 1 graded, best 5.5
53 ❑ Jun 1952 Cover: 0.10 NM value: 160.00
• CGC: 1 graded, best 3.0
54 ❑ Jul 1952 Cover: 0.10 NM value: 160.00
• CGC: 1 graded, best 7.0
55 ❑ Aug 1952 Cover: 0.10 NM value: 160.00
56 ❑ Sep 1952 Cover: 0.10 NM value: 160.00
• CGC: 1 graded, best 6.0
57 ❑ Oct 1952 Cover: 0.10 NM value: 160.00
• CGC: 1 graded, best 7.0
58 ❑ Nov 1952 Cover: 0.10 NM value: 160.00
• CGC: 2 graded, best 9.0
59 ❑ Dec 1952 Cover: 0.10 NM value: 160.00
60 ❑ Jan 1953 Cover: 0.10 NM value: 160.00
61 ❑ Feb 1953 Cover: 0.10 NM value: 140.00
• CGC: 1 graded, best 9.2
62 ❑ Mar 1953 Cover: 0.10 NM value: 140.00
63 ❑ Apr 1953 Cover: 0.10 NM value: 140.00
64 ❑ May 1953 Cover: 0.10 NM value: 140.00
• CGC: 1 graded, best 9.2
65 ❑ Jun 1953 Cover: 0.10 NM value: 140.00
66 ❑ Jul 1953 Cover: 0.10 NM value: 140.00
67 ❑ Aug 1953 Cover: 0.10 NM value: 140.00
• CGC: 1 graded, best 6.0
68 ❑ Sep 1953 Cover: 0.10 NM value: 140.00
69 ❑ Oct 1953 Cover: 0.10 NM value: 140.00
• CGC: 1 graded, best 9.0
70 ❑ Nov 1953 Cover: 0.10 NM value: 140.00
• CGC: 1 graded, best 7.5
★ Appearance of Killer Shark.
71 ❑ Dec 1953 Cover: 0.10 NM value: 175.00
• CGC: 1 graded, best 7.0
★ Origin of Blackhawk.
72 ❑ Jan 1954 Cover: 0.10 NM value: 125.00
73 ❑ Feb 1954 Cover: 0.10 NM value: 125.00
• CGC: 1 graded, best 7.0
74 ❑ Mar 1954 Cover: 0.10 NM value: 125.00
75 ❑ Apr 1954 Cover: 0.10 NM value: 125.00
76 ❑ May 1954 Cover: 0.10 NM value: 125.00
77 ❑ Jun 1954 Cover: 0.10 NM value: 125.00
78 ❑ Jul 1954 Cover: 0.10 NM value: 125.00
79 ❑ Aug 1954 Cover: 0.10 NM value: 125.00
80 ❑ Sep 1954 Cover: 0.10 NM value: 125.00
• CGC: 1 graded, best 7.5
81 ❑ Oct 1954, four-color Cover: 0.10 NM value: 120.00
• CGC: 3 graded, best 7.5
82 ❑ Nov 1954, four-color Cover: 0.10 NM value: 120.00
83 ❑ Dec 1954, four-color Cover: 0.10 NM value: 120.00
84 ❑ Jan 1955, four-color Cover: 0.10 NM value: 120.00
85 ❑ Feb 1955, four-color Cover: 0.10 NM value: 120.00
86 ❑ Mar 1955, four-color Cover: 0.10 NM value: 120.00
87 ❑ Apr 1955, four-color Cover: 0.10 NM value: 115.00
88 ❑ May 1955, four-color Cover: 0.10 NM value: 115.00
• CGC: 1 graded, best 7.5
89 ❑ Jun 1955, four-color Cover: 0.10 NM value: 115.00
• CGC: 1 graded, best 4.5
90 ❑ Jul 1955, four-color Cover: 0.10 NM value: 115.00
91 ❑ Aug 1955, four-color Cover: 0.10 NM value: 115.00
92 ❑ Sep 1955, four-color Cover: 0.10 NM value: 115.00
93 ❑ Oct 1955, four-color Cover: 0.10 NM value: 125.00
★ Origin of Blackhawk.
94 ❑ Nov 1955, four-color Cover: 0.10 NM value: 105.00
• CGC: 1 graded, best 8.5
95 ❑ Dec 1955, four-color Cover: 0.10 NM value: 105.00
96 ❑ Jan 1956, full color Cover: 0.10 NM value: 105.00
97 ❑ Feb 1956, four-color Cover: 0.10 NM value: 105.00
• CGC: 1 graded, best 8.0
98 ❑ Mar 1956, four-color Cover: 0.10 NM value: 105.00
• CGC: 1 graded, best 9.4
99 ❑ Apr 1956, four-color Cover: 0.10 NM value: 105.00
• CGC: 1 graded, best 8.0
100 ❑ May 1956, four-color Cover: 0.10 NM value: 135.00
• CGC: 1 graded, best 8.0
• 100th anniversary issue.
101 ❑ Jun 1956, four-color Cover: 0.10 NM value: 100.00
102 ❑ Jul 1956, four-color Cover: 0.10 NM value: 100.00
103 ❑ Aug 1956, four-color Cover: 0.10 NM value: 100.00
104 ❑ Sep 1956, four-color Cover: 0.10 NM value: 100.00
105 ❑ Oct 1956, four-color Cover: 0.10 NM value: 100.00
• CGC: 1 graded, best 6.0
106 ❑ Nov 1956, four-color Cover: 0.10 NM value: 100.00
• CGC: 1 graded, best 9.0
107 ❑ Dec 1956, four-color Cover: 0.10 NM value: 100.00
• CGC: 1 graded, best 7.5
108 ❑ Jan 1957, four-color Cover: 0.10 NM value: 390.00
• CGC: 5 graded, best 9.2
• DC Begins publishing (formerly Quality)
109 ❑ Feb 1957, four-color Cover: 0.10 NM value: 125.00
• CGC: 1 graded, best 9.0
110 ❑ Mar 1957, four-color Cover: 0.10 NM value: 105.00
• CGC: 1 graded, best 8.5
111 ❑ Apr 1957, four-color Cover: 0.10 NM value: 105.00
112 ❑ May 1957, four-color Cover: 0.10 NM value: 105.00
113 ❑ Jun 1957, four-color Cover: 0.10 NM value: 105.00
114 ❑ Jul 1957, four-color Cover: 0.10 NM value: 105.00
• CGC: 1 graded, best 5.0
115 ❑ Aug 1957, four-color Cover: 0.10 NM value: 105.00
116 ❑ Sep 1957, four-color Cover: 0.10 NM value: 105.00
117 ❑ Oct 1957, four-color Cover: 0.10 NM value: 105.00
118 ❑ Nov 1957, four-color Cover: 0.10 NM value: 125.00
• CGC: 1 graded, best 4.0
A: Frank Frazetta
119 ❑ Dec 1957, four-color Cover: 0.10 NM value: 85.00
120 ❑ Jan 1958, four-color Cover: 0.10 NM value: 85.00
121 ❑ Feb 1958, four-color Cover: 0.10 NM value: 85.00
122 ❑ Mar 1958, four-color Cover: 0.10 NM value: 85.00
123 ❑ Apr 1958, four-color Cover: 0.10 NM value: 85.00
124 ❑ May 1958, four-color Cover: 0.10 NM value: 85.00
125 ❑ Jun 1958, four-color Cover: 0.10 NM value: 85.00
126 ❑ Jul 1958, four-color Cover: 0.10 NM value: 85.00
127 ❑ Aug 1958, four-color Cover: 0.10 NM value: 85.00
128 ❑ Sep 1958 Cover: 0.10 NM value: 85.00
129 ❑ Oct 1958 Cover: 0.10 NM value: 85.00
130 ❑ Nov 1958, full color Cover: 0.10 NM value: 85.00
131 ❑ Dec 1958, four-color Cover: 0.10 NM value: 65.00
132 ❑ Jan 1959 Cover: 0.10 NM value: 65.00
133 ❑ Feb 1959 Cover: 0.10 NM value: 65.00
• CGC: 1 graded, best 6.5
★ 1st Appearance of Lady Blackhawk.
134 ❑ Mar 1959, four-color Cover: 0.10 NM value: 65.00
135 ❑ Apr 1959, four-color Cover: 0.10 NM value: 65.00
• CGC: 1 graded, best 7.0
136 ❑ May 1959, four-color Cover: 0.10 NM value: 65.00
137 ❑ Jun 1959, four-color Cover: 0.10 NM value: 65.00
138 ❑ Jul 1959, four-color Cover: 0.10 NM value: 65.00
139 ❑ Aug 1959, four-color Cover: 0.10 NM value: 65.00
140 ❑ Sep 1959 Cover: 0.10 NM value: 65.00
141 ❑ Oct 1959 Cover: 0.10 NM value: 50.00
142 ❑ Nov 1959, four-color Cover: 0.10 NM value: 50.00
143 ❑ Dec 1959 Cover: 0.10 NM value: 50.00
144 ❑ Jan 1960, four-color Cover: 0.10 NM value: 50.00
Circ: Statement: 316,000
145 ❑ Feb 1960, four-color Cover: 0.10 NM value: 50.00
Circ: Statement: 316,000
146 ❑ Mar 1960 Cover: 0.10 NM value: 50.00
Circ: Statement: 316,000
147 ❑ Apr 1960, four-color Cover: 0.10 NM value: 50.00
Circ: Statement: 316,000
148 ❑ May 1960 Cover: 0.10 NM value: 50.00
Circ: Statement: 316,000
149 ❑ Jun 1960, four-color Cover: 0.10 NM value: 50.00
Circ: Statement: 316,000
150 ❑ Jul 1960 Cover: 0.10 NM value: 48.00
Circ: Statement: 316,000
151 ❑ Aug 1960 Cover: 0.10 NM value: 48.00
Circ: Statement: 316,000 • CGC: 1 graded, best 9.0
152 ❑ Sep 1960, four-color Cover: 0.10 NM value: 48.00
Circ: Statement: 316,000
153 ❑ Oct 1960, four-color Cover: 0.10 NM value: 48.00
Circ: Statement: 316,000
154 ❑ Nov 1960, four-color Cover: 0.10 NM value: 48.00
Circ: Statement: 316,000
155 ❑ Dec 1960, four-color Cover: 0.10 NM value: 48.00
Circ: Statement: 316,000
156 ❑ Jan 1961, four-color Cover: 0.10 NM value: 48.00
Circ: Statement: 305,000
157 ❑ Feb 1961 Cover: 0.10 NM value: 48.00
Circ: Statement: 305,000
158 ❑ Mar 1961, four-color Cover: 0.10 NM value: 48.00
Circ: Statement: 305,000
159 ❑ Apr 1961, four-color Cover: 0.10 NM value: 48.00
Circ: Statement: 305,000
160 ❑ May 1961, four-color Cover: 0.10 NM value: 48.00
Circ: Statement: 305,000 • CGC: 1 graded, best 8.5
161 ❑ Jun 1961, four-color Cover: 0.10 NM value: 48.00
Circ: Statement: 305,000 • CGC: 1 graded, best 7.5
162 ❑ Jul 1961 Cover: 0.10 NM value: 48.00
Circ: Statement: 305,000
163 ❑ Aug 1961, four-color Cover: 0.10 NM value: 48.00
Circ: Statement: 305,000
164 ❑ Sep 1961 Cover: 0.10 NM value: 60.00
Circ: Statement: 305,000 • CGC: 1 graded, best 4.5
★ Origin of Blackhawks.
165 ❑ Oct 1961 Cover: 0.10 NM value: 48.00
Circ: Statement: 305,000
166 ❑ Nov 1961 Cover: 0.10 NM value: 48.00
Circ: Statement: 305,000 • CGC: 1 graded, best 6.0
167 ❑ Dec 1961 Cover: 0.12 NM value: 22.00
Circ: Statement: 305,000
168 ❑ Jan 1962 Cover: 0.12 NM value: 22.00
Circ: Statement: 250,000
169 ❑ Feb 1962 Cover: 0.12 NM value: 22.00
Circ: Statement: 250,000 • CGC: 1 graded, best 5.0
170 ❑ Mar 1962 Cover: 0.12 NM value: 22.00
Circ: Statement: 250,000
171 ❑ Apr 1962 Cover: 0.12 NM value: 22.00
Circ: Statement: 250,000
172 ❑ May 1962 Cover: 0.12 NM value: 22.00
Circ: Statement: 250,000
173 ❑ Jun 1962 Cover: 0.12 NM value: 22.00
Circ: Statement: 250,000 • CGC: 1 graded, best 8.5

Other grades: Multiply prices above by **1.5 for Mint • 2/3 for Very Fine • 1/3 for Fine • 1/5 for Very Good • 1/8 for Good**

174 ❑ Jul 1962 Cover: 0.12 **NM** value: **22.00**
Circ: Statement: **250,000**
175 ❑ Aug 1962 Cover: 0.12 **NM** value: **22.00**
Circ: Statement: **250,000**
176 ❑ Sep 1962 Cover: 0.12 **NM** value: **22.00**
Circ: Statement: **250,000**
177 ❑ Oct 1962 Cover: 0.12 **NM** value: **22.00**
Circ: Statement: **250,000**
178 ❑ Nov 1962 Cover: 0.12 **NM** value: **22.00**
Circ: Statement: **250,000** • **CGC:** 1 graded, best 7.0
179 ❑ Dec 1962 Cover: 0.12 **NM** value: **22.00**
Circ: Statement: **250,000** • **CGC:** 1 graded, best 5.5
180 ❑ Jan 1963 Cover: 0.12 **NM** value: **22.00**
• **CGC:** 1 graded, best 9.2
181 ❑ Feb 1963 Cover: 0.12 **NM** value: **12.00**
• **CGC:** 1 graded, best 9.2
182 ❑ Mar 1963 Cover: 0.12 **NM** value: **12.00**
• **CGC:** 1 graded, best 9.6
183 ❑ Apr 1963 Cover: 0.12 **NM** value: **12.00**
• **CGC:** 1 graded, best 9.4
184 ❑ May 1963 Cover: 0.12 **NM** value: **12.00**
• **CGC:** 2 graded, best 9.4
185 ❑ Jun 1963 Cover: 0.12 **NM** value: **12.00**
• **CGC:** 2 graded, best 9.8
186 ❑ Jul 1963 Cover: 0.12 **NM** value: **12.00**
187 ❑ Aug 1963 Cover: 0.12 **NM** value: **12.00**
188 ❑ Sep 1963 Cover: 0.12 **NM** value: **12.00**
189 ❑ Oct 1963 Cover: 0.12 **NM** value: **12.00**
★ Origin of Blackhawks.
190 ❑ Nov 1963 Cover: 0.12 **NM** value: **12.00**
191 ❑ Dec 1963 Cover: 0.12 **NM** value: **10.00**
• **CGC:** 1 graded, best 9.2
192 ❑ Jan 1964 Cover: 0.12 **NM** value: **10.00**
193 ❑ Feb 1964 Cover: 0.12 **NM** value: **10.00**
• Has 1963 Statement, filed 10/1/63; no circ figures published
194 ❑ Mar 1964 Cover: 0.12 **NM** value: **10.00**
195 ❑ Apr 1964 Cover: 0.12 **NM** value: **10.00**
196 ❑ May 1964 Cover: 0.12 **NM** value: **10.00**
197 ❑ Jun 1964 Cover: 0.12 **NM** value: **10.00**
• new look
198 ❑ Jul 1964, four-color Cover: 0.12 **NM** value: **12.00**
★ Origin of Blackhawks.
199 ❑ Aug 1964 Cover: 0.12 **NM** value: **10.00**
200 ❑ Sep 1964 Cover: 0.12 **NM** value: **10.00**
201 ❑ Oct 1964 Cover: 0.12 **NM** value: **8.00**
202 ❑ Nov 1964 Cover: 0.12 **NM** value: **8.00**
203 ❑ Dec 1964 Cover: 0.12 **NM** value: **8.00**
★ Origin of Chop-Chop.
204 ❑ Jan 1965 Cover: 0.12 **NM** value: **8.00**
205 ❑ Feb 1965 Cover: 0.12 **NM** value: **8.00**
206 ❑ Mar 1965 Cover: 0.12 **NM** value: **8.00**
• **CGC:** 1 graded, best 9.2
• Has 1964 Statement, filed 10/1/64; no circ figures published
207 ❑ Apr 1965 Cover: 0.12 **NM** value: **8.00**
208 ❑ May 1965 Cover: 0.12 **NM** value: **8.00**
209 ❑ Jun 1965 Cover: 0.12 **NM** value: **8.00**
210 ❑ Jul 1965 Cover: 0.12 **NM** value: **8.00**
211 ❑ Aug 1965 Cover: 0.12 **NM** value: **8.00**
• **CGC:** 1 graded, best 9.2
212 ❑ Sep 1965 Cover: 0.12 **NM** value: **8.00**
213 ❑ Oct 1965 Cover: 0.12 **NM** value: **8.00**
214 ❑ Nov 1965 Cover: 0.12 **NM** value: **8.00**
215 ❑ Dec 1965 Cover: 0.12 **NM** value: **8.00**
• **CGC:** 1 graded, best 7.5
216 ❑ Jan 1966 Cover: 0.12 **NM** value: **8.00**
Circ: Statement: **228,453**
217 ❑ Feb 1966 Cover: 0.12 **NM** value: **8.00**
Circ: Statement: **228,453**
218 ❑ Mar 1966 Cover: 0.12 **NM** value: **8.00**
Circ: Statement: **228,453** • **CGC:** 1 graded, best 9.0
219 ❑ Apr 1966 Cover: 0.12 **NM** value: **8.00**
Circ: Statement: **228,453**
220 ❑ May 1966 Cover: 0.12 **NM** value: **8.00**
Circ: Statement: **228,453**
221 ❑ Jun 1966 Cover: 0.12 **NM** value: **8.00**
Circ: Statement: **228,453**
222 ❑ Jul 1966 Cover: 0.12 **NM** value: **8.00**
Circ: Statement: **228,453**
223 ❑ Aug 1966 Cover: 0.12 **NM** value: **8.00**
Circ: Statement: **228,453**
224 ❑ Sep 1966 Cover: 0.12 **NM** value: **8.00**
Circ: Statement: **228,453** • **CGC:** 1 graded, best 9.4
225 ❑ Oct 1966 Cover: 0.12 **NM** value: **8.00**
Circ: Statement: **228,453**
226 ❑ Nov 1966 Cover: 0.12 **NM** value: **8.00**
Circ: Statement: **228,453**
227 ❑ Dec 1966 Cover: 0.12 **NM** value: **8.00**
Circ: Statement: **228,453** • **CGC:** 1 graded, best 9.2
228 ❑ Jan 1967 Cover: 0.12 **NM** value: **8.00**
Circ: Statement: **157,700** • **CGC:** 2 graded, best 9.2
229 ❑ Feb 1967 Cover: 0.12 **NM** value: **8.00**
Circ: Statement: **157,700**
• Has 1966 Statement, filed 10/1/66; avg print run 402,000; avg sales 227,000; avg subs 1,453; avg total paid 228,453; samples 265; max existent 228,478; 43% of run returned
230 ❑ Mar 1967 Cover: 0.12 **NM** value: **8.00**
Circ: Statement: **157,700**
• Blackhawks become super-heroes;New costumes
231 ❑ Apr 1967 Cover: 0.12 **NM** value: **8.00**
Circ: Statement: **157,700** • **CGC:** 2 graded, best 9.4
• Blackhawks as super-heroes
232 ❑ May 1967 Cover: 0.12 **NM** value: **8.00**
Circ: Statement: **157,700**
• Blackhawks as super-heroes
233 ❑ Jun 1967 Cover: 0.12 **NM** value: **8.00**
Circ: Statement: **157,700**
• Blackhawks as super-heroes
234 ❑ Jul 1967 Cover: 0.12 **NM** value: **8.00**
Circ: Statement: **157,700**
• Blackhawks as super-heroes
235 ❑ Aug 1967 Cover: 0.12 **NM** value: **8.00**
Circ: Statement: **157,700** • **CGC:** 1 graded, best 9.4
• Blackhawks as super-heroes
236 ❑ Sep 1967 Cover: 0.12 **NM** value: **8.00**
Circ: Statement: **157,700**
• Blackhawks as super-heroes
237 ❑ Nov 1967 Cover: 0.12 **NM** value: **8.00**
Circ: Statement: **157,700**
• Blackhawks as super-heroes
238 ❑ Jan 1968 Cover: 0.12 **NM** value: **8.00**
• **CGC:** 1 graded, best 9.6
• Blackhawks as super-heroes
239 ❑ Mar 1968 Cover: 0.12 **NM** value: **8.00**
• **CGC:** 3 graded, best 9.6
• Blackhawks as super-heroes
240 ❑ May 1968 Cover: 0.12 **NM** value: **8.00**
• **CGC:** 2 graded, best 9.4
• Blackhawks as super-heroes
241 ❑ Jul 1968 Cover: 0.12 **NM** value: **8.00**
• Blackhawks as super-heroes
242 ❑ Sep 1968 Cover: 0.12 **NM** value: **8.00**
• **CGC:** 1 graded, best 9.2
• Blackhawks back to old costumes
243 ❑ Nov 1968 Cover: 0.12 **NM** value: **8.00**
• **CGC:** 1 graded, best 9.2
Mission Incredible • Last issue of 1960s run
244 ❑ Feb 1976 Cover: 0.25 **NM** value: **4.00**
• **CGC:** 1 graded, best 7.5
Death's Right Hand • New issues begin with old # sequence **A:** George Evans **W:** Steve Skeates
245 ❑ Apr 1976 Cover: 0.30 **NM** value: **4.00**
246 ❑ Jun 1976 Cover: 0.30 **NM** value: **4.00**
247 ❑ Aug 1976 Cover: 0.30 **NM** value: **4.00**
• Bicentennial #25
248 ❑ Sep 1976 Cover: 0.30 **NM** value: **4.00**
249 ❑ Nov 1976 Cover: 0.30 **NM** value: **4.00**
250 ❑ Jan 1977 Cover: 0.30 **NM** value: **4.00**
★ Death of Chuck.
251 ❑ Oct 1982 Cover: 0.60 **NM** value: **4.00**
• **CGC:** 2 graded, best 9.6
252 ❑ Nov 1982 Cover: 0.60 **NM** value: **4.00**
★ Versus War Wheel.
253 ❑ Dec 1982 Cover: 0.60 **NM** value: **4.00**
254 ❑ Jan 1983 Cover: 0.60 **NM** value: **4.00**
255 ❑ Feb 1983 Cover: 0.60 **NM** value: **4.00**
256 ❑ Mar 1983 Cover: 0.60 **NM** value: **4.00**
257 ❑ Apr 1983 Cover: 0.60 **NM** value: **4.00**
C: Howard Chaykin
258 ❑ May 1983 Cover: 0.60 **NM** value: **4.00**
C: Howard Chaykin
259 ❑ Jun 1983 Cover: 0.60 **NM** value: **4.00**
C: Howard Chaykin
260 ❑ Jul 1983 Cover: 0.60 **NM** value: **4.00**
Detached Service Diary **A:** Howard Chaykin **C:** Howard Chaykin **W:** Mark Evanier
261 ❑ Aug 1983 Cover: 0.60 **NM** value: **2.50**
262 ❑ Sep 1983 Cover: 0.60 **NM** value: **2.50**
Der Fuehrer's Face! **A:** Dan Spiegle **C:** Howard Chaykin **W:** Mark Evanier
263 ❑ Oct 1983 Cover: 0.60 **NM** value: **2.50**
C: Gil Kane ★ Versus War Wheel.
264 ❑ Nov 1983 Cover: 0.60 **NM** value: **2.50**
265 ❑ Dec 1983 Cover: 0.75 **NM** value: **2.50**
266 ❑ Jan 1984 Cover: 0.75 **NM** value: **2.50**
267 ❑ Feb 1984 Cover: 0.75 **NM** value: **2.50**
268 ❑ Mar 1984 Cover: 0.75 **NM** value: **2.50**
269 ❑ Apr 1984 Cover: 0.75 **NM** value: **2.50**
★ 1st Appearance of Killer Shark I (General Haifisch).
270 ❑ May 1984 Cover: 0.75 **NM** value: **2.50**
271 ❑ Jul 1984 Cover: 0.75 **NM** value: **2.50**
272 ❑ Sep 1984 Cover: 0.75 **NM** value: **2.50**
273 ❑ Nov 1984 Cover: 0.75 **NM** value: **2.50**
final issue. **C:** Howard Chaykin

BLACKHAWK (2ND SERIES) DC

Janos Prohaska, better known as Blackhawk, was the heroic leader of Blackhawk Squadron during World War II. He swiftly went from hero to villain, when he was accused of having ties to the Communists before the war. Gone were the high-flying days of his past. His next battles would be filled with subterfuge and Cold War paranoia.

In Howard Chaykin's remake of a classic war hero, the line between the good guys and the bad guys is no longer clear — what's certain is that the stakes are higher than ever.

This "prestige format" series created some stir when it was released, due to the suggested depiction of a sexual activity in the first issue, unexpected in a title reviving a classic character from a more innocent time. Retailers in some areas reported that they moved the issue behind the counter with the adult titles, when they discovered the scene.

1 ❑ Mar 1988 Cover: 2.95 **NM** value: **3.50**
Circ: CapCity orders: **49,000**
Blood & Iron • no mature readers advisory **A:** Steve Oliff; Howard Chaykin; Ken Bruzenak **W:** Howard Chaykin
2 ❑ Apr 1988 Cover: 2.95 **NM** value: **3.50**
Circ: CapCity orders: **40,850** • **CGC:** 1 graded, best 9.4
Follow Blackjack's Example, Increase Your Quota For The Front Lines **A:** Steve Oliff; Howard Chaykin; Ken Bruzenak **W:** Howard Chaykin
3 ❑ May 1988 Cover: 2.95 **NM** value: **3.50**
Circ: CapCity orders: **38,450**
Blackout **A:** Steve Oliff; Howard Chaykin; Ken Bruzenak **W:** Howard Chaykin

BLACKHAWK (3RD SERIES) DC

This third Blackhawk series finishes the overhaul of the Blackhawk legend that Howard Chaykin began in Blackhawk (2nd Series).

The series takes place in 1947, two years after the Last Great War. It is a time of rising paranoia over the "Worldwide Communist Conspiracy." It seemed everyone is on the lookout for closet Communists. Even mythical Imperial Comics, which put Blackhawk's wartime adventures into comic-book form, is forced to change his name from Janos Prohaska to "Bart Hawk," toning down his Polish ancestry and "real-life" links to Trotskyism. News of this remake soon reaches the "real" Blackhawks, who find that too many people are willing to forget old heroes when caught up in fear of the "Red Menace."

1 ❑ Mar 1989 Cover: 1.50 **NM** value: **2.00**
Circ: CapCity orders: **21,200** • **CGC:** 2 graded, best 9.4
All In Color For A Crime **A:** Rick Burchett **W:** Martin Pasko
2 ❑ Apr 1989 Cover: 1.50 **NM** value: **1.75**
Circ: CapCity orders: **15,500**
3 ❑ May 1989 Cover: 1.50 **NM** value: **1.75**
Circ: CapCity orders: **13,300**
4 ❑ Jun 1989 Cover: 1.50 **NM** value: **1.75**
Circ: CapCity orders: **12,350**
5 ❑ Aug 1989 Cover: 1.50 **NM** value: **1.75**
Circ: CapCity orders: **10,400**
6 ❑ Sep 1989 Cover: 1.50 **NM** value: **Cover or less**
Circ: CapCity orders: **9,400**
7 ❑ Oct 1989 Cover: 2.50 **NM** value: **Cover or less**
Circ: CapCity orders: **9,100**
• Double-size. **A:** Will Eisner
8 ❑ Nov 1989 Cover: 1.50 **NM** value: **Cover or less**
Circ: CapCity orders: **7,800**
9 ❑ Dec 1989 Cover: 1.50 **NM** value: **Cover or less**
Circ: CapCity orders: **6,700**
10 ❑ Jan 1990 Cover: 1.50 **NM** value: **Cover or less**
Circ: CapCity orders: **6,400**
11 ❑ 1990 Cover: 1.50 **NM** value: **Cover or less**
Circ: CapCity orders: **6,000**
12 ❑ 1990 Cover: 1.75 **NM** value: **Cover or less**
Circ: CapCity orders: **5,650**
13 ❑ 1990 Cover: 1.75 **NM** value: **Cover or less**
14 ❑ 1990 Cover: 1.75 **NM** value: **Cover or less**
Circ: CapCity orders: **5,100**
15 ❑ 1990 Cover: 1.75 **NM** value: **Cover or less**
Circ: CapCity orders: **4,900**
16 ❑ 1990 Cover: 1.75 **NM** value: **Cover or less**
Circ: CapCity orders: **4,900**
Anl 1 ❑ ca. 1989 Cover: 2.95 **NM** value: **Cover or less**
Circ: CapCity orders: **13,300**
SE 1 ❑ ca. 1992 Cover: 3.50 **NM** value: **Cover or less**
Circ: CapCity orders: **6,000**
• Special edition (1992). Blackhawk Hardware • Special **A:** Mike Vosburg **W:** John Ostrander

BLACK HEART: ASSASSIN Iguana

1 ❑ Cover: 2.95 **NM** value: **Cover or less**
A: Rosy Chun **W:** Robert H. Chong ★ 1st Appearance of Black Heart.

BLACK HEART BILLY Slave Labor

1 ❑ Mar 2000, b&w Cover: 2.95 **NM** value: **Cover or less**
Circ: Diamd. preorders: **2,208**
A: Kieron Dwyer; Rick Remender **W:** Kieron Dwyer; Rick Remender

BLACK HOLE Kitchen Sink

1 ❑ Cover: 3.50 **NM** value: **Cover or less**
Circ: CapCity orders: **3,045**
Biology 101; Planet Xeno; SSSSSS **A:** Charles Burns **W:** Charles Burns
2 ❑ Nov 1995 Cover: 3.50 **NM** value: **Cover or less**
3 ❑ Jul 1996 Cover: 3.50 **NM** value: **Cover or less**
4 ❑ Jun 1997 Cover: 3.50 **NM** value: **Cover or less**
Circ: Diamd. preorders: **5,775**
5 ❑ Mar 1998 Cover: 3.95 **NM** value: **Cover or less**
Circ: Diamd. preorders: **5,749**
6 ❑ Dec 1998 Cover: 4.50 **NM** value: **Cover or less**
Circ: Diamd. preorders: **5,302**
7 ❑ ca. 1999 Cover: 4.50 **NM** value: **Cover or less**
Circ: Diamd. preorders: **5,254**
8 ❑ ca. 2000 Cover: 4.50 **NM** value: **Cover or less**
Circ: Diamd. preorders: **5,269**
9 ❑ ca. 2001 Cover: 4.50 **NM** value: **Cover or less**
Circ: Diamd. preorders: **5,147**

Capital City orders are the actual sales of comic books by Capital City Distribution, once one of the largest U.S. sellers of comics to comics shops. Capital City's share of comics shop sales, while not known exactly, increases from around 10-20% in the mid-1980s to 30-35% in the mid-1990s. Capital City's share of comic books sold on newsstands (most Marvels and DCs) will be less.

CGC-graded: Multiply prices above by **33 for 9.9 M • 16 for 9.8 NM/M • 7 for 9.6 NM+ • 5 for 9.4 NM • 2.5 for 9.2 NM- • 1.5 for 9.0 VF/NM**

BLACK HOLE, THE (WALT DISNEY...) Whitman

The Black Hole was Disney's attempt to get a little of the Star Wars action. The resulting movie, while one of the most colorful SF movies to date, lacked interesting characters and had an ending that defied both science and logic.

Disney's comics licensee plowed ahead anyway, with a two-issue adaptation of the film and a two-issue stretch of original stories under the "Beyond the Black Hole" banner. On the "other side," the humans and their robot pal find a world that's, well, pretty much just like the one they left, with the same spooky spaceship haunted by the same spooky evil doctor and the same nasty red robot. A few things were different in this alternate reality, though; like, the big spooky red robot talked, making life a lot easier on the plotter of the comic book...

Sold in three-packs, a fourth issue, advertised in #3, is believed to have been distributed separately. — JJM

1 ❑ Mar 1980 Cover: 0.40 **NM** value: **2.00**
📖 Part 1 of the movie, "The Black Hole" by Walt Disney Productions
2 ❑ May 1980 Cover: 0.40 **NM** value: **1.50**
📖 The conclusion of the movie
3 ❑ Jul 1980 Cover: 0.40 **NM** value: **1.50**
📖 Beyond the Black Hole
4 ❑ Sep 1980 Cover: 0.40 **NM** value: **3.00**
• the Virlights final issue.

BLACK HOOD DC / Impact

1 ❑ Dec 1991 Cover: 1.00 **NM** value: **Cover or less**
Circ: CapCity orders: **34,050**
📖 Justice. No Waiting! ★ Origin of The Black Hood. ★ 1st Appearance of Pirate Blue, The Black Hood (Nathan Cray), The Black Hood (Giles "Hit" Coffee).
2 ❑ Jan 1992 Cover: 1.00 **NM** value: **Cover or less**
Circ: CapCity orders: **18,700**
3 ❑ Feb 1992 Cover: 1.00 **NM** value: **Cover or less**
Circ: CapCity orders: **13,950**
★ 1st Appearance of Tom Sickler, The Creeptures.
4 ❑ Mar 1992 Cover: 1.00 **NM** value: **Cover or less**
Circ: CapCity orders: **11,150**
★ 1st Appearance of Ozone.
5 ❑ Apr 1992 Cover: 1.00 **NM** value: **Cover or less**
Circ: CapCity orders: **9,750**
📖 The Coming of the Crusaders, Part 4
6 ❑ May 1992 Cover: 1.00 **NM** value: **Cover or less**
Circ: CapCity orders: **9,150**
7 ❑ Jun 1992 Cover: 1.25 **NM** value: **Cover or less**
Circ: CapCity orders: **8,250**
8 ❑ Aug 1992 Cover: 1.25 **NM** value: **Cover or less**
Circ: CapCity orders: **8,050**
9 ❑ Sep 1992 Cover: 1.25 **NM** value: **Cover or less**
Circ: CapCity orders: **6,750**
10 ❑ Oct 1992 Cover: 1.25 **NM** value: **Cover or less**
Circ: CapCity orders: **6,250**
11 ❑ Nov 1992 Cover: 1.25 **NM** value: **Cover or less**
Circ: CapCity orders: **5,750**
★ 1st Appearance of Fox, The Fox.
12 ❑ Dec 1992 Cover: 1.25 **NM** value: **Cover or less**
Circ: CapCity orders: **5,600**
final issue.★ Origin of Black Hood.
Anl 1❑ Cover: 2.50 **NM** value: **Cover or less**
Circ: CapCity orders: **8,550**
📖 Earth Quest, Part 6 • trading card

BLACK HOOD (M.L.J.) M.L.J.

9 ❑ Win 1943 Cover: 0.10 **NM** value: **750.00**
10 ❑ Spr 1944 Cover: 0.10 **NM** value: **500.00**
11 ❑ Sum 1944 Cover: 0.10 **NM** value: **400.00**
12 ❑ Fal 1944 Cover: 0.10 **NM** value: **400.00**
13 ❑ Win 1944 Cover: 0.10 **NM** value: **400.00**
14 ❑ Spr 1945 Cover: 0.10 **NM** value: **400.00**
15 ❑ Sum 1945 Cover: 0.10 **NM** value: **300.00**
16 ❑ Fal 1945 Cover: 0.10 **NM** value: **300.00**
• **CGC:** 1 graded, best 6.0
17 ❑ Win 1945 Cover: 0.10 **NM** value: **300.00**
18 ❑ Spr 1946 Cover: 0.10 **NM** value: **300.00**
• **CGC:** 1 graded, best 6.0
19 ❑ Sum 1946 Cover: 0.10 **NM** value: **300.00**
• **CGC:** 1 graded, best 8.0

BLACK HOOD, THE (RED CIRCLE) Archie / Red Circle

1 ❑ Jun 1983 Cover: 1.00 **NM** value: **3.00**
📖 The Mask...and the Man **A:** Alex Toth; Gray Morrow **W:** Cary Burkett
2 ❑ Aug 1983 Cover: 1.00 **NM** value: **2.00**
📖 The Dark Destroyer **A:** Alex Toth; Gray Morrow; Pat Boyette **W:** Gary Cohn
3 ❑ Oct 1983 Cover: 1.00 **NM** value: **2.00**
A: Alex Toth; Gray Morrow

BLACKJACK Dark Angel

1 ❑ Sep 1996 Cover: 2.95 **NM** value: **Cover or less**
📖 Second Bite of the Cobra **A:** Joe Bennett **W:** Alex Simmons
2 ❑ Oct 1996 Cover: 2.95 **NM** value: **Cover or less**
📖 Second Bite of the Cobra **A:** Joe Bennett **W:** Alex Simmons
3 ❑ Jan 1997 Cover: 2.95 **NM** value: **Cover or less**
📖 Second Bite of the Cobra **A:** Joe Bennett; Jack Jadson **W:** Alex Simmons
4 ❑ 1997 Cover: 2.95 **NM** value: **Cover or less**
W: Alex Simmons
SE 1❑ Sep 1998 Cover: 3.50 **NM** value: **Cover or less**
Circ: Diamd. preorders: **2,180**
W: Alex Simmons

BLACK JACK (VIZ) Viz

Bk 1❑ Cover: 15.95 **NM** value: **Cover or less**
• collects serialized story from Manga Vizion **A:** Osamu Tezuka **W:** Osamu Tezuka
SE 1❑ Cover: 3.25 **NM** value: **Cover or less**
📖 Under the Knife **A:** Osamu Tezuka **W:** Osamu Tezuka

BLACKJACK (VOL. 2) Dark Angel

1 ❑ Apr 1997 Cover: 2.95 **NM** value: **Cover or less**
2 ❑ Feb 1998 Cover: 2.95 **NM** value: **Cover or less**

BLACK KISS Vortex

Howard Chaykin (Star Wars, American Flagg!) has always taken chances. With the stylish Black Kiss, he pushed the bounds further than ever before. Black Kiss is a story of sex, corruption, lies, and murder.

The story follows Dagmar, a ruthless woman, as she resorts to any means necessary to reclaim a set of tapes which are being used to blackmail her. Her blackmailer is equally ruthless — and they'll both use anyone and anything to get what they want.

Reminiscent of American Flagg! (but even more intense), Black Kiss is an adults-only experiment by one of the great writer-artists.

The series was collected several times with variations on the title, such as Big Black Kiss and Thick Black Kiss.

1 ❑ Jun 1988 Cover: 1.25 **NM** value: **2.50**
Circ: CapCity orders: **6,700**
A: Howard Chaykin **W:** Howard Chaykin
1-2 ❑ Cover: 1.25 **NM** value: **2.00**
1-3 ❑ Cover: 1.25 **NM** value: **2.00**
2 ❑ Jul 1988 Cover: 1.25 **NM** value: **2.50**
Circ: CapCity orders: **5,475**
A: Howard Chaykin **W:** Howard Chaykin
2-2 ❑ Cover: 1.25 **NM** value: **2.00**
3 ❑ Aug 1988 Cover: 1.25 **NM** value: **2.00**
Circ: CapCity orders: **8,050**
A: Howard Chaykin **W:** Howard Chaykin
4 ❑ Sep 1988 Cover: 1.25 **NM** value: **2.00**
Circ: CapCity orders: **8,000**
polybagged with black insert card covering actual cover. **A:** Howard Chaykin **W:** Howard Chaykin
5 ❑ Oct 1988 Cover: 1.25 **NM** value: **2.00**
Circ: CapCity orders: **9,600**
A: Howard Chaykin **W:** Howard Chaykin
6 ❑ Nov 1988 Cover: 1.25 **NM** value: **2.00**
Circ: CapCity orders: **10,325**
A: Howard Chaykin **W:** Howard Chaykin
7 ❑ Dec 1988 Cover: 1.25 **NM** value: **2.00**
Circ: CapCity orders: **10,975**
A: Howard Chaykin **W:** Howard Chaykin
8 ❑ Jan 1989 Cover: 1.25 **NM** value: **2.00**
Circ: CapCity orders: **11,725**
• indicia says 88 (misprint) **A:** Howard Chaykin **W:** Howard Chaykin
9 ❑ Feb 1989 Cover: 1.25 **NM** value: **2.00**
Circ: CapCity orders: **12,200**
• indicia says 88 (misprint) **A:** Howard Chaykin **W:** Howard Chaykin
10 ❑ Mar 1989 Cover: 1.50 **NM** value: **2.00**
Circ: CapCity orders: **13,100**
• indicia says 88 (misprint) **A:** Howard Chaykin **W:** Howard Chaykin
11 ❑ May 1989 Cover: 1.50 **NM** value: **2.00**
Circ: CapCity orders: **12,800**
A: Howard Chaykin **W:** Howard Chaykin
12 ❑ Jul 1989 Cover: 1.50 **NM** value: **2.00**
Circ: CapCity orders: **12,425**
A: Howard Chaykin **W:** Howard Chaykin

BLACK KNIGHT (ATLAS) Atlas

1 ❑ May 1955 Cover: 0.10 **NM** value: **600.00**
📖 The Menace of Modred the Evil; Untitled (Origin of the Crusader, part 1); The Abduction of King Arthur • First Black Knight
2 ❑ Jul 1955 Cover: 0.10 **NM** value: **400.00**
• **CGC:** 3 graded, best 6.5
📖 Untitled (Black Knight); Tournament of Doom; Untitled (Origin of the Crusader, part 2); The Siege of Camelot
3 ❑ Sep 1955 Cover: 0.10 **NM** value: **300.00**
• **CGC:** 1 graded, best 6.5
📖 The Black Knight Unmasked; Untitled (Black Knight); Untitled (Crusader); Untitled (Black Knight)
4 ❑ Nov 1955 Cover: 0.10 **NM** value: **300.00**
📖 Betrayed; Untitled (Black Knight); Untitled (Crusader); Untitled (Black Knight)
5 ❑ Apr 1956 Cover: 0.10 **NM** value: **300.00**
• **CGC:** 1 graded, best 8.5
📖 Untitled (Black Knight); Men of the Shadows; The Scent of Treason; The Invincible Tartar • Dragon of Kentswood Swamp

BLACK KNIGHT: EXODUS Marvel

1 ❑ Dec 1996 Cover: 2.50 **NM** value: **Cover or less**
Circ: Direct Market orders: **35,500**
One-shot.

BLACK KNIGHT (LTD. SERIES) Marvel

1 ❑ Jun 1990 Cover: 1.50 **NM** value: **2.00**
Circ: CapCity orders: **31,400** • **CGC:** 1 graded, best 9.2
📖 The Rebirth Of The Black Knight **A:** Tony DeZuniga **W:** Roy Thomas; Dann Thomas ★ Origin of Black Knight III (Dane Whitman), Black Knight I (Sir Percy), Black Knight II (Nathan Garrett).
2 ❑ Jul 1990 Cover: 1.50 **NM** value: **Cover or less**
Circ: CapCity orders: **24,800**
★ Appearance of Capt. Britain, Captain Britain.
3 ❑ Aug 1990 Cover: 1.50 **NM** value: **Cover or less**
Circ: CapCity orders: **21,800**
📖 The Black Knight Has a Thousand Eyes... **A:** Rich Buckler; The Slashing Dudes **W:** Roy Thomas; Dann Thomas ★ 1st Appearance of new Valkyrie. ★ Appearance of Doctor Strange.
4 ❑ Sep 1990 Cover: 1.50 **NM** value: **Cover or less**
Circ: CapCity orders: **20,800**
★ Appearance of Doctor Strange, Valkyrie.

BLACK KNIGHT (TOBY) Toby

1 ❑ May 1953 Cover: 0.10 **NM** value: **150.00**
• **CGC:** 1 graded, best 8.0

BLACK LAMB, THE DC / Helix

1 ❑ Nov 1996 Cover: 2.50 **NM** value: **Cover or less**
Circ: Diamd. preorders: **27,469**
📖 The Hated The Haunted The Hunted **A:** Tim Truman **W:** Tim Truman
2 ❑ Dec 1996 Cover: 2.50 **NM** value: **Cover or less**
Circ: Direct Market orders: **21,809**
A: Tim Truman **W:** Tim Truman
3 ❑ Jan 1997 Cover: 2.50 **NM** value: **Cover or less**
Circ: Direct Market orders: **20,102**
📖 Steel Maiden **A:** Tim Truman **W:** Tim Truman
4 ❑ Feb 1997 Cover: 2.50 **NM** value: **Cover or less**
Circ: Diamd. preorders: **18,095**
A: Tim Truman **W:** Tim Truman
5 ❑ Mar 1997 Cover: 2.50 **NM** value: **Cover or less**
Circ: Diamd. preorders: **16,930**
A: Tim Truman **W:** Tim Truman
6 ❑ Apr 1997 Cover: 2.50 **NM** value: **Cover or less**
Circ: Diamd. preorders: **15,700**
A: Tim Truman **W:** Tim Truman

BLACK LIGHTNING (1ST SERIES) DC

Jefferson Pierce was an Olympic decathlon star but he returns to his old neighborhood as a teacher. But the streets have gotten meaner, while Pierce was gone; drug dealers even ply their trade in the high schools. Pierce stands up to them, but, in retaliation, the mob known as "the 100" kills one of his students. After all, they know that the one thing he cares about above all is his students.

He has to fight back, but he can't do so as Jefferson Pierce. With the help of an old friend, he fashions a disguise. Now, as Black Lightning, he's taking back the streets.

An inspiring hero, Black Lightning later became a member of The Outsiders.

1 ❑ Apr 1977 Cover: 0.30 **NM** value: **5.00**
• **CGC:** 9 graded, best 9.6
A: Trevor Von Eeden; Frank Springer **W:** Tony Isabella ★ Origin of Black Lightning. ★ 1st Appearance of Black Lightning.
2 ❑ May 1977 Cover: 0.30 **NM** value: **3.00**
3 ❑ Jul 1977 Cover: 0.35 **NM** value: **3.00**
4 ❑ Sep 1977 Cover: 0.35 **NM** value: **3.00**
5 ❑ Nov 1977 Cover: 0.35 **NM** value: **3.00**
6 ❑ Jan 1978 Cover: 0.35 **NM** value: **2.50**
★ 1st Appearance of Syonide I.
7 ❑ Mar 1978 Cover: 0.35 **NM** value: **2.50**
8 ❑ Apr 1978 Cover: 0.35 **NM** value: **2.50**
9 ❑ May 1978 Cover: 0.35 **NM** value: **2.50**
10 ❑ Jul 1978 Cover: 0.35 **NM** value: **2.50**
11 ❑ Sep 1978 Cover: 0.50 **NM** value: **2.50**
final issue.★ Appearance of The Ray.

BLACK LIGHTNING (2ND SERIES) DC

1 ❑ Feb 1995 Cover: 1.95 **NM** value: **2.50**
Circ: CapCity orders: **16,150**
📖 The Weekend Report **A:** Eddy Newell **W:** Tony Isabella
2 ❑ Mar 1995 Cover: 1.95 **NM** value: **2.00**
Circ: CapCity orders: **10,025**
📖 Teachers **A:** Eddy Newell **W:** Tony Isabella
3 ❑ Apr 1995 Cover: 1.95 **NM** value: **2.00**
Circ: CapCity orders: **8,000**
📖 Students **A:** Eddy Newell **W:** Tony Isabella
4 ❑ May 1995 Cover: 1.95 **NM** value: **2.00**
Circ: CapCity orders: **7,050**
5 ❑ Jun 1995 Cover: 2.25 **NM** value: **Cover or less**
Circ: CapCity orders: **6,375**
6 ❑ Jul 1995 Cover: 2.25 **NM** value: **2.75**
Circ: CapCity orders: **5,600**
★ Appearance of Gangbuster.
7 ❑ Aug 1995 Cover: 2.25 **NM** value: **Cover or less**
Circ: CapCity orders: **5,350**
★ Appearance of Gangbuster.
8 ❑ Sep 1995 Cover: 2.25 **NM** value: **Cover or less**
Circ: CapCity orders: **4,900**
9 ❑ Oct 1995 Cover: 2.25 **NM** value: **Cover or less**
Circ: CapCity orders: **3,700**
10 ❑ Nov 1995 Cover: 2.25 **NM** value: **Cover or less**
11 ❑ Dec 1995 Cover: 2.25 **NM** value: **Cover or less**
12 ❑ Jan 1996 Cover: 2.25 **NM** value: **Cover or less**
13 ❑ Feb 1996 Cover: 2.25 **NM** value: **Cover or less**

📖 To Protect and Serve final issue. **A:** N. Steven Harris; Eddy Newell **W:** David DeVries

BLACK MAGIC (DC) — DC

1 ❑ Nov 1973 Cover: 0.20 **NM** value: **7.00**
• **CGC:** 3 graded, best 9.6
📖 Maniac; The Head of the Family; The Greatest Horror of them All, the Amazing Story of a Beautiful Freak
2 ❑ Dec 1973 Cover: 0.20 **NM** value: **4.00**
• **CGC:** 2 graded, best 9.6
📖 Fool's Paradise; The Cat People; Birth After Death; Those Who are About to Die
3 ❑ Apr 1974 Cover: 0.20 **NM** value: **4.00**
• **CGC:** 2 graded, best 9.6
📖 Nasty Little Man; The Angel of Death
4 ❑ Jun 1974 Cover: 0.20 **NM** value: **4.00**
📖 The Girl the Earth Ate Up!; His Father's Footsteps!; The Man with a Vision (text story); Last Second of Life! **A:** Jack Kirby **W:** Joe Simon
5 ❑ Aug 1974 Cover: 0.20 **NM** value: **4.00**
📖 Strange Old Bird; Up There
6 ❑ Oct 1974 Cover: 0.20 **NM** value: **4.00**
• **CGC:** 1 graded, best 9.2
📖 The Girl Who Walked on Water
7 ❑ Dec 1974 Cover: 0.20 **NM** value: **4.00**
📖 The Cloak
8 ❑ Feb 1975 Cover: 0.20 **NM** value: **4.00**
📖 The Girl in the Grave; Send Us Your Dreams
9 ❑ Apr 1975 Cover: 0.20 **NM** value: **4.00**
📖 The Woman in the Tower

BLACK MAGIC (ECLIPSE) — Eclipse

1 ❑ Cover: 5.00 **NM** value: **Cover or less**
• Japanese, b&w **A:** Masamune Shirow **W:** Masamune Shirow
2 ❑ Cover: 3.50 **NM** value: **Cover or less**
A: Masamune Shirow **W:** Masamune Shirow
3 ❑ Cover: 3.50 **NM** value: **Cover or less**
A: Masamune Shirow **W:** Masamune Shirow
4 ❑ Cover: 3.50 **NM** value: **Cover or less**
A: Masamune Shirow **W:** Masamune Shirow
Bk 1❑ Cover: 16.95 **NM** value: **Cover or less**
• Collects Black Magic (Eclipse) #1-4 **A:** Masamune Shirow **W:** Masamune Shirow

BLACK MAGIC (PRIZE) — Prize

1 ❑ Oct 1950 Cover: 0.10 **NM** value: **625.00**
• **CGC:** 4 graded, best 7.5
📖 Last Second of Life **A:** Jack Kirby **W:** Joe Simon
2 ❑ Dec 1950 Cover: 0.10 **NM** value: **325.00**
• **CGC:** 1 graded, best 9.2
📖 The Scorn of the Faceless People; The Cloak **A:** Jack Kirby **W:** Joe Simon
3 ❑ Feb 1951 Cover: 0.10 **NM** value: **240.00**
📖 A Silver Bullet for Your Heart **A:** Jack Kirby **W:** Joe Simon
4 ❑ Apr 1951 Cover: 0.10 **NM** value: **200.00**
• **CGC:** 2 graded, best 8.5
📖 Voodoo on Tenth Avenue **A:** Jack Kirby **W:** Joe Simon
5 ❑ Jun 1951 Cover: 0.10 **NM** value: **200.00**
📖 The World of Spirits **A:** Jack Kirby **W:** Joe Simon
6 ❑ Aug 1951 Cover: 0.10 **NM** value: **200.00**
• **CGC:** 1 graded, best 6.0
📖 Union with the Dead **A:** Jack Kirby **W:** Joe Simon
7 ❑ Oct 1951 Cover: 0.10 **NM** value: **165.00**
• **CGC:** 1 graded, best 9.4
📖 The Thing in the Fog
8 ❑ Dec 1951 Cover: 0.10 **NM** value: **140.00**
• **CGC:** 3 graded, best 9.0
9 ❑ Feb 1952 Cover: 0.10 **NM** value: **140.00**
10 ❑ Mar 1952 Cover: 0.10 **NM** value: **140.00**
📖 Dead Man's Lode; Seven Years Bad Luck
11 ❑ Apr 1952 Cover: 0.10 **NM** value: **140.00**
• **CGC:** 2 graded, best 8.0
📖 The Girl Who Walked on Water
12 ❑ May 1952 Cover: 0.10 **NM** value: **140.00**
• **CGC:** 1 graded, best 3.5
13 ❑ Jun 1952 Cover: 0.10 **NM** value: **140.00**
📖 Up There; Visions of Nostradamus
14 ❑ Jul 1952 Cover: 0.10 **NM** value: **140.00**
• **CGC:** 1 graded, best 9.4
15 ❑ Aug 1952 Cover: 0.10 **NM** value: **140.00**
📖 Angel of Death
16 ❑ Sep 1952 Cover: 0.10 **NM** value: **140.00**
17 ❑ Oct 1952 Cover: 0.10 **NM** value: **140.00**
18 ❑ Nov 1952 Cover: 0.10 **NM** value: **140.00**
• **CGC:** 2 graded, best 7.5
📖 Nasty Little Man; Come Claim My Corpse; Detour Lorelei Highway
19 ❑ Dec 1952 Cover: 0.10 **NM** value: **125.00**
📖 Sammy's Wonderful Glass
20 ❑ Jan 1953 Cover: 0.10 **NM** value: **125.00**
📖 Birth After Death
21 ❑ Feb 1953 Cover: 0.10 **NM** value: **125.00**
• **CGC:** 1 graded, best 8.5
📖 The Feathered Serpent
22 ❑ Mar 1953 Cover: 0.10 **NM** value: **125.00**
📖 The Monsters on the Lake
23 ❑ Apr 1953 Cover: 0.10 **NM** value: **125.00**
📖 Those Who are About to Die
24 ❑ May 1953 Cover: 0.10 **NM** value: **125.00**
• **CGC:** 1 graded, best 8.0
📖 After I'm Gone
25 ❑ Jun 1953 Cover: 0.10 **NM** value: **140.00**
• **CGC:** 1 graded, best 8.0
📖 Strange Old Bird; The Human Cork; A Beast is in the Streets
26 ❑ Sep 1953 Cover: 0.10 **NM** value: **140.00**
📖 Fool's Paradise; The Sting of Scorpio; The Strange Antics of the Mystic Mirror; Demon Wind
27 ❑ Nov 1953 Cover: 0.10 **NM** value: **300.00**
📖 The Cat People; The Merry Ghosts of Campbell Castle • 1st published Ditko art **A:** Steve Ditko
28 ❑ Jan 1954 Cover: 0.10 **NM** value: **200.00**
📖 An Eye for an Eye; Alive after 5000 Years **A:** Steve Ditko
29 ❑ Mar 1954 Cover: 0.10 **NM** value: **160.00**
📖 The Greatest Horror of them all, the Amazing Story of a Beautiful Freak **A:** Steve Ditko
30 ❑ May 1954 Cover: 0.10 **NM** value: **50.00**
📖 The Head of the Family
31 ❑ Jul 1954 Cover: 0.10 **NM** value: **48.00**
📖 Gargoyle; Slaughter-House; The Half-Men; Hungry as a Wolf
32 ❑ Sep 1954 Cover: 0.10 **NM** value: **44.00**
📖 Maniac
33 ❑ Nov 1954 Cover: 0.10 **NM** value: **44.00**
📖 Lone Shark; The Strangest Facts
34 ❑ Sep 1957 Cover: 0.10 **NM** value: **35.00**
35 ❑ Nov 1957 Cover: 0.10 **NM** value: **35.00**
36 ❑ Jan 1958 Cover: 0.10 **NM** value: **35.00**
37 ❑ Mar 1958 Cover: 0.10 **NM** value: **35.00**
38 ❑ May 1958 Cover: 0.10 **NM** value: **35.00**
📖 The Mystic; The Last Role; The Impossible; Satellite (text story); The Test;
39 ❑ Jul 1958 Cover: 0.10 **NM** value: **35.00**
40 ❑ Sep 1958 Cover: 0.10 **NM** value: **30.00**
41 ❑ Cover: 0.10 **NM** value: **30.00**
42 ❑ Jul 1960 Cover: 0.10 **NM** value: **30.00**
📖 Jasper's Jungle; The Counterpanes (text story); The Man Who Cried Mermaid; Man Reaches Moon!; Those Who Vanish; Strange Obituary (text story); The Night of August 9th **A:** Paul Reinman
43 ❑ Sep 1960 Cover: 0.10 **NM** value: **30.00**
44 ❑ Nov 1960 Cover: 0.10 **NM** value: **30.00**
📖 I Flew Over The Big Wall; Picture Of Mystery; No Time Like The Present; Where Is Murdock?; Beyond The Darkness
45 ❑ Jan 1961 Cover: 0.10 **NM** value: **30.00**
46 ❑ Mar 1961 Cover: 0.10 **NM** value: **28.00**
47 ❑ May 1961 Cover: 0.10 **NM** value: **28.00**
• **CGC:** 1 graded, best 6.5
48 ❑ Jul 1961 Cover: 0.10 **NM** value: **28.00**
49 ❑ Sep 1961 Cover: 0.10 **NM** value: **28.00**
50 ❑ Nov 1961 Cover: 0.10 **NM** value: **28.00**

BLACKMASK — DC

1 ❑ Cover: 4.95 **NM** value: **Cover or less**
Circ: CapCity orders: **7,350**
A: Jim Baikie **W:** Brian Augustyn
2 ❑ Cover: 4.95 **NM** value: **Cover or less**
Circ: CapCity orders: **4,250**
A: Jim Baikie **W:** Brian Augustyn
3 ❑ Cover: 4.95 **NM** value: **Cover or less**
Circ: CapCity orders: **3,700**
A: Jim Baikie **W:** Brian Augustyn

BLACKMASK (EASTERN) — Eastern

1 ❑ Cover: 1.75 **NM** value: **Cover or less**
• Translated by Franz Hankel **A:** Jong-Jin Lee **W:** Jong-Jin Lee

BLACK MIST — Caliber

1 ❑ Jan 1998 Cover: 2.95 **NM** value: **Cover or less**
Circ: Diamd. preorders: **3,725**
📖 Anguish of The Mist **A:** Avido Khahaifa **W:** James Pruett
2 ❑ 1998 Cover: 2.95 **NM** value: **Cover or less**
A: Avido Khahaifa **W:** James Pruett
3 ❑ 1998 Cover: 2.95 **NM** value: **Cover or less**
A: Avido Khahaifa **W:** James Pruett
4 ❑ 1998 Cover: 2.95 **NM** value: **Cover or less**
A: Avido Khahaifa **W:** James Pruett
Bk 1❑ b&w Cover: 12.95 **NM** value: **Cover or less**
• Anguish of the Mist

BLACK MIST: BLOOD OF KALI — Caliber

1 ❑ Cover: 2.95 **NM** value: **Cover or less**
A: Mike Perkins **W:** James Pruett
2 ❑ Cover: 2.95 **NM** value: **Cover or less**
3 ❑ Cover: 2.95 **NM** value: **Cover or less**

BLACKMOON — U.S.Comics

1 ❑ Cover: 1.50 **NM** value: **2.00**
📖 Blackmoon Rising **A:** James C. Hallett **W:** James C. Hallett ★ Origin of Blackmoon.
2 ❑ Cover: 1.50 **NM** value: **2.00**
3 ❑ Cover: 1.75 **NM** value: **2.00**

BLACK OPS — Image

1 ❑ Jan 1996 Cover: 2.50 **NM** value: **Cover or less**
A: Dan Norton **W:** Dan Norton; Shon Bury ★ 1st Appearance of Shire, Geek & H.E.R.B., Redbird.
2 ❑ Feb 1996 Cover: 2.50 **NM** value: **Cover or less**
★ 1st Appearance of Crane.
3 ❑ Mar 1996 Cover: 2.50 **NM** value: **Cover or less**
4 ❑ Apr 1996 Cover: 2.50 **NM** value: **Cover or less**
5/A ❑ Jun 1996 Cover: 2.50 **NM** value: **Cover or less**
5/B ❑ Jun 1996 Cover: 2.50 **NM** value: **Cover or less**
alternate cover.
Bk 1❑ Cover: 14.95 **NM** value: **Cover or less**
• collects #1-5

The CGC numbers printed in individual listings above represent the **number of copies examined** and given a **Universal** grade by CGC and the **best such copy** graded at press time. For current populations, watch for special ***Comics Buyer's Guide*** issues or check **www.cgccomics.com.**

BLACK ORCHID — DC / Vertigo

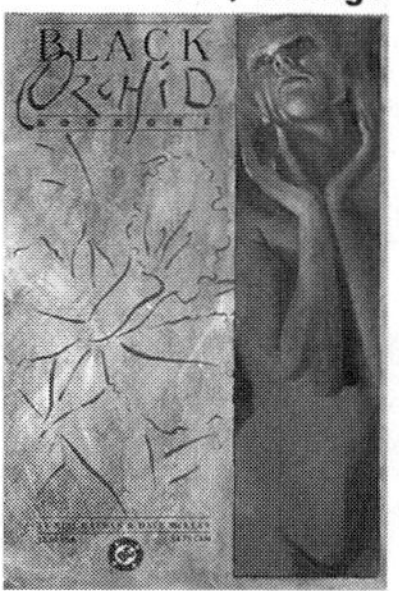

Once, Black Orchid was a superhero. Of course, that was before the Black Orchid mini-series, when she died — and was reborn as something else. She is beyond human now, ethereal and celestial, though she masquerades as a woman when the mood suits her. As a model, an escort, or even as a campaign worker, she wields a strange power of enchantment. To look in her eyes is to lose yourself in them.

But wherever such a thing of beauty exists, men will seek to hunt it down and possess it. In her own way, Black Orchid inspires obsession — even murder.

1 ❑ Sep 1993 Cover: 1.95 **NM** value: **2.50**
Circ: CapCity orders: **32,250** • **CGC:** 4 graded, best 9.6
📖 Sightings **A:** Jill Thompson **W:** Dick Foreman
1/PL❑ Sep 1993 **NM** value: **5.00**
• **CGC:** 1 graded, best 9.6
• Platinum edition. 📖 Sightings **A:** Jill Thompson **W:** Dick Foreman
2 ❑ Oct 1993 Cover: 1.95 **NM** value: **2.25**
Circ: CapCity orders: **16,300**
📖 Uprootings **A:** Jill Thompson **W:** Dick Foreman
3 ❑ Nov 1993 Cover: 1.95 **NM** value: **2.25**
Circ: CapCity orders: **14,550**
📖 The Tainted Zone **A:** Jill Thompson **W:** Dick Foreman
4 ❑ Dec 1993 Cover: 1.95 **NM** value: **2.25**
Circ: CapCity orders: **13,800**
5 ❑ Jan 1994 Cover: 1.95 **NM** value: **2.25**
Circ: CapCity orders: **12,900**
📖 The Mind Fields, Part 1
6 ❑ Feb 1994 Cover: 1.95 **NM** value: **2.00**
Circ: CapCity orders: **12,000**
📖 The God In The Cage **A:** Jill Thompson **W:** Dick Foreman
7 ❑ Mar 1994 Cover: 1.95 **NM** value: **2.00**
Circ: CapCity orders: **11,300**
📖 Upon the Threshold **A:** Rebecca Guay **W:** Dick Foreman
8 ❑ Apr 1994 Cover: 1.95 **NM** value: **2.00**
Circ: CapCity orders: **10,450**
W: Dick Foreman
9 ❑ May 1994 Cover: 1.95 **NM** value: **2.00**
Circ: CapCity orders: **10,200**
📖 The Murmuring Of The Mists, The Whisper If Flowers **A:** Rebecca Guay **W:** Dick Foreman
10 ❑ Jun 1994 Cover: 1.95 **NM** value: **2.00**
Circ: CapCity orders: **9,600**
📖 Florescence **A:** Rebecca Guay **W:** Dick Foreman
11 ❑ Jul 1994 Cover: 1.95 **NM** value: **2.00**
Circ: CapCity orders: **9,200**
📖 Suzy And The Trade Of Fates **A:** Rebecca Guay **W:** Dick Foreman
12 ❑ Aug 1994 Cover: 1.95 **NM** value: **2.00**
Circ: CapCity orders: **8,800**
📖 Mr. Weems Takes a Wife **A:** Rebecca Guay **W:** Dick Foreman
13 ❑ Sep 1994 Cover: 1.95 **NM** value: **2.00**
Circ: CapCity orders: **8,250**
14 ❑ Oct 1994 Cover: 1.95 **NM** value: **2.00**
Circ: CapCity orders: **7,850**
15 ❑ Nov 1994 Cover: 1.95 **NM** value: **2.00**
Circ: CapCity orders: **7,500**
16 ❑ Dec 1994 Cover: 1.95 **NM** value: **2.00**
Circ: CapCity orders: **7,250**
17 ❑ Jan 1995 Cover: 1.95 **NM** value: **Cover or less**
Circ: CapCity orders: **6,700**
📖 A Twisted Season, Part 1 **A:** Rebecca Guay **W:** Dick Foreman
18 ❑ Feb 1995 Cover: 1.95 **NM** value: **Cover or less**
Circ: CapCity orders: **6,100**
📖 Twisted Season, Part 2
19 ❑ Mar 1995 Cover: 1.95 **NM** value: **Cover or less**
Circ: CapCity orders: **5,650**
📖 Twisted Season, Part 3
20 ❑ Apr 1995 Cover: 1.95 **NM** value: **Cover or less**
Circ: CapCity orders: **5,350**
📖 Twisted Season, Part 4
21 ❑ May 1995 Cover: 2.25 **NM** value: **Cover or less**
Circ: CapCity orders: **5,175**
📖 Twisted Season, Part 5
22 ❑ Jun 1995 Cover: 2.25 **NM** value: **Cover or less**
Circ: CapCity orders: **4,975**
📖 Twisted Season, Part 6 final issue.
Anl 1❑ Cover: 3.95 **NM** value: **4.00**
Circ: CapCity orders: **15,400**
📖 The Children's Crusade, Part 2 • Children's Crusade

BLACK ORCHID (MINI-SERIES) — DC

1 ❑ 1988 Cover: 1.95 **NM** value: **5.00**
Circ: CapCity orders: **32,150** • **CGC:** 5 graded, best 9.8
A: Dave McKean **W:** Neil Gaiman
1/PL❑ **NM** value: **6.00**
• Platinum edition. **A:** Dave McKean **W:** Neil Gaiman
2 ❑ 1989 Cover: 1.95 **NM** value: **5.00**
Circ: CapCity orders: **25,300** • **CGC:** 2 graded, best 9.8
A: Dave McKean **W:** Neil Gaiman ★ Appearance of Batman.
3 ❑ 1989 Cover: 1.95 **NM** value: **5.00**
Circ: CapCity orders: **25,700** • **CGC:** 1 graded, best 9.8
A: Dave McKean **W:** Neil Gaiman
Bk 1❑ Cover: 19.95 **NM** value: **Cover or less**
Circ: CapCity orders: **2,000**
• Trade Paperback. • collects Black Orchid (mini-series) #1-3 **A:** Dave McKean **W:** Neil Gaiman

CGC-graded: Multiply prices above by **33 for 9.9 M • 16 for 9.8 NM/M • 7 for 9.6 NM+ • 5 for 9.4 NM • 2.5 for 9.2 NM- • 1.5 for 9.0 VF/NM**

BLACK PANTHER — Marvel

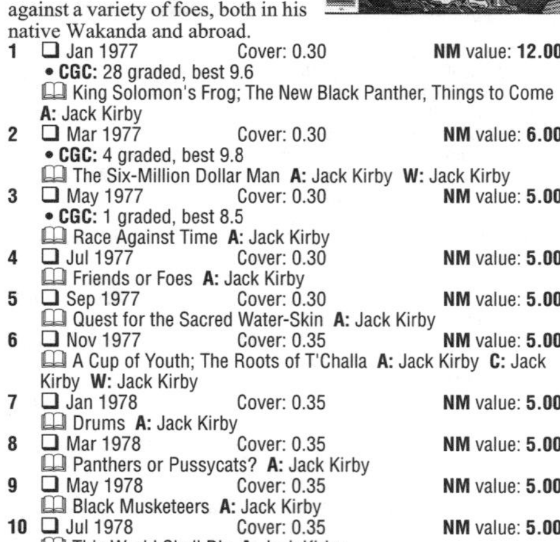

T'Challa is the son of T'Chaka, ruler of the African kingdom of Wakanda. Educated in the U.S., he is forced to return home when his father is killed by perennial Spider-Man villain Klaw. As the new ruler of Wakanda, T'Challa has to undergo a strange initiation rite which leads to his gaining great strength and agility — and taking on the role of Wakanda's protector, The Black Panther.

Black Panther had long been a member of The Avengers, but only in 1977 did he appear in a series of his own. This title pits the Panther against a variety of foes, both in his native Wakanda and abroad.

1 ❑ Jan 1977 Cover: 0.30 **NM** value: **12.00**
• **CGC:** 28 graded, best 9.6
King Solomon's Frog; The New Black Panther, Things to Come **A:** Jack Kirby
2 ❑ Mar 1977 Cover: 0.30 **NM** value: **6.00**
• **CGC:** 4 graded, best 9.8
The Six-Million Dollar Man **A:** Jack Kirby **W:** Jack Kirby
3 ❑ May 1977 Cover: 0.30 **NM** value: **5.00**
• **CGC:** 1 graded, best 8.5
Race Against Time **A:** Jack Kirby
4 ❑ Jul 1977 Cover: 0.30 **NM** value: **5.00**
Friends or Foes **A:** Jack Kirby
5 ❑ Sep 1977 Cover: 0.30 **NM** value: **5.00**
Quest for the Sacred Water-Skin **A:** Jack Kirby
6 ❑ Nov 1977 Cover: 0.35 **NM** value: **5.00**
A Cup of Youth; The Roots of T'Challa **A:** Jack Kirby **C:** Jack Kirby **W:** Jack Kirby
7 ❑ Jan 1978 Cover: 0.35 **NM** value: **5.00**
Drums **A:** Jack Kirby
8 ❑ Mar 1978 Cover: 0.35 **NM** value: **5.00**
Panthers or Pussycats? **A:** Jack Kirby
9 ❑ May 1978 Cover: 0.35 **NM** value: **5.00**
Black Musketeers **A:** Jack Kirby
10 ❑ Jul 1978 Cover: 0.35 **NM** value: **5.00**
This World Shall Die **A:** Jack Kirby
11 ❑ Sep 1978 Cover: 0.35 **NM** value: **4.00**
Kiber the Cruel **A:** Jack Kirby
12 ❑ Nov 1978 Cover: 0.35 **NM** value: **4.00**
The Kiber Clue **A:** Jack Kirby
13 ❑ Jan 1979 Cover: 0.35 **NM** value: **4.00**
What Is, and What Should Never Be **A:** Jack Kirby
14 ❑ Mar 1979 Cover: 0.35 **NM** value: **4.00**
The Beasts in the Jungle **A:** Jerry Bingham
15 ❑ May 1979 Cover: 0.40 **NM** value: **4.00**
Revenge of the Black Panther final issue. **A:** Jack Kirby ★ Appearance of Klaw.

BLACK PANTHER (LTD. SERIES) — Marvel

1 ❑ Jul 1988 Cover: 1.25 **NM** value: **2.00**
Circ: CapCity orders: **23,700**
Cry, The Accursed Country **A:** Denys Cowan **W:** Peter B. Gillis
2 ❑ Aug 1988 Cover: 1.25 **NM** value: **2.00**
Circ: CapCity orders: **18,550**
A: Denys Cowan **W:** Peter B. Gillis
3 ❑ Sep 1988 Cover: 1.25 **NM** value: **2.00**
Circ: CapCity orders: **19,300**
A: Denys Cowan **W:** Peter B. Gillis
4 ❑ Oct 1988 Cover: 1.25 **NM** value: **2.00**
Circ: CapCity orders: **19,300**
A: Denys Cowan **W:** Peter B. Gillis

BLACK PANTHER: PANTHER'S PREY — Marvel

1 ❑ May 1991 Cover: 4.95 **NM** value: **Cover or less**
Circ: CapCity orders: **19,200**
A: Dwayne Turner **W:** Don McGregor
2 ❑ Jun 1991 Cover: 4.95 **NM** value: **Cover or less**
Circ: CapCity orders: **16,600**
A: Dwayne Turner **W:** Don McGregor
3 ❑ Aug 1991 Cover: 4.95 **NM** value: **Cover or less**
Circ: CapCity orders: **14,950**
A: Dwayne Turner **W:** Don McGregor
4 ❑ Oct 1991 Cover: 4.95 **NM** value: **Cover or less**
Circ: CapCity orders: **14,150**
Prey for the Night; Burie Alive; The Price is Blood; Solitaire Showdow; A formal Satellite Announcement; Matrimonial Ractions; Welcome Party; The Snake Eats; Last Chances; Epilogue **A:** Dwayne Turner **W:** Don McGregor

BLACK PANTHER (VOL. 2) — Marvel

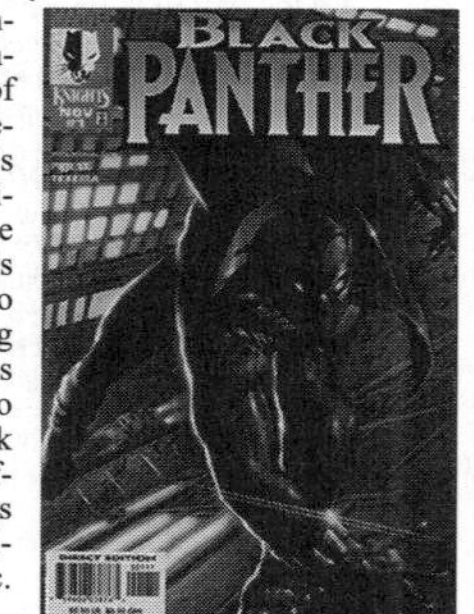

One of the major accomplishments of the Marvel Knights imprint has been the updating of several classic Marvel super-heroes for the modern era. Here, it's The Black Panther, who previously had his own series in the late 1970s, getting the cool '90s spin. The Panther — known also as T'Challa, the mysterious King of Wakanda — must leave his civil-war-torn African nation to investigate a murder in New York City. His adventures in a very different kind of jungle in this series enmesh him in the affairs of villains, both earthly and demonic. He also encounters former super-hero acquaintances, from both The Avengers and The Fantastic Four, and a cast of regulars that includes wildcard government agent Everett K. Ross, a man as quick with a sarcastic remark as a gun.

A team of name creators pitch in, notably writer Christopher Priest and artist Mark Texeira, who lends his richly textured, realistic art to the first several issues.

1 ❑ Nov 1998 Cover: 2.50 **NM** value: **5.00**
Circ: Diamd. preorders: **56,481** • **CGC:** 4 graded, best 9.6
• gatefold summary. The Client **A:** Alitha Martinez; Joe Quesada **W:** Mark Texeira; Christopher Priest
1/SC❑ Nov 1998 Cover: 6.95 **NM** value: **7.00**
• **CGC:** 1 graded, best 9.6
DFE alternate cover. The Client **A:** Alitha Martinez; Joe Quesada **W:** Mark Texeira; Christopher Priest
2/A ❑ Dec 1998 Cover: 2.50 **NM** value: **4.00**
Circ: Diamd. preorders: **50,221**
• gatefold summary. **W:** Christopher Priest
2/B ❑ Dec 1998 Cover: 2.50 **NM** value: **4.00**
• gatefold summary. **W:** Christopher Priest
3 ❑ Jan 1999 Cover: 2.50 **NM** value: **3.00**
Circ: Diamd. preorders: **46,987**
• gatefold summary, A: Fantastic Four **A:** Joe Quesada **W:** Christopher Priest
4 ❑ Feb 1999 Cover: 2.50 **NM** value: **3.00**
Circ: Diamd. preorders: **48,774**
A: Joe Quesada **W:** Christopher Priest ★ Appearance of Mephisto.
5 ❑ Mar 1999 Cover: 2.50 **NM** value: **3.00**
Circ: Diamd. preorders: **44,472**
A: Vince Evans **W:** Christopher Priest ★ Appearance of Mephisto.
6 ❑ Apr 1999 Cover: 2.50 **NM** value: **Cover or less**
Circ: Diamd. preorders: **41,991**
A: Joe Jusko **W:** Christopher Priest ★ Appearance of Kraven the Hunter. ★ Versus Kraven the Hunter.
7 ❑ May 1999 Cover: 2.50 **NM** value: **Cover or less**
Circ: Diamd. preorders: **39,508**
8 ❑ Jun 1999 Cover: 2.50 **NM** value: **Cover or less**
Circ: Diamd. preorders: **40,104**
9 ❑ Jul 1999 Cover: 2.50 **NM** value: **Cover or less**
Circ: Diamd. preorders: **36,980**
10 ❑ Aug 1999 Cover: 2.50 **NM** value: **Cover or less**
Circ: Diamd. preorders: **35,732**
11 ❑ Sep 1999 Cover: 2.50 **NM** value: **Cover or less**
Circ: Diamd. preorders: **35,909**
12 ❑ Oct 1999 Cover: 2.50 **NM** value: **Cover or less**
13 ❑ Dec 1999 Cover: 2.50 **NM** value: **Cover or less**
Circ: Diamd. preorders: **31,486**
14 ❑ Jan 2000 Cover: 2.50 **NM** value: **Cover or less**
Circ: Diamd. preorders: **29,146**
15 ❑ Feb 2000 Cover: 2.50 **NM** value: **Cover or less**
Circ: Diamd. preorders: **30,053**
16 ❑ Mar 2000 Cover: 2.50 **NM** value: **Cover or less**
Circ: Diamd. preorders: **26,029**
17 ❑ Apr 2000 Cover: 2.50 **NM** value: **Cover or less**
Circ: Diamd. preorders: **24,021**
18 ❑ May 2000 Cover: 2.50 **NM** value: **Cover or less**
Circ: Diamd. preorders: **23,829**
19 ❑ Jun 2000 Cover: 2.50 **NM** value: **Cover or less**
Circ: Diamd. preorders: **23,244**
20 ❑ Jul 2000 Cover: 2.50 **NM** value: **Cover or less**
Circ: Diamd. preorders: **23,142**
21 ❑ Aug 2000 Cover: 2.50 **NM** value: **Cover or less**
Circ: Diamd. preorders: **22,714**
22 ❑ Sep 2000 Cover: 2.50 **NM** value: **Cover or less**
Circ: Diamd. preorders: **22,072**
23 ❑ Oct 2000 Cover: 2.50 **NM** value: **Cover or less**
Circ: Diamd. preorders: **20,781**
24 ❑ Nov 2000 Cover: 2.50 **NM** value: **Cover or less**
Circ: Diamd. preorders: **20,539**
Beloved **A:** Walden Wong **W:** M.D. Bright; Christopher Priest
25 ❑ Dec 2000 Cover: 2.50 **NM** value: **Cover or less**
Circ: Diamd. preorders: **22,933**
Maximum Security; Passage **A:** Sal Velluto **W:** Christopher Priest
26 ❑ Jan 2001 Cover: 2.50 **NM** value: **Cover or less**
Circ: Diamd. preorders: **21,416**
Sturm und Drang, A Story of Love and War, Part 1: Echoes **A:** Sal Velluto **W:** Christopher Priest ★ Appearance of Storm.
27 ❑ Feb 2001 Cover: 2.50 **NM** value: **Cover or less**
Circ: Diamd. preorders: **20,932**
Sturm und Drang, A Story of Love and War, Part 2: An Epidemic Insanity **A:** Sal Velluto **W:** Christopher Priest
28 ❑ Mar 2001 Cover: 2.50 **NM** value: **Cover or less**
Circ: Diamd. preorders: **20,728**
Sturm und Drang, A Story of Love and War, Part 3: The Trade of Kings **A:** Sal Velluto **W:** Christopher Priest
29 ❑ Apr 2001 Cover: 2.50 **NM** value: **Cover or less**
Circ: Diamd. preorders: **20,671**
Sturm und Drang, A Story of Love and War, Part 4: The Continuation of Politics by Other Means **A:** Sal Velluto **W:** Christopher Priest
30 ❑ May 2001 Cover: 2.50 **NM** value: **Cover or less**
Circ: Diamd. preorders: **20,952**
The Story Thus Far • World War II story **A:** Norm Breyfogle **W:** Christopher Priest ★ Appearance of Captain America.
31 ❑ Jun 2001 Cover: 2.50 **NM** value: **Cover or less**
Circ: Diamd. preorders: **21,333**
32 ❑ Jul 2001 Cover: 2.50 **NM** value: **Cover or less**
Circ: Diamd. preorders: **21,635**
33 ❑ Aug 2001 Cover: 2.50 **NM** value: **Cover or less**
Circ: Diamd. preorders: **21,826**
34 ❑ Sep 2001 Cover: 2.50 **NM** value: **Cover or less**
Circ: Diamd. preorders: **22,436**
35 ❑ Oct 2001 Cover: 2.50 **NM** value: **Cover or less**
Circ: Diamd. preorders: **22,133**
36 ❑ Nov 2001 Cover: 3.50 **NM** value: **Cover or less**
Circ: Diamd. preorders: **21,105**
37 ❑ Dec 2001 Cover: 2.25 **NM** value: **Cover or less**
Circ: Diamd. preorders: **20,592**
38 ❑ Jan 2002 Cover: 2.50 **NM** value: **Cover or less**
Circ: Diamd. preorders: **21,032**
39 ❑ Feb 2002 Cover: 2.50 **NM** value: **Cover or less**
Circ: Diamd. preorders: **21,039**
40 ❑ Mar 2002 Cover: 2.50 **NM** value: **Cover or less**
Circ: Diamd. preorders: **20,188**

BLACK PEARL, THE — Dark Horse

1 ❑ Sep 1996 Cover: 2.95 **NM** value: **3.50**
Circ: Diamd. preorders: **19,428**
A: H.M. Baker **W:** Eric Johnson; Mark Hamill
2 ❑ Oct 1996 Cover: 2.95 **NM** value: **3.00**
Circ: Diamd. preorders: **14,668**
A: H.M. Baker **W:** Eric Johnson; Mark Hamill
3 ❑ Nov 1996 Cover: 2.95 **NM** value: **3.00**
Circ: Diamd. preorders: **16,097**
A: H.M. Baker **W:** Eric Johnson; Mark Hamill
4 ❑ Dec 1996 Cover: 2.95 **NM** value: **3.00**
Circ: Direct Market orders: **12,894**
A: H.M. Baker **W:** Eric Johnson; Mark Hamill
5 ❑ Jan 1997 Cover: 2.95 **NM** value: **3.00**
Circ: Direct Market orders: **13,124**
final issue. **A:** H.M. Baker **W:** Eric Johnson; Mark Hamill
Bk 1❑ Cover: 16.95 **NM** value: **Cover or less**
• collects series **W:** Mark Hamill

BLACK PHANTOM — AC

Black Phantom originally appeared in Tim Holt's comics as a sexy lady outlaw, but Holt helped her to see the error of her wicked ways and turned her into a masked crimefighter who occasionally rode with him when he took on the alter ego of Redmask of the Rio Grande. The first issue of Black Phantom appeared in 1954, and stories from that title — as well as other Black Phantom tales — are reprinted in this series from Bill Black's AC Comics. The series also features appearances by Holt as Redmask, as well as other Western fare. Incidentally, many of the stories were written by Gardner Fox, the legendary creator of both The Justice Society of America and The Justice League of America.

1 ❑ b&w Cover: 2.50 **NM** value: **Cover or less**
2 ❑ Cover: 2.50 **NM** value: **Cover or less**
3 ❑ b&w Cover: 2.75 **NM** value: **Cover or less**

BLACK PHANTOM (MAGAZINE ENTERPRISES) — Magazine Enterprises

1 ❑ ca. 1954 Cover: 0.10 **NM** value: **250.00**
• **CGC:** 2 graded, best 7.0

BLACK RIDER — Atlas

8 ❑ 1950 Cover: 0.10 **NM** value: **300.00**
9 ❑ 1950 Cover: 0.10 **NM** value: **150.00**
10 ❑ 1950 Cover: 0.10 **NM** value: **150.00**
11 ❑ Nov 1950 Cover: 0.10 **NM** value: **100.00**
• **CGC:** 1 graded, best 8.0
12 ❑ Jan 1951 Cover: 0.10 **NM** value: **100.00**
13 ❑ Mar 1951 Cover: 0.10 **NM** value: **100.00**
14 ❑ May 1951 Cover: 0.10 **NM** value: **100.00**
15 ❑ Jul 1951 Cover: 0.10 **NM** value: **100.00**
16 ❑ Sep 1951 Cover: 0.10 **NM** value: **100.00**
17 ❑ Nov 1951 Cover: 0.10 **NM** value: **100.00**
18 ❑ Jan 1952 Cover: 0.10 **NM** value: **100.00**
19 ❑ Nov 1952 Cover: 0.10 **NM** value: **100.00**
20 ❑ Jan 1953 Cover: 0.10 **NM** value: **100.00**
21 ❑ Mar 1953 Cover: 0.10 **NM** value: **75.00**
22 ❑ May 1953 Cover: 0.10 **NM** value: **75.00**
23 ❑ Jul 1953 Cover: 0.10 **NM** value: **75.00**
24 ❑ Sep 1953 Cover: 0.10 **NM** value: **75.00**
25 ❑ Nov 1953 Cover: 0.10 **NM** value: **75.00**
26 ❑ Jan 1954 Cover: 0.10 **NM** value: **75.00**
27 ❑ Mar 1954 Cover: 0.10 **NM** value: **75.00**

BLACK RIDER RIDES AGAIN!, THE — Atlas

1 ❑ Sep 1957 Cover: 0.10 **NM** value: **125.00**
Legend of the Black Rider; Dual at Dawn; Treachery at Hangman's Bridge • reprints Western Gunfighters #10; reprints Western Gunfighters #11; reprints Western Gunfighters #12 **A:** Jack Kirby

BLACK SABBATH — Rock-It / Malibu

1 ❑ Feb 1994 Cover: 3.95 **NM** value: **Cover or less**

BLACK SCORPION — Special Studio

1 ❑ b&w Cover: 2.75 **NM** value: **Cover or less**
2 ❑ b&w Cover: 2.75 **NM** value: **Cover or less**
3 ❑ b&w Cover: 2.75 **NM** value: **Cover or less**

BLACK SEPTEMBER — Malibu / Ultraverse

8 ❑ Cover: 1.50 **NM** value: **2.00**
• events affect the Infinity issues of the other Ultraverse titles

BLACKSTAR — Imperial

1 ❑ Cover: 1.80 **NM** value: **2.00**
2 ❑ Cover: 1.80 **NM** value: **2.00**

BLACKSTONE — E.C.

E.C. continued the (real-life) character who'd appeared in Street and Smith's Super Magician Comics from the first issue to Vol. 4, #10 (Feb 46) and in Street and Smith's single issue of Black-

Other grades: Multiply prices above by **1.5 for Mint • 2/3 for Very Fine • 1/3 for Fine • 1/5 for Very Good • 1/8 for Good**

stone, Master Magician Comics (Mar 46). The issue also introduced "The Happy Houlihans," which was got its own title at the same time. — Maggie

1 ❑ Fal 1947 Cover: 0.10 **NM** value: **350.00**
• **CGC:** 2 graded, best 7.0
📖 Blackstone fights the Stone Men of Vala!; Introducing-The Happy Houlihans; Blackstone's vanishing coin trick; Blackstone visits the Isle of Doom
2 ❑ May 1948 Cover: 0.10 **NM** value: **250.00**
3 ❑ Jul 1948 Cover: 0.10 **NM** value: **250.00**
• **CGC:** 1 graded, best 7.0
4 ❑ Sep 1948 Cover: 0.10 **NM** value: **250.00**

BLACKSTONE, MASTER MAGICIAN COMICS — Vital Publications

1 ❑ Mar 1946 Cover: 0.10 **NM** value: **175.00**
• **CGC:** 1 graded, best 9.0
2 ❑ May 1946 Cover: 0.10 **NM** value: **125.00**
3 ❑ Jul 1946 Cover: 0.10 **NM** value: **125.00**
• **CGC:** 1 graded, best 8.0

BLACK SUN: X-MEN — Marvel

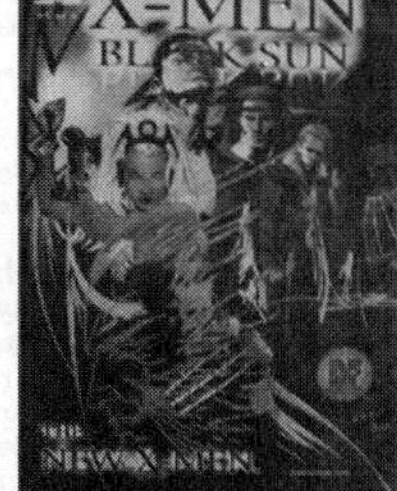

To celebrate the 25th anniversary of the "all-new, all-different" X-Men, Marvel offers this five-issue limited series that features the return of the other-dimensional demon Belasco and Illyana Rasputin, mystic warrior and former member of The New Mutants. Belasco prepares to take over the world, and Marvel's merry mutants stand ready to stop him. Unfortunately, they're going to have to go through each other to get at him — not willingly, of course. That demon-possession'll get you every time. To make this anniversary event even more special, writer Chris Claremont (Fantastic Four) is joined by former X-writers Len Wein (The Incredible Hulk), Roy Thomas (The Avengers), and Louise Simonson (Power Pack).

1 ❑ Nov 2000 Cover: 2.99 **NM** value: **Cover or less**
📖 Skin the Cat! **A:** Thomas Derenick **W:** Chris Claremont
1/A ❑ Nov 2000 Cover: 2.99 **NM** value: **5.00**
Dynamic Forces cover.
2 ❑ Nov 2000 Cover: 2.99 **NM** value: **Cover or less**
📖 X-Men Black Sun Second Spell: Spear the Angel! **A:** Thomas Derenick **W:** Len Wein; Chris Claremont
3 ❑ Nov 2000 Cover: 2.99 **NM** value: **Cover or less**
📖 X-Men Black Sun Third Spell: Bare the Claws! **A:** Karl Waller; Thomas Derenick **W:** Roy Thomas; Chris Claremont
4 ❑ Nov 2000 Cover: 2.99 **NM** value: **Cover or less**
📖 X-Men Black Sun Fourth Spell: Light the Fire! **A:** Alitha Martinez; Thomas Derenick **W:** Louise Simonson; Chris Claremont
5 ❑ Nov 2000 Cover: 2.99 **NM** value: **Cover or less**
📖 X-Men Black Sun Final Spell: Cast the Magik! **A:** Pablo Raimondi; Thomas Derenick **W:** Chris Claremont

BLACK SWAN COMICS — M.L.J.

1 ❑ ca. 1945 Cover: 0.10 **NM** value: **150.00**
• **CGC:** 1 graded, best 9.6

BLACK TERROR, THE (ECLIPSE) — Eclipse

1 ❑ Oct 1989 Cover: 4.95 **NM** value: **Cover or less**
Circ: CapCity orders: **4,225**
A: Dan Brereton **W:** Chuck Dixon; Beau Smith
1/Aut❑Oct 1989 Cover: 3.50 **NM** value: **Cover or less**
A: Dan Brereton **W:** Chuck Dixon; Beau Smith
2 ❑ Mar 1990 Cover: 4.95 **NM** value: **Cover or less**
Circ: CapCity orders: **4,700**
A: Dan Brereton **W:** Chuck Dixon; Beau Smith
2/Aut❑Mar 1990 Cover: 3.50 **NM** value: **Cover or less**
A: Dan Brereton **W:** Chuck Dixon; Beau Smith
3 ❑ Jun 1990 Cover: 4.95 **NM** value: **Cover or less**
Circ: CapCity orders: **4,850**
📖 Seduction of Deceit **A:** Dan Brereton **W:** Chuck Dixon; Beau Smith
3/Aut❑Jun 1990 Cover: 3.50 **NM** value: **Cover or less**
A: Dan Brereton **W:** Chuck Dixon; Beau Smith

BLACK TERROR, THE (VISUAL EDITIONS) — Visual Editions

1 ❑ Win 1942 Cover: 0.10 **NM** value: **1850.00**
2 ❑ Jun 1943 Cover: 0.10 **NM** value: **800.00**
3 ❑ Aug 1943 Cover: 0.10 **NM** value: **640.00**
4 ❑ Nov 1943 Cover: 0.10 **NM** value: **485.00**
5 ❑ Feb 1944 Cover: 0.10 **NM** value: **485.00**
6 ❑ May 1944 Cover: 0.10 **NM** value: **425.00**
7 ❑ Aug 1944 Cover: 0.10 **NM** value: **425.00**
8 ❑ Nov 1944 Cover: 0.10 **NM** value: **425.00**
9 ❑ Feb 1945 Cover: 0.10 **NM** value: **425.00**
10 ❑ May 1945 Cover: 0.10 **NM** value: **425.00**
11 ❑ Aug 1945 Cover: 0.10 **NM** value: **365.00**
12 ❑ Nov 1945 Cover: 0.10 **NM** value: **365.00**
13 ❑ Jan 1946 Cover: 0.10 **NM** value: **365.00**
14 ❑ Apr 1946 Cover: 0.10 **NM** value: **365.00**
15 ❑ Jul 1946 Cover: 0.10 **NM** value: **365.00**
16 ❑ Oct 1946 Cover: 0.10 **NM** value: **315.00**
17 ❑ Jan 1947 Cover: 0.10 **NM** value: **315.00**
18 ❑ Apr 1947 Cover: 0.10 **NM** value: **315.00**
19 ❑ Jul 1947 Cover: 0.10 **NM** value: **315.00**
20 ❑ Oct 1947 Cover: 0.10 **NM** value: **315.00**
21 ❑ Dec 1947 Cover: 0.10 **NM** value: **315.00**
22 ❑ Mar 1948 Cover: 0.10 **NM** value: **265.00**
23 ❑ Jun 1948 Cover: 0.10 **NM** value: **265.00**
24 ❑ Sep 1948 Cover: 0.10 **NM** value: **265.00**
25 ❑ Dec 1948 Cover: 0.10 **NM** value: **265.00**
📖 The Nameless Men!; The Girl Who Cleared Her Name!; Television Trick (text); Homer...Used Car; The Last Chance; The Winston Murder; Cure for Uncle Dan (text); Spectro Master of Magic...The Case of the Jealous Clown! **A:** Mort Meskin **W:** Charles Strong; Donald Hobart
26 ❑ Mar 1949 Cover: 0.10 **NM** value: **265.00**
27 ❑ Jun 1949 Cover: 0.10 **NM** value: **265.00**
final issue.

BLACKTHORNE'S 3 IN 1 — Blackthorne

1 ❑ Cover: 1.75 **NM** value: **Cover or less**
2 ❑ Feb 1987 Cover: 1.75 **NM** value: **Cover or less**

BLACKTHORNE'S HARVEY FLIP BOOK — Blackthorne

1 ❑ b&w Cover: 2.00 **NM** value: **Cover or less**
★ Appearance of Sad Sack, Stumbo.

BLACK WEB — Inks

1 ❑ Cover: 2.95 **NM** value: **Cover or less**
Circ: CapCity orders: **4,165**
📖 The Evil Taste Of Revenge **A:** David Brian Michel **W:** Rebecca Strong ★ Origin of Black Web. ★ 1st Appearance of Black Web.

BLACK WIDOW — Marvel

1 ❑ Jun 1999 Cover: 2.99 **NM** value: **3.50**
Circ: Diamd. preorders: **67,791** • **CGC:** 5 graded, best 9.6
2 ❑ Jul 1999 Cover: 2.99 **NM** value: **3.00**
Circ: Diamd. preorders: **51,831**
3 ❑ Aug 1999 Cover: 2.99 **NM** value: **3.00**
Circ: Diamd. preorders: **51,121**

BLACK WIDOW: THE COLDEST WAR — Marvel

Bk 1❑ Jun 1990 Cover: 9.95 **NM** value: **Cover or less**
Circ: CapCity orders: **7,700**

BLACK WIDOW (VOL. 2) — Marvel

1 ❑ Jan 2001 Cover: 2.99 **NM** value: **Cover or less**
Circ: Diamd. preorders: **39,491** • **CGC:** 3 graded, best 9.6
📖 Breakdown, Part 1; Breakdown **A:** Scott Hampton **W:** Devin Grayson; Greg Rucka
2 ❑ Feb 2001 Cover: 2.99 **NM** value: **Cover or less**
Circ: Diamd. preorders: **34,599** • **CGC:** 1 graded, best 9.6
📖 Breakdown, Part 2 **A:** Scott Hampton **W:** Devin Grayson; Greg Rucka
3 ❑ May 2001 Cover: 2.99 **NM** value: **Cover or less**
Circ: Diamd. preorders: **31,965**
📖 Breakdown, Part 3 **A:** Scott Hampton **W:** Devin Grayson; Greg Rucka

BLACK WIDOW: WEB OF INTRIGUE — Marvel

1 ❑ Jun 1999 Cover: 3.50 **NM** value: **Cover or less**
Circ: Diamd. preorders: **8,880**
• collects Marvel Fanfare #10-13

BLACKWULF — Marvel

1 ❑ Jun 1994 Cover: 2.50 **NM** value: **Cover or less**
Circ: CapCity orders: **23,800**
Embossed cover. 📖 Where Monsters Dwell **A:** Angel Medina **W:** Glenn Herdling
2 ❑ Jul 1994 Cover: 1.50 **NM** value: **Cover or less**
Circ: CapCity orders: **14,900**
3 ❑ Aug 1994 Cover: 1.50 **NM** value: **Cover or less**
Circ: CapCity orders: **11,400**
4 ❑ Sep 1994 Cover: 1.50 **NM** value: **Cover or less**
Circ: CapCity orders: **9,950**
5 ❑ Oct 1994 Cover: 1.50 **NM** value: **Cover or less**
Circ: CapCity orders: **8,150**
6 ❑ Nov 1994 Cover: 1.50 **NM** value: **Cover or less**
Circ: CapCity orders: **7,050**
7 ❑ Dec 1994 Cover: 1.50 **NM** value: **Cover or less**
Circ: CapCity orders: **6,650**
8 ❑ Jan 1995 Cover: 1.50 **NM** value: **Cover or less**
Circ: CapCity orders: **5,600**
9 ❑ Feb 1995 Cover: 1.50 **NM** value: **Cover or less**
Circ: CapCity orders: **5,100**
10 ❑ Mar 1995 Cover: 1.50 **NM** value: **Cover or less**
Circ: CapCity orders: **4,400**
final issue.

BLACK ZEPPELIN (GENE DAY'S...) — Renegade

1 ❑ Apr 1985 Cover: 1.70 **NM** value: **2.00**
📖 The Strip **A:** Gene Day **W:** Gene Day
2 ❑ Cover: 1.70 **NM** value: **2.00**
3 ❑ Cover: 1.70 **NM** value: **2.00**
4 ❑ Cover: 1.70 **NM** value: **2.00**
📖 An Evil Clause
5 ❑ Cover: 2.00 **NM** value: **Cover or less**
📖 Life's End; Gravedigger's Banquet

Diamond preorders are the estimated number of comics sold, prior to their release, to comics shops in North America by Diamond Comic Distributors, the largest distributor. These figures underreport the actual number of circulating copies by the amount of reorders Diamond took (usually 5-10% again of the preorders) and sales by publishers to newsstand and bookstore distributors. For many independent publishers, Diamond's preorders may be quite close to the actual number of copies in circulation.

BLADE (1ST SERIES) — Marvel

A surprise hit movie in the late '90s resurrected fan interest in this '70s character, and Marvel helped kick start it with this tale of the vampire-killer who's not entirely human himself. It begins at Blade's funeral, as he has been recently slain by Dracula, and friends and associates have gathered to lay him to his final rest. But how final is it? Private eye — and vampire — Hannibal King isn't sure, and he enlists the aid of exorcist Daimon Hellstrom to find out. Blade can't be dead, for his dreaded work is still unfinished.

Written by Marv Wolfman and drawn by Gene Colan and Tom Palmer, this one-shot promotional giveaway reprints Blade's origin story from Tomb of Dracula. It's a fast-paced yarn in which a band of heroes (anti-heroes?) battle the forces of the undead, who are led by the evil Deacon Frost, a vampire with even more powers than the average undead. Blade rises to the occasion — but he's not the man he was.

1 ❑ May 1997 **NM** value: **1.50**
• giveaway. 📖 The Final Glory of Deacon Frost **A:** Gene Colan; Tom Palmer **W:** Marv Wolfman ★ Origin of Blade.

BLADE (2ND SERIES) — Marvel

1 ❑ Mar 1998 Cover: 3.50 **NM** value: **Cover or less**
Circ: Diamd. preorders: **25,069**
📖 Crescent City Blues **A:** Gene Colan **W:** Christopher Golden

BLADE (3RD SERIES) — Marvel

1 ❑ Oct 1998 Cover: 5.99 **NM** value: **Cover or less**
Circ: Diamd. preorders: **22,318**
No issue number. One-shot. • gatefold summary. 📖 Blood Allies, Part 1 **A:** Brian Hagan **W:** Don McGregor
2/A ❑ Dec 1998 Cover: 2.99 **NM** value: **Cover or less**
Circ: Diamd. preorders: **21,064**
cover says Nov, indicia says Dec. • gatefold summary. 📖 Blood Allies, Part 2 **A:** Brian Hagan; Bart Sears(cover) **W:** Don McGregor
2/B ❑ Dec 1998 Cover: 2.99 **NM** value: **Cover or less**
📖 Blood Allies, Part 2 **A:** Brian Hagan **W:** Don McGregor
3 ❑ Jan 1999 Cover: 2.99 **NM** value: **Cover or less**
Circ: Diamd. preorders: **17,370**
cover says Dec, indicia says Jan. • gatefold summary. **A:** Brian Hagan **W:** Don McGregor
4 ❑ Cover: 2.99 **NM** value: **Cover or less**
A: Brian Hagan **W:** Don McGregor ★ Appearance of Morbius.

BLADE (4TH SERIES) — Marvel

1 ❑ Nov 1998 Cover: 3.50 **NM** value: **Cover or less**
• gatefold summary. 📖 Blood Allies, Part 1 **A:** Brian Hagan **W:** Don McGregor
2/A ❑ Dec 1998 Cover: 2.99 **NM** value: **Cover or less**
cover says Nov, indicia says Dec. • gatefold summary. 📖 Blood Allies, Part 2 **A:** Brian Hagan; Bart Sears(cover) **W:** Don McGregor
2/B ❑ Dec 1998 Cover: 2.99 **NM** value: **Cover or less**
📖 Blood Allies, Part 2 **A:** Brian Hagan **W:** Don McGregor
3 ❑ Jan 1999 Cover: 2.99 **NM** value: **Cover or less**
cover says Dec, indicia says Jan. • gatefold summary. **A:** Brian Hagan **W:** Don McGregor
4 ❑ Cover: 2.99 **NM** value: **Cover or less**
A: Brian Hagan **W:** Don McGregor ★ Appearance of Morbius.

BLADE (BUCCANEER) — Buccaneer

This black-and-white series from Buccaneer Publications tells the story of a genetically enhanced, sword-wielding ninja-type who has finally left behind the corporation that created him and the government agency he worked for and set out to find his family. Of course, in fiction, you just can't escape those corporations and government agencies; once they've genetically enhanced you, they want you to earn your — um — enhancements. So anti-hero Blade finds himself at once on the run and in pursuit. Not unusual, to be sure, but the early art from such stalwarts as Tony Harris (Starman) and Craig Hamilton (Aquaman) is worth a look.

1 ❑ Cover: 2.00 **NM** value: **Cover or less**
A: Tony Harris **W:** Sean Mercer
2 ❑ Cover: 2.00 **NM** value: **Cover or less**
A: Tony Harris **W:** Sean Mercer

BLADE OF SHURIKEN — Eternity

1 ❑ May 1987 Cover: 1.95 **NM** value: **Cover or less**
📖 The Blade of Shuriken **A:** Reggie Byers **W:** Reggie Byers
2 ❑ Jul 1987 Cover: 1.95 **NM** value: **Cover or less**
A: Reggie Byers **W:** Reggie Byers
3 ❑ Sep 1987 Cover: 1.95 **NM** value: **Cover or less**
A: Reggie Byers **W:** Reggie Byers
4 ❑ Nov 1987 Cover: 1.95 **NM** value: **Cover or less**
A: Reggie Byers **W:** Reggie Byers
5 ❑ Jan 1988 Cover: 1.95 **NM** value: **Cover or less**
A: Reggie Byers **W:** Reggie Byers

Creator Key
W = Writer • A = Artist • C = Cover Artist

CGC-graded: Multiply prices above by **33 for 9.9 M** • **16 for 9.8 NM/M** • **7 for 9.6 NM+** • **5 for 9.4 NM** • **2.5 for 9.2 NM-** • **1.5 for 9.0 VF/NM**

BLADE OF THE IMMORTAL — Dark Horse

Blade of the Immortal tells the story of Manji, a swordsman who was cursed with immortality by another immortal. His escape from immorality — his release from the curse — will be his, if he manages to kill 1,000 evil men. Hiroaki Samura's comic book, influenced by Osamu Tezuka's Dororo (1967 manga, eventual 1969 anime), was one of the best-selling manga in Japan in the 1990s and is faithfully reprinted for the American audience.

The series is fast-paced and well-written and is a fine example of the raw energy manga can transmit.

1 ❑ Jun 1996 Cover: 2.95 **NM** value: **3.50**
A: Hiroaki Samura **W:** Hiroaki Samura

2 ❑ Jul 1996 Cover: 2.95 **NM** value: **3.00**
📖 Conquest, Part 1 **A:** Hiroaki Samura **W:** Hiroaki Samura

3 ❑ Aug 1996 Cover: 2.95 **NM** value: **3.00**
📖 Conquest, Part 2 **A:** Hiroaki Samura **W:** Hiroaki Samura

4 ❑ Sep 1996 Cover: 2.95 **NM** value: **3.00**
📖 Conquest, Part 3 **A:** Hiroaki Samura **W:** Hiroaki Samura

5 ❑ Oct 1996 Cover: 2.95 **NM** value: **3.00**
Circ: Diamd. preorders: **10,831**
📖 Genius, Part 1 **A:** Hiroaki Samura **W:** Hiroaki Samura

6 ❑ Nov 1996 Cover: 2.95 **NM** value: **Cover or less**
Circ: Diamd. preorders: **9,983**
📖 Genius, Part 2 **A:** Hiroaki Samura **W:** Hiroaki Samura

7 ❑ Dec 1996 Cover: 2.95 **NM** value: **Cover or less**
Circ: Direct Market orders: **11,833**
📖 Fanatic, Part 1 **A:** Hiroaki Samura **W:** Hiroaki Samura

8 ❑ Jan 1997 Cover: 2.95 **NM** value: **Cover or less**
Circ: Direct Market orders: **10,431**
📖 Fanatic, Part 2 **A:** Hiroaki Samura **W:** Hiroaki Samura

9 ❑ Apr 1997 Cover: 3.95 **NM** value: **Cover or less**
Circ: Diamd. preorders: **11,448**
• Giant-size. 📖 Call of the Worm, Part 1 **A:** Hiroaki Samura; Sergio Aragonés; Gary Gianni; Jae Lee; Terry Moore **W:** Hiroaki Samura

10 ❑ May 1997 Cover: 3.95 **NM** value: **Cover or less**
Circ: Diamd. preorders: **10,562**
• Giant-size. 📖 Call of the Worm, Part 2 **A:** Hiroaki Samura; Roger Langridge; Kelley Jones; Dick Giordano; Stan Sakai **W:** Hiroaki Samura

11 ❑ Jun 1997 Cover: 3.95 **NM** value: **Cover or less**
Circ: Diamd. preorders: **10,006**
• Giant-size. 📖 Call of the Worm, Part 3 **A:** Hiroaki Samura; Paul Grist; Dan Brereton; Gil Kane; Gene Ha **W:** Hiroaki Samura

12 ❑ Jul 1997 Cover: 2.95 **NM** value: **Cover or less**
Circ: Diamd. preorders: **11,063**
📖 Dreamsong, Part 1 **A:** Hiroaki Samura **W:** Hiroaki Samura

13 ❑ Aug 1997 Cover: 2.95 **NM** value: **Cover or less**
Circ: Diamd. preorders: **11,120**
📖 Dreamsong, Part 2 **A:** Hiroaki Samura **W:** Hiroaki Samura

14 ❑ Sep 1997 Cover: 2.95 **NM** value: **Cover or less**
Circ: Diamd. preorders: **11,403**
📖 Dreamsong, Part 3 **A:** Hiroaki Samura **W:** Hiroaki Samura

15 ❑ Oct 1997 Cover: 2.95 **NM** value: **Cover or less**
Circ: Diamd. preorders: **11,535**
📖 Dreamsong, Part 4 **A:** Hiroaki Samura **W:** Hiroaki Samura

16 ❑ Nov 1997 Cover: 2.95 **NM** value: **Cover or less**
Circ: Diamd. preorders: **11,620**
📖 Dreamsong, Part 5 **A:** Hiroaki Samura **W:** Hiroaki Samura

17 ❑ Dec 1997 Cover: 2.95 **NM** value: **Cover or less**
Circ: Diamd. preorders: **11,327**
📖 Dreamsong, Part 6 **A:** Hiroaki Samura **W:** Hiroaki Samura

18 ❑ Jan 1998 Cover: 2.95 **NM** value: **Cover or less**
Circ: Diamd. preorders: **11,093**
📖 Dreamsong, Part 7 **A:** Hiroaki Samura **W:** Hiroaki Samura

19 ❑ Mar 1998 Cover: 3.95 **NM** value: **Cover or less**
Circ: Diamd. preorders: **10,962**
📖 Rin's Bane, Part 1 **A:** Hiroaki Samura **W:** Hiroaki Samura

20 ❑ Apr 1998 Cover: 3.95 **NM** value: **Cover or less**
Circ: Diamd. preorders: **10,928**
📖 Rin's Bane, Part 2 **A:** Hiroaki Samura **W:** Hiroaki Samura

21 ❑ May 1998 Cover: 2.95 **NM** value: **Cover or less**
Circ: Diamd. preorders: **11,047**
📖 On Silent Wings, Part 1 **A:** Hiroaki Samura **W:** Hiroaki Samura

22 ❑ Jun 1998 Cover: 2.95 **NM** value: **Cover or less**
Circ: Diamd. preorders: **10,673**
📖 On Silent Wings, Part 2 **A:** Hiroaki Samura **W:** Hiroaki Samura

23 ❑ Jul 1998 Cover: 2.95 **NM** value: **Cover or less**
Circ: Diamd. preorders: **10,359**
📖 On Silent Wings, Part 3 **A:** Hiroaki Samura **W:** Hiroaki Samura

24 ❑ Aug 1998 Cover: 2.95 **NM** value: **Cover or less**
Circ: Diamd. preorders: **10,548**
📖 On Silent Wings, Part 4 **A:** Hiroaki Samura **W:** Hiroaki Samura

25 ❑ Sep 1998 Cover: 2.95 **NM** value: **Cover or less**
Circ: Diamd. preorders: **10,581**
📖 On Silent Wings, Part 5 **A:** Hiroaki Samura **W:** Hiroaki Samura

26 ❑ Oct 1998 Cover: 3.95 **NM** value: **Cover or less**
Circ: Diamd. preorders: **10,603**
📖 On Silent Wings, Part 6 **A:** Hiroaki Samura **W:** Hiroaki Samura

27 ❑ Nov 1998 Cover: 2.95 **NM** value: **Cover or less**
Circ: Diamd. preorders: **10,389**
📖 On Silent Wings, Part 7 **A:** Hiroaki Samura **W:** Hiroaki Samura

28 ❑ Dec 1998 Cover: 2.95 **NM** value: **Cover or less**
Circ: Diamd. preorders: **10,200**
📖 On Silent Wings, Part 8 **A:** Hiroaki Samura **W:** Hiroaki Samura

29 ❑ Jan 1999 Cover: 2.95 **NM** value: **Cover or less**
Circ: Diamd. preorders: **10,743**
📖 Dark Shadows, Part 1 **A:** Hiroaki Samura **W:** Hiroaki Samura

30 ❑ Feb 1999 Cover: 2.95 **NM** value: **Cover or less**
Circ: Diamd. preorders: **9,907**
📖 Dark Shadows, Part 2 **A:** Hiroaki Samura **W:** Hiroaki Samura

31 ❑ Mar 1999 Cover: 2.95 **NM** value: **Cover or less**
Circ: Diamd. preorders: **9,999**
📖 Dark Shadows, Part 3 **A:** Hiroaki Samura **W:** Hiroaki Samura

32 ❑ Apr 1999 Cover: 2.95 **NM** value: **Cover or less**
Circ: Diamd. preorders: **10,267**
📖 Dark Shadows, Part 4 **A:** Hiroaki Samura **W:** Hiroaki Samura

33 ❑ May 1999 Cover: 2.95 **NM** value: **Cover or less**
Circ: Diamd. preorders: **9,985**
📖 Dark Shadows, Part 5 **A:** Hiroaki Samura **W:** Hiroaki Samura

34 ❑ Jun 1999 Cover: 3.95 **NM** value: **Cover or less**
Circ: Diamd. preorders: **9,890**
📖 Food **A:** Hiroaki Samura **W:** Hiroaki Samura

35 ❑ Jul 1999 Cover: 2.95 **NM** value: **Cover or less**
Circ: Diamd. preorders: **10,577**
📖 Heart of Darkness, Part 1 **A:** Hiroaki Samura **W:** Hiroaki Samura

36 ❑ Aug 1999 Cover: 2.95 **NM** value: **3.95**
Circ: Diamd. preorders: **9,957**
📖 Heart of Darkness, Part 2 **A:** Hiroaki Samura **W:** Hiroaki Samura

37 ❑ Sep 1999 Cover: 2.95 **NM** value: **3.95**
Circ: Diamd. preorders: **9,784**
📖 Heart of Darkness, Part 3 **A:** Hiroaki Samura **W:** Hiroaki Samura

38 ❑ Oct 1999 Cover: 2.95 **NM** value: **3.95**
Circ: Diamd. preorders: **10,043**
📖 Heart of Darkness, Part 4 **A:** Hiroaki Samura **W:** Hiroaki Samura

39 ❑ Nov 1999 Cover: 2.95 **NM** value: **2.99**
Circ: Diamd. preorders: **9,581**
A: Hiroaki Samura **W:** Hiroaki Samura

40 ❑ Dec 1999 Cover: 2.95 **NM** value: **2.99**
Circ: Diamd. preorders: **10,300**
A: Hiroaki Samura **W:** Hiroaki Samura

41 ❑ Jan 2000 Cover: 2.95 **NM** value: **2.99**
Circ: Diamd. preorders: **9,527**
A: Hiroaki Samura **W:** Hiroaki Samura

42 ❑ Feb 2000 Cover: 3.50 **NM** value: **Cover or less**
Circ: Diamd. preorders: **8,907**
A: Hiroaki Samura **W:** Hiroaki Samura

43 ❑ Mar 2000 Cover: 2.95 **NM** value: **2.99**
Circ: Diamd. preorders: **9,715**
📖 The Gathering, Part 1 **A:** Hiroaki Samura **W:** Hiroaki Samura

44 ❑ Apr 2000 Cover: 2.95 **NM** value: **2.99**
Circ: Diamd. preorders: **9,299**
📖 The Gathering, Part 2 **A:** Hiroaki Samura **W:** Hiroaki Samura

45 ❑ May 2000 Cover: 2.95 **NM** value: **2.99**
Circ: Diamd. preorders: **9,364**
📖 The Gathering, Part 3 **A:** Hiroaki Samura **W:** Hiroaki Samura

46 ❑ Jun 2000 Cover: 2.95 **NM** value: **2.99**
Circ: Diamd. preorders: **9,398**
📖 The Gathering, Part 4 **A:** Hiroaki Samura **W:** Hiroaki Samura

47 ❑ Jul 2000 Cover: 2.95 **NM** value: **2.99**
Circ: Diamd. preorders: **9,362**
📖 The Gathering, Part 5 **A:** Hiroaki Samura **W:** Hiroaki Samura

48 ❑ Aug 2000 Cover: 2.95 **NM** value: **2.99**
Circ: Diamd. preorders: **8,972**
📖 The Gathering, Part 6 **A:** Hiroaki Samura **W:** Hiroaki Samura

49 ❑ Sep 2000 Cover: 2.95 **NM** value: **2.99**
Circ: Diamd. preorders: **9,122**
📖 The Gathering, Part 7 **A:** Hiroaki Samura **W:** Hiroaki Samura

50 ❑ Oct 2000 Cover: 2.99 **NM** value: **Cover or less**
Circ: Diamd. preorders: **9,114**
📖 The Gathering, Part 8 **A:** Hiroaki Samura **W:** Hiroaki Samura

51 ❑ Nov 2000 Cover: 2.99 **NM** value: **Cover or less**
Circ: Diamd. preorders: **8,973**
📖 The Gathering, Part 9 **A:** Hiroaki Samura **W:** Hiroaki Samura

52 ❑ Dec 2000 Cover: 2.99 **NM** value: **Cover or less**
Circ: Diamd. preorders: **8,862**
📖 The Gathering, Part 10 **A:** Hiroaki Samura **W:** Hiroaki Samura

53 ❑ Jan 2001 Cover: 2.99 **NM** value: **Cover or less**
Circ: Diamd. preorders: **8,562**
📖 The Gathering, Part 11 **A:** Hiroaki Samura **W:** Hiroaki Samura

Bk 1❑ Mar 1997 Cover: 12.95 **NM** value: **Cover or less**
📖 Blood of a Thousand • Blood of a Thousand;collects issues #1-6 **A:** Hiroaki Samura **W:** Hiroaki Samura

Bk 2❑ Mar 1998 Cover: 12.95 **NM** value: **Cover or less**
📖 Cry of the Worm • Cry of the Worm, collects issues #7-11 **A:** Hiroaki Samura **W:** Hiroaki Samura

Bk 4❑ Cover: 14.95 **NM** value: **Cover or less**
• On Silent Wings collects issues 19-23

BLADE RUNNER — Marvel

1 ❑ Oct 1982 Cover: 0.60 **NM** value: **1.00**
A: Al Williamson; Carlos Garzon **W:** Archie Goodwin

2 ❑ Nov 1982 Cover: 0.60 **NM** value: **1.00**
A: Al Williamson; Carlos Garzon; Brent Anderson(cover) **W:** Archie Goodwin

Bk 1❑ Cover: 1.75 **NM** value: **Cover or less**

BLADESMEN, THE — Blue Comet

0 ❑ b&w Cover: 2.00 **NM** value: **Cover or less**
A: Dell Barras; Craig A. Stormon **W:** Dell Barras; Craig A. Stormon

1 ❑ b&w Cover: 2.00 **NM** value: **Cover or less**
📖 A Gathering of Hawks **A:** Dell Barras; Craig A. Stormon **W:** Dell Barras; Craig A. Stormon

2 ❑ Cover: 2.25 **NM** value: **Cover or less**
A: Dell Barras; Craig A. Stormon **W:** Dell Barras; Craig A. Stormon

BLADE: THE VAMPIRE-HUNTER — Marvel

1 ❑ Jul 1994 Cover: 2.95 **NM** value: **Cover or less**
Circ: CapCity orders: **25,200**
foil cover. 📖 Dark Visions **A:** Doug Wheatley **W:** Ian Edginton

2 ❑ Aug 1994 Cover: 1.95 **NM** value: **Cover or less**
Circ: CapCity orders: **15,200**
📖 Red Prophet **A:** Doug Wheatley **W:** Ian Edginton

3 ❑ Sep 1994 Cover: 1.95 **NM** value: **Cover or less**
Circ: CapCity orders: **13,150**

4 ❑ Oct 1994 Cover: 1.95 **NM** value: **Cover or less**
Circ: CapCity orders: **11,550**

5 ❑ Nov 1994 Cover: 1.95 **NM** value: **Cover or less**
Circ: CapCity orders: **9,800**

6 ❑ Dec 1994 Cover: 1.95 **NM** value: **Cover or less**
Circ: CapCity orders: **9,000**

7 ❑ Jan 1995 Cover: 1.95 **NM** value: **Cover or less**
Circ: CapCity orders: **7,675**

8 ❑ Feb 1995 Cover: 1.95 **NM** value: **Cover or less**
Circ: CapCity orders: **6,825**

9 ❑ Mar 1995 Cover: 1.95 **NM** value: **Cover or less**
Circ: CapCity orders: **6,050**

10 ❑ Apr 1995 Cover: 1.95 **NM** value: **Cover or less**
Circ: CapCity orders: **5,575**
final issue.

BLADE: VAMPIRE HUNTER — Marvel

1 ❑ Dec 1999 Cover: 3.50 **NM** value: **Cover or less**
📖 Chaos, Part 1 **A:** Bart Sears **W:** Bart Sears

2 ❑ Jan 2000 Cover: 2.50 **NM** value: **Cover or less**
Circ: Diamd. preorders: **29,946**

3 ❑ Feb 2000 Cover: 2.50 **NM** value: **Cover or less**
Circ: Diamd. preorders: **26,206**

4 ❑ Mar 2000 Cover: 2.50 **NM** value: **Cover or less**
Circ: Diamd. preorders: **21,722**

5 ❑ Apr 2000 Cover: 2.50 **NM** value: **Cover or less**
Circ: Diamd. preorders: **19,104**

6 ❑ May 2000 Cover: 2.50 **NM** value: **Cover or less**
Circ: Diamd. preorders: **17,133**

BLAIR WHICH? (SERGIO ARAGONÉS'...) — Dark Horse

1 ❑ Dec 1999 Cover: 2.95 **NM** value: **Cover or less**
A: Sergio Aragonés **W:** Mark Evanier

BLAIR WITCH CHRONICLES, THE — Oni

1 ❑ Mar 2000, b&w Cover: 2.95 **NM** value: **Cover or less**
Circ: Diamd. preorders: **12,034** • **CGC:** 1 graded, best 9.0
📖 The Kearney Interview **A:** Tom Fowler; Guy Davis **W:** Jan Van Meter; Jen Van Meter

2 ❑ Apr 2000 Cover: 2.95 **NM** value: **Cover or less**
Circ: Diamd. preorders: **8,591**
📖 The Offering **A:** Tom Fowler; Bernie Mireault **W:** Jan Van Meter; Jen Van Meter

3 ❑ Jun 2000 Cover: 2.95 **NM** value: **Cover or less**
Circ: Diamd. preorders: **6,853**
A: Tom Fowler **W:** Jan Van Meter; Jen Van Meter

4 ❑ Jul 2000 Cover: 2.95 **NM** value: **Cover or less**
Circ: Diamd. preorders: **6,384**
📖 Fire **A:** Tom Fowler **W:** Jan Van Meter; Jen Van Meter

Bk 1❑ Sep 2000 Cover: 15.95 **NM** value: **Cover or less**
• collects mini-series **W:** Jen Van Meter

BLAIR WITCH: DARK TESTAMENTS — Image

1 ❑ Oct 2000 Cover: 2.95 **NM** value: **Cover or less**
Circ: Diamd. preorders: **9,109**
A: Charles Adlard **W:** Ian Edgington

BLAIR WITCH PROJECT, THE — Oni

The mythos of The Blair Witch Project was elaborately designed before the movie was released, including such information as that Blair Township was founded in 1634, that there were accusations of witchcraft in the late 1700s, that seven children in the area were missing in the early 1940s, and that an assortment of other strange events occurred in the area. The film begins in October 1994, when a college filmmaking project leads a number of people into the woods to make a documentary, and is told via the film, which is recovered a year later.

The Oni Press version had a number of variant editions. — Maggie

1 ❑ Aug 1999 Cover: 2.95 **NM** value: **10.00**
📖 Curse; She Needs Me: Coffin Rock; Left Alone: The Rustin Park Killings • prequel to movie **A:** Bernie Mireault; Guy Davis; Tommy Lee Edwards **W:** Jen Van Meter

1-2 ❑ Cover: 2.95 **NM** value: **Cover or less**

BLANCHE GOES TO HOLLYWOOD — Dark Horse

1 ❑ b&w Cover: 2.95 **NM** value: **Cover or less**
No issue number.

BLANCHE GOES TO NEW YORK — Dark Horse

Blanche Goes to New York is a delightfully genteel combination of piano lessons and demonic invasion. The one-shot special begins when Blanche arrives in 1900s New York to study piano at the home of Professor Pellegrini. The professor is a former intimate of some of the more "radical" composers, such as Debussy, Schoenberg, and Mahler.

As exotic as these piano compositions might sound to the gentle Blanche's ears, it is nothing compared to the strange sounds that sometimes emanate from the lower levels of the house. When Blanche investigates, she finds that the wondrous city of New York harbors some very old secrets.

1 ❑ Nov 1992, b&w Cover: 2.95 **NM** value: **Cover or less**
No issue number. **A:** Rick Geary **W:** Rick Geary

Other grades: Multiply prices above by **1.5 for Mint • 2/3 for Very Fine • 1/3 for Fine • 1/5 for Very Good • 1/8 for Good**

BLARNEY — Discovery
1 ❑ Cover: 2.95 NM value: Cover or less
cardstock cover, b&w.

BLAST CORPS — Dark Horse
1 ❑ Oct 1998 Cover: 2.50 NM value: Cover or less
Circ: Diamd. preorders: 3,695
• based on Nintendo 64 games

BLASTERS SPECIAL — DC
1 ❑ May 1989 Cover: 2.00 NM value: Cover or less
Circ: CapCity orders: 18,700
A: James W. Fry III W: Peter David

BLAST-OFF — Harvey
1 ❑ Oct 1965 Cover: 0.12 NM value: 26.00
📖 Caution! Atoms!; Lunar Goliaths; The Great Moon Mystery A: Joe Simon; Al Williamson; Jack Kirby; Reed Crandall W: Joe Simon; Al Williamson; Jack Kirby; Reed Crandall ★ Appearance of The Three Rocketeers.

BLAZE — Marvel
1 ❑ Aug 1994 Cover: 2.95 NM value: Cover or less
Circ: CapCity orders: 26,950
silver enhanced cover. 📖 A Cold Blast From Ice Box Bob! A: Henry Martinez W: Larry Hama ★ Origin of Johnny Blaze.
2 ❑ Sep 1994 Cover: 1.95 NM value: Cover or less
Circ: CapCity orders: 16,000
3 ❑ Oct 1994 Cover: 1.95 NM value: Cover or less
Circ: CapCity orders: 13,050
4 ❑ Nov 1994 Cover: 1.95 NM value: Cover or less
Circ: CapCity orders: 11,800
5 ❑ Dec 1994 Cover: 1.95 NM value: Cover or less
Circ: CapCity orders: 10,550
6 ❑ Jan 1995 Cover: 1.95 NM value: Cover or less
Circ: CapCity orders: 9,125
7 ❑ Feb 1995 Cover: 1.95 NM value: Cover or less
Circ: CapCity orders: 8,025
8 ❑ Mar 1995 Cover: 1.95 NM value: Cover or less
Circ: CapCity orders: 7,100
9 ❑ Apr 1995 Cover: 1.95 NM value: Cover or less
Circ: CapCity orders: 6,425
10 ❑ May 1995 Cover: 1.95 NM value: Cover or less
Circ: CapCity orders: 5,925
11 ❑ Jun 1995 Cover: 1.95 NM value: Cover or less
Circ: CapCity orders: 5,750
12 ❑ Jul 1995 Cover: 1.95 NM value: Cover or less
Circ: CapCity orders: 5,425
final issue.

BLAZE CARSON — Marvel
1 ❑ Sep 1948 Cover: 0.10 NM value: 175.00
• CGC: 1 graded, best 7.0
3 ❑ Jan 1949 Cover: 0.10 NM value: 125.00
4 ❑ Mar 1949 Cover: 0.10 NM value: 125.00
5 ❑ May 1949 Cover: 0.10 NM value: 125.00
2 ❑ Nov 1948 Cover: 0.10 NM value: 125.00

BLAZE: LEGACY OF BLOOD — Marvel
1 ❑ Dec 1993 Cover: 1.75 NM value: Cover or less
Circ: CapCity orders: 42,300
📖 Legacy Of Blood, Part 1 A: Ron Wagner W: Howard Mackie
2 ❑ Jan 1994 Cover: 1.75 NM value: Cover or less
Circ: CapCity orders: 23,200
3 ❑ Feb 1994 Cover: 1.75 NM value: Cover or less
Circ: CapCity orders: 20,100
4 ❑ Mar 1994 Cover: 1.75 NM value: Cover or less
Circ: CapCity orders: 16,900

BLAZE OF GLORY — Marvel
Wonderment, Montana, where whites, Indians, and freed blacks live together peacefully, has been attacked and isolated by hooded outlaws called Nightriders. In desperation, townspeople recruit several gunfighters to their cause. Despite their reputation as ruthless outlaws, The Rawhide Kid, Kid Colt, The Two-Gun Kid, and The Outlaw Kid do not hesitate to come to the beleaguered town's aid.

Besides the seemingly endless forces of The Nightriders, the four gunslingers must also deal with a bounty hunter known as Gunhawk and a Pinkerton agent named Caleb Hammer. Luckily, they have allies of their own. The local Nez Perce have summoned their champion, Red Wolf, and the mysterious Ghost Rider has also placed the townspeople under his protection.

Subtitled "Last Ride of the Western Heroes," this dark, grim tale by John Ostrander and Leonardo Manco might well be the final chapter for some of Marvel's most popular Western characters.

1 ❑ Feb 2000 Cover: 2.99 NM value: Cover or less
Circ: Diamd. preorders: 21,945
• biweekly mini-series
2 ❑ Feb 2000 Cover: 2.99 NM value: Cover or less
Circ: Diamd. preorders: 19,642
3 ❑ Mar 2000 Cover: 2.99 NM value: Cover or less
Circ: Diamd. preorders: 16,155
4 ❑ Mar 2000 Cover: 2.99 NM value: Cover or less
Circ: Diamd. preorders: 15,976

BLAZING SIXGUNS — Avon
1 ❑ ca. 1952 Cover: 0.10 NM value: 100.00
• CGC: 1 graded, best 7.0

BLAZING BATTLE TALES — Seaboard / Atlas
1 ❑ Jul 1975 Cover: 0.25 NM value: 2.50
• CGC: 2 graded, best 9.4

BLAZING COMBAT — Warren
1 ❑ Oct 1965 Cover: 0.35 NM value: 100.00
• scarcer A: Frank Frazetta(cover)
2 ❑ 1965 Cover: 0.35 NM value: 35.00
A: Frank Frazetta(cover)
3 ❑ 1966 Cover: 0.35 NM value: 35.00
A: Frank Frazetta(cover)
4 ❑ 1966 Cover: 0.35 NM value: 35.00
A: Frank Frazetta(cover)
Anl 1❑ NM value: 50.00

BLAZING COMBAT (APPLE) — Apple
1 ❑ Cover: 4.50 NM value: Cover or less
2 ❑ b&w Cover: 4.50 NM value: Cover or less

BLAZING COMBAT: WORLD WAR I AND WORLD WAR II — Apple
1 ❑ Cover: 3.75 NM value: Cover or less
2 ❑ Jun 1994 Cover: 3.75 NM value: Cover or less

BLAZING FOXHOLES — Eros
1 ❑ Cover: 2.95 NM value: Cover or less
A: Art Wetherell W: Art Wetherell
2 ❑ Cover: 2.95 NM value: Cover or less
A: Art Wetherell W: Art Wetherell
3 ❑ Jan 1995 Cover: 2.95 NM value: Cover or less
📖 The Percy Patrol A: Art Wetherell W: Art Wetherell

BLAZING WEST — ACG
American Comics Group published primarily non-super-hero titles from 1943 to 1967. Although it did venture into super-heroes with Magicman and Nemesis — and super-hero parody with Herbie, the Fat Fury — during the craze inspired by the Batman TV series of the mid-1960s, ACG stayed the course with funny animal, teen humor, horror, science fiction, adventure, and war comics. ACG's Western offerings were The Hooded Horseman and Blazing West.

Blazing West was an anthology title that ran for 22 issues, from 1948 to 1952, and featured such gun-toting stalwarts as "Injun" Jones, a white man who was a friend to the Apache tribe; Bantam Buckaroo, a boy billed as "90 pounds of pure TNT"; Buffalo Belle, a fiery female gunfighter; and The Hooded Horseman, a mysterious, Lone Ranger-type hero who was introduced in #14.

1 ❑ Fal 1948 Cover: 0.10 NM value: 85.00
• CGC: 1 graded, best 9.0
★ 1st Appearance of Injun Jones.
2 ❑ Nov 1948 Cover: 0.10 NM value: 48.00
3 ❑ Jan 1949 Cover: 0.10 NM value: 35.00
4 ❑ Mar 1949 Cover: 0.10 NM value: 35.00
5 ❑ May 1949 Cover: 0.10 NM value: 35.00
6 ❑ Jul 1949 Cover: 0.10 NM value: 28.00
7 ❑ Sep 1949 Cover: 0.10 NM value: 28.00
8 ❑ Nov 1949 Cover: 0.10 NM value: 28.00
9 ❑ Jan 1950 Cover: 0.10 NM value: 28.00
10 ❑ Mar 1950 Cover: 0.10 NM value: 28.00
11 ❑ May 1950 Cover: 0.10 NM value: 22.00
12 ❑ Jul 1950 Cover: 0.10 NM value: 22.00
📖 Injun Jones; Bantam Buckaroo; The Jump (text story); The Apache Kid; Buffalo Belle; The Eyes Have It (text story); Famous Western Feuds: Clay Allison vs. Chunk Colbert; Desert Doom (text story); Texas Tim, Ranger; A Cowboy's Day
13 ❑ Sep 1950 Cover: 0.10 NM value: 22.00
14 ❑ Nov 1950 Cover: 0.10 NM value: 58.00
★ Origin of The Hooded Horseman. ★ 1st Appearance of The Hooded Horseman.
15 ❑ Jan 1951 Cover: 0.10 NM value: 28.00
16 ❑ Mar 1951 Cover: 0.10 NM value: 22.00
17 ❑ May 1951 Cover: 0.10 NM value: 22.00
18 ❑ Jul 1951 Cover: 0.10 NM value: 20.00
19 ❑ Sep 1951 Cover: 0.10 NM value: 20.00
20 ❑ Nov 1951 Cover: 0.10 NM value: 20.00
21 ❑ Feb 1952 Cover: 0.10 NM value: 18.00
22 ❑ Mar 1952 Cover: 0.10 NM value: 18.00

BLAZING WESTERN (AC) — AC
1 ❑ b&w Cover: 2.50 NM value: Cover or less

BLAZING WESTERN (AVALON) — Avalon
1 ❑ Cover: 2.75 NM value: Cover or less
📖 Cheyenne Kid: The Legend of the White Buffalo; You Ride With Crazy Horse; Pecos Justice; Mr. Young of the Boothill Gazette: The Last Round!; Billy the Kid: Sequaqua the Warrior!

BLEAT — Slave Labor
1 ❑ Aug 1995 Cover: 2.95 NM value: Cover or less

BLEEDING HEART — Fantagraphics
1 ❑ Cover: 2.50 NM value: Cover or less
2 ❑ Spr 1992 Cover: 2.50 NM value: Cover or less
3 ❑ Cover: 2.50 NM value: Cover or less
4 ❑ Cover: 2.50 NM value: Cover or less
5 ❑ Aug 1993 Cover: 2.50 NM value: Cover or less

BLINDSIDE — Image
1 ❑ Feb 1998 Cover: 2.50 NM value: Cover or less
• video game magazine in comic-book format. 📖 Video Games of the Stars; Blip Tips I; Blip Tips II; Hall of Fame; Clubhouse; Video Jokes; Player's Choice; News Blips; Game Design; Donkey Kong; Blip Survey A: Bob Camp; Eliot Brown; Gary Brodsky; Roger Elwood; Ron Zalme ★ 1st Appearance of Mario, Donkey Kong.
1/A ❑ Aug 1996 Cover: 2.50 NM value: Cover or less
wraparound cover.
1/B ❑ Aug 1996 Cover: 2.50 NM value: Cover or less
white background cover.
2 ❑ Sep 1996 Cover: 2.50 NM value: Cover or less
Circ: Diamd. preorders: 19,443
3 ❑ Dec 1996 Cover: 2.50 NM value: Cover or less
Circ: Direct Market orders: 12,862
4 ❑ 1997 Cover: 2.50 NM value: Cover or less
5 ❑ 1997 Cover: 2.50 NM value: Cover or less
6 ❑ 1997 Cover: 2.50 NM value: Cover or less
7 ❑ 1997 Cover: 2.50 NM value: Cover or less

BLINK — Marvel
1 ❑ Mar 2001 Cover: 2.99 NM value: Cover or less
• CGC: 4 graded, best 9.8
A: Trevor McCarthy W: Scott Lobdell
2 ❑ Apr 2001 Cover: 2.99 NM value: Cover or less
📖 Through the Looking Glass ... A: Trevor McCarthy W: Scott Lobdell
3 ❑ May 2001 Cover: 2.99 NM value: Cover or less
📖 On the Side of the Angels A: Trevor McCarthy W: Scott Lobdell; Judd Winick
4 ❑ Cover: 2.99 NM value: Cover or less

BLIP — Marvel
In the early 1980s, before video games were able to portray realistic figures in vibrant three-dimensional color, games that relied on a maze-type layout (like Pac-Man and Donkey Kong) were the peak in arcade entertainment. The comparatively simple (by modern standards) graphics and sound effects made a name like Blip appropriate for a comic book dealing with video games. Their incredible popularity did not bode well for the comics industry. It became apparent that much of the money that kids used to set aside for comics was now spent on video games. So with an "If you can't beat 'em ..." attitude, Marvel published this title, which profiled popular teen television stars and the video games they liked. In addition to the celebrity features, Blip also gave readers tips on strategy to help them perfect their techniques.

1 ❑ 1983 Cover: 1.00 NM value: Cover or less
• video game magazine in comic-book format. 📖 Video Games of the Stars; Blip Tips I; Blip Tips II; Hall of Fame; Clubhouse; Video Jokes; Player's Choice; News Blips; Game Design; Donkey Kong; Blip Survey A: Bob Camp; Eliot Brown; Gary Brodsky; Roger Elwood; Ron Zalme W: Rick Parker; Roger Elwood; Ron Zalme; Steven Grant; Eliot Brown Gary Brodsky; George Sullivan ★ 1st Appearance of Mario, Donkey Kong.
2 ❑ Cover: 1.00 NM value: Cover or less
3 ❑ Cover: 1.00 NM value: Cover or less
4 ❑ Cover: 1.00 NM value: Cover or less
5 ❑ Cover: 1.00 NM value: Cover or less
6 ❑ Cover: 1.00 NM value: Cover or less
7 ❑ Cover: 1.00 NM value: Cover or less

BLIP AND THE C.C.A.D.S. — Amazing
1 ❑ Cover: 1.95 NM value: 2.00
2 ❑ Cover: 1.95 NM value: 2.00

BLIP (BARDIC) — Bardic
1 ❑ Feb 1998 Cover: 1.25 NM value: Cover or less
📖 The Caretakers A: Steve Conley; Dave Sim; Bill Knapp; Tara Jenkins; Joe Zabel; Jimmy Gownley; Craig A. Taillefer; Teri S. Wood; Jenni Gregory; Mark Sherman; Michael Cohen; Scott Morse; Carla McNeil; David Yukovich; M'Oak W: Steve Conley; Dave Sim; Bill Knapp; Tara Jenkins; Joe Zabel; Jimmy Gownley; Craig A. Taillefer; Teri S. Wood; Jenni Gregory; Mark Sherman; Michael Cohen; Scott Morse; Carla McNeil; David Yukovich; M'Oak

BLISS ALLEY — Image
1 ❑ Jul 1997 Cover: 2.95 NM value: Cover or less
Circ: Diamd. preorders: 6,840
2 ❑ Sep 1997 Cover: 2.95 NM value: Cover or less
Circ: Diamd. preorders: 4,622
A: William Messner-Loebs W: William Messner-Loebs

BLITE — Fantagraphics
1 ❑ b&w Cover: 2.25 NM value: Cover or less

BLITZ — Nightwynd
1 ❑ Cover: 2.50 NM value: Cover or less
2 ❑ Cover: 2.50 NM value: Cover or less
3 ❑ Cover: 2.50 NM value: Cover or less
4 ❑ Cover: 2.50 NM value: Cover or less

BLITZKRIEG — DC
1 ❑ Jan 1976 Cover: 0.25 NM value: 7.00
• CGC: 10 graded, best 9.6
📖 Enemy A: Ric Estrada W: Robert Kanigher

CGC-graded: Multiply prices above by **33 for 9.9 M • 16 for 9.8 NM/M • 7 for 9.6 NM+ • 5 for 9.4 NM • 2.5 for 9.2 NM- • 1.5 for 9.0 VF/NM**

2 ❑ Mar 1976 Cover: 0.30 **NM** value: **4.00**
• **CGC:** 1 graded, best 9.6

3 ❑ May 1976 Cover: 0.30 **NM** value: **4.00**
• **CGC:** 2 graded, best 9.6
The Execution; The Partisans! **A:** Ric Estrada **W:** Robert Kanigher

4 ❑ Jul 1976 Cover: 0.30 **NM** value: **4.00**
• **CGC:** 1 graded, best 9.4
• Bicentennial #20

5 ❑ Sep 1976 Cover: 0.30 **NM** value: **4.00**
• **CGC:** 1 graded, best 8.0
final issue.

BLOCKADE — Heritage Collection

1 ❑ Cover: 9.95 **NM** value: **Cover or less**
No issue number. • Trade Paperback. • focuses on Civil War naval battles **A:** Wayne Vansant **W:** Wayne Vansant

BLONDE, THE — Fantagraphics / Eros

1 ❑ Cover: 2.50 **NM** value: **Cover or less**
2 ❑ Cover: 2.50 **NM** value: **Cover or less**
3 ❑ Cover: 2.50 **NM** value: **Cover or less**

BLONDE ADDICTION — Blitzweasel

1 ❑ Cover: 2.95 **NM** value: **Cover or less**
A: P.M. Butler **W:** Cynthia Johns; Dave Butler
2 ❑ Cover: 2.95 **NM** value: **Cover or less**
3 ❑ Cover: 2.95 **NM** value: **Cover or less**
4 ❑ Cover: 2.95 **NM** value: **Cover or less**
• flip-book with Blonde Avenger's Subplots

BLONDE AVENGER — Blitzweasel

27/A❑ Cover: 3.95 **NM** value: **Cover or less**
Model Kombat **A:** P.M. Butler **W:** Cindy Johns; Dave R.
27/B❑ Cover: 3.95 **NM** value: **Cover or less**
Photo cover. Model Kombat **A:** P.M. Butler **W:** Cindy Johns; Dave R.

BLONDE AVENGER: CROSSOVER CRAZZEEE — Blitzweasel

1 ❑ Cover: 3.95 **NM** value: **Cover or less**
No issue number. One-shot.

BLONDE AVENGER, THE (MINI-SERIES) — Eros

1 ❑ Cover: 2.75 **NM** value: **Cover or less**
A: P.M. Butler **W:** Cindy Johns; Dave R.
2 ❑ Cover: 2.75 **NM** value: **Cover or less**
A: P.M. Butler **W:** Cindy Johns; Dave R.
3 ❑ Cover: 2.75 **NM** value: **Cover or less**
A: P.M. Butler **W:** Cindy Johns; Dave R.
4 ❑ Apr 1994 Cover: 2.75 **NM** value: **Cover or less**
Maneater **A:** P.M. Butler **W:** Cindy Johns; Dave R.

BLONDE AVENGER MONTHLY — Blitzweasel

1 ❑ Mar 1996, b&w Cover: 2.95 **NM** value: **4.00**
Dangerous Island, Part 1
2 ❑ Cover: 2.95 **NM** value: **3.00**
Dangerous Island, Part 2
3 ❑ Cover: 2.95 **NM** value: **Cover or less**
Dangerous Island, Part 3
4 ❑ Cover: 2.95 **NM** value: **Cover or less**
Dangerous Island, Part 4
5 ❑ Cover: 2.95 **NM** value: **Cover or less**
Dangerous Island, Part 5
6 ❑ Cover: 2.95 **NM** value: **Cover or less**
Dangerous Island, Part 6

BLONDE AVENGER ONE-SHOT SPECIAL: THE SPYING GAME — Blitzweasel

1 ❑ Mar 1996, b&w Cover: 2.95 **NM** value: **Cover or less**
The Spying Game **A:** P.M. Butler **W:** Dave R.; R.A.Jones

BLONDE, THE: BONDAGE PALACE — Fantagraphics / Eros

1 ❑ Cover: 2.95 **NM** value: **Cover or less**
A: Franco Saudelli **W:** Franco Saudelli
2 ❑ Cover: 2.95 **NM** value: **Cover or less**
A: Franco Saudelli **W:** Franco Saudelli
3 ❑ Cover: 2.95 **NM** value: **Cover or less**
A: Franco Saudelli **W:** Franco Saudelli
5 ❑ May 1994 Cover: 2.95 **NM** value: **Cover or less**
A: Franco Saudelli **W:** Franco Saudelli

BLONDE PHANTOM — Timely

12 ❑ ca. 1946 Cover: 0.10 **NM** value: **1000.00**
• **CGC:** 2 graded, best 5.5
13 ❑ ca. 1946 Cover: 0.10 **NM** value: **750.00**
• **CGC:** 4 graded, best 9.4
14 ❑ ca. 1946 Cover: 0.10 **NM** value: **650.00**
• **CGC:** 3 graded, best 9.0
15 ❑ ca. 1947 Cover: 0.10 **NM** value: **650.00**
• **CGC:** 4 graded, best 9.2
16 ❑ ca. 1947 Cover: 0.10 **NM** value: **650.00**
• **CGC:** 8 graded, best 9.4
17 ❑ ca. 1947 Cover: 0.10 **NM** value: **500.00**
18 ❑ ca. 1948 Cover: 0.10 **NM** value: **500.00**
19 ❑ ca. 1948 Cover: 0.10 **NM** value: **500.00**
• **CGC:** 1 graded, best 9.0
20 ❑ ca. 1948 Cover: 0.10 **NM** value: **500.00**
21 ❑ ca. 1949 Cover: 0.10 **NM** value: **500.00**
• **CGC:** 2 graded, best 8.0
22 ❑ ca. 1949 Cover: 0.10 **NM** value: **500.00**
• **CGC:** 1 graded, best 5.0

BLONDIE COMICS — David McKay

The Blondie strip created by Chic Young (1901-1973) has been a part of the American consciousness since it was introduced in 1930. It began as a gag strip about Blondie as a pert flapper, surrounded by suitors — but she married Dagwood Bumstead in 1933, and the strip turned into a family comedy gag-a-day.

Dagwood works for Mr. Dithers, an old blowhard who chews out Dagwood with legendary frequency. Other regular characters include Dagwood and Blondie's children and even their pet dogs. Comic-book appearances included strip reprints and stand-alone stories produced specifically for the comic books.

Originally published by McKay, this series moved first to Harvey, then over to Charlton from #177 on.

1 ❑ Spr 1947 Cover: 0.10 **NM** value: **175.00**
• McKay publishes **A:** Chic Young **W:** Chic Young
2 ❑ Sum 1947 Cover: 0.10 **NM** value: **75.00**
A: Chic Young **W:** Chic Young
3 ❑ Fal 1947 Cover: 0.10 **NM** value: **55.00**
A: Chic Young **W:** Chic Young
4 ❑ Win 1947 Cover: 0.10 **NM** value: **55.00**
A: Chic Young **W:** Chic Young
5 ❑ Spr 1948 Cover: 0.10 **NM** value: **55.00**
A: Chic Young **W:** Chic Young
6 ❑ Cover: 0.10 **NM** value: **32.00**
A: Chic Young **W:** Chic Young
7 ❑ Cover: 0.10 **NM** value: **32.00**
A: Chic Young **W:** Chic Young
8 ❑ Cover: 0.10 **NM** value: **32.00**
A: Chic Young **W:** Chic Young
9 ❑ Cover: 0.10 **NM** value: **32.00**
A: Chic Young **W:** Chic Young
10 ❑ 1949 Cover: 0.10 **NM** value: **32.00**
A: Chic Young **W:** Chic Young
11 ❑ 1949 Cover: 0.10 **NM** value: **24.00**
Dagwood: Special Delivery; Room and Board; Just the Type; Paul Bunyan: Logging off Flat-Top Peak; Blondie: Slow Motion!; Blondie: Monotony in Reverse!; Blondie: A "Bone" Lure!; They'll Do it Every Time **A:** Chic Young; Dow Walling; Gene Ahern; Jimmy Hatlo; Bob Dunn **W:** Chic Young; Dow Walling; Gene Ahern; Jimmy Hatlo; Bob Dunn
12 ❑ 1949 Cover: 0.10 **NM** value: **24.00**
A: Chic Young **W:** Chic Young
13 ❑ 1949 Cover: 0.10 **NM** value: **24.00**
A: Chic Young **W:** Chic Young
14 ❑ 1949 Cover: 0.10 **NM** value: **24.00**
A: Chic Young **W:** Chic Young
15 ❑ 1949 Cover: 0.10 **NM** value: **24.00**
• Last McKay issue **A:** Chic Young **W:** Chic Young
16 ❑ Mar 1950 Cover: 0.10 **NM** value: **24.00**
• Harvey begins publishing **A:** Chic Young **W:** Chic Young
17 ❑ Apr 1950 Cover: 0.10 **NM** value: **16.00**
A: Chic Young **W:** Chic Young
18 ❑ May 1950 Cover: 0.10 **NM** value: **16.00**
A: Chic Young **W:** Chic Young
19 ❑ Jun 1950 Cover: 0.10 **NM** value: **16.00**
A: Chic Young **W:** Chic Young
20 ❑ Jul 1950 Cover: 0.10 **NM** value: **16.00**
A: Chic Young **W:** Chic Young
21 ❑ Aug 1950 Cover: 0.10 **NM** value: **12.00**
A: Chic Young **W:** Chic Young
22 ❑ Sep 1950 Cover: 0.10 **NM** value: **12.00**
A: Chic Young **W:** Chic Young
23 ❑ Oct 1950 Cover: 0.10 **NM** value: **12.00**
A: Chic Young **W:** Chic Young
24 ❑ Nov 1950 Cover: 0.10 **NM** value: **12.00**
A: Chic Young **W:** Chic Young
25 ❑ Dec 1950 Cover: 0.10 **NM** value: **12.00**
A: Chic Young **W:** Chic Young
26 ❑ Jan 1951 Cover: 0.10 **NM** value: **12.00**
• **CGC:** 1 graded, best 9.2
Pin Up; Everyman For Himself **A:** Chic Young **W:** Chic Young
27 ❑ Feb 1951 Cover: 0.10 **NM** value: **12.00**
A: Chic Young **W:** Chic Young
28 ❑ Mar 1951 Cover: 0.10 **NM** value: **12.00**
A: Chic Young **W:** Chic Young
29 ❑ Apr 1951 Cover: 0.10 **NM** value: **12.00**
A: Chic Young **W:** Chic Young
30 ❑ May 1951 Cover: 0.10 **NM** value: **12.00**
A: Chic Young **W:** Chic Young
31 ❑ Jun 1951 Cover: 0.10 **NM** value: **12.00**
A: Chic Young **W:** Chic Young
32 ❑ Jul 1951 Cover: 0.10 **NM** value: **12.00**
A: Chic Young **W:** Chic Young
33 ❑ Aug 1951 Cover: 0.10 **NM** value: **12.00**
A: Chic Young **W:** Chic Young
34 ❑ Sep 1951 Cover: 0.10 **NM** value: **12.00**
A: Chic Young **W:** Chic Young
35 ❑ Oct 1951 Cover: 0.10 **NM** value: **12.00**
Blondie: Between Two Fires; Blondie: Sole Mates; Colonel Potter and the Duchess; Blondie: My Error!; Blondie: Easy Does It!; Grandma; The Sorrowful Dragon (text story); Double Trouble; The Water Lilly and the Frog (text story) **A:** Chic Young; Bill MacLean; Chas Kuhn **W:** Chic Young; Bill MacLean; Chas Kuhn
36 ❑ Nov 1951 Cover: 0.10 **NM** value: **12.00**
37 ❑ Dec 1951 Cover: 0.10 **NM** value: **12.00**
• **CGC:** 1 graded, best 9.2
38 ❑ 1952 Cover: 0.10 **NM** value: **12.00**
39 ❑ 1952 Cover: 0.10 **NM** value: **12.00**
40 ❑ 1952 Cover: 0.10 **NM** value: **12.00**
41 ❑ 1952 Cover: 0.10 **NM** value: **12.00**
42 ❑ 1952 Cover: 0.10 **NM** value: **12.00**
43 ❑ 1952 Cover: 0.10 **NM** value: **12.00**
44 ❑ 1952 Cover: 0.10 **NM** value: **12.00**
45 ❑ 1952 Cover: 0.10 **NM** value: **12.00**
46 ❑ 1952 Cover: 0.10 **NM** value: **12.00**
47 ❑ 1952 Cover: 0.10 **NM** value: **12.00**
48 ❑ Cover: 0.10 **NM** value: **12.00**
49 ❑ Cover: 0.10 **NM** value: **12.00**
50 ❑ 1953 Cover: 0.10 **NM** value: **12.00**
51 ❑ 1953 Cover: 0.10 **NM** value: **9.00**
52 ❑ 1953 Cover: 0.10 **NM** value: **9.00**
53 ❑ 1953 Cover: 0.10 **NM** value: **9.00**
54 ❑ 1953 Cover: 0.10 **NM** value: **9.00**
55 ❑ 1953 Cover: 0.10 **NM** value: **9.00**
56 ❑ 1953 Cover: 0.10 **NM** value: **9.00**
57 ❑ 1953 Cover: 0.10 **NM** value: **9.00**
58 ❑ 1953 Cover: 0.10 **NM** value: **9.00**
59 ❑ Cover: 0.10 **NM** value: **9.00**
60 ❑ Cover: 0.10 **NM** value: **9.00**
61 ❑ Cover: 0.10 **NM** value: **9.00**
62 ❑ Cover: 0.10 **NM** value: **9.00**
63 ❑ Cover: 0.10 **NM** value: **9.00**
64 ❑ Cover: 0.10 **NM** value: **9.00**
65 ❑ Cover: 0.10 **NM** value: **9.00**
66 ❑ Cover: 0.10 **NM** value: **9.00**
67 ❑ Cover: 0.10 **NM** value: **9.00**
68 ❑ Cover: 0.10 **NM** value: **9.00**
69 ❑ Cover: 0.10 **NM** value: **9.00**
70 ❑ 1954 Cover: 0.10 **NM** value: **9.00**
71 ❑ Cover: 0.10 **NM** value: **9.00**
72 ❑ Cover: 0.10 **NM** value: **9.00**
73 ❑ Cover: 0.10 **NM** value: **9.00**
74 ❑ Cover: 0.10 **NM** value: **9.00**
75 ❑ Cover: 0.10 **NM** value: **9.00**
76 ❑ Cover: 0.10 **NM** value: **9.00**
77 ❑ Cover: 0.10 **NM** value: **9.00**
78 ❑ Cover: 0.10 **NM** value: **9.00**
79 ❑ Cover: 0.10 **NM** value: **9.00**
80 ❑ Cover: 0.10 **NM** value: **9.00**
81 ❑ Cover: 0.10 **NM** value: **8.00**
82 ❑ 1955 Cover: 0.10 **NM** value: **8.00**
83 ❑ 1955 Cover: 0.10 **NM** value: **8.00**
84 ❑ 1955 Cover: 0.10 **NM** value: **8.00**
85 ❑ 1955 Cover: 0.10 **NM** value: **8.00**
86 ❑ Cover: 0.10 **NM** value: **8.00**
87 ❑ Cover: 0.10 **NM** value: **8.00**
88 ❑ Cover: 0.10 **NM** value: **8.00**
89 ❑ Cover: 0.10 **NM** value: **8.00**
Quarter Boy; It Pays to Advertise; Star Nite; You Can't Win; Two Faced; Billy and the Grifalon (text); Jacquot the Jester (text) • Includes The Flop Family
90 ❑ Cover: 0.10 **NM** value: **8.00**
Shaved and Clipped
91 ❑ Cover: 0.10 **NM** value: **8.00**
92 ❑ Cover: 0.10 **NM** value: **8.00**
93 ❑ Cover: 0.10 **NM** value: **8.00**
94 ❑ Sep 1956, four-color Cover: 0.10 **NM** value: **8.00**
95 ❑ Cover: 0.10 **NM** value: **8.00**
96 ❑ Cover: 0.10 **NM** value: **8.00**
97 ❑ Cover: 0.10 **NM** value: **8.00**
98 ❑ 1957 Cover: 0.10 **NM** value: **8.00**
99 ❑ 1957 Cover: 0.10 **NM** value: **8.00**
100 ❑ 1957 Cover: 0.10 **NM** value: **9.00**
• 100th anniversary issue.
101 ❑ 1957 Cover: 0.10 **NM** value: **7.00**
102 ❑ 1957 Cover: 0.10 **NM** value: **7.00**
103 ❑ 1957 Cover: 0.10 **NM** value: **7.00**
104 ❑ 1957 Cover: 0.10 **NM** value: **7.00**
105 ❑ 1957 Cover: 0.10 **NM** value: **7.00**
106 ❑ 1957 Cover: 0.10 **NM** value: **7.00**
107 ❑ 1957 Cover: 0.10 **NM** value: **7.00**
108 ❑ 1957 Cover: 0.10 **NM** value: **7.00**
109 ❑ Cover: 0.10 **NM** value: **7.00**
110 ❑ 1958 Cover: 0.10 **NM** value: **7.00**
111 ❑ 1958 Cover: 0.10 **NM** value: **7.00**
112 ❑ 1958 Cover: 0.10 **NM** value: **7.00**
113 ❑ 1958 Cover: 0.10 **NM** value: **7.00**
114 ❑ 1958 Cover: 0.10 **NM** value: **7.00**
115 ❑ 1958 Cover: 0.10 **NM** value: **7.00**
116 ❑ 1958 Cover: 0.10 **NM** value: **7.00**
117 ❑ 1958 Cover: 0.10 **NM** value: **7.00**
118 ❑ 1958 Cover: 0.10 **NM** value: **7.00**
119 ❑ 1958 Cover: 0.10 **NM** value: **7.00**
120 ❑ 1958 Cover: 0.10 **NM** value: **7.00**
121 ❑ Jan 1959 Cover: 0.10 **NM** value: **7.00**
122 ❑ 1959 Cover: 0.10 **NM** value: **7.00**
123 ❑ 1959 Cover: 0.10 **NM** value: **7.00**
124 ❑ 1959 Cover: 0.10 **NM** value: **7.00**
125 ❑ 1959 Cover: 0.10 **NM** value: **8.00**
• Double-size.
126 ❑ 1959 Cover: 0.10 **NM** value: **7.00**
127 ❑ 1959 Cover: 0.10 **NM** value: **7.00**
128 ❑ 1959 Cover: 0.10 **NM** value: **7.00**
129 ❑ 1959 Cover: 0.10 **NM** value: **7.00**
130 ❑ Cover: 0.10 **NM** value: **7.00**
131 ❑ Cover: 0.10 **NM** value: **6.00**
132 ❑ Cover: 0.10 **NM** value: **6.00**
133 ❑ 1960 Cover: 0.10 **NM** value: **6.00**
Circ: Statement: **218,344**
134 ❑ 1960 Cover: 0.10 **NM** value: **6.00**
Circ: Statement: **218,344**
135 ❑ 1960 Cover: 0.10 **NM** value: **6.00**
Circ: Statement: **218,344**
136 ❑ 1960 Cover: 0.10 **NM** value: **6.00**
Circ: Statement: **218,344**

Other grades: Multiply prices above by **1.5 for Mint • 2/3 for Very Fine • 1/3 for Fine • 1/5 for Very Good • 1/8 for Good**

137❑ 1960 Cover: 0.10 **NM** value: **6.00**
Circ: Statement: **218,344**
138❑ 1960 Cover: 0.10 **NM** value: **6.00**
Circ: Statement: **218,344**
139❑ 1960 Cover: 0.10 **NM** value: **6.00**
Circ: Statement: **218,344**
140❑ 1960 Cover: 0.10 **NM** value: **6.00**
Circ: Statement: **218,344**
141❑ **NM** value: **8.00**
142❑ **NM** value: **8.00**
143❑ **NM** value: **8.00**
144❑ Apr 1961 **NM** value: **8.00**
• Has 1960 Statement, filed 10/1/1960; avg total paid circ 218,344
145❑ **NM** value: **8.00**
146❑ **NM** value: **8.00**
147❑ **NM** value: **8.00**
148❑ **NM** value: **8.00**
149❑ **NM** value: **8.00**
150❑ **NM** value: **8.00**
151❑ **NM** value: **8.00**
152❑ **NM** value: **8.00**
153❑ **NM** value: **8.00**
154❑ **NM** value: **8.00**
155❑ **NM** value: **8.00**
156❑ **NM** value: **8.00**
157❑ **NM** value: **8.00**
158❑ **NM** value: **8.00**
159❑ **NM** value: **8.00**
160❑ 1965 **NM** value: **8.00**
161❑ 1965 **NM** value: **8.00**
162❑ 1965 **NM** value: **8.00**
163❑ Nov 1965 Cover: 0.12 **NM** value: **8.00**
164❑ Aug 1966 Cover: 0.12 **NM** value: **8.00**
• King Features Syndicate begins publishing
165❑ 1966 **NM** value: **8.00**
166❑ **NM** value: **8.00**
167❑ **NM** value: **8.00**
168❑ 1967 **NM** value: **4.00**
169❑ 1967 **NM** value: **4.00**
170❑ 1967 **NM** value: **4.00**
171❑ 1967 **NM** value: **4.00**
172❑ 1967 **NM** value: **4.00**
173❑ 1967 **NM** value: **4.00**
174❑ 1967 **NM** value: **4.00**
175❑ Dec 1967 **NM** value: **4.00**
176❑ **NM** value: **4.00**
177❑ Feb 1969 **NM** value: **4.00**
178❑ 1969 **NM** value: **4.00**
179❑ 1969 **NM** value: **4.00**
180❑ 1969 **NM** value: **4.00**
181❑ 1969 **NM** value: **3.00**
182❑ **NM** value: **3.00**
183❑ 1970 **NM** value: **3.00**
184❑ 1970 **NM** value: **3.00**
185❑ 1970 **NM** value: **3.00**
186❑ 1970 **NM** value: **3.00**
187❑ Sep 1970 Cover: 0.15 **NM** value: **3.00**
188❑ **NM** value: **3.00**
189❑ **NM** value: **3.00**
190❑ 1971 **NM** value: **3.00**
191❑ 1971 **NM** value: **3.00**
192❑ 1971 **NM** value: **3.00**
193❑ 1971 **NM** value: **3.00**
194❑ 1971 **NM** value: **3.00**
195❑ **NM** value: **3.00**
196❑ 1972 **NM** value: **3.00**
197❑ 1972 **NM** value: **3.00**
198❑ 1972 **NM** value: **3.00**
199❑ 1972 **NM** value: **3.00**
200❑ Oct 1972 Cover: 0.20 **NM** value: **3.00**
• Anniversary issue.
201❑ Cover: 0.20 **NM** value: **2.50**
202❑ 1973 Cover: 0.20 **NM** value: **2.50**
Circ: Statement: **130,090**
203❑ 1973 Cover: 0.20 **NM** value: **2.50**
Circ: Statement: **130,090**
204❑ 1973 Cover: 0.20 **NM** value: **2.50**
Circ: Statement: **130,090**
205❑ 1973 Cover: 0.20 **NM** value: **2.50**
Circ: Statement: **130,090**
206❑ Sep 1973 Cover: 0.20 **NM** value: **2.50**
Circ: Statement: **130,090**
207❑ 1974 **NM** value: **2.50**
Circ: Statement: **97,750**
208❑ May 1974 **NM** value: **2.50**
Circ: Statement: **97,750**
• Has 1973 Statement; avg total paid circ 130,090
209❑ 1974 **NM** value: **2.50**
Circ: Statement: **97,750**
210❑ 1974 **NM** value: **2.50**
Circ: Statement: **97,750**
211❑ 1974 **NM** value: **2.50**
Circ: Statement: **97,750**
212❑ 1975 **NM** value: **2.50**
213❑ 1975 **NM** value: **2.50**
214❑ Jun 1975 **NM** value: **2.50**
• Has 1974 Statement; avg total paid circ 120,135
215❑ 1975 **NM** value: **2.50**
216❑ 1975 **NM** value: **2.50**
217❑ 1976 Cover: 0.25 **NM** value: **2.50**
📖 Quiet! Dagwood At Work!; A Very Full Day; Getting Into The Act!; It's The Way You Do It **A:** Chic Young **W:** Chic Young
218❑ 1976 **NM** value: **2.50**
219❑ 1976 **NM** value: **2.50**
220❑ 1976 **NM** value: **2.50**
221❑ 1976 **NM** value: **2.50**
222❑ Nov 1976 **NM** value: **2.50**
final issue.

BLOOD — Fantaco

1 ❑ b&w Cover: 3.95 **NM** value: **Cover or less**

BLOOD AND GLORY — Marvel

Captain America has long been the almost untarnished symbol of liberty and justice. Whereas other traditional heroes have turned into grim 'n' gritty vigilantes or morally ambiguous avengers, Captain America has always tried to represent his country with honesty and integrity.

What happens, then, when his government proves unworthy of that trust?

In Blood and Glory, a conspiracy is afoot at the very top levels of government to circumvent the law in order to advance a secret agenda in Central America. When Cap uncovers clues pointing to this conspiracy, he resolves to follow the trail to its source. To stop him, the conspirators turn to the vigilante known as The Punisher, convincing him that Cap is betraying the country he represents. Not long after, the Punisher will focus on Captain America as his next target.

1 ❑ Cover: 5.95 **NM** value: **Cover or less**
Circ: CapCity orders: **28,750**
Embossed cover. 📖 We The People... **A:** Klaus Janson **W:** D.G. Chichester; Margaret Clark ★ Appearance of Punisher.
2 ❑ Cover: 5.95 **NM** value: **Cover or less**
📖 Eternal Vigilance **A:** Klaus Janson **W:** D.G. Chichester; Margaret Clark ★ Appearance of Punisher.
3 ❑ Cover: 5.95 **NM** value: **Cover or less**
📖 Establish the Blessings of Liberty **A:** Klaus Janson **W:** D.G. Chichester; Margaret Clark ★ Appearance of Punisher, Captain America, Terror, Inc..

BLOOD & KISSES — Fantaco

1 ❑ Cover: 3.95 **NM** value: **Cover or less**
A: Leif Jones **W:** Leif Jones
2 ❑ Cover: 3.95 **NM** value: **Cover or less**

BLOOD & ROSES ADVENTURES — Knight Press

Now at Knight Press, Blood & Roses Adventures continues the saga of Christiana Blood and Tamara Rose, two women who travel through time in search of the missing shards of the Time Stone. As the series begins, Blood and Rose have completed their mission and handed over the final shard of the Time-Stone to their Time-Lord contact.

When they make their return to Infinity (the realm of the Time-Lords), they are in for a rude surprise. A fellow agent named Marta has taken control of the Time-Stone and intends to use it to gain ultimate power. Stopping her results in the deaths of several of Blood and Rose's comrades, and in the end they are forced to sever Marta's power by shattering the Time-Stone. With Marta defeated, Blood & Rose find that they are back at their old job: jumping through time and into constant peril to collect the bits of the shattered Time-Stone.

1 ❑ May 1995, b&w Cover: 2.95 **NM** value: **Cover or less**
A: Mark Hester; Bob Hickey **W:** Bob Hickey; Bill Nichols

BLOOD & ROSES: FUTURE PAST TENSE — Sky

1 ❑ Dec 1993 Cover: 2.25 **NM** value: **Cover or less**
Circ: CapCity orders: **3,735**
• Silver logo regular edition. **A:** Brad Gorby **W:** Bob Hickey
1/Ash❑ **NM** value: **3.00**
• ashcan edition. **A:** Brad Gorby **W:** Bob Hickey
1/GO❑ **NM** value: **3.00**
• Gold logo promotional edition. **A:** Brad Gorby **W:** Bob Hickey
2 ❑ Cover: 2.25 **NM** value: **Cover or less**
A: Brad Gorby **W:** Bob Hickey

BLOOD & ROSES: SEARCH FOR THE TIME-STONE — Sky

1 ❑ Cover: 2.50 **NM** value: **Cover or less**
A: Gene Gonzales **W:** Joe Martin; Bob Hickey
1/Ash❑ **NM** value: **3.00**
• ashcan edition.
2 ❑ Cover: 2.50 **NM** value: **Cover or less**

Diamond preorders are the estimated number of comics sold, prior to their release, to comics shops in North America by Diamond Comic Distributors, the largest distributor. These figures underreport the actual number of circulating copies by the amount of reorders Diamond took (usually 5-10% again of the preorders) and sales by publishers to newsstand and bookstore distributors. For many independent publishers, Diamond's preorders may be quite close to the actual number of copies in circulation.

BLOOD AND SHADOWS — DC / Vertigo

This mini-series from Vertigo by novelist Joe R. Lansdale (Jonah Hex: Two-Gun Mojo) is not for the squeamish. Set in east Texas in the 1940s, Blood and Shadows features small-time detective Chet Daly on the trail of a gruesome killer the papers have dubbed "The Skinner."

Initially involved as a favor to his girlfriend, who was worried about her brother's disappearance, Daly embarks on a journey of horror and mysticism. His investigation leads him to the discovery of a cache of grisly trophies and the mythological God of the Razor, a deity governing all things sharp and evil. Daly will risk much to defeat a demon that is entirely beyond his experience, but The God of the Razor has made it personal. This curious blending of the hardboiled private eye genre with the occult leads the reader into territory familiar to Clive Barker fans.

1 ❑ Cover: 5.95 **NM** value: **Cover or less**
A: Mark A. Nelson **W:** Joe Lansdale
2 ❑ Cover: 5.95 **NM** value: **Cover or less**
A: Mark A. Nelson **W:** Joe Lansdale
3 ❑ Cover: 5.95 **NM** value: **Cover or less**
A: Mark A. Nelson **W:** Joe Lansdale
4 ❑ Cover: 5.95 **NM** value: **Cover or less**
A: Mark A. Nelson **W:** Joe Lansdale

BLOOD AND THUNDER — Conquest

1 ❑ b&w Cover: 2.95 **NM** value: **Cover or less**

BLOOD & WATER — Slave Labor

1 ❑ Oct 1991, b&w Cover: 3.95 **NM** value: **Cover or less**

BLOOD: A TALE — Marvel / Epic

1 ❑ Sep 1996 Cover: 3.25 **NM** value: **Cover or less**
Circ: CapCity orders: **13,650** Direct Market orders: **17,000**
📖 Uroborous **A:** Kent Williams **W:** J.M. DeMatteis
2 ❑ Oct 1996 Cover: 3.25 **NM** value: **Cover or less**
Circ: CapCity orders: **11,900** Direct Market orders: **14,250**
📖 Communion **A:** Kent Williams **W:** J.M. DeMatteis
3 ❑ Nov 1996 Cover: 3.25 **NM** value: **Cover or less**
Circ: CapCity orders: **12,800** Direct Market orders: **13,000**
📖 Theophany **A:** Kent Williams **W:** J.M. DeMatteis
4 ❑ Dec 1996 Cover: 3.25 **NM** value: **Cover or less**
Circ: CapCity orders: **13,150** Direct Market orders: **12,500**
A: Kent Williams **W:** J.M. DeMatteis
Bk 1❑ Cover: 15.95 **NM** value: **Cover or less**
Circ: CapCity orders: **1,800**
A: Kent Williams **W:** J.M. DeMatteis

BLOOD: A TALE (VERTIGO) — DC / Vertigo

1 ❑ Nov 1996 Cover: 2.95 **NM** value: **Cover or less**
📖 Uroborous **A:** Kent Williams **W:** J.M. DeMatteis
2 ❑ Dec 1996 Cover: 2.95 **NM** value: **Cover or less**
📖 Communion **A:** Kent Williams **W:** J.M. DeMatteis
3 ❑ Jan 1997 Cover: 2.95 **NM** value: **Cover or less**
📖 Theophany **A:** Kent Williams **W:** J.M. DeMatteis
4 ❑ Feb 1997 Cover: 2.95 **NM** value: **Cover or less**
📖 Ouroborous **A:** Kent Williams **W:** J.M. DeMatteis

BLOODBATH — DC

1 ❑ Dec 1993 Cover: 3.50 **NM** value: **Cover or less**
Circ: CapCity orders: **28,850**
A: Chuck Wojtkiewicz; Bill Willingham **W:** Dan Raspler
2 ❑ Dec 1993 Cover: 3.50 **NM** value: **Cover or less**
Circ: CapCity orders: **27,550**

BLOODBROTHERS — Eternity

1 ❑ Cover: 1.95 **NM** value: **Cover or less**
2 ❑ Cover: 1.95 **NM** value: **Cover or less**
3 ❑ Cover: 1.95 **NM** value: **Cover or less**
4 ❑ Cover: 1.95 **NM** value: **Cover or less**

BLOODCHILDE — Millennium

1 ❑ Dec 1994 Cover: 2.50 **NM** value: **Cover or less**
Circ: CapCity orders: **3,945**
📖 Portrait of a Surreal Killer **A:** O.J. Cariello **W:** Faye Perozich
2 ❑ Feb 1995 Cover: 2.50 **NM** value: **Cover or less**
3 ❑ May 1995 Cover: 2.50 **NM** value: **Cover or less**
4 ❑ Jul 1995 Cover: 2.95 **NM** value: **Cover or less**
W: Neil Gaiman

BLOOD CLUB — Kitchen Sink

1 ❑ full color Cover: 5.95 **NM** value: **Cover or less**
No issue number.
2 ❑ Cover: 5.95 **NM** value: **Cover or less**
• Cover says "Blood Club Featuring Big Baby"

BLOODFANG — Epitath Studios

1 ❑ Cover: 2.50 **NM** value: **Cover or less**

BLOOD FEAST — Eternity

1 ❑ b&w Cover: 2.50 **NM** value: **Cover or less**
tame cover. **A:** Stan Timmons; Mike Matthews **W:** Jack Herman
1/SC❑b&w Cover: 2.50 **NM** value: **Cover or less**
Explicit (photo) cover. **A:** Stan Timmons; Mike Matthews **W:** Jack Herman
2 ❑ b&w Cover: 2.50 **NM** value: **Cover or less**
2/SC❑ Cover: 2.50 **NM** value: **Cover or less**
Explicit (photo) cover.

CGC-graded: Multiply prices above by **33 for 9.9 M • 16 for 9.8 NM/M • 7 for 9.6 NM+ • 5 for 9.4 NM • 2.5 for 9.2 NM- • 1.5 for 9.0 VF/NM**

BLOOD FEAST: THE SCREENPLAY — Eternity

1 ❑ b&w Cover: 4.95 **NM** value: **Cover or less**
No issue number. • not comics

BLOODFIRE — Lightning

Brian Reace was a marine, critically wounded in battle. The only thing that could save his life was an emergency transfusion of the experimental Super Enhancement Formula, so it was used, despite the risks. Brian lived and was even made more powerful as a result of the transfusion. But there was a strange side-effect: His bloodstream became flammable. (Just to make his life even more complex, he also became H.I.V. positive.)

Despite his problems, Brian takes on the identity of Bloodfire and receives a special commission from the president, himself, to work as a super-powered secret agent.

0 ❑ May 1994 Cover: 3.50 **NM** value: **Cover or less**
Circ: CapCity orders: **4,325**
• Giant-size. **A:** Terral Lawrence **W:** Steven Zyskowski ★ Origin of Bloodfire.

1 ❑ Mar 1993, b&w Cover: 3.50 **NM** value: **4.00**
Circ: CapCity orders: **8,770**
• promotional copy **A:** Terral Lawrence ★ Origin of Bloodfire. ★ 1st Appearance of Bloodfire.

1/PL❑ Jun 1993 Cover: 3.50 **NM** value: **Cover or less**
• platinum

1/SC❑ Jun 1993 Cover: 3.50 **NM** value: **Cover or less**
• red foil

2 ❑ Jul 1993 Cover: 2.95 **NM** value: **Cover or less**
A: Terral Lawrence

3 ❑ Aug 1993 Cover: 2.95 **NM** value: **Cover or less**
A: Terral Lawrence

4 ❑ Sep 1993 Cover: 2.95 **NM** value: **Cover or less**
A: Terral Lawrence

5 ❑ Oct 1993 Cover: 2.95 **NM** value: **Cover or less**
Circ: CapCity orders: **5,175**
• trading card **A:** Terral Lawrence

6 ❑ Nov 1993 Cover: 2.95 **NM** value: **Cover or less**
Circ: CapCity orders: **5,125**
📖 Paybacks Are Hell! **A:** Terral Lawrence **W:** Joseph A. Zyskowski; Steven Zyskowski

7 ❑ Dec 1993 Cover: 2.95 **NM** value: **Cover or less**
Circ: CapCity orders: **5,300**

8 ❑ Jan 1994 Cover: 2.95 **NM** value: **Cover or less**
Circ: CapCity orders: **5,250**
★ Origin of Prodigal.

9 ❑ Feb 1994 Cover: 2.95 **NM** value: **Cover or less**
Circ: CapCity orders: **4,125**

10 ❑ Mar 1994 Cover: 2.95 **NM** value: **Cover or less**
Circ: CapCity orders: **3,200**

11 ❑ Apr 1994 Cover: 2.95 **NM** value: **Cover or less**
Circ: CapCity orders: **2,825**

12 ❑ May 1994 Cover: 2.95 **NM** value: **Cover or less**
Circ: CapCity orders: **2,650**

BLOODFIRE/HELLINA — Lightning

1 ❑ Aug 1995 Cover: 3.00 **NM** value: **Cover or less**
Circ: CapCity orders: **5,185**
📖 Common Enemy! **A:** Terral Lawrence **W:** Joseph A. Zyskowski ★ Origin of Hellina.

1/Nude❑ Aug 1995 Cover: 9.95 **NM** value: **Cover or less**
• Nude edition.

1/PL❑ **NM** value: **5.00**
• Platinum edition. 📖 Common Enemy! **A:** Terral Lawrence **W:** Joseph A. Zyskowski ★ Origin of Hellina.

BLOOD GOTHIC — Fantaco

1 ❑ Cover: 4.95 **NM** value: **Cover or less**
📖 The Thrice Cursed Calvin Brewster

2 ❑ Cover: 4.95 **NM** value: **Cover or less**

BLOODHUNTER — Brainstorm

1 ❑ Oct 1996, b&w Cover: 2.95 **NM** value: **Cover or less**
Circ: Diamd. preorders: **22,807**
cardstock cover.

BLOOD IS THE HARVEST — Eclipse

1 ❑ **NM** value: **10.00**
Circ: CapCity orders: **4,750**

2 ❑ Cover: 2.50 **NM** value: **Cover or less**

3 ❑ Cover: 2.50 **NM** value: **Cover or less**

4 ❑ Cover: 2.50 **NM** value: **Cover or less**

BLOOD IS THE HARVEST (ONE-SHOT) — Catechetical Guild

1 ❑ ca. 1950 **NM** value: **750.00**
• **CGC:** 2 graded, best 9.6

BLOOD JUNKIES — Eternity

1 ❑ Cover: 2.50 **NM** value: **Cover or less**

2 ❑ Cover: 2.50 **NM** value: **Cover or less**

BLOOD LEGACY: THE STORY OF RYAN — Image

1 ❑ Jul 2000 Cover: 2.50 **NM** value: **Cover or less**
A: Mark Pajarillo; Eric Basaldua **W:** Kerri Hawkins

2 ❑ Aug 2000 Cover: 2.50 **NM** value: **Cover or less**
A: Mark Pajarillo; Eric Basaldua **W:** Kerri Hawkins

3 ❑ Sep 2000 Cover: 2.50 **NM** value: **Cover or less**
A: Mark Pajarillo; Eric Basaldua **W:** Kerri Hawkins

4 ❑ Nov 2000 Cover: 2.50 **NM** value: **Cover or less**
A: Mark Pajarillo; Eric Basaldua **W:** Kerri Hawkins

BLOODLETTING (1ST SERIES) — Fantaco

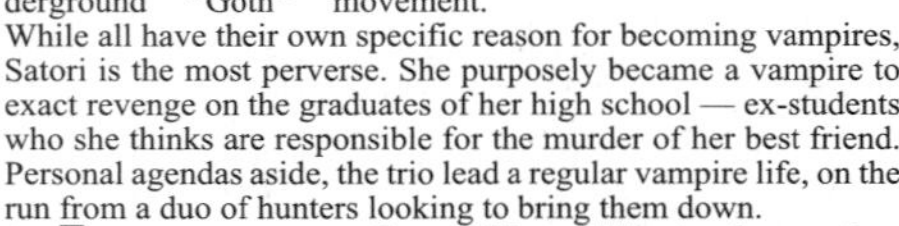

There is no lack for vampire stories in the world of comics. Looking for a traditional Count Dracula tale? It's been done. What about a story starring vampires who hunt other vampires? That's been done, too. Wait a minute. How about a story about ancient vampires living in today's modern world as ultra hip Gen X'ers? Man, has that been done! And the haphazardly thrown-together, black and white Bloodletting is yet another example.

Satori, Max, and Cosette are three "eternally trapped at 20-something-year-old" vampires who roam 1990s California as part of its underground "Goth" movement. While all have their own specific reason for becoming vampires, Satori is the most perverse. She purposely became a vampire to exact revenge on the graduates of her high school — ex-students who she thinks are responsible for the murder of her best friend. Personal agendas aside, the trio lead a regular vampire life, on the run from a duo of hunters looking to bring them down.

1 ❑ Cover: 2.95 **NM** value: **Cover or less**
A: Chyna Clugston **W:** Chyna Clugston

BLOODLETTING (2ND SERIES) — Fantaco

1 ❑ Cover: 3.95 **NM** value: **Cover or less**
A: Chyna Clugston **W:** Chyna Clugston

2 ❑ Cover: 3.95 **NM** value: **Cover or less**
A: Chyna Clugston **W:** Chyna Clugston

BLOODLINES — Aircel

1 ❑ Cover: 1.70 **NM** value: **3.00**
📖 Overture, Part 1 • Aircel publishes **A:** Rob Walton **W:** Rob Walton

2 ❑ Cover: 1.70 **NM** value: **2.50**
📖 Overture, Part 2 **A:** Rob Walton **W:** Rob Walton

3 ❑ Cover: 1.70 **NM** value: **2.50**
📖 Overture, Part 3 • Blackburn begins as publisher **A:** Rob Walton **W:** Rob Walton

4 ❑ Cover: 1.70 **NM** value: **2.50**
A: Rob Walton **W:** Rob Walton

5 ❑ Cover: 1.75 **NM** value: **2.50**
A: Rob Walton **W:** Rob Walton

6 ❑ Cover: 1.75 **NM** value: **2.50**
A: Rob Walton **W:** Rob Walton

BLOODLINES: A TALE FROM THE HEART OF AFRICA — Marvel / Epic

1 ❑ Cover: 5.95 **NM** value: **Cover or less**

BLOODLUST — Slave Labor

"Being a vampire in the modern world can be so confusing. There are many things that you have to adjust to." So begins the saga of Aaron: just an average Joe who happens to get his sustenance from lapping up other people's vital fluids. While serving his evil master (an old man confined to a wheelchair in a run-down tenement), Aaron has to contend with all kinds of social misfits, including many who are just as bloodthirsty as he is, even though they're not members of the undead.

Bloodlust's twisted plot comes courtesy of Dan Vado, with moody black-and-white art by Alex Sheikman with an assist from Nick Grey.

1 ❑ Dec 1990 Cover: 2.25 **NM** value: **Cover or less**
📖 Cross Of The Damned **A:** Alex Sheikman **W:** Dan Vado

BLOOD 'N' GUTS — Aircel

1 ❑ Nov 1990, b&w Cover: 2.50 **NM** value: **Cover or less**
A: Barry Blair **C:** Barry Blair **W:** Barry Blair ★ 1st Appearance of Blood & Guts.

2 ❑ Cover: 2.50 **NM** value: **Cover or less**
A: Barry Blair **W:** Barry Blair

3 ❑ Cover: 2.50 **NM** value: **Cover or less**
A: Barry Blair **W:** Barry Blair

4 ❑ Cover: 2.50 **NM** value: **Cover or less**
A: Barry Blair **W:** Barry Blair

CGC price ratios appearing on the bottom of right-hand pages are for pre-1990 comic books "slabbed" by Comics Guaranty Corp.

They represent the median price offered on eBay above our printed prices for comics in each grade. These are only a guide; individual prices vary by interest in the issue and the number of CGC-graded copies on the market.

BLOOD OF DRACULA — Apple

Ever since Bram Stoker, the vampire known as Dracula has been haunting the world's dreams. The subject of countless books, movies, and comics, it would seem that there would be little that could be added to his legend. Still, Apple Comics does just that in Blood of Dracula.

The series runs as a serial anthology, featuring three stories in each issue. Dracula is shown throughout the ages: hunting for blood in his native land and stalking the streets of America. In one story set in the 1930s, he comes across a moonshiner who is actually a werewolf and who has been creating other werewolves by putting filings from his teeth into the libations he distributes. The wildest concept is Dracula in 2199, where The Lord of the Vampires awakens after a long sleep to find himself in a world ruled by cold, hard science and populated by advanced robots. That world has forgotten the mystical -but Dracula is determined to show them fear.

1 ❑ Cover: 1.75 **NM** value: **2.00**
A: Neil Vokes **W:** Rick Shanklin

2 ❑ Cover: 1.75 **NM** value: **2.00**
A: Neil Vokes **W:** Rick Shanklin

3 ❑ Cover: 1.75 **NM** value: **2.00**
📖 Enter Freely...And Of Your Own Will **A:** Neil Vokes **W:** Rick Shanklin

4 ❑ Cover: 1.75 **NM** value: **2.00**

5 ❑ Cover: 1.75 **NM** value: **2.00**

6 ❑ Cover: 1.95 **NM** value: **2.00**

7 ❑ Cover: 1.95 **NM** value: **2.00**

8 ❑ Cover: 1.95 **NM** value: **2.00**

9 ❑ Cover: 1.95 **NM** value: **2.00**

10 ❑ Cover: 1.95 **NM** value: **2.00**

11 ❑ Cover: 1.95 **NM** value: **2.00**

12 ❑ Cover: 1.95 **NM** value: **2.00**

13 ❑ Cover: 2.25 **NM** value: **Cover or less**
A: Bernie Wrightson

14 ❑ Cover: 2.25 **NM** value: **Cover or less**
A: Bernie Wrightson

15 ❑ Cover: 3.75 **NM** value: **Cover or less**
• flexidisc

16 ❑ Cover: 2.25 **NM** value: **Cover or less**
A: Bernie Wrightson

17 ❑ Cover: 2.25 **NM** value: **Cover or less**
A: Bernie Wrightson

18 ❑ Cover: 2.25 **NM** value: **Cover or less**
A: Bernie Wrightson

19 ❑ Cover: 2.25 **NM** value: **Cover or less**
A: Bernie Wrightson

20 ❑ Cover: 2.25 **NM** value: **Cover or less**
• Final issue?

BLOOD OF THE INNOCENT — Warp

1 ❑ Cover: 2.00 **NM** value: **Cover or less**
Circ: CapCity orders: **4,775**
A: Marc Hempel **W:** Mark Wheatley; Rick Shanklin

2 ❑ Cover: 2.00 **NM** value: **Cover or less**
Circ: CapCity orders: **4,300**
📖 Light of the Sun, Dark of the Moon **A:** Marc Hempel **W:** Mark Wheatley; Rick Shanklin

3 ❑ Cover: 2.00 **NM** value: **Cover or less**
Circ: CapCity orders: **4,275**
A: Marc Hempel **W:** Mark Wheatley; Rick Shanklin

4 ❑ Cover: 2.00 **NM** value: **Cover or less**
Circ: CapCity orders: **4,275**
A: Marc Hempel **W:** Mark Wheatley; Rick Shanklin

BLOOD PACK — DC

1 ❑ Mar 1995 Cover: 1.50 **NM** value: **Cover or less**
Circ: CapCity orders: **11,500**
📖 All Shook Up **A:** Chris Taylor **W:** Charles Moore

2 ❑ Apr 1995 Cover: 1.50 **NM** value: **Cover or less**
Circ: CapCity orders: **7,250**
A: Chris Taylor **W:** Charles Moore ★ Appearance of Superboy.

3 ❑ May 1995 Cover: 1.50 **NM** value: **Cover or less**
Circ: CapCity orders: **5,975**
A: Chris Taylor **W:** Charles Moore

4 ❑ Jun 1995 Cover: 1.50 **NM** value: **Cover or less**
Circ: CapCity orders: **5,225**
A: Chris Taylor **W:** Charles Moore

BLOODPOOL — Image

1 ❑ Aug 1995 Cover: 2.50 **NM** value: **Cover or less**
Circ: CapCity orders: **21,375**
📖 Discharged **A:** Patrick Lee **W:** Mary Jo Duffy

1/SC❑ Aug 1995 Cover: 2.50 **NM** value: **Cover or less**
alternate cover.

2 ❑ Sep 1995 Cover: 2.50 **NM** value: **Cover or less**
Circ: CapCity orders: **12,875**
A: Patrick Lee **W:** Mary Jo Duffy

3 ❑ Oct 1995 Cover: 2.50 **NM** value: **Cover or less**
Circ: CapCity orders: **7,750**
A: Patrick Lee **W:** Mary Jo Duffy

4 ❑ Nov 1995 Cover: 2.50 **NM** value: **Cover or less**
A: Patrick Lee **W:** Mary Jo Duffy

Bk 1❑ Cover: 12.95 **NM** value: **Cover or less**
• collects #1-4;Collects Bloodpool #1-4 **A:** Patrick Lee **W:** Mary Jo Duffy

SE 1❑ Mar 1996 Cover: 2.50 **NM** value: **Cover or less**
• Special

BLOOD REIGN — Fathom

1 ❑ Cover: 2.95 **NM** value: **Cover or less**
A: Tim Tyler **W:** Tim Tyler

2 ❑ Cover: 2.95 **NM** value: **Cover or less**
A: Tim Tyler **W:** Tim Tyler

3 ❑ Oct 1991 Cover: 2.95 **NM** value: **Cover or less**
A: Tim Tyler **W:** Tim Tyler

BLOODSCENT — Comico

1 ❑ Oct 1988 Cover: 2.00 **NM** value: **Cover or less**
Circ: CapCity orders: **5,150**
📖 Bloodscent; Acts of Darkness **A:** Gene Colan; Bernie Mireault **W:** Dean Allen Schreck

BLOODSEED — Marvel

1 ❑ Oct 1993 Cover: 1.95 **NM** value: **Cover or less**
Circ: CapCity orders: **28,400**
A: Liam Sharp **W:** Liam Sharp; Paul Neary ★ 1st Appearance of Bloodseed.

2 ❑ Nov 1993 Cover: 1.95 **NM** value: **Cover or less**
Circ: CapCity orders: **12,400**
Gold cover. • nudity;Final issue (series was rescheduled as 2-issue series) **A:** Liam Sharp **W:** Liam Sharp; Paul Neary

BLOODSHED — Damage!

1 ❑ **NM** value: **2.95**
A: Lionel Ordaz **W:** Gerald Sanchez

1/LE❑ **NM** value: **2.95**
no cover price, b&w. **A:** Lionel Ordaz **W:** Gerald Sanchez

2 ❑ **NM** value: **2.95**
A: Lionel Ordaz **W:** Gerald Sanchez

3 ❑ **NM** value: **2.95**
📖 Lies, Ancuysm / You Know Who You Are!; Oh, The Guilt; Endless, Nameless **A:** Lionel Ordaz **W:** Gerald Sanchez

Ash 1❑ **NM** value: **2.00**

BLOODSHOT — Valiant

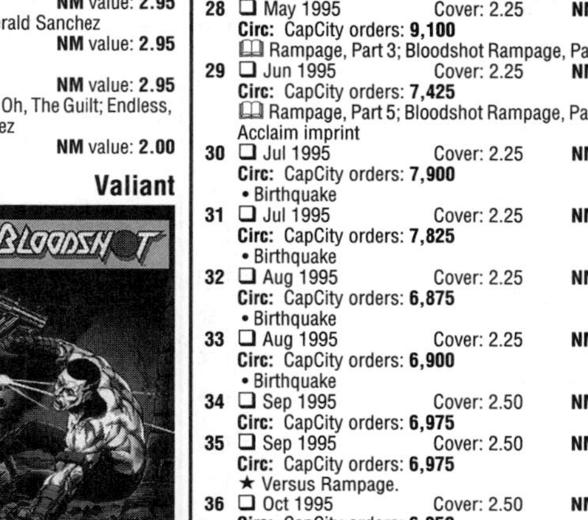

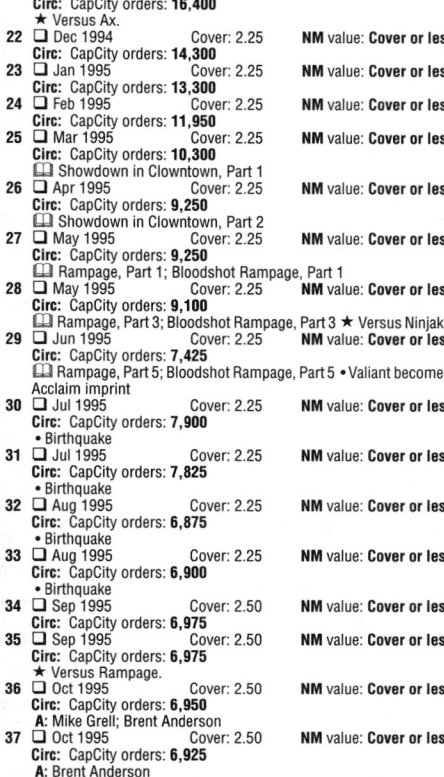

He is a fierce warrior with enhanced reactions, computerized nano-machines in his bloodstream, and a burning need to avenge himself on those who took away his former life. A creation of "Project Rising Spirit," the American branch of Musashi Labs, he was one of a line of enhanced humans being built to serve as weapons of the corporation. His case file bore the name "Bloodshot."

Bloodshot's fate changes, when a boy (who will look familiar to fans of Eternal Warrior) appears and alters the shape of the experiment. When Bloodshot wakes up, he breaks free from Project Rising Spirit. He is now a renegade, an altered human with a shrouded past that apparently involved organized crime. And he's a very, very dangerous person to tangle with.

0 ❑ Mar 1994 Cover: 3.50 **NM** value: **Cover or less**
Circ: CapCity orders: **63,625** • **CGC:** 2 graded, best 9.9
chromium cover, A: Eternal Warrior. ★ Origin of Bloodshot.

0/GO❑Mar 1994 **NM** value: **4.00**
• **CGC:** 1 graded, best 9.8
no cover price. • Gold edition. ★ Origin of Bloodshot. ★ Appearance of Eternal Warrior.

1 ❑ Feb 1993 Cover: 3.50 **NM** value: **Cover or less**
Circ: CapCity orders: **186,500** • **CGC:** 7 graded, best 9.8
Metallic embossed foil cover. 📖 Blood of the Machine **A:** Don Perlin **W:** Kevin VanHook

2 ❑ Mar 1993 Cover: 2.50 **NM** value: **Cover or less**
Circ: CapCity orders: **67,600**
★ Versus X-O Manowar.

3 ❑ Apr 1993 Cover: 2.25 **NM** value: **Cover or less**
Circ: CapCity orders: **61,200**

4 ❑ May 1993 Cover: 2.25 **NM** value: **Cover or less**
Circ: CapCity orders: **71,600**
★ Appearance of Eternal Warrior.

5 ❑ Jun 1993 Cover: 2.25 **NM** value: **Cover or less**
Circ: CapCity orders: **87,100**
★ Appearance of Rai, Eternal Warrior.

6 ❑ Jul 1993 Cover: 2.25 **NM** value: **Cover or less**
Circ: CapCity orders: **90,300**
★ 1st Appearance of Ninjak.

7 ❑ Aug 1993 Cover: 2.25 **NM** value: **Cover or less**
Circ: CapCity orders: **78,100**
★ Appearance of Ninjak.

8 ❑ Sep 1993 Cover: 2.25 **NM** value: **Cover or less**
Circ: CapCity orders: **76,200**

9 ❑ Oct 1993 Cover: 2.25 **NM** value: **Cover or less**
Circ: CapCity orders: **56,800**

10 ❑ Nov 1993 Cover: 2.25 **NM** value: **Cover or less**
Circ: CapCity orders: **51,375**

11 ❑ Dec 1993 Cover: 2.25 **NM** value: **Cover or less**
Circ: CapCity orders: **47,800**

12 ❑ Jan 1994 Cover: 2.25 **NM** value: **Cover or less**
Circ: CapCity orders: **39,625**
📖 Bloodshot's Day Off **A:** Don Perlin **W:** Kevin VanHook

13 ❑ Feb 1994 Cover: 2.25 **NM** value: **Cover or less**
Circ: CapCity orders: **36,500**

14 ❑ Mar 1994 Cover: 2.25 **NM** value: **Cover or less**
Circ: CapCity orders: **29,725**

15 ❑ Apr 1994 Cover: 2.25 **NM** value: **Cover or less**
Circ: CapCity orders: **25,500**

16 ❑ May 1994 Cover: 2.25 **NM** value: **Cover or less**
Circ: CapCity orders: **29,000**
• trading card

17 ❑ Jun 1994 Cover: 2.25 **NM** value: **Cover or less**
Circ: CapCity orders: **21,375**
★ Appearance of H.A.R.D.Corps.

18 ❑ Aug 1994 Cover: 2.25 **NM** value: **Cover or less**
Circ: CapCity orders: **20,025**

19 ❑ Sep 1994 Cover: 2.25 **NM** value: **Cover or less**
Circ: CapCity orders: **18,950**

20 ❑ Oct 1994 Cover: 2.25 **NM** value: **Cover or less**
Circ: CapCity orders: **22,850**
📖 The Chaos Effect: Gamma, Part 1 • Chaos Effect

21 ❑ Nov 1994 Cover: 2.25 **NM** value: **Cover or less**
Circ: CapCity orders: **16,400**
★ Versus Ax.

22 ❑ Dec 1994 Cover: 2.25 **NM** value: **Cover or less**
Circ: CapCity orders: **14,300**

23 ❑ Jan 1995 Cover: 2.25 **NM** value: **Cover or less**
Circ: CapCity orders: **13,300**

24 ❑ Feb 1995 Cover: 2.25 **NM** value: **Cover or less**
Circ: CapCity orders: **11,950**

25 ❑ Mar 1995 Cover: 2.25 **NM** value: **Cover or less**
Circ: CapCity orders: **10,300**
📖 Showdown in Clowntown, Part 1

26 ❑ Apr 1995 Cover: 2.25 **NM** value: **Cover or less**
Circ: CapCity orders: **9,250**
📖 Showdown in Clowntown, Part 2

27 ❑ May 1995 Cover: 2.25 **NM** value: **Cover or less**
Circ: CapCity orders: **9,250**
📖 Rampage, Part 1; Bloodshot Rampage, Part 1

28 ❑ May 1995 Cover: 2.25 **NM** value: **Cover or less**
Circ: CapCity orders: **9,100**
📖 Rampage, Part 3; Bloodshot Rampage, Part 3 ★ Versus Ninjak.

29 ❑ Jun 1995 Cover: 2.25 **NM** value: **Cover or less**
Circ: CapCity orders: **7,425**
📖 Rampage, Part 5; Bloodshot Rampage, Part 5 • Valiant becomes Acclaim imprint

30 ❑ Jul 1995 Cover: 2.25 **NM** value: **Cover or less**
Circ: CapCity orders: **7,900**
• Birthquake

31 ❑ Jul 1995 Cover: 2.25 **NM** value: **Cover or less**
Circ: CapCity orders: **7,825**
• Birthquake

32 ❑ Aug 1995 Cover: 2.25 **NM** value: **Cover or less**
Circ: CapCity orders: **6,875**
• Birthquake

33 ❑ Aug 1995 Cover: 2.25 **NM** value: **Cover or less**
Circ: CapCity orders: **6,900**
• Birthquake

34 ❑ Sep 1995 Cover: 2.50 **NM** value: **Cover or less**
Circ: CapCity orders: **6,975**

35 ❑ Sep 1995 Cover: 2.50 **NM** value: **Cover or less**
Circ: CapCity orders: **6,975**
★ Versus Rampage.

36 ❑ Oct 1995 Cover: 2.50 **NM** value: **Cover or less**
Circ: CapCity orders: **6,950**
A: Mike Grell; Brent Anderson

37 ❑ Oct 1995 Cover: 2.50 **NM** value: **Cover or less**
Circ: CapCity orders: **6,925**
A: Brent Anderson

38 ❑ Nov 1995 Cover: 2.50 **NM** value: **Cover or less**
Circ: CapCity orders: **6,275**

39 ❑ Nov 1995 Cover: 2.50 **NM** value: **Cover or less**
Circ: CapCity orders: **6,300**

40 ❑ Dec 1995 Cover: 2.50 **NM** value: **Cover or less**
Circ: CapCity orders: **5,425**

41 ❑ Dec 1995 Cover: 2.50 **NM** value: **Cover or less**
Circ: CapCity orders: **5,500**

42 ❑ Jan 1996 Cover: 2.50 **NM** value: **Cover or less**
Circ: CapCity orders: **4,450**

43 ❑ Jan 1996 Cover: 2.50 **NM** value: **Cover or less**
Circ: CapCity orders: **4,450**

44 ❑ Feb 1996 Cover: 2.50 **NM** value: **Cover or less**

45 ❑ Mar 1996 Cover: 2.50 **NM** value: **Cover or less**

46 ❑ Apr 1996 Cover: 2.50 **NM** value: **Cover or less**

47 ❑ May 1996 Cover: 2.50 **NM** value: **Cover or less**

48 ❑ May 1996 Cover: 2.50 **NM** value: **Cover or less**

49 ❑ Jun 1996 Cover: 2.50 **NM** value: **Cover or less**

50 ❑ Jul 1996 Cover: 2.50 **NM** value: **Cover or less**

51 ❑ Aug 1996 Cover: 2.50 **NM** value: **Cover or less**
final issue.

YB 1❑ca. 1994 Cover: 3.95 **NM** value: **Cover or less**
Circ: CapCity orders: **20,000**
• Yearbook (annual) #1.

YB 2❑ Cover: 2.95 **NM** value: **Cover or less**
Circ: CapCity orders: **5,975**
• Yearbook (annual) #1.

BLOODSHOT (VOL. 2) — Acclaim

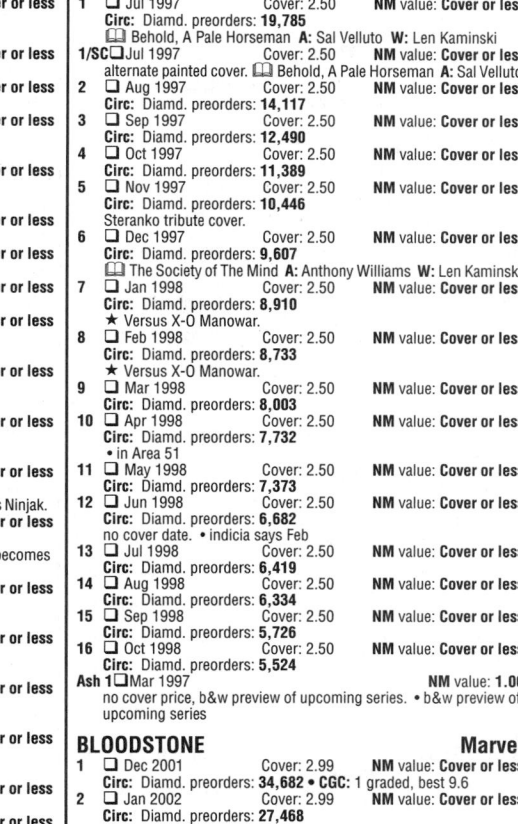

The members of Project Lazarus reanimated a lifeless corpse and, in their desire to create something newer and better than the man they started with, they added cybernetic implants and other biological improvements to increase brain power and physical prowess. They created Bloodshot, the perfect experiment and ultimate weapon. There was just one little problem: Bloodshot was more than the Project bargained for.

Now Bloodshot is free and looking for the answers to his lost past. Though Project: Lazarus may hold the answers to Bloodshot's origin, his former life is linked to New York's crime families. A loose cannon, Bloodshot is now hunted by the Project, the police, and the mob.

1 ❑ Jul 1997 Cover: 2.50 **NM** value: **Cover or less**
Circ: Diamd. preorders: **19,785**
📖 Behold, A Pale Horseman **A:** Sal Velluto **W:** Len Kaminski

1/SC❑Jul 1997 Cover: 2.50 **NM** value: **Cover or less**
alternate painted cover. 📖 Behold, A Pale Horseman **A:** Sal Velluto

2 ❑ Aug 1997 Cover: 2.50 **NM** value: **Cover or less**
Circ: Diamd. preorders: **14,117**

3 ❑ Sep 1997 Cover: 2.50 **NM** value: **Cover or less**
Circ: Diamd. preorders: **12,490**

4 ❑ Oct 1997 Cover: 2.50 **NM** value: **Cover or less**
Circ: Diamd. preorders: **11,389**

5 ❑ Nov 1997 Cover: 2.50 **NM** value: **Cover or less**
Circ: Diamd. preorders: **10,446**
Steranko tribute cover.

6 ❑ Dec 1997 Cover: 2.50 **NM** value: **Cover or less**
Circ: Diamd. preorders: **9,607**
📖 The Society of The Mind **A:** Anthony Williams **W:** Len Kaminski

7 ❑ Jan 1998 Cover: 2.50 **NM** value: **Cover or less**
Circ: Diamd. preorders: **8,910**
★ Versus X-O Manowar.

8 ❑ Feb 1998 Cover: 2.50 **NM** value: **Cover or less**
Circ: Diamd. preorders: **8,733**
★ Versus X-O Manowar.

9 ❑ Mar 1998 Cover: 2.50 **NM** value: **Cover or less**
Circ: Diamd. preorders: **8,003**

10 ❑ Apr 1998 Cover: 2.50 **NM** value: **Cover or less**
Circ: Diamd. preorders: **7,732**
• in Area 51

11 ❑ May 1998 Cover: 2.50 **NM** value: **Cover or less**
Circ: Diamd. preorders: **7,373**

12 ❑ Jun 1998 Cover: 2.50 **NM** value: **Cover or less**
Circ: Diamd. preorders: **6,682**
no cover date. • indicia says Feb

13 ❑ Jul 1998 Cover: 2.50 **NM** value: **Cover or less**
Circ: Diamd. preorders: **6,419**

14 ❑ Aug 1998 Cover: 2.50 **NM** value: **Cover or less**
Circ: Diamd. preorders: **6,334**

15 ❑ Sep 1998 Cover: 2.50 **NM** value: **Cover or less**
Circ: Diamd. preorders: **5,726**

16 ❑ Oct 1998 Cover: 2.50 **NM** value: **Cover or less**
Circ: Diamd. preorders: **5,524**

Ash 1❑Mar 1997 **NM** value: **1.00**
no cover price, b&w preview of upcoming series. • b&w preview of upcoming series

BLOODSTONE — Marvel

1 ❑ Dec 2001 Cover: 2.99 **NM** value: **Cover or less**
Circ: Diamd. preorders: **34,682** • **CGC:** 1 graded, best 9.6

2 ❑ Jan 2002 Cover: 2.99 **NM** value: **Cover or less**
Circ: Diamd. preorders: **27,468**

3 ❑ Feb 2002 Cover: 2.99 **NM** value: **Cover or less**
Circ: Diamd. preorders: **24,560**

BLOODSTRIKE — Image

Created by Rob Liefeld, Bloodstrike is an elite strike force of super-humans. It consists of Fourplay, a four-armed avenger; Tag, a lithe martial artist whose touch causes people to freeze in their tracks; Shogun, a heavily armored walking arsenal; and Deadlock, a Wolverine-like fighter with deadly claws.

The leader of the powerful team is Col. Cabbot, a perfect combination of firepower and strategic thinking. Cabbot is also the brother of the leader of Brigade, another Liefeld-created team — a team that does not always work cooperatively with Bloodstrike, to say the least.

1 ❑ Apr 1993 Cover: 2.95 **NM** value: **3.00**
Circ: CapCity orders: **228,075**
fading blood cover. 📖 Blood Brothers Prelude **A:** Rob Liefeld ★ 1st Appearance of Tag, Deadlock, Shogun, Col. Cabbot, Fourplay.

2 ❑ Jun 1993 Cover: 1.95 **NM** value: **2.00**
Circ: CapCity orders: **137,600**
★ 1st Appearance of Lethal.

3 ❑ Jul 1993 Cover: 1.95 **NM** value: **2.00**
Circ: CapCity orders: **118,850**
📖 Blood Brothers, Part 4

4 ❑ Oct 1993 Cover: 1.95 **NM** value: **2.00**
Circ: CapCity orders: **88,700**
📖 Down Time **A:** Chris Alexander **W:** Keith Giffen

5 ❑ Nov 1993 Cover: 1.95 **NM** value: **2.00**
Circ: CapCity orders: **76,950**
★ 1st Appearance of Noble. ★ Appearance of Supreme.

6 ❑ Dec 1993 Cover: 1.95 **NM** value: **2.00**
Circ: CapCity orders: **68,225**
• Chapel becomes team leader

7 ❑ Jan 1994 Cover: 1.95 **NM** value: **2.00**
Circ: CapCity orders: **58,050**
★ Appearance of Chapel.

8 ❑ Feb 1994 Cover: 1.95 **NM** value: **2.00**
Circ: CapCity orders: **30,550**

9 ❑ Mar 1994 Cover: 1.95 **NM** value: **2.00**
Circ: CapCity orders: **30,225**
📖 Extreme Prejudice, Part 3

10 ❑ Apr 1994 Cover: 1.95 **NM** value: **2.00**
Circ: CapCity orders: **28,850**
📖 Extreme Prejudice, Part 7

11 ❑ Jul 1994 Cover: 1.95 **NM** value: **2.00**
Circ: CapCity orders: **28,025**

12 ❑ Aug 1994 Cover: 1.95 **NM** value: **2.00**
Circ: CapCity orders: **26,025**

13 ❑ Aug 1994 Cover: 2.50 **NM** value: **Cover or less**
Circ: CapCity orders: **24,600**

CGC-graded: Multiply prices above by **33 for 9.9 M • 16 for 9.8 NM/M • 7 for 9.6 NM+ • 5 for 9.4 NM • 2.5 for 9.2 NM- • 1.5 for 9.0 VF/NM**

14 ❑ Sep 1994 Cover: 2.50 **NM** value: **Cover or less**
Circ: CapCity orders: **23,050**
15 ❑ Oct 1994 Cover: 1.95 **NM** value: **2.50**
Circ: CapCity orders: **22,450**
📖 Extreme Sacrifice
16 ❑ Nov 1994 Cover: 2.50 **NM** value: **Cover or less**
Circ: CapCity orders: **19,625**
📖 Extreme Sacrifice
17 ❑ Dec 1994 Cover: 1.95 **NM** value: **2.50**
Circ: CapCity orders: **16,875**
📖 Extreme Sacrifice
18 ❑ Jan 1995 Cover: 2.50 **NM** value: **Cover or less**
Circ: CapCity orders: **19,375**
📖 Extreme Sacrifice; Extreme Sacrifice, Part 2 • polybagged with trading card
19 ❑ Feb 1995 Cover: 2.50 **NM** value: **Cover or less**
Circ: CapCity orders: **14,250**
📖 Extreme Sacrifice Aftermath • polybagged
20 ❑ Mar 1995 Cover: 2.50 **NM** value: **Cover or less**
Circ: CapCity orders: **13,850**
21 ❑ Apr 1995 Cover: 2.50 **NM** value: **Cover or less**
Circ: CapCity orders: **13,025**
22 ❑ May 1995 Cover: 2.50 **NM** value: **Cover or less**
Circ: CapCity orders: **12,900**
23 ❑ **NM** value: **2.50**
24 ❑ **NM** value: **2.50**
25 ❑ May 1994 Cover: 1.95 **NM** value: **Cover or less**
Circ: CapCity orders: **31,150**
• Images of Tomorrow;Published out of sequence as a preview of the future

BLOODSTRIKE ASSASSIN — Image

0 ❑ Oct 1995 Cover: 2.50 **NM** value: **Cover or less**
Circ: CapCity orders: **7,175**
1/A ❑ Jun 1995 Cover: 2.50 **NM** value: **Cover or less**
Circ: CapCity orders: **20,900**
1/B ❑ Jun 1995 Cover: 2.50 **NM** value: **Cover or less**
alternate cover.
2 ❑ Jul 1995 Cover: 2.50 **NM** value: **Cover or less**
Circ: CapCity orders: **15,200**
3 ❑ Aug 1995 Cover: 2.50 **NM** value: **Cover or less**
Circ: CapCity orders: **12,150**
4 ❑ Cover: 2.50 **NM** value: **Cover or less**
Circ: CapCity orders: **9,825**

BLOODSUCKER — Fantagraphics / Eros

All issues are adults only.
1 ❑ b&w Cover: 2.50 **NM** value: **Cover or less**
A: Bob Fingerman **W:** Lydia Lunch

BLOOD SWORD, THE — Jademan

1 ❑ Aug 1988 Cover: 1.95 **NM** value: **2.00**
Circ: CapCity orders: **7,900**
2 ❑ Sep 1988 Cover: 1.95 **NM** value: **2.00**
Circ: CapCity orders: **3,425**
3 ❑ Oct 1988 Cover: 1.95 **NM** value: **2.00**
Circ: CapCity orders: **3,250**
4 ❑ Nov 1988 Cover: 1.95 **NM** value: **2.00**
Circ: CapCity orders: **3,125**
5 ❑ Dec 1988 Cover: 1.95 **NM** value: **2.00**
Circ: CapCity orders: **3,400**
6 ❑ Jan 1989 Cover: 1.95 **NM** value: **2.00**
Circ: CapCity orders: **3,425**
7 ❑ Feb 1989 Cover: 1.95 **NM** value: **2.00**
Circ: CapCity orders: **3,350**
8 ❑ Mar 1989 Cover: 1.95 **NM** value: **2.00**
Circ: CapCity orders: **2,925**
9 ❑ Apr 1989 Cover: 1.95 **NM** value: **2.00**
Circ: CapCity orders: **3,000**
10 ❑ May 1989 Cover: 1.95 **NM** value: **2.00**
Circ: CapCity orders: **3,000**
11 ❑ Jun 1989 Cover: 1.95 **NM** value: **2.00**
Circ: CapCity orders: **2,600**
12 ❑ Jul 1989 Cover: 1.95 **NM** value: **2.00**
Circ: CapCity orders: **2,400**
13 ❑ Aug 1989 Cover: 1.95 **NM** value: **2.00**
Circ: CapCity orders: **2,400**
14 ❑ Sep 1989 Cover: 1.95 **NM** value: **2.00**
Circ: CapCity orders: **2,600**
15 ❑ Oct 1989 Cover: 1.95 **NM** value: **2.00**
Circ: CapCity orders: **2,400**
16 ❑ Nov 1989 Cover: 1.95 **NM** value: **2.00**
Circ: CapCity orders: **2,400**
17 ❑ Dec 1989 Cover: 1.95 **NM** value: **2.00**
Circ: CapCity orders: **2,400**
18 ❑ Jan 1990 Cover: 1.95 **NM** value: **2.00**
Circ: CapCity orders: **2,400**
19 ❑ Feb 1990 Cover: 1.95 **NM** value: **2.00**
Circ: CapCity orders: **2,200**
20 ❑ Mar 1990 Cover: 1.95 **NM** value: **2.00**
Circ: CapCity orders: **2,000**
21 ❑ Apr 1990 Cover: 1.95 **NM** value: **2.00**
Circ: CapCity orders: **2,000**
22 ❑ May 1990 Cover: 1.95 **NM** value: **2.00**
Circ: CapCity orders: **2,000**
23 ❑ Jun 1990 Cover: 1.95 **NM** value: **2.00**
Circ: CapCity orders: **2,000**
24 ❑ Jul 1990 Cover: 1.95 **NM** value: **2.00**
Circ: CapCity orders: **2,000**
25 ❑ Aug 1990 Cover: 1.95 **NM** value: **2.00**
Circ: CapCity orders: **2,000**
26 ❑ Sep 1990 Cover: 1.95 **NM** value: **2.00**
Circ: CapCity orders: **2,000**
27 ❑ Oct 1990 Cover: 1.95 **NM** value: **2.00**
Circ: CapCity orders: **2,000**
28 ❑ Nov 1990 Cover: 1.95 **NM** value: **2.00**
Circ: CapCity orders: **2,000**
29 ❑ Dec 1990 Cover: 1.95 **NM** value: **2.00**
Circ: CapCity orders: **2,000**
30 ❑ Jan 1991 Cover: 1.95 **NM** value: **2.00**
Circ: CapCity orders: **2,000**
31 ❑ Feb 1991 Cover: 1.95 **NM** value: **2.00**
Circ: CapCity orders: **2,000**
32 ❑ Mar 1991 Cover: 1.95 **NM** value: **2.00**
Circ: CapCity orders: **1,800**
33 ❑ Apr 1991 Cover: 1.95 **NM** value: **2.00**
Circ: CapCity orders: **1,800**
34 ❑ May 1991 Cover: 1.95 **NM** value: **2.00**
Circ: CapCity orders: **1,800**
35 ❑ Jun 1991 Cover: 1.95 **NM** value: **2.00**
Circ: CapCity orders: **1,800**
36 ❑ Jul 1991 Cover: 1.95 **NM** value: **2.00**
Circ: CapCity orders: **1,800**
37 ❑ Aug 1991 Cover: 1.95 **NM** value: **2.00**
Circ: CapCity orders: **1,800**
38 ❑ Sep 1991 Cover: 1.95 **NM** value: **2.00**
Circ: CapCity orders: **1,800**
39 ❑ Oct 1991 Cover: 1.95 **NM** value: **2.00**
Circ: CapCity orders: **1,600**
40 ❑ Nov 1991 Cover: 1.95 **NM** value: **2.00**
41 ❑ Dec 1991 Cover: 1.95 **NM** value: **2.00**
42 ❑ Jan 1992 Cover: 1.95 **NM** value: **2.00**

BLOOD SWORD DYNASTY — Jademan

1 ❑ Sep 1989 Cover: 1.25 **NM** value: **1.50**
Circ: CapCity orders: **3,800**
2 ❑ Oct 1989 Cover: 1.25 **NM** value: **1.50**
Circ: CapCity orders: **3,000**
3 ❑ Nov 1989 Cover: 1.25 **NM** value: **1.50**
Circ: CapCity orders: **2,400**
4 ❑ Dec 1989 Cover: 1.25 **NM** value: **1.50**
Circ: CapCity orders: **2,400**
5 ❑ Jan 1990 Cover: 1.25 **NM** value: **1.50**
Circ: CapCity orders: **2,400**
6 ❑ Feb 1990 Cover: 1.25 **NM** value: **1.50**
Circ: CapCity orders: **2,400**
7 ❑ Mar 1990 Cover: 1.25 **NM** value: **1.50**
Circ: CapCity orders: **2,200**
8 ❑ Apr 1990 Cover: 1.25 **NM** value: **1.50**
Circ: CapCity orders: **2,000**
9 ❑ May 1990 Cover: 1.25 **NM** value: **1.50**
Circ: CapCity orders: **1,800**
10 ❑ Jun 1990 Cover: 1.25 **NM** value: **1.50**
Circ: CapCity orders: **1,800**
11 ❑ Jul 1990 Cover: 1.25 **NM** value: **1.50**
Circ: CapCity orders: **1,800**
12 ❑ Aug 1990 Cover: 1.25 **NM** value: **1.50**
Circ: CapCity orders: **1,800**
13 ❑ Sep 1990 Cover: 1.25 **NM** value: **1.50**
Circ: CapCity orders: **1,800**
14 ❑ Oct 1990 Cover: 1.25 **NM** value: **1.50**
Circ: CapCity orders: **1,800**
15 ❑ Nov 1990 Cover: 1.25 **NM** value: **1.50**
Circ: CapCity orders: **1,800**
16 ❑ Dec 1990 Cover: 1.25 **NM** value: **1.50**
Circ: CapCity orders: **1,800**
17 ❑ Jan 1991 Cover: 1.25 **NM** value: **1.50**
Circ: CapCity orders: **1,800**
18 ❑ Feb 1991 Cover: 1.25 **NM** value: **1.50**
Circ: CapCity orders: **1,800**
19 ❑ Mar 1991 Cover: 1.25 **NM** value: **1.50**
Circ: CapCity orders: **1,800**
20 ❑ Apr 1991 Cover: 1.25 **NM** value: **1.50**
Circ: CapCity orders: **1,800**
21 ❑ May 1991 Cover: 1.25 **NM** value: **1.50**
Circ: CapCity orders: **1,600**
22 ❑ Jun 1991 Cover: 1.25 **NM** value: **1.50**
Circ: CapCity orders: **1,600**
23 ❑ Jul 1991 Cover: 1.25 **NM** value: **1.50**
Circ: CapCity orders: **1,600**
24 ❑ Aug 1991 Cover: 1.25 **NM** value: **1.50**
Circ: CapCity orders: **1,600**
25 ❑ Sep 1991 Cover: 1.25 **NM** value: **1.50**
Circ: CapCity orders: **1,600**
26 ❑ Oct 1991 Cover: 1.25 **NM** value: **1.50**
Circ: CapCity orders: **1,600**
27 ❑ Nov 1991 Cover: 1.25 **NM** value: **1.50**
Circ: CapCity orders: **1,600**
28 ❑ Dec 1991 Cover: 1.25 **NM** value: **1.50**
29 ❑ Jan 1992 Cover: 1.25 **NM** value: **1.50**

BLOOD SYNDICATE — DC / Milestone

Deadly gas killed their fellow gang members on the crime-ridden streets of Paris Island, but that which killed others made this bunch strong. The Blood Syndicate is a gang consisting of nine super-powered teens. Among them are Flashback, who can travel back three seconds in time; Fade, who can walk through walls and is not quite in our dimension; Third Rail, who grabs energy from any electrical force and in turn becomes enormous and powerful; Brickhouse, a temperamental woman literally turned into a wall of bricks; Holocaust, who freely blasts fire; and Tek-9, a fountain of deadly firepower. Together they destroy the "white man's poison" of drugs, as the fellow survivors of Paris Island fear, hate, or admire them.

Are they heroes or villains? Milestone comics leaves it to readers to decide for themselves. One thing is for sure: They're a far cry from The Justice League.

1 ❑ Apr 1993 Cover: 1.50 **NM** value: **2.00**
★ 1st Appearance of Blood Syndicate, Rob Chaplik.
1/CS❑ Apr 1993 Cover: 2.95 **NM** value: **3.00**
Circ: CapCity orders: **58,750**
• poster, trading card ★ 1st Appearance of Blood Syndicate, Rob Chaplik.
2 ❑ May 1993 Cover: 1.50 **NM** value: **Cover or less**
Circ: CapCity orders: **24,900**
★ 1st Appearance of Boogieman. ★ Versus Holocaust.
3 ❑ Jun 1993 Cover: 1.50 **NM** value: **Cover or less**
Circ: CapCity orders: **19,050**
★ 1st Appearance of MOM. ★ Appearance of Boogieman.
4 ❑ Jul 1993 Cover: 1.50 **NM** value: **Cover or less**
Circ: CapCity orders: **17,450**
★ Death of Tech-9.
5 ❑ Aug 1993 Cover: 1.50 **NM** value: **Cover or less**
Circ: CapCity orders: **15,000**
★ 1st Appearance of Demon Fox, John Wing, Kwai.
6 ❑ Sep 1993 Cover: 1.50 **NM** value: **Cover or less**
Circ: CapCity orders: **12,750**
7 ❑ Oct 1993 Cover: 1.50 **NM** value: **Cover or less**
Circ: CapCity orders: **11,350**
★ 1st Appearance of Edmund, Cornelia.
8 ❑ Nov 1993 Cover: 1.50 **NM** value: **Cover or less**
Circ: CapCity orders: **9,750**
★ 1st Appearance of Kwai.
9 ❑ Dec 1993 Cover: 1.50 **NM** value: **Cover or less**
Circ: CapCity orders: **9,400**
★ Origin of Blood Syndicate. ★ 1st Appearance of Templo.
10 ❑ Jan 1994 Cover: 2.50 **NM** value: **Cover or less**
Circ: CapCity orders: **12,200**
Metallic ink cover. 📖 Shadow War; Shadow War, Part 4 ★ 1st Appearance of Bubbasaur.
11 ❑ Feb 1994 Cover: 1.50 **NM** value: **Cover or less**
Circ: CapCity orders: **7,950**
• Aquamaria joins Blood Syndicate
12 ❑ Mar 1994 Cover: 1.50 **NM** value: **Cover or less**
Circ: CapCity orders: **7,150**
★ 1st Appearance of The Rat Congress.
13 ❑ Apr 1994 Cover: 1.50 **NM** value: **Cover or less**
Circ: CapCity orders: **6,550**
📖 Infestation, Part 1 **A:** J.H. Williams **W:** Ivan Velez Jr. ★ 1st Appearance of The White Roaches.
14 ❑ May 1994 Cover: 1.50 **NM** value: **Cover or less**
Circ: CapCity orders: **6,250**
📖 Infestation, Part 2 **A:** J.H. Williams **W:** Ivan Velez Jr.
15 ❑ Jun 1994 Cover: 1.50 **NM** value: **Cover or less**
Circ: CapCity orders: **6,200**
📖 Infestation, Part 3 **A:** J.H. Williams **W:** Ivan Velez Jr.
16 ❑ Jul 1994 Cover: 1.50 **NM** value: **Cover or less**
Circ: CapCity orders: **22,900**
📖 Worlds Collide, Part 6 ★ Appearance of Superman.
17 ❑ Aug 1994 Cover: 1.75 **NM** value: **Cover or less**
Circ: CapCity orders: **19,150**
📖 Worlds Collide, Part 13
18 ❑ Sep 1994 Cover: 1.75 **NM** value: **Cover or less**
Circ: CapCity orders: **6,300**
19 ❑ Oct 1994 Cover: 1.75 **NM** value: **Cover or less**
Circ: CapCity orders: **6,450**
20 ❑ Nov 1994 Cover: 1.75 **NM** value: **Cover or less**
Circ: CapCity orders: **5,950**
★ Appearance of Shadow Cabinet.
21 ❑ Dec 1994 Cover: 1.75 **NM** value: **Cover or less**
Circ: CapCity orders: **5,650**
22 ❑ Jan 1995 Cover: 1.75 **NM** value: **Cover or less**
Circ: CapCity orders: **4,850**
📖 Some Dissembly Required **A:** Chris Cross **W:** Ivan Velez Jr.
23 ❑ Feb 1995 Cover: 1.75 **NM** value: **Cover or less**
Circ: CapCity orders: **4,275**
24 ❑ Mar 1995 Cover: 1.75 **NM** value: **Cover or less**
Circ: CapCity orders: **3,900**
25 ❑ Apr 1995 Cover: 2.95 **NM** value: **Cover or less**
Circ: CapCity orders: **3,700**
• Giant-size. • Tech-9 returns
26 ❑ May 1995 Cover: 1.75 **NM** value: **Cover or less**
Circ: CapCity orders: **3,500**
27 ❑ Jun 1995 Cover: 1.75 **NM** value: **Cover or less**
Circ: CapCity orders: **3,500**
28 ❑ Jul 1995 Cover: 2.50 **NM** value: **Cover or less**
Circ: CapCity orders: **3,500**
📖 Good Intentions, Bad Seasons
29 ❑ Aug 1995 Cover: 0.99 **NM** value: **1.00**
Circ: CapCity orders: **4,025**
📖 Long Hot Summer
30 ❑ Sep 1995 Cover: 2.50 **NM** value: **Cover or less**
Circ: CapCity orders: **3,575**
📖 The Long Hot Summer
31 ❑ Oct 1995 Cover: 2.50 **NM** value: **Cover or less**
Circ: CapCity orders: **2,875**
32 ❑ Nov 1995 Cover: 2.50 **NM** value: **Cover or less**
33 ❑ Dec 1995 Cover: 0.99 **NM** value: **Cover or less**
34 ❑ Jan 1996 Cover: 2.50 **NM** value: **Cover or less**
35 ❑ Feb 1996 Cover: 3.50 **NM** value: **Cover or less**
📖 The Beginning of the End final issue. **A:** Wilfred **W:** Dwayne McDuffie; Ivan Velez Jr.

BLOODTHIRST: TERMINUS OPTION — Alpha Productions

1 ❑ b&w Cover: 3.50 **NM** value: **Cover or less**
📖 Masquerade **A:** Delfin Barral **W:** Chris Mills
2 ❑ Cover: 2.50 **NM** value: **Cover or less**
📖 Maelstrom **A:** Delfin Barral **W:** Chris Mills

Other grades: Multiply prices above by **1.5 for Mint • 2/3 for Very Fine • 1/3 for Fine • 1/5 for Very Good • 1/8 for Good**

BLOODTHIRST: THE NIGHTFALL CONSPIRACY — Alpha
1 ❑ Cover: 2.50 **NM** value: **Cover or less**
2 ❑ Cover: 2.50 **NM** value: **Cover or less**

BLOODTHIRSTY PIRATE TALES — Black Swan Press
1 ❑ Cover: 2.50 **NM** value: **Cover or less**
2 ❑ Cover: 2.50 **NM** value: **Cover or less**
3 ❑ Cover: 2.50 **NM** value: **Cover or less**
4 ❑ Fal 1996 Cover: 2.50 **NM** value: **Cover or less**
5 ❑ Spr 1997 Cover: 2.50 **NM** value: **Cover or less**
The Wrecking Annie; Pearl's Rekoning; Legend of the Black Mariah **A:** N. Authur Johnson; Richard Becker **W:** N. Authur Johnson; Richard Becker
6 ❑ Win 1997 Cover: 2.50 **NM** value: **Cover or less**

BLOOD TIES — Full Moon / Milestone
1 ❑ Cover: 2.25 **NM** value: **Cover or less**
Genesis **A:** Eric Adams **W:** Adam Heeter; Evan O'Neal

BLOODWING — Eternity
1 ❑ Jan 1988 Cover: 1.95 **NM** value: **Cover or less**
A: John Gallagher **W:** Bill Spangler
2 ❑ Feb 1988 Cover: 1.95 **NM** value: **Cover or less**
3 ❑ Mar 1988 Cover: 1.95 **NM** value: **Cover or less**
4 ❑ Apr 1988 Cover: 1.95 **NM** value: **Cover or less**
5 ❑ May 1988 Cover: 1.95 **NM** value: **Cover or less**
6 ❑ Cover: 1.95 **NM** value: **Cover or less**

BLOODWULF — Image
Bloodwulf is ultra-violence with a smile on its face — death with a sense of humor. The character was introduced in Image Comics' Darker Image #1 in 1992, although little background was given until this 1995 series was introduced.

Very much like DC Comics' Lobo, Bloodwulf is an intergalactic bad boy, causing a commotion everywhere he goes. This four-issue mini-series opens with a disgruntled Bloodwulf. He hasn't indulged in senseless violence for a while. His wife makes him go find someone to beat up, because he is driving her crazy by loitering around the house. The rest of the series chronicles Bloodwulf's adventures, as he drives around the galaxy on his galactic gun-starship.

1 ❑ Feb 1995 Cover: 2.50 **NM** value: **Cover or less**
Circ: CapCity orders: **18,175**
five different covers. An Ill Wind Breaks **A:** Dick Giordano; Daerick Gröss Jr.; Rob Liefeld(cover) **W:** Andy Mangels
2 ❑ Mar 1995 Cover: 2.50 **NM** value: **Cover or less**
Circ: CapCity orders: **13,625**
A: Daerick Gröss Jr. **W:** Andy Mangels
3 ❑ Apr 1995 Cover: 2.50 **NM** value: **Cover or less**
Circ: CapCity orders: **11,975**
A: Daerick Gröss Jr. **W:** Andy Mangels
4 ❑ May 1995 Cover: 2.50 **NM** value: **Cover or less**
Circ: CapCity orders: **11,850**
A: Daerick Gröss Jr. **W:** Andy Mangels
Smr 1 ❑ Aug 1995 Cover: 2.50 **NM** value: **Cover or less**
Circ: CapCity orders: **10,050**
★ Appearance of Supreme.

BLOODY BONES & BLACKEYED PEAS — Galaxy
1 ❑ Cover: 1.00 **NM** value: **Cover or less**

BLOODYHOT — Parody Press
1 ❑ Cover: 2.50 **NM** value: **2.95**
A: David Neal Miller **W:** Don Chin

BLOODY MARY — DC / Helix
1 ❑ Oct 1996 Cover: 2.25 **NM** value: **Cover or less**
A: Carlos Ezquerra **W:** Garth Ennis
2 ❑ Nov 1996 Cover: 2.25 **NM** value: **Cover or less**
Circ: Diamd. preorders: **27,359**
A: Carlos Ezquerra **W:** Garth Ennis
3 ❑ Dec 1996 Cover: 2.25 **NM** value: **Cover or less**
Circ: Direct Market orders: **24,652**
A: Carlos Ezquerra **W:** Garth Ennis
4 ❑ Jan 1997 Cover: 2.25 **NM** value: **Cover or less**
Circ: Direct Market orders: **21,797**
final issue. **A:** Carlos Ezquerra **W:** Garth Ennis

BLOODY MARY: LADY LIBERTY — DC / Helix
1 ❑ Sep 1997 Cover: 2.50 **NM** value: **Cover or less**
Circ: Diamd. preorders: **20,085**
A: Carlos Ezquerra **W:** Garth Ennis
2 ❑ Oct 1997 Cover: 2.50 **NM** value: **Cover or less**
Circ: Diamd. preorders: **15,648**
A: Carlos Ezquerra **W:** Garth Ennis
3 ❑ Nov 1997 Cover: 2.50 **NM** value: **Cover or less**
Circ: Diamd. preorders: **14,857**
A: Carlos Ezquerra **W:** Garth Ennis
4 ❑ Dec 1997 Cover: 2.50 **NM** value: **Cover or less**
Circ: Diamd. preorders: **14,000**
A: Carlos Ezquerra **W:** Garth Ennis

BLUE — Image
1 ❑ Aug 1999 Cover: 2.50 **NM** value: **Cover or less**
Circ: Diamd. preorders: **10,391**
A: Jason Johnson; Drew Struzan; Edwin Rosell; Greg Aronowitz **W:** Greg Aronowitz
2 ❑ Apr 2000 Cover: 2.50 **NM** value: **Cover or less**
Circ: Diamd. preorders: **5,541**
A: Jason Johnson; Edwin Rosell; Greg Aronowitz **W:** Greg Aronowitz

BLUEBEARD — Slave Labor
1 ❑ b&w Cover: 2.95 **NM** value: **Cover or less**
A: Phil Elliott **W:** James Robinson
2 ❑ b&w Cover: 2.95 **NM** value: **Cover or less**
W: James Robinson
3 ❑ b&w Cover: 2.95 **NM** value: **Cover or less**
W: James Robinson
Bk 1 ❑ b&w Cover: 9.95 **NM** value: **Cover or less**
• collects mini-series **W:** James Robinson
Bk 1-2 ❑ b&w Cover: 12.95 **NM** value: **Cover or less**

BLUE BEETLE (DC) — DC
The Blue Beetle is Ted Kord, a good-hearted man whose evil uncle succeeded in murdering the original Blue Beetle (Dan Garrett). As Garrett died, Kord swears to carry on the name of The Blue Beetle. Although he has no super-powers with which to fight crime, Kord trains his body to perfection, and uses his technical wizardry to create a variety of devices, including "the Bug," his flying vehicle.

Originally a Charlton comics character, The Blue Beetle came to DC with The Question and Captain Atom, during the Crisis on Infinite Earths. He would later become a key member of Justice League International.

1 ❑ Jun 1986 Cover: 0.75 **NM** value: **1.50**
Circ: CapCity orders: **16,350**
Out from The Ashes **A:** Paris Cullins **W:** Len Wein ★ Origin of Blue Beetle. ★ Versus Firefist.
2 ❑ Jul 1986 Cover: 0.75 **NM** value: **1.00**
Circ: CapCity orders: **12,550**
This City's Not For Burning! **A:** Paris Cullins **W:** Len Wein ★ Origin of Firefist. ★ Versus Firefist.
3 ❑ Aug 1986 Cover: 0.75 **NM** value: **1.00**
Circ: CapCity orders: **11,550**
★ Versus Madmen.
4 ❑ Sep 1986 Cover: 0.75 **NM** value: **1.00**
Circ: CapCity orders: **12,500**
★ Versus Doctor Alchemy.
5 ❑ Oct 1986 Cover: 0.75 **NM** value: **1.00**
Circ: CapCity orders: **12,500**
★ Appearance of The Question.
6 ❑ Nov 1986 Cover: 0.75 **NM** value: **1.00**
Circ: CapCity orders: **11,450**
★ Appearance of The Question.
7 ❑ Dec 1986 Cover: 0.75 **NM** value: **1.00**
Circ: CapCity orders: **10,550**
Gang War **A:** Paris Cullins; Dell Barras **W:** Len Wein ★ Appearance of The Question. ★ Death of Muse.
8 ❑ Jan 1987 Cover: 0.75 **NM** value: **1.00**
Circ: CapCity orders: **9,000**
★ Versus Calculator.
9 ❑ Feb 1987 Cover: 0.75 **NM** value: **1.00**
Circ: CapCity orders: **10,500**
• Legends
10 ❑ Mar 1987 Cover: 0.75 **NM** value: **1.00**
Circ: CapCity orders: **13,550**
• Legends ★ Versus Chronos.
11 ❑ Apr 1987 Cover: 0.75 **NM** value: **1.00**
Circ: CapCity orders: **10,650**
★ Appearance of Teen Titans.
12 ❑ May 1987 Cover: 0.75 **NM** value: **1.00**
Circ: CapCity orders: **10,800**
★ Appearance of Teen Titans.
13 ❑ Jun 1987 Cover: 0.75 **NM** value: **1.00**
Circ: CapCity orders: **10,150**
★ Appearance of Teen Titans.
14 ❑ Jul 1987 Cover: 0.75 **NM** value: **1.00**
Circ: CapCity orders: **9,350**
15 ❑ Aug 1987 Cover: 0.75 **NM** value: **1.00**
Circ: CapCity orders: **10,250**
16 ❑ Sep 1987 Cover: 0.75 **NM** value: **1.00**
Circ: CapCity orders: **10,550**
17 ❑ Oct 1987 Cover: 0.75 **NM** value: **1.00**
Circ: CapCity orders: **10,500**
18 ❑ Nov 1987 Cover: 1.00 **NM** value: **Cover or less**
Circ: CapCity orders: **10,250**
19 ❑ Dec 1987 Cover: 1.00 **NM** value: **Cover or less**
Circ: CapCity orders: **9,500**
20 ❑ Jan 1988 Cover: 1.00 **NM** value: **Cover or less**
Circ: CapCity orders: **11,500**
Millennium • Millennium
21 ❑ Feb 1988 Cover: 1.00 **NM** value: **Cover or less**
Circ: CapCity orders: **15,250**
Millennium • Millennium
22 ❑ Mar 1988 Cover: 1.00 **NM** value: **Cover or less**
Circ: CapCity orders: **10,550**
23 ❑ Apr 1988 Cover: 1.00 **NM** value: **Cover or less**
Circ: CapCity orders: **11,200**
24 ❑ May 1988 Cover: 1.00 **NM** value: **Cover or less**
Circ: CapCity orders: **11,900**
final issue.

BLUE BEETLE (FOX) — Fox
1 ❑ Win 1939 Cover: 0.10 **NM** value: **3000.00**
• **CGC:** 3 graded, best 5.5
2 ❑ ca. 1940 Cover: 0.10 **NM** value: **1800.00**
3 ❑ Jul 1940 Cover: 0.10 **NM** value: **1500.00**
4 ❑ Fal 1940 Cover: 0.10 **NM** value: **1000.00**
5 ❑ Jan 1941 Cover: 0.10 **NM** value: **750.00**
6 ❑ Mar 1941 Cover: 0.10 **NM** value: **600.00**
7 ❑ Jun 1941 Cover: 0.10 **NM** value: **600.00**
8 ❑ Aug 1941 Cover: 0.10 **NM** value: **600.00**
9 ❑ Oct 1941 Cover: 0.10 **NM** value: **600.00**
• **CGC:** 1 graded, best 4.0
10 ❑ Dec 1941 Cover: 0.10 **NM** value: **600.00**
11 ❑ Feb 1942 Cover: 0.10 **NM** value: **450.00**
12 ❑ Jun 1942 Cover: 0.10 **NM** value: **450.00**
• **CGC:** 1 graded, best 7.0
13 ❑ Aug 1942 Cover: 0.10 **NM** value: **450.00**
14 ❑ Sep 1942 Cover: 0.10 **NM** value: **450.00**
15 ❑ Oct 1942 Cover: 0.10 **NM** value: **450.00**
16 ❑ Nov 1942 Cover: 0.10 **NM** value: **400.00**
17 ❑ Dec 1942 Cover: 0.10 **NM** value: **400.00**
18 ❑ Jan 1943 Cover: 0.10 **NM** value: **400.00**
19 ❑ Mar 1943 Cover: 0.10 **NM** value: **400.00**
20 ❑ Apr 1943 Cover: 0.10 **NM** value: **400.00**
• **CGC:** 2 graded, best 8.0
21 ❑ May 1943 Cover: 0.10 **NM** value: **350.00**
• **CGC:** 1 graded, best 7.5
22 ❑ Jun 1943 Cover: 0.10 **NM** value: **350.00**
23 ❑ Jul 1943 Cover: 0.10 **NM** value: **350.00**
24 ❑ Aug 1943 Cover: 0.10 **NM** value: **350.00**
• **CGC:** 1 graded, best 9.2
25 ❑ Sep 1943 Cover: 0.10 **NM** value: **350.00**
26 ❑ Oct 1943 Cover: 0.10 **NM** value: **350.00**
• **CGC:** 1 graded, best 9.2
27 ❑ Nov 1943 Cover: 0.10 **NM** value: **350.00**
28 ❑ Dec 1943 Cover: 0.10 **NM** value: **350.00**
29 ❑ Jan 1944 Cover: 0.10 **NM** value: **350.00**
30 ❑ Mar 1944 Cover: 0.10 **NM** value: **350.00**
31 ❑ May 1944 Cover: 0.10 **NM** value: **300.00**
32 ❑ Jul 1944 Cover: 0.10 **NM** value: **300.00**
• **CGC:** 1 graded, best 9.4
33 ❑ Aug 1944 Cover: 0.10 **NM** value: **300.00**
• **CGC:** 1 graded, best 9.6
34 ❑ Sep 1944 Cover: 0.10 **NM** value: **300.00**
• **CGC:** 1 graded, best 7.0
35 ❑ Oct 1944 Cover: 0.10 **NM** value: **300.00**
36 ❑ Nov 1944 Cover: 0.10 **NM** value: **300.00**
37 ❑ ca. 1945 Cover: 0.10 **NM** value: **300.00**
38 ❑ Sum 1945 Cover: 0.10 **NM** value: **300.00**
• **CGC:** 2 graded, best 9.6
39 ❑ Fal 1945 Cover: 0.10 **NM** value: **300.00**
40 ❑ Win 1945 Cover: 0.10 **NM** value: **300.00**
• **CGC:** 2 graded, best 9.2
41 ❑ Mar 1946 Cover: 0.10 **NM** value: **250.00**
• **CGC:** 3 graded, best 9.2
42 ❑ May 1946 Cover: 0.10 **NM** value: **250.00**
43 ❑ Jul 1946 Cover: 0.10 **NM** value: **250.00**
44 ❑ Sep 1947 Cover: 0.10 **NM** value: **250.00**
45 ❑ Jun 1947 Cover: 0.10 **NM** value: **250.00**
• **CGC:** 1 graded, best 9.0
46 ❑ Jul 1947 Cover: 0.10 **NM** value: **250.00**
• **CGC:** 1 graded, best 9.4
47 ❑ Aug 1947 Cover: 0.10 **NM** value: **250.00**
• **CGC:** 2 graded, best 9.6
48 ❑ Sep 1947 Cover: 0.10 **NM** value: **250.00**
• **CGC:** 2 graded, best 9.2
49 ❑ Oct 1947 Cover: 0.10 **NM** value: **250.00**
• **CGC:** 4 graded, best 9.4
50 ❑ Nov 1947 Cover: 0.10 **NM** value: **250.00**
• **CGC:** 2 graded, best 9.4
51 ❑ Dec 1947 Cover: 0.10 **NM** value: **200.00**
• **CGC:** 7 graded, best 9.6
52 ❑ Jan 1948 Cover: 0.10 **NM** value: **200.00**
• **CGC:** 5 graded, best 9.6
53 ❑ Feb 1948 Cover: 0.10 **NM** value: **200.00**
• **CGC:** 1 graded, best 9.2
54 ❑ Mar 1948 Cover: 0.10 **NM** value: **200.00**
• **CGC:** 5 graded, best 9.4
55 ❑ Apr 1948 Cover: 0.10 **NM** value: **200.00**
• **CGC:** 1 graded, best 9.6
56 ❑ May 1948 Cover: 0.10 **NM** value: **200.00**
• **CGC:** 2 graded, best 9.2
57 ❑ Jul 1948 Cover: 0.10 **NM** value: **200.00**
• **CGC:** 2 graded, best 9.2
58 ❑ Apr 1950 Cover: 0.10 **NM** value: **Cover or less**
59 ❑ Jun 1950 Cover: 0.10 **NM** value: **200.00**
• **CGC:** 1 graded, best 8.5
60 ❑ Aug 1950 Cover: 0.10 **NM** value: **200.00**

BLUE BEETLE (VOL. 2) — Charlton
1 ❑ Jun 1967 Cover: 0.12 **NM** value: **45.00**
• **CGC:** 2 graded, best 9.4
A: Steve Ditko
2 ❑ Aug 1967 Cover: 0.12 **NM** value: **30.00**
• **CGC:** 1 graded, best 9.0
A: Steve Ditko
3 ❑ Oct 1967 Cover: 0.12 **NM** value: **20.00**
A: Steve Ditko
4 ❑ Dec 1967 Cover: 0.12 **NM** value: **20.00**
• **CGC:** 3 graded, best 9.2
A: Steve Ditko
5 ❑ Nov 1968 Cover: 0.12 **NM** value: **20.00**
A: Steve Ditko

BLUE BEETLE (VOL. 3) — Charlton
1 ❑ **NM** value: **55.00**
• **CGC:** 9 graded, best 9.8
A: Steve Ditko
2 ❑ **NM** value: **24.00**
• **CGC:** 3 graded, best 9.8
A: Steve Ditko

CGC-graded: Multiply prices above by **33 for 9.9 M • 16 for 9.8 NM/M • 7 for 9.6 NM+ • 5 for 9.4 NM • 2.5 for 9.2 NM- • 1.5 for 9.0 VF/NM**

3 ❑ **NM** value: **18.00**
A: Steve Ditko
4 ❑ **NM** value: **18.00**
• **CGC:** 1 graded, best 7.5
A: Steve Ditko
5 ❑ **NM** value: **18.00**
A: Steve Ditko
50 ❑ **NM** value: **20.00**
• Has 1964 Statement, filed 9/30/64; avg print run 222,967; avg sales 136,021; avg subs 15; avg total paid 136,036; samples 25; max existent 136,061; 39% of run returned **A:** Steve Ditko
51 ❑ **NM** value: **20.00**
A: Steve Ditko
52 ❑ **NM** value: **20.00**
A: Steve Ditko
53 ❑ **NM** value: **20.00**
A: Steve Ditko
54 ❑ **NM** value: **20.00**
A: Steve Ditko

BLUEBERRY — Marvel / Epic

Bk 1❑ Cover: 12.95 **NM** value: **Cover or less**
• Chihuahua Pearl
Bk 2❑ Cover: 14.95 **NM** value: **Cover or less**
• Ballad for a Coffin
Bk 3❑ Cover: 12.95 **NM** value: **Cover or less**
• Angel Face
Bk 4❑ Cover: 12.95 **NM** value: **Cover or less**
• Great Tribe
Bk 5❑ Cover: 12.95 **NM** value: **Cover or less**
Circ: CapCity orders: **1,525**
• End of the Trail

BLUE BOLT — Novelty Press

Early issues of Blue Bolt featured a super-hero of the same name who had the power to control electricity. It was a standard Golden Age super-hero strip in most respects, except that it represented the first creative effort of the groundbreaking team of Joe Simon and Jack Kirby, who would later go on to create Captain America, among many others. Kirby's art in those early issues was raw but charged with intense energy and set the stage for his 50-year reign as the "King" of comics artists. Simon and Kirby soon left the strip, and Blue Bolt became a backup feature in his own title to a plainclothes adventurer named Dick Cole.

Cole and the increasingly innocuous backup features eventually gave way to horror and mystery stories in the late 1940s, and the title was rechristened "Ghostly Weird Tales." Some issues featured classic lurid covers by L.B. Cole.

1 ❑ Jun 1940 Cover: 0.10 **NM** value: **2000.00**
• **CGC:** 1 graded, best 6.5
W: Joe Simon ★ Origin of Blue Bolt. ★ 1st Appearance of Blue Bolt.
2 ❑ Jul 1940 Cover: 0.10 **NM** value: **1050.00**
Blue Bolt • 1st collaboration between Joe Simon & Jack Kirby **A:** Jack Kirby **W:** Joe Simon
3 ❑ Aug 1940 Cover: 0.10 **NM** value: **875.00**
Blue Bolt **A:** Joe Simon; Jack Kirby **W:** Joe Simon
4 ❑ Sep 1940 Cover: 0.10 **NM** value: **700.00**
• **CGC:** 1 graded, best 4.0
Blue Bolt **A:** Joe Simon; Jack Kirby **W:** Joe Simon
5 ❑ Oct 1940 Cover: 0.10 **NM** value: **700.00**
• **CGC:** 1 graded, best 5.0
Blue Bolt **A:** Joe Simon; Bill Everett; Jack Kirby **W:** Joe Simon
6 ❑ Nov 1940 Cover: 0.10 **NM** value: **640.00**
Blue Bolt **A:** Joe Simon; Jack Kirby **W:** Joe Simon ★ Origin of Blue Bolt.
7 ❑ Dec 1940 Cover: 0.10 **NM** value: **640.00**
• **CGC:** 1 graded, best 5.5
Blue Bolt **A:** Joe Simon; Jack Kirby **W:** Joe Simon
8 ❑ Jan 1941 Cover: 0.10 **NM** value: **640.00**
Blue Bolt **A:** Joe Simon; Jack Kirby **W:** Joe Simon
9 ❑ Feb 1941 Cover: 0.10 **NM** value: **640.00**
Blue Bolt **A:** Joe Simon; Jack Kirby **W:** Joe Simon
10 ❑ Mar 1941 Cover: 0.10 **NM** value: **640.00**
Blue Bolt **A:** Joe Simon; Jack Kirby **W:** Joe Simon
11 ❑ Apr 1941 Cover: 0.10 **NM** value: **640.00**
12 ❑ May 1941 Cover: 0.10 **NM** value: **640.00**
13 ❑ Jun 1941 Cover: 0.10 **NM** value: **210.00**
14 ❑ Jul 1941 Cover: 0.10 **NM** value: **150.00**
15 ❑ Aug 1941 Cover: 0.10 **NM** value: **125.00**
16 ❑ Sep 1941 Cover: 0.10 **NM** value: **125.00**
17 ❑ Oct 1941 Cover: 0.10 **NM** value: **125.00**
18 ❑ Nov 1941 Cover: 0.10 **NM** value: **125.00**
• **CGC:** 1 graded, best 8.5
19 ❑ Dec 1941 Cover: 0.10 **NM** value: **100.00**
20 ❑ Jan 1942 Cover: 0.10 **NM** value: **100.00**
21 ❑ Feb 1942 Cover: 0.10 **NM** value: **100.00**
22 ❑ Mar 1942 Cover: 0.10 **NM** value: **100.00**
23 ❑ Apr 1942 Cover: 0.10 **NM** value: **100.00**
24 ❑ May 1942 Cover: 0.10 **NM** value: **100.00**
25 ❑ Jun 1942 Cover: 0.10 **NM** value: **85.00**
26 ❑ Jul 1942 Cover: 0.10 **NM** value: **75.00**
27 ❑ Aug 1942 Cover: 0.10 **NM** value: **75.00**
28 ❑ Sep 1942 Cover: 0.10 **NM** value: **75.00**
29 ❑ Oct 1942 Cover: 0.10 **NM** value: **75.00**
30 ❑ Nov 1942 Cover: 0.10 **NM** value: **75.00**
31 ❑ Dec 1942 Cover: 0.10 **NM** value: **75.00**
32 ❑ Jan 1943 Cover: 0.10 **NM** value: **75.00**
33 ❑ Feb 1943 Cover: 0.10 **NM** value: **75.00**
• **CGC:** 1 graded, best 6.5
34 ❑ Mar 1943 Cover: 0.10 **NM** value: **75.00**
35 ❑ Apr 1943 Cover: 0.10 **NM** value: **75.00**
36 ❑ May 1943 Cover: 0.10 **NM** value: **75.00**
37 ❑ Jun 1943 Cover: 0.10 **NM** value: **85.00**
38 ❑ Jul 1943 Cover: 0.10 **NM** value: **50.00**
39 ❑ Sep 1943 Cover: 0.10 **NM** value: **50.00**
• **CGC:** 1 graded, best 2.5
40 ❑ Nov 1943 Cover: 0.10 **NM** value: **50.00**
41 ❑ Dec 1943 Cover: 0.10 **NM** value: **50.00**
42 ❑ Jan 1944 Cover: 0.10 **NM** value: **50.00**
• **CGC:** 1 graded, best 7.0
43 ❑ Feb 1944 Cover: 0.10 **NM** value: **50.00**
44 ❑ Mar 1944 Cover: 0.10 **NM** value: **50.00**
45 ❑ Apr 1944 Cover: 0.10 **NM** value: **50.00**
46 ❑ May 1944 Cover: 0.10 **NM** value: **50.00**
47 ❑ Jun 1944 Cover: 0.10 **NM** value: **50.00**
48 ❑ Jul 1944 Cover: 0.10 **NM** value: **50.00**
49 ❑ Sep 1944 Cover: 0.10 **NM** value: **40.00**
50 ❑ Nov 1944 Cover: 0.10 **NM** value: **40.00**
51 ❑ Dec 1944 Cover: 0.10 **NM** value: **40.00**
52 ❑ Jan 1945 Cover: 0.10 **NM** value: **40.00**
53 ❑ Feb 1945 Cover: 0.10 **NM** value: **40.00**
54 ❑ Mar 1945 Cover: 0.10 **NM** value: **40.00**
55 ❑ Apr 1945 Cover: 0.10 **NM** value: **40.00**
56 ❑ May 1945 Cover: 0.10 **NM** value: **40.00**
57 ❑ Jun 1945 Cover: 0.10 **NM** value: **35.00**
58 ❑ Aug 1945 Cover: 0.10 **NM** value: **35.00**
59 ❑ Sep 1945 Cover: 0.10 **NM** value: **35.00**
60 ❑ Oct 1945 Cover: 0.10 **NM** value: **35.00**
• **CGC:** 1 graded, best 9.2
61 ❑ Nov 1945 Cover: 0.10 **NM** value: **35.00**
62 ❑ Dec 1945 Cover: 0.10 **NM** value: **35.00**
63 ❑ Feb 1946 Cover: 0.10 **NM** value: **35.00**
64 ❑ Mar 1946 Cover: 0.10 **NM** value: **35.00**
65 ❑ Apr 1946 Cover: 0.10 **NM** value: **35.00**
66 ❑ May 1946 Cover: 0.10 **NM** value: **35.00**
67 ❑ Jun 1946 Cover: 0.10 **NM** value: **30.00**
68 ❑ Jul 1946 Cover: 0.10 **NM** value: **30.00**
69 ❑ Aug 1946 Cover: 0.10 **NM** value: **30.00**
70 ❑ Sep 1946 Cover: 0.10 **NM** value: **30.00**
71 ❑ Oct 1946 Cover: 0.10 **NM** value: **30.00**
72 ❑ Nov 1946 Cover: 0.10 **NM** value: **30.00**
73 ❑ Dec 1946 Cover: 0.10 **NM** value: **30.00**
74 ❑ Jan 1947 Cover: 0.10 **NM** value: **30.00**
75 ❑ Feb 1947 Cover: 0.10 **NM** value: **30.00**
76 ❑ Mar 1947 Cover: 0.10 **NM** value: **30.00**
77 ❑ Apr 1947 Cover: 0.10 **NM** value: **30.00**
78 ❑ May 1947 Cover: 0.10 **NM** value: **30.00**
79 ❑ Jun 1947 Cover: 0.10 **NM** value: **30.00**
80 ❑ Jul 1947 Cover: 0.10 **NM** value: **30.00**
81 ❑ Aug 1947 Cover: 0.10 **NM** value: **30.00**
82 ❑ Sep 1947 Cover: 0.10 **NM** value: **30.00**
83 ❑ Oct 1947 Cover: 0.10 **NM** value: **30.00**
84 ❑ Nov 1947 Cover: 0.10 **NM** value: **30.00**
85 ❑ Dec 1947 Cover: 0.10 **NM** value: **30.00**
86 ❑ Jan 1948 Cover: 0.10 **NM** value: **30.00**
87 ❑ Feb 1948 Cover: 0.10 **NM** value: **30.00**
88 ❑ Mar 1948 Cover: 0.10 **NM** value: **30.00**
89 ❑ Apr 1948 Cover: 0.10 **NM** value: **30.00**
Dick Cole; Rick Richards; Cameraman (text story); Sergeant Spook; Edison Bell; Heathcliff the Hobo; Dink; Blue Bolt the American **A:** Art Helfant; Jack Harmon; Milt Hammer **W:** Art Helfant; Milt Hammer
90 ❑ May 1948 Cover: 0.10 **NM** value: **30.00**
91 ❑ Jun 1948 Cover: 0.10 **NM** value: **30.00**
92 ❑ Jul 1948 Cover: 0.10 **NM** value: **30.00**
93 ❑ Aug 1948 Cover: 0.10 **NM** value: **30.00**
94 ❑ Sep 1948 Cover: 0.10 **NM** value: **30.00**
95 ❑ Oct 1948 Cover: 0.10 **NM** value: **30.00**
• **CGC:** 1 graded, best 8.0
96 ❑ Nov 1948 Cover: 0.10 **NM** value: **30.00**
97 ❑ Jan 1949 Cover: 0.10 **NM** value: **30.00**
98 ❑ Mar 1949 Cover: 0.10 **NM** value: **30.00**
99 ❑ May 1949 Cover: 0.10 **NM** value: **30.00**
• **CGC:** 1 graded, best 9.0
100 ❑ Jul 1949 Cover: 0.10 **NM** value: **30.00**
101 ❑ Sep 1949 Cover: 0.10 **NM** value: **30.00**
102 ❑ Nov 1949 Cover: 0.10 **NM** value: **150.00**
• Star begins as publisher
103 ❑ Jan 1950 Cover: 0.10 **NM** value: **150.00**
• **CGC:** 3 graded, best 7.5
104 ❑ Mar 1950 Cover: 0.10 **NM** value: **150.00**
105 ❑ Apr 1950 Cover: 0.10 **NM** value: **325.00**
• **CGC:** 4 graded, best 9.2
★ Origin of Blue Bolt.
106 ❑ Aug 1950 Cover: 0.10 **NM** value: **250.00**
Blue Bolt • Reprints Blue Bolt #2
107 ❑ Nov 1950 Cover: 0.10 **NM** value: **250.00**
• **CGC:** 2 graded, best 7.0
Blue Bolt • Reprints Blue Bolt #3
108 ❑ Feb 1951 Cover: 0.10 **NM** value: **250.00**
Blue Bolt • Reprints Blue Bolt #4
109 ❑ May 1951 Cover: 0.10 **NM** value: **250.00**
110 ❑ Aug 1951 Cover: 0.10 **NM** value: **250.00**
• **CGC:** 2 graded, best 8.5
111 ❑ Nov 1951 Cover: 0.10 **NM** value: **250.00**
• **CGC:** 4 graded, best 8.0
112 ❑ Feb 1952 Cover: 0.10 **NM** value: **250.00**
113 ❑ May 1952 Cover: 0.10 **NM** value: **250.00**
• **CGC:** 1 graded, best 9.0
114 ❑ Jul 1952 Cover: 0.10 **NM** value: **250.00**
• **CGC:** 1 graded, best 8.5
115 ❑ Sep 1952 Cover: 0.10 **NM** value: **250.00**
• **CGC:** 2 graded, best 7.5
116 ❑ Nov 1952 Cover: 0.10 **NM** value: **250.00**
• **CGC:** 1 graded, best 9.2
117 ❑ Jan 1953 Cover: 0.10 **NM** value: **250.00**
• **CGC:** 1 graded, best 8.0
118 ❑ Mar 1953 Cover: 0.10 **NM** value: **250.00**
• **CGC:** 1 graded, best 9.0
119 ❑ May 1953 Cover: 0.10 **NM** value: **250.00**
• **CGC:** 1 graded, best 9.0
• Series continued as Ghostly Weird Tales #120
Bk 1❑ Cover: 14.95 **NM** value: **Cover or less**
• collects Golden Age stories **A:** Joe Simon; Jack Kirby

BLUE BULLETEER, THE — AC

1 ❑ b&w Cover: 2.25 **NM** value: **2.50**
Double Trouble For Lady Luger! **A:** Bill Lux **W:** Bill Black ★ Origin of Blue Bulleteer.

BLUE CIRCLE — REWL Publications

1 ❑ Jun 1944 Cover: 0.10 **NM** value: **175.00**
• **CGC:** 1 graded, best 7.5
2 ❑ Jul 1944 Cover: 0.10 **NM** value: **125.00**
3 ❑ Sep 1944 Cover: 0.10 **NM** value: **125.00**
4 ❑ Feb 1945 Cover: 0.10 **NM** value: **125.00**
5 ❑ Mar 1945 Cover: 0.10 **NM** value: **100.00**
6 ❑ ca. 1945 Cover: 0.10 **NM** value: **100.00**

BLUE DEVIL — DC

Whiz kid Dan Cassidy creates a blue devil costume with a tough exoskeleton, inner motors that give him great strength, and pyrotechnics for effect. The costume gets him a starring roll in a horror film — but not, unfortunately, the girl he's in love with. When a bumbling actor unleashes a real demon, it is Dan, with the powers his costume gives him, who is the only one who can save cast and crew.

However, the battle with the real demon has one devastating side effect. When Dan gets home, he finds out he has become one with the suit. Though initially horrified, he eventually comes to enjoy his new situation and becomes skilled in use of his rocket-trident weapon.

1 ❑ Jun 1984 Cover: 0.75 **NM** value: **1.50**
★ Origin of Blue Devil.
2 ❑ Jul 1984 Cover: 0.75 **NM** value: **1.00**
★ Versus Shockwave.
3 ❑ Aug 1984 Cover: 0.75 **NM** value: **1.00**
★ Versus Metallo.
4 ❑ Sep 1984 Cover: 0.75 **NM** value: **1.00**
★ Appearance of Zatanna.
5 ❑ Oct 1984 Cover: 0.75 **NM** value: **1.00**
★ Appearance of Zatanna.
6 ❑ Nov 1984 Cover: 0.75 **NM** value: **1.00**
★ 1st Appearance of Bolt.
7 ❑ Dec 1984 Cover: 0.75 **NM** value: **1.00**
★ Versus Bolt. ★ Versus Trickster.
8 ❑ Jan 1985 Cover: 0.75 **NM** value: **1.00**
★ Versus Bolt. ★ Versus Trickster.
9 ❑ Feb 1985 Cover: 0.75 **NM** value: **1.00**
★ Versus Bolt. ★ Versus Trickster.
10 ❑ Mar 1985 Cover: 0.75 **NM** value: **1.00**
11 ❑ Apr 1985 Cover: 0.75 **NM** value: **1.00**
12 ❑ May 1985 Cover: 0.75 **NM** value: **1.00**
Circ: CapCity orders: **9,600**
★ Appearance of Demon.
13 ❑ Jun 1985 Cover: 0.75 **NM** value: **1.00**
Circ: CapCity orders: **9,000**
★ Appearance of Green Lantern, Zatanna.
14 ❑ Jul 1985 Cover: 0.75 **NM** value: **1.00**
Circ: CapCity orders: **8,850**
★ 1st Appearance of Kid Devil.
15 ❑ Aug 1985 Cover: 0.75 **NM** value: **1.00**
Circ: CapCity orders: **8,350**
16 ❑ Sep 1985 Cover: 0.75 **NM** value: **1.00**
Circ: CapCity orders: **8,400**
17 ❑ Oct 1985 Cover: 0.75 **NM** value: **1.00**
Circ: CapCity orders: **10,700**
Crisis on Infinite Earths • Crisis
18 ❑ Nov 1985 Cover: 0.75 **NM** value: **1.00**
Circ: CapCity orders: **11,300**
Crisis on Infinite Earths • Crisis
19 ❑ Dec 1985 Cover: 0.75 **NM** value: **1.00**
Circ: CapCity orders: **8,100**
20 ❑ Jan 1986 Cover: 0.75 **NM** value: **1.00**
Circ: CapCity orders: **7,900**
21 ❑ Feb 1986 Cover: 0.75 **NM** value: **1.00**
Circ: CapCity orders: **8,100**
22 ❑ Mar 1986 Cover: 0.75 **NM** value: **1.00**
Circ: CapCity orders: **8,700**
23 ❑ Apr 1986 Cover: 0.75 **NM** value: **1.00**
Circ: CapCity orders: **7,850**
Caught In the Firestorm ★ Appearance of Firestorm.
24 ❑ May 1986 Cover: 0.75 **NM** value: **1.00**
Circ: CapCity orders: **7,300**
25 ❑ Jun 1986 Cover: 0.75 **NM** value: **1.00**
Circ: CapCity orders: **6,900**
26 ❑ Jul 1986 Cover: 0.75 **NM** value: **1.00**
Circ: CapCity orders: **7,300**
★ Versus Green Gargoyle.
27 ❑ Aug 1986 Cover: 0.75 **NM** value: **1.00**
Circ: CapCity orders: **7,100**
28 ❑ Sep 1986 Cover: 0.75 **NM** value: **1.00**
Circ: CapCity orders: **7,000**
29 ❑ Oct 1986 Cover: 0.75 **NM** value: **1.00**
Circ: CapCity orders: **6,950**
30 ❑ Nov 1986 Cover: 1.25 **NM** value: **Cover or less**
Circ: CapCity orders: **7,250**
• Double-size. ★ Versus Flash's Rogues' Gallery.

Other grades: Multiply prices above by **1.5 for Mint • 2/3 for Very Fine • 1/3 for Fine • 1/5 for Very Good • 1/8 for Good**

31 ❑ Dec 1986 Cover: 1.25 **NM** value: **Cover or less**
Circ: CapCity orders: **7,550**
• Giant-size. final issue.
Anl 1❑Nov 1985 Cover: 1.25 **NM** value: **Cover or less**
Circ: CapCity orders: **9,550**

BLUE HOLE — Christine Shields
1 ❑ Cover: 2.95 **NM** value: **Cover or less**
📖 Sworn to True; Adventures of the Kerosene Boy; Sex Dream # 34; Ruby Hunts Diamonds in the Night; The Pancake Man **A:** Christine Shields **W:** Christine Shields

BLUE LILY, THE — Dark Horse
1 ❑ Mar 1993 Cover: 3.95 **NM** value: **Cover or less**
Circ: CapCity orders: **5,500**
A: Angus McKie **W:** Angus McKie
2 ❑ Cover: 3.95 **NM** value: **Cover or less**
Circ: CapCity orders: **4,025**
A: Angus McKie **W:** Angus McKie
3 ❑ Cover: 3.95 **NM** value: **Cover or less**
Circ: CapCity orders: **3,775**
A: Angus McKie **W:** Angus McKie
4 ❑ Cover: 3.95 **NM** value: **Cover or less**
Circ: CapCity orders: **4,350**
A: Angus McKie **W:** Angus McKie

BLUE LOCO — Kitchen Sink
1 ❑ Feb 1997 Cover: 5.95 **NM** value: **Cover or less**
Circ: Diamd. preorders: **1,814**
cardstock cover.

BLUE MONDAY: ABSOLUTE BEGINNERS — Oni
1 ❑ ca. 2001 Cover: 2.95 **NM** value: **Cover or less**
Circ: Diamd. preorders: **3,813**
2 ❑ ca. 2001 Cover: 2.95 **NM** value: **Cover or less**
Circ: Diamd. preorders: **3,333**
3 ❑ ca. 2001 Cover: 2.95 **NM** value: **Cover or less**
Circ: Diamd. preorders: **3,722**
4 ❑ ca. 2001 Cover: 2.95 **NM** value: **Cover or less**
Circ: Diamd. preorders: **4,171**

BLUE MONDAY: LOVECATS — Oni
1 ❑ ca. 2002 Cover: 2.95 **NM** value: **Cover or less**
Circ: Diamd. preorders: **4,346**

BLUE MONDAY: THE KIDS ARE ALRIGHT — Oni
1 ❑ ca. 2000 Cover: 2.95 **NM** value: **Cover or less**
Circ: Diamd. preorders: **3,387**
2 ❑ ca. 2000 Cover: 2.95 **NM** value: **Cover or less**
Circ: Diamd. preorders: **2,557**
3 ❑ ca. 2000 Cover: 2.95 **NM** value: **Cover or less**
Circ: Diamd. preorders: **3,592**

BLUE MOON — Mu Press
1 ❑ Sep 1992 Cover: 2.50 **NM** value: **Cover or less**
2 ❑ Nov 1992 Cover: 2.50 **NM** value: **Cover or less**
3 ❑ Feb 1993 Cover: 2.50 **NM** value: **Cover or less**
4 ❑ May 1993 Cover: 2.50 **NM** value: **Cover or less**
5 ❑ Dec 1993 Cover: 2.50 **NM** value: **Cover or less**

BLUE MOON: A ONE AND A TWO — Aeon

Reprinting the first two issues of Blue Moon, this trade paperback introduces Lyssa, an ordinary, plain sort of girl who has recurring pirate fantasies. These visions begin to intrude on her life, and soon it seems her parallel existence as a pirate captain on the high seas may be more real than her mundane existence as a single girl trying to make it in the 20th century. But are her friends Larry and Eleanor, who are tinkering with a device improbably named the "discombobulation-otron," responsible for Lyssa's sudden slips into another reality? And will her feelings for the dashing Allen in that other life lead her to a romantic adventure like no other? Peopled by cartoonish characters with a foot in reality, Blue Moon features attractive art in the style of Teri Wood or Phil Foglio but suffers from a slightly discombobulated plot. Perhaps it's that machine acting up again.
Bk 1❑ b&w Cover: 4.95 **NM** value: **Cover or less**
• Collects first two issues of the series **A:** Charlie Wise **W:** Charlie Wise

BLUE MOON (VOL. 2) — Aeon
1 ❑ Aug 1994, b&w Cover: 2.95 **NM** value: **Cover or less**

BLUE RIBBON COMICS — M.L.J.
1 ❑ Nov 1939 Cover: 0.10 **NM** value: **2000.00**
• **CGC:** 2 graded, best 9.4
2 ❑ Dec 1939 Cover: 0.10 **NM** value: **1000.00**
• **CGC:** 1 graded, best 7.5
3 ❑ Jan 1940 Cover: 0.10 **NM** value: **700.00**
4 ❑ Apr 1940 Cover: 0.10 **NM** value: **600.00**
5 ❑ Jul 1940 Cover: 0.10 **NM** value: **600.00**
• **CGC:** 2 graded, best 9.2
6 ❑ Sep 1940 Cover: 0.10 **NM** value: **500.00**
7 ❑ Nov 1940 Cover: 0.10 **NM** value: **500.00**
• **CGC:** 5 graded, best 9.2
8 ❑ Jan 1941 Cover: 0.10 **NM** value: **500.00**
9 ❑ Feb 1941 Cover: 0.10 **NM** value: **500.00**
10 ❑ Mar 1941 Cover: 0.10 **NM** value: **500.00**
• **CGC:** 1 graded, best 7.5
11 ❑ Apr 1941 Cover: 0.10 **NM** value: **450.00**
12 ❑ May 1941 Cover: 0.10 **NM** value: **450.00**
• **CGC:** 1 graded, best 7.0
13 ❑ Jun 1941 Cover: 0.10 **NM** value: **450.00**
• **CGC:** 1 graded, best 2.0
14 ❑ Jul 1941 Cover: 0.10 **NM** value: **450.00**
15 ❑ Aug 1941 Cover: 0.10 **NM** value: **450.00**
16 ❑ Sep 1941 Cover: 0.10 **NM** value: **450.00**
17 ❑ Oct 1941 Cover: 0.10 **NM** value: **450.00**
18 ❑ Nov 1941 Cover: 0.10 **NM** value: **450.00**
19 ❑ Dec 1941 Cover: 0.10 **NM** value: **450.00**
• **CGC:** 1 graded, best 3.5
20 ❑ Jan 1942 Cover: 0.10 **NM** value: **450.00**
21 ❑ Feb 1942 Cover: 0.10 **NM** value: **450.00**
22 ❑ Mar 1942 Cover: 0.10 **NM** value: **450.00**

BLUE RIBBON COMICS (VOL. 2) — Archie / Red Circle
1 ❑ Nov 1983 Cover: 1.50 **NM** value: **2.50**
📖 The Strange New World of The Fly; The Fly Strikes; The Master of Junk-Ri-La!; Tommy Troy Teaches Judo; Come into My Parlor; One of Our Skyscrapers is Missing; Fly Discovers his Buzz Gun; • Red Circle publishes **A:** Joe Simon; Al Williamson; Jack Kirby **C:** Steve Ditko **W:** Joe Simon
2 ❑ Nov 1983 Cover: 1.50 **NM** value: **Cover or less**
A: Alex Nino; Trevor Von Eden; Alex Ni±o **C:** Rich Buckler
3 ❑ Dec 1983 Cover: 1.50 **NM** value: **Cover or less**
4 ❑ Jan 1984 Cover: 1.00 **NM** value: **1.50**
5 ❑ Feb 1984 Cover: 0.75 **NM** value: **1.50**
📖 The Double Life of Private Strong; Spawn of the X-World; Mystery of the Vanished Wreckage; The Menace of the Micro- Men • All reprinted from "The Double Life of Private Strong" #1 ★ Appearance of Steel Sterling.
6 ❑ Mar 1984 Cover: 0.75 **NM** value: **1.50**
7 ❑ Apr 1984 Cover: 0.75 **NM** value: **1.50**
📖 The Fox: Heads or Tales?; The Fox: Heads I Win, Tails You Lose! **A:** Dick Ayers; Tony DeZuniga **W:** Rich Buckler; Stan Timmons
8 ❑ May 1984 Cover: 0.75 **NM** value: **1.50**
9 ❑ Jun 1984 Cover: 0.75 **NM** value: **1.50**
10 ❑ Jul 1984 Cover: 0.75 **NM** value: **1.50**
11 ❑ Aug 1984 Cover: 0.75 **NM** value: **1.50**
12 ❑ Sep 1984 Cover: 0.75 **NM** value: **1.50**
13 ❑ Oct 1984 Cover: 0.75 **NM** value: **1.50**
14 ❑ Dec 1984 Cover: 0.75 **NM** value: **1.50**

BLUE WITCH OF OZ, THE — Dark Horse
Bk 1❑ Oct 1992 Cover: 9.95 **NM** value: **Cover or less**
A: Eric Shanower **W:** Eric Shanower

B-MOVIE PRESENTS — B-Movie
1 ❑ Cover: 1.70 **NM** value: **Cover or less**
📖 Captain Daring: Under a Black Venusian Sky; The World of X-Ray: Midnight Connection **A:** Ken Holewczynski; Mark Paniccia **W:** Ken Holewczynski; Mark Paniccia
2 ❑ Cover: 1.70 **NM** value: **Cover or less**
3 ❑ Cover: 1.70 **NM** value: **Cover or less**
4 ❑ Cover: 1.70 **NM** value: **Cover or less**

BOARD OF SUPERHEROS — Not Available
1 ❑ Cover: 0.50 **NM** value: **Cover or less**
📖 The Amazing Cynical Man Meets The Boss **A:** Matt Feazell **W:** Matt Feazell

BOBBY BENSON'S B-BAR-B RIDERS (MAGAZINE ENTERPRISES) — Magazine Enterprises
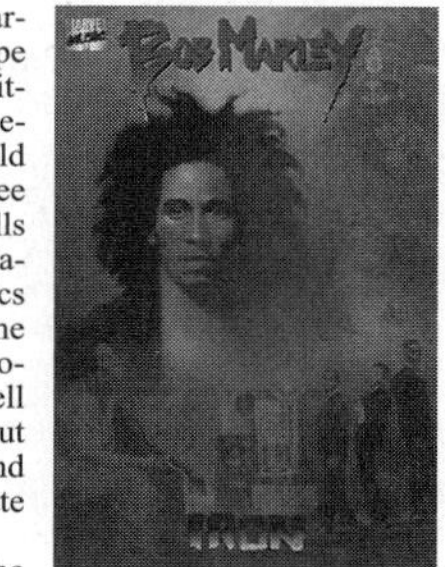

The kids' radio show in the mid-1930s called Bobby Benson's Adventures (aka The H-Bar-O Rangers)was changed into the show known as Bobby Benson and the B-Bar-B Riders beginning in 1949 and running until 1955. Benson (played by Ivan Cury and Clyde Campbell) was a boy who owned the B-Bar-B ranch. Don Knotts played Windy Wales, the handyman and comic relief. Tex Mason (played by Charles Irving and Bob Haig) was the foreman. And Craig McDonnell played Harka, an Indian ranch hand. Plots often involved solving a mystery.

While the comic book couldn't convey the electrifying cry of "Beee-Bar-Beeeeeeee!" that opened each show, it featured terrific Western art by Bob Powell, some Western covers by Frank Frazetta, and appearances of the Western version of The Ghost Rider. — Maggie
1 ❑ May 1950 Cover: 0.10 **NM** value: **300.00**
2 ❑ ca. 1950 Cover: 0.10 **NM** value: **125.00**
3 ❑ ca. 1950 Cover: 0.10 **NM** value: **100.00**
• **CGC:** 1 graded, best 7.5
4 ❑ ca. 1950 Cover: 0.10 **NM** value: **100.00**
5 ❑ Cover: 0.10 **NM** value: **100.00**
6 ❑ ca. 1951 Cover: 0.10 **NM** value: **75.00**
7 ❑ ca. 1951 Cover: 0.10 **NM** value: **75.00**
8 ❑ ca. 1951 Cover: 0.10 **NM** value: **75.00**
9 ❑ ca. 1951 Cover: 0.10 **NM** value: **75.00**
10 ❑ ca. 1951 Cover: 0.10 **NM** value: **75.00**
11 ❑ ca. 1951 Cover: 0.10 **NM** value: **60.00**
12 ❑ Cover: 0.10 **NM** value: **60.00**
13 ❑ ca. 1952 Cover: 0.10 **NM** value: **60.00**
14 ❑ ca. 1952 Cover: 0.10 **NM** value: **60.00**
• **CGC:** 6 graded, best 8.5
15 ❑ ca. 1952 Cover: 0.10 **NM** value: **60.00**
• **CGC:** 1 graded, best 6.0
16 ❑ ca. 1952 Cover: 0.10 **NM** value: **50.00**
17 ❑ ca. 1952 Cover: 0.10 **NM** value: **50.00**
18 ❑ ca. 1952 Cover: 0.10 **NM** value: **50.00**
19 ❑ ca. 1953 Cover: 0.10 **NM** value: **50.00**

BOBBY BENSON'S B-BAR-B RIDERS — AC
AC specializes in repackaging comics created in an earlier day. The 1950's series from Magazine Enterprises was called Bobby Benson's B-Bar-B Riders and was based on the 1949-1955 Western radio show Bobby Benson and the B-Bar-B Riders. — Maggie
1 ❑ Cover: 2.75 **NM** value: **Cover or less**

BOBBY RUCKERS — Art
1 ❑ Cover: 2.95 **NM** value: **Cover or less**
📖 The Falling Woman **A:** David Gwathmey **W:** Bebe Williams

BOB, THE GALACTIC BUM — DC
1 ❑ Feb 1995 Cover: 1.95 **NM** value: **2.00**
Circ: CapCity orders: **8,725**
📖 And the Maggot Cried "Death" **A:** Carlos Ezquerra **W:** Alan Grant; John Wagner
2 ❑ Mar 1995 Cover: 1.95 **NM** value: **2.00**
Circ: CapCity orders: **5,650**
📖 The Piker **A:** Carlos Ezquerra **W:** Alan Grant; John Wagner
3 ❑ Apr 1995 Cover: 1.95 **NM** value: **2.00**
Circ: CapCity orders: **4,825**
A: Carlos Ezquerra **W:** Alan Grant; John Wagner
4 ❑ Jun 1995 Cover: 1.95 **NM** value: **2.00**
Circ: CapCity orders: **4,325**
A: Carlos Ezquerra **W:** Alan Grant; John Wagner

BOB MARLEY, TALE OF THE TUFF GONG — Marvel
Rastafarian musician Bob Marley is revered by a certain type across cultures, drawn by his political activism and dream of a peaceful, just future, all told to the world through music. This series in three parts — Iron, Lion and Zion — tells Marley's story and that of the Jamaican people, with his lyrics dropped in for effect. Though some might call it biased, it is an authorized bio of sorts, and very well done. And if those wondering about the roots of Rastafarianism will find that Iron provides a fairly accurate separate short story at the end.

The roster of contributors to the project include writer Charles E. Hall, cartoonist Peter Kuper, and artists Gene Colan and Mort Todd.
1 ❑ Cover: 5.95 **NM** value: **Cover or less**
📖 Iron; Dread-I-Story **A:** Gene Colan; Tennyson Smith **W:** Charles Hall
2 ❑ Cover: 5.95 **NM** value: **Cover or less**
A: Gene Colan; Tennyson Smith **W:** Charles Hall
3 ❑ Cover: 5.95 **NM** value: **Cover or less**
A: Gene Colan; Tennyson Smith **W:** Charles Hall

"BOB'S" FAVORITE COMICS — Rip Off
All issues are adults only.
1 ❑ b&w Cover: 2.50 **NM** value: **Cover or less**
📖 Car Dog Meets PeeBear; He might be a Subgenius; The Stranger's Parable; Strange Golf; VaVa Voom; The Essence of All Humor; One Go? Too Many!; Double or Nothing; Notre "BoB"; He's "Bob" **A:** Gilbert Shelton; Dona Sangre; H.S. Hall; Ivan Palmer; Ivan Stang; Jay Kinney; Palmer Vreedeez; Byron Werner **W:** Gilbert Shelton; Dona Sangre; H.S. Hall; Ivan Palmer; Ivan Stang; Jay Kinney; Palmer Vreedeez; Byron Werner
1-2 ❑ b&w Cover: 2.50 **NM** value: **Cover or less**
1-3 ❑ b&w Cover: 2.50 **NM** value: **Cover or less**

BOB STEELE WESTERN — AC
1 ❑ b&w Cover: 2.75 **NM** value: **Cover or less**

BODY BAGS — Dark Horse / Blanc Noir
1 ❑ Sep 1996 Cover: 2.95 **NM** value: **5.00**
Circ: Diamd. preorders: **17,062** • **CGC:** 2 graded, best 9.8
📖 Father's Day, Part 1 **A:** Jason Pearson **W:** Jason Pearson
2 ❑ Oct 1996 Cover: 2.95 **NM** value: **6.00**
Circ: Diamd. preorders: **15,830** • **CGC:** 1 graded, best 9.8
📖 Father's Day, Part 2 **A:** Jason Pearson **W:** Jason Pearson
3 ❑ Nov 1996 Cover: 2.95 **NM** value: **4.00**
Circ: Diamd. preorders: **15,907**
📖 Father's Day, Part 3 **A:** Jason Pearson **W:** Jason Pearson
4 ❑ Jan 1997 Cover: 2.95 **NM** value: **3.50**
Circ: Direct Market orders: **17,705** • **CGC:** 1 graded, best 9.6
📖 Father's Day, Part 4 **A:** Jason Pearson **W:** Jason Pearson
Ash 1❑ **NM** value: **3.00**
A: Jason Pearson **W:** Jason Pearson
Bk 1❑ Cover: 12.95 **NM** value: **Cover or less**
📖 Father's Day • collects mini-series **A:** Jason Pearson **W:** Jason Pearson

BODY COUNT (AIRCEL) — Aircel
1 ❑ Cover: 2.25 **NM** value: **Cover or less**
📖 Co-Ed Killers **A:** Dave Cooper **W:** Barry Blair
2 ❑ Cover: 2.25 **NM** value: **Cover or less**
3 ❑ Cover: 2.25 **NM** value: **Cover or less**
4 ❑ Cover: 2.25 **NM** value: **Cover or less**

BODYCOUNT (IMAGE) — Image
1 ❑ Mar 1996 Cover: 2.50 **NM** value: **Cover or less**
A: Simon Bisley **W:** Kevin Eastman
2 ❑ Apr 1996 Cover: 2.50 **NM** value: **Cover or less**
A: Simon Bisley **W:** Kevin Eastman
3 ❑ May 1996 Cover: 2.50 **NM** value: **Cover or less**
A: Simon Bisley **W:** Kevin Eastman

CGC-graded: Multiply prices above by **33 for 9.9 M • 16 for 9.8 NM/M • 7 for 9.6 NM+ • 5 for 9.4 NM • 2.5 for 9.2 NM- • 1.5 for 9.0 VF/NM**

4 ❑ Cover: 2.50 **NM value: Cover or less**
final issue. **A:** Simon Bisley **W:** Kevin Eastman
Bk 1❑ Cover: 17.95 **NM value: Cover or less**
• Casey Jones & Raphael;collects Bodycount mini-series **A:** Simon Bisley **W:** Kevin Eastman

BODY DOUBLES — DC

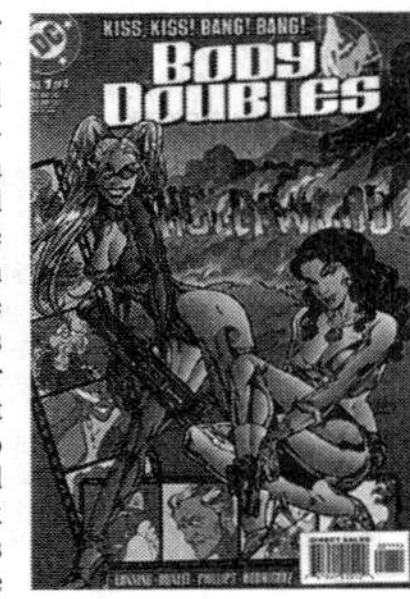

Life isn't easy, when you're a pair of buxom babes who dabble in murder for money. Mixing sex appeal and gratuitous violence, this mini-series (preceded by a one-shot a year earlier) features as its lead characters Bonny Hoffman, the daughter of a mob boss, and Carmen Leno, an ex-adult film actress. The two cold-hearted women work as assassins for "Uncle" Nick "Killer Queen" Hoffman and an outfit called Requiem Inc. They're also being pursued by Agents Goodland and Moore of the FBI. (Think Felix and Oscar with guns.) All of that is nothing compared to the challenge they face, when the Mystress of the Rhormorid arrives on Earth and makes a deal with them to hunt down meta-human women so she can feed on their life force. Cameos by Argent of the Teen Titans, Power Girl, and Wonder Woman provide ample opportunity for gratuitous T&A and fetishistic fight sequences.

1 ❑ Oct 1999 Cover: 2.50 **NM value: Cover or less**
Circ: Diamd. preorders: **18,888**
Girl Power! **A:** Joe Phillips **W:** Andy Lanning; Dan Abnett ★ Appearance of Mystress.
2 ❑ Nov 1999 Cover: 2.50 **NM value: Cover or less**
Circ: Diamd. preorders: **15,049**
A: Joe Phillips **W:** Andy Lanning; Dan Abnett
3 ❑ Dec 1999 Cover: 2.50 **NM value: Cover or less**
Circ: Diamd. preorders: **13,950**
Cold Snap **A:** Joe Phillips **W:** Andy Lanning; Dan Abnett
4 ❑ Jan 2000 Cover: 2.50 **NM value: Cover or less**
Circ: Diamd. preorders: **12,500**
A: Joe Phillips; Jason Rodriguez **W:** Andy Lanning; Dan Abnett

BODY DOUBLES (VILLAINS) — DC

1 ❑ Feb 1998 Cover: 1.95 **NM value: 2.00**
• New Year's Evil

BODYGUARD — Aircel

All issues are adults only.
1 ❑ Sep 1990, b&w Cover: 2.50 **NM value: Cover or less**
Boots 'n All; Stick Shift; Nicked Off; God's Own Game (text piece on cricket); It Ain't Cricket • intro by Todd McFarlane **A:** Glenn Lumsden **C:** Paul Gulacy **W:** David de Vries
2 ❑ Oct 1990, b&w Cover: 2.50 **NM value: Cover or less**
Writer's Block; Clarry's Mum's Lamington Recipe; Cassandra; Easter Bunny; Great White Bait; The Beaver State **A:** Glenn Lumsden **C:** Paul Gulacy **W:** David de Vries
3 ❑ Nov 1990, b&w Cover: 2.50 **NM value: Cover or less**
Bk 1❑ Cover: 9.95 **NM value: Cover or less**

BODY PAINT — Eros

1 ❑ Cover: 2.95 **NM value: Cover or less**
A: Raevyn **W:** Raevyn
2 ❑ Jun 1995 Cover: 2.95 **NM value: Cover or less**
A: Raevyn **W:** Raevyn

BODY SWAP, THE — Roger Mason

1 ❑ **NM value: 2.95**
A: Roger Mason **W:** Roger Mason

BOFFO IN HELL — Neatly Chiseled Features

1 ❑ Cover: 2.50 **NM value: Cover or less**
What Color is the Sky in Your World? **A:** Joe Martin **W:** Joe Martin

BOFFO LAFFS — Paragraphics

1 ❑ Cover: 2.50 **NM value: Cover or less**
first hologram cover.
2 ❑ Cover: 1.95 **NM value: Cover or less**
3 ❑ Cover: 1.95 **NM value: Cover or less**
4 ❑ Cover: 1.95 **NM value: Cover or less**
5 ❑ Cover: 1.95 **NM value: Cover or less**

BOFFY THE VAMPIRE LAYER — Fantagraphics / Eros

1 ❑ ca. 2000 Cover: 2.95 **NM value: Cover or less**
2 ❑ ca. 2000 Cover: 2.95 **NM value: Cover or less**
Circ: Diamd. preorders: **2,119**
3 ❑ ca. 2001 Cover: 2.95 **NM value: Cover or less**
Circ: Diamd. preorders: **1,835**

To find the median price offered on eBay at press time for pre-1990 **CGC-graded comics**, multiply by:

9.9 (M): **33**	8.5 (VF+): **1.25**
9.8(NM/M): **16**	8.0 (VF): **0.85**
9.6 (NM+): **7**	7.5 (VF-): **0.6**
9.4 (NM): **5**	7.0 (F/VF): **0.5**
9.2 (NM-): **2.5**	6.5 (F+): **0.4**
9.0 (VF/NM): **1.5**	6.0 (F-): **0.33**

These are median prices of all CGC comics auctioned on eBay; prices for individual issues will vary.

BOGIE MAN, THE — Fat Man

It's a cold and stormy New Year's eve in Greenock. Rain pours over the roof of the Spinbinnie Hospital, resting place for the mentally insane. There, in an upstairs room, Francis Forbes Clunie is seen dangling from a noose in his room. Only it isn't Clunie, merely a dummy — and the caretaker who rushes in to look after Clunie finds himself bashed over the head by an attacker lurking in the shadows. The caretaker is then stripped of his uniform and keys, and the attacker slips out into the night.

The attacker has the body of Francis Clunie, but, as far as he is concerned, it is Humphrey Bogart who has escaped. That, you see, is the nature of Clunie's ailment. And now Bogie is wandering the streets of Scotland, wearing a trenchcoat and going after "The Fat Man" (a character from the Bogart-starring "The Maltese Falcon").

1 ❑ Cover: 1.95 **NM value: 2.50**
Farewell, My Looney **A:** Robin Smith **W:** Alan Grant; John Wagner
2 ❑ Cover: 1.95 **NM value: 2.50**
The Treasure of The Ford Sierra **A:** Robin Smith **W:** Alan Grant; John Wagner
3 ❑ Cover: 1.95 **NM value: 2.50**
To Huv and Huvnae **A:** Robin Smith **W:** Alan Grant; John Wagner
4 ❑ Cover: 1.95 **NM value: 2.50**
A: Robin Smith **W:** Alan Grant; John Wagner

BOGIE MAN, THE: CHINATOON — Atomeka

1 ❑ Cover: 2.95 **NM value: Cover or less**
Barefoot in the Pork **A:** Robin Smith **W:** Alan Grant; John Wagner
2 ❑ Cover: 2.95 **NM value: Cover or less**
3 ❑ Cover: 2.95 **NM value: Cover or less**
4 ❑ Cover: 2.95 **NM value: Cover or less**

BOGIE MAN, THE (COLLECTION) — DC / Paradox Graphic Mystery

Bk 1❑ b&w Cover: 13.95 **NM value: Cover or less**
• digest-sized. • collects Fat Man and Atomeka series

BOGIE MAN: THE MANHATTAN PROJECT — Tundra

1 ❑ Cover: 4.95 **NM value: Cover or less**
No issue number.

BOG SWAMP DEMON — Hall of Heroes

1 ❑ Aug 1996 Cover: 2.50 **NM value: Cover or less**
Deliverance **A:** Bo Robertson **W:** Ryan Brown; Doug Brammer
2 ❑ Oct 1996 Cover: 2.50 **NM value: Cover or less**
• no indicia
3 ❑ Dec 1996 Cover: 2.50 **NM value: Cover or less**
4 ❑ Mar 1997 Cover: 2.50 **NM value: Cover or less**

BOHOS — Image

1 ❑ May 1998 Cover: 2.95 **NM value: Cover or less**
Circ: Diamd. preorders: **4,583**
cover says Jun, indicia says May. **A:** Jason Waltrip; John Waltrip **W:** Maggie Whorf
2 ❑ Jun 1998 Cover: 2.95 **NM value: Cover or less**
Circ: Diamd. preorders: **4,125**
A: Jason Waltrip; John Waltrip **W:** Maggie Whorf
3 ❑ Jul 1998 Cover: 2.95 **NM value: Cover or less**
Circ: Diamd. preorders: **2,915**
• no month of publication **A:** Jason Waltrip; John Waltrip **W:** Maggie Whorf
Bk 1❑ Cover: 12.95 **NM value: Cover or less**
A: Jason Waltrip; John Waltrip **W:** Maggie Whorf

BO JACKSON VS. MICHAEL JORDAN — Celebrity

1 ❑ Cover: 2.95 **NM value: Cover or less**
A: Scott Harrison; Garrett Berner **W:** Dan Murdock
2 ❑ Cover: 2.95 **NM value: Cover or less**

BOLD ADVENTURE — Pacific

1 ❑ Cover: 1.25 **NM value: 2.00**
Time Force **A:** Rudy Nebres **W:** Bill Dubay
2 ❑ Cover: 1.50 **NM value: 2.00**
3 ❑ Cover: 1.50 **NM value: 2.00**
final issue.

BOLT AND STARFORCE SIX — AC

1 ❑ Jul 1984 Cover: 1.75 **NM value: Cover or less**
A: Rod Whigham **W:** Bill Black

BOLT SPECIAL — AC

1 ❑ Cover: 1.50 **NM value: 2.00**

BOMARC — Nightwynd

1 ❑ Cover: 2.50 **NM value: Cover or less**
2 ❑ Cover: 2.50 **NM value: Cover or less**
3 ❑ Cover: 2.50 **NM value: Cover or less**

The prices seen above do not represent the highest possible prices seen in online auctions, but rather the prices we have seen these issues reliably fetch in a variety of environments (storefront retail, mail order, auction and convention).

BOMBA — DC

The Bomba series of children's adventure novels was written under the penname "Roy Rockwood" in the 1920s and starred a boy castaway who lived in the South American jungle and survived bouts with anacondas, hostile tribes, volcanoes, and the like, before eventually being reunited (in the last volume) with the world from which he'd come as an infant.

Eventually, the series was licensed by Producer Walter Mirisch for a series of feature films starring Johnny Sheffield. Those began to be released starting in 1949. There were 10 films in the series, three more than there were issues of the DC series which ran nearly two decades later. — Maggie

1 ❑ Sep 1967 Cover: 0.12 **NM value: 20.00**
Nightmare! ★ 1st Appearance of Bomba.
2 ❑ Nov 1967 Cover: 0.12 **NM value: 10.00**
3 ❑ Jan 1968 Cover: 0.12 **NM value: 10.00**
4 ❑ Mar 1968 Cover: 0.12 **NM value: 10.00**
5 ❑ May 1968 Cover: 0.12 **NM value: 10.00**
6 ❑ Jul 1968 Cover: 0.12 **NM value: 10.00**
7 ❑ Sep 1968 Cover: 0.12 **NM value: 10.00**
final issue.

BOMBAST — Topps

1 ❑ Apr 1993 Cover: 2.95 **NM value: Cover or less**
Circ: CapCity orders: **59,150**
Bombast Lives • Savage Dragon **A:** John Severin; Dick Ayers **C:** Jack Kirby **W:** Gary Friedrich

BOMBASTIC — Screaming Dodo

1 ❑ Nov 1996 Cover: 2.50 **NM value: Cover or less**
What's Up? **A:** Brian Clopper **W:** Brian Clopper
2 ❑ Feb 1997 Cover: 2.50 **NM value: Cover or less**
A: Brian Clopper **W:** Brian Clopper
3 ❑ May 1997 Cover: 2.50 **NM value: Cover or less**
A: Brian Clopper **W:** Brian Clopper
4 ❑ Aug 1997 Cover: 2.50 **NM value: Cover or less**
A: Brian Clopper **W:** Brian Clopper
5 ❑ Dec 1997 Cover: 2.50 **NM value: Cover or less**
cardstock cover. **A:** Brian Clopper **W:** Brian Clopper

BOMBER COMICS — Elliott Publications

1 ❑ Spr 1944 Cover: 0.10 **NM value: 400.00**
• **CGC:** 1 graded, best 9.4
2 ❑ Sum 1944 Cover: 0.10 **NM value: 300.00**
• **CGC:** 2 graded, best 7.5
3 ❑ Fal 1944 Cover: 0.10 **NM value: 250.00**
• **CGC:** 2 graded, best 8.0
4 ❑ Win 1944 Cover: 0.10 **NM value: 250.00**
• **CGC:** 2 graded, best 7.0

BONANZA — Gold Key

The Cartwright clan — Pa and his sons, half-brothers Adam, Hoss, and Little Joe — helped keep their Nevada ranch safe from cattle rustlers and natural forces on the popular television show that ran from 1959 to 1973. The show was the first Western televised in color and starred Lorne Greene, Pernell Roberts, Dan Blocker, and Michael Landon as a family of men coping with their personal problems and the problems of coordinating the business of ranching and dealing with other ranchers and mining interests in the area. It was one of the most successful TV Westerns.

The comic-book adaptation offered the typical slick Gold Key packaging, with photo covers and stories featuring father and sons facing familiar Western situations.

1 ❑ Dec 1962 Cover: 0.12 **NM value: 110.00**
★ Appearance of Series continued from.
2 ❑ Mar 1963 Cover: 0.12 **NM value: 75.00**
3 ❑ Jun 1963 Cover: 0.12 **NM value: 50.00**
4 ❑ Sep 1963 Cover: 0.12 **NM value: 50.00**
5 ❑ Dec 1963 Cover: 0.12 **NM value: 50.00**
6 ❑ Feb 1964 Cover: 0.12 **NM value: 30.00**
Circ: Statement: **253,547**
7 ❑ Apr 1964 Cover: 0.12 **NM value: 30.00**
Circ: Statement: **253,547**
8 ❑ Jun 1964 Cover: 0.12 **NM value: 30.00**
Circ: Statement: **253,547**
9 ❑ Aug 1964 Cover: 0.12 **NM value: 30.00**
Circ: Statement: **253,547** • **CGC:** 1 graded, best 5.0
10 ❑ Oct 1964 Cover: 0.12 **NM value: 30.00**
Circ: Statement: **253,547**
11 ❑ Dec 1964 Cover: 0.12 **NM value: 20.00**
Circ: Statement: **253,547**
12 ❑ Feb 1965 Cover: 0.12 **NM value: 20.00**
Circ: Statement: **244,042**
13 ❑ Apr 1965 Cover: 0.12 **NM value: 20.00**
Circ: Statement: **244,042**
14 ❑ Jun 1965 Cover: 0.12 **NM value: 20.00**
Circ: Statement: **244,042**
15 ❑ Aug 1965 Cover: 0.12 **NM value: 20.00**
Circ: Statement: **244,042**

Other grades: Multiply prices above by **1.5 for Mint • 2/3 for Very Fine • 1/3 for Fine • 1/5 for Very Good • 1/8 for Good**

16 ❑ Oct 1965 Cover: 0.12 **NM** value: **20.00**
Circ: Statement: **244,042**
17 ❑ Dec 1965 Cover: 0.12 **NM** value: **20.00**
Circ: Statement: **244,042**
18 ❑ Feb 1966 Cover: 0.12 **NM** value: **20.00**
Circ: Statement: **230,033**
Strange Cargo; Dead Set on Winning; Lost Bonanzas of the West: The Scalp Hunters' Ledge (text story); The Gold Brickers; Christmas Gift for Mooney's Gulch; The Best Defense
19 ❑ Apr 1966 Cover: 0.12 **NM** value: **20.00**
Circ: Statement: **230,033**
20 ❑ Jun 1966 Cover: 0.12 **NM** value: **20.00**
Circ: Statement: **230,033**
21 ❑ Aug 1966 Cover: 0.12 **NM** value: **15.00**
Circ: Statement: **230,033**
22 ❑ Oct 1966 Cover: 0.12 **NM** value: **15.00**
Circ: Statement: **230,033**
23 ❑ Feb 1967 Cover: 0.12 **NM** value: **15.00**
Circ: Statement: **225,625**
24 ❑ May 1967 Cover: 0.12 **NM** value: **15.00**
Circ: Statement: **225,625**
25 ❑ Aug 1967 Cover: 0.12 **NM** value: **15.00**
Circ: Statement: **225,625**
The Fugitive; Desert Salvage; Schieffelin's Bonanza (text story); Sore Loser
26 ❑ Nov 1967 Cover: 0.12 **NM** value: **15.00**
Circ: Statement: **225,625**
27 ❑ Feb 1968 Cover: 0.12 **NM** value: **15.00**
28 ❑ May 1968 Cover: 0.12 **NM** value: **15.00**
29 ❑ Aug 1968 Cover: 0.15 **NM** value: **15.00**
30 ❑ Nov 1968 Cover: 0.15 **NM** value: **15.00**
• **CGC:** 1 graded, best 8.5
31 ❑ Feb 1969 Cover: 0.15 **NM** value: **10.00**
32 ❑ May 1969 Cover: 0.15 **NM** value: **10.00**
• **CGC:** 1 graded, best 8.0
33 ❑ Aug 1969 Cover: 0.15 **NM** value: **10.00**
34 ❑ Nov 1969 Cover: 0.15 **NM** value: **10.00**
35 ❑ Feb 1970 Cover: 0.15 **NM** value: **10.00**
36 ❑ May 1970 Cover: 0.15 **NM** value: **10.00**
37 ❑ Aug 1970 Cover: 0.15 **NM** value: **10.00**
• **CGC:** 1 graded, best 8.5
final issue.

BONDAGE CONFESSIONS — Eros

1 ❑ Cover: 2.95 **NM** value: **Cover or less**
A: Dementia **W:** Dementia
2 ❑ Cover: 2.95 **NM** value: **Cover or less**
A: Dementia **W:** Dementia
3 ❑ Cover: 2.95 **NM** value: **Cover or less**
A: Dementia **W:** Dementia
4 ❑ Nov 1998 Cover: 2.95 **NM** value: **Cover or less**
A: Dementia **W:** Dementia

BONDAGE FAIRIES — Antarctic / Venus

1 ❑ Mar 1994 Cover: 2.95 **NM** value: **5.00**
Circ: CapCity orders: **2,695**
A: Kondom **W:** Kondom
1-2 ❑ May 1994 Cover: 2.95 **NM** value: **Cover or less**
1-3 ❑ Aug 1994 Cover: 2.95 **NM** value: **Cover or less**
1-4 ❑ Jan 1995 Cover: 2.95 **NM** value: **Cover or less**
2 ❑ Apr 1994 Cover: 2.95 **NM** value: **4.00**
Circ: CapCity orders: **2,565**
A: Kondom **W:** Kondom
2-2 ❑ Jun 1994 Cover: 2.95 **NM** value: **Cover or less**
2-3 ❑ Oct 1994 Cover: 2.95 **NM** value: **Cover or less**
2-4 ❑ Apr 1995 Cover: 2.95 **NM** value: **Cover or less**
3 ❑ May 1994 Cover: 2.95 **NM** value: **3.25**
Circ: CapCity orders: **2,885**
A: Kondom **W:** Kondom
3-2 ❑ Sep 1994 Cover: 2.95 **NM** value: **Cover or less**
3-3 ❑ Dec 1994 Cover: 2.95 **NM** value: **Cover or less**
4 ❑ Jun 1994 Cover: 2.95 **NM** value: **3.25**
A: Kondom **W:** Kondom
4-2 ❑ Nov 1994 Cover: 2.95 **NM** value: **Cover or less**
4-3 ❑ Jan 1995 Cover: 2.95 **NM** value: **Cover or less**
5 ❑ Jul 1994 Cover: 2.95 **NM** value: **3.25**
A: Kondom **W:** Kondom
5-2 ❑ Nov 1994 Cover: 2.95 **NM** value: **Cover or less**
5-3 ❑ Feb 1995 Cover: 2.95 **NM** value: **Cover or less**
6 ❑ Aug 1994 Cover: 2.95 **NM** value: **Cover or less**
A: Kondom **W:** Kondom
6-2 ❑ Feb 1995 Cover: 2.95 **NM** value: **Cover or less**
Bk 1❑ Cover: 12.95 **NM** value: **Cover or less**
• The Collected Bondage Fairies;Collects Bondage Fairies #1-6 **A:** Kondom **W:** Kondom

BONDAGE FAIRIES EXTREME — Fantagraphics / Eros

1 ❑ Oct 1999 Cover: 3.50 **NM** value: **Cover or less**
Circ: Diamd. preorders: **5,383**
A: Kondom **W:** Kondom
2 ❑ Nov 1999 Cover: 3.50 **NM** value: **Cover or less**
Circ: Diamd. preorders: **4,761**
3 ❑ Dec 1999 Cover: 3.50 **NM** value: **Cover or less**
Circ: Diamd. preorders: **4,773**
4 ❑ Jan 2000 Cover: 3.50 **NM** value: **Cover or less**
Circ: Diamd. preorders: **4,746**
5 ❑ Feb 2000 Cover: 3.50 **NM** value: **Cover or less**
Circ: Diamd. preorders: **4,561**
6 ❑ Mar 2000 Cover: 3.50 **NM** value: **Cover or less**
Circ: Diamd. preorders: **4,885**
7 ❑ Apr 2000 Cover: 3.50 **NM** value: **Cover or less**
Circ: Diamd. preorders: **4,918**
8 ❑ May 2000 Cover: 3.95 **NM** value: **Cover or less**
Circ: Diamd. preorders: **4,956**
9 ❑ Jun 2000 Cover: 3.50 **NM** value: **Cover or less**
Circ: Diamd. preorders: **5,024**
10 ❑ Jul 2000 Cover: 3.50 **NM** value: **Cover or less**
Circ: Diamd. preorders: **4,972**
11 ❑ Sep 2000 Cover: 3.50 **NM** value: **Cover or less**
Circ: Diamd. preorders: **4,804**
12 ❑ Oct 2000 Cover: 3.50 **NM** value: **Cover or less**
Circ: Diamd. preorders: **4,673**
13 ❑ Nov 2000 Cover: 3.95 **NM** value: **Cover or less**
14 ❑ ca. 2000 Cover: 3.50 **NM** value: **Cover or less**

BONDAGE GIRLS AT WAR — Fantagraphics / Eros

1 ❑ 1996 Cover: 2.95 **NM** value: **Cover or less**
A: Ron Wilber **W:** Ron Wilber
2 ❑ 1996 Cover: 2.95 **NM** value: **Cover or less**
A: Ron Wilber **W:** Ron Wilber
3 ❑ 1996 Cover: 2.95 **NM** value: **Cover or less**
A: Ron Wilber **W:** Ron Wilber
4 ❑ 1996 Cover: 2.95 **NM** value: **Cover or less**
A: Ron Wilber **W:** Ron Wilber
5 ❑ Feb 1997 Cover: 2.95 **NM** value: **Cover or less**
A: Ron Wilber **W:** Ron Wilber
6 ❑ ca. 1997 Cover: 2.95 **NM** value: **Cover or less**
Circ: Diamd. preorders: **1,688**

BONE — Cartoon Books

Jeff Smith created a classic funnybook for the 1990s, combining Walt Disney-style art with strong storytelling and characterization. Bone is the story of a little character called Fone Bone. Originally from Boneville, he finds himself, along with other Bone characters Phoney Bone and Smiley Bone, in a village a long way from home. In the course of settling into village life, they discover there are more forces at work than would seem usual in a rural town. Eventually, they come to learn about Stupid, Stupid Rat Creatures, a gigantic dragon, and more. The beautiful village girl Thorn quickly wins Fone Bone's adoration — but she is more than she seems, and so is her grandmother.

Winner of numerous awards, including the 1994 Eisner for Best New Series and the 1995 Eisner for Best Continuing Series, Bone has appeal for young and old alike.

1 ❑ Jul 1991 Cover: 2.95 **NM** value: **115.00**
• **CGC:** 7 graded, best 9.0
• 3000 printed **A:** Jeff Smith **W:** Jeff Smith ★ 1st Appearance of Phoney Bone, Smiley Bone, Fone Bone.
1-2 ❑ Cover: 2.95 **NM** value: **10.00**
1-3 ❑ Cover: 2.95 **NM** value: **3.00**
1-4 ❑ Cover: 2.95 **NM** value: **3.00**
1-5 ❑ Cover: 2.95 **NM** value: **3.00**
1-6 ❑ Cover: 2.95 **NM** value: **3.00**
1-7 ❑ Cover: 2.95 **NM** value: **3.00**
1-8 ❑ Cover: 2.95 **NM** value: **3.00**
1-9 ❑ Cover: 2.95 **NM** value: **3.00**
2 ❑ Sep 1991 Cover: 2.95 **NM** value: **60.00**
• **CGC:** 1 graded, best 9.0
A: Jeff Smith **W:** Jeff Smith ★ 1st Appearance of Thorn.
2-2 ❑ Cover: 2.95 **NM** value: **8.00**
• **CGC:** 1 graded, best 9.2
2-3 ❑ Cover: 2.95 **NM** value: **3.00**
2-4 ❑ Cover: 2.95 **NM** value: **3.00**
2-5 ❑ Cover: 2.95 **NM** value: **3.00**
2-6 ❑ Cover: 2.95 **NM** value: **3.00**
2-7 ❑ Cover: 2.95 **NM** value: **3.00**
2-8 ❑ Cover: 2.95 **NM** value: **3.00**
• Image reprint
3 ❑ Dec 1991 Cover: 2.95 **NM** value: **35.00**
A: Jeff Smith **W:** Jeff Smith
3-2 ❑ Cover: 2.95 **NM** value: **5.00**
3-3 ❑ Cover: 2.95 **NM** value: **3.00**
3-4 ❑ Cover: 2.95 **NM** value: **3.00**
3-5 ❑ Cover: 2.95 **NM** value: **3.00**
3-6 ❑ Cover: 2.95 **NM** value: **3.00**
3-7 ❑ Cover: 2.95 **NM** value: **3.00**
3-8 ❑ Cover: 2.95 **NM** value: **3.00**
• Image reprint
4 ❑ Mar 1992 Cover: 2.95 **NM** value: **25.00**
A: Jeff Smith **W:** Jeff Smith
4-2 ❑ Cover: 2.95 **NM** value: **4.00**
4-3 ❑ Cover: 2.95 **NM** value: **3.00**
4-4 ❑ Cover: 2.95 **NM** value: **3.00**
4-5 ❑ Cover: 2.95 **NM** value: **3.00**
4-6 ❑ Cover: 2.95 **NM** value: **3.00**
5 ❑ Jun 1992 Cover: 2.95 **NM** value: **20.00**
A: Jeff Smith **W:** Jeff Smith
5-2 ❑ Cover: 2.95 **NM** value: **4.00**
5-3 ❑ Cover: 2.95 **NM** value: **3.00**
5-4 ❑ Cover: 2.95 **NM** value: **3.00**
5-5 ❑ Cover: 2.95 **NM** value: **3.00**
5-6 ❑ Cover: 2.95 **NM** value: **3.00**
5-7 ❑ Cover: 2.95 **NM** value: **3.00**
6 ❑ Nov 1992 Cover: 2.95 **NM** value: **12.00**
A: Jeff Smith **W:** Jeff Smith
6-2 ❑ Cover: 2.95 **NM** value: **4.00**
6-3 ❑ Cover: 2.95 **NM** value: **3.00**
6-4 ❑ Cover: 2.95 **NM** value: **3.00**
6-5 ❑ Cover: 2.95 **NM** value: **3.00**
6-6 ❑ Cover: 2.95 **NM** value: **3.00**
7 ❑ Dec 1992 Cover: 2.95 **NM** value: **12.00**
• **CGC:** 1 graded, best 9.4
A: Jeff Smith **W:** Jeff Smith
7-2 ❑ Cover: 2.95 **NM** value: **3.00**
7-3 ❑ Cover: 2.95 **NM** value: **3.00**
7-4 ❑ Cover: 2.95 **NM** value: **3.00**
7-5 ❑ Cover: 2.95 **NM** value: **3.00**
8 ❑ Feb 1993 Cover: 2.95 **NM** value: **10.00**
The Great Cow Race, Part 1 • Eisner award-winning story (1994)
A: Jeff Smith **W:** Jeff Smith
8-2 ❑ Cover: 2.95 **NM** value: **3.00**
8-3 ❑ Cover: 2.95 **NM** value: **3.00**
8-4 ❑ Cover: 2.95 **NM** value: **3.00**
8-5 ❑ Cover: 2.95 **NM** value: **3.00**
8-6 ❑ Cover: 2.95 **NM** value: **3.00**
8-7 ❑ Cover: 2.95 **NM** value: **3.00**
• Image reprint **A:** Jeff Smith **W:** Jeff Smith
9 ❑ Jul 1993 Cover: 2.95 **NM** value: **5.00**
The Great Cow Race, Part 2 • Eisner award-winning story (1994)
A: Jeff Smith **W:** Jeff Smith
9-2 ❑ Cover: 2.95 **NM** value: **3.00**
9-3 ❑ Cover: 2.95 **NM** value: **3.00**
9-4 ❑ Cover: 2.95 **NM** value: **3.00**
10 ❑ Sep 1993 Cover: 2.95 **NM** value: **4.00**
Circ: CapCity orders: **3,400**
The Great Cow Race, Part 3 • Eisner award-winning story (1994)
A: Jeff Smith **W:** Jeff Smith
10-2❑ Cover: 2.95 **NM** value: **3.00**
Circ: CapCity orders: **2,655**
10-3❑ Cover: 2.95 **NM** value: **3.00**
11 ❑ Dec 1993 Cover: 2.95 **NM** value: **4.00**
Circ: CapCity orders: **4,240**
A: Jeff Smith **W:** Jeff Smith
11-2❑ Cover: 2.95 **NM** value: **3.00**
Circ: CapCity orders: **4,395**
12 ❑ Feb 1994 Cover: 2.95 **NM** value: **4.00**
Circ: CapCity orders: **6,350**
A: Jeff Smith **W:** Jeff Smith
12-2❑ Cover: 2.95 **NM** value: **3.00**
Circ: CapCity orders: **4,915**
12-3❑ Cover: 2.95 **NM** value: **3.00**
13 ❑ Mar 1994 Cover: 2.95 **NM** value: **4.00**
Circ: CapCity orders: **11,550**
A: Jeff Smith **W:** Jeff Smith
13-2❑ Cover: 2.95 **NM** value: **3.00**
• Image reprint **A:** Jeff Smith **W:** Jeff Smith
13.5❑ **NM** value: **5.00**
• **CGC:** 1 graded, best 9.4
• Wizard promotional edition. **A:** Jeff Smith **W:** Jeff Smith
13.5/GO❑ **NM** value: **5.00**
• **CGC:** 1 graded, best 9.4
• Gold edition. **A:** Jeff Smith **W:** Jeff Smith
14 ❑ May 1994 Cover: 2.95 **NM** value: **3.00**
A: Jeff Smith **W:** Jeff Smith
14-2❑ Cover: 2.95 **NM** value: **3.00**
• Image reprint **A:** Jeff Smith **W:** Jeff Smith
15 ❑ Aug 1994 Cover: 2.95 **NM** value: **3.00**
Circ: CapCity orders: **16,325**
A: Jeff Smith **W:** Jeff Smith
15-2❑ Cover: 2.95 **NM** value: **3.00**
• Image reprint **A:** Jeff Smith **W:** Jeff Smith
16 ❑ Oct 1994 Cover: 2.95 **NM** value: **3.00**
Circ: CapCity orders: **15,475**
A: Jeff Smith **W:** Jeff Smith
16-2❑ Cover: 2.95 **NM** value: **Cover or less**
• Image reprint **A:** Jeff Smith **W:** Jeff Smith
17 ❑ Jan 1995 Cover: 2.95 **NM** value: **Cover or less**
Circ: CapCity orders: **14,375**
A: Jeff Smith **W:** Jeff Smith
17-2❑ Cover: 2.95 **NM** value: **Cover or less**
• Image reprint **A:** Jeff Smith **W:** Jeff Smith
18 ❑ Apr 1995 Cover: 2.95 **NM** value: **Cover or less**
Circ: CapCity orders: **12,550**
A: Jeff Smith **W:** Jeff Smith
18-2❑ Cover: 2.95 **NM** value: **Cover or less**
• Image reprint **A:** Jeff Smith **W:** Jeff Smith
19 ❑ Jun 1995 Cover: 2.95 **NM** value: **Cover or less**
Circ: CapCity orders: **12,525**
A: Jeff Smith **W:** Jeff Smith
19-2❑ Cover: 2.95 **NM** value: **Cover or less**
• Image reprint **A:** Jeff Smith **W:** Jeff Smith
20 ❑ Oct 1995 Cover: 2.95 **NM** value: **Cover or less**
Circ: CapCity orders: **12,700**
• moves to Image **A:** Jeff Smith **W:** Jeff Smith
20-2❑ Cover: 2.95 **NM** value: **Cover or less**
• Image reprint **A:** Jeff Smith **W:** Jeff Smith
21 ❑ Dec 1995 Cover: 2.95 **NM** value: **Cover or less**
• Image begins as publisher **A:** Jeff Smith **W:** Jeff Smith
22 ❑ Feb 1996 Cover: 2.95 **NM** value: **Cover or less**
A: Jeff Smith **W:** Jeff Smith
23 ❑ May 1996 Cover: 2.95 **NM** value: **Cover or less**
A: Jeff Smith **W:** Jeff Smith ★ 1st Appearance of Baby Rat Creature.
24 ❑ Jun 1996 Cover: 2.95 **NM** value: **Cover or less**
A: Jeff Smith **W:** Jeff Smith
25 ❑ Aug 1996 Cover: 2.95 **NM** value: **Cover or less**
A: Jeff Smith **W:** Jeff Smith
26 ❑ Dec 1996 Cover: 2.95 **NM** value: **Cover or less**
Circ: Direct Market orders: **34,000**
A: Jeff Smith **W:** Jeff Smith
27 ❑ Apr 1997 Cover: 2.95 **NM** value: **Cover or less**
Circ: Diamd. preorders: **32,648**
• Phoney captures Red Dragon;series returns to Cartoon Books **A:** Jeff Smith **W:** Jeff Smith
28 ❑ Aug 1997 Cover: 2.95 **NM** value: **Cover or less**
Circ: Diamd. preorders: **29,100**
• Cartoon Books begins as publisher **A:** Jeff Smith **W:** Jeff Smith
29 ❑ Nov 1997 Cover: 2.95 **NM** value: **Cover or less**
Circ: Diamd. preorders: **25,047**
A: Jeff Smith **W:** Jeff Smith
30 ❑ Jan 1998 Cover: 2.95 **NM** value: **Cover or less**
Circ: Diamd. preorders: **24,791**
A: Jeff Smith **W:** Jeff Smith
31 ❑ Apr 1998 Cover: 2.95 **NM** value: **Cover or less**
Circ: Diamd. preorders: **24,854**
A: Jeff Smith **W:** Jeff Smith

CGC-graded: Multiply prices above by **33 for 9.9 M • 16 for 9.8 NM/M • 7 for 9.6 NM+ • 5 for 9.4 NM • 2.5 for 9.2 NM- • 1.5 for 9.0 VF/NM**

32 ❑ Jun 1998 Cover: 2.95 **NM** value: **Cover or less**
Circ: Diamd. preorders: **23,391**
A: Jeff Smith **W:** Jeff Smith
33 ❑ Aug 1998 Cover: 2.95 **NM** value: **Cover or less**
Circ: Diamd. preorders: **22,743**
A: Jeff Smith **W:** Jeff Smith
34 ❑ Dec 1998 Cover: 2.95 **NM** value: **Cover or less**
Circ: Diamd. preorders: **21,429**
A: Jeff Smith **W:** Jeff Smith
35 ❑ Mar 1999 Cover: 2.95 **NM** value: **Cover or less**
Circ: Diamd. preorders: **21,009**
A: Jeff Smith **W:** Jeff Smith
36 ❑ May 1999 Cover: 2.95 **NM** value: **Cover or less**
Circ: Diamd. preorders: **20,458**
A: Jeff Smith **W:** Jeff Smith
37 ❑ Aug 1999 Cover: 2.95 **NM** value: **Cover or less**
Circ: Diamd. preorders: **20,612**
cover says Sep, indicia says Aug. **A:** Jeff Smith **W:** Jeff Smith
38/A❑ Aug 2000 Cover: 4.95 **NM** value: **Cover or less**
Circ: Diamd. preorders: **25,600**
📖 Endgame **A:** Jeff Smith **C:** Jeff Smith **W:** Jeff Smith
38/B❑ Aug 2000 Cover: 4.95 **NM** value: **Cover or less**
alternate cover. 📖 Endgame **A:** Jeff Smith; Frank Miller(cover) **C:** Frank Miller **W:** Jeff Smith
38/C❑ Aug 2000 Cover: 4.95 **NM** value: **Cover or less**
alternate cover. 📖 Endgame **A:** Jeff Smith; Alex Ross(cover) **C:** Alex Ross **W:** Jeff Smith
39 ❑ Oct 2000 Cover: 2.95 **NM** value: **Cover or less**
Circ: Diamd. preorders: **18,179**
📖 Ghost Circles **A:** Jeff Smith **C:** Jeff Smith **W:** Jeff Smith
40 ❑ Jan 2001 Cover: 2.95 **NM** value: **Cover or less**
Circ: Diamd. preorders: **18,524**
A: Jeff Smith **C:** Jeff Smith **W:** Jeff Smith
41 ❑ Mar 2001 Cover: 2.95 **NM** value: **Cover or less**
Circ: Diamd. preorders: **17,573**
📖 The Dusty Trail to Atheia **A:** Jeff Smith **C:** Jeff Smith **W:** Jeff Smith
42 ❑ May 2001 Cover: 2.95 **NM** value: **Cover or less**
Circ: Diamd. preorders: **17,502**
A: Jeff Smith **W:** Jeff Smith
43 ❑ Jul 2001 Cover: 2.95 **NM** value: **Cover or less**
Circ: Diamd. preorders: **17,038**
A: Jeff Smith **W:** Jeff Smith
44 ❑ Sep 2001 Cover: 2.95 **NM** value: **Cover or less**
A: Jeff Smith **W:** Jeff Smith
Bk 1❑ Cover: 12.95 **NM** value: **Cover or less**
• collects Bone #1-6, b&w;Forward by Will Eisner **A:** Jeff Smith **W:** Jeff Smith
Bk 1/HC❑ Aug 1995 Cover: 19.95 **NM** value: **Cover or less**
hardcover. • collects Bone #1-6, b&w;Forward by Will Eisner **A:** Jeff Smith **W:** Jeff Smith
Bk 1/HC-2❑ Cover: 19.95 **NM** value: **Cover or less**
Bk 2❑ Cover: 12.95 **NM** value: **Cover or less**
• collects Bone #7-12 **A:** Jeff Smith **W:** Jeff Smith
Bk 2/HC❑ Sep 1996 Cover: 22.95 **NM** value: **Cover or less**
hardcover. • collects Bone #7-12 **A:** Jeff Smith **W:** Jeff Smith
Bk 2-2❑ Cover: 14.95 **NM** value: **Cover or less**
Bk 3❑ Cover: 12.95 **NM** value: **Cover or less**
• collects Bone #13-18 **A:** Jeff Smith **W:** Jeff Smith
Bk 3/HC❑ **NM** value: **24.95**
hardcover. • collects Bone #13-18
Bk 4❑ Cover: 16.95 **NM** value: **Cover or less**
• collects Bone #20-27 **A:** Jeff Smith **W:** Jeff Smith
Bk 4/HC❑ Cover: 24.95 **NM** value: **Cover or less**
hardcover. • collects Bone #20-27 **A:** Jeff Smith **W:** Jeff Smith
Bk 5❑ b&w Cover: 14.95 **NM** value: **Cover or less**
Bk 5/HC❑ b&w Cover: 22.95 **NM** value: **Cover or less**
hardcover.
SE 1❑ Cover: 2.00 **NM** value: **Cover or less**
• Special edition.

BONES — Malibu

1 ❑ Cover: 1.95 **NM** value: **Cover or less**
2 ❑ Cover: 1.95 **NM** value: **Cover or less**
3 ❑ Cover: 1.95 **NM** value: **Cover or less**
4 ❑ Nov 1987 Cover: 1.95 **NM** value: **Cover or less**

BONE SAW — Tundra

All issues are adults only.
1 ❑ b&w Cover: 14.95 **NM** value: **Cover or less**

BONESHAKER — Caliber

1 ❑ Cover: 3.50 **NM** value: **Cover or less**
A: Phil Hester **W:** Phil Hester

BONE SOURCEBOOK — Image

1/A ❑ Nov 1995, b&w Cover: 2.00 **NM** value: **Cover or less**
no cover price. • promotional handout
1/B ❑ Nov 1995 Cover: 2.00 **NM** value: **Cover or less**
• San Diego Comic-Con edition.

BONEYARD — NBM

2 ❑ **NM** value: **Cover or less**
3 ❑ **NM** value: **Cover or less**
4 ❑ **NM** value: **Cover or less**
5 ❑ **NM** value: **Cover or less**
1 ❑ ca. 2001 Cover: 2.95 **NM** value: **Cover or less**
Circ: Diamd. preorders: **3,550**

BONEYARD PRESS 1993 TOURBOOK — Boneyard

1 ❑ Cover: 1.50 **NM** value: **Cover or less**
• Distributor giveaway previewing Boneyard Press books. **A:** Hart Fisher **W:** Hart Fisher

BONGO SPECIAL EDITION — Bongo

1 ❑ Cover: 20.00 **NM** value: **Cover or less**
hardcover collection of Simpsons #1, Bartman #1, Itchy&Scratchy #1, Radioactive Man #1 (1000 copies).

BOOF AND THE BRUISE CREW — Image

1 ❑ Jul 1994 Cover: 1.95 **NM** value: **Cover or less**
Circ: CapCity orders: **16,650**
1/A ❑ Jul 1994 Cover: 1.95 **NM** value: **Cover or less**
alternate cover.
2 ❑ Aug 1994 Cover: 1.95 **NM** value: **Cover or less**
Circ: CapCity orders: **11,200**
2/A ❑ Aug 1994 Cover: 1.95 **NM** value: **Cover or less**
alternate cover.
3 ❑ Sep 1994 Cover: 1.95 **NM** value: **Cover or less**
Circ: CapCity orders: **9,650**
📖 Shock Treatment; Model Me Beautiful **A:** Tim Harkins **W:** Beau Smith
3/A ❑ Sep 1994 Cover: 1.95 **NM** value: **Cover or less**
alternate cover. 📖 Shock Treatment; Model Me Beautiful **A:** Tim Harkins
4 ❑ Oct 1994 Cover: 1.95 **NM** value: **Cover or less**
Circ: CapCity orders: **7,650**
5 ❑ Nov 1994 Cover: 1.95 **NM** value: **Cover or less**
Circ: CapCity orders: **5,575**
6 ❑ Dec 1994 Cover: 1.95 **NM** value: **Cover or less**
Circ: CapCity orders: **4,350**

BOOF (ICONOGRAFIX) — Iconografix

1 ❑ b&w Cover: 2.50 **NM** value: **Cover or less**

BOOF (IMAGE) — Image

Todd McFarlane, creator of Spawn, was the driving force behind Boof. The series made its debut in July 1994 and featured the title character, a short, fat warrior from the planet Smashmouth. The thoroughly obnoxious Boof is discovered by a small, 10-year-old boy named Nick, while Nick is playing in the yard. Although he becomes friends with Nick, the same can't be said for Nick's dog, Buddy. They take an instant dislike to each other and are constantly at each other's throats. Boof crash-landed on Earth while trying to return to Smashmouth and now needs a place to hide until he can repair his ship.

This title was scripted by Beau Smith and drawn by John Cleary. Boof can also be seen in the companion title Boof and the Bruise Crew.

1 ❑ Jul 1994 Cover: 1.95 **NM** value: **Cover or less**
Circ: CapCity orders: **20,075**
📖 Boof's N' The Hood; The Buddy System **A:** John Cleary ★ 1st Appearance of Boof.
1/A ❑ Jul 1994 Cover: 1.95 **NM** value: **Cover or less**
alternate cover. 📖 Boof's N' The Hood; The Buddy System **A:** John Cleary ★ 1st Appearance of Boof.
2 ❑ Aug 1994 Cover: 1.95 **NM** value: **Cover or less**
Circ: CapCity orders: **12,750**
2/A ❑ Aug 1994 Cover: 1.95 **NM** value: **Cover or less**
alternate cover.
3 ❑ Sep 1994 Cover: 1.95 **NM** value: **Cover or less**
Circ: CapCity orders: **11,400**
📖 Drivin' This Crazy; Chained Heat **A:** John Cleary **W:** Beau Smith
3/A ❑ Sep 1994 Cover: 1.95 **NM** value: **Cover or less**
alternate cover. 📖 Drivin' This Crazy; Chained Heat **A:** John Cleary
4 ❑ Oct 1994 Cover: 1.95 **NM** value: **Cover or less**
Circ: CapCity orders: **9,600**
5 ❑ Nov 1994 Cover: 1.95 **NM** value: **Cover or less**
Circ: CapCity orders: **7,300**
6 ❑ Dec 1994 Cover: 1.95 **NM** value: **Cover or less**
Circ: CapCity orders: **5,800**

BOOGEYMAN (SERGIO ARAGONÉS'...) — Dark Horse

1 ❑ Jun 1998 Cover: 2.95 **NM** value: **Cover or less**
📖 The Dictator **A:** Sergio Aragonés **W:** Mark Evanier
2 ❑ Jul 1998 Cover: 2.95 **NM** value: **Cover or less**
📖 The Great Prime Evil Forest; The Ship of Fear; The King of Crime; Mr. Diggs **A:** Sergio Aragonés **W:** Mark Evanier
3 ❑ Aug 1998 Cover: 2.95 **NM** value: **Cover or less**
📖 The Unknown Man of Magic!; A Monster in the Barn!; Honest Abe; Mr. Diggs **A:** Sergio Aragonés **W:** Mark Evanier
4 ❑ Sep 1998 Cover: 2.95 **NM** value: **Cover or less**
📖 The Great Conquistador; The Dare; The Boogeyman Will Get You! **A:** Sergio Aragonés **W:** Mark Evanier
Bk 1❑ Jun 1999 Cover: 9.95 **NM** value: **Cover or less**
No issue number. • digest-sized.

BOOGIEMAN, THE — Rion

1 ❑ b&w Cover: 1.50 **NM** value: **Cover or less**
📖 The Boogieman; Pumpkin Head **A:** Dan Berger; Jim Pallotta **W:** Dan Berger; Jim Pallotta

BOOK — Dreamsmith Studios

1 ❑ May 1998, b&w Cover: 3.50 **NM** value: **Cover or less**
Circ: Diamd. preorders: **5,144**

BOOK OF ANGELS — Caliber

1 ❑ ca. 1997, b&w Cover: 3.95 **NM** value: **Cover or less**
Circ: Diamd. preorders: **3,800**
No issue number. cardstock cover.

BOOK OF ANTS — Artisan

1 ❑ Cover: 2.95 **NM** value: **Cover or less**
Circ: Diamd. preorders: **4,001**

BOOK OF BALLADS AND SAGAS, THE — Green Man Press

Green Man Press is the publishing house headed by Charles Vess. Best known as the artist working with such outstanding writers as Neil Gaiman (Sandman, Stardust) and Jeff Smith (Rose), Vess also has produced his own series featuring his (black-and-white) interpretations of a number of (mostly British, mostly fantasy-oriented) folksongs. His versions usually put a different spin on the traditional material, as when his "False Knight on the Road" adds a plot element to what is usually simply performed as a "devil's nine questions" type of song.

Additional material includes a continued saga and Vess' commentary on the world of folk music. — Maggie

1 ❑ 1996b&w Cover: 2.95 **NM** value: **Cover or less**
Circ: CapCity orders: **5,510**
2 ❑ 1996b&w Cover: 2.95 **NM** value: **Cover or less**
3 ❑ Jun 1996, b&w Cover: 3.50 **NM** value: **Cover or less**
4 ❑ Dec 1996, b&w Cover: 3.25 **NM** value: **3.50**
Circ: Direct Market orders: **9,594**
Bk 1❑ Cover: 9.95 **NM** value: **Cover or less**
• Ballads;collects Book of Ballads and Sagas #1-4

BOOK OF FATE, THE — DC

1 ❑ Feb 1997 Cover: 2.25 **NM** value: **Cover or less**
Circ: Diamd. preorders: **19,983**
📖 Lament **A:** Ron Wagner **W:** Keith Giffen ★ Origin of Fate, Jared Stevens.
2 ❑ Mar 1997 Cover: 2.25 **NM** value: **Cover or less**
Circ: Diamd. preorders: **15,116**
📖 Carnal Beckoning **A:** Ron Wagner **W:** Keith Giffen ★ Appearance of Sentinel.
3 ❑ Apr 1997 Cover: 2.25 **NM** value: **Cover or less**
Circ: Diamd. preorders: **13,291**
📖 Caught in the Crossfire! **A:** Ron Wagner **W:** Keith Giffen
4 ❑ May 1997 Cover: 2.25 **NM** value: **Cover or less**
Circ: Diamd. preorders: **12,097**
★ Versus Two-Face.
5 ❑ Jun 1997 Cover: 2.25 **NM** value: **Cover or less**
Circ: Diamd. preorders: **11,400**
6 ❑ Jul 1997 Cover: 2.25 **NM** value: **Cover or less**
Circ: Diamd. preorders: **10,719**
📖 Convergence, Part 1 • continues in Night Force #8
7 ❑ Aug 1997 Cover: 2.25 **NM** value: **Cover or less**
Circ: Diamd. preorders: **9,626**
★ Versus Rats.
8 ❑ Sep 1997 Cover: 2.25 **NM** value: **Cover or less**
Circ: Diamd. preorders: **9,190**
9 ❑ Oct 1997 Cover: 2.25 **NM** value: **Cover or less**
Circ: Diamd. preorders: **8,897**
10 ❑ Nov 1997 Cover: 2.25 **NM** value: **Cover or less**
Circ: Diamd. preorders: **8,552**
11 ❑ Dec 1997 Cover: 2.25 **NM** value: **Cover or less**
Circ: Diamd. preorders: **8,334**
Face cover. 📖 The Perception of Doors **A:** Matt Smith **W:** Keith Giffen; Alan Grant
12 ❑ Jan 1998 Cover: 2.50 **NM** value: **Cover or less**
Circ: Diamd. preorders: **8,241**
📖 One Man's Fate final issue. • final issue, A: Lobo **A:** Keith Giffen **W:** Keith Giffen; Alan Grant ★ Appearance of Lobo.

BOOK OF NIGHT, THE — Dark Horse

1 ❑ Jul 1987 Cover: 1.50 **NM** value: **2.50**
A: Charles Vess **W:** Charles Vess
2 ❑ Aug 1987 Cover: 1.50 **NM** value: **2.00**
A: Charles Vess **W:** Charles Vess
3 ❑ Sep 1987 Cover: 1.75 **NM** value: **2.00**
A: Charles Vess **W:** Charles Vess
Bk 1❑ Sep 1991 Cover: 12.95 **NM** value: **Cover or less**
A: Charles Vess **W:** Charles Vess
Bk 1/LE❑ Sep 1991 Cover: 49.95 **NM** value: **Cover or less**
• Limited edition hardcover. **A:** Charles Vess **W:** Charles Vess

BOOK OF SPELLS — Double Edge

This amateurish mini-series offers a confusing mix of sketchy, unfinished art and a storyline cribbed from a variety of classic fantasy adventures like J. R. R. Tolkien's The Lord of the Rings. Bart and Masloc (an intellectual and a rogue, respectively) are time travelers who are on a quest in a nondescript ancient land peopled by the standard group of miscreants, marauders, and monsters of all races and creeds. There are demons to be fought and, of course, plenty of women to be victimized and saved by the intrepid Masloc. Meanwhile, another adventurer named Peter White faces demonic threats of his own but is aided by a powerful ring of life that will allow him to defeat evil wherever it manifests itself. Although the illustration occasionally makes it difficult to tell, there is some adult content, including excessive violence, nudity, and rough language.

1 ❑ Cover: 2.00 **NM** value: **Cover or less**

Other grades: Multiply prices above by **1.5 for Mint • 2/3 for Very Fine • 1/3 for Fine • 1/5 for Very Good • 1/8 for Good**

2 ❑ Sep 1994 Cover: 2.00 **NM** value: **Cover or less**
The Crook **A:** Mark Levine
3 ❑ Cover: 2.00 **NM** value: **Cover or less**
4 ❑ Cover: 2.00 **NM** value: **Cover or less**

BOOK OF THE DAMNED: A HELLRAISER COMPANION (CLIVE BARKER'S...) Marvel / Epic

1 ❑ Cover: 4.95 **NM** value: **Cover or less**
Circ: CapCity orders: **8,900**
2 ❑ Cover: 4.95 **NM** value: **Cover or less**
Circ: CapCity orders: **7,050**
3 ❑ Cover: 4.95 **NM** value: **Cover or less**
Circ: CapCity orders: **5,100**
Journale **A:** Dave McKean; Bill Sienkiewicz; Paul Johnson; Eliot Brown; Tristan Shane; Dan Lawlis; Jorge Zaffino; John Rheaume **W:** Eliot Brown; John Rozum
4 ❑ Cover: 4.95 **NM** value: **Cover or less**
Circ: CapCity orders: **4,650**

BOOK OF THE DEAD Marvel

1 ❑ Dec 1993 Cover: 1.75 **NM** value: **2.00**
Circ: CapCity orders: **8,050**
Frankenstein! **A:** Mike Ploog **W:** Gary Friedrich
2 ❑ Jan 1994 Cover: 1.75 **NM** value: **2.00**
Circ: CapCity orders: **5,450**
3 ❑ Feb 1994 Cover: 1.75 **NM** value: **2.00**
Circ: CapCity orders: **4,400**
4 ❑ Mar 1994 Cover: 1.75 **NM** value: **2.00**
Circ: CapCity orders: **3,750**
Dance To The Murder **A:** Mike Ploog **W:** Steve Gerber

BOOK OF THE SUBGENIUS, THE Simon & Schuster

1 ❑ Cover: 10.95 **NM** value: **Cover or less**
A: J.R. Dobbs **W:** J.R. Dobbs

BOOK OF THE TAROT Caliber / Tome

1 ❑ b&w Cover: 3.95 **NM** value: **Cover or less**
No issue number.

BOOK OF THOTH, THE Circle Studios

1 ❑ Jun 1995 Cover: 2.50 **NM** value: **Cover or less**

BOOKS OF FAERIE, THE DC / Vertigo

Timothy Hunter, the young magician hero of the Books of Magic, has finally learned his true heritage. The people he knew as his parents were truly just his adoptive parents — his real father is the faerie Tamlin, and his mother is Queen Titania of Faerie.

This three-issue mini-series delves further into the past to explore the origins of Titania herself. Once, she was a human girl named Maryrose, who made the mistake of following the faerie lights while gathering wood in the forest. She was taken in by the kindly faerie queen Dymphia, who raised her as a daughter. All was well until Dymphia's husband returned from war and met the girl (now known as Rosebud). In her, he saw the chance for a new bride — as well as the heir he had never been able to sire with Dymphia. Conveniently, Dymphia was put out of the picture, and Rosebud became the new queen Titania. And Timothy Hunter's story is just beginning.

1 ❑ Mar 1997 Cover: 2.50 **NM** value: **Cover or less**
Circ: Diamd. preorders: **33,013**
The Foundling's Tale **A:** Peter Gross **W:** Bronwyn Carlton ★ Origin of Titania. ★ Appearance of Timothy Hunter, Auberon, Titania.
2 ❑ Apr 1997 Cover: 2.50 **NM** value: **Cover or less**
Circ: Diamd. preorders: **26,810**
The Widow's Tale **A:** Peter Gross **W:** Bronwyn Carlton
3 ❑ May 1997 Cover: 2.50 **NM** value: **Cover or less**
Circ: Diamd. preorders: **27,000**
A: Peter Gross **W:** Bronwyn Carlton
Bk 1❑ Cover: 14.95 **NM** value: **Cover or less**
• collects mini-series and Arcana Annual #1

BOOKS OF FAERIE, THE: AUBERON'S TALE DC / Vertigo

1 ❑ Aug 1998 Cover: 2.50 **NM** value: **Cover or less**
Circ: Diamd. preorders: **21,624**
The Regicide **A:** Peter Gross; Vince Locke **W:** Bronwyn Carlton
2 ❑ Sep 1998 Cover: 2.50 **NM** value: **Cover or less**
Circ: Diamd. preorders: **19,209**
The Pretender **A:** Peter Gross; Vince Locke **W:** Bronwyn Carlton
3 ❑ Oct 1998 Cover: 2.50 **NM** value: **Cover or less**
Circ: Diamd. preorders: **18,533**
The Usurper **A:** Peter Gross; Vince Locke **W:** Bronwyn Carlton
Bk 1❑ Cover: 14.95 **NM** value: **Cover or less**
Sturm and the Silver Treasure • Collects series plus stories from Books of Magic #57, 58, The Books of Magic Annual #1 **A:** Mark Buckingham; Peter Gross; Ryan Kelly; Vince Locke **W:** Bronwyn Carlton

BOOKS OF FAERIE, THE: MOLLY'S STORY DC / Vertigo

1 ❑ Sep 1999 Cover: 2.50 **NM** value: **Cover or less**
Circ: Diamd. preorders: **17,849**
Twilight **A:** Hermann Mejia **W:** John Ney Rieber
2 ❑ Oct 1999 Cover: 2.50 **NM** value: **Cover or less**
Circ: Diamd. preorders: **16,229**
Iron and Thorn **A:** Hermann Mejia **W:** John Ney Rieber
3 ❑ Nov 1999 Cover: 2.50 **NM** value: **Cover or less**
Circ: Diamd. preorders: **15,556**
A: Hermann Mejia **W:** John Ney Rieber
4 ❑ Dec 1999 Cover: 2.50 **NM** value: **Cover or less**
Circ: Diamd. preorders: **15,537**
The Importance of Being Evil **A:** Hermann Mejia **W:** John Ney Rieber

BOOKS OF LORE: SPECIAL EDITION Peregrine Entertainment

1 ❑ Cover: 2.95 **NM** value: **Cover or less**
Circ: Diamd. preorders: **6,622**
cardstock cover, b&w.
1/LE❑ Cover: 12.95 **NM** value: **Cover or less**
• Collector's Edition, bagged with poster and limited and regular editions of #1.
2 ❑ Nov 1997 Cover: 2.95 **NM** value: **Cover or less**

BOOKS OF LORE: STORYTELLER Peregrine Entertainment

1 ❑ Cover: 2.95 **NM** value: **Cover or less**

BOOKS OF LORE: THE KAYNIN GAMBIT Peregrine Entertainment

0 ❑ Dec 1998 Cover: 2.95 **NM** value: **Cover or less**
1 ❑ Nov 1998 Cover: 2.95 **NM** value: **Cover or less**
1/SC❑Nov 1998 Cover: 2.95 **NM** value: **Cover or less**
alternate cover.
2 ❑ Jan 1999 Cover: 2.95 **NM** value: **Cover or less**
Circ: Diamd. preorders: **1,095**
3 ❑ Mar 1999 Cover: 2.95 **NM** value: **Cover or less**
Ash 1❑Jul 1998 Cover: 5.00 **NM** value: **Cover or less**
• b&w preview of Books Of Lore: The Kaynin Gambit

BOOKS OF MAGIC, THE (MINI-SERIES) DC

Young Timothy Hunter was just a regular kid-spectacles and all. Little did he know that he also possessed the potential to become the greatest magician since Merlin. But others knew, and they determined to show him his choices in life. Among them were the Phantom Stranger, John Constantine (Hellblazer), Doctor Occult, and Mister E. They appeared to Timothy and took him on a journey to show him what magic was all about. Guided by each of them, Timothy would travel from England to New York, meeting everyone from the Spectre to Madame Xanadu to Doctor Fate...for that matter, every major occult character in the DC universe. Ultimately, Timothy would have to choose his own path, but in the beginning, it starts with a simple question: "Do you believe in magic?"

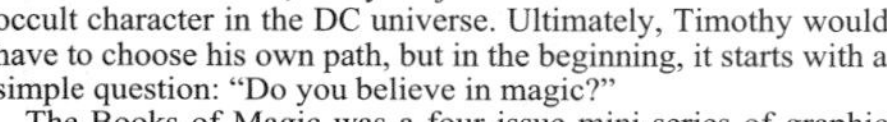

The Books of Magic was a four-issue mini-series of graphic novels graced by the storytelling of Neil Gaiman (Sandman) and stunning painted art by John Bolton.

1 ❑ Dec 1990 Cover: 3.95 **NM** value: **6.00**
Circ: CapCity orders: **22,000**
The Invisible Labyrinth **A:** John Bolton **W:** Neil Gaiman ★ 1st Appearance of Timothy Hunter.
2 ❑ Jan 1991 Cover: 3.95 **NM** value: **5.00**
Circ: CapCity orders: **19,350**
A: John Bolton; Scott Hampton **W:** Neil Gaiman
3 ❑ Feb 1991 Cover: 3.95 **NM** value: **5.00**
Circ: CapCity orders: **17,150**
A: John Bolton; Charles Vess **W:** Neil Gaiman
4 ❑ Mar 1991 Cover: 3.95 **NM** value: **5.00**
Circ: CapCity orders: **17,950**
The Road to Nowhere • Paul Johnson **A:** Paul Johnson **W:** Neil Gaiman
Bk 1❑ Cover: 19.95 **NM** value: **Cover or less**
• Trade Paperback. • Collects issues #1-4 **A:** Paul Johnson **W:** Neil Gaiman

BOOKS OF MAGIC, THE DC / Vertigo

1 ❑ May 1994 Cover: 1.95 **NM** value: **5.00**
Circ: CapCity orders: **21,050** • **CGC:** 1 graded, best 9.2
Bindings, Part 1 **A:** Gary Amaro **W:** John Ney Rieber
1/SI❑ May 1994 Cover: 1.95 **NM** value: **8.00**
• **CGC:** 1 graded, best 9.6
no cover price. • Silver (limited promotional) edition. Bindings, Part 1 **A:** Gary Amaro **W:** John Ney Rieber
2 ❑ Jun 1994 Cover: 1.95 **NM** value: **4.00**
Circ: CapCity orders: **15,800**
Bindings, Part 2 **A:** Gary Amaro **W:** John Ney Rieber
3 ❑ Jul 1994 Cover: 1.95 **NM** value: **4.00**
Circ: CapCity orders: **14,600**
Bindings, Part 3 **W:** John Ney Rieber
4 ❑ Aug 1994 Cover: 1.95 **NM** value: **4.00**
Circ: CapCity orders: **18,050**
Bindings, Part 4 **W:** John Ney Rieber
5 ❑ Sep 1994 Cover: 1.95 **NM** value: **3.00**
Circ: CapCity orders: **16,850**
The Hidden School **A:** Peter Snejbjerg **W:** John Ney Rieber
6 ❑ Oct 1994 Cover: 1.95 **NM** value: **3.00**
Circ: CapCity orders: **17,350**
Sacrifices, Part 1 **A:** Peter Gross **W:** John Ney Rieber
7 ❑ Nov 1994 Cover: 1.95 **NM** value: **3.00**
Circ: CapCity orders: **17,500**
Sacrifices, Part 2 **A:** Peter Gross **W:** John Ney Rieber
8 ❑ Dec 1994 Cover: 1.95 **NM** value: **3.00**
Circ: CapCity orders: **18,100**
Sacrifices, Part 3 **A:** Peter Gross **W:** John Ney Rieber
9 ❑ Jan 1995 Cover: 1.95 **NM** value: **3.00**
Circ: CapCity orders: **17,300**
The Artificial Heart, Part 1 **W:** John Ney Rieber
10 ❑ Feb 1995 Cover: 1.95 **NM** value: **3.00**
Circ: CapCity orders: **16,320**
The Artificial Heart, Part 2 **W:** John Ney Rieber
11 ❑ Mar 1995 Cover: 1.95 **NM** value: **2.50**
Circ: CapCity orders: **15,625**
The Artificial Heart, Part 3 **A:** Gary Amaro **W:** John Ney Rieber
12 ❑ Apr 1995 Cover: 1.95 **NM** value: **2.50**
Circ: CapCity orders: **14,975**
Small Glass Worlds, Part 1 **A:** Peter Snejbjerg **W:** John Ney Rieber
13 ❑ May 1995 Cover: 1.95 **NM** value: **2.50**
Circ: CapCity orders: **14,125**
Small Glass Worlds, Part 2 **A:** Peter Snejbjerg **W:** John Ney Rieber
14 ❑ Jul 1995 Cover: 2.50 **NM** value: **Cover or less**
Circ: CapCity orders: **13,750**
What Fire Leaves Us **A:** Peter Gross **W:** John Ney Rieber
15 ❑ Aug 1995 Cover: 2.50 **NM** value: **Cover or less**
Circ: CapCity orders: **13,950**
Playgrounds, Part 1 **A:** Peter Snejbjerg **W:** John Ney Rieber
16 ❑ Sep 1995 Cover: 2.50 **NM** value: **Cover or less**
Circ: CapCity orders: **12,925**
Playgrounds, Part 2 **A:** Peter Snejbjerg **W:** John Ney Rieber
17 ❑ Oct 1995 Cover: 2.50 **NM** value: **Cover or less**
Circ: CapCity orders: **11,375**
W: John Ney Rieber
18 ❑ Nov 1995 Cover: 2.50 **NM** value: **Cover or less**
W: John Ney Rieber
19 ❑ Dec 1995 Cover: 2.50 **NM** value: **Cover or less**
W: John Ney Rieber
20 ❑ Jan 1996 Cover: 2.50 **NM** value: **Cover or less**
W: John Ney Rieber
21 ❑ Feb 1996 Cover: 2.50 **NM** value: **Cover or less**
Heavy Petting **A:** Peter Gross **W:** John Ney Rieber
22 ❑ Mar 1996 Cover: 2.50 **NM** value: **Cover or less**
Needlepoint **A:** Peter Gross **W:** John Ney Rieber
23 ❑ Apr 1996 Cover: 2.50 **NM** value: **Cover or less**
Red Rover, Red Rover **A:** Peter Gross **W:** John Ney Rieber
24 ❑ May 1996 Cover: 2.50 **NM** value: **Cover or less**
W: John Ney Rieber
25 ❑ Jun 1996 Cover: 2.50 **NM** value: **Cover or less**
W: John Ney Rieber ★ Appearance of appearance. ★ Appearance of appearance.
26 ❑ Jul 1996 Cover: 2.50 **NM** value: **Cover or less**
Rites of Passage **A:** Peter Gross **W:** John Ney Rieber
27 ❑ Aug 1996 Cover: 2.50 **NM** value: **Cover or less**
Rites of Passage; Rites of Passage, Part 1 **W:** John Ney Rieber
28 ❑ Sep 1996 Cover: 2.50 **NM** value: **Cover or less**
Rites of Passage; Rites of Passage, Part 2 **W:** John Ney Rieber
29 ❑ Oct 1996 Cover: 2.50 **NM** value: **Cover or less**
Rites of Passage; Rites of Passage, Part 3 **A:** Peter Snejbjerg; Peter Gross **W:** John Ney Rieber
30 ❑ Nov 1996 Cover: 2.50 **NM** value: **Cover or less**
Circ: Diamd. preorders: **30,757**
Rites of Passage; Rites of Passage, Part 4 **A:** Peter Snejbjerg; Peter Gross **W:** John Ney Rieber
31 ❑ Dec 1996 Cover: 2.50 **NM** value: **Cover or less**
Circ: Direct Market orders: **30,806**
Rites of Passage; Rites of Passage, Part 5 **A:** Peter Snejbjerg **W:** John Ney Rieber
32 ❑ Jan 1997 Cover: 2.50 **NM** value: **Cover or less**
Circ: Direct Market orders: **29,673**
Rites of Passage; Rites of Passage, Part 6 **A:** Peter Snejbjerg **W:** John Ney Rieber
33 ❑ Feb 1997 Cover: 2.50 **NM** value: **Cover or less**
Circ: Diamd. preorders: **28,939**
Rites of Passage; Rites of Passage, Part 7 **A:** Peter Snejbjerg **W:** John Ney Rieber
34 ❑ Mar 1997 Cover: 2.50 **NM** value: **Cover or less**
Circ: Diamd. preorders: **28,708**
Rites of Passage; Rites of Passage, Part 8 **A:** Peter Snejbjerg **W:** John Ney Rieber
35 ❑ Apr 1997 Cover: 2.50 **NM** value: **Cover or less**
Circ: Diamd. preorders: **27,790**
Rites of Passage; Rites of Passage, Part 9 **A:** Peter Snejbjerg **W:** John Ney Rieber
36 ❑ May 1997 Cover: 2.50 **NM** value: **Cover or less**
Circ: Diamd. preorders: **27,730**
Rites of Passage; Rites of Passage, Part 10 **A:** Peter Snejbjerg **W:** John Ney Rieber
37 ❑ Jun 1997 Cover: 2.50 **NM** value: **Cover or less**
Circ: Diamd. preorders: **27,353**
Rites of Passage; Rites of Passage, Part 11 **A:** Peter Snejbjerg **W:** John Ney Rieber
38 ❑ Jul 1997 Cover: 2.50 **NM** value: **Cover or less**
Circ: Diamd. preorders: **26,226**
Rites of Passage
39 ❑ Aug 1997 Cover: 2.50 **NM** value: **Cover or less**
Circ: Diamd. preorders: **26,336**
40 ❑ Sep 1997 Cover: 2.50 **NM** value: **Cover or less**
Circ: Diamd. preorders: **25,188**
41 ❑ Oct 1997 Cover: 2.50 **NM** value: **Cover or less**
Circ: Diamd. preorders: **24,844**
42 ❑ Nov 1997 Cover: 2.50 **NM** value: **Cover or less**
Circ: Diamd. preorders: **24,382**
The Bridge **A:** Jill Thompson **W:** John Ney Rieber
43 ❑ Dec 1997 Cover: 2.50 **NM** value: **Cover or less**
Circ: Diamd. preorders: **24,107**
King of This **A:** Peter Gross **W:** John Ney Rieber
44 ❑ Jan 1998 Cover: 2.50 **NM** value: **Cover or less**
Circ: Diamd. preorders: **23,753**
45 ❑ Feb 1998 Cover: 2.50 **NM** value: **Cover or less**
Circ: Diamd. preorders: **23,218**
Slave of Heavens, Part 1 **W:** John Ney Rieber
46 ❑ Mar 1998 Cover: 2.50 **NM** value: **Cover or less**
Circ: Diamd. preorders: **22,406**
Slave of Heavens, Part 2 **W:** John Ney Rieber

CGC-graded: Multiply prices above by **33 for 9.9 M • 16 for 9.8 NM/M • 7 for 9.6 NM+ • 5 for 9.4 NM • 2.5 for 9.2 NM- • 1.5 for 9.0 VF/NM**

47 ❑ Apr 1998 Cover: 2.50 **NM** value: **Cover or less**
Circ: Diamd. preorders: **21,627**
🕮 Slave of Heavens, Part 3 **A:** Peter Gross; Temujin **W:** John Ney Rieber

48 ❑ May 1998 Cover: 2.50 **NM** value: **Cover or less**
Circ: Diamd. preorders: **21,462**
🕮 Slave of Heavens, Part 4 **W:** John Ney Rieber

49 ❑ Jun 1998 Cover: 2.50 **NM** value: **Cover or less**
Circ: Diamd. preorders: **21,721**
🕮 Slave of Heavens Conclusion **W:** John Ney Rieber

50 ❑ Jul 1998 Cover: 2.50 **NM** value: **Cover or less**
Circ: Diamd. preorders: **23,629**
• preview of issue #51

51 ❑ Aug 1998 Cover: 2.50 **NM** value: **Cover or less**
Circ: Diamd. preorders: **21,391**
🕮 A Thousand Worlds of Tim

52 ❑ Sep 1998 Cover: 2.50 **NM** value: **Cover or less**
Circ: Diamd. preorders: **20,042**

53 ❑ Oct 1998 Cover: 2.50 **NM** value: **Cover or less**
Circ: Diamd. preorders: **19,691**

54 ❑ Nov 1998 Cover: 2.50 **NM** value: **Cover or less**
Circ: Diamd. preorders: **19,412**

55 ❑ Dec 1998 Cover: 2.50 **NM** value: **Cover or less**
Circ: Diamd. preorders: **19,141**
A: Linda Medley

56 ❑ Jan 1999 Cover: 2.50 **NM** value: **Cover or less**
Circ: Diamd. preorders: **18,670**
★ Appearance of Cain.

57 ❑ Feb 1999 Cover: 2.50 **NM** value: **Cover or less**
Circ: Diamd. preorders: **18,086**
• Books of Faerie back-up **A:** Peter Gross; Ryan Kelly **W:** Peter Gross; Bronwyn Carlton

58 ❑ Mar 1999 Cover: 2.50 **NM** value: **Cover or less**
Circ: Diamd. preorders: **18,032**
🕮 Books of Faerie: Auberon Finds a Friend • Books of Faerie back-up **A:** Peter Gross; Cecilia Mejia **W:** Peter Gross; Bronwyn Carlton

59 ❑ Apr 1999 Cover: 2.50 **NM** value: **Cover or less**
Circ: Diamd. preorders: **17,276**
🕮 Books of Faerie: The Kelpie's Love • Books of Faerie back-up **A:** Peter Gross **W:** Peter Gross; Bronwyn Carlton

60 ❑ May 1999 Cover: 2.50 **NM** value: **Cover or less**
Circ: Diamd. preorders: **17,342**
🕮 In Defense of his Country **A:** Peter Gross **W:** Peter Gross

61 ❑ Jun 1999 Cover: 2.50 **NM** value: **Cover or less**
Circ: Diamd. preorders: **17,657**
🕮 All Things Timothy **A:** Peter Gross **W:** Peter Gross

62 ❑ Jul 1999 Cover: 2.50 **NM** value: **Cover or less**
Circ: Diamd. preorders: **17,367**
🕮 Wrong Side of the Tracks • Books of Faerie back-up **A:** Peter Gross; Ryan Kelly **W:** Peter Gross

63 ❑ Aug 1999 Cover: 2.50 **NM** value: **Cover or less**
Circ: Diamd. preorders: **17,002**
🕮 The Good Fella **A:** Gary Amaro **W:** Peter Hogan

64 ❑ Sep 1999 Cover: 2.50 **NM** value: **Cover or less**
Circ: Diamd. preorders: **17,241**
🕮 Heart of the Storm **A:** Peter Gross **W:** Peter Gross

65 ❑ Oct 1999 Cover: 2.50 **NM** value: **Cover or less**
Circ: Diamd. preorders: **16,837**
🕮 The Arrangement **A:** Peter Gross **W:** Peter Gross

66 ❑ Nov 1999 Cover: 2.50 **NM** value: **Cover or less**
Circ: Diamd. preorders: **16,549**
🕮 A Day A Night A Dream; A Day, a Night & a Dream, Part 1 **A:** Peter Gross **W:** Peter Gross

67 ❑ Dec 1999 Cover: 2.50 **NM** value: **Cover or less**
Circ: Diamd. preorders: **16,808**
🕮 A Day, a Night & a Dream, Part 2 **A:** Peter Gross **W:** Peter Gross

68 ❑ Jan 2000 Cover: 2.50 **NM** value: **Cover or less**
Circ: Diamd. preorders: **16,195**
🕮 Pentimento **A:** Peter Gross; Ryan Kelly **W:** Peter Gross

69 ❑ Feb 2000 Cover: 2.50 **NM** value: **Cover or less**
Circ: Diamd. preorders: **15,858**
🕮 Cauldrons & Kettles **A:** Peter Gross **W:** Peter Gross

70 ❑ Mar 2000 Cover: 2.50 **NM** value: **Cover or less**
Circ: Diamd. preorders: **15,716**

71 ❑ Apr 2000 Cover: 2.50 **NM** value: **Cover or less**
Circ: Diamd. preorders: **14,926**

72 ❑ May 2000 Cover: 2.50 **NM** value: **Cover or less**
Circ: Diamd. preorders: **15,322**
🕮 The Lord of the Hunt **A:** John Ridgway **W:** Peter Gross

73 ❑ Jun 2000 Cover: 2.50 **NM** value: **Cover or less**
Circ: Diamd. preorders: **15,062**
🕮 The Closing, Part 1 **A:** Peter Gross **W:** Peter Gross

Anl 1❑ Feb 1997 Cover: 3.95 **NM** value: **Cover or less**
Circ: Diamd. preorders: **27,084**
• 1997 Annual

Anl 2❑ Feb 1998 Cover: 3.95 **NM** value: **Cover or less**
Circ: Diamd. preorders: **20,723**
🕮 Horn • 1998 Annual **A:** Jamie Tolagson **W:** John Ney Rieber

Anl 3❑ Jun 1999 Cover: 3.95 **NM** value: **Cover or less**
Circ: Diamd. preorders: **16,042**
🕮 The Thousand Deaths of Timothy Hunter • 1999 Annual **A:** Kelley Jones; Peter Gross **W:** Peter Gross

Bk 1❑ Cover: 12.95 **NM** value: **Cover or less**
• Trade Paperback. 🕮 I: The Invisible Labyrinth; II: The Shadow World; III: The Land Of Summer's Twilight; IV: The Road To Nowhere • Bindings;collects The Books of Magic #1-4 **A:** Gary Amaro **W:** John Ney Rieber

Bk 2❑ Cover: 17.50 **NM** value: **Cover or less**
• Trade Paperback. • Summonings;collects The Books of Magic #5-13 and Vertigo Rave #1 **W:** John Ney Rieber

Bk 3❑ Cover: 12.95 **NM** value: **Cover or less**
• Trade Paperback. • Reckonings;Collects The Books of Magic #14-20 **W:** John Ney Rieber

Bk 4❑ Cover: 12.95 **NM** value: **Cover or less**
• Trade Paperback. • Transformations;Collects The Books of Magic #21-25 **W:** John Ney Rieber

Bk 5❑ Cover: 14.95 **NM** value: **Cover or less**
• Girl in the Box;collects The Books of Magic #26-32 **A:** Peter Snejbjerg; Peter Gross **W:** John Ney Rieber

BOOM BOOM — Aeon

1 ❑ b&w Cover: 2.50 **NM** value: **Cover or less**
2 ❑ Sep 1994, b&w Cover: 2.50 **NM** value: **Cover or less**

BOONDOGGLE — Knight Press

1 ❑ Mar 1995 Cover: 2.95 **NM** value: **Cover or less**
A: Steve Steglin **W:** Steve Steglin

2 ❑ Cover: 2.95 **NM** value: **Cover or less**
A: Steve Steglin **W:** Steve Steglin

3 ❑ Nov 1995 Cover: 2.95 **NM** value: **Cover or less**
A: Steve Steglin **W:** Steve Steglin

4 ❑ Cover: 2.95 **NM** value: **Cover or less**
A: Steve Steglin **W:** Steve Steglin

SE 1❑ Nov 1996, b&w Cover: 2.95 **NM** value: **Cover or less**
🕮 Here Today Gone Tomorrow **A:** Steve Steglin **W:** Steve Steglin

BOOSTER GOLD — DC

He's a powerful super-hero who can outrun and outfight evil villains with the best of them. Booster also has a good agent — which, in our highly commercialized world, gives Booster the biggest headlines and makes him millions of dollars. Booster sells his likeness to advertising, lunch boxes, and multi-million dollar movie projects. As a result, he enjoys a membership at an exclusive health club, has his own chauffeured limousine, and more fame and glory than Metropolis' other super-hero, Superman.

Who said there was no money to be made in public service?

1 ❑ Feb 1986 Cover: 0.75 **NM** value: **1.25**
Circ: CapCity orders: **13,800**
A: Dan Jurgens ★ 1st Appearance of Booster Gold. ★ Versus Blackguard.

2 ❑ Mar 1986 Cover: 0.75 **NM** value: **1.00**
Circ: CapCity orders: **10,400**
A: Dan Jurgens ★ 1st Appearance of Mindancer.

3 ❑ Apr 1986 Cover: 0.75 **NM** value: **1.00**
Circ: CapCity orders: **10,250**
🕮 The Night Has Two Thousand Eyes **A:** Dan Jurgens

4 ❑ May 1986 Cover: 0.75 **NM** value: **1.00**
Circ: CapCity orders: **10,050**
A: Dan Jurgens

5 ❑ Jun 1986 Cover: 0.75 **NM** value: **1.00**
Circ: CapCity orders: **8,700**
A: Dan Jurgens

6 ❑ Jul 1986 Cover: 0.75 **NM** value: **1.00**
Circ: CapCity orders: **8,950**
A: Dan Jurgens ★ Appearance of Superman.

7 ❑ Aug 1986 Cover: 0.75 **NM** value: **1.00**
Circ: CapCity orders: **8,700**
A: Dan Jurgens ★ Appearance of Superman.

8 ❑ Sep 1986 Cover: 0.75 **NM** value: **1.00**
Circ: CapCity orders: **8,850**
A: Dan Jurgens ★ Appearance of Legion.

9 ❑ Oct 1986 Cover: 0.75 **NM** value: **1.00**
Circ: CapCity orders: **8,650**
A: Dan Jurgens ★ Appearance of Legion.

10 ❑ Nov 1986 Cover: 0.75 **NM** value: **1.00**
Circ: CapCity orders: **8,800**
A: Dan Jurgens

11 ❑ Dec 1986 Cover: 0.75 **NM** value: **1.00**
Circ: CapCity orders: **8,750**
A: Dan Jurgens

12 ❑ Jan 1987 Cover: 0.75 **NM** value: **1.00**
Circ: CapCity orders: **8,250**
A: Dan Jurgens

13 ❑ Feb 1987 Cover: 0.75 **NM** value: **1.00**
Circ: CapCity orders: **8,750**
A: Dan Jurgens

14 ❑ Mar 1987 Cover: 0.75 **NM** value: **1.00**
Circ: CapCity orders: **8,200**
• back to future **A:** Dan Jurgens

15 ❑ Apr 1987 Cover: 0.75 **NM** value: **1.00**
Circ: CapCity orders: **7,950**
A: Dan Jurgens

16 ❑ May 1987 Cover: 0.75 **NM** value: **1.00**
Circ: CapCity orders: **7,400**
A: Dan Jurgens ★ 1st Appearance of Booster Gold International.

17 ❑ Jun 1987 Cover: 0.75 **NM** value: **1.00**
Circ: CapCity orders: **7,500**
A: Dan Jurgens ★ Appearance of CheshireHawk.

18 ❑ Jul 1987 Cover: 0.75 **NM** value: **1.00**
Circ: CapCity orders: **7,600**
A: Dan Jurgens

19 ❑ Aug 1987 Cover: 0.75 **NM** value: **1.00**
Circ: CapCity orders: **8,350**
A: Dan Jurgens ★ Versus Rainbow Raider.

20 ❑ Sep 1987 Cover: 0.75 **NM** value: **1.00**
Circ: CapCity orders: **8,750**
• blind **A:** Dan Jurgens

21 ❑ Oct 1987 Cover: 0.75 **NM** value: **1.00**
Circ: CapCity orders: **8,850**
A: Dan Jurgens

22 ❑ Nov 1987 Cover: 1.00 **NM** value: **Cover or less**
Circ: CapCity orders: **10,450**
A: Dan Jurgens ★ Appearance of Justice League International.

23 ❑ Dec 1987 Cover: 1.00 **NM** value: **Cover or less**
Circ: CapCity orders: **11,100**
A: Dan Jurgens ★ Appearance of Superman.

24 ❑ Jan 1988 Cover: 1.00 **NM** value: **Cover or less**
Circ: CapCity orders: **14,450**
🕮 Millennium • Millennium **A:** Dan Jurgens

25 ❑ Feb 1988 Cover: 1.00 **NM** value: **Cover or less**
Circ: CapCity orders: **15,500**
final issue. • Millennium;Millennium, final issue **A:** Dan Jurgens

BOOTS OF THE OPPRESSOR — Northstar

1 ❑ Cover: 2.95 **NM** value: **Cover or less**

BORDERGUARD — Eternity

1 ❑ Nov 1987 Cover: 1.95 **NM** value: **Cover or less**
🕮 Borderguard, Part 1 **A:** Albert Val **W:** C. J. Henderson; Peter Palmer

2 ❑ Dec 1987 Cover: 1.95 **NM** value: **Cover or less**
🕮 Borderguard, Part 2 **A:** Albert Val **W:** C. J. Henderson; Peter Palmer

BORDER PATROL — P.L. Publishing

1 ❑ Jun 1951 Cover: 0.10 **NM** value: **50.00**
• **CGC:** 1 graded, best 6.5

BORDER WORLDS (VOL. 1) — Kitchen Sink

1 ❑ Jul 1986 Cover: 1.95 **NM** value: **2.00**
🕮 Living In A Space Suit • Reprinted from Megaton Man **A:** Donald Simpson **W:** Donald Simpson

2 ❑ Sep 1986 Cover: 1.95 **NM** value: **2.00**
🕮 Empress Of China **A:** Donald Simpson **W:** Donald Simpson

3 ❑ Nov 1986 Cover: 1.95 **NM** value: **2.00**
🕮 View From the Edge **A:** Donald Simpson **W:** Donald Simpson

4 ❑ Jan 1987 Cover: 1.95 **NM** value: **2.00**
A: Donald Simpson **W:** Donald Simpson

5 ❑ Apr 1987 Cover: 1.95 **NM** value: **2.00**
🕮 Differing World Views **A:** Donald Simpson **W:** Donald Simpson

6 ❑ Jun 1987 Cover: 1.95 **NM** value: **2.00**
A: Donald Simpson **W:** Donald Simpson

7 ❑ Aug 1987 Cover: 2.00 **NM** value: **Cover or less**
final issue. • pages 4-5 transposed **A:** Donald Simpson **W:** Donald Simpson

7/A ❑ Cover: 2.00 **NM** value: **Cover or less**
• Corrected edition. final issue. • corrected **A:** Donald Simpson **W:** Donald Simpson

BORDER WORLDS (VOL. 2) — Kitchen Sink

All issues are adults only.

1 ❑ b&w Cover: 2.00 **NM** value: **Cover or less**
🕮 Marooned **A:** Donald Simpson **W:** Donald Simpson

BORIS' ADVENTURE MAGAZINE — Nicotat

1 ❑ Aug 1988, b&w Cover: 2.00 **NM** value: **Cover or less**

BORIS KARLOFF TALES OF MYSTERY — Gold Key

3 ❑ Apr 1963 Cover: 0.12 **NM** value: **24.00**
• **CGC:** 1 graded, best 8.0

4 ❑ Jul 1963 Cover: 0.12 **NM** value: **20.00**
• **CGC:** 1 graded, best 7.5

5 ❑ Oct 1963 Cover: 0.12 **NM** value: **20.00**
🕮 The Sorcerer's Potion; Possessed; The Master's Touch (text story); A Cage for Hassan; The Enigma of Shanti Devi

6 ❑ Jan 1964 Cover: 0.12 **NM** value: **20.00**
• **CGC:** 1 graded, best 9.0

7 ❑ Sep 1964 Cover: 0.12 **NM** value: **18.00**
• **CGC:** 1 graded, best 8.0

8 ❑ Dec 1965 Cover: 0.12 **NM** value: **18.00**

9 ❑ Mar 1965 Cover: 0.12 **NM** value: **30.00**
A: Wally Wood

10 ❑ Jun 1965 Cover: 0.12 **NM** value: **15.00**
• **CGC:** 1 graded, best 9.0

11 ❑ Sep 1965 Cover: 0.12 **NM** value: **22.00**

12 ❑ Dec 1965 Cover: 0.12 **NM** value: **15.00**
• **CGC:** 1 graded, best 9.0
back cover pin-up. 🕮 The Convention; The Dunce; Mr. Memory; The Barbados Coffins (text story); The Auction

13 ❑ Mar 1966 Cover: 0.12 **NM** value: **12.00**
🕮 The Five Casks of Greed; The Door of Doom!; The Haunted Tanker (text story); The Man Who Lived in Yesterday

14 ❑ Jun 1966 Cover: 0.12 **NM** value: **12.00**
🕮 The Black Stallion of York; The Phone to the Past; Heart's Desire; The Room that Never Grew Old; Text page "The Mystery of Patience Worth"; Murder in Marble; Day of Darkness

15 ❑ Sep 1966 Cover: 0.12 **NM** value: **15.00**
🕮 Captives of the Camera; The Phantom Rescue (text story); The Evil Eye; The Rainmaker; The Building that Came to Life

16 ❑ Dec 1966 Cover: 0.12 **NM** value: **12.00**
17 ❑ Mar 1967 Cover: 0.12 **NM** value: **12.00**
18 ❑ Jun 1967 Cover: 0.12 **NM** value: **12.00**
19 ❑ Sep 1967 Cover: 0.12 **NM** value: **12.00**
20 ❑ Dec 1967 Cover: 0.12 **NM** value: **12.00**
🕮 The Medium; Death and Napoleon's Marshal (text story); Mysteries Beyond the Grave; The Death Bell; The Sleeping Dragon

21 ❑ Mar 1968 Cover: 0.12 **NM** value: **18.00**
🕮 Screaming Skull **A:** Jeff Jones

22 ❑ Jun 1968 Cover: 0.12 **NM** value: **10.00**
• **CGC:** 1 graded, best 9.4

23 ❑ Sep 1968 Cover: 0.15 **NM** value: **10.00**
🕮 Past and Present Danger; Burn, Witch, Burn; The Crystal Ball; The Dream • 10053-809

24 ❑ Dec 1968 Cover: 0.15 **NM** value: **10.00**
25 ❑ Mar 1969 Cover: 0.15 **NM** value: **10.00**
🕮 The Thing Called Illona; The Strangling Pearls (text story); Behemoth; The Metamorphs; Death is the Hunter

26 ❑ Jun 1969 Cover: 0.15 **NM** value: **10.00**
27 ❑ Sep 1969 Cover: 0.15 **NM** value: **10.00**
🕮 Fantasties of the Fog; The Horror in the Velvet Mask (text story); Beware the Angry Lighthouse; Mind Monster

28 ❑ Dec 1969 Cover: 0.15 **NM** value: **10.00**
🕮 Creature of the Swamp; Son of Satan (text story); Golden Seaweed; When Children Speak; Monster Mountain

29 ❑ Feb 1970 Cover: 0.15 **NM** value: **10.00**
30 ❑ May 1970 Cover: 0.15 **NM** value: **10.00**
🕮 The Grotesque One; The Living Skeleton (text story); The Farmer Takes an Ad; Produce Me a Monster

Other grades: Multiply prices above by **1.5 for Mint • 2/3 for Very Fine • 1/3 for Fine • 1/5 for Very Good • 1/8 for Good**

31 ❑ Aug 1970 Cover: 0.15 **NM** value: **8.50**
• **CGC:** 1 graded, best 9.4
32 ❑ Nov 1970 Cover: 0.15 **NM** value: **8.50**
• **CGC:** 1 graded, best 9.6
The Eyes of the Monster; The Cobra God (text story); Satan's Highway; The Goddess of Greed; They Came From the Deep!
33 ❑ Cover: 0.15 **NM** value: **8.50**
34 ❑ Apr 1971 Cover: 0.15 **NM** value: **8.50**
• **CGC:** 2 graded, best 9.8
35 ❑ ca. 1971 Cover: 0.15 **NM** value: **8.50**
36 ❑ Cover: 0.15 **NM** value: **8.50**
37 ❑ Cover: 0.15 **NM** value: **8.50**
38 ❑ Cover: 0.15 **NM** value: **8.50**
39 ❑ Cover: 0.15 **NM** value: **8.50**
40 ❑ Cover: 0.15 **NM** value: **8.50**
41 ❑ Cover: 0.15 **NM** value: **7.50**
42 ❑ ca. 1972 Cover: 0.15 **NM** value: **7.50**
43 ❑ Cover: 0.15 **NM** value: **7.50**
44 ❑ Cover: 0.15 **NM** value: **7.50**
45 ❑ Cover: 0.15 **NM** value: **7.50**
46 ❑ ca. 1973 Cover: 0.15 **NM** value: **7.50**
47 ❑ Jun 1973 Cover: 0.20 **NM** value: **7.50**
48 ❑ Jul 1973 Cover: 0.20 **NM** value: **7.50**
49 ❑ Aug 1973 Cover: 0.20 **NM** value: **7.50**
Blind to Danger; Royal Madness (text story); Daddy's Little Pet; The Yeti Will Get You!; The Hitchhiker • 90053-308
50 ❑ Cover: 0.20 **NM** value: **7.50**
51 ❑ Cover: 0.20 **NM** value: **6.00**
52 ❑ Cover: 0.20 **NM** value: **6.00**
53 ❑ ca. 1974 Cover: 0.20 **NM** value: **6.00**
Molten Fury; Tender Feelings; The Bronco Buster; The Forest Of Evil **A:** Boris Karloff **W:** Boris Karloff
54 ❑ ca. 1974 **NM** value: **6.00**
55 ❑ ca. 1974 Cover: 0.25 **NM** value: **6.00**
56 ❑ ca. 1974 Cover: 0.25 **NM** value: **6.00**
Grandpa's Tall Tales; Text page on "Pibloktoq"; Shadow of a Monster; Forbidden Fruit; A Jagged Orbit
57 ❑ ca. 1974 Cover: 0.25 **NM** value: **6.00**
58 ❑ ca. 1974 Cover: 0.25 **NM** value: **6.00**
59 ❑ Cover: 0.25 **NM** value: **6.00**
60 ❑ Apr 1975 Cover: 0.25 **NM** value: **5.00**
61 ❑ ca. 1975 Cover: 0.25 **NM** value: **5.00**
62 ❑ ca. 1975 Cover: 0.25 **NM** value: **5.00**
63 ❑ ca. 1975 Cover: 0.25 **NM** value: **5.00**
64 ❑ ca. 1975 Cover: 0.25 **NM** value: **5.00**
65 ❑ Cover: 0.25 **NM** value: **5.00**
The Pharaoh's Zoo; No Thing is My Enemy; The Mail-Order Monster; Don't Put it on Paper
66 ❑ Cover: 0.25 **NM** value: **5.00**
67 ❑ Cover: 0.25 **NM** value: **5.00**
68 ❑ Jun 1976 **NM** value: **5.00**
69 ❑ ca. 1976 **NM** value: **5.00**
70 ❑ Sep 1976 Cover: 0.30 **NM** value: **5.00**
71 ❑ ca. 1976 Cover: 0.30 **NM** value: **5.00**
72 ❑ Dec 1976 Cover: 0.30 **NM** value: **5.00**
73 ❑ ca. 1977 Cover: 0.30 **NM** value: **5.00**
74 ❑ Apr 1977 Cover: 0.30 **NM** value: **5.00**
75 ❑ ca. 1977 Cover: 0.30 **NM** value: **3.00**
76 ❑ ca. 1977 Cover: 0.30 **NM** value: **3.00**
77 ❑ ca. 1977 Cover: 0.30 **NM** value: **3.00**
78 ❑ Oct 1977 Cover: 0.30 **NM** value: **3.00**
79 ❑ **NM** value: **3.00**
80 ❑ **NM** value: **3.00**
81 ❑ ca. 1978 **NM** value: **3.00**
82 ❑ ca. 1978 Cover: 0.50 **NM** value: **3.00**
83 ❑ ca. 1978 Cover: 0.50 **NM** value: **3.00**
84 ❑ ca. 1978 **NM** value: **3.00**
85 ❑ ca. 1978 **NM** value: **3.00**
86 ❑ ca. 1978 **NM** value: **3.00**
87 ❑ ca. 1978 **NM** value: **3.00**
88 ❑ **NM** value: **3.00**
89 ❑ Feb 1979 Cover: 0.35 **NM** value: **3.00**
A World in the Making; Afraid of His Own Shadow; A Strange Sense of Humor
90 ❑ ca. 1979 Cover: 0.35 **NM** value: **3.00**
91 ❑ May 1979 **NM** value: **3.00**
92 ❑ ca. 1979 **NM** value: **3.00**
93 ❑ ca. 1979 **NM** value: **3.00**
94 ❑ ca. 1979 **NM** value: **3.00**
95 ❑ Oct 1979 **NM** value: **3.00**
96 ❑ **NM** value: **3.00**
97 ❑ Feb 1980 **NM** value: **3.00**
final issue.

BORIS KARLOFF THRILLER — Gold Key

1 ❑ Oct 1962 Cover: 0.12 **NM** value: **50.00**
• **CGC:** 4 graded, best 9.2
2 ❑ Jan 1963 Cover: 0.12 **NM** value: **35.00**

BORIS THE BEAR — Dark Horse

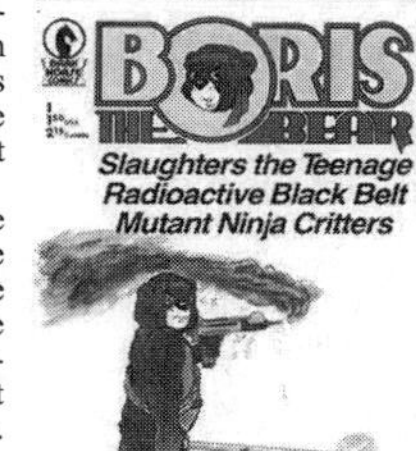

Boris is a comics-collecting teddy bear who lives in a tree fort in his boy, David's, back yard. But this cute little animal isn't like all the others in the funny books: He's got an attitude — and an Uzi.

Once upon a time, critters like the Teenage Mutant Ninja Turtles were recognized as satirical; now, these mutant funny animals have become a genre unto themselves. Boris decides it's time to put things straight — with as much violence as possible.

James Dean Smith's Boris the Bear (with writing assists from Mike Richardson and Randy Stradley) is hilarious, self-effacing, and (of course) more than a little twisted. Those who have become numbed from comic book overload may find this title will sensitize them again. This was one of Dark Horse's earliest titles.

1 ❑ ca. 1986, b&w Cover: 1.50 **NM** value: **3.00**
• **CGC:** 1 graded, best 9.6
Boris The Bear Slaughters The Teenage Radioactive Black Belt Mutant Ninja Critters **A:** James Dean Smith **W:** James Dean Smith; Mike Richardson; Randy Stradley
1-2 ❑ b&w Cover: 1.50 **NM** value: **1.75**
2 ❑ b&w Cover: 1.50 **NM** value: **2.25**
3 ❑ b&w Cover: 1.50 **NM** value: **2.50**
The Secret Hero Of The Super Wars **A:** James Dean Smith **W:** James Dean Smith; Mike Richardson; Randy Stradley
4 ❑ b&w Cover: 1.50 **NM** value: **2.50**
two different covers.
5 ❑ b&w Cover: 1.50 **NM** value: **2.50**
6 ❑ b&w Cover: 1.50 **NM** value: **2.50**
7 ❑ b&w Cover: 1.50 **NM** value: **2.25**
8 ❑ b&w Cover: 1.50 **NM** value: **2.25**
The Return Of The Living Teenage Radioactive Mutant Ninja Critters **A:** James Dean Smith **W:** Mike Richardson
9 ❑ b&w Cover: 1.50 **NM** value: **2.25**
10 ❑ May 1987, b&w Cover: 1.50 **NM** value: **2.25**
11 ❑ Jun 1987, b&w Cover: 1.50 **NM** value: **2.25**
12 ❑ Jul 1987, b&w Cover: 1.75 **NM** value: **2.25**
13 ❑ Nov 1987, b&w Cover: 1.50 **NM** value: **2.25**
14 ❑ Dec 1987, b&w Cover: 1.50 **NM** value: **2.25**
15 ❑ ca. 1988, b&w Cover: 1.50 **NM** value: **2.25**
16 ❑ Mar 1988, b&w Cover: 1.50 **NM** value: **2.25**
17 ❑ ca. 1988, b&w Cover: 1.50 **NM** value: **2.25**
18 ❑ ca. 1988, b&w Cover: 1.50 **NM** value: **2.25**
19 ❑ Sep 1988, b&w Cover: 1.75 **NM** value: **2.25**
20 ❑ Nov 1988, b&w Cover: 1.75 **NM** value: **2.25**
21 ❑ ca. 1989, b&w Cover: 1.75 **NM** value: **2.00**
22 ❑ Apr 1989, b&w Cover: 1.95 **NM** value: **2.00**
23 ❑ May 1989, b&w Cover: 1.95 **NM** value: **2.00**
24 ❑ Jul 1989, b&w Cover: 1.95 **NM** value: **2.00**
25 ❑ b&w Cover: 1.95 **NM** value: **2.00**
26 ❑ Jul 1990, b&w Cover: 1.95 **NM** value: **2.00**
27 ❑ Oct 1990, b&w Cover: 1.95 **NM** value: **2.00**
28 ❑ ca. 1990, b&w Cover: 1.95 **NM** value: **2.00**
29 ❑ Jan 1991, b&w Cover: 1.95 **NM** value: **2.00**
30 ❑ Apr 1991, b&w Cover: 2.50 **NM** value: **Cover or less**
31 ❑ Jun 1991, b&w Cover: 2.25 **NM** value: **2.50**
32 ❑ Jul 1991, b&w Cover: 2.25 **NM** value: **2.50**
33 ❑ Sep 1991, b&w Cover: 2.25 **NM** value: **2.50**
34 ❑ Nov 1991, b&w Cover: 2.25 **NM** value: **2.50**

BORIS THE BEAR INSTANT COLOR CLASSICS — Dark Horse

1 ❑ Jul 1987 Cover: 1.75 **NM** value: **2.00**
Circ: CapCity orders: **6,150**
• Reprints Boris the Bear #1 in color **A:** James Dean Smith **W:** Randy Stradley ★ 1st Appearance of Boris the Bear.
2 ❑ Aug 1987 Cover: 1.95 **NM** value: **2.00**
Circ: CapCity orders: **4,800**
3 ❑ Dec 1987 Cover: 1.95 **NM** value: **2.00**
Circ: CapCity orders: **4,075**

BORN AGAIN — Spire

1 ❑ Cover: 0.39 **NM** value: **3.00**
No issue number. • Chuck Colson

BORN TO BE WILD — Eclipse

Bk 1 ❑ b&w Cover: 10.95 **NM** value: **Cover or less**
A: Todd Dezuniga; Todd McFarlane **C:** Bill Sienkiewicz

BORN TO KILL — Aircel

1 ❑ May 1991, b&w Cover: 2.50 **NM** value: **Cover or less**
A: Barry Blair; Angel de Mioche **C:** Barry Blair **W:** Tang Lung Hum
2 ❑ Cover: 2.50 **NM** value: **Cover or less**
3 ❑ Cover: 2.50 **NM** value: **Cover or less**

BOSTON BOMBERS, THE — Caliber

1 ❑ Cover: 2.50 **NM** value: **Cover or less**
Circ: CapCity orders: **2,850**
The Black Star Strikes **A:** Chris Jones **W:** Ron Fortier
2 ❑ Cover: 2.50 **NM** value: **Cover or less**
Circ: CapCity orders: **1,975**
A: Chris Jones **W:** Ron Fortier
3 ❑ Cover: 2.50 **NM** value: **Cover or less**
A: Chris Jones **W:** Ron Fortier
4 ❑ Cover: 2.50 **NM** value: **Cover or less**
A: Chris Jones **W:** Ron Fortier
5 ❑ Cover: 2.50 **NM** value: **Cover or less**
A: Chris Jones **W:** Ron Fortier
6 ❑ Cover: 2.50 **NM** value: **Cover or less**
A: Chris Jones **W:** Ron Fortier

To find the median price offered on eBay at press time for pre-1990 **CGC-graded comics**, multiply by:

9.9 (M): **33**	8.5 (VF+): **1.25**
9.8(NM/M): **16**	8.0 (VF): **0.85**
9.6 (NM+): **7**	7.5 (VF-): **0.6**
9.4 (NM): **5**	7.0 (F/VF): **0.5**
9.2 (NM-): **2.5**	6.5 (F+): **0.4**
9.0 (VF/NM): **1.5**	6.0 (F-): **0.33**

These are median prices of all CGC comics auctioned on eBay; prices for individual issues will vary.

BOUDOIR — Akbar

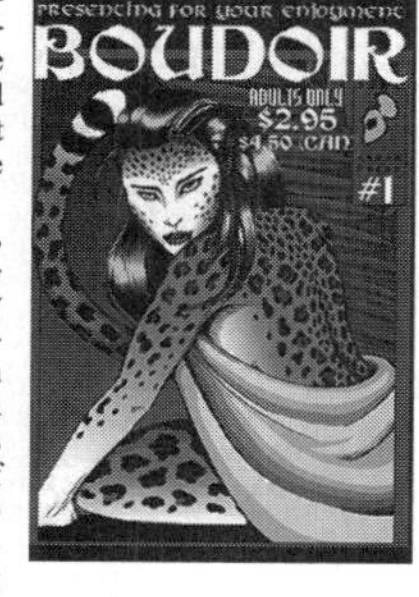

This is the successor to the erotica fanzine that T.L. Graf and her husband published for five issues in the mid-1990s. The previous effort died from a lack of contributions, but Graf decided to try again with the help of Limelight Press in 1999.

The new series, unfortunately, seems little more than a loose collection of standard manga fantasy and pinups. The best of the first issue's efforts is "Metro," in which Tora-Chan's clean pencils add a touch of class to what otherwise is a by-the-numbers erotic fantasy of a boy trying to work up the nerve to talk to a girl he saw at the train station while at the same time picturing the two of them engaging in a lusty encounter.

1 ❑ Cover: 2.95 **NM** value: **Cover or less**
Metro; Pizza Girl; Newlywed Blisse: Undressed Distress **A:** Jeremy Lambros; Tora-Chan **W:** Jeremy Lambros; Tora-Chan ★ 1st Appearance of Pizza Girl.

BOULEVARD OF BROKEN DREAMS — Fantagraphics

1 ❑ Cover: 3.95 **NM** value: **Cover or less**
No issue number.

BOUNCER, THE — Fox

10 ❑ ca. 1944 Cover: 0.10 **NM** value: **150.00**
11 ❑ Sep 1944 Cover: 0.10 **NM** value: **125.00**
12 ❑ Oct 1944 Cover: 0.10 **NM** value: **100.00**
13 ❑ Nov 1944 Cover: 0.10 **NM** value: **100.00**
14 ❑ Spr 1944 Cover: 0.10 **NM** value: **100.00**

BOUND AND GAGGED — Iconografix

1 ❑ Cover: 2.50 **NM** value: **Cover or less**
I, Debunker! **A:** Michael Aushenker **W:** Michael Aushenker

BOUND IN DARKNESS: INFINITY ISSUE — CFD

1 ❑ b&w Cover: 2.50 **NM** value: **Cover or less**

BOUNTY — Caliber

1 ❑ Cover: 2.50 **NM** value: **Cover or less**
Bounty; Navarro **A:** Paul Daly; Brandon Peterson Aubrey Bradford **W:** Paul Daly; Brent Traux; Randall Thayer
2 ❑ Cover: 2.50 **NM** value: **Cover or less**
3 ❑ Cover: 2.50 **NM** value: **Cover or less**

BOUNTY OF ZONE-Z — Sunset Strips

1 ❑ Cover: 2.50 **NM** value: **Cover or less**
No issue number.

BOX — Fantagraphics / Eros

1 ❑ Cover: 2.25 **NM** value: **Cover or less**
2 ❑ Cover: 2.25 **NM** value: **Cover or less**
3 ❑ Cover: 2.25 **NM** value: **Cover or less**
4 ❑ Cover: 2.25 **NM** value: **Cover or less**
5 ❑ Cover: 2.25 **NM** value: **Cover or less**
6 ❑ Cover: 2.25 **NM** value: **Cover or less**

BOXBOY — Slave Labor

1 ❑ Aug 1993 Cover: 1.00 **NM** value: **Cover or less**
Look! It's Boxboy!; The World of Boxboy; Box Envy; That Word!!!!; Hey Boxboy!; Digital Boxboy; I Am My Father! **A:** Dan Vado **W:** Dan Vado
1-2 ❑ May 1995 Cover: 1.25 **NM** value: **Cover or less**
2 ❑ Jul 1995 Cover: 1.25 **NM** value: **Cover or less**
No Restroom for the Weary; I Love Hockey; Angry Voices; What's the Matter With You?!!; The Power of Boxboy; Faith; True Lies; Boxboy Is… **A:** Dan Vado **W:** Dan Vado

BOX OFFICE POISON — Antarctic

Alex Robinson's Box Office Poison is a slice-of-life series featuring characters that many readers will identify with: Sherman, the bookstore clerk; Ed, the struggling cartoonist; Stephen, the history teacher; Dorothy, Sherman's manipulative girlfriend; and Irving Flavor, an elderly cartoonist who created a Batman-like character and was cheated out of the rights and profits.

The long-running story features Sherman's ongoing love-hate relationship with both his job and Dorothy, both of which are cutting into his writing and free time. Meanwhile, Ed tries to help Irving gain some of the recognition he feels the old artist is due for his creation. The soap-opera aspects of the strip are what kept readers coming back for more than four years and more than 20 issues. — Brent

0 ❑ Cover: 2.95 **NM** value: **4.00**
• Collects stories from mini-comics **A:** Alex Robinson **W:** Alex Robinson
1 ❑ Oct 1996 Cover: 3.50 **NM** value: **8.00**
Circ: Diamd. preorders: **2,499**
The Bohemian Girl **A:** Alex Robinson **W:** Alex Robinson
2 ❑ Dec 1996 Cover: 2.95 **NM** value: **5.00**
Boiling Frog **A:** Alex Robinson **W:** Alex Robinson

CGC-graded: Multiply prices above by **33 for 9.9 M • 16 for 9.8 NM/M • 7 for 9.6 NM+ • 5 for 9.4 NM • 2.5 for 9.2 NM- • 1.5 for 9.0 VF/NM**

3 ❑ Feb 1997 Cover: 2.95 **NM** value: **4.00**
Ed-The Ink Stud **A:** Alex Robinson **W:** Alex Robinson

4 ❑ Mar 1997 Cover: 2.95 **NM** value: **4.00**
Ballad of Jane and Stephen **A:** Alex Robinson **W:** Alex Robinson

5 ❑ ca. 1997 Cover: 2.95 **NM** value: **3.00**
A: Alex Robinson **W:** Alex Robinson

6 ❑ ca. 1997 Cover: 2.95 **NM** value: **3.00**
A: Alex Robinson **W:** Alex Robinson

7 ❑ Nov 1997 Cover: 2.95 **NM** value: **3.00**
A: Alex Robinson **W:** Alex Robinson

8 ❑ Feb 1998 Cover: 2.95 **NM value: Cover or less**
cover says Feb 97, indicia says Feb 98. **A:** Alex Robinson **W:** Alex Robinson

9 ❑ Apr 1998 Cover: 2.95 **NM value: Cover or less**
cover says May, indicia says Apr. Bumbles Bounce! **A:** Alex Robinson **W:** Alex Robinson

10 ❑ Jul 1998 Cover: 2.95 **NM value: Cover or less**
When Titans Clash! **A:** Alex Robinson **W:** Alex Robinson

11 ❑ Oct 1998 Cover: 2.95 **NM value: Cover or less**
A: Alex Robinson **W:** Alex Robinson

12 ❑ Dec 1998 Cover: 2.95 **NM value: Cover or less**
wraparound cover. Which Celebrity Will You be Sleeping With?; A Rock in a Pond; House of Tweed **A:** Alex Robinson **W:** Alex Robinson

13 ❑ Feb 1999 Cover: 2.95 **NM** value: **2.99**
Circ: Diamd. preorders: **1,225**
Where will you be in ten years?; In the Company of Guys **A:** Alex Robinson **W:** Alex Robinson

14 ❑ Jun 1999 Cover: 2.99 **NM value: Cover or less**
Grudge!; The End **A:** Alex Robinson **W:** Alex Robinson

15 ❑ Aug 1999 Cover: 2.95 **NM** value: **2.99**
Another Satellite **A:** Alex Robinson **W:** Alex Robinson

16 ❑ 1999 Cover: 2.99 **NM value: Cover or less**
A: Alex Robinson **W:** Alex Robinson

17 ❑ 2000 Cover: 2.99 **NM value: Cover or less**
A: Alex Robinson **W:** Alex Robinson

18 ❑ ca. 2000 Cover: 2.99 **NM value: Cover or less**
A: Alex Robinson **W:** Alex Robinson

20 ❑ Aug 2000, b&w Cover: 2.99 **NM value: Cover or less**
Omen **A:** Alex Robinson **W:** Alex Robinson

Bk 1 ❑ Sep 1998 Cover: 14.95 **NM value: Cover or less**
• collects Box Office Poison #1-6 **A:** Alex Robinson **W:** Alex Robinson

SS 1 ❑ May 1997 Cover: 4.95 **NM value: Cover or less**
• Super Special

BOX OFFICE POISON: KOLOR KARNIVAL — Antarctic

1 ❑ May 1999 Cover: 2.99 **NM** value: **3.50**
Circ: Diamd. preorders: **1,355**
cover says Apr, indicia says May. Temptation • Kolor Karnival **A:** Alex Robinson **W:** Alex Robinson

BOY AND HIS 'BOT, A — Now

1 ❑ Jan 1987 Cover: 1.95 **NM value: Cover or less**
• digest-sized. **A:** Gary Thomas Washington **W:** Gary Thomas Washington

BOY COMICS — Lev Gleason

Product of quality-conscious Lev Gleason Publications and a classic "sleeper" title from the Golden Age, Boy Comics featured the storytelling skills of Charles Biro and the adventures of Crimebuster, a charismatic and interesting boy hero. For the first several issues of Boy Comics, Crimebuster was locked in battle with the terrifying Nazi villain Iron Jaw, perhaps the most evil and hateful character of the entire Golden Age. Young Crimebuster and his pet monkey, Squeeks, often suffered horribly at the hands of Iron Jaw before eventually prevailing. (Iron Jaw kept being killed and then recovering.) Boy Comics eventually lost some of its edge, but CB and Squeeks soldiered on against the minions of the underworld into the 1950s. Backup features included Dilly Duncan, Rocky X, Young Robin Hood, and Bombshell.

3 ❑ Apr 1942 Cover: 0.10 **NM** value: **1500.00**
• **CGC:** 1 graded, best 4.5
• Series continued from Captain Battle #2 **A:** Norman Maurer **W:** Charles Biro ★ Origin of Crimebuster. ★ 1st Appearance of Iron Jaw.

4 ❑ Jun 1942 Cover: 0.10 **NM** value: **600.00**
• **CGC:** 2 graded, best 7.5
Hitler cover.

5 ❑ Aug 1942 Cover: 0.10 **NM** value: **485.00**
• **CGC:** 1 graded, best 4.0

6 ❑ Oct 1942 Cover: 0.10 **NM** value: **900.00**
• **CGC:** 1 graded, best 7.0
★ Origin of Iron Jaw.

7 ❑ Dec 1942 Cover: 0.10 **NM** value: **425.00**
Hitler cover.

8 ❑ Feb 1943 Cover: 0.10 **NM** value: **465.00**
• **CGC:** 1 graded, best 7.0
★ Death of Iron Jaw.

9 ❑ Apr 1943 Cover: 0.10 **NM** value: **425.00**
• **CGC:** 1 graded, best 6.0

10 ❑ Jun 1943 Cover: 0.10 **NM** value: **585.00**
• Return of Iron Jaw

11 ❑ Aug 1943 Cover: 0.10 **NM** value: **300.00**
• **CGC:** 1 graded, best 4.5

12 ❑ Oct 1943 Cover: 0.10 **NM** value: **300.00**
• **CGC:** 1 graded, best 7.0

13 ❑ Dec 1943 Cover: 0.10 **NM** value: **300.00**
• **CGC:** 2 graded, best 8.5

14 ❑ Feb 1944 Cover: 0.10 **NM** value: **300.00**
• **CGC:** 2 graded, best 9.0

15 ❑ Apr 1944 Cover: 0.10 **NM** value: **325.00**
★ Death of Iron Jaw.

16 ❑ Jun 1944 Cover: 0.10 **NM** value: **185.00**
• **CGC:** 1 graded, best 7.0

17 ❑ Aug 1944 Cover: 0.10 **NM** value: **200.00**
• **CGC:** 1 graded, best 9.2
Flag cover.

18 ❑ Oct 1944 Cover: 0.10 **NM** value: **185.00**
• **CGC:** 2 graded, best 9.4

19 ❑ Dec 1944 Cover: 0.10 **NM** value: **185.00**
• **CGC:** 2 graded, best 7.5

20 ❑ Feb 1945 Cover: 0.10 **NM** value: **185.00**
• **CGC:** 1 graded, best 7.5

21 ❑ Apr 1945 Cover: 0.10 **NM** value: **125.00**
• **CGC:** 1 graded, best 9.0

22 ❑ Jun 1945 Cover: 0.10 **NM** value: **125.00**
• **CGC:** 1 graded, best 9.2

23 ❑ Aug 1945 Cover: 0.10 **NM** value: **125.00**
• **CGC:** 1 graded, best 9.2

24 ❑ Oct 1945 Cover: 0.10 **NM** value: **125.00**
• **CGC:** 2 graded, best 9.0

25 ❑ Dec 1945 Cover: 0.10 **NM** value: **125.00**
• **CGC:** 1 graded, best 8.0

26 ❑ Feb 1946 Cover: 0.10 **NM** value: **100.00**
• **CGC:** 2 graded, best 9.4
Crimebuster; Swoop Storm; Real Hero; Young Robin Hood and his Band; Little Dynamite **A:** Norman Maurer; Charles Biro; Alan Mandel; Jack Alderman **W:** Charles Biro

27 ❑ Apr 1946 Cover: 0.10 **NM** value: **100.00**
• **CGC:** 2 graded, best 9.0

28 ❑ Jun 1946 Cover: 0.10 **NM** value: **100.00**
• **CGC:** 1 graded, best 7.5

29 ❑ Aug 1946 Cover: 0.10 **NM** value: **100.00**

30 ❑ Oct 1946 Cover: 0.10 **NM** value: **165.00**
★ Origin of Crimebuster.

31 ❑ Dec 1946 Cover: 0.10 **NM** value: **85.00**
• **CGC:** 1 graded, best 8.0

32 ❑ Feb 1947 Cover: 0.10 **NM** value: **85.00**
• **CGC:** 1 graded, best 9.2

33 ❑ Apr 1947 Cover: 0.10 **NM** value: **85.00**

34 ❑ Jun 1947 Cover: 0.10 **NM** value: **85.00**
• **CGC:** 1 graded, best 8.5

35 ❑ Aug 1947 Cover: 0.10 **NM** value: **85.00**

36 ❑ Oct 1947 Cover: 0.10 **NM** value: **85.00**
• **CGC:** 1 graded, best 8.5

37 ❑ Dec 1947 Cover: 0.10 **NM** value: **85.00**
38 ❑ Feb 1947 Cover: 0.10 **NM** value: **85.00**
39 ❑ Apr 1947 Cover: 0.10 **NM** value: **85.00**
40 ❑ Jun 1947 Cover: 0.10 **NM** value: **85.00**
41 ❑ Aug 1947 Cover: 0.10 **NM** value: **65.00**
42 ❑ Oct 1947 Cover: 0.10 **NM** value: **65.00**
43 ❑ Dec 1947 Cover: 0.10 **NM** value: **65.00**
44 ❑ Feb 1948 Cover: 0.10 **NM** value: **65.00**
45 ❑ Apr 1948 Cover: 0.10 **NM** value: **65.00**
46 ❑ Jun 1948 Cover: 0.10 **NM** value: **65.00**
47 ❑ Aug 1948 Cover: 0.10 **NM** value: **65.00**
48 ❑ Oct 1948 Cover: 0.10 **NM** value: **65.00**
49 ❑ Dec 1948 Cover: 0.10 **NM** value: **65.00**
50 ❑ Feb 1949 Cover: 0.10 **NM** value: **65.00**
51 ❑ Mar 1950 Cover: 0.10 **NM** value: **45.00**
52 ❑ Apr 1950 Cover: 0.10 **NM** value: **45.00**
53 ❑ May 1950 Cover: 0.10 **NM** value: **45.00**
54 ❑ Jun 1950 Cover: 0.10 **NM** value: **45.00**
55 ❑ Jul 1950 Cover: 0.10 **NM** value: **45.00**
56 ❑ Aug 1950 Cover: 0.10 **NM** value: **45.00**
57 ❑ Sep 1950 Cover: 0.10 **NM** value: **45.00**
58 ❑ Oct 1950 Cover: 0.10 **NM** value: **45.00**
• **CGC:** 1 graded, best 8.0
59 ❑ Nov 1950 Cover: 0.10 **NM** value: **45.00**
60 ❑ Dec 1950 Cover: 0.10 **NM** value: **45.00**
61 ❑ Jan 1951 Cover: 0.10 **NM** value: **50.00**
62 ❑ Feb 1951 Cover: 0.10 **NM** value: **50.00**
63 ❑ Mar 1951 Cover: 0.10 **NM** value: **38.00**
64 ❑ Apr 1951 Cover: 0.10 **NM** value: **38.00**
65 ❑ May 1951 Cover: 0.10 **NM** value: **38.00**
66 ❑ Jun 1951 Cover: 0.10 **NM** value: **38.00**
67 ❑ Jul 1951 Cover: 0.10 **NM** value: **38.00**
68 ❑ Aug 1951 Cover: 0.10 **NM** value: **38.00**
69 ❑ Sep 1951 Cover: 0.10 **NM** value: **38.00**
70 ❑ Oct 1951 Cover: 0.10 **NM** value: **38.00**
71 ❑ Nov 1951 Cover: 0.10 **NM** value: **38.00**
72 ❑ Dec 1951 Cover: 0.10 **NM** value: **38.00**
73 ❑ Jan 1952 Cover: 0.10 **NM** value: **38.00**
74 ❑ Feb 1952 Cover: 0.10 **NM** value: **38.00**
75 ❑ Mar 1952 Cover: 0.10 **NM** value: **38.00**
• **CGC:** 1 graded, best 8.5
76 ❑ Apr 1952 Cover: 0.10 **NM** value: **38.00**
77 ❑ May 1952 Cover: 0.10 **NM** value: **38.00**
78 ❑ Jun 1952 Cover: 0.10 **NM** value: **38.00**
79 ❑ Jul 1952 Cover: 0.10 **NM** value: **38.00**
80 ❑ Aug 1952 Cover: 0.10 **NM** value: **38.00**
81 ❑ Sep 1952 Cover: 0.10 **NM** value: **30.00**
82 ❑ Oct 1952 Cover: 0.10 **NM** value: **30.00**
83 ❑ Nov 1952 Cover: 0.10 **NM** value: **30.00**
84 ❑ Dec 1952 Cover: 0.10 **NM** value: **30.00**
85 ❑ Jan 1953 Cover: 0.10 **NM** value: **30.00**
86 ❑ Feb 1953 Cover: 0.10 **NM** value: **30.00**
87 ❑ Mar 1953 Cover: 0.10 **NM** value: **30.00**
88 ❑ Apr 1953 Cover: 0.10 **NM** value: **30.00**
89 ❑ May 1953 Cover: 0.10 **NM** value: **30.00**
90 ❑ Jun 1953 Cover: 0.10 **NM** value: **30.00**
91 ❑ Jul 1953 Cover: 0.10 **NM** value: **30.00**
92 ❑ Aug 1953 Cover: 0.10 **NM** value: **30.00**
93 ❑ Sep 1953 Cover: 0.10 **NM** value: **30.00**
94 ❑ Oct 1953 Cover: 0.10 **NM** value: **30.00**
95 ❑ Nov 1953 Cover: 0.10 **NM** value: **30.00**
96 ❑ Dec 1953 Cover: 0.10 **NM** value: **30.00**
97 ❑ Jan 1954 Cover: 0.10 **NM** value: **30.00**
98 ❑ Feb 1954 Cover: 0.10 **NM** value: **30.00**
99 ❑ Mar 1954 Cover: 0.10 **NM** value: **30.00**
100 ❑ Apr 1954 Cover: 0.10 **NM** value: **30.00**
101 ❑ May 1954 Cover: 0.10 **NM** value: **24.00**
102 ❑ Jun 1954 Cover: 0.10 **NM** value: **24.00**
103 ❑ Jul 1954 Cover: 0.10 **NM** value: **24.00**
104 ❑ ca. 1954 Cover: 0.10 **NM** value: **24.00**
105 ❑ Nov 1954 Cover: 0.10 **NM** value: **24.00**
106 ❑ Dec 1954 Cover: 0.10 **NM** value: **24.00**
107 ❑ ca. 1955 Cover: 0.10 **NM** value: **24.00**
108 ❑ ca. 1955 Cover: 0.10 **NM** value: **24.00**
109 ❑ ca. 1955 Cover: 0.10 **NM** value: **24.00**
110 ❑ ca. 1955 Cover: 0.10 **NM** value: **24.00**
111 ❑ ca. 1955 Cover: 0.10 **NM** value: **24.00**
112 ❑ ca. 1955 Cover: 0.10 **NM** value: **24.00**
113 ❑ ca. 1955 Cover: 0.10 **NM** value: **24.00**
114 ❑ ca. 1955 Cover: 0.10 **NM** value: **24.00**
115 ❑ ca. 1955 Cover: 0.10 **NM** value: **24.00**
116 ❑ ca. 1955 Cover: 0.10 **NM** value: **24.00**
117 ❑ ca. 1955 Cover: 0.10 **NM** value: **24.00**
118 ❑ ca. 1956 Cover: 0.10 **NM** value: **24.00**
119 ❑ Mar 1956 Cover: 0.10 **NM** value: **24.00**
final issue.

BOY COMMANDOS (1ST SERIES) — DC

1 ❑ Win 1942 Cover: 0.10 **NM** value: **4000.00**
• **CGC:** 7 graded, best 7.5
The Town That Couldn't Be Conquered; Heroes Never Die; Satan Wears a Swastika; Ghost Raiders **A:** Jack Kirby **W:** Joe Simon

2 ❑ Spr 1943 Cover: 0.10 **NM** value: **1250.00**
• **CGC:** 2 graded, best 8.0
The Silent People Speak; On the Double M'Lord; The Knights Wore Khaki; Nine Lives for Victory **A:** Jack Kirby **W:** Joe Simon

3 ❑ Sum 1943 Cover: 0.10 **NM** value: **850.00**
• **CGC:** 3 graded, best 9.4
A Film from the Front, Unsensored; The Siege of Troy; Cyril Thwaite Rides Again; The Return of Agent Axis **A:** Jack Kirby **W:** Joe Simon

4 ❑ Fal 1943 Cover: 0.10 **NM** value: **475.00**
• **CGC:** 1 graded, best 7.5
Flames at Dawn; Brooklyn Revere's Ride; Madman at Mt. Cloud; Toinette the Terrible; Bugle of the Brave; Road to Berlin **A:** Jack Kirby **W:** Joe Simon

5 ❑ Win 1943 Cover: 0.10 **NM** value: **475.00**
• **CGC:** 2 graded, best 9.2
Reassignment in Norway; A Town to Remember; The Mysterious Mr. Mulani; Satan to See You **A:** Jack Kirby **W:** Joe Simon

6 ❑ Spr 1944 Cover: 0.10 **NM** value: **475.00**
• **CGC:** 4 graded, best 8.5
News from Belgium; Jackals of Jawnpore; Destiny Writes the Headlines **A:** Jack Kirby **W:** Joe Simon

7 ❑ Sum 1944 Cover: 0.10 **NM** value: **400.00**
• **CGC:** 5 graded, best 9.6
The Shadow of Valhalla **A:** Jack Kirby **W:** Joe Simon

8 ❑ Fal 1944 Cover: 0.10 **NM** value: **400.00**
• **CGC:** 3 graded, best 9.4
A: Jack Kirby **W:** Joe Simon

9 ❑ Win 1944 Cover: 0.10 **NM** value: **400.00**
• **CGC:** 6 graded, best 9.2

10 ❑ Spr 1945 Cover: 0.10 **NM** value: **400.00**
• **CGC:** 3 graded, best 9.6

11 ❑ Sum 1945 Cover: 0.10 **NM** value: **210.00**
• **CGC:** 3 graded, best 9.6

12 ❑ Fal 1945 Cover: 0.10 **NM** value: **210.00**
• **CGC:** 4 graded, best 8.0
Coast Guard Reconnaissance

13 ❑ Win 1945 Cover: 0.10 **NM** value: **210.00**
• **CGC:** 4 graded, best 9.6

14 ❑ Mar 1946 Cover: 0.10 **NM** value: **210.00**
• **CGC:** 2 graded, best 9.2

15 ❑ May 1946 Cover: 0.10 **NM** value: **210.00**
• **CGC:** 3 graded, best 9.4
Crime in Technicolor; Trial of Crimson Scorpion; Roman Holiday

16 ❑ Jun 1946 Cover: 0.10 **NM** value: **210.00**

17 ❑ Sep 1946 Cover: 0.10 **NM** value: **210.00**
• **CGC:** 3 graded, best 9.4
The Stolen Centuries; Terror on the Yangtze; Brooklyn Gets a Haircut

18 ❑ Nov 1946 Cover: 0.10 **NM** value: **210.00**
• **CGC:** 4 graded, best 9.2

19 ❑ Jan 1947 Cover: 0.10 **NM** value: **210.00**
• **CGC:** 2 graded, best 7.0
Saga of Rip Van Carter; Torpedo Pirates; Tenderfoot from Brooklyn

20 ❑ Mar 1947 Cover: 0.10 **NM** value: **210.00**
• **CGC:** 2 graded, best 6.5

21 ❑ May 1947 Cover: 0.10 **NM** value: **175.00**
• **CGC:** 1 graded, best 7.0
The Top of the World; The Script That Was Never Written; The Lady Known as Velvet

22 ❑ Jul 1947 Cover: 0.10 **NM** value: **175.00**
• **CGC:** 1 graded, best 8.5

23 ❑ Sep 1947 Cover: 0.10 **NM** value: **200.00**
• **CGC:** 2 graded, best 9.4
Unlucky Thirteen; The Legion of Forgotten Men; The Sunken World **A:** Jack Kirby **W:** Joe Simon

24 ❑ Nov 1947 Cover: 0.10 **NM** value: **140.00**
Crazy Quilt and the Camouflage Crimes; Enemy with Six Legs; Up, Up, & Away

25 ❑ Jan 1948 Cover: 0.10 **NM** value: **140.00**

26 ❑ Mar 1948 Cover: 0.10 **NM** value: **140.00**
• **CGC:** 1 graded, best .5

27 ❑ May 1948 Cover: 0.10 **NM** value: **140.00**
• **CGC:** 2 graded, best 9.2

Other grades: Multiply prices above by **1.5 for Mint • 2/3 for Very Fine • 1/3 for Fine • 1/5 for Very Good • 1/8 for Good**

The Ape that Plotted Crimes!; The Crimes of Diamond Hand; Sea Voyage (text story); The Case of the Killer Cadet; Shorty **A:** Henry Boltinoff **W:** Thomas Graw

28 ❑ Jul 1948 Cover: 0.10 **NM** value: **140.00**
• **CGC:** 2 graded, best 9.4

29 ❑ Sep 1948 Cover: 0.10 **NM** value: **140.00**
• **CGC:** 1 graded, best 7.5
Case of the Silent Commando; City at the Center of the Earth

30 ❑ Nov 1948 Cover: 0.10 **NM** value: **140.00**
• **CGC:** 1 graded, best 8.5
Triumph of William Tell; Miracle Pitcher

31 ❑ Jan 1949 Cover: 0.10 **NM** value: **125.00**
Solitary Confinement

32 ❑ Mar 1949 Cover: 0.10 **NM** value: **125.00**
• **CGC:** 1 graded, best 8.5
Designer of Doom; Dale Evans, Queen of the Westerns

33 ❑ May 1949 Cover: 0.10 **NM** value: **125.00**
• **CGC:** 1 graded, best 8.5
Houdini from Brooklyn; Color Crimes of Crazy Quilt

34 ❑ Jul 1949 Cover: 0.10 **NM** value: **125.00**
• **CGC:** 2 graded, best 9.2

35 ❑ Sep 1949 Cover: 0.10 **NM** value: **125.00**

36 ❑ Nov 1949 Cover: 0.10 **NM** value: **175.00**
• **CGC:** 1 graded, best 9.0
final issue.★ 1st Appearance of The Atomobile.

BOY COMMANDOS (2ND SERIES) — DC

1 ❑ Oct 1973 Cover: 0.20 **NM** value: **4.00**
The Sphinx Speaks; Heroes Never Die; The Commandos are Coming • Reprinted from Detective Comics #66 ("Sphinx") and Boy Commandos #1 ("Heroes") **A:** Jack Kirby **W:** Joe Simon

2 ❑ Dec 1973 Cover: 0.20 **NM** value: **3.00**
Nine Lives for Victory; News From Belgium final issue. • Reprinted from Boy Commandos #2 & #6 respectively **A:** Jack Kirby **W:** Joe Simon

BOY EXPLORERS COMICS — Harvey

1 ❑ ca. 1946 Cover: 0.10 **NM** value: **400.00**
• **CGC:** 2 graded, best 9.0
Talent for Trouble

2 ❑ ca. 1946 Cover: 0.10 **NM** value: **400.00**
• **CGC:** 1 graded, best .5
The Edge of the World

BOY LOVES GIRL — Lev Gleason

25 ❑ Jul 1952 Cover: 0.10 **NM** value: **25.00**
26 ❑ Aug 1952 Cover: 0.10 **NM** value: **25.00**
27 ❑ Sep 1952 Cover: 0.10 **NM** value: **18.00**
28 ❑ Oct 1952 Cover: 0.10 **NM** value: **18.00**
29 ❑ ca. 1952 Cover: 0.10 **NM** value: **18.00**
30 ❑ Jan 1953 Cover: 0.10 **NM** value: **18.00**
31 ❑ Feb 1953 Cover: 0.10 **NM** value: **18.00**
32 ❑ Mar 1953 Cover: 0.10 **NM** value: **18.00**
33 ❑ Apr 1953 Cover: 0.10 **NM** value: **18.00**
34 ❑ May 1953 Cover: 0.10 **NM** value: **18.00**
35 ❑ Jun 1953 Cover: 0.10 **NM** value: **18.00**
36 ❑ Jul 1953 Cover: 0.10 **NM** value: **18.00**
37 ❑ Aug 1953 Cover: 0.10 **NM** value: **18.00**
38 ❑ Sep 1953 Cover: 0.10 **NM** value: **18.00**
39 ❑ Oct 1953 Cover: 0.10 **NM** value: **18.00**
40 ❑ Nov 1953 Cover: 0.10 **NM** value: **18.00**
41 ❑ Dec 1953 Cover: 0.10 **NM** value: **15.00**
42 ❑ Jan 1954 Cover: 0.10 **NM** value: **15.00**
43 ❑ Feb 1954 Cover: 0.10 **NM** value: **15.00**
44 ❑ Mar 1954 Cover: 0.10 **NM** value: **15.00**
My Desperate Choice; Love on Trial; Detour: Love Ahead; The Wrong Kind Of Charm
45 ❑ Apr 1954 Cover: 0.10 **NM** value: **15.00**
46 ❑ May 1954 Cover: 0.10 **NM** value: **15.00**
47 ❑ ca. 1954 Cover: 0.10 **NM** value: **15.00**
48 ❑ ca. 1954 Cover: 0.10 **NM** value: **15.00**
49 ❑ 1954 Cover: 0.10 **NM** value: **15.00**
50 ❑ Feb 1955 Cover: 0.10 **NM** value: **15.00**
51 ❑ ca. 1955 Cover: 0.10 **NM** value: **12.00**
52 ❑ Cover: 0.10 **NM** value: **12.00**
53 ❑ Cover: 0.10 **NM** value: **12.00**
54 ❑ Cover: 0.10 **NM** value: **12.00**
55 ❑ Cover: 0.10 **NM** value: **12.00**
56 ❑ Cover: 0.10 **NM** value: **12.00**
57 ❑ Jun 1956 Cover: 0.10 **NM** value: **12.00**

BOYS' RANCH (HARVEY) — Harvey

The series didn't last for long, but it marks the pinnacle of Jack Kirby's work on Western comics. With the artistic help of Mort Meskin, the kid-gang team of Dandy ("who finds a fight just as exciting as a pretty gal"), comic-relief Wabash, and the captivating Angel ("there's no halo over Angel — for two very good reasons — and they're both strapped to his hips!") under the care of scout Clay Duncan came to life. It combined the best traits of the Joe Simon-and-Jack Kirby kid-teams and produced at least one outright masterpiece in its less than a year of production: the story of Mother Delilah (in #3).

When Marvel Comics produced a series of other hardcover reprints in 1991, the company reprinted the entirety of the Harvey series in one volume, just because it deserved preservation. — Maggie

1 ❑ Oct 1950 Cover: 0.10 **NM** value: **450.00**
The Man Who Hated Boys; How to Ride a Horse, Lesson 1; Now You Can Make Your Own Pair of Western Moccasins!; Boys' Ranch (Map); Meet Wee Willie Weehawken... The Oldest Boy at Boys' Ranch!; A Very Dangerous Dude; Western Lore from the Boys' Ranch Scrapbook;

2 ❑ Dec 1950 Cover: 0.10 **NM** value: **300.00**
Lead Will Fly at Sunset; How Cowboys Say It; How To Ride a Horse, Lesson 2; Four Massacres (2-page spread); The Original Cowboys; Apache Justice; The Clay Duncan Story!; How to Spin a Rope, Lesson 2

3 ❑ Feb 1951 Cover: 0.10 **NM** value: **275.00**
Mother Delilah; How To Ride a Horse, Lesson 3; Social Night in Town (2-page spread); The Legend of Alby Fleezer!; How Cowboys Say It; Famous Western Fighters: The Texas Rangers; I'll Fight You for Lucy!; How to Spin a Rope, Lesson 3

4 ❑ Apr 1951 Cover: 0.10 **NM** value: **250.00**
The Bugle Blows at Bloody Knife!; How Cowboys Say It; The Deadly Barrel of Clay Duncan's Rifle! (2-page spread); How to Spin a Rope, Lesson 4; Fight to the Finish!; How to Make Your Own Tom-Tom; How To Ride a Horse, Lesson 4; How-To-Make-It Series – Indi

5 ❑ Jun 1951 Cover: 0.10 **NM** value: **250.00**
The Last Mail to Red Fork!; How To Ride a Horse, Lesson 5; The Riders of the Pony Express (2-page spread); Bandits, Bullets and Wild Wild Women!; The Man of Iron; How to Spin a Rope, Lesson 5

6 ❑ Aug 1951 Cover: 0.10 **NM** value: **250.00**
Teeth for the Iron Horse!; How To Ride a Horse, Lesson 6; Remember the Alamo! (2-page spread); "Happy Boy" Carries the Ball!; How Cowboys Say It; How To Spin a Rope, Lesson 6; Indian Attack; Six-Gun Justice

BOYS' RANCH (MARVEL) — Marvel

Bk 1/HC ❑ Cover: 39.95 **NM** value: **Cover or less**
hardcover. • Reprints most of Boys' Ranch #1-6 by Harvey

BOZO — Dell

As the host of a popular TV cartoon show, Bozo the Clown was once a cultural icon known to children across the country. In fact, before the introduction of McDonald's Ronald McDonald, Bozo was possibly the most famous clown in America. In his comics, Bozo is the owner of the Minikin Circus and is known as the world's greatest animal trainer. Of course, he often gets involved in funny and sometimes dangerous adventures, but, with the help of his pal Sparky, things usually turn out OK.

Bozo first appeared in Four Color #285, which is considered the first of seven issues that ran under his own name in the early 1950s. He also starred in four other Four Color issues and had a second series about a decade later, but it only lasted four issues. He was lost to obscurity in comics until 1992, when Innovation released a reprint edition of Four Color #285.

1 ❑ May 1962 Cover: 0.15 **NM** value: **60.00**
• 01-073-207★ Appearance of Series continued from.
2 ❑ Apr 1963 Cover: 0.12 **NM** value: **45.00**
3 ❑ Jul 1963 Cover: 0.12 **NM** value: **45.00**
4 ❑ Jan 1952 Cover: 0.15 **NM** value: **38.00**
• **CGC:** 1 graded, best 8.0
• Bozo The Capital Clown
5 ❑ Apr 1952 Cover: 0.10 **NM** value: **38.00**
6 ❑ Jul 1952 Cover: 0.10 **NM** value: **38.00**
7 ❑ Oct 1952 Cover: 0.10 **NM** value: **38.00**

BOZO THE CLOWN IN 3-D (LARRY HARMON'S) — Blackthorne

1 ❑ Cover: 2.50 **NM** value: **Cover or less**
A: Andy Ice **W:** Hale Lane

1-2 ❑ Cover: 2.50 **NM** value: **Cover or less**
A: Andy Ice **W:** Hale Lane

2 ❑ Cover: 2.50 **NM** value: **Cover or less**

BOZO: THE WORLD'S MOST FAMOUS CLOWN (LARRY HARMON'S...) — Innovation

1 ❑ Cover: 6.95 **NM** value: **Cover or less**
Bozo And The Manikin Circus; Seal Of Approval; Bozo And The Ya-Chi-Ta Lion; Springtime For Bozo, A History Of Bozo • some reprint;Reprints Four Color Comics #285 **A:** Larry Harmon **W:** Larry Harmon

BOZZ CHRONICLES, THE — Marvel / Epic

1 ❑ Dec 1985 Cover: 1.50 **NM** value: **2.00**
Circ: CapCity orders: **7,700**
A: Bret Blevins **W:** David Michelinie ★ Origin of Bozz. ★ 1st Appearance of Bozz.

2 ❑ Feb 1986 Cover: 1.50 **NM** value: **2.00**
Circ: CapCity orders: **7,150**

3 ❑ Apr 1986 Cover: 1.50 **NM** value: **2.00**
Circ: CapCity orders: **7,300**

4 ❑ Jun 1986 Cover: 1.50 **NM** value: **2.00**
Circ: CapCity orders: **7,500**

5 ❑ Aug 1986 Cover: 1.50 **NM** value: **2.00**
Circ: CapCity orders: **7,000**
The Cobblestone Jungle **A:** Bret Blevins **W:** David Michelinie

6 ❑ Oct 1986 Cover: 1.50 **NM** value: **2.00**
Circ: CapCity orders: **6,300**
final issue.

BRADLEYS, THE — Fantagraphics

1 ❑ Apr 1999 Cover: 2.95 **NM** value: **Cover or less**
Circ: Diamd. preorders: **5,808**

2 ❑ May 1999 Cover: 2.95 **NM** value: **Cover or less**
Circ: Diamd. preorders: **4,314**

3 ❑ Jul 1999 Cover: 2.95 **NM** value: **Cover or less**
Circ: Diamd. preorders: **3,757**

BRADY BUNCH — Dell

1 ❑ ca. 1970 Cover: 0.15 **NM** value: **45.00**
• **CGC:** 1 graded, best 9.6

2 ❑ ca. 1970 Cover: 0.15 **NM** value: **30.00**
• **CGC:** 1 graded, best 9.2

BRAGADE — Parody Press

1 ❑ Mar 1993 Cover: 2.50 **NM** value: **Cover or less**
A: H.J. Cho **W:** H.J. Cho

BRAINBANX — DC / Helix

1 ❑ Mar 1997 Cover: 2.50 **NM** value: **Cover or less**
Circ: Diamd. preorders: **16,095**
Down Upon the Darkness **A:** Jason Minor **W:** Elaine Lee

2 ❑ Apr 1997 Cover: 2.50 **NM** value: **Cover or less**
Circ: Diamd. preorders: **10,887**
The Word and the Light **W:** Elaine Lee

3 ❑ May 1997 Cover: 2.50 **NM** value: **Cover or less**
Circ: Diamd. preorders: **9,117**
A: Jason Minor **W:** Elaine Lee

4 ❑ Jun 1997 Cover: 2.50 **NM** value: **Cover or less**
Circ: Diamd. preorders: **7,916**
From You Have I Come Forth **W:** Elaine Lee

5 ❑ Jul 1997 Cover: 2.50 **NM** value: **Cover or less**
Circ: Diamd. preorders: **6,897**
A: Jason Minor **W:** Elaine Lee

6 ❑ Aug 1997 Cover: 2.50 **NM** value: **Cover or less**
Circ: Diamd. preorders: **6,392**
Within Radiant Waters **W:** Elaine Lee

BRAIN BAT 3-D — 3-D Zone

1 ❑ Cover: 3.95 **NM** value: **Cover or less**

BRAINBOMB — Behemoth

Bk 1 ❑ Aug 1999 Cover: 19.95 **NM** value: **Cover or less**

BRAIN BOY — Dell

The series chronicled the adventures of Matt Price, better known as Brain Boy, an agent for a special branch of the Secret Service. Price is recruited by the organization right out of college, because he possesses special mental powers, including mind reading and levitation. He can also control other people's minds. Brain Boy's enemy is an evil dictator named Ricorta, who makes continuous attempts to take over the world. Of Brain Boy's six major adventures, three are against Ricorta. The other three are very different, as he fights dinosaurs, zombies, and a murderous millionaire.

This comic book series began in 1962, following an appearance in Four Color Comics #1330.

2 ❑ Cover: 0.12 **NM** value: **65.00**
★ Appearance of Series numbering continued from.
3 ❑ Cover: 0.12 **NM** value: **50.00**
4 ❑ ca. 1963 Cover: 0.12 **NM** value: **45.00**
5 ❑ Jun 1963 Cover: 0.12 **NM** value: **45.00**
• **CGC:** 1 graded, best 9.2
6 ❑ ca. 1963 Cover: 0.12 **NM** value: **45.00**
• **CGC:** 1 graded, best 9.4
The Mindless Ones; The Devil Worshiper (text story); Mr. Ozimandias: Devil's Acres final issue.

BRAIN CAPERS — Fantagraphics

1 ❑ Cover: 3.95 **NM** value: **Cover or less**

BRAINCHILD

Minneapolis College of Art and Design

2 ❑ b&w **NM** value: **1.00**
no cover price. Electropolis; Robot Dude; Mind's Eye; Boozer; A Proposal; Medusa Jack; Dark; Timothy Meets God; Angel Boy; Wizard; Proeliator Preliator; Flash; Spawn; Realm Denizen; Wal-Mart; Suramu

BRAIN FANTASY — Last Gasp

1 ❑ Cover: 0.50 **NM** value: **3.00**
Drooms Day; Flying Saucer Man; Nimrod O Mighty Hunter; Where Do We Go from Here? **A:** George Metzger; Rick Shubb; Robert Inwood **W:** George Metzger; Rick Shubb; Robert Inwood; David Parker

BRAINGLO — Psi Comics

1 ❑ Cover: 1.75 **NM** value: **Cover or less**

BRAND NEW YORK — Mean

1 ❑ Jul 1997, b&w and redCover: 3.95 **NM** value: **Cover or less**
cardstock cover. **A:** Zoltan **W:** Peter Avanti

2 ❑ Cover: 3.95 **NM** value: **Cover or less**
A: Zoltan **W:** Peter Avanti

Capital City orders are the actual sales of comic books by Capital City Distribution, once one of the largest U.S. sellers of comics to comics shops. Capital City's share of comics shop sales, while not known exactly, increases from around 10-20% in the mid-1980s to 30-35% in the mid-1990s. Capital City's share of comic books sold on newsstands (most Marvels and DCs) will be less.

CGC-graded: Multiply prices above by **33 for 9.9 M • 16 for 9.8 NM/M • 7 for 9.6 NM+ • 5 for 9.4 NM • 2.5 for 9.2 NM- • 1.5 for 9.0 VF/NM**

BRASS — Image

Written by Aron Wiesenfeld with art by Richard Bennett, Brass is one of the more successful combinations of American super-heroes and Japanese-style mecha comics.

The story itself focuses on Herschel Goldstein, a former homeless man who is working his way up from the gutter, starting as a janitor. Things are beginning to work out for him when he learns that the stomach pain he has been feeling for the past few weeks is actually cancer — deadly, inoperable cancer. Thanks to a covert project started three decades earlier, however, he finds salvation of sorts, courtesy of a techno-organic virus. It saves his life, allowing him to transform himself into "something out of a Japanese sitcom. A 12-foot walking Buick with big-ass guns coming out the yin-yang." Goofy as it sounds, Wiesenfeld's writing makes the whole thing work, and Bennett's art gives a great manga feel to the whole project.

1 ❑ Aug 1996 Cover: 2.50 **NM** value: **Cover or less**
A: Richard Bennett **W:** Richard Bennett; Aron Wiesenfeld ★ Origin of Brass. ★ 1st Appearance of Brass.

1/Dlx❑Aug 1996 Cover: 4.50 **NM** value: **Cover or less**
• Folio edition.

2 ❑ Sep 1996 Cover: 2.50 **NM** value: **Cover or less**
A: Richard Bennett **W:** Richard Bennett; Aron Wiesenfeld

3 ❑ May 1997 Cover: 2.50 **NM** value: **Cover or less**
Circ: Diamd. preorders: **28,593**
A: Richard Bennett **W:** Richard Bennett; Aron Wiesenfeld

BRASS (WILDSTORM) — WildStorm

1 ❑ Aug 2000 Cover: 2.50 **NM** value: **Cover or less**
Circ: Diamd. preorders: **15,805**
A: Carlos D'Anda; Richard Bennett **W:** John Arcudi

2 ❑ Sep 2000 Cover: 2.50 **NM** value: **Cover or less**
Circ: Diamd. preorders: **12,351**
A: Carlos D'Anda; Richard Bennett **W:** John Arcudi

3 ❑ Oct 2000 Cover: 2.50 **NM** value: **Cover or less**
Circ: Diamd. preorders: **10,477**
A: Carlos D'Anda; Richard Bennett **W:** John Arcudi

4 ❑ Nov 2000 Cover: 2.50 **NM** value: **Cover or less**
Circ: Diamd. preorders: **9,956**
A: Carlos D'Anda; Richard Bennett **W:** John Arcudi

5 ❑ Dec 2000 Cover: 2.50 **NM** value: **Cover or less**
Circ: Diamd. preorders: **9,509**
A: Carlos D'Anda; Richard Bennett **W:** John Arcudi

6 ❑ Jan 2001 Cover: 2.50 **NM** value: **Cover or less**
Circ: Diamd. preorders: **9,084**
A: Carlos D'Anda; Richard Bennett **W:** John Arcudi

BRATPACK — King Hell

In the city of Slumberg, the masked avengers are lowlifes who terrorize the population and make a mockery of civil rights. But even more despised are their irresponsible teen sidekicks: a "Brat Pack" of bullies and drug abusers who use their "super" status to get their kicks. That is, until leather-masked Doctor Blasphemy decides to wipe them out with a car bomb.

From the acid-tipped pen of Rick Veitch comes this dark, five-part mini-series published by King Hell, told with verve and energy in a dramatic palette of gray wash tones. Brutal, compelling, and darkly humorous, the Brat Pack practices its credo: "Live fast, love hard, and die with your mask on."

1 ❑ Aug 1990, b&w Cover: 2.95 **NM** value: **4.00**
A: Rick Veitch **W:** Rick Veitch ★ 1st Appearance of Doctor Blasphemy, Luna, Kid Vicious, Wild Boy.

1-2 ❑ Cover: 2.95 **NM** value: **3.00**

1-3 ❑ Cover: 2.95 **NM** value: **3.00**

2 ❑ Nov 1990 Cover: 2.95 **NM** value: **Cover or less**
A: Rick Veitch **W:** Rick Veitch

3 ❑ Jan 1991 Cover: 2.95 **NM** value: **Cover or less**
A: Rick Veitch **W:** Rick Veitch

4 ❑ Mar 1991 Cover: 2.95 **NM** value: **Cover or less**
A: Rick Veitch **W:** Rick Veitch

5 ❑ May 1991 Cover: 2.95 **NM** value: **Cover or less**
A: Rick Veitch **W:** Rick Veitch

Bk 1❑ Cover: 15.95 **NM** value: **Cover or less**
• Collects Bratpack #1-5 **A:** Rick Veitch **W:** Rick Veitch

BRAT PACK/MAXIMORTAL SUPER SPECIAL — King Hell

1 ❑ Sep 1996 Cover: 2.95 **NM** value: **Cover or less**
Circ: Diamd. preorders: **6,110**

BRATS BIZARRE — Marvel / Epic

1 ❑ May 1994 Cover: 2.50 **NM** value: **Cover or less**
Circ: CapCity orders: **5,150**

2 ❑ Jun 1994 Cover: 2.50 **NM** value: **Cover or less**
Circ: CapCity orders: **3,200**
📖 Bebe's Bogus Funeral **A:** Anthony Adhikary **W:** Pat Mills; Tony Skinner

3 ❑ Jul 1994 Cover: 2.50 **NM** value: **Cover or less**
Circ: CapCity orders: **2,900**
• trading card

4 ❑ Aug 1994 Cover: 2.50 **NM** value: **Cover or less**
Circ: CapCity orders: **2,800**

BRAVE AND THE BOLD, THE — DC

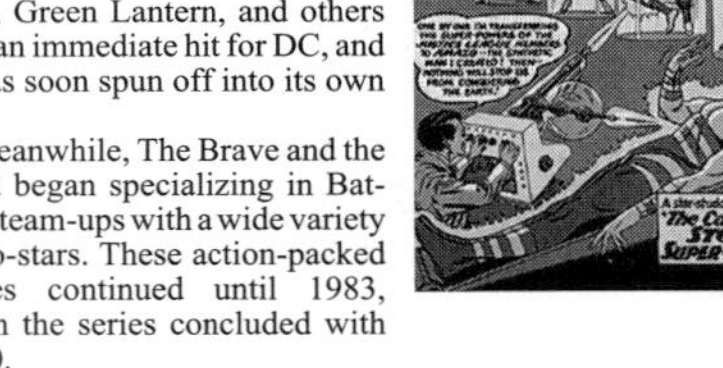

The Brave and the Bold got its start in 1955, featuring Viking Price, Silent Knight, and The Golden Gladiator. It stepped up the action in Mar 60, with issue #28's introduction of a new team, dubbed The Justice League of America. That group, which featured Batman, Superman, Hawkman, Green Lantern, and others was an immediate hit for DC, and it was soon spun off into its own title.

Meanwhile, The Brave and the Bold began specializing in Batman team-ups with a wide variety of co-stars. These action-packed issues continued until 1983, when the series concluded with #200.

1 ❑ Aug 1955 Cover: 0.10 **NM** value: **2500.00**
• **CGC:** 8 graded, best 7.0
• Viking Prince, Golden Gladiator, Silent Knight;Vi **A:** Joe Kubert

2 ❑ Oct 1955 Cover: 0.10 **NM** value: **1075.00**
• **CGC:** 2 graded, best 4.5
• Viking Prince, Golden Gladiator, Silent Knight

3 ❑ Dec 1955 Cover: 0.10 **NM** value: **640.00**
• **CGC:** 4 graded, best 8.5
• Viking Prince, Golden Gladiator, Silent Knight

4 ❑ Feb 1956 Cover: 0.10 **NM** value: **600.00**
• **CGC:** 1 graded, best 6.5
• Viking Prince, Golden Gladiator, Silent Knight

5 ❑ Apr 1956 Cover: 0.10 **NM** value: **600.00**
• **CGC:** 1 graded, best 7.0
• Robin Hood, Silent Knight, Viking Prince

6 ❑ Jun 1956 Cover: 0.10 **NM** value: **400.00**
• **CGC:** 1 graded, best 7.0
• Robin Hood, Silent Knight, Golden Gladiator **A:** Joe Kubert

7 ❑ Aug 1956 Cover: 0.10 **NM** value: **400.00**
• Robin Hood, Silent Knight, Viking Prince **A:** Joe Kubert

8 ❑ Oct 1956 Cover: 0.10 **NM** value: **400.00**
• Robin Hood, Silent Knight, Golden Gladiator **A:** Joe Kubert

9 ❑ Dec 1956 Cover: 0.10 **NM** value: **400.00**
• **CGC:** 3 graded, best 8.5
• Robin Hood, Silent Knight, Viking Prince **A:** Joe Kubert

10 ❑ Feb 1957 Cover: 0.10 **NM** value: **400.00**
• **CGC:** 1 graded, best 2.5
• Robin Hood, Silent Knight, Viking Prince **A:** Joe Kubert

11 ❑ Apr 1957 Cover: 0.10 **NM** value: **320.00**
• Robin Hood, Silent Knight, Viking Prince **A:** Joe Kubert

12 ❑ Jun 1957 Cover: 0.10 **NM** value: **320.00**
• **CGC:** 1 graded, best 9.0
• Robin Hood, Silent Knight, Viking Prince **A:** Joe Kubert

13 ❑ Sep 1957 Cover: 0.10 **NM** value: **320.00**
• Robin Hood, Silent Knight, Viking Prince **A:** Joe Kubert

14 ❑ Nov 1957 Cover: 0.10 **NM** value: **320.00**
• Robin Hood, Silent Knight, Viking Prince **A:** Joe Kubert

15 ❑ Jan 1958 Cover: 0.10 **NM** value: **320.00**
• Robin Hood, Silent Knight, Viking Prince **A:** Joe Kubert

16 ❑ Mar 1958 Cover: 0.10 **NM** value: **320.00**
• **CGC:** 2 graded, best 8.0
• Silent Knight, Viking Prince **A:** Joe Kubert

17 ❑ May 1958 Cover: 0.10 **NM** value: **320.00**
• Silent Knight, Viking Prince **A:** Joe Kubert

18 ❑ Jul 1958 Cover: 0.10 **NM** value: **320.00**
• **CGC:** 1 graded, best 7.5
• Silent Knight, Viking Prince **A:** Joe Kubert

19 ❑ Sep 1958 Cover: 0.10 **NM** value: **320.00**
• **CGC:** 2 graded, best 7.5
• Silent Knight, Viking Prince **A:** Joe Kubert

20 ❑ Nov 1958 Cover: 0.10 **NM** value: **320.00**
• Silent Knight, Viking Prince **A:** Joe Kubert

21 ❑ Jan 1959 Cover: 0.10 **NM** value: **320.00**
• **CGC:** 1 graded, best 7.5
• Silent Knight, Viking Prince **A:** Joe Kubert

22 ❑ Mar 1959 Cover: 0.10 **NM** value: **320.00**
• **CGC:** 4 graded, best 7.0
• Silent Knight, Viking Prince **A:** Joe Kubert

23 ❑ May 1959 Cover: 0.10 **NM** value: **375.00**
• **CGC:** 1 graded, best 7.5
• Viking Prince **A:** Joe Kubert ★ Origin of Viking Prince.

24 ❑ Jul 1959 Cover: 0.10 **NM** value: **320.00**
• Viking Prince **A:** Joe Kubert

25 ❑ Sep 1959 Cover: 0.10 **NM** value: **400.00**
• **CGC:** 1 graded, best 4.0
★ 1st Appearance of The Suicide Squad (Golden Age).

26 ❑ Nov 1959 Cover: 0.10 **NM** value: **300.00**
• **CGC:** 1 graded, best 7.0
★ 2nd Appearance of Suicide Squad.

27 ❑ Jan 1960 Cover: 0.10 **NM** value: **300.00**
Circ: Statement: **214,000** • **CGC:** 1 graded, best 3.0
★ 3rd Appearance of Suicide Squad.

28 ❑ Mar 1960 Cover: 0.10 **NM** value: **5300.00**
Circ: Statement: **214,000** • **CGC:** 50 graded, best 9.4
📖 Starro the Conqueror!; Starro vs. Green Lantern; Starro vs. Wonder Woman and J'onn J'onzz; Starro vs. the Flash; Starro vs. the Justice League of America • Justice League of America **A:** Mike Sekowsky **W:** Gardner Fox ★ 1st Appearance of Justice League of America, Starro the Conqueror, Snapper Carr.

29 ❑ May 1960 Cover: 0.10 **NM** value: **2300.00**
Circ: Statement: **214,000** • **CGC:** 26 graded, best 8.0
📖 Challenge of the Weapons Master! • Justice League of America ★ 2nd Appearance of Justice League of America.

30 ❑ Jul 1960 Cover: 0.10 **NM** value: **2000.00**
Circ: Statement: **214,000** • **CGC:** 26 graded, best 8.0
📖 The Case of the Stolen Super-Powers! • Justice League of America ★ 1st Appearance of Amazo, Professor Ivo. ★ 3rd Appearance of Justice League of America.

31 ❑ Sep 1960 Cover: 0.10 **NM** value: **340.00**
Circ: Statement: **214,000** • **CGC:** 4 graded, best 7.0
★ 1st Appearance of Cave Carson.

32 ❑ Nov 1960 Cover: 0.10 **NM** value: **195.00**
Circ: Statement: **214,000** • **CGC:** 4 graded, best 8.0
• Cave Carson

33 ❑ Jan 1961 Cover: 0.10 **NM** value: **195.00**
Circ: Statement: **245,000** • **CGC:** 2 graded, best 7.5
• Cave Carson

34 ❑ Mar 1961 Cover: 0.10 **NM** value: **1950.00**
Circ: Statement: **245,000** • **CGC:** 59 graded, best 9.4
📖 Creature of a Thousand Shapes **A:** Jack Kirby; Joe Kubert **W:** Gardner Fox ★ 1st Appearance of Thanagar, Byth, Hawkwoman II (Shayera Thal), Hawkman II (Katar Hol).

35 ❑ May 1961 Cover: 0.10 **NM** value: **525.00**
Circ: Statement: **245,000** • **CGC:** 20 graded, best 9.4
📖 Menace of the Matter Master; Valley of Vanishing Man • Hawkman **A:** Jack Kirby; Joe Kubert **W:** Gardner Fox ★ 1st Appearance of Matter Master.

36 ❑ Jul 1961 Cover: 0.10 **NM** value: **400.00**
Circ: Statement: **245,000** • **CGC:** 10 graded, best 9.4
📖 Strange Spells of the Sorcerer; Shadow Thief of Midway • Hawkman **A:** Jack Kirby; Joe Kubert **W:** Gardner Fox ★ 1st Appearance of Shadow-Thief.

37 ❑ Sep 1961 Cover: 0.10 **NM** value: **250.00**
Circ: Statement: **245,000** • **CGC:** 4 graded, best 8.5
• Suicide Squad

38 ❑ Nov 1961 Cover: 0.10 **NM** value: **225.00**
Circ: Statement: **245,000** • **CGC:** 1 graded, best 8.5
• Suicide Squad

39 ❑ Jan 1962 Cover: 0.10 **NM** value: **225.00**
Circ: Statement: **210,000** • **CGC:** 3 graded, best 9.0
• Suicide Squad

40 ❑ Mar 1962 Cover: 0.12 **NM** value: **140.00**
Circ: Statement: **210,000** • **CGC:** 3 graded, best 7.5
• Cave Carson

41 ❑ May 1962 Cover: 0.12 **NM** value: **140.00**
Circ: Statement: **210,000** • **CGC:** 2 graded, best 9.2
• Cave Carson

42 ❑ Jul 1962 Cover: 0.12 **NM** value: **300.00**
Circ: Statement: **210,000** • **CGC:** 19 graded, best 9.2
📖 The Menace of the Dragonfly Raiders **A:** Jack Kirby; Joe Kubert **W:** Gardner Fox ★ Appearance of Hawkman.

43 ❑ Sep 1962 Cover: 0.12 **NM** value: **350.00**
Circ: Statement: **210,000** • **CGC:** 17 graded, best 9.4
📖 The Masked Marauders of Earth **A:** Jack Kirby; Joe Kubert **W:** Gardner Fox ★ Origin of Hawkman (Silver Age). ★ 1st Appearance of Manhawks.

44 ❑ Nov 1962 Cover: 0.12 **NM** value: **260.00**
Circ: Statement: **210,000** • **CGC:** 11 graded, best 9.2
📖 Earth's Impossible Day; The Men Who Moved the World **A:** Jack Kirby; Joe Kubert **W:** Gardner Fox ★ Appearance of Hawkman.

45 ❑ Jan 1963 Cover: 0.12 **NM** value: **50.00**
• **CGC:** 1 graded, best 9.4
• Strange Sports Stories **A:** Carmine Infantino

46 ❑ Mar 1963 Cover: 0.12 **NM** value: **50.00**
• **CGC:** 2 graded, best 9.6
• Strange Sports Stories; Has 1962 Statement, filed 10/1/62; avg total paid circ 210,000 **A:** Carmine Infantino

47 ❑ May 1963 Cover: 0.12 **NM** value: **50.00**
• **CGC:** 2 graded, best 9.6
• Strange Sports Stories **A:** Carmine Infantino

48 ❑ Jul 1963 Cover: 0.12 **NM** value: **50.00**
• **CGC:** 4 graded, best 9.6
• Strange Sports Stories **A:** Carmine Infantino

49 ❑ Sep 1963 Cover: 0.12 **NM** value: **50.00**
• **CGC:** 2 graded, best 9.2
• Strange Sports Stories **A:** Carmine Infantino

50 ❑ Nov 1963 Cover: 0.12 **NM** value: **175.00**
• **CGC:** 7 graded, best 9.6
• Green Arrow;Team-ups begin

51 ❑ Jan 1964 Cover: 0.12 **NM** value: **225.00**
• **CGC:** 11 graded, best 9.6
• Aquaman, Hawkman;Early Hawkman/Aquaman team-up

52 ❑ Mar 1964 Cover: 0.12 **NM** value: **125.00**
• **CGC:** 3 graded, best 7.5
• Sgt. Rock; Has 1963 Statement, filed 10/1/62; no circ figures published **A:** Jack Kirby

53 ❑ May 1964 Cover: 0.12 **NM** value: **125.00**
• **CGC:** 5 graded, best 9.2
• Atom & Flash **A:** Alex Toth

54 ❑ Jul 1964 Cover: 0.12 **NM** value: **265.00**
• **CGC:** 27 graded, best 9.6
★ Origin of Teen Titans. ★ 1st Appearance of Teen Titans.

55 ❑ Sep 1964 Cover: 0.12 **NM** value: **40.00**
• **CGC:** 4 graded, best 9.6
• Metal Men, Atom

56 ❑ Nov 1964 Cover: 0.12 **NM** value: **40.00**
• **CGC:** 5 graded, best 9.6
• Flash★ 1st Appearance of Wynde.

57 ❑ Jan 1965 Cover: 0.12 **NM** value: **145.00**
Circ: Statement: **249,768** • **CGC:** 12 graded, best 9.6
★ Origin of Metamorpho. ★ 1st Appearance of Metamorpho.

58 ❑ Mar 1965 Cover: 0.12 **NM** value: **65.00**
Circ: Statement: **249,768** • **CGC:** 7 graded, best 9.6
• Has 1964 Statement, filed 10/1/64; no circ figures published **A:** Ramona Fradon ★ 2nd Appearance of Metamorpho.

59 ❑ May 1965 Cover: 0.12 **NM** value: **75.00**
Circ: Statement: **249,768** • **CGC:** 11 graded, best 9.8
• Batman;Batman/Green Lantern team-up

60 ❑ Jul 1965 Cover: 0.12 **NM** value: **80.00**
Circ: Statement: **249,768** • **CGC:** 3 graded, best 9.6
• Teen Titans★ 1st Appearance of Wonder Girl (Donna Troy).

Other grades: Multiply prices above by **1.5 for Mint • 2/3 for Very Fine • 1/3 for Fine • 1/5 for Very Good • 1/8 for Good**

61 ❑ Sep 1965 Cover: 0.12 **NM** value: **85.00**
Circ: Statement: **249,768** • **CGC:** 13 graded, best 9.6
Mastermind of Menaces! • Starman, Black Canary **A:** Murphy Anderson ★ Origin of Starman I (Ted Knight), Black Canary.

62 ❑ Nov 1965 Cover: 0.12 **NM** value: **85.00**
Circ: Statement: **249,768** • **CGC:** 15 graded, best 9.6
The Big Super-Hero Hunt! • Starman, Black Canary **A:** Murphy Anderson

63 ❑ Jan 1966 Cover: 0.12 **NM** value: **30.00**
Circ: Statement: **279,406** • **CGC:** 10 graded, best 9.6
• Supergirl

64 ❑ Mar 1966 Cover: 0.12 **NM** value: **55.00**
Circ: Statement: **279,406** • **CGC:** 13 graded, best 9.6
• Batman ★ Appearance of Eclipso.

65 ❑ May 1966 Cover: 0.12 **NM** value: **20.00**
Circ: Statement: **279,406** • **CGC:** 5 graded, best 9.4
• Doom Patrol; Has 1965 Statement; avg total paid circ 249,768

66 ❑ Jul 1966 Cover: 0.12 **NM** value: **20.00**
Circ: Statement: **279,406** • **CGC:** 6 graded, best 9.4
• Metamorpho, Metal Men

67 ❑ Sep 1966 Cover: 0.12 **NM** value: **35.00**
Circ: Statement: **279,406** • **CGC:** 7 graded, best 9.6
• Batman, Flash;Batman in all remaining issues **A:** Carmine Infantino

68 ❑ Nov 1966 Cover: 0.12 **NM** value: **60.00**
Circ: Statement: **279,406** • **CGC:** 16 graded, best 9.6
• Metamorpho ★ Appearance of Joker.

69 ❑ Jan 1967 Cover: 0.12 **NM** value: **25.00**
Circ: Statement: **342,400** • **CGC:** 12 graded, best 9.6
• Green Lantern

70 ❑ Mar 1967 Cover: 0.12 **NM** value: **25.00**
Circ: Statement: **342,400** • **CGC:** 8 graded, best 9.4
• Hawkman; Has 1966 Statement; avg print run 460,000; avg sales 277,000; avg subs 2,406; avg total paid 279,406; samples 265; max existent 279,406; 39% of run returned

71 ❑ May 1967 Cover: 0.12 **NM** value: **25.00**
Circ: Statement: **342,400** • **CGC:** 8 graded, best 9.8
• Green Arrow

72 ❑ Jul 1967 Cover: 0.12 **NM** value: **22.00**
Circ: Statement: **342,400** • **CGC:** 13 graded, best 9.6
• Spectre **A:** Carmine Infantino

73 ❑ Sep 1967 Cover: 0.12 **NM** value: **20.00**
Circ: Statement: **342,400** • **CGC:** 4 graded, best 9.4
• Aquaman, Atom

74 ❑ Nov 1967 Cover: 0.12 **NM** value: **20.00**
Circ: Statement: **342,400** • **CGC:** 3 graded, best 9.6
• Metal Men

75 ❑ Jan 1968 Cover: 0.12 **NM** value: **20.00**
Circ: Statement: **290,900** • **CGC:** 8 graded, best 9.4
• Spectre

76 ❑ Mar 1968 Cover: 0.12 **NM** value: **20.00**
Circ: Statement: **290,900** • **CGC:** 6 graded, best 9.4
• Plastic Man; Has 1967 Statement; avg print run 521,000; avg sales 340,000; avg subs 2,400; avg total paid 342,400; samples 340; max existent 342,400; 34% of run returned

77 ❑ May 1968 Cover: 0.12 **NM** value: **20.00**
Circ: Statement: **290,900** • **CGC:** 4 graded, best 9.2

78 ❑ Jul 1968 Cover: 0.12 **NM** value: **20.00**
Circ: Statement: **290,900** • **CGC:** 7 graded, best 9.6
• Wonder Woman ★ 1st Appearance of Copperhead.

79 ❑ Sep 1968 Cover: 0.12 **NM** value: **40.00**
Circ: Statement: **290,900** • **CGC:** 7 graded, best 9.4
• Deadman **A:** Neal Adams ★ Appearance of Deadman.

80 ❑ Nov 1968 Cover: 0.12 **NM** value: **35.00**
Circ: Statement: **290,900** • **CGC:** 6 graded, best 9.2
• Creeper **A:** Neal Adams ★ Appearance of Creeper.

81 ❑ Jan 1969 Cover: 0.12 **NM** value: **35.00**
Circ: Statement: **242,501** • **CGC:** 2 graded, best 8.0
• Flash **A:** Neal Adams ★ Appearance of Deadman.

82 ❑ Mar 1969 Cover: 0.12 **NM** value: **35.00**
Circ: Statement: **242,501** • **CGC:** 2 graded, best 9.6
• Has 1968 Statement; avg print run 469,000; avg sales 290,000; avg subs 900; avg total paid 290,900; samples 1,286; max existent 290,900; 38% of run returned **A:** Neal Adams ★ Origin of Ocean Master. ★ Appearance of Deadman.

83 ❑ May 1969 Cover: 0.12 **NM** value: **45.00**
Circ: Statement: **242,501** • **CGC:** 2 graded, best 9.4
• Titans **A:** Neal Adams

84 ❑ Jul 1969 Cover: 0.12 **NM** value: **32.00**
Circ: Statement: **242,501** • **CGC:** 9 graded, best 9.4
• Sgt. Rock **A:** Neal Adams

85 ❑ Sep 1969 Cover: 0.15 **NM** value: **32.00**
Circ: Statement: **242,501** • **CGC:** 5 graded, best 9.6
• Green Arrow;Green Arrow gets new costume **A:** Neal Adams

86 ❑ Nov 1969 Cover: 0.15 **NM** value: **32.00**
Circ: Statement: **242,501** • **CGC:** 9 graded, best 9.4
• Deadman **A:** Neal Adams

87 ❑ Jan 1970 Cover: 0.15 **NM** value: **20.00**
Circ: Statement: **211,266** • **CGC:** 4 graded, best 9.4
• Wonder Woman

88 ❑ Mar 1970 Cover: 0.15 **NM** value: **20.00**
Circ: Statement: **211,266** • **CGC:** 5 graded, best 9.4
• Wildcat

89 ❑ May 1970 Cover: 0.15 **NM** value: **20.00**
Circ: Statement: **211,266** • **CGC:** 2 graded, best 9.6
• Phantom Stranger; Has 1969 Statement; avg print run 448,000; avg sales 242,000; avg subs 501; avg total paid 242,501; samples 346; max existent 242,501; 46% of run returned

90 ❑ Jul 1970 Cover: 0.15 **NM** value: **20.00**
Circ: Statement: **211,266** • **CGC:** 4 graded, best 9.4
• Adam Strange

91 ❑ Sep 1970 Cover: 0.15 **NM** value: **18.00**
Circ: Statement: **211,266** • **CGC:** 1 graded, best 9.2
• Black Canary

92 ❑ Nov 1970 Cover: 0.15 **NM** value: **18.00**
Circ: Statement: **211,266** • **CGC:** 1 graded, best 9.2
• Bat Squad

93 ❑ Jan 1971 Cover: 0.15 **NM** value: **30.00**
Circ: Statement: **210,708** • **CGC:** 4 graded, best 9.0
• House of Mystery **A:** Neal Adams

94 ❑ Mar 1971 Cover: 0.15 **NM** value: **18.00**
Circ: Statement: **210,708** • **CGC:** 2 graded, best 9.4
• Titans

95 ❑ May 1971 Cover: 0.15 **NM** value: **11.00**
Circ: Statement: **210,708** • **CGC:** 3 graded, best 9.6
• Plastic Man

96 ❑ Jul 1971 Cover: 0.15 **NM** value: **11.00**
Circ: Statement: **210,708** • **CGC:** 7 graded, best 9.8
• Sgt. Rock

97 ❑ Sep 1971 Cover: 0.25 **NM** value: **11.00**
Circ: Statement: **210,708** • **CGC:** 5 graded, best 9.4
• Wildcat

98 ❑ Nov 1971 Cover: 0.25 **NM** value: **11.00**
Circ: Statement: **210,708** • **CGC:** 3 graded, best 9.4
• Phantom Stranger

99 ❑ Jan 1972 Cover: 0.25 **NM** value: **11.00**
Circ: Statement: **179,819** • **CGC:** 4 graded, best 9.4
• Flash **A:** Nick Cardy

100 ❑ Mar 1972 Cover: 0.25 **NM** value: **30.00**
Circ: Statement: **179,819** • **CGC:** 11 graded, best 9.8
• Double-size. • Green Arrow **A:** Neal Adams

101 ❑ May 1972 Cover: 0.25 **NM** value: **6.00**
Circ: Statement: **179,819** • **CGC:** 5 graded, best 9.6
• Metamorpho; Has 1971 Statement; avg print run 379,166; avg sales 210,708; avg total paid 210,708; office use 333; max existent 211,041; 44% of run returned

102 ❑ Jul 1972 Cover: 0.25 **NM** value: **9.00**
Circ: Statement: **179,819** • **CGC:** 5 graded, best 9.4
• Titans **A:** Neal Adams

103 ❑ Oct 1972 Cover: 0.20 **NM** value: **6.00**
Circ: Statement: **179,819**
• Metal Men

104 ❑ Dec 1972 Cover: 0.20 **NM** value: **6.00**
Circ: Statement: **179,819** • **CGC:** 1 graded, best 7.5
• Deadman **A:** Jim Aparo

105 ❑ Feb 1973 Cover: 0.20 **NM** value: **6.00**
Circ: Statement: **190,047**
• Wonder Woman **A:** Jim Aparo

106 ❑ Apr 1973 Cover: 0.20 **NM** value: **6.00**
Circ: Statement: **190,047** • **CGC:** 2 graded, best 8.5
• Green Arrow; Has 1972 Statement; avg print run 351,000; avg sales 179,609; avg total paid 179,819; samples 523; office use 446; max existent 180,788; 19% of run returned **A:** Jim Aparo

107 ❑ Jul 1973 Cover: 0.20 **NM** value: **6.00**
Circ: Statement: **190,047**
• Black Canary

108 ❑ Sep 1973 Cover: 0.20 **NM** value: **6.00**
Circ: Statement: **190,047** • **CGC:** 3 graded, best 9.6
• Sgt. Rock **A:** Jim Aparo

109 ❑ Nov 1973 Cover: 0.20 **NM** value: **6.00**
Circ: Statement: **190,047**
• Demon **A:** Jim Aparo

110 ❑ Jan 1974 Cover: 0.20 **NM** value: **6.00**
Circ: Statement: **191,722**
• Wildcat **A:** Jim Aparo

111 ❑ Mar 1974 Cover: 0.20 **NM** value: **12.00**
Circ: Statement: **191,722** • **CGC:** 1 graded, best 9.2
• Joker **A:** Jim Aparo

112 ❑ May 1974 Cover: 0.60 **NM** value: **12.00**
Circ: Statement: **191,722** • **CGC:** 3 graded, best 9.6
• Mr. Miracle; Has 1973 Statement; avg print run 367,667; avg sales 189,355; avg subs 692; avg total paid 190,047; samples 100; office use 1,562; max existent 191,709; 48% of run returned

113 ❑ Jul 1974 Cover: 0.60 **NM** value: **12.00**
Circ: Statement: **191,722** • **CGC:** 5 graded, best 9.6
• Metal Men **A:** Jim Aparo

114 ❑ Sep 1974 Cover: 0.60 **NM** value: **12.00**
Circ: Statement: **191,722** • **CGC:** 2 graded, best 9.0
• Aquaman **A:** Jim Aparo

115 ❑ Nov 1974 Cover: 0.60 **NM** value: **12.00**
Circ: Statement: **191,722** • **CGC:** 3 graded, best 9.6
A: Jim Aparo ★ Origin of Viking Prince.

116 ❑ Jan 1975 Cover: 0.60 **NM** value: **12.00**
Circ: Statement: **160,000** • **CGC:** 2 graded, best 9.2
• Spectre **A:** Jim Aparo

117 ❑ Mar 1975 Cover: 0.60 **NM** value: **12.00**
Circ: Statement: **160,000**
• Sgt. Rock;reprints Secret Six #1 **A:** Jim Aparo

118 ❑ Apr 1975 Cover: 0.25 **NM** value: **12.00**
Circ: Statement: **160,000** • **CGC:** 1 graded, best 9.4
• Wildcat, Joker **A:** Jim Aparo

119 ❑ Jun 1975 Cover: 0.25 **NM** value: **4.00**
Circ: Statement: **160,000** • **CGC:** 1 graded, best 9.2
• Man-Bat; Has 1974 Statement; avg print run 380,640; avg sales 190,100; avg subs 1,622; avg total paid 191,722; samples 100; office use 1,485; max existent 193,307; 49% of run returned **A:** Jim Aparo

120 ❑ Jul 1975 Cover: 0.50 **NM** value: **4.00**
Circ: Statement: **160,000** • **CGC:** 1 graded, best 9.6
• Kamandi, 68 pgs., reprints Secret Six #2;Kamandi;reprints Secret Six #2 **A:** Jim Aparo

121 ❑ Sep 1975 Cover: 0.25 **NM** value: **4.00**
Circ: Statement: **160,000** • **CGC:** 1 graded, best 7.5
• Metal Men **A:** Jim Aparo

122 ❑ Oct 1975 Cover: 0.25 **NM** value: **4.00**
Circ: Statement: **160,000**
• Swamp Thing

123 ❑ Dec 1975 Cover: 0.25 **NM** value: **4.00**
Circ: Statement: **160,000**
• Plastic Man, Metamorpho **A:** Jim Aparo

124 ❑ Jan 1976 Cover: 0.25 **NM** value: **4.00**
Circ: Statement: **153,000**
• Sgt. Rock **A:** Jim Aparo

125 ❑ Mar 1976 Cover: 0.25 **NM** value: **4.00**
Circ: Statement: **153,000**
• Flash **A:** Jim Aparo

126 ❑ Apr 1976 Cover: 0.30 **NM** value: **4.00**
Circ: Statement: **153,000**
• Aquaman **A:** Jim Aparo

127 ❑ Jun 1976 Cover: 0.30 **NM** value: **4.00**
Circ: Statement: **153,000**
• Wildcat; Has 1975 Statement; avg print run 358,000; avg sales 158,000; avg subs 2,000; avg total paid 160,000; samples 1,000; office use 2,000; max existent 163,000; 55% of run returned **A:** Jim Aparo

128 ❑ Jul 1976 Cover: 0.30 **NM** value: **4.00**
Circ: Statement: **153,000**
• Mr. Miracle;Bicentennial #19 **A:** Jim Aparo

129 ❑ Sep 1976 Cover: 0.30 **NM** value: **11.00**
Circ: Statement: **153,000** • **CGC:** 2 graded, best 7.5
• Green Arrow/Joker

130 ❑ Oct 1976 Cover: 0.30 **NM** value: **11.00**
Circ: Statement: **153,000** • **CGC:** 2 graded, best 7.5
• Green Arrow/Joker

131 ❑ Dec 1976 Cover: 0.30 **NM** value: **6.00**
Circ: Statement: **153,000**
• Wonder Woman **A:** Jim Aparo ★ Appearance of Catwoman.

132 ❑ Feb 1977 Cover: 0.30 **NM** value: **3.50**
Circ: Statement: **149,791**
• Kung Fu Fighter **A:** Jim Aparo

133 ❑ Apr 1977 Cover: 0.30 **NM** value: **3.50**
Circ: Statement: **149,791**
• Deadman **A:** Jim Aparo

134 ❑ May 1977 Cover: 0.30 **NM** value: **3.50**
Circ: Statement: **149,791**
• Green Lantern; Has 1976 Statement; avg print run 360,000; avg sales 151,000; avg subs 2,000; avg total paid 153,000; samples 1,000; max existent 154,000; 57% of run returned **A:** Jim Aparo

135 ❑ Jul 1977 Cover: 0.35 **NM** value: **3.50**
Circ: Statement: **149,791**
• Metal Men **A:** Jim Aparo

136 ❑ Sep 1977 Cover: 0.35 **NM** value: **3.50**
Circ: Statement: **149,791** • **CGC:** 1 graded, best 9.0
• Green Arrow, Metal Men

137 ❑ Oct 1977 Cover: 0.35 **NM** value: **3.50**
Circ: Statement: **149,791**
• Demon

138 ❑ Nov 1977 Cover: 0.35 **NM** value: **3.50**
Circ: Statement: **149,791**
• Mr. Miracle **A:** Jim Aparo

139 ❑ Jan 1978 Cover: 0.35 **NM** value: **3.50**
Circ: Statement: **121,563**
• Hawkman **A:** Jim Aparo

140 ❑ Mar 1978 Cover: 0.35 **NM** value: **3.50**
Circ: Statement: **121,563**
• Wonder Woman **A:** Jim Aparo

141 ❑ May 1978 Cover: 0.35 **NM** value: **11.00**
Circ: Statement: **121,563** • **CGC:** 3 graded, best 9.8
• Black Canary, Joker; Has 1977 Statement; avg print run 355,507; avg sales 147,912; avg subs 1,879; avg total paid 149,791; samples 400; office use 2,722; max existent 152,913; 57% of run returned

142 ❑ Jul 1978 Cover: 0.35 **NM** value: **3.50**
Circ: Statement: **121,563**
• Aquaman **A:** Jim Aparo

143 ❑ Sep 1978 Cover: 0.50 **NM** value: **3.50**
Circ: Statement: **121,563**
A: Jim Aparo ★ Origin of Human Target.

144 ❑ Nov 1978 Cover: 0.50 **NM** value: **3.50**
Circ: Statement: **121,563**
• Green Arrow **A:** Jim Aparo

145 ❑ Dec 1978 Cover: 0.40 **NM** value: **3.50**
Circ: Statement: **121,563**
• Phantom Stranger **A:** Jim Aparo

146 ❑ Jan 1979 Cover: 0.40 **NM** value: **3.50**
Circ: Statement: **153,034**
• E-2 Batman/Unknown Soldier **A:** Jim Aparo

147 ❑ Feb 1979 Cover: 0.40 **NM** value: **3.50**
Circ: Statement: **153,034**
A: Jim Aparo ★ Appearance of Doctor Light.

148 ❑ Mar 1979 Cover: 0.40 **NM** value: **3.50**
Circ: Statement: **153,034**
• Plastic Man

149 ❑ Apr 1979 Cover: 0.40 **NM** value: **3.50**
Circ: Statement: **153,034** • **CGC:** 4 graded, best 9.6
• Teen Titans; Has 1978 Statement; avg print run 368,255; avg sales 119,955; avg subs 1,608; avg total paid 121,563; samples 105; office use 3,100; max existent 124,768; 66% of run returned **A:** Jim Aparo

150 ❑ May 1979 Cover: 0.40 **NM** value: **3.50**
Circ: Statement: **153,034** • **CGC:** 2 graded, best 9.6
• Superman **A:** Jim Aparo

151 ❑ Jun 1979 Cover: 0.40 **NM** value: **3.50**
Circ: Statement: **153,034**
• Flash **A:** Jim Aparo

152 ❑ Jul 1979 Cover: 0.40 **NM** value: **3.50**
Circ: Statement: **153,034**
• Atom **A:** Jim Aparo

153 ❑ Aug 1979 Cover: 0.40 **NM** value: **3.50**
Circ: Statement: **153,034**
• Red Tornado **A:** Don Newton

154 ❑ Sep 1979 Cover: 0.40 **NM** value: **3.50**
Circ: Statement: **153,034**
• Metamorpho **A:** Jim Aparo

155 ❑ Oct 1979 Cover: 0.40 **NM** value: **3.50**
Circ: Statement: **153,034**
• Green Lantern **A:** Jim Aparo

156 ❑ Nov 1979 Cover: 0.40 **NM** value: **3.50**
Circ: Statement: **153,034**
• Doctor Fate **A:** Don Newton

157 ❑ Dec 1979 Cover: 0.40 **NM** value: **3.50**
Circ: Statement: **153,034**
• Kamandi, continues story from Kamandi #59;Kamandi;continues story from Kamandi #59 **A:** Jim Aparo

158 ❑ Jan 1980 Cover: 0.40 **NM** value: **3.50**
Circ: Statement: **109,180**
• Wonder Woman **A:** Jim Aparo

159 ❑ Feb 1980 Cover: 0.40 **NM** value: **3.50**
Circ: Statement: **109,180**
• Ra's al Ghul **A:** Jim Aparo

CGC-graded: Multiply prices above by **33 for 9.9 M • 16 for 9.8 NM/M • 7 for 9.6 NM+ • 5 for 9.4 NM • 2.5 for 9.2 NM- • 1.5 for 9.0 VF/NM**

160 ❑ Mar 1980 Cover: 0.40 **NM** value: **3.50**
Circ: Statement: **109,180**
• Supergirl **A:** Jim Aparo
161 ❑ Apr 1980 Cover: 0.40 **NM** value: **3.50**
Circ: Statement: **109,180 • CGC:** 1 graded, best 9.4
• Adam Strange; Has 1979 Statement; avg print run 298,166; avg sales 152,252; avg subs 783; avg total paid 153,034; office use 122; max existent 153,157; 49% of run returned **A:** Jim Aparo
162 ❑ May 1980 Cover: 0.40 **NM** value: **3.50**
Circ: Statement: **109,180**
• Sgt. Rock **A:** Jim Aparo
163 ❑ Jun 1980 Cover: 0.40 **NM** value: **3.50**
Circ: Statement: **109,180**
• Black Lightning **A:** Dick Giordano
164 ❑ Jul 1980 Cover: 0.40 **NM** value: **3.50**
Circ: Statement: **109,180**
🕮 The Mystery of the Mobile Museum! • Hawkman **A:** José Luis Garcia-Lopez ★ Appearance of Hawkgirl, Hawkman.
165 ❑ Aug 1980 Cover: 0.40 **NM** value: **3.50**
Circ: Statement: **109,180**
• Man-Bat **A:** Don Newton
166 ❑ Sep 1980 Cover: 0.40 **NM** value: **3.50**
Circ: Statement: **109,180**
• Black Canary **A:** Don Spiegle; Tony DeZuniga ★ 1st Appearance of Nemesis.
167 ❑ Oct 1980 Cover: 0.50 **NM** value: **3.50**
Circ: Statement: **109,180**
• Blackhawk **A:** Dave Cockrum; Dan Adkins
168 ❑ Nov 1980 Cover: 0.50 **NM** value: **3.50**
Circ: Statement: **109,180**
• Green Arrow **A:** Jim Aparo
169 ❑ Dec 1980 Cover: 0.50 **NM** value: **3.50**
Circ: Statement: **109,180**
• Zatanna **A:** Jim Aparo
170 ❑ Jan 1981 Cover: 0.50 **NM** value: **3.50**
Circ: Statement: **92,847**
• Nemesis **A:** Jim Aparo
171 ❑ Feb 1981 Cover: 0.50 **NM** value: **3.50**
Circ: Statement: **92,847**
• Scalphunter **A:** Gene Colan; José Luis Garcia-Lopez
172 ❑ Mar 1981 Cover: 0.50 **NM** value: **3.50**
Circ: Statement: **92,847**
• Firestorm **A:** Carmine Infantino
173 ❑ Apr 1981 Cover: 0.50 **NM** value: **3.50**
Circ: Statement: **92,847**
• Guardians **A:** Jim Aparo
174 ❑ May 1981 Cover: 0.50 **NM** value: **3.50**
Circ: Statement: **92,847**
• Green Lantern; Has 1980 Statement; avg print run 241,477; avg sales 107,850 avg subs 1,330; avg total paid 109,180; samples 127; max existent 112,166; 66% of run returned **A:** Jim Aparo
175 ❑ Jun 1981 Cover: 0.50 **NM** value: **3.50**
Circ: Statement: **92,847**
• Lois Lane **A:** Jim Aparo
176 ❑ Jul 1981 Cover: 0.50 **NM** value: **3.50**
Circ: Statement: **92,847**
• Swamp Thing **A:** Jim Aparo
177 ❑ Aug 1981 Cover: 0.50 **NM** value: **3.50**
Circ: Statement: **92,847**
• Elongated Man **A:** Jim Aparo
178 ❑ Sep 1981 Cover: 0.50 **NM** value: **3.50**
Circ: Statement: **92,847**
• Creeper **A:** Jim Aparo
179 ❑ Oct 1981 Cover: 0.60 **NM** value: **3.50**
Circ: Statement: **92,847 • CGC:** 6 graded, best 9.6
• Legion **A:** Ernie Colon
180 ❑ Nov 1981 Cover: 0.60 **NM** value: **3.00**
Circ: Statement: **92,847**
• Spectre, Nemesis **A:** Jim Aparo
181 ❑ Dec 1981 Cover: 0.60 **NM** value: **3.00**
Circ: Statement: **92,847**
• Hawk & Dove, Nemesis **A:** Jim Aparo
182 ❑ Jan 1982 Cover: 0.60 **NM** value: **3.00**
Circ: Statement: **91,097**
• E-2 Robin **A:** Jim Aparo
183 ❑ Feb 1982 Cover: 0.60 **NM** value: **3.00**
Circ: Statement: **91,097**
• Riddler, Nemesis **A:** Carmine Infantino
184 ❑ Mar 1982 Cover: 0.60 **NM** value: **3.00**
Circ: Statement: **91,097**
• Huntress **A:** Jim Aparo
185 ❑ Apr 1982 Cover: 0.60 **NM** value: **3.00**
Circ: Statement: **91,097**
• Green Lantern
186 ❑ May 1982 Cover: 0.60 **NM** value: **3.00**
Circ: Statement: **91,097**
• Hawkman, Nemesis; Has 1981 Statement; avg print run 241,261; avg sales 91,247; avg subs 1,600; avg total paid 92,847; samples 127; office use 3,997; max existent 96,971; 60% of run returned **A:** Jim Aparo
187 ❑ Jun 1982 Cover: 0.60 **NM** value: **3.00**
Circ: Statement: **91,097 • CGC:** 1 graded, best 6.5
• Metal Men, Nemesis **A:** Jim Aparo
188 ❑ Jul 1982 Cover: 0.60 **NM** value: **3.00**
Circ: Statement: **91,097**
🕮 A Grave As Wide As The World • Rose & Thorn **A:** Jim Aparo **W:** Robert Kanigher
189 ❑ Aug 1982 Cover: 0.60 **NM** value: **3.00**
Circ: Statement: **91,097**
• Thorn, Nemesis **A:** Jim Aparo
190 ❑ Sep 1982 Cover: 0.60 **NM** value: **3.00**
Circ: Statement: **91,097**
• Adam Strange, Nemesis **A:** Jim Aparo
191 ❑ Oct 1982 Cover: 0.60 **NM** value: **8.00**
Circ: Statement: **91,097 • CGC:** 2 graded, best 9.6
• Joker **A:** Jim Aparo ★ Appearance of Penguin, Nemesis.
192 ❑ Nov 1982 Cover: 0.60 **NM** value: **3.00**
Circ: Statement: **91,097**
• Superboy **A:** Jim Aparo ★ Versus Mr. IQ.
193 ❑ Dec 1982 Cover: 0.60 **NM** value: **3.00**
Circ: Statement: **91,097**
A: Jim Aparo ★ Death of Nemesis.
194 ❑ Jan 1984 Cover: 0.60 **NM** value: **3.00**
• Flash;Flash, V: Rainbow Raider, Double-X **A:** Carmine Infantino ★ Versus Double-X. ★ Versus Rainbow Raider.
195 ❑ Feb 1984 Cover: 0.60 **NM** value: **3.00**
• I...Vampire **A:** Jim Aparo
196 ❑ Mar 1984 Cover: 0.60 **NM** value: **3.00**
• Ragman **A:** Jim Aparo
197 ❑ Apr 1984 Cover: 0.60 **NM** value: **4.00**
• CGC: 1 graded, best 9.8
• Catwoman;Wedding of Earth-2 Batman & Earth-2 Catwoman **A:** Joe Simon
198 ❑ May 1984 Cover: 0.60 **NM** value: **3.00**
• Karate Kid; Has 1982 Statement; avg print run 236,457; avg sales 89,457; avg subs 1,640; avg total paid 91,097; samples 677; office use 1,869; max existent 93,643; 60% of run returned
199 ❑ Jun 1984 Cover: 0.60 **NM** value: **3.00**
• Spectre **A:** Ross Andru
200 ❑ Jul 1984 Cover: 1.50 **NM** value: **7.00**
• CGC: 5 graded, best 9.6
• Giant-size. final issue. • E-1 and E-2 Batman **A:** Jim Aparo ★ 1st Appearance of Halo, Katana, Geo-Force, Outsiders.

BRAVE AND THE BOLD, THE (MINI-SERIES) DC

1 ❑ Dec 1991 Cover: 1.75 **NM** value: **2.50**
Circ: CapCity orders: **35,600**
A: Shea Anton Pensa **W:** Mike Grell; Mike Baron
2 ❑ Jan 1992 Cover: 1.75 **NM** value: **2.00**
Circ: CapCity orders: **23,050**
A: Shea Anton Pensa **W:** Mike Grell; Mike Baron
3 ❑ Feb 1992 Cover: 1.75 **NM** value: **2.00**
Circ: CapCity orders: **19,450**
A: Shea Anton Pensa **W:** Mike Grell; Mike Baron
4 ❑ Mar 1992 Cover: 1.75 **NM** value: **Cover or less**
Circ: CapCity orders: **15,450**
A: Shea Anton Pensa **W:** Mike Grell; Mike Baron
5 ❑ May 1992 Cover: 1.75 **NM** value: **Cover or less**
Circ: CapCity orders: **12,650**
A: Shea Anton Pensa **W:** Mike Grell; Mike Baron
6 ❑ Jun 1992 Cover: 1.75 **NM** value: **Cover or less**
Circ: CapCity orders: **11,450**
A: Shea Anton Pensa **W:** Mike Grell; Mike Baron

BRAVE OLD WORLD DC / Vertigo

1 ❑ Feb 2000 Cover: 2.50 **NM** value: **Cover or less**
Circ: Diamd. preorders: **14,728**
🕮 The Century Turns, Abort, Retry, Reboot (Winter) **A:** Guy Davis; Phil Hester **W:** William Messner-Loebs
2 ❑ Mar 2000 Cover: 2.50 **NM** value: **Cover or less**
Circ: Diamd. preorders: **10,797**
🕮 Melting Pot; Manual Override (Spring) **A:** Guy Davis; Phil Hester **W:** William Messner-Loebs
3 ❑ Apr 2000 Cover: 2.50 **NM** value: **Cover or less**
Circ: Diamd. preorders: **9,813**
🕮 A Thousand Natural Shocks; Bugfix (Summer) **A:** Guy Davis; Phil Hester **W:** William Messner-Loebs
4 ❑ May 2000 Cover: 2.50 **NM** value: **Cover or less**
Circ: Diamd. preorders: **9,113**
🕮 Weaker Vessels; Permanent Fatal Errors (Fall) **A:** Guy Davis; Phil Hester **W:** William Messner-Loebs

BRAVESTARR IN 3-D Blackthorne

1 ❑ Cover: 2.50 **NM** value: **Cover or less**
2 ❑ Cover: 2.50 **NM** value: **Cover or less**
Circ: CapCity orders: **1,200**

BRAVO FOR ADVENTURE Dragon Lady

1 ❑ Cover: 5.95 **NM** value: **Cover or less**
A: Alex Toth

BRAVURA PREVIEW BOOK Malibu / Bravura

Malibu Comics made a splash with the 1994 debut of its Bravura line of creator-owned comics. The Bravura Preview comics were used as teasers to introduce readers to the new line.

Bravura's first year included the mystery-horror title 'Breed by Jim Starlin, Howard Chaykin's heroic redux Power & Glory, Walt Simonson's space-adventure title Star Slammers, a new Dreadstar (Malibu) series by Peter David and Ernie Colon, and super-powered action title Edge by Steven Grant and Gil Kane.

1995's preview comic book introduced readers to Bravura's new line-up. Leading off the pack was action-romance Strikeback!, Jim Starlin's 'Breed II, Daniel Brereton's moody Nocturnals, Marv Wolfman's action-packed The Man Called A-X, and Norm Breyfogle's search for meaning in Metaphysique.

0 ❑ **NM** value: **3.00**
🕮 'Breed story; Power and Glory story; Falling from Grace (text); Dreadstar Sketchbook; The Sky is Falling • Coupon redemption promotion **A:** Jim Starlin; Howard Chaykin; Gil Kane; Walt Simonson; Ernie Colon **W:** Jim Starlin; Howard Chaykin; Walt Simonson; Steven Grant
1 ❑ Nov 1993 Cover: 1.50 **NM** value: **Cover or less**
no cover price. • 1994 Preview book
2 ❑ Aug 1994 Cover: 1.50 **NM** value: **Cover or less**
Circ: CapCity orders: **7,675**
(#1 on cover). • 1995 Preview book **W:** Kara Lamb

BREAD & CIRCUSES Moe Press / Bravura

1 ❑ Cover: 2.50 **NM** value: **Cover or less**
🕮 Swimming with Belugas; Me and the Folk Hero; Tough Love **A:** Andy Hartzell **W:** Andy Hartzell

BREAKDOWNS Infinity

1 ❑ Oct 1986 Cover: 1.70 **NM** value: **Cover or less**
• CGC: 1 graded, best 9.4
🕮 Theater of the Absurd; Limaperg; The Curious Cures of Dr. Rafgagh; Psychofrenzy; Bad Nightmare; I 'ate Me Arm! **A:** J.J. Cobb; Russell Runion **W:** J.J. Cobb; Russell Runion

BREAKFAST AFTER NOON Oni

1 ❑ May 2000, b&w Cover: 2.95 **NM** value: **Cover or less**
Circ: Diamd. preorders: **3,637**
A: Andi Watson **W:** Andi Watson
2 ❑ Aug 2000, b&w Cover: 2.95 **NM** value: **Cover or less**
Circ: Diamd. preorders: **2,684**
A: Andi Watson **W:** Andi Watson
3 ❑ Sep 2000, b&w Cover: 2.95 **NM** value: **Cover or less**
Circ: Diamd. preorders: **2,761**
A: Andi Watson **W:** Andi Watson
4 ❑ Nov 2000, b&w Cover: 2.95 **NM** value: **Cover or less**
Circ: Diamd. preorders: **2,469**
A: Andi Watson **W:** Andi Watson
5 ❑ Dec 2000, b&w Cover: 2.95 **NM** value: **Cover or less**
Circ: Diamd. preorders: **2,520**
A: Andi Watson **W:** Andi Watson
6 ❑ Jan 2001, b&w Cover: 2.95 **NM** value: **Cover or less**
Circ: Diamd. preorders: **2,475**
A: Andi Watson **W:** Andi Watson

BREAKNECK BLVD. (MOTION) Motion

0 ❑ Feb 1994, b&w Cover: 2.50 **NM** value: **Cover or less**
1 ❑ Jul 1994, b&w Cover: 2.50 **NM** value: **Cover or less**
★ 1st Appearance of Blu-J, b&w, Blu-J.
2 ❑ Sep 1994, b&w Cover: 2.50 **NM** value: **Cover or less**

BREAKNECK BLVD. (SLAVE LABOR) Slave Labor

Life can be brutally short or endlessly painful on the streets, especially when, like Frank Dunkard, you don't have a clue. Tagged with the moniker Urban Angst, poor Frank winds up in more trouble than he can handle. Ranging from heated arguments with his alcoholic mother to staring down a gun barrel, he raises the tension to almost unnerving levels in every situation. Writer-artist Timothy Markin pulls no punches using frank language, sexual situations, and sharp social commentary while creating a realistic modern-day milieu. Frank uses the tough-guy persona on the street but underneath he knows that some growing up is required. Frank's getting an education at the School of Hard Knocks. It remains to be seen whether he'll survives the semester.

1 ❑ Jul 1995 Cover: 2.95 **NM** value: **Cover or less**
🕮 Feel Every Beat **A:** Timothy Markin **W:** Timothy Markin; Jeremy Mace
2 ❑ Oct 1995 Cover: 2.95 **NM** value: **Cover or less**
🕮 La Femme Incident **A:** Timothy Markin **W:** Timothy Markin; Jeremy Mace
3 ❑ Jan 1996 Cover: 2.95 **NM** value: **Cover or less**
A: Timothy Markin **W:** Timothy Markin; Jeremy Mace
4 ❑ May 1996 Cover: 2.95 **NM** value: **Cover or less**
🕮 A Long Way From Home **A:** Timothy Markin **W:** Timothy Markin; Jeremy Mace
5 ❑ Aug 1996 Cover: 2.95 **NM** value: **Cover or less**
🕮 Ten Percenter **A:** Timothy Markin **W:** Timothy Markin; Jeremy Mace
6 ❑ Dec 1996 Cover: 2.95 **NM** value: **Cover or less**
🕮 More Fire than Flame **A:** Timothy Markin **W:** Timothy Markin; Jeremy Mace

BREAK THE CHAIN Marvel Music

1 ❑ Cover: 6.99 **NM** value: **Cover or less**
Circ: CapCity orders: **3,350**
• polybagged with KRS-1 cassette tape **A:** George Pérez **W:** Gerard Jones

BREAK-THRU Malibu

1 ❑ Dec 1993 Cover: 2.50 **NM** value: **Cover or less**
Circ: CapCity orders: **32,400**
🕮 Break-Thru, Part 1 **A:** George Pérez
1/LE ❑ Dec 1993 Cover: 2.50 **NM** value: **4.00**
• Ultra Limited;foil logo
2 ❑ Jan 1994 Cover: 2.50 **NM** value: **Cover or less**
Circ: CapCity orders: **21,850**
🕮 Break-Thru, Part 13 **A:** George Pérez

BREATHTAKER DC

1 ❑ Jul 1990 Cover: 4.95 **NM** value: **5.00**
Circ: CapCity orders: **11,650**
A: Marc Hempel **W:** Mark Wheatley ★ 1st Appearance of The Man, Breathtaker.
2 ❑ Aug 1990 Cover: 4.95 **NM** value: **5.00**
Circ: CapCity orders: **8,550**
A: Marc Hempel **W:** Mark Wheatley
3 ❑ Sep 1990 Cover: 4.95 **NM** value: **5.00**
Circ: CapCity orders: **7,700**
A: Marc Hempel **W:** Mark Wheatley ★ Origin of Breathtaker.
4 ❑ Oct 1990 Cover: 4.95 **NM** value: **5.00**
Circ: CapCity orders: **6,750**
A: Marc Hempel **W:** Mark Wheatley

Other grades: Multiply prices above by **1.5 for Mint • 2/3 for Very Fine • 1/3 for Fine • 1/5 for Very Good • 1/8 for Good**

Bk 1❑ Cover: 14.95 **NM value: Cover or less**
• Reprints Breathtaker #1-4 with new pages;introduction by Neil Gaiman **A:** Marc Hempel **W:** Mark Wheatley; Neil Gaiman

'BREED — Malibu / Bravura

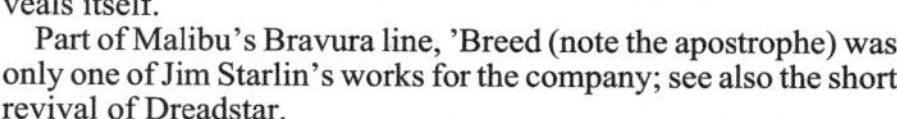

It was just after the second World War when it all began, in a town with the unlikely name of Bucksnort, Texas. (Well, not so unlikely. There's one in Tennessee!) Following a disturbance, a police car is sent to investigate, only to disappear. Army troops enter the town to found a charnel house. The town has only one survivor: a pregnant woman. But who was the father?

Giving birth to a healthy son, the woman lapses into a catatonic state, and the boy is taken by a soldier to raise. Years passed uneventfully, until the boy sees combat in Laos. Then, under fire, his true nature reveals itself.

Part of Malibu's Bravura line, 'Breed (note the apostrophe) was only one of Jim Starlin's works for the company; see also the short revival of Dreadstar.

1 ❑ Jan 1994 Cover: 2.50 **NM value: Cover or less**
Circ: CapCity orders: **38,750**
2 ❑ Feb 1994 Cover: 2.50 **NM value: Cover or less**
Circ: CapCity orders: **20,250**
3 ❑ Mar 1994 Cover: 2.50 **NM value: Cover or less**
Circ: CapCity orders: **18,375**
4 ❑ Apr 1994 Cover: 2.50 **NM value: Cover or less**
Circ: CapCity orders: **20,500**
5 ❑ May 1994 Cover: 2.50 **NM value: Cover or less**
Circ: CapCity orders: **20,625**
6 ❑ Jun 1994 Cover: 2.50 **NM value: Cover or less**
Circ: CapCity orders: **20,125**
Bk 1❑ Cover: 12.95 **NM value: Cover or less**
• Collects 'Breed 1-6 **A:** Jim Starlin **W:** Jim Starlin

BREEDER//CERTAIN.REVOLUTIONS — Visceral

1 ❑ Cover: 0.99 **NM value: Cover or less**
A: Alan Hagen **W:** Davey Perry

'BREED II — Malibu / Bravura

1 ❑ Nov 1994 Cover: 2.95 **NM value: Cover or less**
Circ: CapCity orders: **15,250**
2 ❑ Dec 1994 Cover: 2.95 **NM value: Cover or less**
Circ: CapCity orders: **10,825**
3 ❑ Jan 1995 Cover: 2.95 **NM value: Cover or less**
Circ: CapCity orders: **9,925**
4 ❑ Feb 1995 Cover: 2.95 **NM value: Cover or less**
Circ: CapCity orders: **8,875**
5 ❑ Mar 1995 Cover: 2.95 **NM value: Cover or less**
Circ: CapCity orders: **8,475**
6 ❑ Apr 1995 Cover: 2.95 **NM value: Cover or less**
Circ: CapCity orders: **8,050**

BRENDA STARR — Four Star

13 ❑ Sep 1947 Cover: 0.10 **NM value: 500.00**
• **CGC:** 1 graded, best 8.5
14 ❑ Mar 1948 Cover: 0.10 **NM value: 500.00**
• **CGC:** 4 graded, best 9.4
3 ❑ Jun 1948 Cover: 0.10 **NM value: 450.00**
• **CGC:** 2 graded, best 9.0
4 ❑ Sep 1948 Cover: 0.10 **NM value: 450.00**
• **CGC:** 1 graded, best 8.5
5 ❑ Nov 1948 Cover: 0.10 **NM value: 400.00**
• **CGC:** 1 graded, best 9.2
6 ❑ Jan 1949 Cover: 0.10 **NM value: 400.00**
• **CGC:** 1 graded, best 8.0
7 ❑ Mar 1949 Cover: 0.10 **NM value: 400.00**
• **CGC:** 1 graded, best 8.0
8 ❑ May 1949 Cover: 0.10 **NM value: 400.00**
• **CGC:** 1 graded, best 9.2
9 ❑ Jul 1949 Cover: 0.10 **NM value: 400.00**
• **CGC:** 1 graded, best 9.6
10 ❑ Aug 1949 Cover: 0.10 **NM value: 400.00**
• **CGC:** 1 graded, best 9.8
11 ❑ Oct 1949 Cover: 0.10 **NM value: 400.00**
• **CGC:** 3 graded, best 9.2
12 ❑ Dec 1949 Cover: 0.10 **NM value: 400.00**
• **CGC:** 2 graded, best 9.2

BRENDA STARR (AVALON) — Avalon

1 ❑ Cover: 2.95 **NM value: Cover or less**
A: Dale Messick **W:** Dale Messick
2 ❑ Cover: 2.95 **NM value: Cover or less**
A: Dale Messick **W:** Dale Messick

BRENDA STARR (CHARLTON) — Charlton

13 ❑ Jun 1955 Cover: 0.10 **NM value: 100.00**
• Reprints from newspaper strips **A:** Dale Messick **W:** Dale Messick
14 ❑ Aug 1955 Cover: 0.10 **NM value: 100.00**
• Reprints from newspaper strips **A:** Dale Messick **W:** Dale Messick
15 ❑ Oct 1955 Cover: 0.10 **NM value: 100.00**
final issue. • Reprints from newspaper strips **A:** Dale Messick **W:** Dale Messick

BRENDA STARR CUT-OUTS AND COLORING BOOK — Blackthorne

1 ❑ Cover: 6.95 **NM value: Cover or less**

BRENDA STARR REPORTER (1ST SERIES) — Charlton

13 ❑ Jun 1955 Cover: 0.10 **NM value: 125.00**
• **CGC:** 1 graded, best 8.5
14 ❑ Aug 1955 Cover: 0.10 **NM value: 125.00**
15 ❑ Oct 1955 Cover: 0.10 **NM value: 125.00**

BRENDA STARR REPORTER (2ND SERIES) — Dell

1 ❑ Oct 1963 Cover: 0.12 **NM value: 150.00**
• **CGC:** 2 graded, best 9.4

BRICK BRADFORD — Standard

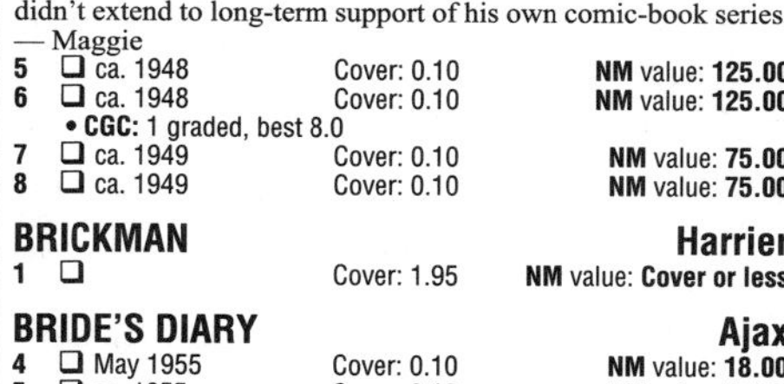

The character began in newspaper comic strips in 1933, written by William Ritt and drawn by Clarence Gray and featured a combination of all sorts of traditional pulp adventures. The main gimmick was Brick's "Time Top," used to get his buddies and him "safely" out of one era's dangers (and into those of another).

Dressed in what critic Coulton Waugh termed a "specially designed cosmosuit, a startling compromise between riding breeches and bell-bottomed trousers, the dynamic adventurer faced crises with aplomb. His prowess, however, didn't extend to long-term support of his own comic-book series. — Maggie

5 ❑ ca. 1948 Cover: 0.10 **NM value: 125.00**
6 ❑ ca. 1948 Cover: 0.10 **NM value: 125.00**
• **CGC:** 1 graded, best 8.0
7 ❑ ca. 1949 Cover: 0.10 **NM value: 75.00**
8 ❑ ca. 1949 Cover: 0.10 **NM value: 75.00**

BRICKMAN — Harrier

1 ❑ Cover: 1.95 **NM value: Cover or less**

BRIDE'S DIARY — Ajax

4 ❑ May 1955 Cover: 0.10 **NM value: 18.00**
5 ❑ ca. 1955 Cover: 0.10 **NM value: 15.00**
6 ❑ Cover: 0.10 **NM value: 15.00**
7 ❑ Cover: 0.10 **NM value: 15.00**
8 ❑ ca. 1956 Cover: 0.10 **NM value: 12.00**
9 ❑ Cover: 0.10 **NM value: 12.00**
10 ❑ Cover: 0.10 **NM value: 12.00**

BRIDE'S SECRETS — Ajax

1 ❑ Mar 1954 Cover: 0.10 **NM value: 45.00**
2 ❑ ca. 1954 Cover: 0.10 **NM value: 25.00**
📖 I Married a Mama's Boy; Belated Kisses; Was My Wedding Band to Tarnish; Runaway Wife
3 ❑ ca. 1954 Cover: 0.10 **NM value: 16.00**
4 ❑ Cover: 0.10 **NM value: 16.00**
5 ❑ Cover: 0.10 **NM value: 16.00**
6 ❑ Cover: 0.10 **NM value: 16.00**
7 ❑ ca. 1955 Cover: 0.10 **NM value: 10.00**
8 ❑ Cover: 0.10 **NM value: 10.00**
9 ❑ Cover: 0.10 **NM value: 10.00**
10 ❑ Cover: 0.10 **NM value: 10.00**
11 ❑ Cover: 0.10 **NM value: 9.00**
12 ❑ Cover: 0.10 **NM value: 9.00**
13 ❑ Cover: 0.10 **NM value: 9.00**
14 ❑ Cover: 0.10 **NM value: 9.00**
15 ❑ Cover: 0.10 **NM value: 9.00**
16 ❑ Cover: 0.10 **NM value: 9.00**
17 ❑ Cover: 0.10 **NM value: 9.00**
18 ❑ Cover: 0.10 **NM value: 9.00**
19 ❑ May 1958 Cover: 0.10 **NM value: 9.00**
final issue.

BRIDGMAN'S CONSTRUCTIVE ANATOMY — A-List

1 ❑ Apr 1998, b&w Cover: 2.95 **NM value: Cover or less**

BRIGADE — Image

After months in space in the Brigade limited series, the team finally makes its way back to its base in Malibu, Calif. Saddened by the death of their friend, Atlas, everyone is feeling a little edgy on arrival. Little do they know that mere moments after they land, another teammate, Stasis, will be cut down in cold blood. Her assassin is none other than Battlestone's brother Cabbot, leader of Bloodstrike.

Sudden death and non-stop action set the pace for this second volume of Brigade. Published as an ongoing series, it was created and coplotted by Image artist Rob Liefeld.

0 ❑ Sep 1993 Cover: 1.95 **NM value: 2.25**
Circ: CapCity orders: **114,075**
gatefold cover. **A:** Jeff Matsuda **W:** Rob Liefeld ★ 1st Appearance of Warcry.
1 ❑ May 1993 Cover: 1.95 **NM value: 2.00**
Circ: CapCity orders: **148,925**
📖 Blood Brothers, Part 1 **A:** Marat Mychaels **W:** Rob Liefeld ★ 1st Appearance of Boone, Hacker.
2 ❑ Jun 1993 Cover: 2.95 **NM value: Cover or less**
Circ: CapCity orders: **105,350**
foil cover. 📖 Blood Brothers, Part 3 **A:** Marat Mychaels **W:** Eric Stephenson; Hank Kanalz
2/A ❑ Jun 1993 Cover: 2.95 **NM value: Cover or less**
alternate cover.
3 ❑ Sep 1993 Cover: 1.95 **NM value: 2.00**
Circ: CapCity orders: **87,525**
📖 Blood Brothers, Part 5 ★ 1st Appearance of Roman.
4 ❑ Oct 1993 Cover: 1.95 **NM value: 2.00**
Circ: CapCity orders: **86,250**
5 ❑ Nov 1993 Cover: 1.95 **NM value: 2.00**
Circ: CapCity orders: **71,250**
6 ❑ Dec 1993 Cover: 1.95 **NM value: Cover or less**
Circ: CapCity orders: **64,200**
★ 1st Appearance of Worlok, Coral.
7 ❑ Feb 1994 Cover: 1.95 **NM value: Cover or less**
Circ: CapCity orders: **32,800**
8 ❑ Mar 1994 Cover: 1.95 **NM value: Cover or less**
Circ: CapCity orders: **31,825**
📖 Extreme Prejudice
9 ❑ Apr 1994 Cover: 1.95 **NM value: Cover or less**
Circ: CapCity orders: **29,925**
📖 Extreme Prejudice, Part 6
10 ❑ Jun 1994 Cover: 1.95 **NM value: Cover or less**
Circ: CapCity orders: **28,875**
11 ❑ Aug 1994 Cover: 2.50 **NM value: Cover or less**
Circ: CapCity orders: **27,675**
★ Appearance of WildC.A.T.s.
12 ❑ Sep 1994 Cover: 2.50 **NM value: Cover or less**
Circ: CapCity orders: **25,450**
★ Appearance of WildC.A.T.s.
13 ❑ Oct 1994 Cover: 1.95 **NM value: 2.50**
Circ: CapCity orders: **23,200**
14 ❑ Nov 1994 Cover: 1.95 **NM value: 2.50**
Circ: CapCity orders: **20,100**
15 ❑ Dec 1994 Cover: 2.50 **NM value: Cover or less**
Circ: CapCity orders: **18,550**
16 ❑ Jan 1995 Cover: 2.50 **NM value: Cover or less**
Circ: CapCity orders: **20,450**
📖 Extreme Sacrifice, Part 4; Extreme Sacrifice, Part 3
17 ❑ Feb 1995 Cover: 2.50 **NM value: Cover or less**
Circ: CapCity orders: **14,850**
📖 Extreme Sacrifice Aftermath
18 ❑ Mar 1995 Cover: 2.50 **NM value: Cover or less**
Circ: CapCity orders: **13,975**
18/SC❑Mar 1995 Cover: 2.50 **NM value: Cover or less**
alternate cover.
19 ❑ Apr 1995 Cover: 2.50 **NM value: Cover or less**
Circ: CapCity orders: **13,100**
★ Appearance of Glory.
20/A❑May 1995 Cover: 2.50 **NM value: Cover or less**
Circ: CapCity orders: **13,175**
★ Appearance of Glory.
20/B❑May 1995 Cover: 2.50 **NM value: Cover or less**
alternate cover. ★ Appearance of Glory, Glory.
21 ❑ Jun 1995 Cover: 2.50 **NM value: Cover or less**
Circ: CapCity orders: **13,750**
• Funeral of Shadowhawk
22 ❑ Jul 1995 Cover: 2.50 **NM value: Cover or less**
Circ: CapCity orders: **14,950**
25 ❑ May 1994 Cover: 1.95 **NM value: Cover or less**
Circ: CapCity orders: **32,325**
• Images of Tomorrow;Published out of sequence as a preview of the future
26 ❑ Jun 1994 Cover: 1.95 **NM value: Cover or less**
Circ: CapCity orders: **30,375**
• Published out of sequence as a preview of the future
27 ❑ Jul 1994 Cover: 2.50 **NM value: Cover or less**
final issue.

BRIGADE (MINI-SERIES) — Image

1 ❑ Aug 1992 Cover: 1.95 **NM value: 2.50**
Circ: CapCity orders: **205,050**
C: Rob Liefeld ★ 1st Appearance of Genocide, Brigade.
1/GO❑Aug 1992 Cover: 5.00 **NM value: Cover or less**
• **CGC:** 1 graded, best 9.2
• Gold edition. ★ 1st Appearance of Genocide, Brigade.
2 ❑ Oct 1992 Cover: 3.50 **NM value: Cover or less**
Circ: CapCity orders: **137,400**
C: Rob Liefeld
2/GO❑Oct 1992 Cover: 3.50 **NM value: Cover or less**
• Gold edition.
3 ❑ Feb 1993 Cover: 1.95 **NM value: 2.00**
Circ: CapCity orders: **116,800**
A: Marat Mychaels **C:** Rob Liefeld **W:** Eric Stephenson ★ 1st Appearance of the Birds of Prey.
4 ❑ Jul 1993 Cover: 2.50 **NM value: Cover or less**
Circ: CapCity orders: **78,725**
• flip side of Youngblood #5

BRIGADE SOURCEBOOK — Image

1 ❑ Aug 1994 Cover: 2.95 **NM value: Cover or less**
Circ: CapCity orders: **18,750**

BRIK HAUSS — Blackthorne

1 ❑ Jul 1987 Cover: 1.75 **NM value: Cover or less**
📖 Brik Hauss and the Nuclear Cat-Astrophe

BRILLIANT BOY — Circus

1 ❑ Jan 1997 Cover: 2.95 **NM value: Cover or less**
2 ❑ Mar 1997 Cover: 2.50 **NM value: Cover or less**
3 ❑ May 1997 Cover: 2.50 **NM value: Cover or less**
4 ❑ Cover: 2.50 **NM value: Cover or less**
5 ❑ Cover: 2.50 **NM value: Cover or less**

CGC-graded: Multiply prices above by **33 for 9.9 M • 16 for 9.8 NM/M • 7 for 9.6 NM+ • 5 for 9.4 NM • 2.5 for 9.2 NM- • 1.5 for 9.0 VF/NM**

BRING BACK THE BAD GUYS — Marvel

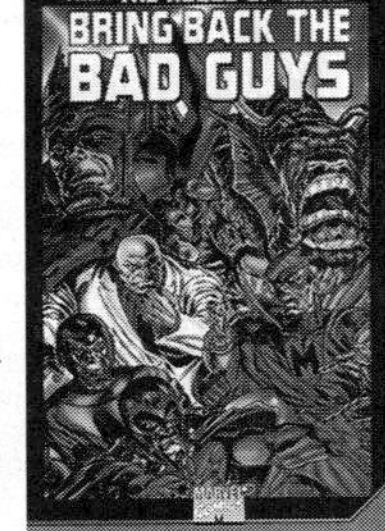

In this sequel to Stan Lee's Bring on the Bad Guys, the House of Ideas again offers a selection of stories introducing some of Marvel Comics' most classic villains.

Magneto, the master of magnetism, is featured in reprints from X-Men (1st Series) #4 and #161. The Kingpin plots against both Spider-Man (Marvel Tales #190) and Daredevil (Daredevil #172). The Avengers face the time-traveling might of Kang the Conqueror in Avengers #8 and Giant-Size Avengers #2. The many-ringed Mandarin battles Iron Man in Tales of Suspense #50 and Iron Man #275. Finally, the cosmos-spanning might of Galactus is displayed in Fantastic Four #341. The trade paperback also reprints the original 10-page story featuring the classic Lee-Kirby monster Fin Fang Foom.

Bring Back the Bad Guys presents the work of Stan Lee, Jack Kirby, John Romita, Don Heck, Steve Englehart, Chris Claremont, Dave Cockrum, Frank Miller, Klaus Janson, John Byrne, Paul Ryan, and Walter Simonson.

1 ❑ May 1998 Cover: 24.99 **NM** value: **Cover or less**
📖 The Brotherhood of Evil Mutants!; Gold Rush!; Spider-Man No More!; Gang War; Kang, the Conqueror; A Blast from the Past!; Fin Fang Foom Part 2; The Hands of the Mandarin!; Dragon Doom!; Galactus; The Ultimate Solution • Reprints X-Men #4, #161, Marvel Tales #190, Daredevil #172, The Avengers #8, GS #2, Tales of Suspense #50, Iron Man #275;The Origin of Galactus **A:** Paul Ryan; Don Heck; Jack Kirby; Frank Miller; Dave Cockrum; John Romita; Walt Simonson **W:** John Byrne; Frank Miller; Walt Simonson; Stan Lee; Chris Claremont; Steve Englehart ★ Appearance of Cyclops, Beast.

BRING ON THE BAD GUYS: ORIGINS OF THE MARVEL COMICS VILLAINS — Marvel

Bk 1❑ Cover: 6.95 **NM** value: **10.00**
📖 Prisoners of Doom; The Origin of Dr. Doom; The Comicg of Loki; The Boyhood of Loki; The Vengeance of the Thunder-God; A Viper in our Midst; The Fantastic Origin of the Red Skull; Lest Tyranny Triumph; The Sentinel and the Spy • (Fireside); all reprint material

BRINKE OF DESTRUCTION — High-Top

1 ❑ Dec 1995 Cover: 2.95 **NM** value: **Cover or less**
1/CS❑ Dec 1995 Cover: 6.99 **NM** value: **Cover or less**
• packaged with audio tape
2 ❑ Cover: 2.95 **NM** value: **Cover or less**
3 ❑ Jan 1997 Cover: 2.95 **NM** value: **Cover or less**
Circ: Direct Market orders: **3,869**
SE 1❑ Cover: 6.95 **NM** value: **Cover or less**

BRINKE OF DESTRUCTION (BVBOOKS) — BV Books

1 ❑ b&w Cover: 2.50 **NM** value: **Cover or less**
A: Bob Hanon **W:** Richard McEnroe

BRINKE OF DISASTER — High-Top

1 ❑ Sep 1996 Cover: 2.25 **NM** value: **Cover or less**
Circ: Diamd. preorders: **3,066**

BRINKE OF ETERNITY — Chaos

1 ❑ Apr 1994 Cover: 2.75 **NM** value: **Cover or less**
Circ: CapCity orders: **9,638** • **CGC:** 6 graded, best 9.8
A: Mike Holliman **W:** Brian Pulido; Brinke Stevens

BRIT-CIT BABES — Fleetway-Quality

1 ❑ Cover: 5.95 **NM** value: **Cover or less**
No issue number. **C:** Brian Bolland

BROADWAY BABES — Avalon

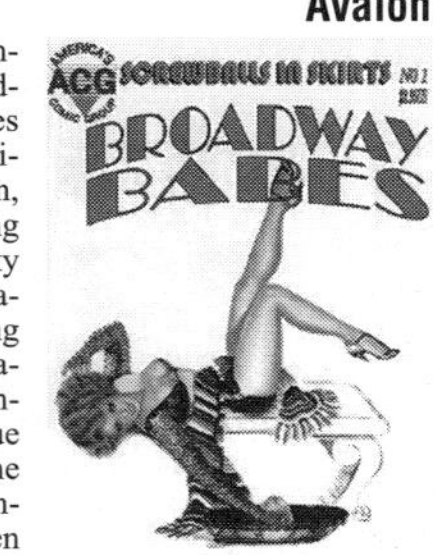

The inane adventures of Moronica are detailed in this black-and-white collection reprinting stories dating from 1950 to 1954. Moronica, a simple-minded young woman, wanders through her life, vexing and perplexing all who are unlucky enough to experience a conversation with her. When she's running a dog laundry, she tosses a live beagle and a stuffed eagle into a washing machine, resulting in a unique kind of "bird dog." At the circus, she gets into a fight with a balloon vendor who won't sell his hat even though it carries a sign that reads "5 cents." No matter what kind of foolish trouble Moronica gets into, her dumb luck always ensure that she lands on her feet, looking like the only one who really understands her wacky situations. It's all extremely reminiscent of the classic "My Friend Irma."

1 ❑ Cover: 2.95 **NM** value: **Cover or less**
📖 Moronica, Miss Nitwit of 1954; Moronica, Miss Nitwit of 1953; Moronica, Miss Nitwit of 1950 • reprints Moronica stories, b&w

BROADWAY VIDEO SPECIAL COLLECTORS EDITION — Broadway

1 ❑ **NM** value: **1.00**
cardstock cover. • Promotional giveaway. • 1150 copies printed

BROID — Eternity

1 ❑ b&w Cover: 2.75 **NM** value: **Cover or less**
2 ❑ Cover: 2.25 **NM** value: **Cover or less**
3 ❑ Cover: 2.25 **NM** value: **Cover or less**
4 ❑ Cover: 2.25 **NM** value: **Cover or less**

BROKEN AXIS — Antarctic

1 ❑ b&w Cover: 2.95 **NM** value: **Cover or less**
📖 History of Silly Wars **A:** Ben Dunn; Ted Nomora **W:** Ted Nomora

BROKEN FENDER (VOL. 2) — Top Shelf Productions

2 ❑ b&w Cover: 2.95 **NM** value: **Cover or less**

BROKEN HALO: IS THERE NOTHING SACRED? — Broken Halos

2 ❑ Oct 1998, b&w Cover: 2.95 **NM** value: **Cover or less**
Circ: Diamd. preorders: **3,397**
A: Darrell C.L. Donald **C:** Tim Vigil **W:** Darrell C.L. Donald
2/Nude❑ Oct 1998, b&w Cover: 4.95 **NM** value: **Cover or less**
• nude cover edition. **A:** Darrell C.L. Donald **C:** Tim Vigil **W:** Darrell C.L. Donald

BROKEN HEROES — Sirius

1 ❑ Mar 1998 Cover: 2.50 **NM** value: **Cover or less**
Circ: Diamd. preorders: **3,942**
2 ❑ Apr 1998 Cover: 2.50 **NM** value: **Cover or less**
Circ: Diamd. preorders: **2,583**
3 ❑ May 1998 Cover: 2.50 **NM** value: **Cover or less**
4 ❑ Jun 1998 Cover: 2.50 **NM** value: **Cover or less**
5 ❑ Jul 1998 Cover: 2.50 **NM** value: **Cover or less**
6 ❑ Aug 1998 Cover: 2.50 **NM** value: **Cover or less**
7 ❑ Sep 1998 Cover: 2.50 **NM** value: **Cover or less**
8 ❑ Oct 1998 Cover: 2.50 **NM** value: **Cover or less**
9 ❑ Nov 1998 Cover: 2.50 **NM** value: **Cover or less**
10 ❑ Dec 1998 Cover: 2.50 **NM** value: **Cover or less**
11 ❑ Jan 1999 Cover: 2.50 **NM** value: **Cover or less**
12 ❑ Feb 1999 Cover: 2.50 **NM** value: **Cover or less**

BRONX — Eternity

1 ❑ Cover: 2.50 **NM** value: **Cover or less**
2 ❑ Cover: 2.50 **NM** value: **Cover or less**
3 ❑ Cover: 2.50 **NM** value: **Cover or less**

BROOKLYN DREAMS — DC / Paradox

1 ❑ Cover: 4.95 **NM** value: **Cover or less**
Circ: CapCity orders: **4,950**
A: Glenn Barr **W:** J.M. DeMatteis
2 ❑ Cover: 4.95 **NM** value: **Cover or less**
Circ: CapCity orders: **4,025**
3 ❑ Cover: 4.95 **NM** value: **Cover or less**
Circ: CapCity orders: **3,475**
4 ❑ Cover: 4.95 **NM** value: **Cover or less**
Circ: CapCity orders: **2,775**

BROTHERHOOD — Marvel

8 ❑ **NM** value: **Cover or less**
1 ❑ Jul 2000 Cover: 2.25 **NM** value: **Cover or less**
Circ: Diamd. preorders: **72,200** • **CGC:** 15 graded, best 9.8
2 ❑ Aug 2000 Cover: 2.25 **NM** value: **Cover or less**
Circ: Diamd. preorders: **68,446** • **CGC:** 1 graded, best 9.6
3 ❑ Sep 2000 Cover: 2.25 **NM** value: **Cover or less**
Circ: Diamd. preorders: **58,728**
4 ❑ Oct 2000 Cover: 2.25 **NM** value: **Cover or less**
Circ: Diamd. preorders: **51,213**
5 ❑ Nov 2000 Cover: 2.25 **NM** value: **Cover or less**
Circ: Diamd. preorders: **43,617**
1st printing.
6 ❑ Dec 2000 Cover: 2.25 **NM** value: **Cover or less**
Circ: Diamd. preorders: **39,775**
7 ❑ Jan 2001 Cover: 2.25 **NM** value: **Cover or less**
Circ: Diamd. preorders: **34,694**

BROTHERMAN — Big City

1 ❑ Cover: 2.00 **NM** value: **Cover or less**
2 ❑ Cover: 2.00 **NM** value: **Cover or less**
3 ❑ Cover: 2.00 **NM** value: **Cover or less**
4 ❑ Cover: 2.00 **NM** value: **Cover or less**
5 ❑ Cover: 2.00 **NM** value: **Cover or less**
6 ❑ Cover: 2.00 **NM** value: **Cover or less**
7 ❑ Cover: 2.00 **NM** value: **Cover or less**
8 ❑ Cover: 2.00 **NM** value: **Cover or less**

BROTHER MAN: DICTATOR OF DISCIPLINE — Big City

11 ❑ Jul 1996 Cover: 2.95 **NM** value: **Cover or less**
• magazine-sized.

BROTHER POWER, THE GEEK — DC

Described on both covers of the short-lived series as "a thing that lives and fights for its soul!" — Brother Power the Geek carried the first-issue cover blurb "Here is the real-life scene of the dangers in hippie-land!"

Written and drawn by Joe Simon, the story opened with put-upon hippies putting bloody clothing on a tailor's dummy, spilling oil on it and leaving it by a radiator. After a couple of seasons pass, the dummy is struck by lightning and brought to life. When it fights back after an attack by motorcycle thugs, the hippies dub the dummy Brother Power. "It's for real, all right, but real what? It doesn't talk ... Is it evil? Good? Or just a geek!" Eventually, it learns to talk: "Man, I tell it like it is now! The sound is groovey! It blows my mind!" Cool? This attempt to convey a hippie character devoted to love and peace became an icon, instead, of failure in conveying the youth culture. — Maggie

1 ❑ Sep 1968 Cover: 0.12 **NM** value: **40.00**
• **CGC:** 5 graded, best 9.4
📖 A Thing is Born **A:** Joe Simon **W:** Joe Simon ★ 1st Appearance of Brother Power, the Geek.
2 ❑ Nov 1968 Cover: 0.12 **NM** value: **25.00**
• **CGC:** 1 graded, best 8.5

BROTHERS, HANG IN THERE, THE — Spire

1 ❑ Cover: 0.49 **NM** value: **3.00**
📖 Hang in There **A:** Al Hartley **W:** Al Hartley

BROTHERS OF THE SPEAR — Gold Key

1 ❑ Cover: 0.15 **NM** value: **20.00**
2 ❑ Cover: 0.15 **NM** value: **10.00**
3 ❑ Dec 1972 Cover: 0.15 **NM** value: **6.00**
📖 Attack of the Veiled Men **A:** Jesse Santos
4 ❑ ca. 1973 Cover: 0.15 **NM** value: **6.00**
5 ❑ ca. 1973 Cover: 0.20 **NM** value: **6.00**
📖 Riders In The Sky
6 ❑ ca. 1973 Cover: 0.20 **NM** value: **4.00**
7 ❑ Cover: 0.20 **NM** value: **4.00**
8 ❑ Cover: 0.20 **NM** value: **4.00**
9 ❑ Jun 1974 Cover: 0.20 **NM** value: **4.00**
10 ❑ ca. 1974 Cover: 0.25 **NM** value: **4.00**
11 ❑ Cover: 0.25 **NM** value: **4.00**
12 ❑ Cover: 0.25 **NM** value: **4.00**
13 ❑ Cover: 0.25 **NM** value: **4.00**
14 ❑ Cover: 0.25 **NM** value: **4.00**
15 ❑ ca. 1975 Cover: 0.25 **NM** value: **4.00**
16 ❑ Nov 1975 Cover: 0.25 **NM** value: **4.00**
17 ❑ Cover: 0.25 **NM** value: **4.00**
• Original series ends (1976)
18 ❑ ca. 1976 Cover: 0.25 **NM** value: **2.50**
• One-shot continuation of series (1982)

BRUCE LEE — Malibu

1 ❑ Jul 1994 Cover: 2.95 **NM** value: **Cover or less**
Circ: CapCity orders: **15,325**
📖 One In Punch **A:** Val Mayerik **W:** Mike Baron
2 ❑ Aug 1994 Cover: 2.95 **NM** value: **Cover or less**
Circ: CapCity orders: **10,750**
A: Val Mayerik **W:** Mike Baron
3 ❑ Sep 1994 Cover: 2.95 **NM** value: **Cover or less**
Circ: CapCity orders: **9,300**
📖 Tinsel Town Rebellion **A:** Val Mayerik **W:** Mike Baron
4 ❑ Oct 1994 Cover: 2.95 **NM** value: **Cover or less**
Circ: CapCity orders: **9,025**
A: Val Mayerik **W:** Mike Baron
5 ❑ Nov 1994 Cover: 2.95 **NM** value: **Cover or less**
Circ: CapCity orders: **7,825**
A: Val Mayerik **W:** Mike Baron
6 ❑ Dec 1994 Cover: 2.95 **NM** value: **Cover or less**
Circ: CapCity orders: **6,775**
A: Val Mayerik **W:** Mike Baron

BRUCE WAYNE: AGENT OF S.H.I.E.L.D. — Marvel / Amalgam

1 ❑ Apr 1996 Cover: 1.95 **NM** value: **Cover or less**
One-shot. 📖 Mission: Destroy Hydra **A:** Cary Nord **W:** Chuck Dixon ★ Origin of Bruce Wayne, Agent of S.H.I.E.L.D..

BRU-HED — Schism

Mike Pascale first drew Bru-Hed in 1986, on the back of the sketchbook of his friend, Dean Armstrong. They both got a laugh out of it at the time, but it was not until seven years later that this funny, beer-swigging character actually appeared in this ashcan test-market edition.

Bru-Hed is a "guy's guy": ultra-conservative, skirt-chasing, obnoxious, and often more than a little gone on "Pudweiser, All-American Beer." Nevertheless, the hero is always ready for action, as readers see for themselves, when he defends the Earth against alien attack by luring the space travelers into his basement. There, they drink all his beer, get loaded, and zap everything in sight.

1 ❑ Mar 1994 Cover: 2.50 **NM** value: **3.50**
📖 Don't Take the World Serious **A:** Mike Pascale; Dean Armstrong(cover) **W:** Mike Pascale ★ 1st Appearance of Bru-Hed, Grrim & Grritty.
1/Ash❑ Cover: 2.50 **NM** value: **4.00**
• Test-Market Ashcan edition. **A:** Mike Pascale; Dean Armstrong(cover) **W:** Mike Pascale ★ 1st Appearance of Bru-Hed, Grrim & Grritty.
1/SC❑ Mar 1994 Cover: 2.50 **NM** value: **Cover or less**
metallic foil logo on cover.
2 ❑ Jul 1994, b&w Cover: 2.50 **NM** value: **Cover or less**
A: Mike Pascale; Dean Armstrong(cover) **W:** Mike Pascale
3 ❑ b&w Cover: 2.50 **NM** value: **Cover or less**
• Pete Bickford thanked on letters page **A:** Mike Pascale; Dean Armstrong(cover) **W:** Mike Pascale ★ Death of Grrim & Grritty.
4 ❑ Cover: 2.50 **NM** value: **Cover or less**
final issue. **A:** Mike Pascale; Dean Armstrong(cover) **W:** Mike Pascale
Ash 1❑ Cover: 2.50 **NM** value: **4.00**
• Test-Market Ashcan edition. • ashcan, b&w **A:** Mike Pascale; Dean Armstrong(cover) ★ 1st Appearance of Bru-Hed, Grrim & Grritty.

Other grades: Multiply prices above by **1.5 for Mint • 2/3 for Very Fine • 1/3 for Fine • 1/5 for Very Good • 1/8 for Good**

Bk 1❑ Cover: 13.95 **NM value: Cover or less**
• The Collected Bru-Hed;Collects Bru-Hed #1-4, Ashcan version of #1 **A:** Mike Pascale; Dean Armstrong(cover) **W:** Mike Pascale; Clifford Meth

BRU-HED'S BREATHTAKING BEAUTIES Schism

1 ❑ Cover: 2.50 **NM value: Cover or less**
Circ: CapCity orders: **2,480**
b&w pin-ups, cardstock cover. **A:** Mike Pascale; Dean Armstrong(cover) **W:** Mike Pascale

BRU-HED'S BUNNIES, BADDIES & BUDDIES Schism

1 ❑ Cover: 2.50 **NM value: Cover or less**
A: Mike Pascale **W:** Mike Pascale

BRU-HED'S GUIDE TO GETTIN' GIRLS NOW! Schism

1 ❑ Cover: 2.95 **NM value: Cover or less**
A: Mike Pascale; Dean Armstrong(cover); Hosho McCreesh **W:** Mike Pascale
2 ❑ Cover: 2.50 **NM value: Cover or less**
A: Mike Pascale; Stefan Damian **W:** Mike Pascale

BRUISER, THE Mythic

1 ❑ **NM value: 2.50**
no cover price, b&w. **A:** Peter Palmiotti; Pia J. Guerra **W:** Angelo Furlan

BRUISER Anthem

1 ❑ Cover: 2.45 **NM value: Cover or less**

BRUNNER'S BEAUTIES Fantagraphics / Eros

1 ❑ Cover: 4.95 **NM value: Cover or less**
No issue number. • pin-ups, adult, b&w

BRUTE, THE Atlas-Seaboard

1 ❑ Feb 1975 Cover: 0.25 **NM value: 2.00**
• **CGC:** 3 graded, best 9.4
📖 Night Of The Brute **A:** Mike Sekowsky **W:** Michael Fleisher ★ Origin of Brute. ★ 1st Appearance of Brute.
2 ❑ Apr 1975 Cover: 0.25 **NM value: 1.00**
3 ❑ Jul 1975 Cover: 0.25 **NM value: 1.00**

BRUTE FORCE Marvel

1 ❑ Aug 1990 Cover: 1.00 **NM value: Cover or less**
Circ: CapCity orders: **15,700**
📖 Fast Feud **A:** José Delbo **W:** Simon Furman ★ Origin of Brute Force. ★ 1st Appearance of Brute Force.
2 ❑ Sep 1990 Cover: 1.00 **NM value: Cover or less**
Circ: CapCity orders: **10,850**
3 ❑ Oct 1990 Cover: 1.00 **NM value: Cover or less**
Circ: CapCity orders: **8,200**
4 ❑ Nov 1990 Cover: 1.00 **NM value: Cover or less**
Circ: CapCity orders: **6,200**

B-36 Paradise Valley

1 ❑ b&w Cover: 3.00 **NM value: Cover or less**
2 ❑ b&w Cover: 3.00 **NM value: Cover or less**
infinity cover.

BUBBLEGUM CRISIS: GRAND MAL Dark Horse

1 ❑ Mar 1994 Cover: 2.50 **NM value: Cover or less**
Circ: CapCity orders: **7,050**
A: Adam Warren **W:** Adam Warren
2 ❑ Apr 1994 Cover: 2.50 **NM value: Cover or less**
Circ: CapCity orders: **5,725**
A: Adam Warren **W:** Adam Warren
3 ❑ May 1994 Cover: 2.50 **NM value: Cover or less**
Circ: CapCity orders: **6,800**
A: Adam Warren **W:** Adam Warren
4 ❑ Jun 1994 Cover: 2.50 **NM value: Cover or less**
Circ: CapCity orders: **6,925**
A: Adam Warren **W:** Adam Warren
Bk 1❑ Cover: 14.95 **NM value: Cover or less**
• Collects Bubblegum Crisis: Grand Mal #1-4 **A:** Adam Warren **W:** Adam Warren

BUCCANEERS Quality

19 ❑ Jan 1950 Cover: 0.10 **NM value: 350.00**
20 ❑ Mar 1950 Cover: 0.10 **NM value: 250.00**
• **CGC:** 1 graded, best 8.5
21 ❑ May 1950 Cover: 0.10 **NM value: 250.00**
22 ❑ Jul 1950 Cover: 0.10 **NM value: 250.00**
23 ❑ Sep 1950 Cover: 0.10 **NM value: 250.00**
• **CGC:** 1 graded, best 4.0
24 ❑ Nov 1950 Cover: 0.10 **NM value: 200.00**
25 ❑ Jan 1951 Cover: 0.10 **NM value: 200.00**
26 ❑ Mar 1951 Cover: 0.10 **NM value: 200.00**
27 ❑ May 1951 Cover: 0.10 **NM value: 200.00**

BUCE N GAR Rak

1 ❑ b&w Cover: 1.75 **NM value: Cover or less**
2 ❑ b&w Cover: 1.75 **NM value: Cover or less**
3 ❑ b&w Cover: 1.75 **NM value: Cover or less**

BUCKAROO BANZAI Marvel

1 ❑ Dec 1984 Cover: 0.75 **NM value: 1.00**
2 ❑ Feb 1985 Cover: 0.75 **NM value: 1.00**

BUCK GODOT, ZAP GUN FOR HIRE Palliard Press

Buck Godot is a rough-and-tumble kind of guy with a heart of gold. He's widely regarded as "the worst-dressed sentient being in the galaxy," although his job as a bodyguard lets him hang around some of the universe's sexiest beings, including the famed Louisa Dem Five. In this extended mini-series (its eight issues were published over the span of three years), Buck joins Louisa to find out why her brothels on Gallimaufry have been doing so very poorly. Along the way, he dodges tax notifiers, battles long-lost relatives, and faces the pandemonium brought on by the sudden appearance of a cheerful floating lizard considered a deity by 3/4 of Gallimaufry's religions.

Buck Godot, Zap Gun for Hire is a continuation of the hard-to-find Buck Godot graphic novels published by Donning/Starblaze. Creator Phil Foglio is famous for his lighthearted storytelling, as seen in Angel and the Ape (2nd Series), a title he did for DC.

1 ❑ Jul 1993 Cover: 2.95 **NM value: 3.50**
📖 The Gallimaufry, Part 1 **A:** Phil Foglio **W:** Phil Foglio
2 ❑ Nov 1993 Cover: 2.95 **NM value: 3.00**
📖 The Gallimaufry, Part 2 **A:** Phil Foglio **W:** Phil Foglio
3 ❑ Apr 1994 Cover: 2.95 **NM value: Cover or less**
📖 The Gallimaufry, Part 3 **A:** Phil Foglio **W:** Phil Foglio
4 ❑ Aug 1994 Cover: 2.95 **NM value: Cover or less**
📖 The Gallimaufry, Part 4 **A:** Phil Foglio **W:** Phil Foglio
5 ❑ Sep 1995 Cover: 2.95 **NM value: Cover or less**
📖 The Gallimaufry, Part 5 **A:** Phil Foglio **W:** Phil Foglio
6 ❑ Oct 1995 Cover: 2.95 **NM value: Cover or less**
📖 The Gallimaufry, Part 6 **A:** Phil Foglio **W:** Phil Foglio
7 ❑ Aug 1997 Cover: 2.95 **NM value: Cover or less**
📖 The Gallimaufry, Part 7 **A:** Phil Foglio **W:** Phil Foglio
8 ❑ Mar 1998 Cover: 3.50 **NM value: Cover or less**
Circ: Diamd. preorders: **3,565**
📖 The Gallimaufry, Part 8 final issue. **A:** Phil Foglio **W:** Phil Foglio

BUCK JONES Dell

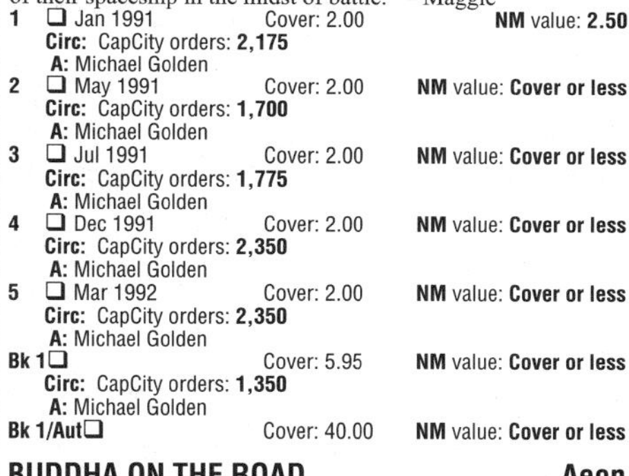

Jones (1889 or 1891-1942) was a movie star who died of burns received in the Cocoanut Grove nightclub fire, which killed more than 400 people. His real name was Charles Frederick Gebhart (or a variant spelling) and he was one of the big stars (with Hoot Gibson, Ken Maynard, and Tom Mix) of silent Western films. He also performed in Wild West shows and circuses and successfully made the transition to talkies. He even starred in a radio series in the later 1930s.

When his Dell comic book was released, it was a decade after his last movie had been released, and many of the readers probably didn't know of the connection to the real actor. By the time of his death, he'd appeared in roughly 150 films (most of them Westerns) from 1918 to 1942. — Maggie

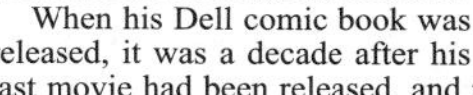

2 ❑ Apr 1951 Cover: 0.10 **NM value: 50.00**
3 ❑ Jul 1951 Cover: 0.10 **NM value: 50.00**
• **CGC:** 1 graded, best 5.5
4 ❑ Oct 1951 Cover: 0.10 **NM value: 50.00**
5 ❑ Jan 1952 Cover: 0.10 **NM value: 50.00**
6 ❑ Apr 1952 Cover: 0.10 **NM value: 45.00**
7 ❑ Jul 1952 Cover: 0.10 **NM value: 45.00**
8 ❑ Oct 1952 Cover: 0.10 **NM value: 45.00**

BUCK ROGERS (EASTERN COLOR) Eastern Color

1 ❑ Win 1940 Cover: 0.10 **NM value: 2500.00**
• **CGC:** 2 graded, best 5.0
2 ❑ Jul 1941 Cover: 0.10 **NM value: 1500.00**
• **CGC:** 2 graded, best 7.5
3 ❑ Dec 1941 Cover: 0.10 **NM value: 1000.00**
• **CGC:** 2 graded, best 6.0
4 ❑ Jul 1942 Cover: 0.10 **NM value: 1000.00**
5 ❑ ca. 1943 Cover: 0.10 **NM value: 750.00**
• **CGC:** 1 graded, best .5
6 ❑ Sep 1943 Cover: 0.10 **NM value: 750.00**

BUCK ROGERS COMICS MODULE TSR

1 ❑ Cover: 2.95 **NM value: Cover or less**
Circ: CapCity orders: **1,850**
📖 Rude Awakening; The Gauntlet (game); Into the 25th Century!
• Listed as 1 of 3 **W:** Kim Mohan; Tom Wham
2 ❑ Cover: 2.95 **NM value: Cover or less**
3 ❑ Cover: 2.95 **NM value: Cover or less**
Circ: CapCity orders: **3,000**
4 ❑ Cover: 2.95 **NM value: Cover or less**
Circ: CapCity orders: **2,750**
5 ❑ Cover: 2.95 **NM value: Cover or less**
Circ: CapCity orders: **2,496**
6 ❑ Cover: 2.95 **NM value: Cover or less**
Circ: CapCity orders: **2,112**
7 ❑ Cover: 2.95 **NM value: Cover or less**
Circ: CapCity orders: **2,112**
8 ❑ Cover: 2.95 **NM value: Cover or less**
Circ: CapCity orders: **1,920**
9 ❑ Cover: 2.95 **NM value: Cover or less**
Circ: CapCity orders: **1,536**

BUCK ROGERS (GOLD KEY/WHITMAN) Gold Key / Whitman

1 ❑ Oct 1964 Cover: 0.15 **NM value: 35.00**
• **CGC:** 2 graded, best 9.6
📖 The Space Slavers • 10/64;Gold Key publishes
2 ❑ Aug 1979 Cover: 0.40 **NM value: 4.00**
📖 Buck Rogers (movie adaptation), Part 1
3 ❑ Sep 1979 Cover: 0.40 **NM value: 4.00**
📖 Buck Rogers (movie adaptation), Part 2
4 ❑ Oct 1979 Cover: 0.40 **NM value: 4.00**
📖 Buck Rogers (movie adaptation), Part 3
5 ❑ Dec 1979 Cover: 0.40 **NM value: 3.00**
6 ❑ Feb 1980 Cover: 0.40 **NM value: 3.00**
7 ❑ Apr 1980 Cover: 0.40 **NM value: 3.00**
• Series begins under Whitman imprint
8 ❑ ca. 1980 Cover: 0.40 **NM value: 3.00**
9 ❑ ca. 1980 Cover: 0.40 **NM value: 3.00**
10 ❑ **NM value: 3.00**
11 ❑ **NM value: 3.00**
12 ❑ **NM value: 3.00**
13 ❑ **NM value: 3.00**
14 ❑ ca. 1981 **NM value: 3.00**
15 ❑ **NM value: 3.00**
16 ❑ **NM value: 3.00**
final issue.

BUCKY O'HARE Continuity

Written by Larry Hama and drawn by Michael Golden, Bucky O'Hare featured the adventures of a kid who (as he announces on the cover of #1) is "trapped in a dimension of funny animals." Bucky is not the kid; he's an anthropomorphic rabbit who's captain of the crew of the S.P.A.C.E. frigate Righteous Indignation in a science-fiction series in which ducks, gorillas, and rabbits battle toads. The kid is Willy DuWitt, a science buff who enters the series concerned about his school science fair project involving a photon accelerator. That's the link between his home in San Francisco and that of the ship of the space-traveling crew, as he joins them to repair the photon accelerator of their spaceship in the midst of battle. — Maggie

1 ❑ Jan 1991 Cover: 2.00 **NM value: 2.50**
Circ: CapCity orders: **2,175**
A: Michael Golden
2 ❑ May 1991 Cover: 2.00 **NM value: Cover or less**
Circ: CapCity orders: **1,700**
A: Michael Golden
3 ❑ Jul 1991 Cover: 2.00 **NM value: Cover or less**
Circ: CapCity orders: **1,775**
A: Michael Golden
4 ❑ Dec 1991 Cover: 2.00 **NM value: Cover or less**
Circ: CapCity orders: **2,350**
A: Michael Golden
5 ❑ Mar 1992 Cover: 2.00 **NM value: Cover or less**
Circ: CapCity orders: **2,350**
A: Michael Golden
Bk 1❑ Cover: 5.95 **NM value: Cover or less**
Circ: CapCity orders: **1,350**
A: Michael Golden
Bk 1/Aut❑ Cover: 40.00 **NM value: Cover or less**

BUDDHA ON THE ROAD Aeon

1 ❑ Aug 1996 Cover: 2.95 **NM value: Cover or less**
A: Colin Upton **W:** Colin Upton
2 ❑ Nov 1996 Cover: 2.95 **NM value: Cover or less**
A: Colin Upton **W:** Colin Upton

BUFFALO BILL Youthful

2 ❑ Oct 1950 Cover: 0.10 **NM value: 75.00**
3 ❑ Dec 1950 Cover: 0.10 **NM value: 45.00**
4 ❑ Feb 1951 Cover: 0.10 **NM value: 45.00**
• **CGC:** 1 graded, best 8.5
5 ❑ Apr 1951 Cover: 0.10 **NM value: 45.00**
6 ❑ Jun 1951 Cover: 0.10 **NM value: 45.00**
7 ❑ Aug 1951 Cover: 0.10 **NM value: 45.00**
8 ❑ Oct 1951 Cover: 0.10 **NM value: 45.00**
9 ❑ Dec 1951 Cover: 0.10 **NM value: 45.00**

BUFFALO BILL JR. Gold Key

7 ❑ Feb 1958 Cover: 0.10 **NM value: 35.00**
• First six issues appeared as Dell Four Color.
8 ❑ May 1958 Cover: 0.10 **NM value: 35.00**
9 ❑ Aug 1958 Cover: 0.10 **NM value: 35.00**
10 ❑ Nov 1958 Cover: 0.10 **NM value: 35.00**
11 ❑ Feb 1959 Cover: 0.10 **NM value: 35.00**
• **CGC:** 1 graded, best 9.6
12 ❑ May 1959 Cover: 0.10 **NM value: 35.00**
13 ❑ Aug 1959 Cover: 0.10 **NM value: 35.00**
• **CGC:** 1 graded, best 9.4

BUFFALO BILL PICTURE STORIES Street & Smith

1 ❑ Jun 1949 Cover: 0.10 **NM value: 75.00**
• **CGC:** 1 graded, best 7.5
2 ❑ Aug 1949 Cover: 0.10 **NM value: 75.00**

BUFFALO WINGS Antarctic

1 ❑ Sep 1993, b&w Cover: 2.50 **NM value: Cover or less**
2 ❑ Nov 1993, b&w Cover: 2.75 **NM value: Cover or less**

CGC-graded: Multiply prices above by **33 for 9.9 M • 16 for 9.8 NM/M • 7 for 9.6 NM+ • 5 for 9.4 NM • 2.5 for 9.2 NM- • 1.5 for 9.0 VF/NM**

BUFFY THE VAMPIRE SLAYER — Dark Horse

In 1992, Kristy Swanson played Buffy Summers in a feature film, where creator Joss Whedon introduced the concept of The Slayer, a young woman whose role is to kill vampires. In March 1997, "Welcome to the Hellmouth" introduced the TV audience to Sunnydale High and Sarah Michelle Gellar as Buffy. In addition, the cast expanded to add such characters as "the Scooby Gang" of Xander Harris and Willow Rosenberg, along with Buffy's new Watcher, Rupert Giles.

A little over a year later, Dark Horse began producing new comic-book stories about the team that spends much of its time patrolling Sunnydale and staking newly risen vampires before they can menace the general population. Care is taken to adhere to appearance and mythos of the TV series and the cast and storyline evolve. —Maggie

0.5 ❑ NM value: **3.00**
• **CGC:** 20 graded, best 9.9
• Wizard promotional edition.

0.5/GO❑ NM value: **8.00**
• Wizard promotional edition. • Gold logo

0.5/PI❑ NM value: **10.00**
• Wizard promotional edition. • Platinum logo

1 ❑ Sep 1998 Cover: 2.95 NM value: **5.00**
Circ: Diamd. preorders: **61,382 • CGC:** 3 graded, best 9.6
• no month of publication

1/A ❑ Sep 1998 Cover: 2.95 NM value: **8.00**
photo cover with foil logo. • Another Universe

1/B ❑ Sep 1998 Cover: 2.95 NM value: **3.00**
photo cover (Buffy holding gate) without foil logo. • Another Universe

1/GO❑Sep 1998 Cover: 2.95 NM value: **7.00**
• **CGC:** 8 graded, best 9.8
art cover with gold foil logo. • Gold logo;gold foil logo

1/SC❑Sep 1998 Cover: 2.95 NM value: **6.00**
• **CGC:** 5 graded, best 9.8
Photo cover.

1-2 ❑ Feb 1999 Cover: 2.95 NM value: **Cover or less**
Circ: Diamd. preorders: **4,039**

2 ❑ Oct 1998 Cover: 2.95 NM value: **4.00**
Circ: Diamd. preorders: **43,717 • CGC:** 2 graded, best 9.6
Halloween **A:** Joe Bennett **W:** Andi Watson

2/SC❑Oct 1998 Cover: 2.95 NM value: **5.00**
Photo cover. Halloween **A:** Joe Bennett **W:** Andi Watson

3 ❑ Nov 1998 Cover: 2.95 NM value: **4.00**
Circ: Diamd. preorders: **47,803**
Cold Turkey • no month of publication **A:** Joe Bennett **W:** Andi Watson

3/SC❑Nov 1998 Cover: 2.95 NM value: **5.00**
Photo cover. Cold Turkey **A:** Joe Bennett **W:** Andi Watson

4 ❑ Dec 1998 Cover: 2.95 NM value: **4.00**
Circ: Diamd. preorders: **51,805**
White Christmas **A:** Hector Gomez **W:** Andi Watson

4/SC❑Dec 1998 Cover: 2.95 NM value: **4.00**
Photo cover. White Christmas **A:** Hector Gomez **W:** Andi Watson

5 ❑ Jan 1999 Cover: 2.95 NM value: **4.00**
Circ: Diamd. preorders: **48,287**
Happy New Year **A:** Hector Gomez **W:** Andi Watson

5/SC❑Jan 1999 Cover: 2.95 NM value: **4.00**
Photo cover. Happy New Year **A:** Hector Gomez **W:** Andi Watson

6 ❑ Feb 1999 Cover: 2.95 NM value: **3.00**
Circ: Diamd. preorders: **44,964**
New Kid on the Block, Part 1 **A:** Hector Gomez **W:** Dan Brereton; Andi Watson

6/SC❑Feb 1999 Cover: 2.95 NM value: **3.00**
Photo cover. New Kid on the Block, Part 1 **A:** Hector Gomez **W:** Dan Brereton; Andi Watson

7 ❑ Mar 1999 Cover: 2.95 NM value: **3.00**
Circ: Diamd. preorders: **44,787**
New Kid on the Block, Part 2 **A:** Hector Gomez **W:** Dan Brereton; Andi Watson

7/SC❑Mar 1999 Cover: 2.95 NM value: **3.00**
• **CGC:** 1 graded, best 9.0
Photo cover. New Kid on the Block, Part 2 **A:** Hector Gomez **W:** Dan Brereton; Andi Watson

8 ❑ Apr 1999 Cover: 2.95 NM value: **3.00**
Circ: Diamd. preorders: **44,975**
The Final Cut **A:** Jason Pearson; Cliff Richards **W:** Andi Watson

8/SC❑Apr 1999 Cover: 2.95 NM value: **3.00**
Photo cover. The Final Cut **A:** Jason Pearson; Cliff Richards **W:** Andi Watson

9 ❑ May 1999 Cover: 2.95 NM value: **Cover or less**
Circ: Diamd. preorders: **42,869**
Hey, Good Lookin' **A:** Joe Bennett **W:** Andi Watson

9/SC❑May 1999 Cover: 2.95 NM value: **Cover or less**
• **CGC:** 1 graded, best 9.4
Photo cover. Hey, Good Lookin' **A:** Joe Bennett **W:** Andi Watson

10 ❑ Jun 1999 Cover: 2.95 NM value: **Cover or less**
Circ: Diamd. preorders: **41,226**
• teen magazine-style cover. Hey, Good Lookin', part 2 **A:** Joe Bennett **W:** Andi Watson

10/SC❑Jun 1999 Cover: 2.95 NM value: **Cover or less**
Photo cover. Hey, Good Lookin', part 2 **A:** Joe Bennett **W:** Andi Watson

11 ❑ Jul 1999 Cover: 2.95 NM value: **Cover or less**
Circ: Diamd. preorders: **39,042**
A Boy Named Sue **A:** Joe Bennett **W:** Andi Watson

11/SC❑Jul 1999 Cover: 2.95 NM value: **Cover or less**
Photo cover. A Boy Named Sue **A:** Joe Bennett **W:** Andi Watson

12 ❑ Aug 1999 Cover: 2.95 NM value: **Cover or less**
Circ: Diamd. preorders: **36,588**
A Nice Girl Like You **A:** Christian Zanier **W:** Christopher Golden

12/SC❑Aug 1999 Cover: 2.95 NM value: **Cover or less**
Photo cover. A Nice Girl Like You **A:** Christian Zanier **W:** Christopher Golden

13 ❑ Sep 1999 Cover: 2.95 NM value: **Cover or less**
Circ: Diamd. preorders: **34,598**
Bad Blood, Part 4 **A:** Cliff Richards **W:** Andi Watson

13/SC❑Sep 1999 Cover: 2.95 NM value: **Cover or less**
Photo cover. Bad Blood, Part 4 **A:** Cliff Richards **W:** Andi Watson

14 ❑ Oct 1999 Cover: 2.95 NM value: **Cover or less**
Circ: Diamd. preorders: **33,948**
Bad Blood, Part 5 **A:** Cliff Richards **W:** Andi Watson

14/SC❑Oct 1999 Cover: 2.95 NM value: **Cover or less**
Photo cover. Bad Blood, Part 5 **A:** Cliff Richards **W:** Andi Watson

15 ❑ Nov 1999 Cover: 2.95 NM value: **Cover or less**
Circ: Diamd. preorders: **31,940**
Bad Blood, Part 6 **A:** Cliff Richards **W:** Andi Watson

15/SC❑Nov 1999 Cover: 2.95 NM value: **Cover or less**
Photo cover. Bad Blood, Part 6 **A:** Cliff Richards **W:** Andi Watson

16 ❑ Dec 1999 Cover: 2.95 NM value: **Cover or less**
Circ: Diamd. preorders: **34,140**
The Food Chain **A:** Christian Zanier **W:** Christopher Golden

16/SC❑Dec 1999 Cover: 2.95 NM value: **Cover or less**
Photo cover. The Food Chain **A:** Christian Zanier **W:** Christopher Golden

17 ❑ Jan 2000 Cover: 2.95 NM value: **Cover or less**
Circ: Diamd. preorders: **28,594**
Bad Blood, Part 7 **A:** Cliff Richards **W:** Andi Watson

17/SC❑Jan 2000 Cover: 2.95 NM value: **Cover or less**
Photo cover. Bad Blood, Part 7 **A:** Cliff Richards **W:** Andi Watson

18 ❑ Feb 2000 Cover: 2.95 NM value: **Cover or less**
Circ: Diamd. preorders: **26,608**

18/SC❑Feb 2000 Cover: 2.95 NM value: **Cover or less**
Photo cover.

19 ❑ Mar 2000 Cover: 2.95 NM value: **Cover or less**
Circ: Diamd. preorders: **26,595**

19/SC❑Mar 2000 Cover: 2.95 NM value: **Cover or less**
Photo cover.

20 ❑ Apr 2000 Cover: 2.95 NM value: **Cover or less**
Circ: Diamd. preorders: **26,158**

20/SC❑Apr 2000 Cover: 2.95 NM value: **Cover or less**
Photo cover.

21 ❑ May 2000 Cover: 2.95 NM value: **Cover or less**
Circ: Diamd. preorders: **25,474**
The Blood of Carthage, Part 1

21/SC❑May 2000 Cover: 2.95 NM value: **Cover or less**
Photo cover. The Blood of Carthage, Part 1

22 ❑ Jun 2000 Cover: 2.95 NM value: **Cover or less**
Circ: Diamd. preorders: **25,504**
The Blood of Carthage, Part 2 **A:** Cliff Richards **W:** Christopher Golden

22/SC❑Jun 2000 Cover: 2.95 NM value: **Cover or less**
Photo cover. The Blood of Carthage, Part 2 **A:** Cliff Richards **W:** Christopher Golden

23 ❑ Jul 2000 Cover: 2.95 NM value: **Cover or less**
Circ: Diamd. preorders: **24,542**
The Blood of Carthage, Part 3 **A:** Cliff Richards **W:** Christopher Golden

23/SC❑Jul 2000 Cover: 2.95 NM value: **Cover or less**
Photo cover. The Blood of Carthage, Part 3 **A:** Cliff Richards **W:** Christopher Golden

24 ❑ Aug 2000 Cover: 2.95 NM value: **Cover or less**
Circ: Diamd. preorders: **12,500**
The Blood of Carthage, Part 4 **A:** Cliff Richards **W:** Christopher Golden

24/SC❑Aug 2000 Cover: 2.95 NM value: **Cover or less**
Circ: Diamd. preorders: **12,787**
Photo cover. The Blood of Carthage, Part 4 **A:** Cliff Richards **W:** Christopher Golden

25 ❑ Sep 2000 Cover: 2.95 NM value: **Cover or less**
Circ: Diamd. preorders: **22,467**
The Blood of Carthage, Part 4 **A:** Cliff Richards **W:** Christopher Golden

25/SC❑Sep 2000 Cover: 2.95 NM value: **Cover or less**
• **CGC:** 1 graded, best 9.4
Photo cover. The Blood of Carthage, Part 4 **A:** Cliff Richards **W:** Christopher Golden

26 ❑ Oct 2000 Cover: 2.99 NM value: **Cover or less**
Circ: Diamd. preorders: **21,308**
The Heart of a Slayer, Part 1 **A:** Cliff Richards **W:** Chris Boal

26/SC❑Oct 2000 Cover: 2.99 NM value: **Cover or less**
Photo cover. The Heart of a Slayer, Part 1 **A:** Cliff Richards **W:** Chris Boal

27 ❑ Nov 2000 Cover: 2.99 NM value: **Cover or less**
Circ: Diamd. preorders: **21,216**
The Heart of a Slayer, Part 2 **A:** Cliff Richards **W:** Chris Boal

27/SC❑Nov 2000 Cover: 2.99 NM value: **Cover or less**
Photo cover. The Heart of a Slayer, Part 2 **A:** Cliff Richards **W:** Chris Boal

28 ❑ Dec 2000 Cover: 2.99 NM value: **Cover or less**
Circ: Diamd. preorders: **20,412**
Cemetery of Lost Love **A:** Cliff Richards **W:** Jim Pascoe; Tom Fassbender

28/SC❑Dec 2000 Cover: 2.99 NM value: **Cover or less**
Photo cover. Cemetery of Lost Love **A:** Cliff Richards **W:** Jim Pascoe; Tom Fassbender

29 ❑ Jan 2001 Cover: 2.99 NM value: **Cover or less**
Circ: Diamd. preorders: **19,559**
Past Lives, Part 2 **A:** Cliff Richards; Christian Zanier **W:** Christopher Golden; Tom Sniegoski

29/SC❑Jan 2001 Cover: 2.99 NM value: **Cover or less**
Photo cover. Past Lives, Part 2 **A:** Cliff Richards; Christian Zanier **W:** Christopher Golden; Tom Sniegoski

30 ❑ Feb 2001 Cover: 2.99 NM value: **Cover or less**
Circ: Diamd. preorders: **18,973**
Past Lives, Part 4 **A:** Cliff Richards **W:** Christopher Golden; Tom Sniegoski

30/SC❑Feb 2001 Cover: 2.99 NM value: **Cover or less**
Photo cover. Past Lives, Part 4 **A:** Cliff Richards **W:** Christopher Golden; Tom Sniegoski

31 ❑ Mar 2001 Cover: 2.99 NM value: **Cover or less**
Circ: Diamd. preorders: **18,487**
Lost and Found **A:** Cliff Richards **W:** Jim Pascoe; Tom Fassbender

31/SC❑Mar 2001 Cover: 2.99 NM value: **Cover or less**
Photo cover. Lost and Found **A:** Cliff Richards **W:** Jim Pascoe; Tom Fassbender

32 ❑ Apr 2001 Cover: 2.99 NM value: **Cover or less**
Circ: Diamd. preorders: **18,378**
Invasion **A:** Cliff Richards **W:** Jim Pascoe; Tom Fassbender

32/SC❑Apr 2001 Cover: 2.99 NM value: **Cover or less**
Photo cover. Invasion **A:** Cliff Richards **W:** Jim Pascoe; Tom Fassbender

33 ❑ May 2001 Cover: 2.99 NM value: **Cover or less**
Circ: Diamd. preorders: **17,995**

33/SC❑May 2001 Cover: 2.99 NM value: **Cover or less**
Photo cover.

34 ❑ Jun 2001 Cover: 2.99 NM value: **Cover or less**
Circ: Diamd. preorders: **17,986**

34/SC❑Jun 2001 Cover: 2.99 NM value: **Cover or less**
Photo cover.

35 ❑ Jul 2001 Cover: 2.99 NM value: **Cover or less**
Circ: Diamd. preorders: **18,715**

35/SC❑Jul 2001 Cover: 2.99 NM value: **Cover or less**
Photo cover.

Anl 1999❑Aug 1999 Cover: 4.95 NM value: **Cover or less**
Circ: Diamd. preorders: **24,484**
Photo cover. The Latest Craze; Bad Dog • squarebound;1999 Annual **A:** Cliff Richards; Jeff Matsuda; Randy Green; Ryan Sook **W:** Christopher Golden; Douglas Petrie; Tom Sniegoski

Bk 1❑ Mar 1999 Cover: 9.95 NM value: **Cover or less**
The Remaining Sunlight • collects #1-3 plus new story

Bk 2❑ Aug 1999 Cover: 10.95 NM value: **Cover or less**
Uninvited Guests

Bk 3❑ Cover: 10.95 NM value: **Cover or less**
Bad Blood

Bk 4❑ Cover: 10.95 NM value: **Cover or less**
Crash Test Demons

Bk 5❑ Cover: 10.95 NM value: **Cover or less**
Pale Reflection

Bk 6❑ Cover: 10.95 NM value: **Cover or less**
The Blood of Carthage

BUFFY THE VAMPIRE SLAYER: ANGEL — Dark Horse

1 ❑ May 1999 Cover: 2.95 NM value: **3.50**
Circ: Diamd. preorders: **42,947**
A: Hector Gomez **W:** Christopher Golden

1/SC❑May 1999 Cover: 2.95 NM value: **3.50**
Photo cover. **A:** Hector Gomez **W:** Christopher Golden

2 ❑ Jun 1999 Cover: 2.95 NM value: **3.00**
Circ: Diamd. preorders: **38,179**
A: Hector Gomez **W:** Christopher Golden

2/SC❑Jun 1999 Cover: 2.95 NM value: **3.00**
Photo cover. **A:** Hector Gomez **W:** Christopher Golden

3 ❑ Jul 1999 Cover: 2.95 NM value: **3.00**
Circ: Diamd. preorders: **35,769**
A: Hector Gomez **W:** Christopher Golden

3/SC❑Jul 1999 Cover: 2.95 NM value: **3.00**
Photo cover. **A:** Hector Gomez **W:** Christopher Golden

Bk 1❑ Cover: 2.95 NM value: **3.00**

BUFFY THE VAMPIRE SLAYER: FOOD CHAIN — Dark Horse

1 ❑ Cover: 16.95 NM value: **Cover or less**

BUFFY THE VAMPIRE SLAYER: GILES — Dark Horse

This one-shot focuses on Buffy's mentor and former official Watcher, Rupert Giles, who returns to England to attend the funeral of his own former mentor, who died under mysterious circumstances. Despite the Watcher's Council's elitist secrecy, Giles soon discovers that his friend sacrificed himself in an attempt to stop the re-emergence of ancient gods of evil. With only one other person, the witch Micaela Tomasi, willing to accept the seriousness of the situation and aid the exiled Watcher, Giles sets out to destroy the nether-beings' human host before a gateway between dimensions can be formed. With the fate of the entire world at stake, the man known to his former comrades as "Ripper" Giles proves that, with or without the Slayer, he's still a force to be reckoned with in the fight against evil.

1 ❑ Oct 2000 Cover: 2.99 NM value: **Cover or less**
Circ: Diamd. preorders: **17,056**
Beyond the Pale **A:** Eric Powell **W:** Christopher Golden; Tom Sniegoski

1/SC❑Oct 2000 Cover: 2.99 NM value: **Cover or less**
Photo cover. Beyond the Pale **A:** Eric Powell **W:** Christopher Golden; Tom Sniegoski

BUFFY THE VAMPIRE SLAYER: JONATHAN — Dark Horse

1 ❑ Jan 2001 Cover: 2.99 NM value: **Cover or less**
Circ: Diamd. preorders: **15,433**
Codename: Comrades **A:** Cliff Richards **W:** Jane Espernson

1/SC❑Jan 2001 Cover: 2.99 NM value: **Cover or less**
Photo cover. Codename: Comrades **A:** Cliff Richards **W:** Jane Espernson

Other grades: Multiply prices above by **1.5 for Mint • 2/3 for Very Fine • 1/3 for Fine • 1/5 for Very Good • 1/8 for Good**

BUFFY THE VAMPIRE SLAYER: LOVER'S WALK — Dark Horse

1 ❑ Feb 2001 Cover: 2.99 **NM** value: **Cover or less**
Circ: Diamd. preorders: **17,535**
Photo cover. 📖 One Small Promise; Punish Me With Kisses; Who Made Who? **A:** Cliff Richards; Eric Powell; Chynna Clugston-Major **W:** Chynna Clugston-Major; Jim Pascoe; Christopher Golden; Jamie S. Rich; Tom Fassbender

BUFFY THE VAMPIRE SLAYER: RING OF FIRE — Dark Horse

1 ❑ Aug 2000 Cover: 9.95 **NM** value: **Cover or less**
Photo cover. **A:** Ryan Sook **W:** Doug Petrie

BUFFY THE VAMPIRE SLAYER: SPIKE AND DRU — Dark Horse

1 ❑ Apr 1999 Cover: 2.95 **NM** value: **Cover or less**
Photo cover. 📖 Spike & Dru Paint the Town Red; The Queen of Hearts **A:** Ryan Sook **W:** Christopher Golden; James Marsters
2 ❑ May 1999 Cover: 2.95 **NM** value: **Cover or less**
3 ❑ Jun 1999 Cover: 2.95 **NM** value: **Cover or less**
📖 All's Fair **A:** Eric Powell **W:** Christopher Golden
3/SC❑ Dec 2000 Cover: 2.95 **NM** value: **Cover or less**
Photo cover. 📖 All's Fair **A:** Eric Powell **W:** Christopher Golden

BUFFY THE VAMPIRE SLAYER: THE ORIGIN — Dark Horse

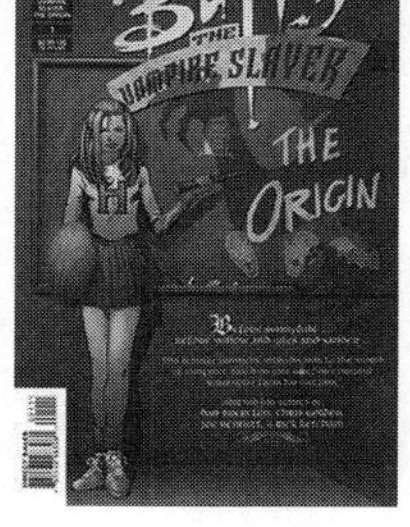

Once in every generation, a Slayer is born. A young woman is raised and trained to hunt the blood-sucking vampires around us. This series tells the origin of this generation's Slayer.

Buffy Summers is just another high-school cheerleader, hanging out with friends, studying, and watching movies, until the day Merrick appears. He explains the strange dreams she has been having; dreams of a Magyar peasant, an Indian princess, and a prostitute in China. In every dream, the girls are fighting monsters. They, too, were Slayers.

Merrick could not find Buffy for many years. She's completely untrained, but time is short. Victims with extensive neck wounds are being discovered and, now, they're rising from the dead. Buffy the Vampire Slayer is all that stands between the vampires and helpless humanity.

1 ❑ Jan 1999 Cover: 2.95 **NM** value: **3.50**
Circ: Diamd. preorders: **49,974**
A: Joe Bennett **W:** Dan Brereton; Christopher Golden
1/LE❑ Jan 1999 Cover: 19.95 **NM** value: **Cover or less**
• Limited edition foil cover. **A:** Joe Bennett **W:** Dan Brereton; Christopher Golden
1/SC❑ Jan 1999 Cover: 2.95 **NM** value: **4.00**
Photo cover. **A:** Joe Bennett **W:** Dan Brereton; Christopher Golden
2 ❑ Feb 1999 Cover: 2.95 **NM** value: **Cover or less**
Circ: Diamd. preorders: **40,797**
A: Joe Bennett **W:** Dan Brereton; Christopher Golden
2/SC❑ Feb 1999 Cover: 2.95 **NM** value: **Cover or less**
Photo cover. **A:** Joe Bennett **W:** Dan Brereton; Christopher Golden
3 ❑ Mar 1999 Cover: 2.95 **NM** value: **Cover or less**
Circ: Diamd. preorders: **41,135**
A: Joe Bennett **W:** Dan Brereton; Christopher Golden
3/SC❑ Mar 1999 Cover: 2.95 **NM** value: **Cover or less**
Photo cover. **A:** Joe Bennett **W:** Dan Brereton; Christopher Golden
Bk 1❑ Cover: 9.95 **NM** value: **Cover or less**
• Collects series **A:** Joe Bennett **W:** Dan Brereton; Christopher Golden

BUFFY THE VAMPIRE SLAYER: WILLOW & TARA — Dark Horse

1 ❑ Apr 2001 Cover: 2.99 **NM** value: **Cover or less**
Circ: Diamd. preorders: **17,761**
A: Terry Moore; Eric Powell **W:** Amber Benson; Christopher Golden
1/SC❑ Apr 2001 Cover: 2.99 **NM** value: **Cover or less**
A: Terry Moore; Eric Powell **W:** Amber Benson; Christopher Golden

BUG & STUMP — Aaargh!

1 ❑ Aut 1993, b&w Cover: 2.95 **NM** value: **Cover or less**
• Australian;Australian, b&w
2 ❑ Spr 1994, b&w Cover: 2.95 **NM** value: **Cover or less**
• Australian;Australian, b&w

BUGBOY — Image

1 ❑ Jun 1998, b&w Cover: 3.95 **NM** value: **Cover or less**
Circ: Diamd. preorders: **2,698**
📖 What I Did on My Vacation; Who Was That Masked Boy? **A:** Mark Lewis **W:** Mark Lewis

B.U.G.G.'S — Acetylene Comics

1 ❑ Cover: 2.25 **NM** value: **Cover or less**
2 ❑ Cover: 2.25 **NM** value: **Cover or less**

BUGHOUSE — Cat-Head

1 ❑ Mar 1954, b&w Cover: 2.95 **NM** value: **Cover or less**
📖 Opening Night **A:** Steve Lafler **W:** Steve Lafler
2 ❑ Nov 1994, b&w Cover: 2.50 **NM** value: **2.95**
A: Steve Lafler **W:** Steve Lafler
3 ❑ Jun 1995, b&w Cover: 2.50 **NM** value: **2.95**
A: Steve Lafler **W:** Steve Lafler
4 ❑ Sep 1954, b&w Cover: 2.75 **NM** value: **2.95**
cardstock cover. **A:** Steve Lafler **W:** Steve Lafler
5 ❑ Spr 1997, b&w Cover: 2.95 **NM** value: **Cover or less**
A: Steve Lafler **W:** Steve Lafler
Bk 1❑ b&w Cover: 12.95 **NM** value: **Cover or less**
• Collects #1-4 with 27 new pages **A:** Steve Lafler **W:** Steve Lafler

BUG-HUNTERS — Trident

In a far future run by corporations, a military expert and software developer must keep tabs on two large and silly robots that leave havoc in their wake. Not that too many people notice: In this world, videogames rule, virtual realities sometimes leak into the real domain, and it's up to this four to hunt down the bugs in the system.

While the pages of this one-shot are sometimes a tad busy, the art itself is clearly rendered.

This graphic novel was put together by the trio of Jerry Paris, Pedro Henry and Garry Leach.

1 ❑ b&w Cover: 5.95 **NM** value: **Cover or less**
No issue number. **A:** Gary Leach; Jerry Paris; Pedro Henry **W:** Gary Leach; Jerry Paris; Pedro Henry

BUG (MARVEL) — Marvel

1 ❑ Mar 1997 Cover: 2.99 **NM** value: **Cover or less**
Circ: Direct Market orders: **22,750**
One-shot. 📖 Apples & Origins **A:** Derec Aucoin **W:** Todd Dezago
★ Versus Annihilus.

BUG (PLANET-X) — Planet-X

1 ❑ Cover: 1.50 **NM** value: **Cover or less**
A: Tony Basilicato **W:** Tony Basilicato

BUGS BUNNY — DC

1 ❑ Jun 1990 Cover: 1.00 **NM** value: **2.00**
Circ: CapCity orders: **14,100**
2 ❑ Jul 1990 Cover: 1.00 **NM** value: **1.50**
Circ: CapCity orders: **8,950**
3 ❑ Aug 1990 Cover: 1.00 **NM** value: **1.50**
Circ: CapCity orders: **7,850**

BUGS BUNNY AND PORKY PIG — Dell

1 ❑ ca. 1965 Cover: 0.25 **NM** value: **25.00**
• **CGC:** 3 graded, best 9.6

BUGS BUNNY (DELL) — Dell

28 ❑ Dec 1952 Cover: 0.10 **NM** value: **35.00**
29 ❑ Feb 1953 Cover: 0.10 **NM** value: **35.00**
30 ❑ Apr 1953 Cover: 0.10 **NM** value: **35.00**
31 ❑ Jun 1953 Cover: 0.10 **NM** value: **35.00**
32 ❑ Aug 1953 Cover: 0.10 **NM** value: **35.00**
33 ❑ Oct 1953 Cover: 0.10 **NM** value: **35.00**
34 ❑ Dec 1953 Cover: 0.10 **NM** value: **35.00**
35 ❑ Feb 1954 Cover: 0.10 **NM** value: **35.00**
36 ❑ Apr 1954 Cover: 0.10 **NM** value: **35.00**
37 ❑ Jun 1954 Cover: 0.10 **NM** value: **35.00**
38 ❑ Aug 1954 Cover: 0.10 **NM** value: **35.00**
39 ❑ Oct 1954 Cover: 0.10 **NM** value: **35.00**
40 ❑ Dec 1954 Cover: 0.10 **NM** value: **35.00**
41 ❑ Feb 1955 Cover: 0.10 **NM** value: **25.00**
42 ❑ Apr 1955 Cover: 0.10 **NM** value: **25.00**
43 ❑ Jun 1955 Cover: 0.10 **NM** value: **25.00**
44 ❑ Aug 1955 Cover: 0.10 **NM** value: **25.00**
45 ❑ Oct 1955 Cover: 0.10 **NM** value: **25.00**
46 ❑ Dec 1955 Cover: 0.10 **NM** value: **25.00**
47 ❑ Feb 1956 Cover: 0.10 **NM** value: **25.00**
48 ❑ Apr 1956 Cover: 0.10 **NM** value: **25.00**
49 ❑ Jun 1956 Cover: 0.10 **NM** value: **25.00**
50 ❑ Aug 1956 Cover: 0.10 **NM** value: **25.00**
51 ❑ Oct 1956 Cover: 0.10 **NM** value: **25.00**
52 ❑ Dec 1956 Cover: 0.10 **NM** value: **25.00**
53 ❑ Feb 1957 Cover: 0.10 **NM** value: **25.00**
54 ❑ Apr 1957 Cover: 0.10 **NM** value: **25.00**
55 ❑ Jun 1957 Cover: 0.10 **NM** value: **25.00**
56 ❑ Aug 1957 Cover: 0.10 **NM** value: **25.00**
57 ❑ Oct 1957 Cover: 0.10 **NM** value: **25.00**
58 ❑ Dec 1957 Cover: 0.10 **NM** value: **25.00**
59 ❑ Feb 1958 Cover: 0.10 **NM** value: **25.00**
60 ❑ Apr 1958 Cover: 0.10 **NM** value: **25.00**
61 ❑ Jun 1958 Cover: 0.10 **NM** value: **20.00**
62 ❑ Aug 1958 Cover: 0.10 **NM** value: **20.00**
63 ❑ Oct 1958 Cover: 0.10 **NM** value: **20.00**
64 ❑ Dec 1958 Cover: 0.10 **NM** value: **20.00**
65 ❑ Feb 1959 Cover: 0.10 **NM** value: **20.00**
66 ❑ Apr 1959 Cover: 0.10 **NM** value: **20.00**
• **CGC:** 1 graded, best 5.0
67 ❑ Jun 1959 Cover: 0.10 **NM** value: **20.00**
68 ❑ Aug 1959 Cover: 0.10 **NM** value: **20.00**
69 ❑ Oct 1959 Cover: 0.10 **NM** value: **20.00**
70 ❑ Dec 1959 Cover: 0.10 **NM** value: **20.00**
71 ❑ Feb 1960 Cover: 0.10 **NM** value: **20.00**
72 ❑ Apr 1960 Cover: 0.10 **NM** value: **20.00**
73 ❑ Jun 1960 Cover: 0.10 **NM** value: **20.00**
74 ❑ Aug 1960 Cover: 0.10 **NM** value: **20.00**
75 ❑ Oct 1960 Cover: 0.10 **NM** value: **20.00**
76 ❑ Dec 1960 Cover: 0.10 **NM** value: **20.00**
77 ❑ Mar 1961 Cover: 0.15 **NM** value: **20.00**
78 ❑ May 1961 Cover: 0.15 **NM** value: **20.00**
79 ❑ Jul 1961 Cover: 0.15 **NM** value: **20.00**
80 ❑ Sep 1961 Cover: 0.15 **NM** value: **20.00**
81 ❑ Nov 1961 Cover: 0.15 **NM** value: **15.00**
82 ❑ Jan 1962 Cover: 0.15 **NM** value: **15.00**
83 ❑ Mar 1962 Cover: 0.15 **NM** value: **15.00**
84 ❑ May 1962 Cover: 0.15 **NM** value: **15.00**
85 ❑ Jul 1962 Cover: 0.15 **NM** value: **15.00**

BUGS BUNNY (GOLD KEY) — Gold Key

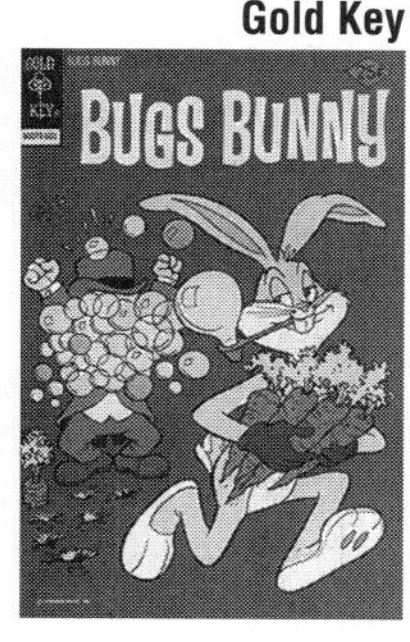

Early issues of Bugs Bunny, the inevitable (and inevitably popular) adaptation of Warner Bros.' wise-cracking rabbit, appeared as Dell Four Colors before becoming an "official" Dell series, and it continued for another two decades as a Gold Key series. Stories in the series alternate between comic shorts of five-to-seven pages and issue-length adventures, sometimes involving many other characters from the Warner Bros. stable. One issue finds all the 'toons at the Great America amusement park, while in another Bugs must save Beep Beep, The Road Runner from the disguised cowboy Leo I. O'Tweecy (Wile E. Coyote spelled sideways.

The series also had supporting characters all its own, including a prospecting uncle and Honey Bunny, a love interest for Bugs.

—JJM

86 ❑ Oct 1962 Cover: 0.25 **NM** value: **6.00**
• **CGC:** 3 graded, best 8.5
87 ❑ Dec 1962 Cover: 0.25 **NM** value: **6.00**
• **CGC:** 2 graded, best 8.0
88 ❑ Mar 1963 Cover: 0.25 **NM** value: **6.00**
• **CGC:** 3 graded, best 8.5
89 ❑ Jun 1963 Cover: 0.12 **NM** value: **6.00**
• **CGC:** 1 graded, best 8.0
90 ❑ Sep 1963 Cover: 0.12 **NM** value: **6.00**
• **CGC:** 1 graded, best 7.0
91 ❑ Dec 1963 Cover: 0.12 **NM** value: **6.00**
92 ❑ Mar 1964 Cover: 0.12 **NM** value: **6.00**
Circ: Statement: **322,317** • **CGC:** 1 graded, best 8.0
93 ❑ May 1964 Cover: 0.12 **NM** value: **6.00**
Circ: Statement: **322,317** • **CGC:** 1 graded, best 8.0
94 ❑ Jul 1964 Cover: 0.12 **NM** value: **6.00**
Circ: Statement: **322,317** • **CGC:** 1 graded, best 7.0
95 ❑ Sep 1964 Cover: 0.12 **NM** value: **6.00**
Circ: Statement: **322,317** • **CGC:** 1 graded, best 8.0
96 ❑ Nov 1964 Cover: 0.12 **NM** value: **6.00**
Circ: Statement: **322,317** • **CGC:** 1 graded, best 7.0
97 ❑ Jan 1965 Cover: 0.12 **NM** value: **6.00**
Circ: Statement: **291,816** • **CGC:** 1 graded, best 7.0
98 ❑ Mar 1965 Cover: 0.12 **NM** value: **6.00**
Circ: Statement: **291,816** • **CGC:** 1 graded, best 6.5
99 ❑ May 1965 Cover: 0.12 **NM** value: **6.00**
Circ: Statement: **291,816** • **CGC:** 1 graded, best 8.0
100❑ Jul 1965 Cover: 0.12 **NM** value: **6.00**
Circ: Statement: **291,816** • **CGC:** 1 graded, best 8.5
101❑ Sep 1965 Cover: 0.12 **NM** value: **5.00**
Circ: Statement: **291,816** • **CGC:** 1 graded, best 5.5
102❑ Nov 1965 Cover: 0.12 **NM** value: **5.00**
Circ: Statement: **291,816** • **CGC:** 1 graded, best 8.0
103❑ Jan 1966 Cover: 0.12 **NM** value: **5.00**
Circ: Statement: **276,949** • **CGC:** 1 graded, best 7.5
104❑ Mar 1966 Cover: 0.12 **NM** value: **5.00**
Circ: Statement: **276,949** • **CGC:** 1 graded, best 8.5
105❑ May 1966 Cover: 0.12 **NM** value: **5.00**
Circ: Statement: **276,949** • **CGC:** 1 graded, best 8.5
106❑ Jul 1966 Cover: 0.12 **NM** value: **5.00**
Circ: Statement: **276,949** • **CGC:** 1 graded, best 8.5
107❑ Sep 1966 Cover: 0.12 **NM** value: **5.00**
Circ: Statement: **276,949** • **CGC:** 1 graded, best 8.0
108❑ Nov 1966 Cover: 0.12 **NM** value: **5.00**
Circ: Statement: **276,949** • **CGC:** 1 graded, best 9.2
109❑ Jan 1967 Cover: 0.12 **NM** value: **5.00**
Circ: Statement: **266,815** • **CGC:** 1 graded, best 7.5
110❑ Mar 1967 Cover: 0.12 **NM** value: **5.00**
Circ: Statement: **266,815** • **CGC:** 1 graded, best 9.2
111❑ May 1967 Cover: 0.12 **NM** value: **5.00**
Circ: Statement: **266,815** • **CGC:** 1 graded, best 9.0
112❑ Jul 1967 Cover: 0.12 **NM** value: **5.00**
Circ: Statement: **266,815** • **CGC:** 1 graded, best 9.2
113❑ Sep 1967 Cover: 0.12 **NM** value: **5.00**
Circ: Statement: **266,815** • **CGC:** 1 graded, best 7.0
114❑ Nov 1967 Cover: 0.12 **NM** value: **5.00**
Circ: Statement: **266,815** • **CGC:** 1 graded, best 6.5
115❑ Jan 1968 Cover: 0.12 **NM** value: **5.00**
• **CGC:** 1 graded, best 6.0
116❑ Mar 1968 Cover: 0.12 **NM** value: **5.00**
• **CGC:** 1 graded, best 7.5
117❑ May 1968 Cover: 0.12 **NM** value: **5.00**
• **CGC:** 1 graded, best 8.0
118❑ Jul 1968 Cover: 0.12 **NM** value: **5.00**
• **CGC:** 1 graded, best 7.0
119❑ Sep 1968 Cover: 0.15 **NM** value: **5.00**
120❑ Nov 1968 Cover: 0.15 **NM** value: **5.00**
121❑ Jan 1969 Cover: 0.15 **NM** value: **3.50**
122❑ Mar 1969 Cover: 0.15 **NM** value: **3.50**
123❑ May 1969 Cover: 0.15 **NM** value: **3.50**
124❑ Jul 1969 Cover: 0.15 **NM** value: **3.50**
125❑ Sep 1969 Cover: 0.15 **NM** value: **3.50**
126❑ Nov 1969 Cover: 0.15 **NM** value: **3.50**
127❑ Jan 1970 Cover: 0.15 **NM** value: **3.50**
Circ: Statement: **268,081**
128❑ Mar 1970 Cover: 0.15 **NM** value: **3.50**
Circ: Statement: **268,081**
129❑ May 1970 Cover: 0.15 **NM** value: **3.50**
Circ: Statement: **268,081**
130❑ Jul 1970 Cover: 0.15 **NM** value: **3.50**
Circ: Statement: **268,081**
131❑ Sep 1970 Cover: 0.15 **NM** value: **3.50**
Circ: Statement: **268,081**

CGC-graded: Multiply prices above by **33 for 9.9 M • 16 for 9.8 NM/M • 7 for 9.6 NM+ • 5 for 9.4 NM • 2.5 for 9.2 NM- • 1.5 for 9.0 VF/NM**

132 ❑ Nov 1970 Cover: 0.15 **NM** value: **3.50**
Circ: Statement: **268,081**
133 ❑ Jan 1971 Cover: 0.15 **NM** value: **3.50**
134 ❑ Mar 1971 Cover: 0.15 **NM** value: **3.50**
• Has 1970 Statement, filed 9/30/70; avg print run 409,457; avg sales 258,000; avg subs 10,081; avg total paid 268,081; samples 603; max existent 268,684; 34% of run returned
135 ❑ May 1971 Cover: 0.15 **NM** value: **3.50**
136 ❑ Jul 1971 Cover: 0.15 **NM** value: **3.50**
137 ❑ Sep 1971 Cover: 0.15 **NM** value: **3.50**
138 ❑ Oct 1971 Cover: 0.15 **NM** value: **3.50**
139 ❑ Dec 1971 Cover: 0.15 **NM** value: **3.50**
140 ❑ Jan 1971 Cover: 0.15 **NM** value: **3.50**
141 ❑ Mar 1972 Cover: 0.15 **NM** value: **3.50**
🕮 Rabbit Luck; Super Citizen; Prize-Winning Pop-Up (text story); Squatter's Rights; Daffy Duck: Code of the North Woods
142 ❑ May 1972 Cover: 0.15 **NM** value: **3.50**
143 ❑ Jul 1972 Cover: 0.15 **NM** value: **3.50**
144 ❑ Sep 1972 Cover: 0.15 **NM** value: **3.50**
145 ❑ Oct 1972 Cover: 0.15 **NM** value: **3.50**
146 ❑ Dec 1972 Cover: 0.15 **NM** value: **3.50**
147 ❑ Jan 1973 Cover: 0.15 **NM** value: **3.50**
148 ❑ Mar 1973 Cover: 0.15 **NM** value: **3.50**
149 ❑ May 1973 Cover: 0.15 **NM** value: **3.50**
150 ❑ Jul 1973 Cover: 0.20 **NM** value: **3.50**
151 ❑ Aug 1973 Cover: 0.20 **NM** value: **2.50**
152 ❑ Sep 1973 Cover: 0.20 **NM** value: **2.50**
153 ❑ Nov 1973 Cover: 0.20 **NM** value: **2.50**
154 ❑ Jan 1974 Cover: 0.20 **NM** value: **2.50**
155 ❑ Mar 1974 Cover: 0.20 **NM** value: **2.50**
156 ❑ May 1974 Cover: 0.20 **NM** value: **2.50**
157 ❑ Jul 1974 Cover: 0.25 **NM** value: **2.50**
158 ❑ Aug 1974 Cover: 0.25 **NM** value: **2.50**
159 ❑ Sep 1974 Cover: 0.25 **NM** value: **2.50**
160 ❑ Nov 1974 Cover: 0.25 **NM** value: **2.50**
161 ❑ Jan 1975 Cover: 0.25 **NM** value: **2.50**
🕮 Fearless Fudd; Haunted Mustache; The Big Catch
162 ❑ Mar 1975 Cover: 0.25 **NM** value: **2.50**
163 ❑ May 1975 Cover: 0.25 **NM** value: **2.50**
164 ❑ Jul 1975 Cover: 0.25 **NM** value: **2.50**
165 ❑ Aug 1975 Cover: 0.25 **NM** value: **2.50**
166 ❑ Sep 1975 Cover: 0.25 **NM** value: **2.50**
167 ❑ Oct 1975 Cover: 0.25 **NM** value: **2.50**
• **CGC:** 4 graded, best 9.4
168 ❑ Nov 1975 Cover: 0.25 **NM** value: **2.50**
169 ❑ Jan 1976 Cover: 0.25 **NM** value: **2.50**
170 ❑ Mar 1976 Cover: 0.25 **NM** value: **2.50**
171 ❑ Apr 1976 Cover: 0.25 **NM** value: **2.50**
172 ❑ May 1976 Cover: 0.25 **NM** value: **2.50**
173 ❑ Jun 1976 Cover: 0.25 **NM** value: **2.50**
174 ❑ Jul 1976 Cover: 0.25 **NM** value: **2.50**
175 ❑ Aug 1976 Cover: 0.30 **NM** value: **2.50**
176 ❑ Sep 1976 Cover: 0.30 **NM** value: **2.50**
177 ❑ Oct 1976 Cover: 0.30 **NM** value: **2.50**
178 ❑ Nov 1976 Cover: 0.30 **NM** value: **2.50**
179 ❑ Dec 1976 Cover: 0.30 **NM** value: **2.50**
180 ❑ Jan 1977 Cover: 0.30 **NM** value: **2.50**
181 ❑ Feb 1977 Cover: 0.30 **NM** value: **2.50**
182 ❑ Mar 1977 Cover: 0.30 **NM** value: **2.50**
183 ❑ Apr 1977 Cover: 0.30 **NM** value: **2.50**
184 ❑ May 1977 Cover: 0.30 **NM** value: **2.50**
185 ❑ Jun 1977 Cover: 0.30 **NM** value: **2.50**
186 ❑ Jul 1977 Cover: 0.30 **NM** value: **2.50**
187 ❑ Aug 1977 Cover: 0.30 **NM** value: **2.50**
188 ❑ Sep 1977 Cover: 0.30 **NM** value: **2.50**
189 ❑ Oct 1977 **NM** value: **2.50**
190 ❑ Nov 1977 **NM** value: **2.50**
191 ❑ Dec 1977 **NM** value: **2.50**
192 ❑ Jan 1978 **NM** value: **2.50**
193 ❑ Feb 1978 **NM** value: **2.50**
194 ❑ Mar 1978 **NM** value: **2.50**
195 ❑ Apr 1978 **NM** value: **2.50**
196 ❑ May 1978 **NM** value: **2.50**
197 ❑ Jun 1978 **NM** value: **2.50**
198 ❑ Jul 1978 Cover: 0.35 **NM** value: **2.50**
199 ❑ Aug 1978 Cover: 0.35 **NM** value: **2.50**
200 ❑ Sep 1978 Cover: 0.35 **NM** value: **2.50**
201 ❑ Oct 1978 Cover: 0.35 **NM** value: **2.00**
202 ❑ Nov 1978 Cover: 0.35 **NM** value: **2.00**
203 ❑ Dec 1978 Cover: 0.35 **NM** value: **2.00**
204 ❑ Jan 1979 Cover: 0.35 **NM** value: **2.00**
205 ❑ Feb 1979 Cover: 0.35 **NM** value: **2.00**
206 ❑ Mar 1979 Cover: 0.35 **NM** value: **2.00**
207 ❑ Apr 1979 **NM** value: **2.00**
208 ❑ May 1979 **NM** value: **2.00**
209 ❑ Jun 1979 Cover: 0.40 **NM** value: **2.00**
210 ❑ Jul 1979 Cover: 0.40 **NM** value: **2.00**
211 ❑ Aug 1979 Cover: 0.40 **NM** value: **2.00**
212 ❑ ca. 1979 Cover: 0.40 **NM** value: **2.00**
213 ❑ **NM** value: **2.00**
214 ❑ **NM** value: **2.00**
215 ❑ **NM** value: **2.00**
216 ❑ **NM** value: **2.00**
217 ❑ **NM** value: **2.00**
218 ❑ **NM** value: **2.00**
219 ❑ **NM** value: **2.00**
220 ❑ **NM** value: **2.00**
221 ❑ Sep 1980 **NM** value: **2.00**
222 ❑ Nov 1980 Cover: 0.50 **NM** value: **2.00**
223 ❑ Jan 1981 Cover: 0.50 **NM** value: **2.00**
224 ❑ Mar 1981 Cover: 0.50 **NM** value: **2.00**
225 ❑ ca. 1981 **NM** value: **2.00**
226 ❑ ca. 1981 **NM** value: **2.00**
227 ❑ ca. 1981 **NM** value: **2.00**
228 ❑ ca. 1981 **NM** value: **2.00**
229 ❑ ca. 1981 **NM** value: **2.00**
230 ❑ ca. 1981 **NM** value: **2.00**
231 ❑ ca. 1981 **NM** value: **2.00**
232 ❑ ca. 1981 **NM** value: **2.00**
233 ❑ ca. 1981 **NM** value: **2.00**
234 ❑ ca. 1981, four-color Cover: 0.60 **NM** value: **2.00**
🕮 Cave Caper, The Goblin Plot **W:** Uncred.
235 ❑ ca. 1982 Cover: 0.60 **NM** value: **2.00**
236 ❑ ca. 1982 Cover: 0.60 **NM** value: **2.00**
237 ❑ ca. 1982 Cover: 0.60 **NM** value: **2.00**
238 ❑ ca. 1982 Cover: 0.60 **NM** value: **2.00**
239 ❑ ca. 1982 Cover: 0.60 **NM** value: **2.00**
240 ❑ ca. 1982 Cover: 0.60 **NM** value: **2.00**
241 ❑ **NM** value: **2.00**
242 ❑ **NM** value: **2.00**
243 ❑ **NM** value: **2.00**
244 ❑ **NM** value: **2.00**
245 ❑ **NM** value: **2.00**
final issue.

BUGS BUNNY MONTHLY, THE — DC

1 ❑ Cover: 1.95 **NM** value: **Cover or less**
2 ❑ Cover: 1.95 **NM** value: **Cover or less**
3 ❑ Cover: 1.95 **NM** value: **Cover or less**
🕮 Hoods in the Woods; The Great Bugsini **A:** Alvaro Flores; Horacio Saavedra **W:** David Cody Weiss; Brett Koth; David Rawson

BUGS BUNNY'S CHRISTMAS FUNNIES — Dell

1 ❑ Hol 1950 Cover: 0.25 **NM** value: **200.00**
2 ❑ Hol 1951 Cover: 0.25 **NM** value: **150.00**
3 ❑ Hol 1952 Cover: 0.25 **NM** value: **150.00**
• **CGC:** 2 graded, best 9.4
4 ❑ Hol 1953 Cover: 0.25 **NM** value: **150.00**
• **CGC:** 2 graded, best 9.2
5 ❑ Hol 1954 Cover: 0.25 **NM** value: **150.00**
6 ❑ Hol 1955 Cover: 0.25 **NM** value: **150.00**
7 ❑ Hol 1956 Cover: 0.25 **NM** value: **125.00**
• **CGC:** 2 graded, best 9.2
8 ❑ Hol 1957 Cover: 0.25 **NM** value: **125.00**
9 ❑ Hol 1958 Cover: 0.25 **NM** value: **125.00**
• **CGC:** 1 graded, best 8.5

BUGS BUNNY'S HALLOWEEN PARADE — Dell

1 ❑ ca. 1953 Cover: 0.25 **NM** value: **150.00**
• **CGC:** 1 graded, best 8.0
2 ❑ ca. 1954 Cover: 0.25 **NM** value: **125.00**
• **CGC:** 1 graded, best 8.5

BUGS BUNNY'S TRICK 'N' TREAT HALLOWEEN FUN — Dell

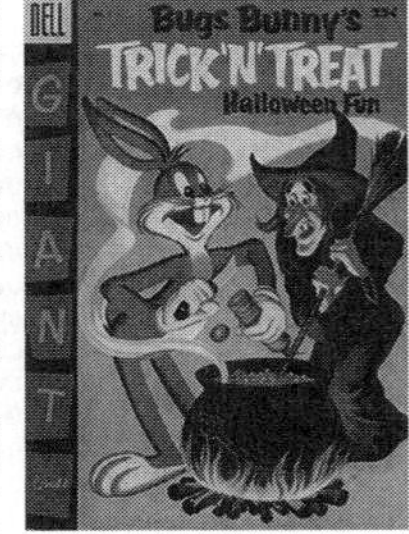

Bugs Bunny's Trick 'n' Treat Halloween Fun is another oversized Dell "giant," bursting at the seams with fun and spooky and usually hilarious antics of Bugs and his familiar crew (Porky Pig, Yosemite Sam, Elmer Fudd, and company). The Halloween issue naturally features ghostly goings-on, witches, haunted houses, and other fearsome frolics. Like the animated cartoons that inspired them, the comic-book adventures of Bugs and his pals features gags in nearly every panel, tied together by a goofy plot that improbably holds together with precise kid-like logic.

As such, they are as easily appreciated by adults as children.

3 ❑ Oct 1955 Cover: 0.25 **NM** value: **85.00**
• **CGC:** 1 graded, best 9.0
🕮 Sylvester's Halloween Scare; Bugs Bunny and Spooky the Spook; Jack-O-Lantern Jamboree; Halloween Hometown Hijinx; The Giant Goblins; Porky's Picture Puzzle Party; The Witches of Creepy Cavern; Mary Jane and Sniffles; Bugs Bunn • Continues from Halloween Parade #2★ Appearance of Elmer Fudd. ★ Appearance of Porky Pig, Petunia Pig, Daffy Duck, Spooky the Spook, Yosemite Sam, Tweety Bird, Bugs Bunny.
4 ❑ Oct 1956 Cover: 0.25 **NM** value: **85.00**
• **CGC:** 1 graded, best 9.6

BUGS BUNNY'S VACATION FUNNIES — Dell

1 ❑ Cover: 0.25 **NM** value: **150.00**
2 ❑ Cover: 0.25 **NM** value: **120.00**
3 ❑ Cover: 0.25 **NM** value: **100.00**
• **CGC:** 1 graded, best 9.4
4 ❑ Jun 1954 Cover: 0.25 **NM** value: **80.00**
• **CGC:** 1 graded, best 9.2
5 ❑ ca. 1955 Cover: 0.25 **NM** value: **80.00**
• **CGC:** 2 graded, best 9.4
🕮 Bugs Bunny's Vacation Advice; Paradise Island; Bugs Bunny's Park Band; Petunia's Rebus Roadmap; Trailer Trouble; Cicero's Dude Ranch Roundup; Games around the World; The King-Size Tweety Bird; Tweety's Vacation Souvenir; Hero for a Day; Chi ★ Appearance of Elmer Fudd, Porky Pig, Petunia Pig, Sylvester Cat, Daffy Duck, Tweety Bird, Cicero Swine, Henry Hawk, Bugs Bunny, Foghorn Leghorn.
6 ❑ ca. 1956 Cover: 0.25 **NM** value: **80.00**
7 ❑ ca. 1957 Cover: 0.25 **NM** value: **80.00**
• **CGC:** 1 graded, best 9.6
8 ❑ Jun 1958 Cover: 0.25 **NM** value: **80.00**
• **CGC:** 1 graded, best 9.2
9 ❑ Jun 1959 Cover: 0.25 **NM** value: **80.00**
• **CGC:** 1 graded, best 9.2

BUGS BUNNY WINTER FUN — Gold Key

1 ❑ Dec 1967 Cover: 0.25 **NM** value: **30.00**
• **CGC:** 1 graded, best 8.5

BUG'S GIFT, A — Discovery

1 ❑ Cover: 1.95 **NM** value: **Cover or less**
🕮 A Bug's Gift **A:** Lynette Weisberg **W:** Scott Deschaine

BUILDING, THE — DC

1 ❑ Cover: 9.95 **NM** value: **Cover or less**
A: Will Eisner **W:** Will Eisner

BULLET CROW, FOWL OF FORTUNE — Eclipse

1 ❑ Cover: 2.00 **NM** value: **Cover or less**
2 ❑ Cover: 2.00 **NM** value: **Cover or less**

BULLETMAN — Fawcett

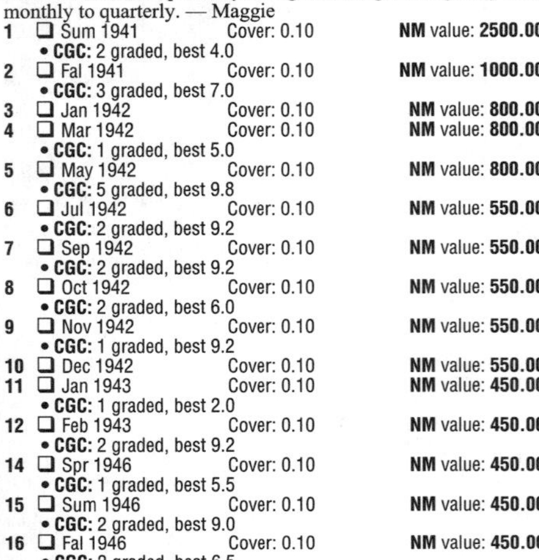

Bulletman (known as "the flying detective") was one of the stars among Fawcett's universe of superheroes and appeared, for example, in Master Comics. His adventures began as the cover feature of the biweekly Nickle Comics #1 (May 17 40), and, when that series ended, he quickly moved to Master Comics (in #7, Oct 40). It was there that his companion, Bulletgirl, was introduced. (She joined him in #13, Apr 41).

The couple's headgear consisted of a sort of "shell" hat, they could fly in their fight against evil, and they were joined by Bulletdog in #10 (Dec 42). Note: There was no #13 in the series, probably owing to a change in frequency from monthly to quarterly. — Maggie

1 ❑ Sum 1941 Cover: 0.10 **NM** value: **2500.00**
• **CGC:** 2 graded, best 4.0
2 ❑ Fal 1941 Cover: 0.10 **NM** value: **1000.00**
• **CGC:** 3 graded, best 7.0
3 ❑ Jan 1942 Cover: 0.10 **NM** value: **800.00**
4 ❑ Mar 1942 Cover: 0.10 **NM** value: **800.00**
• **CGC:** 1 graded, best 5.0
5 ❑ May 1942 Cover: 0.10 **NM** value: **800.00**
• **CGC:** 5 graded, best 9.8
6 ❑ Jul 1942 Cover: 0.10 **NM** value: **550.00**
• **CGC:** 2 graded, best 9.2
7 ❑ Sep 1942 Cover: 0.10 **NM** value: **550.00**
• **CGC:** 2 graded, best 9.2
8 ❑ Oct 1942 Cover: 0.10 **NM** value: **550.00**
• **CGC:** 2 graded, best 6.0
9 ❑ Nov 1942 Cover: 0.10 **NM** value: **550.00**
• **CGC:** 1 graded, best 9.2
10 ❑ Dec 1942 Cover: 0.10 **NM** value: **550.00**
11 ❑ Jan 1943 Cover: 0.10 **NM** value: **450.00**
• **CGC:** 1 graded, best 2.0
12 ❑ Feb 1943 Cover: 0.10 **NM** value: **450.00**
• **CGC:** 2 graded, best 9.2
14 ❑ Spr 1946 Cover: 0.10 **NM** value: **450.00**
• **CGC:** 1 graded, best 5.5
15 ❑ Sum 1946 Cover: 0.10 **NM** value: **450.00**
• **CGC:** 2 graded, best 9.0
16 ❑ Fal 1946 Cover: 0.10 **NM** value: **450.00**
• **CGC:** 2 graded, best 6.5

BULLETPROOF — Known Associates

1 ❑ b&w Cover: 3.95 **NM** value: **Cover or less**

BULLETPROOF COMICS — Wet Paint Graphics

1 ❑ Cover: 2.25 **NM** value: **Cover or less**
2 ❑ May 1999 Cover: 2.25 **NM** value: **Cover or less**
3 ❑ Sep 1999 Cover: 2.25 **NM** value: **Cover or less**

BULLETPROOF MONK — Image

1 ❑ Nov 1998 Cover: 2.95 **NM** value: **Cover or less**
Circ: Diamd. preorders: **6,462**
🕮 Days of Thinking Why **A:** Michael Avon Oeming **W:** Brett Lewis
2 ❑ Dec 1998 Cover: 2.95 **NM** value: **Cover or less**
Circ: Diamd. preorders: **4,090**
🕮 Moments of Present Past **A:** Michael Avon Oeming **W:** Brett Lewis; R.A. Jones
3 ❑ Jan 1999 Cover: 2.95 **NM** value: **Cover or less**
Circ: Diamd. preorders: **3,512**
🕮 Knowing you, Knowing me **A:** Michael Avon Oeming **W:** R.A. Jones

BULLETS AND BRACELETS — Marvel / Amalgam

1 ❑ Apr 1996 Cover: 1.95 **NM** value: **Cover or less**
🕮 Final Trust **A:** Gary Frank **W:** John Ostrander

BULLS-EYE (CHARLTON) — Charlton

6 ❑ Jun 1955 Cover: 0.10 **NM** value: **200.00**
🕮 Tomahawks for Two; Bulls-Eye and the Killer Horse; The Coming of the Sioux; The Man Who Lived Twice **A:** Joe Simon; Jack Kirby **C:** Joe Simon; Jack Kirby
7 ❑ Sep 1955 Cover: 0.10 **NM** value: **200.00**
🕮 Duel in the Sky; The Flaming Arrow; The Stolen Rain God **A:** Joe Simon; Jack Kirby **C:** Joe Simon; Jack Kirby

BULLS-EYE (MAINLINE) — Mainline

1 ❑ Aug 1954 Cover: 0.10 **NM** value: **350.00**
🕮 Bulls-Eye, the Boy; Bulls-Eye, The Youth **A:** Jack Kirby **C:** Jack Kirby
2 ❑ Oct 1954 Cover: 0.10 **NM** value: **300.00**
🕮 Union Jack; Grand Prize **A:** Jack Kirby **C:** Joe Simon; Jack Kirby
3 ❑ Dec 1954 Cover: 0.10 **NM** value: **250.00**
🕮 Devil Bird; On Target; The Ghosts of Dead Center **A:** Jack Kirby **C:** Joe Simon; Jack Kirby
4 ❑ Feb 1955 Cover: 0.10 **NM** value: **250.00**
🕮 The Pinto People; Doom Town **A:** Jack Kirby **C:** Joe Simon; Jack Kirby

Other grades: Multiply prices above by **1.5 for Mint • 2/3 for Very Fine • 1/3 for Fine • 1/5 for Very Good • 1/8 for Good**

5 ❑ Apr 1955 Cover: 0.10 **NM** value: **250.00**
📖 Headhunter; Grandma Tomahawk **A:** Jack Kirby **C:** Joe Simon; Jack Kirby

BULLWINKLE — Dell

1 ❑ **NM** value: **Cover or less**
• **CGC:** 1 graded, best 7.5

BULLWINKLE & ROCKY (BLACKTHORNE) — Blackthorne

1 ❑ Cover: 2.50 **NM** value: **Cover or less**
2 ❑ Cover: 2.50 **NM** value: **Cover or less**
3 ❑ Cover: 2.50 **NM** value: **Cover or less**
3D 1❑ Mar 1987 Cover: 2.50 **NM** value: **Cover or less**
Circ: CapCity orders: **3,908**

BULLWINKLE AND ROCKY (CHARLTON) — Charlton

1 ❑ Jul 1970 Cover: 0.15 **NM** value: **30.00**
• poster
2 ❑ Sep 1970 Cover: 0.15 **NM** value: **18.00**
3 ❑ Nov 1970 Cover: 0.15 **NM** value: **15.00**
4 ❑ Jan 1971 Cover: 0.15 **NM** value: **12.00**
5 ❑ Mar 1971 Cover: 0.15 **NM** value: **12.00**
6 ❑ May 1971 Cover: 0.15 **NM** value: **12.00**
7 ❑ Jul 1971 Cover: 0.15 **NM** value: **12.00**

BULLWINKLE AND ROCKY (GOLD KEY) — Gold Key

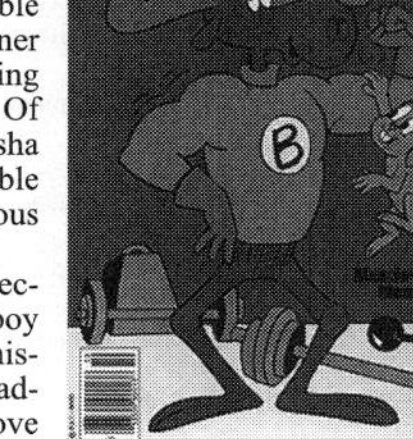

Bullwinkle J. Moose and Rocky the Flying Squirrel star in this humorous series, based on the characters of Jay Ward and Bill Scott's TV shows. As usual, Bullwinkle manages to bumble his way in and out of all manner of trouble, with Rocky offering words of unheeded wisdom. Of course, spies Boris and Natasha are also around to stir up trouble with a variety of nefarious schemes.

Also featured are the intellectual dog Mr. Peabody and his boy Sherman, who travel through history in a series of improbable adventures. And, as if all the above weren't enough laughs for the comics-buying dollar, the title also includes a number of episodes of the ever-popular Fractured Fairy Tales.

1 ❑ Nov 1962 Cover: 0.12 **NM** value: **140.00**
• **CGC:** 3 graded, best 9.0
2 ❑ Feb 1963 Cover: 0.12 **NM** value: **100.00**
• **CGC:** 1 graded, best 7.0
3 ❑ Apr 1972 Cover: 0.15 **NM** value: **40.00**
• **CGC:** 1 graded, best 8.0
4 ❑ Jul 1972 Cover: 0.15 **NM** value: **40.00**
• **CGC:** 1 graded, best 8.5
5 ❑ Sep 1972 Cover: 0.15 **NM** value: **40.00**
• **CGC:** 1 graded, best 8.0
6 ❑ Jan 1973 Cover: 0.15 **NM** value: **28.00**
• **CGC:** 2 graded, best 9.4
7 ❑ Apr 1973 Cover: 0.15 **NM** value: **28.00**
• **CGC:** 1 graded, best 8.0
8 ❑ Jul 1973 Cover: 0.20 **NM** value: **28.00**
• **CGC:** 1 graded, best 8.5
9 ❑ Oct 1973 Cover: 0.20 **NM** value: **28.00**
• **CGC:** 1 graded, best 7.5
10 ❑ Jan 1974 Cover: 0.20 **NM** value: **28.00**
• **CGC:** 2 graded, best 9.2
11 ❑ Apr 1974 Cover: 0.20 **NM** value: **28.00**
• **CGC:** 1 graded, best 7.0
• Last issue of original run
12 ❑ Jun 1976 Cover: 0.25 **NM** value: **14.00**
• Series picks up after hiatus
13 ❑ Sep 1976 Cover: 0.25 **NM** value: **20.00**
14 ❑ Dec 1976 Cover: 0.30 **NM** value: **16.00**
15 ❑ Mar 1977 Cover: 0.30 **NM** value: **9.00**
16 ❑ Jun 1977 Cover: 0.30 **NM** value: **9.00**
17 ❑ Sep 1977 Cover: 0.30 **NM** value: **9.00**
18 ❑ Dec 1977 Cover: 0.30 **NM** value: **9.00**
19 ❑ **NM** value: **9.00**
20 ❑ Cover: 0.40 **NM** value: **9.00**
21 ❑ Cover: 0.40 **NM** value: **7.00**
22 ❑ Cover: 0.40 **NM** value: **7.00**
23 ❑ Oct 1979 Cover: 0.40 **NM** value: **7.00**
📖 Muscle Bound Moose
24 ❑ Dec 1979 Cover: 0.40 **NM** value: **7.00**
25 ❑ Cover: 0.40 **NM** value: **7.00**
final issue.

BULLWINKLE AND ROCKY (STAR) — Marvel / Star

1 ❑ Nov 1987 Cover: 1.00 **NM** value: **1.50**
Circ: CapCity orders: **5,700**
📖 The "Invisible Ray" or "---!" **A:** Ernie Colon **W:** Dave Manak
2 ❑ Jan 1988 Cover: 1.00 **NM** value: **1.25**
Circ: CapCity orders: **3,500**
3 ❑ Mar 1988 Cover: 1.00 **NM** value: **1.25**
Circ: CapCity orders: **3,500**
4 ❑ May 1988 Cover: 1.00 **NM** value: **1.25**
Circ: CapCity orders: **2,900**
5 ❑ Jul 1988 Cover: 1.00 **NM** value: **1.25**
Circ: CapCity orders: **3,100**
6 ❑ Sep 1988 Cover: 1.00 **NM** value: **1.25**
Circ: CapCity orders: **2,700**
7 ❑ Nov 1988 Cover: 1.00 **NM** value: **1.25**
Circ: CapCity orders: **2,400**
8 ❑ Jan 1989 Cover: 1.00 **NM** value: **1.25**
Circ: CapCity orders: **2,300**
📖 Bullwinkle and Rocky: The Moose Who Would be Mayor Or… Be-Caucus You're Mine!; Dudley Do-Right of the Mounties: A Nick in Time; Mr. Know-It-All: The Stand-In; Bullwinkle and Rocky: Don't Rain on my Campaign or Takin' Debate • Marvel publishes **A:** Ernie Colon **W:** Dave Manak
9 ❑ Mar 1989 Cover: 1.00 **NM** value: **1.25**
Circ: CapCity orders: **2,400**
final issue.
Bk 1❑ Cover: 4.95 **NM** value: **Cover or less**

BULLWINKLE FOR PRESIDENT IN 3-D — Blackthorne

1 ❑ Cover: 2.50 **NM** value: **Cover or less**
Circ: CapCity orders: **1,050**

BULLWINKLE MOTHER MOOSE NURSERY POMES — Dell

1 ❑ May 1962 Cover: 0.15 **NM** value: **100.00**
• **CGC:** 1 graded, best 7.0

BUMBERCOMIX — Starhead

1 ❑ **NM** value: **1.00**
• Giveaway from arts festival.

BURGLAR BILL — Trident

1 ❑ b&w Cover: 2.25 **NM** value: **Cover or less**

BURIAL OF THE RATS (BRAM STOKER'S...) — Roger Corman's Cosmic Comics

1 ❑ Cover: 2.50 **NM** value: **Cover or less**
Circ: CapCity orders: **4,150**
A: Francisco Solano Lopez **W:** Jerry Prosser

BURIED TREASURE — Pure Imagination

1 ❑ Cover: 5.95 **NM** value: **Cover or less**
2 ❑ Cover: 5.95 **NM** value: **Cover or less**
3 ❑ Cover: 5.95 **NM** value: **Cover or less**
• moves to Caliber

BURIED TREASURE (2ND SERIES) — Caliber

1 ❑ Cover: 2.50 **NM** value: **Cover or less**
• reprints, b&w **A:** Al Williamson; Frank Frazetta
2 ❑ Cover: 2.50 **NM** value: **Cover or less**
A: Joe Simon; Joe Orlando; Jack Kirby; Wally Wood; Jack Cole
3 ❑ Cover: 2.50 **NM** value: **Cover or less**
• reprints Frankenstein **A:** Frank Frazetta; Wally Wood
4 ❑ Cover: 2.50 **NM** value: **Cover or less**
A: Frank Frazetta

BURKE'S LAW — Dell

The popular TV police drama of the same name ran from 1963 to 1966, starring Gene Barry as Capt. Amos Burke, a suave, handsome, millionaire chief of detectives in Los Angeles. He worked for the police department because he loved the challenge. Often arriving at crime scenes in a Rolls Royce chauffeured by his trusty driver Henry, Burke would proceed to solve murders while spouting truisms he called "Burke's Laws." Meant to capitalize on the popularity of the television show, Burke's adventures were published in comics form starting in 1964, but the stories did not have the advantage the TV series had: an endless series of Hollywood stars eager to perform in bit-part cameos.

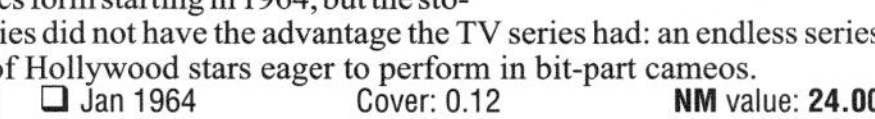

1 ❑ Jan 1964 Cover: 0.12 **NM** value: **24.00**
Photo cover.
2 ❑ ca. 1964 Cover: 0.12 **NM** value: **20.00**
Photo cover.
3 ❑ Mar 1965 Cover: 0.12 **NM** value: **20.00**
• **CGC:** 1 graded, best 7.0
Photo cover.

BURRITO — Accent!

1 ❑ Jan 1995 Cover: 2.50 **NM** value: **Cover or less**
2 ❑ Apr 1995 Cover: 2.50 **NM** value: **2.75**
3 ❑ Jul 1995 Cover: 2.75 **NM** value: **Cover or less**
4 ❑ Nov 1995 Cover: 2.75 **NM** value: **Cover or less**
5 ❑ Jul 1996 Cover: 2.75 **NM** value: **Cover or less**
📖 Discovered?! Is that You Finding Me or Me Finding You **A:** Carlos Saldaña **W:** Carlos Saldaña

BUSHIDO — Eternity

1 ❑ Jul 1988 Cover: 1.95 **NM** value: **Cover or less**
A: Ben Dunn **W:** Bruce Balfour
2 ❑ Cover: 1.95 **NM** value: **Cover or less**
A: Ben Dunn **W:** Bruce Balfour
3 ❑ Cover: 1.95 **NM** value: **Cover or less**
A: Ben Dunn **W:** Bruce Balfour
4 ❑ Cover: 1.95 **NM** value: **Cover or less**
A: Ben Dunn **W:** Bruce Balfour

BUSHIDO BLADE OF ZATOICHI WALRUS — Solson

1 ❑ Cover: 2.00 **NM** value: **Cover or less**

BUSHWHACKED — Eros

1 ❑ Cover: 2.95 **NM** value: **Cover or less**

BUSTER — Crisis

1 ❑ Cover: 2.50 **NM** value: **Cover or less**
2 ❑ Cover: 2.50 **NM** value: **Cover or less**

BUSTER BROWN COMIC BOOK — Buster Brown

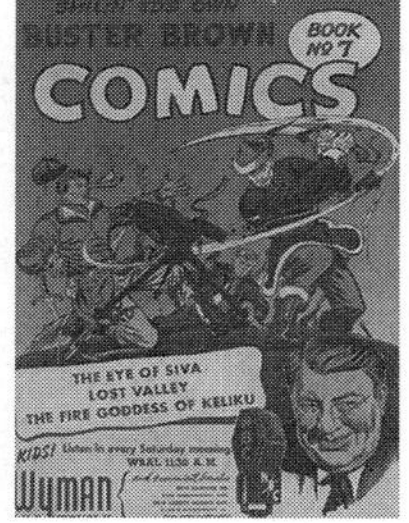

Buster Brown is one of the oldest characters in American comics, dating from 1902, the creation of Yellow Kid pioneer Richard Outcault (1863-1928). While The Yellow Kid was a slum character, Buster was clearly wealthy — but the child of privilege was, nevertheless, naughty. And that's what each strip was built on: the disaster caused by Buster, followed by his promise to be good from that point on.

Outcault had considerable success licensing The Yellow Kid for a number of products, but with Buster Brown he outdid his previous efforts. The best-known of his licenses is one that continues to this day: Buster Brown shoes, where the symbol includes Buster's dog, Tige. The shoe company used this comic book as an additional promotional tool, but its stories did not contain the antics of boy and dog; it was simply an anthology giveaway comic book available in stores selling Buster Brown shoes. The adventure stories were entertaining, and the art was often excellent. — Maggie

1 ❑ ca. 1945 **NM** value: **100.00**
2 ❑ **NM** value: **65.00**
3 ❑ **NM** value: **45.00**
4 ❑ **NM** value: **45.00**
5 ❑ **NM** value: **45.00**
6 ❑ **NM** value: **32.00**
7 ❑ **NM** value: **32.00**
📖 The Fire Goddess of Keliku; The Eye of Siva; Lost Valley **W:** Hobart Donovan
8 ❑ **NM** value: **32.00**
9 ❑ **NM** value: **32.00**
10 ❑ **NM** value: **32.00**
11 ❑ **NM** value: **24.00**
12 ❑ **NM** value: **24.00**
13 ❑ **NM** value: **24.00**
14 ❑ **NM** value: **24.00**
15 ❑ **NM** value: **24.00**
16 ❑ **NM** value: **24.00**
17 ❑ **NM** value: **24.00**
18 ❑ **NM** value: **24.00**
19 ❑ **NM** value: **24.00**
20 ❑ **NM** value: **24.00**
21 ❑ **NM** value: **16.00**
22 ❑ **NM** value: **16.00**
23 ❑ **NM** value: **16.00**
24 ❑ **NM** value: **16.00**
25 ❑ **NM** value: **35.00**
A: Reed Crandall
26 ❑ **NM** value: **16.00**
27 ❑ **NM** value: **16.00**
28 ❑ **NM** value: **16.00**
29 ❑ **NM** value: **35.00**
A: Reed Crandall
30 ❑ **NM** value: **35.00**
📖 Gunga; Smilin' Ed and his Gang Visit the Zoo; Rumpus on Rex **A:** Reed Crandall; Ed McConnell; Ray Willner
31 ❑ **NM** value: **35.00**
A: Reed Crandall
32 ❑ **NM** value: **35.00**
A: Reed Crandall
33 ❑ **NM** value: **35.00**
A: Reed Crandall
34 ❑ **NM** value: **35.00**
A: Reed Crandall
35 ❑ **NM** value: **35.00**
A: Reed Crandall
36 ❑ **NM** value: **35.00**
A: Reed Crandall
37 ❑ **NM** value: **35.00**
A: Reed Crandall
38 ❑ **NM** value: **16.00**
39 ❑ **NM** value: **16.00**
40 ❑ **NM** value: **35.00**
A: Reed Crandall
41 ❑ **NM** value: **35.00**
A: Reed Crandall
42 ❑ **NM** value: **16.00**
43 ❑ **NM** value: **16.00**
final issue.

BUSTER BROWN DRAWING BOOK — Collins Baking Co.

1 ❑ ca. 1904 **NM** value: **500.00**
• **CGC:** 1 graded, best 8.0

BUSTER BROWN OF THE SAFETY PATROL — Custom

1 ❑ **NM** value: **Cover or less**
• **CGC:** 1 graded, best 3.5

BUSTER BUNNY — Standard

1 ❑ Nov 1949 Cover: 0.10 **NM** value: **40.00**
A: Frank Frazetta(text illustration)
2 ❑ Cover: 0.10 **NM** value: **22.00**
3 ❑ Cover: 0.10 **NM** value: **16.00**
4 ❑ Cover: 0.10 **NM** value: **16.00**
5 ❑ Cover: 0.10 **NM** value: **16.00**

CGC-graded: Multiply prices above by **33 for 9.9 M • 16 for 9.8 NM/M • 7 for 9.6 NM+ • 5 for 9.4 NM • 2.5 for 9.2 NM- • 1.5 for 9.0 VF/NM**

6 ❑ Cover: 0.10 **NM** value: **15.00**
7 ❑ Cover: 0.10 **NM** value: **15.00**
Heap Big Trouble
8 ❑ Cover: 0.10 **NM** value: **15.00**
9 ❑ Cover: 0.10 **NM** value: **15.00**
10 ❑ Cover: 0.10 **NM** value: **15.00**
11 ❑ Cover: 0.10 **NM** value: **15.00**
12 ❑ ca. 1951 Cover: 0.10 **NM** value: **15.00**
13 ❑ Cover: 0.10 **NM** value: **15.00**
14 ❑ Cover: 0.10 **NM** value: **15.00**
15 ❑ Cover: 0.10 **NM** value: **15.00**
16 ❑ Cover: 0.10 **NM** value: **15.00**

BUSTER CRABBE (FAMOUS FUNNIES) — Famous Funnies

1 ❑ Nov 1951 Cover: 0.10 **NM** value: **250.00**
2 ❑ Jan 1952 Cover: 0.10 **NM** value: **250.00**
• **CGC:** 1 graded, best 9.2
3 ❑ Mar 1952 Cover: 0.10 **NM** value: **250.00**
4 ❑ May 1952 Cover: 0.10 **NM** value: **200.00**
• **CGC:** 1 graded, best 8.5
5 ❑ Jul 1952 Cover: 0.10 **NM** value: **200.00**
• **CGC:** 1 graded, best 6.5
6 ❑ Sep 1952 Cover: 0.10 **NM** value: **200.00**
7 ❑ Nov 1952 Cover: 0.10 **NM** value: **150.00**
8 ❑ Jan 1953 Cover: 0.10 **NM** value: **150.00**
9 ❑ Mar 1952 Cover: 0.10 **NM** value: **150.00**
10 ❑ May 1953 Cover: 0.10 **NM** value: **125.00**
11 ❑ Jul 1953 Cover: 0.10 **NM** value: **125.00**
12 ❑ Sep 1953 Cover: 0.10 **NM** value: **125.00**

BUSTER CRABBE (LEV GLEASON) — Lev Gleason

Crabbe (1907-1983) acted in a number of genres (Buck Rogers, Flash Gordon, Tarzan, the TV series Captain Gallant of the Foreign Legion), and the comic book was an anthology of stand-alone stories in those genres: a Western, a jungle story, a science-fiction story, a Foreign Legion story. Art on the stories was often excellent. — Maggie

1 ❑ Dec 1953 Cover: 0.10 **NM** value: **125.00**
2 ❑ Feb 1954 Cover: 0.10 **NM** value: **100.00**
3 ❑ Apr 1954 Cover: 0.10 **NM** value: **100.00**
4 ❑ Jun 1954 Cover: 0.10 **NM** value: **10.00**
• **CGC:** 1 graded, best 9.4

BUSTER THE AMAZING BEAR — Ursus Studios

1 ❑ Aug 1992 Cover: 2.50 **NM** value: **Cover or less**
says Aug 93 on cover, Aug 92 in indicia. Rude Awakening • Surprise Poster Insert **A:** Tommy Yune **W:** Tommy Yune
2 ❑ Oct 1993 Cover: 2.50 **NM** value: **Cover or less**
A: Tommy Yune **W:** Tommy Yune
2-2 ❑ Oct 1994 Cover: 2.50 **NM** value: **Cover or less**
3 ❑ Jan 1994 Cover: 2.50 **NM** value: **Cover or less**
A: Tommy Yune **W:** Tommy Yune
4 ❑ May 1994 Cover: 2.95 **NM** value: **Cover or less**
A: Tommy Yune **W:** Tommy Yune
5 ❑ Nov 1994 Cover: 2.50 **NM** value: **Cover or less**
A: Tommy Yune **W:** Tommy Yune

BUSTLINE COMBAT — Eros

1 ❑ May 1999 Cover: 2.95 **NM** value: **Cover or less**
Circ: Diamd. preorders: **39,638**
Tanks for the Mammaries; The Island; Sgt. Flurry and her Howling Harlots! **A:** Dementia **W:** Dementia

BUTCHER, THE — DC

No, not a blood-and-guts series — or even a series about Ernest Borgnine's Marty, though you're forgiven, if that's what you thought.

No, John Butcher is a Native American, and his totem is that of the hawk. And, as he discovers on a butte in the desert, it is his peculiar fate to "rend" snakes.

He makes his first responsibility in adulthood to "rend" the land-developers, who murdered his family in order to mine the mineral-rich desert. He's a warrior, trained not only in the mysticism of nature, but also in the arts of ninja.

A well-executed limited series from DC in 1990, this title owes much to the writing skills of Mike Baron.

1 ❑ May 1990 Cover: 2.50 **NM** value: **Cover or less**
Circ: CapCity orders: **20,400**
A: Shea Anton Pensa **W:** Mike Baron ★ 1st Appearance of John Butcher.
2 ❑ Jun 1990 Cover: 2.50 **NM** value: **Cover or less**
Circ: CapCity orders: **15,200**
A: Shea Anton Pensa **W:** Mike Baron
3 ❑ Jul 1990 Cover: 2.50 **NM** value: **Cover or less**
Circ: CapCity orders: **13,100**
A: Shea Anton Pensa **W:** Mike Baron
4 ❑ Aug 1990 Cover: 2.50 **NM** value: **Cover or less**
Circ: CapCity orders: **13,050**
A: Shea Anton Pensa **W:** Mike Baron
5 ❑ Sep 1990 Cover: 2.50 **NM** value: **Cover or less**
Circ: CapCity orders: **11,450**
A: Shea Anton Pensa **W:** Mike Baron

BUTCHER KNIGHT — Image

1/A ❑ Dec 2000 Cover: 2.50 **NM** value: **Cover or less**
Demon's teeth cover. **A:** Dwayne Turner **W:** Charles Holland
1/B ❑ Dec 2000 Cover: 2.50 **NM** value: **Cover or less**
Woman standing next to demon on cover. **A:** Dwayne Turner **W:** Charles Holland
1/C ❑ Dec 2000 Cover: 2.50 **NM** value: **Cover or less**
Woman posing on demon on cover. **A:** Dwayne Turner **W:** Charles Holland
1/D ❑ Dec 2000 Cover: 2.50 **NM** value: **Cover or less**
White cover. **A:** Dwayne Turner **W:** Charles Holland
2 ❑ Jan 2001 Cover: 2.50 **NM** value: **Cover or less**
Circ: Diamd. preorders: **20,723**
A: Dwayne Turner **W:** Charles Holland
3 ❑ Apr 2001 Cover: 2.50 **NM** value: **Cover or less**
Circ: Diamd. preorders: **14,668**
A: Dwayne Turner **W:** Charles Holland
4 ❑ May 2001 Cover: 2.50 **NM** value: **Cover or less**
Circ: Diamd. preorders: **14,785**
A: Dwayne Turner **W:** Charles Holland

BUTT BISCUIT — Fantagraphics

1 ❑ Cover: 2.25 **NM** value: **Cover or less**
2 ❑ Cover: 2.25 **NM** value: **Cover or less**
3 ❑ Cover: 2.25 **NM** value: **Cover or less**

BUTTERSCOTCH — Fantagraphics / Eros

1 ❑ Cover: 2.50 **NM** value: **Cover or less**
2 ❑ Cover: 2.50 **NM** value: **Cover or less**
3 ❑ Cover: 2.50 **NM** value: **Cover or less**

BUTTON MAN: THE KILLING GAME — Kitchen Sink

1 ❑ Aug 1995 Cover: 15.95 **NM** value: **Cover or less**
• oversized graphic novel.

BUZ SAWYER — Standard

The Buz Sawyer adventure comic strip was created by Roy Crane (1901-1977), following his work on NEA's Wash Tubbs and Captain Easy. The new strip began in 1943, starring a Navy pilot and his gunner buddy, Roscoe Sweeny — and featuring the stylish art of Crane, who used screening to great effect in the black-and-white daily strips. The strip long outlived Crane, but the comic book had only a short run.

He told members of The National Cartoonists Society, "If I had it to do over, I'd never do a Sunday. It's the straw that breaks backs." Nevertheless, Crane was an artist's artist (as witness the number of Crane panels that found their way into other artist's swipe files. — Maggie

1 ❑ Jun 1948 Cover: 0.10 **NM** value: **125.00**
• **CGC:** 2 graded, best 9.0
2 ❑ Cover: 0.10 **NM** value: **75.00**
3 ❑ 1949 Cover: 0.10 **NM** value: **50.00**

BUZ SAWYER QUARTERLY — Dragon Lady

1 ❑ Nov 1986 Cover: 5.95 **NM** value: **Cover or less**
2 ❑ Apr 1987 Cover: 5.95 **NM** value: **Cover or less**
3 ❑ Apr 1987 Cover: 5.95 **NM** value: **Cover or less**

BUZZ — Kitchen Sink

1 ❑ Cover: 2.95 **NM** value: **Cover or less**
2 ❑ Cover: 2.95 **NM** value: **Cover or less**
3 ❑ Cover: 2.95 **NM** value: **Cover or less**
Drink, Clown, Drink!; No Fran; Naked Snack, Part 2; Fetal Elvis; Mutant Book Of The Dead; Zero Skills; Life... It's Wacky; Captain Wireless, Part 2; Sex Roles; Deviant Postcard Set #2 **A:** Charles Burns; Ken Struck; Kevin Atkinson; Dr. Fishmonger; Mack White; Mark Landman; Mark Newgarden; Roy Tompkins **W:** Charles Burns; Ken Struck; Kevin Atkinson; Dr. Fishmonger; Mack White; Mark Landman; Mark Newgarden; Roy Tompkins

BUZZ, THE — Marvel

1 ❑ Jul 2000 Cover: 2.99 **NM** value: **Cover or less**
Comes a Hero! **A:** Sal Buscema; Ron Frenz **W:** Ron Frenz; Tom DeFalco
2 ❑ Aug 2000 Cover: 2.99 **NM** value: **Cover or less**
A: Sal Buscema; Ron Frenz **W:** Ron Frenz; Tom DeFalco
3 ❑ Sep 2000 Cover: 2.99 **NM** value: **Cover or less**
Moments of Truth **A:** Sal Buscema; Ron Frenz **W:** Ron Frenz; Tom DeFalco

BUZZ AND BELL — Platinum

Bk 1 ❑ Cover: 9.95 **NM** value: **Cover or less**
A: Sergio Aragonés

BUZZ AND COLONEL TOAD — Belmont

1 ❑ Cover: 2.50 **NM** value: **Cover or less**
2 ❑ Cover: 2.50 **NM** value: **Cover or less**
3 ❑ Jan 1998 Cover: 2.50 **NM** value: **Cover or less**

BUZZARD — Cat-Head

1 ❑ Cover: 2.75 **NM** value: **3.25**
2 ❑ Oct 1990 Cover: 2.75 **NM** value: **3.25**
3 ❑ Cover: 2.75 **NM** value: **3.25**
4 ❑ Cover: 2.75 **NM** value: **3.25**
5 ❑ Cover: 2.75 **NM** value: **3.25**
6 ❑ Aug 1992 Cover: 2.75 **NM** value: **3.25**
7 ❑ Feb 1993 Cover: 2.95 **NM** value: **3.25**
8 ❑ Cover: 2.95 **NM** value: **3.25**
9 ❑ Cover: 2.95 **NM** value: **3.25**
10 ❑ Cover: 2.95 **NM** value: **3.25**
11 ❑ Cover: 3.25 **NM** value: **Cover or less**
12 ❑ Cover: 3.25 **NM** value: **3.50**
13 ❑ Cover: 3.25 **NM** value: **3.50**
14 ❑ Cover: 3.50 **NM** value: **Cover or less**
C: Mark Martin
15 ❑ Cover: 3.50 **NM** value: **Cover or less**
16 ❑ Cover: 3.50 **NM** value: **Cover or less**
17 ❑ Cover: 3.50 **NM** value: **Cover or less**
18 ❑ Cover: 3.75 **NM** value: **Cover or less**
19 ❑ Cover: 3.75 **NM** value: **Cover or less**
Old Grumpy; Caliente; Troubletown; White Christmas (text story); Ken's Corner; Dorrie; The Best Laid Plans (text story); Modern Comedy; Krazy Kat Theater; 40 Hour Man, Part 12; Ice Cube Therapy **A:** Steve Lafler; James Kochalka; Aleksander Zograf; Heather Shinn; Jeff Roysdon; Lloyd Dangle; Marcellus Hall; Phoebe Gloeckner; Thierry Guitard **W:** Steve Lafler; James Kochalka; Aleksander Zograf; Heather Shinn; Lloyd Dangle; Marcellus Hall; David Greenberger; Stephen Beaupre
20 ❑ Cover: 3.75 **NM** value: **Cover or less**

BUZZBOY — Skydog Press

1 ❑ May 1998 Cover: 2.95 **NM** value: **Cover or less**
2 ❑ Aug 1998 Cover: 2.95 **NM** value: **Cover or less**
3 ❑ Oct 1998 Cover: 2.95 **NM** value: **Cover or less**
4 ❑ Win 1998 Cover: 2.95 **NM** value: **Cover or less**

BUZZ BUZZ COMICS MAGAZINE — Horse

1 ❑ Cover: 4.95 **NM** value: **Cover or less**
A: Paul Pope; Moebius; Jeff Smith; Stephen R. Bissette

BUZZY — DC

When Archie proved the viability of teen humor in comics during World War II, DC was quick to come out with its own competing title, Buzzy. "America's Favorite Teen-Ager" is a good-looking, blond, high-school student facing the hassles of pleasing his girlfriend Suzy and fending off his high-handed rival Wolfie.

Each issue features three or four short vignettes centered on such familiar teen-humor plot devices as Suzie's ill-tempered father, foiling the school principal, Wolfie's schemes to get girls, and so on.

Both the art and writing heavily mine the vein made popular by Archie, which was enough to keep the series going into the mid-1950s.

1 ❑ Win 1944 Cover: 0.10 **NM** value: **125.00**
2 ❑ Spr 1945 Cover: 0.10 **NM** value: **65.00**
3 ❑ Sum 1945 Cover: 0.10 **NM** value: **48.00**
4 ❑ Fal 1945 Cover: 0.10 **NM** value: **40.00**
5 ❑ Win 1945 Cover: 0.10 **NM** value: **40.00**
6 ❑ Mar 1946 Cover: 0.10 **NM** value: **35.00**
7 ❑ May 1946 Cover: 0.10 **NM** value: **35.00**
8 ❑ Jul 1946 Cover: 0.10 **NM** value: **35.00**
9 ❑ Sep 1946 Cover: 0.10 **NM** value: **35.00**
10 ❑ Nov 1946 Cover: 0.10 **NM** value: **35.00**
11 ❑ Jan 1947 Cover: 0.10 **NM** value: **30.00**
12 ❑ Mar 1947 Cover: 0.10 **NM** value: **30.00**
13 ❑ May 1947 Cover: 0.10 **NM** value: **30.00**
14 ❑ Jul 1947 Cover: 0.10 **NM** value: **30.00**
15 ❑ Sep 1947 Cover: 0.10 **NM** value: **30.00**
16 ❑ Nov 1947 Cover: 0.10 **NM** value: **30.00**
17 ❑ Jan 1948 Cover: 0.10 **NM** value: **30.00**
18 ❑ Mar 1948 Cover: 0.10 **NM** value: **30.00**
19 ❑ May 1948 Cover: 0.10 **NM** value: **30.00**
20 ❑ Jul 1948 Cover: 0.10 **NM** value: **30.00**
21 ❑ Sep 1948 Cover: 0.10 **NM** value: **22.00**
22 ❑ Nov 1948 Cover: 0.10 **NM** value: **22.00**
23 ❑ Jan 1949 Cover: 0.10 **NM** value: **22.00**
24 ❑ Mar 1949 Cover: 0.10 **NM** value: **22.00**
25 ❑ May 1949 Cover: 0.10 **NM** value: **22.00**
26 ❑ Jul 1949 Cover: 0.10 **NM** value: **22.00**
27 ❑ Sep 1949 Cover: 0.10 **NM** value: **22.00**
28 ❑ Nov 1949 Cover: 0.10 **NM** value: **22.00**
29 ❑ Jan 1950 Cover: 0.10 **NM** value: **22.00**
30 ❑ Mar 1950 Cover: 0.10 **NM** value: **22.00**
31 ❑ May 1950 Cover: 0.10 **NM** value: **16.00**
32 ❑ Jul 1950 Cover: 0.10 **NM** value: **16.00**
• Scribbly back-up
33 ❑ Sep 1950 Cover: 0.10 **NM** value: **16.00**
34 ❑ Nov 1950 Cover: 0.10 **NM** value: **16.00**
35 ❑ Jan 1951 Cover: 0.10 **NM** value: **16.00**
36 ❑ Mar 1951 Cover: 0.10 **NM** value: **16.00**
37 ❑ May 1951 Cover: 0.10 **NM** value: **16.00**
38 ❑ Jul 1951 Cover: 0.10 **NM** value: **16.00**
39 ❑ Sep 1951 Cover: 0.10 **NM** value: **16.00**
40 ❑ Nov 1951 Cover: 0.10 **NM** value: **16.00**
41 ❑ Jan 1952 Cover: 0.10 **NM** value: **13.00**
42 ❑ Mar 1952 Cover: 0.10 **NM** value: **13.00**
43 ❑ May 1952 Cover: 0.10 **NM** value: **13.00**
44 ❑ Jul 1952 Cover: 0.10 **NM** value: **13.00**
45 ❑ Sep 1952 Cover: 0.10 **NM** value: **13.00**
46 ❑ Nov 1952 Cover: 0.10 **NM** value: **13.00**
47 ❑ Jan 1953 Cover: 0.10 **NM** value: **13.00**
Free Speech-Free For All; Buzzy; Datewise Do's And Don'ts; Laurie; Coby; Stevie
48 ❑ Mar 1953 Cover: 0.10 **NM** value: **13.00**
49 ❑ May 1953 Cover: 0.10 **NM** value: **13.00**
50 ❑ Jul 1953 Cover: 0.10 **NM** value: **13.00**
51 ❑ Sep 1953 Cover: 0.10 **NM** value: **9.00**
52 ❑ Nov 1953 Cover: 0.10 **NM** value: **9.00**
53 ❑ Jan 1954 Cover: 0.10 **NM** value: **9.00**
54 ❑ ca. 1954 Cover: 0.10 **NM** value: **9.00**
55 ❑ ca. 1954 Cover: 0.10 **NM** value: **9.00**
56 ❑ ca. 1954 Cover: 0.10 **NM** value: **9.00**
57 ❑ ca. 1954 Cover: 0.10 **NM** value: **9.00**
58 ❑ Aug 1954 Cover: 0.10 **NM** value: **9.00**
59 ❑ ca. 1954 Cover: 0.10 **NM** value: **9.00**
60 ❑ ca. 1954 Cover: 0.10 **NM** value: **9.00**

Other grades: Multiply prices above by **1.5 for Mint • 2/3 for Very Fine • 1/3 for Fine • 1/5 for Very Good • 1/8 for Good**

61 ❑ Cover: 0.10 **NM** value: **9.00**
62 ❑ Feb 1955 Cover: 0.10 **NM** value: **9.00**
63 ❑ ca. 1955 Cover: 0.10 **NM** value: **9.00**
64 ❑ ca. 1955 Cover: 0.10 **NM** value: **9.00**
65 ❑ Jul 1955 Cover: 0.10 **NM** value: **9.00**
66 ❑ ca. 1955 Cover: 0.10 **NM** value: **9.00**
67 ❑ ca. 1955 Cover: 0.10 **NM** value: **9.00**
68 ❑ Nov 1955 Cover: 0.10 **NM** value: **9.00**
69 ❑ Cover: 0.10 **NM** value: **9.00**
70 ❑ Feb 1956 Cover: 0.10 **NM** value: **9.00**
71 ❑ May 1956 Cover: 0.10 **NM** value: **9.00**
72 ❑ ca. 1956 Cover: 0.10 **NM** value: **9.00**
73 ❑ ca. 1956 Cover: 0.10 **NM** value: **9.00**
74 ❑ Dec 1956 Cover: 0.10 **NM** value: **9.00**
75 ❑ ca. 1957 Cover: 0.10 **NM** value: **9.00**
76 ❑ Oct 1957 Cover: 0.10 **NM** value: **9.00**
77 ❑ Oct 1958 Cover: 0.10 **NM** value: **9.00**
final issue.

BY BIZARRE HANDS — Dark Horse

1 ❑ Apr 1994 Cover: 2.50 **NM** value: **Cover or less**
Circ: CapCity orders: **2,350**
📖 Tight Little Stitches In A Deadman's Back **A:** Phil Hester **W:** Joe Lansdale
2 ❑ May 1994 Cover: 2.50 **NM** value: **Cover or less**
W: Joe Lansdale
3 ❑ 1994 Cover: 2.50 **NM** value: **Cover or less**
W: Joe Lansdale

BY THE TIME I GET TO WAGGA WAGGA — Harrier

1 ❑ Cover: 1.50 **NM** value: **Cover or less**
A: Eddie Campbell

C•23 — Image

Comics fans fear any comic book created to be part of "something else."

Jim Lee's C-23 tells the story of a far future in which the remnants of humanity live in an underground city, The Colony. They send cybernetically enhanced HyperShock Troops to ty to reclaim the Earth's surface from the Angelans, a monstrous race of humanoid insects.

The "something else" concerning comics fans was a collectible card game. C-23 was actually part of an unprecedented effort by the collectible card game business to attract comics readers. The game world was jointly developed by Lee and Wizards of the Coast, and the comic book and card game were simultaneously released. As it turned out, the game itself had few takers, and non-gaming comics fans didn't rush to read a title they perceived as an appendage to a game. Neither comic book nor game lasted long. — JJM

1 ❑ Apr 1998 Cover: 2.50 **NM** value: **Cover or less**
A: Alexander Lozano **W:** Brandon Choi; Jeff Mariotte ★ 1st Appearance of Fluxus, Zum, A-Mortal, The Hyperclan, Armek, Tronix, Primaid, Zenturion, Protex.
2 ❑ May 1998 Cover: 2.50 **NM** value: **Cover or less**
A: Alexander Lozano **W:** Jeff Mariotte
3 ❑ Jun 1998 Cover: 2.50 **NM** value: **Cover or less**
• bound-in card **A:** Alexander Lozano **W:** Jeff Mariotte
4 ❑ Jul 1998 Cover: 2.50 **NM** value: **Cover or less**
A: Alexander Lozano **W:** Jeff Mariotte
5 ❑ Aug 1998 Cover: 2.50 **NM** value: **Cover or less**
A: Alexander Lozano **W:** Jeff Mariotte
6 ❑ Sep 1998 Cover: 2.50 **NM** value: **Cover or less**
A: Alexander Lozano **W:** Jeff Mariotte
7 ❑ Oct 1998 Cover: 2.50 **NM** value: **Cover or less**
A: Alexander Lozano; Richard Corben(cover) **W:** Jeff Mariotte
8 ❑ Nov 1998 Cover: 2.50 **NM** value: **Cover or less**
A: Alexander Lozano **W:** Jeff Mariotte
8/SC❑ Nov 1998 Cover: 2.50 **NM** value: **Cover or less**
alternate cover (group).

CABBOT: BLOODHUNTER — Maximum

1 ❑ Jan 1997 Cover: 2.50 **NM** value: **Cover or less**
Circ: Direct Market orders: **14,344**

CABINET OF DR. CALIGARI, THE — Monster

1 ❑ Apr 1992 Cover: 2.25 **NM** value: **Cover or less**
A: Mike Hoffman **W:** Ian Carney
2 ❑ Jun 1992 Cover: 2.25 **NM** value: **Cover or less**
A: Mike Hoffman **W:** Ian Carney
3 ❑ Sep 1992 Cover: 2.25 **NM** value: **Cover or less**
A: Mike Hoffman **W:** Ian Carney

To find the median price offered on eBay at press time for pre-1990 **CGC-graded comics**, multiply by:

9.9 (M): **33**	8.5 (VF+): **1.25**
9.8(NM/M): **16**	8.0 (VF): **0.85**
9.6 (NM+): **7**	7.5 (VF-): **0.6**
9.4 (NM): **5**	7.0 (F/VF): **0.5**
9.2 (NM-): **2.5**	6.5 (F+): **0.4**
9.0 (VF/NM): **1.5**	6.0 (F-): **0.33**

These are median prices of all CGC comics auctioned on eBay; prices for individual issues will vary.

CABLE — Marvel

He first was seen in our timeline in The New Mutants #87 (Mar 90), but, although he has had remarkable influence on the various mutant teams in the Marvel Universe, readers have only relatively recently begun to discover much about him. They now know that the man known as Cable has another name, Nathan Dayspring, and that he hails from a dark, totalitarian version of our world, centuries in the future. Thanks to the technology of that period, he has the ability to transport himself back in time. He uses that ability to wage a war in time and space, with the ultimate goal of preventing that dark future from occurring.

An immensely popular character since he first appeared, Cable was featured in the two-issue Cable: Blood and Metal, then in 1993 was given this, his first ongoing series. In it readers finally learn many of the answers to the questions they have been asking about this mysterious warrior.

-1 ❑ Jul 1997 Cover: 1.95 **NM** value: **2.25**
• Flashback
1 ❑ May 1993 Cover: 3.50 **NM** value: **4.00**
Circ: CapCity orders: **219,300** Diamd. preorders: **84,396** • **CGC:** 6 graded, best 9.8
Embossed cover.
2 ❑ Jun 1993 Cover: 2.00 **NM** value: **2.50**
Circ: CapCity orders: **127,400**
📖 Mired in Destiny
3 ❑ Jul 1993 Cover: 2.00 **NM** value: **2.50**
Circ: CapCity orders: **99,600**
📖 Twenty Questions
4 ❑ Aug 1993 Cover: 2.00 **NM** value: **2.50**
Circ: CapCity orders: **93,200**
📖 A Leader Among Men
5 ❑ Nov 1993 Cover: 2.00 **NM** value: **2.50**
Circ: CapCity orders: **58,200**
6 ❑ Dec 1993 Cover: 2.00 **NM** value: **2.50**
Circ: CapCity orders: **58,100**
A: Art Thibert **W:** Fabian Nicieza ★ Appearance of Other, Sinsear.
7 ❑ Jan 1994 Cover: 2.00 **NM** value: **2.50**
Circ: Statement: **212,292** CapCity orders: **49,100**
8 ❑ Feb 1994 Cover: 2.00 **NM** value: **2.50**
Circ: Statement: **212,292** CapCity orders: **46,800**
9 ❑ Mar 1994 Cover: 2.00 **NM** value: **2.50**
Circ: Statement: **212,292** CapCity orders: **44,800**
10 ❑ Apr 1994 Cover: 2.00 **NM** value: **2.50**
Circ: Statement: **212,292** CapCity orders: **42,550**
11 ❑ May 1994 Cover: 2.00 **NM** value: **2.25**
Circ: Statement: **212,292** CapCity orders: **41,650**
12 ❑ Jun 1994 Cover: 2.00 **NM** value: **2.25**
Circ: Statement: **212,292** CapCity orders: **40,650**
13 ❑ Jul 1994 Cover: 2.00 **NM** value: **2.25**
Circ: Statement: **212,292** CapCity orders: **39,500**
14 ❑ Aug 1994 Cover: 2.00 **NM** value: **2.25**
Circ: Statement: **212,292** CapCity orders: **37,450**
15 ❑ Sep 1994 Cover: 2.00 **NM** value: **2.25**
Circ: Statement: **212,292** CapCity orders: **36,450**
📖 Shadows
16 ❑ Oct 1994 Cover: 2.00 **NM** value: **2.50**
📖 Final Sanction, Part 2
16/SC❑ Oct 1994 Cover: 3.50 **NM** value: **5.50**
Circ: Statement: **212,292** CapCity orders: **48,400**
📖 Final Sanction, Part 2
17 ❑ Nov 1994 Cover: 1.50 **NM** value: **Cover or less**
17/Dlx❑ Nov 1994 Cover: 1.95 **NM** value: **2.00**
Circ: Statement: **212,292** CapCity orders: **33,750**
• deluxe
18 ❑ Dec 1994 Cover: 1.50 **NM** value: **Cover or less**
18/Dlx❑ Dec 1994 Cover: 1.95 **NM** value: **2.00**
Circ: Statement: **212,292** CapCity orders: **36,000**
• deluxe
19 ❑ Jan 1995 Cover: 1.50 **NM** value: **Cover or less**
19/Dlx❑ Jan 1995 Cover: 1.95 **NM** value: **2.00**
Circ: Statement: **161,714** CapCity orders: **35,550**
• deluxe
20 ❑ Feb 1995 Cover: 1.50 **NM** value: **Cover or less**
20/Dlx❑ Feb 1995 Cover: 1.95 **NM** value: **2.00**
Circ: Statement: **161,714** CapCity orders: **46,825**
📖 An Hour of Last Things • deluxe;A Legion Quest Addendum **A:** Ian Churchill **W:** Jeph Loeb ★ Appearance of X-Men.
21 ❑ Jul 1995 Cover: 1.95 **NM** value: **2.00**
Circ: Statement: **161,714** CapCity orders: **53,650**
• Has 1994 Statement, filed 10/1/94; avg print run 335,217; avg sales 211,025; avg subs 1,267; avg total paid 212,292; samples 125; office use 500; max existent 212,917; 37% of run returned
22 ❑ Aug 1995 Cover: 1.95 **NM** value: **2.00**
Circ: Statement: **161,714** CapCity orders: **51,800**
23 ❑ Sep 1995 Cover: 1.95 **NM** value: **2.00**
Circ: Statement: **161,714**
24 ❑ Oct 1995 Cover: 1.95 **NM** value: **2.00**
Circ: Statement: **149,639**
no issue number on cover.
25 ❑ Nov 1995 Cover: 3.95 **NM** value: **4.00**
Circ: Statement: **149,639** • **CGC:** 1 graded, best 9.6
enhanced wraparound fold-out cardstock cover. • Giant-size. 📖 What Was…What Is… • 25th Issue Extravaganza **A:** Ian Churchill; Joel Thomas **W:** Jeph Loeb
26 ❑ Dec 1995 Cover: 1.95 **NM** value: **2.00**
Circ: Statement: **149,639**
★ Appearance of Weapon X.
27 ❑ Jan 1996 Cover: 1.95 **NM** value: **2.00**
Circ: Statement: **149,639**
• Has 1995 Statement, filed 10/1/95; avg print run 238,637; avg sales 159,928; avg subs 1,786; avg total paid 161,714; samples 750; office use 500; max existent 162,964; 32% of run returned ★ Versus Sugar Man.
28 ❑ Feb 1996 Cover: 1.95 **NM** value: **2.00**
Circ: Statement: **149,639**
★ Versus Sugar Man.
29 ❑ Mar 1996 Cover: 1.95 **NM** value: **2.00**
Circ: Statement: **149,639**
📖 Man In The Mirror **A:** Ian Churchill **W:** Jeph Loeb
30 ❑ Apr 1996 Cover: 1.95 **NM** value: **2.00**
Circ: Statement: **149,639**
📖 For Every Action… • Cable meets X-Man **A:** Ian Churchill **W:** Jeph Loeb ★ Appearance of X-Man.
31 ❑ May 1996 Cover: 1.95 **NM** value: **2.00**
Circ: Statement: **149,639**
★ Versus X-Man.
32 ❑ Jun 1996 Cover: 1.95 **NM** value: **2.25**
Circ: Statement: **149,639**
33 ❑ Jul 1996 Cover: 1.95 **NM** value: **2.25**
Circ: Statement: **149,639**
34 ❑ Aug 1996 Cover: 1.95 **NM** value: **2.25**
Circ: Statement: **149,639**
📖 Onslaught: Phase 1; Onslaught ★ Versus Hulk.
35 ❑ Sep 1996 Cover: 1.95 **NM** value: **Cover or less**
Circ: Statement: **149,639**
📖 Onslaught: Phase 2; Onslaught ★ Versus Apocalypse.
36 ❑ Oct 1996 Cover: 1.95 **NM** value: **Cover or less**
Circ: Statement: **133,041**
37 ❑ Nov 1996 Cover: 1.95 **NM** value: **Cover or less**
Circ: Statement: **133,041** Direct Market orders: **121,750**
★ Appearance of Weapon X.
38 ❑ Dec 1996 Cover: 1.95 **NM** value: **Cover or less**
Circ: Statement: **133,041** Direct Market orders: **119,250**
📖 In Perspective • Has 1996 Statement, filed 10/1/96; avg print run 200,801; avg sales 147,649; avg subs 1,990; avg total paid 149,639; samples 600; office use 125; max existent 150,364; 25% of run returned **A:** Ian Churchill **W:** Jeph Loeb ★ Appearance of Micronauts.
39 ❑ Jan 1997 Cover: 1.95 **NM** value: **Cover or less**
Circ: Statement: **133,041** Direct Market orders: **113,750**
📖 All Things Great And Small **A:** Ian Churchill **W:** Jeph Loeb ★ Appearance of Micronauts.
40 ❑ Feb 1997 Cover: 1.95 **NM** value: **Cover or less**
Circ: Statement: **133,041** Direct Market orders: **106,500**
📖 Into The Dark **A:** Scott Clark **W:** Todd Dezago
41 ❑ Mar 1997 Cover: 1.95 **NM** value: **Cover or less**
Circ: Statement: **133,041** Direct Market orders: **97,500**
📖 Depths of Time **A:** Steve Crespo **W:** Todd Dezago ★ Appearance of Bishop.
42 ❑ Apr 1997 Cover: 1.95 **NM** value: **Cover or less**
Circ: Statement: **133,041** Direct Market orders: **92,500**
📖 Tolerance **A:** Randy Green **W:** Todd Dezago
43 ❑ May 1997 Cover: 1.95 **NM** value: **Cover or less**
Circ: Statement: **133,041** Diamd. preorders: **90,306**
📖 Legend of the Askani'Son; Broken Soldiers **A:** Randy Green; Chap Yaep **W:** Brian Vaughan; Todd Dezago
44 ❑ Jun 1997 Cover: 1.95 **NM** value: **Cover or less**
Circ: Statement: **133,041** Diamd. preorders: **90,032**
📖 Temptation in the Wilderness **A:** Randy Green; Allen Im **W:** James Robinson
45 ❑ Aug 1997 Cover: 1.99 **NM** value: **Cover or less**
Circ: Statement: **133,041** Diamd. preorders: **92,438**
• gatefold summary. • Operation Zero Tolerance
46 ❑ Sep 1997 Cover: 1.99 **NM** value: **Cover or less**
Circ: Statement: **133,041** Diamd. preorders: **87,138**
• gatefold summary. • Operation Zero Tolerance
47 ❑ Oct 1997 Cover: 1.99 **NM** value: **Cover or less**
Circ: Diamd. preorders: **87,256**
• gatefold summary. • Operation Zero Tolerance
48 ❑ Nov 1997 Cover: 1.99 **NM** value: **Cover or less**
Circ: Diamd. preorders: **83,191**
• gatefold summary.
49 ❑ Dec 1997 Cover: 1.99 **NM** value: **Cover or less**
Circ: Diamd. preorders: **82,428**
• gatefold summary. • Has 1997 Statement; avg total paid circ 133,041
50 ❑ Jan 1998 Cover: 1.99 **NM** value: **2.95**
Circ: Diamd. preorders: **87,111**
• Giant-size.
51 ❑ Feb 1998 Cover: 1.99 **NM** value: **Cover or less**
Circ: Diamd. preorders: **75,840**
• gatefold summary.
52 ❑ Mar 1998 Cover: 1.99 **NM** value: **Cover or less**
Circ: Diamd. preorders: **72,277**
• gatefold summary.
53 ❑ Apr 1998 Cover: 1.99 **NM** value: **Cover or less**
Circ: Diamd. preorders: **66,390**
• gatefold summary.
54 ❑ May 1998 Cover: 1.99 **NM** value: **Cover or less**
Circ: Diamd. preorders: **63,834**
• gatefold summary. ★ Appearance of Black Panther. ★ Versus Klaw.
55 ❑ Jun 1998 Cover: 1.99 **NM** value: **Cover or less**
Circ: Diamd. preorders: **63,044**
• gatefold summary. ★ Appearance of Domino.
56 ❑ Jul 1998 Cover: 1.99 **NM** value: **Cover or less**
Circ: Diamd. preorders: **59,145**
• gatefold summary.
57 ❑ Aug 1998 Cover: 1.99 **NM** value: **Cover or less**
Circ: Diamd. preorders: **58,110**
• gatefold summary.
58 ❑ Sep 1998 Cover: 1.99 **NM** value: **Cover or less**
Circ: Diamd. preorders: **54,777**
• gatefold summary.
59 ❑ Oct 1998 Cover: 1.99 **NM** value: **Cover or less**
Circ: Diamd. preorders: **52,183**

CGC-graded: Multiply prices above by **33 for 9.9 M • 16 for 9.8 NM/M • 7 for 9.6 NM+ • 5 for 9.4 NM • 2.5 for 9.2 NM- • 1.5 for 9.0 VF/NM**

• gatefold summary. 📖 The Nemesis Contract, Part 1 ★ Versus Zzzax.

60 ❑ Nov 1998 Cover: 1.99 **NM** value: **Cover or less**
Circ: Diamd. preorders: **50,648**
• gatefold summary. 📖 The Nemesis Contract, Part 2 ★ 1st Appearance of Agent 18.

61 ❑ Nov 1998 Cover: 1.99 **NM** value: **Cover or less**
Circ: Diamd. preorders: **50,087**
• gatefold summary. 📖 The Nemesis Contract, Part 3 • captured by S.H.I.E.L.D.

62 ❑ Dec 1998 Cover: 1.99 **NM** value: **Cover or less**
Circ: Diamd. preorders: **49,745**
• gatefold summary. 📖 The Nemesis Contract, Part 4; Blood Brothers, Part 1 ★ Appearance of Nick Fury.

63 ❑ Jan 1999 Cover: 1.99 **NM** value: **Cover or less**
Circ: Diamd. preorders: **49,126**
• gatefold summary. 📖 Blood Brothers, Part 2 **A:** Stephen Platt ★ Appearance of Stryfe. ★ Versus Stryfe.

64 ❑ Feb 1999 Cover: 1.99 **NM** value: **Cover or less**
Circ: Diamd. preorders: **47,202**
• gatefold summary. **A:** J.O. Ladronn **W:** Joe Casey ★ Origin of Cable. ★ Appearance of Ozymandias.

65 ❑ Mar 1999 Cover: 1.99 **NM** value: **Cover or less**
Circ: Diamd. preorders: **46,701**
A: J.O. Ladronn **W:** Joe Casey ★ 1st Appearance of Acidroid. ★ Appearance of Rachel Summers.

66 ❑ Apr 1999 Cover: 1.99 **NM** value: **Cover or less**
Circ: Diamd. preorders: **46,071**
📖 Sign of the End Times, part 1 **A:** J.O. Ladronn **W:** Joe Casey

67 ❑ May 1999 Cover: 1.99 **NM** value: **Cover or less**
Circ: Diamd. preorders: **45,841**
★ Appearance of Avengers.

68 ❑ Jun 1999 Cover: 1.99 **NM** value: **Cover or less**
Circ: Diamd. preorders: **46,684**
★ Appearance of Avengers.

69 ❑ Jul 1999 Cover: 1.99 **NM** value: **Cover or less**
Circ: Diamd. preorders: **44,969**

70 ❑ Aug 1999 Cover: 1.99 **NM** value: **Cover or less**
Circ: Diamd. preorders: **45,669**

71 ❑ Sep 1999 Cover: 1.99 **NM** value: **Cover or less**
Circ: Diamd. preorders: **51,158**
★ Versus Hound Master.

72 ❑ Oct 1999 Cover: 1.99 **NM** value: **Cover or less**
Circ: Diamd. preorders: **46,151**

73 ❑ Nov 1999 Cover: 1.99 **NM** value: **Cover or less**
Circ: Diamd. preorders: **42,351**

74 ❑ Dec 1999 Cover: 1.99 **NM** value: **Cover or less**
Circ: Diamd. preorders: **43,016**

75 ❑ Jan 2000 Cover: 2.25 **NM** value: **Cover or less**
Circ: Diamd. preorders: **52,060**

76 ❑ Feb 2000 Cover: 2.25 **NM** value: **Cover or less**
Circ: Diamd. preorders: **51,548**

77 ❑ Mar 2000 Cover: 2.25 **NM** value: **Cover or less**
Circ: Diamd. preorders: **57,213**

78 ❑ Apr 2000 Cover: 2.25 **NM** value: **Cover or less**
Circ: Diamd. preorders: **46,993**

79 ❑ May 2000 Cover: 2.25 **NM** value: **Cover or less**
Circ: Diamd. preorders: **55,907**

80 ❑ Jun 2000 Cover: 2.25 **NM** value: **Cover or less**
Circ: Diamd. preorders: **47,465**

81 ❑ Jul 2000 Cover: 2.25 **NM** value: **Cover or less**
Circ: Diamd. preorders: **45,906**

82 ❑ Aug 2000 Cover: 2.25 **NM** value: **Cover or less**
Circ: Diamd. preorders: **44,832**

83 ❑ Sep 2000 Cover: 2.25 **NM** value: **Cover or less**
Circ: Diamd. preorders: **43,010**

84 ❑ Oct 2000 Cover: 2.25 **NM** value: **Cover or less**
Circ: Statement: **47,414** Diamd. preorders: **39,463**

85 ❑ Nov 2000 Cover: 2.25 **NM** value: **Cover or less**
Circ: Statement: **47,414** Diamd. preorders: **39,083**
📖 Undertow **A:** Michael Ryan **W:** Robert Weinberg

86 ❑ Dec 2000 Cover: 2.25 **NM** value: **Cover or less**
Circ: Statement: **47,414** Diamd. preorders: **38,652**
📖 Last Man Standing **A:** Essad Ribic **W:** Robert Weinberg

87 ❑ Jan 2001 Cover: 2.25 **NM** value: **Cover or less**
Circ: Statement: **47,414** Diamd. preorders: **43,969** • **CGC:** 1 graded, best 9.6
📖 Dream's End, Part 2: Life Decisions **A:** Michael Ryan **W:** Robert Weinberg

88 ❑ Feb 2001 Cover: 2.25 **NM** value: **Cover or less**
Circ: Statement: **47,414** Diamd. preorders: **38,155**
📖 Earth Abides **A:** Michael Ryan **W:** Robert Weinberg ★ Appearance of Nightcrawler.

89 ❑ Mar 2001 Cover: 2.25 **NM** value: **Cover or less**
Circ: Statement: **47,414** Diamd. preorders: **37,293**
📖 Dark Tide Rising **A:** Thomas Derenick **W:** Robert Weinberg

90 ❑ Apr 2001 Cover: 2.25 **NM** value: **Cover or less**
Circ: Statement: **47,414** Diamd. preorders: **37,384**
📖 Hearts of Darkness **A:** Michael Ryan **W:** Robert Weinberg

91 ❑ May 2001 Cover: 2.25 **NM** value: **Cover or less**
Circ: Statement: **47,414** Diamd. preorders: **36,467**

92 ❑ Jun 2001 Cover: 2.25 **NM** value: **Cover or less**
Circ: Statement: **47,414** Diamd. preorders: **36,491**

93 ❑ Jul 2001 Cover: 2.25 **NM** value: **Cover or less**
Circ: Statement: **47,414** Diamd. preorders: **36,074**

94 ❑ Aug 2001 Cover: 2.25 **NM** value: **Cover or less**
Circ: Statement: **47,414** Diamd. preorders: **36,209**

95 ❑ Sep 2001 Cover: 2.25 **NM** value: **Cover or less**
Circ: Statement: **47,414** Diamd. preorders: **37,316**

96 ❑ Oct 2001 Cover: 2.25 **NM** value: **Cover or less**
Circ: Diamd. preorders: **37,433**

97 ❑ Nov 2001 Cover: 2.25 **NM** value: **Cover or less**
Circ: Diamd. preorders: **37,062**

98 ❑ Dec 2001 Cover: 2.25 **NM** value: **Cover or less**
Circ: Diamd. preorders: **35,364**

99 ❑ Jan 2002 Cover: 2.25 **NM** value: **Cover or less**
Circ: Diamd. preorders: **35,283**

100 ❑ Feb 2002 Cover: 3.99 **NM** value: **Cover or less**
Circ: Diamd. preorders: **38,932**
• Has 2001 Statement, filed 10/1/2001; avg print run 59,925; avg sales 46,112; avg subs 1,302; avg total paid 47,414; samples 600; max existent 48,014; 20% of run returned

101 ❑ Mar 2002 Cover: 2.25 **NM** value: **Cover or less**
Circ: Diamd. preorders: **33,687**

Anl 1998 ❑ Sep 1998 Cover: 2.99 **NM** value: **Cover or less**
wraparound cover. 📖 Engines of Destruction, Part 1 • Cable/Machine Man '98;continues in Machine Man/Bastion '98

Anl 1999 ❑ Sep 1999 Cover: 3.50 **NM** value: **Cover or less**
Circ: Diamd. preorders: **34,118**
★ Versus Sinister.

CABLE AND THE NEW MUTANTS — Marvel

Bk 1 ❑ Cover: 15.95 **NM** value: **Cover or less**
Circ: CapCity orders: **5,900**

CABLE: BLOOD AND METAL — Marvel

1 ❑ Oct 1992 Cover: 2.50 **NM** value: **3.50**
Circ: CapCity orders: **191,000** • **CGC:** 5 graded, best 9.8
A: John Romita Jr. **W:** Fabian Nicieza

2 ❑ Nov 1992 Cover: 2.50 **NM** value: **3.00**
Circ: CapCity orders: **137,700**
A: John Romita Jr. **W:** Fabian Nicieza

CABLE: SECOND GENESIS — Marvel

1 ❑ Sep 1999 Cover: 3.99 **NM** value: **Cover or less**
Circ: Diamd. preorders: **7,040**
📖 The Beginning of The End; The End of The Beginning; A Force to be Reckoned with • collects New Mutants #1-2 and X-Force #1 **A:** Rob Liefeld **W:** Rob Liefeld; Fabian Nicieza

CABLE TV — Parody

Poor Cable TV! Even though Lizard magazine rated him the most popular comic-book character of December 1992, he's the only one in the top 10 not to have his own comics title. After a sufficiently mysterious period of brooding, he sets off across the space-time continuum to rectify the situation. Instead of getting his own series, however, he winds up an unwilling guest star in just about everybody else's. He bounces from Quantum Creep episodes to fighting off Aliens who want to steal his Pez. From there he jousts with Judge Bread, bops pint-sized Predators, and tangles with a Terminator who reminds him, "I may not have skin ... but I DO have my own series!"

This one-shot starring the head of X-Farce is a funny takeoff on Marvel's Cable and X-Force titles.

1 ❑ b&w Cover: 2.50 **NM** value: **Cover or less**

CADAVERA — Monster

1 ❑ b&w Cover: 1.95 **NM** value: **Cover or less**
2 ❑ b&w Cover: 1.95 **NM** value: **Cover or less**

CADENCE OF THE DIRGE — Gothic

1 ❑ Cover: 2.50 **NM** value: **Cover or less**
A: Brian LeBlanc **W:** Ronnie Prudhomme Jr.

1/SC ❑ Cover: 2.50 **NM** value: **Cover or less**
alternate cover. **A:** Brian LeBlanc; Daniel Presedo(cover) **W:** Ronnie Prudhomme Jr.

CADET GRAY OF WEST POINT — Dell

1 ❑ ca. 1958 **NM** value: **80.00**
• **CGC:** 1 graded, best 8.0

CADILLACS & DINOSAURS — Marvel / Epic

In the 26th century, only a few tribes of humans cling to existence in a world overtaken by huge prehistoric-type creatures, such as the scavenger "Zekes," which look like pteranodons, and enormous cave bears. One of these tribes lives in the City in the Sea, clinging together in the tops of what used to be skyscrapers. In any age, there's always someone who sets himself apart from others. Here it's Jack "Cadillac" Tenrec, a mechanic lovingly restoring an ancient Cadillac, the master and tamer of the wild dinosaur-like creatures of his time, and a courageous peace-keeper and explorer. Others follow his lead and quietly respect him — until Hannah Dundee, an ambassador from another tribe, arrives in town...

This six-issue series reprinted and colorized the classic Xenozoic Tales from Kitchen Sink Press.

1 ❑ Nov 1990 Cover: 2.50 **NM** value: **Cover or less**
Circ: CapCity orders: **9,650** • **CGC:** 2 graded, best 9.8
📖 An Archipelago of Stone • Reprints Xenozoic Tales #1 in color **A:** Mark Schultz **W:** Mark Schultz

2 ❑ Dec 1990 Cover: 2.50 **NM** value: **Cover or less**
Circ: CapCity orders: **8,750**
• Reprints Xenozoic Tales #2 in color **A:** Mark Schultz **W:** Mark Schultz

3 ❑ Jan 1991 Cover: 2.50 **NM** value: **Cover or less**
Circ: CapCity orders: **7,150** • **CGC:** 1 graded, best 9.8
• Reprints Xenozoic Tales #3 in color **A:** Mark Schultz **W:** Mark Schultz

4 ❑ Feb 1991 Cover: 2.50 **NM** value: **Cover or less**
Circ: CapCity orders: **6,600** • **CGC:** 1 graded, best 9.8
• Reprints Xenozoic Tales #4 in color **A:** Mark Schultz **W:** Mark Schultz

5 ❑ Mar 1991 Cover: 2.50 **NM** value: **Cover or less**
Circ: CapCity orders: **5,750** • **CGC:** 1 graded, best 9.8
• Reprints Xenozoic Tales #5 in color **A:** Steve Stiles; Mark Schultz **W:** Mark Schultz

6 ❑ Apr 1991 Cover: 2.50 **NM** value: **Cover or less**
Circ: CapCity orders: **4,950** • **CGC:** 1 graded, best 9.8
• Reprints Xenozoic Tales #6 in color **A:** Mark Schultz **W:** Mark Schultz

3D 1 ❑ Jul 1982 Cover: 3.95 **NM** value: **Cover or less**
• **CGC:** 2 graded, best 9.8
• 100 Page giant. 📖 The Growing Pool **A:** Mark Schultz **W:** Mark Schultz

CADILLACS & DINOSAURS (VOL. 2) — Topps

1 ❑ Feb 1994 Cover: 2.50 **NM** value: **Cover or less**
A: Dick Giordano

1/SC ❑ Feb 1994 Cover: 2.95 **NM** value: **Cover or less**
Circ: CapCity orders: **10,875**
foil cover. **A:** Dick Giordano

2 ❑ Mar 1994 Cover: 2.50 **NM** value: **Cover or less**
A: Dick Giordano

2/Dlx ❑ Mar 1994 Cover: 2.50 **NM** value: **Cover or less**
Circ: CapCity orders: **7,975**
• poster by Moebius **A:** Dick Giordano **C:** William Stout

3 ❑ Apr 1994 Cover: 2.50 **NM** value: **Cover or less**
A: Dick Giordano

3/Dlx ❑ Apr 1994 Cover: 2.50 **NM** value: **Cover or less**
Circ: CapCity orders: **7,850**
• poster **C:** William Stout

4 ❑ Jun 1994 Cover: 2.50 **NM** value: **Cover or less**
📖 Man Eater, Part 1 **A:** Jean-Claude St. Aubin **W:** Roy Thomas

4/SC ❑ Jun 1994 Cover: 2.50 **NM** value: **Cover or less**
Circ: CapCity orders: **7,525**
C: Sam Kieth

5 ❑ Aug 1994 Cover: 2.50 **NM** value: **Cover or less**
Circ: CapCity orders: **5,250**
📖 Man Eater, Part 2

6 ❑ Oct 1994 Cover: 2.50 **NM** value: **Cover or less**
Circ: CapCity orders: **4,800**
📖 Man Eater, Part 3

7 ❑ Dec 1994 Cover: 2.50 **NM** value: **Cover or less**
Circ: CapCity orders: **4,875**
📖 The Wild Ones! **A:** Esteban Maroto

8 ❑ Feb 1995 Cover: 2.50 **NM** value: **Cover or less**
Circ: CapCity orders: **4,400**

9 ❑ Apr 1995 Cover: 2.50 **NM** value: **Cover or less**
Circ: CapCity orders: **5,075**

10 ❑ Jun 1995 Cover: 2.50 **NM** value: **Cover or less**

CAFFEINE — Slave Labor

1 ❑ Jan 1996 Cover: 2.95 **NM** value: **Cover or less**
A: Jim Hill **W:** Jim Hill

2 ❑ Apr 1996 Cover: 2.95 **NM** value: **Cover or less**
A: Jim Hill **W:** Jim Hill

3 ❑ Jul 1996 Cover: 2.95 **NM** value: **Cover or less**
A: Jim Hill **W:** Jim Hill

4 ❑ Nov 1996 Cover: 2.95 **NM** value: **Cover or less**
A: Jim Hill **W:** Jim Hill

5 ❑ Jan 1997 Cover: 2.95 **NM** value: **Cover or less**
A: Jim Hill **W:** Jim Hill

6 ❑ Apr 1997 Cover: 2.95 **NM** value: **Cover or less**
A: Jim Hill **W:** Jim Hill

7 ❑ Jul 1997 Cover: 2.95 **NM** value: **Cover or less**
A: Jim Hill **W:** Jim Hill

8 ❑ Nov 1997 Cover: 2.95 **NM** value: **Cover or less**
A: Jim Hill **W:** Jim Hill

9 ❑ Jan 1998 Cover: 2.95 **NM** value: **Cover or less**
A: Jim Hill

10 ❑ Apr 1998 Cover: 2.95 **NM** value: **Cover or less**
final issue. **A:** Jim Hill

CAGE — Marvel

Once upon a time, a street kid got framed for a narcotics rap. He was sent to Seagate Prison where he signed up for a medical experiment in a desperate try to get his sentence reduced. The experiment changed him, giving him steel-hard strength and amazing strength. When he was released from prison, he decided to call himself "Luke Cage, Hero for Hire" and later "Power Man."

He went into business with another super-hero named Iron Fist, calling their venture "Heroes for Hire." Business was good for a while, but it eventually went sour. Then Iron Fist was killed, and Cage was framed again, this time for murder.

Now he's back — not as Power Man, but as Cage. He's sick of getting fooled with, and he's not going to take it any more.

1 ❑ Apr 1992 Cover: 1.50 **NM** value: **Cover or less**
Circ: Statement: **165,025** CapCity orders: **95,100** • **CGC:** 1 graded, best 9.4

2 ❑ May 1992 Cover: 1.25 **NM** value: **Cover or less**
Circ: Statement: **165,025** CapCity orders: **53,700**

3 ❑ Jun 1992 Cover: 1.25 **NM** value: **Cover or less**
Circ: Statement: **165,025** CapCity orders: **56,400**
★ Appearance of Punisher.

4 ❑ Jul 1992 Cover: 1.25 **NM** value: **Cover or less**
Circ: Statement: **165,025** CapCity orders: **45,900**
★ Appearance of Punisher.

Other grades: Multiply prices above by **1.5 for Mint • 2/3 for Very Fine • 1/3 for Fine • 1/5 for Very Good • 1/8 for Good**

5 ❑ Aug 1992 Cover: 1.25 **NM** value: **Cover or less**
Circ: Statement: **165,025** CapCity orders: **38,200**
🕮 The Evil and the Cure, Part 1

6 ❑ Sep 1992 Cover: 1.25 **NM** value: **Cover or less**
Circ: Statement: **165,025** CapCity orders: **28,800**
🕮 The Evil and the Cure, Part 2

7 ❑ Oct 1992 Cover: 1.25 **NM** value: **Cover or less**
Circ: Statement: **165,025** CapCity orders: **24,500**

8 ❑ Nov 1992 Cover: 1.25 **NM** value: **Cover or less**
Circ: Statement: **165,025** CapCity orders: **20,500**

9 ❑ Dec 1992 Cover: 1.25 **NM** value: **Cover or less**
Circ: Statement: **165,025** CapCity orders: **19,700**

10 ❑ Jan 1993 Cover: 1.25 **NM** value: **Cover or less**
Circ: CapCity orders: **17,900**

11 ❑ Feb 1993 Cover: 1.25 **NM** value: **Cover or less**
Circ: CapCity orders: **16,100**

12 ❑ Mar 1993 Cover: 1.75 **NM** value: **Cover or less**
Circ: CapCity orders: **23,500**
• Iron Fist; Has 1992 Statement, filed 10/1/92; avg print run 239,592; avg sales 164,942; avg subs 83; avg total paid 165,025; samples 63; office use 125; max existent 165,025; 31% of run returned

13 ❑ Apr 1993 Cover: 1.25 **NM** value: **Cover or less**
Circ: CapCity orders: **16,300**

14 ❑ May 1993 Cover: 1.25 **NM** value: **Cover or less**
Circ: CapCity orders: **15,500**

15 ❑ Jun 1993 Cover: 1.25 **NM** value: **Cover or less**
Circ: CapCity orders: **14,600**

16 ❑ Jul 1993 Cover: 1.25 **NM** value: **Cover or less**
Circ: CapCity orders: **13,500**

17 ❑ Aug 1993 Cover: 1.25 **NM** value: **Cover or less**
Circ: CapCity orders: **15,200**
🕮 Infinity Crusade

18 ❑ Sep 1993 Cover: 1.25 **NM** value: **Cover or less**
Circ: CapCity orders: **10,700**
🕮 The Dark, Part 1

19 ❑ Oct 1993 Cover: 1.25 **NM** value: **Cover or less**
Circ: CapCity orders: **9,850**
🕮 The Dark, Part 2 **A:** Brian Pelletier **W:** Marc McLaurin

20 ❑ Nov 1993 Cover: 1.25 **NM** value: **Cover or less**
Circ: CapCity orders: **9,850**
🕮 The Dark, Part 3 final issue.

CAGED HEAT 3000 — Roger Corman's Cosmic Comics

1 ❑ Cover: 2.50 **NM** value: **Cover or less**
🕮 The Big Doll House **A:** Matt Thompson; Ellen Forney **W:** Ellen Forney; Jerry Prosser

2 ❑ Cover: 2.50 **NM** value: **Cover or less**
A: Matt Thompson **W:** Jerry Prosser

CAGES — Tundra

1 ❑ b&w Cover: 3.50 **NM** value: **7.00**
Circ: CapCity orders: **6,050**
A: Dave McKean **W:** Dave McKean

2 ❑ b&w Cover: 3.50 **NM** value: **5.00**
A: Dave McKean **W:** Dave McKean

3 ❑ b&w Cover: 3.50 **NM** value: **4.50**
Circ: CapCity orders: **4,225**
A: Dave McKean **W:** Dave McKean

4 ❑ Cover: 3.95 **NM** value: **4.50**
A: Dave McKean **W:** Dave McKean

5 ❑ Cover: 3.95 **NM** value: **4.50**
Circ: CapCity orders: **4,025**
A: Dave McKean **W:** Dave McKean

6 ❑ Cover: 3.95 **NM** value: **4.50**
Circ: CapCity orders: **3,650**
A: Dave McKean **W:** Dave McKean

7 ❑ Cover: 3.95 **NM** value: **4.00**
Circ: CapCity orders: **4,150**
A: Dave McKean **W:** Dave McKean

8 ❑ Cover: 3.95 **NM** value: **4.00**
Circ: CapCity orders: **3,350**
A: Dave McKean **W:** Dave McKean

9 ❑ Cover: 3.95 **NM** value: **4.95**
A: Dave McKean **W:** Dave McKean

10 ❑ Cover: 4.95 **NM** value: **Cover or less**
final issue. **A:** Dave McKean **W:** Dave McKean

Bk 1❑ Cover: 44.95 **NM** value: **50.00**
A: Dave McKean

CAIN — Harris

1 ❑ Cover: 2.95 **NM** value: **Cover or less**
Circ: CapCity orders: **31,600**
• trading card **A:** Hannibal King **W:** David Quinn

2 ❑ Oct 1993 Cover: 2.95 **NM** value: **Cover or less**
Circ: CapCity orders: **19,825**
two alternate covers. **A:** Hannibal King **C:** Brian Stelfreeze **W:** David Quinn

CALCULATED RISK — Genesis

1 ❑ b&w Cover: 2.00 **NM** value: **Cover or less**

Diamond preorders are the estimated number of comics sold, prior to their release, to comics shops in North America by Diamond Comic Distributors, the largest distributor. These figures underreport the actual number of circulating copies by the amount of reorders Diamond took (usually 5-10% again of the preorders) and sales by publishers to newsstand and bookstore distributors. For many independent publishers, Diamond's preorders may be quite close to the actual number of copies in circulation.

CALIBER CHRISTMAS, A — Caliber

This 64-page anthology features nine Caliber Comics characters in stories that evoke the spirit of Christmas.

As examples of the anthology, in a story featuring Saint Germaine by Gary Reed and Andy Bennett, an old man lies on his hospital deathbed remembering his life, his wife, his children, and his father. Germaine's visit brings back the joy of Christmas and demonstrates the power of memories.

In a Kilroy story by Joe Pruett and Michael Gaydos, an American soldier trapped in North Vietnam gets a second chance at life on Christmas Eve. In a Lifequest story by Matt Vanderpol, Sam explains and demonstrates the joys of giving.

The anthology also contains stories of Legendlore, The Jam, The Apparition, Pakkins' Land, Kaos Moon, and Little White Mouse.

1 ❑ Dec 1989 Cover: 3.95 **NM** value: **5.95**
• **CGC:** 4 graded, best 9.8
🕮 LifeQuest…A Time to Remember; • Crow;sampler **A:** Michael Gaydos; Bernie Mireault; David Boller; Philip Xavier; Paul Sizer; Gene Gonzales; Gary Shipman; Andy Bennett; Matt Vanderpol **W:** Joe Martin; Bernie Mireault; David Boller; Paul Sizer; Gary Shipman; Matt Vanderpol; Gary Reed; James Pruett

CALIBER CORE — Caliber

0 ❑ b&w Cover: 2.95 **NM** value: **Cover or less**
• intro to imprint

Ash 1❑b&w **NM** value: **1.00**
no cover price. • intro to imprint

CALIBER PRESENTS — Caliber

1 ❑ Jan 1989, b&w Cover: 1.95 **NM** value: **6.00**
• **CGC:** 21 graded, best 9.6
• Crow

2 ❑ 1989b&w Cover: 1.95 **NM** value: **2.00**
3 ❑ 1989b&w Cover: 1.95 **NM** value: **2.00**
4 ❑ 1989b&w Cover: 1.95 **NM** value: **2.00**
5 ❑ 1989b&w Cover: 1.95 **NM** value: **2.00**
6 ❑ Aug 1989 Cover: 1.95 **NM** value: **2.00**
🕮 Fugitive; This is only a Test; Cuda; The Bore; Fairie Tails; Eyes of the Hero; Caliber Preview: Frost **A:** James Dean Smith; Tim Vigil; Kevin Van Hook; Guy Davis; Andrew Pepoy; John Dennis; Dan McKinnon; Greg Cravens

7 ❑ Cover: 1.95 **NM** value: **2.00**
8 ❑ Cover: 1.95 **NM** value: **2.00**
9 ❑ Cover: 2.50 **NM** value: **Cover or less**
10 ❑ Cover: 2.95 **NM** value: **Cover or less**
11 ❑ Cover: 2.95 **NM** value: **Cover or less**
12 ❑ Cover: 2.50 **NM** value: **Cover or less**
13 ❑ Cover: 2.95 **NM** value: **Cover or less**
14 ❑ Cover: 2.50 **NM** value: **Cover or less**
15 ❑ Sep 1990 Cover: 3.50 **NM** value: **Cover or less**
• **CGC:** 1 graded, best 9.6
16 ❑ Cover: 3.50 **NM** value: **Cover or less**
17 ❑ Cover: 3.50 **NM** value: **Cover or less**
18 ❑ Cover: 3.50 **NM** value: **Cover or less**
19 ❑ Cover: 3.50 **NM** value: **Cover or less**
20 ❑ Cover: 3.50 **NM** value: **Cover or less**
21 ❑ Cover: 3.50 **NM** value: **Cover or less**
22 ❑ Cover: 3.50 **NM** value: **Cover or less**
23 ❑ Cover: 3.50 **NM** value: **Cover or less**
24 ❑ Cover: 3.50 **NM** value: **Cover or less**
🕮 Mack the Knife, A Night in Paradise, Sharks, Caliber Preview: The Zone Continuum, Puppy Love, Frames Edge **A:** Alan Oldham; Shane Simmons; R.G. Taylor; Bill Widener; Scott Tolson; Starlen Baxter **W:** Alan Oldham; Shane Simmons; Bill Widener; Mark Askwith; Starlen Baxter; Brian McDonald

CALIBER PRESENTS: CINDERELLA ON FIRE — Caliber

1 ❑ b&w Cover: 2.95 **NM** value: **Cover or less**
No issue number.

CALIBER PRESENTS: GENERATOR COMICS — Caliber

1 ❑ b&w Cover: 2.95 **NM** value: **Cover or less**
No issue number.

CALIBER PRESENTS: HYBRID STORIES — Caliber

1 ❑ b&w Cover: 2.95 **NM** value: **Cover or less**
No issue number. 🕮 The Dinner Guest; Baboon Boy; Mount Sinai; Pick Pockets; Role Reversal; Give It Up; **A:** Dominic Bugatto **W:** Franz Kafka

CALIBER PRESENTS: PETIT MAL — Caliber

1 ❑ b&w Cover: 2.95 **NM** value: **Cover or less**
No issue number.

CALIBER PRESENTS: ROMANTIC TALES — Caliber

1 ❑ b&w Cover: 2.95 **NM** value: **Cover or less**
No issue number. 🕮 Princess Leah

CALIBER PRESENTS: SEPULCHER OPUS — Caliber

1 ❑ b&w Cover: 2.95 **NM** value: **Cover or less**
No issue number.

CALIBER PRESENTS: SOMETHING INSIDE — Caliber

1 ❑ b&w Cover: 3.50 **NM** value: **Cover or less**
No issue number. **A:** Laurence Campbell **W:** Paul Carstairs

CALIBER PRESENTS: SUB-ATOMIC SHOCK — Caliber

1 ❑ b&w Cover: 2.95 **NM** value: **Cover or less**
No issue number.

CALIBER SPOTLIGHT — Caliber

Caliber Spotlight is a giant one-shot that previews the publisher's new offerings for 1995. The weighty volume includes sneak previews at Unleashed (by Joe Sinn's Brooks Hagen), Gabriel, and Nowheresville, along with "New Worlds" titles Raven Chronicles, Inferno, Underside, and The Searchers. The last has a particularly interesting premise: Its stars are a team of researchers descended from the key characters in such H.G. Wells and Jules Verne novels as The Island of Doctor Moreau and 20,000 Leagues under the Sea.

With these previews are short stories featuring Caliber's leading characters: A.K.A. Goldfish, Kabuki, Kilroy, and Oz. Altogether, it's an impressive introduction to a publisher regarded as a bright light in black-and-white comics.

1 ❑ May 1995 Cover: 2.95 **NM** value: **Cover or less**
🕮 A.K.A. Goldfish; Kabuki; Raven Chronicles; Inferno; Searchers; Underside; Kilroy Is Here; Oz • b&w anthology with A.K.A. Goldfish, Kabuki, Kilroy is Here, Oz, and previews

CALIBRATIONS — Caliber

1 ❑ b&w Cover: 2.95 **NM** value: **Cover or less**
🕮 Stage Fright; Atmospherics, Part 1 **A:** Ken Meyer Jr.; Jill Thompson **W:** Warren Ellis; Marc Andreyko

2 ❑ Cover: 0.99 **NM** value: **1.00**
🕮 Atmospherics, Part 2

3 ❑ Cover: 0.99 **NM** value: **1.00**
🕮 Atmospherics, Part 3

4 ❑ Cover: 0.99 **NM** value: **1.00**
🕮 Atmospherics, Part 4

5 ❑ Cover: 0.99 **NM** value: **1.00**
🕮 Atmospherics, Part 5

CALIBRATIONS (VOL. 2) — Caliber

1 ❑ Jun 1996 Cover: 0.99 **NM** value: **1.00**
• preview of The Lost and Atmospherics

2 ❑ Jul 1996 Cover: 0.99 **NM** value: **1.00**
3 ❑ Aug 1996 Cover: 0.99 **NM** value: **1.00**
4 ❑ Sep 1996 Cover: 0.99 **NM** value: **1.00**
Circ: Diamd. preorders: **2,926**

5 ❑ Oct 1996 Cover: 0.99 **NM** value: **1.00**
Circ: Diamd. preorders: **2,772**

CALIFORNIA COMICS — California

1 ❑ **NM** value: **5.00**
2 ❑ **NM** value: **4.00**

CALIFORNIA GIRLS — Eclipse

1 ❑ Jun 1987 Cover: 2.00 **NM** value: **Cover or less**
2 ❑ Jul 1987 Cover: 2.00 **NM** value: **Cover or less**
3 ❑ Aug 1987 Cover: 2.00 **NM** value: **Cover or less**
4 ❑ Sep 1987 Cover: 2.00 **NM** value: **Cover or less**
5 ❑ Oct 1987 Cover: 2.00 **NM** value: **Cover or less**
6 ❑ Nov 1987 Cover: 2.00 **NM** value: **Cover or less**
7 ❑ Dec 1987 Cover: 2.00 **NM** value: **Cover or less**
8 ❑ Jan 1988 Cover: 2.00 **NM** value: **Cover or less**
🕮 The Sound of Breaking Glass **A:** Barb Rausch **W:** Trina Robbins

CALIFORNIA RAISINS IN 3-D, THE — Blackthorne

1 ❑ Dec 1987 Cover: 2.50 **NM** value: **Cover or less**
Circ: CapCity orders: **2,450**
• a.k.a. Blackthorne in 3-D #31 **A:** Andy Ice; David Cody Weiss; Chris Miller; Jeff Marghart **W:** Weissworks

1-2 ❑ Cover: 2.50 **NM** value: **Cover or less**
A: Andy Ice; David Cody Weiss; Chris Miller; Jeff Marghart

1-3 ❑ Cover: 2.50 **NM** value: **Cover or less**
A: Andy Ice; David Cody Weiss; Chris Miller; Jeff Marghart

2 ❑ Cover: 2.50 **NM** value: **Cover or less**
Circ: CapCity orders: **1,575**
A: Andy Ice; David Cody Weiss; Chris Miller; Jeff Marghart **W:** Weissworks

3 ❑ Cover: 2.50 **NM** value: **Cover or less**
Circ: CapCity orders: **1,550**
A: Andy Ice; David Cody Weiss; Chris Miller; Jeff Marghart **W:** Weissworks

4 ❑ Cover: 2.50 **NM** value: **Cover or less**
Circ: CapCity orders: **1,150**
A: Andy Ice; David Cody Weiss; Chris Miller; Jeff Marghart **W:** Weissworks

5 ❑ Cover: 2.50 **NM** value: **Cover or less**
A: Andy Ice; David Cody Weiss; Chris Miller; Jeff Marghart **W:** Weissworks

CALIFORNIA RAISINS: ULTIMATE COLLECTION — Blackthorne

Bk 1❑ b&w Cover: 4.95 **NM** value: **Cover or less**

CGC-graded: Multiply prices above by **33 for 9.9 M • 16 for 9.8 NM/M • 7 for 9.6 NM+ • 5 for 9.4 NM • 2.5 for 9.2 NM- • 1.5 for 9.0 VF/NM**

CALIGARI 2050 — Monster

1 ❑ Cover: 2.25 **NM** value: **Cover or less**
2 ❑ Cover: 2.25 **NM** value: **Cover or less**
3 ❑ Cover: 2.25 **NM** value: **Cover or less**

CALLED FROM DARKNESS — Anarchy

1 ❑ Cover: 2.95 **NM** value: **Cover or less**
A: Marc Sandroni **W:** Vinson Watson

CALLING ALL BOYS — Parents' Magazine Institute

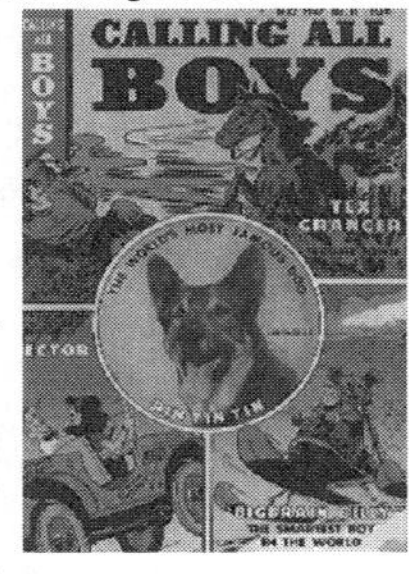

Drawing on the success of the earlier Calling All Girls and Calling All Kids, the publishers of Parents Magazine launched this, the logical extension of the series, in 1946.

Each giant-sized issue brought numerous stories, including the comical exploits of Hector, sports comics featuring Streaky Smith, and the super-smart adventures of "Big Brain Billy." In an unusual move for a comics magazine, it also includes numerous multi-page text stories. Wrapping things up, a "Coach's Corner," written by such sports legends as Joe DiMaggio gave kids tips for improving their playing abilities.

After 17 issues under the Calling All Boys name, the title became known as Tex Granger, after the title's popular Western feature.

1 ❑ Jan 1946 Cover: 0.10 **NM** value: **60.00**
2 ❑ Feb 1946 Cover: 0.10 **NM** value: **28.00**
3 ❑ Apr 1946 Cover: 0.10 **NM** value: **16.00**
4 ❑ May 1946 Cover: 0.10 **NM** value: **14.00**
5 ❑ Jun 1946 Cover: 0.10 **NM** value: **14.00**
6 ❑ Jul 1946 Cover: 0.10 **NM** value: **14.00**
7 ❑ Sep 1946 Cover: 0.10 **NM** value: **14.00**
8 ❑ Oct 1946 Cover: 0.10 **NM** value: **14.00**
9 ❑ Dec 1946 Cover: 0.10 **NM** value: **14.00**
10 ❑ Mar 1947 Cover: 0.10 **NM** value: **28.00**
Gary Cooper cover.
11 ❑ May 1947 Cover: 0.10 **NM** value: **14.00**
Rin Tin Tin photo cover.
12 ❑ Jul 1947 Cover: 0.10 **NM** value: **35.00**
Bob Hope photo cover.
13 ❑ Cover: 0.10 **NM** value: **28.00**
Bing Crosby photo cover.
14 ❑ Nov 1947 Cover: 0.10 **NM** value: **14.00**
15 ❑ Jan 1948 Cover: 0.10 **NM** value: **14.00**
16 ❑ Mar 1948 Cover: 0.10 **NM** value: **14.00**
17 ❑ May 1948 Cover: 0.10 **NM** value: **14.00**
• Series continued in Tex Granger #18

CALLING ALL GIRLS — Parents' Magazine Institute

1 ❑ Sep 1941 Cover: 0.10 **NM** value: **100.00**
2 ❑ 1941 Cover: 0.10 **NM** value: **95.00**
3 ❑ Cover: 0.10 **NM** value: **90.00**
4 ❑ Cover: 0.10 **NM** value: **85.00**
5 ❑ 1942 Cover: 0.10 **NM** value: **80.00**
6 ❑ 1942 Cover: 0.10 **NM** value: **75.00**
7 ❑ 1942 Cover: 0.10 **NM** value: **70.00**
8 ❑ 1942 Cover: 0.10 **NM** value: **65.00**
9 ❑ 1942 Cover: 0.10 **NM** value: **60.00**
10 ❑ 1942 Cover: 0.10 **NM** value: **50.00**
11 ❑ 1942 Cover: 0.10 **NM** value: **50.00**
12 ❑ Cover: 0.10 **NM** value: **50.00**
13 ❑ Cover: 0.10 **NM** value: **50.00**
14 ❑ 1943 Cover: 0.10 **NM** value: **45.00**
15 ❑ 1943 Cover: 0.10 **NM** value: **45.00**
16 ❑ 1943 Cover: 0.10 **NM** value: **45.00**
17 ❑ 1943 Cover: 0.10 **NM** value: **40.00**
18 ❑ 1943 Cover: 0.10 **NM** value: **40.00**
19 ❑ 1943 Cover: 0.10 **NM** value: **40.00**
20 ❑ 1943 Cover: 0.10 **NM** value: **35.00**
21 ❑ 1943 Cover: 0.10 **NM** value: **35.00**
22 ❑ 1943 Cover: 0.10 **NM** value: **35.00**
23 ❑ Nov 1943 Cover: 0.10 **NM** value: **30.00**
24 ❑ 1943 Cover: 0.10 **NM** value: **30.00**
25 ❑ 1944 Cover: 0.10 **NM** value: **30.00**
26 ❑ 1944 Cover: 0.10 **NM** value: **30.00**
27 ❑ 1944 Cover: 0.10 **NM** value: **25.00**
28 ❑ 1944 Cover: 0.10 **NM** value: **25.00**
29 ❑ 1944 Cover: 0.10 **NM** value: **25.00**
30 ❑ 1944 Cover: 0.10 **NM** value: **25.00**
31 ❑ 1944 Cover: 0.10 **NM** value: **25.00**
32 ❑ 1944 Cover: 0.10 **NM** value: **25.00**
33 ❑ 1944 Cover: 0.10 **NM** value: **25.00**
34 ❑ 1944 Cover: 0.10 **NM** value: **25.00**
35 ❑ 1944 Cover: 0.10 **NM** value: **25.00**
36 ❑ 1944 Cover: 0.10 **NM** value: **25.00**
37 ❑ 1945 Cover: 0.10 **NM** value: **25.00**
38 ❑ 1945 Cover: 0.10 **NM** value: **25.00**
39 ❑ 1945 Cover: 0.10 **NM** value: **25.00**
40 ❑ 1945 Cover: 0.10 **NM** value: **20.00**
41 ❑ 1945 Cover: 0.10 **NM** value: **20.00**
42 ❑ 1945 Cover: 0.10 **NM** value: **20.00**
43 ❑ Oct 1945 Cover: 0.10 **NM** value: **20.00**
44 ❑ Dec 1945 Cover: 0.10 **NM** value: **20.00**
45 ❑ Jan 1946 Cover: 0.10 **NM** value: **20.00**
46 ❑ Feb 1946 Cover: 0.10 **NM** value: **20.00**
47 ❑ Mar 1946 Cover: 0.10 **NM** value: **20.00**
48 ❑ Apr 1946 Cover: 0.10 **NM** value: **20.00**
49 ❑ May 1946 Cover: 0.10 **NM** value: **20.00**
50 ❑ Jun 1946 Cover: 0.10 **NM** value: **20.00**
51 ❑ Jul 1946 Cover: 0.10 **NM** value: **20.00**
52 ❑ Aug 1946 Cover: 0.10 **NM** value: **20.00**
53 ❑ Sep 1946 Cover: 0.10 **NM** value: **20.00**
54 ❑ Oct 1946 Cover: 0.10 **NM** value: **20.00**
55 ❑ Nov 1946 Cover: 0.10 **NM** value: **15.00**
56 ❑ Dec 1946 Cover: 0.10 **NM** value: **15.00**
57 ❑ Jan 1947 Cover: 0.10 **NM** value: **15.00**
58 ❑ Feb 1947 Cover: 0.10 **NM** value: **15.00**
59 ❑ Mar 1947 Cover: 0.10 **NM** value: **15.00**
60 ❑ Apr 1947 Cover: 0.10 **NM** value: **15.00**
61 ❑ May 1947 Cover: 0.10 **NM** value: **15.00**
62 ❑ Jun 1947 Cover: 0.10 **NM** value: **15.00**
63 ❑ Jul 1947 Cover: 0.10 **NM** value: **15.00**
64 ❑ Aug 1947 Cover: 0.10 **NM** value: **15.00**
65 ❑ Sep 1947 Cover: 0.10 **NM** value: **15.00**
66 ❑ Oct 1947 Cover: 0.10 **NM** value: **15.00**
67 ❑ Nov 1947 Cover: 0.10 **NM** value: **15.00**
68 ❑ Dec 1947 Cover: 0.10 **NM** value: **15.00**
69 ❑ Jan 1948 Cover: 0.10 **NM** value: **15.00**
70 ❑ Feb 1948 Cover: 0.10 **NM** value: **15.00**
71 ❑ Mar 1948 Cover: 0.10 **NM** value: **15.00**
72 ❑ Apr 1948 Cover: 0.10 **NM** value: **15.00**
73 ❑ May 1948 Cover: 0.10 **NM** value: **15.00**
74 ❑ Jun 1948 Cover: 0.10 **NM** value: **15.00**
75 ❑ Jul 1948 Cover: 0.10 **NM** value: **15.00**
76 ❑ Aug 1948 Cover: 0.10 **NM** value: **15.00**
77 ❑ Sep 1948 Cover: 0.10 **NM** value: **15.00**
78 ❑ Oct 1948 Cover: 0.10 **NM** value: **15.00**
79 ❑ Nov 1948 Cover: 0.10 **NM** value: **15.00**
80 ❑ Dec 1948 Cover: 0.10 **NM** value: **10.00**
81 ❑ Jan 1949 Cover: 0.10 **NM** value: **10.00**
82 ❑ Feb 1949 Cover: 0.10 **NM** value: **10.00**
83 ❑ Mar 1949 Cover: 0.10 **NM** value: **10.00**
84 ❑ Apr 1949 Cover: 0.10 **NM** value: **10.00**
85 ❑ May 1949 Cover: 0.10 **NM** value: **10.00**
86 ❑ Jun 1949 Cover: 0.10 **NM** value: **10.00**
87 ❑ Jul 1949 Cover: 0.10 **NM** value: **10.00**
88 ❑ Aug 1949 Cover: 0.10 **NM** value: **10.00**
89 ❑ Sep 1949 Cover: 0.10 **NM** value: **10.00**

CALLING ALL KIDS — Parents' Magazine Institute

1 ❑ Jan 1946 Cover: 0.10 **NM** value: **55.00**
2 ❑ Mar 1946 Cover: 0.10 **NM** value: **24.00**
3 ❑ May 1946 Cover: 0.10 **NM** value: **16.00**
4 ❑ Jul 1946 Cover: 0.10 **NM** value: **12.00**
5 ❑ Oct 1946 Cover: 0.10 **NM** value: **12.00**
6 ❑ Dec 1946 Cover: 0.10 **NM** value: **12.00**
7 ❑ 1947 Cover: 0.10 **NM** value: **12.00**
8 ❑ 1947 Cover: 0.10 **NM** value: **12.00**
9 ❑ 1947 Cover: 0.10 **NM** value: **12.00**
10 ❑ Aug 1947 Cover: 0.10 **NM** value: **12.00**
11 ❑ 1947 Cover: 0.10 **NM** value: **10.00**
12 ❑ 1947 Cover: 0.10 **NM** value: **10.00**
13 ❑ 1947 Cover: 0.10 **NM** value: **10.00**
14 ❑ Nov 1947 Cover: 0.10 **NM** value: **10.00**
📖 Guess My Name (activity); **W:** Hilda Holt; Jane Sylvester
15 ❑ Dec 1947 Cover: 0.10 **NM** value: **10.00**
16 ❑ Jan 1948 Cover: 0.10 **NM** value: **10.00**
17 ❑ Feb 1948 Cover: 0.10 **NM** value: **10.00**
18 ❑ Apr 1948 Cover: 0.10 **NM** value: **10.00**
19 ❑ Jun 1948 Cover: 0.10 **NM** value: **10.00**
20 ❑ Aug 1948 Cover: 0.10 **NM** value: **10.00**
21 ❑ Oct 1948 Cover: 0.10 **NM** value: **10.00**
22 ❑ Dec 1948 Cover: 0.10 **NM** value: **10.00**
23 ❑ Feb 1949 Cover: 0.10 **NM** value: **10.00**
24 ❑ Apr 1949 Cover: 0.10 **NM** value: **10.00**
25 ❑ Jun 1949 Cover: 0.10 **NM** value: **10.00**
26 ❑ Aug 1949 Cover: 0.10 **NM** value: **10.00**
final issue.

CALL ME PRINCESS — CPM

1 ❑ May 1999 Cover: 2.95 **NM** value: **Cover or less**
Circ: Diamd. preorders: **5,011**
A: Tomoko Taniguchi **W:** Tomoko Taniguchi
1/A ❑ May 1999 Cover: 2.95 **NM** value: **Cover or less**
A: Tomoko Taniguchi; Colleen Doran(cover) **W:** Tomoko Taniguchi

CAMBION — Slave Labor

1 ❑ Dec 1995 Cover: 2.95 **NM** value: **Cover or less**
A: Phil Rittenhouse **W:** Joe Gentile
2 ❑ Feb 1996 Cover: 2.95 **NM** value: **Cover or less**
A: Phil Rittenhouse **W:** Joe Gentile
3 ❑ Feb 1997, b&w Cover: 2.95 **NM** value: **Cover or less**
📖 Rhythm's Gonna Get'cha • Published by Moonstone **A:** Phil Rittenhouse **W:** Joe Gentile

CAMELOT ETERNAL — Caliber

1 ❑ Cover: 2.50 **NM** value: **Cover or less**
📖 Part 1, Avalon Denied, Prologue; After the Fall **A:** Jim Calafiore **W:** Jim Calafiore
2 ❑ Cover: 2.50 **NM** value: **Cover or less**
3 ❑ Cover: 2.50 **NM** value: **Cover or less**
4 ❑ Cover: 2.50 **NM** value: **Cover or less**
5 ❑ Cover: 2.50 **NM** value: **Cover or less**
6 ❑ Cover: 2.50 **NM** value: **Cover or less**
7 ❑ Cover: 2.50 **NM** value: **Cover or less**
8 ❑ Cover: 2.50 **NM** value: **Cover or less**

> The CGC numbers printed in individual listings above represent the **number of copies examined** and given a **Universal** grade by CGC and the **best such copy** graded at press time. For current populations, watch for special ***Comics Buyer's Guide*** issues or check **www.cgccomics.com.**

CAMELOT 3000 — DC

In England's hour of greatest need, King Arthur is resurrected to help repel an alien invasion in this 12-issue maxi-series. Revived by Merlin, Arthur begins a quest to reunite his Knights of the Round Table, but finds that with the passage of centuries, some changes have occurred, including a mutated Sir Percival and a female Tristan, while Lancelot and Guinevere renew their illicit romance.

Arthur's old nemeses Morgan le Fay and Mordred also return in updated forms to bedevil the King. The Brian Bolland-drawn series is also noteworthy for the lengthy delays between latter issues. — Brent

1 ❑ Dec 1982 Cover: 1.00 **NM** value: **2.50**
📖 The Past And Future King! **A:** Brian Bolland **W:** Mike W. Barr
★ Origin of Merlin, Arthur.
2 ❑ Jan 1983 Cover: 1.00 **NM** value: **2.00**
A: Brian Bolland
3 ❑ Feb 1983 Cover: 1.00 **NM** value: **2.00**
A: Brian Bolland
4 ❑ Mar 1983 Cover: 1.00 **NM** value: **2.00**
A: Brian Bolland
5 ❑ Apr 1983 Cover: 1.00 **NM** value: **2.00**
📖 The Tale Of Morgan LeFay **A:** Brian Bolland **W:** Mike W. Barr
6 ❑ Jul 1983 Cover: 1.00 **NM** value: **2.00**
A: Brian Bolland
7 ❑ Aug 1983 Cover: 1.00 **NM** value: **2.00**
A: Brian Bolland
8 ❑ Sep 1983 Cover: 1.00 **NM** value: **2.00**
A: Brian Bolland
9 ❑ Dec 1983 Cover: 1.00 **NM** value: **2.00**
A: Brian Bolland
10 ❑ Mar 1984 Cover: 1.00 **NM** value: **2.00**
A: Brian Bolland
11 ❑ Jul 1984 Cover: 1.00 **NM** value: **2.00**
A: Brian Bolland
12 ❑ Apr 1985 Cover: 1.00 **NM** value: **2.00**
A: Brian Bolland
Bk 1 ❑ Cover: 12.95 **NM** value: **14.95**
Circ: CapCity orders: **3,075**
• Collects Camelot 3000 #1-12

CAMERA COMICS — U.S. Camera

1 ❑ ca. 1944 Cover: 0.10 **NM** value: **150.00**
• **CGC:** 1 graded, best 8.5
2 ❑ Cover: 0.10 **NM** value: **125.00**
3 ❑ Cover: 0.10 **NM** value: **125.00**
4 ❑ Cover: 0.10 **NM** value: **100.00**
5 ❑ Cover: 0.10 **NM** value: **100.00**
6 ❑ Cover: 0.10 **NM** value: **100.00**
7 ❑ Cover: 0.10 **NM** value: **90.00**
8 ❑ Cover: 0.10 **NM** value: **90.00**
9 ❑ Cover: 0.10 **NM** value: **90.00**
10 ❑ Cover: 0.10 **NM** value: **90.00**
11 ❑ Cover: 0.10 **NM** value: **90.00**

CAMP CANDY — Marvel

Based on the animated TV series of the same name, Camp Candy depicts actor John Candy as a counselor and handyman in a summer camp. The comedian is joined in his camp adventures by Binky, Rex, Nurse Molly, and a lot of wisecracking kids.

With the release of the film Uncle Buck, Candy was near the height of his popularity with children when this series was on the air and in stores. Yet, the DIC Enterprises cartoon ran only one year on NBC, the 1989-1990 season.

Camp Candy remains one of the few comics to depict a real-life actor in a cartoon situation in recent years. Candy died of a heart attack in 1994. — JJM

1 ❑ May 1990 Cover: 1.00 **NM** value: **Cover or less**
Circ: CapCity orders: **4,250**
📖 The Return of Headless Harry; The Owimpic Kid **A:** Howie Post **W:** Angelo Decesare
2 ❑ Jun 1990 Cover: 1.00 **NM** value: **Cover or less**
Circ: CapCity orders: **2,600**
📖 The Counterfeit Campers; The Moose Who Loves Me **A:** Howie Post **W:** Angelo Decesare
3 ❑ Jul 1990 Cover: 1.00 **NM** value: **Cover or less**
Circ: CapCity orders: **2,250**
4 ❑ Aug 1990 Cover: 1.00 **NM** value: **Cover or less**
Circ: CapCity orders: **1,600**
5 ❑ Sep 1990 Cover: 1.00 **NM** value: **Cover or less**
6 ❑ Oct 1990 Cover: 1.00 **NM** value: **Cover or less**
Circ: CapCity orders: **1,200**

> **Capital City** orders are the actual sales of comic books by Capital City Distribution, once one of the largest U.S. sellers of comics to comics shops. Capital City's share of comics shop sales, while not known exactly, increases from around 10-20% in the mid-1980s to 30-35% in the mid-1990s. Capital City's share of comic books sold on newsstands (most Marvels and DCs) will be less.

Other grades: Multiply prices above by **1.5 for Mint • 2/3 for Very Fine • 1/3 for Fine • 1/5 for Very Good • 1/8 for Good**

CAMP COMICS
Dell

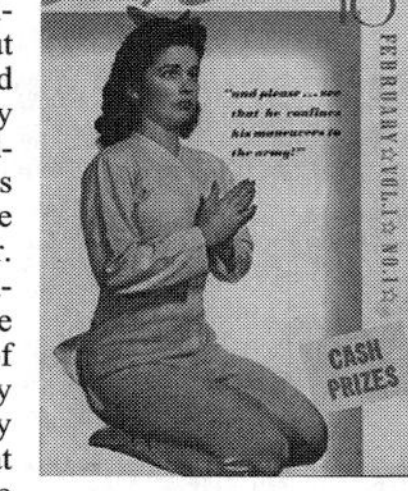

When World War II broke out, Dell — noted for its comics dedicated for young readers — tried out a title to be distributed to the Armed Forces. The stories were clearly aimed at adult males and carried advertising (something else that was not a feature of Dell comics of the day) for cigarettes and shaving gear.

The anthology title featured pin-up photo covers, straight adventure strips, and slapstick comedy, one of the latter features being "Seaman Sy Wheeler" written and drawn by Walt Kelly. It's not clear today what forces led to the cancellation of the title; what is clear is that the war lasted longer than Camp Comics did. — Maggie

1 ❑ Feb 1942 Cover: 0.10 **NM** value: **500.00**
2 ❑ Mar 1942 Cover: 0.10 **NM** value: **450.00**
• **CGC:** 2 graded, best 9.6
3 ❑ Apr 1942 Cover: 0.10 **NM** value: **400.00**

CAMPING WITH BIGFOOT
Slave Labor

1 ❑ Sep 1995 Cover: 2.95 **NM** value: **Cover or less**
A: F. Andrew Taylor **W:** F. Andrew Taylor

CAMPUS LOVES
Quality

1 ❑ Dec 1949 Cover: 0.10 **NM** value: **200.00**
2 ❑ Feb 1950 Cover: 0.10 **NM** value: **150.00**
3 ❑ Apr 1950 Cover: 0.10 **NM** value: **125.00**
4 ❑ Jun 1950 Cover: 0.10 **NM** value: **125.00**
5 ❑ Aug 1950 Cover: 0.10 **NM** value: **100.00**

CAMPUS ROMANCES
Avon

1 ❑ ca. 1949 Cover: 0.10 **NM** value: **150.00**
2 ❑ ca. 1949 Cover: 0.10 **NM** value: **100.00**
3 ❑ ca. 1950 Cover: 0.10 **NM** value: **100.00**

CANADIAN COMICS CAVALCADE
Artworx

1 ❑ b&w Cover: 2.00 **NM** value: **Cover or less**
A: Dean Motter; Ty Templeton; Peter Hsu; Dan Day; Chester Brown; Arn Saba

CANADIAN NINJA
Quebec

1 ❑ Cover: 1.50 **NM** value: **Cover or less**

CANADIAN ROCK SPECIAL
Revolutionary

This black-and-white special from Revolutionary Comics chronicles the — unauthorized — story of Canadian rockers Rush. The art is a bit simple, but the story is the stuff of "VH1: Legends" or "Behind the Music." It begins with early attempts by Geddy Lee, Alex Lifeson, and Neil Peart to form a band, as well as the impact of Led Zeppelin's first album on that band's sound. Rush gained recognition opening for such established acts as Blue Oyster Cult and Nazareth and appearing on "In Concert" and "Don Kirshner's Rock Concert." Of course, the band hit its zenith in the late 1970s and the early 1980s, but it has continued to produce music that gets air-time.

1 ❑ Apr 1994, b&w Cover: 2.50 **NM** value: **Cover or less**
📖 Ex-Poseurs • Rush **A:** Terry Pallot **W:** Jay Allen Sanford

CANCER: THE CRAB BOY
Sabre's Edge

1 ❑ Cover: 2.95 **NM** value: **Cover or less**
2 ❑ Cover: 2.95 **NM** value: **Cover or less**
3 ❑ Cover: 2.95 **NM** value: **Cover or less**
4 ❑ Cover: 2.95 **NM** value: **Cover or less**
5 ❑ Cover: 2.95 **NM** value: **Cover or less**

CANDIDE REVEALED
Fantagraphics / Eros

All issues are adults only.

1 ❑ b&w Cover: 2.25 **NM** value: **Cover or less**

CANDY
Quality

1 ❑ Fal 1944 Cover: 0.10 **NM** value: **300.00**
2 ❑ Win 1944 Cover: 0.10 **NM** value: **200.00**
3 ❑ Spr 1945 Cover: 0.10 **NM** value: **200.00**

CANDY (COMIC MAGAZINES)
Comic Magazines / Eros

1 ❑ Fal 1947 Cover: 0.10 **NM** value: **90.00**
2 ❑ Win 1947 Cover: 0.10 **NM** value: **50.00**
3 ❑ Spr 1948 Cover: 0.10 **NM** value: **35.00**
4 ❑ 1948 Cover: 0.10 **NM** value: **35.00**
5 ❑ 1948 Cover: 0.10 **NM** value: **35.00**
6 ❑ Oct 1948 Cover: 0.10 **NM** value: **25.00**
7 ❑ Cover: 0.10 **NM** value: **25.00**
8 ❑ Cover: 0.10 **NM** value: **25.00**
9 ❑ Cover: 0.10 **NM** value: **25.00**
10 ❑ Cover: 0.10 **NM** value: **25.00**
11 ❑ Cover: 0.10 **NM** value: **20.00**
12 ❑ Cover: 0.10 **NM** value: **20.00**
13 ❑ Cover: 0.10 **NM** value: **20.00**
14 ❑ Cover: 0.10 **NM** value: **20.00**
15 ❑ Cover: 0.10 **NM** value: **20.00**
16 ❑ Cover: 0.10 **NM** value: **20.00**
17 ❑ Cover: 0.10 **NM** value: **20.00**
18 ❑ Cover: 0.10 **NM** value: **20.00**
19 ❑ Cover: 0.10 **NM** value: **20.00**
20 ❑ Cover: 0.10 **NM** value: **20.00**
21 ❑ Cover: 0.10 **NM** value: **16.00**
22 ❑ Cover: 0.10 **NM** value: **16.00**
23 ❑ Cover: 0.10 **NM** value: **16.00**
24 ❑ Cover: 0.10 **NM** value: **16.00**
25 ❑ Cover: 0.10 **NM** value: **16.00**
26 ❑ Cover: 0.10 **NM** value: **16.00**
27 ❑ Cover: 0.10 **NM** value: **16.00**
28 ❑ Cover: 0.10 **NM** value: **16.00**
29 ❑ Cover: 0.10 **NM** value: **16.00**
30 ❑ Cover: 0.10 **NM** value: **16.00**
31 ❑ Cover: 0.10 **NM** value: **14.00**
32 ❑ Cover: 0.10 **NM** value: **14.00**
33 ❑ Cover: 0.10 **NM** value: **14.00**
34 ❑ Cover: 0.10 **NM** value: **14.00**
35 ❑ Cover: 0.10 **NM** value: **14.00**
36 ❑ Cover: 0.10 **NM** value: **14.00**
37 ❑ Cover: 0.10 **NM** value: **14.00**
38 ❑ Cover: 0.10 **NM** value: **14.00**
39 ❑ Cover: 0.10 **NM** value: **14.00**
40 ❑ Cover: 0.10 **NM** value: **12.00**
41 ❑ Cover: 0.10 **NM** value: **12.00**
42 ❑ Cover: 0.10 **NM** value: **12.00**
43 ❑ 1953 Cover: 0.10 **NM** value: **12.00**
44 ❑ 1953 Cover: 0.10 **NM** value: **12.00**
45 ❑ Cover: 0.10 **NM** value: **12.00**
📖 A Lad'n His Lamp; Will Bragg; Masquerade Massacre; Fortune Hunting; Sweep No More, My Lady!; Dressed To Kill
46 ❑ 1954 Cover: 0.10 **NM** value: **12.00**
47 ❑ 1954 Cover: 0.10 **NM** value: **12.00**
48 ❑ May 1954 Cover: 0.10 **NM** value: **12.00**
49 ❑ Cover: 0.10 **NM** value: **12.00**
50 ❑ Cover: 0.10 **NM** value: **12.00**
51 ❑ Cover: 0.10 **NM** value: **10.00**
52 ❑ Cover: 0.10 **NM** value: **10.00**
53 ❑ Cover: 0.10 **NM** value: **10.00**
54 ❑ 1955 Cover: 0.10 **NM** value: **10.00**
55 ❑ 1955 Cover: 0.10 **NM** value: **10.00**
56 ❑ 1955 Cover: 0.10 **NM** value: **10.00**
57 ❑ 1955 Cover: 0.10 **NM** value: **10.00**
58 ❑ 1955 Cover: 0.10 **NM** value: **10.00**
59 ❑ Jan 1956 Cover: 0.10 **NM** value: **10.00**
60 ❑ 1956 Cover: 0.10 **NM** value: **10.00**
61 ❑ 1956 Cover: 0.10 **NM** value: **10.00**
62 ❑ 1956 Cover: 0.10 **NM** value: **10.00**
63 ❑ 1956 Cover: 0.10 **NM** value: **10.00**
64 ❑ Jul 1956 Cover: 0.10 **NM** value: **10.00**
final issue.

CANNIBALIS
Raging Rhino

All issues are adults only.

1 ❑ b&w Cover: 2.95 **NM** value: **Cover or less**

CANNON
Fantagraphics / Eros

Cannon is an action-packed adventure series from comics legend Wally Wood, who drew many fine comics of the Golden Age and had a long run on various E.C. titles.

With the help of Editor Bill Pierson, Wood's 1960s Cannon strip was collected into this eight-issue mini-series for Eros. In it, John Cannon, the United States' top secret agent, travels the globe to stop dictators, assassins, and other threats. In doing so, he is constantly plagued by a pair of female agents: Sue Stevens, a Russian agent trained in a fictional small town to fit in as the perfect American, and Madame Toy, a communist Chinese femme fatale. Both can't seem to stop falling all over Cannon, even as they arrange to have him killed. They are just two of the beauties who seem to follow Cannon around without benefit of clothes — the occasional depiction of which leads to this series' "adults only" rating.

1 ❑ Feb 1991, b&w Cover: 2.75 **NM** value: **Cover or less**
A: Wally Wood **W:** Wally Wood
1-2 ❑ Cover: 2.95 **NM** value: **Cover or less**
2 ❑ Mar 1991, b&w Cover: 2.75 **NM** value: **2.95**
A: Wally Wood **W:** Wally Wood
2-2 ❑ Cover: 2.95 **NM** value: **Cover or less**
3 ❑ Apr 1991 Cover: 2.75 **NM** value: **2.95**
📖 Love, Lust, and Larceny **A:** Wally Wood **W:** Wally Wood ★ Origin of Madame Toy, Sue Stevens.
3-2 ❑ Cover: 2.95 **NM** value: **Cover or less**
4 ❑ May 1991 Cover: 2.75 **NM** value: **2.95**
A: Wally Wood **W:** Wally Wood
5 ❑ Jun 1991 Cover: 2.75 **NM** value: **2.95**
A: Wally Wood **W:** Wally Wood
6 ❑ Jul 1991 Cover: 2.75 **NM** value: **2.95**
A: Wally Wood **W:** Wally Wood
7 ❑ Aug 1991 Cover: 2.75 **NM** value: **2.95**
A: Wally Wood **W:** Wally Wood
8 ❑ Sep 1991 Cover: 2.95 **NM** value: **Cover or less**
A: Wally Wood **W:** Wally Wood

CAPE CITY
Dimension X

1 ❑ b&w Cover: 2.75 **NM** value: **Cover or less**
2 ❑ b&w Cover: 2.75 **NM** value: **Cover or less**

CAPITAL CAPERS PRESENTS
BLT Studios

1 ❑ Oct 1994, b&w Cover: 2.95 **NM** value: **Cover or less**
📖 Socialism Trek: The Search for Health Care **A:** Greg Barrington **W:** Greg Barrington; Dom Loise

CAP'N OATMEAL
All American

1 ❑ b&w Cover: 2.25 **NM** value: **Cover or less**

CAP'N QUICK & A FOOZLE
Eclipse

1 ❑ Jul 1984 Cover: 1.50 **NM** value: **Cover or less**
📖 Together Again…for the First Time **A:** Marshall Rogers **W:** Chris Goldberg ★ Appearance of Stat, Foozle, Doberman, Cap'n Quick, Mel, Granny, The "Great Jones", The Darklydale Dancers.
2 ❑ Mar 1985 Cover: 1.75 **NM** value: **Cover or less**
A: Marshall Rogers **W:** Chris Goldberg
3 ❑ Cover: 1.50 **NM** value: **Cover or less**
• Title changes to The Foozle **A:** Marshall Rogers **W:** Chris Goldberg

CAPTAIN ACTION
Karl Art

0 ❑ Cover: 1.95 **NM** value: **Cover or less**
• preview of ongoing series;Insert in Space Bananas #1 **A:** John Ridgway **W:** Barry Kraus ★ 1st Appearance of Doctor Evil, Captain Action (Karl Art).

CAPTAIN ACTION (DC)
DC

1 ❑ Nov 1968 Cover: 0.12 **NM** value: **40.00**
• **CGC:** 15 graded, best 9.6
A: Wally Wood; Wood **W:** Jim Shooter ★ Origin of Captain Action.
2 ❑ Jan 1969 Cover: 0.12 **NM** value: **25.00**
• **CGC:** 4 graded, best 9.6
A: Gil Kane; Wally Wood **W:** Jim Shooter
3 ❑ Mar 1969 Cover: 0.12 **NM** value: **25.00**
• **CGC:** 4 graded, best 9.6
A: Gil Kane; Wally Wood
4 ❑ May 1969 Cover: 0.12 **NM** value: **25.00**
• **CGC:** 6 graded, best 9.6
A: Gil Kane
5 ❑ Jul 1969 Cover: 0.12 **NM** value: **25.00**
• **CGC:** 2 graded, best 9.2
A: Gil Kane; Wally Wood

CAPTAIN AERO COMICS
Continental

1 ❑ Dec 1941 Cover: 0.10 **NM** value: **1200.00**
2 ❑ Feb 1942 Cover: 0.10 **NM** value: **750.00**
• **CGC:** 1 graded, best 7.0
3 ❑ Mar 1942 Cover: 0.10 **NM** value: **700.00**
• **CGC:** 2 graded, best 8.5
4 ❑ Apr 1942 Cover: 0.10 **NM** value: **700.00**
5 ❑ May 1942 Cover: 0.10 **NM** value: **700.00**
6 ❑ Jun 1942 Cover: 0.10 **NM** value: **650.00**
7 ❑ Jul 1942 Cover: 0.10 **NM** value: **650.00**
8 ❑ Sep 1942 Cover: 0.10 **NM** value: **300.00**
• **CGC:** 1 graded, best 7.5
9 ❑ Nov 1942 Cover: 0.10 **NM** value: **250.00**
10 ❑ Jan 1943 Cover: 0.10 **NM** value: **250.00**
11 ❑ Sep 1943 Cover: 0.10 **NM** value: **200.00**
12 ❑ Nov 1943 Cover: 0.10 **NM** value: **200.00**
13 ❑ Jan 1944 Cover: 0.10 **NM** value: **200.00**
14 ❑ Apr 1944 Cover: 0.10 **NM** value: **175.00**
15 ❑ Jun 1944 Cover: 0.10 **NM** value: **175.00**
• **CGC:** 2 graded, best 7.0
16 ❑ Aug 1944 Cover: 0.10 **NM** value: **175.00**
• **CGC:** 1 graded, best 9.0
17 ❑ Oct 1944 Cover: 0.10 **NM** value: **175.00**
21 ❑ Dec 1944 Cover: 0.10 **NM** value: **150.00**
22 ❑ Apr 1945 Cover: 0.10 **NM** value: **150.00**
23 ❑ Aug 1945 Cover: 0.10 **NM** value: **150.00**
• **CGC:** 2 graded, best 9.2
24 ❑ Nov 1945 Cover: 0.10 **NM** value: **150.00**
• **CGC:** 1 graded, best 9.4
25 ❑ Feb 1946 Cover: 0.10 **NM** value: **150.00**
• **CGC:** 1 graded, best 4.0
26 ❑ Aug 1946 Cover: 0.10 **NM** value: **150.00**
• **CGC:** 3 graded, best 8.0

CAPTAIN AMERICA AND THE CAMPBELL KIDS
Marvel

1 ❑ ca. 1980 **NM** value: **1.00**
• **CGC:** 1 graded, best 9.4
No issue number. • giveaway.

CAPTAIN AMERICA BATTLEBOOK
Marvel

1 ❑ Cover: 3.99 **NM** value: **Cover or less**
A: Jean-Claude St. Aubin; Bill Tucci(cover); Phyllis Novin

CAPTAIN AMERICA COMICS
Marvel

As war raged across Europe in 1941, America watched the action nervously from the sidelines. There were many, however, who yearned to strike back at Hitler. Among these was Joe Simon, who, along with Jack Kirby, created Captain America as an exercise in patriotic wish-fulfillment. The first-issue cover even features Captain America wading through a legion of Nazis to land a hard right cross on Hitler's chin.

Along with the premiere of Captain America himself, this series introduced young sidekick "Bucky" Barnes, a camp mascot who discovered Captain America's secret identity and decided to join him in his adventures. During the war years of 1941-1945, the pair took on Nazis and fifth columnists,

CGC-graded: Multiply prices above by **33 for 9.9 M • 16 for 9.8 NM/M • 7 for 9.6 NM+ • 5 for 9.4 NM • 2.5 for 9.2 NM- • 1.5 for 9.0 VF/NM**

and their fan club, "The Sentinels of Liberty," even turned in numerous neighbors as suspected saboteurs. Once the war was over, however, Cap faded from sight, to be reawakened later in The Avengers #4.

1 ❑ Mar 1941 Cover: 0.10 **NM** value: **59000.00**
• **CGC:** 14 graded, best 9.6
📖 Case #1: Meet Captain America; The Soldier's Soup; Case #2: Sando and Omar; Captain America and the Riddle of the Red Skull; Murder Ltd.; Stories from the Dark Ages • 1st appearance/origin Captain America; Hurricane; Tuk **A:** Joe Simon; Jack Kirby ★ Origin of Captain America I (Rogers). ★ 1st Appearance of Captain America I (Steve Rogers), The Red Skull, Bucky I (Bucky Barnes).

2 ❑ Apr 1941 Cover: 0.10 **NM** value: **11000.00**
• **CGC:** 7 graded, best 8.5
📖 Captain America and the Ageless Orientals Who Wouldn't Die; Trapped in the Nazi Stronghold; The Wax Statue that Struck Death; The Valley of the Mist; (Untitled) • Hurricane **A:** Joe Simon; Jack Kirby

3 ❑ May 1941 Cover: 0.10 **NM** value: **9000.00**
• **CGC:** 8 graded, best 9.4
📖 The Return of the Red Skull; Hunchback of Hollywood and the Movie Murder; The Queer Case of the Murdering Butterfly and the Ancient Mummies; Amazing Spy Adventures; Captain America Foils the Traitor's Revenge (Text) • First Stan Lee work at Marvel **A:** Joe Simon; Jack Kirby

4 ❑ Jun 1941 Cover: 0.10 **NM** value: **5500.00**
• **CGC:** 5 graded, best 8.0
📖 Captain America and the Unholy Legion; Captain America and Ivan the Terrible; The Case of the Fake Money Fiends; Captain America in Horror Hospital; Bomb Sight Thieves **A:** Joe Simon; Jack Kirby

5 ❑ Aug 1941 Cover: 0.10 **NM** value: **5000.00**
• **CGC:** 6 graded, best 8.0
📖 Captain America and the Ringmaster of Death; The Gruesome Secret of the Dragon of Death; Killers of the Bund; The Terror that was Devil's Island **A:** Joe Simon; Jack Kirby

6 ❑ Sep 1941 Cover: 0.10 **NM** value: **4500.00**
• **CGC:** 3 graded, best 5.5
📖 Captain America Battles the Camera Fiend and His Darts of Doom; Meet the Fang, Arch Fiend of the Orient; The Strange Case of Captain America and the Hangman: Who Killed Dr. Vardoff? **A:** Joe Simon; Jack Kirby

7 ❑ Oct 1941 Cover: 0.10 **NM** value: **5000.00**
• **CGC:** 5 graded, best 9.0
Red Skull cover. 📖 Captain America and the Red Skull; Death Loads the Bases; Horror Plays the Scales **A:** Joe Simon; Jack Kirby

8 ❑ Nov 1941 Cover: 0.10 **NM** value: **3500.00**
• **CGC:** 3 graded, best 7.5
📖 The Strange Mystery of the Ruby of the Nile and It's Heritage of Horror; Murder Stalks the Maneuvers; Case of the Black Witch **A:** Joe Simon; Jack Kirby

9 ❑ Dec 1941 Cover: 0.10 **NM** value: **3500.00**
• **CGC:** 2 graded, best 5.0
📖 Captain America and the White Death; Captain America and the Man Who Could Not Die; The Case of the Black Talon **A:** Joe Simon; Jack Kirby

10 ❑ Jan 1942 Cover: 0.10 **NM** value: **3500.00**
• **CGC:** 8 graded, best 9.0
📖 Captain America: A Personal Account of His Smashing a Spy Ambush; Hotel of Horror; The Phantom Hound of Cardiff Moor; Father Time **A:** Joe Simon; Jack Kirby

11 ❑ Feb 1942 Cover: 0.10 **NM** value: **3000.00**
• **CGC:** 3 graded, best 6.5
A: Al Avison

12 ❑ Mar 1942 Cover: 0.10 **NM** value: **3000.00**
• **CGC:** 2 graded, best 6.5
A: Al Avison

13 ❑ Apr 1942 Cover: 0.10 **NM** value: **3200.00**
• **CGC:** 2 graded, best 7.0
A: Al Avison

14 ❑ May 1942 Cover: 0.10 **NM** value: **3000.00**
• **CGC:** 4 graded, best 7.5
A: Al Avison

15 ❑ Jun 1942 Cover: 0.10 **NM** value: **3000.00**
• **CGC:** 3 graded, best 9.0
A: Al Avison

16 ❑ Jul 1942 Cover: 0.10 **NM** value: **3500.00**
• **CGC:** 3 graded, best 6.5
• Red Skull unmasks Captain America **A:** Al Avison

17 ❑ Aug 1942 Cover: 0.10 **NM** value: **2500.00**
• **CGC:** 6 graded, best 9.2
A: Al Avison

18 ❑ Sep 1942 Cover: 0.10 **NM** value: **2000.00**
• **CGC:** 2 graded, best 7.0
A: Al Avison ★ Appearance of Human Torch.

19 ❑ Oct 1942 Cover: 0.10 **NM** value: **2000.00**
• **CGC:** 6 graded, best 8.5
A: Al Avison ★ Appearance of Human Torch.

20 ❑ Nov 1942 Cover: 0.10 **NM** value: **2000.00**
• **CGC:** 2 graded, best 8.5
A: Al Avison ★ Appearance of Sub-Mariner.

21 ❑ Dec 1942 Cover: 0.10 **NM** value: **1800.00**
• **CGC:** 2 graded, best 7.0

22 ❑ Jan 1943 Cover: 0.10 **NM** value: **1800.00**
• **CGC:** 2 graded, best 8.0

22/A❑ Jan 1943 Cover: 0.10 **NM** value: **12000.00**
• 1942 giant-size issue (cover from Captain America #22, contents from Captain America #18 and Marvel .

23 ❑ Feb 1943 Cover: 0.10 **NM** value: **1800.00**
• **CGC:** 4 graded, best 9.0

24 ❑ Mar 1943 Cover: 0.10 **NM** value: **1800.00**
• **CGC:** 1 graded, best 7.5

25 ❑ Apr 1943 Cover: 0.10 **NM** value: **1800.00**
• **CGC:** 3 graded, best 9.4

26 ❑ May 1943 Cover: 0.10 **NM** value: **1600.00**
• **CGC:** 4 graded, best 8.5

27 ❑ Jun 1943 Cover: 0.10 **NM** value: **1600.00**
• **CGC:** 1 graded, best 7.0

28 ❑ Jul 1943 Cover: 0.10 **NM** value: **1600.00**

29 ❑ Aug 1943 Cover: 0.10 **NM** value: **1600.00**
• **CGC:** 1 graded, best 8.0

30 ❑ Sep 1943 Cover: 0.10 **NM** value: **1600.00**
• **CGC:** 6 graded, best 9.0

31 ❑ Oct 1943 Cover: 0.10 **NM** value: **1350.00**
• **CGC:** 1 graded, best 4.0

32 ❑ Nov 1943 Cover: 0.10 **NM** value: **1350.00**
• **CGC:** 4 graded, best 8.5

33 ❑ Dec 1943 Cover: 0.10 **NM** value: **1350.00**
• **CGC:** 2 graded, best 9.2

34 ❑ Jan 1944 Cover: 0.10 **NM** value: **1350.00**
• **CGC:** 2 graded, best 8.0

35 ❑ Feb 1944 Cover: 0.10 **NM** value: **1350.00**
• **CGC:** 2 graded, best 4.0

36 ❑ Mar 1944 Cover: 0.10 **NM** value: **1600.00**
• **CGC:** 2 graded, best 7.5
Hitler cover.

37 ❑ Apr 1944 Cover: 0.10 **NM** value: **1500.00**
• **CGC:** 2 graded, best 9.4
★ Appearance of Red Skull.

38 ❑ May 1944 Cover: 0.10 **NM** value: **1250.00**

39 ❑ Jun 1944 Cover: 0.10 **NM** value: **1250.00**
• **CGC:** 2 graded, best 9.0

40 ❑ Jul 1944 Cover: 0.10 **NM** value: **1250.00**
• **CGC:** 3 graded, best 8.5

41 ❑ Aug 1944 Cover: 0.10 **NM** value: **1150.00**
• **CGC:** 5 graded, best 9.6

42 ❑ Oct 1944 Cover: 0.10 **NM** value: **1150.00**
• **CGC:** 4 graded, best 8.0

43 ❑ Dec 1944 Cover: 0.10 **NM** value: **1150.00**
• **CGC:** 1 graded, best 9.2

44 ❑ Jan 1945 Cover: 0.10 **NM** value: **1150.00**
• **CGC:** 3 graded, best 9.2

45 ❑ Mar 1945 Cover: 0.10 **NM** value: **1150.00**
• **CGC:** 1 graded, best 3.5

46 ❑ Apr 1945 Cover: 0.10 **NM** value: **1150.00**
• **CGC:** 4 graded, best 9.2

47 ❑ Jun 1945 Cover: 0.10 **NM** value: **1150.00**
• **CGC:** 4 graded, best 9.0

48 ❑ Jul 1945 Cover: 0.10 **NM** value: **1150.00**
• **CGC:** 3 graded, best 9.0

49 ❑ Aug 1945 Cover: 0.10 **NM** value: **1150.00**
• **CGC:** 1 graded, best 6.5

50 ❑ Oct 1945 Cover: 0.10 **NM** value: **1150.00**
• **CGC:** 6 graded, best 9.0

51 ❑ Dec 1945 Cover: 0.10 **NM** value: **1150.00**
• **CGC:** 9 graded, best 9.2

52 ❑ Jan 1946 Cover: 0.10 **NM** value: **1150.00**
• **CGC:** 8 graded, best 9.0

53 ❑ Feb 1946 Cover: 0.10 **NM** value: **1150.00**
• **CGC:** 4 graded, best 9.2

54 ❑ Mar 1946 Cover: 0.10 **NM** value: **1150.00**
• **CGC:** 1 graded, best 3.0

55 ❑ Apr 1946 Cover: 0.10 **NM** value: **1150.00**
• **CGC:** 1 graded, best 8.0

56 ❑ May 1946 Cover: 0.10 **NM** value: **1150.00**
• **CGC:** 6 graded, best 9.2

57 ❑ Jul 1946 Cover: 0.10 **NM** value: **1150.00**
• **CGC:** 3 graded, best 9.6

58 ❑ Sep 1946 Cover: 0.10 **NM** value: **1150.00**
• **CGC:** 3 graded, best 9.4

59 ❑ Nov 1946 Cover: 0.10 **NM** value: **2500.00**
• **CGC:** 7 graded, best 9.4
📖 The Private Life of Captain America ★ Origin of Captain America I (Steve Rogers).

60 ❑ Jan 1947 Cover: 0.10 **NM** value: **1150.00**
• **CGC:** 1 graded, best 6.0

61 ❑ Mar 1947 Cover: 0.10 **NM** value: **1800.00**
• **CGC:** 3 graded, best 9.0
Red Skull cover.

62 ❑ May 1947 Cover: 0.10 **NM** value: **1050.00**
• **CGC:** 4 graded, best 9.2

63 ❑ Jul 1947 Cover: 0.10 **NM** value: **1050.00**
• **CGC:** 4 graded, best 9.2

64 ❑ Oct 1947 Cover: 0.10 **NM** value: **1050.00**
• **CGC:** 2 graded, best 8.5

65 ❑ Jan 1948 Cover: 0.10 **NM** value: **1050.00**
• **CGC:** 4 graded, best 8.5

66 ❑ Apr 1948 Cover: 0.10 **NM** value: **1250.00**
• **CGC:** 3 graded, best 6.5
★ Origin of Golden Girl.

67 ❑ Jul 1948 Cover: 0.10 **NM** value: **1150.00**
• **CGC:** 2 graded, best 6.5

68 ❑ Sep 1948 Cover: 0.10 **NM** value: **1150.00**

69 ❑ Nov 1948 Cover: 0.10 **NM** value: **1150.00**
📖 The Golden Girl

70 ❑ Jan 1949 Cover: 0.10 **NM** value: **1150.00**
• **CGC:** 1 graded, best 6.5
📖 Worlds at War

71 ❑ Mar 1949 Cover: 0.10 **NM** value: **1000.00**
• **CGC:** 1 graded, best 5.5
📖 Trapped

72 ❑ May 1949 Cover: 0.10 **NM** value: **1000.00**

73 ❑ Jul 1949 Cover: 0.10 **NM** value: **1000.00**
• **CGC:** 3 graded, best 6.5
📖 The Outcast of Time

74 ❑ Oct 1949 Cover: 0.10 **NM** value: **3500.00**
• **CGC:** 4 graded, best 6.5
📖 The Red Skull Strikes Again • Title: "Captain America Weird Tales"

75 ❑ Feb 1950 Cover: 0.10 **NM** value: **2000.00**
• **CGC:** 6 graded, best 8.5
📖 The Thing in the Chest • Title: "Captain America Weird Tales"

76 ❑ May 1954 Cover: 0.10 **NM** value: **850.00**
• **CGC:** 2 graded, best 7.5
📖 Captain America Strikes; The Betrayers

77 ❑ Jul 1954 Cover: 0.10 **NM** value: **850.00**

78 ❑ Sep 1954 Cover: 0.10 **NM** value: **850.00**
• **CGC:** 2 graded, best 7.5
final issue.

CAPTAIN AMERICA: DEATHLOK LIVES! Marvel

1 ❑ Cover: 4.95 **NM** value: **Cover or less**
📖 One Man in Search of Himself • Reprints from Captain America #286-288 **A:** Mike Zeck **W:** J.M. DeMatteis

CAPTAIN AMERICA: DRUG WAR Marvel

1 ❑ Apr 1993 Cover: 2.00 **NM** value: **Cover or less**
Circ: CapCity orders: **14,900**

CAPTAIN AMERICA GOES TO WAR AGAINST DRUGS Marvel

1 ❑ ca. 1990 **NM** value: **1.00**
• **CGC:** 1 graded, best 8.0
No issue number. • Anti-drug giveaway. 📖 High Heat **A:** Sal Velluto **W:** Peter David

CAPTAIN AMERICA: MEDUSA EFFECT Marvel

1 ❑ Mar 1994 Cover: 2.95 **NM** value: **Cover or less**
Circ: CapCity orders: **10,700**
📖 The Medusa Effect **A:** Rich Buckler; M.C. Wyman **W:** Roy Thomas

CAPTAIN AMERICA/NICK FURY: BLOOD TRUCE Marvel

1 ❑ Feb 1995 Cover: 5.95 **NM** value: **Cover or less**
• prestige format one-shot **A:** Andrew Currie **W:** Howard Chaykin; Ben Schwartz

CAPTAIN AMERICA/NICK FURY: OTHERWORLD WAR Marvel

1 ❑ Cover: 6.95 **NM** value: **Cover or less**

CAPTAIN AMERICA (POCKET BOOKS) Marvel

Bk 1❑ Cover: 2.25 **NM** value: **Cover or less**
Circ: CapCity orders: **10,150**
• (Pocket Books 1979)

Bk 1/HC❑ Cover: 3.95 **NM** value: **Cover or less**
hardcover.

CAPTAIN AMERICA: SENTINEL OF LIBERTY Marvel

Much like Batman: Legends of the Dark Knight, Captain America: Sentinel of Liberty examines various parts of Cap's past from World War II to the present. The short-lived series (perhaps the abbreviation of the subtitle was an indication of its chances?) featured an Invaders story set during World War II co-starring Sub-Mariner and The Human Torch, a 1960s-based story co-starring The Falcon right after he donned Cap's costume to escape a police barricade, and a modern-day story featuring Cap fighting alongside the forces of S.H.I.E.L.D. Some of the stories were poignant, some were silly, but all served to give more insight into what makes Cap the hero that he is. — Brent

1 ❑ Sep 1998 Cover: 1.99 **NM** value: **2.25**
Circ: Diamd. preorders: **89,412**
wraparound cover. • gatefold summary. 📖 Sentinel of Liberty **A:** Ron Garney **W:** Ron Garney; Mark Waid

1/SC❑ Sep 1988 Cover: 2.99 **NM** value: **3.00**
Circ: Diamd. preorders: **10,553**
• Roughcut edition. 📖 Sentinel of Liberty **A:** Ron Garney

2 ❑ Oct 1998 Cover: 1.99 **NM** value: **2.00**
Circ: Diamd. preorders: **79,632**
• gatefold summary. • Invaders **A:** Ron Garney **W:** Ron Garney; Mark Waid

3 ❑ Nov 1998 Cover: 1.99 **NM** value: **2.00**
Circ: Diamd. preorders: **61,835**
• gatefold summary. • Invaders **A:** Ron Garney **W:** Ron Garney; Mark Waid

4 ❑ Dec 1998 Cover: 1.99 **NM** value: **2.00**
Circ: Diamd. preorders: **55,720**
• gatefold summary. • Invaders **A:** Ron Garney **W:** Ron Garney; Mark Waid

5 ❑ Jan 1999 Cover: 1.99 **NM** value: **2.00**
Circ: Diamd. preorders: **49,731**
• gatefold summary. 📖 Tales of Suspense, Part 1 • Tales of Suspense tribute **A:** Ron Garney; Ron Frenz; Dougie Braithwaite **W:** Mark Waid ★ Appearance of S.H.I.E.L.D., Iron Man.

6 ❑ Feb 1999 Cover: 2.99 **NM** value: **Cover or less**
Circ: Diamd. preorders: **45,456**
• double-sized. 📖 Tales of Suspense, Part 2 • Tales of Suspense tribute **A:** Ron Garney; Dougie Braithwaite **W:** Roger Stern; Mark Waid ★ Appearance of Iron Man.

7 ❑ Mar 1999 Cover: 1.99 **NM** value: **2.00**
Circ: Diamd. preorders: **41,498**
• Bicentennial story **A:** Roger Langridge; Ron Frenz **W:** Roger Stern; Vaughan

8 ❑ Apr 1999 Cover: 1.99 **NM** value: **2.00**
Circ: Diamd. preorders: **38,414**
📖 Flashpoint **A:** Cully Hamner **W:** Mark Waid ★ Appearance of Sam Wilson, Falcon.

9 ❑ May 1999 Cover: 1.99 **NM** value: **2.00**
Circ: Diamd. preorders: **35,732**
★ Appearance of Falcon.

10 ❑ Jun 1999 Cover: 1.99 **NM** value: **2.00**
Circ: Diamd. preorders: **34,349**
★ Appearance of Dino Manelli. ★ Versus M.O.D.O.K..

11 ❑ Jul 1999 Cover: 1.99 **NM** value: **2.00**
Circ: Diamd. preorders: **33,050**
★ Versus Human Torch.

Other grades: Multiply prices above by **1.5 for Mint • 2/3 for Very Fine • 1/3 for Fine • 1/5 for Very Good • 1/8 for Good**

12 ❑ Aug 1999 Cover: 2.99 **NM** value: **3.00**
Circ: Diamd. preorders: **31,868**
final issue. ★ Appearance of Bucky.

CAPTAIN AMERICA: SENTINEL OF LIBERTY (NOVEL) Marvel

Bk 1❑ **NM** value: **5.00**
• (Fireside)

CAPTAIN AMERICA: THE LEGEND Marvel

1 ❑ Sep 1996 Cover: 3.95 **NM** value: **Cover or less**
wraparound cover. • background on Cap and his supporting cast

CAPTAIN AMERICA: THE MOVIE SPECIAL Marvel

1 ❑ Cover: 3.50 **NM** value: **Cover or less**
Circ: CapCity orders: **15,100**
No issue number.

CAPTAIN AMERICA (VOL. 1) Marvel

When World War II began, Steve Rogers attempted to enlist in the army, but was turned away because he was considered too frail. Wanting to help any way he could, he offered to serve as a human guinea pig for the experimental Super Soldier Serum. The formula worked, transforming this former 98-pound weakling into the powerhouse known as Captain America.

A star of the Golden Age of comics, Captain America joined the Silver Age when he was revived in The Avengers #4. He soon became the leader of that team, as well as co-starring with Iron Man in Tales of Suspense. Following issue #99, Tales of Suspense spun Iron Man off into a new title, and changed its name to Captain America.

The series ran uninterrupted for years, with writer Mark Gruenwald redefining the series in the 1980s and early 1990s. Writer Mark Waid was returning attention to the title when Marvel booted him off and ended the series to make way for Rob Liefeld's "Heroes Reborn" version.

100 ❑ Apr 1968 Cover: 0.12 **NM** value: **250.00**
Circ: Statement: **273,476** • **CGC:** 214 graded, best 9.9
🕮 This Monster Unmasked • Series continued from Tales of Suspense #99; Has 1967 Statement, filed 10/1/67; avg print run 447,949; avg sales 256,242; avg subs 1,100; avg total paid 257,342; samples 95; max existent 257,437; 43% of run returned **A:** Jack Kirby ★ Appearance of Avengers.

101 ❑ May 1968 Cover: 0.12 **NM** value: **50.00**
Circ: Statement: **273,476** • **CGC:** 39 graded, best 9.6
🕮 When Wakes the Sleeper **A:** Jack Kirby ★ 1st Appearance of 4th Sleeper.

102 ❑ Jun 1968 Cover: 0.12 **NM** value: **35.00**
Circ: Statement: **273,476** • **CGC:** 30 graded, best 9.8
🕮 The Sleeper Strikes **A:** Jack Kirby

103 ❑ Jul 1968 Cover: 0.12 **NM** value: **35.00**
Circ: Statement: **273,476** • **CGC:** 21 graded, best 9.6
🕮 The Weakest Link • Agent 13's identity revealed as Sharon Carter **A:** Jack Kirby ★ Appearance of Red Skull.

104 ❑ Aug 1968 Cover: 0.12 **NM** value: **35.00**
Circ: Statement: **273,476** • **CGC:** 24 graded, best 9.8
🕮 Slave of the Skull **A:** Jack Kirby ★ Versus Red Skull.

105 ❑ Sep 1968 Cover: 0.12 **NM** value: **35.00**
Circ: Statement: **273,476** • **CGC:** 20 graded, best 9.8
🕮 In the Name of Batroc **A:** Jack Kirby ★ Versus Batroc.

106 ❑ Oct 1968 Cover: 0.12 **NM** value: **35.00**
Circ: Statement: **273,476** • **CGC:** 26 graded, best 9.8
🕮 Cap Goes Wild! **A:** Jack Kirby **W:** Stan Lee

107 ❑ Nov 1968 Cover: 0.12 **NM** value: **35.00**
Circ: Statement: **273,476** • **CGC:** 18 graded, best 9.6
🕮 If the Past Be Not Dead ... **A:** Jack Kirby **W:** Stan Lee ★ 1st Appearance of Dr. Faustus, Doctor Faustus. ★ Appearance of Red Skull.

108 ❑ Dec 1968 Cover: 0.12 **NM** value: **35.00**
Circ: Statement: **273,476** • **CGC:** 34 graded, best 9.8
🕮 The Snares of the Trapster **A:** Jack Kirby

109 ❑ Jan 1969 Cover: 0.12 **NM** value: **40.00**
Circ: Statement: **243,798** • **CGC:** 66 graded, best 9.8
🕮 The Hero that Was! **A:** Jack Kirby **W:** Stan Lee ★ Origin of Captain America.

109-2❑ Cover: 0.12 **NM** value: **2.00**
• **CGC:** 1 graded, best 8.5

110 ❑ Feb 1969 Cover: 0.12 **NM** value: **45.00**
Circ: Statement: **243,798** • **CGC:** 37 graded, best 9.8
🕮 No Longer Alone • Rick Jones dons Bucky costume **A:** Jim Steranko ★ 1st Appearance of Viper II (as Madame Hydra), Viper. ★ Appearance of Hulk, Rick Jones.

111 ❑ Mar 1969 Cover: 0.12 **NM** value: **40.00**
Circ: Statement: **243,798** • **CGC:** 39 graded, best 9.6
🕮 Tomorrow You Live, Tonight I Die **A:** Jim Steranko

112 ❑ Apr 1969 Cover: 0.12 **NM** value: **30.00**
Circ: Statement: **243,798** • **CGC:** 9 graded, best 9.8
🕮 Lest We Forget • album; Has 1968 Statement, filed 10/1/68; avg print run 425,200; avg sales 272,186; avg subs 1,290; avg total paid 273,476; samples 400; max existent 273,876; 36% of run returned **A:** George Tuska; Jack Kirby ★ Origin of Viper II (as Madame Hydra), Captain America.

113 ❑ May 1969 Cover: 0.12 **NM** value: **40.00**
Circ: Statement: **243,798** • **CGC:** 30 graded, best 9.8
🕮 The Strange Death of Captain America • Avengers **A:** Jim Steranko

114 ❑ Jun 1969 Cover: 0.12 **NM** value: **16.00**
Circ: Statement: **243,798** • **CGC:** 6 graded, best 9.8
🕮 The Man Behind the Mask **A:** John Romita

115 ❑ Jul 1969 Cover: 0.12 **NM** value: **16.00**
Circ: Statement: **243,798** • **CGC:** 12 graded, best 9.6
🕮 Now Begins the Nightmare

116 ❑ Aug 1969 Cover: 0.15 **NM** value: **16.00**
Circ: Statement: **243,798** • **CGC:** 5 graded, best 9.6
🕮 Far Worse than Death

117 ❑ Sep 1969 Cover: 0.15 **NM** value: **35.00**
Circ: Statement: **243,798** • **CGC:** 12 graded, best 9.4
🕮 The Coming of the Falcon **A:** Gene Colan; Joe Sinnott ★ 1st Appearance of Falcon.

118 ❑ Oct 1969 Cover: 0.15 **NM** value: **14.00**
Circ: Statement: **243,798** • **CGC:** 2 graded, best 9.4
🕮 The Falcon Fights On **A:** Gene Colan; Joe Sinnott **W:** Stan Lee ★ Appearance of Falcon.

119 ❑ Nov 1969 Cover: 0.15 **NM** value: **14.00**
Circ: Statement: **243,798** • **CGC:** 4 graded, best 9.6
🕮 Now Falls The Skull **A:** Gene Colan; Joe Sinnott **W:** Stan Lee ★ Appearance of Falcon.

120 ❑ Dec 1969 Cover: 0.15 **NM** value: **14.00**
Circ: Statement: **243,798** • **CGC:** 4 graded, best 9.4
🕮 Crack Up On Campus **A:** Gene Colan; Joe Sinnott **W:** Stan Lee ★ Appearance of Falcon.

121 ❑ Jan 1970 Cover: 0.15 **NM** value: **10.00**
Circ: Statement: **225,651** • **CGC:** 3 graded, best 9.0
🕮 The Coming Of The Man-Brute **A:** Gene Colan **W:** Stan Lee ★ Origin of Captain America.

122 ❑ Feb 1970 Cover: 0.15 **NM** value: **9.00**
Circ: Statement: **225,651** • **CGC:** 1 graded, best 9.4
🕮 The Sting Of The Scorpion **A:** Gene Colan **W:** Stan Lee

123 ❑ Mar 1970 Cover: 0.15 **NM** value: **9.00**
Circ: Statement: **225,651** • **CGC:** 4 graded, best 9.4
🕮 Suprema, The Deadliest Of The Species **A:** Gene Colan **W:** Stan Lee ★ 1st Appearance of Suprema (later becomes Mother Night).

124 ❑ Apr 1970 Cover: 0.15 **NM** value: **9.00**
Circ: Statement: **225,651** • **CGC:** 2 graded, best 8.0
🕮 Mission: Stop The Cyborg • Has 1969 Statement; avg print run 421,644; avg sales 241,518; avg subs 1,280; avg total paid 243,798; samples 110; max existent 242,908; 42% of run returned **A:** Gene Colan **W:** Stan Lee

125 ❑ May 1970 Cover: 0.15 **NM** value: **9.00**
Circ: Statement: **225,651** • **CGC:** 4 graded, best 9.0
🕮 Captured In Vietnam **A:** Gene Colan **W:** Stan Lee

126 ❑ Jun 1970 Cover: 0.15 **NM** value: **9.00**
Circ: Statement: **225,651** • **CGC:** 2 graded, best 9.6
🕮 The Fate of ... the Falcon! **A:** Gene Colan **W:** Stan Lee ★ 1st Appearance of Diamond Head. ★ Appearance of Falcon.

127 ❑ Jul 1970 Cover: 0.15 **NM** value: **9.00**
Circ: Statement: **225,651** • **CGC:** 2 graded, best 7.5
🕮 Who Calls Me Traitor? **A:** Gene Colan **W:** Stan Lee

128 ❑ Aug 1970 Cover: 0.15 **NM** value: **9.00**
Circ: Statement: **225,651** • **CGC:** 1 graded, best 9.2
🕮 Mission: Stamp Out Satan's Angels! **A:** Gene Colan **W:** Stan Lee

129 ❑ Sep 1970 Cover: 0.15 **NM** value: **9.00**
Circ: Statement: **225,651** • **CGC:** 3 graded, best 9.0
🕮 The Vengeance Of The Red Skull **A:** Gene Colan **W:** Stan Lee

130 ❑ Oct 1970 Cover: 0.15 **NM** value: **9.00**
Circ: Statement: **225,651** • **CGC:** 4 graded, best 9.4
🕮 Up Against The Wall! **A:** Gene Colan **W:** Stan Lee

131 ❑ Nov 1970 Cover: 0.15 **NM** value: **8.00**
Circ: Statement: **225,651** • **CGC:** 22 graded, best 9.6
🕮 Bucky Reborn **A:** Gene Colan **W:** Stan Lee

132 ❑ Dec 1970 Cover: 0.15 **NM** value: **8.00**
Circ: Statement: **225,651** • **CGC:** 6 graded, best 9.4
🕮 The Fearful Secret of Bucky Barnes **A:** Gene Colan **W:** Stan Lee

133 ❑ Jan 1971 Cover: 0.15 **NM** value: **8.00**
Circ: Statement: **209,315** • **CGC:** 40 graded, best 9.8
🕮 Madness In The Slums! • Falcon becomes Captain America's partner **A:** Gene Colan **W:** Stan Lee ★ Origin of M.O.D.O.K..

134 ❑ Feb 1971 Cover: 0.15 **NM** value: **8.00**
Circ: Statement: **209,315** • **CGC:** 2 graded, best 9.4
🕮 They Call Him Stoneface **A:** Gene Colan **W:** Stan Lee

135 ❑ Mar 1971 Cover: 0.15 **NM** value: **8.00**
Circ: Statement: **209,315** • **CGC:** 20 graded, best 9.6
🕮 More Monster Than Man! **A:** Gene Colan **C:** John Romita **W:** Stan Lee

136 ❑ Apr 1971 Cover: 0.15 **NM** value: **8.00**
Circ: Statement: **209,315** • **CGC:** 1 graded, best 7.0
🕮 The World Below • Has 1970 Statement; avg print run 395,862; avg sales 224,651; avg subs 1,000; avg total paid 225,651; samples 0; office use 110; max existent 225,761; 43% of run returned **A:** Gene Colan **W:** Stan Lee

137 ❑ May 1971 Cover: 0.15 **NM** value: **8.00**
Circ: Statement: **209,315** • **CGC:** 3 graded, best 9.6
🕮 To Stalk the Spider-Man **A:** Gene Colan; Bill Everett ★ Appearance of Spider-Man.

138 ❑ Jun 1971 Cover: 0.15 **NM** value: **8.00**
Circ: Statement: **209,315** • **CGC:** 3 graded, best 9.4
🕮 It Happens in Harlem **A:** John Romita ★ Appearance of Spider-Man.

139 ❑ Jul 1971 Cover: 0.15 **NM** value: **8.00**
Circ: Statement: **209,315**
🕮 The Badge And The Betrayal! **A:** Gene Colan; John Romita **W:** Stan Lee

140 ❑ Aug 1971 Cover: 0.15 **NM** value: **8.00**
Circ: Statement: **209,315** • **CGC:** 1 graded, best 9.2
🕮 In the Grip of Gargoyle **A:** John Romita ★ Origin of Grey Gargoyle.

141 ❑ Sep 1971 Cover: 0.15 **NM** value: **6.00**
Circ: Statement: **209,315**
🕮 The Unholy Alliance! **A:** John Romita **W:** Stan Lee

142 ❑ Oct 1971 Cover: 0.15 **NM** value: **6.00**
Circ: Statement: **209,315**
🕮 And In The End... **A:** John Romita **W:** Gary Friedrich ★ Versus Grey Gargoyle.

143 ❑ Nov 1971 Cover: 0.25 **NM** value: **6.00**
Circ: Statement: **209,315** • **CGC:** 3 graded, best 9.6
• Giant-size. 🕮 Power To The People **A:** John Romita **W:** Gary Friedrich

144 ❑ Dec 1971 Cover: 0.20 **NM** value: **6.00**
Circ: Statement: **209,315**
🕮 Hydra Over All **A:** John Romita **W:** Gary Friedrich

145 ❑ Jan 1972 Cover: 0.20 **NM** value: **6.00**
Circ: Statement: **178,193** • **CGC:** 2 graded, best 9.6
🕮 Skyjacked! **A:** Gil Kane **W:** Gary Friedrich

146 ❑ Feb 1972 Cover: 0.20 **NM** value: **6.00**
Circ: Statement: **178,193**
🕮 Mission: Destroy The Femme Force! **A:** Sal Buscema **W:** Gary Friedrich

147 ❑ Mar 1972 Cover: 0.20 **NM** value: **6.00**
Circ: Statement: **178,193**
🕮 And Behold the Hordes of Hydra

148 ❑ Apr 1972 Cover: 0.20 **NM** value: **6.00**
Circ: Statement: **178,193** • **CGC:** 2 graded, best 9.4
🕮 The Big Sleep

149 ❑ May 1972 Cover: 0.20 **NM** value: **6.00**
Circ: Statement: **178,193**
🕮 All The Colors...Of Evil • Has 1971 Statement, filed 9/23/71; avg print run 359,217; avg sales 208,390; avg subs 925; avg total paid 209,315; samples 110; office use 1,630; max existent 211,055; 41% of run returned **A:** Sal Buscema **W:** Gerry Conway

150 ❑ Jun 1972 Cover: 0.20 **NM** value: **6.00**
Circ: Statement: **178,193**
🕮 Mirror, Mirror

151 ❑ Jul 1972 Cover: 0.20 **NM** value: **6.00**
Circ: Statement: **178,193** • **CGC:** 1 graded, best 9.0
🕮 Panic on Park Avenue

152 ❑ Aug 1972 Cover: 0.20 **NM** value: **6.00**
Circ: Statement: **178,193**
🕮 Terror In The Night! **A:** Sal Buscema **W:** Gerry Conway

153 ❑ Sep 1972 Cover: 0.20 **NM** value: **6.00**
Circ: Statement: **178,193**
🕮 Captain America: Hero or Hoax? ★ 1st Appearance of Bucky III (Jack Monroe). ★ 1st Appearance of Captain America IV. ★ Versus Red Skull.

154 ❑ Oct 1972 Cover: 0.20 **NM** value: **6.00**
Circ: Statement: **178,193**
🕮 The Falcon Fights Alone

155 ❑ Nov 1972 Cover: 0.20 **NM** value: **6.00**
Circ: Statement: **178,193**
🕮 The Incredible Origin Of The Other Captain America! **A:** Sal Buscema **W:** Steve Englehart ★ Origin of Captain America II (Jack Monroe), Captain America.

156 ❑ Dec 1972 Cover: 0.20 **NM** value: **6.00**
Circ: Statement: **178,193**
🕮 One into Two Won't Go

157 ❑ Jan 1973 Cover: 0.20 **NM** value: **6.00**
Circ: Statement: **175,738**
🕮 Veni, Vidi, Vici, Viper

158 ❑ Feb 1973 Cover: 0.20 **NM** value: **6.00**
Circ: Statement: **175,738**
🕮 The Crime Wave Breaks

159 ❑ Mar 1973 Cover: 0.20 **NM** value: **6.00**
Circ: Statement: **175,738**
🕮 Turning Point • Has 1972 Statement, filed 9/21/72; avg print run 349,714; avg sales 177,204; avg subs 989; avg total paid 178,193; samples 110; office use 1,128; max existent 179,431; 51% of run returned

160 ❑ Apr 1973 Cover: 0.20 **NM** value: **6.00**
Circ: Statement: **175,738**
🕮 Enter: Solarr ★ 1st Appearance of Solarr.

161 ❑ May 1973 Cover: 0.20 **NM** value: **5.00**
Circ: Statement: **175,738**
🕮 ...If He Loseth His Soul! **A:** Sal Buscema **W:** Steve Englehart

162 ❑ Jun 1973 Cover: 0.20 **NM** value: **5.00**
Circ: Statement: **175,738** • **CGC:** 1 graded, best 7.0
🕮 This Way Lies Madness! **A:** Sal Buscema **W:** Steve Englehart ★ Origin of Sharon Carter.

163 ❑ Jul 1973 Cover: 0.20 **NM** value: **5.00**
Circ: Statement: **175,738** • **CGC:** 1 graded, best 7.5
🕮 Beware Of Serpents! **A:** Sal Buscema **W:** Steve Englehart ★ 1st Appearance of Dave Cox.

164 ❑ Aug 1973 Cover: 0.20 **NM** value: **5.00**
Circ: Statement: **175,738**
🕮 Queen Of The Werewolves! **A:** Alan Weiss **W:** Steve Englehart ★ 1st Appearance of Nightshade.

165 ❑ Sep 1973 Cover: 0.20 **NM** value: **5.00**
Circ: Statement: **175,738**
🕮 The Yellow Claw Strikes **A:** Sal Buscema **W:** Steve Englehart

166 ❑ Oct 1973 Cover: 0.20 **NM** value: **5.00**
Circ: Statement: **175,738**
🕮 Night Of the Lurking Dead! **A:** Sal Buscema **W:** Steve Englehart

167 ❑ Nov 1973 Cover: 0.20 **NM** value: **5.00**
Circ: Statement: **175,738**
🕮 Ashes To Ashes **A:** Sal Buscema **W:** Steve Englehart

168 ❑ Dec 1973 Cover: 0.20 **NM** value: **5.00**
Circ: Statement: **175,738**
🕮 ...And A Phoenix Shall Arise **A:** Sal Buscema **W:** Roy Thomas; Tony Isabella ★ 1st Appearance of Phoenix I (Helmut Zemo). ★ Appearance of Baron Zemo (Helmut). ★ Death of Phoenix I (Helmut Zemo).

169 ❑ Jan 1974 Cover: 0.20 **NM** value: **5.00**
Circ: Statement: **183,344**
🕮 When a Legend Dies ★ 1st Appearance of Moonstone I (Lloyd Bloch)-cameo.

170 ❑ Feb 1974 Cover: 0.20 **NM** value: **5.00**
Circ: Statement: **183,344**
🕮 J'Accuse! **A:** Sal Buscema **W:** Mike Friedrich ★ 1st Appearance of Moonstone I (Lloyd Bloch)-full.

171 ❑ Mar 1974 Cover: 0.20 **NM** value: **5.00**
Circ: Statement: **183,344**
🕮 Bust Out!

172 ❑ Apr 1974 Cover: 0.20 **NM** value: **9.00**
Circ: Statement: **183,344**
🕮 Believe It or Not: The Banshee **A:** Sal Buscema ★ Appearance of X-Men, Banshee.

173 ❑ May 1974 Cover: 0.25 **NM** value: **9.00**
Circ: Statement: **183,344** • **CGC:** 2 graded, best 9.4

CGC-graded: Multiply prices above by **33 for 9.9 M** • **16 for 9.8 NM/M** • **7 for 9.6 NM+** • **5 for 9.4 NM** • **2.5 for 9.2 NM-** • **1.5 for 9.0 VF/NM**

The Sins Of The Secret Empire! • Has 1973 Statement; avg sales 174,934; avg subs 804; avg total paid circ 175,738 **A:** Sal Buscema **W:** Steve Englehart ★ Appearance of X-Men.

174 ❑ Jun 1974 Cover: 0.25 **NM** value: **9.00**
Circ: Statement: **183,344 • CGC:** 2 graded, best 9.4
It's Always Darkest… **A:** Sal Buscema ★ Appearance of X-Men.

175 ❑ Jul 1974 Cover: 0.25 **NM** value: **9.00**
Circ: Statement: **183,344**
…Before the Dawn **A:** Sal Buscema ★ Appearance of X-Men.

176 ❑ Aug 1974 Cover: 0.25 **NM** value: **6.00**
Circ: Statement: **183,344**
Captain America Must Die **A:** Sal Buscema

177 ❑ Sep 1974 Cover: 0.25 **NM** value: **5.00**
Circ: Statement: **183,344**
Lucifer Be Thy Name • recalls origin and quits **A:** Sal Buscema

178 ❑ Oct 1974 Cover: 0.25 **NM** value: **5.00**
Circ: Statement: **183,344**
If the Falcon Should Fall **A:** Sal Buscema

179 ❑ Nov 1974 Cover: 0.25 **NM** value: **5.00**
Circ: Statement: **183,344 • CGC:** 11 graded, best 9.8
Slings And Arrows! **A:** Sal Buscema **W:** Steve Englehart

180 ❑ Dec 1974 Cover: 0.25 **NM** value: **7.00**
Circ: Statement: **183,344**
The Coming of Nomad **A:** Sal Buscema ★ Origin of Nomad. ★ 1st Appearance of Nomad (Steve Rogers), Viper II.

181 ❑ Jan 1975 Cover: 0.25 **NM** value: **6.00**
Circ: Statement: **180,156**
The Mark Of Madness! **A:** Sal Buscema **W:** Steve Englehart ★ Origin of Captain America (new). ★ 1st Appearance of Captain America (new).

182 ❑ Feb 1975 Cover: 0.25 **NM** value: **4.00**
Circ: Statement: **180,156**
Inferno

183 ❑ Mar 1975 Cover: 0.25 **NM** value: **5.00**
Circ: Statement: **180,156**
Nomad No More • Steve Rogers becomes Captain America again ★ Death of Captain America (new).

184 ❑ Apr 1975 Cover: 0.25 **NM** value: **4.00**
Circ: Statement: **180,156 • CGC:** 1 graded, best 9.6
Cap's Back!

185 ❑ May 1975 Cover: 0.25 **NM** value: **4.00**
Circ: Statement: **180,156 • CGC:** 2 graded, best 9.6
Scream the Scarlet Skull • Has 1974 Statement; avg total paid circ 183,344

186 ❑ Jun 1975 Cover: 0.25 **NM** value: **5.00**
Circ: Statement: **180,156 • CGC:** 2 graded, best 9.2
Mind Cage ★ Origin of Falcon (real origin).

187 ❑ Jul 1975 Cover: 0.25 **NM** value: **4.00**
Circ: Statement: **180,156**
The Madness Maze

188 ❑ Aug 1975 Cover: 0.25 **NM** value: **4.00**
Circ: Statement: **180,156**
Druid-War **A:** Sal Buscema **W:** John Warner

189 ❑ Sep 1975 Cover: 0.25 **NM** value: **4.00**
Circ: Statement: **180,156**
Arena For A Fallen Hero **A:** Frank Robbins **W:** Tony Isabella

190 ❑ Oct 1975 Cover: 0.25 **NM** value: **4.00**
Circ: Statement: **180,156**
Nightshade Is Deadlier The Second Time Around! **A:** Frank Robbins **W:** Tony Isabella

191 ❑ Nov 1975 Cover: 0.25 **NM** value: **4.00**
Circ: Statement: **180,156**
The Trial Of The Falcon! **A:** Frank Robbins **W:** Bill Mantlo

192 ❑ Dec 1975 Cover: 0.25 **NM** value: **4.00**
Circ: Statement: **180,156 • CGC:** 1 graded, best 9.4
Mad-Flight! **A:** Frank Robbins **W:** Marv Wolfman ★ 1st Appearance of Karla Sofen (becomes Moonstone).

193 ❑ Jan 1976 Cover: 0.25 **NM** value: **4.00**
Circ: Statement: **165,147 • CGC:** 8 graded, best 9.6
Madbomb, Part 1; Screamer in the Brain! **A:** Jack Kirby **W:** Jack Kirby

194 ❑ Feb 1976 Cover: 0.25 **NM** value: **4.00**
Circ: Statement: **165,147**
Madbomb, Part 2; The Trojan Horde **A:** Jack Kirby **W:** Jack Kirby

195 ❑ Mar 1976 Cover: 0.25 **NM** value: **4.00**
Circ: Statement: **165,147**
Madbomb, Part 3; It's 1984! **A:** Jack Kirby **W:** Jack Kirby

196 ❑ Apr 1976 Cover: 0.25 **NM** value: **4.00**
Circ: Statement: **165,147**
Madbomb, Part 4; Kill-Derby **A:** Jack Kirby **W:** Jack Kirby

197 ❑ May 1976 Cover: 0.25 **NM** value: **4.00**
Circ: Statement: **165,147 • CGC:** 1 graded, best 9.6
Madbomb, Part 5; The Rocks Are Burning! **A:** Jack Kirby **W:** Jack Kirby

198 ❑ Jun 1976 Cover: 0.25 **NM** value: **4.00**
Circ: Statement: **165,147 • CGC:** 2 graded, best 9.6
Madbomb, Part 6; Captain America's Love Story **A:** Jack Kirby **W:** Jack Kirby

199 ❑ Jul 1976 Cover: 0.25 **NM** value: **4.00**
Circ: Statement: **165,147 • CGC:** 7 graded, best 9.8
Madbomb, Part 7; The Man Who Sold the United States **A:** Jack Kirby **W:** Jack Kirby

200 ❑ Aug 1976 Cover: 0.25 **NM** value: **5.00**
Circ: Statement: **165,147 • CGC:** 17 graded, best 9.8
• 200th anniversary issue. Madbomb, Part 8; Dawn's Early Light **A:** Jack Kirby **W:** Jack Kirby

201 ❑ Sep 1976 Cover: 0.30 **NM** value: **3.00**
Circ: Statement: **165,147 • CGC:** 1 graded, best 7.5
The Night People **A:** Jack Kirby **W:** Jack Kirby

202 ❑ Oct 1976 Cover: 0.30 **NM** value: **3.00**
Circ: Statement: **165,147**
Mad, Mad Dimension **A:** Jack Kirby

203 ❑ Nov 1976 Cover: 0.30 **NM** value: **3.00**
Circ: Statement: **165,147 • CGC:** 1 graded, best 8.0
Alamo II **A:** Jack Kirby **W:** Jack Kirby

204 ❑ Dec 1976 Cover: 0.30 **NM** value: **3.00**
Circ: Statement: **165,147 • CGC:** 1 graded, best 9.4
The Unburied One **A:** Jack Kirby **W:** Jack Kirby

205 ❑ Jan 1977 Cover: 0.30 **NM** value: **3.00**
Circ: Statement: **148,370**
Agron Walks The Earth! **A:** Jack Kirby **W:** Jack Kirby

206 ❑ Feb 1977 Cover: 0.30 **NM** value: **3.00**
Circ: Statement: **148,370 • CGC:** 2 graded, best 9.4
Face To Face With The Swine! **A:** Jack Kirby **W:** Jack Kirby ★ 1st Appearance of Donna Maria Puentes.

207 ❑ Mar 1977 Cover: 0.30 **NM** value: **3.00**
Circ: Statement: **148,370**
The Tiger And The Swine! • Has 1976 Statement, filed 9/20/76; avg print run 355,693; avg sales 164,093; avg subs 1,054; avg total paid 165,147; samples 0; office use 2,468; max existent 167,615; 53% of run returned **A:** Jack Kirby **W:** Jack Kirby

208 ❑ Apr 1977 Cover: 0.30 **NM** value: **3.00**
Circ: Statement: **148,370 • CGC:** 2 graded, best 9.6
The River Of Death! **A:** Jack Kirby **W:** Jack Kirby ★ 1st Appearance of Arnim Zola.

209 ❑ May 1977 Cover: 0.30 **NM** value: **3.00**
Circ: Statement: **148,370 • CGC:** 1 graded, best 9.6
Arnim Zola – The Bio-Fanatic! **A:** Jack Kirby **W:** Jack Kirby ★ 1st Appearance of Arnim Zola, Doughboy.

210 ❑ Jun 1977 Cover: 0.30 **NM** value: **3.00**
Circ: Statement: **148,370**
Showdown Day! **A:** Jack Kirby **W:** Jack Kirby

211 ❑ Jul 1977 Cover: 0.30 **NM** value: **3.00**
Circ: Statement: **148,370 • CGC:** 2 graded, best 9.4
Nazi "X"! **A:** Jack Kirby **W:** Jack Kirby

212 ❑ Aug 1977 Cover: 0.30 **NM** value: **3.00**
Circ: Statement: **148,370 • CGC:** 1 graded, best 9.6
The Face Of A Hero **A:** Jack Kirby **W:** Jack Kirby

213 ❑ Sep 1977 Cover: 0.30 **NM** value: **3.00**
Circ: Statement: **148,370 • CGC:** 1 graded, best 9.4
The Night Flyer! **A:** Jack Kirby **W:** Jack Kirby

214 ❑ Oct 1977 Cover: 0.30 **NM** value: **3.00**
Circ: Statement: **148,370**
Falcon **A:** Jack Kirby **W:** Jack Kirby

215 ❑ Nov 1977 Cover: 0.35 **NM** value: **3.00**
Circ: Statement: **148,370**
The Way It Really Was **A:** Gil Kane

216 ❑ Dec 1977 Cover: 0.35 **NM** value: **3.00**
Circ: Statement: **148,370**
The Human Torch Meets Captain America • Reprinted from Strange Tales #114 **A:** Gil Kane

217 ❑ Jan 1978 Cover: 0.35 **NM** value: **3.00**
Circ: Statement: **116,146 • CGC:** 1 graded, best 9.4
The Search for Steve Rogers **A:** John Buscema ★ 1st Appearance of Quasar (Marvel Man), Blue Streak.

218 ❑ Feb 1978 Cover: 0.35 **NM** value: **3.00**
Circ: Statement: **116,146 • CGC:** 1 graded, best 9.4
One Day in Newfoundland **A:** Sal Buscema

219 ❑ Mar 1978 Cover: 0.35 **NM** value: **3.00**
Circ: Statement: **116,146**
The Adventures of Captain America • Has 1977 Statement; avg total paid circ 148,370 **A:** Sal Buscema

220 ❑ Apr 1978 Cover: 0.35 **NM** value: **3.00**
Circ: Statement: **116,146**
The Ameridroid Lives! **A:** Sal Buscema; Gil Kane; John Tartag; Mike Esposito **W:** Don Glut

221 ❑ May 1978 Cover: 0.35 **NM** value: **3.00**
Circ: Statement: **116,146**
Cul-De-Sac **A:** Sal Buscema; Gil Kane; Mike Esposito **W:** Steve Gerber

222 ❑ Jun 1978 Cover: 0.35 **NM** value: **3.00**
Circ: Statement: **116,146**
Monumental Menace **A:** Sal Buscema; John Tartag; Mike Esposito **W:** Steve Gerber

223 ❑ Jul 1978 Cover: 0.35 **NM** value: **3.00**
Circ: Statement: **116,146 • CGC:** 1 graded, best 9.4
Call Me Animus **A:** Sal Buscema; John Byrne; John Tartag; Mike Esposito **W:** Steve Gerber

224 ❑ Aug 1978 Cover: 0.35 **NM** value: **3.00**
Circ: Statement: **116,146**
Saturday Night Furor **A:** Mike Zeck **W:** Peter B. Gillis ★ 1st Appearance of Señor Muerte II (Philip Garcia).

225 ❑ Sep 1978 Cover: 0.35 **NM** value: **3.00**
Circ: Statement: **116,146 • CGC:** 1 graded, best 9.2
Devastation **A:** Sal Buscema **W:** Steve Gerber

226 ❑ Oct 1978 Cover: 0.35 **NM** value: **3.00**
Circ: Statement: **116,146**
Am I Still Captain America? **A:** Sal Buscema; John Tartag; Mike Esposito **W:** Roger McKenzie

227 ❑ Nov 1978 Cover: 0.35 **NM** value: **3.00**
Circ: Statement: **116,146**
This Deadly Gauntlet **A:** Sal Buscema; John Tartag; Mike Esposito **W:** Roger McKenzie

228 ❑ Dec 1978 Cover: 0.35 **NM** value: **3.00**
Circ: Statement: **116,146**
A Serpent Lurks Below **A:** Sal Buscema; John Tartag; Mike Esposito **W:** Roger McKenzie

229 ❑ Jan 1979 Cover: 0.35 **NM** value: **3.00**
Traitors All About Me! **A:** Sal Buscema **W:** Roger McKenzie ★ Appearance of Marvel Man (Quasar).

230 ❑ Feb 1979 Cover: 0.35 **NM** value: **3.00**
Assault on Alcatraz! **A:** Sal Buscema; Don Perlin **W:** Roger Stern; Roger McKenzie ★ Appearance of Hulk. ★ Versus Hulk.

231 ❑ Mar 1979 Cover: 0.35 **NM** value: **3.00**
Aftermath! • Has 1978 Statement, filed 9/25/78; avg print run 329,629; avg sales 109,580; avg subs 6,566; avg total paid 116,146; samples 155; office use1,550; max existent 117,851; 64% of run returned **A:** Sal Buscema; Don Perlin **W:** Roger McKenzie ★ Versus Grand Director.

232 ❑ Apr 1979 Cover: 0.35 **NM** value: **3.00**
• **CGC:** 1 graded, best 9.6
The Flame And The Fury **A:** Sal Buscema; Don Perlin **W:** Jim Shooter; Roger McKenzie

233 ❑ May 1979 Cover: 0.40 **NM** value: **3.00**
Crossfire **A:** Sal Buscema; Don Perlin **W:** Roger McKenzie ★ Death of Sharon Carter.

234 ❑ Jun 1979 Cover: 0.40 **NM** value: **3.00**
Burn, Cap, Burn ★ Appearance of Daredevil.

235 ❑ Jul 1979 Cover: 0.40 **NM** value: **3.00**
To Stalk the Killer Skies **A:** Sal Buscema; Frank Miller; Jack Abel ★ Appearance of Daredevil.

236 ❑ Aug 1979 Cover: 0.40 **NM** value: **3.00**
Death Dive! **A:** Sal Buscema; Don Perlin **W:** Michael Fleisher ★ Death of Captain America IV.

237 ❑ Sep 1979 Cover: 0.40 **NM** value: **3.00**
From The Ashes… • Steve moves to Brooklyn **A:** Sal Buscema; Don Perlin **W:** Roger McKenzie ★ 1st Appearance of Anna Kappelbaum, Joshua Cooper, Copperhead, Mike Farrel.

238 ❑ Oct 1979 Cover: 0.40 **NM** value: **3.00**
Snowfall Fury **A:** John Byrne; Fred Kida **W:** Peter B. Gillis

239 ❑ Nov 1979 Cover: 0.40 **NM** value: **3.00**
Mind-Stains On The Virgin Snow **A:** John Byrne; Fred Kida **W:** Peter B. Gillis

240 ❑ Dec 1979 Cover: 0.40 **NM** value: **3.00**
Gang Wars! **A:** Alan Kupperberg **W:** Alan Kupperberg

241 ❑ Jan 1980 Cover: 0.40 **NM** value: **6.50**
Circ: Statement: **165,498 • CGC:** 19 graded, best 9.6
A: Frank Miller; Frank Miller(cover) ★ Appearance of Punisher.

242 ❑ Feb 1980 Cover: 0.40 **NM** value: **2.50**
Circ: Statement: **165,498**
Facades! **A:** Don Perlin; Joe Sinnott **W:** Steven Grant

243 ❑ Mar 1980 Cover: 0.40 **NM** value: **2.50**
Circ: Statement: **165,498**
The Lazarus Conspiracy **A:** Rich Buckler; George Pérez; Don Perlin **W:** Roger McKenzie

244 ❑ Apr 1980 Cover: 0.40 **NM** value: **2.50**
Circ: Statement: **165,498**
The Way Of All Flesh! **A:** Frank Miller; Don Perlin; Frank Miller(cover) **W:** Roger McKenzie

245 ❑ May 1980 Cover: 0.40 **NM** value: **2.50**
Circ: Statement: **165,498**
The Calypso Connection **A:** Frank Miller; Frank Mil **W:** Roger McKenzie

246 ❑ Jun 1980 Cover: 0.40 **NM** value: **2.50**
Circ: Statement: **165,498**
The Sins Of The Fathers **A:** George Pérez; Jerry Bingham **W:** Peter B. Gillis

247 ❑ Jul 1980 Cover: 0.40 **NM** value: **2.50**
Circ: Statement: **165,498**
By The Dawn's Early Light! **A:** John Byrne **W:** Roger Stern ★ 1st Appearance of Machinesmith.

248 ❑ Aug 1980 Cover: 0.40 **NM** value: **2.50**
Circ: Statement: **165,498 • CGC:** 1 graded, best 9.6
A: John Byrne **W:** Roger Stern ★ 1st Appearance of Bernie Rosenthal.

249 ❑ Sep 1980 Cover: 0.50 **NM** value: **2.50**
Circ: Statement: **165,498 • CGC:** 1 graded, best 9.4
Death, Where Is Thy Sting? **A:** John Byrne **W:** Roger Stern ★ Origin of Machinesmith.

250 ❑ Oct 1980 Cover: 0.50 **NM** value: **2.50**
Circ: Statement: **165,498**
A: John Byrne **W:** Roger Stern

251 ❑ Nov 1980 Cover: 0.50 **NM** value: **2.50**
Circ: Statement: **165,498**
A: John Byrne **W:** Roger Stern

252 ❑ Dec 1980 Cover: 0.50 **NM** value: **2.50**
Circ: Statement: **165,498**
Cold Fire **A:** John Byrne **W:** Roger Stern

253 ❑ Jan 1981 Cover: 0.50 **NM** value: **2.50**
Circ: Statement: **159,647**
Should Old Acquaintance Be Forgot **A:** John Byrne **W:** Roger Stern ★ 1st Appearance of Joe Chapman (becomes Union Jack III). ★ Death of Union Jack II (Brian Falsworth).

254 ❑ Feb 1981 Cover: 0.50 **NM** value: **2.50**
Circ: Statement: **159,647**
Blood On The Moors **A:** John Byrne **W:** Roger Stern ★ Origin of Union Jack III (Joe Chapman). ★ 1st Appearance of Union Jack III (Joe Chapman). ★ Death of Baron Blood, Union Jack I (Lord Falsworth).

255 ❑ Mar 1981 Cover: 0.50 **NM** value: **2.50**
Circ: Statement: **159,647 • CGC:** 3 graded, best 9.8
• 40th anniversary. The Living Legend **A:** John Byrne; Frank Miller; Frank Miller(cover) **W:** Roger Stern ★ Origin of Captain America. ★ 1st Appearance of Sarah Rogers (Steve's mother).

256 ❑ Apr 1981 Cover: 0.50 **NM** value: **2.00**
Circ: Statement: **159,647**
The Ghost Of Greymoor Castle! **A:** Gene Colan **W:** Bill Mantlo

257 ❑ May 1981 Cover: 0.50 **NM** value: **2.00**
Circ: Statement: **159,647**
Deadly Anniversary **A:** Lee Elias **W:** Mike W. Barr ★ Appearance of Hulk.

258 ❑ Jun 1981 Cover: 0.50 **NM** value: **2.00**
Circ: Statement: **159,647**
Blockbuster **A:** Mike Zeck **W:** Chris Claremont; David Michelinie

259 ❑ Jul 1981 Cover: 0.50 **NM** value: **2.00**
Circ: Statement: **159,647**
Rite Of Passage! **A:** Mike Zeck **W:** David Michelinie

260 ❑ Aug 1981 Cover: 0.50 **NM** value: **2.00**
Circ: Statement: **159,647**
Prison Reform! **A:** Alan Kupperberg; Al Milgrom **W:** Al Milgrom

261 ❑ Sep 1981 Cover: 0.50 **NM** value: **2.00**
Circ: Statement: **159,647**
Celluloid Heroes! **A:** Mike Zeck **W:** J.M. DeMatteis

262 ❑ Oct 1981 Cover: 0.50 **NM** value: **2.00**
Circ: Statement: **159,647**
Death of A Legend? **A:** Mike Zeck **W:** J.M. DeMatteis

263 ❑ Nov 1981 Cover: 0.50 **NM** value: **2.00**
Circ: Statement: **159,647**
…The Last Movie **A:** Mike Zeck **W:** J.M. DeMatteis

264 ❑ Dec 1981 Cover: 0.50 **NM** value: **2.00**
Circ: Statement: **159,647**
The American Dreamers! • X-Men cameo **A:** Mike Zeck **W:** J.M. DeMatteis ★ Appearance of X-Men.

265 ❑ Jan 1982 Cover: 0.60 **NM** value: **2.00**
Circ: Statement: **157,214**

Other grades: Multiply prices above by **1.5 for Mint • 2/3 for Very Fine • 1/3 for Fine • 1/5 for Very Good • 1/8 for Good**

📖 Thunderhead **A:** Mike Zeck; John Beatty **W:** David Anthony Kraft ★ Appearance of Nick Fury & Spider-Man.

266 ❑ Feb 1982 Cover: 0.60 **NM** value: **2.00**
Circ: Statement: **157,214** • **CGC:** 2 graded, best 9.8
📖 The Flight From Thunderhead! **A:** Mike Zeck; John Beatty **W:** David Anthony Kraft

267 ❑ Mar 1982 Cover: 0.60 **NM** value: **2.00**
Circ: Statement: **157,214**
📖 The Man Who Made A Difference! **A:** Mike Zeck **W:** J.M. DeMatteis ★ 1st Appearance of Everyman.

268 ❑ Apr 1982 Cover: 0.60 **NM** value: **2.00**
Circ: Statement: **157,214**
📖 Peace On Earth-Good Will To Man **A:** Mike Zeck **W:** J.M. DeMatteis

269 ❑ May 1982 Cover: 0.60 **NM** value: **2.00**
Circ: Statement: **157,214**
📖 A Mind Is A Terrible Thing To Waste **A:** Mike Zeck **W:** J.M. DeMatteis ★ 1st Appearance of Team America.

270 ❑ Jun 1982 Cover: 0.60 **NM** value: **2.00**
Circ: Statement: **157,214**
📖 Someone Who Cares **A:** Mike Zeck **W:** J.M. DeMatteis

271 ❑ Jul 1982 Cover: 0.60 **NM** value: **2.00**
Circ: Statement: **157,214**
📖 The Mystery Of Mr. X **A:** Alan Kupperberg **W:** David Anthony Kraft

272 ❑ Aug 1982 Cover: 0.60 **NM** value: **2.50**
Circ: Statement: **157,214**
📖 Mean Streets **A:** Mike Zeck **W:** J.M. DeMatteis ★ 1st Appearance of Vermin.

273 ❑ Sep 1982 Cover: 0.60 **NM** value: **2.00**
Circ: Statement: **157,214**
📖 Cap And The Howlers...Together Again! **A:** Mike Zeck **W:** David Anthony Kraft

274 ❑ Oct 1982 Cover: 0.60 **NM** value: **2.00**
Circ: Statement: **157,214**
📖 Death Of A Hero! **A:** Mike Zeck **W:** David Anthony Kraft ★ Death of General Samuel "Happy Sam" Sawyer.

275 ❑ Nov 1982 Cover: 0.60 **NM** value: **2.00**
Circ: Statement: **157,214**
📖 Yesterday's Shadows • Bernie Rosenthal learns Cap's identity **A:** Mike Zeck **W:** J.M. DeMatteis

276 ❑ Dec 1982 Cover: 0.60 **NM** value: **3.50**
Circ: Statement: **157,214**
📖 Turning Point • Later becomes Citizen V **A:** Mike Zeck **W:** J.M. DeMatteis ★ 1st Appearance of Baron Zemo II (Helmut Zemo).

277 ❑ Jan 1983 Cover: 0.60 **NM** value: **2.00**
Circ: Statement: **139,674**
📖 In Thy Image **A:** Mike Zeck **W:** J.M. DeMatteis

278 ❑ Feb 1983 Cover: 0.60 **NM** value: **2.00**
Circ: Statement: **139,674**
A: Mike Zeck

279 ❑ Mar 1983 Cover: 0.60 **NM** value: **2.00**
Circ: Statement: **139,674**
📖 Of Monsters And Men **A:** Mike Zeck **W:** J.M. DeMatteis

280 ❑ Apr 1983 Cover: 0.60 **NM** value: **2.00**
Circ: Statement: **139,674**
📖 Sermon Of Straw **A:** Mike Zeck **W:** J.M. DeMatteis

281 ❑ May 1983 Cover: 0.60 **NM** value: **2.00**
Circ: Statement: **139,674**
📖 Before The Fall **A:** Mike Zeck **W:** J.M. DeMatteis ★ Appearance of Jack Monroe.

282 ❑ Jun 1983 Cover: 0.60 **NM** value: **4.00**
Circ: Statement: **139,674** • **CGC:** 1 graded, best 9.6
A: Mike Zeck **W:** J.M. DeMatteis ★ 1st Appearance of Joseph Rogers (Steve's father), Nomad II (Jack Monroe).

282-2 ❑ Cover: 1.75 **NM** value: **2.00**

283 ❑ Jul 1983 Cover: 0.60 **NM** value: **3.00**
Circ: Statement: **139,674**
📖 America The Cursed **A:** Mike Zeck **W:** J.M. DeMatteis ★ 2nd Appearance of Nomad (Jack Monroe).

284 ❑ Aug 1983 Cover: 0.60 **NM** value: **2.00**
Circ: Statement: **139,674**
A: Mike Zeck **W:** J.M. DeMatteis ★ Appearance of Patriot (Jeffrey Mace).

285 ❑ Sep 1983 Cover: 0.60 **NM** value: **2.00**
Circ: Statement: **139,674**
📖 Letting Go **A:** Sal Buscema; Mike Zeck **W:** J.M. DeMatteis ★ Death of Patriot (Jeffrey Mace). ★ Versus Porcupine.

286 ❑ Oct 1983 Cover: 0.60 **NM** value: **3.00**
Circ: Statement: **139,674** • **CGC:** 1 graded, best 9.9
A: Mike Zeck ★ Appearance of Deathlok.

287 ❑ Nov 1983 Cover: 0.60 **NM** value: **3.00**
Circ: Statement: **139,674**
A: Mike Zeck ★ Appearance of Deathlok.

288 ❑ Dec 1983 Cover: 0.60 **NM** value: **3.00**
Circ: Statement: **139,674**
A: Mike Zeck ★ Appearance of Deathlok.

289 ❑ Jan 1984 Cover: 0.60 **NM** value: **2.00**
Circ: Statement: **148,659**
📖 Tomorrow The World? • Assistant Editors' Month **A:** Mike Zeck **W:** J.M. DeMatteis ★ Appearance of Bernie America.

290 ❑ Feb 1984 Cover: 0.60 **NM** value: **2.00**
Circ: Statement: **148,659**
📖 Echoes • Zemo **A:** John Byrne; Ron Frenz **W:** J.M. DeMatteis ★ 1st Appearance of Black Crow (in crow form). ★ Appearance of Mother Night.

291 ❑ Mar 1984 Cover: 0.60 **NM** value: **2.00**
Circ: Statement: **148,659**
📖 To Tame A Tumbler **A:** Herb Trimpe **C:** John Byrne **W:** Bill Mantlo

292 ❑ Apr 1984 Cover: 0.60 **NM** value: **2.00**
Circ: Statement: **148,659**
📖 An American Christmas! **A:** Paul Neary **W:** J.M. DeMatteis ★ Origin of Black Crow. ★ 1st Appearance of Black Crow (in human form).

293 ❑ May 1984 Cover: 0.60 **NM** value: **2.00**
Circ: Statement: **148,659**
📖 Field Of Vision **A:** Paul Neary **W:** J.M. DeMatteis

294 ❑ Jun 1984 Cover: 0.60 **NM** value: **2.00**
Circ: Statement: **148,659**
📖 The Measure Of A Man **A:** Paul Neary **W:** J.M. DeMatteis

295 ❑ Jul 1984 Cover: 0.60 **NM** value: **2.00**
Circ: Statement: **148,659**
📖 The Centre Cannot hold! **A:** Paul Neary **W:** J.M. DeMatteis

296 ❑ Aug 1984 Cover: 0.60 **NM** value: **2.00**
Circ: Statement: **148,659**
📖 Things Fall Apart! **A:** Paul Neary **W:** J.M. DeMatteis

297 ❑ Sep 1984 Cover: 0.60 **NM** value: **2.00**
Circ: Statement: **148,659**
📖 All My Sins Remembered **A:** Paul Neary **W:** J.M. DeMatteis

298 ❑ Oct 1984 Cover: 0.60 **NM** value: **2.00**
Circ: Statement: **148,659**
📖 Sturm Und Drang: The Life And Times Of The Red Skull **A:** Paul Neary **W:** J.M. DeMatteis ★ Origin of Red Skull.

299 ❑ Nov 1984 Cover: 0.60 **NM** value: **2.00**
Circ: Statement: **148,659**
📖 The Bunker **A:** Paul Neary **W:** J.M. DeMatteis ★ Origin of Red Skull.

300 ❑ Dec 1984 Cover: 0.60 **NM** value: **2.00**
Circ: Statement: **148,659**
📖 Das Ende! **A:** Paul Neary; Mike Zeck **W:** J.M. DeMatteis ★ Versus Red Skull.

301 ❑ Jan 1985 Cover: 0.60 **NM** value: **2.00**
Circ: Statement: **169,964**
📖 All Good Things... **A:** Paul Neary **W:** Mike Carlin

302 ❑ Feb 1985 Cover: 0.60 **NM** value: **2.00**
Circ: Statement: **169,964**
📖 ...And Other Strangers! **A:** Paul Neary **W:** Mike Carlin ★ 1st Appearance of Machete.

303 ❑ Mar 1985 Cover: 0.60 **NM** value: **2.00**
Circ: Statement: **169,964**
📖 Double Dare **A:** Paul Neary **W:** Mike Carlin ★ Versus Batroc.

304 ❑ Apr 1985 Cover: 0.65 **NM** value: **2.00**
Circ: Statement: **169,964**

305 ❑ May 1985 Cover: 0.65 **NM** value: **2.00**
Circ: Statement: **169,964** CapCity orders: **11,100**
📖 Walk Upon England! **A:** Paul Neary **W:** Mike Carlin ★ Appearance of Captain Britain.

306 ❑ Jun 1985 Cover: 0.65 **NM** value: **2.00**
Circ: Statement: **169,964** CapCity orders: **11,400**
📖 Summoning! **A:** Paul Neary **W:** Mike Carlin ★ Appearance of Captain Britain.

307 ❑ Jul 1985 Cover: 0.65 **NM** value: **2.00**
Circ: Statement: **169,964** CapCity orders: **11,800**
📖 Stop Making Sense **A:** Paul Neary **W:** Mark Gruenwald ★ 1st Appearance of Madcap.

308 ❑ Aug 1985 Cover: 0.65 **NM** value: **2.00**
Circ: Statement: **169,964** CapCity orders: **19,500**
📖 Secret Wars II; The Body In Question • Secret Wars II **A:** John Byrne; Paul Neary **W:** Mark Gruenwald

309 ❑ Sep 1985 Cover: 0.65 **NM** value: **2.00**
Circ: Statement: **169,964** CapCity orders: **12,400**
📖 Nomad Madcap Cap... • Nomad leaves team **A:** Paul Neary **W:** Mark Gruenwald ★ Origin of Madcap. ★ Versus Madcap.

310 ❑ Oct 1985 Cover: 0.65 **NM** value: **2.00**
Circ: Statement: **169,964** CapCity orders: **12,200**
A: Paul Neary **W:** Mark Gruenwald ★ 1st Appearance of Diamondback, Rattler, Cottonmouth II, Serpent Society, Bushmaster, Asp II (Cleo).

311 ❑ Nov 1985 Cover: 0.65 **NM** value: **2.00**
Circ: Statement: **169,964** CapCity orders: **14,200**
📖 Working... **A:** Paul Neary **W:** Mark Gruenwald ★ Versus Super-Adaptoid.

312 ❑ Dec 1985 Cover: 0.65 **NM** value: **2.00**
Circ: Statement: **169,964** CapCity orders: **11,900**
📖 Deface The Nation **A:** Paul Neary **W:** Mark Gruenwald ★ Origin of Flag-Smasher. ★ 1st Appearance of Flag-Smasher.

313 ❑ Jan 1986 Cover: 0.65 **NM** value: **2.00**
Circ: Statement: **139,482** CapCity orders: **11,600**
📖 Mission: Murder Modok! **A:** John Byrne; Paul Neary **W:** Mark Gruenwald

314 ❑ Feb 1986 Cover: 0.75 **NM** value: **2.00**
Circ: Statement: **139,482** CapCity orders: **12,800**

315 ❑ Mar 1986 Cover: 0.75 **NM** value: **2.00**
Circ: Statement: **139,482** CapCity orders: **12,300**
★ Death of Porcupine. ★ Versus Serpent Society.

316 ❑ Apr 1986 Cover: 0.75 **NM** value: **2.00**
Circ: Statement: **139,482** CapCity orders: **13,000**

317 ❑ May 1986 Cover: 0.75 **NM** value: **2.00**
Circ: Statement: **139,482** CapCity orders: **13,000**

318 ❑ Jun 1986 Cover: 0.75 **NM** value: **2.00**
Circ: Statement: **139,482** CapCity orders: **13,500**
★ Death of The Blue Streak. ★ Death of Death-Adder.

319 ❑ Jul 1986 Cover: 0.75 **NM** value: **2.00**
Circ: Statement: **139,482** CapCity orders: **13,900**
📖 Death Ringer I (Anthony Davis); Death Rapier ★ Death of Bird-Man II (Achil.

320 ❑ Aug 1986 Cover: 0.75 **NM** value: **2.00**
Circ: Statement: **139,482** CapCity orders: **14,300**
★ Versus Scourge.

321 ❑ Sep 1986 Cover: 0.75 **NM** value: **2.00**
Circ: Statement: **139,482** CapCity orders: **13,500**
A: Mike Zeck ★ 1st Appearance of Ultimatum.

322 ❑ Oct 1986 Cover: 0.75 **NM** value: **2.00**
Circ: Statement: **139,482** CapCity orders: **15,600**
★ 1st Appearance of Super-Patriot.

323 ❑ Nov 1986 Cover: 0.75 **NM** value: **2.00**
Circ: Statement: **139,482** CapCity orders: **16,300**
A: Mike Zeck ★ 1st Appearance of Super-Patriot II (later becomes USAgent).

324 ❑ Dec 1986 Cover: 0.75 **NM** value: **2.00**
Circ: Statement: **139,482** CapCity orders: **15,700**
A: Mike Zeck

325 ❑ Jan 1987 Cover: 0.75 **NM** value: **2.00**
Circ: Statement: **147,750** CapCity orders: **15,600**
A: Mike Zeck ★ 1st Appearance of Slug.

326 ❑ Feb 1987 Cover: 0.75 **NM** value: **2.00**
Circ: Statement: **147,750** CapCity orders: **15,600**
A: Mike Zeck

327 ❑ Mar 1987 Cover: 0.75 **NM** value: **2.00**
Circ: Statement: **147,750** CapCity orders: **15,400**
A: Mike Zeck

328 ❑ Apr 1987 Cover: 0.75 **NM** value: **2.00**
Circ: Statement: **147,750** CapCity orders: **16,700**
📖 The Hard Way! **A:** Paul Neary; Mike Zeck; Vince Colletta **W:** Mark Gruenwald ★ Origin of Demolition-Man. ★ 1st Appearance of Demolition-Man.

329 ❑ May 1987 Cover: 0.75 **NM** value: **2.00**
Circ: Statement: **147,750** CapCity orders: **14,100**
A: Mike Zeck

330 ❑ Jun 1987 Cover: 0.75 **NM** value: **2.00**
Circ: Statement: **147,750** CapCity orders: **14,400**
A: Mike Zeck ★ Appearance of D-Man, Demolition-Man.

331 ❑ Jul 1987 Cover: 0.75 **NM** value: **2.00**
Circ: Statement: **147,750** CapCity orders: **14,200**
A: Mike Zeck

332 ❑ Aug 1987 Cover: 0.75 **NM** value: **4.00**
Circ: Statement: **147,750** CapCity orders: **15,900**
• Steve Rogers quits as Captain America **A:** Mike Zeck

333 ❑ Sep 1987 Cover: 0.75 **NM** value: **3.50**
Circ: Statement: **147,750** CapCity orders: **17,300** • **CGC:** 1 graded, best 9.6
• John Walker (Super-Patriot II) becomes Captain America **A:** Mike Zeck ★ 1st Appearance of Captain America VI (John Walker).

334 ❑ Oct 1987 Cover: 0.75 **NM** value: **3.00**
Circ: Statement: **147,750** CapCity orders: **18,900**
A: Mike Zeck ★ 1st Appearance of Bucky IV (Lemar Hoskins).

335 ❑ Nov 1987 Cover: 0.75 **NM** value: **2.50**
Circ: Statement: **147,750** CapCity orders: **22,700**
★ 1st Appearance of Watchdogs.

336 ❑ Dec 1987 Cover: 0.75 **NM** value: **2.50**
Circ: Statement: **147,750** CapCity orders: **22,700**
A: Mike Zeck

337 ❑ Jan 1988 Cover: 0.75 **NM** value: **2.50**
Circ: CapCity orders: **22,700**
A: Mike Zeck ★ 1st Appearance of Fer-de-Lance, The Captain, Puff Adder.

338 ❑ Feb 1988 Cover: 0.75 **NM** value: **2.50**
Circ: CapCity orders: **24,300**
★ Death of Professor Power.

339 ❑ Mar 1988 Cover: 0.75 **NM** value: **2.50**
Circ: CapCity orders: **33,800**
📖 Fall of the Mutants • Fall of Mutants

340 ❑ Apr 1988 Cover: 0.75 **NM** value: **2.50**
Circ: CapCity orders: **26,600**

341 ❑ May 1988 Cover: 0.75 **NM** value: **2.00**
Circ: CapCity orders: **25,100**
★ 1st Appearance of Left-Winger, Rock Python (cameo), Battle Star.
★ Appearance of Iron Man.

342 ❑ Jun 1988 Cover: 0.75 **NM** value: **2.00**
Circ: CapCity orders: **23,900**
★ 1st Appearance of Rock Python (full appearance).

343 ❑ Jul 1988 Cover: 0.75 **NM** value: **2.00**
Circ: CapCity orders: **24,800**
★ 1st Appearance of Quill.

344 ❑ Aug 1988 Cover: 1.50 **NM** value: **2.00**
Circ: CapCity orders: **26,000**
• Giant-size.

345 ❑ Sep 1988 Cover: 0.75 **NM** value: **2.00**
Circ: CapCity orders: **25,500**

346 ❑ Oct 1988 Cover: 0.75 **NM** value: **2.00**
Circ: CapCity orders: **25,000**

347 ❑ Nov 1988 Cover: 0.75 **NM** value: **2.00**
Circ: CapCity orders: **25,000**
📖 Vengeance **A:** Kieron Dwyer **W:** Mark Gruenwald ★ Death of Left-Winger.

348 ❑ Dec 1988 Cover: 0.75 **NM** value: **2.00**
Circ: CapCity orders: **24,900**
★ Versus Flag Smasher.

349 ❑ Jan 1989 Cover: 0.75 **NM** value: **2.00**
Circ: Statement: **178,800** CapCity orders: **24,600**

350 ❑ Feb 1989 Cover: 1.75 **NM** value: **3.00**
Circ: Statement: **178,800** CapCity orders: **32,300**
• Giant-size. • The Captain and Super-Patriot fight for title of Captain America

351 ❑ Mar 1989 Cover: 0.75 **NM** value: **2.00**
Circ: Statement: **178,800** CapCity orders: **26,400**
★ Appearance of Nick Fury. ★ Death of Watchdog.

352 ❑ Apr 1989 Cover: 0.75 **NM** value: **2.00**
Circ: Statement: **178,800** CapCity orders: **25,900**
★ 1st Appearance of Machete. ★ Appearance of Soviet Super Soldiers.

353 ❑ May 1989 Cover: 0.75 **NM** value: **2.00**
Circ: Statement: **178,800** CapCity orders: **26,000**
★ Appearance of Soviet Super Soldiers.

354 ❑ Jun 1989 Cover: 0.75 **NM** value: **2.00**
Circ: Statement: **178,800** CapCity orders: **26,100**
• Super-Patriot becomes USAgent ★ 1st Appearance of U.S. Agent.
★ Appearance of Fabian Stankowitz.

355 ❑ Jul 1989 Cover: 0.75 **NM** value: **1.50**
Circ: Statement: **178,800** CapCity orders: **25,700**
📖 Missing Persons **A:** Rich Buckler **W:** Mark Gruenwald

356 ❑ Aug 1989 Cover: 0.75 **NM** value: **1.50**
Circ: Statement: **178,800** CapCity orders: **27,300**
📖 Camptown Rages! **A:** Al Milgrom **W:** Mark Gruenwald ★ 1st Appearance of Mother Night.

357 ❑ Sep 1989 Cover: 1.00 **NM** value: **1.50**
Circ: Statement: **178,800** CapCity orders: **27,300**
📖 Bloodstone Hunt; The Bloodstone Hunt, Part 1 • CBG Fan Awards parody ballot

358 ❑ Sep 1989 Cover: 1.00 **NM** value: **1.50**
Circ: Statement: **178,800** CapCity orders: **28,400**
📖 The Bloodstone Hunt, Part 2 ★ Appearance of John Jameson.

359 ❑ Oct 1989 Cover: 1.00 **NM** value: **1.50**
Circ: Statement: **178,800** CapCity orders: **26,400**
📖 The Bloodstone Hunt, Part 3 ★ 1st Appearance of Crossbones (cameo).

CGC-graded: Multiply prices above by **33 for 9.9 M • 16 for 9.8 NM/M • 7 for 9.6 NM+ • 5 for 9.4 NM • 2.5 for 9.2 NM- • 1.5 for 9.0 VF/NM**

360 ❑ Oct 1989 Cover: 1.00 **NM** value: **1.50**
Circ: Statement: **178,800** CapCity orders: **26,400**
📖 Bloodstone Hunt, Part 4; The Bloodstone Hunt, Part 4 **A:** Kieron Dwyer **W:** Mark Gruenwald ★ 1st Appearance of Crossbones (full appearance).

361 ❑ Nov 1989 Cover: 1.00 **NM** value: **1.50**
Circ: Statement: **178,800** CapCity orders: **26,100**
📖 The Bloodstone Hunt, Part 5

362 ❑ Nov 1989 Cover: 1.00 **NM** value: **1.50**
Circ: Statement: **178,800** CapCity orders: **26,400**
📖 The Bloodstone Hunt, Part 6

363 ❑ Nov 1989 Cover: 1.00 **NM** value: **1.50**
Circ: Statement: **178,800** CapCity orders: **27,000**

364 ❑ Dec 1989 Cover: 1.00 **NM** value: **1.50**
Circ: Statement: **178,800** CapCity orders: **26,400**

365 ❑ Dec 1989 Cover: 1.00 **NM** value: **1.50**
Circ: Statement: **178,800** CapCity orders: **28,500**
📖 Acts of Vengeance, Part 8 • Acts of Vengeance **A:** Kieron Dwyer **W:** Mark Gruenwald

366 ❑ Jan 1990 Cover: 1.00 **NM** value: **1.50**
Circ: Statement: **170,900** CapCity orders: **29,700**
📖 Acts of Vengeance, Part 17 • Acts of Vengeance

367 ❑ Feb 1990 Cover: 1.00 **NM** value: **1.50**
Circ: Statement: **170,900** CapCity orders: **30,300**
📖 Acts of Vengeance, Part 25 • Acts of Vengeance;Red Skull vs. Magneto

368 ❑ Mar 1990 Cover: 1.00 **NM** value: **1.50**
Circ: Statement: **170,900** CapCity orders: **27,900**
★ Origin of Machinesmith.

369 ❑ Apr 1990 Cover: 1.00 **NM** value: **1.50**
Circ: Statement: **170,900** CapCity orders: **27,300**
★ 1st Appearance of Skeleton Crew.

370 ❑ May 1990 Cover: 1.00 **NM** value: **1.50**
Circ: Statement: **170,900** CapCity orders: **28,800**

371 ❑ Jun 1990 Cover: 1.00 **NM** value: **1.50**
Circ: Statement: **170,900** CapCity orders: **29,100**
📖 Cap's Night Out **A:** Ron Lim **W:** Mark Gruenwald

372 ❑ Jul 1990 Cover: 1.00 **NM** value: **1.50**
Circ: Statement: **170,900** CapCity orders: **32,400**
📖 Streets of Poison

373 ❑ Jul 1990 Cover: 1.00 **NM** value: **1.50**
Circ: Statement: **170,900** CapCity orders: **31,200**
📖 Streets of Poison

374 ❑ Aug 1990 Cover: 1.00 **NM** value: **1.50**
Circ: Statement: **170,900** CapCity orders: **30,300**
📖 Streets of Poison

375 ❑ Aug 1990 Cover: 1.00 **NM** value: **1.50**
Circ: Statement: **170,900** CapCity orders: **30,300**
📖 Streets of Poison

376 ❑ Sep 1990 Cover: 1.00 **NM** value: **1.50**
Circ: Statement: **170,900** CapCity orders: **29,700**
📖 Streets of Poison

377 ❑ Sep 1990 Cover: 1.00 **NM** value: **1.50**
Circ: Statement: **170,900** CapCity orders: **29,400**
📖 Streets of Poison

378 ❑ Oct 1990 Cover: 1.00 **NM** value: **1.50**
Circ: Statement: **170,900** CapCity orders: **28,800**
📖 Streets of Poison

379 ❑ Nov 1990 Cover: 1.00 **NM** value: **1.50**
Circ: Statement: **170,900** CapCity orders: **28,800**
★ Origin of Nefarius. ★ 1st Appearance of Nefarius. ★ Appearance of Quasar. ★ Versus Nefarius.

380 ❑ Dec 1990 Cover: 1.00 **NM** value: **1.50**
Circ: Statement: **170,900** CapCity orders: **29,700**

381 ❑ Jan 1991 Cover: 1.00 **NM** value: **1.50**
Circ: Statement: **177,458** CapCity orders: **29,700**
📖 This Gun's For Hire **A:** Ron Lim **W:** Mark Gruenwald

382 ❑ Feb 1991 Cover: 1.00 **NM** value: **1.50**
Circ: Statement: **177,458** CapCity orders: **28,800**

383 ❑ Mar 1991 Cover: 2.00 **NM** value: **3.00**
Circ: Statement: **177,458** CapCity orders: **37,500** • **CGC:** 5 graded, best 9.8
• 50th anniversary issue. **A:** Jim Lee(cover)

384 ❑ Apr 1991 Cover: 1.00 **NM** value: **1.50**
Circ: Statement: **177,458** CapCity orders: **29,100**
📖 Lair Of the Ice Worm **A:** Ron Lim **W:** Mark Gruenwald ★ Appearance of Jack Frost, Jack Frost.

385 ❑ May 1991 Cover: 1.00 **NM** value: **1.50**
Circ: Statement: **177,458** CapCity orders: **29,700**
📖 Going To The Dogs **A:** Ron Lim **W:** Mark Gruenwald

386 ❑ Jun 1991 Cover: 1.00 **NM** value: **1.50**
Circ: Statement: **177,458** CapCity orders: **30,600**
📖 For Righteousness' Sake **A:** Ron Lim **W:** Mark Gruenwald ★ Appearance of U.S. Agent.

387 ❑ Jul 1991 Cover: 1.00 **NM** value: **1.50**
Circ: Statement: **177,458** CapCity orders: **30,000**
📖 Superia Stratagem; Superia Stratagem, Part 1 • Red Skull back-up stories **A:** Rik Levins **W:** Mark Gruenwald

388 ❑ Jul 1991 Cover: 1.00 **NM** value: **1.50**
Circ: Statement: **177,458** CapCity orders: **29,700**
📖 Superia Stratagem; Superia Stratagem, Part 2 • Red Skull back-up stories **A:** Rik Levins **W:** Mark Gruenwald ★ 1st Appearance of Impala.

389 ❑ Aug 1991 Cover: 1.00 **NM** value: **1.50**
Circ: Statement: **177,458** CapCity orders: **30,900**
📖 Superia Stratagem; Superia Stratagem, Part 3 • Red Skull back-up stories **A:** Rik Levins **W:** Mark Gruenwald

390 ❑ Aug 1991 Cover: 1.00 **NM** value: **1.50**
Circ: Statement: **177,458** CapCity orders: **30,600**
📖 Superia Stratagem; Superia Stratagem, Part 4 **A:** Rik Levins **W:** Mark Gruenwald

391 ❑ Sep 1991 Cover: 1.00 **NM** value: **1.50**
Circ: Statement: **177,458** CapCity orders: **30,900**
📖 Superia Stratagem; Superia Stratagem, Part 5 **A:** Rik Levins **W:** Mark Gruenwald

392 ❑ Sep 1991 Cover: 1.00 **NM** value: **1.50**
Circ: Statement: **177,458** CapCity orders: **30,900**
📖 Superia Stratagem; Superia Stratagem, Part 6 **A:** Rik Levins **W:** Mark Gruenwald

393 ❑ Oct 1991 Cover: 1.00 **NM** value: **1.50**
Circ: Statement: **177,458** CapCity orders: **30,300**
📖 Skullbound **A:** Rik Levins; Larry Alexander **W:** Mark Gruenwald

394 ❑ Nov 1991 Cover: 1.00 **NM** value: **1.50**
Circ: Statement: **177,458** CapCity orders: **29,100**
📖 The Crimson Crusade **A:** Rik Levins **W:** Mark Gruenwald

395 ❑ Dec 1991 Cover: 1.00 **NM** value: **1.50**
Circ: Statement: **177,458** CapCity orders: **29,700**
📖 Rogues In The House **A:** Rik Levins **W:** Mark Gruenwald

396 ❑ Jan 1992 Cover: 1.00 **NM** value: **1.50**
Circ: Statement: **222,175** CapCity orders: **28,500**
★ 1st Appearance of Jack O'Lantern II.

397 ❑ Feb 1992 Cover: 1.25 **NM** value: **1.50**
Circ: Statement: **222,175** CapCity orders: **27,300**

398 ❑ Mar 1992 Cover: 1.25 **NM** value: **1.50**
Circ: Statement: **222,175** CapCity orders: **38,100**
📖 Operation: Galactic Storm, Part 1 • Galactic Storm

399 ❑ Apr 1992 Cover: 1.25 **NM** value: **1.50**
Circ: Statement: **222,175** CapCity orders: **33,600**
📖 Operation: Galactic Storm, Part 8 • Galactic Storm **A:** Rik Levins; Dan Bulanadi **W:** Mark Gruenwald

400 ❑ May 1992 Cover: 2.25 **NM** value: **2.50**
Circ: Statement: **222,175** CapCity orders: **55,200**
Double-gatefold cover. 📖 Operation: Galactic Storm, Part 15; Captain America Joins the Avengers • Galactic Storm;reprints Avengers #4 **A:** Rik Levins; Larry Alexander **W:** Mark Gruenwald ★ Origin of Cutthroat, Diamondback.

401 ❑ Jun 1992 Cover: 1.25 **NM** value: **1.50**
Circ: Statement: **222,175** CapCity orders: **31,800**
📖 Operation: Galactic Storm Aftermath **A:** Rik Levins **W:** Mark Gruenwald

402 ❑ Jul 1992 Cover: 1.25 **NM** value: **1.50**
Circ: Statement: **222,175** CapCity orders: **33,900**
📖 Man & Wolf, Part 1; Man and Wolf, Part 1 **A:** Rik Levins **W:** Mark Gruenwald ★ 1st Appearance of Dredmund Druid. ★ Appearance of Wolverine.

403 ❑ Jul 1992 Cover: 1.25 **NM** value: **1.50**
Circ: Statement: **222,175** CapCity orders: **38,300**
📖 Man & Wolf, Part 2; Man and Wolf, Part 2 **A:** Rik Levins **W:** Mark Gruenwald ★ 2nd Appearance of Dredmund Druid. ★ Appearance of Wolverine.

404 ❑ Aug 1992 Cover: 1.25 **NM** value: **1.50**
Circ: Statement: **222,175**
📖 Man & Wolf, Part 3; Man and Wolf, Part 3 **A:** Rik Levins **W:** Mark Gruenwald ★ Appearance of Wolverine.

405 ❑ Aug 1992 Cover: 1.25 **NM** value: **1.50**
Circ: Statement: **222,175** CapCity orders: **45,500**
📖 Man & Wolf, Part 4; Man and Wolf, Part 4 **A:** Rik Levins **W:** Mark Gruenwald ★ Appearance of Wolverine.

406 ❑ Sep 1992 Cover: 1.25 **NM** value: **1.50**
Circ: Statement: **222,175** CapCity orders: **36,600**
📖 Man & Wolf, Part 5; Man and Wolf, Part 5 **A:** Rik Levins **W:** Mark Gruenwald ★ Appearance of Wolverine.

407 ❑ Sep 1992 Cover: 1.25 **NM** value: **1.50**
Circ: Statement: **222,175** CapCity orders: **40,700**
📖 Man & Wolf, Part 6; Man and Wolf, Part 6 **A:** Rik Levins **W:** Mark Gruenwald ★ Appearance of Wolverine, Cable.

408 ❑ Oct 1992 Cover: 1.25 **NM** value: **1.50**
Circ: Statement: **222,175** CapCity orders: **28,200**
📖 Infinity War **A:** Rik Levins **W:** Mark Gruenwald ★ Death of Cutthroat.

409 ❑ Nov 1992 Cover: 1.25 **NM** value: **1.50**
Circ: Statement: **222,175** CapCity orders: **26,800**
📖 Blood And Diamonds **A:** Rik Levins **W:** Mark Gruenwald

410 ❑ Dec 1992 Cover: 1.25 **NM** value: **1.50**
Circ: Statement: **222,175** CapCity orders: **26,300**

411 ❑ Jan 1993 Cover: 1.25 **NM** value: **1.50**
Circ: Statement: **163,858** CapCity orders: **24,800**
📖 Taking Aim, Part 1 **A:** Rik Levins **W:** Mark Gruenwald

412 ❑ Feb 1993 Cover: 1.25 **NM** value: **1.50**
Circ: Statement: **163,858** CapCity orders: **24,400**
📖 Taking Aim, Part 2 **A:** Rik Levins **W:** Mark Gruenwald

413 ❑ Mar 1993 Cover: 1.25 **NM** value: **1.50**
Circ: Statement: **163,858** CapCity orders: **23,000**
📖 Hostile Takeover **A:** Rik Levins **W:** Mark Gruenwald ★ Versus Modam.

414 ❑ Apr 1993 Cover: 1.25 **NM** value: **1.50**
Circ: Statement: **163,858** CapCity orders: **24,900**
• Savage Land

415 ❑ May 1993 Cover: 1.25 **NM** value: **1.50**
Circ: Statement: **163,858** CapCity orders: **24,200**

416 ❑ Jun 1993 Cover: 1.25 **NM** value: **1.50**
Circ: Statement: **163,858** CapCity orders: **23,600**

417 ❑ Jul 1993 Cover: 1.25 **NM** value: **1.50**
Circ: Statement: **163,858** CapCity orders: **22,900**

418 ❑ Aug 1993 Cover: 1.25 **NM** value: **1.50**
Circ: Statement: **163,858** CapCity orders: **23,100**

419 ❑ Sep 1993 Cover: 1.25 **NM** value: **1.50**
Circ: Statement: **163,858** CapCity orders: **21,900**
★ Appearance of Silver Sable.

420 ❑ Oct 1993 Cover: 1.25 **NM** value: **1.50**
📖 The Faustus Affair, Part 2 **A:** Rik Levins **W:** Mark Gruenwald ★ Appearance of Nomad, Blazing Skull, Viper.

420/CS ❑ Oct 1993 Cover: 2.95 **NM** value: **Cover or less**
Circ: Statement: **163,858** CapCity orders: **19,000**
• Includes copy of Dirt Magazine. 📖 The Faustus Affair, Part 2 **A:** Rik Levins ★ Appearance of Nomad, Blazing Skull, Viper.

421 ❑ Nov 1993 Cover: 1.25 **NM** value: **1.50**
Circ: Statement: **163,858** CapCity orders: **20,700**
📖 The Faustus Affair, Part 4 ★ Appearance of Nomad.

422 ❑ Dec 1993 Cover: 1.25 **NM** value: **1.50**
Circ: Statement: **163,858** CapCity orders: **20,700**

423 ❑ Jan 1994 Cover: 1.25 **NM** value: **1.50**
Circ: Statement: **114,892** CapCity orders: **19,700**
★ Versus Namor.

424 ❑ Feb 1994 Cover: 1.25 **NM** value: **1.50**
Circ: Statement: **114,892** CapCity orders: **19,600**

425 ❑ Mar 1994 Cover: 1.75 **NM** value: **2.50**
• Giant-size. 📖 Fighting Chance; Fighting Chance, Part 1 **A:** Dave Hoover **W:** Mark Gruenwald

425/SC ❑ Mar 1994 Cover: 2.95 **NM** value: **3.25**
Circ: Statement: **114,892** CapCity orders: **38,950**
Foil-embossed cover. • Giant-size. 📖 Fighting Chance; Fighting Chance, Part 1 **A:** Dave Hoover **W:** Mark Gruenwald

426 ❑ Apr 1994 Cover: 1.25 **NM** value: **1.50**
Circ: Statement: **114,892** CapCity orders: **23,250**
📖 Fighting Chance; Fighting Chance, Part 2 **A:** Dave Hoover **W:** Mark Gruenwald

427 ❑ May 1994 Cover: 1.50 **NM** value: **Cover or less**
Circ: Statement: **114,892** CapCity orders: **21,850**
📖 Fighting Chance; Fighting Chance, Part 3 **A:** Dave Hoover **W:** Mark Gruenwald

428 ❑ Jun 1994 Cover: 1.50 **NM** value: **Cover or less**
Circ: Statement: **114,892** CapCity orders: **24,000**
📖 Fighting Chance; Fighting Chance, Part 4 **A:** Dave Hoover **W:** Mark Gruenwald

429 ❑ Jul 1994 Cover: 1.50 **NM** value: **Cover or less**
Circ: Statement: **114,892** CapCity orders: **24,050**
📖 Fighting Chance; Fighting Chance, Part 5 **A:** Dave Hoover **W:** Mark Gruenwald ★ 1st Appearance of Kono the Sumo.

430 ❑ Aug 1994 Cover: 1.50 **NM** value: **Cover or less**
Circ: Statement: **114,892** CapCity orders: **22,800**
📖 Fighting Chance; Fighting Chance, Part 6 **A:** Dave Hoover **W:** Mark Gruenwald

431 ❑ Sep 1994 Cover: 1.50 **NM** value: **Cover or less**
Circ: Statement: **114,892** CapCity orders: **23,000**
📖 Fighting Chance; Fighting Chance, Part 7 **A:** Dave Hoover **W:** Mark Gruenwald ★ 1st Appearance of Free Spirit.

432 ❑ Oct 1994 Cover: 1.50 **NM** value: **Cover or less**
Circ: Statement: **114,892** CapCity orders: **20,800**
📖 Fighting Chance; Fighting Chance, Part 8 **A:** Dave Hoover **W:** Mark Gruenwald

433 ❑ Nov 1994 Cover: 1.50 **NM** value: **Cover or less**
Circ: Statement: **114,892** CapCity orders: **19,600**
📖 Fighting Chance; Fighting Chance, Part 9 **A:** Dave Hoover **W:** Mark Gruenwald

434 ❑ Dec 1994 Cover: 1.50 **NM** value: **Cover or less**
Circ: Statement: **114,892** CapCity orders: **19,100**
📖 Fighting Chance; Fighting Chance, Part 10 **A:** Dave Hoover **W:** Mark Gruenwald ★ 1st Appearance of Jack Flag.

435 ❑ Jan 1995 Cover: 1.50 **NM** value: **Cover or less**
Circ: Statement: **82,258** CapCity orders: **17,750**
📖 Fighting Chance; Fighting Chance, Part 11 **A:** Dave Hoover **W:** Mark Gruenwald ★ Versus new Cobra.

436 ❑ Feb 1995 Cover: 1.50 **NM** value: **Cover or less**
Circ: Statement: **82,258** CapCity orders: **17,875**
📖 Fighting Chance; Fighting Chance, Part 12 **A:** Dave Hoover **W:** Mark Gruenwald

437 ❑ Mar 1995 Cover: 1.50 **NM** value: **Cover or less**
Circ: Statement: **82,258** CapCity orders: **17,650**
📖 Fighting Chance Epilogue

438 ❑ Apr 1995 Cover: 1.50 **NM** value: **Cover or less**
Circ: Statement: **82,258** CapCity orders: **17,275**
★ 1st Appearance of Cap-Armor.

439 ❑ May 1995 Cover: 1.50 **NM** value: **Cover or less**
Circ: Statement: **82,258** CapCity orders: **16,100**
★ Versus Death-Stalker.

440 ❑ Jun 1995 Cover: 1.50 **NM** value: **Cover or less**
Circ: Statement: **82,258** CapCity orders: **16,875**
📖 Taking A.I.M., Part 1

441 ❑ Jul 1995 Cover: 1.50 **NM** value: **Cover or less**
Circ: Statement: **82,258** CapCity orders: **15,575**
📖 Taking A.I.M., Part 3

442 ❑ Aug 1995 Cover: 1.50 **NM** value: **Cover or less**
Circ: Statement: **82,258** CapCity orders: **14,775**

443 ❑ Sep 1995 Cover: 1.50 **NM** value: **Cover or less**
Circ: Statement: **82,258**
★ Death of Captain America.

444 ❑ Oct 1995 Cover: 1.50 **NM** value: **4.00**
Circ: Statement: **82,258**
• Title changes to Steve Rogers, Captain America;Red Skull brings Cap back to life;Return of Sharon Carter **A:** Ron Garney **W:** Mark Waid

445 ❑ Nov 1995 Cover: 1.50 **NM** value: **3.00**
Circ: Statement: **79,676**
📖 Operation Rebirth, Part 1 • Return of Sharon Carter;Cap revived **A:** Ron Garney **W:** Mark Waid

446 ❑ Dec 1995 Cover: 1.50 **NM** value: **3.00**
Circ: Statement: **79,676**
📖 Operation Rebirth, Part 2 **A:** Ron Garney **W:** Mark Waid ★ Appearance of Red Skull.

447 ❑ Jan 1996 Cover: 1.50 **NM** value: **3.00**
Circ: Statement: **79,676**
📖 Operation Rebirth, Part 3 • Has 1995 Statement, filed 10/1/95; avg print run 135,845; avg sales 78,525; avg subs 3,733; avg total paid 82,258; samples 750; office use 500; max existent 83,508; 39% of run returned **A:** Ron Garney **W:** Mark Waid

448 ❑ Feb 1996 Cover: 2.95 **NM** value: **4.00**
Circ: Statement: **79,676**
• Giant-size. 📖 Operation Rebirth, Part 4 **A:** Ron Garney **W:** Mark Waid

449 ❑ Mar 1996 Cover: 1.50 **NM** value: **2.00**
Circ: Statement: **79,676**
A: Ron Garney **W:** Mark Waid

450 ❑ Apr 1996 Cover: 1.50 **NM** value: **2.00**
Circ: Statement: **79,676**
📖 Man Without a Country, Part 1 • Title returns to Captain America;Cap's American citizenship is revoked **A:** Ron Garney **W:** Mark Waid

450/A ❑ Apr 1996 Cover: 1.50 **NM** value: **2.50**
alternate cover. 📖 Man Without a Country, Part 1 **A:** Ron Garney **W:** Mark Waid

451 ❑ May 1996 Cover: 1.50 **NM** value: **2.00**
Circ: Statement: **79,676**
📖 Man Without a Country, Part 2 **A:** Ron Garney **W:** Mark Waid

452 ❑ Jun 1996 Cover: 1.50 **NM** value: **2.00**
Circ: Statement: **79,676**
A: Ron Garney **W:** Mark Waid

Other grades: Multiply prices above by **1.5 for Mint • 2/3 for Very Fine • 1/3 for Fine • 1/5 for Very Good • 1/8 for Good**

453 ❑ Jul 1996 Cover: 1.50 **NM** value: **2.00**
Circ: Statement: **79,676**
• Cap's citizenship restored **A:** Ron Garney **W:** Mark Waid

454 ❑ Aug 1996 Cover: 1.50 **NM** value: **2.00**
Circ: Statement: **79,676**
Sanctuary final issue. **A:** Ron Garney **W:** Mark Waid

Anl 1 ❑ ca. 1971 Cover: 0.25 **NM** value: **18.00**
• **CGC:** 3 graded, best 9.6
• Cover reads "King-Size Special". The Origin of Captain America; Midnight in Greymoor Castle; If This Be Treason; When You Lie Down with Dogs; 30 Minutes to Live • Reprints from Tales of Suspense #63, 69-71, 75

Anl 2 ❑ ca. 1972 Cover: 0.25 **NM** value: **12.00**
• Cover reads "King-Size Special". The Sleeper Shall Awake; Where Walks the Sleeper; The Final Sleep; The Revengers vs. Captain America • Reprints from Tales of Suspense #72-74; Not Brand Ecch #3

Anl 3 ❑ ca. 1976 Cover: 0.50 **NM** value: **4.00**
The Thing from the Black-Hole Star **A:** Jack Kirby

Anl 4 ❑ ca. 1977 Cover: 0.50 **NM** value: **4.00**
• **CGC:** 2 graded, best 9.4
The Great Mutant Massacre **A:** Jack Kirby ★ 1st Appearance of Slither, Crucible (Marvel).

Anl 5 ❑ ca. 1981 Cover: 0.75 **NM** value: **3.00**
A: Frank Miller(cover)

Anl 6 ❑ ca. 1982 Cover: 1.00 **NM** value: **3.00**
The Invaders • Four Caps

Anl 7 ❑ ca. 1983 Cover: 1.00 **NM** value: **3.00**
The Last Enchantment • Cosmic Cube **A:** Brian Postman **W:** Peter B. Gillis ★ Origin of Kubik (Cosmic Cube).

Anl 8 ❑ ca. 1986 Cover: 1.25 **NM** value: **16.00**
Circ: CapCity orders: **19,400** • **CGC:** 37 graded, best 9.8
★ Appearance of Wolverine.

Anl 9 ❑ ca. 1990 Cover: 2.00 **NM** value: **3.00**
Circ: CapCity orders: **35,000**
Terminus Factor; The Terminus Factor, Part 1 ★ Appearance of Iron Man.

Anl 10 ❑ ca. 1991 Cover: 2.00 **NM** value: **2.50**
Von Strucker Gambit; The Von Strucker gambit, Part 3; Brothers; Forgive Our Trespasses; Worth Fighting For **A:** Don Heck; James Brock; Mike Manley; Larry Alexander **W:** Fabian Nicieza; D.G. Chichester; Mark Gruenwald ★ Origin of Captain America, Bushmaster.

Anl 11 ❑ ca. 1992 Cover: 2.25 **NM** value: **2.50**
Circ: CapCity orders: **27,000**
Citizen Kang, Part 1 • Citizen Kang **A:** Rich Yanizeski; James Brock; Eliot Brown; Larry Alexander **W:** Mark Gruenwald

Anl 12 ❑ ca. 1993 Cover: 2.95 **NM** value: **Cover or less**
Circ: CapCity orders: **37,800**
• trading card;Polybagged with trading card ★ 1st Appearance of Battling Bantam.

Anl 13 ❑ ca. 1994 Cover: 2.95 **NM** value: **Cover or less**
Circ: CapCity orders: **14,800**
★ Versus Red Skull.

Ash 1 ❑ Cover: 0.75 **NM** value: **1.00**
• ashcan edition. • no indicia;Mini "Ashcan" preview

Bk 1 ❑ Cover: 4.95 **NM** value: **Cover or less**
Circ: CapCity orders: **4,150**
• Deathlok Lives

Bk 2/HC ❑ Cover: 75.00 **NM** value: **Cover or less**
Circ: CapCity orders: **2,140**
• The Classic Years;slipcased

Bk 3 ❑ Cover: 12.95 **NM** value: **Cover or less**
• War and Remembrance **A:** John Byrne

GS 1 ❑ Cover: 0.50 **NM** value: **14.00**
Captain America; The Army of Assassins Strikes; The Strength of the Sumo; Break-Out in Cell Block 10; The Origin of Captain America • Reprints from Tales of Suspense

SE 1 ❑ Cover: 2.00 **NM** value: **3.00**
Circ: CapCity orders: **5,550**
• Special Edition #1. • reprint of Steranko issues **A:** Jim Steranko **C:** Jim Steranko

SE 2 ❑ Cover: 2.00 **NM** value: **3.00**
• Special Edition #2. • reprint of Steranko issues **A:** Jim Steranko **C:** Jim Steranko

CAPTAIN AMERICA (VOL. 2) Marvel

As sales overall slipped during the mid-1990s, Marvel reached out to two artists who had left to form Image, Rob Liefeld and Jim Lee, handing them control of Captain America, Iron Man, the Avengers, and the Fantastic Four. It was more than just creative chores. The two moved the characters into a "pocket universe," retelling the stories from the beginning, their way.

No series in "Heroes Reborn" generated more controversy than Captain America Vol. 2. Mark Waid's readers on the old series were decidely not Rob Liefeld fans, and Liefeld's take on the Super Soldier angered many. Forget that Cap originally went into suspended animation due to a fall into Arctic waters; in Liefeld's version, an angry Harry Truman had Cap brainwashed after the hero's refusal to accept the atomic bombing of Hiroshima. (Cap's memory is restored as this series begins.)Many readers were offended by the reworking of history — after all, Captain America had actually been shown proudly saluting an atomic cloud in an issue of Young Men. More, however, were bothered by the series' monosyllabic take on storytelling, with one Liefeld issue sporting just a few more panels than pages.

Sales on early issues were impressive by 1996 standards, but Marvel was hoping for numbers more akin to Liefeld's X-Force #1. After a dispute, Liefeld left the series before a year was done.
— JJM

1 ❑ Nov 1996 Cover: 2.95 **NM** value: **3.00**
Circ: Statement: **131,214** Direct Market orders: **274,250** • **CGC:** 2 graded, best 9.6
Captain America jumping forward on cover. Courage • Steve Rogers regains memories of WW II action **A:** Rob Liefeld **W:** Jeph Loeb; Rob Liefeld

1/A ❑ Nov 1996 Cover: 2.95 **NM** value: **3.00**
• **CGC:** 4 graded, best 9.8
Variant cover (flag background). Courage **A:** Rob Liefeld **W:** Jeph Loeb; Rob Liefeld

1/B ❑ Nov 1996 Cover: 25.00 **NM** value: **Cover or less**
Circ: Direct Market orders: **1,500** • **CGC:** 1 graded, best 9.6
variant cover. Courage **A:** Rob Liefeld **W:** Jeph Loeb; Rob Liefeld

2 ❑ Dec 1996 Cover: 1.95 **NM** value: **2.00**
Circ: Statement: **131,214** Direct Market orders: **132,000**
Secrets **A:** Rob Liefeld **W:** Jeph Loeb; Rob Liefeld ★ Appearance of Nick Fury, Red Skull.

3 ❑ Jan 1997 Cover: 1.95 **NM** value: **2.00**
Circ: Statement: **131,214** Direct Market orders: **124,750**
Patriotism **A:** Rob Liefeld **W:** Jeph Loeb; Rob Liefeld ★ Versus Crossbones.

4 ❑ Feb 1997 Cover: 1.95 **NM** value: **Cover or less**
Circ: Statement: **131,214** Direct Market orders: **117,750**
Fire **A:** Rob Liefeld **W:** Jeph Loeb; Rob Liefeld ★ Versus Master Man.

5 ❑ Mar 1997 Cover: 1.95 **NM** value: **Cover or less**
Circ: Statement: **131,214** Direct Market orders: **112,500**
Victory **A:** Rob Liefeld **W:** Jeph Loeb; Rob Liefeld

6 ❑ Apr 1997 Cover: 1.95 **NM** value: **Cover or less**
Circ: Statement: **131,214** Direct Market orders: **116,750**
Industrial Revolution Epilogue; Soldier **A:** Rob Liefeld **W:** Jeph Loeb; Rob Liefeld ★ Appearance of Cable.

7 ❑ May 1997 Cover: 1.95 **NM** value: **Cover or less**
Circ: Statement: **131,214** Diamd. preorders: **109,134**
Crossroads **A:** Joe Phillips **W:** James Robinson ★ Origin of Captain America (Heroes Reborn version).

8 ❑ Jun 1997 Cover: 1.95 **NM** value: **Cover or less**
Circ: Statement: **131,214** Diamd. preorders: **114,668**

9 ❑ Jul 1997 Cover: 1.95 **NM** value: **Cover or less**
Circ: Statement: **131,214** Diamd. preorders: **107,765**

10 ❑ Aug 1997 Cover: 1.99 **NM** value: **Cover or less**
Circ: Statement: **131,214** Diamd. preorders: **108,860**
• gatefold summary. ★ Appearance of Falcon.

11 ❑ Sep 1997 Cover: 1.99 **NM** value: **Cover or less**
Circ: Statement: **131,214** Diamd. preorders: **101,896**
• gatefold summary. ★ Versus Nick Fury.

12 ❑ Oct 1997 Cover: 1.99 **NM** value: **Cover or less**
Circ: Statement: **153,214** Diamd. preorders: **109,168**
cover forms quadtych with Avengers #12. • gatefold summary. Heroes Reunited, Part 4 • Iron Man #12;and Fantastic Four #12

Ash 1 ❑ Mar 1995 Cover: 1.95 **NM** value: **Cover or less**
• Collector's Preview

ASH 1/A ❑ **NM** value: **1.00**
no cover price. • Special Comicon Edition.

CAPTAIN AMERICA (VOL. 3) Marvel

Captain America had been around the block a few times. Since Private Steve Rogers swallowed that super-soldier formula in the secret lab of Dr. Reinstein in 1941, Captain America had fought Nazis, Communists, Hydra, and the Secret Empire; been blown up, frozen solid, thrust headlong into the mid-1960s, and faced off adversity on his own and as a member of the Avengers. But rarely had he faced a more daunting challenge than regaining reader faith and credibility after Rob Liefeld's relaunch in Captain America (Vol. 2).

Fortunately, the creative team of Mark Waid and Ron Garney were up to the task of breathing new life into this American icon. Waid's thought-provoking storyline and Garney's lean, gutsy art drew comparisons to the best work ever done on the character by the likes of Jack Kirby, Jim Steranko and Steve Englehart.

After time passed and a few creator changes transpired, Marvel cancelled the series again, moving Cap, thought dead for a time, into a 2002 limited series, Captain America: Dead Man Running.

1 ❑ Jan 1998 Cover: 2.99 **NM** value: **3.50**
Circ: Statement: **153,214** Diamd. preorders: **197,884** • **CGC:** 5 graded, best 9.8
wraparound cover. • gatefold summary. • follows events in Heroes Return;Cap in Japan **A:** Ron Garney **W:** Mark Waid ★ Versus Lady Deathstrike.

1/A ❑ Jan 1998 Cover: 2.99 **NM** value: **4.00**
• **CGC:** 1 graded, best 9.8
alternate cover. • gatefold summary. • follows events in Heroes Return;Cap in Japan **A:** Ron Garney **W:** Mark Waid ★ Versus Lady Deathstrike.

2 ❑ Feb 1998 Cover: 1.99 **NM** value: **3.00**
Circ: Statement: **153,214** Diamd. preorders: **142,765** • **CGC:** 2 graded, best 9.8
• gatefold summary. • Cap loses his shield; Has 1997 Statement, filed 10/1/97; avg print run 217,181; avg sales 127,974; avg subs 3,240; avg total paid 131,214; samples 324; office use 125; max existent 131,663; 39% of run returned

2/A ❑ Feb 1998 Cover: 1.99 **NM** value: **3.00**
variant cover.

3 ❑ Mar 1998 Cover: 1.99 **NM** value: **2.00**
Circ: Statement: **153,214** Diamd. preorders: **108,291**
• gatefold summary. Museum Piece **A:** Ron Garney **W:** Bob Wiacek ★ 1st Appearance of New shield.

4 ❑ Apr 1998 Cover: 1.99 **NM** value: **2.00**
Circ: Statement: **153,214** Diamd. preorders: **98,004**
• gatefold summary. • true identity of Sensational Hydra revealed ★ Appearance of Hawkeye.

5 ❑ May 1998 Cover: 1.99 **NM** value: **2.00**
Circ: Statement: **153,214** Diamd. preorders: **95,967**
• gatefold summary. • Cap replaced by Skrull ★ Appearance of Thor.

6 ❑ Jun 1998 Cover: 1.99 **NM** value: **2.00**
Circ: Statement: **153,214** Diamd. preorders: **95,929**
• gatefold summary. • Skrulls revealed

7 ❑ Jul 1998 Cover: 1.99 **NM** value: **2.00**
Circ: Statement: **153,214** Diamd. preorders: **91,879**
• gatefold summary. ★ Versus Skrulls.

8 ❑ Aug 1998 Cover: 1.99 **NM** value: **2.00**
Circ: Statement: **153,214** Diamd. preorders: **93,527**
• gatefold summary. Live Kree or Die, Part 2 • Cap's shield destroyed;continues in Quicksilver #10

9 ❑ Sep 1998 Cover: 1.99 **NM** value: **2.00**
Circ: Statement: **94,475** Diamd. preorders: **85,836**
• gatefold summary. • Cap gets new virtual shield

10 ❑ Oct 1998 Cover: 1.99 **NM** value: **2.00**
Circ: Statement: **94,475** Diamd. preorders: **82,993**
• gatefold summary. • Nightmare ★ Versus USAgent.

11 ❑ Nov 1998 Cover: 1.99 **NM** value: **Cover or less**
Circ: Statement: **94,475** Diamd. preorders: **82,697**
• gatefold summary. • Has 1998 Statement, filed 10/1/98; avg print run 226,700; avg sales 150,704; avg subs 2,510; avg total paid 153,214; samples 324; office use 125; max existent 153,663; 32% of run returned ★ Versus Nightmare.

12 ❑ Dec 1998 Cover: 2.99 **NM** value: **Cover or less**
Circ: Statement: **94,475** Diamd. preorders: **81,682**
wraparound cover. • double-sized. ★ Versus Nightmare.

12/LE ❑ Dec 1998 Cover: 24.99 **NM** value: **Cover or less**

13 ❑ Jan 1999 Cover: 1.99 **NM** value: **Cover or less**
Circ: Statement: **94,475** Diamd. preorders: **76,096**
• gatefold summary. **A:** Dougie Braithwaite **W:** Mark Waid ★ Versus A.I.M..

14 ❑ Feb 1999 Cover: 1.99 **NM** value: **Cover or less**
Circ: Statement: **94,475** Diamd. preorders: **72,727**
• gatefold summary. **A:** Dougie Braithwaite **W:** Mark Waid ★ Origin of Red Skull. ★ Appearance of Red Skull.

15 ❑ Mar 1999 Cover: 1.99 **NM** value: **Cover or less**
Circ: Statement: **94,475** Diamd. preorders: **71,398**
A: Andy Kubert **W:** Mark Waid ★ Appearance of Red Skull. ★ Versus Red Skull.

16 ❑ Apr 1999 Cover: 1.99 **NM** value: **Cover or less**
Circ: Statement: **94,475** Diamd. preorders: **66,874**
A: Andy Kubert **W:** Mark Waid ★ Appearance of Red Skull. ★ Versus Red Skull.

17 ❑ May 1999 Cover: 1.99 **NM** value: **Cover or less**
Circ: Statement: **94,475** Diamd. preorders: **66,359**
★ Appearance of Korvac. ★ Death of Red Skull.

18 ❑ Jun 1999 Cover: 1.99 **NM** value: **Cover or less**
Circ: Statement: **94,475** Diamd. preorders: **67,946**
★ Versus Korvac.

19 ❑ Jul 1999 Cover: 1.99 **NM** value: **Cover or less**
Circ: Statement: **94,475** Diamd. preorders: **65,949**
Triumph of the Will **A:** Andy Kubert **W:** Mark Waid ★ Appearance of Sharon Carter, Red Skull.

20 ❑ Aug 1999 Cover: 1.99 **NM** value: **Cover or less**
Circ: Statement: **94,475** Diamd. preorders: **64,855**
• Sgt. Fury back-up (b&w) ★ Appearance of USAgent.

21 ❑ Sep 1999 Cover: 1.99 **NM** value: **Cover or less**
Circ: Statement: **91,046** Diamd. preorders: **63,065**
• Sgt. Fury back-up (b&w) ★ Appearance of Giant-Man, Wasp, Iron Man.

22 ❑ Oct 1999 Cover: 1.99 **NM** value: **Cover or less**
Circ: Statement: **91,046** Diamd. preorders: **59,946**
• Cap's shield restored ★ Versus Klaw.

23 ❑ Nov 1999 Cover: 1.99 **NM** value: **Cover or less**
Circ: Statement: **91,046** Diamd. preorders: **57,292**
• Has 1999 Statement, filed 10/1/99; avg print run 136,050; avg sales 91,851; avg subs 2,624; avg total paid 94,475; samples 1,850; office use 125; max existent 96,450; 30% of run returned

24 ❑ Dec 2000 Cover: 1.99 **NM** value: **2.25**
Circ: Statement: **91,046** Diamd. preorders: **56,171**

25 ❑ Jan 2000 Cover: 2.99 **NM** value: **Cover or less**
Circ: Statement: **91,046** Diamd. preorders: **56,308**
• Giant-size.

26 ❑ Feb 2000 Cover: 1.99 **NM** value: **2.25**
Circ: Statement: **91,046** Diamd. preorders: **55,756**
Twisted Tomorrows, Part 2 **A:** Andy Kubert **W:** Dan Jurgens ★ Appearance of Falcon. ★ Versus Hatemonger.

27 ❑ Mar 2000 Cover: 1.99 **NM** value: **2.25**
Circ: Statement: **91,046** Diamd. preorders: **50,943**

28 ❑ Apr 2000 Cover: 1.99 **NM** value: **2.25**
Circ: Statement: **91,046** Diamd. preorders: **48,272**

29 ❑ May 2000 Cover: 1.99 **NM** value: **2.25**
Circ: Statement: **91,046** Diamd. preorders: **49,057**

30 ❑ Jun 2000 Cover: 2.25 **NM** value: **Cover or less**
Circ: Statement: **91,046** Diamd. preorders: **48,118**
Waste of Dreams **A:** Andy Kubert **W:** Dan Jurgens ★ Appearance of Count Nefaria.

31 ❑ Jul 2000 Cover: 2.25 **NM** value: **Cover or less**
Circ: Statement: **91,046** Diamd. preorders: **47,382**

32 ❑ Aug 2000 Cover: 2.25 **NM** value: **Cover or less**
Circ: Statement: **91,046** Diamd. preorders: **47,442**
Heart • World War II story **A:** Jerry Ordway **C:** Andy Kubert **W:** Dan Jurgens

33 ❑ Sep 2000 Cover: 2.25 **NM** value: **Cover or less**
Circ: Statement: **91,046** Diamd. preorders: **47,745**

34 ❑ Oct 2000 Cover: 2.25 **NM** value: **Cover or less**
Circ: Statement: **51,803** Diamd. preorders: **44,123**

35 ❑ Nov 2000 Cover: 2.25 **NM** value: **Cover or less**
Circ: Statement: **51,803** Diamd. preorders: **44,496**
When Strikes Protocide! **A:** Dan Jurgens **W:** Dan Jurgens ★ Versus Protocide.

36 ❑ Dec 2000 Cover: 2.25 **NM** value: **Cover or less**
Circ: Statement: **51,803** Diamd. preorders: **45,221**

CGC-graded: Multiply prices above by **33 for 9.9 M • 16 for 9.8 NM/M • 7 for 9.6 NM+ • 5 for 9.4 NM • 2.5 for 9.2 NM- • 1.5 for 9.0 VF/NM**

📖 Maximum Security; Maelstrom Within **A:** Dan Jurgens **C:** Dan Jurgens **W:** Dan Jurgens ★ Versus Mercurio.

37 ❑ Jan 2001 Cover: 2.25 **NM** value: **Cover or less**
Circ: Statement: **51,803** Diamd. preorders: **43,191**
📖 Brothers • Has 2000 Statement, filed 10/1/2000; avg print run 120,742; avg sales 88,776; avg subs 2,270; avg total paid 91,046; samples 600; office use 125; max existent 91,771; 24% of run returned **A:** Dan Jurgens **C:** Dan Jurgens **W:** Dan Jurgens ★ Versus Protocide.

38 ❑ Feb 2001 Cover: 2.25 **NM** value: **Cover or less**
Circ: Statement: **51,803** Diamd. preorders: **42,352**
📖 Across the Rubicon **A:** Dan Jurgens **C:** Dan Jurgens **W:** Dan Jurgens ★ Appearance of Protocide.

39 ❑ Mar 2001 Cover: 2.25 **NM** value: **Cover or less**
Circ: Statement: **51,803** Diamd. preorders: **41,074**
📖 A Gulf So Wide **A:** Dan Jurgens **C:** Dan Jurgens **W:** Dan Jurgens

40 ❑ Apr 2001 Cover: 2.25 **NM** value: **Cover or less**
Circ: Statement: **51,803** Diamd. preorders: **40,549**
📖 Fighting Back **A:** Dan Jurgens **C:** Dan Jurgens **W:** Dan Jurgens

41 ❑ May 2001 Cover: 2.25 **NM** value: **Cover or less**
Circ: Statement: **51,803** Diamd. preorders: **39,805**
📖 Duel **A:** Dan Jurgens **C:** Dan Jurgens **W:** Dan Jurgens

42 ❑ Jun 2001 Cover: 2.25 **NM** value: **Cover or less**
Circ: Statement: **51,803** Diamd. preorders: **39,802**

43 ❑ Jul 2001 Cover: 2.25 **NM** value: **Cover or less**
Circ: Statement: **51,803** Diamd. preorders: **39,259**

44 ❑ Aug 2001 Cover: 2.25 **NM** value: **Cover or less**
Circ: Statement: **51,803** Diamd. preorders: **39,628**

45 ❑ Sep 2001 Cover: 2.25 **NM** value: **Cover or less**
Circ: Statement: **51,803** Diamd. preorders: **41,259**

46 ❑ Oct 2001 Cover: 2.25 **NM** value: **Cover or less**
Circ: Diamd. preorders: **41,024**

47 ❑ Nov 2001 Cover: 2.25 **NM** value: **Cover or less**
Circ: Diamd. preorders: **38,136**

48 ❑ Dec 2001 Cover: 2.25 **NM** value: **Cover or less**
Circ: Diamd. preorders: **37,830**

49 ❑ Jan 2002 Cover: 2.25 **NM** value: **Cover or less**
Circ: Diamd. preorders: **38,012**

50 ❑ Feb 2002 Cover: 5.95 **NM** value: **Cover or less**
Circ: Diamd. preorders: **43,001**
• Has 2001 Statement, filed 10/1/2001; avg print run 70,400; avg sales 49,509; avg subs 2,294; avg total paid 51,803; samples 600; office use 0; max existent 52,403; 26% of run returned

Anl 1998❑ca. 1998 Cover: 3.50 **NM** value: **Cover or less**
Circ: Diamd. preorders: **47,352**
wraparound cover.

Anl 1999❑ca. 1999 Cover: 3.50 **NM** value: **Cover or less**
Circ: Diamd. preorders: **40,550**
★ Versus Flag-Smasher.

Anl 2000❑ca. 2000 Cover: 3.50 **NM** value: **Cover or less**
Circ: Diamd. preorders: **33,147**
📖 Who is … Protocide?!; The Test • continued from Captain America #35 **A:** Scot Eaton; Greg Scott **W:** Dan Jurgens; Bill Rosemann ★ Origin of Protocide, Captain America. ★ 1st Appearance of Elite Agents of S.H.I.E.L.D..

CAPTAIN & THE KIDS — United Feature

1 ❑	ca. 1947	Cover: 0.10	**NM** value: **100.00**
2 ❑		Cover: 0.10	**NM** value: **75.00**
3 ❑		Cover: 0.10	**NM** value: **50.00**
4 ❑		Cover: 0.10	**NM** value: **45.00**
5 ❑		Cover: 0.10	**NM** value: **45.00**
6 ❑		Cover: 0.10	**NM** value: **45.00**
7 ❑		Cover: 0.10	**NM** value: **40.00**
8 ❑		Cover: 0.10	**NM** value: **40.00**
9 ❑		Cover: 0.10	**NM** value: **40.00**
10 ❑		Cover: 0.10	**NM** value: **35.00**
11 ❑		Cover: 0.10	**NM** value: **35.00**
12 ❑		Cover: 0.10	**NM** value: **35.00**
13 ❑		Cover: 0.10	**NM** value: **30.00**
14 ❑		Cover: 0.10	**NM** value: **30.00**
15 ❑		Cover: 0.10	**NM** value: **30.00**
16 ❑		Cover: 0.10	**NM** value: **30.00**
17 ❑	ca. 1949	Cover: 0.10	**NM** value: **25.00**
18 ❑		Cover: 0.10	**NM** value: **25.00**
19 ❑		Cover: 0.10	**NM** value: **25.00**
20 ❑		Cover: 0.10	**NM** value: **20.00**
21 ❑	ca. 1951	Cover: 0.10	**NM** value: **20.00**
22 ❑		Cover: 0.10	**NM** value: **20.00**
23 ❑		Cover: 0.10	**NM** value: **20.00**
24 ❑		Cover: 0.10	**NM** value: **20.00**
25 ❑		Cover: 0.10	**NM** value: **15.00**
26 ❑		Cover: 0.10	**NM** value: **15.00**
27 ❑		Cover: 0.10	**NM** value: **15.00**
28 ❑		Cover: 0.10	**NM** value: **15.00**
29 ❑		Cover: 0.10	**NM** value: **15.00**
30 ❑		Cover: 0.10	**NM** value: **10.00**
31 ❑		Cover: 0.10	**NM** value: **10.00**
32 ❑		Cover: 0.10	**NM** value: **10.00**

CAPTAIN ATOM (CHARLTON) — Charlton

Air Force Captain Adam Combine is the victim of a freak nuclear accident, but, instead of being disintegrated by the deadly radiation, he is transformed into a being of pure energy, Captain Atom.

Captain Atom first appeared in Charlton's Space Adventures in 1960, an early entry in the Silver Age super-hero revival. Despite lean and gutsy art by Steve Ditko, Captain Atom could not survive Charlton's mediocre distribution and sank into obscurity. The strip was revived in this series in 1967 under the editorship of Dick Giordano, who brought back Ditko, along with Denny O'Neil and Jim Aparo.

In the mid-1980s, DC bought the rights to the Charlton heroes, using them both as heroes in the DC universe and as the basis for the characters in Alan Moore's Watchmen, where Captain Atom served as the template for Doc Manhattan.

78 ❑ Dec 1965 Cover: 0.12 **NM** value: **60.00**
• **CGC:** 7 graded, best 9.4
• Series continued from Strange Suspense Stories #77 ★ Origin of Captain Atom.

79 ❑ Mar 1966 Cover: 0.12 **NM** value: **40.00**
• **CGC:** 2 graded, best 9.4

80 ❑ May 1966 Cover: 0.12 **NM** value: **40.00**
• **CGC:** 1 graded, best 8.5
📖 Death Knell of the World **A:** Steve Ditko

81 ❑ Jul 1966 Cover: 0.12 **NM** value: **35.00**
• **CGC:** 1 graded, best 8.0

82 ❑ Sep 1966 Cover: 0.12 **NM** value: **35.00**
• **CGC:** 1 graded, best 9.0

83 ❑ Nov 1966 Cover: 0.12 **NM** value: **35.00**
• **CGC:** 1 graded, best 9.0
★ 1st Appearance of Ted Kord (Blue Beetle).

84 ❑ Jan 1967 Cover: 0.12 **NM** value: **35.00**
• **CGC:** 1 graded, best 9.2
★ 1st Appearance of Captain Atom (new).

85 ❑ Mar 1967 Cover: 0.12 **NM** value: **35.00**
• **CGC:** 1 graded, best 9.0

86 ❑ Jun 1967 Cover: 0.12 **NM** value: **35.00**

87 ❑ Aug 1967 Cover: 0.12 **NM** value: **35.00**
📖 The Menace: Of The Fiery Icer • Nightshade back-up story **A:** Steve Ditko **W:** Dave Kaler

88 ❑ Oct 1967 Cover: 0.12 **NM** value: **35.00**
• **CGC:** 1 graded, best 9.0

89 ❑ Dec 1967 Cover: 0.12 **NM** value: **35.00**
• **CGC:** 1 graded, best 9.0
final issue.

CAPTAIN ATOM (DC) — DC

1 ❑ Mar 1987 Cover: 1.00 **NM** value: **2.00**
Circ: CapCity orders: **24,050**
📖 Point of Origin • New costume **A:** Pat Broderick **W:** Cary Bates
★ Origin of Captain Atom.

2 ❑ Apr 1987 Cover: 0.75 **NM** value: **1.50**
Circ: CapCity orders: **17,400**

3 ❑ May 1987 Cover: 0.75 **NM** value: **1.50**
Circ: CapCity orders: **15,100**
★ Origin of Captain Atom (fake origin).

4 ❑ Jun 1987 Cover: 0.75 **NM** value: **1.50**
Circ: CapCity orders: **13,900**

5 ❑ Jul 1987 Cover: 0.75 **NM** value: **1.50**
Circ: CapCity orders: **15,250**
★ Appearance of Firestorm.

6 ❑ Aug 1987 Cover: 0.75 **NM** value: **1.25**
Circ: CapCity orders: **16,400**
★ Versus Doctor Spectro.

7 ❑ Sep 1987 Cover: 0.75 **NM** value: **1.25**
Circ: CapCity orders: **17,150**

8 ❑ Oct 1987 Cover: 0.75 **NM** value: **1.25**
Circ: CapCity orders: **17,400**
★ Appearance of Plastique.

9 ❑ Nov 1987 Cover: 0.75 **NM** value: **1.25**
Circ: CapCity orders: **16,700**

10 ❑ Dec 1987 Cover: 0.75 **NM** value: **1.25**
Circ: CapCity orders: **16,000**

11 ❑ Jan 1988 Cover: 0.75 **NM** value: **1.25**
Circ: CapCity orders: **19,850**
• Millennium ★ Appearance of Firestorm.

12 ❑ Feb 1988 Cover: 0.75 **NM** value: **1.25**
Circ: CapCity orders: **15,500**
★ 1st Appearance of Major Force.

13 ❑ Mar 1988 Cover: 0.75 **NM** value: **1.25**
Circ: CapCity orders: **15,250**

14 ❑ Apr 1988 Cover: 0.75 **NM** value: **1.25**
Circ: CapCity orders: **15,650**

15 ❑ May 1988 Cover: 0.75 **NM** value: **1.25**
Circ: CapCity orders: **14,600**
★ Versus Major Force.

16 ❑ Jun 1988 Cover: 0.75 **NM** value: **1.25**
Circ: CapCity orders: **14,900**
★ Appearance of JLI.

17 ❑ Jul 1988 Cover: 1.00 **NM** value: **1.25**
Circ: CapCity orders: **14,250**
★ Appearance of Swamp Thing.

18 ❑ Aug 1988 Cover: 1.00 **NM** value: **1.25**
Circ: CapCity orders: **13,700**

19 ❑ Sep 1988 Cover: 1.00 **NM** value: **1.25**
Circ: CapCity orders: **13,650**

20 ❑ Oct 1988 Cover: 1.00 **NM** value: **1.25**
Circ: CapCity orders: **14,400**
★ Appearance of Blue Beetle.

21 ❑ Nov 1988 Cover: 1.00 **NM** value: **1.25**
Circ: CapCity orders: **13,150**

22 ❑ Dec 1988 Cover: 1.00 **NM** value: **1.25**
Circ: CapCity orders: **13,100**
• Plastique vs. Nightshade

23 ❑ ca. 1988 Cover: 1.00 **NM** value: **1.25**
Circ: CapCity orders: **12,450**
• no month of publication ★ Versus Ghost.

24 ❑ ca. 1989 Cover: 1.00 **NM** value: **1.25**
Circ: CapCity orders: **14,760**
• Invasion!;no month of publication

25 ❑ Jan 1989 Cover: 1.00 **NM** value: **1.25**
Circ: CapCity orders: **13,100**
• Invasion!;no month of publication

26 ❑ Feb 1989 Cover: 1.00 **NM** value: **1.25**
Circ: CapCity orders: **12,150**
★ Origin of Captain Atom. ★ Appearance of JLA.

27 ❑ Mar 1989 Cover: 1.00 **NM** value: **1.25**
Circ: CapCity orders: **11,850**
📖 Truth and Consequences **A:** Pat Broderick **W:** Cary Bates; Greg Weisman ★ Origin of Captain Atom.

28 ❑ Apr 1989 Cover: 1.00 **NM** value: **1.25**
Circ: CapCity orders: **12,500**
★ Origin of Captain Atom. ★ Versus Ghost.

29 ❑ May 1989 Cover: 1.00 **NM** value: **1.25**
Circ: CapCity orders: **12,300**
📖 A Contrite Heart **A:** Rafael Kayanan **W:** Cary Bates; Greg Weisman

30 ❑ Jun 1989 Cover: 1.00 **NM** value: **1.25**
Circ: CapCity orders: **13,800**
📖 Janus Directive

31 ❑ Jul 1989 Cover: 1.00 **NM** value: **1.25**
Circ: CapCity orders: **12,950**
★ Versus Rocket Red.

32 ❑ Aug 1989 Cover: 1.00 **NM** value: **1.25**
Circ: CapCity orders: **13,200**

33 ❑ Sep 1989 Cover: 1.00 **NM** value: **1.25**
Circ: CapCity orders: **12,700**
• Batman;new costume

34 ❑ Oct 1989 Cover: 1.00 **NM** value: **1.25**
Circ: CapCity orders: **12,650**
★ Versus Doctor Spectro.

35 ❑ Nov 1989 Cover: 1.00 **NM** value: **1.25**
Circ: CapCity orders: **12,000**
• back to old costume ★ Appearance of Major Force.

36 ❑ Dec 1989 Cover: 1.00 **NM** value: **1.25**
Circ: CapCity orders: **12,500**

37 ❑ Jan 1990 Cover: 1.00 **NM** value: **1.25**
Circ: CapCity orders: **12,050**

38 ❑ Feb 1990 Cover: 1.00 **NM** value: **1.25**
Circ: CapCity orders: **11,500**
★ Versus Black Racer.

39 ❑ Mar 1990 Cover: 1.00 **NM** value: **1.25**
Circ: CapCity orders: **11,150**

40 ❑ Apr 1990 Cover: 1.00 **NM** value: **1.25**
Circ: CapCity orders: **10,850**

41 ❑ May 1990 Cover: 1.00 **NM** value: **1.25**
Circ: CapCity orders: **10,950**

42 ❑ Jun 1990 Cover: 1.00 **NM** value: **1.25**
Circ: CapCity orders: **10,650**

43 ❑ Jul 1990 Cover: 1.00 **NM** value: **1.25**
Circ: CapCity orders: **10,350**

44 ❑ Aug 1990 Cover: 1.00 **NM** value: **1.25**
Circ: CapCity orders: **9,800**
★ Appearance of Plastique.

45 ❑ Sep 1990 Cover: 1.00 **NM** value: **1.25**
Circ: CapCity orders: **9,500**

46 ❑ Oct 1990 Cover: 1.00 **NM** value: **1.25**
Circ: CapCity orders: **9,650**
• Superman

47 ❑ Nov 1990 Cover: 1.00 **NM** value: **1.25**
Circ: CapCity orders: **9,900**

48 ❑ Dec 1990 Cover: 1.00 **NM** value: **1.25**
Circ: CapCity orders: **9,250**

49 ❑ Jan 1991 Cover: 1.00 **NM** value: **1.25**
Circ: CapCity orders: **9,150**
• Trial of Plastique

50 ❑ Feb 1991 Cover: 2.00 **NM** value: **Cover or less**
Circ: CapCity orders: **9,800**
• Giant-size. ★ Death of Megala.

51 ❑ Mar 1991 Cover: 1.00 **NM** value: **1.25**
Circ: CapCity orders: **8,950**

52 ❑ Apr 1991 Cover: 1.00 **NM** value: **1.25**
Circ: CapCity orders: **8,600**

53 ❑ May 1991 Cover: 1.00 **NM** value: **1.25**
Circ: CapCity orders: **8,700**

54 ❑ Jun 1991 Cover: 1.00 **NM** value: **1.25**
Circ: CapCity orders: **8,650**

55 ❑ Jul 1991 Cover: 1.00 **NM** value: **1.25**
Circ: CapCity orders: **8,350**

56 ❑ Aug 1991 Cover: 1.00 **NM** value: **1.25**
Circ: CapCity orders: **8,600**

57 ❑ Sep 1991 Cover: 1.00 **NM** value: **1.25**
Circ: CapCity orders: **9,200**
📖 War of the Gods, Part 7 final issue.

Anl 1❑ca. 1988 Cover: 1.25 **NM** value: **1.50**
Circ: CapCity orders: **15,900**
says 88 on cover, 87 in indicia. ★ 1st Appearance of Major Force. ★ Versus Major Force.

Anl 2❑ca. 1989 Cover: 1.50 **NM** value: **Cover or less**
Circ: CapCity orders: **13,050**
★ Versus Queen Bee.

CAPTAIN ATOM (NATIONWIDE) — Nationwide

1 ❑ ca. 1950 Cover: 0.10 **NM** value: **300.00**
• **CGC:** 2 graded, best 8.5

2 ❑	Cover: 0.10	**NM** value: **150.00**
3 ❑	Cover: 0.10	**NM** value: **150.00**
4 ❑	Cover: 0.10	**NM** value: **150.00**
5 ❑	Cover: 0.10	**NM** value: **150.00**
6 ❑	Cover: 0.10	**NM** value: **125.00**
7 ❑	Cover: 0.10	**NM** value: **125.00**

CAPTAIN AWARENESS: ASSAULT ON CAMPUS — 2-D Graphics

1 ❑ Cover: 3.95 **NM** value: **Cover or less**
No issue number. • social issues

CAPTAIN BATTLE — Picture Scoop

3 ❑ Win 1942 Cover: 0.10 **NM** value: **500.00**

4 ❑ Cover: 0.10 **NM** value: **450.00**

5 ❑ Sum 1943 Cover: 0.10 **NM** value: **450.00**
• **CGC:** 1 graded, best 7.5

Other grades: Multiply prices above by **1.5 for Mint • 2/3 for Very Fine • 1/3 for Fine • 1/5 for Very Good • 1/8 for Good**

CAPTAIN BATTLE COMICS — New Friday

1 ❑ Sum 1941 Cover: 0.10 **NM** value: **1200.00**
• **CGC:** 1 graded, best 8.5
2 ❑ Fal 1941 Cover: 0.10 **NM** value: **750.00**

CAPTAIN BATTLE JR. — Lev Gleason

1 ❑ Fal 1943 Cover: 0.10 **NM** value: **900.00**
• **CGC:** 2 graded, best 8.0
2 ❑ Win 1943 Cover: 0.10 **NM** value: **700.00**

CAPTAIN CANUCK — Comely

1 ❑ Jul 1975 Cover: 0.35 **NM** value: **3.00**
W: Richard Comely
2 ❑ Cover: 0.35 **NM** value: **2.00**
• no month of publication
3 ❑ Cover: 0.35 **NM** value: **2.00**
• no month of publication
4 ❑ Aug 1979 Cover: 0.50 **NM** value: **1.50**
• New publisher
5 ❑ Sep 1979 Cover: 0.50 **NM** value: **1.50**
6 ❑ Nov 1979 Cover: 0.50 **NM** value: **1.50**
7 ❑ Jan 1980 Cover: 0.50 **NM** value: **1.50**
8 ❑ Mar 1980 Cover: 0.50 **NM** value: **1.50**
A: George Freeman **W:** Richard Comely; George Freeman
9 ❑ May 1980 Cover: 0.50 **NM** value: **1.50**
says Jun on cover. • May in indicia
10 ❑ Aug 1980 Cover: 0.50 **NM** value: **1.50**
11 ❑ Oct 1980 Cover: 0.50 **NM** value: **1.50**
12 ❑ Dec 1980 Cover: 0.50 **NM** value: **1.50**
13 ❑ Feb 1981 Cover: 0.50 **NM** value: **1.50**
14 ❑ Apr 1981 Cover: 0.50 **NM** value: **1.50**
📖 Fire-Fight; Beyond final issue. **A:** George Freeman; Jean-Claude St. Aubin **W:** George Freeman

CAPTAIN CANUCK (2ND SERIES) — Semple

0/A ❑ Cover: 0.95 **NM** value: **1.50**
Circ: CapCity orders: **4,480**
• English
0/B ❑ Cover: 0.95 **NM** value: **1.50**
• French
1 ❑ Cover: 1.95 **NM** value: **Cover or less**
1/GO❑ Cover: 2.95 **NM** value: **Cover or less**
• gold;trading cards

CAPTAIN CANUCK FIRST SUMMER SPECIAL — Comely

1 ❑ Sep 1980 Cover: 0.95 **NM** value: **1.50**

CAPTAIN CANUCK REBORN — Semple

0 ❑ Sep 1993 Cover: 0.95 **NM** value: **1.50**
A: Richard Comely **W:** Richard Comely
1 ❑ Jan 1994 Cover: 2.50 **NM** value: **Cover or less**
A: Richard Comely; Leonard Kirk **W:** Richard Comely
1/GO❑ Cover: 2.95 **NM** value: **3.00**
• Gold polybagged edition with trading cards.
2 ❑ Jul 1994 Cover: 2.50 **NM** value: **Cover or less**
3 ❑ b&w Cover: 2.50 **NM** value: **Cover or less**
cardstock cover. • strip reprints

CAPTAIN CARROT AND HIS AMAZING ZOO CREW — DC

An irradiated carrot turns mild-mannered cartoon bunny Roger Rabbit (no, not the movie and novel Roger Rabbit)into Captain Carrot, who's out to save the world. He gets by with a little help from his friends: Pig-Iron, actually Peter Porkchops; Fastback, the Reptilian Rocket, a descendant of the Amazing Whatzit; Rubberduck, a stretchy mallard; Alley-Kat-Abra, a feline sorceress; and Yankee Poodle, a Wonder Woman clone. Superman makes an appearance in the first issue. Scott Shaw (who signed his name with an exclamation mark) and Roy Thomas provided many stories resurrecting characters from DC's funny-animal past and integrating them into a funny-animal superhero present day. The back-issue market has rarely valued this series highly, but there's strong reading value to these issues.

1 ❑ Mar 1982 Cover: 0.60 **NM** value: **1.50**
📖 The Pluto Syndrome **A:** Scott Shaw **W:** Roy Thomas ★ Appearance of Superman, Starro.
2 ❑ Apr 1982 Cover: 0.60 **NM** value: **1.00**
A: Alfredo Alcala
3 ❑ May 1982 Cover: 0.60 **NM** value: **1.00**
4 ❑ Jun 1982 Cover: 0.60 **NM** value: **1.00**
5 ❑ Jul 1982 Cover: 0.60 **NM** value: **1.00**
★ Appearance of Oklahoma Bones.
6 ❑ Aug 1982 Cover: 0.60 **NM** value: **1.00**
★ Versus Bunny from Beyond.
7 ❑ Sep 1982 Cover: 0.60 **NM** value: **1.00**
★ Appearance of Bow-zar the Barbarian.
8 ❑ Oct 1982 Cover: 0.60 **NM** value: **1.00**
★ 1st Appearance of Z-Building (Zoo Crew's Headquarters).
9 ❑ Nov 1982 Cover: 0.60 **NM** value: **1.00**
• Masters of the Universe preview ★ Appearance of Terrific Whatzie, Three Mouseketeers.
10 ❑ Dec 1982 Cover: 0.60 **NM** value: **1.00**
11 ❑ Jan 1983 Cover: 0.60 **NM** value: **1.00**
12 ❑ Feb 1983 Cover: 0.60 **NM** value: **1.00**
• 1st Art Adams art;1st Arthur Adams art **A:** Arthur Adams ★ 1st Appearance of Little Cheese.
13 ❑ Mar 1983 Cover: 0.60 **NM** value: **1.00**
14 ❑ Apr 1983 Cover: 0.60 **NM** value: **1.00**
📖 Crisis on Earth-C!, Part 1 • Justa Lotta Animals **A:** Carol Lay; Al Gordon; Scott Shaw **W:** Scott Shaw; E. Nelson Bridwell
15 ❑ May 1983 Cover: 0.60 **NM** value: **1.00**
• Justa Lotta Animals
16 ❑ Jun 1983 Cover: 0.60 **NM** value: **1.00**
17 ❑ Jul 1983 Cover: 0.60 **NM** value: **1.00**
18 ❑ Aug 1983 Cover: 0.60 **NM** value: **1.00**
19 ❑ Sep 1983 Cover: 0.60 **NM** value: **1.00**
★ Versus Frogzilla.
20 ❑ Nov 1983 Cover: 0.60 **NM** value: **1.00**
final issue.★ Appearance of Changeling. ★ Versus Gorilla Grodd.

CAPTAIN CONFEDERACY (EPIC) — Marvel / Epic

1 ❑ Nov 1991 Cover: 1.95 **NM** value: **2.00**
Circ: CapCity orders: **10,000**
📖 Crossroad **A:** Vince Stone **W:** Will Shetterly
2 ❑ Dec 1991 Cover: 1.95 **NM** value: **2.00**
Circ: CapCity orders: **7,800**
A: Vince Stone **W:** Will Shetterly
3 ❑ Jan 1992 Cover: 1.95 **NM** value: **2.00**
Circ: CapCity orders: **5,400**
📖 Hellhound on My Trail **A:** Vince Stone **W:** Will Shetterly
4 ❑ Feb 1992 Cover: 1.95 **NM** value: **2.00**
Circ: CapCity orders: **4,400**
A: Vince Stone **W:** Will Shetterly

CAPTAIN CONFEDERACY (STEELDRAGON) — Steeldragon

1 ❑ Cover: 1.50 **NM** value: **Cover or less**
📖 The Making of a Hero **A:** Vince Stone **W:** Will Shetterly
2 ❑ Cover: 1.50 **NM** value: **Cover or less**
A: Vince Stone **W:** Will Shetterly
3 ❑ Cover: 1.50 **NM** value: **Cover or less**
📖 Beer and Confidences; Ant Boy! **A:** Vince Stone; Matt Feazell **W:** Matt Feazell; Will Shetterly
4 ❑ Cover: 1.50 **NM** value: **Cover or less**
A: Vince Stone **W:** Will Shetterly
5 ❑ Cover: 1.50 **NM** value: **Cover or less**
A: Vince Stone **W:** Will Shetterly
6 ❑ Sum 1987 Cover: 1.50 **NM** value: **Cover or less**
A: Vince Stone **W:** Will Shetterly
7 ❑ Aut 1987 Cover: 1.75 **NM** value: **Cover or less**
A: Vince Stone **W:** Will Shetterly
8 ❑ Win 1987 Cover: 1.75 **NM** value: **Cover or less**
A: Vince Stone **W:** Will Shetterly
9 ❑ Spr 1988 Cover: 1.75 **NM** value: **Cover or less**
A: Vince Stone **W:** Will Shetterly
10 ❑ Jun 1988 Cover: 1.75 **NM** value: **Cover or less**
A: Vince Stone **W:** Will Shetterly
11 ❑ Jun 1988 Cover: 1.75 **NM** value: **Cover or less**
A: Vince Stone **W:** Will Shetterly
12 ❑ Oct 1988 Cover: 1.75 **NM** value: **Cover or less**
A: Vince Stone **W:** Will Shetterly
SE 1❑ Sum 1987 Cover: 1.75 **NM** value: **Cover or less**
A: Vince Stone **W:** Will Shetterly ★ Origin of Captain Confederacy.
SE 2❑ Sum 1987 Cover: 1.75 **NM** value: **Cover or less**
A: Vince Stone **W:** Will Shetterly ★ Origin of Captain Confederacy.

CAPTAIN COSMOS, THE LAST STARVEYOR — Ybor City

1 ❑ Cover: 2.95 **NM** value: **Cover or less**
📖 The Beast from Hyperspace; Captain (text); Captain Cosmos gallery; Biography: Martin C. Warner (text); Frank Thomas, Sherlock Holmes and Tom Corbett, Space Cadet (text) **A:** Joe Staton **W:** Nicola Cutii; Joe Sarno

CAPTAIN CRAFTY — Conception

1 ❑ Jun 1994, b&w wraparound cover. Cover: 2.50 **NM** value: **Cover or less**
2 ❑ Win 1994, b&w wraparound cover. Cover: 2.50 **NM** value: **Cover or less**
2.5 ❑ Apr 1998 Cover: 1.00 **NM** value: **Cover or less**

CAPTAIN CRAFTY COLOR SPECTACULAR — Conception

1 ❑ Aug 1996 wraparound cover. Cover: 2.50 **NM** value: **Cover or less**
2 ❑ Dec 1996 wraparound cover. Cover: 2.50 **NM** value: **Cover or less**

CAPTAIN DINGLEBERRY — Slave Labor

1 ❑ Aug 1998 Cover: 2.95 **NM** value: **Cover or less**
Circ: Diamd. preorders: **3,009**
A: Harper Jaten; Rick Remember **W:** Harper Jaten; Rick Remember
2 ❑ Sep 1998 Cover: 2.95 **NM** value: **Cover or less**
Circ: Diamd. preorders: **1,951**
A: Harper Jaten; Rick Remember **W:** Harper Jaten; Rick Remember
3 ❑ Oct 1998 Cover: 2.95 **NM** value: **Cover or less**
Circ: Diamd. preorders: **1,852**
A: Harper Jaten; Rick Remember **W:** Harper Jaten; Rick Remember
4 ❑ 1998 Cover: 2.95 **NM** value: **Cover or less**
A: Harper Jaten; Rick Remember **W:** Harper Jaten; Rick Remember
5 ❑ Jan 1999 Cover: 2.95 **NM** value: **Cover or less**
📖 Bun Ca-Ca City and the Runsdance Kid **A:** Harper Jaten; Rick Remember **W:** Harper Jaten; Rick Remember
6 ❑ Feb 1999 Cover: 2.95 **NM** value: **Cover or less**
Circ: Diamd. preorders: **1,287**
A: Harper Jaten; Rick Remember **W:** Harper Jaten; Rick Remember

CAPTAIN EASY — Standard

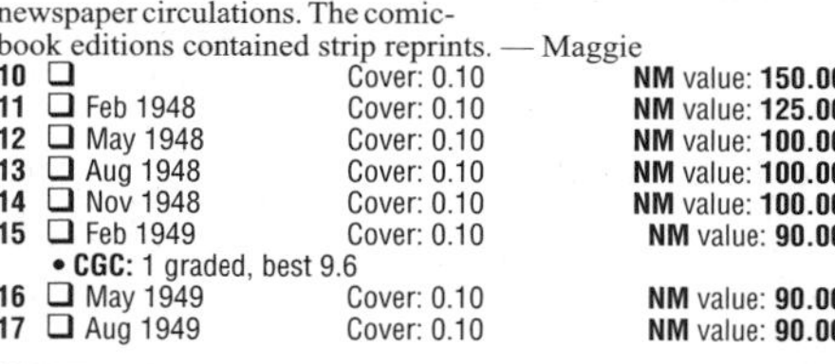

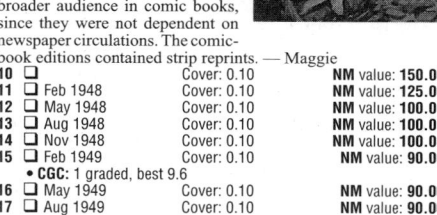

Roy Crane (1901-1977) created a comedy newspaper strip in 1924 focused on his Wash Tubbs character; after five years, he created Captain Easy as an adventuring counterpoint to Tubbs. By 1933, Easy got a Sunday strip. (Crane later told members of the National Cartoonists Society, "If I had it to do over, I'd nver do a Sunday. It's the straw that breaks backs.")

Eventually, Tubbs and Easy were taken over by Les Turner (1899-1988). Easy was among many comic-strip characters who found a broader audience in comic books, since they were not dependent on newspaper circulations. The comic-book editions contained strip reprints. — Maggie

10 ❑ Cover: 0.10 **NM** value: **150.00**
11 ❑ Feb 1948 Cover: 0.10 **NM** value: **125.00**
12 ❑ May 1948 Cover: 0.10 **NM** value: **100.00**
13 ❑ Aug 1948 Cover: 0.10 **NM** value: **100.00**
14 ❑ Nov 1948 Cover: 0.10 **NM** value: **100.00**
15 ❑ Feb 1949 Cover: 0.10 **NM** value: **90.00**
• **CGC:** 1 graded, best 9.6
16 ❑ May 1949 Cover: 0.10 **NM** value: **90.00**
17 ❑ Aug 1949 Cover: 0.10 **NM** value: **90.00**

CAPTAIN ELECTRON — BCSI

1 ❑ full color Cover: 2.25 **NM** value: **Cover or less**
A: Jayson Disbrow

CAPTAIN EO 3-D — Eclipse

1 ❑ Aug 1987 Cover: 3.50 **NM** value: **Cover or less**
Circ: CapCity orders: **4,825**
No issue number. • oversized (11x17).
Bk 1❑ Aug 1987 Cover: 6.95 **NM** value: **Cover or less**
• oversized (11x17).

CAPTAIN FEARLESS COMICS — Holyoke

1 ❑ Aug 1941 **NM** value: **500.00**
• **CGC:** 1 graded, best 9.2
2 ❑ Sep 1941 **NM** value: **300.00**
• **CGC:** 2 graded, best 9.2

CAPTAIN FLIGHT COMICS — Four Star

1 ❑ Mar 1944 Cover: 0.10 **NM** value: **350.00**
2 ❑ May 1944 Cover: 0.10 **NM** value: **200.00**
3 ❑ Jul 1944 Cover: 0.10 **NM** value: **200.00**
4 ❑ Sep 1944 Cover: 0.10 **NM** value: **200.00**
• **CGC:** 1 graded, best 8.0
5 ❑ Dec 1944 Cover: 0.10 **NM** value: **200.00**
• **CGC:** 1 graded, best 7.0
6 ❑ Jan 1945 Cover: 0.10 **NM** value: **150.00**
• **CGC:** 1 graded, best 8.0
7 ❑ Mar 1945 Cover: 0.10 **NM** value: **150.00**
8 ❑ May 1945 Cover: 0.10 **NM** value: **150.00**
9 ❑ Sep 1945 Cover: 0.10 **NM** value: **125.00**
10 ❑ Dec 1945 Cover: 0.10 **NM** value: **125.00**
• **CGC:** 1 graded, best 9.0
11 ❑ Feb 1947 Cover: 0.10 **NM** value: **125.00**
• **CGC:** 2 graded, best 7.5

CAPTAIN FORTUNE — Rip Off

1 ❑ Cover: 2.95 **NM** value: **Cover or less**
📖 Pressure **A:** Ron Fontes **W:** Ron Fontes
2 ❑ Cover: 3.25 **NM** value: **Cover or less**
📖 Treasure Moon, Part 1 **A:** Ron Fontes **W:** Ron Fontes
3 ❑ Cover: 3.25 **NM** value: **Cover or less**
📖 Treasure Moon, Part 2 **A:** Ron Fontes **W:** Ron Fontes
4 ❑ Cover: 3.25 **NM** value: **Cover or less**
📖 Treasure Moon, Part 3 **A:** Ron Fontes **W:** Ron Fontes

CAPTAIN GALLANT — Charlton

Captain Gallant was mainly a comic book advertisement for the television show of the same name which starred action-hero star Buster Crabbe. The series premiered in 1955 and had two versions for the first issue. Heinz Manufacturing Company sponsored the comic and was given its own issue in which Captain Gallant tells all of the kids that they should use Heinz products. To appeal to the kids, the series was narrated by a little boy named Cuffy, the Foreign Legion's mascot who related what a good time it was being the Legion mascot without any irony.

In the Heinz issue, the publisher featured actual pictures of Crabbe and Cuffy. Food trivia buffs who owned the Heinz version of issue #1 also got an ad checklist of the 57 products sold by Heinz (yes, this is where Heinz 57 Sauce got its name).

1 ❑ ca. 1955 Cover: 0.10 **NM** value: **35.00**
📖 Josie Gets Goin'; Marcher On Crever, March On Or Die; Desert Dee-light; A Saddle For Baba; **A:** Don Heck
1/A ❑ ca. 1955 **NM** value: **10.00**
• Heinz giveaway version with ads for Heinz products throughout.
A: Don Heck
2 ❑ ca. 1955 Cover: 0.10 **NM** value: **25.00**
3 ❑ ca. 1956 Cover: 0.10 **NM** value: **25.00**
4 ❑ Sep 1956 Cover: 0.10 **NM** value: **25.00**

CAPTAIN GLORY — Topps

0 ❑ Apr 1993 Cover: 2.95 **NM** value: **Cover or less**
Circ: CapCity orders: **56,575**
• trading card **A:** Steve Ditko; Jack Kirby
1 ❑ Apr 1993 Cover: 2.95 **NM** value: **Cover or less**
A: Steve Ditko; Jack Kirby(cover)

CGC-graded: Multiply prices above by **33 for 9.9 M • 16 for 9.8 NM/M • 7 for 9.6 NM+ • 5 for 9.4 NM • 2.5 for 9.2 NM- • 1.5 for 9.0 VF/NM**

CAPTAIN GRAVITY — Penny-Farthing

1 ❑ Dec 1998 Cover: 2.75 **NM** value: **Cover or less**
Circ: Diamd. preorders: **1,854**
📖 The Curse of Ah Puch **A:** Keith Martin **W:** Stephen Vrattos

1/Aut❑Dec 1998 **NM** value: **3.50**
📖 The Curse of Ah Puch **A:** Keith Martin

2 ❑ Jan 1999 Cover: 2.75 **NM** value: **Cover or less**
Circ: Diamd. preorders: **1,081**
A: Keith Martin **W:** Stephen Vrattos

3 ❑ Feb 1999 Cover: 2.75 **NM** value: **Cover or less**
Circ: Diamd. preorders: **1,157**
A: Keith Martin **W:** Stephen Vrattos

4 ❑ Mar 1999 Cover: 2.75 **NM** value: **Cover or less**
A: Keith Martin **W:** Stephen Vrattos

Bk 1❑ Aug 1999 Cover: 19.95 **NM** value: **Cover or less**
• Trade Paperback. • collects mini-series;polybagged with Captain Gravity: One True Hero #1

CAPTAIN GRAVITY: ONE TRUE HERO — Penny-Farthing

1 ❑ Aug 1999 Cover: 2.95 **NM** value: **Cover or less**
One-shot.

CAPTAIN HARLOCK — Eternity

1 ❑ b&w Cover: 1.95 **NM** value: **2.50**
📖 An Exchange of Futures • Character created by Leiji Matsumoto **A:** Ben Dunn **W:** Robert W. Gibson

2 ❑ Cover: 1.95 **NM** value: **2.50**
A: Ben Dunn **W:** Robert W. Gibson

3 ❑ Cover: 1.95 **NM** value: **2.50**
A: Ben Dunn **W:** Robert W. Gibson

4 ❑ Cover: 1.95 **NM** value: **2.50**
A: Ben Dunn **W:** Robert W. Gibson

5 ❑ Cover: 1.95 **NM** value: **2.50**
A: Ben Dunn **W:** Robert W. Gibson

6 ❑ Cover: 1.95 **NM** value: **2.50**
A: Ben Dunn **W:** Robert W. Gibson

7 ❑ Cover: 1.95 **NM** value: **2.50**
A: Ben Dunn **W:** Robert W. Gibson

8 ❑ Cover: 1.95 **NM** value: **2.50**
A: Ben Dunn **W:** Robert W. Gibson

9 ❑ Cover: 1.95 **NM** value: **2.50**
A: Ben Dunn **W:** Robert W. Gibson

10 ❑ Cover: 1.95 **NM** value: **2.50**
A: Ben Dunn **W:** Robert W. Gibson

11 ❑ Cover: 1.95 **NM** value: **2.50**
A: Ben Dunn **W:** Robert W. Gibson

12 ❑ Cover: 2.25 **NM** value: **2.50**
A: Ben Dunn **W:** Robert W. Gibson

13 ❑ Cover: 2.25 **NM** value: **2.50**
A: Ben Dunn **W:** Robert W. Gibson

Bk 1❑ Cover: 9.95 **NM** value: **Cover or less**
• Captain Harlock Returns

HS 1❑b&w Cover: 2.50 **NM** value: **Cover or less**
• prestige format.

CAPTAIN HARLOCK: DEATHSHADOW RISING — Eternity

1 ❑ Cover: 2.25 **NM** value: **Cover or less**
2 ❑ Cover: 2.25 **NM** value: **Cover or less**
3 ❑ Cover: 2.25 **NM** value: **Cover or less**
4 ❑ Cover: 2.25 **NM** value: **Cover or less**
5 ❑ Cover: 2.25 **NM** value: **Cover or less**
6 ❑ Cover: 2.25 **NM** value: **Cover or less**

CAPTAIN HARLOCK: THE FALL OF THE EMPIRE — Eternity

1 ❑ Cover: 2.50 **NM** value: **Cover or less**
2 ❑ Aug 1992 Cover: 2.50 **NM** value: **Cover or less**
A: Tim Eldred **W:** Robert W. Gibson
3 ❑ Cover: 2.50 **NM** value: **Cover or less**
4 ❑ Cover: 2.50 **NM** value: **Cover or less**

CAPTAIN HARLOCK: THE MACHINE PEOPLE — Eternity

1 ❑ Cover: 2.50 **NM** value: **Cover or less**
Circ: CapCity orders: **3,020**
A: Tim Eldred **W:** Robert W. Gibson

2 ❑ Cover: 2.50 **NM** value: **Cover or less**
A: Tim Eldred **W:** Robert W. Gibson

3 ❑ Cover: 2.50 **NM** value: **Cover or less**
A: Tim Eldred **W:** Robert W. Gibson

4 ❑ Cover: 2.50 **NM** value: **Cover or less**
📖 Flesh and Steel **A:** Tim Eldred

CAPTAIN HARLOCK: THE ORIGINAL TELEVISION SCRIPTS — Eternity

Bk 1❑ b&w Cover: 19.95 **NM** value: **Cover or less**

CAPT. HOLO AND HIS ADVENTURES IN THE HOLOGRAPHIC DIMENSION IN 3-D — Blackthorne

1 ❑ Cover: 2.50 **NM** value: **Cover or less**
Hologram cover. 📖 A blight upon the Land **A:** Andy Ice **W:** Kevin Brown

CAPTAIN JET — Farrell

1 ❑ May 1952 Cover: 0.10 **NM** value: **150.00**
• **CGC:** 1 graded, best 9.0
2 ❑ Jul 1952 Cover: 0.10 **NM** value: **100.00**
3 ❑ Sep 1952 Cover: 0.10 **NM** value: **75.00**
4 ❑ Nov 1952 Cover: 0.10 **NM** value: **50.00**
5 ❑ Jan 1953 Cover: 0.10 **NM** value: **50.00**

CAPTAIN JOHNER & THE ALIENS — Valiant

Some of Valiant Comics' most popular characters were first published by Dell Comics. Captain Johner & The Aliens originally appeared as a backup story in the pages of Magnus, Robot Fighter (Gold Key). Valiant recolored the art and created new covers for the reprinting in 1995.

The story chronicles the adventures of space traveler Captain Johner and his crew. The crew discovers a new planet, where the strange inhabitants welcome the Earthmen. Half of the crew travel with their new alien friends back to Earth. The other half of the crew stays behind to learn alien customs. Certain aliens decid that Captain Johner and his crew are a threat and attempt to disintegrate the contingent left on the planet. Meanwhile, the aliens on Johner's ship actually save him while entering Earth's atmosphere. The whole saga is a morality play about the need for tolerance and how friends can be found in any culture.

1 ❑ May 1995 Cover: 2.95 **NM** value: **Cover or less**
Circ: CapCity orders: **4,500**
cardstock cover. 📖 The Aliens • reprints back-ups from Magnus, Robot Fighter (Gold Key) #1-7 **A:** Russ Manning; Paul Smith(cover) **W:** Russ Manning

2 ❑ May 1995 Cover: 2.95 **NM** value: **Cover or less**
Circ: CapCity orders: **4,225**
cardstock cover. 📖 An Alien Welcome • reprints back-ups from Magnus, Robot Fighter (Gold Key) **A:** Russ Manning **W:** Russ Manning

CAPTAIN JUSTICE — Marvel

1 ❑ ca. 1988 Cover: 1.25 **NM** value: **Cover or less**
Circ: CapCity orders: **11,250**
📖 Once a Hero, Part 1 • TV show **A:** Steve Leialoha **W:** J.M. DeMatteis

2 ❑ ca. 1988 Cover: 1.25 **NM** value: **Cover or less**
Circ: CapCity orders: **9,300**
📖 Once a Hero, Part 2 • TV show **A:** Steve Leialoha **W:** J.M. DeMatteis

CAPTAIN KIDD — Fox

24 ❑ Jun 1949 Cover: 0.10 **NM** value: **100.00**
• **CGC:** 1 graded, best 7.5
25 ❑ ca. 1949 Cover: 0.10 **NM** value: **100.00**

CAPTAIN MARVEL (1ST SERIES) — Marvel

"Captain Marvel" is actually a bit of a misnomer. His full, real name was Captain Mar-Vell, officer of the Intergalactic Kree Fleet. Sent to Earth to investigate the destruction of an ancient Kree sentry by the Fantastic Four, he winds up siding with humanity against all manner of perils, including invasion by his own race.

Adopting the identity of Dr. Walt Lawson, his early adventures centered around Cape Canaveral, home of the U.S. space program at that time. Interestingly enough, the chief of security at that time was one Carol Danvers, who much later would gain similar super-powers, becoming known to the world as Ms. Marvel.

1 ❑ May 1968 Cover: 0.12 **NM** value: **45.00**
• **CGC:** 88 graded, best 9.8
📖 Out of the Holocaust-A Hero! • Indicia: Marvel's Space-Born Superhero: Captain Marvel **A:** Gene Colan **W:** Roy Thomas

2 ❑ Jun 1968 Cover: 0.12 **NM** value: **18.00**
• **CGC:** 21 graded, best 9.8
📖 From The Void Of Space Comes...The Super Skrull! **A:** Gene Colan **W:** Roy Thomas ★ Appearance of Sub-Mariner. ★ Versus Skrull.

3 ❑ Jul 1968 Cover: 0.12 **NM** value: **15.00**
• **CGC:** 6 graded, best 9.8
📖 From the Ashes of Defeat! **A:** Gene Colan **W:** Roy Thomas ★ Versus Skrull.

4 ❑ Aug 1968 Cover: 0.12 **NM** value: **15.00**
• **CGC:** 7 graded, best 9.4
📖 Alien And The Amphibian! **A:** Gene Colan **W:** Roy Thomas ★ Appearance of Sub-Mariner. ★ Versus Sub-Mariner.

5 ❑ Sep 1968 Cover: 0.12 **NM** value: **12.00**
• **CGC:** 1 graded, best 9.0
📖 The Mark of The Metazoid **A:** Don Heck **W:** Arnold Drake

6 ❑ Oct 1968 Cover: 0.12 **NM** value: **9.00**
• **CGC:** 3 graded, best 9.2
📖 In the Path of Solam **A:** Don Heck

7 ❑ Nov 1968 Cover: 0.12 **NM** value: **9.00**
• **CGC:** 2 graded, best 9.4
📖 Die, Town, Die **A:** Don Heck ★ Versus Quasimodo.

8 ❑ Dec 1968 Cover: 0.12 **NM** value: **9.00**
• **CGC:** 3 graded, best 9.4
📖 And Fear Shall Follow **A:** Don Heck ★ 1st Appearance of Aakon (alien race).

9 ❑ Jan 1969 Cover: 0.12 **NM** value: **9.00**
• **CGC:** 4 graded, best 9.4
📖 Between Hammer and Anvil **A:** Don Heck

10 ❑ Feb 1969 Cover: 0.12 **NM** value: **9.00**
• **CGC:** 2 graded, best 9.4
📖 Die, Traitor **A:** Don Heck

11 ❑ Mar 1969 Cover: 0.12 **NM** value: **9.00**
• **CGC:** 2 graded, best 9.2
📖 Rebirth **A:** Dick Ayers **C:** Barry Windsor-Smith **W:** Arnold Drake ★ Death of Una.

12 ❑ Apr 1969 Cover: 0.12 **NM** value: **7.00**
• **CGC:** 2 graded, best 9.0
📖 The Man-Slayer **A:** Dick Ayers **W:** Arnold Drake

13 ❑ May 1969 Cover: 0.12 **NM** value: **7.00**
• **CGC:** 5 graded, best 9.6
📖 Traitors or Heroes?

14 ❑ Jun 1969 Cover: 0.12 **NM** value: **7.00**
• **CGC:** 4 graded, best 9.6
📖 When a Galaxy Beckons ★ Appearance of Iron Man.

15 ❑ Aug 1969 Cover: 0.15 **NM** value: **7.00**
• **CGC:** 2 graded, best 9.2
📖 That Zo Might Live, a Galaxy Must Die

16 ❑ Sep 1969 Cover: 0.15 **NM** value: **7.00**
📖 Behind the Mask of Zo

17 ❑ Oct 1969 Cover: 0.15 **NM** value: **7.00**
📖 And a Child Shall Lead You! • new costume; crossover with Captain America #114-116 **A:** Gil Kane; Dan Adkins **C:** Gil Kane; Dan Adkins **W:** Roy Thomas ★ Origin of Rick Jones retold.

18 ❑ Nov 1969 Cover: 0.15 **NM** value: **7.00**
• **CGC:** 1 graded, best 7.0
📖 Vengeance is Mine

19 ❑ Dec 1969 Cover: 0.15 **NM** value: **7.00**
• **CGC:** 1 graded, best 4.0
📖 The Mad Master of Murder Maze • series goes on hiatus **A:** Gil Kane; Dan Adkins

20 ❑ Jun 1970 Cover: 0.15 **NM** value: **7.00**
• **CGC:** 3 graded, best 9.6
📖 The Hunter and the Holocaust **A:** Gil Kane; Dan Adkins **C:** Gil Kane; Dan Adkins **W:** Roy Thomas

21 ❑ Aug 1970 Cover: 0.15 **NM** value: **7.00**
• **CGC:** 5 graded, best 9.0
📖 Here Comes the Hulk • series goes on hiatus ★ Appearance of Hulk.

22 ❑ Sep 1972 Cover: 0.20 **NM** value: **7.00**
📖 To Live Again • Title changes to Captain Marvel after hiatus ★ Versus Megaton.

23 ❑ Nov 1972 Cover: 0.20 **NM** value: **7.00**
📖 Death at the End of the World ★ Versus Megaton.

24 ❑ Jan 1973 Cover: 0.20 **NM** value: **7.00**
📖 Death in High Places

25 ❑ Mar 1973 Cover: 0.20 **NM** value: **10.00**
• **CGC:** 3 graded, best 9.8
📖 A Taste of Madness • Thanos War begins **A:** Jim Starlin

26 ❑ May 1973 Cover: 0.20 **NM** value: **10.00**
• **CGC:** 3 graded, best 9.4
📖 Betrayal • Thing; Masterlord revealed as Thanos **A:** Jim Starlin ★ Appearance of Thanos.

27 ❑ Jul 1973 Cover: 0.20 **NM** value: **8.00**
• **CGC:** 1 graded, best 9.4
📖 Trapped on Titan • death of Super Skrull **A:** Jim Starlin ★ 1st Appearance of Death (Marvel). ★ Appearance of Thanos.

28 ❑ Sep 1973 Cover: 0.20 **NM** value: **8.00**
• **CGC:** 1 graded, best 9.4
📖 When Titans Collide; A Clash of Titans; Mind-Slave • Avengers **A:** Al Milgrom; Jim Starlin ★ Appearance of Thanos.

29 ❑ Nov 1973 Cover: 0.20 **NM** value: **6.00**
• **CGC:** 2 graded, best 9.4
📖 Metamorphosis • Captain Marvel gets new powers **A:** Al Milgrom; Jim Starlin ★ Origin of Kronos. ★ Appearance of Thanos.

30 ❑ Jan 1974 Cover: 0.20 **NM** value: **6.00**
• **CGC:** 2 graded, best 9.4
📖 To Be Free from Control; A Time for Confrontation; End of an Empire **A:** Al Milgrom; Jim Starlin ★ Appearance of Thanos. ★ Versus Controller.

31 ❑ Mar 1974 Cover: 0.20 **NM** value: **8.00**
• **CGC:** 2 graded, best 9.0
📖 The Beginning of the End • Avengers **A:** Jim Starlin ★ 1st Appearance of ISAAC. ★ Appearance of Thanos.

32 ❑ May 1974 Cover: 0.25 **NM** value: **8.00**
• **CGC:** 2 graded, best 9.4
📖 Thanos the Insane God • Rick Jones vs. Thanos; continued in Avengers #125 **A:** Jim Starlin ★ Origin of Moondragon, Drax. ★ Appearance of Thanos.

33 ❑ Jul 1974 Cover: 0.25 **NM** value: **10.00**
• **CGC:** 2 graded, best 9.4
📖 The God Himself • Thanos War ends; continued from Avengers #125 **A:** Jim Starlin ★ Origin of Thanos.

34 ❑ Sep 1974 Cover: 0.25 **NM** value: **5.00**
📖 Blown Away! • Captain Marvel contracts cancer (will eventually die from it) **A:** Jim Starlin; Jack Abel ★ 1st Appearance of Nitro.

35 ❑ Nov 1974 Cover: 0.25 **NM** value: **3.00**
📖 Deadly Genesis • Ant-Man, Wasp **A:** Alfredo Alcala ★ Versus Living Laser.

36 ❑ Jan 1975 Cover: 0.25 **NM** value: **3.00**
📖 Watching and Waiting • Watcher **A:** Jim Starlin ★ Appearance of Thanos.

37 ❑ Mar 1975 Cover: 0.25 **NM** value: **2.00**
📖 Lift-Off • Watcher

38 ❑ May 1975 Cover: 0.25 **NM** value: **2.00**
📖 No Way Out • Trial of the Watcher

39 ❑ Jul 1975 Cover: 0.25 **NM** value: **2.00**
📖 The Trial of the Watcher • Watcher (Uatu) ★ 1st Appearance of Aron the Rogue Watcher.

40 ❑ Sep 1975 Cover: 0.25 **NM** value: **2.00**
📖 Rocky Mountain 'Bye • Watcher

41 ❑ Nov 1975 Cover: 0.25 **NM** value: **2.00**
📖 Havoc on Homeworld ★ Appearance of Supreme Intelligence. ★ Versus Ronan.

42 ❑ Jan 1976 Cover: 0.25 **NM** value: **2.00**
📖 Shoot-Out at the O.K. Space station ★ Versus Stranger.

43 ❑ Mar 1976 Cover: 0.25 **NM** value: **2.00**
📖 Destroy! Destroy! Screams the Destroyer **A:** Al Milgrom **W:** Steve Englehart ★ Versus Drax.

44 ❑ May 1976 Cover: 0.25 **NM** value: **2.00**
• **CGC:** 1 graded, best 3.5
📖 Death Throws ★ Versus Drax.

Other grades: Multiply prices above by **1.5 for Mint • 2/3 for Very Fine • 1/3 for Fine • 1/5 for Very Good • 1/8 for Good**

45 ❑ Jul 1976 Cover: 0.25 **NM** value: **2.00**
The Bi-Centennial
46 ❑ Sep 1976 Cover: 0.30 **NM** value: **2.00**
Only One Can Win ★ 1st Appearance of Supremor.
47 ❑ Nov 1976 Cover: 0.30 **NM** value: **2.00**
★ Appearance of Human Torch. ★ Versus Sentry Sinister.
48 ❑ Jan 1977 Cover: 0.30 **NM** value: **2.00**
★ 1st Appearance of Cheetah (Esteban Carracus). ★ Versus Cheetah, Sentry Sinister.
49 ❑ Mar 1977 Cover: 0.30 **NM** value: **2.00**
★ Versus Ronan.
50 ❑ May 1977 Cover: 0.30 **NM** value: **2.00**
To Begin Anew! **A:** Al Milgrom **W:** Scott Edelman ★ 1st Appearance of Doctor Minerva. ★ Appearance of Avengers, Adaptoid.
51 ❑ Jul 1977 Cover: 0.30 **NM** value: **2.00**
★ Versus Mercurio.
52 ❑ Sep 1977 Cover: 0.30 **NM** value: **2.00**
53 ❑ Nov 1977 Cover: 0.35 **NM** value: **2.00**
54 ❑ Jan 1978 Cover: 0.35 **NM** value: **2.00**
55 ❑ Mar 1978 Cover: 0.35 **NM** value: **2.00**
★ Versus Death-Grip.
56 ❑ May 1978 Cover: 0.35 **NM** value: **2.00**
Survival Quest! **A:** Pat Broderick **W:** Doug Moench ★ Versus Death-Grip.
57 ❑ Jul 1978 Cover: 0.35 **NM** value: **3.00**
Star Burst • (flashback);(flashback) **A:** Pat Broderick; Bob Wiacek **W:** Roger McKenzie ★ Appearance of Thanos. ★ Versus Thor.
58 ❑ Sep 1978 Cover: 0.35 **NM** value: **2.00**
★ Versus Drax.
59 ❑ Nov 1978 Cover: 0.35 **NM** value: **2.00**
★ 1st Appearance of Elysius. ★ Versus Drax.
60 ❑ Jan 1979 Cover: 0.35 **NM** value: **2.00**
61 ❑ Mar 1979 Cover: 0.35 **NM** value: **2.00**
Chaos And The Pit! **A:** Pat Broderick **W:** Doug Moench
62 ❑ May 1979 Cover: 0.40 **NM** value: **2.00**
final issue.
GS 1❑ Cover: 0.50 **NM** value: **10.00**
And a Child Shall Lead You!; The Hunter and the Holocaust; Here Comes the Hulk • reprinted from Captain Marvel #17, 20 and 21 with some omissions

CAPTAIN MARVEL (2ND SERIES) Marvel

1 ❑ Nov 1989 Cover: 1.50 **NM** value: **Cover or less**
Circ: CapCity orders: **23,200**
One-shot. The Dream Is The Truth • New Captain Marvel (Monica Rambeau) gets her powers back **A:** Doc Bright **W:** Dwayne McDuffie

CAPTAIN MARVEL (3RD SERIES) Marvel

2 ❑ Feb 1994 Cover: 1.75 **NM** value: **Cover or less**

CAPTAIN MARVEL (4TH SERIES) Marvel

1 ❑ Dec 1995 Cover: 2.95 **NM** value: **Cover or less**
enhanced cardstock cover. Sins of the Fathers, Part 1 **A:** Ed Benés **W:** Fabian Nicieza
2 ❑ Jan 1996 Cover: 1.95 **NM** value: **Cover or less**
Sins of the Fathers, Part 2 **A:** Ed Benés **W:** Fabian Nicieza ★ Appearance of Rick and Marlo Jones.
3 ❑ Feb 1996 Cover: 1.95 **NM** value: **Cover or less**
Sins of the Fathers, Part 3 **A:** Ed Benés **W:** Fabian Nicieza
4 ❑ Mar 1996 Cover: 1.95 **NM** value: **Cover or less**
Sins of the Fathers, Part 4 **A:** Ed Benés **W:** Fabian Nicieza
5 ❑ Apr 1996 Cover: 1.95 **NM** value: **Cover or less**
In the Name of God? **A:** Daerick Gr÷ss **W:** Fabian Nicieza
6 ❑ May 1996 Cover: 1.95 **NM** value: **Cover or less**
A: Ed Benés **W:** Fabian Nicieza

CAPTAIN MARVEL (5TH SERIES) Marvel

In a case of deja vu all over again, perennial sidekick Rick Jones found himself once again switching his molecules with a member of the Kree race, in this case Genis, the son of Mar-Vell.

Genis merged with Jones to save Rick's life at the end of Avengers Forever which directly led into this fifth Captain Marvel series.

Written by Peter David, the series has a lot of fun with super-hero conventions, including battle crys with Rick convincing Genis that a certain phrase is heroic when it's more on the order of "Is your refrigerator running?"

David also weaves in appearances by other Marvel characters he's worked on, including The Hulk, Spider-Man 2099, and The Maestro. — Brent

0 ❑ **NM** value: **3.00**
• Wizard promotional edition.
1 ❑ Jan 2000 Cover: 2.95 **NM** value: **3.00**
Circ: Diamd. preorders: **44,221** • **CGC:** 5 graded, best 9.8
Regular cover (space background w/rocks). First Contact **A:** Chris Cross **W:** Peter David
1/A ❑ Jan 2000 Cover: 2.95 **NM** value: **4.00**
Variant cover by Chris Cross (Marvel against white background). First Contact **A:** Chris Cross **W:** Peter David ★ 1st Appearance of 10 ratio.
2 ❑ Feb 2000 Cover: 2.50 **NM** value: **Cover or less**
Circ: Diamd. preorders: **37,035**
Does a Hulk Sit In the Woods? **A:** Chris Cross **W:** Peter David ★ Appearance of Wendigo, Moondragon, Hulk.
3 ❑ Mar 2000 Cover: 2.50 **NM** value: **Cover or less**
Circ: Diamd. preorders: **30,490**
One Down, Wendigo **A:** Chris Cross **W:** Peter David ★ Appearance of Wendigo, Moondragon, Hulk, Drax. ★ Death of Lorraine.
4 ❑ Apr 2000 Cover: 2.50 **NM** value: **Cover or less**
Circ: Diamd. preorders: **28,803**
Other Side of the Drax **A:** Ron Lim **W:** Peter David ★ Appearance of Moondragon, Drax.
5 ❑ May 2000 Cover: 2.50 **NM** value: **Cover or less**
Circ: Diamd. preorders: **29,466**
Visit to an Even Smaller Planet • in microverse **A:** James Fry **W:** Peter David ★ Appearance of Moondragon, Drax.
6 ❑ Jun 2000 Cover: 2.50 **NM** value: **Cover or less**
Circ: Diamd. preorders: **28,987**
It's a Small Universe After All **A:** Chris Cross **W:** Peter David
7 ❑ Jul 2000 Cover: 2.50 **NM** value: **Cover or less**
Circ: Diamd. preorders: **28,401**
8 ❑ Aug 2000 Cover: 2.50 **NM** value: **Cover or less**
Circ: Diamd. preorders: **28,565**
9 ❑ Sep 2000 Cover: 2.50 **NM** value: **Cover or less**
Circ: Diamd. preorders: **28,175**
Anything Can Happen Day **A:** Chris Cross **W:** Peter David ★ Appearance of Super Skrull, Silver Surfer.
10 ❑ Oct 2000 Cover: 2.50 **NM** value: **Cover or less**
Circ: Diamd. preorders: **26,392**
11 ❑ Nov 2000 Cover: 2.50 **NM** value: **Cover or less**
Circ: Diamd. preorders: **26,864** • **CGC:** 1 graded, best 9.6
Together Again for the First Time! **A:** Jim Starlin **W:** Peter David ★ Appearance of Moondragon, Silver Surfer, Mar-Vell.
12 ❑ Dec 2000 Cover: 2.50 **NM** value: **Cover or less**
Circ: Diamd. preorders: **28,029**
Maximum Security; Dead and In Person ... **A:** Chris Cross **W:** Peter David
13 ❑ Jan 2001 Cover: 2.50 **NM** value: **Cover or less**
Circ: Diamd. preorders: **26,378**
Am I Blue? **A:** Chris Cross **W:** Peter David
14 ❑ Feb 2001 Cover: 2.50 **NM** value: **Cover or less**
Circ: Diamd. preorders: **26,433**
Truth or Dare **A:** Patrick Zircher **W:** Fabian Nicieza
15 ❑ Mar 2001 Cover: 2.50 **NM** value: **Cover or less**
Circ: Diamd. preorders: **25,613**
Micro-Management **A:** Chris Cross **W:** Peter David
16 ❑ Apr 2001 Cover: 2.50 **NM** value: **Cover or less**
Circ: Diamd. preorders: **25,047**
Marvel Mania **A:** Chris Cross **W:** Peter David
17 ❑ May 2001 Cover: 2.50 **NM** value: **Cover or less**
Circ: Diamd. preorders: **27,563**
Cheating Death **A:** Jim Starlin **W:** Peter David ★ Appearance of Thor.
18 ❑ Jun 2001 Cover: 2.50 **NM** value: **Cover or less**
Circ: Diamd. preorders: **28,615**
19 ❑ Jul 2001 Cover: 2.50 **NM** value: **Cover or less**
Circ: Diamd. preorders: **27,043**
20 ❑ Aug 2001 Cover: 2.50 **NM** value: **Cover or less**
Circ: Diamd. preorders: **27,130**
21 ❑ Sep 2001 Cover: 2.50 **NM** value: **Cover or less**
Circ: Diamd. preorders: **28,167**
22 ❑ Oct 2001 Cover: 2.50 **NM** value: **Cover or less**
Circ: Diamd. preorders: **27,835**
23 ❑ Nov 2001 Cover: 2.50 **NM** value: **Cover or less**
Circ: Diamd. preorders: **25,678**
24 ❑ Dec 2001 Cover: 2.50 **NM** value: **Cover or less**
Circ: Diamd. preorders: **24,593**
25 ❑ Jan 2002 Cover: 2.50 **NM** value: **Cover or less**
Circ: Diamd. preorders: **24,534**
26 ❑ Feb 2002 Cover: 2.50 **NM** value: **Cover or less**
Circ: Diamd. preorders: **24,438**
27 ❑ Mar 2002 Cover: 2.50 **NM** value: **Cover or less**
Circ: Diamd. preorders: **23,603**
28 ❑ Mar 2002 Cover: 2.50 **NM** value: **Cover or less**
Circ: Diamd. preorders: **22,128**

CAPTAIN MARVEL ADVENTURES Fawcett

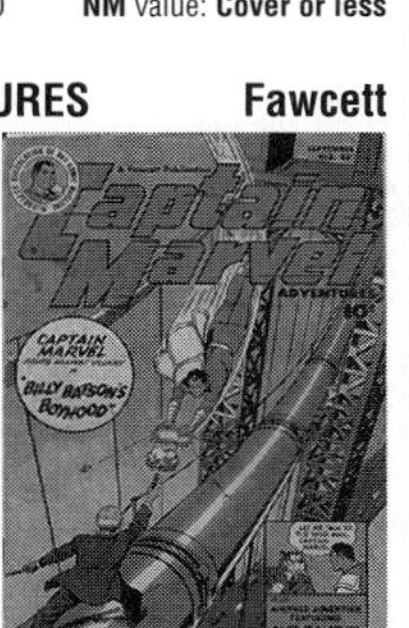

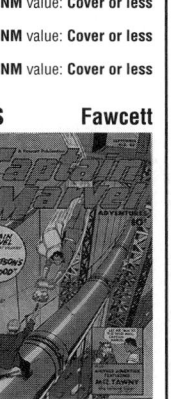

An ancient Egyptian wizard gives newsboy Billy Batson the power to transform himself into the world's mightiest mortal by uttering his magical name, Shazam! As Captain Marvel, he has a hugely successful career during comics' Golden Age and helps keep the world safe from villains like the evil scientist Dr. Sivana and the evil mastermind, Mr. Mind.

The good-humored Captain, co-created by C.C. Beck, made his debut in the first issue of Whiz Comics (numbered #2) in 1940 and quickly added his own series in 1941. Loose, funny, and filled with memorable characters and great stories, Captain Marvel was one of the most significant comic-book series ever created. During the 1940s, his popularity rivaled that of Superman, which prompted a lawsuit claiming that Captain Marvel had infringed on Superman's copyright. In 1953, a consent decree finally put Captain Marvel out of action until DC arranged with Fawcett that DC would publish new stories about The Big Red Cheese.

1 ❑ Spr 1941 Cover: 0.10 **NM** value: **30000.00**
• **CGC:** 3 graded, best 3.5
No number on cover. Capt. Marvel; Capt. Marvel Out West; (untitled); Capt. Marvel Battles the Vampire • Rare **A:** Jack Kirby
2 ❑ Sum 1941 Cover: 0.10 **NM** value: **3500.00**
• **CGC:** 1 graded, best 6.0
3 ❑ Fal 1941 Cover: 0.10 **NM** value: **2000.00**
• **CGC:** 6 graded, best 9.2
4 ❑ Oct 1941 Cover: 0.10 **NM** value: **1400.00**
• **CGC:** 1 graded, best 8.0
5 ❑ Dec 1941 Cover: 0.10 **NM** value: **1100.00**
• **CGC:** 1 graded, best 5.0
6 ❑ Jan 1942 Cover: 0.10 **NM** value: **800.00**
• **CGC:** 2 graded, best 5.5
7 ❑ Feb 1942 Cover: 0.10 **NM** value: **800.00**
• **CGC:** 1 graded, best 8.0
8 ❑ Mar 1942 Cover: 0.10 **NM** value: **750.00**
• **CGC:** 2 graded, best 8.0
9 ❑ Apr 1942 Cover: 0.10 **NM** value: **750.00**
• **CGC:** 2 graded, best 7.5
10 ❑ May 1942 Cover: 0.10 **NM** value: **750.00**
• **CGC:** 2 graded, best 9.2
11 ❑ May 1942 Cover: 0.10 **NM** value: **650.00**
• **CGC:** 2 graded, best 9.0
12 ❑ Jun 1942 Cover: 0.10 **NM** value: **650.00**
• **CGC:** 1 graded, best 7.0
13 ❑ Jul 1942 Cover: 0.10 **NM** value: **650.00**
• **CGC:** 2 graded, best 8.0
14 ❑ Aug 1942 Cover: 0.10 **NM** value: **650.00**
• **CGC:** 4 graded, best 9.0
15 ❑ Sep 1942 Cover: 0.10 **NM** value: **650.00**
• **CGC:** 2 graded, best 8.0
16 ❑ Oct 1942 Cover: 0.10 **NM** value: **625.00**
• **CGC:** 2 graded, best 9.0
17 ❑ Nov 1942 Cover: 0.10 **NM** value: **625.00**
• **CGC:** 4 graded, best 9.4
18 ❑ Dec 1942 Cover: 0.10 **NM** value: **1200.00**
• **CGC:** 6 graded, best 9.0
★ Origin of Mary Marvel. ★ 1st Appearance of Mary Marvel.
19 ❑ Jan 1943 Cover: 0.10 **NM** value: **525.00**
• **CGC:** 2 graded, best 9.4
20 ❑ Jan 1943 Cover: 0.10 **NM** value: **525.00**
21 ❑ Feb 1943 Cover: 0.10 **NM** value: **450.00**
• **CGC:** 1 graded, best 7.0
22 ❑ Mar 1943 Cover: 0.10 **NM** value: **450.00**
• **CGC:** 3 graded, best 9.6
23 ❑ Apr 1943 Cover: 0.10 **NM** value: **650.00**
• **CGC:** 1 graded, best 9.4
★ 1st Appearance of Mr. Mind.
24 ❑ Jun 1943 Cover: 0.10 **NM** value: **400.00**
• **CGC:** 4 graded, best 9.4
25 ❑ Jul 1943 Cover: 0.10 **NM** value: **400.00**
• **CGC:** 1 graded, best 9.4
26 ❑ Aug 1943 Cover: 0.10 **NM** value: **400.00**
Flag cover.
27 ❑ Sep 1943 Cover: 0.10 **NM** value: **350.00**
• **CGC:** 1 graded, best 9.6
28 ❑ Oct 1943 Cover: 0.10 **NM** value: **350.00**
29 ❑ Nov 1943 Cover: 0.10 **NM** value: **350.00**
• **CGC:** 3 graded, best 9.4
30 ❑ Dec 1943 Cover: 0.10 **NM** value: **350.00**
31 ❑ Jan 1944 Cover: 0.10 **NM** value: **300.00**
• **CGC:** 1 graded, best 9.4
32 ❑ Feb 1944 Cover: 0.10 **NM** value: **300.00**
• **CGC:** 3 graded, best 9.0
33 ❑ Mar 1944 Cover: 0.10 **NM** value: **300.00**
• **CGC:** 3 graded, best 9.4
34 ❑ Apr 1944 Cover: 0.10 **NM** value: **300.00**
• **CGC:** 1 graded, best 9.4
35 ❑ May 1944 Cover: 0.10 **NM** value: **300.00**
• **CGC:** 3 graded, best 9.2
36 ❑ Jun 1944 Cover: 0.10 **NM** value: **300.00**
• **CGC:** 1 graded, best 8.5
37 ❑ Jul 1944 Cover: 0.10 **NM** value: **300.00**
38 ❑ Aug 1944 Cover: 0.10 **NM** value: **300.00**
• **CGC:** 2 graded, best 9.4
39 ❑ Aug 1944 Cover: 0.10 **NM** value: **300.00**
• **CGC:** 2 graded, best 9.4
40 ❑ Oct 1944 Cover: 0.10 **NM** value: **300.00**
• **CGC:** 2 graded, best 9.0
41 ❑ Nov 1944 Cover: 0.10 **NM** value: **260.00**
• **CGC:** 2 graded, best 8.5
42 ❑ Jan 1945 Cover: 0.10 **NM** value: **260.00**
• **CGC:** 1 graded, best 9.2
43 ❑ Feb 1945 Cover: 0.10 **NM** value: **260.00**
• **CGC:** 1 graded, best 7.0
★ 1st Appearance of Uncle Marvel.
44 ❑ Mar 1945 Cover: 0.10 **NM** value: **260.00**
• **CGC:** 1 graded, best 6.5
45 ❑ Apr 1945 Cover: 0.10 **NM** value: **230.00**
• **CGC:** 1 graded, best 7.0
46 ❑ May 1945 Cover: 0.10 **NM** value: **230.00**
• **CGC:** 2 graded, best 9.0
47 ❑ Jul 1945 Cover: 0.10 **NM** value: **230.00**
• **CGC:** 2 graded, best 5.5
48 ❑ Aug 1945 Cover: 0.10 **NM** value: **230.00**
• **CGC:** 4 graded, best 8.5
49 ❑ Oct 1945 Cover: 0.10 **NM** value: **230.00**
• **CGC:** 4 graded, best 8.5
50 ❑ Dec 1945 Cover: 0.10 **NM** value: **230.00**
• **CGC:** 13 graded, best 9.6
51 ❑ Jan 1946 Cover: 0.10 **NM** value: **210.00**
• **CGC:** 11 graded, best 9.4
52 ❑ Jan 1946 Cover: 0.10 **NM** value: **210.00**
• **CGC:** 5 graded, best 9.6
53 ❑ Feb 1946 Cover: 0.10 **NM** value: **210.00**
• **CGC:** 2 graded, best 8.5
54 ❑ Feb 1946 Cover: 0.10 **NM** value: **210.00**
• **CGC:** 1 graded, best 9.4
55 ❑ Mar 1946 Cover: 0.10 **NM** value: **210.00**
• **CGC:** 2 graded, best 6.0
56 ❑ Mar 1946 Cover: 0.10 **NM** value: **210.00**
• **CGC:** 2 graded, best 9.6
57 ❑ Mar 1946 Cover: 0.10 **NM** value: **210.00**
58 ❑ Apr 1946 Cover: 0.10 **NM** value: **210.00**
• **CGC:** 1 graded, best .5
59 ❑ Apr 1946 Cover: 0.10 **NM** value: **210.00**
60 ❑ May 1946 Cover: 0.10 **NM** value: **210.00**
61 ❑ May 1946 Cover: 0.10 **NM** value: **200.00**
• **CGC:** 1 graded, best 7.5
62 ❑ Jun 1946 Cover: 0.10 **NM** value: **200.00**
• **CGC:** 1 graded, best 7.0
63 ❑ Jul 1946 Cover: 0.10 **NM** value: **200.00**
64 ❑ Aug 1946 Cover: 0.10 **NM** value: **200.00**
• **CGC:** 1 graded, best 7.0

CGC-graded: Multiply prices above by **33 for 9.9 M • 16 for 9.8 NM/M • 7 for 9.6 NM+ • 5 for 9.4 NM • 2.5 for 9.2 NM- • 1.5 for 9.0 VF/NM**

65 ❑ Sep 1946 Cover: 0.10 **NM** value: **200.00**
• **CGC:** 1 graded, best 6.0
66 ❑ Oct 1946 Cover: 0.10 **NM** value: **200.00**
• **CGC:** 1 graded, best 7.0
67 ❑ Nov 1946 Cover: 0.10 **NM** value: **200.00**
68 ❑ Jan 1947 Cover: 0.10 **NM** value: **200.00**
69 ❑ Feb 1947 Cover: 0.10 **NM** value: **200.00**
• **CGC:** 1 graded, best 8.0
70 ❑ Mar 1947 Cover: 0.10 **NM** value: **200.00**
• **CGC:** 1 graded, best 8.5
71 ❑ Apr 1947 Cover: 0.10 **NM** value: **175.00**
• **CGC:** 1 graded, best 8.0
72 ❑ May 1947 Cover: 0.10 **NM** value: **175.00**
• **CGC:** 1 graded, best 9.0
73 ❑ Jun 1947 Cover: 0.10 **NM** value: **175.00**
74 ❑ Jul 1947 Cover: 0.10 **NM** value: **175.00**
75 ❑ Aug 1947 Cover: 0.10 **NM** value: **175.00**
• **CGC:** 2 graded, best 9.2
76 ❑ Sep 1947 Cover: 0.10 **NM** value: **175.00**
• **CGC:** 1 graded, best 8.0
77 ❑ Oct 1947 Cover: 0.10 **NM** value: **175.00**
78 ❑ Nov 1947 Cover: 0.10 **NM** value: **175.00**
• **CGC:** 3 graded, best 9.4
79 ❑ Dec 1947 Cover: 0.10 **NM** value: **175.00**
★ Origin of Mr. Tawny.
80 ❑ Jan 1948 Cover: 0.10 **NM** value: **175.00**
• **CGC:** 1 graded, best 6.0
81 ❑ Feb 1948 Cover: 0.10 **NM** value: **150.00**
• **CGC:** 1 graded, best 5.0
82 ❑ Mar 1948 Cover: 0.10 **NM** value: **150.00**
• **CGC:** 2 graded, best 9.2
83 ❑ Apr 1948 Cover: 0.10 **NM** value: **150.00**
84 ❑ May 1948 Cover: 0.10 **NM** value: **150.00**
85 ❑ Jun 1948 Cover: 0.10 **NM** value: **150.00**
86 ❑ Jul 1948 Cover: 0.10 **NM** value: **150.00**
87 ❑ Aug 1948 Cover: 0.10 **NM** value: **150.00**
88 ❑ Sep 1948 Cover: 0.10 **NM** value: **150.00**
89 ❑ Oct 1948 Cover: 0.10 **NM** value: **150.00**
90 ❑ Nov 1948 Cover: 0.10 **NM** value: **150.00**
91 ❑ Dec 1948 Cover: 0.10 **NM** value: **135.00**
92 ❑ Jan 1949 Cover: 0.10 **NM** value: **135.00**
93 ❑ Feb 1949 Cover: 0.10 **NM** value: **135.00**
94 ❑ Mar 1949 Cover: 0.10 **NM** value: **135.00**
95 ❑ Apr 1949 Cover: 0.10 **NM** value: **135.00**
📖 Captain Marvel and the Great Polar Ice Cap; The Man Who Wanted To Be Poor; History Goes Wild; His Long Chance
96 ❑ May 1949 Cover: 0.10 **NM** value: **135.00**
97 ❑ Jun 1949 Cover: 0.10 **NM** value: **135.00**
• **CGC:** 1 graded, best 7.5
98 ❑ Jul 1949 Cover: 0.10 **NM** value: **135.00**
99 ❑ Aug 1949 Cover: 0.10 **NM** value: **135.00**
100 ❑ Sep 1949 Cover: 0.10 **NM** value: **325.00**
• 100th anniversary issue. ★ Origin of Captain Marvel (Fawcett).
101 ❑ Oct 1949 Cover: 0.10 **NM** value: **135.00**
102 ❑ Nov 1949 Cover: 0.10 **NM** value: **135.00**
103 ❑ Dec 1949 Cover: 0.10 **NM** value: **135.00**
104 ❑ Jan 1950 Cover: 0.10 **NM** value: **135.00**
105 ❑ Feb 1950 Cover: 0.10 **NM** value: **135.00**
106 ❑ Mar 1950 Cover: 0.10 **NM** value: **135.00**
• **CGC:** 1 graded, best 8.5
107 ❑ Apr 1950 Cover: 0.10 **NM** value: **135.00**
108 ❑ May 1950 Cover: 0.10 **NM** value: **135.00**
• **CGC:** 1 graded, best 2.5
109 ❑ Jun 1950 Cover: 0.10 **NM** value: **135.00**
110 ❑ Jul 1950 Cover: 0.10 **NM** value: **135.00**
111 ❑ Aug 1950 Cover: 0.10 **NM** value: **135.00**
• **CGC:** 1 graded, best 1.8
112 ❑ Sep 1950 Cover: 0.10 **NM** value: **135.00**
• **CGC:** 1 graded, best 2.0
113 ❑ Oct 1950 Cover: 0.10 **NM** value: **135.00**
• **CGC:** 1 graded, best 2.5
114 ❑ Nov 1950 Cover: 0.10 **NM** value: **135.00**
115 ❑ Dec 1950 Cover: 0.10 **NM** value: **135.00**
• **CGC:** 1 graded, best 8.0
116 ❑ Jan 1951 Cover: 0.10 **NM** value: **135.00**
117 ❑ Feb 1951 Cover: 0.10 **NM** value: **135.00**
118 ❑ Mar 1951 Cover: 0.10 **NM** value: **135.00**
• **CGC:** 1 graded, best 7.5
119 ❑ Apr 1951 Cover: 0.10 **NM** value: **135.00**
120 ❑ May 1951 Cover: 0.10 **NM** value: **135.00**
121 ❑ Jun 1951 Cover: 0.10 **NM** value: **200.00**
• **CGC:** 1 graded, best 1.5
★ Origin of Captain Marvel (Fawcett).
122 ❑ Jul 1951 Cover: 0.10 **NM** value: **125.00**
123 ❑ Aug 1951 Cover: 0.10 **NM** value: **125.00**
124 ❑ Sep 1951 Cover: 0.10 **NM** value: **125.00**
• **CGC:** 1 graded, best 3.5
125 ❑ Oct 1951 Cover: 0.10 **NM** value: **125.00**
• **CGC:** 1 graded, best 1.8
126 ❑ Nov 1951 Cover: 0.10 **NM** value: **125.00**
127 ❑ Dec 1951 Cover: 0.10 **NM** value: **125.00**
• **CGC:** 2 graded, best 9.0
128 ❑ Jan 1952 Cover: 0.10 **NM** value: **125.00**
129 ❑ Feb 1952 Cover: 0.10 **NM** value: **125.00**
130 ❑ Mar 1952 Cover: 0.10 **NM** value: **125.00**
• **CGC:** 1 graded, best 3.0
131 ❑ Apr 1952 Cover: 0.10 **NM** value: **125.00**
132 ❑ May 1952 Cover: 0.10 **NM** value: **125.00**
133 ❑ Jun 1952 Cover: 0.10 **NM** value: **125.00**
134 ❑ Jul 1952 Cover: 0.10 **NM** value: **125.00**
135 ❑ Aug 1952 Cover: 0.10 **NM** value: **125.00**
136 ❑ Sep 1952 Cover: 0.10 **NM** value: **125.00**
137 ❑ Oct 1952 Cover: 0.10 **NM** value: **125.00**
• **CGC:** 1 graded, best 1.8
138 ❑ Nov 1952 Cover: 0.10 **NM** value: **125.00**
139 ❑ Dec 1952 Cover: 0.10 **NM** value: **125.00**
140 ❑ Jan 1953 Cover: 0.10 **NM** value: **125.00**
141 ❑ Feb 1953 Cover: 0.10 **NM** value: **110.00**
142 ❑ Mar 1953 Cover: 0.10 **NM** value: **110.00**
143 ❑ Apr 1953 Cover: 0.10 **NM** value: **110.00**
144 ❑ May 1953 Cover: 0.10 **NM** value: **110.00**
145 ❑ Jun 1953 Cover: 0.10 **NM** value: **110.00**
146 ❑ Jul 1953 Cover: 0.10 **NM** value: **110.00**
147 ❑ Aug 1953 Cover: 0.10 **NM** value: **110.00**
148 ❑ Sep 1953 Cover: 0.10 **NM** value: **110.00**
149 ❑ Oct 1953 Cover: 0.10 **NM** value: **110.00**
150 ❑ Nov 1953 Cover: 0.10 **NM** value: **110.00**
• **CGC:** 2 graded, best 7.5
final issue.

CAPTAIN MARVEL JR. — Fawcett

Junior was a teen who had been crippled by Captain Nazi in a story starting in Master Comics #21 (Dec 41), moving to Whiz #25 (Dec 41), and concluding in Master Comics #22 (Jan 42). Junior's life was saved by Captain Marvel, who provided the lad with super-powers to save his life. The method of acquiring those powers was speaking the name of his protector: Captain Marvel. Freddy, like the other Fawcett Marvels, could change back and forth by calling out those words. The most highly collected art was drawn by Mac Raboy, but the lad not only appeared (drawn by other artists, too) with Captain and Mary Marvel in The Marvel Family and his ongoing feature in Master, but he also sustained his own title for more than a decade.

— Maggie

1 ❑ Nov 1942 Cover: 0.10 **NM** value: **4800.00**
• **CGC:** 5 graded, best 7.0
2 ❑ Dec 1942 Cover: 0.10 **NM** value: **1850.00**
★ Appearance of Captain Nazi.
3 ❑ Jan 1943 Cover: 0.10 **NM** value: **1000.00**
• **CGC:** 1 graded, best 6.0
4 ❑ Feb 1943 Cover: 0.10 **NM** value: **1250.00**
Classic cover.
5 ❑ Mar 1943 Cover: 0.10 **NM** value: **850.00**
★ Appearance of Captain Nazi.
6 ❑ Apr 1943 Cover: 0.10 **NM** value: **725.00**
• **CGC:** 2 graded, best 9.0
7 ❑ May 1943 Cover: 0.10 **NM** value: **725.00**
• **CGC:** 1 graded, best 7.5
8 ❑ Jun 1943 Cover: 0.10 **NM** value: **725.00**
9 ❑ Jul 1943 Cover: 0.10 **NM** value: **675.00**
10 ❑ Aug 1943 Cover: 0.10 **NM** value: **675.00**
11 ❑ Sep 1943 Cover: 0.10 **NM** value: **560.00**
• **CGC:** 1 graded, best 9.0
12 ❑ Oct 1943 Cover: 0.10 **NM** value: **560.00**
13 ❑ Nov 1943 Cover: 0.10 **NM** value: **560.00**
• **CGC:** 3 graded, best 9.4
14 ❑ Dec 1943 Cover: 0.10 **NM** value: **560.00**
15 ❑ Jan 1944 Cover: 0.10 **NM** value: **560.00**
16 ❑ Feb 1944 Cover: 0.10 **NM** value: **485.00**
• **CGC:** 1 graded, best 5.5
17 ❑ Mar 1944 Cover: 0.10 **NM** value: **485.00**
18 ❑ Apr 1944 Cover: 0.10 **NM** value: **485.00**
• **CGC:** 2 graded, best 9.4
19 ❑ May 1944 Cover: 0.10 **NM** value: **485.00**
• **CGC:** 1 graded, best 8.5
20 ❑ Jun 1944 Cover: 0.10 **NM** value: **485.00**
21 ❑ Jul 1944 Cover: 0.10 **NM** value: **400.00**
22 ❑ Aug 1944 Cover: 0.10 **NM** value: **400.00**
23 ❑ Sep 1944 Cover: 0.10 **NM** value: **400.00**
24 ❑ Oct 1944 Cover: 0.10 **NM** value: **400.00**
• **CGC:** 1 graded, best 8.0
25 ❑ Nov 1944 Cover: 0.10 **NM** value: **400.00**
26 ❑ Jan 1945 Cover: 0.10 **NM** value: **350.00**
27 ❑ Feb 1945 Cover: 0.10 **NM** value: **350.00**
• **CGC:** 1 graded, best 6.5
28 ❑ Mar 1945 Cover: 0.10 **NM** value: **350.00**
• **CGC:** 1 graded, best 5.0
29 ❑ Apr 1945 Cover: 0.10 **NM** value: **350.00**
• **CGC:** 1 graded, best 9.9
30 ❑ May 1945 Cover: 0.10 **NM** value: **350.00**
• **CGC:** 1 graded, best 7.5
31 ❑ Jul 1945 Cover: 0.10 **NM** value: **290.00**
32 ❑ Sep 1945 Cover: 0.10 **NM** value: **290.00**
33 ❑ Nov 1945 Cover: 0.10 **NM** value: **290.00**
34 ❑ Jan 1946 Cover: 0.10 **NM** value: **290.00**
35 ❑ Feb 1946 Cover: 0.10 **NM** value: **290.00**
• **CGC:** 1 graded, best 8.0
36 ❑ Mar 1946 Cover: 0.10 **NM** value: **250.00**
37 ❑ Apr 1946 Cover: 0.10 **NM** value: **250.00**
• **CGC:** 1 graded, best 7.5
38 ❑ May 1946 Cover: 0.10 **NM** value: **250.00**
39 ❑ Jun 1946 Cover: 0.10 **NM** value: **250.00**
40 ❑ Jul 1946 Cover: 0.10 **NM** value: **250.00**
• **CGC:** 1 graded, best 8.0
41 ❑ Aug 1946 Cover: 0.10 **NM** value: **210.00**
42 ❑ Sep 1946 Cover: 0.10 **NM** value: **210.00**
43 ❑ Oct 1946 Cover: 0.10 **NM** value: **210.00**
44 ❑ Nov 1946 Cover: 0.10 **NM** value: **210.00**
45 ❑ Dec 1946 Cover: 0.10 **NM** value: **210.00**
46 ❑ Feb 1947 Cover: 0.10 **NM** value: **210.00**
47 ❑ Mar 1947 Cover: 0.10 **NM** value: **210.00**
48 ❑ Apr 1947 Cover: 0.10 **NM** value: **210.00**
49 ❑ May 1947 Cover: 0.10 **NM** value: **210.00**
50 ❑ Jun 1947 Cover: 0.10 **NM** value: **210.00**
51 ❑ Jul 1947 Cover: 0.10 **NM** value: **165.00**
• **CGC:** 1 graded, best 5.5
52 ❑ Aug 1947 Cover: 0.10 **NM** value: **165.00**
53 ❑ Sep 1947 Cover: 0.10 **NM** value: **165.00**
54 ❑ Oct 1947 Cover: 0.10 **NM** value: **165.00**
55 ❑ Nov 1947 Cover: 0.10 **NM** value: **165.00**
56 ❑ Dec 1947 Cover: 0.10 **NM** value: **165.00**
• **CGC:** 1 graded, best 4.5
57 ❑ Jan 1948 Cover: 0.10 **NM** value: **165.00**
• **CGC:** 1 graded, best 5.0
58 ❑ Feb 1948 Cover: 0.10 **NM** value: **165.00**
• **CGC:** 1 graded, best 6.0
59 ❑ Mar 1948 Cover: 0.10 **NM** value: **165.00**
60 ❑ Apr 1948 Cover: 0.10 **NM** value: **165.00**
61 ❑ May 1948 Cover: 0.10 **NM** value: **140.00**
62 ❑ Jun 1948 Cover: 0.10 **NM** value: **140.00**
63 ❑ Jul 1948 Cover: 0.10 **NM** value: **140.00**
64 ❑ Aug 1948 Cover: 0.10 **NM** value: **140.00**
65 ❑ Sep 1948 Cover: 0.10 **NM** value: **140.00**
• **CGC:** 1 graded, best 7.0
66 ❑ Oct 1948 Cover: 0.10 **NM** value: **140.00**
• **CGC:** 1 graded, best 5.0
67 ❑ Nov 1948 Cover: 0.10 **NM** value: **140.00**
68 ❑ Dec 1948 Cover: 0.10 **NM** value: **140.00**
69 ❑ Jan 1949 Cover: 0.10 **NM** value: **140.00**
70 ❑ Feb 1949 Cover: 0.10 **NM** value: **140.00**
71 ❑ Mar 1949 Cover: 0.10 **NM** value: **125.00**
72 ❑ Apr 1949 Cover: 0.10 **NM** value: **125.00**
73 ❑ May 1949 Cover: 0.10 **NM** value: **125.00**
74 ❑ Jun 1949 Cover: 0.10 **NM** value: **125.00**
75 ❑ Jul 1949 Cover: 0.10 **NM** value: **125.00**
76 ❑ Aug 1949 Cover: 0.10 **NM** value: **125.00**
77 ❑ Sep 1949 Cover: 0.10 **NM** value: **125.00**
78 ❑ Oct 1949 Cover: 0.10 **NM** value: **125.00**
79 ❑ Nov 1949 Cover: 0.10 **NM** value: **125.00**
80 ❑ Dec 1949 Cover: 0.10 **NM** value: **125.00**
81 ❑ Jan 1950 Cover: 0.10 **NM** value: **110.00**
82 ❑ Feb 1950 Cover: 0.10 **NM** value: **110.00**
83 ❑ Mar 1950 Cover: 0.10 **NM** value: **110.00**
84 ❑ Apr 1950 Cover: 0.10 **NM** value: **110.00**
85 ❑ May 1950 Cover: 0.10 **NM** value: **110.00**
86 ❑ Jun 1950 Cover: 0.10 **NM** value: **110.00**
87 ❑ Jul 1950 Cover: 0.10 **NM** value: **110.00**
88 ❑ Aug 1950 Cover: 0.10 **NM** value: **110.00**
• **CGC:** 1 graded, best 9.4
89 ❑ Sep 1950 Cover: 0.10 **NM** value: **110.00**
90 ❑ Oct 1950 Cover: 0.10 **NM** value: **110.00**
91 ❑ Nov 1950 Cover: 0.10 **NM** value: **100.00**
92 ❑ Dec 1950 Cover: 0.10 **NM** value: **100.00**
• **CGC:** 1 graded, best 3.0
93 ❑ Jan 1951 Cover: 0.10 **NM** value: **100.00**
94 ❑ Feb 1951 Cover: 0.10 **NM** value: **100.00**
95 ❑ Mar 1951 Cover: 0.10 **NM** value: **100.00**
96 ❑ Apr 1951 Cover: 0.10 **NM** value: **100.00**
97 ❑ May 1951 Cover: 0.10 **NM** value: **100.00**
98 ❑ Jun 1951 Cover: 0.10 **NM** value: **100.00**
99 ❑ Jul 1951 Cover: 0.10 **NM** value: **100.00**
100 ❑ Aug 1951 Cover: 0.10 **NM** value: **140.00**
• **CGC:** 1 graded, best 8.0
101 ❑ Sep 1951 Cover: 0.10 **NM** value: **90.00**
102 ❑ Oct 1951 Cover: 0.10 **NM** value: **90.00**
103 ❑ Nov 1951 Cover: 0.10 **NM** value: **90.00**
104 ❑ Dec 1951 Cover: 0.10 **NM** value: **90.00**
105 ❑ Jan 1952 Cover: 0.10 **NM** value: **90.00**
106 ❑ Feb 1952 Cover: 0.10 **NM** value: **90.00**
107 ❑ Mar 1952 Cover: 0.10 **NM** value: **90.00**
108 ❑ Apr 1952 Cover: 0.10 **NM** value: **90.00**
109 ❑ May 1952 Cover: 0.10 **NM** value: **90.00**
110 ❑ Jun 1952 Cover: 0.10 **NM** value: **90.00**
• **CGC:** 1 graded, best 2.0
111 ❑ Jul 1952 Cover: 0.10 **NM** value: **90.00**
112 ❑ Aug 1952 Cover: 0.10 **NM** value: **90.00**
113 ❑ Sep 1952 Cover: 0.10 **NM** value: **90.00**
114 ❑ Oct 1952 Cover: 0.10 **NM** value: **90.00**
115 ❑ Nov 1952 Cover: 0.10 **NM** value: **90.00**
116 ❑ Dec 1952 Cover: 0.10 **NM** value: **90.00**
117 ❑ Feb 1953 Cover: 0.10 **NM** value: **90.00**
118 ❑ Apr 1953 Cover: 0.10 **NM** value: **90.00**
• **CGC:** 1 graded, best 7.5
119 ❑ Jun 1953 Cover: 0.10 **NM** value: **90.00**
• **CGC:** 1 graded, best 4.0

CAPTAIN MARVEL PRESENTS THE TERRIBLE FIVE — M.F.

Brought out to capitalize on the increasing popularity of super-hero comics in the mid-1960s Silver Age, Captain Marvel Presents the Terrible Five was a copyright violation waiting to happen. The titular Captain Marvel was an original character, a "robot from another planet endowed with superior knowledge," with little in common with the Golden Age Fawcett Captain Marvel (legally enjoined from publication at that time) or Marvel's Captain Marvel, who would make his appearance the following year.

Other characters in the book, including Dr. Doom, Dr. Fate, Tiny Man, and a stretchable sleuth named Elastic Man, strayed very close to existing properties as well, and legal action eventually suspended the MF Enterprises' comic business in 1967. The void was quickly filled by dozens of other similar, workmanlike efforts from other second-string companies.

1 ❑ Cover: 0.25 **NM** value: **30.00**
• **CGC:** 1 graded, best 9.4

Other grades: Multiply prices above by **1.5 for Mint • 2/3 for Very Fine • 1/3 for Fine • 1/5 for Very Good • 1/8 for Good**

📖 Professor Doom and His Organization B.I.R.D.; The Return of Atom-Jaw; Dr. Fate and the Missing Hand!; Elasticman and Tinyman; Elasticman Becomes James Goode **A:** Carl Hubbell **W:** Bob Lamont

CAPTAIN MARVEL STORYBOOK — Fawcett

1 ❑ Sum 1947 Cover: 0.10 **NM** value: **400.00**
2 ❑ Win 1947 Cover: 0.10 **NM** value: **300.00**
• **CGC:** 1 graded, best 6.5
3 ❑ Spr 1948 Cover: 0.10 **NM** value: **300.00**
4 ❑ ca. 1949 Cover: 0.10 **NM** value: **300.00**

CAPTAIN MIDNIGHT — Fawcett

In 1939, Captain Midnight was offered as a radio serial as a follow-up to the earlier serial The Air Adventures of Jimmie Allen. The captain was World War I flying ace Captain Red Albright who became known as Captain Midnight because he'd returned from a mission at that hour. Hired to stop the villainies of Ivan Shark (a master criminal who wanted to take over the world), he put together a team to combat his foes. When the country entered World War II, Captain Midnight and his Secret Squadron pursued Nazis and saboteurs. The radio show ended in 1949; Columbia produced a 15-chapter movie serial in 1942; and a TV version ran from 1954 to 1956.

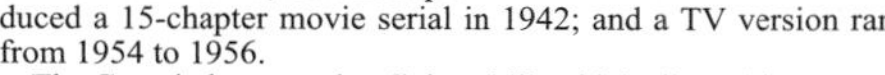

The Captain has amazing flying skill, which allows him to outmaneuver even the most determined Nazi fighter pilot and perform incredible landings on impossible terrain. He also has a "glider-chute" which gives him gliding ability, and a "Doom Beam Torch" which generates heat rays. And, like any self-respecting hero of the age, he has a pair of wards, Chuck Ramsey and Joyce Ryan, as well as a legion of faithful listeners who tune into his radio adventures, decoder rings at the ready. The comic book ran during the years the radio show achieved its peak popularity.

1 ❑ Sep 1942 Cover: 0.10 **NM** value: **2250.00**
• **CGC:** 1 graded, best 4.5
★ Origin of Captain Midnight.
2 ❑ Oct 1942 Cover: 0.10 **NM** value: **1000.00**
3 ❑ Nov 1942 Cover: 0.10 **NM** value: **725.00**
4 ❑ Jan 1943 Cover: 0.10 **NM** value: **725.00**
• **CGC:** 2 graded, best 7.5
5 ❑ Feb 1943 Cover: 0.10 **NM** value: **725.00**
6 ❑ Mar 1943 Cover: 0.10 **NM** value: **565.00**
7 ❑ Apr 1943 Cover: 0.10 **NM** value: **565.00**
• **CGC:** 1 graded, best 7.0
8 ❑ May 1943 Cover: 0.10 **NM** value: **565.00**
9 ❑ Jun 1943 Cover: 0.10 **NM** value: **565.00**
10 ❑ Jul 1943 Cover: 0.10 **NM** value: **565.00**
11 ❑ Aug 1943 Cover: 0.10 **NM** value: **385.00**
• **CGC:** 1 graded, best 7.0
12 ❑ Sep 1943 Cover: 0.10 **NM** value: **385.00**
• **CGC:** 2 graded, best 9.0
13 ❑ Oct 1943 Cover: 0.10 **NM** value: **385.00**
• **CGC:** 1 graded, best 8.5
14 ❑ Nov 1943 Cover: 0.10 **NM** value: **385.00**
• **CGC:** 1 graded, best 9.0
15 ❑ Dec 1943 Cover: 0.10 **NM** value: **385.00**
• **CGC:** 3 graded, best 9.4
16 ❑ Jan 1944 Cover: 0.10 **NM** value: **360.00**
17 ❑ Feb 1944 Cover: 0.10 **NM** value: **360.00**
• **CGC:** 2 graded, best 9.0
18 ❑ Mar 1944 Cover: 0.10 **NM** value: **360.00**
19 ❑ Apr 1944 Cover: 0.10 **NM** value: **360.00**
20 ❑ May 1944 Cover: 0.10 **NM** value: **360.00**
• **CGC:** 1 graded, best 8.5
21 ❑ Jun 1944 Cover: 0.10 **NM** value: **275.00**
• **CGC:** 1 graded, best 9.4
22 ❑ Jul 1944 Cover: 0.10 **NM** value: **275.00**
• **CGC:** 1 graded, best 8.0
23 ❑ Aug 1944 Cover: 0.10 **NM** value: **275.00**
• **CGC:** 2 graded, best 9.4
24 ❑ Sep 1944 Cover: 0.10 **NM** value: **275.00**
• **CGC:** 1 graded, best 9.4
25 ❑ Oct 1944 Cover: 0.10 **NM** value: **275.00**
• **CGC:** 2 graded, best 9.2
26 ❑ Nov 1944 Cover: 0.10 **NM** value: **275.00**
27 ❑ Jan 1945 Cover: 0.10 **NM** value: **275.00**
• **CGC:** 1 graded, best 8.0
28 ❑ Feb 1945 Cover: 0.10 **NM** value: **275.00**
29 ❑ Mar 1945 Cover: 0.10 **NM** value: **275.00**
• **CGC:** 1 graded, best 9.0
30 ❑ Apr 1945 Cover: 0.10 **NM** value: **275.00**
31 ❑ May 1945 Cover: 0.10 **NM** value: **215.00**
32 ❑ Jun 1945 Cover: 0.10 **NM** value: **215.00**
• **CGC:** 1 graded, best 9.6
33 ❑ Jul 1945 Cover: 0.10 **NM** value: **215.00**
• **CGC:** 1 graded, best 9.8
34 ❑ Aug 1945 Cover: 0.10 **NM** value: **215.00**
35 ❑ Sep 1945 Cover: 0.10 **NM** value: **215.00**
36 ❑ Oct 1945 Cover: 0.10 **NM** value: **215.00**
37 ❑ Nov 1945 Cover: 0.10 **NM** value: **215.00**
38 ❑ Feb 1946 Cover: 0.10 **NM** value: **215.00**
39 ❑ Apr 1946 Cover: 0.10 **NM** value: **215.00**
• **CGC:** 2 graded, best 6.0
40 ❑ May 1946 Cover: 0.10 **NM** value: **215.00**
• **CGC:** 1 graded, best 6.0
41 ❑ Jun 1946 Cover: 0.10 **NM** value: **185.00**
• **CGC:** 1 graded, best 9.0
42 ❑ Jul 1946 Cover: 0.10 **NM** value: **185.00**
• **CGC:** 1 graded, best 9.6
43 ❑ Aug 1946 Cover: 0.10 **NM** value: **185.00**
44 ❑ Sep 1946 Cover: 0.10 **NM** value: **185.00**
45 ❑ Oct 1946 Cover: 0.10 **NM** value: **185.00**
46 ❑ Nov 1946 Cover: 0.10 **NM** value: **185.00**
47 ❑ Dec 1946 Cover: 0.10 **NM** value: **185.00**
48 ❑ Feb 1947 Cover: 0.10 **NM** value: **185.00**
49 ❑ Mar 1947 Cover: 0.10 **NM** value: **185.00**
50 ❑ Apr 1947 Cover: 0.10 **NM** value: **185.00**
51 ❑ May 1947 Cover: 0.10 **NM** value: **160.00**
52 ❑ Jun 1947 Cover: 0.10 **NM** value: **160.00**
53 ❑ Jul 1947 Cover: 0.10 **NM** value: **160.00**
• **CGC:** 1 graded, best 9.4
54 ❑ Aug 1947 Cover: 0.10 **NM** value: **160.00**
55 ❑ Sep 1947 Cover: 0.10 **NM** value: **160.00**
• **CGC:** 1 graded, best 9.6
56 ❑ Oct 1947 Cover: 0.10 **NM** value: **160.00**
57 ❑ Nov 1947 Cover: 0.10 **NM** value: **160.00**
📖 The Cross-Country Crime!; Pilot Pete; Aero Patrol; Whipper-Snappers; Johnny Blair in the Air; The Race to Pluto! **A:** Dick Kraus
58 ❑ Dec 1947 Cover: 0.10 **NM** value: **160.00**
59 ❑ Jan 1948 Cover: 0.10 **NM** value: **160.00**
60 ❑ Feb 1948 Cover: 0.10 **NM** value: **160.00**
• **CGC:** 2 graded, best 9.2
61 ❑ Mar 1948 Cover: 0.10 **NM** value: **150.00**
62 ❑ Apr 1948 Cover: 0.10 **NM** value: **150.00**
• **CGC:** 1 graded, best 9.4
63 ❑ May 1948 Cover: 0.10 **NM** value: **150.00**
64 ❑ Jun 1948 Cover: 0.10 **NM** value: **150.00**
65 ❑ Jul 1948 Cover: 0.10 **NM** value: **150.00**
66 ❑ Aug 1948 Cover: 0.10 **NM** value: **150.00**
67 ❑ Fal 1948 Cover: 0.10 **NM** value: **150.00**
• Series continued in Sweethearts #68

CAPTAIN NAUTICUS & THE OCEAN FORCE — Express / Entity

1 ❑ May 1994 Cover: 2.95 **NM** value: **Cover or less**
📖 More Trouble Than You Can Fathom! ★ 1st Appearance of Captain Nauticus.
1/LE❑ Oct 1994 Cover: 2.95 **NM** value: **Cover or less**
• limited promotional edition.
2 ❑ Dec 1994 Cover: 2.95 **NM** value: **Cover or less**
• for The National Maritime Center Authority

CAPTAIN NICE — Gold Key

The TV series starring William Daniels ran for only half a season in 1967; it's not surprising that the comic book only managed a single issue — published after the show had left the air. — Maggie

1 ❑ Nov 1967 Cover: 0.12 **NM** value: **35.00**
• **CGC:** 2 graded, best 7.5
One-shot.

CAPTAIN N: THE GAME MASTER — Valiant

1 ❑ Cover: 1.95 **NM** value: **Cover or less**
Circ: CapCity orders: **3,300**
W: George Caragonne
2 ❑ Cover: 1.95 **NM** value: **Cover or less**
Circ: CapCity orders: **1,800**
📖 The Happy Zone; Villains' Do's and Don'ts; The Item; Just a Dog **A:** Don Hudson **W:** George Caragonne
3 ❑ Cover: 1.95 **NM** value: **Cover or less**
Circ: CapCity orders: **1,500**
W: George Caragonne
4 ❑ Cover: 1.95 **NM** value: **Cover or less**
Circ: CapCity orders: **1,200**
W: George Caragonne
5 ❑ Cover: 1.95 **NM** value: **Cover or less**
6 ❑ Cover: 1.95 **NM** value: **Cover or less**

CAPTAIN OBLIVION — Harrier

1 ❑ Aug 1987 Cover: 1.95 **NM** value: **Cover or less**
📖 Red Ant, White Ant, The Moon, The Moon, The Moon **A:** Glenn Dakin **W:** Glenn Dakin

CAPTAIN PARAGON — AC

1 ❑ Dec 1983 Cover: 1.50 **NM** value: **Cover or less**
📖 The Diamond Connection **A:** Don Secrease **W:** Bill Black
2 ❑ Cover: 1.50 **NM** value: **Cover or less**
3 ❑ Cover: 1.50 **NM** value: **Cover or less**
4 ❑ Cover: 1.50 **NM** value: **Cover or less**

CAPTAIN PARAGON AND THE SENTINELS OF JUSTICE — AC

1 ❑ Cover: 1.75 **NM** value: **Cover or less**
📖 The Shadows of Legends **A:** Greg Guler **W:** Greg Guler; Dan St. John
2 ❑ Cover: 1.75 **NM** value: **Cover or less**
3 ❑ Cover: 1.75 **NM** value: **Cover or less**
4 ❑ Cover: 1.75 **NM** value: **Cover or less**
5 ❑ Cover: 1.50 **NM** value: **1.75**
• Title changes to Sentinels of Justice ★ Origin of Capt. Paragon.
6 ❑ Cover: 1.50 **NM** value: **1.75**

CAPTAIN PHIL — Steeldragon

1 ❑ Cover: 1.50 **NM** value: **Cover or less**

The CGC numbers printed in individual listings above represent the **number of copies examined** and given a **Universal** grade by CGC and the **best such copy** graded at press time. For current populations, watch for special ***Comics Buyer's Guide*** issues or check **www.cgccomics.com.**

CAPTAIN PLANET AND THE PLANETEERS — Marvel

Captain Planet and the Planeteers was adapted almost verbatim from the Saturday morning cartoon series by the same name. Its stars are five kids from around the globe who are given power rings by Gaia ("Mother Earth" herself) so that they can defend the planet from polluters.

Each ring gives its bearer control of one of the classic elements of earth, air, water, and fire. The last ring, given to the Indian boy Ma-Ti, has the power of "heart," linking the others through telepathy. When the rings are used together, they also have the power to summon Captain Planet, a super-hero for the planet. Together, Captain Planet and the young "Planeteers" fight to save the Earth from such villains as the pig-like "Hoggish Greedly" whose schemes have included strip-mining wildlife sanctuaries and shooting trash into space.

1 ❑ Oct 1991 Cover: 1.00 **NM** value: **Cover or less**
Circ: CapCity orders: **16,800**
📖 A Hero for Earth! • TV **A:** José Delbo **C:** Neal Adams **W:** Barry Dutter; Jim Salicrup ★ Origin of the Planeteers.
2 ❑ Nov 1991 Cover: 1.00 **NM** value: **Cover or less**
Circ: CapCity orders: **8,800**
3 ❑ Dec 1991 Cover: 1.00 **NM** value: **Cover or less**
Circ: CapCity orders: **6,600**
4 ❑ Jan 1992 Cover: 1.00 **NM** value: **Cover or less**
Circ: CapCity orders: **5,100**
5 ❑ Feb 1992 Cover: 1.25 **NM** value: **Cover or less**
Circ: CapCity orders: **3,900**
6 ❑ Mar 1992 Cover: 1.25 **NM** value: **Cover or less**
Circ: CapCity orders: **3,100**
7 ❑ Apr 1992 Cover: 1.25 **NM** value: **Cover or less**
Circ: CapCity orders: **2,600**
8 ❑ Jun 1992 Cover: 1.25 **NM** value: **Cover or less**
Circ: CapCity orders: **2,300**
9 ❑ Jul 1992 Cover: 1.25 **NM** value: **Cover or less**
10 ❑ Aug 1992 Cover: 1.25 **NM** value: **Cover or less**
11 ❑ Sep 1992 Cover: 1.25 **NM** value: **Cover or less**
Circ: CapCity orders: **1,900**
12 ❑ Oct 1992 Cover: 1.25 **NM** value: **Cover or less**
final issue.

CAPTAIN POWER AND THE SOLDIERS OF THE FUTURE — Continuity

1 ❑ Dec 1988 Cover: 2.00 **NM** value: **Cover or less**
newsstand cover. • Captain Power standing **A:** Neal Adams **W:** Neal Adams; Peter Stone
1/DM❑ 1988 Cover: 2.00 **NM** value: **Cover or less**
Circ: CapCity orders: **4,550**
direct-sale cover. • Captain Power kneeling **A:** Neal Adams
2 ❑ Jan 1989 Cover: 2.00 **NM** value: **Cover or less**
Circ: CapCity orders: **3,900**
A: Neal Adams **W:** Neal Adams; Peter Stone

CAPTAIN ROCKET — P.L. Publishing

1 ❑ Nov 1951 **NM** value: **350.00**
• **CGC:** 2 graded, best 8.0

CAPTAIN SALVATION — Streetlight

1 ❑ Cover: 1.95 **NM** value: **Cover or less**

CAPTAIN SATAN — Millennium

1 ❑ Cover: 2.95 **NM** value: **Cover or less**
📖 Second Chances • Flip-book format **A:** Chris Hunter; Sean Shaw **W:** Steven Seagle; Terry Collins
2 ❑ Cover: 2.95 **NM** value: **Cover or less**
• Flip-book format

CAPT. SAVAGE AND HIS LEATHERNECK RAIDERS — Marvel

1 ❑ Jan 1968 Cover: 0.12 **NM** value: **14.00**
• **CGC:** 3 graded, best 9.4
A: Dick Ayers ★ Origin of Captain Savage and his Leatherneck Raiders. ★ Appearance of Sgt. Fury.
2 ❑ Mar 1968 Cover: 0.12 **NM** value: **9.00**
• **CGC:** 3 graded, best 9.4
A: Dick Ayers ★ Origin of Hydra. ★ Versus Baron Strucker.
3 ❑ May 1968 Cover: 0.12 **NM** value: **8.00**
• **CGC:** 1 graded, best 7.0
A: Dick Ayers ★ Versus Baron Strucker, Hydra.
4 ❑ Jul 1968 Cover: 0.12 **NM** value: **8.00**
• **CGC:** 1 graded, best 9.2
A: Dick Ayers ★ Versus Baron Strucker.
5 ❑ Aug 1968 Cover: 0.12 **NM** value: **8.00**
• **CGC:** 2 graded, best 9.2
A: Dick Ayers
6 ❑ Sep 1968 Cover: 0.12 **NM** value: **7.00**
📖 Save a Howler **A:** Dick Ayers **W:** Gary Friedrich ★ Appearance of Izzy Cohen.
7 ❑ Oct 1968 Cover: 0.12 **NM** value: **7.00**
📖 Objective: Ben Grimm **A:** Dick Ayers **W:** Archie Goodwin ★ Appearance of Ben Grimm.
8 ❑ Nov 1968 Cover: 0.12 **NM** value: **7.00**
• **CGC:** 1 graded, best 9.2
📖 Foul Ball • (becomes Captain Savage) **A:** Dick Ayers **W:** Gary Friedrich
9 ❑ Dec 1968 Cover: 0.12 **NM** value: **7.00**
📖 The Gun-Runner • Title changes to Captain Savage (and his Battlefield Raiders) **A:** Dick Ayers **W:** Gary Friedrich
10 ❑ Jan 1969 Cover: 0.12 **NM** value: **7.00**
📖 To the Last Man! **A:** Dick Ayers **W:** Gary Friedrich

CGC-graded: Multiply prices above by **33 for 9.9 M • 16 for 9.8 NM/M • 7 for 9.6 NM+ • 5 for 9.4 NM • 2.5 for 9.2 NM- • 1.5 for 9.0 VF/NM**

11 ❑ Feb 1969 Cover: 0.12 **NM** value: **6.00**
Death of a Leatherneck! • Story continued in Sgt. Fury #64 **A:** Dick Ayers **W:** Gary Friedrich ★ Appearance of Sgt. Fury. ★ Death of Baker.

12 ❑ Mar 1969 Cover: 0.12 **NM** value: **6.00**
Pray for Simon Savage! **A:** Dick Ayers

13 ❑ Apr 1969 Cover: 0.12 **NM** value: **6.00**
The Junk-Heap Juggernauts! **A:** Don Heck; Dick Ayers **W:** Arnold Drake

14 ❑ May 1969 Cover: 0.12 **NM** value: **6.00**
Savage's First Mission! **A:** Don Heck; Dick Ayers **W:** Arnold Drake

15 ❑ Jul 1969 Cover: 0.15 **NM** value: **5.00**
• Title changes to Capt. Savage **A:** Dick Ayers

16 ❑ Sep 1969 Cover: 0.15 **NM** value: **5.00**
A: Dick Ayers

17 ❑ Nov 1969 Cover: 0.15 **NM** value: **5.00**
The Unsinkable Jay Little Bear **A:** Dick Ayers

18 ❑ Jan 1970 Cover: 0.15 **NM** value: **5.00**
The High Cost of Fighting! **A:** Dick Ayers **W:** Gary Friedrich

19 ❑ Mar 1970 Cover: 0.15 **NM** value: **5.00**
final issue. **A:** Dick Ayers

CAPTAIN SCIENCE — Youthful

1 ❑ Nov 1950 Cover: 0.10 **NM** value: **750.00**
• **CGC:** 6 graded, best 9.2

2 ❑ Feb 1951 Cover: 0.10 **NM** value: **400.00**
• **CGC:** 3 graded, best 9.6

3 ❑ Apr 1951 Cover: 0.10 **NM** value: **350.00**

4 ❑ Jun 1951 Cover: 0.10 **NM** value: **350.00**
• **CGC:** 7 graded, best 9.2

5 ❑ Aug 1951 Cover: 0.10 **NM** value: **300.00**
• **CGC:** 3 graded, best 9.0

6 ❑ Oct 1951 Cover: 0.10 **NM** value: **300.00**
• **CGC:** 1 graded, best 6.5

7 ❑ Dec 1951 Cover: 0.10 **NM** value: **275.00**
• **CGC:** 1 graded, best 9.0

CAPTAIN'S JOLTING TALES — One Shot

1 ❑ Aug 1991 Cover: 2.95 **NM** value: **Cover or less**

2 ❑ Oct 1991 Cover: 3.50 **NM** value: **Cover or less**

3 ❑ Cover: 3.50 **NM** value: **Cover or less**
• trading card

3/Dlx ❑ Dec 1992 Cover: 3.50 **NM** value: **Cover or less**

4 ❑ Cover: 3.50 **NM** value: **Cover or less**

CAPTAIN STERNN: RUNNING OUT OF TIME — Kitchen Sink

1 ❑ Sep 1993, b&w Cover: 4.95 **NM** value: **5.50**
Circ: CapCity orders: **8,900**
A: Bernie Wrightson **W:** Bernie Wrightson

2 ❑ Dec 1993, b&w Cover: 4.95 **NM** value: **5.00**
Circ: CapCity orders: **7,125**
A: Bernie Wrightson **W:** Bernie Wrightson

3 ❑ Mar 1994 Cover: 4.95 **NM** value: **5.00**
Circ: CapCity orders: **6,250**
A: Bernie Wrightson **W:** Bernie Wrightson

4 ❑ May 1994 Cover: 4.95 **NM** value: **5.00**
A: Bernie Wrightson **W:** Bernie Wrightson

5 ❑ Sep 1994 Cover: 4.95 **NM** value: **5.00**
Circ: CapCity orders: **5,175**
A: Bernie Wrightson **W:** Bernie Wrightson

CAPTAIN STEVE SAVAGE — Avon

1 ❑ ca. 1951 Cover: 0.10 **NM** value: **100.00**
2 ❑ Cover: 0.10 **NM** value: **80.00**
3 ❑ Cover: 0.10 **NM** value: **50.00**
4 ❑ Cover: 0.10 **NM** value: **50.00**
5 ❑ Cover: 0.10 **NM** value: **50.00**
6 ❑ Cover: 0.10 **NM** value: **50.00**
7 ❑ Cover: 0.10 **NM** value: **50.00**
8 ❑ Cover: 0.10 **NM** value: **50.00**
9 ❑ Cover: 0.10 **NM** value: **50.00**
10 ❑ Cover: 0.10 **NM** value: **50.00**
11 ❑ Cover: 0.10 **NM** value: **50.00**
12 ❑ Cover: 0.10 **NM** value: **50.00**
13 ❑ Cover: 0.10 **NM** value: **50.00**

CAPT. STORM — DC

1 ❑ Jun 1964 Cover: 0.12 **NM** value: **25.00**
• **CGC:** 1 graded, best 7.5
Killer Hunt! ★ Origin of Captain Storm.

2 ❑ Aug 1964 Cover: 0.12 **NM** value: **16.00**
• **CGC:** 1 graded, best 9.4

3 ❑ Oct 1964 Cover: 0.12 **NM** value: **16.00**
• **CGC:** 1 graded, best 9.6

4 ❑ Dec 1964 Cover: 0.12 **NM** value: **16.00**
• **CGC:** 1 graded, best 9.2

5 ❑ Feb 1965 Cover: 0.12 **NM** value: **16.00**
6 ❑ Apr 1965 Cover: 0.12 **NM** value: **12.00**
7 ❑ Jun 1965 Cover: 0.12 **NM** value: **10.00**
8 ❑ Aug 1965 Cover: 0.12 **NM** value: **10.00**
9 ❑ Oct 1965 Cover: 0.12 **NM** value: **10.00**
10 ❑ Dec 1965 Cover: 0.12 **NM** value: **10.00**
11 ❑ Feb 1966 Cover: 0.12 **NM** value: **10.00**
12 ❑ Apr 1966 Cover: 0.12 **NM** value: **10.00**
13 ❑ Jun 1966 Cover: 0.12 **NM** value: **10.00**
14 ❑ Aug 1966 Cover: 0.12 **NM** value: **10.00**
15 ❑ Oct 1966 Cover: 0.12 **NM** value: **10.00**
16 ❑ Dec 1966 Cover: 0.12 **NM** value: **8.00**
17 ❑ Feb 1967 Cover: 0.12 **NM** value: **8.00**
18 ❑ Apr 1967 Cover: 0.12 **NM** value: **8.00**
final issue.

CAPTAIN TAX TIME — Paul Haynes Comics

1 ❑ Cover: 3.50 **NM** value: **Cover or less**
A: Ted Collyer; Terry Rotsaert **W:** Ted Collyer; Terry Rotsaert; Paul Haynes

CAPTAIN 3-D — Harvey

1 ❑ Dec 1953 Cover: 0.10 **NM** value: **75.00**
• **CGC:** 6 graded, best 9.0
The Man from the World of D; The Menace of the Living Dolls; Iron Hat McGinty and His Destruction Gang

CAPTAIN THUNDER AND BLUE BOLT — Hero

1 ❑ Cover: 1.95 **NM** value: **Cover or less**
Back to the Beginning **A:** Dell Barras **W:** Roy Thomas; Dann Thomas ★ Origin of Blue Bolt. ★ Appearance of Captain Thunder.

2 ❑ Cover: 1.95 **NM** value: **Cover or less**
Circ: CapCity orders: **2,125**
A: Dell Barras **W:** Roy Thomas; Dann Thomas

3 ❑ Cover: 1.95 **NM** value: **Cover or less**
A: Dell Barras **W:** Roy Thomas; Dann Thomas ★ Origin of Captain Thunder.

4 ❑ Cover: 1.95 **NM** value: **Cover or less**
A: Dell Barras **W:** Roy Thomas; Dann Thomas

5 ❑ Cover: 1.95 **NM** value: **Cover or less**
Circ: CapCity orders: **1,800**
A: Dell Barras **W:** Roy Thomas; Dann Thomas

6 ❑ Cover: 1.95 **NM** value: **Cover or less**
Circ: CapCity orders: **1,650**
A: Dell Barras **W:** Roy Thomas; Dann Thomas

7 ❑ Cover: 1.95 **NM** value: **Cover or less**
Circ: CapCity orders: **1,600**
A: Dell Barras **W:** Roy Thomas; Dann Thomas

8 ❑ Cover: 1.95 **NM** value: **Cover or less**
Circ: CapCity orders: **1,550**
A: Dell Barras **W:** Roy Thomas; Dann Thomas ★ 1st Appearance of King's Gambit.

9 ❑ Cover: 1.95 **NM** value: **Cover or less**
Circ: CapCity orders: **1,450**
A: Dell Barras **W:** Roy Thomas; Dann Thomas

10 ❑ Cover: 1.95 **NM** value: **Cover or less**
Circ: CapCity orders: **1,300**
A: Dell Barras **W:** Roy Thomas; Dann Thomas

CAPTAIN THUNDER AND BLUE BOLT (VOL. 2) — Hero

1 ❑ Aug 1992 Cover: 3.50 **NM** value: **Cover or less**
Blow-Back **A:** Howard Simpson; E.R. Cruz **W:** Roy Thomas; Dann Thomas

2 ❑ Cover: 3.50 **NM** value: **Cover or less**
W: Roy Thomas; Dann Thomas

CAPTAIN VENTURE AND THE LAND BENEATH THE SEA — Gold Key

1 ❑ Oct 1968 Cover: 0.12 **NM** value: **35.00**
• **CGC:** 2 graded, best 9.6

2 ❑ Oct 1969 Cover: 0.15 **NM** value: **30.00**
• **CGC:** 1 graded, best 7.5

CAPTAIN VICTORY AND THE GALACTIC RANGERS — Pacific

Jack Kirby, the artist who created or co-created Captain America, The Fantastic Four, The Incredible Hulk, Thor, and countless others, brings yet another hero into the world with Captain Victory and the Galactic Rangers. "King" Kirby's style shows throughout in the futuristic bent and fantastic weaponry and gadgetry of this series.

Captain Victory, an intergalactic policeman, is always on the lookout for the thieves, criminals, and rogues who roam through outer space. And, once he finds them, he doesn't give up — he always brings them to justice, no matter how, even if it means having his body replaced, if he gets badly hurt in battle.

1 ❑ Nov 1981 Cover: 1.00 **NM** value: **1.50**
• **CGC:** 2 graded, best 9.6
Captain Victory and his Galactic Rangers **A:** Jack Kirby **W:** Jack Kirby ★ 1st Appearance of Mr. Mind.

2 ❑ Jan 1982 Cover: 1.00 **NM** value: **1.25**
• **CGC:** 1 graded, best 9.4
Death-Hive, U.S.A. **A:** Jack Kirby **W:** Jack Kirby

3 ❑ Mar 1982 Cover: 1.00 **NM** value: **1.25**
Encounters of a Savage Kind **A:** Jack Kirby; Neal Adams **W:** Jack Kirby ★ 1st Appearance of Ms. Mystic.

4 ❑ May 1982 Cover: 1.00 **NM** value: **1.25**
The Fighting Airborne; The Goozlebobber • Goozlebobber **A:** Jack Kirby **W:** Jack Kirby

5 ❑ Jul 1982 Cover: 1.00 **NM** value: **1.25**
Our Backs to the Wall; King of the Unwanted • Goozlebobber **A:** Jack Kirby **W:** Jack Kirby

6 ❑ Sep 1982 Cover: 1.00 **NM** value: **1.25**
Victory is Sacrifice; (untitled) • Goozlebobber **A:** Jack Kirby **W:** Jack Kirby

7 ❑ Oct 1982 Cover: 1.00 **NM** value: **1.25**
Wonder Warriors; Ranger Recruit: Martius Klavus • Martius Klavus **A:** Jack Kirby **W:** Jack Kirby

8 ❑ Dec 1982 Cover: 1.00 **NM** value: **1.25**
Zap-Out; The Roman Syndrome • Martius Klavus **A:** Jack Kirby **W:** Jack Kirby

9 ❑ Feb 1983 Cover: 1.00 **NM** value: **1.25**
God's Many Mansions; Martius Klavus and The Unseen World • Martius Klavus **A:** Jack Kirby **W:** Jack Kirby ★ 1st Appearance of Paranex the Fighting Fetus.

10 ❑ Apr 1983 Cover: 1.00 **NM** value: **1.25**
The Voice; Rainmaker **A:** Jack Kirby; Tim Conrad **W:** Jack Kirby; Tim Conrad ★ Appearance of Paranex the Fighting Fetus.

11 ❑ Jun 1983 Cover: 1.00 **NM** value: **1.25**
Meet Big Ugly **A:** Jack Kirby **W:** Jack Kirby ★ Origin of Captain Victory.

12 ❑ Oct 1983 Cover: 1.00 **NM** value: **1.25**
Growing Up with the Lost Ranger **A:** Jack Kirby **W:** Jack Kirby

13 ❑ Jan 1984 Cover: 1.50 **NM** value: **Cover or less**
Gangs of Space • indicia lists title as Captain Victory. **A:** Jack Kirby **W:** Jack Kirby

SE 1 ❑ Oct 1983 Cover: 1.50 **NM** value: **Cover or less**
The Space Musketeers **A:** Jack Kirby **W:** Jack Kirby

CAPTAIN VICTORY AND THE GALACTIC RANGERS (MINI-SERIES) — Jack Kirby

1 ❑ Jul 2000 Cover: 2.95 **NM** value: **Cover or less**
Circ: Diamd. preorders: **5,084**
no cover price. **A:** Jack Kirby **W:** Jeremy Kirby

2 ❑ Sep 2000 Cover: 2.95 **NM** value: **Cover or less**
Circ: Diamd. preorders: **2,843**
A: Jack Kirby **W:** Jeremy Kirby

3 ❑ Nov 2000 Cover: 2.95 **NM** value: **Cover or less**
A: Jack Kirby **W:** Jeremy Kirby

CAPTAIN VIDEO — Fawcett

1 ❑ Feb 1951 Cover: 0.10 **NM** value: **400.00**
• **CGC:** 1 graded, best 6.5

2 ❑ Apr 1951 Cover: 0.10 **NM** value: **325.00**
• **CGC:** 1 graded, best 7.0
Photo cover. Captain Video and the Time When Men Could Not Walk!; Rod Cameron...The Gun Duel!; Captain Video and the Hidden Island; Airfield Al...Relatively Speaking!; The Little Monsters (text); Captain Video and the Legion of Evil • Cited in Seduction of the Innocent: "Morbid fantasies are conjured up for children, like the one that suddenly mankind's legs do not function" **W:** Kermit Welles

3 ❑ Jun 1951 Cover: 0.10 **NM** value: **200.00**

4 ❑ Aug 1951 Cover: 0.10 **NM** value: **200.00**

5 ❑ Oct 1951 Cover: 0.10 **NM** value: **200.00**
• **CGC:** 1 graded, best 8.0

6 ❑ Dec 1951 Cover: 0.10 **NM** value: **200.00**
final issue.

CAPTAIN WINGS COMPACT COMICS — AC

1 ❑ Cover: 3.95 **NM** value: **Cover or less**
2 ❑ Cover: 3.95 **NM** value: **Cover or less**

CAPTAIN ZEPHYR AND THE TIGER WOMAN — Millennium

1 ❑ b&w Cover: 2.95 **NM** value: **Cover or less**
No issue number. cover says The Tiger Woman. • no indicia

CARAVAN KIDD — Dark Horse

Dark Horse Comics is one of the leading American publishers of manga comics. In 1992, it added to its already impressive list of Japanese titles by releasing an English translation of Johji Manabe's Caravan Kidd.

The series is set on a post-apocalyptic Earth where resources are so scarce that traders can charge incredibly high amounts of money for anything. Two of these traders — Babo, a weird little creature, and Wataru, a human boy — are a couple of the best. They make a good living from the needs of others, although Wataru seems to feel a little more sympathy for the needy people who cannot afford their goods. Even Babo becomes strangely likable, however, when they are tricked into following a mysterious woman into the Wastelands. This woman is Mian Toris, an accomplished warrior who is being chased by what seems like the entire Helgebard Empire. As for Babo and Wataru, their troubles are only beginning.

1 ❑ Jul 1992 Cover: 2.50 **NM** value: **Cover or less**
Circ: CapCity orders: **3,400**
A: Johji Manabe **W:** Johji Manabe

2 ❑ Aug 1992 Cover: 2.50 **NM** value: **Cover or less**
Circ: CapCity orders: **2,850**
A: Johji Manabe **W:** Johji Manabe

3 ❑ Sep 1992 Cover: 2.50 **NM** value: **Cover or less**
A: Johji Manabe **W:** Johji Manabe

4 ❑ Oct 1992 Cover: 2.50 **NM** value: **Cover or less**
A: Johji Manabe **W:** Johji Manabe

5 ❑ Nov 1992 Cover: 2.50 **NM** value: **Cover or less**
A: Johji Manabe **W:** Johji Manabe

6 ❑ Dec 1992 Cover: 2.50 **NM** value: **Cover or less**
Circ: CapCity orders: **2,700**
A: Johji Manabe **W:** Johji Manabe

7 ❑ Jan 1993 Cover: 2.50 **NM** value: **Cover or less**
A: Johji Manabe **W:** Johji Manabe

8 ❑ Feb 1993 Cover: 2.50 **NM** value: **Cover or less**
A: Johji Manabe **W:** Johji Manabe

9 ❑ Mar 1993 Cover: 2.50 **NM** value: **Cover or less**
Circ: CapCity orders: **3,100**
A: Johji Manabe **W:** Johji Manabe

10 ❑ Apr 1993 Cover: 2.50 **NM** value: **Cover or less**
Circ: CapCity orders: **2,950**
A: Johji Manabe **W:** Johji Manabe

Bk 1 ❑ b&w Cover: 19.95 **NM** value: **Cover or less**
• collects first series **A:** Johji Manabe **W:** Johji Manabe

CARAVAN KIDD PART 2 — Dark Horse

1 ❑ May 1993 Cover: 2.50 **NM** value: **Cover or less**
Circ: CapCity orders: **3,350**
A: Johji Manabe **W:** Johji Manabe

Other grades: Multiply prices above by **1.5 for Mint • 2/3 for Very Fine • 1/3 for Fine • 1/5 for Very Good • 1/8 for Good**

2 ❑ Jun 1993 Cover: 2.50 **NM** value: **Cover or less**
Circ: CapCity orders: **3,275**
A: Johji Manabe **W:** Johji Manabe
3 ❑ Jul 1993 Cover: 2.95 **NM** value: **Cover or less**
A: Johji Manabe **W:** Johji Manabe
4 ❑ Aug 1993 Cover: 2.50 **NM** value: **Cover or less**
Circ: CapCity orders: **2,850**
A: Johji Manabe **W:** Johji Manabe
5 ❑ Sep 1993 Cover: 2.50 **NM** value: **Cover or less**
A: Johji Manabe **W:** Johji Manabe
6 ❑ Oct 1993 Cover: 2.50 **NM** value: **Cover or less**
A: Johji Manabe **W:** Johji Manabe
7 ❑ Cover: 2.50 **NM** value: **Cover or less**
Circ: CapCity orders: **2,650**
A: Johji Manabe **W:** Johji Manabe
8 ❑ Cover: 2.50 **NM** value: **Cover or less**
Circ: CapCity orders: **2,700**
A: Johji Manabe **W:** Johji Manabe
9 ❑ Mar 1994 Cover: 2.50 **NM** value: **Cover or less**
Circ: CapCity orders: **2,825**
A: Johji Manabe **W:** Johji Manabe
10 ❑ Apr 1994 Cover: 2.50 **NM** value: **Cover or less**
Circ: CapCity orders: **2,850**
A: Johji Manabe **W:** Johji Manabe
Bk 2❑ b&w Cover: 19.95 **NM** value: **Cover or less**
A: Johji Manabe **W:** Johji Manabe

CARAVAN KIDD PART 3 — Dark Horse

1 ❑ May 1994 Cover: 2.50 **NM** value: **Cover or less**
Circ: CapCity orders: **3,625**
A: Johji Manabe **W:** Johji Manabe
2 ❑ Jun 1994 Cover: 2.50 **NM** value: **Cover or less**
Circ: CapCity orders: **3,550**
A: Johji Manabe **W:** Johji Manabe
3 ❑ Jul 1994 Cover: 2.50 **NM** value: **Cover or less**
A: Johji Manabe **W:** Johji Manabe
4 ❑ Aug 1994 Cover: 2.50 **NM** value: **Cover or less**
A: Johji Manabe **W:** Johji Manabe
5 ❑ Sep 1994 Cover: 2.50 **NM** value: **Cover or less**
Circ: CapCity orders: **3,375**
A: Johji Manabe **W:** Johji Manabe
6 ❑ Oct 1994 Cover: 2.50 **NM** value: **Cover or less**
Circ: CapCity orders: **3,325**
A: Johji Manabe **W:** Johji Manabe
7 ❑ Nov 1994 Cover: 2.95 **NM** value: **Cover or less**
Circ: CapCity orders: **3,175**
A: Johji Manabe **W:** Johji Manabe
8 ❑ Dec 1994 Cover: 2.95 **NM** value: **Cover or less**
Circ: CapCity orders: **3,300**
A: Johji Manabe **W:** Johji Manabe
Bk 3❑ b&w Cover: 19.95 **NM** value: **Cover or less**
A: Johji Manabe **W:** Johji Manabe

CARBON KNIGHT — Lunar Studios

1 ❑ Cover: 2.95 **NM** value: **Cover or less**
2 ❑ Cover: 2.95 **NM** value: **Cover or less**

CARE BEARS — Marvel / Star

1 ❑ Nov 1985 Cover: 0.65 **NM** value: **1.00**
Circ: CapCity orders: **3,800**
🕮 The Plot to Steal Summer **A:** Howie Post **W:** Howie Post
2 ❑ Jan 1986 Cover: 0.65 **NM** value: **1.00**
Circ: CapCity orders: **2,400**
3 ❑ Mar 1986 Cover: 0.65 **NM** value: **1.00**
Circ: CapCity orders: **2,300**
4 ❑ May 1986 Cover: 0.75 **NM** value: **1.00**
Circ: CapCity orders: **2,100**
5 ❑ Jul 1986 Cover: 0.75 **NM** value: **1.00**
Circ: CapCity orders: **2,200**
6 ❑ Sep 1986 Cover: 0.75 **NM** value: **1.00**
Circ: CapCity orders: **2,000**
7 ❑ Nov 1986 Cover: 0.75 **NM** value: **1.00**
Circ: CapCity orders: **2,100**
8 ❑ Jan 1987 Cover: 0.75 **NM** value: **1.00**
Circ: Statement: **65,900** CapCity orders: **2,050**
9 ❑ Mar 1987 Cover: 0.75 **NM** value: **1.00**
Circ: Statement: **65,900** CapCity orders: **2,000**
10 ❑ May 1987 Cover: 0.75 **NM** value: **1.00**
Circ: Statement: **65,900** CapCity orders: **1,550**
11 ❑ Jul 1987 Cover: 1.00 **NM** value: **Cover or less**
Circ: Statement: **65,900** CapCity orders: **1,400**
12 ❑ Sep 1987 Cover: 1.00 **NM** value: **Cover or less**
Circ: Statement: **65,900** CapCity orders: **1,450**
13 ❑ Nov 1987 Cover: 1.00 **NM** value: **Cover or less**
Circ: Statement: **65,900**
★ Appearance of Madballs.
14 ❑ Jan 1988 Cover: 1.00 **NM** value: **Cover or less**
Circ: CapCity orders: **1,250**
15 ❑ Mar 1988 Cover: 1.00 **NM** value: **Cover or less**
Circ: CapCity orders: **1,200**
16 ❑ May 1988 Cover: 1.00 **NM** value: **Cover or less**
Circ: CapCity orders: **1,150**
17 ❑ Jul 1988 Cover: 1.00 **NM** value: **Cover or less**
Circ: CapCity orders: **1,000**
18 ❑ Sep 1988 Cover: 1.00 **NM** value: **Cover or less**
Circ: CapCity orders: **1,000**
19 ❑ Nov 1988 Cover: 1.00 **NM** value: **Cover or less**
Circ: CapCity orders: **900**
20 ❑ Jan 1989 Cover: 1.00 **NM** value: **Cover or less**
Circ: CapCity orders: **900**
final issue.

CAREER GIRL ROMANCES — Charlton / Star

24 ❑ Jun 1964 Cover: 0.12 **NM** value: **3.50**
25 ❑ Sep 1964 Cover: 0.12 **NM** value: **3.50**
26 ❑ Cover: 0.12 **NM** value: **3.50**
27 ❑ Cover: 0.12 **NM** value: **3.50**
28 ❑ 1965 Cover: 0.12 **NM** value: **3.50**
29 ❑ 1965 Cover: 0.12 **NM** value: **3.50**
30 ❑ 1965 Cover: 0.12 **NM** value: **3.50**
31 ❑ Nov 1965 Cover: 0.12 **NM** value: **3.50**
32 ❑ Jan 1966 Cover: 0.12 **NM** value: **40.00**
★ Appearance of Elvis Presley.
33 ❑ 1966 Cover: 0.12 **NM** value: **3.00**
34 ❑ 1966 Cover: 0.12 **NM** value: **3.00**
35 ❑ 1966 Cover: 0.12 **NM** value: **3.00**
36 ❑ 1966 Cover: 0.12 **NM** value: **3.00**
37 ❑ 1966 Cover: 0.12 **NM** value: **3.00**
38 ❑ 1967 Cover: 0.12 **NM** value: **3.00**
Circ: Statement: **125,710**
39 ❑ 1967 Cover: 0.12 **NM** value: **3.00**
Circ: Statement: **125,710**
40 ❑ 1967 Cover: 0.12 **NM** value: **3.00**
Circ: Statement: **125,710**
41 ❑ Aug 1967 Cover: 0.12 **NM** value: **3.00**
Circ: Statement: **125,710**
42 ❑ Oct 1967 Cover: 0.12 **NM** value: **3.00**
Circ: Statement: **125,710**
43 ❑ Dec 1967 Cover: 0.12 **NM** value: **3.00**
Circ: Statement: **125,710**
44 ❑ Feb 1968 Cover: 0.12 **NM** value: **3.00**
45 ❑ 1968 Cover: 0.12 **NM** value: **3.00**
46 ❑ Aug 1968 Cover: 0.12 **NM** value: **3.00**
47 ❑ Oct 1968 Cover: 0.12 **NM** value: **3.00**
• **CGC:** 1 graded, best 7.5
48 ❑ Dec 1968 Cover: 0.12 **NM** value: **3.00**
49 ❑ Feb 1969 Cover: 0.12 **NM** value: **3.00**
50 ❑ Apr 1969 Cover: 0.12 **NM** value: **3.00**
🕮 Only Talent for Love; Behind That Leering Smile; The Thief Also Steals Kisses;
51 ❑ Jun 1969 Cover: 0.12 **NM** value: **2.50**
52 ❑ Aug 1969 Cover: 0.15 **NM** value: **2.50**
53 ❑ Oct 1969 Cover: 0.15 **NM** value: **2.50**
54 ❑ Dec 1969 Cover: 0.15 **NM** value: **2.50**
55 ❑ Feb 1970 Cover: 0.15 **NM** value: **2.50**
56 ❑ Apr 1970 Cover: 0.15 **NM** value: **2.50**
57 ❑ Jun 1970 Cover: 0.15 **NM** value: **2.50**
58 ❑ Aug 1970 Cover: 0.15 **NM** value: **2.50**
59 ❑ Oct 1970 Cover: 0.15 **NM** value: **2.50**
60 ❑ Dec 1970 Cover: 0.15 **NM** value: **2.50**
61 ❑ Feb 1971 Cover: 0.15 **NM** value: **2.50**
62 ❑ Apr 1971 Cover: 0.15 **NM** value: **2.50**
63 ❑ Jun 1971 Cover: 0.15 **NM** value: **2.50**
64 ❑ Aug 1971 Cover: 0.20 **NM** value: **2.50**
65 ❑ Oct 1971 Cover: 0.20 **NM** value: **2.50**
66 ❑ Dec 1971 Cover: 0.20 **NM** value: **2.50**
Circ: Statement: **128,030**
67 ❑ Feb 1972 Cover: 0.20 **NM** value: **2.50**
Circ: Statement: **128,030**
68 ❑ Apr 1972 Cover: 0.20 **NM** value: **2.50**
Circ: Statement: **128,030**
69 ❑ Jun 1972 Cover: 0.20 **NM** value: **2.50**
Circ: Statement: **128,030**
70 ❑ Aug 1972 Cover: 0.20 **NM** value: **2.50**
Circ: Statement: **128,030**
71 ❑ Oct 1972 Cover: 0.20 **NM** value: **2.50**
Circ: Statement: **128,030**
72 ❑ Dec 1973 Cover: 0.20 **NM** value: **2.50**
73 ❑ Feb 1973 Cover: 0.20 **NM** value: **2.50**
74 ❑ Apr 1973 Cover: 0.20 **NM** value: **2.50**
• Has 1972 Statement; avg total sales 128,030
75 ❑ Jul 1973 Cover: 0.20 **NM** value: **2.50**
76 ❑ Aug 1973 Cover: 0.20 **NM** value: **2.50**
77 ❑ Oct 1973 Cover: 0.20 **NM** value: **2.50**
78 ❑ Dec 1973 Cover: 0.20 **NM** value: **2.50**
final issue.

CAR 54 WHERE ARE YOU? — Dell

The slapstick sitcom ran from 1961 to 1963 on TV and starred Joe E. Ross as Officer Gunther Toody and Fred Gwynne as Officer Francis Muldoon of New York City's 53rd Precinct. It remains familiar to today's TV audiences, thanks to occasional reruns and the memorable theme.

Some covers featured bits of dialogue over photos of the two; #4, for example, carries the typical speech from Toody: "Ooo, Ooo, Francis! A monkey just drove off with the Captain's car!" And that was about the level of the show — and the comic-book version. Early issues of the comic-book series ran while the show was aired; later issues reprinted the early issues. — Maggie

2 ❑ Aug 1962 Cover: 0.12 **NM** value: **75.00**
3 ❑ Oct 1962 Cover: 0.12 **NM** value: **45.00**
• **CGC:** 1 graded, best 9.2
4 ❑ Dec 1962 Cover: 0.12 **NM** value: **40.00**
• **CGC:** 1 graded, best 9.0
5 ❑ Mar 1963 Cover: 0.12 **NM** value: **40.00**
6 ❑ Jun 1963 Cover: 0.12 **NM** value: **35.00**
• **CGC:** 1 graded, best 9.4
7 ❑ Sep 1963 Cover: 0.12 **NM** value: **35.00**
• **CGC:** 1 graded, best 9.2

CARL AND LARRY CHRISTMAS SPECIAL — Comics Interview

1 ❑ b&w Cover: 2.25 **NM** value: **Cover or less**

CARL BARKS LIBRARY OF WALT DISNEY'S COMICS AND STORIES, THE — Gladstone

1 ❑ Cover: 8.95 **NM** value: **Cover or less**
🕮 The Victory Garden; The Rabbit's Foot; Lifeguard Daze; Good Deeds; The Limber W Guest Ranch **A:** Carl Barks **W:** Carl Barks
1-2 ❑ Cover: 8.95 **NM** value: **Cover or less**

CARMILLA — Aircel

All issues are adults only.
1 ❑ Feb 1991, b&w Cover: 2.50 **NM** value: **Cover or less**
outer paper wrapper to cover nude cover.
2 ❑ Mar 1991, b&w Cover: 2.50 **NM** value: **Cover or less**
3 ❑ Apr 1991, b&w Cover: 2.50 **NM** value: **Cover or less**
4 ❑ b&w Cover: 2.50 **NM** value: **Cover or less**
5 ❑ b&w Cover: 2.50 **NM** value: **Cover or less**
6 ❑ b&w Cover: 2.50 **NM** value: **Cover or less**

CARNAGE — Eternity

1 ❑ Cover: 1.95 **NM** value: **Cover or less**
🕮 Wrath **A:** Richard Kane Ferguson **W:** Richard Kane Ferguson

CARNAGE: IT'S A WONDERFUL LIFE — Marvel

1 ❑ Oct 1996 Cover: 1.95 **NM** value: **Cover or less**

CARNAGE: MINDBOMB — Marvel

Spider-Man's black costume from the Marvel Super Heroes Secret Wars was eventually revealed to be an alien symbiote. When Spider-Man rejected it, it found a new host in Eddie Brock and became the killer Venom. Brock, however, was relatively sane. Not so Cletus Kasady, a maniacal killer who became the villain Carnage when a bit of the symbiote found its way into his bloodstream.

After murdering dozens of people, Carnage was eventually apprehended and brought to Ravencroft, a facility for the most dangerous of the criminally insane. There he lives out his days in a locked vault, waiting for the chance to kill again. In this one-shot special, Carnage is visited by Matthew Kurtz, a shadowy scientist with top-level security clearance. Kurtz is determined to go alone into the cell with Carnage, peer into his mind, and find out what makes him tick. But not even Kurtz is ready to experience the madness he finds there.

1 ❑ Feb 1996 Cover: 2.95 **NM** value: **Cover or less**
One-shot. foil cover. **A:** Kyle Hotz **W:** Warren Ellis

CARNAL COMICS: ANNA MALLE — Re-Visionary

1 ❑ Cover: 2.95 **NM** value: **Cover or less**
🕮 Anna Malle **A:** Larry Nadolsky **W:** Anna Malle

CARNAL COMICS: BRITTANY O'CONNELL — Re-Visionary

1 ❑ Cover: 2.95 **NM** value: **Cover or less**
🕮 Carnal Crowd Pleaser **A:** Mike Sagara; Dennis Clark **W:** Jay Allen Sanford; Brittany O'Connell

CARNAL COMICS: BUNNY BLEU — Revisionary

All issues are adults only.
1 ❑ Sep 1996, b&w Cover: 2.95 **NM** value: **Cover or less**

CARNAL COMICS: CHRISTI LAKE — Re-Visionary

1 ❑ Cover: 3.50 **NM** value: **Cover or less**
Photo cover (nude). 🕮 On the Range **A:** Glenn Morangie **W:** Jay Allen Sanford; Christi Lake

CARNAL COMICS: JEANNA FINE — Re-Visionary

1 ❑ Cover: 2.95 **NM** value: **Cover or less**
🕮 Jeanna Fine: In the Extreme! **A:** Larry Nadolsky **W:** Jay Allen Sanford; Jeanna Fine

CARNAL COMICS: JENNA JAMESON — Re-Visionary

1 ❑ Cover: 2.95 **NM** value: **Cover or less**
🕮 Jenna Jameson: Super-Model **A:** Chuck Bordell **W:** Jay Allen Sanford; Janna Jameson

CARNAL COMICS: JILL KELLY — Re-Visionary

1 ❑ Cover: 3.50 **NM** value: **Cover or less**
Photo cover (nude). 🕮 Back in the Saddle; Time Out **A:** Kevin Breyfogle; Justin Norman **W:** Jay Allen Sanford; Jill Kelly

CARNAL COMICS: JULIA ANN — Re-Visionary

1 ❑ Cover: 2.95 **NM** value: **Cover or less**
🕮 Hollywood Heartbreaker **A:** Pretorius **W:** Jay Allen Sanford; Julia Ann

Capital City orders are the actual sales of comic books by Capital City Distribution, once one of the largest U.S. sellers of comics to comics shops. Capital City's share of comics shop sales, while not known exactly, increases from around 10-20% in the mid-1980s to 30-35% in the mid-1990s. Capital City's share of comic books sold on newsstands (most Marvels and DCs) will be less.

CGC-graded: Multiply prices above by **33 for 9.9 M • 16 for 9.8 NM/M • 7 for 9.6 NM+ • 5 for 9.4 NM • 2.5 for 9.2 NM- • 1.5 for 9.0 VF/NM**

CARNAL COMICS: LEGENDS OF PORN — Re-Visionary

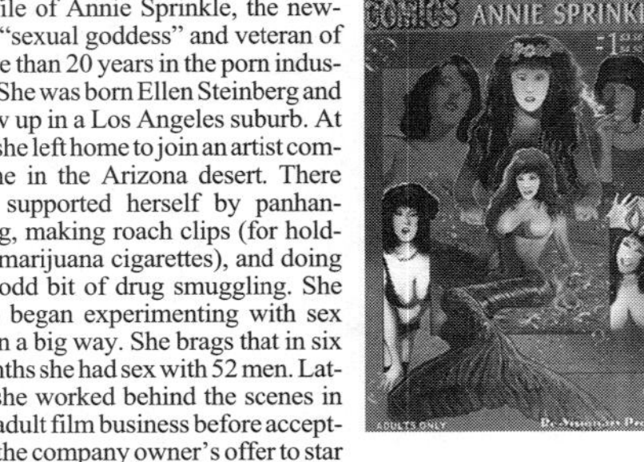

This series got started off with a profile of Annie Sprinkle, the new-age "sexual goddess" and veteran of more than 20 years in the porn industry. She was born Ellen Steinberg and grew up in a Los Angeles suburb. At 17, she left home to join an artist commune in the Arizona desert. There she supported herself by panhandling, making roach clips (for holding marijuana cigarettes), and doing the odd bit of drug smuggling. She also began experimenting with sex — in a big way. She brags that in six months she had sex with 52 men. Later, she worked behind the scenes in the adult film business before accepting the company owner's offer to star in a film. She claimed she chose her stage name by hearing the voice of a ghost named Annie Sprinkle, a woman she thinks died a virgin and is living out her desires through her. Over the years, she earned a reputation as a woman who would try anything, as well as something of a sexual mystic and teacher, by holding workshops on sex.

1 ❑ Cover: 3.50 **NM** value: **Cover or less**
📖 Annie Sprinkle: Two Decades of Boogie Nights! **A:** Kevin Breyfogle; Annie Sprinkle; Jay Allen Sanford **W:** Kevin Breyfogle; Annie Sprinkle; Jay Allen Sanford ★ Origin of Annie Sprinkle.

CARNAL COMICS: LISA ANN — Re-Visionary

1 ❑ Cover: 2.95 **NM** value: **Cover or less**
📖 On My Own **A:** Joe Paradise **W:** Jay Allen Sanford; Lisa Ann

CARNAL COMICS: NICI STERLING — Re-Visionary

1 ❑ Cover: 2.95 **NM** value: **Cover or less**
📖 Nici Sterling: Jewel in the Crown **A:** Paradise **W:** Jay Allen Sanford; Nici Sterling

CARNAL COMICS: PORSCHE LYNN — Re-Visionary

1 ❑ Cover: 2.95 **NM** value: **Cover or less**
📖 Right Here, Right Now **A:** Kevin Breyfogle **W:** Jay Allen Sanford; Porsche Lynn

CARNAL COMICS PRESENTS DEJA SIN: FALLEN ANGEL — Re-Visionary

All issues are adults only.

1 ❑ Jun 1999, b&w Cover: 3.50 **NM** value: **Cover or less**
1/A ❑ Jun 1999, b&w Cover: 3.50 **NM** value: **Cover or less**
📖 Fallen Angel
1/B ❑ Jun 1999, b&w Cover: 3.50 **NM** value: **Cover or less**
Bottoms Up photo cover. 📖 Fallen Angel

CARNAL COMICS PRESENTS DEMI'S WILD KINGDOM ADVENTURE — Re-Visionary

All issues are adults only.

1 ❑ Sep 1999, b&w **NM** value: **3.50**
no cover price.

CARNAL COMICS PRESENTS GINGER LYNN IS TORN — Re-Visionary

All issues are adults only.

Adapted from the adult film, which marked the return of porn legend Ginger Lynn to the genre, this comic features the actress in a torrent of sex, interrupted briefly by story. Ginger, as "Clarisse Bijou" is a soap opera star whose old flame is getting married to another woman. Clarisse manages to score with both the bride and groom-to-be, eventually solving everyone's romantic dilemmas by deciding on a group marriage.

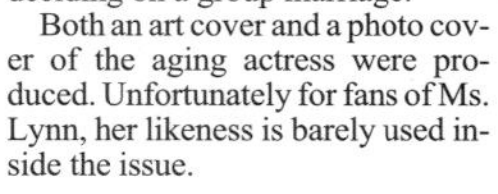

Both an art cover and a photo cover of the aging actress were produced. Unfortunately for fans of Ms. Lynn, her likeness is barely used inside the issue.

1/A ❑ Sep 1999, b&w Cover: 3.50 **NM** value: **Cover or less**
Photo cover. **A:** Beth Ann Rafael; Bugsy; Cookie; Jake Smiley; Justin Norman **W:** Beth Ann Rafael; Bugsy; Cookie; Jake Smiley; Jay Allen Sanford; Justin Norman
1/B ❑ Sep 1999, b&w Cover: 3.50 **NM** value: **Cover or less**
alternate coveradult. **A:** Beth Ann Rafael; Bugsy; Cookie; Jake Smiley; Justin Norman **W:** Beth Ann Rafael; Bugsy; Cookie; Jake Smiley; Jay Allen Sanford; Justin Norman

CARNAL COMICS PRESENTS MARILYN CHAMBERS IS STILL INSATIABLE — Re-Visionary

All issues are adults only.

1/A ❑ Sep 1999, b&w Cover: 3.50 **NM** value: **Cover or less**
Photo cover. **A:** Kevin Breyfogle; Eddie Avon **W:** Jay Allen Sanford
1/B ❑ Sep 1999 Cover: 3.50 **NM** value: **Cover or less**
alternate cover. **A:** Kevin Breyfogle; Eddie Avon **W:** Jay Allen Sanford

CARNAL COMICS PRESENTS PORN STAR FANTASIES — Re-Visionary

1 ❑ Cover: 2.95 **NM** value: **Cover or less**
2 ❑ Cover: 2.95 **NM** value: **Cover or less**
3 ❑ Cover: 2.95 **NM** value: **Cover or less**
📖 The Nubile Noble **A:** Mike Wolfer **W:** Jay Allen Sanford; Sarah-Jane Hamilton
4 ❑ Cover: 2.95 **NM** value: **Cover or less**
5 ❑ Cover: 2.95 **NM** value: **Cover or less**
6 ❑ Cover: 2.95 **NM** value: **Cover or less**
📖 Jasmin St. Claire: Surfer Safari **A:** Fauve **W:** Jay Allen Sanford; Jasmin St. Claire
7 ❑ Cover: 2.95 **NM** value: **Cover or less**
8 ❑ Cover: 2.95 **NM** value: **Cover or less**
9 ❑ Cover: 2.95 **NM** value: **Cover or less**
10 ❑ Cover: 2.95 **NM** value: **Cover or less**
📖 Minka: Island Girl • Minka, Hypatia Lee, Kelly O'Dell, Nightingale **A:** Justin Normal **W:** Jay Allen Sanford; Minka

CARNAL COMICS PRESENTS WICKED WEAPON: OFFICIAL FILM ADAPTATION — Re-Visionary

1 ❑ Cover: 3.50 **NM** value: **Cover or less**
Photo cover. **A:** Kevin Breyfogle **W:** Jay Allen Sanford; Brad Armstrong

CARNAL COMICS: REBECCA BARDOUX — Re-Visionary

1 ❑ Cover: 2.95 **NM** value: **Cover or less**
📖 Giving It All **A:** Larry Nadolsky **W:** Jay Allen Sanford; Rebecca Bardoux

CARNAL COMICS: REBECCA LORD — Re-Visionary

1 ❑ Cover: 2.95 **NM** value: **Cover or less**
📖 French Kiss **A:** Nick Poliwko **W:** Jay Allen Sanford; Rebecca Lord
1/Nude ❑ Cover: 3.50 **NM** value: **Cover or less**
nude photo cover. 📖 French Kiss **A:** Nick Poliwko **W:** Jay Allen Sanford; Rebecca Lord

CARNAL COMICS: SARAH-JANE HAMILTON — Re-Visionary

1 ❑ Mar 1994 Cover: 2.50 **NM** value: **Cover or less**
• Sarah Jane Hamilton
2 ❑ Apr 1994 Cover: 2.50 **NM** value: **Cover or less**
• Sarah Jane Hamilton
3 ❑ Cover: 2.50 **NM** value: **Cover or less**

CARNAL COMICS: SUMMER CUMMINGS & SKYE BLUE — Re-Visionary

1 ❑ Cover: 3.50 **NM** value: **Cover or less**
📖 Summer 'n' Skye: Over the Edge!; The Most Outrageous Show on Earth **A:** Peter Cortez **W:** Jay Allen Sanford; Skye Blue; Summer Cummings

CARNAL COMICS: TAYLOR WANE — Re-Visionary

1 ❑ Cover: 2.95 **NM** value: **Cover or less**

CARNAL COMICS: ZOD — Re-Visionary

1 ❑ Cover: 3.50 **NM** value: **Cover or less**
Photo cover. 📖 World Class Zo'; World Class Zod **A:** Nick Poliwko **W:** Jay Allen Sanford; Zo'
1/Nude ❑ Cover: 3.50 **NM** value: **Cover or less**
Photo cover. 📖 World Class Zod **A:** Nick Poliwko **W:** Jay Allen Sanford; Zo'

CARNEYS, THE — Archie

1 ❑ Sum 1994 Cover: 2.00 **NM** value: **Cover or less**

CARNOSAUR CARNAGE — Atomeka

1 ❑ Cover: 4.95 **NM** value: **Cover or less**
Circ: CapCity orders: **3,000**
📖 The Skin of Hadrosaurs; Battle at the Edge of Time; Big in Japan; Dinosaurs Rool! **A:** John McCrea; Anthony Williams; Kevin Walker; Richard Dolan **W:** Nick Abadzis; Steve White; Brian Williamson; Dan Abnett

CARTOON CARTOONS — DC

1 ❑ Mar 2001 Cover: 1.99 **NM** value: **Cover or less**
Circ: Diamd. preorders: **5,064**
📖 Ed, Edd n Eddy: Last Nail in the Edhouse; Johnny Bravo's Rules to Live By: Tip #12 Johnny on the Spot; Courage the Cowardly Dog: The Gods Must be Nosy; A Sheep in the Big City Shortie; Who are Baboon? **A:** Tim Harkins; Dean Sternecky; Mike Wetterhahn; Mo Willems; Scott Underwood **W:** Frank Strom; Mo Willems; Robbie Busch; Danny Antonucci; Paul Kupperberg
2 ❑ Apr 2001 Cover: 1.99 **NM** value: **Cover or less**
Circ: Diamd. preorders: **3,461**
📖 Ed, Edd n Eddy: Half Bak-Ed; Cow and Chicken: Chicken and the Beanstalk; Johnny Bravo: See no Johnny **A:** Mike Kazaleh; Neal Sternecky; Vincent DePorter **W:** Michael Kraiger; Scott Cunningham; Paul Kupperberg
3 ❑ May 2001 Cover: 1.99 **NM** value: **Cover or less**
Circ: Diamd. preorders: **3,492**
📖 The Big Winner **A:** Robert Pope **W:** Robbie Busch
4 ❑ Jun 2001 Cover: 1.99 **NM** value: **Cover or less**
Circ: Diamd. preorders: **3,076**
5 ❑ Jul 2001 Cover: 1.99 **NM** value: **Cover or less**
Circ: Diamd. preorders: **2,946**
6 ❑ Aug 2001 Cover: 1.99 **NM** value: **Cover or less**
Circ: Diamd. preorders: **3,998**
7 ❑ Sep 2001 Cover: 1.99 **NM** value: **Cover or less**
Circ: Diamd. preorders: **3,057**

The CGC numbers printed in individual listings above represent the **number of copies examined** and given a **Universal** grade by CGC and the **best such copy** graded at press time. For current populations, watch for special ***Comics Buyer's Guide*** issues or check **www.cgccomics.com.**

CARTOON HISTORY OF THE UNIVERSE, THE — Rip Off

This series is no less ambitious than a comics-format distillation of all of known history. Larry Gonick has undertaken the job of relating history through panels, word balloons, and captions, and he succeeds brilliantly. This series is delightful and informative and never gets bogged down in tedious detail.

Gonick has done other comics, including a history of the United States and focused books about particular science fields, but this is his finest work. Gonick presents the concepts of the ancient world in modern one-liners and puns, and the effect keeps the interest up through the sometimes complicated anecdotes.

When the Doubleday collections began in the '90s, this series came into public notice. It's a fine series that perfectly demonstrates the flexibility and potential of the comics medium.

1 ❑ b&w Cover: 2.50 **NM** value: **4.50**
cardstock cover. 📖 The Evolution of Everything **A:** Larry Gonick **W:** Larry Gonick
2 ❑ b&w Cover: 2.50 **NM** value: **3.50**
cardstock cover. **A:** Larry Gonick **W:** Larry Gonick
3 ❑ b&w Cover: 2.50 **NM** value: **3.50**
cardstock cover. **A:** Larry Gonick **W:** Larry Gonick
4 ❑ b&w Cover: 2.50 **NM** value: **3.50**
cardstock cover. **A:** Larry Gonick **W:** Larry Gonick
5 ❑ b&w Cover: 2.50 **NM** value: **3.50**
cardstock cover. **A:** Larry Gonick **W:** Larry Gonick
6 ❑ b&w Cover: 2.50 **NM** value: **Cover or less**
cardstock cover. **A:** Larry Gonick **W:** Larry Gonick
7 ❑ b&w Cover: 2.50 **NM** value: **Cover or less**
cardstock cover. **A:** Larry Gonick **W:** Larry Gonick
8 ❑ b&w Cover: 2.95 **NM** value: **Cover or less**
A: Larry Gonick **W:** Larry Gonick
9 ❑ b&w Cover: 2.95 **NM** value: **Cover or less**
A: Larry Gonick **W:** Larry Gonick
Bk 1 ❑ Cover: 12.95 **NM** value: **Cover or less**
A: Larry Gonick **W:** Larry Gonick
Bk 2 ❑ Cover: 12.95 **NM** value: **Cover or less**
A: Larry Gonick **W:** Larry Gonick

CARTOONIST, THE — Sirius / Dog Star

1 ❑ b&w Cover: 2.95 **NM** value: **Cover or less**
• collects strips **A:** Teri Wood

CARTOON NETWORK — DC

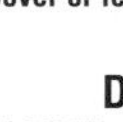

This one-shot was part of a multimillion-dollar giveaway by DC and the Cartoon Network, designed to boost comic-book sales. And, unlike many giveaways, it's a lot of fun. In the first tale, Cow and Chicken learn that honesty is the best policy at the Inferno Scrap Metal yard owned by Se±or Diablo. Next, a wordless Scooby-Doo story features a criminal who is enamored of lovely Daphne. In a third story, Mr. Spacely intends to replace George Jetson with a robot that looks and acts like him — the real merriment begins when "Robogeorge" assumes George Jetson's life for a day. Blessed with simplicity of pace and uncomplicated art and entirely devoid of angst and grit, each story has its own merits. Even though this copy is intended for younger readers, it's enjoyable reading for adults, as well.

1 ❑ **NM** value: **1.00**
No issue number. • Giveaway from DC Comics to promote comics. 📖 Cow and Chicken: Recycling Daze; Scooby Doo: Repeat Offender; The Jetsons: Robo George • Reprints stories from Cartoon Networks Presents #6 **A:** William Wray; Tim Harkins; Glenn Barr **W:** Mike Kraiger; Chris Duffy; Michael Kupperman

CARTOON NETWORK CHRISTMAS SPECTACULAR — Archie

1 ❑ Cover: 2.00 **NM** value: **Cover or less**
📖 Too Much Christmas Spirit; It's A Gift; Mail Must go Through; The Last Christmas Carol; The Top 10 Cultral Events of the Year in Guzzler's Gulch; Don't Badger the Customers!; Quick Draw!; It's a Blunderful Life! ★ Appearance of Scooby-Doo, The Flintstones, The Jetsons, Yogi Bear, Huckleberry Hound, Magilla Gorilla.

CARTOON NETWORK PRESENTS — DC

1 ❑ Aug 1997 Cover: 1.75 **NM** value: **2.00**
Circ: Diamd. preorders: **10,440**
• Dexter's Laboratory, Top Cat
2 ❑ Sep 1997 Cover: 1.75 **NM** value: **Cover or less**
Circ: Diamd. preorders: **9,095**
• Space Ghost, Yogi Bear
3 ❑ Oct 1997 Cover: 1.75 **NM** value: **Cover or less**
Circ: Diamd. preorders: **5,853**
📖 The Twiddle Method; Wally Gator: Fifteen Minutes of Fame • Hanna-Barbera crossover with Mr. Peebles, Ranger Smith, Officer Dibble, Mr. Twiddle, and Colonel Fusby;Wally Gator back-up;Cartoon All-Stars **A:** Gary Fields; Bill Alger **W:** Sam Henderson
4 ❑ Nov 1997 Cover: 1.75 **NM** value: **Cover or less**
Circ: Diamd. preorders: **5,505**

Other grades: Multiply prices above by **1.5 for Mint • 2/3 for Very Fine • 1/3 for Fine • 1/5 for Very Good • 1/8 for Good**

📖 Dial M for Monkey • Dial M for Monkey **A:** Paul Rudish **W:** Paul Rudish; Gennady Tartakovsky

5 ❑ Dec 1997 Cover: 1.95 **NM** value: **Cover or less**
Circ: Diamd. preorders: **5,199**
• Toonami★ Appearance of Birdman, Herculoids.

6 ❑ Jan 1998 Cover: 1.95 **NM** value: **Cover or less**
Circ: Diamd. preorders: **4,719**
📖 Cow and Chicken: Recycling Daze; Scooby Doo: Repeat Offender; The Jetsons: Robo George • Cow and Chicken **A:** William Wray; Tim Harkins; Glenn Barr **W:** Mike Kraiger; Chris Duffy; Michael Kupperman

7 ❑ Feb 1998 Cover: 1.95 **NM** value: **Cover or less**
Circ: Diamd. preorders: **4,390**
• Wacky Races

8 ❑ Mar 1998 Cover: 1.95 **NM** value: **Cover or less**
Circ: Diamd. preorders: **4,149**
📖 The Karate Chump!; Clothes Make the Man! • Fighting Monkies;Johnny Bravo **A:** Anthony Williams; Dave Schwartz **W:** Dwayne McDuffie; Jesse Leon McCann

9 ❑ Apr 1998 Cover: 1.95 **NM** value: **Cover or less**
Circ: Diamd. preorders: **3,478**
• Toonami★ Appearance of Herculoids, Birdman.

10 ❑ May 1998 Cover: 1.95 **NM** value: **Cover or less**
Circ: Diamd. preorders: **3,374**
• Cow & Chicken

11 ❑ Jun 1998 Cover: 1.95 **NM** value: **Cover or less**
Circ: Diamd. preorders: **3,213**
• Wacky Races

12 ❑ Aug 1998 Cover: 1.95 **NM** value: **Cover or less**
Circ: Diamd. preorders: **3,242**
• Cartoon All-Stars;Peter Potamus

13 ❑ Sep 1998 Cover: 1.99 **NM** value: **Cover or less**
Circ: Diamd. preorders: **3,199**
• Toonami, Birdman, Herculoids

14 ❑ Oct 1998 Cover: 1.99 **NM** value: **Cover or less**
Circ: Diamd. preorders: **3,543**
• Cow and Chicken

15 ❑ Nov 1998 Cover: 1.99 **NM** value: **Cover or less**
Circ: Diamd. preorders: **2,867**
• Wacky Races

16 ❑ Dec 1998 Cover: 1.99 **NM** value: **Cover or less**
Circ: Diamd. preorders: **2,898**
• Cartoon All-Stars;Top Cat

17 ❑ Jan 1999 Cover: 1.99 **NM** value: **Cover or less**
Circ: Diamd. preorders: **3,624**
📖 Winter Takes all • Toonami, Herculoids, Galaxy Trio;Toonami **A:** John Delaney **W:** Mike Kraiger

18 ❑ Feb 1999 Cover: 1.99 **NM** value: **Cover or less**
Circ: Diamd. preorders: **2,766**
📖 Treasure Hunt • Cartoon All-Stars;Funtastic Treasure Hunt

19 ❑ Mar 1999 Cover: 1.99 **NM** value: **Cover or less**
Circ: Diamd. preorders: **2,954**
📖 Attack of the 50-Foot Chicken • Cow and Chicken

20 ❑ Apr 1999 Cover: 1.99 **NM** value: **Cover or less**
Circ: Diamd. preorders: **2,570**
• Cartoon All-Stars;Hong Kong Phooey, Atom Ant, Secret Squirrel

21 ❑ May 1999 Cover: 1.99 **NM** value: **Cover or less**
Circ: Diamd. preorders: **2,518**
📖 Cat on a Hot Tin Pooch; Galtar and the Golden Lance: Zorn to the Rescue! • Toonami, Blue Falcon and Dyno-Mutt, Galtar and the Golden Lance;Toonami **A:** John Delaney; Manny Galán **W:** Andy Merrill; Dan Slott

22 ❑ Jun 1999 Cover: 1.99 **NM** value: **Cover or less**
Circ: Diamd. preorders: **2,581**
📖 Night of the Iron Horse; Brain Food; Mighty Magilla • Cartoon All-Stars;Baba Looey **A:** Gary Fields; Bill Alger **W:** Mike Kraiger; Terry Collins ★ Appearance of Yogi Bear, Quick Draw McGraw, Magilla Gorilla, Boo Boo Bear, El Kabonng, Ranger Jones, Ranger Smith.

23 ❑ Jul 1999 Cover: 1.99 **NM** value: **Cover or less**
Circ: Diamd. preorders: **2,677**
📖 Jabberjaw: Gammyjaws; Speed Buggy: Bah, Humbug!; Captain Caveman: Neanderthal Nightmare • Jabberjaw, Speed Buggy, Captain Caveman;Jabberjaw;Speed Buggy;Captain Caveman **A:** John Delaney; Manny Galán **W:** Andy Merrill; Chuck Kim; Terry Collins

24 ❑ Aug 1999 Cover: 1.99 **NM** value: **Cover or less**
Circ: Diamd. preorders: **2,824**
📖 Puppy Power; Goober and the Ghost Chasers: The Video Vanishes • Scrappy-Doo **A:** John Delaney **W:** Terry Collins

SE 1/PL❑ **NM** value: **2.00**
no cover price. • Platinum edition. • Dexter's Laboratory

CARTOON NETWORK PRESENTS SPACE GHOST — Archie

1 ❑ Mar 1997 Cover: 1.50 **NM** value: **Cover or less**
• **CGC:** 3 graded, best 9.8

CARTOON NETWORK STARRING — DC

1 ❑ Sep 1999 Cover: 1.99 **NM** value: **Cover or less**
Circ: Diamd. preorders: **5,630** • **CGC:** 1 graded, best 9.2
• The Powerpuff Girls **A:** Craig McCracken **W:** Craig McCracken; Genndy Tartakovsky

2 ❑ Oct 1999 Cover: 1.99 **NM** value: **Cover or less**
Circ: Diamd. preorders: **4,074**
📖 Johnny in Paradise! **A:** Dan Day **W:** Jess McCann ★ 1st Appearance of Johnny Bravo (in comics).

3 ❑ Nov 1999 Cover: 1.99 **NM** value: **Cover or less**
Circ: Diamd. preorders: **3,434**

4 ❑ Dec 1999 Cover: 1.99 **NM** value: **Cover or less**
Circ: Diamd. preorders: **5,372**
📖 45 Minutes 'til Showtime! • Space Ghost **A:** C. Martin Croker **W:** Andy Merrill

5 ❑ Jan 2000 Cover: 1.99 **NM** value: **Cover or less**
Circ: Diamd. preorders: **6,755**

6 ❑ Feb 2000 Cover: 1.99 **NM** value: **Cover or less**
Circ: Diamd. preorders: **4,103**

7 ❑ Mar 2000 Cover: 1.99 **NM** value: **Cover or less**
Circ: Diamd. preorders: **3,298**

8 ❑ Apr 2000 Cover: 1.99 **NM** value: **Cover or less**
Circ: Diamd. preorders: **3,330**

9 ❑ May 2000 Cover: 1.99 **NM** value: **Cover or less**
Circ: Diamd. preorders: **4,566**
📖 Zorak: Wotta Felon! • Space Ghost **A:** Robert Pope; C. Martin Croker **W:** Andy Merrill

10 ❑ Jun 2000 Cover: 1.99 **NM** value: **Cover or less**
Circ: Diamd. preorders: **3,025**

11 ❑ Jul 2000 Cover: 1.99 **NM** value: **Cover or less**
Circ: Diamd. preorders: **3,052**

12 ❑ Aug 2000 Cover: 1.99 **NM** value: **Cover or less**
Circ: Diamd. preorders: **4,523**

13 ❑ Sep 2000 Cover: 1.99 **NM** value: **Cover or less**
Circ: Diamd. preorders: **2,973**
📖 Weak in the Sneeze; Flaming Desire **A:** Tim Harkins; Gary Fields **W:** Jennifer Moore; Dan Slott; Sean Carolan

14 ❑ Oct 2000 Cover: 1.99 **NM** value: **Cover or less**
Circ: Diamd. preorders: **2,949**
📖 Under My Wheels • Johnny Bravo **A:** Anthony Williams **W:** Frank Strom

15 ❑ Nov 2000 Cover: 1.99 **NM** value: **Cover or less**
Circ: Diamd. preorders: **3,915**
📖 Just Desserts • Space Ghost **A:** Matt Jenkins **W:** Robbie Busch

16 ❑ Dec 2000 Cover: 1.99 **NM** value: **Cover or less**
Circ: Diamd. preorders: **2,860**
📖 Two Dips in the Ocean • Cow and Chicken **A:** Mike Kazaleh **W:** Jess McCann

17 ❑ Jan 2001 Cover: 1.99 **NM** value: **Cover or less**
Circ: Diamd. preorders: **2,936**
📖 Giddy-Up Johnny!; Beach Blanket Bravo; Sheep in the Big City: Shear Terror! • Johnny Bravo **A:** Anthony Williams; Gary Terry; Jonathan Royce **W:** Mo Williams; Paul Kupperberg

18 ❑ Feb 2001 Cover: 1.99 **NM** value: **Cover or less**
Circ: Diamd. preorders: **3,816**
📖 Who Voo-Dooed It?; Lokar, Lothario • Space Ghost **A:** Robert Pope; Penciller **W:** C. Martin Croker; John Rozum

CARTOON QUARTERLY — Gladstone

1 ❑ **NM** value: **5.00**
• Mickey Mouse

CARTOON TALES (DISNEY'S...) — Disney

1 ❑ ca. 1992 Cover: 2.95 **NM** value: **Cover or less**
📖 101 Dalmatians; Lucky's Big Break; Cruella's Very Furry Christmas **A:** Al Hubbard; Willie Ito **W:** Carl Fallberg; Ed Nofziger; Floyd Norman

2 ❑ ca. 1992 Cover: 2.95 **NM** value: **Cover or less**
📖 Just Us Justice Ducks • 21809;Darkwing Duck **A:** John Blair Moore; Gary Martin **W:** Doug Gray; Brian Swenlin; Kevin Campbell

3 ❑ ca. 1992 Cover: 2.95 **NM** value: **Cover or less**
📖 F'Reeze a Jolly Good Fellow!; Contractual Desperation • 21810;Tale Spin: Surprise in the Skies;Reprints stories from Disney's Tale Spin #4, 6 **A:** Hector Saavedra; Oscar Saavedra; Robert Bat; Ruben Torreiro **W:** Bobbi JG Weiss

CARTUNE LAND — Magic Carpet

1 ❑ b&w Cover: 1.50 **NM** value: **Cover or less**
📖 In Other Worlds; the Changeling Earth; Do Not Pull Rope; Children of the Desolation; The Biggest Game; The Stone; Decoys; On the Path to the Sea; The Machine; War with the Machines; Flight into the Desolation; Infinity Road; The Dream Horn **A:** Donnie Jupiter **W:** Donnie Jupiter

2 ❑ Jul 1987, b&w Cover: 1.50 **NM** value: **Cover or less**
📖 Fury of Desolation; Uncle Scourge; The One World; The Stone Meets The Raver; The Time Door; The Changeling Earth; The Girl and The Barbarian; The Origin of Stone **A:** Donnie Jupiter **W:** Donnie Jupiter

CARVERS — Image

"Carve or starve." "Shreddin' like he's pulling a trailer." Hardly dialogue you'd normally read in a comic book, but it happened, all because of snowboarding. Snowboarders have a new vernacular, a hip attitude, baggy pants, and an assortment of colors of hair and goatees. The culture is one of free spirits, a fulfilling lifestyle, and a real individual expression; about being "stoked and amped," which is jargon for thrilled to death and ready to go. Five snowboarders travel through a dimensional portal and are transported to a frozen wasteland. But rise up, crew! They're attacked by spear-carrying, nuclear-bomb-holding Yetis preparing to invade our dimension. Grab some air with the "carvers," as they embark on a mission to save the world in "phat" style!

1 ❑ Oct 1998 Cover: 2.95 **NM** value: **Cover or less**
Circ: Diamd. preorders: **9,244**
📖 Chilling Out **A:** Arnold Pander; Jacob Pander **W:** Robert Loren Flemming

2 ❑ Nov 1998 Cover: 2.95 **NM** value: **Cover or less**
Circ: Diamd. preorders: **7,062**
📖 All Downhill **A:** Arnold Pander; Jacob Pander **W:** Robert Loren Flemming

3 ❑ Dec 1998 Cover: 2.95 **NM** value: **Cover or less**
Circ: Diamd. preorders: **4,646**
📖 End Run **A:** Arnold Pander; Jacob Pander

Bk 1❑ Cover: 9.95 **NM** value: **Cover or less**

CAR WARRIORS — Marvel / Epic

1 ❑ Jun 1991 Cover: 2.25 **NM** value: **Cover or less**
Circ: CapCity orders: **10,200**
A: Steve Dillon **W:** Chuck Dixon

2 ❑ Jul 1991 Cover: 2.25 **NM** value: **Cover or less**
Circ: CapCity orders: **7,100**
A: Steve Dillon **W:** Chuck Dixon

3 ❑ Aug 1991 Cover: 2.25 **NM** value: **Cover or less**
Circ: CapCity orders: **6,600**
A: Steve Dillon **W:** Chuck Dixon

4 ❑ Sep 1991 Cover: 2.25 **NM** value: **Cover or less**
Circ: CapCity orders: **5,700**
A: Steve Dillon **W:** Chuck Dixon

CASANOVA — Aircel

All issues are adults only.

1 ❑ b&w Cover: 2.50 **NM** value: **Cover or less**
2 ❑ b&w Cover: 2.50 **NM** value: **Cover or less**
3 ❑ b&w Cover: 2.50 **NM** value: **Cover or less**
4 ❑ b&w Cover: 2.50 **NM** value: **Cover or less**
5 ❑ b&w Cover: 2.50 **NM** value: **Cover or less**
6 ❑ b&w Cover: 2.50 **NM** value: **Cover or less**
7 ❑ b&w Cover: 2.50 **NM** value: **Cover or less**
8 ❑ b&w Cover: 2.50 **NM** value: **Cover or less**
9 ❑ Nov 1991, b&w Cover: 2.95 **NM** value: **Cover or less**
10 ❑ b&w Cover: 2.95 **NM** value: **Cover or less**

CASE MORGAN, GUMSHOE PRIVATE EYE — Forbidden Fruit

All issues are adults only.

1 ❑ b&w Cover: 2.95 **NM** value: **Cover or less**
2 ❑ b&w Cover: 2.95 **NM** value: **Cover or less**
3 ❑ b&w Cover: 2.95 **NM** value: **Cover or less**
4 ❑ b&w Cover: 2.95 **NM** value: **Cover or less**
5 ❑ b&w Cover: 2.95 **NM** value: **Cover or less**
6 ❑ b&w Cover: 2.95 **NM** value: **Cover or less**
7 ❑ b&w Cover: 2.95 **NM** value: **Cover or less**
8 ❑ b&w Cover: 2.95 **NM** value: **Cover or less**
9 ❑ b&w Cover: 2.95 **NM** value: **Cover or less**
10 ❑ b&w Cover: 2.95 **NM** value: **Cover or less**
11 ❑ b&w Cover: 3.50 **NM** value: **Cover or less**

CASE OF BLIND FEAR, A — Eternity

This black-and-white limited series by writer Martin Powell and artist Seppo Makinen is a worthy sequel to the excellent Scarlet in Gaslight, which brought detective Sherlock Holmes into conflict with Count Dracula. Here, Victorian-era Londoners are reporting mysterious, floating objects and apparitions with visible internal organs — and baffled officials at Scotland Yard have brought in super-sleuth Holmes to get to the bottom of these strange sightings. As it turns out, Holmes is in a battle of wits with none other than Hawley Griffin, the title character of H.G. Wells's The Invisible Man. But what is Griffin's connection with Holmes' partner, Dr. Watson? Curiouser and curiouser, eh?

1 ❑ Jan 1989, b&w Cover: 1.95 **NM** value: **Cover or less**
📖 The Madness • Sherlock Holmes, Invisible Man **A:** Seppo Makkinen **W:** Martin Powell

2 ❑ Apr 1989, b&w Cover: 1.95 **NM** value: **Cover or less**
📖 The Woman • Sherlock Holmes, Invisible Man **A:** Seppo Makkinen **W:** Martin Powell

3 ❑ b&w Cover: 1.95 **NM** value: **Cover or less**
• Sherlock Holmes, Invisible Man

4 ❑ b&w Cover: 1.95 **NM** value: **Cover or less**
• Sherlock Holmes, Invisible Man

Bk 1❑ Cover: 9.95 **NM** value: **Cover or less**
• paperback

CASE OF THE WASTED WATER — Rheem

1 ❑ ca. 1972 **NM** value: **5.00**
• **CGC:** 1 graded, best 9.4

CASES OF SHERLOCK HOLMES — Renegade

1 ❑ May 1986, b&w Cover: 1.70 **NM** value: **2.00**
• Renegade publishes **A:** Dan Day **W:** Sir Arthur Conan Doyle

2 ❑ Jul 1986, b&w Cover: 1.70 **NM** value: **2.00**
📖 The Adventure of the Dancing Men **A:** Dan Day **W:** Sir Arthur Conan Doyle

3 ❑ Sep 1986 Cover: 2.00 **NM** value: **Cover or less**
📖 The Strange Adventure of The Vourdalak **A:** Dan Day **W:** Sir Arthur Conan Doyle

4 ❑ Nov 1986 Cover: 2.00 **NM** value: **Cover or less**
📖 The Adventure of the Six Napoleons **A:** Dan Day **W:** Sir Arthur Conan Doyle

5 ❑ Jan 1987 Cover: 2.00 **NM** value: **Cover or less**
📖 The Adventure of the Engineer's Thumb **A:** Dan Day **W:** Sir Arthur Conan Doyle

6 ❑ Mar 1987 Cover: 2.00 **NM** value: **Cover or less**
A: Dan Day **W:** Sir Arthur Conan Doyle

7 ❑ May 1987 Cover: 2.00 **NM** value: **Cover or less**
A: Dan Day **W:** Sir Arthur Conan Doyle

8 ❑ Jul 1987 Cover: 2.00 **NM** value: **Cover or less**
A: Dan Day **W:** Sir Arthur Conan Doyle

9 ❑ Sep 1987 Cover: 2.00 **NM** value: **Cover or less**
📖 The Adventure of the Copper Beeches **A:** Dan Day **W:** Sir Arthur Conan Doyle

10 ❑ Nov 1987 Cover: 2.00 **NM** value: **Cover or less**
📖 The Adventure of the Greek Interpreter **A:** Dan Day **W:** Sir Arthur Conan Doyle

11 ❑ Jan 1988 Cover: 2.00 **NM** value: **Cover or less**
📖 The Adventure of Black Peter **A:** Dan Day; David Day **W:** Sir Arthur Conan Doyle

CGC-graded: Multiply prices above by **33 for 9.9 M • 16 for 9.8 NM/M • 7 for 9.6 NM+ • 5 for 9.4 NM • 2.5 for 9.2 NM- • 1.5 for 9.0 VF/NM**

12 ❑ Mar 1988 Cover: 2.00 **NM** value: **Cover or less**
A: Dan Day **W:** Sir Arthur Conan Doyle
13 ❑ May 1988 Cover: 2.00 **NM** value: **Cover or less**
📖 The Adventure of the Naval Treaty, Part 1 **A:** Dan Day **W:** Sir Arthur Conan Doyle
14 ❑ Jul 1988 Cover: 2.00 **NM** value: **Cover or less**
📖 The Adventure of the Naval Treaty, Part 2 **A:** Dan Day **W:** Sir Arthur Conan Doyle
15 ❑ Sep 1988 Cover: 2.00 **NM** value: **Cover or less**
📖 The Adventure of Charles Augustus Milverton **A:** Dan Day **W:** Sir Arthur Conan Doyle
16 ❑ Nov 1988, b&w Cover: 2.25 **NM** value: **Cover or less**
• Northstar begins as publisher **A:** Dan Day **W:** Sir Arthur Conan Doyle
17 ❑ Jan 1989, b&w Cover: 2.25 **NM** value: **Cover or less**
📖 The Adventure of the Abbey Grange **A:** Dan Day **W:** Sir Arthur Conan Doyle
18 ❑ Mar 1989, b&w Cover: 2.25 **NM** value: **Cover or less**
📖 The Adventure of the Blue Carbuncle **A:** Dan Day **W:** Sir Arthur Conan Doyle
19 ❑ May 1989 Cover: 2.25 **NM** value: **Cover or less**
📖 The Man With the Twisted Lip **A:** Ronn Sutton
20 ❑ Jul 1989 Cover: 2.25 **NM** value: **Cover or less**
📖 The Red-Headed League **A:** Dan Day; David Day **W:** Sir Arthur Conan Doyle
21 ❑ Sep 1989 Cover: 2.25 **NM** value: **Cover or less**
A: Dan Day
22 ❑ Nov 1989 Cover: 2.25 **NM** value: **Cover or less**
A: Dan Day
23 ❑ Jan 1990 Cover: 2.25 **NM** value: **Cover or less**
A: Dan Day
24 ❑ Mar 1990 Cover: 2.25 **NM** value: **Cover or less**
A: Dan Day

CASEY JONES & RAPHAEL — Mirage

Eschewing a conventional narrative and traditional rules of grammar, spelling, and punctuation, this series from Mirage Publisher Kevin Eastman (Teenage Mutant Ninja Turtles) and Simon Bisley (Lobo) teams up the two action heroes and takes them on a two-fisted trip through the urban underworld.

During an imaginatively rendered barroom brawl, Jones encounters Midnight, a beautiful, voluptuous hitwoman. She's on the run from Johnny Woo Woo, a co-killer who was once almost greased during a job she bungled in Hong Kong. JWW has followed her to New York and catches up with her just in time for the gun-hating Casey to lend her a hand. Could Raph be far behind?

This title also includes a considerably more subdued backup feature, Jim Lawson's Guzzi LeMans.

1 ❑ Oct 1994 Cover: 2.75 **NM** value: **Cover or less**
Circ: CapCity orders: **6,985**
A: Kevin Eastman **W:** Kevin Eastman

CASEY JONES: NORTH BY DOWNEAST — Mirage

1 ❑ May 1994 Cover: 2.75 **NM** value: **Cover or less**
Circ: CapCity orders: **2,655**
A: Rick Veitch **W:** Rick Veitch
2 ❑ Jul 1994 Cover: 2.75 **NM** value: **Cover or less**
Circ: CapCity orders: **3,110**
final issue. **A:** Rick Veitch **W:** Rick Veitch

CASPER ADVENTURE DIGEST — Harvey

1 ❑ Oct 1992 Cover: 1.75 **NM** value: **2.00**
2 ❑ Dec 1992 Cover: 1.75 **NM** value: **Cover or less**
3 ❑ Jan 1993 Cover: 1.75 **NM** value: **Cover or less**
4 ❑ Apr 1993 Cover: 1.75 **NM** value: **Cover or less**
5 ❑ Jul 1993 Cover: 1.75 **NM** value: **Cover or less**
6 ❑ Oct 1993 Cover: 1.75 **NM** value: **Cover or less**
7 ❑ Cover: 1.75 **NM** value: **Cover or less**
8 ❑ Cover: 1.75 **NM** value: **Cover or less**

CASPER AND FRIENDS — Harvey

1 ❑ ca. 1991 Cover: 1.25 **NM** value: **1.50**
Circ: CapCity orders: **2,350**
2 ❑ ca. 1991 Cover: 1.25 **NM** value: **1.50**
3 ❑ ca. 1992 Cover: 1.25 **NM** value: **1.50**
4 ❑ ca. 1992 Cover: 1.25 **NM** value: **1.50**
5 ❑ ca. 1992 Cover: 1.25 **NM** value: **1.50**

CASPER AND FRIENDS MAGAZINE — Marvel

1 ❑ Mar 1997 Cover: 3.99 **NM** value: **Cover or less**
• magazine. ★ Appearance of Casper, Richie Rich, Baby Huey.
2 ❑ May 1997 Cover: 3.99 **NM** value: **Cover or less**
• magazine. ★ Appearance of Casper, Richie Rich, Baby Huey.
3 ❑ Jul 1997 Cover: 3.99 **NM** value: **Cover or less**
• magazine. ★ Appearance of Casper, Richie Rich, Baby Huey.

CASPER AND THE GHOSTLY TRIO — Harvey

1 ❑ Nov 1972 Cover: 0.20 **NM** value: **20.00**
• **CGC:** 1 graded, best 8.5
2 ❑ Jan 1973 Cover: 0.20 **NM** value: **15.00**
3 ❑ Mar 1973 Cover: 0.20 **NM** value: **15.00**
4 ❑ May 1973 Cover: 0.20 **NM** value: **15.00**
5 ❑ Jul 1973 Cover: 0.20 **NM** value: **12.00**
6 ❑ Sep 1973 Cover: 0.20 **NM** value: **12.00**
7 ❑ Nov 1973 Cover: 0.20 **NM** value: **12.00**
8 ❑ Aug 1990 Cover: 1.00 **NM** value: **Cover or less**
9 ❑ Oct 1990 Cover: 1.00 **NM** value: **Cover or less**
10 ❑ Dec 1990 Cover: 1.00 **NM** value: **Cover or less**

CASPER & WENDY — Harvey

1 ❑ Sep 1972 Cover: 0.25 **NM** value: **8.00**
• Alice in Wonderland
2 ❑ Nov 1972 Cover: 0.25 **NM** value: **4.00**
3 ❑ Jan 1973 Cover: 0.25 **NM** value: **4.00**
• **CGC:** 1 graded, best 7.5
4 ❑ Mar 1973 Cover: 0.25 **NM** value: **4.00**
• **CGC:** 1 graded, best 9.4
5 ❑ May 1973 Cover: 0.25 **NM** value: **4.00**
6 ❑ Jul 1973 Cover: 0.25 **NM** value: **3.00**
7 ❑ Sep 1973 Cover: 0.25 **NM** value: **3.00**
8 ❑ Nov 1973 Cover: 0.25 **NM** value: **3.00**

CASPER DIGEST MAGAZINE — Harvey

1 ❑ Cover: 1.75 **NM** value: **2.00**
2 ❑ Cover: 1.75 **NM** value: **2.00**
3 ❑ Cover: 1.75 **NM** value: **2.00**
4 ❑ Cover: 1.75 **NM** value: **2.00**
9 ❑ Sep 1989 Cover: 1.75 **NM** value: **2.00**
10 ❑ Feb 1990 Cover: 1.75 **NM** value: **2.00**
📖 Thanskgiving Parade Special
11 ❑ May 1990 Cover: 1.75 **NM** value: **2.00**
12 ❑ Jul 1990 Cover: 1.75 **NM** value: **2.00**
13 ❑ Aug 1990 Cover: 1.75 **NM** value: **2.00**

CASPER DIGEST MAGAZINE (VOL. 2) — Harvey

1 ❑ Sep 1991 Cover: 1.75 **NM** value: **Cover or less**
2 ❑ Jan 1992 Cover: 1.75 **NM** value: **Cover or less**
3 ❑ Apr 1992 Cover: 1.75 **NM** value: **Cover or less**
4 ❑ Jul 1992 Cover: 1.75 **NM** value: **Cover or less**
• indicia says Casper Digest.
5 ❑ Nov 1992 Cover: 1.75 **NM** value: **Cover or less**
6 ❑ Feb 1993 Cover: 1.75 **NM** value: **Cover or less**
7 ❑ May 1993 Cover: 1.75 **NM** value: **Cover or less**
8 ❑ Aug 1993 Cover: 1.75 **NM** value: **Cover or less**
9 ❑ Nov 1993 Cover: 1.75 **NM** value: **Cover or less**
10 ❑ Feb 1994 Cover: 1.75 **NM** value: **Cover or less**
11 ❑ May 1994 Cover: 1.75 **NM** value: **Cover or less**
12 ❑ Jul 1994 Cover: 1.75 **NM** value: **Cover or less**
13 ❑ Aug 1994 Cover: 1.75 **NM** value: **Cover or less**
14 ❑ Nov 1994 Cover: 1.75 **NM** value: **Cover or less**

CASPER ENCHANTED TALES DIGEST — Harvey

1 ❑ May 1992 Cover: 1.75 **NM** value: **Cover or less**
2 ❑ Sep 1992 Cover: 1.75 **NM** value: **Cover or less**
3 ❑ 1993 Cover: 1.75 **NM** value: **Cover or less**
4 ❑ Jun 1993 Cover: 1.75 **NM** value: **Cover or less**
5 ❑ Sep 1993 Cover: 1.75 **NM** value: **Cover or less**
6 ❑ Dec 1993 Cover: 1.75 **NM** value: **Cover or less**
7 ❑ 1994 Cover: 1.75 **NM** value: **Cover or less**
8 ❑ Jun 1994 Cover: 1.75 **NM** value: **Cover or less**
9 ❑ Aug 1994 Cover: 1.75 **NM** value: **Cover or less**
10 ❑ Oct 1994 Cover: 1.75 **NM** value: **Cover or less**

CASPER GHOSTLAND — Harvey

1 ❑ Win 1958 Cover: 1.25 **NM** value: **Cover or less**

CASPER IN 3-D — Blackthorne

Casper the Friendly Ghost is back, and this time he's leapin' right off the page at ya! But so are such luminaries as Sheena, Queen of the Jungle; Dick Tracy; Bullwinkle and Rocky; Underdog; G.I. Joe; Laurel and Hardy; and — hold onto your seats — the California Raisins. This Casper in 3-D special was part of a larger Blackthorne line of 3-D specials, reprinting the adventures of several classic Harvey Comics characters in their own 3-D titles, including Baby Huey, Little Dot, Playful Little Audrey, and Wendy, the Good Little Witch, as well as movie adaptations for Star Wars, Red Heat, Waxworks, and Moonwalker. There were also issues devoted to horror and science-fiction stories.

1 ❑ Win 1988 Cover: 2.50 **NM** value: **Cover or less**
📖 Roar Lion; Uncle Casper Vs. Uncle Trio; Granny Whammy Socks it to 'Em; Camouflage Expert; The Glass People;

CASPER'S GHOSTLAND — Harvey

1 ❑ Win 1959 **NM** value: **125.00**
• **CGC:** 1 graded, best 6.0
2 ❑ 1960 **NM** value: **55.00**
3 ❑ 1960 **NM** value: **28.00**
4 ❑ 1960 **NM** value: **28.00**
5 ❑ 1960 **NM** value: **28.00**
6 ❑ 1960 **NM** value: **20.00**
7 ❑ 1960 **NM** value: **20.00**
8 ❑ 1961 **NM** value: **20.00**
9 ❑ 1961 **NM** value: **20.00**
10 ❑ Jul 1961 **NM** value: **20.00**
11 ❑ Oct 1961 **NM** value: **15.00**
12 ❑ Jan 1962 **NM** value: **15.00**
13 ❑ Apr 1962 **NM** value: **15.00**
14 ❑ Jul 1962 Cover: 0.25 **NM** value: **15.00**
15 ❑ Oct 1962 Cover: 0.25 **NM** value: **15.00**
16 ❑ Jan 1963 Cover: 0.25 **NM** value: **15.00**
17 ❑ Apr 1963 Cover: 0.25 **NM** value: **15.00**
18 ❑ Jul 1963 Cover: 0.25 **NM** value: **15.00**
19 ❑ Oct 1963 Cover: 0.25 **NM** value: **15.00**
20 ❑ Jan 1964 Cover: 0.25 **NM** value: **15.00**
21 ❑ Apr 1964 Cover: 0.25 **NM** value: **12.00**
22 ❑ Jul 1964 Cover: 0.25 **NM** value: **12.00**
23 ❑ Oct 1964 Cover: 0.25 **NM** value: **12.00**
24 ❑ Jan 1965 Cover: 0.25 **NM** value: **12.00**
25 ❑ Apr 1965 Cover: 0.25 **NM** value: **12.00**
26 ❑ Jul 1965 Cover: 0.25 **NM** value: **12.00**
27 ❑ Oct 1965 Cover: 0.25 **NM** value: **12.00**
28 ❑ Jan 1966 Cover: 0.25 **NM** value: **12.00**
29 ❑ Apr 1966 Cover: 0.25 **NM** value: **12.00**
30 ❑ Jun 1966 Cover: 0.25 **NM** value: **12.00**
31 ❑ Aug 1966 Cover: 0.25 **NM** value: **8.00**
32 ❑ Oct 1966 Cover: 0.25 **NM** value: **8.00**
33 ❑ Dec 1966 Cover: 0.25 **NM** value: **8.00**
34 ❑ Feb 1967 Cover: 0.25 **NM** value: **8.00**
35 ❑ Apr 1967 Cover: 0.25 **NM** value: **8.00**
36 ❑ Jun 1967 Cover: 0.25 **NM** value: **8.00**
37 ❑ Aug 1967 Cover: 0.25 **NM** value: **8.00**
38 ❑ Oct 1967 Cover: 0.25 **NM** value: **8.00**
39 ❑ Dec 1967 Cover: 0.25 **NM** value: **8.00**
40 ❑ Feb 1968 Cover: 0.25 **NM** value: **8.00**
41 ❑ Apr 1968 Cover: 0.25 **NM** value: **6.00**
42 ❑ Jun 1968 Cover: 0.25 **NM** value: **6.00**
43 ❑ Aug 1968 Cover: 0.25 **NM** value: **6.00**
44 ❑ Oct 1968 Cover: 0.25 **NM** value: **6.00**
45 ❑ Dec 1968 Cover: 0.25 **NM** value: **6.00**
46 ❑ Jan 1969 Cover: 0.25 **NM** value: **6.00**
47 ❑ Mar 1969 Cover: 0.25 **NM** value: **6.00**
48 ❑ May 1969 Cover: 0.25 **NM** value: **6.00**
49 ❑ Jul 1969 Cover: 0.25 **NM** value: **6.00**
50 ❑ Sep 1969 Cover: 0.25 **NM** value: **6.00**
51 ❑ Nov 1969 Cover: 0.25 **NM** value: **6.00**
52 ❑ Jan 1970 Cover: 0.25 **NM** value: **6.00**
53 ❑ Mar 1970 Cover: 0.25 **NM** value: **6.00**
54 ❑ May 1970 Cover: 0.25 **NM** value: **6.00**
55 ❑ Jul 1970 Cover: 0.25 **NM** value: **6.00**
56 ❑ Sep 1970 Cover: 0.25 **NM** value: **6.00**
57 ❑ Nov 1970 Cover: 0.25 **NM** value: **6.00**
58 ❑ Jan 1971 Cover: 0.25 **NM** value: **6.00**
59 ❑ Mar 1971 Cover: 0.25 **NM** value: **6.00**
60 ❑ May 1971 Cover: 0.25 **NM** value: **6.00**
61 ❑ Jul 1971 Cover: 0.25 **NM** value: **4.00**
62 ❑ Sep 1971 Cover: 0.25 **NM** value: **4.00**
63 ❑ Nov 1971 Cover: 0.25 **NM** value: **4.00**
64 ❑ Jan 1972 Cover: 0.25 **NM** value: **4.00**
65 ❑ Mar 1972 Cover: 0.25 **NM** value: **4.00**
66 ❑ May 1972 Cover: 0.25 **NM** value: **4.00**
67 ❑ Jul 1972 Cover: 0.25 **NM** value: **4.00**
68 ❑ Sep 1972 Cover: 0.25 **NM** value: **4.00**
69 ❑ Nov 1972 Cover: 0.25 **NM** value: **4.00**
70 ❑ Jan 1973 Cover: 0.25 **NM** value: **4.00**
Circ: Statement: **105,892**
71 ❑ Mar 1973 Cover: 0.25 **NM** value: **4.00**
Circ: Statement: **105,892**
72 ❑ May 1973 Cover: 0.25 **NM** value: **4.00**
Circ: Statement: **105,892**
73 ❑ Jul 1973 Cover: 0.25 **NM** value: **4.00**
Circ: Statement: **105,892**
74 ❑ Sep 1973 Cover: 0.25 **NM** value: **4.00**
Circ: Statement: **105,892**
75 ❑ Nov 1973 Cover: 0.25 **NM** value: **4.00**
Circ: Statement: **105,892**
76 ❑ Jan 1974 Cover: 0.25 **NM** value: **4.00**
Circ: Statement: **121,794**
77 ❑ Mar 1974 Cover: 0.25 **NM** value: **4.00**
Circ: Statement: **121,794**
78 ❑ May 1974 Cover: 0.25 **NM** value: **4.00**
Circ: Statement: **121,794**
• Has 1973 Statement, filed 10/1/73; avg print run 238,213; avg sales 105,877; avg subs 15; avg total paid 105,892; samples 345; max existent 106,237; 55% of run returned
79 ❑ Jul 1974 Cover: 0.25 **NM** value: **4.00**
Circ: Statement: **121,794**
80 ❑ Sep 1974 Cover: 0.25 **NM** value: **4.00**
Circ: Statement: **121,794**
81 ❑ Nov 1974 Cover: 0.25 **NM** value: **3.00**
Circ: Statement: **121,794**
82 ❑ Jan 1975 Cover: 0.25 **NM** value: **3.00**
Circ: Statement: **116,716**
83 ❑ Mar 1975 Cover: 0.25 **NM** value: **3.00**
Circ: Statement: **116,716**
84 ❑ May 1975 Cover: 0.25 **NM** value: **3.00**
Circ: Statement: **116,716**
📖 Papa Piper's Puppets; Where Have Our Friends Gone?; The Tables Are Turned; Birthday Present (text story); First Prize (text story); Spooky: The Try-Out; • Has 1974 Statement; avg total paid circ 121,794
85 ❑ Jul 1975 Cover: 0.25 **NM** value: **3.00**
Circ: Statement: **116,716**
86 ❑ Sep 1975 Cover: 0.25 **NM** value: **3.00**
Circ: Statement: **116,716**
87 ❑ Nov 1975 Cover: 0.25 **NM** value: **3.00**
Circ: Statement: **116,716**
88 ❑ Feb 1976 Cover: 0.25 **NM** value: **3.00**
89 ❑ Apr 1976 Cover: 0.25 **NM** value: **3.00**
90 ❑ Jun 1976 Cover: 0.25 **NM** value: **3.00**
91 ❑ Aug 1976 Cover: 0.25 **NM** value: **3.00**
92 ❑ Oct 1976 Cover: 0.30 **NM** value: **3.00**
93 ❑ Dec 1976 Cover: 0.30 **NM** value: **3.00**
📖 The Return of Goof-Oh; With Your Looks and My Brains; A Gaggle of Geniuses; Spooky: The Ghost Walks at Midnight
94 ❑ Feb 1977 Cover: 0.30 **NM** value: **3.00**
📖 The Wrong Santa Claus; The Littlest Reindeer; Merry Christmas; Spooky: Blessed Be Thy Booing
95 ❑ 1977 Cover: 0.30 **NM** value: **3.00**
96 ❑ 1977 Cover: 0.30 **NM** value: **3.00**
97 ❑ Dec 1977 Cover: 0.30 **NM** value: **3.00**
98 ❑ **NM** value: **3.00**

Other grades: Multiply prices above by **1.5 for Mint • 2/3 for Very Fine • 1/3 for Fine • 1/5 for Very Good • 1/8 for Good**

CASPER SPACE SHIP — Harvey

1 ❑ Aug 1972 Cover: 0.25 NM value: **15.00**
• **CGC:** 1 graded, best 9.2
2 ❑ Oct 1972 Cover: 0.25 NM value: **12.00**
3 ❑ Dec 1972 Cover: 0.25 NM value: **12.00**
4 ❑ Feb 1973 Cover: 0.25 NM value: **10.00**
5 ❑ Apr 1973 Cover: 0.25 NM value: **10.00**

CASPER THE FRIENDLY GHOST (2ND SERIES) — Harvey

Everyone's favorite little ghost continues to spread his message of kindness and goodwill throughout the Enchanted Forest. Although most of the inhabitants of the forest, from talking animals to elves and gnomes, believe in Casper's message of love and peace, there are always a few troublemakers out there. At the top of the list is Casper's own "family," the mischievous Ghostly Trio. But, when the safety of everyone's forest home is at stake, even these supposedly bad guys manage to come to Casper's aid, proving that good will always be stronger than evil.

1 ❑ Mar 1991 Cover: 1.25 NM value: **2.00**
Circ: CapCity orders: **2,750**
2 ❑ May 1991 Cover: 1.25 NM value: **1.50**
Circ: CapCity orders: **1,550**
3 ❑ Jul 1991 Cover: 1.25 NM value: **1.50**
Circ: CapCity orders: **1,175**
4 ❑ Sep 1991 Cover: 1.25 NM value: **1.50**
5 ❑ Nov 1991 Cover: 1.25 NM value: **1.50**
6 ❑ Jan 1992 Cover: 1.25 NM value: **1.50**
7 ❑ Mar 1992 Cover: 1.25 NM value: **1.50**
8 ❑ 1992 Cover: 1.25 NM value: **1.50**
9 ❑ 1992 Cover: 1.25 NM value: **1.50**
10 ❑ 1992 Cover: 1.25 NM value: **1.50**
11 ❑ Dec 1992 Cover: 1.25 NM value: **1.50**
📖 Cloud Nine; The Poifect Boo; The Peculiar Kettle;
12 ❑ 1993 Cover: 1.25 NM value: **1.50**
13 ❑ 1993 Cover: 1.25 NM value: **1.50**
14 ❑ 1993 Cover: 1.25 NM value: **1.50**
15 ❑ Oct 1993 Cover: 1.50 NM value: **Cover or less**
16 ❑ Nov 1993 Cover: 1.50 NM value: **Cover or less**
17 ❑ Dec 1993 Cover: 1.50 NM value: **Cover or less**
18 ❑ Jan 1994 Cover: 1.50 NM value: **Cover or less**
19 ❑ Feb 1994 Cover: 1.50 NM value: **Cover or less**
20 ❑ Mar 1994 Cover: 1.50 NM value: **Cover or less**
21 ❑ Apr 1994 Cover: 1.50 NM value: **Cover or less**
22 ❑ May 1994 Cover: 1.50 NM value: **Cover or less**
23 ❑ Jun 1994 Cover: 1.50 NM value: **Cover or less**
24 ❑ Jul 1994 Cover: 1.50 NM value: **Cover or less**
25 ❑ Aug 1994 Cover: 1.50 NM value: **Cover or less**
26 ❑ Sep 1994 Cover: 1.50 NM value: **Cover or less**
27 ❑ Oct 1994 Cover: 1.50 NM value: **Cover or less**
28 ❑ Nov 1994 Cover: 1.50 NM value: **Cover or less**
📖 The Adventure; The Second Adventure; The Last is the Best: Spooky in Delayed Scaring
GS 1❑ Cover: 2.25 NM value: **Cover or less**
📖 Helpless Hunt; I Am the Spirit of Helpfulness; Showing a Better Spirit; I Hear You; One Strike You're Out; Nobody's Perfect; The Disenchanted Forest; The Towing Witch
GS 2❑ Cover: 2.25 NM value: **Cover or less**
GS 3❑ Cover: 2.25 NM value: **Cover or less**
GS 4❑ Cover: 2.25 NM value: **Cover or less**

CASPER THE FRIENDLY GHOST BIG BOOK — Harvey

1 ❑ Cover: 1.95 NM value: **Cover or less**
2 ❑ Cover: 1.95 NM value: **Cover or less**
📖 The Mysterious Zooky; Tricks Not Treats; The Awful Planet; Brooms Are Better; Halloween Land; A Fright To Remember; Three Little Pigs
3 ❑ Cover: 1.95 NM value: **Cover or less**

CASTLE WAITING — Olio

Linda Medley's black-and-white series takes place in a medieval fantasyland in which human characters interact with fantasy characters, yet stories frequently involve historical elements. Clear, confident, excellent line art combine with topnotch fantasy storytelling; the focal storyline features a young woman looking for a place to have her baby — then meeting other characters and learning more about the people and places around her. Medley excels at depicting the unusual plot element of sheer friendliness.
— Maggie

1 ❑ Cover: 2.95NM value: **9.00**
📖 Bahtalo Drom **A:** Linda Medley **W:** Linda Medley
1-2 ❑ Cover: 2.95 NM value: **Cover or less**
1-3 ❑ Cover: 2.95 NM value: **Cover or less**
2 ❑ Cover: 2.95 NM value: **5.00**
A: Linda Medley **W:** Linda Medley
2-2 ❑ Cover: 2.95 NM value: **Cover or less**
3 ❑ Cover: 2.95 NM value: **4.00**
• Akiko pin-up **A:** Linda Medley **W:** Linda Medley
3-2 ❑ Cover: 2.95 NM value: **Cover or less**
4 ❑ Cover: 2.95 NM value: **3.50**
• Scott Roberts pin-up **A:** Linda Medley **W:** Linda Medley
4-2 ❑ Cover: 2.95 NM value: **Cover or less**
5 ❑ Mar 1998 Cover: 2.95 NM value: **3.50**
Circ: Diamd. preorders: **3,703**
A: Linda Medley **W:** Linda Medley
5-2 ❑ Cover: 2.95 NM value: **Cover or less**
6 ❑ May 1998 Cover: 2.95 NM value: **3.00**
Circ: Diamd. preorders: **3,769**
• profiles of 12 Witches begins **A:** Linda Medley **W:** Linda Medley
7 ❑ Oct 1998 Cover: 2.95 NM value: **Cover or less**
Circ: Diamd. preorders: **4,167**
A: Linda Medley **W:** Linda Medley
8 ❑ Jan 1999 Cover: 2.95 NM value: **Cover or less**
Circ: Diamd. preorders: **4,324**
• Hiatus issue **A:** Linda Medley **W:** Linda Medley
Ash 1❑ NM value: **10.00**
• Limited ashcan edition given away (20 printed). 📖 The Curse of Brambly Hedge **A:** Linda Medley **W:** Linda Medley
Bk 1❑ b&w Cover: 5.95 NM value: **9.00**
No issue number. • prestige format. 📖 The Curse of Brambly Hedge • prequel to ongoing series **A:** Linda Medley **W:** Linda Medley
Bk 1-2❑ Cover: 9.00 NM value: **Cover or less**

CASTLE WAITING (CARTOON) — Cartoon

1 ❑ Jul 2000, b&w Cover: 2.95 NM value: **Cover or less**
Circ: Diamd. preorders: **6,796**
📖 Solicitine, Part 1 • follows events of Olio series **A:** Linda Medley **W:** Linda Medley
2 ❑ Oct 2000 Cover: 2.95 NM value: **Cover or less**
Circ: Diamd. preorders: **5,788**
📖 Solicitine, Part 2 **A:** Linda Medley **W:** Linda Medley
3 ❑ Dec 2000 Cover: 2.95 NM value: **Cover or less**
Circ: Diamd. preorders: **5,699**
📖 Solicitine, Part 3 **A:** Linda Medley **W:** Linda Medley
4 ❑ Mar 2001 Cover: 2.95 NM value: **Cover or less**
Circ: Diamd. preorders: **5,357**
📖 Solicitine, Part 4 **A:** Linda Medley **W:** Linda Medley

CASUAL HEROES — Image

1 ❑ Apr 1996 Cover: 2.25 NM value: **2.50**
📖 I Love Myself Better Than You **A:** Kevin McCarthy **W:** Kevin McCarthy

CAT, THE — Marvel

Greer Grant was a promising biology student, when she married policeman Bill Nelson. When Bill was killed, she decided to go back to work and wound up assisting in the lab of an old colleague, Dr. Tumolo. Tumolo's work was an experimental treatment to perfect the mental and physical powers of women. Although they are supposed to conduct the experiments solely on a previously chosen subject, Dr. Tumolo and Greer agree to subject Greer to the same treatments to see what will develop.

Greer finds herself gaining an amazing mechanical and mental aptitude, as well as increased strength and agility. When Dr. Tumolo is killed and her work is perverted by a criminal madman, Greer takes on the role of The Cat to avenge her death. This, her first series, tells of The Cat's early days, before she (as Tigra) became a member of West Coast Avengers.

1 ❑ Nov 1972 Cover: 0.20 NM value: **20.00**
• **CGC:** 7 graded, best 9.4
📖 Beware The Claws Of The Cat! • (Cat later becomes Tigra);(Cat later becomes Tigra) **A:** Wally Wood; Marie Severin **W:** Linda Fite ★ Origin of Cat. ★ 1st Appearance of Cat.
2 ❑ Jan 1973 Cover: 0.20 NM value: **14.00**
• **CGC:** 4 graded, best 9.4
3 ❑ Apr 1973 Cover: 0.20 NM value: **10.00**
• **CGC:** 3 graded, best 9.2
★ Appearance of Contains letter by Frank Miller (1st Miller.
4 ❑ Jun 1973 Cover: 0.20 NM value: **10.00**
• **CGC:** 1 graded, best 9.4

CAT, THE (AIRCEL) — Aircel

All issues are adults only.
1 ❑ b&w Cover: 2.50 NM value: **Cover or less**
2 ❑ b&w Cover: 2.50 NM value: **Cover or less**

CATALYST: AGENTS OF CHANGE — Dark Horse

1 ❑ Feb 1994 Cover: 2.00 NM value: **Cover or less**
Circ: CapCity orders: **11,675**
cardstock cover with foil logo. 📖 Behind The Golden Curtain **A:** Steve Carr; Tim Hamilton **W:** Eddie Campbell; Pete Ford
2 ❑ Mar 1994 Cover: 2.00 NM value: **Cover or less**
Circ: CapCity orders: **7,475**
W: Eddie Campbell; Pete Ford
3 ❑ Apr 1994 Cover: 2.00 NM value: **Cover or less**
Circ: CapCity orders: **6,975**
📖 Golden Day **A:** Tim Hamilton; Shane Glines **W:** Eddie Campbell; Pete Ford
4 ❑ May 1994 Cover: 2.00 NM value: **Cover or less**
Circ: CapCity orders: **6,850**
📖 and so are Myths Made **A:** Tim Hamilton; Shane Glines **W:** Eddie Campbell; Pete Ford
5 ❑ Cover: 2.00 NM value: **Cover or less**
Circ: CapCity orders: **6,125**
6 ❑ Aug 1994 Cover: 2.00 NM value: **Cover or less**
Circ: CapCity orders: **4,925**
7 ❑ Sep 1994 Cover: 2.00 NM value: **Cover or less**
Circ: CapCity orders: **4,450**
📖 We Lucky Few **A:** Tim Hamilton **W:** Barbara Kesel

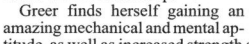

Creator Key
W = Writer • A = Artist • C = Cover Artist

CAT & MOUSE — EF Graphics

1 ❑ Jan 1989 Cover: 2.00 NM value: **Cover or less**
Circ: CapCity orders: **1,575**
• part color
1-2 ❑ Cover: 1.75 NM value: **2.00**

CAT & MOUSE (AIRCEL) — Aircel

1 ❑ Mar 1990, b&w Cover: 2.25 NM value: **2.50**
📖 A Game of Cat & Mouse **A:** Mitch Byrd **W:** Mitch Byrd; Steven Butler; Roland Mann
2 ❑ Apr 1990 Cover: 2.25 NM value: **2.50**
3 ❑ May 1990 Cover: 2.25 NM value: **2.50**
4 ❑ Jun 1990 Cover: 2.25 NM value: **2.50**
5 ❑ Jul 1990 Cover: 2.25 NM value: **2.50**
📖 Working 11 to 7 Really Makes Life a Drag **A:** Mitch Byrd **W:** Roland Mann
6 ❑ Aug 1990 Cover: 2.25 NM value: **2.50**
7 ❑ Sep 1990 Cover: 2.25 NM value: **2.50**
8 ❑ Oct 1990 Cover: 2.25 NM value: **2.50**
📖 Fight From the Inside **A:** Mitch Byrd **W:** Roland Mann
9 ❑ Nov 1990 Cover: 2.25 NM value: **2.50**
10 ❑ Dec 1990 Cover: 2.25 NM value: **2.50**
11 ❑ Jan 1991 Cover: 2.25 NM value: **2.50**
📖 Into the Fire **A:** Mitch Byrd **W:** Roland Mann
12 ❑ Feb 1991 Cover: 2.25 NM value: **2.50**
📖 Dead on Time! **A:** Mitch Byrd **W:** Roland Mann ★ Death of Nail.
13 ❑ Mar 1991 Cover: 2.25 NM value: **2.50**
📖 Good Times Bad Times **A:** Chris Cross; Tim Eldred; Tha Grimlen Jack; Brian Dale **W:** Roland Mann
14 ❑ Apr 1991 Cover: 2.25 NM value: **2.50**
15 ❑ May 1991 Cover: 2.25 NM value: **2.50**
16 ❑ Jun 1991 Cover: 2.25 NM value: **2.50**
17 ❑ Aug 1991 Cover: 2.25 NM value: **2.50**
18 ❑ Sep 1991 Cover: 2.25 NM value: **2.50**
Bk 1❑ Oct 1990 Cover: 9.95 NM value: **Cover or less**
Bk 2❑ Cover: 9.95 NM value: **Cover or less**
• Wearin' 'n' Tearin'

CAT CLAW — Eternity

1 ❑ Sep 1990, b&w Cover: 2.50 NM value: **Cover or less**
★ Origin of Cat Claw.
1-2 ❑ Cover: 2.50 NM value: **Cover or less**
2 ❑ Nov 1990 Cover: 2.50 NM value: **Cover or less**
3 ❑ Jan 1991 Cover: 2.50 NM value: **Cover or less**
4 ❑ Feb 1991 Cover: 2.50 NM value: **Cover or less**
5 ❑ Apr 1991 Cover: 2.50 NM value: **Cover or less**
6 ❑ Jun 1991 Cover: 2.50 NM value: **Cover or less**
7 ❑ Cover: 2.50 NM value: **Cover or less**
8 ❑ Cover: 2.50 NM value: **Cover or less**
9 ❑ Cover: 2.50 NM value: **Cover or less**
Bk 1❑ b&w Cover: 9.95 NM value: **Cover or less**
• Cat Scratch Fever

CATFIGHT — Insomnia

1 ❑ Mar 1995, b&w Cover: 2.75 NM value: **Cover or less**
📖 The Lolli-pop Man Gets Licked! **A:** Terral Lawrence **W:** Steven Zyskowski ★ 1st Appearance of Catfight, The Lolli-pop Man.
1/GO❑ Cover: 5.00 NM value: **Cover or less**
• Gold edition. 📖 The Lolli-pop Man Gets Licked! **A:** Terral Lawrence **W:** Steven Zyskowski ★ 1st Appearance of Catfight, The Lolli-pop Man.

CATFIGHT: DREAM INTO ACTION — Lightning

1 ❑ Mar 1996 Cover: 2.75 NM value: **Cover or less**
• Creed Guest Star **A:** Matt Martin **W:** Joseph Zyskowski ★ Appearance of CreeD, Hellina, Perg.

CATFIGHT: DREAM WARRIOR — Lightning

1 ❑ Cover: 2.75 NM value: **Cover or less**

CATFIGHT: ESCAPE FROM LIMBO — Lightning

1 ❑ Nov 1996 Cover: 2.75 NM value: **Cover or less**
Circ: Direct Market orders: **3,184**
A: O'Clair Albert **W:** Joseph Zyskowski

CATFIGHT: SWEET REVENGE — Lightning

1 ❑ Apr 1997, b&w Cover: 2.95 NM value: **Cover or less**
alternate cover B.

Diamond preorders are the estimated number of comics sold, prior to their release, to comics shops in North America by Diamond Comic Distributors, the largest distributor. These figures underreport the actual number of circulating copies by the amount of reorders Diamond took (usually 5-10% again of the preorders) and sales by publishers to newsstand and bookstore distributors. For many independent publishers, Diamond's preorders may be quite close to the actual number of copies in circulation.

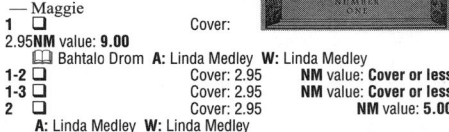

CGC-graded: Multiply prices above by **33 for 9.9 M • 16 for 9.8 NM/M • 7 for 9.6 NM+ • 5 for 9.4 NM • 2.5 for 9.2 NM- • 1.5 for 9.0 VF/NM**

CATHOLIC COMICS (VOL. 2) — Catholic

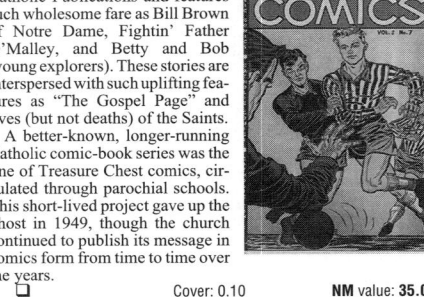

The series was published by Catholic Publications and features such wholesome fare as Bill Brown of Notre Dame, Fightin' Father O'Malley, and Betty and Bob (young explorers). These stories are interspersed with such uplifting features as "The Gospel Page" and lives (but not deaths) of the Saints.

A better-known, longer-running Catholic comic-book series was the line of Treasure Chest comics, circulated through parochial schools. This short-lived project gave up the ghost in 1949, though the church continued to publish its message in comics form from time to time over the years.

1 ❑ Cover: 0.10 **NM** value: **35.00**
2 ❑ Cover: 0.10 **NM** value: **35.00**
3 ❑ Cover: 0.10 **NM** value: **35.00**
4 ❑ Cover: 0.10 **NM** value: **35.00**
5 ❑ Cover: 0.10 **NM** value: **35.00**
6 ❑ Nov 1946 Cover: 0.10 **NM** value: **35.00**
7 ❑ Cover: 0.10 **NM** value: **35.00**
📖 Bill Brown of Notre Dame; Father O'Malley; Jet Plane; Betty and Bob; Angel of Judgement; Pudgy Pig
8 ❑ Cover: 0.10 **NM** value: **35.00**
9 ❑ Cover: 0.10 **NM** value: **35.00**
10 ❑ Cover: 0.10 **NM** value: **35.00**

CATHOLIC PICTORIAL — Catholic Guild

1 ❑ ca. 1947 **NM** value: **25.00**
• **CGC:** 1 graded, best 7.5

CATMAN — AC

1 ❑ Cover: 5.95 **NM** value: **Cover or less**
• AC Ashcan edition. **A:** Bob Fujitani
2 ❑ Cover: 5.95 **NM** value: **Cover or less**
• "AC Ashcan Edition.

CATMAN COMICS — Continental

1 ❑ May 1941 Cover: 0.10 **NM** value: **3000.00**
• **CGC:** 4 graded, best 8.5
2 ❑ Jun 1941 Cover: 0.10 **NM** value: **1000.00**
3 ❑ Jul 1941 Cover: 0.10 **NM** value: **1000.00**
4 ❑ Sep 1941 Cover: 0.10 **NM** value: **1000.00**
• **CGC:** 1 graded, best 6.0
5 ❑ Dec 1941 Cover: 0.10 **NM** value: **750.00**
• **CGC:** 1 graded, best 3.5
6 ❑ Jan 1942 Cover: 0.10 **NM** value: **750.00**
• **CGC:** 1 graded, best 7.0
7 ❑ Feb 1942 Cover: 0.10 **NM** value: **700.00**
8 ❑ Mar 1942 Cover: 0.10 **NM** value: **700.00**
9 ❑ Apr 1942 Cover: 0.10 **NM** value: **700.00**
• **CGC:** 1 graded, best 8.5
10 ❑ May 1942 Cover: 0.10 **NM** value: **650.00**
• **CGC:** 1 graded, best 4.0
11 ❑ Jun 1942 Cover: 0.10 **NM** value: **650.00**
• **CGC:** 1 graded, best 6.0
12 ❑ Jul 1942 Cover: 0.10 **NM** value: **650.00**
• **CGC:** 1 graded, best 5.0
13 ❑ Sep 1942 Cover: 0.10 **NM** value: **650.00**
14 ❑ Oct 1942 Cover: 0.10 **NM** value: **650.00**
15 ❑ Nov 1942 Cover: 0.10 **NM** value: **600.00**
16 ❑ Dec 1942 Cover: 0.10 **NM** value: **600.00**
17 ❑ Jan 1943 Cover: 0.10 **NM** value: **600.00**
18 ❑ Jul 1943 Cover: 0.10 **NM** value: **550.00**
19 ❑ Sep 1943 Cover: 0.10 **NM** value: **550.00**
• **CGC:** 1 graded, best 9.6
20 ❑ Oct 1943 Cover: 0.10 **NM** value: **550.00**
21 ❑ Nov 1943 Cover: 0.10 **NM** value: **500.00**
22 ❑ Dec 1943 Cover: 0.10 **NM** value: **500.00**
23 ❑ Mar 1944 Cover: 0.10 **NM** value: **450.00**
24 ❑ May 1944 Cover: 0.10 **NM** value: **450.00**
25 ❑ Jul 1944 Cover: 0.10 **NM** value: **450.00**
• **CGC:** 1 graded, best 7.0
25-2 ❑ Sep 1944 Cover: 0.10 **NM** value: **500.00**
26 ❑ Nov 1944 Cover: 0.10 **NM** value: **400.00**
27 ❑ Apr 1945 Cover: 0.10 **NM** value: **400.00**
• **CGC:** 2 graded, best 9.0
28 ❑ Jun 1945 Cover: 0.10 **NM** value: **400.00**
• **CGC:** 1 graded, best 7.5
29 ❑ Aug 1945 Cover: 0.10 **NM** value: **400.00**
• **CGC:** 5 graded, best 8.5
30 ❑ Dec 1945 Cover: 0.10 **NM** value: **350.00**
• **CGC:** 1 graded, best 8.5
31 ❑ Jun 1946 Cover: 0.10 **NM** value: **350.00**
• **CGC:** 9 graded, best 9.4
32 ❑ Aug 1946 Cover: 0.10 **NM** value: **350.00**
• **CGC:** 1 graded, best 5.0

CATNIP — Side Show

1 ❑ Cover: 2.95 **NM** value: **Cover or less**
A: Jim Ridings **W:** Jim Ridings

CATSEYE — Manic Press

1 ❑ Dec 1998 Cover: 2.50 **NM** value: **2.95**
A: Karl Alstaetter **W:** Karl Alstaetter
2 ❑ 1999 Cover: 2.50 **NM** value: **Cover or less**
3 ❑ 1999 Cover: 2.50 **NM** value: **Cover or less**
4 ❑ 1999 Cover: 2.50 **NM** value: **Cover or less**
5 ❑ 1999 Cover: 2.50 **NM** value: **Cover or less**
6 ❑ 1999 Cover: 2.50 **NM** value: **Cover or less**
7 ❑ 1999 Cover: 2.50 **NM** value: **Cover or less**
8 ❑ 1999 Cover: 2.50 **NM** value: **Cover or less**

CATSEYE AGENCY — Rip Off

Alien Nation and Blade Runner meet Purina Cat Chow in Catseye Agency — a three-issue, black-and-white mini-series from Rip Off Press. Unfortunately, weaving two of science fiction's cult properties around a weak story is not enough to create quality storytelling. Throw into the mix confusing illustrations and busy inks, and it's a story that detracts from the overall science-fiction experience.

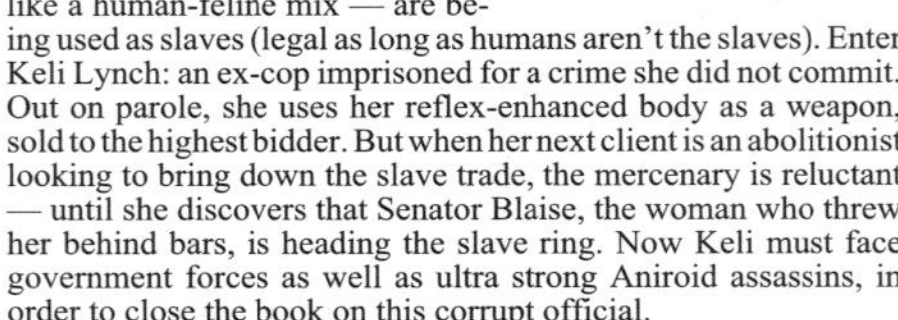

In Catseye Agency, Earth of the future has moved forward in terms of technology and backward in terms of social rights. Aniroids — artificially created beings that look like a human-feline mix — are being used as slaves (legal as long as humans aren't the slaves). Enter Keli Lynch: an ex-cop imprisoned for a crime she did not commit. Out on parole, she uses her reflex-enhanced body as a weapon, sold to the highest bidder. But when her next client is an abolitionist looking to bring down the slave trade, the mercenary is reluctant — until she discovers that Senator Blaise, the woman who threw her behind bars, is heading the slave ring. Now Keli must face government forces as well as ultra strong Aniroid assassins, in order to close the book on this corrupt official.

1 ❑ Sep 1992, b&w Cover: 2.50 **NM** value: **Cover or less**
A: Darren W. Frydendall **W:** James Lomax
2 ❑ Oct 1992, b&w Cover: 2.50 **NM** value: **Cover or less**
A: Darren W. Frydendall **W:** James Lomax

CAT TALES — Eternity

1 ❑ b&w Cover: 2.95 **NM** value: **Cover or less**
• 3-D. • Felix

CAT, T.H.E. (DELL) — Dell

1 ❑ ca. 1967 Cover: 0.12 **NM** value: **18.00**
2 ❑ ca. 1967 Cover: 0.12 **NM** value: **12.00**
3 ❑ ca. 1967 Cover: 0.12 **NM** value: **12.00**
4 ❑ Oct 1967 Cover: 0.12 **NM** value: **12.00**
Photo cover. 📖 The Czars Car Caper!; The 14th Year!; The Furious Feline!;

CATTLE BRAIN — Itchy Eyeball

1 ❑ b&w Cover: 2.75 **NM** value: **Cover or less**
2 ❑ b&w Cover: 2.75 **NM** value: **Cover or less**
3 ❑ b&w Cover: 2.75 **NM** value: **Cover or less**

CATWOMAN (1ST SERIES) — DC

1 ❑ Feb 1989 Cover: 1.50 **NM** value: **5.00**
Circ: CapCity orders: **36,550** Diamd. preorders: **49,413** • **CGC:** 16 graded, best 9.8
📖 Metamorphosis **A:** J.J. Birch **W:** Mindy Newell ★ Origin of Catwoman (new origin).
2 ❑ Mar 1989 Cover: 1.50 **NM** value: **4.00**
Circ: CapCity orders: **28,400** Diamd. preorders: **39,576** • **CGC:** 5 graded, best 9.4
A: J.J. Birch **W:** Mindy Newell
3 ❑ Apr 1989 Cover: 1.50 **NM** value: **3.00**
Circ: CapCity orders: **29,500** Diamd. preorders: **35,795** • **CGC:** 2 graded, best 9.2
A: J.J. Birch **W:** Mindy Newell
4 ❑ May 1989 Cover: 1.50 **NM** value: **3.00**
Circ: CapCity orders: **37,800** Diamd. preorders: **37,237** • **CGC:** 2 graded, best 9.2
A: J.J. Birch **W:** Mindy Newell
Bk 1 ❑ Cover: 9.95 **NM** value: **Cover or less**
Circ: CapCity orders: **4,800**
• Collects Catwoman (Mini-Series) #1-4 **A:** J.J. Birch; Pat Broderick **W:** Mindy Newell

CATWOMAN (2ND SERIES) — DC

The burglar Catwoman, long one of Batman's greatest enemies, enjoyed additional attention following the release of the film Batman Returns and earned her own unlimited series soon afterward.

The series' start finds Batman out of action, thanks to Bane, who's forced his way to the pinnacle of Gotham City's criminal sect. He expects Catwoman to do his dirty work, but it isn't long before she asserts her independence

Early issues of this series gained notoriety in the fan community for their overly voluptuous depiction of Catwoman, whose greatest gravity-defying stunt would seem to be walking upright without falling over. But if you can get past a lightweight gymnast needing a trousseau by the U.S. Army Corps of Engineers, there are some compelling adventure stories to be found here. — JJM

0 ❑ Oct 1994 Cover: 1.50 **NM** value: **2.50**
Circ: CapCity orders: **44,900**
📖 Cat Shadows **A:** Jim Balent **W:** Doug Moench ★ Origin of Catwoman.
1 ❑ Aug 1993 Cover: 1.95 **NM** value: **5.00**
Circ: CapCity orders: **87,450** • **CGC:** 18 graded, best 10.0
📖 Life Lines, Part 1 **A:** Jim Balent **W:** Mary Jo Duffy ★ Origin of Catwoman.
2 ❑ Sep 1993 Cover: 1.50 **NM** value: **3.50**
Circ: CapCity orders: **71,050**
📖 Life Lines, Part 2 **A:** Jim Balent **W:** Mary Jo Duffy
3 ❑ Oct 1993 Cover: 1.50 **NM** value: **3.00**
Circ: CapCity orders: **43,150** • **CGC:** 1 graded, best 9.8
📖 Life Lines, Part 3
4 ❑ Nov 1993 Cover: 1.50 **NM** value: **3.00**
Circ: CapCity orders: **43,700**
📖 Life Lines, Part 4
5 ❑ Dec 1993 Cover: 1.50 **NM** value: **3.00**
Circ: CapCity orders: **39,150**
6 ❑ Jan 1994 Cover: 1.50 **NM** value: **2.50**
Circ: CapCity orders: **50,900**
📖 Knightquest: The Search
7 ❑ Feb 1994 Cover: 1.50 **NM** value: **2.50**
Circ: CapCity orders: **49,200**
📖 Knightquest: The Crusade
8 ❑ Mar 1994 Cover: 1.50 **NM** value: **2.50**
Circ: CapCity orders: **35,050**
📖 Zephyr **A:** Jim Balent **W:** Mary Jo Duffy
9 ❑ Apr 1994 Cover: 1.50 **NM** value: **2.50**
Circ: CapCity orders: **33,600**
10 ❑ May 1994 Cover: 1.50 **NM** value: **2.50**
Circ: CapCity orders: **34,200**
11 ❑ Jun 1994 Cover: 1.50 **NM** value: **2.50**
Circ: CapCity orders: **33,650**
12 ❑ Jul 1994 Cover: 1.50 **NM** value: **2.50**
Circ: CapCity orders: **43,650**
📖 KnightsEnd, Part 6 **A:** Jim Balent **W:** Mary Jo Duffy
13 ❑ Aug 1994 Cover: 1.50 **NM** value: **2.50**
Circ: CapCity orders: **41,300**
📖 KnightsEnd Aftermath; KnightsEnd Aftermath, Part 2
14 ❑ Sep 1994 Cover: 1.50 **NM** value: **2.50**
Circ: CapCity orders: **11,900**
📖 Zero Hour • Zero Hour
15 ❑ Nov 1994 Cover: 1.50 **NM** value: **2.50**
Circ: CapCity orders: **33,450**
16 ❑ Dec 1994 Cover: 1.50 **NM** value: **2.50**
Circ: CapCity orders: **32,100**
17 ❑ Jan 1995 Cover: 1.50 **NM** value: **2.50**
Circ: CapCity orders: **30,600**
18 ❑ Feb 1995 Cover: 1.50 **NM** value: **2.50**
Circ: CapCity orders: **29,875**
19 ❑ Mar 1995 Cover: 1.50 **NM** value: **2.50**
Circ: CapCity orders: **26,575**
20 ❑ Apr 1995 Cover: 1.50 **NM** value: **2.50**
Circ: CapCity orders: **24,800**
21 ❑ May 1995 Cover: 1.95 **NM** value: **2.50**
Circ: CapCity orders: **23,950**
22 ❑ Jul 1995 Cover: 1.95 **NM** value: **2.50**
Circ: CapCity orders: **23,300**
23 ❑ Aug 1995 Cover: 1.95 **NM** value: **2.50**
Circ: CapCity orders: **23,450**
24 ❑ Sep 1995 Cover: 1.95 **NM** value: **2.50**
Circ: CapCity orders: **21,650**
25 ❑ Oct 1995 Cover: 2.95 **NM** value: **3.00**
Circ: CapCity orders: **19,975**
• Giant-size. ★ Appearance of Robin, Psyba-Rats.
26 ❑ Nov 1995 Cover: 1.95 **NM** value: **2.50**
27 ❑ Dec 1995 Cover: 1.95 **NM** value: **2.50**
28 ❑ Jan 1996 Cover: 1.95 **NM** value: **2.50**
29 ❑ Feb 1996 Cover: 1.95 **NM** value: **2.50**
📖 Thieves **A:** Jim Balent; Bob Smith **W:** Chuck Dixon
30 ❑ Mar 1996 Cover: 1.95 **NM** value: **2.50**
📖 The Great Plane Robbery **A:** Jim Balent **W:** Chuck Dixon
31 ❑ Mar 1996 Cover: 1.95 **NM** value: **2.50**
📖 Contagion, Part 5 **A:** Jim Balent **W:** Chuck Dixon
32 ❑ Apr 1996 Cover: 1.95 **NM** value: **3.00**
📖 Contagion, Part 9
33 ❑ May 1996 Cover: 1.95 **NM** value: **3.00**
📖 Devil Does Your Dog Bite
34 ❑ Jun 1996 Cover: 1.95 **NM** value: **2.50**
35 ❑ Jul 1996 Cover: 1.95 **NM** value: **2.50**
36 ❑ Aug 1996 Cover: 1.95 **NM** value: **2.50**
📖 Legacy, Part 2
37 ❑ Sep 1996 Cover: 1.95 **NM** value: **2.50**
38 ❑ Oct 1996 Cover: 1.95 **NM** value: **2.50**
📖 Year Two, Part 1 **A:** Jim Balent **W:** Doug Moench
39 ❑ Nov 1996 Cover: 1.95 **NM** value: **2.50**
Circ: Direct Market orders: **48,593**
📖 Year Two, Part 2 **A:** Jim Balent **W:** Doug Moench
40 ❑ Dec 1996 Cover: 1.95 **NM** value: **2.50**
Circ: Direct Market orders: **48,373**
📖 Year Two, Part 3 **A:** Jim Balent **W:** Doug Moench ★ Versus Two-Face, Penguin.
41 ❑ Jan 1997 Cover: 1.95 **NM** value: **2.00**
Circ: Direct Market orders: **46,183**
📖 Stolen Yesterdays **A:** Jim Balent **W:** Doug Moench
42 ❑ Feb 1997 Cover: 1.95 **NM** value: **2.00**
Circ: Diamd. preorders: **44,718**
📖 She-Cats, Part 1 **A:** Jim Balent **W:** Doug Moench ★ 1st Appearance of Cybercat.
43 ❑ Mar 1997 Cover: 1.95 **NM** value: **2.00**
Circ: Diamd. preorders: **43,363**
📖 She-Cats, Part 2 **A:** Jim Balent **W:** Doug Moench ★ Appearance of She-Cat.
44 ❑ Apr 1997 Cover: 1.95 **NM** value: **2.00**
Circ: Diamd. preorders: **41,363**
45 ❑ May 1997 Cover: 1.95 **NM** value: **2.00**
Circ: Diamd. preorders: **41,275**
📖 Nine Deaths of the Cat
46 ❑ Jun 1997 Cover: 1.95 **NM** value: **2.00**
Circ: Diamd. preorders: **41,325**
★ Versus Two-Face.
47 ❑ Jul 1997 Cover: 1.95 **NM** value: **2.00**
Circ: Diamd. preorders: **40,447**
★ Versus Two-Face.
48 ❑ Aug 1997 Cover: 1.95 **NM** value: **2.00**
Circ: Diamd. preorders: **39,801**
49 ❑ Sep 1997 Cover: 1.95 **NM** value: **2.00**
Circ: Diamd. preorders: **38,617**

Other grades: Multiply prices above by **1.5 for Mint • 2/3 for Very Fine • 1/3 for Fine • 1/5 for Very Good • 1/8 for Good**

50 ❑ Oct 1997 Cover: 2.95 **NM** value: **Cover or less**
Circ: Diamd. preorders: **45,924**
50/A❑ Oct 1997 Cover: 2.95 **NM** value: **Cover or less**
Circ: Diamd. preorders: **9,073**
• yellow logo
50/B❑ Oct 1997 Cover: 2.95 **NM** value: **Cover or less**
• purple logo
51 ❑ Nov 1997 Cover: 1.95 **NM** value: **2.00**
Circ: Diamd. preorders: **38,608**
🕮 Big Game **A:** Jim Balent **W:** Doug Moench ★ Versus Huntress.
52 ❑ Dec 1997 Cover: 1.95 **NM** value: **2.00**
Circ: Diamd. preorders: **38,625**
Face cover. 🕮 The Headhunter: Bigger Game **A:** Jim Balent **W:** Doug Moench
53 ❑ Jan 1998 Cover: 1.95 **NM** value: **2.00**
Circ: Diamd. preorders: **38,149**
54 ❑ Feb 1998 Cover: 1.95 **NM** value: **2.00**
Circ: Diamd. preorders: **37,041**
🕮 Object Relations • self-contained story;1st Devin Grayson script **A:** Jim Balent **W:** Devin Grayson
55 ❑ Mar 1998 Cover: 1.95 **NM** value: **2.00**
Circ: Diamd. preorders: **36,540**
🕮 Shared Mentality • self-contained story **A:** Jim Balent **W:** Devin Grayson
56 ❑ Apr 1998 Cover: 1.95 **NM** value: **2.00**
Circ: Diamd. preorders: **41,833**
🕮 Cataclysm, Part 6 • continues in Robin #52
57 ❑ May 1998 Cover: 1.95 **NM** value: **2.00**
Circ: Diamd. preorders: **41,670**
🕮 Cataclysm, Part 15 • continues in Batman: Arkham Asylum – Tales of Madness #1 ★ Versus Poison Ivy.
58 ❑ Jun 1998 Cover: 1.95 **NM** value: **2.00**
Circ: Diamd. preorders: **37,744**
★ Versus Scarecrow.
59 ❑ Jul 1998 Cover: 1.95 **NM** value: **2.00**
Circ: Diamd. preorders: **36,825**
★ Versus Scarecrow.
60 ❑ Aug 1998 Cover: 1.95 **NM** value: **2.00**
Circ: Diamd. preorders: **37,456**
★ Versus Scarecrow.
61 ❑ Sep 1998 Cover: 1.99 **NM** value: **2.00**
Circ: Diamd. preorders: **35,805**
62 ❑ Oct 1998 Cover: 1.99 **NM** value: **2.00**
Circ: Diamd. preorders: **34,548**
★ Appearance of Nemesis.
63 ❑ Dec 1998 Cover: 1.99 **NM** value: **2.00**
Circ: Diamd. preorders: **34,916**
★ Versus Joker.
64 ❑ Jan 1999 Cover: 1.99 **NM** value: **2.00**
Circ: Diamd. preorders: **34,116**
A: Jim Balent **W:** Devin Grayson ★ Appearance of Joker, Batman. ★ Versus Joker.
65 ❑ Feb 1999 Cover: 1.99 **NM** value: **2.00**
Circ: Diamd. preorders: **33,349**
A: Jim Balent **W:** Devin Grayson ★ Appearance of Scarecrow, Joker, Batman. ★ Versus Joker.
66 ❑ Mar 1999 Cover: 1.99 **NM** value: **2.00**
Circ: Diamd. preorders: **32,302**
🕮 I'll Take Manhattan, Part 1 **A:** Jim Balent **W:** Devin Grayson
67 ❑ Apr 1999 Cover: 1.99 **NM** value: **2.00**
Circ: Diamd. preorders: **30,866**
🕮 I'll Take Manhattan, Part 2 **A:** Jim Balent **W:** Devin Grayson
68 ❑ May 1999 Cover: 1.99 **NM** value: **2.00**
Circ: Diamd. preorders: **31,210**
🕮 I'll Take Manhattan, Part 3 • Lady Vic **A:** Jim Balent **W:** Devin Grayson ★ Versus Body Doubles.
69 ❑ Jun 1999 Cover: 1.99 **NM** value: **2.00**
Circ: Diamd. preorders: **31,623**
🕮 I'll Take Manhattan, Part 4 **A:** Jim Balent **W:** Devin Grayson ★ Appearance of Trickster.
70 ❑ Jul 1999 Cover: 1.99 **NM** value: **Cover or less**
Circ: Diamd. preorders: **30,804**
🕮 I'll Take Manhattan, Part 5 **A:** Jim Balent **W:** Devin Grayson
71 ❑ Aug 1999 Cover: 1.99 **NM** value: **Cover or less**
Circ: Diamd. preorders: **30,668**
🕮 I'll Take Manhattan: Requiem for Selina Kyle **A:** Jim Balent **W:** Devin Grayson
72 ❑ Sep 1999 Cover: 1.99 **NM** value: **Cover or less**
Circ: Diamd. preorders: **32,921**
🕮 The Mission • No Man's Land **A:** Jim Balent **W:** Devin Grayson
73 ❑ Oct 1999 Cover: 1.99 **NM** value: **Cover or less**
Circ: Diamd. preorders: **32,153**
🕮 Ms. Direction • No Man's Land **A:** Jim Balent **W:** John Ostrander
74 ❑ Nov 1999 Cover: 1.99 **NM** value: **Cover or less**
Circ: Diamd. preorders: **31,609**
• No Man's Land
75 ❑ Dec 1999 Cover: 1.99 **NM** value: **Cover or less**
Circ: Diamd. preorders: **33,964**
🕮 The Rules • No Man's Land **A:** Jim Balent
76 ❑ Jan 2000 Cover: 1.99 **NM** value: **Cover or less**
Circ: Diamd. preorders: **33,143**
🕮 Strange Bedfellows • No Man's Land **A:** Jim Balent
77 ❑ Feb 2000 Cover: 1.99 **NM** value: **Cover or less**
Circ: Diamd. preorders: **35,266**
78 ❑ Mar 2000 Cover: 1.99 **NM** value: **Cover or less**
Circ: Diamd. preorders: **30,959**
79 ❑ Apr 2000 Cover: 1.99 **NM** value: **Cover or less**
Circ: Diamd. preorders: **29,689**
🕮 Meet Jane Doe **A:** Staz Johnson **W:** Bronwyn Carlton
80 ❑ May 2000 Cover: 1.99 **NM** value: **Cover or less**
Circ: Diamd. preorders: **29,724**
🕮 Kitten in a Cage **A:** Staz Johnson **W:** Bronwyn Carlton
81 ❑ Jun 2000 Cover: 1.99 **NM** value: **Cover or less**
Circ: Diamd. preorders: **29,017**
A: Staz Johnson **W:** Bronwyn Carlton
82 ❑ Jul 2000 Cover: 1.99 **NM** value: **Cover or less**
Circ: Diamd. preorders: **28,663**
A: Staz Johnson **W:** Bronwyn Carlton
83 ❑ Aug 2000 Cover: 1.99 **NM** value: **Cover or less**
Circ: Diamd. preorders: **28,455**
A: Staz Johnson **W:** Bronwyn Carlton
84 ❑ Sep 2000 Cover: 2.25 **NM** value: **Cover or less**
Circ: Diamd. preorders: **28,825**
🕮 The Lesser of Two Evils **A:** Staz Johnson **W:** Bronwyn Carlton
85 ❑ Oct 2000 Cover: 2.25 **NM** value: **Cover or less**
Circ: Diamd. preorders: **26,255**
🕮 The Cat Came Back **A:** Staz Johnson **W:** Bronwyn Carlton
86 ❑ Nov 2000 Cover: 2.25 **NM** value: **Cover or less**
Circ: Diamd. preorders: **27,088**
🕮 Tears for Fluffy **A:** Cary Nord; Staz Johnson **W:** Bronwyn Carlton
87 ❑ Dec 2000 Cover: 2.25 **NM** value: **Cover or less**
Circ: Diamd. preorders: **26,498**
🕮 Casa De Mujer-Gato **A:** N. Steven Harris **W:** Jordan B. Gorfinkel
88 ❑ Jan 2001 Cover: 2.25 **NM** value: **Cover or less**
Circ: Diamd. preorders: **25,800**
🕮 TK **A:** Cary Nord **W:** Bronwyn Carlton
89 ❑ Feb 2001 Cover: 2.25 **NM** value: **Cover or less**
Circ: Diamd. preorders: **29,195**
🕮 Always Leave 'em Laughing **A:** Craig Rousseau; Staz Johnson **W:** Bronwyn Carlton
90 ❑ Mar 2001 Cover: 2.25 **NM** value: **Cover or less**
Circ: Diamd. preorders: **31,950**
🕮 Office Down, Part 4 **A:** Mike Tilly **W:** Bronwyn Carlton
91 ❑ Apr 2001 Cover: 2.25 **NM** value: **Cover or less**
Circ: Diamd. preorders: **24,463**
🕮 The Short Road **A:** Peter Doherty **W:** Bronwyn Carlton
92 ❑ May 2001 Cover: 2.25 **NM** value: **Cover or less**
Circ: Diamd. preorders: **24,974**
🕮 Tag **A:** Staz Johnson **W:** John Francis Moore
1000000❑ Nov 1998 Cover: 1.99 **NM** value: **2.00**
Circ: Diamd. preorders: **42,024**
Anl 1❑ ca. 1994 Cover: 2.95 **NM** value: **3.50**
Circ: CapCity orders: **29,850**
• Elseworlds
Anl 2❑ ca. 1995 Cover: 3.95 **NM** value: **Cover or less**
Circ: CapCity orders: **18,950**
• Year One
Anl 3❑ ca. 1996 Cover: 2.95 **NM** value: **Cover or less**
• Legends of the Dead Earth
Anl 4❑ ca. 1997 Cover: 3.95 **NM** value: **Cover or less**
Circ: Diamd. preorders: **34,490**
• Pulp Heroes
Bk 1❑ Cover: 9.95 **NM** value: **Cover or less**
• The Catfile;collects Catwoman #15-19;Reprints Catwoman #15-19

CATWOMAN: GUARDIAN OF GOTHAM — DC

1 ❑ ca. 1999 Cover: 5.95 **NM** value: **Cover or less**
Circ: Diamd. preorders: **26,997**
A: Kim Demulder; Jim Blatent **W:** Doug Moench
2 ❑ ca. 1999 Cover: 5.95 **NM** value: **Cover or less**
Circ: Diamd. preorders: **23,650**
A: Kim Demulder; Jim Blatent **W:** Doug Moench

CATWOMAN PLUS — DC

1 ❑ Nov 1997 Cover: 2.95 **NM** value: **Cover or less**
Circ: Diamd. preorders: **31,945**
🕮 Undead…And Loving It!; Wild Things, Part 3 • continues in Robin Plus #2 **A:** Anthony Williams; Andy Lanning **W:** Len Kaminski; Chuck Dixon ★ Appearance of Scream Queen.

CATWOMAN/VAMPIRELLA: THE FURIES — DC

1 ❑ Feb 1997 Cover: 5.95 **NM** value: **Cover or less**
Circ: Diamd. preorders: **56,447**
• prestige format. 🕮 The Furies • crossover with Harris **A:** Jim Balent **W:** Chuck Dixon ★ Appearance of Pantha.

CATWOMAN/WILDCAT — DC

1 ❑ Aug 1998 Cover: 2.50 **NM** value: **Cover or less**
Circ: Diamd. preorders: **33,916**
🕮 2 Against the House **A:** Sergio Cariello **W:** Chuck Dixon; Beau Smith
2 ❑ Sep 1998 Cover: 2.50 **NM** value: **Cover or less**
Circ: Diamd. preorders: **29,921**
3 ❑ Oct 1998 Cover: 2.50 **NM** value: **Cover or less**
Circ: Diamd. preorders: **28,757**
4 ❑ Nov 1998 Cover: 2.50 **NM** value: **Cover or less**
Circ: Diamd. preorders: **27,420**

CAVE BANG — Eros

1 ❑ Oct 1996 Cover: 2.95 **NM** value: **Cover or less**
A: Tayyar Ozkan **W:** Tayyar Ozkan
2 ❑ Jul 2000 Cover: 2.95 **NM** value: **Cover or less**
A: Tayyar Ozkan **W:** Tayyar Ozkan

CAVE GIRL — AC

1 ❑ Cover: 2.95 **NM** value: **Cover or less**
Circ: CapCity orders: **1,800**
★ Origin of Cave Girl.
11 ❑ ca. 1953 **NM** value: **350.00**
• **CGC:** 1 graded, best 3.0
12 ❑ **NM** value: **250.00**
13 ❑ Jul 1954 **NM** value: **250.00**
• **CGC:** 1 graded, best 8.0
14 ❑ **NM** value: **250.00**

CAVE KIDS — Gold Key

1 ❑ Feb 1963 Cover: 0.12 **NM** value: **50.00**
• **CGC:** 2 graded, best 9.4
2 ❑ ca. 1963 Cover: 0.12 **NM** value: **25.00**
3 ❑ Nov 1963 Cover: 0.12 **NM** value: **25.00**
• **CGC:** 1 graded, best 7.5
4 ❑ Mar 1964 Cover: 0.12 **NM** value: **25.00**
• **CGC:** 1 graded, best 6.5
5 ❑ Jun 1964 Cover: 0.12 **NM** value: **25.00**
• **CGC:** 1 graded, best 7.5
6 ❑ Sep 1964 Cover: 0.12 **NM** value: **20.00**
• **CGC:** 1 graded, best 7.5
7 ❑ Dec 1964 Cover: 0.12 **NM** value: **20.00**
• **CGC:** 1 graded, best 8.0
8 ❑ Mar 1965 Cover: 0.12 **NM** value: **20.00**
• **CGC:** 1 graded, best 9.0
9 ❑ Jun 1965 Cover: 0.12 **NM** value: **20.00**
• **CGC:** 1 graded, best 9.0
10 ❑ Sep 1965 Cover: 0.12 **NM** value: **15.00**
• **CGC:** 1 graded, best 8.5
11 ❑ Dec 1965 Cover: 0.12 **NM** value: **15.00**
• **CGC:** 1 graded, best 9.0
12 ❑ Mar 1966 Cover: 0.12 **NM** value: **15.00**
• **CGC:** 1 graded, best 9.0
13 ❑ Jun 1966 Cover: 0.12 **NM** value: **10.00**
• **CGC:** 1 graded, best 8.0
14 ❑ Sep 1966 Cover: 0.12 **NM** value: **10.00**
• **CGC:** 1 graded, best 8.5
15 ❑ Dec 1966 Cover: 0.12 **NM** value: **10.00**
• **CGC:** 1 graded, best 6.0
16 ❑ Mar 1967 Cover: 0.12 **NM** value: **10.00**
• **CGC:** 1 graded, best 8.0

CAVEMAN — Caveman Publishing

1 ❑ Apr 1998 Cover: 3.50 **NM** value: **Cover or less**
2 ❑ Jun 1998 Cover: 3.50 **NM** value: **Cover or less**
3 ❑ Aug 1998 Cover: 3.50 **NM** value: **Cover or less**
4 ❑ Oct 1998 Cover: 3.50 **NM** value: **Cover or less**
GN 1❑ b&w Cover: 9.95 **NM** value: **Cover or less**
🕮 Evolution, Heck! • graphic novel

CAVEWOMAN — Basement

1 ❑ Jan 1994, b&w Cover: 2.95 **NM** value: **55.00**
• **CGC:** 5 graded, best 9.4
2 ❑ ca. 1994, b&w Cover: 2.95 **NM** value: **35.00**
• **CGC:** 1 graded, best 9.4
3 ❑ 1994b&w Cover: 2.95 **NM** value: **25.00**
4 ❑ Nov 1994, b&w Cover: 2.95 **NM** value: **20.00**
5 ❑ b&w Cover: 2.95 **NM** value: **20.00**
6 ❑ b&w Cover: 2.95 **NM** value: **20.00**

CAVEWOMAN: MISSING LINK — Basement

1 ❑ Sep 1997, b&w Cover: 2.95 **NM** value: **Cover or less**
Circ: Diamd. preorders: **6,008**
2 ❑ Nov 1997, b&w Cover: 2.95 **NM** value: **Cover or less**
Circ: Diamd. preorders: **5,097**
Bk 1❑ Nov 1998, b&w Cover: 9.95 **NM** value: **Cover or less**
A: Jim Schumaker **W:** Bradley Walton

CAVEWOMAN: RAIN — Basement

A series that is much better than it might appear at first glance, Cavewoman seems at times part Wonder Woman, part Jurassic Park, and part Night of the Living Dead.

As the second series begins, the town of Marshville has been transported back in time to the age of the dinosaurs. Meriem Cooper (aka Cavewoman) was transported to this age when she was a young girl by her grandfather, using a time machine he'd invented. The idea was to let her escape her abusive mother, but, when her grandfather dies, she is stuck in the prehistoric era for years. When she is 19, however, the entire town of Marshville is transported back to join her. Unfortunately, the townspeople are not nearly as adept at survival in the wilds of prehistory as Meriem and find themselves being picked off, one-by-one, by packs of roving dinosaurs. Luckily, the problem isn't too bad in the heat of summer — but the rainy season is just about to begin.

1 ❑ ca. 1996 Cover: 2.95 **NM** value: **4.00**
• **CGC:** 1 graded, best 9.6
A: Budd Root **W:** Budd Root
1-2 ❑ Cover: 2.95 **NM** value: **Cover or less**
1-3 ❑ Cover: 2.95 **NM** value: **Cover or less**
2 ❑ Cover: 2.95 **NM** value: **3.50**
A: Budd Root **W:** Budd Root
2-2 ❑ Cover: 2.95 **NM** value: **Cover or less**
2-3 ❑ Cover: 2.95 **NM** value: **Cover or less**
3 ❑ ca. 1997 Cover: 2.95 **NM** value: **3.50**
A: Budd Root **W:** Budd Root
3-2 ❑ Cover: 2.95 **NM** value: **Cover or less**
• **CGC:** 1 graded, best 9.2
4 ❑ Cover: 2.95 **NM** value: **3.00**
A: Budd Root **W:** Budd Root
4-2 ❑ Cover: 2.95 **NM** value: **Cover or less**
5 ❑ Nov 1996 Cover: 2.95 **NM** value: **3.00**
Circ: Direct Market orders: **7,164**
A: Budd Root **W:** Budd Root
5-2 ❑ Cover: 2.95 **NM** value: **Cover or less**
6 ❑ Feb 1997 Cover: 2.95 **NM** value: **3.00**
Circ: Diamd. preorders: **6,399**
A: Budd Root **W:** Budd Root
7 ❑ May 1997 Cover: 2.95 **NM** value: **3.00**
Circ: Diamd. preorders: **6,569**
A: Budd Root **W:** Budd Root
8 ❑ Sep 1997 Cover: 2.95 **NM** value: **3.00**
Circ: Diamd. preorders: **6,394**
A: Budd Root **W:** Budd Root

CECIL KUNKLE (2ND SERIES) — Darkline

1 ❑ Cover: 3.50 **NM** value: **Cover or less**
2 ❑ Cover: 3.50 **NM** value: **Cover or less**

CGC-graded: Multiply prices above by **33 for 9.9 M • 16 for 9.8 NM/M • 7 for 9.6 NM+ • 5 for 9.4 NM • 2.5 for 9.2 NM- • 1.5 for 9.0 VF/NM**

3 ❑ b&w Cover: 2.00 **NM** value: **Cover or less**
Santa cover.

CECIL KUNKLE (CHARLES A. WAGNER'S...) Renegade

1 ❑ May 1986, b&w Cover: 1.70 **NM** value: **2.00**
📖 Take Two...They're Good for You! **A:** Charles A. Wagner **W:** Charles A. Wagner

CELEBRITY Horizontal

1 ❑ b&w Cover: 2.50 **NM** value: **Cover or less**
newsprint cover.

CELESTIAL MECHANICS: THE ADVENTURES OF WIDGET WILHELMINA JONES Innovation

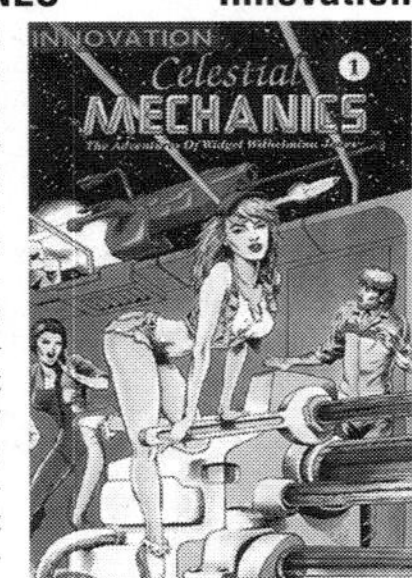

Widget Wilhelmina Jones is a charming rogue and space mechanic who has just done the impossible. By studying the remains of a wrecked spaceship, extrapolating from her own mechanical knowledge, and using imagination, she has managed to duplicate a semantic loophole space drive. This drive is the key to interstellar travel — and a closely guarded trade secret of the Halplex corporation. The way she figures it, she has three choices: use it to break up Halplex's monopoly on space travel; offer to sell it back to Halplex so the secret can remain safe; or go into business for herself. She chooses the last option.

To help her in her scheme, she has enlisted the aid of: her little sister Terebinthia, a cadet in the Halplex-owned Space Patrol; Flange, a gorgeous computer hacker; and Quarkstomper, a fellow rogue who once was the object of Terebinthia's crush. With them, Jones sets out for adventure — with Halplex assassins close behind.

1 ❑ Dec 1990, b&w Cover: 2.75 **NM** value: **Cover or less**
📖 What a Glorious Feeling, I'm Happy Again **A:** Gary Thomas Washington **W:** Kurt Wilcken

2 ❑ Feb 1991, b&w Cover: 2.75 **NM** value: **Cover or less**
📖 We've Talked The Whole Night Through **A:** Gary Thomas Washington **W:** Kurt Wilcken

3 ❑ b&w Cover: 2.75 **NM** value: **Cover or less**
A: Gary Thomas Washington **W:** Kurt Wilcken

CELESTINE Image

1 ❑ May 1996 Cover: 2.50 **NM** value: **Cover or less**
1/SC❑ May 1996 Cover: 2.50 **NM** value: **Cover or less**
alternate cover.
2 ❑ Jun 1996 Cover: 2.50 **NM** value: **Cover or less**

CELL Antarctic

1 ❑ Sep 1996, b&w Cover: 2.95 **NM** value: **Cover or less**
Circ: Diamd. preorders: **4,753**
A: Derek Kirk **W:** Derek Kirk

2 ❑ Nov 1996, b&w Cover: 2.95 **NM** value: **Cover or less**
Circ: Direct Market orders: **2,846**
A: Derek Kirk **W:** Derek Kirk

3 ❑ Jan 1997, b&w Cover: 2.95 **NM** value: **Cover or less**
Circ: Direct Market orders: **2,294**
A: Derek Kirk **W:** Derek Kirk

CENOTAPH Northstar

1 ❑ Cover: 3.95 **NM** value: **Cover or less**
A: Tony Akins **W:** Tony Akins

CENTRIFUGAL BUMBLE-PUPPY Fantagraphics

1 ❑ b&w Cover: 2.25 **NM** value: **Cover or less**
2 ❑ b&w Cover: 2.25 **NM** value: **Cover or less**
3 ❑ b&w Cover: 2.25 **NM** value: **Cover or less**
4 ❑ b&w Cover: 2.25 **NM** value: **Cover or less**
5 ❑ b&w Cover: 2.25 **NM** value: **Cover or less**
6 ❑ b&w Cover: 2.25 **NM** value: **Cover or less**
7 ❑ Cover: 2.25 **NM** value: **Cover or less**
8 ❑ Cover: 2.50 **NM** value: **Cover or less**

CENTURIONS DC

Following World War III, the nations of the world finally band together to form lasting peace. In that climate, Dr. Elias Terror begins an independent research base in the Arctic using technology to make the frozen land habitable. His contributions to science eventually cause the World Council to admit his base as a sovereign state: a move it will later come to regret, since he steals advanced cybernetic technology and uses diplomatic immunity to avoid prosecution. Terror intends to use the technology to transform himself and others into powerful cyborgs and vows to take over the world with his new army.

Hamstrung by politics, the world turns to the Centurions to stop Terror. Powerful already, this team can don special suits of armor by shouting, "PowerXtreme!" The Centurions wage battle against terror on land, in the sea, and in the air.

1 ❑ Jun 1987 Cover: 0.75 **NM** value: **1.00**
Circ: CapCity orders: **10,200**
W: Bob Rozakis ★ Origin of Centurions.

2 ❑ Jul 1987 Cover: 0.75 **NM** value: **1.00**
Circ: CapCity orders: **8,150**
📖 Seeing Is Not Believing! **A:** Don Heck; Al Vey **W:** Bob Rozakis ★ Origin of Centurions.

3 ❑ Aug 1987 Cover: 0.75 **NM** value: **1.00**
Circ: CapCity orders: **7,100**

4 ❑ Sep 1987 Cover: 1.00 **NM** value: **Cover or less**
Circ: CapCity orders: **6,500**

CENTURY: DISTANT SONS Marvel

1 ❑ Feb 1996 Cover: 2.95 **NM** value: **Cover or less**
A: Jim Calafiore **W:** Andy Lanning; Dan Abnett ★ Death of The Broker.

CEREAL KILLINGS Fantagraphics

1 ❑ Mar 1992, b&w Cover: 2.25 **NM** value: **2.50**
A: James Sturm **W:** James Sturm
2 ❑ b&w Cover: 2.25 **NM** value: **2.50**
A: James Sturm **W:** James Sturm
3 ❑ b&w Cover: 2.25 **NM** value: **2.50**
📖 Lost Causes; Slump **A:** James Sturm; Ward Sutton **W:** James Sturm
4 ❑ b&w Cover: 2.50 **NM** value: **Cover or less**
A: James Sturm **W:** James Sturm
5 ❑ b&w Cover: 2.50 **NM** value: **Cover or less**
A: James Sturm **W:** James Sturm

CEREBUS BI-WEEKLY Aardvark-Vanaheim

1 ❑ Dec 1988 Cover: 1.25 **NM** value: **2.00**
A: Dave Sim **W:** Dave Sim ★ Appearance of Reprints Cerebus the Aardvark #1, 1st.
2 ❑ Dec 1988 Cover: 1.25 **NM** value: **1.50**
• Reprints Cerebus the Aardvark #2 **A:** Dave Sim **W:** Dave Sim
3 ❑ Dec 1988 Cover: 1.25 **NM** value: **1.50**
• Reprints Cerebus the Aardvark #3 **A:** Dave Sim **W:** Dave Sim
4 ❑ Jan 1989 Cover: 1.25 **NM** value: **1.50**
• Reprints Cerebus the Aardvark #4 **A:** Dave Sim **W:** Dave Sim
5 ❑ Jan 1989 Cover: 1.25 **NM** value: **1.50**
• Reprints Cerebus the Aardvark #5 **A:** Dave Sim **W:** Dave Sim
6 ❑ Feb 1989 Cover: 1.25 **NM** value: **1.50**
• Reprints Cerebus the Aardvark #6 **A:** Dave Sim **W:** Dave Sim
7 ❑ Feb 1989 Cover: 1.25 **NM** value: **1.50**
• Reprints Cerebus the Aardvark #7 **A:** Dave Sim **W:** Dave Sim
8 ❑ Mar 1989 Cover: 1.25 **NM** value: **1.50**
• Reprints Cerebus the Aardvark #8 **A:** Dave Sim **W:** Dave Sim
9 ❑ Mar 1989 Cover: 1.25 **NM** value: **1.50**
• Reprints Cerebus the Aardvark #9 **A:** Dave Sim **W:** Dave Sim
10 ❑ Apr 1989 Cover: 1.25 **NM** value: **1.50**
• Reprints Cerebus the Aardvark #10 **A:** Dave Sim **W:** Dave Sim
11 ❑ Apr 1989 Cover: 1.25 **NM** value: **1.50**
• Reprints Cerebus the Aardvark #11 **A:** Dave Sim **W:** Dave Sim
12 ❑ May 1989 Cover: 1.25 **NM** value: **1.50**
• Reprints Cerebus the Aardvark #12 **A:** Dave Sim **W:** Dave Sim
13 ❑ May 1989 Cover: 1.25 **NM** value: **1.50**
• Reprints Cerebus the Aardvark #13 **A:** Dave Sim **W:** Dave Sim
14 ❑ May 1989 Cover: 1.25 **NM** value: **1.50**
• Reprints Cerebus the Aardvark #14 **A:** Dave Sim **W:** Dave Sim
15 ❑ Jun 1989 Cover: 1.25 **NM** value: **1.50**
📖 A Day In The Pits • Reprints Cerebus the Aardvark #15 **A:** Dave Sim **W:** Dave Sim
16 ❑ Jun 1989 Cover: 1.25 **NM** value: **1.50**
• Reprints Cerebus the Aardvark #16 **A:** Dave Sim **W:** Dave Sim
17 ❑ Jul 1989 Cover: 1.25 **NM** value: **10.00**
• Reprints Cerebus the Aardvark #17 with new material **A:** Dave Sim; Martin Wagner **W:** Dave Sim; Martin Wagner ★ 1st Appearance of Hepcats.
18 ❑ Jul 1989 Cover: 1.25 **NM** value: **1.50**
• Reprints Cerebus the Aardvark #18 **A:** Dave Sim **W:** Dave Sim
19 ❑ Aug 1989 Cover: 1.25 **NM** value: **1.50**
• Reprints Cerebus the Aardvark #19 **A:** Dave Sim **W:** Dave Sim
20 ❑ Aug 1989 Cover: 1.25 **NM** value: **15.00**
• Reprints Cerebus the Aardvark #20 with new material **A:** Dave Sim; Evan Dorkin **W:** Dave Sim; Evan Dorkin ★ 1st Appearance of Milk & Cheese.
21 ❑ Sep 1989 Cover: 1.25 **NM** value: **1.50**
• Reprints Cerebus the Aardvark #21 **A:** Dave Sim **W:** Dave Sim
22 ❑ Sep 1989 Cover: 1.25 **NM** value: **1.50**
• Reprints Cerebus the Aardvark #22 **A:** Dave Sim **W:** Dave Sim
23 ❑ Oct 1989 Cover: 1.25 **NM** value: **1.50**
• Reprints Cerebus the Aardvark #23 **A:** Dave Sim **W:** Dave Sim
24 ❑ Oct 1989 Cover: 1.25 **NM** value: **1.50**
• Reprints Cerebus the Aardvark #24 **A:** Dave Sim **W:** Dave Sim
25 ❑ Nov 1989 Cover: 1.25 **NM** value: **1.50**
• Reprints Cerebus the Aardvark #25 **A:** Dave Sim **W:** Dave Sim
26 ❑ Nov 1989 Cover: 1.25 **NM** value: **1.50**
• Reprints Cerebus the Aardvark #26 **A:** Dave Sim **W:** Dave Sim

CEREBUS: CHURCH & STATE Aardvark-Vanaheim

1 ❑ Feb 1991 Cover: 2.00 **NM** value: **Cover or less**
• Reprints Cerebus the Aardvark #51 **A:** Dave Sim **W:** Dave Sim
2 ❑ Feb 1991 Cover: 2.00 **NM** value: **Cover or less**
• Reprints Cerebus the Aardvark #52 **A:** Dave Sim **W:** Dave Sim
3 ❑ Mar 1991 Cover: 2.00 **NM** value: **Cover or less**
• Reprints Cerebus the Aardvark #53 **A:** Dave Sim **W:** Dave Sim
4 ❑ Mar 1991 Cover: 2.00 **NM** value: **Cover or less**
• Reprints Cerebus the Aardvark #54 **A:** Dave Sim **W:** Dave Sim
5 ❑ Apr 1991 Cover: 2.00 **NM** value: **Cover or less**
• Reprints Cerebus the Aardvark #55 **A:** Dave Sim **W:** Dave Sim
6 ❑ Apr 1991 Cover: 2.00 **NM** value: **Cover or less**
• Reprints Cerebus the Aardvark #56 **A:** Dave Sim **W:** Dave Sim
7 ❑ May 1991 Cover: 2.00 **NM** value: **Cover or less**
• Reprints Cerebus the Aardvark #57 **A:** Dave Sim **W:** Dave Sim
8 ❑ May 1991 Cover: 2.00 **NM** value: **Cover or less**
• Reprints Cerebus the Aardvark #58 **A:** Dave Sim **W:** Dave Sim
9 ❑ Jun 1991 Cover: 2.00 **NM** value: **Cover or less**
• Reprints Cerebus the Aardvark #59 **A:** Dave Sim **W:** Dave Sim
10 ❑ Jun 1991 Cover: 2.00 **NM** value: **Cover or less**
• Reprints Cerebus the Aardvark #60 **A:** Dave Sim **W:** Dave Sim
11 ❑ Jul 1991 Cover: 2.00 **NM** value: **Cover or less**
• Reprints Cerebus the Aardvark #61 **A:** Dave Sim **W:** Dave Sim
12 ❑ Jul 1991 Cover: 2.00 **NM** value: **Cover or less**
• Reprints Cerebus the Aardvark #62 **A:** Dave Sim **W:** Dave Sim
13 ❑ Aug 1991 Cover: 2.00 **NM** value: **Cover or less**
• Reprints Cerebus the Aardvark #63 **A:** Dave Sim **W:** Dave Sim
14 ❑ Aug 1991 Cover: 2.00 **NM** value: **Cover or less**
• Reprints Cerebus the Aardvark #64 **A:** Dave Sim **W:** Dave Sim
15 ❑ Sep 1991 Cover: 2.00 **NM** value: **Cover or less**
• Reprints Cerebus the Aardvark #65 **A:** Dave Sim; Gerhard **W:** Dave Sim
16 ❑ Sep 1991 Cover: 2.00 **NM** value: **Cover or less**
• Reprints Cerebus the Aardvark #66 **A:** Dave Sim; Gerhard **W:** Dave Sim
17 ❑ Oct 1991 Cover: 2.00 **NM** value: **Cover or less**
• Reprints Cerebus the Aardvark #67 **A:** Dave Sim; Gerhard **W:** Dave Sim
18 ❑ Oct 1991 Cover: 2.00 **NM** value: **Cover or less**
• Reprints Cerebus the Aardvark #68 **A:** Dave Sim; Gerhard **W:** Dave Sim
19 ❑ Nov 1991 Cover: 2.00 **NM** value: **Cover or less**
• Reprints Cerebus the Aardvark #69 **A:** Dave Sim; Gerhard **W:** Dave Sim
20 ❑ Nov 1991 Cover: 2.00 **NM** value: **Cover or less**
📖 Sane As It Ever Was • Reprints Cerebus the Aardvark #70 **A:** Dave Sim; Gerhard **W:** Dave Sim
21 ❑ Dec 1991 Cover: 2.00 **NM** value: **Cover or less**
• Reprints Cerebus the Aardvark #71 **A:** Dave Sim; Gerhard **W:** Dave Sim
22 ❑ Dec 1991 Cover: 2.00 **NM** value: **Cover or less**
• Reprints Cerebus the Aardvark #72 **A:** Dave Sim; Gerhard **W:** Dave Sim
23 ❑ Jan 1992 Cover: 2.00 **NM** value: **Cover or less**
• Reprints Cerebus the Aardvark #73 **A:** Dave Sim; Gerhard **W:** Dave Sim
24 ❑ Jan 1992 Cover: 2.00 **NM** value: **Cover or less**
• Reprints Cerebus the Aardvark #74 **A:** Dave Sim; Gerhard **W:** Dave Sim
25 ❑ Feb 1992 Cover: 2.00 **NM** value: **Cover or less**
• Reprints Cerebus the Aardvark #75 **A:** Dave Sim; Gerhard **W:** Dave Sim
26 ❑ Feb 1992 Cover: 2.00 **NM** value: **Cover or less**
• Reprints Cerebus the Aardvark #76 **A:** Dave Sim; Gerhard **W:** Dave Sim
27 ❑ Mar 1992 Cover: 2.00 **NM** value: **Cover or less**
• Reprints Cerebus the Aardvark #77 **A:** Dave Sim; Gerhard **W:** Dave Sim
28 ❑ Mar 1992 Cover: 2.00 **NM** value: **Cover or less**
• Reprints Cerebus the Aardvark #78 **A:** Dave Sim; Gerhard **W:** Dave Sim
29 ❑ Apr 1992 Cover: 2.00 **NM** value: **Cover or less**
📖 Spinning Straw Into Gold • Reprints Cerebus the Aardvark #79 **A:** Dave Sim; Gerhard **W:** Dave Sim
30 ❑ Apr 1992 Cover: 2.00 **NM** value: **Cover or less**
• Reprints Cerebus the Aardvark #80 **A:** Dave Sim; Gerhard **W:** Dave Sim

CEREBUS COMPANION Win-Mill

1 ❑ Dec 1993 Cover: 3.95 **NM** value: **Cover or less**
Circ: CapCity orders: **2,980**
2 ❑ Dec 1994 Cover: 3.95 **NM** value: **Cover or less**

CEREBUS GUIDE TO SELF PUBLISHING Aardvark-Vanaheim

1 ❑ Nov 1997 Cover: 3.95 **NM** value: **Cover or less**
No issue number. • collects Sim text pieces on the subject from Cerebus

CEREBUS: GUYS PARTY PACK Aardvark-Vanaheim

This giant-size "party pack" reprints Cerebus the Aardvark #201-204. Taken together these issues form the story of a little aardvark on a truly epic bender.

Missing an eye and an ear as a result of his sword fight in Reads, Cerebus has sought solace at the bottom of a bottle. Camping out at the local bar, he's joined by fellow patrons Harrison Starkey and Richard George (a very familiar looking pair), as well as a surly bartender, and Bacchus, the god of alcohol himself. Oh, and somewhere during the midst of the alcoholic stupor, there's a game of Five Bar Gate ("the fastest game in Estarcion"), and a battle for Cerebus' soul featuring Bacchus and Roarin' Rick, the Rare Bit Fiend.

This is one hangover that Cerebus is never going to forget...

1 ❑ Cover: 3.95 **NM** value: **Cover or less**
📖 Guys • Reprints Cerebus the Aardvark #201-204 **A:** Dave Sim; Gerhard **W:** Dave Sim

CEREBUS HIGH SOCIETY Aardvark-Vanaheim

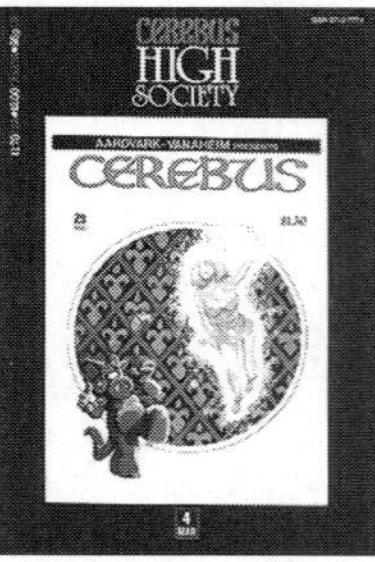

Cerebus High Society continues the reprint program began in Cerebus Biweekly. Issues of this series reprinted #26-50 of Cerebus the Aardvark, the famous "High Society" storyline that brought Sim his first widespread comics fame and which many still consider his most-fully realized run on the title.

"High Society" finds the aardvark barbarian thrust into a world of political intrigue — first as a spoiler, and then as an independent actor. Surrounded by the crafty Astoria, the demented Moon Roach, and a cast of other crazies, Cerebus runs

Other grades: Multiply prices above by **1.5 for Mint • 2/3 for Very Fine • 1/3 for Fine • 1/5 for Very Good • 1/8 for Good**

for Prime Minister against Lord Julius' goat and then must contend with the trials of life after the election.

Each issue of this reprint series includes a page spotlighting the comics talents of various fan contributors. — JJM

1 ❑ Feb 1990 Cover: 1.70 **NM** value: **2.00**
A: Dave Sim **C:** Dave Sim **W:** Dave Sim

2 ❑ Feb 1990 Cover: 1.70 **NM** value: **2.00**

3 ❑ Mar 1990 Cover: 1.70 **NM** value: **2.00**

4 ❑ Mar 1990 Cover: 1.70 **NM** value: **2.00**

5 ❑ Apr 1990 Cover: 1.70 **NM** value: **2.00**

6 ❑ Apr 1990 Cover: 1.70 **NM** value: **2.00**

7 ❑ May 1990 Cover: 1.70 **NM** value: **2.00**

8 ❑ May 1990 Cover: 1.70 **NM** value: **2.00**

9 ❑ Jun 1990 Cover: 1.70 **NM** value: **2.00**

10 ❑ Jun 1990 Cover: 1.70 **NM** value: **2.00**

11 ❑ Jul 1990 Cover: 2.00 **NM** value: **Cover or less**

12 ❑ Jul 1990 Cover: 2.00 **NM** value: **Cover or less**

13 ❑ Aug 1990 Cover: 2.00 **NM** value: **Cover or less**

14 ❑ Aug 1990 Cover: 2.00 **NM** value: **Cover or less**

15 ❑ Sep 1990 Cover: 2.00 **NM** value: **Cover or less**

16 ❑ Sep 1990 Cover: 2.00 **NM** value: **Cover or less**

17 ❑ Oct 1990 Cover: 2.00 **NM** value: **Cover or less**

18 ❑ Oct 1990 Cover: 2.00 **NM** value: **Cover or less**

19 ❑ Nov 1990 Cover: 2.00 **NM** value: **Cover or less**

20 ❑ Nov 1990 Cover: 2.00 **NM** value: **Cover or less**

21 ❑ Dec 1990 Cover: 2.00 **NM** value: **Cover or less**

22 ❑ Dec 1990 Cover: 2.00 **NM** value: **Cover or less**

23 ❑ Jan 1991 Cover: 2.00 **NM** value: **Cover or less**

24 ❑ Jan 1991 Cover: 2.00 **NM** value: **Cover or less**

25 ❑ Feb 1991 Cover: 2.00 **NM** value: **Cover or less**

CEREBUS JAM Aardvark-Vanaheim

1 ❑ Apr 1985 Cover: 2.00 **NM** value: **Cover or less**
📖 In Defense of Fort Columbia; The First Invention of Armor; Squinteye the Sailor; Cerebus Jam

CEREBUS THE AARDVARK Aardvark-Vanaheim

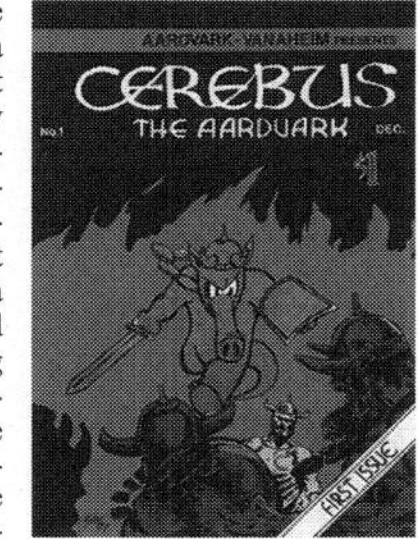

Cerebus, who "stood only five hands high, had a lengthy snout, a long tail and was covered with short gray fur," might seem an unlikely candidate to star in the longest-running independent comic book published today. But since 1977, creator and publisher Dave Sim has put the title character, an aardcark in a fantasy setting that often seemed contemporary, through a dizzying series of career changes: from barbarian to bodyguard, from prime minister to pope, from bum to messiah wanna-be. Sim has, in the course of his nearly finished "300-issue limited series" provided laughter and wrestled with larger dramatic and philosophical themes.

A counterfeit version of #1 exists; it has glossy stock on the inside cover. It still has a significant market value as a historical conversation piece and thus has a listing below. — JJM

0 ❑ Jun 1993, b&w Cover: 2.25 **NM** value: **4.00**
Circ: CapCity orders: **15,500**
• Reprints Cerebus the Aardvark #51, 112/113, 137/138 **A:** Dave Sim **W:** Dave Sim

0/GO❑ **NM** value: **6.00**
Gold logo on cover. • Reprints Cerebus the Aardvark #51, 112/113, 137/138 **A:** Dave Sim **W:** Dave Sim

1 ❑ Dec 1977 Cover: 1.00 **NM** value: **275.00**
• genuine; Low circulation **A:** Dave Sim **W:** Dave Sim ★ 1st Appearance of Cerebus.

1/CF❑ Cover: 1.00 **NM** value: **35.00**
• Counterfeit edition (glossy cover stock on inside cover). • counterfeit; Low circulation **A:** Dave Sim **W:** Dave Sim ★ 1st Appearance of Cerebus.

2 ❑ 1978 Cover: 1.00 **NM** value: **70.00**
• **CGC:** 4 graded, best 9.2
📖 Captive in Boreala **A:** Dave Sim **W:** Dave Sim

3 ❑ 1978 Cover: 1.00 **NM** value: **65.00**
• **CGC:** 4 graded, best 9.4
📖 Song of Red Sophia **A:** Dave Sim **W:** Dave Sim ★ 1st Appearance of Red Sophia.

4 ❑ 1978 Cover: 1.00 **NM** value: **40.00**
• **CGC:** 3 graded, best 9.4
📖 Death's Dark Tread **A:** Dave Sim **W:** Dave Sim ★ 1st Appearance of Elrod the Albino.

5 ❑ Aug 1978 Cover: 1.00 **NM** value: **35.00**
• **CGC:** 2 graded, best 9.4
📖 The Idol **A:** Dave Sim **W:** Dave Sim

6 ❑ Oct 1978 Cover: 1.00 **NM** value: **35.00**
• **CGC:** 5 graded, best 9.6
📖 The Secret **A:** Dave Sim **W:** Dave Sim

7 ❑ Dec 1978 Cover: 1.00 **NM** value: **24.00**
• **CGC:** 5 graded, best 9.6
📖 Black Sun Rising **A:** Dave Sim **W:** Dave Sim

8 ❑ Feb 1979 Cover: 1.00 **NM** value: **24.00**
• **CGC:** 9 graded, best 9.6
📖 Day of the Earth-Pig **A:** Dave Sim **W:** Dave Sim

9 ❑ Apr 1979 Cover: 1.00 **NM** value: **24.00**
• **CGC:** 3 graded, best 9.4
📖 Swords Against Imesh **A:** Dave Sim **W:** Dave Sim

10 ❑ Jun 1979 Cover: 1.00 **NM** value: **24.00**
• **CGC:** 3 graded, best 9.6
📖 Merchant of Unshib **A:** Dave Sim **W:** Dave Sim

11 ❑ Aug 1979 Cover: 1.00 **NM** value: **20.00**
• **CGC:** 3 graded, best 9.4
📖 The Merchant and the Cockroach **A:** Dave Sim **W:** Dave Sim ★ 1st Appearance of Captain Cockroach.

12 ❑ Oct 1979 Cover: 1.00 **NM** value: **20.00**
• **CGC:** 3 graded, best 9.6
📖 Beduin by Night **A:** Dave Sim **W:** Dave Sim

13 ❑ Dec 1979 Cover: 1.00 **NM** value: **20.00**
• **CGC:** 3 graded, best 9.2
📖 Black magiking **A:** Dave Sim **W:** Dave Sim

14 ❑ Mar 1980 Cover: 1.00 **NM** value: **20.00**
• **CGC:** 2 graded, best 9.4
📖 The Walls of Palnu **A:** Dave Sim **W:** Dave Sim

15 ❑ Apr 1980 Cover: 1.00 **NM** value: **20.00**
• **CGC:** 3 graded, best 9.6
📖 A Day In The Pits **A:** Dave Sim **W:** Dave Sim

16 ❑ May 1980 Cover: 1.25 **NM** value: **18.00**
• **CGC:** 2 graded, best 9.4
📖 A Night at the Masque **A:** Dave Sim **W:** Dave Sim

17 ❑ Jun 1980 Cover: 1.25 **NM** value: **18.00**
• **CGC:** 2 graded, best 9.2
📖 Champion **A:** Dave Sim **W:** Dave Sim

18 ❑ Jul 1980 Cover: 1.25 **NM** value: **18.00**
• **CGC:** 1 graded, best 8.5
📖 Fluroc **A:** Dave Sim **W:** Dave Sim

19 ❑ Aug 1980 Cover: 1.25 **NM** value: **18.00**
• **CGC:** 1 graded, best 9.2
📖 She-Devil in the Shadows **A:** Dave Sim **W:** Dave Sim

20 ❑ Sep 1980 Cover: 1.25 **NM** value: **18.00**
📖 Mind Games **A:** Dave Sim **W:** Dave Sim

21 ❑ Oct 1980 Cover: 1.25 **NM** value: **30.00**
• **CGC:** 6 graded, best 9.6
📖 Captain Cockroach • Low circulation **A:** Dave Sim **W:** Dave Sim

22 ❑ Nov 1980 **NM** value: **16.00**
no cover price. 📖 The Death of Elrod **A:** Dave Sim **W:** Dave Sim

23 ❑ Dec 1980 Cover: 1.50 **NM** value: **7.00**
📖 The Beguiling **A:** Dave Sim **W:** Dave Sim

24 ❑ Jan 1981 Cover: 1.50 **NM** value: **7.00**
📖 Swamp Sounds **A:** Dave Sim **W:** Dave Sim

25 ❑ Mar 1981 Cover: 1.50 **NM** value: **7.00**
📖 This Woman, This Thing **A:** Dave Sim **W:** Dave Sim

26 ❑ May 1981 Cover: 1.50 **NM** value: **7.00**
📖 High Society:High Society **A:** Dave Sim **W:** Dave Sim

27 ❑ Jun 1981 Cover: 1.50 **NM** value: **7.00**
📖 High Society: The Kidnapping of An Aardvark **A:** Dave Sim **W:** Dave Sim

28 ❑ Jul 1981 Cover: 1.50 **NM** value: **7.00**
📖 High Society: Mind Game II **A:** Dave Sim **W:** Dave Sim

29 ❑ Aug 1981 Cover: 1.50 **NM** value: **7.00**
📖 High Society: Repercussions **A:** Dave Sim **W:** Dave Sim

30 ❑ Sep 1981 Cover: 1.50 **NM** value: **7.00**
📖 High Society: Debts **A:** Dave Sim **W:** Dave Sim

31 ❑ Oct 1981 Cover: 1.50 **NM** value: **7.00**
• **CGC:** 1 graded, best 9.6
📖 High Society: Chasing Cootie! **A:** Dave Sim **W:** Dave Sim

32 ❑ Nov 1981 Cover: 1.50 **NM** value: **6.00**
📖 High Society: Alliance **A:** Dave Sim **W:** Dave Sim

33 ❑ Dec 1981 Cover: 1.50 **NM** value: **6.00**
📖 High Society: Friction **A:** Dave Sim **W:** Dave Sim

34 ❑ Jan 1982 Cover: 1.50 **NM** value: **6.00**
📖 High Society: Three Days Before **A:** Dave Sim **W:** Dave Sim

35 ❑ Feb 1982 Cover: 1.50 **NM** value: **6.00**
📖 High Society: Two Days Before **A:** Dave Sim **W:** Dave Sim

36 ❑ Mar 1982 Cover: 1.50 **NM** value: **6.00**
📖 High Society: The Night Before **A:** Dave Sim **W:** Dave Sim

37 ❑ Apr 1982 Cover: 1.50 **NM** value: **6.00**
📖 High Society: It's Showtime! **A:** Dave Sim **W:** Dave Sim

38 ❑ May 1982 Cover: 1.50 **NM** value: **6.00**
📖 High Society: Petuniacon, Day Two **A:** Dave Sim **W:** Dave Sim

39 ❑ Jun 1982 Cover: 1.50 **NM** value: **6.00**
📖 High Society: Petuniacon, Day Three **A:** Dave Sim **W:** Dave Sim

40 ❑ Jul 1982 Cover: 1.50 **NM** value: **6.00**
📖 High Society: Campaign; Goat back-up **A:** Dave Sim **W:** Dave Sim

41 ❑ Aug 1982 Cover: 1.50 **NM** value: **5.00**
📖 High Society: Heroes **A:** Dave Sim **W:** Dave Sim

42 ❑ Sep 1982 Cover: 1.50 **NM** value: **5.00**
📖 High Society: Campaign's End **A:** Dave Sim **W:** Dave Sim

43 ❑ Oct 1982 Cover: 1.50 **NM** value: **5.00**
📖 High Society: Election Night **A:** Dave Sim **W:** Dave Sim

44 ❑ Nov 1982 Cover: 1.50 **NM** value: **5.00**
📖 High Society: The Deciding Vote • sideways **A:** Dave Sim **W:** Dave Sim

45 ❑ Dec 1982 Cover: 1.50 **NM** value: **5.00**
📖 High Society: Cerebus' Six Crises, Crisis Number One: The Bureaucratic Rebellion • sideways **A:** Dave Sim **W:** Dave Sim

46 ❑ Jan 1983 Cover: 1.40 **NM** value: **5.00**
📖 High Society: Cerebus' Six Crises: Crisis Number Two: A Night In lest, or Summit Enchanted Evening • sideways **A:** Dave Sim **W:** Dave Sim

47 ❑ Feb 1983 Cover: 1.40 **NM** value: **5.00**
📖 High Society: Cerebus' Six Crises: Crisis Number Three: Balances • sideways **A:** Dave Sim **W:** Dave Sim

48 ❑ Mar 1983 Cover: 1.40 **NM** value: **5.00**
📖 High Society: Cerebus' Six Crises: Crisis Number Four: Upstairs • sideways **A:** Dave Sim **W:** Dave Sim

49 ❑ Apr 1983 Cover: 1.40 **NM** value: **5.00**
📖 High Society: Cerebus' Six Crises: Crisis Number Five: The Last Stand • rotating issue **A:** Dave Sim **W:** Dave Sim

50 ❑ May 1983 Cover: 1.40 **NM** value: **5.00**
📖 High Society: Cerebus' Six Crises: Crisis Number Six: Denouement **A:** Dave Sim **W:** Dave Sim

51 ❑ Jun 1983 Cover: 1.40 **NM** value: **8.00**
📖 Church & State • Low circulation **A:** Dave Sim **W:** Dave Sim

52 ❑ Jul 1983 Cover: 1.40 **NM** value: **5.00**
📖 Church & State **A:** Dave Sim **W:** Dave Sim

53 ❑ Aug 1983 Cover: 1.40 **NM** value: **5.00**
📖 Church & State **A:** Dave Sim **W:** Dave Sim ★ 1st Appearance of Wolveroach (cameo).

54 ❑ Sep 1983 Cover: 1.40 **NM** value: **5.00**
📖 Church & State **A:** Dave Sim **W:** Dave Sim ★ 1st Appearance of Wolveroach (full story). ★ Appearance of Wolveroach.

55 ❑ Oct 1983 Cover: 1.40 **NM** value: **5.00**
📖 Church & State **A:** Dave Sim **W:** Dave Sim ★ Appearance of Wolveroach.

56 ❑ Nov 1983 Cover: 1.40 **NM** value: **5.00**
📖 Church & State **A:** Dave Sim; Jim Valentino **W:** Dave Sim; Jim Valentino ★ 1st Appearance of Normalman. ★ Appearance of Wolveroach.

57 ❑ Dec 1983 Cover: 1.40 **NM** value: **4.00**
📖 Church & State **A:** Dave Sim; Jim Valentino **W:** Dave Sim; Jim Valentino ★ 2nd Appearance of Normalman.

58 ❑ Jan 1984 Cover: 1.70 **NM** value: **4.00**
📖 Church & State **A:** Dave Sim **W:** Dave Sim

59 ❑ Feb 1984 Cover: 1.70 **NM** value: **4.00**
📖 Church & State **A:** Dave Sim **W:** Dave Sim

60 ❑ Mar 1984 Cover: 1.70 **NM** value: **4.00**
📖 Church & State **A:** Dave Sim **W:** Dave Sim

61 ❑ Apr 1984 Cover: 1.70 **NM** value: **5.00**
📖 Church & State • Flaming Carrot **A:** Dave Sim **W:** Dave Sim ★ Appearance of Flaming Carrot.

62 ❑ May 1984 Cover: 1.70 **NM** value: **5.00**
📖 Church & State • Flaming Carrot **A:** Dave Sim **W:** Dave Sim ★ Appearance of Flaming Carrot.

63 ❑ Jun 1984 Cover: 1.70 **NM** value: **3.00**
📖 Church & State **A:** Dave Sim **W:** Dave Sim

64 ❑ Jul 1984 Cover: 1.70 **NM** value: **3.00**
📖 Church & State **A:** Dave Sim **W:** Dave Sim

65 ❑ Aug 1984 Cover: 1.70 **NM** value: **3.00**
📖 Church & State • Gerhard begins as background artist **A:** Dave Sim; Gerhard **W:** Dave Sim

66 ❑ Sep 1984 Cover: 1.70 **NM** value: **3.00**
📖 Church & State **A:** Dave Sim; Gerhard **W:** Dave Sim

67 ❑ Oct 1984 Cover: 1.70 **NM** value: **3.00**
📖 Church & State **A:** Dave Sim; Gerhard **W:** Dave Sim

68 ❑ Nov 1984 Cover: 1.70 **NM** value: **3.00**
📖 Church & State **A:** Dave Sim; Gerhard **W:** Dave Sim

69 ❑ Dec 1984 Cover: 1.70 **NM** value: **3.00**
📖 Church & State **A:** Dave Sim; Gerhard **W:** Dave Sim

70 ❑ Jan 1985 Cover: 1.70 **NM** value: **3.00**
📖 Church & State **A:** Dave Sim; Gerhard **W:** Dave Sim

71 ❑ Feb 1985 Cover: 1.70 **NM** value: **3.00**
📖 Church & State **A:** Dave Sim; Gerhard **W:** Dave Sim

72 ❑ Mar 1985 Cover: 1.70 **NM** value: **3.00**
📖 Church & State **A:** Dave Sim; Gerhard **W:** Dave Sim

73 ❑ Apr 1985 Cover: 1.70 **NM** value: **3.00**
📖 Church & State **A:** Dave Sim; Gerhard **W:** Dave Sim

74 ❑ May 1985 Cover: 1.70 **NM** value: **3.00**
📖 Church & State **A:** Dave Sim; Gerhard **W:** Dave Sim

75 ❑ Jun 1985 Cover: 1.70 **NM** value: **3.00**
📖 Church & State **A:** Dave Sim; Gerhard **W:** Dave Sim

76 ❑ Jul 1985 Cover: 1.70 **NM** value: **3.00**
📖 Church & State **A:** Dave Sim; Gerhard **W:** Dave Sim

77 ❑ Aug 1985 Cover: 1.70 **NM** value: **3.00**
📖 Church & State **A:** Dave Sim; Gerhard **W:** Dave Sim

78 ❑ Sep 1985 Cover: 1.70 **NM** value: **3.00**
📖 Church & State **A:** Dave Sim; Gerhard **W:** Dave Sim

79 ❑ Oct 1985 Cover: 1.70 **NM** value: **3.00**
📖 Church & State **A:** Dave Sim; Gerhard **W:** Dave Sim

80 ❑ Nov 1985 Cover: 1.70 **NM** value: **3.00**
📖 Church & State **A:** Dave Sim; Gerhard **W:** Dave Sim

81 ❑ Dec 1985 Cover: 1.70 **NM** value: **3.00**
📖 Church & State **A:** Dave Sim; Gerhard **W:** Dave Sim

82 ❑ Jan 1986 Cover: 1.70 **NM** value: **3.00**
📖 Church & State **A:** Dave Sim; Gerhard **W:** Dave Sim

83 ❑ Feb 1986 Cover: 1.70 **NM** value: **3.00**
📖 Church & State **A:** Dave Sim; Gerhard **W:** Dave Sim

84 ❑ Mar 1986 Cover: 1.70 **NM** value: **3.00**
📖 Church & State **A:** Dave Sim; Gerhard **W:** Dave Sim

85 ❑ Apr 1986 Cover: 1.70 **NM** value: **3.00**
📖 Church & State **A:** Dave Sim; Gerhard **W:** Dave Sim

86 ❑ May 1986 Cover: 1.70 **NM** value: **3.00**
📖 Church & State **A:** Dave Sim; Gerhard **W:** Dave Sim

87 ❑ Jun 1986 Cover: 1.70 **NM** value: **3.00**
📖 Church & State **A:** Dave Sim; Gerhard **W:** Dave Sim

88 ❑ Jul 1986 Cover: 1.70 **NM** value: **3.00**
📖 Church & State **A:** Dave Sim; Gerhard **W:** Dave Sim

89 ❑ Aug 1986 Cover: 1.70 **NM** value: **3.00**
📖 Church & State **A:** Dave Sim; Gerhard **W:** Dave Sim

90 ❑ Sep 1986 Cover: 1.70 **NM** value: **3.00**
📖 Church & State **A:** Dave Sim; Gerhard **W:** Dave Sim

91 ❑ Oct 1986 Cover: 1.70 **NM** value: **3.00**
📖 Church & State **A:** Dave Sim; Gerhard **W:** Dave Sim

92 ❑ Nov 1986 Cover: 1.70 **NM** value: **3.00**
📖 Church & State **A:** Dave Sim; Gerhard **W:** Dave Sim

93 ❑ Dec 1986 Cover: 1.70 **NM** value: **3.00**
📖 Church & State **A:** Dave Sim; Gerhard **W:** Dave Sim

94 ❑ Jan 1987 Cover: 1.70 **NM** value: **3.00**
📖 Church & State **A:** Dave Sim; Gerhard **W:** Dave Sim

95 ❑ Feb 1987 Cover: 1.70 **NM** value: **3.00**
📖 Church & State **A:** Dave Sim; Gerhard **W:** Dave Sim

96 ❑ Mar 1987 Cover: 1.70 **NM** value: **3.00**
📖 Church & State **A:** Dave Sim; Gerhard **W:** Dave Sim

97 ❑ Apr 1987 Cover: 1.70 **NM** value: **3.00**
📖 Church & State **A:** Dave Sim; Gerhard **W:** Dave Sim

98 ❑ May 1987 Cover: 1.70 **NM** value: **3.00**
📖 Church & State **A:** Dave Sim; Gerhard **W:** Dave Sim

99 ❑ Jun 1987 Cover: 1.70 **NM** value: **3.00**
📖 Church & State **A:** Dave Sim; Gerhard **W:** Dave Sim

100 ❑ Jul 1987 Cover: 1.70 **NM** value: **3.00**
📖 Church & State **A:** Dave Sim; Gerhard **W:** Dave Sim

101 ❑ Aug 1987 Cover: 1.70 **NM** value: **2.50**
📖 Church & State **A:** Dave Sim; Gerhard **W:** Dave Sim

102 ❑ Sep 1987 Cover: 1.70 **NM** value: **2.50**
📖 Church & State **A:** Dave Sim; Gerhard **W:** Dave Sim

103 ❑ Oct 1987 Cover: 1.70 **NM** value: **2.50**
📖 Church & State **A:** Dave Sim; Gerhard **W:** Dave Sim

104 ❑ Nov 1987 Cover: 1.70 **NM** value: **2.50**
📖 Church & State **A:** Dave Sim; Gerhard **W:** Dave Sim ★ Appearance of Flaming Carrot.

105 ❑ Dec 1987 Cover: 1.70 **NM** value: **2.50**
📖 Church & State; Ascension's End, Part 1 **A:** Dave Sim; Gerhard **W:** Dave Sim

CGC-graded: Multiply prices above by **33 for 9.9 M • 16 for 9.8 NM/M • 7 for 9.6 NM+ • 5 for 9.4 NM • 2.5 for 9.2 NM- • 1.5 for 9.0 VF/NM**

106 ❑ Jan 1988 Cover: 2.00 **NM** value: **2.50**
Church & State; Ascension's End, Part 2 **A:** Dave Sim; Gerhard **W:** Dave Sim
107 ❑ Feb 1988 Cover: 2.00 **NM** value: **2.50**
Church & State **A:** Dave Sim; Gerhard **W:** Dave Sim
108 ❑ Mar 1988 Cover: 2.00 **NM** value: **2.50**
Church & State **A:** Dave Sim; Gerhard **W:** Dave Sim
109 ❑ Apr 1988 Cover: 2.00 **NM** value: **2.50**
Church & State **A:** Dave Sim; Gerhard **W:** Dave Sim
110 ❑ May 1988 Cover: 2.00 **NM** value: **2.50**
Church & State **A:** Dave Sim; Gerhard **W:** Dave Sim
111 ❑ Jun 1988 Cover: 2.00 **NM** value: **2.50**
Church & State **A:** Dave Sim; Gerhard **W:** Dave Sim
112 ❑ Jul 1988 Cover: 2.00 **NM** value: **2.50**
• Double-issue #112 and #113 **A:** Dave Sim; Gerhard **W:** Dave Sim
114 ❑ Sep 1988 Cover: 2.00 **NM** value: **2.50**
Jaka's Story, Part 1 **A:** Dave Sim; Gerhard **W:** Dave Sim
115 ❑ Oct 1988 Cover: 2.00 **NM** value: **2.50**
Jaka's Story, Part 2 **A:** Dave Sim; Gerhard **W:** Dave Sim
116 ❑ Nov 1988 Cover: 2.00 **NM** value: **2.50**
Jaka's Story, Part 3 **A:** Dave Sim; Gerhard **W:** Dave Sim
117 ❑ Dec 1988 Cover: 2.00 **NM** value: **2.50**
Jaka's Story, Part 4 **A:** Dave Sim; Gerhard **W:** Dave Sim
118 ❑ Jan 1989 Cover: 2.00 **NM** value: **2.50**
Jaka's Story, Part 5 **A:** Dave Sim; Gerhard **W:** Dave Sim
119 ❑ Feb 1989 Cover: 2.00 **NM** value: **2.50**
Jaka's Story, Part 6 **A:** Dave Sim; Gerhard **W:** Dave Sim
120 ❑ Mar 1989 Cover: 2.00 **NM** value: **2.50**
Jaka's Story, Part 7 **A:** Dave Sim; Gerhard **W:** Dave Sim
121 ❑ Apr 1989 Cover: 2.00 **NM** value: **2.50**
Jaka's Story, Part 8 **A:** Dave Sim; Gerhard **W:** Dave Sim
122 ❑ May 1989 Cover: 2.00 **NM** value: **2.50**
Jaka's Story, Part 9 **A:** Dave Sim; Gerhard **W:** Dave Sim
123 ❑ Jun 1989 Cover: 2.00 **NM** value: **2.50**
Jaka's Story, Part 10 **A:** Dave Sim; Gerhard **W:** Dave Sim
124 ❑ Jul 1989 Cover: 2.00 **NM** value: **2.50**
Jaka's Story, Part 11 **A:** Dave Sim; Gerhard **W:** Dave Sim
125 ❑ Aug 1989 Cover: 2.00 **NM** value: **2.50**
Jaka's Story, Part 12 **A:** Dave Sim; Gerhard **W:** Dave Sim
126 ❑ Sep 1989 Cover: 2.00 **NM** value: **2.50**
Jaka's Story, Part 13 **A:** Dave Sim; Gerhard **W:** Dave Sim
127 ❑ Oct 1989 Cover: 2.00 **NM** value: **2.50**
Jaka's Story, Part 14 **A:** Dave Sim; Gerhard **W:** Dave Sim
128 ❑ Nov 1989 Cover: 2.00 **NM** value: **2.50**
Jaka's Story, Part 15 **A:** Dave Sim; Gerhard **W:** Dave Sim
129 ❑ Dec 1989 Cover: 2.00 **NM** value: **2.50**
Jaka's Story, Part 16 **A:** Dave Sim; Gerhard **W:** Dave Sim
130 ❑ Jan 1990 Cover: 2.00 **NM** value: **2.50**
Jaka's Story, Part 17 **A:** Dave Sim; Gerhard **W:** Dave Sim
131 ❑ Feb 1990 Cover: 2.00 **NM** value: **2.50**
Jaka's Story, Part 18 **A:** Dave Sim; Gerhard **W:** Dave Sim
132 ❑ Mar 1990 Cover: 2.00 **NM** value: **2.50**
Jaka's Story, Part 19 **A:** Dave Sim; Gerhard **W:** Dave Sim
133 ❑ Apr 1990 Cover: 2.00 **NM** value: **2.50**
Jaka's Story, Part 19 **A:** Dave Sim; Gerhard **W:** Dave Sim
134 ❑ May 1990 Cover: 2.00 **NM** value: **2.50**
Jaka's Story, Part 20 **A:** Dave Sim; Gerhard **W:** Dave Sim
135 ❑ Jun 1990 Cover: 2.00 **NM** value: **2.50**
Jaka's Story, Part 21 **A:** Dave Sim; Gerhard **W:** Dave Sim
136 ❑ Jul 1990 Cover: 2.00 **NM** value: **2.50**
Jaka's Story, Part 22 **A:** Dave Sim; Gerhard **W:** Dave Sim
137 ❑ Aug 1990 Cover: 2.25 **NM** value: **2.50**
Jaka's Story, Part 23 **A:** Dave Sim; Gerhard **W:** Dave Sim
138 ❑ Sep 1990 Cover: 2.25 **NM** value: **2.50**
Photo cover. Jaka's Story, Part 24 **A:** Dave Sim; Gerhard **W:** Dave Sim
139 ❑ Oct 1990 Cover: 2.25 **NM** value: **2.50**
Melmoth, Part 0 **A:** Dave Sim; Gerhard **W:** Dave Sim
140 ❑ Nov 1990 Cover: 2.25 **NM** value: **Cover or less**
Melmoth, Part 1 **A:** Dave Sim; Gerhard **W:** Dave Sim
141 ❑ Dec 1990 Cover: 2.25 **NM** value: **Cover or less**
Melmoth, Part 2 **A:** Dave Sim; Gerhard **W:** Dave Sim
142 ❑ Jan 1991 Cover: 2.25 **NM** value: **Cover or less**
Melmoth, Part 3 **A:** Dave Sim; Gerhard **W:** Dave Sim
143 ❑ Feb 1991 Cover: 2.25 **NM** value: **Cover or less**
Melmoth, Part 4 **A:** Dave Sim; Gerhard **W:** Dave Sim
144 ❑ Mar 1991 Cover: 2.25 **NM** value: **Cover or less**
Melmoth, Part 5 **A:** Dave Sim; Gerhard **W:** Dave Sim
145 ❑ Apr 1991 Cover: 2.25 **NM** value: **Cover or less**
Melmoth, Part 6 **A:** Dave Sim; Gerhard **W:** Dave Sim
146 ❑ May 1991 Cover: 2.25 **NM** value: **Cover or less**
Melmoth, Part 7 **A:** Dave Sim; Gerhard **W:** Dave Sim
147 ❑ Jun 1991 Cover: 2.25 **NM** value: **Cover or less**
Melmoth, Part 8 **A:** Dave Sim; Gerhard **W:** Dave Sim
148 ❑ Jul 1991 Cover: 2.25 **NM** value: **Cover or less**
Melmoth, Part 9 **A:** Dave Sim; Gerhard **W:** Dave Sim
149 ❑ Aug 1991 Cover: 2.25 **NM** value: **Cover or less**
Melmoth, Part 10 **A:** Dave Sim; Gerhard **W:** Dave Sim
150 ❑ Sep 1991 Cover: 2.25 **NM** value: **Cover or less**
Melmoth, Part 11 **A:** Dave Sim; Gerhard **W:** Dave Sim
151 ❑ Oct 1991 Cover: 2.25 **NM** value: **Cover or less**
Mothers & Daughters, Part 1 **A:** Dave Sim; Gerhard **W:** Dave Sim
152 ❑ Nov 1991 Cover: 2.25 **NM** value: **Cover or less**
Circ: CapCity orders: **4,775**
Mothers & Daughters, Part 2 **A:** Dave Sim; Gerhard **W:** Dave Sim
153 ❑ Dec 1991 Cover: 2.25 **NM** value: **Cover or less**
Circ: CapCity orders: **4,625**
Mothers & Daughters, Part 3 **A:** Dave Sim; Gerhard **W:** Dave Sim
154 ❑ Jan 1992 Cover: 2.25 **NM** value: **Cover or less**
Circ: CapCity orders: **4,625**
Mothers & Daughters, Part 4 **A:** Dave Sim; Gerhard **W:** Dave Sim
155 ❑ Feb 1992 Cover: 2.25 **NM** value: **Cover or less**
Circ: CapCity orders: **4,550**
Mothers & Daughters, Part 5 **A:** Dave Sim; Gerhard **W:** Dave Sim
156 ❑ Mar 1992 Cover: 2.25 **NM** value: **Cover or less**
Circ: CapCity orders: **4,825**
Mothers & Daughters, Part 6 **A:** Dave Sim; Gerhard **W:** Dave Sim
157 ❑ Apr 1992 Cover: 2.25 **NM** value: **Cover or less**
Circ: CapCity orders: **4,975**
Mothers & Daughters, Part 7 **A:** Dave Sim; Gerhard **W:** Dave Sim
158 ❑ May 1992 Cover: 2.25 **NM** value: **Cover or less**
Circ: CapCity orders: **5,100**
Mothers & Daughters, Part 8 **A:** Dave Sim; Gerhard **W:** Dave Sim
159 ❑ Jun 1992 Cover: 2.25 **NM** value: **Cover or less**
Circ: CapCity orders: **5,175**
Mothers & Daughters, Part 9 **A:** Dave Sim; Gerhard **W:** Dave Sim
160 ❑ Jul 1992 Cover: 2.25 **NM** value: **Cover or less**
Circ: CapCity orders: **5,050**
Mothers & Daughters, Part 10 **A:** Dave Sim; Gerhard **W:** Dave Sim
161 ❑ Aug 1992 Cover: 2.25 **NM** value: **Cover or less**
Circ: CapCity orders: **5,175** • **CGC:** 1 graded, best 9.2
Mothers & Daughters, Part 11 • Bone back-up **A:** Dave Sim; Gerhard **W:** Dave Sim
162 ❑ Sep 1992 Cover: 2.25 **NM** value: **Cover or less**
Circ: CapCity orders: **5,175**
Mothers & Daughters, Part 12 **A:** Dave Sim; Gerhard **W:** Dave Sim
163 ❑ Oct 1992 Cover: 2.25 **NM** value: **Cover or less**
Circ: CapCity orders: **5,350**
Mothers & Daughters, Part 13 **A:** Dave Sim; Gerhard **W:** Dave Sim
164 ❑ Nov 1992 Cover: 2.25 **NM** value: **Cover or less**
Circ: CapCity orders: **5,200**
Mothers & Daughters, Part 14 **A:** Dave Sim; Gerhard **W:** Dave Sim
165 ❑ Dec 1992 Cover: 2.25 **NM** value: **Cover or less**
Circ: CapCity orders: **5,525**
Mothers & Daughters, Part 15 **A:** Dave Sim; Gerhard **W:** Dave Sim
165-2 ❑ Dec 1992 Cover: 2.25 **NM** value: **Cover or less**
166 ❑ Jan 1993 Cover: 2.25 **NM** value: **Cover or less**
Circ: CapCity orders: **5,450**
Mothers & Daughters, Part 16 **A:** Dave Sim; Gerhard **W:** Dave Sim
167 ❑ Feb 1993 Cover: 2.25 **NM** value: **Cover or less**
Circ: CapCity orders: **6,025**
Mothers & Daughters, Part 17 **A:** Dave Sim; Gerhard **W:** Dave Sim
168 ❑ Mar 1993 Cover: 2.25 **NM** value: **Cover or less**
Circ: CapCity orders: **6,150**
Mothers & Daughters, Part 18 **A:** Dave Sim; Gerhard **W:** Dave Sim
169 ❑ Apr 1993 Cover: 2.25 **NM** value: **Cover or less**
Circ: CapCity orders: **6,225**
Mothers & Daughters, Part 19 **A:** Dave Sim; Gerhard **W:** Dave Sim
170 ❑ May 1993 Cover: 2.25 **NM** value: **Cover or less**
Circ: CapCity orders: **6,200**
Mothers & Daughters, Part 20 **A:** Dave Sim; Gerhard **W:** Dave Sim
171 ❑ Jun 1993 Cover: 2.25 **NM** value: **Cover or less**
Circ: CapCity orders: **6,700**
Mothers & Daughters, Part 21 **A:** Dave Sim; Gerhard **W:** Dave Sim
172 ❑ Jul 1993 Cover: 2.25 **NM** value: **Cover or less**
Circ: CapCity orders: **6,325**
Mothers & Daughters, Part 22 **A:** Dave Sim; Gerhard **W:** Dave Sim
173 ❑ Aug 1993 Cover: 2.25 **NM** value: **Cover or less**
Circ: CapCity orders: **6,400**
Mothers & Daughters, Part 23 **A:** Dave Sim; Gerhard **W:** Dave Sim
174 ❑ Sep 1993 Cover: 2.25 **NM** value: **Cover or less**
Circ: CapCity orders: **6,575**
Mothers & Daughters, Part 24 **A:** Dave Sim; Gerhard **W:** Dave Sim
175 ❑ Oct 1993 Cover: 2.25 **NM** value: **Cover or less**
Circ: CapCity orders: **6,850**
Mothers & Daughters, Part 25; Reads, Part 1 **A:** Dave Sim; Gerhard **W:** Dave Sim
176 ❑ Nov 1993 Cover: 2.25 **NM** value: **Cover or less**
Circ: CapCity orders: **6,625**
Mothers & Daughters, Part 26; Reads, Part 2 **A:** Dave Sim; Gerhard **W:** Dave Sim
177 ❑ Dec 1993 Cover: 2.25 **NM** value: **Cover or less**
Circ: CapCity orders: **6,450**
Mothers & Daughters, Part 27; Reads, Part 3 **A:** Dave Sim; Gerhard **W:** Dave Sim
178 ❑ Jan 1994 Cover: 2.25 **NM** value: **Cover or less**
Circ: CapCity orders: **6,475**
Mothers & Daughters, Part 28; Reads, Part 4 **A:** Dave Sim; Gerhard **W:** Dave Sim
179 ❑ Feb 1994 Cover: 2.25 **NM** value: **Cover or less**
Circ: CapCity orders: **6,400**
Mothers & Daughters, Part 29; Reads, Part 5 **A:** Dave Sim; Gerhard **W:** Dave Sim
180 ❑ Mar 1994 Cover: 2.25 **NM** value: **Cover or less**
Circ: CapCity orders: **6,450**
Mothers & Daughters, Part 30; Reads, Part 6 **A:** Dave Sim; Gerhard **W:** Dave Sim
181 ❑ Apr 1994 Cover: 2.25 **NM** value: **Cover or less**
Circ: CapCity orders: **6,375**
Mothers & Daughters, Part 31; Reads, Part 7 **A:** Dave Sim; Gerhard **W:** Dave Sim
182 ❑ May 1994 Cover: 2.25 **NM** value: **Cover or less**
Circ: CapCity orders: **6,545**
Mothers & Daughters, Part 32; Reads, Part 8 **A:** Dave Sim; Gerhard **W:** Dave Sim
183 ❑ Jun 1994 Cover: 2.25 **NM** value: **Cover or less**
Circ: CapCity orders: **6,550**
Mothers & Daughters, Part 33; Reads, Part 9 **A:** Dave Sim; Gerhard **W:** Dave Sim
184 ❑ Jul 1994 Cover: 2.25 **NM** value: **Cover or less**
Circ: CapCity orders: **6,625**
Mothers & Daughters, Part 34; Reads, Part 10 **A:** Dave Sim; Gerhard **W:** Dave Sim
185 ❑ Aug 1994 Cover: 2.25 **NM** value: **Cover or less**
Circ: CapCity orders: **6,500**
Mothers & Daughters, Part 35; Reads, Part 11 **A:** Dave Sim; Gerhard **W:** Dave Sim
186 ❑ Sep 1994 Cover: 2.25 **NM** value: **Cover or less**
Circ: CapCity orders: **6,425**
Mothers & Daughters, Part 36; Reads, Part 12 **A:** Dave Sim; Gerhard **W:** Dave Sim
187 ❑ Oct 1994 Cover: 2.25 **NM** value: **Cover or less**
Circ: CapCity orders: **6,425**
Mothers & Daughters, Part 37 **A:** Dave Sim; Gerhard **W:** Dave Sim
188 ❑ Nov 1994 Cover: 2.25 **NM** value: **Cover or less**
Circ: CapCity orders: **5,920**
Mothers & Daughters, Part 38 **A:** Dave Sim; Gerhard **W:** Dave Sim
189 ❑ Dec 1994 Cover: 2.25 **NM** value: **Cover or less**
Circ: CapCity orders: **5,820**
Mothers & Daughters, Part 39 **A:** Dave Sim; Gerhard **W:** Dave Sim
190 ❑ Jan 1994 Cover: 2.25 **NM** value: **Cover or less**
Circ: CapCity orders: **5,540**
Mothers & Daughters, Part 40 **A:** Dave Sim; Gerhard **W:** Dave Sim
191 ❑ Feb 1994 Cover: 2.25 **NM** value: **Cover or less**
Circ: CapCity orders: **5,350**
Mothers & Daughters **A:** Dave Sim; Gerhard **W:** Dave Sim
192 ❑ Mar 1994 Cover: 2.25 **NM** value: **Cover or less**
Circ: CapCity orders: **5,360**
Mothers & Daughters **A:** Dave Sim; Gerhard **W:** Dave Sim
193 ❑ Apr 1994 Cover: 2.25 **NM** value: **Cover or less**
Circ: CapCity orders: **5,405**
Mothers & Daughters **A:** Dave Sim; Gerhard **W:** Dave Sim
194 ❑ May 1995 Cover: 2.25 **NM** value: **Cover or less**
Circ: CapCity orders: **5,325**
Mothers & Daughters **A:** Dave Sim; Gerhard **W:** Dave Sim
195 ❑ Jun 1995 Cover: 2.25 **NM** value: **Cover or less**
Circ: CapCity orders: **5,165**
Mothers & Daughters **A:** Dave Sim; Gerhard **W:** Dave Sim
196 ❑ Jul 1995 Cover: 2.25 **NM** value: **Cover or less**
Circ: CapCity orders: **5,245**
Mothers & Daughters **A:** Dave Sim; Gerhard **W:** Dave Sim
197 ❑ Aug 1995 Cover: 2.25 **NM** value: **Cover or less**
Circ: CapCity orders: **4,930**
Mothers & Daughters **A:** Dave Sim; Gerhard **W:** Dave Sim
198 ❑ Sep 1995 Cover: 2.25 **NM** value: **Cover or less**
Circ: CapCity orders: **4,615**
Mothers & Daughters **A:** Dave Sim; Gerhard **W:** Dave Sim
199 ❑ Oct 1995 Cover: 2.25 **NM** value: **Cover or less**
Mothers & Daughters **A:** Dave Sim; Gerhard **W:** Dave Sim
200 ❑ Nov 1995 Cover: 2.25 **NM** value: **Cover or less**
Mothers & Daughters • Patty Cake back-up **A:** Dave Sim; Gerhard **W:** Dave Sim
201 ❑ Dec 1995 Cover: 2.25 **NM** value: **Cover or less**
Guys, Part 1 **A:** Dave Sim; Gerhard **W:** Dave Sim
202 ❑ Jan 1996 Cover: 2.25 **NM** value: **Cover or less**
Guys, Part 2 **A:** Dave Sim; Gerhard **W:** Dave Sim
203 ❑ Feb 1996 Cover: 2.25 **NM** value: **Cover or less**
Guys, Part 3 **A:** Dave Sim; Gerhard **W:** Dave Sim
204 ❑ Mar 1996 Cover: 2.25 **NM** value: **Cover or less**
Guys, Part 4 **A:** Dave Sim; Gerhard **W:** Dave Sim
205 ❑ Apr 1996 Cover: 2.25 **NM** value: **Cover or less**
Guys, Part 5 **A:** Dave Sim; Gerhard **W:** Dave Sim
206 ❑ May 1996 Cover: 2.25 **NM** value: **Cover or less**
Guys, Part 6 **A:** Dave Sim; Gerhard **W:** Dave Sim
207 ❑ Jun 1996 Cover: 2.25 **NM** value: **Cover or less**
Guys, Part 7 **A:** Dave Sim; Gerhard **W:** Dave Sim
208 ❑ Jul 1996 Cover: 2.25 **NM** value: **Cover or less**
Guys, Part 8 **A:** Dave Sim; Gerhard **W:** Dave Sim
209 ❑ Aug 1996 Cover: 2.25 **NM** value: **Cover or less**
Guys, Part 9 **A:** Dave Sim; Gerhard **W:** Dave Sim
210 ❑ Sep 1996 Cover: 2.25 **NM** value: **Cover or less**
Circ: Diamd. preorders: **12,190**
Guys, Part 10 **A:** Dave Sim; Gerhard **W:** Dave Sim
211 ❑ Oct 1996 Cover: 2.25 **NM** value: **Cover or less**
Circ: Diamd. preorders: **12,140**
Guys, Part 11 **A:** Dave Sim; Gerhard **W:** Dave Sim
212 ❑ Nov 1996 Cover: 2.25 **NM** value: **Cover or less**
Circ: Direct Market orders: **11,874**
Guys, Part 12 **A:** Dave Sim; Gerhard **W:** Dave Sim
213 ❑ Dec 1996 Cover: 2.25 **NM** value: **Cover or less**
Circ: Direct Market orders: **11,469**
Guys, Part 13 **A:** Dave Sim; Gerhard **W:** Dave Sim
214 ❑ Jan 1997 Cover: 2.25 **NM** value: **Cover or less**
Circ: Direct Market orders: **10,911**
Guys, Part 14 **A:** Dave Sim; Gerhard **W:** Dave Sim
215 ❑ Feb 1997 Cover: 2.25 **NM** value: **Cover or less**
Circ: Diamd. preorders: **10,779**
Guys, Part 15 **A:** Dave Sim; Gerhard **W:** Dave Sim
216 ❑ Mar 1997 Cover: 2.25 **NM** value: **Cover or less**
Circ: Diamd. preorders: **10,129**
Guys, Part 16 **A:** Dave Sim; Gerhard **W:** Dave Sim
217 ❑ Apr 1997 Cover: 2.25 **NM** value: **Cover or less**
Circ: Diamd. preorders: **10,250**
Guys, Part 17 **A:** Dave Sim; Gerhard **W:** Dave Sim
218 ❑ May 1997 Cover: 2.25 **NM** value: **Cover or less**
Circ: Diamd. preorders: **10,789**
Guys, Part 18 **A:** Dave Sim; Gerhard **W:** Dave Sim
219 ❑ Jun 1997 Cover: 2.25 **NM** value: **Cover or less**
Circ: Diamd. preorders: **10,997**
Guys, Part 19 **A:** Dave Sim; Gerhard **W:** Dave Sim
220 ❑ Jul 1997 Cover: 2.25 **NM** value: **Cover or less**
Circ: Diamd. preorders: **10,642**
Rick's Story, Part 1 **A:** Dave Sim; Gerhard **W:** Dave Sim
221 ❑ Aug 1997 Cover: 2.25 **NM** value: **Cover or less**
Circ: Diamd. preorders: **10,322**
Rick's Story, Part 2 **A:** Dave Sim; Gerhard **W:** Dave Sim
222 ❑ Sep 1997 Cover: 2.25 **NM** value: **Cover or less**
Circ: Diamd. preorders: **10,804**
Rick's Story, Part 3 **A:** Dave Sim; Gerhard **W:** Dave Sim
223 ❑ Oct 1997 Cover: 2.25 **NM** value: **Cover or less**
Circ: Diamd. preorders: **10,714**
Rick's Story, Part 4 **A:** Dave Sim; Gerhard **W:** Dave Sim
224 ❑ Nov 1997 Cover: 2.25 **NM** value: **Cover or less**
Circ: Diamd. preorders: **10,688**
Rick's Story, Part 5 **A:** Dave Sim; Gerhard **W:** Dave Sim
225 ❑ Dec 1997 Cover: 2.25 **NM** value: **Cover or less**
Circ: Diamd. preorders: **10,507**
Rick's Story, Part 6 **A:** Dave Sim; Gerhard **W:** Dave Sim
226 ❑ Jan 1998 Cover: 2.25 **NM** value: **Cover or less**
Circ: Diamd. preorders: **10,321**
Rick's Story, Part 7 **A:** Dave Sim; Gerhard **W:** Dave Sim
227 ❑ Feb 1998 Cover: 2.25 **NM** value: **Cover or less**
Circ: Diamd. preorders: **10,012**
Rick's Story, Part 8 **A:** Dave Sim; Gerhard **W:** Dave Sim
228 ❑ Mar 1998 Cover: 2.25 **NM** value: **Cover or less**
Circ: Diamd. preorders: **9,926**
Rick's Story, Part 9 **A:** Dave Sim; Gerhard **W:** Dave Sim
229 ❑ Apr 1998 Cover: 2.25 **NM** value: **Cover or less**
Circ: Diamd. preorders: **10,095**
Rick's Story, Part 10 **A:** Dave Sim; Gerhard **W:** Dave Sim

Other grades: Multiply prices above by **1.5 for Mint • 2/3 for Very Fine • 1/3 for Fine • 1/5 for Very Good • 1/8 for Good**

230 ❑ May 1998 Cover: 2.25 **NM value: Cover or less**
Circ: Diamd. preorders: **9,621**
📖 Rick's Story, Part 11 **A:** Dave Sim; Gerhard **W:** Dave Sim
231 ❑ Jun 1998 Cover: 2.25 **NM value: Cover or less**
Circ: Diamd. preorders: **9,594**
📖 Rick's Story, Part 12 **A:** Dave Sim; Gerhard **W:** Dave Sim
232 ❑ Jul 1998 Cover: 2.25 **NM value: Cover or less**
Circ: Diamd. preorders: **9,388**
📖 Going Home, Part 1 **A:** Dave Sim; Gerhard **W:** Dave Sim
233 ❑ Aug 1998 Cover: 2.25 **NM value: Cover or less**
Circ: Diamd. preorders: **9,038**
📖 Going Home, Part 2 **A:** Dave Sim; Gerhard **W:** Dave Sim
234 ❑ Sep 1998 Cover: 2.25 **NM value: Cover or less**
Circ: Diamd. preorders: **9,120**
📖 Going Home, Part 3 **A:** Dave Sim; Gerhard **W:** Dave Sim
235 ❑ Oct 1998 Cover: 2.25 **NM value: Cover or less**
Circ: Diamd. preorders: **9,149**
📖 Going Home, Part 4 **A:** Dave Sim; Gerhard **W:** Dave Sim
236 ❑ Nov 1998 Cover: 2.25 **NM value: Cover or less**
Circ: Diamd. preorders: **9,121**
📖 Going Home, Part 5 **A:** Dave Sim; Gerhard **W:** Dave Sim
237 ❑ Dec 1998 Cover: 2.25 **NM value: Cover or less**
Circ: Diamd. preorders: **8,984**
📖 Going Home, Part 6 **A:** Dave Sim; Gerhard **W:** Dave Sim
238 ❑ Jan 1999 Cover: 2.25 **NM value: Cover or less**
Circ: Diamd. preorders: **8,869**
📖 Going Home, Part 7 **A:** Dave Sim; Gerhard **W:** Dave Sim
239 ❑ Feb 1999 Cover: 2.25 **NM value: Cover or less**
Circ: Diamd. preorders: **8,700**
📖 Going Home, Part 8 **A:** Dave Sim; Gerhard **W:** Dave Sim
240 ❑ Mar 1999 Cover: 2.25 **NM value: Cover or less**
Circ: Diamd. preorders: **8,703**
📖 Going Home, Part 9 **A:** Dave Sim; Gerhard **W:** Dave Sim
241 ❑ Apr 1999 Cover: 2.25 **NM value: Cover or less**
Circ: Diamd. preorders: **8,891**
📖 Going Home, Part 10 **A:** Dave Sim; Gerhard **W:** Dave Sim
242 ❑ May 1999 Cover: 2.25 **NM value: Cover or less**
Circ: Diamd. preorders: **8,592**
📖 Going Home, Part 11 **A:** Dave Sim; Gerhard **W:** Dave Sim
243 ❑ Jun 1999 Cover: 2.25 **NM value: Cover or less**
Circ: Diamd. preorders: **8,534**
📖 Going Home, Part 12 **A:** Dave Sim; Gerhard **W:** Dave Sim
244 ❑ Jul 1999 Cover: 2.25 **NM value: Cover or less**
Circ: Diamd. preorders: **8,434**
📖 Going Home, Part 13 **A:** Dave Sim; Gerhard **W:** Dave Sim
245 ❑ Aug 1999 Cover: 2.25 **NM value: Cover or less**
Circ: Diamd. preorders: **8,261**
📖 Going Home, Part 14 **A:** Dave Sim; Gerhard **W:** Dave Sim
246 ❑ Sep 1999 Cover: 2.25 **NM value: Cover or less**
Circ: Diamd. preorders: **8,140**
📖 Going Home, Part 15 **A:** Dave Sim; Gerhard **W:** Dave Sim
247 ❑ Oct 1999 Cover: 2.25 **NM value: Cover or less**
Circ: Diamd. preorders: **8,230**
📖 Going Home, Part 16 **A:** Dave Sim; Gerhard **W:** Dave Sim
248 ❑ Nov 1999 Cover: 2.25 **NM value: Cover or less**
Circ: Diamd. preorders: **8,042**
📖 Going Home, Part 17 **A:** Dave Sim; Gerhard **W:** Dave Sim
249 ❑ Dec 1999 Cover: 2.25 **NM value: Cover or less**
Circ: Diamd. preorders: **7,861**
📖 Going Home, Part 18 **A:** Dave Sim; Gerhard **W:** Dave Sim
250 ❑ Jan 2000 Cover: 2.25 **NM value: Cover or less**
Circ: Diamd. preorders: **7,789**
📖 Going Home, Part 19 **A:** Dave Sim; Gerhard **W:** Dave Sim
251 ❑ Feb 2000 Cover: 2.25 **NM value: Cover or less**
Circ: Diamd. preorders: **7,379**
📖 Going Home, Part 20 **A:** Dave Sim; Gerhard **W:** Dave Sim
252 ❑ Mar 2000 Cover: 2.25 **NM value: Cover or less**
Circ: Diamd. preorders: **7,686**
📖 Going Home, Part 21 **A:** Dave Sim; Gerhard **W:** Dave Sim
253 ❑ Apr 2000 Cover: 2.25 **NM value: Cover or less**
Circ: Diamd. preorders: **7,478**
📖 Going Home, Part 22 **A:** Dave Sim; Gerhard **W:** Dave Sim
254 ❑ May 2000 Cover: 2.25 **NM value: Cover or less**
Circ: Diamd. preorders: **7,470**
📖 Going Home, Part 23 **A:** Dave Sim; Gerhard **W:** Dave Sim
255 ❑ Jun 2000 Cover: 2.25 **NM value: Cover or less**
Circ: Diamd. preorders: **7,634**
📖 Going Home, Part 24 **A:** Dave Sim; Gerhard **W:** Dave Sim
256 ❑ Jul 2000 Cover: 2.25 **NM value: Cover or less**
Circ: Diamd. preorders: **7,543**
📖 Going Home, Part 25 **A:** Dave Sim; Gerhard **W:** Dave Sim
257 ❑ Aug 2000 Cover: 2.25 **NM value: Cover or less**
Circ: Diamd. preorders: **7,139**
📖 Going Home, Part 26 **A:** Dave Sim; Gerhard **W:** Dave Sim
258 ❑ Sep 2000 Cover: 2.25 **NM value: Cover or less**
Circ: Diamd. preorders: **7,277**
📖 Going Home, Part 27 **A:** Dave Sim; Gerhard **W:** Dave Sim
259 ❑ Oct 2000 Cover: 2.25 **NM value: Cover or less**
Circ: Diamd. preorders: **7,286**
📖 Going Home, Part 28 **A:** Dave Sim; Gerhard **W:** Dave Sim
260 ❑ Nov 2000 Cover: 2.25 **NM value: Cover or less**
Circ: Diamd. preorders: **7,249**
📖 Going Home, Part 29 **A:** Dave Sim; Gerhard **W:** Dave Sim
261 ❑ Dec 2000 Cover: 2.25 **NM value: Cover or less**
Circ: Diamd. preorders: **6,977**
📖 Going Home, Part 30 **A:** Dave Sim; Gerhard **W:** Dave Sim
262 ❑ Jan 2001 Cover: 2.25 **NM value: Cover or less**
Circ: Diamd. preorders: **7,002**
A: Dave Sim; Gerhard **W:** Dave Sim
263 ❑ Feb 2001 Cover: 2.25 **NM value: Cover or less**
Circ: Diamd. preorders: **6,953**
A: Dave Sim; Gerhard **W:** Dave Sim
264 ❑ Mar 2001 Cover: 2.25 **NM value: Cover or less**
Circ: Diamd. preorders: **6,890**
A: Dave Sim; Gerhard **W:** Dave Sim
265 ❑ Apr 2001 Cover: 2.25 **NM value: Cover or less**
Circ: Diamd. preorders: **6,908**
A: Dave Sim; Gerhard **W:** Dave Sim
266 ❑ May 2001 Cover: 2.25 **NM value: Cover or less**
Circ: Diamd. preorders: **7,011**
A: Dave Sim; Gerhard **W:** Dave Sim
267 ❑ Jun 2001 Cover: 2.25 **NM value: Cover or less**
Circ: Diamd. preorders: **7,123**
A: Dave Sim; Gerhard **W:** Dave Sim
268 ❑ Jul 2001 Cover: 2.25 **NM value: Cover or less**
Circ: Diamd. preorders: **7,565**
A: Dave Sim; Gerhard **W:** Dave Sim
Bk 1 ❑ Cover: 25.00 **NM value: Cover or less**
• Cerebus; "Phone book": Collects Cerebus #1-25 **A:** Dave Sim **W:** Dave Sim
Bk 2 ❑ Cover: 25.00 **NM value: Cover or less**
• High Society "phone book"; Reprints Cerebus the Aardvark #26-50 **A:** Dave Sim **W:** Dave Sim
Bk 3 ❑ Cover: 30.00 **NM value: Cover or less**
• Church & State 1 "phone book"; Reprints Cerebus the Aardvark #52-? **A:** Dave Sim; Gerhard **W:** Dave Sim
Bk 4 ❑ Cover: 30.00 **NM value: Cover or less**
• Church & State 2 "phone book"; Reprints Cerebus the Aardvark #?-111 **A:** Dave Sim; Gerhard **W:** Dave Sim
Bk 5 ❑ Cover: 25.00 **NM value: Cover or less**
• Jaka's Story "phone book"; Reprints Cerebus the Aardvark #114-136 **A:** Dave Sim; Gerhard **W:** Dave Sim
Bk 6 ❑ Cover: 17.00 **NM value: Cover or less**
• Melmoth "phone book": Collects Cerebus the Aardvark #139-150 **A:** Dave Sim; Gerhard **W:** Dave Sim
Bk 7 ❑ Cover: 17.00 **NM value: Cover or less**
• Flight "phone book": Collects Cerebus the Aardvark #151-162 **A:** Dave Sim; Gerhard **W:** Dave Sim
Bk 8 ❑ Cover: 17.00 **NM value: Cover or less**
• Women "phone book"; Reprints Cerebus the Aardvark #163-174 **A:** Dave Sim; Gerhard **W:** Dave Sim
Bk 9 ❑ Cover: 17.00 **NM value: Cover or less**
• Reads "phone book"; Reprints Cerebus the Aardvark #175-186 **A:** Dave Sim; Gerhard **W:** Dave Sim
Bk 10 ❑ Cover: 17.00 **NM value: Cover or less**
• Minds "Phone Book"; Reprints Cerebus the Aardvark #187-200 **A:** Dave Sim; Gerhard **W:** Dave Sim

CEREBUS WORLD TOUR BOOK — Aardvark-Vanaheim

1 ❑ b&w Cover: 2.95 **NM value: Cover or less**
No issue number.

CHADZ FRENDZ — Smiling Face

1 ❑ Jan 1998 Cover: 1.50 **NM value: Cover or less**
📖 Chad The Chicken; Don't Sleep in My Class; Babe's Egg **A:** Fraser D. Graham **W:** Fraser D. Graham

CHAINGANG — Northstar

1 ❑ b&w Cover: 2.50 **NM value: Cover or less**
2 ❑ Cover: 2.50 **NM value: Cover or less**

CHAIN GANG WAR — DC

One of the most disturbing problems with super-heroes is that the people they work so hard to catch — whether it be Doctor Octopus or some street thug — never seem to spend much time in jail. Inevitably, these goons either escape or the legal system lets them off. Either way, they'll be back soon to menace innocent people.

The three people at the heart of the Chain Gang War have a novel solution to this problem. Distrustful of the system, they have taken matters into their own hands. Now, when gangsters such as Carlo Brunetti evade justice, the Chain Gang makes it their business to put things right. But, while vigilantes like The Punisher would just kill these criminals, members of the Chain Gang feel it's important that the villains serve time — in their jail.

1 ❑ Jul 1993 Cover: 2.50 **NM value: Cover or less**
Circ: CapCity orders: **30,500**
Foil embossed cover. 📖 Chain Reaction **A:** Dave Johnson **W:** John Wagner
1/SI ❑ Cover: 2.50 **NM value: 4.00**
• Silver promotional edition. 📖 Chain Reaction **A:** Dave Johnson **W:** John Wagner
2 ❑ Aug 1993 Cover: 1.75 **NM value: 2.00**
Circ: CapCity orders: **11,400**
A: Dave Johnson **W:** John Wagner
3 ❑ Sep 1993 Cover: 1.75 **NM value: 2.00**
Circ: CapCity orders: **8,400**
📖 Weak Link **A:** Dave Johnson **W:** John Wagner
4 ❑ Oct 1993 Cover: 1.75 **NM value: 2.00**
Circ: CapCity orders: **7,000**
W: John Wagner
5 ❑ Nov 1993 Cover: 2.50 **NM value: Cover or less**
Circ: CapCity orders: **12,600**
Embossed cover. **W:** John Wagner ★ Appearance of Deathstroke, Azrael, Batman.
6 ❑ Dec 1993 Cover: 1.75 **NM value: Cover or less**
Circ: CapCity orders: **9,550**
W: John Wagner
7 ❑ Jan 1994 Cover: 1.75 **NM value: Cover or less**
Circ: CapCity orders: **4,600**
📖 Jail Break **A:** Gary Erskine **W:** John Wagner
8 ❑ Feb 1994 Cover: 1.75 **NM value: Cover or less**
Circ: CapCity orders: **4,250**
📖 The Crooked Man, Part 1 **A:** Dave Johnson **W:** John Wagner
9 ❑ Mar 1994 Cover: 1.75 **NM value: Cover or less**
Circ: CapCity orders: **3,550**
📖 The Crooked Man, Part 2 **A:** Frederico Cueva **W:** John Wagner
10 ❑ Apr 1994 Cover: 1.75 **NM value: Cover or less**
Circ: CapCity orders: **3,400**
📖 The Crooked Man, Part 3 **A:** Frederico Cueva **W:** John Wagner
11 ❑ May 1994 Cover: 1.75 **NM value: Cover or less**
Circ: CapCity orders: **3,550**
📖 The Crooked Man, Part 4 **A:** Gary Erskine; Dave Johnson **W:** John Wagner
12 ❑ Jun 1994 Cover: 1.75 **NM value: 2.00**
Circ: CapCity orders: **3,050**
📖 Meltdown final issue. • End of Chain Gang **A:** Dave Johnson **W:** John Wagner ★ Death of Curtis Zecker.

CHAINSAW VIGILANTE — NEC

1 ❑ Cover: 3.25 **NM value: 3.50**
Circ: CapCity orders: **3,865**
📖 Night Of Lumber Equipment And Minor Surgery **A:** Zander Cannon **W:** Zander Cannon ★ Appearance of Tick.
1/A ❑ Cover: 14.00 **NM value: Cover or less**
Orange cover. **A:** Zander Cannon **W:** Zander Cannon
1/B ❑ Cover: 17.00 **NM value: Cover or less**
Gold foil cover. **A:** Zander Cannon **W:** Zander Cannon
1/C ❑ Cover: 25.00 **NM value: Cover or less**
Pseudo-3D "platinum" foil cover. **A:** Zander Cannon **W:** Zander Cannon
2 ❑ Cover: 2.75 **NM value: Cover or less**
A: Zander Cannon **W:** Zander Cannon
3 ❑ Cover: 2.75 **NM value: Cover or less**
A: Zander Cannon **W:** Zander Cannon
Bk 1 ❑ Cover: 5.00 **NM value: Cover or less**
• Chainsaw Vigilante Bonanza **A:** Zander Cannon **W:** Zander Cannon

CHAINS OF CHAOS — Harris

1 ❑ Nov 1994 Cover: 2.95 **NM value: Cover or less**
Circ: CapCity orders: **18,450**
📖 Link One **A:** John Stinman **W:** Tom Sniegoski
2 ❑ Dec 1994 Cover: 2.95 **NM value: Cover or less**
Circ: CapCity orders: **13,075**
A: Caesar **W:** Tom Sniegoski
3 ❑ Jan 1995 Cover: 2.95 **NM value: Cover or less**
Circ: CapCity orders: **14,625**
📖 Link III **A:** Caesar **W:** Tom Sniegoski

CHAKAN — Rak

1 ❑ b&w **NM value: 4.00**

CHALLENGE OF THE UNKNOWN — Ace

6 ❑ Sep 1950 Cover: 0.10 **NM value: 225.00**
• **CGC:** 1 graded, best 8.5

CHALLENGERS OF THE FANTASTIC — Marvel / Amalgam

1 ❑ Jun 1997 Cover: 1.95 **NM value: 2.00**
A: Tom Grummettt; Al Vey(inks) **W:** Karl Kesel

CHALLENGERS OF THE UNKNOWN — DC

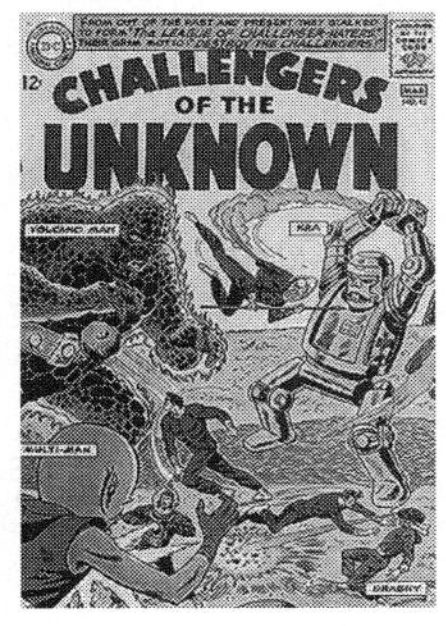

Pilot Ace Morgan, wrestler Rocky Davis, acrobat Red Ryan, and professional diver Professor Haley were strangers en route to an appearance on the "Heroes" radio show. There they were to be honored for their individual acts of heroism. On the way, however, their plane was caught in a violent storm and crashed. The four miraculously survived, but they were changed by the experience. They felt they were living on borrowed time and decided to take on all life's challenges for as long as it lasted. Thus the four strangers became the Challengers of the Unknown, fearless adventurers dedicated to exploring the edges of existence.

The group first debuted in Showcase #6, later going on to star in this long-lived series which ran on-and-off from 1958 to 1978.

1 ❑ May 1958 Cover: 0.10 **NM value: 2000.00**
• **CGC:** 13 graded, best 9.4
📖 The Man Who Tampered with Infinity; The Human Pets **A:** Jack Kirby
2 ❑ Jul 1958 Cover: 0.10 **NM value: 750.00**
• **CGC:** 3 graded, best 8.0
📖 The Traitorous Challenger; The Monster Maker **A:** Jack Kirby
3 ❑ Sep 1958 Cover: 0.10 **NM value: 625.00**
• **CGC:** 2 graded, best 7.5
📖 The Secret of the Sorcerer's Mirror; Menace of the Invincible Challenger **A:** Jack Kirby
4 ❑ Nov 1958 Cover: 0.10 **NM value: 510.00**
• **CGC:** 3 graded, best 9.0
📖 The Wizard of Time **A:** Jack Kirby; Wally Wood
5 ❑ Jan 1959 Cover: 0.10 **NM value: 510.00**
• **CGC:** 3 graded, best 9.0
📖 The Riddle of the Star-Stone **A:** Jack Kirby; Wally Wood
6 ❑ Mar 1959 Cover: 0.10 **NM value: 510.00**
• **CGC:** 2 graded, best 9.0
📖 Captives of the Space Circus; The Sorceress of Forbidden Valley **A:** Jack Kirby; Wally Wood
7 ❑ May 1959 Cover: 0.10 **NM value: 510.00**
• **CGC:** 2 graded, best 9.0
📖 The Beasts from Planet Nine; The Isle of No Return **A:** Jack Kirby; Wally Wood
8 ❑ Jul 1959 Cover: 0.10 **NM value: 510.00**
• **CGC:** 3 graded, best 9.0
📖 The Man Who Stole the Future; The Prisoners of Robot Planet **A:** Jack Kirby; Wally Wood

CGC-graded: Multiply prices above by **33 for 9.9 M • 16 for 9.8 NM/M • 7 for 9.6 NM+ • 5 for 9.4 NM • 2.5 for 9.2 NM- • 1.5 for 9.0 VF/NM**

9 ❑ Sep 1959 Cover: 0.10 **NM** value: **300.00**
• **CGC:** 2 graded, best 7.0
A: Jack Kirby
10 ❑ Nov 1959 Cover: 0.10 **NM** value: **300.00**
A: Jack Kirby
11 ❑ Jan 1960 Cover: 0.10 **NM** value: **200.00**
Circ: Statement: **228,000** • **CGC:** 2 graded, best 8.5
12 ❑ Mar 1960 Cover: 0.10 **NM** value: **200.00**
Circ: Statement: **228,000**
13 ❑ May 1960 Cover: 0.10 **NM** value: **200.00**
Circ: Statement: **228,000**
14 ❑ Jul 1960 Cover: 0.10 **NM** value: **200.00**
Circ: Statement: **228,000**
★ Origin of Multi-Man. ★ 1st Appearance of Multi-Man.
15 ❑ Sep 1960 Cover: 0.10 **NM** value: **200.00**
Circ: Statement: **228,000**
16 ❑ Nov 1960 Cover: 0.10 **NM** value: **120.00**
Circ: Statement: **228,000** • **CGC:** 1 graded, best 9.2
17 ❑ Jan 1961 Cover: 0.10 **NM** value: **120.00**
Circ: Statement: **235,000** • **CGC:** 1 graded, best 9.0
18 ❑ Mar 1961 Cover: 0.10 **NM** value: **120.00**
Circ: Statement: **235,000**
★ 1st Appearance of Cosmo (Challengers of the Unknown's Pet).
19 ❑ May 1961 Cover: 0.10 **NM** value: **120.00**
Circ: Statement: **235,000** • **CGC:** 3 graded, best 7.0
20 ❑ Jul 1961 Cover: 0.10 **NM** value: **120.00**
Circ: Statement: **235,000** • **CGC:** 1 graded, best 9.0
21 ❑ Sep 1961 Cover: 0.10 **NM** value: **70.00**
Circ: Statement: **235,000** • **CGC:** 2 graded, best 7.0
22 ❑ Nov 1961 Cover: 0.10 **NM** value: **70.00**
Circ: Statement: **235,000** • **CGC:** 1 graded, best 8.0
23 ❑ Jan 1962 Cover: 0.12 **NM** value: **70.00**
Circ: Statement: **195,000** • **CGC:** 1 graded, best 9.0
24 ❑ Mar 1962 Cover: 0.12 **NM** value: **70.00**
Circ: Statement: **195,000** • **CGC:** 2 graded, best 9.2
25 ❑ May 1962 Cover: 0.12 **NM** value: **70.00**
Circ: Statement: **195,000** • **CGC:** 2 graded, best 7.0
26 ❑ Jul 1962 Cover: 0.12 **NM** value: **70.00**
Circ: Statement: **195,000** • **CGC:** 2 graded, best 7.5
27 ❑ Sep 1962 Cover: 0.12 **NM** value: **70.00**
Circ: Statement: **195,000** • **CGC:** 3 graded, best 9.0
28 ❑ Nov 1962 Cover: 0.12 **NM** value: **70.00**
Circ: Statement: **195,000** • **CGC:** 1 graded, best 5.5
29 ❑ Jan 1963 Cover: 0.12 **NM** value: **70.00**
• **CGC:** 3 graded, best 9.6
30 ❑ Mar 1963 Cover: 0.12 **NM** value: **70.00**
• **CGC:** 3 graded, best 9.2
• Has 1962 Statement; avg total paid circ 195,000
31 ❑ May 1963 Cover: 0.12 **NM** value: **80.00**
• **CGC:** 3 graded, best 9.2
★ Origin of Challengers of the Unknown.
32 ❑ Jul 1963 Cover: 0.12 **NM** value: **42.00**
• **CGC:** 2 graded, best 9.6
33 ❑ Sep 1963 Cover: 0.12 **NM** value: **42.00**
• **CGC:** 2 graded, best 9.2
34 ❑ Nov 1963 Cover: 0.12 **NM** value: **42.00**
• **CGC:** 3 graded, best 9.4
★ Origin of Multi-Woman. ★ 1st Appearance of Multi-Woman.
35 ❑ Jan 1964 Cover: 0.12 **NM** value: **42.00**
• **CGC:** 2 graded, best 9.4
36 ❑ Mar 1964 Cover: 0.12 **NM** value: **42.00**
• **CGC:** 1 graded, best 9.0
• Has 1963 Statement, filed 10/1/63; no circ figures published
37 ❑ May 1964 Cover: 0.12 **NM** value: **42.00**
• **CGC:** 2 graded, best 9.2
38 ❑ Jul 1964 Cover: 0.12 **NM** value: **42.00**
• **CGC:** 1 graded, best 9.2
39 ❑ Sep 1964 Cover: 0.12 **NM** value: **42.00**
• **CGC:** 1 graded, best 8.5
40 ❑ Nov 1964 Cover: 0.12 **NM** value: **42.00**
• **CGC:** 1 graded, best 8.0
📖 The Super Powers of the Challengers **A:** Bob Brown **W:** F.E. Herron
41 ❑ Jan 1965 Cover: 0.12 **NM** value: **24.00**
Circ: Statement: **220,965** • **CGC:** 1 graded, best 7.5
42 ❑ Mar 1965 Cover: 0.12 **NM** value: **24.00**
Circ: Statement: **220,965** • **CGC:** 1 graded, best 9.4
📖 The League Of Challenger Haters
43 ❑ May 1965 Cover: 0.12 **NM** value: **24.00**
Circ: Statement: **220,965** • **CGC:** 1 graded, best 9.0
• Challengers of the Unknown get new uniforms; Has 1964 Statement, filed 10/1/64; no circ figures published
44 ❑ Jul 1965 Cover: 0.12 **NM** value: **24.00**
Circ: Statement: **220,965** • **CGC:** 1 graded, best 9.0
45 ❑ Sep 1965 Cover: 0.12 **NM** value: **24.00**
Circ: Statement: **220,965** • **CGC:** 2 graded, best 9.4
46 ❑ Nov 1965 Cover: 0.12 **NM** value: **24.00**
Circ: Statement: **220,965**
47 ❑ Jan 1966 Cover: 0.12 **NM** value: **24.00**
Circ: Statement: **210,316**
48 ❑ Mar 1966 Cover: 0.12 **NM** value: **24.00**
Circ: Statement: **210,316** • **CGC:** 1 graded, best 9.4
★ Appearance of The Doom Patrol.
49 ❑ May 1966 Cover: 0.12 **NM** value: **24.00**
Circ: Statement: **210,316** • **CGC:** 1 graded, best 3.0
50 ❑ Jul 1966 Cover: 0.12 **NM** value: **24.00**
Circ: Statement: **210,316**
📖 Final Hour for the Challengers **A:** Bob Brown **W:** F.E. Herron
★ 1st Appearance of Villo.
51 ❑ Sep 1966 Cover: 0.12 **NM** value: **20.00**
Circ: Statement: **210,316** • **CGC:** 1 graded, best 5.0
• Has 1965 Statement; avg print run 347,000; avg sales 220,000; avg subs 965; avg total paid 220,965; samples 142; max existent 221,107; 36% of run returned ★ Appearance of Sea Devils. ★ Versus Sponge Man.
52 ❑ Nov 1966 Cover: 0.12 **NM** value: **20.00**
Circ: Statement: **210,316**
53 ❑ Jan 1967 Cover: 0.12 **NM** value: **20.00**
Circ: Statement: **182,200**
54 ❑ Mar 1967 Cover: 0.12 **NM** value: **20.00**
Circ: Statement: **182,200**
55 ❑ May 1967 Cover: 0.12 **NM** value: **20.00**
Circ: Statement: **182,200**
★ 1st Appearance of Tino Manarry. ★ Death of Red Ryan.
56 ❑ Jul 1967 Cover: 0.12 **NM** value: **20.00**
Circ: Statement: **182,200** • **CGC:** 1 graded, best 9.4
57 ❑ Sep 1967 Cover: 0.12 **NM** value: **20.00**
Circ: Statement: **182,200**
58 ❑ Nov 1967 Cover: 0.12 **NM** value: **20.00**
Circ: Statement: **182,200** • **CGC:** 1 graded, best 9.2
★ Versus Neutro.
59 ❑ Jan 1968 Cover: 0.12 **NM** value: **20.00**
Circ: Statement: **166,450**
60 ❑ Mar 1968 Cover: 0.12 **NM** value: **20.00**
Circ: Statement: **166,450** • **CGC:** 1 graded, best 9.2
• Red Ryan returns
61 ❑ May 1968 Cover: 0.12 **NM** value: **7.00**
Circ: Statement: **166,450**
62 ❑ Jul 1968 Cover: 0.12 **NM** value: **7.00**
Circ: Statement: **166,450** • **CGC:** 1 graded, best 9.6
63 ❑ Sep 1968 Cover: 0.12 **NM** value: **7.00**
Circ: Statement: **166,450**
64 ❑ Nov 1968 Cover: 0.12 **NM** value: **7.00**
Circ: Statement: **166,450**
📖 The Secrets of the Sorcerer's Box • reprints Showcase #6 **A:** Jack Kirby ★ Origin of Challengers of the Unknown.
65 ❑ Jan 1969 Cover: 0.12 **NM** value: **7.00**
Circ: Statement: **140,238**
📖 The Freezing Sun • reprints Showcase #6 **A:** Jack Kirby ★ Origin of Challengers of the Unknown.
66 ❑ Mar 1969 Cover: 0.12 **NM** value: **7.00**
Circ: Statement: **140,238** • **CGC:** 2 graded, best 9.6
67 ❑ May 1969 Cover: 0.12 **NM** value: **7.00**
Circ: Statement: **140,238**
• Has 1968 Statement, filed 10/1/68; avg print run 317,000; avg sales 166,000; avg subs 450; avg total paid 166,450; samples 386; max existent 166,836; 47% of run returned
68 ❑ Jul 1969 Cover: 0.12 **NM** value: **7.00**
Circ: Statement: **140,238** • **CGC:** 1 graded, best 9.4
📖 One Of Us Is A Madman **A:** Jack Sparling; Vince Colletta **W:** Denny O'Neil
69 ❑ Sep 1969 Cover: 0.15 **NM** value: **7.00**
Circ: Statement: **140,238**
★ 1st Appearance of Corinna.
70 ❑ Nov 1969 Cover: 0.15 **NM** value: **7.00**
Circ: Statement: **140,238**
71 ❑ Jan 1970 Cover: 0.15 **NM** value: **7.00**
72 ❑ Mar 1970 Cover: 0.15 **NM** value: **7.00**
73 ❑ May 1970 Cover: 0.15 **NM** value: **7.00**
• Has 1969 Statement, filed 10/1/69; avg print run 290,000; avg sales 140,000; avg subs 238; avg total paid 140,238; samples 246; max existent 140,584; 52% of run returned
74 ❑ Jul 1970 Cover: 0.15 **NM** value: **14.00**
• **CGC:** 1 graded, best 9.6
A: Neal Adams ★ Appearance of Deadman.
75 ❑ Sep 1970 Cover: 0.15 **NM** value: **7.00**
📖 Ultivac is Loose • reprints Showcase #7 **A:** Jack Kirby ★ Versus Ultivac.
76 ❑ Nov 1970 Cover: 0.15 **NM** value: **7.00**
📖 The Traitorous Challenger; The Secret of the Sorcerer's Mirror • Reprints stories from Challengers of the Unknown #2 & #3
77 ❑ Jan 1971 Cover: 0.15 **NM** value: **7.00**
📖 The Menace of the Ancient Vials • reprints Showcase #12
78 ❑ Feb 1973 Cover: 0.20 **NM** value: **7.00**
📖 The Isle of No Return; The Sorceress of Forbidden Valley • Reprints stories from Challengers of the Unknown #6 & #7
79 ❑ Apr 1973 Cover: 0.20 **NM** value: **7.00**
📖 The Monster Maker; The Human Pets • reprints stories from Challengers of the Unknown #1 and 2 **C:** Joe Kubert
80 ❑ Jul 1973 Cover: 0.20 **NM** value: **7.00**
📖 The Day the Earth Blew Up • reprints Showcase #11; series goes on hiatus for four years
81 ❑ Jul 1977 Cover: 0.20 **NM** value: **6.00**
82 ❑ Aug 1977 Cover: 0.20 **NM** value: **5.00**
• **CGC:** 1 graded, best 9.6
★ Appearance of Swamp Thing.
83 ❑ Oct 1977 Cover: 0.20 **NM** value: **5.00**
84 ❑ Dec 1977 Cover: 0.20 **NM** value: **5.00**
85 ❑ Feb 1978 Cover: 0.20 **NM** value: **5.00**
• **CGC:** 2 graded, best 9.6
★ Appearance of Deadman, Swamp Thing.
86 ❑ Apr 1978 Cover: 0.20 **NM** value: **5.00**
★ Appearance of Deadman, Swamp Thing.
87 ❑ Jul 1978 Cover: 0.35 **NM** value: **5.00**
final issue. **A:** Keith Giffen ★ Appearance of Deadman, Swamp Thing, Rip Hunter.

CHALLENGERS OF THE UNKNOWN (2ND SERIES) DC

One of the more interesting attempts to revive the first super-team of the Silver Age, this ongoing series does not include any of the original Challengers of the Unknown (except for guest appearances). Nor is it as lighthearted as the concept that spawned it.

Here, the supernatural is the "unknown" challenged by the new team, composed of racecar driver Clay Brody, pilot Marlon Corbett, software designer Kenn Kawa, and theoretical physicist Brenda Ruskin. Instead of the garish monsters and world-dominating villains their predecessors battled, this quartet encounters sinister elemental forces, killer demons, and other paranormal baddies.

The tone of the series — set largely by the edgy art of John Paul Leon (Earth X, Further Adventures of Cyclops and Phoenix) — is that of a moody thriller. Steven Grant's (Grifter, X-Man) scripts are packed with sophisticated suspense, as much as any of DC's other contemporary horror/fantasy titles (Hellblazer, Swamp Thing, and Night Force, in particular). Ultimately, however, these newer, darker heroes were "living on borrowed time" as much as the originals. Fans of the 1960s series must have felt the absence of the burly guys in yellow jumpsuits, enough so that this revival folded after 18 issues.

1 ❑ Feb 1997 Cover: 2.25 **NM** value: **2.50**
Circ: Diamd. preorders: **25,060** • **CGC:** 2 graded, best 9.4
• new team
2 ❑ Mar 1997 Cover: 2.25 **NM** value: **2.50**
Circ: Diamd. preorders: **18,428**
📖 Undead **A:** John Paul Leon **W:** Len Kaminski; Steven Grant
3 ❑ Apr 1997 Cover: 2.25 **NM** value: **2.50**
Circ: Diamd. preorders: **16,692**
📖 Threshold
4 ❑ May 1997 Cover: 2.25 **NM** value: **2.50**
Circ: Diamd. preorders: **15,770**
★ Origin of Challengers.
5 ❑ Jun 1997 Cover: 2.25 **NM** value: **2.50**
Circ: Diamd. preorders: **14,725**
📖 Private Lives **A:** Bill Reinhold; John Paul Leon **W:** Steven Grant
6 ❑ Jul 1997 Cover: 2.25 **NM** value: **Cover or less**
Circ: Diamd. preorders: **13,566**
📖 Convergenge, Part 3 • concludes in Scare Tactics #8
7 ❑ Aug 1997 Cover: 2.25 **NM** value: **Cover or less**
Circ: Diamd. preorders: **13,038**
📖 Last Days, Part 1 • return of original Challengers
8 ❑ Sep 1997 Cover: 2.25 **NM** value: **Cover or less**
Circ: Diamd. preorders: **12,016**
📖 Last Days, Part 2 ★ Origin of both Challenger teams.
9 ❑ Oct 1997 Cover: 2.25 **NM** value: **Cover or less**
Circ: Diamd. preorders: **11,484**
📖 Last Days, Part 3
10 ❑ Nov 1997 Cover: 2.25 **NM** value: **Cover or less**
Circ: Diamd. preorders: **10,788**
📖 Broken Spirits **A:** Jill Thompson **W:** Steven Grant
11 ❑ Dec 1997 Cover: 2.25 **NM** value: **Cover or less**
Circ: Diamd. preorders: **10,691**
Face cover. 📖 Times Fade Away **A:** John Paul Leon **W:** Steven Grant
12 ❑ Jan 1998 Cover: 2.25 **NM** value: **Cover or less**
Circ: Diamd. preorders: **10,245**
★ Appearance of Batman.
13 ❑ Feb 1998 Cover: 2.25 **NM** value: **Cover or less**
Circ: Diamd. preorders: **9,127**
14 ❑ Mar 1998 Cover: 2.25 **NM** value: **Cover or less**
📖 Dark Waters **A:** Christopher Schenck **W:** Steven Grant
15 ❑ Apr 1998 Cover: 2.25 **NM** value: **3.00**
• Millennium Giants;continues in Superman #134
16 ❑ May 1998 Cover: 2.25 **NM** value: **Cover or less**
Circ: Diamd. preorders: **8,783**
• tales of the original Challengers
17 ❑ Jun 1998 Cover: 2.25 **NM** value: **Cover or less**
Circ: Diamd. preorders: **8,501**
18 ❑ Jul 1998 Cover: 2.50 **NM** value: **Cover or less**
Circ: Diamd. preorders: **8,462**
final issue.

CHALLENGERS OF THE UNKNOWN (MINI-SERIES) DC

1 ❑ Mar 1991 Cover: 1.75 **NM** value: **2.50**
Circ: CapCity orders: **23,500**
📖 The Challengers Must Die **A:** Tim Sale **W:** Jeph Loeb ★ Origin of Challengers of the Unknown (new origin).
2 ❑ Apr 1991 Cover: 1.75 **NM** value: **2.00**
Circ: CapCity orders: **15,200**
3 ❑ May 1991 Cover: 1.75 **NM** value: **2.00**
Circ: CapCity orders: **13,300**
4 ❑ Jun 1991 Cover: 1.75 **NM** value: **2.00**
Circ: CapCity orders: **11,400**
5 ❑ Jul 1991 Cover: 1.75 **NM** value: **2.00**
Circ: CapCity orders: **10,650**
6 ❑ Aug 1991 Cover: 1.75 **NM** value: **2.00**
Circ: CapCity orders: **9,400**
C: Gil Kane
7 ❑ Sep 1991 Cover: 1.75 **NM** value: **2.00**
Circ: CapCity orders: **9,050**
📖 Another World! **A:** Tim Sale **C:** Arthur Adams **W:** Jeph Loeb
8 ❑ Oct 1991 Cover: 1.75 **NM** value: **2.00**
Circ: CapCity orders: **8,150**

CHAMBER OF CHILLS Marvel

2 ❑ Jan 1973 Cover: 0.20 **NM** value: **4.00**
• **CGC:** 1 graded, best 9.2
📖 The Spell of the Dragon
3 ❑ Mar 1973 Cover: 0.20 **NM** value: **4.00**
4 ❑ May 1973 Cover: 0.20 **NM** value: **3.00**
5 ❑ Jul 1973 Cover: 0.20 **NM** value: **3.00**
6 ❑ Sep 1973 Cover: 0.20 **NM** value: **3.00**
7 ❑ Nov 1973 Cover: 0.20 **NM** value: **3.00**
8 ❑ Jan 1974 Cover: 0.20 **NM** value: **3.00**
9 ❑ Mar 1974 Cover: 0.20 **NM** value: **3.00**
10 ❑ May 1974 Cover: 0.25 **NM** value: **3.00**
11 ❑ Jul 1974 Cover: 0.25 **NM** value: **3.00**
📖 Back from the Dead • Reprint story from Tales of Suspense #28
12 ❑ Sep 1974 Cover: 0.25 **NM** value: **3.00**
13 ❑ Nov 1974 Cover: 0.25 **NM** value: **3.00**
14 ❑ Jan 1975 Cover: 0.25 **NM** value: **3.00**
• **CGC:** 1 graded, best 9.4
15 ❑ Mar 1975 Cover: 0.25 **NM** value: **3.00**
• **CGC:** 1 graded, best 9.2
16 ❑ May 1975 Cover: 0.25 **NM** value: **3.00**

Other grades: Multiply prices above by **1.5 for Mint • 2/3 for Very Fine • 1/3 for Fine • 1/5 for Very Good • 1/8 for Good**

17 ❑ Jul 1975 Cover: 0.25 **NM** value: **3.00**
18 ❑ Sep 1975 Cover: 0.25 **NM** value: **3.00**
📖 I Found Monstrom • Reprint story from Tales to Astonish #11
19 ❑ Nov 1975 Cover: 0.25 **NM** value: **3.00**
📖 Look Out, Here Come the Four-Armed Men • Reprint story from Tales to Astonish #26
20 ❑ Jan 1976 Cover: 0.25 **NM** value: **3.00**
21 ❑ Mar 1976 Cover: 0.25 **NM** value: **3.00**
22 ❑ May 1976 Cover: 0.25 **NM** value: **3.00**
📖 He Walked Through Walls • Reprint story from Tales to Astonish #26
23 ❑ Jul 1976 Cover: 0.25 **NM** value: **3.00**
• **CGC:** 1 graded, best 9.0
24 ❑ Sep 1976 Cover: 0.30 **NM** value: **3.00**
25 ❑ Nov 1976 Cover: 0.30 **NM** value: **3.00**

CHAMBER OF CHILLS (HARVEY) — Harvey

1 ❑ Jun 1951 Cover: 0.10 **NM** value: **350.00**
• **CGC:** 2 graded, best 7.5
2 ❑ Aug 1951 Cover: 0.10 **NM** value: **275.00**
• **CGC:** 1 graded, best 8.0
3 ❑ Oct 1951 Cover: 0.10 **NM** value: **275.00**
• **CGC:** 3 graded, best 9.2
4 ❑ Dec 1951 Cover: 0.10 **NM** value: **275.00**
• **CGC:** 2 graded, best 9.0
5 ❑ Feb 1952 Cover: 0.10 **NM** value: **250.00**
• **CGC:** 3 graded, best 9.0
6 ❑ Mar 1952 Cover: 0.10 **NM** value: **250.00**
• **CGC:** 2 graded, best 8.0
7 ❑ Apr 1952 Cover: 0.10 **NM** value: **250.00**
• **CGC:** 1 graded, best 6.5
8 ❑ May 1952 Cover: 0.10 **NM** value: **250.00**
9 ❑ Jun 1952 Cover: 0.10 **NM** value: **250.00**
• **CGC:** 3 graded, best 8.0
10 ❑ Jul 1952 Cover: 0.10 **NM** value: **225.00**
• **CGC:** 4 graded, best 9.2
11 ❑ Aug 1952 Cover: 0.10 **NM** value: **225.00**
• **CGC:** 1 graded, best 9.0
12 ❑ Sep 1952 Cover: 0.10 **NM** value: **225.00**
• **CGC:** 5 graded, best 8.5
13 ❑ Oct 1952 Cover: 0.10 **NM** value: **225.00**
• **CGC:** 4 graded, best 9.4
14 ❑ Nov 1952 Cover: 0.10 **NM** value: **225.00**
• **CGC:** 2 graded, best 9.0
15 ❑ Jan 1953 Cover: 0.10 **NM** value: **225.00**
• **CGC:** 5 graded, best 9.4
16 ❑ Mar 1953 Cover: 0.10 **NM** value: **225.00**
• **CGC:** 3 graded, best 9.0
17 ❑ May 1953 Cover: 0.10 **NM** value: **225.00**
18 ❑ Jul 1953 Cover: 0.10 **NM** value: **225.00**
• **CGC:** 3 graded, best 9.0
19 ❑ Sep 1953 Cover: 0.10 **NM** value: **225.00**
• **CGC:** 6 graded, best 9.0
20 ❑ Nov 1953 Cover: 0.10 **NM** value: **200.00**
• **CGC:** 2 graded, best 9.0
21 ❑ Jan 1954 Cover: 0.10 **NM** value: **200.00**
• **CGC:** 2 graded, best 9.0
22 ❑ Mar 1954 Cover: 0.10 **NM** value: **200.00**
• **CGC:** 2 graded, best 9.2
23 ❑ May 1954 Cover: 0.10 **NM** value: **200.00**
• **CGC:** 4 graded, best 8.5
24 ❑ Jul 1954 Cover: 0.10 **NM** value: **200.00**
• **CGC:** 2 graded, best 9.2
25 ❑ Oct 1954 Cover: 0.10 **NM** value: **200.00**
• **CGC:** 2 graded, best 9.0
26 ❑ Dec 1954 Cover: 0.10 **NM** value: **175.00**
• **CGC:** 1 graded, best 7.0

CHAMBER OF DARKNESS — Marvel

Inspired by the success of the Joe Orlando-edited "mystery" titles at DC in the early 1970s, Marvel launched its own horror and suspense anthology titles like Chamber of Darkness, Tower of Shadows, and others. Many of the chilling stories followed the classic horror comic formulas laid down by E.C. in titles like Tales rom the Crypt (sanitized for the Comics Code, of course) and were illustrated with gusto by some of Marvel's top talents of the time, including John Severin, Gil Kane, John Buscema, and Bernie Wrightson. The Marvel series also mined a richer source for story inspiration, adapting tales from such fantasy and horror pulps of the 1930s as Weird Tales.

1 ❑ Oct 1968 Cover: 0.15 **NM** value: **14.00**
• **CGC:** 9 graded, best 9.6
📖 It's Only Magic!; Mr. Craven Buys His Scream House!; Always Leave 'em Laughing! **A:** John Buscema; Don Heck; Denny O'Neil **W:** Gary Friedrich; Stan Lee
2 ❑ Dec 1968 Cover: 0.15 **NM** value: **5.00**
3 ❑ Feb 1969 Cover: 0.15 **NM** value: **5.00**
• **CGC:** 1 graded, best 8.5
4 ❑ Apr 1969 Cover: 0.15 **NM** value: **20.00**
• **CGC:** 9 graded, best 9.4
📖 The Monster; The Sword and the Sorcerers • Conan try-out **A:** Barry Windsor-Smith
5 ❑ Jun 1969 Cover: 0.15 **NM** value: **4.00**
📖 And Fear Shall Follow
6 ❑ Aug 1969 Cover: 0.15 **NM** value: **4.00**
7 ❑ Oct 1969 Cover: 0.15 **NM** value: **8.00**
• **CGC:** 2 graded, best 9.4
📖 I Found the Abominable Snowman • 1st Bernie Wrightson work; reprints story from Tales to Astonish #13 **A:** Bernie Wrightson
8 ❑ Dec 1969 Cover: 0.15 **NM** value: **4.00**
• **CGC:** 1 graded, best 9.2

CHAMBER OF EVIL — Comax

1 ❑ Cover: 2.95 **NM** value: **Cover or less**
📖 Demon Skull's Revenge **A:** Butch Burcham **W:** Butch Burcham

CHAMP COMICS — Harvey

11 ❑ Oct 1940 Cover: 0.10 **NM** value: **800.00**
• **CGC:** 1 graded, best 6.0
12 ❑ Feb 1941 Cover: 0.10 **NM** value: **750.00**
13 ❑ May 1941 Cover: 0.10 **NM** value: **750.00**
• **CGC:** 1 graded, best 3.5
14 ❑ Jul 1941 Cover: 0.10 **NM** value: **700.00**
15 ❑ Sep 1941 Cover: 0.10 **NM** value: **700.00**
16 ❑ Nov 1941 Cover: 0.10 **NM** value: **650.00**
• **CGC:** 1 graded, best 4.0
17 ❑ Feb 1942 Cover: 0.10 **NM** value: **650.00**
18 ❑ May 1942 Cover: 0.10 **NM** value: **650.00**
19 ❑ Jun 1942 Cover: 0.10 **NM** value: **600.00**
20 ❑ Jul 1942 Cover: 0.10 **NM** value: **600.00**
21 ❑ Aug 1942 Cover: 0.10 **NM** value: **600.00**
22 ❑ Sep 1942 Cover: 0.10 **NM** value: **550.00**
23 ❑ Oct 1942 Cover: 0.10 **NM** value: **550.00**
24 ❑ Dec 1942 Cover: 0.10 **NM** value: **550.00**
25 ❑ Apr 1943 Cover: 0.10 **NM** value: **550.00**

CHAMPION, THE — Special Studio

1 ❑ b&w Cover: 2.50 **NM** value: **Cover or less**
A: Dan Day **W:** Doug Moench

CHAMPION COMICS — Harvey

2 ❑ Dec 1939 Cover: 0.10 **NM** value: **1500.00**
• **CGC:** 2 graded, best 6.5
3 ❑ Jan 1940 Cover: 0.10 **NM** value: **750.00**
4 ❑ Feb 1940 Cover: 0.10 **NM** value: **750.00**
5 ❑ Mar 1940 Cover: 0.10 **NM** value: **700.00**
• **CGC:** 1 graded, best 9.0
6 ❑ Apr 1940 Cover: 0.10 **NM** value: **700.00**
• **CGC:** 1 graded, best 9.0
7 ❑ May 1940 Cover: 0.10 **NM** value: **700.00**
8 ❑ Jun 1940 Cover: 0.10 **NM** value: **650.00**
• **CGC:** 2 graded, best 9.0
9 ❑ Jul 1940 Cover: 0.10 **NM** value: **650.00**
10 ❑ Aug 1940 Cover: 0.10 **NM** value: **650.00**

CHAMPION OF KATARA, THE — Mu Press

1 ❑ Jan 1992, b&w Cover: 2.50 **NM** value: **Cover or less**
2 ❑ Apr 1992 Cover: 2.50 **NM** value: **Cover or less**

CHAMPION OF KATARA — Crack O'Dawn

1 ❑ Cover: 1.50 **NM** value: **Cover or less**

CHAMPION OF KATARA: DUM-DUMS & DRAGONS, THE — Mu

1 ❑ Jun 1995, b&w Cover: 2.95 **NM** value: **Cover or less**
2 ❑ Jul 1995, b&w Cover: 2.95 **NM** value: **Cover or less**
3 ❑ Aug 1995, b&w Cover: 2.95 **NM** value: **Cover or less**

CHAMPIONS CLASSICS — Hero

1 ❑ Cover: 0.90 **NM** value: **1.00**
13 ❑ Oct 1993 Cover: 3.95 **NM** value: **Cover or less**
• b&w reprint
14 ❑ Jan 1994 Cover: 3.95 **NM** value: **Cover or less**
• b&w reprint

CHAMPIONS CLASSICS/FLARE ADVENTURES — Hero

2 ❑ Cover: 2.95 **NM** value: **Cover or less**
• flip-format
3 ❑ Cover: 2.95 **NM** value: **Cover or less**
• flip-format
4 ❑ Cover: 3.50 **NM** value: **Cover or less**
• flip-format
5 ❑ Cover: 3.50 **NM** value: **Cover or less**
• flip-format
6 ❑ Cover: 3.50 **NM** value: **Cover or less**
• flip-format
7 ❑ Cover: 3.50 **NM** value: **Cover or less**
• flip-format

CHAMPIONS (ECLIPSE) — Eclipse

1 ❑ Jun 1986 Cover: 1.25 **NM** value: **1.50**
Circ: CapCity orders: **9,025**
📖 The Curse of the Hellfire Crown ★ 1st Appearance of Rose, Marksman, The Champions (game characters), Giant, Flare, Icestar, Foxbat.
2 ❑ Sep 1986 Cover: 1.25 **NM** value: **1.50**
Circ: CapCity orders: **7,200**
3 ❑ Oct 1986 Cover: 1.25 **NM** value: **1.50**
Circ: CapCity orders: **6,550**
4 ❑ Nov 1986 Cover: 1.25 **NM** value: **1.50**
Circ: CapCity orders: **6,475**
5 ❑ Feb 1987 Cover: 1.25 **NM** value: **1.50**
Circ: CapCity orders: **5,125**
★ Origin of Flare.
6 ❑ Feb 1987 Cover: 1.25 **NM** value: **1.50**
Circ: CapCity orders: **5,025**

Looking for further information about a specific comic book or line of comics? Write a letter to ***Comics Buyer's Guide*** at ohso@krause.com — if we don't know, one of our readers always does!

CHAMPIONS (HERO) — Hero

Champions features several characters who were created for the Champions role-playing game. The game allows players to take the role of a super-hero, matching powers and strategy against a colorful assortment of villains.

The series runs true to the light-hearted spirit of the game and stars: Flare, a young and apparently man-crazy blonde with the ability to harness photonic energy; Icestar, who can create ice out of the water vapor in the air; Rose, an occult investigator; and their leader, Marksman, an experienced soldier.

This title ran for a dozen issues before restarting as The League of Champions #1. As an added bonus for Champions players, many of the lead characters that the group encounters in the comic book are described (with ability scores, etc.) for use with the role-playing game.

1 ❑ Sep 1987 Cover: 1.95 **NM** value: **Cover or less**
2 ❑ Oct 1987 Cover: 1.95 **NM** value: **Cover or less**
3 ❑ Nov 1987 Cover: 1.95 **NM** value: **Cover or less**
4 ❑ Dec 1987 Cover: 1.95 **NM** value: **Cover or less**
5 ❑ Jan 1988 Cover: 1.95 **NM** value: **Cover or less**
6 ❑ Feb 1988 Cover: 1.95 **NM** value: **Cover or less**
7 ❑ Mar 1988 Cover: 1.95 **NM** value: **Cover or less**
8 ❑ May 1988 Cover: 1.95 **NM** value: **Cover or less**
9 ❑ Jun 1988 Cover: 1.95 **NM** value: **Cover or less**
10 ❑ Jul 1988 Cover: 1.95 **NM** value: **Cover or less**
11 ❑ Sep 1988 Cover: 1.95 **NM** value: **Cover or less**
12 ❑ Oct 1988 Cover: 1.95 **NM** value: **Cover or less**
13 ❑ Cover: 1.95 **NM** value: **Cover or less**
14 ❑ Cover: 1.95 **NM** value: **Cover or less**
15 ❑ Cover: 1.95 **NM** value: **Cover or less**

CHAMPIONS, THE (MARVEL) — Marvel

1 ❑ Oct 1975 Cover: 0.25 **NM** value: **12.00**
• **CGC:** 43 graded, best 9.6
📖 The World Still Needs...The Champions! **A:** Don Heck **W:** Tony Isabella ★ Origin of The Champions. ★ 1st Appearance of The Champions. ★ Appearance of Venus.
2 ❑ Jan 1976 Cover: 0.25 **NM** value: **6.00**
• **CGC:** 1 graded, best 9.4
📖 Whom the Gods Would Join
3 ❑ Feb 1976 Cover: 0.25 **NM** value: **6.00**
• **CGC:** 2 graded, best 9.6
📖 Assault on Olympus
4 ❑ Mar 1976 Cover: 0.25 **NM** value: **5.00**
• **CGC:** 2 graded, best 9.4
📖 Murder at Malibu
5 ❑ Apr 1976 Cover: 0.25 **NM** value: **5.00**
• **CGC:** 1 graded, best 9.6
📖 The Economy Is So Bad That... **A:** Don Heck ★ Origin of Rampage (Marvel). ★ 1st Appearance of Rampage (Marvel). ★ Appearance of Ghost Rider.
6 ❑ Jun 1976 Cover: 0.25 **NM** value: **4.00**
• **CGC:** 2 graded, best 9.6
📖 Mad Dogs and Businessmen
7 ❑ Aug 1976 Cover: 0.25 **NM** value: **4.00**
• **CGC:** 2 graded, best 9.4
📖 The Man Who Created the Black Widow
8 ❑ Oct 1976 Cover: 0.30 **NM** value: **4.00**
• **CGC:** 1 graded, best 9.8
📖 Divide and Conquer **A:** Gil Kane
9 ❑ Dec 1976 Cover: 0.30 **NM** value: **4.00**
• **CGC:** 1 graded, best 9.6
📖 The Battle Of Los Angeles **A:** Gil Kane; Bob Hall **W:** Bill Mantlo ★ Versus Darkstar, Titanium Man, Crimson Dynamo.
10 ❑ Jan 1977 Cover: 0.30 **NM** value: **4.00**
📖 One Man's Son Is Another Man's Poison **A:** Dave Cockrum
11 ❑ Feb 1977 Cover: 0.30 **NM** value: **6.00**
📖 The Shadow From the Stars **A:** John Byrne
12 ❑ Mar 1977 Cover: 0.30 **NM** value: **6.00**
📖 The Stranger? **A:** John Byrne **W:** Bill Mantlo
13 ❑ May 1977 Cover: 0.30 **NM** value: **6.00**
📖 The Doom That Went on Forever **A:** John Byrne
14 ❑ Jul 1977 Cover: 0.30 **NM** value: **6.00**
• **CGC:** 2 graded, best 9.4
📖 The Creature Called Swarm **A:** John Byrne ★ 1st Appearance of Swarm.
15 ❑ Sep 1977 Cover: 0.30 **NM** value: **6.00**
• **CGC:** 2 graded, best 9.4
📖 Death Drone **A:** John Byrne
16 ❑ Nov 1977 Cover: 0.35 **NM** value: **6.00**
📖 A World Lost **A:** John Byrne; Bob Hall ★ Appearance of Doctor Doom.
17 ❑ Jan 1978 Cover: 0.35 **NM** value: **6.00**
• **CGC:** 1 graded, best 9.2
📖 The Sentinels Hunt Again final issue. **A:** John Byrne; George Tuska ★ Versus Sentinels.

Capital City orders are the actual sales of comic books by Capital City Distribution, once one of the largest U.S. sellers of comics to comics shops. Capital City's share of comics shop sales, while not known exactly, increases from around 10-20% in the mid-1980s to 30-35% in the mid-1990s. Capital City's share of comic books sold on newsstands (most Marvels and DCs) will be less.

CGC-graded: Multiply prices above by **33 for 9.9 M • 16 for 9.8 NM/M • 7 for 9.6 NM+ • 5 for 9.4 NM • 2.5 for 9.2 NM- • 1.5 for 9.0 VF/NM**

CHAMPION SPORTS — DC

Champion Sports was a short-lived sports series of the mid-1970s. During its three-issue run, it featured stories that ranged from inspirational to frankly unbelievable.

The latter included the tale of a boy who knocks his shoulder out of whack while trying out for a spot in the minor leagues. That injury somehow provides him with incredible pitching ability and a killer fastball that let him strike out the Oakland A's. His moment in the sun is soon over, however, as an auto accident puts him into the hospital, where, "while fixing up other injuries," the doctors decide to also take care of the shoulder that has slipped out of its socket. Without the trick arm, his pitching career is over — but then another injury, years later, leaves him with an arm that can hurl a football almost 100 yards.

1 ❑ Nov 1973 Cover: 0.20 **NM** value: **5.00**
• **CGC:** 1 graded, best 9.4
📖 The Kid Who Beat the Oakland A's; The Little Racer; The First Hurdle

2 ❑ Jan 1974 Cover: 0.20 **NM** value: **3.50**
📖 The Enchanted Bat; Street Fighter; The Animal **A:** Jerry Grandenetti **W:** Joe Simon

3 ❑ Mar 1974 Cover: 0.20 **NM** value: **3.50**
📖 Horse Story; The Saga of Wild Bill Hickok; Jack the Giants Killer **A:** Jerry Grandenetti **W:** Joe Simon

CHAMPS — Fantagraphics

Bk 1❑ Cover: 12.95 **NM** value: **Cover or less**

CHANGE COMMANDER GOKU (1ST SERIES) — Antarctic

1 ❑ Oct 1993 Cover: 2.95 **NM** value: **Cover or less**
📖 Battle Burn, Part 1 **A:** Ippongi Bang **W:** Ippongi Bang ★ Origin of Change Commander Goku. ★ 1st Appearance of Change Commander Goku.

2 ❑ Nov 1993 Cover: 2.95 **NM** value: **Cover or less**
📖 Battle Burn, Part 2 **A:** Ippongi Bang **W:** Ippongi Bang

3 ❑ Dec 1993 Cover: 2.95 **NM** value: **Cover or less**
📖 Battle Burn, Part 3 **A:** Ippongi Bang **W:** Ippongi Bang

4 ❑ Jan 1994 Cover: 2.95 **NM** value: **Cover or less**
📖 Battle Burn, Part 4 **A:** Ippongi Bang **W:** Ippongi Bang ★ 1st Appearance of The True-Brewing Magnetic Man.

5 ❑ Feb 1994 Cover: 2.95 **NM** value: **Cover or less**
📖 Battle Burn, Part 5 **A:** Ippongi Bang **W:** Ippongi Bang

Bk 1❑ Dec 1996, b&w Cover: 12.95 **NM** value: **Cover or less**
• Collected Change Commander Goku;Collects Change Commander Goku (1st Series) #1-5 **A:** Ippongi Bang **W:** Ippongi Bang

CHANGE COMMANDER GOKU 2 — Antarctic

1 ❑ Sep 1996 Cover: 2.95 **NM** value: **Cover or less**
2 ❑ Nov 1996 Cover: 2.95 **NM** value: **Cover or less**
3 ❑ Jan 1997 Cover: 2.95 **NM** value: **Cover or less**
4 ❑ Mar 1997 Cover: 2.95 **NM** value: **Cover or less**

CHANGES — Tundra

1 ❑ Cover: 7.95 **NM** value: **Cover or less**

CHANNEL ZERO — Image

1 ❑ Feb 1998 Cover: 2.95 **NM** value: **Cover or less**
Circ: Diamd. preorders: **4,086**
A: Brian Wood **W:** Brian Wood

2 ❑ Apr 1998 Cover: 2.95 **NM** value: **Cover or less**
Circ: Diamd. preorders: **3,031**
A: Brian Wood **W:** Brian Wood

3 ❑ Jun 1998 Cover: 2.95 **NM** value: **Cover or less**
Circ: Diamd. preorders: **2,475**
A: Brian Wood **W:** Brian Wood

4 ❑ Aug 1998 Cover: 2.95 **NM** value: **Cover or less**
Circ: Diamd. preorders: **2,389**
A: Brian Wood **W:** Brian Wood

5 ❑ Nov 1998 Cover: 2.95 **NM** value: **Cover or less**
Circ: Diamd. preorders: **2,219**
📖 Global Supermarket **A:** Brian Wood **W:** Brian Wood

6 ❑ Feb 1999 Cover: 2.95 **NM** value: **Cover or less**
Circ: Diamd. preorders: **2,067**
A: Brian Wood **W:** Brian Wood

Bk 1❑ Jan 1998 Cover: 14.95 **NM** value: **Cover or less**
No issue number. • Trade Paperback. • collects series;Collects Channel Zero #1-4 **A:** Brian Wood **W:** Brian Wood

CHANNEL ZERO: DUPE — Image

1 ❑ Jan 1999, b&w Cover: 2.95 **NM** value: **Cover or less**
No issue number. **A:** Brian Wood **W:** Brian Wood

CHAOS! BIBLE, THE — Chaos

1 ❑ Nov 1995 Cover: 3.50 **NM** value: **Cover or less**
Circ: CapCity orders: **12,175** • **CGC:** 1 graded, best 9.6
📖 Alien Evil; Root of All Evil **A:** Leonardo Jimenez; Brian Hughes **W:** Brian Pulido

CHAOS! CHRONICLES — Chaos

1 ❑ Feb 2000 Cover: 3.50 **NM** value: **Cover or less**
A: David Brewer; Steven Hughes; Jim Balent; Curtis Arnold; Ken Branch **W:** Brian Pulido; Dave Balance; Judy Evers; Matt Brady; Mike Francis

CHAOS EFFECT, THE: ALPHA — Valiant

In Tibet in 1994, a mysterious black vortex opened in the sky, its dark energies growing until its effects can be felt all across the world. All manner of technology seems to be rendered useless by these forces, while many of those gifted with superpernatural abilities find their powers changed, their abilities enhanced. Not all are changed for the better, however. Solar, Man of the Atom, awakens to find his very essence dissolving. It seems the end of the world is truly at hand, and the planet's most powerful people, heroes and villains alike, may not be enough to stop it.

The two-part epic crosses over into virtually every Valiant title, the Chaos Effect reaching across the globe and even through time to involve everyone from Turok to X-O Manowar to Magnus, the robot fighter. The multi-part tale eventually provides the lead-in to the new ongoing Timewalker series.

1 ❑ ca. 1994 **NM** value: **1.00**
Circ: CapCity orders: **9,463** • **CGC:** 1 graded, best 9.4
no cover price. • giveaway. 📖 Chaos Rules **A:** Bernard Chang **W:** Bob Layton ★ Appearance of Timewalker.

1/GO❑ca. 1994 **NM** value: **1.50**
• Gold edition. 📖 Chaos Rules **A:** Bernard Chang **W:** Bob Layton ★ Appearance of Timewalker.

CHAOS EFFECT, THE: EPILOGUE — Valiant

1 ❑ Dec 1994 Cover: 2.95 **NM** value: **Cover or less**
Circ: CapCity orders: **15,650**
cardstock cover. 📖 In Search of Faith Part 1 • Magnus in 20th century **A:** Louis Small Jr. **W:** Kevin Van Hook ★ Appearance of Faith, Timewalker.

2 ❑ Jan 1995 Cover: 2.95 **NM** value: **Cover or less**
Circ: CapCity orders: **15,450**
cardstock cover. 📖 In Search of Faith Part 2 • Magnus in 20th century **A:** Louis Small Jr. **W:** Kevin Van Hook

CHAOS EFFECT, THE: OMEGA — Valiant

1 ❑ Nov 1994 Cover: 2.25 **NM** value: **Cover or less**
Circ: CapCity orders: **26,350**
cardstock cover. • Magnus to 20th century

1/GO❑Nov 1994 **NM** value: **3.00**
cardstock cover. • Gold edition. • Magnus to 20th century

2 ❑ Nov 1994 Cover: 2.25 **NM** value: **Cover or less**
📖 From Chaos Comes…Order • Omega **A:** Bernard Chang **W:** Bob Layton

2/GO❑Nov 1994 **NM** value: **2.50**
• Gold edition. 📖 From Chaos Comes…Order **A:** Bernard Chang **W:** Bob Layton

CHAOS! GALLERY — Chaos

1 ❑ Aug 1997 Cover: 2.95 **NM** value: **Cover or less**
Circ: Diamd. preorders: **21,638**
• pin-ups

CHAOS! PRESENTS JADE — Chaos

1 ❑ May 2001 Cover: 2.99 **NM** value: **Cover or less**
Circ: Diamd. preorders: **4,928**
A: Ken Lashley **W:** Christopher Golden; Tom Sniegoski

2 ❑ 2001 Cover: 2.99 **NM** value: **Cover or less**
A: Ken Lashley **W:** Christopher Golden; Tom Sniegoski

3 ❑ 2001 Cover: 2.99 **NM** value: **Cover or less**
A: Ken Lashley **W:** Christopher Golden; Tom Sniegoski

4 ❑ 2001 Cover: 2.99 **NM** value: **Cover or less**
A: Ken Lashley **W:** Christopher Golden; Tom Sniegoski

CHAOS! QUARTERLY — Chaos

1 ❑ Cover: 4.95 **NM** value: **5.00**
Circ: CapCity orders: **23,275** • **CGC:** 1 graded, best 9.8
📖 Lady Death; Purgatori; Cremator; Bedlam **A:** Paul Pelletier; Justiniano; Steven Hughes; Louis Small Jr. **W:** Brian Pulido; Christensen; Mark Seifert

2 ❑ Cover: 4.95 **NM** value: **5.00**
📖 Lady Demon; Robo-Evil; Cremator; Bad Girls **A:** Brad Parker; Steven Hughes; Michael Okamoto; Leonardo Jimenez; Boris Vallejo(cover) **W:** Brian Pulido; Christensen; Mark Seifert

3 ❑ Cover: 3.95 **NM** value: **Cover or less**

CHAPEL — Image

1 ❑ Feb 1995 Cover: 2.50 **NM** value: **2.99**
Circ: CapCity orders: **24,300**
A: John Stinsman **W:** Robert Norton

2 ❑ Mar 1995 Cover: 2.50 **NM** value: **Cover or less**
Circ: CapCity orders: **18,650**

2/SC❑Mar 1995 Cover: 2.50 **NM** value: **Cover or less**
alternate cover. • Chapel firing right, white lettering in logo

CHAPEL (MINI-SERIES) — Image

1 ❑ Cover: 2.50 **NM** value: **3.50**
A: Calvin Irving; Thomas Tenney **W:** Brian Witten; Eric Stephenson

2 ❑ Mar 1995 Cover: 2.50 **NM** value: **Cover or less**
A: Calvin Irving **W:** Brian Witten

CHAPEL (VOL. 2) — Image

1 ❑ Aug 1995 Cover: 2.50 **NM** value: **Cover or less**
Circ: CapCity orders: **22,150**
A: Calvin Irving **W:** Brian Witten

1/SC❑Aug 1995 Cover: 2.50 **NM** value: **Cover or less**
alternate cover. **A:** Calvin Irving **W:** Brian Witten

2 ❑ Sep 1995 Cover: 2.50 **NM** value: **Cover or less**
Circ: CapCity orders: **14,575**
A: Calvin Irving **W:** Brian Witten; Eric Stephenson

3 ❑ Oct 1995 Cover: 2.50 **NM** value: **Cover or less**
Circ: CapCity orders: **8,375**
A: Calvin Irving; Shelby Robertson; Richard Horie **W:** Brian Witten; Eric Stephenson

4 ❑ Nov 1995 Cover: 2.50 **NM** value: **Cover or less**
• Babewatch

5 ❑ Dec 1995 Cover: 2.50 **NM** value: **Cover or less**
★ Appearance of Spawn. ★ Versus Spawn.

6 ❑ Feb 1996 Cover: 2.50 **NM** value: **Cover or less**
★ Appearance of Spawn.

7 ❑ Apr 1996 Cover: 2.50 **NM** value: **Cover or less**
📖 Shadow Hunt, Part 2 ★ Versus Shadowhawk.

CHARLEMAGNE — Defiant

Charles Smith has spent all his life fighting for his dreams. When he learns that his brother's plane has gone down in Vietnam, Charles desperately holds onto the hope that he would be found. When the military gives up searching, Charles slips out of his parents' Kentucky home and stows away to Vietnam to find his brother by himself.

Arriving in Vietnam, he comes into contact with Doctor Nguyen, who is instrumental in helping Charles, having spent a year observing, as Charles single-handedly searched the countryside for his brother. At last, word comes, telling where Charles' brother is. The two are finally united — just as an air strike wipes out the village.

Charles' brother dies, and Charles lies in a coma for 18 years, all the while dreaming of being able to help set the world right. When he wakes, he discovers he now possesses the power to do just that.

0 ❑ Feb 1994 Cover: 10.00 **NM** value: **Cover or less**
• giveaway.

1 ❑ Mar 1994 Cover: 3.25 **NM** value: **3.50**
Circ: CapCity orders: **18,400**
📖 Fire Will Come… **A:** Adam Pollina **W:** D.G. Chichester ★ Origin of Charlemagne. ★ 1st Appearance of Charlemagne.

2 ❑ Apr 1994 Cover: 2.50 **NM** value: **Cover or less**
Circ: CapCity orders: **11,700**
📖 The Dance Of Eternity **A:** Adam Pollina **W:** D.G. Chichester ★ Appearance of War Dancer.

3 ❑ May 1994 Cover: 2.50 **NM** value: **Cover or less**
Circ: CapCity orders: **9,725**
📖 Fear Itself **A:** Adam Pollina **W:** D.G. Chichester ★ Appearance of Doctor Michael Alexander.

4 ❑ Jun 1994 Cover: 3.25 **NM** value: **Cover or less**
Circ: CapCity orders: **8,350**

5 ❑ Cover: 2.50 **NM** value: **Cover or less**
Circ: CapCity orders: **7,150**

6 ❑ Cover: 2.50 **NM** value: **Cover or less**
Circ: CapCity orders: **6,350**

7 ❑ Cover: 2.50 **NM** value: **Cover or less**
Circ: CapCity orders: **4,950**

8 ❑ Cover: 2.50 **NM** value: **Cover or less**
final issue.

CHARLES BURNS' MODERN HORROR SKETCHBOOK — Kitchen Sink

1 ❑ Cover: 6.95 **NM** value: **Cover or less**
No issue number.

CHARLIE CHAN (CRESTWOOD) — Crestwood

1 ❑ Jun 1948 Cover: 0.10 **NM** value: **700.00**
• **CGC:** 1 graded, best 7.5
📖 Land of the Leopard Men

2 ❑ Aug 1948 Cover: 0.10 **NM** value: **400.00**
📖 The Vanishing Jewel Salesman

3 ❑ Oct 1948 Cover: 0.10 **NM** value: **400.00**
4 ❑ Dec 1948 Cover: 0.10 **NM** value: **400.00**
5 ❑ Feb 1949 Cover: 0.10 **NM** value: **300.00**
6 ❑ Jun 1955 Cover: 0.10 **NM** value: **300.00**
7 ❑ Sep 1955 Cover: 0.10 **NM** value: **300.00**
8 ❑ Dec 1955 Cover: 0.10 **NM** value: **250.00**
9 ❑ Mar 1956 Cover: 0.10 **NM** value: **250.00**

CHARLIE CHAN (DELL) — Dell

Hawaiian sleuth Charlie Chan was created by novelist Earl Derr Biggers(1884-1933) in 1925 and achieved fame in a series of films starring Warner Oland. Stereotypically Asian, Chan, accompanied by his "Number One Son" and, eventually, others uses fortune-cookie wisdom and keen observation to solve crimes and foil the plans of master criminals.

Chan's career in comics began in the Albert Andriola-drawn newspaper strip started in 1938 and ran until mid-1942. Chan appeared in comic books, both as a feature in anthology titles and as the title character through most of the 1940s and '50s. In 1965, Dell began a new series featuring art by Frank Springer. It ran only two issues.

1 ❑ Dec 1965 Cover: 0.12 **NM** value: **40.00**
• **CGC:** 1 graded, best 9.4
📖 The Touch of Midas **A:** Frank Springer

2 ❑ Mar 1966 Cover: 0.12 **NM** value: **26.00**
A: Frank Springer

Other grades: Multiply prices above by **1.5 for Mint • 2/3 for Very Fine • 1/3 for Fine • 1/5 for Very Good • 1/8 for Good**

CHARLIE CHAN (ETERNITY) — Eternity

1 ❑ Mar 1989 Cover: 1.95 **NM** value: **Cover or less**
• b&w strip reprint
2 ❑ Mar 1989 Cover: 1.95 **NM** value: **Cover or less**
• b&w strip reprint
3 ❑ Apr 1989 Cover: 1.95 **NM** value: **Cover or less**
• b&w strip reprint
4 ❑ May 1989 Cover: 1.95 **NM** value: **Cover or less**
• b&w strip reprint
5 ❑ Jul 1989 Cover: 2.25 **NM** value: **Cover or less**
6 ❑ Aug 1989 Cover: 2.25 **NM** value: **Cover or less**

CHARLIE THE CAVEMAN — Fantasy General

1 ❑ b&w Cover: 1.70 **NM** value: **2.00**

CHARLTON ACTION FEATURING STATIC — Charlton

11 ❑ Oct 1985 Cover: 0.75 **NM** value: **1.50**
12 ❑ Dec 1985 Cover: 0.75 **NM** value: **1.50**

CHARLTON BULLSEYE (VOL. 2) — Charlton

1 ❑ Jun 1981 Cover: 0.50 **NM** value: **3.00**
📖 Blue Beetle & The Question: The Enigma! **A:** Dan Reed **W:** Benjamin Smith
2 ❑ Jul 1981 Cover: 0.60 **NM** value: **2.00**
3 ❑ Sep 1981 Cover: 0.60 **NM** value: **2.00**
4 ❑ Nov 1981 Cover: 0.60 **NM** value: **2.00**
5 ❑ Jan 1982 Cover: 0.60 **NM** value: **2.00**
6 ❑ Mar 1982 Cover: 0.60 **NM** value: **2.00**
7 ❑ May 1982 Cover: 0.60 **NM** value: **2.00**
📖 The Games Of Ragnath **A:** Dan Reed **W:** Benjamin Smith ★ Appearance of Captain Atom.
8 ❑ Jul 1982 Cover: 0.60 **NM** value: **2.00**
📖 Strange Encounter **A:** Mark Heike **W:** Bill Anderson
9 ❑ Sep 1982 Cover: 0.60 **NM** value: **2.00**
📖 Bludd The Ultimate Barbarian **A:** Gene Day **W:** Gene Day
10 ❑ Dec 1982 **NM** value: **1.00**

CHARLTON CLASSICS — Charlton

1 ❑ Apr 1980 Cover: 0.50 **NM** value: **2.00**
2 ❑ Jun 1980 Cover: 0.50 **NM** value: **2.00**
3 ❑ Aug 1980 Cover: 0.50 **NM** value: **2.00**
4 ❑ Oct 1980 Cover: 0.50 **NM** value: **2.00**
5 ❑ Dec 1980 Cover: 0.50 **NM** value: **2.00**
6 ❑ Feb 1981 Cover: 0.50 **NM** value: **2.00**
7 ❑ Apr 1981 Cover: 0.50 **NM** value: **2.00**
8 ❑ Jun 1981 Cover: 0.50 **NM** value: **2.00**
📖 The Boar; The Legend of Hercules; The Thing in the Hole • Hercules; Joe Gill story, Sam Glanzman art credits; Tom Sutton script and art
9 ❑ Aug 1981 Cover: 0.50 **NM** value: **2.00**

CHARLTON PREMIERE — Charlton

1 ❑ Sep 1967 Cover: 0.12 **NM** value: **6.00**
📖 Its The Shape!; Introducing The Tyro Team; The Spookman
2 ❑ Nov 1967 Cover: 0.12 **NM** value: **4.00**
3 ❑ Jan 1968 Cover: 0.12 **NM** value: **4.00**
• **CGC:** 1 graded, best 9.4
4 ❑ May 1968 Cover: 0.12 **NM** value: **4.00**

CHARLTON SPORT LIBRARY: PROFESSIONAL FOOTBALL — Charlton

1 ❑ Win 1969 **NM** value: **50.00**
• **CGC:** 1 graded, best 8.0

CHASE — DC

1 ❑ Feb 1998 Cover: 2.50 **NM** value: **3.00**
Circ: Diamd. preorders: **34,825**
📖 Baptized in Fire • bound-in trading cards **A:** J.H. Williams; Mick Gray **W:** D. Curtis Johnson
2 ❑ Mar 1998 Cover: 2.50 **NM** value: **Cover or less**
Circ: Diamd. preorders: **26,013**
📖 Letdowns **A:** J.H. Williams; Mick Gray **W:** D. Curtis Johnson ★ Appearance of Bolt, Sledge, Killer Frost, Copperhead.
3 ❑ Apr 1998 Cover: 2.50 **NM** value: **Cover or less**
Circ: Diamd. preorders: **20,596**
4 ❑ May 1998 Cover: 2.50 **NM** value: **Cover or less**
Circ: Diamd. preorders: **19,230**
★ Appearance of Clock King.
5 ❑ Jun 1998 Cover: 2.50 **NM** value: **Cover or less**
Circ: Diamd. preorders: **17,835**
★ Appearance of Klarion.
6 ❑ Jul 1998 Cover: 2.50 **NM** value: **Cover or less**
Circ: Diamd. preorders: **16,467**
7 ❑ Aug 1998 Cover: 2.50 **NM** value: **Cover or less**
Circ: Diamd. preorders: **16,361**
8 ❑ Sep 1998 Cover: 2.50 **NM** value: **Cover or less**
Circ: Diamd. preorders: **16,043**
9 ❑ Oct 1998 Cover: 2.50 **NM** value: **Cover or less**
Circ: Diamd. preorders: **15,199**
★ Appearance of Green Lantern.
1000000❑Nov 1998 Cover: 2.50 **NM** value: **Cover or less**
Circ: Diamd. preorders: **20,960**
📖 Don't Believe It! final issue. **A:** J.H. Williams **W:** D. Curtis Johnson

CHASER PLATOON — Aircel

1 ❑ Feb 1991, b&w Cover: 2.25 **NM** value: **Cover or less**
📖 Rhetoric
2 ❑ Mar 1991, b&w Cover: 2.25 **NM** value: **Cover or less**
📖 Reception
3 ❑ Apr 1991, b&w Cover: 2.25 **NM** value: **Cover or less**
📖 Strings
4 ❑ May 1991, b&w Cover: 2.25 **NM** value: **Cover or less**
📖 Last Day
5 ❑ b&w Cover: 2.25 **NM** value: **Cover or less**
6 ❑ b&w Cover: 2.25 **NM** value: **Cover or less**

CHASSIS (VOL. 1) — Millennium / Expand

1 ❑ Cover: 2.95 **NM** value: **Cover or less**
• foil logo **A:** William O'Neill **C:** Adam Hughes **W:** Joshua Dysart; William O'Neill
1-2 ❑ May 1997 Cover: 2.95 **NM** value: **Cover or less**
2 ❑ Cover: 2.95 **NM** value: **Cover or less**
A: William O'Neill **W:** Joshua Dysart; William O'Neill
3 ❑ Apr 1998 Cover: 2.95 **NM** value: **Cover or less**
A: William O'Neill **W:** Joshua Dysart; William O'Neill

CHASSIS (VOL. 2) — Hurricane

Chassis goes for the same sense of fun and adventure that made Speed Racer so successful. The title character, Chassis McBain, is a Grand Prix-winning "aero-run" driver. The sport resembles 1950s-era stock car driving with the notable exception that the cars are all rocket-powered and hover over the ground. The setting for the series seems to be an alternate version of the 1940s in which World War II never happened and Eleanor Roosevelt was president of the U.S.

The action in the series takes place both on and off the race track. In winning one race, Chassis unwittingly makes an enemy of "Cover-girl," a fellow racer whose once-striking beauty has been marred by a tragic accident. Chassis seems to attract danger, but she's also well able to take care of herself. It's an enjoyable, stylish series with broad appeal.

0 ❑ Cover: 2.95 **NM** value: **Cover or less**
1 ❑ Jun 1998 Cover: 2.95 **NM** value: **Cover or less**
📖 Old Ghosts and, New Blood, Part 1 **A:** William O'Neill **C:** Adam Hughes **W:** Joshua Dysart; William O'Neill
2 ❑ Sep 1998 Cover: 2.95 **NM** value: **Cover or less**
📖 Old Ghosts and, New Blood, Part 2 **A:** William O'Neill **W:** Joshua Dysart; William O'Neill
3 ❑ Jan 1999 Cover: 2.95 **NM** value: **Cover or less**
A: William O'Neill **W:** Joshua Dysart; William O'Neill

CHASSIS (VOL. 3) — Image

0 ❑ Apr 1999 Cover: 2.95 **NM** value: **Cover or less**
Circ: Diamd. preorders: **1,742**
• background information
1 ❑ Nov 1999 Cover: 2.95 **NM** value: **Cover or less**
Circ: Diamd. preorders: **9,675**
A: William O'Neill **W:** Joshua Dysart
1/A ❑ Nov 1999 Cover: 2.95 **NM** value: **Cover or less**
Alternate cover with Chassis standing against blueprint background. **A:** William O'Neill **W:** Joshua Dysart
2 ❑ Dec 1999 Cover: 2.95 **NM** value: **Cover or less**
Circ: Diamd. preorders: **6,699**
A: William O'Neill **W:** Joshua Dysart
3 ❑ Mar 2000 Cover: 2.95 **NM** value: **Cover or less**
Circ: Diamd. preorders: **5,026**
A: Tone Rodriguez; William O'Neill **W:** Joshua Dysart
4 ❑ Mar 2000 Cover: 2.95 **NM** value: **Cover or less**
Circ: Diamd. preorders: **4,009**
A: Tone Rodriguez; William O'Neill **W:** Joshua Dysart

CHASTITY — Chaos

0.5 ❑ Jan 2001 Cover: 2.95 **NM** value: **Cover or less**
Circ: Diamd. preorders: **13,309**
A: Adriano Batista **W:** Steven Grant

CHASTITY: LUST FOR LIFE — Chaos

1 ❑ May 1999 Cover: 2.95 **NM** value: **Cover or less**
Circ: Diamd. preorders: **18,805**
2 ❑ Jun 1999 Cover: 2.95 **NM** value: **Cover or less**
Circ: Diamd. preorders: **17,367**

CHASTITY: REIGN OF TERROR — Chaos

1 ❑ Oct 2000 Cover: 2.95 **NM** value: **Cover or less**
A: Luke Ross **W:** Steven Grant

CHASTITY: ROCKED — Chaos

1 ❑ Nov 1998 Cover: 2.95 **NM** value: **Cover or less**
Circ: Diamd. preorders: **32,692**
📖 Lust for Life **A:** Justiniano **W:** Phil Nutman
2 ❑ Dec 1998 Cover: 2.95 **NM** value: **Cover or less**
Circ: Diamd. preorders: **21,178** • **CGC:** 3 graded, best 9.8
📖 The Passenger **A:** Ivan Reis **W:** Phil Nutman
3 ❑ Jan 1999 Cover: 2.95 **NM** value: **Cover or less**
Circ: Diamd. preorders: **20,188**
4 ❑ Feb 1999 Cover: 2.95 **NM** value: **Cover or less**
Circ: Diamd. preorders: **19,651**

Diamond preorders are the estimated number of comics sold, prior to their release, to comics shops in North America by Diamond Comic Distributors, the largest distributor. These figures underreport the actual number of circulating copies by the amount of reorders Diamond took (usually 5-10% again of the preorders) and sales by publishers to newsstand and bookstore distributors. For many independent publishers, Diamond's preorders may be quite close to the actual number of copies in circulation.

CHASTITY: THEATRE OF PAIN — Chaos

In 1976, Chastity, a beautiful, abused teen-ager is living in Toledo, Ohio. She dreams of becoming a professional actress and, when she escapes her troubled home and journeys to London to pursue her goals, she is bitten by a vampire and turned into a creature of the night. Befriended by the mysterious Countess, who allows her to feed on her attacker, Chastity begins learning about her unworldly and bloody abilities. Fortunately for her, Chastity has an ability unique to vampires: She can't be detected by other vampires. But this power becomes a curse, after the Countess and other characters seek to use Chastity for personal gain.

1 ❑ Feb 1997 Cover: 2.95 **NM** value: **Cover or less**
Circ: Diamd. preorders: **48,799** • **CGC:** 26 graded, best 9.9
A: Justiniano **W:** Brian Pulido
1/SC❑Feb 1997 **NM** value: **5.00**
• **CGC:** 3 graded, best 9.8
cardstock cover. • Onyx Premium Edition.
2 ❑ Apr 1997 Cover: 2.95 **NM** value: **Cover or less**
Circ: Diamd. preorders: **28,945**
A: Justiniano **W:** Brian Pulido
3 ❑ Jun 1997 Cover: 2.95 **NM** value: **Cover or less**
Circ: Diamd. preorders: **32,001**
back cover pin-up. **A:** Justiniano **W:** Brian Pulido
3/SC❑Jun 1997 **NM** value: **5.00**
no cover price. • Final Curtain Edition. • Limited Engagement
Bk 1❑ Cover: 9.95 **NM** value: **Cover or less**
• collects mini-series with original sketches **A:** Justiniano **W:** Brian Pulido

CHEAPSKIN — Fantagraphics / Eros

All issues are adults only.

1 ❑ b&w Cover: 2.95 **NM** value: **Cover or less**

CHECKMATE — DC

1 ❑ Apr 1988 Cover: 1.25 **NM** value: **1.50**
Circ: CapCity orders: **22,400**
📖 Opening Gambit **A:** Steve Erwin **W:** Paul Kupperberg ★ Origin of Checkmate.
2 ❑ May 1988 Cover: 1.25 **NM** value: **Cover or less**
Circ: CapCity orders: **15,800**
C: Gil Kane
3 ❑ Jun 1988 Cover: 1.25 **NM** value: **Cover or less**
Circ: CapCity orders: **15,550**
C: Rob Liefeld
4 ❑ Jul 1988 Cover: 1.25 **NM** value: **Cover or less**
Circ: CapCity orders: **17,500**
C: Gil Kane
5 ❑ Aug 1988 Cover: 1.25 **NM** value: **Cover or less**
Circ: CapCity orders: **16,600**
6 ❑ Sep 1988 Cover: 1.25 **NM** value: **Cover or less**
Circ: CapCity orders: **16,400**
7 ❑ Oct 1988 Cover: 1.25 **NM** value: **Cover or less**
Circ: CapCity orders: **15,750**
C: Gil Kane
8 ❑ Nov 1988 Cover: 1.25 **NM** value: **Cover or less**
Circ: CapCity orders: **13,650**
C: Gil Kane ★ Appearance of Black Thorn.
9 ❑ Dec 1988 Cover: 1.25 **NM** value: **Cover or less**
Circ: CapCity orders: **12,550**
10 ❑ Win 1988 Cover: 1.25 **NM** value: **Cover or less**
Circ: CapCity orders: **11,650**
C: Gil Kane
11 ❑ Hol 1988 Cover: 1.25 **NM** value: **Cover or less**
Circ: CapCity orders: **13,250**
• Invasion! First Strike **C:** Gil Kane
12 ❑ Feb 1989 Cover: 1.25 **NM** value: **Cover or less**
Circ: CapCity orders: **12,150**
• Invasion! Aftermath
13 ❑ Mar 1989 Cover: 1.50 **NM** value: **Cover or less**
Circ: CapCity orders: **10,200**
14 ❑ Apr 1989 Cover: 1.50 **NM** value: **Cover or less**
Circ: CapCity orders: **9,850**
★ Appearance of Black Thorn.
15 ❑ May 1989 Cover: 1.50 **NM** value: **Cover or less**
Circ: CapCity orders: **11,600**
📖 Janus Directive, Part 1; The Janus Directive, Part 1 • continues in Suicide Squad #27 **C:** Gil Kane
16 ❑ May 1989 Cover: 1.50 **NM** value: **Cover or less**
Circ: CapCity orders: **11,400**
📖 Janus Directive, Part 3 • continues in Suicide Squad #28 **C:** Gil Kane ★ Appearance of Major Force.
17 ❑ Jun 1989 Cover: 1.50 **NM** value: **Cover or less**
📖 Janus Directive, Part 5 • continues in Manhunter #14 **C:** Gil Kane
18 ❑ Jun 1989 Cover: 1.50 **NM** value: **Cover or less**
Circ: CapCity orders: **11,250**
📖 Janus Directive, Part 9 • continues in Suicide Squad #30 **C:** Gil Kane
19 ❑ Jul 1989 Cover: 1.50 **NM** value: **Cover or less**
Circ: CapCity orders: **10,200**
C: Gil Kane
20 ❑ Aug 1989 Cover: 1.50 **NM** value: **Cover or less**
Circ: CapCity orders: **10,800**
21 ❑ Oct 1989 Cover: 1.50 **NM** value: **Cover or less**
Circ: CapCity orders: **10,250**
22 ❑ Nov 1989 Cover: 1.50 **NM** value: **Cover or less**
Circ: CapCity orders: **9,750**
23 ❑ Dec 1989 Cover: 1.50 **NM** value: **Cover or less**
Circ: CapCity orders: **9,100**

CGC-graded: Multiply prices above by **33 for 9.9 M • 16 for 9.8 NM/M • 7 for 9.6 NM+ • 5 for 9.4 NM • 2.5 for 9.2 NM- • 1.5 for 9.0 VF/NM**

24 ❑ Jan 1990 Cover: 1.50 **NM** value: **Cover or less**
Circ: CapCity orders: **8,900**
25 ❑ Feb 1990 Cover: 1.50 **NM** value: **Cover or less**
Circ: CapCity orders: **8,500**
26 ❑ Cover: 1.50 **NM** value: **Cover or less**
Circ: CapCity orders: **8,200**
27 ❑ Cover: 1.50 **NM** value: **Cover or less**
Circ: CapCity orders: **7,750**
28 ❑ Jun 1990 Cover: 1.50 **NM** value: **Cover or less**
Circ: CapCity orders: **7,600**
29 ❑ Jul 1990 Cover: 1.50 **NM** value: **Cover or less**
Circ: CapCity orders: **7,400**
30 ❑ Aug 1990 Cover: 1.50 **NM** value: **Cover or less**
Circ: CapCity orders: **7,050**
31 ❑ Oct 1990 Cover: 1.50 **NM** value: **Cover or less**
Circ: CapCity orders: **6,750**
32 ❑ Dec 1990 Cover: 1.50 **NM** value: **Cover or less**
Circ: CapCity orders: **6,550**
33 ❑ Cover: 1.50 **NM** value: **Cover or less**
Circ: CapCity orders: **6,650**
final issue.

CHECKMATE (GOLD KEY) — Gold Key

The TV series starring private detectives Anthony George (1925-) and Doug McClure (1935-1995) ran two seasons, from 1960 to 1962. The basis for the series is that the investigators work in San Francisco, working to prevent crimes including killings, instead of to solve already-committed crimes. Their clients come to them in response to perceived threats, in hopes of averting disaster.

However, the comic book about their agency, Checkmate, Inc., ran for only two issues published at the end of the TV series' run. And there's no connection with the DC series of the same name.

— Maggie

1 ❑ ca. 1962 Cover: 0.12 **NM** value: **30.00**
• **CGC:** 1 graded, best 7.0
2 ❑ ca. 1963 Cover: 0.12 **NM** value: **20.00**
• **CGC:** 1 graded, best 7.0

CHECK-UP — Fantagraphics

1 ❑ b&w Cover: 2.75 **NM** value: **Cover or less**

CHEECH WIZARD — Last Gasp

1 ❑ Cover: 0.75 **NM** value: **Cover or less**
A: Vaughn Bodé **W:** Vaughn Bodé

CHEERLEADERS FROM HELL — Caliber

1 ❑ b&w Cover: 2.50 **NM** value: **Cover or less**
A: Mark Bloodworth **W:** Neil Robertson

CHEESE HEADS, THE — Tragedy Strikes

1 ❑ b&w Cover: 2.50 **NM** value: **Cover or less**
• second edition.
1-2 ❑ b&w Cover: 2.95 **NM** value: **Cover or less**
• second edition.
2 ❑ b&w Cover: 2.50 **NM** value: **Cover or less**
3 ❑ Cover: 2.95 **NM** value: **Cover or less**
4 ❑ Cover: 2.95 **NM** value: **Cover or less**
5 ❑ Cover: 2.95 **NM** value: **Cover or less**

CHEESE WEASEL — Side Show

1 ❑ Cover: 2.95 **NM** value: **Cover or less**
Color cover. **A:** Jim Ridings **W:** Jim Ridings
2 ❑ Cover: 2.95 **NM** value: **Cover or less**
Black & white covers begin. **A:** Jim Ridings **W:** Jim Ridings
3 ❑ Cover: 2.95 **NM** value: **Cover or less**
A: Jim Ridings **W:** Jim Ridings
4 ❑ Cover: 2.95 **NM** value: **Cover or less**
A: Jim Ridings **W:** Jim Ridings
5 ❑ Cover: 2.95 **NM** value: **Cover or less**
A: Jim Ridings **W:** Jim Ridings
6 ❑ Cover: 2.95 **NM** value: **Cover or less**
A: Jim Ridings **W:** Jim Ridings
7 ❑ Cover: 2.95 **NM** value: **Cover or less**
A: Jim Ridings **W:** Jim Ridings

CHEESE WEASEL: INNOCENT UNTIL PROVEN GUILTY — Side Show

1 ❑ Cover: 9.95 **NM** value: **Cover or less**
A: Jim Ridings **W:** Jim Ridings

CHEETA POP SCREAM QUEEN — Antarctic / Venus

1 ❑ May 1994 Cover: 2.95 **NM** value: **Cover or less**
A: Frank Strom **W:** Frank Strom
2 ❑ Nov 1994 Cover: 2.95 **NM** value: **Cover or less**
A: Frank Strom **W:** Frank Strom
3 ❑ Jan 1995 Cover: 2.95 **NM** value: **Cover or less**
A: Frank Strom **W:** Frank Strom
4 ❑ Mar 1995 Cover: 2.95 **NM** value: **Cover or less**
📖 Galaxy Marshall Gingaban vs. Claw King **A:** Frank Strom **W:** Frank Strom
5 ❑ May 1995 Cover: 2.95 **NM** value: **Cover or less**
📖 Interview with a Pornstar **A:** Frank Strom **W:** Frank Strom

CHEETA POP (VOL. 2) — Eros

1 ❑ Cover: 2.95 **NM** value: **Cover or less**
A: Frank Strom **W:** Frank Strom
2 ❑ Cover: 2.95 **NM** value: **Cover or less**
A: Frank Strom **W:** Frank Strom

3 ❑ Jan 1996 Cover: 2.95 **NM** value: **Cover or less**
📖 Morality and Monsters **A:** Frank Strom **W:** Frank Strom

CHEMICAL WARFARE — Checker Comics

1 ❑ b&w Cover: 2.50 **NM** value: **2.95**
2 ❑ Sum 1998, b&w Cover: 2.50 **NM** value: **2.95**
3 ❑ Cover: 2.95 **NM** value: **Cover or less**

CHEN -N- SOLLY — Thwack! Pow!

1 ❑ Cover: 0.50 **NM** value: **Cover or less**
A: Garth Haslam **W:** Garth Haslam
2 ❑ Cover: 0.50 **NM** value: **Cover or less**
📖 Reading, Riteing, & 'Rithmatic... **A:** Garth Haslam **W:** Garth Haslam

CHEQUE, MATE, THE — Fantagraphics

1 ❑ b&w Cover: 3.50 **NM** value: **Cover or less**
No issue number.

CHERRY — Last Gasp

All issues are adults only.

Cherry Poptart is the libidinous heroine of this sexy, silly series. Unshaken by the dangers of sex in the modern day, the blonde lives a sort of free-love existence with her fellow schoolmates. That is to say, Cherry gets down and dirty with just about anyone she meets. Created by Larry Welz, this explicit yet hilarious series enjoys the support of a large group of devoted fans.

The art, reminiscent of the adventures of a certain Riverdale gang, gives readers the fantasies they've lusted after for years. A spin-off series, Cherry's Jubilee, allowed other creators to play in Welz' sandbox.

1 ❑ Cover: 2.50 **NM** value: **7.50**
• 1977 **A:** Larry Welz **W:** Larry Welz ★ 1st Appearance of Cherry Poptart.
1-2 ❑ Cover: 2.50 **NM** value: **3.00**
2 ❑ Cover: 2.50 **NM** value: **4.00**
A: Larry Welz **W:** Larry Welz
3 ❑ Cover: 2.50 **NM** value: **4.00**
• Title changes to Cherry;indicia says Cherry (nee Poptart) **A:** Larry Welz **W:** Larry Welz
4 ❑ Cover: 2.50 **NM** value: **3.50**
A: Larry Welz **W:** Larry Welz
5 ❑ Cover: 2.50 **NM** value: **3.50**
A: Larry Welz **W:** Larry Welz
6 ❑ Cover: 2.50 **NM** value: **3.50**
A: Larry Welz **W:** Larry Welz
7 ❑ Cover: 2.50 **NM** value: **3.50**
A: Larry Welz **W:** Larry Welz
8 ❑ Cover: 2.50 **NM** value: **3.50**
📖 Ellie Dee in the Land of Woz • Oz parody Land of Woz **A:** Larry Welz **W:** Larry Welz
9 ❑ Cover: 2.50 **NM** value: **3.50**
A: Larry Welz **W:** Larry Welz
10 ❑ Cover: 2.50 **NM** value: **3.50**
📖 The New Guy; Honor Farm Girls; Charry & Zara Tungi: Rebel Without a Hardon; Hole in One; The Cherry Duke Show **A:** Larry Welz **W:** Larry Welz; Dan Fogel
11 ❑ Cover: 3.50 **NM** value: **3.95**
• 3-D issue;Cherry in 3D **A:** Larry Welz **W:** Larry Welz
11-2❑ Cover: 3.95 **NM** value: **Cover or less**
• Kitchen Sink reprint
12 ❑ Sum 1991 Cover: 2.95 **NM** value: **3.00**
• Cherry goes to Iraq **A:** Larry Welz **W:** Larry Welz
13 ❑ Cover: 2.95 **NM** value: **3.00**
• Last Cherry issue from Last Gasp **A:** Larry Welz **W:** Larry Welz
14 ❑ Feb 1993 Cover: 2.95 **NM** value: **Cover or less**
Circ: CapCity orders: **5,600**
📖 Cherry Does The Time Warp • moves to Kitchen Sink;1st issue at Kitchen Sink **A:** Larry Welz **W:** Larry Welz ★ Origin of Cherry.
15 ❑ Nov 1993 Cover: 2.95 **NM** value: **Cover or less**
Circ: CapCity orders: **5,425**
A: Larry Welz **W:** Larry Welz
16 ❑ Nov 1994 Cover: 2.95 **NM** value: **Cover or less**
Circ: CapCity orders: **5,050**
A: Larry Welz **W:** Larry Welz
17 ❑ Apr 1995 Cover: 2.95 **NM** value: **Cover or less**
Circ: CapCity orders: **4,895**
• TMNT parody **A:** Larry Welz **W:** Larry Welz
18 ❑ Oct 1995 Cover: 2.95 **NM** value: **Cover or less**
A: Larry Welz **W:** Larry Welz
19 ❑ Sep 1996 Cover: 2.95 **NM** value: **Cover or less**
• moves to Cherry Comics **A:** Larry Welz **W:** Larry Welz
20 ❑ Mar 1999 Cover: 2.95 **NM** value: **Cover or less**
Circ: Diamd. preorders: **6,207**
• was Kitchen Sink
Bk 1❑ Apr 1995, b&w Cover: 15.95 **NM** value: **Cover or less**
• collects Cherry #1-3 and stories from Funny Book #1 and Tuff S**t Comics
Bk 2❑ Mar 1994, b&w Cover: 15.95 **NM** value: **Cover or less**
• collects Cherry #4-6

CHERRY DELUXE — Cherry

All issues are adults only.

1 ❑ Aug 1998, b&w Cover: 4.00 **NM** value: **Cover or less**
Circ: Diamd. preorders: **5,581**
W: Neil Gaiman

CHERRY'S JUBILEE — Tundra

1 ❑ Cover: 2.95 **NM** value: **Cover or less**
Circ: CapCity orders: **4,800**

2 ❑ Cover: 2.95 **NM** value: **Cover or less**
3 ❑ Cover: 2.95 **NM** value: **Cover or less**
Circ: CapCity orders: **4,625**
4 ❑ Cover: 2.95 **NM** value: **Cover or less**
Circ: CapCity orders: **4,447**

CHERYL BLOSSOM (1ST SERIES) — Archie

1 ❑ Sep 1995 Cover: 1.50 **NM** value: **2.50**
Circ: CapCity orders: **2,325**
2 ❑ Oct 1995 Cover: 1.50 **NM** value: **2.00**
Circ: CapCity orders: **2,050**
3 ❑ Nov 1995 Cover: 1.50 **NM** value: **2.00**

CHERYL BLOSSOM (2ND SERIES) — Archie

1 ❑ Jul 1996 Cover: 1.50 **NM** value: **2.00**
2 ❑ Aug 1996 Cover: 1.50 **NM** value: **Cover or less**
3 ❑ Sep 1996 Cover: 1.50 **NM** value: **Cover or less**

CHERYL BLOSSOM (3RD SERIES) — Archie

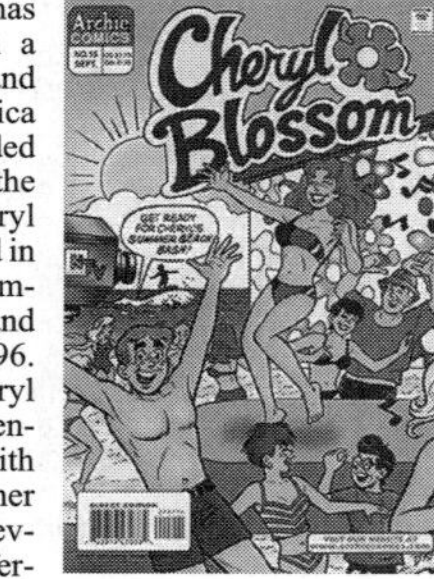

For years, Archie Andrews has had trouble choosing between a beautiful blonde, Betty Cooper, and a stunning brunette, Veronica Lodge. In 1995, his publisher added to his problems by reintroducing the gorgeous redhead named Cheryl Blossom, who'd been introduced in 1982 and who'd starred in two limited series and four specials and earned this ongoing series in 1996. While she's certainly lovely, Cheryl is petulant and demanding of attention; many of her adventures with Archie and the gang focus on her need to be the main attraction at every event and often end very differently from what she had hoped. Amazingly, the Archie creators have come up with a character who makes Veronica, one of comics' original "spoiled little rich girls," seem deep!

1 ❑ Apr 1997 Cover: 1.50 **NM** value: **2.00**
Circ: Diamd. preorders: **5,658**
2 ❑ May 1997 Cover: 1.50 **NM** value: **Cover or less**
Circ: Diamd. preorders: **4,488**
3 ❑ Jun 1997 Cover: 1.50 **NM** value: **Cover or less**
Circ: Diamd. preorders: **4,558**
4 ❑ Aug 1997 Cover: 1.50 **NM** value: **Cover or less**
Circ: Diamd. preorders: **4,927**
5 ❑ Sep 1997 Cover: 1.50 **NM** value: **Cover or less**
Circ: Diamd. preorders: **4,772**
6 ❑ Oct 1997 Cover: 1.50 **NM** value: **Cover or less**
Circ: Diamd. preorders: **4,670**
7 ❑ Nov 1997 Cover: 1.50 **NM** value: **Cover or less**
Circ: Diamd. preorders: **4,780**
8 ❑ Jan 1998 Cover: 1.75 **NM** value: **Cover or less**
Circ: Diamd. preorders: **4,839**
9 ❑ Feb 1998 Cover: 1.75 **NM** value: **Cover or less**
Circ: Diamd. preorders: **4,786**
10 ❑ Mar 1998 Cover: 1.75 **NM** value: **Cover or less**
Circ: Diamd. preorders: **4,474**
11 ❑ Apr 1998 Cover: 1.75 **NM** value: **Cover or less**
Circ: Diamd. preorders: **4,455**
12 ❑ May 1998 Cover: 1.75 **NM** value: **Cover or less**
Circ: Diamd. preorders: **4,123**
13 ❑ Jun 1998 Cover: 1.75 **NM** value: **Cover or less**
Circ: Diamd. preorders: **3,995**
14 ❑ Aug 1998 Cover: 1.75 **NM** value: **Cover or less**
Circ: Diamd. preorders: **4,166**
15 ❑ Sep 1998 Cover: 1.75 **NM** value: **Cover or less**
Circ: Diamd. preorders: **4,089**
cover forms triptych with issue #16 and #17. 📖 Beach Bash; Party Hardly
16 ❑ Oct 1998 Cover: 1.75 **NM** value: **Cover or less**
Circ: Diamd. preorders: **3,799**
17 ❑ Nov 1998 Cover: 1.75 **NM** value: **Cover or less**
Circ: Diamd. preorders: **3,611**
📖 Cheryl-Mania; How Crafty **A:** Dan Parent **W:** Dan Parent
18 ❑ Jan 1999 Cover: 1.75 **NM** value: **Cover or less**
Circ: Diamd. preorders: **3,695**
• Cheryl as super-model with readers' fashions
19 ❑ Feb 1999 Cover: 1.75 **NM** value: **Cover or less**
Circ: Diamd. preorders: **3,620**
20 ❑ Mar 1999 Cover: 1.75 **NM** value: **Cover or less**
Circ: Diamd. preorders: **3,539**
📖 Cinderblossom **A:** Dan Parent **W:** Dan Parent
21 ❑ Apr 1999 Cover: 1.79 **NM** value: **Cover or less**
Circ: Diamd. preorders: **3,411**
📖 Sugar World **A:** Holly Golightly **W:** Holly Golightly
22 ❑ May 1999 Cover: 1.79 **NM** value: **Cover or less**
Circ: Diamd. preorders: **3,288**
📖 Big in Japan **A:** Holly Golightly **W:** Holly Golightly
23 ❑ Jun 1999 Cover: 1.79 **NM** value: **Cover or less**
Circ: Diamd. preorders: **3,062**
24 ❑ Aug 1999 Cover: 1.79 **NM** value: **Cover or less**
Circ: Diamd. preorders: **3,285**
25 ❑ Sep 1999 Cover: 1.79 **NM** value: **Cover or less**
Circ: Diamd. preorders: **3,512**
26 ❑ Oct 1999 Cover: 1.79 **NM** value: **Cover or less**
Circ: Diamd. preorders: **3,299**
27 ❑ Nov 1999 Cover: 1.79 **NM** value: **Cover or less**
Circ: Diamd. preorders: **3,200**

CHERYL BLOSSOM GOES HOLLYWOOD — Archie

1 ❑ Dec 1996 Cover: 1.50 **NM** value: **Cover or less**
Circ: Direct Market orders: **5,328**

Other grades: Multiply prices above by **1.5 for Mint • 2/3 for Very Fine • 1/3 for Fine • 1/5 for Very Good • 1/8 for Good**

She Ought to Be in Pictures, Part 1; She Ought to Be in Pictures, Part 2; She Ought to Be in Pictures, Part 3; She Ought to Be in Pictures, Part 4 **A:** Dan Parent **W:** Dan Parent
2 ❑ Jan 1997 Cover: 1.50 **NM** value: **Cover or less**
Circ: Direct Market orders: **4,894**
A: Dan Parent **W:** Dan Parent
3 ❑ Feb 1997 Cover: 1.50 **NM** value: **Cover or less**
Circ: Diamd. preorders: **4,717**
A: Dan Parent **W:** Dan Parent

CHERYL BLOSSOM SPECIAL — Archie

1 ❑ Cover: 2.00 **NM** value: **Cover or less**
Circ: CapCity orders: **2,400**
2 ❑ Cover: 2.00 **NM** value: **Cover or less**
3 ❑ Cover: 2.00 **NM** value: **Cover or less**
4 ❑ Cover: 2.00 **NM** value: **Cover or less**

CHESTY SANCHEZ — Antarctic

1 ❑ Nov 1995, b&w Cover: 2.95 **NM** value: **Cover or less**
A: Jay; Scott Michaud **W:** Steve Ross
2 ❑ Mar 1996, b&w Cover: 2.95 **NM** value: **Cover or less**
A: Jay; Scott Michaud **W:** Steve Ross
3 ❑ Cover: 2.95 **NM** value: **Cover or less**
A: Jay; Scott Michaud **W:** Steve Ross
SE 1 ❑ Feb 1999, b&w Cover: 5.99 **NM** value: **Cover or less**
cardstock cover. • Super Special Edition. • Super Special;collects two-issue series **A:** Jay; Jayne Wu; Laura Molina; Scott Michaud; Carlos Salda±a **W:** Steve Ross

CHEVAL NOIR — Dark Horse

Cheval Noir is an import-oriented black-and-white collection from top-drawer publisher Dark Horse. "Cheval" means "horse"; "noir" means "black" in French. The anthology features short stories from some of the best comic talents in the world, including Moebius, Daniel Torres, Dave Stevens, and Michael Kaluta. The material is translated and re-lettered (when necessary) for the benefit of an English-speaking audience.

Before it ended its run, the series had encompassed 48 issues in a variety of formats, ranging from standard size (32 pages) to giant size (72 pages) issues.

1 ❑ Aug 1989, b&w Cover: 3.50 **NM** value: **Cover or less**
Lone Sloane; Fever In Urbicand; Fred and Bob; Adele and the Beast; Angel Fusion; Rork **A:** Olivier Vatine; Joel Andreas; Jacques Tardi; Keisuke Goto; Philippe Druillet; Schuiten **C:** Dave Stevens **W:** Joel Andreas; Jacques Tardi; Philippe Druillet; Schuiten; Cailleteau; Hiroyuki Kato
2 ❑ Oct 1989, b&w Cover: 3.50 **NM** value: **Cover or less**
C: Dave Stevens
3 ❑ Cover: 3.50 **NM** value: **Cover or less**
4 ❑ 1990 Cover: 3.50 **NM** value: **Cover or less**
5 ❑ Mar 1990 Cover: 3.50 **NM** value: **Cover or less**
A: Brian Bolland
6 ❑ 1990 Cover: 3.50 **NM** value: **Cover or less**
Sunstroke; Fred and Bob; Robert Redford; The Demon of the Eiffel Tower; Fever In Urbicand; Lone Sloane; Diary of a Fullerette; Rork **A:** Olivier Vatine; Joel Andreas; Rick Geary; Brian Bolland; Jacques Tardi; Peeters; Phil Trumbo; Philippe Druillet **W:** Joel Andreas; Rick Geary; Brian Bolland; Michael W. Kaluta; Jacques Tardi; Philippe Druillet; Schuiten; Cailleteau
7 ❑ 1990 Cover: 3.50 **NM** value: **Cover or less**
C: Dave Stevens
8 ❑ 1990 Cover: 3.50 **NM** value: **Cover or less**
Coutoo, Part 1 **A:** Joel Andreas **W:** Joel Andreas
9 ❑ 1990 Cover: 3.50 **NM** value: **Cover or less**
Coutoo, Part 2 **A:** Joel Andreas **W:** Joel Andreas
10 ❑ 1990 Cover: 3.50 **NM** value: **Cover or less**
Coutoo, Part 3 **A:** Joel Andreas **W:** Joel Andreas
11 ❑ 1990 Cover: 3.50 **NM** value: **Cover or less**
Coutoo, Part 4 **A:** Joel Andreas **W:** Joel Andreas
12 ❑ 1990 Cover: 3.50 **NM** value: **Cover or less**
Coutoo, Part 5 **A:** Joel Andreas **W:** Joel Andreas
13 ❑ 1990 Cover: 3.50 **NM** value: **Cover or less**
14 ❑ Cover: 3.50 **NM** value: **Cover or less**
15 ❑ 1991 Cover: 3.50 **NM** value: **Cover or less**
16 ❑ 1991 Cover: 3.50 **NM** value: **3.75**
• trading cards
17 ❑ 1991 Cover: 3.50 **NM** value: **Cover or less**
• trading cards
18 ❑ 1991 Cover: 3.50 **NM** value: **Cover or less**
• trading cards
19 ❑ 1991 Cover: 3.50 **NM** value: **Cover or less**
• trading cards
20 ❑ 1991 Cover: 3.50 **NM** value: **Cover or less**
21 ❑ 1991 Cover: 3.50 **NM** value: **Cover or less**
22 ❑ 1991 Cover: 3.50 **NM** value: **Cover or less**
23 ❑ 1991 Cover: 3.50 **NM** value: **Cover or less**
24 ❑ 1991 Cover: 3.50 **NM** value: **Cover or less**
25 ❑ 1991 Cover: 3.50 **NM** value: **Cover or less**
26 ❑ Jan 1992 Cover: 3.50 **NM** value: **Cover or less**
27 ❑ Feb 1992 Cover: 2.95 **NM** value: **Cover or less**
28 ❑ Mar 1992 Cover: 2.95 **NM** value: **Cover or less**
29 ❑ Apr 1992 Cover: 2.95 **NM** value: **Cover or less**
30 ❑ May 1992 Cover: 2.95 **NM** value: **Cover or less**
31 ❑ Jun 1992 Cover: 2.95 **NM** value: **Cover or less**
32 ❑ Jul 1992 Cover: 2.95 **NM** value: **Cover or less**
33 ❑ Aug 1992 Cover: 2.95 **NM** value: **Cover or less**
The Angriest Dog in the World; The Man From the Ciguri; Sabotage; In Search of Peter Pan **A:** Moebius; Cosey; Daniel Torres; David Lynch **W:** Moebius; Cosey; Daniel Torres; David Lynch
34 ❑ Sep 1992 Cover: 2.95 **NM** value: **Cover or less**
35 ❑ Oct 1992 Cover: 2.95 **NM** value: **Cover or less**
36 ❑ Nov 1992 Cover: 2.95 **NM** value: **Cover or less**
37 ❑ Dec 1992 Cover: 2.95 **NM** value: **Cover or less**
38 ❑ Jan 1993 Cover: 2.95 **NM** value: **Cover or less**
39 ❑ Feb 1993 Cover: 2.95 **NM** value: **Cover or less**
40 ❑ Mar 1993 Cover: 2.95 **NM** value: **Cover or less**
41 ❑ Apr 1993 Cover: 2.95 **NM** value: **Cover or less**
42 ❑ May 1993 Cover: 2.95 **NM** value: **Cover or less**
43 ❑ Jun 1993 Cover: 2.95 **NM** value: **Cover or less**
44 ❑ Jul 1993 Cover: 2.95 **NM** value: **Cover or less**
45 ❑ Aug 1993 Cover: 2.95 **NM** value: **Cover or less**
46 ❑ Sep 1993 Cover: 2.95 **NM** value: **Cover or less**
47 ❑ Oct 1993 Cover: 2.95 **NM** value: **Cover or less**
48 ❑ Nov 1993 Cover: 2.95 **NM** value: **Cover or less**
49 ❑ Dec 1993 Cover: 2.95 **NM** value: **Cover or less**
50 ❑ Jan 1994 Cover: 2.95 **NM** value: **Cover or less**
final issue.

CHEYENNE — Dell

Cheyenne ran on TV from 1955 to 1963, a popular Western TV starring Clint Walker (1927-) as Cheyenne Bodie, who roamed the West following the Civil War. a cowboy hero. Cheyenne helped the cause of justice by assisting sheriffs and the Army while maintaining his own fierce independence from any organized authority. A sense of freedom and rebelliousness underlies Cheyenne to a greater extent than many more conventional Westerns.

The comic-book version from Dell featured two Cheyenne stories each issue, plus a backup feature, Small Bear, about an Indian boy. There were also one-page text stories and features.

5 ❑ Nov 1957 Cover: 0.10 **NM** value: **32.00**
6 ❑ Feb 1958 Cover: 0.10 **NM** value: **24.00**
7 ❑ May 1958 Cover: 0.10 **NM** value: **24.00**
• **CGC:** 1 graded, best 8.0
8 ❑ Aug 1958 Cover: 0.10 **NM** value: **24.00**
9 ❑ Nov 1958 Cover: 0.10 **NM** value: **24.00**
10 ❑ Feb 1959 Cover: 0.10 **NM** value: **24.00**
11 ❑ May 1959 Cover: 0.10 **NM** value: **18.00**
12 ❑ Aug 1959 Cover: 0.10 **NM** value: **18.00**
13 ❑ Nov 1959 Cover: 0.10 **NM** value: **18.00**
14 ❑ Feb 1960 Cover: 0.10 **NM** value: **18.00**
• **CGC:** 1 graded, best 9.6
15 ❑ Apr 1960 Cover: 0.10 **NM** value: **18.00**
• **CGC:** 1 graded, best 9.6
16 ❑ Jun 1960 Cover: 0.10 **NM** value: **18.00**
• **CGC:** 2 graded, best 9.2
17 ❑ Aug 1960 Cover: 0.10 **NM** value: **18.00**
18 ❑ Oct 1960 Cover: 0.10 **NM** value: **18.00**
• **CGC:** 1 graded, best 8.0
19 ❑ Dec 1960 Cover: 0.10 **NM** value: **18.00**
• **CGC:** 1 graded, best 9.4
20 ❑ Feb 1961 Cover: 0.10 **NM** value: **18.00**
• **CGC:** 1 graded, best 9.6
21 ❑ Apr 1961 Cover: 0.10 **NM** value: **18.00**
22 ❑ Jun 1961 Cover: 0.10 **NM** value: **18.00**
23 ❑ Aug 1961 Cover: 0.10 **NM** value: **18.00**
24 ❑ Oct 1961 Cover: 0.10 **NM** value: **18.00**
• **CGC:** 1 graded, best 9.4
25 ❑ Dec 1961 Cover: 0.10 **NM** value: **18.00**
final issue.

CHEYENNE KID — Charlton

8 ❑ Jul 1957 Cover: 0.10 **NM** value: **30.00**
• Series continued from Wild Frontier #7
9 ❑ Oct 1957 Cover: 0.10 **NM** value: **20.00**
10 ❑ Cover: 0.10 **NM** value: **35.00**
A: Al Williamson; Steve Ditko(cover art)
11 ❑ 1958 Cover: 0.10 **NM** value: **30.00**
• Giant-size. **A:** Al Williamson
12 ❑ 1958 Cover: 0.10 **NM** value: **20.00**
13 ❑ 1958 Cover: 0.10 **NM** value: **20.00**
14 ❑ 1958 Cover: 0.10 **NM** value: **20.00**
15 ❑ Cover: 0.10 **NM** value: **20.00**
16 ❑ Cover: 0.10 **NM** value: **16.00**
17 ❑ 1959 Cover: 0.10 **NM** value: **16.00**
18 ❑ 1959 Cover: 0.10 **NM** value: **16.00**
19 ❑ Cover: 0.10 **NM** value: **16.00**
20 ❑ Cover: 0.10 **NM** value: **16.00**
21 ❑ Cover: 0.10 **NM** value: **14.00**
22 ❑ 1960 Cover: 0.10 **NM** value: **14.00**
23 ❑ 1960 Cover: 0.10 **NM** value: **14.00**
24 ❑ Cover: 0.10 **NM** value: **14.00**
25 ❑ Cover: 0.10 **NM** value: **14.00**
26 ❑ Cover: 0.10 **NM** value: **14.00**
27 ❑ Cover: 0.10 **NM** value: **14.00**
28 ❑ May 1961 Cover: 0.10 **NM** value: **14.00**
29 ❑ Jul 1961 Cover: 0.10 **NM** value: **14.00**
30 ❑ Sep 1961 Cover: 0.10 **NM** value: **14.00**
31 ❑ Nov 1961 Cover: 0.10 **NM** value: **10.00**
• **CGC:** 1 graded, best 5.5
32 ❑ Feb 1962 Cover: 0.10 **NM** value: **10.00**
33 ❑ Apr 1962 Cover: 0.10 **NM** value: **10.00**
34 ❑ Jun 1962 Cover: 0.10 **NM** value: **10.00**
35 ❑ Aug 1962 Cover: 0.12 **NM** value: **10.00**
36 ❑ Oct 1962 Cover: 0.12 **NM** value: **10.00**
37 ❑ Dec 1962 Cover: 0.12 **NM** value: **10.00**
38 ❑ Feb 1963 Cover: 0.12 **NM** value: **10.00**
39 ❑ Apr 1963 Cover: 0.12 **NM** value: **10.00**
40 ❑ Jun 1963 Cover: 0.12 **NM** value: **10.00**
41 ❑ Aug 1963 Cover: 0.12 **NM** value: **8.00**
42 ❑ Dec 1963 Cover: 0.12 **NM** value: **8.00**
43 ❑ Oct 1963 Cover: 0.12 **NM** value: **8.00**
44 ❑ Feb 1964 Cover: 0.12 **NM** value: **8.00**
Circ: Statement: **121,963**
45 ❑ Apr 1964 Cover: 0.12 **NM** value: **8.00**
Circ: Statement: **121,963**
46 ❑ 1964 Cover: 0.12 **NM** value: **8.00**
Circ: Statement: **121,963**
47 ❑ Oct 1964 Cover: 0.12 **NM** value: **8.00**
Circ: Statement: **121,963**
48 ❑ Dec 1964 Cover: 0.12 **NM** value: **8.00**
Circ: Statement: **121,963**
49 ❑ Feb 1965 Cover: 0.12 **NM** value: **8.00**
Circ: Statement: **118,124**
50 ❑ May 1965 Cover: 0.12 **NM** value: **8.00**
Circ: Statement: **118,124**
• Has1964 Statement, filed 9/30/1964; avg print run 187,971; avg sales 121,957; avg subs 6; avg total paid 121,963; samples 26; max existent 121,989; 35% of run returned
51 ❑ Aug 1965 Cover: 0.12 **NM** value: **6.00**
Circ: Statement: **118,124**
52 ❑ Sep 1965 Cover: 0.12 **NM** value: **6.00**
Circ: Statement: **118,124**
53 ❑ Nov 1965 Cover: 0.12 **NM** value: **6.00**
Circ: Statement: **118,124**
54 ❑ Jan 1966 Cover: 0.12 **NM** value: **6.00**
Circ: Statement: **116,320**
55 ❑ Apr 1966 Cover: 0.12 **NM** value: **6.00**
Circ: Statement: **116,320**
56 ❑ Jun 1966 Cover: 0.12 **NM** value: **6.00**
Circ: Statement: **116,320**
57 ❑ Aug 1966 Cover: 0.12 **NM** value: **6.00**
Circ: Statement: **116,320**
58 ❑ Oct 1966 Cover: 0.12 **NM** value: **6.00**
Circ: Statement: **116,320**
59 ❑ Dec 1966 Cover: 0.12 **NM** value: **6.00**
Circ: Statement: **116,320**
60 ❑ Feb 1967 Cover: 0.12 **NM** value: **6.00**
Circ: Statement: **120,328**
61 ❑ May 1967 Cover: 0.12 **NM** value: **6.00**
Circ: Statement: **120,328**
62 ❑ Jul 1967 Cover: 0.12 **NM** value: **6.00**
Circ: Statement: **120,328**
63 ❑ Sep 1967 Cover: 0.12 **NM** value: **6.00**
Circ: Statement: **120,328**
64 ❑ Nov 1967 Cover: 0.12 **NM** value: **6.00**
Circ: Statement: **120,328**
65 ❑ Jan 1968 Cover: 0.12 **NM** value: **6.00**
Circ: Statement: **140,040**
66 ❑ May 1968 Cover: 0.12 **NM** value: **6.00**
Circ: Statement: **140,040**
67 ❑ Jul 1968 Cover: 0.12 **NM** value: **6.00**
Circ: Statement: **140,040**
68 ❑ Sep 1968 Cover: 0.12 **NM** value: **6.00**
Circ: Statement: **140,040**
69 ❑ Nov 1968 Cover: 0.12 **NM** value: **6.00**
Circ: Statement: **140,040**
70 ❑ Jan 1969 Cover: 0.12 **NM** value: **6.00**
71 ❑ Mar 1969 Cover: 0.12 **NM** value: **4.00**
72 ❑ May 1969 Cover: 0.12 **NM** value: **4.00**
73 ❑ Jul 1969 Cover: 0.12 **NM** value: **4.00**
74 ❑ Sep 1969 Cover: 0.15 **NM** value: **4.00**
75 ❑ Nov 1969 Cover: 0.15 **NM** value: **4.00**
76 ❑ Jan 1970 Cover: 0.15 **NM** value: **4.00**
Circ: Statement: **124,045**
77 ❑ Mar 1970 Cover: 0.15 **NM** value: **4.00**
Circ: Statement: **124,045**
78 ❑ May 1970 Cover: 0.15 **NM** value: **4.00**
Circ: Statement: **124,045**
79 ❑ Jul 1970 Cover: 0.15 **NM** value: **4.00**
Circ: Statement: **124,045**
80 ❑ Sep 1970 Cover: 0.15 **NM** value: **4.00**
Circ: Statement: **124,045**
81 ❑ Nov 1970 Cover: 0.15 **NM** value: **4.00**
Circ: Statement: **124,045**
82 ❑ Jan 1971 Cover: 0.15 **NM** value: **4.00**
83 ❑ Mar 1971 Cover: 0.15 **NM** value: **4.00**
84 ❑ May 1971 Cover: 0.15 **NM** value: **4.00**
• Has 1970 Statement, filed 9/30/1970; avg print run 200,000; avg sales 140,000; avg subs 40; avg total paid140,040; samples 300; max existent 140,340; 30% of run returned
85 ❑ Jul 1971 Cover: 0.15 **NM** value: **4.00**
86 ❑ Sep 1971 Cover: 0.15 **NM** value: **4.00**
87 ❑ Nov 1971 Cover: 0.20 **NM** value: **4.00**
87-2 ❑ ca. 1978 Cover: 0.35 **NM** value: **2.00**
• Modern Comics reprints;Modern Comics reprint
88 ❑ Jan 1972 Cover: 0.20 **NM** value: **4.00**
89 ❑ Mar 1972 Cover: 0.20 **NM** value: **4.00**
The Warmaker; How "Rojito" became... Apache Red; Tenderfoot Sheriff: The Cane Gun (text); Rider in the Night **A:** Fred Himes; Sanho Kim **W:** Joe Gill ★ Origin of Apache Red.
89-2 ❑ ca. 1978 Cover: 0.35 **NM** value: **2.00**
The Warmaker; How "Rojito" became... Apache Red; Tenderfoot Sheriff: The Cane Gun (text); Rider in the Night • Modern Comics reprint;Modern Comics reprints **A:** Fred Himes; Sanho Kim; **W:** Joe Gill ★ Origin of Apache Red.
90 ❑ May 1972 Cover: 0.20 **NM** value: **4.00**
The Treaty Breakers; Apache Red; Blood Feud **A:** Sanho Kim **W:** Joe Gill
91 ❑ Jul 1972 Cover: 0.20 **NM** value: **2.50**
92 ❑ Sep 1972 Cover: 0.20 **NM** value: **2.50**
93 ❑ Nov 1972 Cover: 0.20 **NM** value: **2.50**
94 ❑ Jan 1973 Cover: 0.20 **NM** value: **2.50**
95 ❑ Mar 1973 Cover: 0.20 **NM** value: **2.50**
96 ❑ May 1973 Cover: 0.20 **NM** value: **2.50**
• Has 1972 Statement; avg total paid circ 124,045
97 ❑ Jul 1973 Cover: 0.20 **NM** value: **2.50**
98 ❑ Sep 1973 Cover: 0.20 **NM** value: **2.50**
99 ❑ Nov 1973 Cover: 0.20 **NM** value: **2.50**
final issue.

CGC-graded: Multiply prices above by **33 for 9.9 M • 16 for 9.8 NM/M • 7 for 9.6 NM+ • 5 for 9.4 NM • 2.5 for 9.2 NM- • 1.5 for 9.0 VF/NM**

CHIAROSCURO — DC / Vertigo

From the Vertigo line, writers Pat McGreal and David Rawson and artist Chas Truog present a 10-issue account of the life of the Renaissance master Leonardo da Vinci. The story is told from the viewpoint of Salai, Leonardo's amoral, conniving apprentice. The relationship between master and servant, and of art and the artist, is explored, providing a startling and often dark portrait of human natures and desires. The work and research that went into this project is evident, and the specialized subject matter is presented in a reader-friendly, approachable way.

Chiaroscuro is a term relating to the interplay between light and dark in a picture.

1 Jul 1995 Cover: 2.50 **NM** value: **Cover or less**
Circ: CapCity orders: **8,900**
Greater Than Light **A:** Chas Truog **W:** David Rawson; Pat McGreal
2 Aug 1995 Cover: 2.50 **NM** value: **Cover or less**
Circ: CapCity orders: **7,275**
A: Chas Truog **W:** David Rawson; Pat McGreal
3 Sep 1995 Cover: 2.95 **NM** value: **Cover or less**
Circ: CapCity orders: **6,700**
Clearly in Dreams **A:** Chas Truog **W:** David Rawson; Pat McGreal
4 Oct 1995 Cover: 2.95 **NM** value: **Cover or less**
Dispero **A:** Chas Truog **W:** David Rawson; Pat McGreal
5 Nov 1995 Cover: 2.95 **NM** value: **Cover or less**
Limb of Satan **A:** Chas Truog **W:** David Rawson; Pat McGreal
6 Dec 1995 Cover: 2.95 **NM** value: **Cover or less**
A: Chas Truog **W:** David Rawson; Pat McGreal
7 Jan 1996 Cover: 2.95 **NM** value: **Cover or less**
A: Chas Truog **W:** David Rawson; Pat McGreal
8 Feb 1996 Cover: 2.95 **NM** value: **Cover or less**
The Giant **A:** Chas Truog **W:** David Rawson; Pat McGreal
9 Mar 1996 Cover: 2.95 **NM** value: **Cover or less**
The Deluge **A:** Chas Truog **W:** David Rawson; Pat McGreal
10 Apr 1996 Cover: 2.95 **NM** value: **Cover or less**
The Great Bird final issue. **A:** Chas Truog **W:** David Rawson; Pat McGreal

CHI CHIAN — Sirius

1 Oct 1997 Cover: 2.95 **NM** value: **Cover or less**
Circ: Diamd. preorders: **7,045**
2 Dec 1997 Cover: 2.95 **NM** value: **Cover or less**
Circ: Diamd. preorders: **4,237**
2-2 Cover: 2.95 **NM** value: **Cover or less**
2-3 Cover: 2.95 **NM** value: **Cover or less**
3 Feb 1998 Cover: 2.95 **NM** value: **Cover or less**
Circ: Diamd. preorders: **3,499**
4 Apr 1998 Cover: 2.95 **NM** value: **Cover or less**
Circ: Diamd. preorders: **3,026**
5 Jun 1998 Cover: 2.95 **NM** value: **Cover or less**
Circ: Diamd. preorders: **2,688**
6 Aug 1998 Cover: 2.95 **NM** value: **Cover or less**
Circ: Diamd. preorders: **2,325**

CHICK MAGNET — Voluptuous

1 Cover: 2.95 **NM** value: **Cover or less**
A: Anthony Vukojevich **W:** Anthony Vukojevich

CHIEF VICTORIO'S APACHE MASSACRE — Avon

1 ca. 1951 **NM** value: **300.00**
• **CGC:** 3 graded, best 9.0

CHILDHOOD'S END — Image

1 Oct 1997, b&w Cover: 2.95 **NM** value: **Cover or less**
A: Jim Calafiore **W:** Jim Calafiore; Malcolm Bourne
2 Nov 1997 Cover: 2.95 **NM** value: **Cover or less**
• <Never published?> **A:** Jim Calafiore **W:** Jim Calafiore; Malcolm Bourne
3 Dec 1997 Cover: 2.95 **NM** value: **Cover or less**
• <Never published?> **A:** Jim Calafiore **W:** Jim Calafiore; Malcolm Bourne
4 Jan 1998 Cover: 2.95 **NM** value: **Cover or less**
• <Never published?> **A:** Jim Calafiore **W:** Jim Calafiore; Malcolm Bourne
5 Feb 1998 Cover: 2.95 **NM** value: **Cover or less**
• <Never published?> **A:** Jim Calafiore **W:** Jim Calafiore; Malcolm Bourne

CHILDREN OF FIRE — Fantagor

1 Cover: 2.00 **NM** value: **Cover or less**
Circ: CapCity orders: **5,925**
A: Richard Corben **W:** Richard Corben
2 Cover: 2.00 **NM** value: **Cover or less**
Circ: CapCity orders: **4,725**
A: Richard Corben **W:** Richard Corben
3 Cover: 2.00 **NM** value: **Cover or less**
Circ: CapCity orders: **4,200**
A: Richard Corben **W:** Richard Corben

CHILDREN OF THE FALLEN ANGEL — Ace

1 Feb 1997 Cover: 2.95 **NM** value: **Cover or less**
Gothic Moon **A:** Jay Juch **W:** Kevin Santiago

indicates **Story Title** or **Storyline** information.
★ indicates **Character Appearance** information.
W = Writer • A = Artist • C = Cover Artist

CHILDREN OF THE NIGHT — Nightwynd

In a darkling realm, a beautiful demon named Nadia dreams of freedom. With the help of two fellow demons, she hatches a plan.

Back in our world, two boys discover a treasure trunk while walking on the beach. They find a book inside, engraved with mystical symbols, which they take with them to the "sissy ballet class" their parents signed them up for. There, they show it to their teacher, who finds in it a very special dance for the children to try.

But, when the dance begins, they find they cannot stop, even as the ground cracks under them and demons rip through into our world. The dance of death has begun, and Nadia is once more in the realm of the living.

For mortals, the time of fear has begun.

1 b&w Cover: 2.50 **NM** value: **Cover or less**
Dance Of Death
2 b&w Cover: 2.50 **NM** value: **Cover or less**
A: Barry Blair **W:** Peter Palmiotti
3 b&w Cover: 2.50 **NM** value: **Cover or less**
4 b&w Cover: 2.50 **NM** value: **Cover or less**

CHILDREN OF THE VOYAGER — Marvel

1 Sep 1993 Cover: 2.95 **NM** value: **Cover or less**
Circ: CapCity orders: **23,400**
Embossed cover. Shadows & Fog • foil **A:** Paul Johnson **W:** Nick Abadzis
2 Oct 1993 Cover: 1.95 **NM** value: **Cover or less**
Circ: CapCity orders: **7,800**
The Counterfeit Man **A:** Paul Johnson **W:** Nick Abadzis
3 Nov 1993 Cover: 1.95 **NM** value: **Cover or less**
Circ: CapCity orders: **6,050**
Candle Burning Brightly **A:** Paul Johnson **W:** Nick Abadzis
4 Dec 1993 Cover: 1.95 **NM** value: **Cover or less**
Circ: CapCity orders: **5,150**
State Of Grace **A:** Paul Johnson **W:** Nick Abadzis

CHILDREN'S CRUSADE, THE — DC / Vertigo

In 1212, yet another Crusade was ending in bloody failure. As the story goes: A monk cried out, saying that God was not allowing the Christians to prevail, since their souls were already stained with sin. What was needed, he said, was an army of innocents: a children's crusade. The call went out, and 50,000 girls and boys answered. They sailed on 100 ships toward the Holy Land. But on the way, a storm arose and wrecked all but two of the ships, killing 49,000 children in one night. The remaining two ships delivered their passengers into slavery and pain. But for a few of these doomed children, there was salvation, of sorts, as they escaped into another place.

Centuries later, it seems that an entire village of children has also found the doorway into that other world. Just as the Pied Piper stole the children of Hamelin, someone — or something — has caused every child in tiny Flaxdown to disappear — into a mysterious world for lost children.

1 Dec 1993 Cover: 3.95 **NM** value: **4.50**
Circ: CapCity orders: **21,150**
The Children's Crusade, Part 1 **A:** Chris Bachalo **W:** Neil Gaiman
2 Jan 1994 Cover: 3.95 **NM** value: **4.00**
Circ: CapCity orders: **15,900**
The Children's Crusade, Part 7 **A:** Chris Bachalo **W:** Neil Gaiman

CHILDREN WITH GLUE — Blackbird

Bk 1 b&w Cover: 4.95 **NM** value: **Cover or less**
• Shannon Wheeler

CHILD'S PLAY 2: THE OFFICIAL MOVIE ADAPTATION — Innovation

1 Cover: 2.50 **NM** value: **Cover or less**
Circ: CapCity orders: **4,205**
• Adapted from the screenplay by Don Mancini **A:** Darick Robertson **W:** Andy Mangels; Don Mancini
2 Cover: 2.50 **NM** value: **Cover or less**
Circ: CapCity orders: **3,880**
A: Darick Robertson **W:** Andy Mangels; Don Mancini
3 Cover: 2.50 **NM** value: **Cover or less**
Circ: CapCity orders: **3,085**
Andy and the Chucky Factory **A:** Darick Robertson **W:** Andy Mangels; Don Mancini
Bk 1 Cover: 6.95 **NM** value: **Cover or less**
• collection

CHILD'S PLAY 3 — Innovation

1 Cover: 2.50 **NM** value: **Cover or less**
Circ: CapCity orders: **2,665**
2 Cover: 2.50 **NM** value: **Cover or less**
Circ: CapCity orders: **2,105**
3 Cover: 2.50 **NM** value: **Cover or less**
Circ: CapCity orders: **2,110**
Good Guys Wear Blood **A:** Brandon McKinney **W:** Andy Mangels
4 Cover: 2.50 **NM** value: **Cover or less**

CHILD'S PLAY: THE SERIES — Innovation

1 Cover: 2.50 **NM** value: **Cover or less**
Circ: CapCity orders: **4,155**
Night Of The Living Doll **A:** Paul Camilleri **W:** Andy Mangels
2 Cover: 2.50 **NM** value: **Cover or less**
Circ: CapCity orders: **3,925**
3 Cover: 2.50 **NM** value: **Cover or less**
Circ: CapCity orders: **3,340**
4 Cover: 2.50 **NM** value: **Cover or less**
Circ: CapCity orders: **2,500**
5 Cover: 2.50 **NM** value: **Cover or less**
Circ: CapCity orders: **2,290**

CHILI — Marvel

Chili, red-headed rival to Marvel's teen-fashion mainstay Millie the Model, got her own title in 1967 as Marvel, drowning in super-hero titles, tried to keep its female reader base from taking off.

Vain, flighty Chili largely avoids the Archie-like quality inherent in practically all American teen humor comics, offering more witty banter, an element of high-fashion and plain old late-1960s weirdness)

Writer Stan Lee is at his campiest in the scripts for these issues, which sometimes read like Stan's take on a Marx Brothers routine, if you can imagine that!

2 Jun 1969 Cover: 0.15 **NM** value: **12.00**
3 Jul 1969 Cover: 0.15 **NM** value: **8.00**
4 Aug 1969 Cover: 0.15 **NM** value: **8.00**
5 Sep 1969 Cover: 0.15 **NM** value: **8.00**
6 Oct 1969 Cover: 0.15 **NM** value: **6.00**
7 Nov 1969 Cover: 0.15 **NM** value: **6.00**
8 Dec 1969 Cover: 0.15 **NM** value: **6.00**
9 Jan 1970 Cover: 0.15 **NM** value: **6.00**
10 Feb 1970 Cover: 0.15 **NM** value: **8.00**
• **CGC:** 1 graded, best 9.2
11 Mar 1970 Cover: 0.15 **NM** value: **5.00**
12 Apr 1970 Cover: 0.15 **NM** value: **5.00**
13 May 1970 Cover: 0.15 **NM** value: **5.00**
14 Jun 1970 Cover: 0.15 **NM** value: **5.00**
15 Jul 1970 Cover: 0.15 **NM** value: **5.00**
16 Aug 1970 Cover: 0.15 **NM** value: **5.00**
17 Sep 1970 Cover: 0.15 **NM** value: **5.00**
18 Aug 1972 Cover: 0.20 **NM** value: **5.00**
19 Oct 1972 Cover: 0.20 **NM** value: **5.00**
20 Dec 1972 Cover: 0.20 **NM** value: **5.00**
21 Feb 1973 Cover: 0.20 **NM** value: **5.00**
22 Apr 1973 Cover: 0.20 **NM** value: **5.00**
23 Jun 1973 Cover: 0.20 **NM** value: **5.00**
24 Aug 1973 Cover: 0.20 **NM** value: **5.00**
25 Oct 1973 Cover: 0.20 **NM** value: **5.00**
26 Dec 1973 Cover: 0.20 **NM** value: **5.00**
final issue.
SE 1 Dec 1971 Cover: 0.25 **NM** value: **12.00**
• Special edition.

CHILLER — Marvel / Epic

1 Cover: 7.95 **NM** value: **Cover or less**
A: John Ridgway **W:** James D. Hudnall
2 Cover: 7.95 **NM** value: **Cover or less**
A: John Ridgway **W:** James D. Hudnall
Bk 1 Cover: 17.95 **NM** value: **Cover or less**
• collects mini-series **A:** John Ridgway **W:** James D. Hudnall

CHILLING ADVENTURES IN SORCERY — Archie

1 Sep 1972 Cover: 0.20 **NM** value: **15.00**
• **CGC:** 1 graded, best 8.5
2 Cover: 0.20 **NM** value: **15.00**
3 Oct 1973 Cover: 0.20 **NM** value: **10.00**
• **CGC:** 1 graded, best 9.2
4 Dec 1973 Cover: 0.20 **NM** value: **10.00**
5 Feb 1974 Cover: 0.20 **NM** value: **10.00**
• **CGC:** 1 graded, best 9.6

CHILLING TALES — Youthful

13 Dec 1952 **NM** value: **450.00**
• **CGC:** 3 graded, best 8.0
14 Feb 1953 **NM** value: **300.00**
• **CGC:** 1 graded, best 5.5
15 Apr 1953 **NM** value: **300.00**
• **CGC:** 2 graded, best 7.5
16 **NM** value: **250.00**
17 **NM** value: **250.00**
• **CGC:** 1 graded, best 6.5

CHILLING TALES OF HORROR (2ND SERIES) — Stanley

1 Cover: 0.50 **NM** value: **9.00**
2/A Feb 1971 Cover: 0.50 **NM** value: **8.00**
Vampire's Prey; The Swami's Secret; Belt of Evil; The Man who Tried to Live Forever; Day the World Died; Spirit of Frankenstein
2/B Cover: 0.50 **NM** value: **8.00**
3 Cover: 0.50 **NM** value: **6.00**
4 Cover: 0.50 **NM** value: **6.00**
5 Cover: 0.50 **NM** value: **6.00**

CHINAGO AND OTHER STORIES — Tome Press

1 b&w Cover: 2.50 **NM** value: **Cover or less**

CHINA SEA — Nightwynd

1 b&w Cover: 2.50 **NM** value: **Cover or less**
A: Barry Blair **W:** Barry Blair
2 b&w Cover: 2.50 **NM** value: **Cover or less**
A: Barry Blair **W:** Barry Blair
3 b&w Cover: 2.50 **NM** value: **Cover or less**
A: Barry Blair **W:** Barry Blair
4 b&w Cover: 2.50 **NM** value: **Cover or less**
A: Barry Blair **W:** Barry Blair

Other grades: Multiply prices above by **1.5 for Mint • 2/3 for Very Fine • 1/3 for Fine • 1/5 for Very Good • 1/8 for Good**

Bk 1❑ Cover: 6.95 **NM** value: **Cover or less**
• album b&w

CHIPMUNKS & SQUIRRELS — Original Syndicate

1 ❑ Dec 1994 Cover: 5.95 **NM** value: **Cover or less**
📖 The Game of the Name **A:** Michael Auschenker **W:** Michael Auschenker

CHIP 'N' DALE (1ST SERIES) — Dell

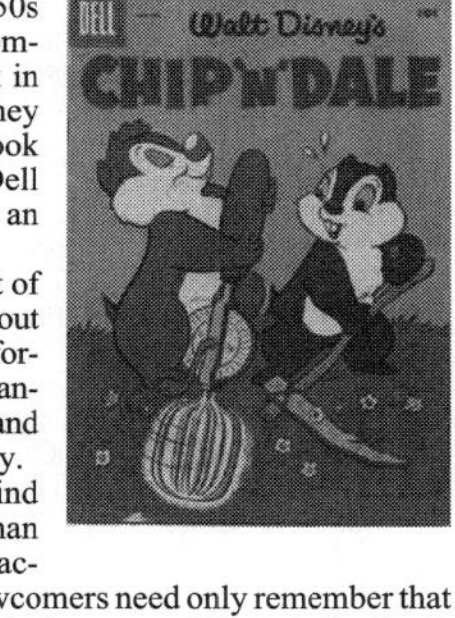

The late 1940s and early 1950s brought a pair of chipmunks to complicate the life of Donald Duck in Disney animated shorts. They popped into their own comic book in the early 1950s, first in three Dell Four Color issues and then into an ongoing title.

Torturing Donald was still part of the series, but stories branched out into the rest of the chipmunks' forested world. Other Disney funny-animal characters, such as L'il Wolf and Br'er Bear, turned up occasionally.

The reader will probably find these episodes more palatable than any of the cartoons, as the characters' shrill voices are absent. Newcomers need only remember that Chip is the smart one with the black nose, and Dale is the dumb one with the red nose. — JJM

#	Date	Cover	NM value
4	❑ Dec 1955	Cover: 0.10	**NM** value: **35.00**
5	❑ Feb 1956	Cover: 0.10	**NM** value: **35.00**
6	❑ Jun 1956	Cover: 0.10	**NM** value: **30.00**
7	❑ Sep 1956	Cover: 0.10	**NM** value: **30.00**
8	❑ Dec 1956	Cover: 0.10	**NM** value: **30.00**
9	❑ Mar 1957	Cover: 0.10	**NM** value: **30.00**
10	❑ Jun 1957	Cover: 0.10	**NM** value: **30.00**
11	❑ Sep 1957	Cover: 0.10	**NM** value: **24.00**
12	❑ Dec 1957	Cover: 0.10	**NM** value: **24.00**
13	❑ Mar 1958	Cover: 0.10	**NM** value: **24.00**
14	❑ Jun 1958	Cover: 0.10	**NM** value: **24.00**
14/A	❑ Jun 1958 • 15¢ price on cover	Cover: 0.15	**NM** value: **75.00**
15	❑ Sep 1958	Cover: 0.10	**NM** value: **24.00**
16	❑ Dec 1958	Cover: 0.10	**NM** value: **24.00**
17	❑ Mar 1959	Cover: 0.10	**NM** value: **24.00**
18	❑ Jun 1959	Cover: 0.10	**NM** value: **24.00**
19	❑ Sep 1959	Cover: 0.10	**NM** value: **24.00**
20	❑ Dec 1959	Cover: 0.10	**NM** value: **24.00**
21	❑ Mar 1960	Cover: 0.10	**NM** value: **20.00**
22	❑ Jun 1960	Cover: 0.10	**NM** value: **20.00**
23	❑ Sep 1960	Cover: 0.10	**NM** value: **20.00**
24	❑ Dec 1960	Cover: 0.10	**NM** value: **20.00**
25	❑ Mar 1961	Cover: 0.10	**NM** value: **20.00**
26	❑ Jun 1961	Cover: 0.10	**NM** value: **20.00**
27	❑ Sep 1961	Cover: 0.10	**NM** value: **20.00**
28	❑ Dec 1961	Cover: 0.10	**NM** value: **20.00**
29	❑ Mar 1962	Cover: 0.10	**NM** value: **20.00**
30	❑ Jun 1962	Cover: 0.10	**NM** value: **20.00**

CHIP 'N' DALE (2ND SERIES) — Gold Key

#	Date	Cover	NM value
1	❑ May 1967	Cover: 0.15	**NM** value: **20.00**
2	❑ Aug 1968	Cover: 0.15	**NM** value: **12.00**
3	❑ Apr 1969	Cover: 0.15	**NM** value: **8.00**
4	❑ Aug 1969	Cover: 0.15	**NM** value: **8.00**
5	❑ Dec 1969	Cover: 0.15	**NM** value: **8.00**
6	❑ Mar 1970	Cover: 0.15	**NM** value: **5.00**
7	❑ Jun 1970	Cover: 0.15	**NM** value: **5.00**
8	❑ Sep 1970	Cover: 0.15	**NM** value: **5.00**
9	❑ Dec 1970	Cover: 0.15	**NM** value: **5.00**
10	❑ Mar 1971	Cover: 0.15	**NM** value: **5.00**
11	❑ Jun 1971	Cover: 0.15	**NM** value: **5.00**
12	❑ Sep 1971	Cover: 0.15	**NM** value: **5.00**
13	❑ Dec 1971	Cover: 0.15	**NM** value: **5.00**
14	❑ Mar 1972	Cover: 0.15	**NM** value: **5.00**
15	❑ May 1972	Cover: 0.15	**NM** value: **5.00**
16	❑ Jul 1972	Cover: 0.15	**NM** value: **5.00**
17	❑ Sep 1972	Cover: 0.15	**NM** value: **5.00**
18	❑ Nov 1972	Cover: 0.15	**NM** value: **5.00**
19	❑ Jan 1973	Cover: 0.15	**NM** value: **5.00**
20	❑ Mar 1973	Cover: 0.15	**NM** value: **5.00**
21	❑ May 1973	Cover: 0.20	**NM** value: **3.00**
22	❑ Jul 1973	Cover: 0.20	**NM** value: **3.00**
23	❑ Sep 1973	Cover: 0.20	**NM** value: **3.00**
24	❑ Nov 1973	Cover: 0.20	**NM** value: **3.00**
25	❑ Jan 1974	Cover: 0.20	**NM** value: **3.00**
26	❑ Mar 1974	Cover: 0.20	**NM** value: **3.00**
27	❑ May 1974	Cover: 0.20	**NM** value: **3.00**
28	❑ Jul 1974	Cover: 0.20	**NM** value: **3.00**
29	❑ Sep 1974	Cover: 0.25	**NM** value: **3.00**
30	❑ Nov 1974	Cover: 0.25	**NM** value: **3.00**
31	❑ Jan 1975	Cover: 0.25	**NM** value: **3.00**
32	❑ Mar 1975	Cover: 0.25	**NM** value: **3.00**
33	❑ May 1975	Cover: 0.25	**NM** value: **3.00**
34	❑ Jul 1975	Cover: 0.25	**NM** value: **3.00**
35	❑ Sep 1975	Cover: 0.25	**NM** value: **3.00**
36	❑ Nov 1975	Cover: 0.25	**NM** value: **3.00**
37	❑ Jan 1976	Cover: 0.25	**NM** value: **3.00**
38	❑ Mar 1976	Cover: 0.25	**NM** value: **3.00**
39	❑ May 1976	Cover: 0.25	**NM** value: **3.00**
40	❑ Jul 1976	Cover: 0.25	**NM** value: **3.00**
41	❑ Aug 1976	Cover: 0.30	**NM** value: **2.50**
42	❑ Sep 1976	Cover: 0.30	**NM** value: **2.50**
43	❑ Nov 1976	Cover: 0.30	**NM** value: **2.50**
44	❑ Jan 1977	Cover: 0.30	**NM** value: **2.50**
45	❑ Mar 1977	Cover: 0.30	**NM** value: **2.50**
46	❑ May 1977	Cover: 0.30	**NM** value: **2.50**
47	❑ Jul 1977	Cover: 0.30	**NM** value: **2.50**
48	❑ Aug 1977	Cover: 0.30	**NM** value: **2.50**
49	❑ Nov 1977	Cover: 0.30	**NM** value: **2.50**
50	❑ Jan 1978	Cover: 0.35	**NM** value: **2.50**
51	❑ Mar 1978	Cover: 0.35	**NM** value: **2.50**
52	❑ May 1978	Cover: 0.35	**NM** value: **2.50**
53	❑ Jul 1978	Cover: 0.35	**NM** value: **2.50**
54	❑ Sep 1978	Cover: 0.35	**NM** value: **2.50**
55	❑ Nov 1978	Cover: 0.35	**NM** value: **2.50**
56	❑ Jan 1979	Cover: 0.35	**NM** value: **2.50**
57	❑ Mar 1979	Cover: 0.35	**NM** value: **2.50**
58	❑ May 1979	Cover: 0.40	**NM** value: **2.50**
59	❑ Jul 1979	Cover: 0.40	**NM** value: **2.50**
60	❑ Aug 1979	Cover: 0.40	**NM** value: **2.50**
61	❑ Sep 1979	Cover: 0.40	**NM** value: **2.50**
62	❑ Oct 1979	Cover: 0.40	**NM** value: **2.50**
63	❑ Nov 1979	Cover: 0.40	**NM** value: **2.50**
64	❑ Feb 1980	Cover: 0.40	**NM** value: **2.50**
65	❑ Apr 1980	Cover: 0.40	**NM** value: **2.50**
66	❑ Jun 1980	Cover: 0.40	**NM** value: **2.50**
67	❑ Aug 1980	Cover: 0.40	**NM** value: **2.50**
68	❑ 1980		**NM** value: **2.50**
69	❑ 1981		**NM** value: **2.50**
70	❑ 1981		**NM** value: **2.50**
71	❑ Jun 1981	Cover: 0.50	**NM** value: **2.50**
72	❑ Aug 1982	Cover: 0.50	**NM** value: **2.50**
73	❑ Oct 1982	Cover: 0.50	**NM** value: **2.50**
74	❑ Dec 1982	Cover: 0.50	**NM** value: **2.50**
75	❑ Feb 1982	Cover: 0.60	**NM** value: **2.50**
76	❑ 1982	Cover: 0.60	**NM** value: **2.50**
77	❑ 1982	Cover: 0.60	**NM** value: **2.50**
78	❑		**NM** value: **2.50**
79	❑		**NM** value: **2.50**
80	❑		**NM** value: **2.50**
81	❑		**NM** value: **2.50**
82	❑		**NM** value: **2.50**
83	❑	Cover: 0.60	**NM** value: **2.50**

CHIP 'N' DALE (ONE-SHOT) — Disney

1 ❑ Cover: 3.50 **NM** value: **Cover or less**
Circ: CapCity orders: **1,750**
No issue number. 📖 Secret Casebook

CHIP 'N' DALE RESCUE RANGERS (DISNEY'S...) — Disney

1 ❑ Jun 1990 Cover: 1.50 **NM** value: **2.00**
Circ: CapCity orders: **8,100**
📖 Rescue Rangers to the Rescue **A:** H. Saavedra; R. Valenti ★ Origin of Rescue Rangers.

2 ❑ Jul 1990 Cover: 1.50 **NM** value: **1.75**
Circ: CapCity orders: **5,600**
★ Origin of Rescue Rangers.

3 ❑ Aug 1990 Cover: 1.50 **NM** value: **1.75**
Circ: CapCity orders: **6,300**

4 ❑ Sep 1990 Cover: 1.50 **NM** value: **1.75**
Circ: CapCity orders: **6,300**
📖 The King of Beasts Caper, Part 2

5 ❑ Oct 1990 Cover: 1.50 **NM** value: **1.75**
Circ: CapCity orders: **6,450**

6 ❑ Nov 1990 Cover: 1.50 **NM** value: **1.75**
Circ: CapCity orders: **5,950**

7 ❑ Dec 1990 Cover: 1.50 **NM** value: **1.75**
Circ: CapCity orders: **5,350**

8 ❑ Jan 1991 Cover: 1.50 **NM** value: **1.75**
Circ: CapCity orders: **5,350**

9 ❑ Feb 1991 Cover: 1.50 **NM** value: **1.75**
Circ: CapCity orders: **5,200**

10 ❑ Mar 1991 Cover: 1.50 **NM** value: **1.75**
Circ: CapCity orders: **5,150**

11 ❑ Apr 1991 Cover: 1.50 **NM** value: **1.75**
Circ: CapCity orders: **4,600**

12 ❑ May 1991 Cover: 1.50 **NM** value: **1.75**
Circ: CapCity orders: **4,400**

13 ❑ Jun 1991 Cover: 1.50 **NM** value: **1.75**
Circ: CapCity orders: **4,300**

14 ❑ Jul 1991 Cover: 1.50 **NM** value: **1.75**
Circ: CapCity orders: **4,300**

15 ❑ Aug 1991 Cover: 1.50 **NM** value: **1.75**
Circ: CapCity orders: **4,200**

16 ❑ Sep 1991 Cover: 1.50 **NM** value: **1.75**
Circ: CapCity orders: **4,250**

17 ❑ Oct 1991 Cover: 1.50 **NM** value: **1.75**
Circ: CapCity orders: **4,150**

18 ❑ Nov 1991 Cover: 1.50 **NM** value: **1.75**
Circ: CapCity orders: **3,950**

19 ❑ Dec 1991 Cover: 1.50 **NM** value: **1.75**
Circ: CapCity orders: **3,750**

CHIPS AND VANILLA — Kitchen Sink

1 ❑ Jun 1988, b&w Cover: 1.75 **NM** value: **Cover or less**

CGC price ratios appearing on the bottom of right-hand pages are for pre-1990 comic books "slabbed" by Comics Guaranty Corp.

They represent the median price offered on eBay above our printed prices for comics in each grade. These are only a guide; individual prices vary by interest in the issue and the number of CGC-graded copies on the market.

CHIRALITY — CPM

All issues are adults only.

Chirality is the third comic-book work by popular Japanese animator Satoshi Urushihara. Urushihara had made his start working on animations for G.I. Joe, A Real American Hero and The Transformers before going freelance to work on Record of Lodoss War and Crying Freeman. In 1990, he moved into comics with Legend of Lemnear and Plastic Little. Chirality, his third series, is the only one so far to remain purely in comics form.

Plot-wise, Chirality is a bit like Battlestar Galactica "writ small." Vic, Shiori, Carol, Patty, and Shizumi are searching for the promised land of Gaia while being menaced by robots who seek to destroy them. Various romances among group members develop (particularly between the shape-shifting Shiori and Carol), as well as great personal enmity from Adam, a former partner who now wants them dead.

1 ❑ Mar 1997 Cover: 2.95 **NM** value: **Cover or less**
Circ: Diamd. preorders: **2,309**
📖 The Reunion **A:** Satoshi Urushihara **W:** Satoshi Urushihara ★ 1st Appearance of Carol, Vic, Shizuma, Shiori.

2 ❑ Apr 1997 Cover: 2.95 **NM** value: **Cover or less**
📖 The Promise • Carol reveals morph power **A:** Satoshi Urushihara **W:** Satoshi Urushihara ★ Origin of Carol. ★ 2nd Appearance of Carol, Vic, Shiori.

3 ❑ May 1997 Cover: 2.95 **NM** value: **Cover or less**
📖 The Decision **A:** Satoshi Urushihara **W:** Satoshi Urushihara ★ 1st Appearance of Patty.

4 ❑ Jun 1997 Cover: 2.95 **NM** value: **Cover or less**
Circ: Diamd. preorders: **3,562**
📖 The Memory **A:** Satoshi Urushihara **W:** Satoshi Urushihara

5 ❑ Jul 1997 Cover: 2.95 **NM** value: **Cover or less**
📖 The Flight **A:** Satoshi Urushihara **W:** Satoshi Urushihara

6 ❑ Aug 1997 Cover: 2.95 **NM** value: **Cover or less**
📖 The Mission **A:** Satoshi Urushihara **W:** Satoshi Urushihara ★ 1st Appearance of Adam.

7 ❑ Sep 1997 Cover: 2.95 **NM** value: **Cover or less**
Circ: Diamd. preorders: **4,002**
📖 An Old Rival **A:** Satoshi Urushihara **W:** Satoshi Urushihara

8 ❑ Oct 1997 Cover: 2.95 **NM** value: **Cover or less**
Circ: Diamd. preorders: **4,130**
📖 Cruelty **A:** Satoshi Urushihara **W:** Satoshi Urushihara

9 ❑ Nov 1997 Cover: 2.95 **NM** value: **Cover or less**
Circ: Diamd. preorders: **4,276**
📖 Anguish **A:** Satoshi Urushihara **W:** Satoshi Urushihara

10 ❑ Dec 1997 Cover: 2.95 **NM** value: **Cover or less**
Circ: Diamd. preorders: **4,179**
📖 Insanity **A:** Satoshi Urushihara **W:** Satoshi Urushihara

11 ❑ Jan 1998 Cover: 2.95 **NM** value: **Cover or less**
Circ: Diamd. preorders: **4,138**
📖 Love **A:** Satoshi Urushihara **W:** Satoshi Urushihara

12 ❑ Feb 1998 Cover: 2.95 **NM** value: **Cover or less**
Circ: Diamd. preorders: **3,917**
A: Satoshi Urushihara **W:** Satoshi Urushihara

13 ❑ Mar 1998 Cover: 2.95 **NM** value: **Cover or less**
Circ: Diamd. preorders: **3,995**
📖 Selection **A:** Satoshi Urushihara **W:** Satoshi Urushihara

14 ❑ Apr 1998 Cover: 2.95 **NM** value: **Cover or less**
Circ: Diamd. preorders: **4,094**
📖 Soul Desire **A:** Satoshi Urushihara **W:** Satoshi Urushihara

15 ❑ May 1998 Cover: 2.95 **NM** value: **Cover or less**
Circ: Diamd. preorders: **3,859**
📖 Love and Loathing **A:** Satoshi Urushihara **W:** Satoshi Urushihara

16 ❑ Jun 1998 Cover: 2.95 **NM** value: **Cover or less**
Circ: Diamd. preorders: **3,826**
📖 Infiltration **A:** Satoshi Urushihara **W:** Satoshi Urushihara

17 ❑ Jul 1998 Cover: 2.95 **NM** value: **Cover or less**
Circ: Diamd. preorders: **4,041**
📖 Eye of the Storm **A:** Satoshi Urushihara **W:** Satoshi Urushihara

18 ❑ Aug 1998 Cover: 2.95 **NM** value: **Cover or less**
Circ: Diamd. preorders: **3,944**
final issue. **A:** Satoshi Urushihara **W:** Satoshi Urushihara

Bk 1❑ b&w Cover: 9.95 **NM** value: **Cover or less**
📖 The Reunion; The Promise; The Decision • collects #1-4 **A:** Satoshi Urushihara **W:** Satoshi Urushihara

Bk 2❑ b&w Cover: 14.95 **NM** value: **Cover or less**
📖 The Memory; The Flight; The Mission; An Old Rival • collects #5-7 **A:** Satoshi Urushihara **W:** Satoshi Urushihara

Bk 3❑ b&w Cover: 14.95 **NM** value: **Cover or less**
A: Satoshi Urushihara **W:** Satoshi Urushihara

Bk 4❑ Jul 2000, b&w Cover: 15.95 **NM** value: **Cover or less**
A: Satoshi Urushihara **W:** Satoshi Urushihara

CHIRÖN — Hammac

1 ❑ b&w Cover: 2.00 **NM** value: **Cover or less**
• Hammac Publications **A:** Marc Sutherland **W:** Jim MacNaughton

2 ❑ b&w Cover: 2.00 **NM** value: **Cover or less**
• Hammac Publications

3 ❑ b&w Cover: 1.95 **NM** value: **2.00**
• Alpha Productions takes over

C.H.I.X. — Image

1 ❑ Jan 1998 Cover: 2.50 **NM** value: **Cover or less**
• Bad Girl parody comic book;Bad Girl paro **A:** Aaron Lopresti; Adam Warren; Terry Dodson; Matt Haley; Ron Randall **W:** Aaron Lopresti; Adam Warren; Terry Dodson; Matt Haley; Ron Randall

1/SC❑ Jan 1998 Cover: 2.50 **NM** value: **5.40**
• X-Ray edition. • Bad Girl parody comic book;Comic Cavalcade alternate

CGC-graded: Multiply prices above by **33 for 9.9 M • 16 for 9.8 NM/M • 7 for 9.6 NM+ • 5 for 9.4 NM • 2.5 for 9.2 NM- • 1.5 for 9.0 VF/NM**

C.H.I.X. THAT TIME FORGOT — Image
1 ❑ Aug 1998 Cover: 2.95 NM value: **Cover or less**
📖 That Time Forgot; Death How Cruel Ye Be **A:** Aaron Lopresti; Terry Dodson; Matt Haley; Paul Ryan; Ron Randall; Jeff Johnson; Hilary Barta **W:** Aaron Lopresti; Terry Dodson; Matt Haley; Ron Randall; Hilary Barta; Gary Martin; Randy Emberlin; Tom Simmons ★ 2nd Appearance of Good Girl.

CHOICE COMICS — Great Comics
1 ❑ Dec 1941 Cover: 0.10 NM value: **1250.00**
• **CGC:** 1 graded, best 7.0
2 ❑ ca. 1942 Cover: 0.10 NM value: **800.00**
3 ❑ Apr 1942 Cover: 0.10 NM value: **750.00**

CHOICES — Angry Isis
1 ❑ Cover: 4.00 NM value: **Cover or less**
No issue number.

CHOKE, THE — Anubis
Anl 1❑Jul 1994 Cover: 2.75 NM value: **Cover or less**
📖 Chains **A:** Vaughn Schultz **W:** Vaughn Schultz

CHOO-CHOO CHARLIE — Gold Key
Good & Plenty Candy was released by the Quaker City confectionery Company in 1893, "the oldest branded candy in the United States." Choo Choo Charlie was a (young-looking) engineer whose train ran on Good & Plenty candy, his first commercials appearing in 1950.

It seemed to stretch credulity that there'd be enough in the concept to provide continuity for a comic book, since there was little more than the opening lines of the commercial's ditty: "Once upon a time there was an engineer. Choo Choo Charlie was his name, we hear. He had an engine and he sure had fun. He used Good & Plenty candy to make his train run." There was only one issue of a Choo-Choo Charlie comic book, which may be one more than anyone could have expected. — Maggie
1 ❑ Dec 1969 Cover: 0.15 NM value: **100.00**
• **CGC:** 6 graded, best 9.2

CHOPPER: EARTH, WIND & FIRE — Fleetway-Quality
1 ❑ Cover: 2.95 NM value: **Cover or less**
cardstock cover.
2 ❑ Cover: 2.95 NM value: **Cover or less**

CHOPPER: SONG OF THE SURFER — Fleetway-Quality
1 ❑ Cover: 9.95 NM value: **Cover or less**

CHOSEN, THE — Martinez
1 ❑ Jul 1995 Cover: 2.50 NM value: **Cover or less**
No issue number. cover indicates Premiere Issue. ★ 1st Appearance of Pache, Santana (super-hero), Rico Chico, Rattler, Santo.

CHRISTIAN COMICS & GAMES MAGAZINE — Aida-Zee
0 ❑ b&w Cover: 3.50 NM value: **Cover or less**
1 ❑ b&w Cover: 3.50 NM value: **Cover or less**

CHRISTINA WINTERS: AGENT OF DEATH — Eros
1 ❑ Cover: 2.95 NM value: **Cover or less**
A: Steve Mannion **W:** Steve Mannion
2 ❑ Mar 1995 Cover: 2.95 NM value: **Cover or less**
A: Steve Mannion **W:** Steve Mannion

CHRISTMAS CLASSICS (WALT KELLY'S...) — Eclipse
1 ❑ Dec 1987 Cover: 1.75 NM value: **Cover or less**
Circ: CapCity orders: **3,475**
📖 Christmas Comes to the Wood Land; The Adventures of Peter Wheat • Peter Wheat **A:** Walt Kelly **W:** Walt Kelly; Maggie Thompson

CHRISTMAS TREASURY, A — Dell
1 ❑ 1954 Cover: 0.25 NM value: **50.00**
• **CGC:** 1 graded, best 9.2
• Dell Giant

CHRISTMAS WITH SUPERSWINE — Fantagraphics
1 ❑ b&w Cover: 2.00 NM value: **Cover or less**

CHRISTMAS WITH THE SUPER-HEROES — DC
1 ❑ Jan 1989 Cover: 2.95 NM value: **3.00**
Circ: CapCity orders: **12,300**
📖 Wanted: Santa Claus – Dead Or Alive **A:** Murphy Anderson; Dick Giordano; Frank Miller; Curt Swan; Steve Mitchell **W:** Denny O'Neil
2 ❑ Dec 1989 Cover: 2.95 NM value: **3.00**
Circ: CapCity orders: **19,400**
A: Gray Morrow; John Byrne; Dick Giordano

CHROMA-TICK, THE — New England
NEC Press is best known for its highly successful and popular black-and-white series The Tick. The company grew at an exponential pace in the late 1980s and early 1990s. As the fan base for the nigh-invulnerable blue guy grew, so did NEC's popularity. In 1992, NEC decided to share the wealth and reprint the early issues of The Tick in color so that Tick fans could enjoy the series fully. The new series was titled The Chroma-Tick.

Issues often feature updated art and new articles by the Tick's creator, writer, and penciller, Ben Edlund. Each issue also offered cards, posters, and other paraphernalia for the fans.
1 ❑ Feb 1992, full color Cover: 3.95 NM value: **Cover or less**
📖 High Rise Hijinx • trading cards;Reprints The Tick #1 in color **A:** Ben Edlund **W:** Ben Edlund
2 ❑ Jun 1992, full color Cover: 3.95 NM value: **Cover or less**
• "Special Edition #2". 📖 High Rise Hijinx • trading cards **W:** Ben Edlund
3 ❑ Aug 1992, full color Cover: 3.50 NM value: **Cover or less**
W: Ben Edlund
4 ❑ Oct 1992, full color Cover: 2.95 NM value: **3.50**
Bush cover. **W:** Ben Edlund
4/A ❑ Oct 1992 Cover: 2.95 NM value: **3.50**
Perot cover. **W:** Ben Edlund
4/B ❑ Oct 1992 Cover: 2.95 NM value: **3.50**
Clinton cover. **W:** Ben Edlund
5 ❑ full color Cover: 2.95 NM value: **3.50**
W: Ben Edlund
6 ❑ full color Cover: 3.50 NM value: **4.50**
W: Ben Edlund
7 ❑ Cover: 3.50 NM value: **Cover or less**
8 ❑ Cover: 3.50 NM value: **Cover or less**
📖 A Matter of Cosmic Import **A:** Ben Edlund **W:** Ben Edlund
9 ❑ Cover: 3.50 NM value: **Cover or less**

CHROME — Hot Comics
1 ❑ Oct 1986 Cover: 1.50 NM value: **Cover or less**
Circ: CapCity orders: **8,550**
📖 Shadow of the Torturer **A:** Kelley Jones **W:** Peter B. Gillis
2 ❑ Cover: 1.50 NM value: **Cover or less**
Circ: CapCity orders: **5,275**
3 ❑ Cover: 1.50 NM value: **Cover or less**
Circ: CapCity orders: **6,600**

CHROMIUM MAN, THE — Triumphant
Kaanar was once a powerful warrior in the Riot Guard and a force throughout the Empire. After countless years of battle, he tries to put it all behind him, taking up the life of a farmer on Kaabari. There he meets his wife Laayana and thinks he has found peace at last.

But it is not to be. The people of Kaabari have grown tired of empire rule and have finally gathered the courage to gather for a protest. After all, there hasn't been a military presence on Kaabari for five years. The protesters could not have guessed that their peaceful demonstration would be broken up by a detachment of Riot Gear, the enforcers of the Empire. The soldiers sweep down with swiftness and brutality, taking hundreds prisoner and killing the others. When Kaanar realizes that his wife is among those taken, he is forced to shift back into his armored form as the Chromium Man and rejoin a battle that he thought was long behind him.
0 ❑ Apr 1994 Cover: 2.50 NM value: **Cover or less**
Circ: CapCity orders: **4,238**
1 ❑ Jan 1994 Cover: 2.50 NM value: **Cover or less**
Circ: CapCity orders: **7,825**
1/Ash❑1994 Cover: 2.50 NM value: **Cover or less**
• ashcan edition. **A:** Adam Pollina **W:** John Riley
2 ❑ 1994 Cover: 2.50 NM value: **Cover or less**
Circ: CapCity orders: **4,825**
• indicia not updated through issue #7;says Jan 94;Violent Past
3 ❑ 1994 Cover: 2.50 NM value: **Cover or less**
Circ: CapCity orders: **5,480**
4 ❑ 1994 Cover: 2.50 NM value: **Cover or less**
Circ: CapCity orders: **6,660**
📖 Bonds And Choices • Unleashed! **A:** Adam Pollina **W:** John Riley
5 ❑ 1994 Cover: 2.50 NM value: **Cover or less**
Circ: CapCity orders: **5,665**
• Unleashed!
6 ❑ 1994 Cover: 2.50 NM value: **Cover or less**
Circ: CapCity orders: **4,670**
📖 The Courier, Part 1
7 ❑ 1994 Cover: 2.50 NM value: **Cover or less**
Circ: CapCity orders: **4,255**
8 ❑ Mar 1994 Cover: 2.50 NM value: **Cover or less**
Circ: CapCity orders: **3,355**
9 ❑ Mar 1994 Cover: 2.50 NM value: **Cover or less**
Circ: CapCity orders: **2,824**
10 ❑ May 1994 Cover: 2.50 NM value: **Cover or less**
Circ: CapCity orders: **2,350**
11 ❑ Cover: 2.50 NM value: **Cover or less**
12 ❑ Cover: 2.50 NM value: **Cover or less**
13 ❑ Cover: 2.50 NM value: **Cover or less**
14 ❑ Cover: 2.50 NM value: **Cover or less**
15 ❑ Cover: 2.50 NM value: **Cover or less**

CHROMIUM MAN, THE: VIOLENT PAST — Triumphant
1 ❑ Cover: 2.50 NM value: **Cover or less**
Circ: CapCity orders: **4,550**
📖 Violent Past, Part 1 **A:** Steven Harris **W:** John Riley
2 ❑ Cover: 2.50 NM value: **Cover or less**
Circ: CapCity orders: **4,400**
A: Steven Harris **W:** John Riley

CHRONIC APATHY — Illiterature Press
1 ❑ Aug 1995, b&w Cover: 2.95 NM value: **Cover or less**
2 ❑ Sep 1995, b&w Cover: 2.95 NM value: **Cover or less**
3 ❑ Oct 1995, b&w Cover: 2.95 NM value: **Cover or less**
4 ❑ Dec 1995, b&w Cover: 2.95 NM value: **Cover or less**

CHRONIC IDIOCY — Caliber
1 ❑ b&w Cover: 2.50 NM value: **Cover or less**
A: Dave Cooper **W:** Dave Cooper
2 ❑ b&w Cover: 2.50 NM value: **Cover or less**
A: Dave Cooper **W:** Dave Cooper
3 ❑ b&w Cover: 2.50 NM value: **Cover or less**
A: Dave Cooper **W:** Dave Cooper

CHRONICLES OF CORUM, THE — First
1 ❑ Cover: 1.75 NM value: **2.00**
Circ: CapCity orders: **7,675**
A: Mike Mignola **W:** Mike Baron
2 ❑ Cover: 1.75 NM value: **2.00**
Circ: CapCity orders: **5,850**
3 ❑ Cover: 1.75 NM value: **2.00**
Circ: CapCity orders: **5,600**
4 ❑ Cover: 1.75 NM value: **2.00**
Circ: CapCity orders: **5,900**
5 ❑ Cover: 1.75 NM value: **2.00**
Circ: CapCity orders: **6,000**
6 ❑ Cover: 1.75 NM value: **2.00**
Circ: CapCity orders: **5,625**
7 ❑ Cover: 1.75 NM value: **2.00**
Circ: CapCity orders: **5,325**
8 ❑ Cover: 1.75 NM value: **2.00**
Circ: CapCity orders: **5,475**
9 ❑ Cover: 1.75 NM value: **2.00**
Circ: CapCity orders: **4,775**
10 ❑ Cover: 1.75 NM value: **2.00**
Circ: CapCity orders: **4,450**
11 ❑ Cover: 1.75 NM value: **2.00**
Circ: CapCity orders: **4,025**
12 ❑ Cover: 1.95 NM value: **2.00**
Circ: CapCity orders: **3,650**

CHRONICLES OF CRIME AND MYSTERY: SHERLOCK HOLMES — Northstar
1 ❑ b&w Cover: 2.25 NM value: **Cover or less**

CHRONICLES OF PANDA KHAN, THE — Abacus
1 ❑ Cover: 1.50 NM value: **Cover or less**
A: Dave Garcia **W:** Monica Sharp
2 ❑ Cover: 2.00 NM value: **Cover or less**
A: Dave Garcia **W:** Monica Sharp
3 ❑ Cover: 2.00 NM value: **Cover or less**
A: Dave Garcia **W:** Monica Sharp
4 ❑ Cover: 2.00 NM value: **Cover or less**
A: Dave Garcia **W:** Monica Sharp

CHRONOS — DC
Walker Gabriel struggles with a killer, as an energy portal surrounds them and suddenly he finds himself in Smallville, Kansas, in the 1800s catching a ride on a horse-drawn wagon with a man named Kent. So begins the time-travelling adventures of the new Chronos.

One of The Atom's foes during the Silver Age was the time-traveling villain, Chronos. In 1998, a new character, Walker Gabriel, appropriates the name with the approval of the original Chronos. In addition to moving through time to satisfy himself (like seeing the Beatles in Hamburg in 1960), Gabriel is making a tidy profit as a high-tech thief, until his employer attempts to make him the fall guy in the murder of a Linear Man. The concept of affecting history has made the time traveler a venerable character type in comics, and this series involves itself intricately in DC's past.
1 ❑ Mar 1998 Cover: 2.50 NM value: **Cover or less**
Circ: Diamd. preorders: **23,249**
📖 Time Out of Time **A:** Paul Guinan **W:** John Francis Moore
2 ❑ Apr 1998 Cover: 2.50 NM value: **Cover or less**
Circ: Diamd. preorders: **16,362**
📖 Down on the Farm **A:** Paul Guinan **W:** John Francis Moore
3 ❑ May 1998 Cover: 2.50 NM value: **Cover or less**
Circ: Diamd. preorders: **14,533**
4 ❑ Jun 1998 Cover: 2.50 NM value: **Cover or less**
Circ: Diamd. preorders: **13,168**
★ Death of original Chronos.
5 ❑ Jul 1998 Cover: 2.50 NM value: **Cover or less**
Circ: Diamd. preorders: **11,614**

Other grades: Multiply prices above by **1.5 for Mint • 2/3 for Very Fine • 1/3 for Fine • 1/5 for Very Good • 1/8 for Good**

6 ❑ Aug 1998 Cover: 2.50 **NM value: Cover or less**
Circ: Diamd. preorders: **10,876**
• funeral of original Chronos★ Appearance of Tattooed Man.
7 ❑ Sep 1998 Cover: 2.50 **NM value: Cover or less**
Circ: Diamd. preorders: **10,630**
8 ❑ Oct 1998 Cover: 2.50 **NM value: Cover or less**
Circ: Diamd. preorders: **9,576**
9 ❑ Dec 1998 Cover: 2.50 **NM value: Cover or less**
Circ: Diamd. preorders: **9,511**
★ Appearance of Destiny.
10 ❑ Jan 1999 Cover: 2.50 **NM value: Cover or less**
Circ: Diamd. preorders: **9,384**
A: Paul Guinan **W:** John Francis Moore ★ Appearance of Azrael.
11 ❑ Feb 1999 Cover: 2.50 **NM value: Cover or less**
Circ: Diamd. preorders: **9,375**
final issue. **A:** Paul Guinan **W:** John Francis Moore
1000000❑Nov 1998 Cover: 2.50 **NM value: Cover or less**
Circ: Diamd. preorders: **18,436**
★ Appearance of Hourman.

CHRONOWAR — Dark Horse / Manga
1 ❑ Aug 1996, b&w Cover: 2.95 **NM value: Cover or less**
A: Kazumasa Takayama **W:** Kazumasa Takayama
2 ❑ Sep 1996, b&w Cover: 2.95 **NM value: Cover or less**
Circ: Diamd. preorders: **11,903**
A: Kazumasa Takayama **W:** Kazumasa Takayama
3 ❑ Oct 1996, b&w Cover: 2.95 **NM value: Cover or less**
Circ: Diamd. preorders: **10,740**
A: Kazumasa Takayama **W:** Kazumasa Takayama
4 ❑ Nov 1996, b&w Cover: 2.95 **NM value: Cover or less**
Circ: Direct Market orders: **9,597**
A: Kazumasa Takayama **W:** Kazumasa Takayama
5 ❑ Dec 1996, b&w Cover: 2.95 **NM value: Cover or less**
Circ: Direct Market orders: **8,748**
A: Kazumasa Takayama **W:** Kazumasa Takayama
6 ❑ Jan 1997, b&w Cover: 2.95 **NM value: Cover or less**
Circ: Direct Market orders: **8,010**
A: Kazumasa Takayama **W:** Kazumasa Takayama
7 ❑ Feb 1997, b&w Cover: 2.95 **NM value: Cover or less**
Circ: Diamd. preorders: **7,558**
A: Kazumasa Takayama **W:** Kazumasa Takayama
8 ❑ Mar 1997, b&w Cover: 2.95 **NM value: Cover or less**
Circ: Diamd. preorders: **7,305**
A: Kazumasa Takayama **W:** Kazumasa Takayama
9 ❑ Apr 1997, b&w Cover: 2.95 **NM value: Cover or less**
Circ: Diamd. preorders: **7,150**
A: Kazumasa Takayama **W:** Kazumasa Takayama

CHUCKLING WHATSIT, THE — Fantagraphics
Bk 1❑ Oct 1997, b&w Cover: 16.95 **NM value: Cover or less**
• collects serial from Zero Zero

CHUCK NORRIS — Marvel / Star
1 ❑ Jan 1987 Cover: 0.75 **NM** value: **1.50**
Circ: CapCity orders: **6,650**
📖 The Super Cruiser **A:** Steve Ditko **W:** Mary Jo Duffy
2 ❑ Mar 1987 Cover: 0.75 **NM** value: **1.25**
A: Steve Ditko
3 ❑ May 1987 Cover: 0.75 **NM** value: **1.25**
Circ: CapCity orders: **4,000**
A: Steve Ditko
4 ❑ Jul 1987 Cover: 0.75 **NM** value: **1.25**
Circ: CapCity orders: **2,400**
5 ❑ Sep 1997 Cover: 0.75 **NM** value: **1.25**
Circ: CapCity orders: **2,200**

CHUK THE BARBARIC — Avatar
3 ❑ Cover: 1.25 **NM value: Cover or less**
no color cover.

CHYNA — Chaos
1 ❑ Sep 2000 Cover: 2.95 **NM value: Cover or less**
Circ: Diamd. preorders: **13,313**
📖 Guilt and Innocence **A:** Eddy Barrows **W:** Steven Grant

CINDER AND ASHE — DC
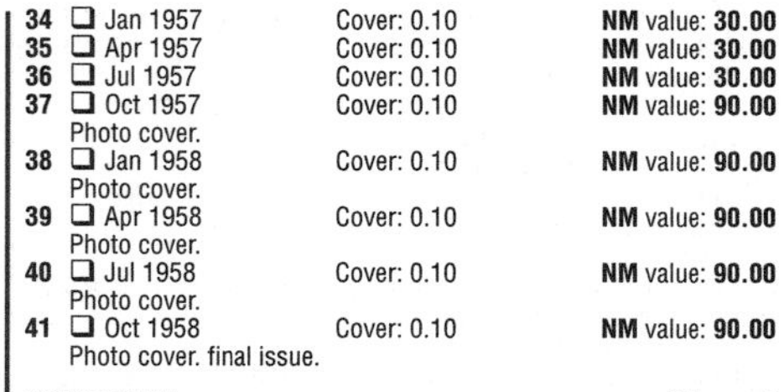

Cinder and Ashe was a four-issue mini-series by Gerry Conway and Jose L. Garcia Lopez. Cinder is an red-headed woman of mixed heritage who grew up in war-torn Vietnam. Jake Ashe is a Cajun who served in that war in hopes of finding his real father. Instead, he met Cinder, his future partner.

Today, Cinder and Ashe are investigators working out of New Orleans, but their latest case feels a bit like going back to war. A farmer named Wilson Starger hires them to find his missing daughter, Jennifer. However, the more they look into the case, the stranger things become. Their employer turns out to be a cipher — a man without a credit record, driver's license, or official presence of any kind. Moreover, the people they contact regarding the case exhibit a nasty tendency to turn up dead.

1 ❑ May 1988 Cover: 1.75 **NM value: Cover or less**
Circ: CapCity orders: **17,200**
A: José Luis Garcia-Lopez **W:** Gerry Conway
2 ❑ Jun 1988 Cover: 1.75 **NM value: Cover or less**
Circ: CapCity orders: **12,950**
A: José Luis Garcia-Lopez **W:** Gerry Conway
3 ❑ Jul 1988 Cover: 1.75 **NM value: Cover or less**
Circ: CapCity orders: **12,050**
4 ❑ Aug 1988 Cover: 1.75 **NM value: Cover or less**
Circ: CapCity orders: **11,650**

CINDERELLA LOVE — Ziff-Davis
1 ❑ ca. 1950 Cover: 0.10 **NM** value: **60.00**
• Listed as #10 (1950)
2 ❑ Apr 1951 Cover: 0.10 **NM** value: **35.00**
• Listed as #11 (1951)
3 ❑ Sep 1951 Cover: 0.10 **NM** value: **28.00**
• Listed as #12 (1951)
4 ❑ Oct 1951 Cover: 0.10 **NM** value: **24.00**
5 ❑ Dec 1951 Cover: 0.10 **NM** value: **24.00**
6 ❑ Feb 1952 Cover: 0.10 **NM** value: **24.00**
7 ❑ Apr 1952 Cover: 0.10 **NM** value: **24.00**
8 ❑ Jun 1952 Cover: 0.10 **NM** value: **24.00**
📖 Doctor In My Heart; A Record Breaking Affair; Good-bye, My Love; Sleight of Heart;
9 ❑ Aug 1952 Cover: 0.10 **NM** value: **24.00**
10 ❑ Oct 1952 Cover: 0.10 **NM** value: **24.00**
11 ❑ ca. 1952 Cover: 0.10 **NM** value: **20.00**
12 ❑ Oct 1953 Cover: 0.10 **NM** value: **20.00**
13 ❑ Feb 1954 Cover: 0.10 **NM** value: **20.00**
14 ❑ Apr 1954 Cover: 0.10 **NM** value: **20.00**
15 ❑ Aug 1954 Cover: 0.10 **NM** value: **20.00**
25 ❑ Dec 1954 Cover: 0.10 **NM** value: **20.00**
26 ❑ Feb 1955 Cover: 0.10 **NM** value: **20.00**
27 ❑ Apr 1955 Cover: 0.10 **NM** value: **20.00**
28 ❑ Aug 1955 Cover: 0.10 **NM** value: **20.00**
29 ❑ Oct 1955 Cover: 0.10 **NM** value: **20.00**
final issue.

CIRCLE UNLEASHED, THE — Epoch
1 ❑ May 1995 Cover: 3.00 **NM value: Cover or less**
📖 Sacrifice **A:** Donald McQuay **W:** Donald McQuay

CIRCLE WEAVE, THE: APPRENTICE TO A GOD — Abalone Press
1 ❑ b&w Cover: 2.00 **NM value: Cover or less**
2 ❑ b&w Cover: 2.00 **NM value: Cover or less**
📖 Into the Storm **A:** Matthew Kalleigh; Robert Lewis **W:** Matthew Kalleigh; Robert Lewis

CIRCUS THE COMIC RIOT — Globe
1 ❑ Jun 1938 **NM** value: **6000.00**
• **CGC:** 2 graded, best 8.5

CIRCUS WORLD — Hammac
1 ❑ b&w Cover: 2.50 **NM value: Cover or less**
📖 Tryouts **A:** Jim Mc Naughton **W:** Barry Longyear
2 ❑ Cover: 2.50 **NM value: Cover or less**
3 ❑ Cover: 2.50 **NM value: Cover or less**

CISCO KID, THE — Dell
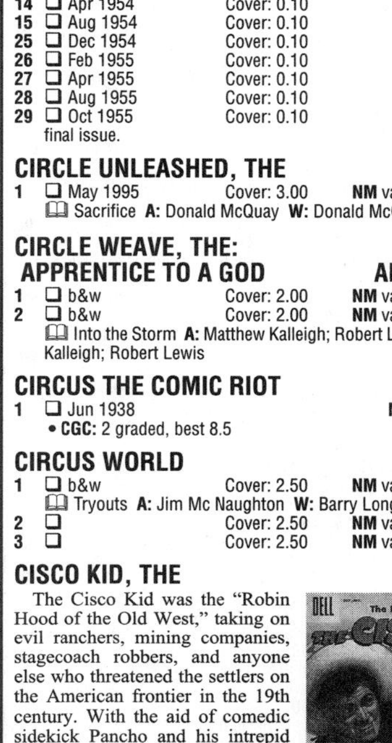

The Cisco Kid was the "Robin Hood of the Old West," taking on evil ranchers, mining companies, stagecoach robbers, and anyone else who threatened the settlers on the American frontier in the 19th century. With the aid of comedic sidekick Pancho and his intrepid horse Diablo, Cisco patrolled the plains and high desert in pulp magazines, paperbacks, movies, TV, and radio shows — and comic books during the 1940s and '50s.

After a tryout in Dell's Four Color Comics, Cisco and Pancho (and their horses) graduated to a feature series that ran throughout the 1950s. Issues often featured realistically painted covers that stood out on the newsstands next to many of the competing titles. Readers would get two complete Cisco Kid tales in each book, along with a lighter backup story featuring Pancho or the horses.

2 ❑ Jan 1951 Cover: 0.10 **NM** value: **100.00**
★ Appearance of Series continued from.
3 ❑ Mar 1951 Cover: 0.10 **NM** value: **85.00**
4 ❑ Jun 1951 Cover: 0.10 **NM** value: **80.00**
5 ❑ Sep 1951 Cover: 0.10 **NM** value: **80.00**
6 ❑ Nov 1951 Cover: 0.10 **NM** value: **75.00**
7 ❑ Jan 1952 Cover: 0.10 **NM** value: **75.00**
8 ❑ Mar 1952 Cover: 0.10 **NM** value: **75.00**
9 ❑ May 1952 Cover: 0.10 **NM** value: **75.00**
10 ❑ Jul 1952 Cover: 0.10 **NM** value: **75.00**
11 ❑ Sep 1952 Cover: 0.10 **NM** value: **55.00**
12 ❑ Nov 1952 Cover: 0.10 **NM** value: **55.00**
13 ❑ Jan 1953 Cover: 0.10 **NM** value: **55.00**
14 ❑ Mar 1953 Cover: 0.10 **NM** value: **55.00**
15 ❑ May 1953 Cover: 0.10 **NM** value: **55.00**
• **CGC:** 1 graded, best 9.4
16 ❑ Jul 1953 Cover: 0.10 **NM** value: **55.00**
17 ❑ Sep 1953 Cover: 0.10 **NM** value: **55.00**
18 ❑ Nov 1953 Cover: 0.10 **NM** value: **55.00**
• **CGC:** 1 graded, best 9.4
19 ❑ Jan 1954 Cover: 0.10 **NM** value: **55.00**
20 ❑ Mar 1954 Cover: 0.10 **NM** value: **55.00**
21 ❑ May 1954 Cover: 0.10 **NM** value: **45.00**
22 ❑ Jul 1954 Cover: 0.10 **NM** value: **45.00**
23 ❑ Sep 1954 Cover: 0.10 **NM** value: **45.00**
24 ❑ Nov 1954 Cover: 0.10 **NM** value: **45.00**
25 ❑ Jan 1954 Cover: 0.10 **NM** value: **45.00**
26 ❑ Mar 1955 Cover: 0.10 **NM** value: **45.00**
27 ❑ May 1955 Cover: 0.10 **NM** value: **45.00**
28 ❑ Jul 1955 Cover: 0.10 **NM** value: **45.00**
29 ❑ Oct 1955 Cover: 0.10 **NM** value: **45.00**
30 ❑ Jan 1956 Cover: 0.10 **NM** value: **45.00**
31 ❑ Apr 1956 Cover: 0.10 **NM** value: **30.00**
32 ❑ Jul 1956 Cover: 0.10 **NM** value: **30.00**
33 ❑ Oct 1956 Cover: 0.10 **NM** value: **30.00**
📖 The Cisco Kid: Bad Medicine; The Chase (text); Pedro: The Missing Mustache; The Cisco Kid: The Alarm
34 ❑ Jan 1957 Cover: 0.10 **NM** value: **30.00**
35 ❑ Apr 1957 Cover: 0.10 **NM** value: **30.00**
36 ❑ Jul 1957 Cover: 0.10 **NM** value: **30.00**
37 ❑ Oct 1957 Cover: 0.10 **NM** value: **90.00**
Photo cover.
38 ❑ Jan 1958 Cover: 0.10 **NM** value: **90.00**
Photo cover.
39 ❑ Apr 1958 Cover: 0.10 **NM** value: **90.00**
Photo cover.
40 ❑ Jul 1958 Cover: 0.10 **NM** value: **90.00**
Photo cover.
41 ❑ Oct 1958 Cover: 0.10 **NM** value: **90.00**
Photo cover. final issue.

CITIZEN V — Marvel
1 ❑ Jun 2001 Cover: 2.99 **NM value: Cover or less**
Circ: Diamd. preorders: **28,832**
2 ❑ Jul 2001 Cover: 2.99 **NM value: Cover or less**
Circ: Diamd. preorders: **25,722**
3 ❑ Aug 2001 Cover: 2.99 **NM value: Cover or less**
Circ: Diamd. preorders: **23,619**

CITIZEN V & THE V BATTALION: EVERLASTING — Marvel
1 ❑ Apr 2001 Cover: 2.99 **NM value: Cover or less**
Circ: Diamd. preorders: **19,715**

CITIZEN V BATTLEBOOK — Marvel
1 ❑ Cover: 3.99 **NM value: Cover or less**
A: Jean-Claude St. Aubin; Bill Tucci(cover)

CITY OF SILENCE — Image
1 ❑ May 2000 Cover: 2.50 **NM value: Cover or less**
Circ: Diamd. preorders: **23,122**
A: Gary Erskine **W:** Warren Ellis
2 ❑ Jun 2000 Cover: 2.50 **NM value: Cover or less**
Circ: Diamd. preorders: **17,529**
A: Gary Erskine **W:** Warren Ellis
3 ❑ Jul 2000 Cover: 2.50 **NM value: Cover or less**
Circ: Diamd. preorders: **14,864**
A: Gary Erskine **W:** Warren Ellis

CITY OF THE LIVING DEAD — Avon
1 ❑ ca. 1952 Cover: 0.10 **NM** value: **300.00**
• **CGC:** 2 graded, best 9.4

CITY PEOPLE NOTEBOOK — DC
1 ❑ Cover: 9.95 **NM value: Cover or less**
• DC Edition. **A:** Will Eisner **W:** Will Eisner

CLAIRE VOYANT — Leader
The newspaper strip by Jack Sparling began in 1943 and ran until 1948, featuring the adventures of a young woman first introduced in a lifeboat suffering from amnesia. The strip outlived the comic book. — Maggie

1 ❑ 1946 Cover: 0.10 **NM** value: **500.00**
2 ❑ ca. 1946 Cover: 0.10 **NM** value: **400.00**
• **CGC:** 5 graded, best 9.6
3 ❑ 1946 Cover: 0.10 **NM** value: **400.00**
4 ❑ 1947 Cover: 0.10 **NM** value: **400.00**
• **CGC:** 1 graded, best 7.0

CLAIR VOYANT — Lightning
1 ❑ Jun 1996, b&w Cover: 3.50 **NM value: Cover or less**

CLAN APIS — Active Synapse
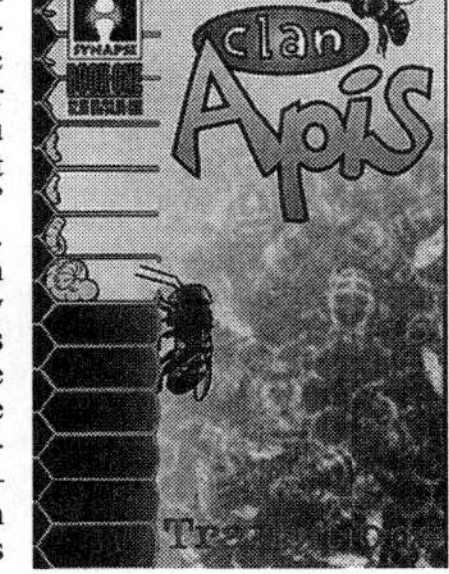

On the letters/editorial page in the back of this charming and educational independent comic book, writer-artist Jay Hosler says, "It is [my] hope to give you all a peak (sic) at the magic that exists right your own backyard." So what's it all about? Well, bees. That's right. Bees. Drawing on his own expertise about honey bees, scientist Hosler constructs a wonderful story about the place of these glorious insects in the world and their social order, focusing on one particular group — the Clan Apis — and one bee in that clan. One episode finds young Nyuki afraid of the transformation from larva to honey bee. A mentor of sorts, Dvorah comforts Nyuki, reminding her that she will become a part of a much larger organization, that the transformation is necessary for her to understand her place in the complex order of things. Great stuff from a deserving Xeric Grant recipient!

1 ❑ b&w Cover: 2.95 **NM value: Cover or less**
• educational comic about bees **A:** Jay Hosler **W:** Jay Hosler
2 ❑ Cover: 2.95 **NM value: Cover or less**
3 ❑ Cover: 2.95 **NM value: Cover or less**
4 ❑ Cover: 2.95 **NM value: Cover or less**
5 ❑ Apr 1999, b&w Cover: 3.95 **NM value: Cover or less**

CLANDESTINE — Marvel
1 ❑ Oct 1994 Cover: 2.95 **NM** value: **3.00**
Circ: CapCity orders: **31,850**
foil cover. 📖 Family Reunion, Part 1 **A:** Alan Davis **W:** Alan Davis
★ 1st Appearance of Imp, The Crimson Crusader.
2 ❑ Nov 1994 Cover: 2.50 **NM value: Cover or less**
Circ: CapCity orders: **19,550**
wraparound cover. 📖 Family Reunion, Part 2 **A:** Alan Davis **W:** Alan Davis

CGC-graded: Multiply prices above by **33 for 9.9 M • 16 for 9.8 NM/M • 7 for 9.6 NM+ • 5 for 9.4 NM • 2.5 for 9.2 NM- • 1.5 for 9.0 VF/NM**

3 ❑ Dec 1994 Cover: 2.50 **NM** value: **Cover or less**
Circ: CapCity orders: **18,000**
A: Alan Davis **W:** Alan Davis

4 ❑ Jan 1995 Cover: 2.50 **NM** value: **Cover or less**
Circ: CapCity orders: **16,675**
A: Alan Davis **W:** Alan Davis

5 ❑ Feb 1995 Cover: 2.50 **NM** value: **Cover or less**
Circ: CapCity orders: **14,500**
A: Alan Davis **W:** Alan Davis

6 ❑ Mar 1995 Cover: 2.50 **NM** value: **Cover or less**
Circ: CapCity orders: **13,425**
A: Alan Davis **W:** Alan Davis

7 ❑ Apr 1995 Cover: 2.50 **NM** value: **Cover or less**
Circ: CapCity orders: **12,375**
A: Alan Davis **W:** Alan Davis

8 ❑ May 1995 Cover: 2.50 **NM** value: **Cover or less**
Circ: CapCity orders: **11,650**
A: Alan Davis **W:** Alan Davis

9 ❑ Jun 1995 Cover: 2.50 **NM** value: **Cover or less**
Circ: CapCity orders: **10,250**

10 ❑ Jul 1995 Cover: 2.50 **NM** value: **Cover or less**
Circ: CapCity orders: **9,600**

11 ❑ Aug 1995 Cover: 2.50 **NM** value: **Cover or less**
Circ: CapCity orders: **8,825**

12 ❑ Sep 1995 Cover: 2.50 **NM** value: **Cover or less**
final issue.

Ash 1❑Oct 1994 Cover: 1.50 **NM** value: **Cover or less**
Circ: CapCity orders: **9,150**
• Preview

CLASH — DC

1 ❑ ca. 1991 Cover: 4.95 **NM** value: **Cover or less**
Circ: CapCity orders: **11,900**
A: Adam Kubert **W:** Tom Veitch

2 ❑ ca. 1991 Cover: 4.95 **NM** value: **Cover or less**
Circ: CapCity orders: **8,050**
The Power And The Glory **A:** Adam Kubert **W:** Tom Veitch

3 ❑ ca. 1991 Cover: 4.95 **NM** value: **Cover or less**
Circ: CapCity orders: **7,100**
A: Adam Kubert **W:** Tom Veitch

CLASSIC ADVENTURE STRIPS — Dragon Lady

1 ❑ May 1985 Cover: 2.95 **NM** value: **4.00**
• King of the Royal Mounted

2 ❑ Jul 1985 Cover: 2.95 **NM** value: **4.00**
• Red Ryder

3 ❑ Sep 1985 Cover: 2.95 **NM** value: **4.00**
• Dickie Dare, Flash Gordon

4 ❑ Nov 1985 Cover: 2.95 **NM** value: **4.00**
• Buz Sawyer;Johnny Hazard;Steve Canyon **A:** Frank Robbins; Roy Crane **W:** Frank Robbins; Roy Crane

5 ❑ Jan 1986 Cover: 2.95 **NM** value: **4.00**
• Wash Tubbs **A:** Roy Crane **W:** Roy Crane

6 ❑ Mar 1986 Cover: 2.95 **NM** value: **4.00**
• Mandrake the Magician, Johnny Hazard, Rip Kirby

7 ❑ Jul 1986 Cover: 2.95 **NM** value: **4.00**
• Buz Sawyer

8 ❑ Oct 1986 Cover: 2.95 **NM** value: **4.00**

9 ❑ Jan 1987 Cover: 2.95 **NM** value: **4.00**

10 ❑ Apr 1987 Cover: 2.95 **NM** value: **4.00**
Buck Rogers vs. Dr. Modor **A:** Murphy Anderson **W:** Murphy Anderson

CLASSIC ALEX TOTH ZORRO, THE — Image

1 ❑ Jul 1998 Cover: 15.95 **NM** value: **Cover or less**
• Trade Paperback. Presenting Señor Zorro; Zorro's Secret Passage; The Ghost of the Mission; Garcia's Secret; The King's Emissary; A Day Day for Bernardo; The Little Zorro; The Visitor; A Double for Diego • reprints Eclipse collection **A:** Alex Toth **W:** Alex Toth

2 ❑ Aug 1998 Cover: 15.95 **NM** value: **Cover or less**
• Trade Paperback. The Eagle's Brood; Gypsy Warning; The Enchanted Bell; The Marauders of Monterey; The Runaway Witness; Friend Indeed • reprints Eclipse collection **A:** Alex Toth **W:** Alex Toth

CLASSIC GIRLS — Eternity

1 ❑ b&w Cover: 2.50 **NM** value: **Cover or less**
2 ❑ b&w Cover: 2.50 **NM** value: **Cover or less**
3 ❑ b&w Cover: 2.50 **NM** value: **Cover or less**
4 ❑ b&w Cover: 2.50 **NM** value: **Cover or less**

CLASSIC JONNY QUEST: SKULL & DOUBLE CROSSBONES — Illustrated Productions

1 ❑ Mar 1996 **NM** value: **1.00**
no cover price. • smaller than normal size comic book. • inserted with Jonny Quest videos

CLASSIC JONNY QUEST: THE QUETONG MISSILE MYSTERY — Illustrated Productions

1 ❑ Mar 1996 **NM** value: **1.00**
no cover price. • smaller than normal size comic book. • inserted with Jonny Quest videos

CLASSIC PUNISHER — Marvel

1 ❑ Dec 1989, b&w Cover: 4.95 **NM** value: **Cover or less**
• prestige format. • Reprints Punisher stories from Marvel Preview #2, Marvel Super Action #1★ Origin of the Punisher.

CLASSICS DESECRATED — NBM

1 ❑ b&w Cover: 8.95 **NM** value: **Cover or less**

CLASSICS ILLUSTRATED (FIRST) — First

In 1941, Albert L. Kanter hit upon the idea of using comic books to introduce children to the joy of reading. He adapted some of the great classics of literature into comic-book form, then sold his creation, Classic Comics, to parents and educators. After a shaky start, the series changed its name to Classics Illustrated and went on to become one of the best-loved comics series of all time.

In 1990, First Comics reintroduced the series in a deluxe, beautifully illustrated format with entirely new adaptations. This new series makes the old favorites fresh again, breathing new life into this great line of comics.

1 ❑ Feb 1990 Cover: 3.75 **NM** value: **4.00**
Circ: CapCity orders: **8,075**
The Raven • Raven **A:** Gahan Wilson **W:** Edgar Allan Poe

2 ❑ Feb 1990 Cover: 3.75 **NM** value: **4.00**
Circ: CapCity orders: **6,400**
Great Expectations • Great Expectations **A:** Rick Geary

3 ❑ Feb 1990 Cover: 3.75 **NM** value: **4.00**
Circ: CapCity orders: **7,150**
Through the Looking Glass • Through the Looking Glass **A:** Kyle Baker

4 ❑ Feb 1990 Cover: 3.75 **NM** value: **4.00**
Circ: CapCity orders: **9,000 • CGC:** 1 graded, best 9.8
Moby Dick • Moby Dick **A:** Bill Sienkiewicz; Bill Sienkiewicz(cover)

5 ❑ Mar 1990 Cover: 3.75 **NM** value: **4.00**
Circ: CapCity orders: **10,700**
Hamlet • Hamlet **A:** Tom Mandrake **W:** Steven Grant

6 ❑ Mar 1990 Cover: 3.75 **NM** value: **4.00**
Circ: CapCity orders: **10,550**
The Scarlet Letter • Scarlet Letter **A:** P. Craig Russell; Jill Thompson; P. Craig Russel **W:** P. Craig Russel

7 ❑ Apr 1990 Cover: 3.75 **NM** value: **4.00**
Circ: CapCity orders: **9,350**
The Count of Monte Cristo • Count of Monte Cristo **A:** Don Spiegle; Dan Spiegle **W:** Steven Grant

8 ❑ Apr 1990 Cover: 3.75 **NM** value: **4.00**
Circ: CapCity orders: **9,750**
Dr. Jekyll and Mr. Hyde • Doctor Jekyll & Mr. Hyde **A:** Jack Kirby; John K. Snyder III **W:** John K. Snyder III

9 ❑ May 1990 Cover: 3.75 **NM** value: **4.00**
Circ: CapCity orders: **11,725**
Tom Sawyer • Tom Sawyer **A:** Mike Ploog

10 ❑ Jun 1990 Cover: 3.75 **NM** value: **4.00**
Circ: CapCity orders: **10,650**
Call of the Wild • Call of the Wild **A:** Ricardo Villagran

11 ❑ Jul 1990 Cover: 3.75 **NM** value: **4.00**
Circ: CapCity orders: **10,900**
Rip Van Winkle • Rip Van Winkle **A:** Jeffrey Busch

12 ❑ Aug 1990 Cover: 3.75 **NM** value: **4.00**
Circ: CapCity orders: **9,900**
The Island of Dr. Moreau • Island of Doctor Moreau **A:** Eric Vincent

13 ❑ Oct 1990 Cover: 3.75 **NM** value: **4.00**
Circ: CapCity orders: **8,550**
Wuthering Heights • Wuthering Heights **A:** Rick Geary

14 ❑ Sep 1990 Cover: 3.75 **NM** value: **4.00**
Circ: CapCity orders: **8,350**
Fall of the House of Usher • Fall of the House of Usher **A:** P. Craig Russell; Jay Geldhof

15 ❑ Nov 1990 Cover: 3.75 **NM** value: **4.00**
Circ: CapCity orders: **7,150**
The Gift of the Magi • Gift of Magi **A:** Gary Gianni

16 ❑ Dec 1990 Cover: 3.75 **NM** value: **4.00**
Circ: CapCity orders: **8,025**
A Christmas Carol • Christmas Carol **A:** Joe Staton **W:** Joe Staton

17 ❑ 1991 Cover: 3.75 **NM** value: **4.00**
Circ: CapCity orders: **6,925**
Treasure Island • Treasure Island **A:** Pat Boyette

18 ❑ 1991 Cover: 3.95 **NM** value: **4.00**
Circ: CapCity orders: **6,600**
The Devil's Dictionary • Jungle **A:** Peter Kuper

19 ❑ Feb 1991 Cover: 3.95 **NM** value: **4.00**
Circ: CapCity orders: **6,475**
Secret Agent • Secret Agent **A:** John K. Snyder III **W:** John K. Snyder III

20 ❑ Mar 1991 Cover: 3.95 **NM** value: **4.00**
Circ: CapCity orders: **6,300**
The Invisible Man • Invisible Man **A:** Rick Geary

21 ❑ 1991 Cover: 3.95 **NM** value: **4.00**
Circ: CapCity orders: **5,825**
Cyrano de Bergerac • Cyrano de Bergerac **A:** Kyle Baker

22 ❑ 1991 Cover: 3.95 **NM** value: **4.00**
Circ: CapCity orders: **5,600**
The Jungle Book • Jungle Books **A:** Jeffrey Busch

23 ❑ Apr 1991 Cover: 3.95 **NM** value: **4.00**
Circ: CapCity orders: **5,250**
Swiss Family Robinson • Robinson Crusoe **A:** Pat Boyette

24 ❑ May 1991 Cover: 3.95 **NM** value: **4.00**
Circ: CapCity orders: **5,250**
Rime of the Ancient Mariner • Rime of Ancient Mariner **A:** Dean Motter

25 ❑ May 1991 Cover: 3.95 **NM** value: **4.00**
Circ: CapCity orders: **5,950**
Ivanhoe • Ivanhoe **A:** Ray Lago

26 ❑ Jun 1991 Cover: 3.95 **NM** value: **4.00**
Circ: CapCity orders: **4,975**
Aesop's Fables • Aesop's Fables **A:** Eric Vincent

27 ❑ Cover: 3.95 **NM** value: **4.00**
Circ: CapCity orders: **4,875**
The Jungle • Jungle **A:** Peter Kuper

CLASSICS ILLUSTRATED (GILBERTON) — Gilberton

In 1941, Albert E. Kanter introduced Classic Comics, later renamed Classics Illustrated. Kanter's idea was to use the comic-book form to make great literature accessible to readers who might never otherwise make the effort. Whether his idea represented a watering-down of the classics, as some critics claimed, it was an amazingly popular move. Most of the 169 comics in this series were reprinted numerous times, with 23rd printings being relatively common. Their popularity even extended to schools, where the colorful, well-written adaptations must have seemed a welcome alternative to reading lengthy texts.

Kanter later introduced Classics Illustrated Junior, adapting children's literature for younger readers. The series also gave rise to numerous imitations over the years.

For collectors, their popularity is particularly problematic, since various reprintings were not clearly marked. The best clue to figuring out which printing a given issue is lies in the highest reorder number (HRN) from the series order form on the back of each copy.

We extend our thanks to Classics Illustrated authority Dan Malan, who has painstakingly determined the distinguishing characteristics of each printing and who has generously allowed us to use this information here. If you'd like to learn more about this remarkable series, we would encourage you to refer to his definitive "The Complete Guide to Classics Collectibles," available in four volumes from: Malan Classical Enterprises, 7519 Lindbergh Dr., St. Louis, MO 63117 (314) 781-2319. In later years, other publishers reprinted issues, usually with new covers or coloring.

1 ❑ Cover: 0.10 **NM** value: **4300.00**
The Three Musketeers
1-2 ❑ **HRN:** 10 **NM** value: **250.00**
1-3 ❑ **HRN:** 15 **NM** value: **125.00**
1-4 ❑ **HRN:** 18 **NM** value: **100.00**
1-5 ❑ **HRN:** 21 **NM** value: **90.00**
1-6 ❑ **HRN:** 28 **NM** value: **75.00**
1-7 ❑ **HRN:** 36 **NM** value: **35.00**
1-8 ❑ **HRN:** 60 **NM** value: **24.00**
1-9 ❑ **HRN:** 64 **NM** value: **20.00**
1-10❑ **HRN:** 78 **NM** value: **18.00**
1-11❑ **HRN:** 93 **NM** value: **18.00**
1-12❑ **HRN:** 114 **NM** value: **12.00**
1-13❑ **HRN:** 134 **NM** value: **12.00**
1-14❑ **HRN:** 143 **NM** value: **12.00**
1-15❑ **HRN:** 150 **NM** value: **12.00**
1-16❑ **HRN:** 149 **NM** value: **5.00**
1-17❑ **HRN:** 167 **NM** value: **5.00**
1-18❑ **HRN:** 167 Apr 1964 **NM** value: **5.00**
1-19❑ **HRN:** 167 Jan 1965 **NM** value: **5.00**
1-20❑ **HRN:** 167 Mar 1965 **NM** value: **5.00**
1-21❑ **HRN:** 167 Jan 1967 **NM** value: **5.00**
1-22❑ **HRN:** 166 Spr 1969 Cover: 0.25 **NM** value: **5.00**
1-23❑ **HRN:** 169 Spr 1971 **NM** value: **5.00**
2 ❑ Cover: 0.10 **NM** value: **1700.00**
Ivanhoe
2-2 ❑ **HRN:** 10 **NM** value: **230.00**
2-3 ❑ **HRN:** 15 **NM** value: **125.00**
2-4 ❑ **HRN:** 18 **NM** value: **100.00**
2-5 ❑ **HRN:** 21 **NM** value: **90.00**
2-6 ❑ **HRN:** 28 **NM** value: **75.00**
2-7 ❑ **HRN:** 36 **NM** value: **35.00**
2-8 ❑ **HRN:** 60 **NM** value: **24.00**
2-9 ❑ **HRN:** 64 **NM** value: **20.00**
2-10❑ **HRN:** 78 **NM** value: **18.00**
2-11❑ **HRN:** 89 **NM** value: **16.00**
2-12❑ **HRN:** 106 **NM** value: **12.00**
2-13❑ **HRN:** 121 **NM** value: **12.00**
2-14❑ **HRN:** 136 **NM** value: **12.00**
2-15❑ **HRN:** 142 **NM** value: **5.00**
2-16❑ **HRN:** 153 **NM** value: **5.00**
2-17❑ **HRN:** 149 **NM** value: **5.00**
2-18❑ **HRN:** 167 **NM** value: **5.00**
2-19❑ **HRN:** 167 May 1964 **NM** value: **5.00**
2-20❑ **HRN:** 167 Jan 1965 **NM** value: **5.00**
2-21❑ **HRN:** 167 Mar 1966 **NM** value: **5.00**
2/A-22❑ **HRN:** 166 Sep 1967 **NM** value: **5.00**
2/B-22❑ **HRN:** 166 **NM** value: **35.00**
2-23❑ **HRN:** 166 Cover: 0.25 **NM** value: **5.00**
2-24❑ **HRN:** 169 **NM** value: **5.00**
2-25❑ **HRN:** 169 **NM** value: **5.00**
3 ❑ Cover: 0.10 **NM** value: **1200.00**
The Count of Monte Cristo
3-2 ❑ **HRN:** 10 **NM** value: **225.00**
3-3 ❑ **HRN:** 15 **NM** value: **125.00**
3-4 ❑ **HRN:** 18 **NM** value: **100.00**
3-5 ❑ **HRN:** 20 **NM** value: **90.00**
3-6 ❑ **HRN:** 21 **NM** value: **85.00**
3-7 ❑ **HRN:** 28 **NM** value: **75.00**
3-8 ❑ **HRN:** 36 **NM** value: **35.00**
3-9 ❑ **HRN:** 60 **NM** value: **24.00**
3-10❑ **HRN:** 62 **NM** value: **20.00**
3-11❑ **HRN:** 71 **NM** value: **18.00**
3-12❑ **HRN:** 87 **NM** value: **16.00**
3-13❑ **HRN:** 113 **NM** value: **12.00**
3-14❑ **HRN:** 135 **NM** value: **12.00**
3-15❑ **HRN:** 143 **NM** value: **12.00**
3-16❑ **HRN:** 153 **NM** value: **5.00**
3-17❑ **HRN:** 161 **NM** value: **5.00**
3-18❑ **HRN:** 167 **NM** value: **5.00**
3-19❑ **HRN:** 167 Jul 1964 **NM** value: **5.00**

Other grades: Multiply prices above by **1.5 for Mint • 2/3 for Very Fine • 1/3 for Fine • 1/5 for Very Good • 1/8 for Good**

3-20❑ **HRN:** 167 Jul 1965 **NM** value: **5.00**
3-21❑ **HRN:** 167 Jul 1966 **NM** value: **5.00**
3-22❑ **HRN:** 166 Cover: 0.25 **NM** value: **5.00**
3-23❑ **HRN:** 169 **NM** value: **5.00**
4 ❑ Cover: 0.10 **NM** value: **1000.00**
The Last of the Mohicans
4-2 ❑ **HRN:** 12 **NM** value: **225.00**
4-3 ❑ **HRN:** 15 **NM** value: **125.00**
4-4 ❑ **HRN:** 20 **NM** value: **100.00**
4-5 ❑ **HRN:** 21 **NM** value: **90.00**
4-6 ❑ **HRN:** 28 **NM** value: **75.00**
4-7 ❑ **HRN:** 36 **NM** value: **35.00**
4-8 ❑ **HRN:** 60 **NM** value: **24.00**
4-9 ❑ **HRN:** 64 **NM** value: **20.00**
4-10❑ **HRN:** 78 **NM** value: **18.00**
4-11❑ **HRN:** 89 **NM** value: **16.00**
4-12❑ **HRN:** 117 **NM** value: **12.00**
4-13❑ **HRN:** 135 **NM** value: **12.00**
4-14❑ **HRN:** 141 **NM** value: **10.00**
4-15❑ **HRN:** 150 **NM** value: **10.00**
4-16❑ **HRN:** 161 **NM** value: **5.00**
4-17❑ **HRN:** 167 **NM** value: **5.00**
4-18❑ **HRN:** 167 Jun 1964 **NM** value: **5.00**
4-19❑ **HRN:** 167 Aug 1965 **NM** value: **5.00**
4-20❑ **HRN:** 167 Aug 1967 **NM** value: **5.00**
4-21❑ **HRN:** 166 Cover: 0.25 **NM** value: **5.00**
4-22❑ **HRN:** 169 Spr 1969 **NM** value: **5.00**
5 ❑ Cover: 0.10 **NM** value: **1150.00**
Moby Dick
5/A ❑ Cover: 0.10 **NM** value: **1900.00**
Moby Dick • Rare variation, free promo
5/B ❑ Cover: 0.10 **NM** value: **1900.00**
Moby Dick • Rare variation, free promo
5-2 ❑ **HRN:** 10 **NM** value: **230.00**
5-3 ❑ **HRN:** 15 **NM** value: **175.00**
5-4 ❑ **HRN:** 18 **NM** value: **160.00**
5-5 ❑ **HRN:** 20 **NM** value: **125.00**
5-6 ❑ **HRN:** 21 **NM** value: **100.00**
5-7 ❑ **HRN:** 28 **NM** value: **90.00**
5-8 ❑ **HRN:** 36 **NM** value: **40.00**
5-9 ❑ **HRN:** 60 **NM** value: **25.00**
5-10❑ **HRN:** 62 **NM** value: **20.00**
5-11❑ **HRN:** 71 **NM** value: **20.00**
5-12❑ **HRN:** 87 **NM** value: **12.00**
5-13❑ **HRN:** 118 **NM** value: **12.00**
5-14❑ **HRN:** 131 **NM** value: **12.00**
5-15❑ **HRN:** 138 **NM** value: **5.00**
5-16❑ **HRN:** 148 **NM** value: **5.00**
5-17❑ **HRN:** 158 **NM** value: **5.00**
5-18❑ **HRN:** 167 **NM** value: **5.00**
5-19❑ **HRN:** 167 Jun 1964 **NM** value: **5.00**
5-20❑ **HRN:** 167 Jul 1965 **NM** value: **5.00**
5-21❑ **HRN:** 167 Mar 1966 **NM** value: **5.00**
5-22❑ **HRN:** 167 Sep 1967 **NM** value: **5.00**
5-23❑ **HRN:** 166 Cover: 0.25 **NM** value: **5.00**
5-24❑ **HRN:** 169 **NM** value: **5.00**
6 ❑ Cover: 0.10 **NM** value: **1000.00**
A Tale of Two Cities
6-2 ❑ **HRN:** 14 **NM** value: **225.00**
6-3 ❑ **HRN:** 18 **NM** value: **175.00**
6-4 ❑ **HRN:** 20 **NM** value: **125.00**
6-5 ❑ **HRN:** 28 **NM** value: **75.00**
6-6 ❑ **HRN:** 51 **NM** value: **40.00**
6-7 ❑ **HRN:** 64 **NM** value: **25.00**
6-8 ❑ **HRN:** 78 **NM** value: **20.00**
6-9 ❑ **HRN:** 89 **NM** value: **12.00**
6-10❑ **HRN:** 117 **NM** value: **12.00**
6-11❑ **HRN:** 132 **NM** value: **12.00**
6-12❑ **HRN:** 140 **NM** value: **5.00**
6-13❑ **HRN:** 147 **NM** value: **5.00**
6-14❑ **HRN:** 152 **NM** value: **5.00**
6-15❑ **HRN:** 153 **NM** value: **5.00**
6-16❑ **HRN:** 149 **NM** value: **5.00**
6-17❑ **HRN:** 167 **NM** value: **5.00**
6-18❑ **HRN:** 167 Jun 1964 **NM** value: **5.00**
6-19❑ **HRN:** 167 Aug 1965 **NM** value: **5.00**
6-20❑ **HRN:** 166 Jun 1967 **NM** value: **5.00**
6-21❑ **HRN:** 166 Fal 1968 Cover: 0.25 **NM** value: **5.00**
6-22❑ **HRN:** 169 Sum 1970 **NM** value: **5.00**
7 ❑ Cover: 0.10 **NM** value: **775.00**
Robin Hood
7-2 ❑ **HRN:** 12 **NM** value: **200.00**
7-3 ❑ **HRN:** 18 **NM** value: **160.00**
7-4 ❑ **HRN:** 20 **NM** value: **125.00**
7-5 ❑ **HRN:** 22 **NM** value: **100.00**
7-6 ❑ **HRN:** 28 **NM** value: **90.00**
7-7 ❑ **HRN:** 51 **NM** value: **40.00**
7-8 ❑ **HRN:** 64 **NM** value: **25.00**
7-9 ❑ **HRN:** 78 **NM** value: **20.00**
7-10❑ **HRN:** 97 **NM** value: **20.00**
7-11❑ **HRN:** 106 **NM** value: **14.00**
7-12❑ **HRN:** 121 **NM** value: **14.00**
7-13❑ **HRN:** 129 **NM** value: **12.00**
7-14❑ **HRN:** 136 **NM** value: **12.00**
7-15❑ **HRN:** 143 **NM** value: **5.00**
7-16❑ **HRN:** 153 **NM** value: **5.00**
7-17❑ **HRN:** 164 **NM** value: **5.00**
7-18❑ **HRN:** 167 **NM** value: **5.00**
7-19❑ **HRN:** 167 Jun 1964 **NM** value: **5.00**
7-20❑ **HRN:** 167 Mar 1965 **NM** value: **5.00**
7-21❑ **HRN:** 167 Jul 1965 **NM** value: **5.00**
7-22❑ **HRN:** 16 Dec 1967 **NM** value: **5.00**
7-23❑ **HRN:** 169 Sum 1969Cover: 0.25 **NM** value: **5.00**
8 ❑ Cover: 0.10 **NM** value: **1500.00**
Arabian Nights
8-2 ❑ **HRN:** 17 **NM** value: **500.00**
8-3 ❑ **HRN:** 20 **NM** value: **400.00**
8/A-4❑ **HRN:** 28 **NM** value: **325.00**
8/B-4❑ **HRN:** 28 **NM** value: **325.00**
8-5 ❑ **HRN:** 51 **NM** value: **175.00**
8-6 ❑ **HRN:** 64 **NM** value: **125.00**
8-7 ❑ **HRN:** 78 **NM** value: **110.00**
8-8 ❑ **HRN:** 164 **NM** value: **100.00**
9 ❑ Mar 1943 **NM** value: **700.00**
Slick & Glossy Cover. Les Miserables
9/A ❑ Mar 1943 **NM** value: **750.00**
Rough & Pulpy cover. Les Miserables
9/B ❑ Mar 1943 **NM** value: **750.00**
Rough & Pulpy cover. Les Miserables
9-2 ❑ **HRN:** 14 **NM** value: **175.00**
9-3 ❑ **HRN:** 18 Mar 1944 **NM** value: **150.00**
9-4 ❑ **HRN:** 20 **NM** value: **125.00**
9-5 ❑ **HRN:** 28 **NM** value: **90.00**
9-6 ❑ **HRN:** 51 **NM** value: **40.00**
9-7 ❑ **HRN:** 71 **NM** value: **25.00**
9-8 ❑ **HRN:** 87 **NM** value: **25.00**
9-9 ❑ **HRN:** 161 **NM** value: **20.00**
9-10❑ **HRN:** 167 Sep 1963 **NM** value: **12.00**
9-11❑ **HRN:** 167 Dec 1965 **NM** value: **12.00**
9-12❑ **HRN:** 166 Cover: 0.25 **NM** value: **10.00**
10/A❑ Cover: 0.10 **NM** value: **650.00**
Violet/Purple cover. Robinson Crusoe
10/B❑ Cover: 0.10 **NM** value: **685.00**
Blue/Gray cover. Robinson Crusoe
10/A-2❑ **HRN:** 14 **NM** value: **225.00**
10/B-2❑ **HRN:** 14 **NM** value: **200.00**
10-3❑ **HRN:** 18 **NM** value: **125.00**
10-4❑ **HRN:** 20 **NM** value: **110.00**
10-5❑ **HRN:** 28 **NM** value: **85.00**
10-6❑ **HRN:** 51 **NM** value: **40.00**
10-7❑ **HRN:** 64 **NM** value: **25.00**
10-8❑ **HRN:** 78 **NM** value: **20.00**
10-9❑ **HRN:** 97 **NM** value: **14.00**
10-10❑ **HRN:** 114 **NM** value: **12.00**
10-11❑ **HRN:** 130 **NM** value: **12.00**
10-12❑ **HRN:** 140 **NM** value: **12.00**
10-13❑ **HRN:** 153 **NM** value: **5.00**
10-14❑ **HRN:** 164 **NM** value: **5.00**
10-15❑ **HRN:** 167 **NM** value: **5.00**
10-16❑ **HRN:** 167 Jul 1964 **NM** value: **5.00**
10-17❑ **HRN:** 167 May 1965 **NM** value: **5.00**
10-18❑ **HRN:** 167 Jun 1966 **NM** value: **5.00**
10-19❑ **HRN:** 166 Fal 1968 Cover: 0.25 **NM** value: **5.00**
10-20❑ **HRN:** 166 **NM** value: **5.00**
10-21❑ **HRN:** 169 Sum 1970 **NM** value: **5.00**
11 ❑ May 1943 Cover: 0.10 **NM** value: **700.00**
Don Quixote
11-2❑ **HRN:** 18 **NM** value: **200.00**
11-3❑ **HRN:** 21 **NM** value: **125.00**
11-4❑ **HRN:** 28 **NM** value: **90.00**
11-5❑ **HRN:** 110 **NM** value: **25.00**
11-6❑ **HRN:** 156 **NM** value: **12.00**
11-7❑ **HRN:** 165 **NM** value: **5.00**
11-8❑ **HRN:** 167 Jan 1964 **NM** value: **5.00**
11-9❑ **HRN:** 167 Nov 1965 **NM** value: **5.00**
11-10❑ **HRN:** 166 Cover: 0.25 **NM** value: **5.00**
12 ❑ Cover: 0.10 **NM** value: **700.00**
Rip Van Winkle and the Headless Horseman
12-2❑ **HRN:** 15 **NM** value: **200.00**
12-3❑ **HRN:** 20 **NM** value: **125.00**
12-4❑ **HRN:** 22 **NM** value: **100.00**
12-5❑ **HRN:** 28 **NM** value: **90.00**
12-6❑ **HRN:** 60 **NM** value: **40.00**
12-7❑ **HRN:** 62 **NM** value: **24.00**
12-8❑ **HRN:** 71 **NM** value: **16.00**
12-9❑ **HRN:** 89 **NM** value: **16.00**
12-10❑ **HRN:** 118 **NM** value: **12.00**
12-11❑ **HRN:** 132 **NM** value: **12.00**
12-12❑ **HRN:** 150 **NM** value: **12.00**
12-13❑ **HRN:** 158 **NM** value: **5.00**
12-14❑ **HRN:** 167 **NM** value: **5.00**
12-15❑ **HRN:** 167 Dec 1963 **NM** value: **5.00**
12-16❑ **HRN:** 167 Jun 1965 **NM** value: **5.00**
12-17❑ **HRN:** 167 Apr 1966 **NM** value: **5.00**
12-18❑ **HRN:** 166 Cover: 0.25 **NM** value: **5.00**
12-19❑ **HRN:** 169 Sum 1970 **NM** value: **5.00**
13 ❑ Cover: 0.10 **NM** value: **950.00**
Dr. Jekyll and Mr. Hyde
13-2❑ **HRN:** 15 **NM** value: **225.00**
13-3❑ **HRN:** 20 **NM** value: **175.00**
13-4❑ **HRN:** 28 **NM** value: **120.00**
13-5❑ **HRN:** 60 **NM** value: **40.00**
13-6❑ **HRN:** 62 **NM** value: **24.00**
13-7❑ **HRN:** 71 **NM** value: **16.00**
13-8❑ **HRN:** 87 **NM** value: **16.00**
13-9❑ **HRN:** 112 **NM** value: **16.00**
13-10❑ **HRN:** 153 **NM** value: **5.00**
13-11❑ **HRN:** 161 **NM** value: **5.00**
13-12❑ **HRN:** 167 **NM** value: **5.00**
13-13❑ **HRN:** 167 Aug 1964 **NM** value: **5.00**
13-14❑ **HRN:** 167 Nov 1965 **NM** value: **5.00**
13-15❑ **HRN:** 166 Cover: 0.25 **NM** value: **5.00**
13-16❑ **HRN:** 169 **NM** value: **5.00**
14 ❑ Cover: 0.10 **NM** value: **1550.00**
Westward Ho!
14-2❑ **HRN:** 15 **NM** value: **500.00**
14-3❑ **HRN:** 21 **NM** value: **375.00**
14-4❑ **HRN:** 28 **NM** value: **300.00**
14-5❑ **HRN:** 53 **NM** value: **250.00**
15 ❑ Cover: 0.10 **NM** value: **550.00**
Uncle Tom's Cabin
15-2❑ **HRN:** 15 **NM** value: **200.00**
15-3❑ **HRN:** 21 **NM** value: **125.00**
15-4❑ **HRN:** 28 **NM** value: **80.00**
15-5❑ **HRN:** 53 **NM** value: **35.00**
15-6❑ **HRN:** 71 **NM** value: **24.00**
15-7❑ **HRN:** 89 Cover: 0.15 **NM** value: **20.00**
15-8❑ **HRN:** 117 **NM** value: **16.00**
15-9❑ **HRN:** 128 **NM** value: **12.00**
15-10❑ **HRN:** 137 **NM** value: **5.00**
15-11❑ **HRN:** 146 **NM** value: **5.00**
15-12❑ **HRN:** 154 **NM** value: **5.00**
15-13❑ **HRN:** 161 **NM** value: **5.00**
15-14❑ **HRN:** 167 **NM** value: **5.00**
15-15❑ **HRN:** 167 Jun 1964 **NM** value: **5.00**
15-16❑ **HRN:** 167 May 1965 **NM** value: **5.00**
15-17❑ **HRN:** 166 May 1967 **NM** value: **5.00**
15-18❑ **HRN:** 166 **NM** value: **5.00**
15-19❑ **HRN:** 169 Sum 1970 **NM** value: **5.00**
16 ❑ Cover: 0.10 **NM** value: **550.00**
Gulliver's Travels
16-2❑ **HRN:** 18 **NM** value: **175.00**
16-3❑ **HRN:** 22 **NM** value: **125.00**
16-4❑ **HRN:** 28 **NM** value: **75.00**
16-5❑ **HRN:** 60 **NM** value: **30.00**
16-6❑ **HRN:** 62 **NM** value: **20.00**
16-7❑ **HRN:** 78 Cover: 0.15 **NM** value: **16.00**
16-8❑ **HRN:** 89 **NM** value: **12.00**
16-9❑ **HRN:** 155 **NM** value: **12.00**
16-10❑ **HRN:** 165 **NM** value: **5.00**
16-11❑ **HRN:** 167 May 1964 **NM** value: **5.00**
16-12❑ **HRN:** 167 Nov 1965 **NM** value: **5.00**
16-13❑ **HRN:** 166 **NM** value: **5.00**
16-14❑ **HRN:** 169 **NM** value: **5.00**
17 ❑ Cover: 0.10 **NM** value: **550.00**
The Deerslayer
17/A-2❑ **HRN:** 18 **NM** value: **175.00**
17/B-2❑ **HRN:** 18 **NM** value: **125.00**
17-3❑ **HRN:** 22 **NM** value: **75.00**
17-4❑ **HRN:** 28 **NM** value: **25.00**
17-5❑ **HRN:** 60 **NM** value: **20.00**
17-6❑ **HRN:** 64 **NM** value: **16.00**
17-7❑ **HRN:** 85 Cover: 0.15 **NM** value: **16.00**
17-8❑ **HRN:** 118 **NM** value: **12.00**
17-9❑ **HRN:** 132 **NM** value: **12.00**
17-10❑ **HRN:** 167 Nov 1966 **NM** value: **12.00**
17-11❑ **HRN:** 166 Cover: 0.25 **NM** value: **10.00**
17-12❑ **HRN:** 169 Spr 1971 **NM** value: **10.00**
18/A❑ Cover: 0.10 **NM** value: **650.00**
The Hunchback of Notre Dame • Published by Gilberton Co.
18/B❑ Cover: 0.10 **NM** value: **650.00**
The Hunchback of Notre Dame • Published by Island Publishers
18-2❑ **HRN:** 18 **NM** value: **200.00**
18-3❑ **HRN:** 22 **NM** value: **130.00**
18-4❑ **HRN:** 28 **NM** value: **100.00**
18-5❑ **HRN:** 60 **NM** value: **35.00**
18-6❑ **HRN:** 62 **NM** value: **24.00**
18-7❑ **HRN:** 78 Cover: 0.15 **NM** value: **20.00**
18/A-8❑ **HRN:** 89 **NM** value: **16.00**
18/B-8❑ **HRN:** 89 **NM** value: **16.00**
18-9❑ **HRN:** 118 **NM** value: **16.00**
18-10❑ **HRN:** 140 **NM** value: **16.00**
18-11❑ **HRN:** 146 **NM** value: **16.00**
18-12❑ **HRN:** 158 **NM** value: **16.00**
18-13❑ **HRN:** 165 **NM** value: **5.00**
18-14❑ **HRN:** 167 Sep 1963 **NM** value: **5.00**
18-15❑ **HRN:** 167 Oct 1964 **NM** value: **5.00**
18-16❑ **HRN:** 167 Apr 1966 **NM** value: **5.00**
18-17❑ **HRN:** 166 Cover: 0.25 **NM** value: **5.00**
18-18❑ **HRN:** 169 Spr 1970 **NM** value: **5.00**
19/A❑ Cover: 0.10 **NM** value: **435.00**
Huckleberry Finn • Published by Gilberton Co.
19/B❑ Cover: 0.10 **NM** value: **435.00**
Huckleberry Finn • Published by Island Publishers
19-2❑ **HRN:** 18 Cover: 0.15 **NM** value: **185.00**
19-3❑ **HRN:** 22 **NM** value: **125.00**
19-4❑ **HRN:** 28 **NM** value: **80.00**
19-5❑ **HRN:** 60 **NM** value: **30.00**
19-6❑ **HRN:** 62 **NM** value: **24.00**
19-7❑ **HRN:** 78 **NM** value: **16.00**
19-8❑ **HRN:** 89 **NM** value: **16.00**
19-9❑ **HRN:** 117 **NM** value: **12.00**
19-10❑ **HRN:** 131 **NM** value: **12.00**
19-11❑ **HRN:** 140 **NM** value: **5.00**
19-12❑ **HRN:** 150 **NM** value: **5.00**
19-13❑ **HRN:** 158 **NM** value: **5.00**
19-14❑ **HRN:** 165 **NM** value: **5.00**
19-15❑ **HRN:** 167 **NM** value: **5.00**
19-16❑ **HRN:** 167 Jun 1964 **NM** value: **5.00**
19-17❑ **HRN:** 167 Jun 1965 **NM** value: **5.00**
19-18❑ **HRN:** 167 Oct 1965 **NM** value: **5.00**
19-19❑ **HRN:** 166 Sep 1967 **NM** value: **5.00**
19-20❑ **HRN:** 166 Cover: 0.25 **NM** value: **5.00**
19-21❑ **HRN:** 169 Sum 1970 **NM** value: **5.00**
20/A❑ Cover: 0.10 **NM** value: **400.00**
The Corsican Brothers • Published by Gilberton Co.
20/B❑ Cover: 0.10 **NM** value: **400.00**
The Corsican Brothers • Published by The Courier
20/C❑ Cover: 0.10 **NM** value: **400.00**
The Corsican Brothers • Published by Long Island Independent
20/D❑ Cover: 0.10 **NM** value: **400.00**
The Corsican Brothers • Published by Gilberton Co. & Long Island Independent, Rare
20-2❑ **HRN:** 22 **NM** value: **150.00**
20-3❑ **HRN:** 28 **NM** value: **125.00**
20-4❑ **HRN:** 60 **NM** value: **80.00**
20/A-5❑ **HRN:** 62 **NM** value: **60.00**
20/B-5❑ **HRN:** 62 **NM** value: **60.00**
20-6❑ **HRN:** 78 Cover: 0.15 **NM** value: **50.00**
20-7❑ **HRN:** 97 **NM** value: **35.00**
21/A❑ Cover: 0.10 **NM** value: **800.00**
3 Famous Mysteries • Published by Gilberton Co.
21/B❑ Cover: 0.10 **NM** value: **800.00**
3 Famous Mysteries • Published by Island Publishers

CGC-graded: Multiply prices above by **33 for 9.9 M • 16 for 9.8 NM/M • 7 for 9.6 NM+ • 5 for 9.4 NM • 2.5 for 9.2 NM- • 1.5 for 9.0 VF/NM**

21/C❑ Cover: 0.10 NM value: 800.00
3 Famous Mysteries • Published by The Courier
21-2❑ HRN: 22 NM value: 250.00
21-3❑ HRN: 30 NM value: 185.00
21-4❑ HRN: 62 NM value: 140.00
21-5❑ HRN: 70 NM value: 125.00
21-6❑ HRN: 85 Cover: 0.15 NM value: 100.00
21-7❑ HRN: 114 NM value: 100.00
22/A❑ Cover: 0.10 NM value: 350.00
The Pathfinder • Published by Gilberton Co.
22/B❑ Cover: 0.10 NM value: 325.00
The Pathfinder • Published by Island Publishers
22/C❑ Cover: 0.10 NM value: 325.00
The Pathfinder • Published by Queens Home News
22-2❑ HRN: 30 NM value: 24.00
22-3❑ HRN: 60 NM value: 20.00
22-4❑ HRN: 70 NM value: 16.00
22-5❑ HRN: 85 Cover: 0.15 NM value: 14.00
22-6❑ HRN: 118 NM value: 12.00
22-7❑ HRN: 132 NM value: 12.00
22-8❑ HRN: 146 NM value: 12.00
22-9❑ HRN: 167 Nov 1963 NM value: 12.00
22-10❑ HRN: 167 Dec 1965 NM value: 12.00
22-11❑ HRN: 166 Aug 1967 NM value: 12.00
23 ❑ Cover: 0.10 NM value: 325.00
Oliver Twist
23/A-2❑ HRN: 30 NM value: 130.00
23/B-2❑ HRN: 30 NM value: 90.00
23-3❑ HRN: 60 NM value: 30.00
23-4❑ HRN: 62 NM value: 24.00
23-5❑ HRN: 71 NM value: 20.00
23-6❑ HRN: 85 Cover: 0.15 NM value: 16.00
23-7❑ HRN: 94 NM value: 12.00
23-8❑ HRN: 118 NM value: 12.00
23-9❑ HRN: 136 NM value: 12.00
23-10❑ HRN: 150 NM value: 10.00
23-11❑ HRN: 164 NM value: 5.00
23-12❑ HRN: 164 NM value: 5.00
23-13❑ HRN: 167 NM value: 5.00
23-14❑ HRN: 167 Aug 1964 NM value: 5.00
23-15❑ HRN: 167 Dec 1965 NM value: 5.00
23-16❑ HRN: 166 NM value: 5.00
23-17❑ HRN: 166 NM value: 5.00
24 ❑ Cover: 0.10 NM value: 300.00
A Connecticut Yankee in King Arthur's Court
24-2❑ HRN: 30 NM value: 75.00
24-3❑ HRN: 60 NM value: 25.00
24-4❑ HRN: 62 NM value: 24.00
24-5❑ HRN: 71 NM value: 16.00
24-6❑ HRN: 87 NM value: 16.00
24-7❑ HRN: 121 NM value: 16.00
24-8❑ HRN: 140 NM value: 16.00
24-9❑ HRN: 53 NM value: 12.00
24-10❑ HRN: 164 NM value: 5.00
24-11❑ HRN: 167 NM value: 5.00
24-12❑ HRN: 167 Jul 1964 NM value: 5.00
24-13❑ HRN: 167 Jun 1966 NM value: 5.00
24-14❑ HRN: 166 Cover: 0.25 NM value: 5.00
24-15❑ HRN: 169 Spr 1971 NM value: 5.00
25 ❑ Cover: 0.10 NM value: 300.00
Two Years Before the Mast
25-2❑ NM value: 85.00
Two Years Before the Mast • 2nd printing, HRN 30
25-3❑ NM value: 30.00
Two Years Before the Mast • 3rd printing, HRN 60
25-4❑ NM value: 24.00
Two Years Before the Mast • 4th printing, HRN 62
25-5❑ NM value: 16.00
Two Years Before the Mast • 5th printing, HRN 71
25-6❑ NM value: 16.00
Two Years Before the Mast • 6th printing, HRN 85
25-7❑ NM value: 14.00
Two Years Before the Mast • 7th printing, HRN 114
25-8❑ NM value: 12.00
Two Years Before the Mast • 8th printing, HRN 156
25-9❑ Dec 1963 NM value: 5.00
Two Years Before the Mast • 9th printing, HRN 167
25-10❑ Dec 1965 NM value: 5.00
Two Years Before the Mast • 10th printing, HRN 167
25-11❑ Sep 1967 NM value: 5.00
Two Years Before the Mast • 11th printing, HRN 166
25-12❑ Cover: 0.25 NM value: 5.00
Two Years Before the Mast • 12th printing, HRN 169; Winter, 1969
26 ❑ Cover: 0.10 NM value: 775.00
Frankenstein
26/A-2❑ HRN: 30 NM value: 250.00
26/B-2❑ HRN: 30 NM value: 250.00
26-3❑ HRN: 60 NM value: 60.00
26-4❑ HRN: 62 NM value: 60.00
26-5❑ HRN: 71 NM value: 30.00
26/A-6❑ HRN: 82 Cover: 0.15 NM value: 25.00
26/B-6❑ HRN: 82 Cover: 0.15 NM value: 35.00
26-7❑ HRN: 117 NM value: 20.00
26-8❑ HRN: 146 NM value: 20.00
26-9❑ HRN: 152 NM value: 30.00
26-10❑ HRN: 153 NM value: 5.00
26-11❑ HRN: 160 NM value: 5.00
26-12❑ HRN: 165 NM value: 5.00
26-13❑ HRN: 167 NM value: 5.00
26-14❑ HRN: 167 Jun 1964 NM value: 5.00
26-15❑ HRN: 167 Jun 1965 NM value: 5.00
26-16❑ HRN: 167 Oct 1965 NM value: 5.00
26-17❑ HRN: 166 Sep 1967 NM value: 5.00
26-18❑ HRN: 169 Jun 1969 Cover: 0.25 NM value: 5.00
26-19❑ HRN: 169 Mar 1971 NM value: 5.00
27 ❑ Cover: 0.10 NM value: 300.00
The Adventures of Marco Polo
27-2❑ HRN: 30 NM value: 90.00
27-3❑ HRN: 70 NM value: 24.00
27-4❑ HRN: 87 Cover: 0.15 NM value: 16.00
27-5❑ HRN: 117 NM value: 12.00
27-6❑ HRN: 154 NM value: 12.00
27-7❑ HRN: 165 NM value: 5.00
27-8❑ HRN: 167 Apr 1964 NM value: 5.00
27-9❑ HRN: 167 Jun 1966 NM value: 5.00
27-10❑ HRN: 169 Jun 1969 Cover: 0.25 NM value: 5.00
28 ❑ Cover: 0.10 NM value: 300.00
Michael Strogoff
28-2❑ HRN: 51 NM value: 90.00
28-3❑ HRN: 115 NM value: 16.00
28-4❑ HRN: 155 NM value: 12.00
28-5❑ HRN: 167 Nov 1963 NM value: 12.00
28-6❑ HRN: 167 Aug 1966 NM value: 10.00
28-7❑ HRN: 169 Jun 1969 Cover: 0.25 NM value: 10.00
29 ❑ Cover: 0.10 NM value: 450.00
The Prince and the Pauper
29-2❑ HRN: 60 NM value: 25.00
29-3❑ HRN: 62 NM value: 22.00
29-4❑ HRN: 71 NM value: 16.00
29-5❑ HRN: 93 NM value: 16.00
29-6❑ HRN: 114 NM value: 12.00
29-7❑ HRN: 128 NM value: 12.00
29-8❑ HRN: 138 NM value: 5.00
29-9❑ HRN: 150 NM value: 5.00
29-10❑ HRN: 164 NM value: 5.00
29-11❑ HRN: 167 NM value: 5.00
29-12❑ HRN: 167 Jul 1964 NM value: 5.00
29-13❑ HRN: 167 Nov 1965 NM value: 5.00
29-14❑ HRN: 166 NM value: 5.00
29-15❑ HRN: 169 Jun 1969 Cover: 0.25 NM value: 5.00
30 ❑ Cover: 0.10 NM value: 285.00
The Moonstone
30-2❑ HRN: 60 NM value: 32.00
30-3❑ HRN: 70 NM value: 30.00
30-4❑ HRN: 155 NM value: 30.00
30-5❑ HRN: 165 NM value: 16.00
30-6❑ HRN: 167 Jan 1964 NM value: 5.00
30-7❑ HRN: 167 Sep 1965 NM value: 5.00
30-8❑ HRN: 166 NM value: 5.00
31 ❑ Cover: 0.10 NM value: 250.00
The Black Arrow
31-2❑ HRN: 51 NM value: 30.00
31-3❑ HRN: 64 NM value: 16.00
31-4❑ HRN: 87 Cover: 0.15 NM value: 14.00
31-5❑ HRN: 108 NM value: 12.00
31-6❑ HRN: 125 NM value: 12.00
31-7❑ HRN: 131 NM value: 12.00
31-8❑ HRN: 140 NM value: 5.00
31-9❑ HRN: 148 NM value: 5.00
31-10❑ HRN: 161 NM value: 5.00
31-11❑ HRN: 167 NM value: 5.00
31-12❑ HRN: 167 Jul 1964 NM value: 5.00
31-13❑ HRN: 167 Nov 1965 NM value: 5.00
31-14❑ HRN: 166 Cover: 0.25 NM value: 5.00
32 ❑ Cover: 0.10 NM value: 300.00
Lorna Doone
32-2❑ HRN: 53 NM value: 40.00
32-3❑ HRN: 85 Cover: 0.15 NM value: 25.00
32-4❑ HRN: 118 NM value: 16.00
32-5❑ HRN: 138 NM value: 16.00
32-6❑ HRN: 150 NM value: 5.00
32-7❑ HRN: 165 NM value: 5.00
32-8❑ HRN: 167 Jan 1964 NM value: 5.00
32-9❑ HRN: 167 Nov 1965 NM value: 5.00
32-10❑ HRN: 166 NM value: 5.00
33 ❑ NM value: 1000.00
The Adventures of Sherlock Holmes
33-2❑ HRN: 53 NM value: 375.00
33-3❑ HRN: 71 NM value: 285.00
33/A-4❑ HRN: 89 NM value: 230.00
33/B-4❑ HRN: 89 NM value: 230.00
34 ❑ NM value: 275.00
Mysterious Island
34-2❑ HRN: 60 NM value: 30.00
34-3❑ HRN: 62 NM value: 24.00
34-4❑ HRN: 71 NM value: 20.00
34-5❑ HRN: 78 NM value: 20.00
34-6❑ HRN: 92 NM value: 16.00
34-7❑ HRN: 117 NM value: 12.00
34-8❑ HRN: 140 NM value: 12.00
34-9❑ HRN: 156 NM value: 5.00
34-10❑ HRN: 167 Oct 1963 NM value: 5.00
34-11❑ HRN: 167 May 1964 NM value: 5.00
34-12❑ HRN: 167 Jun 1966 NM value: 5.00
34-13❑ HRN: 166 NM value: 5.00
35 ❑ Cover: 0.10 NM value: 300.00
The Last Days of Pompeii
35-2❑ HRN: 161 Mar 1961 Cover: 0.15 NM value: 24.00
35-3❑ HRN: 167 Jan 1964 NM value: 10.00
35-4❑ HRN: 167 Jul 1966 NM value: 10.00
35-5❑ HRN: 169 Mar 1970 Cover: 0.25 NM value: 10.00
36 ❑ Cover: 0.10 NM value: 200.00
Typee
36-2❑ NM value: 35.00
Typee • 2nd printing, HRN 64
36-3❑ NM value: 16.00
Typee • 3rd printing, HRN 155
36-4❑ Sep 1963 NM value: 10.00
Typee • 4th printing, HRN 167
36-5❑ Jul 1964 NM value: 5.00
Typee • 5th printing, HRN 167
36-6❑ Jun 1969 Cover: 0.15 NM value: 5.00
Typee • 6th printing, HRN 169
37 ❑ Cover: 0.10 NM value: 150.00
The Pioneers
37/A-2❑ HRN: 62 NM value: 24.00
37/B-2❑ HRN: 62 Cover: 0.10 NM value: 45.00
37-3❑ HRN: 70 NM value: 16.00
37-4❑ HRN: 92 NM value: 12.00
37-5❑ HRN: 118 NM value: 12.00
37-6❑ HRN: 131 NM value: 10.00
37-7❑ HRN: 132 NM value: 10.00
37-8❑ HRN: 153 NM value: 10.00
37-9❑ HRN: 167 May 1964 NM value: 5.00
37-10❑ HRN: 167 Jun 1966 NM value: 5.00
37-11❑ HRN: 166 Cover: 0.25 NM value: 5.00
38 ❑ Cover: 0.10 NM value: 175.00
Adventures of Cellini
38-2❑ HRN: 164 NM value: 20.00
38-3❑ HRN: 167 Dec 1963 NM value: 20.00
38-4❑ HRN: 167 Jul 1966 NM value: 16.00
38-5❑ HRN: 169 Cover: 0.25 NM value: 16.00
39 ❑ Cover: 0.10 NM value: 200.00
Jane Eyre
39-2❑ HRN: 60 NM value: 25.00
39-3❑ HRN: 62 NM value: 20.00
39-4❑ HRN: 71 NM value: 20.00
39-5❑ HRN: 92 Cover: 0.15 NM value: 20.00
39-6❑ HRN: 118 NM value: 14.00
39-7❑ HRN: 142 NM value: 14.00
39-8❑ HRN: 154 NM value: 14.00
39-9❑ HRN: 165 NM value: 14.00
39-10❑ HRN: 167 Dec 1963 NM value: 14.00
39-11❑ HRN: 167 Apr 1965 NM value: 14.00
39-12❑ HRN: 167 Aug 1966 NM value: 14.00
39-13❑ HRN: 166 NM value: 14.00
40 ❑ Cover: 0.10 NM value: 550.00
Mysteries
40-2❑ HRN: 62 NM value: 235.00
40-3❑ HRN: 75 NM value: 160.00
40-4❑ HRN: 95 Cover: 0.15 NM value: 125.00
41 ❑ Cover: 0.10 NM value: 350.00
Twenty Years After
41-2❑ HRN: 62 NM value: 25.00
41-3❑ HRN: 78 Cover: 0.15 NM value: 20.00
41-4❑ HRN: 156 NM value: 5.00
41-5❑ HRN: 167 Dec 1963 NM value: 5.00
41-6❑ HRN: 167 Nov 1966 NM value: 5.00
41-7❑ HRN: 169 Mar 1970 Cover: 0.25 NM value: 5.00
42 ❑ Cover: 0.10 NM value: 160.00
Swiss Family Robinson
42/A-2❑ HRN: 62 NM value: 30.00
42/B-2❑ HRN: 62 NM value: 40.00
42-3❑ HRN: 75 NM value: 20.00
42-4❑ HRN: 93 NM value: 14.00
42-5❑ HRN: 117 NM value: 14.00
42-6❑ HRN: 131 NM value: 12.00
42-7❑ HRN: 137 NM value: 12.00
42-8❑ HRN: 141 NM value: 12.00
42-9❑ HRN: 152 NM value: 12.00
42-10❑ HRN: 158 NM value: 5.00
42-11❑ HRN: 165 NM value: 5.00
42-12❑ HRN: 167 Dec 1963 NM value: 5.00
42-13❑ HRN: 167 Apr 1965 NM value: 5.00
42-14❑ HRN: 167 May 1966 NM value: 5.00
42-15❑ HRN: 166 Nov 1967 NM value: 5.00
42-16❑ HRN: 169 Mar 1970 NM value: 5.00
43 ❑ Nov 1947 Cover: 0.10 NM value: 650.00
• CGC: 3 graded, best 7.0
Great Expectations • Mentioned in Seduction of the Innocent (p311: "...Oh, Don't cut my throat, sir!")
43-2❑ HRN: 62 ca. 1949 NM value: 435.00
• CGC: 1 graded, best 9.0
44/A❑ Cover: 0.10 NM value: 525.00
Mysteries of Paris • Printed on newsprint;Mentioned in Seduction of the Innocent (p323 "...blood shows beneath the bandage of a man whose eyes have been gouged out.")
44/B❑ Cover: 0.10 NM value: 525.00
Mysteries of Paris • Printed on white, heavier paper;Mentioned in Seduction of the Innocent (p323 "...blood shows beneath the bandage of a man whose eyes have been gouged out.")
44/A-2❑ HRN: 62 NM value: 200.00
44/B-2❑ HRN: 62 NM value: 200.00
44-3❑ HRN: 78 Cover: 0.15 NM value: 125.00
45 ❑ Cover: 0.10 NM value: 90.00
Tom Brown's School Days
45-2❑ HRN: 64 NM value: 30.00
45-3❑ HRN: 161 NM value: 12.00
45-4❑ HRN: 167 Feb 1964 NM value: 5.00
45-5❑ HRN: 167 Oct 1966 NM value: 5.00
45-6❑ HRN: 166 Aug 1966 Cover: 0.25 NM value: 5.00
46 ❑ Cover: 0.10 NM value: 100.00
Kidnapped
46/A-2❑ HRN: 62 NM value: 30.00
46/B-2❑ HRN: 62 Cover: 0.10 NM value: 55.00
46-3❑ HRN: 78 Cover: 0.15 NM value: 18.00
46-4❑ HRN: 87 NM value: 16.00
46-5❑ HRN: 118 NM value: 12.00
46-6❑ HRN: 131 NM value: 12.00
46-7❑ HRN: 140 NM value: 5.00
46-8❑ HRN: 150 NM value: 5.00
46-9❑ HRN: 156 NM value: 5.00
46-10❑ HRN: 164 NM value: 5.00
46-11❑ HRN: 167 NM value: 5.00
46-12❑ HRN: 167 Mar 1964 NM value: 5.00
46-13❑ HRN: 167 Jun 1965 NM value: 5.00
46-14❑ HRN: 167 Dec 1965 NM value: 5.00
46-15❑ HRN: 166 Nov 1967 NM value: 5.00
46-16❑ HRN: 166 Dec 1969 Cover: 0.25 NM value: 5.00
46-17❑ HRN: 169 Jun 1970 NM value: 5.00
47 ❑ Cover: 0.10 NM value: 90.00
Twenty Thousand Leagues Under The Sea
47-2❑ HRN: 64 NM value: 30.00
47-3❑ HRN: 78 Cover: 0.15 NM value: 16.00

Other grades: Multiply prices above by **1.5 for Mint • 2/3 for Very Fine • 1/3 for Fine • 1/5 for Very Good • 1/8 for Good**

47-4❑ HRN: 94 NM value: 14.00
47-5❑ HRN: 118 NM value: 12.00
47-6❑ HRN: 128 NM value: 12.00
47-7❑ HRN: 133 NM value: 12.00
47-8❑ HRN: 140 NM value: 5.00
47-9❑ HRN: 148 NM value: 5.00
47-10❑ HRN: 156 NM value: 5.00
47-11❑ HRN: 165 NM value: 5.00
47-12❑ HRN: 167 Mar 1964 NM value: 5.00
47-13❑ HRN: 167 Aug 1965 NM value: 5.00
47-14❑ HRN: 167 May 1967 NM value: 5.00
47-15❑ HRN: 166 NM value: 5.00
47-16❑ HRN: 169 Mar 1970Cover: 0.25 NM value: 5.00
48 ❑ Cover: 0.10 NM value: 85.00
David Copperfield
48-2❑ HRN: 64 NM value: 30.00
48-3❑ HRN: 87 Cover: 0.15 NM value: 16.00
48-4❑ HRN: 121 NM value: 14.00
48-5❑ HRN: 130 NM value: 10.00
48-6❑ HRN: 140 NM value: 5.00
48-7❑ HRN: 148 NM value: 5.00
48-8❑ HRN: 156 NM value: 5.00
48-9❑ HRN: 167 NM value: 5.00
48-10❑ HRN: 167 Apr 1964 NM value: 5.00
48-11❑ HRN: 167 Jun 1965 NM value: 5.00
48-12❑ HRN: 166 May 1967 NM value: 5.00
48-13❑ HRN: 166 NM value: 5.00
48-14❑ HRN: 166 Mar 1969Cover: 0.25 NM value: 5.00
48-15❑ HRN: 169 Dec 1969 NM value: 5.00
49 ❑ Cover: 0.10 NM value: 175.00
Alice in Wonderland
49-2❑ HRN: 64 NM value: 40.00
49/A-3❑ HRN: 85 Cover: 0.15 NM value: 30.00
49/B-3❑ HRN: 85 Cover: 0.15 NM value: 30.00
49-4❑ HRN: 155 NM value: 24.00
49-5❑ HRN: 165 NM value: 20.00
49-6❑ HRN: 167 Mar 1964 NM value: 20.00
49-7❑ HRN: 167 Jun 1966 NM value: 10.00
49/A-8❑ HRN: 166 Sep 1968 NM value: 10.00
49/B-8❑ HRN: 166 Sep 1968 NM value: 10.00
50/A❑ Cover: 0.10 NM value: 100.00
Adventures of Tom Sawyer • Date: August, 1948 (Correct date)
50/B❑ Cover: 0.10 NM value: 100.00
Adventures of Tom Sawyer • Date: September, 1948 (Printing error)
50/C❑ Cover: 0.10 NM value: 100.00
Outside back cover is blue & yellow (very rare). Adventures of Tom Sawyer • Date: September, 1948 (Printing error)
50-2❑ HRN: 64 NM value: 20.00
50-3❑ HRN: 78 Cover: 0.15 NM value: 14.00
50-4❑ HRN: 94 NM value: 12.00
50-5❑ HRN: 117 NM value: 12.00
50-6❑ HRN: 132 NM value: 12.00
50-7❑ HRN: 140 NM value: 12.00
50-8❑ HRN: 150 NM value: 12.00
50-9❑ HRN: 164 NM value: 12.00
50-10❑ HRN: 167 NM value: 5.00
50-11❑ HRN: 167 Jan 1965 NM value: 5.00
50-12❑ HRN: 167 May 1966 NM value: 5.00
50-13❑ HRN: 166 Dec 1967 NM value: 5.00
50-14❑ HRN: 169 Sep 1969Cover: 0.25 NM value: 5.00
50-15❑ HRN: 169 Dec 1971 NM value: 5.00
51/A❑ Sep 1948 Cover: 0.10 NM value: 80.00
Christmas Carol illustration on inside back cover. The Spy
51/B❑ Sep 1948 Cover: 0.10 NM value: 80.00
Man In The Iron Mask illustration on inside back cover. The Spy
51/C❑ Aug 1948 Cover: 0.10 NM value: 80.00
The Spy
51/D❑ Aug 1948 Cover: 0.10 NM value: 95.00
Outside back cover – blue & yellow. The Spy
51-2❑ HRN: 89 NM value: 24.00
51-3❑ HRN: 121 NM value: 19.00
51-4❑ HRN: 139 NM value: 14.00
51-5❑ HRN: 156 NM value: 12.00
51-6❑ HRN: 167 Mar 1964 NM value: 10.00
51-7❑ HRN: 167 Jul 1966 NM value: 5.00
51/A-8❑ HRN: 166 Dec 1969Cover: 0.25 NM value: 5.00
51/B-8❑ HRN: 166 Dec 1969Cover: 0.25 NM value: 5.00
52 ❑ NM value: 75.00
The House of Seven Gables
52-2❑ HRN: 89 NM value: 20.00
52-3❑ HRN: 121 NM value: 14.00
52-4❑ HRN: 142 NM value: 14.00
52-5❑ HRN: 156 NM value: 5.00
52-6❑ HRN: 165 NM value: 5.00
52-7❑ HRN: 167 May 1964 NM value: 5.00
52-8❑ HRN: 167 Mar 1966 NM value: 5.00
52-9❑ HRN: 166 NM value: 5.00
52-10❑ HRN: 169 Mar 1970 NM value: 5.00
53 ❑ Cover: 0.10 NM value: 115.00
A Christmas Carol
54 ❑ Cover: 0.10 NM value: 100.00
Man in the Iron Mask
54-2❑ HRN: 93 Cover: 0.15 NM value: 35.00
54/A-3❑ HRN: 111 NM value: 28.00
54/B-3❑ HRN: 111 NM value: 28.00
54-4❑ HRN: 142 NM value: 16.00
54-5❑ HRN: 154 NM value: 8.00
54-6❑ HRN: 165 NM value: 8.00
54-7❑ HRN: 167 May 1964 NM value: 8.00
54-8❑ HRN: 167 Mar 1966 NM value: 8.00
54/A-9❑ HRN: 166 Dec 1969Cover: 0.25 NM value: 8.00
54/B-9❑ HRN: 166 Dec 1969Cover: 0.25 NM value: 8.00
55 ❑ Cover: 0.10 NM value: 75.00
Silas Marner
55-2❑ HRN: 75 NM value: 25.00
55-3❑ HRN: 97 NM value: 12.00
55-4❑ HRN: 121 NM value: 12.00
55-5❑ HRN: 130 NM value: 5.00
55-6❑ HRN: 140 NM value: 5.00
55-7❑ HRN: 154 NM value: 5.00
55-8❑ HRN: 165 NM value: 5.00
55-9❑ HRN: 167 Feb 1964 NM value: 5.00
55-10❑ HRN: 167 Jun 1965 NM value: 5.00
55-11❑ HRN: 166 May 1967 NM value: 5.00
55/A-12❑ HRN: 166 Dec 1969Cover: 0.25 NM value: 5.00
55/B-12❑ HRN: 166 Dec 1969Cover: 0.25 NM value: 5.00
56 ❑ Feb 1949 Cover: 0.10 NM value: 125.00
The Toilers of the Sea
56-2❑ HRN: 165 NM value: 24.00
56-3❑ HRN: 167 Mar 1964 NM value: 18.00
56-4❑ HRN: 167 Oct 1966 NM value: 18.00
57 ❑ Mar 1949 Cover: 0.10 NM value: 80.00
The Song of Hiawatha A: Alex A. Blum W: Henry Wadsworth Longfellow
57-2❑ HRN: 75 NM value: 24.00
57-3❑ HRN: 94 Mar 1949 Cover: 0.15 NM value: 16.00
57-4❑ HRN: 118 NM value: 16.00
57-5❑ HRN: 134 NM value: 12.00
57-6❑ HRN: 139 NM value: 12.00
57-7❑ HRN: 154 NM value: 12.00
57-8❑ HRN: 167 NM value: 5.00
57-9❑ HRN: 167 Sep 1964 NM value: 5.00
57-10❑ HRN: 167 Oct 1965 NM value: 5.00
57-11❑ HRN: 166 Sep 1968Cover: 0.25 NM value: 5.00
58 ❑ Cover: 0.10 NM value: 75.00
The Prairie
58/A-2❑ HRN: 62 NM value: 35.00
58/B-2❑ HRN: 62 NM value: 35.00
58-3❑ HRN: 78 Cover: 0.15 NM value: 16.00
58-4❑ HRN: 114 NM value: 12.00
58-5❑ HRN: 131 NM value: 12.00
58-6❑ HRN: 132 NM value: 12.00
58-7❑ HRN: 146 NM value: 12.00
58-8❑ HRN: 155 NM value: 5.00
58-9❑ HRN: 167 May 1964 NM value: 5.00
58-10❑ HRN: 167 Apr 1966 NM value: 5.00
58-11❑ HRN: 169 Sum 1969Cover: 0.25 NM value: 5.00
59 ❑ Cover: 0.10 NM value: 100.00
Wuthering Heights
59-2❑ HRN: 85 Cover: 0.15 NM value: 35.00
59-3❑ HRN: 156 NM value: 14.00
59-4❑ HRN: 167 Jan 1964 NM value: 5.00
59-5❑ HRN: 167 Oct 1966 NM value: 5.00
59-6❑ HRN: 169 Sum 1969Cover: 0.25 NM value: 5.00
60 ❑ NM value: 90.00
Black Beauty
60-2❑ HRN: 62 NM value: 30.00
60-3❑ HRN: 85 NM value: 20.00
60-4❑ HRN: 158 NM value: 12.00
60-5❑ HRN: 167 Feb 1964 NM value: 12.00
60-6❑ HRN: 167 Mar 1966 NM value: 10.00
60-7❑ NM value: 10.00
61/A❑ Jul 1949 Cover: 0.10 NM value: 85.00
Top front cover – deep purple. The Woman in White
61/B❑ Cover: 0.10 NM value: 85.00
Top Front cover – pink. The Woman in White
61-2❑ HRN: 156 NM value: 16.00
61-3❑ HRN: 167 Jan 1964 NM value: 14.00
61-4❑ HRN: 166 Cover: 0.25 NM value: 14.00
62 ❑ Aug 1949 Cover: 0.10 NM value: 75.00
Western Stories
62-2❑ HRN: 89 Cover: 0.15 NM value: 24.00
62-3❑ HRN: 121 NM value: 16.00
62-4❑ HRN: 137 NM value: 12.00
62-5❑ HRN: 152 NM value: 5.00
62-6❑ HRN: 167 Oct 1963 NM value: 5.00
62-7❑ HRN: 167 Jun 1964 NM value: 5.00
62-8❑ HRN: 167 Nov 1966 NM value: 5.00
62-9❑ HRN: 166 Cover: 0.25 NM value: 5.00
63 ❑ Cover: 0.10 NM value: 85.00
The Man Without A Country
63-2❑ HRN: 78 Cover: 0.15 NM value: 25.00
63-3❑ HRN: 156 NM value: 16.00
63-4❑ HRN: 165 NM value: 10.00
63-5❑ HRN: 167 Mar 1964 NM value: 5.00
63-6❑ HRN: 167 Aug 1966 NM value: 5.00
63-7❑ HRN: 169 Sum 1969Cover: 0.25 NM value: 5.00
64 ❑ Cover: 0.10 NM value: 85.00
Treasure Island
64/A-2❑ HRN: 82 Cover: 0.15 NM value: 25.00
64/B-2❑ HRN: 82 Cover: 0.15 NM value: 25.00
64-3❑ HRN: 117 NM value: 16.00
64-4❑ HRN: 131 NM value: 12.00
64-5❑ HRN: 138 NM value: 5.00
64-6❑ HRN: 146 NM value: 5.00
64-7❑ HRN: 158 NM value: 5.00
64-8❑ HRN: 165 NM value: 5.00
64-9❑ HRN: 167 NM value: 5.00
64-10❑ HRN: 167 Jun 1964 NM value: 5.00
64-11❑ HRN: 167 Dec 1965 NM value: 5.00
64-12❑ HRN: 166 Oct 1967 NM value: 5.00
64-13❑ HRN: 169 Spr 1969Cover: 0.25 NM value: 5.00
64-14❑ NM value: 5.00
65 ❑ Cover: 0.10 NM value: 75.00
Benjamin Franklin
65-2❑ HRN: 131 NM value: 24.00
65-3❑ HRN: 154 NM value: 16.00
65-4❑ HRN: 167 Feb 1964 NM value: 5.00
65-5❑ HRN: 167 Apr 1966 NM value: 5.00
65-6❑ HRN: 169 Fal 1969 Cover: 0.25 NM value: 5.00
66 ❑ Dec 1949 Cover: 0.10 NM value: 175.00
The Cloister and the Hearth
67 ❑ Cover: 0.10 NM value: 70.00
The Scottish Chiefs
67-2❑ HRN: 85 Cover: 0.15 NM value: 24.00
67-3❑ HRN: 118 NM value: 14.00
67-4❑ HRN: 136 NM value: 12.00
67-5❑ HRN: 154 NM value: 5.00
67-6❑ HRN: 167 Nov 1963 NM value: 5.00
67-7❑ HRN: 167 Aug 1965 NM value: 5.00
68 ❑ Cover: 0.10 NM value: 70.00
Julius Caesar
68-2❑ HRN: 85 Cover: 0.15 NM value: 24.00
68-3❑ HRN: 108 NM value: 16.00
68-4❑ HRN: 156 NM value: 16.00
68-5❑ HRN: 165 NM value: 16.00
68-6❑ HRN: 167 Feb 1964 NM value: 5.00
68-7❑ HRN: 167 Nov 1965 NM value: 5.00
68-8❑ HRN: 166 Jul 1967 NM value: 5.00
68-9❑ HRN: 169 Spr 1969 NM value: 5.00
69 ❑ Cover: 0.10 NM value: 75.00
Around the World in 80 Days
69-2❑ HRN: 87 Cover: 0.15 NM value: 25.00
69-3❑ HRN: 125 NM value: 20.00
69-4❑ HRN: 136 NM value: 12.00
69-5❑ HRN: 146 NM value: 5.00
69-6❑ HRN: 152 NM value: 5.00
69-7❑ HRN: 164 NM value: 5.00
69-8❑ HRN: 167 NM value: 5.00
69-9❑ HRN: 167 Jul 1967 NM value: 5.00
69-10❑ HRN: 167 Nov 1965 NM value: 5.00
69-11❑ HRN: 166 Jul 1967 NM value: 5.00
69-12❑ HRN: 169 Spr 1969Cover: 0.25 NM value: 5.00
70 ❑ Cover: 0.10 NM value: 60.00
The Pilot
70-2❑ HRN: 92 Cover: 0.15 NM value: 20.00
70-3❑ HRN: 125 NM value: 14.00
70-4❑ HRN: 156 NM value: 14.00
70-5❑ HRN: 167 Feb 1964 NM value: 12.00
70-6❑ HRN: 167 May 1966 NM value: 5.00
71 ❑ May 1950 Cover: 0.10 NM value: 100.00
The Man Who Laughs
71-2❑ HRN: 165 NM value: 50.00
71-3❑ HRN: 167 Apr 1964 NM value: 35.00
72 ❑ Cover: 0.10 NM value: 60.00
The Oregon Trail
72-2❑ HRN: 89 Cover: 0.15 NM value: 25.00
72-3❑ HRN: 121 NM value: 18.00
72-4❑ HRN: 131 NM value: 12.00
72-5❑ HRN: 140 NM value: 5.00
72-6❑ HRN: 150 NM value: 5.00
72-7❑ HRN: 164 NM value: 5.00
72-8❑ HRN: 167 NM value: 5.00
72-9❑ HRN: 167 Aug 1964 NM value: 5.00
72-10❑ HRN: 167 Oct 1965 NM value: 5.00
72-11❑ HRN: 166 NM value: 5.00
73 ❑ Jul 1950 Cover: 0.10 NM value: 200.00
The Black Tulip
74 ❑ Cover: 0.10 NM value: 200.00
Mr. Midshipman Easy
75 ❑ Cover: 0.10 NM value: 60.00
The Lady of the Lake
75-2❑ HRN: 85 NM value: 28.00
75-3❑ HRN: 118 NM value: 16.00
75-4❑ HRN: 139 NM value: 12.00
75-5❑ HRN: 154 NM value: 5.00
75-6❑ HRN: 165 NM value: 5.00
75-7❑ HRN: 167 Apr 1964 NM value: 5.00
75-8❑ HRN: 167 May 1966 NM value: 5.00
75-9❑ HRN: 169 Spr 1969 NM value: 5.00
76 ❑ Cover: 0.10 NM value: 55.00
The Prisoner of Zenda
76-2❑ HRN: 85 NM value: 24.00
76-3❑ HRN: 111 NM value: 16.00
76-4❑ HRN: 128 NM value: 12.00
76-5❑ HRN: 152 NM value: 5.00
76-6❑ HRN: 165 NM value: 5.00
76-7❑ HRN: 167 Apr 1964 NM value: 5.00
76-8❑ HRN: 167 Sep 1966 NM value: 5.00
76-9❑ HRN: 169 Fal 1969 NM value: 5.00
77 ❑ Cover: 0.10 NM value: 55.00
The Iliad
77-2❑ HRN: 87 NM value: 24.00
77-3❑ HRN: 121 NM value: 16.00
77-4❑ HRN: 139 NM value: 12.00
77-5❑ HRN: 150 NM value: 5.00
77-6❑ HRN: 165 NM value: 5.00
77-7❑ HRN: 167 Oct 1963 NM value: 5.00
77-8❑ HRN: 167 Jul 1964 NM value: 5.00
77-9❑ HRN: 167 May 1966 NM value: 5.00
77-10❑ HRN: 166 NM value: 5.00
78 ❑ Cover: 0.10 NM value: 75.00
Joan of Arc
78-2❑ HRN: 87 NM value: 25.00
78-3❑ HRN: 113 NM value: 16.00
78-4❑ HRN: 128 NM value: 12.00
78-5❑ HRN: 140 NM value: 5.00
78-6❑ HRN: 150 NM value: 5.00
78-7❑ HRN: 159 NM value: 5.00
78-8❑ HRN: 167 NM value: 5.00
78-9❑ HRN: 167 Dec 1963 NM value: 5.00
78-10❑ HRN: 167 Jun 1965 NM value: 5.00
78-11❑ HRN: 166 Jun 1967 NM value: 5.00
78-12❑ HRN: 166 NM value: 5.00
79 ❑ Cover: 0.10 NM value: 55.00
Cyrano de Bergerac
79-2❑ HRN: 85 NM value: 24.00
79-3❑ HRN: 118 NM value: 16.00
79-4❑ HRN: 133 NM value: 12.00
79-5❑ HRN: 156 NM value: 5.00
79-6❑ HRN: 167 Aug 1964 NM value: 5.00
80 ❑ NM value: 55.00
White Fang

CGC-graded: Multiply prices above by 33 for 9.9 M • 16 for 9.8 NM/M • 7 for 9.6 NM+ • 5 for 9.4 NM • 2.5 for 9.2 NM- • 1.5 for 9.0 VF/NM

80-2❑ **HRN:** 87 Cover: 0.10 **NM** value: **24.00**
80-3❑ **HRN:** 125 **NM** value: **16.00**
80-4❑ **HRN:** 132 **NM** value: **12.00**
80-5❑ **HRN:** 140 **NM** value: **5.00**
80-6❑ **HRN:** 153 **NM** value: **5.00**
80-7❑ **HRN:** 167 **NM** value: **5.00**
80-8❑ **HRN:** 167 Sep 1964 **NM** value: **5.00**
80-9❑ **HRN:** 167 Jul 1965 **NM** value: **5.00**
80-10❑ **HRN:** 166 Jul 1967 **NM** value: **5.00**
80-11❑ **HRN:** 169 Fal 1969 **NM** value: **5.00**
81 ❑ Cover: 0.15 **NM** value: **45.00**
🕮 The Odyssey
81-2❑ **HRN:** 167 Aug 1964 **NM** value: **12.00**
81-3❑ **HRN:** 167 Oct 1966 **NM** value: **12.00**
81-4❑ **HRN:** 169 Spr 1969 **NM** value: **12.00**
82 ❑ Cover: 0.15 **NM** value: **35.00**
🕮 The Master of Ballantrae
82-2❑ **HRN:** 167 Aug 1964 **NM** value: **12.00**
82-3❑ **HRN:** 166 Fal 1968 **NM** value: **12.00**
83 ❑ Cover: 0.15 **NM** value: **35.00**
🕮 The Jungle Book
83-2❑ **HRN:** 110 **NM** value: **10.00**
83-3❑ **HRN:** 125 **NM** value: **5.00**
83-4❑ **HRN:** 134 **NM** value: **5.00**
83-5❑ **HRN:** 142 **NM** value: **5.00**
83-6❑ **HRN:** 150 **NM** value: **5.00**
83-7❑ **HRN:** 159 **NM** value: **5.00**
83-8❑ **HRN:** 167 **NM** value: **5.00**
83-9❑ **HRN:** 167 Mar 1965 **NM** value: **5.00**
83-10❑ **HRN:** 167 Nov 1965 **NM** value: **5.00**
83-11❑ **HRN:** 167 May 1966 **NM** value: **5.00**
83-12❑ **HRN:** 166 **NM** value: **5.00**
84 ❑ Cover: 0.15 **NM** value: **75.00**
🕮 The Gold Bug and Other Stories
84-2❑ **HRN:** 167 **NM** value: **35.00**
85 ❑ Cover: 0.15 **NM** value: **25.00**
🕮 The Sea Wolf
85-2❑ **HRN:** 121 **NM** value: **5.00**
85-3❑ **HRN:** 132 **NM** value: **5.00**
85-4❑ **HRN:** 141 **NM** value: **5.00**
85-5❑ **HRN:** 161 **NM** value: **5.00**
85-6❑ **HRN:** 167 Feb 1964 **NM** value: **5.00**
85-7❑ **HRN:** 167 Nov 1965 **NM** value: **5.00**
85-8❑ **HRN:** 169 Fal 1969 **NM** value: **5.00**
86 ❑ Cover: 0.15 **NM** value: **25.00**
🕮 Under Two Flags
86-2❑ **HRN:** 117 **NM** value: **5.00**
86-3❑ **HRN:** 139 **NM** value: **5.00**
86-4❑ **HRN:** 158 **NM** value: **5.00**
86-5❑ **HRN:** 167 Feb 1964 **NM** value: **5.00**
86-6❑ **HRN:** 167 Aug 1966 **NM** value: **5.00**
86-7❑ **HRN:** 169 Sum 1969 **NM** value: **5.00**
87 ❑ Cover: 0.15 **NM** value: **25.00**
🕮 A Midsummer Night's Dream
87-2❑ **HRN:** 161 **NM** value: **5.00**
87-3❑ **HRN:** 167 Apr 1964 **NM** value: **5.00**
87-4❑ **HRN:** 167 May 1966 **NM** value: **5.00**
87-5❑ **HRN:** 169 Sum 1969Cover: 0.25 **NM** value: **5.00**
88 ❑ Cover: 0.15 **NM** value: **25.00**
🕮 Men of Iron
88-2❑ **HRN:** 154 **NM** value: **5.00**
88-3❑ **HRN:** 167 Jan 1964 **NM** value: **5.00**
88-4❑ **HRN:** 166 **NM** value: **5.00**
89 ❑ Cover: 0.25 **NM** value: **30.00**
🕮 Crime and Punishment
89-2❑ **HRN:** 152 **NM** value: **8.00**
89-3❑ **HRN:** 167 Apr 1964 **NM** value: **5.00**
89-4❑ **HRN:** 167 May 1966 **NM** value: **5.00**
89-5❑ **HRN:** 169 Fal 1969 **NM** value: **5.00**
90 ❑ **NM** value: **20.00**
🕮 Green Mansions
90-2❑ **HRN:** 148 Cover: 0.15 **NM** value: **8.00**
90-3❑ **HRN:** 165 **NM** value: **5.00**
90-4❑ **HRN:** 167 Apr 1964 **NM** value: **5.00**
90-5❑ **HRN:** 167 Sep 1966 **NM** value: **5.00**
90-6❑ **HRN:** 169 Sum 1969Cover: 0.25 **NM** value: **5.00**
91 ❑ Cover: 0.15 **NM** value: **24.00**
🕮 Call of the Wild
91-2❑ **HRN:** 112 **NM** value: **12.00**
91-3❑ **HRN:** 125 **NM** value: **5.00**
91-4❑ **HRN:** 134 **NM** value: **5.00**
91-5❑ **HRN:** 143 **NM** value: **5.00**
91-6❑ **HRN:** 165 **NM** value: **5.00**
91-7❑ **HRN:** 167 **NM** value: **5.00**
91-8❑ **HRN:** 167 Apr 1965 **NM** value: **5.00**
91-9❑ **HRN:** 167 Mar 1966 **NM** value: **5.00**
91-10❑ **HRN:** 166 Nov 1967 **NM** value: **5.00**
91-11❑ **HRN:** 169 Spr 1970 **NM** value: **5.00**
92/A❑ Cover: 0.15 **NM** value: **20.00**
🕮 The Courtship of Miles Standish • Print normal
92/B❑ Cover: 0.15 **NM** value: **20.00**
Outside back cover – "cracked plate" reorder list #47-49. 🕮 The Courtship of Miles Standish
92-2❑ **HRN:** 165 **NM** value: **5.00**
92-3❑ **HRN:** 167 Mar 1964 **NM** value: **5.00**
92-4❑ **HRN:** 166 May 1967 **NM** value: **5.00**
92-5❑ **HRN:** 169 **NM** value: **5.00**
93 ❑ Cover: 0.15 **NM** value: **22.00**
🕮 Pudd'nhead Wilson
93-2❑ **HRN:** 165 **NM** value: **8.00**
93-3❑ **HRN:** 167 Mar 1964 **NM** value: **5.00**
93-4❑ **HRN:** 166 Cover: 0.25 **NM** value: **5.00**
94 ❑ Cover: 0.15 **NM** value: **22.00**
🕮 David Balfour
94-2❑ **HRN:** 167 May 1965 **NM** value: **5.00**
94-3❑ **HRN:** 166 Cover: 0.25 **NM** value: **5.00**
95/A❑ **HRN:** 96 Cover: 0.15 **NM** value: **45.00**
🕮 All Quiet on the Western Front
95/B❑ **HRN:** 99 Cover: 0.15 **NM** value: **45.00**
🕮 All Quiet on the Western Front
95-2❑ **HRN:** 167 Oct 1964 **NM** value: **14.00**
95-3❑ **HRN:** 167 Nov 1966 **NM** value: **10.00**
96 ❑ Cover: 0.15 **NM** value: **20.00**
🕮 Daniel Boone
96-2❑ **HRN:** 117 **NM** value: **5.00**
96-3❑ **HRN:** 128 **NM** value: **5.00**
96-4❑ **HRN:** 132 **NM** value: **5.00**
96-5❑ **HRN:** 134 **NM** value: **5.00**
96-6❑ **HRN:** 158 **NM** value: **5.00**
96-7❑ **HRN:** 167 Jan 1964 **NM** value: **5.00**
96-8❑ **HRN:** 167 May 1965 **NM** value: **5.00**
96-9❑ **HRN:** 167 Nov 1966 **NM** value: **5.00**
96-10❑ **HRN:** 166 Cover: 0.25 **NM** value: **5.00**
97 ❑ Cover: 0.15 **NM** value: **20.00**
🕮 King Solomon's Mines
97-2❑ **HRN:** 118 **NM** value: **5.00**
97-3❑ **HRN:** 131 **NM** value: **5.00**
97-4❑ **HRN:** 141 **NM** value: **5.00**
97-5❑ **HRN:** 158 **NM** value: **5.00**
97-6❑ **HRN:** 167 Feb 1964 **NM** value: **5.00**
97-7❑ **HRN:** 167 Sep 1965 **NM** value: **5.00**
97-8❑ **HRN:** 169 Sum 1969Cover: 0.25 **NM** value: **5.00**
98 ❑ Cover: 0.15 **NM** value: **25.00**
🕮 The Red Badge of Courage
98-2❑ **HRN:** 118 **NM** value: **8.00**
98-3❑ **HRN:** 132 **NM** value: **5.00**
98-4❑ **HRN:** 142 **NM** value: **5.00**
98-5❑ **HRN:** 152 **NM** value: **5.00**
98-6❑ **HRN:** 161 **NM** value: **5.00**
98-7❑ **HRN:** 167 **NM** value: **5.00**
98-8❑ **HRN:** 167 Sep 1964 **NM** value: **5.00**
98-9❑ **HRN:** 167 Oct 1965 **NM** value: **5.00**
98-10❑ **HRN:** 166 Cover: 0.25 **NM** value: **5.00**
99 ❑ Cover: 0.15 **NM** value: **25.00**
🕮 Hamlet
99-2❑ **HRN:** 121 **NM** value: **5.00**
99-3❑ **HRN:** 141 **NM** value: **5.00**
99-4❑ **HRN:** 158 **NM** value: **5.00**
99-5❑ **HRN:** 167 **NM** value: **5.00**
99-6❑ **HRN:** 167 May 1965 **NM** value: **5.00**
99-7❑ **HRN:** 166 Apr 1967 **NM** value: **5.00**
99-8❑ **HRN:** 169 Spr 1969 Cover: 0.25 **NM** value: **5.00**
100❑ Cover: 0.15 **NM** value: **22.00**
🕮 Mutiny on the Bounty
100-2❑ **HRN:** 117 **NM** value: **5.00**
100-3❑ **HRN:** 132 **NM** value: **5.00**
100-4❑ **HRN:** 142 **NM** value: **5.00**
100-5❑ **HRN:** 155 **NM** value: **5.00**
100-6❑ **HRN:** 167 **NM** value: **5.00**
100-7❑ **HRN:** 167 May 1964 **NM** value: **5.00**
100-8❑ **HRN:** 167 Mar 1966 **NM** value: **5.00**
100-9❑ **HRN:** 169 Spr 1970 **NM** value: **5.00**
101❑ Cover: 0.15 **NM** value: **22.00**
🕮 William Tell **A:** Maurice Del Bourgo **W:** Fred Schiller
101-2❑ **HRN:** 118 **NM** value: **5.00**
101-3❑ **HRN:** 141 **NM** value: **5.00**
101-4❑ **HRN:** 158 **NM** value: **5.00**
101-5❑ **HRN:** 167 **NM** value: **5.00**
101-6❑ **HRN:** 167 Nov 1964 **NM** value: **5.00**
101-7❑ **HRN:** 166 Apr 1967 **NM** value: **5.00**
101-8❑ **HRN:** 169 Dec 1969Cover: 0.25 **NM** value: **5.00**
102❑ Cover: 0.15 **NM** value: **40.00**
🕮 The White Company
102-2❑ **HRN:** 165 **NM** value: **18.00**
102-3❑ **HRN:** 167 Apr 1964 **NM** value: **15.00**
103❑ Cover: 0.15 **NM** value: **22.00**
🕮 Men Against the Sea
103-2❑ **HRN:** 114 **NM** value: **5.00**
103-3❑ **HRN:** 131 **NM** value: **5.00**
103-4❑ **HRN:** 158 **NM** value: **5.00**
103-5❑ **HRN:** 149 **NM** value: **5.00**
103-6❑ **HRN:** 167 Mar 1964 **NM** value: **5.00**
104❑ Cover: 0.15 **NM** value: **20.00**
🕮 Bring 'Em Back Alive
104-2❑ **HRN:** 118 **NM** value: **5.00**
104-3❑ **HRN:** 133 **NM** value: **5.00**
104-4❑ **HRN:** 150 **NM** value: **5.00**
104-5❑ **HRN:** 158 **NM** value: **5.00**
104-6❑ **HRN:** 167 Oct 1963 **NM** value: **5.00**
104-7❑ **HRN:** 167 Sep 1965 **NM** value: **5.00**
104-8❑ **HRN:** 169 Cover: 0.25 **NM** value: **5.00**
105❑ Cover: 0.15 **NM** value: **24.00**
🕮 From the Earth to the Moon
105-2❑ **HRN:** 118 **NM** value: **5.00**
105-3❑ **HRN:** 132 **NM** value: **5.00**
105-4❑ **HRN:** 141 **NM** value: **5.00**
105-5❑ **HRN:** 146 **NM** value: **5.00**
105-6❑ **HRN:** 156 **NM** value: **5.00**
105-7❑ **HRN:** 167 **NM** value: **5.00**
105-8❑ **HRN:** 167 May 1964 **NM** value: **5.00**
105-9❑ **HRN:** 167 May 1965 **NM** value: **5.00**
105/A-10❑ **HRN:** 166 Oct 1967 **NM** value: **5.00**
105/B-10❑ **HRN:** 166 Oct 1967 **NM** value: **5.00**
105-11❑ **HRN:** 169 Sum 1969Cover: 0.25 **NM** value: **5.00**
105-12❑ **HRN:** 169 Spr 1971 **NM** value: **5.00**
106❑ Cover: 0.15 **NM** value: **20.00**
🕮 Buffalo Bill
106-2❑ **HRN:** 118 **NM** value: **5.00**
106-3❑ **HRN:** 132 **NM** value: **5.00**
106-4❑ **HRN:** 142 **NM** value: **5.00**
106-5❑ **HRN:** 161 **NM** value: **5.00**
106-6❑ **HRN:** 167 Mar 1964 **NM** value: **5.00**
106-7❑ **HRN:** 166 Aug 1967 **NM** value: **5.00**
106-8❑ **HRN:** 169 Sep 1969 **NM** value: **5.00**
107❑ **NM** value: **20.00**
🕮 King of the Khyber Rifles
107-2❑ **HRN:** 118 **NM** value: **5.00**
107-3❑ **HRN:** 146 **NM** value: **5.00**
107-4❑ **HRN:** 158 **NM** value: **5.00**
107-5❑ **HRN:** 167 **NM** value: **5.00**
107-6❑ **HRN:** 167 Oct 1966 **NM** value: **5.00**
108/A❑ Cover: 0.15 **NM** value: **22.00**
🕮 Knights of the Round Table
108/B❑ Cover: 0.15 **NM** value: **30.00**
🕮 Knights of the Round Table • The Talisman (scarce)
108-2❑ **HRN:** 117 **NM** value: **5.00**
108-3❑ **HRN:** 153 **NM** value: **5.00**
108-4❑ **HRN:** 165 **NM** value: **5.00**
108-5❑ **HRN:** 167 Apr 1964 **NM** value: **5.00**
108-6❑ **HRN:** 167 Apr 1967Cover: 0.25 **NM** value: **5.00**
108-7❑ **HRN:** 169 Sum 1969 **NM** value: **5.00**
109❑ Cover: 0.15 **NM** value: **22.00**
🕮 Pitcairn's Island
109-2❑ **HRN:** 165 **NM** value: **10.00**
109-3❑ **HRN:** 167 Mar 1964 **NM** value: **8.00**
109-4❑ **HRN:** 166 Jun 1967 **NM** value: **8.00**
110❑ Aug 1953 Cover: 0.15 **NM** value: **80.00**
🕮 A Study in Scarlet
110-2❑ **HRN:** 165 **NM** value: **60.00**
111❑ Cover: 0.15 **NM** value: **30.00**
🕮 The Talisman
111-2❑ **HRN:** 165 **NM** value: **8.00**
111-3❑ **HRN:** 167 May 1964 **NM** value: **5.00**
111-4❑ **HRN:** 166 Fal 1968 Cover: 0.25 **NM** value: **5.00**
112❑ Cover: 0.15 **NM** value: **25.00**
🕮 Adventures of Kit Carson
112-2❑ **HRN:** 129 **NM** value: **5.00**
112-3❑ **HRN:** 141 **NM** value: **5.00**
112-4❑ **HRN:** 152 **NM** value: **5.00**
112-5❑ **HRN:** 161 **NM** value: **5.00**
112-6❑ **HRN:** 167 **NM** value: **5.00**
112-7❑ **HRN:** 167 Feb 1967 **NM** value: **5.00**
112-8❑ **HRN:** 167 **NM** value: **5.00**
112-9❑ **HRN:** 166 Cover: 0.25 **NM** value: **5.00**
113❑ Cover: 0.15 **NM** value: **50.00**
🕮 The Forty-Five Guardsmen
113-2❑ **HRN:** 166 Jul 1963 **NM** value: **30.00**
114❑ Cover: 0.15 **NM** value: **50.00**
🕮 The Red Rover
114-2❑ **HRN:** 166 Jul 1963 **NM** value: **30.00**
115❑ Cover: 0.15 **NM** value: **50.00**
🕮 How I Found Livingstone
115-2❑ **HRN:** 167 Jan 1967 **NM** value: **25.00**
116❑ Cover: 0.15 **NM** value: **50.00**
🕮 The Bottle Imp
116-2❑ **HRN:** 167 Jan 1967 **NM** value: **25.00**
117❑ Cover: 0.15 **NM** value: **45.00**
🕮 Captains Courageous
117-2❑ **HRN:** 167 Feb 1967 **NM** value: **18.00**
117-3❑ **HRN:** 169 Fal 1970 **NM** value: **16.00**
118❑ Cover: 0.15 **NM** value: **50.00**
🕮 Rob Roy
118-2❑ **HRN:** 167 Feb 1967 **NM** value: **25.00**
119❑ Cover: 0.15 **NM** value: **50.00**
🕮 Soldiers In Fortune **W:** Richard Harding Davis
119-2❑ **HRN:** 166 Mar 1967 **NM** value: **16.00**
119-3❑ **HRN:** 169 Spr 1970 **NM** value: **12.00**
120❑ Cover: 0.15 **NM** value: **45.00**
🕮 The Hurricane
120-2❑ **HRN:** 166 Mar 1967 **NM** value: **22.00**
121❑ Cover: 0.15 **NM** value: **22.00**
🕮 Wild Bill Hickok
121-2❑ **HRN:** 132 **NM** value: **5.00**
121-3❑ **HRN:** 141 **NM** value: **5.00**
121-4❑ **HRN:** 154 **NM** value: **5.00**
121-5❑ **HRN:** 167 **NM** value: **5.00**
121-6❑ **HRN:** 167 Aug 1964 **NM** value: **5.00**
121-7❑ **HRN:** 166 Apr 1967 **NM** value: **5.00**
121-8❑ **HRN:** 169 **NM** value: **5.00**
122❑ Cover: 0.15 **NM** value: **22.00**
🕮 The Mutineers
122-2❑ **HRN:** 136 **NM** value: **5.00**
122-3❑ **HRN:** 146 **NM** value: **5.00**
122-4❑ **HRN:** 158 **NM** value: **5.00**
122-5❑ **HRN:** 167 Nov 1963 **NM** value: **5.00**
122-6❑ **HRN:** 167 Mar 1965 **NM** value: **5.00**
122-7❑ **HRN:** 166 Aug 1967 **NM** value: **5.00**
123❑ Cover: 0.15 **NM** value: **22.00**
🕮 Fang and Claw
123-2❑ **HRN:** 133 **NM** value: **5.00**
123-3❑ **HRN:** 143 **NM** value: **5.00**
123-4❑ **HRN:** 154 **NM** value: **5.00**
123-5❑ **HRN:** 167 **NM** value: **5.00**
123-6❑ **HRN:** 167 Sep 1965 **NM** value: **5.00**
124❑ Cover: 0.15 **NM** value: **35.00**
🕮 The War of the Worlds
124-2❑ **HRN:** 131 **NM** value: **12.00**
124-3❑ **HRN:** 141 **NM** value: **8.00**
124-4❑ **HRN:** 148 **NM** value: **8.00**
124-5❑ **HRN:** 156 **NM** value: **6.00**
124-6❑ **HRN:** 165 **NM** value: **6.00**
124-7❑ **HRN:** 167 **NM** value: **6.00**
124-8❑ **HRN:** 167 Nov 1964 **NM** value: **6.00**
124-9❑ **HRN:** 167 Nov 1965 **NM** value: **6.00**
124-10❑ **HRN:** 166 Cover: 0.25 **NM** value: **6.00**
124-11❑ **HRN:** 169 Sum 1970 **NM** value: **6.00**
125❑ Cover: 0.15 **NM** value: **20.00**
🕮 The Ox Bow Incident
125-2❑ **HRN:** 142 **NM** value: **5.00**
125-3❑ **HRN:** 152 **NM** value: **5.00**
125-4❑ **HRN:** 149 **NM** value: **5.00**
125-5❑ **HRN:** 167 **NM** value: **5.00**
125-6❑ **HRN:** 167 Nov 1964 **NM** value: **5.00**
125-7❑ **HRN:** 166 Apr 1967 **NM** value: **5.00**

Other grades: Multiply prices above by **1.5 for Mint • 2/3 for Very Fine • 1/3 for Fine • 1/5 for Very Good • 1/8 for Good**

125-8❑ **HRN:** 169 Win 1969Cover: 0.25 **NM** value: **5.00**
126❑ Cover: 0.15 **NM** value: **20.00**
The Downfall
126-2❑ **HRN:** 167 Aug 1964 **NM** value: **5.00**
126-3❑ **HRN:** 166 **NM** value: **5.00**
127❑ Jul 1955 Cover: 0.15 **NM** value: **20.00**
The King of the Mountains **A:** N.J. Notel **W:** Edmond About
127-2❑ **HRN:** 167 Jun 1964 **NM** value: **5.00**
127-3❑ **HRN:** 166 Fal 1968 **NM** value: **5.00**
128❑ Cover: 0.15 **NM** value: **25.00**
Macbeth
128-2❑ **HRN:** 143 **NM** value: **5.00**
128-3❑ **HRN:** 158 **NM** value: **5.00**
128-4❑ **HRN:** 167 **NM** value: **5.00**
128-5❑ **HRN:** 167 Jun 1964 **NM** value: **5.00**
128-6❑ **HRN:** 166 Apr 1967 **NM** value: **5.00**
128-7❑ **HRN:** 166 Cover: 0.25 **NM** value: **5.00**
128-8❑ **HRN:** 169 Spr 1970 **NM** value: **5.00**
129❑ Nov 1955 Cover: 0.15 **NM** value: **60.00**
• **CGC:** 1 graded, best 5.0
Davy Crockett
129-2❑ **HRN:** 167 Sep 1966 **NM** value: **35.00**
130❑ Cover: 0.15 **NM** value: **25.00**
Caesar's Conquests
130-2❑ **HRN:** 142 **NM** value: **5.00**
130-3❑ **HRN:** 152 **NM** value: **5.00**
130-4❑ **HRN:** 149 **NM** value: **5.00**
130-5❑ **HRN:** 167 **NM** value: **5.00**
130-6❑ **HRN:** 167 Oct 1964 **NM** value: **5.00**
130-7❑ **HRN:** 167 Apr 1966 **NM** value: **5.00**
131❑ Cover: 0.15 **NM** value: **20.00**
The Covered Wagon
131-2❑ **HRN:** 143 **NM** value: **5.00**
131-3❑ **HRN:** 152 **NM** value: **5.00**
131-4❑ **HRN:** 158 **NM** value: **5.00**
131-5❑ **HRN:** 167 **NM** value: **5.00**
131-6❑ **HRN:** 167 Nov 1964 **NM** value: **5.00**
131-7❑ **HRN:** 167 Apr 1966 **NM** value: **5.00**
131-8❑ **HRN:** 169 Cover: 0.25 **NM** value: **5.00**
132❑ Cover: 0.15 **NM** value: **22.00**
The Dark Frigate **W:** Charles Boardman Hawes
132-2❑ **HRN:** 150 **NM** value: **5.00**
132-3❑ **HRN:** 167 Jan 1964 **NM** value: **5.00**
132-4❑ **HRN:** 166 May 1967 **NM** value: **5.00**
133❑ Cover: 0.15 **NM** value: **35.00**
The Time Machine
133-2❑ **HRN:** 142 **NM** value: **10.00**
133-3❑ **HRN:** 152 **NM** value: **8.00**
133-4❑ **HRN:** 158 **NM** value: **8.00**
133-5❑ **HRN:** 167 **NM** value: **8.00**
133-6❑ **HRN:** 167 Jun 1964 **NM** value: **5.00**
133-7❑ **HRN:** 167 Mar 1966 **NM** value: **5.00**
133-8❑ **HRN:** 166 Dec 1967 **NM** value: **5.00**
133-9❑ **HRN:** 169 Cover: 0.25 **NM** value: **5.00**
134❑ Cover: 0.15 **NM** value: **25.00**
Romeo & Juliet
134-2❑ **HRN:** 161 **NM** value: **5.00**
134-3❑ **HRN:** 167 Sep 1963 **NM** value: **5.00**
134-4❑ **HRN:** 167 May 1965 **NM** value: **5.00**
134-5❑ **HRN:** 166 Jun 1967 **NM** value: **5.00**
134-6❑ **HRN:** 166 **NM** value: **5.00**
135❑ Cover: 0.15 **NM** value: **20.00**
Waterloo
135-2❑ **HRN:** 153 **NM** value: **5.00**
135-3❑ **HRN:** 167 **NM** value: **5.00**
135-4❑ **HRN:** 167 Sep 1964 **NM** value: **5.00**
135-5❑ **HRN:** 166 Cover: 0.25 **NM** value: **5.00**
136❑ Cover: 0.15 **NM** value: **20.00**
Lord Jim
136-2❑ **HRN:** 165 **NM** value: **5.00**
136-3❑ **HRN:** 167 Mar 1964 **NM** value: **5.00**
136-4❑ **HRN:** 167 Sep 1966 **NM** value: **5.00**
136-5❑ **HRN:** 169 Sum 1969 **NM** value: **5.00**
137❑ Cover: 0.15 **NM** value: **20.00**
The Little Savage
137-2❑ **HRN:** 148 **NM** value: **5.00**
137-3❑ **HRN:** 156 **NM** value: **5.00**
137-4❑ **HRN:** 167 **NM** value: **5.00**
137-5❑ **HRN:** 167 Oct 1964 **NM** value: **5.00**
137-6❑ **HRN:** 166 Aug 1967 **NM** value: **5.00**
137-7❑ **HRN:** 169 Spr 1970 **NM** value: **5.00**
138❑ Cover: 0.15 **NM** value: **35.00**
A Journey to the Center of the Earth
138-2❑ **HRN:** 146 **NM** value: **5.00**
138-3❑ **HRN:** 156 **NM** value: **5.00**
138-4❑ **HRN:** 158 **NM** value: **5.00**
138-5❑ **HRN:** 167 **NM** value: **5.00**
138-6❑ **HRN:** 167 Jun 1964 **NM** value: **5.00**
138-7❑ **HRN:** 167 Apr 1966 **NM** value: **5.00**
138-8❑ **HRN:** 166 **NM** value: **5.00**
139❑ **NM** value: **20.00**
In the Reign of Terror **W:** G.A. Henty
139-2❑ **HRN:** 154 **NM** value: **5.00**
139-3❑ **HRN:** 167 **NM** value: **5.00**
139-4❑ **HRN:** 167 Jul 1964 **NM** value: **5.00**
139-5❑ **HRN:** 166 Cover: 0.25 **NM** value: **5.00**
140❑ Cover: 0.15 **NM** value: **20.00**
On Jungle Trails
140-2❑ **HRN:** 150 **NM** value: **5.00**
140-3❑ **HRN:** 160 **NM** value: **5.00**
140-4❑ **HRN:** 167 Sep 1963 **NM** value: **5.00**
140-5❑ **HRN:** 167 Sep 1965 **NM** value: **5.00**
141❑ Cover: 0.15 **NM** value: **25.00**
Castle Dangerous
141-2❑ **HRN:** 152 **NM** value: **5.00**
141-3❑ **HRN:** 167 **NM** value: **5.00**
141-4❑ **HRN:** 166 Jul 1966 **NM** value: **5.00**
142❑ Cover: 0.15 **NM** value: **25.00**
Abraham Lincoln
142-2❑ **HRN:** 154 **NM** value: **5.00**
142-3❑ **HRN:** 158 **NM** value: **5.00**
142-4❑ **HRN:** 167 Oct 1963 **NM** value: **5.00**
142-5❑ **HRN:** 167 Jul 1965 **NM** value: **5.00**
142-6❑ **HRN:** 166 Nov 1965 **NM** value: **5.00**
142-7❑ **HRN:** 169 Fal 1969 **NM** value: **5.00**
143❑ Cover: 0.15 **NM** value: **20.00**
Kim
143-2❑ **HRN:** 165 **NM** value: **5.00**
143-3❑ **HRN:** 167 Nov 1963 **NM** value: **5.00**
143-4❑ **HRN:** 167 Aug 1965 **NM** value: **5.00**
143-5❑ **HRN:** 169 **NM** value: **5.00**
144❑ Cover: 0.15 **NM** value: **30.00**
The First Men in the Moon
144-2❑ **HRN:** 153 **NM** value: **5.00**
144-3❑ **HRN:** 161 **NM** value: **5.00**
144-4❑ **HRN:** 167 **NM** value: **5.00**
144-5❑ **HRN:** 167 Dec 1965 **NM** value: **5.00**
144-6❑ **HRN:** 167 Fal 1968 **NM** value: **5.00**
144-7❑ **HRN:** 166 Cover: 0.25 **NM** value: **5.00**
145❑ Cover: 0.15 **NM** value: **22.00**
The Crisis
145-2❑ **HRN:** 156 **NM** value: **5.00**
145-3❑ **HRN:** 167 Oct 1963 **NM** value: **5.00**
145-4❑ **HRN:** 167 Mar 1965 **NM** value: **5.00**
145-5❑ **HRN:** 166 **NM** value: **5.00**
146❑ **NM** value: **22.00**
With Fire and Sword
146-2❑ **HRN:** 156 **NM** value: **5.00**
146-3❑ **HRN:** 167 Nov 1963 **NM** value: **5.00**
146-4❑ **HRN:** 167 Mar 1965 **NM** value: **5.00**
147❑ Cover: 0.15 **NM** value: **22.00**
Ben-Hur
147-2❑ **HRN:** 152 **NM** value: **22.00**
147-3❑ **HRN:** 153 **NM** value: **5.00**
147-4❑ **HRN:** 158 **NM** value: **5.00**
147-5❑ **HRN:** 167 **NM** value: **5.00**
147-6❑ **HRN:** 167 Feb 1965 **NM** value: **5.00**
147-7❑ **HRN:** 167 Sep 1966 **NM** value: **5.00**
147/A-8❑ **HRN:** 166 Fal 1968Cover: 0.25 **NM** value: **5.00**
147/B-8❑ **HRN:** 166 Fal 1968Cover: 0.25 **NM** value: **5.00**
148❑ Cover: 0.15 **NM** value: **22.00**
The Buccaneer
148-2❑ **NM** value: **5.00**
148-3❑ **HRN:** 167 **NM** value: **5.00**
148-4❑ **HRN:** 167 Sep 1965 **NM** value: **5.00**
148-5❑ **HRN:** 169 Sum 1969Cover: 0.25 **NM** value: **5.00**
149❑ Cover: 0.15 **NM** value: **22.00**
Off on a Comet
149-2❑ **HRN:** 155 **NM** value: **5.00**
149-3❑ **HRN:** 149 **NM** value: **5.00**
149-4❑ **HRN:** 167 Dec 1963 **NM** value: **5.00**
149-5❑ **HRN:** 167 Feb 1965 **NM** value: **5.00**
149-6❑ **HRN:** 167 Oct 1966 **NM** value: **5.00**
149-7❑ **HRN:** 166 Fal 1968 Cover: 0.25 **NM** value: **5.00**
150❑ Cover: 0.15 **NM** value: **40.00**
The Virginian
150-2❑ **HRN:** 164 **NM** value: **12.00**
150-3❑ **HRN:** 167 Oct 1963 **NM** value: **12.00**
150-4❑ **HRN:** 167 Dec 1965 **NM** value: **12.00**
151❑ Cover: 0.15 **NM** value: **40.00**
Won By the Sword
151-2❑ **HRN:** 164 **NM** value: **12.00**
151-3❑ **HRN:** 167 Oct 1963 **NM** value: **12.00**
151-4❑ **HRN:** 166 Jul 1967 **NM** value: **10.00**
152❑ Cover: 0.15 **NM** value: **40.00**
Wild Animals I Have Known
152/A-2❑ **HRN:** 149 **NM** value: **12.00**
152/B-2❑ **HRN:** 149 **NM** value: **12.00**
152/C-2❑ **HRN:** 149 **NM** value: **12.00**
152-3❑ **HRN:** 167 Sep 1963 **NM** value: **5.00**
152-4❑ **HRN:** 167 Aug 1965 **NM** value: **5.00**
152-5❑ **HRN:** 169 Fal 1969 **NM** value: **5.00**
153❑ Cover: 0.15 **NM** value: **40.00**
The Invisible Man
153/A-2❑ **HRN:** 149 **NM** value: **8.00**
153/B-2❑ **HRN:** 149 **NM** value: **5.00**
153-3❑ **HRN:** 167 **NM** value: **5.00**
153-4❑ **HRN:** 167 Feb 1965 **NM** value: **5.00**
153-5❑ **HRN:** 167 Sep 1966 **NM** value: **5.00**
153-6❑ **HRN:** 166 **NM** value: **5.00**
153-7❑ **HRN:** 169 **NM** value: **5.00**
154❑ Cover: 0.15 **NM** value: **35.00**
The Conspiracy Of Pontiac
154-2❑ **HRN:** 167 Nov 1963 **NM** value: **12.00**
154-3❑ **HRN:** 167 Jul 1964 **NM** value: **12.00**
154-4❑ **HRN:** 166 Dec 1967Cover: 0.25 **NM** value: **12.00**
155❑ Cover: 0.15 **NM** value: **25.00**
The Lion of the North **W:** G.A. Henty
155-2❑ **HRN:** 167 Jan 1964 **NM** value: **5.00**
155-3❑ **HRN:** 166 **NM** value: **5.00**
156❑ Cover: 0.15 **NM** value: **25.00**
The Conquest of Mexico
156-2❑ **HRN:** 167 Jan 1964 **NM** value: **5.00**
156-3❑ **HRN:** 166 Aug 1967 **NM** value: **5.00**
156-4❑ **HRN:** 169 Spr 1970 **NM** value: **5.00**
157❑ Cover: 0.15 **NM** value: **35.00**
Lives of the Hunted
157-2❑ **HRN:** 167 Feb 1964 **NM** value: **12.00**
157-3❑ **HRN:** 166 Oct 1967 **NM** value: **12.00**
158❑ Cover: 0.15 **NM** value: **35.00**
The Conspirators
158-2❑ **HRN:** 167 Jul 1964 **NM** value: **12.00**
158-3❑ **HRN:** 166 Oct 1967 **NM** value: **12.00**
159❑ Cover: 0.15 **NM** value: **35.00**
The Octopus
159-2❑ **HRN:** 167 Feb 1964 **NM** value: **12.00**
159-3❑ **HRN:** 166 Cover: 0.25 **NM** value: **12.00**
160/A❑ **HRN:** 159 Jan 1961Cover: 0.15 **NM** value: **35.00**
The Food of the Gods
160/B❑ **HRN:** 160 Cover: 0.15 **NM** value: **35.00**
The Food of the Gods
160-2❑ **HRN:** 167 Jan 1964 **NM** value: **12.00**
160-3❑ **HRN:** 166 Jun 1967 **NM** value: **12.00**
161❑ Cover: 0.15 **NM** value: **35.00**
Cleopatra
161-2❑ **HRN:** 167 Jan 1964 **NM** value: **12.00**
161-3❑ **HRN:** 166 Aug 1967 **NM** value: **12.00**
162❑ Cover: 0.15 **NM** value: **35.00**
Robur the Conqueror
162-2❑ **HRN:** 167 Jul 1964 **NM** value: **12.00**
162-3❑ **HRN:** 166 Aug 1967 **NM** value: **12.00**
163❑ Cover: 0.15 **NM** value: **35.00**
Master of the World
163-2❑ **HRN:** 167 Jan 1965 **NM** value: **12.00**
163-3❑ **HRN:** 166 Cover: 0.25 **NM** value: **12.00**
164❑ Cover: 0.15 **NM** value: **35.00**
The Cossack Chief
164-2❑ **HRN:** 167 Apr 1965 **NM** value: **12.00**
164-3❑ **HRN:** 166 Fal 1968 Cover: 0.25 **NM** value: **12.00**
165❑ Dec 1961 Cover: 0.15 **NM** value: **35.00**
The Queen's Necklace
165-2❑ **HRN:** 167 Apr 1965 **NM** value: **12.00**
165-3❑ **HRN:** 166 Fal 1968 Cover: 0.25 **NM** value: **12.00**
166❑ Cover: 0.15 **NM** value: **60.00**
Tigers and Traitors
166-2❑ **HRN:** 167 Feb 1964 **NM** value: **16.00**
166-3❑ **HRN:** 167 Nov 1966 **NM** value: **16.00**
167❑ Aug 1962 Cover: 0.15 **NM** value: **65.00**
• **CGC:** 1 graded, best 7.5
Faust
167-2❑ **HRN:** 167 Feb 1964 **NM** value: **24.00**
167-3❑ **HRN:** 166 Jun 1967 **NM** value: **24.00**
168❑ Cover: 0.25 **NM** value: **75.00**
In Freedom's Cause
169❑ May 1969 Cover: 0.25 **NM** value: **65.00**
Negro Americans: The Early Years
169-2❑ **HRN:** 169 **NM** value: **25.00**

CLASSICS ILLUSTRATED JUNIOR Gilberton

Following the success of Classics Illustrated, the publisher decided to broaden the line in 1953 by launching a series based on popular fairy tales. Alice's Adventures in Wonderland had been tried in the earlier Classics Illustrated series, but the somewhat older readers of that line did not receive it well. The new series of Classics Illustrated Junior editions proved popular, however, and soon was reprinted to almost the same extent that the main series had been.

Among the (public domain) stories adapted were The Little Mermaid, The Frog Prince, Rapunzel, Jack and the Beanstalk, Cinderella, and Pinocchio. From a collector's point of view, the Junior editions are a bargain, with almost all later printings selling for just a few dollars, in comparison to the princely prices that issues of Classics Illustrated often command.

501❑ Oct 1953 Cover: 0.15 **NM** value: **70.00**
Snow White and the Seven Dwarves
501-2❑ **HRN:** 524 **NM** value: **5.00**
501-3❑ **HRN:** 541 **NM** value: **5.00**
501-4❑ **NM** value: **5.00**
501-5❑ **HRN:** 565 **NM** value: **5.00**
501-6❑ **HRN:** 568 **NM** value: **5.00**
501-7❑ **HRN:** 576 **NM** value: **5.00**
501-8❑ **HRN:** 576 Nov 1966 **NM** value: **5.00**
501-9❑ **HRN:** 576 **NM** value: **5.00**
502❑ Nov 1953 Cover: 0.15 **NM** value: **40.00**
The Ugly Duckling
502-2❑ **HRN:** 524 **NM** value: **5.00**
502-3❑ **HRN:** 544 **NM** value: **5.00**
502-4❑ **HRN:** 563 **NM** value: **5.00**
502-5❑ **HRN:** 568 **NM** value: **5.00**
502-6❑ **HRN:** 575 **NM** value: **5.00**
502-7❑ **HRN:** 576 Oct 1964 **NM** value: **5.00**
502-8❑ **HRN:** 576 Dec 1966 **NM** value: **5.00**
502-9❑ **HRN:** 576 Sum 1969 **NM** value: **5.00**
503❑ Dec 1953 Cover: 0.15 **NM** value: **25.00**
Cinderella
503-2❑ **HRN:** 524 **NM** value: **5.00**
503-3❑ **HRN:** 541 **NM** value: **5.00**
503-4❑ **NM** value: **5.00**
503-5❑ **HRN:** 565 **NM** value: **5.00**
503-6❑ **HRN:** 568 **NM** value: **5.00**
503-7❑ **HRN:** 574 **NM** value: **5.00**
503-8❑ **HRN:** 576 **NM** value: **5.00**
503-9❑ **HRN:** 576 Apr 1964 **NM** value: **5.00**
503-10❑ **HRN:** 576 Jun 1966 **NM** value: **5.00**
503-11❑ **HRN:** 576 Spr 1969 **NM** value: **5.00**
504❑ Jan 1954 Cover: 0.15 **NM** value: **18.00**
The Pied Piper
504-2❑ **HRN:** 523 **NM** value: **5.00**
504-3❑ **HRN:** 526 **NM** value: **5.00**
504-4❑ **HRN:** 544 **NM** value: **5.00**
504-5❑ **HRN:** 563 **NM** value: **5.00**
504-6❑ **HRN:** 568 **NM** value: **5.00**
504-7❑ **HRN:** 576 **NM** value: **5.00**
504-8❑ **HRN:** 576 Nov 1966 **NM** value: **5.00**
504-9❑ **HRN:** 576 Sum 1969 **NM** value: **5.00**
505❑ Feb 1954 Cover: 0.15 **NM** value: **18.00**
Sleeping Beauty

CGC-graded: Multiply prices above by **33 for 9.9 M • 16 for 9.8 NM/M • 7 for 9.6 NM+ • 5 for 9.4 NM • 2.5 for 9.2 NM- • 1.5 for 9.0 VF/NM**

505-2❑ HRN: 524 NM value: 5.00
505-3❑ HRN: 548 NM value: 5.00
505-4❑ HRN: 559 NM value: 5.00
505-5❑ HRN: 568 NM value: 5.00
505-6❑ HRN: 574 NM value: 5.00
505-7❑ HRN: 576 Mar 1964 NM value: 5.00
505-8❑ HRN: 576 Oct 1966 NM value: 5.00
505-9❑ HRN: 576 Fal 1969 NM value: 5.00
506 ❑ Mar 1954 Cover: 0.15 NM value: 15.00
The Three Little Pigs
506-2❑ HRN: 523 NM value: 5.00
506-3❑ HRN: 560 NM value: 5.00
506-4❑ HRN: 568 NM value: 5.00
506-5❑ HRN: 575 NM value: 5.00
506-6❑ HRN: 576 Oct 1964 NM value: 5.00
506-7❑ HRN: 576 Jun 1967 NM value: 5.00
506-8❑ HRN: 577 Spr 1971 NM value: 5.00
507 ❑ Apr 1954 Cover: 0.15 NM value: 15.00
Jack and the Beanstalk
507-2❑ HRN: 526 NM value: 5.00
507-3❑ HRN: 559 NM value: 5.00
507-4❑ HRN: 568 NM value: 5.00
507-5❑ HRN: 575 NM value: 5.00
507-6❑ HRN: 576 Jun 1964 NM value: 5.00
507-7❑ HRN: 576 Jan 1967 NM value: 5.00
507-8❑ HRN: 576 Sum 1969 NM value: 5.00
508 ❑ May 1954 Cover: 0.15 NM value: 15.00
Goldilocks and the Three Bears
508-2❑ HRN: 526 NM value: 5.00
508-3❑ HRN: 563 NM value: 5.00
508-4❑ HRN: 568 NM value: 5.00
508-5❑ HRN: 576 Mar 1964 NM value: 5.00
508-6❑ HRN: 576 Jun 1966 NM value: 5.00
508-7❑ HRN: 577 NM value: 5.00
509 ❑ Jun 1954 Cover: 0.15 NM value: 15.00
Beauty and the Beast
509-2❑ HRN: 527 NM value: 5.00
509-3❑ HRN: 552 NM value: 5.00
509-4❑ HRN: 563 NM value: 5.00
509-5❑ HRN: 568 NM value: 5.00
509-6❑ HRN: 576 Mar 1964 NM value: 5.00
509-7❑ HRN: 576 Jul 1966 NM value: 5.00
509-8❑ HRN: 576 Sum 1969 NM value: 5.00
510 ❑ Jul 1954 Cover: 0.15 NM value: 15.00
Little Red Riding Hood
510-2❑ HRN: 527 NM value: 5.00
510-3❑ HRN: 563 NM value: 5.00
510-4❑ HRN: 574 NM value: 5.00
510-5❑ HRN: 576 Nov 1964 NM value: 5.00
510-6❑ HRN: 576 Mar 1967 NM value: 5.00
510-7❑ HRN: 576 Fal 1969 NM value: 5.00
511 ❑ Aug 1954 Cover: 0.15 NM value: 15.00
Puss in Boots
511-2❑ HRN: 526 NM value: 15.00
511-3❑ HRN: 565 NM value: 5.00
511-4❑ HRN: 574 NM value: 5.00
511-5❑ HRN: 576 Mar 1964 NM value: 5.00
511-6❑ HRN: 576 Feb 1967 NM value: 5.00
511-7❑ HRN: 576 Sum 1969 NM value: 5.00
512 ❑ Sep 1954 Cover: 0.15 NM value: 15.00
Rumpelstiltskin
512-2❑ HRN: 526 NM value: 15.00
512-3❑ HRN: 560 NM value: 15.00
512-4❑ NM value: 15.00
512-5❑ HRN: 576 May 1964 NM value: 15.00
512-6❑ HRN: 576 Jan 1967 NM value: 15.00
512-7❑ HRN: 576 Fal 1969 NM value: 15.00
513 ❑ Nov 1954 Cover: 0.15 NM value: 25.00
Pinocchio
513-2❑ HRN: 530 NM value: 6.00
513-3❑ HRN: 550 NM value: 6.00
513-4❑ HRN: 563 NM value: 6.00
513-5❑ HRN: 568 NM value: 6.00
513-6❑ HRN: 576 Dec 1963 NM value: 5.00
513-7❑ HRN: 576 Aug 1965 NM value: 5.00
513-8❑ HRN: 576 May 1967 NM value: 5.00
513-9❑ HRN: 576 Fal 1969 NM value: 5.00
514 ❑ Jan 1955 Cover: 0.15 NM value: 20.00
The Steadfast Tin Soldier
514-2❑ HRN: 530 NM value: 6.00
514-3❑ HRN: 560 NM value: 6.00
514-4❑ HRN: 562 NM value: 5.00
514-5❑ HRN: 568 NM value: 5.00
515 ❑ Mar 1955 Cover: 0.15 NM value: 15.00
Johnny Appleseed
515-2❑ HRN: 530 NM value: 5.00
515-3❑ HRN: 563 NM value: 5.00
515-4❑ HRN: 568 NM value: 5.00
515-5❑ HRN: 576 Jan 1964 NM value: 5.00
515-6❑ HRN: 576 Sep 1966 NM value: 5.00
515-7❑ HRN: 576 Spr 1969 NM value: 5.00
516 ❑ May 1955 Cover: 0.15 NM value: 25.00
Aladdin and his Lamp
516-2❑ HRN: 530 NM value: 6.00
516-3❑ HRN: 563 NM value: 6.00
516-4❑ HRN: 574 NM value: 6.00
516-5❑ HRN: 576 May 1964 NM value: 5.00
516-6❑ HRN: 576 Oct 1966 NM value: 5.00
516-7❑ HRN: 576 Spr 1969 NM value: 5.00
517 ❑ Jul 1955 Cover: 0.15 NM value: 15.00
The Emperor's New Clothes
517-2❑ HRN: 538 NM value: 5.00
517-3❑ HRN: 563 NM value: 5.00
517-4❑ HRN: 574 NM value: 5.00
517-5❑ HRN: 576 Jan 1967 NM value: 5.00
517-6❑ HRN: 576 Sum 1969 NM value: 5.00
518 ❑ Sep 1955 Cover: 0.15 NM value: 15.00
The Golden Goose
518-2❑ HRN: 565 NM value: 5.00
518-3❑ HRN: 574 NM value: 5.00
518-4❑ HRN: 576 Nov 1965 NM value: 5.00
518-5❑ HRN: 577 NM value: 5.00
519 ❑ Oct 1955 Cover: 0.15 NM value: 20.00
Paul Bunyan
519-2❑ HRN: 527 NM value: 6.00
519-3❑ HRN: 538 NM value: 6.00
519-4❑ HRN: 557 NM value: 6.00
519-5❑ HRN: 565 NM value: 5.00
519-6❑ HRN: 568 NM value: 5.00
519-7❑ HRN: 575 NM value: 5.00
519-8❑ HRN: 576 NM value: 5.00
519-9❑ HRN: 576 May 1964 NM value: 5.00
519-10❑ HRN: 576 Dec 1966 NM value: 5.00
519-11❑ HRN: 576 Fal 1969 NM value: 5.00
520 ❑ Nov 1955 Cover: 0.15 NM value: 20.00
Thumbelina
520-2❑ HRN: 552 NM value: 6.00
520-3❑ HRN: 563 NM value: 6.00
520-4❑ HRN: 568 NM value: 6.00
520-5❑ HRN: 576 NM value: 5.00
520-6❑ HRN: 576 Jun 1967 NM value: 5.00
520-7❑ HRN: 576 Fal 1969 NM value: 5.00
521 ❑ Dec 1955 Cover: 0.15 NM value: 12.00
The King of the Golden River
521-2❑ HRN: 556 NM value: 4.00
521-3❑ HRN: 565 NM value: 4.00
521-4❑ HRN: 574 NM value: 4.00
521-5❑ HRN: 576 Nov 1964 NM value: 4.00
521-6❑ HRN: 576 Fal 1969 NM value: 4.00
522 ❑ Jan 1956 Cover: 0.15 NM value: 12.00
The Nightingale
522-2❑ HRN: 565 NM value: 4.00
522-3❑ HRN: 574 NM value: 4.00
522-4❑ HRN: 576 Oct 1965 NM value: 4.00
522-5❑ HRN: 576 NM value: 4.00
523 ❑ Feb 1956 Cover: 0.15 NM value: 12.00
The Gallant Tailor
523-2❑ HRN: 5 NM value: 4.00
523-3❑ HRN: 5 NM value: 4.00
523-4❑ HRN: 5 NM value: 4.00
523-5❑ HRN: 5 NM value: 4.00
524 ❑ Mar 1956 Cover: 0.15 NM value: 12.00
The Wild Swans
524-2❑ HRN: 540 NM value: 4.00
524-3❑ HRN: 560 NM value: 4.00
524-4❑ HRN: 568 NM value: 4.00
524-5❑ HRN: 576 NM value: 4.00
524-6❑ HRN: 576 Feb 1967 NM value: 4.00
525 ❑ Apr 1956 Cover: 0.15 NM value: 18.00
The Little Mermaid
525-2❑ HRN: 547 NM value: 5.00
525-3❑ HRN: 563 NM value: 5.00
525-4❑ HRN: 571 NM value: 5.00
525-5❑ HRN: 576 Dec 1964 NM value: 5.00
525-6❑ HRN: 576 Jan 1966 NM value: 5.00
526 ❑ May 1956 Cover: 0.15 NM value: 12.00
The Frog Prince
526-2❑ HRN: 550 NM value: 4.00
526-3❑ HRN: 563 NM value: 4.00
526-4❑ HRN: 568 NM value: 4.00
526-5❑ HRN: 576 Apr 1964 NM value: 4.00
526-6❑ HRN: 576 Feb 1967 NM value: 4.00
527 ❑ Jun 1956 Cover: 0.15 NM value: 12.00
The Golden-Haired Giant
527-2❑ HRN: 560 NM value: 4.00
527-3❑ HRN: 568 NM value: 4.00
527-4❑ HRN: 576 Jan 1964 NM value: 4.00
527-5❑ HRN: 576 Mar 1967 NM value: 4.00
527-6❑ HRN: 576 NM value: 4.00
528 ❑ Jul 1956 Cover: 0.15 NM value: 12.00
The Penny Prince
528-2❑ HRN: 557 NM value: 4.00
528-3❑ HRN: 565 NM value: 4.00
528-4❑ HRN: 568 NM value: 4.00
528-5❑ HRN: 576 Nov 1963 NM value: 4.00
528-6❑ HRN: 576 Jul 1967 NM value: 4.00
529 ❑ Aug 1956 Cover: 0.15 NM value: 12.00
The Magic Servants
529-2❑ HRN: 559 NM value: 4.00
529-3❑ HRN: 568 NM value: 4.00
530 ❑ Sep 1956 Cover: 0.15 NM value: 12.00
The Golden Bird
530-2❑ HRN: 556 NM value: 4.00
530-3❑ HRN: 560 NM value: 4.00
530-4❑ HRN: 576 Aug 1965 NM value: 4.00
530-5❑ HRN: 576 NM value: 4.00
531 ❑ Oct 1956 Cover: 0.15 NM value: 12.00
The Dancing Princess
531-2❑ HRN: 556 NM value: 4.00
531-3❑ HRN: 565 NM value: 4.00
531-4❑ HRN: 571 NM value: 4.00
531-5❑ HRN: 576 Jul 1964 NM value: 4.00
531-6❑ HRN: 576 Feb 1967 NM value: 4.00
532 ❑ Nov 1956 Cover: 0.15 NM value: 15.00
Rapunzel
532-2❑ HRN: 559 NM value: 5.00
532-3❑ HRN: 567 NM value: 5.00
532-4❑ HRN: 575 NM value: 5.00
532-5❑ HRN: 576 NM value: 5.00
532-6❑ HRN: 576 Dec 1965 NM value: 5.00
532-7❑ HRN: 577 NM value: 5.00
533 ❑ Dec 1956 Cover: 0.15 NM value: 12.00
The Magic Fountain
533-2❑ HRN: 556 NM value: 4.00
533-3❑ HRN: 562 NM value: 4.00
533-4❑ HRN: 576 Dec 1964 NM value: 4.00
533-5❑ HRN: 576 NM value: 4.00
534 ❑ Jan 1957 Cover: 0.15 NM value: 12.00
The Golden Touch
534-2❑ HRN: 556 NM value: 4.00
534-4❑ HRN: 576 Dec 1964 NM value: 4.00
534-5❑ HRN: 576 NM value: 4.00
535 ❑ Feb 1957 Cover: 0.15 NM value: 25.00
The Wizard of Oz
535-2❑ HRN: 557 NM value: 8.00
535-3❑ HRN: 565 NM value: 6.00
535-4❑ HRN: 571 NM value: 6.00
535-5❑ HRN: 576 Dec 1964 NM value: 6.00
535-6❑ HRN: 576 Oct 1966 NM value: 6.00
535-7❑ HRN: 577 Spr 1971 NM value: 6.00
536 ❑ Mar 1957 Cover: 0.15 NM value: 12.00
The Chimney Sweep
536-2❑ HRN: 556 NM value: 4.00
536-3❑ HRN: 563 NM value: 4.00
536-4❑ HRN: 574 NM value: 4.00
536-5❑ HRN: 575 Mar 1966 NM value: 4.00
536-6❑ HRN: 576 Mar 1967 NM value: 4.00
537 ❑ Apr 1957 Cover: 0.15 NM value: 12.00
The Three Fairies
537-2❑ HRN: 559 NM value: 4.00
537-3❑ HRN: 568 NM value: 4.00
537-4❑ HRN: 576 May 1964 NM value: 4.00
537-5❑ HRN: 576 Feb 1967 NM value: 4.00
538 ❑ May 1957 Cover: 0.15 NM value: 12.00
Silly Hans
538-2❑ HRN: 565 NM value: 4.00
538-3❑ HRN: 574 NM value: 4.00
538-4❑ HRN: 576 Sep 1964 NM value: 4.00
538-5❑ HRN: 576 NM value: 4.00
539 ❑ Jun 1957 Cover: 0.15 NM value: 12.00
The Enchanted Fish
539-2❑ HRN: 556 NM value: 4.00
539-3❑ HRN: 562 NM value: 4.00
539-4❑ HRN: 574 NM value: 4.00
539-5❑ HRN: 576 Aug 1965 NM value: 4.00
539-6❑ HRN: 577 NM value: 4.00
540 ❑ Jul 1957 Cover: 0.15 NM value: 12.00
The Tinder-Box
540-2❑ HRN: 556 NM value: 4.00
540-3❑ HRN: 559 NM value: 4.00
540-4❑ HRN: 567 NM value: 4.00
540-5❑ HRN: 576 Sep 1965 NM value: 4.00
540-6❑ HRN: 577 NM value: 4.00
541 ❑ Aug 1957 Cover: 0.15 NM value: 15.00
Snow White and Rose Red
541-2❑ HRN: 556 NM value: 5.00
541-3❑ HRN: 561 NM value: 5.00
541-4❑ HRN: 576 Sep 1965 NM value: 5.00
541-5❑ HRN: 576 NM value: 5.00
542 ❑ Sep 1957 NM value: 12.00
The Donkey's Tale
542-2❑ HRN: 563 Cover: 0.15 NM value: 4.00
542-3❑ HRN: 574 NM value: 4.00
542-4❑ HRN: 576 Oct 1965 NM value: 4.00
542-5❑ HRN: 577 NM value: 4.00
543 ❑ Oct 1957 NM value: 12.00
The House in the Woods
543-2❑ HRN: 556 Cover: 0.15 NM value: 4.00
543-3❑ HRN: 563 NM value: 4.00
543-4❑ HRN: 576 Dec 1964 NM value: 4.00
543-5❑ HRN: 576 Feb 1967 NM value: 4.00
544 ❑ Nov 1957 Cover: 0.15 NM value: 24.00
The Golden Fleece
544-2❑ HRN: 556 NM value: 8.00
544-3❑ HRN: 565 NM value: 8.00
544-4❑ HRN: 575 NM value: 7.00
544-5❑ HRN: 576 Oct 1964 NM value: 7.00
544-6❑ HRN: 576 NM value: 7.00
545 ❑ Dec 1957 Cover: 0.15 NM value: 12.00
The Glass Mountain
545-2❑ HRN: 556 NM value: 4.00
545-3❑ HRN: 563 NM value: 4.00
545-4❑ HRN: 575 NM value: 4.00
545-5❑ HRN: 576 NM value: 4.00
546 ❑ Jan 1958 Cover: 0.15 NM value: 12.00
The Elves and the Shoemaker
546-2❑ HRN: 556 NM value: 4.00
546-3❑ HRN: 565 NM value: 4.00
546-4❑ HRN: 576 Sep 1964 NM value: 4.00
546-5❑ HRN: 576 NM value: 4.00
547 ❑ Feb 1958 Cover: 0.15 NM value: 12.00
The Wishing Table
547-2❑ HRN: 565 NM value: 4.00
547-3❑ HRN: 575 NM value: 4.00
547-4❑ HRN: 576 Nov 1964 NM value: 4.00
547-5❑ HRN: 576 Mar 1967 NM value: 4.00
548 ❑ Mar 1958 Cover: 0.15 NM value: 12.00
The Magic Pitcher
548-2❑ HRN: 556 NM value: 4.00
548-3❑ HRN: 563 NM value: 4.00
548-4❑ HRN: 568 NM value: 4.00
548-5❑ HRN: 576 Jul 1964 NM value: 4.00
548-6❑ HRN: 576 NM value: 4.00
549 ❑ Apr 1958 Cover: 0.15 NM value: 12.00
Simple Kate
549-2❑ HRN: 563 NM value: 4.00
549-3❑ HRN: 568 NM value: 4.00
549-4❑ HRN: 575 NM value: 4.00
549-5❑ HRN: 576 Dec 1965 NM value: 4.00
549-6❑ HRN: 576 Spr 1969 NM value: 4.00
550 ❑ May 1958 Cover: 0.15 NM value: 12.00
The Singing Donkey A: Stan Campbell
550-2❑ HRN: 563 NM value: 4.00
550-3❑ HRN: 568 NM value: 4.00

Other grades: Multiply prices above by **1.5 for Mint • 2/3 for Very Fine • 1/3 for Fine • 1/5 for Very Good • 1/8 for Good**

550-4❑ **HRN:** 576 Apr 1964 **NM** value: **4.00**
550-5❑ **HRN:** 576 Fal 1968 **NM** value: **4.00**
551 ❑ Jun 1958 Cover: 0.15 **NM** value: **12.00**
📖 The Queen Bee
551-2❑ **HRN:** 568 **NM** value: **4.00**
551-3❑ **HRN:** 575 **NM** value: **4.00**
551-4❑ **HRN:** 576 Jul 1965 **NM** value: **4.00**
551-5❑ **HRN:** 577 **NM** value: **4.00**
552 ❑ Jul 1958 Cover: 0.15 **NM** value: **12.00**
📖 The Three Little Dwarfs; Aesop's Fables: The Woodcutters and the Ax
552-2❑ **HRN:** 563 Cover: 0.15 **NM** value: **4.00**
552-3❑ **HRN:** 571 Cover: 0.15 **NM** value: **4.00**
552-4❑ **HRN:** 576 Nov 1963 **NM** value: **4.00**
552-5❑ **HRN:** 576 Sep 1966 **NM** value: **4.00**
553 ❑ Aug 1958 Cover: 0.15 **NM** value: **12.00**
📖 King Thrushbeard
553-2❑ **HRN:** 562 **NM** value: **4.00**
553-3❑ **HRN:** 567 **NM** value: **4.00**
553-4❑ **HRN:** 575 **NM** value: **4.00**
553-5❑ **HRN:** 576 Mar 1965 **NM** value: **4.00**
553-6❑ **HRN:** 576 **NM** value: **4.00**
554 ❑ Sep 1958 Cover: 0.15 **NM** value: **12.00**
📖 The Enchanted Deer
554-2❑ **HRN:** 558 **NM** value: **4.00**
554-3❑ **HRN:** 565 **NM** value: **4.00**
554-4❑ **HRN:** 575 **NM** value: **4.00**
554-5❑ **HRN:** 576 Apr 1964 **NM** value: **4.00**
554-6❑ **HRN:** 576 Aug 1967 **NM** value: **4.00**
555 ❑ Oct 1958 Cover: 0.15 **NM** value: **12.00**
📖 The 3 Golden Apples
555-2❑ **HRN:** 568 **NM** value: **4.00**
555-3❑ **HRN:** 576 **NM** value: **4.00**
555-4❑ **HRN:** 576 Sep 1966 **NM** value: **4.00**
556 ❑ Nov 1958 Cover: 0.15 **NM** value: **12.00**
📖 The Elf Mound
556-2❑ **HRN:** 568 **NM** value: **4.00**
556-3❑ **HRN:** 575 **NM** value: **4.00**
556-4❑ **HRN:** 576 Mar 1965 **NM** value: **4.00**
556-5❑ **HRN:** 576 Fal 1968 **NM** value: **4.00**
557 ❑ Dec 1958 Cover: 0.15 **NM** value: **12.00**
📖 Silly Willy
557-2❑ **HRN:** 568 **NM** value: **4.00**
557-3❑ **HRN:** 574 **NM** value: **4.00**
557-4❑ **HRN:** 576 Oct 1964 **NM** value: **4.00**
557-5❑ **HRN:** 576 Fal 1968 **NM** value: **4.00**
558 ❑ Feb 1959 Cover: 0.15 **NM** value: **12.00**
📖 The Magic Dish
558-2❑ **HRN:** 556 **NM** value: **4.00**
558-3❑ **HRN:** 574 **NM** value: **4.00**
558-4❑ **HRN:** 576 Sep 1966 **NM** value: **4.00**
559 ❑ Apr 1959 Cover: 0.15 **NM** value: **12.00**
📖 The Japanese Lantern
559-2❑ **HRN:** 574 **NM** value: **4.00**
559-3❑ **HRN:** 576 Dec 1964 **NM** value: **4.00**
559-4❑ **HRN:** 576 Jan 1967 **NM** value: **4.00**
560 ❑ Jun 1959 Cover: 0.15 **NM** value: **12.00**
📖 The Doll Princess
560-2❑ **HRN:** 574 **NM** value: **4.00**
560-3❑ **HRN:** 576 Dec 1964 **NM** value: **4.00**
560-4❑ **HRN:** 576 Apr 1967 **NM** value: **4.00**
561 ❑ Aug 1959 Cover: 0.15 **NM** value: **12.00**
📖 Hans Humdrum
561-2❑ **HRN:** 574 **NM** value: **4.00**
561-3❑ **HRN:** 576 Mar 1965 **NM** value: **4.00**
561-4❑ **HRN:** 576 Fal 1968 **NM** value: **4.00**
562 ❑ Oct 1959 Cover: 0.15 **NM** value: **12.00**
📖 The Enchanted Pony
562-2❑ **HRN:** 574 **NM** value: **4.00**
562-3❑ **HRN:** 576 Sep 1964 **NM** value: **4.00**
562-4❑ **HRN:** 576 Mar 1967 **NM** value: **4.00**
563 ❑ Dec 1959 Cover: 0.15 **NM** value: **12.00**
📖 The Wishing Well
563-2❑ **HRN:** 574 **NM** value: **4.00**
563-3❑ **HRN:** 576 Jan 1964 **NM** value: **4.00**
563-4❑ **HRN:** 576 Spr 1969 **NM** value: **4.00**
564 ❑ Feb 1960 Cover: 0.15 **NM** value: **12.00**
📖 The Salt Mountain
564-2❑ **HRN:** 574 **NM** value: **4.00**
564-3❑ **HRN:** 576 Jan 1965 **NM** value: **4.00**
564-4❑ **HRN:** 576 Mar 1967 **NM** value: **4.00**
565 ❑ Apr 1960 Cover: 0.15 **NM** value: **12.00**
📖 The Silly Princess
565-2❑ **HRN:** 575 **NM** value: **4.00**
565-3❑ **HRN:** 576 Jan 1965 **NM** value: **4.00**
565-4❑ **HRN:** 576 **NM** value: **4.00**
566 ❑ Jun 1960 Cover: 0.15 **NM** value: **12.00**
📖 Clumsy Hans
566-2❑ **HRN:** 575 **NM** value: **4.00**
566-3❑ **HRN:** 576 Jan 1965 **NM** value: **4.00**
566-4❑ **HRN:** 576 **NM** value: **4.00**
567 ❑ Aug 1960 Cover: 0.15 **NM** value: **12.00**
📖 The Bearskin Soldier
567-2❑ **HRN:** 575 **NM** value: **4.00**
567-3❑ **HRN:** 576 Feb 1965 **NM** value: **4.00**
567-4❑ **HRN:** 576 May 1967 **NM** value: **4.00**
567-5❑ **HRN:** 576 **NM** value: **4.00**
568 ❑ Oct 1960 Cover: 0.15 **NM** value: **12.00**
📖 The Happy Hedgehog
568-2❑ **HRN:** 575 **NM** value: **4.00**
568-3❑ **HRN:** 576 Feb 1965 **NM** value: **4.00**
568-4❑ **HRN:** 576 May 1967 **NM** value: **4.00**
569 ❑ Dec 1960 Cover: 0.15 **NM** value: **12.00**
📖 The Three Giants
569-2❑ **HRN:** 575 **NM** value: **4.00**
569-3❑ **HRN:** 576 Feb 1965 **NM** value: **4.00**
569-4❑ **HRN:** 576 Fal 1968 **NM** value: **4.00**
570 ❑ Feb 1961 Cover: 0.15 **NM** value: **12.00**
📖 The Pearl Princess
570-2❑ **HRN:** 575 **NM** value: **4.00**
570-3❑ **HRN:** 576 Feb 1965 **NM** value: **4.00**
570-4❑ **HRN:** 577 **NM** value: **4.00**
571 ❑ Apr 1961 Cover: 0.15 **NM** value: **12.00**
📖 How Fire Came to the Indians
571-2❑ **HRN:** 576 **NM** value: **4.00**
571-3❑ **HRN:** 576 Nov 1966 **NM** value: **4.00**
571-4❑ **HRN:** 576 Spr 1969 **NM** value: **4.00**
572 ❑ Jun 1961 Cover: 0.15 **NM** value: **12.00**
📖 The Drummer Boy
572-2❑ **HRN:** 576 **NM** value: **4.00**
572-3❑ **HRN:** 576 Jan 1967 **NM** value: **4.00**
573 ❑ Aug 1961 Cover: 0.15 **NM** value: **12.00**
📖 The Crystal Ball
573-2❑ **HRN:** 576 Oct 1963 **NM** value: **4.00**
573-3❑ **HRN:** 576 Aug 1966 **NM** value: **4.00**
574 ❑ **NM** value: **12.00**
📖 Brightboots
574-2❑ **HRN:** 576 Nov 1964 **NM** value: **4.00**
574-3❑ **HRN:** 576 **NM** value: **4.00**
575 ❑ Feb 1962 Cover: 0.15 **NM** value: **12.00**
📖 The Fearless Prince
575-2❑ **HRN:** 576 Feb 1964 **NM** value: **4.00**
575-3❑ **HRN:** 576 Nov 1966 **NM** value: **4.00**
576 ❑ Jun 1962 Cover: 0.15 **NM** value: **12.00**
📖 The Princess Who Saw Everything
576-2❑ **HRN:** 576 Dec 1963 **NM** value: **4.00**
576-3❑ **HRN:** 576 Mar 1967 **NM** value: **4.00**
577 ❑ Cover: 0.15 **NM** value: **25.00**
📖 The Runaway Dumpling • Winter, 1969

CLASSICS ILLUSTRATED SPECIAL ISSUE Gilberton

129 ❑ Dec 1955 Cover: 0.35 **NM** value: **50.00**
📖 The Story of Jesus
132 ❑ Jun 1956 Cover: 0.35 **NM** value: **45.00**
📖 The Story of America
135 ❑ Dec 1956 Cover: 0.35 **NM** value: **35.00**
📖 The Ten Commandments
138 ❑ **HRN:** 137 Jun 1957 Cover: 0.35 **NM** value: **35.00**
📖 Adventures in Science
138-2❑ **HRN:** 149 Jun 1957 Cover: 0.35 **NM** value: **25.00**
138-3❑ **HRN:** 149 Dec 1961 Cover: 0.35 **NM** value: **35.00**
141 ❑ Dec 1957 Cover: 0.35 **NM** value: **40.00**
📖 The Rough Rider
144 ❑ Jun 1958 Cover: 0.35 **NM** value: **40.00**
📖 Blazing the Trails West
147 ❑ Dec 1958 Cover: 0.35 **NM** value: **40.00**
📖 Crossing the Rockies
150 ❑ Jun 1959 Cover: 0.35 **NM** value: **40.00**
📖 Royal Canadian Police
153 ❑ Dec 1959 Cover: 0.35 **NM** value: **40.00**
📖 Men, Guns & Cattle
156 ❑ Jun 1960 Cover: 0.35 **NM** value: **40.00**
📖 The Atomic Age
159 ❑ Dec 1960 Cover: 0.35 **NM** value: **40.00**
📖 Rockets, Jets and Missiles
162 ❑ Jun 1961 Cover: 0.35 **NM** value: **75.00**
📖 War Between the States
165 ❑ Dec 1961 Cover: 0.35 **NM** value: **45.00**
📖 To the Stars
166 ❑ ca. 1962 Cover: 0.35 **NM** value: **50.00**
📖 World War II
167 ❑ Jul 1962 Cover: 0.35 **NM** value: **50.00**
📖 Prehistoric World

CLASSICS ILLUSTRATED STUDY GUIDE Acclaim

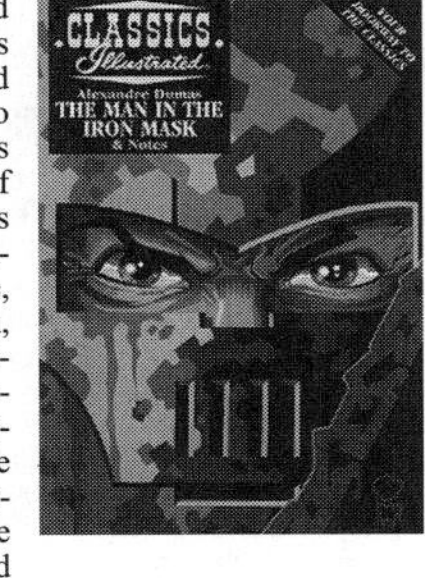

Publisher Acclaim Comics billed these digest-size recolored reprints of the original Classics Illustrated comics as something similar to CliffsNotes. Not only are readers treated to comic-book versions of such notable literary works as Romeo & Juliet, A Tale of Two Cities, The Hunchback of Notre Dame, and A Midsummer Night's Dream, they are also provided with analytical essays, biographies of the authors, study questions, and character sketches. Without a doubt, these are handy introductions to the literary classics and may encourage young readers to venture beyond comic books.

1 ❑ 1997 Cover: 4.99 **NM** value: **Cover or less**
No issue number. • All Quiet on the Western Front
2 ❑ 1997 Cover: 4.99 **NM** value: **Cover or less**
No issue number. • Around the World in 80 Days
3 ❑ Sep 1997 Cover: 4.99 **NM** value: **Cover or less**
No issue number. • The Call of the Wild
4 ❑ 1997 Cover: 4.99 **NM** value: **Cover or less**
No issue number. • Captains Courageous
5 ❑ 1997 Cover: 4.99 **NM** value: **Cover or less**
No issue number. • A Christmas Carol
6 ❑ 1997 Cover: 4.99 **NM** value: **Cover or less**
No issue number. • The Count of Monte Cristo
7 ❑ Aug 1997 Cover: 4.99 **NM** value: **Cover or less**
No issue number. • David Copperfield
8 ❑ 1997 Cover: 4.99 **NM** value: **Cover or less**
No issue number. • Doctor Jekyll and Mr. Hyde
9 ❑ 1997 Cover: 5.25 **NM** value: **Cover or less**
No issue number. • Don Quixote
10 ❑ 1997 Cover: 4.99 **NM** value: **Cover or less**
No issue number. • Faust
11 ❑ 1997 Cover: 4.99 **NM** value: **Cover or less**
No issue number. • Frankenstein
12 ❑ 1997 Cover: 4.99 **NM** value: **Cover or less**
No issue number. • Great Expectations
13 ❑ Sep 1997 Cover: 4.99 **NM** value: **Cover or less**
No issue number. • The Hunchback of Notre Dame
14 ❑ 1997 Cover: 4.99 **NM** value: **Cover or less**
No issue number. • The Iliad
15 ❑ 1997 Cover: 4.99 **NM** value: **Cover or less**
No issue number. • The Invisible Man
16 ❑ Aug 1997 Cover: 4.99 **NM** value: **Cover or less**
No issue number. • Julius Caesar
17 ❑ Aug 1997 Cover: 4.99 **NM** value: **Cover or less**
No issue number. • The Jungle Book
18 ❑ 1997 Cover: 4.99 **NM** value: **Cover or less**
No issue number. • Kidnapped
19 ❑ 1997 Cover: 4.99 **NM** value: **Cover or less**
No issue number. • Kim
20 ❑ 1997 Cover: 4.99 **NM** value: **Cover or less**
No issue number. • The Last of the Mohicans
21 ❑ Sep 1997 Cover: 4.99 **NM** value: **Cover or less**
No issue number. • Lord Jim
22 ❑ Aug 1997 Cover: 4.99 **NM** value: **Cover or less**
No issue number. • The Man in the Iron Mask
23 ❑ 1997 Cover: 4.99 **NM** value: **Cover or less**
No issue number. • The Master of Ballantrae
24 ❑ Apr 1997 Cover: 4.99 **NM** value: **Cover or less**
No issue number. • A Midsummer Night's Dream
25 ❑ Apr 1997 Cover: 4.99 **NM** value: **Cover or less**
No issue number. • Moby Dick
26 ❑ 1997 Cover: 4.99 **NM** value: **Cover or less**
No issue number. • new adaptation of Narrative of the Life of Frederick Douglass
27 ❑ 1997 Cover: 4.99 **NM** value: **Cover or less**
No issue number. • The Prince and the Pauper
28 ❑ Aug 1997 Cover: 4.99 **NM** value: **Cover or less**
No issue number. 📖 Pudd'nhead Wilson • Pudd'nhead Wilson **A:** Henry C. Kiefer; Clem Robbins(cover) **W:** Andrew Jay Hoffman; Mark Twain
29 ❑ Sep 1997 Cover: 4.99 **NM** value: **Cover or less**
No issue number. • Robinson Crusoe
30 ❑ 1997 Cover: 4.99 **NM** value: **Cover or less**
No issue number. • new adaptation of The Scarlet Pimpernel
31 ❑ 1997 Cover: 4.99 **NM** value: **Cover or less**
No issue number. • Silas Marner
32 ❑ 1997 Cover: 4.99 **NM** value: **Cover or less**
No issue number. • War of the Worlds
33 ❑ 1997 Cover: 4.99 **NM** value: **Cover or less**
No issue number. • Wuthering Heights
34 ❑ Feb 1997 Cover: 4.99 **NM** value: **Cover or less**
No issue number. 📖 Romeo and Juliet **A:** George Evans **W:** Susan Schwartz; William Shakespeare
35 ❑ 1997 Cover: 4.99 **NM** value: **Cover or less**
36 ❑ Feb 1997 Cover: 4.99 **NM** value: **Cover or less**
No issue number. 📖 Crime and Punishment **A:** Rudolph Palais **W:** Andrew J. Hoffman; Fyodor Dostoyevsky
37 ❑ Jul 1997 Cover: 4.99 **NM** value: **Cover or less**
No issue number. 📖 Gulliver's Travels **A:** Lillian Chestney **W:** Dan Kushner; Gregory Feeley; Jonathan Swift
38 ❑ Feb 1997 Cover: 4.99 **NM** value: **Cover or less**
No issue number. 📖 Tom Sawyer **A:** Aldo Rubano **W:** Andrew Jay Hoffman; H. Miller; Mark Twain

CLASSIC STAR WARS Dark Horse

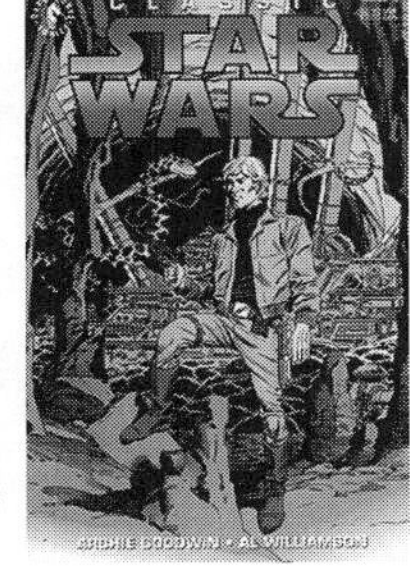

Among the adaptations spawned by Star Wars, one of the overlooked greats is a daily newspaper strip that continued the adventures of Luke Skywalker, Han Solo, and the rest of the characters seeking to save the galaxy from the tyranny of the Empire.

More than a decade later, Dark Horse Comics brought the Archie Goodwin/Al Williamson run on that strip back in comic-book form as Classic Star Wars. Dark Horse does a reasonably good job of converting the newspaper strip into comic book form, removing redundant panels and coloring the artwork (with Williamson's participation).

Strip enthusiasts will still long for a reprint work that preserves the original form, but this will do in the meantime. A later Dark Horse series, Classic Star Wars: The Early Adventures, reprinted Russ Manning's strips.

1 ❑ Aug 1992 Cover: 2.50 **NM** value: **4.00**
Circ: CapCity orders: **19,975** • **CGC:** 2 graded, best 9.4
2 ❑ Sep 1992 Cover: 2.50 **NM** value: **3.50**
Circ: CapCity orders: **16,500**
3 ❑ Oct 1992 Cover: 2.50 **NM** value: **3.50**
Circ: CapCity orders: **16,250**
4 ❑ Nov 1992 Cover: 2.50 **NM** value: **3.25**
Circ: CapCity orders: **16,850**
5 ❑ Dec 1992 Cover: 2.50 **NM** value: **3.25**
Circ: CapCity orders: **17,050**
A: Al Williamson **W:** Archie Goodwin
6 ❑ Jan 1993 Cover: 2.50 **NM** value: **3.00**
Circ: CapCity orders: **16,375**
A: Al Williamson **W:** Archie Goodwin
7 ❑ Feb 1993 Cover: 2.50 **NM** value: **3.00**
Circ: CapCity orders: **17,550**
A: Al Williamson **W:** Archie Goodwin
8 ❑ Apr 1993 Cover: 2.50 **NM** value: **3.00**
Circ: CapCity orders: **19,375**
• trading card **A:** Al Williamson **W:** Archie Goodwin
9 ❑ May 1993 Cover: 2.50 **NM** value: **3.00**
Circ: CapCity orders: **14,925**
A: Al Williamson **W:** Archie Goodwin

CGC-graded: Multiply prices above by **33 for 9.9 M** • **16 for 9.8 NM/M** • **7 for 9.6 NM+** • **5 for 9.4 NM** • **2.5 for 9.2 NM-** • **1.5 for 9.0 VF/NM**

10 ❑ Jun 1993 Cover: 2.50 **NM** value: **3.00**
Circ: CapCity orders: **14,450**
11 ❑ Aug 1993 Cover: 2.50 **NM** value: **3.00**
Circ: CapCity orders: **13,425**
12 ❑ Sep 1993 Cover: 2.50 **NM** value: **3.00**
Circ: CapCity orders: **12,350**
13 ❑ Oct 1993 Cover: 2.50 **NM** value: **3.00**
Circ: CapCity orders: **12,050**
14 ❑ Nov 1993 Cover: 2.50 **NM** value: **3.00**
Circ: CapCity orders: **12,375**
15 ❑ Jan 1994 Cover: 2.50 **NM** value: **3.00**
Circ: CapCity orders: **11,775**
16 ❑ Feb 1994 Cover: 2.50 **NM** value: **3.00**
Circ: CapCity orders: **10,975**
17 ❑ Mar 1994 Cover: 2.50 **NM** value: **3.00**
Circ: CapCity orders: **10,550**
18 ❑ Apr 1994 Cover: 2.50 **NM** value: **3.00**
19 ❑ May 1994 Cover: 2.50 **NM** value: **3.00**
Circ: CapCity orders: **11,450**
20 ❑ Jun 1994 Cover: 3.50 **NM** value: **Cover or less**
Circ: CapCity orders: **12,475**
• Giant-size. final issue.
Bk 2❑ Jul 1995 Cover: 16.95 **NM** value: **Cover or less**
• collects Classic Star Wars #8-14
Bk 3❑ Cover: 19.95 **NM** value: **Cover or less**
• Escape To Hoth;collects Classic Star Wars #15-20

CLASSIC STAR WARS: A LONG TIME AGO — Dark Horse

1 ❑ Mar 1999 Cover: 12.95 **NM** value: **Cover or less**
2 ❑ Apr 1999 Cover: 12.95 **NM** value: **Cover or less**
A: Al Williamson; Michael Golden; Carmine Infantino; Gene Day; Walt Simonson; Terry Austin; & Tom Palmer **W:** Archie Goodwin; Mike W. Barr
3 ❑ May 1999 Cover: 12.95 **NM** value: **Cover or less**
no cover price. **A:** Walt Simonson **W:** David Michelinie
4 ❑ Jun 1999 Cover: 12.95 **NM** value: **Cover or less**
no cover price. **A:** Ron Frenz; Gene Day **W:** David Michelinie; Jo Duffy
5 ❑ Jul 1999 Cover: 12.95 **NM** value: **Cover or less**
no cover price. **A:** Carmine Infantino; Walt Simonson **W:** David Michelinie
6 ❑ Aug 1999 Cover: 12.95 **NM** value: **Cover or less**
A: Cynthia Martin; Tom Palmer; Art Nichols; Ron Frenz; Bob McLeod **W:** Jo Duffy; Linda Grant; Randy Stradley

CLASSIC STAR WARS: A NEW HOPE — Dark Horse

1 ❑ Jun 1994 Cover: 3.95 **NM** value: **Cover or less**
Circ: CapCity orders: **19,500**
• prestige format. • Collects Star Wars (Marvel) #1-3 **A:** Howard Chaykin **W:** Roy Thomas
2 ❑ Jul 1994 Cover: 3.95 **NM** value: **Cover or less**
Circ: CapCity orders: **15,750**
• prestige format. • Collects Star Wars (Marvel) #4-6 **A:** Howard Chaykin **W:** Roy Thomas
Bk 1❑ Nov 1995 Cover: 9.95 **NM** value: **Cover or less**
• collects the two-issue series

CLASSIC STAR WARS: DEVILWORLDS — Dark Horse

1 ❑ Aug 1996 Cover: 2.50 **NM** value: **Cover or less**
A: Alan Davis **W:** Alan Moore
2 ❑ Sep 1996 Cover: 2.50 **NM** value: **Cover or less**
Circ: Diamd. preorders: **31,545**
📖 Rust Never Sleeps **A:** Alan Davis **W:** Alan Moore

CLASSIC STAR WARS: HAN SOLO AT STARS' END — Dark Horse

1 ❑ Mar 1997 Cover: 2.95 **NM** value: **Cover or less**
Circ: Diamd. preorders: **32,810**
cardstock cover. • adapts Brian Daley novel **A:** Alfredo Alcala **W:** Archie Goodwin
2 ❑ Apr 1997 Cover: 2.95 **NM** value: **Cover or less**
Circ: Diamd. preorders: **28,503**
cardstock cover. • adapts Brian Daley novel **A:** Alfredo Alcala **W:** Archie Goodwin
3 ❑ May 1997 Cover: 2.95 **NM** value: **Cover or less**
Circ: Diamd. preorders: **27,711**
cardstock cover. • adapts Brian Daley novel **A:** Alfredo Alcala **W:** Archie Goodwin
Bk 1❑ Sep 1997 Cover: 6.95 **NM** value: **Cover or less**
• collects adaptation of Brian Daley novel

CLASSIC STAR WARS: RETURN OF THE JEDI — Dark Horse

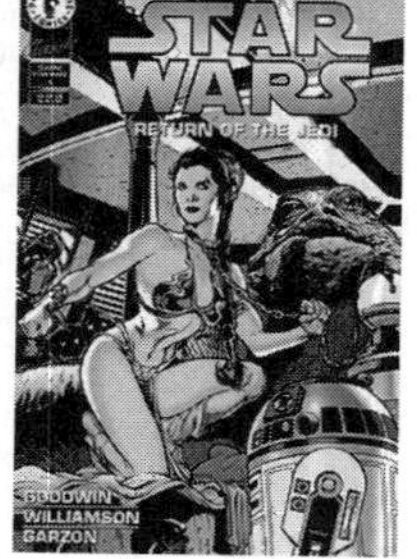

This prestige format limited series begins with an Adam Hughes cover featuring Princess Leia in her slave-girl bikini and proceeds to reprint Marvel Comics' terrific adaptation of the third film in the original Star Wars trilogy. Once again, comics legends Archie Goodwin (Iron Man, Manhunter) and Al Williamson (Forbidden Worlds, Weird Science) are at the creative helm and take readers on a beautiful, breathtaking journey through an equally imaginative film.

As with the previous Classic Star Wars reprint series from Dark Horse, sketches from the film round out each issue.

1 ❑ Oct 1994 Cover: 3.50 **NM** value: **Cover or less**
Circ: CapCity orders: **16,300**
• polybagged with trading card **A:** Al Williamson; Carlos Garzon **W:** Archie Goodwin
2 ❑ Cover: 3.95 **NM** value: **Cover or less**
Circ: CapCity orders: **13,850**
A: Al Williamson; Carlos Garzon **W:** Archie Goodwin
Bk 1❑ Nov 1995 Cover: 9.95 **NM** value: **Cover or less**
• collects the two-issue series

CLASSIC STAR WARS: THE EARLY ADVENTURES — Dark Horse

1 ❑ Aug 1994 Cover: 2.50 **NM** value: **Cover or less**
Circ: CapCity orders: **16,325**
A: Russ Manning **W:** Russ Manning
2 ❑ Sep 1994 Cover: 2.50 **NM** value: **Cover or less**
Circ: CapCity orders: **13,975**
A: Rick Hoberg; Russ Manning **W:** Russ Manning
3 ❑ Oct 1994 Cover: 2.50 **NM** value: **Cover or less**
Circ: CapCity orders: **14,150**
A: Russ Manning
4 ❑ Nov 1994 Cover: 2.50 **NM** value: **Cover or less**
Circ: CapCity orders: **12,750**
A: Russ Manning
5 ❑ Dec 1994 Cover: 2.50 **NM** value: **Cover or less**
Circ: CapCity orders: **11,975**
A: Russ Manning
6 ❑ Jan 1995 Cover: 2.50 **NM** value: **Cover or less**
Circ: CapCity orders: **11,200**
A: Russ Manning
7 ❑ Feb 1995 Cover: 2.50 **NM** value: **Cover or less**
Circ: CapCity orders: **10,700**
A: Russ Manning
8 ❑ Mar 1995 Cover: 2.50 **NM** value: **Cover or less**
Circ: CapCity orders: **10,825**
9 ❑ Apr 1995 Cover: 2.50 **NM** value: **Cover or less**
Circ: CapCity orders: **10,900**
Bk 1❑ May 1997 Cover: 19.95 **NM** value: **Cover or less**
• collects series

CLASSIC STAR WARS: THE EMPIRE STRIKES BACK — Dark Horse

1 ❑ Aug 1994 Cover: 3.95 **NM** value: **Cover or less**
Circ: CapCity orders: **15,750**
• prestige format. **A:** Al Williamson **W:** Archie Goodwin
2 ❑ Sep 1994 Cover: 3.95 **NM** value: **Cover or less**
Circ: CapCity orders: **13,850**
• prestige format. **A:** Al Williamson **W:** Archie Goodwin
Bk 1❑ Nov 1995 Cover: 9.95 **NM** value: **Cover or less**
• collects mini-series

CLASSIC STAR WARS: THE VANDELHELM MISSION — Dark Horse

1 ❑ Mar 1995 Cover: 2.50 **NM** value: **Cover or less**
Circ: CapCity orders: **12,425** Diamd. preorders: **4,891**
A: Al Williamson **W:** Archie Goodwin

CLASSIC TERRY & THE PIRATES — Avalon

1 ❑ Cover: 2.95 **NM** value: **Cover or less**
📖 A Letter from Home **A:** Milton Caniff; Warren Sattler **W:** Milton Caniff
2 ❑ Cover: 2.95 **NM** value: **Cover or less**
A: Milton Caniff **W:** Milton Caniff
3 ❑ Cover: 2.95 **NM** value: **Cover or less**
A: Milton Caniff **W:** Milton Caniff
4 ❑ Cover: 2.95 **NM** value: **Cover or less**
A: Milton Caniff **W:** Milton Caniff
5 ❑ Cover: 2.95 **NM** value: **Cover or less**
A: Milton Caniff **W:** Milton Caniff

CLASSIC X-MEN — Marvel

It may seem incomprehensible today, but in the early 1970s, the X-Men were a moribund group, never really scoring with readers. The introduction of a new, more exciting team of X-Men changed all that. By 1986, it was clear that the new X-Men were a major hit, if not yet the phenomenon they were by the 1990s. As such, Marvel decided the time was right to begin reprinting their adventures-sometimes in slightly modified form-beginning from their early adventures in Giant-Size X-Men #1.

This series was one of the most popular reprint titles, starting in 1986, and running for forty-five issues before changing names to X-Men Classic, and continuing until 1995. In addition to the reprints, Classic X-Men also includes new backup stories by Chris CLaremont and John Bolton, filling in the blanks in the continuity. These are, often enough, worth the price of admission.

1 ❑ Sep 1986 Cover: 1.00 **NM** value: **6.00**
Circ: CapCity orders: **58,100** • **CGC:** 4 graded, best 9.6
C: Arthur Adams
2 ❑ Oct 1986 Cover: 1.00 **NM** value: **3.50**
Circ: CapCity orders: **47,700** • **CGC:** 1 graded, best 9.2
📖 The Doomsmith Scenario!; First Friends • Reprints X-Men (1st Series) #94 **A:** John Bolton; Dave Cockrum **C:** Arthur Adams **W:** Len Wein; Chris Claremont
3 ❑ Nov 1986 Cover: 1.00 **NM** value: **3.00**
Circ: CapCity orders: **48,600**
C: Arthur Adams
4 ❑ Dec 1986 Cover: 1.00 **NM** value: **3.00**
Circ: CapCity orders: **43,800**
C: Arthur Adams
5 ❑ Jan 1987 Cover: 1.00 **NM** value: **3.00**
Circ: CapCity orders: **37,800**
C: Arthur Adams
6 ❑ Feb 1987 Cover: 1.00 **NM** value: **2.50**
Circ: CapCity orders: **36,000**
C: Arthur Adams
7 ❑ Mar 1987 Cover: 1.00 **NM** value: **2.50**
Circ: CapCity orders: **34,600**
C: Arthur Adams
8 ❑ Apr 1987 Cover: 1.00 **NM** value: **2.50**
Circ: CapCity orders: **34,200**
C: Arthur Adams
9 ❑ May 1987 Cover: 1.00 **NM** value: **2.50**
Circ: CapCity orders: **31,600**
C: Arthur Adams
10 ❑ Jun 1987 Cover: 1.00 **NM** value: **2.50**
Circ: CapCity orders: **30,800**
C: Arthur Adams
11 ❑ Jul 1987 Cover: 1.00 **NM** value: **2.50**
Circ: CapCity orders: **29,800**
12 ❑ Aug 1987 Cover: 1.00 **NM** value: **2.50**
Circ: CapCity orders: **30,500**
C: Arthur Adams
13 ❑ Sep 1987 Cover: 1.00 **NM** value: **2.50**
Circ: CapCity orders: **32,800**
C: Arthur Adams
14 ❑ Oct 1987 Cover: 1.00 **NM** value: **2.50**
Circ: CapCity orders: **33,100**
C: Arthur Adams
15 ❑ Nov 1987 Cover: 1.00 **NM** value: **2.50**
Circ: CapCity orders: **32,300**
C: Arthur Adams
16 ❑ Dec 1987 Cover: 1.00 **NM** value: **2.50**
Circ: CapCity orders: **30,600**
C: Arthur Adams
17 ❑ Jan 1988 Cover: 1.00 **NM** value: **2.50**
Circ: CapCity orders: **30,500**
18 ❑ Feb 1988 Cover: 1.00 **NM** value: **2.50**
Circ: CapCity orders: **31,500**
C: Arthur Adams
19 ❑ Mar 1988 Cover: 1.00 **NM** value: **2.50**
Circ: CapCity orders: **31,100**
C: Arthur Adams
20 ❑ Apr 1988 Cover: 1.00 **NM** value: **2.50**
Circ: CapCity orders: **32,100**
C: Arthur Adams
21 ❑ May 1988 Cover: 1.00 **NM** value: **2.50**
Circ: CapCity orders: **30,200**
C: Arthur Adams
22 ❑ Jun 1988 Cover: 1.00 **NM** value: **2.50**
Circ: CapCity orders: **28,900**
A: Frank Miller **C:** Arthur Adams
23 ❑ Jul 1988 Cover: 1.00 **NM** value: **2.50**
Circ: CapCity orders: **29,600**
C: Arthur Adams
24 ❑ Aug 1988 Cover: 1.00 **NM** value: **2.50**
Circ: CapCity orders: **29,200**
25 ❑ Sep 1988 Cover: 1.00 **NM** value: **2.50**
Circ: CapCity orders: **28,700**
26 ❑ Oct 1988 Cover: 1.25 **NM** value: **2.50**
Circ: CapCity orders: **29,400**
27 ❑ Nov 1988 Cover: 1.25 **NM** value: **2.50**
Circ: CapCity orders: **29,000**
28 ❑ Dec 1988 Cover: 1.25 **NM** value: **2.50**
Circ: CapCity orders: **28,700**
29 ❑ Jan 1989 Cover: 1.25 **NM** value: **2.50**
Circ: Statement: **181,090** CapCity orders: **28,800**
30 ❑ Feb 1989 Cover: 1.25 **NM** value: **2.00**
Circ: Statement: **181,090** CapCity orders: **27,600**
31 ❑ Mar 1989 Cover: 1.25 **NM** value: **2.00**
Circ: Statement: **181,090** CapCity orders: **27,800**
📖 There's Something Awful on Muir Island; Spigot at the End of the Universe • Reprints X-Men (1st Series) #125 **A:** John Bolton; John Byrne **W:** Ann Nocenti; Chris Claremont
32 ❑ Apr 1989 Cover: 1.25 **NM** value: **2.00**
Circ: Statement: **181,090** CapCity orders: **27,100**
33 ❑ May 1989 Cover: 1.25 **NM** value: **2.00**
Circ: Statement: **181,090** CapCity orders: **26,800**
34 ❑ Jun 1989 Cover: 1.25 **NM** value: **2.00**
Circ: Statement: **181,090** CapCity orders: **26,400**
35 ❑ Jul 1989 Cover: 1.25 **NM** value: **2.00**
Circ: Statement: **181,090** CapCity orders: **26,900**
36 ❑ Aug 1989 Cover: 1.25 **NM** value: **2.00**
Circ: Statement: **181,090** CapCity orders: **27,500**
37 ❑ Sep 1989 Cover: 1.25 **NM** value: **2.00**
Circ: Statement: **181,090** CapCity orders: **27,000**
38 ❑ Oct 1989 Cover: 1.25 **NM** value: **2.00**
Circ: Statement: **181,090** CapCity orders: **27,800**
39 ❑ Nov 1989 Cover: 1.25 **NM** value: **2.00**
Circ: Statement: **181,090** CapCity orders: **28,000**
40 ❑ Nov 1989 Cover: 1.25 **NM** value: **2.00**
Circ: Statement: **181,090** CapCity orders: **28,100**
41 ❑ Dec 1989 Cover: 1.25 **NM** value: **2.00**
Circ: Statement: **181,090** CapCity orders: **26,700**
42 ❑ Dec 1989 Cover: 1.25 **NM** value: **2.00**
Circ: Statement: **181,090** CapCity orders: **26,400**
43 ❑ Jan 1990 Cover: 1.75 **NM** value: **2.00**
Circ: Statement: **157,274** CapCity orders: **28,100**
44 ❑ Feb 1990 Cover: 1.25 **NM** value: **2.00**
Circ: Statement: **157,274** CapCity orders: **25,900**
45 ❑ Mar 1990 Cover: 1.25 **NM** value: **2.00**
Circ: Statement: **157,274** CapCity orders: **25,500**
• Series continues as X-Men Classic;Series continued in X-Men Classic #46

CLAUS — Draco

1 ❑ Dec 1997 Cover: 2.95 **NM** value: **Cover or less**

Other grades: Multiply prices above by **1.5 for Mint • 2/3 for Very Fine • 1/3 for Fine • 1/5 for Very Good • 1/8 for Good**

CLAWS — Conquest
1 ❑ b&w Cover: 2.95 **NM** value: **Cover or less**

CLAW THE UNCONQUERED — DC
1 ❑ Jun 1975 Cover: 0.25 **NM** value: **2.00**
• **CGC:** 8 graded, best 9.6
🕮 The Sword And The silent Scream **A:** Ernie Chua **W:** David Michelinie ★ 1st Appearance of Claw the Unconquered.
2 ❑ Aug 1975 Cover: 0.25 **NM** value: **1.50**
3 ❑ Oct 1975 Cover: 0.25 **NM** value: **1.25**
4 ❑ Dec 1975 Cover: 0.25 **NM** value: **1.00**
5 ❑ Feb 1976 Cover: 0.25 **NM** value: **1.00**
6 ❑ Apr 1976 Cover: 0.25 **NM** value: **1.00**
7 ❑ Jun 1976 Cover: 0.30 **NM** value: **1.00**
8 ❑ Aug 1976 Cover: 0.30 **NM** value: **1.00**
• Bicentennial #18
9 ❑ Oct 1976 Cover: 0.30 **NM** value: **1.00**
★ Origin of Claw the Unconquered.
10 ❑ May 1978 Cover: 0.35 **NM** value: **1.00**
11 ❑ Jul 1978 Cover: 0.35 **NM** value: **1.00**
12 ❑ Sep 1978 Cover: 0.35 **NM** value: **1.00**
final issue.

CLEM: MALL SECURITY — Spit Take
0 ❑ b&w Cover: 2.00 **NM** value: **Cover or less**

CLEOPATRA — Rip Off
All issues are adults only.
1 ❑ Feb 1992, b&w Cover: 2.50 **NM** value: **Cover or less**
No issue number.

CLERKS: THE COMIC BOOK — Oni
Independent filmmaker and comic book fan Kevin Smith got a lot of buzz going with the release of Clerks. This film was an irreverent look at the so-called lives of a pair of clerks at a convenience store and the adjoining video rental outlet. The dull, mind-numbing work is punctuated by customers who range from creepy to partially insane. For laughs, video store clerk Randall delights in making up ways to torture the customers, such as ignoring the posted store hours or making customers battle for the last copy of The Mighty Ducks.

Clerks: The Comic Book, is a continuation of the movie. Here, Randall convinces his fellow clerk, Dante, to join with him in trying to corner the market on Star Wars toys. It's rude, full of in-jokes, and all the funnier for the way it nails the fanboyish craziness surrounding the comic and toy markets.

1 ❑ Feb 1998 Cover: 2.95 **NM** value: **8.00**
Circ: Diamd. preorders: **15,949** • **CGC:** 2 graded, best 9.8
A: Jim Mahfood **W:** Kevin Smith
1-2 ❑ Cover: 2.95 **NM** value: **Cover or less**
1-3 ❑ Cover: 2.95 **NM** value: **Cover or less**
1-4 ❑ May 1998 Cover: 2.95 **NM** value: **Cover or less**
2 ❑ Cover: 2.95 **NM** value: **Cover or less**
HS 1❑ Dec 1998, b&w Cover: 2.95 **NM** value: **3.50**
Circ: Diamd. preorders: **41,036** • **CGC:** 3 graded, best 9.8
• Double-size. **A:** Jim Mahfood **C:** Arthur Adams **W:** Kevin Smith

CLIFFHANGER! — Image
1 ❑ ca. 1997 **NM** value: **3.00**

CLIFFHANGER COMICS — AC
1 ❑ b&w Cover: 2.50 **NM** value: **Cover or less**
2 ❑ b&w Cover: 2.50 **NM** value: **Cover or less**

CLIFFHANGER COMICS (2ND SERIES) — AC
1 ❑ b&w Cover: 2.75 **NM** value: **Cover or less**
• new and reprint
2 ❑ Aug 1990, b&w Cover: 2.75 **NM** value: **Cover or less**
• new and reprint

CLIMAX — Gillmor
1 ❑ Jul 1955 Cover: 0.10 **NM** value: **80.00**
2 ❑ Sep 1955 Cover: 0.10 **NM** value: **60.00**
🕮 The Painter!; The Witness!; Double Car Crosser (text story); Cold Cash!; The Treasure; Penalty! **A:** Sal Trapani **W:** Sal Trapani

CLIMAXXX — Aircel
All issues are adults only.
1 ❑ Apr 1991, full color Cover: 3.50 **NM** value: **Cover or less**
Circ: CapCity orders: **3,410**
2 ❑ May 1991, full color Cover: 3.50 **NM** value: **Cover or less**
Circ: CapCity orders: **2,280**
3 ❑ Jun 1991, full color Cover: 3.50 **NM** value: **Cover or less**
Circ: CapCity orders: **2,120**
4 ❑ Jul 1991, full color Cover: 3.50 **NM** value: **Cover or less**

CLINT — Trigon
1 ❑ Sep 1986 Cover: 2.50 **NM** value: **Cover or less**
🕮 Baby the Reign Must Fall **A:** Ken Meyer **W:** Donald Chin
2 ❑ Jan 1987 Cover: 2.50 **NM** value: **Cover or less**
🕮 Magnun Force **A:** Ken Meyer **W:** Donald Chin

CLINT: THE HAMSTER TRIUMPHANT — Eclipse
1 ❑ b&w Cover: 1.50 **NM** value: **Cover or less**
2 ❑ b&w Cover: 1.50 **NM** value: **Cover or less**

CLIVE BARKER, ILLUSTRATOR — Eclipse
Bk 1❑ Cover: 19.95 **NM** value: **Cover or less**
A: Pat Broderick
Bk 1/HC❑ Cover: 39.95 **NM** value: **Cover or less**
hardcover.

CLOAK & DAGGER — Marvel
Continued from the Cloak & Dagger limited series, this title follows the two hapless teenagers-turned-mutant-super-heroes from Spectacular Spider-Man #64 on their continuing quest for justice.

Having realized that they had fallen to the criminals' level, by acting as judge, jury, and executioner, they now seek mainly to save addicts from their addictions. They save the full power of their power for those who deal the drugs and prey on children.

Dark and occasionally compelling, Cloak & Dagger spins a tale of innocence lost on the mean streets of New York City. While Cloak and Dagger are heroes, they are also tragic as they fight their unwinnable war.

1 ❑ Jul 1985 Cover: 0.65 **NM** value: **2.00**
Circ: CapCity orders: **41,300**
A: Tony DeZuniga
2 ❑ Sep 1985 Cover: 0.65 **NM** value: **1.50**
Circ: CapCity orders: **33,700**
🕮 Standing In The Shadows **A:** Rick Leonardi; Tony DeZuniga **W:** Bill Mantlo
3 ❑ Nov 1985 Cover: 0.65 **NM** value: **1.50**
Circ: CapCity orders: **27,800**
A: Tony DeZuniga ★ Appearance of Spider-Man.
4 ❑ Jan 1986 Cover: 0.65 **NM** value: **1.50**
Circ: CapCity orders: **28,300**
• Secret Wars II **A:** Todd Dezuniga
5 ❑ Mar 1985 Cover: 0.75 **NM** value: **1.25**
Circ: CapCity orders: **22,900**
A: Tony DeZuniga ★ Origin of Mayhem. ★ 1st Appearance of Mayhem.
6 ❑ May 1985 Cover: 0.75 **NM** value: **1.25**
Circ: CapCity orders: **21,000**
A: Tony DeZuniga
7 ❑ Jul 1985 Cover: 0.75 **NM** value: **1.25**
Circ: CapCity orders: **19,100**
A: Tony DeZuniga
8 ❑ Sep 1985 Cover: 0.75 **NM** value: **1.25**
Circ: CapCity orders: **17,300**
A: Tony DeZuniga
9 ❑ Nov 1985 Cover: 0.75 **NM** value: **1.25**
Circ: CapCity orders: **21,400**
A: Arthur Adams; Tony DeZuniga
10 ❑ Jan 1986 Cover: 0.75 **NM** value: **1.25**
Circ: CapCity orders: **16,300**
A: Tony DeZuniga
11 ❑ Mar 1986 Cover: 1.25 **NM** value: **1.50**
Circ: CapCity orders: **15,700**
• Giant-size. final issue. **A:** Tony DeZuniga

CLOAK AND DAGGER IN PREDATOR AND PREY — Marvel
1 ❑ Cover: 5.95 **NM** value: **Cover or less**
No issue number. One-shot. • prestige format.

CLOAK & DAGGER (LTD. SERIES) — Marvel
1 ❑ Oct 1983 Cover: 0.60 **NM** value: **2.95**
• **CGC:** 1 graded, best 9.8
🕮 The Priest **A:** Rick Leonardi; Tony DeZuniga **W:** Bill Mantlo ★ 1st Appearance of Brigid O'Reilly.
2 ❑ Nov 1983 Cover: 0.60 **NM** value: **2.95**
🕮 Bellyful of Blues! **A:** Rick Leonardi; Tony DeZuniga **W:** Bill Mantlo
3 ❑ Dec 1983 Cover: 0.60 **NM** value: **2.00**
🕮 Dark is My Love, and Deadly! **A:** Rick Leonardi; Tony DeZuniga **W:** Bill Mantlo
4 ❑ Jan 1984 Cover: 0.60 **NM** value: **2.00**
🕮 True Confessions **A:** Rick Leonardi; Tony DeZuniga **W:** Bill Mantlo ★ Origin of Cloak & Dagger.

CLOAK AND DAGGER (ZIFF-DAVIS) — Ziff-Davis
1 ❑ ca. 1953 Cover: 0.10 **NM** value: **100.00**
• **CGC:** 1 graded, best 6.5

CLOCK! — Top Shelf
3 ❑ b&w Cover: 2.95 **NM** value: **Cover or less**

CLOCKWORK ANGELS — Image
This black-and-white digest comic book from writer-artist Lea Hernandez is called "Scientific Romance" by acclaimed writer Warren Ellis (StormWatch, Excalibur, The Authority), who also describes its creator as "obviously barking mad" for "producing comics for girls." And he means that in the best possible way.

This sequel to Hernandez' Cathedral Child follows Temperance, a woman who can read the final thoughts of the dead, and her companion Amy, as they become embroiled in a plot involving a murderer and his accomplice in New Orleans in 1897. Will Amy's gentle nature mean the end of the heroines? What miracle is she destined to perform that will outstrip anything Temperance has ever conceived of doing? This second volume of the "Texas Steampunk" saga is must reading.

1 ❑ b&w Cover: 10.95 **NM** value: **Cover or less**
• digest-sized.
Bk 1❑ Cover: 10.95 **NM** value: **Cover or less**
A: Lea Hernandez **W:** Warren Ellis; Lea Hernandez

CLONEZONE SPECIAL — Dark Horse
1 ❑ b&w Cover: 2.00 **NM** value: **Cover or less**
🕮 The Zone: Shakedown **A:** Neil Vokes **W:** Mike Baron

CLOVER HONEY — Fantagraphics
Bk 1❑ Dec 1995, b&w Cover: 12.95 **NM** value: **Cover or less**
No issue number. • Trade Paperback.

CLOWN: NOBODY'S LAUGHING NOW, THE — Fleetway-Quality
1 ❑ Cover: 4.95 **NM** value: **Cover or less**
No issue number.

CLOWNS — Yahoo Pro / Quality
1 ❑ Cover: 0.50 **NM** value: **3.00**
🕮 Simon the Pieman; Clowns; Armin Kill-a-Brew **A:** Dave Geiser **W:** Dave Geiser

CLOWNS, THE — Dark Horse
1 ❑ Apr 1998, b&w Cover: 2.95 **NM** value: **Cover or less**
Circ: Diamd. preorders: **7,099**
No issue number. 🕮 Pagliacci • adapts Leoncavallo opera **A:** P. Craig Russell; Galen Showman **W:** P. Craig Russell

CLUE COMICS — Hillman
1 ❑ Jan 1943 Cover: 0.10 **NM** value: **750.00**
• **CGC:** 1 graded, best 9.0
2 ❑ Feb 1943 Cover: 0.10 **NM** value: **300.00**
• **CGC:** 1 graded, best 9.8
3 ❑ Mar 1943 Cover: 0.10 **NM** value: **300.00**
• **CGC:** 1 graded, best 9.6
4 ❑ Jun 1943 Cover: 0.10 **NM** value: **250.00**
5 ❑ Sep 1943 Cover: 0.10 **NM** value: **250.00**
• **CGC:** 2 graded, best 9.4
6 ❑ Dec 1943 Cover: 0.10 **NM** value: **250.00**
• **CGC:** 2 graded, best 9.2
7 ❑ Mar 1944 Cover: 0.10 **NM** value: **200.00**
• **CGC:** 1 graded, best 9.0
8 ❑ Fal 1944 Cover: 0.10 **NM** value: **200.00**
• **CGC:** 3 graded, best 9.6
9 ❑ Win 1944 Cover: 0.10 **NM** value: **200.00**
• **CGC:** 1 graded, best 7.0
10 ❑ Oct 1946 Cover: 0.10 **NM** value: **175.00**
• **CGC:** 2 graded, best 9.6
11 ❑ Dec 1946 Cover: 0.10 **NM** value: **175.00**
12 ❑ Feb 1947 Cover: 0.10 **NM** value: **175.00**
13 ❑ Mar 1947 Cover: 0.10 **NM** value: **150.00**
🕮 king of the Bank Robbers
14 ❑ Apr 1947 Cover: 0.10 **NM** value: **150.00**
• **CGC:** 1 graded, best 8.0
🕮 A Clue for You; On Stage for Murder; The Short, Dangerous Life of Packy Smith • Detective Powell; Gun Master
15 ❑ May 1947 Cover: 0.10 **NM** value: **150.00**
🕮 The Battle for Packy Smith; Flowers for Roma; The Case of the Superstitious Slayers • Gun Master

CLUTCHING HAND — ACG
1 ❑ Jul 1954 **NM** value: **275.00**
• **CGC:** 1 graded, best 8.0

CLYDE CRASHCUP — Dell
1 ❑ Aug 1963 Cover: 0.12 **NM** value: **125.00**
• **CGC:** 2 graded, best 9.0
2 ❑ 1963 Cover: 0.12 **NM** value: **100.00**
3 ❑ May 1964 Cover: 0.12 **NM** value: **100.00**
• **CGC:** 1 graded, best 9.2
4 ❑ Jun 1964 Cover: 0.12 **NM** value: **100.00**
• **CGC:** 3 graded, best 9.0
5 ❑ Sep 1964 Cover: 0.12 **NM** value: **100.00**

C-M-O COMICS — Chicago Mail Order
1 ❑ ca. 1942 **NM** value: **1000.00**
2 ❑ ca. 1942 **NM** value: **1000.00**
• **CGC:** 2 graded, best 7.5

COBALT 60 — Tundra
1 ❑ Cover: 4.95 **NM** value: **Cover or less**
2 ❑ Cover: 4.95 **NM** value: **Cover or less**

COBALT BLUE — Power
1 ❑ Jan 1978 Cover: 0.50 **NM** value: **2.00**
A: Mike Gustovich

COBALT BLUE (INNOVATION) — Innovation
1 ❑ Sep 1989 Cover: 1.95 **NM** value: **2.00**
Circ: CapCity orders: **3,550**
A: Mike Gustovich
2 ❑ Oct 1989 Cover: 1.95 **NM** value: **2.00**
Circ: CapCity orders: **2,975**
A: Mike Gustovich
GN 1❑ Cover: 5.95 **NM** value: **Cover or less**
• Graphic novel **A:** Keith Pollard

COBRA — Viz
1 ❑ Cover: 2.95 **NM** value: **Cover or less**
A: Buichi Terasawa **W:** Buichi Terasawa
2 ❑ Cover: 2.95 **NM** value: **Cover or less**
A: Buichi Terasawa **W:** Buichi Terasawa
3 ❑ Cover: 2.95 **NM** value: **Cover or less**
A: Buichi Terasawa **W:** Buichi Terasawa
4 ❑ Cover: 2.95 **NM** value: **Cover or less**
A: Buichi Terasawa **W:** Buichi Terasawa
5 ❑ Cover: 2.95 **NM** value: **Cover or less**
A: Buichi Terasawa **W:** Buichi Terasawa

CGC-graded: Multiply prices above by **33 for 9.9 M • 16 for 9.8 NM/M • 7 for 9.6 NM+ • 5 for 9.4 NM • 2.5 for 9.2 NM- • 1.5 for 9.0 VF/NM**

6 ❑ Cover: 2.95 **NM** value: **Cover or less**
A: Buichi Terasawa **W:** Buichi Terasawa
7 ❑ Cover: 3.25 **NM** value: **Cover or less**
A: Buichi Terasawa **W:** Buichi Terasawa
8 ❑ Cover: 3.25 **NM** value: **Cover or less**
A: Buichi Terasawa **W:** Buichi Terasawa
9 ❑ Cover: 3.25 **NM** value: **Cover or less**
A: Buichi Terasawa **W:** Buichi Terasawa
10 ❑ Cover: 3.25 **NM** value: **Cover or less**
A: Buichi Terasawa **W:** Buichi Terasawa
11 ❑ Cover: 3.25 **NM** value: **Cover or less**
A: Buichi Terasawa **W:** Buichi Terasawa
12 ❑ Cover: 3.25 **NM** value: **Cover or less**
A: Buichi Terasawa **W:** Buichi Terasawa

COCOMALT BIG BOOK OF COMICS — Harry A. Chesler

1 ❑ ca. 1938 **NM** value: **1400.00**
• **CGC:** 1 graded, best 7.5

CODA — Coda

1 ❑ Cover: 2.00 **NM** value: **Cover or less**
Circ: CapCity orders: **6,520**
A: Frank Panucci **W:** Frank Panucci
2 ❑ Cover: 2.00 **NM** value: **Cover or less**
A: Frank Panucci **W:** Frank Panucci
3 ❑ Cover: 2.00 **NM** value: **Cover or less**
A: Frank Panucci **W:** Frank Panucci
4 ❑ Cover: 2.00 **NM** value: **Cover or less**
A: Frank Panucci **W:** Frank Panucci

CODE BLUE — Image

1 ❑ Apr 1998 Cover: 2.95 **NM** value: **Cover or less**
Circ: Diamd. preorders: **3,995**
A: Jimmie Robinson **W:** Jimmie Robinson

CODENAME: DANGER — Lodestone

1 ❑ Aug 1985 Cover: 1.50 **NM** value: **2.00**
Circ: CapCity orders: **8,100**
📖 Double Or Nothing **A:** Rich Buckler **W:** Robert Loren Flemming
2 ❑ Oct 1985 Cover: 1.50 **NM** value: **1.75**
Circ: CapCity orders: **5,275**
W: Robert Loren Flemming
3 ❑ Jan 1986 Cover: 1.50 **NM** value: **1.75**
Circ: CapCity orders: **4,875**
📖 I.O.U. **A:** Paul Smith **W:** Robert Loren Flemming
4 ❑ May 1986 Cover: 1.50 **NM** value: **1.75**
Circ: CapCity orders: **4,550**

CODENAME: FIREARM — Malibu

Written by James Robinson, Firearm was one of the best of Malibu's Ultraverse titles in the initial run. In late 1995, Malibu relaunched its universe, eventually reincarnating Firearm in this new "Codename: Firearm" series.

Alec Swann, the original Firearm, appears in issues #0-2 as part of a backup story, but, otherwise, the series is devoted to the adventures of Jimmy Hitch. Jimmy is a covert agent and sniper working in the service of the Lodge, just one of those average, everyday secret organizations.

0 ❑ ca. 1995 Cover: 2.95 **NM** value: **Cover or less**
Circ: CapCity orders: **4,900**
📖 Idle Thoughts, Part 1 **A:** Gary Erskine **W:** James Robinson
1 ❑ ca. 1995 Cover: 2.95 **NM** value: **Cover or less**
Circ: CapCity orders: **4,850**
📖 The Adversary; Idle Thoughts, Part 2 **A:** Gary Erskine; Gabriel Gecko **W:** James Robinson; David Quinn
2 ❑ ca. 1995 Cover: 2.95 **NM** value: **Cover or less**
📖 Idle Thoughts, Part 3 **A:** Gary Erskine **W:** James Robinson
3 ❑ ca. 1995 Cover: 2.95 **NM** value: **Cover or less**
4 ❑ ca. 1995 Cover: 2.95 **NM** value: **Cover or less**
5 ❑ ca. 1995 Cover: 2.95 **NM** value: **Cover or less**

CODENAME: GENETIX — Marvel

1 ❑ Feb 1993 Cover: 1.75 **NM** value: **Cover or less**
Circ: CapCity orders: **22,200**
📖 Nature Of The Beast, Part 1 **A:** Phil Gascoine **W:** Andy Lanning; Graham Marks ★ 1st Appearance of Genetix.
2 ❑ Mar 1993 Cover: 1.75 **NM** value: **Cover or less**
📖 Nature Of The Beast, Part 2 **A:** Phil Gascoine **W:** Andy Lanning; Graham Marks ★ Appearance of Wolverine.
3 ❑ Apr 1993 Cover: 1.75 **NM** value: **Cover or less**
📖 Nature Of The Beast, Part 3 **A:** Phil Gascoine **W:** Andy Lanning; Graham Marks ★ Appearance of Wolverine.
4 ❑ May 1993 Cover: 1.75 **NM** value: **Cover or less**
📖 Nature Of The Beast, Part 4 **A:** Phil Gascoine **W:** Andy Lanning; Graham Marks

CODE NAME NINJA — Solson

1 ❑ b&w Cover: 2.00 **NM** value: **Cover or less**
📖 Silent Steps of the Ninja **A:** Enie Guanlao; Mike Shaw **W:** Monroe Arnold

CODENAME: SCORPIO — Antarctic

1 ❑ Oct 1996, b&w Cover: 2.95 **NM** value: **Cover or less**
Circ: Diamd. preorders: **5,783**
A: Esad T. Rubic **W:** Miljenko Horvatic
2 ❑ Apr 1997, b&w Cover: 2.95 **NM** value: **Cover or less**
A: Esad T. Rubic **W:** Miljenko Horvatic
3 ❑ Jul 1997, b&w Cover: 2.95 **NM** value: **Cover or less**
Circ: Diamd. preorders: **1,664**
A: Esad T. Rubic **W:** Miljenko Horvatic
4 ❑ Sep 1997, b&w Cover: 2.95 **NM** value: **Cover or less**
A: Esad T. Rubic **W:** Miljenko Horvatic

CODENAME: SPITFIRE — Marvel

10 ❑ Jul 1987 Cover: 0.75 **NM** value: **1.00**
• Series continued from Spitfire and the Troubleshooters #9
11 ❑ Aug 1987 Cover: 0.75 **NM** value: **1.00**
12 ❑ Sep 1987 Cover: 0.75 **NM** value: **1.00**
13 ❑ Oct 1987 Cover: 0.75 **NM** value: **1.00**

CODENAME: STRIKEFORCE — Spectrum

1 ❑ Jun 1984 Cover: 1.00 **NM** value: **1.50**
📖 Strikeforce! **A:** Tom Morgan **W:** Fred Schiller

CODENAME: STRYKE FORCE — Image

0 ❑ Jun 1995 Cover: 2.50 **NM** value: **Cover or less**
Circ: CapCity orders: **18,525**
indicia says Jun, cover says Jul. **A:** Anthony Winn **W:** Mike Heisler
1 ❑ Jan 1994 Cover: 2.95 **NM** value: **Cover or less**
Circ: CapCity orders: **65,075**
A: Brandon Peterson **W:** Marc Silvestri
1/GO ❑ Jan 1994 Cover: 2.95 **NM** value: **4.00**
• **CGC:** 2 graded, best 9.8
• Gold promotional edition. **A:** Brandon Peterson **W:** Marc Silvestri
1/SC ❑ Jan 1994 Cover: 2.95 **NM** value: **4.00**
• blue embossed edition.
2 ❑ Mar 1994 Cover: 1.95 **NM** value: **Cover or less**
Circ: CapCity orders: **41,075**
3 ❑ Apr 1994 Cover: 1.95 **NM** value: **Cover or less**
Circ: CapCity orders: **34,550**
4 ❑ Jun 1994 Cover: 1.95 **NM** value: **Cover or less**
Circ: CapCity orders: **32,900**
5 ❑ Jul 1994 Cover: 1.95 **NM** value: **Cover or less**
6 ❑ Aug 1994 Cover: 1.95 **NM** value: **Cover or less**
Circ: CapCity orders: **30,750**
7 ❑ Oct 1994 Cover: 1.95 **NM** value: **Cover or less**
Circ: CapCity orders: **24,800**
8/A ❑ Nov 1994 Cover: 1.95 **NM** value: **Cover or less**
same cover. • different poster
8/B ❑ Nov 1994 Cover: 1.95 **NM** value: **Cover or less**
same cover. • different poster
8/C ❑ Nov 1994 Cover: 1.95 **NM** value: **Cover or less**
same cover. • different poster
9 ❑ Dec 1994 Cover: 1.95 **NM** value: **Cover or less**
Circ: CapCity orders: **22,725**
10 ❑ Jan 1995 Cover: 1.95 **NM** value: **Cover or less**
Circ: CapCity orders: **20,775**
11 ❑ Mar 1995 Cover: 1.95 **NM** value: **Cover or less**
Circ: CapCity orders: **17,375**
12 ❑ Apr 1995 Cover: 1.95 **NM** value: **Cover or less**
Circ: CapCity orders: **16,925**
13 ❑ May 1995 Cover: 2.25 **NM** value: **Cover or less**
Circ: CapCity orders: **16,450**
14 ❑ Aug 1995 Cover: 2.25 **NM** value: **Cover or less**
Circ: CapCity orders: **16,700**
Bk 1 ❑ Apr 1995 Cover: 9.95 **NM** value: **Cover or less**
• collects #1-3

CODE OF HONOR — Marvel

Code of Honor may be the most faithful descendent of the blockbuster hit Marvels. Like that series, Code of Honor takes a "man in the street" look at a world filled with super-heroes and features beautifully painted art throughout. Earlier follow-ups seemed more like attempts to cash in with high-priced special editions than efforts at serious storytelling.

Thanks to the efforts of veteran writer Chuck Dixon, Code of Honor is a pleasant return to form. It focuses on more recent events in the Marvel universe, as seen through the eyes of New York's police force. Reading more like a cop drama with super-heroes in the background, it brings pathos and humanity to a genre that often seems to consist of little more than people in colorful costumes flying around and hitting each other.

1 ❑ Jan 1997 Cover: 5.95 **NM** value: **Cover or less**
Circ: Direct Market orders: **47,625**
A: Brad Parker; Tristan Shane **W:** Chuck Dixon
2 ❑ Mar 1997 Cover: 5.95 **NM** value: **Cover or less**
Circ: Direct Market orders: **38,000**
📖 Verdicts **A:** Vince Evans; Terese Nielsen **W:** Chuck Dixon
3 ❑ Apr 1997 Cover: 5.95 **NM** value: **Cover or less**
Circ: Direct Market orders: **37,000**
📖 The Street **A:** Paul Lee; Daerick Gröss Jr.; Bob Wakelin **W:** Chuck Dixon
4 ❑ May 1997 Cover: 5.95 **NM** value: **Cover or less**
Circ: Diamd. preorders: **33,904**
📖 Sirens **A:** Brad Parker **W:** Chuck Dixon

CODE XIII — Comcat

1 ❑ Cover: 6.95 **NM** value: **Cover or less**
📖 The Day of the Black Sun
2 ❑ Cover: 6.95 **NM** value: **Cover or less**
📖 Where the Indian Walks
3 ❑ Cover: 6.95 **NM** value: **Cover or less**
📖 The Tears of Hell
4 ❑ Cover: 6.95 **NM** value: **Cover or less**
📖 S.P.A.D.S.
5 ❑ Cover: 6.95 **NM** value: **Cover or less**
📖 Total Red

CODY OF THE PONY EXPRESS — Charlton

8 ❑ Nov 1955 Cover: 0.10 **NM** value: **35.00**
• continues from Bulls-Eye (Charlton) #7
9 ❑ Feb 1956 Cover: 0.10 **NM** value: **25.00**
10 ❑ Jul 1956 Cover: 0.10 **NM** value: **25.00**

CODY STARBUCK — Star*Reach

1 ❑ Cover: 2.00 **NM** value: **Cover or less**
A: Howard Chaykin

CO-ED SEXXTASY — Eros

1 ❑ Dec 1999 Cover: 3.50 **NM** value: **Cover or less**
Circ: Diamd. preorders: **3,333**
A: Makota Fujisaki **W:** Makota Fujisaki
2 ❑ Jan 2000 Cover: 3.50 **NM** value: **Cover or less**
Circ: Diamd. preorders: **3,206**
A: Makota Fujisaki **W:** Makota Fujisaki
3 ❑ Feb 2000 Cover: 3.50 **NM** value: **Cover or less**
Circ: Diamd. preorders: **3,033**
A: Makota Fujisaki **W:** Makota Fujisaki
4 ❑ Mar 2000 Cover: 3.95 **NM** value: **Cover or less**
Circ: Diamd. preorders: **3,159**
A: Makota Fujisaki **W:** Makota Fujisaki
5 ❑ Apr 2000 Cover: 3.50 **NM** value: **Cover or less**
Circ: Diamd. preorders: **3,202**
A: Makota Fujisaki **W:** Makota Fujisaki
6 ❑ May 2000 Cover: 3.50 **NM** value: **Cover or less**
Circ: Diamd. preorders: **3,405**
A: Makota Fujisaki **W:** Makota Fujisaki
7 ❑ Jun 2000 Cover: 3.50 **NM** value: **Cover or less**
Circ: Diamd. preorders: **3,406**
A: Makota Fujisaki **W:** Makota Fujisaki
8 ❑ Jul 2000 Cover: 3.95 **NM** value: **Cover or less**
Circ: Diamd. preorders: **3,323**
A: Makota Fujisaki **W:** Makota Fujisaki
9 ❑ Aug 2000 Cover: 3.50 **NM** value: **Cover or less**
Circ: Diamd. preorders: **3,141**
A: Makota Fujisaki **W:** Makota Fujisaki
10 ❑ Sep 2000 Cover: 3.50 **NM** value: **Cover or less**
Circ: Diamd. preorders: **3,251**
A: Makota Fujisaki **W:** Makota Fujisaki
11 ❑ Oct 2000 Cover: 3.50 **NM** value: **Cover or less**
Circ: Diamd. preorders: **3,120**
📖 The Travails of Miss Yukiko Kurisono **A:** Makota Fujisaki **W:** Makota Fujisaki

COFFEE WORLD — World

1 ❑ Cover: 1.50 **NM** value: **Cover or less**
📖 Cup 'a Joe; Too Much Coffee Man; A Saving Grace; Nine One One; My Cuppeth Runneth Overeth; The Alan Bland Story **A:** Scott Saavedra; Shannon Wheeler; Gheena; Ian Smith; Rick Pinchera; Stan Shaw; Tom Buss; Tyson Smith **W:** Scott Saavedra; Shannon Wheeler; Gheena; Ian Smith; Rick Pinchera; Stan Shaw; Tom Buss; Tyson Smith

COFFIN, THE — Oni

Who says super-heroes are the living embodiment of good? Who says they're even living to begin with? Sure, comics have had their share of inanimate characters (The Vision, The Red Tornado, Machine Man, et al.), but none compare to Phil Hester and Mike Huddleston's title creation The Coffin. The black-and-white, four-issue limited series of the same name manages to balance carefully between the super-hero, science-fiction, and horror genres, all the while telling a classic tale of heroism and redemption.

Dr. Ashar Ahmed is a scientist driven by his work. Obsessed with conquering death, the researcher has developed an impermeable polymer — one that can capture and encase an ascending soul. To that end, the entity trapped inside lives an eternal life in a mechanical body. But, when the man funding these experiments has Ahmed murdered — confiscating the research for his own evil uses — the doctor traps his soul in a human-shaped suit (nicknamed "the coffin"). With a new lease on "life," Ahmed looks to undo the damage created by his once-selfish existence. But his murderous financier and Hell itself have different plans for the doctor.

1 ❑ Sep 2000, b&w Cover: 2.95 **NM** value: **Cover or less**
Circ: Diamd. preorders: **4,071**
A: Mike Huddleston **W:** Phil Hester

COFFIN BLOOD — Monster

1 ❑ b&w Cover: 3.95 **NM** value: **Cover or less**

COLD BLOODED — Northstar

1 ❑ b&w Cover: 2.95 **NM** value: **Cover or less**
A: Kyle Holtz **W:** Rafael Nieves

COLD-BLOODED CHAMELEON COMMANDOS — Blackthorne

1 ❑ Cover: 1.75 **NM** value: **Cover or less**
A: Michael Kelley; William Clausen **W:** Michael Kelley; William Clausen ★ Origin of The Cold-Blooded Chameleon Commandos. ★ 1st Appearance of The Cold-Blooded Chameleon Commandos.
2 ❑ Cover: 1.75 **NM** value: **Cover or less**
A: Michael Kelley; William Clausen **W:** Michael Kelley; William Clausen

Other grades: Multiply prices above by **1.5 for Mint • 2/3 for Very Fine • 1/3 for Fine • 1/5 for Very Good • 1/8 for Good**

3 ☐ Cover: 1.75 **NM value: Cover or less**
A: Michael Kelley; William Clausen **W:** Michael Kelley; William Clausen

4 ☐ Cover: 1.75 **NM value: Cover or less**
A: Michael Kelley; William Clausen **W:** Michael Kelley; William Clausen

5 ☐ Cover: 1.75 **NM value: Cover or less**
A: Michael Kelley; William Clausen **W:** Michael Kelley; William Clausen

COLD BLOODED: THE BURNING KISS — Northstar

1 ☐ Nov 1993 Cover: 4.95 **NM value: Cover or less**
cardstock cover.

COLD EDEN — Legacy

4 ☐ Nov 1995, b&w Cover: 2.35 **NM value: Cover or less**
cover says Feb 96, indicia says Nov 95.

COLE BLACK — Rocky Hartberg

1 ☐ Cover: 1.50 **NM value: Cover or less**
📖 Just Another Bimbo In A Monkey Suit **A:** Rocky Hartberg **W:** Rocky Hartberg

2 ☐ Cover: 1.50 **NM value: Cover or less**
📖 Days of Wine and Rodents **A:** Rocky Hartberg **W:** Rocky Hartberg

3 ☐ Cover: 1.50 **NM value: Cover or less**
📖 The Big Squeeze **A:** Rocky Hartberg **W:** Rocky Hartberg

4 ☐ Cover: 1.50 **NM value: Cover or less**
📖 Three Clicks of the Heel **A:** Rocky Hartberg **W:** Rocky Hartberg

5 ☐ Cover: 1.50 **NM value: Cover or less**
A: Rocky Hartberg **W:** Rocky Hartberg

COLE BLACK (VOL. 2) — Hartberg

1 ☐ Cover: 1.50 **NM value: Cover or less**
📖 Fallen Star **A:** Rocky Hartberg **W:** Rocky Hartberg

2 ☐ Cover: 1.50 **NM value: Cover or less**
📖 Harem Holiday **A:** Rocky Hartberg **W:** Rocky Hartberg

3 ☐ Cover: 1.50 **NM value: Cover or less**
A: Rocky Hartberg **W:** Rocky Hartberg

COLLECTION — Eternity

1 ☐ Cover: 2.95 **NM value: Cover or less**
A: Kevin Farrell **W:** Kevin Farrell

COLLECTOR'S DRACULA, THE — Millennium

1 ☐ Cover: 3.95 **NM value: Cover or less**
📖 Nosferatu: Plague of Terror; Blood War; Portrait of Dracula; Young Dracula; Vampire Bat; The Last of The Vampires; The Hunt **A:** Rik Levins; John Bolton; Brian Michael Bendis; David Mack; Wendy Snow-Lang; Sean Shaw; Bob Curran; Daerick Gross; Mark Ellis; Bob Lewis **W:** Rik Levins; Wendy Snow-Lang; Mark Ellis; Paul Davis; Bob Lewis; J. Harker

2 ☐ Cover: 3.95 **NM value: Cover or less**

COLLECTORS GUIDE TO THE ULTRAVERSE — Malibu / Ultraverse

1 ☐ Aug 1994 Cover: 0.99 **NM value: 1.00**

COLLIER'S — Fantagraphics

1 ☐ b&w Cover: 2.75 **NM value: Cover or less**
2 ☐ b&w Cover: 3.25 **NM value: Cover or less**

COLONIA — Colonia Press

Young Jack and his two uncles find themselves cast adrift after a mysterious storm sinks their boat off the coast of Massachusetts. They're quite happy when they're rescued, until they realize they have been saved by what appears to be a group of pirates in an ancient galleon. Their escape from the privateers is only the beginning of their adventures, however. While his uncles seem oblivious to the unusual circumstances of their situation, Jack slowly adjusts to the notion that they may have been somehow cast back in time, to the era of Columbus. But after encounters with a talking duck, a strange fish-man, and Spanish Conquistadors with removable heads, Jack soon realizes that time travel is the least of their problems.

Jeff Nicholson provides some interesting fantasy tales here in a series marred only by its irregular schedule of release.

1 ☐ Oct 1998, b&w Cover: 2.95 **NM value: Cover or less**
Circ: Diamd. preorders: **2,119**
A: Jeff Nicholson **W:** Jeff Nicholson

1-2 ☐ b&w Cover: 2.95 **NM value: Cover or less**

2 ☐ b&w Cover: 2.95 **NM value: Cover or less**
A: Jeff Nicholson **W:** Jeff Nicholson

3 ☐ b&w Cover: 2.95 **NM value: Cover or less**
A: Jeff Nicholson **W:** Jeff Nicholson

COLORS IN BLACK — Dark Horse

1 ☐ Mar 1995 Cover: 2.95 **NM value: Cover or less**
Circ: CapCity orders: **3,325**
📖 The Life That Jack Built; The Red Hot Pizza Girl; Passion Play **A:** Christopher Schenck; Scott Tolson **W:** Scott Tolson; Jason R. Lamb

2 ☐ 1995 Cover: 2.95 **NM value: Cover or less**
Circ: CapCity orders: **2,075**

3 ☐ 1995 Cover: 2.95 **NM value: Cover or less**
4 ☐ 1995 Cover: 2.95 **NM value: Cover or less**

COLOSSAL SHOW — Gold Key

1 ☐ Oct 1969 **NM value: 40.00**
• **CGC:** 1 graded, best 8.0

COLOSSUS — Marvel

1 ☐ Oct 1997 Cover: 2.99 **NM value: Cover or less**
Circ: Diamd. preorders: **60,604**
gatefold cover. • gatefold summary. 📖 A Most Dangerous Game
A: Bryan Hitch **W:** Ben Raab

COLOSSUS BATTLEBOOK — Marvel

1 ☐ Cover: 3.99 **NM value: Cover or less**

COLOSSUS COMICS — Sun

1 ☐ Mar 1940 Cover: 0.10 **NM value: 4000.00**
• **CGC:** 1 graded, best 9.4

COLOSSUS: GOD'S COUNTRY — Marvel

1 ☐ Cover: 6.95 **NM value: Cover or less**
Circ: CapCity orders: **10,725**
One-shot. • prestige format.

COLOUR OF MAGIC, THE (TERRY PRATCHETT'S...) — Innovation

1 ☐ Cover: 2.50 **NM value: Cover or less**
Circ: CapCity orders: **2,985**

2 ☐ Cover: 2.50 **NM value: Cover or less**
Circ: CapCity orders: **2,450**

3 ☐ Cover: 2.50 **NM value: Cover or less**
Circ: CapCity orders: **2,885**

4 ☐ Cover: 2.50 **NM value: Cover or less**
Circ: CapCity orders: **2,795**

COLT — Kz Comics

1 ☐ Cover: 0.95 **NM value: 1.25**
2 ☐ Cover: 0.95 **NM value: 1.25**
3 ☐ Cover: 0.95 **NM value: 1.25**
4 ☐ Cover: 0.95 **NM value: 1.25**

COLT .45 — Dell

The Warner Bros. TV series featuring Wayde Preston (1929-1992, whose last role was as "Jack" in the 1991 Captain America film) as Christopher Colt ran from 1957 to 1960. Colt was a government agent working under cover in the West, and the TV show eventually added the character of Christopher's cousin Sam Colt Jr.(Donald May).

The Dell comic-book version ran from 1958 to 1961. Sometimes, plot descriptions appeared on the cover, as with #5: "Chris Colt tries to stop a hate-filled man from starting a war in Cannon Town!" When there are good photo covers, it increases the appeal of this sort of title to TV fans. — Maggie

4 ☐ Feb 1960 Cover: 0.10 **NM value: 35.00**
• **CGC:** 1 graded, best 9.0

5 ☐ May 1960 Cover: 0.10 **NM value: 35.00**
• **CGC:** 1 graded, best 9.2

6 ☐ Aug 1960 Cover: 0.10 **NM value: 30.00**
7 ☐ Nov 1960 Cover: 0.10 **NM value: 20.00**
8 ☐ Feb 1961 Cover: 0.10 **NM value: 20.00**
• **CGC:** 2 graded, best 9.4

9 ☐ May 1961 Cover: 0.10 **NM value: 20.00**

COLT SPECIAL — AC

1 ☐ Aug 1985 Cover: 1.50 **NM value: Cover or less**

COLUMBUS — Dark Horse

1 ☐ b&w Cover: 2.50 **NM value: Cover or less**
A: Jaxon **W:** Starlen Baxter

COLVILLE — King Ink

1 ☐ Sep 1997, b&w Cover: 3.00 **NM value: Cover or less**
No issue number.

COMBAT (ATLAS) — Atlas

1 ☐ Jun 1952 Cover: 0.10 **NM value: 150.00**
• **CGC:** 1 graded, best 5.5

2 ☐ Jul 1952 Cover: 0.10 **NM value: 80.00**
3 ☐ Aug 1952 Cover: 0.10 **NM value: 80.00**
4 ☐ Sep 1952 Cover: 0.10 **NM value: 75.00**
5 ☐ Oct 1952 Cover: 0.10 **NM value: 75.00**
6 ☐ Nov 1952 Cover: 0.10 **NM value: 70.00**
7 ☐ Dec 1952 Cover: 0.10 **NM value: 70.00**
8 ☐ Jan 1953 Cover: 0.10 **NM value: 70.00**
9 ☐ Feb 1953 Cover: 0.10 **NM value: 65.00**
10 ☐ Mar 1953 Cover: 0.10 **NM value: 65.00**
11 ☐ Apr 1953 Cover: 0.10 **NM value: 65.00**

COMBAT CASEY — Sports Action

6 ☐ Jan 1953 Cover: 0.10 **NM value: 40.00**
• **CGC:** 1 graded, best 5.0
• Series continued from War Combat #5

7 ☐ Mar 1953 Cover: 0.10 **NM value: 34.00**
8 ☐ May 1953 Cover: 0.10 **NM value: 26.00**
9 ☐ Jul 1953 Cover: 0.10 **NM value: 26.00**
10 ☐ Sep 1953 Cover: 0.10 **NM value: 26.00**
11 ☐ Nov 1953 Cover: 0.10 **NM value: 20.00**
12 ☐ Dec 1953 Cover: 0.10 **NM value: 20.00**
13 ☐ Jan 1954 Cover: 0.10 **NM value: 20.00**
14 ☐ Feb 1954 Cover: 0.10 **NM value: 20.00**
15 ☐ Apr 1954 Cover: 0.10 **NM value: 20.00**
16 ☐ Jun 1954 Cover: 0.10 **NM value: 20.00**
17 ☐ Aug 1954 Cover: 0.10 **NM value: 20.00**
18 ☐ Oct 1954 Cover: 0.10 **NM value: 20.00**
19 ☐ Dec 1954 Cover: 0.10 **NM value: 20.00**
20 ☐ Feb 1955 Cover: 0.10 **NM value: 20.00**
21 ☐ Apr 1955 Cover: 0.10 **NM value: 20.00**
📖 The Tanks are Coming!; Basic Training! **A:** Robert Q. Sale

22 ☐ Jun 1955 Cover: 0.10 **NM value: 20.00**
23 ☐ Aug 1955 Cover: 0.10 **NM value: 20.00**
24 ☐ Oct 1955 Cover: 0.10 **NM value: 20.00**
25 ☐ Dec 1955 Cover: 0.10 **NM value: 20.00**
26 ☐ Feb 1956 Cover: 0.10 **NM value: 20.00**
27 ☐ Apr 1956 Cover: 0.10 **NM value: 20.00**
28 ☐ Jun 1956 Cover: 0.10 **NM value: 20.00**
29 ☐ Aug 1956 Cover: 0.10 **NM value: 20.00**
30 ☐ Oct 1956 Cover: 0.10 **NM value: 20.00**
31 ☐ Dec 1956 Cover: 0.10 **NM value: 20.00**
32 ☐ Feb 1957 Cover: 0.10 **NM value: 20.00**
33 ☐ Apr 1957 Cover: 0.10 **NM value: 20.00**
34 ☐ Jun 1957 Cover: 0.10 **NM value: 20.00**
final issue.

COMBAT (DELL) — Dell

Dell's Combat series differed from many war comics in sticking to the actual facts of various battles, rather than merely using them as a backdrop against which fictionalized stories were told. In that respect, many of the stories are similar to those in some of E.C.'s war titles, though the art in the Dell title was not up to that in the E.C. series. Certainly, Combat did its share of dramatization, but by and large the real story was in the daring plans and individual courage that turned the tide of battle. These ranged from the British commando assault on the German U-Boat base at Saint-Nazaire to John F. Kennedy's exploits as the commander of PT-109.

1 ☐ Cover: 0.12 **NM value: 40.00**
2 ☐ Cover: 0.12 **NM value: 18.00**
3 ☐ Cover: 0.12 **NM value: 18.00**
4 ☐ Cover: 0.12 **NM value: 25.00**
• John F. Kennedy story

5 ☐ Cover: 0.12 **NM value: 16.00**
6 ☐ Cover: 0.12 **NM value: 12.00**
7 ☐ Cover: 0.12 **NM value: 12.00**
8 ☐ Cover: 0.12 **NM value: 12.00**
📖 Monte Cassino

9 ☐ Cover: 0.12 **NM value: 12.00**
10 ☐ Cover: 0.12 **NM value: 9.00**
11 ☐ Cover: 0.12 **NM value: 9.00**
12 ☐ Cover: 0.12 **NM value: 9.00**
13 ☐ Cover: 0.12 **NM value: 9.00**
14 ☐ Cover: 0.12 **NM value: 9.00**
15 ☐ Cover: 0.12 **NM value: 9.00**
16 ☐ Cover: 0.12 **NM value: 9.00**
17 ☐ Cover: 0.12 **NM value: 9.00**
18 ☐ Cover: 0.12 **NM value: 9.00**
19 ☐ Cover: 0.12 **NM value: 9.00**
• Saint-Nazairre

20 ☐ **NM value: 9.00**
21 ☐ **NM value: 8.00**
22 ☐ **NM value: 8.00**
23 ☐ **NM value: 8.00**
24 ☐ **NM value: 8.00**
25 ☐ **NM value: 8.00**
26 ☐ **NM value: 8.00**
27 ☐ **NM value: 8.00**
28 ☐ **NM value: 6.00**
29 ☐ **NM value: 6.00**
30 ☐ **NM value: 6.00**
31 ☐ **NM value: 6.00**
32 ☐ **NM value: 6.00**
33 ☐ **NM value: 6.00**
34 ☐ **NM value: 6.00**
35 ☐ **NM value: 6.00**
36 ☐ **NM value: 6.00**
37 ☐ **NM value: 6.00**
38 ☐ **NM value: 6.00**
39 ☐ **NM value: 6.00**
40 ☐ **NM value: 6.00**
final issue.

COMBAT (IMAGE) — Image

1 ☐ Jan 1996 Cover: 2.50 **NM value: Cover or less**
A: Mark Pajarillo **W:** Brian Witten; Cy Voris

2 ☐ Jan 1996 Cover: 2.50 **NM value: Cover or less**
A: Mark Pajarillo **W:** Brian Witten; Cy Voris

To find prices for other grades for comic books not graded by CGC, multiply the above prices by:

Mint: 150%	VF-: 55%	VG-: 17%
NM/M:125%	F/VF: 48%	G+: 14%
NM+: 110%	F+: 40%	**Good: 12.5%**
NM-: 90%	**Fine: 33.3%**	G-: 11%
VF/NM: 83%	F-: 30%	FR/G: 10%
VF+: 75%	VG/F: 25%	**Fair: 8%**
Very Fine: 66.6%	VG+: 23%	**Poor: 2%**
	Very Good: 20%	

CGC-graded: Multiply prices above by **33 for 9.9 M • 16 for 9.8 NM/M • 7 for 9.6 NM+ • 5 for 9.4 NM • 2.5 for 9.2 NM- • 1.5 for 9.0 VF/NM**

COMBAT KELLY (1ST SERIES) — Marvel

With its first issue released in November 1951, Combat Kelly was an action-filled war title set during the Korean War, which the U.S. was then fighting. The star of the series is a rough-and-tumble Irishman who takes on the "Quilted Horde" (North Koreans) armed with his M-1 Garande rifle and unlimited courage. He is backed up by similarly fearless dogfaces, including "Cookie," an unimpressive-looking lad who in one story is shown single-handedly wiping out an entire Communist platoon.

At the same time E.C. was producing the thought-provokingly brilliant Frontline Combat, this series satisfied itself portraying brawling shoot-em-ups.

1 ❑ Nov 1951 Cover: 0.10 **NM** value: **100.00**
• **CGC:** 1 graded, best 8.5
★ 1st Appearance of Combat Kelly.
2 ❑ Jan 1952 Cover: 0.10 **NM** value: **50.00**
• **CGC:** 1 graded, best 4.5
3 ❑ Mar 1952 Cover: 0.10 **NM** value: **35.00**
4 ❑ May 1952 Cover: 0.10 **NM** value: **30.00**
5 ❑ 1952 Cover: 0.10 **NM** value: **30.00**
6 ❑ 1952 Cover: 0.10 **NM** value: **30.00**
7 ❑ 1952 Cover: 0.10 **NM** value: **30.00**
8 ❑ Dec 1952 Cover: 0.10 **NM** value: **30.00**
9 ❑ Jan 1953 Cover: 0.10 **NM** value: **30.00**
10 ❑ Feb 1953 Cover: 0.10 **NM** value: **30.00**
11 ❑ Cover: 0.10 **NM** value: **24.00**
12 ❑ Cover: 0.10 **NM** value: **24.00**
13 ❑ Cover: 0.10 **NM** value: **24.00**
14 ❑ Cover: 0.10 **NM** value: **24.00**
15 ❑ Cover: 0.10 **NM** value: **24.00**
16 ❑ Cover: 0.10 **NM** value: **24.00**
17 ❑ Cover: 0.10 **NM** value: **27.00**
📖 Combat Casey; Ten Li'l Reds; ★ Appearance of Combat Casey.
18 ❑ Cover: 0.10 **NM** value: **18.00**
19 ❑ Cover: 0.10 **NM** value: **18.00**
20 ❑ Cover: 0.10 **NM** value: **18.00**
21 ❑ Cover: 0.10 **NM** value: **18.00**
Transvestite cover.
22 ❑ Cover: 0.10 **NM** value: **18.00**
23 ❑ Cover: 0.10 **NM** value: **18.00**
24 ❑ Cover: 0.10 **NM** value: **18.00**
25 ❑ Cover: 0.10 **NM** value: **18.00**
26 ❑ Cover: 0.10 **NM** value: **18.00**
27 ❑ Cover: 0.10 **NM** value: **18.00**
28 ❑ Cover: 0.10 **NM** value: **18.00**
29 ❑ Cover: 0.10 **NM** value: **18.00**
30 ❑ Cover: 0.10 **NM** value: **18.00**
31 ❑ Cover: 0.10 **NM** value: **15.00**
32 ❑ Cover: 0.10 **NM** value: **15.00**
33 ❑ Cover: 0.10 **NM** value: **15.00**
34 ❑ Cover: 0.10 **NM** value: **15.00**
35 ❑ Cover: 0.10 **NM** value: **15.00**
36 ❑ Cover: 0.10 **NM** value: **15.00**
37 ❑ Jun 1956 Cover: 0.10 **NM** value: **15.00**
38 ❑ Aug 1956 Cover: 0.10 **NM** value: **15.00**
39 ❑ Oct 1956 Cover: 0.10 **NM** value: **15.00**
40 ❑ Dec 1956 Cover: 0.10 **NM** value: **15.00**
41 ❑ Feb 1957 Cover: 0.10 **NM** value: **15.00**
42 ❑ Apr 1957 Cover: 0.10 **NM** value: **15.00**
43 ❑ Jun 1957 Cover: 0.10 **NM** value: **15.00**
44 ❑ Aug 1957 Cover: 0.10 **NM** value: **15.00**
final issue.

COMBAT KELLY (2ND SERIES) — Marvel

1 ❑ Jun 1972 Cover: 0.20 **NM** value: **8.00**
• **CGC:** 1 graded, best 9.2
📖 Stop the Luftwaffe…Win the War! • Combat Kelly becomes leader of Dum-Dum Dugan's Deadly Dozen (from Sgt. Fury #98) **A:** Dick Ayers **W:** Gary Friedrich ★ Origin of Combat Kelly.
2 ❑ Aug 1972 Cover: 0.20 **NM** value: **5.00**
📖 Lonely Are The Brave; **A:** Dick Ayers **W:** Gary Friedrich
3 ❑ Oct 1972 Cover: 0.20 **NM** value: **5.00**
A: Dick Ayers ★ Origin of Combat Kelly.
4 ❑ Dec 1972 Cover: 0.20 **NM** value: **3.00**
A: Dick Ayers ★ Appearance of Sgt. Fury and his Howling Commandos.
5 ❑ Feb 1973 Cover: 0.20 **NM** value: **3.00**
A: Dick Ayers
6 ❑ Apr 1973 Cover: 0.20 **NM** value: **3.00**
A: Dick Ayers
7 ❑ Jun 1973 Cover: 0.20 **NM** value: **3.00**
A: Dick Ayers
8 ❑ Aug 1973 Cover: 0.20 **NM** value: **3.00**
A: Dick Ayers
9 ❑ Oct 1973 Cover: 0.20 **NM** value: **3.00**
• **CGC:** 1 graded, best 9.6
final issue. • Combat Kelly leaves team **A:** Dick Ayers ★ Death of Deadly Dozen.

COMBAT ZONE — Avalon

1 ❑ b&w Cover: 2.95 **NM** value: **Cover or less**

COME AGAIN — Eros

1 ❑ Feb 1997 Cover: 2.95 **NM** value: **Cover or less**
Circ: Diamd. preorders: **1,712**
A: Rick McCollum **W:** Cathleen Hurley
2 ❑ May 1997 Cover: 2.95 **NM** value: **Cover or less**
A: Rick McCollum; Bill Cavalier **W:** Cathleen Hurley

COMEDY COMICS — Timely

9 ❑ Apr 1942 Cover: 0.10 **NM** value: **2000.00**
10 ❑ Jun 1942 Cover: 0.10 **NM** value: **1500.00**
11 ❑ Sep 1942 Cover: 0.10 **NM** value: **500.00**
12 ❑ Nov 1942 Cover: 0.10 **NM** value: **500.00**
13 ❑ Jan 1943 Cover: 0.10 **NM** value: **500.00**
14 ❑ Mar 1943 Cover: 0.10 **NM** value: **400.00**
15 ❑ May 1943 Cover: 0.10 **NM** value: **400.00**
• **CGC:** 1 graded, best 7.5
16 ❑ Jul 1943 Cover: 0.10 **NM** value: **400.00**
17 ❑ Sep 1943 Cover: 0.10 **NM** value: **300.00**
18 ❑ Nov 1943 Cover: 0.10 **NM** value: **300.00**
19 ❑ Jan 1944 Cover: 0.10 **NM** value: **300.00**
20 ❑ Mar 1944 Cover: 0.10 **NM** value: **300.00**
21 ❑ May 1944 Cover: 0.10 **NM** value: **200.00**
22 ❑ Jul 1944 Cover: 0.10 **NM** value: **200.00**
23 ❑ Sep 1944 Cover: 0.10 **NM** value: **200.00**
24 ❑ Nov 1944 Cover: 0.10 **NM** value: **200.00**
25 ❑ Jan 1945 Cover: 0.10 **NM** value: **150.00**
26 ❑ Mar 1945 Cover: 0.10 **NM** value: **150.00**
27 ❑ May 1945 Cover: 0.10 **NM** value: **150.00**
28 ❑ Jul 1945 Cover: 0.10 **NM** value: **100.00**
29 ❑ Sep 1945 Cover: 0.10 **NM** value: **100.00**
30 ❑ Nov 1945 Cover: 0.10 **NM** value: **100.00**
31 ❑ Jan 1946 Cover: 0.10 **NM** value: **100.00**
32 ❑ Mar 1946 Cover: 0.10 **NM** value: **75.00**
33 ❑ May 1946 Cover: 0.10 **NM** value: **75.00**
34 ❑ Jul 1946 Cover: 0.10 **NM** value: **75.00**

COMET, THE (IMPACT) — DC / Impact

1 ❑ Jul 1991 Cover: 1.00 **NM** value: **Cover or less**
Circ: CapCity orders: **41,100**
📖 First Flight **A:** Tom Lyle **W:** Tom Lyle ★ Origin of Comet.
2 ❑ Aug 1991 Cover: 1.00 **NM** value: **Cover or less**
Circ: CapCity orders: **25,400**
★ 1st Appearance of Lance Perry, Applejack.
3 ❑ Sep 1991 Cover: 1.00 **NM** value: **Cover or less**
Circ: CapCity orders: **20,000**
4 ❑ Oct 1991 Cover: 1.00 **NM** value: **Cover or less**
Circ: CapCity orders: **19,200**
★ 1st Appearance of Inferno. ★ Versus Black Hood.
5 ❑ Nov 1991 Cover: 1.00 **NM** value: **Cover or less**
Circ: CapCity orders: **17,050**
★ 1st Appearance of The Hangman (as Roger Adams).
6 ❑ Dec 1991 Cover: 1.00 **NM** value: **Cover or less**
Circ: CapCity orders: **16,900**
★ 1st Appearance of The Hangman (in costume), Hangman.
7 ❑ Jan 1992 Cover: 1.00 **NM** value: **Cover or less**
Circ: CapCity orders: **13,900**
★ 1st Appearance of The Wolf, Bob Phantom.
8 ❑ Feb 1992 Cover: 1.00 **NM** value: **Cover or less**
Circ: CapCity orders: **12,450**
📖 Shattered Secrets **A:** Tom Lyle **W:** Mark Waid ★ 1st Appearance of The Black Witch. ★ Versus Web.
9 ❑ Mar 1992 Cover: 1.00 **NM** value: **Cover or less**
Circ: CapCity orders: **10,300**
10 ❑ Apr 1992 Cover: 1.00 **NM** value: **Cover or less**
Circ: CapCity orders: **9,050**
📖 The Coming Of The Crusaders, Part 2 • trading card
11 ❑ May 1992 Cover: 1.00 **NM** value: **Cover or less**
Circ: CapCity orders: **8,900**
12 ❑ Jun 1992 Cover: 1.00 **NM** value: **Cover or less**
Circ: CapCity orders: **8,250**
13 ❑ Jul 1992 Cover: 1.00 **NM** value: **Cover or less**
Circ: CapCity orders: **7,750**
14 ❑ Aug 1992 Cover: 1.25 **NM** value: **Cover or less**
Circ: CapCity orders: **7,850**
15 ❑ Sep 1992 Cover: 1.25 **NM** value: **Cover or less**
Circ: CapCity orders: **6,350**
16 ❑ Oct 1992 Cover: 1.25 **NM** value: **Cover or less**
Circ: CapCity orders: **6,100**
17 ❑ Nov 1992 Cover: 1.25 **NM** value: **Cover or less**
Circ: CapCity orders: **5,700**
18 ❑ Dec 1992 Cover: 1.25 **NM** value: **Cover or less**
Circ: CapCity orders: **5,400**
final issue.
Anl 1❑ Cover: 2.50 **NM** value: **Cover or less**
Circ: CapCity orders: **8,400**
📖 Earth Quest, Part 3 • trading card

COMET MAN — Marvel

1 ❑ Feb 1987 Cover: 1.00 **NM** value: **Cover or less**
Circ: CapCity orders: **22,900**
📖 The Coming Of The Comet Man **A:** Kelley Jones; Gerry Talaoc **W:** Bill Mumy; Miguel Ferrer ★ Origin of Comet Man. ★ 1st Appearance of Comet Man.
2 ❑ Mar 1987 Cover: 1.00 **NM** value: **Cover or less**
Circ: CapCity orders: **17,400**
3 ❑ Apr 1987 Cover: 1.00 **NM** value: **Cover or less**
Circ: CapCity orders: **16,600**
📖 When The Truth Is Found To Be Lies **A:** Kelley Jones **W:** Bill Mumy; Miguel Ferrer
4 ❑ May 1987 Cover: 1.00 **NM** value: **Cover or less**
Circ: CapCity orders: **13,700**
5 ❑ Jun 1987 Cover: 1.00 **NM** value: **Cover or less**
Circ: CapCity orders: **12,600**
6 ❑ Jul 1987 Cover: 1.00 **NM** value: **Cover or less**
Circ: CapCity orders: **12,500**
final issue.

Statement of Ownership figures are the average number of copies originally sold, as cited by the publisher to the U.S. Postal Service. These estimate **all** sales, in comics shops and on newsstands.

COMET, THE (RED CIRCLE) — Archie / Red Circle

The Comet, created by Jack Cole (Plastic Man), made his debut in the first issue of Pep Comics in 1940. He was John Dickering, a research scientist who used himself as a guinea pig to test the effects of man-made gasses on the human nervous system. The cumulative effects of his experiments turned him into a violent engine of destruction with powerful eye beams that he controlled with a visor (pre-dating Cyclops of The X-Men by about 20 years). Soon, the super-hero format of Pep was relinquished to Archie, but the character returned in this series in 1983. Four decades earlier, he may have ruthlessly killed thugs and murderers, but he has had a change of heart in this version and is haunted by his previous behavior.

1 ❑ Oct 1983 Cover: 1.00 **NM** value: **Cover or less**
📖 Comet **A:** Carmine Infantino **W:** Bill Dubay ★ Origin of Comet.
2 ❑ Dec 1983 Cover: 1.00 **NM** value: **Cover or less**
A: Carmine Infantino

COMET TALES — Rocket

1 ❑ Cover: 1.00 **NM** value: **Cover or less**
2 ❑ Cover: 1.00 **NM** value: **Cover or less**
3 ❑ Cover: 1.00 **NM** value: **Cover or less**

COMIC ALBUM — Dell

1 ❑ Mar 1958 Cover: 0.10 **NM** value: **100.00**
• **CGC:** 1 graded, best 7.5
2 ❑ Jun 1958 Cover: 0.10 **NM** value: **50.00**
• **CGC:** 1 graded, best 8.5
3 ❑ Sep 1958 Cover: 0.10 **NM** value: **75.00**
• **CGC:** 2 graded, best 8.5
4 ❑ Dec 1958 Cover: 0.10 **NM** value: **30.00**
5 ❑ Mar 1959 Cover: 0.10 **NM** value: **30.00**
6 ❑ Jun 1959 Cover: 0.10 **NM** value: **30.00**
7 ❑ Sep 1959 Cover: 0.10 **NM** value: **40.00**
• **CGC:** 1 graded, best 9.2
8 ❑ Dec 1959 Cover: 0.10 **NM** value: **30.00**
9 ❑ Mar 1960 Cover: 0.10 **NM** value: **30.00**
10 ❑ Jun 1960 Cover: 0.10 **NM** value: **30.00**
• **CGC:** 1 graded, best 9.0
11 ❑ Sep 1960 Cover: 0.10 **NM** value: **40.00**
12 ❑ Dec 1960 Cover: 0.10 **NM** value: **30.00**
13 ❑ Mar 1961 Cover: 0.10 **NM** value: **30.00**
14 ❑ Jun 1961 Cover: 0.15 **NM** value: **30.00**
15 ❑ Sep 1961 Cover: 0.15 **NM** value: **40.00**
16 ❑ Dec 1961 Cover: 0.15 **NM** value: **80.00**
• **CGC:** 1 graded, best 9.2
17 ❑ Mar 1962 Cover: 0.15 **NM** value: **40.00**
18 ❑ Jun 1962 Cover: 0.15 **NM** value: **80.00**

COMIC BOOK — Marvel / Spumco

1 ❑ ca. 1996 Cover: 5.95 **NM** value: **6.95**
Circ: Direct Market orders: **11,750**
• oversized anthology. 📖 Jimmy the Turtle Food Collector **A:** John K. **W:** Jim Smith
2 ❑ ca. 1997 Cover: 5.95 **NM** value: **6.95**
• oversized anthology.

COMIC BOOK CONFIDENTIAL — Sphinx

1 ❑ **NM** value: **2.00**
No issue number. • giveaway promo for documentary film of same name.

COMIC BOOK HEAVEN — Slave Labor

1 ❑ Cover: 1.95 **NM** value: **2.00**
2 ❑ Cover: 1.95 **NM** value: **2.00**

COMIC BOOK TALENT SEARCH, THE — Silverwolf

1 ❑ Feb 1987 Cover: 1.50 **NM** value: **Cover or less**

COMIC CAPERS — Timely

1 ❑ ca. 1944 Cover: 0.10 **NM** value: **150.00**
2 ❑ ca. 1944 Cover: 0.10 **NM** value: **120.00**
3 ❑ ca. 1945 Cover: 0.10 **NM** value: **100.00**
4 ❑ ca. 1945 Cover: 0.10 **NM** value: **100.00**
5 ❑ ca. 1945 Cover: 0.10 **NM** value: **75.00**
6 ❑ ca. 1946 Cover: 0.10 **NM** value: **75.00**

COMIC CAVALCADE — DC

The anthology title began as self-contained stories of a number of DC's super-heroes in something of a companion anthology to the World's Finest Comics' assemblage of Superman, Batman, and Robin. Flash, Green Lantern, and Wonder Woman initially starred in the 15-cent giant Comic Cavalcade – but the popularity of those characters wasn't enough to support the series. Also, much like World's Finest, while the three heroes would appear together on the cover, they had separate adventures inside.

At the end of 1948, funny animals took it over, and Fox, Crow, Dodo, Frog, and Nutsy Squirrel romped where heroes had once fought evil. — Maggie

Other grades: Multiply prices above by **1.5 for Mint • 2/3 for Very Fine • 1/3 for Fine • 1/5 for Very Good • 1/8 for Good**

1 ❑ Win 1942 Cover: 0.15 **NM** value: **7500.00**
• **CGC:** 6 graded, best 6.5
2 ❑ Spr 1943 Cover: 0.15 **NM** value: **2000.00**
• **CGC:** 1 graded, best 4.0
The Seal-Men's War on Santa Claus • Sandman
3 ❑ Sum 1943 Cover: 0.15 **NM** value: **1500.00**
4 ❑ Fal 1943 Cover: 0.15 **NM** value: **1200.00**
5 ❑ Win 1943 Cover: 0.15 **NM** value: **1200.00**
• **CGC:** 3 graded, best 7.0
6 ❑ Spr 1944 Cover: 0.15 **NM** value: **1000.00**
• **CGC:** 1 graded, best 6.5
7 ❑ Sum 1944 Cover: 0.15 **NM** value: **1000.00**
8 ❑ Fal 1944 Cover: 0.15 **NM** value: **1000.00**
9 ❑ Win 1944 Cover: 0.15 **NM** value: **1000.00**
The Subsea Pirates; One Hundred Years of Co-operation; A Tale of a City; The Baker Kneaded Dough (text story); Filipinos are People; A Ride in the Sky; The Tale of the Winged Horse ★ Appearance of Wonder Woman.
10 ❑ Spr 1945 Cover: 0.15 **NM** value: **1000.00**
• **CGC:** 1 graded, best 6.5
11 ❑ Sum 1945 Cover: 0.15 **NM** value: **800.00**
• **CGC:** 1 graded, best 9.4
12 ❑ Fal 1945 Cover: 0.15 **NM** value: **800.00**
• **CGC:** 1 graded, best 3.5
13 ❑ Win 1945 Cover: 0.15 **NM** value: **1000.00**
• **CGC:** 2 graded, best 8.0
14 ❑ Apr 1946 Cover: 0.15 **NM** value: **800.00**
• **CGC:** 2 graded, best 8.5
15 ❑ Jun 1946 Cover: 0.15 **NM** value: **800.00**
• **CGC:** 1 graded, best 9.0
16 ❑ Aug 1946 Cover: 0.15 **NM** value: **800.00**
• **CGC:** 1 graded, best 9.2
17 ❑ Oct 1946 Cover: 0.15 **NM** value: **800.00**
• **CGC:** 1 graded, best 9.0
18 ❑ Dec 1946 Cover: 0.15 **NM** value: **800.00**
• **CGC:** 2 graded, best 9.0
19 ❑ Feb 1947 Cover: 0.15 **NM** value: **800.00**
• **CGC:** 2 graded, best 9.0
20 ❑ Apr 1947 Cover: 0.15 **NM** value: **800.00**
• **CGC:** 2 graded, best 9.2
21 ❑ Jun 1947 Cover: 0.15 **NM** value: **750.00**
• **CGC:** 1 graded, best 8.5
22 ❑ Aug 1947 Cover: 0.15 **NM** value: **750.00**
• **CGC:** 1 graded, best 7.0
23 ❑ Oct 1947 Cover: 0.15 **NM** value: **750.00**
• **CGC:** 2 graded, best 7.5
24 ❑ Dec 1947 Cover: 0.15 **NM** value: **950.00**
• **CGC:** 3 graded, best 8.0
25 ❑ Feb 1948 Cover: 0.15 **NM** value: **700.00**
• **CGC:** 2 graded, best 9.0
26 ❑ Apr 1948 Cover: 0.15 **NM** value: **700.00**
• **CGC:** 3 graded, best 9.6
27 ❑ Jun 1948 Cover: 0.15 **NM** value: **700.00**
• **CGC:** 1 graded, best 8.5
28 ❑ Aug 1948 Cover: 0.15 **NM** value: **700.00**
• **CGC:** 1 graded, best 6.0
29 ❑ Oct 1948 Cover: 0.15 **NM** value: **750.00**
• **CGC:** 2 graded, best 8.0
30 ❑ Dec 1948 Cover: 0.15 **NM** value: **300.00**
31 ❑ Feb 1949 Cover: 0.15 **NM** value: **300.00**
32 ❑ Apr 1949 Cover: 0.15 **NM** value: **300.00**
33 ❑ Jun 1949 Cover: 0.15 **NM** value: **300.00**
34 ❑ Aug 1949 Cover: 0.15 **NM** value: **250.00**
35 ❑ Oct 1949 Cover: 0.15 **NM** value: **250.00**
36 ❑ Dec 1949 Cover: 0.15 **NM** value: **250.00**
37 ❑ Feb 1950 Cover: 0.15 **NM** value: **200.00**
38 ❑ Apr 1950 Cover: 0.15 **NM** value: **200.00**
• **CGC:** 1 graded, best 5.0
39 ❑ Jun 1950 Cover: 0.15 **NM** value: **200.00**
• **CGC:** 1 graded, best 5.0
40 ❑ Aug 1950 Cover: 0.15 **NM** value: **150.00**
41 ❑ Oct 1950 Cover: 0.15 **NM** value: **150.00**
42 ❑ Dec 1950 Cover: 0.15 **NM** value: **150.00**
43 ❑ Feb 1951 Cover: 0.15 **NM** value: **100.00**
44 ❑ Apr 1951 Cover: 0.15 **NM** value: **100.00**
45 ❑ Jun 1951 Cover: 0.15 **NM** value: **75.00**
46 ❑ Aug 1951 Cover: 0.15 **NM** value: **75.00**
47 ❑ Oct 1951 Cover: 0.15 **NM** value: **75.00**
• **CGC:** 1 graded, best 9.6
48 ❑ Dec 1951 Cover: 0.15 **NM** value: **75.00**
• **CGC:** 1 graded, best 9.0
49 ❑ Feb 1952 Cover: 0.15 **NM** value: **75.00**
50 ❑ Apr 1952 Cover: 0.15 **NM** value: **75.00**
51 ❑ Jun 1952 Cover: 0.15 **NM** value: **70.00**
52 ❑ Aug 1952 Cover: 0.15 **NM** value: **70.00**
53 ❑ Oct 1952 Cover: 0.15 **NM** value: **70.00**
54 ❑ Dec 1952 Cover: 0.15 **NM** value: **70.00**
55 ❑ Feb 1953 Cover: 0.15 **NM** value: **70.00**
56 ❑ Apr 1953 Cover: 0.15 **NM** value: **70.00**
57 ❑ Jun 1953 Cover: 0.15 **NM** value: **70.00**
58 ❑ Aug 1953 Cover: 0.15 **NM** value: **70.00**
59 ❑ Oct 1953 Cover: 0.15 **NM** value: **70.00**
60 ❑ Dec 1953 Cover: 0.15 **NM** value: **65.00**
61 ❑ Feb 1954 Cover: 0.15 **NM** value: **65.00**
62 ❑ Apr 1954 Cover: 0.15 **NM** value: **65.00**
63 ❑ Jun 1954 Cover: 0.15 **NM** value: **65.00**
• **CGC:** 1 graded, best 4.5

COMIC CLOCK (OSCAR AND FRIDAY'S...) — Fawcett
1 ❑ Cover: 0.10 **NM** value: **10.00**

COMIC LAND — Fact and Fiction Publications
1 ❑ Mar 1946 **NM** value: **100.00**
• **CGC:** 2 graded, best 8.5

COMICO BLACK BOOK, THE — Comico
This one-shot book recaps Comico's first five years in existence. It gives one-page descriptions about every title it published from 1983 to 1987. The impressive publishing history includes the titles Grendel (1st Series), Slaughterman, AZ, Primer, Grendel (2nd series), Jonny Quest, Justice Machine, Mage, Robotech: The Macross Saga, Robotech Masters, Robotech — The New Generation, Jonny Quest Classics, Star Blazers, The Fish Police, Gumby's Summer Fun Special, Robotech 3-D, Ginger Fox, Jezebel Jade, Mage II, and Max Headroom.
Comico's editorial lineup at the time contained many who would later go on to become super-stars in the world of comics. Among them: Art Adams (Hellboy), Mike Baron (Nexus), Mike W. Barr, Steve Bisette, Bret Blevins, Chris Claremont (Uncanny X-Men), Harlan Ellison, Tony Isabella, Alan Moore (Watchmen), and Chuck Dixon.
1 ❑ Cover: 1.50 **NM** value: **2.00**
A: Arthur Adams **W:** Maggie Brenner

COMICO CHRISTMAS SPECIAL — Comico
1 ❑ Dec 1988 Cover: 2.50 **NM** value: **Cover or less**
Circ: CapCity orders: **5,400**
A: Steve Rude **C:** Dave Stevens

COMICO COLLECTION — Comico
1 ❑ Cover: 9.95 **NM** value: **Cover or less**
• 10 comics & Grendel: Devil's Vagary

COMICS — Dell
1 ❑ Mar 1937 Cover: 0.10 **NM** value: **1500.00**
• **CGC:** 2 graded, best 9.0
2 ❑ Apr 1937 Cover: 0.10 **NM** value: **750.00**
3 ❑ 1937 Cover: 0.10 **NM** value: **600.00**
4 ❑ 1937 Cover: 0.10 **NM** value: **600.00**
5 ❑ 1937 Cover: 0.10 **NM** value: **600.00**
6 ❑ 1937 Cover: 0.10 **NM** value: **600.00**
7 ❑ 1938 Cover: 0.10 **NM** value: **600.00**
8 ❑ 1938 Cover: 0.10 **NM** value: **600.00**
9 ❑ 1938 Cover: 0.10 **NM** value: **600.00**
10 ❑ 1938 Cover: 0.10 **NM** value: **500.00**
11 ❑ 1938 Cover: 0.10 **NM** value: **500.00**

COMICS AND STORIES — Dark Horse
1 ❑ Apr 1996 Cover: 2.95 **NM** value: **Cover or less**
• Wolf & Red
2 ❑ May 1996 Cover: 2.95 **NM** value: **Cover or less**
3 ❑ Jun 1996 Cover: 2.95 **NM** value: **Cover or less**
Duck and Cover; Son of King Size Canar; Bird is the Word! • Bad Luck Blackie **A:** Tom King; Jay Stephens; Bill Morrison **W:** Mark Martin; Jay Stephens; Scott Shaw
4 ❑ Jan 1997 Cover: 2.95 **NM** value: **Cover or less**
Circ: Diamd. preorders: **3,116**
Kaboom!; Farm Harm • Screwball Squirrel **A:** Mark Martin; Tony Millionaire **W:** Mark Martin; Tony Millionaire

COMICS ARE DEAD — Slap Happy
1 ❑ 1999b&w Cover: 4.95 **NM** value: **Cover or less**

COMICS ARTIST SHOWCASE, THE — Showcase
1 ❑ Cover: 1.00 **NM** value: **Cover or less**
No Such Thing as Demond; A Tiger's Tale; The Fierce Leopardman; Wishing **A:** Adam Woolridge; Anthony Breaux; Kevin Grays; Matthew Rollwagen; Steven Pe **W:** Adam Woolridge; Kevin Grays; Matthew Rollwagen

COMICS' GREATEST WORLD — Dark Horse
1 ❑ Jun 1993 Cover: 1.00 **NM** value: **Cover or less**
• preview copy of Comics' Greatest World: X;1500 printed

COMICS' GREATEST WORLD - ARCADIA — Dark Horse
Dark Horse kicked off its Comics' Greatest World series with this weekly mini-series.
Arcadia is a corrupt city, overrun with organized crime. Into this oppressive climate comes X, Pit Bulls, Ghost, and Monster. Each of these characters was introduced in a separate issue, with only X and Ghost eventually moving on to their own titles.

X is a costumed vigilante whose primary mission is to clean up the political corruption in his city, while Ghost is a female spectre who returns from the dead armed with twin revolvers. The series continues in Comics' Greatest World: Golden City. — Brent
1 ❑ Jun 1993 Cover: 1.00 **NM** value: **2.00**
• X;Arcadia, Week 1 **A:** Chris Warner; Lee Weeks; Frank Miller(cover) **W:** Mike Richardson; Jerry Prosser ★ 1st Appearance of X.
1/LE❑ Jun 1993 Cover: 1.00 **NM** value: **2.50**
enhanced cardstock cover. • limited edition for Heroes World Distribution. • X **A:** Chris Warner; Lee Weeks; Frank Miller(cover) **W:** Mike Richardson; Jerry Prosser
2 ❑ Cover: 1.00 **NM** value: **Cover or less**
• Pit Bulls;Arcadia, Week 2 **A:** Joe Phillips; Lee Weeks **W:** Mike Richardson; Jerry Prosser
3 ❑ Jun 1993 Cover: 1.00 **NM** value: **3.00**
• **CGC:** 2 graded, best 8.5
• Ghost;Arcadia, Week 3 **A:** Adam Hughes; Lee Weeks **W:** Mike Richardson; Jerry Prosser ★ 1st Appearance of Ghost.
4 ❑ Cover: 1.00 **NM** value: **Cover or less**
• Monster;continues in Comics' Greatest World – Golden City;Arcadia, Week 4 **A:** Derek Thompson; Lee Weeks **W:** Mike Richardson; Jerry Prosser
Bk 1❑ **NM** value: **6.00**
• Collected edition. • Collects series **A:** Derek Thompson; Lee Weeks **W:** Mike Richardson; Jerry Prosser

COMICS' GREATEST WORLD - CINNABAR FLATS — Dark Horse
1 ❑ Jun 1993 Cover: 1.00 **NM** value: **Cover or less**
• Division 13;Vortex, Week 1 **A:** Doug Mahnke; Lee Weeks **W:** Mike Richardson; Randy Stradley
1/A ❑ Aug 1993 **NM** value: **2.50**
cardstock cover. • limited edition for American Distribution. • Division 13;Vortex, Week 1 **A:** Doug Mahnke; Lee Weeks **W:** Mike Richardson; Randy Stradley
1/LE❑ Aug 1993 **NM** value: **2.50**
cardstock cover. • limited edition. • Division 13
2 ❑ Jun 1993 Cover: 1.00 **NM** value: **Cover or less**
• Hero Zero;Vortex, Week 2 **A:** Doug Mahnke; Lee Weeks **W:** Mike Richardson; Randy Stradley
3 ❑ Jun 1993 Cover: 1.00 **NM** value: **Cover or less**
• King Tiger;Vortex, Week 3 **A:** Doug Mahnke; Lee Weeks **W:** Mike Richardson; Randy Stradley
4 ❑ Jun 1993 Cover: 1.00 **NM** value: **Cover or less**
• Out of the Vortex;continues in Out of the Vortex (Comics' Greatest World...);continues in Comics' Greatest World – Out of the Vortex;Vortex, Week 4 **A:** Doug Mahnke; Lee Weeks **W:** Mike Richardson; Randy Stradley
Bk 1❑ Jun 1993 **NM** value: **6.00**
• Collected edition. • Collects series **A:** Doug Mahnke; Lee Weeks **W:** Mike Richardson; Randy Stradley

COMICS' GREATEST WORLD - GOLDEN CITY — Dark Horse
1 ❑ Jul 1993 Cover: 1.00 **NM** value: **Cover or less**
Circ: CapCity orders: **41,725**
• Rebel;Golden City, Week 1 **A:** Lee Weeks **C:** Joe Orlando **W:** Mike Richardson
1/LE❑ Cover: 1.00 **NM** value: **2.50**
enhanced cardstock cover. • limited edition for Heroes World Distribution. • Rebel;Golden City, Week 1 **A:** Lee Weeks **C:** Joe Orlando **W:** Mike Richardson
2 ❑ Cover: 1.00 **NM** value: **Cover or less**
Circ: CapCity orders: **40,575**
• Mecha;Golden City, Week 2 **A:** Chuck Wojtkiewicz; Lee Weeks **W:** Mike Richardson; Barbara Kesel
3 ❑ Jul 1993 Cover: 1.00 **NM** value: **Cover or less**
Circ: CapCity orders: **40,525**
• Titan;Golden City, Week 3 **A:** Brian Apthorp; Lee Weeks **C:** Walt Simonson **W:** Mike Richardson; Barbara Kesel
4 ❑ Aug 1993 Cover: 1.00 **NM** value: **Cover or less**
Circ: CapCity orders: **40,375**
Catalyst • continues in Comics' Greatest World – Steel Harbor;Catalyst: Agents of Change;Golden City, Week 4 **A:** Jan Duursema; Lee Weeks **W:** Mike Richardson; Barbara Kesel
Bk 1❑ **NM** value: **6.00**
no cover price. • Collected edition. • Collects series **A:** Jan Duursema; Lee Weeks **W:** Mike Richardson; Barbara Kesel

COMICS' GREATEST WORLD - STEEL HARBOR — Dark Horse
The third major location in the Comics' Greatest World universe, Steel Harbor was once a booming industrial center that has been hit hard by recession. A spiraling crime rate leads such Steel Harbor citizens as Barb Kopetski (aka Barb Wire) to take matters into their own hands and fight crime at the street level. Barb Wire is aided by The Machine, a cyborg who can monitor the entire city with his artificial parts. In its third week, the mini-series focused on one of Steel Harbor's street gangs, The Wolf Gang, a group of super-powered gangbangers, who join Barb Wire and company to take out Steel Harbor's more corrupt elements. They're aided in the final issue by the psychic Motorhead. The series continues in Comics' Greatest World: Cinnabar Flats. — Brent

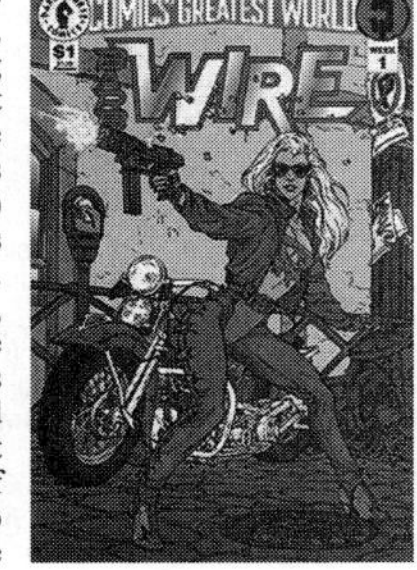

1 ❑ Aug 1993 Cover: 1.00 **NM** value: **2.50**
Circ: CapCity orders: **38,125**
• Barb Wire;Steel Harbor, Week 1 **A:** Paul Gulacy; Lee Weeks **W:** Chris Warner; Mike Richardson ★ 1st Appearance of Barb Wire.
2 ❑ Cover: 1.00 **NM** value: **Cover or less**
Circ: CapCity orders: **38,475**
• The Machine;Steel Harbor, Week 2 **A:** Ted Naifeh; Lee Weeks **W:** Chris Warner; Mike Richardson
3 ❑ Aug 1993 Cover: 1.00 **NM** value: **Cover or less**
Circ: CapCity orders: **37,275**
• Wolf Gang;Steel Harbor, Week 3 **A:** Lee Weeks; Clem Robins **W:** Chris Warner; Mike Richardson
4 ❑ Aug 1993 Cover: 1.00 **NM** value: **Cover or less**
Circ: CapCity orders: **37,550**

CGC-graded: Multiply prices above by **33 for 9.9 M • 16 for 9.8 NM/M • 7 for 9.6 NM+ • 5 for 9.4 NM • 2.5 for 9.2 NM- • 1.5 for 9.0 VF/NM**

• Motorhead;continues in Comics' Greatest World – Cinnabar Flats;Steel Harbor, Week 4 **A:** Vince Giarrano; Lee Weeks **W:** Chris Warner; Mike Richardson
Bk 1 ❑ **NM** value: **6.00**
• Collected edition. • Collects series **A:** Vince Giarrano; Lee Weeks **W:** Chris Warner; Mike Richardson

COMICS MAGAZINE — Comics Magazine

1 ❑ May 1936 Cover: 0.10 **NM** value: **10000.00**
• **CGC:** 1 graded, best 7.5
2 ❑ Jun 1936 Cover: 0.10 **NM** value: **2500.00**
3 ❑ Jul 1936 Cover: 0.10 **NM** value: **1500.00**
4 ❑ Aug 1936 Cover: 0.10 **NM** value: **1500.00**
5 ❑ Sep 1936 Cover: 0.10 **NM** value: **1500.00**

COMICS 101 PRESENTS — Cheap Thrills

1 ❑ Aug 1994, b&w **NM** value: **1.50**
No issue number. two covers. • one inside the other

COMICS ON PARADE — United Features

Comics on Parade was one of the very first comic books to reach the newsstands, making its debut in 1938. Published by United Features Syndicate, Comics on Parade focused on a different comic strip character each issue, reprinting 64 pages worth of color Sundays and dailies.

Among the features were Tarzan by Hal Foster and Burne Hogarth; The Captain and the Kids; Little Mary Mixup; Dynamite Dunn; Tailspin Tommy; Nancy and Fritzi Ritz; and Li'l Abner. All came from the United Features stable, and several made the successful transition to titles of their own.

1 ❑ Apr 1938 Cover: 0.10 **NM** value: **2800.00**
• **CGC:** 1 graded, best 8.5
2 ❑ May 1938 Cover: 0.10 **NM** value: **1050.00**
3 ❑ Jun 1938 Cover: 0.10 **NM** value: **775.00**
4 ❑ Jul 1938 Cover: 0.10 **NM** value: **600.00**
5 ❑ Aug 1938 Cover: 0.10 **NM** value: **600.00**
• **CGC:** 2 graded, best 6.5
6 ❑ Sep 1938 Cover: 0.10 **NM** value: **420.00**
7 ❑ Oct 1938 Cover: 0.10 **NM** value: **420.00**
8 ❑ Nov 1938 Cover: 0.10 **NM** value: **420.00**
9 ❑ Dec 1938 Cover: 0.10 **NM** value: **325.00**
• Li'l Abner
10 ❑ Jan 1939 Cover: 0.10 **NM** value: **325.00**
11 ❑ Feb 1939 Cover: 0.10 **NM** value: **285.00**
12 ❑ Mar 1939 Cover: 0.10 **NM** value: **285.00**
13 ❑ Apr 1939 Cover: 0.10 **NM** value: **285.00**
14 ❑ May 1939 Cover: 0.10 **NM** value: **285.00**
15 ❑ Jun 1939 Cover: 0.10 **NM** value: **285.00**
• **CGC:** 1 graded, best 8.5
16 ❑ Jul 1939 Cover: 0.10 **NM** value: **260.00**
17 ❑ Aug 1939 Cover: 0.10 **NM** value: **260.00**
• **CGC:** 1 graded, best 7.5
18 ❑ Sep 1939 Cover: 0.10 **NM** value: **260.00**
19 ❑ Oct 1939 Cover: 0.10 **NM** value: **260.00**
• **CGC:** 1 graded, best 8.0
20 ❑ Nov 1939 Cover: 0.10 **NM** value: **260.00**
21 ❑ Dec 1939 Cover: 0.10 **NM** value: **230.00**
22 ❑ Jan 1940 Cover: 0.10 **NM** value: **230.00**
23 ❑ Feb 1940 Cover: 0.10 **NM** value: **230.00**
24 ❑ Mar 1940 Cover: 0.10 **NM** value: **230.00**
25 ❑ Apr 1940 Cover: 0.10 **NM** value: **230.00**
26 ❑ Jun 1940 Cover: 0.10 **NM** value: **210.00**
27 ❑ Aug 1940 Cover: 0.10 **NM** value: **210.00**
28 ❑ Oct 1940 Cover: 0.10 **NM** value: **210.00**
29 ❑ Dec 1940 Cover: 0.10 **NM** value: **210.00**
30 ❑ Feb 1941 Cover: 0.10 **NM** value: **210.00**
• Li'l Abner
31 ❑ Apr 1941 Cover: 0.10 **NM** value: **135.00**
• The Captain and the Kids **A:** Rudolph Dirks **W:** Rudolph Dirks
32 ❑ Jun 1941 Cover: 0.10 **NM** value: **135.00**
33 ❑ Aug 1941 Cover: 0.10 **NM** value: **135.00**
• Li'l Abner
34 ❑ Oct 1941 Cover: 0.10 **NM** value: **135.00**
• The Captain and the Kids **A:** Rudolph Dirks **W:** Rudolph Dirks
35 ❑ Dec 1941 Cover: 0.10 **NM** value: **135.00**
36 ❑ Mar 1942 Cover: 0.10 **NM** value: **100.00**
• Li'l Abner
37 ❑ Jun 1942 Cover: 0.10 **NM** value: **100.00**
• The Captain and the Kids **A:** Rudolph Dirks **W:** Rudolph Dirks
38 ❑ Sep 1942 Cover: 0.10 **NM** value: **100.00**
• Nancy and Fritzi Ritz
39 ❑ Dec 1942 Cover: 0.10 **NM** value: **100.00**
• Li'l Abner
40 ❑ Mar 1943 Cover: 0.10 **NM** value: **100.00**
• The Captain and the Kids **A:** Rudolph Dirks **W:** Rudolph Dirks
41 ❑ Jun 1943 Cover: 0.10 **NM** value: **75.00**
• Nancy and Fritzi Ritz
42 ❑ Sep 1943 Cover: 0.10 **NM** value: **75.00**
• Li'l Abner
43 ❑ Dec 1943 Cover: 0.10 **NM** value: **75.00**
• The Captain and the Kids **A:** Rudolph Dirks **W:** Rudolph Dirks
44 ❑ Mar 1944 Cover: 0.10 **NM** value: **75.00**
• Nancy and Fritzi Ritz
45 ❑ Jun 1944 Cover: 0.10 **NM** value: **75.00**
• Li'l Abner
46 ❑ Sep 1944 Cover: 0.10 **NM** value: **75.00**
• The Captain and the Kids **A:** Rudolph Dirks **W:** Rudolph Dirks
47 ❑ Dec 1944 Cover: 0.10 **NM** value: **75.00**
• Nancy and Fritzi Ritz
48 ❑ Mar 1945 Cover: 0.10 **NM** value: **75.00**
• Li'l Abner
49 ❑ Jun 1945 Cover: 0.10 **NM** value: **75.00**
• The Captain and the Kids **A:** Rudolph Dirks **W:** Rudolph Dirks
50 ❑ Sep 1945 Cover: 0.10 **NM** value: **75.00**
• Nancy and Fritzi Ritz
51 ❑ Dec 1945 Cover: 0.10 **NM** value: **60.00**
• Li'l Abner
52 ❑ Mar 1946 Cover: 0.10 **NM** value: **60.00**
• The Captain and the Kids **A:** Rudolph Dirks **W:** Rudolph Dirks
53 ❑ Jun 1946 Cover: 0.10 **NM** value: **60.00**
• Nancy and Fritzi Ritz
54 ❑ Sep 1946 Cover: 0.10 **NM** value: **60.00**
• Li'l Abner
55 ❑ Dec 1946 Cover: 0.10 **NM** value: **60.00**
• Nancy and Fritzi Ritz
56 ❑ Mar 1947 Cover: 0.10 **NM** value: **60.00**
• The Captain and the Kids **A:** Rudolph Dirks **W:** Rudolph Dirks
57 ❑ Jun 1947 Cover: 0.10 **NM** value: **60.00**
• Nancy and Fritzi Ritz
58 ❑ Sep 1947 Cover: 0.10 **NM** value: **60.00**
• Li'l Abner
59 ❑ Dec 1947 Cover: 0.10 **NM** value: **60.00**
• The Captain and the Kids **A:** Rudolph Dirks **W:** Rudolph Dirks
60 ❑ Mar 1948 Cover: 0.10 **NM** value: **60.00**
• Nancy and Fritzi Ritz
61 ❑ Jun 1948 Cover: 0.10 **NM** value: **50.00**
• Nancy and Fritzi Ritz
62 ❑ Sep 1948 Cover: 0.10 **NM** value: **50.00**
• Nancy and Fritzi Ritz
63 ❑ Dec 1948 Cover: 0.10 **NM** value: **50.00**
• Nancy and Fritzi Ritz
64 ❑ Feb 1949 Cover: 0.10 **NM** value: **50.00**
• Nancy and Fritzi Ritz
65 ❑ Apr 1949 Cover: 0.10 **NM** value: **50.00**
• Nancy and Fritzi Ritz
66 ❑ Jun 1949 Cover: 0.10 **NM** value: **50.00**
• Nancy and Fritzi Ritz
67 ❑ Aug 1949 Cover: 0.10 **NM** value: **50.00**
• Nancy and Fritzi Ritz
68 ❑ Oct 1949 Cover: 0.10 **NM** value: **50.00**
• Nancy and Fritzi Ritz
69 ❑ Dec 1949 Cover: 0.10 **NM** value: **50.00**
• Nancy and Fritzi Ritz
70 ❑ Feb 1950 Cover: 0.10 **NM** value: **50.00**
• Nancy and Fritzi Ritz
71 ❑ Apr 1950 Cover: 0.10 **NM** value: **50.00**
• Nancy
72 ❑ Jun 1950 Cover: 0.10 **NM** value: **50.00**
• Nancy
73 ❑ Aug 1950 Cover: 0.10 **NM** value: **50.00**
• Nancy
74 ❑ Oct 1950 Cover: 0.10 **NM** value: **50.00**
• Nancy
75 ❑ Dec 1950 Cover: 0.10 **NM** value: **50.00**
• Nancy
76 ❑ Feb 1951 Cover: 0.10 **NM** value: **50.00**
• Nancy
77 ❑ Apr 1951 Cover: 0.10 **NM** value: **50.00**
• Nancy and Sluggo
78 ❑ Jun 1951 Cover: 0.10 **NM** value: **50.00**
• Nancy and Sluggo
79 ❑ Aug 1951 Cover: 0.10 **NM** value: **50.00**
• Nancy and Sluggo
80 ❑ Oct 1951 Cover: 0.10 **NM** value: **50.00**
• Nancy and Sluggo
81 ❑ Dec 1951 Cover: 0.10 **NM** value: **36.00**
• Nancy and Sluggo
82 ❑ Feb 1952 Cover: 0.10 **NM** value: **36.00**
• Nancy and Sluggo
83 ❑ Apr 1952 Cover: 0.10 **NM** value: **36.00**
• Nancy and Sluggo
84 ❑ Jun 1952 Cover: 0.10 **NM** value: **36.00**
• Nancy and Sluggo
85 ❑ Aug 1952 Cover: 0.10 **NM** value: **36.00**
• Nancy and Sluggo
86 ❑ Oct 1952 Cover: 0.10 **NM** value: **36.00**
• Nancy and Sluggo
87 ❑ Dec 1952 Cover: 0.10 **NM** value: **36.00**
• Nancy and Sluggo
88 ❑ Feb 1953 Cover: 0.10 **NM** value: **36.00**
• Nancy and Sluggo
89 ❑ Apr 1953 Cover: 0.10 **NM** value: **36.00**
• Nancy and Sluggo
90 ❑ Jun 1953 Cover: 0.10 **NM** value: **36.00**
• Nancy and Sluggo
91 ❑ Aug 1953 Cover: 0.10 **NM** value: **36.00**
• Nancy and Sluggo
92 ❑ Oct 1953 Cover: 0.10 **NM** value: **36.00**
• Nancy and Sluggo
93 ❑ Dec 1953 Cover: 0.10 **NM** value: **36.00**
• Nancy and Sluggo
94 ❑ Feb 1954 Cover: 0.10 **NM** value: **36.00**
• Nancy and Sluggo
95 ❑ Apr 1954 Cover: 0.10 **NM** value: **36.00**
• Nancy and Sluggo
96 ❑ May 1954 Cover: 0.10 **NM** value: **36.00**
• Nancy and Sluggo
97 ❑ Jun 1954 Cover: 0.10 **NM** value: **36.00**
• Nancy and Sluggo
98 ❑ Jul 1954 Cover: 0.10 **NM** value: **36.00**
• Nancy and Sluggo
99 ❑ Aug 1954 Cover: 0.10 **NM** value: **36.00**
• Nancy and Sluggo
100 ❑ Sep 1954 Cover: 0.10 **NM** value: **36.00**
• Nancy and Sluggo
101 ❑ Oct 1954 Cover: 0.10 **NM** value: **36.00**
• Nancy and Sluggo
102 ❑ Nov 1954 Cover: 0.10 **NM** value: **36.00**
• Nancy and Sluggo
103 ❑ Dec 1954 Cover: 0.10 **NM** value: **36.00**
• Nancy and Sluggo
104 ❑ Feb 1955 Cover: 0.10 **NM** value: **36.00**
• Nancy and Sluggo
SE 1 ❑ Sum 1948 Cover: 0.10 **NM** value: **36.00**
• The Captain and the Kids **A:** Rudolph Dirks **W:** Rudolph Dirks

COMICS READING LIBRARIES — King

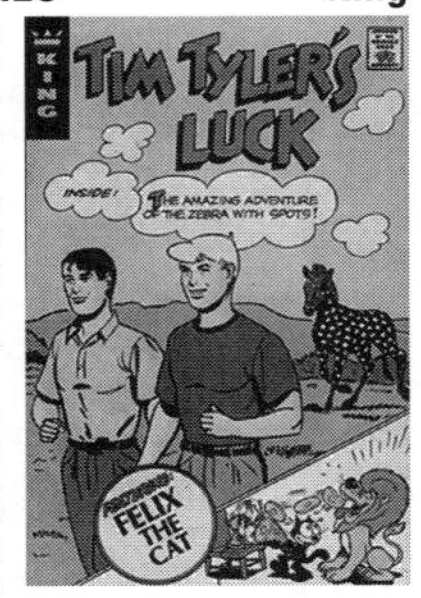

Comics Reading Libraries were a series of give-away comic books produced by King Features Syndicate and publisher Charlton Comics. The comics focused on such favorite King characters as Beetle Bailey, Blondie, Popeye, and The Phantom. The stories in which those chracters appeared were told with simplified text, to help youngsters learn to read.

Between the stories were games, exercises, and features focusing on word use, punctuation, grammar, and facts about books. Issues were given away at schools and libraries throughout the 1970s to encourage reading for fun.

1 ❑ ca. 1974 **NM** value: **8.00**
📖 Tiger: False Alarm; Tiger: Dog Days!; Trixie; Tiger: The Music Lover; Quincy Goes to Camp; Tiger: Notes to You!; Quincy: Clean Sweep?; Trixie and Dawg • Comics Reading Library presents Tiger, and Quincy **A:** Bud Blake ★ Appearance of Tiger, Quincy, Granny, Trixie, Punkinhead, Dawg, Viola, Stripe.
2 ❑ **NM** value: **6.00**
• Comics Reading Library presents Beetle Bailey, Blondie, and Popeye
3 ❑ **NM** value: **6.00**
• Comics Reading Library presents Blondie, and Beetle Bailey
4 ❑ **NM** value: **6.00**
• Comics Reading Library presents Tim Tyler's Luck, and Felix the Cat
5 ❑ **NM** value: **6.00**
• Comics Reading Library presents Quincy, and Henry
6 ❑ **NM** value: **9.00**
• Comics Reading Library presents The Phantom, and Mandrake
7 ❑ **NM** value: **6.00**
• Comics Reading Library presents Popeye, and Little King
8 ❑ **NM** value: **10.00**
• Comics Reading Library presents Prince Valiant, and Flash Gordon
9 ❑ **NM** value: **6.00**
• Comics Reading Library presents Hagar the Horrible, and Boner's Ark
10 ❑ **NM** value: **6.00**
• Comics Reading Library presents Redeye, and Tiger
11 ❑ **NM** value: **6.00**
• Comics Reading Library presents Blondie, and Hi & Lois
12 ❑ **NM** value: **6.00**
• Comics Reading Library presents Popeye
13 ❑ **NM** value: **6.00**
• Comics Reading Library presents Beetle Bailey, and Little King
14 ❑ **NM** value: **6.00**
• Comics Reading Library presents Quincy, and Hamlet
15 ❑ **NM** value: **6.00**
• Comics Reading Library presents The Phantom, and The Genius
16 ❑ **NM** value: **6.00**
• Comics Reading Library presents Flash Gordon, and Mandrake

COMICS REVUE — Comics Interview

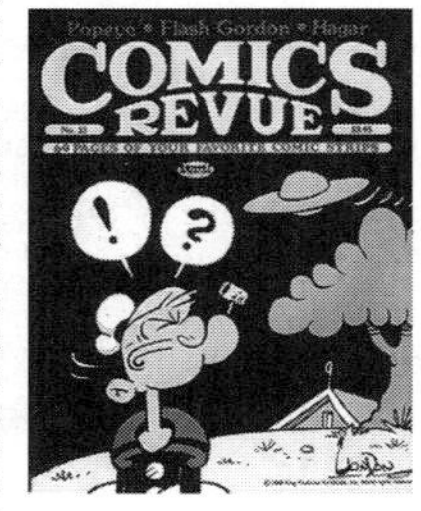

Rick Norwood's magazine boasts that it is "the only monthly magazine in America devoted entirely to comic strips." And so it is. Norwood has specialized for some time in providing strip reprints, and his focus on continuity strips makes the publication a haven for fans and collectors of what seems at times to be a dying art form. The focus here is on classic strips as well as current ones, and material reprinted ranges from Milt Caniff's Steve Canyon and Warren Tufts' Casey Ruggles to Russ Manning's run on Tarzan and Stan Lee's Amazing Spider-Man.

There are also such comedy strips as George Herriman's Krazy Kat and Crockett Johnson's Barnaby. It's a treasure trove of material, much of which is unavailable elsewhere. — Maggie

1 ❑ ca. 1986 **NM** value: **8.00**
2 ❑ ca. 1986 **NM** value: **6.00**
3 ❑ ca. 1986 **NM** value: **6.00**
4 ❑ ca. 1986 **NM** value: **6.00**
5 ❑ ca. 1986 **NM** value: **6.00**
6 ❑ ca. 1986 **NM** value: **5.00**
7 ❑ ca. 1986 **NM** value: **5.00**
8 ❑ ca. 1986 **NM** value: **5.00**
9 ❑ ca. 1986 **NM** value: **5.00**
10 ❑ ca. 1986 **NM** value: **5.00**
11 ❑ ca. 1986 **NM** value: **4.00**
12 ❑ ca. 1986 **NM** value: **4.00**
13 ❑ ca. 1987 **NM** value: **4.00**
14 ❑ ca. 1987 **NM** value: **4.00**
15 ❑ ca. 1987 **NM** value: **4.00**
16 ❑ ca. 1987 **NM** value: **4.00**
17 ❑ ca. 1987 **NM** value: **4.00**
18 ❑ ca. 1987 **NM** value: **4.00**
19 ❑ ca. 1987 **NM** value: **4.00**

Other grades: Multiply prices above by **1.5 for Mint • 2/3 for Very Fine • 1/3 for Fine • 1/5 for Very Good • 1/8 for Good**

20 ❑ ca. 1987 NM value: **4.00**
21 ❑ ca. 1987 NM value: **4.00**
22 ❑ ca. 1987 NM value: **4.00**
23 ❑ ca. 1987 NM value: **4.00**
24 ❑ ca. 1987 NM value: **4.00**
25 ❑ ca. 1988 Cover: 3.50 NM value: **4.00**
26 ❑ ca. 1988 NM value: **4.00**
27 ❑ ca. 1988 NM value: **4.00**
28 ❑ ca. 1988 NM value: **4.00**
29 ❑ ca. 1988 NM value: **4.00**
30 ❑ ca. 1988 NM value: **4.00**
Milton Caniff tribute
31 ❑ ca. 1988 NM value: **5.00**
32 ❑ ca. 1988 NM value: **5.00**
33 ❑ ca. 1988 NM value: **5.00**
34 ❑ ca. 1988 NM value: **5.00**
35 ❑ ca. 1988 Cover: 3.95 NM value: **5.00**
36 ❑ ca. 1988 NM value: **5.00**
37 ❑ ca. 1989 NM value: **5.00**
38 ❑ ca. 1989 NM value: **5.00**
39 ❑ ca. 1989 Cover: 4.95 NM value: **5.00**
40 ❑ ca. 1989 Cover: 4.95 NM value: **5.00**
41 ❑ ca. 1989 Cover: 4.95 NM value: **5.00**
42 ❑ ca. 1989 Cover: 4.95 NM value: **5.00**
43 ❑ ca. 1989 Cover: 4.95 NM value: **5.00**
44 ❑ ca. 1989 Cover: 4.95 NM value: **5.00**
45 ❑ ca. 1989 Cover: 4.95 NM value: **5.00**
46 ❑ ca. 1990 Cover: 4.95 NM value: **5.00**
47 ❑ ca. 1990 Cover: 4.95 NM value: **5.00**
48 ❑ ca. 1990 Cover: 4.95 NM value: **5.00**
49 ❑ ca. 1990 Cover: 4.95 NM value: **5.00**
50 ❑ ca. 1990 Cover: 4.95 NM value: **5.00**
51 ❑ ca. 1990 Cover: 4.95 NM value: **5.00**
52 ❑ ca. 1990 Cover: 4.95 NM value: **5.00**
53 ❑ ca. 1990 Cover: 4.95 NM value: **5.00**
54 ❑ ca. 1990 Cover: 4.95 NM value: **5.00**
55 ❑ ca. 1990 Cover: 4.95 NM value: **5.00**
56 ❑ ca. 1990 Cover: 4.95 NM value: **5.00**
57 ❑ ca. 1990 Cover: 4.95 NM value: **5.00**
58 ❑ ca. 1991 Cover: 4.95 NM value: **5.00**
59 ❑ ca. 1991 Cover: 4.95 NM value: **5.00**
60 ❑ ca. 1991 Cover: 4.95 NM value: **5.00**
61 ❑ ca. 1991 Cover: 4.95 NM value: **5.00**
62 ❑ ca. 1991 Cover: 4.95 NM value: **5.00**
63 ❑ ca. 1991 Cover: 4.95 NM value: **5.00**
64 ❑ ca. 1991 Cover: 4.95 NM value: **5.00**
65 ❑ ca. 1991 Cover: 4.95 NM value: **5.00**
66 ❑ ca. 1991 Cover: 4.95 NM value: **5.00**
67 ❑ ca. 1991 Cover: 4.95 NM value: **5.00**
• Tarzan
68 ❑ ca. 1991 Cover: 4.95 NM value: **5.00**
• Gasoline Alley
69 ❑ ca. 1991 Cover: 4.95 NM value: **5.00**
70 ❑ ca. 1992 Cover: 4.95 NM value: **5.00**
71 ❑ ca. 1992 Cover: 4.95 NM value: **5.00**
72 ❑ ca. 1992 Cover: 4.95 NM value: **5.00**
73 ❑ ca. 1992 Cover: 4.95 NM value: **5.00**
74 ❑ ca. 1992 Cover: 4.95 NM value: **5.00**
75 ❑ ca. 1992 Cover: 4.95 NM value: **5.00**
76 ❑ ca. 1992 Cover: 4.95 NM value: **5.00**
77 ❑ ca. 1992 Cover: 4.95 NM value: **5.00**
78 ❑ ca. 1992 Cover: 4.95 NM value: **5.00**
79 ❑ ca. 1992 Cover: 4.95 NM value: **5.00**
80 ❑ ca. 1992 Cover: 4.95 NM value: **5.00**
81 ❑ ca. 1992 Cover: 4.95 NM value: **5.00**
82 ❑ ca. 1993 Cover: 5.95 NM value: **6.00**
83 ❑ ca. 1993 Cover: 5.95 NM value: **6.00**
84 ❑ ca. 1993 Cover: 5.95 NM value: **6.00**
85 ❑ ca. 1993 Cover: 5.95 NM value: **6.00**
86 ❑ ca. 1993 Cover: 5.95 NM value: **6.00**
87 ❑ ca. 1993 Cover: 5.95 NM value: **6.00**
88 ❑ ca. 1993 Cover: 5.95 NM value: **6.00**
89 ❑ ca. 1993 Cover: 5.95 NM value: **6.00**
90 ❑ ca. 1993 Cover: 5.95 NM value: **6.00**
91 ❑ ca. 1993 Cover: 5.95 NM value: **6.00**
92 ❑ ca. 1993 Cover: 5.95 NM value: **6.00**
93 ❑ ca. 1993 Cover: 5.95 NM value: **6.00**
94 ❑ ca. 1994 Cover: 5.95 NM value: **6.00**
95 ❑ ca. 1994 Cover: 5.95 NM value: **6.00**
96 ❑ ca. 1994 Cover: 5.95 NM value: **6.00**
• Amazing Spider-Man
97 ❑ ca. 1994 Cover: 5.95 NM value: **6.00**
98 ❑ ca. 1994 Cover: 5.95 NM value: **6.00**
99 ❑ ca. 1994 Cover: 5.95 NM value: **Cover or less**
100 ❑ ca. 1994 Cover: 5.95 NM value: **Cover or less**
101 ❑ ca. 1994 Cover: 5.95 NM value: **Cover or less**
102 ❑ ca. 1994 Cover: 5.95 NM value: **Cover or less**
103 ❑ ca. 1994 Cover: 5.95 NM value: **Cover or less**
104 ❑ ca. 1994 Cover: 5.95 NM value: **Cover or less**
105 ❑ ca. 1994 Cover: 5.95 NM value: **Cover or less**
106 ❑ ca. 1995 Cover: 5.95 NM value: **Cover or less**
107 ❑ ca. 1995 Cover: 5.95 NM value: **Cover or less**
108 ❑ ca. 1995 Cover: 5.95 NM value: **Cover or less**
109 ❑ ca. 1995 Cover: 5.95 NM value: **Cover or less**
110 ❑ ca. 1995 Cover: 5.95 NM value: **Cover or less**
111 ❑ ca. 1995 Cover: 5.95 NM value: **Cover or less**
112 ❑ ca. 1995 Cover: 5.95 NM value: **Cover or less**
113 ❑ ca. 1995 Cover: 5.95 NM value: **Cover or less**
114 ❑ ca. 1995 Cover: 5.95 NM value: **Cover or less**
115 ❑ ca. 1995 Cover: 5.95 NM value: **Cover or less**
116 ❑ ca. 1995 Cover: 5.95 NM value: **Cover or less**
117 ❑ ca. 1995 Cover: 5.95 NM value: **Cover or less**
118 ❑ ca. 1996 Cover: 5.95 NM value: **Cover or less**
119 ❑ ca. 1996 Cover: 5.95 NM value: **Cover or less**
120 ❑ ca. 1996 Cover: 5.95 NM value: **Cover or less**
121 ❑ ca. 1996 Cover: 5.95 NM value: **Cover or less**
122 ❑ ca. 1996 Cover: 5.95 NM value: **Cover or less**
123 ❑ ca. 1996 Cover: 5.95 NM value: **Cover or less**
124 ❑ ca. 1996 Cover: 5.95 NM value: **Cover or less**
125 ❑ ca. 1996 Cover: 5.95 NM value: **Cover or less**
126 ❑ ca. 1996 Cover: 5.95 NM value: **Cover or less**
127 ❑ ca. 1996 Cover: 5.95 NM value: **Cover or less**
128 ❑ ca. 1996 Cover: 5.95 NM value: **Cover or less**
129 ❑ ca. 1996 Cover: 5.95 NM value: **Cover or less**
130 ❑ ca. 1997 Cover: 5.95 NM value: **Cover or less**
131 ❑ ca. 1997 Cover: 5.95 NM value: **Cover or less**
132 ❑ ca. 1997 Cover: 5.95 NM value: **Cover or less**
133 ❑ ca. 1997 Cover: 5.95 NM value: **Cover or less**
134 ❑ ca. 1997 Cover: 5.95 NM value: **Cover or less**
135 ❑ ca. 1997 Cover: 5.95 NM value: **Cover or less**
136 ❑ ca. 1997 Cover: 5.95 NM value: **Cover or less**
137 ❑ ca. 1997 Cover: 5.95 NM value: **Cover or less**
138 ❑ ca. 1997 Cover: 5.95 NM value: **Cover or less**
139 ❑ ca. 1997 Cover: 5.95 NM value: **Cover or less**
140 ❑ ca. 1997 Cover: 5.95 NM value: **Cover or less**
141 ❑ ca. 1997 Cover: 5.95 NM value: **Cover or less**
142 ❑ ca. 1998 Cover: 5.95 NM value: **Cover or less**
143 ❑ ca. 1998 Cover: 5.95 NM value: **Cover or less**
144 ❑ ca. 1998 Cover: 5.95 NM value: **Cover or less**
145 ❑ ca. 1998 Cover: 5.95 NM value: **Cover or less**
146 ❑ ca. 1998 Cover: 5.95 NM value: **Cover or less**
147 ❑ ca. 1998 Cover: 5.95 NM value: **Cover or less**
148 ❑ ca. 1998 Cover: 5.95 NM value: **Cover or less**
149 ❑ ca. 1998 Cover: 5.95 NM value: **Cover or less**
150 ❑ ca. 1998 Cover: 5.95 NM value: **Cover or less**
151 ❑ ca. 1998 Cover: 5.95 NM value: **Cover or less**
152 ❑ ca. 1998 Cover: 5.95 NM value: **Cover or less**
153 ❑ ca. 1998 Cover: 5.95 NM value: **Cover or less**
154 ❑ ca. 1998 Cover: 5.95 NM value: **Cover or less**
155 ❑ ca. 1999 Cover: 5.95 NM value: **Cover or less**
156 ❑ ca. 1999 Cover: 5.95 NM value: **Cover or less**
157 ❑ ca. 1999 Cover: 5.95 NM value: **Cover or less**
158 ❑ ca. 1999 Cover: 5.95 NM value: **Cover or less**
159 ❑ ca. 1999 Cover: 5.95 NM value: **Cover or less**
160 ❑ ca. 1999 Cover: 5.95 NM value: **Cover or less**
161 ❑ ca. 1999 Cover: 5.95 NM value: **Cover or less**
162 ❑ ca. 1999 Cover: 5.95 NM value: **Cover or less**
163 ❑ ca. 1999 Cover: 5.95 NM value: **Cover or less**
164 ❑ ca. 1999 Cover: 5.95 NM value: **Cover or less**
165 ❑ ca. 1999 Cover: 5.95 NM value: **Cover or less**
166 ❑ ca. 1999 Cover: 5.95 NM value: **Cover or less**
167 ❑ ca. 2000 Cover: 5.95 NM value: **Cover or less**
168 ❑ ca. 2000 Cover: 5.95 NM value: **Cover or less**
169 ❑ ca. 2000 Cover: 5.95 NM value: **Cover or less**
170 ❑ ca. 2000 Cover: 5.95 NM value: **Cover or less**
171 ❑ ca. 2000 Cover: 5.95 NM value: **Cover or less**
172 ❑ ca. 2000 Cover: 5.95 NM value: **Cover or less**
173 ❑ ca. 2000 Cover: 5.95 NM value: **Cover or less**
174 ❑ ca. 2000 Cover: 5.95 NM value: **Cover or less**
175 ❑ ca. 2000 Cover: 5.95 NM value: **Cover or less**
176 ❑ ca. 2000 Cover: 5.95 NM value: **Cover or less**
177 ❑ ca. 2000 Cover: 5.95 NM value: **Cover or less**
178 ❑ ca. 2000 Cover: 5.95 NM value: **Cover or less**
179 ❑ ca. 2001 Cover: 5.95 NM value: **Cover or less**
180 ❑ ca. 2001 Cover: 5.95 NM value: **Cover or less**
181 ❑ ca. 2001 Cover: 5.95 NM value: **Cover or less**
182 ❑ ca. 2001 Cover: 5.95 NM value: **Cover or less**
183 ❑ ca. 2001 Cover: 5.95 NM value: **Cover or less**
184 ❑ ca. 2001 Cover: 5.95 NM value: **Cover or less**
185 ❑ ca. 2001 Cover: 5.95 NM value: **Cover or less**
186 ❑ ca. 2001 Cover: 5.95 NM value: **Cover or less**
187 ❑ ca. 2001 Cover: 5.95 NM value: **Cover or less**
188 ❑ ca. 2001 Cover: 5.95 NM value: **Cover or less**
189 ❑ ca. 2001 Cover: 5.95 NM value: **Cover or less**
190 ❑ ca. 2001 Cover: 5.95 NM value: **Cover or less**

COMICS THAT ATE MY BRAIN, THE — Eternity
Bk 1 ❑ b&w Cover: 9.95 NM value: **Cover or less**

COMICSTRIPS (PETER KUPER'S...) — Tundra
1 ❑ Cover: 6.95 NM value: **Cover or less**
A: Peter Kuper **W:** Peter Kuper

COMING OF APHRODITE — Hero
1 ❑ b&w Cover: 3.95 NM value: **Cover or less**

COMIX BOOK — Marvel
1 ❑ ca. 1974 Cover: 1.00 NM value: **10.00**
The Bir • 1974 **A:** Tim Boxell **W:** Tim Boxell; Howard Cruse; Kim Deitch; Evert; Vince Davis
2 ❑ ca. 1974 Cover: 1.00 NM value: **8.00**
3 ❑ ca. 1975 Cover: 1.00 NM value: **8.00**
4 ❑ ca. 1975 Cover: 1.00 NM value: **5.00**
5 ❑ ca. 1975 Cover: 1.00 NM value: **5.00**

COMMANDER BATTLE AND THE ATOMIC SUB — ACG
1 ❑ NM value: **400.00**
• **CGC:** 1 graded, best 6.5
2 ❑ NM value: **200.00**
3 ❑ NM value: **200.00**
4 ❑ NM value: **200.00**
5 ❑ NM value: **150.00**
6 ❑ NM value: **150.00**
7 ❑ NM value: **150.00**

COMMAND REVIEW — Thoughts & Images
1 ❑ Jul 1986, b&w Cover: 4.00 NM value: **Cover or less**
• collects stories from Albedo #1-4
2 ❑ Aug 1987, b&w Cover: 4.00 NM value: **Cover or less**
• collects stories from Albedo #5-8
3 ❑ b&w Cover: 5.00 NM value: **Cover or less**
4 ❑ Jan 1994 Cover: 4.95 NM value: **Cover or less**
• (former Thoughts & Imagess title)

COMMIES FROM MARS — Last Gasp

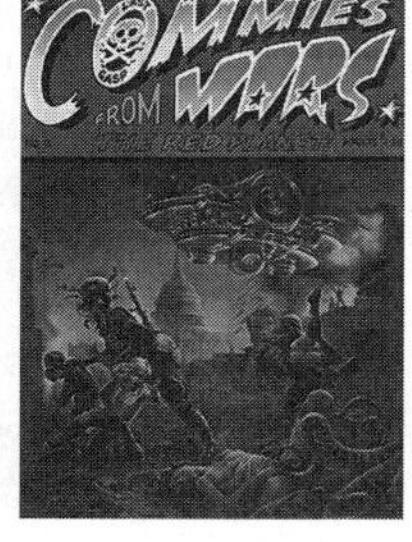

You didn't think they called it "the red planet" because of the color of its soil, did you?

Begun in the late 1970s and published sporadically until the mid-1980s, Commies from Mars is an unusual, funny comic book. It combines a fondness for alien invader science-fiction with good, old-fashioned anti-Communist paranoia and a hippie's love of sex, jokes, and sly humor.

Ted Boxell was the organizing force behind this anthology series, and he invited a collection of underground comix artists to contribute short stories to each issue. Although all submissions were based on the theme of Communist invaders from Mars, each has its own take on the subject. Expect to see everything from depictions of President Reagan as a Martian lizard creature to lowbrow alien sex strips to devilish tales of Martians using our own stupidity to help them destroy our world.

1 ❑ Cover: 1.50 NM value: **2.00**
A: Tim Boxell **W:** Tim Boxell
2 ❑ Cover: 1.50 NM value: **2.00**
Snak?; The Treaty; The Adventures of Alan Rabbit; 12001, A Spaced Outessy **A:** Tim Boxell; J. Michael Leonard; Rich Larson; Doug Hansen; Hunt Emerson **W:** Tim Boxell; J. Michael Leonard; Rich Larson; Doug Hansen; Hunt Emerson
3 ❑ Cover: 1.50 NM value: **2.00**
A: Tim Boxell **W:** Tim Boxell
4 ❑ Cover: 1.50 NM value: **2.00**
A: Tim Boxell **W:** Tim Boxell
5 ❑ Cover: 1.50 NM value: **2.00**
A: Tim Boxell **W:** Tim Boxell
6 ❑ Cover: 2.50 NM value: **Cover or less**
Life Drags on on the New Martian Earth; Counterpoint; Melcher for President; Free Press; A Sailor's Dream; Rage Riley; A Fatal Fondness! **A:** Tim Boxell; Rich Larson; Kenneth Huey; Shawn Kerri **W:** Tim Boxell; Rich Larson; Kenneth Huey; Shawn Kerri
Bk 1 ❑ Cover: 9.95 NM value: **Cover or less**
• Commies from Mars, the Collected Works;Reprints best of Commies From Mars #1-4;Introduction by Jerry Garcia

COMMUNION — Fantagraphics / Eros
All issues are adults only.
1 ❑ b&w Cover: 2.75 NM value: **Cover or less**

COMPLEAT ALIENS, THE — Dark Horse
1/HC ❑ Sep 1993 Cover: 150.00 NM value: **Cover or less**
• Hardover limited edition. • Collects Aliens, Aliens II, Dark Horse Presents Aliens, and Aliens: Earth War

COMPLETE CHEECH WIZARD — Rip Off
1 ❑ Oct 1986, b&w Cover: 2.25 NM value: **Cover or less**
• Vaughn BodT **A:** Vaughn Bodé
2 ❑ Jan 1987, b&w Cover: 2.25 NM value: **Cover or less**
• Vaughn BodT **A:** Vaughn Bodé
3 ❑ May 1987, b&w and colorCover: 2.50 NM value: **Cover or less**
• Vaughn BodT **A:** Vaughn Bodé
4 ❑ Nov 1987, b&w and colorCover: 2.50 NM value: **Cover or less**
• Vaughn BodT **A:** Vaughn Bodé

COMPLETE CLASSIC ALEX TOTH ZORRO, THE — Image
1 ❑ May 1999 Cover: 18.95 NM value: **Cover or less**
No issue number. • Trade Paperback.

COMPLETE COMICS — Timely
2 ❑ Win 1944 Cover: 0.10 NM value: **1000.00**
• **CGC:** 3 graded, best 8.5

COMPLETE CRUMB COMICS, THE — Fantagraphics
1 ❑ Oct 1987 Cover: 12.95 NM value: **Cover or less**
A: Robert Crumb **W:** Robert Crumb
2 ❑ NM value: **12.95**
A: Robert Crumb **W:** Robert Crumb
2/HC ❑ Cover: 35.00 NM value: **Cover or less**
hardcover. **A:** Robert Crumb **W:** Robert Crumb
3 ❑ NM value: **12.95**
A: Robert Crumb **W:** Robert Crumb
4 ❑ NM value: **12.95**
A: Robert Crumb **W:** Robert Crumb
5 ❑ NM value: **12.95**
A: Robert Crumb **W:** Robert Crumb
6 ❑ NM value: **12.95**
A: Robert Crumb **W:** Robert Crumb
7 ❑ NM value: **12.95**
A: Robert Crumb **W:** Robert Crumb
8 ❑ NM value: **12.95**
A: Robert Crumb **W:** Robert Crumb
9 ❑ NM value: **12.95**
A: Robert Crumb **W:** Robert Crumb
10 ❑ NM value: **12.95**
A: Robert Crumb **W:** Robert Crumb
11 ❑ NM value: **12.95**
A: Robert Crumb **W:** Robert Crumb
12 ❑ Mar 1997, b&w Cover: 18.95 NM value: **Cover or less**
A: Robert Crumb **W:** Robert Crumb

COMPLETELY BAD BOYS — Fantagraphics
1 ❑ b&w Cover: 2.50 NM value: **Cover or less**

CGC-graded: Multiply prices above by **33 for 9.9 M • 16 for 9.8 NM/M • 7 for 9.6 NM+ • 5 for 9.4 NM • 2.5 for 9.2 NM- • 1.5 for 9.0 VF/NM**

COMPLETE MYSTERY — Marvel

1 ❑ Aug 1948 Cover: 0.10 **NM** value: **350.00**
• **CGC:** 1 graded, best 8.5
2 ❑ Oct 1948 Cover: 0.10 **NM** value: **300.00**
3 ❑ Dec 1948 Cover: 0.10 **NM** value: **300.00**
4 ❑ Feb 1949 Cover: 0.10 **NM** value: **300.00**

COMPLETE POGO COMICS, THE — Eclipse

1 ❑ Cover: 8.95 **NM** value: **Cover or less**
Circ: CapCity orders: **1,825**
A: Walt Kelly
2 ❑ Cover: 8.95 **NM** value: **Cover or less**
Circ: CapCity orders: **1,500**
A: Walt Kelly
3 ❑ Cover: 8.95 **NM** value: **Cover or less**
A: Walt Kelly
4 ❑ Cover: 8.95 **NM** value: **Cover or less**
A: Walt Kelly

COMPLETE ROG 2000, THE — Pacific

1 ❑ Cover: 2.95 **NM** value: **Cover or less**

COMPOST COMICS — Gasparotti

1 ❑ Cover: 0.50 **NM** value: **3.00**
Scientific Comics; The Thing in The Garden; Nature's Memory; Doctor Atomic and His Chicken Mobile; The Old Potato Hag; The Fretile Crescent **A:** George Metzger; Hector Tellez; Larry Todd; R.T. Reece; T.P. Gasparotti **W:** George Metzger; Hector Tellez; Larry Todd; R.T. Reece; T.P. Gasparotti

COMRADES OF WAR — Dead Air

1 ❑ Cover: 2.15 **NM** value: **2.25**
Fresh Meat **A:** Glen Lannon **W:** Gordon McEachern
2 ❑ Cover: 2.15 **NM** value: **2.25**
A: Glen Lannon **W:** Gordon McEachern

CONAN — Marvel

Robert E. Howard's Conan the Barbarian, first brought to comics in the early 1970s, has an updated look-and attitude-in this series.

Slashing and hacking at his targets, whether they're fellow gladiators or giant spiders, is just the natural course of action for this Cimmerian, who has much more cunning and intelligence than the corrupt, corpulent despots who think he serves them. Though he appears to be nothing more than an ignorant barbarian, he has plans and schemes that belie his unrefined appearance. In addition to his strength and skill with a sword, this muscular hero has a sense of humor that serves him as well.

1 ❑ Aug 1995 Cover: 2.95 **NM** value: **Cover or less**
Circ: CapCity orders: **12,850**
cardstock cover. Song Of The Death Pits **A:** Barry Crain **W:** Larry Hama
2 ❑ Sep 1995 Cover: 2.95 **NM** value: **Cover or less**
cardstock cover. The Treasure of Harach Gnar **A:** Barry Crain **W:** Larry Hama
3 ❑ Oct 1995 Cover: 2.95 **NM** value: **Cover or less**
cardstock cover.
4 ❑ Nov 1995 Cover: 2.95 **NM** value: **Cover or less**
cardstock cover. ★ Appearance of Rune.
5 ❑ Dec 1995 Cover: 2.95 **NM** value: **Cover or less**
cardstock cover. **A:** Doug Wheatley **W:** Larry Hama ★ Appearance of yeti.
6 ❑ Jan 1996 Cover: 2.95 **NM** value: **Cover or less**
cardstock cover.
7 ❑ Feb 1996 Cover: 2.95 **NM** value: **Cover or less**
★ Versus Man of Iron.
8 ❑ Mar 1996 Cover: 2.95 **NM** value: **Cover or less**
cardstock cover.
9 ❑ Apr 1996 Cover: 2.95 **NM** value: **Cover or less**
cardstock cover. God Fall **A:** Joe Bennett **W:** Dan Abnett
10 ❑ May 1996 Cover: 2.95 **NM** value: **Cover or less**
cardstock cover. Queen of the Amazons **A:** Enrique Alcatena **W:** Larry Hama
11 ❑ Jun 1996 Cover: 2.95 **NM** value: **Cover or less**
cardstock cover.
12 ❑ Jul 1996 Cover: 2.95 **NM** value: **Cover or less**
final issue.
Bk 1❑ Cover: 1.95 **NM** value: **Cover or less**
Bk 2❑ Cover: 1.95 **NM** value: **Cover or less**
Bk 3❑ Cover: 1.95 **NM** value: **Cover or less**
Bk 4❑ Cover: 1.95 **NM** value: **Cover or less**
Bk 5❑ Cover: 2.25 **NM** value: **Cover or less**
Bk 6❑ Cover: 2.25 **NM** value: **Cover or less**

CONAN CLASSIC — Marvel

1 ❑ Jun 1994 Cover: 1.50 **NM** value: **Cover or less**
Circ: CapCity orders: **10,950**
The Coming of Conan • Reprints Conan the Barbarian #1 **A:** Barry Windsor-Smith **W:** Roy Thomas ★ Origin of Conan. ★ 1st Appearance of Conan.
2 ❑ Jul 1994 Cover: 1.50 **NM** value: **Cover or less**
Circ: CapCity orders: **8,200**
W: Roy Thomas
3 ❑ Aug 1994 Cover: 1.50 **NM** value: **Cover or less**
Circ: CapCity orders: **7,700**
W: Roy Thomas
4 ❑ Sep 1994 Cover: 1.50 **NM** value: **Cover or less**
Circ: CapCity orders: **7,100**
W: Roy Thomas
5 ❑ Oct 1994 Cover: 1.50 **NM** value: **Cover or less**
Circ: CapCity orders: **6,500**
W: Roy Thomas
6 ❑ Nov 1994 Cover: 1.50 **NM** value: **Cover or less**
Circ: CapCity orders: **5,900**
W: Roy Thomas
7 ❑ Dec 1994 Cover: 1.50 **NM** value: **Cover or less**
Circ: CapCity orders: **5,600**
W: Roy Thomas
8 ❑ Jan 1995 Cover: 1.50 **NM** value: **Cover or less**
Circ: CapCity orders: **5,100**
W: Roy Thomas
9 ❑ Feb 1995 Cover: 1.50 **NM** value: **Cover or less**
Circ: CapCity orders: **4,625**
W: Roy Thomas
10 ❑ Mar 1995 Cover: 1.50 **NM** value: **Cover or less**
Circ: CapCity orders: **4,300**
W: Roy Thomas
11 ❑ Apr 1995 Cover: 1.50 **NM** value: **Cover or less**
Circ: CapCity orders: **3,975**
final issue. **W:** Roy Thomas

CONAN: DEATH COVERED IN GOLD — Marvel

1 ❑ Sep 1999 Cover: 2.99 **NM** value: **Cover or less**
Circ: Diamd. preorders: **19,012**
3 ❑ Nov 1999 Cover: 2.99 **NM** value: **Cover or less**
Circ: Diamd. preorders: **15,116**

CONAN: FLAME AND THE FIEND — Marvel

1 ❑ Aug 2000 Cover: 2.99 **NM** value: **Cover or less**
Circ: Diamd. preorders: **15,355**
A: Geof Isherwood **W:** Roy Thomas
2 ❑ Sep 2000 Cover: 2.99 **NM** value: **Cover or less**
Circ: Diamd. preorders: **13,855**
A: Geof Isherwood **W:** Roy Thomas
3 ❑ Oct 2000 Cover: 2.99 **NM** value: **Cover or less**
Circ: Diamd. preorders: **12,691**
A: Geof Isherwood **W:** Roy Thomas

CONAN OF THE ISLES — Marvel

Bk 1❑ Cover: 8.95 **NM** value: **Cover or less**

CONAN: RETURN OF STYRM — Marvel

Conan is brought in as an unwilling savior of the town of Valdover in this three-issue mini-series. Apparently, he killed the mercenaries who were scheduled to save the town from the ravages of the dragon Styrm. As a result, the sorceress in charge of the town used a combination of threats and bribes to secure his word to save the town, instead.

Writer Matt Nixon stretches things out, giving penciller Paolo Parente plenty of pointless battle scenes to draw during the course of the series, which neither thrill nor advance the plot. The sorceress, it seems, is perfectly willing to grind through dozens of assassin helpers in order to get Conan's aid — throwing them away in a succession of meaningless battles with Conan in order "to prove his worth." At three giant-sized issues, the series seems easily two and a half issues too long to communicate this by-the-book tale.

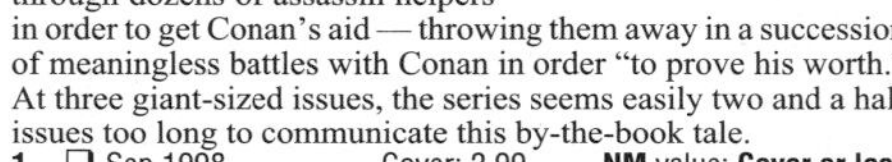

1 ❑ Sep 1998 Cover: 2.99 **NM** value: **Cover or less**
Circ: Diamd. preorders: **17,400**
• gatefold summary. **A:** Paolo Parente **W:** Matt Nixon
2 ❑ Oct 1998 Cover: 2.99 **NM** value: **Cover or less**
Circ: Diamd. preorders: **15,409**
• gatefold summary. **A:** Paolo Parente **W:** Matt Nixon
3 ❑ Nov 1998 Cover: 2.99 **NM** value: **Cover or less**
Circ: Diamd. preorders: **15,013**
• gatefold summary. **A:** Paolo Parente **W:** Matt Nixon

CONAN: RIVER OF BLOOD — Marvel

1 ❑ Jun 1998 Cover: 2.50 **NM** value: **Cover or less**
Circ: Diamd. preorders: **18,132**
2 ❑ Jul 1998 Cover: 2.50 **NM** value: **Cover or less**
Circ: Diamd. preorders: **15,970**
3 ❑ Aug 1998 Cover: 2.50 **NM** value: **Cover or less**
Circ: Diamd. preorders: **15,832**

CONAN SAGA — Marvel

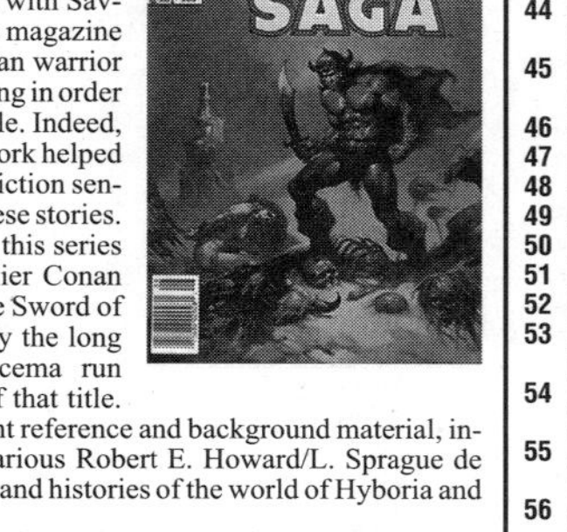

Launched in 1987, Conan Saga became the third black-and-white, magazine-sized comic to feature the adventures of Conan. As with Savage Sword of Conan, this magazine proved that the Cimmerian warrior does not need color printing in order to be vivid and memorable. Indeed, the black-and-white artwork helped to evoke a grittier, pulp-fiction sensibility well-suited for these stories.

The tales contained in this series were reprints of the earlier Conan the Barbarian and Savage Sword of Conan series, particularly the long Roy Thomas/John Buscema run which was a highlight of that title. In addition, issues brought reference and background material, including indices of the various Robert E. Howard/L. Sprague de Camp novel adaptations, and histories of the world of Hyboria and its chief characters.

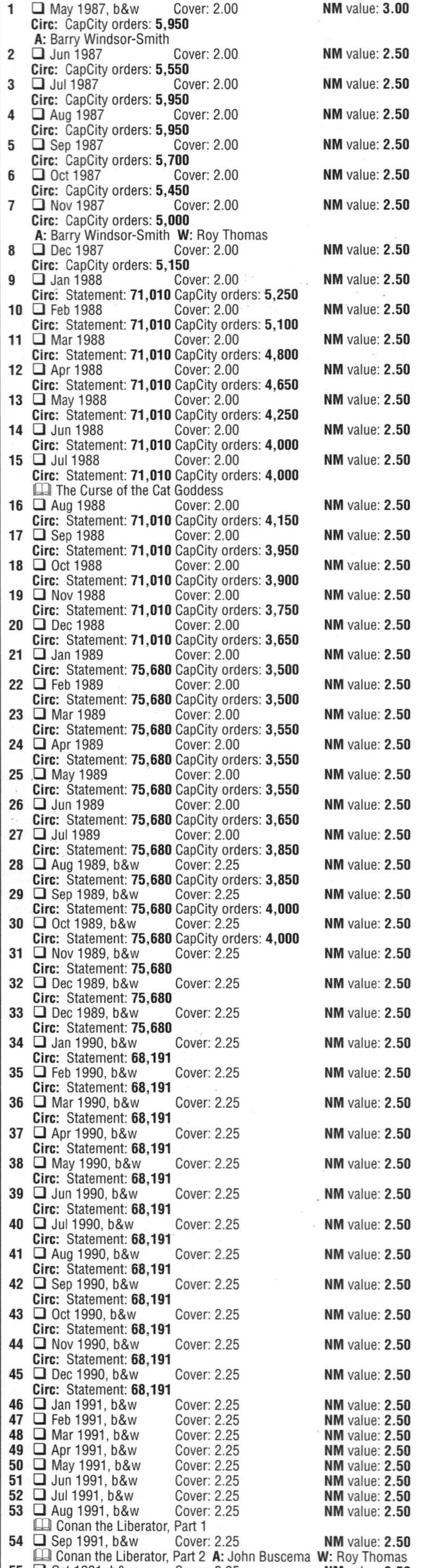

1 ❑ May 1987, b&w Cover: 2.00 **NM** value: **3.00**
Circ: CapCity orders: **5,950**
A: Barry Windsor-Smith
2 ❑ Jun 1987 Cover: 2.00 **NM** value: **2.50**
Circ: CapCity orders: **5,550**
3 ❑ Jul 1987 Cover: 2.00 **NM** value: **2.50**
Circ: CapCity orders: **5,950**
4 ❑ Aug 1987 Cover: 2.00 **NM** value: **2.50**
Circ: CapCity orders: **5,950**
5 ❑ Sep 1987 Cover: 2.00 **NM** value: **2.50**
Circ: CapCity orders: **5,700**
6 ❑ Oct 1987 Cover: 2.00 **NM** value: **2.50**
Circ: CapCity orders: **5,450**
7 ❑ Nov 1987 Cover: 2.00 **NM** value: **2.50**
Circ: CapCity orders: **5,000**
A: Barry Windsor-Smith **W:** Roy Thomas
8 ❑ Dec 1987 Cover: 2.00 **NM** value: **2.50**
Circ: CapCity orders: **5,150**
9 ❑ Jan 1988 Cover: 2.00 **NM** value: **2.50**
Circ: Statement: **71,010** CapCity orders: **5,250**
10 ❑ Feb 1988 Cover: 2.00 **NM** value: **2.50**
Circ: Statement: **71,010** CapCity orders: **5,100**
11 ❑ Mar 1988 Cover: 2.00 **NM** value: **2.50**
Circ: Statement: **71,010** CapCity orders: **4,800**
12 ❑ Apr 1988 Cover: 2.00 **NM** value: **2.50**
Circ: Statement: **71,010** CapCity orders: **4,650**
13 ❑ May 1988 Cover: 2.00 **NM** value: **2.50**
Circ: Statement: **71,010** CapCity orders: **4,250**
14 ❑ Jun 1988 Cover: 2.00 **NM** value: **2.50**
Circ: Statement: **71,010** CapCity orders: **4,000**
15 ❑ Jul 1988 Cover: 2.00 **NM** value: **2.50**
Circ: Statement: **71,010** CapCity orders: **4,000**
The Curse of the Cat Goddess
16 ❑ Aug 1988 Cover: 2.00 **NM** value: **2.50**
Circ: Statement: **71,010** CapCity orders: **4,150**
17 ❑ Sep 1988 Cover: 2.00 **NM** value: **2.50**
Circ: Statement: **71,010** CapCity orders: **3,950**
18 ❑ Oct 1988 Cover: 2.00 **NM** value: **2.50**
Circ: Statement: **71,010** CapCity orders: **3,900**
19 ❑ Nov 1988 Cover: 2.00 **NM** value: **2.50**
Circ: Statement: **71,010** CapCity orders: **3,750**
20 ❑ Dec 1988 Cover: 2.00 **NM** value: **2.50**
Circ: Statement: **71,010** CapCity orders: **3,650**
21 ❑ Jan 1989 Cover: 2.00 **NM** value: **2.50**
Circ: Statement: **75,680** CapCity orders: **3,500**
22 ❑ Feb 1989 Cover: 2.00 **NM** value: **2.50**
Circ: Statement: **75,680** CapCity orders: **3,500**
23 ❑ Mar 1989 Cover: 2.00 **NM** value: **2.50**
Circ: Statement: **75,680** CapCity orders: **3,550**
24 ❑ Apr 1989 Cover: 2.00 **NM** value: **2.50**
Circ: Statement: **75,680** CapCity orders: **3,550**
25 ❑ May 1989 Cover: 2.00 **NM** value: **2.50**
Circ: Statement: **75,680** CapCity orders: **3,550**
26 ❑ Jun 1989 Cover: 2.00 **NM** value: **2.50**
Circ: Statement: **75,680** CapCity orders: **3,650**
27 ❑ Jul 1989 Cover: 2.00 **NM** value: **2.50**
Circ: Statement: **75,680** CapCity orders: **3,850**
28 ❑ Aug 1989, b&w Cover: 2.25 **NM** value: **2.50**
Circ: Statement: **75,680** CapCity orders: **3,850**
29 ❑ Sep 1989, b&w Cover: 2.25 **NM** value: **2.50**
Circ: Statement: **75,680** CapCity orders: **4,000**
30 ❑ Oct 1989, b&w Cover: 2.25 **NM** value: **2.50**
Circ: Statement: **75,680** CapCity orders: **4,000**
31 ❑ Nov 1989, b&w Cover: 2.25 **NM** value: **2.50**
Circ: Statement: **75,680**
32 ❑ Dec 1989, b&w Cover: 2.25 **NM** value: **2.50**
Circ: Statement: **75,680**
33 ❑ Dec 1989, b&w Cover: 2.25 **NM** value: **2.50**
Circ: Statement: **75,680**
34 ❑ Jan 1990, b&w Cover: 2.25 **NM** value: **2.50**
Circ: Statement: **68,191**
35 ❑ Feb 1990, b&w Cover: 2.25 **NM** value: **2.50**
Circ: Statement: **68,191**
36 ❑ Mar 1990, b&w Cover: 2.25 **NM** value: **2.50**
Circ: Statement: **68,191**
37 ❑ Apr 1990, b&w Cover: 2.25 **NM** value: **2.50**
Circ: Statement: **68,191**
38 ❑ May 1990, b&w Cover: 2.25 **NM** value: **2.50**
Circ: Statement: **68,191**
39 ❑ Jun 1990, b&w Cover: 2.25 **NM** value: **2.50**
Circ: Statement: **68,191**
40 ❑ Jul 1990, b&w Cover: 2.25 **NM** value: **2.50**
Circ: Statement: **68,191**
41 ❑ Aug 1990, b&w Cover: 2.25 **NM** value: **2.50**
Circ: Statement: **68,191**
42 ❑ Sep 1990, b&w Cover: 2.25 **NM** value: **2.50**
Circ: Statement: **68,191**
43 ❑ Oct 1990, b&w Cover: 2.25 **NM** value: **2.50**
Circ: Statement: **68,191**
44 ❑ Nov 1990, b&w Cover: 2.25 **NM** value: **2.50**
Circ: Statement: **68,191**
45 ❑ Dec 1990, b&w Cover: 2.25 **NM** value: **2.50**
Circ: Statement: **68,191**
46 ❑ Jan 1991, b&w Cover: 2.25 **NM** value: **2.50**
47 ❑ Feb 1991, b&w Cover: 2.25 **NM** value: **2.50**
48 ❑ Mar 1991, b&w Cover: 2.25 **NM** value: **2.50**
49 ❑ Apr 1991, b&w Cover: 2.25 **NM** value: **2.50**
50 ❑ May 1991, b&w Cover: 2.25 **NM** value: **2.50**
51 ❑ Jun 1991, b&w Cover: 2.25 **NM** value: **2.50**
52 ❑ Jul 1991, b&w Cover: 2.25 **NM** value: **2.50**
53 ❑ Aug 1991, b&w Cover: 2.25 **NM** value: **2.50**
Conan the Liberator, Part 1
54 ❑ Sep 1991, b&w Cover: 2.25 **NM** value: **2.50**
Conan the Liberator, Part 2 **A:** John Buscema **W:** Roy Thomas
55 ❑ Oct 1991, b&w Cover: 2.25 **NM** value: **2.50**
Conan the Liberator, Part 3 **A:** John Buscema **W:** Roy Thomas
56 ❑ Nov 1991, b&w Cover: 2.25 **NM** value: **2.50**
Conan the Liberator, Part 4 **A:** John Buscema **W:** Roy Thomas

Other grades: Multiply prices above by **1.5 for Mint • 2/3 for Very Fine • 1/3 for Fine • 1/5 for Very Good • 1/8 for Good**

57 ❑ Dec 1991, b&w Cover: 2.25 **NM** value: **2.50**
📖 The Scarlet Citadel **A:** Frank Brunner **W:** Roy Thomas
58 ❑ Jan 1992, b&w Cover: 2.25 **NM** value: **2.50**
Circ: CapCity orders: **3,700**
59 ❑ Feb 1992, b&w Cover: 2.25 **NM** value: **2.50**
Circ: CapCity orders: **3,650**
60 ❑ Mar 1992, b&w Cover: 2.25 **NM** value: **2.50**
Circ: CapCity orders: **3,450**
📖 The Star of Khorala **A:** John Buscema **W:** Roy Thomas
61 ❑ Apr 1992, b&w Cover: 2.25 **NM** value: **2.50**
Circ: CapCity orders: **3,350**
📖 The Sword of Skelos **A:** John Buscema **W:** Roy Thomas
62 ❑ May 1992, b&w Cover: 2.25 **NM** value: **2.50**
Circ: CapCity orders: **3,400**
📖 The Eye of Erlik **A:** John Buscema **W:** Roy Thomas
63 ❑ Jun 1992, b&w Cover: 2.25 **NM** value: **2.50**
Circ: CapCity orders: **3,500**
📖 For the Throne of Zamboula **A:** John Buscema **W:** Roy Thomas
64 ❑ Jul 1992, b&w Cover: 2.25 **NM** value: **2.50**
Circ: CapCity orders: **3,350**
📖 The City of Skulls **A:** Mike Vosburg **W:** Roy Thomas
65 ❑ Aug 1992, b&w Cover: 2.25 **NM** value: **2.50**
Circ: CapCity orders: **3,600**
📖 The Ivory Goddess **A:** John Buscema **W:** Roy Thomas
66 ❑ Sep 1992, b&w Cover: 2.25 **NM** value: **2.50**
Circ: CapCity orders: **3,400**
📖 The Phoenix on the Sword **A:** Vincente Alcazar **W:** Roy Thomas
67 ❑ Oct 1992, b&w Cover: 2.25 **NM** value: **2.50**
Circ: CapCity orders: **3,350**
68 ❑ Nov 1992, b&w Cover: 2.25 **NM** value: **2.50**
Circ: CapCity orders: **3,400**
📖 Bride of the Conqueror **A:** John Buscema **W:** Roy Thomas
69 ❑ Dec 1992, b&w Cover: 2.25 **NM** value: **2.50**
Circ: CapCity orders: **3,200**
70 ❑ Jan 1993, b&w Cover: 2.25 **NM** value: **2.50**
Circ: CapCity orders: **3,200**
71 ❑ Feb 1993, b&w Cover: 2.25 **NM** value: **2.50**
Circ: CapCity orders: **3,300**
📖 Revenge of the Barbarian **A:** John Buscema **W:** Roy Thomas
72 ❑ Mar 1993, b&w Cover: 2.25 **NM** value: **2.50**
Circ: CapCity orders: **3,250**
A: John Buscema **W:** Roy Thomas
73 ❑ Apr 1993, b&w Cover: 2.25 **NM** value: **2.50**
Circ: CapCity orders: **3,400**
A: John Buscema **W:** Roy Thomas
74 ❑ May 1993, b&w Cover: 2.25 **NM** value: **2.50**
Circ: CapCity orders: **3,500**
A: John Buscema **W:** Roy Thomas
75 ❑ Jun 1993 Cover: 3.95 **NM** value: **4.00**
Circ: CapCity orders: **4,350**
• poster, handbook
76 ❑ Jul 1993, b&w Cover: 2.25 **NM** value: **Cover or less**
Circ: CapCity orders: **3,600**
77 ❑ Aug 1993, b&w Cover: 2.25 **NM** value: **Cover or less**
Circ: CapCity orders: **3,700**
📖 The Warrior and the Were-Woman
78 ❑ Sep 1993, b&w Cover: 2.25 **NM** value: **Cover or less**
Circ: CapCity orders: **3,600**
79 ❑ Oct 1993, b&w Cover: 2.25 **NM** value: **Cover or less**
Circ: CapCity orders: **3,450**
📖 Red Sonja: Balek Lives!; The Tower of Blood; Of Flame and the Fiend; The Last Ballad of Laza-Lanti • Reprints Conan the Barbarian #43-45 **A:** Ernie Chan; John Buscema; Frank Thorne; Neal Adams("Crusty Bunkers") **W:** Bruce Jones; Roy Thomas ★ Appearance of Red Sonja.
80 ❑ Nov 1993, b&w Cover: 2.25 **NM** value: **Cover or less**
Circ: CapCity orders: **3,450**
📖 The Trail of the Bloodstained God **A:** John Buscema **W:** Roy Thomas
81 ❑ Dec 1993, b&w Cover: 2.25 **NM** value: **Cover or less**
Circ: CapCity orders: **3,600**
📖 The Curse of the Conjurer **A:** John Buscema **W:** Roy Thomas
82 ❑ Jan 1994, b&w Cover: 2.25 **NM** value: **Cover or less**
Circ: CapCity orders: **3,500**
📖 The Oracle of Ophir **A:** John Buscema **W:** Roy Thomas
83 ❑ Feb 1994, b&w Cover: 3.00 **NM** value: **Cover or less**
Circ: CapCity orders: **3,500**
84 ❑ Mar 1994, b&w Cover: 2.25 **NM** value: **Cover or less**
Circ: CapCity orders: **3,350**
85 ❑ Apr 1994, b&w Cover: 2.25 **NM** value: **Cover or less**
Circ: CapCity orders: **3,300**
86 ❑ May 1994, b&w Cover: 2.25 **NM** value: **Cover or less**
Circ: CapCity orders: **3,300**
📖 Talons of the Man-Tiger **A:** John Buscema **W:** Roy Thomas
87 ❑ Jun 1994, b&w Cover: 2.25 **NM** value: **Cover or less**
Circ: CapCity orders: **3,300**
📖 The City in the Storm **A:** John Buscema **W:** Roy Thomas
88 ❑ Jul 1994, b&w Cover: 2.25 **NM** value: **Cover or less**
Circ: CapCity orders: **3,350**
📖 Vengeance in Asgalun **A:** John Buscema **W:** Roy Thomas
89 ❑ Aug 1994, b&w Cover: 2.25 **NM** value: **Cover or less**
Circ: CapCity orders: **3,525**
📖 The Battle at the Black Walls **A:** John Buscema **W:** Roy Thomas
90 ❑ Sep 1994, b&w Cover: 2.25 **NM** value: **Cover or less**
Circ: CapCity orders: **3,450**
91 ❑ Oct 1994, b&w Cover: 2.25 **NM** value: **Cover or less**
Circ: CapCity orders: **3,450**
📖 The Sorceress of the Swamp **A:** Howard Chaykin **W:** Roy Thomas
92 ❑ Nov 1994, b&w Cover: 2.25 **NM** value: **Cover or less**
Circ: CapCity orders: **3,250**
📖 Two Against the Hawk City **A:** John Buscema **W:** Roy Thomas
93 ❑ Dec 1994, b&w Cover: 2.25 **NM** value: **Cover or less**
Circ: CapCity orders: **3,100**
📖 The Queen and the Corsairs **A:** John Buscema **W:** Roy Thomas
94 ❑ Jan 1995, b&w Cover: 2.25 **NM** value: **Cover or less**
Circ: CapCity orders: **3,025**
📖 Savage Doings in Shem! **A:** John Buscema **W:** Roy Thomas
95 ❑ Feb 1995, b&w Cover: 2.25 **NM** value: **Cover or less**
Circ: CapCity orders: **2,825**
📖 Prelude to Death **A:** John Buscema **W:** Roy Thomas
96 ❑ Mar 1995, b&w Cover: 2.25 **NM** value: **Cover or less**
Circ: CapCity orders: **2,725**
📖 The Devil has Many Legs!; The Men Who Drink Blood • Reprints Conan the Barbarian #101-103 in black and white **A:** John Buscema **W:** Roy Thomas
97 ❑ Apr 1995, b&w Cover: 2.25 **NM** value: **Cover or less**
Circ: CapCity orders: **2,525**
📖 A War of Wizards! final issue. **A:** John Buscema **W:** Roy Thomas

CONAN: SCARLET SWORD — Marvel

1 ❑ Dec 1998 Cover: 2.99 **NM** value: **Cover or less**
Circ: Diamd. preorders: **15,195**
• gatefold summary. **A:** Stefano Raffaele **W:** Roy Thomas
2 ❑ Jan 1999 Cover: 2.99 **NM** value: **Cover or less**
Circ: Diamd. preorders: **14,107**
• gatefold summary. **A:** Stefano Raffaele **W:** Roy Thomas
3 ❑ Feb 1999 Cover: 2.99 **NM** value: **Cover or less**
Circ: Diamd. preorders: **13,535**
A: Stefano Raffaele **W:** Roy Thomas

CONAN THE ADVENTURER — Marvel

For a "dead" title, Conan showed an awful lot of life in the early 1990s. After nearly 300 issues, the centerpiece Conan the Barbarian was canceled in 1994, only to have the character reappear months later in Conan the Adventurer, Conan Classic, Conan Saga, Conan, etc. For its part, Conan the Adventurer related tales of a youthful Conan just starting out on the barbarian life that would eventually result in him being crowned Conan the King.

This short-lived series was meant to complement an animated cartoon series of the same name.

1 ❑ Jun 1994 Cover: 2.50 **NM** value: **Cover or less**
Circ: CapCity orders: **23,700**
Embossed foil cover. 📖 Barbarians at the Gate • foil embossed **A:** Rafael Kayanan **W:** Roy Thomas
2 ❑ Jul 1994 Cover: 1.50 **NM** value: **Cover or less**
Circ: CapCity orders: **15,000**
A: Rafael Kayanan **W:** Roy Thomas
3 ❑ Aug 1994 Cover: 1.50 **NM** value: **Cover or less**
Circ: CapCity orders: **14,500**
A: Rafael Kayanan **W:** Roy Thomas
4 ❑ Sep 1994 Cover: 1.50 **NM** value: **Cover or less**
Circ: CapCity orders: **14,300**
📖 Between Twin Terrors **A:** Rafael Kayanan **W:** Roy Thomas
5 ❑ Oct 1994 Cover: 1.50 **NM** value: **Cover or less**
Circ: CapCity orders: **13,250**
A: Rafael Kayanan **W:** Roy Thomas
6 ❑ Nov 1994 Cover: 1.50 **NM** value: **Cover or less**
Circ: CapCity orders: **12,200**
📖 The Slavers **W:** Roy Thomas
7 ❑ Dec 1994 Cover: 1.50 **NM** value: **Cover or less**
Circ: CapCity orders: **11,450**
📖 The Choosers of the Slain! **W:** Roy Thomas
8 ❑ Jan 1995 Cover: 1.50 **NM** value: **Cover or less**
Circ: CapCity orders: **10,350**
A: Rafael Kayanan **W:** Roy Thomas
9 ❑ Feb 1995 Cover: 1.50 **NM** value: **Cover or less**
Circ: CapCity orders: **9,450**
A: Rafael Kayanan **W:** Roy Thomas
10 ❑ Mar 1995 Cover: 1.50 **NM** value: **Cover or less**
Circ: CapCity orders: **8,475**
A: Rafael Kayanan **W:** Roy Thomas
11 ❑ Apr 1995 Cover: 1.50 **NM** value: **Cover or less**
Circ: CapCity orders: **7,825**
A: Rafael Kayanan **W:** Roy Thomas
12 ❑ May 1995 Cover: 1.50 **NM** value: **Cover or less**
Circ: CapCity orders: **7,500**
A: Rafael Kayanan **W:** Roy Thomas
13 ❑ Jun 1995 Cover: 1.50 **NM** value: **Cover or less**
Circ: CapCity orders: **7,175**
A: Rafael Kayanan **W:** Roy Thomas
14 ❑ Jul 1995 Cover: 1.50 **NM** value: **Cover or less**
Circ: CapCity orders: **6,725**
final issue. **A:** Rafael Kayanan **W:** Roy Thomas

CONAN THE BARBARIAN — Marvel

Known variously as "Conan of Cimmeria," "Amra" (the Lion), or merely "Conan," his sword and skills are the stuff of legends. In his adventures, first written for the pulps by Robert E. Howard, he has fought gods and devils, monsters and men. He has led armies and sailed the seas as a pirate captain with the beautiful Belit at his side. He has fought with, and beside, fellow Howard creations the legendary Kull of Atlantis and the she-devil with a sword Red Sonja. In the end, he became King Conan, as he always knew he would.

With his popularity revived by a series of paperbacks collecting the pulp adventures, Conan the Barbarian is one of the best-known sword-and-sorcery characters of all time. The popularity of the Marvel comics series led to other media outlets, including a pair of motion pictures starring Arnold Schwarzenegger.

1 ❑ Oct 1970 Cover: 0.15 **NM** value: **150.00**
• **CGC:** 209 graded, best 9.8
📖 The Coming of Conan! **A:** Barry Windsor-Smith **W:** Roy Thomas ★ Origin of Conan. ★ 1st Appearance of Conan. ★ Appearance of Kull.
2 ❑ Dec 1970 Cover: 0.15 **NM** value: **45.00**
• **CGC:** 48 graded, best 9.8
📖 Lair of the Beast-Men • Howard story **A:** Barry Windsor-Smith **W:** Roy Thomas
3 ❑ Feb 1971 Cover: 0.15 **NM** value: **55.00**
• **CGC:** 78 graded, best 9.6
📖 The Twilight of the Grim, Grey God • low dist.; Howard story **A:** Tom Sutton; Barry Windsor-Smith **W:** Roy Thomas
4 ❑ Apr 1971 Cover: 0.15 **NM** value: **24.00**
• **CGC:** 32 graded, best 9.6
📖 The Tower of the Elephant • Howard story **A:** Tom Sutton; Sal Buscema; Barry Windsor-Smith **W:** Roy Thomas; Robert E. Howard
5 ❑ May 1971 Cover: 0.15 **NM** value: **20.00**
• **CGC:** 21 graded, best 9.6
📖 Zukala's Daughter • Howard story **A:** Tom Sutton; Barry Windsor-Smith **W:** Roy Thomas
6 ❑ Jun 1971 Cover: 0.15 **NM** value: **20.00**
• **CGC:** 16 graded, best 9.6
📖 Devil-Wings Over Shadizar **A:** Barry Windsor-Smith **W:** Roy Thomas
7 ❑ Jul 1971 Cover: 0.15 **NM** value: **20.00**
• **CGC:** 25 graded, best 9.8
📖 The Lurker Within • Howard story **A:** Barry Windsor-Smith **W:** Roy Thomas ★ 1st Appearance of Thoth Amon.
8 ❑ Aug 1971 Cover: 0.15 **NM** value: **20.00**
• **CGC:** 11 graded, best 9.8
📖 The Keepers of the Crypt • Howard story **A:** Barry Windsor-Smith **W:** Roy Thomas
9 ❑ Aug 1971 Cover: 0.15 **NM** value: **20.00**
• **CGC:** 20 graded, best 9.6
📖 The Garden of Fear • Howard story **A:** Barry Windsor-Smith **W:** Roy Thomas
10 ❑ Oct 1971 Cover: 0.25 **NM** value: **16.00**
• **CGC:** 14 graded, best 9.6
• Giant-size. 📖 Beware the Wrath of Anu: Men of the Shadows; The King and the Oak • Howard story **A:** Barry Windsor-Smith **W:** Roy Thomas ★ Appearance of King Kull.
11 ❑ Nov 1971 Cover: 0.25 **NM** value: **16.00**
• **CGC:** 6 graded, best 9.6
• Giant-size. 📖 Rogues in the House; The Talons of Thak • Howard story **A:** Barry Windsor-Smith **W:** Roy Thomas
12 ❑ Dec 1971 Cover: 0.20 **NM** value: **15.00**
• **CGC:** 5 graded, best 9.8
📖 The Dweller in the Dark; The Blood of the Dragon **A:** Barry Windsor-Smith **W:** Roy Thomas
13 ❑ Jan 1972 Cover: 0.20 **NM** value: **15.00**
• **CGC:** 9 graded, best 9.6
📖 Web of the Spider-God **A:** Barry Windsor-Smith **W:** Roy Thomas
14 ❑ Mar 1972 Cover: 0.20 **NM** value: **12.00**
• **CGC:** 15 graded, best 9.6
📖 A Sword Called Stormbringer • Michael Moorcock characters **A:** Barry Windsor-Smith **W:** Roy Thomas ★ 1st Appearance of Elric.
15 ❑ May 1972 Cover: 0.20 **NM** value: **12.00**
• **CGC:** 13 graded, best 9.6
📖 The Green Empress of Melnibone • Michael Moorcock characters **A:** Barry Windsor-Smith **W:** Roy Thomas ★ Appearance of Elric.
16 ❑ Jul 1972 Cover: 0.20 **NM** value: **10.00**
• **CGC:** 7 graded, best 9.6
📖 The Frost Giant's Daughter; The Sword and the Sorcerers • reprinted from Savage Tales #1 and Chamber of Darkness #4 **A:** Tom Sutton; Barry Windsor-Smith **W:** Roy Thomas
17 ❑ Aug 1972 Cover: 0.20 **NM** value: **5.00**
• **CGC:** 4 graded, best 9.6
📖 The Gods of Bal-Sagoth • Howard story **A:** Gil Kane **W:** Roy Thomas
18 ❑ Aug 1972 Cover: 0.20 **NM** value: **5.00**
• **CGC:** 5 graded, best 9.4
📖 The Thing in the Temple • Howard story **A:** Gil Kane **W:** Roy Thomas
19 ❑ Oct 1972 Cover: 0.20 **NM** value: **8.00**
• **CGC:** 8 graded, best 9.6
📖 Hawks from the Sea **A:** Barry Windsor-Smith **W:** Roy Thomas
20 ❑ Nov 1972 Cover: 0.20 **NM** value: **8.00**
• **CGC:** 7 graded, best 9.6
📖 The Black Hound of Vengeance **A:** Barry Windsor-Smith **W:** Roy Thomas
21 ❑ Dec 1972 Cover: 0.20 **NM** value: **8.00**
• **CGC:** 12 graded, best 9.6
📖 The Monster of the Monoliths • Howard story **A:** Barry Windsor-Smith **W:** Roy Thomas
22 ❑ Jan 1973 Cover: 0.20 **NM** value: **8.00**
• **CGC:** 14 graded, best 9.6
📖 The Coming of Conan • reprinted from Conan the Barbarian #1 **A:** Barry Windsor-Smith **W:** Roy Thomas
23 ❑ Feb 1973 Cover: 0.20 **NM** value: **20.00**
• **CGC:** 21 graded, best 9.8
📖 The Shadow of the Vulture • Howard story **A:** Tom Sutton; Barry Windsor-Smith; Gil Kane **W:** Roy Thomas ★ 1st Appearance of Red Sonja.
24 ❑ Mar 1973 Cover: 0.20 **NM** value: **8.00**
• **CGC:** 30 graded, best 9.8
📖 The Song of Red Sonja • Red Sonja;1st full Red Sonja story **A:** Barry Windsor-Smith **W:** Roy Thomas ★ Appearance of Red Sonja.
25 ❑ Apr 1973 Cover: 0.20 **NM** value: **4.00**
• **CGC:** 1 graded, best 9.6
📖 The Mirrors of Kharam-Akkad • Howard story **A:** Tom Sutton; John Buscema; Gil Kane **W:** Roy Thomas
26 ❑ May 1973 Cover: 0.20 **NM** value: **3.00**
📖 The Hour Of The Griffin **A:** John Buscema **W:** Roy Thomas
27 ❑ Jun 1973 Cover: 0.20 **NM** value: **3.00**
📖 The Blood Of Bel-Hissar • Howard story **A:** John Buscema **W:** Roy Thomas
28 ❑ Jul 1973 Cover: 0.20 **NM** value: **3.00**

Moon Of Zimbabwe • Howard story **A:** Tom Sutton; John Buscema; Gil Kane **W:** Roy Thomas

29 ❑ Aug 1973 Cover: 0.20 **NM** value: **3.00**
Two Against Turan • Howard story **A:** Tom Sutton; John Buscema; Gil Kane **W:** Roy Thomas

30 ❑ Sep 1973 Cover: 0.20 **NM** value: **3.00**
The Hand Of Negral • Howard story **A:** Tom Sutton; John Buscema; Gil Kane **W:** Roy Thomas

31 ❑ Oct 1973 Cover: 0.20 **NM** value: **2.00**
The Shadow In The tomb **A:** John Buscema **W:** Roy Thomas

32 ❑ Nov 1973 Cover: 0.20 **NM** value: **2.00**
Flame Winds Of Lost Khitai • Norvell Page story **A:** John Buscema **W:** Roy Thomas

33 ❑ Dec 1973 Cover: 0.20 **NM** value: **2.00**
Death And Seven Wizards • Norvell Page story **A:** John Buscema **W:** Roy Thomas

34 ❑ Jan 1974 Cover: 0.20 **NM** value: **2.00**
The Temptress In The Tower Of Flame • Norvell Page story **A:** John Buscema **W:** Roy Thomas

35 ❑ Feb 1974 Cover: 0.20 **NM** value: **2.00**
The Hell Spawn Of Kara-Shehr • Howard story **A:** John Buscema **W:** Roy Thomas

36 ❑ Mar 1974 Cover: 0.20 **NM** value: **2.00**
Beware The Hyrkanians Bearing Gifts • Lin Carter/L.Sprague deCamp story **A:** John Buscema **W:** Roy Thomas

37 ❑ Apr 1974 Cover: 0.20 **NM** value: **3.00**
• **CGC:** 3 graded, best 9.4
Curse Of The Golden Skull • Lin Carter/L.Sprague deCamp story **A:** Tom Sutton; Neal Adams **W:** Roy Thomas

38 ❑ May 1974 Cover: 0.25 **NM** value: **2.00**
Night-Lurker! • Howard story **W:** Roy Thomas

39 ❑ Jun 1974 Cover: 0.25 **NM** value: **2.00**
Dragon From The Inland Sea! **A:** John Buscema **W:** Roy Thomas

40 ❑ Jul 1974 Cover: 0.25 **NM** value: **2.00**
The Fiend From The Forgotten City **A:** Rich Buckler **W:** Roy Thomas

41 ❑ Aug 1974 Cover: 0.25 **NM** value: **2.00**
The Garden Of Death And Life **A:** John Buscema; Gil Kane **W:** Roy Thomas

42 ❑ Sep 1974 Cover: 0.25 **NM** value: **2.00**
Night Of The Gargoyle • Howard story **A:** John Buscema; Gil Kane **W:** Roy Thomas

43 ❑ Oct 1974 Cover: 0.25 **NM** value: **2.00**
Tower Of Blood • Red Sonja **A:** John Buscema; Gil Kane **W:** Roy Thomas

44 ❑ Nov 1974 Cover: 0.25 **NM** value: **2.00**
Of Flame And The Fiend • Red Sonja **A:** John Buscema **W:** Roy Thomas

45 ❑ Dec 1974 Cover: 0.25 **NM** value: **2.00**
The Last Ballad Of Laza-Lanti **A:** Neal Adams **W:** Roy Thomas

46 ❑ Jan 1975 Cover: 0.25 **NM** value: **2.00**
The Curse Of The Conjurer **A:** John Buscema **W:** Roy Thomas

47 ❑ Feb 1975 Cover: 0.25 **NM** value: **2.00**
Goblins In The Moonlight **A:** John Buscema **W:** Roy Thomas

48 ❑ Mar 1975 Cover: 0.25 **NM** value: **2.00**
The Rats Dance At Ravengard **A:** John Buscema **W:** Roy Thomas ★ Origin of Conan.

49 ❑ Apr 1975 Cover: 0.25 **NM** value: **2.00**
Wolf-Woman! **A:** John Buscema **W:** Roy Thomas

50 ❑ May 1975 Cover: 0.25 **NM** value: **2.00**
The Dweller In The Pool **A:** John Buscema **W:** Roy Thomas

51 ❑ Jun 1975 Cover: 0.25 **NM** value: **1.50**
Man Born Of Demon! **A:** John Buscema **W:** Roy Thomas ★ Versus Unos.

52 ❑ Jul 1975 Cover: 0.25 **NM** value: **1.50**
The Altar And The Scorpion **A:** John Buscema **W:** Roy Thomas

53 ❑ Aug 1975 Cover: 0.25 **NM** value: **1.50**
Brothers Of The Blade **A:** John Buscema **W:** Roy Thomas

54 ❑ Sep 1975 Cover: 0.25 **NM** value: **1.50**
The Oracle Of Ophir **A:** John Buscema **W:** Roy Thomas

55 ❑ Oct 1975 Cover: 0.25 **NM** value: **1.50**
Shadow On The Land! **A:** John Buscema **W:** Roy Thomas

56 ❑ Nov 1975 Cover: 0.25 **NM** value: **1.50**
The Strange High Tower In The Mist! **A:** John Buscema **W:** Roy Thomas

57 ❑ Dec 1975 Cover: 0.25 **NM** value: **1.50**
Incident in Argos **A:** Mike Ploog **W:** Roy Thomas

58 ❑ Jan 1976 Cover: 0.25 **NM** value: **2.00**
Queen Of The Black Coast! **A:** John Buscema **W:** Roy Thomas ★ 2nd Appearance of BTlit.

59 ❑ Feb 1976 Cover: 0.25 **NM** value: **2.00**
The Ballad Of BTlit **A:** John Buscema **W:** Roy Thomas ★ Origin of BTlit.

60 ❑ Mar 1976 Cover: 0.25 **NM** value: **1.50**
Riders Of The River-Dragons **A:** John Buscema **W:** Roy Thomas

61 ❑ Apr 1976 Cover: 0.25 **NM** value: **1.50**
On The Track Of The She-Pirate **A:** John Buscema **W:** Roy Thomas

62 ❑ May 1976 Cover: 0.25 **NM** value: **1.50**
Lord Of The Lions **A:** John Buscema **W:** Roy Thomas

63 ❑ Jun 1976 Cover: 0.25 **NM** value: **1.50**
• **CGC:** 1 graded, best 8.0
Death Among The Ruins **A:** John Buscema **W:** Roy Thomas

64 ❑ Jul 1976 Cover: 0.25 **NM** value: **1.50**
• **CGC:** 1 graded, best 9.4
The Secret Of Skull River **A:** Al Milgrom; Jim Starlin **W:** Roy Thomas

65 ❑ Aug 1976 Cover: 0.25 **NM** value: **1.50**
• **CGC:** 1 graded, best 9.4
Fiends Of The Feathered Serpent! **A:** John Buscema; Gil Kane **W:** Roy Thomas

66 ❑ Sep 1976 Cover: 0.30 **NM** value: **1.50**
A: John Buscema; Gil Kane **W:** Roy Thomas ★ Versus Dagon.

67 ❑ Oct 1976 Cover: 0.30 **NM** value: **1.50**
Talons Of The Man Tiger! • Red Sonja **A:** John Buscema; Gil Kane **W:** Roy Thomas ★ Appearance of Red Sonja.

68 ❑ Nov 1976 Cover: 0.30 **NM** value: **1.50**
• (continued from Marvel Feature #7);(continued from Marvel Feature #7) **A:** John Buscema; Gil Kane **W:** Roy Thomas ★ Appearance of Red Sonja.

69 ❑ Dec 1976 Cover: 0.30 **NM** value: **1.50**
• **CGC:** 1 graded, best 9.6
The Demon Out Of The Deep! **W:** Roy Thomas

70 ❑ Jan 1977 Cover: 0.30 **NM** value: **1.50**
• **CGC:** 1 graded, best 9.8
A: John Buscema **W:** Roy Thomas

71 ❑ Feb 1977 Cover: 0.30 **NM** value: **1.50**
The Secret Of Ashtoreth! **A:** John Buscema **W:** Roy Thomas

72 ❑ Mar 1977 Cover: 0.30 **NM** value: **1.50**
Vengeance In Asgalun **A:** John Buscema **W:** Roy Thomas

73 ❑ Apr 1977 Cover: 0.30 **NM** value: **1.50**
He Who Waits -In the Well Of Skelos **A:** John Buscema **W:** Roy Thomas

74 ❑ May 1977 Cover: 0.30 **NM** value: **1.50**
The Battle At The Black Walls! **A:** John Buscema **W:** Roy Thomas

75 ❑ Jun 1977 Cover: 0.30 **NM** value: **1.50**
• **CGC:** 1 graded, best 7.5
Hawk Riders Of Harach! **A:** John Buscema **W:** Roy Thomas

76 ❑ Jul 1977 Cover: 0.30 **NM** value: **1.50**
Swordless In Stygia **A:** John Buscema **W:** Roy Thomas

77 ❑ Aug 1977 Cover: 0.30 **NM** value: **1.50**
• **CGC:** 1 graded, best 8.0
When Giants Walk The Earth **A:** John Buscema **W:** Roy Thomas

78 ❑ Sep 1977 Cover: 0.30 **NM** value: **1.50**
Curse Of The Undead Man **A:** John Buscema **W:** Roy Thomas

79 ❑ Oct 1977 Cover: 0.30 **NM** value: **1.50**
The Lost Valley Of Iskander **A:** Howard Chaykin **W:** Roy Thomas

80 ❑ Nov 1977 Cover: 0.35 **NM** value: **1.50**
Trial By Combat! **A:** Howard Chaykin **W:** Roy Thomas

81 ❑ Dec 1977 Cover: 0.35 **NM** value: **1.50**
The Eye Of The Serpent **A:** Howard Chaykin **W:** Roy Thomas

82 ❑ Jan 1978 Cover: 0.35 **NM** value: **1.50**
The Sorceress Of The Swamp! **A:** Howard Chaykin **W:** Roy Thomas

83 ❑ Feb 1978 Cover: 0.35 **NM** value: **1.50**
The Dance Of The Skull **A:** Howard Chaykin **W:** Roy Thomas

84 ❑ Mar 1978 Cover: 0.35 **NM** value: **1.50**
Two Against The Hawk City! **A:** John Buscema **W:** Roy Thomas ★ 1st Appearance of Zula.

85 ❑ Apr 1978 Cover: 0.35 **NM** value: **1.50**
Of Swordsmen And Sorcerers! **A:** John Buscema **W:** Roy Thomas ★ Origin of Zula.

86 ❑ May 1978 Cover: 0.35 **NM** value: **1.50**
The Devourer Of The Dead **A:** John Buscema **W:** Roy Thomas

87 ❑ Jun 1978 Cover: 0.35 **NM** value: **1.50**
Demons At The Summit! • Reprints Savage Sword of Conan #3 in color **A:** John Buscema **W:** Roy Thomas

88 ❑ Jul 1978 Cover: 0.35 **NM** value: **1.50**
The Queen And The Corsairs! • Return of Belit;Return of BTlit **A:** John Buscema **W:** Roy Thomas

89 ❑ Aug 1978 Cover: 0.35 **NM** value: **1.50**
The Sword And the Serpent **A:** John Buscema **W:** Roy Thomas ★ Versus Thoth-Amon.

90 ❑ Sep 1978 Cover: 0.35 **NM** value: **1.50**
The Diadem Of The Giant-Kings! **A:** John Buscema **W:** Roy Thomas

91 ❑ Oct 1978 Cover: 0.35 **NM** value: **1.50**
Savage Doings In Shem! **A:** John Buscema **W:** Roy Thomas

92 ❑ Nov 1978 Cover: 0.35 **NM** value: **1.50**
The Thing in the Crypt **A:** John Buscema **W:** Roy Thomas

93 ❑ Dec 1978 Cover: 0.35 **NM** value: **1.50**
The Rage And Revenge • Belit regains throne;BTlit regains throne **A:** John Buscema **W:** Roy Thomas

94 ❑ Jan 1979 Cover: 0.35 **NM** value: **1.50**
The Beast-King Of Abombi! **A:** John Buscema **W:** Roy Thomas

95 ❑ Feb 1979 Cover: 0.35 **NM** value: **1.50**
The Return Of Amra! **A:** John Buscema **W:** Roy Thomas

96 ❑ Mar 1979 Cover: 0.35 **NM** value: **1.50**
The Long Night Of Fang And Talon!, Part 1 **A:** John Buscema **W:** Roy Thomas

97 ❑ Apr 1979 Cover: 0.35 **NM** value: **1.50**
The Long Night Of Fang And Talon!, Part 2 **A:** John Buscema **W:** Roy Thomas

98 ❑ May 1979 Cover: 0.40 **NM** value: **1.50**
• **CGC:** 1 graded, best 9.8
Sea-Woman **A:** John Buscema **W:** Roy Thomas

99 ❑ Jun 1979 Cover: 0.40 **NM** value: **1.50**
Devil Crabs Of the Dark Cliffs! **A:** John Buscema **W:** Roy Thomas

100 ❑ Jul 1979 Cover: 0.60 **NM** value: **2.00**
• **CGC:** 11 graded, best 9.8
• Double-size issue. Death On The Black Coast **A:** Tom Sutton; John Buscema **W:** Roy Thomas ★ Death of Belit. ★ Death of BTlit.

101 ❑ Aug 1979 Cover: 0.40 **NM** value: **1.00**
The Devil Has Many Legs **A:** John Buscema **W:** Roy Thomas

102 ❑ Sep 1979 Cover: 0.40 **NM** value: **1.00**
The Men Who Drink Blood **A:** John Buscema **W:** Roy Thomas

103 ❑ Oct 1979 Cover: 0.40 **NM** value: **1.00**
Bride Of The Vampire! **A:** John Buscema **W:** Roy Thomas

104 ❑ Nov 1979 Cover: 0.40 **NM** value: **1.00**
The Vale Of Lost Women **A:** John Buscema **W:** Roy Thomas

105 ❑ Dec 1979 Cover: 0.40 **NM** value: **1.00**
Whispering Shadows **A:** John Buscema **W:** Roy Thomas

106 ❑ Jan 1980 Cover: 0.40 **NM** value: **1.00**
Circ: Statement: **215,243**
Chaos In The Land Called Kush!0 **A:** John Buscema **W:** Roy Thomas

107 ❑ Feb 1980 Cover: 0.40 **NM** value: **1.00**
Circ: Statement: **215,243**
Demon Of The Night! **A:** John Buscema **W:** Roy Thomas

108 ❑ Mar 1980 Cover: 0.40 **NM** value: **1.00**
Circ: Statement: **215,243**
The Moon-Eaters Of Darfar! **A:** John Buscema **W:** Roy Thomas

109 ❑ Apr 1980 Cover: 0.40 **NM** value: **1.00**
Circ: Statement: **215,243**
Sons Of The Bear God! **A:** John Buscema **W:** Roy Thomas

110 ❑ May 1980 Cover: 0.40 **NM** value: **1.00**
Circ: Statement: **215,243**
Beware The Bear Of Heaven **A:** John Buscema **W:** Roy Thomas

111 ❑ Jun 1980 Cover: 0.40 **NM** value: **1.00**
Circ: Statement: **215,243**
Cimmerian Against A City **A:** John Buscema **W:** Roy Thomas

112 ❑ Jul 1980 Cover: 0.40 **NM** value: **1.00**
Circ: Statement: **215,243**
Buryat Besieged! **A:** John Buscema **W:** Roy Thomas

113 ❑ Aug 1980 Cover: 0.40 **NM** value: **1.00**
Circ: Statement: **215,243**
A Devil In The Family! **A:** John Buscema **W:** Roy Thomas

114 ❑ Sep 1980 Cover: 0.50 **NM** value: **1.00**
Circ: Statement: **215,243**
The Shadow Of The Beast! **A:** John Buscema **W:** Roy Thomas

115 ❑ Oct 1980 Cover: 0.75 **NM** value: **1.50**
Circ: Statement: **215,243**
• double-sized. A War Of Wizards **A:** John Buscema **W:** Roy Thomas

116 ❑ Nov 1980 Cover: 0.50 **NM** value: **1.00**
Circ: Statement: **215,243**
A Crawler On The Midst! **A:** John Buscema; Neal Adams **W:** Len Wein

117 ❑ Dec 1980 Cover: 0.50 **NM** value: **1.00**
Circ: Statement: **215,243**
The Corridor f Mullah Kajar **A:** John Buscema **W:** Larry Hama

118 ❑ Jan 1981 Cover: 0.50 **NM** value: **1.00**
Circ: Statement: **184,448**
Valley Of Forever Night **A:** John Buscema **W:** J.M. DeMatteis

119 ❑ Feb 1981 Cover: 0.50 **NM** value: **1.00**
Circ: Statement: **184,448**
The Voice Of One Long Gone **A:** John Buscema **W:** J.M. DeMatteis

120 ❑ Mar 1981 Cover: 0.50 **NM** value: **1.00**
Circ: Statement: **184,448**
Hand Of Erlik! **A:** John Buscema **W:** J.M. DeMatteis

121 ❑ Apr 1981 Cover: 0.50 **NM** value: **1.00**
Circ: Statement: **184,448**
The Price Of Perfection • Has 1980 Statement, filed 10/1/80; avg print run 402,906; avg sales 208,664; avg subs 6,579; avg total paid 215,243; samples 716; office use 2,679; max existent 218,638; 46% of run returned **A:** John Buscema **W:** J.M. DeMatteis

122 ❑ May 1981 Cover: 0.50 **NM** value: **1.00**
Circ: Statement: **184,448**
The City Where Time Stood Still **A:** John Buscema **W:** J.M. DeMatteis

123 ❑ Jun 1981 Cover: 0.50 **NM** value: **1.00**
Circ: Statement: **184,448**
The Horror Beneath The Hills **A:** John Buscema **W:** J.M. DeMatteis

124 ❑ Jul 1981 Cover: 0.50 **NM** value: **1.00**
Circ: Statement: **184,448**
The Eternity War! **A:** John Buscema **W:** J.M. DeMatteis

125 ❑ Aug 1981 Cover: 0.50 **NM** value: **1.00**
Circ: Statement: **184,448**
The Witches Of Nexxx **A:** John Buscema **W:** J.M. DeMatteis

126 ❑ Sep 1981 Cover: 0.50 **NM** value: **1.00**
Circ: Statement: **184,448**
The Blood Red Eye Of Truth **A:** John Buscema **W:** J.M. DeMatteis

127 ❑ Oct 1981 Cover: 0.50 **NM** value: **1.00**
Circ: Statement: **184,448**
The Snow Haired Woman Of The Wastes **A:** John Buscema **W:** J.M. DeMatteis

128 ❑ Nov 1981 Cover: 0.50 **NM** value: **1.00**
Circ: Statement: **184,448**
And Life Sprang Forth From These **A:** Gil Kane **C:** Gil Kane **W:** J.M. DeMatteis

129 ❑ Dec 1981 Cover: 0.50 **NM** value: **1.00**
Circ: Statement: **184,448**

130 ❑ Jan 1982 Cover: 0.60 **NM** value: **1.00**
Circ: Statement: **197,495**
The Quest Ends! **A:** Gil Kane **W:** J.M. DeMatteis

131 ❑ Feb 1982 Cover: 0.60 **NM** value: **1.00**
Circ: Statement: **197,495**
The Ring Of Rhax **A:** Gil Kane **W:** J.M. DeMatteis

132 ❑ Mar 1982 Cover: 0.60 **NM** value: **1.00**
Circ: Statement: **197,495**
Games Of Gharn **A:** Gil Kane **W:** Bruce Jones

133 ❑ Apr 1982 Cover: 0.60 **NM** value: **1.00**
Circ: Statement: **197,495**
The Witch Of Windsor **A:** Gil Kane **W:** Bruce Jones

134 ❑ May 1982 Cover: 0.60 **NM** value: **1.00**
Circ: Statement: **197,495**
A Hitch In Time • Has 1981 Statement, filed 10/1/81; avg print run 376,659; avg sales 177,007; avg subs 7,441; avg total paid 184,448; samples 644; office use 3,876; max existent 188,968; 50% of run returned **A:** Gil Kane **W:** Bruce Jones

135 ❑ Jun 1982 Cover: 0.60 **NM** value: **1.00**
Circ: Statement: **197,495**
The Forest Of The Night **A:** Marc Silvestri **W:** Steven Grant

136 ❑ Jul 1982 Cover: 0.60 **NM** value: **1.00**
Circ: Statement: **197,495**
The River Of Death **A:** John Buscema **W:** Bruce Jones

137 ❑ Aug 1982 Cover: 0.60 **NM** value: **1.00**
Circ: Statement: **197,495**
Titan's Gambit **A:** Alfredo Alcala **W:** Bruce Jones

138 ❑ Sep 1982 Cover: 0.60 **NM** value: **1.00**
Circ: Statement: **197,495**
The Isle Of The Dead **A:** Val Mayerik **W:** Bruce Jones

139 ❑ Oct 1982 Cover: 0.60 **NM** value: **1.00**
Circ: Statement: **197,495**
In The Lair Of The Damned **A:** Val Mayerik **W:** Bruce Jones

140 ❑ Nov 1982 Cover: 0.60 **NM** value: **1.00**
Circ: Statement: **197,495** • **CGC:** 1 graded, best 9.6
Spider Isle **A:** John Buscema **W:** Bruce Jones

141 ❑ Dec 1982 Cover: 0.60 **NM** value: **1.00**
Circ: Statement: **197,495**
The Web Tightens **A:** John Buscema **W:** Bruce Jones

Other grades: Multiply prices above by **1.5 for Mint • 2/3 for Very Fine • 1/3 for Fine • 1/5 for Very Good • 1/8 for Good**

142 ❑ Jan 1983 Cover: 0.60 **NM** value: **1.00**
Circ: Statement: **206,434**
📖 The Maze, The Man, The Monster **A:** John Buscema **W:** Bruce Jones
143 ❑ Feb 1983 Cover: 0.60 **NM** value: **1.00**
Circ: Statement: **206,434**
📖 Life Among The Dead **A:** John Buscema **W:** Bruce Jones
144 ❑ Mar 1983 Cover: 0.60 **NM** value: **1.00**
Circ: Statement: **206,434**
📖 The Blade And The Beast **A:** John Buscema **W:** Bruce Jones
145 ❑ Apr 1983 Cover: 0.60 **NM** value: **1.00**
Circ: Statement: **206,434**
📖 Son Of Cimmeria • Has 1982 Statement, filed 10/1/82; avg print run 394,289; avg sales 186,541; avg subs 10,954; avg total paid 197,495; samples 727; office use 3,772; max existent 201,994; 49% of run returned **A:** John Buscema **W:** Bruce Jones
146 ❑ May 1983 Cover: 0.60 **NM** value: **1.00**
Circ: Statement: **206,434**
📖 Night Of The Three Sisters! **A:** John Buscema **W:** Mary Jo Duffy
147 ❑ Jun 1983 Cover: 0.60 **NM** value: **1.00**
Circ: Statement: **206,434**
📖 Tower Of Mitra! **A:** John Buscema **W:** Bruce Jones
148 ❑ Jul 1983 Cover: 0.60 **NM** value: **1.00**
Circ: Statement: **206,434**
📖 The Plague Of Forlek **A:** John Buscema **W:** Bruce Jones
149 ❑ Aug 1983 Cover: 0.60 **NM** value: **1.00**
Circ: Statement: **206,434**
📖 Deathmark **A:** John Buscema **W:** Bruce Jones
150 ❑ Sep 1983 Cover: 0.60 **NM** value: **1.00**
Circ: Statement: **206,434**
📖 Tower Of Flame! **A:** John Buscema **W:** Michael Fleisher
151 ❑ Oct 1983 Cover: 0.60 **NM** value: **1.00**
Circ: Statement: **206,434**
📖 Vale Of Death! **A:** John Buscema **W:** Michael Fleisher
152 ❑ Nov 1983 Cover: 0.60 **NM** value: **1.00**
Circ: Statement: **206,434**
📖 The Dark Blade Of Jergal Zadh! **A:** John Buscema **W:** Michael Fleisher
153 ❑ Dec 1983 Cover: 0.60 **NM** value: **1.00**
Circ: Statement: **206,434**
📖 The Bird Men Of Akah Ma'at! **A:** John Buscema **W:** Michael Fleisher
154 ❑ Jan 1984 Cover: 0.60 **NM** value: **1.00**
Circ: Statement: **205,751**
📖 The Man Bats Of Ur-Xanarrh! • Assistant Editors' Month **A:** Gary Kwapisz **W:** Michael Fleisher
155 ❑ Feb 1984 Cover: 0.60 **NM** value: **1.00**
Circ: Statement: **205,751**
📖 The Anger Of Conan **A:** John Buscema **W:** Michael Fleisher
156 ❑ Mar 1984 Cover: 0.60 **NM** value: **1.00**
Circ: Statement: **205,751**
📖 The Curse! **A:** John Buscema **W:** Michael Fleisher
157 ❑ Apr 1984 Cover: 0.60 **NM** value: **1.00**
Circ: Statement: **205,751**
📖 The Wizard **A:** John Buscema **W:** Michael Fleisher
158 ❑ May 1984 Cover: 0.60 **NM** value: **1.00**
Circ: Statement: **205,751**
📖 Night Of The Wolf **A:** John Buscema **W:** Michael Fleisher
159 ❑ Jun 1984 Cover: 0.60 **NM** value: **1.00**
Circ: Statement: **205,751**
📖 Cauldron Of The Doomed! • Has 1983 Statement, filed 10/5/83; avg print run 418,034; avg sales 194,818; avg subs 11,616; avg total paid 206,434; samples 806; office use 3,370; max existent 210,610; 50% of run returned **A:** John Buscema **W:** Michael Fleisher
160 ❑ Jul 1984 Cover: 0.60 **NM** value: **1.00**
Circ: Statement: **205,751**
📖 Veil of Darkness **A:** Bob Camp **W:** Michael Fleisher
161 ❑ Aug 1984 Cover: 0.60 **NM** value: **1.00**
Circ: Statement: **205,751**
📖 The House Of Skulls! **A:** John Buscema **W:** Michael Fleisher
162 ❑ Sep 1984 Cover: 0.60 **NM** value: **1.00**
Circ: Statement: **205,751**
📖 Destroyer In The Flame **A:** John Buscema **W:** Michael Fleisher
163 ❑ Oct 1984 Cover: 0.60 **NM** value: **1.00**
Circ: Statement: **205,751**
📖 Cavern Of The Vines Of Doom! **A:** John Buscema **W:** Michael Fleisher
164 ❑ Nov 1984 Cover: 0.60 **NM** value: **1.00**
Circ: Statement: **205,751**
📖 The Jeweled Sword Of Tem **A:** Gary Kwapisz **W:** Larry Yakata
165 ❑ Dec 1984 Cover: 0.60 **NM** value: **1.00**
Circ: Statement: **205,751**
📖 Temple Of The Dragon **A:** John Buscema **W:** Michael Fleisher
166 ❑ Jan 1985 Cover: 0.60 **NM** value: **1.00**
Circ: Statement: **176,397**
📖 Blood Of The Titan **A:** John Buscema **W:** Michael Fleisher
167 ❑ Feb 1985 Cover: 0.60 **NM** value: **1.00**
Circ: Statement: **176,397**
📖 The Creature From Time's Dawn! **A:** John Buscema **C:** Michael W. Kaluta **W:** Michael Fleisher
168 ❑ Mar 1985 Cover: 0.60 **NM** value: **1.00**
Circ: Statement: **176,397**
📖 The Bird-Woman And The Beast! **A:** John Buscema **W:** Michael Fleisher
169 ❑ Apr 1985 Cover: 0.65 **NM** value: **1.00**
Circ: Statement: **176,397**
• Has 1984 Statement, filed 9/28/84; avg print run 410,058; avg sales 193,531; avg subs 12,220; avg total paid 205,751; samples 147; office use 3,152; max existent 209,050; 49% of run returned **A:** John Buscema **W:** Michael Fleisher
170 ❑ May 1985 Cover: 0.65 **NM** value: **1.00**
Circ: Statement: **176,397** CapCity orders: **8,300**
📖 Dominion Of The Dead! **A:** John Buscema **W:** Michael Fleisher
171 ❑ Jun 1985 Cover: 0.65 **NM** value: **1.00**
Circ: Statement: **176,397** CapCity orders: **8,100**
📖 Barbarian Death Song **A:** John Buscema **W:** Michael Fleisher
172 ❑ Jul 1985 Cover: 0.65 **NM** value: **1.00**
Circ: Statement: **176,397** CapCity orders: **9,400**
A: John Buscema **W:** Michael Fleisher
173 ❑ Aug 1985 Cover: 0.65 **NM** value: **1.00**
Circ: Statement: **176,397** CapCity orders: **8,300**
📖 Honor Among Thieves **A:** John Buscema **W:** James Owsley
174 ❑ Sep 1985 Cover: 0.65 **NM** value: **1.00**
Circ: Statement: **176,397** CapCity orders: **9,200**
📖 Children Of The Night **A:** John Buscema **W:** James Owsley
175 ❑ Oct 1985 Cover: 0.65 **NM** value: **1.00**
Circ: Statement: **176,397** CapCity orders: **7,800**
📖 The Scarlet Personage! **A:** John Buscema **W:** James Owsley
176 ❑ Nov 1985 Cover: 0.65 **NM** value: **1.00**
Circ: Statement: **176,397** CapCity orders: **7,700**
📖 Argos Rain **A:** John Buscema **W:** James Owsley
177 ❑ Dec 1985 Cover: 0.65 **NM** value: **1.00**
Circ: Statement: **176,397** CapCity orders: **7,600**
📖 Well of Souls! **A:** John Buscema **W:** James Owsley
178 ❑ Jan 1986 Cover: 0.65 **NM** value: **1.00**
Circ: Statement: **151,351** CapCity orders: **7,400**
📖 Death Hunt **A:** John Buscema **W:** James Owsley
179 ❑ Feb 1986 Cover: 0.75 **NM** value: **1.00**
Circ: Statement: **151,351** CapCity orders: **7,900**
📖 The End Of All There Is **A:** John Buscema **W:** James Owsley
180 ❑ Mar 1986 Cover: 0.75 **NM** value: **1.00**
Circ: Statement: **151,351** CapCity orders: **7,700**
A: John Buscema **W:** James Owsley
181 ❑ Apr 1986 Cover: 0.75 **NM** value: **1.00**
Circ: Statement: **151,351** CapCity orders: **8,000**
📖 Maddoc's Reign • Has 1985 Statement, filed 10/1/85; avg print run 358,966; avg sales 162,397; avg subs 14,000; avg total paid 176,397; samples 140; office use 873; max existent 177,410; 51% of run returned **A:** John Buscema **W:** James Owsley
182 ❑ May 1986 Cover: 0.75 **NM** value: **1.00**
Circ: Statement: **151,351** CapCity orders: **8,000**
📖 Testament **A:** John Buscema **W:** James Owsley
183 ❑ Jun 1986 Cover: 0.75 **NM** value: **1.00**
Circ: Statement: **151,351** CapCity orders: **7,800**
📖 Blood Dawn **A:** John Buscema **W:** James Owsley
184 ❑ Jul 1986 Cover: 0.75 **NM** value: **1.00**
Circ: Statement: **151,351** CapCity orders: **8,100**
185 ❑ Aug 1986 Cover: 0.75 **NM** value: **1.00**
Circ: Statement: **151,351** CapCity orders: **8,000**
186 ❑ Sep 1986 Cover: 0.75 **NM** value: **1.00**
Circ: Statement: **151,351** CapCity orders: **8,000**
📖 The Crimson Brotherhood **A:** Michael Docherty **W:** Don Kraar
187 ❑ Oct 1986 Cover: 0.75 **NM** value: **1.00**
Circ: Statement: **151,351** CapCity orders: **8,300**
📖 Resurrection **A:** John Buscema **W:** James Owsley
188 ❑ Nov 1986 Cover: 0.75 **NM** value: **1.00**
Circ: Statement: **151,351** CapCity orders: **8,600**
189 ❑ Dec 1986 Cover: 0.75 **NM** value: **1.00**
Circ: Statement: **151,351** CapCity orders: **8,500**
190 ❑ Jan 1987 Cover: 0.75 **NM** value: **1.00**
Circ: Statement: **135,041** CapCity orders: **8,500**
191 ❑ Feb 1987 Cover: 0.75 **NM** value: **1.00**
Circ: Statement: **135,041** CapCity orders: **8,700**
192 ❑ Mar 1987 Cover: 0.75 **NM** value: **1.00**
Circ: Statement: **135,041** CapCity orders: **8,500**
193 ❑ Apr 1987 Cover: 0.75 **NM** value: **1.00**
Circ: Statement: **135,041** CapCity orders: **8,800**
• Has 1986 Statement, filed 10/6/86; avg print run 338,553; avg sales 141,759; avg subs 9,592; avg total paid 151,351; samples 225; office use 1,989; max existent 153,565; 55% of run returned
194 ❑ May 1987 Cover: 1.00 **NM** value: **Cover or less**
Circ: Statement: **135,041** CapCity orders: **8,400**
📖 Victory **A:** Val Semeiks **W:** James Owsley
195 ❑ Jun 1987 Cover: 1.00 **NM** value: **Cover or less**
Circ: Statement: **135,041** CapCity orders: **8,400**
196 ❑ Jul 1987 Cover: 1.00 **NM** value: **Cover or less**
Circ: Statement: **135,041** CapCity orders: **8,600**
197 ❑ Aug 1987 Cover: 1.00 **NM** value: **Cover or less**
Circ: Statement: **135,041** CapCity orders: **9,200**
📖 Stand **A:** Val Semeiks **W:** James Owsley
198 ❑ Sep 1987 Cover: 1.00 **NM** value: **Cover or less**
Circ: Statement: **135,041** CapCity orders: **10,000**
199 ❑ Oct 1987 Cover: 1.00 **NM** value: **Cover or less**
Circ: Statement: **135,041** CapCity orders: **10,500**
200 ❑ Nov 1987 Cover: 1.50 **NM** value: **Cover or less**
Circ: Statement: **135,041** CapCity orders: **12,150**
• 200th issue anniversary. 📖 The Fall Of Acheron **A:** Val Semeiks **W:** James Owsley
201 ❑ Dec 1987 Cover: 1.00 **NM** value: **Cover or less**
Circ: Statement: **135,041** CapCity orders: **10,600**
202 ❑ Jan 1988 Cover: 1.00 **NM** value: **Cover or less**
Circ: Statement: **109,350** CapCity orders: **10,750**
203 ❑ Feb 1988 Cover: 1.00 **NM** value: **Cover or less**
Circ: Statement: **109,350** CapCity orders: **10,900**
204 ❑ Mar 1988 Cover: 1.00 **NM** value: **Cover or less**
Circ: Statement: **109,350** CapCity orders: **11,000**
205 ❑ Apr 1988 Cover: 1.00 **NM** value: **Cover or less**
Circ: Statement: **109,350** CapCity orders: **11,200**
206 ❑ May 1988 Cover: 1.00 **NM** value: **Cover or less**
Circ: Statement: **109,350** CapCity orders: **10,600**
207 ❑ Jun 1988 Cover: 1.00 **NM** value: **Cover or less**
Circ: Statement: **109,350** CapCity orders: **9,900**
208 ❑ Jul 1988 Cover: 1.00 **NM** value: **Cover or less**
Circ: Statement: **109,350** CapCity orders: **10,000**
209 ❑ Aug 1988 Cover: 1.00 **NM** value: **Cover or less**
Circ: Statement: **109,350** CapCity orders: **10,300**
210 ❑ Sep 1988 Cover: 1.00 **NM** value: **Cover or less**
Circ: Statement: **109,350** CapCity orders: **10,200**
211 ❑ Oct 1988 Cover: 1.00 **NM** value: **Cover or less**
Circ: Statement: **109,350** CapCity orders: **10,100**
212 ❑ Nov 1988 Cover: 1.00 **NM** value: **Cover or less**
Circ: Statement: **109,350** CapCity orders: **9,900**
213 ❑ Dec 1988 Cover: 1.00 **NM** value: **Cover or less**
Circ: Statement: **109,350** CapCity orders: **10,100**
214 ❑ Jan 1989 Cover: 1.00 **NM** value: **Cover or less**
Circ: Statement: **98,917** CapCity orders: **9,500**
215 ❑ Feb 1989 Cover: 1.00 **NM** value: **Cover or less**
Circ: Statement: **98,917** CapCity orders: **9,400**
216 ❑ Mar 1989 Cover: 1.00 **NM** value: **Cover or less**
Circ: Statement: **98,917** CapCity orders: **9,400**
217 ❑ Apr 1989 Cover: 1.00 **NM** value: **Cover or less**
Circ: Statement: **98,917** CapCity orders: **9,500**
218 ❑ May 1989 Cover: 1.00 **NM** value: **Cover or less**
Circ: Statement: **98,917** CapCity orders: **9,400**
219 ❑ Jun 1989 Cover: 1.00 **NM** value: **Cover or less**
Circ: Statement: **98,917** CapCity orders: **9,600**
220 ❑ Jul 1989 Cover: 1.00 **NM** value: **Cover or less**
Circ: Statement: **98,917** CapCity orders: **9,400**
221 ❑ Aug 1989 Cover: 1.00 **NM** value: **Cover or less**
Circ: Statement: **98,917** CapCity orders: **9,800**
222 ❑ Sep 1989 Cover: 1.00 **NM** value: **Cover or less**
Circ: Statement: **98,917** CapCity orders: **9,600**
223 ❑ Oct 1989 Cover: 1.00 **NM** value: **Cover or less**
Circ: Statement: **98,917** CapCity orders: **9,600**
📖 The Wheel Of Life And Death **A:** Gary Kwapisz **W:** Michael Fleisher
224 ❑ Nov 1989 Cover: 1.00 **NM** value: **Cover or less**
Circ: Statement: **98,917** CapCity orders: **9,600**
225 ❑ Nov 1989 Cover: 1.00 **NM** value: **Cover or less**
Circ: Statement: **98,917** CapCity orders: **9,800**
226 ❑ Dec 1989 Cover: 1.00 **NM** value: **Cover or less**
Circ: Statement: **98,917** CapCity orders: **9,500**
227 ❑ Dec 1989 Cover: 1.00 **NM** value: **Cover or less**
Circ: Statement: **98,917** CapCity orders: **9,400**
228 ❑ Jan 1990 Cover: 1.00 **NM** value: **Cover or less**
Circ: Statement: **97,699** CapCity orders: **9,600**
229 ❑ Feb 1990 Cover: 1.00 **NM** value: **Cover or less**
Circ: Statement: **97,699** CapCity orders: **9,600**
230 ❑ Mar 1990 Cover: 1.00 **NM** value: **Cover or less**
Circ: Statement: **97,699** CapCity orders: **9,600**
231 ❑ Apr 1990 Cover: 1.00 **NM** value: **Cover or less**
Circ: Statement: **97,699** CapCity orders: **9,100**
232 ❑ May 1990 Cover: 1.00 **NM** value: **Cover or less**
Circ: Statement: **97,699** CapCity orders: **12,300**
• starts over **A:** Ron Lim
233 ❑ Jun 1990 Cover: 1.00 **NM** value: **Cover or less**
Circ: Statement: **97,699** CapCity orders: **11,200**
A: Ron Lim
234 ❑ Jul 1990 Cover: 1.00 **NM** value: **Cover or less**
Circ: Statement: **97,699** CapCity orders: **11,300**
A: Ron Lim
235 ❑ Aug 1990 Cover: 1.00 **NM** value: **Cover or less**
Circ: Statement: **97,699** CapCity orders: **11,400**
A: Ron Lim
236 ❑ Sep 1990 Cover: 1.00 **NM** value: **Cover or less**
Circ: Statement: **97,699** CapCity orders: **11,400**
A: Ron Lim
237 ❑ Oct 1990 Cover: 1.00 **NM** value: **Cover or less**
Circ: Statement: **97,699** CapCity orders: **11,100**
238 ❑ Nov 1990 Cover: 1.00 **NM** value: **Cover or less**
Circ: Statement: **97,699** CapCity orders: **11,100**
239 ❑ Dec 1990 Cover: 1.00 **NM** value: **Cover or less**
Circ: Statement: **97,699** CapCity orders: **10,600**
240 ❑ Jan 1991 Cover: 1.00 **NM** value: **Cover or less**
Circ: CapCity orders: **10,200**
📖 The End Must Come **A:** Gary Hartle **W:** Justin Arthur
241 ❑ Feb 1991 Cover: 1.00 **NM** value: **1.50**
Circ: CapCity orders: **11,800**
A: Todd McFarlane(cover) **C:** Todd McFarlane
242 ❑ Mar 1991 Cover: 1.00 **NM** value: **1.50**
Circ: CapCity orders: **10,800**
A: Jim Lee(cover) **C:** Jim Lee
243 ❑ Apr 1991 Cover: 1.00 **NM** value: **Cover or less**
Circ: CapCity orders: **10,300**
• Red Sonja
244 ❑ May 1991 Cover: 1.00 **NM** value: **Cover or less**
Circ: CapCity orders: **11,300**
• Red Sonja
245 ❑ Jun 1991 Cover: 1.00 **NM** value: **Cover or less**
Circ: CapCity orders: **11,200**
• Red Sonja
246 ❑ Jul 1991 Cover: 1.00 **NM** value: **Cover or less**
Circ: CapCity orders: **11,600**
• Red Sonja
247 ❑ Aug 1991 Cover: 1.00 **NM** value: **Cover or less**
Circ: CapCity orders: **12,000**
• Red Sonja
248 ❑ Sep 1991 Cover: 1.00 **NM** value: **Cover or less**
Circ: CapCity orders: **11,900**
• Red Sonja
249 ❑ Oct 1991 Cover: 1.00 **NM** value: **Cover or less**
Circ: CapCity orders: **12,000**
• Red Sonja
250 ❑ Nov 1991 Cover: 1.50 **NM** value: **Cover or less**
Circ: CapCity orders: **12,900**
• 250th issue anniversary.
251 ❑ Dec 1991 Cover: 1.00 **NM** value: **Cover or less**
Circ: CapCity orders: **11,300**
252 ❑ Jan 1992 Cover: 1.00 **NM** value: **Cover or less**
Circ: CapCity orders: **11,800**
253 ❑ Feb 1992 Cover: 1.25 **NM** value: **Cover or less**
Circ: CapCity orders: **11,400**
254 ❑ Mar 1992 Cover: 1.25 **NM** value: **Cover or less**
Circ: CapCity orders: **10,200**
255 ❑ Apr 1992 Cover: 1.25 **NM** value: **Cover or less**
Circ: CapCity orders: **9,700**
256 ❑ May 1992 Cover: 1.25 **NM** value: **Cover or less**
Circ: CapCity orders: **9,600**
257 ❑ Jun 1992 Cover: 1.25 **NM** value: **Cover or less**
Circ: CapCity orders: **9,900**
★ Versus Thoth-Amon.
258 ❑ Jul 1992 Cover: 1.25 **NM** value: **Cover or less**
Circ: CapCity orders: **9,800**
• returns to Cimmeria
259 ❑ Aug 1992 Cover: 1.25 **NM** value: **Cover or less**
Circ: CapCity orders: **9,700**
260 ❑ Sep 1992 Cover: 1.25 **NM** value: **Cover or less**
Circ: CapCity orders: **8,700**

CGC-graded: Multiply prices above by **33 for 9.9 M • 16 for 9.8 NM/M • 7 for 9.6 NM+ • 5 for 9.4 NM • 2.5 for 9.2 NM- • 1.5 for 9.0 VF/NM**

261 ❑ Oct 1992 Cover: 1.25 **NM** value: **Cover or less**
Circ: CapCity orders: **8,700**
262 ❑ Nov 1992 Cover: 1.25 **NM** value: **Cover or less**
Circ: CapCity orders: **8,500**
263 ❑ Dec 1992 Cover: 1.25 **NM** value: **Cover or less**
Circ: CapCity orders: **8,400**
264 ❑ Jan 1993 Cover: 1.25 **NM** value: **Cover or less**
Circ: CapCity orders: **8,100**
265 ❑ Feb 1993 Cover: 1.25 **NM** value: **Cover or less**
Circ: CapCity orders: **8,200**
266 ❑ Mar 1993 Cover: 1.25 **NM** value: **Cover or less**
Circ: CapCity orders: **8,200**
267 ❑ Apr 1993 Cover: 1.25 **NM** value: **Cover or less**
Circ: CapCity orders: **9,500**
268 ❑ May 1993 Cover: 1.25 **NM** value: **Cover or less**
Circ: CapCity orders: **9,500**
269 ❑ Jun 1993 Cover: 1.25 **NM** value: **Cover or less**
Circ: CapCity orders: **9,400**
270 ❑ Jul 1993 Cover: 1.25 **NM** value: **Cover or less**
Circ: CapCity orders: **9,600**
271 ❑ Aug 1993 Cover: 1.25 **NM** value: **Cover or less**
Circ: CapCity orders: **9,300**
272 ❑ Sep 1993 Cover: 1.25 **NM** value: **Cover or less**
Circ: CapCity orders: **8,750**
273 ❑ Oct 1993 Cover: 1.25 **NM** value: **Cover or less**
Circ: CapCity orders: **8,100**
📖 Conan the Punisher **A:** Michael Docherty **W:** Roy Thomas ★ Appearance of Lord of the Purple Lotus.
274 ❑ Nov 1993 Cover: 1.25 **NM** value: **Cover or less**
Circ: CapCity orders: **8,600**
275 ❑ Dec 1993 Cover: 2.50 **NM** value: **Cover or less**
Circ: CapCity orders: **10,100**
final issue.
Anl 1 ❑ ca. 1973 Cover: 0.35 **NM** value: **6.00**
• **CGC:** 4 graded, best 9.2
• Cover reads "King-Size Special". 📖 Lair of the Beast-Men; The Tower of the Elephant • Reprints Conan the Barbarian #2 and 4 **A:** Barry Windsor-Smith
Anl 2 ❑ Jan 1976 Cover: 0.50 **NM** value: **4.00**
📖 Conan The Cimmerian **A:** John Buscema; Barry Windsor-Smith **W:** Roy Thomas; Robert E. Howard
Anl 3 ❑ ca. 1977 Cover: 0.60 **NM** value: **2.00**
📖 At The Mountain Of The Moon God • Reprints Savage Sword of Conan #2 **A:** John Buscema; Howard Chaykin; Neal Adams **W:** Roy Thomas ★ Appearance of King Kull.
Anl 4 ❑ ca. 1978 Cover: 0.60 **NM** value: **2.00**
📖 The Return Of The Conqueror! • King Conan story **A:** John Buscema **W:** Roy Thomas
Anl 5 ❑ ca. 1979 Cover: 0.75 **NM** value: **2.00**
📖 Bride Of The Conqueror **A:** John Buscema **W:** Roy Thomas
Anl 6 ❑ ca. 1981 Cover: 0.75 **NM** value: **2.00**
📖 King Of The Forgotten People **A:** John Buscema **W:** Roy Thomas
Anl 7 ❑ ca. 1982 Cover: 1.00 **NM** value: **1.50**
📖 Conan of the Isles **A:** John Buscema **W:** Roy Thomas
Anl 8 ❑ ca. 1983 Cover: 1.00 **NM** value: **1.50**
📖 Dark Night Of The White Queen **A:** Val Mayerik **W:** James Owsley
Anl 9 ❑ ca. 1984 Cover: 1.00 **NM** value: **1.50**
📖 Wrath Of The Shambling God! **A:** Ernie Chan **W:** Michael Fleisher
Anl 10 ❑ ca. 1985 Cover: 1.25 **NM** value: **Cover or less**
Circ: CapCity orders: **7,800**
📖 Scorched Earth **A:** Ernie Chan **W:** James Owsley
Anl 11 ❑ ca. 1986 Cover: 1.25 **NM** value: **Cover or less**
Circ: CapCity orders: **11,100**
📖 Bride Of The Orulist **A:** Ernie Chan **W:** James Owsley
Anl 12 ❑ ca. 1987 Cover: 1.25 **NM** value: **Cover or less**
📖 Legion of the Dead **A:** Vince Giarrano **W:** Val Semeiks; James Owsley
GS 1 ❑ Sep 1974 Cover: 0.50 **NM** value: **4.00**
📖 The Hour of the Dragon; The Stranger from Hell; When Mountains Reel; The Twilight of the Grim, Grey God • New stories; reprints Conan the Barbarian #3 ★ 1st Appearance of BTlit.
GS 2 ❑ Dec 1974 Cover: 0.50 **NM** value: **3.00**
📖 Conan Bound!; The Haunter of the Pits; Zukala's Daughter • New stories; reprints Conan the Barbarian #5 **A:** Gil Kane **W:** Roy Thomas
GS 3 ❑ Apr 1975 Cover: 0.50 **NM** value: **3.00**
📖 To Tarantia-And The Tower; The Trial in the Temple; Devil Wings Over Shadizar • New stories; reprints Conan the Barbarian #6 **A:** Gil Kane **W:** Roy Thomas
GS 4 ❑ Jun 1975 Cover: 0.50 **NM** value: **3.00**
📖 Swords Of The South; The Lurker Within • New story; reprints Conan the Barbarian #7 **A:** Gil Kane **W:** Roy Thomas
GS 5 ❑ ca. 1975 Cover: 0.50 **NM** value: **3.00**
📖 A Sword Called Stormbringer; The Green Empress of Melnibone; The Blood of the Dragon • reprints Conan the Barbarian #12, 14 and 15 **A:** Barry Windsor-Smith **W:** Roy Thomas
SE 1 ❑ Cover: 2.50 **NM** value: **Cover or less**
📖 Red Nails **A:** Barry Windsor-Smith **W:** Roy Thomas

CONAN THE BARBARIAN MOVIE SPECIAL Marvel

As a child, Conan watched helplessly as his parents and all the adults of his tribe were brutally slaughtered. He and the other children were taken captive and spent years at hard labor. Many of the other children died from their harsh treatment, but Conan, fueled by thoughts of revenge, grew strong and thrived. Eventually, he was sold again and trained as a pit-fighter. He excelled, becoming even stronger as he mastered the art of personal combat. His skills enabled him to overcome his masters and escape to freedom. Dubbed a barbarian by the vicious raiders who had held him in captivity, Conan now wanders the world seeking those responsible for the death of his tribe. With the help of Subotai, a thief and master archer, and the beautiful warrior Valeria, Conan must match his sword against the zealous followers of the snake-god Set.

This special adapts the movie starring Arnold Schwarzenegger, James Earl Jones, and Sandahl Bergman.

1 ❑ Oct 1982 Cover: 0.60 **NM** value: **1.00**
A: John Buscema **W:** John Buscema; Michael Fleisher
2 ❑ Nov 1982 Cover: 0.60 **NM** value: **1.00**
A: John Buscema **W:** John Buscema; Michael Fleisher

CONAN THE BARBARIAN: THE USURPER Marvel

1 ❑ Dec 1997 Cover: 2.50 **NM** value: **Cover or less**
Circ: Diamd. preorders: **28,845**
gatefold cover. • gatefold summary. **A:** Steve Lieber **W:** Chuck Dixon
2 ❑ Jan 1998 Cover: 2.50 **NM** value: **Cover or less**
Circ: Diamd. preorders: **25,707**
• gatefold summary. **A:** Steve Lieber **W:** Chuck Dixon
3 ❑ Feb 1988 Cover: 2.50 **NM** value: **Cover or less**
Circ: Diamd. preorders: **24,118**
A: Steve Lieber **W:** Chuck Dixon
4 ❑ Mar 1988 Cover: 2.50 **NM** value: **Cover or less**
A: Steve Lieber **W:** Chuck Dixon

CONAN THE BARBARIAN (VOL. 2) Marvel

1 ❑ Jul 1997 Cover: 2.50 **NM** value: **Cover or less**
Circ: Diamd. preorders: **31,545**
2 ❑ Aug 1997 Cover: 2.50 **NM** value: **Cover or less**
Circ: Diamd. preorders: **25,114**
3 ❑ Oct 1997 Cover: 2.50 **NM** value: **Cover or less**
Circ: Diamd. preorders: **23,668**

CONAN THE DESTROYER Marvel

Conan, the sword-wielding barbarian, has accepted the role of bodyguard for a young girl, who is on a quest for a mystical talisman. Taramis, queen of Shadizar, has promised Conan his own kingdom, and the resurrection of his dead love, Valeria, if he helps the girl retrieve the ancient horn of the god Dagoth. With the horn, the queen hopes to revive the dormant god, and rule with him as his immortal consort.

But Taramis has lied to both the girl and Conan. The barbarian is marked for death once the horn is retrieved, and it is the young girl's fate to be sacrificed during the revival of Dagoth. Conan, however, has never been one to accept a preordained destiny, and with the help of his comrades-in-arms, he manages to foil Taramis' plots and defeat the newly awakened god.

The two-issue series is based on the second Conan movie, starring Arnold Schwarzenegger.

1 ❑ Jan 1985 Cover: 0.75 **NM** value: **1.00**
A: Bob Camp **W:** Roy Thomas
2 ❑ Mar 1985 Cover: 0.75 **NM** value: **1.00**
A: Bob Camp **W:** Roy Thomas

CONAN: THE HORN OF AZOTH Marvel

Bk 1 ❑ Cover: 8.95 **NM** value: **Cover or less**
Circ: CapCity orders: **2,800**

CONAN THE KING Marvel

Beginning with issue #20, and continuing until its conclusion with issue #55, King Conan ran under the new title Conan the King. It continued the adventures of the former barbarian, now having risen to become the lord of Aquilonia.

This second phase of the series concentrated more heavily on the conflict between Conan's two sons, Conn and Taurus. Taurus was second-born, less courageous, and athletically inferior to his brother, and was accordingly less favored by his father. This embittered him, and he turned to dark magicks in order to gain a measure of revenge. He even went so far as to ally himself with a sorcerer who sought to slay his father and older brother. Ultimately, his treachery was revealed and he was defeated, but not before bringing untold woe to his family.

20 ❑ Jan 1984 Cover: 1.00 **NM** value: **1.50**
Circ: Statement: **141,537**
• Continued from King Conan #19
21 ❑ Mar 1984 Cover: 1.00 **NM** value: **1.50**
Circ: Statement: **141,537**
C: Michael W. Kaluta
22 ❑ May 1984 Cover: 1.00 **NM** value: **1.50**
Circ: Statement: **141,537**
• Has 1983 Statement, filed 10/5/83; avg print run 293,838; avg sales 139,132; avg subs 2,537; avg total paid 141,669; samples 649; office use 1,302; max existent 143,620; 51% of run returned **C:** Michael W. Kaluta
23 ❑ Jul 1984 Cover: 1.00 **NM** value: **1.50**
Circ: Statement: **141,537**
C: Michael W. Kaluta
24 ❑ Sep 1984 Cover: 1.00 **NM** value: **1.50**
Circ: Statement: **141,537**
C: Michael W. Kaluta
25 ❑ Nov 1984 Cover: 1.00 **NM** value: **1.50**
Circ: Statement: **141,537**
C: Michael W. Kaluta
26 ❑ Jan 1985 Cover: 1.00 **NM** value: **1.50**
Circ: Statement: **120,335**
C: Michael W. Kaluta
27 ❑ Mar 1985 Cover: 1.00 **NM** value: **1.50**
Circ: Statement: **120,335**
C: Michael W. Kaluta
28 ❑ May 1985 Cover: 1.25 **NM** value: **1.50**
Circ: Statement: **120,335** CapCity orders: **8,000**
• Has 1984 Statement; avg total paid circ 141,537 **C:** Michael W. Kaluta
29 ❑ Jul 1985 Cover: 1.25 **NM** value: **1.50**
Circ: Statement: **120,335** CapCity orders: **7,700**
C: Michael W. Kaluta
30 ❑ Sep 1985 Cover: 1.25 **NM** value: **1.50**
Circ: Statement: **120,335** CapCity orders: **7,600**
C: Michael W. Kaluta
31 ❑ Nov 1985 Cover: 1.25 **NM** value: **1.50**
Circ: Statement: **120,335** CapCity orders: **7,700**
C: Michael W. Kaluta
32 ❑ Jan 1986 Cover: 1.25 **NM** value: **1.50**
Circ: CapCity orders: **7,100**
33 ❑ Mar 1986 Cover: 1.25 **NM** value: **1.50**
Circ: CapCity orders: **7,400**
34 ❑ May 1986 Cover: 1.25 **NM** value: **1.50**
Circ: CapCity orders: **7,700**
📖 Tower of Death • Has 1985 Statement, filed 10/1/85; avg print run 272,260; avg sales 115,135; avg subs 5,200; avg total paid 120,335; samples 145; office use 369; max existent 120,849; 55% of run returned
35 ❑ Jul 1986 Cover: 1.25 **NM** value: **1.50**
Circ: CapCity orders: **7,600**
36 ❑ Sep 1986 Cover: 1.25 **NM** value: **1.50**
Circ: CapCity orders: **7,500**
37 ❑ Nov 1986 Cover: 1.25 **NM** value: **1.50**
Circ: CapCity orders: **8,700**
38 ❑ Jan 1987 Cover: 1.25 **NM** value: **1.50**
Circ: CapCity orders: **7,800**
39 ❑ Mar 1987 Cover: 1.25 **NM** value: **1.50**
Circ: CapCity orders: **8,000**
40 ❑ May 1987 Cover: 1.25 **NM** value: **1.50**
Circ: CapCity orders: **7,600**
41 ❑ Jul 1987 Cover: 1.25 **NM** value: **1.50**
Circ: CapCity orders: **7,700**
42 ❑ Sep 1987 Cover: 1.25 **NM** value: **1.50**
Circ: CapCity orders: **8,800**
43 ❑ Nov 1987 Cover: 1.25 **NM** value: **1.50**
Circ: CapCity orders: **9,150**
44 ❑ Jan 1988 Cover: 1.25 **NM** value: **1.50**
Circ: CapCity orders: **9,200**
45 ❑ Mar 1988 Cover: 1.25 **NM** value: **1.50**
Circ: CapCity orders: **9,300**
46 ❑ May 1988 Cover: 1.50 **NM** value: **Cover or less**
Circ: CapCity orders: **8,900**
47 ❑ Jul 1988 Cover: 1.50 **NM** value: **Cover or less**
Circ: CapCity orders: **8,400**
48 ❑ Sep 1988 Cover: 1.50 **NM** value: **Cover or less**
Circ: CapCity orders: **8,700**
49 ❑ Nov 1988 Cover: 1.50 **NM** value: **Cover or less**
Circ: CapCity orders: **8,300**
50 ❑ Jan 1989 Cover: 1.50 **NM** value: **Cover or less**
Circ: CapCity orders: **8,300**
51 ❑ Mar 1989 Cover: 1.50 **NM** value: **Cover or less**
Circ: CapCity orders: **8,200**
52 ❑ May 1989 Cover: 1.50 **NM** value: **Cover or less**
Circ: CapCity orders: **8,100**
53 ❑ Jul 1989 Cover: 1.50 **NM** value: **Cover or less**
Circ: CapCity orders: **8,200**
54 ❑ Sep 1989 Cover: 1.50 **NM** value: **Cover or less**
Circ: CapCity orders: **8,100**
55 ❑ Nov 1989 Cover: 1.50 **NM** value: **Cover or less**
Circ: CapCity orders: **8,200**
final issue.

CONAN: THE LORD OF THE SPIDERS Marvel

1 ❑ Mar 1998 Cover: 2.50 **NM** value: **Cover or less**
Circ: Diamd. preorders: **19,190**
gatefold cover. • gatefold summary. 📖 The Webs We Weave **A:** Stefano Raffaele **W:** Roy Thomas
2 ❑ Apr 1998 Cover: 2.50 **NM** value: **Cover or less**
Circ: Diamd. preorders: **17,450**
• gatefold summary. **A:** Stefano Raffaele **W:** Roy Thomas
3 ❑ May 1998 Cover: 2.50 **NM** value: **Cover or less**
Circ: Diamd. preorders: **22,334**
• gatefold summary. **A:** Stefano Raffaele **W:** Roy Thomas

CONAN-THE MOVIE Marvel

Bk 1 ❑ Cover: 1.75 **NM** value: **Cover or less**
• (Marvel 1982)

CONAN: THE RAVAGERS OUT OF TIME Marvel

Bk 1 ❑ Cover: 9.95 **NM** value: **Cover or less**

CONAN THE REAVER Marvel

Bk 1 ❑ Cover: 6.50 **NM** value: **Cover or less**
Circ: CapCity orders: **6,050**

CONAN THE ROGUE Marvel

Bk 1 ❑ Cover: 9.95 **NM** value: **Cover or less**
Circ: CapCity orders: **2,600**

CONAN THE SAVAGE Marvel

1 ❑ Aug 1995 Cover: 2.95 **NM** value: **Cover or less**
Circ: CapCity orders: **9,125**
• b&w magazine.

Other grades: Multiply prices above by **1.5 for Mint • 2/3 for Very Fine • 1/3 for Fine • 1/5 for Very Good • 1/8 for Good**

2 ❑ Sep 1995 Cover: 2.95 **NM** value: **Cover or less**
• b&w magazine. 🕮 Stalker in the Snows, Part 1
3 ❑ Oct 1995 Cover: 2.95 **NM** value: **Cover or less**
• b&w magazine. 🕮 Stalker in the Snows, Part 2
4 ❑ Nov 1995 Cover: 2.95 **NM** value: **Cover or less**
• b&w magazine. 🕮 Stalker in the Snows, Part 3 • indicia gives title as Conan★ Versus Rune.
5 ❑ Dec 1995 Cover: 2.95 **NM** value: **Cover or less**
• b&w magazine. 🕮 Stalkers of the Snows, Part 4 **A:** Val Mayerik **W:** Mike Baron
6 ❑ Jan 1996 Cover: 2.95 **NM** value: **Cover or less**
• b&w magazine.
7 ❑ Feb 1996 Cover: 2.95 **NM** value: **Cover or less**
• b&w magazine.
8 ❑ Mar 1996 Cover: 2.95 **NM** value: **Cover or less**
• b&w magazine. 🕮 Ivory; Fate **A:** Val Mayerik; Neil Hansen **W:** Neil Hansen; Mike Baron
9 ❑ Apr 1996 Cover: 2.95 **NM** value: **Cover or less**
• b&w magazine.
10 ❑ May 1996 Cover: 2.95 **NM** value: **Cover or less**
• b&w magazine.
11 ❑ Jun 1996 Cover: 2.95 **NM** value: **Cover or less**
12 ❑ Jul 1996 Cover: 2.95 **NM** value: **Cover or less**

CONAN: THE SKULL OF SET — Marvel

Bk 1❑ Cover: 8.95 **NM** value: **Cover or less**

CONAN VS. RUNE — Marvel

1 ❑ Nov 1995 Cover: 2.95 **NM** value: **Cover or less**
One-shot. 🕮 The Dark God **A:** Barry Windsor-Smith **W:** Barry Windsor-Smith

CONCRETE — Dark Horse

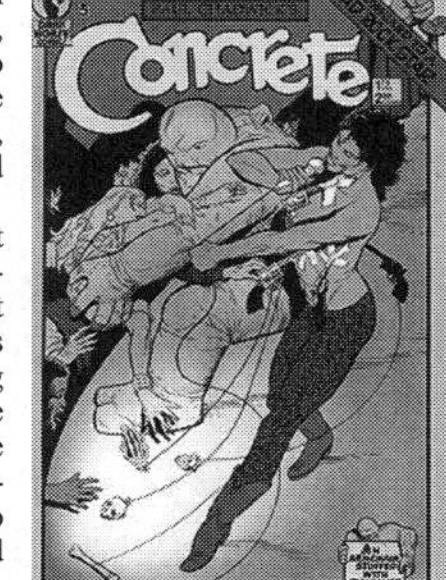

When Ronald Lithgow's brain was transplanted into its new, rocky body, he was on his way to instant stardom. As Concrete, he has become the talk of the town, and is taking to his newfound fame like a duck to water.

He may look like the Thing, but the lovable Concrete is no brawler. Instead, he tries his hand at more "normal" pursuits, such as rescuing mine workers and trying to swim the Atlantic Ocean. Since Concrete is also a writer, he records these experiences on paper, eventually turning them into books. These pursuits, combined with his penchant for publicity, would seem to almost guarantee the books to be best-sellers.

A well-written and intelligent character, Concrete first appeared in the pages of Dark Horse Presents #1. This first solo book continues that tradition of fine storytelling and exquisitely detailed art.

1 ❑ Mar 1987 Cover: 1.50 **NM** value: **5.00**
• **CGC:** 1 graded, best 8.0
🕮 A Stone Among Stones **A:** Paul Chadwick **W:** Paul Chadwick
1-2 ❑ Cover: 1.50 **NM** value: **2.00**
2 ❑ Jun 1987 Cover: 1.50 **NM** value: **3.00**
A: Paul Chadwick **W:** Paul Chadwick
3 ❑ Aug 1987 Cover: 1.50 **NM** value: **3.00**
A: Paul Chadwick **W:** Paul Chadwick ★ Origin of Concrete.
4 ❑ Oct 1987 Cover: 1.75 **NM** value: **2.50**
A: Paul Chadwick **W:** Paul Chadwick ★ Origin of Concrete.
5 ❑ Dec 1987 Cover: 1.75 **NM** value: **2.50**
A: Paul Chadwick **W:** Paul Chadwick
6 ❑ Feb 1988 Cover: 1.75 **NM** value: **2.50**
A: Paul Chadwick **W:** Paul Chadwick
7 ❑ Apr 1988 Cover: 1.75 **NM** value: **2.50**
A: Paul Chadwick **W:** Paul Chadwick
8 ❑ Jun 1988 Cover: 1.75 **NM** value: **2.50**
A: Paul Chadwick **W:** Paul Chadwick
9 ❑ Sep 1988 Cover: 1.75 **NM** value: **2.50**
A: Paul Chadwick **W:** Paul Chadwick
10 ❑ Cover: 1.75 **NM** value: **2.00**
final issue. **A:** Paul Chadwick **W:** Paul Chadwick
Bk 1❑ Cover: 24.95 **NM** value: **Cover or less**
• Complete Concrete **A:** Paul Chadwick **W:** Paul Chadwick
Hero 1❑ **NM** value: **1.00**
• Hero Special edition. 🕮 Moving A Big Rock • Included with Hero Illustrated #23 **A:** Paul Chadwick **W:** Paul Chadwick

CONCRETE: A NEW LIFE — Dark Horse

1 ❑ Oct 1989 Cover: 2.95 **NM** value: **Cover or less**
• b&w reprint **A:** Paul Chadwick ★ Origin of Concrete.

CONCRETE CELEBRATES EARTH DAY — Dark Horse

1 ❑ Apr 1990 Cover: 3.50 **NM** value: **Cover or less**
Circ: CapCity orders: **9,400**
🕮 Like Disneyland, Only Toxic; Earth Streams; A Billion Conscious Acts; The Still Planet • Moebius **A:** Charles Vess; Moebius; Paul Chadwick **W:** Charles Vess; Moebius; Paul Chadwick

CONCRETE COLOR SPECIAL — Dark Horse

1 ❑ Feb 1989 Cover: 2.95 **NM** value: **Cover or less**
Circ: CapCity orders: **8,350**
🕮 The Damp Descent; Lifestyles of the Rich and Famous; Under the Desert Stars • reprint in color **A:** Paul Chadwick **W:** Paul Chadwick

CONCRETE: ECLECTICA — Dark Horse

1 ❑ Apr 1993 Cover: 2.95 **NM** value: **Cover or less**
Circ: CapCity orders: **8,025**
wraparound cover from 1992 WonderCon program book. **A:** Paul Chadwick **W:** Paul Chadwick
2 ❑ May 1993 Cover: 2.95 **NM** value: **Cover or less**
Circ: CapCity orders: **6,700**
wraparound cover. **A:** Paul Chadwick **W:** Paul Chadwick

CONCRETE: FRAGILE CREATURE — Dark Horse

1 ❑ Jun 1991, full color Cover: 2.50 **NM** value: **Cover or less**
Circ: CapCity orders: **9,225**
wraparound cover. **A:** Paul Chadwick **W:** Paul Chadwick
2 ❑ Jul 1991, full color Cover: 2.50 **NM** value: **Cover or less**
Circ: CapCity orders: **8,800**
wraparound cover. **A:** Paul Chadwick **W:** Paul Chadwick
3 ❑ Aug 1991, full color Cover: 2.50 **NM** value: **Cover or less**
Circ: CapCity orders: **8,050**
wraparound cover. **A:** Paul Chadwick **W:** Paul Chadwick
4 ❑ Feb 1992, full color Cover: 2.50 **NM** value: **Cover or less**
Circ: CapCity orders: **8,725**
wraparound cover. **A:** Paul Chadwick **W:** Paul Chadwick
Bk 1❑ Cover: 15.95 **NM** value: **Cover or less**
A: Paul Chadwick **W:** Paul Chadwick

CONCRETE JUNGLE: THE LEGEND OF THE BLACK LION — Acclaim

1 ❑ Apr 1998 Cover: 2.50 **NM** value: **Cover or less**
Circ: Diamd. preorders: **8,683**
🕮 Speaking in Tongues **A:** James W. Fry III **W:** Christopher Priest

CONCRETE: KILLER SMILE — Dark Horse / Legend

1 ❑ Jul 1994 Cover: 2.95 **NM** value: **Cover or less**
Circ: CapCity orders: **11,675**
A: Paul Chadwick **W:** Paul Chadwick
2 ❑ Aug 1994 Cover: 2.95 **NM** value: **Cover or less**
Circ: CapCity orders: **9,550**
A: Paul Chadwick **W:** Paul Chadwick
3 ❑ Sep 1994 Cover: 2.95 **NM** value: **Cover or less**
Circ: CapCity orders: **9,200**
A: Paul Chadwick **W:** Paul Chadwick
4 ❑ Oct 1994 Cover: 2.95 **NM** value: **Cover or less**
Circ: CapCity orders: **9,475**
A: Paul Chadwick **W:** Paul Chadwick
Bk 1❑ Oct 1995 Cover: 16.95 **NM** value: **Cover or less**
No issue number. • Trade Paperback. • collects mini-series **A:** Paul Chadwick **W:** Paul Chadwick

CONCRETE: LAND & SEA — Dark Horse

1 ❑ Feb 1989, b&w Cover: 2.95 **NM** value: **Cover or less**
wraparound cardstock cover. • reprints first two Concrete stories with additional material **A:** Paul Chadwick

CONCRETE: ODD JOBS — Dark Horse

1 ❑ Jul 1990 Cover: 3.50 **NM** value: **Cover or less**
• b&w reprint;Collects Concrete #5-6 **A:** Paul Chadwick **W:** Paul Chadwick

CONCRETE: SHORT STORIES 1986-1989 — Dark Horse

Bk 1❑ Dec 1990 Cover: 15.95 **NM** value: **Cover or less**
• 1986-1989;collects stories from Dark Horse Presents and elsewhere **A:** Paul Chadwick **W:** Paul Chadwick

CONCRETE: SHORT STORIES 1990-1995 — Dark Horse

Bk 1❑ Jan 1996 Cover: 14.95 **NM** value: **Cover or less**
No issue number. • Trade Paperback. • collects various stories from myriad sources **A:** Paul Chadwick **W:** Paul Chadwick

CONCRETE: STRANGE ARMOR — Dark Horse

1 ❑ Dec 1997 Cover: 2.95 **NM** value: **Cover or less**
A: Paul Chadwick **W:** Paul Chadwick ★ Origin of Concrete.
2 ❑ Jan 1998 Cover: 2.95 **NM** value: **Cover or less**
A: Paul Chadwick **W:** Paul Chadwick ★ Origin of Concrete.
3 ❑ Mar 1998 Cover: 2.95 **NM** value: **Cover or less**
A: Paul Chadwick **W:** Paul Chadwick ★ Origin of Concrete.
4 ❑ Apr 1998 Cover: 2.95 **NM** value: **Cover or less**
A: Paul Chadwick **W:** Paul Chadwick ★ Origin of Concrete.
5 ❑ May 1998 Cover: 2.95 **NM** value: **Cover or less**
A: Paul Chadwick **W:** Paul Chadwick ★ Origin of Concrete.
Bk 1❑ Oct 1998 Cover: 16.95 **NM** value: **Cover or less**
A: Paul Chadwick **W:** Paul Chadwick ★ Origin of Concrete.

CONCRETE: THINK LIKE A MOUNTAIN — Dark Horse / Legend

Uncommon in its quality and uncompromising in its principles, Paul Chadwick's Concrete has become one of the most popular "prestige" comic titles of the 1990s. In the six-part "Think Like a Mountain" mini-series, the stone-faced but lovable Concrete and a band of Earth First! Activists attempt to prevent the logging of an ancient forest in the Pacific Northwest. "Think Like a Mountain" thoughtfully explores environmental activism, civil disobedience, and the high cost of living according to one's ideals.

Chadwick is a superb graphic storyteller who carefully balances plot, characterization, and heavy duty political propaganda while avoiding the kind of self-righteous tedium that usually results when comics self-consciously tackle important issues. Geoff Darrow's detail-rich covers round out the high quality package from Dark Horse.

1 ❑ Mar 1996, b&w Cover: 2.95 **NM** value: **Cover or less**
No issue number. • promotional giveaway for mini-series. 🕮 Green Fire **A:** Paul Chadwick **W:** Paul Chadwick
2 ❑ Apr 1996 Cover: 2.95 **NM** value: **Cover or less**
🕮 Hidden Graveyard **A:** Paul Chadwick **W:** Paul Chadwick
3 ❑ May 1996 Cover: 2.95 **NM** value: **Cover or less**
🕮 Arms and Boxes **A:** Paul Chadwick **W:** Paul Chadwick
4 ❑ Jun 1996 Cover: 2.95 **NM** value: **Cover or less**
🕮 Weight of the World **A:** Paul Chadwick **W:** Paul Chadwick
5 ❑ Jul 1996 Cover: 2.95 **NM** value: **Cover or less**
🕮 Nightwork **A:** Paul Chadwick **W:** Paul Chadwick
6 ❑ Aug 1996 Cover: 2.95 **NM** value: **Cover or less**
🕮 Charismatic Megafauna **A:** Paul Chadwick; Geof Darrow(cover) **W:** Paul Chadwick
Ash 1❑b&w **NM** value: **1.00**
No issue number. • promotional giveaway for mini-series. **A:** Paul Chadwick; Geof Darrow(cover) **W:** Paul Chadwick
Bk 1❑ Apr 1997 Cover: 17.95 **NM** value: **Cover or less**
A: Paul Chadwick; Geof Darrow(cover) **W:** Paul Chadwick

CONDOM-MAN — Aaaahh!!

1 ❑ Cover: 3.95 **NM** value: **Cover or less**
• Gold ink limited edition. **A:** Chris Swafford **W:** Chris Swafford

CONDORMAN (WALT DISNEY) — Whitman

1 ❑ Nov 1981 Cover: 0.50 **NM** value: **1.00**
2 ❑ Dec 1981 Cover: 0.50 **NM** value: **1.00**
🕮 Conclusion
3 ❑ Jan 1982 Cover: 0.50 **NM** value: **1.00**

CONEHEADS — Marvel

1 ❑ Jun 1994 Cover: 1.75 **NM** value: **Cover or less**
Circ: CapCity orders: **9,800**
🕮 Homecoming **A:** Tom Richmond **W:** Terry Collins
2 ❑ Jul 1994 Cover: 1.75 **NM** value: **Cover or less**
Circ: CapCity orders: **6,000**
3 ❑ Aug 1994 Cover: 1.75 **NM** value: **Cover or less**
Circ: CapCity orders: **4,350**
4 ❑ Sep 1994 Cover: 1.75 **NM** value: **Cover or less**

CONFESSIONS OF A CEREAL EATER — NBM

Rob "Rocco" Maisch has lived an average life. But it's rather amazing how vividly he remembers it. This series provides true stories from his life, arranged in random order over roughly 30 years.

As examples of the tales, in "Daniel's Den" Rob and his friends experience all the trials and tribulations of attending a rock show at a club. In "Movin' In" the author tells the story of the rivalry and hi-jinks between two adjacent college dorms. And in "Scott's Jock," he experiences the joys and embarrassment of purchasing his first jock strap with his father.

As the author states in his introduction, "Some are a bit nostalgic while others hold the grim fascination of a really outstanding train wreck. Hopefully, they are all funny to various twisted degrees."

1 ❑ 2000 b&w Cover: 2.95 **NM** value: **Cover or less**
🕮 Daniel's Den; Movin' In; Scott's Jock; Two In a Canoe **A:** James Vining; Nick Rummel; Robyn Chapman; Brett Weldele **C:** Scott Hampton **W:** Rob Maisch
2 ❑ 2000 b&w Cover: 2.95 **NM** value: **Cover or less**
🕮 A Quiet Evening at Home; Bailey Daze: Rat Tales; Father of the Year; Gym Wimps **A:** Darryl Jones; Lee Oaks; Paul Hudson; Rob Epps; Bret Weldele **C:** Brett Weldele **W:** Rob Maisch
3 ❑ 2000 b&w Cover: 2.95 **NM** value: **Cover or less**
🕮 Yule Be Sorry; Junkers; The Bells; The Ramon Campaign **A:** James Vining; Lee Oaks **C:** Lee Oaks **W:** Rob Maisch

CONFESSIONS OF A TEENAGE VAMPIRE: THE TURNING — Scholastic

1 ❑ Jul 1997 Cover: 4.99 **NM** value: **Cover or less**
No issue number. • digest.

CONFESSIONS OF A TEENAGE VAMPIRE: ZOMBIE SATURDAY NIGHT — Scholastic

1 ❑ Jul 1997 Cover: 4.99 **NM** value: **Cover or less**
No issue number. • digest.

CONFESSIONS OF ROMANCE — Star

7 ❑ Nov 1953 Cover: 0.10 **NM** value: **75.00**
8 ❑ Feb 1954 Cover: 0.10 **NM** value: **65.00**
9 ❑ May 1954 Cover: 0.10 **NM** value: **75.00**
10 ❑ Aug 1954 Cover: 0.10 **NM** value: **50.00**
• **CGC:** 1 graded, best 7.0
11 ❑ Nov 1954 Cover: 0.10 **NM** value: **50.00**

CONFESSOR, THE (DEMONICUS EX DEO) — Dark Matter

1 ❑ b&w Cover: 2.95 **NM** value: **Cover or less**
🕮 Purgation

CONFRONTATION, THE — Sacred Origin

1 ❑ Jul 1997 Cover: 2.95 **NM** value: **Cover or less**
🕮 The Journey **A:** R. Brad Garlich **W:** Johnny M. Lopez
2 ❑ Oct 1997 Cover: 2.95 **NM** value: **Cover or less**
🕮 Genesis **A:** R. Brad Garlich; Sella Garlich **W:** Johnny M. Lopez
3 ❑ 1997 Cover: 2.95 **NM** value: **Cover or less**
4 ❑ 1998 Cover: 2.95 **NM** value: **Cover or less**
SE 1❑ **NM** value: **5.00**
• Convention exclusive edition. **A:** John Donahue **W:** Johnny M. Lopez

CGC-graded: Multiply prices above by **33 for 9.9 M • 16 for 9.8 NM/M • 7 for 9.6 NM+ • 5 for 9.4 NM • 2.5 for 9.2 NM- • 1.5 for 9.0 VF/NM**

CONGO BILL (DC) — DC

Though his adventures ran for years as a back-up feature in Action Comics, the jungle explorer failed to support a similar run as star of his own title. The series ran only about a year, as the Comics Code was introduced and the publisher hunted for genres that would still provide adventure stories for young readers. Clearly in the same genre as Alex Raymond's Jungle Jim comic strip, it featured a white adventurer in African jungles. Over the years, Congo Bill acted as guardian to Janu, the Jungle Boy (orphaned son of a jungle guide) and eventually acquired a ring which let him trade identities for an hour at a time with Congorilla, a golden gorilla. Congorilla first appeared in Action Comics #248 (Jan 59), several years after this series ended. — Maggie

1 ❑ Aug 1954 Cover: 0.10 **NM** value: **800.00**
• **CGC:** 1 graded, best 2.5
2 ❑ Oct 1954 Cover: 0.10 **NM** value: **650.00**
• **CGC:** 2 graded, best 8.0
3 ❑ Dec 1954 Cover: 0.10 **NM** value: **500.00**
• **CGC:** 1 graded, best 6.5
4 ❑ Feb 1955 Cover: 0.10 **NM** value: **500.00**
• **CGC:** 1 graded, best 4.0
5 ❑ Apr 1955 Cover: 0.10 **NM** value: **450.00**
6 ❑ Jun 1955 Cover: 0.10 **NM** value: **450.00**
• **CGC:** 1 graded, best 6.5
7 ❑ Aug 1955 Cover: 0.10 **NM** value: **450.00**
• **CGC:** 1 graded, best 6.0

CONGO BILL (VERTIGO) — DC / Vertigo

1 ❑ Oct 1999 Cover: 2.95 **NM** value: **Cover or less**
Circ: Diamd. preorders: **12,774**
📖 The Message **A:** Danijel Zeelj **W:** Scott Cunningham
2 ❑ Nov 1999 Cover: 2.95 **NM** value: **Cover or less**
Circ: Diamd. preorders: **10,265**
A: Danijel Zeelj **W:** Scott Cunningham
3 ❑ Dec 1999 Cover: 2.95 **NM** value: **Cover or less**
Circ: Diamd. preorders: **8,752**
📖 The Darkness **A:** Danijel Zeelj **W:** Scott Cunningham
4 ❑ Jan 2000 Cover: 2.95 **NM** value: **Cover or less**
Circ: Diamd. preorders: **7,786**
📖 The Beast **A:** Danijel Zeelj **W:** Scott Cunningham

CONGORILLA — DC

1 ❑ Nov 1992 Cover: 1.75 **NM** value: **2.00**
Circ: CapCity orders: **14,350**
📖 Now I Lay Me Down to Sleep... **A:** Neil Vokes **W:** Steve Englehart
2 ❑ Dec 1992 Cover: 1.75 **NM** value: **Cover or less**
Circ: CapCity orders: **8,700**
A: Neil Vokes **W:** Steve Englehart
3 ❑ Jan 1993 Cover: 1.75 **NM** value: **Cover or less**
Circ: CapCity orders: **7,250**
A: Neil Vokes **W:** Steve Englehart
4 ❑ Feb 1993 Cover: 1.75 **NM** value: **Cover or less**
Circ: CapCity orders: **6,450**
A: Neil Vokes **W:** Steve Englehart

CONJURORS — DC

1 ❑ Apr 1999 Cover: 2.95 **NM** value: **Cover or less**
Circ: Diamd. preorders: **17,628**
📖 The Birth of Magic • Elseworlds story **A:** Eduardo Barreto **W:** Chuck Dixon ★ Appearance of Challengers of the Unknown, Deadman, Phantom Stranger.
2 ❑ May 1999 Cover: 2.95 **NM** value: **Cover or less**
Circ: Diamd. preorders: **14,783**
📖 The Death of Magic • Elseworlds story **A:** Eduardo Barreto **W:** Chuck Dixon
3 ❑ Jun 1999 Cover: 2.95 **NM** value: **Cover or less**
Circ: Diamd. preorders: **14,167**
📖 Magic and Machine • Elseworlds story **A:** Eduardo Barreto **W:** Chuck Dixon

CONQUEROR — Harrier

1 ❑ Aug 1984 Cover: 1.75 **NM** value: **Cover or less**
2 ❑ Oct 1984 Cover: 1.75 **NM** value: **Cover or less**
📖 Ladies' Night; Local Problem; Fl'ff's Machine **A:** Dave Gibbons(cover) **W:** Eddie Campbell
3 ❑ Dec 1984 Cover: 1.75 **NM** value: **Cover or less**
4 ❑ Feb 1985 Cover: 1.75 **NM** value: **Cover or less**
5 ❑ Apr 1985 Cover: 1.75 **NM** value: **Cover or less**
6 ❑ Jun 1985 Cover: 1.75 **NM** value: **Cover or less**
7 ❑ Aug 1985 Cover: 1.75 **NM** value: **Cover or less**
8 ❑ Oct 1985 Cover: 1.75 **NM** value: **Cover or less**
9 ❑ Dec 1985 Cover: 1.75 **NM** value: **Cover or less**
SE 1 ❑ Cover: 1.95 **NM** value: **Cover or less**
• Special edition (1987). 📖 Unicorn on Winchester; Mark of the Beast; Mine...For Keeps; Lisellan Tea Party **A:** Art Wetherell; Dave Harwood; Tom Abell **W:** Eddie Campbell; Brian Cuffe; Martin Lock; Rob Sharp

CONQUEROR OF THE BARREN EARTH — DC

1 ❑ Feb 1983 Cover: 0.75 **NM** value: **1.00**
📖 The Ravager **A:** Ron Randall **W:** Gary Cohn
2 ❑ Mar 1983 Cover: 0.75 **NM** value: **1.00**
3 ❑ Apr 1983 Cover: 0.75 **NM** value: **1.00**
4 ❑ May 1983 Cover: 0.75 **NM** value: **1.00**

CONQUEROR UNIVERSE — Harrier

1 ❑ Cover: 2.75 **NM** value: **Cover or less**
📖 Castle in the Air; Sacrifice; The Naming; The Conqueror Experiment; Captain Thunder; A short History **A:** Mike Collins; Andrew Nixon; Dave Harwood; David A. Roach; Graham Bleatman; Ken Hopgood; Tony O'Donnell **W:** Martin Lock

CONSERVATION CORPS — Archie

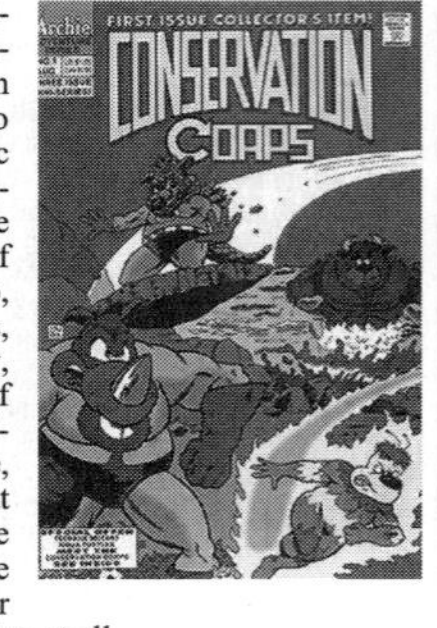

Appearing first in Teenage Mutant Ninja Turtles Meet the Conservation Corps, the Conservation Corps is a team of do-gooders who have dedicated their super-heroic lives to the preservation of the environment. They are: The Stone Hedgehog, England's master of earth and rock; Water Buffalo, North America's lord of the oceans, lakes, rivers, and streams; Firefly, South America's commander of heat and fire; and Greenhorn, Africa's ruler of flora and fauna. Sure, the concept's a wee bit hokey, but this is a fun group. And, hey, the kids can learn about the importance of protecting the environment for future generations — not a bad thing at all.

1 ❑ Aug 1993 Cover: 1.25 **NM** value: **Cover or less**
Circ: CapCity orders: **2,825**
📖 Lost & Found **A:** Dan Nakrosis; Paul Castiglia **W:** Dan Nakrosis; Paul Castiglia
2 ❑ Sep 1993 Cover: 1.25 **NM** value: **Cover or less**
3 ❑ Nov 1993 Cover: 1.25 **NM** value: **Cover or less**

CONSPIRACY — Marvel

1 ❑ Feb 1998 Cover: 2.99 **NM** value: **Cover or less**
Circ: Diamd. preorders: **39,336**
📖 Show & Tell **A:** Igor Kordey **W:** Dan Abnett
2 ❑ Mar 1998 Cover: 2.99 **NM** value: **Cover or less**
Circ: Diamd. preorders: **36,804**
📖 Print the Legend **A:** Igor Kordey **W:** Dan Abnett

CONSPIRACY COMICS — Revolutionary

1 ❑ Oct 1991 Cover: 2.50 **NM** value: **Cover or less**
• Marilyn Monroe
2 ❑ Feb 1992, b&w Cover: 2.50 **NM** value: **Cover or less**
• John F. Kennedy
3 ❑ Jul 1992, b&w Cover: 2.50 **NM** value: **Cover or less**
• Robert F. Kennedy

CONSTELLATION GRAPHICS — Stages

1 ❑ Cover: 1.50 **NM** value: **Cover or less**
2 ❑ Cover: 1.50 **NM** value: **Cover or less**

CONSTRUCT — Caliber

1 ❑ **NM** value: **2.95**
2 ❑ **NM** value: **2.95**
3 ❑ **NM** value: **2.95**
4 ❑ **NM** value: **2.95**
5 ❑ **NM** value: **2.95**

CONTACT COMICS — Aviation

1 ❑ Jul 1944 Cover: 0.10 **NM** value: **400.00**
2 ❑ Sep 1944 Cover: 0.10 **NM** value: **375.00**
3 ❑ Nov 1944 Cover: 0.10 **NM** value: **375.00**
4 ❑ Jan 1945 Cover: 0.10 **NM** value: **325.00**
5 ❑ Mar 1945 Cover: 0.10 **NM** value: **325.00**
6 ❑ May 1945 Cover: 0.10 **NM** value: **325.00**
7 ❑ Jul 1945 Cover: 0.10 **NM** value: **275.00**
8 ❑ Sep 1945 Cover: 0.10 **NM** value: **275.00**
• **CGC:** 1 graded, best 9.2
9 ❑ Nov 1945 Cover: 0.10 **NM** value: **250.00**
10 ❑ Jan 1946 Cover: 0.10 **NM** value: **250.00**
• **CGC:** 1 graded, best 9.4
11 ❑ Mar 1946 Cover: 0.10 **NM** value: **250.00**
12 ❑ Jul 1946 Cover: 0.10 **NM** value: **250.00**
• **CGC:** 6 graded, best 8.0

CONTAMINATED ZONE, THE — Brave New Words

1 ❑ Apr 1991, b&w Cover: 2.50 **NM** value: **Cover or less**
📖 The Status of Bio-Level 5 **A:** Matt Howarth **W:** Matt Howarth
2 ❑ 1991b&w Cover: 2.50 **NM** value: **Cover or less**
A: Matt Howarth **W:** Matt Howarth
3 ❑ 1991b&w Cover: 2.50 **NM** value: **Cover or less**
A: Matt Howarth **W:** Matt Howarth

CONTEMPORARY BIO-GRAPHICS — Revolutionary

1 ❑ Dec 1991, b&w Cover: 2.50 **NM** value: **Cover or less**
📖 Don't Start the Revolution Without Smilin' Stan Lee • Stan Lee **A:** Blackwell **W:** Jay Allen Sanford
2 ❑ Apr 1992, b&w Cover: 2.50 **NM** value: **Cover or less**
• Boris Yeltsin
3 ❑ May 1992, b&w Cover: 2.50 **NM** value: **Cover or less**
• Gene Roddenberry
4 ❑ Jun 1992 Cover: 2.50 **NM** value: **Cover or less**
• Pee Wee Herman
5 ❑ Sep 1992, b&w Cover: 2.50 **NM** value: **Cover or less**
• David Lynch
6 ❑ Oct 1992 Cover: 2.50 **NM** value: **Cover or less**
• Ross Perot
7 ❑ Dec 1992, b&w Cover: 2.50 **NM** value: **Cover or less**
• Spike Lee
8 ❑ Jun 1993, b&w Cover: 2.50 **NM** value: **Cover or less**
• Image story

CONTENDER COMICS SPECIAL — Contender

1 ❑ b&w **NM** value: **1.00**

CONTEST OF CHAMPIONS II — Marvel

Reprising the classic 1980s three-issue limited series, with a five-issue one, Chris Claremont and Oscar Jiminez introduce the Coterie, a space-faring race of gamemasters that values physical competition, who transport most of the Marvel super-heroes from the Earth to their ship to test their skills against one another. In exchange for providing this entertaining display for the Coterie, the heroes will earn for the Earth the accumulated knowledge the aliens have gathered in their travels. On the surface, it sound like a good deal, but is something more sinister going on behind the scenes? Iron Man certainly believes so, when he finds the entire place crawling with "nanites" and the Coterie's offer too good to be true. Before he gets the opportunity to investigate, he's forced to fight the X-Men's Psylocke and the members of X-Force.

An early dose of 1980s nostalgia here that, while interesting, doesn't quite have the simple charm of the original.

1 ❑ Sep 1999 Cover: 2.50 **NM** value: **Cover or less**
Circ: Diamd. preorders: **59,130**
📖 The Gathering • Iron Man vs. Psylocke;Iron Man vs. X-Force **A:** Oscar Jimenez **W:** Chris Claremont
2 ❑ Sep 1999 Cover: 2.50 **NM** value: **Cover or less**
Circ: Diamd. preorders: **53,920**
• Human Torch vs. Spider-Girl, Storm, She-Hulk;Mr. Fantastic vs. Hulk **A:** Oscar Jimenez **W:** Chris Claremont
3 ❑ Oct 1999 Cover: 2.50 **NM** value: **Cover or less**
Circ: Diamd. preorders: **47,092**
• Thor vs. Storm;Cable vs. Scarlet Witch;New Warriors vs. Slingers **A:** Oscar Jimenez **W:** Chris Claremont
4 ❑ Nov 1999 Cover: 2.50 **NM** value: **Cover or less**
Circ: Diamd. preorders: **46,365**
• Black Panther vs Captain America **A:** Oscar Jimenez **W:** Chris Claremont
5 ❑ Nov 1999 Cover: 2.50 **NM** value: **Cover or less**
Circ: Diamd. preorders: **47,347**
• Rogue vs Warbird **A:** Oscar Jimenez **W:** Chris Claremont

CONTINUUM — Continuity

1 ❑ Oct 1988 **NM** value: **2.50**

CONTRACTORS — Eclipse

1 ❑ b&w Cover: 2.00 **NM** value: **Cover or less**
A: Jun-87; Ken Macklin **W:** Ken Macklin

CONTRACT WITH GOD, A (DC) — DC

1 ❑ Cover: 12.95 **NM** value: **Cover or less**
📖 A Contract With God; The Street Singer; The Super; Cookalein **A:** Will Eisner **W:** Will Eisner

CONVOCATIONS-A MAGIC: THE GATHERING GALLERY — Acclaim / Armada

1 ❑ Jan 1995 Cover: 2.50 **NM** value: **Cover or less**
Circ: CapCity orders: **8,600**
reproduces covers from several Magic mini-series. • pin-ups **W:** Michael W. Kaluta; Mike Dringenberg; Gerard Lee; Juda Tverski; Pete Venters; Tobin Dorn

COOCHY COOTY MEN'S COMICS — Print Mint

1 ❑ Cover: 0.50 **NM** value: **3.00**
A: Robert Williams **W:** Robert Williams

COO COO COMICS — Animated / Armada

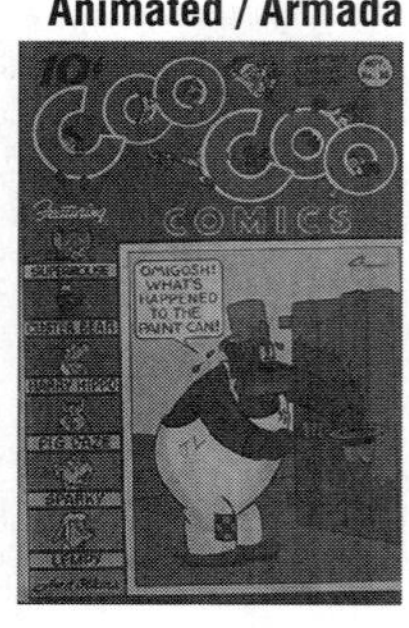

Coo Coo Comics was a funny animal comic book whose creators hit on an obvious and entertaining combination: funny animals and super-heroes. Super Mouse made his debut in Coo Coo Comics #1 and entertained readers as the lead story for almost the entire 10-year run of the title. (Hoppy the Marvel Bunny didn't appear for another two months.) Backing up this super-powered rodent are Tuffy, a tom cat with a resemblance to Warner Brothers' famous feline Sylvester; Dodger, a "squoil" from Brooklyn; Samuel Spaniel, a goofy pooch; and Bruno Bear, a slow-witted country bumpkin with a taste for honey.

Also featured in each issue are several text-only stories of about a page each, with a single spot illustration across the top. Some of these illustrations, especially in the middle issues, were the (very early) work of Frank Frazetta, the acclaimed fantasy artist.

1 ❑ Oct 1942 Cover: 0.10 **NM** value: **160.00**
★ Origin of Supermouse. ★ 1st Appearance of Supermouse.
2 ❑ Dec 1942 Cover: 0.10 **NM** value: **65.00**
3 ❑ Feb 1943 Cover: 0.10 **NM** value: **40.00**
📖 Kuddly Kubs: The Pest Busters; Winken, Blinken, & Nod; Jack Rabbit's Jackpot; Willie Woodchuck's Relations (text story); Kenny; A Cat's Tail (text story); Bernie the Fox; Basil the Bold; The Left-Handed Rabbit (text story); Earl the Squirrel **A:** D. Williams; Dressler; Joe Oriolo; Tom Golden; Bob Naylod **W:** Joe Oriolo; Tom Golden; Bob Naylod; Charles Strong; Chuck Stanley; Kelvin McKay
4 ❑ Apr 1943 Cover: 0.10 **NM** value: **40.00**
5 ❑ May 1943 Cover: 0.10 **NM** value: **40.00**
6 ❑ Jul 1943 Cover: 0.10 **NM** value: **34.00**

Other grades: Multiply prices above by **1.5 for Mint • 2/3 for Very Fine • 1/3 for Fine • 1/5 for Very Good • 1/8 for Good**

7 ❑ Sep 1943 Cover: 0.10 **NM** value: **34.00**
8 ❑ Nov 1943 Cover: 0.10 **NM** value: **34.00**
9 ❑ Jan 1944 Cover: 0.10 **NM** value: **34.00**
10 ❑ Mar 1944 Cover: 0.10 **NM** value: **34.00**
11 ❑ May 1944 Cover: 0.10 **NM** value: **28.00**
12 ❑ Jul 1944 Cover: 0.10 **NM** value: **28.00**
13 ❑ Sep 1944 Cover: 0.10 **NM** value: **28.00**
14 ❑ Nov 1944 Cover: 0.10 **NM** value: **28.00**
15 ❑ Jan 1945 Cover: 0.10 **NM** value: **28.00**
16 ❑ Mar 1945 Cover: 0.10 **NM** value: **28.00**
17 ❑ May 1945 Cover: 0.10 **NM** value: **28.00**
18 ❑ Jul 1945 Cover: 0.10 **NM** value: **28.00**
19 ❑ Sep 1945 Cover: 0.10 **NM** value: **28.00**
20 ❑ Nov 1945 Cover: 0.10 **NM** value: **28.00**
21 ❑ Jan 1946 Cover: 0.10 **NM** value: **24.00**
22 ❑ Feb 1946 Cover: 0.10 **NM** value: **24.00**
23 ❑ Mar 1946 Cover: 0.10 **NM** value: **24.00**
24 ❑ Apr 1946 Cover: 0.10 **NM** value: **24.00**
25 ❑ May 1946 Cover: 0.10 **NM** value: **24.00**
26 ❑ Jun 1946 Cover: 0.10 **NM** value: **24.00**
27 ❑ Jul 1946 Cover: 0.10 **NM** value: **24.00**
28 ❑ Aug 1946 Cover: 0.10 **NM** value: **24.00**
29 ❑ Sep 1946 Cover: 0.10 **NM** value: **24.00**
30 ❑ Nov 1946 Cover: 0.10 **NM** value: **24.00**
31 ❑ Jan 1947 Cover: 0.10 **NM** value: **20.00**
32 ❑ Mar 1947 Cover: 0.10 **NM** value: **20.00**
33 ❑ May 1947 Cover: 0.10 **NM** value: **20.00**
34 ❑ Jul 1947 Cover: 0.10 **NM** value: **35.00**
A: Frank Frazetta(text illustration); Al Hubbard; Jack Bradbury **W:** Jack Bradbury; Alison Leslie; Donald Hobart; Jack Cosgrief; Lily K. Scott
35 ❑ Sep 1947 Cover: 0.10 **NM** value: **35.00**
A: Frank Frazetta(text illustration)
36 ❑ Nov 1947 Cover: 0.10 **NM** value: **35.00**
A: Frank Frazetta(text illustration)
37 ❑ Jan 1948 Cover: 0.10 **NM** value: **35.00**
A: Frank Frazetta(text illustration)
38 ❑ Mar 1948 Cover: 0.10 **NM** value: **35.00**
A: Frank Frazetta(text illustration)
39 ❑ May 1948 Cover: 0.10 **NM** value: **35.00**
A: Frank Frazetta(text illustration)
40 ❑ Jul 1948 Cover: 0.10 **NM** value: **35.00**
A: Frank Frazetta(text illustration)
41 ❑ Sep 1948 Cover: 0.10 **NM** value: **85.00**
A: Frank Frazetta
42 ❑ Nov 1948 Cover: 0.10 **NM** value: **75.00**
A: Frank Frazetta
43 ❑ Jan 1949 Cover: 0.10 **NM** value: **40.00**
A: Frank Frazetta(text illustration)
44 ❑ Mar 1949 Cover: 0.10 **NM** value: **40.00**
A: Frank Frazetta(text illustration)
45 ❑ May 1949 Cover: 0.10 **NM** value: **40.00**
A: Frank Frazetta(text illustration)
46 ❑ Jul 1949 Cover: 0.10 **NM** value: **40.00**
A: Frank Frazetta(text illustration)
47 ❑ Sep 1949 Cover: 0.10 **NM** value: **75.00**
A: Frank Frazetta
48 ❑ Nov 1949 Cover: 0.10 **NM** value: **40.00**
A: Frank Frazetta(text illustration)
49 ❑ Jan 1950 Cover: 0.10 **NM** value: **60.00**
• 3-D. **A:** Frank Frazetta(text illustration)
50 ❑ Mar 1950 Cover: 0.10 **NM** value: **50.00**
• 3-D. **A:** Frank Frazetta(text illustration)
51 ❑ May 1950 Cover: 0.10 **NM** value: **50.00**
• 3-D.
52 ❑ Jul 1950 Cover: 0.10 **NM** value: **18.00**
53 ❑ Sep 1950 Cover: 0.10 **NM** value: **18.00**
54 ❑ Nov 1950 Cover: 0.10 **NM** value: **18.00**
55 ❑ Jan 1951 Cover: 0.10 **NM** value: **18.00**
56 ❑ Mar 1951 Cover: 0.10 **NM** value: **18.00**
57 ❑ May 1951 Cover: 0.10 **NM** value: **18.00**
58 ❑ Jul 1951 Cover: 0.10 **NM** value: **18.00**
59 ❑ Sep 1951 Cover: 0.10 **NM** value: **18.00**
60 ❑ Nov 1951 Cover: 0.10 **NM** value: **18.00**
61 ❑ Jan 1952 Cover: 0.10 **NM** value: **18.00**
62 ❑ Mar 1952 Cover: 0.10 **NM** value: **18.00**

COOKIE — ACG

1 ❑ Apr 1946 Cover: 0.10 **NM** value: **90.00**
2 ❑ Aug 1946 Cover: 0.10 **NM** value: **48.00**
3 ❑ Oct 1946 Cover: 0.10 **NM** value: **35.00**
4 ❑ Jan 1947 Cover: 0.10 **NM** value: **35.00**
5 ❑ Feb 1947 Cover: 0.10 **NM** value: **35.00**
6 ❑ Apr 1947 Cover: 0.10 **NM** value: **25.00**
7 ❑ Jun 1947 Cover: 0.10 **NM** value: **25.00**
8 ❑ Aug 1947 Cover: 0.10 **NM** value: **25.00**
9 ❑ Oct 1947 Cover: 0.10 **NM** value: **25.00**
10 ❑ Dec 1947 Cover: 0.10 **NM** value: **25.00**
11 ❑ Feb 1948 Cover: 0.10 **NM** value: **22.00**
12 ❑ Apr 1948 Cover: 0.10 **NM** value: **22.00**
13 ❑ Jun 1948 Cover: 0.10 **NM** value: **22.00**
14 ❑ Aug 1948 Cover: 0.10 **NM** value: **22.00**
15 ❑ Oct 1948 Cover: 0.10 **NM** value: **22.00**
16 ❑ Dec 1948 Cover: 0.10 **NM** value: **22.00**
17 ❑ Feb 1949 Cover: 0.10 **NM** value: **22.00**
18 ❑ Apr 1949 Cover: 0.10 **NM** value: **22.00**
19 ❑ Jun 1949 Cover: 0.10 **NM** value: **22.00**
20 ❑ Aug 1949 Cover: 0.10 **NM** value: **22.00**
21 ❑ Oct 1949 Cover: 0.10 **NM** value: **18.00**
22 ❑ Dec 1949 Cover: 0.10 **NM** value: **18.00**
23 ❑ Feb 1950 Cover: 0.10 **NM** value: **18.00**
24 ❑ Apr 1950 Cover: 0.10 **NM** value: **18.00**
25 ❑ Jun 1950 Cover: 0.10 **NM** value: **18.00**
26 ❑ Aug 1950 Cover: 0.10 **NM** value: **18.00**
27 ❑ Oct 1950 Cover: 0.10 **NM** value: **18.00**
28 ❑ Dec 1950 Cover: 0.10 **NM** value: **18.00**
29 ❑ Feb 1951 Cover: 0.10 **NM** value: **18.00**
30 ❑ Apr 1951 Cover: 0.10 **NM** value: **18.00**
31 ❑ Jun 1951 Cover: 0.10 **NM** value: **18.00**
32 ❑ Aug 1951 Cover: 0.10 **NM** value: **18.00**
33 ❑ Oct 1951 Cover: 0.10 **NM** value: **18.00**
34 ❑ Dec 1951 Cover: 0.10 **NM** value: **18.00**
35 ❑ Feb 1952 Cover: 0.10 **NM** value: **18.00**
36 ❑ Apr 1952 Cover: 0.10 **NM** value: **18.00**
37 ❑ Jun 1952 Cover: 0.10 **NM** value: **18.00**
38 ❑ Aug 1952 Cover: 0.10 **NM** value: **18.00**
39 ❑ Oct 1952 Cover: 0.10 **NM** value: **18.00**
40 ❑ Dec 1952 Cover: 0.10 **NM** value: **18.00**
41 ❑ Feb 1953 Cover: 0.10 **NM** value: **16.00**
42 ❑ ca. 1953 Cover: 0.10 **NM** value: **16.00**
Two's Company-Three's Revoltin'! (text story);
43 ❑ Jun 1953 Cover: 0.10 **NM** value: **16.00**
44 ❑ Sep 1953 Cover: 0.10 **NM** value: **16.00**
45 ❑ Nov 1953 Cover: 0.10 **NM** value: **16.00**
46 ❑ Jan 1954 Cover: 0.10 **NM** value: **16.00**
47 ❑ Feb 1954 Cover: 0.10 **NM** value: **16.00**
48 ❑ Apr 1954 Cover: 0.10 **NM** value: **16.00**
49 ❑ Jun 1954 Cover: 0.10 **NM** value: **16.00**
50 ❑ Aug 1954 Cover: 0.10 **NM** value: **16.00**
51 ❑ Oct 1954 Cover: 0.10 **NM** value: **16.00**
52 ❑ Dec 1954 Cover: 0.10 **NM** value: **16.00**
53 ❑ ca. 1955 Cover: 0.10 **NM** value: **16.00**
54 ❑ ca. 1955 Cover: 0.10 **NM** value: **16.00**
55 ❑ Aug 1955 Cover: 0.10 **NM** value: **16.00**
final issue.

COOL WORLD — DC

1 ❑ Apr 1992 Cover: 1.75 **NM** value: **Cover or less**
Circ: CapCity orders: **5,400**
2 ❑ May 1992 Cover: 1.75 **NM** value: **Cover or less**
Circ: CapCity orders: **4,700**
3 ❑ Jun 1992 Cover: 1.75 **NM** value: **Cover or less**
Circ: CapCity orders: **4,900**
4 ❑ Sep 1992 Cover: 1.75 **NM** value: **Cover or less**
Circ: CapCity orders: **4,300**

COOL WORLD MOVIE ADAPTATION — DC

1 ❑ Cover: 3.50 **NM** value: **Cover or less**
Circ: CapCity orders: **7,200**
No issue number. **A:** Alan Kupperberg **W:** Michael Eury

COP CALLED TRACY, A — Avalon

Modern comics fans whose papers don't carry the strip may best know him from the Warren Beatty film, but Avalon remembers the daily comic strip in which Dick Tracy got his start in 1931 and reprints those early Chester Gould (1900-1985) stories in this title. Here, the square-jawed, straitlaced hero, a master detective with guns, gadgets, and an unflappable demeanor at his disposal, meets a beautiful woman whose amnesia might be hiding more than her identity. It might also be protecting a murderer. Tracy tries to get to the bottom of the ever-deepening mystery, while shadowy criminals try to stop him and bodies begin to pile up. Will he be next?

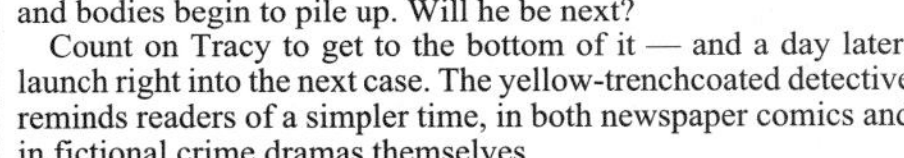

Count on Tracy to get to the bottom of it — and a day later, launch right into the next case. The yellow-trenchcoated detective reminds readers of a simpler time, in both newspaper comics and in fictional crime dramas themselves.

1 ❑ Cover: 2.95 **NM** value: **Cover or less**
Dick Tracy **A:** Chester Gould **W:** Chester Gould
2 ❑ Cover: 2.95 **NM** value: **Cover or less**
Dick Tracy **A:** Chester Gould **W:** Chester Gould
3 ❑ Cover: 2.95 **NM** value: **Cover or less**
Dick Tracy **A:** Chester Gould **W:** Chester Gould
4 ❑ Cover: 2.95 **NM** value: **Cover or less**
Dick Tracy **A:** Chester Gould **W:** Chester Gould
5 ❑ Cover: 2.95 **NM** value: **Cover or less**
Dick Tracy **A:** Chester Gould **W:** Chester Gould
6 ❑ Cover: 2.95 **NM** value: **Cover or less**
Dick Tracy **A:** Chester Gould **W:** Chester Gould
7 ❑ Cover: 2.95 **NM** value: **Cover or less**
Dick Tracy **A:** Chester Gould **W:** Chester Gould
8 ❑ Cover: 2.95 **NM** value: **Cover or less**
Dick Tracy **A:** Chester Gould **W:** Chester Gould
9 ❑ Cover: 2.95 **NM** value: **Cover or less**
Dick Tracy **A:** Chester Gould **W:** Chester Gould
10 ❑ Cover: 2.95 **NM** value: **Cover or less**
Dick Tracy **A:** Chester Gould **W:** Chester Gould
11 ❑ Cover: 2.95 **NM** value: **Cover or less**
Dick Tracy **A:** Chester Gould **W:** Chester Gould
12 ❑ Cover: 2.95 **NM** value: **Cover or less**
Dick Tracy **A:** Chester Gould **W:** Chester Gould
13 ❑ Cover: 2.95 **NM** value: **Cover or less**
Dick Tracy **A:** Chester Gould **W:** Chester Gould
14 ❑ Cover: 2.95 **NM** value: **Cover or less**
Dick Tracy **A:** Chester Gould **W:** Chester Gould
15 ❑ Cover: 2.95 **NM** value: **Cover or less**
Dick Tracy **A:** Chester Gould **W:** Chester Gould
16 ❑ Cover: 2.95 **NM** value: **Cover or less**
Dick Tracy **A:** Chester Gould **W:** Chester Gould

COPS — DC

1 ❑ Aug 1988 Cover: 1.50 **NM** value: **Cover or less**
Circ: CapCity orders: **15,000**
• Giant-size. Bad Vibes **A:** Pat Broderick; Pablo Marcos **W:** Doug Moench ★ Origin of COPS. ★ 1st Appearance of COPS.
2 ❑ Sep 1988 Cover: 1.00 **NM** value: **Cover or less**
Circ: CapCity orders: **11,650**
3 ❑ Oct 1988 Cover: 1.00 **NM** value: **Cover or less**
Circ: CapCity orders: **11,950**
4 ❑ Nov 1988 Cover: 1.00 **NM** value: **Cover or less**
Circ: CapCity orders: **9,650**
5 ❑ Dec 1988 Cover: 1.00 **NM** value: **Cover or less**
Circ: CapCity orders: **8,500**
6 ❑ Win 1988 Cover: 1.00 **NM** value: **Cover or less**
Circ: CapCity orders: **7,650**
Ms. Demeanor's Capital Crime • Winter, 1988 **A:** Pat Broderick; Pablo Marcos **W:** Doug Moench
7 ❑ Hol 1988 Cover: 1.00 **NM** value: **Cover or less**
Circ: CapCity orders: **6,550**
• Holdays, 1988
8 ❑ Jan 1989 Cover: 1.00 **NM** value: **Cover or less**
Circ: CapCity orders: **6,200**
9 ❑ Feb 1989 Cover: 1.00 **NM** value: **Cover or less**
Circ: CapCity orders: **6,250**
10 ❑ Mar 1989 Cover: 1.00 **NM** value: **Cover or less**
Circ: CapCity orders: **5,750**
11 ❑ Apr 1989 Cover: 1.00 **NM** value: **Cover or less**
Circ: CapCity orders: **5,250**
12 ❑ May 1989 Cover: 1.00 **NM** value: **Cover or less**
Circ: CapCity orders: **5,000**
13 ❑ Jun 1989 Cover: 1.00 **NM** value: **Cover or less**
Circ: CapCity orders: **4,700**
14 ❑ Jul 1989 Cover: 1.00 **NM** value: **Cover or less**
Circ: CapCity orders: **4,400**
15 ❑ Aug 1989 Cover: 1.00 **NM** value: **Cover or less**
Circ: CapCity orders: **4,250**
final issue.

COPS: THE JOB — Marvel

1 ❑ Jun 1992 Cover: 1.25 **NM** value: **Cover or less**
Circ: CapCity orders: **14,400**
First Day **A:** Mike Harris **W:** Larry Hama; Joe Jusko
2 ❑ Jul 1992 Cover: 1.25 **NM** value: **Cover or less**
Circ: CapCity orders: **9,300**
3 ❑ Aug 1992 Cover: 1.25 **NM** value: **Cover or less**
Circ: CapCity orders: **8,000**
4 ❑ Sep 1992 Cover: 1.25 **NM** value: **Cover or less**
Circ: CapCity orders: **6,300**
Repercussions **A:** Mike Harris **W:** Larry Hama; Joe Jusko

COPYBOOK TALES, THE — Slave Labor

Jamie was always an avid comic fan, and the flashbacks to his childhood strongly contrast his innocence and fervor then, with the harsher realities of his grown-up life. One scene in particular should strike a chord with any fan: young Jamie lamenting the impossibility of ever selling his comic-book collection, side by side with a scene of adult-Jamie fervently counting his cash after just such a deed.

There are no super-heroes with dazzling powers in this book, no building-smashing battle scenes, and no maniacal villains with plans of world conquest. There is, however, solid writing combined with quality art. It's a great story about an average guy with big dreams, trying to make it in a world designed to smash hopes on the rocks.

Copybook Tales started as a mini publication, where it proved popular enough to make it to standard format.

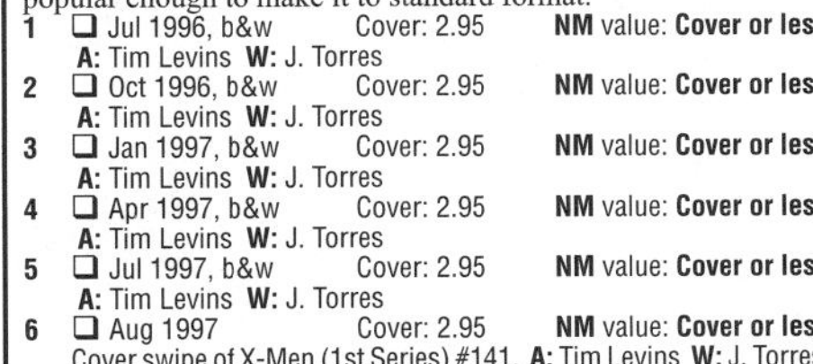

1 ❑ Jul 1996, b&w Cover: 2.95 **NM** value: **Cover or less**
A: Tim Levins **W:** J. Torres
2 ❑ Oct 1996, b&w Cover: 2.95 **NM** value: **Cover or less**
A: Tim Levins **W:** J. Torres
3 ❑ Jan 1997, b&w Cover: 2.95 **NM** value: **Cover or less**
A: Tim Levins **W:** J. Torres
4 ❑ Apr 1997, b&w Cover: 2.95 **NM** value: **Cover or less**
A: Tim Levins **W:** J. Torres
5 ❑ Jul 1997, b&w Cover: 2.95 **NM** value: **Cover or less**
A: Tim Levins **W:** J. Torres
6 ❑ Aug 1997 Cover: 2.95 **NM** value: **Cover or less**
Cover swipe of X-Men (1st Series) #141. **A:** Tim Levins **W:** J. Torres

CORBAN THE BARBEARIAN — Me Comix

1 ❑ Cover: 1.50 **NM** value: **Cover or less**
2 ❑ Cover: 1.50 **NM** value: **Cover or less**

CORBEN SPECIAL, A — Pacific

1 ❑ Cover: 1.50 **NM** value: **Cover or less**
• Adapted From Edgar Allan Poe **A:** Richard Corben **W:** Richard Corben

CORBO — Sword in Stone

1 ❑ Cover: 1.75 **NM** value: **Cover or less**

CORMAC MAC ART — Dark Horse

1 ❑ Jul 1989, b&w Cover: 1.95 **NM** value: **Cover or less**
Circ: CapCity orders: **4,900**
A: E.R. Cruz; John Bolton(cover) **W:** Roy Thomas; Dann Thomas
2 ❑ Aug 1989, b&w Cover: 1.95 **NM** value: **Cover or less**
Circ: CapCity orders: **3,475**
A: E.R. Cruz; John Bolton(cover) **W:** Roy Thomas; Dann Thomas
3 ❑ Mar 1990, b&w Cover: 1.95 **NM** value: **Cover or less**
Circ: CapCity orders: **2,800**
A: E.R. Cruz; John Bolton(cover) **W:** Roy Thomas; Dann Thomas
4 ❑ Apr 1990, b&w Cover: 1.95 **NM** value: **Cover or less**
A: E.R. Cruz; John Bolton(cover) **W:** Roy Thomas; Dann Thomas

CGC-graded: Multiply prices above by **33 for 9.9 M • 16 for 9.8 NM/M • 7 for 9.6 NM+ • 5 for 9.4 NM • 2.5 for 9.2 NM- • 1.5 for 9.0 VF/NM**

CORNY'S FETISH — Dark Horse

1 ❑ Apr 1998, b&w Cover: 4.95 **NM** value: **Cover or less**
Circ: Diamd. preorders: **3,130**
No issue number. One-shot.

CORPORATE CRIME COMICS — Kitchen Sink

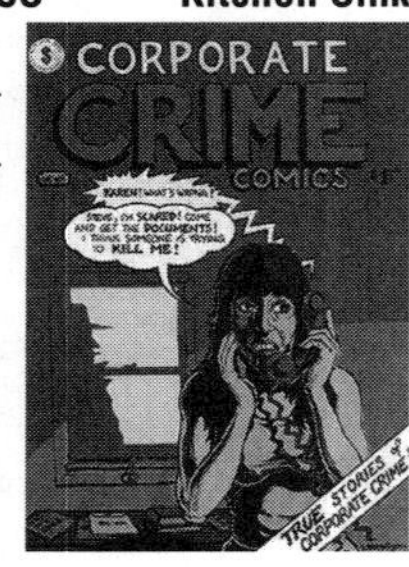

Corporate Crime Comics takes aim at the abuses of large corporations. Working with a collection of artists and writers, Editor Leonard Rifas tells tales from the killing of nuclear plant worker Karen Silkwood to episodes of false advertising and tax dodges. Jaded consumers of today will likely find new grounds for cynicism when reading about events like the Triangle Fire of 1911 that killed 146 garment workers, when their unsafe sweatshop building caught fire — trapping the workers who were normally locked inside during the workday to discourage them from leaving early. Governmental abuse also figures heavily into many of the stories, such as the famous Teapot Dome scandal and a 1954 scheme to void Aristotle Onassis' Jidda Agreement, an oil-shipping deal that had offended the wealthy AramCo oil company.

1 ❑ **NM** value: **2.50**
2 ❑ **NM** value: **2.50**

CORTEZ AND THE FALL OF THE AZTECS — Tome

1 ❑ b&w Cover: 2.95 **NM** value: **Cover or less**
2 ❑ b&w Cover: 2.95 **NM** value: **Cover or less**

CORUM: THE BULL AND THE SPEAR — First

1 ❑ Cover: 1.95 **NM** value: **Cover or less**
Circ: CapCity orders: **4,400**
📖 The Past Through Tomorrow **A:** Jill Thompson **W:** Mark Shainblum
2 ❑ Cover: 1.95 **NM** value: **Cover or less**
Circ: CapCity orders: **3,650**
3 ❑ Cover: 1.95 **NM** value: **Cover or less**
Circ: CapCity orders: **3,450**
4 ❑ Cover: 1.95 **NM** value: **Cover or less**
Circ: CapCity orders: **3,400**

CORVUS REX: A LEGACY OF SHADOWS — Crow

1 ❑ Feb 1996, b&w Cover: 1.95 **NM** value: **Cover or less**
No issue number. • Prologue **A:** Dave Morris; Ian Morris **W:** Dave Morris; Ian Morris

COSMIC BOOK, THE — Ace

1 ❑ Cover: 1.95 **NM** value: **Cover or less**
Circ: CapCity orders: **2,375**
📖 Encounter; Tonango's Folly; UFO and the Perts vs. Experts; Fatal Evolution; A Mystery!; Empire; ...Of Gods and Bondage! **A:** Fred Himes; Alex Toth; Pat Boyette; Wally Wood; Mike Himes **W:** Fred Himes; Alex Toth; Pat Boyette; Wally Wood; Mike Himes

COSMIC BOY — DC

Rokk Krinn is a member of the Legionnaires, a team of super-heroes in the far-distant future. As the story begins, he is stalked, not by some cosmic super-villain, but by a mere mortal named Lydda Jath. Lydda has developed a crush on Rokk and has persuaded her bio-engineer father to scrape up limited superpowers for her so she can join the Legionnaires. After a few months, in a new identity as Night Girl, she can't compete and the Legionnaires reject her — but she has what she wanted: Rokk, aka Cosmic Boy.

When the Time Institute borrows a time bubble, Cosmic Boy and Night Girl decide to vacation in the 20th century together. Unfortunately, something goes terribly wrong during the trip, and they end up on an Earth where superheroes like themselves are almost universally despised.

1 ❑ Dec 1986 Cover: 0.75 **NM** value: **1.00**
Circ: CapCity orders: **24,050**
📖 Those Who Will Not Learn The Lessons Of History • Legends Spin-Off, Part 4 **A:** Keith Giffen; Bob Smith **W:** Paul Levitz
2 ❑ Jan 1987 Cover: 0.75 **NM** value: **1.00**
Circ: CapCity orders: **17,850**
• Legends Spin-Off, Part 8
3 ❑ Feb 1987 Cover: 0.75 **NM** value: **1.00**
Circ: CapCity orders: **16,950**
• Legends Spin-Off, Part 13
4 ❑ Mar 1987 Cover: 0.75 **NM** value: **1.00**
Circ: CapCity orders: **17,600**
• Legends Spin-Off, Part 20 ★ Versus Time Trapper.

COSMIC HEROES — Eternity

1 ❑ b&w Cover: 1.95 **NM** value: **Cover or less**
• Buck Rogers
2 ❑ b&w Cover: 1.95 **NM** value: **Cover or less**
• Buck Rogers
3 ❑ b&w Cover: 1.95 **NM** value: **Cover or less**
• Buck Rogers
4 ❑ b&w Cover: 1.95 **NM** value: **Cover or less**
• Buck Rogers
5 ❑ b&w Cover: 1.95 **NM** value: **Cover or less**
• Buck Rogers
6 ❑ b&w Cover: 1.95 **NM** value: **Cover or less**
• Buck Rogers
7 ❑ Cover: 2.25 **NM** value: **Cover or less**
8 ❑ Cover: 2.25 **NM** value: **Cover or less**
9 ❑ Cover: 2.95 **NM** value: **Cover or less**
10 ❑ Cover: 3.50 **NM** value: **Cover or less**
11 ❑ Cover: 3.95 **NM** value: **Cover or less**

COSMIC KLITI — Fantagraphics / Eros

All issues are adults only.
1 ❑ b&w Cover: 2.25 **NM** value: **Cover or less**
A: Gray Morrow

COSMIC ODYSSEY — DC

1 ❑ Nov 1988 Cover: 3.50 **NM** value: **Cover or less**
Circ: CapCity orders: **35,400**
📖 Discovery **A:** Mike Mignola **W:** Jim Starlin ★ Appearance of Superman, Batman. ★ Versus Darkseid.
2 ❑ Dec 1988 Cover: 3.50 **NM** value: **Cover or less**
Circ: CapCity orders: **26,850**
A: Mike Mignola **W:** Jim Starlin
3 ❑ Dec 1988 Cover: 3.50 **NM** value: **Cover or less**
Circ: CapCity orders: **25,300**
📖 Decisions **A:** Mike Mignola **W:** Jim Starlin
4 ❑ Jan 1989 Cover: 3.50 **NM** value: **Cover or less**
Circ: CapCity orders: **25,500**
A: Mike Mignola **W:** Jim Starlin

COSMIC POWERS — Marvel

1 ❑ Mar 1994 Cover: 2.50 **NM** value: **Cover or less**
Circ: CapCity orders: **26,950**
• Thanos
2 ❑ Apr 1994 Cover: 2.50 **NM** value: **Cover or less**
Circ: CapCity orders: **18,650**
• Terrax
3 ❑ May 1994 Cover: 2.50 **NM** value: **Cover or less**
Circ: CapCity orders: **17,050**
• Jack of Hearts & Ganymede
4 ❑ Jun 1994 Cover: 2.50 **NM** value: **Cover or less**
Circ: CapCity orders: **18,150**
📖 Legacy
5 ❑ Jul 1994 Cover: 2.50 **NM** value: **Cover or less**
Circ: CapCity orders: **18,350**
• Morg
6 ❑ Aug 1994 Cover: 2.50 **NM** value: **Cover or less**
Circ: CapCity orders: **17,650**
final issue. • Tyrant **A:** Scot Eaton **W:** Ron Marz

COSMIC POWERS UNLIMITED — Marvel

1 ❑ May 1995 Cover: 3.95 **NM** value: **Cover or less**
Circ: CapCity orders: **16,425**
A: Steve Carr; Scott Benefiel; Ron Lim **W:** Ron Marz ★ Appearance of Captain Marvel I (Mar-Vell).
2 ❑ Aug 1995 Cover: 3.95 **NM** value: **Cover or less**
Circ: CapCity orders: **11,750**
cover says Sep. • indicia says Aug
3 ❑ Dec 1995 Cover: 3.95 **NM** value: **Cover or less**
4 ❑ Feb 1996 Cover: 3.95 **NM** value: **Cover or less**
5 ❑ May 1996 Cover: 3.95 **NM** value: **Cover or less**

COSMIC RAY — Image

1/A ❑ Jun 1999 Cover: 2.95 **NM** value: **Cover or less**
Circ: Diamd. preorders: **8,922**
green sunglasses cover. 📖 The Resurection of Cosmic Ray **A:** Stephen Blue **W:** Stephen Blue
1/B ❑ Jun 1999 Cover: 2.95 **NM** value: **Cover or less**
Murderer or Hero cover. **A:** Stephen Blue **W:** Stephen Blue
2 ❑ Aug 1999 Cover: 2.95 **NM** value: **Cover or less**
Circ: Diamd. preorders: **4,277**
A: Stephen Blue **W:** Stephen Blue
3 ❑ Oct 1999 Cover: 2.95 **NM** value: **Cover or less**
Circ: Diamd. preorders: **2,430**
A: Stephen Blue **W:** Stephen Blue

COSMIC STELLER REBELLERS — Hammac

1 ❑ Cover: 1.50 **NM** value: **Cover or less**
2 ❑ Cover: 1.50 **NM** value: **Cover or less**

COSMO CAT — Fox

1 ❑ ca. 1946 Cover: 0.10 **NM** value: **100.00**
2 ❑ ca. 1946 Cover: 0.10 **NM** value: **80.00**
3 ❑ ca. 1946 Cover: 0.10 **NM** value: **80.00**
4 ❑ ca. 1946 Cover: 0.10 **NM** value: **80.00**
5 ❑ ca. 1947 Cover: 0.10 **NM** value: **80.00**

COSMOS — Micmac

1 ❑ Cover: 2.00 **NM** value: **Cover or less**

COTTON CANDY AUTOPSY — DC / Piranha

Bk 1 ❑ b&w Cover: 12.95 **NM** value: **Cover or less**

COUGAR, THE — Atlas-Seaboard

1 ❑ Apr 1975 Cover: 0.25 **NM** value: **2.00**
• **CGC:** 4 graded, best 9.6
2 ❑ Jul 1975 Cover: 0.25 **NM** value: **2.00**
★ Origin of Cougar.

COUNTDOWN — WildStorm

1 ❑ Jun 2000 Cover: 2.95 **NM** value: **Cover or less**
Circ: Diamd. preorders: **12,578**
A: Aaron Lopresti **W:** Jeff Mariotte
2 ❑ Jul 2000 Cover: 2.95 **NM** value: **Cover or less**
Circ: Diamd. preorders: **10,321**
A: Aaron Lopresti **W:** Jeff Mariotte
3 ❑ Aug 2000 Cover: 2.95 **NM** value: **Cover or less**
Circ: Diamd. preorders: **8,917**
A: Aaron Lopresti **W:** Jeff Mariotte
4 ❑ Sep 2000 Cover: 2.95 **NM** value: **Cover or less**
Circ: Diamd. preorders: **7,640**
A: Aaron Lopresti **W:** Jeff Mariotte
5 ❑ Oct 2000 Cover: 2.95 **NM** value: **Cover or less**
Circ: Diamd. preorders: **6,041**
A: Aaron Lopresti **W:** Jeff Mariotte
6 ❑ Nov 2000 Cover: 2.95 **NM** value: **Cover or less**
Circ: Diamd. preorders: **5,871**
A: Aaron Lopresti **W:** Jeff Mariotte
7 ❑ Dec 2000 Cover: 2.95 **NM** value: **Cover or less**
Circ: Diamd. preorders: **5,262**
A: Aaron Lopresti **W:** Jeff Mariotte
8 ❑ Jan 2001 Cover: 2.95 **NM** value: **Cover or less**
Circ: Diamd. preorders: **5,108**
A: Aaron Lopresti **W:** Jeff Mariotte

COUNT DUCKULA — Marvel

1 ❑ Jan 1989 Cover: 1.00 **NM** value: **1.50**
Circ: CapCity orders: **6,600**
★ Origin of Count Duckula.
2 ❑ Feb 1989 Cover: 1.00 **NM** value: **Cover or less**
Circ: CapCity orders: **3,700**
3 ❑ Mar 1989 Cover: 1.00 **NM** value: **Cover or less**
Circ: CapCity orders: **3,400**
📖 Love at First Bite; Danger Mouse...A Twisted Tail **A:** Warren Kremer **W:** Michael Gallagher ★ 1st Appearance of Danger Mouse. ★ Appearance of Penfold.
4 ❑ Apr 1989 Cover: 1.00 **NM** value: **Cover or less**
Circ: CapCity orders: **2,900**
• Danger Mouse
5 ❑ May 1989 Cover: 1.00 **NM** value: **Cover or less**
Circ: CapCity orders: **2,450**
• Danger Mouse
6 ❑ Jun 1989 Cover: 1.00 **NM** value: **Cover or less**
Circ: CapCity orders: **2,400**
• Danger Mouse
7 ❑ Jul 1989 Cover: 1.00 **NM** value: **Cover or less**
Circ: CapCity orders: **2,150**
• Danger Mouse
8 ❑ Aug 1989 Cover: 1.00 **NM** value: **Cover or less**
Circ: CapCity orders: **2,350**
• Geraldo Rivera
9 ❑ Sep 1989 Cover: 1.00 **NM** value: **Cover or less**
Circ: CapCity orders: **2,500**
10 ❑ Oct 1989 Cover: 1.00 **NM** value: **Cover or less**
Circ: CapCity orders: **1,900**
11 ❑ Nov 1989 Cover: 1.00 **NM** value: **Cover or less**
Circ: CapCity orders: **2,000**
12 ❑ Dec 1989 Cover: 1.00 **NM** value: **Cover or less**
Circ: CapCity orders: **1,800**
13 ❑ Jan 1990 Cover: 1.00 **NM** value: **Cover or less**
14 ❑ Feb 1990 Cover: 1.00 **NM** value: **Cover or less**
Circ: CapCity orders: **1,250**
15 ❑ Mar 1990 Cover: 1.00 **NM** value: **Cover or less**
Circ: CapCity orders: **1,350**

COUNTERPARTS — Tundra

Counterparts is a three-issue mini-series written by Stefan Petrucha of X-Files fame. The series is set in a warped future when people are addicted to TPGs (Temporary Personality Grafts). If you don't like the person you are, simply change your personality. However, people sometimes experience terrible side effects, like complete personality loss.

Such is the case with Hieronymous Jones. After his case is listed as incurable, his wife takes him to a TPG specialist who claims that he can reverse the effects. The treatments seem to have no effect on Jones, so his wife takes a TPG, turning her into a heartless wench who leaves him. After she leaves, Jones "wakes up" and realizes that the treatments have caused his legs, torso, head, and arms to detach, each having have its own personality.

1 ❑ Jan 1993, b&w Cover: 2.95 **NM** value: **Cover or less**
📖 The Sum of the Parts **A:** Barry Crain **W:** Stefan Petrucha
2 ❑ Mar 1993, b&w Cover: 2.95 **NM** value: **Cover or less**
A: Barry Crain **W:** Stefan Petrucha
3 ❑ Cover: 2.95 **NM** value: **Cover or less**
A: Barry Crain **W:** Stefan Petrucha

COUPLE OF WINOS, A — Fantagraphics

1 ❑ b&w Cover: 2.25 **NM** value: **Cover or less**

COURAGE COMICS — J. Edward

1 ❑ **NM** value: **75.00**
2 ❑ ca. 1945 **NM** value: **75.00**
• **CGC:** 1 graded, best 5.5
3 ❑ **NM** value: **75.00**

COURAGEOUS MAN ADVENTURES — Moordam

1 ❑ b&w Cover: 2.95 **NM** value: **Cover or less**
• Mr. Beat back-up
2 ❑ b&w Cover: 2.95 **NM** value: **Cover or less**
📖 Spunky's Evil Twin!; The Security Secrets of the Silo of Sanctuary! **A:** George Broderick Jr. **W:** George Broderick Jr.
3 ❑ Cover: 2.95 **NM** value: **Cover or less**

Creator Key
W = Writer • A = Artist • C = Cover Artist

Other grades: Multiply prices above by **1.5 for Mint • 2/3 for Very Fine • 1/3 for Fine • 1/5 for Very Good • 1/8 for Good**

COURTSHIP OF EDDIE'S FATHER — Dell

The successful sitcom ran from 1969 to 1972 and starred Bill Bixby (1934-1993), later to star in The Incredible Hulk. In this case, however, he was the widower father of Eddie (played by Brandon Cruz), and in show after show Eddie tried to pair his dad with an appropriate mate. The show was preceded by the Mark Toby novel of the same name and a 1963 film (directed by Vincente Minnelli, starring Glenn Ford, Shirley Jones, and Ronny Howard). Obviously, the show was more successful than the comic-book version, which didn't even survive to appear on the newsstand throughout the duration of the prime-time series. — Maggie

1 ❑ Jan 1970 Cover: 0.15 **NM** value: **40.00**
• **CGC:** 1 graded, best 9.0
2 ❑ May 1970 Cover: 0.15 **NM** value: **30.00**

COUTOO — Dark Horse

1 ❑ b&w Cover: 3.50 **NM** value: **Cover or less**
No issue number. One-shot. **A:** Joel Andreas **W:** Joel Andreas

COVEN, THE — Awesome

1/A ❑ Aug 1997 Cover: 2.50 **NM** value: **3.00**
Circ: Diamd. preorders: **52,094**
"Butt" cover. 📖 Murder in the First **A:** Ian Churchill; Rob Liefeld(cover) **W:** Jeph Loeb
1/B ❑ Aug 1997 Cover: 2.50 **NM** value: **4.00**
Man with flaming hands on cover. 📖 Murder in the First • Red border **A:** Ian Churchill **W:** Jeph Loeb
1/C ❑ Aug 1997 Cover: 2.50 **NM** value: **6.00**
"Wizard Authentic" cover. 📖 Murder in the First **A:** Ian Churchill **W:** Jeph Loeb
1/D ❑ Aug 1997 Cover: 2.50 **NM** value: **3.00**
Team on cover. 📖 Murder in the First • White border **A:** Ian Churchill **W:** Jeph Loeb
1/E ❑ Aug 1997 Cover: 2.50 **NM** value: **5.00**
• **CGC:** 6 graded, best 10.0
Chromium cover otherwise same as 1/A. • Dynamic Forces edition. 📖 Murder in the First **A:** Ian Churchill; Rob Liefeld(cover) **W:** Jeph Loeb
1/F ❑ Aug 1997 Cover: 2.50 **NM** value: **4.00**
• 1ø Edition. 📖 Murder in the First • Flip book with Kaboom 1+ **A:** Ian Churchill **W:** Jeph Loeb
1/G ❑ Aug 1997 **NM** value: **5.00**
"Flame Hands" cover. 📖 Murder in the First **A:** Ian Churchill **W:** Jeph Loeb
1-2 ❑ 1997 Cover: 2.50 **NM** value: **Cover or less**
• "Fan Appreciation Edition". 📖 Murder in the First • Is really 2nd Printing **A:** Ian Churchill **W:** Jeph Loeb
2 ❑ Sep 1997 Cover: 2.50 **NM** value: **4.00**
Circ: Diamd. preorders: **21,503**
A: Ian Churchill **W:** Jeph Loeb
2/GO❑Sep 1997 **NM** value: **5.00**
• Gold edition limited to 5000 copies. **A:** Ian Churchill **W:** Jeph Loeb
3 ❑ Oct 1997 Cover: 2.50 **NM** value: **3.00**
Circ: Diamd. preorders: **24,411**
A: Ian Churchill **W:** Jeph Loeb
3/A ❑ Oct 1997 **NM** value: **4.00**
Red foil logo on cover. **A:** Ian Churchill **W:** Jeph Loeb
4 ❑ Nov 1998 Cover: 2.50 **NM** value: **3.00**
Circ: Diamd. preorders: **27,975**
A: Ian Churchill **W:** Jeph Loeb
5 ❑ Jan 1998 Cover: 2.50 **NM** value: **3.00**
Circ: Diamd. preorders: **30,919**
A: Ian Churchill **W:** Jeph Loeb
5/A ❑ Jan 1998 **NM** value: **3.00**
Variant cover, woman, ghouls standing in water. **A:** Ian Churchill **W:** Jeph Loeb
6 ❑ Feb 1998 Cover: 2.50 **NM** value: **Cover or less**
Circ: Diamd. preorders: **28,812**
A: Ian Churchill **W:** Jeph Loeb
Bk 1❑ Cover: 4.95 **NM** value: **Cover or less**
• Collects issues #1-2 **A:** Ian Churchill **W:** Jeph Loeb

COVEN: DARK ORIGINS — Awesome

1 ❑ Jun 1999 Cover: 2.50 **NM** value: **Cover or less**
Circ: Diamd. preorders: **28,191**

COVEN, THE: FANTOM — Awesome

1 ❑ Feb 1998 Cover: 2.50 **NM** value: **3.00**
Circ: Diamd. preorders: **18,433**
A: Ian Churchill **W:** Jeph Loeb
1/GO❑Feb 1998 **NM** value: **4.00**
• **CGC:** 1 graded, best 9.4
• Gold logo **A:** Ian Churchill **W:** Jeph Loeb

COVEN OF ANGELS — Jitterbug

1 ❑ Nov 1995 Cover: 2.95 **NM** value: **5.00**
2 ❑ Cover: 2.95 **NM** value: **6.00**
📖 Buffalo Girls; Clown Story; The Garden of Earthly Delights; Alyssa (The Untamed); Baby Oil; The Kauffman Index; Litany **A:** Nathan MacDicken; Jacob Saariaho; Joseph Michael Linsner(cover); Rob Schrab; Brian Wanamaker **W:** Eliza Travisano; Kristen Brennan
Ash 1❑ **NM** value: **10.00**
• Ashcan edition with Linsner cover. **A:** Joseph Michael Linsner(cover)

📖 indicates **Story Title** or **Storyline** information.
★ indicates **Character Appearance** information.

COVEN 13 — No Mercy

A recently abandoned abattoir used by an occult group for animal sacrifices in cult rituals has attracted the attention of three voluptuous witches on motorcycles. Angel, Penny, and Lizzie are long on attitude backed up by supernatural abilities and, by their own admission, "Out to save the world."

Written by Rikki Rocket, the drummer for the rock group Poison, this title includes many elements of Rocket's interest: beautiful women, motorcycles, witchcraft, and animal protection. Although it is the impetus for the story, the animal-protection aspect seems to be an anomalous presence in an otherwise-standard "Bad Girl" title. But Rocket's membership in the group "Last Chance of Animals" explains its incorporation.

The art by Matt Busch evokes the look of a fumetti. Real-life models were used as photo references, then scanned into a computer and enhanced with special effects to render a finished page that is strikingly realistic. Although this art is memorable, the photo-realism tends to limit the characters to a set of stock expressions.

1 ❑ Aug 1997 Cover: 2.50 **NM** value: **Cover or less**
Circ: Diamd. preorders: **5,225**
A: Matt Busch **W:** Rikki Rockett

COVENTRY — Fantagraphics

1 ❑ Nov 1996, b&w Cover: 3.95 **NM** value: **Cover or less**
Circ: Direct Market orders: **6,413**
cardstock cover. 📖 The Frogs of God
2 ❑ Mar 1997, b&w Cover: 3.95 **NM** value: **Cover or less**
Circ: Diamd. preorders: **4,874**
cardstock cover. 📖 Thirteen Dead Guys Named Bob **A:** Bill Willingham **W:** Bill Willingham
3 ❑ Jul 1997, b&w Cover: 3.95 **NM** value: **Cover or less**
Circ: Diamd. preorders: **5,210**
cardstock cover. 📖 Later That Same Day

COVEN, THE (VOL. 2) — Awesome

1 ❑ Jan 1999 Cover: 2.50 **NM** value: **Cover or less**
Circ: Diamd. preorders: **45,296**
regular cover. • Woman with glowing gloves facing forward **A:** Ian Churchill **W:** Jeph Loeb
1/A ❑ Jan 1999 Cover: 2.50 **NM** value: **5.00**
Two team-members flying on cover with white Coven logo. • Chrome ("Covenchrome") edition with certificate of authenticity. **A:** Ian Churchill **W:** Jeph Loeb
1/B ❑ Jan 1999 Cover: 2.50 **NM** value: **3.00**
Variant "scratch" cover by Ian Churchill. **A:** Ian Churchill **W:** Jeph Loeb
1/C ❑ Jan 1999 Cover: 2.50 **NM** value: **3.00**
• Gold edition. **A:** Ian Churchill **W:** Jeph Loeb
1/D ❑ Jan 1999 Cover: 2.50 **NM** value: **3.00**
"Spellcaster" cover by Rob Liefeld. **A:** Ian Churchill **W:** Jeph Loeb
1/E ❑ Jan 1999 Cover: 2.50 **NM** value: **Cover or less**
"Black Mass" cover by Ian Churchill. **A:** Ian Churchill **W:** Jeph Loeb
1/F ❑ Jan 1999 Cover: 2.50 **NM** value: **4.00**
Dynamic Forces exclusive cover with two women surfing. **A:** Ian Churchill **W:** Jeph Loeb
2 ❑ Feb 1999 Cover: 2.50 **NM** value: **Cover or less**
Circ: Diamd. preorders: **26,795**
A: Ian Churchill **W:** Jeph Loeb
3 ❑ Mar 1999 Cover: 2.50 **NM** value: **Cover or less**
Circ: Diamd. preorders: **24,174**
A: Ian Churchill **W:** Jeph Loeb
4 ❑ Apr 1999 Cover: 2.50 **NM** value: **Cover or less**
Circ: Diamd. preorders: **23,036**
A: Ian Churchill **W:** Jeph Loeb

COW — MonsterPants

1 ❑ Cover: 1.99 **NM** value: **Cover or less**
📖 Galactic Glamour; The Puppeteer; Charlie Chaplin; The Bunny; Faery Chasm; Oliver the One-Eyed Boy; The Little Fried Egg; Incident at Teplitz; Summer Vacation **A:** Aleksander Zograf; Danielle Ste. Just; Jaime Morgan Roberts; James Felix McKenney; Kathy Doyle; Mick Cusimano **W:** Danielle Ste. Just; Jaime Morgan Roberts; James Felix McKenney; Kathy Doyle; Mick Cusimano; Bradford Scobie; Leonardi Rizzi
2 ❑ Cover: 1.99 **NM** value: **Cover or less**
3 ❑ Cover: 1.99 **NM** value: **Cover or less**
A: Alan W. Limacher; Aleksander Zograf; Danielle Ste. Just; Jake Wyckoff; Miss Lasko-Gross; Pete Sickman-Garner; Rick Limacher; Tyson Smith; Chad Verrill **W:** Michael T. Gilbert; Danielle Ste. Just; Ian Smith; Jake Wyckoff; James Felix McKenney; Miss Lasko-Gross; Pete Sickman-Garner; Rick Limacher; Chad Verrill; Gordana Basta

To find the median price offered on eBay at press time for pre-1990 **CGC-graded comics**, multiply by:

9.9 (M): **33**	8.5 (VF+): **1.25**
9.8(NM/M): **16**	8.0 (VF): **0.85**
9.6 (NM+): **7**	7.5 (VF-): **0.6**
9.4 (NM): **5**	7.0 (F/VF): **0.5**
9.2 (NM-): **2.5**	6.5 (F+): **0.4**
9.0 (VF/NM): **1.5**	6.0 (F-): **0.33**

These are median prices of all CGC comics auctioned on eBay; prices for individual issues will vary.

COW-BOY — Ogre Press

Clan Apis' creator Jay Hosler did a comic strip which appeared for some time in Comics Buyer's Guide. It featured the comedy adventures of a costumed hero who wore the mask of a cow's head and used spray from udders dangling from the costume's front. Only one issue starring Cow-Boy as its title character appeared and focused on the character's origin, but keep in mind that the writer-artist did win a Xeric Grant (for Clan Apis). Hosler's cruder style in Cow-Boy is appropriate to the parodies he writes. — Maggie

1 ❑ b&w Cover: 4.00 **NM** value: **Cover or less**
★ Origin of Cow-Boy.

COWBOY LOVE — Avalon

1 ❑ b&w Cover: 2.95 **NM** value: **Cover or less**

COWBOY WESTERN — Charlton

17 ❑ Jul 1948 Cover: 0.10 **NM** value: **125.00**
18 ❑ Sep 1948 Cover: 0.10 **NM** value: **100.00**
19 ❑ Nov 1948 Cover: 0.10 **NM** value: **100.00**
20 ❑ Jan 1949 Cover: 0.10 **NM** value: **100.00**
21 ❑ Mar 1949 Cover: 0.10 **NM** value: **100.00**
22 ❑ May 1949 Cover: 0.10 **NM** value: **90.00**
23 ❑ Jul 1949 Cover: 0.10 **NM** value: **90.00**
24 ❑ Sep 1949 Cover: 0.10 **NM** value: **90.00**
25 ❑ Nov 1949 Cover: 0.10 **NM** value: **90.00**
26 ❑ Jan 1950 Cover: 0.10 **NM** value: **85.00**
27 ❑ Mar 1950 Cover: 0.10 **NM** value: **85.00**
28 ❑ May 1950 Cover: 0.10 **NM** value: **85.00**
29 ❑ Jul 1950 Cover: 0.10 **NM** value: **85.00**
30 ❑ Sep 1950 Cover: 0.10 **NM** value: **85.00**
31 ❑ Nov 1950 Cover: 0.10 **NM** value: **80.00**
32 ❑ Jan 1951 Cover: 0.10 **NM** value: **80.00**
33 ❑ Mar 1951 Cover: 0.10 **NM** value: **80.00**
34 ❑ May 1951 Cover: 0.10 **NM** value: **80.00**
35 ❑ Jul 1951 Cover: 0.10 **NM** value: **80.00**
36 ❑ Sep 1951 Cover: 0.10 **NM** value: **75.00**
37 ❑ Nov 1951 Cover: 0.10 **NM** value: **75.00**
38 ❑ Jan 1952 Cover: 0.10 **NM** value: **75.00**
39 ❑ Mar 1952 Cover: 0.10 **NM** value: **75.00**
46 ❑ ca. 1953 Cover: 0.10 **NM** value: **60.00**
47 ❑ ca. 1954 Cover: 0.10 **NM** value: **60.00**
48 ❑ ca. 1954 Cover: 0.10 **NM** value: **60.00**
49 ❑ May 1954 Cover: 0.10 **NM** value: **60.00**
50 ❑ Jul 1954 Cover: 0.10 **NM** value: **50.00**
• **CGC:** 3 graded, best 9.0
51 ❑ Sep 1954 Cover: 0.10 **NM** value: **50.00**
52 ❑ Nov 1954 Cover: 0.10 **NM** value: **50.00**
53 ❑ Jan 1955 Cover: 0.10 **NM** value: **50.00**
54 ❑ Mar 1955 Cover: 0.10 **NM** value: **50.00**
55 ❑ May 1955 Cover: 0.10 **NM** value: **50.00**
56 ❑ Jul 1955 Cover: 0.10 **NM** value: **50.00**
57 ❑ Sep 1955 Cover: 0.10 **NM** value: **50.00**
58 ❑ Nov 1955 Cover: 0.10 **NM** value: **50.00**
59 ❑ Jan 1956 Cover: 0.10 **NM** value: **50.00**
60 ❑ Mar 1956 Cover: 0.10 **NM** value: **50.00**
61 ❑ May 1956 Cover: 0.10 **NM** value: **45.00**
62 ❑ Jul 1956 Cover: 0.10 **NM** value: **45.00**
63 ❑ Sep 1956 Cover: 0.10 **NM** value: **45.00**
64 ❑ Nov 1956 Cover: 0.10 **NM** value: **45.00**
65 ❑ Jan 1957 Cover: 0.10 **NM** value: **45.00**
66 ❑ Mar 1957 Cover: 0.10 **NM** value: **45.00**
67 ❑ May 1957 Cover: 0.10 **NM** value: **45.00**
• **CGC:** 1 graded, best 7.5

COWGIRL ROMANCES — Fiction House

1 ❑ ca. 1950 Cover: 0.10 **NM** value: **200.00**
📖 The Range of Singing Guns; Ride Fast for Wyoming; Beneath the Outlaw Moon
2 ❑ ca. 1950 Cover: 0.10 **NM** value: **150.00**
📖 The Lady of Lawless Range; Montana Rides the Gun-Trail; Ranch of Golden Dreams
3 ❑ ca. 1951 Cover: 0.10 **NM** value: **125.00**
📖 Daughter of the Devil's Brand; Maverick Guns from Arizona
4 ❑ ca. 1951 Cover: 0.10 **NM** value: **100.00**
📖 The Bride Wore Buckskin
5 ❑ ca. 1951 Cover: 0.10 **NM** value: **100.00**
📖 The Taming of Lone-Star Lou; Stampede for Wyoming
6 ❑ ca. 1951 Cover: 0.10 **NM** value: **100.00**
📖 Rose of Mustang Mesa; A Wife for Don Diablo
7 ❑ ca. 1951 Cover: 0.10 **NM** value: **75.00**
📖 Nobody Loves a Gun Man; The Range of Twisted Brands
8 ❑ ca. 1951 Cover: 0.10 **NM** value: **75.00**
📖 Wild Beauty; Six-Gun Wedding
9 ❑ ca. 1952 Cover: 0.10 **NM** value: **75.00**
📖 Gun-Feud Sweethearts; Love Wears a Bogus Brand
10 ❑ ca. 1952 Cover: 0.10 **NM** value: **50.00**
📖 Two Hearts Against the Vigilantes; The No-Girl of Stampede Valley
11 ❑ ca. 1952 Cover: 0.10 **NM** value: **50.00**
📖 Love Is Where You Find It
12 ❑ ca. 1952 Cover: 0.10 **NM** value: **50.00**
📖 Send Back My Love; The Ranch of Riddles

COW PUNCHER — Avon

1 ❑ 1947 Cover: 0.10 **NM** value: **300.00**
• **CGC:** 1 graded, best 8.5
2 ❑ 1947 Cover: 0.10 **NM** value: **200.00**
3 ❑ ca. 1947 Cover: 0.10 **NM** value: **100.00**
• **CGC:** 3 graded, best 7.5

CGC-graded: Multiply prices above by **33 for 9.9 M • 16 for 9.8 NM/M • 7 for 9.6 NM+ • 5 for 9.4 NM • 2.5 for 9.2 NM- • 1.5 for 9.0 VF/NM**

4 ❑ 1948 Cover: 0.10 **NM** value: **100.00**
📖 The Devil's Scourge
5 ❑ 1948 Cover: 0.10 **NM** value: **100.00**
📖 Prince of Pioneers
6 ❑ 1948 Cover: 0.10 **NM** value: **75.00**
7 ❑ 1948 Cover: 0.10 **NM** value: **75.00**

COYOTE — Marvel / Epic

1 ❑ Apr 1983 Cover: 1.50 **NM** value: **2.50**
A: Steve Leialoha **W:** Steve Englehart ★ Origin of Coyote.
2 ❑ Jun 1983 Cover: 1.50 **NM** value: **2.00**
3 ❑ Sep 1983 Cover: 1.50 **NM** value: **2.00**
4 ❑ Jan 1984 Cover: 1.50 **NM** value: **Cover or less**
5 ❑ Apr 1984 Cover: 1.50 **NM** value: **Cover or less**
6 ❑ Jun 1984 Cover: 1.50 **NM** value: **Cover or less**
7 ❑ Jul 1984 Cover: 1.50 **NM** value: **Cover or less**
A: Steve Ditko
8 ❑ Oct 1984 Cover: 1.50 **NM** value: **Cover or less**
A: Steve Ditko
9 ❑ Dec 1984 Cover: 1.50 **NM** value: **Cover or less**
A: Steve Ditko
10 ❑ Jan 1985 Cover: 1.50 **NM** value: **Cover or less**
11 ❑ Mar 1985 Cover: 1.50 **NM** value: **2.50**
Circ: CapCity orders: **5,250** • **CGC:** 2 graded, best 9.4
• 1st Todd McFarlane art **A:** Todd McFarlane
12 ❑ May 1985 Cover: 1.50 **NM** value: **2.00**
Circ: CapCity orders: **5,200**
A: Todd McFarlane
13 ❑ Jul 1985 Cover: 1.50 **NM** value: **2.00**
Circ: CapCity orders: **5,050**
A: Todd McFarlane
14 ❑ Sep 1985 Cover: 1.50 **NM** value: **Cover or less**
Circ: CapCity orders: **5,900** • **CGC:** 1 graded, best 9.6
A: Todd McFarlane ★ Appearance of Badger.
15 ❑ Nov 1985 Cover: 1.50 **NM** value: **Cover or less**
Circ: CapCity orders: **4,450**
16 ❑ Jan 1986 Cover: 1.50 **NM** value: **Cover or less**
Circ: CapCity orders: **4,450**

CRABBS — Cat-Head

1 ❑ b&w Cover: 3.75 **NM** value: **Cover or less**

CRACKAJACK FUNNIES — Dell

This was one of the pioneering comics put out, as comics companies felt their way into the new world of periodical four-color publishing. To provide content, the publisher began by going to existing comic strips and collecting them in each issue.

Such New York World-Telegram strips as Roy Crane's Wash Tubbs, Gene Ahern's Our Boarding House, Abe Martin's Boots, and Merrill Blosser's Freckles kicked off the series. Later content included Red Ryder, Ellery Queen, Tarzan, and The Owl. The Owl, in fact, was not only the only costumed hero in the series, he was also quickly cover-featured and continued that way through most of his appearances in the title. — Maggie

1 ❑ Jun 1938 Cover: 0.10 **NM** value: **1800.00**
2 ❑ Jul 1938 Cover: 0.10 **NM** value: **900.00**
3 ❑ Aug 1938 Cover: 0.10 **NM** value: **650.00**
4 ❑ Sep 1938 Cover: 0.10 **NM** value: **500.00**
5 ❑ Oct 1938 Cover: 0.10 **NM** value: **500.00**
6 ❑ Nov 1938 Cover: 0.10 **NM** value: **450.00**
7 ❑ Dec 1938 Cover: 0.10 **NM** value: **450.00**
8 ❑ Jan 1939 Cover: 0.10 **NM** value: **450.00**
9 ❑ Mar 1939 Cover: 0.10 **NM** value: **450.00**
10 ❑ Apr 1939 Cover: 0.10 **NM** value: **350.00**
11 ❑ May 1939 Cover: 0.10 **NM** value: **350.00**
12 ❑ Jun 1939 Cover: 0.10 **NM** value: **350.00**
13 ❑ Jul 1939 Cover: 0.10 **NM** value: **350.00**
14 ❑ Aug 1939 Cover: 0.10 **NM** value: **350.00**
15 ❑ Sep 1939 Cover: 0.10 **NM** value: **350.00**
16 ❑ Oct 1939 Cover: 0.10 **NM** value: **350.00**
17 ❑ Nov 1939 Cover: 0.10 **NM** value: **350.00**
18 ❑ Dec 1939 Cover: 0.10 **NM** value: **350.00**
19 ❑ Jan 1940 Cover: 0.10 **NM** value: **350.00**
20 ❑ Feb 1940 Cover: 0.10 **NM** value: **250.00**
21 ❑ Mar 1940 Cover: 0.10 **NM** value: **250.00**
• **CGC:** 1 graded, best 9.6
22 ❑ Apr 1940 Cover: 0.10 **NM** value: **250.00**
23 ❑ May 1940 Cover: 0.10 **NM** value: **250.00**
24 ❑ Jun 1940 Cover: 0.10 **NM** value: **250.00**
25 ❑ Jul 1940 Cover: 0.10 **NM** value: **250.00**
26 ❑ Aug 1940 Cover: 0.10 **NM** value: **200.00**
27 ❑ Sep 1940 Cover: 0.10 **NM** value: **200.00**
28 ❑ Oct 1940 Cover: 0.10 **NM** value: **200.00**
29 ❑ Nov 1940 Cover: 0.10 **NM** value: **200.00**
30 ❑ Dec 1940 Cover: 0.10 **NM** value: **175.00**
31 ❑ Jan 1941 Cover: 0.10 **NM** value: **175.00**
32 ❑ Feb 1941 Cover: 0.10 **NM** value: **175.00**
33 ❑ Mar 1941 Cover: 0.10 **NM** value: **175.00**
34 ❑ Apr 1941 Cover: 0.10 **NM** value: **175.00**
35 ❑ May 1941 Cover: 0.10 **NM** value: **175.00**
36 ❑ Jun 1941 Cover: 0.10 **NM** value: **175.00**
37 ❑ Jul 1941 Cover: 0.10 **NM** value: **175.00**
38 ❑ Aug 1941 Cover: 0.10 **NM** value: **175.00**
39 ❑ Sep 1941 Cover: 0.10 **NM** value: **175.00**
40 ❑ Oct 1941 Cover: 0.10 **NM** value: **150.00**
41 ❑ Nov 1941 Cover: 0.10 **NM** value: **150.00**
42 ❑ Dec 1941 Cover: 0.10 **NM** value: **150.00**
43 ❑ Jan 1942 Cover: 0.10 **NM** value: **150.00**

CRACKBRAINED COMIX — Crackbrained

1 ❑ Cover: 2.00 **NM** value: **Cover or less**
2 ❑ Cover: 2.00 **NM** value: **Cover or less**
3 ❑ Cover: 2.00 **NM** value: **Cover or less**
📖 The Biscuit; Observe; Probosco; The Enhancer **A:** Barrie Lynn; Jim Richardson; Chris Larson **W:** Barrie Lynn; Jim Richardson; Chris Larson; Allen Richardson

CRACK BUSTERS — Showcase

1 ❑ Cover: 1.95 **NM** value: **Cover or less**
2 ❑ Cover: 1.95 **NM** value: **Cover or less**
📖 Enter: The Mechanic! **A:** Dave Schwartz **W:** Paul Simione

CRACK COMICS — Quality

When the anthology title was known as Crack Comics, it featured costumed heroes; when it changed to Crack Western (after 62 issues), it dropped them all. With early issues probably most collected because of the work of artist Lou Fine on The Black Condor, there were other features of interest, including stories of varying lengths in the "Alias the Spider" feature and five-page shorts of Pen Miller (a cartoonist detective), which ran in #23-60, and Madam Fatal (who, despite the name, was a man).

As was often the case in such anthologies, several of the continuing features were comedy shorts (like "Rube Goldberg's Side Show" and "Slap Happy Pappy"). — Maggie

1 ❑ May 1940 Cover: 0.10 **NM** value: **5000.00**
• **CGC:** 2 graded, best 6.5
2 ❑ Jul 1940 Cover: 0.10 **NM** value: **2500.00**
3 ❑ Aug 1940 Cover: 0.10 **NM** value: **1500.00**
4 ❑ Sep 1940 Cover: 0.10 **NM** value: **1250.00**
5 ❑ Oct 1940 Cover: 0.10 **NM** value: **950.00**
6 ❑ Nov 1940 Cover: 0.10 **NM** value: **950.00**
7 ❑ Dec 1940 Cover: 0.10 **NM** value: **950.00**
8 ❑ Jan 1941 Cover: 0.10 **NM** value: **950.00**
9 ❑ Feb 1941 Cover: 0.10 **NM** value: **950.00**
10 ❑ Mar 1941 Cover: 0.10 **NM** value: **950.00**
11 ❑ Apr 1941 Cover: 0.10 **NM** value: **850.00**
12 ❑ May 1941 Cover: 0.10 **NM** value: **850.00**
13 ❑ Jun 1941 Cover: 0.10 **NM** value: **850.00**
14 ❑ Jul 1941 Cover: 0.10 **NM** value: **850.00**
• **CGC:** 1 graded, best 8.5
15 ❑ Aug 1941 Cover: 0.10 **NM** value: **850.00**
16 ❑ Sep 1941 Cover: 0.10 **NM** value: **850.00**
17 ❑ Oct 1941 Cover: 0.10 **NM** value: **850.00**
18 ❑ Nov 1941 Cover: 0.10 **NM** value: **850.00**
19 ❑ Dec 1941 Cover: 0.10 **NM** value: **850.00**
20 ❑ Jan 1942 Cover: 0.10 **NM** value: **850.00**
21 ❑ Feb 1942 Cover: 0.10 **NM** value: **675.00**
22 ❑ Mar 1942 Cover: 0.10 **NM** value: **675.00**
23 ❑ May 1942 Cover: 0.10 **NM** value: **675.00**
24 ❑ Jul 1942 Cover: 0.10 **NM** value: **675.00**
25 ❑ Sep 1942 Cover: 0.10 **NM** value: **600.00**
26 ❑ Nov 1942 Cover: 0.10 **NM** value: **600.00**
• **CGC:** 1 graded, best 5.0
27 ❑ Jan 1943 Cover: 0.10 **NM** value: **850.00**
• **CGC:** 1 graded, best 4.0
28 ❑ Mar 1943 Cover: 0.10 **NM** value: **400.00**
29 ❑ May 1943 Cover: 0.10 **NM** value: **400.00**
• **CGC:** 2 graded, best 9.2
30 ❑ Aug 1943 Cover: 0.10 **NM** value: **400.00**
31 ❑ Oct 1943 Cover: 0.10 **NM** value: **250.00**
• **CGC:** 1 graded, best 9.6
32 ❑ Dec 1943 Cover: 0.10 **NM** value: **250.00**
• **CGC:** 1 graded, best 1.0
33 ❑ Spr 1944 Cover: 0.10 **NM** value: **250.00**
• **CGC:** 2 graded, best 9.4
34 ❑ Sum 1944 Cover: 0.10 **NM** value: **250.00**
35 ❑ Aut 1944 Cover: 0.10 **NM** value: **250.00**
• **CGC:** 2 graded, best 8.5
36 ❑ Win 1944 Cover: 0.10 **NM** value: **250.00**
37 ❑ Spr 1945 Cover: 0.10 **NM** value: **250.00**
38 ❑ Sum 1945 Cover: 0.10 **NM** value: **250.00**
39 ❑ Aut 1945 Cover: 0.10 **NM** value: **250.00**
• **CGC:** 2 graded, best 9.2
40 ❑ Win 1945 Cover: 0.10 **NM** value: **225.00**
• **CGC:** 1 graded, best 7.5
41 ❑ Spr 1946 Cover: 0.10 **NM** value: **225.00**
42 ❑ Sum 1946 Cover: 0.10 **NM** value: **225.00**
43 ❑ Jul 1946 Cover: 0.10 **NM** value: **225.00**
44 ❑ Sep 1946 Cover: 0.10 **NM** value: **225.00**
45 ❑ Nov 1946 Cover: 0.10 **NM** value: **225.00**
46 ❑ Jan 1947 Cover: 0.10 **NM** value: **225.00**
• **CGC:** 1 graded, best 4.0
47 ❑ Mar 1947 Cover: 0.10 **NM** value: **225.00**
48 ❑ May 1947 Cover: 0.10 **NM** value: **225.00**
• **CGC:** 1 graded, best 4.0
49 ❑ Jul 1947 Cover: 0.10 **NM** value: **225.00**
50 ❑ Sep 1947 Cover: 0.10 **NM** value: **225.00**
• **CGC:** 1 graded, best 2.5
51 ❑ Nov 1947 Cover: 0.10 **NM** value: **225.00**
52 ❑ Jan 1948 Cover: 0.10 **NM** value: **225.00**
53 ❑ Mar 1948 Cover: 0.10 **NM** value: **225.00**
• **CGC:** 1 graded, best 1.8
54 ❑ May 1948 Cover: 0.10 **NM** value: **225.00**
55 ❑ Jul 1948 Cover: 0.10 **NM** value: **200.00**
56 ❑ Sep 1948 Cover: 0.10 **NM** value: **200.00**
57 ❑ Nov 1948 Cover: 0.10 **NM** value: **200.00**
• **CGC:** 1 graded, best 7.0
58 ❑ Jan 1949 Cover: 0.10 **NM** value: **200.00**
59 ❑ Mar 1949 Cover: 0.10 **NM** value: **200.00**
• **CGC:** 2 graded, best 7.0
60 ❑ May 1949 Cover: 0.10 **NM** value: **150.00**
61 ❑ Jul 1949 Cover: 0.10 **NM** value: **150.00**
62 ❑ Sep 1949 Cover: 0.10 **NM** value: **150.00**
• **CGC:** 1 graded, best 5.5

CRACKED — Globe

1 ❑ Feb 1958 Cover: 0.25 **NM** value: **125.00**
2 ❑ Apr 1958 Cover: 0.25 **NM** value: **60.00**
3 ❑ Jun 1958 Cover: 0.25 **NM** value: **35.00**
4 ❑ Aug 1958 Cover: 0.25 **NM** value: **35.00**
5 ❑ Oct 1958 Cover: 0.25 **NM** value: **35.00**
6 ❑ Dec 1958 Cover: 0.25 **NM** value: **20.00**
7 ❑ Feb 1959 Cover: 0.25 **NM** value: **20.00**
8 ❑ 1959 Cover: 0.25 **NM** value: **20.00**
9 ❑ 1959 Cover: 0.25 **NM** value: **20.00**
10 ❑ 1959 Cover: 0.25 **NM** value: **20.00**
11 ❑ 1959 Cover: 0.25 **NM** value: **12.00**
12 ❑ Cover: 0.25 **NM** value: **12.00**
13 ❑ Cover: 0.25 **NM** value: **12.00**
14 ❑ Jun 1960 Cover: 0.25 **NM** value: **12.00**
📖 Old Ideas for New Panel Shows
15 ❑ 1960 Cover: 0.25 **NM** value: **12.00**
16 ❑ 1960 Cover: 0.25 **NM** value: **12.00**
17 ❑ Cover: 0.25 **NM** value: **12.00**
18 ❑ 1961 Cover: 0.25 **NM** value: **12.00**
19 ❑ 1961 Cover: 0.25 **NM** value: **12.00**
20 ❑ 1961 Cover: 0.25 **NM** value: **12.00**
21 ❑ Cover: 0.25 **NM** value: **10.00**
22 ❑ 1962 Cover: 0.25 **NM** value: **10.00**
23 ❑ 1962 Cover: 0.25 **NM** value: **10.00**
24 ❑ 1962 Cover: 0.25 **NM** value: **10.00**
25 ❑ Jul 1962 Cover: 0.25 **NM** value: **10.00**
26 ❑ Cover: 0.25 **NM** value: **10.00**
27 ❑ Cover: 0.25 **NM** value: **10.00**
28 ❑ 1963 Cover: 0.25 **NM** value: **10.00**
29 ❑ 1963 Cover: 0.25 **NM** value: **10.00**
30 ❑ 1963 Cover: 0.25 **NM** value: **10.00**
31 ❑ Sep 1963 Cover: 0.25 **NM** value: **8.00**
32 ❑ Cover: 0.25 **NM** value: **8.00**
33 ❑ Cover: 0.25 **NM** value: **8.00**
34 ❑ Cover: 0.25 **NM** value: **8.00**
35 ❑ 1964 Cover: 0.25 **NM** value: **8.00**
36 ❑ 1964 Cover: 0.25 **NM** value: **8.00**
37 ❑ 1964 Cover: 0.25 **NM** value: **8.00**
38 ❑ 1964 Cover: 0.25 **NM** value: **8.00**
39 ❑ Cover: 0.25 **NM** value: **8.00**
40 ❑ Cover: 0.25 **NM** value: **8.00**
41 ❑ Cover: 0.25 **NM** value: **8.00**
42 ❑ Cover: 0.25 **NM** value: **8.00**
43 ❑ May 1965 Cover: 0.25 **NM** value: **8.00**
44 ❑ **NM** value: **8.00**
45 ❑ **NM** value: **8.00**
46 ❑ **NM** value: **8.00**
47 ❑ **NM** value: **8.00**
48 ❑ **NM** value: **8.00**
49 ❑ **NM** value: **8.00**
50 ❑ **NM** value: **8.00**
51 ❑ **NM** value: **5.00**
52 ❑ **NM** value: **5.00**
53 ❑ **NM** value: **5.00**
54 ❑ **NM** value: **5.00**
55 ❑ **NM** value: **5.00**
56 ❑ **NM** value: **5.00**
57 ❑ **NM** value: **5.00**
58 ❑ **NM** value: **5.00**
59 ❑ **NM** value: **5.00**
60 ❑ **NM** value: **5.00**
61 ❑ **NM** value: **5.00**
62 ❑ **NM** value: **5.00**
63 ❑ **NM** value: **5.00**
64 ❑ **NM** value: **5.00**
65 ❑ **NM** value: **5.00**
66 ❑ **NM** value: **5.00**
67 ❑ **NM** value: **5.00**
68 ❑ **NM** value: **5.00**
69 ❑ **NM** value: **5.00**
70 ❑ **NM** value: **5.00**
71 ❑ **NM** value: **5.00**
72 ❑ **NM** value: **5.00**
73 ❑ **NM** value: **5.00**
74 ❑ **NM** value: **5.00**
75 ❑ **NM** value: **5.00**
76 ❑ **NM** value: **5.00**
77 ❑ **NM** value: **5.00**
78 ❑ **NM** value: **5.00**
79 ❑ **NM** value: **5.00**
80 ❑ **NM** value: **5.00**
81 ❑ **NM** value: **5.00**
82 ❑ **NM** value: **5.00**
83 ❑ **NM** value: **5.00**
84 ❑ **NM** value: **5.00**
85 ❑ **NM** value: **5.00**
86 ❑ **NM** value: **5.00**
87 ❑ **NM** value: **5.00**
88 ❑ **NM** value: **5.00**
89 ❑ **NM** value: **5.00**
90 ❑ **NM** value: **5.00**
91 ❑ **NM** value: **5.00**
92 ❑ **NM** value: **5.00**
93 ❑ **NM** value: **5.00**
94 ❑ **NM** value: **5.00**
95 ❑ **NM** value: **5.00**
96 ❑ **NM** value: **5.00**
97 ❑ **NM** value: **5.00**
98 ❑ **NM** value: **5.00**

Other grades: Multiply prices above by **1.5 for Mint • 2/3 for Very Fine • 1/3 for Fine • 1/5 for Very Good • 1/8 for Good**

99 ☐ Mar 1972 Cover: 0.40 **NM** value: **5.00**
100 ☐ May 1972 Cover: 0.40 **NM** value: **5.00**
101 ☐ Jul 1972 Cover: 0.40 **NM** value: **4.00**
102 ☐ Aug 1972 Cover: 0.40 **NM** value: **4.00**
103 ☐ Sep 1972 Cover: 0.40 **NM** value: **4.00**
104 ☐ Oct 1972 Cover: 0.40 **NM** value: **4.00**
105 ☐ Nov 1972 Cover: 0.40 **NM** value: **4.00**
106 ☐ Jan 1973 Cover: 0.40 **NM** value: **4.00**
107 ☐ Mar 1973 Cover: 0.40 **NM** value: **4.00**
108 ☐ May 1973 Cover: 0.40 **NM** value: **4.00**
109 ☐ Jul 1973 Cover: 0.40 **NM** value: **4.00**
110 ☐ Aug 1973 Cover: 0.40 **NM** value: **4.00**
111 ☐ Sep 1973 Cover: 0.40 **NM** value: **4.00**
112 ☐ Oct 1973 Cover: 0.40 **NM** value: **4.00**
113 ☐ Nov 1973 Cover: 0.40 **NM** value: **4.00**
114 ☐ Jan 1974 Cover: 0.40 **NM** value: **4.00**
115 ☐ Mar 1974 Cover: 0.40 **NM** value: **4.00**
116 ☐ May 1974 Cover: 0.40 **NM** value: **4.00**
117 ☐ Jul 1974 Cover: 0.40 **NM** value: **4.00**
118 ☐ Aug 1974 Cover: 0.40 **NM** value: **4.00**
119 ☐ Sep 1974 Cover: 0.40 **NM** value: **4.00**
120 ☐ Oct 1974 Cover: 0.40 **NM** value: **4.00**
121 ☐ Nov 1974 Cover: 0.40 **NM** value: **4.00**
122 ☐ Jan 1975 **NM** value: **4.00**
Circ: Statement: **413,481**
123 ☐ Mar 1975 Cover: 0.50 **NM** value: **4.00**
Circ: Statement: **413,481**
124 ☐ May 1975 Cover: 0.50 **NM** value: **4.00**
Circ: Statement: **413,481**
125 ☐ Jul 1975 Cover: 0.50 **NM** value: **4.00**
Circ: Statement: **413,481**
126 ☐ Aug 1975 Cover: 0.50 **NM** value: **4.00**
Circ: Statement: **413,481**
127 ☐ Sep 1975 Cover: 0.50 **NM** value: **4.00**
Circ: Statement: **413,481**
128 ☐ Oct 1975 Cover: 0.50 **NM** value: **4.00**
Circ: Statement: **413,481**
129 ☐ Nov 1975 Cover: 0.50 **NM** value: **4.00**
Circ: Statement: **413,481**
130 ☐ Jan 1976 Cover: 0.50 **NM** value: **4.00**
Circ: Statement: **441,245**
131 ☐ Mar 1976 Cover: 0.50 **NM** value: **4.00**
Circ: Statement: **441,245**
132 ☐ May 1976 Cover: 0.50 **NM** value: **4.00**
Circ: Statement: **441,245**
133 ☐ Jul 1976 Cover: 0.50 **NM** value: **4.00**
Circ: Statement: **441,245**
134 ☐ Aug 1976 Cover: 0.50 **NM** value: **4.00**
Circ: Statement: **441,245**
135 ☐ Sep 1976 Cover: 0.50 **NM** value: **4.00**
Circ: Statement: **441,245**
136 ☐ Oct 1976 Cover: 0.50 **NM** value: **4.00**
Circ: Statement: **441,245**
137 ☐ Nov 1976 Cover: 0.50 **NM** value: **4.00**
Circ: Statement: **441,245**
138 ☐ Dec 1976 Cover: 0.50 **NM** value: **4.00**
Circ: Statement: **441,245**
139 ☐ Jan 1977 Cover: 0.50 **NM** value: **4.00**
Circ: Statement: **473,801**
140 ☐ Mar 1977 Cover: 0.50 **NM** value: **4.00**
Circ: Statement: **473,801**
• Has 1976 Statement; avg total paid circ 441,245
141 ☐ May 1977 Cover: 0.50 **NM** value: **4.00**
Circ: Statement: **473,801**
142 ☐ Jul 1977 Cover: 0.50 **NM** value: **4.00**
Circ: Statement: **473,801**
143 ☐ Aug 1977 Cover: 0.50 **NM** value: **4.00**
Circ: Statement: **473,801**
144 ☐ Sep 1977 Cover: 0.60 **NM** value: **4.00**
Circ: Statement: **473,801**
145 ☐ Oct 1977 Cover: 0.60 **NM** value: **4.00**
Circ: Statement: **473,801**
146 ☐ Nov 1977 Cover: 0.60 **NM** value: **4.00**
Circ: Statement: **473,801**
147 ☐ Dec 1977 Cover: 0.60 **NM** value: **4.00**
Circ: Statement: **473,801**
148 ☐ Jan 1978 Cover: 0.60 **NM** value: **4.00**
Circ: Statement: **463,085**
149 ☐ Mar 1978 Cover: 0.60 **NM** value: **4.00**
Circ: Statement: **463,085**
• Has 1977 Statement; avg total paid circ 473,801
150 ☐ May 1978 Cover: 0.60 **NM** value: **4.00**
Circ: Statement: **463,085**
151 ☐ Jul 1978 Cover: 0.60 **NM** value: **3.00**
Circ: Statement: **463,085**
152 ☐ Aug 1978 Cover: 0.60 **NM** value: **3.00**
Circ: Statement: **463,085**
153 ☐ Sep 1978 Cover: 0.60 **NM** value: **3.00**
Circ: Statement: **463,085**
154 ☐ Oct 1978 Cover: 0.60 **NM** value: **3.00**
Circ: Statement: **463,085**
155 ☐ Nov 1978 Cover: 0.60 **NM** value: **3.00**
Circ: Statement: **463,085**
156 ☐ Dec 1978 Cover: 0.60 **NM** value: **3.00**
Circ: Statement: **463,085**
157 ☐ Jan 1979 Cover: 0.60 **NM** value: **3.00**
Circ: Statement: **434,946**
158 ☐ Mar 1979 Cover: 0.60 **NM** value: **3.00**
Circ: Statement: **434,946**
• Has 1978 Statement; avg print run 861,114; avg sales 458,583; avg subs 4,502; avg total paid 463,085; samples 126; office use 700; max existent 463,911; 46% of run returned
159 ☐ May 1979 Cover: 0.60 **NM** value: **5.00**
Circ: Statement: **434,946**
160 ☐ Jul 1979 Cover: 0.60 **NM** value: **3.00**
Circ: Statement: **434,946**
161 ☐ Aug 1979 Cover: 0.60 **NM** value: **3.00**
Circ: Statement: **434,946**
162 ☐ Sep 1979 Cover: 0.75 **NM** value: **3.00**
Circ: Statement: **434,946**
163 ☐ Oct 1979 Cover: 0.75 **NM** value: **3.00**
Circ: Statement: **434,946**
164 ☐ Nov 1979 Cover: 0.75 **NM** value: **3.00**
Circ: Statement: **434,946**
165 ☐ Dec 1979 Cover: 0.75 **NM** value: **3.00**
Circ: Statement: **434,946**
166 ☐ Jan 1980 Cover: 0.75 **NM** value: **3.00**
167 ☐ Mar 1980 Cover: 0.75 **NM** value: **3.00**
• Has 1979 Statement; avg print run 797,757; avg sales 430,316; avg subs 4,630; avg total paid 434,946; samples 114; office use 718; max existent 435,778; 45% of run returned
168 ☐ May 1980 Cover: 0.75 **NM** value: **3.00**
169 ☐ Jul 1980 Cover: 0.75 **NM** value: **3.00**
170 ☐ Aug 1980 Cover: 0.75 **NM** value: **3.00**
171 ☐ Sep 1980 Cover: 0.75 **NM** value: **3.00**
172 ☐ Oct 1980 Cover: 0.75 **NM** value: **3.00**
173 ☐ Nov 1980 Cover: 0.75 **NM** value: **3.00**
174 ☐ Dec 1980 Cover: 0.75 **NM** value: **3.00**
175 ☐ Jan 1981 Cover: 0.75 **NM** value: **3.00**
Circ: Statement: **341,762**
176 ☐ Mar 1981 Cover: 0.75 **NM** value: **3.00**
Circ: Statement: **341,762**
177 ☐ May 1981 Cover: 0.75 **NM** value: **3.00**
Circ: Statement: **341,762**
178 ☐ Jul 1981 Cover: 0.75 **NM** value: **3.00**
Circ: Statement: **341,762**
179 ☐ Aug 1981 Cover: 0.75 **NM** value: **3.00**
Circ: Statement: **341,762**
180 ☐ Sep 1981 Cover: 0.90 **NM** value: **3.00**
Circ: Statement: **341,762**
181 ☐ Oct 1981 Cover: 0.90 **NM** value: **3.00**
Circ: Statement: **341,762**
182 ☐ Nov 1981 Cover: 0.90 **NM** value: **3.00**
Circ: Statement: **341,762**
183 ☐ Dec 1981 Cover: 0.90 **NM** value: **3.00**
Circ: Statement: **341,762**
184 ☐ Jan 1982 Cover: 0.90 **NM** value: **3.00**
185 ☐ Mar 1982 Cover: 0.90 **NM** value: **3.00**
• Has 1981 Statement, filed 10/1/81; avg print run 701,270; avg sales 338,695; avg subs 3,067; avg total paid 341,762; samples 120; office use 680; max existent 342,562; 51% of run returned
186 ☐ May 1982 Cover: 0.90 **NM** value: **3.00**
187 ☐ Jul 1982 Cover: 0.90 **NM** value: **3.00**
188 ☐ Aug 1982 Cover: 0.90 **NM** value: **3.00**
189 ☐ Sep 1982 Cover: 1.00 **NM** value: **3.00**
190 ☐ Oct 1982 Cover: 1.00 **NM** value: **3.00**
191 ☐ Nov 1982 Cover: 1.00 **NM** value: **3.00**
192 ☐ Jan 1983 Cover: 1.00 **NM** value: **3.00**
Circ: Statement: **272,581**
193 ☐ Mar 1983 Cover: 1.00 **NM** value: **3.00**
Circ: Statement: **272,581**
194 ☐ May 1983 Cover: 1.00 **NM** value: **3.00**
Circ: Statement: **272,581**
195 ☐ Jul 1983 Cover: 1.00 **NM** value: **3.00**
Circ: Statement: **272,581**
196 ☐ Aug 1983 Cover: 1.00 **NM** value: **3.00**
Circ: Statement: **272,581**
197 ☐ Sep 1983 Cover: 1.00 **NM** value: **3.00**
Circ: Statement: **272,581**
198 ☐ Oct 1983 Cover: 1.00 **NM** value: **3.00**
Circ: Statement: **272,581**
199 ☐ Nov 1983 Cover: 1.00 **NM** value: **3.00**
Circ: Statement: **272,581**
200 ☐ Dec 1983 **NM** value: **3.00**
Circ: Statement: **272,581**
201 ☐ Jan 1984 **NM** value: **2.50**
Circ: Statement: **238,595**
202 ☐ Mar 1984 **NM** value: **2.50**
Circ: Statement: **238,595**
203 ☐ May 1984 **NM** value: **2.50**
Circ: Statement: **238,595**
204 ☐ Jul 1984 **NM** value: **2.50**
Circ: Statement: **238,595**
205 ☐ Aug 1984 **NM** value: **2.50**
Circ: Statement: **238,595**
206 ☐ Sep 1984 Cover: 1.25 **NM** value: **2.50**
Circ: Statement: **238,595**
207 ☐ Oct 1984 Cover: 1.25 **NM** value: **2.50**
Circ: Statement: **238,595**
208 ☐ Nov 1984 Cover: 1.25 **NM** value: **2.50**
Circ: Statement: **238,595**
209 ☐ Jan 1985 Cover: 1.25 **NM** value: **2.50**
210 ☐ Mar 1985 Cover: 1.25 **NM** value: **2.50**
211 ☐ May 1985 Cover: 1.25 **NM** value: **2.50**
212 ☐ Jul 1985 Cover: 1.25 **NM** value: **2.50**
213 ☐ Aug 1985 Cover: 1.25 **NM** value: **2.50**
214 ☐ Sep 1985 Cover: 1.25 **NM** value: **2.50**
215 ☐ Oct 1985 Cover: 1.25 **NM** value: **2.50**
216 ☐ Nov 1985 Cover: 1.25 **NM** value: **2.50**
217 ☐ Dec 1985 Cover: 1.25 **NM** value: **2.50**
218 ☐ Jan 1986 Cover: 1.25 **NM** value: **2.50**
Circ: Statement: **197,047**
219 ☐ Mar 1986 Cover: 1.25 **NM** value: **2.50**
Circ: Statement: **197,047**
Sylvester P. Smythe as Rambo
220 ☐ May 1986 Cover: 1.25 **NM** value: **2.50**
Circ: Statement: **197,047**
221 ☐ Jul 1986 Cover: 1.25 **NM** value: **2.50**
Circ: Statement: **197,047**
222 ☐ Aug 1986 Cover: 1.25 **NM** value: **2.50**
Circ: Statement: **197,047**
223 ☐ Sep 1986 Cover: 1.25 **NM** value: **2.50**
Circ: Statement: **197,047**
224 ☐ Oct 1986 Cover: 1.25 **NM** value: **2.50**
Circ: Statement: **197,047**
225 ☐ Nov 1986 Cover: 1.25 **NM** value: **2.50**
Circ: Statement: **197,047**
226 ☐ Mar 1987 Cover: 1.25 **NM** value: **2.50**
Circ: Statement: **182,654**
227 ☐ May 1987 **NM** value: **2.50**
Circ: Statement: **182,654**
228 ☐ Jul 1987 Cover: 1.35 **NM** value: **2.50**
Circ: Statement: **182,654**
229 ☐ Aug 1987 Cover: 1.35 **NM** value: **2.50**
Circ: Statement: **182,654**
230 ☐ Sep 1987 Cover: 1.35 **NM** value: **2.50**
Circ: Statement: **182,654**
231 ☐ Oct 1987 Cover: 1.35 **NM** value: **2.50**
Circ: Statement: **182,654**
232 ☐ Nov 1987 Cover: 1.35 **NM** value: **2.50**
Circ: Statement: **182,654**
233 ☐ Jan 1988 **NM** value: **2.50**
234 ☐ Mar 1988 **NM** value: **2.50**
235 ☐ May 1988 **NM** value: **2.50**
236 ☐ Jul 1988 **NM** value: **2.50**
237 ☐ Aug 1988 **NM** value: **2.50**
238 ☐ Sep 1988 **NM** value: **2.50**
239 ☐ Oct 1988 **NM** value: **2.50**
240 ☐ Nov 1988 **NM** value: **2.50**
241 ☐ Dec 1988 **NM** value: **2.50**
242 ☐ Jan 1989 **NM** value: **2.50**
243 ☐ Mar 1989 **NM** value: **2.50**
244 ☐ May 1989 **NM** value: **2.50**
245 ☐ Jul 1989 **NM** value: **2.50**
246 ☐ Aug 1989 Cover: 1.49 **NM** value: **2.50**
247 ☐ Sep 1989 Cover: 1.49 **NM** value: **2.50**
248 ☐ Oct 1989 Cover: 1.49 **NM** value: **2.50**
249 ☐ Nov 1989 Cover: 1.49 **NM** value: **2.50**
250 ☐ Dec 1989 **NM** value: **2.50**
251 ☐ Jan 1990 **NM** value: **2.00**
252 ☐ Mar 1990 **NM** value: **2.00**
253 ☐ May 1990 **NM** value: **2.00**
254 ☐ Jul 1990 **NM** value: **2.00**
255 ☐ Aug 1990 **NM** value: **2.00**
256 ☐ Sep 1990 **NM** value: **2.00**
257 ☐ Oct 1990 **NM** value: **2.00**
258 ☐ Nov 1990 Cover: 1.75 **NM** value: **2.00**
259 ☐ Dec 1990 Cover: 1.75 **NM** value: **2.00**
260 ☐ Jan 1991 Cover: 1.75 **NM** value: **2.00**
261 ☐ Mar 1991 Cover: 1.75 **NM** value: **2.00**
262 ☐ May 1991 Cover: 1.75 **NM** value: **2.00**
263 ☐ Jul 1991 Cover: 1.75 **NM** value: **2.00**
264 ☐ Aug 1991 Cover: 1.75 **NM** value: **2.00**
265 ☐ Sep 1991 Cover: 1.75 **NM** value: **2.00**
266 ☐ Oct 1991 Cover: 1.75 **NM** value: **2.00**
267 ☐ Nov 1991 Cover: 1.75 **NM** value: **2.00**
268 ☐ Dec 1991 Cover: 1.75 **NM** value: **2.00**
269 ☐ Jan 1992 Cover: 1.75 **NM** value: **2.00**
270 ☐ Mar 1992 Cover: 1.75 **NM** value: **2.00**
271 ☐ May 1992 Cover: 1.75 **NM** value: **2.00**
272 ☐ Jul 1992 Cover: 1.75 **NM** value: **2.00**
273 ☐ Aug 1992 Cover: 1.75 **NM** value: **2.00**
274 ☐ Sep 1992 Cover: 1.75 **NM** value: **2.00**
275 ☐ Oct 1992 Cover: 1.75 **NM** value: **2.00**
276 ☐ Nov 1992 Cover: 1.75 **NM** value: **2.00**
277 ☐ Dec 1992 Cover: 1.75 **NM** value: **2.00**
278 ☐ Jan 1993 Cover: 1.75 **NM** value: **2.00**
279 ☐ Mar 1993 Cover: 1.75 **NM** value: **2.00**
280 ☐ May 1993 Cover: 1.75 **NM** value: **2.00**
281 ☐ Jul 1993 Cover: 1.75 **NM** value: **2.00**
282 ☐ Aug 1993 Cover: 1.75 **NM** value: **2.00**
283 ☐ Sep 1993 Cover: 1.75 **NM** value: **2.00**
284 ☐ Oct 1993 Cover: 1.75 **NM** value: **2.00**
285 ☐ Nov 1993 Cover: 1.75 **NM** value: **2.00**
286 ☐ Dec 1993 Cover: 1.75 **NM** value: **2.00**
287 ☐ Jan 1994 Cover: 1.75 **NM** value: **2.00**
288 ☐ Mar 1994 Cover: 1.75 **NM** value: **2.00**
289 ☐ May 1994 Cover: 1.75 **NM** value: **2.00**
290 ☐ Jul 1994 Cover: 1.75 **NM** value: **2.00**
291 ☐ Aug 1994 Cover: 1.75 **NM** value: **2.00**
• b&w magazine.
292 ☐ Sep 1994 Cover: 1.75 **NM** value: **2.00**
• b&w magazine.
293 ☐ Oct 1994 Cover: 1.75 **NM** value: **2.00**
294 ☐ Nov 1994 Cover: 1.75 **NM** value: **2.00**
• b&w magazine.
295 ☐ Dec 1994 Cover: 1.95 **NM** value: **2.00**
• b&w magazine.
296 ☐ Jan 1995 Cover: 1.95 **NM** value: **2.00**
• b&w magazine.
297 ☐ Mar 1995 Cover: 1.95 **NM** value: **2.00**
• b&w magazine.
298 ☐ May 1995 Cover: 1.95 **NM** value: **2.00**
299 ☐ Jul 1995 Cover: 1.95 **NM** value: **2.00**
300 ☐ Aug 1995 Cover: 1.95 **NM** value: **2.00**
301 ☐ Sep 1995 Cover: 1.95 **NM** value: **2.00**
302 ☐ Oct 1995 Cover: 1.95 **NM** value: **2.00**
• b&w magazine.
303 ☐ Nov 1995 **NM** value: **2.00**
304 ☐ Dec 1995 **NM** value: **2.00**
305 ☐ Jan 1996 **NM** value: **2.00**
306 ☐ Mar 1996 Cover: 1.99 **NM** value: **2.00**
• b&w magazine.
307 ☐ 1996 Cover: 1.99 **NM** value: **2.00**
308 ☐ 1996 Cover: 1.99 **NM** value: **2.00**
309 ☐ 1996 Cover: 1.99 **NM** value: **2.00**
310 ☐ 1996 Cover: 1.99 **NM** value: **2.00**
311 ☐ 1996 Cover: 1.99 **NM** value: **2.00**
312 ☐ Cover: 1.99 **NM** value: **2.00**
313 ☐ Cover: 1.99 **NM** value: **2.00**
314 ☐ Cover: 1.99 **NM** value: **2.00**
315 ☐ Cover: 1.99 **NM** value: **2.00**
316 ☐ Cover: 1.99 **NM** value: **2.00**
317 ☐ Cover: 1.99 **NM** value: **2.00**
318 ☐ Cover: 1.99 **NM** value: **2.00**

CGC-graded: Multiply prices above by **33 for 9.9 M • 16 for 9.8 NM/M • 7 for 9.6 NM+ • 5 for 9.4 NM • 2.5 for 9.2 NM- • 1.5 for 9.0 VF/NM**

319 ❑ Cover: 1.99 **NM** value: **2.00**
320 ❑ Cover: 1.99 **NM** value: **2.00**
321 ❑ Cover: 1.99 **NM** value: **2.00**
322 ❑ Cover: 1.99 **NM** value: **2.00**
323 ❑ Cover: 1.99 **NM** value: **2.00**
324 ❑ Cover: 1.99 **NM** value: **2.00**
325 ❑ Cover: 1.99 **NM** value: **2.00**
326 ❑ Cover: 1.99 **NM** value: **2.00**
327 ❑ Cover: 1.99 **NM** value: **2.00**
328 ❑ Cover: 1.99 **NM** value: **2.00**
📖 King of the Ill; If the Simpsons Starred in a TV Drama; Joe Camel Ads to Keep You Smoking; Schlubber; Mouth Park • Simpsons, South Park, King of the Hill parody **A:** John Severin; Gary Fields; Don Orehek; Frank Cummings; Gunnar Johnson; Mike Ricigliano; Walt Brogan; Brian Bolinger **W:** Gunnar Johnson; Mike Ricigliano; Chris Gennusa; Greg Grabianski; Joseph O'Brien; Sherry Johnson; Todd Jackson; Walt Silverstone
329 ❑ Cover: 1.99 **NM** value: **2.00**
330 ❑ Cover: 1.99 **NM** value: **2.00**
331 ❑ Cover: 1.99 **NM** value: **2.00**
332 ❑ Cover: 1.99 **NM** value: **2.00**
333 ❑ Cover: 1.99 **NM** value: **2.00**
334 ❑ Cover: 1.99 **NM** value: **2.00**
335 ❑ Cover: 1.99 **NM** value: **2.00**
336 ❑ Cover: 1.99 **NM** value: **2.00**
337 ❑ Cover: 1.99 **NM** value: **2.00**
338 ❑ Cover: 1.99 **NM** value: **2.00**
339 ❑ Cover: 1.99 **NM** value: **2.00**
340 ❑ Cover: 1.99 **NM** value: **2.00**
341 ❑ Cover: 1.99 **NM** value: **2.00**
342 ❑ Cover: 1.99 **NM** value: **2.00**
343 ❑ Cover: 1.99 **NM** value: **2.00**

CRACKED COLLECTORS' EDITION — Globe

4 ❑ Cover: 0.50 **NM** value: **10.00**
5 ❑ Cover: 0.50 **NM** value: **8.00**
6 ❑ Cover: 0.50 **NM** value: **6.00**
7 ❑ Cover: 0.50 **NM** value: **6.00**
8 ❑ 1975 Cover: 0.50 **NM** value: **6.00**
9 ❑ 1975 Cover: 0.50 **NM** value: **6.00**
10 ❑ 1975 Cover: 0.50 **NM** value: **6.00**
11 ❑ 1975 Cover: 0.50 **NM** value: **5.00**
12 ❑ 1975 Cover: 0.50 **NM** value: **5.00**
13 ❑ 1976 Cover: 0.50 **NM** value: **5.00**
14 ❑ 1976 Cover: 0.50 **NM** value: **5.00**
15 ❑ 1976 Cover: 0.50 **NM** value: **5.00**
16 ❑ 1976 Cover: 0.60 **NM** value: **5.00**
17 ❑ 1976 **NM** value: **5.00**
18 ❑ 1976 **NM** value: **5.00**
19 ❑ **NM** value: **5.00**
20 ❑ **NM** value: **5.00**
21 ❑ **NM** value: **5.00**
22 ❑ **NM** value: **5.00**
23 ❑ **NM** value: **5.00**
24 ❑ **NM** value: **5.00**
25 ❑ **NM** value: **5.00**
26 ❑ **NM** value: **5.00**
27 ❑ **NM** value: **5.00**
28 ❑ **NM** value: **5.00**
29 ❑ **NM** value: **5.00**
30 ❑ **NM** value: **5.00**
31 ❑ **NM** value: **4.00**
32 ❑ **NM** value: **4.00**
33 ❑ **NM** value: **4.00**
34 ❑ **NM** value: **4.00**
35 ❑ **NM** value: **4.00**
36 ❑ **NM** value: **4.00**
37 ❑ **NM** value: **4.00**
38 ❑ **NM** value: **4.00**
39 ❑ **NM** value: **4.00**
40 ❑ **NM** value: **4.00**
41 ❑ **NM** value: **4.00**
42 ❑ **NM** value: **4.00**
43 ❑ **NM** value: **4.00**
44 ❑ **NM** value: **4.00**
45 ❑ **NM** value: **4.00**
46 ❑ **NM** value: **4.00**
47 ❑ **NM** value: **4.00**
48 ❑ **NM** value: **4.00**
49 ❑ **NM** value: **4.00**
50 ❑ **NM** value: **4.00**
51 ❑ **NM** value: **3.00**
52 ❑ **NM** value: **3.00**
53 ❑ **NM** value: **3.00**
54 ❑ **NM** value: **3.00**
55 ❑ **NM** value: **3.00**
56 ❑ **NM** value: **3.00**
57 ❑ **NM** value: **3.00**
58 ❑ **NM** value: **3.00**
59 ❑ **NM** value: **3.00**
60 ❑ **NM** value: **3.00**
61 ❑ **NM** value: **3.00**
62 ❑ **NM** value: **3.00**
63 ❑ **NM** value: **3.00**
64 ❑ **NM** value: **3.00**
65 ❑ **NM** value: **3.00**
66 ❑ **NM** value: **3.00**
67 ❑ **NM** value: **3.00**
68 ❑ **NM** value: **3.00**
69 ❑ **NM** value: **3.00**
70 ❑ **NM** value: **3.00**
71 ❑ **NM** value: **3.00**
72 ❑ Sep 1987 Cover: 1.35 **NM** value: **3.00**
73 ❑ Jan 1988 Cover: 2.75 **NM** value: **3.00**
74 ❑ **NM** value: **3.00**
75 ❑ **NM** value: **3.00**
76 ❑ **NM** value: **3.00**
77 ❑ **NM** value: **3.00**
78 ❑ **NM** value: **3.00**
79 ❑ **NM** value: **3.00**
80 ❑ **NM** value: **3.00**
81 ❑ **NM** value: **3.00**
82 ❑ **NM** value: **3.00**
83 ❑ **NM** value: **3.00**
84 ❑ **NM** value: **3.00**
85 ❑ **NM** value: **3.00**
86 ❑ **NM** value: **3.00**
87 ❑ **NM** value: **3.00**
88 ❑ **NM** value: **3.00**
89 ❑ **NM** value: **3.00**
90 ❑ **NM** value: **3.00**
91 ❑ **NM** value: **3.00**
92 ❑ **NM** value: **3.00**
93 ❑ **NM** value: **3.00**
94 ❑ **NM** value: **3.00**
95 ❑ **NM** value: **3.00**
96 ❑ **NM** value: **3.00**
97 ❑ **NM** value: **3.00**
98 ❑ **NM** value: **3.00**
99 ❑ **NM** value: **3.00**
100 ❑ **NM** value: **3.00**
101 ❑ Jan 1995 Cover: 1.95 **NM** value: **3.00**
• b&w magazine.

CRAP — Fantagraphics

1 ❑ Aug 1993 Cover: 2.50 **NM** value: **Cover or less**
2 ❑ Nov 1993 Cover: 2.50 **NM** value: **Cover or less**
3 ❑ Feb 1994 Cover: 2.50 **NM** value: **Cover or less**
4 ❑ May 1994 Cover: 2.50 **NM** value: **Cover or less**
5 ❑ Aug 1994 Cover: 2.50 **NM** value: **Cover or less**

CRASH COMICS — Tem Publishing

1 ❑ May 1940 Cover: 0.10 **NM** value: **2500.00**
📖 The Solar Legion
2 ❑ Jul 1940 Cover: 0.10 **NM** value: **1200.00**
📖 The Solar Legion
3 ❑ Aug 1940 Cover: 0.10 **NM** value: **1000.00**
📖 The Solar Legion
4 ❑ Sep 1940 Cover: 0.10 **NM** value: **2500.00**
• **CGC:** 1 graded, best 3.0
5 ❑ Nov 1940 Cover: 1.00 **NM** value: **1000.00**
• **CGC:** 1 graded, best 4.0

CRASH DUMMIES — Harvey

And you thought the Crash Dummies just made your cars safer?

Ha! They're also toys and cartoon characters! In this series from Harvey Comics, the Dummies find themselves in a number of comedic situations — Dummies in space, Dummies as super-heroes, Dummies at Christmas, etc. Never mind that in the real world they're merely inanimate punching bags, albeit heroically sacrificing themselves to protect the rest of the population. Here, they manage to be — well — heroes, saving the day and managing a pretty good punchline at the end of every adventure. Good stuff for the kiddies!

1 ❑ 1994 Cover: 1.50 **NM** value: **Cover or less**
Circ: CapCity orders: **4,375**
2 ❑ 1994 Cover: 1.50 **NM** value: **Cover or less**
3 ❑ Jun 1994 Cover: 1.50 **NM** value: **Cover or less**
📖 The Space Dummies; My Daddy The Junkman **A:** Bill Vallely **W:** Angelo Decesare

CRASH METRO & THE STAR SQUAD — Oni Press

1 ❑ May 1999, b&w Cover: 2.95 **NM** value: **Cover or less**
Circ: Diamd. preorders: **5,650**

CRASH RYAN — Marvel / Epic

Christopher C. "Crash" Ryan was once a respected airline pilot, until the day his engine caught fire and he had to land in a windswept field. Despite his courageous struggle to control his failing plane, it struck hard and burned, killing many of the passengers. Crash's license was revoked, and the only job he could get was ferrying air mail in the jungles of Central America.

Then one day, making a routine run, Crash sees two strange planes chasing a third. All three look like something out of a science-fiction novel, with propulsion systems unlike anything he's ever seen. The attacking planes force their quarry down, before turning on Crash, who manages to outmaneuver them, even in his old biplane. Investigating the downed plane, Crash encounters an old friend and is drawn into a jet-age struggle...

1 ❑ Oct 1984 Cover: 1.50 **NM** value: **Cover or less**
📖 Doomsday Eve **A:** Ron Harris **W:** Ron Harris
2 ❑ Nov 1984 Cover: 1.50 **NM** value: **Cover or less**
📖 Doomsday **A:** Ron Harris **W:** Ron Harris
3 ❑ Dec 1984 Cover: 1.50 **NM** value: **Cover or less**
📖 Fortress Japan! **A:** Ron Harris **W:** Ron Harris
4 ❑ Jan 1985 Cover: 1.50 **NM** value: **Cover or less**
📖 The Final Battle! **A:** Ron Harris **W:** Ron Harris

CRASH TEST DUMMIES — Harvey

1 ❑ Cover: 1.50 **NM** value: **Cover or less**
2 ❑ Cover: 1.50 **NM** value: **Cover or less**
3 ❑ Cover: 1.50 **NM** value: **Cover or less**

CRAY BABY ADVENTURES SPECIAL, THE — Electric Milk

1 ❑ Cover: 2.95 **NM** value: **Cover or less**
A: Art Baltazar **W:** Art Baltazar

CRAY-BABY ADVENTURES, THE: WRATH OF THE PEDIDDLERS — Destination Entertainment

1 ❑ b&w Cover: 2.95 **NM** value: **Cover or less**
A: Art Baltazar **W:** Art Baltazar

CRAZY (ATLAS) — Atlas

1 ❑ Dec 1953 Cover: 0.10 **NM** value: **200.00**
2 ❑ Jan 1954 Cover: 0.10 **NM** value: **150.00**
📖 The Beast from a Million Billion Trillion Squillion Fathoms!
3 ❑ Feb 1954 Cover: 0.10 **NM** value: **125.00**
• **CGC:** 1 graded, best 7.0
4 ❑ Mar 1954 Cover: 0.10 **NM** value: **125.00**
5 ❑ Apr 1954 Cover: 0.10 **NM** value: **125.00**
6 ❑ May 1954 Cover: 0.10 **NM** value: **125.00**
7 ❑ Jun 1954 Cover: 0.10 **NM** value: **125.00**

CRAZY BOB — Blackbird

1 ❑ b&w Cover: 2.75 **NM** value: **Cover or less**
2 ❑ b&w Cover: 2.00 **NM** value: **Cover or less**

CRAZYFISH PREVIEW — Crazyfish

1 ❑ **NM** value: **0.50**
2 ❑ **NM** value: **0.50**
📖 Soulwind; Supermodels Don't Know Kung Fu; Littlegreyman **A:** C.S. Morse; Lauren Faust **W:** C.S. Morse; Lauren Faust

CRAZY (MAGAZINE) — Marvel

As Marvel under its Atlas imprint launched Mad imitation Crazy in its comic-book days, so it imitated Mad magazine's format via its Crazy black-and-white magazine. It lasted longer than its comic-book version: a decade.

Of course, there's the typical movie parodies, and Marvel seemed to have a better sense than Mad of what films its particular readers were interested in. Mad would concentrate more on super-heroes and SF movies in the late 1990s, but Crazy did it from the start.

Crazy had its own running features in characters such as Teen Hulk and Obnoxio the Clown, who would later cross over with the X-Men in his own one-shot comic book. Marvel even sent up its own "Dark Phoenix Saga" from The X-Men in a late issue, actually offending a few of that title's way-too-serious fans.

Put Cracked and Not Brand Ecch in a blender, and you've got Crazy. Don't miss Steve Skeates' "How the Kitten Lost His Nose" from this series, an overlooked classic of children's literature. —JJM

1 ❑ 1973 Cover: 0.40 **NM** value: **10.00**
2 ❑ 1973 Cover: 0.40 **NM** value: **6.00**
3 ❑ Mar 1973 Cover: 0.40 **NM** value: **5.00**
4 ❑ May 1973 Cover: 0.40 **NM** value: **5.00**
5 ❑ Cover: 0.40 **NM** value: **5.00**
6 ❑ Cover: 0.40 **NM** value: **3.00**
7 ❑ Cover: 0.40 **NM** value: **3.00**
8 ❑ Cover: 0.50 **NM** value: **3.00**
9 ❑ Cover: 0.50 **NM** value: **3.00**
10 ❑ Cover: 0.50 **NM** value: **3.00**
11 ❑ Cover: 0.50 **NM** value: **3.00**
12 ❑ Cover: 0.50 **NM** value: **3.00**
13 ❑ Cover: 0.50 **NM** value: **3.00**
14 ❑ Cover: 0.50 **NM** value: **3.00**
15 ❑ Cover: 0.50 **NM** value: **3.00**
16 ❑ Cover: 0.50 **NM** value: **2.00**
17 ❑ Cover: 0.50 **NM** value: **2.00**
18 ❑ Cover: 0.50 **NM** value: **2.00**
19 ❑ Cover: 0.50 **NM** value: **2.00**
20 ❑ **NM** value: **2.00**
21 ❑ **NM** value: **1.50**
22 ❑ **NM** value: **1.50**
23 ❑ **NM** value: **1.50**
24 ❑ **NM** value: **1.50**
25 ❑ 1977 **NM** value: **1.50**
Circ: Statement: **123,494**
26 ❑ 1977 **NM** value: **1.50**
Circ: Statement: **123,494**
27 ❑ 1977 **NM** value: **1.50**
Circ: Statement: **123,494**
28 ❑ 1977 **NM** value: **1.50**
Circ: Statement: **123,494**
29 ❑ 1977 **NM** value: **1.50**
Circ: Statement: **123,494**
30 ❑ 1977 **NM** value: **1.50**
Circ: Statement: **123,494**
31 ❑ 1977 **NM** value: **1.50**
Circ: Statement: **123,494**
32 ❑ Dec 1977 Cover: 0.60 **NM** value: **1.50**
Circ: Statement: **123,494**
33 ❑ Cover: 0.60 **NM** value: **1.50**
34 ❑ Cover: 0.60 **NM** value: **1.50**
35 ❑ 1978 Cover: 0.60 **NM** value: **1.50**
• Has 1977 Statement; avg total paid circ 123,494

Other grades: Multiply prices above by **1.5 for Mint • 2/3 for Very Fine • 1/3 for Fine • 1/5 for Very Good • 1/8 for Good**

36 ❑ 1978 Cover: 0.60 **NM** value: **1.50**
37 ❑ 1978 Cover: 0.60 **NM** value: **1.50**
38 ❑ 1978 Cover: 0.60 **NM** value: **1.50**
39 ❑ 1978 **NM** value: **1.50**
40 ❑ 1978 **NM** value: **1.50**
41 ❑ 1978 **NM** value: **1.50**
42 ❑ 1978 **NM** value: **1.50**
43 ❑ 1978 **NM** value: **1.50**
44 ❑ 1978 **NM** value: **1.50**
45 ❑ 1978 **NM** value: **1.50**
46 ❑ 1979 **NM** value: **1.50**
47 ❑ 1979 **NM** value: **1.50**
48 ❑ 1979 **NM** value: **1.50**
49 ❑ 1979 **NM** value: **1.50**
50 ❑ 1979 **NM** value: **1.50**
51 ❑ 1979 **NM** value: **1.50**
52 ❑ 1979 **NM** value: **1.50**
53 ❑ 1979 **NM** value: **1.50**
54 ❑ 1979 **NM** value: **1.50**
55 ❑ 1979 **NM** value: **1.50**
56 ❑ 1979 **NM** value: **1.50**
57 ❑ 1979 **NM** value: **1.50**
58 ❑ Jan 1980 Cover: 1.25 **NM** value: **1.50**
59 ❑ Feb 1980 **NM** value: **1.50**
60 ❑ Mar 1980 **NM** value: **1.50**
61 ❑ Apr 1980 **NM** value: **1.50**
62 ❑ May 1980 **NM** value: **1.50**
63 ❑ Jun 1980 **NM** value: **1.50**
64 ❑ Jul 1980 Cover: 1.25 **NM** value: **1.50**
65 ❑ Aug 1980 **NM** value: **1.50**
66 ❑ Sep 1980 **NM** value: **1.50**
📖 mpire Strikes Back (parody); The Creatures in the Volcano • "Creatures" parodizes Journy into Mystery #51
67 ❑ Oct 1980 **NM** value: **1.50**
68 ❑ Nov 1980 **NM** value: **1.50**
69 ❑ Dec 1980 **NM** value: **1.50**
70 ❑ Jan 1981 **NM** value: **1.50**
Circ: Statement: **118,000**
71 ❑ Feb 1981 **NM** value: **1.50**
Circ: Statement: **118,000**
72 ❑ Mar 1981 **NM** value: **1.50**
Circ: Statement: **118,000**
73 ❑ Apr 1981 **NM** value: **1.50**
Circ: Statement: **118,000**
74 ❑ May 1981 **NM** value: **1.50**
Circ: Statement: **118,000**
75 ❑ Jun 1981 **NM** value: **1.50**
Circ: Statement: **118,000**
76 ❑ Jul 1981 **NM** value: **1.50**
Circ: Statement: **118,000**
77 ❑ Aug 1981 **NM** value: **1.50**
Circ: Statement: **118,000**
78 ❑ Sep 1981 **NM** value: **1.50**
Circ: Statement: **118,000**
79 ❑ Oct 1981 Cover: 1.25 **NM** value: **1.50**
Circ: Statement: **118,000**
80 ❑ Nov 1981 Cover: 0.90 **NM** value: **1.50**
Circ: Statement: **118,000**
81 ❑ Dec 1981 Cover: 0.90 **NM** value: **1.50**
Circ: Statement: **118,000**
82 ❑ Jan 1982 Cover: 1.25 **NM** value: **1.50**
📖 Spider-Man Tackles the Torch • parodizes Amazing Spider-Man #8
83 ❑ Feb 1982 Cover: 0.90 **NM** value: **1.50**
• Raiders of the Lost Ark parody
84 ❑ Mar 1982 Cover: 0.90 **NM** value: **1.50**
85 ❑ Apr 1982 Cover: 1.25 **NM** value: **1.50**
86 ❑ May 1982 Cover: 0.90 **NM** value: **1.50**
87 ❑ Jun 1982 Cover: 0.90 **NM** value: **1.50**
88 ❑ Jul 1982 Cover: 0.90 **NM** value: **1.50**
89 ❑ Aug 1982 Cover: 0.90 **NM** value: **1.50**
90 ❑ Sep 1982 Cover: 0.90 **NM** value: **1.50**
91 ❑ Oct 1982 Cover: 1.25 **NM** value: **1.50**
• Blade Runner parody
92 ❑ Dec 1982 Cover: 1.25 **NM** value: **1.50**
• Star Trek II parody
93 ❑ Feb 1983 Cover: 1.25 **NM** value: **1.50**
94 ❑ Apr 1983 Cover: 1.25 **NM** value: **1.50**

CRAZYMAN — Continuity

1 ❑ Apr 1992 Cover: 3.95 **NM** value: **Cover or less**
Circ: CapCity orders: **9,625**
enhanced cover.
2 ❑ May 1992 Cover: 2.50 **NM** value: **Cover or less**
Circ: CapCity orders: **7,625**
A: Brian Bolland **C:** Neal Adams
3 ❑ Jul 1992 Cover: 2.50 **NM** value: **Cover or less**
Circ: CapCity orders: **3,075**

CRAZYMAN (2ND SERIES) — Continuity

1 ❑ May 1993 Cover: 3.95 **NM** value: **Cover or less**
Circ: CapCity orders: **8,625**
• Die-cut comic book
2 ❑ Dec 1993 Cover: 2.50 **NM** value: **Cover or less**
Circ: CapCity orders: **7,200**
3 ❑ Dec 1993 Cover: 2.50 **NM** value: **Cover or less**
Circ: CapCity orders: **6,975**
A: Dan Barry **W:** Peter Stone
4 ❑ Jan 1994 Cover: 2.50 **NM** value: **Cover or less**
Circ: CapCity orders: **7,750**
• indicia says #3

CRAZY, MAN, CRAZY — Charlton

1 ❑ **NM** value: **Cover or less**
2 ❑ **NM** value: **Cover or less**

CRAZY (MARVEL) — Marvel

When Marvel began reprinting its classic stories, it was only a matter of time before the company got around to Not Brand Echh, its broad humor and super-hero parody series from the late 1960s. Not Brand Echh lampooned Marvel and DC super-hero comics with wit aimed squarely at the recognizable species that had evolved during the Marvel Silver Age, comicus fanboyus, and may not hold the same enchantment for later readers. However, many of the genuinely funny moments in the series were powered by the riotous art of Marie Severin. What might have been fresh and funny the first time around apparently proved less popular in reprint format, and Crazy lasted a scant three issues.

1 ❑ Feb 1973 Cover: 0.20 **NM** value: **12.00**
• **CGC:** 1 graded, best 8.0
• reprints Not Brand Ecch
2 ❑ Apr 1973 Cover: 0.20 **NM** value: **7.00**
📖 The Human Scorch Has to Meet the Family • reprints Not Brand Ecch #6
3 ❑ Jun 1973 Cover: 0.20 **NM** value: **7.00**
📖 The Origin of the Fantastical Four final issue. • reprints Not Brand Ecch #7

CREATURE — Antarctic

1 ❑ Oct 1997, b&w Cover: 2.95 **NM** value: **Cover or less**
📖 A Deadly Silence **A:** Don Walker **W:** Don Walker
2 ❑ Dec 1997, b&w Cover: 2.95 **NM** value: **Cover or less**
📖 All Hell **A:** Don Walker **W:** Don Walker

CREATURE COMMANDOS — DC

1 ❑ May 2000 Cover: 2.50 **NM** value: **Cover or less**
Circ: Diamd. preorders: **15,541**
📖 A Spear of Silence **A:** Scot Eaton **W:** Timothy Truman
2 ❑ Jun 2000 Cover: 2.50 **NM** value: **Cover or less**
Circ: Diamd. preorders: **12,340**
📖 From Here to Heaven is a Scar **A:** Scot Eaton **W:** Timothy Truman
3 ❑ Jul 2000 Cover: 2.50 **NM** value: **Cover or less**
Circ: Diamd. preorders: **11,213**
A: Scot Eaton **W:** Timothy Truman
4 ❑ Aug 2000 Cover: 2.50 **NM** value: **Cover or less**
Circ: Diamd. preorders: **10,335**
A: Scot Eaton **W:** Timothy Truman
5 ❑ Sep 2000 Cover: 2.50 **NM** value: **Cover or less**
Circ: Diamd. preorders: **9,629**
A: Scot Eaton **W:** Timothy Truman
6 ❑ Oct 2000 Cover: 2.50 **NM** value: **Cover or less**
Circ: Diamd. preorders: **8,584**
📖 The Last Wall of the Castle **A:** Scot Eaton **W:** Timothy Truman
7 ❑ Nov 2000 Cover: 2.50 **NM** value: **Cover or less**
Circ: Diamd. preorders: **8,215**
📖 The Other Side of this Life **A:** Scot Eaton **W:** Timothy Truman
8 ❑ Dec 2000 Cover: 2.50 **NM** value: **Cover or less**
Circ: Diamd. preorders: **8,198**
📖 War Movie **A:** Scot Eaton **W:** Timothy Truman

CREATURE FEATURES — Mojo

1 ❑ b&w Cover: 4.95 **NM** value: **Cover or less**
• prestige format one-shot

CREATURE FEATURES (ART ADAMS'...) — Dark Horse

1 ❑ Aug 1996 Cover: 13.95 **NM** value: **Cover or less**
No issue number. • Trade Paperback. **A:** Arthur Adams **W:** Arthur Adams

CREATURES OF THE ID — Caliber

1 ❑ Jan 1990, b&w Cover: 2.95 **NM** value: **15.00**
• **CGC:** 2 graded, best 9.2
A: Bernie Mireault; Mike Allred; Bernie Mierault; Jeffrey Lang **W:** Bernie Mireault; Mike Allred; Jeffrey Lang ★ 1st Appearance of Madman (Frank Einstein).

CREATURES ON THE LOOSE — Marvel

Beginning with issue #10, the series, "Tower of Shadows" became "Creatures on the Loose," trading in its stock of science-fiction/horror stories for sword and sorcery. Its first issue brought us a new character, King Kull featuring the art of Bernie Wrightson. Kull, a barbarian warrior from the lost continent of Atlantis, was very popular and later appeared in a number of series bearing his name.

Back at Creatures on the Loose, the sword and sorcery storylines continued. Issue #16 introduced us to Gullivar Jones, Warrior of Mars. In an action-filled storyline based very loosely on Edward L. Arnold's Lieut. Gulliver Jones: His Vacation (1905) and reminiscent of Edgar Rice Burroughs, Gullivar fought a host of otherworldly menaces, saving alien women from the jaws of certain death.

Later experiments at COTL included Thongor, and lastly, Man-wolf. Unfortunately, neither of these caught on, and Creatures on the Loose ceased with issue #37.

10 ❑ Mar 1971 Cover: 0.15 **NM** value: **15.00**
• **CGC:** 7 graded, best 9.6
📖 The Skull of Silence; Trull! The Inhuman! • Title changes to Creatures on the Loose;first King Kull story;Series continued from Tower of Shadows #9; "Trull" reprints story from Tales to Astonish #21 **A:** Bernie Wrightson; Jack Kirby; Dick Ayers **W:** Roy Thomas; Stan Lee
11 ❑ May 1971 Cover: 0.15 **NM** value: **3.00**
📖 The Unbelievable Menace of Moomba • reprints story from Tales to Astonish #23
12 ❑ Jul 1971 Cover: 0.15 **NM** value: **3.00**
📖 I Was Captured By Korilla • reprints story from Journey into Mystery #69
13 ❑ Sep 1971 Cover: 0.15 **NM** value: **3.00**
📖 I Was Captured By the Creature from Krogarr; Midnight on Haunted Hill • reprints stories from Tales to Astonish #25 & #28
14 ❑ Nov 1971 Cover: 0.20 **NM** value: **3.00**
📖 What Happened in Dead Storage? • reprints story from Tales to Astonish #33
15 ❑ Jan 1972 Cover: 0.20 **NM** value: **3.00**
📖 Spragg, Conqueror of the Human Race
16 ❑ Mar 1972 Cover: 0.20 **NM** value: **3.00**
📖 Warrior of Mars; The Impossible Tunnel; The Frightened Man **A:** Gil Kane **W:** Roy Thomas ★ Origin of Gullivar Jones, Warrior of Mars.
17 ❑ May 1972 Cover: 0.20 **NM** value: **3.00**
📖 River Of The Dead! **A:** Gil Kane **W:** Roy Thomas ★ Appearance of Gullivar Jones, Warrior of Mars.
18 ❑ Jul 1972 Cover: 0.20 **NM** value: **3.00**
📖 Wasteland...On A Weirdling World! **A:** Ross Andru; Sam Grainger **W:** George Effinger; Gerry Conway ★ Appearance of Gullivar Jones, Warrior of Mars.
19 ❑ Sep 1972 Cover: 0.20 **NM** value: **3.00**
📖 The Long Road to Nowhere! **A:** Jim Mooney; Wayne Boring **W:** George Alex Effinger ★ Appearance of Gullivar Jones, Warrior of Mars.
20 ❑ Nov 1972 Cover: 0.20 **NM** value: **4.00**
📖 What Price Victory? **A:** Gray Morrow **W:** George Alec Effinger ★ Appearance of Gullivar Jones, Warrior of Mars.
21 ❑ Jan 1973 Cover: 0.20 **NM** value: **4.00**
📖 Two Worlds to Win **A:** Jim Steranko(cover) ★ Appearance of Gullivar Jones, Warrior of Mars.
22 ❑ Mar 1973 Cover: 0.20 **NM** value: **3.00**
• **CGC:** 2 graded, best 8.5
📖 Thongor, Warrior of Lost Lemuria ★ Appearance of Thongor.
23 ❑ May 1973 Cover: 0.20 **NM** value: **3.00**
📖 Where Broods the Demon! **A:** Val Mayerik **W:** George Effinger ★ Appearance of Thongor.
24 ❑ Jul 1973 Cover: 0.20 **NM** value: **3.00**
📖 Red Swords, Black Wings! **A:** Val Mayerik **W:** George Alec Effinger; Lin Carter ★ Appearance of Thongor.
25 ❑ Sep 1973 Cover: 0.20 **NM** value: **3.00**
📖 The Wizard of Lemuria! **A:** Val Mayerik **W:** George Alec Effinger; Lin Carter; Tony Isabella ★ Appearance of Thongor.
26 ❑ Nov 1973 Cover: 0.20 **NM** value: **3.00**
📖 Tower of the Serpent Women! **A:** Val Mayerik **W:** Gardner F. Fox ★ Appearance of Thongor.
27 ❑ Jan 1974 Cover: 0.20 **NM** value: **3.00**
📖 In the Crypts of Yamath! **A:** Val Mayerik **W:** Gardner F. Fox ★ Appearance of Thongor.
28 ❑ Mar 1974 Cover: 0.20 **NM** value: **3.00**
📖 Mountain Thunder! **A:** Vincente Alcazar **W:** Steve Gerber ★ Appearance of Thongor.
29 ❑ May 1974 Cover: 0.25 **NM** value: **3.00**
📖 Lord of Chaos! **A:** Vincente Alcazar **W:** Steve Gerber ★ Appearance of Thongor.
30 ❑ Jul 1974 Cover: 0.25 **NM** value: **3.00**
• **CGC:** 1 graded, best 9.4
📖 Full Moon, Dark Fear ★ Appearance of Man-Wolf.
31 ❑ Sep 1974 Cover: 0.25 **NM** value: **3.00**
📖 The Beast Within! **A:** George Tuska **W:** Doug Moench ★ Appearance of Man-Wolf.
32 ❑ Nov 1974 Cover: 0.25 **NM** value: **3.00**
📖 Moon of the Hunter ★ Appearance of Man-Wolf.
33 ❑ Jan 1975 Cover: 0.25 **NM** value: **3.00**
• **CGC:** 1 graded, best 9.2
📖 Deathgame ★ Appearance of Man-Wolf.
34 ❑ Mar 1975 Cover: 0.25 **NM** value: **3.00**
📖 Night Flight ★ Appearance of Man-Wolf.
35 ❑ May 1975 Cover: 0.25 **NM** value: **3.00**
📖 Wolfquest ★ Appearance of Man-Wolf.
36 ❑ Jul 1975 Cover: 0.25 **NM** value: **3.00**
📖 Weirdstone ★ Appearance of Man-Wolf.
37 ❑ Sep 1975 Cover: 0.25 **NM** value: **3.00**
📖 Moonbound ★ Appearance of Man-Wolf.
KS 1❑ **NM** value: **5.00**
• King-size special.

CREECH, THE — Image

1 ❑ Oct 1997 Cover: 1.95 **NM** value: **Cover or less**
Circ: Diamd. preorders: **94,015**
📖 A Vision of Death **A:** Greg Capullo **W:** Greg Capullo ★ Origin of Creech.
1/A ❑ Oct 1997 Cover: 1.95 **NM** value: **Cover or less**
alternate cover.
2 ❑ Nov 1997 Cover: 2.50 **NM** value: **Cover or less**
Circ: Diamd. preorders: **60,844**
📖 Awakening **A:** Greg Capullo **W:** Greg Capullo
3 ❑ Dec 1997 Cover: 2.50 **NM** value: **Cover or less**
Circ: Diamd. preorders: **51,649**
📖 The Resurrection **A:** Greg Capullo **W:** Greg Capullo
Bk 1❑ Cover: 9.95 **NM** value: **Cover or less**
A: Greg Capullo **W:** Greg Capullo

CREED (1ST SERIES) — Hall of Heroes

1 ❑ **NM** value: **5.00**
• **CGC:** 2 graded, best 9.2
A: Trent Kaniuga **W:** Trent Kaniuga
2 ❑ Dec 1994 **NM** value: **4.00**
• **CGC:** 2 graded, best 9.8
📖 Heaven Seed **A:** Trent Kaniuga **W:** Trent Kaniuga
Bk 1❑ May 1997 Cover: 5.95 **NM** value: **Cover or less**
• The Void;collects first CreeD series **A:** Trent Kaniuga **W:** Trent Kaniuga
Bk 1/LE❑May 1997 Cover: 9.95 **NM** value: **Cover or less**
• limited edition. • The Void;collects first CreeD series **A:** Trent Kaniuga **W:** Trent Kaniuga

CGC-graded: Multiply prices above by **33 for 9.9 M • 16 for 9.8 NM/M • 7 for 9.6 NM+ • 5 for 9.4 NM • 2.5 for 9.2 NM- • 1.5 for 9.0 VF/NM**

CREED (2ND SERIES) — Lightning

1 ❑ Sep 1995, b&w Cover: 3.00 **NM** value: **Cover or less**
Circ: CapCity orders: **2,920**
• reprints Hall of Heroes #1 and #2 with corrections;Black and white **A:** Trent Kaniuga **W:** Trent Kaniuga
1/A ❑ Sep 1995, full color **NM** value: **2.75**
A: Trent Kaniuga **W:** Trent Kaniuga
1/B ❑ Sep 1995 **NM** value: **2.75**
• Purple edition. **A:** Trent Kaniuga **W:** Trent Kaniuga
1/PL❑ Sep 1995 Cover: 3.00 **NM** value: **4.00**
enhanced cover. • Collector's edition. **A:** Trent Kaniuga **W:** Trent Kaniuga
2 ❑ Jan 1996 Cover: 3.00 **NM** value: **Cover or less**
A: Trent Kaniuga **W:** Trent Kaniuga
2/PL❑ Jan 1996 Cover: 3.00 **NM** value: **9.95**
alternate cover. • Platinum edition. **A:** Trent Kaniuga **W:** Trent Kaniuga
3 ❑ Jul 1996 Cover: 3.00 **NM** value: **Cover or less**
• bagged with trading card **A:** Trent Kaniuga **W:** Trent Kaniuga
3/PL❑ Cover: 3.00 **NM** value: **Cover or less**
• Platinum edition.

CREED: CRANIAL DISORDER — Lightning

1 ❑ Nov 1996 Cover: 3.00 **NM** value: **Cover or less**
Circ: Direct Market orders: **6,513**
2 ❑ Nov 1996 Cover: 3.00 **NM** value: **Cover or less**
Circ: Direct Market orders: **4,642**
alternate cover, cover says Dec, indicia says Nov.
3 ❑ Apr 1997 Cover: 2.95 **NM** value: **3.00**
Circ: Diamd. preorders: **4,552**
alternate cover.

CREED: MECHANICAL EVOLUTION — Gearbox

1 ❑ Sep 2000 Cover: 2.95 **NM** value: **Cover or less**
Circ: Diamd. preorders: **2,404**
A: Trent Kaniuga **W:** Trent Kaniuga

CREED/TEENAGE MUTANT NINJA TURTLES — Lightning

1 ❑ May 1996 Cover: 3.00 **NM** value: **Cover or less**
📖 Dream Stone **A:** Trent Kaniuga **W:** Trent Kaniuga

CREED: THE GOOD SHIP AND THE NEW JOURNEY HOME — Lightning

1 ❑ Jul 1997, b&w Cover: 2.95 **NM** value: **Cover or less**
Circ: Diamd. preorders: **4,490**

CREED USE YOUR DELUSION — Avatar

1 ❑ Jan 1998 Cover: 3.00 **NM** value: **Cover or less**
Circ: Diamd. preorders: **4,072**
A: Trent Kaniuga **W:** Trent Kaniuga
2 ❑ Feb 1998 Cover: 3.00 **NM** value: **Cover or less**
Circ: Diamd. preorders: **3,399**
A: Trent Kaniuga **W:** Trent Kaniuga

CREEPER, THE — DC

1 ❑ Dec 1997 Cover: 2.50 **NM** value: **Cover or less**
Circ: Diamd. preorders: **29,357**
📖 Screaming to Get Out **A:** Shawn Martinbrough **W:** Len Kaminski
2 ❑ Jan 1998 Cover: 2.50 **NM** value: **Cover or less**
Circ: Diamd. preorders: **20,830**
A: Shawn Martinbrough **W:** Len Kaminski
3 ❑ Feb 1998 Cover: 2.50 **NM** value: **Cover or less**
Circ: Diamd. preorders: **17,481**
A: Shawn Martinbrough **W:** Len Kaminski
4 ❑ Mar 1998 Cover: 2.50 **NM** value: **Cover or less**
Circ: Diamd. preorders: **14,363**
A: Shawn Martinbrough **W:** Len Kaminski
5 ❑ Apr 1998 Cover: 2.50 **NM** value: **Cover or less**
Circ: Diamd. preorders: **11,847**
A: Shawn Martinbrough **W:** Len Kaminski
6 ❑ May 1998 Cover: 2.50 **NM** value: **Cover or less**
Circ: Diamd. preorders: **10,999**
A: Shawn Martinbrough **W:** Len Kaminski
7 ❑ Jun 1998 Cover: 2.50 **NM** value: **Cover or less**
Circ: Diamd. preorders: **11,496**
A: Shawn Martinbrough **W:** Len Kaminski ★ Versus Joker.
8 ❑ Jul 1998 Cover: 2.50 **NM** value: **Cover or less**
Circ: Diamd. preorders: **10,816**
A: Shawn Martinbrough **W:** Len Kaminski ★ Appearance of Batman.
9 ❑ Aug 1998 Cover: 2.50 **NM** value: **Cover or less**
Circ: Diamd. preorders: **9,188**
A: Shawn Martinbrough **W:** Len Kaminski
10 ❑ Sep 1998 Cover: 2.50 **NM** value: **Cover or less**
Circ: Diamd. preorders: **8,569**
A: Shawn Martinbrough **W:** Len Kaminski
11 ❑ Oct 1998 Cover: 2.50 **NM** value: **Cover or less**
Circ: Diamd. preorders: **7,944**
A: Shawn Martinbrough **W:** Len Kaminski
1000000❑ Nov 1998 Cover: 2.50 **NM** value: **Cover or less**
Circ: Diamd. preorders: **15,803**
📖 Insanitation final issue. **A:** Shawn Martinbrough **W:** Len Kaminski

CREEPSVILLE — Go-Go

1 ❑ b&w Cover: 2.95 **NM** value: **Cover or less**
📖 Creepsville; Invasion of the Martianmen • trading cards **A:** Frank Kurtz **W:** Frank Kurtz
2 ❑ b&w Cover: 2.95 **NM** value: **Cover or less**
• trading cards
3 ❑ Cover: 2.25 **NM** value: **2.95**
4 ❑ Cover: 2.25 **NM** value: **2.95**
5 ❑ Cover: 2.25 **NM** value: **2.95**

CREEPY (MAGAZINE) — Warren

When the Comics Code brought down E.C. comics in the mid-1950s, fans of horror comics faced the prospect of substandard, watered-down fare instead of a steady diet of well-illustrated gore. James Warren answered their prayers in 1965 with Creepy, a black-and-white magazine (so not subject to the Code). It offered chilling tales in the E.C. tradition, told by such master artists and writers from the classic days as Frank Frazetta, Wally Wood, Reed Crandall, Al Williamson, and John Severin, plus Alex Toth, Neal Adams, and Bernie Wrightson.

Creepy was an anthology title, with four or five stories per issue "narrated" by the ghoulish "Uncle Creepy." Editor Archie Goodwin made Creepy and its companion, Eerie, a showcase of storytelling talent through the first several years. After Goodwin's departure, Creepy slipped a bit but continued to be an unusual and influential publication into the 1980s.

1 ❑ 1964 Cover: 0.35 **NM** value: **60.00**
2 ❑ 1965 Cover: 0.35 **NM** value: **35.00**
3 ❑ 1965 Cover: 0.35 **NM** value: **18.00**
4 ❑ 1965 Cover: 0.35 **NM** value: **15.00**
5 ❑ Oct 1965 Cover: 0.35 **NM** value: **15.00**
6 ❑ Dec 1965 Cover: 0.35 **NM** value: **12.00**
7 ❑ Feb 1966 Cover: 0.35 **NM** value: **12.00**
8 ❑ Apr 1966 Cover: 0.35 **NM** value: **12.00**
9 ❑ Jun 1966 Cover: 0.35 **NM** value: **18.00**
• 1st published work by Bernie Wrightson **A:** Bernie Wrightson
10 ❑ Aug 1966 Cover: 0.35 **NM** value: **12.00**
11 ❑ Oct 1967 Cover: 0.35 **NM** value: **10.00**
12 ❑ Dec 1967 Cover: 0.35 **NM** value: **10.00**
13 ❑ Feb 1967 Cover: 0.35 **NM** value: **10.00**
14 ❑ Apr 1967 Cover: 0.35 **NM** value: **12.00**
A: Neal Adams
15 ❑ Jun 1967 Cover: 0.40 **NM** value: **9.00**
A: Frank Frazetta(cover)
16 ❑ Aug 1967 Cover: 0.40 **NM** value: **9.00**
A: Frank Frazetta(cover)
17 ❑ Oct 1967 Cover: 0.40 **NM** value: **9.00**
18 ❑ Dec 1967 Cover: 0.40 **NM** value: **9.00**
19 ❑ Feb 1968 Cover: 0.40 **NM** value: **9.00**
20 ❑ Apr 1968 Cover: 0.40 **NM** value: **9.00**
21 ❑ Jun 1968 Cover: 0.40 **NM** value: **7.00**
22 ❑ Aug 1968 Cover: 0.40 **NM** value: **7.00**
23 ❑ Oct 1968 Cover: 0.40 **NM** value: **7.00**
24 ❑ Dec 1969 Cover: 0.40 **NM** value: **7.00**
25 ❑ Feb 1969 Cover: 0.40 **NM** value: **7.00**
26 ❑ Apr 1969 Cover: 0.40 **NM** value: **7.00**
27 ❑ Jun 1969 **NM** value: **7.00**
28 ❑ Aug 1969 Cover: 0.50 **NM** value: **7.00**
29 ❑ Oct 1969 Cover: 0.50 **NM** value: **7.00**
30 ❑ Dec 1969 Cover: 0.50 **NM** value: **7.00**
31 ❑ Feb 1970 Cover: 0.50 **NM** value: **7.00**
32 ❑ Apr 1970 Cover: 0.50 **NM** value: **7.00**
33 ❑ Jun 1970 Cover: 0.50 **NM** value: **7.00**
34 ❑ Aug 1970 Cover: 0.60 **NM** value: **7.00**
35 ❑ Sep 1970 Cover: 0.60 **NM** value: **7.00**
36 ❑ Nov 1970 Cover: 0.60 **NM** value: **7.00**
37 ❑ Jan 1971 Cover: 0.60 **NM** value: **7.00**
38 ❑ Mar 1971 Cover: 0.60 **NM** value: **7.00**
39 ❑ May 1971 Cover: 0.60 **NM** value: **7.00**
40 ❑ Jul 1971 Cover: 0.60 **NM** value: **7.00**
41 ❑ Sep 1971 Cover: 0.60 **NM** value: **6.00**
42 ❑ Nov 1971 Cover: 0.60 **NM** value: **6.00**
43 ❑ Jan 1972 Cover: 0.75 **NM** value: **6.00**
44 ❑ Mar 1972 Cover: 0.75 **NM** value: **6.00**
45 ❑ Feb 1973 Cover: 0.75 **NM** value: **6.00**
46 ❑ 1972 **NM** value: **6.00**
47 ❑ 1972 **NM** value: **6.00**
48 ❑ Oct 1972 Cover: 1.00 **NM** value: **9.00**
• 1973 annual
49 ❑ Nov 1972 Cover: 0.75 **NM** value: **6.00**
50 ❑ 1973 **NM** value: **6.00**
51 ❑ Mar 1973 Cover: 1.00 **NM** value: **6.00**
52 ❑ 1973 **NM** value: **6.00**
53 ❑ 1973 **NM** value: **6.00**
54 ❑ 1973 **NM** value: **6.00**
55 ❑ 1973 **NM** value: **9.00**
• 1974 annual
56 ❑ Sep 1973 Cover: 1.00 **NM** value: **5.00**
57 ❑ Nov 1973 Cover: 0.75 **NM** value: **5.00**
58 ❑ Dec 1973 Cover: 0.75 **NM** value: **5.00**
59 ❑ Jan 1974 Cover: 1.00 **NM** value: **5.00**
Circ: Statement: **96,085**
60 ❑ Feb 1974 Cover: 1.00 **NM** value: **5.00**
Circ: Statement: **96,085**
61 ❑ Apr 1974 Cover: 1.00 **NM** value: **5.00**
Circ: Statement: **96,085**
62 ❑ May 1974 Cover: 1.00 **NM** value: **5.00**
Circ: Statement: **96,085**
63 ❑ Jul 1974 Cover: 1.00 **NM** value: **5.00**
Circ: Statement: **96,085**
64 ❑ Aug 1974 Cover: 1.25 **NM** value: **5.00**
Circ: Statement: **96,085**
65 ❑ Sep 1974 Cover: 1.25 **NM** value: **8.00**
Circ: Statement: **96,085**
• 1975 annual
66 ❑ Nov 1974 Cover: 1.00 **NM** value: **5.00**
Circ: Statement: **96,085**
67 ❑ Dec 1974 Cover: 1.00 **NM** value: **5.00**
Circ: Statement: **96,085**
68 ❑ Jan 1975 Cover: 1.25 **NM** value: **5.00**
Circ: Statement: **97,450**
69 ❑ Feb 1975 Cover: 1.00 **NM** value: **5.00**
Circ: Statement: **97,450**
70 ❑ Apr 1975 Cover: 1.00 **NM** value: **5.00**
Circ: Statement: **97,450**
• Has 1974 Statement; avg total paid circ 96,085
71 ❑ May 1975 Cover: 1.00 **NM** value: **5.00**
Circ: Statement: **97,450**
72 ❑ Jul 1975 Cover: 1.00 **NM** value: **5.00**
Circ: Statement: **97,450**
73 ❑ Aug 1975 Cover: 1.25 **NM** value: **5.00**
Circ: Statement: **97,450**
74 ❑ Oct 1975 Cover: 1.25 **NM** value: **5.00**
Circ: Statement: **97,450**
75 ❑ Nov 1975 Cover: 1.00 **NM** value: **5.00**
Circ: Statement: **97,450**
76 ❑ Jan 1976 Cover: 1.00 **NM** value: **5.00**
Circ: Statement: **85,985**
77 ❑ Feb 1976 Cover: 1.25 **NM** value: **5.00**
Circ: Statement: **85,985**
• Has 1975 Statement, filed 10/1/75; avg print run 176,240; avg sales 96,930; avg subs 520; avg total paid 97,450; samples 90; office use 43452; max existent 140,992; 20% of run returned **A:** Sanjulian(cover)
78 ❑ Mar 1976 Cover: 1.00 **NM** value: **5.00**
Circ: Statement: **85,985**
79 ❑ May 1976 Cover: 1.00 **NM** value: **5.00**
Circ: Statement: **85,985**
📖 As Ye Sow; Kui; The Super-Abnormal Phenomena Survival Kit; The Shadow of the Axe; Pliny Marsh; The Pit in the Floor • Has Dave Sim, Russ Heath story **A:** Alex Toth; Bernie Wrightson; John Severin; Russ Heath; Luis Bermejo; Martin Salvador; Sanjulian(cover) **W:** Dave Sim; Alex Toth; Bruce Jones; Gerry Boudreau; Jim Stenstrum
80 ❑ Jun 1976 Cover: 1.00 **NM** value: **5.00**
Circ: Statement: **85,985**
81 ❑ Jul 1976 Cover: 1.00 **NM** value: **5.00**
Circ: Statement: **85,985**
82 ❑ Aug 1976 Cover: 1.25 **NM** value: **5.00**
Circ: Statement: **85,985**
83 ❑ Oct 1976 Cover: 1.50 **NM** value: **5.00**
Circ: Statement: **85,985**
84 ❑ Nov 1977 Cover: 1.25 **NM** value: **5.00**
Circ: Statement: **85,985**
85 ❑ Jan 1977 Cover: 1.25 **NM** value: **5.00**
Circ: Statement: **92,565**
86 ❑ Feb 1977 Cover: 1.25 **NM** value: **5.00**
Circ: Statement: **92,565**
• Has 1976 Statement, filed 10/1/76; avg print run 155,400; avg sales 85,470; avg subs 515; avg total paid 85,985; samples 75; office use 38,260; max existent 124,320; 20% of run returned
87 ❑ Mar 1977 Cover: 1.50 **NM** value: **5.00**
Circ: Statement: **92,565**
88 ❑ May 1977 Cover: 1.25 **NM** value: **5.00**
Circ: Statement: **92,565**
89 ❑ Jun 1977 Cover: 1.50 **NM** value: **5.00**
Circ: Statement: **92,565**
90 ❑ Jul 1977 Cover: 1.25 **NM** value: **5.00**
Circ: Statement: **92,565**
91 ❑ Aug 1977 Cover: 1.50 **NM** value: **5.00**
Circ: Statement: **92,565**
📖 The Shadow of the Axe (reprinted from #79)
92 ❑ Oct 1977 Cover: 2.00 **NM** value: **5.00**
Circ: Statement: **92,565**
93 ❑ Nov 1977 Cover: 1.50 **NM** value: **5.00**
Circ: Statement: **92,565**
94 ❑ Jan 1978 Cover: 1.25 **NM** value: **5.00**
95 ❑ Feb 1978 Cover: 1.50 **NM** value: **5.00**
• Has 1977 Statement, filed 11/30/77; avg print run 167,400; avg sales 92,100; avg subs 465; avg total paid 92,565; samples 85; office use 41,270; max existent 133,920; 20% of run returned
96 ❑ Mar 1978 Cover: 1.25 **NM** value: **5.00**
97 ❑ May 1978 Cover: 1.50 **NM** value: **5.00**
98 ❑ Jun 1978 Cover: 1.25 **NM** value: **5.00**
99 ❑ Jul 1978 Cover: 1.25 **NM** value: **5.00**
100 ❑ Aug 1978 Cover: 2.00 **NM** value: **5.00**
101 ❑ Sep 1978 Cover: 1.50 **NM** value: **4.00**
102 ❑ Oct 1978 Cover: 1.75 **NM** value: **4.00**
103 ❑ Nov 1978 Cover: 1.25 **NM** value: **4.00**
104 ❑ Jan 1979 Cover: 1.25 **NM** value: **4.00**
105 ❑ Feb 1979 Cover: 1.50 **NM** value: **4.00**
106 ❑ Mar 1979 Cover: 1.50 **NM** value: **4.00**
107 ❑ May 1979 Cover: 1.50 **NM** value: **4.00**
108 ❑ Jun 1979 Cover: 1.50 **NM** value: **4.00**
109 ❑ Jul 1979 Cover: 1.50 **NM** value: **4.00**
110 ❑ Aug 1979 Cover: 1.75 **NM** value: **4.00**
111 ❑ Sep 1979 Cover: 1.75 **NM** value: **4.00**
112 ❑ Oct 1979 Cover: 2.00 **NM** value: **4.00**
113 ❑ Nov 1979 Cover: 1.50 **NM** value: **4.00**
114 ❑ Jan 1980 Cover: 1.50 **NM** value: **4.00**
115 ❑ Feb 1980 Cover: 1.75 **NM** value: **4.00**
116 ❑ Mar 1980 Cover: 1.75 **NM** value: **4.00**
117 ❑ May 1980 Cover: 1.75 **NM** value: **4.00**
118 ❑ Jun 1980 Cover: 1.75 **NM** value: **4.00**
119 ❑ Jul 1980 Cover: 1.75 **NM** value: **4.00**
120 ❑ Aug 1980 Cover: 1.75 **NM** value: **4.00**
121 ❑ Sep 1980 Cover: 1.75 **NM** value: **4.00**
122 ❑ Oct 1980 Cover: 1.75 **NM** value: **4.00**
123 ❑ Nov 1980 Cover: 1.75 **NM** value: **4.00**
124 ❑ Jan 1981 Cover: 1.75 **NM** value: **4.00**
125 ❑ Feb 1981 Cover: 1.95 **NM** value: **4.00**
126 ❑ Mar 1981 Cover: 2.00 **NM** value: **4.00**
127 ❑ May 1981 Cover: 2.00 **NM** value: **4.00**
128 ❑ Jun 1981 Cover: 2.00 **NM** value: **4.00**
129 ❑ Jul 1981 Cover: 2.00 **NM** value: **4.00**
130 ❑ Aug 1981 Cover: 2.00 **NM** value: **4.00**
131 ❑ Sep 1981 Cover: 2.00 **NM** value: **4.00**
132 ❑ Oct 1981 Cover: 2.00 **NM** value: **4.00**

133 ❑ Nov 1981 Cover: 2.00 **NM** value: **4.00**
134 ❑ Jan 1982 Cover: 2.00 **NM** value: **4.00**
135 ❑ Feb 1982 Cover: 2.00 **NM** value: **4.00**
136 ❑ Mar 1982 Cover: 2.00 **NM** value: **4.00**
137 ❑ May 1982 Cover: 2.00 **NM** value: **4.00**
138 ❑ Jun 1982 Cover: 2.00 **NM** value: **4.00**
139 ❑ Jul 1982 Cover: 2.25 **NM** value: **4.00**
140 ❑ Aug 1982 Cover: 2.25 **NM** value: **4.00**
141 ❑ Sep 1982 Cover: 2.25 **NM** value: **4.00**
142 ❑ Oct 1982 Cover: 2.50 **NM** value: **4.00**
143 ❑ Nov 1982 Cover: 2.25 **NM** value: **4.00**
144 ❑ Jan 1983 Cover: 2.25 **NM** value: **6.00**
• Giant-size. **A:** Frank Frazetta(cover)
145 ❑ Feb 1983 Cover: 2.25 **NM** value: **4.00**
146 ❑ ca. 1985 Cover: 2.95 **NM** value: **6.00**
• Giant-size. final issue.
Anl 1971 ❑ ca. 1971 **NM** value: **7.00**
• 1971 Yearbook.
Anl 1972 ❑ ca. 1972 **NM** value: **7.00**
• 1972 Yearbook.
YB 1968 ❑ ca. 1968 **NM** value: **10.00**
• 1968 Yearbook.
YB 1969 ❑ ca. 1969 Cover: 2.95 **NM** value: **10.00**
• 1969 Yearbook.
YB 1970 ❑ ca. 1970 Cover: 2.95 **NM** value: **10.00**
• 1970 Yearbook.

CREEPY TALES — Pinnacle

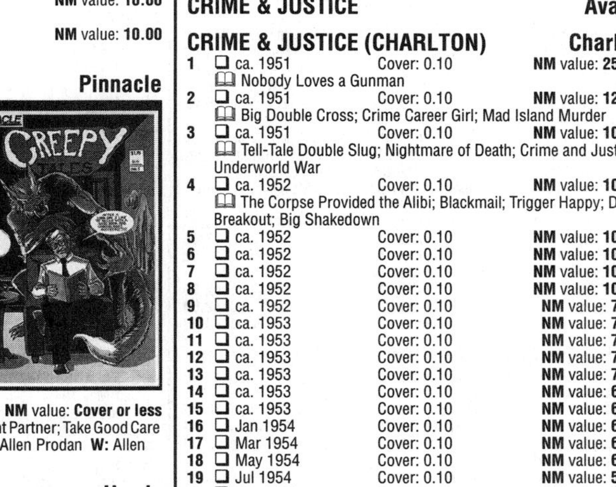

Certainly not as creepy as such predecessors as Tales from the Crypt, Creepy, Eerie, or even The House of Mystery, Creepy Tales delivers in-your-face stories "that portray unusual events," but they lack the subtle nuances and the beautiful art of its earlier inspirations.

Without a doubt, the stories show promise, but their heavy-handed irony makes them simplistic, and the rough, sketchy art makes some of the storytelling hard to follow. Still, "promise" is the important concept in these independents; we need to see where the future of comics is coming from.

1 ❑ 1975 Cover: 1.75 **NM** value: **Cover or less**
📖 The Dinosaur Doctor; Hounded; …Silent Partner; Take Good Care of Kitty **A:** Seppo Makkinen; Alan Larsen; Allen Prodan **W:** Allen Prodan; James Mission; Martin Powell

CREEPY: THE CLASSIC YEARS — Harris

Bk 1 ❑ Cover: 12.95 **NM** value: **Cover or less**
• reprints Warren material

CREEPY: THE LIMITED SERIES — Dark Horse

1 ❑ ca. 1992, b&w Cover: 3.95 **NM** value: **4.00**
Circ: CapCity orders: **7,550**
• prestige format.
2 ❑ ca. 1992, b&w Cover: 3.95 **NM** value: **4.00**
Circ: CapCity orders: **4,250**
• prestige format. **W:** Kurt Busiek
3 ❑ ca. 1992, b&w Cover: 3.95 **NM** value: **4.00**
Circ: CapCity orders: **3,250**
• prestige format. 📖 The Cast Without a Program; Fair Ground; House Party; Do You Know the Beast Man? **A:** James W. Fry III; Jackson Guice; Jim Mooney; Mike Manley; Colleen Doran **W:** Richard Howell; Mary Jo Duffy; Peter David
4 ❑ ca. 1992, b&w Cover: 3.95 **NM** value: **4.00**
Circ: CapCity orders: **3,050**
• prestige format.
FB 1993 ❑ ca. 1993 Cover: 3.95 **NM** value: **12.00**
Circ: CapCity orders: **5,025**
• 1993 "Fearbook";Relaunch of Vampirella for '90s **W:** Kurt Busiek
★ Appearance of Vampirella.

CREEPY THINGS — Charlton

Comics with a supernatural theme enjoyed a surge in popularity in the 1960s and '70s. Attempting to cash in on this trend, Charlton Comics released Creepy Things. With its spooky parade of mutant frogs, practitioners of black magic, vampires, and other strange creatures, this title hoped to attract fans of what came to be called "mystery comics," since "horror comics" were discouraged by the Comics Code. Although the first issue did not have one, later issues had a recurring narrator who set the mood for each tale. This was a common theme for this sort of publication as seen in such other titles as House of Mystery and Tales from the Crypt.

1 ❑ Jul 1975 Cover: 0.25 **NM** value: **5.00**
📖 Read the Signs; The Lurker in the Pit; Indian Summer; The Well **A:** Dick Piscopa; F. Nieto **W:** Dick Piscopa; F. Nieto
2 ❑ Oct 1975 Cover: 0.25 **NM** value: **3.00**
📖 The Greatest Treasure; …A Spell of Misery; A Trap; Slimes Slogs and Glumps **A:** Mike Zeck; Rich Larson; F. Nieto **W:** Joe Gill; Nicola Cutii; Joe Molloy
3 ❑ Dec 1975 Cover: 0.25 **NM** value: **3.00**
4 ❑ Feb 1976 Cover: 0.25 **NM** value: **3.00**
5 ❑ Apr 1976 Cover: 0.25 **NM** value: **3.00**
6 ❑ Jun 1976 Cover: 0.25 **NM** value: **3.00**

CREMATOR — Chaos

1 ❑ Dec 1998 Cover: 2.95 **NM** value: **Cover or less**
Circ: Diamd. preorders: **17,994**
📖 Welcome to Hell! **A:** Leonardo Jimenez **W:** Leonardo Jimenez; Brian Pulido
2 ❑ Dec 1999 Cover: 2.95 **NM** value: **Cover or less**
Circ: Diamd. preorders: **13,683**
wraparound cover. **A:** Leonardo Jimenez **W:** Leonardo Jimenez; Brian Pulido
3 ❑ Jan 1999 Cover: 2.95 **NM** value: **Cover or less**
Circ: Diamd. preorders: **13,981**
A: Leonardo Jimenez **W:** Leonardo Jimenez; Brian Pulido
4 ❑ Feb 1999 Cover: 2.95 **NM** value: **Cover or less**
Circ: Diamd. preorders: **12,446**
A: Leonardo Jimenez **W:** Leonardo Jimenez; Brian Pulido
5 ❑ Apr 1999 Cover: 2.95 **NM** value: **Cover or less**
Circ: Diamd. preorders: **11,335**
A: Leonardo Jimenez **W:** Leonardo Jimenez; Brian Pulido

CRESCENT — B-Line

0 ❑ May 1996 **NM** value: **1.00**

CRIME & JUSTICE — Avalon

CRIME & JUSTICE (CHARLTON) — Charlton

1 ❑ ca. 1951 Cover: 0.10 **NM** value: **250.00**
📖 Nobody Loves a Gunman
2 ❑ ca. 1951 Cover: 0.10 **NM** value: **125.00**
📖 Big Double Cross; Crime Career Girl; Mad Island Murder
3 ❑ ca. 1951 Cover: 0.10 **NM** value: **100.00**
📖 Tell-Tale Double Slug; Nightmare of Death; Crime and Justice; Underworld War
4 ❑ ca. 1952 Cover: 0.10 **NM** value: **100.00**
📖 The Corpse Provided the Alibi; Blackmail; Trigger Happy; Death Breakout; Big Shakedown
5 ❑ ca. 1952 Cover: 0.10 **NM** value: **100.00**
6 ❑ ca. 1952 Cover: 0.10 **NM** value: **100.00**
7 ❑ ca. 1952 Cover: 0.10 **NM** value: **100.00**
8 ❑ ca. 1952 Cover: 0.10 **NM** value: **100.00**
9 ❑ ca. 1952 Cover: 0.10 **NM** value: **75.00**
10 ❑ ca. 1953 Cover: 0.10 **NM** value: **75.00**
11 ❑ ca. 1953 Cover: 0.10 **NM** value: **75.00**
12 ❑ ca. 1953 Cover: 0.10 **NM** value: **75.00**
13 ❑ ca. 1953 Cover: 0.10 **NM** value: **75.00**
14 ❑ ca. 1953 Cover: 0.10 **NM** value: **65.00**
15 ❑ ca. 1953 Cover: 0.10 **NM** value: **65.00**
16 ❑ Jan 1954 Cover: 0.10 **NM** value: **65.00**
17 ❑ Mar 1954 Cover: 0.10 **NM** value: **65.00**
18 ❑ May 1954 Cover: 0.10 **NM** value: **65.00**
19 ❑ Jul 1954 Cover: 0.10 **NM** value: **50.00**
20 ❑ Sep 1954 Cover: 0.10 **NM** value: **50.00**
• **CGC:** 5 graded, best 9.4
21 ❑ Nov 1954 Cover: 0.10 **NM** value: **50.00**
• **CGC:** 5 graded, best 8.5

CRIME AND PUNISHMENT — Lev Gleason

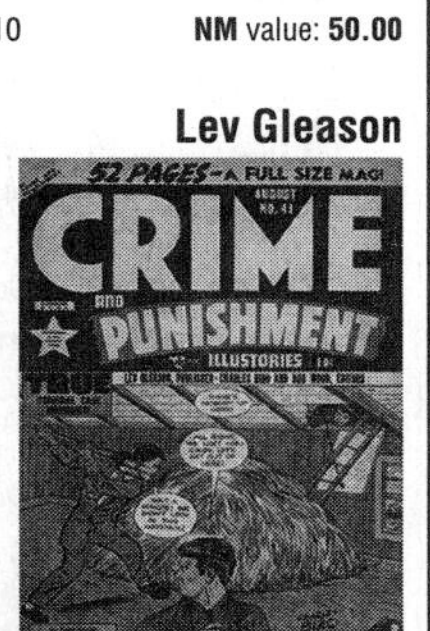

The crime comics of the late 1940s were the stage for intense, complex, and disturbing stories told in comic-book form. Possibly the greatest of all the crime comics publishers was Lev Gleason, who pioneered the genre with the groundbreaking Crime Does Not Pay and other titles, including Crime and Punishment.

Like their counterparts in film noir movies of the period, comic-book criminals rarely, if ever, escape ultimate punishment for their misdeeds. Nevertheless, the emphasis on their activities and personalities make the criminals into the focal point of many stories. Editor-artist Charles Biro had a real feel for the moral geography of the criminal classes, and his stories in Gleason's magazines had an authenticity and sociological rigor that others often lacked. The Comics Code obliterated much of the ambiguity (and drama) of crime comics and doomed the genre in the mid-1950s.

1 ❑ Apr 1948 Cover: 0.10 **NM** value: **150.00**
• **CGC:** 2 graded, best 8.0
2 ❑ May 1948 Cover: 0.10 **NM** value: **75.00**
3 ❑ Jun 1948 Cover: 0.10 **NM** value: **50.00**
• **CGC:** 1 graded, best 9.0
4 ❑ Jul 1948 Cover: 0.10 **NM** value: **50.00**
5 ❑ Aug 1948 Cover: 0.10 **NM** value: **50.00**
6 ❑ Sep 1948 Cover: 0.10 **NM** value: **45.00**
7 ❑ Oct 1948 Cover: 0.10 **NM** value: **45.00**
8 ❑ Nov 1948 Cover: 0.10 **NM** value: **45.00**
9 ❑ Dec 1948 Cover: 0.10 **NM** value: **45.00**
10 ❑ Jan 1949 Cover: 0.10 **NM** value: **45.00**
11 ❑ Feb 1949 Cover: 0.10 **NM** value: **38.00**
12 ❑ Mar 1949 Cover: 0.10 **NM** value: **38.00**
13 ❑ Apr 1949 Cover: 0.10 **NM** value: **38.00**
14 ❑ May 1949 Cover: 0.10 **NM** value: **38.00**
15 ❑ Jun 1949 Cover: 0.10 **NM** value: **38.00**
16 ❑ Jul 1949 Cover: 0.10 **NM** value: **38.00**
17 ❑ Aug 1949 Cover: 0.10 **NM** value: **38.00**
18 ❑ Sep 1949 Cover: 0.10 **NM** value: **38.00**
19 ❑ Oct 1949 Cover: 0.10 **NM** value: **38.00**
20 ❑ Nov 1949 Cover: 0.10 **NM** value: **38.00**
21 ❑ Dec 1949 Cover: 0.10 **NM** value: **34.00**
22 ❑ Jan 1950 Cover: 0.10 **NM** value: **34.00**
23 ❑ Feb 1950 Cover: 0.10 **NM** value: **34.00**
24 ❑ Mar 1950 Cover: 0.10 **NM** value: **34.00**
25 ❑ Apr 1950 Cover: 0.10 **NM** value: **34.00**
26 ❑ May 1950 Cover: 0.10 **NM** value: **34.00**
27 ❑ Jun 1950 Cover: 0.10 **NM** value: **34.00**
28 ❑ Jul 1950 Cover: 0.10 **NM** value: **34.00**
29 ❑ Aug 1950 Cover: 0.10 **NM** value: **34.00**
📖 Danton's Masks; He Walks in Terror; The Bodyguard
30 ❑ Sep 1950 Cover: 0.10 **NM** value: **34.00**
📖 The Sargeant's Story; Mob in Exile; The Suspect; Death Takes a Ride
31 ❑ Oct 1950 Cover: 0.10 **NM** value: **28.00**
📖 Belson's Ghost; When the Lights Went Out; Death Rides the 5:15
32 ❑ Nov 1950 Cover: 0.10 **NM** value: **28.00**
📖 Blind as a Bat; Don't Let Johnny Go; Death from the Fairway; Hotel Hood
33 ❑ Dec 1950 Cover: 0.10 **NM** value: **28.00**
📖 3 Frightened People; The Case of the Elusive Suspect; Detour to Death
34 ❑ Jan 1951 Cover: 0.10 **NM** value: **28.00**
35 ❑ Feb 1951 Cover: 0.10 **NM** value: **28.00**
📖 Trapped; The Black Bag; The Case of the Orange-Pickers' Payroll
36 ❑ Mar 1951 Cover: 0.10 **NM** value: **28.00**
37 ❑ Apr 1951 Cover: 0.10 **NM** value: **28.00**
38 ❑ May 1951 Cover: 0.10 **NM** value: **28.00**
📖 Scourge of the Bookies; Number 28 Motham Square; The Shake-down Murder Case
39 ❑ Jun 1951 Cover: 0.10 **NM** value: **55.00**
📖 Five Dopes; Murderers Circle; Coonan's Comeback; Death Goes to College • Drug story
40 ❑ Jul 1951 Cover: 0.10 **NM** value: **28.00**
41 ❑ Aug 1951 Cover: 0.10 **NM** value: **28.00**
📖 Mission: Gem 'Em!; Flight From Fury; The Cop From Hell's Kitchen; The Case of the Elusive Go-Between **A:** Al McWilliams; Alex Kotsky; Charles Biro(cover); Fred Guardineer
42 ❑ Sep 1951 Cover: 0.10 **NM** value: **28.00**
43 ❑ Oct 1951 Cover: 0.10 **NM** value: **28.00**
44 ❑ Nov 1951 Cover: 0.10 **NM** value: **28.00**
45 ❑ Dec 1951 Cover: 0.10 **NM** value: **55.00**
• Drug story
46 ❑ Jan 1952 Cover: 0.10 **NM** value: **28.00**
47 ❑ Feb 1952 Cover: 0.10 **NM** value: **28.00**
📖 Backfire!; Gangland's First Law; The Last Confession (text story); Insurance Dirt; A Triple Double Cross? **A:** Al McWilliams; Charles Biro(cover)
48 ❑ Mar 1952 Cover: 0.10 **NM** value: **28.00**
49 ❑ Apr 1952 Cover: 0.10 **NM** value: **28.00**
50 ❑ May 1952 Cover: 0.10 **NM** value: **28.00**
51 ❑ Jun 1952 Cover: 0.10 **NM** value: **28.00**
52 ❑ Jul 1952 Cover: 0.10 **NM** value: **28.00**
📖 Go-Between; Million Dollar Hoodlum?; The Hard Rock Boys (text story); The Big Send-Off; A Stoolie's Reward **A:** William Overgard
53 ❑ Aug 1952 Cover: 0.10 **NM** value: **28.00**
📖 The Blonde Who Couldn't Lose…But Did!; The Clover Snatch; The Big Haul (text story); Escape to Doom; Return From a Ride **A:** Dick Rockwell; Fred Guardineer
54 ❑ Sep 1952 Cover: 0.10 **NM** value: **28.00**
55 ❑ Oct 1952 Cover: 0.10 **NM** value: **28.00**
56 ❑ Nov 1952 Cover: 0.10 **NM** value: **28.00**
• **CGC:** 1 graded, best 5.5
57 ❑ Dec 1952 Cover: 0.10 **NM** value: **28.00**
58 ❑ Jan 1953 Cover: 0.10 **NM** value: **28.00**
59 ❑ Feb 1953 Cover: 0.10 **NM** value: **100.00**
• Cited in Seduction of the Innocent ("Comic Book Philosophy")
60 ❑ 1953 Cover: 0.10 **NM** value: **24.00**
61 ❑ 1953 Cover: 0.10 **NM** value: **24.00**
62 ❑ 1953 Cover: 0.10 **NM** value: **24.00**
63 ❑ 1953 Cover: 0.10 **NM** value: **24.00**
📖 Genna Brothers; Harry "The Artist" Hamilton; Lucky Lane
64 ❑ 1953 Cover: 0.10 **NM** value: **24.00**
65 ❑ Jan 1954 Cover: 0.10 **NM** value: **24.00**
66 ❑ Mar 1954 Cover: 0.10 **NM** value: **175.00**
• 3-D.
67 ❑ May 1954 Cover: 0.10 **NM** value: **135.00**
• **CGC:** 1 graded, best 7.5
• 3-D.
68 ❑ Jul 1954 Cover: 0.10 **NM** value: **135.00**
• 3-D.
69 ❑ Oct 1954 Cover: 0.10 **NM** value: **55.00**
• **CGC:** 1 graded, best 5.5
• Drug story
70 ❑ 1954 Cover: 0.10 **NM** value: **24.00**
71 ❑ 1955 Cover: 0.10 **NM** value: **24.00**
72 ❑ 1955 Cover: 0.10 **NM** value: **24.00**
73 ❑ 1955 Cover: 0.10 **NM** value: **24.00**
74 ❑ Aug 1955 Cover: 0.10 **NM** value: **24.00**
final issue.

CRIME AND PUNISHMENT MARSHAL LAW TAKES MANHATTAN — Marvel / Epic

1 ❑ Cover: 4.95 **NM** value: **Cover or less**
No issue number. One-shot. • prestige format. **A:** Kevin O'Neill **W:** Pat Mills

CRIMEBUSTER — AC

0 ❑ Cover: 2.95 **NM** value: **Cover or less**
📖 Back From The Dead-Again! **A:** Mark Heike; Brad Gorby; Bill Black; Christopher Allen; Eric Coile; Richard Rome **W:** Bill Black

The CGC numbers printed in individual listings above represent the **number of copies examined** and given a **Universal** grade by CGC and the **best such copy** graded at press time. For current populations, watch for special ***Comics Buyer's Guide*** issues or check **www.cgccomics.com.**

CGC-graded: Multiply prices above by **33 for 9.9 M** • **16 for 9.8 NM/M** • **7 for 9.6 NM+** • **5 for 9.4 NM** • **2.5 for 9.2 NM-** • **1.5 for 9.0 VF/NM**

CRIMEBUSTER (AVALON) — Avalon

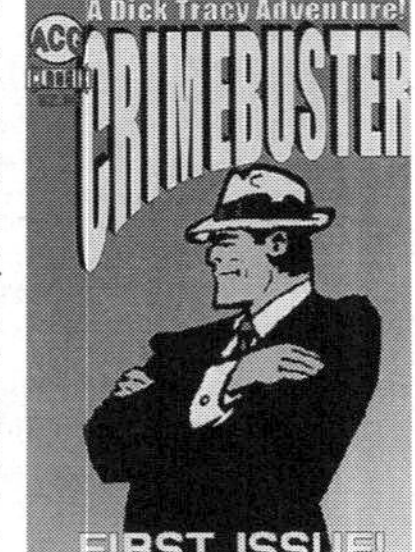

There's Chester Gould's classic rendition of his square-jawed, straight-laced, police detective Dick Tracy — and then there's the versions done by guys who just write and draw like him. These 1980s strips, by Dick Locher and Max Collins, manage to capture the action, drama, and humor of Gould's character without much difficulty. A typical adventure has the detective investigating a friend's financial investor, named (in classic Tracy style) Uppward Lee-Mobile, who claims he can provide a 40%return on an investment. Sounds great, but will the investor himself survive to collect? Fortunately the man in the snapbrim hat and trenchcoat is on the scene to investigate.

Avalon (with cover logo ACG), which reprints the Gould classics in another series, has collected and reprinted these daily strips in black-and-white. A variety of backup features are included.

1 ❑ Cover: 2.95 **NM** value: **Cover or less**
📖 The Saga of Uppward Lee-Mobile; Mr. Blanque **A:** Chester Gould **W:** Chester Gould

CRIMEBUSTER CLASSICS — AC

1 ❑ Cover: 3.50 **NM** value: **Cover or less**

CRIME CAN'T WIN — Marvel / Epic

1 ❑ Sep 1950 Cover: 0.10 **NM** value: **90.00**
#41 on cover (series numbering continued from Cindy Smith).
2 ❑ Dec 1950 Cover: 0.10 **NM** value: **70.00**
#42 on cover (series numbering continued from Cindy Smith). 📖 Sewer Rat!; The Man with Two Lives!; One Was Betrayed!; Escape!
3 ❑ Feb 1951 Cover: 0.10 **NM** value: **65.00**
#43 on cover (series numbering continued from Cindy Smith). 📖 The Criminal Who Reached for another World!; Slim Miller's Lucky Number!; Chicago's Strangest Murder; Horror in Gaul-1527!
4 ❑ Apr 1951 Cover: 0.10 **NM** value: **50.00**
📖 Too Many Crooks!; The Long Ride!; The Madman of Milan!; His Brother's Keeper!
5 ❑ Jun 1951 Cover: 0.10 **NM** value: **50.00**
📖 The Last Ride of George Kroll!; The Big Caper!; Phil Emery's Greed!; Meet the Octopus!
6 ❑ Aug 1951 Cover: 0.10 **NM** value: **50.00**
📖 The West Coast Terror!; Mission: Murder!; Behind Prison Bars!; The Confession!
7 ❑ Oct 1951 Cover: 0.10 **NM** value: **50.00**
8 ❑ Dec 1951 Cover: 0.10 **NM** value: **50.00**
9 ❑ Feb 1952 Cover: 0.10 **NM** value: **50.00**
10 ❑ Apr 1952 Cover: 0.10 **NM** value: **50.00**
📖 Dragnet!; Innocent Bystander!; The Gorilla Strikes!; The Hot-Car Racket!
11 ❑ Jun 1952 Cover: 0.10 **NM** value: **45.00**
12 ❑ Cover: 0.10 **NM** value: **45.00**
final issue.

CRIME CLASSICS — Eternity

1 ❑ Jul 1988 Cover: 1.95 **NM** value: **Cover or less**
📖 The Riddle of the Sealed Box • The Shadow **A:** Vernon Greene **W:** Maxwell Grant
2 ❑ Jul 1988 Cover: 1.95 **NM** value: **Cover or less**
• The Shadow **A:** Vernon Greene **W:** Maxwell Grant
3 ❑ Aug 1988 Cover: 1.95 **NM** value: **Cover or less**
• The Shadow **A:** Vernon Greene **W:** Maxwell Grant
4 ❑ Sep 1989 Cover: 1.95 **NM** value: **Cover or less**
• The Shadow **A:** Vernon Greene **W:** Maxwell Grant
5 ❑ Jan 1989 Cover: 1.95 **NM** value: **Cover or less**
• The Shadow **A:** Vernon Greene **W:** Maxwell Grant
6 ❑ Feb 1989 Cover: 1.95 **NM** value: **Cover or less**
• The Shadow **A:** Vernon Greene **W:** Maxwell Grant
7 ❑ Mar 1989 Cover: 1.95 **NM** value: **Cover or less**
• The Shadow **A:** Vernon Greene **W:** Maxwell Grant
8 ❑ Apr 1989 Cover: 1.95 **NM** value: **Cover or less**
• The Shadow **A:** Vernon Greene **W:** Maxwell Grant
9 ❑ May 1989 Cover: 1.95 **NM** value: **Cover or less**
• The Shadow **A:** Vernon Greene **W:** Maxwell Grant
10 ❑ Jun 1989 Cover: 1.95 **NM** value: **Cover or less**
• The Shadow **A:** Vernon Greene **W:** Maxwell Grant
11 ❑ Aug 1989 Cover: 1.95 **NM** value: **Cover or less**
• The Shadow **A:** Vernon Greene **W:** Maxwell Grant
12 ❑ Sep 1989 Cover: 2.25 **NM** value: **Cover or less**
• The Shadow **A:** Vernon Greene **W:** Maxwell Grant
13 ❑ Oct 1989 Cover: 2.25 **NM** value: **Cover or less**
• The Shadow **A:** Vernon Greene **W:** Maxwell Grant

CRIME CLINIC — Slave Labor

2 ❑ May 1995 Cover: 2.95 **NM** value: **Cover or less**

CRIME CLINIC (ZIFF-DAVIS) — Ziff-Davis

1 ❑ Jul 1951 Cover: 0.10 **NM** value: **200.00**
• **CGC:** 1 graded, best 8.5
📖 Mad Dog of Manhattan
2 ❑ Sep 1951 Cover: 0.10 **NM** value: **150.00**
📖 The Dummy Killer; Big Brother's Heartbreak; Murderer's Nightmare
3 ❑ Win 1951 Cover: 0.10 **NM** value: **150.00**
📖 The Haunting Cure; The Man Who Wanted to Die; Feet of Clay
4 ❑ Spr 1952 Cover: 0.10 **NM** value: **150.00**
📖 Big Shot in the Big House; The Heart of a Con; Nobody Cheats a Hangman
5 ❑ Sum 1952 Cover: 0.10 **NM** value: **150.00**
📖 No Second Chance; The Lady Killer

CRIME DETECTIVE COMICS (VOL. 1) — Hillman

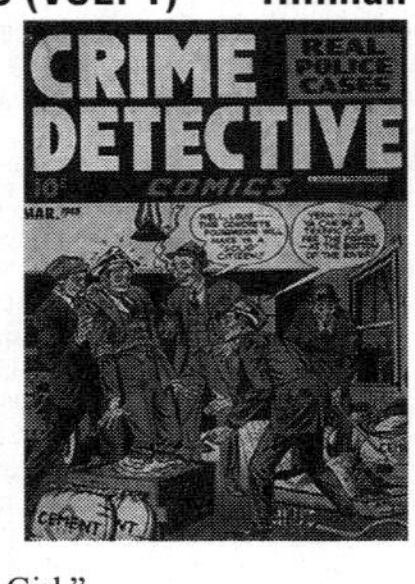

Like so many crime comics of its day, Crime Detective Comics bore a legend on its front cover, "This magazine is dedicated to the prevention of crime. We hope that within its pages the youth of America will learn to know crime for what it really is: a sad, black, dead-end road of fools and tears." Despite such sentiments, however, the criminals in Crime Detective Comics must have seemed glamorous in their own way. And, although they inevitably met their comeuppance in the end, it was the criminal who got all the adventure, money, and the attention of the inevitable "Bad Girl."

Critics such as Dr. Fredric Wertham (author of Seduction of the Innocent) began attacking crime comics during the 1940s, and, by the time #9 of this series appeared, Crime Detective Comics was ready to take a jab back by portraying the doctor, bound and gagged, on the cover.

1 ❑ Mar 1948 Cover: 0.10 **NM** value: **140.00**
2 ❑ May 1948 Cover: 0.10 **NM** value: **65.00**
3 ❑ Jul 1948 Cover: 0.10 **NM** value: **48.00**
4 ❑ Sep 1948 Cover: 0.10 **NM** value: **48.00**
5 ❑ Nov 1948 Cover: 0.10 **NM** value: **55.00**
A: Bernie Krigstein
6 ❑ Jan 1949 Cover: 0.10 **NM** value: **48.00**
📖 Little Mountain of Muscle; French Fried Ice; Buda Godman: Queen of Gem Thieves; Big Operator; The Girl Who Sold Lace (text story); Like Peas in a Pod; A Death in the Family **A:** Al McWilliams; Paul Parker; Leonard Starr
7 ❑ Mar 1949 Cover: 0.10 **NM** value: **48.00**
8 ❑ May 1949 Cover: 0.10 **NM** value: **48.00**
9 ❑ Jul 1949 Cover: 0.10 **NM** value: **145.00**
Anti-Wertham cover cited in Seduction of the Innocent.
10 ❑ Sep 1949 Cover: 0.10 **NM** value: **42.00**
11 ❑ Nov 1949 Cover: 0.10 **NM** value: **42.00**
12 ❑ Jan 1950 Cover: 0.10 **NM** value: **42.00**

CRIME DETECTIVE COMICS (VOL. 2) — Hillman

1 ❑ Mar 1950 Cover: 0.10 **NM** value: **45.00**
A: Bernie Krigstein
2 ❑ May 1950 Cover: 0.10 **NM** value: **30.00**
3 ❑ Jul 1950 Cover: 0.10 **NM** value: **30.00**
4 ❑ Sep 1950 Cover: 0.10 **NM** value: **40.00**
A: Bernie Krigstein
5 ❑ Nov 1950 Cover: 0.10 **NM** value: **28.00**
6 ❑ Jan 1951 Cover: 0.10 **NM** value: **28.00**
7 ❑ Mar 1951 Cover: 0.10 **NM** value: **40.00**
A: Bernie Krigstein
8 ❑ May 1951 Cover: 0.10 **NM** value: **28.00**
9 ❑ Jul 1951 Cover: 0.10 **NM** value: **28.00**
10 ❑ Sep 1951 Cover: 0.10 **NM** value: **28.00**
📖 The Meatball Wears A Holster; The Bottle And Beckett; A Friend From The Old Country; The Black Waltz; The Badge; The Cabbage Can Wait; One Little Tip
11 ❑ Nov 1951 Cover: 0.10 **NM** value: **28.00**
12 ❑ Jan 1952 Cover: 0.10 **NM** value: **28.00**

CRIME DETECTIVE COMICS (VOL. 3) — Hillman

1 ❑ Mar 1952 Cover: 0.10 **NM** value: **28.00**
2 ❑ May 1952 Cover: 0.10 **NM** value: **28.00**
📖 Orders From Center; Something For Mother; A Playful Engineer; The Little Enemy (text story); The Siege of Sidney Street; The Patchwork Gentleman
3 ❑ Jul 1952 Cover: 0.10 **NM** value: **28.00**
4 ❑ Sep 1952 Cover: 0.10 **NM** value: **28.00**
5 ❑ Nov 1952 Cover: 0.10 **NM** value: **28.00**
6 ❑ Jan 1953 Cover: 0.10 **NM** value: **28.00**
7 ❑ Mar 1953 Cover: 0.10 **NM** value: **28.00**
8 ❑ May 1953 Cover: 0.10 **NM** value: **28.00**

CRIME DETECTOR — Timor

1 ❑ Jan 1954 Cover: 0.10 **NM** value: **50.00**
2 ❑ Mar 1954 Cover: 0.10 **NM** value: **32.00**
3 ❑ May 1954 Cover: 0.10 **NM** value: **26.00**
4 ❑ Jul 1954 Cover: 0.10 **NM** value: **26.00**
5 ❑ Sep 1954 Cover: 0.10 **NM** value: **45.00**

CRIME DOES NOT PAY — Lev Gleason

This is the comic book that got the entire crime comics genre rolling — and may have unwittingly contributed to the formation of the Comics Code years later. It began when Bob Wood and Charles Biro were swapping yarns in a bar and decided that gangsters and criminals would provide a neverending flow of new stories for a comic book. Grabbing the name from a popular series of MGM live-action shorts of the 1930s, the pair conspired to rename Silver Streak to Crime Does Not Pay, one of the earliest, and most lurid, crime comics of all time.

The allure of the series was in its graphic and violent stories, drawing material from sources as far back as the middle ages, but concentrating mostly on gangsters of the 1930s. Biro's ghostly "Mr. Crime" narrated many early episodes. This character was a duplicitous advisor to criminals, egging on the thugs — until their inevitable comeuppance in the final page.

22 ❑ Jul 1942 Cover: 0.10 **NM** value: **1550.00**
• **CGC:** 1 graded, best 7.0
• Series continued from Silver Streak Comics #21
23 ❑ Sep 1942 Cover: 0.10 **NM** value: **1000.00**
• **CGC:** 2 graded, best 9.0
24 ❑ Nov 1942 Cover: 0.10 **NM** value: **750.00**
• **CGC:** 6 graded, best 9.2
★ 1st Appearance of Mr. Crime.
25 ❑ Jan 1943 Cover: 0.10 **NM** value: **400.00**
• **CGC:** 2 graded, best 8.0
26 ❑ Mar 1943 Cover: 0.10 **NM** value: **400.00**
27 ❑ May 1943 Cover: 0.10 **NM** value: **400.00**
• **CGC:** 1 graded, best 9.0
28 ❑ Jul 1943 Cover: 0.10 **NM** value: **400.00**
• **CGC:** 2 graded, best 9.0
29 ❑ Sep 1943 Cover: 0.10 **NM** value: **400.00**
30 ❑ Nov 1943 Cover: 0.10 **NM** value: **400.00**
• **CGC:** 2 graded, best 8.5
31 ❑ Jan 1944 Cover: 0.10 **NM** value: **250.00**
• **CGC:** 2 graded, best 8.0
32 ❑ Mar 1944 Cover: 0.10 **NM** value: **250.00**
• **CGC:** 1 graded, best 4.5
33 ❑ May 1944 Cover: 0.10 **NM** value: **250.00**
• **CGC:** 8 graded, best 9.0
34 ❑ Jul 1944 Cover: 0.10 **NM** value: **250.00**
• **CGC:** 1 graded, best 9.2
35 ❑ Sep 1944 Cover: 0.10 **NM** value: **250.00**
• **CGC:** 1 graded, best 9.2
36 ❑ Nov 1944 Cover: 0.10 **NM** value: **250.00**
• **CGC:** 2 graded, best 5.0
37 ❑ Jan 1945 Cover: 0.10 **NM** value: **250.00**
• **CGC:** 1 graded, best 9.0
38 ❑ Mar 1945 Cover: 0.10 **NM** value: **250.00**
39 ❑ May 1945 Cover: 0.10 **NM** value: **250.00**
• **CGC:** 1 graded, best 6.5
40 ❑ Jul 1945 Cover: 0.10 **NM** value: **250.00**
• **CGC:** 1 graded, best 9.0
41 ❑ Sep 1945 Cover: 0.10 **NM** value: **185.00**
★ Origin of Mr. Common Sense. ★ 1st Appearance of Mr. Common Sense.
42 ❑ Nov 1945 Cover: 0.10 **NM** value: **165.00**
• **CGC:** 2 graded, best 7.5
43 ❑ Jan 1946 Cover: 0.10 **NM** value: **110.00**
• **CGC:** 8 graded, best 9.4
44 ❑ Mar 1946 Cover: 0.10 **NM** value: **110.00**
45 ❑ May 1946 Cover: 0.10 **NM** value: **110.00**
• **CGC:** 2 graded, best 9.4
46 ❑ Jul 1946 Cover: 0.10 **NM** value: **110.00**
47 ❑ Sep 1946 Cover: 0.10 **NM** value: **110.00**
48 ❑ Nov 1946 Cover: 0.10 **NM** value: **110.00**
• **CGC:** 1 graded, best 5.5
49 ❑ Jan 1947 Cover: 0.10 **NM** value: **110.00**
50 ❑ Mar 1947 Cover: 0.10 **NM** value: **110.00**
51 ❑ May 1947 Cover: 0.10 **NM** value: **75.00**
• **CGC:** 1 graded, best 9.0
52 ❑ Jun 1947 Cover: 0.10 **NM** value: **75.00**
• **CGC:** 1 graded, best 8.5
53 ❑ Jul 1947 Cover: 0.10 **NM** value: **75.00**
• **CGC:** 1 graded, best 9.0
54 ❑ Aug 1947 Cover: 0.10 **NM** value: **75.00**
55 ❑ Sep 1947 Cover: 0.10 **NM** value: **75.00**
56 ❑ Oct 1947 Cover: 0.10 **NM** value: **75.00**
57 ❑ Nov 1947 Cover: 0.10 **NM** value: **75.00**
58 ❑ Dec 1947 Cover: 0.10 **NM** value: **75.00**
59 ❑ Jan 1948 Cover: 0.10 **NM** value: **75.00**
• **CGC:** 1 graded, best 3.0
60 ❑ Feb 1948 Cover: 0.10 **NM** value: **75.00**
• **CGC:** 1 graded, best 7.0
61 ❑ Mar 1948 Cover: 0.10 **NM** value: **60.00**
62 ❑ Apr 1948 Cover: 0.10 **NM** value: **60.00**
63 ❑ May 1948 Cover: 0.10 **NM** value: **60.00**
64 ❑ Jun 1948 Cover: 0.10 **NM** value: **60.00**
📖 Walter Legenza: The Gangster; On the Level; Robert James; Will Quantrill: General of an Army of Murderers!; Death Stalks in the Night (text story); Who Dunnit? **A:** Bob Fujitani; George Tuska; Charles Biro(cover) **W:** C.H. Moore
65 ❑ Jul 1948 Cover: 0.10 **NM** value: **60.00**
66 ❑ Aug 1948 Cover: 0.10 **NM** value: **60.00**
67 ❑ Sep 1948 Cover: 0.10 **NM** value: **60.00**
68 ❑ Oct 1948 Cover: 0.10 **NM** value: **60.00**
• **CGC:** 1 graded, best 9.4
69 ❑ Nov 1948 Cover: 0.10 **NM** value: **60.00**
70 ❑ Dec 1948 Cover: 0.10 **NM** value: **60.00**
71 ❑ Jan 1949 Cover: 0.10 **NM** value: **50.00**
72 ❑ Feb 1949 Cover: 0.10 **NM** value: **50.00**
73 ❑ Mar 1949 Cover: 0.10 **NM** value: **50.00**
74 ❑ Apr 1949 Cover: 0.10 **NM** value: **50.00**
75 ❑ May 1949 Cover: 0.10 **NM** value: **50.00**
76 ❑ Jun 1949 Cover: 0.10 **NM** value: **50.00**
77 ❑ Jul 1949 Cover: 0.10 **NM** value: **50.00**
78 ❑ Aug 1949 Cover: 0.10 **NM** value: **50.00**
79 ❑ Sep 1949 Cover: 0.10 **NM** value: **50.00**
80 ❑ Oct 1949 Cover: 0.10 **NM** value: **50.00**
81 ❑ Nov 1949 Cover: 0.10 **NM** value: **42.00**
82 ❑ Dec 1949 Cover: 0.10 **NM** value: **42.00**
C: Charles Biro
83 ❑ Jan 1950 Cover: 0.10 **NM** value: **42.00**
84 ❑ Feb 1950 Cover: 0.10 **NM** value: **42.00**
85 ❑ Mar 1950 Cover: 0.10 **NM** value: **42.00**
86 ❑ Apr 1950 Cover: 0.10 **NM** value: **42.00**
87 ❑ May 1950 Cover: 0.10 **NM** value: **42.00**
88 ❑ Jun 1950 Cover: 0.10 **NM** value: **42.00**
89 ❑ Jul 1950 Cover: 0.10 **NM** value: **42.00**
• **CGC:** 1 graded, best 8.0
90 ❑ Aug 1950 Cover: 0.10 **NM** value: **42.00**
91 ❑ Sep 1950 Cover: 0.10 **NM** value: **35.00**
• **CGC:** 1 graded, best 8.5
92 ❑ Oct 1950 Cover: 0.10 **NM** value: **35.00**

Other grades: Multiply prices above by **1.5 for Mint • 2/3 for Very Fine • 1/3 for Fine • 1/5 for Very Good • 1/8 for Good**

93 ❑ Nov 1950 Cover: 0.10 **NM** value: **35.00**
• **CGC:** 1 graded, best 8.0
Painted cover. 📖 The Ostrich Murder Case; Parcel Post; Go Home and Wait for Death! **A:** Bob Fujitani; Fred Guardineer; Tony DiPreta
94 ❑ Dec 1950 Cover: 0.10 **NM** value: **35.00**
95 ❑ Feb 1951 Cover: 0.10 **NM** value: **35.00**
96 ❑ Mar 1951 Cover: 0.10 **NM** value: **35.00**
97 ❑ Apr 1951 Cover: 0.10 **NM** value: **35.00**
98 ❑ May 1951 Cover: 0.10 **NM** value: **35.00**
99 ❑ Jun 1951 Cover: 0.10 **NM** value: **35.00**
100 ❑ Jul 1951 Cover: 0.10 **NM** value: **35.00**
101 ❑ Aug 1951 Cover: 0.10 **NM** value: **32.00**
Painted cover. 📖 Cain Versus Able; The Case of the Crooked Politician; Murder Bait (text story); Murder is a Stranger; Say it With Bullets! **A:** Bob Fujitani; Robert Q. Sale; Dick Rockwell; Fred Guardineer
102 ❑ Sep 1951 Cover: 0.10 **NM** value: **32.00**
103 ❑ Oct 1951 Cover: 0.10 **NM** value: **32.00**
• **CGC:** 1 graded, best 8.0
104 ❑ Nov 1951 Cover: 0.10 **NM** value: **32.00**
105 ❑ Dec 1951 Cover: 0.10 **NM** value: **32.00**
106 ❑ Jan 1952 Cover: 0.10 **NM** value: **32.00**
107 ❑ Feb 1952 Cover: 0.10 **NM** value: **32.00**
📖 It's Not Easy to Quit!; The State Versus "Rock" Madden; Pattern for Punks (text story); The Man Who Ordered His Own Rub-Out **A:** Bob Fujitani; Charles Biro; Scourge of the Waterfront; Tony DiPreta
108 ❑ Mar 1952 Cover: 0.10 **NM** value: **32.00**
109 ❑ Apr 1952 Cover: 0.10 **NM** value: **32.00**
110 ❑ May 1952 Cover: 0.10 **NM** value: **32.00**
111 ❑ Jun 1952 Cover: 0.10 **NM** value: **30.00**
📖 The Eyewitness; The Fatal Switch; Pete Carney; "Country Adams" • "Country" Adams **A:** Bob Fujitani; Fred Guardineer
112 ❑ Jul 1952 Cover: 0.10 **NM** value: **30.00**
113 ❑ Aug 1952 Cover: 0.10 **NM** value: **30.00**
114 ❑ Sep 1952 Cover: 0.10 **NM** value: **30.00**
115 ❑ Oct 1952 Cover: 0.10 **NM** value: **30.00**
📖 Trapped by the Dead; The Criminal Who Wanted to Punish Himself; The Late Tour (text story); Terror On Loon Street; The Lone Witness
116 ❑ Nov 1952 Cover: 0.10 **NM** value: **30.00**
117 ❑ Dec 1952 Cover: 0.10 **NM** value: **30.00**
• **CGC:** 1 graded, best 6.0
118 ❑ Jan 1953 Cover: 0.10 **NM** value: **30.00**
• **CGC:** 1 graded, best 6.0
119 ❑ Feb 1953 Cover: 0.10 **NM** value: **30.00**
📖 Mad Dog Coll: The Mad Gunman; The Hatchet Man; Test Your Judgment (text story); Partners in Corruption
120 ❑ Mar 1953 Cover: 0.10 **NM** value: **30.00**
📖 The Brady Gang: Midwestern Gunmen On a Kill-Crazy Spree!; Cut Rate Murder; The Assassination of Big Angie **A:** A. Wenzel
121 ❑ Apr 1953 Cover: 0.10 **NM** value: **30.00**
📖 Irving "Waxey" Gordon; Marty Aarons "Bugs"; Duke Jarboe **A:** Dick Rockwell
122 ❑ May 1953 Cover: 0.10 **NM** value: **30.00**
123 ❑ Jun 1953 Cover: 0.10 **NM** value: **30.00**
📖 Hymie Weiss: Dynamo of Hate; "Lucky Joe" Masseria; Who Killed Boss Faber? **A:** Dick Rockwell
124 ❑ Jul 1953 Cover: 0.10 **NM** value: **30.00**
125 ❑ Aug 1953 Cover: 0.10 **NM** value: **30.00**
📖 Frank Nash; The End of the Line; The Case of the X-Rayed Killer
126 ❑ Sep 1953 Cover: 0.10 **NM** value: **30.00**
📖 Killer From The Sticks; Kill-Crazy Fred Banjo Blore; Violence
127 ❑ Oct 1953 Cover: 0.10 **NM** value: **30.00**
128 ❑ Nov 1953 Cover: 0.10 **NM** value: **30.00**
📖 Chuck Dorset's Race Against Death; The Map (text story); The High Cost of Dying; Lucky Kid Abel's Two Chances to Die **A:** Bob Brown
129 ❑ Dec 1953 Cover: 0.10 **NM** value: **30.00**
130 ❑ Jan 1954 Cover: 0.10 **NM** value: **30.00**
131 ❑ Feb 1954 Cover: 0.10 **NM** value: **25.00**
132 ❑ Mar 1954 Cover: 0.10 **NM** value: **25.00**
133 ❑ Apr 1954 Cover: 0.10 **NM** value: **25.00**
134 ❑ May 1954 Cover: 0.10 **NM** value: **25.00**
135 ❑ Jun 1954 Cover: 0.10 **NM** value: **25.00**
136 ❑ Jul 1954 Cover: 0.10 **NM** value: **25.00**
• **CGC:** 1 graded, best 6.5
137 ❑ Sep 1954 Cover: 0.10 **NM** value: **25.00**
138 ❑ Oct 1954 Cover: 0.10 **NM** value: **25.00**
139 ❑ Nov 1954 Cover: 0.10 **NM** value: **25.00**
140 ❑ Dec 1954 Cover: 0.10 **NM** value: **25.00**
141 ❑ Jan 1955 Cover: 0.10 **NM** value: **25.00**
• **CGC:** 1 graded, best 8.0
142 ❑ Feb 1955 Cover: 0.10 **NM** value: **25.00**
143 ❑ Mar 1955 Cover: 0.10 **NM** value: **25.00**
• **CGC:** 1 graded, best 4.0
144 ❑ Apr 1955 Cover: 0.10 **NM** value: **25.00**
145 ❑ May 1955 Cover: 0.10 **NM** value: **25.00**
146 ❑ Jun 1955 Cover: 0.10 **NM** value: **25.00**
final issue.

CRIME EXPOSED — Marvel

1 ❑ Dec 1950 Cover: 0.10 **NM** value: **150.00**
• **CGC:** 1 graded, best 6.0
2 ❑ Feb 1951 Cover: 0.10 **NM** value: **100.00**
3 ❑ Apr 1951 Cover: 0.10 **NM** value: **75.00**
4 ❑ Jun 1951 Cover: 0.10 **NM** value: **75.00**
5 ❑ Aug 1951 Cover: 0.10 **NM** value: **75.00**
6 ❑ Sep 1951 Cover: 0.10 **NM** value: **75.00**
7 ❑ Oct 1951 Cover: 0.10 **NM** value: **75.00**
8 ❑ Nov 1951 Cover: 0.10 **NM** value: **75.00**
9 ❑ Dec 1951 Cover: 0.10 **NM** value: **75.00**
10 ❑ Mar 1952 Cover: 0.10 **NM** value: **60.00**
11 ❑ Apr 1952 Cover: 0.10 **NM** value: **60.00**
12 ❑ May 1952 Cover: 0.10 **NM** value: **60.00**
13 ❑ Jun 1952 Cover: 0.10 **NM** value: **60.00**
14 ❑ Jul 1952 Cover: 0.10 **NM** value: **60.00**

CRIME FILES — Standard

5 ❑ Jul 1952 Cover: 0.10 **NM** value: **175.00**
6 ❑ Sep 1952 Cover: 0.10 **NM** value: **100.00**

CRIME MUST LOSE — Timely

4 ❑ Oct 1950 Cover: 0.10 **NM** value: **150.00**
5 ❑ ca. 1951 Cover: 0.10 **NM** value: **150.00**
📖 Tough Guy!; Fall Guy!; End of the Road!; The Fake!
6 ❑ ca. 1951 Cover: 0.10 **NM** value: **150.00**
📖 The Body in Compartment A!; No Bars Could Hold Him!; The Blue People!; The Talking Corpse!
7 ❑ ca. 1951 Cover: 0.10 **NM** value: **125.00**
8 ❑ ca. 1951 Cover: 0.10 **NM** value: **125.00**
9 ❑ ca. 1951 Cover: 0.10 **NM** value: **125.00**
10 ❑ ca. 1952 Cover: 0.10 **NM** value: **125.00**
11 ❑ ca. 1952 Cover: 0.10 **NM** value: **100.00**
12 ❑ ca. 1952 Cover: 0.10 **NM** value: **100.00**

CRIME MUST PAY THE PENALTY — Current

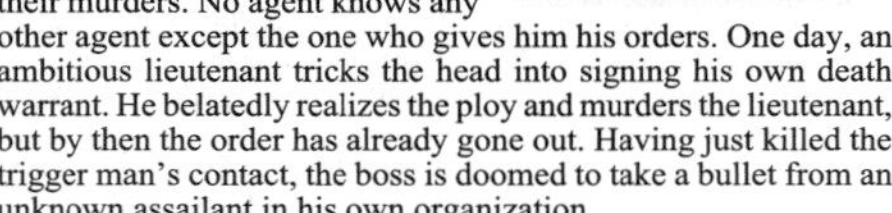

Crime Must Pay the Penalty was wonderfully lurid crime comic of the late 1049s and early 1950s. Like so many other crime comics of the time, this title purported to tell "true cases of actual crimes!" noting, of course, that certain names had been changed to protect the innocent.

Despite its "true cases" claim, many of the stories have a striking resemblance to old mystery story chestnuts. For instance, "Signed in His Own Blood" tells of an assassination ring whose agents follow a strict chain of secrecy in conducting their murders. No agent knows any other agent except the one who gives him his orders. One day, an ambitious lieutenant tricks the head into signing his own death warrant. He belatedly realizes the ploy and murders the lieutenant, but by then the order has already gone out. Having just killed the trigger man's contact, the boss is doomed to take a bullet from an unknown assailant in his own organization.

1 ❑ ca. 1948 Cover: 0.10 **NM** value: **145.00**
#33 on cover (1948).
2 ❑ Jun 1948 Cover: 0.10 **NM** value: **90.00**
3 ❑ Aug 1948 Cover: 0.10 **NM** value: **75.00**
4 ❑ Oct 1948 Cover: 0.10 **NM** value: **75.00**
• **CGC:** 1 graded, best 9.2
• Transvestite story
5 ❑ Dec 1948 Cover: 0.10 **NM** value: **50.00**
6 ❑ Feb 1949 Cover: 0.10 **NM** value: **50.00**
7 ❑ Apr 1949 Cover: 0.10 **NM** value: **50.00**
8 ❑ Jun 1949 Cover: 0.10 **NM** value: **70.00**
• Transvestite story
9 ❑ Aug 1949 Cover: 0.10 **NM** value: **50.00**
10 ❑ Oct 1949 Cover: 0.10 **NM** value: **50.00**
11 ❑ Dec 1949 Cover: 0.10 **NM** value: **40.00**
12 ❑ Feb 1950 Cover: 0.10 **NM** value: **40.00**
13 ❑ Apr 1950 Cover: 0.10 **NM** value: **40.00**
14 ❑ Jun 1950 Cover: 0.10 **NM** value: **40.00**
15 ❑ Aug 1950 Cover: 0.10 **NM** value: **40.00**
16 ❑ Oct 1950 Cover: 0.10 **NM** value: **40.00**
17 ❑ Dec 1950 Cover: 0.10 **NM** value: **40.00**
18 ❑ Feb 1951 Cover: 0.10 **NM** value: **40.00**
19 ❑ Apr 1951 Cover: 0.10 **NM** value: **40.00**
20 ❑ Jun 1951 Cover: 0.10 **NM** value: **40.00**
21 ❑ Aug 1951 Cover: 0.10 **NM** value: **35.00**
22 ❑ Oct 1951 Cover: 0.10 **NM** value: **35.00**
23 ❑ Dec 1951 Cover: 0.10 **NM** value: **35.00**
24 ❑ Feb 1952 Cover: 0.10 **NM** value: **35.00**
25 ❑ Apr 1952 Cover: 0.10 **NM** value: **35.00**
26 ❑ Jun 1952 Cover: 0.10 **NM** value: **35.00**
📖 Pathway to an Early Grave; The Killers who Wouldn't Forget; Big Gun of the Goon Squad; Dangerous Partner (text story); In His Father's Crimson Footsteps
27 ❑ Aug 1952 Cover: 0.10 **NM** value: **35.00**
28 ❑ Oct 1952 Cover: 0.10 **NM** value: **35.00**
29 ❑ Dec 1952 Cover: 0.10 **NM** value: **35.00**
30 ❑ Feb 1953 Cover: 0.10 **NM** value: **35.00**
31 ❑ Apr 1953 Cover: 0.10 **NM** value: **30.00**
32 ❑ 1953 Cover: 0.10 **NM** value: **30.00**
33 ❑ 1953 Cover: 0.10 **NM** value: **30.00**
34 ❑ 1953 Cover: 0.10 **NM** value: **30.00**
35 ❑ Cover: 0.10 **NM** value: **30.00**
36 ❑ 1954 Cover: 0.10 **NM** value: **30.00**
37 ❑ 1954 Cover: 0.10 **NM** value: **30.00**
38 ❑ 1954 Cover: 0.10 **NM** value: **30.00**
39 ❑ 1954 Cover: 0.10 **NM** value: **30.00**
40 ❑ 1954 Cover: 0.10 **NM** value: **30.00**
41 ❑ 1954 Cover: 0.10 **NM** value: **55.00**
• Drug story
42 ❑ Cover: 0.10 **NM** value: **30.00**
43 ❑ Cover: 0.10 **NM** value: **30.00**
44 ❑ Apr 1955 Cover: 0.10 **NM** value: **30.00**
45 ❑ 1955 Cover: 0.10 **NM** value: **30.00**
46 ❑ 1955 Cover: 0.10 **NM** value: **30.00**
• Series continued in Penalty #47

CRIME MYSTERIES — Ribage

1 ❑ May 1952 Cover: 0.10 **NM** value: **450.00**
2 ❑ Jul 1952 Cover: 0.10 **NM** value: **300.00**
3 ❑ Sep 1952 Cover: 0.10 **NM** value: **300.00**
4 ❑ Nov 1952 Cover: 0.10 **NM** value: **400.00**
• **CGC:** 1 graded, best 7.0
5 ❑ Jan 1953 Cover: 0.10 **NM** value: **200.00**
📖 The Claws of the Green Girl
6 ❑ Mar 1953 Cover: 0.10 **NM** value: **200.00**
7 ❑ May 1953 Cover: 0.10 **NM** value: **200.00**
📖 Sons of Satan
8 ❑ Jul 1953 Cover: 0.10 **NM** value: **200.00**
📖 Death Stalks the Crown
9 ❑ Sep 1953 Cover: 0.10 **NM** value: **200.00**
📖 You Are the Murderer!
10 ❑ Nov 1953 Cover: 0.10 **NM** value: **200.00**
📖 The Hoax of Death
11 ❑ Jan 1954 Cover: 0.10 **NM** value: **175.00**
📖 The Strangler
12 ❑ Mar 1954 Cover: 0.10 **NM** value: **175.00**
13 ❑ May 1954 Cover: 0.10 **NM** value: **175.00**
14 ❑ Jul 1954 Cover: 0.10 **NM** value: **175.00**
📖 Painted in Blood
15 ❑ Sep 1954 Cover: 0.10 **NM** value: **175.00**
• **CGC:** 1 graded, best 7.5
📖 Feast of the Dead

CRIME ON THE WATERFRONT — Realistic Comics

4 ❑ May 1952 Cover: 0.10 **NM** value: **200.00**
• **CGC:** 4 graded, best 8.5

CRIME PATROL — E.C.

The E.C. Pre-Trend title was a continuation of International Crime Patrol, which in its turn had been a continuation of International Comics. Many of the covers of Crime Patrol carried the notice "REAL stories from POLICE records!" and carried art by Johnny Craig. Artists on the title included Craig, Henry C. Kiefer, and Al Feldstein.

The title began an evolution into the horror field with "Return from the Grave!" in #15, which featured the first appearance of E.C.'s Crypt-Keeper, created by Al Feldstein. Both #15 and #16 replaced the "Police Records" captions with a "Crypt of Terror" notation on the cover. With the 17th issue, it became The Crypt of Terror. —Maggie

7 ❑ Sum 1948 Cover: 0.10 **NM** value: **600.00**
• **CGC:** 5 graded, best 9.2
8 ❑ Fal 1948 Cover: 0.10 **NM** value: **575.00**
• **CGC:** 2 graded, best 9.0
9 ❑ Win 1948 Cover: 0.10 **NM** value: **575.00**
• **CGC:** 5 graded, best 6.5
10 ❑ Feb 1949 Cover: 0.10 **NM** value: **550.00**
• **CGC:** 6 graded, best 9.0
11 ❑ Apr 1949 Cover: 0.10 **NM** value: **500.00**
• **CGC:** 1 graded, best 7.5
12 ❑ Jun 1949 Cover: 0.10 **NM** value: **500.00**
• **CGC:** 2 graded, best 4.5
13 ❑ Aug 1949 Cover: 0.10 **NM** value: **500.00**
• **CGC:** 4 graded, best 9.0
14 ❑ Oct 1949 Cover: 0.10 **NM** value: **500.00**
• **CGC:** 3 graded, best 8.5
15 ❑ Dec 1949 Cover: 0.10 **NM** value: **2000.00**
• **CGC:** 9 graded, best 9.6
16 ❑ Feb 1950 Cover: 0.10 **NM** value: **1500.00**
• **CGC:** 9 graded, best 9.6

CRIME PATROL (GEMSTONE) — Gemstone

1 ❑ Apr 2000 Cover: 2.50 **NM** value: **Cover or less**
Circ: Diamd. preorders: **3,095**
📖 Captain Crime!; Death by Rocket Bomb!; Slaughter from the Sky!; Madelon • Reprints Crime Patrol #1 (#7) **A:** Johnny Craig; Sheldon Moldoff **W:** Sheldon Moldoff
2 ❑ May 2000 Cover: 2.50 **NM** value: **Cover or less**
Circ: Diamd. preorders: **2,761**
📖 The Deadly Grease Monkey; The Alibi; Igor the Archer; The Case of the Kissing Killer • Reprints Crime Patrol #2 (#8) **A:** Henry C. Kiefer; Ann Brewster; Ed Waldman **W:** Henry C. Kiefer; Ann Brewster; Ed Waldman
3 ❑ Jun 2000 Cover: 2.50 **NM** value: **Cover or less**
Circ: Diamd. preorders: **2,818**
📖 The Slaughter Syndicate; Madelon; Crooked as a Corkscrew!; Double-Crossed • Reprints Crime Patrol #3 (#9) **A:** Al Feldstein; Johnny Craig; Ann Brewster **W:** Al Feldstein; Johnny Craig; Ann Brewster
4 ❑ Jul 2000 Cover: 2.50 **NM** value: **Cover or less**
Circ: Diamd. preorders: **2,649**
📖 Dance-Hall Racket; The Ace of Spades; The Ten O-Clock Burglars (text story); The Horse Painter • Reprints Crime Patrol #4 **A:** Al Feldstein; Henry C. Kiefer; Al Feldstein(cover); Stan Ash **W:** Al Feldstein; Henry C. Kiefer; Stan Ash
5 ❑ Aug 2000 Cover: 2.50 **NM** value: **Cover or less**
Circ: Diamd. preorders: **2,685**
📖 Kidnappers; The Werewolf's Curse!; Fast-Draw Fay • Reprints Crime Patrol #5 **A:** Al Feldstein; Henry C. Kiefer; Howard Larson **W:** Al Feldstein; Henry C. Kiefer; Howard Larson
Anl 1 ❑ ca. 2000 Cover: 13.50 **NM** value: **Cover or less**
• Collects issues #1-5

CRIME PAYS — Boneyard

1 ❑ Oct 1996, b&w Cover: 3.95 **NM** value: **Cover or less**
★ Appearance of Bill the Bull.
2 ❑ Sep 1997 Cover: 2.95 **NM** value: **Cover or less**
📖 Bar Slut; Crime Pays **A:** Jay Bruce Bogle; Sean Pchanko **W:** Hart Fisher

CRIME REPORTER — St. John

1 ❑ Aug 1948 Cover: 0.10 **NM** value: **400.00**
2 ❑ Oct 1948 Cover: 0.10 **NM** value: **600.00**
• **CGC:** 2 graded, best 7.5
3 ❑ Dec 1948 Cover: 0.10 **NM** value: **300.00**

CGC-graded: Multiply prices above by **33 for 9.9 M • 16 for 9.8 NM/M • 7 for 9.6 NM+ • 5 for 9.4 NM • 2.5 for 9.2 NM- • 1.5 for 9.0 VF/NM**

CRIMES BY WOMEN **Fox**

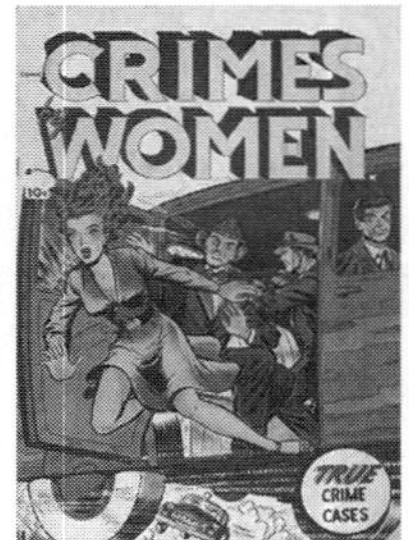

Violence, vice, and really tight dresses — it didn't take the geniuses at Fox Features Syndicate long to discover the winning formula for Crimes by Women, a notable contribution to both the crime comics and cheesecake genres popular in the late 1940s and 1950s. Purporting to detail "true crime cases," Crimes by Women spotlighted the careers of notorious femmes fatales like Bonnie Parker (of "and Clyde" fame) plus assorted gun molls, fast women, black widow killers, and good girls gone wrong. Crimes by Women adopted the characteristic crime comics' tone that all these crimes were "so very, very wrong," while the art lavished detail on every feminine curve and blood-spattered massacre. Unfortunately, the same qualities that made Crimes by Women a hit also ran it afoul of the Comics Code, and the title was among those swept from the stands in 1954.

1 ❑ Jun 1948 Cover: 0.10 **NM** value: **850.00**
• **CGC:** 1 graded, best 9.2

2 ❑ Aug 1948 Cover: 0.10 **NM** value: **500.00**
• **CGC:** 1 graded, best 5.5

3 ❑ Oct 1948 Cover: 0.10 **NM** value: **400.00**
• **CGC:** 1 graded, best 6.5

4 ❑ Dec 1948 Cover: 0.10 **NM** value: **350.00**

5 ❑ Feb 1949 Cover: 0.10 **NM** value: **350.00**

6 ❑ Apr 1949 Cover: 0.10 **NM** value: **300.00**

7 ❑ Jun 1949 Cover: 0.10 **NM** value: **300.00**

8 ❑ Aug 1949 Cover: 0.10 **NM** value: **300.00**

9 ❑ Oct 1949 Cover: 0.10 **NM** value: **300.00**

10 ❑ Dec 1949 Cover: 0.10 **NM** value: **300.00**

11 ❑ Feb 1950 Cover: 0.10 **NM** value: **260.00**

12 ❑ Apr 1950 Cover: 0.10 **NM** value: **260.00**

13 ❑ 1950 Cover: 0.10 **NM** value: **260.00**

14 ❑ 1951 Cover: 0.10 **NM** value: **260.00**

15 ❑ Aug 1951 Cover: 0.10 **NM** value: **260.00**

54 ❑ Cover: 0.10 **NM** value: **150.00**
📖 The Kitty Sarlo story; Nitro Nellie, a True Crime Story; The Diamond of Kor-El-MaÑiñoor; Man Trap; The Diamond of Kor-El-Maninoor final issue. • Continued from My Love Secret #53 **A:** Jimmy Maxwell **W:** Jimmy Maxwell

CRIME SMASHER **Fawcett**

1 ❑ ca. 1949 Cover: 0.10 **NM** value: **265.00**
📖 The Trapping of Public Enemy No. 1!; The Last Request; The Unlucky Rabbit's Foot; Richard Richard: The Lumber Camp Mystery; Sherlock Monk

CRIME-SMASHER (BLUE COMET) **Blue Comet**

SE 1 ❑ Jul 1987 Cover: 1.80 **NM** value: **2.00**
📖 Genesis 27 **A:** Glenn Wong **W:** Roy Thomas; Dann Thomas

CRIME SUSPENSTORIES (E.C.) **E.C.**

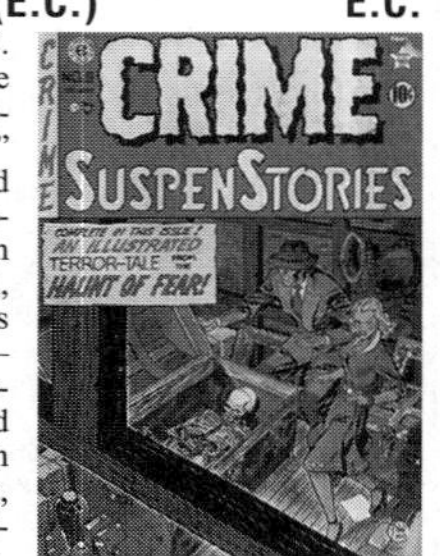

The first two issues of this E.C. title carried the cover message "Featuring a New Trend in magazines ... Startling tales of tension!" Several following issues boasted there was a complete story in the issue: "An illustrated terror-tale from The Haunt of Fear!" The eventual, ongoing subtitle was, "Jolting tales of tension in the EC tradition!" — a caption shared with Shock SuspenStories. Stories of violence and suspense were illustrated by such E.C. standards as Johnny Craig, Reed Crandall, Jack Davis, Will Elder, George Evans, Al Feldstein, Graham Ingels, Jack Kamen, Bernie Krigstein, Harvey Kurtzman, Joe Orlando, Al Williamson, and Wally Wood. The series came to an end with the Comics Magazine Association of America's implementation of the Comics Code, which forbade much of its type of story in newsstand comics. — Maggie

1 ❑ Oct 1950 Cover: 0.10 **NM** value: **800.00**
• **CGC:** 6 graded, best 9.4
📖 Murder May Boomerang; Reward (text story); A Snapshot of Death; Double Indemnity (text story); High Tide **A:** Harvey Kurtzman; Johnny Craig; Wally Wood; Graham Ingels **W:** Harvey Kurtzman; Johnny Craig; Wally Wood; Graham Ingels

1/A ❑ Oct 1950 Cover: 0.10 **NM** value: **1000.00**
• **CGC:** 4 graded, best 9.0
Printing change with the #15 blackened out on cover with #1 printed over it. 📖 Murder May Boomerang; Reward (text story); A Snapshot of Death; Double Indemnity (text story); High Tide **A:** Harvey Kurtzman; Johnny Craig; Wally Wood; Graham Ingels **W:** Harvey Kurtzman; Johnny Craig; Wally Wood; Graham Ingels

2 ❑ Dec 1950 Cover: 0.10 **NM** value: **475.00**
• **CGC:** 9 graded, best 9.8
📖 Dead Ringer; A Moment of Madness; Perfect Murder (text story); The Corpse in the Crematorium; Contract for Death

3 ❑ Feb 1951 Cover: 0.10 **NM** value: **315.00**
• **CGC:** 7 graded, best 9.8
📖 Poison; The Giggling Killer; Faced With Horror; Blood Red Wine

4 ❑ Apr 1951 Cover: 0.10 **NM** value: **315.00**
• **CGC:** 4 graded, best 9.8
📖 Backlash; Premium Overdue; Seaweed (text story); Conniver; Heads-Up **A:** Johnny Craig; Jack Kamen; Jack Davis; Graham Ingels **W:** Johnny Craig; Jack Kamen; Jack Davis; Graham Ingels

5 ❑ Jun 1951 Cover: 0.10 **NM** value: **315.00**
• **CGC:** 4 graded, best 9.6
📖 The Sewer; Mr. Biddy...Lady Killer; The Gullible One; Partially Dissolved

6 ❑ Aug 1951 Cover: 0.10 **NM** value: **235.00**
• **CGC:** 8 graded, best 9.8
📖 A Toast...To Death!; Out of my Mind!; The Switch; Jury Duty!

7 ❑ Oct 1951 Cover: 0.10 **NM** value: **235.00**
• **CGC:** 4 graded, best 9.8
📖 Hatchet-Killer!; Revenge!; Phonies; Horror Under the Big Top!

8 ❑ Dec 1951 Cover: 0.10 **NM** value: **235.00**
• **CGC:** 5 graded, best 9.6
📖 Out of the Frying Pan...; A Trace of Murder!; The Escaped Maniac!; Partnership Dissolved!

9 ❑ Feb 1952 Cover: 0.10 **NM** value: **235.00**
• **CGC:** 7 graded, best 9.8
📖 Understudy to a Corpse!; Medicine!; Cut!; A Tree Grows in Borneo!

10 ❑ Apr 1952 Cover: 0.10 **NM** value: **235.00**
• **CGC:** 3 graded, best 9.4
📖 ...Rocks in His Head!; Lady Killer; Missed by Two Heirs!; Friend to Our Boys!

11 ❑ Jun 1952 Cover: 0.10 **NM** value: **185.00**
• **CGC:** 5 graded, best 9.6
📖 Stiff Punishment!; One Man's Poison!; Big Money (text story); Two for One!; Four for One!; A Fool and His Honey Are Soon Parted!

12 ❑ Aug 1952 Cover: 0.10 **NM** value: **185.00**
• **CGC:** 3 graded, best 9.6
📖 The Execution!; Murder the Lover!; Murder the Husband!; Trap! (text story); Snooze to Me!; Paralyzed!

13 ❑ Oct 1952 Cover: 0.10 **NM** value: **210.00**
• **CGC:** 3 graded, best 9.6
📖 Hear no Evil!; First Impulse!; Second Chance?; Freak! (text story); A Question of Time!!; Forty Whacks!

14 ❑ Dec 1952 Cover: 0.10 **NM** value: **185.00**
• **CGC:** 8 graded, best 9.6
📖 Sweet Dreams!; The Perfect Place!; The Electric Chair; The Hangman's Noose; The Guillotine!; Private Performance!

15 ❑ Feb 1953 Cover: 0.10 **NM** value: **185.00**
• **CGC:** 4 graded, best 9.4
📖 When the Cat's Away...; The Screaming Woman!; The EC Caper (text piece); Water, Water Everywhere...; ...And Not a Drop to Drink!; Hail and Heart-y!

16 ❑ Apr 1953 Cover: 0.10 **NM** value: **190.00**
• **CGC:** 8 graded, best 9.6
📖 Rendezvous!; Fission Bait!; Come Clean!; Who's Next? **A:** Al Williamson; Joe Orlando; Johnny Craig; Jack Kamen **W:** Al Williamson; Joe Orlando; Johnny Craig; Jack Kamen

17 ❑ Jun 1953 Cover: 0.10 **NM** value: **235.00**
• **CGC:** 8 graded, best 9.8
📖 Touch and Go!; One for the Money...; Fired!; ...Two for the Show! **A:** Al Williamson; Johnny Craig; Frank Frazetta; Bill Elder; Jack Kamen **W:** Al Williamson; Johnny Craig; Frank Frazetta; Bill Elder; Jack Kamen; Ray Bradbury

18 ❑ Aug 1953 Cover: 0.10 **NM** value: **170.00**
• **CGC:** 5 graded, best 9.6
📖 Fall Guy for Murder; Juice for the Record!; Frozen Assets!; From Here to Insanity **A:** Johnny Craig; Bill Elder; Reed Crandall; Jack Kamen **W:** Johnny Craig; Bill Elder; Reed Crandall; Jack Kamen

19 ❑ Oct 1953 Cover: 0.10 **NM** value: **170.00**
• **CGC:** 4 graded, best 9.6
📖 The Killer; Wined-Up!; About Phase; Murder May Boomerang **A:** George Evans; Johnny Craig; Reed Crandall **W:** George Evans; Johnny Craig; Reed Crandall

20 ❑ Dec 1953 Cover: 0.10 **NM** value: **215.00**
• **CGC:** 5 graded, best 9.4
Graphic hanging cover cited in Seduction of the Innocent. 📖 Fire Trap!; The Welchers; Double Jepardy; Plane Murder

21 ❑ Mar 1954 Cover: 0.10 **NM** value: **115.00**
• **CGC:** 4 graded, best 9.6
📖 Mother's Day; In the Groove; Understudies!; Blood Brothers

22 ❑ May 1954 Cover: 0.10 **NM** value: **145.00**
• **CGC:** 5 graded, best 9.6
📖 In Each and Every Package; Monotony; Cinder Block; Sight Unseen

23 ❑ Jul 1954 Cover: 0.10 **NM** value: **145.00**
• **CGC:** 4 graded, best 9.6
📖 This'll Kill You!; Standing Room only; Return Blow; Last Resort

24 ❑ Sep 1954 Cover: 0.10 **NM** value: **115.00**
• **CGC:** 6 graded, best 9.6
📖 Double-Crossed; Crushed Ice; Food for Thought; More Blessed to Give... **A:** Joe Orlando; Bernie Krigstein; Reed Crandall; Jack Kamen

25 ❑ Nov 1954 Cover: 0.10 **NM** value: **115.00**
• **CGC:** 3 graded, best 9.2
📖 Three for the Money; Dog Food; Key Chain; The Squealer **A:** George Evans; Bernie Krigstein; Reed Crandall; Jack Kamen

26 ❑ Jan 1955 Cover: 0.10 **NM** value: **115.00**
• **CGC:** 5 graded, best 9.4
📖 The Fixer; Dead Center; The Firebug; Comeback **A:** Joe Orlando; Reed Crandall; Jack Kamen

27 ❑ Mar 1955 Cover: 0.10 **NM** value: **115.00**
• **CGC:** 5 graded, best 9.4
📖 Maniac at Large; Just Her Speed; Where There's Smoke...; Good Boy final issue. **A:** George Evans; Bernie Krigstein; Jack Kamen; Graham Ingels

CRIME SUSPENSTORIES (RCP) **Gemstone**

1 ❑ Nov 1992 Cover: 1.50 **NM** value: **2.00**
Circ: CapCity orders: **4,200**
📖 Murder May Boomerang; Reward (text story); A Snapshot of Death; Double Indemnity (text story); High Tide • Reprints Crime SuspenStories (EC) #1 **A:** Harvey Kurtzman; Johnny Craig; Wally Wood; Graham Ingels **W:** Harvey Kurtzman; Johnny Craig; Wally Wood; Graham Ingels

2 ❑ Nov 1992 Cover: 1.50 **NM** value: **2.00**
Circ: CapCity orders: **3,800**
📖 Dead Ringer; A Moment of Madness; Perfect Murder (text story); The Corpse in the Crematorium; Contract for Death • Reprints Crime SuspenStories (EC) #2

3 ❑ Feb 1993 Cover: 1.50 **NM** value: **2.00**
Circ: Statement: **17,191** CapCity orders: **3,500**
📖 Poison; The Giggling Killer; Faced With Horror; Blood Red Wine • Reprints Crime SuspenStories (EC) #3

4 ❑ May 1993 Cover: 2.00 **NM** value: **Cover or less**
Circ: Statement: **17,191** CapCity orders: **3,500**
📖 Backlash; Premium Overdue; Seaweed (text story); Conniver; Heads-Up • Reprints Crime SuspenStories (EC) #4 **A:** Johnny Craig; Jack Kamen; Jack Davis; Graham Ingels **W:** Johnny Craig; Jack Kamen; Jack Davis; Graham Ingels

5 ❑ Aug 1993 Cover: 2.00 **NM** value: **Cover or less**
Circ: Statement: **17,191**
📖 The Sewer; Mr. Biddy...Lady Killer; The Gullible One; Partially Dissolved • Reprints Crime SuspenStories (EC) #5

6 ❑ Nov 1993 Cover: 2.00 **NM** value: **Cover or less**
Circ: Statement: **17,191** CapCity orders: **2,875**
📖 A Toast...To Death!; Out of my Mind!; The Switch; Jury Duty! • Reprints Crime SuspenStories (EC) #6

7 ❑ Feb 1994 Cover: 2.00 **NM** value: **Cover or less**
Circ: Statement: **8,669** CapCity orders: **2,625**
📖 Hatchet-Killer!; Revenge!; Phonies; Horror Under the Big Top! • Reprints Crime SuspenStories (EC) #7

8 ❑ May 1994 Cover: 2.00 **NM** value: **Cover or less**
Circ: Statement: **8,669** CapCity orders: **2,650**
📖 Out of the Frying Pan...; A Trace of Murder!; The Escaped Maniac!; Partnership Dissolved! • Reprints Crime SuspenStories (EC) #8

9 ❑ Aug 1994 Cover: 2.00 **NM** value: **Cover or less**
Circ: Statement: **8,669** CapCity orders: **2,550**
📖 Understudy to a Corpse!; Medicine!; Cut!; A Tree Grows in Borneo! • Reprints Crime SuspenStories (EC) #9

10 ❑ Nov 1994 Cover: 2.00 **NM** value: **Cover or less**
Circ: Statement: **8,669** CapCity orders: **2,475**
📖 ...Rocks in His Head!; Lady Killer; Missed by Two Heirs!; Friend to Our Boys! • Reprints Crime SuspenStories (EC) #10

11 ❑ Feb 1995 Cover: 2.00 **NM** value: **Cover or less**
Circ: Statement: **7,137** CapCity orders: **2,380**
📖 Stiff Punishment!; One Man's Poison!; Big Money (text story); Two for One!; Four for One!; A Fool and His Honey Are Soon Parted! • Reprints Crime SuspenStories (EC) #11

12 ❑ May 1995 Cover: 2.00 **NM** value: **Cover or less**
Circ: Statement: **7,137**
📖 The Execution!; Murder the Lover!; Murder the Husband!; Trap! (text story); Snooze to Me!; Paralyzed! • Reprints Crime SuspenStories (EC) #12

13 ❑ Aug 1995 Cover: 2.00 **NM** value: **Cover or less**
Circ: Statement: **7,137** CapCity orders: **2,175**
📖 Hear no Evil!; First Impulse!; Second Chance?; Freak! (text story); A Question of Time!!; Forty Whacks! • Reprints Crime SuspenStories (EC) #13

14 ❑ Nov 1995 Cover: 2.00 **NM** value: **Cover or less**
Circ: Statement: **7,137**
📖 Sweet Dreams!; The Perfect Place!; The Electric Chair; The Hangman's Noose; The Guillotine!; Private Performance! • Reprints Crime SuspenStories (EC) #14;

15 ❑ Feb 1996 Cover: 2.00 **NM** value: **Cover or less**
Circ: Statement: **5,729**
📖 When the Cat's Away...; The Screaming Woman!; The EC Caper (text piece); Water, Water Everywhere...; ...And Not a Drop to Drink!; Hail and Heart-y! • Ray Bradbury story;Reprints Crime SuspenStories (EC) #15; Has 1995 Statement; avg print run 10,037; avg sales 6,634; avg subs 503; avg total paid 7,137; max existent 7,137; 0% of run returned

16 ❑ May 1996 Cover: 2.50 **NM** value: **Cover or less**
Circ: Statement: **5,729**
📖 Rendezvous!; Fission Bait!; Come Clean!; Who's Next? • Reprints Crime SuspenStories (EC) #16 **A:** Al Williamson; Joe Orlando; Johnny Craig; Jack Kamen **W:** Al Williamson; Joe Orlando; Johnny Craig; Jack Kamen

17 ❑ Aug 1996 Cover: 2.50 **NM** value: **Cover or less**
Circ: Statement: **5,729**
📖 Touch and Go!; One for the Money...; Fired!; ...Two for the Show! • Ray Bradbury story;Reprints Crime SuspenStories (EC) #17; Has 1996 Statement, filed 9/15/96; avg print run 7,065; avg sales 5,261; avg subs 468; avg total paid 5,729; office use 1,336; max existent 7,065; % of run returned **A:** Al Williamson; Johnny Craig; Frank Frazetta; Bill Elder; Jack Kamen **W:** Al Williamson; Johnny Craig; Frank Frazetta; Bill Elder; Jack Kamen; Ray Bradbury

18 ❑ Nov 1996 Cover: 2.50 **NM** value: **Cover or less**
Circ: Statement: **5,729** Direct Market orders: **4,790**
📖 Fall Guy for Murder; Juice for the Record!; Frozen Assets!; From Here to Insanity • Reprints Crime SuspenStories (EC) #18 **A:** Johnny Craig; Bill Elder; Reed Crandall; Jack Kamen **W:** Johnny Craig; Bill Elder; Reed Crandall; Jack Kamen

19 ❑ Feb 1997 Cover: 2.50 **NM** value: **Cover or less**
Circ: Statement: **5,243** Diamd. preorders: **4,714**
📖 The Killer; Wined-Up!; About Phase; Murder May Boomerang • Reprints Crime SuspenStories (EC) #19 **A:** George Evans; Johnny Craig; Reed Crandall **W:** George Evans; Johnny Craig; Reed Crandall

20 ❑ May 1997 Cover: 2.50 **NM** value: **Cover or less**
Circ: Statement: **5,243** Diamd. preorders: **4,813**
• Reprints Crime SuspenStories (EC) #20

21 ❑ Aug 1997 Cover: 2.50 **NM** value: **Cover or less**
Circ: Statement: **5,243** Diamd. preorders: **4,326**
• Reprints Crime SuspenStories (EC) #21

22 ❑ Nov 1997 Cover: 2.50 **NM** value: **Cover or less**
Circ: Statement: **5,243** Diamd. preorders: **4,405**
• Reprints Crime SuspenStories (EC) #22; Has X Statement, filed 1997; avg total paid circ 5,243

23 ❑ Feb 1998 Cover: 2.50 **NM** value: **Cover or less**
Circ: Diamd. preorders: **4,229**
• Reprints Crime SuspenStories (EC) #23

24 ❑ May 1998 Cover: 2.50 **NM** value: **Cover or less**
Circ: Diamd. preorders: **4,292**

🕮 Double-Crossed; Crushed Ice; Food for Thought; More Blessed to Give... • Reprints Crime SuspenStories (EC) #24 **A:** Joe Orlando; Bernie Krigstein; Reed Crandall; Jack Kamen

25 ❑ Aug 1998 Cover: 2.50 **NM** value: **Cover or less**
Circ: Diamd. preorders: **3,420**
🕮 Three for the Money; Dog Food; Key Chain; The Squealer • Reprints Crime SuspenStories (EC) #25 **A:** George Evans; Bernie Krigstein; Reed Crandall; Jack Kamen

26 ❑ Nov 1998 Cover: 2.50 **NM** value: **Cover or less**
Circ: Diamd. preorders: **3,747**
🕮 The Fixer; Dead Center; The Firebug; Comeback • Reprints Crime SuspenStories (EC) #26 **A:** Joe Orlando; Reed Crandall; Jack Kamen

27 ❑ Feb 1999 Cover: 2.50 **NM** value: **Cover or less**
Circ: Diamd. preorders: **3,621**
🕮 Maniac at Large; Just Her Speed; Where There's Smoke...; Good Boy • Reprints Crime SuspenStories (EC) #27 **A:** George Evans; Bernie Krigstein; Jack Kamen; Graham Ingels

Anl 1❑ Cover: 8.95 **NM** value: **Cover or less**
• Reprints Crime SuspenStories (EC) #1-5

Anl 2❑ Cover: 9.95 **NM** value: **Cover or less**
• Reprints Crime SuspenStories (EC) #6-10

Anl 3❑ Cover: 9.95 **NM** value: **Cover or less**
• Reprints Crime SuspenStories (EC) #11-15

Anl 4❑ Cover: 10.50 **NM** value: **Cover or less**
• Reprints Crime SuspenStories (EC) #15-19

Anl 5❑ Cover: 10.95 **NM** value: **Cover or less**
• Reprints Crime SuspenStories (EC) #20-23

Anl 6❑ Cover: 10.95 **NM** value: **Cover or less**
• Reprints Crime SuspenStories (EC) #24-27

CRIMINALS ON THE RUN — Premium

1 ❑ ca. 1948 Cover: 0.10 **NM** value: **250.00**
2 ❑ ca. 1948 Cover: 0.10 **NM** value: **200.00**
3 ❑ ca. 1948 Cover: 0.10 **NM** value: **200.00**
4 ❑ ca. 1949 Cover: 0.10 **NM** value: **200.00**
5 ❑ ca. 1949 Cover: 0.10 **NM** value: **175.00**
6 ❑ ca. 1949 Cover: 0.10 **NM** value: **175.00**
7 ❑ ca. 1949 Cover: 0.10 **NM** value: **175.00**
8 ❑ ca. 1949 Cover: 0.10 **NM** value: **175.00**
9 ❑ ca. 1949 Cover: 0.10 **NM** value: **175.00**
10 ❑ ca. 1949 Cover: 0.10 **NM** value: **175.00**

CRIMSON — Image / Cliffhanger

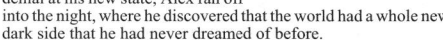

Crimson is a vampire tale that rises against the odds to give a very cool, contemporary spin on the old vampire legends.

The story features young Alex Elder, a teenager who had been going through a dark period leading up to the fateful night when he and three friends were ambushed in Central Park by a group of vampires. Alex was saved from complete dismemberment by the intervention of Ekimus, a creature almost as old as the world itself. Although Ekimus had saved Alex from extinction, he could not prevent Alex from being turned into a vampire. Raging with denial at his new state, Alex ran off into the night, where he discovered that the world had a whole new dark side that he had never dreamed of before.

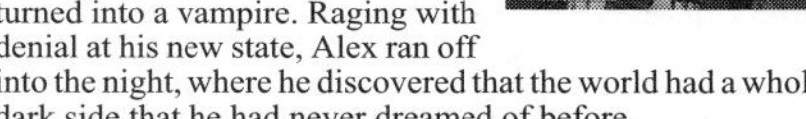

1 ❑ May 1998 Cover: 2.50 **NM** value: **3.50**
Circ: Diamd. preorders: **71,010** • **CGC:** 8 graded, best 9.8
Several figures on cover, one in cowboy hat smoking. 🕮 Dawn to Dusk **A:** Humberto Ramos **W:** Brian Augustyn; Humberto Ramos; Francisco Haghenbeck; Oscar Pinto

1/A ❑ May 1998 Cover: 4.50 **NM** value: **Cover or less**
Circ: Diamd. preorders: **37,492** • **CGC:** 3 graded, best 9.6
Boy covered in blood/rain. 🕮 Dawn to Dusk **A:** Humberto Ramos; Adam Warren(cover) **W:** Brian Augustyn; Humberto Ramos; Francisco Haghenbeck; Oscar Pinto

1/B ❑ May 1998 Cover: 2.50 **NM** value: **15.00**
• **CGC:** 9 graded, best 9.8
chromium cover. • Three figures on ledge

1/C ❑ May 1998 Cover: 2.50 **NM** value: **15.00**
chromium cover. • Dynamic Forces chromium edition with certificate of authenticity. • Boy in graveyard

2 ❑ May 1998 Cover: 2.50 **NM** value: **3.00**
Circ: Diamd. preorders: **67,115**
🕮 Unlife Story **A:** Humberto Ramos **W:** Brian Augustyn; Humberto Ramos; Francisco Haghenbeck; Oscar Pinto

2/A ❑ Jun 1998 Cover: 2.50 **NM** value: **15.00**
alternate cover (vampire). 🕮 Unlife Story **A:** Humberto Ramos **W:** Brian Augustyn; Humberto Ramos; Francisco Haghenbeck; Oscar Pinto

2/B ❑ Jun 1998 Cover: 2.50 **NM** value: **15.00**
• Crimson chrome edition. 🕮 Unlife Story **A:** Humberto Ramos **W:** Brian Augustyn; Humberto Ramos; Francisco Haghenbeck; Oscar Pinto

3 ❑ Jun 1998 Cover: 2.50 **NM** value: **3.00**
Circ: Diamd. preorders: **60,043**
🕮 Payment in Blood **A:** Humberto Ramos **W:** Brian Augustyn; Humberto Ramos; Francisco Haghenbeck; Oscar Pinto

3/A ❑ Jul 1998 Cover: 2.50 **NM** value: **4.00**
alternate cover (red background).

4 ❑ Jul 1998 Cover: 2.50 **NM** value: **Cover or less**
Circ: Diamd. preorders: **62,786**
🕮 The Children of Judas, Part 1 **A:** Humberto Ramos **W:** Brian Augustyn; Humberto Ramos; Francisco Haghenbeck; Oscar Pinto

5 ❑ Aug 1998 Cover: 2.50 **NM** value: **Cover or less**
Circ: Diamd. preorders: **64,751**
🕮 The Children of Judas, Part 2 **A:** Brian Augustyn; Humberto Ramos; Francisco Haghenbeck; Oscar Pinto **W:** Brian Augustyn; Humberto Ramos; Francisco Haghenbeck; Oscar Pinto

6 ❑ Sep 1998 Cover: 2.50 **NM** value: **Cover or less**
Circ: Diamd. preorders: **62,056**
🕮 The Children of Judas, Part 3, Running Mates **A:** Brian Augustyn; Humberto Ramos; Francisco Haghenbeck; Oscar Pinto **W:** Brian Augustyn; Humberto Ramos; Francisco Haghenbeck; Oscar Pinto

7 ❑ Dec 1998 Cover: 2.50 **NM** value: **Cover or less**
🕮 Hark **A:** Humberto Ramos **W:** Brian Augustyn; Humberto Ramos; Francisco Haghenbeck; Oscar Pinto

7/A ❑ Nov 1998 Cover: 2.50 **NM** value: **25.00**
DFE Hard-to-Get Foil covers pack. **A:** Humberto Ramos **W:** Brian Augustyn; Humberto Ramos

7/B ❑ Dec 1998 Cover: 2.50 **NM** value: **3.00**
alternate cover (angels).

7/C ❑ Dec 1998 Cover: 2.50 **NM** value: **3.00**
alternate cover (archway).

8 ❑ Dec 1999 Cover: 2.50 **NM** value: **Cover or less**
Circ: Diamd. preorders: **58,382**
A: Humberto Ramos **W:** Brian Augustyn; Humberto Ramos

9 ❑ Mar 1999 Cover: 2.50 **NM** value: **Cover or less**
Circ: Diamd. preorders: **57,502**
🕮 Raptus **A:** Humberto Ramos **W:** Brian Augustyn

10 ❑ May 1999 Cover: 2.50 **NM** value: **Cover or less**
Circ: Diamd. preorders: **53,589**
🕮 Lamentum **A:** Humberto Ramos **W:** Brian Augustyn

11 ❑ Jun 1999 Cover: 2.50 **NM** value: **Cover or less**
Circ: Diamd. preorders: **52,257**
🕮 Memoria **A:** Humberto Ramos **W:** Brian Augustyn

12 ❑ Aug 1999 Cover: 2.50 **NM** value: **Cover or less**
Circ: Diamd. preorders: **51,049**
🕮 Cantus Excio **A:** Humberto Ramos **W:** Brian Augustyn

13 ❑ Dec 1999 Cover: 2.50 **NM** value: **Cover or less**
Circ: Diamd. preorders: **45,537**
🕮 Life Sentence **A:** Humberto Ramos **W:** Brian Augustyn; Humberto Ramos; Francisco Haghenbeck; Oscar Pinto

14 ❑ Jan 2000 Cover: 2.50 **NM** value: **Cover or less**
Circ: Diamd. preorders: **43,127**
🕮 U-Turn **A:** Humberto Ramos **W:** Brian Augustyn; Humberto Ramos; Francisco Haghenbeck; Oscar Pinto

15 ❑ Feb 2000 Cover: 2.50 **NM** value: **Cover or less**
Circ: Diamd. preorders: **41,473**
A: Humberto Ramos **W:** Brian Augustyn; Humberto Ramos; Francisco Haghenbeck; Oscar Pinto

16 ❑ Mar 2000 Cover: 2.50 **NM** value: **Cover or less**
Circ: Diamd. preorders: **40,334**
A: Humberto Ramos **W:** Brian Augustyn; Humberto Ramos; Francisco Haghenbeck; Oscar Pinto

17 ❑ Apr 2000 Cover: 2.50 **NM** value: **Cover or less**
Circ: Diamd. preorders: **38,629**
🕮 Twisted Paths **A:** Humberto Ramos **W:** Brian Augustyn; Humberto Ramos; Francisco Haghenbeck; Oscar Pinto

18 ❑ Jul 2000 Cover: 2.50 **NM** value: **Cover or less**
Circ: Diamd. preorders: **38,007**
A: Humberto Ramos

19 ❑ Sep 2000 Cover: 2.50 **NM** value: **Cover or less**
Circ: Diamd. preorders: **38,014**
A: Humberto Ramos

20 ❑ Oct 2000 Cover: 2.50 **NM** value: **Cover or less**
Circ: Diamd. preorders: **35,022**
🕮 The Fire This Time **A:** Humberto Ramos **W:** Brian Augustyn

21 ❑ Nov 2000 Cover: 2.50 **NM** value: **Cover or less**
Circ: Diamd. preorders: **34,617**
🕮 Blood and Tears **A:** Humberto Ramos **W:** Brian Augustyn; Humberto Ramos; Francisco Haghenbeck; Oscar Pinto

22 ❑ Dec 2000 Cover: 2.50 **NM** value: **Cover or less**
Circ: Diamd. preorders: **34,234**
🕮 The Cleansing Fire **A:** Humberto Ramos **W:** Brian Augustyn; Humberto Ramos; Francisco Haghenbeck; Oscar Pinto

23 ❑ Jan 2001 Cover: 2.50 **NM** value: **Cover or less**
Circ: Diamd. preorders: **40,439**
🕮 The Narrowing Gyre **A:** Humberto Ramos **W:** Brian Augustyn; Humberto Ramos; Francisco Haghenbeck; Oscar Pinto

24 ❑ Apr 2001 Cover: 2.50 **NM** value: **Cover or less**
Circ: Diamd. preorders: **33,450**
🕮 Excelsus Dei **A:** Humberto Ramos **W:** Brian Augustyn; Humberto Ramos; Francisco Haghenbeck; Oscar Pinto

Bk 1❑ Sep 1999 Cover: 12.95 **NM** value: **Cover or less**
No issue number. 🕮 Dawn to Dusk; Unlife Story; Payment in Blood; The Children of Judas • Collects Crimson #1-6;Loyalty and Loss trade paperback

Bk 2❑ **NM** value: **12.95**

Bk 3❑ Cover: 14.95 **NM** value: **Cover or less**
• Earth Angel;Collects Crimson #13-18 **A:** Humberto Ramos **W:** Brian Augustyn

SE 1❑ Cover: 6.95 **NM** value: **Cover or less**
A: Humberto Ramos **W:** Brian Augustyn

SE 1/A❑ **NM** value: **12.95**
European cover. **A:** Humberto Ramos **W:** Brian Augustyn

SE 1/Aut❑ **NM** value: **19.95**
DFE alternate cover. **A:** Humberto Ramos **W:** Brian Augustyn

SE 1/SC❑ **NM** value: **10.00**
DFE alternate cover. **A:** Humberto Ramos **W:** Brian Augustyn

CRIMSON AVENGER — DC

1 ❑ Jun 1988 Cover: 1.00 **NM** value: **1.50**
Circ: CapCity orders: **18,450**
🕮 The Dark Cross Conspiracy, Part 1 **A:** Greg Brooks **W:** Roy Thomas; Dann Thomas

2 ❑ Jul 1988 Cover: 1.00 **NM** value: **1.50**
Circ: CapCity orders: **14,500**
🕮 The Dark Cross Conspiracy, Part 2 **A:** Greg Brooks **W:** Roy Thomas; Dann Thomas

3 ❑ Aug 1988 Cover: 1.00 **NM** value: **1.50**
Circ: CapCity orders: **12,450**
🕮 The Dark Cross Conspiracy, Part 3 **A:** Greg Brooks; Mike Gustovich **W:** Roy Thomas; Dann Thomas

4 ❑ Sep 1988 Cover: 1.00 **NM** value: **1.50**
Circ: CapCity orders: **11,350**
🕮 The Dark Cross Conspiracy, Part 4 **A:** Greg Brooks; Mike Gustovich **W:** Roy Thomas; Dann Thomas

CRIMSON DREAMS — Crimson

1 ❑ Cover: 2.00 **NM** value: **Cover or less**
2 ❑ Cover: 2.00 **NM** value: **Cover or less**
3 ❑ Cover: 2.00 **NM** value: **Cover or less**
4 ❑ Cover: 2.00 **NM** value: **Cover or less**
5 ❑ Cover: 2.00 **NM** value: **Cover or less**
6 ❑ Cover: 2.00 **NM** value: **Cover or less**
7 ❑ Cover: 2.00 **NM** value: **Cover or less**
8 ❑ Cover: 2.00 **NM** value: **Cover or less**
9 ❑ Cover: 2.00 **NM** value: **Cover or less**
10 ❑ Cover: 2.00 **NM** value: **Cover or less**
11 ❑ Cover: 2.00 **NM** value: **Cover or less**

CRIMSON LETTERS — Adventure

1 ❑ Cover: 2.25 **NM** value: **Cover or less**
• Adventurers b&w

CRIMSON NUN, THE — Antarctic

1 ❑ May 1997 Cover: 2.95 **NM** value: **Cover or less**
Circ: Diamd. preorders: **12,958**
🕮 Old Enemies, New Friends **A:** Bob Diaz **W:** Brian Farrens

2 ❑ Jul 1997 Cover: 2.95 **NM** value: **Cover or less**
Circ: Diamd. preorders: **8,629**
🕮 Into The Interior **A:** Bob Diaz **W:** Brian Farrens

3 ❑ Sep 1997 Cover: 2.95 **NM** value: **Cover or less**
Circ: Diamd. preorders: **7,059**
🕮 The Mountains of Death **A:** Bob Diaz **W:** Brian Farrens

4 ❑ Nov 1997 Cover: 2.95 **NM** value: **Cover or less**
Circ: Diamd. preorders: **6,274**
🕮 Stranger Than Fiction **A:** Bob Diaz **W:** Brian Farrens

CRIMSON PLAGUE — Event

1 ❑ Jun 1997 Cover: 2.95 **NM** value: **Cover or less**
Circ: Diamd. preorders: **29,006**
A: George Pérez **W:** George Pérez

1/LE❑ Jun 1997 Cover: 10.00 **NM** value: **Cover or less**
• alternate limited edition only sold at 1997 Heroes Con. **A:** George Pérez **W:** George Pérez

CRIMSON PLAGUE (GEORGE PÉREZ'S...) — Image

1 ❑ Jun 2000 Cover: 2.95 **NM** value: **Cover or less**
Circ: Diamd. preorders: **29,006**
A: George Pérez **W:** George Pérez

2 ❑ Aug 2000 Cover: 2.50 **NM** value: **Cover or less**
Circ: Diamd. preorders: **23,680**
A: George Pérez **W:** George Pérez

CRIMSON: SCARLET X BLOOD ON THE MOON — DC / Cliffhanger

1 ❑ Oct 1999 Cover: 3.95 **NM** value: **Cover or less**
Circ: Diamd. preorders: **39,242**
One-shot. **A:** Carlos Meglia **W:** Brian Augustyn; Humberto Ramos; Francisco Haghenbeck; Oscar Pinto

CRIMSON SOURCEBOOK — WildStorm

1 ❑ Nov 1999 Cover: 2.95 **NM** value: **Cover or less**
Circ: Diamd. preorders: **30,202**
A: German Garcia; Jason Pearson; Humberto Ramos; David Mack; Mike Wier **W:** Brian Augustyn; Francisco Haghenbeck

CRISIS ON INFINITE EARTHS — DC

This 12-issue maxi-series brought together almost every DC character ever created and destroyed most of the alternate Earths. A must-have for serious fans, this title attempted to clear up inconsistencies in DC continuity and provided an epic, bitter-sweet story to boot. Among the heroes who came to their final end were Supergirl, Dove, the Barry Allen Flash, the Crime Syndicate of Earth-3, and Immortal Man. The heroes and villains left after the Crisis settled in one merged Earth, allowing for more interaction between DC heroes in the future.

Unfortunately, the destruction of the alternate Earths created several new problems for DC, since the old stories that took place on them had to be explained or "retconned" ("retroactive continuity") away. To this day, fans have trouble making sense of the post-Crisis timelines of star-spanning DC groups like The Legion of Super-Heroes. This eventually necessitated DC's Zero Hour series, meant to clean up their continuity for good.

1 ❑ Apr 1985 Cover: 0.75 **NM** value: **4.00**
• **CGC:** 80 graded, best 9.9
wraparound cover. 🕮 The Summoning! **A:** George Pérez **W:** Marv Wolfman ★ 1st Appearance of Blue Beetle in DC universe. ★ Death of Crime Syndicate, Alex Luthor.

2 ❑ May 1985 Cover: 0.75 **NM** value: **3.00**
Circ: CapCity orders: **43,350** • **CGC:** 5 graded, best 9.4
A: George Pérez **W:** Marv Wolfman ★ 1st Appearance of Anti-Monitor (as shadow, voice).

3 ❑ Jun 1985 Cover: 0.75 **NM** value: **2.50**
Circ: CapCity orders: **42,050** • **CGC:** 3 graded, best 9.6
A: George Pérez **W:** Marv Wolfman ★ 1st Appearance of Nighthawk (modern). ★ Death of Gunner, Kid Psycho, Johnny Cloud, Losers, Sarge, Captain Storm, Nighthawk.

4 ❑ Jul 1985 Cover: 0.75 **NM** value: **2.50**
Circ: CapCity orders: **44,450** • **CGC:** 4 graded, best 9.6
A: George Pérez **W:** Marv Wolfman ★ 1st Appearance of Lady Quark, Doctor Light II. ★ Death of The Monitor, Lord Volt, Liana.

5 ❑ Aug 1985 Cover: 0.75 **NM** value: **2.50**

CGC-graded: Multiply prices above by **33 for 9.9 M • 16 for 9.8 NM/M • 7 for 9.6 NM+ • 5 for 9.4 NM • 2.5 for 9.2 NM- • 1.5 for 9.0 VF/NM**

Circ: CapCity orders: **42,350** • **CGC:** 2 graded, best 9.8
A: George Pérez **W:** Marv Wolfman ★ 1st Appearance of Anti-Monitor (fully shown).
6 ❑ Sep 1985 Cover: 0.75 **NM** value: **2.50**
Circ: CapCity orders: **41,500** • **CGC:** 4 graded, best 9.8
A: George Pérez **W:** Marv Wolfman ★ 1st Appearance of New Wildcat.
7 ❑ Oct 1985 Cover: 1.25 **NM** value: **4.00**
Circ: CapCity orders: **50,150** • **CGC:** 54 graded, best 9.8
• Double-size. **A:** George Pérez **W:** Marv Wolfman ★ Origin of Monitor, DC Multiverse, Anti-Monitor, the DC Multiverse. ★ Death of Supergirl.
8 ❑ Nov 1985 Cover: 0.75 **NM** value: **6.00**
Circ: CapCity orders: **41,400** • **CGC:** 41 graded, best 9.8
A: George Pérez **W:** Marv Wolfman ★ Death of Flash II (Barry Allen).
9 ❑ Dec 1985 Cover: 0.75 **NM** value: **3.00**
Circ: CapCity orders: **39,300** • **CGC:** 2 graded, best 9.2
A: George Pérez **W:** Marv Wolfman ★ 1st Appearance of Doctor Spectro in DC universe. ★ Death of five of six renegade Guardians, Lex Luthor (Earth-2).
10 ❑ Jan 1986 Cover: 0.75 **NM** value: **3.00**
Circ: CapCity orders: **38,350** • **CGC:** 3 graded, best 9.6
A: George Pérez **W:** Marv Wolfman ★ Death of Icicle, Aquagirl, Immortal Man, Mirror Master, Maaldor, Starman 3, Chemo, Psimon, Shaggy Man.
11 ❑ Feb 1986 Cover: 0.75 **NM** value: **3.00**
Circ: CapCity orders: **41,650** • **CGC:** 3 graded, best 9.4
A: George Pérez **W:** Marv Wolfman ★ 1st Appearance of Ghost (at DC). ★ Death of Angle-Man.
12 ❑ Mar 1986 Cover: 1.25 **NM** value: **4.00**
Circ: CapCity orders: **42,650** • **CGC:** 10 graded, best 9.6
A: George Pérez **W:** Marv Wolfman
Bk 1❑ Cover: 99.95 **NM** value: **Cover or less**
Hard-cover. • Collects issues #1-12 **W:** Marv Wolfman
Bk 1/Aut❑ Cover: 250.00 **NM** value: **Cover or less**
Hard-cover. • Collects issues #1-12 **W:** Marv Wolfman
Bk 1/HC❑ Cover: 99.95 **NM** value: **Cover or less**
Hard-cover. • Collects issues #1-12 **W:** Marv Wolfman

CRISP — Crisp Biscuit
1 ❑ Apr 1997 Cover: 1.95 **NM** value: **3.00**
📖 Littlefellas; Colin the Adorable Baby Rhino; A Note on the Forthcoming Apocalypse **A:** Robert Wells **W:** Robert Wells
2 ❑ Apr 1998 Cover: 1.95 **NM** value: **3.00**
📖 A Perfect Weekend **A:** Robert Wells **W:** Robert Wells

CRISP BISCUIT — Crisp Biscuit
1 ❑ Jul 1991 Cover: 1.10 **NM** value: **2.00**
📖 Murtle; She's Back; I Met Her at the Funeral; Beach Hero; T2Mar! **A:** Robert Wells; Jan Wiacek; Jason Micallef **W:** Robert Wells; Jan Wiacek; Jason Micallef

CRITICAL ERROR — Dark Horse
1 ❑ Jul 1992 Cover: 2.50 **NM** value: **Cover or less**
Circ: CapCity orders: **6,225**
No issue number. 📖 Critical Error • color reprint of silent story from The Art of John Byrne **A:** John Byrne **W:** John Byrne

CRITICAL MASS — Marvel / Epic
1 ❑ Jan 1989 Cover: 4.95 **NM** value: **Cover or less**
Circ: CapCity orders: **8,100**
📖 Extracting the Control Rods **A:** Bill Sienkiewicz; Gray Morrow; Kevin O'neil **W:** D.G. Chichester; Margaret Clark
2 ❑ Feb 1989 Cover: 4.95 **NM** value: **Cover or less**
Circ: CapCity orders: **6,450**
3 ❑ Mar 1989 Cover: 4.95 **NM** value: **Cover or less**
Circ: CapCity orders: **6,300**
4 ❑ Apr 1989 Cover: 4.95 **NM** value: **Cover or less**
Circ: CapCity orders: **5,700**
5 ❑ May 1989 Cover: 4.95 **NM** value: **Cover or less**
Circ: CapCity orders: **5,050**
6 ❑ Jun 1989 Cover: 4.95 **NM** value: **Cover or less**
Circ: CapCity orders: **4,600**
7 ❑ Jul 1989 Cover: 5.95 **NM** value: **Cover or less**
Circ: CapCity orders: **4,200**

CRITTERS — Fantagraphics
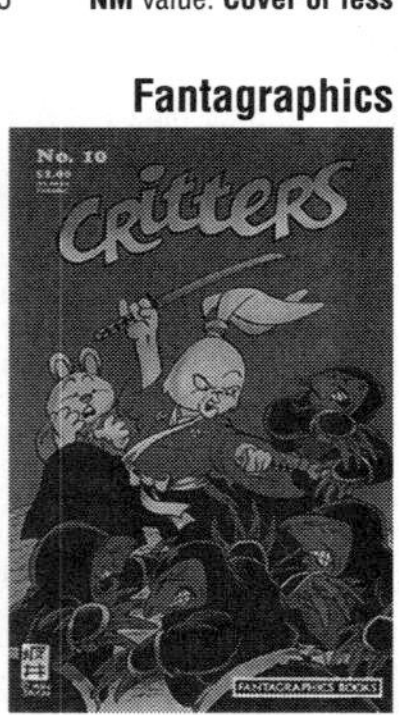

The popularity of the funny-animal adventure comic book Albedo from Thoughts and Images suggested to many that the "anthropomorhic" genre didn't have to be solely about humor. Many creators in the mid-1980s placed funny-animal characters in a variety of situations, and Fantagraphics provided one of the major showcases with Critters.

The anthology contains stories by such noted writer-artists as Joshua Quagmire, Stan Sakai, and Arn Saba, among many more. Cutey Bunny, Usagi Yojimbo, and Neil the Horse completists will need to add the series to their wantlists. — Maggie

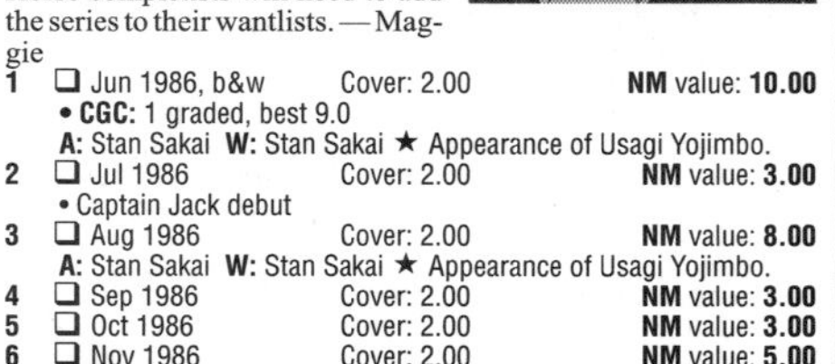
1 ❑ Jun 1986, b&w Cover: 2.00 **NM** value: **10.00**
• **CGC:** 1 graded, best 9.0
A: Stan Sakai **W:** Stan Sakai ★ Appearance of Usagi Yojimbo.
2 ❑ Jul 1986 Cover: 2.00 **NM** value: **3.00**
• Captain Jack debut
3 ❑ Aug 1986 Cover: 2.00 **NM** value: **8.00**
A: Stan Sakai **W:** Stan Sakai ★ Appearance of Usagi Yojimbo.
4 ❑ Sep 1986 Cover: 2.00 **NM** value: **3.00**
5 ❑ Oct 1986 Cover: 2.00 **NM** value: **3.00**
6 ❑ Nov 1986 Cover: 2.00 **NM** value: **5.00**
A: Stan Sakai **W:** Stan Sakai ★ Appearance of Usagi Yojimbo.
7 ❑ Dec 1986 Cover: 2.00 **NM** value: **5.00**
A: Stan Sakai **W:** Stan Sakai ★ Appearance of Usagi Yojimbo.
8 ❑ Jan 1987 Cover: 2.00 **NM** value: **3.00**
9 ❑ Feb 1987 Cover: 2.00 **NM** value: **3.00**
10 ❑ Mar 1987 Cover: 2.00 **NM** value: **4.00**
📖 Usagi Yojimbo: Homecoming; Gnuff: The Ultimate ...rva; Lionheart, Part 3; Gnuff: The Ultimate ørva **A:** Stan Sakai; Freddy Milton; Tom Stazer **W:** Stan Sakai; Freddy Milton; Tom Stazer ★ Appearance of Usagi Yojimbo.
11 ❑ Apr 1987 Cover: 2.00 **NM** value: **3.00**
12 ❑ May 1987 Cover: 2.00 **NM** value: **3.00**
13 ❑ Jun 1987 Cover: 2.00 **NM** value: **3.00**
📖 The Great Race; Birthright II: Chapter II; The History of Surfing • Gnuff story;Birthright II story **A:** Steven A. Gallacci; Mark Armstrong; Freddy Milton **W:** Steven A. Gallacci; Mark Armstrong; Freddy Milton
14 ❑ Jul 1987 Cover: 2.00 **NM** value: **3.00**
★ Appearance of Usagi Yojimbo.
15 ❑ Aug 1987 Cover: 2.00 **NM** value: **3.00**
16 ❑ Sep 1987 Cover: 2.00 **NM** value: **3.00**
17 ❑ Oct 1987 Cover: 2.00 **NM** value: **3.00**
18 ❑ Nov 1987 Cover: 2.00 **NM** value: **3.00**
• indicia says Sep 87
19 ❑ Dec 1987 Cover: 2.00 **NM** value: **3.00**
20 ❑ Jan 1988 Cover: 2.00 **NM** value: **3.00**
21 ❑ Feb 1988 Cover: 2.00 **NM** value: **2.50**
22 ❑ Mar 1988 Cover: 2.00 **NM** value: **2.50**
Watchmen parody cover. • indicia repeated from issue #21
23 ❑ Apr 1988 Cover: 3.95 **NM** value: **Cover or less**
W: Alan Moore
24 ❑ May 1988 Cover: 2.00 **NM** value: **2.50**
25 ❑ Jun 1988 Cover: 2.00 **NM** value: **2.50**
26 ❑ Jul 1988 Cover: 2.00 **NM** value: **2.50**
27 ❑ Aug 1988 Cover: 2.00 **NM** value: **2.50**
28 ❑ Sep 1988 Cover: 2.00 **NM** value: **2.50**
29 ❑ Oct 1988 Cover: 2.00 **NM** value: **2.50**
30 ❑ Nov 1988 Cover: 2.00 **NM** value: **2.50**
31 ❑ Dec 1988 Cover: 2.00 **NM** value: **2.50**
32 ❑ Jan 1989 Cover: 2.00 **NM** value: **2.50**
33 ❑ Feb 1989 Cover: 2.00 **NM** value: **2.50**
34 ❑ Mar 1989 Cover: 2.00 **NM** value: **2.50**
35 ❑ Apr 1989 Cover: 2.00 **NM** value: **2.50**
36 ❑ May 1989 Cover: 2.00 **NM** value: **2.50**
37 ❑ Jun 1989 Cover: 2.00 **NM** value: **2.50**
38 ❑ Jul 1989 Cover: 2.75 **NM** value: **Cover or less**
• Usagi Yojimbo **A:** Donna Barr **W:** Donna Barr ★ 1st Appearance of Stinz.
39 ❑ Aug 1989 Cover: 2.00 **NM** value: **2.50**
• Fission Chicken
40 ❑ Aug 1989 Cover: 2.00 **NM** value: **2.50**
📖 Gnuff
41 ❑ Sep 1989 Cover: 2.00 **NM** value: **Cover or less**
• Platypus
42 ❑ Sep 1989 Cover: 2.00 **NM** value: **Cover or less**
• Captain Jack
43 ❑ 1989 Cover: 2.00 **NM** value: **Cover or less**
44 ❑ 1989 Cover: 2.00 **NM** value: **Cover or less**
45 ❑ 1989 Cover: 2.00 **NM** value: **Cover or less**
46 ❑ 1989 Cover: 2.00 **NM** value: **Cover or less**
47 ❑ 1990 Cover: 2.00 **NM** value: **Cover or less**
48 ❑ 1990 Cover: 2.00 **NM** value: **Cover or less**
49 ❑ 1990 Cover: 2.00 **NM** value: **Cover or less**
50 ❑ 1990 Cover: 4.95 **NM** value: **Cover or less**
final issue.
SE 1❑ Jan 1988 Cover: 2.00 **NM** value: **Cover or less**
• Special #1★ Appearance of Usagi Yojimbo.

CRITTURS — Mu Press
0 ❑ Nov 1992 Cover: 2.50 **NM** value: **Cover or less**

CROMWELL STONE — Dark Horse
1 ❑ b&w Cover: 3.50 **NM** value: **Cover or less**
Circ: CapCity orders: **3,250**
No issue number. **A:** Joel Andreas **W:** Joel Andreas

CROSS — Dark Horse
0 ❑ Oct 1995 Cover: 2.95 **NM** value: **Cover or less**
1 ❑ Nov 1995 Cover: 2.95 **NM** value: **Cover or less**
📖 Genesis **A:** Shannon Londin-Gallant **W:** Chet Williamson; Andrew Vachss
2 ❑ Dec 1995 Cover: 2.95 **NM** value: **Cover or less**
📖 The Bet **A:** Shannon Londin-Gallant **W:** Chet Williamson; Andrew Vachss
3 ❑ Jan 1996 Cover: 2.95 **NM** value: **Cover or less**
A: Shannon Londin-Gallant **W:** Chet Williamson; Andrew Vachss
4 ❑ Feb 1996 Cover: 2.95 **NM** value: **Cover or less**
A: Shannon Londin-Gallant **W:** Chet Williamson; Andrew Vachss
5 ❑ Mar 1996 Cover: 2.95 **NM** value: **Cover or less**
A: Shannon Londin-Gallant **W:** Chet Williamson; Andrew Vachss
6 ❑ Apr 1996 Cover: 2.95 **NM** value: **Cover or less**
A: Shannon Londin-Gallant **W:** Chet Williamson; Andrew Vachss

Diamond preorders are the estimated number of comics sold, prior to their release, to comics shops in North America by Diamond Comic Distributors, the largest distributor. These figures underreport the actual number of circulating copies by the amount of reorders Diamond took (usually 5-10% again of the preorders) and sales by publishers to newsstand and bookstore distributors. For many independent publishers, Diamond's preorders may be quite close to the actual number of copies in circulation.

CROSS AND THE SWITCHBLADE, THE — Spire
This Christian comic tells the true story of David Wilkerson, a preacher who traveled from a small town in Pennsylvania to New York City to preach to inner-city youth gangs.

He is shocked by the drug usage, sex, and violence of the big city. With the money raised by his congregation running out, he almost loses faith when he is unable to even speak to gang members who are being sentenced to jail for murder. But he finds hope again in the streets, in the life of a hardened gang member named Nicky Cruz.

Cruz has allegedly knifed 16 people, and at first, Cruz and his gang threaten Wilkerson. But the preacher is determined to persevere. The story climaxes with a tense mass prayer rally filled with rival gang members.
1 ❑ Cover: 0.35 **NM** value: **3.00**
• Based on the book, The Cross and the Switchblade **A:** Al Hartley **W:** Al Hartley; David Wilkerson; Elizabeth Sherrill; John Sherrill

CROSSED SWORDS — K-Z
1 ❑ Dec 1986 Cover: 0.95 **NM** value: **1.00**
A: Andrew J. Barrett **W:** Tom Zjaba

CROSSFIRE — Eclipse
1 ❑ May 1984 Cover: 1.50 **NM** value: **2.50**
📖 The Long, Hard Climb To Oblivion **A:** Don Spiegle; Dan Spiegle **W:** Dan Spiegle; Mark Evanier
2 ❑ Jun 1984 Cover: 1.50 **NM** value: **1.75**
A: Don Spiegle
3 ❑ Jul 1984 Cover: 1.50 **NM** value: **1.75**
A: Don Spiegle
4 ❑ Aug 1984 Cover: 1.50 **NM** value: **1.75**
A: Don Spiegle
5 ❑ Sep 1984 Cover: 1.50 **NM** value: **1.75**
A: Don Spiegle
6 ❑ Nov 1984 Cover: 1.50 **NM** value: **1.75**
A: Don Spiegle
7 ❑ Dec 1984 Cover: 1.50 **NM** value: **1.75**
A: Don Spiegle
8 ❑ Jan 1985 Cover: 1.50 **NM** value: **1.75**
Circ: CapCity orders: **3,450**
A: Don Spiegle
9 ❑ Mar 1985 Cover: 1.50 **NM** value: **1.75**
Circ: CapCity orders: **3,675**
A: Don Spiegle
10 ❑ Apr 1985 Cover: 1.50 **NM** value: **1.75**
Circ: CapCity orders: **3,550**
A: Don Spiegle
11 ❑ May 1985 Cover: 1.50 **NM** value: **1.75**
Circ: CapCity orders: **3,675**
A: Don Spiegle
12 ❑ Jun 1985 Cover: 1.50 **NM** value: **1.75**
Circ: CapCity orders: **4,300**
Marilyn Monroe cover. • Marilyn Monroe story **A:** Don Spiegle **C:** Dave Stevens
13 ❑ Jul 1985 Cover: 1.75 **NM** value: **Cover or less**
Circ: CapCity orders: **3,675**
A: Don Spiegle
14 ❑ Aug 1985 Cover: 1.75 **NM** value: **Cover or less**
Circ: CapCity orders: **3,525**
A: Don Spiegle
15 ❑ Oct 1985 Cover: 1.75 **NM** value: **Cover or less**
Circ: CapCity orders: **3,400**
A: Don Spiegle
16 ❑ Jan 1986 Cover: 1.75 **NM** value: **Cover or less**
Circ: CapCity orders: **3,475**
A: Don Spiegle; Brent Anderson(cover)
17 ❑ Mar 1986 Cover: 1.75 **NM** value: **Cover or less**
Circ: CapCity orders: **3,550**
A: Don Spiegle
18 ❑ Jan 1987 Cover: 2.00 **NM** value: **Cover or less**
• Black & white issues begin
19 ❑ Feb 1987 Cover: 2.00 **NM** value: **Cover or less**
20 ❑ Mar 1987 Cover: 2.00 **NM** value: **Cover or less**
21 ❑ Apr 1987 Cover: 2.00 **NM** value: **Cover or less**
22 ❑ Jun 1987 Cover: 2.00 **NM** value: **Cover or less**
23 ❑ Jul 1987 Cover: 2.00 **NM** value: **Cover or less**
24 ❑ Aug 1987 Cover: 2.00 **NM** value: **Cover or less**
25 ❑ Oct 1987 Cover: 2.00 **NM** value: **Cover or less**
26 ❑ Feb 1988 Cover: 2.00 **NM** value: **Cover or less**
final issue.

CROSSFIRE AND RAINBOW — Eclipse
1 ❑ Jun 1986 Cover: 1.25 **NM** value: **Cover or less**
Circ: CapCity orders: **6,725**
📖 Jay Endicott, This is Your Sex Life! **A:** Dan Spiegle **W:** Mark Evanier
2 ❑ Jul 1986 Cover: 1.25 **NM** value: **Cover or less**
Circ: CapCity orders: **5,550**
A: Dan Spiegle **W:** Mark Evanier
3 ❑ Aug 1986 Cover: 1.25 **NM** value: **Cover or less**
Circ: CapCity orders: **5,475**
A: Dan Spiegle **W:** Mark Evanier
4 ❑ Sep 1986 Cover: 1.25 **NM** value: **Cover or less**
Circ: CapCity orders: **5,550**
A: Dan Spiegle **C:** Dave Stevens **W:** Mark Evanier

Other grades: Multiply prices above by **1.5 for Mint • 2/3 for Very Fine • 1/3 for Fine • 1/5 for Very Good • 1/8 for Good**

CROSSGEN CHRONICLES — CrossGen

The series provides freestanding stories of the CrossGeneration universe, usually set before the action of the ongoing titles. The first issue gives brief glimpses into each series at that point (Jun 00) and background on the publishing company itself. After that, however, issues are more focused. For example, #2 is set in the past of Scion; #3 shows how relationships developed leading up to the ongoing series of Meridian; #4 features the first meeting of Samandahl Rey and Tchlusarud of Sigil; #5 takes place on Mystic's Ciress; and #6 is a story from the past of Elysia of The First.
— Maggie

1 ❑ Jun 2000 Cover: 3.95 **NM** value: **Cover or less**
Circ: Diamd. preorders: **25,172** • **CGC:** 14 graded, best 9.8
• lead-in to ongoing CrossGen series;background info on creators and series
2 ❑ Mar 2001 Cover: 3.95 **NM** value: **Cover or less**
• **CGC:** 6 graded, best 9.8
3 ❑ Jun 2001 Cover: 3.95 **NM** value: **Cover or less**
4 ❑ Sep 2001 Cover: 3.95 **NM** value: **Cover or less**
5 ❑ Dec 2001 Cover: 3.95 **NM** value: **Cover or less**
6 ❑ Mar 2002 Cover: 3.95 **NM** value: **Cover or less**

CROSSGEN SAMPLER — CrossGen

1 ❑ Feb 2000 **NM** value: **1.00**
• **CGC:** 4 graded, best 9.8
no cover price. • previews of upcoming series

CROSSROADS — First

1 ❑ Jul 1988 Cover: 3.25 **NM** value: **3.50**
Circ: CapCity orders: **8,975**
• Sable, Whisper;Whisper, Sable
2 ❑ Aug 1988 Cover: 3.25 **NM** value: **3.50**
Circ: CapCity orders: **8,225**
📖 Payback • Sable, Badger **A:** Angel Medina **W:** Mike Baron
3 ❑ Sep 1988 Cover: 3.25 **NM** value: **3.50**
Circ: CapCity orders: **7,575**
• Badger, Luther Ironheart
4 ❑ Oct 1988 Cover: 3.25 **NM** value: **3.50**
Circ: CapCity orders: **7,975**
• Grimjack, Judah;Grimjack, Judah Maccabee
5 ❑ Nov 1988 Cover: 3.25 **NM** value: **3.50**
Circ: CapCity orders: **8,050**
• Grimjack, Nexus, Dreadstar

CROW, THE (CALIBER) — Caliber

Pain. Fear. Irony. Despair. Death. The Crow may be the ultimate comic book about loss. It's James O'Barr's incredibly intense tale of about having it all — and having it torn away from you.

It's about a couple named Eric and Shelley, two people who were romantically and completely in love. They were to be married, but had the bad fortune to have their car break down at the wrong place and at the wrong time. A band of wilding punks came upon them and shot Eric in the head, then brutalized and killed Shelley. In his final moments, however, Eric saw a crow...a crow who somehow ferried his soul back from death to allow him his revenge.

One of the rare comics that was successfully translated to the silver screen, the film itself was marked by the tragic accidental death of star Brandon Lee, son of Bruce Lee.

1 ❑ Feb 1989 Cover: 1.95 **NM** value: **35.00**
• **CGC:** 15 graded, best 9.6
• b&w (10, 000 print run) **A:** James O'Barr **W:** James O'Barr ★ Origin of The Crow.
1-2 ❑ Cover: 1.95 **NM** value: **5.00**
• 2nd Printing (5, 000 print run) **A:** James O'Barr **W:** James O'Barr ★ Origin of The Crow.
1-3 ❑ Cover: 1.95 **NM** value: **4.00**
• 3rd printing (5, 000 print run) **A:** James O'Barr **W:** James O'Barr ★ Origin of The Crow.
2 ❑ Mar 1989 Cover: 1.95 **NM** value: **25.00**
• **CGC:** 10 graded, best 9.6
• (7000 print run) **A:** James O'Barr **W:** James O'Barr
2-2 ❑ Dec 1989 Cover: 1.95 **NM** value: **5.00**
• 2nd Printing (5, 000 print run) **A:** James O'Barr **W:** James O'Barr
2-3 ❑ Jun 1990 Cover: 1.95 **NM** value: **4.00**
• 3rd printing (5, 000 print run) **A:** James O'Barr **W:** James O'Barr
3 ❑ Cover: 1.95 **NM** value: **20.00**
• **CGC:** 5 graded, best 9.4
• (5000 print run) **A:** James O'Barr **W:** James O'Barr
3-2 ❑ Cover: 1.95 **NM** value: **5.00**
• 2nd Printing (5, 000 print run) **A:** James O'Barr **W:** James O'Barr
4 ❑ Cover: 1.95 **NM** value: **20.00**
• **CGC:** 6 graded, best 9.4
• only printing (12, 000 print run) **A:** James O'Barr **W:** James O'Barr
Bk 1❑ Cover: 15.95 **NM** value: **Cover or less**
• Collects The Crow #1-4 **A:** James O'Barr **W:** James O'Barr

CROW, THE: CITY OF ANGELS — Kitchen Sink

1 ❑ Jul 1996 Cover: 2.95 **NM** value: **Cover or less**
• adapts movie **A:** Dean Ormston; Tim Bradstreet(cover) **W:** John Wagner
1/SC❑Jul 1996 Cover: 2.95 **NM** value: **Cover or less**
Photo cover. • adapts movie
2 ❑ Aug 1996 Cover: 2.95 **NM** value: **Cover or less**
• adapts movie **A:** Dean Ormston **W:** John Wagner
2/SC❑Aug 1996 Cover: 2.95 **NM** value: **Cover or less**
Photo cover. • adapts movie
3 ❑ Sep 1996 Cover: 2.95 **NM** value: **Cover or less**
Circ: Diamd. preorders: **22,951**
final issue. **A:** Dean Ormston **W:** John Wagner
3/SC❑Sep 1996 Cover: 2.95 **NM** value: **Cover or less**
Circ: Diamd. preorders: **18,308**
photo cover (head shot of Crow). final issue.

CROW, THE: DEAD TIME — Kitchen Sink

1 ❑ Jan 1996, b&w Cover: 2.95 **NM** value: **Cover or less**
A: Alex Maleev **W:** James O'Barr; John Wagner
2 ❑ Feb 1996 Cover: 2.95 **NM** value: **Cover or less**
A: Alex Maleev **W:** James O'Barr; John Wagner
3 ❑ Mar 1996 Cover: 2.95 **NM** value: **Cover or less**
A: Alex Maleev **W:** James O'Barr; John Wagner
Bk 1❑ Jan 1997, b&w Cover: 10.95 **NM** value: **Cover or less**
• collects mini-series

CROW, THE: FLESH & BLOOD — Kitchen Sink

1 ❑ May 1996, b&w Cover: 2.95 **NM** value: **Cover or less**
2 ❑ Jun 1996, b&w Cover: 2.95 **NM** value: **Cover or less**
3 ❑ Jul 1996, b&w Cover: 2.95 **NM** value: **Cover or less**

CROW, THE (IMAGE) — Image

1 ❑ Feb 1999 Cover: 2.50 **NM** value: **3.00**
Circ: Diamd. preorders: **42,723**
📖 Resurrection **A:** Jamie Tolagson **W:** Jon J. Muth
1/A ❑ Feb 1999 Cover: 2.50 **NM** value: **3.00**
• **CGC:** 2 graded, best 9.6
📖 Resurrection • gravestones **A:** Jamie Tolagson **W:** Jon J. Muth
2 ❑ Mar 1999 Cover: 2.50 **NM** value: **Cover or less**
Circ: Diamd. preorders: **30,720**
📖 Shadows **A:** Jamie Tolagson; Kent Williams(cover) **W:** Jon J. Muth
3 ❑ Apr 1999 Cover: 2.50 **NM** value: **Cover or less**
Circ: Diamd. preorders: **28,959**
📖 Death **A:** Jamie Tolagson; Kent Williams(cover) **W:** Jon J. Muth
4 ❑ May 1999 Cover: 2.50 **NM** value: **Cover or less**
Circ: Diamd. preorders: **26,854**
📖 The Line Between the Devil's Teeth **A:** Tommy Lee Edwards **W:** Jon J. Muth
5 ❑ Jun 1999 Cover: 2.50 **NM** value: **Cover or less**
Circ: Diamd. preorders: **23,665**
📖 In the Skin of An Angel Part 1 **A:** Paul Lee **W:** Jon J. Muth
6 ❑ Jul 1999 Cover: 2.50 **NM** value: **Cover or less**
Circ: Diamd. preorders: **21,461**
📖 In the Skin of An Angel Part 2 **A:** Paul Lee **W:** Jon J. Muth
7 ❑ Aug 1999 Cover: 2.50 **NM** value: **Cover or less**
Circ: Diamd. preorders: **19,367**
📖 Touch of Evil, Part 1 **A:** Michael Gaydos **W:** Jon J. Muth
8 ❑ Sep 1999 Cover: 2.50 **NM** value: **Cover or less**
Circ: Diamd. preorders: **17,718**
📖 Touch of Evil, Part 2 **W:** Jon J. Muth; John Kuramoto
9 ❑ Oct 1999 Cover: 2.50 **NM** value: **Cover or less**
Circ: Diamd. preorders: **16,955**
📖 Ashes to Ashes, Part 1 **A:** Jamie Tollagson **W:** Jon J. Muth; John Kuramoto
10 ❑ Nov 1999 Cover: 2.50 **NM** value: **Cover or less**
Circ: Diamd. preorders: **15,232**
📖 Ashes to Ashes, Part 2 **A:** Paul Lee **W:** Jon J. Muth; John Kuramoto

CROWN COMICS — Golfing

1 ❑ 1945 Cover: 0.10 **NM** value: **250.00**
2 ❑ 1945 Cover: 0.10 **NM** value: **200.00**
3 ❑ 1945 Cover: 0.10 **NM** value: **200.00**
4 ❑ 1946 Cover: 0.10 **NM** value: **200.00**
5 ❑ 1946 Cover: 0.10 **NM** value: **200.00**
6 ❑ Jun 1946 Cover: 0.10 **NM** value: **200.00**
• **CGC:** 1 graded, best 9.4
7 ❑ Fal 1946 Cover: 0.10 **NM** value: **175.00**
• **CGC:** 1 graded, best 3.0
8 ❑ Feb 1947 Cover: 0.10 **NM** value: **175.00**
• **CGC:** 1 graded, best 8.5
9 ❑ May 1947 Cover: 0.10 **NM** value: **150.00**
10 ❑ 1947 Cover: 0.10 **NM** value: **150.00**
11 ❑ 1947 Cover: 0.10 **NM** value: **125.00**
12 ❑ 1948 Cover: 0.10 **NM** value: **125.00**
13 ❑ 1948 Cover: 0.10 **NM** value: **125.00**
14 ❑ 1948 Cover: 0.10 **NM** value: **125.00**
15 ❑ Nov 1948 Cover: 0.10 **NM** value: **100.00**
16 ❑ Jan 1949 Cover: 0.10 **NM** value: **100.00**
17 ❑ Mar 1949 Cover: 0.10 **NM** value: **100.00**
18 ❑ May 1949 Cover: 0.10 **NM** value: **100.00**
• **CGC:** 1 graded, best 8.5
19 ❑ Jul 1949 Cover: 0.10 **NM** value: **100.00**

CROW OF THE BEARCLAN — Blackthorne

1 ❑ Oct 1986 Cover: 1.50 **NM** value: **Cover or less**
A: Ken Hooper; Edward A. Luena **W:** Ken Hooper; Shepherd Hendrix; Edward A. Luena; Greg Espinoza
2 ❑ 1987 Cover: 1.50 **NM** value: **Cover or less**
3 ❑ 1987 Cover: 1.50 **NM** value: **Cover or less**
4 ❑ 1987 Cover: 1.75 **NM** value: **Cover or less**
5 ❑ 1987 Cover: 1.75 **NM** value: **Cover or less**
6 ❑ Mar 1988 Cover: 1.75 **NM** value: **Cover or less**

CROW, THE (TUNDRA) — Tundra

1 ❑ Jan 1992, b&w Cover: 4.95 **NM** value: **Cover or less**
Circ: CapCity orders: **4,825**
• prestige format.
2 ❑ Mar 1992, b&w Cover: 4.95 **NM** value: **Cover or less**
• prestige format.
3 ❑ May 1992, b&w Cover: 4.95 **NM** value: **Cover or less**
Circ: CapCity orders: **6,950**
• prestige format.
4 ❑ Cover: 4.95 **NM** value: **Cover or less**

CROW, THE: WAKING NIGHTMARES — Kitchen Sink

1 ❑ Jan 1997, b&w Cover: 2.95 **NM** value: **Cover or less**
Circ: Diamd. preorders: **30,010**
2 ❑ Jan 1998, b&w Cover: 2.95 **NM** value: **Cover or less**
Circ: Diamd. preorders: **12,048**
3 ❑ Feb 1998, b&w Cover: 2.95 **NM** value: **Cover or less**
Circ: Diamd. preorders: **10,790**
4 ❑ May 1998, b&w Cover: 2.95 **NM** value: **Cover or less**
Circ: Diamd. preorders: **20,775**

CROW, THE: WILD JUSTICE — Kitchen Sink

1 ❑ Oct 1996, b&w Cover: 2.95 **NM** value: **Cover or less**
Circ: Diamd. preorders: **28,376**
2 ❑ Nov 1996, b&w Cover: 2.95 **NM** value: **Cover or less**
Circ: Direct Market orders: **34,166**
3 ❑ Dec 1996, b&w Cover: 2.95 **NM** value: **Cover or less**
Circ: Direct Market orders: **30,274**

CROZONIA — Image

1 ❑ Cover: 2.95 **NM** value: **Cover or less**
📖 The Tales From Crozonia **A:** Jim Su **W:** Jim Su; Dan Merisanu

CRUCIAL FICTION — Fantagraphics

1 ❑ b&w Cover: 2.50 **NM** value: **Cover or less**
2 ❑ b&w Cover: 2.25 **NM** value: **Cover or less**
3 ❑ b&w Cover: 2.25 **NM** value: **Cover or less**

CRUCIBLE — DC / Impact

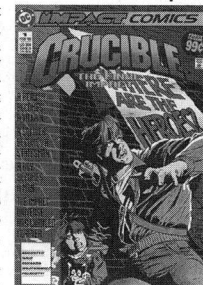

Appearing months after the last of the Impact titles were cancelled, Crucible is either a tribute to fallen heroes or the ushering in of a new era. It all takes place six months after the fall of the Crusaders. In that final story, The Comet, branded a criminal, was revealed to have been killed. The Crusaders, who had banded together to capture him decided that this was the final straw and disbanded. They stepped into interdimensional doors meant to take them home and disappeared. They were not seen again.

Now, a boy named Nathan Cray wears the Black Hood, fighting crime in a world otherwise without heroes. Meanwhile, renegade agents of The Web who go by the name of The Tomorrow Men have stumbled on The Crucible. This is a strange place which drifts free in the time continuum, letting them view the past and future. Looking through time, they plan to control the future — and manipulating Cray is the first step in doing so.

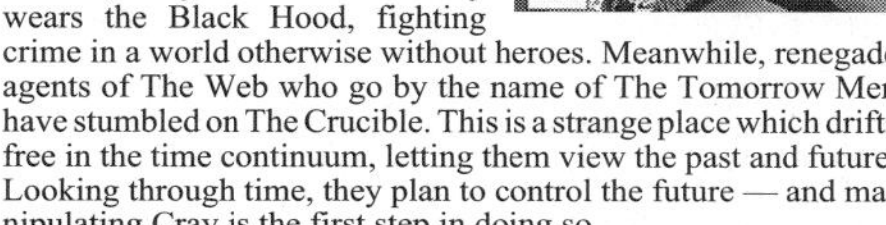

1 ❑ Feb 1993 Cover: 0.99 **NM** value: **1.50**
Circ: CapCity orders: **16,500**
📖 Hood Winked **A:** Joe Quesada **W:** Brian Augustyn; Mark Waid
2 ❑ Mar 1993 Cover: 1.25 **NM** value: **Cover or less**
Circ: CapCity orders: **9,450**
3 ❑ Apr 1993 Cover: 1.25 **NM** value: **Cover or less**
Circ: CapCity orders: **8,650**
4 ❑ May 1993 Cover: 1.25 **NM** value: **Cover or less**
Circ: CapCity orders: **8,800**
5 ❑ Jun 1993 Cover: 1.25 **NM** value: **Cover or less**
Circ: CapCity orders: **7,750**
6 ❑ Jul 1993 Cover: 1.25 **NM** value: **Cover or less**
Circ: CapCity orders: **7,400**
final issue.

CRUEL AND UNUSUAL — DC / Vertigo

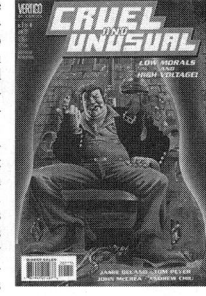

Bobbie Flint has been given the dirtiest job in the world. After a scandal, she was forced to leave her job at the Salvation Channel. Marion Meach, her obese and filthy-minded boss, has blackmailed her into becoming the warden of his god-forsaken prison in the Everglades.

The for-profit prison is automated and has almost no staff, but thanks to government regulation and fines, it's sinking into the red. The "ratburner" electric chair sets two out of three death-row inmates on fire, and the main prison industry consists of raising and skinning alligators, but Bobbie somehow has to make the place turn a profit.

Bobbie may not know anything about prisons, but she knows all about the power of television. Now if she can only survive, she's going to turn things around, and at the same time pay back Marion Meach in spades.

1 ❑ Jun 1999 Cover: 2.95 **NM** value: **Cover or less**
Circ: Diamd. preorders: **14,271**
A: John McCrea **W:** Jamie Delano; Tom Peyer
2 ❑ Jul 1999 Cover: 2.95 **NM** value: **Cover or less**
Circ: Diamd. preorders: **11,732**
A: John McCrea **W:** Jamie Delano; Tom Peyer
3 ❑ Aug 1999 Cover: 2.95 **NM** value: **Cover or less**
Circ: Diamd. preorders: **11,054**
A: John McCrea **W:** Jamie Delano; Tom Peyer
4 ❑ Sep 1999 Cover: 2.95 **NM** value: **Cover or less**
Circ: Diamd. preorders: **10,453**
A: John McCrea **W:** Jamie Delano; Tom Peyer

CRUEL & UNUSUAL PUNISHMENT — Starhead

All issues are adults only.
1 ❑ Nov 1993, b&w Cover: 2.75 **NM** value: **Cover or less**
2 ❑ Oct 1994, b&w Cover: 2.95 **NM** value: **Cover or less**

CGC-graded: Multiply prices above by **33 for 9.9 M** • **16 for 9.8 NM/M** • **7 for 9.6 NM+** • **5 for 9.4 NM** • **2.5 for 9.2 NM-** • **1.5 for 9.0 VF/NM**

CRUEL WORLD — Fantagraphics

1 ❑ b&w Cover: 3.50 **NM** value: **Cover or less**

CRUSADER FROM MARS — Ziff-Davis

1 ❑ ca. 1952 Cover: 0.10 **NM** value: **650.00**
2 ❑ Fal 1952 Cover: 0.10 **NM** value: **450.00**
• **CGC:** 1 graded, best 9.2

CRUSADERS, THE — DC / Impact

1 ❑ May 1992 Cover: 1.00 **NM** value: **Cover or less**
Circ: CapCity orders: **17,600**
📖 Blast From The Past **A:** Rags Morales **W:** Brian Augustyn; Mark Waid ★ 1st Appearance of Kalathar, Captain Commando, The American Crusaders, The Crusaders (Impact).
2 ❑ Jun 1992 Cover: 1.00 **NM** value: **Cover or less**
Circ: CapCity orders: **10,500**
3 ❑ Jul 1992 Cover: 1.00 **NM** value: **Cover or less**
Circ: CapCity orders: **9,250**
📖 Slaves of New York **A:** Rags Morales **W:** Brian Augustyn; Mark Waid
4 ❑ Aug 1992 Cover: 1.00 **NM** value: **Cover or less**
Circ: CapCity orders: **9,200**
5 ❑ Sep 1992 Cover: 1.00 **NM** value: **Cover or less**
Circ: CapCity orders: **7,600**
6 ❑ Oct 1992 Cover: 1.00 **NM** value: **Cover or less**
Circ: CapCity orders: **6,650**
7 ❑ Nov 1992 Cover: 1.00 **NM** value: **Cover or less**
Circ: CapCity orders: **6,150**
📖 Childhood's End, Part 3 **A:** Chuck Wojtkiewicz **W:** Paul Kupperberg
8 ❑ Dec 1992 Cover: 1.00 **NM** value: **Cover or less**
Circ: CapCity orders: **5,300**
final issue.

CRUSADERS — Guild

1 ❑ **NM** value: **1.00**
• Title continued in Southern Nights #2

CRUSADERS, THE (CHICK) — Chick / Impact

1 ❑ Cover: 0.59 **NM** value: **2.00**
📖 Operation Bucharest **A:** Jack T. Chick **W:** Jack T. Chick
2 ❑ Cover: 0.59 **NM** value: **2.00**
📖 The Broken Cross **A:** Jack T. Chick **W:** Jack T. Chick
3 ❑ ca. 1974 Cover: 0.59 **NM** value: **2.00**
📖 Scar Face **A:** Jack T. Chick **W:** Jack T. Chick
4 ❑ Cover: 0.59 **NM** value: **2.00**
📖 Exorcists **A:** Jack T. Chick **W:** Jack T. Chick
5 ❑ Cover: 0.59 **NM** value: **2.00**
📖 Chaos **A:** Jack T. Chick **W:** Jack T. Chick
6 ❑ Cover: 0.59 **NM** value: **2.00**
📖 Primal Man? **A:** Jack T. Chick **W:** Jack T. Chick
7 ❑ Cover: 0.59 **NM** value: **2.00**
📖 The Ark **A:** Jack T. Chick **W:** Jack T. Chick
8 ❑ Cover: 0.59 **NM** value: **2.00**
📖 The Gift **A:** Jack T. Chick **W:** Jack T. Chick
9 ❑ Cover: 0.59 **NM** value: **2.00**
📖 Angel of Light **A:** Jack T. Chick **W:** Jack T. Chick
10 ❑ Cover: 0.59 **NM** value: **2.00**
📖 Spellbound? **A:** Jack T. Chick **W:** Jack T. Chick
11 ❑ Cover: 0.59 **NM** value: **2.00**
📖 Sabotage? **A:** Jack T. Chick **W:** Jack T. Chick
12 ❑ Cover: 0.59 **NM** value: **2.00**
📖 Alberto **A:** Jack T. Chick **W:** Jack T. Chick
13 ❑ Cover: 0.59 **NM** value: **2.00**
📖 Double-Cross **A:** Jack T. Chick **W:** Jack T. Chick
14 ❑ Cover: 0.59 **NM** value: **2.00**
📖 The Godfathers **A:** Jack T. Chick **W:** Jack T. Chick
15 ❑ Cover: 0.59 **NM** value: **2.00**
📖 The Force **A:** Jack T. Chick **W:** Jack T. Chick
16 ❑ Cover: 0.59 **NM** value: **2.00**
📖 The Four Horseman **A:** Jack T. Chick **W:** Jack T. Chick

CRUSADES, THE — Vertigo / Impact

1 ❑ May 2001 Cover: 2.50 **NM** value: **Cover or less**
Circ: Diamd. preorders: **15,764**
📖 The First Crusade AD 2001 **A:** Kelley Jones **W:** Kelley Jones; Steven T. Seagle
2 ❑ Jun 2001 Cover: 2.50 **NM** value: **Cover or less**
Circ: Diamd. preorders: **14,442**
📖 The First Crusade AD 2001 **A:** Kelley Jones **W:** Kelley Jones; Steven T. Seagle
3 ❑ Jul 2001 Cover: 2.50 **NM** value: **Cover or less**
Circ: Diamd. preorders: **14,278**
4 ❑ Aug 2001 Cover: 2.50 **NM** value: **Cover or less**
Circ: Diamd. preorders: **14,466**
5 ❑ Sep 2001 Cover: 2.50 **NM** value: **Cover or less**
Circ: Diamd. preorders: **14,746**

CRUSADES, THE: URBAN DECREE — Vertigo / Impact

1 ❑ Apr 2001 Cover: 3.95 **NM** value: **Cover or less**
Circ: Diamd. preorders: **12,101**
A: Kelley Jones **W:** Steven T. Seagle

CRUSH — Aeon

1 ❑ Nov 1995, b&w Cover: 2.95 **NM** value: **Cover or less**
cardstock cover.
2 ❑ Dec 1995, b&w Cover: 2.95 **NM** value: **Cover or less**
cardstock cover.
3 ❑ Jan 1996, b&w Cover: 2.95 **NM** value: **Cover or less**
cardstock cover.
4 ❑ Feb 1996, b&w Cover: 2.95 **NM** value: **Cover or less**
cardstock cover.

CRUSH, THE — Image

Image Comics and Motown Machineworks struck a deal in 1995 that enabled Image to produce comics based on characters created by Motown. "The Crush" is about an inner-city vigilante named Dr. Pratt, who works as a psychiatrist by day. Pratt has become disgusted with the direction in which the world is headed and decides to do something about it personally. He is sought after by the police as a murderer because he kills his victims by crushing their heads. Crush's main targets are drug dealers and violent street criminals as opposed to the super-powered villains that other heroes battle.

The Crush premiered in January of 1996. Other Motown Machineworks/Image collaborations include Man Against Time and Casual Heroes, both of which also debuted in 1996.

1 ❑ Jan 1996 Cover: 2.25 **NM** value: **Cover or less**
cover says Mar, indicia says Jan. **A:** N. Steven Harris **W:** Mike Baron ★ 1st Appearance of The Crush.
2 ❑ Apr 1996 Cover: 2.25 **NM** value: **Cover or less**
W: Mike Baron
3 ❑ May 1996 Cover: 2.25 **NM** value: **Cover or less**
W: Mike Baron
4 ❑ Jun 1996 Cover: 2.25 **NM** value: **Cover or less**
W: Mike Baron
5 ❑ Jul 1996 Cover: 2.25 **NM** value: **Cover or less**
W: Mike Baron

CRUST — Top Shelf

1 ❑ b&w Cover: 3.00 **NM** value: **Cover or less**
no cover date.

CRUX — CrossGen

1 ❑ May 2001 Cover: 2.95 **NM** value: **Cover or less**
• **CGC:** 2 graded, best 9.8
2 ❑ Jun 2001 Cover: 2.95 **NM** value: **Cover or less**
3 ❑ Jul 2001 Cover: 2.95 **NM** value: **Cover or less**
4 ❑ Aug 2001 Cover: 2.95 **NM** value: **Cover or less**
5 ❑ Sep 2001 Cover: 2.95 **NM** value: **Cover or less**
6 ❑ Oct 2001 Cover: 2.95 **NM** value: **Cover or less**
7 ❑ Nov 2001 Cover: 2.95 **NM** value: **Cover or less**
8 ❑ Dec 2001 Cover: 2.95 **NM** value: **Cover or less**
9 ❑ Jan 2002 Cover: 2.95 **NM** value: **Cover or less**
10 ❑ Feb 2002 Cover: 2.95 **NM** value: **Cover or less**
11 ❑ Mar 2002 Cover: 2.95 **NM** value: **Cover or less**

CRY FOR DAWN — Cry for Dawn

All issues are adults only.

Released into relative obscurity in 1989, Cry for Dawn became the cause celebre of comics fans in the mid-1990s. Joseph Michael Linsner's Dawn first appeared in this horror anthology and was destined to become one of the most famous of the "bad girl" characters when that craze took off.

What's surprising to most is that the red-haired, scantily clad, title character appears only peripherally in this anthology. She's less than a host to the series — really more a recurring image. What makes the title really memorable are the visceral stories by Joe Monks and other writers, with finely rendered artwork by Linsner. No urban horror is too creepy for them, and they are masters at molding fantasies of sex and death into a horrifying whole.

1 ❑ Apr 1989, b&w Cover: 2.25 **NM** value: **80.00**
• **CGC:** 15 graded, best 9.4
📖 Rainstorms & Maniacs; Tokens; Paint it Black; Esque; Bring me a Dream; Kids Meal **A:** Joseph Michael Linsner **W:** Joseph Michael Linsner; Joseph M. Monks; Michael Patricks ★ 1st Appearance of Dawn.
1/A ❑ **NM** value: **15.00**
• Black light edition. 📖 Rainstorms & Maniacs; Tokens; Paint it Black; Esque; Bring me a Dream; Kids Meal **A:** Joseph Michael Linsner **W:** Joseph Michael Linsner; Joseph M. Monks; Michael Patricks
1/CF❑ Cover: 2.25 **NM** value: **15.00**
Has blotchy tones on cover. 📖 Rainstorms & Maniacs; Tokens; Paint it Black; Esque; Bring me a Dream; Kids Meal • Counterfeit version of #1 **A:** Joseph Michael Linsner **W:** Joseph Michael Linsner; Joseph M. Monks; Michael Patricks
1-2 ❑ Cover: 2.25 **NM** value: **50.00**
1-3 ❑ Cover: 2.25 **NM** value: **40.00**
• **CGC:** 1 graded, best 9.6
2 ❑ ca. 1990 Cover: 2.25 **NM** value: **60.00**
• **CGC:** 9 graded, best 9.8
A: Joseph Michael Linsner
2-2 ❑ Cover: 2.25 **NM** value: **25.00**
3 ❑ Cover: 2.25 **NM** value: **50.00**
• **CGC:** 12 graded, best 9.6
A: Joseph Michael Linsner
4 ❑ Win 1991 Cover: 2.25 **NM** value: **30.00**
• **CGC:** 8 graded, best 9.6
A: Joseph Michael Linsner
4/AUT❑Win 1991 Cover: 2.25 **NM** value: **50.00**
A: Joseph Michael Linsner
5 ❑ b&w Cover: 2.25 **NM** value: **25.00**
• **CGC:** 9 graded, best 9.6
A: Joseph Michael Linsner
5/AUT❑ Cover: 2.25 **NM** value: **40.00**
A: Joseph Michael Linsner
5-2 ❑ Cover: 2.25 **NM** value: **12.00**
6 ❑ Fal 1991, b&w Cover: 2.25 **NM** value: **25.00**
• **CGC:** 5 graded, best 9.8
A: Joseph Michael Linsner
6/AUT❑Fal 1991 Cover: 2.25 **NM** value: **30.00**
A: Joseph Michael Linsner
7 ❑ b&w Cover: 2.25 **NM** value: **20.00**
Circ: CapCity orders: **3,610** • **CGC:** 4 graded, best 9.6
A: Joseph Michael Linsner
7/AUT❑ Cover: 2.25 **NM** value: **25.00**
A: Joseph Michael Linsner
8 ❑ Win 1992, b&w Cover: 2.25 **NM** value: **20.00**
Circ: CapCity orders: **5,145** • **CGC:** 4 graded, best 9.6
A: Joseph Michael Linsner
8/AUT❑Win 1992 Cover: 2.25 **NM** value: **25.00**
• **CGC:** 1 graded, best 9.4
A: Joseph Michael Linsner
9 ❑ Spr 1992, b&w Cover: 2.25 **NM** value: **20.00**
Circ: CapCity orders: **4,850** • **CGC:** 7 graded, best 9.4
A: Joseph Michael Linsner
9/AUT❑Spr 1992 Cover: 2.25 **NM** value: **25.00**
• **CGC:** 2 graded, best 9.4
A: Joseph Michael Linsner

CRYING FREEMAN PART 1 — Viz

Yo Hinomura was a brilliant young potter, Emu Hino was a beautiful, lonely painter. Their lives were forever changed by the Chinese Mafia known as the 108 Dragons. He was unwillingly recruited to be their premier assassin, Crying Freeman. She witnessed one of his murders. Now she knows she is next!

This story is a compelling tale of crime and police politics, double crosses, deals with the devil, and a young couple who must determine what the price is of their love.

Ryoichi Ikegami is known for his lifelike style of drawing. He has also worked on Sanctuary, and Mai: The Psychic Girl, among others. Writer Kazuo Koike has produced many other works, including Lone Wolf and Cub. He also has a renowned manga artist school which produced Lum: Urusei Yatsura creator Rumiko Takahashi and Fist of the North Star artist Tetsuo Hara.

1 ❑ 1989 Cover: 3.50 **NM** value: **6.00**
📖 Mr. Yo • 1st appearance of Crying Freeman **A:** Ryoichi Ikegami **W:** Kazuo Koike ★ Origin of The 108 Dragons, Emu Hino. ★ 1st Appearance of Koh Tokugen, Yo Hinomura a.k.a. Crying Freeman, Emu Hino.
2 ❑ Cover: 3.50 **NM** value: **5.00**
📖 Mr. Yo **A:** Ryoichi Ikegami **W:** Kazuo Koike ★ 1st Appearance of Detective Nitta, Ryuji "The Blade". ★ 2nd Appearance of Koh Tokugen, Yo Hinomura a.k.a. Crying Freeman, Emu Hino.
3 ❑ Cover: 3.50 **NM** value: **5.00**
📖 Mr. Yo **A:** Ryoichi Ikegami **W:** Kazuo Koike ★ 2nd Appearance of Detective Nitta, Ryuji "The Blade". ★ Appearance of Koh Tokugen, Yo Hinomura a.k.a. Crying Freeman, Emu Hino.
4 ❑ 1990 Cover: 3.50 **NM** value: **4.00**
📖 Mr. Yo **A:** Ryoichi Ikegami **W:** Kazuo Koike ★ Origin of Crying Freeman. ★ 1st Appearance of Rushichiryu a.k.a. The Seven Crying Dragons a.k.a. Father Dragon. ★ Appearance of Koh Tokugen, Yo Hinomura a.k.a. Crying Freeman, Emu Hino.
5 ❑ 1990 Cover: 3.50 **NM** value: **4.00**
📖 Mr. Yo • Crying Freeman gets tattooed **A:** Ryoichi Ikegami **W:** Kazuo Koike ★ 1st Appearance of Fuh Fung Ling a.k.a. The Tigress a.k.a. Mother Tiger. ★ 2nd Appearance of Father Dragon. ★ Appearance of Yo Hinomura a.k.a. Crying Freeman.
6 ❑ 1990 Cover: 3.50 **NM** value: **4.00**
📖 Mr. Yo **A:** Ryoichi Ikegami **W:** Kazuo Koike ★ 2nd Appearance of Mother Tiger. ★ Appearance of Koh Tokugen, Yo Hinomura a.k.a. Crying Freeman, Emu Hino, Ryuji "The Blade".
7 ❑ 1990 Cover: 3.50 **NM** value: **4.00**
📖 Mr. Yo; Fallen Flower; Flowing Water **A:** Ryoichi Ikegami **W:** Kazuo Koike ★ Appearance of Detective Nitta.
8 ❑ 1990 Cover: 3.50 **NM** value: **4.00**
📖 Fallen Flower; Flowing Water **A:** Ryoichi Ikegami **W:** Kazuo Koike ★ 2nd Appearance of Kimie Hanada. ★ Appearance of Koh Tokugen, Mother Tiger, Detective Nitta, Yo Hinomura a.k.a. Crying Freeman, Emu Hino.
Bk 1❑ Cover: 16.95 **NM** value: **Cover or less**
• Portrait of a Killer Vol. 1

CRYING FREEMAN PART 2 — Viz

1 ❑ 1990 Cover: 3.50 **NM** value: **4.00**
📖 The Tiger Orchid **A:** Ryoichi Ikegami **W:** Kazuo Koike ★ Appearance of Father Dragon, Koh Tokugen, Mother Tiger, Crying Freeman, Emu Hino.
2 ❑ Cover: 3.50 **NM** value: **4.00**
📖 The Tiger Orchid **A:** Ryoichi Ikegami **W:** Kazuo Koike ★ Appearance of Crying Freeman.
3 ❑ Cover: 3.50 **NM** value: **4.00**
📖 The Tiger Orchid; The Wind and the Crane **A:** Ryoichi Ikegami **W:** Kazuo Koike ★ 1st Appearance of Kitche. ★ 2nd Appearance of Ivory Fan. ★ Appearance of Father Dragon, Koh Tokugen, Fu Ching Lan, Mother Tiger, Crying Freeman.
4 ❑ Cover: 3.75 **NM** value: **4.00**
📖 The Wind and the Crane; The Marital Vows **A:** Ryoichi Ikegami **W:** Kazuo Koike ★ 2nd Appearance of Kitche. ★ Appearance of Ivory Fan, Koh Tokugen, Fu Ching Lan, Crying Freeman. ★ Death of Koh Tokugen, Kitche.

Other grades: Multiply prices above by **1.5 for Mint • 2/3 for Very Fine • 1/3 for Fine • 1/5 for Very Good • 1/8 for Good**

5 ❑ Cover: 3.95 **NM value: 4.00**
🕮 The Separation of Dragon and the Tiger; The Killing Ring **A:** Ryoichi Ikegami **W:** Kazuo Koike ★ 1st Appearance of Shikebaro. ★ 2nd Appearance of the Ten Planets, Old Man Mars. ★ Appearance of Ivory Fan, Crying Freeman.
6 ❑ Cover: 3.95 **NM value: 4.00**
🕮 The Killing Ring **A:** Ryoichi Ikegami **W:** Kazuo Koike ★ Appearance of Crying Freeman. ★ Death of Old Man Venus, Old Man Earth, Old Man Jupiter, Old Man Saturn, Old Man Mars.
7 ❑ Cover: 3.95 **NM value: 4.00**
🕮 The Killing Ring **A:** Ryoichi Ikegami **W:** Kazuo Koike ★ Death of Shikeb.
8 ❑ Cover: 3.95 **NM value: 4.00**
🕮 Sister **A:** Ryoichi Ikegami **W:** Kazuo Koike ★ Appearance of Ivory Fan, Fu Ching Lan, Crying Freeman.
9 ❑ 1991 Cover: 3.95 **NM value: 4.00**
🕮 Sister **A:** Ryoichi Ikegami **W:** Kazuo Koike ★ Origin of Muramasa. ★ 1st Appearance of Goken Ishida. ★ 2nd Appearance of Professor Mikage, Muramasa. ★ Appearance of Ivory Fan, Fu Ching Lan, Crying Freeman.
Bk 2❑ Cover: 16.95 NM value: **Cover or less**
• Portrait of a Killer Vol. 2

CRYING FREEMAN PART 3 — Viz

1 ❑ 1991full color Cover: 4.95 **NM value: 5.50**
Circ: CapCity orders: **5,500**
🕮 Tohgoku Oshu • 1st issue in color **A:** Ryoichi Ikegami **W:** Kazuo Koike ★ 1st Appearance of Tohgoku Oshu. ★ 2nd Appearance of Goken Ishida. ★ Appearance of Fu Ching Lan, Dark Eyes, Crying Freeman, Kimie Hanada, Muramasa.
2 ❑ full color Cover: 4.95 **NM value: 5.00**
Circ: CapCity orders: **4,750**
🕮 Tohgoku Oshu • color **A:** Ryoichi Ikegami **W:** Kazuo Koike ★ 2nd Appearance of Tohgoku Oshu. ★ Appearance of Ivory Fan, Fu Ching Lan, Dark Eyes, Crying Freeman, Kimie Hanada.
3 ❑ full color Cover: 4.95 **NM value: 5.00**
Circ: CapCity orders: **4,625**
🕮 Tohgoku Oshu • color **A:** Ryoichi Ikegami **W:** Kazuo Koike ★ Appearance of Ivory Fan, Crying Freeman, Kimie Hanada, Tohgoku Oshu.
4 ❑ full color Cover: 4.95 **NM value: 5.00**
Circ: CapCity orders: **4,350**
🕮 Tohgoku Oshu • color **A:** Ryoichi Ikegami **W:** Kazuo Koike ★ Appearance of Crying Freeman, Kimie Hanada, Tohgoku Oshu.
5 ❑ full color Cover: 4.95 **NM value: 5.00**
Circ: CapCity orders: **4,200**
🕮 Tohgoku Oshu • color **A:** Ryoichi Ikegami **W:** Kazuo Koike
6 ❑ full color Cover: 4.95 **NM value: 5.00**
Circ: CapCity orders: **3,550**
🕮 Tohgoku Oshu • color **A:** Ryoichi Ikegami **W:** Kazuo Koike ★ 2nd Appearance of Master Naiji, Kumagaism. ★ Appearance of Detective Nitta, Crying Freeman, Kimie Hanada, Tohgoku Oshu.
7 ❑ full color Cover: 4.95 **NM value: 5.00**
Circ: CapCity orders: **3,500**
🕮 Tohgoku Oshu • color **A:** Ryoichi Ikegami **W:** Kazuo Koike ★ Appearance of Detective Nitta, Crying Freeman, Master Naiji, Kimie Hanada, Tohgoku Oshu.
8 ❑ full color Cover: 4.95 **NM value: 5.00**
Circ: CapCity orders: **3,325**
🕮 Nothing Ventured, Nothing Gained • color **A:** Ryoichi Ikegami **W:** Kazuo Koike ★ Appearance of Master Naiji.
9 ❑ full color Cover: 4.95 **NM value: 5.00**
Circ: CapCity orders: **3,150**
🕮 Nothing Ventured, Nothing Gained • color **A:** Ryoichi Ikegami **W:** Kazuo Koike ★ Appearance of Ivory Fan, Detective Nitta, Crying Freeman, Master Naiji, Kimie Hanada, Mr. Imaida, Tohgoku Oshu. ★ Death of Detective Nitta.
10 ❑ 1992full color Cover: 4.95 **NM value: 5.00**
Circ: CapCity orders: **3,550**
🕮 Nothing Ventured, Nothing Gained • color **A:** Ryoichi Ikegami **W:** Kazuo Koike ★ Appearance of Fu Ching Lan, Dark Eyes, Crying Freeman, Master Naiji, Kimie Hanada, Tohgoku Oshu, Muramasa. ★ Death of Master Naiji, Tohgoku Oshu.
Bk 3❑ Cover: 14.95 NM value: **Cover or less**
• Shades of Death Vol. 1
Bk 4❑ Cover: 14.95 NM value: **Cover or less**
• Shades of Death Vol. 2

CRYING FREEMAN PART 4 — Viz

1 ❑ Cover: 4.95 **NM value: 5.00**
Circ: CapCity orders: **3,000**
🕮 The Pomegranate **A:** Ryoichi Ikegami **W:** Kazuo Koike ★ 1st Appearance of Wong Da Ren, Wong Shaku. ★ Appearance of Fu Ching Lan, Crying Freeman.
2 ❑ Cover: 4.95 **NM value: 5.00**
Circ: CapCity orders: **3,275**
🕮 The Pomegranate **A:** Ryoichi Ikegami **W:** Kazuo Koike ★ 1st Appearance of Lucky Boyd. ★ 2nd Appearance of Wong Da Ren, Wong Shaku. ★ Appearance of Crying Freeman.
3 ❑ Cover: 4.95 **NM value: 5.00**
Circ: CapCity orders: **3,300**
🕮 The Pomegranate **A:** Ryoichi Ikegami **W:** Kazuo Koike ★ 1st Appearance of Wong Woh-Pei, Wong parents. ★ 2nd Appearance of Lucky Boyd. ★ Appearance of Ivory Fan, Crying Freeman.
4 ❑ Cover: 2.75 **NM value: 3.00**
Circ: CapCity orders: **3,125**
🕮 The Pomegranate **A:** Ryoichi Ikegami **W:** Kazuo Koike ★ 1st Appearance of Larry Buck. ★ 2nd Appearance of Wong Woh-Pei. ★ Appearance of Ivory Fan, Crying Freeman, Lucky Boyd.
5 ❑ Cover: 2.75 **NM value: 3.00**
Circ: CapCity orders: **3,075**
🕮 The Pomegranate **A:** Ryoichi Ikegami **W:** Kazuo Koike ★ Origin of Kidnappers Organization. ★ 1st Appearance of Nina Heaven. ★ 2nd Appearance of Larry Buck. ★ Appearance of Ivory Fan, Crying Freeman, Wong Woh-Pei.
6 ❑ Cover: 2.75 **NM value: 3.00**
Circ: CapCity orders: **3,075**
🕮 The Pomegranate **A:** Ryoichi Ikegami **W:** Kazuo Koike ★ Origin of Nina Heaven. ★ 2nd Appearance of Nina Heaven, Wong parents. ★ Appearance of Ivory Fan, Fu Ching Lan, Dark Eyes, Crying Freeman, Wong Woh-Pei, Muramasa.
7 ❑ Cover: 2.75 **NM value: 3.00**
Circ: CapCity orders: **2,950**
🕮 The Pomegranate **A:** Ryoichi Ikegami **W:** Kazuo Koike ★ Appearance of Ivory Fan, Nina Heaven, Fu Ching Lan, Crying Freeman, Larry Buck, Wong Woh-Pei.
8 ❑ Cover: 2.75 **NM value: 3.00**
Circ: CapCity orders: **2,825**
🕮 The Pomegranate **A:** Ryoichi Ikegami **W:** Kazuo Koike ★ Appearance of Ivory Fan, Nina Heaven, Fu Ching Lan, Crying Freeman, Larry Buck, Wong Woh-Pei, Muramasa. ★ Death of Nina Heaven, Larry Buck.
Bk 5❑ Sep 1994 Cover: 14.95 NM value: **Cover or less**
• Journey to Freedom Vol. 1

CRYING FREEMAN PART 5 — Viz

1 ❑ b&w Cover: 2.75 NM value: **Cover or less**
Circ: CapCity orders: **3,150**
🕮 Journey to Freedom **A:** Ryoichi Ikegami **W:** Kazuo Koike ★ 1st Appearance of Kitaro Tachibana, Yuhei Wadashima, Kimiryu Fumiyama (full). ★ Appearance of Crying Freeman.
2 ❑ b&w Cover: 2.75 NM value: **Cover or less**
Circ: CapCity orders: **2,975**
🕮 Journey to Freedom **A:** Ryoichi Ikegami **W:** Kazuo Koike ★ 1st Appearance of Choko Tateoka, Yujin Fumiyama (full). ★ 2nd Appearance of Kimiryu Fumiyama, Kitaro Tachibana, Yuhei Wadashima. ★ Appearance of Crying Feeman.
3 ❑ b&w Cover: 2.75 NM value: **Cover or less**
Circ: CapCity orders: **2,850**
🕮 Journey to Freedom **A:** Ryoichi Ikegami **W:** Kazuo Koike ★ 2nd Appearance of Choko Tateoka, Yujin Fumiyama. ★ Appearance of Kimiryu Fumiyama, Crying Freeman. ★ Death of Choko Tateoka.
4 ❑ b&w Cover: 2.75 NM value: **Cover or less**
Circ: CapCity orders: **2,950**
🕮 Journey to Freedom **A:** Ryoichi Ikegami **W:** Kazuo Koike ★ 1st Appearance of Kyutche, Mr. Tsunaike. ★ Appearance of Kitaro Tachibana. ★ Appearance of Dark Eyes. ★ Appearance of Crying Freeman. ★ Appearance of Yuhei Wadashima. ★ Death of Yuhei Wadashima.
5 ❑ b&w Cover: 2.75 NM value: **Cover or less**
Circ: CapCity orders: **3,050**
🕮 Journey to Freedom **A:** Ryoichi Ikegami **W:** Kazuo Koike ★ 2nd Appearance of Kyutche. ★ 2nd Appearance of Mr. Tsunaike. ★ Appearance of Crying Freeman. ★ Death of Kyutche.
6 ❑ b&w Cover: 2.75 NM value: **Cover or less**
Circ: CapCity orders: **2,900**
🕮 Journey to Freedom **A:** Ryoichi Ikegami **W:** Kazuo Koike ★ 1st Appearance of Romanof (cameo). ★ Appearance of Crying Freeman. ★ Appearance of Mr. Tsunaike.
7 ❑ b&w Cover: 2.75 NM value: **Cover or less**
Circ: CapCity orders: **2,775**
🕮 Journey to Freedom **A:** Ryoichi Ikegami **W:** Kazuo Koike ★ 1st Appearance of Romanof (full). ★ Appearance of Crying Freeman. ★ Appearance of Mr. Tsunaike.
8 ❑ b&w Cover: 2.75 NM value: **Cover or less**
🕮 Journey to Freedom **A:** Ryoichi Ikegami **W:** Kazuo Koike ★ 2nd Appearance of Romanof. ★ Appearance of Crying Freeman, Mr. Tsunaike. ★ Death of Romanof, Mr. Tsunaike.
9 ❑ b&w Cover: 2.75 NM value: **Cover or less**
🕮 Journey to Freedom **A:** Ryoichi Ikegami **W:** Kazuo Koike ★ 1st Appearance of Rie Katase as an adult. ★ 1st Appearance of Yo Hinomura a.k.a. Crying Freeman as a boy (cameo), Rie Katase as a girl (cameo). ★ Appearance of Crying Freeman.
10 ❑ b&w Cover: 2.75 NM value: **Cover or less**
Circ: CapCity orders: **2,575**
🕮 Journey to Freedom **A:** Ryoichi Ikegami **W:** Kazuo Koike ★ 2nd Appearance of Rie Katase. ★ Appearance of Ivory Fan. ★ Appearance of Crying Freeman.
11 ❑ b&w Cover: 2.75 NM value: **Cover or less**
Bk 6❑ Cover: 14.95 NM value: **Cover or less**
• Journey to Freedom Vol. 2

CRYING FREEMAN PERFECT COLLECTION — Viz

Bk 1❑ Cover: 19.95 NM value: **Cover or less**
• Portrait of a Killer
Bk 2❑ Cover: 19.95 NM value: **Cover or less**
• Shades of Death
Bk 3❑ Cover: 19.95 NM value: **Cover or less**
• The Killing Ring
Bk 4❑ Cover: 19.95 NM value: **Cover or less**
• A Taste of Revenge
Bk 5❑ Cover: 17.95 NM value: **Cover or less**
• Abduction in Chinatown

CRYPT — Image

1 ❑ Aug 1995 Cover: 2.50 NM value: **Cover or less**
Circ: CapCity orders: **19,775**
A: Shelby Robertson **W:** Robert Napton
2 ❑ Oct 1995 Cover: 2.50 NM value: **Cover or less**
Circ: CapCity orders: **12,875**
A: Shelby Robertson **W:** Robert Napton

Capital City orders are the actual sales of comic books by Capital City Distribution, once one of the largest U.S. sellers of comics to comics shops. Capital City's share of comics shop sales, while not known exactly, increases from around 10-20% in the mid-1980s to 30-35% in the mid-1990s. Capital City's share of comic books sold on newsstands (most Marvels and DCs) will be less.

CRYPT, THE — Aaaargh!

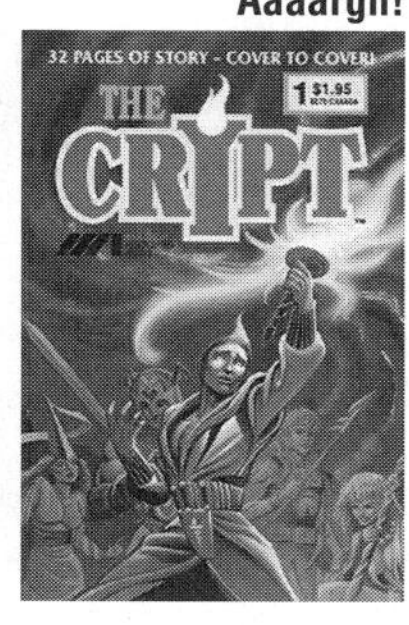

The Crypt is a black-and-white series that chronicles the adventures of a group of teen-agers in a forgotten land. The teen-agers are Sean Gallagher, a 14-year-old boy; Sean's older brother, Steven; Casey, Steven's girlfriend; Josh, a football jock; and Becky, Casey's girlfriend. The teens explore an ancient crypt in which they lose Sean. Steven and Josh go to look for him and find that they have accidentally stumbled upon a strange new world of fantasy. The girls soon join the boys and they band together in an effort to locate Sean. Along the way, the teens fight monsters, save princesses, and meet wise sorcerers.
1 ❑ Cover: 1.95 NM value: **Cover or less**
A: Marc Hempel; Damon Willis; Mark Wheatley(inks) **W:** Gregory Krolczyk

CRYPTIC TALES — Showcase

1 ❑ Cover: 1.95 NM value: **Cover or less**

CRYPTIC WRITINGS OF MEGADETH — Chaos

1 ❑ Sep 1997 Cover: 2.95 NM value: **Cover or less**
Circ: Diamd. preorders: **21,038** • **CGC:** 1 graded, best 9.6
alternate cardstock cover. • Necro Limited Premium Edition. 🕮 Skull Beneath the Skin; Rattlehead; Looking Down the Cross • comics adaptation of Megadeath songs **A:** David Brewer; Robert Brown; Justiniano **W:** Brian Pulido; Dave Mustaine; Mike Flippin
2 ❑ Dec 1997 Cover: 2.95 NM value: **Cover or less**
Circ: Diamd. preorders: **18,618**
• comics adaptation of Megadeath songs **A:** David Brewer; Robert Brown; Justiniano **W:** Brian Pulido; Dave Mustaine; Mike Flippin
Bk 1❑ Dec 1998 Cover: 12.95 NM value: **Cover or less**
• premium edition. • collects mini-series **A:** David Brewer; Robert Brown; Justiniano **W:** Brian Pulido; Dave Mustaine; Mike Flippin
Bk 1/Dlx❑ Cover: 25.00 NM value: **Cover or less**
• Tour Edition. • Leather-bound **A:** David Brewer; Robert Brown; Justiniano **W:** Brian Pulido; Dave Mustaine; Mike Flippin
Bk 1/LE❑ Cover: 50.00 NM value: **Cover or less**
• Tour Edition. **A:** David Brewer; Robert Brown; Justiniano **W:** Brian Pulido; Dave Mustaine; Mike Flippin

CRYPT OF C*M — Eros

1 ❑ Feb 1999 Cover: 2.95 NM value: **Cover or less**
🕮 The Cumback!; Mr. Keys; The Gizfreek! **A:** Dementia **W:** Dementia

CRYPT OF DAWN — Sirius

1 ❑ Oct 1996 Cover: 2.95 **NM value: 4.00**
Circ: Diamd. preorders: **54,576** • **CGC:** 1 graded, best 9.8
🕮 Enter the Crypt; Vicariosity; Tombstone Girls; Rhyder the Blind Beast; Reflections **A:** Saverio Tenuta; Joseph Michael Linsner; Fillbach Brothers **W:** Joseph Michael Linsner; Robb Horan
1/LE❑ Oct 1996 **NM value: 14.00**
• **CGC:** 1 graded, best 9.6
2 ❑ Apr 1997 Cover: 2.95 **NM value: 3.00**
Circ: Diamd. preorders: **44,335**
🕮 Five Minutes of My Life; The Fool of the Web; Mother Instinct; Rapid Eye Movements, Part 1 **A:** David Mack; Joseph Michael Linsner; Roel; Ronald Russell Roach **W:** David Mack; Patricia Breen; Ronald Russell Roach; John Finnegan
3 ❑ Feb 1998 Cover: 2.95 **NM value: 3.00**
4 ❑ Jun 1998 Cover: 2.95 NM value: **Cover or less**
Circ: Diamd. preorders: **26,471**
• color story
5 ❑ Nov 1998 Cover: 2.95 NM value: **Cover or less**
Circ: Diamd. preorders: **21,850**
6 ❑ Mar 1999 Cover: 2.95 NM value: **Cover or less**
• **CGC:** 1 graded, best 9.6
Bk 1❑ Cover: 19.95 NM value: **Cover or less**
🕮 The Best of the Crypt of Dawn • collects mini-series

CRYPT OF SHADOWS — Marvel

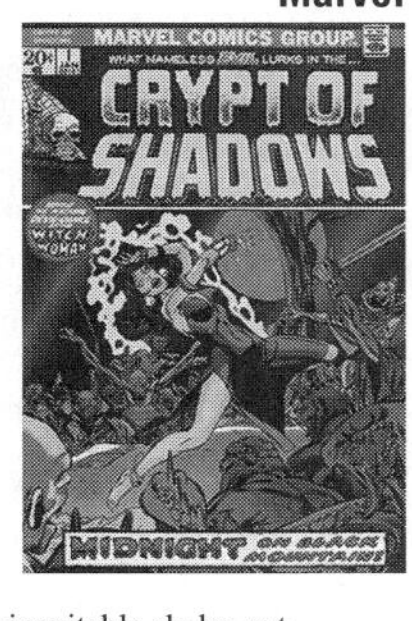

Crypt of Shadows was one of the many horror titles Marvel published in the early 1970s. The Comics Code had relaxed its earlier prohibitions against depicting monsters and ghouls, giving Marvel a chance to reprint reams of material which had lain fallow for years.

The series started out on a strong note, reprinting the classic "Midnight on Black Mountain" from Adventures into Terror #7. Unfortunately, the stories that followed were not compelling enough to win the necessary readers away from DC. The 1970s were tough times in the horror comic business, and Crypt of Shadows fell victim to the inevitable shake-out.
1 ❑ Jan 1973 Cover: 0.20 **NM value: 6.00**
• **CGC:** 1 graded, best 8.5
🕮 Midnight On Black Mountain • Reprints Adventures into Terror #7 **A:** Basil Wolverton
2 ❑ Mar 1973 Cover: 0.20 **NM value: 4.00**
3 ❑ May 1973 Cover: 0.20 **NM value: 4.00**
4 ❑ Jul 1973 Cover: 0.20 **NM value: 3.50**
5 ❑ Sep 1973 Cover: 0.20 **NM value: 3.50**
6 ❑ Oct 1973 Cover: 0.20 **NM value: 3.00**
7 ❑ Nov 1973 Cover: 0.20 **NM value: 3.00**

CGC-graded: Multiply prices above by **33 for 9.9 M • 16 for 9.8 NM/M • 7 for 9.6 NM+ • 5 for 9.4 NM • 2.5 for 9.2 NM- • 1.5 for 9.0 VF/NM**

8 ❑ Jan 1974 Cover: 0.20 **NM** value: **3.00**
9 ❑ Mar 1974 Cover: 0.20 **NM** value: **3.00**
10 ❑ May 1974 Cover: 0.25 **NM** value: **3.00**
• **CGC:** 1 graded, best 9.2
11 ❑ Jul 1974 Cover: 0.25 **NM** value: **2.50**
12 ❑ Sep 1974 Cover: 0.25 **NM** value: **2.50**
13 ❑ Oct 1974 Cover: 0.25 **NM** value: **2.50**
14 ❑ Nov 1974 Cover: 0.25 **NM** value: **2.50**
15 ❑ Jan 1975 Cover: 0.25 **NM** value: **2.50**
• **CGC:** 1 graded, best 9.4
16 ❑ Mar 1975 Cover: 0.25 **NM** value: **2.50**
17 ❑ May 1975 Cover: 0.25 **NM** value: **2.50**
18 ❑ Jul 1975 Cover: 0.25 **NM** value: **2.50**
I Dared to Look Into The Beyond • Reprints Tales to Astonish #11
19 ❑ Sep 1975 Cover: 0.25 **NM** value: **2.50**
20 ❑ Oct 1975 Cover: 0.25 **NM** value: **2.50**
The Martian Who Stole A City • Reptints Tales of Suspense #29
21 ❑ Nov 1975 Cover: 0.25 **NM** value: **2.50**

CRYPT OF TERROR — E.C.

The E.C. New Trend title was a continuation of the company's Crime Patrol series and had as its "host" The Crypt-Keeper, who had been introduced in the earlier series' issue #15. Picking up Crime Patrol's numbering with #17, the title changed again with #20 to Tales from the Crypt.

The covers of all three issues told readers that the series introduced "A New Trend in Magazines...Illustrated Suspenstories We Dare You to Read!" E.C. creators featured in the series' short run included Al Feldstein, Harvey Kurtzman, Wally Wood, Johnny Craig, Graham Ingels, and George Roussos. — Maggie

17 ❑ Apr 1950 Cover: 0.10 **NM** value: **1000.00**
• **CGC:** 13 graded, best 9.6
18 ❑ Jun 1950 Cover: 0.10 **NM** value: **800.00**
• **CGC:** 10 graded, best 9.8
19 ❑ Aug 1950 Cover: 0.10 **NM** value: **750.00**
• **CGC:** 11 graded, best 9.8

CRYSTAL BALLS — Eros

1 ❑ Cover: 2.95 **NM** value: **Cover or less**
2 ❑ Sep 1995 Cover: 2.95 **NM** value: **Cover or less**
The Bridge **A:** Noppie Noppenberger **W:** Noppie Noppenberger

CRYSTAL BREEZE UNLEASHED — High Impact

All issues are adults only.
1 ❑ Oct 1996, b&w Cover: 3.00 **NM** value: **Cover or less**
Circ: Diamd. preorders: **5,979**
no cover price.

CRYSTAL SKULL FILES, THE — Ink & Feathers

1 ❑ Cover: 11.95 **NM** value: **Cover or less**
The Crystal Skull Files, a First Amendment Fable for all ages; Squirrelman: Interlude; Fein-Man; The Confederacy; How to succeed in Cartooning without Getting Slapped Too HardAshpile; **A:** Jim Ridings; Andy Hall; Eric T. Gradberg; Kevin P. Craver **W:** Jim Ridings; Andy Hall; Eric T. Gradberg; Kevin P. Craver

CRYSTAL WAR, THE — Atlantis

1 ❑ Cover: 3.50 **NM** value: **Cover or less**
A: Mats Engesten **W:** James Watson

CTHULHU (H.P. LOVECRAFT'S...) — Millennium

1 ❑ Cover: 2.50 **NM** value: **Cover or less**
Circ: CapCity orders: **10,575**
The Festival, Part 1 **A:** Brian Michael Bendis **W:** R.J.M. Lofficier; H.P. Lovecraft; Roy Thomas
1/CS❑ Cover: 3.50 **NM** value: **Cover or less**
The Festival, Part 1 • trading cards **A:** Brian Michael Bendis **W:** R.J.M. Lofficier; H.P. Lovecraft; Roy Thomas
2 ❑ Cover: 2.50 **NM** value: **Cover or less**
The Festival, Part 2 • trading cards **A:** Brian Michael Bendis **W:** R.J.M. Lofficier; H.P. Lovecraft; Roy Thomas
3 ❑ Cover: 2.50 **NM** value: **Cover or less**
Circ: CapCity orders: **6,150**
The Festival, Part 3 **A:** Brian Michael Bendis **W:** R.J.M. Lofficier; H.P. Lovecraft; Roy Thomas

CTHULHU: THE WHISPER IN DARKNESS (H.P. LOVECRAFT'S...) — Millennium

1 ❑ Cover: 6.95 **NM** value: **Cover or less**
No issue number.

CUCKOO — Green Door

1 ❑ b&w Cover: 2.75 **NM** value: **Cover or less**
cardstock cover.
2 ❑ Win 1996, b&w Cover: 2.75 **NM** value: **Cover or less**
cardstock cover.
3 ❑ Spr 1997, b&w Cover: 2.75 **NM** value: **Cover or less**
cardstock cover.
4 ❑ Sum 1997, b&w Cover: 2.75 **NM** value: **Cover or less**
cardstock cover.
5 ❑ Fal 1997, b&w Cover: 2.75 **NM** value: **Cover or less**
cardstock cover.

CUD — Fantagraphics

All issues are adults only.
1 ❑ b&w Cover: 2.25 **NM** value: **2.50**
2 ❑ b&w Cover: 2.50 **NM** value: **Cover or less**
3 ❑ b&w Cover: 2.50 **NM** value: **Cover or less**
4 ❑ b&w Cover: 2.50 **NM** value: **Cover or less**
5 ❑ b&w Cover: 2.50 **NM** value: **Cover or less**
6 ❑ b&w Cover: 2.50 **NM** value: **Cover or less**
7 ❑ Aug 1994, b&w Cover: 2.50 **NM** value: **Cover or less**

CUDA B.C. — Rebel

1 ❑ Cover: 2.00 **NM** value: **Cover or less**

CUD COMICS — Dark Horse

Cud Comics is a humor title that features the adventures of Eno and Plum, a young couple facing all the trials and dilemmas that other couples deal with when one of them has no life and likes it that way. Cud Comics is drawn by Terry LaBan in the big-foot style of underground comics like The Fabulous Furry Freak Brothers.

The comedy relies on the risque and scatological subject matter common to underground comics from the 1970s. For example, Eno finds fortune and prosperity by becoming an amazingly successful sperm donor — because it's based on an activity at which he excels.

The series also features backup stories about Eno and Plum's friends, including expletive-wielding, thoroughly pierced friend, Angie O'Plastey.

1 ❑ Nov 1995, b&w Cover: 2.95 **NM** value: **Cover or less**
A: Terry Laban **W:** Terry Laban
2 ❑ Jan 1996, b&w Cover: 2.95 **NM** value: **Cover or less**
A: Terry Laban **W:** Terry Laban
3 ❑ Mar 1996, b&w Cover: 2.95 **NM** value: **Cover or less**
A: Terry Laban **W:** Terry Laban
4 ❑ Jun 1996 Cover: 2.95 **NM** value: **Cover or less**
A: Terry Laban **W:** Terry Laban
5 ❑ Sep 1996, b&w Cover: 2.95 **NM** value: **Cover or less**
Circ: Diamd. preorders: **3,950**
Eno and Plum: The Old Folks at Home; Most Girls Like Dick; The Author: Sparky and Me; Seymour Riverpeace: Are we Recovering Yet? **A:** Terry Laban **W:** Terry Laban
6 ❑ Dec 1996, b&w Cover: 2.95 **NM** value: **Cover or less**
Circ: Direct Market orders: **3,814**
A: Terry Laban **W:** Terry Laban
7 ❑ Apr 1997, b&w Cover: 2.95 **NM** value: **Cover or less**
Circ: Diamd. preorders: **3,714**
A: Terry Laban **W:** Terry Laban
8 ❑ Sep 1997, b&w Cover: 2.95 **NM** value: **Cover or less**
A: Terry Laban **W:** Terry Laban
Ash 1❑ **NM** value: **1.00**
A: Terry Laban **W:** Terry Laban ★ Appearance of Ashcan promotional giveaway from comic con.
Bk 1❑ Cover: 12.95 **NM** value: **Cover or less**
A: Terry Laban **W:** Terry Laban

CUIRASS — Harrier

1 ❑ b&w Cover: 1.95 **NM** value: **Cover or less**

CULTURAL JET LAG — Fantagraphics

1 ❑ b&w Cover: 2.50 **NM** value: **Cover or less**

CUPID'S REVENGE — Eros

1 ❑ Cover: 2.95 **NM** value: **Cover or less**
A: Luiz Antonio Aguiar **W:** Luiz Antonio Aguiar
2 ❑ Cover: 2.95 **NM** value: **Cover or less**
A: Luiz Antonio Aguiar **W:** Luiz Antonio Aguiar

CURIO SHOPPE, THE — Phoenix Press

1 ❑ Mar 1995, b&w Cover: 2.50 **NM** value: **Cover or less**
Serendipity; The Big Boner; Microcosm; To Ask a Question; Balance; Nothing is Real; Recumbent; Does It Get Any Better Than This? (Oh, Please, Oh, Please?!!); Toadstools **A:** Robin Bougie; John MacLeod; Michael Hegg; Rebecca Dart; S.E. Mills; Thomas Strating; Tyim Courts **W:** Robin Bougie; John MacLeod; Michael Hegg; Rebecca Dart; S.E. Mills; Tyim Courts; Brett Bogart; Chad Rubie

CURSED WORLDS SOURCE BOOK — Blue Comet

1 ❑ Cover: 2.95 **NM** value: **Cover or less**

CURSE OF DRACULA, THE — Dark Horse

1 ❑ Jul 1998 Cover: 2.95 **NM** value: **Cover or less**
Go to Hell! **A:** Matt Wagner; Gene Colan **W:** Marv Wolfman
2 ❑ Aug 1998 Cover: 2.95 **NM** value: **Cover or less**
A: Matt Wagner; Gene Colan **W:** Marv Wolfman
3 ❑ Sep 1998 Cover: 2.95 **NM** value: **Cover or less**
A: Gene Colan **W:** Marv Wolfman

CURSE OF DREADWOLF — Lightning

1 ❑ Sep 1994, b&w Cover: 2.75 **NM** value: **Cover or less**
Deadly Vision; Homecoming; Running with the Pack! **A:** Paul Abrams **W:** Joseph A. Zyskowsky

CURSE OF RUNE — Malibu

1 ❑ May 1995 Cover: 2.50 **NM** value: **Cover or less**
Circ: CapCity orders: **9,175**
Connections **A:** Kyle Hotz **W:** Chris Ulm

CURSE OF THE MOLEMEN — Kitchen Sink

1 ❑ full color Cover: 2.95 **NM** value: **4.95**
A: Charles Burns **W:** Charles Burns

CURSE OF THE SHE-CAT — AC

1 ❑ Feb 1989, b&w Cover: 2.50 **NM** value: **Cover or less**

Statement of Ownership figures are the average number of copies originally sold, as cited by the publisher to the U.S. Postal Service. These estimate **all** sales, in comics shops and on newsstands.

CURSE OF THE SPAWN — Image

The spinoff to Image's popular Spawn series attempts to marry the Spawn legend with futuristic Gothic horror.

As the legend goes, every 400 years, a new Hellspawn arises. In this future, "a time of damnation given form" also known as the "Antithesis," the few remaining humans flee from zombie soldiers and a variety of other random horrors. One such is the Dessicator, a creature which sucks all cellular moisture from the living. There's also a living-dead Catholic cardinal.

Former human soldier Daniel Llanso comes back to life as Hellspawn, a skeleton (with the odd bit of muscle) that wreaks vengeance and has to suffer about his existence and memories. The end effect is a grudge-fest among skeletons with claws and machine guns, interspersed with occasional agonized-skull close-ups.

1 ❑ Sep 1996 Cover: 1.95 **NM** value: **4.00**
Circ: Diamd. preorders: **158,929** • **CGC:** 6 graded, best 9.8
Dark Future • b&w promo **A:** Dwayne Turner **W:** Alan McElroy
1/A ❑ Sep 1996 Cover: 1.95 **NM** value: **3.00**
1/B ❑ Sep 1996, b&w Cover: 1.95 **NM** value: **3.00**
• **CGC:** 6 graded, best 9.8
2 ❑ Oct 1996 Cover: 1.95 **NM** value: **3.00**
Circ: Diamd. preorders: **136,955**
A: Dwayne Turner **W:** Alan McElroy
3 ❑ Nov 1996 Cover: 1.95 **NM** value: **3.00**
Circ: Direct Market orders: **131,658**
A: Dwayne Turner **W:** Alan McElroy
4 ❑ Dec 1996 Cover: 1.95 **NM** value: **2.50**
Circ: Direct Market orders: **133,490**
Damnation War **A:** Dwayne Turner **W:** Alan McElroy
5 ❑ Dec 1996 Cover: 1.95 **NM** value: **2.50**
Circ: Direct Market orders: **117,944**
Suture **A:** Dwayne Turner **W:** Alan McElroy
6 ❑ Feb 1997 Cover: 1.95 **NM** value: **2.50**
Circ: Diamd. preorders: **106,744**
A: Dwayne Turner **W:** Alan McElroy
7 ❑ Mar 1997 Cover: 1.95 **NM** value: **2.50**
Circ: Diamd. preorders: **98,256**
A: Dwayne Turner **W:** Alan McElroy
8 ❑ Apr 1997 Cover: 1.95 **NM** value: **2.50**
Circ: Diamd. preorders: **94,039**
Carnival of Souls **A:** Dwayne Turner **W:** Alan McElroy
9 ❑ May 1997 Cover: 1.95 **NM** value: **2.50**
Circ: Diamd. preorders: **133,933**
A: Dwayne Turner **W:** Alan McElroy ★ Appearance of Angela.
10 ❑ Jun 1997 Cover: 1.95 **NM** value: **2.50**
Circ: Diamd. preorders: **99,130**
A: Dwayne Turner **W:** Alan McElroy ★ Appearance of Angela.
11 ❑ Aug 1997 Cover: 1.95 **NM** value: **2.50**
Circ: Diamd. preorders: **94,186**
A: Dwayne Turner **W:** Alan McElroy ★ Appearance of Angela.
12 ❑ Sep 1997 Cover: 1.95 **NM** value: **2.50**
Circ: Diamd. preorders: **94,880**
Photo cover. **A:** Dwayne Turner **W:** Alan McElroy
13 ❑ Oct 1997 Cover: 1.95 **NM** value: **2.50**
Circ: Diamd. preorders: **97,451**
Heart of Darkness **A:** Dwayne Turner **W:** Alan McElroy
14 ❑ Nov 1997 Cover: 1.95 **NM** value: **2.50**
Circ: Diamd. preorders: **101,887**
Apocalypse When **A:** Dwayne Turner **W:** Alan McElroy
15 ❑ Dec 1997 Cover: 1.95 **NM** value: **2.50**
Circ: Diamd. preorders: **101,150**
Sympathy for an Angel, Part 1 **A:** Dwayne Turner **W:** Brian Haberlin
16 ❑ Jan 1998 Cover: 1.95 **NM** value: **2.00**
Circ: Diamd. preorders: **94,211**
Sympathy for an Angel, Part 2 **A:** Dwayne Turner **W:** Brian Haberlin
17 ❑ Feb 1998 Cover: 1.95 **NM** value: **2.00**
Circ: Diamd. preorders: **86,314**
Twist of Fate **A:** Dwayne Turner **W:** Alan McElroy
18 ❑ Mar 1998 Cover: 1.95 **NM** value: **2.00**
Circ: Diamd. preorders: **79,083**
Gutshot **A:** Dwayne Turner **W:** Alan McElroy
19 ❑ Apr 1998 Cover: 1.95 **NM** value: **2.00**
Circ: Diamd. preorders: **76,561**
Curse the Curse **A:** Dwayne Turner **W:** Alan McElroy
20 ❑ May 1998 Cover: 1.95 **NM** value: **2.00**
Circ: Diamd. preorders: **75,796**
Dark Myth **A:** Dwayne Turner **W:** Alan McElroy
21 ❑ Jun 1998 Cover: 1.95 **NM** value: **2.00**
Circ: Diamd. preorders: **70,854**
Chaos Cometh **A:** Dwayne Turner **W:** Alan McElroy
22 ❑ Jul 1998 Cover: 1.95 **NM** value: **2.00**
Circ: Diamd. preorders: **67,521**
Deadland **A:** Dwayne Turner **W:** Alan McElroy
23 ❑ Aug 1998 Cover: 1.95 **NM** value: **2.00**
Circ: Diamd. preorders: **63,770**
Overt-Resurrection **A:** Dwayne Turner **W:** Alan McElroy
24 ❑ Sep 1998 Cover: 1.95 **NM** value: **Cover or less**
Circ: Diamd. preorders: **59,671**
Overt-Hell **A:** Clayton Crain **W:** Alan McElroy
25 ❑ Oct 1998 Cover: 1.95 **NM** value: **Cover or less**
Circ: Diamd. preorders: **58,558**
Heart of Hell **A:** Clayton Crain **W:** Alan McElroy
26 ❑ Nov 1998 Cover: 1.95 **NM** value: **Cover or less**
Circ: Diamd. preorders: **57,078**
Brother's Keeper **A:** Clayton Crain **W:** Alan McElroy

Other grades: Multiply prices above by **1.5 for Mint • 2/3 for Very Fine • 1/3 for Fine • 1/5 for Very Good • 1/8 for Good**

27 ❑ Dec 1998 Cover: 1.95 **NM value: Cover or less**
Circ: Diamd. preorders: **54,859**
Return of the Suture, Part 1, Ghosts **A:** Clayton Crain **W:** Alan McElroy
28 ❑ Feb 1999 Cover: 1.95 **NM value: Cover or less**
Circ: Diamd. preorders: **52,773**
Return of the Suture, Part 2, Bleed **A:** Clayton Crain; Todd McFarlane(inks) **W:** Alan McElroy
29 ❑ Mar 1999 Cover: 1.95 **NM value: Cover or less**
Circ: Diamd. preorders: **49,853**
Last Rites **A:** Clayton Crain; Todd McFarlane(inks) **W:** Alan McElroy
Bk 1❑ Cover: 9.95 **NM value: Cover or less**
Sacrifice of the Soul **A:** Dwayne Turner; Dan Miki **W:** Alan McElroy
Bk 2❑ Cover: 9.95 **NM value: Cover or less**
• Blood & Sutures;Collects Curse of the Spawn #5-8 **A:** Dwayne Turner **W:** Alan McElroy
Bk 3❑ **NM value: 9.95**
Bk 4❑ Cover: 10.95 **NM value: Cover or less**
• Lost Values;Collects Curse of the Spawn #12-14, 22-24 **A:** Dwayne Turner; Chance Wolf; Danny Miki; Jason Gorder; Jonathan Glapion **W:** Alan McElroy

CURSE OF THE WEIRD — Marvel

Weird horror/science-fiction comics ruled supreme during the 1950s, a time when super-heroes were in decline, and before the Comics Code Authority cast a chilling hand on the sorts of tales that could be told. Marvel (then known as Atlas Comics) certainly did more than its share of these stories in titles such as Venus, Adventures into Terror, and Astonishing Tales. Although not quite as gripping as the famous EC titles like Tales From the Crypt, these were nevertheless notable as some of the early work of comics legends Steve Ditko and Basil Wolverton.

Throwing everything else it could find onto the racks in the glut of 1993, Marvel also went back to the vaults to dredge up its old classics. One result was this series and its sister title Monster Menace. Here can be found ghosts, reanimated heads of Nazi scientists, and great floating eyeballs. Enjoy!

1 ❑ Dec 1993 Cover: 1.25 **NM value: 1.50**
Circ: CapCity orders: **8,950**
Do Not Panic!; The Brain; The Eye Of Doom; The Man Who Owned A Ghost • Reprints stories from Adventures in Terror #4, Astonishing Tales #10, others **A:** Russ Heath
2 ❑ Jan 1994 Cover: 1.25 **NM value: 1.50**
Circ: CapCity orders: **5,100**
The Ghost Of Grismore Castle!; Bat's Tale; Innocent Bystander; The Unsolid Man; No Sign Of Life
3 ❑ Feb 1994 Cover: 1.25 **NM value: 1.50**
Circ: CapCity orders: **4,150**
4 ❑ Mar 1994 Cover: 1.25 **NM value: 1.50**
Circ: CapCity orders: **3,350**
final issue.

CURSE OF THE ZOMBIE — Marvel
4 ❑ Cover: 1.25 **NM value: Cover or less**

CUTEGIRL — Not Available
1 ❑ Cover: 0.50 **NM value: Cover or less**
A: Matt Feazell **W:** Matt Feazell
2 ❑ Cover: 0.50 **NM value: Cover or less**
CuteGirl Finds A Pet; The Never Ending Struggle **A:** Matt Feazell **W:** Matt Feazell

CUTIE PIE — Junior Readers' Guild
1 ❑ May 1955 Cover: 0.10 **NM value: 24.00**
A: Gene Fawcette **W:** Gene Fawcette
2 ❑ Oct 1955 Cover: 0.10 **NM value: 14.00**
A: Gene Fawcette **W:** Gene Fawcette
3 ❑ Cover: 0.10 **NM value: 14.00**
A: Gene Fawcette **W:** Gene Fawcette
4 ❑ Cover: 0.10 **NM value: 14.00**
A: Gene Fawcette **W:** Gene Fawcette
5 ❑ Cover: 0.10 **NM value: 14.00**
Bonin' Up (Or Down); Not on the Menu!; The Present With a Future (text story); Copy...The Cat's Meow; The Story Teller; Just the Type; **A:** Gene Fawcette **W:** Gene Fawcette

CUTTING EDGE — Marvel
1 ❑ Dec 1995 Cover: 2.95 **NM value: Cover or less**
Ghosts of the Future • continued from The Incredible Hulk #436;continues in The Incredible Hulk #437 **A:** Paul Pelletier; Angel Medina **W:** William Messner-Loebs ★ Appearance of Talbot, Hulk, Omnibus.

CYBER 7 — Eclipse
1 ❑ b&w Cover: 2.00 **NM value: Cover or less**
• Japanese
2 ❑ b&w Cover: 2.00 **NM value: Cover or less**
• Japanese
3 ❑ b&w Cover: 2.00 **NM value: Cover or less**
• Japanese
4 ❑ b&w Cover: 2.00 **NM value: Cover or less**
• Japanese
5 ❑ b&w Cover: 2.00 **NM value: Cover or less**
• Japanese
6 ❑ b&w Cover: 2.00 **NM value: Cover or less**
• Japanese
7 ❑ b&w Cover: 2.00 **NM value: Cover or less**
• Japanese

CYBER 7 BOOK TWO — Eclipse
1 ❑ b&w Cover: 2.00 **NM value: Cover or less**
• Japanese
2 ❑ b&w Cover: 2.00 **NM value: Cover or less**
• Japanese
3 ❑ b&w Cover: 2.00 **NM value: Cover or less**
• Japanese
4 ❑ b&w Cover: 2.00 **NM value: Cover or less**
• Japanese
5 ❑ b&w Cover: 2.00 **NM value: Cover or less**
• Japanese
6 ❑ b&w Cover: 2.00 **NM value: Cover or less**
• Japanese
7 ❑ b&w Cover: 2.00 **NM value: Cover or less**
• Japanese
8 ❑ b&w Cover: 2.00 **NM value: Cover or less**
• Japanese
9 ❑ b&w Cover: 2.00 **NM value: Cover or less**
• Japanese
10 ❑ b&w Cover: 2.00 **NM value: Cover or less**
• Japanese

CYBER CITY: PART 1 — CPM

Sengoku Syunsuke, Merrill "Benten" Yanagawa, and Gabimaru "Goggles" Rikiya are all hardened criminals serving multiple life terms for crimes ranging from murder to anime piracy. The state, however, needs people with their skills, and offers them a deal. If they agree to act as cyber police, tracking down criminals in the Cyber City of Oedo, they can have their sentences reduced by a few years for each felon caught.

Their biggest challenge comes when 50,000 people are held hostage in a Cyber City skyscraper by terrorists. Sengoku is given 24 hours to stop the terrorists, or else their "employers" would explode the collars he and his friends forced to wear around their necks. Fun job!

1 ❑ Sep 1995 Cover: 2.95 **NM value: Cover or less**
• adapts anime **A:** Tim Eldred **W:** Akinori Endo
2 ❑ Sep 1995 Cover: 2.95 **NM value: Cover or less**
• adapts anime **A:** Tim Eldred **W:** Akinori Endo

CYBER CITY: PART 2 — CPM
1 ❑ Oct 1995 Cover: 2.95 **NM value: Cover or less**
• adapts anime **A:** Tim Eldred **W:** Akinori Endo
2 ❑ Nov 1995 Cover: 2.95 **NM value: Cover or less**
• adapts anime **A:** Tim Eldred **W:** Akinori Endo

CYBER CITY: PART 3 — CPM
1 ❑ Dec 1995 Cover: 2.95 **NM value: Cover or less**
• adapts anime **A:** Tim Eldred **W:** Akinori Endo
2 ❑ Jan 1996 Cover: 2.95 **NM value: Cover or less**
• adapts anime **A:** Tim Eldred **W:** Akinori Endo

CYBERCOM, HEART OF THE BLUE MESA — Matrix
1 ❑ Dec 1987, b&w Cover: 2.00 **NM value: Cover or less**
First Impressions **A:** Monique Renée **W:** Monique Renée

CYBER CRUSH: ROBOTS IN REVOLT — Fleetway-Quality
1 ❑ Cover: 1.95 **NM value: Cover or less**
Circ: CapCity orders: **2,850**
Death on the Orient Express; Robo-Hunter **A:** Ian Gibson; Jose Ferrer **W:** Pat Mills; T.B. Grover
2 ❑ Cover: 1.95 **NM value: Cover or less**
Circ: CapCity orders: **1,875**
3 ❑ Cover: 1.95 **NM value: Cover or less**
4 ❑ Cover: 1.95 **NM value: Cover or less**
5 ❑ Cover: 1.95 **NM value: Cover or less**
6 ❑ Cover: 1.95 **NM value: Cover or less**
7 ❑ Cover: 1.95 **NM value: Cover or less**
8 ❑ Cover: 1.95 **NM value: Cover or less**
9 ❑ Cover: 1.95 **NM value: Cover or less**
10 ❑ Cover: 1.95 **NM value: Cover or less**
11 ❑ Cover: 1.95 **NM value: Cover or less**
12 ❑ Cover: 1.95 **NM value: Cover or less**
13 ❑ Cover: 1.95 **NM value: Cover or less**
14 ❑ Cover: 1.95 **NM value: Cover or less**

CYBERELLA — DC / Helix

Cyberella is, in the words of creator Howard Chaykin, "about a lot of things I consider pretty important: television, advertising, capitalism run rampant, image over substance, and, let's not forget, the ever-popular personal betrayal." That's basically the essence of DC's free-wheeling, near-future, corporate hellworld satire.

Cyberella began as the fictional creation of entertainment conglomerate Macrocorp: a 1920s cartoon character called Li'l Ella who morphed, over the years into a net-based role-playing game used for behavioral control in the 21st century. Enter Sunny Winston, a feisty young woman with an unusual gift for strategy and connections to the evil head of Macrocorp. Add a well-timed freak power surge, and suddenly Macrocorp's got a whole lot of trouble.

This was part of Helix, DC's attempt to launch a science-fiction comics line. Unfortunately, the cyberpunk-dominated line didn't snag enough traditional SF fans to keep it going.

1 ❑ Sep 1996 Cover: 2.25 **NM value: Cover or less**
Silent Weapons, Quiet Wars, Part 1 **A:** Don Cameron **W:** Howard Chaykin
2 ❑ Oct 1996 Cover: 2.25 **NM value: Cover or less**
Silent Weapons, Quiet Wars, Part 2 **A:** Don Cameron **W:** Howard Chaykin
3 ❑ Nov 1996 Cover: 2.25 **NM value: Cover or less**
Circ: Direct Market orders: **18,087**
Silent Weapons, Quiet Wars, Part 3 **A:** Don Cameron **W:** Howard Chaykin
4 ❑ Dec 1996 Cover: 2.25 **NM value: Cover or less**
Circ: Direct Market orders: **16,047**
Silent Weapons, Quiet Wars, Part 4 **A:** Don Cameron **W:** Howard Chaykin
5 ❑ Jan 1997 Cover: 2.25 **NM value: Cover or less**
Circ: Diamd. preorders: **14,314**
Silent Weapons, Quiet Wars, Part 5 **A:** Don Cameron **W:** Howard Chaykin
6 ❑ Feb 1997 Cover: 2.25 **NM value: Cover or less**
Circ: Diamd. preorders: **12,328**
Silent Weapons, Quiet Wars, Part 6 **A:** Don Cameron **W:** Howard Chaykin
7 ❑ Mar 1997 Cover: 2.50 **NM value: Cover or less**
Circ: Diamd. preorders: **10,987**
Silent Weapons, Quiet Wars, Part 7 **A:** Don Cameron **W:** Howard Chaykin
8 ❑ Apr 1997 Cover: 2.50 **NM value: Cover or less**
Circ: Diamd. preorders: **9,728**
A: Don Cameron **W:** Howard Chaykin
9 ❑ May 1997 Cover: 2.50 **NM value: Cover or less**
Circ: Diamd. preorders: **8,890**
Program Change, or My Mom, My Enemy **A:** Don Cameron; Butch Lukic **W:** Don Cameron
10 ❑ Jun 1997 Cover: 2.50 **NM value: Cover or less**
Circ: Diamd. preorders: **8,548**
11 ❑ Jul 1997 Cover: 2.50 **NM value: Cover or less**
Circ: Diamd. preorders: **7,230**
12 ❑ Aug 1997 Cover: 2.50 **NM value: Cover or less**
Circ: Diamd. preorders: **6,847**
final issue.

CYBERFARCE — Parody
1 ❑ b&w Cover: 2.50 **NM value: Cover or less**
A: Bill Maus **W:** Don Chin

CYBER FEMMES — Spoof / Quality
1 ❑ Cover: 2.95 **NM value: Cover or less**
A: Adam Pollina **W:** Mike Halbleib

CYBERFORCE ORIGINS — Image
1 ❑ Jan 1995 Cover: 2.50 **NM value: Cover or less**
Circ: CapCity orders: **27,225** • **CGC:** 2 graded, best 9.8
★ Origin of Cyblade.
1/GO❑ **NM value: 4.00**
• Gold edition. ★ Origin of Cyblade.
1-2 ❑ Mar 1996 Cover: 0.99 **NM value: 1.25**
2 ❑ Feb 1995 Cover: 2.50 **NM value: Cover or less**
Circ: CapCity orders: **22,425**
★ Origin of Stryker.
3 ❑ Nov 1995 Cover: 2.50 **NM value: Cover or less**
Circ: CapCity orders: **17,450**
A: Randy Queen **W:** Marc Silvestri; Randy Queen; Brian Selzer ★ Origin of Impact.

CYBERFORCE, STRYKE FORCE: OPPOSING FORCES — Image
1 ❑ Sep 1995 Cover: 2.50 **NM value: Cover or less**
Circ: CapCity orders: **30,000**
A: Billy Tan Mung Khoy **W:** Steve Gerber
2 ❑ Oct 1995 Cover: 2.50 **NM value: Cover or less**
Circ: CapCity orders: **23,950**

CYBERFORCE UNIVERSE SOURCEBOOK — Image
1 ❑ Aug 1994 Cover: 2.50 **NM value: Cover or less**
Circ: CapCity orders: **29,925**
2 ❑ Feb 1995 Cover: 2.50 **NM value: Cover or less**
Circ: CapCity orders: **19,525**
A: Aaron Sowd; Billy Tan; Marc Silvestri; Michael Turner; Brian Haberlin **W:** Brian Selzer; David Wohl

CYBERFORCE (VOL. 1) — Image

Cyberforce, one of the first titles out of the Image Comics line, features beautiful art by Marc Silvestri and introduces Image's first line of mutant super-heroes.

Cyberforce battles to fight discrimination and violence against mutants as well as injustice in general. The team includes the four-armed cyborg Stryker, Ripclaw, Heatwave, Cyblade, and—after the team rescues her in the first issue—Velocity.

Popular for a time, these mutants turned out not to do for Image what the X-Men did for Marvel. A second seris ran for 35 issues (under both Image and Top Cow, after Silvestri briefly left) before running out of gas.

1 ❑ Oct 1992 Cover: 1.95 **NM value: 4.00**

Circ: CapCity orders: **125,900** • **CGC:** 32 graded, best 9.9

CGC-graded: Multiply prices above by **33 for 9.9 M** • **16 for 9.8 NM/M** • **7 for 9.6 NM+** • **5 for 9.4 NM** • **2.5 for 9.2 NM-** • **1.5 for 9.0 VF/NM**

The Tin Men Of War, Part 1 **A:** Marc Silvestri **W:** Eric Silvestri ★ 1st Appearance of Cyberforce.
2 ❑ Mar 1993 Cover: 1.95 **NM** value: **2.50**
Circ: CapCity orders: **89,275**
The Tin Men Of War, Part 2 **A:** Marc Silvestri **W:** Eric Silvestri
3 ❑ May 1993 Cover: 1.95 **NM** value: **2.00**
Circ: CapCity orders: **87,875**
A: Marc Silvestri **W:** Eric Silvestri ★ Appearance of Pitt.
4 ❑ Jul 1993 Cover: 2.50 **NM** value: **Cover or less**
Circ: CapCity orders: **89,800**
foil cover. **A:** Marc Silvestri **W:** Eric Silvestri
Bk 1❑ Cover: 12.95 **NM** value: **Cover or less**
• Cyberforce: Tin Men of War **A:** Marc Silvestri **W:** Eric Silvestri

CYBERFORCE (VOL. 2) — Image

0 ❑ Sep 1993 Cover: 1.95 **NM** value: **2.50**
Circ: CapCity orders: **189,950** • **CGC:** 1 graded, best 9.8
A: Walt Simonson **W:** Walt Simonson ★ Origin of Cyberforce.
1 ❑ Nov 1993 Cover: 1.95 **NM** value: **2.50**
Circ: CapCity orders: **106,550** • **CGC:** 1 graded, best 9.4
A: Marc Silvestri **W:** Marc Silvestri; Eric Silvestri
1/GO❑ **NM** value: **4.00**
• Gold edition. **A:** Marc Silvestri **W:** Marc Silvestri; Eric Silvestri
1-2 ❑ Nov 1993 Cover: 0.99 **NM** value: **1.25**
2 ❑ Feb 1994 Cover: 1.95 **NM** value: **2.50**
Circ: CapCity orders: **71,950**
Killer Instinct, Part 2
2/PL❑ Feb 1994 **NM** value: **3.00**
• **CGC:** 1 graded, best 9.4
• Platinum edition. • foil-embossed outer wrap
3 ❑ Mar 1994 Cover: 1.95 **NM** value: **2.50**
Circ: CapCity orders: **52,925**
Killer Instinct, Part 4
3/GO❑ Mar 1994 **NM** value: **3.00**
• Gold edition. Killer Instinct, Part 4
4 ❑ Apr 1994 Cover: 1.95 **NM** value: **2.50**
Circ: CapCity orders: **48,600**
5 ❑ Jun 1994 Cover: 1.95 **NM** value: **2.50**
Circ: CapCity orders: **52,375**
6 ❑ Jul 1994 Cover: 1.95 **NM** value: **2.00**
Circ: CapCity orders: **57,650**
7 ❑ Sep 1994 Cover: 1.95 **NM** value: **2.00**
Circ: CapCity orders: **50,800**
8 ❑ Oct 1994 Cover: 2.50 **NM** value: **2.75**
Circ: CapCity orders: **40,700**
• Image X-Month **A:** Todd McFarlane
9 ❑ Dec 1994 Cover: 1.95 **NM** value: **2.50**
Circ: CapCity orders: **38,350** • **CGC:** 1 graded, best 9.6
10 ❑ Feb 1995 Cover: 1.95 **NM** value: **2.50**
Circ: CapCity orders: **32,325**
10/GO❑ Feb 1995 **NM** value: **3.00**
• Gold edition.
10/PL❑ Feb 1995 **NM** value: **3.00**
• Platinum edition.
10/SC❑ Feb 1995 Cover: 1.95 **NM** value: **3.00**
alternate cover.
11 ❑ Mar 1995 Cover: 1.95 **NM** value: **2.50**
Circ: CapCity orders: **30,625**
12 ❑ Apr 1995 Cover: 1.95 **NM** value: **2.50**
Circ: CapCity orders: **30,625**
13 ❑ Jun 1995 Cover: 2.25 **NM** value: **2.50**
Circ: CapCity orders: **30,075**
14 ❑ Jul 1995 Cover: 2.25 **NM** value: **2.50**
Circ: CapCity orders: **30,225**
15 ❑ Aug 1995 Cover: 2.25 **NM** value: **2.50**
Circ: CapCity orders: **30,475**
16 ❑ Nov 1995 Cover: 2.25 **NM** value: **2.50**
Circ: CapCity orders: **24,650**
17 ❑ Dec 1995 Cover: 2.25 **NM** value: **Cover or less**
Circ: CapCity orders: **16,300**
A: David Finch **W:** Marc Silvestri; Brian Haberlin
18 ❑ Jan 1996 Cover: 2.25 **NM** value: **2.50**
18/A❑ Jan 1996 Cover: 2.25 **NM** value: **2.50**
alternate cover.
19 ❑ Feb 1996 Cover: 2.50 **NM** value: **Cover or less**
20 ❑ Mar 1996 Cover: 2.50 **NM** value: **Cover or less**
21 ❑ May 1996 Cover: 2.50 **NM** value: **Cover or less**
22 ❑ May 1996 Cover: 2.50 **NM** value: **Cover or less**
23 ❑ Jun 1996 Cover: 2.50 **NM** value: **Cover or less**
24 ❑ Jun 1996 Cover: 2.50 **NM** value: **Cover or less**
25 ❑ Aug 1996 Cover: 3.95 **NM** value: **Cover or less**
enhanced wraparound cardstock cover.
26 ❑ Sep 1996 Cover: 2.50 **NM** value: **Cover or less**
27 ❑ Oct 1996 Cover: 2.50 **NM** value: **Cover or less**
Circ: Diamd. preorders: **52,780**
27/SC❑ Oct 1996 Cover: 2.50 **NM** value: **Cover or less**
alternate cover. **C:** Joe Quesada; Jimmy Palmiotti ★ Appearance of Ash.
28 ❑ Nov 1996 Cover: 2.50 **NM** value: **Cover or less**
Circ: Direct Market orders: **42,694**
★ Appearance of Gabriel (from Ash).
29 ❑ Dec 1996 Cover: 2.50 **NM** value: **Cover or less**
Circ: Direct Market orders: **40,490**
A: David Finch; Michael Turner; D-Baron **W:** Brian Holguin
30 ❑ Feb 1997 Cover: 2.50 **NM** value: **Cover or less**
Circ: Diamd. preorders: **44,109**
Devil's Reign Interlude; Devil's Reign **A:** Scott Lee **W:** Brian Holguin
31 ❑ Mar 1997 Cover: 2.50 **NM** value: **Cover or less**
Circ: Diamd. preorders: **37,920**
32 ❑ Apr 1997 Cover: 2.50 **NM** value: **Cover or less**
Circ: Diamd. preorders: **37,596**
33 ❑ May 1997 Cover: 2.50 **NM** value: **Cover or less**
Circ: Diamd. preorders: **35,969**
34 ❑ Jul 1997 Cover: 2.50 **NM** value: **Cover or less**
Circ: Diamd. preorders: **31,524**
35 ❑ Sep 1997 Cover: 2.50 **NM** value: **Cover or less**
Circ: Diamd. preorders: **30,669**
Anl 1❑ Mar 1995 Cover: 2.50 **NM** value: **Cover or less**
Circ: CapCity orders: **24,675**
Anl 2❑ Aug 1996 Cover: 2.50 **NM** value: **2.95**
Bk 2❑ May 1995 Cover: 9.95 **NM** value: **Cover or less**
• Trade Paperback. • collects Cyberforce #4-7

CYBERFROG: 3RD ANNIVERSARY SPECIAL — Harris

1 ❑ Jan 1997 Cover: 2.50 **NM** value: **Cover or less**
Circ: Diamd. preorders: **5,133**
A: Ethan Van Sciver **W:** Ethan Van Sciver
2 ❑ Feb 1997 Cover: 2.50 **NM** value: **Cover or less**
Circ: Diamd. preorders: **4,722**
A: Ethan Van Sciver **W:** Ethan Van Sciver

CYBERFROG (HARRIS) — Harris

"Oh no! That big armored frog just turned G-Funk's head into strawberry jam! And it looks like we're next!"

Yes, just when you thought you had read it all, from butt-kicking nuns (Warrior Nun Areala) to cigar-chomping ducks (Howard the Duck), in leaps CyberFrog. Springing into action without any discernable origin story, he's a sociopathic, death-dealing amphibian who fights evil and takes great delight in figuring out how many different ways he can dismember the bad guys.

Created and drawn by Ethan Van Sciver, CyberFrog had a brief run at indie publisher Hall of Heroes before moving to Harris Comics. With a decidedly hip style and gleefully hyperviolent style, it found a dedicated fan base and became a minor cult hit.

0 ❑ Mar 1997 Cover: 2.95 **NM** value: **5.00**
Circ: Diamd. preorders: **7,963**
Yo Mama is...An Alien **A:** Ethan Van Sciver **W:** Ethan Van Sciver
0/A ❑ Mar 1997 Cover: 2.95 **NM** value: **8.00**
Art Adams cover. Yo Mama is...An Alien **A:** Ethan Van Sciver **W:** Ethan Van Sciver
1 ❑ Feb 1996 Cover: 2.95 **NM** value: **5.00**
Directing Traffik **A:** Ethan Van Sciver **W:** Ethan Van Sciver
2 ❑ 1996 Cover: 2.95 **NM** value: **4.00**
Torn Together **A:** Ethan Van Sciver **W:** Ethan Van Sciver
3 ❑ 1996 Cover: 2.95 **NM** value: **3.50**
Deathfly By Night **A:** Ethan Van Sciver **W:** Ethan Van Sciver
4 ❑ 1996 Cover: 2.95 **NM** value: **3.50**
The Afterlife of Riley **A:** Ethan Van Sciver **W:** Ethan Van Sciver

CYBERFROG: RESERVOIR FROG — Harris

1 ❑ Sep 1996 Cover: 2.95 **NM** value: **Cover or less**
Circ: Diamd. preorders: **11,402**
Eric Larsen/Ethan Van Sciver cover art. Getting To Hate You **A:** Ethan Van Sciver **W:** Ethan Van Sciver
1/A ❑ Cover: 2.95 **NM** value: **Cover or less**
Ethan Van Sciver Cover Art. Getting To Hate You **A:** Ethan Van Sciver **W:** Ethan Van Sciver
2 ❑ Oct 1996 Cover: 2.95 **NM** value: **Cover or less**
Circ: Diamd. preorders: **9,830**
Ethan Van Sciver Cover Art. Infestation **A:** Ethan Van Sciver **W:** Ethan Van Sciver
2/A ❑ Cover: 2.95 **NM** value: **Cover or less**
Ethan Van Sciver Cover Art. Infestation **A:** Ethan Van Sciver **W:** Ethan Van Sciver

CYBERFROG VS CREED — Harris

1 ❑ Jul 1997 Cover: 2.95 **NM** value: **Cover or less**
Circ: Diamd. preorders: **8,282**
A: Trent Kaniuga; Ethan Van Sciver **W:** Ethan Van Sciver

CYBERHAWKS — Pyramid

1 ❑ b&w Cover: 1.80 **NM** value: **Cover or less**
2 ❑ b&w Cover: 1.80 **NM** value: **Cover or less**

CYBERLUST — Aircel

All issues are adults only.
1 ❑ b&w Cover: 2.95 **NM** value: **Cover or less**
2 ❑ b&w Cover: 2.95 **NM** value: **Cover or less**
3 ❑ b&w Cover: 2.95 **NM** value: **Cover or less**

CYBERNARY — Image

1 ❑ Nov 1995 Cover: 2.50 **NM** value: **Cover or less**
Duet **A:** Jeff Rebner **W:** Steve Gerber
2 ❑ Dec 1995 Cover: 2.50 **NM** value: **Cover or less**
Down Memory Lane **A:** Jeff Rebner **W:** Steve Gerber
3 ❑ Jan 1996 Cover: 2.50 **NM** value: **Cover or less**
A: Jeff Rebner **W:** Steve Gerber
4 ❑ Feb 1996 Cover: 2.50 **NM** value: **Cover or less**
A: Jeff Rebner **W:** Steve Gerber
5 ❑ Mar 1996 Cover: 2.50 **NM** value: **Cover or less**
A: Jeff Rebner **W:** Steve Gerber

> The CGC numbers printed in individual listings above represent the **number of copies examined** and given a **Universal** grade by CGC and the **best such copy** graded at press time. For current populations, watch for special ***Comics Buyer's Guide*** issues or check **www.cgccomics.com.**

CYBERPUNK (BOOK 1) — Innovation

Topo is a cyberpunk, a "juggler" who gets his thrills playing on a worldwide computer network. But unlike the Internet junkies of today, the jugglers in this game actually plug their minds directly into the network, controlling their movements through brainwaves and entering a new reality within the computer.

In this first Cyberpunk book, writer Scott Rockwell spins an engaging tale of alienation, corruption, and ultra-high technology. Topo must enter the network to save a former lover, Juno, who has fallen into the clutches of Roi, the depraved head of a ruthless corporation. As he "jacks in" to battle Roi's electronic defenses, he discovers that Roi has actually wiped out Juno's mind, transferring it into the computer. Unless he can defeat Roi on the electronic playing field, Juno will be lost to him forever.

This story was reprinted as the Cyberpunk Graphic Novel.

1 ❑ Cover: 1.95 **NM** value: **Cover or less**
Circ: CapCity orders: **4,950**
A: Darryl Banks; Ken Steacy(cover) **W:** Scott Rockwell
2 ❑ Cover: 1.95 **NM** value: **Cover or less**
Circ: CapCity orders: **4,025**
A: Darryl Banks; Ken Steacy(cover) **W:** Scott Rockwell
Bk 1❑ Cover: 6.95 **NM** value: **Cover or less**

CYBERPUNK (BOOK 2) — Innovation

1 ❑ Cover: 2.25 **NM** value: **Cover or less**
Circ: CapCity orders: **4,275**
A: Doug Talalla **W:** Scott Rockwell
2 ❑ Cover: 2.25 **NM** value: **Cover or less**
A: Doug Talalla **W:** Scott Rockwell
Bk 1❑ Cover: 6.95 **NM** value: **Cover or less**

CYBERPUNK GRAPHIC NOVEL — Innovation

1 ❑ Cover: 6.95 **NM** value: **Cover or less**
A: Darryl Banks; Ken Steacy(cover) **W:** Scott Rockwell

CYBERPUNK: THE SERAPHIM FILES — Innovation

1 ❑ Cover: 2.50 **NM** value: **Cover or less**
Circ: CapCity orders: **4,000**
A: Doug Talalla **W:** Chris Todd
2 ❑ Cover: 2.50 **NM** value: **Cover or less**
Circ: CapCity orders: **2,840**
A: Doug Talalla **W:** Chris Todd
Bk 1❑ Cover: 6.95 **NM** value: **Cover or less**
• Cyberpunk: The Seraphim Project;Collects Cyberpunk: The Seraphim Files

CYBERPUNX — Image

1/A ❑ Mar 1996 Cover: 2.50 **NM** value: **Cover or less**
Circ: Diamd. preorders: **13,993**
Woman with purple/white costume at bottom of cover. **A:** Ching Lau; Rob Liefeld(cover) **W:** Rob Liefeld; Robert Loren Flemming
1/B ❑ Mar 1996 Cover: 2.50 **NM** value: **Cover or less**
Man with green hair at bottom of cover. **A:** Ching Lau; Stephen Platt(cover) **W:** Rob Liefeld; Robert Loren Flemming
1/C ❑ Mar 1996 Cover: 2.50 **NM** value: **Cover or less**
variant cover. **A:** Ching Lau; Roger Cruz(cover) **W:** Rob Liefeld; Robert Loren Flemming
1/D ❑ Mar 1996 Cover: 2.50 **NM** value: **Cover or less**
variant cover. **A:** Ching Lau **W:** Rob Liefeld; Robert Loren Flemming

CYBERRAD (1ST SERIES) — Continuity

A frightened, confused teenager flees for his life when pursued by a pair of powerful and deadly robots. With no memory of his own identity, the boy has no idea why they've chosen him as their target. But what's most surprising is the fact that he's not only surviving their assault, he's actually able to fight back.

The resulting battle only raises more questions: Why are they so intent on killing him? Who's responsible for their lethal programming? Is he some kind of robot or cyborg himself? His attackers seem to know all the answers, which only makes his situation worse. If the youth doesn't fight back, he'll definitely die. But if he succeeds in defeating his attackers, he may never learn the answers he so desperately needs.

Neal Adams, who also provided the layouts for several issues, created the character.

1 ❑ Jan 1991 Cover: 2.00 **NM** value: **Cover or less**
Circ: CapCity orders: **30,475**
A: Richard Bennett; Terry Shoemaker **W:** Peter Stone
2 ❑ Apr 1991 Cover: 2.00 **NM** value: **Cover or less**
Circ: CapCity orders: **23,325**
A: Richard Bennett; Terry Shoemaker **W:** Peter Stone
3 ❑ May 1991 Cover: 2.00 **NM** value: **Cover or less**
Circ: CapCity orders: **29,175**
W: Peter Stone
4 ❑ Jun 1991 Cover: 2.00 **NM** value: **Cover or less**
W: Peter Stone
5 ❑ Cover: 2.00 **NM** value: **Cover or less**
glow cover. **W:** Peter Stone

Other grades: Multiply prices above by **1.5 for Mint • 2/3 for Very Fine • 1/3 for Fine • 1/5 for Very Good • 1/8 for Good**

6 ❑ Nov 1991 Cover: 2.00 **NM** value: **Cover or less**
• foldout poster **W:** Peter Stone
7 ❑ Mar 1992 Cover: 2.00 **NM** value: **Cover or less**
W: Peter Stone

CYBERRAD (2ND SERIES) — Continuity
1 ❑ Nov 1992 Cover: 2.00 **NM** value: **Cover or less**
Circ: CapCity orders: **12,300**
Hologram cover. **A:** Richard Bennett **W:** Peter Stone

CYBERRAD DEATHWATCH 2000 — Continuity
1 ❑ Apr 1993 Cover: 2.50 **NM** value: **Cover or less**
• trading card **A:** Neal Adams; Richard Bennett **W:** Neal Adams; Peter Stone
2 ❑ Jul 1993 Cover: 2.50 **NM** value: **Cover or less**
• trading card;indicia drops Deathwatch 2000 **A:** Neal Adams; Richard Bennett **W:** Neal Adams; Peter Stone

CYBER REALITY COMIX — Wonder Comix
1 ❑ Fal 1994 Cover: 3.95 **NM** value: **Cover or less**
Arena; Leah; Origins **A:** Nils Osmar **W:** Nils Osmar
2 ❑ Win 1995 Cover: 3.95 **NM** value: **Cover or less**

CYBERSEXATION — Antarctic / Venus
All issues are adults only.
1 ❑ Mar 1997, b&w Cover: 2.95 **NM** value: **Cover or less**
Cyberfux **A:** Paul H. Way **W:** Paul H. Way

CYBERSPACE 3000 — Marvel
Cyberspace 3000 takes place in a setting that's pretty close to that of Star Trek: Deep Space Nine, which was launching at around the same time. Everything happens on Sol III, an orbiting space station that's home to a variety of different Earth and alien races. Each in turn has its own peculiar religions and customs.

Commanded by Captain Jennifer Cabre-Rios, it seems to hold together somehow, until the day a mysterious energy grabs hold of the station and causes half the station to disappear. While everyone on board begins to panic, the captain must somehow regain control — as well as deal with the unexpected menace of Galactus!

1 ❑ Jul 1993 Cover: 2.95 **NM** value: **Cover or less**
Circ: CapCity orders: **55,400**
Glow-in-the-dark cover. Judgment Day **A:** Steve Tappin **W:** Gary Russell
2 ❑ Aug 1993 Cover: 1.75 **NM** value: **Cover or less**
Circ: CapCity orders: **23,400**
A: Steve Tappin **W:** Gary Russell
3 ❑ Sep 1993 Cover: 1.75 **NM** value: **Cover or less**
Circ: CapCity orders: **16,600**
A: Steve Tappin **W:** Gary Russell
4 ❑ Oct 1993 Cover: 1.75 **NM** value: **Cover or less**
Circ: CapCity orders: **12,200**
A: Steve Tappin **W:** Gary Russell ★ Appearance of Galactus, Dark Angel, Silver Surfer.
5 ❑ Nov 1993 Cover: 1.75 **NM** value: **Cover or less**
Circ: CapCity orders: **8,600**
Bad Habits! **A:** Steve Tappin **W:** Gary Russell
6 ❑ Dec 1993 Cover: 1.75 **NM** value: **Cover or less**
Circ: CapCity orders: **7,500**
A: Steve Tappin **W:** Gary Russell
7 ❑ Jan 1994 Cover: 1.75 **NM** value: **Cover or less**
Circ: CapCity orders: **5,300**
A: Steve Tappin **W:** Gary Russell
8 ❑ Feb 1994 Cover: 1.75 **NM** value: **Cover or less**
Circ: CapCity orders: **4,350**
final issue. **A:** Steve Tappin **W:** Gary Russell

CYBERSUIT ARKADYNE — Ianus
1 ❑ b&w Cover: 2.50 **NM** value: **Cover or less**
2 ❑ b&w Cover: 2.50 **NM** value: **Cover or less**
3 ❑ Jun 1992, b&w Cover: 2.50 **NM** value: **Cover or less**
4 ❑ Cover: 2.50 **NM** value: **Cover or less**
5 ❑ Cover: 2.50 **NM** value: **Cover or less**
6 ❑ Cover: 2.50 **NM** value: **Cover or less**

CYBERTRASH AND THE DOG — Silverline
1 ❑ May 1998 Cover: 2.95 **NM** value: **Cover or less**

CYBERZONE — Jet-Black Grafiks
1 ❑ Jul 1994 Cover: 2.50 **NM** value: **3.00**
A: Jimmie Robinson **W:** Jimmie Robinson
2 ❑ Sep 1994 Cover: 2.50 **NM** value: **Cover or less**
A: Jimmie Robinson **W:** Jimmie Robinson
3 ❑ Dec 1994 Cover: 2.50 **NM** value: **Cover or less**
A: Jimmie Robinson **W:** Jimmie Robinson
4 ❑ Mar 1995 Cover: 2.50 **NM** value: **Cover or less**
A: Jimmie Robinson **W:** Jimmie Robinson
5 ❑ May 1995 Cover: 2.50 **NM** value: **Cover or less**
A: Jimmie Robinson **W:** Jimmie Robinson
6 ❑ Sep 1995 Cover: 2.50 **NM** value: **Cover or less**
A: Jimmie Robinson **W:** Jimmie Robinson
7 ❑ Feb 1996 Cover: 2.50 **NM** value: **Cover or less**
A: Jimmie Robinson **W:** Jimmie Robinson
8 ❑ Cover: 2.50 **NM** value: **Cover or less**
final issue. **A:** Jimmie Robinson **W:** Jimmie Robinson

CYBLADE/GHOST RIDER — Marvel
1 ❑ Jan 1997 Cover: 2.95 **NM** value: **Cover or less**
• **CGC:** 1 graded, best 9.6
Devil's Reign, Part 2 • crossover with Top Cow;continues in Ghost Rider/Ballistic **A:** David Finch; Anthony Chun **W:** Ivan Velez Jr.

CYBLADE/SHI: THE BATTLE FOR INDEPENDENTS — Image
1 ❑ Cover: 2.95 **NM** value: **5.00**
Circ: CapCity orders: **71,975** • **CGC:** 35 graded, best 9.8
A: Marc Silvestri; Anthony Winn **W:** Marc Silvestri; Bill Tucci; Brian Haberlin; David Wohl ★ 1st Appearance of Witchblade.
1/A ❑ Cover: 2.95 **NM** value: **6.00**
• **CGC:** 16 graded, best 9.8
alternate cover. • crossover;concludes in Shi/Cyblade: The Battle for Independents #2 **A:** Marc Silvestri; Anthony Winn **W:** Marc Silvestri; Bill Tucci; Brian Haberlin; David Wohl ★ 1st Appearance of Witchblade, Witchblade.
1/B ❑ Cover: 2.95 **NM** value: **6.00**
• crossover;concludes in Shi/Cyblade: The Battle for Independents #2;San Diego Preview **A:** Marc Silvestri; Anthony Winn **W:** Marc Silvestri; Bill Tucci; Brian Haberlin; David Wohl
1/CS❑ **NM** value: **30.00**
• boxed set;crossover with Crusade;also contains Shi/Cyblade: The Battle for Independents #2
Ash 1❑ **NM** value: **2.00**
• preview of crossover with Crusade

CYBRID — Maximum
1 ❑ Jul 1995 Cover: 2.95 **NM** value: **Cover or less**
Circ: CapCity orders: **15,575**
Chrysalis, Part 1 **A:** Sam Liu **W:** Rob Liefeld; Garrett Omata

CYCLE OF FIRE — Paragon
Bk 1❑ b&w Cover: 9.95 **NM** value: **Cover or less**
• Dragonfly

CYCLOPS — Marvel
1 ❑ Oct 2000 Cover: 2.50 **NM** value: **Cover or less**
Circ: Diamd. preorders: **69,007** • **CGC:** 1 graded, best 9.8
2 ❑ Nov 2000 Cover: 2.50 **NM** value: **Cover or less**
Circ: Diamd. preorders: **56,343**
3 ❑ Dec 2000 Cover: 2.50 **NM** value: **Cover or less**
Circ: Diamd. preorders: **49,445**
4 ❑ Jan 2001 Cover: 2.50 **NM** value: **Cover or less**
Circ: Diamd. preorders: **46,854**

CYCOPS — Comics Interview
1 ❑ Jun 1988, b&w Cover: 1.95 **NM** value: **Cover or less**
Cyclops Blues **A:** Brian Stelfreeze **W:** Julie Lee Woodcock
2 ❑ Sum 1988, b&w Cover: 1.95 **NM** value: **Cover or less**
A: Brian Stelfreeze
3 ❑ b&w Cover: 1.95 **NM** value: **Cover or less**
A: Brian Stelfreeze
Bk 1❑ Cover: 8.95 **NM** value: **Cover or less**
• album **A:** Brian Stelfreeze **W:** Julie Lee Woodcock
Bk 1/Aut❑ Cover: 35.00 **NM** value: **Cover or less**

CY-GOR — Image
First appearing in Spawn #38, Cy-Gor was once Mike Konieczny, who volunteered to be the guinea pig in Dr. Frederick Willheim's cybernetic supersoldier project. He lost a good bit of his humanity in the process. Willheim fused bionic parts to the body of an ape, because a human body could not withstand the pain. In order to make sure that the supersoldier was somewhat human, Konieczny's consciousness was supposed to be transferred to the cybernetic gorilla's body. (Cy-Gor, get it?)

Things didn't go as planned, if this can be called a plan. Rather than an amalgam that's 80% human and 20% animal, Cy-Gor is a superstrong gorilla with an amazingly high IQ. Writer Rick Veitch and artist Joel Thomas (Prime) explore what happens when this big fella busts loose in this limited series.

1 ❑ Jul 1999 Cover: 2.50 **NM** value: **Cover or less**
Fire in Mind **A:** Joel Thomas **W:** Rick Veitch
2 ❑ Aug 1999 Cover: 2.50 **NM** value: **Cover or less**
Fire in Mind, Part 2 **A:** Joel Thomas **W:** Rick Veitch
3 ❑ Sep 1999 Cover: 2.50 **NM** value: **Cover or less**
Needles and Pins **A:** Joel Thomas **W:** Rick Veitch
4 ❑ Oct 1999 Cover: 2.50 **NM** value: **Cover or less**
Exquisite Corpse **A:** Joel Thomas **W:** Rick Veitch
5 ❑ Nov 1999 Cover: 2.50 **NM** value: **Cover or less**
Then One Foggy Christmas Eve **A:** Joel Thomas **W:** Rick Veitch

CYLINDERHEAD — Slave Labor
1 ❑ Feb 1989, b&w Cover: 1.95 **NM** value: **Cover or less**
A: Eric Bowman **W:** Eric Bowman

CYNDER — Immortelle
1 ❑ Cover: 2.50 **NM** value: **3.00**
Circ: CapCity orders: **8,345**
A: David Hernandez; Rob Liefeld **W:** Michael A. Hernandez ★ Origin of Cynder. ★ 1st Appearance of Cynder.
2 ❑ Cover: 2.50 **NM** value: **3.00**
Circ: CapCity orders: **6,095**
A: David Hernandez; Bill Tucci **W:** David Hernandez; Michael A. Hernandez
3 ❑ Cover: 2.50 **NM** value: **Cover or less**
W: David Hernandez; Michael A. Hernandez
Anl 1❑Nov 1996 Cover: 2.95 **NM** value: **3.00**
Circ: Direct Market orders: **3,463**
W: David Hernandez; Michael A. Hernandez

CYNDER/HELLINA SPECIAL — Immortelle
1 ❑ Nov 1996 Cover: 2.95 **NM** value: **Cover or less**
Circ: Direct Market orders: **5,605**
A: Leandro Ng **W:** David A. Hernandez

CYNTHERITA — Side Show
1 ❑ Cover: 2.95 **NM** value: **Cover or less**
A: Jim Ridings **W:** Jim Ridings

CYPHER — Gibbs Smith
Bk 1/HC❑b&w Cover: 18.95 **NM** value: **Cover or less**
hardcover.

CZAR CHASM — C&T
1 ❑ b&w Cover: 2.00 **NM** value: **Cover or less**
2 ❑ b&w Cover: 2.00 **NM** value: **Cover or less**

DADAVILLE — Caliber
1 ❑ b&w Cover: 2.95 **NM** value: **Cover or less**

DAEMON MASK — Amazing
1 ❑ Cover: 1.95 **NM** value: **Cover or less**
The Crimson Wings of Silence **A:** Russ Martin **W:** Stuart Hopen

DAEMONSTORM — Caliber
1 ❑ Jan 1997, b&w Cover: 3.95 **NM** value: **Cover or less**
Circ: Diamd. preorders: **12,460**
A: Don Hillsman **C:** Todd McFarlane **W:** Joe Martin
Ash 1❑b&w Cover: 0.99 **NM** value: **1.00**
No issue number. • preview of upcoming series **A:** Don Hillsman **W:** Joe Martin

DAFFY — Dell / Gold Key/Whitman
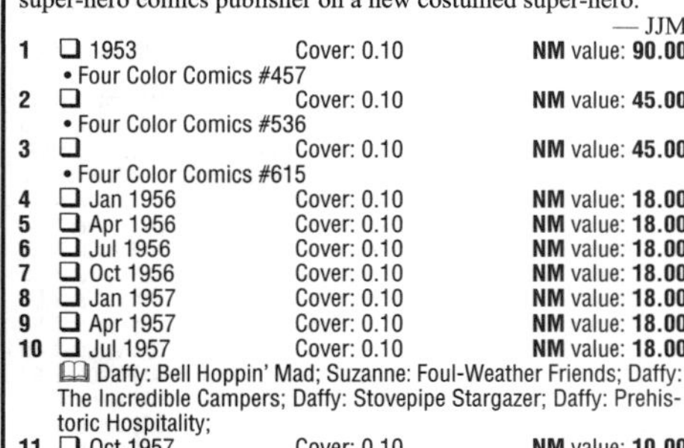

After three issues in Dell's Four Color, Warner Bros. cartoon star Daffy Duck got his own series in 1951, called, simply, Daffy. The series would make the swicth to Gold Key in the early 1960s, with later issues coming out under the Whitman imprint.Stories in these comics depict Daffy as rather less hyperactive than his cartoon counterpart, though he is often looking for a cheap meal or a fast way to get rich. Elmer Fudd and Yosemite Sam are occasional guest stars.

Some of the new Gold Key stories in the 1970s were suspprisingly media savvy, given the insular nature of many cartoon comics. In one story, Daffy plays a lost detective who forgets to take a left at Sesame Street by the big canary; in another, Daffy tries to sell a super-hero comics publisher on a new costumed super-hero.

— JJM

1 ❑ 1953 Cover: 0.10 **NM** value: **90.00**
• Four Color Comics #457
2 ❑ Cover: 0.10 **NM** value: **45.00**
• Four Color Comics #536
3 ❑ Cover: 0.10 **NM** value: **45.00**
• Four Color Comics #615
4 ❑ Jan 1956 Cover: 0.10 **NM** value: **18.00**
5 ❑ Apr 1956 Cover: 0.10 **NM** value: **18.00**
6 ❑ Jul 1956 Cover: 0.10 **NM** value: **18.00**
7 ❑ Oct 1956 Cover: 0.10 **NM** value: **18.00**
8 ❑ Jan 1957 Cover: 0.10 **NM** value: **18.00**
9 ❑ Apr 1957 Cover: 0.10 **NM** value: **18.00**
10 ❑ Jul 1957 Cover: 0.10 **NM** value: **18.00**
Daffy: Bell Hoppin' Mad; Suzanne: Foul-Weather Friends; Daffy: The Incredible Campers; Daffy: Stovepipe Stargazer; Daffy: Prehistoric Hospitality;
11 ❑ Oct 1957 Cover: 0.10 **NM** value: **10.00**
12 ❑ Jan 1958 Cover: 0.15 **NM** value: **10.00**
13 ❑ Apr 1958 **NM** value: **10.00**
14 ❑ Jul 1958 Cover: 0.10 **NM** value: **10.00**
15 ❑ Oct 1958 Cover: 0.10 **NM** value: **10.00**
16 ❑ Jan 1959 Cover: 0.10 **NM** value: **10.00**
17 ❑ Apr 1959 Cover: 0.10 **NM** value: **10.00**
18 ❑ Jul 1959 Cover: 0.10 **NM** value: **10.00**
19 ❑ Oct 1959 Cover: 0.10 **NM** value: **10.00**
20 ❑ Jan 1960 Cover: 0.10 **NM** value: **10.00**
21 ❑ Apr 1960 Cover: 0.10 **NM** value: **6.00**
22 ❑ Jul 1960 **NM** value: **6.00**
23 ❑ Oct 1960 **NM** value: **6.00**
24 ❑ Mar 1961 **NM** value: **6.00**
25 ❑ Jun 1961 **NM** value: **6.00**
26 ❑ Sep 1961 **NM** value: **6.00**
27 ❑ Dec 1961 Cover: 0.15 **NM** value: **6.00**
28 ❑ 1962 Cover: 0.15 **NM** value: **6.00**
29 ❑ 1962 Cover: 0.15 **NM** value: **6.00**
30 ❑ Jul 1962 Cover: 0.15 **NM** value: **6.00**
31 ❑ 1962 **NM** value: **6.00**
32 ❑ 1963 **NM** value: **6.00**
33 ❑ Jun 1963 Cover: 0.12 **NM** value: **6.00**
• Has 1962 Statement, filed 10/1/62; no circ figures published
34 ❑ Sep 1963 Cover: 0.12 **NM** value: **6.00**
35 ❑ Nov 1963 Cover: 0.12 **NM** value: **6.00**
36 ❑ Mar 1964 Cover: 0.12 **NM** value: **6.00**
37 ❑ Jun 1964 Cover: 0.12 **NM** value: **6.00**
38 ❑ Sep 1964 Cover: 0.12 **NM** value: **6.00**
39 ❑ Dec 1964 Cover: 0.12 **NM** value: **6.00**
40 ❑ Mar 1965 Cover: 0.12 **NM** value: **6.00**
Circ: Statement: **243,825**
41 ❑ Jun 1965 Cover: 0.12 **NM** value: **4.00**
Circ: Statement: **243,825**
42 ❑ Sep 1965 Cover: 0.12 **NM** value: **4.00**
Circ: Statement: **243,825**

CGC-graded: Multiply prices above by **33 for 9.9 M • 16 for 9.8 NM/M • 7 for 9.6 NM+ • 5 for 9.4 NM • 2.5 for 9.2 NM- • 1.5 for 9.0 VF/NM**

43 ❑ Dec 1965 Cover: 0.12 **NM** value: **4.00**
Circ: Statement: **243,825**
44 ❑ Mar 1966 Cover: 0.12 **NM** value: **4.00**
Circ: Statement: **254,750**
45 ❑ Jun 1966 Cover: 0.12 **NM** value: **4.00**
Circ: Statement: **254,750**
46 ❑ Sep 1966 Cover: 0.12 **NM** value: **4.00**
Circ: Statement: **254,750**
47 ❑ Dec 1966 Cover: 0.12 **NM** value: **4.00**
Circ: Statement: **254,750**
48 ❑ Mar 1967 Cover: 0.12 **NM** value: **4.00**
Circ: Statement: **212,225**
49 ❑ Jun 1967 Cover: 0.12 **NM** value: **4.00**
Circ: Statement: **212,225**
• Has 1966 Statement, filed 9/28/66; avg print run 383,497; avg sales 254,375; avg subs 375; avg total paid 254,750; samples 552; max existent 255,302; 33% of run returned
50 ❑ Sep 1967 Cover: 0.12 **NM** value: **4.00**
Circ: Statement: **212,225**
51 ❑ Dec 1967 Cover: 0.12 **NM** value: **4.00**
Circ: Statement: **212,225**
52 ❑ Mar 1968 Cover: 0.12 **NM** value: **4.00**
📖 Ye Old Rocking Chair
53 ❑ Jun 1968 Cover: 0.12 **NM** value: **4.00**
54 ❑ Sep 1968 Cover: 0.15 **NM** value: **4.00**
55 ❑ Dec 1968 Cover: 0.15 **NM** value: **4.00**
56 ❑ Mar 1969 Cover: 0.15 **NM** value: **4.00**
57 ❑ May 1969 Cover: 0.15 **NM** value: **4.00**
58 ❑ Jul 1969 Cover: 0.15 **NM** value: **4.00**
59 ❑ Sep 1969 Cover: 0.15 **NM** value: **4.00**
60 ❑ Nov 1969 Cover: 0.15 **NM** value: **4.00**
61 ❑ Jan 1970 Cover: 0.15 **NM** value: **3.00**
Circ: Statement: **204,688**
62 ❑ Mar 1970 Cover: 0.15 **NM** value: **3.00**
Circ: Statement: **204,688**
63 ❑ May 1970 Cover: 0.15 **NM** value: **3.00**
Circ: Statement: **204,688**
64 ❑ Jul 1970 Cover: 0.15 **NM** value: **3.00**
Circ: Statement: **204,688**
65 ❑ Sep 1970 Cover: 0.15 **NM** value: **3.00**
Circ: Statement: **204,688**
66 ❑ Nov 1970 Cover: 0.15 **NM** value: **3.00**
Circ: Statement: **204,688**
67 ❑ Jan 1971 Cover: 0.15 **NM** value: **3.00**
Circ: Statement: **192,856**
68 ❑ Mar 1971 Cover: 0.15 **NM** value: **3.00**
Circ: Statement: **192,856**
• Has 1970 Statement, filed 9/30/70; avg print run 375,269; avg sales 204,500; avg subs 188; avg total paid 204,688; samples 601; max existent 205,289; 45% of run returned
69 ❑ May 1971 Cover: 0.15 **NM** value: **3.00**
Circ: Statement: **192,856**
70 ❑ Jul 1971 Cover: 0.15 **NM** value: **3.00**
Circ: Statement: **192,856**
71 ❑ Sep 1971 Cover: 0.15 **NM** value: **3.00**
Circ: Statement: **192,856**
72 ❑ Nov 1971 Cover: 0.15 **NM** value: **3.00**
Circ: Statement: **192,856**
73 ❑ Jan 1972 Cover: 0.15 **NM** value: **3.00**
74 ❑ Mar 1972 Cover: 0.15 **NM** value: **3.00**
• Has 1971 Statement, filed 9/30/71; avg print run 316,863; avg sales 192,400; avg subs 456; avg total paid 192,856; samples 503; office use 199; max existent 193,558; 39% of run returned
75 ❑ May 1972 Cover: 0.15 **NM** value: **3.00**
76 ❑ Jul 1972 Cover: 0.15 **NM** value: **3.00**
77 ❑ Aug 1972 Cover: 0.15 **NM** value: **3.00**
78 ❑ Oct 1972 Cover: 0.15 **NM** value: **3.00**
79 ❑ Dec 1972 Cover: 0.15 **NM** value: **3.00**
80 ❑ Feb 1973 Cover: 0.15 **NM** value: **3.00**
81 ❑ Apr 1973 Cover: 0.15 **NM** value: **2.00**
82 ❑ Jun 1973 Cover: 0.20 **NM** value: **2.00**
83 ❑ Aug 1973 Cover: 0.20 **NM** value: **2.00**
84 ❑ Oct 1973 Cover: 0.20 **NM** value: **2.00**
85 ❑ Dec 1973 Cover: 0.20 **NM** value: **2.00**
86 ❑ Feb 1974 Cover: 0.20 **NM** value: **2.00**
87 ❑ Apr 1974 Cover: 0.20 **NM** value: **2.00**
88 ❑ Jun 1974 Cover: 0.20 **NM** value: **2.00**
89 ❑ Aug 1974 Cover: 0.25 **NM** value: **2.00**
90 ❑ Oct 1974 Cover: 0.25 **NM** value: **2.00**
91 ❑ Dec 1974 Cover: 0.25 **NM** value: **2.00**
92 ❑ Feb 1975 Cover: 0.25 **NM** value: **2.00**
93 ❑ Apr 1975 Cover: 0.25 **NM** value: **2.00**
94 ❑ Jun 1975 Cover: 0.25 **NM** value: **2.00**
95 ❑ Aug 1975 Cover: 0.25 **NM** value: **2.00**
96 ❑ Sep 1975 Cover: 0.25 **NM** value: **2.00**
97 ❑ Oct 1975 Cover: 0.25 **NM** value: **2.00**
• **CGC:** 5 graded, best 9.4
98 ❑ Dec 1975 Cover: 0.25 **NM** value: **2.00**
99 ❑ Feb 1976 Cover: 0.25 **NM** value: **2.00**
100 ❑ Apr 1976 Cover: 0.25 **NM** value: **2.00**
101 ❑ Jun 1976 Cover: 0.25 **NM** value: **1.50**
102 ❑ Jul 1976 Cover: 0.25 **NM** value: **1.50**
103 ❑ Aug 1976 Cover: 0.25 **NM** value: **1.50**
104 ❑ Oct 1976 Cover: 0.30 **NM** value: **1.50**
105 ❑ Dec 1976 Cover: 0.30 **NM** value: **1.50**
106 ❑ Feb 1977 Cover: 0.30 **NM** value: **1.50**
107 ❑ Apr 1977 Cover: 0.30 **NM** value: **1.50**
108 ❑ Jun 1977 Cover: 0.30 **NM** value: **1.50**
109 ❑ Jul 1977 Cover: 0.30 **NM** value: **1.50**
110 ❑ Aug 1977 Cover: 0.30 **NM** value: **1.50**
111 ❑ Oct 1977 Cover: 0.30 **NM** value: **1.50**
112 ❑ Dec 1977 Cover: 0.35 **NM** value: **1.50**
113 ❑ Feb 1978 Cover: 0.35 **NM** value: **1.50**
114 ❑ Apr 1978 Cover: 0.35 **NM** value: **1.50**
115 ❑ Jun 1978 Cover: 0.35 **NM** value: **1.50**
116 ❑ Jul 1978 Cover: 0.35 **NM** value: **1.50**
117 ❑ Aug 1978 Cover: 0.35 **NM** value: **1.50**
118 ❑ Oct 1978 Cover: 0.35 **NM** value: **1.50**
119 ❑ Dec 1978 Cover: 0.35 **NM** value: **1.50**
120 ❑ Feb 1979 Cover: 0.35 **NM** value: **1.50**
121 ❑ Apr 1979 Cover: 0.40 **NM** value: **1.50**
122 ❑ Jun 1979 Cover: 0.40 **NM** value: **1.50**
123 ❑ Aug 1979 Cover: 0.40 **NM** value: **1.50**
124 ❑ Oct 1979 Cover: 0.40 **NM** value: **1.50**
125 ❑ Dec 1979 Cover: 0.40 **NM** value: **1.50**
126 ❑ Feb 1980 Cover: 0.40 **NM** value: **1.50**
127 ❑ Apr 1980 Cover: 0.40 **NM** value: **1.50**
128 ❑ Jun 1980 Cover: 0.40 **NM** value: **1.50**
129 ❑ Aug 1980 Cover: 0.40 **NM** value: **1.50**
130 ❑ Oct 1980 Cover: 0.40 **NM** value: **1.50**
131 ❑ Dec 1980 Cover: 0.40 **NM** value: **1.50**
132 ❑ Jan 1981 Cover: 0.40 **NM** value: **1.50**
133 ❑ Feb 1981 Cover: 0.50 **NM** value: **1.50**
134 ❑ Mar 1981 Cover: 0.50 **NM** value: **1.50**
135 ❑ Jul 1981 Cover: 0.50 **NM** value: **1.50**
136 ❑ Nov 1981 Cover: 0.50 **NM** value: **1.50**
137 ❑ Dec 1981 Cover: 0.50 **NM** value: **1.50**
138 ❑ Jan 1982 Cover: 0.50 **NM** value: **1.50**
139 ❑ Feb 1982 Cover: 0.60 **NM** value: **1.50**
140 ❑ Mar 1982 Cover: 0.60 **NM** value: **1.50**
141 ❑ Apr 1982 Cover: 0.60 **NM** value: **1.50**
142 ❑ 1982 Cover: 0.60 **NM** value: **1.50**
143 ❑ 1982 Cover: 0.60 **NM** value: **1.50**
144 ❑ 1983 Cover: 0.60 **NM** value: **1.50**
145 ❑ 1983 Cover: 0.60 **NM** value: **1.50**
final issue.

DAFFY QADDAFI — Comics Unlimited

1 ❑ 1986b&w Cover: 1.75 **NM** value: **2.00**
📖 A Dictator's Nightmare in Wonderland • Nancy Reagan cameo ★ Appearance of Oliver North, Moammar Qaddafi, Daffy Duck, Ronald Reagan.

DAGAR DESERT HAWK — Fox

14 ❑ Feb 1948 Cover: 0.10 **NM** value: **500.00**
• **CGC:** 3 graded, best 8.5
📖 Monsters of Mura; The Red Vulture
15 ❑ Apr 1948 Cover: 0.10 **NM** value: **400.00**
• **CGC:** 1 graded, best 8.5
📖 Curse of the Lost Pharoh; Vortex of Death
16 ❑ Jun 1948 Cover: 0.10 **NM** value: **300.00**
• **CGC:** 1 graded, best 6.5
📖 The Wretched Antmen!; Murder, Mutiny and a Blonde!; Bombay Bombshell
17 ❑ 1948 Cover: 0.10 **NM** value: **300.00**
18 ❑ 1948 Cover: 0.10 **NM** value: **300.00**
19 ❑ Aug 1948 Cover: 0.10 **NM** value: **300.00**
📖 Pyramid of Doom!; Death Ray!; The Plot!; Hangman!
20 ❑ Oct 1948 Cover: 0.10 **NM** value: **300.00**
21 ❑ Dec 1948 Cover: 0.10 **NM** value: **300.00**
• **CGC:** 1 graded, best 6.5
📖 The Ghost of Fate
22 ❑ Feb 1949 Cover: 0.10 **NM** value: **300.00**
• **CGC:** 2 graded, best 7.5
23 ❑ Apr 1949 Cover: 0.10 **NM** value: **300.00**

DAGAR THE INVINCIBLE (TALES OF SWORD AND SORCERY...) — Gold Key

Dagar is a sword-wielding barbarian and the last survivor of the nation of Tulgonia. Tulgonia had been wiped out by the armies of Scorpio, a world-conquering fiend. On that day, Dagar swore he would not rest until he had gained his revenge.

Although similar in many ways to Robert E. Howard's Conan the Barbarian, Gold Key's Dagar is even less motivated by altruism. When first meeting Graylin, the beautiful woman who would later become his companion, Dagar was content to ride by while she was being carried off by huge bats. It was only later on that he reconsidered and rushed to her rescue!

1 ❑ Oct 1972 Cover: 0.15 **NM** value: **8.00**
📖 The Sword Of Dagar ★ Origin of Dagar. ★ 1st Appearance of Scorpio, Ostellon.
2 ❑ Jan 1973 Cover: 0.15 **NM** value: **4.00**
3 ❑ Apr 1973 Cover: 0.15 **NM** value: **3.00**
📖 The Wrath Of The Vampires ★ 1st Appearance of Graylin.
4 ❑ Jul 1973 Cover: 0.20 **NM** value: **3.00**
5 ❑ Oct 1973 Cover: 0.20 **NM** value: **3.00**
6 ❑ Jan 1974 Cover: 0.20 **NM** value: **2.50**
• Dark Gods story
7 ❑ Apr 1974 Cover: 0.20 **NM** value: **2.50**
8 ❑ Jul 1974 Cover: 0.20 **NM** value: **2.50**
9 ❑ Oct 1974 Cover: 0.25 **NM** value: **2.50**
10 ❑ Jan 1975 Cover: 0.25 **NM** value: **2.50**
11 ❑ Apr 1975 Cover: 0.25 **NM** value: **2.00**
12 ❑ Jul 1975 Cover: 0.25 **NM** value: **2.00**
13 ❑ Oct 1975 Cover: 0.25 **NM** value: **2.00**
14 ❑ Jan 1976 Cover: 0.25 **NM** value: **2.00**
15 ❑ Apr 1976 Cover: 0.25 **NM** value: **2.00**
16 ❑ Jul 1976 Cover: 0.25 **NM** value: **2.00**
17 ❑ Oct 1976 Cover: 0.30 **NM** value: **2.00**
18 ❑ Dec 1976 Cover: 0.30 **NM** value: **2.00**
• Final issue of original run (1976)
19 ❑ Apr 1982 Cover: 0.60 **NM** value: **2.00**
📖 The Sword Of Dagar • One-shot revival: 1982;Reprints Dagar #1★ Origin of Dagar.

DAGWOOD COMICS (CHIC YOUNG'S...) — Harvey

The Blondie strip created by Chic Young (1901-1973) has been a part of the American consciousness since it was introduced in 1930. It began as a gag strip about Blondie as a pert flapper, surrounded by suitors — but she married Dagwood Bumstead in 1933, and the strip turned into a family comedy gag-a-day.

Dagwood works for Mr. Dithers, an old blowhard who chews out Dagwood with legendary frequency. And Dagwood took over as more of the focal point of the daily strip than was Blondie, who had gone from being a gadabout to taking on the role of tolerant wife. Dagwood was the bumbling star who spent his days being browbeaten by his tyrannical boss and in his off-time doing his absolute best to catch up on his sleep and awaking to consume a "Dagwood sandwich," a towering mountain of food between two slices of bread that is a defining joy in his life.

1 ❑ Sep 1950 Cover: 0.10 **NM** value: **75.00**
2 ❑ Nov 1950 Cover: 0.10 **NM** value: **40.00**
3 ❑ Jan 1951 Cover: 0.10 **NM** value: **30.00**
4 ❑ Mar 1951 Cover: 0.10 **NM** value: **30.00**
5 ❑ Apr 1951 Cover: 0.10 **NM** value: **30.00**
• **CGC:** 1 graded, best 4.5
6 ❑ May 1951 Cover: 0.10 **NM** value: **25.00**
7 ❑ Jun 1951 Cover: 0.10 **NM** value: **25.00**
📖 A Dog-Gone Tale; No He **A:** Chic Young; Bill Zaboly; Jimmy Hatlo; O. Soglow **W:** Chic Young; Jimmy Hatlo; O. Soglow; Tom Sims
8 ❑ Jul 1951 Cover: 0.10 **NM** value: **25.00**
9 ❑ Aug 1951 Cover: 0.10 **NM** value: **25.00**
10 ❑ Sep 1951 Cover: 0.10 **NM** value: **25.00**
11 ❑ Oct 1951 Cover: 0.10 **NM** value: **20.00**
12 ❑ Nov 1951 Cover: 0.10 **NM** value: **20.00**
13 ❑ Dec 1951 Cover: 0.10 **NM** value: **20.00**
📖 Handy Hideout; Women's Ways; It's the Law; Bad Dream; Umbrella Justice
14 ❑ Jan 1952 Cover: 0.10 **NM** value: **20.00**
15 ❑ Feb 1952 Cover: 0.10 **NM** value: **20.00**
16 ❑ Mar 1952 Cover: 0.10 **NM** value: **20.00**
17 ❑ Apr 1952 Cover: 0.10 **NM** value: **20.00**
• **CGC:** 1 graded, best 6.0
18 ❑ May 1952 Cover: 0.10 **NM** value: **20.00**
19 ❑ Jun 1952 Cover: 0.10 **NM** value: **20.00**
20 ❑ Jul 1952 Cover: 0.10 **NM** value: **20.00**
21 ❑ Aug 1952 Cover: 0.10 **NM** value: **16.00**
22 ❑ Sep 1952 Cover: 0.10 **NM** value: **16.00**
23 ❑ Oct 1952 Cover: 0.10 **NM** value: **16.00**
24 ❑ Nov 1952 Cover: 0.10 **NM** value: **16.00**
25 ❑ Dec 1952 Cover: 0.10 **NM** value: **16.00**
26 ❑ Jan 1953 Cover: 0.10 **NM** value: **16.00**
27 ❑ Feb 1953 Cover: 0.10 **NM** value: **16.00**
28 ❑ Mar 1953 Cover: 0.10 **NM** value: **16.00**
29 ❑ Apr 1953 Cover: 0.10 **NM** value: **16.00**
30 ❑ May 1953 Cover: 0.10 **NM** value: **16.00**
31 ❑ Jun 1953 Cover: 0.10 **NM** value: **14.00**
32 ❑ Jul 1953 Cover: 0.10 **NM** value: **14.00**
33 ❑ Aug 1953 Cover: 0.10 **NM** value: **14.00**
34 ❑ Sep 1953 Cover: 0.10 **NM** value: **14.00**
35 ❑ Oct 1953 Cover: 0.10 **NM** value: **14.00**
36 ❑ Nov 1953 Cover: 0.10 **NM** value: **14.00**
37 ❑ Dec 1953 Cover: 0.10 **NM** value: **14.00**
38 ❑ Jan 1954 Cover: 0.10 **NM** value: **14.00**
39 ❑ Feb 1954 Cover: 0.10 **NM** value: **14.00**
40 ❑ Mar 1954 Cover: 0.10 **NM** value: **14.00**
• **CGC:** 1 graded, best 5.5
41 ❑ Apr 1954 Cover: 0.10 **NM** value: **14.00**
42 ❑ May 1954 Cover: 0.10 **NM** value: **14.00**
43 ❑ Jun 1954 Cover: 0.10 **NM** value: **14.00**
44 ❑ Jul 1954 Cover: 0.10 **NM** value: **14.00**
45 ❑ Aug 1954 Cover: 0.10 **NM** value: **14.00**
46 ❑ Sep 1954 Cover: 0.10 **NM** value: **14.00**
47 ❑ Nov 1954 Cover: 0.10 **NM** value: **14.00**
48 ❑ Dec 1954 Cover: 0.10 **NM** value: **14.00**
49 ❑ Jan 1955 Cover: 0.10 **NM** value: **14.00**
50 ❑ Feb 1955 Cover: 0.10 **NM** value: **14.00**
51 ❑ Mar 1955 Cover: 0.10 **NM** value: **12.00**
52 ❑ Apr 1955 Cover: 0.10 **NM** value: **12.00**
53 ❑ May 1955 Cover: 0.10 **NM** value: **12.00**
54 ❑ Jun 1955 Cover: 0.10 **NM** value: **12.00**
55 ❑ Jul 1955 Cover: 0.10 **NM** value: **12.00**
56 ❑ Aug 1955 Cover: 0.10 **NM** value: **12.00**
57 ❑ Sep 1955 Cover: 0.10 **NM** value: **12.00**
58 ❑ Oct 1955 Cover: 0.10 **NM** value: **12.00**
59 ❑ Nov 1955 Cover: 0.10 **NM** value: **12.00**
60 ❑ Dec 1955 Cover: 0.10 **NM** value: **12.00**
61 ❑ Jan 1956 Cover: 0.10 **NM** value: **12.00**
62 ❑ Feb 1956 Cover: 0.10 **NM** value: **12.00**
63 ❑ Mar 1956 Cover: 0.10 **NM** value: **12.00**
64 ❑ Apr 1956 Cover: 0.10 **NM** value: **12.00**
65 ❑ May 1956 Cover: 0.10 **NM** value: **12.00**
66 ❑ Jun 1956 Cover: 0.10 **NM** value: **12.00**
67 ❑ Jul 1956 Cover: 0.10 **NM** value: **12.00**
68 ❑ Aug 1956 Cover: 0.10 **NM** value: **12.00**
69 ❑ Sep 1956 Cover: 0.10 **NM** value: **12.00**
70 ❑ Oct 1956 Cover: 0.10 **NM** value: **12.00**
71 ❑ Nov 1956 Cover: 0.10 **NM** value: **9.00**
72 ❑ Dec 1956 Cover: 0.10 **NM** value: **9.00**
73 ❑ Jan 1957 Cover: 0.10 **NM** value: **9.00**
74 ❑ Feb 1957 Cover: 0.10 **NM** value: **9.00**
75 ❑ Mar 1957 Cover: 0.10 **NM** value: **9.00**

Other grades: Multiply prices above by **1.5 for Mint • 2/3 for Very Fine • 1/3 for Fine • 1/5 for Very Good • 1/8 for Good**

76 ❑ Apr 1957 Cover: 0.10 **NM** value: **9.00**
77 ❑ May 1957 Cover: 0.10 **NM** value: **9.00**
78 ❑ Jun 1957 Cover: 0.10 **NM** value: **9.00**
79 ❑ Jul 1957 Cover: 0.10 **NM** value: **9.00**
80 ❑ Aug 1957 Cover: 0.10 **NM** value: **9.00**
81 ❑ Sep 1957 Cover: 0.10 **NM** value: **7.00**
82 ❑ Oct 1957 Cover: 0.10 **NM** value: **7.00**
83 ❑ Nov 1957 Cover: 0.10 **NM** value: **7.00**
84 ❑ Dec 1957 Cover: 0.10 **NM** value: **7.00**
85 ❑ Jan 1958 Cover: 0.10 **NM** value: **7.00**
86 ❑ Feb 1958 Cover: 0.10 **NM** value: **7.00**
87 ❑ Mar 1958 Cover: 0.10 **NM** value: **7.00**
88 ❑ Apr 1958 Cover: 0.10 **NM** value: **7.00**
89 ❑ May 1958 Cover: 0.10 **NM** value: **7.00**
90 ❑ Jun 1958 Cover: 0.10 **NM** value: **7.00**
91 ❑ Jul 1958 Cover: 0.10 **NM** value: **7.00**
92 ❑ Aug 1958 Cover: 0.10 **NM** value: **7.00**
93 ❑ Sep 1958 Cover: 0.10 **NM** value: **7.00**
94 ❑ Oct 1958 Cover: 0.10 **NM** value: **7.00**
95 ❑ Dec 1958 Cover: 0.10 **NM** value: **7.00**
96 ❑ Jan 1959 Cover: 0.10 **NM** value: **7.00**
97 ❑ Feb 1959 Cover: 0.10 **NM** value: **7.00**
98 ❑ Mar 1959 Cover: 0.10 **NM** value: **7.00**
99 ❑ Apr 1959 Cover: 0.10 **NM** value: **7.00**
100 ❑ May 1959 Cover: 0.10 **NM** value: **7.00**
101 ❑ Jun 1959 Cover: 0.10 **NM** value: **6.00**
102 ❑ Jul 1959 Cover: 0.10 **NM** value: **6.00**
103 ❑ Aug 1959 Cover: 0.10 **NM** value: **6.00**
104 ❑ Sep 1959 Cover: 0.10 **NM** value: **6.00**
105 ❑ Oct 1959 Cover: 0.10 **NM** value: **6.00**
106 ❑ 1959 Cover: 0.10 **NM** value: **6.00**
107 ❑ Cover: 0.10 **NM** value: **6.00**
108 ❑ 1960 Cover: 0.10 **NM** value: **6.00**
Circ: Statement: **118,819**
109 ❑ 1960 Cover: 0.10 **NM** value: **6.00**
Circ: Statement: **118,819**
110 ❑ 1960 Cover: 0.10 **NM** value: **6.00**
Circ: Statement: **118,819**
111 ❑ 1960 Cover: 0.10 **NM** value: **6.00**
Circ: Statement: **118,819**
112 ❑ 1960 Cover: 0.10 **NM** value: **6.00**
Circ: Statement: **118,819**
113 ❑ 1960 Cover: 0.10 **NM** value: **6.00**
Circ: Statement: **118,819**
114 ❑ 1960 Cover: 0.10 **NM** value: **6.00**
Circ: Statement: **118,819**
115 ❑ Sep 1960 Cover: 0.10 **NM** value: **6.00**
Circ: Statement: **118,819**
116 ❑ Cover: 0.10 **NM** value: **6.00**
117 ❑ ca. 1961 Cover: 0.10 **NM** value: **6.00**
118 ❑ ca. 1961 Cover: 0.10 **NM** value: **6.00**
119 ❑ May 1961 Cover: 0.10 **NM** value: **6.00**
• Has 1960 Statement, filed 10/1/60; avg total paid circ 188,819
120 ❑ Jul 1961 Cover: 0.10 **NM** value: **6.00**
121 ❑ Sep 1961 Cover: 0.10 **NM** value: **5.00**
122 ❑ Oct 1961 Cover: 0.25 **NM** value: **5.00**
123 ❑ Nov 1961 Cover: 0.10 **NM** value: **5.00**
124 ❑ Jan 1962 Cover: 0.10 **NM** value: **5.00**
• **CGC:** 2 graded, best 9.4
125 ❑ Mar 1962 Cover: 0.10 **NM** value: **5.00**
• **CGC:** 2 graded, best 9.4
126 ❑ May 1962 Cover: 0.10 **NM** value: **5.00**
• **CGC:** 1 graded, best 9.0
127 ❑ Jul 1962 Cover: 0.10 **NM** value: **5.00**
• **CGC:** 2 graded, best 9.4
128 ❑ Sep 1962 Cover: 0.10 **NM** value: **5.00**
• **CGC:** 1 graded, best 9.0
129 ❑ Oct 1962 Cover: 0.10 **NM** value: **5.00**
• **CGC:** 2 graded, best 9.2
130 ❑ Nov 1962 Cover: 0.10 **NM** value: **5.00**
• **CGC:** 1 graded, best 8.5
131 ❑ Cover: 0.10 **NM** value: **5.00**
132 ❑ 1963 Cover: 0.10 **NM** value: **5.00**
133 ❑ 1963 Cover: 0.10 **NM** value: **5.00**
134 ❑ 1963 Cover: 0.10 **NM** value: **5.00**
135 ❑ Cover: 0.10 **NM** value: **5.00**
136 ❑ **NM** value: **5.00**
137 ❑ Sep 1964 Cover: 0.25 **NM** value: **5.00**
138 ❑ 1965 **NM** value: **5.00**
139 ❑ Sep 1965 Cover: 0.25 **NM** value: **5.00**
140 ❑ Nov 1965 Cover: 0.25 **NM** value: **5.00**
final issue.

DAHMER'S ZOMBIE SQUAD — Boneyard

1 ❑ Feb 1993 Cover: 3.95 **NM** value: **Cover or less**
A: Nelson Danielson **W:** Hart Fisher

DAI KAMIKAZE! — Now

1 ❑ Jun 1987 Cover: 3.00 **NM** value: **Cover or less**
Circ: CapCity orders: **3,350**
📖 Generations **A:** Gigdeon **W:** Brian Augustyn; Len Strazewski
1-2 ❑ Sep 1987 Cover: 1.75 **NM** value: **Cover or less**
2 ❑ Jul 1987 Cover: 1.50 **NM** value: **Cover or less**
Circ: CapCity orders: **2,175**
3 ❑ Aug 1987 Cover: 1.50 **NM** value: **Cover or less**
Circ: CapCity orders: **2,175**
4 ❑ Oct 1987 Cover: 1.50 **NM** value: **Cover or less**
Circ: CapCity orders: **2,000**
5 ❑ Nov 1987 Cover: 1.75 **NM** value: **Cover or less**
Circ: CapCity orders: **2,500**
6 ❑ Dec 1987 Cover: 1.75 **NM** value: **Cover or less**
Circ: CapCity orders: **2,750**
7 ❑ Jan 1988 Cover: 1.75 **NM** value: **Cover or less**
Circ: CapCity orders: **2,875**
8 ❑ Feb 1988 Cover: 1.75 **NM** value: **Cover or less**
Circ: CapCity orders: **2,450**
9 ❑ Apr 1988 Cover: 1.75 **NM** value: **Cover or less**
Circ: CapCity orders: **1,975**
10 ❑ Apr 1988 Cover: 1.75 **NM** value: **Cover or less**
Circ: CapCity orders: **1,650**
11 ❑ Jun 1988 Cover: 1.75 **NM** value: **Cover or less**
Circ: CapCity orders: **1,650**
12 ❑ Jul 1988 Cover: 1.75 **NM** value: **Cover or less**
Circ: CapCity orders: **1,375**

DAIKAZU — Ground Zero

1 ❑ b&w Cover: 1.50 **NM** value: **Cover or less**
1-2 ❑ Cover: 1.50 **NM** value: **Cover or less**
2 ❑ b&w Cover: 1.50 **NM** value: **Cover or less**
2-2 ❑ Cover: 1.50 **NM** value: **Cover or less**
3 ❑ b&w Cover: 1.50 **NM** value: **Cover or less**
4 ❑ b&w Cover: 1.50 **NM** value: **Cover or less**
5 ❑ b&w Cover: 1.50 **NM** value: **Cover or less**
6 ❑ b&w Cover: 1.50 **NM** value: **Cover or less**
7 ❑ b&w Cover: 1.50 **NM** value: **Cover or less**
8 ❑ Cover: 1.75 **NM** value: **Cover or less**

DAILY BUGLE — Marvel

1 ❑ Dec 1996, b&w Cover: 2.50 **NM** value: **Cover or less**
Circ: Direct Market orders: **40,250**
📖 Front Page **A:** Karl Kerschl **W:** Paul Grist
2 ❑ Jan 1997, b&w Cover: 2.50 **NM** value: **Cover or less**
Circ: Direct Market orders: **33,250**
📖 Scoop **A:** Karl Kerschl **W:** Paul Grist
3 ❑ Feb 1997, b&w Cover: 2.50 **NM** value: **Cover or less**
Circ: Direct Market orders: **28,000**
📖 Deadline final issue. **A:** Karl Kerschl **W:** Paul Grist

DAILY PLANET INVASION! EXTRA — DC

1 ❑ Cover: 2.00 **NM** value: **Cover or less**
Circ: CapCity orders: **16,200**
• newspaper

DAIMONS — Cry for Dawn

1 ❑ Cover: 2.50 **NM** value: **Cover or less**
A: Richard Kane Ferguson **W:** Richard Kane Ferguson

DAISY AND DONALD — Gold Key

Filled with stories featuring the relationships between Donald and Daisy Duck, the series occasionally provided reprints of stories by writer-artist Carl Barks. Much of the emphasis was on Daisy and her romantic intentions regarding Donald, but many stories also dealt with the difficulties in being Donald's girlfriend — which are plenty, if you know Donald.

Women's Lib even filters into some of their disagreements, although the Duckburg brand is decidedly tame. In one story reflective of the times, Donald gets caught up in the Citizen's Band radio fad, driving Daisy to distraction as he drives her around, trying to lend traffic tips to truckers and help the police chase criminals. As usual, Donald winds up in jail, which means that Daisy, the empowered 1970s woman, can use his CB to tell her friends about the latest dress sales! — JJM

1 ❑ May 1973 Cover: 0.15 **NM** value: **12.00**
📖 Dinner Date, The Beauty Business, The Shutterbug Duck • Reprints story from Walt Disney's Comics #308 **A:** Carl Barks ★ Appearance of June, May, April.
2 ❑ Aug 1973 Cover: 0.20 **NM** value: **6.00**
3 ❑ Nov 1973 Cover: 0.20 **NM** value: **4.00**
4 ❑ Jan 1974 Cover: 0.20 **NM** value: **4.00**
📖 The Giant Cowry Shell • Reprints story from Walt Disney's Comics #224 **A:** Carl Barks
5 ❑ May 1974 Cover: 0.20 **NM** value: **4.00**
6 ❑ Aug 1974 Cover: 0.25 **NM** value: **4.00**
7 ❑ Nov 1974 Cover: 0.25 **NM** value: **4.00**
8 ❑ Jan 1975 Cover: 0.25 **NM** value: **4.00**
9 ❑ Mar 1975 Cover: 0.25 **NM** value: **4.00**
10 ❑ May 1975 Cover: 0.25 **NM** value: **4.00**
11 ❑ Jul 1975 Cover: 0.25 **NM** value: **3.00**
12 ❑ Sep 1975 Cover: 0.25 **NM** value: **3.00**
13 ❑ Nov 1975 Cover: 0.25 **NM** value: **3.00**
14 ❑ Jan 1976 Cover: 0.25 **NM** value: **3.00**
15 ❑ Mar 1976 Cover: 0.25 **NM** value: **3.00**
16 ❑ May 1976 Cover: 0.25 **NM** value: **3.00**
17 ❑ Jul 1976 Cover: 0.25 **NM** value: **3.00**
18 ❑ Aug 1976 Cover: 0.25 **NM** value: **3.00**
19 ❑ Sep 1976 Cover: 0.30 **NM** value: **3.00**
20 ❑ Nov 1976 Cover: 0.30 **NM** value: **3.00**
21 ❑ Jan 1977 Cover: 0.30 **NM** value: **3.00**
22 ❑ Mar 1977 Cover: 0.30 **NM** value: **3.00**
23 ❑ May 1977 Cover: 0.30 **NM** value: **3.00**
24 ❑ Jul 1977 Cover: 0.30 **NM** value: **3.00**
25 ❑ Aug 1977 Cover: 0.30 **NM** value: **3.00**
26 ❑ Sep 1977 Cover: 0.30 **NM** value: **3.00**
27 ❑ Nov 1977 Cover: 0.30 **NM** value: **3.00**
28 ❑ Jan 1978 Cover: 0.35 **NM** value: **3.00**
29 ❑ Mar 1978 Cover: 0.35 **NM** value: **3.00**
30 ❑ May 1978 Cover: 0.35 **NM** value: **3.00**
31 ❑ Jul 1978 Cover: 0.35 **NM** value: **2.00**
32 ❑ Aug 1978 Cover: 0.35 **NM** value: **2.00**
33 ❑ Sep 1978 Cover: 0.35 **NM** value: **2.00**
34 ❑ Nov 1978 Cover: 0.35 **NM** value: **2.00**
35 ❑ Jan 1979 Cover: 0.35 **NM** value: **2.00**
36 ❑ Mar 1979 Cover: 0.35 **NM** value: **2.00**
37 ❑ May 1979 Cover: 0.40 **NM** value: **2.00**
38 ❑ Jul 1979 Cover: 0.40 **NM** value: **2.00**
39 ❑ Aug 1979 Cover: 0.40 **NM** value: **2.00**
40 ❑ Sep 1979 Cover: 0.40 **NM** value: **2.00**
41 ❑ Nov 1979 Cover: 0.40 **NM** value: **2.00**
42 ❑ Mar 1980 Cover: 0.40 **NM** value: **2.00**
43 ❑ Apr 1980 Cover: 0.40 **NM** value: **2.00**
44 ❑ May 1980 Cover: 0.40 **NM** value: **2.00**
45 ❑ Jun 1980 Cover: 0.40 **NM** value: **2.00**
46 ❑ **NM** value: **2.00**
47 ❑ **NM** value: **2.00**
• **CGC:** 1 graded, best 7.5
48 ❑ **NM** value: **2.00**
49 ❑ **NM** value: **2.00**
50 ❑ **NM** value: **2.00**
51 ❑ **NM** value: **2.00**
52 ❑ **NM** value: **2.00**
53 ❑ Feb 1982 Cover: 0.60 **NM** value: **2.00**
54 ❑ Cover: 0.60 **NM** value: **2.00**
55 ❑ Cover: 0.60 **NM** value: **2.00**
56 ❑ Cover: 0.60 **NM** value: **2.00**
57 ❑ Cover: 0.60 **NM** value: **2.00**
58 ❑ Cover: 0.60 **NM** value: **2.00**
59 ❑ Cover: 0.60 **NM** value: **2.00**

DAISY AND HER PUPS COMICS — Harvey

1 ❑ Cover: 0.10 **NM** value: **12.00**
• (#21, 1951)
2 ❑ Cover: 0.10 **NM** value: **9.00**
• (#22, 1951)
3 ❑ Cover: 0.10 **NM** value: **9.00**
📖 The Worm Turns; Bullies Beware!; Playful Pups; Timid Hero (text story); Fun at the Zoo; Prize Dog (text story); The Little King • (#23, 1951) **A:** Chic Young; O. Soglow; Paul McCarthy **W:** Chic Young; O. Soglow; Paul McCarthy
4 ❑ Cover: 0.10 **NM** value: **9.00**
• (#24, 1952)
5 ❑ Cover: 0.10 **NM** value: **9.00**
• (#25, 1952)
6 ❑ Cover: 0.10 **NM** value: **8.00**
• (#26, 1952)
7 ❑ Cover: 0.10 **NM** value: **8.00**
• (#27, 1952)
8 ❑ Cover: 0.10 **NM** value: **8.00**
9 ❑ Cover: 0.10 **NM** value: **8.00**
10 ❑ Cover: 0.10 **NM** value: **8.00**
11 ❑ Cover: 0.10 **NM** value: **6.00**
12 ❑ Cover: 0.10 **NM** value: **6.00**
13 ❑ Cover: 0.10 **NM** value: **6.00**
14 ❑ Cover: 0.10 **NM** value: **6.00**
15 ❑ Cover: 0.10 **NM** value: **6.00**
16 ❑ Cover: 0.10 **NM** value: **6.00**
17 ❑ Cover: 0.10 **NM** value: **6.00**
18 ❑ Cover: 0.10 **NM** value: **6.00**
• Final issue?

DAKKON BLACKBLADE — Acclaim

1 ❑ Cover: 5.95 **NM** value: **Cover or less**

DAKOTA NORTH — Marvel

1 ❑ Jun 1986 Cover: 0.75 **NM** value: **1.00**
Circ: CapCity orders: **14,200**
📖 Design for Dying **A:** Tony Salmons **W:** Martha Thomases
2 ❑ Aug 1986 Cover: 0.75 **NM** value: **1.00**
Circ: CapCity orders: **9,300**
A: Tony Salmons **W:** Martha Thomases
3 ❑ Oct 1986 Cover: 0.75 **NM** value: **1.00**
Circ: CapCity orders: **8,200**
A: Tony Salmons **W:** Martha Thomases
4 ❑ Dec 1986 Cover: 0.75 **NM** value: **1.00**
Circ: CapCity orders: **7,300**
A: Tony Salmons **W:** Martha Thomases
5 ❑ Feb 1987 Cover: 0.75 **NM** value: **1.00**
Circ: CapCity orders: **6,400**
A: Tony Salmons **W:** Martha Thomases

DALE EVANS COMICS — DC

Dale Evans (born Lucille Wood Smith, 1912-2001), the real-life wife of Roy Rogers (born Leonard Franklin Slye, 1911-1998), starred in many films with him, usually as the romantic interest. Her popularity was such that she starred in her own comic-book series under both the Dell and DC imprint. Moreover, many of the stories were drawn by such outstanding artists as Alex Toth, Warren Tufts, and Russ Manning. The Dell title is found at a different spot in the alphabet (with the title Queen of the West, Dale Evans) and ran in the 1950s.

But prior to that, while her husband's license went to Dell, her adventures came from DC. And Toth art appeared in the DC title, as well.

1 ❑ Sep 1948 Cover: 0.10 **NM** value: **800.00**
• **CGC:** 2 graded, best 9.4
• Photo cover
2 ❑ Nov 1948 Cover: 0.10 **NM** value: **600.00**
• Photo cover
3 ❑ Jan 1949 Cover: 0.10 **NM** value: **500.00**
4 ❑ Mar 1949 Cover: 0.10 **NM** value: **250.00**
• **CGC:** 2 graded, best 9.2
• Photo cover
5 ❑ May 1949 Cover: 0.10 **NM** value: **250.00**
• **CGC:** 2 graded, best 9.2
• Photo cover

CGC-graded: Multiply prices above by **33 for 9.9 M • 16 for 9.8 NM/M • 7 for 9.6 NM+ • 5 for 9.4 NM • 2.5 for 9.2 NM- • 1.5 for 9.0 VF/NM**

6 ❑ Jul 1949 Cover: 0.10 **NM** value: **250.00**
• **CGC:** 3 graded, best 9.0
• Photo cover
7 ❑ Sep 1949 Cover: 0.10 **NM** value: **250.00**
• **CGC:** 3 graded, best 9.2
• Photo cover
8 ❑ Nov 1949 Cover: 0.10 **NM** value: **250.00**
• **CGC:** 3 graded, best 9.6
• Photo cover
9 ❑ Jan 1950 Cover: 0.10 **NM** value: **250.00**
• **CGC:** 2 graded, best 9.4
• Photo cover
10 ❑ Mar 1950 Cover: 0.10 **NM** value: **250.00**
• **CGC:** 2 graded, best 9.6
• Photo cover
11 ❑ May 1950 Cover: 0.10 **NM** value: **100.00**
• **CGC:** 1 graded, best 9.0
• Photo cover
12 ❑ Jul 1950 Cover: 0.10 **NM** value: **100.00**
• **CGC:** 1 graded, best 7.0
• Photo cover
13 ❑ Sep 1950 Cover: 0.10 **NM** value: **100.00**
• **CGC:** 1 graded, best 8.0
• Photo cover
14 ❑ Nov 1950 Cover: 0.10 **NM** value: **100.00**
• **CGC:** 1 graded, best 9.6
• Photo cover
15 ❑ Jan 1951 Cover: 0.10 **NM** value: **100.00**
• **CGC:** 2 graded, best 8.0
16 ❑ Mar 1951 Cover: 0.10 **NM** value: **100.00**
• **CGC:** 2 graded, best 8.0
17 ❑ May 1951 Cover: 0.10 **NM** value: **100.00**
• **CGC:** 1 graded, best 9.0
18 ❑ Jul 1951 Cover: 0.10 **NM** value: **100.00**
19 ❑ Sep 1951 Cover: 0.10 **NM** value: **100.00**
• **CGC:** 1 graded, best 7.5
20 ❑ Nov 1951 Cover: 0.10 **NM** value: **100.00**
• **CGC:** 2 graded, best 9.2
21 ❑ Jan 1952 Cover: 0.10 **NM** value: **100.00**
• **CGC:** 1 graded, best 9.0
22 ❑ Mar 1952 Cover: 0.10 **NM** value: **100.00**
23 ❑ May 1952 Cover: 0.10 **NM** value: **100.00**
• **CGC:** 1 graded, best 8.0
24 ❑ Jul 1952 Cover: 0.10 **NM** value: **100.00**
• **CGC:** 1 graded, best 4.5

DALE KUPER'S SKETCHBOOK — Green Bay

1 ❑ Cover: 2.00 **NM** value: **Cover or less**
No issue number.

DALGODA — Fantagraphics

1 ❑ Aug 1984 Cover: 2.25 **NM** value: **Cover or less**
Factions **A:** Dennis Fujitake **W:** Jan Strnad
2 ❑ Dec 1984 Cover: 1.50 **NM** value: **Cover or less**
3 ❑ Feb 1985 Cover: 1.50 **NM** value: **Cover or less**
4 ❑ Apr 1985 Cover: 1.50 **NM** value: **Cover or less**
5 ❑ Jun 1985 Cover: 2.00 **NM** value: **Cover or less**
Circ: CapCity orders: **4,975**
6 ❑ Oct 1985 Cover: 2.00 **NM** value: **Cover or less**
Circ: CapCity orders: **5,300**
7 ❑ Jan 1986 Cover: 2.00 **NM** value: **Cover or less**
Circ: CapCity orders: **4,650**
The Canine Mutiny, Part 1; Journey
8 ❑ Apr 1986 Cover: 2.00 **NM** value: **Cover or less**
Circ: CapCity orders: **4,525**

DALKIEL: THE PROPHECY — Verotik

All issues are adults only.
1 ❑ Aug 1998 Cover: 3.95 **NM** value: **Cover or less**
Circ: Diamd. preorders: **7,936**
No issue number. cardstock cover.

D-ALPHA — Aircel

All issues are adults only.
Bk 1 ❑ b&w Cover: 9.95 **NM** value: **Cover or less**

DALTON BOYS — Avon

1 ❑ Jan 1951 Cover: 0.10 **NM** value: **100.00**
• **CGC:** 1 graded, best 9.4

DAM — Dam

1 ❑ Cover: 2.95 **NM** value: **Cover or less**
Richi Itch; Zuperman; Vegetable Boy; Carni **A:** Alex Chpunoff **W:** Alex Chpunoff

DAMAGE — DC

Grant Emerson was always the new kid on the block. In the last four years of his life, his family had to move eight times due to his father's job at Solinex. Grant had gotten used to fitting in wherever his family went. Still, the latest school was proving to be something of a problem. Grant had made the mistake of being liked by an over-muscled athlete's girlfriend. As a result, the aforementioned caveman attempted to push Grant's head through the pavement. A coach stopped the fight before it could go anywhere and the thug stormed off. In frustration, Grant slammed on the hood of a car...a slam which demolished the car!

It was then that Grant's superhuman ability to store and use kinetic energy first revealed itself: when you hit him, he could hit back. Harder. Suddenly Grant knew he wasn't going to be fitting in with the other kids...and he would discover that his parents weren't exactly ordinary either!

0 ❑ Oct 1994 Cover: 1.95 **NM** value: **2.00**
Circ: CapCity orders: **14,350**
Back Again • Follows Damage #6 **A:** Bill Marimon **W:** Tom Joyner
1 ❑ Apr 1994 Cover: 1.75 **NM** value: **2.00**
Circ: CapCity orders: **19,550**
Damage **A:** Bill Marimon **W:** Tom Joyner
2 ❑ May 1994 Cover: 1.75 **NM** value: **2.00**
Circ: CapCity orders: **9,850**
3 ❑ Jun 1994 Cover: 1.75 **NM** value: **Cover or less**
Circ: CapCity orders: **7,850**
4 ❑ Jul 1994 Cover: 1.75 **NM** value: **Cover or less**
Circ: CapCity orders: **8,800**
5 ❑ Aug 1994 Cover: 1.95 **NM** value: **Cover or less**
Circ: CapCity orders: **8,300**
• Iron Munro
6 ❑ Sep 1994 Cover: 1.95 **NM** value: **Cover or less**
Circ: CapCity orders: **9,750**
• Zero Hour ★ Appearance of New Titans.
7 ❑ Nov 1994 Cover: 1.95 **NM** value: **Cover or less**
Circ: CapCity orders: **7,950**
8 ❑ Dec 1994 Cover: 1.95 **NM** value: **Cover or less**
Circ: CapCity orders: **8,250**
Fragments, Part 1 **A:** Bill Marimon **W:** Tom Joyner
9 ❑ Jan 1995 Cover: 1.95 **NM** value: **Cover or less**
Circ: CapCity orders: **8,250**
Fragments, Part 2 ★ Appearance of Iron Munro.
10 ❑ Feb 1995 Cover: 1.95 **NM** value: **Cover or less**
Circ: CapCity orders: **7,425**
Fragments, Part 3 ★ Appearance of Iron Munro.
11 ❑ Mar 1995 Cover: 1.95 **NM** value: **Cover or less**
Circ: CapCity orders: **6,925**
Fragments, Part 4
12 ❑ Apr 1995 Cover: 1.95 **NM** value: **Cover or less**
Circ: CapCity orders: **6,450**
13 ❑ Jun 1995 Cover: 1.95 **NM** value: **2.25**
Circ: CapCity orders: **5,875**
Picking Up the Pieces, Part 1
14 ❑ Jul 1995 Cover: 2.25 **NM** value: **Cover or less**
Circ: CapCity orders: **5,775**
Picking Up the Pieces, Part 2 ★ Appearance of Ray.
15 ❑ Aug 1995 Cover: 2.25 **NM** value: **Cover or less**
Circ: CapCity orders: **5,725**
Picking Up the Pieces, Part 3
16 ❑ Sep 1995 Cover: 2.25 **NM** value: **Cover or less**
Circ: CapCity orders: **6,175**
The Siege of The Zi Charam, Part 4
17 ❑ Oct 1995 Cover: 2.25 **NM** value: **Cover or less**
Circ: CapCity orders: **4,450**
18 ❑ Nov 1995 Cover: 2.25 **NM** value: **Cover or less**
Underworld Unleashed • Underworld Unleashed
19 ❑ Dec 1995 Cover: 2.25 **NM** value: **Cover or less**
20 ❑ Jan 1996 Cover: 2.25 **NM** value: **Cover or less**
final issue.

DAMAGE CONTROL (VOL. 1) — Marvel

Damage Control has been called, "Marvel's Most Sensible Series." That's because it answers the question of who does all the cleaning up after The Avengers battle giant robots and destroy half the city as a result. The answer is Damage Control: a group of building contractors specializing in super-powered battle damage.

While the rest of the city quakes when it hears that Doctor Octopus is going out for revenge against Spider-Man, Damage Control is used to handling these things in stride. The only scary part for Damage Control is when there's trouble with the insurance settlement.

1 ❑ May 1989 Cover: 1.00 **NM** value: **1.50**
Circ: CapCity orders: **26,500**
A Restoration Remedy **A:** Ernie Colon **W:** Dwayne McDuffie ★ Appearance of Spider-Man, Thor.
2 ❑ Jun 1989 Cover: 1.00 **NM** value: **Cover or less**
Circ: CapCity orders: **20,600**
A: Ernie Colon **W:** Dwayne McDuffie ★ Appearance of Doctor Doom.
3 ❑ Jul 1989 Cover: 1.00 **NM** value: **Cover or less**
Circ: CapCity orders: **19,700**
A: Ernie Colon **W:** Dwayne McDuffie ★ Appearance of Iron Man.
4 ❑ Aug 1989 Cover: 1.00 **NM** value: **Cover or less**
Circ: CapCity orders: **21,700**
• Inferno **A:** Ernie Colon **W:** Dwayne McDuffie ★ Appearance of Wolverine.

DAMAGE CONTROL (VOL. 2) — Marvel

1 ❑ Dec 1989 Cover: 1.00 **NM** value: **1.50**
Circ: CapCity orders: **25,100**
No Vault Insurance • Acts of Vengeance **A:** Ernie Colon **W:** Dwayne McDuffie ★ Appearance of Captain America, Thor.
2 ❑ Dec 1989 Cover: 1.00 **NM** value: **Cover or less**
Circ: CapCity orders: **22,600**
Acts of Vengeance, Part 15 • Acts of Vengeance **A:** Ernie Colon **W:** Dwayne McDuffie ★ Appearance of Punisher.
3 ❑ Jan 1990 Cover: 1.00 **NM** value: **Cover or less**
Circ: CapCity orders: **22,000**
Acts of Vengeance, Part 23 • Acts of Vengeance **A:** Ernie Colon **W:** Dwayne McDuffie ★ Appearance of She-Hulk.
4 ❑ Feb 1990 Cover: 1.00 **NM** value: **Cover or less**
Circ: CapCity orders: **22,400**
• Acts of Vengeance **A:** Ernie Colon **W:** Dwayne McDuffie ★ Appearance of Punisher, Shield, Captain America, Thor.

DAMAGE CONTROL (VOL. 3) — Marvel

1 ❑ Jun 1991 Cover: 1.25 **NM** value: **1.50**
Circ: CapCity orders: **24,500**
The Sure Thing **A:** Kyle Baker **W:** Dwayne McDuffie ★ Appearance of Spider-Man.
2 ❑ Jul 1991 Cover: 1.25 **NM** value: **Cover or less**
Circ: CapCity orders: **19,100**
★ Appearance of Hulk.
3 ❑ Aug 1991 Cover: 1.25 **NM** value: **Cover or less**
Circ: CapCity orders: **17,500**
The Movie **A:** Ernie Colon **W:** Dwayne McDuffie ★ Appearance of Galactus, Silver Surfer.
4 ❑ Sep 1991 Cover: 1.25 **NM** value: **Cover or less**
Circ: CapCity orders: **13,700**
★ Appearance of Silver Surfer.

DAME PATROL — Spoof

1 ❑ b&w Cover: 2.95 **NM** value: **Cover or less**

DAMLOG — Pyramid

1 ❑ b&w Cover: 1.80 **NM** value: **2.00**

DAMNATION — Fantagraphics

1 ❑ Sum 1994, b&w Cover: 2.95 **NM** value: **Cover or less**
• magazine.

DAMNED — Image

1 ❑ Jun 1997 Cover: 2.50 **NM** value: **Cover or less**
Circ: Diamd. preorders: **24,975**
A: Mike Zeck **W:** Steven Grant
2 ❑ Jul 1997 Cover: 2.50 **NM** value: **Cover or less**
Circ: Diamd. preorders: **15,829**
A: Mike Zeck **W:** Steven Grant
3 ❑ Aug 1997 Cover: 2.50 **NM** value: **Cover or less**
Circ: Diamd. preorders: **12,997**
A: Mike Zeck **W:** Steven Grant
4 ❑ Sep 1997 Cover: 2.50 **NM** value: **Cover or less**
Circ: Diamd. preorders: **10,894**
final issue. **A:** Mike Zeck **W:** Steven Grant

DAMONSTREIK — Imperial

1 ❑ Cover: 1.95 **NM** value: **Cover or less**
Books of the Jihad Saga, Part 2 **A:** Brian Garber **W:** Mike Olchewsky
2 ❑ Cover: 1.95 **NM** value: **Cover or less**
A: Brian Garber **W:** Mike Olchewsky

DAMSELVIS, DAUGHTER OF HELVIS SUPERMAG — Eros

1 ❑ Cover: 3.50 **NM** value: **Cover or less**

DANCE OF DEATH, THE — Tome Press

1 ❑ b&w Cover: 2.95 **NM** value: **Cover or less**
A: Hans Holbein

DANCE OF LIFEY DEATH — Dark Horse

1 ❑ Jan 1994 Cover: 3.95 **NM** value: **Cover or less**
No issue number. **A:** Eddie Campbell **W:** Eddie Campbell

DANCE PARTY DOA — Slave Labor

All issues are adults only.
1 ❑ Nov 1993 Cover: 3.95 **NM** value: **Cover or less**
Dance Party D.O.A.; Kake Gunther vs. the NFL; The Cat's Deadly Challenge; The Near Future; The Body of Christ **A:** Ted Couldron **W:** Ted Couldron

DANCES WITH DEMONS — Marvel

1 ❑ Sep 1993 Cover: 2.95 **NM** value: **Cover or less**
Circ: CapCity orders: **23,100**
Embossed foil cover. **A:** Charles Adlard **W:** Simon Jowett
2 ❑ Oct 1993 Cover: 1.95 **NM** value: **Cover or less**
Circ: CapCity orders: **7,700**
A: Charles Adlard **W:** Simon Jowett ★ Appearance of Manitou.
3 ❑ Nov 1993 Cover: 1.95 **NM** value: **Cover or less**
Circ: CapCity orders: **6,250**
4 ❑ Dec 1993 Cover: 1.95 **NM** value: **Cover or less**
Circ: CapCity orders: **5,300**

DANDY COMICS — E.C.

This was a "funny animal" and "bigfoot" title that E.C. produced as an "entertaining comic" in its early days, as the company experimented to find a variety of comic books that would bring readership. "Dandy" is a rabbit, "Tumbles" is a clown, and "Handy Andy" is a bigfoot human. Andy (usually dressed in a sweater with an "H" on the chest) quickly took over the cover spot, which typically showed him getting into some life-threatening situation without realizing the doom that was about to befall him.

Despite its targeting of young readers, Dandy carried ads for such E.C. titles as Picture Stories from the Bible and even Moon Girl. — Maggie

1 ❑ Spr 1947 Cover: 0.10 **NM** value: **200.00**
• **CGC:** 2 graded, best 8.5
Dandy; Tumbles; Bull Bowser; Doppus O'Tool; Tuffy; Young George Washington
2 ❑ Sum 1947 Cover: 0.10 **NM** value: **200.00**
• **CGC:** 2 graded, best 9.2
Dandy; Baffy Bill and Molly; Ruff and Reddy; Tumbles;

Other grades: Multiply prices above by **1.5 for Mint • 2/3 for Very Fine • 1/3 for Fine • 1/5 for Very Good • 1/8 for Good**

3 ❑ Jul 1947 Cover: 0.10 NM value: 125.00
• CGC: 2 graded, best 7.5
Dandy; Bull Bowser; Tumbles; Handy Andy
4 ❑ Sep 1947 Cover: 0.10 NM value: 125.00
• CGC: 5 graded, best 8.0
Handy Andy; Tuffy; Tumbles; Homecoming Day; Dandy
5 ❑ Nov 1947 Cover: 0.10 NM value: 125.00
• CGC: 5 graded, best 8.5
Handy Andy; Baffy Bill and Molly; Tumbles; Dandy
6 ❑ Jan 1948 Cover: 0.10 NM value: 125.00
• CGC: 3 graded, best 8.0
Handy Andy; Randy the Elephant; Tumbles; Dandy
7 ❑ Spr 1948 Cover: 0.10 NM value: 125.00
• CGC: 4 graded, best 9.0
The Plot; Handy Andy; Tumbles; Tuffy and Clarence; Dandy

DANGER (CHARLTON) — Charlton

1 ❑ Jan 1954 Cover: 0.10 NM value: 100.00
2 ❑ Mar 1954 Cover: 0.10 NM value: 75.00
3 ❑ May 1954 Cover: 0.10 NM value: 75.00
4 ❑ Jul 1954 Cover: 0.10 NM value: 75.00
5 ❑ Sep 1954 Cover: 0.10 NM value: 75.00
6 ❑ Nov 1954 Cover: 0.10 NM value: 75.00
Secret Agent in New York; Trigger Happy Killer
7 ❑ Jan 1955 Cover: 0.10 NM value: 75.00
Khyber Incident
8 ❑ Mar 1955 Cover: 0.10 NM value: 75.00
Kill! Kill! Kill!; Crash in the Alps!; Murder in the Rue Pigalle
9 ❑ May 1955 Cover: 0.10 NM value: 75.00
Intrigue
10 ❑ Jul 1955 Cover: 0.10 NM value: 75.00
Trouble in Morocco
11 ❑ Sep 1955 Cover: 0.10 NM value: 75.00
12 ❑ Jun 1955 Cover: 0.10 NM value: 75.00
13 ❑ Aug 1955 Cover: 0.10 NM value: 75.00
14 ❑ Oct 1955 Cover: 0.10 NM value: 75.00

DANGER COMICS — Danger Comics

1 ❑ b&w Cover: 2.25 NM value: Cover or less
2 ❑ b&w Cover: 2.25 NM value: Cover or less

DANGER FUNNIES — Cry for Dawn

1 ❑ Cover: 2.50 NM value: Cover or less
A: Lance Tooks W: Lance Tooks

DANGER GIRL — Image / Cliffhanger

Danger Girl was the first title with the Cliffhanger! imprint, a creator-owned line of books from WildStorm Studios.

An expert marksman and scholar of ancient civilizations, Abbey Chase is recruited into Danger Girl, a team of female operatives from around the world assembled to battle the Fourth Reich, a union of bizarre, yet dangerous, would-be world conquerors.

Chase joins Natalia Kassle, Sydney Savage, and Silicon Valerie, ordinary women with extraordinary skills, and their leader Deuce, an ex-agent for the British secret service.

Renowned for his attractive women and youthful, fun art, J. Scott Campbell depicts the attitude of the action/comedy movie genre on the printed page.

Unfortunately as the delays between each issue's release got longer and longer, reader apathy increased to the point that the release of the final issue was mostly a non-event.

1 ❑ Mar 1998 Cover: 2.95 NM value: 4.00
Circ: Diamd. preorders: 109,618 • CGC: 30 graded, best 9.9
Dangerously Yours A: J. Scott Campbell W: Andy Hartnell
1/A ❑ Mar 1998 Cover: 2.50 NM value: 15.00
• CGC: 41 graded, best 9.8
chromium cover. Dangerously Yours A: J. Scott Campbell W: Andy Hartnell
1/B ❑ Mar 1998 Cover: 2.50 NM value: 45.00
• magazine-sized. Dangerously Yours A: J. Scott Campbell W: Andy Hartnell
1/C ❑ Mar 1998 Cover: 2.95 NM value: 15.00
• CGC: 7 graded, best 9.8
• Tour Edition. Dangerously Yours • Woman holding rifle, white background A: J. Scott Campbell W: Andy Hartnell
1/D ❑ Mar 1988 NM value: 80.00
Chromium a-go-go cover. Dangerously Yours A: J. Scott Campbell W: Andy Hartnell
2 ❑ May 1998 Cover: 2.50 NM value: 4.00
Circ: Diamd. preorders: 82,250 • CGC: 8 graded, best 9.8
Dangerous Liaisons A: J. Scott Campbell W: Andy Hartnell
2/A ❑ May 1998 Cover: 2.50 NM value: 20.00
Special holochrome cover. Dangerous Liaisons A: J. Scott Campbell W: Andy Hartnell
2/B ❑ May 1988 NM value: 35.00
Dynamic Forces cover, later recalled. Dangerous Liaisons A: J. Scott Campbell W: Andy Hartnell
2/GO❑ May 1998 Cover: 2.50 NM value: 8.00
Dangerous Liaisons • Gold logo A: J. Scott Campbell W: Andy Hartnell
3 ❑ Aug 1998 Cover: 2.50 NM value: 3.00
Circ: Diamd. preorders: 120,587
White background, 3 girls on cover. Dangerous Curves A: J. Scott Campbell W: Andy Hartnell
3/A ❑ Aug 1998 Cover: 2.50 NM value: 3.00
Girls surrounding guy, knife cover. Dangerous Curves A: J. Scott Campbell W: Andy Hartnell
3/B ❑ Aug 1998 Cover: 2.50 NM value: 3.00
"Filled to the Brim with Danger" cover. Dangerous Curves A: J. Scott Campbell W: Andy Hartnell
4 ❑ Dec 1998 Cover: 2.50 NM value: 3.00
Circ: Diamd. preorders: 95,034
Maximum Danger A: J. Scott Campbell W: Andy Hartnell
4/A ❑ Dec 1998 Cover: 2.50 NM value: 3.00
alternate cover (purple background).
5 ❑ Jul 1999 Cover: 2.50 NM value: Cover or less
Circ: Diamd. preorders: 101,181
Damgerous When Wet A: J. Scott Campbell W: J. Scott Campbell; Andy Hartnell
5/A ❑ Jul 1999 NM value: 10.00
• Dynamic Forces variant;Woman in red bikini
5/B ❑ Jul 1999 NM value: 10.00
• Dynamic Forces variant;Woman in blue bikini
6 ❑ Dec 1999 Cover: 2.50 NM value: Cover or less
Circ: Diamd. preorders: 102,341
Dangerous Destinies A: J. Scott Campbell W: J. Scott Campbell; Andy Hartnell
6/A ❑ Dec 1999 Cover: 2.50 NM value: 19.95
• DFE gold foil edition. Dangerous Destinies A: J. Scott Campbell W: J. Scott Campbell; Andy Hartnell
6/GO❑ Dec 1999 Cover: 2.50 NM value: 10.00
• DFE gold foil edition. Dangerous Destinies A: J. Scott Campbell W: J. Scott Campbell; Andy Hartnell
7 ❑ Feb 2001 Cover: 5.95 NM value: Cover or less
Circ: Diamd. preorders: 67,302
Into the Danger Zone A: J. Scott Campbell W: J. Scott Campbell; Andy Hartnell
Ash 1❑ NM value: 5.00
• CGC: 2 graded, best 9.6
• Preview edition. Prelude to Danger A: J. Scott Campbell W: Andy Hartnell
Ash 1/GO❑ NM value: 10.00
• CGC: 1 graded, best 9.6
• Preview edition. Prelude to Danger • Gold logo A: J. Scott Campbell W: Andy Hartnell
Bk 1❑ Aug 1998 Cover: 5.95 NM value: Cover or less
Circ: Diamd. preorders: 6,145
Collects issues Preview, #1, plus variant covers and sketches. • prestige format. The Dangerous Collection • The Dangerous Collection A: J. Scott Campbell W: Andy Hartnell
Bk 2❑ Nov 1998 Cover: 5.95 NM value: Cover or less
Circ: Diamd. preorders: 7,396
Collects issues #2-3, plus variant covers and sketches. • prestige format. The Dangerous Collection • The Dangerous Collection A: J. Scott Campbell W: Andy Hartnell
Bk 3❑ Dec 1999 Cover: 5.95 NM value: Cover or less
Circ: Diamd. preorders: 11,611
Collects issues #4-5, plus variant covers and sketches. The Dangerous Collection A: J. Scott Campbell W: Andy Hartnell

DANGER GIRLS — Animagic / Cliffhanger

1 ❑ Cover: 2.95 NM value: Cover or less

DANGER IS OUR BUSINESS — Toby

1 ❑ Dec 1953 Cover: 0.10 NM value: 200.00
2 ❑ Feb 1954 Cover: 0.10 NM value: 100.00
3 ❑ Apr 1954 Cover: 0.10 NM value: 75.00
4 ❑ Jun 1954 Cover: 0.10 NM value: 75.00
5 ❑ Aug 1954 Cover: 0.10 NM value: 75.00
6 ❑ Oct 1954 Cover: 0.10 NM value: 75.00
7 ❑ Dec 1954 Cover: 0.10 NM value: 75.00
8 ❑ Feb 1955 Cover: 0.10 NM value: 75.00
9 ❑ Apr 1955 Cover: 0.10 NM value: 75.00
10 ❑ Jun 1955 Cover: 0.10 NM value: 75.00

DANGERMAN — Patchwork / Legend

1 ❑ Cover: 2.75 NM value: Cover or less
A: David Lee Ingersoll W: Mark Ahlquist

DANGEROUS TIMES — Evolution

1 ❑ Cover: 1.75 NM value: Cover or less
The Last Survivor of Mona A: James Fletcher W: Alexei Kondrateiv
1-2 ❑ Cover: 1.75 NM value: Cover or less
2 ❑ Cover: 1.75 NM value: Cover or less
2-2 ❑ Cover: 1.75 NM value: Cover or less
3 ❑ Cover: 1.95 NM value: Cover or less
The Stone and the Icon A: Jordan Raskin W: Alexei Kondrateiv
3-2 ❑ Cover: 1.95 NM value: Cover or less
4 ❑ Cover: 1.95 NM value: Cover or less
One Key Many Doors A: Vince Mielcarek W: Margie Saaski
4-2 ❑ Cover: 1.95 NM value: Cover or less
5 ❑ Cover: 1.95 NM value: Cover or less
5-2 ❑ Cover: 1.95 NM value: Cover or less
6 ❑ Cover: 1.95 NM value: Cover or less
Class Struggle A: Vince Mielcarek W: Margie Saaski
6-2 ❑ Cover: 2.25 NM value: Cover or less

DANGER RANGER — Checker

1 ❑ Sum 1998 Cover: 1.95 NM value: Cover or less
Service of a Villain A: Dave Berkebile W: Mark Thompson
2 ❑ 1998 Cover: 1.95 NM value: Cover or less

DANGER (SUPER) — Super

12 ❑ ca. 1964 Cover: 0.12 NM value: 12.00
Black Dwarf; The Gay Desperado; Prehistoric Pete; Nemo in Adventureland; Lucky Coyne
13 ❑ ca. 1964 Cover: 0.12 NM value: 12.00
14 ❑ ca. 1964 Cover: 0.12 NM value: 12.00
15 ❑ ca. 1964 Cover: 0.12 NM value: 12.00
16 ❑ ca. 1964 Cover: 0.12 NM value: 12.00
Young Americans; Johnny Rebel; Monkey Shines; Yankee Girl; Life of Riley

DANGER TRAIL — DC

This short-lived espionage series has the distinction of being one of the few DC series prior to 1967 to run fewer than six issues. Starring intrepid secret agent King Faraday the 1950-51 series dealt with fairly pedestrian situations and banked on the public's interest with all things spy-related at the time to sell the series. Unfortunately, intrigue and spycraft are difficult to portray on the illustrated page and even art by Alex Toth couldn't help the series, which was canceled after only five issues.

Today, collectors seek it out for its rarity. Several of the stories were later reprinted in Showcase #50 and #51 under the title "I, Spy!" — Brent

1 ❑ Jul 1950 Cover: 0.10 NM value: 800.00
• CGC: 2 graded, best 6.5
Hunters of the Whispering Gallery!; Appointment in Paris!; 3 Steps to Mr. Sandino!; Mystery of the Highland Queen! A: Alex Toth
2 ❑ Sep 1950 Cover: 0.10 NM value: 600.00
• CGC: 1 graded, best 5.5
Hangman's House; Trouble in Trinidad; Shadows Over London A: Alex Toth
3 ❑ Nov 1950 Cover: 0.10 NM value: 800.00
• CGC: 4 graded, best 7.5
Thunder Over Thailand; Battle Flag of the Foreign Legion; Hawaiian River God; Ghost Ship of the South Seas • Very rare A: Alex Toth
4 ❑ Feb 1951 Cover: 0.10 NM value: 450.00
• CGC: 3 graded, best 7.0
Reign of the Scarlet Umbrella!; Vengeance of the Matterhorn; The Vanishing Island; End of the Arctic A: Alex Toth
5 ❑ Mar 1951 Cover: 0.10 NM value: 450.00
• CGC: 3 graded, best 9.2
Rendezvous in Rio; South of the Equator final issue. A: Alex Toth

DANGER TRAIL (MINI-SERIES) — DC

1 ❑ Apr 1993 Cover: 1.50 NM value: Cover or less
Circ: CapCity orders: 147,000
The Serpent In The Garden File! A: Carmine Infantino W: Len Wein
2 ❑ May 1993 Cover: 1.50 NM value: Cover or less
Circ: CapCity orders: 8,500
A: Carmine Infantino W: Len Wein
3 ❑ Jun 1993 Cover: 1.50 NM value: Cover or less
Circ: CapCity orders: 6,450
A: Carmine Infantino W: Len Wein
4 ❑ Jul 1993 Cover: 1.50 NM value: Cover or less
Circ: CapCity orders: 5,650
A: Carmine Infantino W: Len Wein

DANGER UNLIMITED — Dark Horse / Legend

1 ❑ Feb 1994 Cover: 2.00 NM value: Cover or less
Circ: CapCity orders: 23,250
The Phoenix Agenda, Part 1 A: John Byrne W: John Byrne ★ 1st Appearance of Miss Mirage, Torch of Liberty, Hunk, Thermal, Doc Danger, Danger Unlimited.
2 ❑ Mar 1994 Cover: 2.50 NM value: Cover or less
Circ: CapCity orders: 16,300
The Phoenix Agenda, Part 2 A: John Byrne W: John Byrne
3 ❑ Apr 1994 Cover: 2.50 NM value: Cover or less
Circ: CapCity orders: 14,600
The Phoenix Agenda, Part 3 A: John Byrne W: John Byrne ★ Origin of Caucus. ★ 1st Appearance of Caucus.
4 ❑ May 1994 Cover: 2.50 NM value: Cover or less
Circ: CapCity orders: 15,500
The Phoenix Agenda, Part 4 A: John Byrne W: John Byrne
Bk 1❑ Apr 1995 Cover: 14.95 NM value: Cover or less
• Collects Danger Unlimited #1-4
Bk 1/LE❑ Cover: 59.95 NM value: Cover or less
• Limited edition hardcover. • Collects Danger Unlimited #1-4

DANGLE — Cat-Head

1 ❑ b&w Cover: 2.75 NM value: Cover or less

DANIEL BOONE — Gold Key

1 ❑ Jan 1965 Cover: 0.12 NM value: 65.00
2 ❑ May 1965 Cover: 0.12 NM value: 28.00
3 ❑ Nov 1965 Cover: 0.12 NM value: 22.00
4 ❑ Feb 1966 Cover: 0.12 NM value: 22.00
5 ❑ May 1966 Cover: 0.12 NM value: 22.00
6 ❑ Aug 1966 Cover: 0.12 NM value: 15.00
7 ❑ Nov 1966 Cover: 0.12 NM value: 15.00
8 ❑ Feb 1967 Cover: 0.12 NM value: 15.00
9 ❑ May 1967 Cover: 0.12 NM value: 15.00
10 ❑ Aug 1967 Cover: 0.12 NM value: 15.00
11 ❑ Nov 1967 Cover: 0.12 NM value: 15.00
12 ❑ Feb 1968 Cover: 0.12 NM value: 15.00
The War Wampum; The Oldest Warrior (text story); Zacchariah Yankee Peddler: The Lucky Charm; The Smuggled Flintlocks
13 ❑ Oct 1968 Cover: 0.15 NM value: 15.00
14 ❑ Jan 1969 Cover: 0.15 NM value: 15.00
15 ❑ Apr 1969 Cover: 0.15 NM value: 15.00
final issue.

DAN'L BOONE — Magazine Enterprises

1 ❑ Sep 1955 Cover: 0.10 NM value: 75.00
2 ❑ Oct 1955 Cover: 0.10 NM value: 50.00
3 ❑ Sep 1956 Cover: 0.10 NM value: 50.00
4 ❑ Nov 1956 Cover: 0.10 NM value: 50.00
5 ❑ Jan 1957 Cover: 0.10 NM value: 50.00
6 ❑ 1957 Cover: 0.10 NM value: 50.00
7 ❑ 1957 Cover: 0.10 NM value: 50.00
8 ❑ 1957 Cover: 0.10 NM value: 50.00

CGC-graded: Multiply prices above by **33 for 9.9 M • 16 for 9.8 NM/M • 7 for 9.6 NM+ • 5 for 9.4 NM • 2.5 for 9.2 NM- • 1.5 for 9.0 VF/NM**

DANNY BLAZE **Charlton**

1 ❑ ca. 1955 Cover: 0.10 **NM** value: **35.00**

2 ❑ ca. 1955 Cover: 0.10 **NM** value: **18.00**

DAN PANIC FUNNIES **Panic**

1 ❑ Cover: 1.75 **NM** value: **Cover or less**

DANSE **Blackthorne**

1 ❑ Cover: 2.00 **NM** value: **Cover or less**

DANTE'S INFERNO **Tome Press**

1 ❑ b&w Cover: 3.50 **NM** value: **Cover or less**
A: Dore

2 ❑ b&w Cover: 3.50 **NM** value: **Cover or less**
A: Dore

DAN TURNER: ACE IN THE HOLE **Eternity**

1 ❑ b&w Cover: 2.50 **NM** value: **Cover or less**

DAN TURNER: DARK STAR OF DEATH **Eternity**

1 ❑ b&w Cover: 2.50 **NM** value: **Cover or less**

DAN TURNER: HOMICIDE HUNCH **Eternity**

1 ❑ Jul 1991, b&w Cover: 2.50 **NM** value: **Cover or less**

DAN TURNER: LIGHTS! CAMERA! MURDER! **Eternity**

Bk 1❑ Aug 1990, b&w Cover: 7.95 **NM** value: **Cover or less**

DAN TURNER: STAR CHAMBER **Eternity**

1 ❑ Sep 1991, b&w Cover: 2.50 **NM** value: **Cover or less**

DAPIEK ABSAROKA: THE KILLER OF CROWS **Tome Press**

1 ❑ b&w Cover: 2.50 **NM** value: **Cover or less**

DARBY O'GILL AND THE LITTLE PEOPLE **Gold Key**

The 1959 Disney movie is probably best noted as the eighth movie with Sean Connery (1930-), and he played the romantic interest (Michael McBride) for Janet Munro (1934-1972). O'Gill was a colorful character telling stories of leprechauns who finds himself entangled in the fantasy. The typical Disney formula of a fantastic discovery that no one will believe (O'Gill's encounters with the wee folk) eventually leads to romance for Munro and Connery and a dream come true for O'Gill.

Also of note is Connery's singing in the film. James Bond might whistle, but he would never belt out a fine Irish ballad. — Maggie

1 ❑ Jan 1970 Cover: 0.15 **NM** value: **100.00**
• **CGC:** 1 graded, best 9.2
No issue number. • Four Color Comics #1024

D'ARC TANGENT **Ffantasy Ffactory**

1 ❑ Aug 1982 Cover: 2.00 **NM** value: **Cover or less**
Clues and Omens **A:** Phil Foglio; Freff **W:** Phil Foglio; Freff

DARE **Monster**

1 ❑ Cover: 2.75 **NM** value: **Cover or less**
Circ: CapCity orders: **4,200**

2 ❑ Cover: 2.75 **NM** value: **Cover or less**

3 ❑ Cover: 2.50 **NM** value: **Cover or less**

DAREDEVIL **Marvel**

Matt Murdock was the son of a second-rate fighter named "Battlin' Jack" Murdock. But although his own life was spent in physical combat, Jack Murdock insisted that Matt avoid fighting, and concentrate instead on his studies. It wasn't easy. The neighborhood kids called him a coward and even nicknamed him "Daredevil" to poke fun at him.

Then fate intervenes in the form of a truck laden with radioactive cargo, headed for an unsuspecting man. Matt runs into the street to save the man, but is hit by the truck himself. Blinded by the accident, he finds his other senses growing far more acute. He even develops a radar sense that lets him "see" objects in the world around him.

When his father was killed for refusing to throw a fight, Matt decides he can hold back no longer — becoming Daredevil, "the Man Without Fear."

Daredevil's record is uneven. Not as popular as some of Stan Lee's other creations, the series has seen many lackluster stretches — including, infamously, a ludicrous storyline involving Matt posing as his own nonexistent, sighted twin brother. But Frank Miller reinvents the character from scratch beginning in #158, generating what is now considered to be the definitive version.

-1 ❑ Jul 1997 Cover: 1.99 **NM** value: **2.25**
Circ: Diamd. preorders: **38,641**
• Flashback

1 ❑ Apr 1964 Cover: 0.12 **NM** value: **1800.00**
• **CGC:** 209 graded, best 9.6
The Origin of Daredevil • 1st appearance/origin of Daredevil **A:** Bill Everett ★ Origin of Daredevil. ★ 1st Appearance of Karen Page, Battling Jack Murdock, Daredevil, Foggy Nelson. ★ Death of Battling Jack Murdock.

2 ❑ Jun 1964 Cover: 0.12 **NM** value: **500.00**
• **CGC:** 69 graded, best 9.6
The Evil Menace of Electro **A:** Joe Orlando ★ Appearance of Fantastic Four. ★ Versus Electro.

3 ❑ Aug 1964 Cover: 0.12 **NM** value: **325.00**
• **CGC:** 47 graded, best 9.8
Daredevil Battles the Owl **A:** Joe Orlando ★ Origin of Owl. ★ 1st Appearance of Owl.

4 ❑ Oct 1964 Cover: 0.12 **NM** value: **260.00**
• **CGC:** 36 graded, best 9.4
Killgrave, the Unbelievable Purple Man! **A:** Joe Orlando ★ Origin of The Purple Man. ★ 1st Appearance of The Purple Man. ★ Versus Killgrave.

5 ❑ Dec 1964 Cover: 0.12 **NM** value: **200.00**
• **CGC:** 39 graded, best 9.6
The Mysterious Masked Matador! **A:** Wally Wood ★ Versus Masked Matador.

6 ❑ Feb 1965 Cover: 0.12 **NM** value: **145.00**
• **CGC:** 34 graded, best 9.6
Trapped by the Fellowship of Fear **A:** Wally Wood ★ 1st Appearance of Mister Fear I (Zoltan Drago). ★ Versus Fellowship of Fear.

7 ❑ Apr 1965 Cover: 0.12 **NM** value: **200.00**
• **CGC:** 43 graded, best 9.4
In Mortal Combat with the Sub-Mariner **A:** Wally Wood ★ 1st Appearance of red costume. ★ Appearance of Sub-Mariner.

8 ❑ Jun 1965 Cover: 0.12 **NM** value: **135.00**
• **CGC:** 45 graded, best 9.6
The Stiltman Cometh **A:** Wally Wood ★ Origin of Stilt Man. ★ 1st Appearance of Stilt Man.

9 ❑ Aug 1965 Cover: 0.12 **NM** value: **130.00**
• **CGC:** 62 graded, best 9.8
That He May See! **A:** Wally Wood

10 ❑ Oct 1965 Cover: 0.12 **NM** value: **130.00**
• **CGC:** 46 graded, best 9.6
While the City Sleeps! **A:** Wally Wood ★ 1st Appearance of Frog-Man I (Francois LeBlanc), Ani-Men, Cat-Man I (Townshend Horgan), Bird-Man I (Henry Hawk), Ape-Man I (Gordon "Monk" Keefer).

11 ❑ Dec 1965 Cover: 0.12 **NM** value: **85.00**
• **CGC:** 21 graded, best 9.6
A Time to Unmask **A:** Jack Kirby; John Romita

12 ❑ Jan 1966 Cover: 0.12 **NM** value: **85.00**
• **CGC:** 16 graded, best 9.6
Sightless In a Saveage Land ★ 2nd Appearance of Ka-Zar.

13 ❑ Feb 1966 Cover: 0.12 **NM** value: **85.00**
• **CGC:** 26 graded, best 9.6
The Secret of Ka-Zar's Origin ★ Origin of Ka-Zar.

14 ❑ Mar 1966 Cover: 0.12 **NM** value: **85.00**
• **CGC:** 17 graded, best 9.6
If This Be Justice... ★ Appearance of Ka-Zar.

15 ❑ Apr 1966 Cover: 0.12 **NM** value: **85.00**
• **CGC:** 31 graded, best 9.6
And Men Shall Call Him... Ox!

16 ❑ May 1966 Cover: 0.12 **NM** value: **90.00**
• **CGC:** 24 graded, best 9.8
Enter: Spider-Man ★ 1st Appearance of Masked Marauder. ★ Appearance of Spider-Man.

17 ❑ Jun 1966 Cover: 0.12 **NM** value: **90.00**
• **CGC:** 24 graded, best 9.8
None Are So Blind ★ Appearance of Spider-Man.

18 ❑ Jul 1966 Cover: 0.12 **NM** value: **50.00**
• **CGC:** 22 graded, best 9.6
There Shall Come a Gladiator! **A:** John Romita ★ Origin of Gladiator I (Melvin Potter). ★ 1st Appearance of Gladiator I (Melvin Potter).

19 ❑ Aug 1966 Cover: 0.12 **NM** value: **50.00**
• **CGC:** 11 graded, best 9.6
Alone Against the Underworld! **A:** John Romita ★ Appearance of Gladiator I (Melvin Potter), Gladiator I (Melvin Potter).

20 ❑ Sep 1966 Cover: 0.12 **NM** value: **45.00**
• **CGC:** 15 graded, best 9.8
The Verdict is Death! **A:** Gene Colan ★ Versus Owl.

21 ❑ Oct 1966 Cover: 0.12 **NM** value: **34.00**
• **CGC:** 12 graded, best 9.6
The Trap Is Sprung **A:** Gene Colan ★ Versus Owl.

22 ❑ Nov 1966 Cover: 0.12 **NM** value: **34.00**
• **CGC:** 10 graded, best 9.6
The Tri-Man Lives! **A:** Gene Colan **W:** Stan Lee

23 ❑ Dec 1966 Cover: 0.12 **NM** value: **34.00**
• **CGC:** 5 graded, best 9.6
Daredevil Goes Wild **A:** Gene Colan

24 ❑ Jan 1967 Cover: 0.12 **NM** value: **34.00**
Circ: Statement: **275,361** • **CGC:** 13 graded, best 9.6
The Mystery of the Midnight Stalker **A:** Gene Colan ★ Appearance of Ka-Zar.

25 ❑ Feb 1967 Cover: 0.12 **NM** value: **34.00**
Circ: Statement: **275,361** • **CGC:** 16 graded, best 9.6
Enter the Leap Frog! **A:** Gene Colan

26 ❑ Mar 1967 Cover: 0.12 **NM** value: **34.00**
Circ: Statement: **275,361** • **CGC:** 7 graded, best 9.6
Stilt-Man Strikes Again! **A:** Gene Colan

27 ❑ Apr 1967 Cover: 0.12 **NM** value: **38.00**
Circ: Statement: **275,361** • **CGC:** 23 graded, best 9.6
Matt Murdock Must Die! **A:** Gene Colan ★ Appearance of Spider-Man.

28 ❑ May 1967 Cover: 0.12 **NM** value: **34.00**
Circ: Statement: **275,361** • **CGC:** 22 graded, best 9.6
Thou Shalt Not Covet Thy Neighbor's Planet! **A:** Gene Colan

29 ❑ Jun 1967 Cover: 0.12 **NM** value: **34.00**
Circ: Statement: **275,361** • **CGC:** 6 graded, best 9.6
Unmasked! **A:** Gene Colan **W:** Stan Lee

30 ❑ Jul 1967 Cover: 0.12 **NM** value: **34.00**
Circ: Statement: **275,361** • **CGC:** 13 graded, best 9.6
If There Should Be a Thunder God! **A:** Gene Colan ★ Appearance of Thor.

31 ❑ Aug 1967 Cover: 0.12 **NM** value: **28.00**
Circ: Statement: **275,361** • **CGC:** 4 graded, best 9.8
Blind Man's Bluff • Cobra **A:** Gene Colan

32 ❑ Sep 1967 Cover: 0.12 **NM** value: **28.00**
Circ: Statement: **275,361** • **CGC:** 12 graded, best 9.8
To Fight the Impossible Fight **A:** Gene Colan

33 ❑ Oct 1967 Cover: 0.12 **NM** value: **28.00**
Circ: Statement: **275,361** • **CGC:** 5 graded, best 9.6
Behold The Beetle **A:** Gene Colan **W:** Stan Lee

34 ❑ Nov 1967 Cover: 0.12 **NM** value: **28.00**
Circ: Statement: **275,361** • **CGC:** 14 graded, best 9.6
To Squash a Beetle **A:** Gene Colan

35 ❑ Dec 1967 Cover: 0.12 **NM** value: **28.00**
Circ: Statement: **275,361** • **CGC:** 11 graded, best 9.6
Daredevil Dies First! **A:** Gene Colan ★ Appearance of Invisible Girl. ★ Versus Trapster.

36 ❑ Jan 1968 Cover: 0.12 **NM** value: **28.00**
Circ: Statement: **292,423** • **CGC:** 10 graded, best 9.8
The Name of the Game is Mayhem! **A:** Gene Colan ★ Appearance of Fantastic Four, Doctor Doom.

37 ❑ Feb 1968 Cover: 0.12 **NM** value: **28.00**
Circ: Statement: **292,423** • **CGC:** 11 graded, best 9.4
Don't Look Now, But It's Doctor Doom **A:** Gene Colan ★ Appearance of Doctor Doom. ★ Versus Doctor Doom.

38 ❑ Mar 1968 Cover: 0.12 **NM** value: **28.00**
Circ: Statement: **292,423** • **CGC:** 9 graded, best 9.6
The Living Prison! • Has 1967 Statement, filed 10/1/67; avg print run 457,293; avg sales 273,961; avg subs 1,400; avg total paid 275,361; samples 95; max existent 275,456; 40% of run returned **A:** Gene Colan **W:** Stan Lee ★ Appearance of Fantastic Four, Doctor Doom.

39 ❑ Apr 1968 Cover: 0.12 **NM** value: **28.00**
Circ: Statement: **292,423** • **CGC:** 5 graded, best 9.4
The Exterminator and the Super-Powered Unholy Three **A:** Gene Colan ★ 1st Appearance of Exterminator (later Death-Stalker).

40 ❑ May 1968 Cover: 0.12 **NM** value: **28.00**
Circ: Statement: **292,423** • **CGC:** 7 graded, best 9.6
The Fallen Hero **A:** Gene Colan **W:** Stan Lee

41 ❑ Jun 1968 Cover: 0.12 **NM** value: **28.00**
Circ: Statement: **292,423** • **CGC:** 5 graded, best 9.8
The Death Of Mike Murdock! **A:** Gene Colan **W:** Stan Lee ★ Death of Mike Murdock (Daredevil's "twin brother").

42 ❑ Jul 1968 Cover: 0.12 **NM** value: **28.00**
Circ: Statement: **292,423** • **CGC:** 5 graded, best 9.6
Nobody Laughs at the Jester **A:** Gene Colan ★ 1st Appearance of Jester.

43 ❑ Aug 1968 Cover: 0.12 **NM** value: **24.00**
Circ: Statement: **292,423** • **CGC:** 20 graded, best 9.6
In Combat With Captain America! **A:** Gene Colan ★ Origin of Daredevil. ★ Versus Captain America.

44 ❑ Sep 1968 Cover: 0.12 **NM** value: **20.00**
Circ: Statement: **292,423** • **CGC:** 8 graded, best 9.6
I, Murderer! **A:** Gene Colan

45 ❑ Oct 1968 Cover: 0.12 **NM** value: **20.00**
Circ: Statement: **292,423** • **CGC:** 15 graded, best 9.8
Photo cover. The Dismal Dregs of Defeat! **A:** Gene Colan

46 ❑ Nov 1968 Cover: 0.12 **NM** value: **20.00**
Circ: Statement: **292,423** • **CGC:** 7 graded, best 9.4
The Final Jest! **A:** Gene Colan

47 ❑ Dec 1968 Cover: 0.12 **NM** value: **20.00**
Circ: Statement: **292,423** • **CGC:** 13 graded, best 9.4
Brother, Take My Hand **A:** Gene Colan

48 ❑ Jan 1969 Cover: 0.12 **NM** value: **20.00**
Circ: Statement: **245,422** • **CGC:** 7 graded, best 9.6
Farewell to Foggy! **A:** Gene Colan

49 ❑ Feb 1969 Cover: 0.12 **NM** value: **20.00**
Circ: Statement: **245,422** • **CGC:** 14 graded, best 9.8
Daredevil Drops Out **A:** Gene Colan ★ 1st Appearance of Samuel "Starr" Saxon.

50 ❑ Mar 1969 Cover: 0.12 **NM** value: **22.00**
Circ: Statement: **245,422** • **CGC:** 6 graded, best 9.9
If In Battle I Fail • Has 1968 Statement, filed 10/1/68; avg print run 435,200; avg sales 290,703; avg subs 1,720; avg total paid 292,423; samples 400; max existent 292,823; 33% of run returned **A:** Barry Windsor-Smith

51 ❑ Apr 1969 Cover: 0.12 **NM** value: **22.00**
Circ: Statement: **245,422** • **CGC:** 9 graded, best 9.6
Run, Murdock, Run! **A:** Barry Windsor-Smith ★ Appearance of Captain America.

52 ❑ May 1969 Cover: 0.12 **NM** value: **22.00**
Circ: Statement: **245,422** • **CGC:** 5 graded, best 9.6
The Night of the Panther! **A:** Barry Windsor-Smith ★ Appearance of Black Panther.

53 ❑ Jun 1969 Cover: 0.12 **NM** value: **25.00**
Circ: Statement: **245,422** • **CGC:** 8 graded, best 9.6
As It Was in the Beginning **A:** Gene Colan ★ Origin of Daredevil.

54 ❑ Jul 1969 Cover: 0.15 **NM** value: **15.00**
Circ: Statement: **245,422** • **CGC:** 5 graded, best 9.6
Call Him Fear **A:** Gene Colan ★ 1st Appearance of Mister Fear II (Samuel "Starr" Saxon). ★ Appearance of Spider-Man.

55 ❑ Aug 1969 Cover: 0.15 **NM** value: **15.00**
Circ: Statement: **245,422** • **CGC:** 1 graded, best 9.4
Cry Coward! **A:** Gene Colan

56 ❑ Sep 1969 Cover: 0.15 **NM** value: **15.00**
Circ: Statement: **245,422** • **CGC:** 3 graded, best 9.4
And Death Came Riding! **A:** Gene Colan

57 ❑ Oct 1969 Cover: 0.15 **NM** value: **15.00**
Circ: Statement: **245,422** • **CGC:** 5 graded, best 9.6
In the Midst of Life! • Daredevil reveals identity to Karen Page **A:** Gene Colan

58 ❑ Nov 1969 Cover: 0.15 **NM** value: **15.00**
Circ: Statement: **245,422** • **CGC:** 6 graded, best 9.4
Spin-Out on Fifth Avenue! **A:** Gene Colan

59 ❑ Dec 1969 Cover: 0.15 **NM** value: **15.00**
Circ: Statement: **245,422** • **CGC:** 5 graded, best 9.6
The Torpedo Will Get You If You Don't Watch Out **A:** Gene Colan

Other grades: Multiply prices above by **1.5 for Mint • 2/3 for Very Fine • 1/3 for Fine • 1/5 for Very Good • 1/8 for Good**

60 Jan 1970 Cover: 0.15 **NM** value: **12.00**
Circ: Statement: **212,935 • CGC:** 3 graded, best 9.6
Showdown at Sea! **A:** Gene Colan

61 Feb 1970 Cover: 0.15 **NM** value: **12.00**
Circ: Statement: **212,935 • CGC:** 6 graded, best 9.8
Trapped by the Trio of Doom **A:** Gene Colan

62 Mar 1970 Cover: 0.15 **NM** value: **12.00**
Circ: Statement: **212,935 • CGC:** 3 graded, best 9.4
Quoth the Nighthhawk, Nevermore! • Has 1969 Statement, filed 10/1/69; avg print run 418,160; avg sales 244,470; avg subs 952; avg total paid 245,422; samples 110; max existent 245,532; 41% of run returned **A:** Gene Colan ★ Origin of Nighthawk II (Kyle Richmond).

63 Apr 1970 Cover: 0.15 **NM** value: **12.00**
Circ: Statement: **212,935 • CGC:** 4 graded, best 9.4
The Girl or the Gladiator? **A:** Gene Colan

64 May 1970 Cover: 0.15 **NM** value: **12.00**
Circ: Statement: **212,935 • CGC:** 1 graded, best 9.6
Suddenly, the Stunt-Master! **A:** Gene Colan

65 Jun 1970 Cover: 0.15 **NM** value: **12.00**
Circ: Statement: **212,935 • CGC:** 2 graded, best 9.4
The Killing of Brother Brimstone **A:** Gene Colan

66 Jul 1970 Cover: 0.15 **NM** value: **12.00**
Circ: Statement: **212,935 • CGC:** 3 graded, best 9.6
And One Cried Murder **A:** Gene Colan **W:** Roy Thomas

67 Aug 1970 Cover: 0.15 **NM** value: **12.00**
Circ: Statement: **212,935 • CGC:** 3 graded, best 9.6
Stilt-Man Stalks the Soundstage **A:** Gene Colan

68 Sep 1970 Cover: 0.15 **NM** value: **12.00**
Circ: Statement: **212,935 • CGC:** 2 graded, best 9.6
Phoenix and the Fighter **A:** Gene Colan

69 Oct 1970 Cover: 0.15 **NM** value: **12.00**
Circ: Statement: **212,935 • CGC:** 3 graded, best 9.0
A Life on the Line **A:** Gene Colan ★ 1st Appearance of William Carver (Thunderbolt).

70 Nov 1970 Cover: 0.15 **NM** value: **12.00**
Circ: Statement: **212,935 • CGC:** 1 graded, best 9.0
The Tribune **A:** Gene Colan **W:** Gary Friedrich

71 Dec 1970 Cover: 0.15 **NM** value: **12.00**
Circ: Statement: **212,935 • CGC:** 2 graded, best 8.5
If an Eye Offend Thee! **A:** Gene Colan

72 Jan 1971 Cover: 0.15 **NM** value: **9.00**
Circ: Statement: **199,872 • CGC:** 4 graded, best 9.6
Lo! The Lord of the Leopards **A:** Gene Colan ★ 1st Appearance of Tagak the Leopard Lord.

73 Feb 1971 Cover: 0.15 **NM** value: **9.00**
Circ: Statement: **199,872 • CGC:** 3 graded, best 9.6
Behold the Brotherhood **A:** Gene Colan

74 Mar 1971 Cover: 0.15 **NM** value: **9.00**
Circ: Statement: **199,872 • CGC:** 3 graded, best 9.8
In the Country of the Blind • Has 1970 Statement, filed 10/1/70; avg print run 385,433; avg sales 211,888; avg subs 1,047; avg total paid 212,935; samples 0; office use 110; max existent 213,045; 45% of run returned **A:** Gene Colan

75 Apr 1971 Cover: 0.15 **NM** value: **9.00**
Circ: Statement: **199,872 • CGC:** 2 graded, best 9.2
Now Rides the Ghost of El Condor **A:** Gene Colan

76 May 1971 Cover: 0.15 **NM** value: **9.00**
Circ: Statement: **199,872 • CGC:** 4 graded, best 9.4
The Deathmarch of El Condor **A:** Gene Colan

77 Jun 1971 Cover: 0.15 **NM** value: **9.00**
Circ: Statement: **199,872 • CGC:** 11 graded, best 9.6
And So Enters the Amazing Spider-Man **A:** Gene Colan

78 Jul 1971 Cover: 0.15 **NM** value: **9.00**
Circ: Statement: **199,872 • CGC:** 2 graded, best 9.4
The Horns of the Bull! **A:** Gene Colan

79 Aug 1971 Cover: 0.15 **NM** value: **9.00**
Circ: Statement: **199,872 • CGC:** 2 graded, best 9.4
Murder Cries Man-Bull! **A:** Gene Colan

80 Sep 1971 Cover: 0.15 **NM** value: **9.00**
Circ: Statement: **199,872 • CGC:** 3 graded, best 9.6
In the Eyes of the Owl **A:** Gene Colan

81 Nov 1971 Cover: 0.25 **NM** value: **9.00**
Circ: Statement: **199,872 • CGC:** 6 graded, best 9.6
And Death is a Woman Called Widow • giant; reprints story from Strange Tales #132 **A:** Gene Colan

82 Dec 1971 Cover: 0.20 **NM** value: **9.00**
Circ: Statement: **199,872 • CGC:** 1 graded, best 9.2
Now Send the Scorpion **A:** Gene Colan

83 Jan 1972 Cover: 0.20 **NM** value: **9.00**
Circ: Statement: **180,765 • CGC:** 2 graded, best 9.6
The Widow Accused **A:** Barry Windsor-Smith ★ Versus Mr. Hyde.

84 Feb 1972 Cover: 0.20 **NM** value: **9.00**
Circ: Statement: **180,765 • CGC:** 1 graded, best 9.2
Night Of The Assassin **A:** Gene Colan **W:** Gerry Conway

85 Mar 1972 Cover: 0.20 **NM** value: **9.00**
Circ: Statement: **180,765 • CGC:** 4 graded, best 9.6
Night Flight

86 Apr 1972 Cover: 0.20 **NM** value: **9.00**
Circ: Statement: **180,765 • CGC:** 1 graded, best 9.4
Once Upon a Time, The Ox

87 May 1972 Cover: 0.20 **NM** value: **9.00**
Circ: Statement: **180,765 • CGC:** 1 graded, best 9.2
From Stage Left, Enter Electro! • Has 1971 Statement, filed 9/23/71; avg print run 328,258; avg sales 198,891; avg subs 981; avg total paid 199,872; samples 110; office use 1,250; max existent 201,232; 39% of run returned

88 Jun 1972 Cover: 0.20 **NM** value: **9.00**
Circ: Statement: **180,765**
Call Him Killgrave **A:** Gene Colan **W:** Gerry Conway ★ Origin of Black Widow.

89 Jul 1972 Cover: 0.20 **NM** value: **9.00**
Circ: Statement: **180,765 • CGC:** 1 graded, best 9.4
Crisis!

90 Aug 1972 Cover: 0.20 **NM** value: **9.00**
Circ: Statement: **180,765 • CGC:** 3 graded, best 9.8
The Sinister Secret of Project Four

91 Sep 1972 Cover: 0.20 **NM** value: **9.00**
Circ: Statement: **180,765 • CGC:** 4 graded, best 9.8
Fear is the Key ★ 1st Appearance of Mister Fear III (Larry Cranston).

92 Oct 1972 Cover: 0.20 **NM** value: **9.00**
Circ: Statement: **180,765 • CGC:** 1 graded, best 9.4
On The Eve Of The Talon **A:** Gene Colan **W:** Gerry Conway

93 Nov 1972 Cover: 0.20 **NM** value: **9.00**
Circ: Statement: **180,765 • CGC:** 2 graded, best 9.6
A Power Corrupt!

94 Dec 1972 Cover: 0.20 **NM** value: **9.00**
Circ: Statement: **180,765 • CGC:** 2 graded, best 9.4
He Can Crush the World

95 Jan 1973 Cover: 0.20 **NM** value: **9.00**
Circ: Statement: **168,379 • CGC:** 2 graded, best 9.6
Bullfight on the Bay

96 Feb 1973 Cover: 0.20 **NM** value: **9.00**
Circ: Statement: **168,379 • CGC:** 2 graded, best 9.4
The Widow Will Make You Pay

97 Mar 1973 Cover: 0.20 **NM** value: **9.00**
Circ: Statement: **168,379 • CGC:** 1 graded, best 9.6
He Who Saves • Has 1972 Statement, filed 9/21/72; avg print run 325,103; avg sales 179,772; avg subs 993; avg total paid 180,765; samples 110; office use 1,119; max existent 181,994; 44% of run returned **A:** Gene Colan **W:** Gerry Conway ★ 1st Appearance of Dark Messiah, Disciples of Doom.

98 Apr 1973 Cover: 0.20 **NM** value: **9.00**
Circ: Statement: **168,379 • CGC:** 2 graded, best 9.6
Let There Be Death

99 May 1973 Cover: 0.20 **NM** value: **9.00**
Circ: Statement: **168,379 • CGC:** 1 graded, best 9.6
The Mark of Hawkeye • story continues in Avengers #110

100 Jun 1973 Cover: 0.20 **NM** value: **15.00**
Circ: Statement: **168,379 • CGC:** 6 graded, best 9.6
• 100th anniversary issue. Mind Storm **A:** Gene Colan ★ 1st Appearance of Angar the Screamer.

101 Jul 1973 Cover: 0.20 **NM** value: **6.00**
Circ: Statement: **168,379**
Vengeance in the Sky Diamonds

102 Aug 1973 Cover: 0.20 **NM** value: **6.00**
Circ: Statement: **168,379 • CGC:** 1 graded, best 9.2
Stilt-Man Stalks The City **A:** Syd Shores **W:** Chris Claremont

103 Sep 1973 Cover: 0.20 **NM** value: **6.00**
Circ: Statement: **168,379 • CGC:** 3 graded, best 9.4
...Then Came Ramrod! **A:** Don Heck **W:** Steve Gerber ★ Origin of Ramrod I. ★ 1st Appearance of Ramrod I.

104 Oct 1973 Cover: 0.20 **NM** value: **6.00**
Circ: Statement: **168,379**
Prey of the Hunter

105 Nov 1973 Cover: 0.20 **NM** value: **6.00**
Circ: Statement: **168,379**
Menace from the Moons of Saturn ★ Origin of Moondragon. ★ 1st Appearance of Moondragon. ★ Appearance of Thanos.

106 Dec 1973 Cover: 0.20 **NM** value: **6.00**
Circ: Statement: **168,379**
Life Be Not Proud! **A:** Don Heck **W:** Steve Gerber ★ 1st Appearance of Black Spectre (female group). ★ Appearance of Black Widow.

107 Jan 1974 Cover: 0.20 **NM** value: **6.00**
Circ: Statement: **161,910 • CGC:** 2 graded, best 9.4
Blind Man's Bluff **A:** Sal Buscema; Bob Brown **W:** Steve Gerber ★ Appearance of Captain Marvel.

108 Mar 1974 Cover: 0.20 **NM** value: **6.00**
Circ: Statement: **161,910**
Cry...Beetle! • Marvel Value Stamp A/22 (Man-Thing) **A:** Bob Brown **W:** Steve Gerber

109 May 1974 Cover: 0.25 **NM** value: **6.00**
Circ: Statement: **161,910**
Dying for Dollars • Story continues in Marvel Two-In-One #3; Has 1973 Statement, filed 9/25/73; avg print run 345,283; avg sales 169,909; avg subs 760; avg total paid 168,379; samples 150; office use 161; max existent 170,980; 51% of run returned

110 Jun 1974 Cover: 0.25 **NM** value: **6.00**
Circ: Statement: **161,910**
Birthright! • Marvel Value Stamp **A:** Gene Colan **W:** Steve Gerber

111 Jul 1974 Cover: 0.25 **NM** value: **6.00**
Circ: Statement: **161,910**
Sword of the Samurai ★ 1st Appearance of Silver Samurai.

112 Aug 1974 Cover: 0.25 **NM** value: **6.00**
Circ: Statement: **161,910**
Death of a Nation?

113 Sep 1974 Cover: 0.25 **NM** value: **6.00**
Circ: Statement: **161,910**
When Strikes the Gladiator

114 Oct 1974 Cover: 0.25 **NM** value: **6.00**
Circ: Statement: **161,910 • CGC:** 1 graded, best 8.5
A Quiet Night In The Swamp • Marvel Value Stamp A/7 (Werewolf) **A:** Bob Brown **W:** Steve Gerber ★ 1st Appearance of Death-Stalker.

115 Nov 1974 Cover: 0.25 **NM** value: **6.00**
Circ: Statement: **161,910 • CGC:** 1 graded, best 9.2
Death Stalks The City! • Marvel Value Stamp A/35 (Killraven) **A:** Bob Brown **W:** Steve Gerber

116 Dec 1974 Cover: 0.25 **NM** value: **6.00**
Circ: Statement: **161,910**
Two Flew Over the Owl's Nest

117 Jan 1975 Cover: 0.25 **NM** value: **6.00**
Circ: Statement: **159,591 • CGC:** 1 graded, best 9.4
Mind Tap! • Marvel Value Stamp A/88 (The Leader) **A:** Bob Brown **W:** Chris Claremont

118 Feb 1975 Cover: 0.25 **NM** value: **6.00**
Circ: Statement: **159,591**
Circus Spelled Sideways Is Death! • Marvel Value Stamp A/28 (Hawkeye) **A:** Don Heck **W:** Gerry Conway ★ 1st Appearance of Blackwing.

119 Mar 1975 Cover: 0.25 **NM** value: **6.00**
Circ: Statement: **159,591 • CGC:** 2 graded, best 9.4
They're Tearing Down Fogwell's Gym

120 Apr 1975 Cover: 0.25 **NM** value: **6.00**
Circ: Statement: **159,591 • CGC:** 2 graded, best 9.4
...And A Hydra New Year! • Marvel Value Stamp A/99 (Sandman) **A:** Bob Brown **W:** Tony Isabella

121 May 1975 Cover: 0.25 **NM** value: **4.00**
Circ: Statement: **159,591 • CGC:** 1 graded, best 9.2
Foggy Nelson, Agent Of Shield • Has 1974 Statement, filed 9/13/74; avg print run 311,000; avg sales 161,098; avg subs 812; avg total paid 161,910; samples 0; office use 1,832; max existent 163,742; 47% of run returned **A:** Bob Brown **W:** Tony Isabella

122 Jun 1975 Cover: 0.25 **NM** value: **4.00**
Circ: Statement: **159,591 • CGC:** 1 graded, best 9.4
Hydra-And-Seek **A:** Bob Brown **W:** Tony Isabella

123 Jul 1975 Cover: 0.25 **NM** value: **4.00**
Circ: Statement: **159,591**
Holocaust In The Halls Of Hydra! **A:** Bob Brown **W:** Tony Isabella

124 Aug 1975 Cover: 0.25 **NM** value: **4.00**
Circ: Statement: **159,591 • CGC:** 1 graded, best 9.4
In the Coils of the Copperhead **A:** Gene Colan; Klaus Janson ★ 1st Appearance of Blake Tower, Copperhead.

125 Sep 1975 Cover: 0.25 **NM** value: **4.00**
Circ: Statement: **159,591 • CGC:** 1 graded, best 9.4
Vengeance is the Copperhead **A:** Klaus Janson

126 Oct 1975 Cover: 0.25 **NM** value: **4.00**
Circ: Statement: **159,591**
Flight of the Torpedo **A:** Klaus Janson ★ 1st Appearance of Torpedo.

127 Nov 1975 Cover: 0.25 **NM** value: **4.00**
Circ: Statement: **159,591**
You Killed that Man, Torpedo, and Now You're Going to Pay! **A:** Klaus Janson

128 Dec 1975 Cover: 0.25 **NM** value: **4.00**
Circ: Statement: **159,591**
Death Stalks The Stairway To The Stars! **A:** Klaus Janson; Bob Brown **W:** Marv Wolfman

129 Jan 1976 Cover: 0.25 **NM** value: **4.00**
Circ: Statement: **134,319**
Man-Bull in a China-Town **A:** Klaus Janson

130 Feb 1976 Cover: 0.25 **NM** value: **4.00**
Circ: Statement: **134,319 • CGC:** 1 graded, best 9.6
Look Out Daredevil, Here Comes the Death-Man **A:** Klaus Janson

131 Mar 1976 Cover: 0.25 **NM** value: **18.00**
Circ: Statement: **134,319 • CGC:** 19 graded, best 9.6
Watch Out for Bullseye • First Bullseye **A:** Klaus Janson ★ Origin of Bullseye.

132 Apr 1976 Cover: 0.25 **NM** value: **4.00**
Circ: Statement: **134,319 • CGC:** 1 graded, best 9.0
Bullseye Rules Supreme

133 May 1976 Cover: 0.25 **NM** value: **3.00**
Circ: Statement: **134,319 • CGC:** 2 graded, best 9.4
Mind-Wave and His Fearsome Think-Tank ★ 1st Appearance of Mind-Wave.

134 Jun 1976 Cover: 0.25 **NM** value: **3.00**
Circ: Statement: **134,319**
There's Trouble in N.Y.C.

135 Jul 1976 Cover: 0.25 **NM** value: **3.00**
Circ: Statement: **134,319**
What Is Happening? **A:** Bob Brown **W:** Marv Wolfman

136 Aug 1976 Cover: 0.25 **NM** value: **3.00**
Circ: Statement: **134,319**
A Hanging For A Hero! **A:** John Buscema **W:** Marv Wolfman

137 Sep 1976 Cover: 0.30 **NM** value: **3.00**
Circ: Statement: **134,319**
The Murder Maze Strikes Twice! **A:** John Buscema **W:** Marv Wolfman

138 Oct 1976 Cover: 0.30 **NM** value: **3.00**
Circ: Statement: **134,319**
Where Is Karen Page? **A:** John Byrne **W:** Marv Wolfman ★ Appearance of Ghost Rider, Death's Head (monster).

139 Nov 1976 Cover: 0.30 **NM** value: **3.00**
Circ: Statement: **134,319**
A Night in the Life **A:** Sal Buscema

140 Dec 1976 Cover: 0.30 **NM** value: **3.00**
Circ: Statement: **134,319**
Death Times Two **A:** Sal Buscema **W:** Bill Mantlo

141 Jan 1977 Cover: 0.30 **NM** value: **3.00**
Circ: Statement: **125,079 • CGC:** 1 graded, best 9.6
Target: Death **A:** Gil Kane

142 Feb 1977 Cover: 0.30 **NM** value: **3.00**
Circ: Statement: **125,079 • CGC:** 1 graded, best 9.4
The Concrete Jungle! **A:** John Buscema ★ Versus Cobra, Mr. Hyde.

143 Mar 1977 Cover: 0.30 **NM** value: **3.00**
Circ: Statement: **125,079**
Hyde And Go Seek • Has 1976 Statement; avg total paid circ 134,319 **A:** Bob Brown **W:** Marv Wolfman

144 Apr 1977 Cover: 0.30 **NM** value: **3.00**
Circ: Statement: **125,079**
Man-Bull Means Mayhem!

145 May 1977 Cover: 0.30 **NM** value: **3.00**
Circ: Statement: **125,079**
Danger Rides The Bitter Wind **A:** George Tuska; Jim Mooney **W:** Jim Shooter

146 Jun 1977 Cover: 0.30 **NM** value: **3.00**
Circ: Statement: **125,079**
Duel! **A:** Gil Kane ★ Appearance of Bullseye. ★ Versus Bullseye.

147 Jul 1977 Cover: 0.30 **NM** value: **3.00**
Circ: Statement: **125,079**
Breaking Point **A:** Gil Kane; Klaus Janson **W:** Jim Shooter

148 Sep 1977 Cover: 0.30 **NM** value: **3.00**
Circ: Statement: **125,079 • CGC:** 1 graded, best 9.0
Manhunt **A:** Gil Kane; Klaus Janson

149 Nov 1977 Cover: 0.35 **NM** value: **3.00**
Circ: Statement: **125,079**
Catspaw **A:** Carmine Infantino; Klause Janson

150 Jan 1978 Cover: 0.35 **NM** value: **3.00**
• **CGC:** 1 graded, best 9.0
Catastrophe **A:** Carmine Infantino; Klaus Janson **W:** Jim Shooter ★ 1st Appearance of Paladin.

151 Mar 1978 Cover: 0.35 **NM** value: **3.00**
• **CGC:** 1 graded, best 9.4

CGC-graded: Multiply prices above by **33 for 9.9 M • 16 for 9.8 NM/M • 7 for 9.6 NM+ • 5 for 9.4 NM • 2.5 for 9.2 NM- • 1.5 for 9.0 VF/NM**

Crisis! • Daredevil reveals identity to Heather Glenn **A:** Gil Kane; Klaus Janson **W:** Roger McKenzie

152 ❑ May 1978 Cover: 0.35 **NM** value: **3.00**
Prisoner • Has 1977 Statement, filed 9/20/77; avg print run 312,799; avg sales 123,155; avg subs 1,924; avg total paid 125,079; samples 200; office use 1,120; max existent 126,399; 60% of run returned **A:** Carmine Infantino; Klaus Janson **W:** Roger McKenzie ★ Appearance of Paladin.

153 ❑ Jul 1978 Cover: 0.35 **NM** value: **3.00**
Betrayal! ★ 1st Appearance of Ben Urich.

154 ❑ Sep 1978 Cover: 0.35 **NM** value: **3.00**
Arena! **A:** Gene Colan **W:** Roger McKenzie

155 ❑ Nov 1978 Cover: 0.35 **NM** value: **3.00**
The Man Without Fear? • Black Widow returns **A:** Frank Robbins **W:** Roger McKenzie

156 ❑ Jan 1979 Cover: 0.35 **NM** value: **3.00**
Ring Of Death! **A:** Gene Colan **W:** Roger McKenzie ★ Appearance of 1960's Daredevil.

157 ❑ Mar 1979 Cover: 0.35 **NM** value: **3.00**
• **CGC:** 2 graded, best 9.4
The Ungrateful Dead **A:** Gene Colan; Klaus Janson **W:** Mary Jo Duffy ★ 1st Appearance of Bird-Man II (Achille DiBacco), Cat-Man II (Sebastian Patane), Ape-Man II (Roy McVey).

158 ❑ May 1979 Cover: 0.40 **NM** value: **30.00**
• **CGC:** 101 graded, best 9.8
A Grave Mistake! • First Miller Daredevil **A:** Frank Miller ★ Origin of Death-Stalker. ★ Death of Cat-Man II (Sebastian Patane). ★ Death of Ape-Man II (Roy McVey). ★ Death of Death-Stalker. ★ Versus Deathstalker.

159 ❑ Jul 1979 Cover: 0.40 **NM** value: **16.00**
• **CGC:** 23 graded, best 9.8
Market for Murder! **A:** Frank Miller ★ Appearance of Bullseye. ★ Versus Bullseye.

160 ❑ Sep 1979 Cover: 0.40 **NM** value: **9.00**
• **CGC:** 8 graded, best 9.6
In the Hands of Bullseye **A:** Frank Miller ★ Versus Bullseye.

161 ❑ Nov 1979 Cover: 0.40 **NM** value: **9.00**
• **CGC:** 10 graded, best 9.6
To Dare the Devil **A:** Frank Miller ★ Versus Bullseye.

162 ❑ Jan 1980 Cover: 0.40 **NM** value: **3.00**
• **CGC:** 2 graded, best 9.4
Requiem for A Pug **A:** Steve Ditko

163 ❑ Mar 1980 Cover: 0.40 **NM** value: **6.00**
• **CGC:** 5 graded, best 9.6
Blind Alley! **A:** Frank Miller

164 ❑ May 1980 Cover: 0.40 **NM** value: **6.00**
• **CGC:** 12 graded, best 9.8
Expose! **A:** Frank Miller

165 ❑ Jul 1980 Cover: 0.40 **NM** value: **6.00**
• **CGC:** 3 graded, best 9.6
Arms of the Octopus **A:** Frank Miller

166 ❑ Sep 1980 Cover: 0.50 **NM** value: **6.00**
• **CGC:** 3 graded, best 9.6
Til Death Do Us Part **A:** Frank Miller

167 ❑ Nov 1980 Cover: 0.50 **NM** value: **6.00**
• **CGC:** 6 graded, best 9.6
The Mauler **A:** Frank Miller

168 ❑ Jan 1981 Cover: 0.50 **NM** value: **24.00**
Circ: Statement: **130,239** • **CGC:** 101 graded, best 9.6
Elektra! • First Elektra **A:** Frank Miller **W:** Frank Miller ★ Origin of Elektra. ★ 1st Appearance of Elektra.

169 ❑ Mar 1981 Cover: 0.50 **NM** value: **8.00**
Circ: Statement: **130,239** • **CGC:** 5 graded, best 9.6
Devils! **A:** Frank Miller **W:** Frank Miller ★ Appearance of Elektra. ★ Versus Bullseye.

170 ❑ May 1981 Cover: 0.50 **NM** value: **8.00**
Circ: Statement: **130,239** • **CGC:** 7 graded, best 9.6
The Kingpin Must Die **A:** Frank Miller **W:** Frank Miller ★ Versus Bullseye.

171 ❑ Jun 1981 Cover: 0.50 **NM** value: **5.00**
Circ: Statement: **130,239** • **CGC:** 3 graded, best 9.4
In the Kingpin's Clutches **A:** Frank Miller **W:** Frank Miller

172 ❑ Jul 1981 Cover: 0.50 **NM** value: **5.00**
Circ: Statement: **130,239** • **CGC:** 7 graded, best 9.8
Gangwar **A:** Frank Miller **W:** Frank Miller

173 ❑ Aug 1981 Cover: 0.50 **NM** value: **5.00**
Circ: Statement: **130,239** • **CGC:** 7 graded, best 9.8
Lady Killer! **A:** Frank Miller **W:** Frank Miller

174 ❑ Sep 1981 Cover: 0.50 **NM** value: **5.00**
Circ: Statement: **130,239** • **CGC:** 18 graded, best 9.8
The Assassination of Matt Murdock **A:** Frank Miller **W:** Frank Miller

175 ❑ Oct 1981 Cover: 0.50 **NM** value: **5.00**
Circ: Statement: **130,239** • **CGC:** 17 graded, best 9.8
Gauntlet **A:** Frank Miller **W:** Frank Miller

176 ❑ Nov 1981 Cover: 0.50 **NM** value: **5.00**
Circ: Statement: **130,239** • **CGC:** 13 graded, best 9.8
Hunters! **A:** Frank Miller **W:** Frank Miller ★ 1st Appearance of Stick. ★ Appearance of Elektra.

177 ❑ Dec 1981 Cover: 0.50 **NM** value: **5.00**
Circ: Statement: **130,239** • **CGC:** 9 graded, best 9.9
Where Angles Fear To Tread **A:** Frank Miller **W:** Frank Miller ★ Appearance of Elektra.

178 ❑ Jan 1982 Cover: 0.60 **NM** value: **5.00**
Circ: Statement: **180,199** • **CGC:** 12 graded, best 9.8
Paper Chase **A:** Frank Miller **W:** Frank Miller ★ Appearance of Elektra.

179 ❑ Feb 1982 Cover: 0.60 **NM** value: **5.00**
Circ: Statement: **180,199** • **CGC:** 13 graded, best 9.8
Spiked **A:** Frank Miller **W:** Frank Miller ★ Appearance of Elektra.

180 ❑ Mar 1982 Cover: 0.60 **NM** value: **5.00**
Circ: Statement: **180,199** • **CGC:** 32 graded, best 9.8
The Damned! **A:** Frank Miller **W:** Frank Miller ★ Appearance of Elektra.

181 ❑ Apr 1982 Cover: 1.00 **NM** value: **7.00**
Circ: Statement: **180,199** • **CGC:** 134 graded, best 9.8
• double-sized. Last Hand • Punisher cameo out of costume; Has 1981 Statement, filed 10/1/81; avg print run 276,812; avg sales 124,520; avg subs 5,719; avg total paid 130,239; samples 526; office use 1,794; max existent 132,559; 52% of run returned **A:** Frank Miller **W:** Frank Miller ★ Death of Elektra. ★ Versus Bullseye.

182 ❑ May 1982 Cover: 0.60 **NM** value: **4.00**
Circ: Statement: **180,199** • **CGC:** 32 graded, best 9.8
She's Alive **A:** Frank Miller **W:** Frank Miller ★ Appearance of Punisher. ★ Versus Punisher.

183 ❑ Jun 1982 Cover: 0.60 **NM** value: **4.00**
Circ: Statement: **180,199** • **CGC:** 11 graded, best 9.8
Child's Play **A:** Frank Miller **W:** Frank Miller; Roger McKenzie ★ Appearance of Punisher. ★ Versus Punisher.

184 ❑ Jul 1982 Cover: 0.60 **NM** value: **4.00**
Circ: Statement: **180,199** • **CGC:** 25 graded, best 9.8
Good Guys Wear Red **A:** Frank Miller **W:** Frank Miller ★ Appearance of Punisher. ★ Versus Punisher.

185 ❑ Aug 1982 Cover: 0.60 **NM** value: **2.50**
Circ: Statement: **180,199** • **CGC:** 5 graded, best 9.8
Guts **A:** Frank Miller; Klaus Janson **W:** Frank Miller

186 ❑ Sep 1982 Cover: 0.60 **NM** value: **2.50**
Circ: Statement: **180,199** • **CGC:** 7 graded, best 9.8
Stilts **A:** Frank Miller; Klaus Janson **W:** Frank Miller

187 ❑ Oct 1982 Cover: 0.60 **NM** value: **2.50**
Circ: Statement: **180,199** • **CGC:** 8 graded, best 9.8
Overkill **A:** Frank Miller; Klaus Janson **W:** Frank Miller ★ Appearance of Black Widow.

188 ❑ Nov 1982 Cover: 0.60 **NM** value: **2.50**
Circ: Statement: **180,199** • **CGC:** 10 graded, best 9.6
The Widow's Bite **A:** Frank Miller; Klaus Janson **W:** Frank Miller

189 ❑ Dec 1982 Cover: 0.60 **NM** value: **3.00**
Circ: Statement: **180,199** • **CGC:** 5 graded, best 9.8
Siege **A:** Frank Miller; Klaus Janson **W:** Frank Miller ★ Death of Stick.

190 ❑ Jan 1983 Cover: 1.00 **NM** value: **3.00**
Circ: Statement: **259,013** • **CGC:** 10 graded, best 9.8
• Double-size. Resurrection **A:** Frank Miller; Klaus Janson **W:** Frank Miller ★ Origin of Elektra. ★ Appearance of Elektra.

191 ❑ Feb 1983 Cover: 0.60 **NM** value: **2.00**
Circ: Statement: **259,013** • **CGC:** 7 graded, best 9.8
A: Frank Miller **W:** Frank Miller

192 ❑ Mar 1983 Cover: 0.60 **NM** value: **2.00**
Circ: Statement: **259,013**
Promises **A:** Klaus Janson **W:** Alan Brennert

193 ❑ Apr 1983 Cover: 0.60 **NM** value: **2.00**
Circ: Statement: **259,013**
Bitsy's Revenge **A:** Klaus Janson **W:** Larry Hama

194 ❑ May 1983 Cover: 0.60 **NM** value: **2.00**
Circ: Statement: **259,013**
Judgement • Has 1982 Statement, filed 10/11/82; avg print run 309,482; avg sales 174,361; avg subs 5,838; avg total paid 180,199; samples 613; office use 2,904; max existent 183,716; 41% of run returned **A:** Klaus Jackson; Klaus Janson **W:** Denny O'Neil

195 ❑ Jun 1983 Cover: 0.60 **NM** value: **2.00**
Circ: Statement: **259,013**
Betrayal **A:** Klaus Jackson; Klaus Janson **W:** Denny O'Neil

196 ❑ Jun 1983 Cover: 0.60 **NM** value: **6.00**
Circ: Statement: **259,013** • **CGC:** 31 graded, best 9.8
Enemies **A:** Klaus Jackson; Klaus Janson **W:** Denny O'Neil ★ Appearance of Wolverine.

197 ❑ Aug 1983 Cover: 0.60 **NM** value: **2.00**
Circ: Statement: **259,013**
Journey **A:** Klaus Jackson **W:** Denny O'Neil ★ Versus Bullseye.

198 ❑ Sep 1983 Cover: 0.60 **NM** value: **2.00**
Circ: Statement: **259,013**
Touch Of A Stranger **A:** William Johnson **W:** Denny O'Neil

199 ❑ Oct 1983 Cover: 0.60 **NM** value: **2.00**
Circ: Statement: **259,013**
Daughter Of A Dark Wind **A:** William Johnson **W:** Denny O'Neil

200 ❑ Nov 1983 Cover: 0.60 **NM** value: **2.00**
Circ: Statement: **259,013** • **CGC:** 1 graded, best 9.6
Redemption **A:** William Johnson **C:** John Byrne **W:** Denny O'Neil ★ Versus Bullseye.

201 ❑ Dec 1983 Cover: 0.60 **NM** value: **2.00**
Circ: Statement: **259,013**
The Day The Devil Didn't Dare! **A:** William Johnson **W:** Denny O'Neil ★ Appearance of Black Widow.

202 ❑ Jan 1984 Cover: 0.60 **NM** value: **2.00**
Circ: Statement: **233,580**
Savages **A:** William Johnson **W:** Denny O'Neil

203 ❑ Feb 1984 Cover: 0.60 **NM** value: **2.00**
Circ: Statement: **233,580**
Trumps! **A:** Geof Isherwood **W:** Steven Grant ★ 1st Appearance of Trump.

204 ❑ Mar 1984 Cover: 0.60 **NM** value: **2.00**
Circ: Statement: **233,580**
Vengeance Of The Victim! **A:** Luke McDonnell **W:** Denny O'Neil

205 ❑ Apr 1984 Cover: 0.60 **NM** value: **2.00**
Circ: Statement: **233,580**
The Gael! **A:** William Johnson **W:** Denny O'Neil

206 ❑ May 1984 Cover: 0.60 **NM** value: **2.00**
Circ: Statement: **233,580**
Every Good And Perfect Gift… **A:** David Mazzucchelli **W:** Denny O'Neil

207 ❑ Jun 1984 Cover: 0.60 **NM** value: **2.00**
Circ: Statement: **233,580**
Ultimatum! • Has 1983 Statement, filed 10/4/83; avg print run 402,372; avg sales 251,742; avg subs 771; avg total paid 259,013; samples 732; office use 3,206; max existent 256,451; 35% of run returned **A:** William Johnson **W:** Denny O'Neil

208 ❑ Jul 1984 Cover: 0.60 **NM** value: **2.00**
Circ: Statement: **233,580**
The Deadliest Night Of My Life! **A:** David Mazzucchelli **W:** Arthur Byron Cover; Harlan Ellison

209 ❑ Aug 1984 Cover: 0.60 **NM** value: **2.00**
Circ: Statement: **233,580**
Blast From The Past! **A:** David Mazzucchelli **W:** Arthur Byron Cover

210 ❑ Sep 1984 Cover: 0.60 **NM** value: **2.00**
Circ: Statement: **233,580**
Survivor! **A:** David Mazzucchelli **W:** Denny O'Neil

211 ❑ Oct 1984 Cover: 0.60 **NM** value: **2.00**
Circ: Statement: **233,580**
This Hungry God **A:** David Mazzucchelli **W:** Denny O'Neil

212 ❑ Nov 1984 Cover: 0.60 **NM** value: **2.00**
Circ: Statement: **233,580**
Lies **A:** David Mazzucchelli **W:** Denny O'Neil

213 ❑ Dec 1984 Cover: 0.60 **NM** value: **2.00**
Circ: Statement: **233,580**
The Blindness Men Wish For **A:** David Mazzucchelli **W:** Denny O'Neil

214 ❑ Jan 1985 Cover: 0.60 **NM** value: **2.00**
Circ: Statement: **177,884**
The Crumbling **A:** David Mazzucchelli **W:** Denny O'Neil

215 ❑ Feb 1985 Cover: 0.60 **NM** value: **2.00**
Circ: Statement: **177,884**
Prophecy **A:** David Mazzucchelli **W:** Denny O'Neil ★ Appearance of Two-Gun Kid.

216 ❑ Mar 1985 Cover: 0.60 **NM** value: **2.00**
Circ: Statement: **177,884**
The Second Secret **A:** David Mazzucchelli **W:** Denny O'Neil

217 ❑ Apr 1985 Cover: 0.65 **NM** value: **2.00**
Circ: Statement: **177,884**
The Sight Stealer **A:** David Mazzucchelli **C:** Frank Miller **W:** Denny O'Neil

218 ❑ May 1985 Cover: 0.65 **NM** value: **2.00**
Circ: Statement: **177,884** CapCity orders: **14,600**
All My Laurels You Have Riven Away! **A:** Sal Buscema **W:** Denny O'Neil

219 ❑ Jun 1985 Cover: 0.65 **NM** value: **2.00**
Circ: Statement: **177,884** CapCity orders: **17,000**
Badlands • Has 1984 Statement, filed 9/28/84; avg print run 362,550; avg sales 225,219; avg subs 8,361; avg total paid 233,580; samples 140; office use 2,609; max existent 236,329; 35% of run returned **A:** Sal Buscema; Frank Miller **W:** Frank Miller

220 ❑ Jul 1985 Cover: 0.65 **NM** value: **2.00**
Circ: Statement: **177,884** CapCity orders: **15,100**
Fog **A:** David Mazzucchelli **W:** Denny O'Neil

221 ❑ Aug 1985 Cover: 0.65 **NM** value: **2.00**
Circ: Statement: **177,884** CapCity orders: **15,300**
Behold My Vengeance! **A:** David Mazzucchelli **W:** Denny O'Neil

222 ❑ Sep 1985 Cover: 0.65 **NM** value: **2.00**
Circ: Statement: **177,884** CapCity orders: **15,600**
Fear In A Handful Of Dust **A:** David Mazzucchelli **W:** Denny O'Neil ★ Appearance of Black Widow.

223 ❑ Oct 1985 Cover: 0.65 **NM** value: **2.00**
Circ: Statement: **177,884** CapCity orders: **25,200**
The Price • Secret Wars II **A:** David Mazzucchelli **W:** Jim Shooter; Denny O'Neil

224 ❑ Nov 1985 Cover: 0.65 **NM** value: **2.00**
Circ: Statement: **177,884** CapCity orders: **15,600**
Abe **A:** Geof Isherwood; Dan Jurgens **W:** James Owsley ★ Versus Sunturion.

225 ❑ Dec 1985 Cover: 0.65 **NM** value: **2.00**
Circ: Statement: **177,884** CapCity orders: **16,000**
…And Then you Die! **A:** David Mazzucchelli **W:** Denny O'Neil ★ Versus Vulture.

226 ❑ Jan 1986 Cover: 0.65 **NM** value: **2.00**
Circ: Statement: **189,959** CapCity orders: **15,700**
Warriors **A:** Frank Miller; David Mazzucchelli; Dennis Janke **W:** Frank Miller; Denny O'Neil

227 ❑ Feb 1986 Cover: 0.75 **NM** value: **2.00**
Circ: Statement: **189,959** CapCity orders: **22,000** • **CGC:** 4 graded, best 9.8
W: Frank Miller ★ Appearance of Kingpin.

228 ❑ Mar 1986 Cover: 0.75 **NM** value: **2.00**
Circ: Statement: **189,959** CapCity orders: **20,000** • **CGC:** 1 graded, best 9.6
W: Frank Miller

229 ❑ Apr 1986 Cover: 0.75 **NM** value: **2.00**
Circ: Statement: **189,959** CapCity orders: **22,600** • **CGC:** 1 graded, best 9.6
W: Frank Miller ★ 1st Appearance of Sister Maggie.

230 ❑ May 1986 Cover: 0.75 **NM** value: **2.00**
Circ: Statement: **189,959** CapCity orders: **24,100**
• Has 1985 Statement, filed 10/1/85; avg print run 318,767; avg sales 170,592; avg subs 7,292; avg total paid 177,884; samples 140; office use 767; max existent 178,791; 44% of run returned **W:** Frank Miller

231 ❑ Jun 1986 Cover: 0.75 **NM** value: **2.00**
Circ: Statement: **189,959** CapCity orders: **24,800**
W: Frank Miller

232 ❑ Jul 1986 Cover: 0.75 **NM** value: **2.00**
Circ: Statement: **189,959** CapCity orders: **26,700**
God And Country **A:** David Mazzucchelli **W:** Frank Miller

233 ❑ Aug 1986 Cover: 0.75 **NM** value: **2.00**
Circ: Statement: **189,959** CapCity orders: **27,600**
Armageddon **A:** David Mazzucchelli **W:** Frank Miller

234 ❑ Sep 1986 Cover: 0.75 **NM** value: **2.00**
Circ: Statement: **189,959** CapCity orders: **20,700**
Madcasting **A:** Steve Ditko **W:** Mark Gruenwald

235 ❑ Oct 1986 Cover: 0.75 **NM** value: **2.00**
Circ: Statement: **189,959** CapCity orders: **29,900**
A Safe Place **A:** Steve Ditko **W:** Danny Fingeroth

236 ❑ Nov 1986 Cover: 0.75 **NM** value: **2.00**
Circ: Statement: **189,959** CapCity orders: **28,700**
American Dreamer **A:** Barry Windsor-Smith **W:** Ann Nocenti

237 ❑ Dec 1986 Cover: 0.75 **NM** value: **2.00**
Circ: Statement: **189,959** CapCity orders: **24,600**
Context! **A:** Louis Williams **W:** John Harkness

238 ❑ Jan 1987 Cover: 0.75 **NM** value: **3.00**
Circ: Statement: **188,642** CapCity orders: **27,200**
Mutant Massacre; It Comes With The Claws **A:** Sal Buscema **W:** Ann Nocenti ★ Appearance of Sabretooth.

239 ❑ Feb 1987 Cover: 0.75 **NM** value: **2.00**
Circ: Statement: **188,642** CapCity orders: **23,100**

Other grades: Multiply prices above by **1.5 for Mint** • **2/3 for Very Fine** • **1/3 for Fine** • **1/5 for Very Good** • **1/8 for Good**

📖 Bad Plumbing! **A:** Louis Williams **C:** Arthur Adams **W:** Ann Nocenti
240 ☐ Mar 1987 Cover: 0.75 **NM** value: **2.00**
Circ: Statement: **188,642** CapCity orders: **23,400**
📖 The Face You Deserve **A:** Louis Williams **W:** Ann Nocenti
241 ☐ Apr 1987 Cover: 0.75 **NM** value: **2.00**
Circ: Statement: **188,642** CapCity orders: **22,500**
📖 Black Christmas • Has 1986 Statement, filed 10/6/86; avg print run 316,462; avg sales 183,142; avg subs 6,817; avg total paid 189,959; samples 225; office use 1,847; max existent 192,031; 39% of run returned **A:** Todd McFarlane **W:** Ann Nocenti
242 ☐ May 1987 Cover: 0.75 **NM** value: **2.00**
Circ: Statement: **188,642** CapCity orders: **21,600**
📖 Caviar Killer **A:** Keith Pollard **W:** Ann Nocenti
243 ☐ Jun 1987 Cover: 0.75 **NM** value: **2.00**
Circ: Statement: **188,642** CapCity orders: **21,400**
📖 Don't Touch Me **A:** Louis Williams **W:** Ann Nocenti
244 ☐ Jul 1987 Cover: 0.75 **NM** value: **2.00**
Circ: Statement: **188,642** CapCity orders: **20,900**
📖 Touch Me **A:** Louis Williams **W:** Ann Nocenti
245 ☐ Aug 1987 Cover: 0.75 **NM** value: **2.00**
Circ: Statement: **188,642** CapCity orders: **21,800**
📖 Burn! **A:** Chuck Patton **W:** Ann Nocenti ★ Appearance of Black Panther.
246 ☐ Sep 1987 Cover: 0.75 **NM** value: **2.00**
Circ: Statement: **188,642** CapCity orders: **22,200**
📖 Bad Guy **A:** Tom Morgan **W:** James Owsley
247 ☐ Oct 1987 Cover: 0.75 **NM** value: **2.00**
Circ: Statement: **188,642** CapCity orders: **22,500**
📖 The Backwards Man **A:** Keith Pollard **W:** Ann Nocenti
248 ☐ Nov 1987 Cover: 0.75 **NM** value: **4.00**
Circ: Statement: **188,642** CapCity orders: **23,200**
★ Appearance of Wolverine.
249 ☐ Dec 1987 Cover: 0.75 **NM** value: **4.00**
Circ: Statement: **188,642** CapCity orders: **26,400** • **CGC:** 4 graded, best 9.0
★ Appearance of Wolverine.
250 ☐ Jan 1988 Cover: 0.75 **NM** value: **2.00**
Circ: Statement: **182,310** CapCity orders: **23,300**
★ 1st Appearance of Bullet.
251 ☐ Feb 1988 Cover: 0.75 **NM** value: **2.00**
Circ: Statement: **182,310** CapCity orders: **24,400**
📖 Save The Planet! **A:** John Romita Jr. **W:** Ann Nocenti
252 ☐ Mar 1988 Cover: 1.25 **NM** value: **3.00**
Circ: Statement: **182,310** CapCity orders: **36,400**
• double-sized. 📖 Ground Zero • Fall of Mutants **A:** John Romita Jr. **W:** Ann Nocenti
253 ☐ Apr 1988 Cover: 0.75 **NM** value: **2.00**
Circ: Statement: **182,310** CapCity orders: **25,700**
254 ☐ May 1988 Cover: 0.75 **NM** value: **6.00**
Circ: Statement: **182,310** CapCity orders: **24,700** • **CGC:** 2 graded, best 9.6
📖 Typhoid! • 1&0: Typhoid Mary **A:** John Romita Jr. **W:** Ann Nocenti ★ Origin of Typhoid Mary. ★ 1st Appearance of Typhoid Mary.
255 ☐ Jun 1988 Cover: 0.75 **NM** value: **3.50**
Circ: Statement: **182,310** CapCity orders: **24,150**
📖 Temptation! **A:** John Romita Jr. **W:** Ann Nocenti ★ 2nd Appearance of Typhoid Mary.
256 ☐ Jul 1988 Cover: 0.75 **NM** value: **2.50**
Circ: Statement: **182,310** CapCity orders: **25,300**
📖 Blindspots • 3: Typhoid Mary; Has 1987 Statement; avg print run 313,353; avg sales 182,167; avg subs 6,475; avg total paid 188,642; samples 136; office use 1,262; max existent 190,040; 39% of run returned **A:** John Romita Jr. **W:** Ann Nocenti ★ Appearance of 3rd.
257 ☐ Aug 1988 Cover: 0.75 **NM** value: **3.00**
Circ: Statement: **182,310** CapCity orders: **30,300** • **CGC:** 2 graded, best 9.6
📖 The Bully **A:** John Romita Jr. **W:** Ann Nocenti ★ Appearance of Punisher.
258 ☐ Sep 1988 Cover: 0.75 **NM** value: **2.00**
Circ: Statement: **182,310** CapCity orders: **27,500**
📖 I Heard The Jungle Breathe **A:** Ron Lim **W:** Fabian Nicieza ★ Origin of Bengal. ★ 1st Appearance of Bengal.
259 ☐ Oct 1988 Cover: 0.75 **NM** value: **2.00**
Circ: Statement: **182,310** CapCity orders: **29,500**
★ Appearance of Typhoid Mary.
260 ☐ Nov 1988 Cover: 1.50 **NM** value: **2.50**
Circ: Statement: **182,310** CapCity orders: **29,400**
• double-sized.
261 ☐ Dec 1988 Cover: 0.75 **NM** value: **2.00**
Circ: Statement: **182,310** CapCity orders: **28,800**
📖 Meltdown! **A:** John Romita Jr. **W:** Ann Nocenti ★ Appearance of Human Torch.
262 ☐ Jan 1989 Cover: 0.75 **NM** value: **2.00**
Circ: Statement: **190,358** CapCity orders: **32,700**
📖 I Found A Me In A Gloomy Hood, Astray… • Inferno **A:** John Romita Jr. **W:** Ann Nocenti
263 ☐ Feb 1989 Cover: 0.75 **NM** value: **2.00**
Circ: Statement: **190,358** CapCity orders: **33,400**
📖 In Bitterness Not Far From Death… • Inferno **A:** John Romita Jr. **W:** Ann Nocenti
264 ☐ Mar 1989 Cover: 0.75 **NM** value: **2.00**
Circ: Statement: **190,358** CapCity orders: **35,900**
📖 Baby Boom! **A:** Steve Ditko **W:** Ann Nocenti
265 ☐ Apr 1989 Cover: 0.75 **NM** value: **2.00**
Circ: Statement: **190,358** CapCity orders: **32,300**
📖 We Again Beheld The Stars • Inferno; Has 1988 Statement, filed 10/1/88; avg print run 292,070; avg sales 177,510; avg subs 4,800; avg total paid 182,310; samples 130; office use 860; max existent 183,300; 37% of run returned **A:** John Romita Jr. **W:** Ann Nocenti
266 ☐ May 1989 Cover: 0.75 **NM** value: **2.00**
Circ: Statement: **190,358**
📖 A Beer With The Devil **A:** John Romita Jr. **W:** Ann Nocenti
267 ☐ Jun 1989 Cover: 0.75 **NM** value: **2.00**
Circ: Statement: **190,358** CapCity orders: **30,500**
📖 Cremains **A:** John Romita Jr. **W:** Ann Nocenti
268 ☐ Jul 1989 Cover: 0.75 **NM** value: **2.00**
Circ: Statement: **190,358** CapCity orders: **31,600**
📖 Golden Rut **A:** John Romita Jr. **W:** Ann Nocenti
269 ☐ Aug 1989 Cover: 0.75 **NM** value: **2.00**
Circ: Statement: **190,358** CapCity orders: **29,600**
📖 Lone Stranger **A:** John Romita Jr. **W:** Ann Nocenti
270 ☐ Sep 1989 Cover: 1.00 **NM** value: **2.00**
Circ: Statement: **190,358** CapCity orders: **29,400**
📖 Blackheart! **A:** John Romita Jr. **W:** Ann Nocenti ★ Origin of Blackheart. ★ 1st Appearance of Blackheart. ★ Appearance of Spider-Man.
271 ☐ Oct 1989 Cover: 1.00 **NM** value: **1.50**
Circ: Statement: **190,358** CapCity orders: **29,700**
📖 Genetrix **A:** John Romita Jr. **W:** Ann Nocenti
272 ☐ Nov 1989 Cover: 1.00 **NM** value: **1.50**
Circ: Statement: **190,358** CapCity orders: **29,700**
★ 1st Appearance of Shotgun II.
273 ☐ Nov 1989 Cover: 1.00 **NM** value: **1.50**
Circ: Statement: **190,358** CapCity orders: **30,300**
274 ☐ Dec 1989 Cover: 1.00 **NM** value: **1.50**
Circ: Statement: **190,358** CapCity orders: **29,300**
📖 Bombs And Lemonade **A:** John Romita Jr. **W:** Ann Nocenti
275 ☐ Dec 1989 Cover: 1.00 **NM** value: **1.50**
Circ: Statement: **190,358** CapCity orders: **30,800**
📖 Acts of Vengeance • Acts of Vengeance **A:** John Romita Jr. **W:** Ann Nocenti
276 ☐ Jan 1990 Cover: 1.00 **NM** value: **1.50**
Circ: Statement: **169,805** CapCity orders: **31,700**
📖 Acts of Vengeance • Acts of Vengeance **A:** John Romita Jr. **W:** Ann Nocenti
277 ☐ Feb 1990 Cover: 1.00 **NM** value: **1.50**
Circ: Statement: **169,805** CapCity orders: **28,700**
📖 Of Crowns And Horns **A:** Rick Leonardi **W:** Ann Nocenti
278 ☐ Mar 1990 Cover: 1.00 **NM** value: **1.50**
Circ: Statement: **169,805** CapCity orders: **29,100**
📖 The Deadly Seven **A:** John Romita Jr. **W:** Ann Nocenti
279 ☐ Apr 1990 Cover: 1.00 **NM** value: **1.50**
Circ: Statement: **169,805** CapCity orders: **28,500**
📖 Before The Flame **A:** John Romita Jr. **W:** Ann Nocenti
280 ☐ May 1990 Cover: 1.00 **NM** value: **1.50**
Circ: Statement: **169,805** CapCity orders: **27,900**
📖 Twilight Of The Idols **A:** John Romita Jr. **W:** Ann Nocenti
281 ☐ Jun 1990 Cover: 1.00 **NM** value: **1.50**
Circ: Statement: **169,805** CapCity orders: **27,000**
📖 Heaven Is Knowing Who You Are • Silver Surfer cameo; Has 1989 Statement, filed 11/1/89; avg print run 291,386; avg sales 185,438; avg subs 4,920; avg total paid 190,358; samples 130; office use 600; max existent 191,088; 34% of run returned **A:** John Romita Jr. **W:** Ann Nocenti
282 ☐ Jul 1990 Cover: 1.00 **NM** value: **1.50**
Circ: Statement: **169,805** CapCity orders: **27,000**
★ Appearance of Silver Surfer.
283 ☐ Aug 1990 Cover: 1.00 **NM** value: **1.50**
Circ: Statement: **169,805** CapCity orders: **27,000**
📖 The American Nightmare **A:** Mark Bagley **W:** Ann Nocenti ★ Appearance of Captain America.
284 ☐ Sep 1990 Cover: 1.00 **NM** value: **1.50**
Circ: Statement: **169,805** CapCity orders: **25,800**
📖 The Outsiders **A:** Lee Weeks **W:** Ann Nocenti
285 ☐ Oct 1990 Cover: 1.00 **NM** value: **1.50**
Circ: Statement: **169,805** CapCity orders: **25,800**
📖 The Shadowman **A:** Lee Weeks **W:** Ann Nocenti
286 ☐ Nov 1990 Cover: 1.00 **NM** value: **1.50**
Circ: Statement: **169,805** CapCity orders: **25,500**
📖 The Thief **A:** Greg Capullo **W:** Ann Nocenti
287 ☐ Dec 1990 Cover: 1.00 **NM** value: **1.50**
Circ: Statement: **169,805** CapCity orders: **25,800**
📖 The Fighter **A:** Lee Weeks **W:** Ann Nocenti
288 ☐ Jan 1991 Cover: 1.00 **NM** value: **1.50**
Circ: Statement: **166,303** CapCity orders: **25,800**
📖 The Student **A:** Lee Weeks **W:** Ann Nocenti
289 ☐ Feb 1991 Cover: 1.00 **NM** value: **1.50**
Circ: Statement: **166,303** CapCity orders: **25,200**
📖 The Hero **A:** Kieron Dwyer **W:** Ann Nocenti
290 ☐ Mar 1991 Cover: 1.00 **NM** value: **1.50**
Circ: Statement: **166,303** CapCity orders: **25,500**
📖 Bullseye! • Has 1990 Statement, filed 10/1/90; avg print run 282,982; avg sales 165,025; avg subs 4,780; avg total paid 169,805; samples 150; office use 600; max existent 170,555; 40% of run returned **A:** Kieron Dwyer **W:** Ann Nocenti
291 ☐ Apr 1991 Cover: 1.00 **NM** value: **1.50**
Circ: Statement: **166,303** CapCity orders: **24,600**
📖 All The News That Fits **A:** Lee Weeks **W:** Ann Nocenti
292 ☐ May 1991 Cover: 1.00 **NM** value: **1.50**
Circ: Statement: **166,303** CapCity orders: **48,600**
📖 Body Count **A:** Lee Weeks **W:** D.G. Chichester ★ Appearance of Punisher.
293 ☐ Jun 1991 Cover: 1.00 **NM** value: **1.50**
Circ: Statement: **166,303** CapCity orders: **48,300**
📖 Murder By Numbers **A:** Lee Weeks **W:** D.G. Chichester ★ Appearance of Punisher.
294 ☐ Jul 1991 Cover: 1.00 **NM** value: **1.50**
Circ: Statement: **166,303** CapCity orders: **54,000**
📖 The Infernal Mysteries **A:** Lee Weeks **W:** D.G. Chichester
295 ☐ Aug 1991 Cover: 1.00 **NM** value: **1.50**
Circ: Statement: **166,303** CapCity orders: **54,600**
📖 Through The Eyes Of The Enemy **A:** Lee Weeks **W:** D.G. Chichester ★ Appearance of Ghost Rider.
296 ☐ Sep 1991 Cover: 1.00 **NM** value: **1.50**
Circ: Statement: **166,303** CapCity orders: **44,700**
📖 Balancing Act **A:** Ron Garney **W:** D.G. Chichester
297 ☐ Oct 1991 Cover: 1.00 **NM** value: **1.50**
Circ: Statement: **166,303** CapCity orders: **39,600**
📖 Last Rites, Part 1 **A:** Lee Weeks **W:** D.G. Chichester ★ Appearance of Typhoid Mary. ★ Versus Typhoid Mary.
298 ☐ Nov 1991 Cover: 1.00 **NM** value: **1.50**
Circ: Statement: **166,303** CapCity orders: **33,300**
📖 Last Rites, Part 2 **A:** Lee Weeks **W:** D.G. Chichester
299 ☐ Dec 1991 Cover: 1.00 **NM** value: **1.50**
Circ: Statement: **166,303** CapCity orders: **36,900**
📖 Last Rites, Part 3 **A:** Lee Weeks **W:** D.G. Chichester
300 ☐ Jan 1992 Cover: 2.00 **NM** value: **3.00**
Circ: CapCity orders: **108,300** • **CGC:** 6 graded, best 9.8
• double-sized. 📖 Last Rites, Part 4 • Kingpin deposed **A:** Lee Weeks **W:** D.G. Chichester
301 ☐ Feb 1992 Cover: 1.25 **NM** value: **1.50**
Circ: CapCity orders: **32,700**
★ Versus Owl.
302 ☐ Mar 1992 Cover: 1.25 **NM** value: **1.50**
Circ: CapCity orders: **30,900**
📖 Nocturnal Hunter **A:** M.C. Wyman **W:** D.G. Chichester ★ Versus Owl.
303 ☐ Apr 1992 Cover: 1.25 **NM** value: **1.50**
Circ: CapCity orders: **28,400**
📖 Dark And Deliverance **A:** M.C. Wyman **W:** D.G. Chichester ★ Versus Owl.
304 ☐ May 1992 Cover: 1.25 **NM** value: **1.50**
Circ: CapCity orders: **26,900**
📖 34 Hours **A:** Ron Garney **W:** D.G. Chichester
305 ☐ Jun 1992 Cover: 1.25 **NM** value: **1.50**
Circ: CapCity orders: **30,300**
📖 Under The Knife **A:** Scott McDaniel **W:** D.G. Chichester ★ 1st Appearance of Surgeon General.
306 ☐ Jul 1992 Cover: 1.25 **NM** value: **1.50**
Circ: CapCity orders: **31,700**
📖 Emergency Procedure **A:** Scott McDaniel **W:** D.G. Chichester
307 ☐ Aug 1992 Cover: 1.25 **NM** value: **1.50**
Circ: CapCity orders: **36,800**
📖 Dead Man's Hand, Part 1 **A:** Scott McDaniel **W:** D.G. Chichester
308 ☐ Sep 1992 Cover: 1.25 **NM** value: **1.50**
Circ: CapCity orders: **30,000**
📖 Dead Man's Hand, Part 4
309 ☐ Oct 1992 Cover: 1.25 **NM** value: **1.50**
Circ: CapCity orders: **29,100**
📖 Dead Man's Hand, Part 7; Cards on the Table **A:** Scott McDaniel **W:** D.G. Chichester
310 ☐ Nov 1992 Cover: 1.25 **NM** value: **1.50**
Circ: CapCity orders: **25,300**
📖 Devil De Rouge **A:** Scott McDaniel **W:** Glenn Herdling
311 ☐ Dec 1992 Cover: 1.25 **NM** value: **1.50**
Circ: CapCity orders: **24,200**
📖 Soul Search **A:** Scott McDaniel **W:** Glenn Herdling
312 ☐ Jan 1993 Cover: 1.25 **NM** value: **1.50**
Circ: CapCity orders: **22,900**
📖 Hot Flashes **A:** Scott McDaniel **W:** D.G. Chichester
313 ☐ Feb 1993 Cover: 1.25 **NM** value: **1.50**
Circ: CapCity orders: **22,800**
📖 So Cold It Burns **A:** Scott McDaniel **W:** D.G. Chichester
314 ☐ Mar 1993 Cover: 1.25 **NM** value: **1.50**
Circ: CapCity orders: **20,600**
📖 Shock Treatment **A:** Scott McDaniel **W:** D.G. Chichester
315 ☐ Apr 1993 Cover: 1.25 **NM** value: **1.50**
Circ: CapCity orders: **22,500**
📖 Shock Therapy **A:** Scott McDaniel **W:** D.G. Chichester ★ Versus Mr. Fear.
316 ☐ May 1993 Cover: 1.25 **NM** value: **1.50**
Circ: CapCity orders: **20,500**
📖 Fare Play **A:** Kevin Kobasic **W:** D.G. Chichester
317 ☐ Jun 1993 Cover: 1.25 **NM** value: **1.50**
Circ: CapCity orders: **19,200**
📖 Grease Is The Word **A:** Scott McDaniel **W:** D.G. Chichester ★ Versus Stiltman.
318 ☐ Jul 1993 Cover: 1.25 **NM** value: **1.50**
Circ: CapCity orders: **19,300**
📖 Grease Monkeys **A:** Scott McDaniel **W:** D.G. Chichester ★ Versus Stiltman. ★ Versus Devil-Man.
319 ☐ Aug 1993 Cover: 1.25 **NM** value: **4.00**
Circ: CapCity orders: **20,700**
• first printing (white);Elektra returns **A:** Scott McDaniel **W:** D.G. Chichester
319-2 ☐ Aug 1993 Cover: 1.25 **NM** value: **Cover or less**
320 ☐ Sep 1993 Cover: 1.25 **NM** value: **3.50**
Circ: CapCity orders: **19,800**
📖 Fall from Grace; Fall From Grace, Part 1 • red costume destroyed;New costume **A:** Scott McDaniel **W:** D.G. Chichester ★ Appearance of Silver Sable.
321 ☐ Oct 1993 Cover: 2.00 **NM** value: **2.50**
📖 Fall from Grace; Fall From Grace, Part 2 **A:** Scott McDaniel **W:** D.G. Chichester
321/SC ☐ Oct 1993 Cover: 2.00 **NM** value: **3.00**
Circ: CapCity orders: **37,700**
Special glow-in-the-dark cover. 📖 Fall from Grace; Fall From Grace, Part 2 **A:** Scott McDaniel **W:** D.G. Chichester
322 ☐ Nov 1993 Cover: 1.25 **NM** value: **2.00**
Circ: CapCity orders: **28,200**
📖 Fall from Grace; Fall From Grace, Part 3 **A:** Scott McDaniel **W:** D.G. Chichester
323 ☐ Dec 1993 Cover: 1.25 **NM** value: **2.00**
Circ: CapCity orders: **41,150**
📖 Fall from Grace; Fall From Grace, Part 4 **A:** Scott McDaniel **W:** D.G. Chichester ★ Versus Venom.
324 ☐ Jan 1994 Cover: 1.25 **NM** value: **2.00**
Circ: Statement: **145,292** CapCity orders: **43,100**
📖 Fall From Grace, Part 5 **A:** Scott McDaniel **W:** D.G. Chichester
325 ☐ Feb 1994 Cover: 2.50 **NM** value: **3.00**
Circ: Statement: **145,292** CapCity orders: **60,975**
• Double-size. 📖 Fall From Grace, Part 6 • poster **A:** Scott McDaniel **W:** D.G. Chichester ★ Death of Hellspawn.
326 ☐ Mar 1994 Cover: 1.25 **NM** value: **1.50**
Circ: Statement: **145,292** CapCity orders: **41,550**
📖 Tree of Knowledge; Tree of Knowledge, Part 1 **A:** Scott McDaniel **W:** D.G. Chichester
327 ☐ Apr 1994 Cover: 1.25 **NM** value: **1.50**
Circ: Statement: **145,292** CapCity orders: **36,250**
📖 Tree of Knowledge, Part 2 **A:** Scott McDaniel **W:** D.G. Chichester
328 ☐ May 1994 Cover: 1.25 **NM** value: **1.50**
Circ: Statement: **145,292** CapCity orders: **32,000**
📖 Tree of Knowledge, Part 3 **A:** Scott McDaniel **W:** D.G. Chichester
329 ☐ Jun 1994 Cover: 1.50 **NM** value: **Cover or less**
Circ: Statement: **145,292** CapCity orders: **34,400**
📖 Tree of Knowledge, Part 4 **A:** Scott McDaniel **W:** D.G. Chichester

CGC-graded: Multiply prices above by **33 for 9.9 M • 16 for 9.8 NM/M • 7 for 9.6 NM+ • 5 for 9.4 NM • 2.5 for 9.2 NM- • 1.5 for 9.0 VF/NM**

330 ❑ Jul 1994 Cover: 1.50 **NM** value: **Cover or less**
Circ: Statement: **145,292** CapCity orders: **34,350**
📖 Tree of Knowledge, Part 5 • Gambit **A:** Scott McDaniel **W:** D.G. Chichester

331 ❑ Aug 1994 Cover: 1.50 **NM** value: **Cover or less**
Circ: Statement: **145,292** CapCity orders: **29,550**
📖 Tree of Knowledge

332 ❑ Sep 1994 Cover: 1.50 **NM** value: **Cover or less**
Circ: Statement: **145,292** CapCity orders: **29,100**

333 ❑ Oct 1994 Cover: 1.50 **NM** value: **Cover or less**
Circ: Statement: **145,292** CapCity orders: **24,850**
📖 Fathoms Of Humanity, Part 1

334 ❑ Nov 1994 Cover: 1.50 **NM** value: **Cover or less**
Circ: Statement: **145,292** CapCity orders: **22,700**
📖 Fathoms Of Humanity, Part 2

335 ❑ Dec 1994 Cover: 1.50 **NM** value: **Cover or less**
Circ: Statement: **145,292** CapCity orders: **21,150**
📖 Fathoms Of Humanity, Part 3 **A:** Tom Grindberg **W:** Greg Wright

336 ❑ Jan 1995 Cover: 1.50 **NM** value: **Cover or less**
Circ: Statement: **64,453** CapCity orders: **18,125**
📖 Fathoms Of Humanity, Part 4

337 ❑ Feb 1995 Cover: 1.50 **NM** value: **Cover or less**
Circ: Statement: **64,453** CapCity orders: **16,800**
📖 Fathoms Of Humanity, Part 5

338 ❑ Mar 1995 Cover: 1.50 **NM** value: **Cover or less**
Circ: Statement: **64,453** CapCity orders: **15,750**
📖 Wages of Sin, Part 1 • Has 1994 Statement, filed 10/1/94; avg print run 458,000; avg sales 143,417; avg subs 1,875; avg total paid 145,292; samples 125; office use 500; max existent 145,804; 68% of run returned

339 ❑ Apr 1995 Cover: 1.50 **NM** value: **Cover or less**
Circ: Statement: **64,453** CapCity orders: **14,550**

340 ❑ May 1995 Cover: 1.50 **NM** value: **Cover or less**
Circ: Statement: **64,453** CapCity orders: **14,175**

341 ❑ Jun 1995 Cover: 1.50 **NM** value: **Cover or less**
Circ: Statement: **64,453** CapCity orders: **13,975**

342 ❑ Jul 1995 Cover: 1.50 **NM** value: **Cover or less**
Circ: Statement: **64,453** CapCity orders: **13,475**

343 ❑ Aug 1995 Cover: 1.50 **NM** value: **Cover or less**
Circ: Statement: **64,453** CapCity orders: **12,725**

344 ❑ Sep 1995 Cover: 1.95 **NM** value: **2.00**
Circ: Statement: **64,453**
• Yellow and red-costumed Daredevil returns

345 ❑ Oct 1995 Cover: 1.95 **NM** value: **2.00**
Circ: Statement: **64,453**
• Red-costumed Daredevil returns;OverPower card inserted

346 ❑ Nov 1995 Cover: 1.95 **NM** value: **2.00**
Circ: Statement: **64,453**

347 ❑ Dec 1995 Cover: 1.95 **NM** value: **2.00**
Circ: Statement: **64,453**
• Identity of both Daredevils revealed **A:** Ron Wagner **W:** J.M. DeMatteis

348 ❑ Jan 1996 Cover: 1.95 **NM** value: **2.00**
Circ: Statement: **57,739**
cover says Dec, indicia says Jan. 📖 Purgatorio ★ Appearance of Sister Maggie, Stick.

349 ❑ Feb 1996 Cover: 1.95 **NM** value: **2.00**
Circ: Statement: **57,739**
📖 Paradiso ★ Appearance of Sister Maggie, Stick.

350 ❑ Mar 1996 Cover: 2.95 **NM** value: **Cover or less**
Circ: Statement: **57,739**
• Giant-size. 📖 Paradiso • Daredevil switches back to red costume **A:** Ron Wagner **W:** Ivan Velez Jr.; J.M. DeMatteis

350/SC ❑ Mar 1996 Cover: 3.50 **NM** value: **Cover or less**
gold ink on cover. • Giant-size. 📖 Paradiso • Daredevil switches back to red costume **A:** Ron Wagner **W:** Ivan Velez Jr.; J.M. DeMatteis

351 ❑ Apr 1996 Cover: 1.95 **NM** value: **2.00**
Circ: Statement: **57,739**
📖 Helping Hands **A:** Shawn McManus **W:** John Rozum ★ 1st Appearance of The Vice Cop.

352 ❑ May 1996 Cover: 1.95 **NM** value: **2.00**
Circ: Statement: **57,739**
📖 Smoky Mirrors **A:** Shawn McManus **W:** Ben Raab ★ Appearance of Bullseye. ★ Versus Bullseye.

353 ❑ Jun 1996 Cover: 1.95 **NM** value: **2.00**
Circ: Statement: **57,739**
★ Versus Mr. Hyde.

354 ❑ Jul 1996 Cover: 1.50 **NM** value: **Cover or less**
Circ: Statement: **57,739**
★ Appearance of Spider-Man.

355 ❑ Aug 1996 Cover: 1.50 **NM** value: **Cover or less**
Circ: Statement: **57,739**
★ Versus Pyro.

356 ❑ Sep 1996 Cover: 1.50 **NM** value: **Cover or less**
Circ: Statement: **50,256**
★ Versus Enforcers.

357 ❑ Oct 1996 Cover: 1.50 **NM** value: **Cover or less**
Circ: Statement: **50,256**
★ Versus Enforcers.

358 ❑ Nov 1996 Cover: 1.50 **NM** value: **Cover or less**
Circ: Statement: **50,256** Direct Market orders: **39,500**
• Has 1996 Statement, filed 10/1/96; avg print run 85,682; avg sales 56,564; avg subs 1,175; avg total paid 57,739; samples 600; office use 125; max existent 58,464; 32% of run returned★ Versus Mysterio.

359 ❑ Dec 1996 Cover: 1.50 **NM** value: **Cover or less**
Circ: Statement: **50,256** Direct Market orders: **38,500**
📖 The Devil You Know! **A:** Cary Nord **W:** Karl Kesel

360 ❑ Jan 1997 Cover: 1.50 **NM** value: **Cover or less**
Circ: Statement: **50,256** Direct Market orders: **38,000**
📖 Alone Against The Absorbing Man! **A:** Cary Nord **W:** Karl Kesel ★ Versus Absorbing Man.

361 ❑ Feb 1997 Cover: 1.50 **NM** value: **Cover or less**
Circ: Statement: **50,256** Direct Market orders: **37,250**
📖 Unfinished Business **A:** Cary Nord **W:** Karl Kesel ★ Appearance of Black Widow.

362 ❑ Mar 1997 Cover: 1.99 **NM** value: **Cover or less**
Circ: Statement: **50,256** Direct Market orders: **36,000**
📖 Never Look Back **A:** Cary Nord **W:** Karl Kesel

363 ❑ Apr 1997 Cover: 1.99 **NM** value: **Cover or less**
Circ: Statement: **50,256** Direct Market orders: **37,250**
📖 The City That Never Sleeps **A:** Gene Colan **W:** Karl Kesel ★ 1st Appearance of Insomnia. ★ Versus Insomnia.

364 ❑ May 1997 Cover: 1.99 **NM** value: **Cover or less**
Circ: Statement: **50,256** Diamd. preorders: **35,905**
📖 No Rest for the Wicked! **A:** Cary Nord **W:** Karl Kesel

365 ❑ Jun 1997 Cover: 1.99 **NM** value: **Cover or less**
Circ: Statement: **50,256** Diamd. preorders: **34,680**
📖 A Question of Trust **A:** Cary Nord **W:** Joe Kelly ★ Versus Molten Man.

366 ❑ Aug 1997 Cover: 1.99 **NM** value: **Cover or less**
Circ: Statement: **50,256** Diamd. preorders: **32,532**
• gatefold summary.

367 ❑ Sep 1997 Cover: 1.99 **NM** value: **Cover or less**
Circ: Statement: **39,814** Diamd. preorders: **31,709**
• gatefold summary.

368 ❑ Oct 1997 Cover: 1.99 **NM** value: **Cover or less**
Circ: Statement: **39,814** Diamd. preorders: **31,108**
• gatefold summary. ★ Versus Omega Red.

369 ❑ Nov 1997 Cover: 1.99 **NM** value: **Cover or less**
Circ: Statement: **39,814** Diamd. preorders: **30,352**
• gatefold summary.

370 ❑ Dec 1997 Cover: 1.99 **NM** value: **Cover or less**
Circ: Statement: **39,814** Diamd. preorders: **30,325**
• gatefold summary. 📖 Fallout • Has 1997 Statement, filed 10/1/97; avg print run 74,167; avg sales 50,148; avg subs 108; avg total paid 50,256; samples 161; office use 125; max existent 50,542; 32% of run returned★ Appearance of Black Widow.

371 ❑ Jan 1998 Cover: 1.99 **NM** value: **Cover or less**
Circ: Statement: **39,814** Diamd. preorders: **29,419**
• gatefold summary. • Ghost Rider

372 ❑ Feb 1998 Cover: 1.99 **NM** value: **Cover or less**
Circ: Statement: **39,814** Diamd. preorders: **28,471**
• gatefold summary. ★ Appearance of Ghost Rider.

373 ❑ Mar 1998 Cover: 1.99 **NM** value: **Cover or less**
Circ: Statement: **39,814** Diamd. preorders: **27,092**
• gatefold summary.

374 ❑ Apr 1998 Cover: 1.99 **NM** value: **Cover or less**
Circ: Statement: **39,814** Diamd. preorders: **26,174**
• gatefold summary.

375 ❑ May 1998 Cover: 2.99 **NM** value: **Cover or less**
Circ: Statement: **39,814** Diamd. preorders: **27,222**
• Giant-size. ★ Versus Mr. Fear.

376 ❑ Jun 1998 Cover: 1.99 **NM** value: **Cover or less**
Circ: Statement: **39,814** Diamd. preorders: **28,321**
Matt sent deep undercover, regains eyesight. • gatefold summary. 📖 Flying Blind, Part 1

377 ❑ Jul 1998 Cover: 1.99 **NM** value: **Cover or less**
Circ: Statement: **39,814** Diamd. preorders: **26,455**
• gatefold summary. 📖 Flying Blind, Part 2 • Matt as Laurent Levasseur with new costume

378 ❑ Aug 1998 Cover: 1.99 **NM** value: **Cover or less**
Circ: Statement: **39,814** Diamd. preorders: **26,629**
• gatefold summary. 📖 Flying Blind, Part 3

379 ❑ Sep 1998 Cover: 1.99 **NM** value: **Cover or less**
Circ: Statement: **39,814** Diamd. preorders: **25,513**
• gatefold summary. 📖 Flying Blind, Part 4 • Matt regains his identity and loses sight

380 ❑ Oct 1998 Cover: 2.99 **NM** value: **Cover or less**
Circ: Statement: **39,814** Diamd. preorders: **25,597** • **CGC:** 1 graded, best 9.6
• Giant-size. final issue.★ Appearance of Kingpin.

Anl 1 ❑ Sep 1967 Cover: 0.25 **NM** value: **25.00**
• **CGC:** 16 graded, best 9.6
• Cover reads "King-Size Special". 📖 Elektro and the Emissaries of Evil! **A:** Gene Colan

Anl 2 ❑ Feb 1971 Cover: 0.25 **NM** value: **9.00**
• **CGC:** 3 graded, best 9.8
• Cover reads "King-Size Special".

Anl 3 ❑ Cover: 0.25 **NM** value: **9.00**
• Cover reads "King-Size Special". 📖 Enter Spider-Man; None Are So Blind • Reprints Daredevil #16-17

Anl 4 ❑ Cover: 0.50 **NM** value: **5.00**
📖 The Name of the Game is Death; And Who Shall Save the Panthers?

Anl 5 ❑ Cover: 2.00 **NM** value: **4.00**
Cover # of 4 seems to be a mistake. 📖 A Friend In Need; Role Reversal; The Rescue; The Redeemed And The Condemned; Saga of The Serpent Crown, Chapter VII • Atlantis Attacks;1989 annual **A:** Mark Bagley; John Romita Jr.; Whilce Portacio **W:** Greg Wright; Gerry Conway; Peter Sanderson

Anl 6 ❑ Cover: 2.00 **NM** value: **3.00**
Circ: CapCity orders: **36,300**
📖 Predator; Truth Or Dare; Innocent Bystander?; Two Schizos • Lifeform **A:** Gary Hartle; Tom Sutton; Michael Bair; Cam Kennedy **W:** Greg Wright

Anl 7 ❑ Cover: 2.00 **NM** value: **2.50**
Circ: CapCity orders: **39,200**
📖 Crippling Death; Malicious Justice-Or Injustice; The Dark Lady; Guns Don't Kill • Von Strucker Gambit **A:** Ron Garney; Don Hudson; Larry Alexander **W:** Greg Wright; Eric Fein ★ Origin of Crippler. ★ 1st Appearance of Crippler.

Anl 8 ❑ Cover: 2.25 **NM** value: **2.50**
Circ: CapCity orders: **30,600**
📖 System Bytes; The System Bytes, Part 2 **A:** M.C. Wyman **W:** Greg Wright

Anl 9 ❑ Cover: 2.95 **NM** value: **Cover or less**
Circ: CapCity orders: **36,800**
📖 Devouring Madness, On the Clock, Resurrections • trading card **W:** Greg Wright; Glenn Headling ★ Origin of Devourer. ★ 1st Appearance of Devourer.

Anl 10 ❑ Cover: 2.95 **NM** value: **Cover or less**

Anl 1997 ❑ Sep 1997 Cover: 2.99 **NM** value: **Cover or less**
Circ: Diamd. preorders: **45,329**
• gatefold summary. • Daredevil/Deadpool '97;combined annuals for Daredevil and Deadpool

Bk 1 ❑ Cover: 6.95 **NM** value: **Cover or less**
• In Love and War

Bk 2 ❑ Cover: 19.95 **NM** value: **Cover or less**
• Fall From Grace;Collects Daredevil #319-325

Bk 3 ❑ Feb 1988 Cover: 19.95 **NM** value: **Cover or less**
📖 • Fall from Grace;collects the storyline from Daredevil #319-325

Bk 3/HC ❑ Cover: 22.90 **NM** value: **Cover or less**
• Born Again

Bk 4 ❑ Feb 1988 Cover: 9.95 **NM** value: **Cover or less**
📖 Born Again

GS 1 ❑ Cover: 0.50 **NM** value: **8.00**

DAREDEVIL/BATMAN — Marvel

1 ❑ ca. 1997 Cover: 5.99 **NM** value: **Cover or less**
Circ: Diamd. preorders: **63,958**
No issue number. • prestige format. 📖 Eye For An Eye • crossover with DC **A:** Scott McDaniel **W:** D.G. Chichester

DAREDEVIL/BLACK WIDOW: ABATTOIR — Marvel

1 ❑ Cover: 14.95 **NM** value: **Cover or less**
A: Joe Chiodo **W:** Jim Starlin

DAREDEVIL CHRONICLES, THE — Fantaco

1 ❑ Cover: 1.50 **NM** value: **2.00**
📖 D.D.'s Fact **A:** Fred Hembeck; George Pérez; John Byrne; Joe Staton; Michael T. Gilbert; Klaus Janson; Trina Robbins; Dave Simons; Steve Leialoha; Spain Rodriguez **W:** Fred Hembeck; Michael T. Gilbert; Joey Cavalieri; John Skerchock III; Mitch Cohn; Peter Sanderson; Rocco Nigro; Steve Webb

DAREDEVIL (LEV GLEASON) — Lev Gleason

Daredevil Comics began as an above-average Golden Age superhero title from quality-conscious Lev Gleason Publishing. Under the guidance of writer-artist Charles Biro, Daredevil evolved into a costume-hero venue for a variety of comics stories.

Armed with only his courage, ability, and uncanny skill with a boomerang, masked acrobat Daredevil made his debut in Silver Streak #6 (1940), taking on one of the most fearsome villains of the Golden Age, the Claw. Their epic battle spilled into the pages of Daredevil Comics in 1941, and Daredevil's solo adventures lasted for 31 action-packed issues.

At that point, Biro introduced a gang of kids called the Little Wise Guys. When one of the kids died in the course of one of the stories, it was a rare moment in comics of the days. Eventually, Daredevil unmasked and became a mentor to the kids, who eventually pushed the title character out of his own comic book.

1 ❑ Jul 1941 Cover: 0.10 **NM** value: **9000.00**
• **CGC:** 3 graded, best 7.5

2 ❑ Aug 1941 Cover: 0.10 **NM** value: **2600.00**
• **CGC:** 1 graded, best 3.0

3 ❑ Sep 1941 Cover: 0.10 **NM** value: **1500.00**
• **CGC:** 2 graded, best 9.4

4 ❑ Oct 1941 Cover: 0.10 **NM** value: **1200.00**

5 ❑ Nov 1941 Cover: 0.10 **NM** value: **1025.00**

6 ❑ Dec 1941 Cover: 0.10 **NM** value: **880.00**

7 ❑ Feb 1942 Cover: 0.10 **NM** value: **775.00**

8 ❑ Mar 1942 Cover: 0.10 **NM** value: **700.00**

9 ❑ Apr 1942 Cover: 0.10 **NM** value: **700.00**

10 ❑ May 1942 Cover: 0.10 **NM** value: **700.00**

11 ❑ Jun 1942 Cover: 0.10 **NM** value: **625.00**
• **CGC:** 1 graded, best 4.5

12 ❑ Aug 1942 Cover: 0.10 **NM** value: **950.00**
• **CGC:** 2 graded, best 8.0
★ Origin of The Claw.

13 ❑ Oct 1942 Cover: 0.10 **NM** value: **825.00**
• **CGC:** 1 graded, best 5.0
★ 1st Appearance of The Little Wise Guys.

14 ❑ Dec 1942 Cover: 0.10 **NM** value: **475.00**
• **CGC:** 1 graded, best 7.5

15 ❑ Feb 1943 Cover: 0.10 **NM** value: **575.00**

16 ❑ Apr 1943 Cover: 0.10 **NM** value: **425.00**

17 ❑ Jun 1943 Cover: 0.10 **NM** value: **425.00**

18 ❑ Aug 1943 Cover: 0.10 **NM** value: **975.00**
• **CGC:** 3 graded, best 8.0
★ Origin of Daredevil (Golden Age, New Origin).

19 ❑ Oct 1943 Cover: 0.10 **NM** value: **365.00**

20 ❑ Nov 1943 Cover: 0.10 **NM** value: **365.00**

21 ❑ Jan 1944 Cover: 0.10 **NM** value: **560.00**
• **CGC:** 1 graded, best 7.5
• The Claw begins

22 ❑ Feb 1944 Cover: 0.10 **NM** value: **275.00**

23 ❑ Apr 1944 Cover: 0.10 **NM** value: **275.00**

24 ❑ May 1944 Cover: 0.10 **NM** value: **275.00**
• **CGC:** 1 graded, best 9.0

25 ❑ Jun 1944 Cover: 0.10 **NM** value: **275.00**

26 ❑ Aug 1944 Cover: 0.10 **NM** value: **275.00**

27 ❑ Nov 1944 Cover: 0.10 **NM** value: **275.00**
• **CGC:** 1 graded, best 6.0

28 ❑ Jan 1945 Cover: 0.10 **NM** value: **275.00**
• **CGC:** 1 graded, best 9.2

29 ❑ Mar 1945 Cover: 0.10 **NM** value: **275.00**
• **CGC:** 1 graded, best 6.0

30 ❑ May 1945 Cover: 0.10 **NM** value: **275.00**
• **CGC:** 1 graded, best 9.0

31 ❑ Jul 1945 Cover: 0.10 **NM** value: **585.00**
• **CGC:** 3 graded, best 9.0
★ Death of The Claw.

32 ❑ Sep 1945 Cover: 0.10 **NM** value: **200.00**
• **CGC:** 2 graded, best 8.5

33 ❑ Nov 1945 Cover: 0.10 **NM** value: **200.00**

Other grades: Multiply prices above by **1.5 for Mint • 2/3 for Very Fine • 1/3 for Fine • 1/5 for Very Good • 1/8 for Good**

34 ❑ Jan 1946 Cover: 0.10 NM value: 200.00
• CGC: 4 graded, best 9.0
35 ❑ Mar 1946 Cover: 0.10 NM value: 200.00
• CGC: 3 graded, best 8.0
36 ❑ May 1946 Cover: 0.10 NM value: 200.00
37 ❑ Jul 1946 Cover: 0.10 NM value: 200.00
38 ❑ Sep 1946 Cover: 0.10 NM value: 275.00
★ Origin of Daredevil (Golden Age, New Origin).
39 ❑ Nov 1946 Cover: 0.10 NM value: 200.00
40 ❑ Jan 1947 Cover: 0.10 NM value: 200.00
41 ❑ Mar 1947 Cover: 0.10 NM value: 150.00
• CGC: 1 graded, best 9.2
42 ❑ May 1947 Cover: 0.10 NM value: 150.00
• CGC: 1 graded, best 9.0
43 ❑ Jul 1947 Cover: 0.10 NM value: 150.00
44 ❑ Sep 1947 Cover: 0.10 NM value: 150.00
• CGC: 1 graded, best 8.5
45 ❑ Nov 1947 Cover: 0.10 NM value: 150.00
• CGC: 1 graded, best 6.5
46 ❑ Jan 1948 Cover: 0.10 NM value: 150.00
47 ❑ Mar 1948 Cover: 0.10 NM value: 150.00
48 ❑ May 1948 Cover: 0.10 NM value: 150.00
49 ❑ Jul 1948 Cover: 0.10 NM value: 150.00
50 ❑ Sep 1948 Cover: 0.10 NM value: 150.00
• CGC: 1 graded, best 5.0
51 ❑ Nov 1948 Cover: 0.10 NM value: 115.00
52 ❑ Jan 1949 Cover: 0.10 NM value: 115.00
53 ❑ Mar 1949 Cover: 0.10 NM value: 115.00
54 ❑ May 1949 Cover: 0.10 NM value: 115.00
55 ❑ Jul 1949 Cover: 0.10 NM value: 115.00
56 ❑ Sep 1949 Cover: 0.10 NM value: 115.00
57 ❑ Nov 1949 Cover: 0.10 NM value: 115.00
58 ❑ Jan 1950 Cover: 0.10 NM value: 115.00
📖 Daredevil and the Little Wise Guys: In Their Race Against the Tricky Robbers!; Daredevil and the Little Wise Guys: Pee Wee's Case Against the Conceited Football Star!; Sniffer A: Norman Maurer; Carl Hubbell W: Carl Hubbell; Charles Biro
59 ❑ Feb 1950 Cover: 0.10 NM value: 115.00
60 ❑ Mar 1950 Cover: 0.10 NM value: 115.00
61 ❑ Apr 1950 Cover: 0.10 NM value: 90.00
62 ❑ May 1950 Cover: 0.10 NM value: 90.00
63 ❑ Jun 1950 Cover: 0.10 NM value: 90.00
64 ❑ Jul 1950 Cover: 0.10 NM value: 90.00
65 ❑ Aug 1950 Cover: 0.10 NM value: 90.00
66 ❑ Sep 1950 Cover: 0.10 NM value: 90.00
67 ❑ Oct 1950 Cover: 0.10 NM value: 90.00
68 ❑ Nov 1950 Cover: 0.10 NM value: 90.00
69 ❑ Dec 1950 Cover: 0.10 NM value: 90.00
• Daredevil features end
70 ❑ Jan 1951 Cover: 0.10 NM value: 60.00
71 ❑ Feb 1951 Cover: 0.10 NM value: 60.00
72 ❑ Mar 1951 Cover: 0.10 NM value: 60.00
73 ❑ Apr 1951 Cover: 0.10 NM value: 60.00
74 ❑ May 1951 Cover: 0.10 NM value: 60.00
75 ❑ Jun 1951 Cover: 0.10 NM value: 60.00
76 ❑ Jul 1951 Cover: 0.10 NM value: 60.00
77 ❑ Aug 1951 Cover: 0.10 NM value: 60.00
78 ❑ Sep 1951 Cover: 0.10 NM value: 60.00
79 ❑ Oct 1951 Cover: 0.10 NM value: 70.00
• Daredevil features begin again
80 ❑ Nov 1951 Cover: 0.10 NM value: 70.00
81 ❑ Dec 1951 Cover: 0.10 NM value: 55.00
82 ❑ Jan 1952 Cover: 0.10 NM value: 55.00
83 ❑ Feb 1952 Cover: 0.10 NM value: 55.00
84 ❑ Mar 1952 Cover: 0.10 NM value: 55.00
85 ❑ Apr 1952 Cover: 0.10 NM value: 55.00
86 ❑ May 1952 Cover: 0.10 NM value: 55.00
87 ❑ Jun 1952 Cover: 0.10 NM value: 55.00
88 ❑ Jul 1952 Cover: 0.10 NM value: 55.00
89 ❑ Aug 1952 Cover: 0.10 NM value: 55.00
90 ❑ Sep 1952 Cover: 0.10 NM value: 55.00
91 ❑ Oct 1952 Cover: 0.10 NM value: 55.00
92 ❑ Nov 1952 Cover: 0.10 NM value: 55.00
93 ❑ Dec 1952 Cover: 0.10 NM value: 55.00
94 ❑ Jan 1953 Cover: 0.10 NM value: 55.00
95 ❑ Feb 1953 Cover: 0.10 NM value: 55.00
96 ❑ Mar 1953 Cover: 0.10 NM value: 55.00
97 ❑ Apr 1953 Cover: 0.10 NM value: 55.00
98 ❑ May 1953 Cover: 0.10 NM value: 55.00
99 ❑ Jun 1953 Cover: 0.10 NM value: 55.00
100 ❑ Jul 1953 Cover: 0.10 NM value: 60.00
101 ❑ Aug 1953 Cover: 0.10 NM value: 45.00
102 ❑ Sep 1953 Cover: 0.10 NM value: 45.00
103 ❑ Oct 1953 Cover: 0.10 NM value: 45.00
• CGC: 1 graded, best 7.0
104 ❑ Nov 1953 Cover: 0.10 NM value: 45.00
105 ❑ Dec 1953 Cover: 0.10 NM value: 45.00
106 ❑ Jan 1954 Cover: 0.10 NM value: 45.00
107 ❑ Feb 1954 Cover: 0.10 NM value: 45.00
108 ❑ Mar 1954 Cover: 0.10 NM value: 45.00
109 ❑ Apr 1954 Cover: 0.10 NM value: 45.00
110 ❑ May 1954 Cover: 0.10 NM value: 45.00
111 ❑ 1954 Cover: 0.10 NM value: 45.00
112 ❑ 1954 Cover: 0.10 NM value: 45.00
113 ❑ 1954 Cover: 0.10 NM value: 45.00
114 ❑ Cover: 0.10 NM value: 45.00
115 ❑ Cover: 0.10 NM value: 45.00
116 ❑ Cover: 0.10 NM value: 45.00
117 ❑ Cover: 0.10 NM value: 45.00
118 ❑ 1955 Cover: 0.10 NM value: 45.00
119 ❑ 1955 Cover: 0.10 NM value: 45.00
120 ❑ 1955 Cover: 0.10 NM value: 45.00
121 ❑ 1955 Cover: 0.10 NM value: 36.00
122 ❑ 1955 Cover: 0.10 NM value: 36.00
123 ❑ 1955 Cover: 0.10 NM value: 36.00
124 ❑ 1955 Cover: 0.10 NM value: 36.00
125 ❑ 1955 Cover: 0.10 NM value: 36.00
126 ❑ Cover: 0.10 NM value: 36.00
127 ❑ Cover: 0.10 NM value: 36.00
128 ❑ Cover: 0.10 NM value: 36.00
129 ❑ Cover: 0.10 NM value: 36.00
130 ❑ 1956 Cover: 0.10 NM value: 36.00
131 ❑ 1956 Cover: 0.10 NM value: 36.00
132 ❑ 1956 Cover: 0.10 NM value: 36.00
133 ❑ Aug 1956 Cover: 0.10 NM value: 36.00
134 ❑ Sep 1956 Cover: 0.10 NM value: 36.00
final issue.

DAREDEVIL: MARKED FOR DEATH — Marvel

Bk 1 ❑ Cover: 13.45 NM value: Cover or less
Circ: CapCity orders: 650

DAREDEVIL: NINJA — Marvel

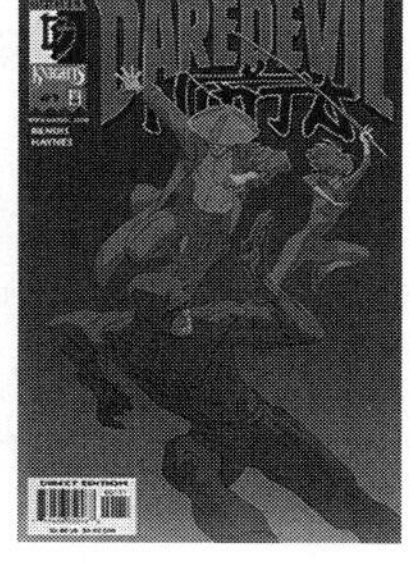

Matt Murdock, the blind lawyer known as Daredevil, has not slept well in years. How, then, was a ninja able to steal a treasured object from beneath his nose one night?

Murdock's martial arts Sensei was a man named Stick, who trained him to live with his blindness and to control his senses. Ultimately, Stick sacrificed himself to save Murdock from the deadly ninja clan known as the Hand. Now, a ninja has managed to steal the only memento Murdock had from his Sensei — the old man's staff. Murdock is determined to retrieve the staff, and to find out what mystery lies behind its theft.

1 ❑ Dec 2000 Cover: 2.99 NM value: Cover or less
Circ: Diamd. preorders: 43,843
A: David Self; Rob Haynes W: Brian Michael Bendis
2 ❑ Jan 2001 Cover: 2.99 NM value: Cover or less
Circ: Diamd. preorders: 38,576
A: David Self W: Brian Michael Bendis
3 ❑ May 2001 Cover: 2.99 NM value: Cover or less
Circ: Diamd. preorders: 36,702
A: David Self W: Brian Michael Bendis

DAREDEVIL/PUNISHER: CHILD'S PLAY — Marvel

1 ❑ Cover: 4.95 NM value: Cover or less
Circ: CapCity orders: 10,175
📖 Child's Play A: Frank Miller W: Frank Miller

DAREDEVIL/SHI — Marvel

1 ❑ Feb 1997 Cover: 2.99 NM value: 3.00
Circ: Direct Market orders: 62,500
📖 None are so Blind; Blind Faith • crossover with Crusade A: Jamal Igle; Al Williamson(inks) W: Bill Tucci; Peter Gutierrez; Christopher Golden; Tom Sniegoski

DAREDEVIL/SPIDER-MAN — Marvel

1 ❑ Jan 2001 Cover: 2.99 NM value: Cover or less
Circ: Diamd. preorders: 49,117 • CGC: 2 graded, best 9.6
📖 Unusual Suspects, Part 1; Unusual Suspects A: Phil Winslade W: Paul Jenkins
2 ❑ Feb 2001 Cover: 2.99 NM value: Cover or less
Circ: Diamd. preorders: 43,406 • CGC: 1 graded, best 9.8
📖 Unusual Suspects, Part 2: The Sting A: Phil Winslade W: Paul Jenkins
3 ❑ Mar 2001 Cover: 2.99 NM value: Cover or less
Circ: Diamd. preorders: 40,089 • CGC: 2 graded, best 9.6
📖 Unusual Suspects, Part 3: Bad Boys Don't Cry A: Phil Winslade W: Paul Jenkins
4 ❑ Apr 2001 Cover: 2.99 NM value: Cover or less
Circ: Diamd. preorders: 38,833
📖 Unusual Suspects, Part 4: Things Get Worse A: Phil Winslade W: Paul Jenkins

DAREDEVIL THE MAN WITHOUT FEAR — Marvel

1 ❑ Oct 1993 Cover: 2.95 NM value: 4.00
Circ: CapCity orders: 56,400 • CGC: 1 graded, best 9.6
Partial foil cover. A: Al Williamson; John Romita Jr. W: Frank Miller
★ Origin of Daredevil.
2 ❑ Nov 1993 Cover: 2.95 NM value: 4.00
Circ: CapCity orders: 46,300 • CGC: 1 graded, best 9.8
Partial foil cover. A: Al Williamson; John Romita Jr. W: Frank Miller
3 ❑ Dec 1993 Cover: 2.95 NM value: 4.00
Circ: CapCity orders: 46,700 • CGC: 1 graded, best 9.8
cardstock cover. A: Al Williamson; John Romita Jr. W: Frank Miller
4 ❑ Jan 1994 Cover: 2.95 NM value: 3.50
Circ: CapCity orders: 47,900 • CGC: 1 graded, best 9.6
Partial foil cover. A: Al Williamson; John Romita Jr. W: Frank Miller
5 ❑ Feb 1994 Cover: 2.95 NM value: 3.50
Circ: CapCity orders: 53,800 • CGC: 1 graded, best 9.8
cardstock cover. A: Al Williamson; John Romita Jr. W: Frank Miller
Bk 1 ❑ Cover: 15.95 NM value: Cover or less
• Collects Daredevil The Man Without Fear #1-5 A: John Romita Jr. W: Frank Miller

Capital City orders are the actual sales of comic books by Capital City Distribution, once one of the largest U.S. sellers of comics to comics shops. Capital City's share of comics shop sales, while not known exactly, increases from around 10-20% in the mid-1980s to 30-35% in the mid-1990s. Capital City's share of comic books sold on newsstands (most Marvels and DCs) will be less.

DAREDEVIL VS. VAPORA — Marvel

Despite the hokey title, this one-shot, produced in association with the Gas Appliance Manufacturers Association, is a good example of a public service comic done right. It begins as Daredevil saves a badly burned girl from a blazing apartment building. Later, the owner of the apartment turns to Daredevil's alter ego, Matt Murdock, for help in defending against an arson lawsuit. As it turns out, it wasn't the owner who started the blaze, but gas fumes from a can of gas used by the girl's father to remove some tiles. The deadly vapors, personified here as a ghostly figure called "Vapora," appear elsewhere as a woman uses gas to remove a carpet stain, and as two boys use it inside to clean their motorbikes.

Since gas fumes are heavier than air, they tend to drift in an invisible fog until they reach a spark of other source of ignition. It's a silent, deadly hazard that can easily be avoided using the lessons taught here.

1 ❑ Cover: 1.25 NM value: Cover or less
📖 A Season for Tears • Fire-prevention comic A: Mike Harris W: Mindy Newell

DAREDEVIL (VOL. 2) — Marvel

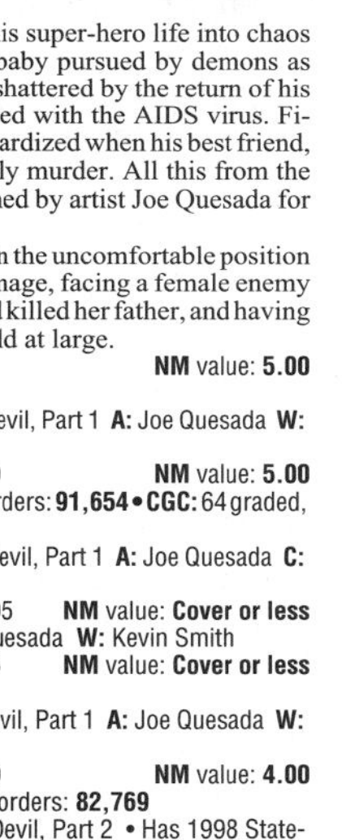

Although Matt Murdock has been blind since childhood, his other senses are heightened to a paranormal degree, allowing him to "see" far more than most people. He can read heat patterns in the air, feel vibratory echoes off the objects around him, even hear a subtle change in a heartbeat. It is with these abilities, as well as his superb agility and fighting skill, that he fights crime as Daredevil, the Man Without Fear.

This second series, bearing the Marvel Knights logo, is darker and more mysterious than the previous run, exposing Daredevil to the terrifying world of the supernatural.

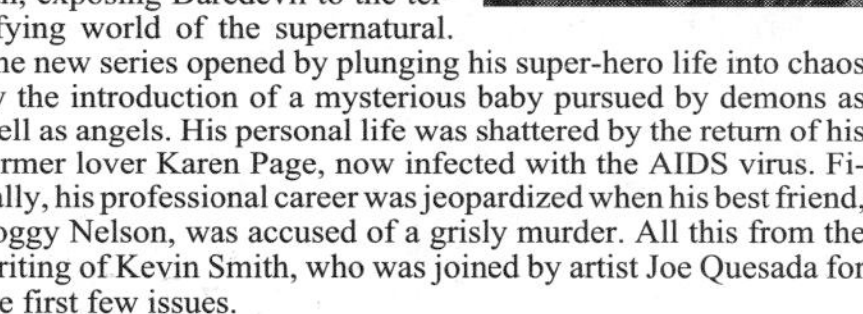

The new series opened by plunging his super-hero life into chaos by the introduction of a mysterious baby pursued by demons as well as angels. His personal life was shattered by the return of his former lover Karen Page, now infected with the AIDS virus. Finally, his professional career was jeopardized when his best friend, Foggy Nelson, was accused of a grisly murder. All this from the writing of Kevin Smith, who was joined by artist Joe Quesada for the first few issues.

Later story arcs put Matt Murdock in the uncomfortable position of suing his alter-ego for property damage, facing a female enemy who was convinced that Daredevil had killed her father, and having his identity revealed to the underworld at large.

0.5 ❑ Nov 1998 NM value: 5.00
• CGC: 22 graded, best 9.8
• gatefold summary. 📖 Guardian Devil, Part 1 A: Joe Quesada W: Kevin Smith
1 ❑ Nov 1998 Cover: 2.50 NM value: 5.00
Circ: Statement: 99,970 Diamd. preorders: 91,654 • CGC: 64 graded, best 9.8
• gatefold summary. 📖 Guardian Devil, Part 1 A: Joe Quesada C: Kevin Smith W: Kevin Smith
1/LE ❑ Nov 1998 Cover: 29.95 NM value: Cover or less
📖 Guardian Devil, Part 1 A: Joe Quesada W: Kevin Smith
1/SC ❑ Nov 1998 Cover: 6.95 NM value: Cover or less
• CGC: 12 graded, best 9.8
DFE alternate cover. 📖 Guardian Devil, Part 1 A: Joe Quesada W: Kevin Smith
2/A ❑ Dec 1998 Cover: 2.50 NM value: 4.00
Circ: Statement: 99,970 Diamd. preorders: 82,769
• gatefold summary. 📖 Guardian Devil, Part 2 • Has 1998 Statement, filed 10/1/98; avg print run 59,408; avg sales 38,193; avg subs 1,621; avg total paid 39,814; samples 161; office use 125; max existent 40,100; 33% of run returned A: Joe Quesada C: Kevin Smith W: Kevin Smith
2/B ❑ Dec 1998 Cover: 2.50 NM value: 4.00
Circ: Statement: 99,970
📖 Guardian Devil, Part 2 A: Joe Quesada W: Kevin Smith
3 ❑ Jan 1999 Cover: 2.50 NM value: 3.00
Circ: Statement: 99,970 Diamd. preorders: 81,686 • CGC: 2 graded, best 9.6
• gatefold summary. 📖 Guardian Devil, Part 3, Dystopia • Matt quits law firm A: Joe Quesada C: Kevin Smith W: Kevin Smith ★ Appearance of Karen Page, Foggy Nelson.
4 ❑ Feb 1999 Cover: 2.50 NM value: 3.00
Circ: Statement: 99,970 Diamd. preorders: 83,414 • CGC: 1 graded, best 9.6
📖 Guardian Devil, Part 4 A: Joe Quesada W: Kevin Smith
5 ❑ Mar 1999 Cover: 2.50 NM value: 3.00
Circ: Statement: 99,970 Diamd. preorders: 83,669 • CGC: 3 graded, best 9.6
📖 Guardian Devil, Part 5 A: Joe Quesada W: Kevin Smith ★ Appearance of Mephisto, Doctor Strange. ★ Death of Karen Page. ★ Versus Bullseye.
6 ❑ Apr 1999 Cover: 2.50 NM value: 3.00
Circ: Statement: 99,970 Diamd. preorders: 79,591 • CGC: 1 graded, best 9.2
📖 Guardian Devil, Part 6 A: Joe Quesada W: Kevin Smith ★ Versus Mysterio.

CGC-graded: Multiply prices above by **33 for 9.9 M • 16 for 9.8 NM/M • 7 for 9.6 NM+ • 5 for 9.4 NM • 2.5 for 9.2 NM- • 1.5 for 9.0 VF/NM**

7 ❑ May 1999 Cover: 2.50 **NM** value: **Cover or less**
Circ: Statement: **99,970** Diamd. preorders: **81,311** • **CGC:** 1 graded, best 9.6
W: Kevin Smith ★ Death of Mysterio.

8 ❑ Jun 1999 Cover: 2.50 **NM** value: **Cover or less**
Circ: Statement: **99,970** Diamd. preorders: **86,046** • **CGC:** 1 graded, best 9.6
• Karen's funeral **W:** Kevin Smith ★ Appearance of Spider-Man.

9 ❑ Dec 1999 Cover: 2.50 **NM** value: **Cover or less**
Circ: Diamd. preorders: **73,707** • **CGC:** 1 graded, best 9.6
• Has 1999 Statement, filed 10/1/99; avg print run 118,742; avg sales 98,457; avg subs 1,513; avg total paid 99,970; samples 600; office use 125; max existent 100,695; 15% of run returned

10 ❑ 2000 Cover: 2.99 **NM** value: **Cover or less**
Circ: Diamd. preorders: **74,555**

11 ❑ 2000 Cover: 2.99 **NM** value: **Cover or less**
Circ: Diamd. preorders: **66,447**

12 ❑ 2000 Cover: 2.99 **NM** value: **Cover or less**
Circ: Diamd. preorders: **75,640**

13 ❑ Oct 2000 Cover: 2.99 **NM** value: **Cover or less**
Circ: Statement: **78,867** Diamd. preorders: **66,489**
📖 Trial and Error • Trial of Kingpin

14 ❑ Mar 2001 Cover: 2.99 **NM** value: **Cover or less**
Circ: Statement: **78,867** Diamd. preorders: **63,772** • **CGC:** 1 graded, best 9.6
📖 An Object in Motion **A:** David Ross; Joe Quesada **W:** David Mack

15 ❑ Apr 2001 Cover: 2.99 **NM** value: **Cover or less**
Circ: Statement: **78,867** Diamd. preorders: **61,501**
📖 Parts of a Hole, Conclusion **A:** David Ross **W:** David Mack

16 ❑ May 2001 Cover: 2.99 **NM** value: **Cover or less**
Circ: Statement: **78,867** Diamd. preorders: **64,208** • **CGC:** 1 graded, best 9.8

17 ❑ Jun 2001 Cover: 2.99 **NM** value: **Cover or less**
Circ: Statement: **78,867** Diamd. preorders: **64,026**

18 ❑ Jul 2001 Cover: 2.99 **NM** value: **Cover or less**
Circ: Statement: **78,867** Diamd. preorders: **62,970**

19 ❑ Aug 2001 Cover: 2.99 **NM** value: **Cover or less**
Circ: Statement: **78,867** Diamd. preorders: **62,321**

20 ❑ Sep 2001 Cover: 2.99 **NM** value: **Cover or less**
Circ: Statement: **78,867** Diamd. preorders: **61,926**

21 ❑ Oct 2001 Cover: 2.99 **NM** value: **Cover or less**
Circ: Diamd. preorders: **61,262**

22 ❑ 2001 Cover: 2.99 **NM** value: **Cover or less**
23 ❑ 2001 Cover: 2.99 **NM** value: **Cover or less**
24 ❑ Nov 2001 Cover: 2.99 **NM** value: **Cover or less**
Circ: Diamd. preorders: **55,448**

25 ❑ Dec 2001 Cover: 2.99 **NM** value: **Cover or less**
Circ: Diamd. preorders: **55,505**

26 ❑ Jan 2002 Cover: 2.99 **NM** value: **Cover or less**
Circ: Diamd. preorders: **56,566** • **CGC:** 3 graded, best 9.8

27 ❑ Feb 2002 Cover: 2.99 **NM** value: **Cover or less**
Circ: Diamd. preorders: **53,115**

28 ❑ Mar 2002 Cover: 2.99 **NM** value: **Cover or less**
Circ: Diamd. preorders: **53,451**
• Has 2001 Statement, filed 10/1/2001; avg print run 104,786; avg sales 76,461; avg subs 2,406; avg total paid 78,867; samples 600; office use 0; max existent 79,467; 24% of run returned

29 ❑ Apr 2002 Cover: 2.99 **NM** value: **Cover or less**
Circ: Diamd. preorders: **51,534**

Bk 1❑ Jan 1999 Cover: 9.95 **NM** value: **Cover or less**
• collects #1-3 plus sketchbook

DAREDEVIL: YELLOW — Marvel

1 ❑ Aug 2001 Cover: 3.50 **NM** value: **Cover or less**
Circ: Diamd. preorders: **74,761** • **CGC:** 54 graded, best 9.9

2 ❑ Sep 2001 Cover: 3.50 **NM** value: **Cover or less**
Circ: Diamd. preorders: **70,149**

3 ❑ Oct 2001 Cover: 3.50 **NM** value: **Cover or less**
Circ: Diamd. preorders: **70,877**

4 ❑ Nov 2001 Cover: 3.50 **NM** value: **Cover or less**
Circ: Diamd. preorders: **64,025**

5 ❑ Dec 2001 Cover: 3.50 **NM** value: **Cover or less**
Circ: Diamd. preorders: **60,437**

6 ❑ Jan 2002 Cover: 3.50 **NM** value: **Cover or less**
Circ: Diamd. preorders: **59,446**

DARERAT/TADPOLE — Mighty Pumpkin

1 ❑ Feb 1987, b&w Cover: 1.95 **NM** value: **Cover or less**
• parody of Frank Miller's Daredevil work;flip book with Tadpole: Prankster back-up;color poster

DARE THE IMPOSSIBLE — Fleetway-Quality

1 ❑ Cover: 1.95 **NM** value: **2.00**
2 ❑ Cover: 1.95 **NM** value: **2.00**
📖 Waterworld
3 ❑ Cover: 1.95 **NM** value: **2.00**
4 ❑ Cover: 1.95 **NM** value: **2.00**
5 ❑ Cover: 1.95 **NM** value: **2.00**
6 ❑ Cover: 1.95 **NM** value: **2.00**
7 ❑ Cover: 1.95 **NM** value: **2.00**
8 ❑ Cover: 1.95 **NM** value: **2.00**
9 ❑ Cover: 1.95 **NM** value: **2.00**
10 ❑ Cover: 1.95 **NM** value: **2.00**
11 ❑ Cover: 1.95 **NM** value: **2.00**
12 ❑ Cover: 1.95 **NM** value: **2.00**
13 ❑ Cover: 1.95 **NM** value: **2.00**
14 ❑ Cover: 1.95 **NM** value: **2.00**
📖 The Servant Awakes
15 ❑ Cover: 1.95 **NM** value: **2.00**
• Final issue?

DARIA JONTAK — JMJ

1 ❑ Jan 2001 Cover: 4.99 **NM** value: **Cover or less**
A: Matt Busch **W:** Matt Busch

DARING ADVENTURES — I.W.

9 ❑ ca. 1963 Cover: 0.12 **NM** value: **20.00**
• **CGC:** 1 graded, best 8.5
10 ❑ ca. 1963 Cover: 0.12 **NM** value: **20.00**
11 ❑ ca. 1964 Cover: 0.12 **NM** value: **20.00**
12 ❑ ca. 1964 Cover: 0.12 **NM** value: **40.00**
13 ❑ ca. 1964 Cover: 0.12 **NM** value: **20.00**
14 ❑ ca. 1964 Cover: 0.12 **NM** value: **20.00**
15 ❑ ca. 1964 Cover: 0.12 **NM** value: **20.00**
16 ❑ ca. 1964 Cover: 0.12 **NM** value: **20.00**
17 ❑ ca. 1964 Cover: 0.12 **NM** value: **20.00**
18 ❑ ca. 1964 Cover: 0.12 **NM** value: **20.00**

DARING ADVENTURES — B Comics

1 ❑ 1993 Cover: 1.50 **NM** value: **2.00**
2 ❑ Jul 1993 Cover: 2.00 **NM** value: **Cover or less**
3 ❑ 1993 Cover: 2.00 **NM** value: **Cover or less**

DARING ESCAPES — Image

1 ❑ Sep 1998 Cover: 2.50 **NM** value: **Cover or less**
Circ: Diamd. preorders: **24,667**
📖 Heart of the Matter **A:** Alan Weiss; Art Nichols **W:** Andrew Grossberg; Tom Orzechowski

1/SC❑Sep 1998 Cover: 2.50 **NM** value: **Cover or less**
alternate cover.

2 ❑ Oct 1998 Cover: 2.50 **NM** value: **Cover or less**
Circ: Diamd. preorders: **14,154**
📖 Matters of Heart **A:** Alan Weiss; Jim Fern **W:** Andrew Grossberg; Tom Orzechowski

3 ❑ Nov 1998 Cover: 2.50 **NM** value: **Cover or less**
Circ: Diamd. preorders: **11,745**

4 ❑ Dec 1998 Cover: 2.50 **NM** value: **Cover or less**
Circ: Diamd. preorders: **8,285**

DARING HERO — King-Ganteaume

1 ❑ Cover: 0.06 **NM** value: **16.00**
📖 The Flying Sharks; Dambuster; Red Jarrett

2 ❑ Cover: 0.06 **NM** value: **10.00**
📖 Inspector Janvier Meets the Black Rose!; Hootshaw; Betrayed!; Holly Vine: Hollywood Detective • Alternate pages in color

3 ❑ Cover: 0.06 **NM** value: **10.00**
📖 Devlin of the Red Devils; Lofty Gaunt; Salvage Pirates

DARING LOVE — Gilmore

1 ❑ ca. 1953 Cover: 0.10 **NM** value: **500.00**

DARING MYSTERY COMICS — Timely

1 ❑ Jan 1940 Cover: 0.10 **NM** value: **18000.00**
2 ❑ Feb 1940 Cover: 0.10 **NM** value: **2500.00**
3 ❑ Apr 1940 Cover: 0.10 **NM** value: **2500.00**
4 ❑ May 1940 Cover: 0.10 **NM** value: **2500.00**
• **CGC:** 2 graded, best 8.0
5 ❑ Jun 1940 Cover: 0.10 **NM** value: **2500.00**
• **CGC:** 2 graded, best 8.0
6 ❑ Sep 1940 Cover: 0.10 **NM** value: **2500.00**
7 ❑ Apr 1941 Cover: 0.10 **NM** value: **2500.00**
• **CGC:** 3 graded, best 7.0
8 ❑ Jan 1942 Cover: 0.10 **NM** value: **2500.00**
10 ❑ Win 1944 Cover: 0.10 **NM** value: **8000.00**
• **CGC:** 1 graded, best 8.0
11 ❑ Sum 1945 Cover: 0.10 **NM** value: **5000.00**
• **CGC:** 6 graded, best 9.4
12 ❑ Fal 1945 Cover: 0.10 **NM** value: **2500.00**
• **CGC:** 4 graded, best 7.0

DARING NEW ADVENTURES OF SUPERGIRL, THE — DC

Supergirl, a super-human Kryptonian hidden behind the facade of a shy brunette teen, found her way to Earth as a 15-year-old and quickly hooked up with her cousin, Superman. Since Superman has crime in Metropolis pretty much under control, after graduating from high school, Supergirl finds herself battling villains in San Francisco and Chicago.

This brief series shortened its name to Supergirl in 1983 but ended its run altogether less than a year later. Supergirl went back to making occasional appearances as a guest super-heroine, eventually dying in Crisis on Infinite Earths #7.

1 ❑ Nov 1982 Cover: 0.60 **NM** value: **2.50**
• **CGC:** 9 graded, best 9.8
📖 A Very Strange And Special Girl **A:** Carmine Infantino **W:** Paul Kupperberg ★ Origin of Supergirl. ★ 1st Appearance of Psi.

2 ❑ Dec 1982 Cover: 0.60 **NM** value: **2.00**
• **CGC:** 3 graded, best 9.8

3 ❑ Jan 1983 Cover: 0.60 **NM** value: **2.00**
• **CGC:** 1 graded, best 9.6
★ 1st Appearance of The Council.

4 ❑ Feb 1983 Cover: 0.60 **NM** value: **1.50**
★ 1st Appearance of The Gang.

5 ❑ Mar 1983 Cover: 0.60 **NM** value: **1.50**
• **CGC:** 1 graded, best 9.8

6 ❑ Apr 1983 Cover: 0.60 **NM** value: **1.50**
★ 1st Appearance of Matrix-Prime.

7 ❑ May 1983 Cover: 0.60 **NM** value: **1.50**
• **CGC:** 1 graded, best 9.8

8 ❑ Jun 1983 Cover: 0.60 **NM** value: **1.50**
• **CGC:** 1 graded, best 9.9
★ 1st Appearance of Reactron. ★ Appearance of The Doom Patrol.

9 ❑ Jul 1983 Cover: 0.60 **NM** value: **1.50**
★ Appearance of The Doom Patrol.

10 ❑ Aug 1983 Cover: 0.60 **NM** value: **1.50**
11 ❑ Sep 1983 Cover: 0.60 **NM** value: **1.50**
12 ❑ Oct 1983 Cover: 0.60 **NM** value: **1.50**
13 ❑ Nov 1983 Cover: 0.60 **NM** value: **1.50**
• New costume;Series continues after this issue as "Supergirl" ★ 1st Appearance of Blackstarr.

DARK, THE — Continuüm

1 ❑ Jan 1995 Cover: 2.00 **NM** value: **Cover or less**
A: Mark D. Bright; Dan Panosian

1/A ❑ Jan 1995 Cover: 2.50 **NM** value: **Cover or less**
enhanced cover.

2 ❑ Feb 1995 Cover: 2.25 **NM** value: **Cover or less**
A: Larry Stroman; Rick Bryant

3 ❑ Mar 1995 Cover: 2.50 **NM** value: **Cover or less**
A: Mark D. Bright; Dan Panosian; Robert Campanella; Jerry Acerno

4 ❑ Apr 1995 Cover: 2.50 **NM** value: **Cover or less**
A: Mark D. Bright **C:** George Pérez

DARK ADVENTURES — Darkline

1 ❑ Cover: 1.25 **NM** value: **Cover or less**
2 ❑ Cover: 1.75 **NM** value: **Cover or less**
3 ❑ Cover: 1.50 **NM** value: **Cover or less**
Circ: CapCity orders: **1,360**
4 ❑ Cover: 1.25 **NM** value: **Cover or less**
★ 1st Appearance of Terror Knight.

DARK AGES — Alternate Concepts

1 ❑ Cover: 3.75 **NM** value: **Cover or less**
📖 Swords in Charahand; Scot the Marauder! Stupid Knights; Thunder **A:** Chas Gillen(back cover); Earl Green; Linc Polderman; Marty Webber; Richard Tomasic **W:** Linc Polderman; Richard Tomasic; John Barrett; Johnny Lauck

DARK ANGEL (1ST SERIES) — Boneyard

1 ❑ May 1997, b&w Cover: 2.95 **NM** value: **Cover or less**
A: Hart Fisher **W:** Hart Fisher

2 ❑ Sep 1991 Cover: 2.25 **NM** value: **Cover or less**
📖 Jack the Green **A:** Hart Fisher **W:** Hart Fisher

3 ❑ Oct 1991 Cover: 2.25 **NM** value: **Cover or less**
📖 The Marking **A:** Hart Fisher **W:** Hart Fisher

DARK ANGEL (2ND SERIES) — Marvel

When Ranulph Haldane was suddenly (err...) removed from the board of MyS-TECH, his daughter, Shevaun, is ready to assume his place. Over the years, Shevaun has learned of the abuses and dark dealings that MyS-TECH has indulged in over the years, and she makes it her mission to put things right. She's aided in this quest by a strange encounter with Darkangel, the Angel of Death. He cloaks her in a costume made from the very fabric of the universe, a costume which adds greatly to her own mystical powers. Shevaun Haldane thus becomes Hell's Angel — an otherworldly avenger and MyS-TECH's worst nightmare.

Formerly known as Hell's Angel, the series changed names with #6 in response to a lawsuit brought against Marvel by the Hell's Angels motorcycle club.

6 ❑ Dec 1992 Cover: 1.75 **NM** value: **Cover or less**
📖 Bad Blood • Title changes to Dark Angel;Series continued from Hell's Angel #5 **A:** Gary Frank **W:** Simon Furman ★ Appearance of Excalibur.

7 ❑ Jan 1993 Cover: 1.75 **NM** value: **Cover or less**
Circ: CapCity orders: **15,000**
📖 Model Soldiers, Part 1 **A:** Duke Mighten **W:** Gary Russell ★ Appearance of Psylocke.

8 ❑ Feb 1993 Cover: 1.75 **NM** value: **Cover or less**
Circ: CapCity orders: **13,800**
📖 Model Soldiers, Part 2 **A:** Duke Mighten **W:** Gary Russell ★ Appearance of Psylocke.

9 ❑ Apr 1993 Cover: 1.75 **NM** value: **Cover or less**
Circ: CapCity orders: **12,200**
📖 Assassination, Part 1 **A:** Dell Barras **W:** Bernie Jaye

10 ❑ May 1993 Cover: 1.75 **NM** value: **Cover or less**
Circ: CapCity orders: **12,200**

11 ❑ Jun 1993 Cover: 1.75 **NM** value: **Cover or less**
Circ: CapCity orders: **11,800**

12 ❑ Jul 1993 Cover: 1.75 **NM** value: **Cover or less**
Circ: CapCity orders: **10,800**

13 ❑ Aug 1993 Cover: 1.75 **NM** value: **Cover or less**
Circ: CapCity orders: **9,800**

14 ❑ Sep 1993 Cover: 1.75 **NM** value: **Cover or less**
Circ: CapCity orders: **7,100**

15 ❑ Oct 1993 Cover: 1.75 **NM** value: **Cover or less**
Circ: CapCity orders: **6,200**
A: Salvador Larroca **W:** Bernie Jaye ★ Appearance of Death's Head II, Techno Wizards.

16 ❑ Nov 1993 Cover: 1.75 **NM** value: **Cover or less**
Circ: CapCity orders: **5,600**

17 ❑ Dec 1993 Cover: 1.75 **NM** value: **Cover or less**
Circ: CapCity orders: **4,950**
final issue.

DARK ANGEL (3RD SERIES) — Boneyard

1 ❑ 1997 Cover: 4.95 **NM** value: **Cover or less**
📖 No Time for Tears; Lubricant; Whore **A:** Matt Roach; Jason Morgan; Joe Janovski **W:** Hart Fisher; Joe Janovski; Bill Yukich

2 ❑ Aug 1997 Cover: 1.95 **NM** value: **Cover or less**
📖 A Quiet Prequel **A:** James Helkowski **W:** Hart Fisher

3 ❑ Sep 1997 Cover: 1.95 **NM** value: **Cover or less**
A: James Helkowski **W:** Hart Fisher

Other grades: Multiply prices above by **1.5 for Mint** • **2/3 for Very Fine** • **1/3 for Fine** • **1/5 for Very Good** • **1/8 for Good**

DARK ANGEL: DEATH DREAMS — Boneyard

1 ❑ Cover: 2.75 **NM value: Cover or less**
📖 The Duffy Bag; No Time For Tears (text story); **A:** Hart Fisher; Daniel Presidio **W:** Hart Fisher

DARK ANGEL: PHOENIX RESURRECTION — Image

1 ❑ May 2000 Cover: 2.95 **NM value: Cover or less**
Circ: Diamd. preorders: **22,400** • **CGC:** 1 graded, best 9.8
A: Kia Asamiya **W:** Kia Asamiya
2 ❑ Aug 2000 Cover: 2.95 **NM value: Cover or less**
Circ: Diamd. preorders: **16,338**
A: Kia Asamiya **W:** Kia Asamiya
3 ❑ Mar 2001 Cover: 2.95 **NM value: Cover or less**
Circ: Diamd. preorders: **15,655**
A: Kia Asamiya **W:** Kia Asamiya

DARK ASSASSIN — Silverwolf

1 ❑ Feb 1987 Cover: 1.50 **NM value: Cover or less**
A: Paul Martin **W:** Kris Silver

DARK, THE (AUGUST HOUSE) — August House

1 ❑ May 1995 Cover: 2.50 **NM value: Cover or less**
Circ: CapCity orders: **2,430**
enhanced cover.

DARKCHYLDE BATTLEBOOK — WildStorm

1/A ❑ Cover: 3.99 **NM value: Cover or less**
• Randy Queen maneuver card **A:** Randy Queen **W:** Rick Leonardi
1/B ❑ Cover: 3.99 **NM value: Cover or less**
• Billy Tucci maneuver card **A:** Randy Queen; Billy Tucci(cover) **W:** Rick Leonardi

DARKCHYLDE (IMAGE) — Image

0/A ❑ Mar 1998 Cover: 2.50 **NM value: Cover or less**
Circ: Diamd. preorders: **60,598**
A: Randy Queen **W:** Randy Queen
0/B ❑ Mar 1998 Cover: 2.50 **NM value: Cover or less**
A: Randy Queen **W:** Randy Queen
0/C ❑ Mar 1998 Cover: 2.50 **NM value: Cover or less**
A: Randy Queen **W:** Randy Queen
0.5 ❑ Aug 1997 **NM value: 4.00**
• Wizard 1/2 edition. • purple background, girl sitting on skull **A:** Randy Queen **W:** Randy Queen
0.5/SC❑Aug 1997 **NM value: 4.00**
• Wizard 1/2 edition. • Black background, demoness **A:** Randy Queen **W:** Randy Queen
1 ❑ Cover: 2.50 **NM value: 5.00**
• **CGC:** 4 graded, best 9.8
A: Randy Queen **W:** Randy Queen
1/AE❑ **NM value: 5.00**
• **CGC:** 2 graded, best 9.6
• American Entertainment variant **A:** Randy Queen **W:** Randy Queen
1/B ❑ Cover: 2.50 **NM value: 6.00**
• **CGC:** 2 graded, best 9.8
• Magazine-style variant. **A:** Randy Queen **W:** Randy Queen
1/C ❑ Cover: 2.50 **NM value: 5.00**
• **CGC:** 2 graded, best 9.6
📖 A Treasury of Sorrows • San Diego Comic-Con variant (Darkchylde with wings standing on front);Flip-book with Glory/Angela #1 **A:** Randy Queen **W:** Randy Queen
2 ❑ Cover: 2.50 **NM value: 3.50**
A: Randy Queen **W:** Randy Queen
2/A ❑ **NM value: 3.50**
• **CGC:** 1 graded, best 9.2
Spider-Web/Moon variant cover. **A:** Randy Queen **W:** Randy Queen
3 ❑ Cover: 2.50 **NM value: 3.00**
A: Randy Queen **W:** Randy Queen
3/A ❑ **NM value: 3.00**
• **CGC:** 2 graded, best 9.6
• All-white variant **A:** Randy Queen **W:** Randy Queen
4/A ❑ Mar 1997 Cover: 2.50 **NM value: 3.00**
Circ: Diamd. preorders: **55,520**
• was Maximum Press title;Image begins as publisher **A:** Randy Queen **W:** Randy Queen
4/B ❑ Mar 1997 Cover: 2.50 **NM value: 3.00**
• **CGC:** 4 graded, best 9.6
alternate cover. • "Fear" Edition. • Image begins as publisher **A:** Randy Queen **W:** Randy Queen
5/A ❑ Sep 1997 Cover: 2.50 **NM value: Cover or less**
Circ: Diamd. preorders: **54,234**
variant cover. **A:** Randy Queen **W:** Randy Queen
5/B ❑ Sep 1997 Cover: 2.50 **NM value: Cover or less**
alternate cover. **A:** Randy Queen **W:** Randy Queen
5/C ❑ Sep 1997 Cover: 2.50 **NM value: Cover or less**
alternate cover. **A:** Randy Queen **W:** Randy Queen
Ash 1❑ **NM value: 3.00**
• Preview edition. **A:** Randy Queen **W:** Randy Queen
Ash 1/GO❑ **NM value: 5.00**
• Preview edition. • Gold logo **A:** Randy Queen **W:** Randy Queen
Ash 1/LE❑ **NM value: 7.00**
A: Randy Queen **W:** Randy Queen
Bk 1❑ Cover: 19.95 **NM value: Cover or less**
• The Descent;polybagged with '98 preview;Collects Darkchylde #1-5 **A:** Randy Queen **W:** Randy Queen

DARKCHYLDE (MAXIMUM) — Maximum

1 ❑ Jun 1996 Cover: 2.50 **NM value: 5.00**
2 ❑ Jul 1996 Cover: 2.50 **NM value: 3.50**
3 ❑ Sep 1996 Cover: 2.50 **NM value: 3.00**

DARKCHYLDE/PAINKILLER JANE — WildStorm

Ash 1❑ **NM value: 4.00**

DARKCHYLDE REMASTERED — Image

0 ❑ Mar 1998 Cover: 2.50 **NM value: Cover or less**
1/A ❑ May 1997 Cover: 2.50 **NM value: Cover or less**
Circ: Diamd. preorders: **44,511**
• reprints Darkchylde #1 with corrections
1/B ❑ May 1997 Cover: 2.50 **NM value: Cover or less**
Circ: Diamd. preorders: **4,626**
alternate cover. • reprints Darkchylde #1 with corrections
2 ❑ Sep 1998 Cover: 2.50 **NM value: Cover or less**
Circ: Diamd. preorders: **19,390**
• reprints Darkchylde #2 with corrections
3 ❑ Nov 1998 Cover: 2.50 **NM value: Cover or less**
Circ: Diamd. preorders: **18,697**
• reprints Darkchylde #3 with corrections

DARKCHYLDE SKETCHBOOK — Image

1 ❑ ca. 1998 **NM value: 5.00**
A: Randy Queen

DARKCHYLDE SUMMER SWIMSUIT SPECTACULAR — DC / Wildstorm

1 ❑ Aug 1999 Cover: 3.95 **NM value: Cover or less**
Circ: Diamd. preorders: **28,698**
• pin-ups **A:** Nelson DeCastro; Joe Chiodo; Jason Johnson; Ron Adrian; J.G. Jones; Jim Lee; Mike Wieringo; Tommy Yune; Rod Pereira; Peter Vale; Randy Queen; Andy Kuhm

DARKCHYLDE SWIMSUIT ILLUSTRATED — Image

Seemingly inspired by the Marvel Swimsuit Special and Lady Death in Lingerie pinup-style books that preceded it, this one-shot features Randy Queen's mysterious heroine, Ariel Chylde, in a potpourri of provocative poses, wearing a variety of thongs and nominal tops. This special fills the gap between the end of the Darkchylde limited series and the beginning of the ongoing series. Several noteworthy artists are represented in this collection, including Jim Lee, Mike Wieringo, Brandon Peterson, Ethan Van Sciver, and Joe Chiodo.

Certainly, an adequate package for fans of "Bad Girl Art."

1 ❑ ca. 1998 Cover: 2.50 **NM value: 3.00**
Circ: Diamd. preorders: **36,320**
• pin-ups **A:** Ethan Van Sciver; Jim Lee; Brandon Peterson; Steve Firchow; Mike Wieringo; Keu Cha; Randy Queen; Chance Wolf; Jeff Piterelli
1/GO❑ **NM value: 4.00**
• Gold logo **A:** Ethan Van Sciver; Jim Lee; Brandon Peterson; Steve Firchow; Mike Wieringo; Keu Cha; Randy Queen; Chance Wolf; Jeff Piterelli

DARKCHYLDE THE DIARY — Image

1/A ❑ Jun 1997 Cover: 2.50 **NM value: Cover or less**
• pin-ups with diary entries
1/B ❑ Jun 1997 Cover: 2.50 **NM value: Cover or less**
alternate cover. • pin-ups with diary entries
1/C ❑ Jun 1997 Cover: 2.50 **NM value: Cover or less**
alternate cover. • pin-ups with diary entries
1/D ❑ Jun 1997 Cover: 2.50 **NM value: Cover or less**
alternate cover. • pin-ups with diary entries

DARKCHYLDE: THE LEGACY — Image

1 ❑ Aug 1998 Cover: 2.50 **NM value: 3.00**
Circ: Diamd. preorders: **83,417**
cardstock cover. **A:** Randy Queen **W:** Randy Queen
1/A ❑ Aug 1998 **NM value: 15.00**
DFE alternate chrome cover. **A:** Randy Queen **W:** Randy Queen
1/SC❑Aug 1998 **NM value: 12.00**
DFE alternate chrome cover. **A:** Randy Queen **W:** Randy Queen
2 ❑ Dec 1998 Cover: 2.50 **NM value: Cover or less**
Circ: Diamd. preorders: **53,858**
A: Randy Queen **W:** Randy Queen
2/SC❑Dec 1998 Cover: 2.50 **NM value: 3.00**
alternate cover. **A:** Randy Queen **W:** Randy Queen
3 ❑ Jun 1999 Cover: 2.50 **NM value: Cover or less**
Circ: Diamd. preorders: **40,982**
A: Randy Queen **W:** Randy Queen

DARK CITY CHRONICLES — Culture

1 ❑ Cover: 3.50 **NM value: Cover or less**
📖 To Feel Human **A:** Christian Zanier **W:** Christian Zanier

DARK CLAW ADVENTURES — DC / Amalgam

Mix Wolverine with Batman Adventures and what do you get? A square-jawed, caped crusader with extensible claws and a mutant healing factor! Yes, the Dark Claw adventures is yet another Amalgam one-shot, blending familiar Marvel and DC characters into new "amalgams" as part of a special joint-publishing exercise between the two giant comic companies.

In this one-shot special, Logan (a.k.a. the Dark Claw) is being stalked by a cyborg assassin with adamantium claws. Who is this cyberfemme fatale? None other than Talia, the daughter of Ra's A-Pocalypse, a villain killed by Dark Claw years ago. Once Talia was a sweetheart of Logan's, but now she's upgraded her weaponry and wants revenge!

1 ❑ Jun 1997 Cover: 1.95 **NM value: Cover or less**
Circ: Diamd. preorders: **130,403** • **CGC:** 1 graded, best 9.4
📖 Face to Face **A:** Rick Burchett; Ty Templeton **W:** Ty Templeton

DARK COMICS — Imperial

1 ❑ Cover: 1.80 **NM value: 2.00**

DARK CONVENTION BOOK, THE — Continuüm

1 ❑ Cover: 1.95 **NM value: Cover or less**

DARK CROSSINGS — Image

1 ❑ Jun 2000 Cover: 5.95 **NM value: Cover or less**
Circ: Diamd. preorders: **37,045**
📖 Dark Clouds Rising **A:** Dwayne Tucker **W:** Charles Holland
2 ❑ Oct 2000 Cover: 5.95 **NM value: Cover or less**
📖 Dark Clouds Overhead **A:** Dwayne Tucker **W:** Charles Holland

DARK CROSSINGS: DARK CLOUDS OVERHEAD — Image

1 ❑ Jun 2000 Cover: 5.95 **NM value: Cover or less**
cover says Dark Crossings: Dark Clouds Rising. • prestige format. **A:** Dwayne Tucker **W:** Charles Holland ★ Appearance of Witchblade, Tomb Raider, Darkness.

DARK CRYSTAL, THE — Marvel

1 ❑ Apr 1983 Cover: 0.60 **NM value: 1.25**
A: Bret Blevins **W:** David Anthony Kraft
2 ❑ May 1983 Cover: 0.60 **NM value: 1.25**

DARK DESTINY — Alpha

1 ❑ Nov 1994 Cover: 3.50 **NM value: Cover or less**
📖 Giant in the Earth **A:** Seppo Makkinen **W:** Martin Powell

DARKDEVIL — Marvel

1 ❑ Nov 2000 Cover: 2.99 **NM value: Cover or less**
📖 From the Abyss …!; The Cursed! **A:** Al Milgrom; Ron Frenz **W:** Ron Frenz; Tom DeFalco
2 ❑ Dec 2000 Cover: 2.99 **NM value: Cover or less**
📖 The Cursed! **A:** Al Milgrom; Ron Frenz **W:** Ron Frenz; Tom DeFalco
3 ❑ Jan 2001 Cover: 2.99 **NM value: Cover or less**
📖 Fathers of the Sin! **A:** Al Milgrom; Ron Frenz **W:** Ron Frenz; Tom DeFalco

DARK DOMINION — Defiant

1 ❑ Oct 1993 Cover: 2.50 **NM value: Cover or less**
Circ: CapCity orders: **64,900**
📖 Haunts of the Very Rich, Part 1; The Gathering Darkness **A:** Joe James **W:** Len Wein ★ 1st Appearance of Chasm, Doctor Michael Alexander.
2 ❑ Nov 1993 Cover: 2.50 **NM value: Cover or less**
Circ: CapCity orders: **32,375**
3 ❑ Dec 1993 Cover: 2.50 **NM value: Cover or less**
Circ: CapCity orders: **23,100**
📖 A Man's Home **A:** Joe James **W:** Joe James; Jim Shooter; Janet Jackson; Jim Wein
4 ❑ Jan 1994 Cover: 2.50 **NM value: Cover or less**
Circ: CapCity orders: **17,775**
📖 Bad Moon Rising **A:** Charles Adlard **W:** Janet Jackson
5 ❑ Feb 1994 Cover: 2.50 **NM value: Cover or less**
Circ: CapCity orders: **14,225**
📖 Family Skeletons, Part 1 **A:** Joe James **W:** Len Wein
6 ❑ Mar 1994 Cover: 2.50 **NM value: Cover or less**
Circ: CapCity orders: **11,625**
📖 Family Skeletons, Part 2 **A:** Louis Small Jr. **W:** Len Wein
7 ❑ Apr 1994 Cover: 2.50 **NM value: Cover or less**
Circ: CapCity orders: **10,275**
📖 Once a Hero, Part 1 **A:** J.G. Jones **W:** Len Wein
8 ❑ May 1994 Cover: 2.50 **NM value: Cover or less**
Circ: CapCity orders: **9,100**
📖 Once a Hero, Part 2 **A:** J.G. Jones **W:** Len Wein
9 ❑ Jun 1994 Cover: 2.50 **NM value: Cover or less**
Circ: CapCity orders: **7,725**
📖 Once a Hero, Part 3 **A:** J.G. Jones **W:** Len Wein
10 ❑ Jul 1994 Cover: 2.50 **NM value: Cover or less**
Circ: CapCity orders: **6,775**
11 ❑ Aug 1994 Cover: 2.50 **NM value: Cover or less**
Circ: CapCity orders: **5,850**
12 ❑ Sep 1994 Cover: 2.50 **NM value: Cover or less**
Circ: CapCity orders: **5,100**
13 ❑ Oct 1994 Cover: 2.50 **NM value: Cover or less**
final issue.

DARKER IMAGE — Image

As the name implies, Darker Image is a look into the more shadowy reaches of the Image universe. A sampler series, it showcases some of the top talent at Image.

Included is Jim Lee's Deathblow — Commander Michael Cray — a former SEAL and special operative, and easily one of the deadliest men alive.

Rob Liefeld provides a look at the character Bloodwulf, a slightly more literate take on ultraviolence a la Lobo.

Also included is Sam Kieth's Maxx, a strange, purple, toothy behemoth with an odd backstory that was only completely explored in his own title. The point here, however, was to give potential readers a look at some of what Image had to offer at the time.

1 ❑ Mar 1993 Cover: 2.50 **NM value: Cover or less**
Circ: CapCity orders: **257,125** • **CGC:** 13 graded, best 9.6
★ 1st Appearance of Maxx, Deathblow.
1/GO❑Mar 1993 Cover: 2.50 **NM value: 4.00**
• Gold logo★ 1st Appearance of Maxx, Deathblow.

CGC-graded: Multiply prices above by **33 for 9.9 M • 16 for 9.8 NM/M • 7 for 9.6 NM+ • 5 for 9.4 NM • 2.5 for 9.2 NM- • 1.5 for 9.0 VF/NM**

1/LE❑ Mar 1993 **NM** value: **4.00**
• White limited edition cover. ★ 1st Appearance of Maxx, Deathblow.

DARKER SIDE OF SEX — Eros

1 ❑ Cover: 2.95 **NM** value: **Cover or less**
A: Rick McCollum; Bill Cavalier **W:** Cathleen Hurley
2 ❑ Cover: 2.95 **NM** value: **Cover or less**
A: Rick McCollum; Bill Cavalier **W:** Cathleen Hurley
3 ❑ Cover: 2.95 **NM** value: **Cover or less**
A: Rick McCollum; Bill Cavalier **W:** Cathleen Hurley

DARKEWOOD — Aircel

1 ❑ full color Cover: 2.00 **NM** value: **Cover or less**
Circ: CapCity orders: **5,000**
A: Gordon Derry **W:** Gordon Derry
2 ❑ full color Cover: 2.00 **NM** value: **Cover or less**
Circ: CapCity orders: **3,675**
A: Gordon Derry **W:** Gordon Derry
3 ❑ full color Cover: 2.00 **NM** value: **Cover or less**
Circ: CapCity orders: **2,800**
A: Gordon Derry **W:** Gordon Derry
4 ❑ full color Cover: 2.00 **NM** value: **Cover or less**
Circ: CapCity orders: **2,450**
A: Gordon Derry **W:** Gordon Derry
5 ❑ full color Cover: 2.00 **NM** value: **Cover or less**
Circ: CapCity orders: **2,450**
A: Gordon Derry **W:** Gordon Derry

DARK FANTASIES — Dark Fantasy

1 ❑ Cover: 2.95 **NM** value: **Cover or less**
Circ: CapCity orders: **4,470**
2 ❑ Cover: 2.95 **NM** value: **Cover or less**
Circ: CapCity orders: **3,645**
3 ❑ Cover: 2.95 **NM** value: **Cover or less**
Circ: CapCity orders: **3,380**
📖 ...Someplace Better; The Center Piece; Third Generation **A:** Eric Olive; John Sutton; Rick Rieger; Trev Utz **W:** Eric Olive; Trev Utz; Erik Robson; Rick and Bill Rieger

DARK FANTASY — Apple

1 ❑ Sep 1992, b&w Cover: 2.75 **NM** value: **Cover or less**
📖 Ph'tillph'tarr; Retrospectacle; Guests **A:** Kevin Schnaper **W:** Kevin Schnaper

DARKFORCE — Omega 7

1 ❑ Cover: 2.50 **NM** value: **Cover or less**
2 ❑ Cover: 3.50 **NM** value: **Cover or less**
• indicia indicates 1992 copyright, probably not year of publication

DARK FRINGE, THE — Brainstorm

2 ❑ Dec 1996, b&w Cover: 2.95 **NM** value: **Cover or less**

DARK FRINGE, THE: SPIRITS OF THE DEAD — Brainstorm

"Spirits of the Dead" is the second installment of the "Dark Fringe" saga and brainchild of creator Eman Torre, who wrote and inked the comics. This series centers on retired police officer Allen Stone. He was once an exemplary cop, but his life and soul are destroyed, when his wife, Helen, is seemingly murdered by the target of his investigation, a mysterious assassin known only as Garrett.

Stone now struggles to keep his personal demons in check, to find the real players in his corrupt city, and to ponder such questions as why he trusts the man who stood above his dead wife's body and who Garrett is.

Stark contrasting of shadows and light, heavy inks, and a chiseled rendering add to the book's characterization and crime noir element. Unusual art causes backgrounds to appear warped and askew, further adding to the story's paranoid, conspiracy-laden feel.

1 ❑ Cover: 2.95 **NM** value: **Cover or less**
📖 The Dark Fringe: Act 2, Part 1 **A:** John Kissee **W:** Eman R. Torre

DARK GAUNTLET, THE — Tarescent

1 ❑ Cover: 2.00 **NM** value: **Cover or less**
2 ❑ Cover: 2.00 **NM** value: **Cover or less**
3 ❑ Cover: 2.00 **NM** value: **Cover or less**
4 ❑ Cover: 2.00 **NM** value: **Cover or less**

DARK GUARD — Marvel

1 ❑ Oct 1993 Cover: 2.25 **NM** value: **2.95**
Circ: CapCity orders: **14,700**
Prism cover. 📖 Tour Of Duty **A:** Carlos Pacheco **W:** Dan Abnett ★ 1st Appearance of The Time Guardian.
2 ❑ Nov 1993 Cover: 1.75 **NM** value: **Cover or less**
Circ: CapCity orders: **6,700**
3 ❑ Dec 1993 Cover: 1.75 **NM** value: **Cover or less**
Circ: CapCity orders: **5,550**
📖 Escalation! **A:** Carlos Pacheco **W:** Dan Abnett
4 ❑ Jan 1994 Cover: 1.75 **NM** value: **Cover or less**
Circ: CapCity orders: **4,650**
5 ❑ Cover: 1.75 **NM** value: **Cover or less**
Circ: CapCity orders: **3,400**
final issue.

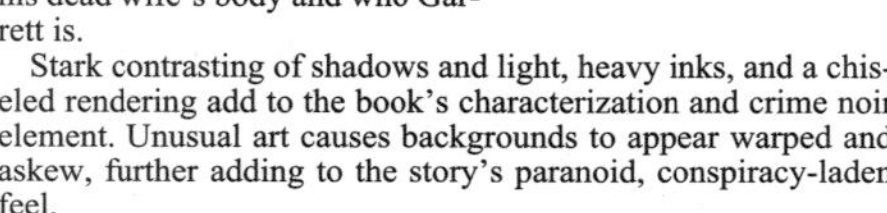

Creator Key
W = Writer • A = Artist • C = Cover Artist

DARKHAWK — Marvel

It was an ebony amulet of unknown origin. Chris Powell found it in an old amusement park, and it changed his life forever. He found that he could use the amulet to change himself into Darkhawk, a shadowy warrior of tremendous power. Now, Chris has sworn to use that power to fight crime.

Although the origin of the character seems pretty traditional, his super-powers seem less super than many in the field. For example, Darkhawk is anything but bulletproof. When wounded, however, he can heal himself entirely by changing back into Chris, then back again into Darkhawk.

1 ❑ Mar 1991 Cover: 1.00 **NM** value: **2.00**
Circ: CapCity orders: **66,900 • CGC:** 3 graded, best 9.6
📖 Dawn of the Darkhawk **A:** Mike Manley **W:** Danny Fingeroth ★ Origin of Darkhawk. ★ 1st Appearance of Darkhawk. ★ Appearance of Hobgoblin.
2 ❑ Apr 1991 Cover: 1.00 **NM** value: **1.50**
Circ: CapCity orders: **55,500**
A: Mike Manley **W:** Danny Fingeroth ★ Appearance of Hobgoblin, Spider-Man.
3 ❑ May 1991 Cover: 1.00 **NM** value: **1.50**
Circ: CapCity orders: **51,900**
A: Mike Manley **W:** Danny Fingeroth ★ Appearance of Hobgoblin, Spider-Man.
4 ❑ Jun 1991 Cover: 1.00 **NM** value: **1.50**
Circ: CapCity orders: **38,900**
A: Mike Manley **W:** Danny Fingeroth
5 ❑ Jul 1991 Cover: 1.00 **NM** value: **1.50**
Circ: CapCity orders: **39,200**
A: Mike Manley **W:** Danny Fingeroth
6 ❑ Aug 1991 Cover: 1.00 **NM** value: **1.50**
Circ: CapCity orders: **42,000**
A: Mike Manley **W:** Danny Fingeroth ★ Appearance of Daredevil, Captain America.
7 ❑ Sep 1991 Cover: 1.00 **NM** value: **1.50**
Circ: CapCity orders: **38,700**
A: Mike Manley **W:** Danny Fingeroth
8 ❑ Oct 1991 Cover: 1.00 **NM** value: **1.50**
Circ: CapCity orders: **39,900**
A: Mike Manley **W:** Danny Fingeroth
9 ❑ Nov 1991 Cover: 1.00 **NM** value: **1.50**
Circ: CapCity orders: **51,900**
📖 Honor Among Psychotics **A:** Mike Manley **W:** Danny Fingeroth ★ Appearance of Punisher.
10 ❑ Dec 1991 Cover: 1.00 **NM** value: **1.50**
Circ: CapCity orders: **42,800**
A: Mike Manley **W:** Danny Fingeroth
11 ❑ Jan 1992 Cover: 1.00 **NM** value: **1.50**
Circ: Statement: **209,433** CapCity orders: **40,700**
A: Mike Manley **W:** Danny Fingeroth
12 ❑ Feb 1992 Cover: 1.25 **NM** value: **1.50**
Circ: Statement: **209,433** CapCity orders: **39,200**
A: Mike Manley **W:** Danny Fingeroth ★ Versus Tombstone.
13 ❑ Mar 1992 Cover: 1.25 **NM** value: **1.50**
Circ: Statement: **209,433** CapCity orders: **43,800**
A: Mike Manley **W:** Danny Fingeroth ★ Appearance of Venom.
14 ❑ Apr 1992 Cover: 1.25 **NM** value: **1.50**
Circ: Statement: **209,433** CapCity orders: **39,700**
A: Mike Manley **W:** Danny Fingeroth ★ Appearance of Venom.
15 ❑ May 1992 Cover: 1.25 **NM** value: **Cover or less**
Circ: Statement: **209,433** CapCity orders: **37,300**
A: Mike Manley **W:** Danny Fingeroth
16 ❑ Jun 1992 Cover: 1.25 **NM** value: **Cover or less**
Circ: Statement: **209,433** CapCity orders: **37,900**
A: Mike Manley **W:** Danny Fingeroth ★ Versus Peristrike Force.
17 ❑ Jul 1992 Cover: 1.25 **NM** value: **Cover or less**
Circ: Statement: **209,433** CapCity orders: **38,700**
A: Mike Manley **W:** Danny Fingeroth ★ Versus Peristrike Force.
18 ❑ Aug 1992 Cover: 1.25 **NM** value: **Cover or less**
Circ: Statement: **209,433** CapCity orders: **38,100**
A: Mike Manley **W:** Danny Fingeroth
19 ❑ Sep 1992 Cover: 1.25 **NM** value: **Cover or less**
Circ: Statement: **209,433** CapCity orders: **35,000**
A: Mike Manley **W:** Danny Fingeroth
20 ❑ Oct 1992 Cover: 1.25 **NM** value: **Cover or less**
Circ: Statement: **209,433** CapCity orders: **33,600**
A: Mike Manley **W:** Danny Fingeroth
21 ❑ Nov 1992 Cover: 1.25 **NM** value: **Cover or less**
Circ: Statement: **209,433** CapCity orders: **32,700**
📖 Return to Forever, Part 1 **A:** Mike Manley **W:** Danny Fingeroth ★ Origin of Darkhawk.
22 ❑ Dec 1992 Cover: 1.25 **NM** value: **Cover or less**
Circ: Statement: **209,433** CapCity orders: **32,600**
📖 Return to Forever, Part 2 **A:** Mike Manley **W:** Danny Fingeroth ★ Appearance of Ghost Rider.
23 ❑ Jan 1993 Cover: 1.25 **NM** value: **Cover or less**
Circ: Statement: **248,000** CapCity orders: **29,000**
📖 Return to Forever, Part 3 **A:** Mike Manley **W:** Danny Fingeroth
24 ❑ Feb 1993 Cover: 1.25 **NM** value: **Cover or less**
Circ: Statement: **248,000** CapCity orders: **26,800**
📖 Return to Forever, Part 4 **A:** Mike Manley **W:** Danny Fingeroth
25 ❑ Mar 1993 Cover: 2.95 **NM** value: **Cover or less**
Circ: Statement: **248,000** CapCity orders: **75,200**
foil cover. • Double-size. 📖 Return to Forever, Part 5 • Has 1992 Statement, filed 10/1/92; avg print run 290,333; avg sales 205,608; avg subs 3,825; avg total paid 209,433; samples 250; office use 500; max existent 210,183; 28% of run returned **A:** Mike Manley **W:** Danny Fingeroth ★ Origin of Darkhawk armor.
26 ❑ Apr 1993 Cover: 1.25 **NM** value: **Cover or less**
Circ: Statement: **248,000** CapCity orders: **25,800**
27 ❑ May 1993 Cover: 1.25 **NM** value: **Cover or less**
Circ: Statement: **248,000** CapCity orders: **25,800**
28 ❑ Jun 1993 Cover: 1.25 **NM** value: **Cover or less**
Circ: Statement: **248,000** CapCity orders: **24,000**
📖 Time To Kill **A:** Tod Smith **W:** Danny Fingeroth
29 ❑ Jul 1993 Cover: 1.25 **NM** value: **Cover or less**
Circ: Statement: **248,000** CapCity orders: **23,600**
30 ❑ Aug 1993 Cover: 1.25 **NM** value: **Cover or less**
Circ: Statement: **248,000** CapCity orders: **25,500**
31 ❑ Sep 1993 Cover: 1.25 **NM** value: **Cover or less**
Circ: Statement: **248,000** CapCity orders: **24,100**
32 ❑ Oct 1993 Cover: 1.25 **NM** value: **Cover or less**
Circ: Statement: **248,000** CapCity orders: **18,800**
A: Tod Smith **W:** Danny Fingeroth
33 ❑ Nov 1993 Cover: 1.25 **NM** value: **Cover or less**
Circ: Statement: **248,000** CapCity orders: **18,550**
34 ❑ Dec 1993 Cover: 1.25 **NM** value: **Cover or less**
Circ: Statement: **248,000** CapCity orders: **17,000**
35 ❑ Jan 1994 Cover: 1.25 **NM** value: **Cover or less**
Circ: Statement: **115,442** CapCity orders: **17,500**
📖 Operation Symbiote, Part 1 ★ Appearance of Venom.
36 ❑ Feb 1994 Cover: 1.25 **NM** value: **Cover or less**
Circ: Statement: **115,442** CapCity orders: **16,350**
📖 Operation Symbiote, Part 2 ★ Appearance of Venom.
37 ❑ Mar 1994 Cover: 1.25 **NM** value: **Cover or less**
Circ: Statement: **115,442** CapCity orders: **14,700**
📖 Operation Symbiote, Part 3 ★ Appearance of Venom.
38 ❑ Apr 1994 Cover: 1.25 **NM** value: **Cover or less**
Circ: Statement: **115,442** CapCity orders: **13,300**
📖 Amulet Quest, Part 1
39 ❑ May 1994 Cover: 1.50 **NM** value: **Cover or less**
Circ: Statement: **115,442** CapCity orders: **12,400**
📖 Amulet Quest, Part 2
40 ❑ Jun 1994 Cover: 1.50 **NM** value: **Cover or less**
Circ: Statement: **115,442** CapCity orders: **12,100**
📖 Amulet Quest, Part 3
41 ❑ Jul 1994 Cover: 1.50 **NM** value: **Cover or less**
Circ: Statement: **115,442** CapCity orders: **11,950**
📖 Amulet Quest, Part 4
42 ❑ Aug 1994 Cover: 1.50 **NM** value: **Cover or less**
Circ: Statement: **115,442** CapCity orders: **11,550**
43 ❑ Sep 1994 Cover: 1.50 **NM** value: **Cover or less**
Circ: Statement: **115,442** CapCity orders: **10,700**
44 ❑ Oct 1994 Cover: 1.50 **NM** value: **Cover or less**
Circ: Statement: **115,442** CapCity orders: **10,050**
45 ❑ Nov 1994 Cover: 1.50 **NM** value: **Cover or less**
Circ: Statement: **115,442** CapCity orders: **9,450**
46 ❑ Dec 1994 Cover: 1.50 **NM** value: **Cover or less**
Circ: Statement: **115,442** CapCity orders: **9,050**
47 ❑ Jan 1995 Cover: 1.50 **NM** value: **Cover or less**
Circ: CapCity orders: **8,525**
48 ❑ Feb 1995 Cover: 1.50 **NM** value: **Cover or less**
Circ: CapCity orders: **7,750**
49 ❑ Mar 1995 Cover: 1.50 **NM** value: **Cover or less**
Circ: CapCity orders: **7,000**
• Has 1994 Statement, filed 10/1/94; avg print run 116,067; avg sales 113,558; avg subs 1,883; avg total paid 115,441; samples 125; office use 500; max existent 116,066; 0% of run returned
50 ❑ Apr 1995 Cover: 2.50 **NM** value: **Cover or less**
Circ: CapCity orders: **7,950**
• Giant-size. final issue.
Anl 1❑ Cover: 2.25 **NM** value: **2.50**
Anl 2❑ Cover: 2.95 **NM** value: **Cover or less**
Circ: CapCity orders: **37,700**
📖 Dreamkiller; Force Of Evil; Taking A Stand; Savage Is The Night **A:** Aaron Lopresti; Scott Kolins; Don Cameron; Larry Alexander **W:** Danny Fingeroth ★ 1st Appearance of Dreamkiller.
Anl 3❑ Cover: 2.95 **NM** value: **Cover or less**
Circ: CapCity orders: **9,150**

DARKHOLD — Marvel

1/CS❑ Oct 1992 Cover: 2.75 **NM** value: **Cover or less**
Circ: CapCity orders: **90,200**
📖 Rise of the Midnight Sons, Part 4 • Midnight Sons **A:** Richard Case **W:** Chris Cooper ★ 1st Appearance of Darkhold Redeemers.
2 ❑ Nov 1992 Cover: 1.75 **NM** value: **Cover or less**
Circ: CapCity orders: **43,800**
📖 For God and Country **A:** Richard Case **W:** Chris Cooper
3 ❑ Dec 1992 Cover: 1.75 **NM** value: **Cover or less**
Circ: CapCity orders: **35,300**
4 ❑ Jan 1993 Cover: 1.75 **NM** value: **Cover or less**
Circ: CapCity orders: **29,300**
📖 Cry N' Garai! **A:** Norman Felchle **W:** Chris Cooper ★ Appearance of Sabretooth.
5 ❑ Feb 1993 Cover: 1.75 **NM** value: **Cover or less**
Circ: CapCity orders: **28,200**
📖 The Living Dead **A:** Al Bigley; Richard Case **W:** Chris Cooper ★ Appearance of Punisher.
6 ❑ Mar 1993 Cover: 1.75 **NM** value: **Cover or less**
Circ: CapCity orders: **18,800**
📖 Duel **A:** Richard Case **W:** Chris Cooper
7 ❑ Mar 1993 Cover: 1.75 **NM** value: **Cover or less**
Circ: CapCity orders: **17,700**
📖 Day Of Infamy **A:** Rurik Tyler **W:** Chris Cooper
8 ❑ Apr 1993 Cover: 1.75 **NM** value: **Cover or less**
Circ: CapCity orders: **16,600**
📖 Betrayal, Part 1 **A:** Rurik Tyler **W:** Chris Cooper
9 ❑ May 1993 Cover: 1.75 **NM** value: **Cover or less**
Circ: CapCity orders: **14,400**
📖 Betrayal, Part 2
10 ❑ Jun 1993 Cover: 1.75 **NM** value: **Cover or less**
Circ: CapCity orders: **13,300**
📖 Betrayal, Part 3
11 ❑ Jul 1993 Cover: 1.75 **NM** value: **Cover or less**
Circ: CapCity orders: **39,200**
Double-cover. 📖 Midnight Massacre, Part 3 **A:** Rurik Tyler **W:** Chris Cooper

Other grades: Multiply prices above by **1.5 for Mint • 2/3 for Very Fine • 1/3 for Fine • 1/5 for Very Good • 1/8 for Good**

12 ❑ Aug 1993 Cover: 1.75 **NM** value: **Cover or less**
Circ: CapCity orders: **10,600**
For Want Of A Soul! **A:** Rurik Tyler **W:** Chris Cooper
13 ❑ Sep 1993 Cover: 1.75 **NM** value: **Cover or less**
Circ: CapCity orders: **10,100**
Stalker In The House • Missing CCA approval stamp **A:** Rurik Tyler **W:** Chris Cooper ★ Appearance of Missing Link.
14 ❑ Oct 1993 Cover: 1.75 **NM** value: **Cover or less**
Circ: CapCity orders: **9,600**
15 ❑ Nov 1993 Cover: 1.75 **NM** value: **Cover or less**
Circ: CapCity orders: **20,600**
Siege of Darkness, Part 4
16 ❑ Dec 1993 Cover: 1.75 **NM** value: **Cover or less**
Circ: CapCity orders: **15,600**
Siege of Darkness, Part 12 final issue. **A:** Rurik Tyler **W:** Chris Cooper

DARK HORSE CLASSICS — Dark Horse

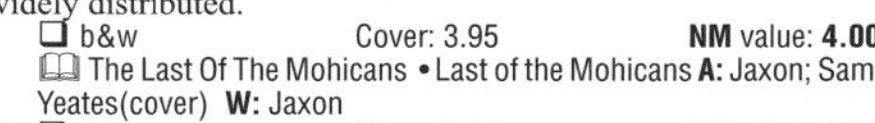

Following the past examples of Gilberton, First, and others, Dark Horse brought great classics of literature to the readers in a comic-book format in this series.

Dark Horse adapts such works as "The Last of the Mohicans," James Fenimore Cooper's tales of adventure and betrayal during the French and Indian war.

Like Classics Illustrated before it, Dark Horse here uses the comics medium to make great literature accessible to people who might otherwise never read the classics. Unlike Classics Illustrated's original incarnation, however, the Dark Horse equivalents were nowhere near as widely distributed.

1 ❑ b&w Cover: 3.95 **NM** value: **4.00**
The Last Of The Mohicans • Last of the Mohicans **A:** Jaxon; Sam Yeates(cover) **W:** Jaxon
2 ❑ b&w Cover: 3.95 **NM** value: **4.00**
20,000 Leagues Under the Sea • 20, 000 Leagues **W:** Gary Gianni; Jules Verne

DARK HORSE CLASSICS: ALIENS VERSUS PREDATOR — Dark Horse

1 ❑ Feb 1997 Cover: 2.95 **NM** value: **Cover or less**
Circ: Diamd. preorders: **8,279**
Reprints Aliens Vs. Predator #1 with new cover. **A:** Phil Norwood **W:** Randy Stradley
2 ❑ Mar 1997 Cover: 2.95 **NM** value: **Cover or less**
Circ: Diamd. preorders: **6,629**
Reprints Aliens Vs. Predator #2 with new cover. **A:** Phil Norwood; Michael Dubisch(cover) **W:** Randy Stradley
3 ❑ Apr 1997 Cover: 2.95 **NM** value: **Cover or less**
Circ: Diamd. preorders: **6,317**
Reprints Aliens Vs. Predator #3 with new cover. **A:** Phil Norwood; Michael Dubisch(cover) **W:** Randy Stradley
4 ❑ May 1997 Cover: 2.95 **NM** value: **Cover or less**
Circ: Diamd. preorders: **5,973**
Reprints Aliens Vs. Predator #4 with new cover. **A:** Phil Norwood **W:** Randy Stradley
5 ❑ Jun 1997 Cover: 2.95 **NM** value: **Cover or less**
Circ: Diamd. preorders: **5,585**
Reprints Aliens Vs. Predator #5 with new cover. **A:** Phil Norwood **W:** Randy Stradley
6 ❑ Jul 1997 Cover: 2.95 **NM** value: **Cover or less**
Circ: Diamd. preorders: **5,293**
Reprints Aliens Vs. Predator #6 with new cover. **A:** Phil Norwood **W:** Randy Stradley

DARK HORSE CLASSICS: GODZILLA — Dark Horse

1 ❑ Apr 1998 Cover: 2.95 **NM** value: **Cover or less**
Circ: Diamd. preorders: **5,474**
A: Arthur Adams **W:** Arthur Adams; Randy Stradley

DARK HORSE CLASSICS: GODZILLA: KING OF THE MONSTERS — Dark Horse

1 ❑ Jul 1998 Cover: 2.95 **NM** value: **Cover or less**
Circ: Diamd. preorders: **7,226**
A: Ron Randall; Stephen R. Bissette **W:** Stephen R. Bissette; Randy Stradley
2 ❑ Aug 1998 Cover: 2.95 **NM** value: **Cover or less**
Circ: Diamd. preorders: **4,765**
Blast from the Past • Can G-Force Survive? In the Grip of Godzilla! **A:** Bobby Rubio; Rich Suchy **W:** Stephen R. Bissette; Randy Stradley
3 ❑ Sep 1998 Cover: 2.95 **NM** value: **Cover or less**
Circ: Diamd. preorders: **4,175**
Dramatization • No Blast from the Past-Godzilla Rules! **A:** Brandon McKinney **W:** Kevin Maguire
4 ❑ Oct 1998 Cover: 2.95 **NM** value: **Cover or less**
Circ: Diamd. preorders: **3,582**
A: Ron Randall; Stephen R. Bissette **W:** Stephen R. Bissette; Randy Stradley
5 ❑ Nov 1998 Cover: 2.95 **NM** value: **Cover or less**
Circ: Diamd. preorders: **3,179**
6 ❑ Dec 1998 Cover: 2.95 **NM** value: **Cover or less**
Circ: Diamd. preorders: **2,792**

The prices seen above do not represent the highest possible prices seen in online auctions, but rather the prices we have seen these issues reliably fetch in a variety of environments (storefront retail, mail order, auction and convention).

DARK HORSE CLASSICS: STAR WARS: DARK EMPIRE — Dark Horse

The deaths of Darth Vader and the Emperor in The Return of the Jedi seemed to have ended the conflict for Luke Skywalker, Han Solo, and Leia Organa. But the overwhelming popularity of Star Wars, more than the machinations of the villains, allows no respite in fighting for the Alliance; thus this reprinted six-issue mini-series from Dark Horse.

Six years after the defeat of the Empire at Endor, Leia and her husband Han Solo are on a mission to rescue Luke and Lando Calrissian from the Imperial home world where they crashed. Arriving in the midst of a heated battle, the clash ends abruptly, when Luke emerges from the ruins of the Imperial Palace, and with the consummate skill of a Jedi Knight, downs the Imperial Walkers. The ensuing celebration is short-lived when Luke insists on staying to battle the vast evil he feels is approaching.

Many fans feel that this could easily have formed the basis of Episode 7 of George Lucas' overarcing story.

1 ❑ Mar 1997 Cover: 2.95 **NM** value: **Cover or less**
Circ: Diamd. preorders: **13,132**
The Destiny of a Jedi **A:** Cam Kennedy **W:** Tom Veitch
2 ❑ Apr 1997 Cover: 2.95 **NM** value: **Cover or less**
Circ: Diamd. preorders: **12,342**
Devastator of Worlds **A:** Cam Kennedy **W:** Tom Veitch
3 ❑ May 1997 Cover: 2.95 **NM** value: **Cover or less**
Circ: Diamd. preorders: **12,087**
The Battle for Calamari **A:** Cam Kennedy **W:** Tom Veitch
4 ❑ Jun 1997 Cover: 2.95 **NM** value: **Cover or less**
Circ: Diamd. preorders: **11,257**
Confrontation on the Smugglers' Moon **A:** Cam Kennedy **W:** Tom Veitch
5 ❑ Jul 1997 Cover: 2.95 **NM** value: **Cover or less**
Circ: Diamd. preorders: **10,721**
Emperor Reborn **A:** Cam Kennedy **W:** Tom Veitch
6 ❑ Aug 1997 Cover: 2.95 **NM** value: **Cover or less**
Circ: Diamd. preorders: **10,129**
The Fate of a Galaxy **A:** Cam Kennedy **W:** Tom Veitch

DARK HORSE CLASSICS: TERROR OF GODZILLA — Dark Horse

1 ❑ Aug 1998 Cover: 2.95 **NM** value: **Cover or less**
Circ: Diamd. preorders: **4,523**
• Translation by Mike Richardson and Randy Stradley of Viz Communications **A:** Kazuhisa Iwata **W:** Kazuhisa Iwata
2 ❑ Sep 1998 Cover: 2.95 **NM** value: **Cover or less**
Circ: Diamd. preorders: **3,935**
• Translation by Mike Richardson and Randy Stradley of Viz Communications **A:** Kazuhisa Iwata **W:** Kazuhisa Iwata
3 ❑ Oct 1998 Cover: 2.95 **NM** value: **Cover or less**
Circ: Diamd. preorders: **3,437**
• Translation by Mike Richardson and Randy Stradley of Viz Communications **A:** Kazuhisa Iwata **W:** Kazuhisa Iwata
4 ❑ Nov 1998 Cover: 2.95 **NM** value: **Cover or less**
Circ: Diamd. preorders: **3,166**
5 ❑ Dec 1998 Cover: 2.95 **NM** value: **Cover or less**
Circ: Diamd. preorders: **2,800**
6 ❑ Jan 1999 Cover: 2.95 **NM** value: **Cover or less**
Circ: Diamd. preorders: **2,536**

DARK HORSE COMICS — Dark Horse

1 ❑ Aug 1992 Cover: 2.50 **NM** value: **3.50**
Circ: CapCity orders: **32,705** • **CGC:** 1 graded, best 9.2
wraparound gatefold cover. Predator: Rite of Passage, Part 1; Time Cop: A Man Out of Time, Part 1; Renegade Part 1 • Predator, RoboCop, Time Cop, Renegade **A:** Vince Giarrano; Rick Leonardi; John Paul Leon; Phil Hester **W:** Mark Verheiden; Chris Claremont; Ian Edginton; John Arcudi ★ 1st Appearance of Time Cop.
2 ❑ Sep 1992 Cover: 2.50 **NM** value: **Cover or less**
Circ: CapCity orders: **21,325**
Aliens: Horror Show, Part 1; Time Cop: A Man Out of Time, Part 3; Indiana Jones and the Shrine of the Sea Devil, Part 1; Robocop, Part 3 • RoboCop, Renegade, Time Cop, Predator **A:** Vince Giarrano; Rick Leonardi; John Paul Leon; Phil Hester **W:** Mark Verheiden; Chris Claremont; Ian Edginton; John Arcudi
3 ❑ Oct 1992 Cover: 2.50 **NM** value: **Cover or less**
Circ: CapCity orders: **18,425**
Time Cop: A Man Out of Time, Part 2; Renegade, Part 2; Robocop, Part 2 • Aliens: Horror Show, RoboCop, Indiana Jones, Time Cop;RoboCop, Indiana Jones, Time Cop, Aliens: Horror Show
4 ❑ Nov 1992 Cover: 2.50 **NM** value: **Cover or less**
Circ: CapCity orders: **16,625**
Predator: Blood Feud, Part 1; Mad Dogs, Part 1; Indiana Jones and the Shrine of the Sea Devil, Part 2; Horror Show, Part 2 • Aliens, Predator, Indiana Jones, Mad Dogs
5 ❑ Dec 1992 Cover: 2.50 **NM** value: **Cover or less**
Circ: CapCity orders: **14,525**
Aliens: Horror Show, Part 3; Predator: Blood Feud, Part 2; Mad Dogs, Part 2; Indiana Jones and the Shrine of the Sea Devil, Part 3 • Aliens, Predator, Indiana Jones, Mad Dogs **A:** Andy Dimitt; Gary Gianni; David Roach; Leo Durañona **W:** Gary Gianni; John Arcudi; Neal Barrett Jr.; Sarah Byam
6 ❑ Jan 1993 Cover: 2.50 **NM** value: **Cover or less**
Circ: CapCity orders: **12,500**
Robocop: Invasions, Part 1; Mad Dogs, Part 3; Predator: Blood Feud, Part 3; Indiana Jones And The Shrine Of The Sea Devil, Part 4 • RoboCop, Predator, Indiana Jones, Mad Dogs **A:** Gary Gianni; Andrew Dimitt; Nick Gnazzo; Leopoldo Dura±ona **W:** Gary Gianni; Steven Grant; John Arcudi; Neal Barrett Jr.
7 ❑ Feb 1993 Cover: 2.50 **NM** value: **5.00**
Circ: CapCity orders: **19,375**
Star Wars: Tales of the Jedi, Part 1; Mad Dogs, Part 4; Robocop: Invasions, Part 2; Predator: Blood Feud, Part 4 • RoboCop, Star Wars, Mad Dogs, Predator **A:** Andy Dimitt; Nick Gnazzo; Janine Johnston; Leo Durañona **W:** Steven Grant; Tom Veitch; John Arcudi; Neal Barrett Jr.
8 ❑ Mar 1993 Cover: 2.50 **NM** value: **5.00**
Circ: CapCity orders: **15,975**
James Bond: Light of My Death, Part 1 • RoboCop, James Bond, Star Wars ★ 1st Appearance of X.
9 ❑ Apr 1993 Cover: 2.50 **NM** value: **4.00**
Circ: CapCity orders: **14,975**
James Bond: Light of My Death, Part 2 • James Bond, Star Wars, RoboCop ★ 2nd Appearance of X.
10 ❑ May 1993 Cover: 2.50 **NM** value: **3.00**
Circ: CapCity orders: **12,050**
Godzilla: Blast From the Past, Part 1; Predator: The Pride at Nghasa, Part 1; James Bond: Light of My Death, Part 3 • X, Predator, Godzilla, James Bond
11 ❑ Jul 1993 Cover: 2.50 **NM** value: **Cover or less**
Circ: CapCity orders: **10,475**
Aliens: Taste; Godzilla: Blast From the Past, Part 2; Predator: The Pride at Nghasa, Part 2; James Bond: Light of My Death, Part 4 • Predator, Godzilla, James Bond, Aliens
12 ❑ Aug 1993 Cover: 2.50 **NM** value: **Cover or less**
Circ: CapCity orders: **9,200**
Predator: The Pride at Nghasa, Part 3 • Aliens, Predator
13 ❑ Sep 1993 Cover: 2.50 **NM** value: **Cover or less**
Circ: CapCity orders: **9,200**
The Mark: Taking Back the Streets, Part 1; Predator: Bad Blood, Part 2; The Thing From Another World: Questionable Research, Part 1 • Aliens, Predator, Thing from Another World **A:** Ted Naifeh; Brad Rader; Derek Thompson **W:** Evan Dorkin; Edward Martin III; Mike W. Barr
14 ❑ Oct 1993 Cover: 2.50 **NM** value: **Cover or less**
Circ: CapCity orders: **8,475**
The Mark: Taking Back the Streets, Part 1; Predator: Bad Blood, Part 3; The Thing From Another World: Questionable Research, Part 2 • Predator, The Mark, Thing from Another World **A:** Ted Naifeh; Brad Rader; Derek Thompson **W:** Evan Dorkin; Edward Martin III; Mike W. Barr
15 ❑ Nov 1993 Cover: 2.50 **NM** value: **Cover or less**
Circ: CapCity orders: **8,850**
The Thing From Another World: Questionable Research, Part 2 **A:** Ted Naifeh **W:** Edward Martin III
16 ❑ Dec 1993 Cover: 2.50 **NM** value: **Cover or less**
Circ: CapCity orders: **7,775**
The Thing From Another World: Questionable Research, Part 4; Predator: The Hunted City, Part 1 **A:** Ted Naifeh **W:** Edward Martin III
17 ❑ Jan 1994 Cover: 2.50 **NM** value: **Cover or less**
Circ: CapCity orders: **9,275**
Alien, Part 1; Star Wars: Droids, Part 1; Predator: The Hunted City, Part 2
18 ❑ Feb 1994 Cover: 2.50 **NM** value: **Cover or less**
Circ: CapCity orders: **8,100**
Alien, Part 2; Star Wars: Droids, Part 2; Predator: The Hunted City, Part 3 • Aliens, Star Wars: Droids, Predator
19 ❑ Mar 1994 Cover: 2.50 **NM** value: **Cover or less**
Circ: CapCity orders: **8,225**
Alien, Part 3; Star Wars: Droids, Part 3 • X, Aliens, Star Wars: Droids
20 ❑ Apr 1994 Cover: 2.50 **NM** value: **Cover or less**
Circ: CapCity orders: **6,925**
21 ❑ May 1994 Cover: 2.50 **NM** value: **Cover or less**
Circ: CapCity orders: **6,450**
22 ❑ Jun 1994 Cover: 2.50 **NM** value: **Cover or less**
Circ: CapCity orders: **6,875**
23 ❑ Jul 1994 Cover: 2.50 **NM** value: **Cover or less**
Circ: CapCity orders: **6,275**
• Aliens, The Machine
24 ❑ Aug 1994 Cover: 2.50 **NM** value: **Cover or less**
Circ: CapCity orders: **5,500**
25 ❑ Sep 1994 Cover: 2.50 **NM** value: **Cover or less**
Circ: CapCity orders: **5,850**
• Flip-book. James Bond: Minute of Midnight; Aliens Vs. Predator: Blood Time final issue.

DARK HORSE DOWN UNDER — Dark Horse

Dark Horse showcases some of the best comics talent from Australia in this three-issue mini-series. Starting off the bunch is "The Undertaker" by Gary Chaloner and Ashley Wood. It's a chilling tale of madness and murder, as a madman who grew up in a graveyard goes hunting the serial killer who murdered his family and drove him over the edge.

Among other stories featured here are cosmic fairy tale "Aquarine" and Eddie Campbell's "The Crafty Bastard Sisyphus." Campbell is famous for his "Deadface" tales of Greek gods walking the modern world. He adds to that tradition with this new story of how the cunning Sisyphus tangles with Zeus and cheats death time and time again.

1 ❑ Jun 1994, b&w Cover: 2.50 **NM** value: **Cover or less**
Circ: CapCity orders: **3,025**

CGC-graded: Multiply prices above by **33 for 9.9 M • 16 for 9.8 NM/M • 7 for 9.6 NM+ • 5 for 9.4 NM • 2.5 for 9.2 NM- • 1.5 for 9.0 VF/NM**

The Undertaker: Dead Reckoning, Part 1; Aquarine; That Crafty Bastard Sisyphus **A:** Eddie Campbell; Ashley Wood; Fil Barlow **W:** Eddie Campbell; Gary Chaloner; Fil Barlow

2 ❑ Aug 1994, b&w Cover: 2.50 **NM value: Cover or less**
The Undertaker: Dead Reckoning, Part 2

3 ❑ Oct 1994, b&w Cover: 2.50 **NM value: Cover or less**
The Undertaker: Dead Reckoning, Part 3; Jace Riegel: The Scimitar Mutiny; Half-Caste **A:** Ashley Wood; Pete Mullins; Steve Carter **W:** Gary Chaloner; Antoinette Rydyr; John Passfield

DARK HORSE FUTURES — Dark Horse

1 ❑ **NM value: 1.00**
no cover price. • ads;Preview of 1989 Dark Horse titles

DARK HORSE MAVERICK 2000 — Dark Horse

0 ❑ Jul 2000 Cover: 3.95 **NM value: Cover or less**
Circ: Diamd. preorders: **13,384**
Mercy!; Concrete: Family Night; Ancient Joe; Norway!; Body Bags: Well, It's About Time!; Deep-Dig; Western Wind **A:** Jason Pearson; Frank Miller; Stan Sakai; C. Scott Morse; Paul Chadwick; Dylan Horrocks; Brian Ralph **W:** Jason Pearson; Frank Miller; Stan Sakai; C. Scott Morse; Paul Chadwick; Dylan Horrocks; Brian Ralph

DARK HORSE MONSTERS — Dark Horse

1 ❑ Feb 1997 Cover: 2.95 **NM value: Cover or less**
Circ: Diamd. preorders: **9,265**
Burn Out; Jungle of the Giants; Mike and Viv Go to Vegas!; Monster Island • Reprinted from Dark Horse Presents #33 & #47 **A:** Vince Mielcarek; Tim Truman; Mike Wolfer; Jack Pollock **W:** Vince Mielcarek; Tim Truman; Mike Wolfer; Jack Pollock; Benjamin Truman

DARK HORSE PRESENTS — Dark Horse

Marvel had Marvel Comics Presents; DC had DC Comics Presents; and independent publisher Dark Horse Comics had...well, you can guess.

Dark Horse Presents wasn't just a clone of the big two's try-out books. For one, it was published in a hefty black-and-white format, packing two or three times as many stories into each issue as any of its competitors. Also, the range of stories is, well, frankly amazing! A single issue may start with a terrible spoof of Dark Horse itself, move on to a gritty true-crime drama such as Sin City, switch over to a fairy tale adapted from Oscar Wilde, cut loose with a Predator tale, then return to part two of the spoof.

1 ❑ Jul 1986 Cover: 2.25 **NM value: 6.00**
• **CGC:** 3 graded, best 9.4
Black Cross; Lifestyles of the Rich and Famous; Mindwalk; Brighter! **A:** Chris Warner; Paul Chadwick; Randy Emberlin **W:** Chris Warner; Paul Chadwick; Randy Stradley ★ 1st Appearance of Concrete. ★ Appearance of Black Cross.

1-2 ❑ Cover: 2.25 **NM value: Cover or less**
1-3 ❑ Cover: 2.25 **NM value: Cover or less**
1-4 ❑ Cover: 2.25 **NM value: Cover or less**
2 ❑ Cover: 1.50 **NM value: 3.00**
★ 2nd Appearance of Concrete.
3 ❑ Nov 1986 Cover: 1.50 **NM value: 2.50**
★ Appearance of Concrete.
4 ❑ Jan 1987 Cover: 1.50 **NM value: 2.50**
★ Appearance of Concrete.
5 ❑ Feb 1987 Cover: 1.50 **NM value: 2.00**
★ Appearance of Concrete.
6 ❑ Apr 1987 Cover: 1.50 **NM value: 2.00**
★ Appearance of Concrete.
7 ❑ May 1987 Cover: 1.50 **NM value: 2.00**
8 ❑ Jun 1987 Cover: 1.50 **NM value: 2.00**
★ Appearance of Concrete.
9 ❑ Jul 1987 Cover: 2.25 **NM value: Cover or less**
10 ❑ Sep 1987 Cover: 1.75 **NM value: 4.50**
★ 1st Appearance of The Mask. ★ Appearance of Concrete.
11 ❑ Oct 1987 Cover: 2.25 **NM value: 3.50**
• **CGC:** 1 graded, best 8.0
★ 2nd Appearance of The Mask.
12 ❑ Nov 1987 Cover: 1.75 **NM value: 2.50**
★ Appearance of Concrete. ★ Appearance of The Mask.
13 ❑ Dec 1987 Cover: 1.75 **NM value: 2.50**
★ Appearance of The Mask.
14 ❑ Jan 1987 Cover: 1.75 **NM value: 3.00**
★ Appearance of Concrete, The Mask.
15 ❑ Feb 1988 Cover: 1.75 **NM value: 2.50**
★ Appearance of The Mask.
16 ❑ Mar 1988 Cover: 1.75 **NM value: 3.00**
★ Appearance of Concrete, The Mask.
17 ❑ Apr 1988 Cover: 1.75 **NM value: 2.00**
• Spume, Muzzi & Woim, Roachmill
18 ❑ Jun 1988 Cover: 1.75 **NM value: 3.50**
★ Appearance of Concrete, The Mask.
19 ❑ Jul 1988 Cover: 1.75 **NM value: 2.50**
★ Appearance of The Mask.
20 ❑ Aug 1988 Cover: 2.95 **NM value: 3.00**
• Double Size. ★ Appearance of Flaming Carrot, Concrete, The Mask.
21 ❑ Aug 1988 Cover: 1.75 **NM value: 2.50**
★ Appearance of The Mask.
22 ❑ Sep 1988 Cover: 1.75 **NM value: 2.50**
★ 1st Appearance of Duckman.
23 ❑ Oct 1988 Cover: 1.75 **NM value: 2.00**
24 ❑ Nov 1988 Cover: 1.75 **NM value: 6.00**
• **CGC:** 8 graded, best 9.8
• Aliens ★ Origin of Aliens. ★ 1st Appearance of Aliens.
25 ❑ Dec 1988 Cover: 1.75 **NM value: 2.00**
26 ❑ Jan 1989 Cover: 1.75 **NM value: 2.00**
27 ❑ Feb 1989 Cover: 1.75 **NM value: 2.00**
28 ❑ Mar 1989 Cover: 2.95 **NM value: 3.00**
• Double Size. • Concrete, Mr. Monster
29 ❑ Apr 1989 Cover: 1.75 **NM value: 2.00**
30 ❑ May 1989 Cover: 1.75 **NM value: 2.00**
31 ❑ Jul 1989 Cover: 1.75 **NM value: 2.00**
• Duckman
32 ❑ Jul 1989 Cover: 3.50 **NM value: Cover or less**
• Giant-size. ★ Appearance of Concrete.
33 ❑ Aug 1989 Cover: 2.25 **NM value: 2.50**
• Giant-size.
34 ❑ Aug 1989 Cover: 1.75 **NM value: 3.00**
Aliens; Zone; Race Of Scorpions • Aliens;Aliens story **A:** Phil Norwood; Mike Kraiger; Leopoldo Dura±ona **W:** Mike Kraiger; Leopoldo Dura±ona; Randy Stradley
35 ❑ Dec 1989 Cover: 1.95 **NM value: 3.00**
• Predator, Heartbreakers, A Tough Nut To Crack, Aliens
36 ❑ Oct 1989 Cover: 1.95 **NM value: 3.00**
regular cover. • Aliens vs. Predator
36/A ❑ Oct 1989 Cover: 1.95 **NM value: 4.00**
• **CGC:** 1 graded, best 9.0
Painted cover. • Aliens vs. Predator
37 ❑ Nov 1989 Cover: 1.95 **NM value: 2.50**
38 ❑ Apr 1990 Cover: 1.95 **NM value: 2.00**
Concrete: Fire At Twilight; Mary: The Elephant; Delia & Celia: A Pyre For Ethrod **A:** Gary Davis; Paul Chadwick; Ed The Geek **W:** Gary Davis; Paul Chadwick; Ed The Geek ★ Appearance of Concrete.
39 ❑ May 1990 Cover: 1.95 **NM value: 2.00**
40 ❑ Jun 1990 Cover: 2.95 **NM value: 3.00**
• Giant-size. **A:** Matt Wagner
41 ❑ Jul 1990 Cover: 2.95 **NM value: Cover or less**
42 ❑ Aug 1990 Cover: 1.95 **NM value: 3.00**
Aliens; Kings In Disguise; The Argosy • Aliens **A:** Bruce Zick; Dan Burr; Willie Schubert **W:** Bruce Zick; Paul Guinan; James Vance
43 ❑ Sep 1990 Cover: 1.95 **NM value: 3.00**
• Aliens
44 ❑ Oct 1990 Cover: 1.95 **NM value: 2.00**
45 ❑ Nov 1990 Cover: 1.95 **NM value: 2.00**
A: Matt Wagner
46 ❑ Nov 1990 Cover: 1.95 **NM value: 2.00**
• Predator, Bacchus, Crash Ryan
47 ❑ Jan 1991 Cover: 1.95 **NM value: 2.00**
• monsters
48 ❑ Feb 1991 Cover: 1.95 **NM value: 2.00**
Harlequin • Black Cross, Roachmill, Concrete, Mr. Monster **A:** Stefano Guadiano **W:** Stephen Csutoras
49 ❑ Mar 1991 Cover: 1.95 **NM value: 2.00**
Restless Sleep **A:** Steve Pugh; Stefano Gaudiano; Earl Geler **W:** Ian Edginton; John Arcudi; Stephen Csutoras
50 ❑ Apr 1991 Cover: 1.95 **NM value: 2.00**
51 ❑ Jun 1991 Cover: 1.95 **NM value: 2.00**
Sin City, Part 2; Harlequin, Part 4; Heartbreakers, Part 2 **A:** Frank Miller; Paul Guinan; Stefano Gaudiano **W:** Frank Miller; Paul Guinan; Anina Bennett; Stephen Csutoras
52 ❑ Jul 1991 Cover: 1.95 **NM value: 2.00**
Sin City **A:** Frank Miller **W:** Frank Miller
53 ❑ Aug 1991 Cover: 1.95 **NM value: 2.00**
Sin City **A:** Frank Miller **W:** Frank Miller
54 ❑ Sep 1991 Cover: 2.25 **NM value: 3.00**
Sin City **A:** Gray Morrow; John Byrne; Frank Miller **W:** John Byrne ★ 1st Appearance of Next Men.
55 ❑ Oct 1991 Cover: 2.25 **NM value: Cover or less**
Sin City, Part 5; Sin City, Part 6 **A:** John Byrne; Frank Miller **W:** John Byrne; Frank Miller ★ 2nd Appearance of Next Men.
56 ❑ Nov 1991 Cover: 3.95 **NM value: Cover or less**
• Double-size. Aliens: Genocide (prelude); Sin City • Aliens **A:** John Byrne; Frank Miller **W:** Frank Miller
57 ❑ Dec 1991 Cover: 3.50 **NM value: Cover or less**
• Giant-size. Sin City **A:** John Byrne; Frank Miller **W:** Frank Miller
58 ❑ Jan 1992 Cover: 1.95 **NM value: 2.00**
Sin City **A:** Frank Miller **W:** Frank Miller
59 ❑ Feb 1992 Cover: 2.25 **NM value: 2.50**
Sin City; Alien Fire; The Baggage Coach Ahead **A:** Eric Vincent; Rick Geary; Frank Miller **W:** Rick Geary; Frank Miller; Anthony Smith
60 ❑ Mar 1992 Cover: 2.25 **NM value: 2.50**
Sin City **A:** Frank Miller **W:** Frank Miller
61 ❑ Apr 1992 Cover: 2.25 **NM value: 2.50**
Sin City **A:** Frank Miller **W:** Frank Miller
62 ❑ May 1992 Cover: 2.25 **NM value: 2.50**
Sin City **A:** Frank Miller **W:** Frank Miller
63 ❑ Jun 1992 Cover: 2.25 **NM value: 2.50**
Circ: CapCity orders: **7,250**
Marie Dakar, The Creep, Abandonment Games **A:** Mike Hoffman; Dale Eaglesham; Moebius **W:** Frank Miller; Moebius; Douglas M. Wheeler; John Arcudi
64 ❑ Jul 1992 Cover: 2.25 **NM value: 2.50**
Circ: CapCity orders: **6,025**
65 ❑ Sep 1992 Cover: 2.25 **NM value: 2.50**
Circ: CapCity orders: **6,600**
66 ❑ Sep 1992 Cover: 2.25 **NM value: 2.50**
Circ: CapCity orders: **6,275**
Concrete; Dr. Giggles, Part 3; An Accidental Death Part 2; Alec • Concrete, Doctor Giggles, An Accidental Death;Concrete, Dr. Giggles, An Accidental Death **A:** Eddie Campbell; Eric Shanower; Paul Chadwick; Alan Burrows **W:** Eddie Campbell; Ed Brubaker; Paul Chadwick; Manny Coto
67 ❑ Nov 1992 Cover: 3.95 **NM value: Cover or less**
Circ: CapCity orders: **9,950**
• Double-size issue. Zoo-Lou vs. Editor, Part 1; Zoo-Lou vs. Editor, Part 2; An Accidental Death, Part 3; Nestrobber: Money For Nothing; Predator: Race War, Part 1; Alec; The Selfish Giant **A:** Eddie Campbell; Tom McWeeney; P. Craig Russell; Jordan Raskin; Eric Shanower; Maya Sakamoto; Rich Hedden **W:** Eddie Campbell; Tom McWeeney; Ed Brubaker; Mary Jo Duffy; Rich Hedden; Andrew Vachss; Oscar Wilde ★ Appearance of Zoo-Lou.
68 ❑ Dec 1992 Cover: 2.25 **NM value: 2.50**
Circ: CapCity orders: **9,425**
Predator: Race War (prelude) • Predator: Race War
69 ❑ Feb 1993 Cover: 2.25 **NM value: 2.50**
Circ: CapCity orders: **10,475**
Predator: Race War, Part 1; Nestrobber: Survival Skills; Paieolove, Part 2; Alec • Predator: Race War **A:** Eddie Campbell; Jordan Raskin; Gary Davis; Maya Sakamoto **W:** Eddie Campbell; Gary Davis; Mary Jo Duffy; Andrew Vachss
70 ❑ Mar 1993 Cover: 2.25 **NM value: 2.50**
Circ: CapCity orders: **7,100**
The Madwoman of the Sacred Heart, Part 1
71 ❑ Apr 1993 Cover: 2.25 **NM value: 2.50**
Circ: CapCity orders: **6,875**
The Madwoman of the Sacred Heart, Part 2; Dominique: The Hardest Part, Part 1
72 ❑ Apr 1993 Cover: 2.25 **NM value: 2.50**
Circ: CapCity orders: **6,850**
The Madwoman of the Sacred Heart, Part 3; Eudaemon, Part 1; Dominique: The Hardest Part, Part 2
73 ❑ Jun 1993 Cover: 2.25 **NM value: 2.50**
Circ: CapCity orders: **6,425**
The Madwoman of the Sacred Heart, Part 4; Eudaemon, Part 2; Dominique: The Hardest Part, Part 3 **A:** Jim Balent; Moebius; Nelson **W:** Mark A. Nelson; Alexandro Jodorowsky; Charles Moore; Lisa Moore
74 ❑ Jun 1993 Cover: 2.25 **NM value: 2.50**
Circ: CapCity orders: **6,350**
The Madwoman of the Sacred Heart, Part 5; Eudaemon, Part 3; The Chairman, Part 1 **A:** Andrew Robinson; Moebius; Nelson **W:** Mark A. Nelson; Alexandro Jodorowsky; Charles Moore
75 ❑ Jul 1993 Cover: 2.25 **NM value: 2.50**
Circ: CapCity orders: **6,600**
The Madwoman of the Sacred Heart, Part 6; The Chairman, Part 2; Sovay **A:** Andrew Robinson; Charles Vess; Moebius **W:** Alexandro Jodorowsky; Charles De Lint; Charles Moore
76 ❑ Aug 1993 Cover: 2.25 **NM value: 2.50**
Circ: CapCity orders: **5,575**
The Madwoman of the Sacred Heart, Part 7; The Chairman, Part 3
77 ❑ Sep 1993 Cover: 2.25 **NM value: 2.50**
Circ: CapCity orders: **4,800**
A: Steve Lieber
78 ❑ Oct 1993 Cover: 2.25 **NM value: 2.50**
Circ: CapCity orders: **4,825**
79 ❑ Nov 1993 Cover: 2.25 **NM value: 2.50**
Circ: CapCity orders: **4,600**
80 ❑ Dec 1993 Cover: 2.25 **NM value: 3.00**
Circ: CapCity orders: **6,750** • **CGC:** 1 graded, best 9.4
81 ❑ Jan 1994 Cover: 2.25 **NM value: 2.50**
Circ: CapCity orders: **4,000**
82 ❑ Feb 1994 Cover: 2.25 **NM value: 2.50**
Circ: CapCity orders: **3,775**
83 ❑ Mar 1994 Cover: 2.25 **NM value: 2.50**
Circ: CapCity orders: **3,850**
84 ❑ Apr 1994 Cover: 2.50 **NM value: Cover or less**
Circ: CapCity orders: **4,000**
85 ❑ May 1994 Cover: 2.50 **NM value: Cover or less**
Circ: CapCity orders: **4,000**
The Eighth Wonder, Part 1; Star Riders, Part 1
86 ❑ Jun 1994 Cover: 2.50 **NM value: Cover or less**
Circ: CapCity orders: **3,850**
The Eighth Wonder, Part 2; Star Riders, Part 2
87 ❑ Jul 1994 Cover: 2.50 **NM value: Cover or less**
Circ: CapCity orders: **4,675**
Hermes Versus The Eyeball Kid, Part 1; The Eighth Wonder, Part 3; Star Riders, Part 3; The Chairman, Part 3; The Madwoman of the Sacred Heart, Part 7 **A:** Eddie Campbell; Andrew Robinson; Moebius **W:** Eddie Campbell; Alexandro Jodorowsky; Charles Moore
88 ❑ Aug 1994 Cover: 2.50 **NM value: Cover or less**
Circ: CapCity orders: **5,725**
• Hellboy **A:** Steve Lieber
89 ❑ Sep 1994 Cover: 2.50 **NM value: Cover or less**
Circ: CapCity orders: **5,700**
• Hellboy
90 ❑ Oct 1994 Cover: 2.50 **NM value: Cover or less**
Circ: CapCity orders: **6,025**
91 ❑ Nov 1994 Cover: 2.50 **NM value: Cover or less**
Circ: CapCity orders: **6,025**
Blackheart, Part 1
92 ❑ Dec 1994 Cover: 2.50 **NM value: Cover or less**
Circ: CapCity orders: **4,125**
Blackheart, Part 2; Too Much Coffee Man, Part 1 ★ Appearance of Too Much Coffee Man.
93 ❑ Jan 1995 Cover: 2.50 **NM value: Cover or less**
Circ: CapCity orders: **4,150**
Blackheart, Part 3; Cud, Part 1; Too Much Coffee Man, Part 2 ★ Appearance of Too Much Coffee Man.
94 ❑ Feb 1995 Cover: 2.50 **NM value: Cover or less**
Circ: CapCity orders: **3,675**
Cud, Part 2; Too Much Coffee Man, Part 3
95 ❑ Mar 1995 Cover: 2.50 **NM value: Cover or less**
Circ: CapCity orders: **3,550**
Cud, Part 3; Too Much Coffee Man, Part 4 ★ Appearance of Too Much Coffee Man.
96 ❑ Apr 1995 Cover: 2.50 **NM value: Cover or less**
Circ: CapCity orders: **3,250**
97 ❑ May 1995 Cover: 2.50 **NM value: Cover or less**
Circ: CapCity orders: **3,075**
98 ❑ Jun 1995 Cover: 2.50 **NM value: Cover or less**
Circ: CapCity orders: **3,000**
99 ❑ Jul 1995 Cover: 2.50 **NM value: Cover or less**
Circ: CapCity orders: **3,175**
100.1 ❑ Aug 1995 Cover: 2.50 **NM value: Cover or less**
Circ: CapCity orders: **8,775**
• Issue 100 #1 **A:** Frank Miller **C:** Frank Miller **W:** Frank Miller
100.2 ❑ Aug 1995 Cover: 2.50 **NM value: Cover or less**
Circ: CapCity orders: **8,575**
Hellboy cover and story. • Issue 100 #2
100.3 ❑ Aug 1995 Cover: 2.50 **NM value: Cover or less**
Circ: CapCity orders: **7,775**
Concrete cover and story. • Issue 100 #3

Other grades: Multiply prices above by **1.5 for Mint • 2/3 for Very Fine • 1/3 for Fine • 1/5 for Very Good • 1/8 for Good**

100.4❑Aug 1995 Cover: 2.50 **NM** value: **Cover or less**
Circ: CapCity orders: **7,775**
• Martha Washington story;Issue 100 #4 **C:** Dave Gibbons **W:** Frank Miller

100.5❑Aug 1995 Cover: 2.50 **NM** value: **Cover or less**
Circ: CapCity orders: **8,350**
• Issue 100 #5 **C:** Mike Allred; Laura Allred

101 ❑ Sep 1995 Cover: 2.50 **NM** value: **Cover or less**
Circ: CapCity orders: **5,100**
★ Appearance of Aliens.

102 ❑ Oct 1995 Cover: 2.50 **NM** value: **Cover or less**

103 ❑ Nov 1995 Cover: 2.95 **NM** value: **Cover or less**
• Kirby centerfold;Mr. Painter, One-Trick Rip-Off, The Pink Tornado, Hairball

104 ❑ Dec 1995 Cover: 2.95 **NM** value: **Cover or less**

105 ❑ Jan 1996 Cover: 2.95 **NM** value: **Cover or less**

106 ❑ Feb 1996 Cover: 2.95 **NM** value: **Cover or less**

107 ❑ Mar 1996 Cover: 2.95 **NM** value: **Cover or less**

108 ❑ Apr 1996 Cover: 2.95 **NM** value: **Cover or less**

109 ❑ May 1996 Cover: 2.95 **NM** value: **Cover or less**

110 ❑ Jun 1996 Cover: 2.95 **NM** value: **Cover or less**

111 ❑ Jul 1996 Cover: 2.95 **NM** value: **Cover or less**

112 ❑ Aug 1996 Cover: 2.95 **NM** value: **Cover or less**

113 ❑ Sep 1996 Cover: 2.95 **NM** value: **Cover or less**
Circ: Diamd. preorders: **6,456**
📖 Lowlife, Part 1; Trypto the Acid Dog, Part 1 **A:** Ed Brubaker; Steve Leialoha **W:** Bill Mumy; Ed Brubaker; Miguel Ferrer

114 ❑ Oct 1996 Cover: 2.95 **NM** value: **Cover or less**
Circ: Diamd. preorders: **14,184**
📖 Star Slammers: Fever Dream; Lowlife, Part 2; Lance Blastoff; Trypto the Acid Dog, Part 2 • Star Slammers, Lance Blastoff, Lowlife, Trypto the Acid Dog **A:** Frank Miller; Walt Simonson; Ed Brubaker; Steve Leialoha **W:** Frank Miller; Bill Mumy; Walt Simonson; Ed Brubaker; Miguel Ferrer

115 ❑ Nov 1996 Cover: 2.95 **NM** value: **Cover or less**
Circ: Direct Market orders: **7,272**
📖 Lowlife, Part 3; Trypto the Acid Dog, Part 3; Dr. Spin, Part 1 • Doctor Spin, The Creep, Lowlife, Trypto the Acid Dog **A:** Roger Langridge; Ed Brubaker; Steve Leialoha **C:** Frank Miller **W:** Bill Mumy; Ed Brubaker; Gordon Rennie; Miguel Ferrer

116 ❑ Dec 1996 Cover: 2.95 **NM** value: **Cover or less**
Circ: Direct Market orders: **6,574**
📖 Trypto the Acid Dog, Part 4; Dr. Spin, Part 2 • Fat Dog Mendoza, Trypto the Acid Dog, Doctor Spin **A:** Roger Langridge; Steve Leialoha **W:** Bill Mumy; Gordon Rennie; Miguel Ferrer

117 ❑ Jan 1997 Cover: 2.95 **NM** value: **Cover or less**
Circ: Diamd. preorders: **8,585**
📖 Aliens: Headhunters; Dr. Spin, Part 3; Trypto the Acid Dog, Part 5 • Aliens, Trypto the Acid Dog, Doctor Spin **A:** Roger Langridge; Gene Colan; Steve Leialoha **W:** Bill Mumy; Gordon Rennie; Miguel Ferrer; Mike W. Barr

118 ❑ Feb 1997 Cover: 2.95 **NM** value: **Cover or less**
Circ: Diamd. preorders: **13,183**
📖 Hectic Planet; Dr. Spin • Monkeyman & O'Brien, Hectic Planet, Trypto the Acid Dog, Doctor Spin **A:** Roger Langridge; Evan Dorkin; Steve Leialoha; L. Lois Buhalis **W:** Arthur Adams; Evan Dorkin; Bill Mumy; Gordon Rennie; Miguel Ferrer

119 ❑ Mar 1997 Cover: 2.95 **NM** value: **Cover or less**
Circ: Diamd. preorders: **11,313**
📖 Trout, Part 1; Hectic Planet, Part 2; Monkeyman & O'Brien, Part 2; Predator • Monkeyman & O'Brien, Hectic Planet, Trout, Predator **A:** Arthur Adams; Scott Kolins; Evan Dorkin; Troy Nixey **W:** Arthur Adams; Evan Dorkin; Troy Nixey; Mike W. Barr

120 ❑ Apr 1997 Cover: 2.95 **NM** value: **Cover or less**
Circ: Diamd. preorders: **9,314**
• One Last Job, The Lords of Misrule, Trout, Hectic Planet

121 ❑ May 1997 Cover: 2.95 **NM** value: **Cover or less**
Circ: Diamd. preorders: **6,914**
• Jack Zero, Aliens, The Lords of Misrule, Trout

122 ❑ Jun 1997 Cover: 2.95 **NM** value: **Cover or less**
Circ: Diamd. preorders: **6,109**
• Jack Zero, Imago, Trout, The Lords of Misrule

123 ❑ Jul 1997 Cover: 2.95 **NM** value: **Cover or less**
Circ: Diamd. preorders: **5,601**
📖 Imago, Part 2; Trout; Jack Zero • Imago, Jack Zero, Trout **A:** Troy Nixey; Brian O'Connell; Arnold Pander **W:** Troy Nixey; Arnold Pander; John Arcudi; Zero Boy

124 ❑ Aug 1997 Cover: 2.95 **NM** value: **Cover or less**
Circ: Diamd. preorders: **7,026**
• Predator, Jack Zero, Outside, Inside

125 ❑ Sep 1997 Cover: 2.95 **NM** value: **Cover or less**
Circ: Diamd. preorders: **7,647**
📖 The Nocturnals, Part 1; Jack Zero; Side Trip **A:** Jason Lutes; Dan Brereton; Arnold Pander **W:** Jason Lutes; Dan Brereton; Arnold Pander; Zero Boy

126 ❑ Oct 1997 Cover: 2.95 **NM** value: **Cover or less**
Circ: Diamd. preorders: **7,381**
📖 The Nocturnals, Part 2; Last Night I Dreamed; Sniper-Hunter for Hire; Skeleton Key; Phineas Page, the Bookshelf Phantom; Matalfer, Part 1; Starship Troopers; A Hole in the Head **A:** Dan Brereton; Bernie Mireault; Andi Watson; Tommy Lee Edwards; Rich Hedden; Vince Roucher; Rupert Bottenberg; Scott Gillis; Steven Weissman. Stan Manoukia **W:** Dan Brereton; Andi Watson; Stan Manoukian; Jan Strnad; Rich Hedden; Steven Weissman; Vince Roucher; Diana Schutz; Jeff DeMos

127 ❑ Nov 1997 Cover: 2.95 **NM** value: **Cover or less**
Circ: Diamd. preorders: **6,579**
📖 The Nocturnals, Part 3; Metalfer; Stiltskin; Blue Monday • Nocturnals, Metalfer, Stiltskin, Blue Monday **A:** Dan Brereton; Stan Manoukian; Chynna Clugston-Major; Shane Oakley **W:** Dan Brereton; Stan Manoukian; Chynna Clugston-Major; Shane Oakley

128 ❑ Jan 1998 Cover: 2.95 **NM** value: **Cover or less**
Circ: Diamd. preorders: **5,104**
📖 Dan & Larry: Don't Do That!, Part 1; Metalfer, Part 3; Stiltskin, Part 2 • Dan & Larry, Metalfer, Stiltskin **A:** Dave Cooper; Shane Oakley; Vince Roucher **W:** Dave Cooper; Stan Manoukian; Shane Oakley

129 ❑ Feb 1998 Cover: 2.95 **NM** value: **Cover or less**
Circ: Diamd. preorders: **5,344**

130 ❑ Mar 1998 Cover: 2.95 **NM** value: **Cover or less**
Circ: Diamd. preorders: **4,824**
• Dan & Larry, Wanted Man, Mary Walker: The Woman

131 ❑ Apr 1998 Cover: 2.95 **NM** value: **Cover or less**
Circ: Diamd. preorders: **5,854**
• Girl Crazy, The Fall, Dan & Larry, Boogie Picker

132 ❑ Apr 1998 Cover: 2.95 **NM** value: **Cover or less**
Circ: Diamd. preorders: **7,433**
• The Fall, Dan & Larry, Dirty Pair

133 ❑ May 1998 Cover: 2.95 **NM** value: **Cover or less**
Circ: Diamd. preorders: **7,366**
• Carson of Venus, The Fall, Dirty Pair, Blue Monday

134 ❑ Jul 1998 Cover: 2.95 **NM** value: **Cover or less**
Circ: Diamd. preorders: **7,479**

135 ❑ Sep 1998 Cover: 2.95 **NM** value: **3.50**
Circ: Diamd. preorders: **4,988**
📖 The Fall, Part 5; The Ark, Part 4; The Mark; Carson of Venus • Carson of Venus, The Mark, The Fall, The Ark **A:** Jason Lutes; Peter Doherty; Ron Randall; Ivan Reis **W:** Ed Brubaker; Mark Verheiden; Dark Macan; Mike W. Barr

136 ❑ Oct 1998 Cover: 2.95 **NM** value: **Cover or less**
Circ: Diamd. preorders: **4,610**
📖 The Ark, Part 3; Spirit of the Badlander • The Ark, Spirit of the Badlander **A:** Sergio Cariello; Ron Randall **W:** Mark Verheiden; Beau Smith

137 ❑ Nov 1998 Cover: 2.95 **NM** value: **Cover or less**
Circ: Diamd. preorders: **5,470**
• Predator, The Ark, My Vagabond Days

138 ❑ Dec 1998 Cover: 2.95 **NM** value: **Cover or less**
Circ: Diamd. preorders: **5,406**
• Terminator, The Moth, My Vagabond Days

139 ❑ Jan 1999 Cover: 2.95 **NM** value: **Cover or less**
Circ: Diamd. preorders: **4,252**
• Roachmill, Saint Slayer

140 ❑ Feb 1999 Cover: 2.95 **NM** value: **Cover or less**
Circ: Diamd. preorders: **5,571**
• Aliens, Usagi Yojimbo, Saint Slayer

141 ❑ Mar 1999 Cover: 2.95 **NM** value: **Cover or less**
Circ: Diamd. preorders: **17,628**
📖 Buffy the Vampire Slayer: Hello Moon; Buffy the Vampire Slayer: Cursed; Buffy the Vampire Slayer: Dead Love • Buffy the Vampire Slayer **A:** Hector Gomez; David Perrin; Joe Bennett **W:** Dan Brereton; Andi Watson; Christopher Golden

142 ❑ Apr 1999 Cover: 2.95 **NM** value: **Cover or less**
Circ: Diamd. preorders: **8,922**
📖 The Book Room Horror; The Devil's Footprints: Worm Song; The Keyhole • Codex Arcana **A:** Vince Giarrano; Galen Showman; Ryan Sook **W:** Mike Mignola; Scott Allie; Welles Hartley ★ 1st Appearance of Doctor Gosburo Coffin.

143 ❑ May 1999 Cover: 2.95 **NM** value: **Cover or less**
Circ: Diamd. preorders: **6,903**
📖 Tarzan: Tales of Pellucidar • Tarzan: Tales of Pellucidar **A:** Thomas Yates **W:** Tom Yeates; Stephen R. Bissette

144 ❑ Jun 1999 Cover: 2.95 **NM** value: **Cover or less**
Circ: Diamd. preorders: **5,027**
• The Vortex, Burglar Girls, Galactic Jack

145 ❑ Jul 1999 Cover: 2.95 **NM** value: **Cover or less**
Circ: Diamd. preorders: **5,361**
• Burglar Girls

146 ❑ Sep 1999 Cover: 2.95 **NM** value: **Cover or less**
Circ: Diamd. preorders: **5,849**
• Aliens vs Predator

147 ❑ Oct 1999 Cover: 2.95 **NM** value: **Cover or less**
Circ: Diamd. preorders: **5,393**
• Ragnok

148 ❑ Oct 1999 Cover: 2.95 **NM** value: **Cover or less**
Circ: Diamd. preorders: **6,509**

149 ❑ Dec 1999 Cover: 2.95 **NM** value: **Cover or less**
Circ: Diamd. preorders: **4,762**

150 ❑ Jan 2000 Cover: 4.50 **NM** value: **Cover or less**
Circ: Diamd. preorders: **10,068**
• Giant-size. 📖 Buffy the Vampire Slayer: Killing Time; Concrete: Sympathy from a Devil; L'il Devil Chef: Trouble in Lunchland; The Nevermen: Death ome Quietly, Part 3; Dirges in the Dark; The Fish Police: Fish City 2 Nite **A:** Cliff Richards; Jack Pollack; Steve Moncuse; Guy Davis; Paul Chadwick; Chris Brunner **W:** Jack Pollack; Steve Moncuse; Paul Chadwick; Chris Brunner; Doug Petrie; Philip Amara

151 ❑ Feb 2000 Cover: 2.95 **NM** value: **Cover or less**
Circ: Diamd. preorders: **9,142**
A: Cliff Richards; Jack Pollack; Steve Moncuse; Guy Davis; Paul Chadwick; Chris Brunner **W:** Jack Pollack; Steve Moncuse; Paul Chadwick; Chris Brunner; Doug Petrie; Philip Amara

152 ❑ Mar 2000 Cover: 2.95 **NM** value: **Cover or less**
Circ: Diamd. preorders: **4,442**
A: Cliff Richards; Jack Pollack; Steve Moncuse; Guy Davis; Paul Chadwick; Chris Brunner **W:** Jack Pollack; Steve Moncuse; Paul Chadwick; Chris Brunner; Doug Petrie; Philip Amara

153 ❑ Apr 2000 Cover: 2.95 **NM** value: **Cover or less**
Circ: Diamd. preorders: **6,552**
A: Cliff Richards; Jack Pollack; Steve Moncuse; Guy Davis; Paul Chadwick; Chris Brunner **W:** Jack Pollack; Steve Moncuse; Paul Chadwick; Chris Brunner; Doug Petrie; Philip Amara

154 ❑ May 2000 Cover: 2.95 **NM** value: **Cover or less**
Circ: Diamd. preorders: **6,080**
A: Cliff Richards; Jack Pollack; Steve Moncuse; Guy Davis; Paul Chadwick; Chris Brunner **W:** Jack Pollack; Steve Moncuse; Paul Chadwick; Chris Brunner; Doug Petrie; Philip Amara

155 ❑ Jun 2000 Cover: 2.95 **NM** value: **Cover or less**
Circ: Diamd. preorders: **6,306**
A: Cliff Richards; Jack Pollack; Steve Moncuse; Guy Davis; Paul Chadwick; Chris Brunner **W:** Jack Pollack; Steve Moncuse; Paul Chadwick; Chris Brunner; Doug Petrie; Philip Amara

156 ❑ Jul 2000 Cover: 2.95 **NM** value: **Cover or less**
Circ: Diamd. preorders: **4,335**
A: Cliff Richards; Jack Pollack; Steve Moncuse; Guy Davis; Paul Chadwick; Chris Brunner **W:** Jack Pollack; Steve Moncuse; Paul Chadwick; Chris Brunner; Doug Petrie; Philip Amara

157 ❑ Sep 2000, b&w Cover: 2.95 **NM** value: **Cover or less**
Circ: Diamd. preorders: **4,414**
📖 Witch's Son, Part 2; The Goon **A:** Cliff Richards; Jack Pollack; Steve Moncuse; Guy Davis; Paul Chadwick; Chris Brunner **W:** Jack Pollack; Steve Moncuse; Paul Chadwick; Chris Brunner; Doug Petrie; Philip Amara

Anl 1997❑Feb 1998, b&w Cover: 4.95 **NM** value: **Cover or less**
cover says 1997, indicia says 1998. 📖 Body Bags; The American: The Big Deal; The Oven Traveler; Aliens: Tourist Season; The Adventures of Rheumy Peepers and Chunky Highlights; The Stiff; Four Cats **A:** Jason Pearson; Chris Marrinan; Paul Pope; Gray Morrow; Mike Allred; Scott Musgrove; Renée French **W:** Jason Pearson; Paul Pope; Jay Stephens; Mark Verheiden; Beau Smith; John Arcudi; Penn Jillette

Anl 1998❑Sep 1998, b&w Cover: 4.95 **NM** value: **Cover or less**
Circ: Diamd. preorders: **14,205**
📖 Hellboy: The Right Hand of Doom; Phineas Page; Buffy the Vampire Slayer: MacGuffins; Skeleton Key: Witch; The Ark, Part 1; My Vagabond Days; Infirmary • Hellboy, Buffy, Skeleton Key, The Ark, My Vagabond Days, Infirmary **A:** John Bolton; Mike Mignola; Luke Ross; Ron Randall; Andi Watson; Pia Guerra; Stefano Gaudiano; Steven Weissman **W:** Mike Mignola; Andi Watson; Mark Verheiden; Steven Weissman; J.L. Van Meter; Matthew Burke; Steven Seagle

Anl 1999❑Aug 1999 Cover: 4.95 **NM** value: **Cover or less**
Circ: Diamd. preorders: **14,949**
📖 Xena Warrior Princess: The Worm; Hellboy: Pancakes; Usagi Yojimbo: A Funny Thing Happened on the Way to the Tournament; Ghost: My Sister's Keeper; Groo: Groo for Sale; Concrete: Orange Glow; Star Wars: Luke Skywalker: Walkabout; The Mask: Angry Young Mask • Dark Horse Jr. **A:** Phil Norwood; Sergio Aragonés; Mike Mignola; Rick Geary; Christian Zanier; Stan Sakai; Paul Chadwick; Joyce Chin **W:** Phil Norwood; Sergio Aragonés; Mike Mignola; Rick Geary; Stan Sakai; Paul Chadwick; Mark Evanier; John Wagner; Mike Kennedy

Anl 2000❑Jun 2000 Cover: 4.95 **NM** value: **Cover or less**
Circ: Diamd. preorders: **12,644**
• Flip-book. 📖 Gabrielle: Atlas Shrugged; Silhouette: Haunted Past; Bombshell: Blowing Your Cookies; Buffy the Vampire Slayer: Take Back the Night; Star Wars: Aurra Sing: Aurra's Song **A:** Mike Deodato; Chris Brunner; Isaac Buckminster Owens; Jim Pascoe; Mark Henry **W:** Jim Pascoe; Dean R. Motter; Ian Edginton; Mike Kennedy; Peter David; Tom Fassbender

Bk 1❑ Apr 1991, b&w Cover: 9.95 **NM** value: **Cover or less**
• Fifth Anniversary Special. • Martha Washington, Concrete **A:** Frank Miller

DARK HORSE PRESENTS: ALIENS — Dark Horse

This 1992 special collected and colorized Aliens appearances from Dark Horse Presents. The first of the five stories, "Theory of Alien Propagation," is a primer on the Aliens' ghastly breeding and hunting practices, speculating on their origins, and concluding with their threat to Earth.

Paul Guinan and Anina Bennett's two-part Aliens story is the most effective of the bunch, relating the tale of a treasure-hunting expedition into an Alien pyramid, revealing a terrible presence within the mausoleum. the Simon Bisley-illustrated "Reapers" is perhaps the least effective, although it does boast Bisley's art, as well as a humorous flourish at the end. The special is concluded with "The Alien," a final chapter in Aliens: Earth War in which mankind arranges to repopulate an Earth overrun by Aliens.

0 ❑ **NM** value: **5.00**
• Platinum

1 ❑ ca. 1992 Cover: 4.95 **NM** value: **Cover or less**
Circ: CapCity orders: **17,425** • **CGC:** 6 graded, best 9.9
📖 Theory of Alien Propagation; Advent; Terminus; Reapers; The Alien • color reprints;Reprints Aliens stories from Dark Horse Presents **A:** Tony Akins; Simon Bisley; Paul Guinan; Mark A. Nelson **W:** Paul Guinan; Mark Verheiden; Anina Bennett; John Arcudi

DARK ISLAND — Davdez

1 ❑ May 1998, b&w Cover: 2.95 **NM** value: **Cover or less**

2 ❑ Jun 1998, b&w Cover: 2.50 **NM** value: **2.95**

3 ❑ Jul 1998, b&w Cover: 2.50 **NM** value: **Cover or less**

DARK KNIGHT ARCHIVES — DC

1 ❑ Cover: 39.95 **NM** value: **Cover or less**
• Reprints Batman #1-4

2 ❑ Cover: 59.95 **NM** value: **Cover or less**
• Reprints Batman #5-8

DARKLIGHT: PRELUDE — Sirius

1 ❑ Jan 1994, b&w Cover: 2.95 **NM** value: **Cover or less**
A: Teri Sue Wood **W:** Teri Sue Wood

2 ❑ b&w Cover: 2.95 **NM** value: **Cover or less**
A: Teri Sue Wood **W:** Teri Sue Wood

3 ❑ b&w Cover: 2.95 **NM** value: **Cover or less**
A: Teri Sue Wood **W:** Teri Sue Wood

DARKLON THE MYSTIC — Pacific

1 ❑ Nov 1983 Cover: 1.50 **NM** value: **Cover or less**
📖 The Price; Retribution; He Who Waits in Shadow!; Duel; **A:** Jim Starlin **W:** Jim Starlin

CGC-graded: Multiply prices above by **33 for 9.9 M • 16 for 9.8 NM/M • 7 for 9.6 NM+ • 5 for 9.4 NM • 2.5 for 9.2 NM- • 1.5 for 9.0 VF/NM**

DARKMAN (MAGAZINE) Marvel

"Now crime has a new enemy and justice has a new face." That is the tag line for one of the more well-done revenge-motif action movies of the 1990s. Sporting a splendid painting by Joe Jusko, cover artist extraordinary, this black and white magazine collects the three-issue adaptation — Darkman (Vol. 1) — of the 1990 movie starring Liam Neeson and Frances McDormand.

Scripted by Ralph Macchio and pencilled by Bob Hall, this chronicles the descent of an innocent to the depths of murderous despair when mobsters destroy his life. Dr. Peyton Westlake develops a synthetic skin replacement that unfortunately breaks down after a couple of hours in direct light. Consequently, when Westlake uses it to repair his disfigured face, he needs to remain in shadows. His nom de guerre as Darkman reflects the rise of the dark aspects of human nature in his own personality.

1 ❑ Sep 1990, b&w Cover: 2.25 **NM** value: **Cover or less**
• Magazine size. **A:** Mark Texeira; Bob Hall **W:** Ralph Macchio

DARK MANSION OF FORBIDDEN LOVE, THE DC

Part Gothic romance, part mystery, each issue of this series gives readers a full-length story featuring a damsel with a dark secret to uncover or hide. Such a story is "The Secret of the Missing Bride," the tale of a young woman who examines her friend's mysterious death and discovers that her friend married into a family whose sinister secrets included neglected children and murdered in-laws, hidden in the rooms of their mansion.

After four issues, this series changed its format from romance-suspense to simply mystery, becoming simply "Forbidden Tales of Dark Mansion."

1 ❑ Sep 1971 Cover: 0.25 **NM** value: **35.00**
• **CGC:** 16 graded, best 9.4
📖 The Mystery Of The Missing Bride **A:** Tony DeZuniga
2 ❑ Nov 1971 Cover: 0.25 **NM** value: **20.00**
• **CGC:** 2 graded, best 9.4
3 ❑ Jan 1972 Cover: 0.25 **NM** value: **20.00**
• **CGC:** 3 graded, best 9.2
4 ❑ Mar 1972 Cover: 0.25 **NM** value: **20.00**
• **CGC:** 3 graded, best 9.8
• Series continued in Forbidden Tales of Dark Mansion #5

DARKMAN (VOL. 1) Marvel

1 ❑ Oct 1990 Cover: 1.50 **NM** value: **2.25**
Circ: CapCity orders: **11,700**
A: Mark Texeira; Bob Hall **W:** Ralph Macchio
2 ❑ Nov 1990 Cover: 1.50 **NM** value: **Cover or less**
Circ: CapCity orders: **9,700**
A: Bob Hall **W:** Ralph Macchio
3 ❑ Dec 1990 Cover: 1.50 **NM** value: **Cover or less**
Circ: CapCity orders: **8,900**
A: Bob Hall **W:** Ralph Macchio

DARKMAN (VOL. 2) Marvel

1 ❑ Apr 1993 Cover: 3.95 **NM** value: **Cover or less**
Circ: CapCity orders: **23,400**
📖 Dark Obsession **A:** Javier Saltares **W:** Kurt Busiek
2 ❑ May 1993 Cover: 2.95 **NM** value: **Cover or less**
Circ: CapCity orders: **13,800**
A: Javier Saltares **W:** Kurt Busiek
3 ❑ Jun 1993 Cover: 2.95 **NM** value: **Cover or less**
Circ: CapCity orders: **10,500**
📖 Dancin' In The Dark **A:** Javier Saltares **W:** Kurt Busiek
4 ❑ Jul 1993 Cover: 2.95 **NM** value: **Cover or less**
Circ: CapCity orders: **9,400**
W: Kurt Busiek
5 ❑ Aug 1993 Cover: 2.95 **NM** value: **Cover or less**
Circ: CapCity orders: **8,000**
W: Kurt Busiek
6 ❑ Sep 1993 Cover: 2.95 **NM** value: **Cover or less**
Circ: CapCity orders: **6,400**
final issue. **W:** Kurt Busiek

DARKMINDS Image

The city of Macropolis has seven million inhabitants packed into a city that stands five miles high. Here, a killer named Paradox has slain dozens of people — all in a singularly grisly manner, leaving no clues behind other than a telltale symbol carved into the victims' bodies. Agent Nagawa of the Special Investigations Unit, so far has been unable to stop the killer and has been assigned a new partner as a result: Agent Nakiko, a beautiful level-two cyborg. In addition to stunning physical attributes, Nakiko is an expert in psionic investigation. While her psychic abilities lead to awkward moments (such as noting when her partner is ogling her), it gives her the ability to seek out the killer by reading the minds of his dead victims.

Dreamwave Productions introduced this title in 1998, successfully employing manga stylings in a high-tech, horror thriller.

0.5 ❑ May 1999 Cover: 2.50 **NM** value: **Cover or less**
Circ: Diamd. preorders: **32,889**
📖 Electric Dream **A:** Patrick Lee **W:** Ken Siu Chong
1 ❑ Jul 1998 Cover: 2.50 **NM** value: **4.00**
Circ: Diamd. preorders: **37,653**
📖 A Deadly Paradox **A:** Patrick Lee **W:** Adrian Tsang; Patrick Lee
1/GO❑Aug 1998 **NM** value: **5.00**
• **CGC:** 4 graded, best 9.9
• DFE gold foil edition. 📖 A Deadly Paradox **A:** Patrick Lee **W:** Adrian Tsang; Patrick Lee
1/SC❑Jul 1998 Cover: 2.50 **NM** value: **5.00**
• **CGC:** 4 graded, best 9.6
alternate cover (solo figure). **A:** Patrick Lee **W:** Adrian Tsang; Patrick Lee
1-2 ❑ Cover: 2.50 **NM** value: **Cover or less**
2 ❑ Aug 1998 Cover: 2.50 **NM** value: **3.50**
Circ: Diamd. preorders: **21,615**
📖 The Neon Dragons **A:** Patrick Lee **W:** Adrian Tsang; Patrick Lee
2/SC❑Aug 1998 Cover: 2.50 **NM** value: **3.50**
alternate cover. **A:** Patrick Lee **W:** Adrian Tsang; Patrick Lee
3 ❑ Sep 1998 Cover: 2.50 **NM** value: **3.00**
Circ: Diamd. preorders: **33,198**
📖 Face of a Killer **A:** Patrick Lee **W:** Adrian Tsang; Patrick Lee
3/SC❑Sep 1998 Cover: 2.50 **NM** value: **3.00**
alternate cover. **A:** Patrick Lee **W:** Adrian Tsang; Patrick Lee
4 ❑ Oct 1998 Cover: 2.50 **NM** value: **3.00**
Circ: Diamd. preorders: **37,761**
cover says Dec, indicia says Oct. 📖 Deadly Intentions **A:** Patrick Lee **W:** Adrian Tsang; Patrick Lee
5 ❑ Nov 1998 Cover: 2.50 **NM** value: **3.00**
Circ: Diamd. preorders: **37,679**
📖 Unlikely Friends, Unlikely Enemies **A:** Patrick Lee **W:** Adrian Tsang; Patrick Lee
6 ❑ Dec 1998 Cover: 2.50 **NM** value: **3.00**
Circ: Diamd. preorders: **37,809**
📖 Opposing Forces **A:** Patrick Lee **W:** Adrian Tsang; Patrick Lee
7 ❑ Feb 1999 Cover: 2.50 **NM** value: **Cover or less**
Circ: Diamd. preorders: **35,771**
📖 The Darkest Mind **A:** Patrick Lee **W:** Adrian Tsang; Patrick Lee
8 ❑ Apr 1999 Cover: 2.50 **NM** value: **Cover or less**
Circ: Diamd. preorders: **33,103**
A: Patrick Lee **W:** Adrian Tsang; Patrick Lee
Bk 1❑ Jan 1999 Cover: 7.95 **NM** value: **Cover or less**
• Collected edition. • collects #1-3 **A:** Patrick Lee **W:** Adrian Tsang; Patrick Lee
Bk 2❑ Mar 1999 Cover: 7.95 **NM** value: **Cover or less**
• Collected edition. • collects #4-6 **A:** Patrick Lee **W:** Adrian Tsang; Patrick Lee
Bk 3❑ May 1999 Cover: 5.95 **NM** value: **Cover or less**
• Collected edition. • collects #7-8 **A:** Patrick Lee **W:** Adrian Tsang; Patrick Lee

DARKMINDS (VOL. 2) Image

0 ❑ Jul 2000 Cover: 2.50 **NM** value: **Cover or less**
Circ: Diamd. preorders: **22,169**
📖 The Bullet **A:** Sigmund Torre; James Raiz **W:** Ken Sui Chong
1 ❑ Feb 2000 Cover: 2.50 **NM** value: **Cover or less**
Circ: Diamd. preorders: **37,011**
📖 The More Things Change… **A:** Omar Dogan **W:** Omar Dogan; Pat Lee; Erik Ko; Ken Sui Chong
2 ❑ Mar 2000 Cover: 2.50 **NM** value: **Cover or less**
Circ: Diamd. preorders: **29,157**
3 ❑ Apr 2000 Cover: 2.50 **NM** value: **Cover or less**
Circ: Diamd. preorders: **27,221**
4 ❑ May 2000 Cover: 2.50 **NM** value: **Cover or less**
Circ: Diamd. preorders: **23,560**
5 ❑ Jun 2000 Cover: 2.50 **NM** value: **Cover or less**
Circ: Diamd. preorders: **23,115**
📖 The Prize **A:** Omar Dogan **W:** Omar Dogan; Pat Lee; Erik Ko; Ken Siu Chong
6 ❑ Sep 2000 Cover: 2.50 **NM** value: **Cover or less**
Circ: Diamd. preorders: **19,683**
📖 9mm Answers **A:** Sigmund Torre **W:** Ken Siu-Chong
7 ❑ Oct 2000 Cover: 2.50 **NM** value: **Cover or less**
Circ: Diamd. preorders: **18,767**
📖 The Hunger **A:** Sigmund Torre **W:** Ken Siu-Chong
8 ❑ Nov 2000 Cover: 2.50 **NM** value: **Cover or less**
Circ: Diamd. preorders: **18,480**
📖 Born Again **A:** Sigmund Torre **W:** Ken Siu-Chong
9 ❑ Feb 2001 Cover: 2.50 **NM** value: **Cover or less**
Circ: Diamd. preorders: **17,853**
📖 A Million and One **A:** Sigmund Torre **W:** Ken Siu-Chong
10 ❑ Apr 2001 Cover: 2.50 **NM** value: **Cover or less**
Circ: Diamd. preorders: **17,329**
📖 Final Bow **A:** Sigmund Torre **W:** Ken Siu-Chong

DARKMINDS/WITCHBLADE Image

1 ❑ Aug 2000 Cover: 5.95 **NM** value: **Cover or less**
A: Pat Lee; James Raiz **W:** David Wohl

DARK MOON PROPHESY Dark Moon Productions

1 ❑ May 1995 **NM** value: **1.00**
No issue number. • free color and b&w preview of Dark Moon line

DARK MYSTERIES Master Publications

1 ❑ Jun 1951 Cover: 0.10 **NM** value: **500.00**
• **CGC:** 5 graded, best 9.2
📖 The Curse of the Sea Witch; The Ghoul of Death
2 ❑ Aug 1951 Cover: 0.10 **NM** value: **300.00**
• **CGC:** 3 graded, best 8.5
📖 The Monster's Ghost; Vampire Fangs of Doom
3 ❑ Nov 1951 Cover: 0.10 **NM** value: **200.00**
• **CGC:** 2 graded, best 9.4
📖 Ghosts from the Unknown; Terror of the Unwilling Witch
4 ❑ Dec 1951 Cover: 0.10 **NM** value: **200.00**
• **CGC:** 1 graded, best 7.0
📖 The Corpse That Came Alive!
5 ❑ Feb 1952 Cover: 0.10 **NM** value: **200.00**
• **CGC:** 1 graded, best 8.0
📖 Horror of the Ghostly Crew; Vampire's Curse
6 ❑ Apr 1952 Cover: 0.10 **NM** value: **200.00**
📖 If the Noose Fits, Wear It!
7 ❑ Jun 1952 Cover: 0.10 **NM** value: **200.00**
📖 Terror of the Cards of Death; The Vampire Corpse
8 ❑ Aug 1952 Cover: 0.10 **NM** value: **200.00**
• **CGC:** 2 graded, best 8.5
📖 Terror of the Ghostly Trail
9 ❑ Oct 1952 Cover: 0.10 **NM** value: **200.00**
📖 Witch's Feast at Dawn; Terror of the Voodoo Ghouls
10 ❑ Feb 1953 Cover: 0.10 **NM** value: **200.00**
• **CGC:** 1 graded, best 4.5
📖 Terror of the Burning Witch
11 ❑ Apr 1953 Cover: 0.10 **NM** value: **200.00**
📖 The River of Blood!
12 ❑ Jun 1953 Cover: 0.10 **NM** value: **200.00**
• **CGC:** 3 graded, best 9.0
📖 The Horror of the Talking Dead!
13 ❑ Aug 1953 Cover: 0.10 **NM** value: **200.00**
📖 The Terror of the Hungry Cats
14 ❑ Oct 1953 Cover: 0.10 **NM** value: **200.00**
• **CGC:** 3 graded, best 7.0
📖 Fingers of Doom!
15 ❑ Dec 1953 Cover: 0.10 **NM** value: **200.00**
• **CGC:** 1 graded, best 7.5
📖 Terror of the Vampire's Teeth
16 ❑ Feb 1954 Cover: 0.10 **NM** value: **150.00**
• **CGC:** 2 graded, best 8.0
📖 Horror of the Walking Dead
17 ❑ Apr 1954 Cover: 0.10 **NM** value: **150.00**
18 ❑ Jun 1954 Cover: 0.10 **NM** value: **150.00**
• **CGC:** 2 graded, best 9.2
19 ❑ Aug 1954 Cover: 0.10 **NM** value: **150.00**
• **CGC:** 7 graded, best 9.4
20 ❑ Oct 1954 Cover: 0.10 **NM** value: **150.00**
• **CGC:** 1 graded, best 7.0
21 ❑ Dec 1954 Cover: 0.10 **NM** value: **150.00**
• **CGC:** 4 graded, best 9.0
📖 Sinister Secret
22 ❑ Mar 1955 Cover: 0.10 **NM** value: **100.00**
📖 The Hand of Destiny
23 ❑ May 1955 Cover: 0.10 **NM** value: **100.00**
📖 The Mardenburg Curse
24 ❑ Jul 1955 Cover: 0.10 **NM** value: **100.00**
📖 Give a Man Enough Rope

DARK NEMESIS (VILLAINS) DC

1 ❑ Feb 1998 Cover: 1.95 **NM** value: **Cover or less**
• New Year's Evil

DARKNESS, THE Top Cow / Image

0 ❑ Cover: 2.50 **NM** value: **3.00**
0.5 ❑ ca. 1996 Cover: 2.95 **NM** value: **3.00**
Circ: Direct Market orders: **19,445**
• Wizard mail-away promotion **A:** Marc Silvestri **W:** Garth Ennis
0.5/SC❑ca. 1996 **NM** value: **5.00**
Christmas cover. • Wizard mail-away promotion
0.5-2❑Mar 2001 Cover: 2.95 **NM** value: **Cover or less**
A: Billy Tan; Marc Silvestri **W:** Billy Tan; Marc Silvestri
1 ❑ Dec 1996 Cover: 2.50 **NM** value: **4.00**
Circ: Direct Market orders: **84,647** • **CGC:** 25 graded, best 9.8
📖 Coming of Age **A:** Marc Silvestri **W:** Garth Ennis
1/A ❑ Dec 1996 Cover: 2.50 **NM** value: **4.00**
• **CGC:** 32 graded, best 9.8
Dark cover variant. 📖 Marc Silvestri **A:** Marc Silvestri **W:** Marc Silvestri
1/B ❑ Dec 1996 **NM** value: **5.00**
• Wizard Ace edition. 📖 Marc Silvestri **A:** Marc Silvestri **W:** Marc Silvestri
1/C ❑ Dec 1996 **NM** value: **4.00**
• **CGC:** 11 graded, best 9.9
• Fan club edition. 📖 Marc Silvestri **A:** Marc Silvestri **W:** Marc Silvestri
1/GO❑Dec 1996 **NM** value: **6.00**
• Gold edition. 📖 Coming of Age **A:** Marc Silvestri **W:** Garth Ennis
1/PL❑Dec 1996 **NM** value: **10.00**
• **CGC:** 5 graded, best 9.6
• Platinum edition. 📖 Coming of Age **A:** Marc Silvestri **W:** Garth Ennis
2 ❑ Jan 1997 Cover: 2.50 **NM** value: **4.00**
Circ: Diamd. preorders: **69,498** • **CGC:** 2 graded, best 9.4
📖 Underworld **A:** Marc Silvestri **W:** Garth Ennis
3 ❑ Mar 1997 Cover: 2.50 **NM** value: **3.00**
Circ: Diamd. preorders: **86,357** • **CGC:** 1 graded, best 9.6
📖 Almost an Angel **A:** Marc Silvestri **W:** Garth Ennis
4 ❑ May 1997 Cover: 2.50 **NM** value: **3.00**
Circ: Diamd. preorders: **87,834**
📖 Brought to Light **A:** Marc Silvestri **W:** Garth Ennis
5 ❑ Jun 1997 Cover: 2.50 **NM** value: **3.00**
Circ: Diamd. preorders: **90,877**
📖 Apocalypse Shortly **A:** Marc Silvestri **W:** Garth Ennis
6 ❑ Jul 1997 Cover: 2.50 **NM** value: **3.00**
Circ: Diamd. preorders: **92,859**
📖 End of an Era **A:** Marc Silvestri **W:** Garth Ennis
7 ❑ Aug 1997 Cover: 2.50 **NM** value: **Cover or less**
Circ: Diamd. preorders: **92,196**
📖 Coming of Age **A:** Marc Silvestri **W:** Garth Ennis
7/A ❑ Aug 1997 Cover: 2.50 **NM** value: **Cover or less**
Variant cover with Michael Turner and babes. 📖 Coming of Age **A:** Marc Silvestri **W:** Garth Ennis
8 ❑ Oct 1997 Cover: 2.50 **NM** value: **Cover or less**
Circ: Diamd. preorders: **106,081**
📖 Coming of Age **A:** Marc Silvestri; Joe Benitez(cover) **W:** Garth Ennis

Other grades: Multiply prices above by **1.5 for Mint • 2/3 for Very Fine • 1/3 for Fine • 1/5 for Very Good • 1/8 for Good**

8/A ❑ Oct 1997 Cover: 2.50 **NM** value: **Cover or less**
alternate cover. 📖 Coming of Age **A:** Marc Silvestri **W:** Garth Ennis
8/B ❑ Oct 1997 Cover: 2.50 **NM** value: **Cover or less**
alternate cover.
8/C ❑ Oct 1997 Cover: 2.50 **NM** value: **Cover or less**
alternate cover.
9 ❑ Nov 1997 Cover: 2.50 **NM** value: **Cover or less**
Circ: Diamd. preorders: **105,404**
📖 Family Ties, Part 2 **A:** Marc Silvestri **W:** Garth Ennis
9/A ❑ Nov 1997 Cover: 2.50 **NM** value: **Cover or less**
alternate cover. 📖 Family Ties, Part 2
10 ❑ Dec 1997 Cover: 2.50 **NM** value: **Cover or less**
Circ: Diamd. preorders: **104,599**
📖 Family Ties, Part 3 **A:** Marc Silvestri **W:** Garth Ennis
10/A❑ Dec 1997 Cover: 2.50 **NM** value: **Cover or less**
alternate cover (gold). 📖 Family Ties, Part 3
10/B❑ Dec 1997 Cover: 2.50 **NM** value: **Cover or less**
alternate cover (gold). 📖 Family Ties, Part 3
11/A❑ Jan 1998 Cover: 2.50 **NM** value: **9.00**
Circ: Diamd. preorders: **357,006**
chromium cover. 📖 Brought to Light **A:** Marc Silvestri **W:** Garth Ennis
11/B❑ Jan 1998 Cover: 2.50 **NM** value: **Cover or less**
📖 Brought to Light **A:** Marc Silvestri; Joe Benitez(cover) **W:** Garth Ennis
11/C❑ Jan 1998 Cover: 2.50 **NM** value: **Cover or less**
📖 Brought to Light **A:** Marc Silvestri; Billy Tan(cover) **W:** Garth Ennis
11/D❑ Jan 1998 Cover: 2.50 **NM** value: **Cover or less**
📖 Brought to Light **A:** Marc Silvestri; David Finch(cover) **W:** Garth Ennis
11/E❑ Jan 1998 Cover: 2.50 **NM** value: **Cover or less**
📖 Brought to Light **A:** Marc Silvestri; Michael Turner(cover) **W:** Garth Ennis
11/F❑ Jan 1998 Cover: 2.50 **NM** value: **Cover or less**
📖 Brought to Light **A:** Marc Silvestri; Whilce Portacio(cover) **W:** Garth Ennis
11/G❑ Jan 1998 Cover: 2.50 **NM** value: **Cover or less**
📖 Brought to Light **A:** Marc Silvestri; Dale Keown(cover) **W:** Garth Ennis
11/H❑ Jan 1998 Cover: 2.50 **NM** value: **Cover or less**
📖 Brought to Light **A:** Marc Silvestri; Brandon Peterson(cover) **W:** Garth Ennis
11/I❑ Jan 1998 Cover: 2.50 **NM** value: **Cover or less**
📖 Brought to Light **A:** Marc Silvestri; Greg Hildebrandt(cover); Tim Hildebrandt(cover) **W:** Garth Ennis
11/J❑ Jan 1998 Cover: 2.50 **NM** value: **Cover or less**
📖 Brought to Light **A:** Marc Silvestri; Nathan Cabrera(cover) **W:** Garth Ennis
12 ❑ Feb 1998 Cover: 2.50 **NM** value: **Cover or less**
Circ: Diamd. preorders: **94,587**
A: Clarence Lansang; Cedric Nocon; Billy Tan; Richard Bennett; Marc Silvestri **W:** Malachy Coney; Garth Ennis
13 ❑ Mar 1998 Cover: 2.50 **NM** value: **Cover or less**
Circ: Diamd. preorders: **88,113**
14 ❑ Apr 1998 Cover: 2.50 **NM** value: **Cover or less**
Circ: Diamd. preorders: **89,925**
15 ❑ Jun 1998 Cover: 2.50 **NM** value: **Cover or less**
Circ: Diamd. preorders: **79,803**
16 ❑ Jul 1998 Cover: 2.50 **NM** value: **Cover or less**
Circ: Diamd. preorders: **78,631**
📖 Family Ties, Part 2 **A:** Joe Benitez **W:** Malachy Coney
17 ❑ Sep 1998 Cover: 2.50 **NM** value: **Cover or less**
Circ: Diamd. preorders: **73,977** • **CGC:** 1 graded, best 9.6
A: David Finch; Clarence Lansang; Cedric Nocon; Joe Benitez **W:** Malachy Coney ★ Origin of Magdalena.
18 ❑ Nov 1998 Cover: 2.50 **NM** value: **Cover or less**
Circ: Diamd. preorders: **68,534**
A: Joe Benitez **W:** Malachy Coney
19 ❑ Jan 1999 Cover: 2.50 **NM** value: **Cover or less**
Circ: Diamd. preorders: **66,445**
A: Joe Benitez **W:** Joe Banitez; Marcia Chen
20/A❑ Apr 1999 Cover: 2.50 **NM** value: **Cover or less**
Circ: Diamd. preorders: **68,718**
Regular Cover (with Darklings). **A:** David Finch; Joe Benitez; Joe Weems V(cover); Matt Nelson(cover) **W:** Malachy Coney; Marcia Chen
20/B❑ Apr 1999 Cover: 2.50 **NM** value: **Cover or less**
alternate cover. **A:** David Finch; Joe Benitez; Joe Weems V(cover); Marc Silvestri(cover); Matt Nelson(cover) **W:** Malachy Coney; Marcia Chen
20/C❑ Apr 1999 Cover: 2.50 **NM** value: **Cover or less**
Alternate Cover (With Darklings). **A:** David Finch; Joe Benitez; Joe Weems V(cover); Liquid!(cover); Marc Silvestri(cover) **W:** Malachy Coney; Marcia Chen
21 ❑ May 1999 Cover: 2.50 **NM** value: **Cover or less**
Circ: Diamd. preorders: **59,045**
A: David Finch; Clarence Lansang **W:** Malachy Coney
22 ❑ Jun 1999 Cover: 2.50 **NM** value: **Cover or less**
Circ: Diamd. preorders: **55,023**
A: Clarence Lansang; Ken Lashley **W:** Malachy Coney
23 ❑ Jul 1999 Cover: 2.50 **NM** value: **Cover or less**
Circ: Diamd. preorders: **54,054**
A: Joe Benitez **W:** Scott Lobdell
24 ❑ Aug 1999 Cover: 2.50 **NM** value: **Cover or less**
Circ: Diamd. preorders: **52,091**
A: Ken Lashley; Joe Benitez **W:** Scott Lobdell
25 ❑ Sep 1999 Cover: 3.99 **NM** value: **Cover or less**
Circ: Diamd. preorders: **54,214**
A: Joe Benitez **W:** Scott Lobdell
25/A❑ 1999 **NM** value: **20.00**
• **CGC:** 20 graded, best 10.0
• Chrome variant
26 ❑ Oct 1999 Cover: 2.50 **NM** value: **Cover or less**
Circ: Diamd. preorders: **46,765**
A: Clarence Lansang **W:** Scott Lobdell
27 ❑ Oct 1999 Cover: 2.50 **NM** value: **Cover or less**
Circ: Diamd. preorders: **44,140**
A: Clarence Lansang **W:** Scott Lobdell
28 ❑ Jan 2000 Cover: 2.50 **NM** value: **Cover or less**
Circ: Diamd. preorders: **45,749**
A: Clarence Lansang **W:** Scott Lobdell
29 ❑ 2000 Cover: 2.50 **NM** value: **Cover or less**
Circ: Diamd. preorders: **40,237**
A: Clarence Lansang **W:** Scott Lobdell
30 ❑ Apr 2000 Cover: 2.50 **NM** value: **Cover or less**
Circ: Diamd. preorders: **38,788**
A: Clarence Lansang **W:** Scott Lobdell
31 ❑ 2000 Cover: 2.50 **NM** value: **Cover or less**
Circ: Diamd. preorders: **37,001**
32 ❑ Jul 2000 Cover: 2.50 **NM** value: **Cover or less**
Circ: Diamd. preorders: **35,148**
33 ❑ Aug 2000 Cover: 2.50 **NM** value: **Cover or less**
Circ: Diamd. preorders: **34,511**
A: Brian Ching **W:** Scott Lobdell
34 ❑ Oct 2000 Cover: 2.50 **NM** value: **Cover or less**
Circ: Diamd. preorders: **33,060**
A: Clayton Crain **W:** Scott Lobdell
35 ❑ Nov 2000 Cover: 2.50 **NM** value: **Cover or less**
Circ: Diamd. preorders: **32,596**
A: Clayton Crain **W:** Scott Lobdell
36 ❑ Dec 2000 Cover: 2.50 **NM** value: **Cover or less**
Circ: Diamd. preorders: **31,651**
A: Clayton Crain **W:** Scott Lobdell
37 ❑ Feb 2001 Cover: 2.50 **NM** value: **Cover or less**
Circ: Diamd. preorders: **30,441**
A: Mark Pajarillo; Brian Denham; Eric Basaldua; Joel Gomez **W:** Scott Lobdell
38 ❑ Apr 2001 Cover: 2.50 **NM** value: **Cover or less**
Circ: Diamd. preorders: **29,722**
A: Brett Booth **W:** Scott Lobdell
39 ❑ May 2001 Cover: 2.50 **NM** value: **Cover or less**
Circ: Diamd. preorders: **29,353**
A: David Finch **W:** David Wohl
40 ❑ Cover: 2.50 **NM** value: **Cover or less**
Circ: Diamd. preorders: **34,758**
Ash 1❑ Jul 1996 **NM** value: **4.00**
• **CGC:** 2 graded, best 9.6
No issue number. no cover price. • preview of upcoming series
ASH 1/A❑ **NM** value: **3.00**
• Prelude;"Wizard Authentic" variant
Bk 1❑ Jun 1997 Cover: 4.95 **NM** value: **Cover or less**
Circ: Diamd. preorders: **24,660**
• Collected Editions #1. • Reprints The Darkness #1-2 **A:** Joe Benitez **W:** Malachy Coney; Garth Ennis
Bk 2❑ Sep 1997 Cover: 4.95 **NM** value: **Cover or less**
• Collected Editions #2. • Reprints The Darkness #3-4 **W:** Garth Ennis
Bk 3❑ Dec 1997 Cover: 4.95 **NM** value: **Cover or less**
• Collected Editions #3. • slipcase;Reprints The Darkness #5-6 **A:** Marc Silvestri **W:** Garth Ennis
Bk 4❑ Feb 1998 Cover: 4.95 **NM** value: **Cover or less**
Circ: Diamd. preorders: **10,774**
• Collected Editions #4. • Reprints The Darkness #7-8 **A:** Marc Silvestri **W:** Garth Ennis
Bk 5❑ Sep 1999 Cover: 5.95 **NM** value: **Cover or less**
• prestige format. • Reprints The Darkness #11-12 **A:** Clarence Lansang; Cedric Nocon; Joe Benitez; Richard Bennett; Marc Silvestri **W:** Malachy Coney; Garth Ennis
Bk 6❑ Apr 1998 Cover: 5.95 **NM** value: **Cover or less**
• Collected Editions #6. • Reprints The Darkness #13-14 **A:** Joe Benitez **W:** Malachy Coney; Garth Ennis
Dlx 1❑ Cover: 14.95 **NM** value: **Cover or less**
• Deluxe edition. • Reprints The Darkness #1-6;Slipcased **A:** Joe Benitez; Marc Silvestri **W:** Malachy Coney; Garth Ennis

DARKNESS/BATMAN, THE — Image
1 ❑ Aug 1999 Cover: 5.95 **NM** value: **Cover or less**
Circ: Diamd. preorders: **73,784**
A: Jeph Loeb **W:** Scott Lobdell

DARKNESS INFINITY — Image
1 ❑ Aug 1999 Cover: 3.50 **NM** value: **Cover or less**
Circ: Diamd. preorders: **41,701**
A: Roger Cruz **W:** Scott Lobdell

DARKNESS/PAINKILLER JANE — Image
Ash 1❑ **NM** value: **3.00**
ASH 1/A❑ **NM** value: **3.00**
variant cover.

DARKNESS, THE: SPEAR OF DESTINY — Image
1 ❑ Apr 2000 Cover: 12.95 **NM** value: **Cover or less**
• Collects The Darkness #15-18 **A:** Joe Benitez **W:** Malachy Coney

DARKNESS/WITCHBLADE SPECIAL — Image
Jackie Estacado decides to turn state's evidence and give up his life as a hitman. Unfortunately, he is kidnapped from protective custody by Cull, leader of the Necrobi, an ancient race feeding on human souls. NYPD Detective Sara Pezzini (Witchblade) and rogue FBI agent Carla Denton follow Jackie into the underground world of the Necrobi. The good news is Jackie possesses the Darkness and Sara controls the Witchblade. The bad news is Jackie supposedly killed Carla's father years ago and she is selling them out to Cull.

The story is concluded in The Darkness #28.

1 ❑ Dec 1999 Cover: 3.95 **NM** value: **Cover or less**
Circ: Diamd. preorders: **48,219**
A: Keu Cha **W:** Scott Lobdell; Christina Z

DARK OZ — Arrow
1 ❑ Cover: 2.75 **NM** value: **Cover or less**
2 ❑ Cover: 2.75 **NM** value: **Cover or less**
3 ❑ Cover: 2.75 **NM** value: **Cover or less**
4 ❑ Cover: 2.75 **NM** value: **Cover or less**
5 ❑ Cover: 2.75 **NM** value: **Cover or less**
• indicia says 97, a misprint

DARK PERIL — Quantum
1 ❑ Cover: 2.95 **NM** value: **Cover or less**
• Flip-book. 📖 Kill the Driver: Greener Grass **A:** Mike Christiansen; Rich Larson **W:** David Watkins
2 ❑ Cover: 2.95 **NM** value: **Cover or less**
3 ❑ Cover: 2.95 **NM** value: **Cover or less**
4 ❑ Cover: 2.95 **NM** value: **Cover or less**

DARK RAT — Maverick Pulp Comix
1 ❑ Sep 1997, b&w Cover: 2.50 **NM** value: **Cover or less**

DARK REALM — Image
1 ❑ Oct 2000 Cover: 2.95 **NM** value: **Cover or less**
Circ: Diamd. preorders: **14,816**
A: Taeson Chang **W:** Eddie Yu; Robert Chong
2 ❑ Dec 2000 Cover: 2.95 **NM** value: **Cover or less**
Circ: Diamd. preorders: **9,999**
A: Taeson Chang **W:** Eddie Yu; Robert Chong
3 ❑ Feb 2001 Cover: 2.95 **NM** value: **Cover or less**
Circ: Diamd. preorders: **8,763**
A: Taeson Chang **W:** Eddie Yu; Robert Chong

DARK REGIONS — White Wolf
1 ❑ Feb 1987 Cover: 1.75 **NM** value: **Cover or less**
📖 The Magic Stream; Ignor Ant; Chuk the Barbarian **A:** Rick McCollum; M.A. Kennedy; Mark Gustafson **W:** M.A. Kennedy; Tom Fallwell
2 ❑ Cover: 1.75 **NM** value: **Cover or less**
3 ❑ May 1987 Cover: 1.75 **NM** value: **Cover or less**

DARKSEED AND OTHER DEFAMATIONS — Boneyard
All issues are adults only.
1 ❑ b&w Cover: 3.95 **NM** value: **Cover or less**

DARKSEID VS. GALACTUS: THE HUNGER — DC / Marvel
1 ❑ Cover: 4.95 **NM** value: **Cover or less**
Circ: CapCity orders: **22,400**
No issue number. One-shot. • prestige format. **A:** John Byrne **W:** John Byrne

DARKSEID (VILLAINS) — DC
Darkseid is gone — lost alongside Ares, Arzaz, and The Nameless One, when they tried to steal the power of the Source. Instead, this nearly limitless power took them prisoner, holding them in a great wall that protects the heart of the Source from those who would steal its power.

But, although Darkseid is no longer master of the world Apokolips, his shadow looms large over the planet. Darkseid's former advisors and servants wage a terrible war to determine who will control the planet's destiny.

But, at the height of the battle, a great stone statue of Darkseid begins to move of its own accord.

This one-shot was part of a series of "New Year's Evil" specials released in early 1998.

1 ❑ Feb 1998 Cover: 1.95 **NM** value: **Cover or less**
📖 Shadows in a Greater Darkness • New Year's Evil **A:** Sal Buscema; Kieron Grant **W:** John Byrne

DARK SHADOWS (GOLD KEY) — Gold Key
Dark Shadows was a creepy Gothic soap opera that began daily afternoon broadcasts in 1966 and ran until 1971. It started with the arrival in the village of Collinsport of a young woman who cameto work for the wealthy Collins family and it featured a mix of deep family secrets until another character arrived on the scene: It was Barnabas Collins, and viewers soon learned that he was a vampire. As the series went more and more deeply into fantasy themes, the series became ritual viewing for a growing afternoon audience and Barnabas became the focus of the series. For those who wanted more stories about their favorite characters, Gold Key dutifully adapted the show in a fairly long-lived series. Lush painted covers and images of Barnabas' brooding face provided the bait that lured readers into this title. It is devotedly collected today by fans of the series, which has been extensively rerun on the Sci-Fi Channel.

1 ❑ Mar 1969 Cover: 0.25 **NM** value: **125.00**
• based on TV series
1/A ❑ **NM** value: **50.00**
• based on TV series;with poster;Without poster
2 ❑ Aug 1969 Cover: 0.15 **NM** value: **55.00**
• **CGC:** 1 graded, best 9.2

CGC-graded: Multiply prices above by **33 for 9.9 M** • **16 for 9.8 NM/M** • **7 for 9.6 NM+** • **5 for 9.4 NM** • **2.5 for 9.2 NM-** • **1.5 for 9.0 VF/NM**

3 ❑ Nov 1969 Cover: 0.15 **NM** value: **50.00**
• **CGC:** 4 graded, best 9.6

4 ❑ Feb 1970 Cover: 0.15 **NM** value: **40.00**

5 ❑ May 1970 Cover: 0.15 **NM** value: **40.00**

6 ❑ Aug 1970 Cover: 0.15 **NM** value: **32.00**

7 ❑ Nov 1970 Cover: 0.15 **NM** value: **32.00**

8 ❑ Feb 1971 Cover: 0.15 **NM** value: **32.00**
• **CGC:** 4 graded, best 9.4

9 ❑ May 1971 Cover: 0.15 **NM** value: **32.00**
• **CGC:** 1 graded, best 9.4

10 ❑ Aug 1971 Cover: 0.15 **NM** value: **32.00**

11 ❑ Nov 1971 Cover: 0.15 **NM** value: **30.00**

12 ❑ Feb 1972 Cover: 0.15 **NM** value: **30.00**

13 ❑ Apr 1972 Cover: 0.15 **NM** value: **30.00**

14 ❑ Jun 1972 Cover: 0.15 **NM** value: **30.00**
Painted cover. The Mystic Painting, Part 1, A Tragedy Recalled; The Mystic Painting, Part 2, Stain of Guilt

15 ❑ Aug 1972 Cover: 0.15 **NM** value: **30.00**

16 ❑ Oct 1972 Cover: 0.15 **NM** value: **24.00**

17 ❑ Dec 1972 Cover: 0.15 **NM** value: **24.00**

18 ❑ Feb 1973 Cover: 0.15 **NM** value: **24.00**

19 ❑ Apr 1973 Cover: 0.15 **NM** value: **24.00**

20 ❑ Jun 1973 Cover: 0.20 **NM** value: **24.00**

21 ❑ Aug 1973 Cover: 0.20 **NM** value: **18.00**

22 ❑ Oct 1973 Cover: 0.20 **NM** value: **18.00**

23 ❑ Dec 1973 Cover: 0.20 **NM** value: **18.00**

24 ❑ Feb 1974 Cover: 0.20 **NM** value: **18.00**

25 ❑ Apr 1974 Cover: 0.20 **NM** value: **18.00**

26 ❑ Jun 1974 Cover: 0.20 **NM** value: **18.00**

27 ❑ Aug 1974 Cover: 0.25 **NM** value: **18.00**

28 ❑ Oct 1974 Cover: 0.25 **NM** value: **18.00**

29 ❑ Dec 1974 Cover: 0.25 **NM** value: **18.00**

30 ❑ Feb 1975 Cover: 0.25 **NM** value: **18.00**

31 ❑ Apr 1975 Cover: 0.25 **NM** value: **15.00**

32 ❑ Jun 1975 Cover: 0.25 **NM** value: **15.00**

33 ❑ Aug 1975 Cover: 0.25 **NM** value: **15.00**

34 ❑ Cover: 0.25 **NM** value: **15.00**

35 ❑ Feb 1975 Cover: 0.25 **NM** value: **15.00**

Bk 1❑ **NM** value: **35.00**
• Synopsis of TV Episodes

DARK SHADOWS (INNOVATION) — Innovation

1 ❑ Jun 1992 Cover: 2.50 **NM** value: **3.00**
Circ: CapCity orders: **14,120**
A Time Of Innocence…And Confidences • TV series **A:** E. Silas Smith **W:** David Campiti; Scott Rockwell

2 ❑ Aug 1992 Cover: 2.50 **NM** value: **Cover or less**
Circ: CapCity orders: **9,415**
• TV series

3 ❑ Nov 1992 Cover: 2.50 **NM** value: **Cover or less**
Circ: CapCity orders: **4,440**
• TV series

4 ❑ Spr 1993 Cover: 2.50 **NM** value: **Cover or less**
Circ: CapCity orders: **7,685**
• TV series

5 ❑ Jun 1993 Cover: 2.50 **NM** value: **Cover or less**
Circ: CapCity orders: **8,790**
Lost in Thought, Part 1 • Book 2, #1 **A:** Hector Gomez(cover); Jose Pimentel **W:** Maggie Thompson

6 ❑ Cover: 2.50 **NM** value: **Cover or less**
Circ: CapCity orders: **6,595**
Lost in Thought, Part 2 • Book 2, #2 **A:** Hector Gomez(cover); Jose Pimentel **W:** Maggie Thompson

7 ❑ Cover: 2.50 **NM** value: **Cover or less**
Circ: CapCity orders: **6,455**
• Book 2, #3 **A:** Hector Gomez(cover); Jose Pimentel **W:** Maggie Thompson

8 ❑ Cover: 2.50 **NM** value: **Cover or less**
Circ: CapCity orders: **5,325**
• Book 2, #4 **A:** Hector Gomez(cover); Jose Pimentel **W:** Maggie Thompson

9 ❑ Cover: 2.50 **NM** value: **Cover or less**
Circ: CapCity orders: **5,900**
A Motion and a Spirit • Book 3 #1 **A:** Felipe Echevarria **W:** Scott Rockwell

DARK SHADOWS (STEINWAY/AJAX) — Steinway

1 ❑ Oct 1957 Cover: 0.10 **NM** value: **100.00**

2 ❑ Jan 1958 Cover: 0.10 **NM** value: **80.00**
• **CGC:** 1 graded, best 7.5

DARK SHRINE — Antarctic Press

1 ❑ May 1999 Cover: 2.99 **NM** value: **Cover or less**
A: Shelby Robertson **W:** Shelby Robertson

2 ❑ Jun 1999 Cover: 2.50 **NM** value: **Cover or less**
A: Shelby Robertson **W:** Shelby Robertson

DARKSIDE — Darkline

1 ❑ Cover: 1.50 **NM** value: **2.99**
… A Time for Nightmare **A:** Ching Lau; Mark Pajarillo; Michael Chang **W:** Rob Liefeld; Robert Napton ★ Appearance of Avengelyne.

DARKSTAR — Rebel

1 ❑ b&w Cover: 2.25 **NM** value: **Cover or less**
A: Scott Frantz **W:** Scott Frantz

2 ❑ b&w Cover: 2.25 **NM** value: **Cover or less**
A: Scott Frantz **W:** Scott Frantz

The prices seen above do not represent the highest possible prices seen in online auctions, but rather the prices we have seen these issues reliably fetch in a variety of environments (storefront retail, mail order, auction and convention).

DARKSTARS, THE — DC

Agent Colos of the Darkstars, an intergalactic security-for-hire force, is a burned-out, unenthusiastic cop who has seen too many senseless deaths. His unscrupulous boss gives him an assignment to fight a war against drugs on Earth. His mission is to stop the distribution of a terrible crack cocaine-like drug called Loco. This drug is being introduced to our world by extraterrestrials just as greedy as, if not greedier than, our very own drug lords.

Darkstars is a well-scripted work of fiction that adds a new twist to the battle between good and evil. Shown to readers through the eyes of a cynic, the story shows how very subjective the difference between the two can be.

0 ❑ Oct 1994 Cover: 1.95 **NM** value: **2.00**
Circ: CapCity orders: **11,800**
Wayward Son • Series continued in Darkstars #24 **A:** Mike Collins **W:** Michael Jan Friedman ★ Origin of Darkstars.

1 ❑ Oct 1992 Cover: 1.75 **NM** value: **Cover or less**
Circ: CapCity orders: **21,950**
Mean Streets **A:** Larry Stroman **W:** Michael Jan Friedman ★ 1st Appearance of Darkstars.

2 ❑ Nov 1992 Cover: 1.75 **NM** value: **Cover or less**
Circ: CapCity orders: **14,100**

3 ❑ Dec 1992 Cover: 1.75 **NM** value: **Cover or less**
Circ: CapCity orders: **11,400**

4 ❑ Jan 1993 Cover: 1.75 **NM** value: **Cover or less**
Circ: CapCity orders: **14,150**

5 ❑ Feb 1993 Cover: 1.75 **NM** value: **Cover or less**
Circ: CapCity orders: **14,600**
★ Appearance of Hawkwoman, Hawkman.

6 ❑ Mar 1993 Cover: 1.75 **NM** value: **Cover or less**
Circ: CapCity orders: **13,450**
★ Appearance of Hawkman.

7 ❑ Apr 1993 Cover: 1.75 **NM** value: **Cover or less**
Circ: CapCity orders: **15,800**

8 ❑ May 1993 Cover: 1.75 **NM** value: **Cover or less**
Circ: CapCity orders: **13,950**

9 ❑ Jun 1993 Cover: 1.75 **NM** value: **Cover or less**
Circ: CapCity orders: **13,250**

10 ❑ Jun 1993 Cover: 1.75 **NM** value: **Cover or less**
Circ: CapCity orders: **12,800**

11 ❑ Aug 1993 Cover: 1.75 **NM** value: **Cover or less**
Circ: CapCity orders: **18,650**
Trinity

12 ❑ Sep 1993 Cover: 1.75 **NM** value: **Cover or less**
Circ: CapCity orders: **14,700**
Trinity

13 ❑ Oct 1993 Cover: 1.75 **NM** value: **Cover or less**
Circ: CapCity orders: **10,200**

14 ❑ Nov 1993 Cover: 1.75 **NM** value: **Cover or less**
Circ: CapCity orders: **9,850**

15 ❑ Dec 1993 Cover: 1.75 **NM** value: **Cover or less**
Circ: CapCity orders: **9,400**

16 ❑ Jan 1994 Cover: 1.75 **NM** value: **Cover or less**
Circ: CapCity orders: **8,500**

17 ❑ Feb 1994 Cover: 1.75 **NM** value: **Cover or less**
Circ: CapCity orders: **6,900**

18 ❑ Mar 1994 Cover: 1.75 **NM** value: **Cover or less**
Circ: CapCity orders: **6,300**
Eve of Destruction, Part 1

19 ❑ Apr 1994 Cover: 1.75 **NM** value: **Cover or less**
Circ: CapCity orders: **5,600**
• Flash

20 ❑ May 1994 Cover: 1.75 **NM** value: **Cover or less**
Circ: CapCity orders: **5,400**
• Flash

21 ❑ Jun 1994 Cover: 1.75 **NM** value: **Cover or less**
Circ: CapCity orders: **6,350**

22 ❑ Jul 1994 Cover: 1.95 **NM** value: **Cover or less**
Circ: CapCity orders: **6,450**
Tangled Webs **A:** Mike Collins **W:** Michael Jan Friedman

23 ❑ Aug 1994 Cover: 1.95 **NM** value: **Cover or less**
Circ: CapCity orders: **6,450**
• Series continued in Darkstars #0, Donna Troy joins Darkstars

24 ❑ Sep 1994 Cover: 1.95 **NM** value: **Cover or less**
Circ: CapCity orders: **8,300**
• Zero Hour

25 ❑ Nov 1994 Cover: 1.95 **NM** value: **Cover or less**
Circ: CapCity orders: **6,050**

26 ❑ Dec 1994 Cover: 1.95 **NM** value: **Cover or less**
Circ: CapCity orders: **6,200**

27 ❑ Jan 1995 Cover: 1.95 **NM** value: **Cover or less**
Circ: CapCity orders: **6,250**

28 ❑ Feb 1995 Cover: 1.95 **NM** value: **Cover or less**
Circ: CapCity orders: **5,550**

29 ❑ Mar 1995 Cover: 1.95 **NM** value: **Cover or less**
Circ: CapCity orders: **5,175**

30 ❑ Apr 1995 Cover: 1.95 **NM** value: **Cover or less**
Circ: CapCity orders: **5,250**

31 ❑ Jun 1995 Cover: 2.25 **NM** value: **Cover or less**
Circ: CapCity orders: **4,500**

32 ❑ Jul 1995 Cover: 2.25 **NM** value: **Cover or less**
Circ: CapCity orders: **5,275**

33 ❑ Aug 1995 Cover: 2.25 **NM** value: **Cover or less**
Circ: CapCity orders: **4,875**

34 ❑ Sep 1995 Cover: 2.25 **NM** value: **Cover or less**
Circ: CapCity orders: **5,750**
The Siege of The Zi Charam, Part 3

35 ❑ Oct 1995 Cover: 2.25 **NM** value: **Cover or less**
Circ: CapCity orders: **4,225**

36 ❑ Nov 1995 Cover: 2.25 **NM** value: **Cover or less**
★ Appearance of Flash.

37 ❑ Dec 1995 Cover: 2.25 **NM** value: **Cover or less**
★ Versus Guy Gardner.

38 ❑ Jan 1996 Cover: 2.25 **NM** value: **Cover or less**
final issue.

DARK TALES OF DAILY HORROR — Antarctic

1 ❑ Feb 1994, b&w Cover: 2.95 **NM** value: **Cover or less**

DARK VISIONS — Pyramid

1 ❑ Nov 1986 Cover: 1.70 **NM** value: **2.00**
The Nightstalker; Dirty Needles; The Wanderer **A:** Tim Tyler; Brad Moore **W:** Tim Tyler; Brad Moore; David Curl

2 ❑ Cover: 1.70 **NM** value: **2.00**

DARK, THE (VOL. 2) — Continuüm

1 ❑ Jun 1993 Cover: 1.95 **NM** value: **2.00**
Circ: CapCity orders: **4,400**

1/SC❑Jun 1993 Cover: 1.95 **NM** value: **2.00**
red foil cover. **C:** Bart Sears

1-2 ❑ Jun 1993 Cover: 1.95 **NM** value: **2.00**

2 ❑ Jul 1993 Cover: 1.95 **NM** value: **2.00**
Circ: CapCity orders: **3,950**

3 ❑ Aug 1993 Cover: 1.95 **NM** value: **2.00**
Circ: CapCity orders: **2,575**
foil cover. **A:** Mark Bright; George Pérez; Todd Lidstone; George Pérez(cover) **C:** Chris Gossett **W:** Joseph Naftali

3/Aut❑Aug 1993 Cover: 1.95 **NM** value: **2.00**
foil cover. **A:** George Pérez **W:** Joseph Naftali

4 ❑ Sep 1993 Cover: 1.95 **NM** value: **2.00**
Circ: CapCity orders: **3,825**

5 ❑ Feb 1994 Cover: 1.95 **NM** value: **2.00**

6 ❑ Mar 1994 Cover: 1.95 **NM** value: **2.00**

7 ❑ Jul 1994 Cover: 1.95 **NM** value: **2.00**
Circ: CapCity orders: **2,865**

7-2 ❑ Jul 1994 Cover: 1.95 **NM** value: **2.00**

DARKWING DUCK — Disney

1 ❑ Cover: 1.50 **NM** value: **Cover or less**

2 ❑ Cover: 1.50 **NM** value: **Cover or less**

3 ❑ Cover: 1.50 **NM** value: **Cover or less**

4 ❑ Cover: 1.50 **NM** value: **Cover or less**

DARKWING DUCK LIMITED SERIES (DISNEY'S…) — Disney

1 ❑ Nov 1991 Cover: 1.50 **NM** value: **Cover or less**
Circ: CapCity orders: **11,350**
Brawl in the Family, Part 1 **A:** John Blair Moore **W:** John Blair Moore

2 ❑ Cover: 1.50 **NM** value: **Cover or less**
Circ: CapCity orders: **6,750**

3 ❑ Cover: 1.50 **NM** value: **Cover or less**
Circ: CapCity orders: **6,050**

4 ❑ Cover: 1.50 **NM** value: **Cover or less**
Circ: CapCity orders: **6,350**

DARK WOLF — Eternity

1 ❑ 1988 b&w Cover: 1.95 **NM** value: **Cover or less**

2 ❑ 1988 b&w Cover: 1.95 **NM** value: **Cover or less**

3 ❑ 1988 b&w Cover: 1.95 **NM** value: **Cover or less**

4 ❑ 1988 b&w Cover: 1.95 **NM** value: **Cover or less**

5 ❑ Jun 1988, b&w Cover: 1.95 **NM** value: **Cover or less**
Destruction **A:** Butch Burcham **W:** R.A. Jones

6 ❑ 1988 b&w Cover: 1.95 **NM** value: **Cover or less**

7 ❑ 1988 b&w Cover: 1.95 **NM** value: **Cover or less**

8 ❑ 1988 b&w Cover: 1.95 **NM** value: **Cover or less**

9 ❑ b&w Cover: 1.95 **NM** value: **Cover or less**

10 ❑ b&w Cover: 1.95 **NM** value: **Cover or less**

11 ❑ b&w Cover: 1.95 **NM** value: **Cover or less**

12 ❑ b&w Cover: 1.95 **NM** value: **Cover or less**

13 ❑ b&w Cover: 1.95 **NM** value: **Cover or less**

14 ❑ b&w Cover: 1.95 **NM** value: **Cover or less**

Anl 1❑b&w Cover: 2.25 **NM** value: **Cover or less**

Bk 1❑ b&w Cover: 7.95 **NM** value: **Cover or less**

DARK WOLF (VOL. 2) — Malibu

1 ❑ Cover: 1.95 **NM** value: **Cover or less**

2 ❑ Cover: 1.95 **NM** value: **Cover or less**

3 ❑ Cover: 1.95 **NM** value: **Cover or less**

4 ❑ Cover: 1.95 **NM** value: **Cover or less**

DARK WORLD — Millennium

1 ❑ Cover: 3.25 **NM** value: **Cover or less**
Circ: CapCity orders: **3,890**
A: O.J. Cariello; Jae Lee; Daniel Presedo; Sandra Chang; Michal Dutkiewicz; Collen Doran; Daerick Gross; Mike Okamoto **W:** Kim Elizabeth

DARQUE PASSAGES — Valiant

1 ❑ Jan 1994 Cover: 2.00 **NM** value: **Cover or less**

DARQUE PASSAGES (VOL. 2) — Acclaim

1 ❑ Apr 1998 Cover: 2.50 **NM** value: **Cover or less**
Circ: Diamd. preorders: **13,870**

2 ❑ Jan 1998 Cover: 2.50 **NM** value: **Cover or less**
Circ: Diamd. preorders: **11,394**
no cover date. • indicia says Jan

3 ❑ Feb 1998 Cover: 2.50 **NM** value: **Cover or less**
Circ: Diamd. preorders: **9,917**
no cover date. • indicia says Feb

DARQUE RAZOR — London Night

1 ❑ Oct 1997 Cover: 3.00 **NM** value: **Cover or less**
Circ: Diamd. preorders: **5,216**
A: Albert Holaso **W:** Dan Membeila

Other grades: Multiply prices above by **1.5 for Mint • 2/3 for Very Fine • 1/3 for Fine • 1/5 for Very Good • 1/8 for Good**

DART — Image

1 ❑ Feb 1996 Cover: 2.50 **NM** value: **Cover or less**
1/A ❑ Feb 1996 Cover: 2.50 **NM** value: **Cover or less**
alternate cover.
2 ❑ Apr 1996 Cover: 2.50 **NM** value: **Cover or less**
A: Jozef Szekeres **W:** Bruce Love; Julie Ditrich
3 ❑ May 1996 Cover: 2.50 **NM** value: **Cover or less**

DARTMAN — Northeastern Press

1 ❑ Cover: 2.00 **NM** value: **Cover or less**

DATA 6 — Artist's Unlimited

1 ❑ Cover: 1.95 **NM** value: **Cover or less**

DATE WITH DEBBI — DC

1 ❑ Feb 1969 Cover: 0.12 **NM** value: **15.00**
• **CGC:** 2 graded, best 9.0
2 ❑ Apr 1969 Cover: 0.12 **NM** value: **10.00**
3 ❑ Jun 1969 Cover: 0.15 **NM** value: **10.00**
4 ❑ Aug 1969 Cover: 0.15 **NM** value: **10.00**
5 ❑ Oct 1969 Cover: 0.15 **NM** value: **10.00**
6 ❑ Dec 1969 Cover: 0.15 **NM** value: **10.00**
7 ❑ Feb 1970 Cover: 0.15 **NM** value: **10.00**
8 ❑ Apr 1970 Cover: 0.15 **NM** value: **10.00**
9 ❑ Jun 1970 Cover: 0.15 **NM** value: **10.00**
10 ❑ Aug 1970 Cover: 0.15 **NM** value: **10.00**
11 ❑ Oct 1970 Cover: 0.15 **NM** value: **10.00**
12 ❑ Dec 1970 Cover: 0.15 **NM** value: **10.00**
13 ❑ Feb 1971 Cover: 0.25 **NM** value: **12.00**
14 ❑ Apr 1971 Cover: 0.25 **NM** value: **12.00**
15 ❑ Jun 1971 Cover: 0.25 **NM** value: **12.00**
16 ❑ Aug 1971 Cover: 0.25 **NM** value: **12.00**
17 ❑ Oct 1971 Cover: 0.25 **NM** value: **12.00**
18 ❑ ca. 1972 Cover: 0.20 **NM** value: **10.00**

DATE WITH JUDY, A — DC

A Date with Judy began as a summer replacement radio show for The Bob Hope Show in 1941 and continued as a comedy summer replacement until it gained enough strength to become a regular show starring Louise Erickson as the teen whose boyfriend was Oogie Pringle and much of whose life focused on dating. There was even a movie in 1948 (starring Jane Powell as Judy with Elizabeth Taylor as Carol Pringle). The show went off the air in 1950 but found a home on TV from 1951 to 1953 with a different cast.

The comedy comic book was durable, starting before the film was released and continuing for seven years after the show had left other media. Early issues featured a drawing of Judy at a radio microphone and carried the line "Radio's famous coast-to-coast favorite." — Maggie

1 ❑ Oct 1947 Cover: 0.10 **NM** value: **110.00**
2 ❑ Dec 1947 Cover: 0.10 **NM** value: **90.00**
• **CGC:** 1 graded, best 9.4
3 ❑ Feb 1948 Cover: 0.10 **NM** value: **45.00**
• **CGC:** 1 graded, best 9.6
4 ❑ Apr 1948 Cover: 0.10 **NM** value: **45.00**
• **CGC:** 1 graded, best 9.2
5 ❑ Jun 1948 Cover: 0.10 **NM** value: **45.00**
6 ❑ Aug 1948 Cover: 0.10 **NM** value: **32.00**
7 ❑ Oct 1948 Cover: 0.10 **NM** value: **32.00**
8 ❑ Dec 1948 Cover: 0.10 **NM** value: **32.00**
9 ❑ Feb 1949 Cover: 0.10 **NM** value: **32.00**
10 ❑ Apr 1949 Cover: 0.10 **NM** value: **32.00**
11 ❑ Jun 1949 Cover: 0.10 **NM** value: **20.00**
12 ❑ Aug 1949 Cover: 0.10 **NM** value: **20.00**
13 ❑ Oct 1949 Cover: 0.10 **NM** value: **20.00**
14 ❑ Dec 1949 Cover: 0.10 **NM** value: **20.00**
15 ❑ Feb 1950 Cover: 0.10 **NM** value: **20.00**
16 ❑ Apr 1950 Cover: 0.10 **NM** value: **20.00**
17 ❑ Jun 1950 Cover: 0.10 **NM** value: **20.00**
18 ❑ Aug 1950 Cover: 0.10 **NM** value: **20.00**
19 ❑ Oct 1950 Cover: 0.10 **NM** value: **20.00**
20 ❑ Dec 1950 Cover: 0.10 **NM** value: **20.00**
21 ❑ Feb 1951 Cover: 0.10 **NM** value: **16.00**
22 ❑ Apr 1951 Cover: 0.10 **NM** value: **16.00**
23 ❑ Jun 1951 Cover: 0.10 **NM** value: **16.00**
24 ❑ Aug 1951 Cover: 0.10 **NM** value: **16.00**
25 ❑ Oct 1951 Cover: 0.10 **NM** value: **16.00**
26 ❑ Dec 1951 Cover: 0.10 **NM** value: **16.00**
27 ❑ Feb 1952 Cover: 0.10 **NM** value: **16.00**
28 ❑ Apr 1952 Cover: 0.10 **NM** value: **16.00**
29 ❑ Jun 1952 Cover: 0.10 **NM** value: **16.00**
30 ❑ Aug 1952 Cover: 0.10 **NM** value: **16.00**
31 ❑ Oct 1952 Cover: 0.10 **NM** value: **16.00**
32 ❑ Dec 1952 Cover: 0.10 **NM** value: **16.00**
33 ❑ Feb 1953 Cover: 0.10 **NM** value: **16.00**
34 ❑ Apr 1953 Cover: 0.10 **NM** value: **16.00**
35 ❑ Jun 1953 Cover: 0.10 **NM** value: **16.00**
36 ❑ Aug 1953 Cover: 0.10 **NM** value: **16.00**
37 ❑ Oct 1953 Cover: 0.10 **NM** value: **16.00**
38 ❑ Dec 1953 Cover: 0.10 **NM** value: **16.00**
39 ❑ Feb 1954 Cover: 0.10 **NM** value: **16.00**
40 ❑ Apr 1954 Cover: 0.10 **NM** value: **16.00**
41 ❑ Jun 1954 Cover: 0.10 **NM** value: **14.00**
42 ❑ Aug 1954 Cover: 0.10 **NM** value: **14.00**
• A Taxing Situation (text story)
43 ❑ Oct 1954 Cover: 0.10 **NM** value: **14.00**
44 ❑ Dec 1954 Cover: 0.10 **NM** value: **14.00**
45 ❑ Feb 1955 Cover: 0.10 **NM** value: **14.00**
46 ❑ Apr 1955 Cover: 0.10 **NM** value: **14.00**
47 ❑ Jun 1955 Cover: 0.10 **NM** value: **14.00**
48 ❑ Aug 1955 Cover: 0.10 **NM** value: **14.00**
49 ❑ Oct 1955 Cover: 0.10 **NM** value: **14.00**
50 ❑ Dec 1955 Cover: 0.10 **NM** value: **14.00**
51 ❑ Feb 1956 Cover: 0.10 **NM** value: **14.00**
52 ❑ Apr 1956 Cover: 0.10 **NM** value: **14.00**
53 ❑ Jul 1956 Cover: 0.10 **NM** value: **14.00**
54 ❑ Sep 1956 Cover: 0.10 **NM** value: **14.00**
55 ❑ Nov 1956 Cover: 0.10 **NM** value: **14.00**
56 ❑ Jan 1957 Cover: 0.10 **NM** value: **14.00**
57 ❑ Mar 1957 Cover: 0.10 **NM** value: **14.00**
58 ❑ May 1957 Cover: 0.10 **NM** value: **14.00**
59 ❑ Jul 1957 Cover: 0.10 **NM** value: **14.00**
60 ❑ Sep 1957 Cover: 0.10 **NM** value: **14.00**
61 ❑ Nov 1957 Cover: 0.10 **NM** value: **9.00**
62 ❑ Jan 1958 Cover: 0.10 **NM** value: **9.00**
63 ❑ Mar 1958 Cover: 0.10 **NM** value: **9.00**
64 ❑ May 1958 Cover: 0.10 **NM** value: **9.00**
65 ❑ Jul 1958 Cover: 0.10 **NM** value: **9.00**
66 ❑ Sep 1958 Cover: 0.10 **NM** value: **9.00**
67 ❑ Nov 1958 Cover: 0.10 **NM** value: **9.00**
68 ❑ Jan 1959 Cover: 0.10 **NM** value: **9.00**
69 ❑ Mar 1959 Cover: 0.10 **NM** value: **9.00**
70 ❑ May 1959 Cover: 0.10 **NM** value: **9.00**
71 ❑ Jul 1959 Cover: 0.10 **NM** value: **9.00**
72 ❑ Sep 1959 Cover: 0.10 **NM** value: **9.00**
73 ❑ Nov 1959 Cover: 0.10 **NM** value: **9.00**
74 ❑ Jan 1960 Cover: 0.10 **NM** value: **9.00**
75 ❑ Mar 1960 Cover: 0.10 **NM** value: **9.00**
76 ❑ May 1960 Cover: 0.10 **NM** value: **9.00**
77 ❑ Jul 1960 Cover: 0.10 **NM** value: **9.00**
78 ❑ Sep 1960 Cover: 0.10 **NM** value: **9.00**
79 ❑ Nov 1961 Cover: 0.10 **NM** value: **9.00**
final issue.

DATE WITH MILLIE, A — Atlas

1 ❑ Oct 1956 Cover: 0.10 **NM** value: **125.00**
2 ❑ Dec 1956 Cover: 0.10 **NM** value: **75.00**
3 ❑ Feb 1957 Cover: 0.10 **NM** value: **75.00**
4 ❑ Apr 1957 Cover: 0.10 **NM** value: **75.00**
5 ❑ Jun 1957 Cover: 0.10 **NM** value: **75.00**
6 ❑ Aug 1957 Cover: 0.10 **NM** value: **75.00**
7 ❑ Oct 1957 Cover: 0.10 **NM** value: **75.00**

DATE WITH MILLIE, A (VOL. 2) — Atlas

1 ❑ Oct 1959 Cover: 0.10 **NM** value: **75.00**
2 ❑ Dec 1959 Cover: 0.10 **NM** value: **50.00**
3 ❑ Feb 1960 Cover: 0.10 **NM** value: **50.00**
4 ❑ Apr 1960 Cover: 0.10 **NM** value: **50.00**
5 ❑ Jun 1960 Cover: 0.10 **NM** value: **50.00**
6 ❑ Aug 1960 Cover: 0.10 **NM** value: **50.00**
7 ❑ Oct 1960 Cover: 0.10 **NM** value: **50.00**

DATE WITH PATSY, A — Atlas

1 ❑ Sep 1957 Cover: 0.10 **NM** value: **60.00**

DAUGHTERS OF FLY IN MY EYE — Eclipse

Bk 1❑ b&w Cover: 9.95 **NM** value: **Cover or less**

DAUGHTERS OF TIME 3-D — 3-D Zone

1 ❑ Cover: 3.95 **NM** value: **Cover or less**
No issue number. **A:** Kurt Schaffenberger **C:** Steve Ditko

DAVID CASSIDY — Charlton

1 ❑ Feb 1972 Cover: 0.20 **NM** value: **25.00**
Photo cover. 📖 Stop Thief…I Love U; David's Deepest Problem; Will the Real David Cassidy Stand Up?
2 ❑ Mar 1972 Cover: 0.20 **NM** value: **16.00**
3 ❑ May 1972 Cover: 0.20 **NM** value: **16.00**
4 ❑ Cover: 0.20 **NM** value: **16.00**
5 ❑ Aug 1972 Cover: 0.20 **NM** value: **16.00**
6 ❑ Sep 1972 Cover: 0.20 **NM** value: **14.00**
7 ❑ Oct 1972 Cover: 0.20 **NM** value: **14.00**
8 ❑ Cover: 0.20 **NM** value: **14.00**
9 ❑ Dec 1972 Cover: 0.20 **NM** value: **14.00**
10 ❑ Cover: 0.20 **NM** value: **12.00**
11 ❑ Mar 1973 Cover: 0.20 **NM** value: **12.00**
12 ❑ May 1973 Cover: 0.20 **NM** value: **12.00**
13 ❑ Jul 1973 Cover: 0.20 **NM** value: **12.00**
14 ❑ Sep 1973 Cover: 0.20 **NM** value: **12.00**
final issue.

DAVID CHELSEA IN LOVE — Eclipse

1 ❑ b&w Cover: 3.50 **NM** value: **Cover or less**
2 ❑ b&w Cover: 3.50 **NM** value: **Cover or less**
3 ❑ b&w Cover: 3.50 **NM** value: **Cover or less**
4 ❑ b&w Cover: 3.50 **NM** value: **Cover or less**

DAVY CROCKETT — Gold Key

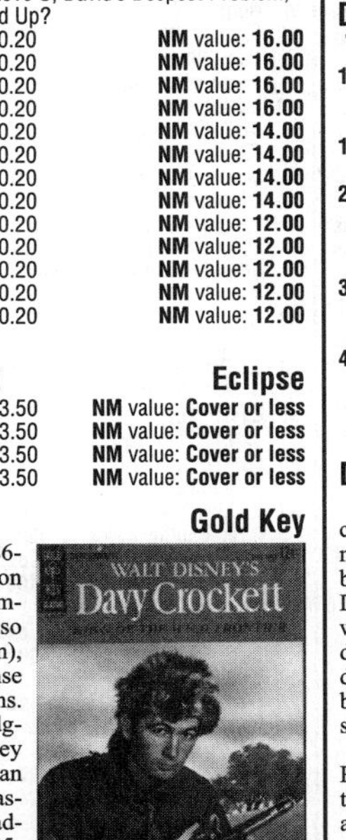

Although Davy Crockett (1786-1836) was a real historical person (which meant any comic-book company that wanted to do so could also publish a comic book about him), this title was produced under license from the Walt Disney organizations. As one of the episodes in its fledgling Disneyland TV series, Disney broadcast "Davy Crockett, Indian Fighter" Dec. 15, 1954. The astounding success of Crockett's adventures starring Fess Parker (1925-) led to their release as theatrical features and kicked off a runaway merchandising success. This comic-book version of Crockett, then, featured the characters as they were depicted on TV. — Maggie

1 ❑ ca. 1963 Cover: 0.12 **NM** value: **100.00**
• **CGC:** 1 graded, best 6.5
2 ❑ Nov 1969 Cover: 0.12 **NM** value: **20.00**

DAWN — Sirius Entertainment

0.5 ❑ ca. 1996 **NM** value: **5.00**
• Wizard mail-away
0.5/SC❑ca. 1996 **NM** value: **22.00**
"Hey Kids" Variant cover. • Wizard mail-away
1 ❑ Jun 1995 Cover: 2.95 **NM** value: **6.00**
Circ: CapCity orders: **44,700** • **CGC:** 21 graded, best 9.8
📖 Lucifer's Halo, Part 1 **A:** Joseph Michael Linsner
1/A ❑ Jun 1995 Cover: 10.00 **NM** value: **12.00**
• **CGC:** 18 graded, best 10.0
"Black light" cover. • blacklight edition. 📖 Lucifer's Halo, Part 1 **A:** Joseph Michael Linsner
1/B ❑ Jun 1995 **NM** value: **15.00**
• **CGC:** 5 graded, best 9.8
• "White Trash" edition. 📖 Lucifer's Halo, Part 1 **A:** Joseph Michael Linsner
1/C ❑ Jun 1995 **NM** value: **15.00**
• **CGC:** 3 graded, best 9.8
• "Look Sharp" edition. 📖 Lucifer's Halo, Part 1 **A:** Joseph Michael Linsner
2 ❑ Sep 1995 Cover: 2.95 **NM** value: **5.00**
Circ: CapCity orders: **28,925**
📖 Lucifer's Halo, Part 1 **A:** Joseph Michael Linsner
2/A ❑ Sep 1995 Cover: 10.00 **NM** value: **25.00**
• Mystery Book **A:** Joseph Michael Linsner
3 ❑ ca. 1996 Cover: 2.95 **NM** value: **5.00**
A: Joseph Michael Linsner
3/A ❑ ca. 1996 Cover: 2.95 **NM** value: **25.00**
A: Joseph Michael Linsner
4 ❑ ca. 1996 Cover: 2.95 **NM** value: **4.00**
A: Joseph Michael Linsner
4/A ❑ ca. 1996 Cover: 2.95 **NM** value: **20.00**
A: Joseph Michael Linsner
5 ❑ Sep 1996 Cover: 2.95 **NM** value: **3.00**
Circ: Diamd. preorders: **63,210**
A: Joseph Michael Linsner
5/A ❑ Sep 1996 Cover: 2.95 **NM** value: **15.00**
A: Joseph Michael Linsner
6 ❑ Oct 1996 Cover: 2.95 **NM** value: **4.00**
Circ: Diamd. preorders: **55,364** • **CGC:** 1 graded, best 9.4
A: Joseph Michael Linsner
6/A ❑ Oct 1996 Cover: 2.95 **NM** value: **15.00**
A: Joseph Michael Linsner
Bk 1❑ Cover: 19.95 **NM** value: **Cover or less**
A: Joseph Michael Linsner

DAWN HUNTER — AC

0 ❑ Cover: 2.95 **NM** value: **Cover or less**
Photo cover.

DAWN OF THE AGE OF APOCALYPSE — Marvel

1 ❑ Cover: 8.95 **NM** value: **Cover or less**
Gold foil cover. 📖 Hour of Last Things; Alpha; The Chosen • Reprints X-Men: Alpha, Cable #20, Age of Apocalypse: The Chosen **A:** Salvador Larocca; Ian Churchill; Steve Epting; Riger Cruz **W:** Jeph Loeb; Scott Lobdell; Howard Mackie; Mark Waid

DAWN TENTH ANNIVERSARY SPECIAL — Sirius Entertainment

1 ❑ Sep 1999 Cover: 2.95 **NM** value: **Cover or less**
Circ: Diamd. preorders: **24,632**

DAWN: THE RETURN OF THE GODDESS — Sirius Entertainment

1 ❑ Apr 1999 Cover: 2.95 **NM** value: **Cover or less**
Circ: Diamd. preorders: **42,820** • **CGC:** 5 graded, best 9.8
A: Joseph Michael Linsner **W:** Joseph Michael Linsner
1/LE❑ Apr 1999 Cover: 25.00 **NM** value: **Cover or less**
A: Joseph Michael Linsner **W:** Joseph Michael Linsner
2 ❑ May 1999 Cover: 2.95 **NM** value: **Cover or less**
Circ: Diamd. preorders: **36,063**
📖 Access; Jaynis Goldbaum's Last Dance **A:** Joseph Michael Linsner; FillbSch Bros **W:** Joseph Michael Linsner
3 ❑ Nov 1999 Cover: 2.95 **NM** value: **Cover or less**
Circ: Diamd. preorders: **33,410** • **CGC:** 1 graded, best 9.6
A: Joseph Michael Linsner **W:** Joseph Michael Linsner
4 ❑ Jul 2000 Cover: 2.95 **NM** value: **Cover or less**
Circ: Diamd. preorders: **30,154** • **CGC:** 1 graded, best 9.6
📖 Atrocity; Ascension **A:** Joseph Michael Linsner **W:** Joseph Michael Linsner

DAY BROTHERS PRESENT — Caliber

This collection of stories mixes classically narrated horror with more modern science fiction. The black-and-white drawings of the Day brothers are dark and brooding, while still involving a high level of detail. Their art maintains their own distinctive quality with each story but is designed to complement the style of each individual writer.

While this series from Caliber Press is meant to be a showcase for the artistic ability of Dan, David, and Gene Day, the stories themselves are well scripted. Obvious effort seems to have been put forth to find writers whose abilities would add to the visual impact of this monthly magazine.

1 ❑ Cover: 2.50 **NM** value: **Cover or less**
A: Dan Day

CGC-graded: Multiply prices above by **33 for 9.9 M** • **16 for 9.8 NM/M** • **7 for 9.6 NM+** • **5 for 9.4 NM** • **2.5 for 9.2 NM-** • **1.5 for 9.0 VF/NM**

2 ❑ Cover: 2.50 **NM** value: **Cover or less**
Hellstorm Locust; The Fly; Morella • Horror **A:** Dan Day **W:** Gordon Derry; Rich Margopoulos; Randy Sauve
3 ❑ Cover: 2.50 **NM** value: **Cover or less**
Goo is Gracious; Pyre!; Shroud of Tattered Grey **A:** Dan Day **W:** Gene Day
4 ❑ Cover: 2.50 **NM** value: **Cover or less**
A: Dan Day

DAYDREAMERS — Marvel

1 ❑ Aug 1997 Cover: 2.50 **NM** value: **Cover or less**
Circ: Diamd. preorders: **36,307**
• gatefold summary. Once Upon a Time... • teams Howard the Duck, Man-Thing, Franklin Richards, Leech, Artie, and Tana **A:** Martin Egeland **W:** Andy Jozefowiez; J.M. DeMatteis; Todd Dezago
2 ❑ Sep 1997 Cover: 2.50 **NM** value: **Cover or less**
Circ: Diamd. preorders: **28,642**
• gatefold summary. Across the Universe **A:** Martin Egeland **W:** George Broderick Jr.; J.M. DeMatteis
3 ❑ Oct 1997 Cover: 2.50 **NM** value: **Cover or less**
Circ: Diamd. preorders: **28,369**
• gatefold summary. Dark Eyes **A:** Martin Egeland **W:** Andy Jozefowiez; J.M. DeMatteis; Todd Dezago

DAY I SWAPPED MY DAD FOR TWO GOLDFISH, THE — White Wolf / Borealis

Bk 1❑ Cover: 14.99 **NM** value: **Cover or less**
No issue number. • Trade Paperback. **W:** Neil Gaiman

DAY OF JUDGMENT — DC

1 ❑ Nov 1999 Cover: 2.95 **NM** value: **Cover or less**
Circ: Diamd. preorders: **59,241**
The Summoning **A:** Matt Smith **W:** Geoff Johns
2 ❑ Nov 1999 Cover: 2.50 **NM** value: **Cover or less**
Circ: Diamd. preorders: **55,425**
Lost Souls **A:** Matt Smith **W:** Geoff Johns
3 ❑ Nov 1999 Cover: 2.50 **NM** value: **Cover or less**
Circ: Diamd. preorders: **54,520**
A: Matt Smith **W:** Geoff Johns
4 ❑ Nov 1999 Cover: 2.50 **NM** value: **Cover or less**
Circ: Diamd. preorders: **54,142**
A: Matt Smith **W:** Geoff Johns ★ Death of Enchantress.
5 ❑ Nov 1999 Cover: 2.50 **NM** value: **Cover or less**
Circ: Diamd. preorders: **54,096** • **CGC:** 2 graded, best 9.4
• Hal Jordan becomes Spectre **A:** Matt Smith **W:** Geoff Johns

DAY OF JUDGMENT SECRET FILES — DC

1 ❑ Nov 1999 Cover: 4.95 **NM** value: **Cover or less**
Circ: Diamd. preorders: **30,326**
• background on participants in event

DAY OF THE DEFENDERS — Marvel

1 ❑ Mar 2001 Cover: 3.50 **NM** value: **Cover or less**
Circ: Diamd. preorders: **10,288**
No issue number. The Monarch and the Mystic!; ... Where Stalks the Nightcrawler!; The Day of the Defenders! **A:** Herb Trimpe; Ross Andru; Marie Severin **W:** Roy Thomas ★ 1st Appearance of The Defenders.

DAYS GO BY LIKE BROKEN RECORDS, THE — Slave Labor

Bk 1❑ Sep 1995 Cover: 15.95 **NM** value: **Cover or less**
• digest-sized reprint of No Hope #1-6.

DAYS OF DARKNESS — Apple

1 ❑ b&w Cover: 2.75 **NM** value: **Cover or less**
2 ❑ b&w Cover: 2.75 **NM** value: **Cover or less**
3 ❑ b&w Cover: 2.75 **NM** value: **Cover or less**
4 ❑ b&w Cover: 2.75 **NM** value: **Cover or less**
5 ❑ b&w Cover: 2.75 **NM** value: **Cover or less**
Bk 1❑ b&w Cover: 14.95 **NM** value: **Cover or less**
• collects series

DAYS OF WRATH — Apple

1 ❑ b&w Cover: 2.75 **NM** value: **Cover or less**
2 ❑ b&w Cover: 2.75 **NM** value: **Cover or less**
3 ❑ b&w Cover: 2.75 **NM** value: **Cover or less**
4 ❑ Jun 1994, b&w Cover: 2.75 **NM** value: **Cover or less**

DAYTONA 500 STORY — Vortex

1 ❑ full color Cover: 2.00 **NM** value: **Cover or less**
Circ: CapCity orders: **4,015**

DAZZLER — Marvel

1 ❑ Mar 1981 Cover: 0.50 **NM** value: **2.00**
Circ: Statement: **296,166** • **CGC:** 31 graded, best 9.8
So Bright This Star • direct;First Marvel direct market-only comic **A:** John Romita Jr. **W:** Tom DeFalco ★ Origin of Dazzler. ★ Appearance of X-Men.
2 ❑ Apr 1981 Cover: 0.50 **NM** value: **1.50**
Circ: Statement: **296,166**
Where Demons Fear to Dwell **A:** John Romita Jr.; Alfredo Alcala **W:** Tom DeFalco ★ Appearance of X-Men.
3 ❑ May 1981 Cover: 0.50 **NM** value: **1.00**
Circ: Statement: **296,166**
The Jewels of Doom! **A:** Alan Kupperberg; John Romita Jr.; Brent Anderson(cover) **W:** Tom DeFalco ★ Appearance of Doctor Doom. ★ Versus Doctor Doom.
4 ❑ Jun 1981 Cover: 0.50 **NM** value: **1.00**
Circ: Statement: **296,166**
Here Nightmares Abide! **A:** Frank Springer **W:** Tom DeFalco ★ Versus Doctor Doom.
5 ❑ Jul 1981 Cover: 0.50 **NM** value: **1.00**
Circ: Statement: **296,166**
Tell Joey I Love Him ★ 1st Appearance of Blue Shield.
6 ❑ Aug 1981 Cover: 0.50 **NM** value: **1.00**
Circ: Statement: **296,166**
The Hulk May Be Hazardous to Your Health
7 ❑ Sep 1981 Cover: 0.50 **NM** value: **1.00**
Circ: Statement: **296,166**
Fort Apache, The Hulk
8 ❑ Oct 1981 Cover: 0.50 **NM** value: **1.00**
Circ: Statement: **296,166**
Hell is For Harry
9 ❑ Nov 1981 Cover: 0.50 **NM** value: **1.00**
Circ: Statement: **296,166**
The Sound and the Fury
10 ❑ Dec 1981 Cover: 0.50 **NM** value: **1.00**
Circ: Statement: **296,166**
In the Darkness, A Light ★ Appearance of Galactus.
11 ❑ Jan 1982 Cover: 0.60 **NM** value: **1.00**
Circ: Statement: **166,657**
Lest Ye Be Judged ★ Appearance of Galactus.
12 ❑ Feb 1982 Cover: 0.60 **NM** value: **1.00**
Circ: Statement: **166,657**
Endless Hate
13 ❑ Mar 1982 Cover: 0.60 **NM** value: **1.00**
Circ: Statement: **166,657**
Trial and Terror
14 ❑ Apr 1982 Cover: 0.60 **NM** value: **1.00**
Circ: Statement: **166,657**
Without Getting Killed or Caught • Has 1981 Statement, filed 10/1/81; avg print run 477,445; avg sales 295,740; avg subs 426; avg total paid 296,166; samples 543; office use 2,118; max existent 298,827; 37% of run returned
15 ❑ May 1982 Cover: 0.60 **NM** value: **1.00**
Circ: Statement: **166,657**
A: Bill Sienkiewicz; Frank Springer
16 ❑ Jun 1982 Cover: 0.60 **NM** value: **1.00**
Circ: Statement: **166,657**
A: Bill Sienkiewicz; Frank Springer
17 ❑ Jul 1982 Cover: 0.60 **NM** value: **1.00**
Circ: Statement: **166,657**
• Angel **A:** Frank Springer
18 ❑ Aug 1982 Cover: 0.60 **NM** value: **1.00**
Circ: Statement: **166,657**
A: Bill Sienkiewicz; Frank Frazetta; Frank Springer
19 ❑ Sep 1982 Cover: 0.60 **NM** value: **1.00**
Circ: Statement: **166,657**
20 ❑ Oct 1982 Cover: 0.60 **NM** value: **1.00**
Circ: Statement: **166,657**
21 ❑ Nov 1982 Cover: 1.00 **NM** value: **Cover or less**
Circ: Statement: **166,657**
Photo cover. • Double-size.
22 ❑ Dec 1982 Cover: 0.60 **NM** value: **1.00**
Circ: Statement: **166,657**
★ Appearance of Rogue. ★ Versus Rogue.
23 ❑ Jan 1983 Cover: 0.60 **NM** value: **1.00**
Circ: Statement: **134,764**
24 ❑ Feb 1983 Cover: 0.60 **NM** value: **1.00**
Circ: Statement: **134,764**
25 ❑ Mar 1983 Cover: 0.60 **NM** value: **1.00**
Circ: Statement: **134,764**
26 ❑ May 1983 Cover: 0.60 **NM** value: **1.00**
Circ: Statement: **134,764**
• Has 1982 Statement, filed 10/1/82; avg print run 396,560; avg sales 160,527; avg subs 6,130; avg total paid 166,657; samples 599; office use 2,042; max existent 169,298; 57% of run returned
27 ❑ Jul 1983 Cover: 0.60 **NM** value: **1.00**
Circ: Statement: **134,764**
A: Bill Sienkiewicz(cover) **C:** Bill Sienkiewicz
28 ❑ Sep 1983 Cover: 0.60 **NM** value: **1.00**
Circ: Statement: **134,764**
A: Bill Sienkiewicz(cover) **C:** Bill Sienkiewicz ★ Appearance of Rogue.
29 ❑ Nov 1983 Cover: 0.60 **NM** value: **1.00**
Circ: Statement: **134,764**
Photo cover. **A:** Bill Sienkiewicz(cover)
30 ❑ Jan 1984 Cover: 0.60 **NM** value: **1.00**
A: Bill Sienkiewicz(cover) **C:** Bill Sienkiewicz
31 ❑ Mar 1984 Cover: 0.60 **NM** value: **1.00**
A: Bill Sienkiewicz(cover) **C:** Bill Sienkiewicz
32 ❑ Jun 1984 Cover: 0.60 **NM** value: **1.00**
• Has 1983 Statement, filed 10/6/83; avg print run 280,641; avg sales 123,119; avg subs 11,645; avg total paid 134,764; samples 690; office use 4,397; max existent 139,851; 50% of run returned **C:** Bill Sienkiewicz ★ Appearance of Inhumans.
33 ❑ Aug 1984 Cover: 0.60 **NM** value: **1.00**
C: Bill Sienkiewicz
34 ❑ Oct 1984 Cover: 0.60 **NM** value: **1.00**
C: Bill Sienkiewicz
35 ❑ Jan 1985 Cover: 0.60 **NM** value: **1.00**
C: Bill Sienkiewicz
36 ❑ Mar 1985 Cover: 0.60 **NM** value: **1.00**
C: John Byrne
37 ❑ May 1985 Cover: 0.65 **NM** value: **1.00**
Circ: CapCity orders: **7,400**
38 ❑ Jul 1985 Cover: 0.65 **NM** value: **1.00**
Circ: CapCity orders: **13,100**
★ Appearance of X-Men.
39 ❑ Sep 1985 Cover: 0.65 **NM** value: **1.00**
Circ: CapCity orders: **9,400**
40 ❑ Nov 1985 Cover: 0.65 **NM** value: **1.00**
Circ: CapCity orders: **19,100**
Secret Wars II • Secret Wars II
41 ❑ Jan 1986 Cover: 0.65 **NM** value: **1.00**
Circ: CapCity orders: **9,600**
42 ❑ Mar 1986 Cover: 0.75 **NM** value: **1.00**
Circ: CapCity orders: **10,800**
final issue.

DC CHALLENGE — DC

1 ❑ Nov 1985 Cover: 1.25 **NM** value: **1.50**
Circ: CapCity orders: **17,050**
Outbreak! **A:** Gene Colan; Bob Smith **W:** Mark Evanier
2 ❑ Dec 1985 Cover: 1.25 **NM** value: **1.50**
Circ: CapCity orders: **13,750**
A: Chuck Patton; Mike DeCarlo **W:** Len Wein
3 ❑ Jan 1986 Cover: 1.25 **NM** value: **1.50**
Circ: CapCity orders: **12,900**
Viking Vengeance **A:** Carmine Infantino; Bob Smith **W:** Doug Moench
4 ❑ Feb 1986 Cover: 1.25 **NM** value: **1.50**
Circ: CapCity orders: **12,850**
A: Gil Kane; Klaus Janson **W:** Paul Levitz
5 ❑ Mar 1986 Cover: 1.25 **NM** value: **1.50**
Circ: CapCity orders: **11,850**
A: Dave Gibbons; Mark Farmer **W:** Mike W. Barr
6 ❑ Apr 1986 Cover: 1.25 **NM** value: **1.50**
Circ: CapCity orders: **10,450**
A Matter of Anti-Matter **A:** Dan Jurgens; Larry Mahlstedt **W:** Elliott S! Maggin
7 ❑ May 1986 Cover: 1.25 **NM** value: **1.50**
Circ: CapCity orders: **10,400**
A: Joe Staton; Steve Mitchell **W:** Paul Kupperberg
8 ❑ Jun 1986 Cover: 1.25 **NM** value: **1.50**
Circ: CapCity orders: **6,750**
A: Rick Hoberg; Dick Giordano **W:** Gerry Conway
9 ❑ Jul 1986 Cover: 1.25 **NM** value: **1.50**
Circ: CapCity orders: **9,700**
A: Karl Kesel; Don Heck **W:** Roy Thomas
10 ❑ Aug 1986 Cover: 1.25 **NM** value: **1.50**
Circ: CapCity orders: **9,150**
A: Curt Swan; Terry Austin **W:** Dan Mishkin
11 ❑ Sep 1986 Cover: 1.25 **NM** value: **1.50**
Circ: CapCity orders: **9,350**
A: Keith Giffen; Romeo Tanghal **W:** Marv Wolfman
12 ❑ Oct 1986 Cover: 1.25 **NM** value: **1.50**
Circ: CapCity orders: **10,300**
A: George Pérez; Terry Austin

DC COMICS PRESENTS — DC

This series might have been more aptly named "DC Comics Presents Superman and..." since each issue featured Superman in a new adventure, teamed up with popular DC characters such as Batgirl, Green Lantern, Robin, and Swamp Thing. Over the years, DC used this series to introduce several new characters, including Superwoman, Ambush Bug, and The Global Guardians.

The series also had the distinction of serving as the home for at least two 16-page preview issues of upcoming DC series. A New Teen Titans preview appeared in #26 and an Atari Force preview ran in #53. The series ended just after the events of Crisis on Infinite Earths and prior to the Superman revamp in 1986.

1 ❑ Jul 1978 Cover: 0.35 **NM** value: **3.00**
• **CGC:** 23 graded, best 9.6
• Flash **A:** José Luis Garcia-Lopez; Dan Adkins
2 ❑ Sep 1978 Cover: 0.50 **NM** value: **3.00**
• **CGC:** 4 graded, best 9.8
• Flash **A:** José Luis Garcia-Lopez; Dan Adkins
3 ❑ Oct 1978 Cover: 0.50 **NM** value: **2.00**
• Adam Strange **A:** José Luis Garcia-Lopez
4 ❑ Dec 1978 Cover: 0.40 **NM** value: **2.00**
Sun-Stroke • Metal Men **A:** José Luis Garcia-Lopez
5 ❑ Jan 1979 Cover: 0.40 **NM** value: **2.00**
Circ: Statement: **135,657**
• Aquaman **A:** Murphy Anderson
6 ❑ Feb 1979 Cover: 0.40 **NM** value: **2.00**
Circ: Statement: **135,657**
• Green Lantern **A:** Curt Swan
7 ❑ Mar 1979 Cover: 0.40 **NM** value: **2.00**
Circ: Statement: **135,657**
• Red Tornado **A:** Dick Dillin
8 ❑ Apr 1979 Cover: 0.40 **NM** value: **2.00**
Circ: Statement: **135,657**
• Swamp Thing **A:** Murphy Anderson
9 ❑ May 1979 Cover: 0.40 **NM** value: **2.00**
Circ: Statement: **135,657**
• Wonder Woman **A:** Joe Staton
10 ❑ Jun 1979 Cover: 0.40 **NM** value: **2.00**
Circ: Statement: **135,657**
• Sgt. Rock **A:** Joe Staton
11 ❑ Jul 1979 Cover: 0.40 **NM** value: **2.00**
Circ: Statement: **135,657**
• Hawkman **A:** Joe Staton
12 ❑ Aug 1979 Cover: 0.40 **NM** value: **2.00**
Circ: Statement: **135,657**
• Mr. Miracle **A:** Rich Buckler; Dick Giordano
13 ❑ Sep 1979 Cover: 0.40 **NM** value: **2.00**
Circ: Statement: **135,657**
To Live in Peace – Nevermore • Legion;Legion of Super-Heroes **A:** Dick Giordano; Dick Dillin
14 ❑ Oct 1979 Cover: 0.40 **NM** value: **1.50**
Circ: Statement: **135,657**
Judge, Jury... and No Justice • Superboy **A:** Dick Giordano; Dick Dillin
15 ❑ Nov 1979 Cover: 0.40 **NM** value: **1.50**
Circ: Statement: **135,657**
• Atom **A:** Joe Staton
16 ❑ Dec 1979 Cover: 0.40 **NM** value: **1.50**
Circ: Statement: **135,657**
• Black Lightning
17 ❑ Jan 1980 Cover: 0.40 **NM** value: **1.50**
Circ: Statement: **132,411**
• Firestorm **A:** José Luis Garcia-Lopez

Other grades: Multiply prices above by **1.5 for Mint • 2/3 for Very Fine • 1/3 for Fine • 1/5 for Very Good • 1/8 for Good**

18 ❑ Feb 1980 Cover: 0.40 **NM** value: **1.50**
Circ: Statement: **132,411**
• Zatanna **A:** Dick Dillin

19 ❑ Mar 1980 Cover: 0.40 **NM** value: **1.50**
Circ: Statement: **132,411**
• Batgirl **A:** Joe Staton

20 ❑ Apr 1980 Cover: 0.40 **NM** value: **1.50**
Circ: Statement: **132,411**
• Green Arrow; Has 1979 Statement; avg print run 308,590; avg sales 135,144; avg subs 513; avg total paid 135,657; office use 121; max existent 135,778; 56% of run returned **A:** José Luis Garcia-Lopez

21 ❑ May 1980 Cover: 0.40 **NM** value: **1.50**
Circ: Statement: **132,411**
• Elongated Man **A:** Joe Staton

22 ❑ Jun 1980 Cover: 0.40 **NM** value: **1.50**
Circ: Statement: **132,411**
• Captain Comet

23 ❑ Jul 1980 Cover: 0.40 **NM** value: **1.50**
Circ: Statement: **132,411**
• Doctor Fate **A:** Joe Staton

24 ❑ Aug 1980 Cover: 0.40 **NM** value: **1.50**
Circ: Statement: **132,411**
• Deadman **A:** José Luis Garcia-Lopez

25 ❑ Sep 1980 Cover: 0.50 **NM** value: **1.50**
Circ: Statement: **132,411**
• Phantom Stranger

26 ❑ Oct 1980 Cover: 0.50 **NM** value: **8.00**
Circ: Statement: **132,411** • **CGC:** 13 graded, best 9.4
Between Friend and Foe; Where Nightmares Begin; Whatever Happened to Sargon the Sorcerer • Green Lantern **A:** Jim Starlin; George Pérez; Kim Demulder; José Delbo **W:** Jim Starlin; Julius Schwartz; Marv Wolfman ★ 1st Appearance of New Teen Titans, Raven, Starfire II (Koriand'r), Cyborg.

27 ❑ Nov 1980 Cover: 0.50 **NM** value: **2.50**
Circ: Statement: **132,411**
• Martian Manhunter;Congorilla back-up **A:** Jim Starlin ★ 1st Appearance of Mongul.

28 ❑ Dec 1980 Cover: 0.50 **NM** value: **1.50**
Circ: Statement: **132,411**
• Supergirl;Johnny Thunder Lawman back-up **A:** Jim Starlin ★ Versus Mongul.

29 ❑ Jan 1981 Cover: 0.50 **NM** value: **1.50**
Circ: Statement: **127,399**
• Spectre **A:** Jim Starlin; Romeo Tanghal

30 ❑ Feb 1981 Cover: 0.50 **NM** value: **1.50**
Circ: Statement: **127,399**
• Black Canary **A:** Curt Swan

31 ❑ Mar 1981 Cover: 0.50 **NM** value: **1.50**
Circ: Statement: **127,399**
• Robin;Robotman back-up **A:** Dick Giordano; José Luis Garcia-Lopez

32 ❑ Apr 1981 Cover: 0.50 **NM** value: **1.50**
Circ: Statement: **127,399**
• Wonder Woman

33 ❑ May 1981 Cover: 0.50 **NM** value: **1.50**
Circ: Statement: **127,399**
• Captain Marvel; Has 1980 Statement, filed 10/1/80; avg print run 339,485 ; avg sales 130,600; avg subs 1,811; avg total paid 132,411; samples 127; office use 3,103; max existent 135,514; 60% of run returned

34 ❑ Jun 1981 Cover: 0.50 **NM** value: **1.50**
Circ: Statement: **127,399**
• Marvel Family

35 ❑ Jul 1981 Cover: 0.50 **NM** value: **1.50**
Circ: Statement: **127,399**
• Man-Bat **A:** Curt Swan

36 ❑ Aug 1981 Cover: 0.50 **NM** value: **1.50**
Circ: Statement: **127,399**
• Starman **A:** Jim Starlin

37 ❑ Sep 1981 Cover: 0.50 **NM** value: **1.50**
Circ: Statement: **127,399**
• Hawkgirl;Rip Hunter back-up **A:** Jim Starlin; Romeo Tanghal

38 ❑ Oct 1981 Cover: 0.60 **NM** value: **1.50**
Circ: Statement: **127,399**
• Flash★ Death of Crimson Avenger.

39 ❑ Nov 1981 Cover: 0.60 **NM** value: **1.50**
Circ: Statement: **127,399**
A: Jim Starlin ★ Appearance of Toyman.

40 ❑ Dec 1981 Cover: 0.60 **NM** value: **1.50**
Circ: Statement: **127,399**
• Metamorpho

41 ❑ Jan 1982 Cover: 0.60 **NM** value: **2.25**
Circ: Statement: **126,805** • **CGC:** 1 graded, best 9.6
• Joker★ 1st Appearance of new Wonder Woman, Joker.

42 ❑ Feb 1982 Cover: 0.60 **NM** value: **1.25**
Circ: Statement: **126,805**
• Unknown Soldier;Golden Age Sandman back-up

43 ❑ Mar 1982 Cover: 0.60 **NM** value: **1.25**
Circ: Statement: **126,805**
• Legion **A:** Curt Swan

44 ❑ Apr 1982 Cover: 0.60 **NM** value: **2.25**
Circ: Statement: **126,805**
• Dial 'H' for Hero★ Appearance of Joker.

45 ❑ May 1982 Cover: 0.60 **NM** value: **1.25**
Circ: Statement: **126,805**
• Firestorm; Has 1981 Statement; avg print run 304,620; avg sales 125,286; avg subs 2,113; avg total paid 127,399; samples 127; office use 2,750; max existent 130,149; 57% of run returned **A:** Rich Buckler

46 ❑ Jun 1982 Cover: 0.60 **NM** value: **1.25**
Circ: Statement: **126,805**
★ 1st Appearance of Global Guardians.

47 ❑ Jul 1982 Cover: 0.60 **NM** value: **1.25**
Circ: Statement: **126,805** • **CGC:** 2 graded, best 8.5
★ 1st Appearance of Masters of Universe.

48 ❑ Aug 1982 Cover: 0.60 **NM** value: **1.25**
Circ: Statement: **126,805**
• Aquaman;Black Pirate back-up;Aquaman, Black Pirate back-up

49 ❑ Sep 1982 Cover: 0.60 **NM** value: **1.25**
Circ: Statement: **126,805**
• Captain Marvel **A:** Rich Buckler

50 ❑ Oct 1982 Cover: 0.60 **NM** value: **1.25**
Circ: Statement: **126,805**
When You Wish Upon a Planetoid • Clark Kent **A:** Curt Swan

51 ❑ Nov 1982 Cover: 0.60 **NM** value: **1.25**
Circ: Statement: **126,805**
• Atom **A:** Frank McLaughlin

52 ❑ Dec 1982 Cover: 0.60 **NM** value: **2.50**
Circ: Statement: **126,805**
• Doom Patrol **A:** Keith Giffen ★ 1st Appearance of Ambush Bug.

53 ❑ Jan 1983 Cover: 0.60 **NM** value: **1.00**
Circ: Statement: **119,559** • **CGC:** 1 graded, best 9.4
• House of Mystery★ 1st Appearance of Atari Force.

54 ❑ Feb 1983 Cover: 0.60 **NM** value: **1.00**
Circ: Statement: **119,559**
• Green Arrow, Black Canary **A:** Don Newton

55 ❑ Mar 1983 Cover: 0.60 **NM** value: **1.00**
Circ: Statement: **119,559**
• Air Wave★ Appearance of Superboy. ★ Versus Parasite.

56 ❑ Apr 1983 Cover: 0.60 **NM** value: **1.00**
Circ: Statement: **119,559**
• Power Girl **A:** Curt Swan ★ 1st Appearance of Maaldor the Darklord.

57 ❑ May 1983 Cover: 0.60 **NM** value: **1.00**
Circ: Statement: **119,559**
• Atomic Knights; Has 1982 Statement; avg print run 313,643; avg sales 124,572; avg subs 2,233; avg total paid 126,805; samples 677; office use 3,043; max existent 129,848; 58% of run returned

58 ❑ Jun 1983 Cover: 0.60 **NM** value: **1.00**
Circ: Statement: **119,559**
• Robin, Elongated Man **A:** Curt Swan **C:** Gil Kane ★ 1st Appearance of The Untouchables (DC).

59 ❑ Jul 1983 Cover: 0.60 **NM** value: **1.00**
Circ: Statement: **119,559**
Ambush Bug II • Legion of Super-Heroes, Ambush Bug **A:** Keith Giffen

60 ❑ Aug 1983 Cover: 0.60 **NM** value: **1.00**
Circ: Statement: **119,559**
• Guardians of the Universe

61 ❑ Sep 1983 Cover: 0.60 **NM** value: **1.00**
Circ: Statement: **119,559**
The Once-and-Future War! • OMAC

62 ❑ Oct 1983 Cover: 0.60 **NM** value: **1.00**
Circ: Statement: **119,559**
• Freedom Fighters

63 ❑ Nov 1983 Cover: 0.60 **NM** value: **1.00**
Circ: Statement: **119,559**
• Amethyst **A:** Don Spiegle

64 ❑ Dec 1983 Cover: 0.75 **NM** value: **1.00**
Circ: Statement: **119,559**
• Kamandi

65 ❑ Jan 1984 Cover: 0.75 **NM** value: **1.00**
Circ: Statement: **93,457** • **CGC:** 1 graded, best 9.6
• Madame Xanadu

66 ❑ Feb 1984 Cover: 0.75 **NM** value: **1.00**
Circ: Statement: **93,457** • **CGC:** 1 graded, best 9.6
• Demon **A:** Jack Kirby ★ 1st Appearance of Blackbriar Thorn.

67 ❑ Mar 1984 Cover: 0.75 **NM** value: **1.00**
Circ: Statement: **93,457**
• Santa Claus★ Versus Toyman.

68 ❑ Apr 1984 Cover: 0.75 **NM** value: **1.00**
Circ: Statement: **93,457**
• Vixen; Has 1983 Statement; avg print run 295,908; avg sales 118,397; avg subs 1,162; avg total paid 119,559; samples 739; office use 2,512; max existent 122,071; 59% of run returned **A:** Murphy Anderson; Curt Swan

69 ❑ May 1984 Cover: 0.75 **NM** value: **1.00**
Circ: Statement: **93,457**
• Blackhawk **A:** Irv Novick

70 ❑ Jun 1984 Cover: 0.75 **NM** value: **1.00**
Circ: Statement: **93,457**
• Metal Men

71 ❑ Jul 1984 Cover: 0.75 **NM** value: **1.00**
Circ: Statement: **93,457**
• Bizarro **A:** Curt Swan

72 ❑ Aug 1984 Cover: 0.75 **NM** value: **1.50**
Circ: Statement: **93,457** • **CGC:** 2 graded, best 9.4
• Phantom Stranger, Joker

73 ❑ Sep 1984 Cover: 0.75 **NM** value: **1.00**
Circ: Statement: **93,457** • **CGC:** 1 graded, best 9.6
• Flash **A:** Carmine Infantino

74 ❑ Oct 1984 Cover: 0.75 **NM** value: **1.00**
Circ: Statement: **93,457**
• Hawkman

75 ❑ Nov 1984 Cover: 0.75 **NM** value: **1.00**
Circ: Statement: **93,457**
• Arion

76 ❑ Dec 1984 Cover: 0.75 **NM** value: **1.00**
Circ: Statement: **93,457**
• Wonder Woman★ Appearance of Monitor.

77 ❑ Jan 1985 Cover: 0.75 **NM** value: **3.00**
Circ: Statement: **89,571**
• Animal Man, Dolphin, Congorilla, Cave Carson, Immortal Man, Rip Hunter, Rick Flagg★ 1st Appearance of The Forgotten Villains.

78 ❑ Feb 1985 Cover: 0.75 **NM** value: **3.00**
Circ: Statement: **89,571**
• Animal Man, Dolphin, Congorilla, Cave Carson, Immortal Man, Rip Hunter, Rick Flagg

79 ❑ Mar 1985 Cover: 0.75 **NM** value: **1.00**
Circ: Statement: **89,571**
• Clark Kent

80 ❑ Apr 1985 Cover: 0.75 **NM** value: **1.00**
Circ: Statement: **89,571**
• Legion;

81 ❑ May 1985 Cover: 0.75 **NM** value: **1.00**
Circ: Statement: **89,571** CapCity orders: **6,600**
• Ambush Bug; Has 1984 Statement; avg print run 260,013; avg sales 92,515; avg subs 942; avg total paid 93,457; samples 236; office use 1,882; max existent 95,339; 63% of run returned★ Versus Kobra.

82 ❑ Jun 1985 Cover: 0.75 **NM** value: **1.00**
Circ: Statement: **89,571** CapCity orders: **5,150**
• Adam Strange

83 ❑ Jul 1985 Cover: 0.75 **NM** value: **1.00**
Circ: Statement: **89,571** CapCity orders: **5,900**
• Outsiders

84 ❑ Aug 1985 Cover: 0.75 **NM** value: **1.00**
Circ: Statement: **89,571** CapCity orders: **5,200** • **CGC:** 1 graded, best 9.6
Give Me Power, Give Me Your World! • Challengers of the Unknown

85 ❑ Sep 1985 Cover: 0.75 **NM** value: **8.00**
Circ: Statement: **89,571** CapCity orders: **8,450** • **CGC:** 1 graded, best 9.8
• Swamp Thing **W:** Alan Moore

86 ❑ Oct 1985 Cover: 0.75 **NM** value: **1.00**
Circ: Statement: **89,571** CapCity orders: **9,500**
• Crisis;Supergirl★ Versus Blackstarr.

87 ❑ Nov 1985 Cover: 1.25 **NM** value: **Cover or less**
Circ: Statement: **89,571** CapCity orders: **10,700**
• Crisis★ 1st Appearance of Superboy of Earth-Prime.

88 ❑ Dec 1985 Cover: 0.75 **NM** value: **1.00**
Circ: Statement: **89,571** CapCity orders: **7,200**
• Crisis

89 ❑ Jan 1986 Cover: 0.75 **NM** value: **1.00**
Circ: CapCity orders: **6,100**
• Omega Men

90 ❑ Feb 1986 Cover: 0.75 **NM** value: **1.00**
Circ: CapCity orders: **6,700**
• Firestorm★ Origin of Captain Atom.

91 ❑ Mar 1986 Cover: 0.75 **NM** value: **1.00**
Circ: CapCity orders: **6,800**
• Captain Comet

92 ❑ Apr 1986 Cover: 0.75 **NM** value: **1.00**
Circ: CapCity orders: **7,200**
• Vigilante; Has 1985 Statement; avg print run 237,532; avg sales 88,631; avg subs 940; avg total paid 91,089; samples 122; office use 1,518; max existent 91,089; 62% of run returned

93 ❑ May 1986 Cover: 0.75 **NM** value: **1.00**
Circ: CapCity orders: **5,850**
• Plastic Man, Elongated Man, Elastic Lad

94 ❑ Jun 1986 Cover: 0.75 **NM** value: **1.00**
Circ: CapCity orders: **6,900**
• Harbinger, Lady Quark, Pariah

95 ❑ Jul 1986 Cover: 0.75 **NM** value: **1.00**
Circ: CapCity orders: **6,800**
• Hawkman

96 ❑ Aug 1986 Cover: 0.75 **NM** value: **1.00**
Circ: CapCity orders: **6,550**
• Blue Devil

97 ❑ Sep 1986 Cover: 1.25 **NM** value: **Cover or less**
Circ: CapCity orders: **9,300**
• Double-size. ★ Appearance of Bizarro, Mxyzptlk. ★ Versus Phantom Zone Criminals.

Anl 1❑ca. 1982 Cover: 1.00 **NM** value: **3.00**
• Superman & E-2 Superman **A:** Rich Buckler

Anl 2❑ca. 1983 Cover: 1.00 **NM** value: **3.00**
★ Origin of Superwoman. ★ 1st Appearance of Superwoman.

Anl 3❑ca. 1984 Cover: 1.25 **NM** value: **3.00**
• Doctor Sivana gains the Shazam! powers

Anl 4❑ca. 1985 Cover: 1.25 **NM** value: **3.00**
Circ: CapCity orders: **6,650**
★ Appearance of Superwoman.

DC GRAPHIC NOVEL — DC

1 ❑ Cover: 5.95 **NM** value: **Cover or less**
• Star Raiders **A:** José Luis Garcia-Lopez **W:** Elliott S! Maggin

2 ❑ Cover: 5.95 **NM** value: **Cover or less**
• Warlords

3 ❑ Cover: 5.95 **NM** value: **Cover or less**
• Medusa Chain **A:** Ernie Colon

4 ❑ Cover: 5.95 **NM** value: **Cover or less**
• Hunger Dogs **A:** Jack Kirby

5 ❑ Cover: 5.95 **NM** value: **Cover or less**
• Me and Joe Priest

6 ❑ Cover: 6.95 **NM** value: **Cover or less**
• Metalzoic

7 ❑ Cover: 5.95 **NM** value: **Cover or less**
• Space Clusters

DC/MARVEL: ALL ACCESS — DC

Axel Asher has a tough job. During the Marvel versus DC/DC versus Marvel series, he learned that he had the ability to act as a bridge between the two universes. In his role as Access, he's sort of a cosmic hall monitor, charged with keeping the two universes separate, lest they merge and form another Amalgam universe like the one that occurred midway through that series.

Axel's powers derive from his nature as a "shard" of two cosmic entities who define the Marvel and DC universes. There are other shards in existence, but most are unaware of their true identity, or their role. Axel, however, is aware of his role, and takes it very seriously indeed. In the first issue of this four-issue mini-series, he is tasked with setting things right when Marvel's Venom appears in DC's city of Metropolis, and comes to blows with Superman. Bringing Venom back where he belongs means putting himself in the line of fire, with no super-powers to protect him.

1 ❑ Dec 1996 Cover: 2.95 **NM** value: **Cover or less**
Circ: Direct Market orders: **150,664**

CGC-graded: Multiply prices above by **33 for 9.9 M • 16 for 9.8 NM/M • 7 for 9.6 NM+ • 5 for 9.4 NM • 2.5 for 9.2 NM- • 1.5 for 9.0 VF/NM**

🕮 The Crossing! • crossover with Marvel **A:** Jackson Guice; Joe Rubinstein **W:** Ron Marz ★ Appearance of Superman, Spider-Man, Venom.

2 ❑ Jan 1997 Cover: 1.95 **NM** value: **2.95**
Circ: Diamd. preorders: **122,718**
🕮 Two Sides of the Same Coin • crossover with Marvel **A:** Jackson Guice; Joe Rubinstein **W:** Ron Marz ★ Appearance of Jubilee, Robin, Two-Face, Scorpion.

3 ❑ Jan 1997 Cover: 1.95 **NM** value: **2.95**
Circ: Diamd. preorders: **118,963**
🕮 In The Doctor's House • crossover with Marvel **A:** Jackson Guice; Joe Rubinstein **W:** Ron Marz ★ Appearance of Jubilee, Robin, Batman, Doctor Strange, Scorpion, JLA, X-Men.

4 ❑ Feb 1997 Cover: 2.95 **NM** value: **Cover or less**
Circ: Diamd. preorders: **88,850**
final issue. • crossover with Marvel **A:** Jackson Guice; Joe Rubinstein **W:** Ron Marz ★ Appearance of JLA, X-Men, Doctor Strangefate, Amalgam universe.

DC/MARVEL CROSSOVER CLASSICS DC-Marvel

1 ❑ Cover: 14.95 **NM** value: **Cover or less**

DC/MARVEL: CROSSOVER CLASSICS II DC / Marvel

1 ❑ Cover: 14.95 **NM** value: **Cover or less**
• collects Batman/Punisher: Lake of Fire, Punisher/Batman: Deadly Knights, Superman/Silver Surfer: Pop, and Batman/Captain America

DC 100 PAGE SUPER SPECTACULAR DC

Cataloging this 19-issue reprint title from DC — which began with #4 and ended with #22 — was a tough task because issues 7-13 are dual-numbered. While they are issues of DC 100 Page Super Spectacular, they are also Superman (1st Series) #245, Adventure Comics #416, Batman #238, Our Army at War #242, Flash (1st Series) #214, Superboy (1st Series) #185, and Superman (1st Series) #252.

Still, in spite of the confusion, this series was jam-packed with classic Golden Age and Silver Age material like the first meeting of the Justice League and the Justice Society; the origin of Two-Face; and early appearances of The Spectre, Kid Eternity, Johnny Quick, Hawkman, Starman, and The Sandman. Just the covers of these comics — primarily by Neal Adams and Nick Cardy — make them worth owning ... especially Adams' "World's Greatest Super-Heroes" (#6) and "World's Greatest Flying Heroes" (#13).

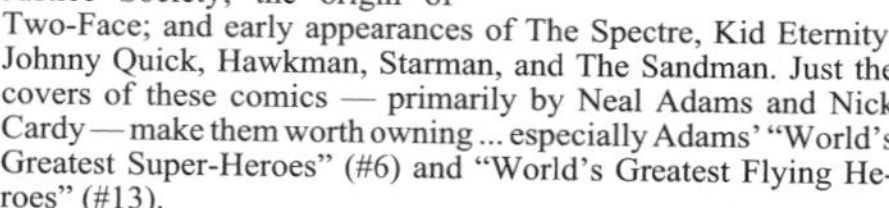

4 ❑ ca. 1971 Cover: 0.50 **NM** value: **100.00**
• **CGC:** 17 graded, best 9.4
back cover pin-up. • Weird Mystery Tales

5 ❑ ca. 1971 Cover: 0.50 **NM** value: **325.00**
• **CGC:** 10 graded, best 9.2
back cover pin-up. 🕮 Made For Love; How Do I Know When I'm Really in Love?; My Shameful Past; My Sister Stole My Man; The Other Girl; The Wrong Kind of Love; Didn't Want His Love; Goodbye, Lover; Happy Ending • Love Stories **A:** Bob Oksner; Win Mortimer; Mort Drucker; Mike Sekowsky; Art Saaf; Ric Estrada; Jay Scott Pike; Norman Nodell; Tony Abruzzi; Vince Colletta **W:** Jack Miller

5-2 ❑ Cover: 6.95 **NM** value: **Cover or less**
• Replica edition. 🕮 Made For Love; How Do I Know When I'm Really in Love?; My Shameful Past; My Sister Stole My Man; The Other Girl; The Wrong Kind of Love; Didn't Want His Love; Goodbye, Lover; Happy Ending • Love Stories **A:** Bob Oksner; Win Mortimer; Mort Drucker; Mike Sekowsky; Art Saaf; Ric Estrada; Jay Scott Pike; Norman Nodell; Tony Abruzzi; Vince Colletta **W:** Jack Miller

6 ❑ ca. 1971 Cover: 0.50 **NM** value: **100.00**
• **CGC:** 17 graded, best 9.4
wraparound cover. • World's Greatest Super-Heroes;reprints JLA #21-22

7 ❑ Dec 1971 Cover: 0.50 **NM** value: **35.00**
back cover pin-up. • really DC-7;a.k.a. Superman #245

8 ❑ Jan 1972 Cover: 0.50 **NM** value: **50.00**
wraparound cover. • really DC-8;a.k.a. Batman #238

9 ❑ Feb 1972 Cover: 0.50 **NM** value: **50.00**
Sgt. Rock, wraparound cover. • really DC-9;a.k.a. Our Army at War #242

10 ❑ Mar 1972 Cover: 0.50 **NM** value: **35.00**
wraparound cover. • really DC-10;a.k.a. Adventure Comics #416;Supergirl

11 ❑ Apr 1972 Cover: 0.50 **NM** value: **35.00**
wraparound cover. • really DC-11;a.k.a. Flash #214

12 ❑ May 1972 Cover: 0.50 **NM** value: **35.00**
• **CGC:** 1 graded, best 5.0
wraparound cover. • really DC-12;a.k.a. Superboy #185

13 ❑ Jun 1972 Cover: 0.50 **NM** value: **35.00**
wraparound cover. • really DC-13;a.k.a. Superman #252

14 ❑ Feb 1973 Cover: 0.50 **NM** value: **30.00**
• **CGC:** 3 graded, best 9.4
wraparound cover. • really DC-14;Batman

15 ❑ Mar 1973 Cover: 0.50 **NM** value: **30.00**
• **CGC:** 7 graded, best 9.8
back cover pin-up. • really DC-15;Superboy

16 ❑ Apr 1973 Cover: 0.50 **NM** value: **25.00**
• **CGC:** 2 graded, best 8.5
back cover cover gallery. • really DC-16;Sgt. Rock

17 ❑ Jun 1973 Cover: 0.50 **NM** value: **25.00**
• **CGC:** 4 graded, best 9.2
back cover cover gallery. • really DC-17;JLA **A:** Joe Simon

18 ❑ Jul 1973 Cover: 0.50 **NM** value: **25.00**
• **CGC:** 2 graded, best 9.4
back cover cover gallery. • Superman's 35th anniversary. • really DC-18

19 ❑ Aug 1973 Cover: 0.50 **NM** value: **25.00**
• **CGC:** 3 graded, best 9.4
back cover pin-up. 🕮 Tarzan and the Elephants' Guardian; Prisoners in Opar; Jane's Own Story: How I Met Tarzan; Tarzan in Tembo-Haven; Behind the Scenes at D.C.; People in Tarzan's Africa • really DC-19;Tarzan **A:** Russ Manning **C:** Joe Kubert **W:** Edgar Rice Burroughs

20 ❑ Sep 1973 Cover: 0.50 **NM** value: **25.00**
• **CGC:** 9 graded, best 9.4
back cover cover gallery. • really DC-20;Batman ★ Origin of Two-Face.

21 ❑ Oct 1973 Cover: 0.50 **NM** value: **25.00**
• **CGC:** 4 graded, best 9.4
back cover cover gallery. • really DC-21;Superboy

22 ❑ Nov 1973 Cover: 0.50 **NM** value: **7.50**
• **CGC:** 2 graded, best 9.4
• really DC-22;Flash;Super Specs become part of individual series beginning with Shazam! #8

DC ONE MILLION DC

1 ❑ Nov 1998 Cover: 2.95 **NM** value: **Cover or less**
Circ: Diamd. preorders: **85,739**
🕮 Riders on the Storm **A:** Val Semeiks **W:** Grant Morrison

1/SC ❑ Nov 1998 Cover: 14.99 **NM** value: **Cover or less**
🕮 Riders on the Storm **A:** Val Semeiks **W:** Grant Morrison

2 ❑ Nov 1998 Cover: 2.95 **NM** value: **Cover or less**
Circ: Diamd. preorders: **81,743**
A: Val Semeiks **W:** Grant Morrison

3 ❑ Nov 1998 Cover: 2.95 **NM** value: **Cover or less**
Circ: Diamd. preorders: **80,587**
🕮 Solaris Rising **A:** Val Semeiks **W:** Grant Morrison

4 ❑ Nov 1998 Cover: 2.95 **NM** value: **Cover or less**
Circ: Diamd. preorders: **79,955**

Bk 1 ❑ Aug 1999 Cover: 14.95 **NM** value: **Cover or less**
No issue number. • Trade Paperback. 🕮 System's Finest; Tales of the Legion of Executive Familiars; The Divided Self; Head Games; Deep Cover; Day in the Lives; Crisis One Million • collects DC One Million #1-4, Green Lantern #1,000,000, Starman #1,000,000, JLA #1,000,000, Resurrection Man #1,000,000, and Superman: Man of Tomorrow #1, 000, 000 **A:** Norm Breyfogle; Cully Hamner; Flint Henry; Drew Johnson; Georges Jeanty; Mike Wieringo; Dusty Abell **W:** Andy Lanning; Mark Schultz; Chuck Dixon; Grant Morrison; Dan Abnett; Ian Edginton; Mark Millar

GS 1 ❑ Aug 1999 Cover: 4.95 **NM** value: **Cover or less**
Circ: Diamd. preorders: **30,110**
🕮 System's Finest; Tales of the Legion of Executive Familiars; The Divided Self; Head Games; Deep Cover; Day in the Lives; Crisis One Million **A:** Norm Breyfogle; Cully Hamner; Flint Henry; Drew Johnson; Georges Jeanty; Mike Wieringo; Dusty Abell **W:** Andy Lanning; Mark Schultz; Chuck Dixon; Grant Morrison; Dan Abnett; Ian Edginton; Mark Millar

DC SAMPLER DC

1 ❑ Sep 1983 Cover: 1.00 **NM** value: **Cover or less**

2 ❑ Sep 1984 **NM** value: **1.00**
no cover price. • Promotional giveaway. • Atari Force, etc. **A:** Fred Hembeck; José Garcia Lopez **W:** Gerry Conway

3 ❑ **NM** value: **1.00**
no cover price. • Promotional giveaway. • The Saga of the Swamp Thing, etc. **A:** Fred Hembeck; John Totleben; Steve Bissette **C:** Fred Hembeck **W:** Alan Moore

DC SCIENCE FICTION GRAPHIC NOVEL DC

1 ❑ Cover: 5.95 **NM** value: **Cover or less**
• Hell on Earth

2 ❑ Cover: 5.95 **NM** value: **Cover or less**
• Nightwings

3 ❑ Cover: 5.95 **NM** value: **Cover or less**
🕮 Frost and Fire

4 ❑ Cover: 5.95 **NM** value: **Cover or less**
• Merchants Venus

5 ❑ Cover: 5.95 **NM** value: **Cover or less**
🕮 Demon with a Glass Hand

6 ❑ Cover: 5.95 **NM** value: **Cover or less**
• Magic Goes Away

7 ❑ Cover: 5.95 **NM** value: **Cover or less**
• Sand Kings

DC SILVER AGE CLASSICS ACTION COMICS DC

In the early 1990s, DC reprinted several significant comics from the 1950s and 1960s as part of an overall Silver Age Classics line. The reprint of Action Comics #252 represented Supergirl's first appearance along with text material discussing the character's impact on the DC universe and Superman mythos.

Other reprints in the series included Showcase #4 (the first Silver Age Flash), Showcase #22 (the first Silver Age Green Lantern), Detective Comics #255 (the first Martian Manhunter), and Adventure Comics #247 (first Legion of Super-Heroes). One new issue was published with Sugar & Spike #99, which included text information from CBG Editor Maggie Thompson. —Brent

252 ❑ Cover: 1.00 **NM** value: **Cover or less**
🕮 The Menace of Metallo!; Congo Bill Dies at Dawn; The Supergirl from Krypton; • reprints Action Comics #252 **A:** Howard Sherman; Al Plastino **W:** Otto Binder; Robert Berstein ★ Origin of Supergirl.

DC SILVER AGE CLASSICS ADVENTURE COMICS DC

247 ❑ Cover: 1.00 **NM** value: **Cover or less**
🕮 The Legion of Super- Heroes; The 13 Superstition Arrows; Aquaman's Super Sea-Squad; • reprints Adventure Comics #247 **A:** Ramona Fradon; George Papp **W:** Otto Binder ★ Origin of Legion.

DC SILVER AGE CLASSICS DETECTIVE COMICS DC

225 ❑ Cover: 1.00 **NM** value: **Cover or less**
🕮 If I Were Batman; The Money That Came to Life!; Introducing John Jones Manhunter from Mars • reprints Detective Comics #225 **A:** Bob Kane **W:** Bob Kane ★ 1st Appearance of J'onn J'onzz.

327 ❑ Cover: 1.00 **NM** value: **Cover or less**
🕮 The Mystery of The Menacing Mask; Ten Miles to Nowhere • reprints Detective Comics #327 **A:** Carmine Infantino; Joe Giella **W:** Gardner Fox; John Broome ★ 1st Appearance of new Batman.

DC SILVER AGE CLASSICS GREEN LANTERN DC

76 ❑ Cover: 1.00 **NM** value: **Cover or less**
• reprints Green Lantern #76 ★ Origin of Green Lantern/Green Arrow team.

DC SILVER AGE CLASSICS HOUSE OF SECRETS DC

92 ❑ Cover: 1.00 **NM** value: **Cover or less**
🕮 Swamp Thing; After I Die; It's Better to Give; Trick or Treat • reprints House of Secrets #92 **A:** Alan Weiss; Bernie Wrightson; Dick Dillin; Tony DeZuniga; Bill Draut **W:** Dick Dillin; Len Wein; Mark Evanier; Mary Skrenes ★ 1st Appearance of Swamp Thing.

DC SILVER AGE CLASSICS SHOWCASE DC

4 ❑ Cover: 1.00 **NM** value: **Cover or less**
🕮 Mystery of the Human Thunderbolt!; The Man Who Broke the Time Barrier!; • reprints Showcase #4 **A:** Carmine Infantino; Joe Kubert **W:** John Broome; Robert Kanigher ★ Origin of Flash.

22 ❑ Cover: 1.00 **NM** value: **Cover or less**
🕮 SOS Green LanternSecret of the Flaming Spear!; Menace of the Runaway Missile!; • reprints Showcase #22 **A:** Gil Kane; Joe Giella **W:** John Broome ★ Origin of Green Lantern.

DC SILVER AGE CLASSICS SUGAR & SPIKE DC

99 ❑ Cover: 1.00 **NM** value: **2.00**
• not a reprint;first publication of Sugar and Spike #99

DC SILVER AGE CLASSICS THE BRAVE AND THE BOLD DC

28 ❑ Cover: 1.00 **NM** value: **1.25**
🕮 Justice League Of America: Starro The Conqueror! • reprints The Braveand the Bold #28 **A:** Mike Sekowsky **W:** Gardner Fox ★ 1st Appearance of JLA, The Justice League of America.

DC SNEAK PREVIEW DC

1 ❑ **NM** value: **1.00**
🕮 Vengeance from the Stars • Featuring JSA, Green Lantern **A:** Mark D. Bright; Rick Burchett **W:** Keith Giffen; Len Strazewski

DC SPECIAL DC

DC Special consisted of a series of double-sized issues spotlighting different parts of the DC universe. One issue, for example, might consist of adventure stories from the early days of The Brave and the Bold, featuring such characters as The Viking Prince, The Silent Knight, and Robin Hood. Other issues focused on topics ranging from strange sports tales to the origins of Golden Age heroes.

Virtually all of this material was reprinted from early DC comics, but at prices ranging from a quarter to 60 cents for many pages of reading, DC Special was a superior reading bargain.

1 ❑ Dec 1968 Cover: 0.25 **NM** value: **14.00**
• **CGC:** 9 graded, best 9.6
• Flash, Batman, Adam Strange **A:** Carmine Infantino

2 ❑ Mar 1969 Cover: 0.25 **NM** value: **8.00**
• **CGC:** 4 graded, best 9.4
• teen

3 ❑ Jun 1969 Cover: 0.25 **NM** value: **8.00**
• **CGC:** 5 graded, best 9.4
🕮 Special Delivery Death! • Green Arrow, Black Canary

4 ❑ Sep 1969 Cover: 0.25 **NM** value: **8.00**
• **CGC:** 1 graded, best 9.6

5 ❑ Dec 1969 Cover: 0.25 **NM** value: **8.00**
• **CGC:** 3 graded, best 9.4

6 ❑ Mar 1970 Cover: 0.25 **NM** value: **8.00**
• **CGC:** 2 graded, best 9.4

7 ❑ Jun 1970 Cover: 0.25 **NM** value: **8.00**
• **CGC:** 1 graded, best 9.6
• Strange Sports

8 ❑ Sep 1970 Cover: 0.25 **NM** value: **8.00**
• Wanted

9 ❑ Dec 1970 Cover: 0.25 **NM** value: **8.00**

10 ❑ Feb 1971 Cover: 0.25 **NM** value: **8.00**
• **CGC:** 2 graded, best 9.2

11 ❑ Apr 1971 Cover: 0.25 **NM** value: **8.00**
• **CGC:** 3 graded, best 9.6
• Monsters

12 ❑ Jun 1971 Cover: 0.25 **NM** value: **8.00**
• **CGC:** 3 graded, best 9.2

Other grades: Multiply prices above by **1.5 for Mint • 2/3 for Very Fine • 1/3 for Fine • 1/5 for Very Good • 1/8 for Good**

📖 Battle For The Dragon Ship; The Ice Dragon; The Viking And The Mermaid; The Silent Night: Duel In Forest Perilous; The Golden Gladiator: The Thunder Of The Chariots; Robin Hood: Three Arrows Against Doom • Viking Prince **A:** Joe Kubert; Russ Heath; Irv Novick **W:** Robert Kanigher

13 ❑ Aug 1971 Cover: 0.25 **NM** value: **8.00**
• Strange Sports

14 ❑ Oct 1971 Cover: 0.25 **NM** value: **8.00**
• **CGC:** 1 graded, best 9.4
• Giant-size. 📖 The Toyman's Castle; The Heat Is In For Captain Cold; The Bird Sayings Crimes! • Wanted: The World's Most Dangerous Villains

15 ❑ Dec 1971 Cover: 0.25 **NM** value: **10.00**
• **CGC:** 2 graded, best 9.2
• Giant-size. • Plastic Man reprints ★ Origin of Woozy Winks, Plastic Man (Golden Age).

16 ❑ Spr 1975 Cover: 0.50 **NM** value: **6.00**
• **CGC:** 4 graded, best 9.6
📖 Batman Battles the Living Beast-Bomb!; Wonder Woman – Gorilla!; The Reign of the Super-Gorilla!; Titano the Super-Ape! • Gorillas **A:** Carmine Infantino; Ross Andru; Joe Giella; Mike Esposito; Wayne Boring **W:** Gardner Fox; John Broome; Otto Binder; Robert Kanigher

17 ❑ Sum 1975 Cover: 0.50 **NM** value: **6.00**

18 ❑ Nov 1975 Cover: 0.50 **NM** value: **6.00**
• **CGC:** 2 graded, best 9.2
• Earth-Shaking Stories

19 ❑ Jan 1976 Cover: 0.50 **NM** value: **6.00**
• **CGC:** 2 graded, best 9.2

20 ❑ Mar 1976 Cover: 0.50 **NM** value: **6.00**
• **CGC:** 2 graded, best 9.4
• Green Lantern

21 ❑ May 1976 Cover: 0.50 **NM** value: **6.00**
• **CGC:** 4 graded, best 9.4
• Monsters, War That Time Forgot

22 ❑ Jul 1976 Cover: 0.50 **NM** value: **6.00**
• Three Musketeers, Robin Hood

23 ❑ Sep 1976 Cover: 0.50 **NM** value: **6.00**
• Three Musketeers, Robin Hood

24 ❑ Oct 1976 Cover: 0.50 **NM** value: **6.00**
• Robin Hood, Viking Prince

25 ❑ Dec 1976 Cover: 0.50 **NM** value: **6.00**
• Robin Hood, Viking Prince

26 ❑ Feb 1977 Cover: 0.50 **NM** value: **6.00**
• Enemy Ace

27 ❑ Apr 1977 Cover: 0.50 **NM** value: **6.00**
• Captain Comet

28 ❑ Jun 1977 Cover: 0.60 **NM** value: **6.00**
• **CGC:** 1 graded, best 9.4
• Batman

29 ❑ Sep 1977 Cover: 0.60 **NM** value: **6.00**
• **CGC:** 2 graded, best 9.6
A: Bob Layton; Joe Staton ★ Origin of Justice Society of America (Secret Origin).

DC SPECIAL BLUE RIBBON DIGEST — DC

1 ❑ Apr 1980 Cover: 0.95 **NM** value: **4.00**
• Legion of Super Heroes

2 ❑ Jun 1980 Cover: 0.95 **NM** value: **3.00**
• Flash

3 ❑ Aug 1980 Cover: 0.95 **NM** value: **3.00**
• Justice Society

4 ❑ Oct 1980 Cover: 0.95 **NM** value: **3.00**
• Green Lantern

5 ❑ Dec 1980 Cover: 0.95 **NM** value: **3.00**
• Secret Origins

6 ❑ Jan 1981 Cover: 0.95 **NM** value: **3.00**
• **CGC:** 1 graded, best 9.0
📖 Death Held the Lantern High; The Phatom Hangman; The Most Fearful Villain of the Supernatural; Death Weaves a Web • House of Mystery **A:** Ernie Chan; Lee Elias; Sam Glanzman; Rico Rival; Tony DeZuniga; Frank Redondo; Jim Aparo; Jerry Grandienetti; Rubeny; A. Alcala; J. Lofamia; J. Noriega; John Calnan **W:** Leo Dorfman; Len Wein; Carl Wessler; George Kashdan; Murray Boltinoff

7 ❑ Mar 1981 Cover: 0.95 **NM** value: **3.00**
• Flying Tigers, Haunted Tank, War That Time Forgot, Enemy Ace

8 ❑ Apr 1981 Cover: 0.95 **NM** value: **3.00**
• Legion

9 ❑ May 1981 Cover: 0.95 **NM** value: **3.00**
• The Atom

10 ❑ Jun 1981 Cover: 0.95 **NM** value: **3.00**
• Warlord

11 ❑ Jul 1981 Cover: 0.95 **NM** value: **3.00**
• Justice League, Justice Society, Seven Soldiers

12 ❑ Aug 1981 Cover: 0.95 **NM** value: **3.00**
• Haunted Tank

13 ❑ Sep 1981 Cover: 0.95 **NM** value: **3.00**
• Strange Sports

14 ❑ Oct 1981 Cover: 0.95 **NM** value: **3.00**
• Science Fiction

15 ❑ Nov 1981 Cover: 0.95 **NM** value: **3.00**
• Superboy, Green Lantern, Batman

16 ❑ Dec 1981 Cover: 0.95 **NM** value: **3.00**
• Green Lantern/Green Arrow

17 ❑ Jan 1982 Cover: 0.95 **NM** value: **3.00**
• **CGC:** 1 graded, best 9.2
• Mystery

18 ❑ Feb 1982 Cover: 0.95 **NM** value: **3.00**
• Sgt. Rock

19 ❑ Mar 1982 Cover: 0.95 **NM** value: **3.00**
📖 The Doom Patrol; The Brotherhood of Evil; Mento – the Man Who Split the Doom Patrol; The Enemy Within the Doom Patrol • Reprints My Greatest Adventure #80 and Doom Patrol #86, 90 and 91

20 ❑ Apr 1982 Cover: 0.95 **NM** value: **8.00**
• **CGC:** 3 graded, best 9.6
• Mystery

21 ❑ May 1982 Cover: 0.95 **NM** value: **3.00**
• War **A:** Jack Kirby

22 ❑ Jun 1982 Cover: 0.95 **NM** value: **3.00**
• Secret Origins

23 ❑ Jul 1982 Cover: 0.95 **NM** value: **3.00**
• Green Arrow

DC SPECIAL SERIES — DC

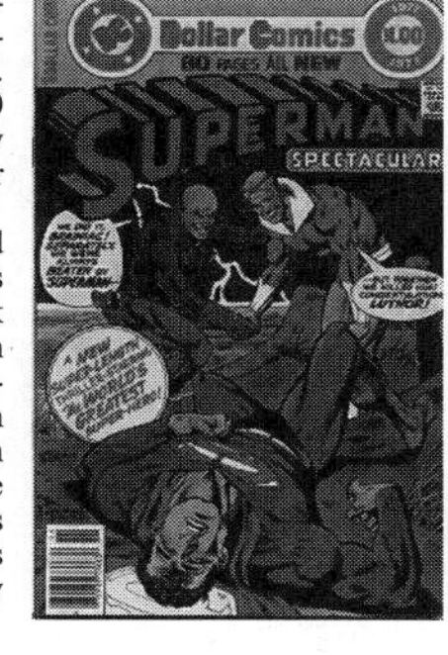

DC Special Series was a giant-sized reprint series that ran sporadically between 1977 and 1981. Its huge issues (as many as 100 pages) reprised many of the early adventures of Batman, Doctor Fate, Superman, and others.

The title's highlights included its reprints of Bernie Wrightson's Swamp Thing stories, Frank Miller's first Batman story in #21, and an almost unprecedented inter-company crossover in #27 that pitted DC's Batman against Marvel's Incredible Hulk. Considering the contents and the price (even the price as back issues), this is a good way to experience many old stories.

1 ❑ Sep 1977 Cover: 1.00 **NM** value: **5.00**
• **CGC:** 6 graded, best 9.8
• 5-Star Super-Hero Spectacular; Super-heroes **A:** Frank McLaughlin; Mike Nasser; Dick Dillin; John Romita; Irv Novick

2 ❑ Sep 1977 Cover: 0.60 **NM** value: **4.00**
📖 Dark Genesis!; The Man who Wanted Forever • Swamp Thing reprint; Swamp Thing **A:** Bernie Wrightson **W:** Len Wein

3 ❑ Oct 1977 Cover: 0.60 **NM** value: **3.00**
• Sgt. Rock **A:** Jack Kirby

4 ❑ Oct 1977 **NM** value: **3.00**
• Unexpected Annual

5 ❑ Nov 1977 Cover: 1.00 **NM** value: **3.00**
📖 The Second Coming of Superman; The First Coming of Superman; A God Walks Among Us; The Fall and Rise of Sonzrr • a.k.a. Superman Spectacular; first DC Dollar Comic; Superman, Luthor ★ Appearance of Superman, Luthor, Brainiac.

6 ❑ Nov 1977 Cover: 0.60 **NM** value: **3.00**
• JLA

7 ❑ Dec 1977 Cover: 0.60 **NM** value: **3.00**
• Ghosts

8 ❑ Feb 1978 Cover: 0.60 **NM** value: **3.00**
• **CGC:** 1 graded, best 9.6
• Brave & Bold **A:** Dick Giordano

9 ❑ Mar 1978 Cover: 1.00 **NM** value: **12.00**
• **CGC:** 1 graded, best 9.4
• Wonder Woman vs. Hitler **A:** Steve Ditko; Dick Ayers; Russ Heath

10 ❑ Apr 1978 Cover: 0.60 **NM** value: **3.00**
• Super-Heroes **A:** Mike Nasser

11 ❑ May 1978 Cover: 1.00 **NM** value: **3.00**
• **CGC:** 1 graded, best 8.0
• Flash; a.k.a. Flash Spectacular **A:** Murphy Anderson; Wally Wood; Kurt Schaffenberger; Irv Novick ★ Appearance of Johnny Quick.

12 ❑ Jun 1978 Cover: 1.00 **NM** value: **3.00**
• Secrets of Haunted House

13 ❑ Jul 1978 Cover: 1.00 **NM** value: **3.00**
• Sgt. Rock

14 ❑ Jul 1978 Cover: 0.60 **NM** value: **3.00**
• Swamp Thing reprint

15 ❑ Aug 1978 Cover: 1.00 **NM** value: **3.00**
• Batman, Ra's al Ghul

16 ❑ Sep 1978 Cover: 1.00 **NM** value: **14.00**
• **CGC:** 3 graded, best 9.4
A: Russ Heath ★ Death of Jonah Hex.

17 ❑ Sep 1979 Cover: 1.00 **NM** value: **2.00**
• Swamp Thing reprint

18 ❑ Oct 1979 Cover: 0.95 **NM** value: **2.00**
• digest Sgt. Rock.

19 ❑ Oct 1979 Cover: 0.95 **NM** value: **2.50**
• digest. • Secret Origins ★ Origin of Wonder Woman.

20 ❑ Jan 1980 Cover: 1.00 **NM** value: **2.50**
📖 The Lurker In Tunnel 13!; The Stalker From Beyond!; The Man Who Would Not Die! • Swamp Thing reprint; a.k.a. Original Swamp Thing Saga **A:** Bernie Wrightson **W:** Len Wein

21 ❑ Mar 1980 Cover: 1.00 **NM** value: **12.00**
• **CGC:** 2 graded, best 9.4
• Batman; Legion; 1st Frank Miller Batman **A:** Frank Miller

22 ❑ Sep 1980 **NM** value: **3.00**
• G.I. Combat

23 ❑ Feb 1981 Cover: 0.75 **NM** value: **3.00**
• digest. • Flash

24 ❑ Feb 1981 Cover: 0.75 **NM** value: **3.00**
• Flash

25 ❑ Sum 1981 Cover: 2.95 **NM** value: **3.00**
• treasury-sized. • Superman II movie adaptation

26 ❑ Sum 1981 Cover: 2.50 **NM** value: **3.00**
• treasury-sized. 📖 Fortress of Fear! • Superman's Fortress **A:** Ross Andru; Romeo Tanghal **W:** Roy Thomas

27 ❑ Dec 1981 Cover: 2.50 **NM** value: **10.00**
• treasury-sized. final issue. • Batman vs. The Incredible Hulk

DC SPOTLIGHT — DC

1 ❑ Sep 1985 **NM** value: **1.00**
C: José Luis Garcia-Lopez

DC SUPER-STARS — DC

1 ❑ Mar 1976 Cover: 0.50 **NM** value: **6.00**
• **CGC:** 6 graded, best 9.6
• Double-size. 📖 Monster Bait; Introducing the Teen Titans; Tales of the Titans (text story) • Teen Titans reprint **A:** Nick Cardy **W:** E. Nelson Bridwell

2 ❑ Apr 1976 Cover: 0.50 **NM** value: **3.00**
• Double-size. • Space

3 ❑ May 1976 Cover: 0.50 **NM** value: **4.00**
• **CGC:** 2 graded, best 9.6
• Superman; Reprints Legion of Super-Heroes story from Adventure Comics #354 and #355 **A:** Curt Swan ★ Appearance of Legion of Super-Heroes.

4 ❑ Jun 1976 Cover: 0.50 **NM** value: **2.00**
• **CGC:** 1 graded, best 9.2

5 ❑ Jul 1976 Cover: 0.50 **NM** value: **2.00**
• **CGC:** 1 graded, best 9.0
• Flash; Bicentennial #33

6 ❑ Aug 1976 Cover: 0.50 **NM** value: **2.00**
• **CGC:** 1 graded, best 9.4

7 ❑ Sep 1976 Cover: 0.50 **NM** value: **2.00**

8 ❑ Oct 1976 Cover: 0.50 **NM** value: **4.00**
• **CGC:** 1 graded, best 9.4
• Reprints Showcase #15

9 ❑ Nov 1976 Cover: 0.50 **NM** value: **2.00**
• Man Behind the Gun

10 ❑ Dec 1976 Cover: 0.50 **NM** value: **5.00**
• Sports stories and Batman story ★ Appearance of Joker.

11 ❑ Jan 1977 Cover: 0.50 **NM** value: **2.00**

12 ❑ Feb 1977 Cover: 0.50 **NM** value: **2.00**
• **CGC:** 1 graded, best 9.2

13 ❑ Mar 1977 Cover: 0.50 **NM** value: **2.00**
• **CGC:** 1 graded, best 9.0
A: Sergio Aragonés

14 ❑ May 1977 Cover: 0.50 **NM** value: **4.00**
★ Origin of Doctor Light, Braniac, Two-Face, Grodd, Shark.

15 ❑ Jul 1977 Cover: 0.50 **NM** value: **4.00**
• war stories

16 ❑ Sep 1977 Cover: 0.60 **NM** value: **3.00**
• **CGC:** 1 graded, best 9.4
A: Don Newton; Bob Layton ★ 1st Appearance of Star Hunters, The Star Hunters.

17 ❑ Nov 1977 Cover: 0.60 **NM** value: **4.00**
• **CGC:** 1 graded, best 9.4
📖 Green Arrow; The Legion Of Super-Heroes; From Each Ending…A Beginning! • Secret Origins; Revealed that Earth-2 Batman had married Earth-2 Catwoman; Legion story **A:** Bob Layton; Mike Grell; Joe Staton; Juan Ortiz **W:** Bob Layton; Joe Staton; Paul Levitz; Denny O'Neil; Jack Harris ★ Origin of Green Arrow, The Huntress II (Helena Wayne). ★ 1st Appearance of Huntress II (Helena Wayne), The Huntress II (Helena Wayne).

18 ❑ Jan 1978 Cover: 0.60 **NM** value: **2.00**
• Deadman, Phantom Stranger

DC 2000 — DC

1 ❑ Sep 2000 Cover: 6.95 **NM** value: **Cover or less**
Circ: Diamd. preorders: **33,652**

2 ❑ Oct 2000 Cover: 6.95 **NM** value: **Cover or less**
Circ: Diamd. preorders: **29,027**
A: Val Semeiks **W:** Tom Peyer

DCU HEROES SECRET FILES — DC

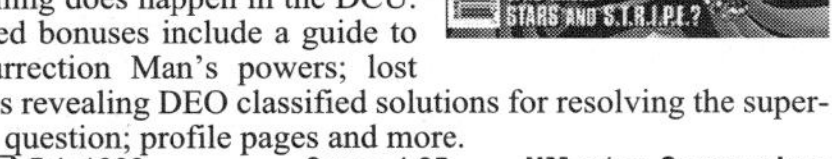

This mysterious one-shot explores the secrets of some of DC's most unusual heroes! In the lead story, the Department of Extranormal Operations sends agent Cameron Chase accompanied by Sarge Steel on an unusual assignment: conducting surveillance and gathering information on super-heroes. However, the cases of Captain Marvel, Hitman, and Resurrection Man don't make this job easy for them. Agent Chase embarrassingly learns firsthand that characters routinely use deception and guile because anything does happen in the DCU. Added bonuses include a guide to Resurrection Man's powers; lost pages revealing DEO classified solutions for resolving the super-hero question; profile pages and more.

1 ❑ Feb 1999 Cover: 4.95 **NM** value: **Cover or less**
Circ: Diamd. preorders: **23,275**
📖 Spies Like Us; A Guide to Resurrection Man's Powers; Lost Pages
A: Derec Aucoin **W:** D. Curtis Johnson

DC UNIVERSE CHRISTMAS, A — DC

1 ❑ Cover: 19.95 **NM** value: **Cover or less**
📖 Batman: Wanted: Santa Claus-Dead or Alive!; The Flash: Present Tense; Wonder Woman: The Story of Fir Balsam; Superman: The Gift
A: Jack Burnl **W:** Brian Augustyn; John Byrne; Dan Jurgens; Paul Levitz; Chuck Dixon; Jerry Siegel; Len Wein; Bob Haney; Denny O'Neill; Devin Grayson; Mark Waid; Paul Dini; William Moulton Marston

DC UNIVERSE HOLIDAY BASH — DC

1 ❑ Jan 1997 Cover: 3.95 **NM** value: **Cover or less**
Circ: Diamd. preorders: **29,774**
• Preview edition. 📖 Superman: The Benefaction of Peace; Catwoman: Bearing Gifts We Traverse Afar; Green Lantern: The Vessel; Flash: Present Tense; Orion & Highfather: A High Father Christmas; Demon: Satan's Little Helper; Batman: Just Another Night • Holiday special for 1996 season **A:** Roger Robinson; Sal Buscema; Paul Ryan; Graham Nolan; Ty Templeton; Kevin Nowlan; Jesse Delperdang **W:** Michael Jan Friedman; Brian Augustyn; Ty Templeton; Walt Simonson; Jim Aparo; Barry Jameson; Denny O'Neil; Mark Waid

2 ❑ Jan 1998 Cover: 3.95 **NM** value: **4.95**
Circ: Diamd. preorders: **19,485**
• prestige format. • Holiday special for 1997 season

3 ❑ Jan 1999 Cover: 4.95 **NM** value: **Cover or less**
Circ: Diamd. preorders: **17,233**
• Signed edition. • Holiday special for 1998 season

CGC-graded: Multiply prices above by **33 for 9.9 M • 16 for 9.8 NM/M • 7 for 9.6 NM+ • 5 for 9.4 NM • 2.5 for 9.2 NM- • 1.5 for 9.0 VF/NM**

DC UNIVERSE: TRINITY — DC

1 ❑ Aug 1993 Cover: 2.95 **NM** value: **Cover or less**
Circ: CapCity orders: **33,400**
foil cover. ★ Appearance of Green Lantern, L.E.G.I.O.N., Darkstars.
2 ❑ Sep 1993 Cover: 2.95 **NM** value: **Cover or less**
Circ: CapCity orders: **21,400**
foil cover.

DC UNIVERSE VILLAINS SECRET FILES — DC

1 ❑ Apr 1999 Cover: 4.95 **NM** value: **Cover or less**
Circ: Diamd. preorders: **20,574**
📖 The Evil We Do **A:** Eric Canete **W:** D. Curtis Johnson

DEAD, THE — Arrow

1 ❑ Cover: 2.95 **NM** value: **Cover or less**
1/A ❑ Cover: 2.95 **NM** value: **Cover or less**
alternate cover.
2 ❑ Cover: 2.95 **NM** value: **Cover or less**
3 ❑ Cover: 2.95 **NM** value: **Cover or less**

DEAD, THE (2ND SERIES) — Arrow

1 ❑ Cover: 2.95 **NM** value: **Cover or less**
📖 Gerald's Game, Part 1 **A:** Matt Mason **W:** Randy Zimmerman; Ralph Griffith

DEAD & BURIED? — Malibu

Bk 1❑ b&w Cover: 9.95 **NM** value: **Cover or less**
• Trade Paperback.

DEADBEATS — Claypool

Deadbeats is a black-and-white vampire soap opera clearly out of the (pardon the expression) mold formed by Dark Shadows. It begins when four teens are found murdered in Mystic Grove, Conn. In time, it becomes clear that a band of vampires who call themselves the Deadbeats are responsible. Not long after the attack, they "recruit" a new member to their band, Michael-Evan Southland ("Southie"), the runaway son of the mayor of Mystic Grove. He, in turn, is made their leader, although it's clear that the original vampire crew has sinister designs that they are not letting him in on.

Opposing the Deadbeats are a motley band of vampire-hunters, including paranormal investigator Dr. V. V. Ralston (the Van Helsing — or Dr. Julia Hoffman — of the bunch) and brave-but-foolish kids Kirby Collier and Jo Isles.

The Deadbeats shines, due to its clear art, solid storytelling, and eclectic sensibility.

1 ❑ Jun 1992 Cover: 2.50 **NM** value: **4.00**
A: Richard Howell **W:** Richard Howell
2 ❑ Jul 1992 Cover: 2.50 **NM** value: **3.00**
📖 They All Laughed! **A:** Richard Howell **W:** Richard Howell
3 ❑ Sep 1992 Cover: 2.50 **NM** value: **3.00**
📖 Pawns **A:** Richard Howell **W:** Richard Howell
4 ❑ Oct 1992 Cover: 2.50 **NM** value: **3.00**
A: Richard Howell **W:** Richard Howell
5 ❑ Sep 1993 Cover: 2.50 **NM** value: **3.00**
A: Richard Howell **W:** Richard Howell
6 ❑ Mar 1994 Cover: 2.50 **NM** value: **Cover or less**
A: Richard Howell **W:** Richard Howell
7 ❑ Jun 1994 Cover: 2.50 **NM** value: **Cover or less**
A: Richard Howell **W:** Richard Howell
8 ❑ Aug 1994 Cover: 2.50 **NM** value: **Cover or less**
📖 The Experiment **A:** Richard Howell **W:** Richard Howell
9 ❑ Nov 1994 Cover: 2.50 **NM** value: **Cover or less**
10 ❑ Jan 1995 Cover: 2.50 **NM** value: **Cover or less**
11 ❑ Mar 1995 Cover: 2.50 **NM** value: **Cover or less**
12 ❑ May 1995 Cover: 2.50 **NM** value: **Cover or less**
13 ❑ Jul 1995 Cover: 2.50 **NM** value: **Cover or less**
14 ❑ Sep 1995 Cover: 2.50 **NM** value: **Cover or less**
15 ❑ Nov 1995 Cover: 2.50 **NM** value: **Cover or less**
16 ❑ Jan 1996 Cover: 2.50 **NM** value: **Cover or less**
17 ❑ Mar 1996 Cover: 2.50 **NM** value: **Cover or less**
18 ❑ May 1996 Cover: 2.50 **NM** value: **Cover or less**
19 ❑ Jul 1996 Cover: 2.50 **NM** value: **Cover or less**
20 ❑ Sep 1996 Cover: 2.50 **NM** value: **Cover or less**
21 ❑ Nov 1996 Cover: 2.50 **NM** value: **Cover or less**
22 ❑ Jan 1997 Cover: 2.50 **NM** value: **Cover or less**
23 ❑ Mar 1997 Cover: 2.50 **NM** value: **Cover or less**
24 ❑ May 1997 Cover: 2.50 **NM** value: **Cover or less**
25 ❑ Jul 1997 Cover: 2.50 **NM** value: **Cover or less**
26 ❑ Sep 1997 Cover: 2.50 **NM** value: **Cover or less**
📖 The Southland Family Saga! **A:** Ricardo Villagran **W:** Richard Howell
27 ❑ Nov 1997 Cover: 2.50 **NM** value: **Cover or less**
📖 Misery Loves Butchery! **A:** Ricardo Villagran **W:** Richard Howell
28 ❑ Jan 1998 Cover: 2.50 **NM** value: **Cover or less**
📖 Burying Dodger! **A:** Richard Howell; Ricardo Villagran **W:** Richard Howell
29 ❑ Mar 1998 Cover: 2.50 **NM** value: **Cover or less**
30 ❑ May 1998 Cover: 2.50 **NM** value: **Cover or less**
31 ❑ Jul 1998 Cover: 2.50 **NM** value: **Cover or less**
32 ❑ Oct 1998 Cover: 2.50 **NM** value: **Cover or less**
33 ❑ Dec 1998 Cover: 2.50 **NM** value: **Cover or less**
34 ❑ Feb 1999 Cover: 2.50 **NM** value: **Cover or less**
35 ❑ Apr 1999 Cover: 2.50 **NM** value: **Cover or less**
36 ❑ Jun 1999 Cover: 2.50 **NM** value: **Cover or less**
37 ❑ Aug 1999 Cover: 2.50 **NM** value: **Cover or less**
38 ❑ Oct 1999 Cover: 2.50 **NM** value: **Cover or less**
39 ❑ Dec 1999 Cover: 2.50 **NM** value: **Cover or less**
• **CGC:** 1 graded, best 9.4
40 ❑ Feb 2000 Cover: 2.50 **NM** value: **Cover or less**
41 ❑ Apr 2000 Cover: 2.50 **NM** value: **Cover or less**
📖 Guys' Night Out!
42 ❑ Jun 2000 Cover: 2.50 **NM** value: **Cover or less**
📖 Dark Dealings!
43 ❑ Aug 2000 Cover: 2.50 **NM** value: **Cover or less**
📖 Dodging the Bullet! **A:** Ricardo Villagran **W:** Richard Howell
Bk 1❑ b&w Cover: 12.95 **NM** value: **Cover or less**
📖 New in Town • collects Deadbeats #1-6, Phantom of Fear City #1 and #3, and Soulsearchers #2

DEADBOLT — Hall of Heroes

1 ❑ Sep 1993 Cover: 2.50 **NM** value: **Cover or less**
• **CGC:** 1 graded, best 9.0
📖 Desolation **A:** Trent Kaniuga **W:** Trent Kaniuga

DEAD BOYS — London Night

1 ❑ Sep 1996 Cover: 3.00 **NM** value: **3.95**
Circ: Diamd. preorders: **5,962**
• Giant-size. • Preview of Morbid Angel in back-up story★ 1st Appearance of Dead Boys.

DEAD CLOWN — Malibu

Malibu put together a series intended to combine the feel of Tales from the Crypt with The Tick.

Using Petrol-global's patented process, JoJo the clown is enhanced to the point at which he can juggle chainsaws for days without tiring or dive into a bucket from a speeding jet. JoJo is to be the first of an army of super-clowns to entertain troops for whatever war would may come along. But something goes wrong, and, after he dies, his decayed body rises from the sludge. Not one to let an opportunity slip away, Bull Davidovich instead uses JoJo as a corporate icon: Ghastly the Dead Clown. However, Dead Clown's first movie is trash before it is even released, and his comic book is toned down to drivel. Fed up with life as a dead clown, JoJo tackles life on his own, despite corporate stooges and hired heroes trying to bring him back to the company.

1 ❑ Oct 1996 Cover: 2.50 **NM** value: **Cover or less**
Circ: CapCity orders: **5,075**
📖 Kill-Krazy Klown **A:** Joel Thomas **W:** Chris Ulm
2 ❑ Cover: 2.50 **NM** value: **Cover or less**
Circ: CapCity orders: **3,500**
3 ❑ Feb 1994 Cover: 2.50 **NM** value: **Cover or less**
Circ: CapCity orders: **2,325**

DEAD CORPS(E) — DC / Helix

1 ❑ Sep 1998 Cover: 2.50 **NM** value: **Cover or less**
Circ: Diamd. preorders: **9,769**
📖 Suckers of Mars **A:** Steve Pugh **W:** Christopher Hinz
2 ❑ Oct 1998 Cover: 2.50 **NM** value: **Cover or less**
Circ: Diamd. preorders: **7,775**
📖 Out of the Coffin: The Death of C.J. Rataan **A:** Steve Pugh **W:** Christopher Hinz
3 ❑ Nov 1998 Cover: 2.50 **NM** value: **Cover or less**
Circ: Diamd. preorders: **6,481**
A: Steve Pugh **W:** Christopher Hinz
4 ❑ Dec 1998 Cover: 2.50 **NM** value: **Cover or less**
Circ: Diamd. preorders: **5,738**
A: Steve Pugh **W:** Christopher Hinz

DEAD END CRIME STORIES — Kirby Publications

1 ❑ Apr 1949 **NM** value: **300.00**
• **CGC:** 2 graded, best 5.0

DEADENDERS — Vertigo

In a post-apocalyptic future, the citizens of New Bethlehem enjoy a life of luxury, complete with controlled weather, purified air, and artificially generated sunlight. They are the lucky minority, however. Most people are forever exiled behind the electrified fences of the outer sectors, forced to live in the squalor and perpetual darkness called New Bedlam. For them, life cannot get any worse.

But for Beezer, a disenchanted youth involved in minor drug deals and car-jackings, it's as if his whole world has shattered. In addition to the natural hardships of the outer sectors, Beezer gets dumped by his girlfriend and discovers he's adopted, all in the same evening. And, for some reason, he's suddenly wanted by the City Corps, licensed thugs for the inner-city government.

As his life spins out of control, Beezer begins suffering from strange and compelling visions of the world the way it was before the Cataclysm.

1 ❑ Mar 2000 Cover: 2.50 **NM** value: **Cover or less**
Circ: Diamd. preorders: **8,299**
📖 Stealing the Sun, Part 1 **A:** Warren Pleece **W:** Ed Brubaker
2 ❑ Apr 2000 Cover: 2.50 **NM** value: **Cover or less**
Circ: Diamd. preorders: **15,201**
📖 Stealing the Sun, Part 2 **A:** Warren Pleece **W:** Ed Brubaker
3 ❑ May 2000 Cover: 2.50 **NM** value: **Cover or less**
Circ: Diamd. preorders: **10,213**
📖 Stealing the Sun, Part 3 **A:** Warren Pleece **W:** Ed Brubaker
4 ❑ Jun 2000 Cover: 2.50 **NM** value: **Cover or less**
Circ: Diamd. preorders: **9,588**
A: Warren Pleece **W:** Ed Brubaker
5 ❑ Jul 2000 Cover: 2.50 **NM** value: **Cover or less**
Circ: Diamd. preorders: **8,936**
📖 Suspended Between Now and Then, Part 1 **A:** Warren Pleece **W:** Ed Brubaker
6 ❑ Aug 2000 Cover: 2.50 **NM** value: **Cover or less**
Circ: Diamd. preorders: **8,521**
📖 Suspended Between Now and Then, Part 2 **A:** Warren Pleece **W:** Ed Brubaker
7 ❑ Sep 2000 Cover: 2.50 **NM** value: **Cover or less**
Circ: Diamd. preorders: **8,247**
📖 Suspended Between Now and Then, Part 3 **A:** Warren Pleece **W:** Ed Brubaker
8 ❑ Oct 2000 Cover: 2.50 **NM** value: **Cover or less**
Circ: Diamd. preorders: **7,614**
📖 My Secret Affair **A:** Warren Pleece **W:** Ed Brubaker
9 ❑ Nov 2000 Cover: 2.50 **NM** value: **Cover or less**
Circ: Diamd. preorders: **7,725**
📖 More Fun in the New World **A:** Warren Pleece **W:** Ed Brubaker
10 ❑ Dec 2000 Cover: 2.50 **NM** value: **Cover or less**
📖 On a Clear Day You Can See Forever **A:** Warren Pleece **W:** Ed Brubaker
11 ❑ Jan 2001 Cover: 2.50 **NM** value: **Cover or less**
Circ: Diamd. preorders: **7,374**
📖 The Good News of the Cataclysm **A:** Warren Pleece **W:** Ed Brubaker
12 ❑ Feb 2001 Cover: 2.50 **NM** value: **Cover or less**
Circ: Diamd. preorders: **7,246**
📖 At This Point in Time **A:** Warren Pleece **W:** Ed Brubaker
13 ❑ Mar 2001 Cover: 2.50 **NM** value: **Cover or less**
Circ: Diamd. preorders: **6,893**
📖 Only for Seconds **A:** Warren Pleece **W:** Ed Brubaker
14 ❑ Apr 2001 Cover: 2.50 **NM** value: **Cover or less**
Circ: Diamd. preorders: **6,777**
📖 Smashing Time, Part 1 **A:** Warren Pleece **W:** Ed Brubaker
15 ❑ May 2001 Cover: 2.50 **NM** value: **Cover or less**
Circ: Diamd. preorders: **6,662**
📖 Smashing Time, Part 2 **A:** Warren Pleece **W:** Ed Brubaker
Bk 1❑ Cover: 9.95 **NM** value: **Cover or less**
• Trade Paperback. 📖 Stealing the Sun **A:** Warren Pleece **W:** Ed Brubaker

DEAD-EYE WESTERN COMICS — Hillman

1 ❑ Nov 1948 Cover: 0.10 **NM** value: **80.00**
• **CGC:** 1 graded, best 8.0
2 ❑ Jan 1949 Cover: 0.10 **NM** value: **60.00**
3 ❑ Mar 1949 Cover: 0.10 **NM** value: **40.00**
4 ❑ May 1949 Cover: 0.10 **NM** value: **40.00**
5 ❑ Cover: 0.10 **NM** value: **30.00**
6 ❑ Cover: 0.10 **NM** value: **30.00**
7 ❑ Cover: 0.10 **NM** value: **30.00**
8 ❑ Jan 1950 Cover: 0.10 **NM** value: **30.00**
9 ❑ Mar 1950 Cover: 0.10 **NM** value: **30.00**
10 ❑ May 1950 Cover: 0.10 **NM** value: **30.00**
11 ❑ Jul 1950 Cover: 0.10 **NM** value: **30.00**
12 ❑ Sep 1950 Cover: 0.10 **NM** value: **30.00**
13 ❑ Cover: 0.10 **NM** value: **30.00**
14 ❑ Cover: 0.10 **NM** value: **30.00**
15 ❑ Cover: 0.10 **NM** value: **30.00**
16 ❑ Cover: 0.10 **NM** value: **30.00**
17 ❑ Cover: 0.10 **NM** value: **30.00**
18 ❑ Cover: 0.10 **NM** value: **30.00**
19 ❑ Cover: 0.10 **NM** value: **30.00**
20 ❑ Cover: 0.10 **NM** value: **30.00**
21 ❑ Cover: 0.10 **NM** value: **30.00**
22 ❑ Cover: 0.10 **NM** value: **30.00**
23 ❑ Cover: 0.10 **NM** value: **30.00**
24 ❑ Cover: 0.10 **NM** value: **30.00**
25 ❑ Cover: 0.10 **NM** value: **30.00**

DEADFACE — Harrier

1 ❑ **NM** value: **5.00**
2 ❑ **NM** value: **4.00**
3 ❑ **NM** value: **3.00**
4 ❑ **NM** value: **3.00**
5 ❑ **NM** value: **3.00**
6 ❑ **NM** value: **2.50**
7 ❑ **NM** value: **2.50**
8 ❑ **NM** value: **2.50**

DEADFACE: DOING THE ISLANDS WITH BACCHUS — Dark Horse

1 ❑ Jul 1991, b&w Cover: 2.95 **NM** value: **Cover or less**
A: Eddie Campbell **W:** Eddie Campbell
2 ❑ Aug 1991, b&w Cover: 2.95 **NM** value: **Cover or less**
A: Eddie Campbell **W:** Eddie Campbell
3 ❑ Sep 1991, b&w Cover: 2.95 **NM** value: **Cover or less**
A: Eddie Campbell **W:** Eddie Campbell

DEADFACE: EARTH, WATER, AIR, AND FIRE — Dark Horse

1 ❑ 1992b&w Cover: 2.50 **NM** value: **Cover or less**
📖 Dust in the Eyes **A:** Wes Kublick **W:** Eddie Campbell
2 ❑ 1992b&w Cover: 2.50 **NM** value: **Cover or less**
A: Eddie Campbell **W:** Eddie Campbell
3 ❑ 1992b&w Cover: 2.50 **NM** value: **Cover or less**
A: Eddie Campbell **W:** Eddie Campbell
4 ❑ 1992b&w Cover: 2.50 **NM** value: **Cover or less**
📖 Staring At The Sun **A:** Eddie Campbell **W:** Eddie Campbell

DEADFACE: IMMORTALITY ISN'T FOREVER — Dark Horse

Bk 1❑ b&w Cover: 14.95 **NM** value: **Cover or less**
A: Eddie Campbell

Other grades: Multiply prices above by **1.5 for Mint • 2/3 for Very Fine • 1/3 for Fine • 1/5 for Very Good • 1/8 for Good**

DEADFISH BEDEVILED
All American

1 ❑ b&w Cover: 2.25 **NM value: Cover or less**

DEADFORCE (ANTARCTIC)
Antarctic Press

1 ❑ May 1999, b&w Cover: 2.99 **NM value: Cover or less**
Circ: Diamd. preorders: **2,734**
🕮 Death and Redemption **A:** Roy Burdine **W:** Roy Burdine
2 ❑ Jun 1999 Cover: 2.99 **NM value: Cover or less**
A: Roy Burdine **W:** Roy Burdine
Ash 1❑ **NM value: 1.00**
A: Roy Burdine **W:** Roy Burdine

DEADFORCE (STUDIONOIR)
Studio Noir

1 ❑ Jul 1996, b&w Cover: 2.50 **NM value: Cover or less**

DEAD GRRRL: DEAD AT 21
Boneyard

1 ❑ Apr 1998 Cover: 2.95 **NM value: Cover or less**
A: Dan plegel **W:** Julia Truman

DEAD HEAT, THE
All American

1 ❑ b&w Cover: 1.95 **NM value: Cover or less**

DEAD IN THE WEST
Dark Horse

All issues are adults only.

East Texas. 1876. The late stage is fighting its way across the countryside outside Mud Creek. It makes a rest stop, and the boy riding shotgun goes into the bushes to do his business. That's when he sees the spider.

The next anyone sees of the stage, it is sitting — empty — in the middle of Mud Creek. Its former passengers now spend their days in root cellars and shallow graves — and walk by night.

The Reverend Jebediah Mercer has also come to town. An itinerant drunkard, he is selling redemption. He feels his mission is to save Mud Creek with a Bible and a revolver. But he will soon learn that Mud Creek, an East Texas city of the Old West, has already earned its damnation.

1 ❑ Oct 1993, b&w Cover: 3.95 **NM value: Cover or less**
Circ: CapCity orders: **6,175**
A: Jaxon **W:** Joe Lansdale; Neal Barrett Jr.
2 ❑ Mar 1994, b&w Cover: 3.95 **NM value: Cover or less**
A: Jaxon **W:** Joe Lansdale; Neal Barrett Jr.

DEAD KID ADVENTURES
Knight

1 ❑ Jul 1998 Cover: 2.95 **NM value: Cover or less**
A: Mary Bierbaum; Tom Bierbaum **W:** Mary Bierbaum; Tom Bierbaum

DEAD KING: BURNT
Chaos

1 ❑ May 1998 Cover: 2.95 **NM value: Cover or less**
Circ: Diamd. preorders: **15,319**
A: David Brewer **W:** Hart Fisher
2 ❑ Jun 1998 Cover: 2.95 **NM value: Cover or less**
Circ: Diamd. preorders: **12,015**
A: David Brewer **W:** Hart Fisher
3 ❑ Jul 1998 Cover: 2.95 **NM value: Cover or less**
Circ: Diamd. preorders: **12,039**
A: David Brewer **W:** Hart Fisher
4 ❑ Aug 1998 Cover: 2.95 **NM value: Cover or less**
Circ: Diamd. preorders: **12,049**
A: David Brewer **W:** Hart Fisher
Bk 1❑ Cover: 12.95 **NM value: Cover or less**
A: David Brewer **W:** Hart Fisher

DEADLANDS: ONE SHOT
Image

Bk 1❑ Aug 1999 Cover: 6.95 **NM value: Cover or less**
A: Richard Pollard; Kevin Sharp **W:** Matt Forbeck

DEADLIEST CREATURE ON EARTH...MAN, THE
Nicotat

1 ❑ b&w Cover: 2.00 **NM value: Cover or less**

DEADLIEST HEROES OF KUNG FU, THE
Marvel

1 ❑ b&w Cover: 1.00 **NM value: Cover or less**
• magazine.

DEADLINE USA
Dark Horse

1 ❑ Sep 1991, b&w Cover: 2.95 **NM value: 3.95**
2 ❑ b&w Cover: 2.95 **NM value: 3.95**
3 ❑ b&w Cover: 2.95 **NM value: 3.95**
4 ❑ Cover: 3.95 **NM value: Cover or less**
🕮 Nail Boss; Timulo; Devil Chef; A-Men; Beryl The Bitch; Wired World; Syd Serene; Young Kafka; Johnny Nemo; The Number 8 Bus To Hell; Tortilla Baby; Hot Triggers **A:** Philip Bond; Brett Ewins; Dave Cooper; Phil Hester; Jack Pollock; Scott Musgrove; Anonyman; Brian Iverson; D'Israeli; Julie Hollings; Molly Eyre; Shaky Kane **W:** Philip Bond; Dave Cooper; Phil Hester; Jack Pollock; Peter Milligan; Scott Musgrove; Anonyman; Brian Iverson; D'Israeli; Julie Hollings; Molly Eyre; Shaky Kane
5 ❑ Cover: 3.95 **NM value: Cover or less**
🕮 Young Kafka; Wired World; Devil Chef; Timulo; Milk And Cheese; Hugo Tate; A-Men; Music Feature-Seaweed; Johnny Nemo; Ingrate; How Jenny Left Earth; Atomic Baby; Gwar **A:** Evan Dorkin; Philip Bond; Brett Ewins; Dave Cooper; Phil Hester; Hunter Jackson; Jack Pollock; Nick Abadzis; Brian Iverson; D'Israeli; Rob Moran; Shaky Kane **W:** Evan Dorkin; Philip Bond; Dave Cooper; Phil Hester; Jack Pollock; Nick Abadzis; Peter Milligan; Brian Iverson; Dan Yell; D'Israeli; Richard White; Rob Moran; Shaky Kane ★ Appearance of Gwar.
6 ❑ Cover: 3.95 **NM value: Cover or less**
7 ❑ Cover: 3.95 **NM value: Cover or less**
8 ❑ Cover: 3.95 **NM value: Cover or less**
final issue.

DEADLY DUO, THE
Image

1 ❑ Nov 1994 Cover: 2.50 **NM value: Cover or less**
Circ: CapCity orders: **23,400**
2 ❑ Dec 1994 Cover: 2.50 **NM value: Cover or less**
Circ: CapCity orders: **17,100**
3 ❑ Jan 1995 Cover: 2.50 **NM value: Cover or less**
Circ: CapCity orders: **12,625**

DEADLY DUO, THE (2ND SERIES)
Image

1 ❑ Jul 1995 Cover: 2.50 **NM value: Cover or less**
Circ: CapCity orders: **19,450**
A: John Cleary **W:** Eric Larsen
2 ❑ Aug 1995 Cover: 2.50 **NM value: Cover or less**
Circ: CapCity orders: **11,475**
A: John Cleary **W:** Eric Larsen
3 ❑ Sep 1995 Cover: 2.50 **NM value: Cover or less**
Circ: CapCity orders: **10,025**
A: Andy Smith **W:** Eric Larsen
4 ❑ Oct 1995 Cover: 2.50 **NM value: Cover or less**
Circ: CapCity orders: **8,275**

DEADLY FOES OF SPIDER-MAN
Marvel

Shocker, The Rhino, The Beetle, Hydro-Man, Speed-Demon, and Boomerang have formed The Sinister Syndicate, in an effort to work together more efficiently as a team rather than devote their strengths to solo endeavors that inevitably put them right back in jail. Led by The Beetle, the group's first mission is a robbery at the Federal Reserve Bank. Unfortunately, the crime doesn't come off as smoothly as planned due to Spider-Man's interference and Boomerang is back in jail once again. The Beetle keeps the rest of the group together and uses legal methods to get Boomerang out of jail, all the while planning several more heists to placate the group's mysterious benefactor.

A typical Spidey adventure, this mini-series focuses more on the villains than the hero. — Brent

1 ❑ May 1991 Cover: 1.00 **NM value: 1.50**
Circ: CapCity orders: **71,400**
🕮 Punishment And Crime • Punisher, Rhino, Kingpin, others appear **A:** Al Milgrom; Kerry Gammill **W:** Danny Fingeroth
2 ❑ Jun 1991 Cover: 1.00 **NM value: 1.50**
Circ: CapCity orders: **52,900**
🕮 The Price Of Justice **A:** Al Milgrom; Kerry Gammill **W:** Danny Fingeroth
3 ❑ Jul 1991 Cover: 1.00 **NM value: 1.50**
Circ: CapCity orders: **54,500**
🕮 Shattered Dreams **A:** Al Milgrom **W:** Danny Fingeroth
4 ❑ Aug 1991 Cover: 1.00 **NM value: 1.50**
Circ: CapCity orders: **56,500**
🕮 While The City Screams **A:** Al Milgrom **W:** Danny Fingeroth

DEADLY HANDS OF KUNG FU
Marvel

1 ❑ Apr 1974 Cover: 0.75 **NM value: 15.00**
2 ❑ Jun 1974 Cover: 0.75 **NM value: 7.00**
3 ❑ Aug 1974 Cover: 0.75 **NM value: 5.00**
4 ❑ Sep 1974 Cover: 0.75 **NM value: 5.00**
5 ❑ Oct 1974 Cover: 0.75 **NM value: 5.00**
6 ❑ Nov 1974 Cover: 0.75 **NM value: 4.00**
7 ❑ Dec 1974 Cover: 0.75 **NM value: 4.00**
8 ❑ Jan 1975 Cover: 0.75 **NM value: 4.00**
9 ❑ Feb 1975 Cover: 0.75 **NM value: 4.00**
10 ❑ Mar 1975 Cover: 0.75 **NM value: 4.00**
11 ❑ Apr 1975 Cover: 0.75 **NM value: 4.00**
12 ❑ May 1975 Cover: 0.75 **NM value: 4.00**
13 ❑ Jun 1975 Cover: 0.75 **NM value: 4.00**
14 ❑ Jul 1975 Cover: 0.75 **NM value: 4.00**
15 ❑ Aug 1975 Cover: 1.25 **NM value: 4.00**
16 ❑ Sep 1975 Cover: 1.00 **NM value: 4.00**
17 ❑ Oct 1975 Cover: 1.00 **NM value: 4.00**
18 ❑ Nov 1975 Cover: 1.00 **NM value: 4.00**
19 ❑ Dec 1975 Cover: 1.00 **NM value: 4.00**
20 ❑ Jan 1976 Cover: 1.00 **NM value: 4.00**
21 ❑ Feb 1976 Cover: 1.00 **NM value: 3.00**
22 ❑ Mar 1976 Cover: 1.00 **NM value: 3.00**
23 ❑ Apr 1976 Cover: 1.00 **NM value: 3.00**
24 ❑ May 1976 Cover: 1.00 **NM value: 3.00**
25 ❑ Jun 1976 Cover: 1.00 **NM value: 3.00**
26 ❑ Jul 1976 Cover: 1.00 **NM value: 3.00**
27 ❑ Aug 1976 Cover: 1.00 **NM value: 3.00**
28 ❑ Sep 1976 Cover: 1.00 **NM value: 3.00**
29 ❑ Oct 1976 Cover: 1.00 **NM value: 3.00**
30 ❑ Nov 1976 Cover: 1.00 **NM value: 3.00**
31 ❑ Dec 1976 Cover: 1.00 **NM value: 3.00**
32 ❑ Jan 1977 Cover: 1.00 **NM value: 3.00**
33 ❑ Feb 1977 Cover: 1.00 **NM value: 3.00**
SE 1❑ Cover: 1.00 **NM value: 3.00**

The prices seen above do not represent the highest possible prices seen in online auctions, but rather the prices we have seen these issues reliably fetch in a variety of environments (storefront retail, mail order, auction and convention).

DEADMAN (1ST SERIES)
DC

"Boston" Brand is a circus aerialist, risking his life two shows a night without a net. As Deadman, he thrills the audience, until he is suddenly gunned down in the middle of his act. Deadman is dead.

Then, an Indian god named Rama Kushna takes pity on the acrobat, bringing his spirit back from the great beyond. Boston is given the power to inhabit the bodies of others and is granted a final wish: to be able to find the man who killed him.

First appearing in the pages of Strange Adventures #205, Deadman is one of the last great lights in that title's twilight days. This, his first self-titled series, brings back those early adventures.

1 ❑ May 1985 Cover: 1.75 **NM value: 2.50**
🕮 Who Has Been Lying In My Grave **A:** Carmine Infantino; Neal Adams **W:** Arnold Drake
2 ❑ Jun 1985 Cover: 1.75 **NM value: 2.00**
A: Neal Adams
3 ❑ Jul 1985 Cover: 1.75 **NM value: 2.00**
A: Neal Adams
4 ❑ Aug 1985 Cover: 1.75 **NM value: 2.00**
A: Neal Adams
5 ❑ Sep 1985 Cover: 1.75 **NM value: 2.00**
A: Neal Adams
6 ❑ Oct 1985 Cover: 1.75 **NM value: 2.00**
A: Neal Adams
7 ❑ Nov 1985 Cover: 1.75 **NM value: 2.00**
A: Neal Adams

DEADMAN (2ND SERIES)
DC

1 ❑ Mar 1986 Cover: 0.75 **NM value: 2.00**
Circ: CapCity orders: **12,950**
🕮 Return...To Forever! **A:** José Luis Garcia-Lopez **W:** Andy Helfer
2 ❑ Apr 1986 Cover: 0.75 **NM value: 2.00**
Circ: CapCity orders: **11,650**
A: José Luis Garcia-Lopez
3 ❑ May 1986 Cover: 0.75 **NM value: 2.00**
Circ: CapCity orders: **11,150**
A: José Luis Garcia-Lopez
4 ❑ Jun 1986 Cover: 0.75 **NM value: 2.00**
Circ: CapCity orders: **11,950**
A: José Luis Garcia-Lopez

DEADMAN: EXORCISM
DC

1 ❑ Cover: 4.95 **NM value: Cover or less**
Circ: CapCity orders: **13,050**
• prestige format.
2 ❑ Cover: 4.95 **NM value: Cover or less**
Circ: CapCity orders: **10,650**
• prestige format. **A:** Kelley Jones **W:** Mike Baron

DEADMAN: LOST SOULS
DC

Bk 1❑ Cover: 19.95 **NM value: Cover or less**
• collects Deadman: Love after Death #1 and 2 and Deadman: Exorcism #1 and 2

DEADMAN: LOVE AFTER DEATH
DC

1 ❑ Dec 1989 Cover: 3.95 **NM value: Cover or less**
Circ: CapCity orders: **21,300**
• prestige format. **A:** Kelley Jones **W:** Mike Baron
2 ❑ Jan 1990 Cover: 3.95 **NM value: Cover or less**
Circ: CapCity orders: **18,900**
• prestige format. **A:** Kelley Jones **W:** Mike Baron

DEAD MAN WALKING
Boneyard

1 ❑ Cover: 2.75 **NM value: Cover or less**
A: Guy Burwell **W:** Bill Yukich

DEAD MEAT
Fleetway-Quality

1 ❑ Cover: 2.95 **NM value: Cover or less**
A: Simon Jacob **W:** Michael Cook
2 ❑ Cover: 2.95 **NM value: Cover or less**
A: Simon Jacob **W:** Michael Cook
3 ❑ Cover: 2.95 **NM value: Cover or less**
A: Simon Jacob **W:** Michael Cook

DEAD MUSE, THE
Fantagraphics

1 ❑ b&w Cover: 3.95 **NM value: Cover or less**
No issue number.

DEAD OF NIGHT
Marvel

1 ❑ Dec 1973 Cover: 0.20 **NM value: 7.50**
• **CGC:** 6 graded, best 9.6
🕮 The Ghost Still Walks; House of Fear; My Brother the Ghoul; He Dwells in a Dungeon **A:** Joe Sinnott; Hank Chapman **W:** Joe Sinnott; Hank Chapman
2 ❑ Feb 1974 Cover: 0.20 **NM value: 5.00**
3 ❑ Apr 1974 Cover: 0.20 **NM value: 5.00**
4 ❑ Jun 1974 Cover: 0.20 **NM value: 4.00**
5 ❑ Aug 1974 Cover: 0.20 **NM value: 4.00**
6 ❑ Oct 1974 Cover: 0.20 **NM value: 4.00**
7 ❑ Dec 1974 Cover: 0.20 **NM value: 4.00**
8 ❑ Feb 1975 Cover: 0.20 **NM value: 4.00**
• **CGC:** 1 graded, best 9.0
9 ❑ Apr 1975 Cover: 0.20 **NM value: 4.00**
10 ❑ Jun 1975 Cover: 0.20 **NM value: 4.00**
• **CGC:** 1 graded, best 9.4
11 ❑ Aug 1975 Cover: 0.25 **NM value: 4.00**
• **CGC:** 3 graded, best 9.2
final issue. ★ 1st Appearance of Scarecrow.

CGC-graded: Multiply prices above by **33 for 9.9 M • 16 for 9.8 NM/M • 7 for 9.6 NM+ • 5 for 9.4 NM • 2.5 for 9.2 NM- • 1.5 for 9.0 VF/NM**

DEAD OR ALIVE-A CYBERPUNK WESTERN — Dark Horse

1 ❑ Apr 1998 Cover: 2.50 **NM** value: **Cover or less**
Circ: Diamd. preorders: **6,011**
A: Alberto Ponticelli **W:** Tatjana

2 ❑ May 1998 Cover: 2.50 **NM** value: **Cover or less**
Circ: Diamd. preorders: **4,722**
A: Alberto Ponticelli **W:** Tatjana

3 ❑ Jun 1998 Cover: 2.50 **NM** value: **Cover or less**
Circ: Diamd. preorders: **4,485**
A: Alberto Ponticelli **W:** Tatjana

4 ❑ Jul 1998 Cover: 2.50 **NM** value: **Cover or less**
Circ: Diamd. preorders: **4,503**
A: Alberto Ponticelli **W:** Tatjana

DEADPAN — Ichor

1 ❑ Mar 1995 Cover: 3.95 **NM** value: **Cover or less**
📖 If We Shadows Have Offended... **A:** Theron Smith **W:** Dave R.

DEADPOOL — Marvel

After appearances in The New Mutants #98 (Feb 91) and two mini-series, the sarcastic, wisecracking mercenary, Wade Wilson, aka Deadpool, has been granted his own ongoing series. As a result of an experimental cancer cure at the Weapon X project (an integral element in the origin of Wolverine) Wilson has Wolverine's mutant self-healing ability and an unflattering skin condition. Although the skin condition isn't much help when he's on a case, his rapid banter and self-deprecating comments make this title a lot of fun and is reminiscent of the early Spider-Man stories minus the self-doubt of Peter Parker.

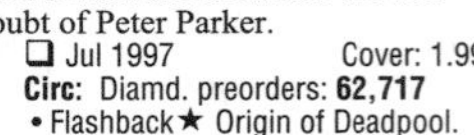

-1 ❑ Jul 1997 Cover: 1.99 **NM** value: **2.25**
Circ: Diamd. preorders: **62,717**
• Flashback ★ Origin of Deadpool.

0 ❑ **NM** value: **1.50**
• Included as giveaway with Wizard Magazine. 📖 You Only Die Twice **A:** Yancey Labat **W:** Joe Kelly

1 ❑ Jan 1997 Cover: 2.99 **NM** value: **4.00**
Circ: Statement: **98,401** Direct Market orders: **112,500** • **CGC:** 1 graded, best 9.4
wraparound cover.

2 ❑ Feb 1997 Cover: 1.99 **NM** value: **3.00**
Circ: Statement: **98,401** Direct Market orders: **82,000**
📖 Operation: That Wacky Doctor's Game! **W:** Joe Kelly

3 ❑ Mar 1997 Cover: 1.99 **NM** value: **2.50**
Circ: Statement: **98,401** Direct Market orders: **72,750**
★ Appearance of Siryn.

4 ❑ Apr 1997 Cover: 1.99 **NM** value: **2.50**
Circ: Statement: **98,401** Direct Market orders: **68,000**
★ Appearance of Hulk. ★ Versus Hulk.

5 ❑ May 1997 Cover: 1.99 **NM** value: **2.00**
Circ: Statement: **98,401** Diamd. preorders: **64,157**

6 ❑ Jun 1997 Cover: 1.99 **NM** value: **2.00**
Circ: Statement: **98,401** Diamd. preorders: **64,593**

7 ❑ Aug 1997 Cover: 1.99 **NM** value: **2.00**
Circ: Statement: **98,401** Diamd. preorders: **59,623**
• gatefold summary.

8 ❑ Sep 1997 Cover: 1.99 **NM** value: **2.00**
Circ: Statement: **98,401** Diamd. preorders: **55,787**
• gatefold summary. 📖 Hey, It's Deadpool! **A:** Ed McGuinness **W:** Joe Kelly

9 ❑ Oct 1997 Cover: 1.99 **NM** value: **2.00**
Circ: Diamd. preorders: **55,138**
• gatefold summary. **A:** Ed McGuinness **W:** Joe Kelly

10 ❑ Nov 1997 Cover: 1.99 **NM** value: **2.00**
Circ: Diamd. preorders: **54,443**
• gatefold summary. 📖 Stumped! • back-up feature on making of Deadpool #11 **A:** Ed McGuinness **W:** Joe Kelly ★ Appearance of Great Lakes Avengers.

11 ❑ Dec 1997 Cover: 2.99 **NM** value: **Cover or less**
Circ: Diamd. preorders: **53,729**
• gatefold summary. 📖 Why is it, to Save me, I Must Kill You? • Deadpool and Blind Al interact with Amazing Spider-Man #47; Has 1997 Statement, filed 10/1/97; avg print run 151,600; avg sales 98,060; avg subs 341; avg total paid 98,401; samples 34; office use 125; max existent 98,560; 35% of run returned **A:** Ed McGuinness **W:** Joe Kelly ★ Appearance of Great Lakes Avengers.

12 ❑ Jan 1998 Cover: 1.99 **NM** value: **2.00**
Circ: Diamd. preorders: **52,437**
• gatefold summary. 📖 The Doctor is Skinned • parody of Faces of the DC Universe month **A:** Kevin Lau; Ed McGuinness **W:** Joe Kelly

13 ❑ Feb 1998 Cover: 1.99 **NM** value: **2.00**
Circ: Diamd. preorders: **49,922**
• gatefold summary.

14 ❑ Mar 1998 Cover: 1.99 **NM** value: **2.00**
Circ: Diamd. preorders: **47,086**
• gatefold summary.

15 ❑ Apr 1998 Cover: 1.99 **NM** value: **2.00**
Circ: Diamd. preorders: **44,630**
• gatefold summary.

16 ❑ May 1998 Cover: 1.99 **NM** value: **2.00**
Circ: Diamd. preorders: **43,440**
• gatefold summary.

17 ❑ Jun 1998 Cover: 1.99 **NM** value: **2.00**
Circ: Diamd. preorders: **43,557**
• gatefold summary.

18 ❑ Jul 1998 Cover: 1.99 **NM** value: **2.00**
Circ: Diamd. preorders: **41,834**
• gatefold summary. ★ Versus Ajax.

19 ❑ Aug 1998 Cover: 1.99 **NM** value: **2.00**
Circ: Diamd. preorders: **42,030**
• gatefold summary. ★ Versus Ajax.

20 ❑ Sep 1998 Cover: 1.99 **NM** value: **2.00**
Circ: Diamd. preorders: **40,257**
• gatefold summary.

21 ❑ Oct 1998 Cover: 1.99 **NM** value: **2.00**
Circ: Diamd. preorders: **38,936**
• gatefold summary.

22 ❑ Nov 1998 Cover: 1.99 **NM** value: **2.00**
Circ: Diamd. preorders: **39,081**
• gatefold summary. ★ Appearance of Cable.

23 ❑ Dec 1998 Cover: 2.99 **NM** value: **Cover or less**
Circ: Diamd. preorders: **39,296**
wraparound cover. • gatefold summary. 📖 Dead Reckoning, Part 1 **A:** Walter McDaniel **W:** Joe Kelly

24 ❑ Jan 1999 Cover: 1.99 **NM** value: **Cover or less**
Circ: Diamd. preorders: **39,062**
• gatefold summary. 📖 Dead Reckoning, Part 2 **A:** Walter McDaniel **W:** Joe Kelly ★ Appearance of Tiamat, Cosmic Messiah.

25 ❑ Feb 1999 Cover: 1.99 **NM** value: **2.99**
Circ: Diamd. preorders: **39,703**
📖 Dead Reckoning, Part 3 **A:** Walter McDaniel **W:** Joe Kelly ★ Appearance of Tiamat. ★ Appearance of Captain America.

26 ❑ Mar 1999 Cover: 1.99 **NM** value: **Cover or less**
Circ: Diamd. preorders: **38,303**
📖 Dead Reckoning Aftermath **A:** P. Woods **W:** Joe Kelly

27 ❑ Apr 1999 Cover: 1.99 **NM** value: **Cover or less**
Circ: Diamd. preorders: **36,739**
A: P. Woods **W:** Joe Kelly ★ Appearance of Wolverine. ★ Versus Doc Bong.

28 ❑ May 1999 Cover: 1.99 **NM** value: **Cover or less**
Circ: Diamd. preorders: **36,776**

29 ❑ Jun 1999 Cover: 1.99 **NM** value: **Cover or less**
Circ: Diamd. preorders: **36,977**

30 ❑ Jul 1999 Cover: 1.99 **NM** value: **Cover or less**
Circ: Diamd. preorders: **35,805**

31 ❑ Aug 1999 Cover: 1.99 **NM** value: **Cover or less**
Circ: Diamd. preorders: **35,360**

32 ❑ Sep 1999 Cover: 1.99 **NM** value: **Cover or less**
Circ: Diamd. preorders: **34,585**

33 ❑ Oct 1999 Cover: 1.99 **NM** value: **Cover or less**
Circ: Diamd. preorders: **33,173**

34 ❑ Nov 1999 Cover: 1.99 **NM** value: **Cover or less**
Circ: Diamd. preorders: **31,945**

35 ❑ Dec 1999 Cover: 1.99 **NM** value: **2.25**
Circ: Diamd. preorders: **31,908**

36 ❑ Jan 2000 Cover: 1.99 **NM** value: **2.25**
Circ: Diamd. preorders: **30,046**

37 ❑ Feb 2000 Cover: 1.99 **NM** value: **2.25**
Circ: Diamd. preorders: **31,790**

38 ❑ Mar 2000 Cover: 1.99 **NM** value: **2.25**
Circ: Diamd. preorders: **28,981**

39 ❑ Apr 2000 Cover: 1.99 **NM** value: **2.25**
Circ: Diamd. preorders: **27,246**

40 ❑ May 2000 Cover: 1.99 **NM** value: **2.25**
Circ: Diamd. preorders: **28,162**

41 ❑ Jun 2000 Cover: 2.25 **NM** value: **Cover or less**
Circ: Diamd. preorders: **27,621**

42 ❑ Jul 2000 Cover: 2.25 **NM** value: **Cover or less**
Circ: Diamd. preorders: **27,605**

43 ❑ Aug 2000 Cover: 2.25 **NM** value: **Cover or less**
Circ: Diamd. preorders: **27,724**

44 ❑ Sep 2000 Cover: 2.25 **NM** value: **Cover or less**
Circ: Diamd. preorders: **27,734**

45 ❑ Oct 2000 Cover: 2.25 **NM** value: **Cover or less**
Circ: Statement: **31,093** Diamd. preorders: **25,903**

46 ❑ Nov 2000 Cover: 2.25 **NM** value: **Cover or less**
Circ: Statement: **31,093** Diamd. preorders: **27,473**
📖 Cruel Summer, Part 1 **A:** Paul Chadwick **W:** Jimmy Palmiotti

47 ❑ Dec 2000 Cover: 2.25 **NM** value: **Cover or less**
Circ: Statement: **31,093** Diamd. preorders: **27,266**
📖 Cruel Summer, Part 2 **A:** Paul Chadwick **W:** Jimmy Palmiotti

48 ❑ Jan 2001 Cover: 2.25 **NM** value: **Cover or less**
Circ: Statement: **31,093** Diamd. preorders: **27,257**
📖 Cruel Summer, Part 3 **A:** Paul Chadwick **W:** Jimmy Palmiotti

49 ❑ Feb 2001 Cover: 2.25 **NM** value: **Cover or less**
Circ: Statement: **31,093** Diamd. preorders: **26,401**
📖 Cat Magnet **A:** Michael Lopez **W:** Jimmy Palmiotti; Buddy Scalera

50 ❑ Mar 2001 Cover: 2.25 **NM** value: **Cover or less**
Circ: Statement: **31,093** Diamd. preorders: **25,797**
📖 The Promise, Part 1 **A:** Darick Robertson **W:** Jimmy Palmiotti; Buddy Scalera

51 ❑ Apr 2001 Cover: 2.25 **NM** value: **Cover or less**
Circ: Statement: **31,093** Diamd. preorders: **24,673**
Detective Comics #39 cover homage. 📖 The Promise, Part 2 **A:** Darick Robertson **W:** Jimmy Palmiotti; Buddy Scalera ★ Appearance of Kid Deadpool.

52 ❑ May 2001 Cover: 2.25 **NM** value: **Cover or less**
Circ: Statement: **31,093** Diamd. preorders: **24,346**
📖 Talk of the Town **A:** Anthony Williams **W:** Jimmy Palmiotti; Buddy Scalera

Anl 1998❑ca. 1988 Cover: 2.99 **NM** value: **Cover or less**
wraparound cover. • gatefold summary. • Deadpool/Death '98

Bk 1❑ Cover: 14.95 **NM** value: **Cover or less**
• Deadpool: Mission Improbable

DEADPOOL: AGENT OF WEAPON X — Marvel

1 ❑ Cover: 2.25 **NM** value: **Cover or less**
2 ❑ Cover: 2.25 **NM** value: **Cover or less**
3 ❑ Cover: 2.25 **NM** value: **Cover or less**
4 ❑ Cover: 2.25 **NM** value: **Cover or less**

DEADPOOL: FUNERAL FOR A FREAK — Marvel

1 ❑ Cover: 2.25 **NM** value: **Cover or less**
2 ❑ Cover: 2.25 **NM** value: **Cover or less**

DEADPOOL (LTD. SERIES) — Marvel

1 ❑ Aug 1994 Cover: 2.50 **NM** value: **4.00**
Circ: CapCity orders: **117,500** • **CGC:** 10 graded, best 10.0
W: Mark Waid

2 ❑ Sep 1994 Cover: 2.50 **NM** value: **3.00**
Circ: CapCity orders: **59,000**
W: Mark Waid

3 ❑ Oct 1994 Cover: 2.50 **NM** value: **3.00**
Circ: CapCity orders: **50,100**
📖 Deadpool Sandwich **A:** Ian Churchill; Ken Lashley **W:** Mark Waid

4 ❑ Nov 1994 Cover: 2.50 **NM** value: **3.00**
Circ: CapCity orders: **51,800**
W: Mark Waid

Bk 1❑ Jun 1997 Cover: 12.99 **NM** value: **Cover or less**
• Trade Paperback. • collects mini-series

DEADPOOL TEAM-UP — Marvel

Deadpool has been hired to save a life? In this Sanctuary-type team-up, a Yakuza boss has created a midget-sized, yet deadly, Deadpool clone known as Widdle Wade. After Widdle Wade murders a Yakuza lieutenant, the little assassin goes after Wade Wilson's former sumo wrestling coach.

Japanese culture plays a stong role in building the plot. For instance, families are bound by their shared belief in reputation, obligation, and responsibility, as well as religious and societal values that stress honor, courage, and politeness. When selfish men pervert the tenets to serve their own dubious intentions, innocent as well as not-so-innocent people become cultural outcasts. And Deadpool doesn't know that, when these values become more important than friendship, everyone loses.

It's a good idea to pay close attention while reading the issues, since almost every panel includes tongue-in-cheek humor.

1 ❑ Dec 1998 Cover: 2.99 **NM** value: **Cover or less**
Circ: Diamd. preorders: **28,081**
• gatefold summary. 📖 Turning Japanese...or Little Demon Inside • Secret Wars II tie-in **A:** Pete Woods **W:** James Felder ★ Appearance of Widdle Wade.

DEADPOOL: THE CIRCLE CHASE — Marvel

1 ❑ Aug 1993 Cover: 2.50 **NM** value: **Cover or less**
Circ: CapCity orders: **55,050**
Embossed cover. 📖 The Circle Chase, Round 1 **A:** Joe Madureira **W:** Fabian Nicieza

2 ❑ Sep 1993 Cover: 2.00 **NM** value: **Cover or less**
Circ: CapCity orders: **41,700**

3 ❑ Oct 1993 Cover: 2.00 **NM** value: **Cover or less**
Circ: CapCity orders: **36,750**

4 ❑ Nov 1993 Cover: 2.00 **NM** value: **Cover or less**
Circ: CapCity orders: **34,450**

DEADSHOT — DC

Floyd Lawton, aka Deadshot, first appeared in Batman #59 (Jun 50). Like Bruce Wayne, Lawton is raised in a rich family which is destroyed when his parents are gunned down by criminals. Unlike Wayne, however, Lawton's rage leads him to a life of crime.

In a story called "The Man Who Replaced Batman," he appears in a black mask and tuxedo and began using his marksmanship skills to round up criminals. He figures if he can upstage and get rid of Batman, he'll then be free to control Gotham City's underworld. Batman stops him, however, and Deadshot disappears until 1977. He then reappears in his current costume, fighting — and losing to — Batman several times. In jail he is approached by Amanda Waller and Rick Flag in Legends #2, recruiting Lawton to join The Suicide Squad. But it seems Lawton agreed out of a desire more to get killed than to escape jail. This mini-series finally begins to explain.

1 ❑ Nov 1988 Cover: 1.00 **NM** value: **1.50**
Circ: CapCity orders: **19,400**
📖 Die But Once **A:** Kim Yale **W:** John Ostrander ★ Origin of Deadshot.

2 ❑ Dec 1988 Cover: 1.00 **NM** value: **1.25**
Circ: CapCity orders: **15,000**
A: Kim Yale **W:** John Ostrander

3 ❑ Win 1988 Cover: 1.00 **NM** value: **1.25**
Circ: CapCity orders: **13,800**
A: Kim Yale **W:** John Ostrander

4 ❑ Hol 1988 Cover: 1.00 **NM** value: **1.25**
Circ: CapCity orders: **13,500**
A: Kim Yale **W:** John Ostrander

DEADTIME STORIES — New Comics

1 ❑ Oct 1987, b&w Cover: 1.75 **NM** value: **Cover or less**
📖 The Prospector Luckiest Strike!; A Toast to Mr. Dalyrimple; No Place Like Home **A:** Norm Breyfogle; Arthur Adams; Steve Rude; Stephen Bissette **W:** Norm Breyfogle; Stephen Bissette; Jan and Bob Stine; Suzanne Lord

DEADWALKERS — Aircel

1/A ❑ Jan 1991 Cover: 2.50 **NM** value: **Cover or less**
"gross" cover. 📖 One of the Living **A:** John Grigni **W:** Christopher Weppler

Other grades: Multiply prices above by **1.5 for Mint • 2/3 for Very Fine • 1/3 for Fine • 1/5 for Very Good • 1/8 for Good**

1/B ❑ Jan 1991 Cover: 2.50 **NM** value: **Cover or less**
"not-so-gross" cover.
2 ❑ Feb 1991 Cover: 2.50 **NM** value: **Cover or less**
A: John Grigni **W:** Christopher Weppler
3 ❑ Mar 1991 Cover: 2.50 **NM** value: **Cover or less**
A: John Grigni **W:** Christopher Weppler
4 ❑ Apr 1991 Cover: 2.50 **NM** value: **Cover or less**
A: John Grigni **W:** Christopher Weppler

DEAD WHO WALK — Realistic Comics

1 ❑ ca. 1952 Cover: 0.10 **NM** value: **250.00**
• **CGC:** 5 graded, best 9.2

DEADWORLD ARCHIVES — Caliber

1 ❑ b&w Cover: 2.50 **NM** value: **Cover or less**
2 ❑ b&w Cover: 2.50 **NM** value: **Cover or less**
3 ❑ b&w Cover: 2.50 **NM** value: **Cover or less**

DEADWORLD: BITS AND PIECES — Caliber

1 ❑ b&w Cover: 2.95 **NM** value: **Cover or less**

DEADWORLD CHRONICLES: PLAGUE — Caliber

1 ❑ Cover: 2.95 **NM** value: **Cover or less**

DEADWORLD: NECROPOLIS — Caliber

1 ❑ Cover: 3.95 **NM** value: **Cover or less**
C: Linsner

DEADWORLD: TO KILL A KING — Caliber

1 ❑ Cover: 2.95 **NM** value: **Cover or less**
• Sinergy as flip-book **A:** Ron McCain **W:** Kyle Garrettt
1/LE❑ Cover: 5.95 **NM** value: **Cover or less**
• limited edition.
2 ❑ Cover: 2.95 **NM** value: **Cover or less**
3 ❑ Cover: 2.95 **NM** value: **Cover or less**

DEADWORLD (VOL. 1) — Arrow

When Pandora's Box is mixed with Night of the Living Dead, the result is Deadworld. Zombies walk the Earth. Worse, a very few of these zombies are intelligent and, as a result, are far more deadly. Few humans still remain, as a group of teens tries to get to safety. Time and time again, the youngsters think they have found their new "home," only to be attacked by the zombie's leader, King Zombie, and his undead followers. The kids eventually discover that the key to solving this mess is a portal to other dimensions that they must somehow close. The series concludes with a climactic battle in which King Zombie is partially defeated and the remaining humans move north to find shelter.

This black-and-white title began its first run with Arrow Comics in 1986. It ran 26 issues over six years before beginning a second run at Caliber.

1 ❑ b&w Cover: 1.50 **NM** value: **3.00**
📖 Eye Of The Zombie • Arrow publishes **A:** Vincent Locke **W:** Stuart Kerr
2 ❑ **NM** value: **2.50**
3 ❑ **NM** value: **2.50**
4 ❑ **NM** value: **2.50**
5 ❑ **NM** value: **2.50**
6 ❑ **NM** value: **2.50**
7 ❑ **NM** value: **2.50**
8 ❑ **NM** value: **2.50**
9 ❑ **NM** value: **2.50**
10 ❑ b&w Cover: 2.50 **NM** value: **Cover or less**
• Caliber begins as publisher
11 ❑ b&w Cover: 2.50 **NM** value: **Cover or less**
12 ❑ b&w Cover: 2.50 **NM** value: **Cover or less**
13 ❑ b&w Cover: 2.50 **NM** value: **Cover or less**
14 ❑ b&w Cover: 2.50 **NM** value: **Cover or less**
15 ❑ b&w Cover: 2.50 **NM** value: **Cover or less**
16 ❑ b&w Cover: 2.50 **NM** value: **Cover or less**
17 ❑ b&w Cover: 2.50 **NM** value: **Cover or less**
18 ❑ b&w Cover: 2.50 **NM** value: **Cover or less**
19 ❑ b&w Cover: 2.50 **NM** value: **Cover or less**
20 ❑ b&w Cover: 2.50 **NM** value: **Cover or less**
21 ❑ b&w Cover: 2.50 **NM** value: **Cover or less**
22 ❑ b&w Cover: 2.50 **NM** value: **Cover or less**
23 ❑ b&w Cover: 2.50 **NM** value: **Cover or less**
24 ❑ b&w Cover: 2.50 **NM** value: **Cover or less**
25 ❑ b&w Cover: 2.50 **NM** value: **Cover or less**
26 ❑ b&w Cover: 3.50 **NM** value: **Cover or less**
final issue.
Bk 1❑ Cover: 9.95 **NM** value: **Cover or less**

DEADWORLD (VOL. 2) — Caliber

1 ❑ b&w Cover: 5.95 **NM** value: **Cover or less**
• Giant-size. 📖 Dead Credits **A:** Troy Nixey **W:** Randall Thayer
2 ❑ b&w Cover: 2.95 **NM** value: **3.00**
3 ❑ b&w Cover: 2.95 **NM** value: **3.00**
4 ❑ b&w Cover: 2.95 **NM** value: **3.00**
5 ❑ b&w Cover: 2.95 **NM** value: **3.00**
6 ❑ b&w Cover: 2.95 **NM** value: **3.00**
7 ❑ b&w Cover: 2.95 **NM** value: **Cover or less**
8 ❑ b&w Cover: 2.95 **NM** value: **Cover or less**
9 ❑ b&w Cover: 2.95 **NM** value: **Cover or less**
10 ❑ b&w Cover: 2.95 **NM** value: **Cover or less**
11 ❑ b&w Cover: 2.95 **NM** value: **Cover or less**
12 ❑ b&w Cover: 2.95 **NM** value: **Cover or less**
13 ❑ b&w Cover: 2.95 **NM** value: **Cover or less**
14 ❑ b&w Cover: 2.95 **NM** value: **Cover or less**
15 ❑ b&w Cover: 2.95 **NM** value: **Cover or less**

DEAR JULIA — Black Eye

1 ❑ **NM** value: **2.95**
A: Brian Biggs **W:** Brian Biggs
2 ❑ **NM** value: **2.95**
A: Brian Biggs **W:** Brian Biggs
3 ❑ **NM** value: **2.95**
A: Brian Biggs **W:** Brian Biggs
4 ❑ **NM** value: **2.95**
A: Brian Biggs **W:** Brian Biggs

DEAR LONELY HEART — Artful Publications

1 ❑ ca. 1951 Cover: 0.10 **NM** value: **70.00**
2 ❑ Oct 1951 Cover: 0.10 **NM** value: **40.00**
3 ❑ Dec 1951 Cover: 0.10 **NM** value: **40.00**
4 ❑ Feb 1951 Cover: 0.10 **NM** value: **40.00**
5 ❑ Apr 1951 Cover: 0.10 **NM** value: **80.00**
6 ❑ Jun 1952 Cover: 0.10 **NM** value: **40.00**
• **CGC:** 1 graded, best 7.5
7 ❑ Aug 1952 Cover: 0.10 **NM** value: **40.00**
8 ❑ Oct 1952 Cover: 0.10 **NM** value: **40.00**

DEAR LONELY HEARTS — Comic Media

1 ❑ Aug 1953 Cover: 0.10 **NM** value: **40.00**
📖 Six Months to Live
2 ❑ Oct 1953 Cover: 0.10 **NM** value: **25.00**
📖 Date Hungry; Price of Passion
3 ❑ Dec 1953 Cover: 0.10 **NM** value: **25.00**
4 ❑ Feb 1954 Cover: 0.10 **NM** value: **25.00**
5 ❑ Apr 1954 Cover: 0.10 **NM** value: **25.00**
6 ❑ Jun 1954 Cover: 0.10 **NM** value: **25.00**
7 ❑ Aug 1954 Cover: 0.10 **NM** value: **25.00**
8 ❑ Oct 1954 Cover: 0.10 **NM** value: **25.00**

DEARLY BELOVED — Ziff-Davis

1 ❑ ca. 1952 Cover: 0.10 **NM** value: **75.00**
📖 To Love and to Cherish; Hurricane of Love • Photo cover

DEATH^3 — Marvel

Set in a flawed future, this four-part series exhibits strong parallels to Mary Shelley's Frankenstein. Just as in that classic, this story is told through the letters and journal of the scientist who creates a half-man, half-monster. There's one chilling difference, however. Whereas Dr. Frankenstein sought to destroy his creation in the name of morality, the doctor in this case, Evelyn Necker, the creator of Death's Head II, has no conscience whatsoever. Instead, she creates cyborgs to perfect her creation, and kills for the needed human parts.

It's yet another Marvel UK title unnecessarily brought over and relabeled for the North American market in the early 1990s glut.

1 ❑ Sep 1993 Cover: 2.95 **NM** value: **Cover or less**
Circ: CapCity orders: **32,100**
Embossed cover. ★ Origin of Death Metal. ★ 1st Appearance of Death Metal.
2 ❑ Oct 1993 Cover: 1.75 **NM** value: **Cover or less**
Circ: CapCity orders: **13,800**
A: Dell Barras **W:** Dan Abnett ★ Appearance of Kingpin, Thing, Iron Man. ★ Appearance of Ghost Rider. ★ Appearance of Doctor Octopus. ★ Appearance of Charnel.
3 ❑ Nov 1993 Cover: 1.75 **NM** value: **Cover or less**
Circ: CapCity orders: **11,800**
4 ❑ Dec 1993 Cover: 1.75 **NM** value: **Cover or less**
Circ: CapCity orders: **8,700**

DEATH & CANDY — Fantagraphics

The indicia of Death & Candy states, "No similarity between any of the names, characters, persons and institutions and those of any living or dead person is intended and any similarity that may exist is purely coincidental." In the case of Death & Candy such similarity wouldn't be coincidental, it would be astounding.

In "Car-Boy's Garden," the bodies of the parents of Car-Boy, whose head is shaped like a car, are buried in a compost heap in his basement. When he disposes of a leftover piece of meat in the same compost heap it roots and flourishes as a sentient meat tree. Then things get very bizarre.

"The Evacuation" is the story of a man visiting his family after a long absence. His family home is now an archaeological dig. He has been gone a long time and his family is different than he remembers them.

These are the abstract expressionist visions of Swedish underground artist Max Andersson. His symbolism, like his artwork, is something less than subtle.

1 ❑ Win 1999 Cover: 3.95 **NM** value: **Cover or less**
📖 Car-Boy's Garden; The Excavation; Wreck-Boy: The Inside Bomb; Car Boy's **A:** Max Andersson **W:** Max Andersson

DEATH & TAXES: THE REAL COSTS OF LIVING — Parody

1 ❑ b&w Cover: 2.50 **NM** value: **Cover or less**
A: Tatsuya Ishida **W:** Mat Gertler

DEATHANGEL — Lightning

1/A ❑ Dec 1997 Cover: 2.95 **NM** value: **Cover or less**
A: John Cleary **W:** John Cleary
1/B ❑ Dec 1997 Cover: 2.95 **NM** value: **Cover or less**
alternate cover. **A:** John Cleary **W:** John Cleary

DEATHBLOW — Image

Commander Cray of the S.O.G. (Special Operations Group) is Deathblow. He's one of the deadliest men alive-a virtual killing machine who does America's dirty work at home and abroad.

Many have tried — and failed — to kill him over the years. But now, inoperable cancer of the brain is about to do what no man could. Knowing that his days are numbered brings a new recklessness — and a certain penitence to this dealer of death.

Issues of this title also included a backup book: Cybernary. There, a dark group of man-machines held court in their own shadowy underworld.

0 ❑ Aug 1996 Cover: 2.95 **NM** value: **Cover or less**
1 ❑ Apr 1993 Cover: 2.50 **NM** value: **3.00**
Circ: CapCity orders: **299,975** • **CGC:** 5 graded, best 9.8
Black varnish cover. 📖 Confessions • Cybernary #1 as flip-book **A:** Jim Lee **W:** Jim Lee; Brandon Choi; Steve Gerber ★ 1st Appearance of Cybernary.
2 ❑ Aug 1993 Cover: 1.75 **NM** value: **2.50**
Circ: CapCity orders: **168,000** • **CGC:** 1 graded, best 9.6
• Cybernary #2 as flip-book **A:** Jim Lee; Nick Manabat **W:** Jim Lee; Brandon Choi; Steve Gerber
3 ❑ Feb 1994 Cover: 1.75 **NM** value: **3.00**
Circ: CapCity orders: **138,950**
• Cybernary #3 as flip-book ★ 1st Appearance of Cisco.
4 ❑ Apr 1994 Cover: 1.75 **NM** value: **2.00**
Circ: CapCity orders: **36,875**
5 ❑ May 1994 Cover: 1.95 **NM** value: **2.00**
Circ: CapCity orders: **37,100**
5/A ❑ May 1994 Cover: 1.95 **NM** value: **4.00**
alternate cover. • Variant cover edition.
6 ❑ Jun 1994 Cover: 1.95 **NM** value: **Cover or less**
Circ: CapCity orders: **36,575**
7 ❑ Jul 1994 Cover: 1.95 **NM** value: **Cover or less**
Circ: CapCity orders: **32,950**
8 ❑ Aug 1994 Cover: 1.95 **NM** value: **Cover or less**
Circ: CapCity orders: **32,200**
9 ❑ Oct 1994 Cover: 1.95 **NM** value: **Cover or less**
Circ: CapCity orders: **29,600**
📖 Dark Angel Saga, Part 9
10 ❑ Nov 1994 Cover: 2.50 **NM** value: **Cover or less**
Circ: CapCity orders: **28,400**
wraparound cover.
11 ❑ Dec 1994 Cover: 2.50 **NM** value: **Cover or less**
Circ: CapCity orders: **25,025**
12 ❑ Jan 1995 Cover: 2.50 **NM** value: **Cover or less**
Circ: CapCity orders: **24,225**
13 ❑ Feb 1995 Cover: 2.50 **NM** value: **Cover or less**
Circ: CapCity orders: **20,075**
14 ❑ Mar 1995 Cover: 2.50 **NM** value: **Cover or less**
Circ: CapCity orders: **19,275**
15 ❑ Apr 1995 Cover: 2.50 **NM** value: **Cover or less**
Circ: CapCity orders: **18,500**
16 ❑ May 1995 Cover: 2.50 **NM** value: **Cover or less**
📖 WildStorm Rising, Part 6 • bound-in trading cards
16/SC❑May 1995 Cover: 2.50 **NM** value: **Cover or less**
Circ: CapCity orders: **27,800**
17 ❑ Jun 1995 Cover: 2.50 **NM** value: **Cover or less**
Circ: CapCity orders: **18,225**
A: Rubi Rouleau **W:** Brandon Choi
17/A❑Jun 1995 Cover: 2.50 **NM** value: **3.00**
• Chicago Comicon limited edition.
18 ❑ Jul 1995 Cover: 2.50 **NM** value: **Cover or less**
Circ: CapCity orders: **17,675**
19 ❑ Sep 1995 Cover: 2.50 **NM** value: **Cover or less**
Circ: CapCity orders: **17,150**
20 ❑ Oct 1995 Cover: 2.50 **NM** value: **Cover or less**
Circ: CapCity orders: **18,925**
📖 Brothers-in-Arms, Part 1
21 ❑ Nov 1995 Cover: 2.50 **NM** value: **Cover or less**
Circ: CapCity orders: **11,650**
📖 Brothers-in-Arms, Part 2 ★ Appearance of Gen13.
22 ❑ Dec 1995 Cover: 2.50 **NM** value: **Cover or less**
📖 Brothers-in-Arms, Part 3
23 ❑ Jan 1996 Cover: 2.50 **NM** value: **Cover or less**
📖 Brothers-in-Arms, Part 4
24 ❑ Feb 1996 Cover: 2.50 **NM** value: **Cover or less**
📖 Brothers-in-Arms, Part 5 ★ Appearance of Grifter.
25 ❑ Mar 1996 Cover: 2.50 **NM** value: **Cover or less**
📖 Brothers-in-Arms, Part 6
26 ❑ Mar 1996 Cover: 2.50 **NM** value: **Cover or less**
📖 Fire from Heaven Prelude 3
27 ❑ Apr 1996 Cover: 2.50 **NM** value: **Cover or less**
📖 Fire from Heaven, Part 8
28 ❑ Jul 1996 Cover: 2.50 **NM** value: **Cover or less**
📖 Fire from Heaven Finale 3

CGC-graded: Multiply prices above by **33 for 9.9 M • 16 for 9.8 NM/M • 7 for 9.6 NM+ • 5 for 9.4 NM • 2.5 for 9.2 NM- • 1.5 for 9.0 VF/NM**

28/SC❑Jul 1996 Cover: 2.50 **NM** value: **Cover or less**
alternate cover. 🕮 Fire from Heaven Finale 3
29 ❑ Aug 1996 Cover: 2.50 **NM** value: **Cover or less**
final issue.
Bk 1❑ Dec 1999 Cover: 19.95 **NM** value: **Cover or less**
• Sinners and Saints;Collects Deathblow #1-12 **A:** Tim Sale; Jim Lee **W:** Jim Lee; Brandon Choi

DEATHBLOW: BYBLOWS — WildStorm

1 ❑ Nov 1999 Cover: 2.95 **NM** value: **Cover or less**
Circ: Diamd. preorders: **21,017**
A: Jim Baikie **W:** Alan Moore
2 ❑ Dec 1999 Cover: 2.95 **NM** value: **Cover or less**
Circ: Diamd. preorders: **18,632**
A: Jim Baikie **W:** Alan Moore
3 ❑ Jan 2000 Cover: 2.95 **NM** value: **Cover or less**
Circ: Diamd. preorders: **14,714**
A: Jim Baikie **W:** Alan Moore

DEATHBLOW/WOLVERINE — Image

1 ❑ Sep 1996 Cover: 2.50 **NM** value: **Cover or less**
Circ: Diamd. preorders: **95,838 • CGC:** 1 graded, best 9.6
• crossover with Marvel **A:** Aron Wiesenfeld **W:** Aron Wiesenfeld
2 ❑ Feb 1997 Cover: 2.50 **NM** value: **Cover or less**
final issue. • crossover with Marvel **A:** Aron Wiesenfeld **W:** Aron Wiesenfeld
Bk 1❑ Aug 1997 Cover: 8.95 **NM** value: **Cover or less**
• collects mini-series

DEATH BY CHOCOLATE — Sleeping Giant

1 ❑ Mar 1996, b&w Cover: 2.50 **NM** value: **Cover or less**
No issue number.

DEATH BY CHOCOLATE: SIR GEOFFREY AND THE CHOCOLATE CAR — Sleeping Giant

1 ❑ b&w Cover: 2.50 **NM** value: **Cover or less**
No issue number.

DEATH BY CHOCOLATE: THE METABOLATORS — Sleeping Giant

1 ❑ b&w Cover: 2.50 **NM** value: **Cover or less**
No issue number.

DEATH BY ECSTASY — Adventure

Bk 1❑ b&w Cover: 9.95 **NM** value: **Cover or less**

DEATH CRAZED TEENAGE SUPERHEROES — Arf! Arf!

1 ❑ Cover: 1.50 **NM** value: **Cover or less**
A: Jim Erskine **W:** Jim Erskine
2 ❑ Cover: 1.50 **NM** value: **Cover or less**
🕮 D.O.A. **A:** Jim Erskine **W:** Jim Erskine

DEATH DEALER — Verotik

What happens when you put a heavy metal rock star, a seasoned fantasy painter, and a popular comic-book illustrator together? You get a prestige format entitled Death Dealer with a cover by Frank Frazetta that inspired a story by Glen Danzig and interior illustrations by Simon Bisley. Death Dealer contains plenty of gratuitous violence, but the story it tells is intriguing.

Death Dealer gives the origin of one of Frazetta's most popular characters. A barbaric warrior followed a black horse into an area where he could almost smell death in the air. It was in this place that the barbarian found the helmet of the Death Dealer. After fighting off a sabre-toothed tiger, the warrior was possessed by the helmet. He was shown the helmet's previous life and begins to understand why the helmet craves revenge against its previous masters. When wearing the helmet, the warrior becomes almost invincible.

Aside from the character's name and the possessive helmet, the comics series has little connection to a series of prose novels written by Jim Silke based on Frazetta's illustrations.

1 ❑ Jul 1995 Cover: 5.95 **NM** value: **6.00**
Circ: CapCity orders: **21,400 • CGC:** 1 graded, best 9.6
A: Frank Frazetta(cover)
2 ❑ May 1996 Cover: 6.95 **NM** value: **Cover or less**
3 ❑ Apr 1997 Cover: 6.95 **NM** value: **Cover or less**
Circ: Diamd. preorders: **25,958**
4 ❑ Jul 1997 Cover: 6.95 **NM** value: **Cover or less**

DEATH DREAMS OF DRACULA — Apple

1 ❑ b&w Cover: 2.50 **NM** value: **Cover or less**
🕮 Have You Seen Me?; Slash! **A:** Ernie Guanlao; Mark Wheatley; Brad Vancata **W:** Mark Wheatley; Rick Shanklin
2 ❑ b&w Cover: 2.50 **NM** value: **Cover or less**
3 ❑ b&w Cover: 2.50 **NM** value: **Cover or less**
4 ❑ b&w Cover: 2.50 **NM** value: **Cover or less**

DEATH GALLERY, A — DC / Vertigo

1 ❑ Cover: 2.95 **NM** value: **3.00**
Circ: CapCity orders: **28,600**
• portraits

DEATH HAWK — Adventure

1 ❑ b&w Cover: 1.95 **NM** value: **Cover or less**
🕮 Dreams Alone **A:** Rik Levins **W:** Mark Ellis
2 ❑ b&w Cover: 1.95 **NM** value: **Cover or less**
🕮 To Enshrine the Past **A:** Rik Levins **W:** Mark Ellis
3 ❑ b&w Cover: 1.95 **NM** value: **Cover or less**

DEATH HUNT — Eternity

1 ❑ b&w Cover: 1.95 **NM** value: **Cover or less**
A: Scott Hanna **W:** C.J. Henderson; Peter Palmer

DEATHLOK (1ST SERIES) — Marvel

Deathlok first appeared in Astonishing Tales #25, a cyborg killing machine whose brain belonged to human Luther Manning. After a run in Astonishing Tales, Deathlok faded from view, appearing sporadically in various issues of Marvel Team-Up, Captain America, and others. Finally, in Marvel Comics Presents #62, his brain was destroyed when the onboard computer electrocuted him.

In 1990, Marvel revisited the Deathlok project in this four-issue graphic novel limited series. Cybertek Systems (the applied cybernetics division of Roxxon Oil) have decided to continue with their failed Deathlok project. The only problem: they need a new brain for the system. That little difficulty is solved when Michael Collins, head of their computer systems division discovered that his "prosthetics" project was actually a weapons system. Michael, a pacifist, threatens to quit. Instead, he was captured — and woke up as the new Deathlok cyborg!

1 ❑ Jul 1990 Cover: 3.95 **NM** value: **Cover or less**
Circ: CapCity orders: **25,350 • CGC:** 5 graded, best 9.8
🕮 The Brains Of The Outfit **A:** Jackson Guice; Joe Jusko(cover) **W:** Greg Wright; Dwayne McDuffie ★ Origin of Deathlok II (Mike Collins). ★ 1st Appearance of Deathlok II (Mike Collins).
2 ❑ Aug 1990 Cover: 3.95 **NM** value: **Cover or less**
Circ: CapCity orders: **19,750**
A: Jackson Guice; Joe Jusko(cover) **W:** Greg Wright; Dwayne McDuffie
3 ❑ Sep 1990 Cover: 3.95 **NM** value: **Cover or less**
Circ: CapCity orders: **17,800**
A: Jackson Guice; Joe Jusko(cover) **W:** Greg Wright; Dwayne McDuffie
4 ❑ Oct 1990 Cover: 3.95 **NM** value: **Cover or less**
Circ: CapCity orders: **19,000**
A: Jackson Guice; Joe Jusko(cover) **W:** Greg Wright; Dwayne McDuffie

DEATHLOK (2ND SERIES) — Marvel

1 ❑ Jul 1991 Cover: 1.75 **NM** value: **2.50**
Circ: CapCity orders: **93,200**
Silver ink cover. 🕮 The Wolf Is At The Door **A:** Denys Cowan **W:** Greg Wright; Dwayne McDuffie
2 ❑ Aug 1991 Cover: 1.75 **NM** value: **2.00**
Circ: CapCity orders: **60,100**
🕮 The Souls Of Cyber-Folk, Part 1 **A:** Denys Cowan **W:** Dwayne McDuffie ★ Appearance of Forge.
3 ❑ Sep 1991 Cover: 1.75 **NM** value: **2.00**
Circ: CapCity orders: **55,500**
🕮 The Souls Of Cyber-Folk, Part 2 **A:** Denys Cowan **W:** Dwayne McDuffie ★ Versus Doctor Doom.
4 ❑ Oct 1991 Cover: 1.75 **NM** value: **2.00**
Circ: CapCity orders: **62,600**
🕮 The Souls Of Cyber-Folk, Part 3 **A:** Denys Cowan **W:** Dwayne McDuffie
5 ❑ Nov 1991 Cover: 1.75 **NM** value: **2.00**
Circ: CapCity orders: **66,800**
🕮 The Souls Of Cyber-Folk, Part 4 • X-Men & Fantastic Four X-over **A:** Denys Cowan **W:** Dwayne McDuffie
6 ❑ Dec 1991 Cover: 1.75 **NM** value: **2.00**
Circ: CapCity orders: **84,300**
🕮 Similar Machines, Part 1 • Punisher x-over **A:** Denys Cowan; Mike Manley **W:** Greg Wright
7 ❑ Jan 1992 Cover: 1.75 **NM** value: **2.00**
Circ: CapCity orders: **69,000**
🕮 Similar Machines, Part 2 • Punisher x-over **A:** Denys Cowan **W:** Greg Wright
8 ❑ Feb 1992 Cover: 1.75 **NM** value: **2.00**
Circ: CapCity orders: **45,900**
🕮 The Ultimate War Machine • Punisher x-over **A:** John Herbert **W:** Greg Wright
9 ❑ Mar 1992 Cover: 1.75 **NM** value: **2.00**
Circ: CapCity orders: **58,200**
🕮 Nightmares of Vengeance **A:** Denys Cowan **W:** Greg Wright ★ Appearance of Ghost Rider. ★ Versus Ghost Rider.
10 ❑ Apr 1992 Cover: 1.75 **NM** value: **2.00**
Circ: CapCity orders: **48,300**
🕮 Wake Up! It's Time to Die! **A:** Denys Cowan **W:** Greg Wright ★ Appearance of Ghost Rider. ★ Versus Ghost Rider.
11 ❑ May 1992 Cover: 1.75 **NM** value: **Cover or less**
Circ: CapCity orders: **38,100**
🕮 Welcome to the Terrordome **A:** Denys Cowan **W:** Dwayne McDuffie ★ 1st Appearance of High-Tech.
12 ❑ Jun 1992 Cover: 1.75 **NM** value: **Cover or less**
Circ: CapCity orders: **36,600**
🕮 Biohazard Agenda, Part 1 **A:** Denys Cowan; Mike Manley **W:** Dwayne McDuffie
13 ❑ Jul 1992 Cover: 1.75 **NM** value: **Cover or less**
Circ: CapCity orders: **36,700**
🕮 Biohazard Agenda, Part 2 **A:** Denys Cowan **W:** Dwayne McDuffie
14 ❑ Aug 1992 Cover: 1.75 **NM** value: **Cover or less**
Circ: CapCity orders: **33,600**
🕮 Biohazard Agenda, Part 3 **A:** Mike Manley **W:** Dwayne McDuffie ★ Origin of Deathlok III (Luther Manning).
15 ❑ Sep 1992 Cover: 1.75 **NM** value: **Cover or less**
Circ: CapCity orders: **28,200**
🕮 Biohazard Agenda, Part 4 **A:** Denys Cowan **W:** Dwayne McDuffie
16 ❑ Oct 1992 Cover: 1.75 **NM** value: **Cover or less**
Circ: CapCity orders: **35,700**
🕮 Infinity War **A:** Walter McDaniel **W:** Dwayne McDuffie
17 ❑ Nov 1992 Cover: 1.75 **NM** value: **Cover or less**
Circ: CapCity orders: **24,600**
🕮 CyberWar, Part 1 **A:** Walter McDaniel **W:** Dwayne McDuffie
18 ❑ Dec 1992 Cover: 1.75 **NM** value: **Cover or less**
Circ: CapCity orders: **21,900**
🕮 CyberWar, Part 2 **A:** Walter McDaniel **W:** Dwayne McDuffie
19 ❑ Jan 1993 Cover: 2.25 **NM** value: **Cover or less**
Circ: CapCity orders: **28,300**
foil cover. 🕮 CyberWar, Part 3 **A:** Walter McDaniel **W:** Greg Wright ★ Origin of Siege. ★ 1st Appearance of Siege.
20 ❑ Feb 1993 Cover: 1.75 **NM** value: **Cover or less**
Circ: CapCity orders: **20,900**
🕮 CyberWar, Part 4 **A:** J.J. Birch; Tom Raney **W:** Greg Wright
21 ❑ Mar 1993 Cover: 1.75 **NM** value: **Cover or less**
Circ: CapCity orders: **19,100**
🕮 CyberWar, Part 5 **A:** Walter McDaniel **W:** Greg Wright
22 ❑ Apr 1993 Cover: 1.75 **NM** value: **Cover or less**
Circ: CapCity orders: **19,500**
23 ❑ May 1993 Cover: 1.75 **NM** value: **Cover or less**
Circ: CapCity orders: **19,000**
🕮 And We Are Not Saved! **A:** Walter McDaniel **W:** Dwayne McDuffie
24 ❑ Jun 1993 Cover: 1.75 **NM** value: **Cover or less**
Circ: CapCity orders: **17,600**
🕮 And All Fashionable Vices Pass For Virtues **A:** Grant Miehm **W:** Dwayne McDuffie
25 ❑ Jul 1993 Cover: 2.95 **NM** value: **Cover or less**
• CGC: 1 graded, best 9.4
foil cover. ★ Appearance of Black Panther.
26 ❑ Aug 1993 Cover: 1.75 **NM** value: **Cover or less**
Circ: CapCity orders: **17,250**
27 ❑ Sep 1993 Cover: 1.75 **NM** value: **Cover or less**
Circ: CapCity orders: **13,900**
28 ❑ Oct 1993 Cover: 1.75 **NM** value: **Cover or less**
Circ: CapCity orders: **14,800**
• Infinity Crusade crossover **A:** Kevin Kobasic **W:** Greg Wright ★ Appearance of Timestream. ★ Appearance of Goddess.
29 ❑ Nov 1993 Cover: 1.75 **NM** value: **Cover or less**
Circ: CapCity orders: **13,700**
30 ❑ Dec 1993 Cover: 1.75 **NM** value: **Cover or less**
Circ: CapCity orders: **12,550**
31 ❑ Jan 1994 Cover: 1.75 **NM** value: **Cover or less**
Circ: CapCity orders: **11,200**
🕮 Cyberstrike, Part 1
32 ❑ Feb 1994 Cover: 1.75 **NM** value: **Cover or less**
Circ: CapCity orders: **10,050**
🕮 Cyberstrike, Part 2
33 ❑ Mar 1994 Cover: 1.75 **NM** value: **Cover or less**
Circ: CapCity orders: **9,200**
🕮 Cyberstrike, Part 3
34 ❑ Apr 1994 Cover: 1.75 **NM** value: **Cover or less**
Circ: CapCity orders: **8,600**
🕮 Cyberstrike, Part 4 final issue.
Anl 1❑ca. 1992 Cover: 2.50 **NM** value: **Cover or less**
Circ: CapCity orders: **33,400**
🕮 Timestream **A:** Jackson Guice **W:** Greg Wright
Anl 2❑ca. 1993 Cover: 2.95 **NM** value: **Cover or less**
Circ: CapCity orders: **14,700**
• Polybagged **A:** John Hebert **W:** Evan Skolnick ★ Origin of Tracer. ★ 1st Appearance of Tracer.
SE 1❑ May 1991 Cover: 2.00 **NM** value: **Cover or less**
Circ: CapCity orders: **16,100**
• reprints Deathlok (1st series) #1
SE 2❑ Jun 1991 Cover: 2.00 **NM** value: **Cover or less**
Circ: CapCity orders: **11,900**
• reprints Deathlok (1st series) #2
SE 3❑ Jun 1991 Cover: 2.00 **NM** value: **Cover or less**
Circ: CapCity orders: **11,800**
• reprints Deathlok (1st series) #3
SE 4❑ Jun 1991 Cover: 2.00 **NM** value: **Cover or less**
Circ: CapCity orders: **11,800**
• reprints Deathlok (1st series) #4

DEATHLOK (3RD SERIES) — Marvel

1 ❑ Sep 1999 Cover: 1.99 **NM** value: **2.00**
Circ: Diamd. preorders: **44,807**
🕮 The Crawl From Small Things Part 1 **A:** Leonardo Manco **W:** Joe Casey; Leonardo Manco
2 ❑ Oct 1999 Cover: 1.99 **NM** value: **Cover or less**
Circ: Diamd. preorders: **40,608**
3 ❑ Nov 1999 Cover: 1.99 **NM** value: **Cover or less**
Circ: Diamd. preorders: **28,874**
4 ❑ Nov 1999 Cover: 1.99 **NM** value: **Cover or less**
Circ: Diamd. preorders: **27,647**
5 ❑ Dec 1999 Cover: 1.99 **NM** value: **Cover or less**
Circ: Diamd. preorders: **26,272**

DEATHMARK — Lightning

1 ❑ Dec 1994, b&w Cover: 2.95 **NM** value: **Cover or less**

Capital City orders are the actual sales of comic books by Capital City Distribution, once one of the largest U.S. sellers of comics to comics shops. Capital City's share of comics shop sales, while not known exactly, increases from around 10-20% in the mid-1980s to 30-35% in the mid-1990s. Capital City's share of comic books sold on newsstands (most Marvels and DCs) will be less.

Other grades: Multiply prices above by **1.5 for Mint • 2/3 for Very Fine • 1/3 for Fine • 1/5 for Very Good • 1/8 for Good**

DEATHMATE — Image / Valiant

Deathmate combines the talents and comics universes of Image and Valiant for the first time.The origin of this great crossover begins in 2062. Solar, Man of the Atom, had long been keeping his lover, Gayle, young and alive using his powers. He finally agrees to let her die, but in his grief over the loss he suffers a schizoid episode, actually splitting into two separate beings. He then enters the place called Unreality where he encounters WildC.A.T.s' Void. Living vessels of the energy from two different worlds, the two are drawn to each other — even though joining together might spell doom for the entire universe.

Back in 1993, the Geomancer Geoff awakes from a dream to find the world changed. Valiant characters such as Bloodshot and Shadowman exist side by side with Youngblood. But this new world has no future — it will be destroyed by the deadly mating of Solar and Void, 70 years from now...

In addition to its use of colors to denote issues rather than numbers, the series is also noteworthy for the first appearance of Gen13.

1 ❑ Sep 1993 Cover: 2.95 **NM** value: **Cover or less**
Circ: CapCity orders: **226,000** • **CGC:** 2 graded, best 9.6
silver cover. 📖 A Love To End All Time • crossover;Prologue **A:** Barry Windsor-Smith **W:** Bob Layton

1/GO❑Sep 1993 Cover: 4.95 **NM** value: **Cover or less**
• Gold cover (limited promotional edition). 📖 A Love To End All Time • gold;Prologue **A:** Barry Windsor-Smith **W:** Bob Layton

2 ❑ Sep 1993 Cover: 4.95 **NM** value: **Cover or less**
Circ: CapCity orders: **149,075** • **CGC:** 16 graded, best 9.8
• Black **A:** Whilce Portacio; Brett Booth; Jim Lee; Brandon Peterson; Marc Silvestri; Scott Clark; Greg Capullo; Jeffrey Scott **W:** Eric Silvestri ★ 1st Appearance of Fairchild, Burn-Out, Gen13 (full), Freefall.

2/GO❑Sep 1993 Cover: 2.95 **NM** value: **6.00**
• **CGC:** 3 graded, best 9.9
• Gold edition. ★ 1st Appearance of Gen13 (full).

3 ❑ Sep 1993 Cover: 4.95 **NM** value: **Cover or less**
Circ: CapCity orders: **157,800**
cover says Oct, indicia says Sep. 📖 Jerked Through Time • Yellow **A:** Bernard Chang **W:** Mike Baron

3/GO❑Sep 1993 Cover: 2.95 **NM** value: **6.00**
• Gold edition. 📖 Jerked Through Time • Yellow **A:** Bernard Chang **W:** Mike Baron

4 ❑ Oct 1993 Cover: 4.95 **NM** value: **Cover or less**
Circ: CapCity orders: **156,100**
📖 Battlestone vs. Magnus Outlaw! • Blue **A:** Jim Calafiore **W:** John Ostrander

4/GO❑Oct 1993 Cover: 4.95 **NM** value: **6.00**
• **CGC:** 1 graded, best 9.4
• Gold edition. • Blue

5 ❑ Nov 1993 Cover: 4.95 **NM** value: **Cover or less**
Circ: CapCity orders: **149,750**
• Red

5/GO❑Nov 1993 Cover: 4.95 **NM** value: **6.00**
• Gold edition. • Red

6 ❑ Feb 1994 Cover: 2.95 **NM** value: **Cover or less**
Circ: CapCity orders: **133,950** • **CGC:** 1 graded, best 9.4
silver cover. 📖 Armageddon Interuptus • Epilogue **A:** Marc Silvestri **W:** Bob Layton

6/GO❑Feb 1994 Cover: 4.95 **NM** value: **Cover or less**
• Gold edition.

DEATH METAL — Marvel

1 ❑ Jan 1994 Cover: 1.95 **NM** value: **Cover or less**
Circ: CapCity orders: **10,900**
2 ❑ Feb 1994 Cover: 1.95 **NM** value: **Cover or less**
3 ❑ Mar 1994 Cover: 1.95 **NM** value: **Cover or less**
4 ❑ Apr 1994 Cover: 1.95 **NM** value: **Cover or less**

DEATH METAL VS. GENETIX — Marvel

1 ❑ Dec 1993 Cover: 2.95 **NM** value: **Cover or less**
Circ: CapCity orders: **9,000**
📖 Offspring, Part 1 **A:** Paco Diaz **W:** Simon Furman
2 ❑ Jan 1994 Cover: 2.95 **NM** value: **Cover or less**
Circ: CapCity orders: **4,850**
📖 Offspring, Part 2 **A:** Paco Diaz **W:** Simon Furman

DEATH OF ANGEL GIRL, THE — Angel

1 ❑ Cover: 2.95 **NM** value: **Cover or less**
📖 A war in Hell **A:** Demitrio Campos **W:** Lloyd Chasseur

DEATH OF ANTISOCIALMAN, THE — Not Available

Matt Feazell is perhaps the best known of the mini-comics publishers. Mini-comics are typically produced by photocopying the pages on standard 8.5" by 11" paper, then folding or cutting them into 1/4-sized pamphlets. Usually mini-comics are something of a "last resort," used as a means for individual artists to publish their work without having any sort of budget. Feazell, on the other hand, has found them an ideal format for his work, which is marked by wacky humor and a minimalist, stick-figure art style. As such, he has made an ongoing practice of putting out mini-comics despite the success of his more conventionally published comics The Amazing Cynicalman and Ert!

In The Death of Antisocialman, Feazell gives readers an apparent oxymoron: the minicomic epic. Spoofing the drawn-out "death" of Superman, Feazell and writer Walt Lockley take a dozen or so issues to kill off Cynicalman's nemesis, the dreaded Antisocialman.

1 ❑ Cover: 0.50 **NM** value: **Cover or less**
A: Matt Feazell **W:** Walt Lockley
2 ❑ Cover: 0.50 **NM** value: **Cover or less**
A: Matt Feazell **W:** Walt Lockley
3 ❑ Cover: 0.50 **NM** value: **Cover or less**
A: Matt Feazell **W:** Walt Lockley
4 ❑ Cover: 0.50 **NM** value: **Cover or less**
A: Matt Feazell **W:** Walt Lockley
5 ❑ Cover: 0.50 **NM** value: **Cover or less**
A: Matt Feazell **W:** Walt Lockley
6 ❑ Cover: 0.50 **NM** value: **Cover or less**
A: Matt Feazell **W:** Walt Lockley
7 ❑ Cover: 0.50 **NM** value: **Cover or less**
A: Matt Feazell **W:** Walt Lockley
8 ❑ Cover: 0.50 **NM** value: **Cover or less**
A: Matt Feazell **W:** Walt Lockley
9 ❑ Cover: 0.50 **NM** value: **Cover or less**
A: Matt Feazell **W:** Walt Lockley
10 ❑ Cover: 0.50 **NM** value: **Cover or less**
A: Matt Feazell **W:** Walt Lockley

DEATH OF HARI KARI, THE — Blackout

0 ❑ Jun 1997 Cover: 2.95 **NM** value: **Cover or less**
Circ: Diamd. preorders: **5,729**
A: Kenneth Lilly **W:** Tom Virkaitis

DEATH OF LADY VAMPRÉ — Blackout

1 ❑ Cover: 2.95 **NM** value: **Cover or less**
Circ: CapCity orders: **6,325**
★ Origin of Lady VamprT.

DEATH OF STUPIDMAN, THE — Parody Press

Parody Press! does a wonderful job at living up to its name. Case in point: The imprint's take on one of the most shocking stories to ever hit the racks, The Death of Superman. But the publisher does not stop with just a straight parody. Rather, it goes on to mock several other industry conventions, such as variant covers, buxom super-heroines, and the inevitable return from the grave for most of the medium's deceased heroes.

What makes The Death of Stupidman so entertaining is not only its blatant attack on the original story, but the targeting of other equally ridiculous themes and characters in the vein of comics. Heroes from all three major publishers — DC, Marvel, and Image — pop up to lend Stupidman a hand in battle against the deadly Gloomsday (a monster made entirely of cereal). Following The Death of Superman closely, Parody Press! used a plethora of puns, some funny, some groaners, to make their point.

1 ❑ Cover: 3.50 **NM** value: **Cover or less**
📖 Gloomsday **A:** Bill Maus **W:** Bill Maus

DEATH OF SUPERBABE — Spoof

1 ❑ b&w Cover: 3.95 **NM** value: **Cover or less**

DEATH OF SUPERMAN — DC

Bk 1❑ Cover: 4.95 **NM** value: **Cover or less**
• **CGC:** 1 graded, best 9.9
• collects storyline
Bk 1/PL❑ **NM** value: **20.00**
• Platinum edition. • Limited to 5000 copies

DEATH OF VAMPIRELLA — Harris

1 ❑ Feb 1997 **NM** value: **15.00**
• **CGC:** 3 graded, best 9.8
chromium cover. • Memorial Edition. • Green logo
1/SC❑Feb 1997 **NM** value: **15.00**
• Holofoil chromium edition. • 750 copies printed;Yellow logo

DEATH RACE 2020 — Cosmic

1 ❑ Apr 1995 Cover: 2.50 **NM** value: **Cover or less**
Circ: CapCity orders: **4,595**
• sequel to Corman film **A:** Kevin O'Neill **W:** Pat Mills; Tony Skinner
2 ❑ May 1995 Cover: 2.50 **NM** value: **Cover or less**
Circ: CapCity orders: **3,100**
📖 Bride of Frankenstein **A:** Kevin O'Neill **W:** Pat Mills; Tony Skinner
5 ❑ Aug 1995 Cover: 2.50 **NM** value: **Cover or less**
Circ: CapCity orders: **2,725**
A: Kevin O'Neill **W:** Pat Mills; Tony Skinner

DEATH RATTLE (VOL. 2) — Kitchen Sink

1 ❑ full color Cover: 2.00 **NM** value: **Cover or less**
Circ: CapCity orders: **4,600**
📖 Killer Planet; Ill Bred; Tom Quick's Revenge **A:** Charles Burns; Rand Holmes; Charles Dallas **W:** Charles Burns; Rand Holmes; Charles Dallas
2 ❑ full color Cover: 2.00 **NM** value: **Cover or less**
Circ: CapCity orders: **3,150**
📖 God's Bosom; A Quagmire of Occult Stories; And Here He Is...the Artist Himself **A:** Rand Holmes; Jaxon; Will Eisner **W:** Rand Holmes; Jaxon; Will Eisner
3 ❑ full color Cover: 2.00 **NM** value: **Cover or less**
Circ: CapCity orders: **3,075**
📖 A Dead Man's Chest; Bulto the Cosmic Slug; Mind Siege! **A:** Steve Stiles; Jaxon; Doug Hansen **W:** Steve Stiles; Jaxon; Doug Hansen
4 ❑ full color Cover: 2.00 **NM** value: **Cover or less**
Circ: CapCity orders: **2,900**
📖 The Power of Prayer; Bulto; Sight Unseen; Killing Time **A:** Rand Holmes; Jaxon; Sam Kieth; Doug Erb **W:** Jaxon; Sam Kieth; Doug Erb; Mike Baron; John Holland
5 ❑ full color Cover: 2.00 **NM** value: **Cover or less**
Circ: CapCity orders: **2,875**
6 ❑ b&w Cover: 2.00 **NM** value: **Cover or less**
📖 Road Kill; Catcalls; Bulto...The Cosmic Slug, Part 4 • Black and white;Listed as #5 in indicia **A:** Rand Holmes; Jaxon; Stephen R. Bissette **W:** Jaxon; Jan Strnad; Tom Veitch
7 ❑ b&w Cover: 2.00 **NM** value: **Cover or less**
📖 This Old House; The Blue Boot; Ed Gein and the Left Hand of God; Workshop **A:** Bill Hartwig; Kenneth Whitfield; Spain Rodriguez **W:** Kenneth Whitfield; Spain Rodriguez; Dave Schreiner
8 ❑ Dec 1986 Cover: 2.00 **NM** value: **Cover or less**
• **CGC:** 5 graded, best 9.6
★ 1st Appearance of Xenozoic.
9 ❑ Jan 1987 Cover: 2.00 **NM** value: **Cover or less**
10 ❑ Mar 1987 Cover: 2.00 **NM** value: **Cover or less**
A: Al Williamson; Frank Frazetta; Wally Wood
11 ❑ May 1987 Cover: 2.00 **NM** value: **Cover or less**
12 ❑ Jul 1987 Cover: 2.00 **NM** value: **Cover or less**
13 ❑ Nov 1987 Cover: 2.00 **NM** value: **Cover or less**
14 ❑ Jan 1988 Cover: 2.00 **NM** value: **Cover or less**
15 ❑ Mar 1988 Cover: 2.00 **NM** value: **Cover or less**
📖 The Big Day Off; The Priest Killer; The Good Listener **A:** Jaxon; Donald Simpson; Bill Hartwig **W:** Jaxon; John Wooley; P.S. Mueller
16 ❑ May 1988 Cover: 2.00 **NM** value: **Cover or less**
17 ❑ Jul 1988 Cover: 2.00 **NM** value: **Cover or less**
📖 Slide, Sinner, Slide; Bulto: Screams of Delight **A:** Rand Holmes; Jaxon **W:** Jaxon; Jim Millaway; John Wooley
18 ❑ Oct 1988 Cover: 2.00 **NM** value: **Cover or less**
📖 Bulto: The Cow Camp; The Old Wisconsin That I Knew; Small Acts of Revenge; When I Grow Up **A:** Ron Wilber; Doug Potter; Jaxon; Bill Hartwig **C:** Frank Miller **W:** Jaxon; Gerard Jones; P.S. Mueller; Steve Rasnic Tem

DEATH RATTLE (VOL. 3) — Kitchen Sink

1 ❑ Oct 1995, b&w Cover: 2.95 **NM** value: **Cover or less**
📖 The Probability Chamber; The Day I Lost My Head; Cut-Up; The Alcoholic Janitor; The Kiss **A:** Brian Biggs; Tim Eldred; Roger Petersen; Mark A. Nelson; Zane Campbell **W:** Brian Biggs; Tim Eldred; Mark A. Nelson; Mark Schultz; Zane Campbell
1-2 ❑ Nov 1995, b&w Cover: 2.95 **NM** value: **Cover or less**
2 ❑ Dec 1995, b&w Cover: 2.95 **NM** value: **Cover or less**
3 ❑ Feb 1996 Cover: 2.95 **NM** value: **Cover or less**
4 ❑ Apr 1996 Cover: 2.95 **NM** value: **Cover or less**
5 ❑ Jun 1996, b&w Cover: 2.95 **NM** value: **Cover or less**
6 ❑ Cover: 2.95 **NM** value: **Cover or less**

DEATHROW — Heroic / Blue Comet

1 ❑ Sep 1993, b&w Cover: 3.50 **NM** value: **Cover or less**
★ 1st Appearance of X-187.

DEATH'S HEAD — Marvel

1 ❑ Dec 1988 Cover: 1.75 **NM** value: **Cover or less**
Circ: CapCity orders: **10,600**
📖 Death's Head Revisited **A:** Bryan Hitch **W:** Simon Furman
2 ❑ Jan 1989 Cover: 1.75 **NM** value: **Cover or less**
Circ: CapCity orders: **7,700**
3 ❑ Feb 1989 Cover: 1.75 **NM** value: **Cover or less**
Circ: CapCity orders: **6,300**
4 ❑ Mar 1989 Cover: 1.75 **NM** value: **Cover or less**
Circ: CapCity orders: **5,450**
5 ❑ Apr 1989 Cover: 1.75 **NM** value: **Cover or less**
Circ: CapCity orders: **4,750**
6 ❑ May 1989 Cover: 1.75 **NM** value: **Cover or less**
Circ: CapCity orders: **4,400**
7 ❑ Jun 1989 Cover: 1.75 **NM** value: **Cover or less**
Circ: CapCity orders: **4,000**
8 ❑ Jul 1989 Cover: 1.75 **NM** value: **Cover or less**
Circ: CapCity orders: **4,400**
📖 Death's Head Revisited **A:** Bryan Hitch **W:** Simon Furman ★ Appearance of Doctor Who.
9 ❑ Aug 1989 Cover: 1.75 **NM** value: **Cover or less**
Circ: CapCity orders: **6,050**
W: Simon Furman ★ Appearance of Fantastic 4.
10 ❑ Sep 1989 Cover: 1.75 **NM** value: **Cover or less**
Circ: CapCity orders: **5,500**
final issue. **W:** Simon Furman ★ Appearance of Iron Man of 2020.

DEATH'S-HEAD (CRYSTAL) — Crystal

1 ❑ Cover: 1.95 **NM** value: **Cover or less**

DEATH'S HEAD II & THE ORIGIN OF DIE-CUT — Marvel

1 ❑ Aug 1993 Cover: 2.95 **NM** value: **Cover or less**
Circ: CapCity orders: **14,550**
foil cover. 📖 The First Cut **A:** John Royle **W:** Glenn Dakin ★ Origin of Die Cut.
2 ❑ Sep 1993 Cover: 1.75 **NM** value: **Cover or less**
Circ: CapCity orders: **10,000**
📖 Death and Perfection **A:** John Royle **W:** Glenn Dakin ★ Origin of Die Cut.

DEATH'S HEAD II GOLD — Marvel

1 ❑ Cover: 3.95 **NM** value: **Cover or less**
Circ: CapCity orders: **18,900**
foil cover.

CGC-graded: Multiply prices above by **33 for 9.9 M • 16 for 9.8 NM/M • 7 for 9.6 NM+ • 5 for 9.4 NM • 2.5 for 9.2 NM- • 1.5 for 9.0 VF/NM**

DEATH'S HEAD II (VOL. 1) Marvel

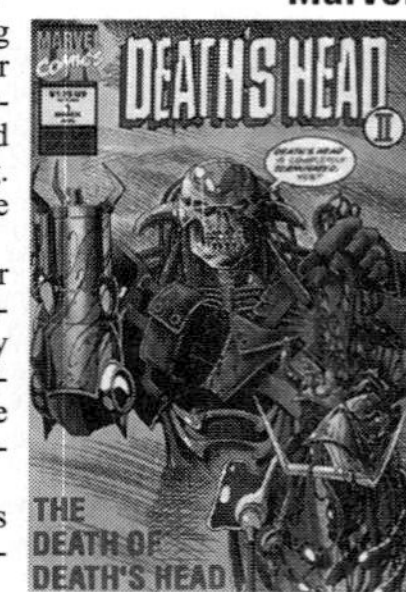

In the year 2020, the remaining heroes of Earth will fight a monster the likes of which they've never before faced. Its name is Charnel, and its purpose is to kill everything. Nothing can stand against it and live long.

Eventually the aging Doctor Strange, Daredevil, Punisher, Wolverine, and others are joined by Death's Head II, a schizophrenic cyborg killing machine in a desperate last stand against the ultimate enemy.

The Death's Head family got its start in the United Kingdom-published Marvel comics.

1 ❑ Mar 1992 Cover: 1.75 **NM** value: **2.50**
Circ: CapCity orders: **37,300**
🕮 The Wild Hunt, Part 1 **A:** Liam Sharp **W:** Dan Abnett ★ 1st Appearance of Death's Head II. ★ Death of Death's Head.

1-2 ❑ Mar 1992 Cover: 1.75 **NM** value: **Cover or less**

2 ❑ Apr 1992 Cover: 1.75 **NM** value: **2.00**
Circ: CapCity orders: **22,500**
🕮 Reed Richards Dies Tonight **A:** Liam Sharp **W:** Dan Abnett

2-2 ❑ Apr 1992 Cover: 1.75 **NM** value: **Cover or less**

3 ❑ May 1992 Cover: 1.75 **NM** value: **2.00**
Circ: CapCity orders: **23,500**
★ 1st Appearance of Tuck.

4 ❑ Jun 1992 Cover: 1.75 **NM** value: **2.00**
Circ: CapCity orders: **39,900**
★ Appearance of Wolverine. ★ Appearance of Captain America.

DEATH'S HEAD II (VOL. 2) Marvel

1 ❑ Dec 1992 Cover: 1.75 **NM** value: **2.00**
Circ: CapCity orders: **105,900**
gatefold cover. 🕮 The Lotus FX, Part 1 **A:** Liam Sharp; Bryan Hitch; Cam Smith; Andy Lanning **W:** Dan Abnett ★ Appearance of X-Men.

2 ❑ Jan 1993 Cover: 1.75 **NM** value: **2.00**
Circ: CapCity orders: **62,400**
🕮 The Lotus FX, Part 2 **A:** Liam Sharp **W:** Dan Abnett ★ Appearance of X-Men.

3 ❑ Feb 1993 Cover: 1.75 **NM** value: **2.00**
Circ: CapCity orders: **52,900**
🕮 The Lotus FX, Part 3 **A:** Liam Sharp **W:** Dan Abnett ★ Appearance of X-Men.

4 ❑ Mar 1993 Cover: 1.75 **NM** value: **2.00**
Circ: CapCity orders: **52,500**
★ Appearance of X-Men.

5 ❑ Apr 1993 Cover: 1.75 **NM** value: **Cover or less**
Circ: CapCity orders: **45,200**

6 ❑ May 1993 Cover: 1.95 **NM** value: **Cover or less**
Circ: CapCity orders: **39,200**
🕮 Borgs 'n the Hood! **A:** Simon Colby **W:** Dan Abnett

7 ❑ Jun 1993 Cover: 1.95 **NM** value: **Cover or less**
Circ: CapCity orders: **35,000**

8 ❑ Jul 1993 Cover: 1.95 **NM** value: **Cover or less**
Circ: CapCity orders: **28,300**

9 ❑ Aug 1993 Cover: 1.95 **NM** value: **Cover or less**
Circ: CapCity orders: **24,700**

10 ❑ Sep 1993 Cover: 1.95 **NM** value: **Cover or less**
Circ: CapCity orders: **19,900**

11 ❑ Oct 1993 Cover: 1.95 **NM** value: **Cover or less**
Circ: CapCity orders: **16,700**
A: Simon Coleby **W:** Dan Abnett ★ 1st Appearance of Death's Head III. ★ Appearance of Doctor Necker, Charnel.

12 ❑ Nov 1993 Cover: 1.95 **NM** value: **Cover or less**
Circ: CapCity orders: **14,300**

13 ❑ Dec 1993 Cover: 1.95 **NM** value: **Cover or less**
Circ: CapCity orders: **12,200**

14 ❑ Jan 1994 Cover: 2.95 **NM** value: **Cover or less**
Circ: CapCity orders: **11,700**
foil cover. • Prelude to Death's Head Gold #1

15 ❑ Feb 1994 Cover: 1.95 **NM** value: **Cover or less**
Circ: CapCity orders: **9,250**

16 ❑ Mar 1994 Cover: 1.95 **NM** value: **Cover or less**
Circ: CapCity orders: **7,450**
final issue.

DEATH SHRIKE Brainstorm

Knighthawk Securities' famous aerie in beautiful Oklahoma City houses their paranormal task force division of super-heroes brought together by Albrecht Cardinal. Robert Overstreet was only one of many people Cardinal dreamed of finding. Overstreet enrolled in the Knighthawk Training Academy, where he was taught to use his psychokinetic abilities to become Death Shrike. Named after one of the most deadly of birds who hunts and kills for pleasure, Shrike must come to terms with the death of his father, the mistrust of his team mates, and Cardinal's own prophecy of betrayal and the death of his glorious achievement.

1 ❑ Jul 1993, b&w Cover: 2.95 **NM** value: **Cover or less**
🕮 Man of Sorrow **A:** Allan Jacobson **W:** Allan Jacobson

DEATHSNAKE, THE Eros

1 ❑ 1994 Cover: 2.95 **NM** value: **Cover or less**
A: John Blackburn **W:** John Blackburn

2 ❑ Oct 1994 Cover: 2.95 **NM** value: **Cover or less**
A: John Blackburn **W:** John Blackburn

DEATHSTROKE THE TERMINATOR DC

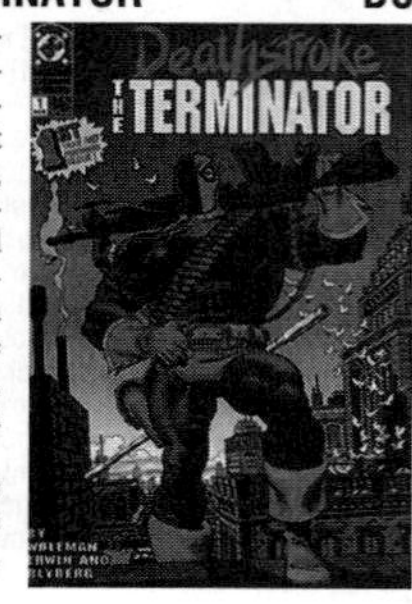

Trained as a soldier, Slade Wilson volunteered to imbibe an experimental formula designed to help resist enemy truth serums. That formula, a derivative of A.C.T.H., sent Slade into a screaming rampage, snapping steel bonds that held him into place. He was soon sedated, however, and lapsed into a coma that lasted months. When he awoke again, he had the powers, agility, and healing factor that make him Deathstroke the Terminator.

First appearing in the pages of the New Teen Titans, Deathstroke eventually crossed over into this, his first solo series.

0 ❑ Oct 1994 Cover: 1.95 **NM** value: **2.00**
Circ: CapCity orders: **13,300**
• Title changes to Deathstroke the Hunted

1 ❑ Aug 1991 Cover: 1.75 **NM** value: **3.00**
Circ: CapCity orders: **47,800 • CGC:** 1 graded, best 9.2
🕮 Full Cycle, Part 1 **A:** Steve Erwin **W:** Marv Wolfman ★ Origin of Deathstroke the Terminator.

1-2 ❑ Cover: 1.75 **NM** value: **Cover or less**

2 ❑ Sep 1991 Cover: 1.75 **NM** value: **2.00**
Circ: CapCity orders: **30,950**
🕮 Full Cycle, Part 2

3 ❑ Oct 1991 Cover: 1.75 **NM** value: **2.00**
Circ: CapCity orders: **34,300**
🕮 Full Cycle, Part 3

4 ❑ Nov 1991 Cover: 1.75 **NM** value: **2.00**
Circ: CapCity orders: **36,050**
🕮 Full Cycle, Part 4 ★ Versus Ravager.

5 ❑ Dec 1991 Cover: 1.75 **NM** value: **2.00**
Circ: CapCity orders: **35,850**

6 ❑ Jan 1992 Cover: 1.75 **NM** value: **2.00**
Circ: CapCity orders: **34,000**
🕮 City of Assassins, Part 1

7 ❑ Feb 1992 Cover: 1.75 **NM** value: **2.00**
Circ: CapCity orders: **32,300**
🕮 City of Assassins, Part 2 • Batman

8 ❑ Mar 1992 Cover: 1.75 **NM** value: **2.00**
Circ: CapCity orders: **28,700**
🕮 City of Assassins, Part 3 • Batman

9 ❑ Apr 1992 Cover: 1.75 **NM** value: **2.00**
Circ: CapCity orders: **25,500**
🕮 City of Assassins, Part 4 • Batman ★ 1st Appearance of Vigilante III (Pat Trayce).

10 ❑ Jun 1992 Cover: 1.75 **NM** value: **2.00**
Circ: CapCity orders: **23,400**
🕮 Guns and Roses, Part 1 **A:** Art Nichols **W:** Marv Wolfman

11 ❑ Jun 1992 Cover: 1.75 **NM** value: **2.00**
Circ: CapCity orders: **24,650**
🕮 Guns and Roses, Part 2 • Vigilante

12 ❑ Jul 1992 Cover: 1.75 **NM** value: **2.00**
Circ: CapCity orders: **25,450**

13 ❑ Aug 1992 Cover: 1.75 **NM** value: **2.00**
Circ: CapCity orders: **28,400**

14 ❑ Sep 1992 Cover: 1.75 **NM** value: **2.00**
🕮 Total Chaos, Part 1

15 ❑ Oct 1992 Cover: 1.75 **NM** value: **2.00**
Circ: CapCity orders: **24,000**
🕮 Total Chaos, Part 4

16 ❑ Nov 1992 Cover: 1.75 **NM** value: **2.00**
Circ: CapCity orders: **23,450**
🕮 Total Chaos, Part 7 ★ Death of Deathstroke the Terminator.

17 ❑ Dec 1992 Cover: 1.75 **NM** value: **2.00**
Circ: CapCity orders: **22,600**
🕮 Titans Sell-Out, Part 2 • Deathstroke the Terminator revived

18 ❑ Jan 1993 Cover: 1.75 **NM** value: **2.00**
Circ: CapCity orders: **20,150**

19 ❑ Feb 1993 Cover: 1.75 **NM** value: **2.00**
Circ: CapCity orders: **20,500**
• Quarac destroyed

20 ❑ Mar 1993 Cover: 1.75 **NM** value: **Cover or less**
Circ: CapCity orders: **19,150**

21 ❑ Apr 1993 Cover: 1.75 **NM** value: **Cover or less**
Circ: CapCity orders: **19,400**

22 ❑ May 1993 Cover: 1.75 **NM** value: **Cover or less**
Circ: CapCity orders: **18,150**

23 ❑ May 1993 Cover: 1.75 **NM** value: **Cover or less**
Circ: CapCity orders: **18,150**

24 ❑ Jun 1993 Cover: 1.75 **NM** value: **Cover or less**
Circ: CapCity orders: **17,000**

25 ❑ Jun 1993 Cover: 1.75 **NM** value: **Cover or less**
Circ: CapCity orders: **16,900**

26 ❑ Jul 1993 Cover: 1.75 **NM** value: **Cover or less**
Circ: CapCity orders: **15,650**

27 ❑ Aug 1993 Cover: 1.75 **NM** value: **Cover or less**
Circ: CapCity orders: **14,400**
🕮 World Tour, Part 1

28 ❑ Sep 1993 Cover: 1.75 **NM** value: **Cover or less**
Circ: CapCity orders: **12,850**
🕮 World Tour, Part 2

29 ❑ Oct 1993 Cover: 1.75 **NM** value: **Cover or less**
Circ: CapCity orders: **12,150**
🕮 World Tour, Part 3

30 ❑ Nov 1993 Cover: 1.75 **NM** value: **Cover or less**
Circ: CapCity orders: **11,300**
🕮 World Tour, Part 4

31 ❑ Dec 1993 Cover: 1.75 **NM** value: **Cover or less**
Circ: CapCity orders: **10,450**
🕮 World Tour, Part 5

32 ❑ Jan 1994 Cover: 1.75 **NM** value: **Cover or less**
Circ: CapCity orders: **9,850**
🕮 World Tour, Part 6

33 ❑ Feb 1994 Cover: 1.75 **NM** value: **Cover or less**
Circ: CapCity orders: **9,000**
🕮 World Tour, Part 7

34 ❑ Mar 1994 Cover: 1.75 **NM** value: **Cover or less**
Circ: CapCity orders: **8,200**
🕮 World Tour, Part 8

35 ❑ Apr 1994 Cover: 1.75 **NM** value: **Cover or less**
Circ: CapCity orders: **7,700**

36 ❑ May 1994 Cover: 1.75 **NM** value: **Cover or less**
Circ: CapCity orders: **7,350**

37 ❑ Jun 1994 Cover: 1.75 **NM** value: **Cover or less**
Circ: CapCity orders: **7,150**
🕮 Sins of the Father! **A:** Jaxon Renick **W:** Marv Wolfman

38 ❑ Jul 1994 Cover: 1.95 **NM** value: **Cover or less**
Circ: CapCity orders: **7,050**
★ Appearance of Vigilante.

39 ❑ Aug 1994 Cover: 1.95 **NM** value: **Cover or less**
Circ: CapCity orders: **7,100**
• Title becomes "Deathstroke the Hunted"

40 ❑ Sep 1994 Cover: 1.95 **NM** value: **Cover or less**
Circ: CapCity orders: **6,750**
🕮 The Hunted, Part 1

41 ❑ Nov 1994 Cover: 1.95 **NM** value: **Cover or less**
Circ: CapCity orders: **7,150**
🕮 The Hunted, Part 2

42 ❑ Dec 1994 Cover: 1.95 **NM** value: **Cover or less**
Circ: CapCity orders: **7,250**
🕮 The Hunted, Part 3

43 ❑ Jan 1995 Cover: 1.95 **NM** value: **Cover or less**
Circ: CapCity orders: **7,100**
🕮 The Hunted, Part 4 **A:** Sergio Cariello **W:** Marv Wolfman

44 ❑ Feb 1995 Cover: 1.95 **NM** value: **Cover or less**
Circ: CapCity orders: **6,600**
🕮 The Hunted, Part 5

45 ❑ Mar 1995 Cover: 1.95 **NM** value: **Cover or less**
Circ: CapCity orders: **6,225**
🕮 The Hunted, Part 6

46 ❑ Apr 1995 Cover: 1.95 **NM** value: **Cover or less**
Circ: CapCity orders: **5,725**

47 ❑ May 1995 Cover: 1.95 **NM** value: **Cover or less**
Circ: CapCity orders: **5,625**

48 ❑ Jun 1995 Cover: 2.25 **NM** value: **Cover or less**
Circ: CapCity orders: **6,525**

49 ❑ Jul 1995 Cover: 2.25 **NM** value: **Cover or less**
Circ: CapCity orders: **6,450**

50 ❑ Aug 1995 Cover: 3.50 **NM** value: **Cover or less**
Circ: CapCity orders: **6,900**
• Giant-size. • Title changes to Deathstroke

51 ❑ Sep 1995 Cover: 2.25 **NM** value: **Cover or less**
Circ: CapCity orders: **5,825**

52 ❑ Oct 1995 Cover: 2.25 **NM** value: **Cover or less**
Circ: CapCity orders: **4,950**
★ Appearance of Hawkman.

53 ❑ Nov 1995 Cover: 2.25 **NM** value: **Cover or less**

54 ❑ Dec 1995 Cover: 2.25 **NM** value: **Cover or less**

55 ❑ Jan 1996 Cover: 2.25 **NM** value: **Cover or less**
🕮 Night of the Karrion, Part 1

56 ❑ Feb 1996 Cover: 2.25 **NM** value: **Cover or less**
🕮 Night of the Karrion!, Part 2 **A:** Mike Huddleston **W:** Marv Wolfman

57 ❑ Mar 1996 Cover: 2.25 **NM** value: **Cover or less**
🕮 Night of the Karrion, Part 3 **A:** Mike Huddleston **W:** Marv Wolfman

58 ❑ Apr 1996 Cover: 2.25 **NM** value: **Cover or less**
🕮 Bad Blood **A:** Tom Grindberg; Alan Caldwell **W:** Marv Wolfman ★ Versus Joker.

59 ❑ May 1996 Cover: 2.25 **NM** value: **Cover or less**

60 ❑ Jun 1996 Cover: 2.25 **NM** value: **Cover or less**
final issue.

Anl 1 ❑ ca. 1992 Cover: 3.50 **NM** value: **Cover or less**
Circ: CapCity orders: **26,900**
🕮 Eclipso: The Darkness Within, Part 13 • Eclipso;1992 Annual **A:** Phil Jimenez; Gabriel Morrissette **W:** David Cody Weiss; Marv Wolfman ★ Appearance of Vigilante.

Anl 2 ❑ ca. 1993 Cover: 3.50 **NM** value: **Cover or less**
Circ: CapCity orders: **18,250**
🕮 Bloodlines • Bloodlines ★ 1st Appearance of Gunfire.

Anl 3 ❑ ca. 1994 Cover: 3.95 **NM** value: **Cover or less**
Circ: CapCity orders: **7,800**
• Elseworlds

Anl 4 ❑ 1995 Cover: 3.95 **NM** value: **Cover or less**
Circ: CapCity orders: **6,350**
🕮 The Web of Eternal Vows

DEATH TALKS ABOUT LIFE DC / Vertigo

This free comic book was originally published as a special six-page insert in DC's various Vertigo books. It starred Sandman's Death — portrayed here as a young woman — with a very serious message for today's youth.

Death, along with a cameo by John Constantine (Hellblazer), gave explicit instructions about avoiding AIDS. Included is a frank discussion of condoms, safe sex, and other topics that, as the cover warned, "some people might find offensive." To these people, Death warns, "Just don't read it. After all, the most it could do is save your life."

1 ❑ **NM** value: **2.00**
• **CGC:** 1 graded, best 9.2
A: Dave McKean **W:** Neil Gaiman

Other grades: Multiply prices above by **1.5 for Mint • 2/3 for Very Fine • 1/3 for Fine • 1/5 for Very Good • 1/8 for Good**

DEATH: THE HIGH COST OF LIVING DC / Vertigo

1 ❑ Mar 1993 Cover: 1.95 **NM** value: **4.00**
Circ: CapCity orders: **72,550** • **CGC:** 6 graded, best 9.8
A: Chris Bachalo **W:** Neil Gaiman

1/PL❑ **NM** value: **9.00**
• **CGC:** 3 graded, best 9.4
• Platinum edition. **A:** Chris Bachalo **W:** Neil Gaiman

2 ❑ Apr 1993 Cover: 1.95 **NM** value: **3.50**
Circ: CapCity orders: **50,850**
A: Chris Bachalo **W:** Neil Gaiman

3 ❑ May 1993 Cover: 1.95 **NM** value: **3.00**
Circ: CapCity orders: **47,750**
• regular edition. **A:** Chris Bachalo **W:** Neil Gaiman

3/A ❑ May 1993 Cover: 1.95 **NM** value: **3.00**
• with error

Bk 1❑ Cover: 12.95 **NM** value: **Cover or less**
Circ: CapCity orders: **4,050**
• Trade Paperback. • Collects Death: The High Cost of Living #1-3 **A:** Chris Bachalo **W:** Neil Gaiman

Bk 1/HC❑ Cover: 19.95 **NM** value: **Cover or less**
Circ: CapCity orders: **4,500**
• Hardcover edition. • Collects Death: The High Cost of Living #1-3 **A:** Chris Bachalo **W:** Neil Gaiman

DEATH: THE TIME OF YOUR LIFE DC / Vertigo

1 ❑ Apr 1996 Cover: 2.95 **NM** value: **4.00**
• **CGC:** 1 graded, best 8.5
📖 Things You Just Do When You're Bored **A:** Chris Bachalo **W:** Neil Gaiman

2 ❑ May 1996 Cover: 2.95 **NM** value: **3.50**
📖 Imaginary Solutions **A:** Chris Bachalo **W:** Neil Gaiman

3 ❑ Jun 1996 Cover: 2.95 **NM** value: **3.50**
📖 The Time Of Your Life **A:** Chris Bachalo **W:** Neil Gaiman

Bk 1❑ Cover: 12.95 **NM** value: **Cover or less**
• collects mini-series and material from Vertigo card set and A Death Gallery;Collects Death: The Time of Your Life #1-3 **A:** Chris Bachalo **W:** Neil Gaiman

Bk 1/HC❑ Cover: 19.95 **NM** value: **Cover or less**
• Hardcover edition. • Collects Death: The High Cost of Living #1-3 **A:** Chris Bachalo **W:** Neil Gaiman

DEATH VALLEY Charlton

1 ❑ Oct 1953 Cover: 0.10 **NM** value: **50.00**
📖 Inferno; Deadly Double Cross; Long Winded Killer; Trail of Vengeance

2 ❑ Dec 1954 Cover: 0.10 **NM** value: **20.00**
📖 Fools Gold; Bloody Sheriff; Baby-Faced Killer

3 ❑ Feb 1954 Cover: 0.10 **NM** value: **20.00**
4 ❑ Apr 1954 Cover: 0.10 **NM** value: **20.00**
5 ❑ Jun 1954 Cover: 0.10 **NM** value: **20.00**
6 ❑ Aug 1954 Cover: 0.10 **NM** value: **20.00**
7 ❑ Jun 1955 Cover: 0.10 **NM** value: **20.00**
8 ❑ Aug 1955 Cover: 0.10 **NM** value: **20.00**
9 ❑ Oct 1955 Cover: 0.10 **NM** value: **20.00**
10 ❑ Dec 1955 Cover: 0.10 **NM** value: **20.00**
11 ❑ Feb 1956 Cover: 0.10 **NM** value: **20.00**
12 ❑ Apr 1956 Cover: 0.10 **NM** value: **20.00**
13 ❑ Jun 1956 Cover: 0.10 **NM** value: **20.00**
14 ❑ Aug 1956 Cover: 0.10 **NM** value: **20.00**

DEATH WARMED OVER Cat-Head

All issues are adults only.

1 ❑ b&w Cover: 2.75 **NM** value: **Cover or less**

DEATHWATCH Harrier

1 ❑ Jul 1987 Cover: 1.95 **NM** value: **Cover or less**
📖 Deathbringer; A Dark Summer; Halloween; Death's Watch; Comes a Time **A:** Art Wetherell **W:** Art Wetherell

DEATHWIND Artline

1 ❑ Cover: 2.50 **NM** value: **Cover or less**
★ 1st Appearance of Deathwind.

DEATHWISH Milestone / DC

1 ❑ Dec 1994 Cover: 2.50 **NM** value: **Cover or less**
Circ: CapCity orders: **9,150**
📖 This Ain't No Cryin' Game **A:** J.H. Williams III **W:** Adam Blaustein; Yves Fezzani

2 ❑ Jan 1995 Cover: 2.50 **NM** value: **Cover or less**
Circ: CapCity orders: **5,500**
A: J.H. Williams III **W:** Adam Blaustein; Yves Fezzani

3 ❑ Feb 1995 Cover: 2.50 **NM** value: **Cover or less**
Circ: CapCity orders: **4,275**
A: J.H. Williams III **W:** Adam Blaustein; Yves Fezzani

4 ❑ Mar 1995 Cover: 2.50 **NM** value: **Cover or less**
Circ: CapCity orders: **3,700**
📖 Silence of the Rahm **A:** J.H. Williams III **W:** Adam Blaustein; Yves Fezzani

To find prices for other grades for comic books not graded by CGC, multiply the above prices by:

Mint: 150%	VF-: 55%	VG-: 17%
NM/M:125%	F/VF: 48%	G+: 14%
NM+: 110%	F+: 40%	**Good: 12.5%**
NM-: 90%	**Fine: 33.3%**	G-: 11%
VF/NM: 83%	F-: 30%	FR/G: 10%
VF+: 75%	VG/F: 25%	**Fair: 8%**
Very Fine: 66.6%	VG+: 23%	**Poor: 2%**
	Very Good: 20%	

DEATHWORLD Adventure

Imagine a planet where every living creature is trying to kill you. A planet with twice Earth's gravity where the climate goes from arctic to tropical in a single day and the beaches offer 30-foot tides and volcanic activity. A planet where plants and animals are armor-plated, poisonous, and fang-mouthed. This is the planet Pyrrus, also known as Deathworld.

Now the man who can't lose, a psionic gambler named Jason dinAlt, has taken the ultimate roll of the dice. He has traveled to Pyrrus to experience Deathworld firsthand. If he can survive the trip from the ship to the adaptation clinic, he'll be gambling with his life every minute of the day.

This mini-series is adapted from the novel by Harry Harrison.

1 ❑ Nov 1990, b&w Cover: 2.50 **NM** value: **Cover or less**
A: Marc Campos **W:** John Holland
2 ❑ Dec 1990, b&w Cover: 2.50 **NM** value: **Cover or less**
A: Marc Campos **W:** John Holland
3 ❑ Jan 1991, b&w Cover: 2.50 **NM** value: **Cover or less**
A: Marc Campos **W:** John Holland
4 ❑ Feb 1991, b&w Cover: 2.50 **NM** value: **Cover or less**
A: Marc Campos **W:** John Holland
Bk 1❑ Cover: 9.95 **NM** value: **Cover or less**

DEATHWORLD BOOK II Adventure

1 ❑ Apr 1991, b&w Cover: 2.50 **NM** value: **Cover or less**
A: Marc Campos **W:** John Holland
2 ❑ May 1991, b&w Cover: 2.50 **NM** value: **Cover or less**
A: Marc Campos **W:** John Holland
3 ❑ Jun 1991, b&w Cover: 2.50 **NM** value: **Cover or less**
A: Marc Campos **W:** John Holland
4 ❑ Jul 1991, b&w Cover: 2.50 **NM** value: **Cover or less**
A: Marc Campos **W:** John Holland

DEATHWORLD BOOK III Adventure

1 ❑ Aug 1991, b&w Cover: 2.50 **NM** value: **Cover or less**
A: Marc Campos **W:** John Holland
2 ❑ Sep 1991, b&w Cover: 2.50 **NM** value: **Cover or less**
A: Marc Campos **W:** John Holland
3 ❑ Nov 1991, b&w Cover: 2.50 **NM** value: **Cover or less**
A: Marc Campos **W:** John Holland
4 ❑ Dec 1991, b&w Cover: 2.50 **NM** value: **Cover or less**
A: Marc Campos **W:** John Holland

DEATH WRECK Marvel

1 ❑ Jan 1994 Cover: 1.95 **NM** value: **Cover or less**
Circ: CapCity orders: **11,100**
A: Stewart Johnson **W:** Craig Houston ★ Origin of Death-Wreck. ★ 1st Appearance of Death-Wreck.
2 ❑ Feb 1994 Cover: 1.95 **NM** value: **Cover or less**
Circ: CapCity orders: **4,550**
3 ❑ Mar 1994 Cover: 1.95 **NM** value: **Cover or less**
Circ: CapCity orders: **3,150**
4 ❑ Apr 1994 Cover: 1.95 **NM** value: **Cover or less**
Circ: CapCity orders: **3,200**
6 ❑ Jun 1994 Cover: 1.95 **NM** value: **Cover or less**
7 ❑ Jul 1994 Cover: 1.95 **NM** value: **Cover or less**

DEBBIE DEAN, CAREER GIRL Civil Service Publications

1 ❑ Apr 1945 Cover: 0.10 **NM** value: **60.00**
• **CGC:** 1 graded, best 9.4

DEBBIE DOES COMICS Aircel

All issues are adults only.

1 ❑ b&w Cover: 2.95 **NM** value: **Cover or less**

DEBBIE DOES DALLAS Aircel

All issues are adults only.

1 ❑ Mar 1991 Cover: 2.50 **NM** value: **Cover or less**
1/3D❑ Cover: 3.95 **NM** value: **Cover or less**
1-2 ❑ Cover: 2.50 **NM** value: **Cover or less**
2 ❑ Apr 1991 Cover: 2.50 **NM** value: **Cover or less**
3 ❑ May 1991 Cover: 2.50 **NM** value: **Cover or less**
4 ❑ Jun 1991 Cover: 2.50 **NM** value: **Cover or less**
5 ❑ Jul 1991 Cover: 2.50 **NM** value: **Cover or less**
6 ❑ 1991 Cover: 2.50 **NM** value: **Cover or less**
7 ❑ Oct 1991 Cover: 2.50 **NM** value: **Cover or less**
8 ❑ Nov 1991 Cover: 2.50 **NM** value: **Cover or less**
9 ❑ Dec 1991 Cover: 2.95 **NM** value: **Cover or less**
10 ❑ 1992 Cover: 2.95 **NM** value: **Cover or less**
11 ❑ 1992 Cover: 2.95 **NM** value: **Cover or less**
12 ❑ 1992 Cover: 2.95 **NM** value: **Cover or less**
13 ❑ 1992 Cover: 2.95 **NM** value: **Cover or less**
14 ❑ 1992 Cover: 2.95 **NM** value: **Cover or less**
15 ❑ Cover: 2.95 **NM** value: **Cover or less**
16 ❑ Cover: 2.95 **NM** value: **Cover or less**
17 ❑ Cover: 2.95 **NM** value: **Cover or less**
18 ❑ Cover: 2.95 **NM** value: **Cover or less**
Bk 1❑ Cover: 14.95 **NM** value: **Cover or less**

DEBBI'S DATES DC

1 ❑ May 1969 Cover: 0.12 **NM** value: **30.00**
• **CGC:** 2 graded, best 9.2
2 ❑ Jul 1969 Cover: 0.15 **NM** value: **18.00**
3 ❑ Sep 1969 Cover: 0.15 **NM** value: **18.00**
4 ❑ Nov 1969 Cover: 0.15 **NM** value: **18.00**
5 ❑ Jan 1970 Cover: 0.15 **NM** value: **18.00**
6 ❑ Mar 1970 Cover: 0.15 **NM** value: **30.00**
7 ❑ May 1970 Cover: 0.15 **NM** value: **18.00**
8 ❑ Jul 1970 Cover: 0.15 **NM** value: **18.00**
9 ❑ Sep 1970 Cover: 0.15 **NM** value: **18.00**
10 ❑ Nov 1970 Cover: 0.15 **NM** value: **18.00**
11 ❑ Jan 1971 Cover: 0.15 **NM** value: **18.00**

DECADE OF DARK HORSE, A Dark Horse

Ten short years after starting out with Dark Horse Presents and Boris the Bear, Dark Horse Comics had grown into one of the most influential comic-book publishers in the country. Building on the concept of creator-owned stories, Dark Horse had attracted some of the best writers and artists in the business. And with the addition of series based on licensed characters from popular movies such as Indiana Jones, Star Wars, and The Terminator, the small company from Oregon had become a major player.

This four-issue series is an unabashed celebration of Dark Horse's first decade, but it is definitely not a reprint title. These all-new stories, from creators like Frank Miller, Matt Wagner, and others, showcase titles such as Grendel, Predator, Aliens, and Sin City.

1 ❑ Jul 1996, b&w and colorCover: 2.95 **NM** value: **Cover or less**
📖 Sin City: Daddy's Little Girl; Predator: 1718; Grendel: The Devil's Week • Sin City, Predator, Grendel stories **A:** Matt Wagner; Frank Miller; Igor Kordey **W:** Matt Wagner; Frank Miller; Henry Gilroy

2 ❑ Aug 1996 Cover: 2.95 **NM** value: **Cover or less**
📖 Star Wars: This Crumb For Hire; Ghost: Sweet Things; Trekker: Mercy Killing • Star Wars, Ghost, Trekker stories **A:** Allen Nunis; Scott Benefiel; Ron Randall **W:** Ron Randall; Eric Luke; Ryder Windham

3 ❑ Sep 1996, b&w and colorCover: 2.95 **NM** value: **Cover or less**
Circ: Diamd. preorders: **18,293**
📖 Aliens: Lucky; Nexus: All and Sundra; Outlanders: The Kahm Family at Home; The Mask: Night of the Return of the Living Ipkiss...Kinda • Aliens, Outlanders, Nexus, The Mask stories **A:** Doug Mahnke; Steve Rude; Johji Manabe; Mark A. Nelson **W:** Johji Manabe; Mark Verheiden; Mike Baron; John Arcudi

4 ❑ Oct 1996 Cover: 2.95 **NM** value: **Cover or less**
Circ: Diamd. preorders: **17,258**
📖 Concrete: World Beneath the Skin; Black Cross; Exon Depot; Godzilla: The Origin of a Species • b&w and color, Concrete, Black Cross, Exon Depot, Godzilla stories, final issue **A:** Scott Kolins; Chris Warner; Masamune Shirow; Paul Chadwick **W:** Chris Warner; Masamune Shirow; Paul Chadwick; Randy Stradley ★ Origin of Godzilla.

Bk 1❑ Apr 1997 Cover: 12.95 **NM** value: **Cover or less**
• Decade;collects stories from A Decade of Dark Horse

DECAPITATOR (RANDY BOWEN'S...) Dark Horse

1 ❑ Jun 1998 Cover: 2.95 **NM** value: **Cover or less**
A: Doug Mahnke; Gary Erskine; Stan Manoukian; John Stokes; Robert McCallum; Vince Roucher **W:** Norm DePlume; Randy Bowen
2 ❑ Jul 1998 Cover: 2.95 **NM** value: **Cover or less**
W: Norm DePlume; Randy Bowen
3 ❑ Aug 1998 Cover: 2.95 **NM** value: **Cover or less**
Circ: Diamd. preorders: **6,534**
W: Norm DePlume; Randy Bowen
4 ❑ Sep 1998 Cover: 2.95 **NM** value: **Cover or less**
Circ: Diamd. preorders: **5,903**
W: Norm DePlume; Randy Bowen

DECEPTION, THE Image

1 ❑ ca. 1999 Cover: 2.95 **NM** value: **Cover or less**
Circ: Diamd. preorders: **2,796**
📖 Vanishing Act **A:** Jeff Parker **W:** Bill Spangler
2 ❑ ca. 1999 Cover: 2.95 **NM** value: **Cover or less**
Circ: Diamd. preorders: **1,724**
📖 Magic Words **A:** Jeff Parker **W:** Bill Spangler
3 ❑ ca. 1999 Cover: 2.95 **NM** value: **Cover or less**
Circ: Diamd. preorders: **1,895**
📖 Quicker than the Eye **A:** Jeff Parker **W:** Bill Spangler

DECORATOR, THE Fantagraphics / Eros

All issues are adults only.

1 ❑ b&w Cover: 2.50 **NM** value: **Cover or less**

DECOY Penny-Farthing Press

1 ❑ Mar 1999 Cover: 2.75 **NM** value: **Cover or less**
Circ: Diamd. preorders: **1,909**
A: Courtney Huddleston **W:** Courtney Huddleston; Eli Williams
1/Aut❑Mar 1999 Cover: 3.25 **NM** value: **Cover or less**
• Auographed edition. **A:** Courtney Huddleston **W:** Courtney Huddleston; Eli Williams
2 ❑ Apr 1999 Cover: 2.75 **NM** value: **Cover or less**
A: Courtney Huddleston **W:** Courtney Huddleston; Eli Williams
3 ❑ May 1999 Cover: 2.75 **NM** value: **Cover or less**
A: Courtney Huddleston **W:** Courtney Huddleston; Eli Williams
4 ❑ Jun 1999 Cover: 2.75 **NM** value: **Cover or less**
A: Courtney Huddleston **W:** Courtney Huddleston; Eli Williams

DEE DEE Fantagraphics/Eros

All issues are adults only.

1 ❑ Jul 1996, b&w Cover: 2.95 **NM** value: **Cover or less**

For up-to-the-week CGC ratios, consult the current issue of **Comics Buyer's Guide**.

CGC-graded: Multiply prices above by **33 for 9.9 M** • **16 for 9.8 NM/M** • **7 for 9.6 NM+** • **5 for 9.4 NM** • **2.5 for 9.2 NM-** • **1.5 for 9.0 VF/NM**

DEEP, THE — Marvel

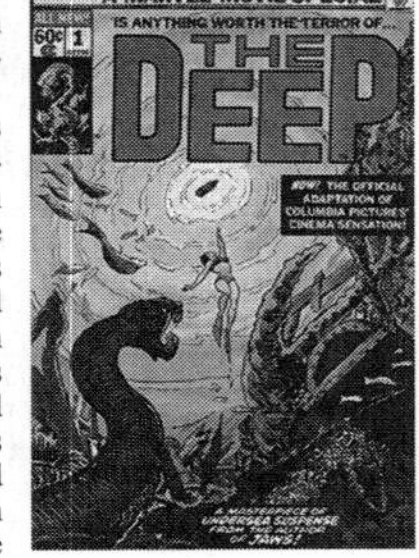

This Marvel Movie Special adapts the Columbia Pictures film based on Peter Benchley's action-packed novel.

During 1943, the Goliath was transporting ammunition and medical supplies when she broke up on a reef and went to the bottom of the sea off Saint David's Island. Years later, in 1977, David Sanders and Gail Berke are exploring the sunken hull when they discover mysterious ampules of some unknown drug and a strange medallion. Soon, others are chasing them, and David and Gail are in over their heads with deadly drug runners and treasure hunters. They discover the fact that "the sea is a tease ... she loves to fool you" — but sometimes she gives up her secrets to those who never give up.

1 ❑ Nov 1977 Cover: 0.60 **NM** value: **1.50**
• **CGC:** 1 graded, best 9.4
A: Carmine Infantino **W:** Doug Moench

DEEP 3D COMIX — Kitchen Sink

1 ❑ Cover: 1.00 **NM** value: **Cover or less**
Super Everythingman; The Computer Saves the Planet; At The Flies

DEEP BLACK — Chaos

1/A ❑ Aug 1997 **NM** value: **2.00**
no cover price. • b&w pencilled pin-ups
1/B ❑ Aug 1997 **NM** value: **2.00**
all-white cardstock cover. • b&w pencilled pin-ups

DEEP DIMENSION HORROR — AC

1 ❑ b&w Cover: 2.95 **NM** value: **Cover or less**
• Simulated 3-D

DEEPEST DIMENSION — Revolutionary

1 ❑ Jun 1993 Cover: 2.50 **NM** value: **Cover or less**
2 ❑ Aug 1993 Cover: 2.50 **NM** value: **Cover or less**
Sea Change **A:** Larry Nadolsky **W:** George Clayton Johnson

DEEP GIRL — Ariel Bordeaux

1 ❑ Cover: 2.50 **NM** value: **Cover or less**
2 ❑ Cover: 2.50 **NM** value: **Cover or less**
3 ❑ Cover: 2.50 **NM** value: **Cover or less**
4 ❑ Cover: 2.50 **NM** value: **Cover or less**
5 ❑ Cover: 2.50 **NM** value: **Cover or less**
Violet; I Am Ellsbette and…; RollerSkates; Alike-A-Look; Tit Chat **W:** Ariel Bordeaux

DEEP TERROR — Avalon

This anthology of seafaring horror stories sets sail with a classic horror-comics feel, as the tales are introduced and narrated by an array of creepy characters. The sense of foreboding is compounded by the stark and moody black-and-white art, heavy with shadows. Whether it's a yarn about a man who managed to die on both the Titanic and the Lusitania, or about the supernatural link between a pirate and his treasure — one that calls him from beyond the grave — this comic book shows that ghosts, and the evil that drives them on, are not things solely locked to the shore.

1 ❑ b&w Cover: 2.95 **NM** value: **Cover or less**
The Legacy; Pay the Price…Twice!; The Treasure; The Final Blow! **A:** Tom Sutton; Pat Boyette; Castellon Alascia **W:** Pat Boyette; Joe Gill; Castellon Alascia

DEE VEE — Dee Vee Press

1 ❑ Feb 1997 Cover: 2.95 **NM** value: **Cover or less**
Circ: Diamd. preorders: **2,439**
Alec (a new work in progress); Vital Reality Six Ways to Tell a Loved One…; Montague Hale: Dreams Burn down; Zooniverse; Mythogyny; The Animal Kingdom; Dogshit; Human-a Gastric Approach; The Muse Leaves; Dee Vee; Devious **A:** Eddie Campbell; Fil Barlow; Pete Mullins; Tonia Walden; Bruce Mutard; Daren White; Helen Maier; Louise Pieper; Marcus Moore; Michael Evans; Ralph Kidson; Tony Single **W:** Eddie Campbell; Fil Barlow; Pete Mullins; Tonia Walden; Bruce Mutard; Daren White; Helen Maier; Louise Pieper; Marcus Moore; Michael Evans; Ralph Kidson; Tony Single
5 ❑ Feb 1998, b&w Cover: 2.95 **NM** value: **Cover or less**
wraparound cover.
6 ❑ Apr 1998, b&w Cover: 2.95 **NM** value: **Cover or less**
wraparound cover.
7 ❑ Jun 1998, b&w Cover: 2.95 **NM** value: **Cover or less**
wraparound cover.

DEFCON 4 — Image

1/A ❑ Feb 1996 Cover: 2.50 **NM** value: **Cover or less**
wraparound cover. **A:** Matt Broome **W:** Matt Broome; Jeff Mariotte
1/B ❑ Feb 1996 Cover: 2.50 **NM** value: **Cover or less**
alternate wraparound cover. **A:** Matt Broome **W:** Matt Broome; Jeff Mariotte
2 ❑ Mar 1996 Cover: 2.50 **NM** value: **Cover or less**
3 ❑ Jun 1996 Cover: 2.50 **NM** value: **Cover or less**
cover says May, indicia says Jun. **A:** Matt Broome **W:** Matt Broome; Jeff Mariotte
4 ❑ Sep 1996 Cover: 2.50 **NM** value: **Cover or less**
A: Matt Broome **W:** Matt Broome; Jeff Mariotte
5 ❑ 1996 Cover: 2.50 **NM** value: **Cover or less**
A: Matt Broome **W:** Matt Broome; Jeff Mariotte

DEFENDERS, THE — Marvel

Originally, the Defenders were Doctor Strange, the Sub-Mariner, and the Incredible Hulk. Soon, however, this star-crossed "non-team" began what would have been a never-ending series of personnel replacements. Nighthawk, Hellcat, Valkyrie, Moondragon, the Gargoyle, and countless others at one point called themselves Defenders.

The list of their foes was equally long, and as the series progressed, grew increasingly mystical in nature. J.M. DeMatteis brings in the Son of Satan to date Hellcat (Patsy Walker, formerly star of one of Marvel's humor comics), who herself wonders about her diabolical parentage. In another story, Valkyrie dies and the Defenders have to go to Asgard to bring her back. Before becoming the "New" Defenders, the title's cultivated a dark, quirky personality all its own.

Everyone wants to revive the Defenders, but no one seems to be able to figure it out. The Secret Defenders and a second volume followed, both ending relatively quickly.

1 ❑ Aug 1972 Cover: 0.20 **NM** value: **50.00**
• **CGC:** 76 graded, best 9.6
I Slay By the Stars! • Team consists of Doctor Strange, Hulk, and Sub-Mariner **A:** Sal Buscema **W:** Steve Englehart
2 ❑ Oct 1972 Cover: 0.20 **NM** value: **25.00**
• **CGC:** 2 graded, best 9.4
The Secret of the Silver Surfer • Silver Surfer joins Defenders **A:** Sal Buscema ★ Appearance of Silver Surfer.
3 ❑ Dec 1972 Cover: 0.20 **NM** value: **20.00**
Four Against the Gods • Black Knight **A:** Sal Buscema; Jim Mooney ★ Appearance of Silver Surfer.
4 ❑ Feb 1973 Cover: 0.20 **NM** value: **20.00**
The New Defender • Valkyrie joins Defenders **A:** Frank McLaughlin; Sal Buscema
5 ❑ Apr 1973 Cover: 0.20 **NM** value: **20.00**
• **CGC:** 3 graded, best 9.4
World Without End **A:** Frank McLaughlin; Sal Buscema ★ Death of Omegatron.
6 ❑ Jun 1973 Cover: 0.20 **NM** value: **15.00**
• **CGC:** 2 graded, best 9.4
The Dreams of Death **A:** Frank McLaughlin; Sal Buscema
7 ❑ Aug 1973 Cover: 0.20 **NM** value: **15.00**
• **CGC:** 1 graded, best 9.2
The War Below the Waves • Hawkeye **A:** Sal Buscema ★ Appearance of Hawkeye.
8 ❑ Sep 1973 Cover: 0.20 **NM** value: **15.00**
• **CGC:** 2 graded, best 9.4
If Atlantis Should Fall: The Deception • Avengers and Defenders vs. Loki and Dormammu, part 2 – continues in Avengers #116 (continued from Avengers #115)★ Appearance of Avengers.
9 ❑ Oct 1973 Cover: 0.20 **NM** value: **15.00**
• **CGC:** 3 graded, best 9.4
Divide and Conquer; The Invincible Iron Man vs. Hawkeye the Archer; Dr. Strange vs. the Black Panther and Mantis • Avengers and Defenders vs. Loki and Dormammu, part 4 – continues in Avengers #117★ Appearance of Avengers.
10 ❑ Nov 1973 Cover: 0.20 **NM** value: **20.00**
• **CGC:** 22 graded, best 9.6
Breakthrough; The Incredible Hulk vs. the Mighty Thor; United We Stand • Avengers and Defenders vs. Loki and Dormammu, part 6 – continues in Avengers #118★ Appearance of Avengers.
11 ❑ Dec 1973 Cover: 0.20 **NM** value: **7.00**
• **CGC:** 1 graded, best 9.0
A Dark and Stormy Knight • Avengers and Defenders vs. Loki and Dormammu, part 8, continued from Avengers #118; Hawkeye, Silver Surfer and Sub-Mariner leave Defenders★ Appearance of Avengers.
12 ❑ Feb 1974 Cover: 0.20 **NM** value: **7.00**
• **CGC:** 4 graded, best 9.6
The Titan Strikes Back
13 ❑ May 1974 Cover: 0.25 **NM** value: **7.00**
• **CGC:** 1 graded, best 9.2
For Sale: One Planet, Slightly Used • Nighthawk★ 1st Appearance of Nebulon.
14 ❑ Jul 1974 Cover: 0.25 **NM** value: **7.00**
And Who Shall Inherit the Earth? • Nighthawk joins Defenders
15 ❑ Sep 1974 Cover: 0.25 **NM** value: **10.00**
• **CGC:** 2 graded, best 8.0
Panic Beneath the Earth • Professor X; Nighthawk new cosume★ Appearance of Magneto. ★ Versus Magneto.
16 ❑ Oct 1974 Cover: 0.25 **NM** value: **8.00**
• **CGC:** 2 graded, best 8.5
Alpha, The Ultimate Mutant • Professor X, Magneto **A:** Sal Buscema **W:** Len Wein ★ Appearance of Magneto.
17 ❑ Nov 1974 Cover: 0.25 **NM** value: **5.00**
• **CGC:** 1 graded, best 8.0
Power Play • Luke Cage★ 1st Appearance of Bulldozer.
18 ❑ Dec 1974 Cover: 0.25 **NM** value: **5.00**
• **CGC:** 1 graded, best 9.0
Rampage! • Luke Cage★ Origin of Bulldozer. ★ Versus Wrecking Crew.
19 ❑ Jan 1975 Cover: 0.25 **NM** value: **5.00**
• **CGC:** 1 graded, best 9.4
Doomball! • Luke Cage **A:** Sal Buscema; Klaus Janson **W:** Chris Claremont
20 ❑ Feb 1975 Cover: 0.25 **NM** value: **5.00**
The Woman She Was • origin of Valkyrie **A:** Sal Buscema ★ Appearance of Thing.
21 ❑ Mar 1975 Cover: 0.25 **NM** value: **5.00**
Enter: The Headmen **A:** Sal Buscema
22 ❑ Apr 1975 Cover: 0.25 **NM** value: **5.00**
Fangs of Fire and Blood **A:** Sal Buscema
23 ❑ May 1975 Cover: 0.25 **NM** value: **5.00**
…The Snakes Shall Inherit The Earth • Yellowjacket **A:** Sal Buscema **W:** Steve Gerber
24 ❑ Jun 1975 Cover: 0.25 **NM** value: **5.00**
-In The Jaws Of The Serpent • Luke Cage, Daredevil, Daimon Hellstorm, Yellowjacket **A:** Sal Buscema **W:** Steve Gerber ★ Appearance of Daredevil. ★ Appearance of Son of Satan.
25 ❑ Jul 1975 Cover: 0.25 **NM** value: **5.00**
The Serpent Sheds Its Skin • Luke Cage, Daredevil, Daimon Hellstorm, Yellowjacket★ Appearance of Daredevil.
26 ❑ Aug 1975 Cover: 0.25 **NM** value: **6.00**
Savage Time ★ Appearance of Guardians of the Galaxy.
27 ❑ Sep 1975 Cover: 0.25 **NM** value: **6.00**
• **CGC:** 2 graded, best 9.6
Three Worlds to Conquer • Guardians of the Galaxy★ 1st Appearance of Starhawk II (Aleta)-cameo. ★ Appearance of Guardians of the Galaxy.
28 ❑ Oct 1975 Cover: 0.25 **NM** value: **6.00**
My Mother, the Badoon • Guardians of the Galaxy, Starhawk★ 1st Appearance of Starhawk II (Aleta)-full. ★ Appearance of Guardians of the Galaxy.
29 ❑ Nov 1975 Cover: 0.25 **NM** value: **6.00**
Let My Planet Go • Guardians of the Galaxy, Starhawk★ Appearance of Guardians of the Galaxy.
30 ❑ Dec 1975 Cover: 0.25 **NM** value: **4.00**
Gold Diggers of Fear
31 ❑ Jan 1976 Cover: 0.25 **NM** value: **4.00**
Nighthawk's Brain
32 ❑ Feb 1976 Cover: 0.25 **NM** value: **4.00**
Musical Minds; My Life and Times; Step Into My Parlor ★ Origin of Nighthawk II (Kyle Richmond).
33 ❑ Mar 1976 Cover: 0.25 **NM** value: **4.00**
Webbed Hands, Warm Heart
34 ❑ Apr 1976 Cover: 0.25 **NM** value: **4.00**
I Think We're All Bozos In This Book! **A:** Sal Buscema; Jim Mooney **W:** Steve Gerber ★ Versus Nebulon.
35 ❑ May 1976 Cover: 0.25 **NM** value: **4.00**
Bring Back My Body to Me, to Me ★ 1st Appearance of Red Guardian II (Doctor Tanja Belinskya).
36 ❑ Jun 1976 Cover: 0.25 **NM** value: **4.00**
A Garden Of Earthly Demise! **A:** Sal Buscema; Klaus Janson **W:** Steve Gerber
37 ❑ Jul 1976 Cover: 0.25 **NM** value: **4.00**
• **CGC:** 1 graded, best 9.2
Evil in Bloom **A:** Sal Buscema; Klaus Janson
38 ❑ Aug 1976 Cover: 0.25 **NM** value: **4.00**
• **CGC:** 1 graded, best 8.5
Exile to Oblivion **A:** Sal Buscema; Klaus Janson **W:** Steve Gerber
39 ❑ Sep 1976 Cover: 0.30 **NM** value: **4.00**
• **CGC:** 1 graded, best 9.0
Riot in Cellblock 12 **A:** Sal Buscema; Klaus Janson
40 ❑ Oct 1976 Cover: 0.30 **NM** value: **4.00**
Love, Anarchy, And, Oh Yes… The Assassin! **A:** Sal Buscema; Klaus Janson **W:** Steve Gerber
41 ❑ Nov 1976 Cover: 0.30 **NM** value: **3.00**
A: Sal Buscema; Klaus Janson
42 ❑ Dec 1976 Cover: 0.30 **NM** value: **3.00**
A: Keith Giffen; Klaus Janson
43 ❑ Jan 1977 Cover: 0.30 **NM** value: **3.00**
A: Keith Giffen; Klaus Janson
44 ❑ Feb 1977 Cover: 0.30 **NM** value: **3.00**
• Hellcat joins Defenders **A:** Keith Giffen; Klaus Janson
45 ❑ Mar 1977 Cover: 0.30 **NM** value: **3.00**
A: Keith Giffen; Klaus Janson
46 ❑ Apr 1977 Cover: 0.30 **NM** value: **3.00**
A: Keith Giffen; Klaus Janson
47 ❑ May 1977 Cover: 0.30 **NM** value: **3.00**
• Moon Knight **A:** Keith Giffen; Klaus Janson
48 ❑ Jun 1977 Cover: 0.30 **NM** value: **3.00**
• **CGC:** 1 graded, best 9.4
Sinister Savior! **A:** Keith Giffen; Dan Green **W:** David Anthony Kraft ★ Origin of Zodiac II.
49 ❑ Jul 1977 Cover: 0.30 **NM** value: **3.00**
A: Keith Giffen ★ Origin of Zodiac II.
50 ❑ Aug 1977 Cover: 0.30 **NM** value: **3.00**
A: Keith Giffen ★ Origin of Zodiac II.
51 ❑ Sep 1977 Cover: 0.30 **NM** value: **2.50**
• **CGC:** 1 graded, best 9.2
A Round With The Ringer! • Moon Knight **A:** Keith Giffen **W:** David Anthony Kraft ★ 1st Appearance of Ringer I (Anthony Davis). ★ Appearance of Moon Knight.
52 ❑ Oct 1977 Cover: 0.30 **NM** value: **2.50**
• **CGC:** 1 graded, best 8.5
Defender Of The Realm! **A:** Keith Giffen; Chic Stone **W:** David Anthony Kraft ★ Origin of Presence. ★ 1st Appearance of Presence. ★ Appearance of Hulk. ★ Versus Sub-Mariner.
53 ❑ Nov 1977 Cover: 0.35 **NM** value: **2.50**
• **CGC:** 1 graded, best 9.0
A: Michael Golden ★ 1st Appearance of Lunatik.
54 ❑ Dec 1977 Cover: 0.35 **NM** value: **2.50**
• **CGC:** 1 graded, best 9.4
A Study in Survival! **A:** Michael Golden; Keith Giffen **W:** David Anthony Kraft
55 ❑ Jan 1978 Cover: 0.35 **NM** value: **2.50**
• **CGC:** 1 graded, best 9.2
★ Origin of Red Guardian II (Doctor Tanja Belinskya).
56 ❑ Feb 1978 Cover: 0.35 **NM** value: **2.50**
• **CGC:** 1 graded, best 9.2

Other grades: Multiply prices above by **1.5 for Mint • 2/3 for Very Fine • 1/3 for Fine • 1/5 for Very Good • 1/8 for Good**

57 ❑ Mar 1978 Cover: 0.35 **NM** value: **2.50**
• **CGC:** 1 graded, best 9.4
58 ❑ Apr 1978 Cover: 0.35 **NM** value: **2.50**
• **CGC:** 1 graded, best 9.0
59 ❑ May 1978 Cover: 0.35 **NM** value: **2.50**
• **CGC:** 1 graded, best 9.4
60 ❑ Jun 1978 Cover: 0.35 **NM** value: **2.50**
• **CGC:** 1 graded, best 9.0
61 ❑ Jul 1978 Cover: 0.35 **NM** value: **2.50**
• **CGC:** 1 graded, best 9.2
62 ❑ Aug 1978 Cover: 0.35 **NM** value: **2.50**
Membership Madness! **A:** Sal Buscema; Jim Mooney **W:** David Anthony Kraft
63 ❑ Sep 1978 Cover: 0.35 **NM** value: **2.50**
64 ❑ Oct 1978 Cover: 0.35 **NM** value: **2.50**
65 ❑ Nov 1978 Cover: 0.35 **NM** value: **2.50**
Of Ambitions And Giant Amoebas **A:** Don Perlin; Bruce D. **W:** David Anthony Kraft
66 ❑ Dec 1978 Cover: 0.35 **NM** value: **2.50**
67 ❑ Jan 1979 Cover: 0.35 **NM** value: **2.50**
Circ: Statement: **152,101**
We, The Unliving **A:** Ed Hannigan **W:** Ed Hannigan
68 ❑ Feb 1979 Cover: 0.35 **NM** value: **2.50**
Circ: Statement: **152,101**
Valhalla Can Wait! **A:** Herb Trimpe **W:** Ed Hannigan; David Anthony Kraft
69 ❑ Mar 1979 Cover: 0.35 **NM** value: **2.50**
Circ: Statement: **152,101**
The Anything Man! **A:** Herb Trimpe **W:** Mary Jo Duffy
70 ❑ Apr 1979 Cover: 0.35 **NM** value: **2.50**
Circ: Statement: **152,101**
Catch A Falling Lunatik! **A:** Herb Trimpe **W:** Ed Hannigan ★ Appearance of Lunatik. ★ Versus Lunatik.
71 ❑ May 1979 Cover: 0.40 **NM** value: **2.50**
Circ: Statement: **152,101**
Stranger And Stranger In A Strange Land **A:** Herb Trimpe; Jack Abel **W:** Ed Hannigan ★ Origin of Lunatik.
72 ❑ Jun 1979 Cover: 0.40 **NM** value: **2.50**
Circ: Statement: **152,101**
Up From The Sky! **A:** Herb Trimpe **W:** Ed Hannigan ★ Appearance of Lunatik.
73 ❑ Jul 1979 Cover: 0.40 **NM** value: **2.50**
Circ: Statement: **152,101**
Of Wizards, Shadows, And Kings **A:** Herb Trimpe **W:** Ed Hannigan ★ Appearance of Foolkiller II (Greg Salinger).
74 ❑ Aug 1979 Cover: 0.40 **NM** value: **2.50**
Circ: Statement: **152,101**
Fools Rush In! • Nighthawk II resigns from Defenders **A:** Herb Trimpe **W:** Ed Hannigan ★ Appearance of Foolkiller II (Greg Salinger).
75 ❑ Sep 1979 Cover: 0.40 **NM** value: **2.50**
Circ: Statement: **152,101**
Poetic Justice **A:** Herb Trimpe **W:** Ed Hannigan ★ Appearance of Foolkiller II (Greg Salinger).
76 ❑ Oct 1979 Cover: 0.40 **NM** value: **2.50**
Circ: Statement: **152,101**
Little Triggers **A:** Herb Trimpe **W:** Steven Grant ★ Origin of Omega.
77 ❑ Nov 1979 Cover: 0.40 **NM** value: **2.50**
Circ: Statement: **152,101**
Waiting For The End Of The World **A:** Herb Trimpe **W:** Steven Grant ★ Death of James-Michael Starling (Omega the Unknown's counterpart).
78 ❑ Dec 1979 Cover: 0.40 **NM** value: **2.00**
Circ: Statement: **152,101**
The Return Of The Original Defenders • Original Defenders return **A:** Herb Trimpe **W:** Ed Hannigan
79 ❑ Jan 1980 Cover: 0.40 **NM** value: **2.00**
Circ: Statement: **151,520**
Chains Of Love **A:** Herb Trimpe; Ed Hannigan **W:** Ed Hannigan
80 ❑ Feb 1980 Cover: 0.40 **NM** value: **2.00**
Circ: Statement: **151,520**
Once A Defender **A:** Herb Trimpe **W:** Ed Hannigan
81 ❑ Mar 1980 Cover: 0.40 **NM** value: **2.00**
Circ: Statement: **151,520**
War In Ogeon! • Has 1979 Statement; avg print run 313,612; avg sales 149,551; avg subs 2,550; avg total paid 152,101; samples 2,394; max existent 154,495; 51% of run returned **A:** Herb Trimpe; Jack Abel **W:** Ed Hannigan
82 ❑ Apr 1980 Cover: 0.40 **NM** value: **2.00**
Circ: Statement: **151,520**
Wizard Death! **A:** Don Perlin **W:** Ed Hannigan
83 ❑ May 1980 Cover: 0.40 **NM** value: **2.00**
Circ: Statement: **151,520**
End Of The Tunnel **A:** Don Perlin **W:** Ed Hannigan
84 ❑ Jun 1980 Cover: 0.40 **NM** value: **2.00**
Circ: Statement: **151,520**
Battle Royal **A:** Don Perlin **W:** Ed Hannigan
85 ❑ Jul 1980 Cover: 0.40 **NM** value: **2.00**
Circ: Statement: **151,520**
86 ❑ Aug 1980 Cover: 0.40 **NM** value: **2.00**
Circ: Statement: **151,520**
87 ❑ Sep 1980 Cover: 0.50 **NM** value: **2.00**
Circ: Statement: **151,520**
Inquest **A:** Pablo Marcos; Don Perlin **W:** Ed Hannigan
88 ❑ Oct 1980 Cover: 0.50 **NM** value: **2.00**
Circ: Statement: **151,520**
Lord Of The Whales **A:** Pablo Marcos; Don Perlin **W:** Ed Hannigan
89 ❑ Nov 1980 Cover: 0.50 **NM** value: **2.00**
Circ: Statement: **151,520**
A Death In The Family! **A:** Pablo Marcos; Don Perlin **W:** Ed Hannigan
90 ❑ Dec 1980 Cover: 0.50 **NM** value: **2.00**
Circ: Statement: **151,520**
Mind Over Mandrill! • Daredevil **A:** Pablo Marcos; Don Perlin; Joe Sinnott **W:** Ed Hannigan
91 ❑ Jan 1981 Cover: 0.50 **NM** value: **2.00**
Circ: Statement: **124,985**
Defiance! • Daredevil **A:** Pablo Marcos; Don Perlin; Joe Sinnott **W:** Ed Hannigan
92 ❑ Feb 1981 Cover: 0.50 **NM** value: **2.00**
Circ: Statement: **124,985**
A: Don Perlin; Joe Sinnott
93 ❑ Mar 1981 Cover: 0.50 **NM** value: **2.00**
Circ: Statement: **124,985**
The Woman Behind The Man! **A:** Don Perlin; Joe Sinnott **W:** J.M. DeMatteis
94 ❑ Apr 1981 Cover: 0.50 **NM** value: **2.00**
Circ: Statement: **124,985**
Beware...The Six-Fingered Man! • Has 1980 Statement; avg print run 306,034; avg sales 148,915; avg subs 2,605; avg total paid 151,520; samples 2,571; max existent 154,091; 50% of run returned **A:** Don Perlin; Joe Sinnott **W:** J.M. DeMatteis ★ 1st Appearance of Gargoyle.
95 ❑ May 1981 Cover: 0.50 **NM** value: **2.00**
Circ: Statement: **124,985**
The Vampire Strikes Back! **A:** Don Perlin; Joe Sinnott **W:** J.M. DeMatteis ★ Origin of Gargoyle. ★ Appearance of Dracula.
96 ❑ Jun 1981 Cover: 0.50 **NM** value: **2.50**
Circ: Statement: **124,985**
A: Don Perlin; Joe Sinnott ★ Appearance of Ghost Rider.
97 ❑ Jul 1981 Cover: 0.50 **NM** value: **2.00**
Circ: Statement: **124,985**
Slouching Toward Bethlehem **A:** Don Perlin; Joe Sinnott **W:** J.M. DeMatteis
98 ❑ Aug 1981 Cover: 0.50 **NM** value: **2.00**
Circ: Statement: **124,985**
The Hand Closes! **A:** Don Perlin; Joe Sinnott **W:** J.M. DeMatteis
99 ❑ Sep 1981 Cover: 0.50 **NM** value: **2.00**
Circ: Statement: **124,985**
Final Conflict **A:** Don Perlin; Joe Sinnott
100 ❑ Oct 1981 Cover: 0.75 **NM** value: **2.00**
Circ: Statement: **124,985** • **CGC:** 1 graded, best 9.6
• Giant-size. • giant **A:** Don Perlin; Joe Sinnott
101 ❑ Nov 1981 Cover: 0.50 **NM** value: **1.50**
Circ: Statement: **124,985**
A: Don Perlin; Joe Sinnott ★ Appearance of Silver Surfer.
102 ❑ Dec 1981 Cover: 0.50 **NM** value: **1.50**
Circ: Statement: **124,985**
Mind Games! **A:** Don Perlin; Joe Sinnott; Jack Abel **W:** J.M. DeMatteis
103 ❑ Jan 1982 Cover: 0.60 **NM** value: **1.50**
Circ: Statement: **135,926**
A: Don Perlin; Joe Sinnott ★ Origin of Null the Living Darkness. ★ 1st Appearance of Null the Living Darkness.
104 ❑ Feb 1982 Cover: 0.60 **NM** value: **1.50**
Circ: Statement: **135,926**
A: Don Perlin; Joe Sinnott
105 ❑ Mar 1982 Cover: 0.60 **NM** value: **1.50**
Circ: Statement: **135,926**
A: Don Perlin; Joe Sinnott
106 ❑ Apr 1982 Cover: 0.60 **NM** value: **1.50**
Circ: Statement: **135,926**
• Has 1981 Statement, filed 10/1/81; avg print run 284,952; avg sales 122,000; avg subs 2,985; avg total paid 124,985; samples 601; office use 3,535; max existent 129,121; 55% of run returned **A:** Don Perlin ★ Appearance of Daredevil. ★ Death of Nighthawk II (Kyle Richmond).
107 ❑ May 1982 Cover: 0.60 **NM** value: **1.50**
Circ: Statement: **135,926**
On Death And Dying... **A:** Don Perlin; Joe Sinnott **W:** J.M. DeMatteis ★ Appearance of Enchantress.
108 ❑ Jun 1982 Cover: 0.60 **NM** value: **1.50**
Circ: Statement: **135,926**
The Wasteland! **A:** Don Perlin **W:** J.M. DeMatteis
109 ❑ Jul 1982 Cover: 0.60 **NM** value: **1.50**
Circ: Statement: **135,926**
110 ❑ Aug 1982 Cover: 0.60 **NM** value: **1.50**
Circ: Statement: **135,926**
...Hunger... **A:** Don Perlin **W:** J.M. DeMatteis
111 ❑ Sep 1982 Cover: 0.60 **NM** value: **1.50**
Circ: Statement: **135,926**
Fathers And Daughters **A:** Don Perlin **W:** J.M. DeMatteis
112 ❑ Oct 1982 Cover: 0.60 **NM** value: **1.50**
Circ: Statement: **135,926**
Strange Visitor From Another Planet! **A:** Don Perlin **W:** J.M. DeMatteis ★ 1st Appearance of Power Princess, Nuke I (Albert Gaines).
113 ❑ Nov 1982 Cover: 0.60 **NM** value: **1.50**
Circ: Statement: **135,926**
114 ❑ Dec 1982 Cover: 0.60 **NM** value: **1.50**
Circ: Statement: **135,926**
Dance Of Darkness/Dance Of Light! **A:** Don Perlin **W:** J.M. DeMatteis
115 ❑ Jan 1983 Cover: 0.60 **NM** value: **1.50**
Circ: Statement: **130,463**
A Very Wrong Turn! **A:** Don Perlin **W:** J.M. DeMatteis
116 ❑ Feb 1983 Cover: 0.60 **NM** value: **1.50**
Circ: Statement: **130,463**
Two By Two **A:** Don Perlin **W:** J.M. DeMatteis
117 ❑ Mar 1983 Cover: 0.60 **NM** value: **1.50**
Circ: Statement: **130,463**
The Gift **A:** Don Perlin **W:** J.M. DeMatteis
118 ❑ Apr 1983 Cover: 0.60 **NM** value: **1.50**
Circ: Statement: **130,463**
The Double! **A:** Don Perlin **W:** J.M. DeMatteis
119 ❑ May 1983 Cover: 0.60 **NM** value: **1.50**
Circ: Statement: **130,463**
• Has 1982 Statement, filed 10/11/82; avg print run 268,644; avg sales 131,461; avg subs 4,465; avg total paid135,926X; samples 700; office use 1,592; max existent 138,218; 49% of run returned★ 1st Appearance of Yandroth II.
120 ❑ Jun 1983 Cover: 0.60 **NM** value: **1.50**
Circ: Statement: **130,463**
121 ❑ Jul 1983 Cover: 0.60 **NM** value: **1.50**
Circ: Statement: **130,463**
122 ❑ Aug 1983 Cover: 0.60 **NM** value: **1.50**
Circ: Statement: **130,463**
Things To Come! **A:** Don Perlin; Brent Anderson(cover) **W:** J.M. DeMatteis
123 ❑ Sep 1983 Cover: 0.60 **NM** value: **1.50**
Circ: Statement: **130,463**
of Elves And Androids! **A:** Don Perlin **W:** J.M. DeMatteis ★ 1st Appearance of Cloud.
124 ❑ Oct 1983 Cover: 0.60 **NM** value: **1.50**
Circ: Statement: **130,463**
125 ❑ Nov 1983 Cover: 1.00 **NM** value: **1.50**
Circ: Statement: **130,463**
• double-sized. Hello, I Must Be Going. (Or...Mad Dogs And Elvishmen!) • New Team begins: Valkyrie, Beast, Iceman, Angel, Gargoyle, and Moondragon **A:** Don Perlin **C:** Bill Sienkiewicz **W:** J.M. DeMatteis ★ 1st Appearance of Mad-Dog.
126 ❑ Dec 1983 Cover: 0.60 **NM** value: **1.50**
Circ: Statement: **130,463**
State Of The Union! **A:** Alan Kupperberg **W:** J.M. DeMatteis ★ Origin of Leviathan I (Edward Cobert). ★ 1st Appearance of Leviathan I (Edward Cobert).
127 ❑ Jan 1984 Cover: 0.60 **NM** value: **1.50**
Circ: Statement: **133,723**
Cloud Hidden! **A:** Sal Buscema **W:** J.M. DeMatteis
128 ❑ Feb 1984 Cover: 0.60 **NM** value: **1.50**
Circ: Statement: **133,723**
Assault On The Empire! **A:** Alan Kupperberg **W:** J.M. DeMatteis
129 ❑ Mar 1984 Cover: 0.60 **NM** value: **1.50**
Circ: Statement: **133,723**
Countdown! **A:** Don Perlin; Kim Demulder **W:** J.M. DeMatteis ★ Appearance of New Mutants. ★ Versus New Mutants.
130 ❑ Apr 1984 Cover: 0.60 **NM** value: **1.50**
Circ: Statement: **133,723**
And In The End! **A:** Mike Zeck **W:** J.M. DeMatteis
131 ❑ May 1984 Cover: 0.60 **NM** value: **1.00**
Circ: Statement: **133,723**
If This Be Walrus...! **A:** Alan Kupperberg **W:** Peter B. Gillis
132 ❑ Jun 1984 Cover: 0.60 **NM** value: **1.00**
Circ: Statement: **133,723**
The Phantom Of Gamma-Ray Flats! • Has 1983 Statement, filed 10/3/83; avg print run 262,471; avg sales 124,636; avg subs 5,827; avg total paid 130,463; samples 764; office use 1,720; max existent 132,947; 49% of run returned **A:** Don Perlin **W:** Peter B. Gillis
133 ❑ Jul 1984 Cover: 0.60 **NM** value: **1.00**
Circ: Statement: **133,723**
★ 1st Appearance of Manslaughter (cameo).
134 ❑ Aug 1984 Cover: 0.60 **NM** value: **1.00**
Circ: Statement: **133,723**
Manslaughter! **A:** Don Perlin **W:** Peter B. Gillis ★ 1st Appearance of Manslaughter (full appearance).
135 ❑ Sep 1984 Cover: 0.60 **NM** value: **1.00**
Circ: Statement: **133,723**
The Fire At Heaven's Gate! **A:** Don Perlin **W:** Peter B. Gillis
136 ❑ Oct 1984 Cover: 0.60 **NM** value: **1.00**
Circ: Statement: **133,723**
Bodies And Souls! **A:** Don Perlin **W:** Peter B. Gillis
137 ❑ Nov 1984 Cover: 0.60 **NM** value: **1.00**
Circ: Statement: **133,723**
Hearts And Minds! **A:** Don Perlin **W:** Peter B. Gillis
138 ❑ Dec 1984 Cover: 0.60 **NM** value: **1.00**
Circ: Statement: **133,723**
Three Women **A:** Don Perlin **W:** Peter B. Gillis ★ Origin of Moondragon.
139 ❑ Jan 1985 Cover: 0.60 **NM** value: **1.00**
Hungry Like The Wolf! • Series continues as The New Defenders **A:** Don Perlin **W:** Peter B. Gillis
140 ❑ Feb 1985 Cover: 0.60 **NM** value: **1.00**
The Heartbreak Kid! **A:** Don Perlin **W:** Peter B. Gillis
141 ❑ Mar 1985 Cover: 0.60 **NM** value: **1.00**
142 ❑ Apr 1985 Cover: 0.65 **NM** value: **1.00**
M.O.N.S.T.E.R.! **A:** Don Perlin **C:** Arthur Adams **W:** Peter B. Gillis
143 ❑ May 1985 Cover: 0.65 **NM** value: **1.00**
Circ: CapCity orders: **10,700**
Another Runner... • Has 1984 Statement, filed 9/28/84; avg print run 259,210; avg sales 127,957; avg subs 5,766; avg total paid 133,723; samples 140; office use 2,652; max existent 136,515; 47% of run returned **A:** Don Perlin **W:** Peter B. Gillis ★ Origin of Moondragon. ★ 1st Appearance of Runner, Dragon of the Moon, Andromeda.
144 ❑ Jun 1985 Cover: 0.65 **NM** value: **1.00**
Circ: CapCity orders: **10,500**
Dragon Midnight **A:** Don Perlin **W:** Peter B. Gillis
145 ❑ Jul 1985 Cover: 0.65 **NM** value: **1.00**
Circ: CapCity orders: **10,500**
★ Appearance of Johnny Blaze.
146 ❑ Aug 1985 Cover: 0.65 **NM** value: **1.00**
Circ: CapCity orders: **11,100**
Fun! **A:** Luke McDonnell **W:** Peter B. Gillis
147 ❑ Sep 1985 Cover: 0.65 **NM** value: **1.00**
Circ: CapCity orders: **10,700**
Sgt. Fury and His Howling Defenders on both cover and in indicia. ...And Games! **A:** Don Perlin **W:** Peter B. Gillis
148 ❑ Oct 1985 Cover: 0.65 **NM** value: **1.00**
Circ: CapCity orders: **10,600**
The Kickshaws Consignment **A:** Sal Buscema; Art Nichols **W:** Peter B. Gillis
149 ❑ Nov 1985 Cover: 0.65 **NM** value: **1.00**
Circ: CapCity orders: **10,300**
Lonely An A Cloud-! **A:** Don Perlin **W:** Peter B. Gillis ★ Origin of Andromeda.
150 ❑ Dec 1985 Cover: 1.25 **NM** value: **Cover or less**
Circ: CapCity orders: **11,200**
• double-sized. The Stars In Their Courses! **A:** Don Perlin **W:** Peter B. Gillis ★ Origin of Cloud.
151 ❑ Jan 1986 Cover: 0.65 **NM** value: **1.00**
Circ: CapCity orders: **10,200**
Second Degree Manslaughter **A:** Don Perlin **W:** Peter B. Gillis
152 ❑ Feb 1986 Cover: 1.25 **NM** value: **Cover or less**
Circ: CapCity orders: **20,100**

CGC-graded: Multiply prices above by **33 for 9.9 M • 16 for 9.8 NM/M • 7 for 9.6 NM+ • 5 for 9.4 NM • 2.5 for 9.2 NM- • 1.5 for 9.0 VF/NM**

• double-sized. Secret Wars II final issue. • Secret Wars II **A:** Don Perlin **W:** Peter B. Gillis ★ Origin of Manslaughter.
Anl 1 ❑ Nov 1976 Cover: 0.50 **NM** value: **6.00**
• **CGC:** 4 graded, best 9.6
A: Jim Starlin ★ Origin of Hulk.
GS 1 ❑ Jul 1974 Cover: 0.50 **NM** value: **6.00**
The Way They Were!; Banished To Outer Space; Bird of Prey; To Catch a Magician; The Once and Again Dooms; The Peerless Power of the Silver Surfer • Original material with reprints from Incredible Hulk #3, Sub-Mariner #41, Strange Tales #145 and Fantastic Four Annual #5 **A:** Jim Starlin **W:** Tony Isabella ★ Appearance of Silver Surfer.
GS 2 ❑ Oct 1974 Cover: 0.50 **NM** value: **4.00**
H as in Hulk, Hell and Holocaust; Satanspawn; Soulgame; Untitled (Sub-Mariner); Untitled (Black Knight); Beyond the Purple Veil • Original material with reprints from Young Men #25, Black Knight #4 and Strange Tales #119
GS 3 ❑ ca. 1975 Cover: 0.50 **NM** value: **4.00**
Games Godlings Play!; The World Destroyers; The House of Shadows; • Original material with reprints from Sub-Mariner #38 and Strange Tales #120 **A:** Don Newton; Jim Starlin; Jim Mooney; Dan Adkins **W:** Steve Gerber ★ 1st Appearance of Korvac.
GS 4 ❑ Apr 1975 Cover: 0.50 **NM** value: **4.00**
Too Cold A Night For Dying!; Flight of the Yellowjacket; Hearts in Darkness; Untitled (Sub-Mariner): Witchcraft in the Wax Museum • Original material with reprints from Human Torch #4 and Strange Tales #121 **A:** Don Heck **W:** Steve Gerber
GS 5 ❑ Jul 1975 Cover: 0.50 **NM** value: **4.00**
Eelar Moves Mysterious Ways!; Quoth the Nighthawk, 'Nevermore!' • Original material with partial reprint of Daredevil #62 **A:** Don Heck **W:** Steve Gerber

DEFENDERS (VOL. 2) — Marvel

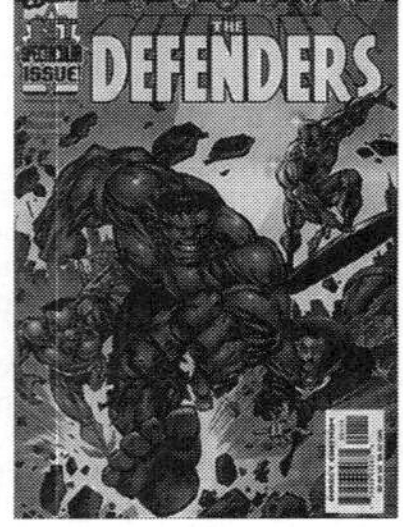

In 2001, comics' only non-team returned — written by Kurt Busiek and Erik Larsen, with Larsen and Klaus Janson providing art.

Much like their original team-up in Marvel Feature #7, this series began with Doctor Strange, Sub-Mariner, The Hulk, and The Silver Surfer (who joined the original team after that initial event) being reluctantly brought together to combat the renewed threat of other-dimensional sorcerer Yandroth, who cursed them to continue to work together with his dying breath. Other former team members Nighthawk, Hellcat, and the Valkyrie also returned, although they were not bound by Yandroth's curse.

At the series' end, the main quartet, tired of being summoned willy-nilly to combat various threats, took matters into their own hands to ensure that such world-shattering events would no longer occur. Readers can follow the story in The Order. — Brent

1 ❑ Mar 2001 Cover: 2.99 **NM** value: **Cover or less**
Circ: Statement: **39,833** Diamd. preorders: **44,861** • **CGC:** 4 graded, best 9.8
Once More, The End of the World ... **A:** Erik Larsen **W:** Kurt Busiek ★ Appearance of Hulk, Doctor Strange, Silver Surfer, Hellcat, Sub-Mariner, Nighthawk.
2 ❑ Apr 2001 Cover: 2.25 **NM** value: **Cover or less**
Circ: Statement: **39,833** Diamd. preorders: **40,429**
The Curse **A:** Erik Larsen **W:** Kurt Busiek
3 ❑ May 2001 Cover: 2.25 **NM** value: **Cover or less**
Circ: Statement: **39,833** Diamd. preorders: **34,932**
The Armies of the Slain **A:** Erik Larsen **W:** Kurt Busiek
4 ❑ Jun 2001 Cover: 2.25 **NM** value: **Cover or less**
Circ: Statement: **39,833** Diamd. preorders: **34,469**
5 ❑ Jul 2001 Cover: 2.25 **NM** value: **Cover or less**
Circ: Statement: **39,833** Diamd. preorders: **33,049**
6 ❑ Aug 2001 Cover: 2.25 **NM** value: **Cover or less**
Circ: Statement: **39,833** Diamd. preorders: **31,459**
7 ❑ Sep 2001 Cover: 2.25 **NM** value: **Cover or less**
Circ: Statement: **39,833** Diamd. preorders: **31,098**
8 ❑ Oct 2001 Cover: 2.25 **NM** value: **Cover or less**
Circ: Diamd. preorders: **29,950**
9 ❑ Nov 2001 Cover: 2.25 **NM** value: **Cover or less**
Circ: Diamd. preorders: **26,450**
10 ❑ Dec 2001 Cover: 2.25 **NM** value: **Cover or less**
Circ: Diamd. preorders: **25,008**
11 ❑ Jan 2002 Cover: 2.25 **NM** value: **Cover or less**
Circ: Diamd. preorders: **24,324**
12 ❑ Feb 2002 Cover: 3.50 **NM** value: **Cover or less**
Circ: Diamd. preorders: **23,681**
• Has 2001 Statement, filed 10/1/2001; avg print run 41,700; avg sales 39,539; avg subs 294; avg total paid 39,833; samples 600; office use 1,267; max existent 41,700; 0% of run returned

DEFENDERS OF DYNATRON CITY — Marvel

1 ❑ Feb 1992 Cover: 1.25 **NM** value: **Cover or less**
Circ: CapCity orders: **10,000**
A: Frank Cirocco **W:** Steve Purcell; Gary Winnick
2 ❑ Mar 1992 Cover: 1.25 **NM** value: **Cover or less**
Circ: CapCity orders: **5,100**
A: Frank Cirocco
3 ❑ Apr 1992 Cover: 1.25 **NM** value: **Cover or less**
Circ: CapCity orders: **4,400**
A: Frank Cirocco
4 ❑ May 1992 Cover: 1.25 **NM** value: **Cover or less**
Circ: CapCity orders: **3,600**
A: Frank Cirocco
5 ❑ Jun 1992 Cover: 1.25 **NM** value: **Cover or less**
Circ: CapCity orders: **3,400**
This Island: Radium **A:** Frank Cirocco **W:** Steve Purcell
6 ❑ Jul 1992 Cover: 1.25 **NM** value: **Cover or less**
A: Frank Cirocco

DEFENDERS OF THE EARTH — Marvel / Star

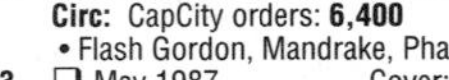

1 ❑ Jan 1987 Cover: 0.75 **NM** value: **1.00**
Circ: CapCity orders: **8,150**
• Flash Gordon, Mandrake, Phantom
2 ❑ Mar 1987 Cover: 0.75 **NM** value: **1.00**
Circ: CapCity orders: **6,400**
• Flash Gordon, Mandrake, Phantom
3 ❑ May 1987 Cover: 0.75 **NM** value: **1.00**
Circ: CapCity orders: **4,100**
• Flash Gordon, Mandrake, Phantom
4 ❑ Jul 1987 Cover: 1.00 **NM** value: **Cover or less**
Circ: CapCity orders: **3,200**
final issue.

DEFENSELESS DEAD, THE — Adventure

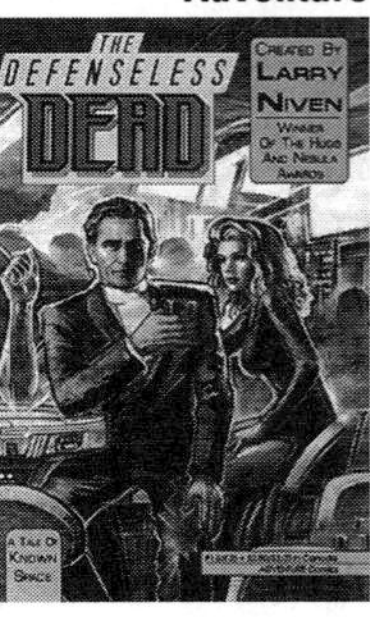

With Bill Spangler scripting and Terry Tidwell and Steven Stiles providing the art, Adventure Comics adapts the acclaimed novella "The Defenseless Dead" by Hugo and Nebula Award winner Larry Niven into a three-issue mini-series.

The time is 2124 A.D. and Amalgamated Regional Militia (A.R.M.) agent Gil Hamilton is entangled in the case to end all cases. Revolving around the world of cryogenically frozen humans and the illegal trade of body parts on the black market, Hamilton must solve a kidnapping before it happens and uncover why a dead man is trying to murder him. All in a day's work for this futuristic detective.

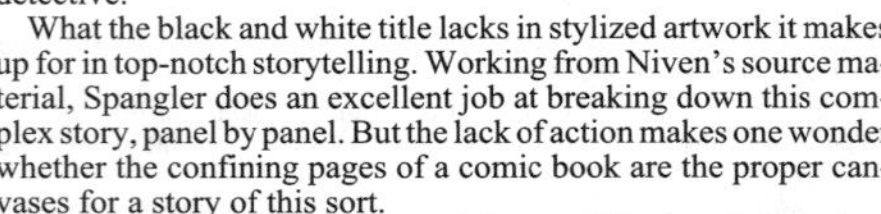

What the black and white title lacks in stylized artwork it makes up for in top-notch storytelling. Working from Niven's source material, Spangler does an excellent job at breaking down this complex story, panel by panel. But the lack of action makes one wonder whether the confining pages of a comic book are the proper canvases for a story of this sort.

1 ❑ Feb 1991, b&w Cover: 2.50 **NM** value: **Cover or less**
• based on Larry Niven story **A:** Terry Tidwell **W:** Bill Spangler; Larry Niven
2 ❑ ca. 1991, b&w Cover: 2.50 **NM** value: **Cover or less**
• based on Larry Niven story **A:** Terry Tidwell **W:** Bill Spangler; Larry Niven
3 ❑ ca. 1991, b&w Cover: 2.50 **NM** value: **Cover or less**
• based on Larry Niven story **A:** Terry Tidwell **W:** Bill Spangler; Larry Niven

DEFIANT GENESIS — Defiant

1 ❑ Oct 1993 **NM** value: **1.00**
no cover price.

DEFINITION — Slave Labor

Since the publication of Awkward, which chronicled her freshman year of high school, creator Ariel Schrag has been looking at herself through a microscope, analyzing and questioning her life as a teen-ager. Definition presents Ariel's sophomore year and proves that there are more complicated things in life than high school chemistry — although that can be pretty hard, too.

Whether she's turning 16 and wrestling with her own sexuality, hanging out with friends, getting crushed against the stage at a No Doubt concert, or ingesting massive amounts of drugs and alcohol, Ariel's autobiographical tale is an honest and refreshing look at a wide variety of tumultuous issues facing teens today.

Ariel's story continues in Potential, which tackles her junior year.

1 ❑ Aug 1997, b&w Cover: 12.95 **NM** value: **Cover or less**
No issue number. • Oversized. **A:** Ariel Schrag **W:** Ariel Schrag

DEITY: REVELATIONS — Image

1 ❑ Jul 1999 Cover: 2.95 **NM** value: **Cover or less**
Circ: Diamd. preorders: **16,976**
• Woman on floating skateboard, figures in background **A:** Karl Altstaetter **W:** Robert Napton; Karl Altstaetter
1/A ❑ Jul 1999 Cover: 2.95 **NM** value: **Cover or less**
variant cover: woman holding her face on cover. **A:** Karl Altstaetter **W:** Robert Napton; Karl Altstaetter
1/B ❑ Jul 1999 Cover: 2.95 **NM** value: **Cover or less**
variant cover. **A:** Karl Altstaetter **W:** Robert Napton; Karl Altstaetter
2 ❑ Sep 1999 Cover: 2.95 **NM** value: **Cover or less**
Circ: Diamd. preorders: **13,607**
variant cover. **A:** Karl Altstaetter **W:** Robert Napton; Karl Altstaetter
3 ❑ Nov 1999 Cover: 2.95 **NM** value: **Cover or less**
Circ: Diamd. preorders: **11,729**
A: Karl Altstaetter **W:** Robert Napton; Karl Altstaetter
4 ❑ Jan 2000 Cover: 2.95 **NM** value: **Cover or less**
Circ: Diamd. preorders: **10,308**
A: Karl Altstaetter **W:** Robert Napton; Karl Altstaetter

indicates **Story Title** or **Storyline** information.
★ indicates **Character Appearance** information.
W = Writer • A = Artist • C = Cover Artist

DEITY (VOL. 1) — Image

OK, so you're a young woman named Jamie, and it's your birthday. You're celebrating with friends in a dance club. Unbeknownst to you, a war is being fought between forces that want to kill you and forces that want to protect you. "Why?" you ask. Well, there's more to you than meets the eye. You stand to inherit the godlike power of Queen Xandra, and the evil Ma'Shiva wants to make sure that doesn't happen.

Don't worry. Once this struggle lands in your lap, you won't have to go it alone. Xandra has sent the Red Flag Troopers Diamond Diaz and Lucius Ego to protect you, and they've linked up with Master Chow Lone and his grandson Tommy, super-cool members of the Shaolin Temple.

Deity is quite a ride from creators Karl Altstaetter and Robert Napton; lots of action fills the pages of this limited series.

0 ❑ May 1998 Cover: 6.00 **NM** value: **Cover or less**
Circ: Diamd. preorders: **8,888**
Flip cover. • exclusive New Dimension Comics edition. **A:** Karl Altstaetter **W:** Robert Napton; Karl Altstaetter
0/A ❑ May 1998 Cover: 2.95 **NM** value: **3.00**
A: Karl Altstaetter **W:** Robert Napton; Karl Altstaetter
1 ❑ Sep 1997 Cover: 2.95 **NM** value: **4.00**
Circ: Diamd. preorders: **7,143**
White background on cover. **A:** Karl Altstaetter **W:** Robert Napton; Karl Altstaetter
1/A ❑ Sep 1997 Cover: 2.95 **NM** value: **5.00**
variant cover. **A:** Karl Altstaetter **W:** Robert Napton; Karl Altstaetter
2 ❑ Oct 1997 Cover: 2.95 **NM** value: **Cover or less**
Circ: Diamd. preorders: **4,614**
Regular cover (power blasts). **A:** Karl Altstaetter **W:** Robert Napton; Karl Altstaetter
2/A ❑ Oct 1997 Cover: 2.95 **NM** value: **3.50**
variant cover. • Brandishing gun, sword **A:** Karl Altstaetter **W:** Robert Napton; Karl Altstaetter
3 ❑ Nov 1997 Cover: 2.95 **NM** value: **Cover or less**
Circ: Diamd. preorders: **4,763**
Regular cover (brown background, bandages on face). **A:** Karl Altstaetter **W:** Robert Napton; Karl Altstaetter
3/A ❑ Nov 1997 Cover: 2.95 **NM** value: **3.50**
variant cover. • Cyborg girl **A:** Karl Altstaetter **W:** Robert Napton; Karl Altstaetter
4 ❑ Dec 1997 Cover: 2.95 **NM** value: **Cover or less**
Circ: Diamd. preorders: **4,632**
A: Karl Altstaetter **W:** Robert Napton; Karl Altstaetter
4/A ❑ Dec 1997 Cover: 2.95 **NM** value: **3.00**
variant cover. **A:** Karl Altstaetter **W:** Robert Napton; Karl Altstaetter
5 ❑ Feb 1998 Cover: 2.95 **NM** value: **Cover or less**
Circ: Diamd. preorders: **4,879**
A: Karl Altstaetter **W:** Robert Napton; Karl Altstaetter
5/A ❑ Feb 1998 Cover: 2.95 **NM** value: **3.00**
variant cover. **A:** Karl Altstaetter **W:** Robert Napton; Karl Altstaetter
6 ❑ Apr 1998 Cover: 2.95 **NM** value: **Cover or less**
Circ: Diamd. preorders: **5,032**
Girl with backpack on cover. **A:** Karl Altstaetter **W:** Robert Napton; Karl Altstaetter
6/A ❑ Apr 1998 Cover: 2.95 **NM** value: **3.00**
variant cover. **A:** Karl Altstaetter **W:** Robert Napton; Karl Altstaetter
Bk 1 ❑ Apr 1999 Cover: 10.95 **NM** value: **Cover or less**
• Collects Deity #1-3 **A:** Karl Altstaetter **W:** Robert Napton; Karl Altstaetter
Bk 2 ❑ May 1999 Cover: 10.95 **NM** value: **Cover or less**
• Collects Deity #4-6 **A:** Karl Altstaetter **W:** Robert Napton; Karl Altstaetter

DEITY (VOL. 2) — Image

1 ❑ Sep 1998 Cover: 2.95 **NM** value: **Cover or less**
Circ: Diamd. preorders: **15,018**
• Flipbook preview of Catseye **A:** Karl Altstaetter **W:** Robert Napton; Karl Altstaetter
1/A ❑ Sep 1998 Cover: 2.95 **NM** value: **Cover or less**
Variant cover with blue background, wielding sword. **A:** Karl Altstaetter; Rob Liefeld(cover) **W:** Robert Napton; Karl Altstaetter
1/B ❑ Sep 1998 Cover: 2.95 **NM** value: **Cover or less**
Variant cover with monster threatening. **A:** Karl Altstaetter **W:** Robert Napton; Karl Altstaetter
1/C ❑ Sep 1998 Cover: 2.95 **NM** value: **Cover or less**
Variant cover with gratuitous bathing suit, cleavage. **A:** Karl Altstaetter **W:** Robert Napton; Karl Altstaetter
2 ❑ Nov 1998 Cover: 2.95 **NM** value: **Cover or less**
Circ: Diamd. preorders: **14,040**
A: Karl Altstaetter **W:** Robert Napton; Karl Altstaetter
3 ❑ Jan 1999 Cover: 2.95 **NM** value: **Cover or less**
Circ: Diamd. preorders: **12,408**
A: Karl Altstaetter **W:** Robert Napton; Karl Altstaetter
4 ❑ Jan 1999 Cover: 2.95 **NM** value: **Cover or less**
Circ: Diamd. preorders: **14,256**
A: Karl Altstaetter **W:** Robert Napton; Karl Altstaetter
5 ❑ May 1999 Cover: 2.95 **NM** value: **Cover or less**
Circ: Diamd. preorders: **12,519**
A: Karl Altstaetter **W:** Robert Napton; Karl Altstaetter
Ash 1 ❑ Jun 1998 Cover: 2.95 **NM** value: **Cover or less**
• Special Preview edition. **A:** Karl Altstaetter **W:** Robert Napton; Karl Altstaetter

DEJA VU — Fantaco

1 ❑ Nov 2000 Cover: 2.95 **NM** value: **Cover or less**
Circ: Diamd. preorders: **2,607**
A: Bernie Wrightson; Michael W. Kaluta

Other grades: Multiply prices above by **1.5 for Mint • 2/3 for Very Fine • 1/3 for Fine • 1/5 for Very Good • 1/8 for Good**

DELIA CHARM — Red Menace
1 ❑ Cover: 2.95 **NM** value: **Cover or less**
2 ❑ Cover: 2.95 **NM** value: **Cover or less**

DELIRIUM — Metro
1 ❑ Cover: 2.00 **NM** value: **Cover or less**

DELLA VISION — Atlas
1 ❑ Apr 1955 Cover: 0.10 **NM** value: **50.00**
2 ❑ Jun 1955 Cover: 0.10 **NM** value: **50.00**
3 ❑ Aug 1955 Cover: 0.10 **NM** value: **50.00**

DELL GIANT COMICS — Dell
21 ❑ Sep 1959 Cover: 0.25 **NM** value: **100.00**
• **CGC:** 1 graded, best 9.0
22 ❑ ca. 1959 Cover: 0.25 **NM** value: **75.00**
• **CGC:** 1 graded, best 4.0
23 ❑ Oct 1959 Cover: 0.25 **NM** value: **90.00**
• **CGC:** 1 graded, best 9.4
24 ❑ Nov 1959 Cover: 0.25 **NM** value: **75.00**
• **CGC:** 3 graded, best 9.6
25 ❑ Nov 1959 Cover: 0.25 **NM** value: **90.00**
• **CGC:** 1 graded, best 9.4
26 ❑ Dec 1959 Cover: 0.25 **NM** value: **200.00**
• **CGC:** 3 graded, best 9.4
27 ❑ ca. 1959 Cover: 0.35 **NM** value: **90.00**
28 ❑ Feb 1960 Cover: 0.25 **NM** value: **90.00**
29 ❑ Apr 1960 Cover: 0.25 **NM** value: **90.00**
• **CGC:** 2 graded, best 9.6
30 ❑ Jun 1960 Cover: 0.25 **NM** value: **90.00**
• **CGC:** 3 graded, best 9.4
31 ❑ Jul 1960 Cover: 0.25 **NM** value: **120.00**
• **CGC:** 2 graded, best 9.6
32 ❑ Aug 1960 Cover: 0.25 **NM** value: **120.00**
33 ❑ Sep 1960 Cover: 0.25 **NM** value: **120.00**
• **CGC:** 2 graded, best 9.6
34 ❑ Aug 1960 Cover: 0.25 **NM** value: **150.00**
• **CGC:** 1 graded, best 4.5
35 ❑ Oct 1960 Cover: 0.25 **NM** value: **120.00**
• **CGC:** 1 graded, best 7.0
36 ❑ Oct 1960 Cover: 0.25 **NM** value: **90.00**
• **CGC:** 1 graded, best 9.4
37 ❑ Nov 1960 Cover: 0.25 **NM** value: **120.00**
38 ❑ Nov 1960 Cover: 0.25 **NM** value: **120.00**
• **CGC:** 3 graded, best 9.2
39 ❑ Dec 1960 Cover: 0.25 **NM** value: **90.00**
• **CGC:** 2 graded, best 9.8
40 ❑ Dec 1960 Cover: 0.25 **NM** value: **120.00**
• **CGC:** 4 graded, best 9.8
41 ❑ Dec 1960 Cover: 0.25 **NM** value: **90.00**
• **CGC:** 2 graded, best 9.6
42 ❑ Apr 1961 Cover: 0.25 **NM** value: **75.00**
43 ❑ May 1961 Cover: 0.25 **NM** value: **75.00**
• **CGC:** 3 graded, best 9.6
44 ❑ Jul 1961 Cover: 0.25 **NM** value: **120.00**
• **CGC:** 2 graded, best 9.6
45 ❑ Aug 1961 Cover: 0.25 **NM** value: **75.00**
• **CGC:** 1 graded, best 9.0
46 ❑ Aug 1961 Cover: 0.25 **NM** value: **75.00**
47 ❑ Aug 1961 Cover: 0.25 **NM** value: **75.00**
• **CGC:** 2 graded, best 9.6
48 ❑ ca. 1961 Cover: 0.25 **NM** value: **200.00**
• **CGC:** 6 graded, best 9.6
49 ❑ ca. 1961 Cover: 0.25 **NM** value: **75.00**
• **CGC:** 2 graded, best 7.0
50 ❑ Oct 1961 Cover: 0.25 **NM** value: **75.00**
• **CGC:** 2 graded, best 9.6
51 ❑ Nov 1961 Cover: 0.25 **NM** value: **75.00**
• **CGC:** 1 graded, best 8.0
52 ❑ Nov 1961 Cover: 0.25 **NM** value: **75.00**
• **CGC:** 4 graded, best 9.8
53 ❑ Dec 1961 Cover: 0.25 **NM** value: **75.00**
• **CGC:** 3 graded, best 9.4
54 ❑ Dec 1961 Cover: 0.25 **NM** value: **75.00**
• **CGC:** 3 graded, best 9.6
55 ❑ Sep 1961 Cover: 0.25 **NM** value: **75.00**
• **CGC:** 5 graded, best 9.6

DELL JUNIOR TREASURY — Dell
1 ❑ Jul 1955 Cover: 0.15 **NM** value: **90.00**
2 ❑ Oct 1955 Cover: 0.15 **NM** value: **60.00**
3 ❑ Jan 1956 Cover: 0.15 **NM** value: **60.00**
4 ❑ Apr 1956 Cover: 0.15 **NM** value: **60.00**
5 ❑ Jul 1956 Cover: 0.15 **NM** value: **60.00**
• **CGC:** 1 graded, best 8.0
6 ❑ Oct 1956 Cover: 0.15 **NM** value: **60.00**
• **CGC:** 1 graded, best 7.0
7 ❑ Jan 1957 Cover: 0.10 **NM** value: **60.00**
8 ❑ Apr 1957 Cover: 0.10 **NM** value: **60.00**
• **CGC:** 1 graded, best 9.0
9 ❑ Jul 1957 Cover: 0.10 **NM** value: **60.00**
10 ❑ Oct 1957 Cover: 0.10 **NM** value: **60.00**

DELTA SQUADRON — Anderpol
1 ❑ Cover: 2.00 **NM** value: **Cover or less**

DELTA TENN — Entertainment
1 ❑ Jul 1987 Cover: 1.50 **NM** value: **Cover or less**
2 ❑ Sep 1987 Cover: 1.50 **NM** value: **Cover or less**
3 ❑ Nov 1987 Cover: 1.50 **NM** value: **Cover or less**
4 ❑ Jan 1988 Cover: 1.50 **NM** value: **Cover or less**
5 ❑ Mar 1988 Cover: 1.50 **NM** value: **Cover or less**
6 ❑ May 1988 Cover: 1.50 **NM** value: **Cover or less**
7 ❑ Jul 1988 Cover: 1.50 **NM** value: **Cover or less**
8 ❑ Sep 1988 Cover: 1.50 **NM** value: **Cover or less**
9 ❑ b&w Cover: 1.50 **NM** value: **Cover or less**
10 ❑ b&w Cover: 1.50 **NM** value: **Cover or less**

DELTA, THE ULTIMATE DIFFERENCE — Apex One
1 ❑ Oct 1997, b&w **NM** value: **2.00**
no cover price.
2 ❑ Fal 1998, b&w Cover: 2.95 **NM** value: **Cover or less**
cardstock cover.

DEMENTED PERVERT — Print Mint
1 ❑ Cover: 0.50 **NM** value: **3.00**
2 ❑ Cover: 0.50 **NM** value: **3.00**
📖 An Adolescent Comes of Age; Masterbation a Sticky Subject; Hung Low; Lester Fester **A:** Dave Geiser **W:** Dave Geiser

DEMENTED: SCORPION CHILD — DMF
1 ❑ Nov 2000 Cover: 2.95 **NM** value: **Cover or less**
📖 Boiling Water Clean **A:** Jaime Antonio **W:** Jaime Antonio
2 ❑ Dec 2000 Cover: 2.95 **NM** value: **Cover or less**
A: Jaime Antonio **W:** Jaime Antonio
3 ❑ Jan 2001 Cover: 2.95 **NM** value: **Cover or less**
A: Jaime Antonio **W:** Jaime Antonio
4 ❑ Feb 2001 Cover: 2.95 **NM** value: **Cover or less**
A: Jaime Antonio **W:** Jaime Antonio
5 ❑ Mar 2001 Cover: 2.95 **NM** value: **Cover or less**
A: Jaime Antonio **W:** Jaime Antonio

DEMI'S WILD KINGDOM ADVENTURE — Opus
All issues are adults only.
1 ❑ Mar 2000, b&w Cover: 9.95 **NM** value: **Cover or less**
• squarebound

DEMI THE DEMONESS — Rip Off
This adult comic-book series from Rip Off Press stars a sexy demoness with a more-than-healthy libido. Notably, this series serves as the launching point for a remarkable "Adventure" special edition that combined erotica with interactive fiction.

When the readers reach the end of a paragraph or page, they can then decide what they want to happen next. This style of branched storytelling became well-known when R.A. Montgomery's Choose Your Own Adventure books were sold in children's bookstores in the 1980s. But in this series, the tone is decidedly not for kids, as Demi the Demoness experiences sexual pleasure with Egyptian cat gods, mortal men, and flying horses.

1 ❑ Mar 1993 Cover: 2.95 **NM** value: **Cover or less**
A: Steven S. Crompton **W:** Anita
2 ❑ Nov 1993 Cover: 2.95 **NM** value: **Cover or less**
3 ❑ Mar 1995 Cover: 2.95 **NM** value: **Cover or less**
• flip-book with Kit-Ra back-up
4 ❑ Cover: 3.25 **NM** value: **Cover or less**
★ 1st Appearance of Imed the Angelic.
SE 1 ❑ Cover: 5.95 **NM** value: **Cover or less**
• "Choose your own adventure"-style special

DEMOLITION MAN — DC
1 ❑ Nov 1993 Cover: 1.75 **NM** value: **Cover or less**
Circ: CapCity orders: **7,800**
📖 Send a Maniac to Catch One! **A:** Rod Whigham **W:** Gary Cohn
2 ❑ Dec 1993 Cover: 1.75 **NM** value: **Cover or less**
Circ: CapCity orders: **6,850**
A: Rod Whigham **W:** Gary Cohn
3 ❑ Jan 1994 Cover: 1.75 **NM** value: **Cover or less**
Circ: CapCity orders: **5,200**
📖 The Man Who Remade The World! **A:** Rod Whigham **W:** Gary Cohn
4 ❑ Feb 1994 Cover: 1.75 **NM** value: **Cover or less**
Circ: CapCity orders: **4,300**
A: Rod Whigham **W:** Gary Cohn

DEMON, THE (1ST SERIES) — DC
Demonologist Jason Blood has been studying the occult for years. One day, he adventures into an old castle and discovers a dusty tomb. Upon reading the inscription on it, he unleashes Etrigan, a demon that has been lurking dormant inside him for centuries.

Etrigan was first summoned to this plane by Merlin the magician, to help him fight Morgaine le Fay back in the days of Camelot. Afterward, the demon has been suppressed in the form of Jason Blood, who has wandered through life ignorant of his true nature.

Today, Etrigan and Jason exist in a strange symbiosis, able to shift between identities at will. As The Demon, he possesses great strength, which he uses to fight a variety of human and supernatural foes. In this first series, he has not yet taken up the practice of always speaking in rhyme, an annoying habit at best.

1 ❑ Aug 1972 Cover: 0.20 **NM** value: **10.00**
• **CGC:** 13 graded, best 9.4
📖 Unleash the One Who Waits • 1st Demon **A:** Jack Kirby ★ Origin of Etrigan. ★ 1st Appearance of Jason Blood, Etrigan, Randu Singh.
2 ❑ Oct 1972 Cover: 0.20 **NM** value: **6.00**
• **CGC:** 3 graded, best 9.4
📖 My Tomb in Castle Branek **A:** Jack Kirby
3 ❑ Nov 1972 Cover: 0.20 **NM** value: **5.00**
• **CGC:** 3 graded, best 9.4
📖 Reincarnators • Batman **A:** Jack Kirby **W:** Jack Kirby
4 ❑ Dec 1972 Cover: 0.20 **NM** value: **5.00**
• **CGC:** 1 graded, best 9.4
📖 The Creature From the Beyond **A:** Jack Kirby
5 ❑ Jan 1973 Cover: 0.20 **NM** value: **4.00**
• **CGC:** 2 graded, best 9.4
📖 Merlin's World, Demon's Wrath **A:** Jack Kirby
6 ❑ Feb 1973 Cover: 0.20 **NM** value: **4.00**
📖 The Howler **A:** Jack Kirby
7 ❑ Mar 1973 Cover: 0.20 **NM** value: **4.00**
📖 A Witch Boy **A:** Jack Kirby ★ 1st Appearance of Klarion the Witch Boy.
8 ❑ Apr 1973 Cover: 0.20 **NM** value: **4.00**
📖 Phantom of the Sewers **A:** Jack Kirby
9 ❑ Jun 1973 Cover: 0.20 **NM** value: **4.00**
• **CGC:** 1 graded, best 7.5
📖 Whatever Happened to Farley Fairfax? **A:** Jack Kirby
10 ❑ Jul 1973 Cover: 0.20 **NM** value: **4.00**
📖 The Thing That Screams **A:** Jack Kirby
11 ❑ Aug 1973 Cover: 0.20 **NM** value: **4.00**
📖 Baron Von Evilstein **A:** Jack Kirby
12 ❑ Sep 1973 Cover: 0.20 **NM** value: **4.00**
📖 Rebirth of Evil **A:** Jack Kirby
13 ❑ Oct 1973 Cover: 0.20 **NM** value: **4.00**
📖 The Night of the Demon **A:** Jack Kirby
14 ❑ Nov 1973 Cover: 0.20 **NM** value: **4.00**
📖 Witchboy **A:** Jack Kirby
15 ❑ Dec 1973 Cover: 0.20 **NM** value: **4.00**
📖 The One Who Vanished **A:** Jack Kirby
16 ❑ Jan 1974 Cover: 0.20 **NM** value: **4.00**
📖 The Immortal Enemy **A:** Jack Kirby

DEMON, THE (2ND SERIES) — DC
1 ❑ Jan 1987 Cover: 0.75 **NM** value: **1.50**
Circ: CapCity orders: **25,500**
📖 Direction From The Darkness **A:** Matt Wagner **W:** Matt Wagner
2 ❑ Feb 1987 Cover: 0.75 **NM** value: **1.00**
Circ: CapCity orders: **20,500**
A: Matt Wagner
3 ❑ Mar 1987 Cover: 0.75 **NM** value: **1.00**
Circ: CapCity orders: **19,650**
A: Matt Wagner
4 ❑ Apr 1987 Cover: 0.75 **NM** value: **1.00**
Circ: CapCity orders: **17,600**
📖 Begins Our Tale of Woe **A:** Matt Wagner **W:** Matt Wagner

DEMON, THE (3RD SERIES) — DC
0 ❑ Oct 1994 Cover: 1.95 **NM** value: **2.00**
Circ: CapCity orders: **11,750**
★ Origin of Jason Blood, Etrigan.
1 ❑ Jul 1990 Cover: 1.50 **NM** value: **4.00**
Circ: CapCity orders: **30,550**
📖 Lost Souls **A:** Val Semeiks **W:** Alan Grant
2 ❑ Aug 1990 Cover: 1.50 **NM** value: **2.50**
Circ: CapCity orders: **22,150**
3 ❑ Sep 1990 Cover: 1.50 **NM** value: **2.50**
Circ: CapCity orders: **23,700**
• Batman
4 ❑ Oct 1990 Cover: 1.50 **NM** value: **2.25**
Circ: CapCity orders: **21,350**
5 ❑ Nov 1990 Cover: 1.50 **NM** value: **2.25**
Circ: CapCity orders: **20,550**
6 ❑ Dec 1990 Cover: 1.50 **NM** value: **2.25**
Circ: CapCity orders: **20,200**
7 ❑ Jan 1991 Cover: 1.50 **NM** value: **2.25**
Circ: CapCity orders: **18,900**
8 ❑ Feb 1991 Cover: 1.50 **NM** value: **2.25**
Circ: CapCity orders: **21,750**
• Batman
9 ❑ Mar 1991 Cover: 1.50 **NM** value: **2.25**
Circ: CapCity orders: **16,350**
10 ❑ Apr 1991 Cover: 1.50 **NM** value: **2.25**
Circ: CapCity orders: **15,300**
11 ❑ May 1991 Cover: 1.50 **NM** value: **3.00**
Circ: CapCity orders: **17,100**
12 ❑ Jun 1991 Cover: 1.50 **NM** value: **2.50**
Circ: CapCity orders: **31,550**
★ Appearance of Lobo.
13 ❑ Jul 1991 Cover: 1.50 **NM** value: **2.50**
Circ: CapCity orders: **28,950**
★ Appearance of Lobo.
14 ❑ Aug 1991 Cover: 1.50 **NM** value: **2.50**
Circ: CapCity orders: **28,900**
★ Appearance of Lobo.
15 ❑ Sep 1991 Cover: 1.50 **NM** value: **2.50**
Circ: CapCity orders: **32,400**
★ Appearance of Lobo.
16 ❑ Oct 1991 Cover: 1.50 **NM** value: **2.00**
Circ: CapCity orders: **18,700**
17 ❑ Nov 1991 Cover: 1.50 **NM** value: **2.00**
Circ: CapCity orders: **23,500**
📖 War of the Gods, Part 19 • War of the Gods
18 ❑ Dec 1991 Cover: 1.50 **NM** value: **2.00**
Circ: CapCity orders: **17,200**
19 ❑ Jan 1992 Cover: 2.50 **NM** value: **Cover or less**
Circ: CapCity orders: **18,750**
• Double-size. • Lobo poster
20 ❑ Feb 1992 Cover: 1.50 **NM** value: **2.00**
Circ: CapCity orders: **15,150**
21 ❑ Mar 1992 Cover: 1.50 **NM** value: **2.00**
Circ: CapCity orders: **17,600**
22 ❑ Apr 1992 Cover: 1.50 **NM** value: **2.00**
Circ: CapCity orders: **15,650**
23 ❑ May 1992 Cover: 1.50 **NM** value: **2.00**
Circ: CapCity orders: **16,400**
• Robin

CGC-graded: Multiply prices above by **33 for 9.9 M • 16 for 9.8 NM/M • 7 for 9.6 NM+ • 5 for 9.4 NM • 2.5 for 9.2 NM- • 1.5 for 9.0 VF/NM**

24 ❑ Jun 1992 Cover: 1.50 **NM** value: **2.00**
Circ: CapCity orders: **17,700**
• Robin
25 ❑ Jul 1992 Cover: 1.50 **NM** value: **Cover or less**
Circ: CapCity orders: **13,350**
26 ❑ Aug 1992 Cover: 1.50 **NM** value: **Cover or less**
Circ: CapCity orders: **14,450**
27 ❑ Sep 1992 Cover: 1.50 **NM** value: **Cover or less**
Circ: CapCity orders: **12,200**
28 ❑ Oct 1992 Cover: 1.75 **NM** value: **Cover or less**
Circ: CapCity orders: **11,900**
• Superman
29 ❑ Nov 1992 Cover: 1.75 **NM** value: **Cover or less**
Circ: CapCity orders: **11,550**
30 ❑ Dec 1992 Cover: 1.75 **NM** value: **Cover or less**
Circ: CapCity orders: **10,600**
31 ❑ Jan 1993 Cover: 1.75 **NM** value: **Cover or less**
Circ: CapCity orders: **13,650**
32 ❑ Feb 1993 Cover: 1.75 **NM** value: **Cover or less**
Circ: CapCity orders: **12,600**
33 ❑ Mar 1993 Cover: 1.75 **NM** value: **Cover or less**
Circ: CapCity orders: **12,600**
34 ❑ Apr 1993 Cover: 1.75 **NM** value: **Cover or less**
Circ: CapCity orders: **12,850**
• Lobo
35 ❑ May 1993 Cover: 1.75 **NM** value: **Cover or less**
Circ: CapCity orders: **12,600**
• Lobo
36 ❑ Jun 1993 Cover: 1.75 **NM** value: **Cover or less**
Circ: CapCity orders: **11,750**
37 ❑ Jul 1993 Cover: 1.75 **NM** value: **Cover or less**
Circ: CapCity orders: **10,700**
38 ❑ Aug 1993 Cover: 1.75 **NM** value: **Cover or less**
Circ: CapCity orders: **10,200**
39 ❑ Sep 1993 Cover: 1.75 **NM** value: **Cover or less**
Circ: CapCity orders: **9,350**
40 ❑ Oct 1993 Cover: 1.75 **NM** value: **Cover or less**
Circ: CapCity orders: **10,800**
41 ❑ Nov 1993 Cover: 1.75 **NM** value: **Cover or less**
Circ: CapCity orders: **8,650**
📖 Castle of the Damned **A:** Kevin Altieri **W:** Kevin Altieri
42 ❑ Dec 1993 Cover: 1.75 **NM** value: **Cover or less**
Circ: CapCity orders: **8,150 • CGC:** 1 graded, best 9.0
43 ❑ Jan 1994 Cover: 1.75 **NM** value: **8.00**
Circ: CapCity orders: **8,100**
W: Garth Ennis ★ Appearance of Hitman.
44 ❑ Feb 1994 Cover: 1.75 **NM** value: **8.00**
Circ: CapCity orders: **7,350 • CGC:** 1 graded, best 9.6
W: Garth Ennis ★ Appearance of Hitman.
45 ❑ Mar 1994 Cover: 1.75 **NM** value: **8.00**
Circ: CapCity orders: **6,600**
W: Garth Ennis ★ Appearance of Hitman.
46 ❑ Apr 1994 Cover: 1.75 **NM** value: **Cover or less**
Circ: CapCity orders: **6,150 • CGC:** 1 graded, best 9.4
★ Appearance of Haunted Tank.
47 ❑ May 1994 Cover: 1.75 **NM** value: **Cover or less**
Circ: CapCity orders: **6,000**
★ Appearance of Haunted Tank.
48 ❑ Jun 1994 Cover: 1.75 **NM** value: **1.95**
Circ: CapCity orders: **5,800**
49 ❑ Jul 1994 Cover: 1.95 **NM** value: **Cover or less**
Circ: CapCity orders: **5,950**
50 ❑ Aug 1994 Cover: 2.95 **NM** value: **Cover or less**
Circ: CapCity orders: **7,850**
• Giant-size.
51 ❑ Sep 1994 Cover: 1.95 **NM** value: **Cover or less**
Circ: CapCity orders: **5,750**
52 ❑ Nov 1994 Cover: 1.95 **NM** value: **Cover or less**
Circ: CapCity orders: **5,550**
📖 Suffer the Children, Part 1 **A:** John McCrea **W:** Garth Ennis ★ Appearance of Hitman.
53 ❑ Dec 1994 Cover: 1.95 **NM** value: **Cover or less**
Circ: CapCity orders: **5,400**
📖 Suffer the Children, Part 2 **A:** John McCrea **W:** Garth Ennis ★ Appearance of Hitman.
54 ❑ Jan 1995 Cover: 1.95 **NM** value: **Cover or less**
Circ: CapCity orders: **5,350**
📖 Suffer the Children, Part 3 **A:** John McCrea **W:** Garth Ennis ★ Appearance of Hitman.
55 ❑ Feb 1995 Cover: 1.95 **NM** value: **Cover or less**
Circ: CapCity orders: **5,000**
56 ❑ Mar 1995 Cover: 1.95 **NM** value: **Cover or less**
Circ: CapCity orders: **4,525**
57 ❑ Apr 1995 Cover: 1.95 **NM** value: **Cover or less**
Circ: CapCity orders: **4,350**
58 ❑ May 1995 Cover: 1.95 **NM** value: **Cover or less**
Circ: CapCity orders: **4,125**
final issue.
Anl 1❑ca. 1992 Cover: 3.00 **NM** value: **Cover or less**
Circ: CapCity orders: **19,050**
📖 Eclipso: The Darkness Within, Part 7 • Eclipso
Anl 2❑ca. 1993 Cover: 3.50 **NM** value: **12.00**
Circ: CapCity orders: **14,700 • CGC:** 5 graded, best 9.6
📖 Bloodlines ★ 1st Appearance of Hitman.

DEMON BEAST INVASION — CPM / Bare Bear

All issues are adults only.
1 ❑ Oct 1996, b&w Cover: 2.95 **NM** value: **Cover or less**
Circ: Diamd. preorders: **4,396**
wraparound cover. **A:** Dave Cooper **W:** Johji Maki

DEMON BEAST INVASION: THE FALLEN — CPM / Bare Bear

All issues are adults only.
1 ❑ Sep 1998, b&w Cover: 2.95 **NM** value: **Cover or less**
Circ: Diamd. preorders: **2,861**
2 ❑ Oct 1998, b&w Cover: 2.95 **NM** value: **Cover or less**
Circ: Diamd. preorders: **2,509**

DEMONBLADE — New Comics

1 ❑ b&w Cover: 1.95 **NM** value: **Cover or less**

DEMON DREAMS — Pacific

Demon Dreams highlights the work of Arthur Suydam. A veteran of DC's House of Secrets, Suydam later went on to create The New Adventures of Cholly and Flytrap, a story about two wandering adventurers in a post-apocalyptic world. He is, perhaps, best known for his work in Heavy Metal, from which many of these stories are adapted.

Suydam's stories are classic adult horror, vaguely reminiscent of H.P. Lovecraft. Among the best in Demon Dreams is "Bad Breath," the tale of a man with chronic halitosis who finds a cure — and a sure-fire way to woo women — when a demon springs to life within him.

1 ❑ Feb 1984 Cover: 1.50 **NM** value: **Cover or less**
📖 Bad Breath; Christmas Carol **A:** Arthur Suydam **W:** Arthur Suydam
2 ❑ May 1984 Cover: 1.50 **NM** value: **Cover or less**
📖 The Toll Bridge; Mama's Place; Food for the Children; Mudwog **A:** Arthur Suydam **W:** Arthur Suydam

DEMON DREAMS OF DR. DREW — AC

1 ❑ Cover: 2.95 **NM** value: **Cover or less**

DEMONGATE — Sirius

1 ❑ May 1996 Cover: 2.50 **NM** value: **Cover or less**
A: Bao Lin Hum; Steve Blevins **W:** Bao Lin Hum; Steve Blevins
2 ❑ Jun 1996 Cover: 2.50 **NM** value: **Cover or less**
3 ❑ Jul 1996 Cover: 2.50 **NM** value: **Cover or less**
4 ❑ 1996 Cover: 2.50 **NM** value: **Cover or less**
5 ❑ Oct 1996 Cover: 2.50 **NM** value: **Cover or less**
Circ: Diamd. preorders: **3,699**
A: Bao Lin Hum; Colin Chan **W:** Bao Lin Hum; Colin Chan
6 ❑ Nov 1996 Cover: 2.50 **NM** value: **Cover or less**
Circ: Direct Market orders: **3,717**
7 ❑ Dec 1996 Cover: 2.50 **NM** value: **Cover or less**
Circ: Direct Market orders: **3,327**
8 ❑ Jan 1997 Cover: 2.50 **NM** value: **Cover or less**
Circ: Diamd. preorders: **3,228**
9 ❑ Feb 1997, b&w Cover: 2.50 **NM** value: **Cover or less**
Circ: Diamd. preorders: **2,901**

DEMON GUN — Crusade

1 ❑ Jun 1996, b&w Cover: 2.95 **NM** value: **Cover or less**
📖 To Whom Vengeance Belong **A:** Barry Orkin **W:** Gary Cohn
2 ❑ Sep 1996, b&w Cover: 2.95 **NM** value: **Cover or less**
3 ❑ Jan 1997, b&w Cover: 2.95 **NM** value: **Cover or less**
Circ: Diamd. preorders: **5,020**

DEMON-HUNTER — Atlas-Seaboard

1 ❑ Sep 1975 Cover: 0.25 **NM** value: **2.00**
• **CGC:** 2 graded, best 9.4
📖 The Harvester of Eyes! **A:** Rich Buckler **W:** Rich Buckler; David Anthony Kraft ★ 1st Appearance of Gideon Cross.

DEMON HUNTER (AIRCEL) — Aircel

1 ❑ Mar 1989, b&w Cover: 1.95 **NM** value: **Cover or less**
A: Barry Blair **W:** Barry Blair
2 ❑ Apr 1989, b&w Cover: 1.95 **NM** value: **Cover or less**
A: Barry Blair **W:** Barry Blair
3 ❑ May 1989, b&w Cover: 1.95 **NM** value: **Cover or less**
A: Barry Blair **W:** Barry Blair
4 ❑ Jun 1989, b&w Cover: 1.95 **NM** value: **Cover or less**
A: Barry Blair **W:** Barry Blair

DEMON HUNTER (DAVDEZ) — Davdez

1 ❑ Aug 1998 Cover: 2.50 **NM** value: **Cover or less**

DEMONIC TOYS — Eternity

1 ❑ Jan 1992 Cover: 2.50 **NM** value: **Cover or less**
2 ❑ Cover: 2.50 **NM** value: **Cover or less**
3 ❑ Cover: 2.50 **NM** value: **Cover or less**
4 ❑ Cover: 2.50 **NM** value: **Cover or less**

DEMONIQUE — London Night

London Night brings its unique brand of gritty, "from the streets" storytelling to the pages of Demonique. Creators Sky Owens, Michael Shustock, and Chris Fry bring action to life within the black-and-white pages of this four-issue mini-series.

Accepting what he believes to be a piece of cake "soft mission," mercenary-for-hire Viper agrees to escort Monika Bachman (aka Demonique) from a monastery in Germany to a research corporation in the United States. It seems that this near-genius 23-year-old has a "gift" that the American government would like to study: a gift of a vampiric nature. Gruesome murders, strange happenings, and some of the underworld's most dangerous creatures await the two fugitives at every turn. It doesn't take long before Viper's so-called "soft mission" turns into one of the most dangerous assignments he has ever accepted. Coming face-to-face with horrific demons, the mercenary realizes that his very cargo may just be the most dangerous monster of them all.

1 ❑ Oct 1994, b&w Cover: 3.00 **NM** value: **Cover or less**
Circ: CapCity orders: **2,560**
A: Sky Owens **W:** Sky Owens; Michael Shustock
2 ❑ 1995 Cover: 3.00 **NM** value: **Cover or less**
3 ❑ 1995 Cover: 3.00 **NM** value: **Cover or less**
4 ❑ 1995 Cover: 3.00 **NM** value: **Cover or less**

DEMON REALM — Medeia

0 ❑ Cover: 2.50 **NM** value: **Cover or less**
A: Donald Kramer **W:** Gregory Skopis

DEMONS & DARK ELVES — Weirdworx

1 ❑ b&w Cover: 2.95 **NM** value: **Cover or less**

DEMON'S BLOOD — Odyssey

1 ❑ Cover: 1.70 **NM** value: **2.00**

DEMONSLAYER — Image

1 ❑ Nov 1999 Cover: 2.95 **NM** value: **Cover or less**
Circ: Diamd. preorders: **17,597**
📖 Jaklyn's Tale, Part 1 **A:** Marat Mychaels **W:** Marat Mychaels
2 ❑ Dec 1999 Cover: 2.95 **NM** value: **Cover or less**
Circ: Diamd. preorders: **14,063**
📖 Jaklyn's Tale, Part 2 **A:** Marat Mychaels **W:** Marat Mychaels
3 ❑ Jan 2000 Cover: 2.95 **NM** value: **Cover or less**
Circ: Diamd. preorders: **11,837**
📖 Jaklyn's Tale, Part 3 **A:** Marat Mychaels **W:** Marat Mychaels

DEMONSLAYER (VOL. 2) — Image

1 ❑ Jun 2000 Cover: 2.95 **NM** value: **Cover or less**
Circ: Diamd. preorders: **12,300**
📖 Into Hell, Part 1 **A:** Marat Mychaels **W:** Marat Mychaels
2 ❑ Jul 2000 Cover: 2.95 **NM** value: **Cover or less**
Circ: Diamd. preorders: **9,933**
📖 Into Hell, Part 2 **A:** Marat Mychaels **W:** Marat Mychaels
3 ❑ Aug 2000 Cover: 2.95 **NM** value: **Cover or less**
Circ: Diamd. preorders: **9,588**
📖 Into Hell, Part 3 **A:** Marat Mychaels **W:** Marat Mychaels

DEMON'S TAILS — Adventure

1 ❑ b&w Cover: 2.50 **NM** value: **Cover or less**
2 ❑ b&w Cover: 2.50 **NM** value: **Cover or less**
3 ❑ b&w Cover: 2.50 **NM** value: **Cover or less**
4 ❑ b&w Cover: 2.50 **NM** value: **Cover or less**

DEMON WARRIOR, THE — Eastern

1 ❑ Aug 1987, b&w Cover: 1.50 **NM** value: **Cover or less**
A: Jae Lee **W:** Jae Lee
2 ❑ 1987b&w Cover: 1.50 **NM** value: **Cover or less**
A: Jae Lee **W:** Jae Lee
3 ❑ 1987b&w Cover: 1.50 **NM** value: **Cover or less**
A: Jae Lee **W:** Jae Lee
4 ❑ 1988b&w Cover: 1.50 **NM** value: **Cover or less**
A: Jae Lee **W:** Jae Lee

DEN — Fantagor

1 ❑ Cover: 2.00 **NM** value: **3.00**
Circ: CapCity orders: **5,525**
A: Richard Corben
2 ❑ Cover: 2.00 **NM** value: **3.00**
Circ: CapCity orders: **4,500**
A: Richard Corben
3 ❑ Cover: 2.00 **NM** value: **3.00**
Circ: CapCity orders: **4,475**
A: Richard Corben
4 ❑ Cover: 2.00 **NM** value: **3.00**
Circ: CapCity orders: **4,475**
A: Richard Corben
5 ❑ Cover: 2.00 **NM** value: **3.00**
Circ: CapCity orders: **4,050**
A: Richard Corben
6 ❑ Cover: 2.00 **NM** value: **2.50**
Circ: CapCity orders: **4,325**
📖 Den, Giant Below; Hunter; The Late Show, The Scarey One **A:** Richard Corben; Simon Revelstroke; Bruce Jones; Stan Dresser **W:** Richard Corben; Bruce Jones; Stan Dresser
7 ❑ Cover: 2.00 **NM** value: **2.50**
Circ: CapCity orders: **4,100**
📖 Den, The Phoenix Fallen; Sea Serpents; Dat was Den, Dis is Now **A:** Richard Corben; Bruce Jones; Brian Buniak; Stan Dresser **W:** Richard Corben; Simon Revelstroke; Bruce Jones; Brian Buniak; Stan Dresser
8 ❑ Cover: 2.00 **NM** value: **2.50**
Circ: CapCity orders: **4,300**
📖 Shuffled Seeds Scattered; The Cure; Such Pretty Little Toes; Damsel in Dragon Dress **A:** Richard Corben; Bruce Jones **W:** Richard Corben; Bruce Jones; Jan Strnad; Doug Moench
9 ❑ Cover: 2.00 **NM** value: **2.50**
Circ: CapCity orders: **4,225**
📖 Strange Nativity; The Drinkers of Dust; Possessed; The Wreck of The Katerra-Dan; To Meet the Faces You Meet **A:** Richard Corben; Alex Nino; Alex Ni±o **W:** Richard Corben; Jan Strnad
10 ❑ Cover: 2.00 **NM** value: **2.50**
Circ: CapCity orders: **4,200**
A: Richard Corben

The prices seen above do not represent the highest possible prices seen in online auctions, but rather the prices we have seen these issues reliably fetch in a variety of environments (storefront retail, mail order, auction and convention).

Other grades: Multiply prices above by **1.5 for Mint • 2/3 for Very Fine • 1/3 for Fine • 1/5 for Very Good • 1/8 for Good**

DENIZENS OF DEEP CITY — Kitchen Sink

Denizens of Deep City is a story about a city and the people who live there. Admittedly quirky, it still has got all the basics conflicts of comicdom. There is crime, as a mellow man comes home and finds his TV has been kidnapped. It has class struggle, as a woman finds that her new apartment doesn't have a medicine cabinet, and that the landlord she signed a five-year lease with couldn't care less. She then organizes a protest march for medicine cabinets in apartments. It has love, as a policeman sent to break up the medicine cabinet march falls for the lovely protest organizer. Finally, there's death, when the accountant, who could never sleep without watching Johnny Carson, goes crazy and shoots the newspaper boy.

And heck, that's only the first issue!

1 ❑ ca. 1988, b&w Cover: 2.00 **NM** value: **Cover or less**
A: Doug Potter **W:** Doug Potter
2 ❑ ca. 1988, b&w Cover: 2.00 **NM** value: **Cover or less**
A: Doug Potter **W:** Doug Potter
3 ❑ ca. 1988, b&w Cover: 2.00 **NM** value: **Cover or less**
A: Doug Potter **W:** Doug Potter
4 ❑ ca. 1988, b&w Cover: 2.00 **NM** value: **Cover or less**
A: Doug Potter **W:** Doug Potter
5 ❑ ca. 1988, b&w Cover: 2.00 **NM** value: **Cover or less**
A: Doug Potter **W:** Doug Potter
6 ❑ ca. 1988, b&w Cover: 2.00 **NM** value: **Cover or less**
A: Doug Potter **W:** Doug Potter
7 ❑ ca. 1988, b&w Cover: 2.00 **NM** value: **Cover or less**
A: Doug Potter **W:** Doug Potter
8 ❑ ca. 1988, b&w Cover: 2.00 **NM** value: **Cover or less**
A: Doug Potter **W:** Doug Potter
9 ❑ ca. 1988 Cover: 2.00 **NM** value: **Cover or less**
A: Doug Potter **W:** Doug Potter

DENNIS THE MENACE AND HIS DOG RUFF — Fawcett

1 ❑ Sum 1961 Cover: 0.15 **NM** value: **20.00**
• **CGC:** 1 graded, best 3.5

DENNIS THE MENACE AND HIS FRIENDS — Fawcett

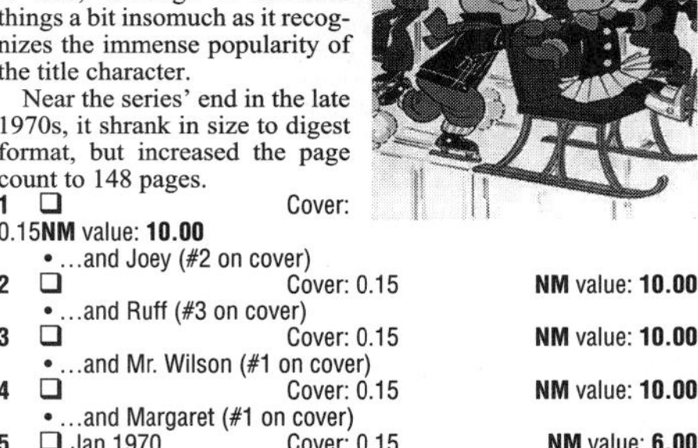

This series reprinted earlier Dennis the Menace adventures, particularly those involving his various friends: his dog Ruff, best pal Joey, arch-nemesis Margaret (she's a girrrrlll!), and his next-door neighbor Mr. Wilson. The strips here were "reprinted by popular demand," a claim which is true, although it stretches things a bit insomuch as it recognizes the immense popularity of the title character.

Near the series' end in the late 1970s, it shrank in size to digest format, but increased the page count to 148 pages.

1 ❑ Cover: 0.15**NM** value: **10.00**
• ...and Joey (#2 on cover)
2 ❑ Cover: 0.15 **NM** value: **10.00**
• ...and Ruff (#3 on cover)
3 ❑ Cover: 0.15 **NM** value: **10.00**
• ...and Mr. Wilson (#1 on cover)
4 ❑ Cover: 0.15 **NM** value: **10.00**
• ...and Margaret (#1 on cover)
5 ❑ Jan 1970 Cover: 0.15 **NM** value: **6.00**
Õand Margaret (#5 on cover).
6 ❑ Jun 1970 Cover: 0.15 **NM** value: **4.00**
• Joey
7 ❑ Aug 1970 Cover: 0.15 **NM** value: **4.00**
8 ❑ Oct 1970 Cover: 0.15 **NM** value: **4.00**
9 ❑ Jan 1971 Cover: 0.15 **NM** value: **4.00**
10 ❑ Jun 1971 Cover: 0.15 **NM** value: **4.00**
11 ❑ Aug 1971 Cover: 0.15 **NM** value: **3.00**
12 ❑ Oct 1971 Cover: 0.15 **NM** value: **3.00**
• Mr. Wilson
13 ❑ Jan 1972 Cover: 0.25 **NM** value: **3.00**
• Margaret
14 ❑ Jun 1972 Cover: 0.25 **NM** value: **3.00**
15 ❑ Aug 1972 Cover: 0.25 **NM** value: **3.00**
• Ruff
16 ❑ Oct 1972 Cover: 0.25 **NM** value: **3.00**
• Mr. Wilson
17 ❑ Jan 1973 Cover: 0.25 **NM** value: **3.00**
18 ❑ Jun 1973 Cover: 0.25 **NM** value: **3.00**
• Joey
19 ❑ Aug 1973 Cover: 0.25 **NM** value: **3.00**
A Full House; Hairy Tale; One for the Books; In the Good old Simmer Time; Jigsaw Puzzle; Barber Shop Harmony; Ruff Stuff; Tinted Vision
20 ❑ Oct 1973 Cover: 0.25 **NM** value: **3.00**
21 ❑ Jan 1974 Cover: 0.25 **NM** value: **3.00**
22 ❑ Jun 1974 Cover: 0.25 **NM** value: **3.00**
• Joey
23 ❑ Aug 1974 Cover: 0.25 **NM** value: **3.00**
24 ❑ Oct 1974 **NM** value: **3.00**
25 ❑ Jan 1975 **NM** value: **3.00**
26 ❑ Jun 1975 **NM** value: **3.00**
27 ❑ Aug 1975 **NM** value: **3.00**
28 ❑ Oct 1975 **NM** value: **3.00**
29 ❑ Jan 1976 Cover: 0.30 **NM** value: **3.00**
Charge!; Up in the Air; The All Star Cast; • ...and Margaret (#29)
30 ❑ Jun 1976 Cover: 0.30 **NM** value: **3.00**
31 ❑ Aug 1976 Cover: 0.30 **NM** value: **2.50**
32 ❑ Oct 1976 **NM** value: **2.50**
33 ❑ Jan 1977 **NM** value: **2.50**
34 ❑ Jun 1977 **NM** value: **2.50**
35 ❑ Aug 1977 Cover: 0.35 **NM** value: **2.50**
• Ruff
36 ❑ Oct 1977 Cover: 0.35 **NM** value: **2.50**
37 ❑ Oct 1977 Cover: 0.95 **NM** value: **2.50**
38 ❑ Apr 1978 Cover: 0.95 **NM** value: **2.50**
• digest size begins.
39 ❑ Jun 1978 Cover: 0.95 **NM** value: **2.50**
40 ❑ Aug 1978 Cover: 0.95 **NM** value: **2.50**
41 ❑ Oct 1978 Cover: 0.95 **NM** value: **2.50**
Girly Whirly; Be My Valentine; Happy Jump Year; Fairy 'Nuff; All Washington'd Up; House Broken; Dennis the Menace, All American Boy; Dennis and the Little Lady; The Mystery Pet; The Compact Car Caper • Reprints first Margaret story; Screamy Mimi story; Chub story
42 ❑ Apr 1979 Cover: 0.95 **NM** value: **2.50**
43 ❑ Jun 1979 Cover: 0.95 **NM** value: **2.50**
The Cooky Caper; The Mirthquake; Cadet Capers; The Wild Watermelon Chase; On the Spot; Gopher Goofy; The Mystery Man; The Curly Bird; The Ski's The Limit; Dreamy Dennis; alphabet stories C-Z • Reprints 24 of 26 Dennis Alphabet stories, omitting A and B
44 ❑ Jul 1979 Cover: 0.95 **NM** value: **2.50**
45 ❑ Oct 1979 Cover: 0.95 **NM** value: **2.50**
46 ❑ Apr 1980 Cover: 0.95 **NM** value: **2.50**
final issue.

DENNIS THE MENACE AND HIS PAL JOEY — Fawcett

1 ❑ ca. 1961 Cover: 0.10 **NM** value: **40.00**

DENNIS THE MENACE BIG BONUS SERIES — Fawcett

10 ❑ Feb 1980 Cover: 0.40 **NM** value: **3.00**
11 ❑ Apr 1980 Cover: 0.40 **NM** value: **3.00**

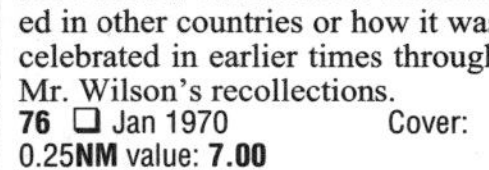

DENNIS THE MENACE BONUS MAGAZINE SERIES — Fawcett

This series is a continuation of the Dennis the Menace (Giants) series that ran from 1955-1969. Like its predecessor, it's a collection of giant-sized reprints of various Dennis the Menace strips from years past, primarily focused around larger themes such as Dennis visiting Washington, D.C. (a popular pastime) or celebrating various holidays. In addition to celebrating the holidays in the U.S., some issues showed how Christmas is celebrated in other countries or how it was celebrated in earlier times through Mr. Wilson's recollections.

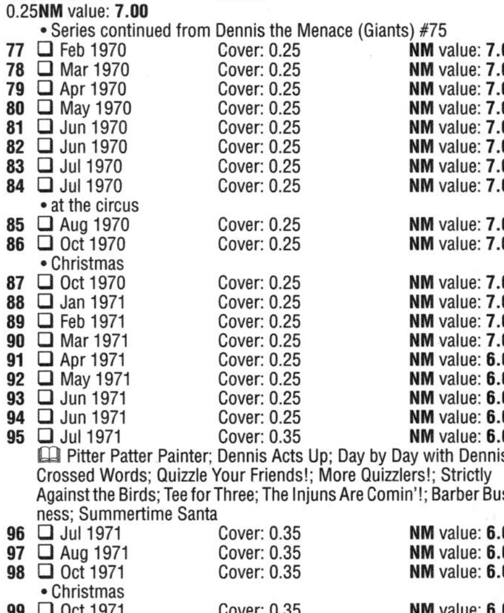

76 ❑ Jan 1970 Cover: 0.25**NM** value: **7.00**
• Series continued from Dennis the Menace (Giants) #75
77 ❑ Feb 1970 Cover: 0.25 **NM** value: **7.00**
78 ❑ Mar 1970 Cover: 0.25 **NM** value: **7.00**
79 ❑ Apr 1970 Cover: 0.25 **NM** value: **7.00**
80 ❑ May 1970 Cover: 0.25 **NM** value: **7.00**
81 ❑ Jun 1970 Cover: 0.25 **NM** value: **7.00**
82 ❑ Jun 1970 Cover: 0.25 **NM** value: **7.00**
83 ❑ Jul 1970 Cover: 0.25 **NM** value: **7.00**
84 ❑ Jul 1970 Cover: 0.25 **NM** value: **7.00**
• at the circus
85 ❑ Aug 1970 Cover: 0.25 **NM** value: **7.00**
86 ❑ Oct 1970 Cover: 0.25 **NM** value: **7.00**
• Christmas
87 ❑ Oct 1970 Cover: 0.25 **NM** value: **7.00**
88 ❑ Jan 1971 Cover: 0.25 **NM** value: **7.00**
89 ❑ Feb 1971 Cover: 0.25 **NM** value: **7.00**
90 ❑ Mar 1971 Cover: 0.25 **NM** value: **7.00**
91 ❑ Apr 1971 Cover: 0.25 **NM** value: **6.00**
92 ❑ May 1971 Cover: 0.25 **NM** value: **6.00**
93 ❑ Jun 1971 Cover: 0.25 **NM** value: **6.00**
94 ❑ Jun 1971 Cover: 0.25 **NM** value: **6.00**
95 ❑ Jul 1971 Cover: 0.35 **NM** value: **6.00**
Pitter Patter Painter; Dennis Acts Up; Day by Day with Dennis; Crossed Words; Quizzle Your Friends!; More Quizzlers!; Strictly Against the Birds; Tee for Three; The Injuns Are Comin'!; Barber Business; Summertime Santa
96 ❑ Jul 1971 Cover: 0.35 **NM** value: **6.00**
97 ❑ Aug 1971 Cover: 0.35 **NM** value: **6.00**
98 ❑ Oct 1971 Cover: 0.35 **NM** value: **6.00**
• Christmas
99 ❑ Oct 1971 Cover: 0.35 **NM** value: **6.00**
100 ❑ Jan 1972 Cover: 0.35 **NM** value: **6.00**
101 ❑ Feb 1972 Cover: 0.35 **NM** value: **6.00**
102 ❑ Mar 1972 Cover: 0.35 **NM** value: **6.00**
Wish I Was
103 ❑ Apr 1972 Cover: 0.35 **NM** value: **6.00**
• Short Stuff Special
104 ❑ May 1972 Cover: 0.35 **NM** value: **6.00**
105 ❑ Jun 1972 Cover: 0.35 **NM** value: **6.00**
106 ❑ Jun 1972 Cover: 0.35 **NM** value: **6.00**
107 ❑ Jul 1972 Cover: 0.35 **NM** value: **6.00**
108 ❑ Jul 1972 Cover: 0.35 **NM** value: **6.00**
109 ❑ Aug 1972 Cover: 0.35 **NM** value: **6.00**
110 ❑ Oct 1972 Cover: 0.35 **NM** value: **6.00**
• Christmas
111 ❑ Oct 1972 Cover: 0.35 **NM** value: **6.00**
• Christmas
112 ❑ Jan 1973 Cover: 0.35 **NM** value: **6.00**
Circ: Statement: **145,565**
• Go-Go Special
113 ❑ Feb 1973 Cover: 0.35 **NM** value: **6.00**
Circ: Statement: **145,565**
Tangled Tales
114 ❑ Mar 1973 Cover: 0.35 **NM** value: **6.00**
Circ: Statement: **145,565**
Hawaii
115 ❑ Apr 1973 Cover: 0.35 **NM** value: **6.00**
Circ: Statement: **145,565**
116 ❑ May 1973 Cover: 0.35 **NM** value: **6.00**
Circ: Statement: **145,565**
117 ❑ Jun 1973 Cover: 0.35 **NM** value: **6.00**
Circ: Statement: **145,565**
118 ❑ Jun 1973 Cover: 0.35 **NM** value: **6.00**
Circ: Statement: **145,565**
119 ❑ Jul 1973 Cover: 0.35 **NM** value: **6.00**
Circ: Statement: **145,565**
• Summer Number and state flags
120 ❑ Jul 1973 Cover: 0.35 **NM** value: **6.00**
Circ: Statement: **145,565**
121 ❑ Aug 1973 Cover: 0.35 **NM** value: **5.00**
Circ: Statement: **145,565**
Way-Out Stories
122 ❑ Oct 1973 Cover: 0.35 **NM** value: **5.00**
Circ: Statement: **145,565**
123 ❑ Oct 1973 Cover: 0.35 **NM** value: **5.00**
Circ: Statement: **145,565**
124 ❑ Jan 1974 Cover: 0.35 **NM** value: **5.00**
Circ: Statement: **134,084**
• Has 1973 Statement; avg total paid circ 145,565
125 ❑ Feb 1974 Cover: 0.35 **NM** value: **5.00**
Circ: Statement: **134,084**
126 ❑ Mar 1974 Cover: 0.35 **NM** value: **5.00**
Circ: Statement: **134,084**
127 ❑ Apr 1974 Cover: 0.35 **NM** value: **5.00**
Circ: Statement: **134,084**
128 ❑ May 1974 Cover: 0.35 **NM** value: **5.00**
Circ: Statement: **134,084**
129 ❑ Jun 1974 Cover: 0.35 **NM** value: **5.00**
Circ: Statement: **134,084**
130 ❑ Jun 1974 Cover: 0.35 **NM** value: **5.00**
Circ: Statement: **134,084**
131 ❑ Jul 1974 Cover: 0.35 **NM** value: **5.00**
Circ: Statement: **134,084**
132 ❑ Jul 1974 Cover: 0.35 **NM** value: **5.00**
Circ: Statement: **134,084**
133 ❑ Aug 1974 Cover: 0.35 **NM** value: **5.00**
Circ: Statement: **134,084**
134 ❑ Oct 1974 Cover: 0.35 **NM** value: **5.00**
Circ: Statement: **134,084**
• Christmas
135 ❑ Oct 1974 Cover: 0.35 **NM** value: **5.00**
Circ: Statement: **134,084**
136 ❑ Jan 1975 Cover: 0.35 **NM** value: **5.00**
Crazy Daze • Has 1974 Statement; avg total paid circ 134,084
137 ❑ Feb 1975 Cover: 0.35 **NM** value: **5.00**
138 ❑ Mar 1975 Cover: 0.35 **NM** value: **5.00**
139 ❑ Apr 1975 Cover: 0.35 **NM** value: **5.00**
140 ❑ May 1975 Cover: 0.35 **NM** value: **5.00**
Big Deal
141 ❑ Jun 1975 Cover: 0.35 **NM** value: **5.00**
142 ❑ Jun 1975 Cover: 0.35 **NM** value: **5.00**
143 ❑ Jul 1975 Cover: 0.35 **NM** value: **5.00**
144 ❑ Jul 1975 Cover: 0.35 **NM** value: **5.00**
Welcome to Washington!; Down in Historic Virginia; The White House; The Capitol
145 ❑ Aug 1975 Cover: 0.35 **NM** value: **5.00**
146 ❑ Oct 1975 Cover: 0.35 **NM** value: **5.00**
• Christmas
147 ❑ Oct 1975 Cover: 0.35 **NM** value: **5.00**
148 ❑ Jan 1976 Cover: 0.35 **NM** value: **5.00**
Circ: Statement: **114,499**
149 ❑ Feb 1976 Cover: 0.35 **NM** value: **5.00**
Circ: Statement: **114,499**
150 ❑ Mar 1976 Cover: 0.35 **NM** value: **5.00**
Circ: Statement: **114,499**
151 ❑ Apr 1976 Cover: 0.35 **NM** value: **4.00**
Circ: Statement: **114,499**
152 ❑ May 1976 Cover: 0.35 **NM** value: **4.00**
Circ: Statement: **114,499**
153 ❑ Jun 1976 Cover: 0.35 **NM** value: **4.00**
Circ: Statement: **114,499**
154 ❑ Jun 1976 Cover: 0.35 **NM** value: **4.00**
Circ: Statement: **114,499**
155 ❑ Jul 1976 Cover: 0.35 **NM** value: **4.00**
Circ: Statement: **114,499**
156 ❑ Jul 1976 Cover: 0.35 **NM** value: **4.00**
Circ: Statement: **114,499**
157 ❑ Aug 1976 Cover: 0.35 **NM** value: **4.00**
Circ: Statement: **114,499**
158 ❑ Oct 1976 Cover: 0.35 **NM** value: **4.00**
Circ: Statement: **114,499**
159 ❑ Oct 1976 Cover: 0.35 **NM** value: **4.00**
Circ: Statement: **114,499**
160 ❑ Jan 1977 Cover: 0.35 **NM** value: **4.00**
161 ❑ 1977 Cover: 0.35 **NM** value: **4.00**
162 ❑ 1977 Cover: 0.35 **NM** value: **4.00**
• Has 1976 Statement; avg total paid circ 114,499
163 ❑ 1977 Cover: 0.35 **NM** value: **4.00**
164 ❑ 1977 Cover: 0.35 **NM** value: **4.00**
165 ❑ 1977 Cover: 0.35 **NM** value: **4.00**

CGC-graded: Multiply prices above by **33 for 9.9 M • 16 for 9.8 NM/M • 7 for 9.6 NM+ • 5 for 9.4 NM • 2.5 for 9.2 NM- • 1.5 for 9.0 VF/NM**

166 ❑ 1977 Cover: 0.35 NM value: 4.00
167 ❑ Jun 1977 Cover: 0.35 NM value: 4.00
168 ❑ 1977 Cover: 0.35 NM value: 4.00
169 ❑ 1977 Cover: 0.35 NM value: 4.00
170 ❑ 1977 Cover: 0.35 NM value: 4.00
171 ❑ 1977 Cover: 0.35 NM value: 3.00
172 ❑ Jan 1978 Cover: 0.35 NM value: 3.00
173 ❑ Feb 1978 Cover: 0.35 NM value: 3.00
174 ❑ Mar 1978 Cover: 0.35 NM value: 3.00
175 ❑ Apr 1978 NM value: 3.00
176 ❑ May 1978 NM value: 3.00
177 ❑ Jun 1978 NM value: 3.00
178 ❑ Jun 1978 NM value: 3.00
179 ❑ Jul 1978 NM value: 3.00
180 ❑ Jul 1978 NM value: 3.00
181 ❑ Aug 1978 NM value: 3.00
182 ❑ Oct 1978 NM value: 3.00
183 ❑ Oct 1978 NM value: 3.00
184 ❑ Jan 1979 NM value: 3.00
Circ: Statement: 73,552
185 ❑ Feb 1979 Cover: 0.40 NM value: 3.00
Circ: Statement: 73,552
186 ❑ Mar 1979 Cover: 0.40 NM value: 3.00
Circ: Statement: 73,552
187 ❑ Apr 1979 Cover: 0.40 NM value: 3.00
Circ: Statement: 73,552
188 ❑ May 1979 Cover: 0.40 NM value: 3.00
Circ: Statement: 73,552
189 ❑ Jun 1979 Cover: 0.40 NM value: 3.00
Circ: Statement: 73,552
190 ❑ Jun 1979 Cover: 0.40 NM value: 3.00
Circ: Statement: 73,552
191 ❑ Jul 1979 Cover: 0.40 NM value: 3.00
Circ: Statement: 73,552
192 ❑ Jul 1979 Cover: 0.40 NM value: 3.00
Circ: Statement: 73,552
193 ❑ Aug 1979 Cover: 0.40 NM value: 3.00
Circ: Statement: 73,552
194 ❑ Oct 1979 Cover: 0.40 NM value: 3.00
Circ: Statement: 73,552
final issue.

DENNIS THE MENACE (FAWCETT) Standard

Dennis Mitchell is a five-year-old with blonde hair, a bouncy personality, and a childish innocence. Why then does his neighbor Mr. Wilson fear his presence, and his parents, Henry and Alice, throw up their hands in exasperation whenever they contemplate his day's activities?

Because Dennis Mitchell is Dennis the Menace — a charmer of a kid with an uncanny talent for accidentally causing trouble. But for all this, he remains a lovable tyke, familiar to anyone who has ever had a five-year-old of their own.

The late Hank Ketcham's cartoon creation has been a popular favorite since it first appeared in the funny pages in 1951. It gave rise to numerous comic series, books, and even screen and stage plays.

1 ❑ Aug 1953 Cover: 0.10 NM value: 350.00
• CGC: 1 graded, best 7.0
★ 1st Appearance of Dennis the Menace, Mr. Wilson, Ruff.
2 ❑ 1953 Cover: 0.10 NM value: 125.00
📖 Angel with a Sweet Tooth; Pee Bee Kappa (Boy Genius); Dennis the Menace vs. The Public Library; Chub; Crazy over Horses, Horses, Horse…; Space-Happy; Dennis the Arteest
3 ❑ Mar 1954 Cover: 0.10 NM value: 85.00
4 ❑ May 1954 Cover: 0.10 NM value: 70.00
5 ❑ Jul 1954 Cover: 0.10 NM value: 70.00
6 ❑ Sep 1954 Cover: 0.10 NM value: 60.00
7 ❑ Nov 1954 Cover: 0.10 NM value: 60.00
9 ❑ Mar 1955 Cover: 0.10 NM value: 60.00
10 ❑ May 1955 Cover: 0.10 NM value: 60.00
11 ❑ Jul 1955 Cover: 0.10 NM value: 45.00
12 ❑ Sep 1955 Cover: 0.10 NM value: 45.00
13 ❑ Nov 1955 Cover: 0.10 NM value: 45.00
14 ❑ Jan 1956 Cover: 0.10 NM value: 45.00
15 ❑ Mar 1956 Cover: 0.10 NM value: 45.00
16 ❑ May 1956 Cover: 0.10 NM value: 45.00
17 ❑ Jul 1956 Cover: 0.10 NM value: 45.00
18 ❑ Sep 1956 Cover: 0.10 NM value: 45.00
19 ❑ Nov 1956 Cover: 0.10 NM value: 45.00
20 ❑ Jan 1957 Cover: 0.10 NM value: 45.00
21 ❑ Mar 1957 Cover: 0.10 NM value: 35.00
22 ❑ May 1957 Cover: 0.10 NM value: 35.00
23 ❑ Jul 1957 Cover: 0.10 NM value: 35.00
24 ❑ Sep 1957 Cover: 0.10 NM value: 35.00
25 ❑ Nov 1957 Cover: 0.10 NM value: 35.00
26 ❑ Jan 1958 Cover: 0.10 NM value: 35.00
27 ❑ Mar 1958 Cover: 0.10 NM value: 35.00
28 ❑ May 1958 Cover: 0.10 NM value: 35.00
29 ❑ Jul 1958 Cover: 0.10 NM value: 35.00
30 ❑ Sep 1958 Cover: 0.10 NM value: 35.00
📖 Breakfast; Hocus Focus; Tiny Terror (text story); Punky; The Inside Story
31 ❑ Nov 1958 Cover: 0.10 NM value: 25.00
32 ❑ Cover: 0.10 NM value: 25.00
33 ❑ 1959 Cover: 0.10 NM value: 25.00
34 ❑ 1959 Cover: 0.10 NM value: 25.00
35 ❑ 1959 Cover: 0.10 NM value: 25.00
36 ❑ 1959 Cover: 0.10 NM value: 25.00
37 ❑ 1959 Cover: 0.10 NM value: 25.00
38 ❑ Sep 1959 Cover: 0.10 NM value: 25.00
39 ❑ Nov 1959 Cover: 0.10 NM value: 25.00
40 ❑ Jan 1960 Cover: 0.10 NM value: 25.00
41 ❑ Mar 1960 Cover: 0.10 NM value: 16.00
42 ❑ May 1960 Cover: 0.10 NM value: 16.00
43 ❑ 1960 Cover: 0.10 NM value: 16.00
44 ❑ 1960 Cover: 0.10 NM value: 16.00
45 ❑ Sep 1960 Cover: 0.10 NM value: 16.00
46 ❑ 1960 Cover: 0.10 NM value: 16.00
47 ❑ Cover: 0.10 NM value: 16.00
48 ❑ Cover: 0.10 NM value: 16.00
49 ❑ 1961 Cover: 0.10 NM value: 16.00
50 ❑ 1961 Cover: 0.10 NM value: 16.00
51 ❑ 1961 Cover: 0.10 NM value: 12.00
52 ❑ 1961 Cover: 0.10 NM value: 12.00
53 ❑ 1961 Cover: 0.10 NM value: 12.00
54 ❑ Cover: 0.10 NM value: 12.00
55 ❑ Cover: 0.10 NM value: 12.00
56 ❑ 1962 Cover: 0.10 NM value: 12.00
57 ❑ 1962 Cover: 0.15 NM value: 12.00
58 ❑ 1962 Cover: 0.15 NM value: 12.00
59 ❑ NM value: 12.00
60 ❑ Jul 1962 Cover: 0.12 NM value: 12.00
61 ❑ 1962 Cover: 0.12 NM value: 12.00
62 ❑ 1962 Cover: 0.12 NM value: 12.00
63 ❑ Cover: 0.12 NM value: 12.00
64 ❑ Cover: 0.12 NM value: 12.00
65 ❑ Mar 1963 Cover: 0.12 NM value: 12.00
66 ❑ May 1963 Cover: 0.12 NM value: 12.00
67 ❑ Jul 1963 Cover: 0.12 NM value: 12.00
68 ❑ Sep 1963 Cover: 0.12 NM value: 12.00
69 ❑ Nov 1963 Cover: 0.12 NM value: 12.00
70 ❑ Jan 1964 Cover: 0.12 NM value: 12.00
71 ❑ Mar 1964 Cover: 0.12 NM value: 9.00
72 ❑ May 1964 Cover: 0.12 NM value: 9.00
73 ❑ Jul 1964 Cover: 0.12 NM value: 9.00
74 ❑ Sep 1964 Cover: 0.12 NM value: 9.00
75 ❑ Nov 1964 Cover: 0.12 NM value: 9.00
76 ❑ Jan 1965 Cover: 0.12 NM value: 9.00
77 ❑ Mar 1965 Cover: 0.12 NM value: 9.00
78 ❑ May 1965 Cover: 0.12 NM value: 9.00
79 ❑ Jul 1965 Cover: 0.12 NM value: 9.00
📖 It's Spring! It's Spring! The Bird is on the Wing! My Word! Absurd! The Wing is on the Bird!; Spilling the Beans; No Schooling
80 ❑ Sep 1965 Cover: 0.12 NM value: 9.00
81 ❑ Nov 1965 Cover: 0.12 NM value: 9.00
82 ❑ Jan 1966 Cover: 0.12 NM value: 9.00
83 ❑ Mar 1966 Cover: 0.12 NM value: 9.00
84 ❑ May 1966 Cover: 0.12 NM value: 9.00
85 ❑ Jul 1966 Cover: 0.12 NM value: 9.00
86 ❑ Sep 1966 Cover: 0.12 NM value: 9.00
87 ❑ Nov 1966 Cover: 0.12 NM value: 9.00
88 ❑ Jan 1967 Cover: 0.12 NM value: 9.00
Circ: Statement: 308,736
89 ❑ Mar 1967 Cover: 0.12 NM value: 9.00
Circ: Statement: 308,736
90 ❑ May 1967 Cover: 0.12 NM value: 9.00
Circ: Statement: 308,736
91 ❑ Jul 1967 Cover: 0.12 NM value: 5.00
Circ: Statement: 308,736
92 ❑ Sep 1967 Cover: 0.12 NM value: 5.00
Circ: Statement: 308,736
93 ❑ Nov 1967 Cover: 0.12 NM value: 5.00
Circ: Statement: 308,736
94 ❑ Jan 1968 Cover: 0.12 NM value: 5.00
95 ❑ Mar 1968 Cover: 0.12 NM value: 5.00
• Has 1967 Statement, filed 10/1/67; avg print run 572,878; avg sales 308,308; avg subs 428; avg total paid 308,736; samples 368; max existent 309,104; 46% of run returned
96 ❑ May 1968 Cover: 0.12 NM value: 5.00
97 ❑ Jul 1968 Cover: 0.12 NM value: 5.00
98 ❑ Sep 1968 Cover: 0.12 NM value: 5.00
99 ❑ Nov 1968 Cover: 0.12 NM value: 5.00
100 ❑ Jan 1969 NM value: 5.00
101 ❑ Mar 1969 NM value: 4.00
102 ❑ May 1969 NM value: 4.00
103 ❑ Jul 1969 NM value: 4.00
104 ❑ Sep 1969 Cover: 0.15 NM value: 4.00
105 ❑ Nov 1969 Cover: 0.15 NM value: 4.00
106 ❑ Jan 1970 Cover: 0.15 NM value: 4.00
107 ❑ Mar 1970 Cover: 0.15 NM value: 4.00
108 ❑ May 1970 Cover: 0.15 NM value: 4.00
109 ❑ Jul 1970 Cover: 0.15 NM value: 4.00
110 ❑ Sep 1970 Cover: 0.15 NM value: 4.00
111 ❑ Nov 1970 Cover: 0.15 NM value: 4.00
112 ❑ Jan 1971 Cover: 0.15 NM value: 4.00
113 ❑ Mar 1971 Cover: 0.15 NM value: 4.00
114 ❑ May 1971 Cover: 0.15 NM value: 4.00
115 ❑ Jul 1971 Cover: 0.15 NM value: 4.00
116 ❑ Sep 1971 Cover: 0.15 NM value: 4.00
• anti-pollution issue
117 ❑ Nov 1971 Cover: 0.15 NM value: 4.00
118 ❑ Jan 1972 Cover: 0.25 NM value: 4.00
119 ❑ Mar 1972 Cover: 0.25 NM value: 4.00
120 ❑ May 1972 Cover: 0.25 NM value: 4.00
121 ❑ Jul 1972 Cover: 0.25 NM value: 3.00
122 ❑ Sep 1972 Cover: 0.25 NM value: 3.00
📖 Spirit of '72
123 ❑ Nov 1972 Cover: 0.25 NM value: 3.00
Circ: Statement: 174,521
124 ❑ Jan 1973 Cover: 0.25 NM value: 3.00
Circ: Statement: 174,521
125 ❑ Mar 1973 Cover: 0.25 NM value: 3.00
Circ: Statement: 174,521
126 ❑ May 1973 Cover: 0.25 NM value: 3.00
Circ: Statement: 174,521
★ Appearance of Gina.
127 ❑ Jul 1973 Cover: 0.25 NM value: 3.00
Circ: Statement: 174,521
128 ❑ Sep 1973 Cover: 0.25 NM value: 3.00
Circ: Statement: 174,521
129 ❑ Nov 1973 Cover: 0.25 NM value: 3.00
Circ: Statement: 178,203
130 ❑ Jan 1974 Cover: 0.25 NM value: 3.00
Circ: Statement: 178,203
131 ❑ Mar 1974 Cover: 0.25 NM value: 3.00
Circ: Statement: 178,203
• Has 1973 Statement; avg total paid circ 174,521
132 ❑ May 1974 Cover: 0.25 NM value: 3.00
Circ: Statement: 178,203
133 ❑ Jul 1974 Cover: 0.25 NM value: 3.00
Circ: Statement: 178,203
134 ❑ Sep 1974 Cover: 0.25 NM value: 3.00
Circ: Statement: 178,203
135 ❑ Nov 1974 Cover: 0.25 NM value: 3.00
136 ❑ Jan 1975 Cover: 0.25 NM value: 3.00
137 ❑ Mar 1975 Cover: 0.25 NM value: 3.00
• Has 1974 Statement; avg total paid circ 178,203
138 ❑ May 1975 Cover: 0.25 NM value: 3.00
139 ❑ Jul 1975 Cover: 0.25 NM value: 3.00
140 ❑ Sep 1975 Cover: 0.25 NM value: 3.00
• at Winchester mansion
141 ❑ Nov 1975 Cover: 0.25 NM value: 2.00
142 ❑ Jan 1976 NM value: 2.00
143 ❑ Mar 1976 Cover: 0.30 NM value: 2.00
144 ❑ May 1976 Cover: 0.30 NM value: 2.00
145 ❑ Jun 1976 Cover: 0.30 NM value: 2.00
146 ❑ Jul 1976 Cover: 0.30 NM value: 2.00
147 ❑ Sep 1976 Cover: 0.30 NM value: 2.00
148 ❑ Nov 1976 Cover: 0.30 NM value: 2.00
149 ❑ Jan 1977 NM value: 2.00
Circ: Statement: 187,202
150 ❑ Mar 1977 NM value: 2.00
Circ: Statement: 187,202
151 ❑ May 1977 Cover: 0.35 NM value: 2.00
Circ: Statement: 187,202
152 ❑ Jul 1977 Cover: 0.35 NM value: 2.00
Circ: Statement: 187,202
153 ❑ Sep 1977 Cover: 0.35 NM value: 2.00
Circ: Statement: 187,202
154 ❑ Nov 1977 Cover: 0.35 NM value: 2.00
Circ: Statement: 187,202
155 ❑ Jan 1978 Cover: 0.35 NM value: 2.00
156 ❑ Mar 1978 Cover: 0.35 NM value: 2.00
157 ❑ May 1978 Cover: 0.35 NM value: 2.00
158 ❑ Jul 1978 Cover: 0.35 NM value: 2.00
159 ❑ Sep 1978 Cover: 0.35 NM value: 2.00
📖 Welcome to the Pumpkin Festival; The Week Watcher
160 ❑ Nov 1978 Cover: 0.35 NM value: 2.00
161 ❑ Jan 1979 Cover: 0.35 NM value: 2.00
162 ❑ Mar 1979 Cover: 0.35 NM value: 2.00
163 ❑ May 1979 Cover: 0.35 NM value: 2.00
164 ❑ Jul 1979 Cover: 0.35 NM value: 2.00
165 ❑ Sep 1979 Cover: 0.35 NM value: 2.00
166 ❑ Nov 1979 Cover: 0.35 NM value: 2.00
final issue.

DENNIS THE MENACE (GIANTS) Fawcett

These giant-sized specials were produced more or less quarterly for almost 15 years between 1955 and 1969. That was the heyday for Dennis the Menace, an innocently mischievous kid whose antics continually threatened to drive his parents to distraction. Dennis is definitely the product of a less jaded era. The "menace" part of his name is due more to youthful high spirits than to any malevolent intention. His parents were continually exasperated by him, underneath, one suspected that they were just as charmed as the reader was.

Along with the various Christmas and summer specials, many of the issues of this series followed Dennis and his family as they went on vacation. These vacation specials made a point of mixing education with hilarity, pointing out the historic and cultural landmarks that Dennis visited.

This series was continued as Dennis the Menace Bonus Magazine Series.

2 ❑ 1956 Cover: 0.25 NM value: 60.00
3 ❑ 1956 Cover: 0.25 NM value: 60.00
4 ❑ 1957 Cover: 0.25 NM value: 60.00
5 ❑ 1957 Cover: 0.25 NM value: 60.00
6 ❑ 1958 Cover: 0.25 NM value: 60.00
• ...In Hawaii
6/A ❑ 1959 NM value: 60.00
• Christmas issue
7 ❑ 1959 Cover: 0.25 NM value: 50.00
8 ❑ 1960 Cover: 0.25 NM value: 50.00
9 ❑ Sum 1961 Cover: 0.25 NM value: 50.00
• CGC: 1 graded, best 9.2
10 ❑ 1961 Cover: 0.25 NM value: 50.00
11 ❑ 1962 Cover: 0.25 NM value: 50.00
12 ❑ 1962 Cover: 0.25 NM value: 50.00
13 ❑ 1963 Cover: 0.25 NM value: 35.00
14 ❑ 1963 Cover: 0.25 NM value: 35.00
15 ❑ 1963 Cover: 0.25 NM value: 35.00
16 ❑ 1963 Cover: 0.25 NM value: 35.00
17 ❑ 1963 Cover: 0.25 NM value: 35.00
18 ❑ 1963 Cover: 0.25 NM value: 35.00
19 ❑ 1963 Cover: 0.25 NM value: 35.00
20 ❑ 1964 Cover: 0.25 NM value: 35.00
21 ❑ 1964 Cover: 0.25 NM value: 20.00
22 ❑ 1964 Cover: 0.25 NM value: 20.00
23 ❑ 1964 Cover: 0.25 NM value: 20.00
24 ❑ 1964 Cover: 0.25 NM value: 20.00
25 ❑ 1964 Cover: 0.25 NM value: 20.00
26 ❑ 1964 Cover: 0.25 NM value: 20.00
27 ❑ Cover: 0.25 NM value: 20.00
28 ❑ Cover: 0.25 NM value: 20.00
29 ❑ 1965 Cover: 0.25 NM value: 20.00

30 ❑ 1965 Cover: 0.25 **NM** value: **15.00**
31 ❑ 1965 Cover: 0.25 **NM** value: **15.00**
32 ❑ 1965 Cover: 0.25 **NM** value: **15.00**
33 ❑ 1965 Cover: 0.25 **NM** value: **15.00**
34 ❑ 1965 Cover: 0.25 **NM** value: **15.00**
35 ❑ 1965 Cover: 0.25 **NM** value: **15.00**
• gatefold summary.
36 ❑ Cover: 0.25 **NM** value: **15.00**
37 ❑ 1966 Cover: 0.25 **NM** value: **15.00**
38 ❑ 1966 Cover: 0.25 **NM** value: **15.00**
39 ❑ 1966 Cover: 0.25 **NM** value: **15.00**
40 ❑ 1966 Cover: 0.25 **NM** value: **15.00**
• ...Visits Washington D.C., 1966
41 ❑ Cover: 0.25 **NM** value: **12.00**
42 ❑ Cover: 0.25 **NM** value: **12.00**
43 ❑ Cover: 0.25 **NM** value: **12.00**
44 ❑ 1967 Cover: 0.25 **NM** value: **12.00**
45 ❑ 1967 Cover: 0.25 **NM** value: **12.00**
46 ❑ 1967 Cover: 0.25 **NM** value: **12.00**
47 ❑ 1967 Cover: 0.25 **NM** value: **12.00**
48 ❑ 1967 Cover: 0.25 **NM** value: **12.00**
49 ❑ 1967 Cover: 0.25 **NM** value: **12.00**
50 ❑ 1967 Cover: 0.25 **NM** value: **12.00**
51 ❑ 1967 Cover: 0.25 **NM** value: **10.00**
52 ❑ Jan 1968 Cover: 0.25 **NM** value: **10.00**
53 ❑ Feb 1968 Cover: 0.25 **NM** value: **10.00**
54 ❑ Mar 1968 Cover: 0.25 **NM** value: **10.00**
55 ❑ Apr 1968 Cover: 0.25 **NM** value: **10.00**
56 ❑ May 1968 Cover: 0.25 **NM** value: **10.00**
57 ❑ Jun 1968 Cover: 0.25 **NM** value: **10.00**
58 ❑ Jul 1968 Cover: 0.25 **NM** value: **10.00**
59 ❑ Aug 1968 Cover: 0.25 **NM** value: **10.00**
60 ❑ Sep 1968 Cover: 0.25 **NM** value: **10.00**
61 ❑ Oct 1968 Cover: 0.25 **NM** value: **9.00**
62 ❑ Nov 1968 Cover: 0.25 **NM** value: **9.00**
63 ❑ Dec 1968 Cover: 0.25 **NM** value: **9.00**
64 ❑ Jan 1969 Cover: 0.25 **NM** value: **9.00**
65 ❑ Feb 1969 Cover: 0.25 **NM** value: **9.00**
66 ❑ Mar 1969 Cover: 0.25 **NM** value: **9.00**
67 ❑ Apr 1969 Cover: 0.25 **NM** value: **9.00**
68 ❑ May 1969 Cover: 0.25 **NM** value: **9.00**
69 ❑ Jun 1969 Cover: 0.25 **NM** value: **9.00**
70 ❑ Jul 1969 Cover: 0.25 **NM** value: **9.00**
71 ❑ Aug 1969 Cover: 0.25 **NM** value: **9.00**
72 ❑ Sep 1969 Cover: 0.25 **NM** value: **9.00**
📖 Dennis Visits Santa Claus
73 ❑ Oct 1969 Cover: 0.25 **NM** value: **9.00**
74 ❑ Nov 1969 Cover: 0.25 **NM** value: **9.00**
75 ❑ Dec 1969 Cover: 0.25 **NM** value: **9.00**
• Series continued in Dennis the Menace Bonus Magazine Series #76.
SE 1❑ ca. 1955 **NM** value: **95.00**
• Giant Vacation Special (Summer, 1955);First issue of this series
SE 2❑ ca. 1955 **NM** value: **80.00**
• Christmas, 1955 Special

DENNIS THE MENACE (MARVEL) — Marvel

1 ❑ Nov 1981 Cover: 0.50 **NM** value: **2.00**
2 ❑ Dec 1981 Cover: 0.50 **NM** value: **1.50**
3 ❑ Jan 1982 Cover: 0.60 **NM** value: **1.50**
4 ❑ Feb 1982 Cover: 0.60 **NM** value: **1.50**
5 ❑ Mar 1982 Cover: 0.60 **NM** value: **1.50**
6 ❑ Apr 1982 Cover: 0.60 **NM** value: **1.50**
7 ❑ May 1982 Cover: 0.60 **NM** value: **1.50**
8 ❑ Jun 1982 Cover: 0.60 **NM** value: **1.50**
9 ❑ Jul 1982 Cover: 0.60 **NM** value: **1.50**
10 ❑ Aug 1982 Cover: 0.60 **NM** value: **1.50**
11 ❑ Sep 1982 Cover: 0.60 **NM** value: **1.50**
12 ❑ Oct 1982 Cover: 0.60 **NM** value: **1.50**
13 ❑ Nov 1982 Cover: 0.60 **NM** value: **1.50**

DENTAL HYGIENE FUNNIES — Slave Labor

1 ❑ Cover: 1.00 **NM** value: **Cover or less**
📖 Loof Toof; Tooth Fairy **A:** TK Talbert **W:** TK Talbert

DEPRESSOR, THE — Being

1 ❑ Cover: 2.50 **NM** value: **Cover or less**
★ 1st Appearance of The Depressor.

DEPUTY DAWG — Gold Key

The Terrytoons character was a Southern deputy whose career, unusually, began in television (on The Deputy Dawg Show) in 1960 and then made the transition to theatrical release — even as the character continued on TV.

His animated popularity did not really translate to long-term popularity in comic-book form, however. He appeared in two issues of Dell's Four Color (#1238 and #1299, from 1961 and 1962 respectively), and had the cover spot on many issues of New Terrytoons in the 1960s. This later from Gold Key would be his first series all to himself, and it ran but a single issue. — Maggie

1 ❑ Aug 1965 Cover: 0.12 **NM** value: **100.00**
• **CGC:** 1 graded, best 9.0

DER VANDALE — Innervision

1 ❑ b&w Cover: 2.50 **NM** value: **Cover or less**
A: Fred Antonacci **W:** Richard Brindisi
1/SC❑ b&w Cover: 2.50 **NM** value: **Cover or less**
alternate cover.
2 ❑ Cover: 2.50 **NM** value: **Cover or less**
3 ❑ Cover: 2.50 **NM** value: **Cover or less**

DESCENDANTS OF TOSHIN — Arrow

1 ❑ Apr 1999, b&w Cover: 2.95 **NM** value: **Cover or less**
No issue number.

DESCENDING ANGELS — Millennium

1 ❑ Cover: 2.95 **NM** value: **Cover or less**

Circ: CapCity orders: **2,105**
📖 The Arrival; Nothing Good; Petals on The Blade **A:** Adam DeKraker; Louis Small Jr.; Ron Sutton **W:** Scott Rockwell; Faye Perozich; Mitchel Reichgut

DESERT PEACH, THE — Thoughts & Images

The gravedigging unit attached to General Erwin "the Desert Fox" Rommel's division is filled with the oddest misfits the German army has: a lost soul who believes he must take care of a pet land mine; a Naziphile who never joined the party because it was "too expensive"; and a Jew who joined the Nazi party in its early stages as camouflage (and for the free drinks) but believes in none of its policies. Commander of them all is Pfirsich Rommel, the Desert Peach. Although a Nazi, Pfirsich is a decidedly decent human being. He's also gay, although trying not to let senior officers find out. This title follows the oddball antics of this military unit and their gentle leader as they try to survive the war and keep it as humane as possible.

Donna Barr has the ability to tickle the funny bone and touch the heart with her wonderful stories and beautiful, expressive drawing. She is also known for her work on The Dreamery and Stinz.

1 ❑ Jul 1988, b&w Cover: 2.00 **NM** value: **10.00**
📖 Who Is This Man • Thoughts & Images publishes **A:** Donna Barr **W:** Donna Barr
2 ❑ Feb 1989, b&w Cover: 2.00 **NM** value: **6.00**
📖 The Bar Fight **A:** Donna Barr **W:** Donna Barr
3 ❑ Jan 1990, b&w Cover: 2.00 **NM** value: **4.00**
📖 Surf's Up • Goes to Mu Press **A:** Donna Barr **W:** Donna Barr
4 ❑ Mar 1990, b&w Cover: 2.00 **NM** value: **4.00**
📖 Is There a Nazi in the House? • First Mu Issue **A:** Donna Barr **W:** Donna Barr

DESERT PEACH — Mu

5 ❑ Jun 1990, b&w Cover: 2.00 **NM** value: **4.00**
📖 Flights of Fancy **A:** Donna Barr **W:** Donna Barr
6 ❑ Aug 1990, b&w Cover: 2.00 **NM** value: **4.00**
📖 A Day Like Any Other **A:** Donna Barr **W:** Donna Barr
7 ❑ Sep 1990 Cover: 2.25 **NM** value: **3.00**
📖 Spoiled Fruit **A:** Donna Barr **W:** Donna Barr
8 ❑ Nov 1990 Cover: 2.25 **NM** value: **3.00**
📖 Dressing Down **A:** Donna Barr **W:** Donna Barr
9 ❑ Dec 1990 Cover: 2.25 **NM** value: **3.00**
📖 Scourge of Love **A:** Donna Barr **W:** Donna Barr
10 ❑ Feb 1991 Cover: 2.50 **NM** value: **3.00**
📖 Two-Timers **A:** Donna Barr **W:** Donna Barr
11 ❑ Jun 1991 Cover: 2.25 **NM** value: **3.00**
📖 Straight and Narrow **A:** Donna Barr **W:** Donna Barr
12 ❑ Aug 1991 Cover: 2.25 **NM** value: **2.50**
📖 Menschenkind **A:** Donna Barr **W:** Donna Barr
13 ❑ Oct 1991 Cover: 2.50 **NM** value: **Cover or less**
📖 Nobody **A:** Donna Barr **W:** Donna Barr
14 ❑ Dec 1991 Cover: 2.50 **NM** value: **Cover or less**
📖 Surprise, Surprise **A:** Donna Barr **W:** Donna Barr
15 ❑ Feb 1992 Cover: 2.50 **NM** value: **Cover or less**
📖 The Triangle Trade **A:** Donna Barr **W:** Donna Barr
16 ❑ Apr 1992 Cover: 2.50 **NM** value: **Cover or less**
📖 Plight of the Phoenix **A:** Donna Barr **W:** Donna Barr
17 ❑ Aug 1992, b&w Cover: 3.95 **NM** value: **Cover or less**
• Giant-size. 📖 Culture Clash **A:** Donna Barr **W:** Donna Barr
18 ❑ Aug 1992, b&w Cover: 2.50 **NM** value: **Cover or less**
📖 Programme to the Musical • Last Mu Press issue **A:** Donna Barr **W:** Donna Barr
19 ❑ ca. 1993, b&w Cover: 4.95 **NM** value: **Cover or less**
📖 Self-Propelled Target • aka Desert Peach: Self-Propelled Target;Aeon begins publishing **A:** Donna Barr **W:** Donna Barr
20 ❑ ca. 1993, b&w Cover: 4.95 **NM** value: **Cover or less**
📖 Fever Dream • aka Desert Peach: Fever Dream **A:** Donna Barr **W:** Donna Barr
21 ❑ Jun 1994, b&w Cover: 4.95 **NM** value: **Cover or less**
📖 The Good Uncle **A:** Donna Barr **W:** Donna Barr
22 ❑ Nov 1994, b&w Cover: 4.95 **NM** value: **Cover or less**
📖 Lady Luck **A:** Donna Barr **W:** Donna Barr
23 ❑ Jun 1995, b&w Cover: 2.95 **NM** value: **Cover or less**
• a.k.a. The Desert Peach: Visions **A:** Donna Barr **W:** Donna Barr
24 ❑ Sep 1995, b&w Cover: 2.95 **NM** value: **Cover or less**
• a.k.a. The Desert Peach: Ups and Downs **A:** Donna Barr **W:** Donna Barr
25 ❑ ca. 1996 Cover: 2.95 **NM** value: **Cover or less**
📖 Beautiful • Last Aeon issue; moves to A Fine Line **A:** Donna Barr **W:** Donna Barr
26 ❑ ca. 1997, b&w Cover: 2.95 **NM** value: **Cover or less**
cardstock cover. 📖 Miki • a.k.a. The Desert Peach: Miki; first issue from A Fine Line **A:** Donna Barr **W:** Donna Barr
27 ❑ ca. 1997 Cover: 2.95 **NM** value: **Cover or less**
📖 New and Different **A:** Donna Barr **W:** Donna Barr
28 ❑ Aug 1998 Cover: 2.95 **NM** value: **Cover or less**
1st printing. 📖 Tongue **A:** Donna Barr **W:** Donna Barr
29 ❑ Apr 2000 Cover: 2.95 **NM** value: **Cover or less**
📖 Out of the East **A:** Donna Barr **W:** Donna Barr
30 ❑ Jun 2001 Cover: 2.95 **NM** value: **Cover or less**
📖 Headaches **A:** Donna Barr **W:** Donna Barr
Bk 1❑ Feb 1993 Cover: 9.95 **NM** value: **12.95**
📖 Beginnings • Peach Slices; Collects Desert Peach #1-3 **A:** Donna Barr **W:** Donna Barr
Bk 2❑ 1992 Cover: 9.95 **NM** value: **12.95**
📖 Politics, Pilots and Puppies • Politics, Pilots and Puppies; Collects Desert Peach #4-6 **A:** Donna Barr **W:** Donna Barr
Bk 2-2❑ Cover: 9.95 **NM** value: **Cover or less**
Bk 2-3❑ Jan 1994 Cover: 12.95 **NM** value: **Cover or less**
Bk 3❑ Jan 1994 Cover: 12.95 **NM** value: **Cover or less**
📖 Foreign Relations • Collects Desert Peach #7-9 **A:** Donna Barr **W:** Donna Barr
Bk 4❑ May 1994 Cover: 12.95 **NM** value: **Cover or less**
1st printing. 📖 Baby Games • Collects Desert Peach #10-12 **A:** Donna Barr **W:** Donna Barr
Bk 5❑ Aug 1994 Cover: 12.95 **NM** value: **Cover or less**
📖 Belief Systems • Collects Desert Peach #13-15 **A:** Donna Barr **W:** Donna Barr
Bk 6❑ Nov 1994 Cover: 14.95 **NM** value: **Cover or less**
📖 Marriage and Mayhem • Collects Desert Peach #16, 17, 19 **A:** Donna Barr **W:** Donna Barr
Bk 7❑ Cover: 9.95 **NM** value: **Cover or less**
📖 Peach Slices • Collects various Desert Peach stories **A:** Donna Barr **W:** Donna Barr

DESERT STORM JOURNAL — Apple

1 ❑ Cover: 2.75 **NM** value: **Cover or less**
Hussein on cover. 📖 Read My Lips: No More Vietnams **A:** Rose Lomax **W:** Don Lomax
1/A ❑ Cover: 2.75 **NM** value: **Cover or less**
Schwartzkopf on cover. **A:** Rose Lomax **W:** Don Lomax
2 ❑ b&w Cover: 2.75 **NM** value: **Cover or less**
W: Don Lomax
3 ❑ b&w Cover: 2.75 **NM** value: **Cover or less**
W: Don Lomax
4 ❑ b&w Cover: 2.75 **NM** value: **Cover or less**
W: Don Lomax
5 ❑ b&w Cover: 2.75 **NM** value: **Cover or less**
W: Don Lomax
6 ❑ b&w Cover: 2.75 **NM** value: **Cover or less**
W: Don Lomax
7 ❑ b&w Cover: 2.75 **NM** value: **Cover or less**
W: Don Lomax
8 ❑ b&w Cover: 2.75 **NM** value: **Cover or less**
W: Don Lomax

DESERT STREAMS — DC / Piranha

1 ❑ Cover: 5.95 **NM** value: **Cover or less**

DESPAIR — Print Mint

1 ❑ ca. 1969 Cover: 0.10 **NM** value: **10.00**
• **CGC:** 2 graded, best 9.4

DESPERADO — Lev Gleason

1 ❑ Jun 1948 Cover: 0.10 **NM** value: **80.00**
• **CGC:** 2 graded, best 9.0
2 ❑ 1948 Cover: 0.10 **NM** value: **40.00**
3 ❑ 1948 Cover: 0.10 **NM** value: **30.00**
4 ❑ 1948 Cover: 0.10 **NM** value: **30.00**
5 ❑ 1948 Cover: 0.10 **NM** value: **30.00**
6 ❑ 1948 Cover: 0.10 **NM** value: **30.00**
7 ❑ 1949 Cover: 0.10 **NM** value: **30.00**
8 ❑ 1949 Cover: 0.10 **NM** value: **30.00**

DESPERADOES — Image

1 ❑ Sep 1997 Cover: 2.50 **NM** value: **Cover or less**
Circ: Diamd. preorders: **12,487**
📖 A Moment's Sunlight **A:** John Cassaday **W:** Jeff Mariotte
1-2 ❑ Sep 1997 Cover: 2.50 **NM** value: **Cover or less**
2 ❑ Oct 1997 Cover: 2.95 **NM** value: **Cover or less**
Circ: Diamd. preorders: **9,825**
📖 The Gathering Gloom **A:** John Cassaday **W:** Jeff Mariotte
3 ❑ Nov 1997 Cover: 2.95 **NM** value: **Cover or less**
Circ: Diamd. preorders: **9,242**
📖 Heroes and Villains **A:** John Cassaday **W:** Jeff Mariotte
4 ❑ Dec 1997 Cover: 2.95 **NM** value: **Cover or less**
Circ: Diamd. preorders: **9,948**
📖 The Dance **A:** John Cassaday **W:** Jeff Mariotte
5 ❑ Jun 1998 Cover: 2.95 **NM** value: **Cover or less**
Circ: Diamd. preorders: **10,157**
📖 Blankenship's Arm **A:** John Cassaday **W:** Jeff Mariotte
Bk 1❑ Cover: 16.95 **NM** value: **Cover or less**
📖 A Moment's Sunlight • A Moment's Sunlight;Collects Desperadoes #1-5 **A:** John Cassaday **W:** Jeff Mariotte

DESPERADOES: EPIDEMIC! — DC / Wildstorm

1 ❑ Nov 1999 Cover: 5.95 **NM** value: **Cover or less**
Circ: Diamd. preorders: **9,148**
No issue number. • prestige format. **A:** John Lucas; John Cassaday **W:** Jeff Mariotte

DESPERATE TIMES — Image

Chris Eliopoulos first came to the attention of comics fans for his skills as a letterer, on titles including the Savage Dragon. (He also designed the logo which Comics Buyer's Guide magazine began using in 2001.) Eliopoulos branches out in Desperate Times, an often very funny comic book.

Using an uncluttered, cartoony style, he tells the story of slackers, politically correct "PC Police," and other assorted oddballs as they deal with life, love, and daytime television. Some of the funniest gags come from the covers themselves, which gleefully mock sexist sales techniques and other over-the-top comic book stereotypes.

1 ❑ Jun 1998 Cover: 2.95 **NM** value: **Cover or less**
Circ: Diamd. preorders: **4,930**
A: Chris Eliopoulos; Erik Larsen **W:** Chris Eliopoulos

CGC-graded: Multiply prices above by **33 for 9.9 M • 16 for 9.8 NM/M • 7 for 9.6 NM+ • 5 for 9.4 NM • 2.5 for 9.2 NM- • 1.5 for 9.0 VF/NM**

2 ❑ Aug 1998 Cover: 2.95 **NM** value: **Cover or less**
Circ: Diamd. preorders: **4,076**
A: Chris Eliopoulos **W:** Chris Eliopoulos
3 ❑ Oct 1998 Cover: 2.95 **NM** value: **Cover or less**
Circ: Diamd. preorders: **3,197**
A: Chris Eliopoulos **W:** Chris Eliopoulos
4 ❑ Dec 1998 Cover: 2.95 **NM** value: **Cover or less**
Circ: Diamd. preorders: **2,870**
A: Chris Eliopoulos **W:** Chris Eliopoulos
Bk 1❑ Oct 1999 Cover: 14.95 **NM** value: **Cover or less**

DESTINATION MOON — Export Publishing
1 ❑ ca. 1950 Cover: 0.10 **NM** value: **500.00**

DESTINY: A CHRONICLE OF DEATHS FORETOLD — DC / Vertigo
1 ❑ ca. 1997 Cover: 5.95 **NM** value: **Cover or less**
Circ: Diamd. preorders: **30,922**
• prestige format. **A:** Kent Williams **W:** Alisa Kwitney
2 ❑ ca. 1997 Cover: 5.95 **NM** value: **Cover or less**
Circ: Diamd. preorders: **27,179**
• prestige format. 📖 Black Death **A:** Kent Williams **W:** Alisa Kwitney
3 ❑ ca. 1997 Cover: 5.95 **NM** value: **Cover or less**
Circ: Diamd. preorders: **25,511**
• prestige format. **A:** Kent Williams **W:** Alisa Kwitney

DESTINY ANGEL — Dark Fantasy
1 ❑ Cover: 3.95 **NM** value: **Cover or less**
📖 Magic Bullet, Part 1 **A:** Ben Fogletto **W:** Allan Coberly

DESTROY!! — Eclipse
Scott McCloud, the Zot creator who would later evolve into a comics art theorist with his Understanding Comics from Tundra (and later, Kitchen Sink) produced this one-shot, oversized commentary on plotless super-hero comics for Eclipse in 1986. The entire issue consists of little more than a bludgeoning super-powered character on a rampage. We don't know about comics in general, but McCloud certainly shows he "understands" comic books about wanton destruction in this effort.

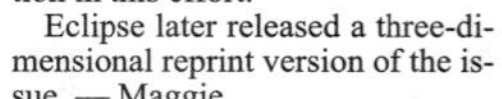

Eclipse later released a three-dimensional reprint version of the issue. — Maggie

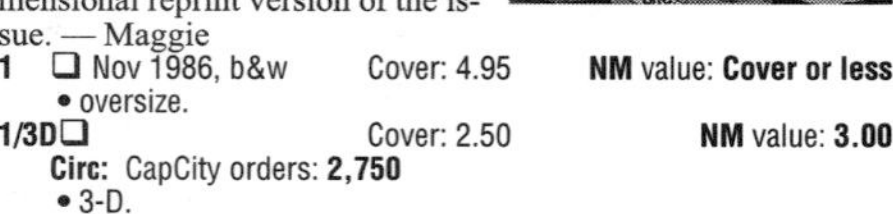

1 ❑ Nov 1986, b&w Cover: 4.95 **NM** value: **Cover or less**
• oversize.
1/3D❑ Cover: 2.50 **NM** value: **3.00**
Circ: CapCity orders: **2,750**
• 3-D.

DESTROY ALL COMICS — Slave Labor
1 ❑ Nov 1994 Cover: 3.50 **NM** value: **Cover or less**
• Oversized.
2 ❑ Feb 1995 Cover: 3.50 **NM** value: **Cover or less**
• Oversized.
3 ❑ Aug 1995 Cover: 3.50 **NM** value: **Cover or less**
• Oversized.
4 ❑ Jan 1996 Cover: 3.50 **NM** value: **Cover or less**
• Oversized.
5 ❑ Apr 1996 Cover: 3.50 **NM** value: **Cover or less**
• Oversized.

DESTROYER DUCK — Eclipse
1 ❑ Feb 1982 Cover: 1.50 **NM** value: **5.00**
• **CGC:** 7 graded, best 9.6
📖 It's Got the Whole World In Its Hand! **A:** Sergio Aragonés; Val Mayerik; Jack Kirby **W:** Mark Evanier; Steve Gerber ★ Origin of Destroyer Duck. ★ 1st Appearance of Groo, Destroyer Duck.
2 ❑ Jan 1983 Cover: 1.50 **NM** value: **Cover or less**
• **CGC:** 1 graded, best 8.0
📖 The Starling, Part 1; Mommie Noises! **A:** Val Mayerik; Jack Kirby **W:** Jerry Siegel; Steve Gerber
3 ❑ Jun 1983 Cover: 1.50 **NM** value: **Cover or less**
📖 Pheromones!; The Starling, Part 2 **A:** Val Mayerik; Jack Kirby **W:** Jerry Siegel; Steve Gerber
4 ❑ Oct 1983 Cover: 1.50 **NM** value: **Cover or less**
📖 Spineless Wonders; The Starling, Part 3 **A:** Val Mayerik; Jack Kirby **W:** Jerry Siegel; Steve Gerber
5 ❑ Dec 1983 Cover: 1.50 **NM** value: **Cover or less**
📖 Shatterer of Worlds!; The Starling, Part 4 **A:** Val Mayerik; Jack Kirby **W:** Jerry Siegel; Buzz Dixon; Steve Gerber
6 ❑ Mar 1984 Cover: 1.50 **NM** value: **Cover or less**
📖 The Starling, Part 5 **A:** Val Mayerik **W:** Jerry Siegel; Steve Gerber
7 ❑ May 1984 Cover: 1.50 **NM** value: **Cover or less**
📖 The Vault of Virus!; The Starling, Part 6 final issue. **A:** Val Mayerik; Gary Kato; Frank Miller(cover) **W:** Jerry Siegel; Buzz Dixon

DESTROYER, THE (MAGAZINE) — Marvel
1 ❑ Nov 1989 Cover: 2.25 **NM** value: **Cover or less**
📖 His Name is Remo **A:** Lee Weeks **W:** Will Murray ★ Origin of Remo Williams.
2 ❑ Dec 1989 Cover: 2.25 **NM** value: **Cover or less**
📖 Golden Rule **A:** Mike Manley **W:** Will Murray
3 ❑ Dec 1989 Cover: 2.25 **NM** value: **Cover or less**
4 ❑ Jan 1990 Cover: 2.25 **NM** value: **Cover or less**
📖 Mass Hysteria; How the Thieving Ninja Came to Be **A:** Steve Ditko; Tom Morgan **W:** Will Murray
5 ❑ Feb 1990 Cover: 2.25 **NM** value: **Cover or less**
📖 The Fist of Gallah; How Remo Came to Sinanju **A:** Lee Weeks **W:** Will Murray
6 ❑ Mar 1990 Cover: 2.25 **NM** value: **Cover or less**
7 ❑ Apr 1990 Cover: 2.25 **NM** value: **Cover or less**
📖 Stone Killer **A:** Rik Levins; Chris Ivy **W:** Will Murray
8 ❑ May 1990 Cover: 2.25 **NM** value: **Cover or less**
📖 America is Worth a Life **A:** Brett Blevins; Lee Weeks **W:** Will Murray

DESTROYER, THE (VALIANT) — Valiant
1 ❑ Apr 1995 Cover: 2.95 **NM** value: **Cover or less**
Circ: CapCity orders: **12,500**
cover says #0. 📖 A Place of Our Own **A:** Mike Manley **W:** Kevin VanHook

DESTROYER, THE (VOL. 2) — Marvel
1 ❑ Mar 1991 Cover: 1.95 **NM** value: **Cover or less**
📖 Drive-By Heaven **A:** Lee Weeks **W:** Will Murray

DESTROYER, THE (VOL. 3) — Marvel
Remo Williams, the title character in this series, is a cross between the Master of Kung Fu and the Punisher. Remo is already skilled in the martial arts and street fighting in general, but when he hooks up with Chiun, a master of body and matter control, Remo becomes virtually unbeatable.

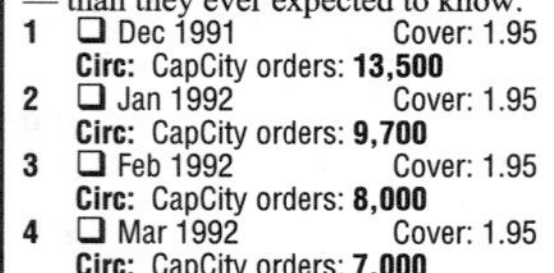

Remo and Chiun, agents of a secret anti-terrorist organization called Cure, are called upon to "negotiate" with some ruthless terrorists and find out who they're working for. Remo shows that he has a far more effective way of getting information out of criminals than the legal methods allow. But when he and Chiun track down their lead, they find out much more — about their opponent and themselves — than they ever expected to know.
1 ❑ Dec 1991 Cover: 1.95 **NM** value: **Cover or less**
Circ: CapCity orders: **13,500**
2 ❑ Jan 1992 Cover: 1.95 **NM** value: **Cover or less**
Circ: CapCity orders: **9,700**
3 ❑ Feb 1992 Cover: 1.95 **NM** value: **Cover or less**
Circ: CapCity orders: **8,000**
4 ❑ Mar 1992 Cover: 1.95 **NM** value: **Cover or less**
Circ: CapCity orders: **7,000**

DESTRUCTOR, THE — Atlas-Seaboard
1 ❑ Feb 1975 Cover: 0.25 **NM** value: **2.00**
• **CGC:** 5 graded, best 9.6
📖 ..The Birth Of A Hero **A:** Steve Ditko; Wally Wood **W:** Archie Goodwin ★ Origin of Destructor.
2 ❑ Apr 1975 Cover: 0.25 **NM** value: **1.50**
A: Steve Ditko; Wally Wood(inker) **W:** Archie Goodwin
3 ❑ Jun 1975 Cover: 0.25 **NM** value: **1.50**
A: Steve Ditko **W:** Archie Goodwin
4 ❑ Aug 1975 Cover: 0.25 **NM** value: **1.50**

DETECTIVE, THE — Sunset Strips
1 ❑ Cover: 2.95 **NM** value: **Cover or less**
A: Cindy Goff **W:** Cindy Goff
2 ❑ Cover: 2.95 **NM** value: **Cover or less**
A: Cindy Goff **W:** Cindy Goff
3 ❑ Cover: 2.95 **NM** value: **Cover or less**
📖 Clutches of the Past **A:** Cindy Goff **W:** Cindy Goff
4 ❑ Cover: 2.95 **NM** value: **Cover or less**
A: Cindy Goff **W:** Cindy Goff
5 ❑ Cover: 2.95 **NM** value: **Cover or less**
A: Cindy Goff **W:** Cindy Goff
6 ❑ Cover: 2.95 **NM** value: **Cover or less**
A: Cindy Goff **W:** Cindy Goff
7 ❑ Cover: 2.95 **NM** value: **Cover or less**
A: Cindy Goff **W:** Cindy Goff
8 ❑ Cover: 2.95 **NM** value: **Cover or less**
A: Cindy Goff **W:** Cindy Goff
9 ❑ Cover: 2.95 **NM** value: **Cover or less**
A: Cindy Goff **W:** Cindy Goff
10 ❑ Cover: 2.95 **NM** value: **Cover or less**
A: Cindy Goff **W:** Cindy Goff
11 ❑ Cover: 2.95 **NM** value: **Cover or less**
A: Cindy Goff **W:** Cindy Goff
12 ❑ Cover: 2.95 **NM** value: **Cover or less**
A: Cindy Goff **W:** Cindy Goff

DETECTIVE, THE: CHRONICLES OF MAX FACCIONI — Caliber
1 ❑ Cover: 2.95 **NM** value: **Cover or less**
📖 The Punch **A:** Cindy Goff **W:** Cindy Goff

DETECTIVE COMICS — DC
The legend of Batman started in Detective Comics #27 (May 39). It was there that the remarkable young Bruce Wayne, heir to the Wayne fortune, saw his parents gunned down by a mugger. The experience changed him forever, and, when he was grown, he began leading a double life. By day, he is an idle playboy, but by night he patrols Gotham City as Batman, a caped crusader who takes on the aspect of a bat in order to frighten criminals.

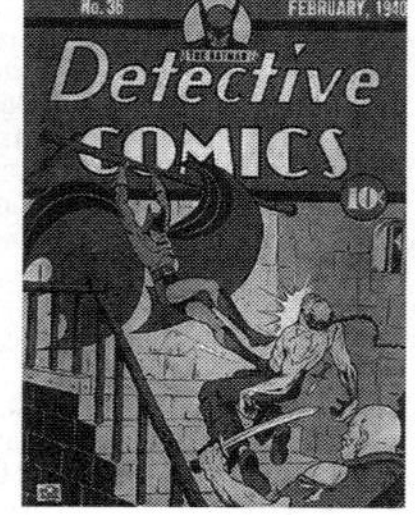

In the more than 60 years that have followed, Detective Comics has been the flagship title of DC's comic line. Indeed, it is from Detective Comics that DC (formerly National Periodical Publications) derives its name.
0 ❑ Oct 1994 Cover: 1.50 **NM** value: **2.50**
Circ: CapCity orders: **57,200**
📖 Choice Of Weapons **A:** Graham Nolan **W:** Chuck Dixon ★ Origin of Batarangs, Batmobile, Batman.
1 ❑ Mar 1937 Cover: 0.10 **NM** value: **61000.00**
• **CGC:** 2 graded, best 6.5
• (also many other detective heroes);(also many other detective heroes) ★ 1st Appearance of Slam Bradley.
2 ❑ Apr 1937 Cover: 0.10 **NM** value: **14500.00**
• **CGC:** 1 graded, best 9.0
3 ❑ May 1937 Cover: 0.10 **NM** value: **9500.00**
4 ❑ Jun 1937 Cover: 0.10 **NM** value: **6000.00**
5 ❑ Jul 1937 Cover: 0.10 **NM** value: **6000.00**
6 ❑ Aug 1937 Cover: 0.10 **NM** value: **3950.00**
• **CGC:** 2 graded, best 4.5
7 ❑ Sep 1937 Cover: 0.10 **NM** value: **3950.00**
• **CGC:** 1 graded, best 6.5
8 ❑ Oct 1937 Cover: 0.10 **NM** value: **5100.00**
• **CGC:** 6 graded, best 5.5
Mr. Chang cover.
9 ❑ Nov 1937 Cover: 0.10 **NM** value: **3850.00**
• **CGC:** 1 graded, best 4.0
10 ❑ Dec 1937 Cover: 0.10 **NM** value: **3850.00**
• **CGC:** 4 graded, best 6.0
11 ❑ Jan 1938 Cover: 0.10 **NM** value: **3850.00**
• **CGC:** 1 graded, best 6.0
12 ❑ Feb 1938 Cover: 0.10 **NM** value: **3850.00**
• **CGC:** 4 graded, best 7.0
13 ❑ Mar 1938 Cover: 0.10 **NM** value: **3850.00**
• **CGC:** 2 graded, best 5.5
14 ❑ Apr 1938 Cover: 0.10 **NM** value: **3850.00**
• **CGC:** 3 graded, best 7.0
15 ❑ May 1938 Cover: 0.10 **NM** value: **3850.00**
• **CGC:** 1 graded, best 4.5
16 ❑ Jun 1938 Cover: 0.10 **NM** value: **3850.00**
• **CGC:** 1 graded, best 3.5
17 ❑ Jul 1938 Cover: 0.10 **NM** value: **3850.00**
• **CGC:** 4 graded, best 6.5
★ 1st Appearance of Fu Manchu.
18 ❑ Aug 1938 Cover: 0.10 **NM** value: **4700.00**
• **CGC:** 1 graded, best 4.0
Fu Manchu cover. • Fu Manchu, Slam Bradley, Speed Saunders, Buck Marshall, Spy, Larry Steele, Cosmo
19 ❑ Sep 1938 Cover: 0.10 **NM** value: **3850.00**
• **CGC:** 2 graded, best 4.0
20 ❑ Oct 1938 Cover: 0.10 **NM** value: **5500.00**
• **CGC:** 5 graded, best 7.5
★ 1st Appearance of The Crimson Avenger.
21 ❑ Nov 1938 Cover: 0.10 **NM** value: **2950.00**
• **CGC:** 1 graded, best 4.0
22 ❑ Dec 1938 Cover: 0.10 **NM** value: **3850.00**
• **CGC:** 1 graded, best 3.5
Crimson Avenger cover. • The Crimson Avenger
23 ❑ Jan 1939 Cover: 0.10 **NM** value: **2950.00**
• **CGC:** 1 graded, best 5.5
• Speed Saunders
24 ❑ Feb 1939 Cover: 0.10 **NM** value: **2950.00**
25 ❑ Mar 1939 Cover: 0.10 **NM** value: **2950.00**
• **CGC:** 1 graded, best 3.0
26 ❑ Apr 1939 Cover: 0.10 **NM** value: **2950.00**
• **CGC:** 4 graded, best 9.0
27 ❑ May 1939 Cover: 0.10 **NM** value: **170000.00**
• **CGC:** 6 graded, best 8.0
📖 The Bat-Man: The Case of the Chemical Syndicate; Speed Saunders Ace Investigator and t **A:** Bob Kane; Joe Shuster; Bill Alger; Fred Guardineer; Hugh Fleming; James Chambers; Paul Gustavson; Sven Elven **W:** Bill Alger; Bill Finger; Fred Guardineer; Hugh Fleming; James Chambers; Jerry Siegel; Paul Gustavson; Sven Elven; Tom Hickey; Paul Dean; Sax Rohmer ★ 1st Appearance of Commissioner Gordon, Batman.
28 ❑ Jun 1939 Cover: 0.10 **NM** value: **18000.00**
• **CGC:** 2 graded, best 9.0
★ 2nd Appearance of Batman.
29 ❑ Jul 1939 Cover: 0.10 **NM** value: **25000.00**
• **CGC:** 5 graded, best 9.6
Batman cover. ★ 1st Appearance of Doctor Death. ★ Appearance of 3rd.
30 ❑ Aug 1939 Cover: 0.10 **NM** value: **6000.00**
• **CGC:** 1 graded, best 8.5
31 ❑ Sep 1939 Cover: 0.10 **NM** value: **25000.00**
• **CGC:** 8 graded, best 8.0
Batman cover.
32 ❑ Oct 1939 Cover: 0.10 **NM** value: **5500.00**
• **CGC:** 7 graded, best 6.5
• Slam Bradley, Speed Saunders, Buck Marshall, Larry Steele backups
33 ❑ Nov 1939 Cover: 0.10 **NM** value: **33000.00**
• **CGC:** 10 graded, best 9.0
★ Origin of Batman.
34 ❑ Dec 1939 Cover: 0.10 **NM** value: **4500.00**
• **CGC:** 7 graded, best 9.2
35 ❑ Jan 1940 Cover: 0.10 **NM** value: **7400.00**
• **CGC:** 1 graded, best 8.5
36 ❑ Feb 1940 Cover: 0.10 **NM** value: **5500.00**
• **CGC:** 4 graded, best 8.0
★ 1st Appearance of Hugo Strange.
37 ❑ Mar 1940 Cover: 0.10 **NM** value: **5300.00**
• **CGC:** 4 graded, best 9.0
38 ❑ Apr 1940 Cover: 0.10 **NM** value: **30000.00**
• **CGC:** 8 graded, best 8.0
★ 1st Appearance of Robin I (Dick Grayson).
39 ❑ May 1940 Cover: 0.10 **NM** value: **5000.00**
• **CGC:** 5 graded, best 8.0
★ 2nd Appearance of Robin I (Dick Grayson).
40 ❑ Jun 1940 Cover: 0.10 **NM** value: **5600.00**
• **CGC:** 6 graded, best 9.0

• Joker ★ 1st Appearance of Clayface I (Basil Karlo). ★ Appearance of Joker.
41 ❑ Jul 1940 Cover: 0.10 **NM** value: **2950.00**
• **CGC:** 7 graded, best 9.0
42 ❑ Aug 1940 Cover: 0.10 **NM** value: **1900.00**
• **CGC:** 2 graded, best 5.0
43 ❑ Sep 1940 Cover: 0.10 **NM** value: **1900.00**
• **CGC:** 2 graded, best 7.5
44 ❑ Oct 1940 Cover: 0.10 **NM** value: **1900.00**
• **CGC:** 7 graded, best 9.4
45 ❑ Nov 1940 Cover: 0.10 **NM** value: **2850.00**
• **CGC:** 9 graded, best 9.6
★ Appearance of Joker.
46 ❑ Dec 1940 Cover: 0.10 **NM** value: **1600.00**
• **CGC:** 3 graded, best 5.0
47 ❑ Jan 1941 Cover: 0.10 **NM** value: **1600.00**
• **CGC:** 4 graded, best 7.5
48 ❑ Feb 1941 Cover: 0.10 **NM** value: **1600.00**
• **CGC:** 4 graded, best 7.5
49 ❑ Mar 1941 Cover: 0.10 **NM** value: **1600.00**
• **CGC:** 3 graded, best 8.0
50 ❑ Apr 1941 Cover: 0.10 **NM** value: **1600.00**
• **CGC:** 5 graded, best 8.0
51 ❑ May 1941 Cover: 0.10 **NM** value: **1175.00**
• **CGC:** 6 graded, best 9.0
52 ❑ Jun 1941 Cover: 0.10 **NM** value: **1175.00**
• **CGC:** 4 graded, best 9.0
53 ❑ Jul 1941 Cover: 0.10 **NM** value: **1175.00**
• **CGC:** 4 graded, best 9.4
54 ❑ Aug 1941 Cover: 0.10 **NM** value: **1175.00**
• **CGC:** 7 graded, best 9.0
55 ❑ Sep 1941 Cover: 0.10 **NM** value: **1175.00**
• **CGC:** 4 graded, best 5.5
56 ❑ Oct 1941 Cover: 0.10 **NM** value: **1175.00**
• **CGC:** 6 graded, best 9.2
57 ❑ Nov 1941 Cover: 0.10 **NM** value: **1175.00**
• **CGC:** 3 graded, best 9.0
58 ❑ Dec 1941 Cover: 0.10 **NM** value: **3200.00**
• **CGC:** 7 graded, best 9.4
★ 1st Appearance of Penguin.
59 ❑ Jan 1942 Cover: 0.10 **NM** value: **1500.00**
• **CGC:** 6 graded, best 8.0
★ 2nd Appearance of Penguin.
60 ❑ Feb 1942 Cover: 0.10 **NM** value: **1300.00**
• **CGC:** 2 graded, best 5.0
★ 1st Appearance of Air Wave I (Larry Jordan). ★ Appearance of Joker.
61 ❑ Mar 1942 Cover: 0.10 **NM** value: **1050.00**
• **CGC:** 2 graded, best 4.0
📖 The Three Racketeers
62 ❑ Apr 1942 Cover: 0.10 **NM** value: **1750.00**
• **CGC:** 9 graded, best 9.0
• Joker ★ Appearance of Joker.
63 ❑ May 1942 Cover: 0.10 **NM** value: **1050.00**
• **CGC:** 6 graded, best 8.0
• Mr. Baffle ★ 1st Appearance of Mr. Baffle.
64 ❑ Jun 1942 Cover: 0.10 **NM** value: **3000.00**
• **CGC:** 7 graded, best 7.0
📖 The Boy Commandos • 1st appearance/origin of the Boy Commandos **A:** Joe Simon; Jack Kirby **W:** Joe Simon; Jack Kirby ★ Origin of Boy Commandos. ★ 1st Appearance of Boy Commandos. ★ Appearance of Joker.
65 ❑ Jul 1942 Cover: 0.10 **NM** value: **1900.00**
• **CGC:** 5 graded, best 7.0
• Boy Commandos ★ Appearance of Boy Commandos.
66 ❑ Aug 1942 Cover: 0.10 **NM** value: **2750.00**
• **CGC:** 5 graded, best 8.0
📖 Two-Face • Boy Commandos ★ Origin of Two-Face. ★ 1st Appearance of Two-Face.
67 ❑ Sep 1942 Cover: 0.10 **NM** value: **1550.00**
• **CGC:** 2 graded, best 9.0
📖 Crime's Early Bird • Boy Commandos ★ Appearance of Penguin.
68 ❑ Oct 1942 Cover: 0.10 **NM** value: **1200.00**
• **CGC:** 3 graded, best 7.5
📖 The Man who Led a Double Life • Boy Commandos ★ Appearance of Two-Face.
69 ❑ Nov 1942 Cover: 0.10 **NM** value: **1300.00**
• **CGC:** 6 graded, best 9.6
📖 The Harlequin's Hoax! • Boy Commandos ★ Appearance of Joker.
70 ❑ Dec 1942 Cover: 0.10 **NM** value: **900.00**
• **CGC:** 7 graded, best 9.6
📖 Man Who Could Read Minds • Boy Commandos
71 ❑ Jan 1943 Cover: 0.10 **NM** value: **1000.00**
• **CGC:** 8 graded, best 8.0
📖 A Crime A Day! • Boy Commandos ★ Appearance of Joker.
72 ❑ Feb 1943 Cover: 0.10 **NM** value: **800.00**
• **CGC:** 1 graded, best 7.5
📖 License for Larceny • Boy Commandos
73 ❑ Mar 1943 Cover: 0.10 **NM** value: **800.00**
• **CGC:** 7 graded, best 9.2
📖 Return of the Scarecrow • Boy Commandos
74 ❑ Apr 1943 Cover: 0.10 **NM** value: **800.00**
• **CGC:** 2 graded, best 9.6
• Boy Commandos ★ 1st Appearance of Tweedledee & Tweedledum.
75 ❑ May 1943 Cover: 0.10 **NM** value: **800.00**
• **CGC:** 3 graded, best 9.4
📖 Robber Baron • Boy Commandos
76 ❑ Jun 1943 Cover: 0.10 **NM** value: **1250.00**
• **CGC:** 7 graded, best 9.2
📖 Slay 'Em With Flowers! • Boy Commandos ★ Appearance of Joker.
77 ❑ Jul 1943 Cover: 0.10 **NM** value: **800.00**
📖 Crime Clinic • Boy Commandos
78 ❑ Aug 1943 Cover: 0.10 **NM** value: **800.00**
• **CGC:** 1 graded, best 8.5
• Boy Commandos
79 ❑ Sep 1943 Cover: 0.10 **NM** value: **800.00**
• **CGC:** 3 graded, best 7.5
📖 Destiny's Auction • Boy Commandos
80 ❑ Oct 1943 Cover: 0.10 **NM** value: **950.00**
• **CGC:** 6 graded, best 9.4
📖 The End of Two-Face • Boy Commandos ★ Appearance of Two-Face.
81 ❑ Nov 1943 Cover: 0.10 **NM** value: **725.00**
• **CGC:** 5 graded, best 9.6
📖 The Cavalier • Boy Commandos ★ 1st Appearance of Cavalier.
82 ❑ Dec 1943 Cover: 0.10 **NM** value: **725.00**
• **CGC:** 4 graded, best 9.0
📖 Quarterback of Crime • Boy Commandos
83 ❑ Jan 1944 Cover: 0.10 **NM** value: **750.00**
• **CGC:** 2 graded, best 9.0
• Boy Commandos ★ Appearance of New.
84 ❑ Feb 1944 Cover: 0.10 **NM** value: **725.00**
• **CGC:** 3 graded, best 9.4
📖 Artists in Villainy
85 ❑ Mar 1944 Cover: 0.10 **NM** value: **950.00**
• **CGC:** 6 graded, best 9.6
• Joker ★ Appearance of Joker.
86 ❑ Apr 1944 Cover: 0.10 **NM** value: **725.00**
• **CGC:** 3 graded, best 9.2
87 ❑ May 1944 Cover: 0.10 **NM** value: **725.00**
• **CGC:** 5 graded, best 9.2
• Penguin
88 ❑ Jun 1944 Cover: 0.10 **NM** value: **725.00**
• **CGC:** 3 graded, best 9.4
89 ❑ Jul 1944 Cover: 0.10 **NM** value: **725.00**
• **CGC:** 7 graded, best 9.6
📖 The Cavalier of Crime Retruns • Boy Commandos
90 ❑ Aug 1944 Cover: 0.10 **NM** value: **725.00**
• **CGC:** 4 graded, best 9.6
• Cover has War Bond appeal
91 ❑ Sep 1944 Cover: 0.10 **NM** value: **850.00**
• **CGC:** 6 graded, best 9.2
📖 The Case of the Practical Joker • Joker ★ Appearance of Joker.
92 ❑ Oct 1944 Cover: 0.10 **NM** value: **600.00**
• **CGC:** 6 graded, best 9.2
93 ❑ Nov 1944 Cover: 0.10 **NM** value: **600.00**
• **CGC:** 4 graded, best 8.0
94 ❑ Dec 1944 Cover: 0.10 **NM** value: **600.00**
• **CGC:** 9 graded, best 9.4
95 ❑ Jan 1945 Cover: 0.10 **NM** value: **600.00**
• **CGC:** 5 graded, best 9.2
96 ❑ Feb 1945 Cover: 0.10 **NM** value: **600.00**
• **CGC:** 7 graded, best 9.0
• Cover has War Bond appeal
97 ❑ Mar 1945 Cover: 0.10 **NM** value: **600.00**
• **CGC:** 3 graded, best 9.0
98 ❑ Apr 1945 Cover: 0.10 **NM** value: **600.00**
• **CGC:** 5 graded, best 9.2
99 ❑ May 1945 Cover: 0.10 **NM** value: **850.00**
• **CGC:** 5 graded, best 8.5
• Penguin ★ Appearance of Penguin.
100 ❑ Jun 1945 Cover: 0.10 **NM** value: **900.00**
• **CGC:** 11 graded, best 9.2
• 100th anniversary issue.
101 ❑ Jul 1945 Cover: 0.10 **NM** value: **560.00**
• **CGC:** 4 graded, best 8.5
War bonds cover.
102 ❑ Aug 1945 Cover: 0.10 **NM** value: **800.00**
• **CGC:** 4 graded, best 9.2
📖 The House that Was Held For Ransom! ★ Appearance of Joker.
103 ❑ Sep 1945 Cover: 0.10 **NM** value: **560.00**
• **CGC:** 5 graded, best 9.6
📖 Trouble Incorporated! **A:** Jack Burnley **W:** Alvin Schwartz
104 ❑ Oct 1945 Cover: 0.10 **NM** value: **560.00**
• **CGC:** 5 graded, best 9.2
📖 The Battle of the Billboards! **A:** Dick Sprang **W:** Alvin Schwartz
105 ❑ Nov 1945 Cover: 0.10 **NM** value: **560.00**
• **CGC:** 6 graded, best 7.5
📖 The Batman Goes Broke! **A:** Win Mortimer **W:** Don Cameron
106 ❑ Dec 1945 Cover: 0.10 **NM** value: **560.00**
• **CGC:** 3 graded, best 9.2
📖 The Phantom of the Library! **A:** Bob Kane **W:** Don Cameron
107 ❑ Jan 1946 Cover: 0.10 **NM** value: **560.00**
• **CGC:** 9 graded, best 9.4
📖 The Mountain of the Moon! **A:** Win Mortimer **W:** Don Cameron
108 ❑ Feb 1946 Cover: 0.10 **NM** value: **560.00**
• **CGC:** 7 graded, best 9.0
📖 The Goat of Gotham City! • Batplane **A:** Dick Sprang **W:** Don Cameron
109 ❑ Mar 1946 Cover: 0.10 **NM** value: **760.00**
• **CGC:** 9 graded, best 9.4
📖 The House that Jokes Built! **A:** Win Mortimer **W:** Don Cameron ★ Appearance of Joker.
110 ❑ Apr 1946 Cover: 0.10 **NM** value: **540.00**
• **CGC:** 5 graded, best 9.4
📖 Batman and Robin in Scotland Yard! **A:** Win Mortimer **W:** Don Cameron
111 ❑ May 1946 Cover: 0.10 **NM** value: **540.00**
• **CGC:** 16 graded, best 9.6
📖 Coaltown, U.S.A. **A:** Win Mortimer **W:** Don Cameron
112 ❑ Jun 1946 Cover: 0.10 **NM** value: **540.00**
• **CGC:** 7 graded, best 9.6
📖 The Case Without a Crime! **A:** Win Mortimer **W:** Alvin Schwartz
113 ❑ Jul 1946 Cover: 0.10 **NM** value: **540.00**
• **CGC:** 6 graded, best 9.2
📖 Crime on the Half-Shell! **A:** Dick Sprang **W:** Bill Finger
114 ❑ Aug 1946 Cover: 0.10 **NM** value: **750.00**
• **CGC:** 4 graded, best 9.8
📖 Acrostic of Crime! **A:** Win Mortimer **W:** Don Cameron ★ Appearance of Joker.
115 ❑ Sep 1946 Cover: 0.10 **NM** value: **540.00**
• **CGC:** 6 graded, best 9.6
📖 The Man Who Lived in a Glass House! **A:** Win Mortimer **W:** Don Cameron
116 ❑ Oct 1946 Cover: 0.10 **NM** value: **540.00**
• **CGC:** 3 graded, best 9.4
📖 The Rescue of Robin Hood! **A:** Win Mortimer **W:** Don Cameron
117 ❑ Nov 1946 Cover: 0.10 **NM** value: **540.00**
• **CGC:** 8 graded, best 9.6
📖 Steeplejack's Showdown! **A:** Bob Kane **W:** Don Cameron
118 ❑ Dec 1946 Cover: 0.10 **NM** value: **750.00**
• **CGC:** 7 graded, best 9.0
📖 The Royal Flush Crimes! • Joker **A:** Howard Sherman **W:** Alvin Schwartz ★ Appearance of Joker.
119 ❑ Jan 1947 Cover: 0.10 **NM** value: **540.00**
• **CGC:** 2 graded, best 9.0
📖 The Case of the Famous Foes! **A:** Dick Sprang **W:** Bill Finger
120 ❑ Feb 1947 Cover: 0.10 **NM** value: **800.00**
• **CGC:** 4 graded, best 9.0
📖 Fowl Play • Penguin ★ Appearance of Penguin.
121 ❑ Mar 1947 Cover: 0.10 **NM** value: **540.00**
• **CGC:** 3 graded, best 9.6
122 ❑ Apr 1946 Cover: 0.10 **NM** value: **975.00**
• **CGC:** 7 graded, best 9.0
📖 The Black Cat Crimes • Proto-Catwoman ★ Appearance of Catwoman.
123 ❑ May 1947 Cover: 0.10 **NM** value: **540.00**
• **CGC:** 7 graded, best 9.2
124 ❑ Jun 1947 Cover: 0.10 **NM** value: **710.00**
• **CGC:** 4 graded, best 8.5
📖 The Crime Parade ★ Appearance of Joker.
125 ❑ Jul 1947 Cover: 0.10 **NM** value: **540.00**
• **CGC:** 1 graded, best 6.5
📖 The Citadel of Crime
126 ❑ Aug 1947 Cover: 0.10 **NM** value: **540.00**
• **CGC:** 7 graded, best 9.4
• Penguin ★ Appearance of Penguin.
127 ❑ Sep 1947 Cover: 0.10 **NM** value: **540.00**
• **CGC:** 7 graded, best 9.2
📖 Pygmies in Giantland
128 ❑ Oct 1947 Cover: 0.10 **NM** value: **710.00**
• **CGC:** 11 graded, best 9.4
📖 Crimes in Reverse • Joker ★ Appearance of Joker.
129 ❑ Nov 1947 Cover: 0.10 **NM** value: **540.00**
• **CGC:** 5 graded, best 9.0
130 ❑ Dec 1947 Cover: 0.10 **NM** value: **540.00**
• **CGC:** 2 graded, best 8.5
131 ❑ Jan 1948 Cover: 0.10 **NM** value: **450.00**
• **CGC:** 1 graded, best 7.0
📖 The Underworld Surgeon
132 ❑ Feb 1948 Cover: 0.10 **NM** value: **450.00**
• **CGC:** 1 graded, best 9.4
📖 The Human Key
133 ❑ Mar 1948 Cover: 0.10 **NM** value: **450.00**
• **CGC:** 6 graded, best 8.0
📖 The Man Who Could See the Future
134 ❑ Apr 1948 Cover: 0.10 **NM** value: **450.00**
• **CGC:** 3 graded, best 9.0
• Boy Commandos
135 ❑ May 1948 Cover: 0.10 **NM** value: **450.00**
• **CGC:** 4 graded, best 9.2
136 ❑ Jun 1948 Cover: 0.10 **NM** value: **450.00**
137 ❑ Jul 1948 Cover: 0.10 **NM** value: **600.00**
• **CGC:** 4 graded, best 7.5
📖 The Rebus Crimes • Joker ★ Appearance of Joker.
138 ❑ Aug 1948 Cover: 0.10 **NM** value: **850.00**
• **CGC:** 1 graded, best 5.0
📖 The Invisible Crime ★ Origin of Robotman.
139 ❑ Sep 1948 Cover: 0.10 **NM** value: **450.00**
• **CGC:** 2 graded, best 9.4
📖 Crimes in Jade
140 ❑ Oct 1948 Cover: 0.10 **NM** value: **3650.00**
• **CGC:** 12 graded, best 8.0
📖 The Riddler ★ 1st Appearance of Riddler.
141 ❑ Nov 1948 Cover: 0.10 **NM** value: **485.00**
• **CGC:** 2 graded, best 9.2
📖 The Gallery of Public Heroes
142 ❑ Dec 1948 Cover: 0.10 **NM** value: **925.00**
• **CGC:** 2 graded, best 9.2
📖 The Riddler's Puzzle Contest • Boy Commandos ★ 2nd Appearance of Riddler.
143 ❑ Jan 1949 Cover: 0.10 **NM** value: **485.00**
• **CGC:** 1 graded, best 5.0
📖 The Pied Piper of Peril
144 ❑ Feb 1949 Cover: 0.10 **NM** value: **485.00**
📖 The Mystery Broadcast • Kay Kyser team-up
145 ❑ Mar 1949 Cover: 0.10 **NM** value: **485.00**
• **CGC:** 2 graded, best 9.0
146 ❑ Apr 1949 Cover: 0.10 **NM** value: **485.00**
• **CGC:** 1 graded, best 4.0
147 ❑ May 1949 Cover: 0.10 **NM** value: **485.00**
• **CGC:** 1 graded, best 6.5
📖 Tiger Shark
148 ❑ Jun 1949 Cover: 0.10 **NM** value: **485.00**
• **CGC:** 1 graded, best 7.5
📖 The Experiment of Professor Zero
149 ❑ Jul 1949 Cover: 0.10 **NM** value: **625.00**
• **CGC:** 8 graded, best 9.4
📖 The Sound-Effect Crimes • Joker ★ Appearance of Joker.
150 ❑ Aug 1949 Cover: 0.10 **NM** value: **500.00**
151 ❑ Sep 1949 Cover: 0.10 **NM** value: **550.00**
• **CGC:** 4 graded, best 9.6
• Pow-Wow Smith back-up ★ Origin of Pow Wow Smith. ★ 1st Appearance of Pow Wow Smith.
152 ❑ Oct 1949 Cover: 0.10 **NM** value: **485.00**
• **CGC:** 1 graded, best 9.0
• Pow-Wow Smith back-up; Vicki Vale story
153 ❑ Nov 1949 Cover: 0.10 **NM** value: **485.00**
• **CGC:** 2 graded, best 7.0
★ 1st Appearance of Roy Raymond, TV Detective.
154 ❑ Dec 1949 Cover: 0.10 **NM** value: **485.00**
• **CGC:** 4 graded, best 8.0
• Pow-Wow Smith back-up

CGC-graded: Multiply prices above by **33 for 9.9 M • 16 for 9.8 NM/M • 7 for 9.6 NM+ • 5 for 9.4 NM • 2.5 for 9.2 NM- • 1.5 for 9.0 VF/NM**

155 ❑ Jan 1950 Cover: 0.10 **NM** value: **485.00**
• **CGC:** 5 graded, best 9.2
Bruce Wayne, Private Detective • Pow-Wow Smith back-up
156 ❑ Feb 1950 Cover: 0.10 **NM** value: **575.00**
• **CGC:** 1 graded, best 5.5
Batmobile of 1950 • New Batmobile; Pow-Wow Smith back-up
157 ❑ Mar 1950 Cover: 0.10 **NM** value: **450.00**
• **CGC:** 4 graded, best 9.6
• Pow-Wow Smith back-up
158 ❑ Apr 1950 Cover: 0.10 **NM** value: **450.00**
• **CGC:** 4 graded, best 8.0
• DC's Dr. Doom; Pow-Wow Smith back-up
159 ❑ May 1950 Cover: 0.10 **NM** value: **450.00**
• **CGC:** 4 graded, best 9.0
• Pow-Wow Smith back-up
160 ❑ Jun 1950 Cover: 0.10 **NM** value: **450.00**
• **CGC:** 1 graded, best 7.5
The Globe-Trotter of Crime • Pow-Wow Smith back-up
161 ❑ Jul 1950 Cover: 0.10 **NM** value: **485.00**
• **CGC:** 6 graded, best 9.4
• Pow-Wow Smith back-up
162 ❑ Aug 1950 Cover: 0.10 **NM** value: **485.00**
• **CGC:** 3 graded, best 7.0
The Law of the Iron Road • Pow-Wow Smith back-up
163 ❑ Sep 1950 Cover: 0.10 **NM** value: **485.00**
• **CGC:** 3 graded, best 9.4
• Pow-Wow Smith back-up
164 ❑ Oct 1950 Cover: 0.10 **NM** value: **485.00**
• **CGC:** 4 graded, best 9.2
Untold Tales of the Bat-Signal • Pow-Wow Smith back-up
165 ❑ Nov 1950 Cover: 0.10 **NM** value: **485.00**
• **CGC:** 3 graded, best 8.0
The Strange Costumes of Batman • Pow-Wow Smith back-up
166 ❑ Dec 1950 Cover: 0.10 **NM** value: **485.00**
• **CGC:** 1 graded, best 3.5
The Man with a Million Faces • Pow-Wow Smith back-up
167 ❑ Jan 1951 Cover: 0.10 **NM** value: **485.00**
• **CGC:** 2 graded, best 8.0
168 ❑ Feb 1951 Cover: 0.10 **NM** value: **3100.00**
• **CGC:** 5 graded, best 9.2
The Man Behind the Red Hood • Pow-Wow Smith back-up ★ Origin of Joker.
169 ❑ Mar 1951 Cover: 0.10 **NM** value: **470.00**
• **CGC:** 3 graded, best 8.0
170 ❑ Apr 1951 Cover: 0.10 **NM** value: **470.00**
• **CGC:** 2 graded, best 9.6
The Flying Dutchman II • Pow-Wow Smith back-up
171 ❑ May 1951 Cover: 0.10 **NM** value: **650.00**
• **CGC:** 5 graded, best 9.0
The Penguin • Pow-Wow Smith back-up ★ Appearance of Penguin.
172 ❑ Jun 1951 Cover: 0.10 **NM** value: **470.00**
• **CGC:** 4 graded, best 9.6
The Outlaw Who Had Nine Lives • Pow-Wow Smith back-up
173 ❑ Jul 1951 Cover: 0.10 **NM** value: **470.00**
• **CGC:** 2 graded, best 8.0
The Batman's Double • Pow-Wow Smith back-up
174 ❑ Aug 1951 Cover: 0.10 **NM** value: **470.00**
• **CGC:** 3 graded, best 9.4
175 ❑ Sep 1951 Cover: 0.10 **NM** value: **470.00**
• **CGC:** 1 graded, best 7.0
The Underworld Bank • Pow-Wow Smith back-up
176 ❑ Oct 1951 Cover: 0.10 **NM** value: **470.00**
• **CGC:** 3 graded, best 9.6
177 ❑ Nov 1951 Cover: 0.10 **NM** value: **360.00**
• **CGC:** 1 graded, best 9.4
The Robberies in the Bat-Cave • Pow-Wow Smith back-up
178 ❑ Dec 1951 Cover: 0.10 **NM** value: **360.00**
• **CGC:** 4 graded, best 9.6
179 ❑ Jan 1952 Cover: 0.10 **NM** value: **360.00**
Buce Wayne, Mayor of Gotham City • Pow-Wow Smith back-up
180 ❑ Feb 1952 Cover: 0.10 **NM** value: **410.00**
• **CGC:** 2 graded, best 9.2
The Joker's Millions • Pow-Wow Smith back-up ★ Appearance of Joker.
181 ❑ Mar 1952 Cover: 0.10 **NM** value: **360.00**
• **CGC:** 1 graded, best 9.0
The Amazing Crimes of the Human Magnet
182 ❑ Apr 1952 Cover: 0.10 **NM** value: **360.00**
• **CGC:** 3 graded, best 5.5
183 ❑ May 1952 Cover: 0.10 **NM** value: **360.00**
• **CGC:** 3 graded, best 6.0
The Famous Name Crimes • Pow-Wow Smith back-up
184 ❑ Jun 1952 Cover: 0.10 **NM** value: **360.00**
• **CGC:** 4 graded, best 9.8
The Human Firefly • Pow-Wow Smith back-up ★ 1st Appearance of Firefly.
185 ❑ Jul 1952 Cover: 0.10 **NM** value: **360.00**
• **CGC:** 1 graded, best 9.4
The Secret of Batman's Utility Belt • Batman's Utility Belt explained; Pow-Wow Smith back-up
186 ❑ Aug 1952 Cover: 0.10 **NM** value: **360.00**
The Flying Bat-Cave • Pow-Wow Smith back-up
187 ❑ Sep 1952 Cover: 0.10 **NM** value: **400.00**
• **CGC:** 1 graded, best 3.0
The Double Crimes of Two-Face • Pow-Wow Smith back-up ★ Appearance of Two-Face.
188 ❑ Oct 1952 Cover: 0.10 **NM** value: **360.00**
Doom in the Bat-Cave • Pow-Wow Smith back-up
189 ❑ Nov 1952 Cover: 0.10 **NM** value: **360.00**
• **CGC:** 2 graded, best 6.0
Undersea Hideout • Pow-Wow Smith back-up
190 ❑ Dec 1952 Cover: 0.10 **NM** value: **550.00**
• **CGC:** 1 graded, best 7.0
★ Origin of Batman.
191 ❑ Jan 1953 Cover: 0.10 **NM** value: **360.00**
• **CGC:** 1 graded, best 7.5
The Man with a License to Kill! • Pow-Wow Smith back-up
192 ❑ Feb 1953 Cover: 0.10 **NM** value: **360.00**
• **CGC:** 1 graded, best 2.5
The Phantom Eye of Gotham City • Pow-Wow Smith back-up
193 ❑ Mar 1953 Cover: 0.10 **NM** value: **410.00**
The Joker's Journal • Pow-Wow Smith back-up ★ Appearance of Joker.
194 ❑ Apr 1953 Cover: 0.10 **NM** value: **360.00**
• **CGC:** 1 graded, best 8.0
The Stolen Bank • Pow-Wow Smith back-up
195 ❑ May 1953 Cover: 0.10 **NM** value: **360.00**
• **CGC:** 2 graded, best 8.5
The Original Batman • Pow-Wow Smith back-up
196 ❑ Jun 1953 Cover: 0.10 **NM** value: **360.00**
• **CGC:** 4 graded, best 8.5
The City Without Guns • Pow-Wow Smith back-up
197 ❑ Jul 1953 Cover: 0.10 **NM** value: **360.00**
• **CGC:** 3 graded, best 7.5
The League Against Batman • Pow-Wow Smith back-up
198 ❑ Aug 1953 Cover: 0.10 **NM** value: **360.00**
• **CGC:** 3 graded, best 8.0
199 ❑ Sep 1953 Cover: 0.10 **NM** value: **360.00**
• **CGC:** 1 graded, best 9.2
200 ❑ Oct 1953 Cover: 0.10 **NM** value: **525.00**
• **CGC:** 2 graded, best 5.5
• 200th anniversary issue. • Pow-Wow Smith back-up
201 ❑ Nov 1953 Cover: 0.10 **NM** value: **360.00**
• **CGC:** 1 graded, best 7.5
The Human Target • Impossible but True back-up
202 ❑ Dec 1953 Cover: 0.10 **NM** value: **360.00**
• **CGC:** 4 graded, best 8.0
Millionaire Island • Roy Raymond back-up
203 ❑ Jan 1954 Cover: 0.10 **NM** value: **400.00**
• **CGC:** 2 graded, best 8.0
Crimes of the Catwoman • Roy Raymond back-up ★ Appearance of Catwoman.
204 ❑ Feb 1954 Cover: 0.10 **NM** value: **360.00**
• **CGC:** 2 graded, best 3.0
The Man Who Could Live Forever! • Roy Raymond back-up
205 ❑ Mar 1954 Cover: 0.10 **NM** value: **525.00**
• **CGC:** 2 graded, best 8.0
The Origin of the Batcave • Roy Raymond back-up ★ Origin of Batcave.
206 ❑ Apr 1954 Cover: 0.10 **NM** value: **360.00**
• **CGC:** 1 graded, best 9.0
The Trapper of Gotham City • Roy Raymond back-up
207 ❑ May 1954 Cover: 0.10 **NM** value: **360.00**
• **CGC:** 1 graded, best 8.0
208 ❑ Jun 1954 Cover: 0.10 **NM** value: **360.00**
• **CGC:** 1 graded, best 8.0
209 ❑ Jul 1954 Cover: 0.10 **NM** value: **360.00**
• **CGC:** 1 graded, best 8.5
The Man Who Shadowed Batman • Roy Raymond back-up
210 ❑ Aug 1954 Cover: 0.10 **NM** value: **360.00**
• **CGC:** 4 graded, best 9.2
211 ❑ Sep 1954 Cover: 0.10 **NM** value: **400.00**
• **CGC:** 1 graded, best 7.0
The Jungle Cat-Queen ★ Appearance of Catwoman.
212 ❑ Oct 1954 Cover: 0.10 **NM** value: **360.00**
The Puppet Master
213 ❑ Nov 1954 Cover: 0.10 **NM** value: **450.00**
• **CGC:** 1 graded, best 7.5
The Mysterious Mirror Man
214 ❑ Dec 1954 Cover: 0.10 **NM** value: **330.00**
• **CGC:** 2 graded, best 7.5
215 ❑ Jan 1955 Cover: 0.10 **NM** value: **330.00**
• **CGC:** 1 graded, best 2.0
The Batmen of All Nations
216 ❑ Feb 1955 Cover: 0.10 **NM** value: **330.00**
• **CGC:** 2 graded, best 9.0
The Bbatman of Tomorrow
217 ❑ Mar 1955 Cover: 0.10 **NM** value: **330.00**
• **CGC:** 1 graded, best 7.0
The Mental Giant of Gotham City
218 ❑ Apr 1955 Cover: 0.10 **NM** value: **330.00**
219 ❑ May 1955 Cover: 0.10 **NM** value: **330.00**
• **CGC:** 1 graded, best 7.5
Gotham City's Strangest Race
220 ❑ Jun 1955 Cover: 0.10 **NM** value: **330.00**
• **CGC:** 1 graded, best 7.0
The Mystery of the Second Batman and Robin Team
221 ❑ Jul 1955 Cover: 0.10 **NM** value: **330.00**
The Thousand-and-One Escapes of Batman and Robin
222 ❑ Aug 1955 Cover: 0.10 **NM** value: **330.00**
• **CGC:** 2 graded, best 8.0
The Great Batman Swindle
223 ❑ Sep 1955 Cover: 0.10 **NM** value: **330.00**
• **CGC:** 1 graded, best 4.5
The Batman Dime Museum
224 ❑ Oct 1955 Cover: 0.10 **NM** value: **330.00**
• **CGC:** 1 graded, best 6.0
The Batman Machine
225 ❑ Nov 1955 Cover: 0.10 **NM** value: **5500.00**
• **CGC:** 16 graded, best 7.5
If I were Batman; Roy Raymond, TV Detective: The Money that Came to Life; Casey the Cop; Varsity Vic; Four Tricks of the Detective's Trade; The Strange Experiment of Dr. Erdell; Homer **A:** Henry Boltinoff; Joe Certa; Ruben Moreira; Sheldon Moldoff **W:** Henry Boltinoff; Edmond Hamilton; Jack Miller; Joe Samachson ★ Origin of Martian Manhunter. ★ 1st Appearance of Martian Manhunter.
226 ❑ Dec 1955 Cover: 0.10 **NM** value: **1300.00**
• **CGC:** 2 graded, best 8.0
★ Origin of Martian Manhunter.
227 ❑ Jan 1956 Cover: 0.10 **NM** value: **460.00**
• **CGC:** 1 graded, best 1.0
228 ❑ Feb 1956 Cover: 0.10 **NM** value: **460.00**
229 ❑ Mar 1956 Cover: 0.10 **NM** value: **460.00**
• **CGC:** 3 graded, best 7.5
230 ❑ Apr 1956 Cover: 0.10 **NM** value: **500.00**
• Martian Manhunter ★ 1st Appearance of Mad Hatter II (uses alias Jervis Tetch).
231 ❑ May 1956 Cover: 0.10 **NM** value: **325.00**
• **CGC:** 3 graded, best 8.0
★ Origin of Martian Manhunter.
232 ❑ Jun 1956 Cover: 0.10 **NM** value: **275.00**
• **CGC:** 1 graded, best 9.0
233 ❑ Jul 1956 Cover: 0.10 **NM** value: **1200.00**
• **CGC:** 4 graded, best 9.0
★ Origin of Batwoman. ★ 1st Appearance of Batwoman.
234 ❑ Aug 1956 Cover: 0.10 **NM** value: **300.00**
• **CGC:** 1 graded, best 8.0
235 ❑ Sep 1956 Cover: 0.10 **NM** value: **565.00**
• **CGC:** 1 graded, best 9.0
★ Origin of Batman.
236 ❑ Oct 1956 Cover: 0.10 **NM** value: **325.00**
• **CGC:** 1 graded, best 8.5
237 ❑ Nov 1956 Cover: 0.10 **NM** value: **275.00**
• **CGC:** 2 graded, best 8.0
238 ❑ Dec 1956 Cover: 0.10 **NM** value: **275.00**
• **CGC:** 4 graded, best 9.0
239 ❑ Jan 1957 Cover: 0.10 **NM** value: **275.00**
• **CGC:** 2 graded, best 8.5
240 ❑ Feb 1957 Cover: 0.10 **NM** value: **275.00**
241 ❑ Mar 1957 Cover: 0.10 **NM** value: **210.00**
• **CGC:** 4 graded, best 7.5
242 ❑ Apr 1957 Cover: 0.10 **NM** value: **210.00**
• **CGC:** 1 graded, best 8.0
243 ❑ May 1957 Cover: 0.10 **NM** value: **210.00**
• **CGC:** 1 graded, best 6.5
244 ❑ Jun 1957 Cover: 0.10 **NM** value: **210.00**
• **CGC:** 2 graded, best 9.0
245 ❑ Jul 1957 Cover: 0.10 **NM** value: **210.00**
• **CGC:** 1 graded, best 8.5
246 ❑ Aug 1957 Cover: 0.10 **NM** value: **210.00**
★ 1st Appearance of Diane Meade (Martian Manhunter's girlfriend).
247 ❑ Sep 1957 Cover: 0.10 **NM** value: **210.00**
★ 1st Appearance of Professor Ivo.
248 ❑ Oct 1957 Cover: 0.10 **NM** value: **210.00**
• **CGC:** 3 graded, best 8.0
249 ❑ Nov 1957 Cover: 0.10 **NM** value: **210.00**
★ Appearance of Batwoman.
250 ❑ Dec 1957 Cover: 0.10 **NM** value: **210.00**
251 ❑ Jan 1958 Cover: 0.10 **NM** value: **210.00**
252 ❑ Feb 1958 Cover: 0.10 **NM** value: **210.00**
• **CGC:** 1 graded, best 8.5
253 ❑ Mar 1958 Cover: 0.10 **NM** value: **210.00**
• **CGC:** 1 graded, best 7.5
254 ❑ Apr 1958 Cover: 0.10 **NM** value: **210.00**
• **CGC:** 3 graded, best 8.0
255 ❑ May 1958 Cover: 0.10 **NM** value: **210.00**
• **CGC:** 2 graded, best 8.5
256 ❑ Jun 1958 Cover: 0.10 **NM** value: **210.00**
• **CGC:** 4 graded, best 8.0
257 ❑ Jul 1958 Cover: 0.10 **NM** value: **210.00**
258 ❑ Aug 1958 Cover: 0.10 **NM** value: **210.00**
259 ❑ Sep 1958 Cover: 0.10 **NM** value: **210.00**
• **CGC:** 3 graded, best 9.0
★ 1st Appearance of Calendar Man.
260 ❑ Oct 1958 Cover: 0.10 **NM** value: **210.00**
261 ❑ Nov 1958 Cover: 0.10 **NM** value: **165.00**
★ 1st Appearance of Doctor Double X.
262 ❑ Dec 1958 Cover: 0.10 **NM** value: **165.00**
263 ❑ Jan 1959 Cover: 0.10 **NM** value: **165.00**
• **CGC:** 2 graded, best 6.5
264 ❑ Feb 1959 Cover: 0.10 **NM** value: **165.00**
265 ❑ Mar 1959 Cover: 0.10 **NM** value: **275.00**
• **CGC:** 6 graded, best 9.0
★ Origin of Batman. ★ Appearance of Joker.
266 ❑ Apr 1959 Cover: 0.10 **NM** value: **165.00**
• **CGC:** 3 graded, best 9.2
267 ❑ May 1959 Cover: 0.10 **NM** value: **210.00**
• **CGC:** 2 graded, best 8.5
★ Origin of Bat-Mite. ★ 1st Appearance of Bat-Mite.
268 ❑ Jun 1959 Cover: 0.10 **NM** value: **165.00**
• **CGC:** 2 graded, best 9.4
269 ❑ Jul 1959 Cover: 0.10 **NM** value: **165.00**
• **CGC:** 5 graded, best 9.4
270 ❑ Aug 1959 Cover: 0.10 **NM** value: **165.00**
• **CGC:** 2 graded, best 9.0
271 ❑ Sep 1959 Cover: 0.10 **NM** value: **175.00**
• **CGC:** 2 graded, best 9.4
★ Origin of Martian Manhunter.
272 ❑ Oct 1959 Cover: 0.10 **NM** value: **125.00**
• **CGC:** 1 graded, best 9.4
273 ❑ Nov 1959 Cover: 0.10 **NM** value: **160.00**
• **CGC:** 3 graded, best 9.0
• Martian Manhunter reveals his identity
274 ❑ Dec 1959 Cover: 0.10 **NM** value: **125.00**
• **CGC:** 1 graded, best 7.0
275 ❑ Jan 1960 Cover: 0.10 **NM** value: **125.00**
Circ: Statement: **314,000** • **CGC:** 2 graded, best 8.5
276 ❑ Feb 1960 Cover: 0.10 **NM** value: **125.00**
Circ: Statement: **314,000** • **CGC:** 3 graded, best 9.0
★ Appearance of Bat-Mite, Batwoman.
277 ❑ Mar 1960 Cover: 0.10 **NM** value: **125.00**
Circ: Statement: **314,000** • **CGC:** 6 graded, best 9.0
278 ❑ Apr 1960 Cover: 0.10 **NM** value: **125.00**
Circ: Statement: **314,000** • **CGC:** 1 graded, best 6.5
279 ❑ May 1960 Cover: 0.10 **NM** value: **125.00**
Circ: Statement: **314,000**
280 ❑ Jun 1960 Cover: 0.10 **NM** value: **125.00**
Circ: Statement: **314,000** • **CGC:** 1 graded, best 9.0
281 ❑ Jul 1960 Cover: 0.10 **NM** value: **100.00**
Circ: Statement: **314,000** • **CGC:** 2 graded, best 9.0
282 ❑ Aug 1960 Cover: 0.10 **NM** value: **100.00**
Circ: Statement: **314,000** • **CGC:** 2 graded, best 8.5
283 ❑ Sep 1960 Cover: 0.10 **NM** value: **100.00**
Circ: Statement: **314,000** • **CGC:** 1 graded, best 7.5

Other grades: Multiply prices above by **1.5 for Mint • 2/3 for Very Fine • 1/3 for Fine • 1/5 for Very Good • 1/8 for Good**

284 ❑ Oct 1960 Cover: 0.10 **NM** value: **100.00**
Circ: Statement: **314,000** • **CGC:** 3 graded, best 9.0
285 ❑ Nov 1960 Cover: 0.10 **NM** value: **100.00**
Circ: Statement: **314,000** • **CGC:** 2 graded, best 6.5
★ Appearance of Batwoman.
286 ❑ Dec 1960 Cover: 0.10 **NM** value: **100.00**
Circ: Statement: **314,000** • **CGC:** 2 graded, best 8.5
★ Appearance of Batwoman.
287 ❑ Jan 1961 Cover: 0.10 **NM** value: **100.00**
Circ: Statement: **325,000** • **CGC:** 2 graded, best 9.2
★ Origin of Martian Manhunter.
288 ❑ Feb 1961 Cover: 0.10 **NM** value: **100.00**
Circ: Statement: **325,000** • **CGC:** 4 graded, best 8.0
289 ❑ Mar 1961 Cover: 0.10 **NM** value: **100.00**
Circ: Statement: **325,000** • **CGC:** 2 graded, best 6.0
290 ❑ Apr 1961 Cover: 0.10 **NM** value: **100.00**
Circ: Statement: **325,000**
291 ❑ May 1961 Cover: 0.10 **NM** value: **100.00**
Circ: Statement: **325,000** • **CGC:** 2 graded, best 9.2
292 ❑ Jun 1961 Cover: 0.10 **NM** value: **100.00**
Circ: Statement: **325,000** • **CGC:** 1 graded, best 9.2
★ Appearance of Batwoman.
293 ❑ Jul 1961 Cover: 0.10 **NM** value: **100.00**
Circ: Statement: **325,000** • **CGC:** 4 graded, best 9.2
294 ❑ Aug 1961 Cover: 0.10 **NM** value: **100.00**
Circ: Statement: **325,000** • **CGC:** 1 graded, best 9.4
295 ❑ Sep 1961 Cover: 0.10 **NM** value: **100.00**
Circ: Statement: **325,000**
296 ❑ Oct 1961 Cover: 0.10 **NM** value: **100.00**
Circ: Statement: **325,000** • **CGC:** 1 graded, best 4.5
297 ❑ Nov 1961 Cover: 0.10 **NM** value: **100.00**
Circ: Statement: **325,000** • **CGC:** 2 graded, best 8.5
298 ❑ Dec 1961 Cover: 0.12 **NM** value: **225.00**
Circ: Statement: **325,000** • **CGC:** 10 graded, best 9.2
★ 1st Appearance of Clayface II (Matt Hagen).
299 ❑ Jan 1962 Cover: 0.12 **NM** value: **70.00**
Circ: Statement: **265,000** • **CGC:** 3 graded, best 9.2
300 ❑ Feb 1962 Cover: 0.12 **NM** value: **70.00**
Circ: Statement: **265,000** • **CGC:** 1 graded, best 6.5
301 ❑ Mar 1962 Cover: 0.12 **NM** value: **65.00**
Circ: Statement: **265,000** • **CGC:** 3 graded, best 9.0
• Has 1961 Statement; avg total paid circ 325,000
302 ❑ Apr 1962 Cover: 0.12 **NM** value: **54.00**
Circ: Statement: **265,000**
★ Appearance of Batwoman.
303 ❑ May 1962 Cover: 0.12 **NM** value: **54.00**
Circ: Statement: **265,000** • **CGC:** 1 graded, best 8.5
304 ❑ Jun 1962 Cover: 0.12 **NM** value: **54.00**
Circ: Statement: **265,000** • **CGC:** 3 graded, best 9.6
305 ❑ Jul 1962 Cover: 0.12 **NM** value: **54.00**
Circ: Statement: **265,000** • **CGC:** 2 graded, best 9.4
306 ❑ Aug 1962 Cover: 0.12 **NM** value: **54.00**
Circ: Statement: **265,000** • **CGC:** 3 graded, best 9.2
307 ❑ Sep 1962 Cover: 0.12 **NM** value: **54.00**
Circ: Statement: **265,000** • **CGC:** 1 graded, best 9.4
★ Appearance of Batwoman.
308 ❑ Oct 1962 Cover: 0.12 **NM** value: **54.00**
Circ: Statement: **265,000** • **CGC:** 3 graded, best 9.0
309 ❑ Nov 1962 Cover: 0.12 **NM** value: **54.00**
Circ: Statement: **265,000** • **CGC:** 4 graded, best 9.4
★ Appearance of Batwoman.
310 ❑ Dec 1962 Cover: 0.12 **NM** value: **54.00**
Circ: Statement: **265,000** • **CGC:** 5 graded, best 9.4
311 ❑ Jan 1963 Cover: 0.12 **NM** value: **54.00**
• **CGC:** 1 graded, best 7.5
★ 1st Appearance of Cat-Man (DC). ★ Appearance of Batwoman.
312 ❑ Feb 1963 Cover: 0.12 **NM** value: **54.00**
• **CGC:** 2 graded, best 9.2
313 ❑ Mar 1963 Cover: 0.12 **NM** value: **54.00**
• **CGC:** 1 graded, best 9.4
314 ❑ Apr 1963 Cover: 0.12 **NM** value: **54.00**
• **CGC:** 3 graded, best 9.4
315 ❑ May 1963 Cover: 0.12 **NM** value: **54.00**
• **CGC:** 5 graded, best 8.5
316 ❑ Jun 1963 Cover: 0.12 **NM** value: **54.00**
• **CGC:** 3 graded, best 9.2
317 ❑ Jul 1963 Cover: 0.12 **NM** value: **54.00**
• **CGC:** 6 graded, best 9.6
318 ❑ Aug 1963 Cover: 0.12 **NM** value: **54.00**
• **CGC:** 4 graded, best 9.2
★ Appearance of Batwoman.
319 ❑ Sep 1963 Cover: 0.12 **NM** value: **54.00**
• **CGC:** 2 graded, best 9.4
320 ❑ Oct 1963 Cover: 0.12 **NM** value: **54.00**
• **CGC:** 4 graded, best 9.2
321 ❑ Nov 1963 Cover: 0.12 **NM** value: **54.00**
• **CGC:** 5 graded, best 9.2
★ Appearance of Batwoman.
322 ❑ Dec 1963 Cover: 0.12 **NM** value: **54.00**
• **CGC:** 3 graded, best 9.4
323 ❑ Jan 1964 Cover: 0.12 **NM** value: **54.00**
• **CGC:** 1 graded, best 9.0
324 ❑ Feb 1964 Cover: 0.12 **NM** value: **54.00**
• Has 1963 Statement, filed 10/1/63; no circ figures published
325 ❑ Mar 1964 Cover: 0.12 **NM** value: **54.00**
• **CGC:** 1 graded, best 9.4
★ Appearance of Batwoman.
326 ❑ Apr 1964 Cover: 0.12 **NM** value: **54.00**
• **CGC:** 4 graded, best 9.2
327 ❑ May 1964 Cover: 0.12 **NM** value: **75.00**
• **CGC:** 6 graded, best 9.0
• 25th anniversary. • symbol change;300th Batman in Detective Comics **A:** Carmine Infantino
328 ❑ Jun 1964 Cover: 0.12 **NM** value: **85.00**
• **CGC:** 2 graded, best 9.2
★ Death of Alfred.
329 ❑ Jul 1964 Cover: 0.12 **NM** value: **40.00**
330 ❑ Aug 1964 Cover: 0.12 **NM** value: **40.00**
• **CGC:** 1 graded, best 9.0
331 ❑ Sep 1964 Cover: 0.12 **NM** value: **35.00**
• **CGC:** 3 graded, best 9.4
332 ❑ Oct 1964 Cover: 0.12 **NM** value: **38.00**
• **CGC:** 3 graded, best 9.2
★ Appearance of Joker.
333 ❑ Nov 1964 Cover: 0.12 **NM** value: **30.00**
• **CGC:** 2 graded, best 9.2
334 ❑ Dec 1964 Cover: 0.12 **NM** value: **30.00**
• **CGC:** 2 graded, best 9.4
★ Appearance of Joker.
335 ❑ Jan 1965 Cover: 0.12 **NM** value: **30.00**
Circ: Statement: **304,414** • **CGC:** 1 graded, best 5.0
336 ❑ Feb 1965 Cover: 0.12 **NM** value: **30.00**
Circ: Statement: **304,414**
337 ❑ Mar 1965 Cover: 0.12 **NM** value: **30.00**
Circ: Statement: **304,414** • **CGC:** 1 graded, best 8.5
• Has 1964 Statement, filed 10/1/64; no circ figures published
338 ❑ Apr 1965 Cover: 0.12 **NM** value: **30.00**
Circ: Statement: **304,414** • **CGC:** 1 graded, best 8.0
339 ❑ May 1965 Cover: 0.12 **NM** value: **30.00**
Circ: Statement: **304,414**
340 ❑ Jun 1965 Cover: 0.12 **NM** value: **30.00**
Circ: Statement: **304,414**
341 ❑ Jul 1965 Cover: 0.12 **NM** value: **40.00**
Circ: Statement: **304,414** • **CGC:** 4 graded, best 9.0
★ Appearance of Joker.
342 ❑ Aug 1965 Cover: 0.12 **NM** value: **30.00**
Circ: Statement: **304,414** • **CGC:** 5 graded, best 9.4
343 ❑ Sep 1965 Cover: 0.12 **NM** value: **28.00**
Circ: Statement: **304,414** • **CGC:** 3 graded, best 9.4
344 ❑ Oct 1965 Cover: 0.12 **NM** value: **28.00**
Circ: Statement: **304,414** • **CGC:** 3 graded, best 9.2
345 ❑ Nov 1965 Cover: 0.12 **NM** value: **28.00**
Circ: Statement: **304,414** • **CGC:** 1 graded, best 9.0
★ 1st Appearance of Blockbuster.
346 ❑ Dec 1965 Cover: 0.12 **NM** value: **28.00**
Circ: Statement: **304,414** • **CGC:** 3 graded, best 9.2
347 ❑ Jan 1966 Cover: 0.12 **NM** value: **28.00**
Circ: Statement: **404,339** • **CGC:** 1 graded, best 9.0
348 ❑ Feb 1966 Cover: 0.12 **NM** value: **28.00**
Circ: Statement: **404,339** • **CGC:** 2 graded, best 9.2
349 ❑ Mar 1966 Cover: 0.12 **NM** value: **28.00**
Circ: Statement: **404,339** • **CGC:** 2 graded, best 9.2
350 ❑ Apr 1966 Cover: 0.12 **NM** value: **28.00**
Circ: Statement: **404,339** • **CGC:** 3 graded, best 9.4
351 ❑ May 1966 Cover: 0.12 **NM** value: **28.00**
Circ: Statement: **404,339** • **CGC:** 2 graded, best 9.4
★ 1st Appearance of Cluemaster.
352 ❑ Jun 1966 Cover: 0.12 **NM** value: **28.00**
Circ: Statement: **404,339** • **CGC:** 4 graded, best 9.4
• Elongated Man back-up
353 ❑ Jul 1966 Cover: 0.12 **NM** value: **28.00**
Circ: Statement: **404,339** • **CGC:** 4 graded, best 9.4
• Has 1965 Statement, filed 10/1/65; avg print run 485,000; avg sales 302,000; avg subs 2,414; avg total paid 304,414; samples 142; max existent 304,556; 37% of run returned
354 ❑ Aug 1966 Cover: 0.12 **NM** value: **28.00**
Circ: Statement: **404,339** • **CGC:** 7 graded, best 9.4
★ 1st Appearance of Doctor Tzin-Tzin.
355 ❑ Sep 1966 Cover: 0.12 **NM** value: **28.00**
Circ: Statement: **404,339** • **CGC:** 3 graded, best 9.6
356 ❑ Oct 1966 Cover: 0.12 **NM** value: **28.00**
Circ: Statement: **404,339** • **CGC:** 5 graded, best 9.6
• Alfred returns
357 ❑ Nov 1966 Cover: 0.12 **NM** value: **28.00**
Circ: Statement: **404,339** • **CGC:** 8 graded, best 9.6
358 ❑ Dec 1966 Cover: 0.12 **NM** value: **28.00**
Circ: Statement: **404,339** • **CGC:** 7 graded, best 9.4
★ 1st Appearance of Spellbinder.
359 ❑ Jan 1967 Cover: 0.12 **NM** value: **75.00**
Circ: Statement: **425,700** • **CGC:** 30 graded, best 9.6
★ 1st Appearance of Batgirl (Barbara Gordon).
360 ❑ Feb 1967 Cover: 0.12 **NM** value: **28.00**
Circ: Statement: **425,700** • **CGC:** 7 graded, best 9.6
• Has 1966 Statement, filed 10/1/66; avg print run 617,000; avg sales 402,000; avg subs 2,339; avg total paid 404,339; max existent 404,339; 0% of run returned
361 ❑ Mar 1967 Cover: 0.12 **NM** value: **28.00**
Circ: Statement: **425,700** • **CGC:** 6 graded, best 9.4
362 ❑ Apr 1967 Cover: 0.12 **NM** value: **28.00**
Circ: Statement: **425,700** • **CGC:** 4 graded, best 9.4
★ Appearance of Riddler.
363 ❑ May 1967 Cover: 0.12 **NM** value: **28.00**
Circ: Statement: **425,700** • **CGC:** 3 graded, best 9.4
★ Appearance of Batgirl (Barbara Gordon).
364 ❑ Jun 1967 Cover: 0.12 **NM** value: **28.00**
Circ: Statement: **425,700** • **CGC:** 6 graded, best 9.2
★ Appearance of Batgirl (Barbara Gordon).
365 ❑ Jul 1967 Cover: 0.12 **NM** value: **40.00**
Circ: Statement: **425,700** • **CGC:** 9 graded, best 9.6
★ Appearance of Joker.
366 ❑ Aug 1967 Cover: 0.12 **NM** value: **28.00**
Circ: Statement: **425,700** • **CGC:** 2 graded, best 9.6
367 ❑ Sep 1967 Cover: 0.12 **NM** value: **28.00**
Circ: Statement: **425,700** • **CGC:** 3 graded, best 9.6
368 ❑ Oct 1967 Cover: 0.12 **NM** value: **28.00**
Circ: Statement: **425,700** • **CGC:** 2 graded, best 9.2
369 ❑ Nov 1967 Cover: 0.12 **NM** value: **44.00**
Circ: Statement: **425,700** • **CGC:** 5 graded, best 9.2
• Robin teams with Batgirl;Elongated Man back-up **A:** Neal Adams
370 ❑ Dec 1967 Cover: 0.12 **NM** value: **28.00**
Circ: Statement: **425,700** • **CGC:** 3 graded, best 9.4
• Elongated Man **A:** Gil Kane; Bernie Krigstein
371 ❑ Jan 1968 Cover: 0.12 **NM** value: **28.00**
Circ: Statement: **309,850** • **CGC:** 9 graded, best 9.6
★ Appearance of Batgirl (Barbara Gordon).
372 ❑ Feb 1968 Cover: 0.12 **NM** value: **22.00**
Circ: Statement: **309,850** • **CGC:** 5 graded, best 9.6
373 ❑ Mar 1968 Cover: 0.12 **NM** value: **22.00**
Circ: Statement: **309,850** • **CGC:** 2 graded, best 9.8
• Has 1967 Statement; avg print run 665,000; avg total paid 425,700★ Appearance of Riddler.
374 ❑ Apr 1968 Cover: 0.12 **NM** value: **22.00**
Circ: Statement: **309,850**
375 ❑ May 1968 Cover: 0.12 **NM** value: **22.00**
Circ: Statement: **309,850**
376 ❑ Jun 1968 Cover: 0.12 **NM** value: **22.00**
Circ: Statement: **309,850** • **CGC:** 2 graded, best 9.4
• Elongated Man back-up
377 ❑ Jul 1968 Cover: 0.12 **NM** value: **22.00**
Circ: Statement: **309,850** • **CGC:** 5 graded, best 9.4
378 ❑ Aug 1968 Cover: 0.12 **NM** value: **22.00**
Circ: Statement: **309,850** • **CGC:** 8 graded, best 9.4
379 ❑ Sep 1968 Cover: 0.12 **NM** value: **22.00**
Circ: Statement: **309,850** • **CGC:** 3 graded, best 9.2
380 ❑ Oct 1968 Cover: 0.12 **NM** value: **22.00**
Circ: Statement: **309,850** • **CGC:** 5 graded, best 9.2
381 ❑ Nov 1968 Cover: 0.12 **NM** value: **22.00**
Circ: Statement: **309,850** • **CGC:** 7 graded, best 9.4
382 ❑ Dec 1968 Cover: 0.12 **NM** value: **22.00**
Circ: Statement: **309,850** • **CGC:** 5 graded, best 9.6
383 ❑ Jan 1969 Cover: 0.12 **NM** value: **22.00**
Circ: Statement: **221,267** • **CGC:** 5 graded, best 9.6
384 ❑ Feb 1969 Cover: 0.12 **NM** value: **22.00**
Circ: Statement: **221,267** • **CGC:** 4 graded, best 9.4
• Has 1968 Statement, filed 10/1/68; avg print run 570,000; avg sales 309,000; avg subs 850; avg total paid 309,850; samples 386; max existent 310,236; 46% of run returned
385 ❑ Mar 1969 Cover: 0.12 **NM** value: **22.00**
Circ: Statement: **221,267** • **CGC:** 7 graded, best 9.4
386 ❑ Apr 1969 Cover: 0.12 **NM** value: **22.00**
Circ: Statement: **221,267** • **CGC:** 3 graded, best 9.6
387 ❑ May 1969 Cover: 0.12 **NM** value: **45.00**
Circ: Statement: **221,267** • **CGC:** 8 graded, best 9.4
• Reprints Detective Comics #27★ 1st Appearance of Batman.
388 ❑ Jun 1969 Cover: 0.15 **NM** value: **25.00**
Circ: Statement: **221,267** • **CGC:** 6 graded, best 9.6
★ Appearance of Joker.
389 ❑ Jul 1969 Cover: 0.15 **NM** value: **16.00**
Circ: Statement: **221,267** • **CGC:** 4 graded, best 9.4
390 ❑ Aug 1969 Cover: 0.15 **NM** value: **16.00**
Circ: Statement: **221,267** • **CGC:** 4 graded, best 9.4
391 ❑ Sep 1969 Cover: 0.15 **NM** value: **13.00**
Circ: Statement: **221,267** • **CGC:** 2 graded, best 8.5
392 ❑ Oct 1969 Cover: 0.15 **NM** value: **13.00**
Circ: Statement: **221,267** • **CGC:** 3 graded, best 9.2
📖 The Gal Most Likely to Be…Batman's Widow!; Robin: Strike! **A:** Murphy Anderson; Gil Kane; Bob Brown; Joe Giella **W:** Frank Robbins; Mike Friedrich ★ 1st Appearance of Jason Bard.
393 ❑ Nov 1969 Cover: 0.15 **NM** value: **13.00**
Circ: Statement: **221,267** • **CGC:** 1 graded, best 9.4
394 ❑ Dec 1969 Cover: 0.15 **NM** value: **13.00**
Circ: Statement: **221,267** • **CGC:** 3 graded, best 9.4
395 ❑ Jan 1970 Cover: 0.15 **NM** value: **20.00**
Circ: Statement: **209,630** • **CGC:** 2 graded, best 9.4
A: Murphy Anderson; Dick Giordano; Neal Adams; Gil Kane
396 ❑ Feb 1970 Cover: 0.15 **NM** value: **13.00**
Circ: Statement: **209,630** • **CGC:** 5 graded, best 9.8
A: Gil Kane **C:** Neal Adams ★ Appearance of Batgirl.
397 ❑ Mar 1970 Cover: 0.15 **NM** value: **20.00**
Circ: Statement: **209,630** • **CGC:** 2 graded, best 9.0
• Has 1969 Statement, filed 10/1/69; avg print run 459,000; avg sales 221,000; avg subs 267; avg total paid 221,267; samples 346; max existent 221,613; 52% of run returned **A:** Neal Adams
398 ❑ Apr 1970 Cover: 0.15 **NM** value: **13.00**
Circ: Statement: **209,630** • **CGC:** 4 graded, best 9.4
399 ❑ May 1970 Cover: 0.15 **NM** value: **13.00**
Circ: Statement: **209,630** • **CGC:** 3 graded, best 9.4
400 ❑ Jun 1970 Cover: 0.15 **NM** value: **45.00**
Circ: Statement: **209,630** • **CGC:** 23 graded, best 9.4
A: Gene Colan; Neal Adams ★ Origin of Man-Bat. ★ 1st Appearance of Man-Bat.
401 ❑ Jul 1970 Cover: 0.15 **NM** value: **10.00**
Circ: Statement: **209,630** • **CGC:** 1 graded, best 9.0
402 ❑ Aug 1970 Cover: 0.15 **NM** value: **20.00**
Circ: Statement: **209,630** • **CGC:** 4 graded, best 9.6
A: Neal Adams
403 ❑ Sep 1970 Cover: 0.15 **NM** value: **10.00**
Circ: Statement: **209,630** • **CGC:** 6 graded, best 9.6
• Robin **A:** Gil Kane **C:** Neal Adams
404 ❑ Oct 1970 Cover: 0.15 **NM** value: **18.00**
Circ: Statement: **209,630** • **CGC:** 3 graded, best 9.4
• Batgirl **A:** Dick Giordano; Neal Adams; Gil Kane
405 ❑ Nov 1970 Cover: 0.15 **NM** value: **10.00**
Circ: Statement: **209,630** • **CGC:** 3 graded, best 9.2
406 ❑ Dec 1970 Cover: 0.15 **NM** value: **10.00**
Circ: Statement: **209,630** • **CGC:** 1 graded, best 9.2
407 ❑ Jan 1971 Cover: 0.15 **NM** value: **20.00**
Circ: Statement: **199,112** • **CGC:** 7 graded, best 9.6
A: Neal Adams ★ Appearance of Man-Bat.
408 ❑ Feb 1971 Cover: 0.15 **NM** value: **20.00**
Circ: Statement: **199,112** • **CGC:** 7 graded, best 9.8
A: Neal Adams
409 ❑ Mar 1971 Cover: 0.15 **NM** value: **10.00**
Circ: Statement: **199,112** • **CGC:** 1 graded, best 9.4
A: Dick Giordano; Irv Novick **C:** Neal Adams
410 ❑ Apr 1971 Cover: 0.15 **NM** value: **20.00**
Circ: Statement: **199,112** • **CGC:** 5 graded, best 9.6
• Batgirl **A:** Don Heck; Dick Giordano; Neal Adams
411 ❑ May 1971 Cover: 0.15 **NM** value: **10.00**
Circ: Statement: **199,112** • **CGC:** 2 graded, best 9.4
★ 1st Appearance of Talia.
412 ❑ Jun 1971 Cover: 0.15 **NM** value: **10.00**
Circ: Statement: **199,112** • **CGC:** 2 graded, best 9.4
413 ❑ Jul 1971 Cover: 0.15 **NM** value: **10.00**
Circ: Statement: **199,112** • **CGC:** 3 graded, best 9.2

CGC-graded: Multiply prices above by **33 for 9.9 M** • **16 for 9.8 NM/M** • **7 for 9.6 NM+** • **5 for 9.4 NM** • **2.5 for 9.2 NM-** • **1.5 for 9.0 VF/NM**

414 ❑ Aug 1971 Cover: 0.15 **NM** value: **10.00**
Circ: Statement: **199,112 • CGC:** 5 graded, best 9.4
• Giant-size.
415 ❑ Sep 1971 Cover: 0.25 **NM** value: **10.00**
Circ: Statement: **199,112 • CGC:** 7 graded, best 9.6
• Giant-size.
416 ❑ Oct 1971 Cover: 0.25 **NM** value: **10.00**
Circ: Statement: **199,112 • CGC:** 5 graded, best 9.6
• Giant-size.
417 ❑ Nov 1971 Cover: 0.25 **NM** value: **10.00**
Circ: Statement: **199,112 • CGC:** 2 graded, best 8.5
• Giant-size.
418 ❑ Dec 1971 Cover: 0.25 **NM** value: **10.00**
Circ: Statement: **199,112 • CGC:** 2 graded, best 9.4
• Giant-size.
419 ❑ Jan 1972 Cover: 0.25 **NM** value: **10.00**
Circ: Statement: **158,638 • CGC:** 4 graded, best 9.4
• Giant-size.
420 ❑ Feb 1972 Cover: 0.25 **NM** value: **10.00**
Circ: Statement: **158,638 • CGC:** 3 graded, best 9.6
• Giant-size.
421 ❑ Mar 1972 Cover: 0.25 **NM** value: **10.00**
Circ: Statement: **158,638 • CGC:** 5 graded, best 9.8
• Giant-size. • Batgirl story; Has 1971 Statement, filed 10/1/71; avg print run 371,666; avg sales 199,040; avg subs 72; avg total paid 199,112; office use 844; max existent 199,956; 46% of run returned **A:** Don Heck
422 ❑ Apr 1972 Cover: 0.25 **NM** value: **10.00**
Circ: Statement: **158,638 • CGC:** 2 graded, best 8.0
• Giant-size.
423 ❑ May 1972 Cover: 0.25 **NM** value: **10.00**
Circ: Statement: **158,638 • CGC:** 4 graded, best 9.4
• Giant-size.
424 ❑ Jun 1972 Cover: 0.25 **NM** value: **10.00**
Circ: Statement: **158,638 • CGC:** 5 graded, best 9.6
• Giant-size.
425 ❑ Jul 1972 Cover: 0.20 **NM** value: **9.00**
Circ: Statement: **158,638 • CGC:** 6 graded, best 9.4
426 ❑ Aug 1972 Cover: 0.20 **NM** value: **9.00**
Circ: Statement: **158,638**
427 ❑ Sep 1972 Cover: 0.20 **NM** value: **9.00**
Circ: Statement: **158,638**
428 ❑ Oct 1972 Cover: 0.20 **NM** value: **9.00**
Circ: Statement: **158,638**
📖 The Invisible Thie of Bleakhill Manor **A:** Dick Dillin **W:** E. Nelson Bridwell
429 ❑ Nov 1972 Cover: 0.20 **NM** value: **9.00**
Circ: Statement: **158,638 • CGC:** 1 graded, best 9.2
430 ❑ Dec 1972 Cover: 0.20 **NM** value: **9.00**
Circ: Statement: **158,638 • CGC:** 2 graded, best 9.6
431 ❑ Jan 1973 Cover: 0.20 **NM** value: **9.00**
Circ: Statement: **153,942 • CGC:** 7 graded, best 9.6
432 ❑ Feb 1973 Cover: 0.20 **NM** value: **9.00**
Circ: Statement: **153,942 • CGC:** 2 graded, best 9.4
433 ❑ Mar 1973 Cover: 0.20 **NM** value: **9.00**
Circ: Statement: **153,942 • CGC:** 2 graded, best 9.4
• Has 1972 Statement; avg total paid circ 158,638
434 ❑ Apr 1973 Cover: 0.20 **NM** value: **9.00**
Circ: Statement: **153,942**
📖 Riddle of the Red-Handed Robber **A:** Rich Buckler **W:** E. Nelson Bridwell ★ 1st Appearance of The Spook.
435 ❑ Jul 1973 Cover: 0.20 **NM** value: **9.00**
Circ: Statement: **153,942 • CGC:** 1 graded, best 9.4
436 ❑ Sep 1973 Cover: 0.20 **NM** value: **9.00**
Circ: Statement: **153,942 • CGC:** 5 graded, best 9.4
437 ❑ Nov 1973 Cover: 0.20 **NM** value: **15.00**
Circ: Statement: **153,942 • CGC:** 7 graded, best 9.4
A: Walt Simonson; Jim Aparo ★ 1st Appearance of Manhunter.
438 ❑ Jan 1974 Cover: 0.50 **NM** value: **14.00**
Circ: Statement: **145,832 • CGC:** 11 graded, best 9.4
• Manhunter **A:** Walt Simonson
439 ❑ Mar 1974 Cover: 0.50 **NM** value: **12.00**
Circ: Statement: **145,832 • CGC:** 7 graded, best 9.6
• Manhunter **A:** Walt Simonson ★ Origin of Manhunter.
440 ❑ May 1974 Cover: 0.60 **NM** value: **12.00**
Circ: Statement: **145,832 • CGC:** 6 graded, best 9.4
• Manhunter; Has 1973 Statement; avg total paid circ 153,942 **A:** Walt Simonson
441 ❑ Jul 1974 Cover: 0.60 **NM** value: **12.00**
Circ: Statement: **145,832 • CGC:** 11 graded, best 9.8
• Manhunter **A:** Walt Simonson
442 ❑ Sep 1974 Cover: 0.60 **NM** value: **12.00**
Circ: Statement: **145,832 • CGC:** 10 graded, best 9.6
• Manhunter **A:** Walt Simonson
443 ❑ Nov 1974 Cover: 0.60 **NM** value: **14.00**
Circ: Statement: **145,832 • CGC:** 7 graded, best 9.4
A: Walt Simonson ★ Death of Manhunter.
444 ❑ Jan 1975 Cover: 0.60 **NM** value: **12.00**
Circ: Statement: **146,000 • CGC:** 9 graded, best 9.4
445 ❑ Mar 1975 Cover: 0.60 **NM** value: **12.00**
Circ: Statement: **146,000 • CGC:** 6 graded, best 9.6
446 ❑ Apr 1975 Cover: 0.25 **NM** value: **8.00**
Circ: Statement: **146,000 • CGC:** 1 graded, best 9.6
📖 Slaughter in Silver; The Mystery of the Flyaway Car • Hawkman back-up **A:** Rich Buckler; Jim Aparo **W:** Len Wein; E. Nelson Bridwell ★ 1st Appearance of Sterling Silversmith.
447 ❑ May 1975 Cover: 0.25 **NM** value: **8.00**
Circ: Statement: **146,000 • CGC:** 3 graded, best 9.6
• Has 1974 Statement; avg total paid circ 145,832
448 ❑ Jun 1975 Cover: 0.25 **NM** value: **8.00**
Circ: Statement: **146,000 • CGC:** 1 graded, best 9.4
449 ❑ Jul 1975 Cover: 0.25 **NM** value: **8.00**
Circ: Statement: **146,000**
450 ❑ Aug 1975 Cover: 0.25 **NM** value: **8.00**
Circ: Statement: **146,000 • CGC:** 3 graded, best 9.2
451 ❑ Sep 1975 Cover: 0.25 **NM** value: **8.00**
Circ: Statement: **146,000 • CGC:** 2 graded, best 9.4
452 ❑ Oct 1975 Cover: 0.25 **NM** value: **8.00**
Circ: Statement: **146,000 • CGC:** 2 graded, best 9.0
📖 The Case of the Ancient Weapons • Hawkman back-up **A:** José Luis Garcia-Lopez **W:** E. Nelson Bridwell
453 ❑ Nov 1975 Cover: 0.25 **NM** value: **8.00**
Circ: Statement: **146,000**
454 ❑ Dec 1975 Cover: 0.25 **NM** value: **8.00**
Circ: Statement: **146,000**
📖 The Catch-Me-If-You-Can Crooks **A:** José Luis Garcia-Lopez **W:** E. Nelson Bridwell
455 ❑ Jan 1976 Cover: 0.25 **NM** value: **8.00**
Circ: Statement: **148,800 • CGC:** 1 graded, best 9.4
📖 Battle of the Backfiring Weapons **A:** José Luis Garcia-Lopez **W:** E. Nelson Bridwell
456 ❑ Feb 1976 Cover: 0.25 **NM** value: **8.00**
Circ: Statement: **148,800**
457 ❑ Mar 1976 Cover: 0.30 **NM** value: **9.00**
Circ: Statement: **148,800**
• Elongated Man back-up ★ Origin of Batman.
458 ❑ Apr 1976 Cover: 0.30 **NM** value: **8.00**
Circ: Statement: **148,800 • CGC:** 3 graded, best 9.4
459 ❑ May 1976 Cover: 0.30 **NM** value: **8.00**
Circ: Statement: **148,800**
460 ❑ Jun 1976 Cover: 0.30 **NM** value: **8.00**
Circ: Statement: **148,800 • CGC:** 1 graded, best 9.2
461 ❑ Jul 1976 Cover: 0.30 **NM** value: **8.00**
Circ: Statement: **148,800**
• Bicentennial #29
462 ❑ Aug 1976 Cover: 0.30 **NM** value: **8.00**
Circ: Statement: **148,800**
463 ❑ Sep 1976 Cover: 0.30 **NM** value: **8.00**
Circ: Statement: **148,800**
★ 1st Appearance of Black Spider, the Calculator.
464 ❑ Oct 1976 Cover: 0.30 **NM** value: **8.00**
Circ: Statement: **148,800 • CGC:** 1 graded, best 9.4
465 ❑ Nov 1976 Cover: 0.30 **NM** value: **8.00**
Circ: Statement: **148,800**
• Elongated Man **A:** Tony DeZuniga
466 ❑ Dec 1976 Cover: 0.30 **NM** value: **13.00**
Circ: Statement: **148,800 • CGC:** 1 graded, best 9.4
A: Tony DeZuniga; Marshall Rogers
467 ❑ Jan 1977 Cover: 0.30 **NM** value: **13.00**
Circ: Statement: **125,743**
📖 The Man Who Skyjacked Hawkman **A:** Tony DeZuniga; Marshall Rogers **W:** Bob Rozakis
468 ❑ Mar 1977 Cover: 0.30 **NM** value: **13.00**
Circ: Statement: **125,743 • CGC:** 4 graded, best 9.4
A: Tony DeZuniga; Marshall Rogers
469 ❑ May 1977 Cover: 0.30 **NM** value: **8.00**
Circ: Statement: **125,743 • CGC:** 7 graded, best 9.6
📖 ...By Death's Eerie Light!; The Origin of Dr. Phosphorus • Has 1976 Statement; avg total paid circ 148,800 **A:** Al Milgrom; Walt Simonson; Marshall Rogers **W:** Steve Englehart ★ 1st Appearance of Doctor Phosphorus.
470 ❑ Jun 1977 Cover: 0.35 **NM** value: **8.00**
Circ: Statement: **125,743 • CGC:** 2 graded, best 9.2
📖 The Master Plan of Dr. Phosphorus! **A:** Al Milgrom; Walt Simonson; Marshall Rogers **W:** Steve Englehart ★ Appearance of Hugo Strange.
471 ❑ Aug 1977 Cover: 0.35 **NM** value: **13.00**
Circ: Statement: **125,743 • CGC:** 3 graded, best 9.6
📖 The Dead Yet Live **A:** Walt Simonson; Marshall Rogers **W:** Steve Englehart ★ Appearance of Hugo Strange.
472 ❑ Sep 1977 Cover: 0.35 **NM** value: **13.00**
Circ: Statement: **125,743 • CGC:** 5 graded, best 9.6
📖 I Am the Batman **A:** Marshall Rogers **W:** Steve Englehart
473 ❑ Oct 1977 Cover: 0.35 **NM** value: **13.00**
Circ: Statement: **125,743 • CGC:** 3 graded, best 9.4
📖 The Malay Penguin **A:** Marshall Rogers **W:** Steve Englehart
474 ❑ Dec 1977 Cover: 0.35 **NM** value: **14.00**
Circ: Statement: **125,743 • CGC:** 4 graded, best 9.6
📖 The Deadshot Ricochet **A:** Marshall Rogers **W:** Steve Englehart
475 ❑ Feb 1978 Cover: 0.35 **NM** value: **24.00**
Circ: Statement: **129,792 • CGC:** 10 graded, best 9.6
📖 The Laughing Fish **A:** Marshall Rogers **W:** Steve Englehart ★ Appearance of Joker.
476 ❑ Mar 1978 Cover: 0.35 **NM** value: **24.00**
Circ: Statement: **129,792 • CGC:** 19 graded, best 9.6
📖 Sign of the Joker! **A:** Marshall Rogers **W:** Steve Englehart ★ Appearance of Joker.
477 ❑ May 1978 Cover: 0.35 **NM** value: **13.00**
Circ: Statement: **129,792 • CGC:** 4 graded, best 9.6
• Has 1977 Statement; avg total paid circ 125,743 **A:** Marshall Rogers
478 ❑ Jul 1978 Cover: 0.35 **NM** value: **13.00**
Circ: Statement: **129,792 • CGC:** 2 graded, best 9.6
📖 The Coming of...Clayface III! **A:** Marshall Rogers **W:** Steve Englehart ★ 1st Appearance of Clayface III (Preston Payne).
479 ❑ Sep 1978 Cover: 0.50 **NM** value: **13.00**
Circ: Statement: **129,792 • CGC:** 1 graded, best 9.0
📖 True Heroes Never Die...; If a Man be Made of Clay...! **A:** Rich Buckler; Marshall Rogers **W:** Len Wein ★ 1st Appearance of The Fadeaway Man.
480 ❑ Nov 1978 Cover: 0.50 **NM** value: **8.00**
Circ: Statement: **129,792 • CGC:** 1 graded, best 9.4
📖 The Case of the Off-Key Crimes **A:** Don Newton; Murphy Anderson **W:** Len Wein
481 ❑ Dec 1978 Cover: 1.00 **NM** value: **12.00**
Circ: Statement: **129,792**
• Double-size. **A:** Don Newton; Jim Starlin; P. Craig Russell; Marshall Rogers; Dan Adkins
482 ❑ Feb 1979 Cover: 1.00 **NM** value: **9.00**
Circ: Statement: **79,872 • CGC:** 3 graded, best 9.4
• Double-size. **A:** Jim Starlin; Howard Chaykin; Dick Giordano; P. Craig Russell
483 ❑ Apr 1979 Cover: 1.00 **NM** value: **10.00**
Circ: Statement: **79,872 • CGC:** 2 graded, best 9.6
• Double-size. **A:** Don Newton; Michael Golden; Dick Giordano; Dan Adkins ★ 1st Appearance of Maxie Zeus.
484 ❑ Jun 1979 Cover: 1.00 **NM** value: **7.00**
Circ: Statement: **79,872 • CGC:** 1 graded, best 7.5
• Double-size. ★ Origin of Robin I (Dick Grayson).
485 ❑ Aug 1979 Cover: 1.00 **NM** value: **6.00**
Circ: Statement: **79,872 • CGC:** 1 graded, best 9.6
• Double-size.
486 ❑ Oct 1979 Cover: 1.00 **NM** value: **6.00**
Circ: Statement: **79,872**
• Double-size.
487 ❑ Dec 1979 Cover: 1.00 **NM** value: **6.00**
Circ: Statement: **79,872**
• Double-size.
488 ❑ Feb 1980 Cover: 1.00 **NM** value: **6.00**
Circ: Statement: **64,635 • CGC:** 1 graded, best 9.2
• Double-size.
489 ❑ Apr 1980 Cover: 1.00 **NM** value: **6.00**
Circ: Statement: **64,635**
• Double-size. • Batgirl forgets Batman and Robin's secret identities; Has 1979 Statement, filed 10/1/79; avg print run 220,259; avg sales 78,686; avg subs 1,186; avg total paid 79,872; office use 123; max existent 79,995; 64% of run returned
490 ❑ May 1980 Cover: 1.00 **NM** value: **6.00**
Circ: Statement: **64,635 • CGC:** 1 graded, best 9.4
• Double-size.
491 ❑ Jun 1980 Cover: 1.00 **NM** value: **6.00**
Circ: Statement: **64,635**
• Double-size.
492 ❑ Jul 1980 Cover: 1.00 **NM** value: **6.00**
Circ: Statement: **64,635 • CGC:** 1 graded, best 9.4
• Double-size.
493 ❑ Aug 1980 Cover: 1.00 **NM** value: **6.00**
Circ: Statement: **64,635 • CGC:** 1 graded, best 9.6
• Double-size.
494 ❑ Sep 1980 Cover: 1.00 **NM** value: **6.00**
Circ: Statement: **64,635**
• Double-size. ★ 1st Appearance of Crime Doctor.
495 ❑ Oct 1980 Cover: 1.00 **NM** value: **6.00**
Circ: Statement: **64,635**
• Double-size.
496 ❑ Nov 1980 Cover: 0.50 **NM** value: **6.00**
Circ: Statement: **64,635**
497 ❑ Dec 1980 Cover: 0.50 **NM** value: **6.00**
Circ: Statement: **64,635**
498 ❑ Jan 1981 Cover: 0.50 **NM** value: **6.00**
Circ: Statement: **89,710**
499 ❑ Feb 1981 Cover: 0.50 **NM** value: **6.00**
Circ: Statement: **89,710**
500 ❑ Mar 1981 Cover: 1.50 **NM** value: **10.00**
Circ: Statement: **89,710 • CGC:** 11 graded, best 9.8
• 500th anniversary issue. 📖 The Strange Death of Dr. Erdel **A:** Carmine Infantino; Dick Giordano; Tom Yeates; Joe Kubert; Walt Simonson **W:** Paul Levitz ★ Appearance of Deadman, Slam Bradley, Hawkman, Robin.
501 ❑ Apr 1981 Cover: 0.50 **NM** value: **5.00**
Circ: Statement: **89,710**
502 ❑ May 1981 Cover: 0.50 **NM** value: **5.00**
Circ: Statement: **89,710**
• Has 1980 Statement, filed 10/1/80; avg print run 227,127; avg sales 63,607; avg subs 1,028; avg total paid 64,635; samples 127; office use 2,583; max existent 67,345; 70% of run returned
503 ❑ Jun 1981 Cover: 0.50 **NM** value: **5.00**
Circ: Statement: **89,710**
A: Jim Starlin
504 ❑ Jul 1981 Cover: 0.50 **NM** value: **8.00**
Circ: Statement: **89,710**
A: Jim Starlin ★ Appearance of Joker.
505 ❑ Aug 1981 Cover: 0.50 **NM** value: **5.00**
Circ: Statement: **89,710**
506 ❑ Sep 1981 Cover: 0.50 **NM** value: **5.00**
Circ: Statement: **89,710**
507 ❑ Oct 1981 Cover: 0.60 **NM** value: **5.00**
Circ: Statement: **89,710**
508 ❑ Nov 1981 Cover: 0.60 **NM** value: **5.00**
Circ: Statement: **89,710**
509 ❑ Dec 1981 Cover: 0.60 **NM** value: **5.00**
Circ: Statement: **89,710**
510 ❑ Jan 1982 Cover: 0.60 **NM** value: **5.00**
Circ: Statement: **85,049**
511 ❑ Feb 1982 Cover: 0.60 **NM** value: **5.00**
Circ: Statement: **85,049**
★ 1st Appearance of Mirage (DC).
512 ❑ Mar 1982 Cover: 0.60 **NM** value: **5.00**
Circ: Statement: **85,049 • CGC:** 2 graded, best 9.6
513 ❑ Apr 1982 Cover: 0.60 **NM** value: **5.00**
Circ: Statement: **85,049**
514 ❑ May 1982 Cover: 0.60 **NM** value: **5.00**
Circ: Statement: **85,049**
📖 Haven!
515 ❑ Jun 1982 Cover: 0.60 **NM** value: **5.00**
Circ: Statement: **85,049**
516 ❑ Jul 1982 Cover: 0.60 **NM** value: **5.00**
Circ: Statement: **85,049**
517 ❑ Aug 1982 Cover: 0.60 **NM** value: **5.00**
Circ: Statement: **85,049**
518 ❑ Sep 1982 Cover: 0.60 **NM** value: **5.00**
Circ: Statement: **85,049**
★ 1st Appearance of Velvet Tiger.
519 ❑ Oct 1982 Cover: 0.60 **NM** value: **5.00**
Circ: Statement: **85,049**
520 ❑ Nov 1982 Cover: 0.60 **NM** value: **5.00**
Circ: Statement: **85,049**
521 ❑ Dec 1982 Cover: 0.60 **NM** value: **5.00**
Circ: Statement: **85,049**
522 ❑ Jan 1983 Cover: 0.60 **NM** value: **5.00**
Circ: Statement: **80,725**
523 ❑ Feb 1983 Cover: 0.60 **NM** value: **5.00**
Circ: Statement: **80,725**
524 ❑ Mar 1983 Cover: 0.60 **NM** value: **6.00**
Circ: Statement: **80,725**
★ 2nd Appearance of Jason Todd.

Other grades: Multiply prices above by **1.5 for Mint • 2/3 for Very Fine • 1/3 for Fine • 1/5 for Very Good • 1/8 for Good**

525 ❑ Apr 1983 Cover: 0.60 **NM** value: **5.00**
Circ: Statement: **80,725**

526 ❑ May 1983 Cover: 1.50 **NM** value: **14.00**
Circ: Statement: **80,725** • **CGC:** 6 graded, best 9.6
A: Don Newton; Alfredo Alcala ★ Appearance of Batman's 500th.

527 ❑ Jun 1983 Cover: 0.60 **NM** value: **3.50**
Circ: Statement: **80,725**
• Has 1982 Statement, filed 10/1/82; avg print run 234,094; avg sales 83,180; avg subs 1,869; avg total paid 85,049; samples 677; office use 2,957; max existent 88,683; 62% of run returned

528 ❑ Jul 1983 Cover: 0.60 **NM** value: **3.50**
Circ: Statement: **80,725**

529 ❑ Aug 1983 Cover: 0.60 **NM** value: **3.50**
Circ: Statement: **80,725**

530 ❑ Sep 1983 Cover: 0.60 **NM** value: **3.50**
Circ: Statement: **80,725** • **CGC:** 1 graded, best 9.4

531 ❑ Oct 1983 Cover: 0.60 **NM** value: **3.00**
Circ: Statement: **80,725**

532 ❑ Nov 1983 Cover: 0.60 **NM** value: **7.00**
Circ: Statement: **80,725** • **CGC:** 1 graded, best 9.8
★ Appearance of Joker.

533 ❑ Dec 1983 Cover: 0.75 **NM** value: **3.00**
Circ: Statement: **80,725**

534 ❑ Jan 1984 Cover: 0.75 **NM** value: **3.00**
Circ: Statement: **77,275**
★ Versus Poison Ivy.

535 ❑ Feb 1984 Cover: 0.75 **NM** value: **7.00**
Circ: Statement: **77,275**
★ 2nd Appearance of Robin II (Jason Todd). ★ Versus Crazy Quilt.

536 ❑ Mar 1984 Cover: 0.75 **NM** value: **3.50**
Circ: Statement: **77,275**
★ Versus Deadshot.

537 ❑ Apr 1984 Cover: 0.75 **NM** value: **3.50**
Circ: Statement: **77,275**
📖 Down Below

538 ❑ May 1984 Cover: 0.75 **NM** value: **3.50**
Circ: Statement: **77,275**
★ Versus Catman.

539 ❑ Jun 1984 Cover: 0.75 **NM** value: **3.50**
Circ: Statement: **77,275**
📖 Boxing ★ Versus Catman.

540 ❑ Jul 1984 Cover: 0.75 **NM** value: **3.50**
Circ: Statement: **77,275** • **CGC:** 1 graded, best 9.6
★ Versus Scarecrow.

541 ❑ Aug 1984 Cover: 0.75 **NM** value: **3.50**
Circ: Statement: **77,275**

542 ❑ Sep 1984 Cover: 0.75 **NM** value: **3.50**
Circ: Statement: **77,275** • **CGC:** 1 graded, best 9.2
★ Versus Nocturna.

543 ❑ Oct 1984 Cover: 0.75 **NM** value: **3.50**
Circ: Statement: **77,275**

544 ❑ Nov 1984 Cover: 0.75 **NM** value: **3.50**
Circ: Statement: **77,275**

545 ❑ Dec 1984 Cover: 0.75 **NM** value: **3.50**
Circ: Statement: **77,275**

546 ❑ Jan 1985 Cover: 0.75 **NM** value: **3.50**
Circ: Statement: **66,739**

547 ❑ Feb 1985 Cover: 0.75 **NM** value: **3.50**
Circ: Statement: **66,739**

548 ❑ Mar 1985 Cover: 0.75 **NM** value: **3.50**
Circ: Statement: **66,739**

549 ❑ Apr 1985 Cover: 0.75 **NM** value: **3.50**
Circ: Statement: **66,739** • **CGC:** 1 graded, best 9.4
W: Alan Moore

550 ❑ May 1985 Cover: 0.75 **NM** value: **3.50**
Circ: Statement: **66,739** CapCity orders: **6,000**
• Green Arrow back-up **W:** Alan Moore

551 ❑ Jun 1985 Cover: 0.75 **NM** value: **3.50**
Circ: Statement: **66,739** CapCity orders: **5,950**
★ Versus Calendar Man.

552 ❑ Jul 1985 Cover: 0.75 **NM** value: **3.50**
Circ: Statement: **66,739** CapCity orders: **6,300**

553 ❑ Aug 1985 Cover: 0.75 **NM** value: **3.50**
Circ: Statement: **66,739** CapCity orders: **6,400**
★ Versus Black Mask.

554 ❑ Sep 1985 Cover: 0.75 **NM** value: **3.50**
Circ: Statement: **66,739** CapCity orders: **6,500**

555 ❑ Oct 1985 Cover: 0.75 **NM** value: **3.50**
Circ: Statement: **66,739** CapCity orders: **6,450** • **CGC:** 1 graded, best 9.0
★ Versus Mirror Master. ★ Versus Captain Boomerang.

556 ❑ Nov 1985 Cover: 0.75 **NM** value: **3.50**
Circ: Statement: **66,739** CapCity orders: **6,450**

557 ❑ Dec 1985 Cover: 0.75 **NM** value: **3.50**
Circ: Statement: **66,739** CapCity orders: **6,350**

558 ❑ Jan 1986 Cover: 0.75 **NM** value: **3.50**
Circ: Statement: **70,319** CapCity orders: **6,350**

559 ❑ Feb 1986 Cover: 0.75 **NM** value: **3.50**
Circ: Statement: **70,319** CapCity orders: **6,650**
★ Appearance of Catwoman, Green Arrow, Black Canary.

560 ❑ Mar 1986 Cover: 0.75 **NM** value: **3.50**
Circ: Statement: **70,319** CapCity orders: **6,700**
★ 1st Appearance of Steelclaw.

561 ❑ Apr 1986 Cover: 0.75 **NM** value: **3.50**
Circ: Statement: **70,319** CapCity orders: **6,800**

562 ❑ May 1986 Cover: 0.75 **NM** value: **3.50**
Circ: Statement: **70,319** CapCity orders: **7,000**

563 ❑ Jun 1986 Cover: 0.75 **NM** value: **3.50**
Circ: Statement: **70,319** CapCity orders: **7,050**
★ Versus Two-Face.

564 ❑ Jul 1986 Cover: 0.75 **NM** value: **3.50**
Circ: Statement: **70,319** CapCity orders: **7,350**
★ Death of Steelclaw. ★ Versus Two-Face.

565 ❑ Aug 1986 Cover: 0.75 **NM** value: **3.50**
Circ: Statement: **70,319** CapCity orders: **7,600**

566 ❑ Sep 1986 Cover: 0.75 **NM** value: **3.50**
Circ: Statement: **70,319** CapCity orders: **8,450**
★ Appearance of Joker.

567 ❑ Oct 1986 Cover: 0.75 **NM** value: **3.50**
Circ: Statement: **70,319** CapCity orders: **10,400** • **CGC:** 1 graded, best 9.6
A: Jim Starlin **W:** Harlan Ellison

568 ❑ Nov 1986 Cover: 0.75 **NM** value: **3.50**
Circ: Statement: **70,319** CapCity orders: **14,000**
• Legends

569 ❑ Dec 1986 Cover: 0.75 **NM** value: **6.00**
Circ: Statement: **70,319** CapCity orders: **10,750** • **CGC:** 2 graded, best 9.8
★ Appearance of Catwoman, Joker. ★ Versus Joker.

570 ❑ Jan 1987 Cover: 0.75 **NM** value: **6.00**
Circ: Statement: **128,475** CapCity orders: **12,250** • **CGC:** 2 graded, best 9.4
★ Appearance of Joker.

571 ❑ Feb 1987 Cover: 0.75 **NM** value: **3.50**
Circ: Statement: **128,475** CapCity orders: **14,350**
★ Versus Scarecrow.

572 ❑ Mar 1987 Cover: 1.25 **NM** value: **4.00**
Circ: Statement: **128,475** CapCity orders: **21,350** • **CGC:** 2 graded, best 9.6
• Giant-size. ★ Appearance of Slam Bradley.

573 ❑ Apr 1987 Cover: 0.75 **NM** value: **3.00**
Circ: Statement: **128,475** CapCity orders: **14,850**
★ Versus Mad Hatter.

574 ❑ May 1987 Cover: 0.75 **NM** value: **3.00**
Circ: Statement: **128,475** CapCity orders: **14,200** • **CGC:** 1 graded, best 8.0
★ Origin of Batman.

575 ❑ Jun 1987 Cover: 0.75 **NM** value: **6.00**
Circ: Statement: **128,475** CapCity orders: **22,850** • **CGC:** 6 graded, best 9.8
📖 Year Two; Batman: Year 2, Part 1

576 ❑ Jul 1987 Cover: 0.75 **NM** value: **4.00**
Circ: Statement: **128,475** CapCity orders: **23,100** • **CGC:** 9 graded, best 9.8
📖 Year Two; Batman: Year 2, Part 2 **A:** Todd McFarlane

577 ❑ Aug 1987 Cover: 0.75 **NM** value: **4.00**
Circ: Statement: **128,475** CapCity orders: **25,350** • **CGC:** 16 graded, best 9.8
📖 Year Two; Batman: Year 2, Part 3 **A:** Todd McFarlane

578 ❑ Sep 1987 Cover: 0.75 **NM** value: **4.00**
Circ: Statement: **128,475** CapCity orders: **31,150** • **CGC:** 6 graded, best 9.8
📖 Year Two; Batman: Year 2, Part 4 **A:** Todd McFarlane

579 ❑ Oct 1987 Cover: 0.75 **NM** value: **2.00**
Circ: Statement: **128,475** CapCity orders: **23,850**
★ Versus Two-Face.

580 ❑ Nov 1987 Cover: 0.75 **NM** value: **2.00**
Circ: Statement: **128,475** CapCity orders: **23,650**
★ Versus Two-Face.

581 ❑ Dec 1987 Cover: 0.75 **NM** value: **2.00**
Circ: Statement: **128,475** CapCity orders: **22,250**
★ Versus Two-Face.

582 ❑ Jan 1988 Cover: 0.75 **NM** value: **2.00**
Circ: CapCity orders: **26,500**
• Millennium

583 ❑ Feb 1988 Cover: 0.75 **NM** value: **2.00**
Circ: CapCity orders: **20,350**
★ 1st Appearance of Ventriloquist.

584 ❑ Mar 1988 Cover: 0.75 **NM** value: **2.00**
Circ: CapCity orders: **19,200**

585 ❑ Apr 1988 Cover: 0.75 **NM** value: **2.00**
Circ: CapCity orders: **19,700**

586 ❑ May 1988 Cover: 0.75 **NM** value: **2.00**
Circ: CapCity orders: **19,100**
★ Versus Rat-catcher.

587 ❑ Jun 1988 Cover: 0.75 **NM** value: **2.00**
Circ: CapCity orders: **18,300**

588 ❑ Jul 1988 Cover: 0.75 **NM** value: **2.00**
Circ: CapCity orders: **18,650**

589 ❑ Aug 1988 Cover: 0.75 **NM** value: **2.00**
Circ: CapCity orders: **19,300**
• Bonus Book #5

590 ❑ Sep 1988 Cover: 0.75 **NM** value: **2.00**
Circ: CapCity orders: **19,250**

591 ❑ Oct 1988 Cover: 0.75 **NM** value: **2.00**
Circ: CapCity orders: **19,700**

592 ❑ Nov 1988 Cover: 0.75 **NM** value: **2.00**
Circ: CapCity orders: **19,100**

593 ❑ Dec 1988 Cover: 0.75 **NM** value: **2.00**

594 ❑ Dec 1988 Cover: 0.75 **NM** value: **2.00**
Circ: CapCity orders: **19,600**
★ 1st Appearance of Joe Potato.

595 ❑ Jan 1989 Cover: 0.75 **NM** value: **2.00**
Circ: CapCity orders: **22,250**
• Bonus Book;Invasion!

596 ❑ Jan 1989 Cover: 0.75 **NM** value: **2.00**
Circ: CapCity orders: **20,550**

597 ❑ Feb 1989 Cover: 0.75 **NM** value: **2.00**
Circ: CapCity orders: **20,650**

598 ❑ Mar 1989 Cover: 2.95 **NM** value: **3.00**
Circ: CapCity orders: **40,200** • **CGC:** 3 graded, best 9.6
• Double-size. 📖 Blind Justice; Blind Justice, Part 1 **C:** Sam Hamm

599 ❑ Apr 1989 Cover: 0.75 **NM** value: **2.50**
Circ: CapCity orders: **39,600**
📖 Blind Justice; Blind Justice, Part 2

600 ❑ May 1989 Cover: 2.95 **NM** value: **3.00**
Circ: CapCity orders: **62,050** • **CGC:** 4 graded, best 9.8
• Double-size. 📖 Blind Justice; Blind Justice, Part 3 **A:** Frank Miller(pin-up) **C:** Sam Hamm

601 ❑ Jun 1989 Cover: 0.75 **NM** value: **2.00**
Circ: CapCity orders: **40,900**
📖 Tulpa, Part 1 ★ Appearance of Demon.

602 ❑ Jul 1989 Cover: 0.75 **NM** value: **2.00**
Circ: CapCity orders: **41,650**
📖 Tulpa, Part 2 **A:** Norm Breyfogle **W:** Alan Grant ★ Appearance of Demon.

603 ❑ Aug 1989 Cover: 0.75 **NM** value: **2.00**
Circ: CapCity orders: **49,950**
📖 Tulpa, Part 3 **A:** Norm Breyfogle **W:** Alan Grant ★ Appearance of Demon.

604 ❑ Sep 1989 Cover: 1.00 **NM** value: **2.00**
Circ: CapCity orders: **84,150** • **CGC:** 1 graded, best 9.6
📖 Mud Pack; The Mud Pack, Part 1 • poster **A:** Norm Breyfogle **W:** Alan Grant

605 ❑ Sep 1989 Cover: 1.00 **NM** value: **2.00**
Circ: CapCity orders: **80,400**
📖 Mud Pack; The Mud Pack, Part 2 **A:** Norm Breyfogle **W:** Alan Grant

606 ❑ Oct 1989 Cover: 1.00 **NM** value: **2.00**
Circ: CapCity orders: **78,900**
📖 Mud Pack; The Mud Pack, Part 3 **A:** Norm Breyfogle **W:** Alan Grant

607 ❑ Oct 1989 Cover: 1.00 **NM** value: **2.00**
Circ: CapCity orders: **77,150**
📖 Mud Pack; The Mud Pack, Part 4 **A:** Norm Breyfogle **W:** Alan Grant

608 ❑ Nov 1989 Cover: 1.00 **NM** value: **2.00**
Circ: CapCity orders: **69,350** • **CGC:** 1 graded, best 9.2
📖 Letters To The Editor **A:** Norm Breyfogle **W:** Alan Grant ★ 1st Appearance of Anarky.

609 ❑ Dec 1989 Cover: 1.00 **NM** value: **2.00**
Circ: CapCity orders: **39,300**
📖 Facts About Bats **A:** Norm Breyfogle **W:** Alan Grant ★ 2nd Appearance of Anarky.

610 ❑ Jan 1990 Cover: 1.00 **NM** value: **2.00**
Circ: CapCity orders: **72,100**
• Penguin

611 ❑ Feb 1990 Cover: 1.00 **NM** value: **1.50**
Circ: CapCity orders: **68,250**
• Penguin

612 ❑ Mar 1990 Cover: 1.00 **NM** value: **1.50**
Circ: CapCity orders: **66,700**
• Catman, Catwoman

613 ❑ Apr 1990 Cover: 1.00 **NM** value: **1.50**
Circ: CapCity orders: **61,000**

614 ❑ May 1990 Cover: 1.00 **NM** value: **1.50**
Circ: CapCity orders: **58,400**

615 ❑ Jun 1990 Cover: 1.00 **NM** value: **1.50**
Circ: CapCity orders: **72,650**
• Penguin

616 ❑ Jun 1990 Cover: 1.00 **NM** value: **1.50**
Circ: CapCity orders: **60,150**

617 ❑ Jul 1990 Cover: 1.00 **NM** value: **1.50**
Circ: CapCity orders: **75,400**
★ Appearance of Joker.

618 ❑ Jul 1990 Cover: 1.00 **NM** value: **1.50**
Circ: CapCity orders: **60,250**
📖 Rite of Passage, Part 1 **A:** Norm Breyfogle **W:** Alan Grant

619 ❑ Aug 1990 Cover: 1.00 **NM** value: **1.50**
Circ: CapCity orders: **53,950**
📖 Rite of Passage, Part 2 **A:** Norm Breyfogle **W:** Alan Grant

620 ❑ Aug 1990 Cover: 1.00 **NM** value: **1.50**
Circ: CapCity orders: **53,850**
📖 Rite of Passage, Part 3 **A:** Norm Breyfogle **W:** Alan Grant

621 ❑ Sep 1990 Cover: 1.00 **NM** value: **1.50**
Circ: CapCity orders: **51,050**

622 ❑ Oct 1990 Cover: 1.00 **NM** value: **1.50**
Circ: CapCity orders: **52,250**
📖 The Demon Within, Part 1 **A:** Flint Henry **C:** Dick Sprang **W:** John Ostrander

623 ❑ Nov 1990 Cover: 1.00 **NM** value: **1.50**
Circ: CapCity orders: **48,050**
📖 The Demon Within, Part 2 **A:** Flint Henry **C:** Dick Sprang **W:** John Ostrander

624 ❑ Dec 1990 Cover: 1.00 **NM** value: **1.50**
Circ: CapCity orders: **49,500**
📖 The Demon Within, Part 3 **A:** Flint Henry **C:** Dick Sprang **W:** John Ostrander

625 ❑ Jan 1991 Cover: 1.00 **NM** value: **1.50**
Circ: CapCity orders: **47,350**

626 ❑ Feb 1991 Cover: 1.00 **NM** value: **1.50**
Circ: CapCity orders: **45,600**

627 ❑ Mar 1991 Cover: 2.95 **NM** value: **3.00**
Circ: CapCity orders: **66,900** • **CGC:** 1 graded, best 9.2
• giant★ Appearance of Batman's 600th.

628 ❑ Apr 1991 Cover: 1.00 **NM** value: **1.50**
Circ: CapCity orders: **44,150**

629 ❑ May 1991 Cover: 1.00 **NM** value: **1.50**
Circ: CapCity orders: **43,200**

630 ❑ Jun 1991 Cover: 1.00 **NM** value: **1.50**
Circ: CapCity orders: **43,550**

631 ❑ Jul 1991 Cover: 1.00 **NM** value: **1.50**
Circ: CapCity orders: **42,250**

632 ❑ Jul 1991 Cover: 1.00 **NM** value: **1.50**
Circ: CapCity orders: **42,150**

633 ❑ Aug 1991 Cover: 1.00 **NM** value: **1.50**
Circ: CapCity orders: **41,900**

634 ❑ Aug 1991 Cover: 1.00 **NM** value: **1.50**
Circ: CapCity orders: **41,900**

635 ❑ Sep 1991 Cover: 1.00 **NM** value: **1.50**
Circ: CapCity orders: **40,200**

636 ❑ Sep 1991 Cover: 1.00 **NM** value: **1.50**
Circ: CapCity orders: **40,700**

637 ❑ Oct 1991 Cover: 1.00 **NM** value: **1.50**
Circ: CapCity orders: **39,550**

638 ❑ Nov 1991 Cover: 1.00 **NM** value: **1.50**
Circ: CapCity orders: **36,850**
📖 The Bomb **A:** Jim Aparo **W:** Peter Milligan

639 ❑ Dec 1991 Cover: 1.00 **NM** value: **1.50**
Circ: CapCity orders: **38,900**

640 ❑ Jan 1992 Cover: 1.00 **NM** value: **1.50**
Circ: CapCity orders: **37,300**

641 ❑ Feb 1992 Cover: 1.00 **NM** value: **1.50**
Circ: CapCity orders: **36,900**

CGC-graded: Multiply prices above by **33 for 9.9 M • 16 for 9.8 NM/M • 7 for 9.6 NM+ • 5 for 9.4 NM • 2.5 for 9.2 NM- • 1.5 for 9.0 VF/NM**

Destroyer, Part 3 • Anton Furst's Gotham City designs **A:** Jim Aparo **W:** Alan Grant

642 ❑ Mar 1992 Cover: 1.00 **NM** value: **1.50**
Circ: CapCity orders: **33,900**
★ Versus Scarface.

643 ❑ Apr 1992 Cover: 1.00 **NM** value: **1.50**
Circ: CapCity orders: **30,200**

644 ❑ May 1992 Cover: 1.00 **NM** value: **1.50**
Circ: CapCity orders: **30,450**
Electric City, Part 1

645 ❑ Jun 1992 Cover: 1.25 **NM** value: **1.50**
Circ: CapCity orders: **32,400**
Electric City, Part 2

646 ❑ Jul 1992 Cover: 1.25 **NM** value: **1.50**
Circ: CapCity orders: **32,550**
Electric City, Part 3 **A:** Tom Lyle **W:** Chuck Dixon

647 ❑ Aug 1992 Cover: 1.25 **NM** value: **1.50**
Circ: CapCity orders: **33,850**

648 ❑ Aug 1992 Cover: 1.25 **NM** value: **1.50**
Circ: CapCity orders: **33,550**

649 ❑ Sep 1992 Cover: 1.25 **NM** value: **1.50**
Circ: CapCity orders: **31,100**

650 ❑ Sep 1992 Cover: 1.25 **NM** value: **1.50**
Circ: CapCity orders: **30,700**

651 ❑ Oct 1992 Cover: 1.25 **NM** value: **1.50**

652 ❑ Oct 1992 Cover: 1.25 **NM** value: **1.50**
Circ: CapCity orders: **32,050**
★ Appearance of The Huntress III (Helena Bertinelli).

653 ❑ Nov 1992 Cover: 1.25 **NM** value: **1.50**
Circ: CapCity orders: **28,300**
★ Appearance of The Huntress III (Helena Bertinelli).

654 ❑ Dec 1992 Cover: 1.25 **NM** value: **1.50**
Circ: CapCity orders: **26,650**
The General, Part 1

655 ❑ Jan 1993 Cover: 1.25 **NM** value: **1.50**
Circ: CapCity orders: **25,850**
The General, Part 2 ★ Versus Ulysses.

656 ❑ Feb 1993 Cover: 1.25 **NM** value: **3.00**
Circ: CapCity orders: **26,450**
The General, Part 3 ★ Appearance of Bane.

657 ❑ Mar 1993 Cover: 1.25 **NM** value: **3.00**
Circ: CapCity orders: **26,550**

658 ❑ Apr 1993 Cover: 1.25 **NM** value: **3.00**
Circ: CapCity orders: **27,950**
Deciphered **A:** Michael Netzer **W:** Chuck Dixon

659 ❑ May 1993 Cover: 1.25 **NM** value: **2.50**
Circ: CapCity orders: **31,950**
Knightfall, Part 2 **A:** Norm Breyfogle **W:** Chuck Dixon

659-2 ❑ May 1993 Cover: 1.25 **NM** value: **Cover or less**

660 ❑ May 1993 Cover: 1.25 **NM** value: **2.00**
Circ: CapCity orders: **32,050**
Knightfall, Part 4 **A:** Jim Balent **W:** Chuck Dixon

661 ❑ Jun 1993 Cover: 1.25 **NM** value: **2.00**
Circ: CapCity orders: **39,900**
Knightfall, Part 6 **A:** Graham Nolan **W:** Chuck Dixon

662 ❑ Jun 1993 Cover: 1.25 **NM** value: **2.00**
Circ: CapCity orders: **39,750**
Knightfall, Part 8 **A:** Graham Nolan **W:** Chuck Dixon

663 ❑ Jul 1993 Cover: 1.25 **NM** value: **2.00**
Circ: CapCity orders: **79,950**
Knightfall, Part 10 **A:** Graham Nolan **W:** Chuck Dixon

664 ❑ Aug 1993 Cover: 1.25 **NM** value: **2.00**
Circ: CapCity orders: **81,700**
Knightfall, Part 12 **A:** Graham Nolan **W:** Chuck Dixon

665 ❑ Aug 1993 Cover: 1.25 **NM** value: **2.00**
Circ: CapCity orders: **124,750**
Knightfall, Part 16 **A:** Graham Nolan **W:** Chuck Dixon

666 ❑ Sep 1993 Cover: 1.25 **NM** value: **2.00**
Circ: CapCity orders: **113,475**
Knightfall, Part 18 **A:** Graham Nolan **W:** Chuck Dixon

667 ❑ Oct 1993 Cover: 1.25 **NM** value: **1.50**
Circ: CapCity orders: **120,050**
Knightquest: The Crusade **A:** Graham Nolan **W:** Chuck Dixon

668 ❑ Nov 1993 Cover: 1.25 **NM** value: **1.50**
Circ: CapCity orders: **89,200**
Knightquest: The Crusade

669 ❑ Dec 1993 Cover: 1.25 **NM** value: **1.50**
Circ: CapCity orders: **81,450**
Knightquest: The Crusade **A:** Graham Nolan **W:** Chuck Dixon

670 ❑ Jan 1994 Cover: 1.25 **NM** value: **1.50**
Circ: CapCity orders: **79,700**
Knightquest: The Crusade ★ Versus Mr. Freeze.

671 ❑ Feb 1994 Cover: 1.50 **NM** value: **Cover or less**
Circ: CapCity orders: **72,050**
Knightquest: The Crusade

672 ❑ Mar 1994 Cover: 1.50 **NM** value: **Cover or less**
Circ: CapCity orders: **60,550**
Knightquest: The Crusade

673 ❑ Apr 1994 Cover: 1.50 **NM** value: **Cover or less**
Circ: CapCity orders: **54,050**
Knightquest: The Crusade; Knightquest ★ Versus Joker.

674 ❑ May 1994 Cover: 1.50 **NM** value: **Cover or less**
Circ: CapCity orders: **50,300**
Knightquest: The Crusade; Knightquest

675 ❑ Jun 1994 Cover: 1.50 **NM** value: **Cover or less**
Knightquest: The Crusade; Knightquest **A:** Graham Nolan **W:** Chuck Dixon

675/PL ❑ Jun 1994 **NM** value: **3.00**
no cover price. • Platinum edition.

675/SC ❑ Jun 1994 Cover: 2.95 **NM** value: **Cover or less**
Circ: CapCity orders: **66,200** • **CGC:** 1 graded, best 9.6
Special cover. • premium edition. Knightquest: The Crusade; Knightquest

676 ❑ Jul 1994 Cover: 2.50 **NM** value: **Cover or less**
Circ: CapCity orders: **50,900**
• Giant-size. KnightsEnd, Part 3

677 ❑ Aug 1994 Cover: 1.50 **NM** value: **Cover or less**
Circ: CapCity orders: **52,150**
KnightsEnd, Part 9 ★ Versus Nightwing.

678 ❑ Sep 1994 Cover: 1.50 **NM** value: **Cover or less**
Circ: CapCity orders: **45,850**
• Zero Hour ★ Origin of Batman.

679 ❑ Nov 1994 Cover: 1.50 **NM** value: **Cover or less**
Circ: CapCity orders: **44,800**
Prodigal, Part 3 ★ Versus Ratcatcher.

680 ❑ Dec 1994 Cover: 1.50 **NM** value: **Cover or less**
Circ: CapCity orders: **43,350**
Prodigal, Part 7 ★ Versus Two-Face.

681 ❑ Jan 1995 Cover: 1.50 **NM** value: **Cover or less**
Circ: CapCity orders: **41,200**
Prodigal, Part 11 **A:** Graham Nolan **W:** Chuck Dixon

682 ❑ Feb 1995 Cover: 1.50 **NM** value: **Cover or less**

682/SC ❑ Feb 1995 Cover: 2.50 **NM** value: **Cover or less**
Circ: CapCity orders: **45,625**
enhanced cover.

683 ❑ Mar 1995 Cover: 1.50 **NM** value: **Cover or less**
Circ: CapCity orders: **37,000**
★ Versus Penguin.

684 ❑ Apr 1995 Cover: 1.50 **NM** value: **Cover or less**
Circ: CapCity orders: **35,225**

685 ❑ May 1995 Cover: 1.50 **NM** value: **Cover or less**
Circ: CapCity orders: **34,625**
A: Steve Lieber

686 ❑ Jun 1995 Cover: 1.95 **NM** value: **2.00**
Circ: CapCity orders: **32,900**
War of the Dragons, Part 3 **A:** Steve Lieber **W:** Chuck Dixon ★ Appearance of Huntress. ★ Appearance of Nightwing.

687 ❑ Jul 1995 Cover: 1.95 **NM** value: **2.00**
Circ: CapCity orders: **31,225**

688 ❑ Aug 1995 Cover: 1.95 **NM** value: **2.00**
Circ: CapCity orders: **31,675**

689 ❑ Sep 1995 Cover: 1.95 **NM** value: **2.00**
Circ: CapCity orders: **29,325**

690 ❑ Oct 1995 Cover: 1.95 **NM** value: **2.00**
Circ: CapCity orders: **24,950**
★ Versus Firefly.

691 ❑ Nov 1995 Cover: 1.95 **NM** value: **2.00**
Underworld Unleashed • Underworld Unleashed ★ Versus Spellbinder.

692 ❑ Dec 1995 Cover: 1.95 **NM** value: **2.00**
• Underworld Unleashed

693 ❑ Jan 1996 Cover: 1.95 **NM** value: **2.00**
Systemic Shock **A:** Staz Johnson; James Hodgkins **W:** Chuck Dixon ★ 1st Appearance of Allergent. ★ Appearance of Poison Ivy.

694 ❑ Feb 1996 Cover: 1.95 **NM** value: **2.00**
Violent Reactions **A:** Staz Johnson; James Hodgkins **W:** Chuck Dixon ★ Appearance of Poison Ivy. ★ Versus Allergent.

695 ❑ Mar 1996 Cover: 1.95 **NM** value: **2.00**
Contagion, Part 2 **A:** Tommy Lee Edwards **W:** Chuck Dixon

696 ❑ Apr 1996 Cover: 1.95 **NM** value: **2.00**
Contagion, Part 8 **A:** Graham Nolan **W:** Chuck Dixon

697 ❑ Jun 1996 Cover: 1.95 **NM** value: **2.00**
★ Versus Two-Face.

698 ❑ Jul 1996 Cover: 1.95 **NM** value: **2.00**
★ Versus Two-Face.

699 ❑ Jul 1996 Cover: 1.95 **NM** value: **2.00**

700 ❑ Aug 1996 Cover: 2.95 **NM** value: **3.50**
• Anniversary issue. Legacy, Part 1

700/SC ❑ Aug 1996 Cover: 4.95 **NM** value: **5.00**
• Anniversary issue. Legacy, Part 1 • cardstock outer wrapper

701 ❑ Sep 1996 Cover: 1.95 **NM** value: **2.00**
Legacy, Part 6 ★ Versus Bane.

702 ❑ Oct 1996 Cover: 1.95 **NM** value: **2.00**
Legacy Epilogue **A:** Graham Nolan **W:** Chuck Dixon

703 ❑ Nov 1996 Cover: 1.95 **NM** value: **2.00**
Circ: Direct Market orders: **68,980**
Howling in the Dark • Final Night **A:** Graham Nolan **W:** Chuck Dixon

704 ❑ Dec 1996 Cover: 1.95 **NM** value: **2.00**
Circ: Direct Market orders: **64,168**
Rocket Scientist • self-contained story **A:** Graham Nolan **W:** Chuck Dixon

705 ❑ Jan 1997 Cover: 1.95 **NM** value: **2.00**
Circ: Diamd. preorders: **62,097**
Badd Girls **A:** Graham Nolan **W:** Chuck Dixon ★ Versus Riddler. ★ Versus Cluemaster.

706 ❑ Feb 1997 Cover: 1.95 **NM** value: **2.00**
Circ: Diamd. preorders: **59,429**
Lethal Pursuits **A:** Graham Nolan **W:** Chuck Dixon ★ Appearance of Riddler. ★ Versus Riddler.

707 ❑ Mar 1997 Cover: 1.95 **NM** value: **2.00**
Circ: Diamd. preorders: **57,379**
Riddled **A:** Graham Nolan **W:** Chuck Dixon ★ Versus Riddler.

708 ❑ Apr 1997 Cover: 1.95 **NM** value: **2.00**
Circ: Diamd. preorders: **54,835**
The Death Lottery, Part 1 **A:** Bill Sienkiewicz; Graham Nolan **W:** Chuck Dixon

709 ❑ May 1997 Cover: 1.95 **NM** value: **2.00**
Circ: Diamd. preorders: **54,450**
The Death Lottery, Part 2 **A:** Bill Sienkiewicz; Graham Nolan **W:** Chuck Dixon

710 ❑ Jun 1997 Cover: 1.95 **NM** value: **2.00**
Circ: Diamd. preorders: **55,388**

711 ❑ Jul 1997 Cover: 1.95 **NM** value: **2.00**
Circ: Diamd. preorders: **52,745**

712 ❑ Aug 1997 Cover: 1.95 **NM** value: **2.00**
Circ: Diamd. preorders: **53,415**

713 ❑ Sep 1997 Cover: 1.95 **NM** value: **2.00**
Circ: Diamd. preorders: **51,212**

714 ❑ Oct 1997 Cover: 1.95 **NM** value: **2.00**
Circ: Diamd. preorders: **51,431**
★ Versus Firefly.

715 ❑ Nov 1997 Cover: 1.95 **NM** value: **2.00**
Circ: Diamd. preorders: **50,352**
Days of Fire **A:** Graham Nolan; Eduardo Barreto **W:** Chuck Dixon ★ Appearance of J'onn J'onzz.

716 ❑ Dec 1997 Cover: 1.95 **NM** value: **2.00**
Circ: Diamd. preorders: **49,959**
Face cover. Death Comes Home **A:** Jim Aparo **W:** Chuck Dixon

717 ❑ Jan 1998 Cover: 1.95 **NM** value: **2.00**
Circ: Diamd. preorders: **48,325**

718 ❑ Feb 1998 Cover: 1.95 **NM** value: **2.00**
Circ: Diamd. preorders: **47,374**
★ Versus Finch.

719 ❑ Mar 1998 Cover: 1.95 **NM** value: **2.50**
Circ: Diamd. preorders: **46,120**
Cataclysm Prelude; Cataclysm

720 ❑ Apr 1998 Cover: 1.95 **NM** value: **3.50**
Circ: Diamd. preorders: **49,044**
Cataclysm, Part 5 • continues in Catwoman #56

721 ❑ May 1998 Cover: 1.95 **NM** value: **3.00**
Circ: Diamd. preorders: **49,158**
Cataclysm, Part 14; Cataclysm • continues in Catwoman #57

722 ❑ Jun 1998 Cover: 1.95 **NM** value: **2.50**
Circ: Diamd. preorders: **48,579**
• Aftershock

723 ❑ Jul 1998 Cover: 1.95 **NM** value: **2.00**
Circ: Diamd. preorders: **48,529**
Brotherhood of the Fist, Part 2 • continues in Robin #55

724 ❑ Aug 1998 Cover: 1.95 **NM** value: **2.00**
Circ: Diamd. preorders: **47,075**
• Aftershock

725 ❑ Sep 1998 Cover: 1.99 **NM** value: **2.00**
Circ: Diamd. preorders: **45,251**
• Aftershock

726 ❑ Oct 1998 Cover: 1.99 **NM** value: **Cover or less**
Circ: Diamd. preorders: **44,941**
• Aftershock ★ Appearance of Joker.

727 ❑ Dec 1998 Cover: 1.99 **NM** value: **Cover or less**
Circ: Diamd. preorders: **44,288**
Fight or Flight, Part 1 • Road to No Man's Land ★ Appearance of Nightwing. ★ Appearance of Robin.

728 ❑ Jan 1999 Cover: 1.99 **NM** value: **Cover or less**
Circ: Diamd. preorders: **42,989**
Fight or Flight, Part 2; Road to No Man's Land • Road to No Man's Land **A:** Will Rosado **W:** Chuck Dixon ★ Appearance of Nightwing. ★ Appearance of Robin.

729 ❑ Feb 1999 Cover: 1.99 **NM** value: **Cover or less**
Circ: Diamd. preorders: **42,408**
Fight or Flight, Part 3; Road to No Man's Land • Road to No Man's Land **A:** Will Rosado **W:** Chuck Dixon ★ Appearance of Nightwing, Robin, Commissioner Gordan.

730 ❑ Mar 1999 Cover: 1.99 **NM** value: **Cover or less**
Circ: Diamd. preorders: **45,813**
No Law and a New Order, Part 4; No Man's Land, Part 1 • No Man's Land **A:** Alex Maleev ★ Appearance of Scarface.

731 ❑ Apr 1999 Cover: 1.99 **NM** value: **Cover or less**
Circ: Diamd. preorders: **43,212**
Fear of Faith, Part 4 • No Man's Land ★ Appearance of Scarecrow, Huntress.

732 ❑ May 1999 Cover: 1.99 **NM** value: **Cover or less**
Circ: Diamd. preorders: **46,103**
Mosaic, Part 2 • No Man's Land **A:** Frank Teran **W:** Greg Rucka ★ Appearance of Batgirl.

733 ❑ Jun 1999 Cover: 1.99 **NM** value: **Cover or less**
Circ: Diamd. preorders: **49,120**
Crisis of Faith; Shades of Grey • No Man's Land **A:** Phil Winslade **W:** Bob Gale

734 ❑ Jul 1999 Cover: 1.99 **NM** value: **Cover or less**
Circ: Diamd. preorders: **49,913**
Mark of Cain, Part 2 • No Man's Land **A:** Damian Scott **W:** Kelley Puckett ★ Appearance of Batgirl.

735 ❑ Aug 1999 Cover: 1.99 **NM** value: **Cover or less**
Circ: Diamd. preorders: **50,061**
Fruit of the Earth, Part 3 • No Man's Land **A:** Bill Sienkiewicz; Dan Jurgens **W:** Greg Rucka ★ Appearance of Poison Ivy. ★ Versus Clayface.

736 ❑ Sep 1999 Cover: 1.99 **NM** value: **Cover or less**
Circ: Diamd. preorders: **50,739**
Homecoming • No Man's Land **A:** Mike Deodato **W:** Larry Hama

737 ❑ Oct 1999 Cover: 1.99 **NM** value: **Cover or less**
Circ: Diamd. preorders: **54,575**
The Code, Part 2 • No Man's Land **A:** Tom Morgan **W:** Bronwyn Carlton ★ Versus Joker. ★ Versus Harley Quinn.

738 ❑ Nov 1999 Cover: 1.99 **NM** value: **Cover or less**
Circ: Diamd. preorders: **49,793**
• No Man's Land

739 ❑ Dec 1999 Cover: 1.99 **NM** value: **Cover or less**
Circ: Diamd. preorders: **51,104**
Jurisprudence, Part 2 • No Man's Land **A:** Damian Scott **W:** Greg Rucka

740 ❑ Jan 2000 Cover: 1.99 **NM** value: **Cover or less**
Circ: Diamd. preorders: **50,966**
Shellgame, Part 2 • No Man's Land **A:** Sergio Cariello **W:** Greg Rucka

741 ❑ Feb 2000 Cover: 1.99 **NM** value: **Cover or less**
Circ: Diamd. preorders: **55,285**

742 ❑ Mar 2000 Cover: 1.99 **NM** value: **Cover or less**
Circ: Diamd. preorders: **48,822**

743 ❑ Apr 2000 Cover: 1.99 **NM** value: **Cover or less**
Circ: Diamd. preorders: **46,188**
Evolution, Part 1 **A:** Shawn Martinbrough **W:** Greg Rucka

744 ❑ May 2000 Cover: 1.99 **NM** value: **Cover or less**
Circ: Diamd. preorders: **48,032**
Evolution, Part 2 **A:** Shawn Martinbrough **W:** Greg Rucka

745 ❑ Jun 2000 Cover: 1.99 **NM** value: **Cover or less**
Circ: Diamd. preorders: **48,664**
Evolution, Part 3 **A:** Shawn Martinbrough **W:** Greg Rucka

746 ❑ Jul 2000 Cover: 1.99 **NM** value: **Cover or less**
Circ: Diamd. preorders: **49,115**

747 ❑ Aug 2000 Cover: 1.99 **NM** value: **Cover or less**
Circ: Diamd. preorders: **48,720**

748 ❑ Sep 2000 Cover: 1.99 **NM** value: **Cover or less**
Circ: Diamd. preorders: **47,701**
Urban Renewal, Part 1 **W:** Greg Rucka

Other grades: Multiply prices above by **1.5 for Mint • 2/3 for Very Fine • 1/3 for Fine • 1/5 for Very Good • 1/8 for Good**

749 ❑ Oct 2000 Cover: 2.50 **NM value: Cover or less**
Circ: Diamd. preorders: **44,320**
📖 Urban Renewal, Part 2 **A:** Phil Hester **W:** Greg Rucka
750 ❑ Nov 2000 Cover: 4.95 **NM value: Cover or less**
Circ: Diamd. preorders: **45,796**
• Giant-size. 📖 Dependence **A:** Shawn Martinbrough **W:** Greg Rucka
751 ❑ Dec 2000 Cover: 2.50 **NM value: Cover or less**
Circ: Diamd. preorders: **43,281**
📖 A Walk in the Park, Part 1 **A:** Shawn Martinbrough **W:** Greg Rucka
752 ❑ Jan 2001 Cover: 2.50 **NM value: Cover or less**
Circ: Diamd. preorders: **42,827**
📖 A Walk in the Park, Part 2 **A:** Shawn Martinbrough **W:** Greg Rucka
753 ❑ Feb 2001 Cover: 2.50 **NM value: Cover or less**
Circ: Diamd. preorders: **44,487**
📖 The Adventures of Copernicus Dent: The Janus Double-Down!; Dead in the Water, Part 8 **A:** Steve Mannion; Jeff Johnson; Brad Rader **W:** Greg Rucka; Jordan B. Gorfinkel
754 ❑ Mar 2001 Cover: 2.50 **NM value: Cover or less**
Circ: Diamd. preorders: **44,889**
📖 Officer Down, Part 6; The Jacobian, Part 9 **A:** Mike Collins; Jeff Johnson **W:** Jordan B. Gorfinkel; Nunzio Defilippis
755 ❑ Apr 2001 Cover: 2.50 **NM value: Cover or less**
Circ: Diamd. preorders: **41,141**
📖 Here's Your Hat, What's Your Hurry? **A:** Shawn Martinbrough **W:** Greg Rucka
756 ❑ May 2001 Cover: 2.50 **NM value: Cover or less**
Circ: Diamd. preorders: **47,221** • **CGC:** 2 graded, best 9.8
📖 Lord of the Ring **A:** Coy Turnbull **W:** Greg Rucka
757 ❑ Jun 2001 Cover: 2.50 **NM value: Cover or less**
Circ: Diamd. preorders: **41,594**
758 ❑ Jul 2001 Cover: 2.50 **NM value: Cover or less**
Circ: Diamd. preorders: **41,048**
759 ❑ Aug 2001 Cover: 2.50 **NM value: Cover or less**
Circ: Diamd. preorders: **43,020**
760 ❑ Sep 2001 Cover: 2.50 **NM value: Cover or less**
Circ: Diamd. preorders: **43,505**
1000000 ❑ Nov 1998 Cover: 1.99 **NM value: Cover or less**
Circ: Diamd. preorders: **52,120**
1000000/SC ❑ Nov 1998 Cover: 14.99 **NM value: Cover or less**
Anl 1 ❑ ca. 1988 Cover: 1.50 **NM value: 5.00**
• **CGC:** 1 graded, best 9.0
★ Versus Penguin.
Anl 2 ❑ ca. 1989 Cover: 2.00 **NM value: 4.00**
Circ: CapCity orders: **58,500**
📖 Blood Secrets • Who's Who entries
Anl 3 ❑ ca. 1990 Cover: 2.00 **NM value: 2.50**
Anl 4 ❑ ca. 1991 Cover: 2.00 **NM value: 2.50**
Circ: CapCity orders: **53,100**
📖 Armageddon 2001, Part 12 • Armageddon 2001
Anl 5 ❑ ca. 1992 Cover: 2.00 **NM value: 2.75**
Circ: CapCity orders: **35,550**
• Eclipso ★ Versus Joker.
Anl 6 ❑ 1993 Cover: 2.50 **NM value: Cover or less**
Circ: CapCity orders: **36,900**
📖 Not Fade Away **A:** Jim Balent **W:** Chuck Dixon ★ 1st Appearance of Geist.
Anl 7 ❑ ca. 1994 Cover: 2.95 **NM value: Cover or less**
Circ: CapCity orders: **29,900**
• Elseworlds
Anl 8 ❑ ca. 1995 Cover: 3.95 **NM value: Cover or less**
Circ: CapCity orders: **24,075**
• Year One ★ Origin of Riddler.
Anl 9 ❑ ca. 1996 Cover: 2.95 **NM value: Cover or less**
📖 War Bat • Legends of the Dead Earth; 1996 annual **A:** Flint Henry **W:** Chuck Dixon
Anl 10 ❑ ca. 1997 Cover: 3.95 **NM value: Cover or less**
Circ: Diamd. preorders: **41,541**
• Pulp Heroes
Bk 1 ❑ Jan 2000 Cover: 12.95 **NM value: Cover or less**
📖 Collects Detective Comics #469-479 • Strange Apparitions **A:** Walt Simonson; Marshall Rogers **W:** Steve Englehart
Bk 1 ❑ Aug 1999 Cover: 14.95 **NM value: Cover or less**
📖 A Remembrance of Threatening Green • Collects series **A:** Marshall Rogers **W:** Don McGregor

DETECTIVE EYE — Centaur

1 ❑ Nov 1940 Cover: 0.10 **NM value: 1600.00**
2 ❑ Dec 1940 Cover: 0.10 **NM value: 1000.00**
• **CGC:** 1 graded, best 9.4

DETECTIVE PICTURE STORIES — Comics Magazine

1 ❑ Dec 1936 Cover: 0.10 **NM value: 3000.00**
• **CGC:** 1 graded, best 4.5
2 ❑ Jan 1937 Cover: 0.10 **NM value: 1500.00**
3 ❑ Feb 1937 Cover: 0.10 **NM value: 800.00**
4 ❑ Mar 1937 Cover: 0.10 **NM value: 800.00**
5 ❑ Apr 1937 Cover: 0.10 **NM value: 800.00**
• **CGC:** 1 graded, best 2.5

DETECTIVES, THE — Alpha Productions

1 ❑ Apr 1993, b&w Cover: 4.95 **NM value: Cover or less**

DETECTIVES, INC.: A TERROR OF DYING DREAMS — Eclipse

1 ❑ Jun 1987 Cover: 1.75 **NM value: 2.00**
• sepia **A:** Gene Colan
2 ❑ Sep 1987 Cover: 1.75 **NM value: 2.00**
Circ: CapCity orders: **3,475**
• sepia **A:** Gene Colan
3 ❑ Dec 1987 Cover: 1.75 **NM value: 2.00**
Circ: CapCity orders: **3,325**
• sepia **A:** Gene Colan
Bk 1 ❑ Cover: 19.95 **NM value: Cover or less**

DETECTIVES INC. (MICRO-SERIES) — Eclipse

1 ❑ Apr 1985 Cover: 1.75 **NM value: 2.00**
📖 A Terror of Dying Dreams; Cheerful Lies and Desperate Truths **A:** Marshall Rogers **W:** Don McGregor
2 ❑ Apr 1985 Cover: 1.75 **NM value: 2.00**
📖 A Hostile Poolside Universe **A:** Marshall Rogers **W:** Don McGregor

DETENTION COMICS — DC

1 ❑ Oct 1996 Cover: 3.50 **NM value: Cover or less**
One-shot. 📖 Mama's Boy; The Lesson; Home • Robin, Superboy, and Warrior stories **A:** Norm Breyfogle; Ron Lim; Joe Philip **W:** Denny O'Neil; Ron Marz; Ruben Diaz

DETONATOR — Chaos

1 ❑ Dec 1994 Cover: 2.75 **NM value: Cover or less**
Circ: CapCity orders: **12,650**
📖 Fear the Hero **A:** Steven Hughes **W:** Brian Pulido
2 ❑ Jan 1994 Cover: 2.75 **NM value: Cover or less**
Circ: CapCity orders: **7,475**
📖 Reunion **A:** Steven Hughes **W:** Brian Pulido ★ Origin of Detonator. ★ Death of Mindbender.

DETOUR — Alternative Press

1 ❑ Oct 1997, b&w Cover: 2.95 **NM value: Cover or less**
Circ: Diamd. preorders: **2,124**

DETROIT! MURDER CITY COMIX — Kent Myers

1 ❑ 1993, b&w Cover: 2.50 **NM value: Cover or less**
2 ❑ 1994, b&w Cover: 2.50 **NM value: Cover or less**
3 ❑ 1994, b&w Cover: 2.50 **NM value: Cover or less**
4 ❑ Jun 1994, b&w Cover: 2.95 **NM value: Cover or less**
5 ❑ Aug 1994, b&w Cover: 2.95 **NM value: Cover or less**
6 ❑ Jan 1995, b&w Cover: 2.95 **NM value: Cover or less**
📖 German Secret Weapon! **A:** Kent Myers; Rick Metcalf **W:** Kent Myers; Rick Metcalf ★ Appearance of Iggy Pop.
7 ❑ May 1995, b&w Cover: 2.95 **NM value: Cover or less**

DEVASTATOR — Image

1 ❑ ca. 1998, b&w Cover: 2.95 **NM value: Cover or less**
Circ: Diamd. preorders: **5,104**
A: Greg Horn **W:** James D. Hudnall
2 ❑ ca. 1998, b&w Cover: 2.95 **NM value: Cover or less**
Circ: Diamd. preorders: **2,881**
A: Greg Horn **W:** James D. Hudnall
3 ❑ ca. 1998 Cover: 2.95 **NM value: Cover or less**
Circ: Diamd. preorders: **2,211**
A: Greg Horn **W:** James D. Hudnall

DEVIANT — Antarctic / Venus

All issues are adults only.
1 ❑ Mar 1999, b&w Cover: 2.99 **NM value: Cover or less**
📖 A Comic Book Journal of Strange Sexual Practices **A:** Robin Bougie **W:** Robin Bougie

DEVIL CHEF — Dark Horse

1 ❑ Jul 1994, b&w Cover: 2.50 **NM value: Cover or less**
A: Jack Pollack **W:** Jack Pollack

DEVIL DINOSAUR — Marvel

"Moon Boy" is a chimpanzee-like ancestor of man. Unlike most of his kind, he is unafraid of the night, thus earning this peculiar name among his people.

One night while exploring, he comes across a group of larger man-apes who've trapped a mother dinosaur beneath a fiery volcano. The volcano erupts suddenly, scattering the man-apes. However, Moon Boy remains and discovers a young offspring of the mother dinosaur. He leads it to safety and tends to its wounds. Soon, they became friends, with Moon Boy using his intelligence, and Devil Dinosaur using its great strength to survive together in a savage world.

One of Jack Kirby's creations for Marvel in 1970s, the series was appreciated by fans of the King and regarded as campy and outdated by others.

1 ❑ Apr 1978 Cover: 0.35 **NM value: 5.00**
• **CGC:** 23 graded, best 9.9
📖 Devil Dinosaur and Moon Boy **A:** Jack Kirby **W:** Jack Kirby ★ Origin of Devil Dinosaur. ★ 1st Appearance of Devil Dinosaur, Moon Boy.
2 ❑ May 1978 Cover: 0.35 **NM value: 3.00**
📖 Devil's War **A:** Jack Kirby
3 ❑ Jun 1978 Cover: 0.35 **NM value: 2.00**
• **CGC:** 1 graded, best 9.8
📖 Giant **A:** Jack Kirby
4 ❑ Jul 1978 Cover: 0.35 **NM value: 2.00**
• **CGC:** 1 graded, best 9.6
📖 Object from the Sky **A:** Jack Kirby
5 ❑ Aug 1978 Cover: 0.35 **NM value: 2.00**
📖 Journey to the Center of the Ants **A:** Jack Kirby
6 ❑ Sep 1978 Cover: 0.35 **NM value: 2.00**
📖 Eev **A:** Jack Kirby
7 ❑ Oct 1978 Cover: 0.35 **NM value: 2.00**
📖 Demon Tree **A:** Jack Kirby
8 ❑ Nov 1978 Cover: 0.35 **NM value: 2.00**
📖 Dino-Riders **A:** Jack Kirby
9 ❑ Dec 1978 Cover: 0.35 **NM value: 2.00**
📖 The Witch and the Warp final issue. **A:** Jack Kirby

DEVIL DINOSAUR SPRING FLING — Marvel

1 ❑ Jun 1997 Cover: 2.99 **NM value: Cover or less**
Circ: Diamd. preorders: **14,664**
One-shot. ★ Appearance of Moon-Boy.

DEVIL-DOG DUGAN — Atlas

1 ❑ Jul 1956 Cover: 0.10 **NM value: 60.00**
2 ❑ Sep 1956 Cover: 0.10 **NM value: 40.00**
3 ❑ Nov 1956 Cover: 0.10 **NM value: 30.00**

DEVIL DOGS — Street & Smith

1 ❑ ca. 1942 Cover: 0.10 **NM value: 200.00**

DEVILINA — Atlas-Seaboard

1 ❑ Jan 1975, b&w Cover: 0.75 **NM value: 9.00**
• magazine.
2 ❑ May 1975, b&w Cover: 0.75 **NM value: 12.00**
• magazine.

DEVIL JACK — Doom Theater

1 ❑ Cover: 2.95 **NM value: Cover or less**
Circ: CapCity orders: **3,610**
A: Tim Tyler **W:** Tim Tyler

DEVIL KIDS — Harvey

Casper and Spooky are ghosts; Wendy's a witch. Hot Stuff is a little devil. Fortunately, the Moral Majority never heard of Harvey Comics — and certainly not the title, Devil Kids, which features the pitchfork-weilding, diaper-wearing devil child and his friends. Of course, premise aside, the comics are otherwise as wholesome as comics come, with Hot Stuff learning patience and other virtues in various stories.

In addition to 19 years in Devil Kids, Hot Stuff's own title saw 177 issues published sporadically over a period of 34 years. Other titles included Hot Stuff Sizzlers and Creepy Caves.

1 ❑ Jul 1962 Cover: 0.12 **NM value: 65.00**
• **CGC:** 1 graded, best 9.4
2 ❑ Sep 1962 Cover: 0.12 **NM value: 40.00**
3 ❑ Nov 1962 Cover: 0.12 **NM value: 30.00**
4 ❑ Jan 1963 Cover: 0.12 **NM value: 18.00**
5 ❑ Mar 1963 Cover: 0.12 **NM value: 18.00**
6 ❑ May 1963 Cover: 0.12 **NM value: 12.00**
7 ❑ Jul 1963 Cover: 0.12 **NM value: 12.00**
8 ❑ Sep 1963 Cover: 0.12 **NM value: 12.00**
9 ❑ Nov 1963 Cover: 0.12 **NM value: 12.00**
10 ❑ Jan 1964 Cover: 0.12 **NM value: 12.00**
11 ❑ Mar 1964 Cover: 0.12 **NM value: 8.00**
12 ❑ May 1964 Cover: 0.12 **NM value: 8.00**
13 ❑ Jul 1964 Cover: 0.12 **NM value: 8.00**
14 ❑ Sep 1964 Cover: 0.12 **NM value: 8.00**
15 ❑ Nov 1964 Cover: 0.12 **NM value: 8.00**
16 ❑ Jan 1965 Cover: 0.12 **NM value: 8.00**
17 ❑ Mar 1965 Cover: 0.12 **NM value: 8.00**
18 ❑ May 1965 Cover: 0.12 **NM value: 8.00**
19 ❑ Jul 1965 Cover: 0.12 **NM value: 8.00**
20 ❑ Sep 1965 Cover: 0.12 **NM value: 8.00**
21 ❑ Nov 1965 Cover: 0.12 **NM value: 6.00**
22 ❑ Jan 1966 Cover: 0.12 **NM value: 6.00**
23 ❑ Mar 1966 Cover: 0.12 **NM value: 6.00**
24 ❑ May 1966 Cover: 0.12 **NM value: 6.00**
25 ❑ Jul 1966 Cover: 0.12 **NM value: 6.00**
26 ❑ Sep 1966 Cover: 0.12 **NM value: 6.00**
27 ❑ Nov 1966 Cover: 0.12 **NM value: 6.00**
28 ❑ Jan 1967 Cover: 0.12 **NM value: 6.00**
29 ❑ Mar 1967 Cover: 0.12 **NM value: 6.00**
30 ❑ May 1967 Cover: 0.12 **NM value: 6.00**
31 ❑ Jul 1967 Cover: 0.12 **NM value: 5.00**
32 ❑ Sep 1967 Cover: 0.12 **NM value: 5.00**
33 ❑ Nov 1967 Cover: 0.12 **NM value: 5.00**
34 ❑ 1968 Cover: 0.12 **NM value: 5.00**
35 ❑ Sep 1968 Cover: 0.12 **NM value: 5.00**
36 ❑ Nov 1968 Cover: 0.12 **NM value: 5.00**
37 ❑ 1969 Cover: 0.12 **NM value: 5.00**
38 ❑ 1969 Cover: 0.12 **NM value: 5.00**
39 ❑ 1969 Cover: 0.12 **NM value: 5.00**
40 ❑ Jun 1969 Cover: 0.15 **NM value: 5.00**
41 ❑ 1969 Cover: 0.25 **NM value: 4.00**
42 ❑ 1969 Cover: 0.25 **NM value: 4.00**
43 ❑ 1970 Cover: 0.25 **NM value: 4.00**
44 ❑ 1970 Cover: 0.25 **NM value: 4.00**
45 ❑ 1970 Cover: 0.25 **NM value: 4.00**
46 ❑ 1970 Cover: 0.25 **NM value: 4.00**
47 ❑ Dec 1970 Cover: 0.25 **NM value: 4.00**
48 ❑ 1971 Cover: 0.25 **NM value: 4.00**
49 ❑ 1971 Cover: 0.25 **NM value: 4.00**
50 ❑ 1971 Cover: 0.25 **NM value: 4.00**
51 ❑ Sep 1971 Cover: 0.25 **NM value: 4.00**
52 ❑ Cover: 0.25 **NM value: 4.00**
53 ❑ Mar 1972 Cover: 0.25 **NM value: 4.00**
54 ❑ 1972 Cover: 0.25 **NM value: 4.00**
55 ❑ 1972 Cover: 0.25 **NM value: 4.00**
56 ❑ 1972 Cover: 0.20 **NM value: 4.00**
57 ❑ Dec 1972 Cover: 0.20 **NM value: 4.00**
58 ❑ Feb 1973 Cover: 0.20 **NM value: 4.00**
59 ❑ Apr 1973 Cover: 0.20 **NM value: 4.00**
60 ❑ Jun 1973 Cover: 0.20 **NM value: 4.00**
61 ❑ Aug 1973 Cover: 0.20 **NM value: 3.00**
62 ❑ Oct 1973 Cover: 0.20 **NM value: 3.00**
63 ❑ Dec 1973 Cover: 0.20 **NM value: 3.00**
64 ❑ 1974 Cover: 0.20 **NM value: 3.00**
65 ❑ 1974 Cover: 0.20 **NM value: 3.00**
66 ❑ 1974 Cover: 0.25 **NM value: 3.00**

CGC-graded: Multiply prices above by **33 for 9.9 M • 16 for 9.8 NM/M • 7 for 9.6 NM+ • 5 for 9.4 NM • 2.5 for 9.2 NM- • 1.5 for 9.0 VF/NM**

67 ❑ 1974 Cover: 0.25 **NM** value: **3.00**
68 ❑ 1974 Cover: 0.25 **NM** value: **3.00**
69 ❑ Apr 1975 Cover: 0.25 **NM** value: **3.00**
70 ❑ Jun 1975 Cover: 0.25 **NM** value: **3.00**
71 ❑ Aug 1975 Cover: 0.25 **NM** value: **3.00**
72 ❑ Oct 1975 Cover: 0.25 **NM** value: **3.00**
73 ❑ Dec 1975 Cover: 0.25 **NM** value: **3.00**
74 ❑ Feb 1976 Cover: 0.25 **NM** value: **3.00**
75 ❑ Apr 1976 Cover: 0.25 **NM** value: **3.00**
76 ❑ Jun 1976 Cover: 0.25 **NM** value: **3.00**
77 ❑ Aug 1976 Cover: 0.25 **NM** value: **3.00**
78 ❑ Oct 1976 Cover: 0.30 **NM** value: **3.00**
79 ❑ Dec 1976 Cover: 0.30 **NM** value: **3.00**
80 ❑ Feb 1977 Cover: 0.30 **NM** value: **2.00**
81 ❑ Apr 1977 Cover: 0.30 **NM** value: **2.00**
📖 The Mystery of the Missing Mountain; Oh, No, Not Again!; The Mountain Thief; Little Angel (text); Stumbo...Hide Our Giant
82 ❑ Jun 1977 Cover: 0.30 **NM** value: **2.00**
83 ❑ Aug 1977 Cover: 0.30 **NM** value: **2.00**
84 ❑ 1977 Cover: 0.30 **NM** value: **2.00**
85 ❑ 1977 Cover: 0.30 **NM** value: **2.00**
86 ❑ Jan 1978 Cover: 0.30 **NM** value: **2.00**
87 ❑ Mar 1978 Cover: 0.30 **NM** value: **2.00**
88 ❑ May 1978 Cover: 0.30 **NM** value: **2.00**
89 ❑ Jul 1978 Cover: 0.30 **NM** value: **2.00**
90 ❑ 1978 Cover: 0.35 **NM** value: **2.00**
91 ❑ Dec 1978 Cover: 0.35 **NM** value: **2.00**
92 ❑ Feb 1979 Cover: 0.35 **NM** value: **2.00**
93 ❑ 1979 Cover: 0.35 **NM** value: **2.00**
94 ❑ 1979 Cover: 0.35 **NM** value: **2.00**
95 ❑ Sep 1979 Cover: 0.35 **NM** value: **2.00**
96 ❑ Nov 1979 Cover: 0.40 **NM** value: **2.00**
97 ❑ Feb 1980 Cover: 0.40 **NM** value: **2.00**
98 ❑ Apr 1980 Cover: 0.40 **NM** value: **2.00**
99 ❑ Jun 1980 Cover: 0.40 **NM** value: **2.00**
100 ❑ Aug 1980 Cover: 0.40 **NM** value: **2.00**
101 ❑ Oct 1980 Cover: 0.50 **NM** value: **2.00**
102 ❑ Dec 1980 Cover: 0.50 **NM** value: **2.00**
103 ❑ Feb 1981 Cover: 0.50 **NM** value: **2.00**
104 ❑ Apr 1981 Cover: 0.50 **NM** value: **2.00**
105 ❑ Jun 1981 Cover: 0.50 **NM** value: **2.00**
106 ❑ Aug 1981 Cover: 0.50 **NM** value: **2.00**
107 ❑ Oct 1981 Cover: 0.50 **NM** value: **2.00**

DEVILMAN — Verotik

1 ❑ Jun 1995 Cover: 2.95 **NM** value: **3.50**
Circ: CapCity orders: **7,990**
📖 The Late Spring of Vienna **A:** Go Nagai **W:** Go Nagai
2 ❑ Cover: 2.95 **NM** value: **3.00**
Circ: CapCity orders: **7,500**
3 ❑ Cover: 2.95 **NM** value: **3.00**
Circ: CapCity orders: **7,075**
4 ❑ Cover: 2.95 **NM** value: **Cover or less**
Circ: CapCity orders: **6,025**
5 ❑ Cover: 2.95 **NM** value: **Cover or less**
6 ❑ **NM** value: **3.50**

DEVIL'S ANGEL, THE — Fantagraphics / Eros

1 ❑ Cover: 2.95 **NM** value: **Cover or less**
A: Frank Thorne **W:** Frank Thorne

DEVIL'S BITE — Boneyard

1 ❑ Cover: 2.95 **NM** value: **Cover or less**
A: Hart Fisher **W:** Hart Fisher
2 ❑ Cover: 2.95 **NM** value: **Cover or less**
📖 The Duffel Bag • Indicia lists as #1 **A:** Hart Fisher; Eric Gnoeff; Joseph Vargo(cover) **W:** Hart Fisher

DEVIL'S BRIGADE, THE — Avalon

Yanks, Brits, Germans, Italians... all brought together in battle during World War II, in various parts of the world. But to British Major Terrance Graeme, the war is simple-and he and his tank, Mother, are ready to face all challenges, and keep the name of the defiant Devil's Brigade alive in the hearts of his countrymen. Joined by an American Major and his men, the small force confronts a battle they must win, against the notorious Major Albert Krueger ("Smiling Albert"). Krueger has made his name from his destruction of Allied tanks, but Graeme is determined to see the man smile for the last time.

These and other such tales of heroism and struggle during war are at the heart of this classic series from the 1960s, collected and reprinted in black-and-white by Avalon.

1 ❑ Cover: 2.95 **NM** value: **Cover or less**

DEVIL'S REIGN — Image

0.5 ❑ ca. 1996 **NM** value: **3.00**
• **CGC:** 8 graded, best 9.8
• Wizard mail-in
0.5/Aut❑ ca. 1996 **NM** value: **6.00**
0.5/Pl❑ ca. 1996 **NM** value: **5.00**
• Platinum edition.

DEVLIN — Maximum

1 ❑ Apr 1996 Cover: 2.50 **NM** value: **Cover or less**
★ Appearance of Avengelyne.

DEVLIN DEMON: NOT FOR NORMAL CHILDREN — Dublin

1 ❑ Cover: 2.95 **NM** value: **Cover or less**

DEVLIN WAUGH: SWIMMING IN BLOOD — Fleetway-Quality

Bk 1❑ Cover: 9.95 **NM** value: **Cover or less**

DEWEY DESADE — Item / Quality

1 ❑ Cover: 3.50 **NM** value: **Cover or less**
2 ❑ Cover: 3.50 **NM** value: **Cover or less**
Ash 1❑ **NM** value: **0.25**
• Promotional, mini-ashcan (4 x 2) **W:** Dan Couto

DEXTER COMICS — Dearfield

1 ❑ Jul 1948 Cover: 0.10 **NM** value: **45.00**
2 ❑ Oct 1948 Cover: 0.10 **NM** value: **40.00**
3 ❑ Jan 1949 Cover: 0.10 **NM** value: **40.00**
4 ❑ Apr 1949 Cover: 0.10 **NM** value: **40.00**
5 ❑ Jul 1949 Cover: 0.10 **NM** value: **40.00**

DEXTER'S LABORATORY — DC

Based on the Cartoon Network series, Dexter's Laboratory is true to its source material. Here, as on TV, Dexter is a boy who uses science and technology to deal with all the typical childhood problems; for example, cybernetic armor is the perfect cure for those dodgeball fears. In his first issue, Dexter became — what else? — a super-hero in grand style via his (Jack) Kirbytron 2000. Artist Genndy Tatakovsky seems to have loads of fun rendering Dexter's lab in standard Kirby circuitry. Ah, but how will our hero fare against the evil Deestructa, a comic-book version of his meddling older sister DeeDee? Find out in this fun adaptation of a truly inspired animated series.

1 ❑ Sep 1999 Cover: 1.99 **NM** value: **2.50**
Circ: Diamd. preorders: **6,534** • **CGC:** 1 graded, best 9.0
📖 Wow! Comic Relief **A:** Genndy Tartakovsky **W:** Craig McCracken; Genndy Tartakovsky
2 ❑ Oct 1999 Cover: 1.99 **NM** value: **2.00**
Circ: Diamd. preorders: **4,817**
📖 Let's Save thw World, You Jerk! **A:** Genndy Tartakovsky **W:** Craig McCracken; Genndy Tartakovsky ★ Appearance of Mandark.
3 ❑ Nov 1999 Cover: 1.99 **NM** value: **2.00**
Circ: Diamd. preorders: **4,277**
• Dexter's robot takes his place
4 ❑ Dec 1999 Cover: 1.99 **NM** value: **2.00**
Circ: Diamd. preorders: **4,523**
📖 Meanwhile... **A:** John Delaney **W:** Dan Slott
5 ❑ Jan 2000 Cover: 1.99 **NM** value: **2.00**
Circ: Diamd. preorders: **4,369**
6 ❑ Feb 2000 Cover: 1.99 **NM** value: **2.00**
Circ: Diamd. preorders: **4,187**
7 ❑ Mar 2000 Cover: 1.99 **NM** value: **2.00**
Circ: Diamd. preorders: **3,685**
8 ❑ Apr 2000 Cover: 1.99 **NM** value: **2.00**
Circ: Diamd. preorders: **3,430**
📖 Dee-Dee Fo-Fum **A:** John Delaney **W:** John Rozum
9 ❑ May 2000 Cover: 1.99 **NM** value: **2.00**
Circ: Diamd. preorders: **3,492**
📖 ...Perfect Chemistry!! **A:** Chris Savino **W:** John Rozum
10 ❑ Jun 2000 Cover: 1.99 **NM** value: **2.00**
Circ: Diamd. preorders: **3,491**
11 ❑ Jul 2000 Cover: 1.99 **NM** value: **Cover or less**
Circ: Diamd. preorders: **3,511**
12 ❑ Aug 2000 Cover: 1.99 **NM** value: **Cover or less**
Circ: Diamd. preorders: **3,687**
13 ❑ Sep 2000 Cover: 1.99 **NM** value: **Cover or less**
Circ: Diamd. preorders: **3,551**
📖 What: Funny?; Forget me Not **A:** John Delaney; Mike Stern **W:** Dave Roman; Brian Swenlin
14 ❑ Oct 2000 Cover: 1.99 **NM** value: **Cover or less**
Circ: Diamd. preorders: **3,462**
📖 Teacher's Pet **A:** Chris Savino **W:** Dan Slott
15 ❑ Nov 2000 Cover: 1.99 **NM** value: **Cover or less**
Circ: Diamd. preorders: **3,471**
📖 Totally Tanked **A:** Bill Wray **W:** Bobbi JG Weiss
16 ❑ Dec 2000 Cover: 1.99 **NM** value: **Cover or less**
Circ: Diamd. preorders: **3,466**
📖 Dee-Dee's Pony Tale **A:** John Delaney **W:** John Rozum
17 ❑ Jan 2001 Cover: 1.99 **NM** value: **Cover or less**
Circ: Diamd. preorders: **3,411**
📖 Dexter's New Clothes **A:** John Delaney **W:** Dave Roman; Brian Swenlin
18 ❑ Feb 2001 Cover: 1.99 **NM** value: **Cover or less**
Circ: Diamd. preorders: **3,323**
📖 Doot-Doot-Doot! **A:** John Delaney **W:** James Denning
19 ❑ Mar 2001 Cover: 1.99 **NM** value: **Cover or less**
Circ: Diamd. preorders: **3,277**
📖 Spoon **A:** Chris Savino **W:** Bobbi JG Weiss
20 ❑ Apr 2001 Cover: 1.99 **NM** value: **Cover or less**
Circ: Diamd. preorders: **3,272**
📖 Journey to the Center of Dee-Dee **A:** John Delaney **W:** Jennifer Moore; Sean Carolan
21 ❑ May 2001 Cover: 1.99 **NM** value: **Cover or less**
Circ: Diamd. preorders: **3,320**
📖 The Big Move **A:** Eduardo Savid **W:** Bobbi JG Weiss
22 ❑ Jun 2001 Cover: 1.99 **NM** value: **Cover or less**
Circ: Diamd. preorders: **3,389**
23 ❑ Jul 2001 Cover: 1.99 **NM** value: **Cover or less**
Circ: Diamd. preorders: **3,392**
24 ❑ Aug 2001 Cover: 1.99 **NM** value: **Cover or less**
Circ: Diamd. preorders: **3,603**
25 ❑ Sep 2001 Cover: 1.99 **NM** value: **Cover or less**
Circ: Diamd. preorders: **12,658**

DHAMPIRE: STILLBORN — DC / Vertigo

1 ❑ Sep 1996 Cover: 5.95 **NM** value: **Cover or less**
Circ: Diamd. preorders: **18,418**
• prestige format. **A:** Paul Lee **W:** Nancy A. Collins

DIA DE LOS MUERTOS (SERGIO ARAGONÉS'...) — Dark Horse

Beloved humorist and comics-scene fixture Sergio Aragones (perpetrator of Groo the Wanderer and many hysterical bits in Mad) takes his turn as righteous satirist in Dia De Los Muertos. This provocative 1998 Dark Horse one-shot takes aim at American cultural imperialism in the form of obnoxious tourists, megalomaniac capitalists, and theme-park consumerism. Aragones couches his earnest critique in a fable of a small town in Mexico that performs a unique ritual every year on the Day of the Dead (Dia De Los Muertos, November 1). Attempts by heavy-handed Americans to exploit this ceremony for profit backfire in a most gruesome (or "Groo"some) manner.

1 ❑ Oct 1998 Cover: 2.95 **NM** value: **Cover or less**
No issue number. One-shot. • Day of the Dead stories **A:** Sergio Aragonés **W:** Sergio Aragonés; Mark Evanier

DIARY OF A DOMINATRIX — Fantagraphics / Eros

All issues are adults only.
1 ❑ b&w Cover: 2.95 **NM** value: **Cover or less**
A: Molly Kiely **W:** Molly Kiely

DIARY OF EMILY K., THE — Fantagraphics / Eros

All issues are adults only.
1 ❑ b&w Cover: 2.50 **NM** value: **Cover or less**

DIARY OF HORROR — Avon

1 ❑ Dec 1952 Cover: 0.10 **NM** value: **250.00**
• **CGC:** 4 graded, best 7.5

DIATOM — Photographics

1 ❑ Apr 1995, b&w Cover: 4.95 **NM** value: **Cover or less**
• prestige format. • fumetti **A:** Michael Vollmer **W:** Michael Vollmer
2 ❑ Cover: 4.95 **NM** value: **Cover or less**
A: Michael Vollmer **W:** Michael Vollmer
3 ❑ Cover: 4.95 **NM** value: **Cover or less**
📖 Cap'n Ice **A:** Michael Vollmer **W:** Michael Vollmer

DICK COLE — Curtis Publishing

1 ❑ Dec 1948 Cover: 0.10 **NM** value: **200.00**
2 ❑ Feb 1949 Cover: 0.10 **NM** value: **120.00**
3 ❑ Apr 1949 Cover: 0.10 **NM** value: **120.00**
• **CGC:** 1 graded, best 9.2
4 ❑ Jun 1949 Cover: 0.10 **NM** value: **120.00**
5 ❑ Aug 1949 Cover: 0.10 **NM** value: **120.00**
6 ❑ Oct 1949 Cover: 0.10 **NM** value: **120.00**
• **CGC:** 1 graded, best 7.5
7 ❑ Dec 1949 Cover: 0.10 **NM** value: **120.00**
8 ❑ Feb 1950 Cover: 0.10 **NM** value: **120.00**
9 ❑ Apr 1950 Cover: 0.10 **NM** value: **120.00**
10 ❑ Jun 1950 Cover: 0.10 **NM** value: **120.00**

DICK DANGER — Olsen

1 ❑ Jan 1998 Cover: 2.95 **NM** value: **Cover or less**
📖 The Star of Bengala; Dick Danger's Crime-Quiz **A:** W.W. Owen **W:** W.W. Owen
2 ❑ Cover: 2.95 **NM** value: **Cover or less**
3 ❑ Cover: 2.95 **NM** value: **Cover or less**
4 ❑ Cover: 2.95 **NM** value: **Cover or less**
5 ❑ Cover: 2.95 **NM** value: **Cover or less**

DICK HERCULES OF ST. MARKHAM'S — Sports Cartoons

1 ❑ Cover: 0.06 **NM** value: **20.00**
2 ❑ Cover: 0.06 **NM** value: **10.00**
3 ❑ Cover: 0.06 **NM** value: **6.00**
📖 Dangerous Pursuit
4 ❑ Cover: 0.06 **NM** value: **6.00**
5 ❑ Cover: 0.06 **NM** value: **6.00**
6 ❑ Cover: 0.06 **NM** value: **6.00**
7 ❑ Cover: 0.06 **NM** value: **6.00**
final issue.

DICKIE DARE — Eastern

1 ❑ ca. 1942 Cover: 0.10 **NM** value: **300.00**
2 ❑ ca. 1942 Cover: 0.10 **NM** value: **200.00**
3 ❑ ca. 1942 Cover: 0.10 **NM** value: **200.00**
4 ❑ ca. 1942 Cover: 0.10 **NM** value: **200.00**

DICKS — Caliber

1 ❑ Apr 1997 Cover: 2.95 **NM** value: **Cover or less**
Circ: Diamd. preorders: **15,358**
2 ❑ Jun 1997 Cover: 2.95 **NM** value: **Cover or less**
Circ: Diamd. preorders: **11,666**
3 ❑ Aug 1997 Cover: 2.95 **NM** value: **Cover or less**
Circ: Diamd. preorders: **9,900**
4 ❑ Nov 1997 Cover: 2.95 **NM** value: **Cover or less**
Circ: Diamd. preorders: **7,608**

DICK TRACY 3-D — Blackthorne

1 ❑ Jul 1986 Cover: 2.00 **NM** value: **2.50**
Circ: CapCity orders: **3,500**
📖 Ocean Death Trap! **A:** Chester Gould **W:** Chester Gould

DICK TRACY ADVENTURES (GLADSTONE) — Gladstone

1 ❑ Sep 1991 Cover: 4.95 **NM** value: **Cover or less**
Circ: CapCity orders: **2,800**
A: Chester Gould **C:** Joe Sinnott **W:** Chester Gould ★ Versus B.B. Eyes.

Other grades: Multiply prices above by **1.5 for Mint • 2/3 for Very Fine • 1/3 for Fine • 1/5 for Very Good • 1/8 for Good**

DICK TRACY ADVENTURES (HAMILTON)

Hamilton

1 ❑ b&w Cover: 3.95 **NM** value: **Cover or less**

DICK TRACY (BLACKTHORNE) **Blackthorne**

1 ❑ Jun 1986 Cover: 6.95 **NM** value: **Cover or less**
2 ❑ Jun 1986 Cover: 6.95 **NM** value: **Cover or less**
3 ❑ Jul 1986 Cover: 6.95 **NM** value: **Cover or less**
4 ❑ Aug 1986 Cover: 6.95 **NM** value: **Cover or less**
5 ❑ Oct 1986 Cover: 6.95 **NM** value: **Cover or less**
6 ❑ Oct 1986 Cover: 6.95 **NM** value: **Cover or less**
7 ❑ Dec 1986 Cover: 6.95 **NM** value: **Cover or less**
8 ❑ Jan 1987 Cover: 6.95 **NM** value: **Cover or less**
9 ❑ Jan 1987 Cover: 6.95 **NM** value: **Cover or less**
10 ❑ Feb 1987 Cover: 6.95 **NM** value: **Cover or less**
11 ❑ Mar 1987 Cover: 6.95 **NM** value: **Cover or less**
12 ❑ Apr 1987 Cover: 6.95 **NM** value: **Cover or less**
13 ❑ May 1987 Cover: 6.95 **NM** value: **Cover or less**
14 ❑ Jun 1987 Cover: 6.95 **NM** value: **Cover or less**
15 ❑ Jul 1987 Cover: 6.95 **NM** value: **Cover or less**
16 ❑ Aug 1987 Cover: 6.95 **NM** value: **Cover or less**
17 ❑ Sep 1987 Cover: 6.95 **NM** value: **Cover or less**
18 ❑ Sep 1987 Cover: 6.95 **NM** value: **Cover or less**
★ Versus Pruneface.
19 ❑ Oct 1987 Cover: 6.95 **NM** value: **Cover or less**
★ Versus Pruneface.
20 ❑ Oct 1987 Cover: 6.95 **NM** value: **Cover or less**
★ Versus Pruneface.
21 ❑ Nov 1987 Cover: 6.95 **NM** value: **Cover or less**
22 ❑ Nov 1987 Cover: 6.95 **NM** value: **Cover or less**
23 ❑ Nov 1987 Cover: 6.95 **NM** value: **Cover or less**
24 ❑ Dec 1987 Cover: 6.95 **NM** value: **Cover or less**
★ Versus Flattop.
Bk 1 ❑ Sep 1990 Cover: 12.95 **NM** value: **Cover or less**
• The Trilogy collection

DICK TRACY COMICS MONTHLY **Harvey**

Harvey picked up the license for a Dick Tracy comic book from the Dell title, continuing its numbering, too. Harvey ran strip reprints, including much classic material.

When the Comics Magazine Association of America began to apply its Comics Code content restrictions to the material by Chester Gould (1900-1985), which had already appeared in family newspapers), its censorship guidelines led to panels in which some of the drawings had simply been removed.

Nevertheless, Harvey continued the title for several years under the restrictions. Later reprints would restore the missing panels. — Maggie

25 ❑ Mar 1950 Cover: 0.10 **NM** value: **110.00**
• Series continued from Dick Tracy (Dell)#24 **A:** Chester Gould **W:** Chester Gould
26 ❑ Apr 1950 Cover: 0.10 **NM** value: **85.00**
A: Chester Gould **W:** Chester Gould
27 ❑ May 1950 Cover: 0.10 **NM** value: **85.00**
A: Chester Gould **W:** Chester Gould
28 ❑ Jun 1950 Cover: 0.10 **NM** value: **85.00**
A: Chester Gould **W:** Chester Gould
29 ❑ Jul 1950 Cover: 0.10 **NM** value: **85.00**
• **CGC:** 1 graded, best 2.5
A: Chester Gould **W:** Chester Gould
30 ❑ Aug 1950 Cover: 0.10 **NM** value: **85.00**
A: Chester Gould **W:** Chester Gould
31 ❑ Sep 1950 Cover: 0.10 **NM** value: **85.00**
A: Chester Gould **W:** Chester Gould
32 ❑ Oct 1950 Cover: 0.10 **NM** value: **85.00**
A: Chester Gould **W:** Chester Gould
33 ❑ Nov 1950 Cover: 0.10 **NM** value: **85.00**
A: Chester Gould **W:** Chester Gould
34 ❑ Dec 1950 Cover: 0.10 **NM** value: **85.00**
A: Chester Gould **W:** Chester Gould
35 ❑ Jan 1951 Cover: 0.10 **NM** value: **85.00**
A: Chester Gould **W:** Chester Gould
36 ❑ Feb 1951 Cover: 0.10 **NM** value: **85.00**
A: Chester Gould **W:** Chester Gould
37 ❑ Mar 1951 Cover: 0.10 **NM** value: **85.00**
• **CGC:** 1 graded, best 9.0
A: Chester Gould **W:** Chester Gould
38 ❑ Apr 1951 Cover: 0.10 **NM** value: **85.00**
• **CGC:** 1 graded, best 9.0
A: Chester Gould **W:** Chester Gould
39 ❑ May 1951 Cover: 0.10 **NM** value: **85.00**
A: Chester Gould **W:** Chester Gould
40 ❑ Jun 1951 Cover: 0.10 **NM** value: **85.00**
A: Chester Gould **W:** Chester Gould
41 ❑ Jul 1951 Cover: 0.10 **NM** value: **85.00**
A: Chester Gould **W:** Chester Gould
42 ❑ Aug 1951 Cover: 0.10 **NM** value: **70.00**
A: Chester Gould **W:** Chester Gould
43 ❑ Sep 1951 Cover: 0.10 **NM** value: **70.00**
A: Chester Gould **W:** Chester Gould
44 ❑ Oct 1951 Cover: 0.10 **NM** value: **70.00**
A: Chester Gould **W:** Chester Gould
45 ❑ Nov 1951 Cover: 0.10 **NM** value: **70.00**
A: Chester Gould **W:** Chester Gould
46 ❑ Dec 1951 Cover: 0.10 **NM** value: **70.00**
A: Chester Gould **W:** Chester Gould
47 ❑ Jan 1952 Cover: 0.10 **NM** value: **70.00**
A: Chester Gould **W:** Chester Gould
48 ❑ Feb 1952 Cover: 0.10 **NM** value: **70.00**
A: Chester Gould **W:** Chester Gould
49 ❑ Mar 1952 Cover: 0.10 **NM** value: **70.00**
A: Chester Gould **W:** Chester Gould
50 ❑ Apr 1952 Cover: 0.10 **NM** value: **70.00**
A: Chester Gould **W:** Chester Gould
51 ❑ May 1952 Cover: 0.10 **NM** value: **60.00**
A: Chester Gould **W:** Chester Gould
52 ❑ Jun 1952 Cover: 0.10 **NM** value: **60.00**
A: Chester Gould **W:** Chester Gould
53 ❑ Jul 1952 Cover: 0.10 **NM** value: **60.00**
A: Chester Gould **W:** Chester Gould
54 ❑ Aug 1952 Cover: 0.10 **NM** value: **60.00**
A: Chester Gould **W:** Chester Gould
55 ❑ Sep 1952 Cover: 0.10 **NM** value: **60.00**
• **CGC:** 1 graded, best 9.0
A: Chester Gould **W:** Chester Gould
56 ❑ Oct 1952 Cover: 0.10 **NM** value: **60.00**
A: Chester Gould **W:** Chester Gould
57 ❑ Nov 1952 Cover: 0.10 **NM** value: **60.00**
A: Chester Gould **W:** Chester Gould
58 ❑ Dec 1952 Cover: 0.10 **NM** value: **60.00**
A: Chester Gould **W:** Chester Gould
59 ❑ Jan 1953 Cover: 0.10 **NM** value: **60.00**
A: Chester Gould **W:** Chester Gould
60 ❑ Feb 1953 Cover: 0.10 **NM** value: **60.00**
A: Chester Gould **W:** Chester Gould
61 ❑ Mar 1953 Cover: 0.10 **NM** value: **52.00**
A: Chester Gould **W:** Chester Gould
62 ❑ Apr 1953 Cover: 0.10 **NM** value: **52.00**
A: Chester Gould **W:** Chester Gould
63 ❑ May 1953 Cover: 0.10 **NM** value: **52.00**
A: Chester Gould **W:** Chester Gould
64 ❑ Jun 1953 Cover: 0.10 **NM** value: **52.00**
A: Chester Gould **W:** Chester Gould
65 ❑ Jul 1953 Cover: 0.10 **NM** value: **52.00**
A: Chester Gould **W:** Chester Gould
66 ❑ Aug 1953 Cover: 0.10 **NM** value: **52.00**
A: Chester Gould **W:** Chester Gould
67 ❑ Sep 1953 Cover: 0.10 **NM** value: **52.00**
A: Chester Gould **W:** Chester Gould
68 ❑ Oct 1953 Cover: 0.10 **NM** value: **52.00**
• **CGC:** 1 graded, best 9.2
A: Chester Gould **W:** Chester Gould
69 ❑ Nov 1953 Cover: 0.10 **NM** value: **52.00**
A: Chester Gould **W:** Chester Gould
70 ❑ Dec 1953 Cover: 0.10 **NM** value: **52.00**
A: Chester Gould **W:** Chester Gould
71 ❑ Jan 1954 Cover: 0.10 **NM** value: **45.00**
A: Chester Gould **W:** Chester Gould
72 ❑ Feb 1954 Cover: 0.10 **NM** value: **45.00**
A: Chester Gould **W:** Chester Gould
73 ❑ Mar 1954 Cover: 0.10 **NM** value: **45.00**
A: Chester Gould **W:** Chester Gould
74 ❑ Apr 1954 Cover: 0.10 **NM** value: **45.00**
A: Chester Gould **W:** Chester Gould
75 ❑ May 1954 Cover: 0.10 **NM** value: **45.00**
A: Chester Gould **W:** Chester Gould
76 ❑ Jun 1954 Cover: 0.10 **NM** value: **45.00**
A: Chester Gould **W:** Chester Gould
77 ❑ Jul 1954 Cover: 0.10 **NM** value: **45.00**
A: Chester Gould **W:** Chester Gould
78 ❑ Aug 1954 Cover: 0.10 **NM** value: **45.00**
A: Chester Gould **W:** Chester Gould
79 ❑ Sep 1954 Cover: 0.10 **NM** value: **45.00**
A: Chester Gould **W:** Chester Gould
80 ❑ Oct 1954 Cover: 0.10 **NM** value: **45.00**
A: Chester Gould **W:** Chester Gould
81 ❑ Nov 1954 Cover: 0.10 **NM** value: **40.00**
A: Chester Gould **W:** Chester Gould
82 ❑ Dec 1954 Cover: 0.10 **NM** value: **40.00**
A: Chester Gould **W:** Chester Gould
83 ❑ Jan 1955 Cover: 0.10 **NM** value: **40.00**
A: Chester Gould **W:** Chester Gould
84 ❑ Feb 1955 Cover: 0.10 **NM** value: **40.00**
A: Chester Gould **W:** Chester Gould
85 ❑ Mar 1955 Cover: 0.10 **NM** value: **40.00**
A: Chester Gould **W:** Chester Gould
86 ❑ Apr 1955 Cover: 0.10 **NM** value: **40.00**
A: Chester Gould **W:** Chester Gould
87 ❑ May 1955 Cover: 0.10 **NM** value: **40.00**
A: Chester Gould **W:** Chester Gould
88 ❑ Jun 1955 Cover: 0.10 **NM** value: **40.00**
A: Chester Gould **W:** Chester Gould
89 ❑ Jul 1955 Cover: 0.10 **NM** value: **40.00**
A: Chester Gould **W:** Chester Gould
90 ❑ Aug 1955 Cover: 0.10 **NM** value: **40.00**
A: Chester Gould **W:** Chester Gould
91 ❑ Sep 1955 Cover: 0.10 **NM** value: **32.00**
A: Chester Gould **W:** Chester Gould
92 ❑ Oct 1955 Cover: 0.10 **NM** value: **32.00**
Dick Tracy and Kincaid Problem **A:** Chester Gould **W:** Chester Gould
93 ❑ Nov 1955 Cover: 0.10 **NM** value: **32.00**
A: Chester Gould **W:** Chester Gould
94 ❑ Dec 1955 Cover: 0.10 **NM** value: **32.00**
A: Chester Gould **W:** Chester Gould
95 ❑ Jan 1956 Cover: 0.10 **NM** value: **32.00**
A: Chester Gould **W:** Chester Gould
96 ❑ Feb 1956 Cover: 0.10 **NM** value: **32.00**
A: Chester Gould **W:** Chester Gould
97 ❑ Mar 1956 Cover: 0.10 **NM** value: **32.00**
A: Chester Gould **W:** Chester Gould
98 ❑ Apr 1956 Cover: 0.10 **NM** value: **32.00**
A: Chester Gould **W:** Chester Gould
99 ❑ May 1956 Cover: 0.10 **NM** value: **32.00**
A: Chester Gould **W:** Chester Gould
100 ❑ Jun 1956 Cover: 0.10 **NM** value: **32.00**
A: Chester Gould **W:** Chester Gould
101 ❑ Jul 1956 Cover: 0.10 **NM** value: **28.00**
A: Chester Gould **W:** Chester Gould
102 ❑ Aug 1956 Cover: 0.10 **NM** value: **28.00**
A: Chester Gould **W:** Chester Gould
103 ❑ Sep 1956 Cover: 0.10 **NM** value: **28.00**
A: Chester Gould **W:** Chester Gould
104 ❑ Oct 1956 Cover: 0.10 **NM** value: **28.00**
A: Chester Gould **W:** Chester Gould
105 ❑ Nov 1956 Cover: 0.10 **NM** value: **28.00**
A: Chester Gould **W:** Chester Gould
106 ❑ Dec 1956 Cover: 0.10 **NM** value: **28.00**
A: Chester Gould **W:** Chester Gould
107 ❑ Jan 1957 Cover: 0.10 **NM** value: **28.00**
A: Chester Gould **W:** Chester Gould
108 ❑ Feb 1957 Cover: 0.10 **NM** value: **28.00**
A: Chester Gould **W:** Chester Gould
109 ❑ Mar 1957 Cover: 0.10 **NM** value: **28.00**
• **CGC:** 1 graded, best 8.0
A: Chester Gould **W:** Chester Gould
110 ❑ Apr 1957 Cover: 0.10 **NM** value: **28.00**
A: Chester Gould **W:** Chester Gould
111 ❑ May 1957 Cover: 0.10 **NM** value: **26.00**
• **CGC:** 1 graded, best 9.4
A: Chester Gould **W:** Chester Gould
112 ❑ Jun 1957 Cover: 0.10 **NM** value: **26.00**
• **CGC:** 1 graded, best 9.4
A: Chester Gould **W:** Chester Gould
113 ❑ Jul 1957 Cover: 0.10 **NM** value: **26.00**
A: Chester Gould **W:** Chester Gould
114 ❑ Aug 1957 Cover: 0.10 **NM** value: **26.00**
A: Chester Gould **W:** Chester Gould
115 ❑ Sep 1957 Cover: 0.10 **NM** value: **26.00**
A: Chester Gould **W:** Chester Gould
116 ❑ Oct 1957 Cover: 0.10 **NM** value: **26.00**
A: Chester Gould **W:** Chester Gould
117 ❑ Nov 1957 Cover: 0.10 **NM** value: **26.00**
A: Chester Gould **W:** Chester Gould
118 ❑ Dec 1957 Cover: 0.10 **NM** value: **26.00**
A: Chester Gould **W:** Chester Gould
119 ❑ Jan 1957 Cover: 0.10 **NM** value: **26.00**
A: Chester Gould **W:** Chester Gould
120 ❑ Feb 1957 Cover: 0.10 **NM** value: **26.00**
Mumbles Quartette **A:** Chester Gould **W:** Chester Gould
121 ❑ Mar 1957 Cover: 0.10 **NM** value: **24.00**
A: Chester Gould **W:** Chester Gould
122 ❑ Apr 1957 Cover: 0.10 **NM** value: **24.00**
A: Chester Gould **W:** Chester Gould
123 ❑ May 1957 Cover: 0.10 **NM** value: **24.00**
A: Chester Gould **W:** Chester Gould
124 ❑ Jun 1957 Cover: 0.10 **NM** value: **24.00**
A: Chester Gould **W:** Chester Gould
125 ❑ Jul 1957 Cover: 0.10 **NM** value: **24.00**
A: Chester Gould **W:** Chester Gould
126 ❑ Aug 1957 Cover: 0.10 **NM** value: **24.00**
A: Chester Gould **W:** Chester Gould
127 ❑ Sep 1957 Cover: 0.10 **NM** value: **24.00**
A: Chester Gould **W:** Chester Gould
128 ❑ Oct 1957 Cover: 0.10 **NM** value: **24.00**
The Case Against the Juvenile Delinquent **A:** Chester Gould **W:** Chester Gould
129 ❑ Nov 1957 Cover: 0.10 **NM** value: **24.00**
A: Chester Gould **W:** Chester Gould
130 ❑ Dec 1957 Cover: 0.10 **NM** value: **24.00**
A: Chester Gould **W:** Chester Gould
131 ❑ Feb 1959 Cover: 0.10 **NM** value: **22.00**
• **CGC:** 1 graded, best 9.4
The Strange Case of Flattop's Conscience **A:** Chester Gould **W:** Chester Gould
132 ❑ Mar 1959 Cover: 0.10 **NM** value: **22.00**
• **CGC:** 2 graded, best 9.0
A: Chester Gould **W:** Chester Gould
133 ❑ 1959 Cover: 0.10 **NM** value: **22.00**
A: Chester Gould **W:** Chester Gould
134 ❑ 1959 Cover: 0.10 **NM** value: **22.00**
A: Chester Gould **W:** Chester Gould
135 ❑ 1959 Cover: 0.10 **NM** value: **22.00**
A: Chester Gould **W:** Chester Gould
136 ❑ Oct 1959 Cover: 0.10 **NM** value: **22.00**
• **CGC:** 1 graded, best 9.2
The Mystery of the Iron Room **A:** Chester Gould **W:** Chester Gould
137 ❑ Dec 1959 Cover: 0.10 **NM** value: **22.00**
• **CGC:** 1 graded, best 9.0
Dick Tracy: The Law Versus Dick Tracy! **A:** Chester Gould **W:** Chester Gould
138 ❑ Feb 1960 Cover: 0.10 **NM** value: **22.00**
A: Chester Gould **W:** Chester Gould
139 ❑ Apr 1960 Cover: 0.10 **NM** value: **22.00**
A: Chester Gould **W:** Chester Gould
140 ❑ Jun 1960 Cover: 0.10 **NM** value: **22.00**
A: Chester Gould **W:** Chester Gould
141 ❑ Aug 1960 Cover: 0.10 **NM** value: **28.00**
• Giant-size. **A:** Chester Gould **W:** Chester Gould
142 ❑ Oct 1960 Cover: 0.10 **NM** value: **28.00**
• Giant-size. **A:** Chester Gould **W:** Chester Gould
143 ❑ Dec 1960 Cover: 0.10 **NM** value: **28.00**
• Giant-size. **A:** Chester Gould **W:** Chester Gould
144 ❑ Feb 1961 Cover: 0.10 **NM** value: **28.00**
• Giant-size. **A:** Chester Gould **W:** Chester Gould
145 ❑ Apr 1961 Cover: 0.10 **NM** value: **28.00**
• Giant-size. final issue. **A:** Chester Gould **W:** Chester Gould
GIVE 1 ❑ **NM** value: **15.00**
• ESSO Giveaway. The Case Of The Purloined Sirloin **A:** Chester Gould **W:** Chester Gould

CGC-graded: Multiply prices above by **33 for 9.9 M • 16 for 9.8 NM/M • 7 for 9.6 NM+ • 5 for 9.4 NM • 2.5 for 9.2 NM- • 1.5 for 9.0 VF/NM**

DICK TRACY CRIMEBUSTER — Avalon

Police detective Dick Tracy is one of the classic newspaper strips, originating in a violent urban setting of the 1930s and continuing into the next century. Dick Tracy's world, consisting of weird villains and bizarre, often brutal situations, is the constant that defines the strip. Creator Chester Gould, set the formula and the writers and artists that succeeded him follow it faithfully.

Partnered with artist, Dick Locher, who mimicked Gould's distinctive style, Max Allen Collins, co-creator of Ms. Tree, assumed the writing chores for the strip in the 1980s. This title from Avalon collected those strips for reprinting in a comic book format.

1 ❑ Cover: 2.95 **NM** value: **Cover or less**
A: Dick Locher; Max Allan Collins **W:** Dick Locher; Max Allan Collins
2 ❑ Cover: 2.95 **NM** value: **Cover or less**
3 ❑ Cover: 2.95 **NM** value: **Cover or less**
4 ❑ Cover: 2.95 **NM** value: **Cover or less**

DICK TRACY DETECTIVE — Avalon

1 ❑ Cover: 2.95 **NM** value: **Cover or less**
A: Chester Gould **W:** Chester Gould
2 ❑ Cover: 2.95 **NM** value: **Cover or less**
📖 Sleet Before the Storm **A:** Chester Gould **W:** Chester Gould
3 ❑ Cover: 2.95 **NM** value: **Cover or less**
📖 Is Ketchum Dead **A:** Chester Gould **W:** Chester Gould
4 ❑ Cover: 2.95 **NM** value: **Cover or less**
A: Chester Gould **W:** Chester Gould

DICK TRACY (DISNEY) — Disney

1 ❑ Cover: 2.95 **NM** value: **Cover or less**
📖 Big City Blues • newsstand format **A:** Kyle Baker **W:** John Moore
1/DM ❑ Cover: 4.95 **NM** value: **Cover or less**
Circ: CapCity orders: **10,675**
• prestige format. 📖 Big City Blues
2 ❑ Cover: 2.95 **NM** value: **Cover or less**
📖 vs. the Underworld • newsstand format
2/DM ❑ Cover: 5.95 **NM** value: **Cover or less**
Circ: CapCity orders: **7,275**
• prestige format. 📖 vs. the Underworld **A:** Kyle Baker **W:** John Moore
3 ❑ Cover: 2.95 **NM** value: **Cover or less**
📖 Movie Adaptation • newsstand format
3/DM ❑ Cover: 5.95 **NM** value: **Cover or less**
Circ: CapCity orders: **7,050**
• prestige format.
Bk 1 ❑ Sep 1990 Cover: 12.95 **NM** value: **Cover or less**
• prestige format. 📖 Big City Blues • The Trilogy collection **A:** Kyle Baker **W:** John Moore

DICK TRACY MONTHLY (BLACKTHORNE) — Blackthorne

1 ❑ May 1986 Cover: 2.00 **NM** value: **Cover or less**
2 ❑ Jun 1986 Cover: 2.00 **NM** value: **Cover or less**
3 ❑ Jul 1986 Cover: 2.00 **NM** value: **Cover or less**
4 ❑ Aug 1986 Cover: 2.00 **NM** value: **Cover or less**
5 ❑ Sep 1986 Cover: 2.00 **NM** value: **Cover or less**
6 ❑ Oct 1986 Cover: 2.00 **NM** value: **Cover or less**
7 ❑ Nov 1986 Cover: 2.00 **NM** value: **Cover or less**
8 ❑ Dec 1986 Cover: 2.00 **NM** value: **Cover or less**
9 ❑ Jan 1987 Cover: 2.00 **NM** value: **Cover or less**
10 ❑ Feb 1987 Cover: 2.00 **NM** value: **Cover or less**
11 ❑ Mar 1987 Cover: 2.00 **NM** value: **Cover or less**
12 ❑ Apr 1987 Cover: 2.00 **NM** value: **Cover or less**
• no month in indicia
13 ❑ May 1987 Cover: 2.00 **NM** value: **Cover or less**
14 ❑ Jun 1987 Cover: 2.00 **NM** value: **Cover or less**
15 ❑ Jul 1987 Cover: 2.00 **NM** value: **Cover or less**
16 ❑ 1988 Cover: 2.00 **NM** value: **Cover or less**
17 ❑ 1988 Cover: 2.00 **NM** value: **Cover or less**
18 ❑ 1988 Cover: 2.00 **NM** value: **Cover or less**
19 ❑ 1988 Cover: 2.00 **NM** value: **Cover or less**
20 ❑ 1988 Cover: 2.00 **NM** value: **Cover or less**
21 ❑ 1988 Cover: 2.00 **NM** value: **Cover or less**
22 ❑ 1988 Cover: 2.00 **NM** value: **Cover or less**
23 ❑ 1988 Cover: 2.00 **NM** value: **Cover or less**
24 ❑ 1988 Cover: 2.00 **NM** value: **Cover or less**
25 ❑ 1988 Cover: 2.00 **NM** value: **Cover or less**
• Series continues as Dick Tracy Weekly

DICK TRACY MONTHLY (DELL) — Dell

1 ❑ Jan 1948 Cover: 0.10 **NM** value: **350.00**
• **CGC:** 1 graded, best 3.0
2 ❑ Feb 1948 Cover: 0.10 **NM** value: **250.00**
3 ❑ Mar 1948 Cover: 0.10 **NM** value: **250.00**
4 ❑ Apr 1948 Cover: 0.10 **NM** value: **250.00**
5 ❑ May 1948 Cover: 0.10 **NM** value: **250.00**
6 ❑ Jun 1948 Cover: 0.10 **NM** value: **250.00**
7 ❑ Jul 1948 Cover: 0.10 **NM** value: **250.00**
8 ❑ Aug 1948 Cover: 0.10 **NM** value: **250.00**
9 ❑ Sep 1948 Cover: 0.10 **NM** value: **250.00**
10 ❑ Oct 1948 Cover: 0.10 **NM** value: **250.00**
11 ❑ Nov 1948 Cover: 0.10 **NM** value: **150.00**
12 ❑ Dec 1948 Cover: 0.10 **NM** value: **150.00**
13 ❑ Jan 1949 Cover: 0.10 **NM** value: **150.00**
14 ❑ Feb 1949 Cover: 0.10 **NM** value: **150.00**
• **CGC:** 1 graded, best 7.5
15 ❑ Mar 1949 Cover: 0.10 **NM** value: **150.00**
16 ❑ Apr 1949 Cover: 0.10 **NM** value: **150.00**
17 ❑ May 1949 Cover: 0.10 **NM** value: **150.00**
18 ❑ Jun 1949 Cover: 0.10 **NM** value: **150.00**
19 ❑ Jul 1949 Cover: 0.10 **NM** value: **150.00**
20 ❑ Aug 1949 Cover: 0.10 **NM** value: **150.00**
21 ❑ Sep 1949 Cover: 0.10 **NM** value: **150.00**
• **CGC:** 1 graded, best 7.5
22 ❑ Oct 1949 Cover: 0.10 **NM** value: **150.00**
23 ❑ Nov 1949 Cover: 0.10 **NM** value: **150.00**
24 ❑ Dec 1949 Cover: 0.10 **NM** value: **150.00**
• Series continues as Dick Tracy Comics Monthly, from Harvey

DICK TRACY SPECIAL — Blackthorne

1 ❑ Jan 1988 Cover: 2.95 **NM** value: **Cover or less**
★ Origin of Tracy.
2 ❑ Mar 1988 Cover: 2.95 **NM** value: **Cover or less**
★ Origin of Tracy.
3 ❑ May 1988 Cover: 2.95 **NM** value: **Cover or less**
★ Origin of Tracy.

DICK TRACY: THE EARLY YEARS — Blackthorne

1 ❑ Aug 1987 Cover: 6.95 **NM** value: **Cover or less**
2 ❑ Oct 1987 Cover: 6.95 **NM** value: **Cover or less**
3 ❑ Apr 1988 Cover: 6.95 **NM** value: **Cover or less**
4 ❑ Cover: 2.95 **NM** value: **Cover or less**

DICK TRACY UNPRINTED STORIES — Blackthorne

1 ❑ Sep 1987 Cover: 2.95 **NM** value: **Cover or less**
A: Chester Gould **W:** Chester Gould
2 ❑ Nov 1987 Cover: 2.95 **NM** value: **Cover or less**
A: Chester Gould **W:** Chester Gould
3 ❑ Jan 1988 Cover: 2.95 **NM** value: **Cover or less**
A: Chester Gould **W:** Chester Gould
4 ❑ Jun 1988 Cover: 4.95 **NM** value: **Cover or less**
A: Chester Gould **W:** Chester Gould ★ Death of Flattop Jr..

DICK TRACY WEEKLY — Blackthorne

26 ❑ Jan 1988 Cover: 2.00 **NM** value: **Cover or less**
27 ❑ Jan 1988 Cover: 2.00 **NM** value: **Cover or less**
28 ❑ Jan 1988 Cover: 2.00 **NM** value: **Cover or less**
29 ❑ Jan 1988 Cover: 2.00 **NM** value: **Cover or less**
30 ❑ Feb 1988 Cover: 2.00 **NM** value: **Cover or less**
31 ❑ Feb 1988 Cover: 2.00 **NM** value: **Cover or less**
32 ❑ Feb 1988 Cover: 2.00 **NM** value: **Cover or less**
33 ❑ Feb 1988 Cover: 2.00 **NM** value: **Cover or less**
34 ❑ Mar 1988 Cover: 2.00 **NM** value: **Cover or less**
35 ❑ Mar 1988 Cover: 2.00 **NM** value: **Cover or less**
36 ❑ Mar 1988 Cover: 2.00 **NM** value: **Cover or less**
37 ❑ Mar 1988 Cover: 2.00 **NM** value: **Cover or less**
38 ❑ Jun 1988 Cover: 2.00 **NM** value: **Cover or less**
39 ❑ Jun 1988 Cover: 2.00 **NM** value: **Cover or less**
40 ❑ Jun 1988 Cover: 2.00 **NM** value: **Cover or less**
41 ❑ Jun 1988 Cover: 2.00 **NM** value: **Cover or less**
42 ❑ Jul 1988 Cover: 2.00 **NM** value: **Cover or less**
43 ❑ Jul 1988 Cover: 2.00 **NM** value: **Cover or less**
44 ❑ Jul 1988 Cover: 2.00 **NM** value: **Cover or less**
45 ❑ Jul 1988 Cover: 2.00 **NM** value: **Cover or less**
46 ❑ Aug 1988 Cover: 2.00 **NM** value: **Cover or less**
47 ❑ Aug 1988 Cover: 2.00 **NM** value: **Cover or less**
48 ❑ Aug 1988 Cover: 2.00 **NM** value: **Cover or less**
49 ❑ Aug 1988 Cover: 2.00 **NM** value: **Cover or less**
50 ❑ Sep 1988 Cover: 2.00 **NM** value: **Cover or less**
51 ❑ Sep 1988 Cover: 2.00 **NM** value: **Cover or less**
52 ❑ Sep 1988 Cover: 2.00 **NM** value: **Cover or less**
53 ❑ Sep 1988 Cover: 2.00 **NM** value: **Cover or less**
54 ❑ Oct 1988 Cover: 2.00 **NM** value: **Cover or less**
55 ❑ Oct 1988 Cover: 2.00 **NM** value: **Cover or less**
56 ❑ Oct 1988 Cover: 2.00 **NM** value: **Cover or less**
57 ❑ Oct 1988 Cover: 2.00 **NM** value: **Cover or less**
58 ❑ Oct 1988 Cover: 2.00 **NM** value: **Cover or less**
59 ❑ Oct 1988 Cover: 2.00 **NM** value: **Cover or less**
60 ❑ Nov 1988 Cover: 2.00 **NM** value: **Cover or less**
61 ❑ Nov 1988 Cover: 2.00 **NM** value: **Cover or less**
62 ❑ Nov 1988 Cover: 2.00 **NM** value: **Cover or less**
63 ❑ Nov 1988 Cover: 2.00 **NM** value: **Cover or less**
64 ❑ Nov 1988 Cover: 2.00 **NM** value: **Cover or less**
65 ❑ Nov 1988 Cover: 2.00 **NM** value: **Cover or less**
66 ❑ Dec 1988 Cover: 2.00 **NM** value: **Cover or less**
67 ❑ Dec 1988 Cover: 2.00 **NM** value: **Cover or less**
68 ❑ Dec 1988 Cover: 2.00 **NM** value: **Cover or less**
69 ❑ Dec 1988 Cover: 2.00 **NM** value: **Cover or less**
70 ❑ Jan 1989 Cover: 2.00 **NM** value: **Cover or less**
71 ❑ Jan 1989 Cover: 2.00 **NM** value: **Cover or less**
72 ❑ Jan 1989 Cover: 2.00 **NM** value: **Cover or less**
73 ❑ Jan 1989 Cover: 2.00 **NM** value: **Cover or less**
74 ❑ Feb 1989 Cover: 2.00 **NM** value: **Cover or less**
75 ❑ Feb 1989 Cover: 2.00 **NM** value: **Cover or less**
76 ❑ Feb 1989 Cover: 2.00 **NM** value: **Cover or less**
77 ❑ Feb 1989 Cover: 2.00 **NM** value: **Cover or less**
78 ❑ Mar 1989 Cover: 2.00 **NM** value: **Cover or less**
79 ❑ Mar 1989 Cover: 2.00 **NM** value: **Cover or less**
80 ❑ Mar 1989 Cover: 2.00 **NM** value: **Cover or less**
81 ❑ Mar 1989 Cover: 2.00 **NM** value: **Cover or less**
82 ❑ Apr 1989 Cover: 2.00 **NM** value: **Cover or less**
83 ❑ Apr 1989 Cover: 2.00 **NM** value: **Cover or less**
84 ❑ Apr 1989 Cover: 2.00 **NM** value: **Cover or less**
85 ❑ Apr 1989 Cover: 2.00 **NM** value: **Cover or less**
86 ❑ May 1989 Cover: 2.00 **NM** value: **Cover or less**
87 ❑ May 1989 Cover: 2.00 **NM** value: **Cover or less**
88 ❑ May 1989 Cover: 2.00 **NM** value: **Cover or less**
89 ❑ May 1989 Cover: 2.00 **NM** value: **Cover or less**
90 ❑ Jun 1989 Cover: 2.00 **NM** value: **Cover or less**
91 ❑ Jun 1989 Cover: 2.00 **NM** value: **Cover or less**
92 ❑ Jun 1989 Cover: 2.00 **NM** value: **Cover or less**
93 ❑ Jun 1989 Cover: 2.00 **NM** value: **Cover or less**
94 ❑ Aug 1989 Cover: 2.00 **NM** value: **Cover or less**
95 ❑ Aug 1989 Cover: 2.00 **NM** value: **Cover or less**
96 ❑ Aug 1989 Cover: 2.00 **NM** value: **Cover or less**
97 ❑ Aug 1989 Cover: 2.00 **NM** value: **Cover or less**
★ 1st Appearance of Moon Maid.
98 ❑ Sep 1989 Cover: 2.00 **NM** value: **Cover or less**
99 ❑ Sep 1989 Cover: 2.00 **NM** value: **Cover or less**

DICK WAD — Slave Labor

All issues are adults only.
1 ❑ Sep 1993, b&w Cover: 2.50 **NM** value: **Cover or less**
A: Evan Dorkin

DICK WINGATE OF THE UNITED STATES NAVY — Toby

1 ❑ ca. 1953 **NM** value: **50.00**
• **CGC:** 1 graded, best 5.5

DIEBOLD — Silent Partners

1 ❑ 1996b&w Cover: 2.95 **NM** value: **Cover or less**
2 ❑ 1996b&w Cover: 2.95 **NM** value: **Cover or less**

DIE-CUT — Marvel

1 ❑ Nov 1993 Cover: 2.50 **NM** value: **Cover or less**
Circ: CapCity orders: **20,500**
diecut cover. 📖 Beastswarm: The Howling **A:** Bernard Custodio **W:** Glenn Dakin
2 ❑ Dec 1993 Cover: 1.75 **NM** value: **Cover or less**
Circ: CapCity orders: **8,350**
A: Bernard Custodio **W:** Glenn Dakin
3 ❑ Jan 1994 Cover: 1.75 **NM** value: **Cover or less**
Circ: CapCity orders: **6,850**
A: Bernard Custodio **W:** Glenn Dakin
4 ❑ Feb 1994 Cover: 1.75 **NM** value: **Cover or less**
Circ: CapCity orders: **4,750**
A: Bernard Custodio **W:** Glenn Dakin

DIE-CUT VS. G-FORCE — Marvel

1 ❑ Nov 1993 Cover: 2.75 **NM** value: **Cover or less**
Holo-Grafx cover. 📖 Grave Incisions **A:** John Royle **W:** John Freeman
2 ❑ Dec 1993 Cover: 2.75 **NM** value: **Cover or less**
Circ: CapCity orders: **8,300**
foil cover. **A:** John Royle **W:** John Freeman

DIESEL — Antarctic

1 ❑ Apr 1997 Cover: 2.95 **NM** value: **Cover or less**
Circ: Diamd. preorders: **5,575**
📖 Master of Dragon **A:** Joe Weltjens **W:** Joe Weltjens

DIFFERENT BEAT COMICS — Fantagraphics

1 ❑ b&w Cover: 3.50 **NM** value: **Cover or less**
📖 Kids These Days; Me & Her; In God We Trust; Say, Man…; The Devil Made Her Do It; Something That Happened To Tom Reynolds; Scratchy Screwballs; Let The Punishment Fit The Crime; Frank; The He That Walks; The Rose Colored Man; Milt Goes To Work **A:** Dan Clowes; J.R. Williams; Peter Bagge; Robert Crumb; Jim Woodring; Gilbert Hernandez; Jaime Hernandez; Roberta Gregory; Peter Kuper; Pat Moriarty; Terry Laban; Dame Darcy; Jeremy Eaton **W:** Dan Clowes; J.R. Williams; Peter Bagge; Robert Crumb; Jim Woodring; Gilbert Hernandez; Jaime Hernandez; Roberta Gregory; Peter Kuper; Pat Moriarty; Terry Laban; Dame Darcy; Jeremy Eaton

DIGGERS, THE — C&T

1 ❑ b&w Cover: 1.50 **NM** value: **Cover or less**

DIGIMON DIGITAL MONSTERS — Dark Horse

1 ❑ May 2000 Cover: 2.95 **NM** value: **Cover or less**
Circ: Diamd. preorders: **17,354**
A: Daniel Hdr
2 ❑ May 2000 Cover: 2.95 **NM** value: **Cover or less**
Circ: Diamd. preorders: **15,435**
A: Andy Kuhn
3 ❑ May 2000 Cover: 2.95 **NM** value: **Cover or less**
Circ: Diamd. preorders: **10,915**
A: Nigel Dobbyn
4 ❑ May 2000 Cover: 2.95 **NM** value: **Cover or less**
Circ: Diamd. preorders: **10,745**
A: Ryan Hill
5 ❑ Aug 2000 Cover: 2.95 **NM** value: **Cover or less**
Circ: Diamd. preorders: **7,120**
A: Daniel Hdr
6 ❑ Sep 2000 Cover: 2.95 **NM** value: **Cover or less**
Circ: Diamd. preorders: **7,074**
A: Andy Kuhn
7 ❑ Sep 2000 Cover: 2.95 **NM** value: **Cover or less**
Circ: Diamd. preorders: **5,610**
A: Nigel Dobbyn
8 ❑ Sep 2000 Cover: 2.95 **NM** value: **Cover or less**
Circ: Diamd. preorders: **5,600**
A: Nigel Dobbyn
9 ❑ Sep 2000 Cover: 2.99 **NM** value: **Cover or less**
Circ: Diamd. preorders: **4,992**
A: Daniel Hdr
10 ❑ Oct 2000 Cover: 2.99 **NM** value: **Cover or less**
Circ: Diamd. preorders: **4,983**
A: Andy Kuhn
11 ❑ Nov 2000 Cover: 2.99 **NM** value: **Cover or less**
Circ: Diamd. preorders: **4,282**
A: Nigel Dobbyn
12 ❑ Nov 2000 Cover: 2.99 **NM** value: **Cover or less**
Circ: Diamd. preorders: **4,268**
A: Nigel Dobbyn

DIGITAL DRAGON — Peregrine Entertainment

1 ❑ Jan 1999, b&w Cover: 2.95 **NM** value: **Cover or less**
2 ❑ Apr 1999, b&w Cover: 2.95 **NM** value: **Cover or less**

Other grades: Multiply prices above by **1.5 for Mint • 2/3 for Very Fine • 1/3 for Fine • 1/5 for Very Good • 1/8 for Good**

DIGITEK — Marvel

1 ❑ Dec 1992 Cover: 1.95 **NM** value: **Cover or less**
Circ: CapCity orders: **24,400**
A Shock to the System, Part 1 **A:** Dermot Power **W:** Andy Lanning; John Tomlinson
2 ❑ Jan 1993 Cover: 1.95 **NM** value: **Cover or less**
Circ: CapCity orders: **16,200**
A Shock to the System, Part 2 **A:** Dermot Power **W:** Andy Lanning; John Tomlinson
3 ❑ Feb 1993 Cover: 2.25 **NM** value: **Cover or less**
Circ: CapCity orders: **14,200**
A Shock to the System, Part 3 **A:** Dermot Power **W:** Andy Lanning; John Tomlinson
4 ❑ Mar 1993 Cover: 2.25 **NM** value: **Cover or less**
Circ: CapCity orders: **12,700**
A Shock to the System, Part 4 **A:** Dermot Power **W:** Andy Lanning; John Tomlinson

DIK SKYCAP — Rip Off

1 ❑ Dec 1991, b&w Cover: 2.50 **NM** value: **Cover or less**
2 ❑ May 1992, b&w Cover: 2.50 **NM** value: **Cover or less**

DILEMMA PRESENTS — Dilemma

1 ❑ Oct 1994, b&w Cover: 2.50 **NM** value: **Cover or less**
2 ❑ b&w Cover: 2.50 **NM** value: **Cover or less**
• Flip-book.
3 ❑ Apr 1995, b&w Cover: 2.50 **NM** value: **Cover or less**
• Flip-book.
4 ❑ b&w Cover: 2.50 **NM** value: **Cover or less**
• Flip-book.

DILLY — Lev Gleason

1 ❑ May 1953 Cover: 0.10 **NM** value: **20.00**
• **CGC:** 1 graded, best 5.5
2 ❑ Jul 1953 Cover: 0.10 **NM** value: **15.00**
3 ❑ Sep 1953 Cover: 0.10 **NM** value: **15.00**

DILTON'S STRANGE SCIENCE — Archie

1 ❑ May 1989 Cover: 0.75 **NM** value: **2.00**
2 ❑ Aug 1989 Cover: 0.75 **NM** value: **1.50**
3 ❑ Nov 1989 Cover: 0.75 **NM** value: **1.50**
4 ❑ Feb 1990 Cover: 0.75 **NM** value: **1.50**
5 ❑ May 1990 Cover: 0.75 **NM** value: **1.50**

DIME COMICS — Newsbook

1 ❑ ca. 1945 Cover: 0.10 **NM** value: **375.00**
• **CGC:** 1 graded, best 8.0

DIMENSION 5 — Edge

All issues are adults only.
1 ❑ Oct 1995, b&w Cover: 3.95 **NM** value: **Cover or less**

DIMENSION X — Karl Art

This large format title brings readers the sort of high quality, end-of-the-world science-fiction that has seldom been seen since the 1950s. In many ways, it's reminiscent of such classic titles as Weird Fantasy and Weird Science.

The series starts off with "The Blood of the Universe," in which a doctor treats a patient who has been experiencing mental flashes from other worlds. A childhood car accident seems to have unlocked some sort of mental door in the man, exposing his mind to another realm of existence. As the doctor continues her examination, she finds her own mind affected in a similar manner. When she finally learns the terrible secret at the heart of the universe, she is driven to commit murder in order to protect the sanity of every person on Earth.

1 ❑ b&w Cover: 3.50 **NM** value: **Cover or less**

DIMENSION Z — Pyramid

1 ❑ Cover: 1.70 **NM** value: **2.00**
2 ❑ Cover: 1.70 **NM** value: **2.00**

DIMM COMICS PRESENTS — Dimm

Ash 0❑ Jan 1996, b&w **NM** value: **1.00**
• ashcan promotional comic
Ash 1❑ May 1996, b&w **NM** value: **1.00**
• ashcan promotional comic

DIM-WITTED DARRYL — Slave Labor

Written and illustrated by Michael Bresnahan, this black-and-white mature-readers funnybook consists of short stories about Darryl, the "world's dumbest mammal." This 28-year-old fourth-grader has plenty of misadventures, and the series delivers a boatload of dim-witted hijinks and slapstick tomfoolery.

Much of the humor centers on Darryl's inability to understand adult subject matter such as sex and death. Readers can peer in on Darryl's home life and see how his friends and neighbors react to his stupidity. The results are occasionally very funny.

1 ❑ Jun 1998, b&w Cover: 2.95 **NM** value: **Cover or less**
Savory Meat; A Colorful World; Schizophrenic Lenny: They are Here! **A:** Michael Bresnahan **W:** Michael Bresnahan
2 ❑ Cover: 2.95 **NM** value: **Cover or less**
A: Michael Bresnahan **W:** Michael Bresnahan
3 ❑ Cover: 2.95 **NM** value: **Cover or less**
A: Michael Bresnahan **W:** Michael Bresnahan

DING DONG — Compix

1 ❑ Jul 1946 Cover: 0.10 **NM** value: **250.00**
2 ❑ Sep 1946 Cover: 0.10 **NM** value: **150.00**
3 ❑ Nov 1946 Cover: 0.10 **NM** value: **100.00**
4 ❑ Jan 1947 Cover: 0.10 **NM** value: **100.00**
5 ❑ Mar 1947 Cover: 0.10 **NM** value: **100.00**

DINGLEDORFS, THE — Skylight

1 ❑ b&w Cover: 2.75 **NM** value: **Cover or less**

DINKY DUCK — St. John

1 ❑ 1951 Cover: 0.10 **NM** value: **100.00**
2 ❑ 1952 Cover: 0.10 **NM** value: **80.00**
3 ❑ 1952 Cover: 0.10 **NM** value: **50.00**
4 ❑ 1952 Cover: 0.10 **NM** value: **50.00**
5 ❑ 1953 Cover: 0.10 **NM** value: **50.00**
6 ❑ 1953 Cover: 0.10 **NM** value: **30.00**
7 ❑ 1953 Cover: 0.10 **NM** value: **30.00**
8 ❑ 1954 Cover: 0.10 **NM** value: **30.00**
9 ❑ 1954 Cover: 0.10 **NM** value: **20.00**
10 ❑ 1954 Cover: 0.10 **NM** value: **20.00**
11 ❑ Nov 1954 Cover: 0.10 **NM** value: **20.00**
12 ❑ Jan 1955 Cover: 0.10 **NM** value: **20.00**
13 ❑ Mar 1955 Cover: 0.10 **NM** value: **15.00**
14 ❑ May 1955 Cover: 0.10 **NM** value: **15.00**
15 ❑ Jul 1955 Cover: 0.10 **NM** value: **15.00**
16 ❑ Sep 1955 Cover: 0.10 **NM** value: **10.00**
17 ❑ ca. 1957 Cover: 0.10 **NM** value: **10.00**
18 ❑ ca. 1957 Cover: 0.10 **NM** value: **10.00**
19 ❑ ca. 1958 Cover: 0.10 **NM** value: **10.00**

DINKY ON THE ROAD — Blind Bat Press

1 ❑ Jun 1994, b&w Cover: 1.95 **NM** value: **Cover or less**

DINO ISLAND — Mirage

1 ❑ Feb 1993 Cover: 2.75 **NM** value: **Cover or less**
Circ: CapCity orders: **4,025**
covers form diptych.
2 ❑ Mar 1993 Cover: 2.75 **NM** value: **Cover or less**
Circ: CapCity orders: **2,800**
covers form diptych. **A:** Jim Lawson **W:** Jim Lawson

DINO-RIDERS — Marvel

1 ❑ Mar 1989 Cover: 1.00 **NM** value: **1.50**
Circ: CapCity orders: **10,200**
2 ❑ Apr 1989 Cover: 1.00 **NM** value: **1.50**
Circ: CapCity orders: **5,400**
3 ❑ May 1989 Cover: 1.00 **NM** value: **1.50**
Circ: CapCity orders: **3,800**

DINOSAUR BOP — Monster

1 ❑ b&w Cover: 2.50 **NM** value: **Cover or less**
2 ❑ b&w Cover: 2.50 **NM** value: **Cover or less**

DINOSAUR ISLAND — Monster

1 ❑ b&w Cover: 2.25 **NM** value: **2.50**

DINOSAUR MANSION — Edge

1 ❑ b&w Cover: 2.95 **NM** value: **Cover or less**
• no indicia

DINOSAUR REX — Upshot

1 ❑ full color Cover: 2.00 **NM** value: **Cover or less**
Circ: CapCity orders: **4,600**
2 ❑ b&w Cover: 2.00 **NM** value: **Cover or less**
Circ: CapCity orders: **3,000**
3 ❑ b&w Cover: 2.00 **NM** value: **Cover or less**
Circ: CapCity orders: **3,100**

DINOSAURS — Hollywood

1 ❑ Cover: 2.95 **NM** value: **3.00**
Circ: CapCity orders: **4,700**
• TV based
2 ❑ Cover: 2.95 **NM** value: **3.00**
Circ: CapCity orders: **3,050**
• TV based

DINOSAURS ATTACK! — Eclipse

1 ❑ Cover: 3.95 **NM** value: **Cover or less**
Circ: CapCity orders: **5,500**
The Timescan Disaster • trading cards **A:** Herb Trimpe **W:** Gary Gerani
2 ❑ Cover: 3.95 **NM** value: **Cover or less**
Circ: CapCity orders: **4,225**
3 ❑ Cover: 3.95 **NM** value: **Cover or less**

DINOSAURS, A CELEBRATION — Marvel / Epic

1 ❑ ca. 1992 Cover: 4.95 **NM** value: **Cover or less**
• Horns and Heavy Armor
2 ❑ ca. 1992 Cover: 4.95 **NM** value: **Cover or less**
• Bone heads and Duck-bills
3 ❑ ca. 1992 Cover: 4.95 **NM** value: **Cover or less**
Lizard-Hipped and Bird Hipped Dinosaurs; The Dinosaur Family Tree; Order: Oviraptosauria; Order: Ornithomimosauria; Order: Prosauropoda; Order: Sauropoda; Dinosaur Neighbors: Crocodilians; The Jurassic Period • Egg stealers and Earth shakers **A:** Anthony Williams; Liam Sharp; Richard Dolan; Gary Leach; Andrew Currie; Dougie Braithwaite; Lesley Dalton; Steve White; Una Fricker; Chris Foss **W:** Steve White; Euan Peters; Mike Howgate; Nicholas J. Vince
4 ❑ ca. 1992 Cover: 4.95 **NM** value: **Cover or less**
• Terrible Claws and Tyrants

DINOSAURS FOR HIRE: DINOSAURS RULE! — Eternity

1 ❑ Cover: 5.95 **NM** value: **Cover or less**
• Dinosaurs Rule!

DINOSAURS FOR HIRE (ETERNITY) — Eternity

Prevented from running a strip called Elvis for Hire, featuring clones of Elvis working for the FBI, Tom Mason switched the central characters to dinosaurs, and publication ensued just in time to catch the crest of the Teenage Mutant Ninja Turtles craze. This is one of the better cash-ins, with a strong sense of irony and more than a sly poke at the comics industry. Archie (a Tyrannosaurus Rex), Lorenzo (a Triceratops), Reese (a Stegosaurus) and Cyrano (a Pterodactyl) are U.S. government agents loaded with guns and gags and out to fight criminals. The original black-and-white series is a little shaky in places, relying on too many knock-back jokes from TMNT and weak art, but the run really kicks in with the second series.

1 ❑ Mar 1988, b&w Cover: 1.95 **NM** value: **2.00**
Rolling Thunder Lizards **A:** Bryon Carson **W:** Tom Mason
1/3D❑ Cover: 2.95 **NM** value: **Cover or less**
• 3-D.
1-2 ❑ Mar 1988 Cover: 1.95 **NM** value: **Cover or less**
2 ❑ Jun 1988 Cover: 1.95 **NM** value: **Cover or less**
3 ❑ Cover: 1.95 **NM** value: **Cover or less**
4 ❑ Cover: 1.95 **NM** value: **Cover or less**
5 ❑ Cover: 1.95 **NM** value: **Cover or less**
6 ❑ Cover: 1.95 **NM** value: **Cover or less**
7 ❑ Cover: 1.95 **NM** value: **Cover or less**
8 ❑ Cover: 1.95 **NM** value: **Cover or less**
9 ❑ Cover: 1.95 **NM** value: **Cover or less**

DINOSAURS FOR HIRE FALL CLASSIC — Eternity

1 ❑ Nov 1988, b&w Cover: 2.25 **NM** value: **Cover or less**
• Fall Classic;Elvis **A:** Nigel Tully **W:** Tom Mason

DINOSAURS FOR HIRE: GUNS 'N' LIZARDS — Eternity

1 ❑ Cover: 5.95 **NM** value: **Cover or less**
• Guns 'n' Lizards

DINOSAURS FOR HIRE (MALIBU) — Malibu

1 ❑ Feb 1993 Cover: 1.95 **NM** value: **Cover or less**
Circ: CapCity orders: **17,750**
2 ❑ Mar 1993 Cover: 1.95 **NM** value: **Cover or less**
Circ: CapCity orders: **7,675**
3 ❑ Apr 1993 Cover: 1.95 **NM** value: **Cover or less**
Circ: CapCity orders: **10,000**
★ Appearance of Ex-Mutants.
4 ❑ May 1993 Cover: 1.95 **NM** value: **Cover or less**
Circ: CapCity orders: **10,725**
5 ❑ Jun 1993 Cover: 2.50 **NM** value: **Cover or less**
Circ: CapCity orders: **8,500**
★ Versus Poacher.
6 ❑ Jul 1993 Cover: 2.50 **NM** value: **Cover or less**
Circ: CapCity orders: **8,250**
Jurassic Park parody cover.
7 ❑ Aug 1993 Cover: 2.50 **NM** value: **Cover or less**
Circ: CapCity orders: **7,700**
★ Versus Turret, Hunter of Dinosaurs.
8 ❑ Sep 1993 Cover: 2.50 **NM** value: **Cover or less**
Circ: CapCity orders: **8,650**
Genesis, Part 2; The Extinction Agenda! **A:** Leonard Kirk **W:** Tom Mason
9 ❑ Oct 1993 Cover: 2.50 **NM** value: **Cover or less**
Circ: CapCity orders: **7,975**
Genesis, Part 5
10 ❑ Nov 1993 Cover: 2.50 **NM** value: **Cover or less**
Circ: CapCity orders: **6,300**
Comics' Greatest World parody cover. Genesis
11 ❑ Dec 1993 Cover: 2.50 **NM** value: **Cover or less**
Circ: CapCity orders: **4,825**
Genesis
12 ❑ Feb 1994 Cover: 2.50 **NM** value: **Cover or less**
Circ: CapCity orders: **4,175**
Ultraverse parody cover. Genesis

DIPPY DUCK — Atlas

1 ❑ Oct 1957 Cover: 0.10 **NM** value: **40.00**

DIRECTORY TO A NONEXISTENT UNIVERSE — Eclipse

1 ❑ Dec 1987 Cover: 2.00 **NM** value: **Cover or less**
Circ: CapCity orders: **1,925**
A: Kerry Callen **W:** Kerry Callen

DIRE WOLVES: A CHRONICLE OF THE DEADWORLD — Caliber

1 ❑ b&w Cover: 3.95 **NM** value: **Cover or less**

DIRTBAG — Twist N Shout

1 ❑ Cover: 2.95 **NM** value: **Cover or less**
A: Richard Johnson **W:** Richard Johnson
2 ❑ Cover: 2.95 **NM** value: **Cover or less**
A: Richard Johnson **W:** Richard Johnson
3 ❑ Cover: 2.95 **NM** value: **Cover or less**
A: Richard Johnson **W:** Richard Johnson
4 ❑ Cover: 2.95 **NM** value: **Cover or less**
A: Richard Johnson **W:** Richard Johnson
5 ❑ Cover: 2.95 **NM** value: **Cover or less**
A: Richard Johnson **W:** Richard Johnson
6 ❑ Cover: 2.95 **NM** value: **Cover or less**

Crowd Control; Deeno in Tourist Trap; Bill the Clown; The X-FliesGraham Lousy Day **A:** Roger Langridge; Richard Johnson; Bebe Williams; Mark Stafford **W:** Roger Langridge; Richard Johnson; Bebe Williams; Mark Stafford

7 ❑ Cover: 2.95 **NM** value: **Cover or less**
If It ain't Broke, Fix It; true Takes from the Periphery; The Monorail Rider; Life Bytes; Billie the Clown in Military Intelligence; If You See Bill on the Road, Kill Him **A:** Roger Langridge; Richard Johnson; Bebe Williams; Fabian Nicieza **W:** Roger Langridge; Richard Johnson; Bebe Williams; Fabian Nicieza

DIRTY DOZEN, THE — Dell

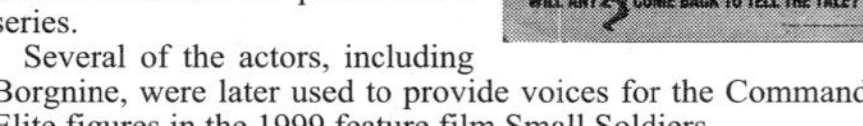

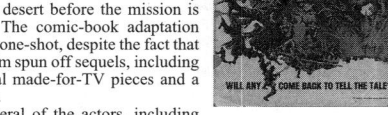

The 1967 film starring Lee Marvin, Ernest Borgnine, Robert Ryan, Charles Bronson, Richard Jaeckel, George Kennedy, and Jim Brown told the story of a group of prisoners who are used in fighting World War II. Their mission, to infiltrate a Nazi fortress and assasinate top Nazi leaders, will result in pardons for them if successful and death if they try to desert before the mission is over. The comic-book adaptation was a one-shot, despite the fact that the film spun off sequels, including several made-for-TV pieces and a series.

Several of the actors, including Borgnine, were later used to provide voices for the Commando Elite figures in the 1999 feature film Small Soldiers.

— Maggie

1 ❑ Oct 1967 Cover: 0.12 **NM** value: **25.00**
• **CGC:** 3 graded, best 9.4
• 12-180-710

DIRTY PAIR — Eclipse

1 ❑ Dec 1988, b&w Cover: 2.00 **NM** value: **6.00**
Cory! Emerson **A:** Adam Warren **W:** Adam Warren
2 ❑ Jan 1989, b&w Cover: 2.00 **NM** value: **4.00**
3 ❑ Feb 1989, b&w Cover: 2.00 **NM** value: **4.00**
4 ❑ Mar 1989, b&w Cover: 2.00 **NM** value: **4.00**
Bk 1 ❑ Sep 1998, b&w Cover: 12.95 **NM** value: **Cover or less**
• collects mini-series

DIRTY PAIR (4TH SERIES) — Viz

1 ❑ Cover: 4.95 **NM** value: **Cover or less**
Circ: CapCity orders: **6,225**
To Kill a Computer
2 ❑ Cover: 4.95 **NM** value: **Cover or less**
Circ: CapCity orders: **5,250**
3 ❑ Cover: 4.95 **NM** value: **Cover or less**
Circ: CapCity orders: **4,775**
4 ❑ Cover: 4.95 **NM** value: **Cover or less**
Circ: CapCity orders: **4,725**
Come Out, Come Out, Assassin
5 ❑ Cover: 4.95 **NM** value: **Cover or less**
Circ: CapCity orders: **4,375**
Address for Danger

DIRTY PAIR: DANGEROUS ACQUAINTANCES — Dark Horse / Manga

1 ❑ b&w Cover: 2.95 **NM** value: **Cover or less**
A: Adam Warren **W:** Adam Warren
2 ❑ b&w Cover: 2.95 **NM** value: **Cover or less**
A: Adam Warren **W:** Adam Warren
3 ❑ b&w Cover: 2.95 **NM** value: **Cover or less**
A: Adam Warren **W:** Adam Warren
4 ❑ b&w Cover: 2.95 **NM** value: **Cover or less**
A: Adam Warren **W:** Adam Warren
5 ❑ b&w Cover: 2.95 **NM** value: **Cover or less**
A: Adam Warren **W:** Adam Warren
Bk 1 ❑ Jun 1997, b&w Cover: 12.95 **NM** value: **14.95**
• collects mini-series;Collects Dirty Pair: Dangerous Acquaintances #1-5 **A:** Adam Warren **W:** Adam Warren
Bk 1/HC ❑ Cover: 75.00 **NM** value: **Cover or less**
• Limited edition hardcover. **A:** Adam Warren **W:** Adam Warren

DIRTY PAIR, THE: FATAL BUT NOT SERIOUS — Dark Horse / Manga

In the year 2141, the human race has spread out in the form of galactic colonies which are governed by the United Galactica, a unified peace force. However, crime still exists in the future, so when the trouble gets too rough, "Trouble Consultants," teams of specially trained police operatives, are brought in. Two of the best of these agents are "the Lovely Angels," two women who, although they are very good, always find some way to destroy plenty of property in the process. This destruction gives them the hated nickname, "the Dirty Pair."

This is the first of several Dark Horse limited series starring the manga-influenced, but American-made characters.

1 ❑ Jul 1995 Cover: 2.95 **NM** value: **Cover or less**
Circ: CapCity orders: **7,700**
A: Adam Warren **W:** Adam Warren
2 ❑ Aug 1995 Cover: 2.95 **NM** value: **Cover or less**
Circ: CapCity orders: **6,075**
A: Adam Warren **W:** Adam Warren
3 ❑ Sep 1995 Cover: 2.95 **NM** value: **Cover or less**
Circ: CapCity orders: **5,550**
A: Adam Warren **W:** Adam Warren
4 ❑ Oct 1995 Cover: 2.95 **NM** value: **Cover or less**
A: Adam Warren **W:** Adam Warren
5 ❑ Nov 1995 Cover: 2.95 **NM** value: **Cover or less**
A: Adam Warren **W:** Adam Warren
Bk 1 ❑ Aug 1996 Cover: 14.95 **NM** value: **Cover or less**
A: Adam Warren **W:** Adam Warren

DIRTY PAIR II — Eclipse

1 ❑ May 1989, b&w **NM** value: **2.50**
2 ❑ Aug 1989, b&w **NM** value: **2.50**
3 ❑ Nov 1989 **NM** value: **2.50**
4 ❑ Feb 1990 **NM** value: **2.50**
5 ❑ May 1990 **NM** value: **2.50**

DIRTY PAIR III — Eclipse

1 ❑ Aug 1990, b&w **NM** value: **2.25**
2 ❑ Nov 1990, b&w **NM** value: **2.25**
3 ❑ Feb 1991 **NM** value: **2.25**
4 ❑ May 1991 **NM** value: **2.25**
5 ❑ Aug 1991 **NM** value: **2.25**

DIRTY PAIR, THE: RUN FROM THE FUTURE — Dark Horse / Manga

1 ❑ Jan 2000 Cover: 2.95 **NM** value: **Cover or less**
Circ: Diamd. preorders: **17,149**
Smart Clothes, Foolish Criminals **A:** Adam Warren **W:** Adam Warren
1/A ❑ Jan 2000 Cover: 2.95 **NM** value: **Cover or less**
Alternate cover by Adam Warren. Smart Clothes, Foolish Criminals **A:** Adam Warren **W:** Adam Warren
2 ❑ Feb 2000 Cover: 2.95 **NM** value: **Cover or less**
Circ: Diamd. preorders: **14,097**
A: Adam Warren **W:** Adam Warren
3 ❑ Mar 2000 Cover: 2.95 **NM** value: **Cover or less**
Circ: Diamd. preorders: **14,719**
A: Adam Warren **W:** Adam Warren
4 ❑ Apr 2000 Cover: 2.95 **NM** value: **Cover or less**
Circ: Diamd. preorders: **15,867**
A: Adam Warren **W:** Adam Warren

DIRTY PAIR, THE: SIM HELL — Dark Horse / Manga

1 ❑ 1993b&w Cover: 2.50 **NM** value: **2.95**
Circ: CapCity orders: **9,000**
A: Adam Warren **W:** Adam Warren
2 ❑ 1993b&w Cover: 2.50 **NM** value: **2.95**
Circ: CapCity orders: **7,075**
A: Adam Warren **W:** Adam Warren
3 ❑ 1993b&w Cover: 2.50 **NM** value: **2.95**
A: Adam Warren **W:** Adam Warren
4 ❑ 1993b&w Cover: 2.50 **NM** value: **2.95**
A: Adam Warren **W:** Adam Warren
5 ❑ 1993 Cover: 2.95 **NM** value: **Cover or less**
A: Adam Warren **W:** Adam Warren
Bk 1 ❑ Cover: 13.95 **NM** value: **Cover or less**
• Collects series **A:** Adam Warren **W:** Adam Warren
Bk 1-2 ❑ Mar 1996 Cover: 13.95 **NM** value: **Cover or less**

DIRTY PAIR, THE: SIM HELL REMASTERED — Dark Horse / Manga

1 ❑ May 2001 Cover: 2.99 **NM** value: **Cover or less**
Circ: Diamd. preorders: **9,732**
A: Adam Warren **W:** Adam Warren

DIRTY PAIR, THE: START THE VIOLENCE — Dark Horse

1/A ❑ Sep 1999 Cover: 2.95 **NM** value: **Cover or less**
Circ: Diamd. preorders: **15,282**
Jason Pearson cover. **A:** Adam Warren; Jason Pearson(cover) **W:** Adam Warren
1/B ❑ Sep 1999 Cover: 2.95 **NM** value: **Cover or less**
variant cover. **A:** Adam Warren **W:** Adam Warren

DIRTY PICTURES — Aircel

All issues are adults only.

1 ❑ Apr 1991, b&w Cover: 2.50 **NM** value: **Cover or less**
2 ❑ b&w Cover: 2.50 **NM** value: **Cover or less**
3 ❑ b&w Cover: 2.50 **NM** value: **Cover or less**

DIRTY PLOTTE — Drawn and Quarterly

1 ❑ Cover: 2.50 **NM** value: **Cover or less**
A: Julie Doucet **W:** Julie Doucet
2 ❑ Cover: 2.50 **NM** value: **Cover or less**
A: Julie Doucet **W:** Julie Doucet
3 ❑ Cover: 2.50 **NM** value: **Cover or less**
A: Julie Doucet **W:** Julie Doucet
4 ❑ Cover: 2.50 **NM** value: **Cover or less**
A: Julie Doucet **W:** Julie Doucet
5 ❑ Cover: 2.50 **NM** value: **Cover or less**
A: Julie Doucet **W:** Julie Doucet
6 ❑ Cover: 2.50 **NM** value: **Cover or less**
A: Julie Doucet **W:** Julie Doucet
7 ❑ Cover: 2.95 **NM** value: **Cover or less**
A: Julie Doucet **W:** Julie Doucet
8 ❑ Cover: 2.95 **NM** value: **Cover or less**
A: Julie Doucet **W:** Julie Doucet
9 ❑ Cover: 2.95 **NM** value: **Cover or less**
A: Julie Doucet **W:** Julie Doucet
10 ❑ Nov 1996 Cover: 3.50 **NM** value: **Cover or less**
Circ: Direct Market orders: **3,077**
A: Julie Doucet **W:** Julie Doucet

DISASTERS OF WAR, THE — Caliber / Tome

1 ❑ b&w Cover: 3.50 **NM** value: **Cover or less**

DISAVOWED — WildStorm

1 ❑ Mar 2000 Cover: 2.50 **NM** value: **Cover or less**
Circ: Diamd. preorders: **14,340**
A: Tommy Lee Edwards **W:** Brandon Choi; Mike Heisler
2 ❑ Apr 2000 Cover: 2.50 **NM** value: **Cover or less**
Circ: Diamd. preorders: **9,818**
Point of View **A:** Tommy Lee Edwards **W:** Brandon Choi; Mike Heisler
3 ❑ May 2000 Cover: 2.50 **NM** value: **Cover or less**
Circ: Diamd. preorders: **8,258**
Smoke and Mirrors **A:** Tommy Lee Edwards **W:** Brandon Choi; Mike Heisler

DISCIPLES, THE — Image

1 ❑ Apr 2001 Cover: 2.95 **NM** value: **Cover or less**
Circ: Diamd. preorders: **11,126** • **CGC:** 1 graded, best 9.8
A: Laurence Campbell **W:** Chris Dows; Colin Clayton

DISHMAN — Eclipse

Poking fun at the super-hero genre by concocting heroes with silly powers is a time-honored tradition. John MacLeod's Dishman, however, is unique in that he gives his hero a really stupid super-power, then refuses to play it for laughs. The result is both interesting and profoundly depressing.

The title character is Paul Mahler, a school teacher about to be married. He's just packing up his old house, including the Fiestaware dishes he'd been using for the past 10 years — which were radioactive at a low level (an actual fact, according to an article in Macleans on May 4, 1981!). As he finishes cleaning up, he wishes that the dishes in the sink were clean, and, as if by magic, they are cleaned, and put away instantly. Unfortunately, that's the whole extent of his super-power! Mahler still feels obliged to become a crimefighter, and as a result, he quickly loses his reputation, his fiancee, and his self-respect.

1 ❑ Sep 1988, b&w Cover: 2.50 **NM** value: **Cover or less**
Dishman Hands **A:** John MacLeod **W:** John MacLeod ★ Origin of Dishman. ★ 1st Appearance of Dishman.

DISNEY AFTERNOON, THE — Marvel

1 ❑ Nov 1994 Cover: 1.50 **NM** value: **Cover or less**
Circ: CapCity orders: **8,550**
Kitchen Clean-up; The Paint Job; Welcome to Gumbeaux • Darkwing Duck, Bonkers, Goof Troop, Tailspin **A:** Andres Klacik; John Blair Moore Cosme Quartieri **W:** John Blair Moore; Janet Gilbert; Roger Brown
2 ❑ Dec 1994 Cover: 1.50 **NM** value: **Cover or less**
Circ: CapCity orders: **5,250**
3 ❑ Jan 1995 Cover: 1.50 **NM** value: **Cover or less**
Circ: CapCity orders: **4,275**
4 ❑ Feb 1995 Cover: 1.50 **NM** value: **Cover or less**
Circ: CapCity orders: **3,450**
5 ❑ Mar 1995 Cover: 1.50 **NM** value: **Cover or less**
Circ: CapCity orders: **2,875**
6 ❑ Apr 1995 Cover: 1.50 **NM** value: **Cover or less**
Circ: CapCity orders: **2,375**
7 ❑ May 1995 Cover: 1.50 **NM** value: **Cover or less**
Circ: CapCity orders: **2,250**
8 ❑ Jun 1995 Cover: 1.50 **NM** value: **Cover or less**
Circ: CapCity orders: **2,050**
9 ❑ Jul 1995 Cover: 1.50 **NM** value: **Cover or less**
10 ❑ Aug 1995 Cover: 1.50 **NM** value: **Cover or less**
final issue.

DISNEY COMIC HITS — Marvel

1 ❑ Oct 1995 Cover: 1.50 **NM** value: **2.00**
Circ: Statement: **60,732**
• Pocahontas
2 ❑ Nov 1995 Cover: 1.50 **NM** value: **Cover or less**
Circ: Statement: **60,732**
• Timon and Pumbaa
3 ❑ Dec 1995 Cover: 1.50 **NM** value: **Cover or less**
Circ: Statement: **60,732**
Pocahontas **A:** Cosmé Quartieri **W:** Barbara Slate ★ Appearance of Pocahontas, Captain John Smith.
4 ❑ Jan 1996 Cover: 2.50 **NM** value: **Cover or less**
Circ: Statement: **60,732**
• Adapts Toy Story
5 ❑ Feb 1996 Cover: 1.50 **NM** value: **Cover or less**
Circ: Statement: **60,732**
Toy Story: Andy's Sleep Over; Beauty & The Beast: Magical Memories!; Pocahontas: Holiday Harmony; Timon & Pumbaa: Mall I Want for Christmas • Winter Wonderland **A:** Cosmé Quartieri **W:** Barbara Slate
6 ❑ Mar 1996 Cover: 1.50 **NM** value: **Cover or less**
Circ: Statement: **60,732**
Aladdin: Faking Thunderbirds **A:** Eduardo Savid **W:** Buzz Dixon
7 ❑ Apr 1996 Cover: 1.50 **NM** value: **Cover or less**
Circ: Statement: **60,732**
Pocahontas: Nature's Way **A:** Cosmé Quartieri **W:** Barbara Slate
8 ❑ May 1996 Cover: 1.50 **NM** value: **Cover or less**
Circ: Statement: **60,732**
9 ❑ Jun 1996 Cover: 1.50 **NM** value: **Cover or less**
Circ: Statement: **60,732**
10 ❑ Jul 1996 Cover: 2.50 **NM** value: **Cover or less**
Circ: Statement: **60,732**
Hunchback of Notre Dame • adapts Hunchback of Notre Dame
11 ❑ Aug 1996 Cover: 1.50 **NM** value: **Cover or less**
Circ: Statement: **60,732**
• Hunchback of Notre Dame

Other grades: Multiply prices above by **1.5 for Mint • 2/3 for Very Fine • 1/3 for Fine • 1/5 for Very Good • 1/8 for Good**

12 ❑ Sep 1996 Cover: 1.50 **NM** value: **Cover or less**
Circ: Statement: **60,732**
• The Little Mermaid

13 ❑ Oct 1996 Cover: 1.50 **NM** value: **Cover or less**
Circ: Direct Market orders: **6,500**
📖 Aladdin and the King of Thieves • adapts Aladdin and the King of Thieves **A:** Scott Rosema **W:** Jack Enyart

14 ❑ Nov 1996 Cover: 1.50 **NM** value: **Cover or less**
📖 Timon & Pumbaa: Once Upon a Timon • Timon & Pumbaa **A:** Cosmé Quartieri **W:** Kayte Kuch; Sheryl Scarborough

15 ❑ Dec 1996 Cover: 1.50 **NM** value: **Cover or less**
Circ: Direct Market orders: **7,750**
• Toy Story adventures; Has 1996 Statement, filed 10/1/96; avg print run 110,779; avg sales 32,455; avg subs 28,277; avg total paid 60,732; samples 600; office use 125; max existent 61,457; 45% of run returned

16 ❑ Jan 1997 Cover: 1.50 **NM** value: **Cover or less**
Circ: Direct Market orders: **7,250**
• adapts 101 Dalmations

DISNEY COMICS ALBUM — Disney

Bk 1❑ Cover: 6.95 **NM** value: **Cover or less**
Circ: CapCity orders: **2,600**
• Donald, Gyro **A:** Carl Barks

Bk 2❑ Cover: 6.95 **NM** value: **Cover or less**
• Uncle Scrooge **A:** Carl Barks

Bk 3❑ Cover: 7.95 **NM** value: **Cover or less**
• Donald Duck **A:** Carl Barks

Bk 4❑ Cover: 7.95 **NM** value: **Cover or less**
• Mickey Mouse vs. Phantom Blot **A:** Floyd Gottfredson

Bk 5❑ Cover: 7.95 **NM** value: **Cover or less**
• Chip 'n' Dale

Bk 6❑ Cover: 7.95 **NM** value: **Cover or less**
• Uncle Scrooge **A:** Carl Barks

Bk 7❑ Cover: 6.95 **NM** value: **Cover or less**
• Donald Duck **A:** Carl Barks

Bk 8❑ Cover: 7.95 **NM** value: **Cover or less**
• Super Goof

DISNEYLAND BIRTHDAY PARTY — Dell

1 ❑ Oct 1958 Cover: 0.25 **NM** value: **500.00**
• **CGC:** 1 graded, best 7.0
📖 Uncle Scrooge and Gyro (Untitled)

DISNEYLAND BIRTHDAY PARTY (WALT DISNEY'S...) — Gladstone

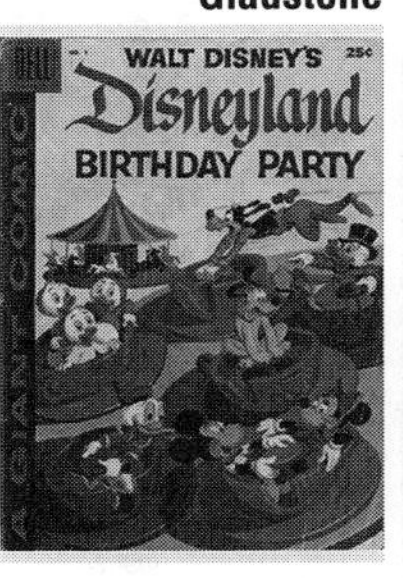

In honor of the 30th anniversary of the Disneyland theme park, Gladstone Publishing reprinted this special edition from 1958, the park's third year. It also marked the beginning of Gladstone's assumption of the publishing chores for many of Disney's other titles.

This issue is a selection of stories that are told as part of a guided tour of the "Happiest Place on Earth," with tales selected to highlight the specific attractions of the park, such as Frontierland, the Snow White ride, Adventureland, and the Peter Pan ride.

Disney's best-known character, Mickey Mouse, acts as tour guide for Donald Duck's nephews, Huey, Dewey, and Louie, as well as his own young nephews, Mortie and Ferdie. The stars of the various stories include such popular characters as Goofy, Uncle Scrooge, and Mr. Toad. This edition also features a special cover with a drawing by the definitive "Duck Man," Carl Barks, superimposed over a photograph of Disneyland.

1 ❑ ca. 1985 Cover: 2.50 **NM** value: **10.00**
• Reprints Disneyland Birthday Party (Giant), Uncle Scrooge Goes to Disneyland **A:** Carl Barks

1/A ❑ **NM** value: **10.00**
• digest.

DISNEY MOVIE BOOK — Disney

1 ❑ Cover: 7.95 **NM** value: **Cover or less**
• Roger Rabbit in Tummy Trouble

DISNEY'S ACTION CLUB — Acclaim

1 ❑ Cover: 4.50 **NM** value: **Cover or less**
• digest. • Hercules, Hunchback, Lion King, Aladdin, Toy Story, Mighty Ducks

2 ❑ Cover: 4.50 **NM** value: **Cover or less**
📖 The Mighty Ducks: Puck Power; The Hunchback of Notre Dame: Misfortunes of War; The Lion King:

3 ❑ Cover: 4.50 **NM** value: **Cover or less**
📖 Aladdin: Monkey Business; Timon & Pumbaa: After Hours; Mighty Ducks: Word Hunt; Toy Story: Skirting Disaster; Hercules: A Stone's Throw Away; The Hunchback of Notre Dame: The Yoke's on You **A:** Howard Simpson; Jackson Guice; Gonzalo Mayo; Carlos Mota; Brian Kong **W:** Jack Enyart; Kayte Kuch; Lee Nordling; Michael Gallagher; Roger Brown; Sheryl Scarborough

4 ❑ Cover: 4.50 **NM** value: **Cover or less**
• digest. 📖 Mighty Ducks: Rough Stuff; Find Aladdin; Toy Story: A Sticky Situation; Hercules: Working From Dawn to Dusk • Mighty Ducks, Toy Story, Aladdin, Hercules stories **A:** Jackson Guice; Brian Kong; Nelson Luty; Rusty Haller **W:** Rurik Tyler; Clay Griffith; Susan Griffith

5 ❑ Cover: 4.50 **NM** value: **Cover or less**
6 ❑ Cover: 4.50 **NM** value: **Cover or less**
7 ❑ Jun 1997 Cover: 4.50 **NM** value: **Cover or less**
Circ: Diamd. preorders: **3,536**

DISNEY'S COLOSSAL COMICS — Disney

1 ❑ Cover: 2.00 **NM** value: **Cover or less**

DISNEY'S COLOSSAL COMICS COLLECTION — Disney

1 ❑ Cover: 1.95 **NM** value: **2.00**
2 ❑ Cover: 1.95 **NM** value: **2.00**
3 ❑ Cover: 1.95 **NM** value: **2.00**
4 ❑ Cover: 1.95 **NM** value: **2.00**
5 ❑ Cover: 1.95 **NM** value: **2.00**
6 ❑ Cover: 1.95 **NM** value: **2.00**
7 ❑ Cover: 1.95 **NM** value: **2.00**
8 ❑ Cover: 1.95 **NM** value: **2.00**
9 ❑ Cover: 1.95 **NM** value: **2.00**
10 ❑ Cover: 1.95 **NM** value: **2.00**

DISNEY'S COMICS IN 3-D — Disney

1 ❑ Cover: 2.95 **NM** value: **Cover or less**
Circ: CapCity orders: **6,550**
A: Carl Barks; Floyd Gottfredson; Don Rosa

DISNEY'S ENCHANTING STORIES — Acclaim

1 ❑ Cover: 4.50 **NM** value: **Cover or less**

2 ❑ Cover: 4.50 **NM** value: **Cover or less**
📖 River of Youth; Service with a Smile; Fly Now, Pay Later; Snow Problem; Prince, The Wonder Dog • Pocahontas **A:** George Wildman; Gonzalo Mayo; Jose Delbo; Peter Pachoumis; Nathaniel Pallant; Rich Hoover **W:** Trina Robbins; Bob Budiansky; Jack Enyart; Kayte Kuch; Michael Gallagher; Sheryl Scarborough

3 ❑ Cover: 4.50 **NM** value: **Cover or less**
📖 The Book Crook; Meg's Mismatched Monograms; Scenti Mental Journey; The Best Gift; Grumpy Birthday to You; Leash Flaws • Beauty & The Beast **A:** Don Perlin; Cosme Quartieri; Gonzalo Mayo; Jose Delbo; Tod Smith **W:** Rurik Tyler; Trina Robbins; Clay & Susan Griffin; Kayte Kuch; Michael Gallagher; Sheryl Scarborough

4 ❑ Cover: 4.50 **NM** value: **Cover or less**
📖 Star Search; Clean-up Time; The Gargoyle of my Dreams; Out-Foxed; • 101 Dalmations **A:** Gonzalo Mayo; Carlos Mota; Tod Smith **W:** Bob Budiansky; Clay & Susan Griffin; Kayte Kuch; Sheryl Scarborough

DISOBEDIENT DAISY — Fantagraphics / Eros

All issues are adults only.

1 ❑ Aug 1995, b&w Cover: 2.95 **NM** value: **Cover or less**
A: Jim Cheff **W:** Jim Cheff

2 ❑ Oct 1995, b&w Cover: 2.95 **NM** value: **Cover or less**
A: Jim Cheff **W:** Jim Cheff

DISTANT SOIL, A (1ST SERIES) — Warp

A Distant Soil is the story of Jason and Lianna Scott. Held in a psychic research institute since they were children, they finally manage to escape by utilizing powers they had just discovered in themselves. Soon afterward, they encounter Rieken and D'Mer, humanoids from another world, who have come to enlist the kids' aid in freeing their galaxy from the enslaving power of the planet Ovanon. Lianna learns that she is an Avatar, potentially the most powerful psychic in the universe. Jason is a Disruptor, able to control the flow of electricity in people and things. So long as these two are alive, Ovanon's power is in jeopardy.

A Distant Soil originally appeared as a preview in Elfquest #16, and went on to become a regular series for Elfquest publisher Warp Graphics. Later, creator Colleen Doran decided to begin self-publishing with her new company Aria Press.

1 ❑ 1983 Cover: 1.50 **NM** value: **10.00**
A: Colleen Doran **W:** Colleen Doran

2 ❑ 1984 Cover: 1.50 **NM** value: **6.00**
A: Colleen Doran **W:** Colleen Doran

3 ❑ 1984 Cover: 1.50 **NM** value: **5.00**
A: Colleen Doran **W:** Colleen Doran

4 ❑ 1984 Cover: 1.50 **NM** value: **5.00**
A: Colleen Doran **W:** Colleen Doran

5 ❑ 1985 Cover: 1.50 **NM** value: **5.00**
A: Colleen Doran **W:** Colleen Doran

6 ❑ Jun 1985 Cover: 1.50 **NM** value: **4.00**
• Standard comic size. 📖 The Chronicles of Panda Khan **A:** Dave Garcia; Colleen Doran **W:** Dave Garcia; Colleen Doran; Monica Sharp
★ 1st Appearance of Panda Khan.

7 ❑ Sep 1985 Cover: 1.50 **NM** value: **4.00**
A: Colleen Doran **W:** Colleen Doran

8 ❑ Dec 1985 Cover: 1.50 **NM** value: **4.00**
A: Colleen Doran **W:** Colleen Doran

9 ❑ Mar 1986 Cover: 1.50 **NM** value: **4.00**
A: Colleen Doran **W:** Colleen Doran

DISTANT SOIL, A (2ND SERIES) — Aria

1 ❑ 1991 Cover: 1.75 **NM** value: **6.00**
A: Colleen Doran **W:** Colleen Doran

1-2 ❑ Cover: 1.75 **NM** value: **3.00**
1-3 ❑ Cover: 1.75 **NM** value: **2.00**
1-4 ❑ Cover: 1.75 **NM** value: **Cover or less**
2 ❑ Cover: 1.75 **NM** value: **4.00**
A: Colleen Doran **W:** Colleen Doran

2-2 ❑ Cover: 1.75 **NM** value: **2.50**
3 ❑ 1992 Cover: 1.75 **NM** value: **4.00**
A: Colleen Doran **W:** Colleen Doran

3-2 ❑ Cover: 1.75 **NM** value: **2.50**
4 ❑ 1993 Cover: 1.75 **NM** value: **3.00**
📖 Knights of the Angel **A:** Colleen Doran **W:** Colleen Doran

4-2 ❑ Cover: 1.75 **NM** value: **2.00**
5 ❑ 1993 Cover: 1.75 **NM** value: **2.50**
📖 Knights of the Angel **A:** Colleen Doran **W:** Colleen Doran

6 ❑ Cover: 1.75 **NM** value: **2.00**
📖 Knights of the Angel **A:** Colleen Doran **W:** Colleen Doran

7 ❑ 1994 Cover: 1.75 **NM** value: **2.00**
A: Colleen Doran **W:** Colleen Doran

8 ❑ Jun 1994 Cover: 1.75 **NM** value: **2.00**
A: Colleen Doran **W:** Colleen Doran

9 ❑ 1994 Cover: 2.50 **NM** value: **Cover or less**
📖 Knights of the Angel, Part 4 **A:** Colleen Doran **W:** Colleen Doran

10 ❑ Cover: 2.50 **NM** value: **Cover or less**
A: Colleen Doran **W:** Colleen Doran

11 ❑ Apr 1995 Cover: 2.50 **NM** value: **Cover or less**
A: Colleen Doran **W:** Colleen Doran

12 ❑ Nov 1995 Cover: 2.50 **NM** value: **Cover or less**
A: Colleen Doran **W:** Colleen Doran

13 ❑ Jun 1996 Cover: 2.50 **NM** value: **2.95**
📖 Ascension, Part 1 **A:** Colleen Doran **W:** Colleen Doran

14 ❑ Aug 1996 Cover: 2.50 **NM** value: **2.95**
📖 Ascension, Part 2 **A:** Colleen Doran **W:** Colleen Doran

15 ❑ Aug 1996 Cover: 2.95 **NM** value: **Cover or less**
📖 Ascension, Part 3 • Image begins as publisher **A:** Colleen Doran **W:** Colleen Doran

16 ❑ Oct 1996 Cover: 2.95 **NM** value: **Cover or less**
Circ: Diamd. preorders: **10,104**
📖 Ascension, Part 4 **A:** Colleen Doran **W:** Colleen Doran

17 ❑ Dec 1996 Cover: 2.95 **NM** value: **Cover or less**
Circ: Direct Market orders: **8,478**
📖 Ascension, Part 5 **A:** Colleen Doran **W:** Colleen Doran

18 ❑ Feb 1997 Cover: 2.95 **NM** value: **Cover or less**
Circ: Diamd. preorders: **7,004**
A: Colleen Doran **W:** Colleen Doran

19 ❑ Apr 1997 Cover: 2.95 **NM** value: **Cover or less**
Circ: Diamd. preorders: **6,832**
A: Colleen Doran **W:** Colleen Doran

20 ❑ Jun 1997 Cover: 2.95 **NM** value: **Cover or less**
Circ: Diamd. preorders: **6,324**
A: Colleen Doran **W:** Colleen Doran

21 ❑ Sep 1997 Cover: 2.95 **NM** value: **Cover or less**
Circ: Diamd. preorders: **5,910**
A: Colleen Doran **W:** Colleen Doran

22 ❑ Dec 1997 Cover: 2.95 **NM** value: **Cover or less**
Circ: Diamd. preorders: **5,435**
A: Colleen Doran **W:** Colleen Doran

23 ❑ Feb 1998 Cover: 2.95 **NM** value: **Cover or less**
Circ: Diamd. preorders: **5,116**
📖 Ascension **A:** Colleen Doran **W:** Colleen Doran

24 ❑ Apr 1998 Cover: 2.95 **NM** value: **Cover or less**
Circ: Diamd. preorders: **4,678**
A: Colleen Doran **W:** Colleen Doran

25 ❑ Jun 1998 Cover: 3.95 **NM** value: **Cover or less**
Circ: Diamd. preorders: **7,829**
• double-sized. 📖 Troll Bridge **A:** Colleen Doran **W:** Colleen Doran; Neil Gaiman

25/LE❑Jun 1998 Cover: 10.00 **NM** value: **Cover or less**
• 15th anniversary issue. 📖 Troll Bridge **A:** Colleen Doran **W:** Colleen Doran; Neil Gaiman

26 ❑ Nov 1998 Cover: 2.95 **NM** value: **Cover or less**
Circ: Diamd. preorders: **4,437**
Christmas cover. • not Christmas story **A:** Colleen Doran **W:** Colleen Doran

27 ❑ Apr 1999 Cover: 2.95 **NM** value: **Cover or less**
Circ: Diamd. preorders: **4,554**
A: Colleen Doran **W:** Colleen Doran

28 ❑ Jul 1999 Cover: 3.95 **NM** value: **Cover or less**
Circ: Diamd. preorders: **4,076**
A: Colleen Doran **W:** Colleen Doran

29 ❑ Dec 1999 Cover: 3.95 **NM** value: **Cover or less**
Circ: Diamd. preorders: **4,286**
A: Colleen Doran **W:** Colleen Doran

30 ❑ Aug 2000 Cover: 3.95 **NM** value: **Cover or less**
Circ: Diamd. preorders: **3,973**
A: Colleen Doran **W:** Colleen Doran

31 ❑ Jan 2001 Cover: 3.95 **NM** value: **Cover or less**
Circ: Diamd. preorders: **3,634**
📖 A World for Dreaming **A:** Colleen Doran **W:** Colleen Doran; Jan Strnad

32 ❑ May 2001 Cover: 3.95 **NM** value: **Cover or less**
Circ: Diamd. preorders: **3,476**
A: Colleen Doran **W:** Colleen Doran

33 ❑ Aug 2001 Cover: 3.95 **NM** value: **Cover or less**
Circ: Diamd. preorders: **3,685**
A: Colleen Doran **W:** Colleen Doran

Bk 1❑ Cover: 18.95 **NM** value: **Cover or less**
• The Gathering;Collects A Distant Soil #1-12 **A:** Colleen Doran **W:** Colleen Doran; Neil Gaiman

Bk 1/HC❑ Cover: 18.95 **NM** value: **Cover or less**
• Collects A Distant Soil #1-12 **A:** Colleen Doran **W:** Colleen Doran; Neil Gaiman

Bk 1/LE❑ Cover: 18.95 **NM** value: **Cover or less**
• Hardcover limited edition (#1-100). • Collects A Distant Soil #1-12 **A:** Colleen Doran **W:** Colleen Doran; Neil Gaiman

Bk 2❑ Cover: 18.95 **NM** value: **Cover or less**
• The Ascendant;Collects A Distant Soil #13-25 **A:** Colleen Doran **W:** Colleen Doran; Neil Gaiman

Bk 3❑ Cover: 6.95 **NM** value: **Cover or less**
• Immigrant Song

Bk 4❑ Cover: 19.95 **NM** value: **Cover or less**
• Knights of the Angel

DITKO PACKAGE — Ditko

1 ❑ Cover: 8.95 **NM** value: **Cover or less**
No issue number. • squarebound

DIVA GRAFIX & STORIES — Starhead

All issues are adults only.

CGC-graded: Multiply prices above by **33 for 9.9 M • 16 for 9.8 NM/M • 7 for 9.6 NM+ • 5 for 9.4 NM • 2.5 for 9.2 NM- • 1.5 for 9.0 VF/NM**

1 ❑ Nov 1993, b&w Cover: 3.95 **NM** value: **Cover or less**
A: Ellen Forney; Dame Darcy; Fiona Smyth **W:** Ellen Forney; Dame Darcy; Fiona Smyth
2 ❑ b&w Cover: 3.95 **NM** value: **Cover or less**
A: Roberta Gregory **W:** Roberta Gregory; Donna Barr

DIVAS — Caliber

1 ❑ b&w Cover: 2.50 **NM** value: **Cover or less**
2 ❑ b&w Cover: 2.50 **NM** value: **Cover or less**
3 ❑ b&w Cover: 2.50 **NM** value: **Cover or less**
4 ❑ b&w Cover: 2.50 **NM** value: **Cover or less**

DIVINE INTERVENTION/GEN13 — DC / Wildstorm

1 ❑ Nov 1999 Cover: 2.50 **NM** value: **Cover or less**
Circ: Diamd. preorders: **34,892**

DIVINE INTERVENTION/WILDCATS — DC / Wildstorm

1 ❑ Nov 1999 Cover: 2.50 **NM** value: **Cover or less**
Circ: Diamd. preorders: **36,977**

DIVINE RIGHT — Image

Max Faraday, a 20-year-old physics undergraduate, has trouble talking to women, has few friends, and works as a pizza delivery man to fund college. It isn't until demonic hounds attempt to kill him and his buddy Devon that his problems really begin.

Max downloads from the Internet an encrypted file stolen by I.O. Agent Christie Blaze. Upon reading it, Max becomes the conduit for the Creation Equation, a power that holds the secrets of the universe. Allied with Blaze and the Fallen, a trio of warriors on the side of Good and Order, he races against the Rath, a force of pure evil bent on bringing on Armageddon.

Jim Lee's explosive, richly detailed pencils and real life dialogue bring a genuine identity to Faraday. Although wrought with insecurities, he has the courage of a true hero, but is that enough to save both his friends and the world?

1 ❑ Sep 1997 Cover: 2.50 **NM** value: **4.00**
Circ: Diamd. preorders: **80,548**
📖 Blaze of Glory **A:** Jim Lee **W:** Jim Lee
1/A ❑ Sep 1997 Cover: 2.50 **NM** value: **4.00**
variant cover. 📖 Blaze of Glory **A:** Jim Lee **W:** Jim Lee
1/B ❑ Sep 1997 Cover: 2.50 **NM** value: **3.00**
• **CGC:** 1 graded, best 9.6
📖 Blaze of Glory • American Entertainment variant;Christy Blaze with flag in background **A:** Jim Lee; Jim Lee(cover) **W:** Jim Lee
1/C ❑ Sep 1997 Cover: 2.50 **NM** value: **3.00**
• Bagged edition. 📖 Blaze of Glory **A:** Jim Lee; Jim Lee(cover) **W:** Jim Lee
1/D ❑ Sep 1997 Cover: 2.50 **NM** value: **Cover or less**
alternate cover. • Spanish edition.
1/E ❑ Sep 1997 Cover: 2.50 **NM** value: **Cover or less**
• Voyager pack with preview of Stormwatch
2 ❑ Oct 1997 Cover: 2.50 **NM** value: **3.00**
Circ: Diamd. preorders: **71,050**
Sword battle scene on cover. 📖 Disco Inferno **A:** Jim Lee **W:** Jim Lee
2/SC ❑ Oct 1997 Cover: 2.50 **NM** value: **Cover or less**
alternate cover. • fight scene
3 ❑ Nov 1997 Cover: 2.50 **NM** value: **Cover or less**
Circ: Diamd. preorders: **72,642**
📖 Enemies of the State **A:** Jim Lee **W:** Jim Lee ★ Appearance of Fairchild.
3/SC ❑ Nov 1997 Cover: 2.50 **NM** value: **Cover or less**
no cover price on outer cover.
4 ❑ Dec 1997 Cover: 2.50 **NM** value: **Cover or less**
Circ: Diamd. preorders: **69,087**
White cover w/blue figure (no Fairchild). 📖 The Love Connection **A:** Jim Lee **W:** Jim Lee
4/SC ❑ Dec 1997 Cover: 2.50 **NM** value: **Cover or less**
Variant cover (Fairchild). 📖 The Love Connection **A:** Jim Lee **W:** Jim Lee
5 ❑ Feb 1998 Cover: 2.50 **NM** value: **Cover or less**
Circ: Diamd. preorders: **60,151**
📖 Party Crashers **A:** Jim Lee **W:** Jim Lee
5/SC ❑ Feb 1998 Cover: 5.40 **NM** value: **Cover or less**
• Pacific Comicon variant cover edition. 📖 Party Crashers **A:** Jim Lee **W:** Jim Lee
6 ❑ Aug 1998 Cover: 2.50 **NM** value: **Cover or less**
Circ: Diamd. preorders: **62,407**
📖 Truth or Consequences **A:** Jim Lee **W:** Jim Lee
7 ❑ Dec 1998 Cover: 2.50 **NM** value: **Cover or less**
Circ: Diamd. preorders: **55,664**
📖 Firewall Online **A:** Jim Lee **W:** Jim Lee
8 ❑ Jan 1999 Cover: 2.50 **NM** value: **Cover or less**
Circ: Diamd. preorders: **56,938**
📖 Into the Hollow Realm, Part 1 **A:** Jim Lee **W:** Jim Lee; Scott Lobdell
8/SC ❑ Jan 1999 Cover: 2.50 **NM** value: **Cover or less**
alternate cover.
9 ❑ Jul 1999 Cover: 2.50 **NM** value: **Cover or less**
Circ: Diamd. preorders: **47,999**
📖 The Fall of the Hollow Realm **A:** Jim Lee **W:** Jim Lee; Scott Lobdell
10 ❑ Oct 1999 Cover: 2.50 **NM** value: **Cover or less**
Circ: Diamd. preorders: **46,123**
📖 Happily Ever After **A:** Jim Lee **W:** Jim Lee; Scott Lobdell
11 ❑ Nov 1999 Cover: 2.50 **NM** value: **Cover or less**
Circ: Diamd. preorders: **42,320**
📖 Destiny Interruptus **A:** Jim Lee **W:** Jim Lee; Scott Lobdell
Ash 1 ❑ Jul 1997 **NM** value: **4.00**
Team on cover. **A:** Jim Lee; Scott Williams **W:** Jim Lee ★ 1st Appearance of Divine Right.
ASH 1/A ❑ Jul 1997 **NM** value: **4.00**
variant cover. • Faraday typing, woman's leg in foreground **A:** Jim Lee; Scott Williams **W:** Jim Lee ★ 1st Appearance of Divine Right.
Bk 1 ❑ Dec 1997 Cover: 5.95 **NM** value: **Cover or less**
• prestige format. • Divine Right Collected Ed.;Collects Divine Right #1-2 **A:** Jim Lee **W:** Jim Lee
Bk 2 ❑ Nov 1998 Cover: 5.95 **NM** value: **Cover or less**
• prestige format. • Divine Right Collected Ed.;Collects Divine Right #3-4 **A:** Jim Lee **W:** Jim Lee
Bk 3 ❑ Sep 1999 Cover: 5.95 **NM** value: **Cover or less**
Circ: Diamd. preorders: **5,405**
• prestige format. • Divine Right Collected Ed.;Collects Divine Right #5-6 **A:** Jim Lee **W:** Jim Lee

DIVISION 13 — Dark Horse

1 ❑ Sep 1994 Cover: 2.50 **NM** value: **Cover or less**
Circ: CapCity orders: **8,825**
A: Alexander Morrissey **W:** Keith Giffen
2 ❑ Oct 1994 Cover: 2.50 **NM** value: **Cover or less**
Circ: CapCity orders: **5,625**
A: Chris Alexander **W:** Keith Giffen
3 ❑ Dec 1994 Cover: 2.50 **NM** value: **Cover or less**
Circ: CapCity orders: **4,575**

DIXIE DUGAN — Columbia

The character of Dixie was introduced in a novel by J.P. McEvoy (1897-1958) in 1928. Her character was spun into a movie and a Broadway play, and she appeared in her own newspaper strip by the end of the following year. The strip ran for more than 30 years.

Her comic-book appearances didn't last nearly that long, the Columbia version running from 1942 to around the end of the decade. While the stories were basically innocent, they were suggestive for the era; several cover gags depict men falling all over themselves to get a better look at Dixie. The first issue features a crossover with Joe Palooka.

A handful of later issues from Prize are believed to exist, but were still being tracked down at press time. — Maggie

1 ❑ ca. 1942 Cover: 0.10 **NM** value: **150.00**
2 ❑ ca. 1943 Cover: 0.10 **NM** value: **75.00**
3 ❑ ca. 1944 Cover: 0.10 **NM** value: **75.00**
4 ❑ ca. 1944 Cover: 0.10 **NM** value: **75.00**
5 ❑ ca. 1945 Cover: 0.10 **NM** value: **75.00**
6 ❑ ca. 1945 Cover: 0.10 **NM** value: **75.00**
7 ❑ ca. 1945 Cover: 0.10 **NM** value: **75.00**
8 ❑ Cover: 0.10 **NM** value: **75.00**
9 ❑ Cover: 0.10 **NM** value: **75.00**
10 ❑ Cover: 0.10 **NM** value: **75.00**
11 ❑ Cover: 0.10 **NM** value: **75.00**
12 ❑ Cover: 0.10 **NM** value: **75.00**
13 ❑ Cover: 0.10 **NM** value: **75.00**
📖 Untitled stories

DIZZY DAMES — ACG

1 ❑ Sep 1952 Cover: 0.10 **NM** value: **80.00**
2 ❑ Nov 1952 Cover: 0.10 **NM** value: **60.00**
3 ❑ Jan 1953 Cover: 0.10 **NM** value: **40.00**
4 ❑ Mar 1953 Cover: 0.10 **NM** value: **40.00**
5 ❑ May 1953 Cover: 0.10 **NM** value: **40.00**
6 ❑ Jul 1953 Cover: 0.10 **NM** value: **40.00**

DIZZY DAMES SPECIAL EDITION — Avalon

1 ❑ Cover: 2.99 **NM** value: **Cover or less**
📖 Broadway Babes; Starlet O'Hara in Hollywood; Man-Huntin' Minnie of Delta Pu; Screwball S'al

DIZZY DON COMICS — F.E. Howard

1 ❑ ca. 1942 Cover: 0.10 **NM** value: **75.00**
2 ❑ ca. 1942 Cover: 0.10 **NM** value: **40.00**
4 ❑ ca. 1942 Cover: 0.10 **NM** value: **30.00**
5 ❑ ca. 1942 Cover: 0.10 **NM** value: **30.00**
6 ❑ ca. 1942 Cover: 0.10 **NM** value: **30.00**
7 ❑ ca. 1943 Cover: 0.10 **NM** value: **30.00**
8 ❑ ca. 1943 Cover: 0.10 **NM** value: **30.00**
9 ❑ ca. 1943 Cover: 0.10 **NM** value: **30.00**
10 ❑ ca. 1943 Cover: 0.10 **NM** value: **30.00**
11 ❑ ca. 1944 Cover: 0.10 **NM** value: **30.00**
12 ❑ ca. 1944 Cover: 0.10 **NM** value: **30.00**
13 ❑ ca. 1944 Cover: 0.10 **NM** value: **30.00**
14 ❑ ca. 1944 Cover: 0.10 **NM** value: **30.00**
15 ❑ ca. 1945 Cover: 0.10 **NM** value: **30.00**
16 ❑ ca. 1945 Cover: 0.10 **NM** value: **30.00**
17 ❑ ca. 1945 Cover: 0.10 **NM** value: **30.00**
18 ❑ ca. 1945 Cover: 0.10 **NM** value: **30.00**
19 ❑ ca. 1946 Cover: 0.10 **NM** value: **30.00**
20 ❑ ca. 1946 Cover: 0.10 **NM** value: **20.00**
21 ❑ ca. 1946 Cover: 0.10 **NM** value: **20.00**
22 ❑ ca. 1946 Cover: 0.10 **NM** value: **20.00**

DIZZY DON COMICS (VOL. 2) — F.E. Howard

3 ❑ Apr 1947 Cover: 0.10 **NM** value: **40.00**

DJANGO AND ANGEL — Caliber

1 ❑ b&w Cover: 2.50 **NM** value: **Cover or less**
A: Riba **W:** Av Donne Avenell
2 ❑ b&w Cover: 2.50 **NM** value: **Cover or less**
3 ❑ b&w Cover: 2.50 **NM** value: **Cover or less**
4 ❑ b&w Cover: 2.50 **NM** value: **Cover or less**
5 ❑ b&w Cover: 2.50 **NM** value: **Cover or less**

DNAGENTS — Eclipse

1 ❑ Mar 1983 Cover: 1.50 **NM** value: **2.50**
• **CGC:** 1 graded, best 9.4
2 ❑ Apr 1983 Cover: 1.50 **NM** value: **2.00**
📖 Stalked! **A:** Will Meugniot **W:** Mark Evanier
3 ❑ May 1983 Cover: 1.50 **NM** value: **2.00**
📖 Somewhat Alive! **A:** Will Meugniot **W:** Mark Evanier
4 ❑ Jul 1983 Cover: 1.50 **NM** value: **2.00**
5 ❑ Aug 1983 Cover: 1.50 **NM** value: **2.00**
6 ❑ Oct 1983 Cover: 1.50 **NM** value: **1.75**
7 ❑ Nov 1983 Cover: 1.50 **NM** value: **1.75**
8 ❑ Jan 1984 Cover: 1.50 **NM** value: **1.75**
9 ❑ Feb 1984 Cover: 1.50 **NM** value: **1.75**
10 ❑ Mar 1984 Cover: 1.50 **NM** value: **1.75**
11 ❑ May 1984 Cover: 1.50 **NM** value: **1.75**
12 ❑ May 1984 Cover: 1.50 **NM** value: **1.75**
13 ❑ Jun 1984 Cover: 1.25 **NM** value: **1.75**
14 ❑ Jul 1984 Cover: 1.50 **NM** value: **1.75**
15 ❑ Aug 1984 Cover: 1.25 **NM** value: **1.75**
A: Erik Larsen
16 ❑ Sep 1984 Cover: 1.25 **NM** value: **1.75**
17 ❑ Dec 1984 Cover: 1.50 **NM** value: **1.75**
18 ❑ Jan 1985 Cover: 1.50 **NM** value: **1.75**
19 ❑ Feb 1985 Cover: 1.50 **NM** value: **1.75**
20 ❑ Mar 1985 Cover: 1.50 **NM** value: **1.75**
21 ❑ Apr 1985 Cover: 1.50 **NM** value: **1.75**
22 ❑ May 1985 Cover: 1.50 **NM** value: **1.75**
23 ❑ Jun 1985 Cover: 1.50 **NM** value: **1.75**
24 ❑ Jul 1985 Cover: 1.50 **NM** value: **1.75**
C: Dave Stevens
3D 1 ❑ Jan 1986 Cover: 2.25 **NM** value: **2.50**
Circ: CapCity orders: **6,900**
• 3-Dminensional DNAgents

DNAGENTS SUPER SPECIAL — Antarctic

1 ❑ Apr 1994, b&w Cover: 3.50 **NM** value: **Cover or less**

DOC CARTER VD COMICS — Health

1 ❑ ca. 1949 **NM** value: **100.00**

DOC CHAOS: THE STRANGE ATTRACTOR — Vortex

1 ❑ Apr 1990 Cover: 3.00 **NM** value: **Cover or less**
Circ: CapCity orders: **1,860**
📖 The Lust for Order Part 1 **A:** Steve Sampson **W:** David Au Thorpe
2 ❑ 1990 Cover: 3.00 **NM** value: **Cover or less**
Circ: CapCity orders: **1,330**
📖 The Lust for Order Part 2 **A:** Steve Sampson **W:** David Au Thorpe
3 ❑ 1990 Cover: 3.00 **NM** value: **Cover or less**
📖 The Lust for Order Part 3 **A:** Steve Sampson **W:** David Au Thorpe

DOC SAMSON — Marvel

1 ❑ Jan 1996 Cover: 1.95 **NM** value: **Cover or less**
W: Evan Skolnick ★ Appearance of Hulk.
2 ❑ Feb 1996 Cover: 1.95 **NM** value: **Cover or less**
📖 Body Double **A:** Ken Lashley; Roberto Flores; Steve Geiger **W:** Evan Skolnick ★ Appearance of She-Hulk.
3 ❑ Mar 1996 Cover: 1.95 **NM** value: **Cover or less**
📖 Copycats **A:** Andrew Wildman; Roberto Flores **W:** Evan Skolnick ★ Versus Punisher.
4 ❑ Apr 1996 Cover: 1.95 **NM** value: **Cover or less**
📖 The Final Analysis **A:** Andrew Wildman; Roberto Flores; Joe Bennett **W:** Evan Skolnick ★ Appearance of Polaris.

DOC SAVAGE COMICS — Street & Smith

1 ❑ May 1940 Cover: 0.10 **NM** value: **2500.00**
• **CGC:** 3 graded, best 9.0
2 ❑ Oct 1940 Cover: 0.10 **NM** value: **800.00**
• **CGC:** 1 graded, best 9.6
3 ❑ Feb 1941 Cover: 0.10 **NM** value: **600.00**
4 ❑ May 1941 Cover: 0.10 **NM** value: **400.00**
• **CGC:** 2 graded, best 7.0
5 ❑ Aug 1941 Cover: 0.10 **NM** value: **400.00**
6 ❑ Nov 1941 Cover: 0.10 **NM** value: **300.00**
• **CGC:** 1 graded, best 7.0
7 ❑ Mar 1942 Cover: 0.10 **NM** value: **300.00**
• **CGC:** 1 graded, best 7.5
8 ❑ Jun 1942 Cover: 0.10 **NM** value: **200.00**
9 ❑ Sep 1942 Cover: 0.10 **NM** value: **200.00**
10 ❑ Nov 1942 Cover: 0.10 **NM** value: **200.00**
• **CGC:** 1 graded, best 7.5
11 ❑ Jan 1943 Cover: 0.10 **NM** value: **200.00**
12 ❑ Feb 1943 Cover: 0.10 **NM** value: **150.00**
13 ❑ Mar 1943 Cover: 0.10 **NM** value: **150.00**
• **CGC:** 2 graded, best 8.5
14 ❑ Apr 1943 Cover: 0.10 **NM** value: **150.00**
15 ❑ May 1943 Cover: 0.10 **NM** value: **100.00**
16 ❑ Jun 1943 Cover: 0.10 **NM** value: **100.00**
17 ❑ Jul 1943 Cover: 0.10 **NM** value: **100.00**
• **CGC:** 1 graded, best 9.2
18 ❑ Aug 1943 Cover: 0.10 **NM** value: **100.00**
• **CGC:** 1 graded, best 7.5
19 ❑ Sep 1943 Cover: 0.10 **NM** value: **100.00**
• **CGC:** 1 graded, best 6.5
20 ❑ Oct 1943 Cover: 0.10 **NM** value: **100.00**
• **CGC:** 1 graded, best 6.5

DOC SAVAGE: CURSE OF THE FIRE GOD — Dark Horse

1 ❑ Sep 1995 Cover: 2.95 **NM** value: **Cover or less**
Circ: CapCity orders: **4,575**
A: Pat Broderick; Steve Vance **W:** Steve Vance
2 ❑ Oct 1995 Cover: 2.95 **NM** value: **Cover or less**
A: Pat Broderick; Steve Vance **W:** Steve Vance

Other grades: Multiply prices above by **1.5 for Mint • 2/3 for Very Fine • 1/3 for Fine • 1/5 for Very Good • 1/8 for Good**

3 ❑ Nov 1995 Cover: 2.95 **NM** value: **Cover or less**
A: Pat Broderick; Steve Vance **W:** Steve Vance
4 ❑ Dec 1995 Cover: 2.95 **NM** value: **Cover or less**
A: Pat Broderick; Steve Vance **W:** Steve Vance

DOC SAVAGE (DC) — DC

Doctor Clark Savage Jr. is one of the most famous characters from 1930s pulp fiction. Raised by his father to be the perfect man, Savage has talents ranging from performing microsurgery to stopping terrorists. He is aided in his adventures by a cast of colorful operatives who are themselves masters of various disciplines.

In the 1988 Doc Savage mini-series, Doc went on a cross-time chase after Nazi scientist Heinz Wessel. Emerging in the present day, he found that although he has maintained his youth, his operatives are now old men. Moreover, Savage discovers he is now a grandfather, with Clark Savage IV showing every sign of following in his illustrious footsteps.

1 ❑ Nov 1988 Cover: 1.75 **NM** value: **2.00**
Circ: CapCity orders: **18,800**
📖 Fire In The Sky!; The Discord Makers, Part 1 **A:** Rod Whigham; Steve Montano **W:** Denny O'Neil
2 ❑ Dec 1988 Cover: 1.75 **NM** value: **2.00**
Circ: CapCity orders: **14,500**
📖 The Discord Makers, Part 2 **A:** Rod Whigham; Steve Montano **W:** Denny O'Neil
3 ❑ Dec 1988 Cover: 1.75 **NM** value: **2.00**
Circ: CapCity orders: **13,000**
4 ❑ Jan 1989 Cover: 1.75 **NM** value: **2.00**
Circ: CapCity orders: **12,050**
5 ❑ Jan 1989 Cover: 1.75 **NM** value: **2.00**
Circ: CapCity orders: **11,400**
6 ❑ Mar 1989 Cover: 1.75 **NM** value: **2.00**
Circ: CapCity orders: **10,700**
7 ❑ Apr 1989 Cover: 1.75 **NM** value: **2.00**
Circ: CapCity orders: **10,000**
8 ❑ May 1989 Cover: 1.75 **NM** value: **2.00**
Circ: CapCity orders: **9,500**
9 ❑ Jun 1989 Cover: 1.75 **NM** value: **2.00**
Circ: CapCity orders: **9,100**
10 ❑ Jul 1989 Cover: 1.75 **NM** value: **2.00**
Circ: CapCity orders: **8,700**
11 ❑ Aug 1989 Cover: 1.75 **NM** value: **2.00**
Circ: CapCity orders: **8,550**
★ Versus John Sunlight.
12 ❑ Sep 1989 Cover: 1.75 **NM** value: **2.00**
Circ: CapCity orders: **8,200**
★ Versus John Sunlight.
13 ❑ Oct 1989 Cover: 2.00 **NM** value: **Cover or less**
Circ: CapCity orders: **8,450**
★ Versus John Sunlight.
14 ❑ Nov 1989 Cover: 2.00 **NM** value: **Cover or less**
Circ: CapCity orders: **7,750**
★ Versus John Sunlight.
15 ❑ Dec 1989 Cover: 2.00 **NM** value: **Cover or less**
Circ: CapCity orders: **7,500**
16 ❑ Jan 1990 Cover: 2.00 **NM** value: **Cover or less**
Circ: CapCity orders: **7,770**
17 ❑ Feb 1990 Cover: 2.00 **NM** value: **Cover or less**
Circ: CapCity orders: **8,800**
• Shadow
18 ❑ Mar 1990 Cover: 2.00 **NM** value: **Cover or less**
Circ: CapCity orders: **8,450**
• Shadow
19 ❑ May 1990 Cover: 2.00 **NM** value: **Cover or less**
Circ: CapCity orders: **7,150**
📖 Air Lord
20 ❑ Jun 1990 Cover: 2.00 **NM** value: **Cover or less**
Circ: CapCity orders: **7,750**
📖 Air Lord
21 ❑ Jul 1990 Cover: 2.00 **NM** value: **Cover or less**
Circ: CapCity orders: **7,750**
📖 Air Lord
22 ❑ Aug 1990 Cover: 2.00 **NM** value: **Cover or less**
Circ: CapCity orders: **7,350**
23 ❑ Sep 1990 Cover: 2.00 **NM** value: **Cover or less**
Circ: CapCity orders: **7,100**
24 ❑ Oct 1990 Cover: 2.00 **NM** value: **Cover or less**
Circ: CapCity orders: **6,650**
final issue.
Anl 1❑ca. 1989 Cover: 3.50 **NM** value: **Cover or less**
Circ: CapCity orders: **9,450**

DOC SAVAGE: DEVIL'S THOUGHTS — Millennium

1 ❑ Cover: 2.50 **NM** value: **Cover or less**
Circ: CapCity orders: **7,400**
A: Steve Stiles **W:** Charles Moore
2 ❑ Cover: 2.50 **NM** value: **Cover or less**
Circ: CapCity orders: **6,625**
3 ❑ Cover: 2.50 **NM** value: **Cover or less**
Circ: CapCity orders: **5,600**

DOC SAVAGE: DOOM DYNASTY — Millennium

1 ❑ full color Cover: 2.50 **NM** value: **Cover or less**
Circ: CapCity orders: **8,225**
A: Mike Wieringo **W:** Terry Collins
2 ❑ full color Cover: 2.50 **NM** value: **Cover or less**
Circ: CapCity orders: **6,675**
A: Mike Wieringo **W:** Terry Collins

DOC SAVAGE (GOLD KEY) — Gold Key

1 ❑ Nov 1966 Cover: 0.12 **NM** value: **35.00**
• **CGC:** 3 graded, best 9.0
📖 The Thousand-Headed Man • 10192-611

DOC SAVAGE: MANUAL OF BRONZE — Millennium

Pulp fiction favorite Doc Savage made his first appearance in The Man of Bronze in Doc Savage Magazine #1, way back in 1933. Pulp publishers Street & Smith also published a short-lived comics series in the 1940s, while Marvel and DC published comics versions in the 1970s and 1980s, respectively. In the early 1990s, Millennium Publications brought the bronze warrior back to comics readers. Not only did they publish several stories, they also released the Manual of Bronze, which was a compendium of information about the character.

Whatever a fan wanted to know about Doc Savage, they could find in this manual. The book contained vital statistics about all of the main characters. These included everything from the exact height of Doc Savage (six feet, eight inches tall), to blueprints for all the bases, vehicles, and weapons used by Savage and his allies.

1 ❑ Aug 1992 Cover: 2.50 **NM** value: **Cover or less**
Circ: CapCity orders: **7,650**
A: Melissa Martin **W:** Mark Ellis; Paul Davis

DOC SAVAGE (MARVEL) — Marvel

1 ❑ Oct 1972 Cover: 0.20 **NM** value: **6.00**
📖 The Man Of Bronze! • adapts Man of Bronze **A:** Ross Andru; Jim Mooney **W:** Steve Englehart
2 ❑ Dec 1972 Cover: 0.20 **NM** value: **3.50**
• adapts Man of Bronze
3 ❑ Feb 1973 Cover: 0.20 **NM** value: **3.00**
• adapts Death in Silver
4 ❑ Apr 1973 Cover: 0.20 **NM** value: **3.00**
• adapts Death in Silver
5 ❑ Jun 1973 Cover: 0.20 **NM** value: **3.00**
• adapts The Monsters
6 ❑ Aug 1973 Cover: 0.20 **NM** value: **3.00**
📖 Where Giants Walk! • adapts The Monsters **A:** Ross Andru **C:** Gil Kane **W:** Gardner F. Fox
7 ❑ Oct 1973 Cover: 0.20 **NM** value: **3.00**
• adapts Brand of the Werewolf
8 ❑ Jan 1974 Cover: 0.20 **NM** value: **3.00**
• adapts Brand of the Werewolf
GS 1❑ca. 1975 Cover: 0.50 **NM** value: **6.00**
• Reprints Doc Savage (Marvel) #1-2

DOC SAVAGE (MARVEL MAGAZINE) — Marvel

With renewed interest in the character sparked by the Doc Savage movie, Marvel kicked off this quarterly black-and-white Doc Savage magazine in 1975. Doc Savage, of course, is the legendary "Man of Bronze," and one of the original pulp fiction action heroes. The title presents new stories by writer Doug Moench, along with film features, interviews with people involved with the creation of Doc Savage, and reviews of the original Doc Savage magazines and novels.

In its eight-issue run, this magazine showed Clark Savage Jr. and his friends, the Amazing Five, saving the world from a variety of madmen. Wherever adventure took him, Savage was always ready to meet it using his intellect and fighting skills to win the day.

1 ❑ Aug 1975 Cover: 1.00 **NM** value: **4.00**
• **CGC:** 5 graded, best 9.4
2 ❑ Oct 1975 Cover: 1.00 **NM** value: **3.00**
3 ❑ Jan 1976 Cover: 1.00 **NM** value: **3.00**
• **CGC:** 1 graded, best 9.0
4 ❑ Apr 1976 Cover: 1.00 **NM** value: **3.00**
• **CGC:** 1 graded, best 9.4
5 ❑ Jul 1976 Cover: 1.00 **NM** value: **3.00**
6 ❑ Oct 1976 Cover: 1.00 **NM** value: **3.00**
7 ❑ Jan 1977 Cover: 1.00 **NM** value: **3.00**
8 ❑ Spr 1977 Cover: 1.00 **NM** value: **3.00**

DOC SAVAGE (MINI-SERIES) — DC

1 ❑ Nov 1987 Cover: 1.75 **NM** value: **2.00**
Circ: CapCity orders: **25,750**
📖 Into The Silver Pyramid **A:** Adam Kubert; Andy Kubert **W:** Denny O'Neil
2 ❑ Dec 1987 Cover: 1.75 **NM** value: **2.00**
Circ: CapCity orders: **20,700**
A: Adam Kubert; Andy Kubert
3 ❑ Jan 1988 Cover: 1.75 **NM** value: **2.00**
Circ: CapCity orders: **19,000**
A: Adam Kubert; Andy Kubert
4 ❑ Feb 1988 Cover: 1.75 **NM** value: **2.00**
Circ: CapCity orders: **19,250**
A: Adam Kubert; Andy Kubert

DOC SAVAGE: REPEL — Millennium

1 ❑ Cover: 2.50 **NM** value: **Cover or less**
Circ: CapCity orders: **5,125**
• only issue ever released

DOC SAVAGE: THE MAN OF BRONZE — Millennium

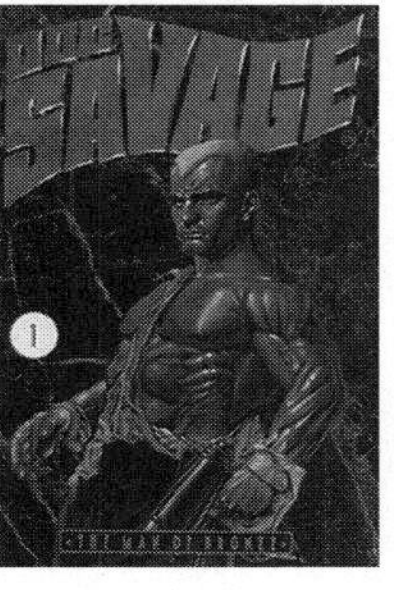

Doc Savage, "the Man of Bronze" was created in 1933 by Lester Dent, writing under the name of Kenneth Robeson. Savage was arguably one of the two most important characters of the 1930s pulps (the other was The Shadow), serving as the inspiration to countless characters which followed. These include Superman, Batman, Indiana Jones, Buckaroo Banzai, and countless others.

After 182 novels published in the 1930s and 1940s, Savage fell from popularity, and the magazine that spawned him ceased publishing in 1949. Marvel picked up the character for a 1972 color, and a 1975 black-and-white series, with mixed results. The rights then moved over to DC in the 1980s, which tried to place the hero in the modern world, again with unsatisfying results. Millennium's treatment in Doc Savage: The Man of Bronze seems to come closest to the original, capturing all the action, humanity, and humor of the original novels.

1 ❑ full color Cover: 2.50 **NM** value: **Cover or less**
Circ: CapCity orders: **17,250**
📖 The Monarch Of Armageddon **A:** Darryl Banks **W:** Mark Ellis
2 ❑ Cover: 2.50 **NM** value: **Cover or less**
Circ: CapCity orders: **10,925**
📖 The Monarch Of Armageddon **A:** Darryl Banks **C:** Doug Wildey **W:** Mark Ellis
3 ❑ Cover: 2.50 **NM** value: **Cover or less**
Circ: CapCity orders: **8,850**
4 ❑ Cover: 2.50 **NM** value: **Cover or less**
Circ: CapCity orders: **8,175**

DOC STEARN...MR. MONSTER — Eclipse

1 ❑ Jan 1985 Cover: 1.75 **NM** value: **2.50**
📖 Triumphant Unleashed • Reprints Mr. Monster story from Vanguard Illustrated #7 **A:** Greg Fox **W:** John Riley ★ 1st Appearance of Mr. Monster.
2 ❑ Aug 1985 Cover: 1.75 **NM** value: **2.00**
C: Dave Stevens
3 ❑ Oct 1985 Cover: 1.75 **NM** value: **2.00**
4 ❑ Dec 1985 Cover: 1.75 **NM** value: **2.00**
5 ❑ Feb 1986 Cover: 1.75 **NM** value: **2.00**
6 ❑ Jun 1986 Cover: 1.75 **NM** value: **2.00**
7 ❑ Dec 1986 Cover: 1.75 **NM** value: **2.00**
8 ❑ Mar 1987 Cover: 1.75 **NM** value: **2.00**
📖 The Case of the Reluctant Werewolf **A:** Michael T. Gilbert **W:** Michael T. Gilbert
9 ❑ Apr 1987 Cover: 1.75 **NM** value: **2.00**
📖 The Hemo Horror **A:** Michael T. Gilbert **W:** Michael T. Gilbert ★ Appearance of Wolff & Byrd.
10 ❑ Jun 1987 Cover: 1.75 **NM** value: **2.00**
📖 Swamp Monster; Rot; The Riddle of the Recalcitrant Refuse final issue. • 6-D **A:** Jeff Bonivert; Basil Wolverton; Michael T. Gilbert **W:** Basil Wolverton; Michael T. Gilbert; Alan Moore

DR. ANDY — Alliance

1 ❑ Aug 1994, b&w Cover: 2.50 **NM** value: **Cover or less**

DR. ANTHONY KING, HOLLYWOOD LOVE DOCTOR — Minoan

1 ❑ 1952 Cover: 0.10 **NM** value: **55.00**
2 ❑ 1952 Cover: 0.10 **NM** value: **32.00**
3 ❑ 1953 Cover: 0.10 **NM** value: **32.00**
4 ❑ May 1954 Cover: 0.10 **NM** value: **32.00**
📖 Winter and Spring; The Lover Who Had No Face; Who Am I?; The Redhead and Formula X final issue.

DR. ATOMIC — Last Gasp

1 ❑ Cover: 0.50 **NM** value: **5.00**
📖 Dr. Atomic and His Spaceship; Dr. Atomic Invents the Iron Pig; Let a Smile be Your Umbrella; The Great Bank Robber; A Horny Old Geezer; Divine Comedy; Dr. Atomic Meets The Space Brothers **A:** Larry S. Todd **W:** Larry S. Todd
2 ❑ Cover: 0.50 **NM** value: **4.00**
📖 The Giant Grass of Bangagong Valley; **A:** Larry S. Todd **W:** Larry S. Todd
3 ❑ Cover: 0.50 **NM** value: **4.00**
📖 Dr. Atomic Meets The Lochness Monster; Dr. Atomic and Mr. Hyde; Dr. Atomic and the Flying Saucers; Pot Bust; Let's Go Hang Gliding with Dr. Atomic **A:** Larry S. Todd **W:** Larry S. Todd
4 ❑ Cover: 0.50 **NM** value: **3.00**
📖 The Pipe and the Dope Book **A:** Larry S. Todd **W:** Larry S. Todd
5 ❑ Cover: 0.50 **NM** value: **3.00**
📖 The Astral Flashlight; Kids Grow Giant Psychedelic Mushrooms 6 Feet Tall; Robot's Reward **A:** Larry S. Todd **W:** Larry S. Todd
6 ❑ Cover: 0.50 **NM** value: **3.00**
📖 The Chariots of The Sun; **A:** Larry S. Todd **W:** Larry S. Todd

DOCTOR BANG — Rip Off

1 ❑ Feb 1992, b&w Cover: 2.50 **NM** value: **Cover or less**

DOCTOR BOOGIE — Media Arts

1 ❑ Cover: 1.75 **NM** value: **Cover or less**
Circ: CapCity orders: **2,550**
📖 Doctor Boogie vs. The Dirt Blobs **A:** Dan McHugh; Peter Gullerud **W:** Dave Newell

DOCTOR CHAOS — Triumphant

1 ❑ Cover: 2.50 **NM** value: **Cover or less**
Circ: CapCity orders: **8,145**

CGC-graded: Multiply prices above by **33 for 9.9 M • 16 for 9.8 NM/M • 7 for 9.6 NM+ • 5 for 9.4 NM • 2.5 for 9.2 NM- • 1.5 for 9.0 VF/NM**

📖 The Demon of Destiny Drive; The Yellow Death; My Fears; Invaders From Mars? • Unleashed! **A:** Jeff Bonivert; William Messner-Loebs; Michael T. Gilbert **W:** Jeff Bonivert; William Messner-Loebs; Michael T. Gilbert

2 ❑ Cover: 2.50 **NM** value: **Cover or less**
Circ: CapCity orders: **6,465**
📖 Bubble Bath of the Damned!; Stretching Things; The Olde Curiosity Shoppe • Unleashed! **A:** Keith Giffen; Donald Simpson; Michael T. Gilbert; Brian Buniak **W:** Keith Giffen; Michael T. Gilbert; Brian Preger

3 ❑ Jan 1994 Cover: 2.50 **NM** value: **Cover or less**
Circ: CapCity orders: **4,085**
📖 Mr. Monster's Bedtime Story, The One Who Lurks! **A:** Michael T. Gilbert; Mark Pacella **W:** Michael T. Gilbert; Randall A. Frew

4 ❑ Feb 1994 Cover: 2.50 **NM** value: **Cover or less**
Circ: CapCity orders: **3,490**
📖 Automatic Terror Machine; On the Job **A:** William Wray; Michael T. Gilbert; Mark Pacella **W:** Michael T. Gilbert; Scott Deschaine

5 ❑ Mar 1994 Cover: 2.50 **NM** value: **Cover or less**
Circ: CapCity orders: **2,705**
📖 Mr. Monster's Vacation; Mr. Monster's Nursery Digest: Up in the Air; Guilty as Hell! **A:** Gerald Forton; Michael T. Gilbert; Batton Lash **W:** Michael T. Gilbert; Batton Lash

6 ❑ Mar 1994 Cover: 2.50 **NM** value: **Cover or less**
Circ: CapCity orders: **2,269**
A: Donald Simpson; Michael T. Gilbert **W:** Michael T. Gilbert

7 ❑ 1994 Cover: 2.50 **NM** value: **Cover or less**
Circ: CapCity orders: **1,885**

8 ❑ 1994 Cover: 2.50 **NM** value: **Cover or less**
9 ❑ 1994 Cover: 2.50 **NM** value: **Cover or less**
10 ❑ 1994 Cover: 2.50 **NM** value: **Cover or less**
11 ❑ 1994 Cover: 2.50 **NM** value: **Cover or less**
12 ❑ 1994 Cover: 2.50 **NM** value: **Cover or less**

DOCTOR CYBORG — Attention!

1 ❑ b&w Cover: 2.95 **NM** value: **Cover or less**
A: Marc Hempel; Damon Willis; Mark Wheatley **W:** Allan Gross ★ 1st Appearance of Doctor Cyborg.

1/Ash❑b&w Cover: 0.99 **NM** value: **1.00**
No issue number. • Preview edition of Doctor Cyborg #1. • preview of series **A:** Marc Hempel; Damon Willis; Mark Wheatley **W:** Allan Gross ★ 1st Appearance of Doctor Cyborg.

2 ❑ b&w Cover: 2.95 **NM** value: **Cover or less**
3 ❑ b&w Cover: 2.95 **NM** value: **Cover or less**

DOCTOR DOOM'S REVENGE — Marvel

1 ❑ ca. 1989 **NM** value: **1.00**
• **CGC:** 1 graded, best 9.0
No issue number. • giveaway comic included with computer game from Paragon Software.

DOCTOR FATE — DC

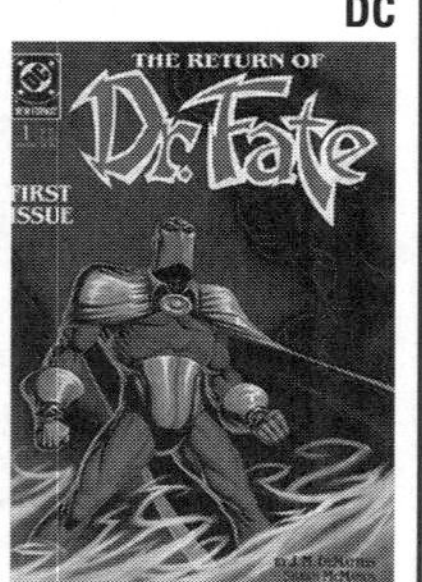

Doctor Fate has been a DC character since the 1940s, when he was introduced in More Fun Comics #55. Although the appearance he presents to the world has remained the same, a number of people have worn the mask. In this series, it's a young boy named Eric, who was artificially aged by the Lord of Order to take on the role of Dr. Fate. But Dr. Fate was always meant to be two people, and it was only when the soul of Eric's stepmother, Linda, was added to his that they formed the first true Dr. Fate.

These two people can join together to become a sorcerous force for order in the continuing war against chaos. This leads to a strange dilemma: a man with the soul of a boy becomes joined, literally body and soul, with a woman who was once his stepmother, and is now more of a soulmate. The strange tension of this relationship notwithstanding, Dr. Fate has a job to do, saving the world from all manner of supernatural perils.

1 ❑ Dec 1988 Cover: 1.25 **NM** value: **2.00**
Circ: CapCity orders: **23,600** • **CGC:** 2 graded, best 9.0
📖 The Return Of Doctor Faith **A:** Shawn McManus **W:** J.M. DeMatteis

2 ❑ Jan 1989 Cover: 1.25 **NM** value: **Cover or less**
Circ: CapCity orders: **17,700**
3 ❑ Jan 1989 Cover: 1.25 **NM** value: **Cover or less**
Circ: CapCity orders: **16,750**
4 ❑ Feb 1989 Cover: 1.25 **NM** value: **Cover or less**
Circ: CapCity orders: **17,550**
5 ❑ Apr 1989 Cover: 1.25 **NM** value: **Cover or less**
Circ: CapCity orders: **16,350**
6 ❑ May 1989 Cover: 1.75 **NM** value: **Cover or less**
Circ: CapCity orders: **15,850**
7 ❑ Jun 1989 Cover: 1.75 **NM** value: **Cover or less**
Circ: CapCity orders: **15,850**
8 ❑ Jul 1989 Cover: 1.75 **NM** value: **Cover or less**
Circ: CapCity orders: **15,050**
9 ❑ Aug 1989 Cover: 1.75 **NM** value: **Cover or less**
Circ: CapCity orders: **14,550**
10 ❑ Sep 1989 Cover: 1.75 **NM** value: **Cover or less**
Circ: CapCity orders: **14,100**
11 ❑ Nov 1989 Cover: 1.75 **NM** value: **Cover or less**
Circ: CapCity orders: **12,750**
12 ❑ Dec 1989 Cover: 1.75 **NM** value: **Cover or less**
Circ: CapCity orders: **12,350**
13 ❑ Jan 1990 Cover: 1.75 **NM** value: **Cover or less**
Circ: CapCity orders: **12,050**
14 ❑ Feb 1990 Cover: 1.75 **NM** value: **Cover or less**
Circ: CapCity orders: **11,850**
15 ❑ Mar 1990 Cover: 1.50 **NM** value: **Cover or less**
Circ: CapCity orders: **11,650**
★ Appearance of JLI.
16 ❑ Apr 1990 Cover: 1.50 **NM** value: **Cover or less**
Circ: CapCity orders: **11,350**
17 ❑ May 1990 Cover: 1.50 **NM** value: **Cover or less**
Circ: CapCity orders: **11,250**
18 ❑ Jun 1990 Cover: 1.50 **NM** value: **Cover or less**
Circ: CapCity orders: **11,150**
19 ❑ Jul 1990 Cover: 1.50 **NM** value: **Cover or less**
Circ: CapCity orders: **11,100**
20 ❑ Aug 1990 Cover: 1.50 **NM** value: **Cover or less**
Circ: CapCity orders: **10,550**
21 ❑ Oct 1990 Cover: 1.50 **NM** value: **Cover or less**
Circ: CapCity orders: **10,350**
22 ❑ Nov 1990 Cover: 1.50 **NM** value: **Cover or less**
Circ: CapCity orders: **10,050**
23 ❑ Dec 1990 Cover: 1.50 **NM** value: **Cover or less**
Circ: CapCity orders: **9,950**
24 ❑ Jan 1991 Cover: 1.50 **NM** value: **Cover or less**
Circ: CapCity orders: **9,750**
25 ❑ Feb 1991 Cover: 1.50 **NM** value: **Cover or less**
Circ: CapCity orders: **12,250**
★ 1st Appearance of Doctor Fate (New).
26 ❑ Mar 1991 Cover: 1.50 **NM** value: **Cover or less**
Circ: CapCity orders: **10,150**
27 ❑ Apr 1991 Cover: 1.50 **NM** value: **Cover or less**
Circ: CapCity orders: **9,200**
28 ❑ May 1991 Cover: 1.50 **NM** value: **Cover or less**
Circ: CapCity orders: **9,200**
29 ❑ Jun 1991 Cover: 1.50 **NM** value: **Cover or less**
Circ: CapCity orders: **9,400**
30 ❑ Jul 1991 Cover: 1.50 **NM** value: **Cover or less**
Circ: CapCity orders: **9,400**
31 ❑ Aug 1991 Cover: 1.50 **NM** value: **Cover or less**
Circ: CapCity orders: **9,150**
32 ❑ Sep 1991 Cover: 1.75 **NM** value: **Cover or less**
Circ: CapCity orders: **15,450**
📖 War of the Gods, Part 8 • War of the Gods
33 ❑ Oct 1991 Cover: 1.75 **NM** value: **Cover or less**
Circ: CapCity orders: **14,450**
📖 War of the Gods, Part 14 • War of the Gods
34 ❑ Nov 1991 Cover: 1.75 **NM** value: **Cover or less**
Circ: CapCity orders: **9,450**
35 ❑ Dec 1991 Cover: 1.75 **NM** value: **Cover or less**
Circ: CapCity orders: **9,200**
36 ❑ Jan 1992 Cover: 1.75 **NM** value: **Cover or less**
Circ: CapCity orders: **9,650**
37 ❑ Feb 1992 Cover: 1.75 **NM** value: **Cover or less**
Circ: CapCity orders: **9,200**
38 ❑ Mar 1992 Cover: 1.75 **NM** value: **Cover or less**
Circ: CapCity orders: **9,300**
39 ❑ Apr 1992 Cover: 1.75 **NM** value: **Cover or less**
Circ: CapCity orders: **7,950**
40 ❑ May 1992 Cover: 1.75 **NM** value: **Cover or less**
Circ: CapCity orders: **8,000**
41 ❑ Jun 1992 Cover: 1.75 **NM** value: **Cover or less**
Circ: CapCity orders: **8,300**
📖 Balances final issue. **A:** Peter Gross **W:** William Messner-Loebs
Anl 1❑Nov 1989 Cover: 2.95 **NM** value: **Cover or less**
Circ: CapCity orders: **14,800**

DOCTOR FATE (MINI-SERIES) — DC

1 ❑ Jul 1987 Cover: 1.50 **NM** value: **2.00**
Circ: CapCity orders: **20,250**
📖 Cycles **A:** Keith Giffen **W:** J.M. DeMatteis
2 ❑ Aug 1987 Cover: 1.50 **NM** value: **2.00**
Circ: CapCity orders: **17,950**
📖 Asylum **A:** Keith Giffen **W:** J.M. DeMatteis
3 ❑ Sep 1987 Cover: 1.50 **NM** value: **2.00**
Circ: CapCity orders: **19,050**
A: Keith Giffen **W:** J.M. DeMatteis
4 ❑ Oct 1987 Cover: 1.50 **NM** value: **2.00**
Circ: CapCity orders: **20,250**
📖 Incarnations **A:** Keith Giffen **W:** J.M. DeMatteis ★ 1st Appearance of Doctor Fate II (Eric Strauss & Linda Strauss). ★ Death of Doctor Fate I (Kent Nelson).

DOCTOR FAUSTUS — Anarchy

1 ❑ b&w Cover: 2.95 **NM** value: **Cover or less**
A: Vinton Heuck **W:** Michael O'Connell
2 ❑ b&w Cover: 2.95 **NM** value: **Cover or less**
A: Tomas Sisneros **W:** Michael O'Connell
Ash 1❑ **NM** value: **2.00**
• ashcan, b&w

DOCTOR FRANKENSTEIN'S HOUSE OF 3-D — 3-D Zone

1 ❑ Cover: 3.95 **NM** value: **Cover or less**
• Oversized.

DR. FU MANCHU — I.W.

1 ❑ ca. 1964 Cover: 0.12 **NM** value: **50.00**
• **CGC:** 1 graded, best 8.0

Capital City orders are the actual sales of comic books by Capital City Distribution, once one of the largest U.S. sellers of comics to comics shops. Capital City's share of comics shop sales, while not known exactly, increases from around 10-20% in the mid-1980s to 30-35% in the mid-1990s. Capital City's share of comic books sold on newsstands (most Marvels and DCs) will be less.

DR. GIGGLES — Dark Horse

Dr. Giggles is the blood-strewn adaptation of the movie of the same name. It all takes place in the town of Moorehigh, where in 1941, the town doctor went crazy and embarked on a killing spree. Dr. Rendell brutally slew person after person. Four of the bodies were never even recovered. Town legend has it that they were hidden in the walls of his now-abandoned house.

Fifty years later, it seems that someone new is playing doctor. An escapee from a mental ward has decided to carry on Rendell's deadly legacy, performing ghastly operations on the unwilling townsfolk. The action here is completely over the top, as seems to be the writer's intent. The story is full of blood and black humor. It's a horror comedy of a sort for those with a strong stomach.

1 ❑ 1992 Cover: 2.50 **NM** value: **Cover or less**
Circ: CapCity orders: **6,225**
📖 Discharge Granted **A:** Kent Burles **W:** Steven Grant
2 ❑ 1992 Cover: 2.50 **NM** value: **Cover or less**
Circ: CapCity orders: **5,000**
A: Kent Burles **W:** Steven Grant

DOCTOR GORPON — Eternity

1 ❑ b&w Cover: 2.50 **NM** value: **Cover or less**
📖 Hands of Death **A:** Marc Hansen **W:** Marc Hansen
2 ❑ b&w Cover: 2.50 **NM** value: **Cover or less**
A: Marc Hansen **W:** Marc Hansen
3 ❑ Aug 1991, b&w Cover: 2.50 **NM** value: **Cover or less**
A: Marc Hansen **W:** Marc Hansen

DR. GOYLE SPECIAL — Arrow

1 ❑ b&w Cover: 2.95 **NM** value: **Cover or less**

DR. KILDARE — Dell

2 ❑ 1962 Cover: 0.12 **NM** value: **50.00**
3 ❑ Oct 1962 Cover: 0.12 **NM** value: **50.00**
4 ❑ Dec 1962 Cover: 0.12 **NM** value: **50.00**
5 ❑ Mar 1963 Cover: 0.12 **NM** value: **50.00**
6 ❑ Jun 1963 Cover: 0.12 **NM** value: **50.00**
7 ❑ Sep 1963 Cover: 0.12 **NM** value: **50.00**
8 ❑ Oct 1964 Cover: 0.12 **NM** value: **50.00**
9 ❑ Apr 1965 Cover: 0.12 **NM** value: **50.00**
• **CGC:** 1 graded, best 9.0

DOCTOR MID-NITE — DC

This prestige format mini-series introduces a new Doctor Mid-Nite to the DC universe. After completing his residency under Dr. Charles McNider, the Golden Age Doctor Mid-Nite, our modern-day hero (who will eventually join the 2000 version of the Justice Society of America) succeeds in both the medical profession and in his elective endeavors as a super-hero.

Created by Matt Wagner of Grendel and Mage fame, this Doctor Mid-Nite is a bit grimmer than the original, but he is nonetheless intriguing; far from the one-note, stone-faced vigilante-type that became popular in the 1980s. Wagner's Doc even makes use of his medical training in his super-heroing.

1 ❑ ca. 1999 Cover: 5.95 **NM** value: **Cover or less**
Circ: Diamd. preorders: **25,330**
• D.O.A. **A:** John K. Snyder III **W:** Matt Wagner
2 ❑ ca. 1999 Cover: 5.95 **NM** value: **Cover or less**
Circ: Diamd. preorders: **20,428**
A: John K. Snyder III **W:** Matt Wagner ★ Appearance of Mouthpiece, Terrible Trio, Black Shadow, Note-Lite.
3 ❑ ca. 1999 Cover: 5.95 **NM** value: **Cover or less**
Circ: Diamd. preorders: **20,983**
A: John K. Snyder III **W:** Matt Wagner
Bk 1❑ ca. 1999 Cover: 19.95 **NM** value: **Cover or less**
• Collects series **A:** John K. Snyder III **W:** Matt Wagner

DR. RADIUM AND THE GIZMOS OF BOOLA-BOOLA — Slave Labor

1 ❑ Jan 1992, b&w Cover: 4.95 **NM** value: **Cover or less**
No issue number.

DR. RADIUM, MAN OF SCIENCE — Slave Labor

1 ❑ Oct 1992, b&w Cover: 2.50 **NM** value: **Cover or less**
2 ❑ Jan 1993, b&w Cover: 2.50 **NM** value: **Cover or less**
3 ❑ Jul 1993 Cover: 2.95 **NM** value: **Cover or less**
4 ❑ Jan 1994 Cover: 2.95 **NM** value: **Cover or less**
5 ❑ Jan 1995, b&w Cover: 2.95 **NM** value: **Cover or less**

DR. ROBOT SPECIAL — Dark Horse

1 ❑ Apr 2000 Cover: 2.95 **NM** value: **Cover or less**
A: Bernie E. Mireault **W:** Bernie E. Mireault

Other grades: Multiply prices above by **1.5 for Mint • 2/3 for Very Fine • 1/3 for Fine • 1/5 for Very Good • 1/8 for Good**

DOCTOR SOLAR, MAN OF THE ATOM — Gold Key

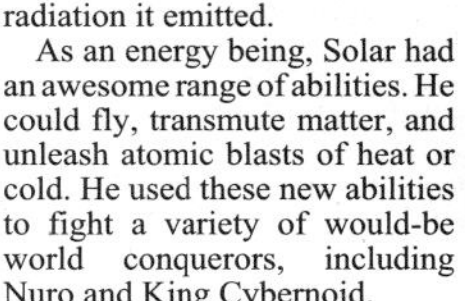
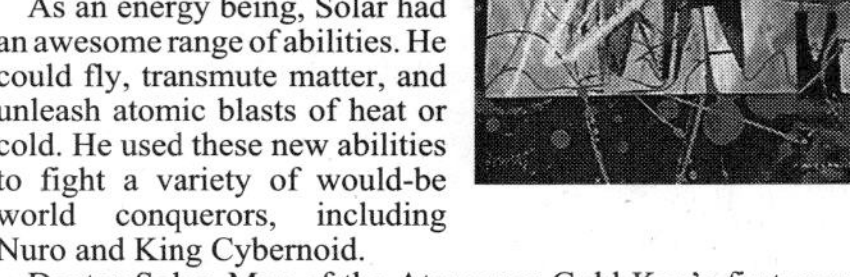

Working in a research laboratory in Atom Valley, Doctor Solar was caught in a premature atomic explosion. The blast had the effect of converting his body into pure energy. At the same time, he retained his consciousness. Later, he would learn to reform his body, and use a special cadmium-lined suit to control the radiation it emitted.

As an energy being, Solar had an awesome range of abilities. He could fly, transmute matter, and unleash atomic blasts of heat or cold. He used these new abilities to fight a variety of would-be world conquerors, including Nuro and King Cybernoid.

Doctor Solar, Man of the Atom was Gold Key's first comics title. Originally published from the early 1960s to the early 1980s, it enjoyed a renaissance in the early '90s when new publisher Valiant licensed the character. Updated, Solar, Man of the Atom became a cornerstone of the Valiant universe.

1 ❑ Oct 1962 Cover: 0.12 **NM** value: **100.00**
• **CGC:** 13 graded, best 9.6
• 1st Gold Key comic★ Origin of Doctor Solar. ★ 1st Appearance of Doctor Solar (out of costume).

2 ❑ Dec 1962 Cover: 0.12 **NM** value: **45.00**
• **CGC:** 2 graded, best 9.0
★ 1st Appearance of Professor Harbinger.

3 ❑ Mar 1963 Cover: 0.12 **NM** value: **30.00**
• **CGC:** 2 graded, best 9.6

4 ❑ Jun 1963 Cover: 0.12 **NM** value: **30.00**
• **CGC:** 1 graded, best 9.4

5 ❑ Sep 1963 Cover: 0.12 **NM** value: **30.00**
★ 1st Appearance of Doctor Solar (in costume).

6 ❑ Nov 1963 Cover: 0.12 **NM** value: **22.00**

7 ❑ Mar 1964 Cover: 0.12 **NM** value: **22.00**
Circ: Statement: **247,315**
Painted cover. Keys of Kn

8 ❑ Jul 1964 Cover: 0.12 **NM** value: **22.00**
Circ: Statement: **247,315**

9 ❑ Oct 1964 Cover: 0.12 **NM** value: **22.00**
Circ: Statement: **247,315**

10 ❑ Jan 1965 Cover: 0.12 **NM** value: **22.00**
Circ: Statement: **226,720**

11 ❑ Mar 1965 Cover: 0.12 **NM** value: **16.00**
Circ: Statement: **226,720**

12 ❑ May 1965 Cover: 0.12 **NM** value: **16.00**
Circ: Statement: **226,720**
• makes multiple versions of self

13 ❑ Jul 1965 Cover: 0.12 **NM** value: **16.00**
Circ: Statement: **226,720** • **CGC:** 1 graded, best 7.5

14 ❑ Sep 1965 Cover: 0.12 **NM** value: **16.00**
Circ: Statement: **226,720**
Painted cover. Solar's Midas Touch, Part 1; Solar's Science Forum; Professor Harbinger: The Angry Waves; Solar's Midas Touch, Part 2

15 ❑ Dec 1965 Cover: 0.12 **NM** value: **20.00**
Circ: Statement: **226,720** • **CGC:** 1 graded, best 9.2
★ Origin of Doctor Solar.

16 ❑ Jun 1966 Cover: 0.12 **NM** value: **16.00**
Circ: Statement: **224,936**
Painted cover. Secrets of Atom Valley; The War of the Suns, Part 1; Secrets of Atom Valley: Birth of a Death Ray; Solar's Science Forum; Professor Harbinger: Mysteries of Light; The War of the Suns, Part 2; Secrets of Atom Valley: Security Guard

17 ❑ Sep 1966 Cover: 0.12 **NM** value: **16.00**
Circ: Statement: **224,936**

18 ❑ Dec 1966 Cover: 0.12 **NM** value: **16.00**
Circ: Statement: **224,936** • **CGC:** 1 graded, best 9.2

19 ❑ Apr 1967 Cover: 0.12 **NM** value: **16.00**
Circ: Statement: **208,135**

20 ❑ Jul 1967 Cover: 0.12 **NM** value: **16.00**
Circ: Statement: **208,135**

21 ❑ Oct 1967 Cover: 0.12 **NM** value: **12.00**
Circ: Statement: **208,135**

22 ❑ Jan 1968 Cover: 0.12 **NM** value: **12.00**
23 ❑ Apr 1968 Cover: 0.12 **NM** value: **12.00**
24 ❑ Jul 1968 Cover: 0.12 **NM** value: **12.00**
25 ❑ Oct 1968 Cover: 0.15 **NM** value: **12.00**
26 ❑ Jan 1969 Cover: 0.15 **NM** value: **12.00**
27 ❑ Apr 1969 Cover: 0.15 **NM** value: **12.00**
• End of original series

28 ❑ Apr 1981 Cover: 0.50 **NM** value: **3.50**
• Series begins again (1981)

29 ❑ 1981 Cover: 0.50 **NM** value: **3.50**
30 ❑ Feb 1982 Cover: 0.60 **NM** value: **3.50**
★ Appearance of Magnus, Robot Fighter (Gold Key).

31 ❑ Mar 1982 Cover: 0.60 **NM** value: **3.50**
final issue.★ Appearance of Magnus, Robot Fighter (Gold Key).

DR. SPECK — Bug Books

1 ❑ b&w Cover: 2.95 **NM** value: **Cover or less**
2 ❑ b&w Cover: 2.95 **NM** value: **Cover or less**
3 ❑ b&w Cover: 2.95 **NM** value: **Cover or less**
4 ❑ b&w Cover: 2.95 **NM** value: **Cover or less**

DOCTOR STRANGE (1ST SERIES) — Marvel

Strange Tales was the original home to Doctor Strange, an arrogant surgeon who loses the use of his hands and learns the mystic arts from The Ancient One. First appearing in #110 of that title, Strange grew in power until he had earned the title of Earth's Sorceror Supreme.

Strange shared Strange Tales with Nick Fury for a time, until Fury spun off into his own series and Marvel's greatest magician took over Strange Tales with #169. Sadly, the Strange Tales children fared worse than the titles fissioned from Marvel's other double features, Tales of Suspense and Tales to Astonish: Neither Fury nor this renamed series, now written by Roy Thomas, lasted long. A new Doctor Strange series returned in 1974. — JJM

169 ❑ Jun 1968 Cover: 0.12 **NM** value: **100.00**
Circ: Statement: **266,422** • **CGC:** 141 graded, best 9.8
The Coming of ... Dr. Strange! • Series continued from Strange Tales #168 **A:** Dan Adkins **W:** Roy Thomas ★ Origin of Doctor Strange.

170 ❑ Jul 1968 Cover: 0.12 **NM** value: **35.00**
Circ: Statement: **266,422** • **CGC:** 20 graded, best 9.6
To Dream, Perchance to Die **A:** Dan Adkins ★ Versus Nightmare.

171 ❑ Aug 1968 Cover: 0.12 **NM** value: **30.00**
Circ: Statement: **266,422** • **CGC:** 13 graded, best 9.6
In the Shadow of Death **A:** Dan Adkins

172 ❑ Sep 1968 Cover: 0.12 **NM** value: **30.00**
Circ: Statement: **266,422** • **CGC:** 7 graded, best 9.4
I, Dormammu **A:** Gene Colan ★ Versus Dormammu.

173 ❑ Oct 1968 Cover: 0.12 **NM** value: **30.00**
Circ: Statement: **266,422** • **CGC:** 18 graded, best 9.6
While a World Awaits **A:** Gene Colan ★ Versus Dormammu.

174 ❑ Nov 1968 Cover: 0.12 **NM** value: **30.00**
Circ: Statement: **266,422** • **CGC:** 7 graded, best 9.8
The Power And The Pendulum **A:** Gene Colan **W:** Roy Thomas ★ 1st Appearance of Satannish.

175 ❑ Dec 1968 Cover: 0.12 **NM** value: **30.00**
Circ: Statement: **266,422** • **CGC:** 4 graded, best 9.2
Unto Us The Sons Of Satannish! **A:** Gene Colan **W:** Roy Thomas

176 ❑ Jan 1969 Cover: 0.12 **NM** value: **30.00**
• **CGC:** 6 graded, best 9.6
O Grave Where is Thy Victory **A:** Gene Colan **W:** Roy Thomas

177 ❑ Feb 1969 Cover: 0.12 **NM** value: **25.00**
• **CGC:** 5 graded, best 9.4
The Cult and the Curse **A:** Gene Colan ★ 1st Appearance of new costume.

178 ❑ Mar 1969 Cover: 0.12 **NM** value: **25.00**
• **CGC:** 7 graded, best 9.8
With One Beside Him **A:** Gene Colan ★ Appearance of Black Knight.

179 ❑ Apr 1969 Cover: 0.12 **NM** value: **25.00**
• **CGC:** 6 graded, best 9.4
The Wondrous World of Doctor Strange • reprints Amazing Spider-Man Annual #2; Has 1968 Statement, filed 10/1/68; avg print run 430,100; avg sales 265,547; avg subs 875; avg total paid 266,422; samples 400; max existent 266,822; 38% of run returned **A:** Steve Ditko ★ Appearance of Spider-Man.

180 ❑ May 1969 Cover: 0.12 **NM** value: **25.00**
• **CGC:** 2 graded, best 9.4
Photo cover. Eternity, Eternity **A:** Gene Colan ★ Appearance of Eternity.

181 ❑ Jun 1969 Cover: 0.12 **NM** value: **25.00**
• **CGC:** 2 graded, best 9.0
If a World Should Die Before I Wake **A:** Gene Colan

182 ❑ Sep 1969 Cover: 0.15 **NM** value: **25.00**
• **CGC:** 2 graded, best 9.6
And Juggernaut Makes Three **A:** Gene Colan ★ Versus Juggernaut.

183 ❑ Nov 1969 Cover: 0.15 **NM** value: **25.00**
• **CGC:** 1 graded, best 9.4
They Walk By Night **A:** Gene Colan

DOCTOR STRANGE (2ND SERIES) — Marvel

Doctor Strange finally gets to start a series from #1 in 1974, and he quickly makes his mark. Jim Starlin takes the Sorceror Supreme on a gut-wrenching, dimension-spanning journey through death in the "Silver Dagger" storyline, one of the all-time Dr. Strange classics.

But into the late 1970s and early 1980s, the master of the mystic arts would continually run afoul of his greatest enemy — a comics-buying market whose interest in magickal realms had greatly cooled over the years. The series came out bimonthly for much of its run, preventing it from gaining much traction. By 1987, Strange suffered the worst indignity of all — a return to starring in just one half of a newly relaunched Strange Tales, with Cloak and Dagger, no less! — JJM

1 ❑ Jun 1974 Cover: 0.25 **NM** value: **25.00**
• **CGC:** 28 graded, best 9.8
Through An Orb Darkly **A:** Frank Brunner; Dick Giordano; Dave Brunner(cover) **W:** Steve Englehart

2 ❑ Aug 1974 Cover: 0.25 **NM** value: **12.00**
• **CGC:** 6 graded, best 9.6
A Separate Reality **A:** Frank Brunner; Dick Giordano **W:** Steve Englehart ★ 1st Appearance of Silver Dagger. ★ Appearance of Defenders.

3 ❑ Sep 1974 Cover: 0.25 **NM** value: **6.00**
Amidst the Madness • reprints with changes Strange Tales #126 and 127 **A:** Frank Brunner; Dick Giordano ★ Versus Dormammu.

4 ❑ Oct 1974 Cover: 0.25 **NM** value: **6.00**
• **CGC:** 1 graded, best 8.0
Where Bound'ries Decay **A:** Frank Brunner; Dick Giordano

5 ❑ Nov 1974 Cover: 0.25 **NM** value: **6.00**
Cloak and Dagger **A:** Frank Brunner; Dick Giordano ★ Origin of Silver Dagger.

6 ❑ Dec 1974 Cover: 0.25 **NM** value: **5.00**
• **CGC:** 1 graded, best 9.6
Lift High the Veil of Tears **A:** Gene Colan

7 ❑ Apr 1975 Cover: 0.25 **NM** value: **5.00**
The Demon Fever **A:** Gene Colan

8 ❑ Jun 1975 Cover: 0.25 **NM** value: **5.00**
• **CGC:** 1 graded, best 9.8
Rights of Passage **A:** Gene Colan ★ Origin of Clea.

9 ❑ Aug 1975 Cover: 0.25 **NM** value: **5.00**
Consummation **A:** Gene Colan ★ Origin of Clea.

10 ❑ Oct 1975 Cover: 0.25 **NM** value: **5.00**
Alone Against Eternity **A:** Gene Colan

11 ❑ Dec 1975 Cover: 0.25 **NM** value: **3.00**
Shadowplay! **A:** Gene Colan

12 ❑ Feb 1976 Cover: 0.25 **NM** value: **3.00**
Final Curtain **A:** Gene Colan

13 ❑ Apr 1967 Cover: 0.25 **NM** value: **3.00**
Planet Earth Is No More **A:** Gene Colan

14 ❑ May 1976 Cover: 0.25 **NM** value: **3.00**
• **CGC:** 1 graded, best 8.0
The Tomb of Dr. Strange **A:** Gene Colan

15 ❑ Jun 1976 Cover: 0.25 **NM** value: **3.00**
• **CGC:** 1 graded, best 9.0
Where There's Smoke... **A:** Gene Colan **W:** Steve Englehart

16 ❑ Jul 1976 Cover: 0.25 **NM** value: **3.00**
Beelzebub on Parade **A:** Gene Colan

17 ❑ Aug 1976 Cover: 0.25 **NM** value: **3.00**
Utopia Rising **A:** Gene Colan

18 ❑ Sep 1976 Cover: 0.30 **NM** value: **3.00**
The Dragon Is Dead **A:** Gene Colan

19 ❑ Oct 1976 Cover: 0.30 **NM** value: **3.00**
Lo, the Powers Changeth **A:** Gene Colan; Alfredo Alcala ★ 1st Appearance of Xander.

20 ❑ Dec 1976 Cover: 0.30 **NM** value: **3.00**
Call Him: Xander the Merciless

21 ❑ Feb 1977 Cover: 0.30 **NM** value: **2.50**
The Coming of ... Dr. Strange! • reprinted from Doctor Strange (1st series) #169★ Origin of Doctor Strange.

22 ❑ Apr 1977 Cover: 0.30 **NM** value: **2.50**
Mind Trip

23 ❑ Jun 1977 Cover: 0.30 **NM** value: **2.50**
Into the Quadriverse

24 ❑ Aug 1977 Cover: 0.30 **NM** value: **2.50**
A Change Cometh

25 ❑ Oct 1977 Cover: 0.30 **NM** value: **2.50**
Doctor Strange versus Doctor Strange ?!

26 ❑ Dec 1977 Cover: 0.35 **NM** value: **2.00**
The Return of the Ancient One

27 ❑ Feb 1978 Cover: 0.35 **NM** value: **2.00**
I, the In-Betweener

28 ❑ Apr 1978 Cover: 0.35 **NM** value: **2.00**
29 ❑ Jun 1978 Cover: 0.35 **NM** value: **2.00**
He Who Stalks! **A:** Tom Sutton **W:** Roger Stern

30 ❑ Aug 1978 Cover: 0.35 **NM** value: **2.00**
A Gathering Of Fear! **A:** Tom Sutton **W:** Roger Stern

31 ❑ Oct 1978 Cover: 0.35 **NM** value: **2.00**
A Death For Immorality **A:** Ricardo Villamonte; Tom Sutton **W:** Don McGregor

32 ❑ Dec 1978 Cover: 0.35 **NM** value: **2.00**
The Dream Weaver **A:** Alan Kupperberg; Rudy Nebres **W:** Roger Stern

33 ❑ Feb 1979 Cover: 0.35 **NM** value: **2.00**
All My Dreams Against Me **A:** Ralph Macchio **W:** Roger Stern

34 ❑ Apr 1979 Cover: 0.35 **NM** value: **2.00**
35 ❑ Jun 1979 Cover: 0.40 **NM** value: **2.00**
36 ❑ Aug 1979 Cover: 0.40 **NM** value: **2.00**
The Man Who Knew Stephen Sanders! **A:** Gene Colan; Dan Green **W:** Roger Stern

37 ❑ Oct 1979 Cover: 0.40 **NM** value: **2.00**
38 ❑ Dec 1979 Cover: 0.40 **NM** value: **2.00**
Eye Of The Beholder **A:** Gene Colan; Dan Green **W:** Chris Claremont

39 ❑ Feb 1980 Cover: 0.40 **NM** value: **2.00**
Circ: Statement: **105,427**

40 ❑ Apr 1980 Cover: 0.40 **NM** value: **2.00**
Circ: Statement: **105,427**

41 ❑ Jun 1980 Cover: 0.40 **NM** value: **2.00**
Circ: Statement: **105,427**

42 ❑ Aug 1980 Cover: 0.40 **NM** value: **2.00**
Circ: Statement: **105,427**

43 ❑ Oct 1980 Cover: 0.50 **NM** value: **2.00**
Circ: Statement: **105,427**

44 ❑ Dec 1980 Cover: 0.50 **NM** value: **2.00**
Circ: Statement: **105,427**

45 ❑ Feb 1981 Cover: 0.50 **NM** value: **2.00**
Circ: Statement: **98,255**

46 ❑ Apr 1981 Cover: 0.50 **NM** value: **2.00**
Circ: Statement: **98,255**
• Has 1980 Statement, filed 10/1/80; avg print run 239,583; avg sales 102,225; avg subs 3,202; avg total paid 105,427; samples 572; office use 2,370; max existent 108,369; 55% of run returned **A:** Frank Miller(cover)

47 ❑ Jun 1981 Cover: 0.50 **NM** value: **2.00**
Circ: Statement: **98,255**

48 ❑ Aug 1981 Cover: 0.50 **NM** value: **2.00**
Circ: Statement: **98,255**
★ Appearance of Brother Voodoo.

CGC-graded: Multiply prices above by **33 for 9.9 M • 16 for 9.8 NM/M • 7 for 9.6 NM+ • 5 for 9.4 NM • 2.5 for 9.2 NM- • 1.5 for 9.0 VF/NM**

49 ❑ Oct 1981 Cover: 0.50 **NM** value: **2.00**
Circ: Statement: **98,255**
★ Appearance of Baron Mordo.

50 ❑ Dec 1981 Cover: 0.50 **NM** value: **2.00**
Circ: Statement: **98,255**
★ Appearance of Baron Mordo.

51 ❑ Feb 1982 Cover: 0.60 **NM** value: **2.00**
Circ: Statement: **119,651**
A Time For Love, A Time For Hate! **W:** Roger Stern

52 ❑ Apr 1982 Cover: 0.60 **NM** value: **2.00**
Circ: Statement: **119,651**
• Has 1981 Statement; avg print run 227,094; avg sales 94,024; avg subs 4,231; avg total paid 98,255; samples 2,918; max existent 101,173; 55% of run returned **W:** Roger Stern

53 ❑ Jun 1982 Cover: 0.60 **NM** value: **2.00**
Circ: Statement: **119,651**

54 ❑ Aug 1982 Cover: 0.60 **NM** value: **2.00**
Circ: Statement: **119,651**
A: Paul Smith; Brent Anderson

55 ❑ Oct 1982 Cover: 0.60 **NM** value: **2.00**
Circ: Statement: **119,651**
A: Paul Smith

56 ❑ Dec 1982 Cover: 0.60 **NM** value: **2.00**
Circ: Statement: **119,651** • **CGC:** 1 graded, best 9.2
A: Paul Smith

57 ❑ Feb 1983 Cover: 0.60 **NM** value: **2.00**
Gather My Disciples Before Me! **A:** Kevin Nowlan **W:** Roger Stern

58 ❑ Apr 1983 Cover: 0.60 **NM** value: **2.00**
...At Loose Ends! **A:** Dan Green **W:** Roger Stern

59 ❑ Jun 1983 Cover: 0.60 **NM** value: **2.00**
Children Of The Night! • Has 1982 Statement, filed 10/11/82; avg print run 240,964; avg sales 114,293; avg subs 5,358; avg total paid 119,651; samples 657; office use 2,727; max existent 123,035; 49% of run returned **A:** Dan Green **W:** Roger Stern

60 ❑ Aug 1983 Cover: 0.60 **NM** value: **2.00**
A: Dan Green **W:** Roger Stern ★ Appearance of Dracula.

61 ❑ Oct 1983 Cover: 0.60 **NM** value: **2.00**
Power Be The Prize **A:** Dan Green **W:** Roger Stern ★ Appearance of Dracula.

62 ❑ Dec 1983 Cover: 0.60 **NM** value: **2.00**
Deliver Us From Evil! **A:** Steve Leialoha **W:** Roger Stern ★ Appearance of Dracula.

63 ❑ Feb 1984 Cover: 0.60 **NM** value: **2.00**
Circ: Statement: **121,574**
Cry Of The Spirit **A:** Carl Potts **W:** Carl Potts

64 ❑ Apr 1984 Cover: 0.60 **NM** value: **2.00**
Circ: Statement: **121,574**
Art Rage **A:** Tony Salmons **W:** Ann Nocenti

65 ❑ Jun 1984 Cover: 0.60 **NM** value: **2.00**
Circ: Statement: **121,574**
Charlatan **A:** Paul Smith **W:** Roger Stern

66 ❑ Aug 1984 Cover: 0.60 **NM** value: **2.00**
Circ: Statement: **121,574**
The Chosen One **A:** Paul Smith **W:** Roger Stern

67 ❑ Oct 1984 Cover: 0.60 **NM** value: **2.00**
Circ: Statement: **121,574**
Private Eyes **A:** Steve Leialoha **W:** Roger Stern

68 ❑ Dec 1984 Cover: 0.60 **NM** value: **2.00**
Circ: Statement: **121,574**
Sword And Sorcery **A:** Paul Smith **W:** Roger Stern

69 ❑ Feb 1985 Cover: 0.60 **NM** value: **2.00**
Sea Cruise **A:** Paul Smith **W:** Roger Stern

70 ❑ Apr 1985 Cover: 0.65 **NM** value: **2.00**
Deadly Exchange **A:** Bret Blevins **W:** Roger Stern

71 ❑ Jun 1985 Cover: 0.65 **NM** value: **2.00**
Circ: CapCity orders: **11,750**
Into The Dark Dimension **A:** Paul Smith **W:** Roger Stern ★ Origin of Umar.

72 ❑ Aug 1985 Cover: 0.65 **NM** value: **2.00**
Circ: CapCity orders: **13,050**
Secret Origin **A:** Paul Smith **W:** Roger Stern

73 ❑ Oct 1985 Cover: 0.65 **NM** value: **2.00**
Circ: CapCity orders: **13,125**
Final Triumph **A:** Paul Smith **W:** Roger Stern

74 ❑ Dec 1985 Cover: 0.65 **NM** value: **2.00**
Circ: CapCity orders: **11,700**
And Now...The Beyonder • Secret Wars II **A:** Mark Badger **W:** Peter B. Gillis ★ 1st Appearance of Ecstasy.

75 ❑ Feb 1986 Cover: 0.75 **NM** value: **2.00**
Circ: CapCity orders: **12,300**
Souls In Torment! **A:** Sal Buscema **W:** Roger Stern ★ Origin of Wong (Doctor Strange's manservant).

76 ❑ Apr 1986 Cover: 0.75 **NM** value: **2.00**
Circ: CapCity orders: **11,850**
What Song The Sirens Sang! **A:** Mark Badger; Chris Warner **W:** Peter B. Gillis

77 ❑ Jun 1986 Cover: 0.75 **NM** value: **2.00**
Circ: CapCity orders: **10,000**
Khat? **A:** Chris Warner **W:** Peter B. Gillis

78 ❑ Aug 1986 Cover: 0.75 **NM** value: **2.00**
Circ: CapCity orders: **10,275**
• New costume

79 ❑ Oct 1986 Cover: 0.75 **NM** value: **2.00**
Circ: CapCity orders: **9,725**
Fata Morganna! **A:** Chris Warner **W:** Peter B. Gillis

80 ❑ Dec 1986 Cover: 0.75 **NM** value: **2.00**
Don't Pay the Ferryman! **A:** Chris Warner **W:** Peter B. Gillis

81 ❑ Feb 1987 Cover: 0.75 **NM** value: **2.00**
The Tongues Of Men And Angels...! final issue. **A:** Chris Warner **W:** Peter B. Gillis

Anl 1❑ ca. 1976 Cover: 0.50 **NM** value: **2.00**
And There Will Be Worlds Anew; A Planet in Turmoil; A City Born in Tears

GS 1❑ ca. 1975 Cover: 0.50 **NM** value: **5.00**
Nightmare; The Mystic and the Machine; Nothing Can Halt Voltorg; This Dream, This Doom; Exile • reprints Dr. Strange stories from Strange Tales #164-168

SE 1❑ Mar 1983 Cover: 2.50 **NM** value: **3.00**
Through An Orb Darkly; A Separate Reality; Where Bound'ries Decay; Cloak And Dagger **A:** Frank Brunner **W:** Steve Englehart

DOCTOR STRANGE (3RD SERIES) — Marvel

1 ❑ Feb 1999 Cover: 2.99 **NM** value: **Cover or less**
Circ: Diamd. preorders: **47,701**
The Flight of Bones **A:** Tony Harris **W:** Tony Harris; Dan Jolley

2 ❑ Mar 1999 Cover: 2.99 **NM** value: **Cover or less**
Circ: Diamd. preorders: **38,067**
The Flight of Bones **A:** Tony Harris **W:** Tony Harris; Dan Jolley

3 ❑ Apr 1999 Cover: 2.99 **NM** value: **Cover or less**
Circ: Diamd. preorders: **33,931**
The Flight of Bones **A:** Tony Harris **W:** Tony Harris; Dan Jolley
★ Appearance of Jonathan White.

4 ❑ May 1999 Cover: 2.99 **NM** value: **Cover or less**
Circ: Diamd. preorders: **32,873**
The Flight of Bones **A:** Tony Harris **W:** Tony Harris; Dan Jolley

DOCTOR STRANGE AND DOCTOR DOOM: TRIUMPH AND TORMENT — Marvel

One of the best graphic novels ever to come from Marvel, Roger Stern's Triumph and Torment does something unusual for a one-shot: It actually resolves a major ongoing issue for a major character in the Marvel Universe. At the same time, it provides definitive depictions of both Doctor Strange and Doctor Doom — and in a slick hardcover package with lustrous art by Mike Mignola and Mark Badger to boot!

The aged Genghis calls the world's greatest sorcerors to a contest, and Doctor Strange is up to the challenge. What he doesn't expect is that Doctor Doom is one of them — and that soon, he'll be assisting Doom in the villain's lifelong quest, freeing his mother's soul from the clutches of the demon Mephisto!

Clever and well-written, with a keen understanding of the characters. Top-notch. — JJM

1 ❑ Oct 1989 Cover: 17.95 **NM** value: **Cover or less**
Circ: CapCity orders: **10,800**
hardcover. **A:** Mark Badger; Mike Mignola **W:** Roger Stern

DOCTOR STRANGE CLASSICS — Marvel

1 ❑ Mar 1984 Cover: 1.50 **NM** value: **2.00**
A: Steve Ditko

2 ❑ Apr 1984 Cover: 1.50 **NM** value: **2.00**
A: Steve Ditko

3 ❑ May 1984 Cover: 1.50 **NM** value: **2.00**
C: Arthur Adams

4 ❑ Jun 1984 Cover: 1.50 **NM** value: **2.00**

DOCTOR STRANGEFATE — DC / Amalgam

1 ❑ Apr 1996 Cover: 1.95 **NM** value: **Cover or less**
Circ: Diamd. preorders: **4,170**
The Decrees Of Fate **A:** José Luis Garcia-Lopez **W:** Ron Marz
★ Appearance of Access.

DOCTOR STRANGE/GHOST RIDER SPECIAL — Marvel

1 ❑ Apr 1991 Cover: 1.50 **NM** value: **Cover or less**
Circ: CapCity orders: **19,350**
Strange Tales Part II • reprints Doctor Strange #28;Continued from Ghost Rider # 12 **A:** Chris Marrinan **W:** Roy Thomas; Dann Thomas

DOCTOR STRANGE (MASS-MARKET PAPERBACKS) — Marvel

Bk 1❑ ca. 1979 Cover: 2.25 **NM** value: **2.50**
• Pocket Books

Bk 2❑ Cover: 2.25 **NM** value: **2.50**
• Pocket Books

DOCTOR STRANGE: MASTER OF THE MYSTIC ARTS — Marvel

Bk 1❑ Cover: 3.95 **NM** value: **Cover or less**
• Fireside

DOCTOR STRANGE: SHAMBALLA — Marvel

1 ❑ ca. 1986 Cover: 5.95 **NM** value: **Cover or less**

DOCTOR STRANGE: SORCERER SUPREME — Marvel

Doctor Strange is a great character, and just about everybody thinks he ought to have an ongoing series. He gets them, but they just never tend to last very long. After his original series, borne out of Strange Tales, went bimonthly and then folded, Marvel dropped a bit of indignity on the Doc by restarting Strange Tales and sticking him with 1980s hit characters (but now mostly forgotten) Cloak & Dagger as co-stars — hardly Nick Fury! As times improved, Marvel restored Doc to his own private practice in Doctor Strange, Sorceror Supreme.

The series, most notable editorially for Strange's extended war with vampires, is actually most famous for a lawsuit. The cover to #15 depicts a young woman, who, it turns out, was really gospel singer Amy Grant — who wasn't thrilled at appearing in "The Vampiric Verses."

Late issues in the series are completely off the wall, as Marvel tried to make Doc more hip and Sandman-like. It didn't work. — JJM

1 ❑ Nov 1988 Cover: 1.25 **NM** value: **3.00**
Circ: CapCity orders: **22,400** • **CGC:** 4 graded, best 10.0
Love is the Spell...The Spell is Death! **A:** Richard Case **W:** Peter B. Gillis

2 ❑ Jan 1989 Cover: 1.50 **NM** value: **2.00**
Circ: Statement: **73,300** CapCity orders: **20,600** • **CGC:** 1 graded, best 9.6
• Inferno

3 ❑ Mar 1989 Cover: 1.50 **NM** value: **2.00**
Circ: Statement: **73,300** CapCity orders: **18,600**

4 ❑ May 1989 Cover: 1.50 **NM** value: **Cover or less**
Circ: Statement: **73,300** CapCity orders: **18,400**

5 ❑ Jul 1989 Cover: 1.50 **NM** value: **Cover or less**
Circ: Statement: **73,300** CapCity orders: **17,700**

6 ❑ Aug 1989 Cover: 1.50 **NM** value: **Cover or less**
Circ: Statement: **73,300** CapCity orders: **17,000**

7 ❑ Sep 1989 Cover: 1.50 **NM** value: **Cover or less**
Circ: Statement: **73,300** CapCity orders: **17,250**

8 ❑ Oct 1989 Cover: 1.50 **NM** value: **Cover or less**
Circ: Statement: **73,300** CapCity orders: **18,000**
★ Origin of Satannish, Mephisto.

9 ❑ Nov 1989 Cover: 1.50 **NM** value: **Cover or less**
Circ: Statement: **73,300** CapCity orders: **18,350**

10 ❑ Dec 1989 Cover: 1.50 **NM** value: **Cover or less**
Circ: Statement: **73,300** CapCity orders: **18,600**
★ Appearance of Morbius.

11 ❑ Dec 1989 Cover: 1.50 **NM** value: **Cover or less**
Circ: Statement: **73,300** CapCity orders: **19,200**
Acts of Vengeance • Acts of Vengeance ★ Appearance of Hobgoblin.

12 ❑ Dec 1989 Cover: 1.50 **NM** value: **Cover or less**
Circ: Statement: **73,300** CapCity orders: **19,000**
Acts of Vengeance • Acts of Vengeance

13 ❑ Jan 1990 Cover: 1.50 **NM** value: **Cover or less**
Circ: Statement: **80,209** CapCity orders: **23,850**
Acts of Vengeance • Acts of Vengeance

14 ❑ Feb 1990 Cover: 1.50 **NM** value: **Cover or less**
Circ: Statement: **80,209** CapCity orders: **19,650**
• vampires

15 ❑ Mar 1990 Cover: 1.50 **NM** value: **3.00**
Circ: Statement: **80,209** CapCity orders: **19,750**
Amy Grant cover (unauthorized, caused Marvel to be sued). • vampires

16 ❑ Apr 1990 Cover: 1.50 **NM** value: **Cover or less**
Circ: Statement: **80,209** CapCity orders: **19,400**
• vampires

17 ❑ May 1990 Cover: 1.50 **NM** value: **Cover or less**
Circ: Statement: **80,209** CapCity orders: **20,050**
• vampires

18 ❑ Jun 1990 Cover: 1.50 **NM** value: **Cover or less**
Circ: Statement: **80,209** CapCity orders: **19,850**
• vampires

19 ❑ Jul 1990 Cover: 1.50 **NM** value: **Cover or less**
Circ: Statement: **80,209** CapCity orders: **19,850**
A: Gene Colan

20 ❑ Aug 1990 Cover: 1.50 **NM** value: **Cover or less**
Circ: Statement: **80,209** CapCity orders: **18,950**

21 ❑ Sep 1990 Cover: 1.50 **NM** value: **Cover or less**
Circ: Statement: **80,209** CapCity orders: **18,900**

22 ❑ Oct 1990 Cover: 1.50 **NM** value: **Cover or less**
Circ: Statement: **80,209** CapCity orders: **18,150**
★ Origin of Umar.

23 ❑ Nov 1990 Cover: 1.50 **NM** value: **Cover or less**
Circ: Statement: **80,209** CapCity orders: **17,200**

24 ❑ Dec 1990 Cover: 1.50 **NM** value: **Cover or less**
Circ: Statement: **80,209** CapCity orders: **17,750**

25 ❑ Jan 1991 Cover: 1.50 **NM** value: **Cover or less**
Circ: Statement: **71,417** CapCity orders: **17,300**

26 ❑ Feb 1991 Cover: 1.50 **NM** value: **Cover or less**
Circ: Statement: **71,417** CapCity orders: **17,600**
• werewolf

27 ❑ Mar 1991 Cover: 1.50 **NM** value: **Cover or less**
Circ: Statement: **71,417** CapCity orders: **17,200**
• werewolf

28 ❑ Apr 1991 Cover: 1.50 **NM** value: **Cover or less**
Circ: Statement: **71,417** CapCity orders: **37,350**
• Ghost Rider x-over

29 ❑ May 1991 Cover: 1.75 **NM** value: **Cover or less**
Circ: Statement: **71,417** CapCity orders: **17,450**

30 ❑ Jun 1991 Cover: 1.75 **NM** value: **Cover or less**
Circ: Statement: **71,417** CapCity orders: **16,650**

31 ❑ Jul 1991 Cover: 1.75 **NM** value: **Cover or less**
Circ: Statement: **71,417** CapCity orders: **39,150**
Infinity Gauntlet • Infinity Gauntlet

32 ❑ Aug 1991 Cover: 1.75 **NM** value: **Cover or less**
Circ: Statement: **71,417** CapCity orders: **36,000**
Infinity Gauntlet • Infinity Gauntlet

33 ❑ Sep 1991 Cover: 1.75 **NM** value: **Cover or less**
Circ: Statement: **71,417** CapCity orders: **37,600**
Infinity Gauntlet • Infinity Gauntlet

34 ❑ Oct 1991 Cover: 1.75 **NM** value: **Cover or less**
Circ: Statement: **71,417** CapCity orders: **32,500**
Infinity Gauntlet • Infinity Gauntlet

35 ❑ Nov 1991 Cover: 1.75 **NM** value: **Cover or less**
Circ: Statement: **71,417** CapCity orders: **31,500**
Infinity Gauntlet • Infinity Gauntlet

36 ❑ Dec 1991 Cover: 1.75 **NM** value: **Cover or less**
Circ: Statement: **71,417** CapCity orders: **32,600**
• Infinity Gauntlet;Prelude to Warlock & the Infinity Watch #1

37 ❑ Jan 1992 Cover: 1.75 **NM** value: **Cover or less**
Circ: Statement: **109,514** CapCity orders: **20,200**

38 ❑ Feb 1992 Cover: 1.75 **NM** value: **Cover or less**
Circ: Statement: **109,514** CapCity orders: **19,100**

39 ❑ Mar 1992 Cover: 1.75 **NM** value: **Cover or less**
Circ: Statement: **109,514** CapCity orders: **19,300**

40 ❑ Apr 1992 Cover: 1.75 **NM** value: **Cover or less**
Circ: Statement: **109,514** CapCity orders: **17,000**

Other grades: Multiply prices above by **1.5 for Mint • 2/3 for Very Fine • 1/3 for Fine • 1/5 for Very Good • 1/8 for Good**

41 ❑ May 1992 Cover: 1.75 **NM** value: **Cover or less**
Circ: Statement: **109,514** CapCity orders: **26,600**
• Wolverine

42 ❑ Jun 1992 Cover: 1.75 **NM** value: **Cover or less**
Circ: Statement: **109,514** CapCity orders: **34,800**
Infinity War • Galactus **A:** Geof Isherwood **W:** Roy Thomas

43 ❑ Jul 1992 Cover: 1.75 **NM** value: **Cover or less**
Circ: Statement: **109,514** CapCity orders: **35,100**
Infinity War

44 ❑ Aug 1992 Cover: 1.75 **NM** value: **Cover or less**
Circ: Statement: **109,514** CapCity orders: **33,300**
Infinity War

45 ❑ Sep 1992 Cover: 1.75 **NM** value: **Cover or less**
Circ: Statement: **109,514** CapCity orders: **35,100**
Infinity War

46 ❑ Oct 1992 Cover: 1.75 **NM** value: **Cover or less**
Circ: Statement: **109,514** CapCity orders: **32,100**
Infinity War

47 ❑ Nov 1992 Cover: 1.75 **NM** value: **Cover or less**
Circ: Statement: **109,514** CapCity orders: **29,300**
Infinity War

48 ❑ Dec 1992 Cover: 1.75 **NM** value: **Cover or less**
Circ: Statement: **109,514** CapCity orders: **19,800**

49 ❑ Jan 1993 Cover: 1.75 **NM** value: **Cover or less**
Circ: CapCity orders: **17,700**

50 ❑ Feb 1993 Cover: 2.95 **NM** value: **Cover or less**
Circ: CapCity orders: **63,800**
Prism cover. The Heart Of Darkness • Prelude to Secret Defenders #1 **A:** Geof Isherwood **W:** Len Kaminski

51 ❑ Mar 1993 Cover: 1.75 **NM** value: **Cover or less**
Circ: CapCity orders: **17,600**
• Has 1992 Statement, filed 10/1/92; avg print run 110,238; avg sales 107,939; avg subs 1,575; avg total paid 109,514; samples 240; office use 484; max existent 110238; 0% of run returned

52 ❑ Apr 1993 Cover: 1.75 **NM** value: **Cover or less**
Circ: CapCity orders: **18,500**

53 ❑ May 1993 Cover: 1.75 **NM** value: **Cover or less**
Circ: CapCity orders: **18,200**

54 ❑ Jun 1993 Cover: 1.75 **NM** value: **Cover or less**
Circ: CapCity orders: **22,300**

55 ❑ Jul 1993 Cover: 1.75 **NM** value: **Cover or less**
Circ: CapCity orders: **21,200**

56 ❑ Aug 1993 Cover: 1.75 **NM** value: **Cover or less**
Circ: CapCity orders: **20,700**

57 ❑ Sep 1993 Cover: 1.75 **NM** value: **Cover or less**
Circ: CapCity orders: **15,800**

58 ❑ Oct 1993 Cover: 1.75 **NM** value: **Cover or less**
Circ: CapCity orders: **14,700**
A: Geof Isherwood **W:** Geof Isherwood ★ Appearance of Urthona.

59 ❑ Nov 1993 Cover: 1.75 **NM** value: **Cover or less**
Circ: CapCity orders: **13,500**

60 ❑ Dec 1993 Cover: 1.75 **NM** value: **Cover or less**
Circ: CapCity orders: **22,750**
Spot varnish cover. Siege of Darkness, Part 7

61 ❑ Jan 1994 Cover: 1.75 **NM** value: **Cover or less**
Circ: Statement: **51,485** CapCity orders: **19,000**
Siege of Darkness, Part 15

62 ❑ Feb 1994 Cover: 1.75 **NM** value: **Cover or less**
Circ: Statement: **51,485** CapCity orders: **18,200**

63 ❑ Mar 1994 Cover: 1.75 **NM** value: **Cover or less**
Circ: Statement: **51,485** CapCity orders: **16,250**

64 ❑ Apr 1994 Cover: 1.75 **NM** value: **Cover or less**
Circ: Statement: **51,485**

65 ❑ May 1994 Cover: 1.95 **NM** value: **Cover or less**
Circ: Statement: **51,485** CapCity orders: **16,250**

66 ❑ Jun 1994 Cover: 1.95 **NM** value: **Cover or less**
Circ: Statement: **51,485** CapCity orders: **15,750**

67 ❑ Jul 1994 Cover: 1.95 **NM** value: **Cover or less**
Circ: Statement: **51,485** CapCity orders: **15,500**

68 ❑ Aug 1994 Cover: 1.95 **NM** value: **Cover or less**
Circ: Statement: **51,485** CapCity orders: **14,100**

69 ❑ Sep 1994 Cover: 1.95 **NM** value: **Cover or less**
Circ: Statement: **51,485** CapCity orders: **14,100**

70 ❑ Oct 1994 Cover: 1.95 **NM** value: **Cover or less**
Circ: Statement: **51,485** CapCity orders: **12,800**
★ Appearance of Hulk.

71 ❑ Nov 1994 Cover: 1.95 **NM** value: **Cover or less**
Circ: Statement: **51,485** CapCity orders: **1,200**
★ Appearance of Hulk.

72 ❑ Dec 1994 Cover: 1.95 **NM** value: **Cover or less**
Circ: Statement: **51,485** CapCity orders: **1,200**
Last Rites, Part 1

73 ❑ Jan 1995 Cover: 1.95 **NM** value: **Cover or less**
Circ: Statement: **23,861** CapCity orders: **11,900**
Last Rites, Part 2

74 ❑ Feb 1995 Cover: 1.95 **NM** value: **Cover or less**
Circ: Statement: **23,861** CapCity orders: **19,300**
Last Rites, Part 3

75 ❑ Mar 1995 Cover: 2.50 **NM** value: **Cover or less**
• Giant-size. Last Rites, Part 4

75/SC❑ Mar 1995 Cover: 3.50 **NM** value: **Cover or less**
Circ: Statement: **23,861** CapCity orders: **12,500**
• Giant-size. Last Rites, Part 4

76 ❑ Apr 1995 Cover: 1.95 **NM** value: **Cover or less**
Circ: Statement: **23,861** CapCity orders: **12,000**

77 ❑ May 1995 Cover: 1.95 **NM** value: **Cover or less**
Circ: Statement: **23,861** CapCity orders: **11,800**

78 ❑ Jun 1995 Cover: 1.95 **NM** value: **Cover or less**
Circ: Statement: **23,861** CapCity orders: **11,400**

79 ❑ Jul 1995 Cover: 1.95 **NM** value: **Cover or less**
Circ: Statement: **23,861** CapCity orders: **12,200**

80 ❑ Aug 1995 Cover: 1.95 **NM** value: **Cover or less**
Circ: Statement: **23,861** CapCity orders: **12,700**
• indicia changes to Doctor Strange, Sorcerer Supreme for remainder of run

81 ❑ Sep 1995 Cover: 1.95 **NM** value: **Cover or less**
Circ: Statement: **23,861** CapCity orders: **12,500**

82 ❑ Oct 1995 Cover: 1.95 **NM** value: **Cover or less**
Circ: Statement: **23,861**

83 ❑ Nov 1995 Cover: 1.95 **NM** value: **Cover or less**

84 ❑ Dec 1995 Cover: 1.95 **NM** value: **Cover or less**
The Homecoming, Part 1 **A:** Mark Buckingham **W:** J.M. DeMatteis ★ Appearance of Mordo.

85 ❑ Jan 1996 Cover: 1.95 **NM** value: **Cover or less**
The Homecoming, Part 2 • Has 1995 Statement, filed 10/1/95; avg print run 35,133; avg sales 22,950; avg subs 911; avg total paid 23,861; samples 750; office use 500; max existent 25,111; 29% of run returned **A:** Pascual Ferry **W:** J.M. DeMatteis ★ Origin of Mordo.

86 ❑ Feb 1996 Cover: 1.95 **NM** value: **Cover or less**
The Homecoming, Part 3 **A:** Mark Buckingham **W:** J.M. DeMatteis

87 ❑ Mar 1996 Cover: 1.95 **NM** value: **Cover or less**
The Homecoming, Part 4 **A:** Mark Buckingham **W:** J.M. DeMatteis ★ Death of Mordo.

88 ❑ Apr 1996 Cover: 1.95 **NM** value: **Cover or less**
Fall of the Tempo, Part 1

89 ❑ May 1996 Cover: 1.95 **NM** value: **Cover or less**
Fall of the Tempo, Part 2

90 ❑ Jun 1996 Cover: 1.95 **NM** value: **Cover or less**
final issue.

Anl 2❑ ca. 1992 Cover: 2.25 **NM** value: **Cover or less**
Circ: CapCity orders: **23,600**
Return of Defenders; Return of the Defenders, Part 4; His Master's Foes; Rintrah: Future Master Of The Mystic Arts; Baron Blood: First Blood; Clea: Raiders OF The Purple Evil **A:** Gary Hartle; Dave Hoover; M.C. Wyman; Francisco Solano Lopez **W:** R.J.M. Lofficier; Roy Thomas

Anl 3❑ ca. 1993 Cover: 2.95 **NM** value: **Cover or less**
Circ: CapCity orders: **25,900**
• trading card

Anl 4❑ ca. 1994 Cover: 2.95 **NM** value: **Cover or less**
Circ: CapCity orders: **12,900**
Strangers Among Us

Ash 1❑ ca. 1995, b&w Cover: 0.75 **NM** value: **Cover or less**
• no indicia

DR. STRANGE VS. DRACULA — Marvel

1 ❑ Mar 1994 Cover: 1.75 **NM** value: **Cover or less**
Circ: CapCity orders: **8,150**
A: Gene Colan; Tom Palmer **W:** Marv Wolfman

DOCTOR STRANGE: WHAT IS IT THAT DISTURBS YOU STEPHEN? — Marvel

1 ❑ Oct 1997 Cover: 5.99 **NM** value: **Cover or less**
• squarebound **A:** P. Craig Russell

DR. TOMORROW — Acclaim

During the early days of World War II, Bart Simms acquired technology from the future, including a computer with a massive amount of historical and technical information about the remainder of the century, allowing the young man to become the futuristic hero Dr. Tomorrow.

Simms used his knowledge throughout the next several decades to thwart various nefarious schemes and publisher Acclaim used famous artists of the respective eras such as Gil Kane for the 1960s to provide covers. An interesting time paradox series and great art throughout. — Brent

1 ❑ May 1997 Cover: 2.50 **NM** value: **Cover or less**
Circ: Diamd. preorders: **13,794**
Age of Tomorrow **A:** Don Perlin **W:** Bob Layton

2 ❑ Jun 1997 Cover: 2.50 **NM** value: **Cover or less**
Circ: Diamd. preorders: **11,257**
A: Don Perlin **W:** Bob Layton ★ Versus Teutonic Knight.

3 ❑ Jul 1997 Cover: 2.50 **NM** value: **Cover or less**
Circ: Diamd. preorders: **10,384**
A: Don Perlin **W:** Bob Layton ★ Versus Nazi X-O.

4 ❑ Aug 1997 Cover: 2.50 **NM** value: **Cover or less**
Circ: Diamd. preorders: **9,970**
Tomorrow Ends Today **A:** Jim Hall **W:** Bob Layton

5 ❑ Sep 1997 Cover: 2.50 **NM** value: **Cover or less**
Circ: Diamd. preorders: **9,334**
A: Don Perlin **W:** Bob Layton ★ Death of Cappy.

6 ❑ Oct 1997 Cover: 2.50 **NM** value: **Cover or less**
Circ: Diamd. preorders: **8,919**
A: Don Perlin **W:** Bob Layton ★ 1st Appearance of Mushroom Cloud.

7 ❑ Nov 1997 Cover: 2.50 **NM** value: **Cover or less**
Circ: Diamd. preorders: **8,516**
• Tomorrow and Mushroom Cloud go to Vietnam **A:** Don Perlin **W:** Bob Layton

8 ❑ Dec 1997 Cover: 2.50 **NM** value: **Cover or less**
Circ: Diamd. preorders: **8,195**
A: Don Perlin **C:** Gil Kane **W:** Bob Layton ★ Versus Warmaster.

9 ❑ Jan 1998 Cover: 2.50 **NM** value: **Cover or less**
Circ: Diamd. preorders: **7,582**
no cover date. • indicia says Jan 98 **A:** Don Perlin **W:** Bob Layton

10 ❑ Feb 1998 Cover: 2.50 **NM** value: **Cover or less**
Circ: Diamd. preorders: **6,999**
no cover date. • indicia says Jan 98 **A:** Don Perlin **W:** Bob Layton

11 ❑ Mar 1998 Cover: 2.50 **NM** value: **Cover or less**
Circ: Diamd. preorders: **7,035**
A: Don Perlin **W:** Bob Layton

12 ❑ Apr 1998 Cover: 2.50 **NM** value: **Cover or less**
Circ: Diamd. preorders: **7,167**
A: Don Perlin **W:** Bob Layton

DOCTOR WEIRD — Caliber / Big Bang

1 ❑ Oct 1994, b&w Cover: 2.95 **NM** value: **Cover or less**
Circ: CapCity orders: **2,685**
Where Monsters Dwell **A:** David Zimmerman **W:** Ed DeGeorge

2 ❑ May 1995, b&w Cover: 2.95 **NM** value: **Cover or less**

SE 1❑ Feb 1994, b&w Cover: 3.95 **NM** value: **Cover or less**
Circ: CapCity orders: **2,445**

DR. WEIRD (VOL. 2) — October

1 ❑ Oct 1997 Cover: 2.95 **NM** value: **Cover or less**
Wasteland **A:** Billy Hodge **W:** Ed DeGeorge

2 ❑ Jul 1998 Cover: 2.95 **NM** value: **Cover or less**

DOCTOR WHO — Marvel

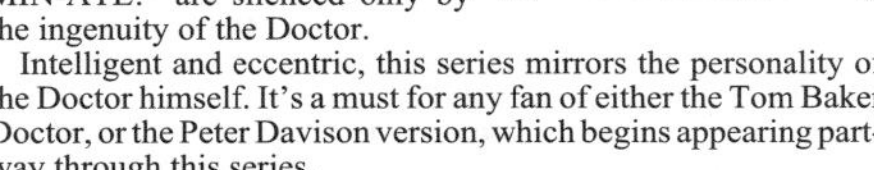

Inspired by the longest-running science-fiction show in television history, Doctor Who reprints tales of the world's favorite Time Lord from Britain's Doctor Who Magazine.

Traveling across time in his slightly-malfunctioning TARDIS (a time machine that looks, in the Doctor's case, like a blue police box), the Doctor constantly finds himself pitted against evil monsters of all shapes and sizes. These have included the infamous Daleks, evil robot-like creatures whose shrill mechanical cries of "EX-TER-MIN-ATE!" are silenced only by the ingenuity of the Doctor.

Intelligent and eccentric, this series mirrors the personality of the Doctor himself. It's a must for any fan of either the Tom Baker Doctor, or the Peter Davison version, which begins appearing partway through this series.

1 ❑ Oct 1997 Cover: 1.50 **NM** value: **2.50**
• **CGC:** 2 graded, best 9.8
• BBC TV series;Reprint from Doctor Who Monthly (British) **A:** Dave Gibbons **W:** Pat Mills; Wagner

2 ❑ Nov 1984 Cover: 1.50 **NM** value: **2.00**
Revenge Of Wrath • Reprint from Doctor Who Monthly (British) **A:** Dave Gibbons **W:** Pat Mills; Wagner

3 ❑ Dec 1984 Cover: 1.50 **NM** value: **2.00**
Dogs Of Doom • Reprint from Doctor Who Monthly (British) **A:** Dave Gibbons **W:** Pat Mills; Wagner

4 ❑ Jan 1985 Cover: 1.50 **NM** value: **2.00**
• Reprint from Doctor Who Monthly (British)

5 ❑ Feb 1985 Cover: 1.50 **NM** value: **2.00**
• Reprint from Doctor Who Monthly (British)

6 ❑ Mar 1985 Cover: 1.50 **NM** value: **2.00**
• Reprint from Doctor Who Monthly (British)

7 ❑ Apr 1985 Cover: 1.50 **NM** value: **2.00**
• Reprint from Doctor Who Monthly (British)

8 ❑ May 1985 Cover: 1.50 **NM** value: **2.00**
Circ: CapCity orders: **9,300**
• Reprint from Doctor Who Monthly (British)

9 ❑ Jun 1985 Cover: 1.50 **NM** value: **2.00**
Circ: CapCity orders: **8,850**
• Reprint from Doctor Who Monthly (British)

10 ❑ Jul 1985 Cover: 1.50 **NM** value: **2.00**
Circ: CapCity orders: **8,300**
• Reprint from Doctor Who Monthly (British)

11 ❑ Aug 1985 Cover: 1.50 **NM** value: **Cover or less**
Circ: CapCity orders: **7,500**
• Reprint from Doctor Who Monthly (British)

12 ❑ Sep 1985 Cover: 1.50 **NM** value: **Cover or less**
Circ: CapCity orders: **7,600**
• Reprint from Doctor Who Monthly (British)

13 ❑ Oct 1985 Cover: 1.50 **NM** value: **Cover or less**
Circ: CapCity orders: **8,900**
• Reprint from Doctor Who Monthly (British)

14 ❑ Nov 1985 Cover: 1.50 **NM** value: **Cover or less**
Circ: CapCity orders: **7,700**
• Reprint from Doctor Who Monthly (British)

15 ❑ Dec 1985 Cover: 1.50 **NM** value: **Cover or less**
Circ: CapCity orders: **7,200**
• Reprint from Doctor Who Monthly (British)

16 ❑ Jan 1986 Cover: 1.50 **NM** value: **Cover or less**
Circ: CapCity orders: **6,450**
• Reprint from Doctor Who Monthly (British)

17 ❑ Feb 1986 Cover: 1.50 **NM** value: **Cover or less**
Circ: CapCity orders: **6,700**
• Reprint from Doctor Who Monthly (British)

18 ❑ Mar 1986 Cover: 1.50 **NM** value: **Cover or less**
Circ: CapCity orders: **6,150**
• Reprint from Doctor Who Monthly (British)

19 ❑ Apr 1986 Cover: 1.50 **NM** value: **Cover or less**
Circ: CapCity orders: **6,250**
Stars Fell on Stockbridge; Touchdown on Deneb • Reprint from Doctor Who Monthly (British)

20 ❑ May 1986 Cover: 1.50 **NM** value: **Cover or less**
Circ: CapCity orders: **6,100**
• Reprint from Doctor Who Monthly (British)

21 ❑ Jun 1986 Cover: 1.50 **NM** value: **Cover or less**
Circ: CapCity orders: **5,850**
• Reprint from Doctor Who Monthly (British)

22 ❑ Jul 1986 Cover: 1.50 **NM** value: **Cover or less**
Circ: CapCity orders: **6,050**
• Reprint from Doctor Who Monthly (British)

23 ❑ Aug 1986 Cover: 1.50 **NM** value: **Cover or less**
Circ: CapCity orders: **5,700**
• Reprint from Doctor Who Monthly (British)

CGC-graded: Multiply prices above by **33 for 9.9 M • 16 for 9.8 NM/M • 7 for 9.6 NM+ • 5 for 9.4 NM • 2.5 for 9.2 NM- • 1.5 for 9.0 VF/NM**

DR. WHO AND THE DALEKS — Dell

Doctor Who, the classic British science fiction television program, was first introduced to audiences in the United States way back in 1966, thanks to an issue of Dell's Movie Classics comics. The time-traveling doctor is here shown in his earliest incarnation, with his son and two grandchildren coming along for the rollicking adventures through time and space. Using the Tardis, the Doctor's time machine (which appears from the outside to be an old London telephone booth), the crew encounters the fearsome Daleks, evil robots bent on enslaving the earth. Doctor Who has remained popular through the years and has made many other appearances in comics since this landmark issue.

1 ❑ Cover: 0.12 **NM** value: **50.00**
• **CGC:** 1 graded, best 4.5
Photo cover from movie. 🕮 Dr. Who and the Daleks

DR. WIRTHAM'S COMIX & STORIES — Clifford Neal

1 ❑ **NM** value: **2.00**
2 ❑ **NM** value: **2.00**
3 ❑ **NM** value: **5.00**
4 ❑ Cover: 1.50 **NM** value: **Cover or less**
5 ❑ Cover: 2.00 **NM** value: **Cover or less**
• Flip book with #6
6 ❑ Cover: 2.00 **NM** value: **Cover or less**
• Flip book with #5
7 ❑ Cover: 2.50 **NM** value: **Cover or less**
🕮 Sicky Claws Conquers the Weird Dicks!; Mother Goose; White Feather; The Harvest; Miss Story; In Our Midst; Binary Systems Analysis Primer; Jungle Sugar • Flip book with #8 **A:** Eric Vincent; Robert Williams; Doug Potter; Joe Zabel; Mark A. Nelson; Jay Kinney; Oisif Egaux; Rickey Grimes **W:** Eric Vincent; Robert Williams; Doug Potter; Joe Zabel; Mark A. Nelson; Jay Kinney; Oisif Egaux; Rickey Grimes
8 ❑ Cover: 2.50 **NM** value: **Cover or less**
🕮 Shooty Beagle Goes to the Mall; Obsession; Sleezeball; The Marilyn File; Marilyn Monroe: A Hollywood Fantasy; Crime Does Not Pay; Murder, Morphine, and Mother • Flip book with #7 **A:** Gary Dumm; Mike Roberts; Don Lomax; Terry Beatty; Greg Budgett; Mike Matthews **W:** Gary Dumm; Mike Roberts; Terry Beatty; Greg Budgett; Mike Matthews; Bruce V. Kalnins

DR. WONDER — Old Town

1 ❑ Jun 1996, b&w Cover: 2.95 **NM** value: **Cover or less**
🕮 Terror in the Town Square!; The Writer (text story); The Final Showdown **A:** Dick Ayers; Irwin Hasen **W:** David Allikas ★ Origin of Doctor Wonder.
2 ❑ Jul 1996, b&w Cover: 2.95 **NM** value: **Cover or less**
3 ❑ Aug 1996, b&w Cover: 2.95 **NM** value: **Cover or less**
4 ❑ Oct 1996, b&w Cover: 2.95 **NM** value: **Cover or less**
5 ❑ Fal 1997, b&w Cover: 2.95 **NM** value: **Cover or less**
• magazine-sized. 🕮 Fan Page (t **A:** Dick Ayers; Mark Voger **W:** Scott Saavedra; Mark Voger; Brian Saner-Lamken; Craig Shutt; David Allikas; Jacob Gilbert; Jim Lawless; Mike Giacoia

DOCTOR ZERO — Marvel / Epic

1 ❑ Apr 1988 Cover: 1.25 **NM** value: **1.50**
Circ: CapCity orders: **22,400**
🕮 Shadows Of Troy **A:** Denys Cowan; Bill Sienkiewicz(cover) **C:** Bill Sienkiewicz **W:** D.G. Chichester; Margaret Clark
2 ❑ Jun 1988 Cover: 1.25 **NM** value: **1.50**
Circ: CapCity orders: **17,000**
C: Bill Sienkiewicz
3 ❑ Aug 1988 Cover: 1.25 **NM** value: **1.50**
Circ: CapCity orders: **14,900**
4 ❑ Oct 1988 Cover: 1.50 **NM** value: **Cover or less**
Circ: CapCity orders: **11,446**
5 ❑ Dec 1988 Cover: 1.50 **NM** value: **Cover or less**
Circ: CapCity orders: **10,250**
6 ❑ Feb 1989 Cover: 1.50 **NM** value: **Cover or less**
Circ: CapCity orders: **8,800**
7 ❑ Apr 1989 Cover: 1.50 **NM** value: **Cover or less**
Circ: CapCity orders: **7,700**
🕮 man Is But A Dream Of A Shadow **A:** Dan Spiegle **W:** D.G. Chichester; Margaret Clark
8 ❑ Jun 1989 Cover: 1.50 **NM** value: **Cover or less**
Circ: CapCity orders: **7,100**
final issue.

DR. ZOMB'S HOUSE OF FREAKS — Starhead

1 ❑ b&w Cover: 2.75 **NM** value: **Cover or less**
A: Art Penn **W:** Art Penn

DOC WEIRD'S THRILL BOOK — Pure Imagination

1 ❑ Cover: 1.75 **NM** value: **2.00**
A: Al Williamson; Alex Toth; Frank Frazetta; Bob Powell; Mike Peppe; Virgil Finlay
2 ❑ Cover: 1.75 **NM** value: **2.00**
• Jack Cole **A:** Wally Wood; Jack Cole
3 ❑ Cover: 2.00 **NM** value: **Cover or less**
A: Wally Wood

Statement of Ownership figures are the average number of copies originally sold, as cited by the publisher to the U.S. Postal Service. These estimate **all** sales, in comics shops and on newsstands.

DODEKAIN — Antarctic

Sixty years ago, a young scientist was forced to escape to Earth from his homeworld during an unprovoked attack by an extra-terrestrial race. At the moment of his world's destruction, the bitter seeds of revenge were planted within his heart. Driven by images of his world's destruction, the scientist began constructing a fearful instrument of retribution.

The refugee ages into a local mad scientist known as Dr. G, who patiently awaits the arrival of his long-time enemy. When the Zogelians attack Earth, Dr. G responds by unleashing the gargantuan robot Dodekain. However, the mad scientist yields control of the larger than earth-sized robot to an emotional 12-year old. Somehow Takuma Ippongi must avenge the destruction of a planet without destroying his own in the process.

1 ❑ Nov 1994, b&w Cover: 2.95 **NM** value: **Cover or less**
A: Masayuki Fujihara **W:** Masayuki Fujihara
2 ❑ Dec 1994, b&w Cover: 2.95 **NM** value: **Cover or less**
A: Masayuki Fujihara **W:** Masayuki Fujihara
3 ❑ Jan 1995, b&w Cover: 2.95 **NM** value: **Cover or less**
A: Masayuki Fujihara **W:** Masayuki Fujihara
4 ❑ Feb 1995, b&w Cover: 2.95 **NM** value: **Cover or less**
A: Masayuki Fujihara **W:** Masayuki Fujihara
5 ❑ Mar 1995, b&w Cover: 2.95 **NM** value: **Cover or less**
A: Masayuki Fujihara **W:** Masayuki Fujihara
6 ❑ Apr 1995, b&w Cover: 2.95 **NM** value: **Cover or less**
A: Masayuki Fujihara **W:** Masayuki Fujihara
7 ❑ May 1995, b&w Cover: 2.95 **NM** value: **Cover or less**
A: Masayuki Fujihara **W:** Masayuki Fujihara
8 ❑ Jun 1995, b&w Cover: 2.95 **NM** value: **Cover or less**
final issue. **A:** Masayuki Fujihara **W:** Masayuki Fujihara

DO-DO — Nationwide

1 ❑ ca. 1950 Cover: 0.05 **NM** value: **100.00**
• **CGC:** 2 graded, best 9.2
2 ❑ ca. 1950 Cover: 0.05 **NM** value: **100.00**
3 ❑ ca. 1950 Cover: 0.05 **NM** value: **100.00**
4 ❑ ca. 1950 Cover: 0.05 **NM** value: **100.00**
5 ❑ ca. 1951 Cover: 0.05 **NM** value: **100.00**
6 ❑ ca. 1951 Cover: 0.05 **NM** value: **100.00**
7 ❑ ca. 1951 Cover: 0.05 **NM** value: **100.00**

DOG — Rebel

1 ❑ b&w Cover: 2.25 **NM** value: **Cover or less**
2 ❑ b&w Cover: 2.25 **NM** value: **Cover or less**

DOG BOY — Fantagraphics

1 ❑ Cover: 1.75 **NM** value: **2.00**
A: Steve Lafler **W:** Steve Lafler
2 ❑ Cover: 1.75 **NM** value: **Cover or less**
A: Steve Lafler **W:** Steve Lafler
3 ❑ May 1987 Cover: 1.75 **NM** value: **Cover or less**
🕮 The Brainstorm **A:** Steve Lafler **W:** Steve Lafler
4 ❑ Cover: 1.75 **NM** value: **Cover or less**
A: Steve Lafler **W:** Steve Lafler
5 ❑ Cover: 1.75 **NM** value: **Cover or less**
A: Steve Lafler **W:** Steve Lafler
6 ❑ Cover: 1.75 **NM** value: **Cover or less**
A: Steve Lafler **W:** Steve Lafler
7 ❑ Sep 1987 Cover: 1.75 **NM** value: **Cover or less**
A: Steve Lafler **W:** Steve Lafler
8 ❑ Cover: 1.75 **NM** value: **Cover or less**
A: Steve Lafler **W:** Steve Lafler
9 ❑ Cover: 1.75 **NM** value: **Cover or less**
A: Steve Lafler **W:** Steve Lafler

DOG MOON — DC / Vertigo

1 ❑ Cover: 6.95 **NM** value: **Cover or less**
No issue number. One-shot. **A:** Tim Truman **W:** Robert Hunter

DOGPATCH COMICS (AL CAPP'S ...) — Toby

1 ❑ Jun 1949 Cover: 0.10 **NM** value: **120.00**
2 ❑ Aug 1949 Cover: 0.10 **NM** value: **80.00**
3 ❑ Oct 1949 Cover: 0.10 **NM** value: **80.00**
4 ❑ Dec 1949 Cover: 0.10 **NM** value: **80.00**

DOGS OF WAR — Defiant

1 ❑ Apr 1994 Cover: 2.50 **NM** value: **Cover or less**
Circ: CapCity orders: **13,950**
🕮 Reassignment **A:** Georges Jeanty **W:** Jim Shooter; Art Holcomb
2 ❑ May 1994 Cover: 2.50 **NM** value: **Cover or less**
Circ: CapCity orders: **9,375**
🕮 What Makes Brothers… **A:** Georges Jeanty **W:** Art Holcomb
3 ❑ Jun 1994 Cover: 2.50 **NM** value: **Cover or less**
Circ: CapCity orders: **7,450**
🕮 I've Got A Little List… **A:** Georges Jeanty **W:** Jim Shooter; Art Holcomb
4 ❑ Jul 1994 Cover: 2.50 **NM** value: **Cover or less**
Circ: CapCity orders: **6,100**
5 ❑ Aug 1994 Cover: 2.50 **NM** value: **Cover or less**
Circ: CapCity orders: **4,975**
6 ❑ Sep 1994 Cover: 2.50 **NM** value: **Cover or less**
Circ: CapCity orders: **4,050**
7 ❑ Oct 1994 Cover: 2.50 **NM** value: **Cover or less**
8 ❑ Nov 1994 Cover: 2.50 **NM** value: **Cover or less**
final issue.

DOG SOUP — Dog Soup

1 ❑ b&w Cover: 2.50 **NM** value: **Cover or less**

DOGS-O-WAR — Crusade

1 ❑ Jun 1996, b&w Cover: 2.95 **NM** value: **Cover or less**
2 ❑ Jul 1996, b&w Cover: 2.95 **NM** value: **Cover or less**
3 ❑ Jan 1997, b&w Cover: 2.95 **NM** value: **Cover or less**
final issue.

DOG T.A.G.S.: TRAINED ANIMAL GUN SQUADRON — Bugged Out

1 ❑ Jun 1993, b&w Cover: 1.95 **NM** value: **Cover or less**

DOIN' TIME WITH OJ — Boneyard

1 ❑ Dec 1994, b&w Cover: 2.95 **NM** value: **3.50**
A: Nelson Danielson **W:** Hart Fisher; Nelson Danielson

DOJINSHI — Antarctic

1 ❑ Oct 1992, b&w Cover: 2.95 **NM** value: **Cover or less**
2 ❑ Dec 1992, b&w Cover: 2.95 **NM** value: **Cover or less**
3 ❑ Feb 1993, b&w Cover: 2.95 **NM** value: **Cover or less**
4 ❑ Apr 1993, b&w Cover: 2.95 **NM** value: **Cover or less**

DOLL — Rip Off

All issues are adults only.

Guy Colwell created this adults-only series, which somehow manages to be sleazy and highbrow at the same time. Its star character is a sort of life-sized, robotic sex-slave — "a real live doll." Doll is loaned out by two psychologists to be a sex-surrogate for their patients.

Now comes the really weird part: Colwell uses the rather graphic sex scenes as a metaphor for more "normal" male-female relationships. In the midst of sex scenes with Doll, the patients carry out monologues wondering whether all male-female relationships are based on dominance, whether women have been perversely socialized to demean non-dominant men, etc. In short, it's the sort of discussion you'd expect to find in a women's studies class, carried out in what otherwise would be a sleaze-mag. To say the least, it's a strange juxtaposition.

1 ❑ Feb 1989, b&w Cover: 2.50 **NM** value: **3.00**
A: Guy Colwell **W:** Guy Colwell
2 ❑ Mar 1989, b&w Cover: 2.50 **NM** value: **Cover or less**
A: Guy Colwell **W:** Guy Colwell
3 ❑ May 1989, b&w Cover: 2.50 **NM** value: **Cover or less**
A: Guy Colwell **W:** Guy Colwell
4 ❑ Feb 1990, b&w Cover: 2.50 **NM** value: **Cover or less**
A: Guy Colwell **W:** Guy Colwell
5 ❑ Mar 1991, b&w Cover: 2.50 **NM** value: **Cover or less**
A: Guy Colwell **W:** Guy Colwell
6 ❑ May 1991, b&w Cover: 2.50 **NM** value: **Cover or less**
A: Guy Colwell **W:** Guy Colwell
7 ❑ Jun 1991, b&w Cover: 2.50 **NM** value: **Cover or less**
A: Guy Colwell **W:** Guy Colwell
8 ❑ Sep 1992, b&w Cover: 2.95 **NM** value: **Cover or less**
A: Guy Colwell **W:** Guy Colwell
Bk 1❑ Cover: 9.95 **NM** value: **Cover or less**
A: Guy Colwell **W:** Guy Colwell
Bk 2❑ Cover: 15.95 **NM** value: **Cover or less**
A: Guy Colwell **W:** Guy Colwell

DOLL MAN (BELL) — Bell Features

24 ❑ ca. 1949 Cover: 0.10 **NM** value: **Cover or less**
25 ❑ ca. 1949 Cover: 0.10 **NM** value: **Cover or less**
26 ❑ ca. 1949 Cover: 0.10 **NM** value: **Cover or less**
27 ❑ ca. 1949 Cover: 0.10 **NM** value: **Cover or less**
28 ❑ ca. 1949 Cover: 0.10 **NM** value: **Cover or less**
29 ❑ ca. 1949 Cover: 0.10 **NM** value: **Cover or less**
30 ❑ ca. 1949 Cover: 0.10 **NM** value: **Cover or less**

DOLLMAN (MINI-SERIES) — Eternity

1 ❑ Nov 1991, full color Cover: 2.50 **NM** value: **Cover or less**
Circ: CapCity orders: **2,940**
🕮 The Brain From Beyond • movie tie-in **A:** Marc Campos **W:** Bill Spangler ★ 1st Appearance of Dollman (Brick Bardo).
2 ❑ 1992full color Cover: 2.50 **NM** value: **Cover or less**
Circ: CapCity orders: **1,870**
• movie tie-in **A:** Marc Campos **W:** Bill Spangler
3 ❑ 1992full color Cover: 2.50 **NM** value: **Cover or less**
• movie tie-in **A:** Marc Campos **W:** Bill Spangler
4 ❑ 1992full color Cover: 2.50 **NM** value: **Cover or less**
🕮 Blaze Of Glory • movie tie-in **A:** Marc Campos **W:** Bill Spangler

DOLL MAN QUARTERLY — Quality

When the Silver Age Atom was created, it reminded many long-time comics collectors of this Golden Age super-hero. Doll Man came out of the Will Eisner studio, drawn at first by Lou Fine. The costumed crime-fighter shrank from his civilian identity as Darrel Dane to combat the crooks as The Doll Man and was introduced in Feature Comics #27 (Dec 39), where he appeared in (appropriately) short stories (starting as four-pagers, the length slowly growing over the months to nine-pagers, then 11-pagers, then 13, eventually shrinking back to 11-pagers by the time of the series' end in 1950). But he was given his own title, initially a quarterly, in Fall 1941, and he'd starred in 47 issues by the end of 1953.

— Maggie

Other grades: Multiply prices above by **1.5 for Mint • 2/3 for Very Fine • 1/3 for Fine • 1/5 for Very Good • 1/8 for Good**

1 ❑ Fal 1941 Cover: 0.10 **NM** value: **2000.00**
• **CGC:** 2 graded, best 7.5
2 ❑ Spr 1942 Cover: 0.10 **NM** value: **1000.00**
3 ❑ Sum 1942 Cover: 0.10 **NM** value: **600.00**
4 ❑ Win 1942 Cover: 0.10 **NM** value: **300.00**
5 ❑ Spr 1943 Cover: 0.10 **NM** value: **300.00**
• **CGC:** 1 graded, best 8.0
6 ❑ Sum 1943 Cover: 0.10 **NM** value: **300.00**
• **CGC:** 1 graded, best 9.4
7 ❑ Fal 1943 Cover: 0.10 **NM** value: **300.00**
8 ❑ Spr 1946 Cover: 0.10 **NM** value: **1000.00**
• **CGC:** 3 graded, best 9.2
9 ❑ Sum 1946 Cover: 0.10 **NM** value: **300.00**
10 ❑ Fal 1946 Cover: 0.10 **NM** value: **200.00**
11 ❑ Win 1946 Cover: 0.10 **NM** value: **200.00**
12 ❑ Spr 1947 Cover: 0.10 **NM** value: **200.00**
13 ❑ Sum 1947 Cover: 0.10 **NM** value: **200.00**
14 ❑ Fal 1947 Cover: 0.10 **NM** value: **200.00**
15 ❑ Win 1947 Cover: 0.10 **NM** value: **200.00**
16 ❑ Spr 1948 Cover: 0.10 **NM** value: **200.00**
• **CGC:** 1 graded, best .5
17 ❑ Jul 1948 Cover: 0.10 **NM** value: **200.00**
18 ❑ Sep 1948 Cover: 0.10 **NM** value: **200.00**
• **CGC:** 2 graded, best 8.0
19 ❑ Nov 1948 Cover: 0.10 **NM** value: **200.00**
• **CGC:** 2 graded, best 7.0
20 ❑ Jan 1949 Cover: 0.10 **NM** value: **150.00**
21 ❑ Mar 1949 Cover: 0.10 **NM** value: **150.00**
• **CGC:** 1 graded, best 6.0
22 ❑ May 1949 Cover: 0.10 **NM** value: **150.00**
23 ❑ Jul 1949 Cover: 0.10 **NM** value: **150.00**
24 ❑ Sep 1949 Cover: 0.10 **NM** value: **150.00**
25 ❑ Nov 1949 Cover: 0.10 **NM** value: **150.00**
• **CGC:** 2 graded, best 8.0
26 ❑ Jan 1950 Cover: 0.10 **NM** value: **130.00**
• **CGC:** 1 graded, best 8.5
27 ❑ Mar 1950 Cover: 0.10 **NM** value: **130.00**
• **CGC:** 1 graded, best 8.5
28 ❑ May 1950 Cover: 0.10 **NM** value: **130.00**
29 ❑ Jul 1950 Cover: 0.10 **NM** value: **130.00**
30 ❑ Sep 1950 Cover: 0.10 **NM** value: **130.00**
• **CGC:** 1 graded, best 3.5
31 ❑ Dec 1950 Cover: 0.10 **NM** value: **120.00**
32 ❑ Feb 1951 Cover: 0.10 **NM** value: **120.00**
• **CGC:** 1 graded, best 7.5
33 ❑ Apr 1951 Cover: 0.10 **NM** value: **120.00**
• **CGC:** 1 graded, best 6.0
34 ❑ Jun 1951 Cover: 0.10 **NM** value: **120.00**
35 ❑ Aug 1951 Cover: 0.10 **NM** value: **120.00**
36 ❑ Oct 1951 Cover: 0.10 **NM** value: **120.00**
37 ❑ Dec 1951 Cover: 0.10 **NM** value: **130.00**
38 ❑ Feb 1952 Cover: 0.10 **NM** value: **120.00**
• **CGC:** 1 graded, best 8.5
39 ❑ Apr 1952 Cover: 0.10 **NM** value: **120.00**
40 ❑ Jun 1952 Cover: 0.10 **NM** value: **120.00**
• **CGC:** 1 graded, best 8.0
41 ❑ Aug 1952 Cover: 0.10 **NM** value: **120.00**
42 ❑ Oct 1952 Cover: 0.10 **NM** value: **120.00**
43 ❑ Dec 1952 Cover: 0.10 **NM** value: **120.00**
44 ❑ Feb 1953 Cover: 0.10 **NM** value: **100.00**
45 ❑ Apr 1953 Cover: 0.10 **NM** value: **100.00**
46 ❑ Jun 1953 Cover: 0.10 **NM** value: **100.00**
47 ❑ Oct 1953 Cover: 0.10 **NM** value: **100.00**

DOLL PARTS — Sirius

1 ❑ Oct 2000, b&w Cover: 2.95 **NM** value: **Cover or less**
Circ: Diamd. preorders: **2,101**
A: Shawn Pacheco **W:** Mike L. Taylor

DOLLS — Sirius

1 ❑ Jun 1996 Cover: 2.95 **NM** value: **Cover or less**
A: Saverio Tenuta **W:** Lorenzo Bartoli

DOLLY — Approved

1 ❑ Jul 1951 Cover: 0.10 **NM** value: **25.00**

DOLLY DILL — Marvel

1 ❑ ca. 1945 Cover: 0.10 **NM** value: **75.00**

DOLLZ, THE — Image

1 ❑ Apr 2001 Cover: 2.95 **NM** value: **Cover or less**
Circ: Diamd. preorders: **38,335** • **CGC:** 1 graded, best 9.8
A: Randy Green **W:** Randy Green; Tom Sniegoski

DOME: GROUND ZERO, THE — DC / Helix

1 ❑ Cover: 7.95 **NM** value: **Cover or less**
No issue number. • prestige format. • computer-generated

DOMINATION FACTOR: AVENGERS — Marvel

1 ❑ Nov 1999 Cover: 2.50 **NM** value: **Cover or less**
says 1.2 on cover, 1 in indicia.
2 ❑ Nov 1999 Cover: 2.50 **NM** value: **Cover or less**
says 2.4 on cover, 2 in indicia. 🕮 Strange Tales **A:** Dennis Jahnke **W:** Jerry Ordway

DOMINATION FACTOR: FANTASTIC FOUR — Marvel

1 ❑ Dec 1999 Cover: 2.50 **NM** value: **Cover or less**
cover forms diptych with Domination Factor: Avengers #1. 🕮 Arrival **A:** Bob McLeod **W:** Dan Jurgens
2 ❑ Dec 1999 Cover: 2.50 **NM** value: **Cover or less**
says 2.3 on cover, 2 in indicia. 🕮 Flashback Times Four **A:** Bob McLeod **W:** Dan Jurgens

DOMINION — Eclipse

Earth has become a sewer. Most plant life has died, the atmosphere has become a poisonous bacterial soup, and people cannot walk out of doors without wearing oxygen masks. The population is restive and crime has grown rampant. Who is there to restore order? The Tank Police.

The Tank Police's orders are to capture the Super Criminal Buaku and his gang, which includes the sensual cat sisters Annapuma and Unipuma. Can they stop Buaku and restore the planet to health?

Masamune Shirow displays his concern for the environment in this lively series. He is also the creator of Appleseed and Orion.

1 ❑ ca. 1990, b&w Cover: 2.00 **NM** value: **3.00**
• Japanese **A:** Masamune Shirow **W:** Masamune Shirow
2 ❑ ca. 1990, b&w Cover: 2.00 **NM** value: **2.50**
• Japanese **A:** Masamune Shirow **W:** Masamune Shirow
3 ❑ ca. 1991, b&w Cover: 2.00 **NM** value: **2.50**
• Japanese **A:** Masamune Shirow **W:** Masamune Shirow
4 ❑ ca. 1991, b&w Cover: 2.00 **NM** value: **Cover or less**
• Japanese **A:** Masamune Shirow **W:** Masamune Shirow
5 ❑ ca. 1991, b&w Cover: 2.00 **NM** value: **Cover or less**
• Japanese **A:** Masamune Shirow **W:** Masamune Shirow
6 ❑ ca. 1991, b&w Cover: 2.00 **NM** value: **Cover or less**
• Japanese **A:** Masamune Shirow **W:** Masamune Shirow
Bk 1 ❑ ca. 1991 Cover: 14.95 **NM** value: **Cover or less**
• Collects Dominion #1-6 **A:** Masamune Shirow **W:** Masamune Shirow

DOMINION: CONFLICT 1 — Dark Horse / Manga

1 ❑ Mar 1996, b&w Cover: 2.95 **NM** value: **Cover or less**
A: Masamune Shirow **W:** Masamune Shirow
2 ❑ Apr 1996, b&w Cover: 2.95 **NM** value: **Cover or less**
A: Masamune Shirow **W:** Masamune Shirow
3 ❑ May 1996, b&w Cover: 2.95 **NM** value: **Cover or less**
A: Masamune Shirow **W:** Masamune Shirow
4 ❑ Jun 1996, b&w Cover: 2.95 **NM** value: **Cover or less**
A: Masamune Shirow **W:** Masamune Shirow
5 ❑ Jul 1996, b&w Cover: 2.95 **NM** value: **Cover or less**
A: Masamune Shirow **W:** Masamune Shirow
6 ❑ Aug 1996, b&w Cover: 2.95 **NM** value: **Cover or less**
final issue. **A:** Masamune Shirow **W:** Masamune Shirow
Bk 1 ❑ Aug 1996, b&w Cover: 2.95 **NM** value: **14.95**
• Collects Dominion: Conflict 1 #1-6 **A:** Masamune Shirow **W:** Masamune Shirow

DOMINION: PHANTOM OF THE AUDIENCE — Dark Horse

1 ❑ Cover: 2.50 **NM** value: **Cover or less**
Circ: CapCity orders: **4,700**
No issue number.

DOMINIQUE: FAMILY MATTERS — Caliber

1 ❑ b&w Cover: 2.95 **NM** value: **Cover or less**
A: Gene Gonzales **W:** Charles Moore; Lisa Moore

DOMINIQUE: KILLZONE — Caliber

1 ❑ b&w Cover: 2.95 **NM** value: **Cover or less**
One-shot. **A:** Casey Jones; Michael Perkins **W:** Charles Moore; Lisa Moore

DOMINIQUE: PROTECT AND SERVE — Caliber

1 ❑ b&w Cover: 2.95 **NM** value: **Cover or less**
One-shot.

DOMINIQUE: WHITE KNUCKLE DRIVE — Caliber

1 ❑ b&w Cover: 2.95 **NM** value: **Cover or less**
One-shot. **A:** Matthew Smith **W:** Charles Moore; Lisa Moore

DOMINO — Marvel

1 ❑ Jan 1997 Cover: 1.95 **NM** value: **2.00**
Circ: Direct Market orders: **83,250**
🕮 Rise and Fall **A:** David Perrin **W:** Ben Raab
2 ❑ Feb 1997 Cover: 1.95 **NM** value: **2.00**
Circ: Direct Market orders: **68,000**
A: David Perrin **W:** Ben Raab ★ Versus Deathstrike.
3 ❑ Mar 1997 Cover: 1.95 **NM** value: **2.00**
Circ: Direct Market orders: **59,000**
🕮 Hard Luck **A:** David Perrin **W:** Ben Raab

DOMINO CHANCE — Chance

1 ❑ May 1982, b&w Cover: 1.50 **NM** value: **2.50**
1-2 ❑ b&w Cover: 1.50 **NM** value: **Cover or less**
2 ❑ Jul 1982, b&w Cover: 1.50 **NM** value: **2.00**
3 ❑ Sep 1982, b&w Cover: 1.50 **NM** value: **2.00**
4 ❑ 1983b&w Cover: 1.50 **NM** value: **2.00**
5 ❑ Jul 1983, b&w Cover: 1.50 **NM** value: **2.00**
6 ❑ 1984b&w Cover: 1.50 **NM** value: **2.00**
7 ❑ 1984b&w Cover: 1.50 **NM** value: **2.00**
★ 1st Appearance of Gizmo.
8 ❑ 1985b&w Cover: 1.50 **NM** value: **2.00**
★ 2nd Appearance of Gizmo.
9 ❑ 1985b&w Cover: 1.50 **NM** value: **2.00**

DOMINO CHANCE: ROACH EXTRAORDINAIRE — Amazing

1 ❑ Cover: 1.95 **NM** value: **Cover or less**

DOMINO LADY — Fantagraphics / Eros

All issues are adults only.

Ellen Patrick has been fighting organized crime as the Domino Lady ever since her father, Owen Patrick, a law-abiding politician, was murdered by the mob. She's devoted her life to the fight, enlisting the help of her butler, Delgyn Hoyt, who had been serving the Patrick family for years.

In this mini-series, she turns her sights on a mad scientist who has unleashed a blood craving dinosaur into the city. The scientist controls the beast by way of a magic flute. Domino Lady must acquire the flute if she hopes to save the city.

Domino Lady is an action-oriented mini-series, for adults only.

1 ❑ Dec 1990, b&w Cover: 1.95 **NM** value: **Cover or less**
A: Ron Wilber **W:** Ron Wilber
2 ❑ Jan 1991, b&w Cover: 1.95 **NM** value: **Cover or less**
A: Ron Wilber **W:** Ron Wilber
3 ❑ Mar 1991, b&w Cover: 1.95 **NM** value: **Cover or less**
A: Ron Wilber **W:** Ron Wilber

DOMINO LADY'S JUNGLE ADVENTURE — Fantagraphics / Eros

All issues are adults only.

1 ❑ b&w Cover: 2.50 **NM** value: **2.75**
A: Ron Wilber **W:** Ron Wilber
2 ❑ b&w Cover: 2.75 **NM** value: **Cover or less**
A: Ron Wilber **W:** Ron Wilber
3 ❑ Nov 1992, b&w Cover: 2.75 **NM** value: **Cover or less**
A: Ron Wilber **W:** Ron Wilber

DOMU: A CHILD'S DREAM — Dark Horse / Manga

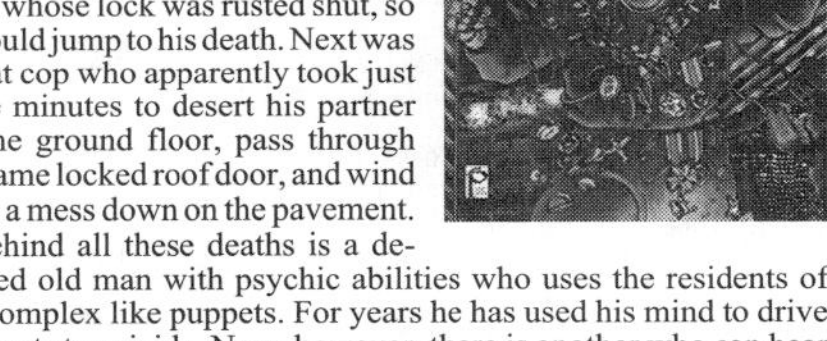

Something is preying on the residents of the Tsutsumi Public Housing Complex. In the past three years, two dozen residents have met with mysterious ends: suicides, possible murders, or deaths that were simply unexplained. Among the most recent was a man who calmly walked up to the roof and passed through a door whose lock was rusted shut, so he could jump to his death. Next was a beat cop who apparently took just three minutes to desert his partner on the ground floor, pass through the same locked roof door, and wind up in a mess down on the pavement.

Behind all these deaths is a deranged old man with psychic abilities who uses the residents of the complex like puppets. For years he has used his mind to drive residents to suicide. Now, however, there is another who can hear his mental commands and stand against them: a little girl with powers of her own. The two are destined for battle in this three-issue mini-series by Akira's Katsuhiro Otomo.

1 ❑ Cover: 5.95 **NM** value: **Cover or less**
Circ: CapCity orders: **6,350**
A: Katsuhiro Otomo **W:** Katsuhiro Otomo
2 ❑ Cover: 5.95 **NM** value: **Cover or less**
Circ: CapCity orders: **4,775**
A: Katsuhiro Otomo **W:** Katsuhiro Otomo
3 ❑ May 1995 Cover: 5.95 **NM** value: **Cover or less**
Circ: CapCity orders: **4,875**
A: Katsuhiro Otomo **W:** Katsuhiro Otomo
Bk 1 ❑ Feb 1996, b&w Cover: 17.95 **NM** value: **Cover or less**
• Collects Domu: A Child's Dream #1-3 **A:** Katsuhiro Otomo **W:** Katsuhiro Otomo

DONALD AND MICKEY — Gladstone

19 ❑ Sep 1993 Cover: 1.50 **NM** value: **Cover or less**
Circ: CapCity orders: **4,850**
A: Carl Barks
20 ❑ Nov 1993 Cover: 2.95 **NM** value: **Cover or less**
Circ: CapCity orders: **5,025**
A: Carl Barks
21 ❑ Jan 1994 Cover: 1.50 **NM** value: **Cover or less**
Circ: CapCity orders: **4,425**
A: Carl Barks; William Van Horn
22 ❑ Mar 1994 Cover: 1.50 **NM** value: **Cover or less**
Circ: CapCity orders: **4,200**
A: Carl Barks
23 ❑ May 1994 Cover: 1.50 **NM** value: **Cover or less**
Circ: CapCity orders: **3,850**
A: Carl Barks
24 ❑ Jul 1994 Cover: 1.50 **NM** value: **Cover or less**
Circ: CapCity orders: **3,850**
A: Carl Barks
25 ❑ Sep 1994 Cover: 2.95 **NM** value: **Cover or less**
Circ: CapCity orders: **3,875**
26 ❑ Nov 1994 Cover: 1.50 **NM** value: **Cover or less**
Circ: CapCity orders: **3,750**
• newsstand distribution by Marvel
27 ❑ Jan 1995 Cover: 1.50 **NM** value: **Cover or less**
Circ: Statement: **71,769** CapCity orders: **3,750**
28 ❑ Mar 1995 Cover: 1.50 **NM** value: **Cover or less**
Circ: Statement: **71,769** CapCity orders: **3,575**
29 ❑ May 1995 Cover: 1.50 **NM** value: **Cover or less**
Circ: Statement: **71,769** CapCity orders: **3,350**
30 ❑ Jul 1995 Cover: 1.50 **NM** value: **Cover or less**
Circ: Statement: **71,769** CapCity orders: **3,300**

CGC-graded: Multiply prices above by **33 for 9.9 M • 16 for 9.8 NM/M • 7 for 9.6 NM+ • 5 for 9.4 NM • 2.5 for 9.2 NM- • 1.5 for 9.0 VF/NM**

DONALD AND MICKEY IN DISNEYLAND — Dell

1 ❑ May 1958 Cover: 0.25 **NM** value: **100.00**
• **CGC:** 1 graded, best 9.4

DONALD AND SCROOGE — Disney

1 ❑ ca. 1992 Cover: 1.75 **NM** value: **Cover or less**
2 ❑ ca. 1992 Cover: 1.75 **NM** value: **Cover or less**
3 ❑ ca. 1992 Cover: 1.75 **NM** value: **Cover or less**
Bk 1 ❑ ca. 1992 Cover: 8.95 **NM** value: **Cover or less**
A: Don Rosa

DONALD DUCK ADVENTURES (DISNEY) — Disney

1 ❑ Jun 1990 Cover: 1.50 **NM** value: **2.50**
Circ: CapCity orders: **11,650**
The Money Pit **A:** Don Rosa **W:** Don Rosa
2 ❑ Jul 1990 Cover: 1.50 **NM** value: **2.00**
Circ: CapCity orders: **8,050**
A: Carl Barks; William Van Horn
3 ❑ Aug 1990 Cover: 1.50 **NM** value: **2.00**
Circ: CapCity orders: **8,600**
A: William Van Horn
4 ❑ Sep 1990 Cover: 1.50 **NM** value: **2.00**
Circ: CapCity orders: **8,300**
A: Carl Barks; William Van Horn
5 ❑ Oct 1990 Cover: 1.50 **NM** value: **2.00**
Circ: CapCity orders: **8,650**
A: William Van Horn
6 ❑ Nov 1990 Cover: 1.50 **NM** value: **2.00**
Circ: CapCity orders: **7,500**
A: William Van Horn
7 ❑ Dec 1990 Cover: 1.50 **NM** value: **2.00**
Circ: CapCity orders: **7,100**
A: William Van Horn
8 ❑ Jan 1991 Cover: 1.50 **NM** value: **2.00**
Circ: Statement: **61,910** CapCity orders: **7,300**
A: William Van Horn
9 ❑ Feb 1991 Cover: 1.50 **NM** value: **2.00**
Circ: Statement: **61,910** CapCity orders: **7,400**
• reprint of 1: Uncle Scrooge **A:** Carl Barks
10 ❑ Mar 1991 Cover: 1.50 **NM** value: **2.00**
Circ: Statement: **61,910** CapCity orders: **6,800**
A: William Van Horn
11 ❑ Apr 1991 Cover: 1.50 **NM** value: **2.00**
Circ: Statement: **61,910** CapCity orders: **6,150**
Mad #1 cover parody.
12 ❑ May 1991 Cover: 1.50 **NM** value: **2.00**
Circ: Statement: **61,910** CapCity orders: **5,850**
13 ❑ Jun 1991 Cover: 1.50 **NM** value: **2.00**
Circ: Statement: **61,910** CapCity orders: **5,650**
A: William Van Horn
14 ❑ Jul 1991 Cover: 1.50 **NM** value: **2.00**
Circ: Statement: **61,910** CapCity orders: **5,600**
A: Carl Barks
15 ❑ Aug 1991 Cover: 1.50 **NM** value: **2.00**
Circ: Statement: **61,910** CapCity orders: **5,550**
A: William Van Horn
16 ❑ Sep 1991 Cover: 1.50 **NM** value: **2.00**
Circ: Statement: **61,910** CapCity orders: **5,550**
17 ❑ Oct 1991 Cover: 1.50 **NM** value: **2.00**
Circ: Statement: **61,910** CapCity orders: **5,550**
Time Tetrad, Part 1
18 ❑ Nov 1991 Cover: 1.50 **NM** value: **2.00**
Circ: Statement: **61,910** CapCity orders: **5,300**
That Ol' Soft Soap **A:** William Van Horn
19 ❑ Dec 1991 Cover: 1.50 **NM** value: **2.00**
Circ: Statement: **61,910** CapCity orders: **5,000**
A: William Van Horn
20 ❑ Jan 1992 Cover: 1.50 **NM** value: **2.00**
Circ: CapCity orders: **5,000**
A: William Van Horn
21 ❑ Feb 1992 Cover: 1.50 **NM** value: **Cover or less**
Circ: CapCity orders: **5,750**
• golden Christmas tree **A:** Carl Barks
22 ❑ Mar 1992 Cover: 1.50 **NM** value: **Cover or less**
Circ: CapCity orders: **5,450**
A: Don Rosa
23 ❑ Apr 1992 Cover: 1.50 **NM** value: **Cover or less**
Circ: CapCity orders: **5,100**
A: Carl Barks
24 ❑ May 1992 Cover: 1.50 **NM** value: **Cover or less**
Circ: CapCity orders: **5,300**
A: Don Rosa
25 ❑ Jun 1992 Cover: 1.50 **NM** value: **Cover or less**
Circ: CapCity orders: **5,300**
• map piece
26 ❑ Jul 1992 Cover: 1.50 **NM** value: **Cover or less**
Circ: CapCity orders: **5,800**
• map piece **A:** Carl Barks
27 ❑ Aug 1992 Cover: 1.50 **NM** value: **Cover or less**
Circ: CapCity orders: **5,400**
• map piece **A:** Carl Barks
28 ❑ Sep 1992 Cover: 1.50 **NM** value: **Cover or less**
Circ: CapCity orders: **5,550**
• Olympics
29 ❑ Oct 1992 Cover: 1.50 **NM** value: **Cover or less**
Circ: CapCity orders: **5,000**
30 ❑ Nov 1992 Cover: 1.50 **NM** value: **Cover or less**
Circ: CapCity orders: **4,600**
31 ❑ Dec 1992 Cover: 1.50 **NM** value: **Cover or less**
Circ: CapCity orders: **4,650**
32 ❑ Jan 1993 Cover: 1.50 **NM** value: **Cover or less**
Circ: Statement: **159,310** CapCity orders: **4,500**
33 ❑ Feb 1993 Cover: 1.50 **NM** value: **Cover or less**
Circ: Statement: **159,310** CapCity orders: **4,500**
34 ❑ Mar 1993 Cover: 1.50 **NM** value: **Cover or less**
Circ: Statement: **159,310** CapCity orders: **5,150**
• Return of Super-Duck **A:** Don Rosa
35 ❑ Apr 1993 Cover: 1.50 **NM** value: **Cover or less**
Circ: Statement: **159,310** CapCity orders: **4,450**
A: Carl Barks
36 ❑ May 1993 Cover: 1.50 **NM** value: **Cover or less**
Circ: Statement: **159,310** CapCity orders: **4,850**
A: Carl Barks
37 ❑ Jun 1993 Cover: 1.50 **NM** value: **Cover or less**
Circ: Statement: **159,310** CapCity orders: **5,400**
A: Carl Barks; Don Rosa
38 ❑ Jul 1993 Cover: 1.50 **NM** value: **Cover or less**
Circ: Statement: **159,310** CapCity orders: **4,900**
39 ❑ Aug 1993 Cover: 1.50 **NM** value: **Cover or less**
Circ: Statement: **159,310**
40 ❑ Sep 1993 Cover: 1.50 **NM** value: **Cover or less**
Circ: Statement: **159,310**
41 ❑ Oct 1993 Cover: 1.50 **NM** value: **Cover or less**
Circ: Statement: **159,310**
42 ❑ Nov 1993 Cover: 1.50 **NM** value: **Cover or less**
Circ: Statement: **159,310**
C: Carl Barks
43 ❑ 1993 Cover: 1.50 **NM** value: **Cover or less**
Circ: Statement: **159,310**
44 ❑ Dec 1993 Cover: 1.50 **NM** value: **Cover or less**
Circ: Statement: **159,310**
• Gladstone resumes publishing its series

DONALD DUCK ADVENTURES (GLADSTONE) — Gladstone

1 ❑ Nov 1987 Cover: 0.95 **NM** value: **2.50**
Circ: CapCity orders: **6,900**
A: Carl Barks
2 ❑ Jan 1988 Cover: 0.95 **NM** value: **2.00**
Circ: Statement: **74,809** CapCity orders: **5,325**
A: Carl Barks
3 ❑ Mar 1988 Cover: 0.95 **NM** value: **2.00**
Circ: Statement: **74,809** CapCity orders: **5,925**
Lost in the Andes **A:** Carl Barks
4 ❑ May 1988 Cover: 0.95 **NM** value: **2.00**
Circ: Statement: **74,809** CapCity orders: **5,425**
A: Carl Barks
5 ❑ Jul 1988 Cover: 0.95 **NM** value: **2.00**
Circ: Statement: **74,809** CapCity orders: **5,550**
A: Carl Barks; Don Rosa
6 ❑ Aug 1988 Cover: 0.95 **NM** value: **1.50**
Circ: Statement: **74,809** CapCity orders: **5,350**
A: Carl Barks
7 ❑ Sep 1988 Cover: 0.95 **NM** value: **1.50**
Circ: Statement: **74,809** CapCity orders: **5,700**
A: Carl Barks
8 ❑ Oct 1988 Cover: 0.95 **NM** value: **1.50**
Circ: Statement: **74,809** CapCity orders: **6,350**
A: Carl Barks; Don Rosa
9 ❑ Nov 1988 Cover: 0.95 **NM** value: **1.50**
Circ: Statement: **74,809** CapCity orders: **5,900**
A: Carl Barks
10 ❑ Dec 1988 Cover: 0.95 **NM** value: **1.50**
Circ: Statement: **74,809** CapCity orders: **5,700**
A: Carl Barks
11 ❑ Feb 1989 Cover: 0.95 **NM** value: **1.50**
Circ: Statement: **68,887** CapCity orders: **6,800**
A: Carl Barks
12 ❑ May 1989 Cover: 1.50 **NM** value: **Cover or less**
Circ: Statement: **68,887** CapCity orders: **7,900**
Return to Plain Awful **A:** Carl Barks; Don Rosa
13 ❑ Jul 1989 Cover: 1.50 **NM** value: **Cover or less**
Circ: Statement: **68,887** CapCity orders: **6,250**
A: Carl Barks **C:** Don Rosa
14 ❑ Aug 1989 Cover: 1.50 **NM** value: **Cover or less**
Circ: Statement: **68,887** CapCity orders: **7,500**
A: Carl Barks
15 ❑ Sep 1989 Cover: 1.50 **NM** value: **Cover or less**
Circ: Statement: **68,887** CapCity orders: **6,450**
A: Carl Barks
16 ❑ Oct 1989 Cover: 1.50 **NM** value: **Cover or less**
Circ: Statement: **68,887** CapCity orders: **6,850**
A: Carl Barks
17 ❑ Nov 1989 Cover: 1.50 **NM** value: **Cover or less**
Circ: Statement: **68,887** CapCity orders: **6,400**
A: Carl Barks
18 ❑ Dec 1989 Cover: 1.50 **NM** value: **Cover or less**
Circ: Statement: **68,887** CapCity orders: **6,650**
No Such Varmint **A:** Carl Barks
19 ❑ Feb 1990 Cover: 1.50 **NM** value: **Cover or less**
Circ: CapCity orders: **6,550**
• Has 1991 Statement, filed 10/1/91; avg print run 157,681; avg sales 56,652; avg subs 5,658; avg total paid 61,910; samples 174; office use 5,440; max existent 67,924; 58% of run returned **A:** Carl Barks
20 ❑ Apr 1990 Cover: 1.50 **NM** value: **Cover or less**
Circ: CapCity orders: **6,550**
Old Castle's Secret • series goes on hiatus during Disney run **A:** Carl Barks
21 ❑ Aug 1993 Cover: 1.50 **NM** value: **Cover or less**
Circ: CapCity orders: **5,150**
A: Carl Barks **C:** Don Rosa
22 ❑ Oct 1993 Cover: 1.50 **NM** value: **Cover or less**
Circ: CapCity orders: **5,000**
The Pixilated Parrot **A:** Carl Barks
23 ❑ Dec 1993 Cover: 1.50 **NM** value: **Cover or less**
Circ: CapCity orders: **5,000**
C: Don Rosa
24 ❑ Feb 1994 Cover: 1.50 **NM** value: **Cover or less**
Circ: CapCity orders: **5,850**
The Black Moon **A:** William Van Horn
25 ❑ Apr 1994 Cover: 1.50 **NM** value: **Cover or less**
Circ: CapCity orders: **4,475**
26 ❑ Jun 1994 Cover: 2.95 **NM** value: **Cover or less**
Circ: CapCity orders: **4,350**
A: Carl Barks
27 ❑ Aug 1994 Cover: 1.50 **NM** value: **Cover or less**
Circ: CapCity orders: **5,725**
28 ❑ Oct 1994 Cover: 1.50 **NM** value: **Cover or less**
Circ: CapCity orders: **4,225**
cover uses portion of Barks painting. Sheriff of Bullet Valley **A:** Carl Barks
29 ❑ Dec 1994 Cover: 1.50 **NM** value: **Cover or less**
Circ: CapCity orders: **4,250**
• newsstand distribution by Marvel
30 ❑ Feb 1995 Cover: 2.95 **NM** value: **Cover or less**
Circ: Statement: **76,397** CapCity orders: **5,025**
Christmas for Shacktown **A:** Carl Barks
31 ❑ Apr 1995 Cover: 1.50 **NM** value: **Cover or less**
Circ: Statement: **76,397** CapCity orders: **3,925**
32 ❑ Jun 1995 Cover: 1.50 **NM** value: **Cover or less**
Circ: Statement: **76,397** CapCity orders: **3,850**
33 ❑ Aug 1995 Cover: 1.95 **NM** value: **Cover or less**
Circ: Statement: **76,397** CapCity orders: **3,725**
The Golden Helmet **A:** Carl Barks
34 ❑ Oct 1995 Cover: 1.50 **NM** value: **Cover or less**
Circ: Statement: **76,397** CapCity orders: **5,325**
newsprint covers begin.
35 ❑ Dec 1995 Cover: 1.50 **NM** value: **Cover or less**
Circ: Statement: **76,397** CapCity orders: **4,825**
36 ❑ Feb 1996 Cover: 1.50 **NM** value: **Cover or less**
Circ: Statement: **41,070**
37 ❑ Apr 1996 Cover: 1.50 **NM** value: **Cover or less**
Circ: Statement: **41,070**
38 ❑ Jun 1996 Cover: 1.50 **NM** value: **Cover or less**
Circ: Statement: **41,070**
39 ❑ Aug 1996 Cover: 1.50 **NM** value: **Cover or less**
Circ: Statement: **41,070**
40 ❑ Oct 1996 Cover: 1.50 **NM** value: **Cover or less**
Circ: Statement: **41,070**
41 ❑ Dec 1996 Cover: 1.50 **NM** value: **Cover or less**
Circ: Statement: **41,070** Direct Market orders: **7,399**
42 ❑ Feb 1997 Cover: 1.50 **NM** value: **Cover or less**
Circ: Statement: **33,272**
43 ❑ Apr 1997 Cover: 1.50 **NM** value: **Cover or less**
Circ: Statement: **33,272** Diamd. preorders: **7,358**
newsprint covers end.
44 ❑ Jun 1997 Cover: 1.95 **NM** value: **Cover or less**
Circ: Statement: **33,272** Diamd. preorders: **6,658**
45 ❑ Aug 1997 Cover: 1.95 **NM** value: **Cover or less**
Circ: Statement: **33,272** Diamd. preorders: **6,657**
46 ❑ Oct 1997 Cover: 1.95 **NM** value: **Cover or less**
Circ: Statement: **33,272** Diamd. preorders: **6,689**
47 ❑ Dec 1997 Cover: 1.95 **NM** value: **Cover or less**
Circ: Statement: **33,272** Diamd. preorders: **6,590**
Trick or Treat **A:** Carl Barks
48 ❑ Feb 1998 Cover: 1.95 **NM** value: **Cover or less**
Circ: Diamd. preorders: **5,474**
final issue. • Has 1997 Statement, filed 9/4/97; avg print run 64,620; avg sales 29,240; avg subs 3,332; avg total paid 244; samples 244; office use 1,598 ; max existent 34,414; 46% of run returned

DONALD DUCK ALBUM (WALT DISNEY'S) — Dell

1 ❑ May 1961 Cover: 0.10 **NM** value: **45.00**
• **CGC:** 1 graded, best 5.5
• FC 1182

DONALD DUCK & MICKEY MOUSE — Gladstone

1 ❑ Sep 1995 Cover: 1.50 **NM** value: **Cover or less**
Circ: Statement: **71,769** CapCity orders: **4,200**
2 ❑ Nov 1995 Cover: 1.50 **NM** value: **Cover or less**
Circ: Statement: **71,769** CapCity orders: **3,350**
3 ❑ Jan 1996 Cover: 1.50 **NM** value: **Cover or less**
4 ❑ Mar 1996 Cover: 1.50 **NM** value: **Cover or less**
5 ❑ May 1996 Cover: 1.50 **NM** value: **Cover or less**
6 ❑ Jul 1996 Cover: 1.50 **NM** value: **Cover or less**
7 ❑ Sep 1996 Cover: 1.50 **NM** value: **Cover or less**

DONALD DUCK BEACH PARTY (WALT DISNEY'S...) — Dell

1 ❑ ca. 1954 Cover: 0.25 **NM** value: **100.00**
• **CGC:** 3 graded, best 9.2
Rival Boatmen • Reprints story from Walt Disney's Comics #45
2 ❑ Jul 1955 Cover: 0.25 **NM** value: **65.00**
• **CGC:** 1 graded, best 6.5
3 ❑ 1956 Cover: 0.25 **NM** value: **55.00**
4 ❑ 1957 Cover: 0.25 **NM** value: **55.00**
5 ❑ ca. 1958 Cover: 0.25 **NM** value: **55.00**
• **CGC:** 2 graded, best 9.4
The Gem Jam
6 ❑ 1959 Cover: 0.25 **NM** value: **55.00**

DONALD DUCK DIGEST — Gladstone

1 ❑ **NM** value: **3.50**
Circ: CapCity orders: **2,675**
2 ❑ **NM** value: **3.00**
Circ: CapCity orders: **2,450**
3 ❑ **NM** value: **3.00**
Circ: CapCity orders: **2,750**
4 ❑ **NM** value: **3.00**
Circ: CapCity orders: **1,650**
5 ❑ **NM** value: **3.00**
Circ: CapCity orders: **1,275**

DONALD DUCK FUN BOOK — Dell

1 ❑ ca. 1953 Cover: 0.25 **NM** value: **500.00**
2 ❑ Oct 1954 Cover: 0.25 **NM** value: **500.00**
• **CGC:** 1 graded, best 9.0

DONALD DUCK IN DISNEYLAND — Dell

1 ❑ Sep 1955 Cover: 0.25 **NM** value: **150.00**
• **CGC:** 3 graded, best 9.2

Other grades: Multiply prices above by **1.5 for Mint • 2/3 for Very Fine • 1/3 for Fine • 1/5 for Very Good • 1/8 for Good**

DONALD DUCK (WALT DISNEY'S...)

Dell / Gold Key

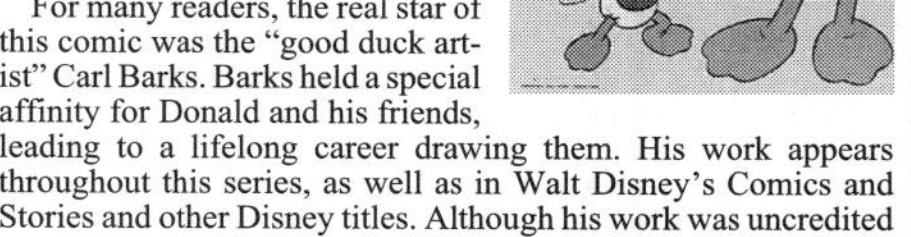

Walt Disney's Donald Duck first appeared in the 1934 animated short, The Wise Little Hen, where his lisping voice was said to have been inspired by a real-life Disney producer (who never caught on to the "homage" being paid him!). From there he went on to star in numerous cartoons and comic strips. This solo series grew out of his earlier appearances in Four Color Comics.

For many readers, the real star of this comic was the "good duck artist" Carl Barks. Barks held a special affinity for Donald and his friends, leading to a lifelong career drawing them. His work appears throughout this series, as well as in Walt Disney's Comics and Stories and other Disney titles. Although his work was uncredited in the stories themselves, it's recognizable by its sheer quality, as well as the vivid imagination and playfulness Barks brought to the series.

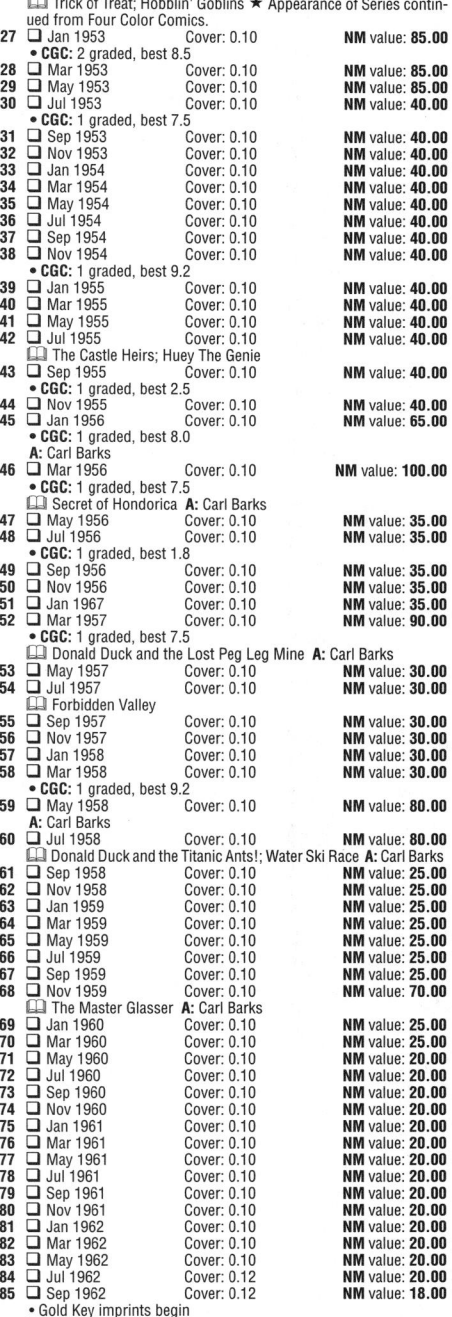

26 ❑ Nov 1952 Cover: 0.10 **NM** value: **250.00**
• **CGC:** 1 graded, best 5.5
📖 Trick of Treat; Hobblin' Goblins ★ Appearance of Series continued from Four Color Comics.

27 ❑ Jan 1953 Cover: 0.10 **NM** value: **85.00**
• **CGC:** 2 graded, best 8.5

28 ❑ Mar 1953 Cover: 0.10 **NM** value: **85.00**

29 ❑ May 1953 Cover: 0.10 **NM** value: **85.00**

30 ❑ Jul 1953 Cover: 0.10 **NM** value: **40.00**
• **CGC:** 1 graded, best 7.5

31 ❑ Sep 1953 Cover: 0.10 **NM** value: **40.00**

32 ❑ Nov 1953 Cover: 0.10 **NM** value: **40.00**

33 ❑ Jan 1954 Cover: 0.10 **NM** value: **40.00**

34 ❑ Mar 1954 Cover: 0.10 **NM** value: **40.00**

35 ❑ May 1954 Cover: 0.10 **NM** value: **40.00**

36 ❑ Jul 1954 Cover: 0.10 **NM** value: **40.00**

37 ❑ Sep 1954 Cover: 0.10 **NM** value: **40.00**

38 ❑ Nov 1954 Cover: 0.10 **NM** value: **40.00**
• **CGC:** 1 graded, best 9.2

39 ❑ Jan 1955 Cover: 0.10 **NM** value: **40.00**

40 ❑ Mar 1955 Cover: 0.10 **NM** value: **40.00**

41 ❑ May 1955 Cover: 0.10 **NM** value: **40.00**

42 ❑ Jul 1955 Cover: 0.10 **NM** value: **40.00**
📖 The Castle Heirs; Huey The Genie

43 ❑ Sep 1955 Cover: 0.10 **NM** value: **40.00**
• **CGC:** 1 graded, best 2.5

44 ❑ Nov 1955 Cover: 0.10 **NM** value: **40.00**

45 ❑ Jan 1956 Cover: 0.10 **NM** value: **65.00**
• **CGC:** 1 graded, best 8.0
A: Carl Barks

46 ❑ Mar 1956 Cover: 0.10 **NM** value: **100.00**
• **CGC:** 1 graded, best 7.5
📖 Secret of Hondorica **A:** Carl Barks

47 ❑ May 1956 Cover: 0.10 **NM** value: **35.00**

48 ❑ Jul 1956 Cover: 0.10 **NM** value: **35.00**
• **CGC:** 1 graded, best 1.8

49 ❑ Sep 1956 Cover: 0.10 **NM** value: **35.00**

50 ❑ Nov 1956 Cover: 0.10 **NM** value: **35.00**

51 ❑ Jan 1967 Cover: 0.10 **NM** value: **35.00**

52 ❑ Mar 1957 Cover: 0.10 **NM** value: **90.00**
• **CGC:** 1 graded, best 7.5
📖 Donald Duck and the Lost Peg Leg Mine **A:** Carl Barks

53 ❑ May 1957 Cover: 0.10 **NM** value: **30.00**

54 ❑ Jul 1957 Cover: 0.10 **NM** value: **30.00**
📖 Forbidden Valley

55 ❑ Sep 1957 Cover: 0.10 **NM** value: **30.00**

56 ❑ Nov 1957 Cover: 0.10 **NM** value: **30.00**

57 ❑ Jan 1958 Cover: 0.10 **NM** value: **30.00**

58 ❑ Mar 1958 Cover: 0.10 **NM** value: **30.00**
• **CGC:** 1 graded, best 9.2

59 ❑ May 1958 Cover: 0.10 **NM** value: **80.00**
A: Carl Barks

60 ❑ Jul 1958 Cover: 0.10 **NM** value: **80.00**
📖 Donald Duck and the Titanic Ants!; Water Ski Race **A:** Carl Barks

61 ❑ Sep 1958 Cover: 0.10 **NM** value: **25.00**

62 ❑ Nov 1958 Cover: 0.10 **NM** value: **25.00**

63 ❑ Jan 1959 Cover: 0.10 **NM** value: **25.00**

64 ❑ Mar 1959 Cover: 0.10 **NM** value: **25.00**

65 ❑ May 1959 Cover: 0.10 **NM** value: **25.00**

66 ❑ Jul 1959 Cover: 0.10 **NM** value: **25.00**

67 ❑ Sep 1959 Cover: 0.10 **NM** value: **25.00**

68 ❑ Nov 1959 Cover: 0.10 **NM** value: **70.00**
📖 The Master Glasser **A:** Carl Barks

69 ❑ Jan 1960 Cover: 0.10 **NM** value: **25.00**

70 ❑ Mar 1960 Cover: 0.10 **NM** value: **25.00**

71 ❑ May 1960 Cover: 0.10 **NM** value: **20.00**

72 ❑ Jul 1960 Cover: 0.10 **NM** value: **20.00**

73 ❑ Sep 1960 Cover: 0.10 **NM** value: **20.00**

74 ❑ Nov 1960 Cover: 0.10 **NM** value: **20.00**

75 ❑ Jan 1961 Cover: 0.10 **NM** value: **20.00**

76 ❑ Mar 1961 Cover: 0.10 **NM** value: **20.00**

77 ❑ May 1961 Cover: 0.10 **NM** value: **20.00**

78 ❑ Jul 1961 Cover: 0.10 **NM** value: **20.00**

79 ❑ Sep 1961 Cover: 0.10 **NM** value: **20.00**

80 ❑ Nov 1961 Cover: 0.10 **NM** value: **20.00**

81 ❑ Jan 1962 Cover: 0.10 **NM** value: **20.00**

82 ❑ Mar 1962 Cover: 0.10 **NM** value: **20.00**

83 ❑ May 1962 Cover: 0.10 **NM** value: **20.00**

84 ❑ Jul 1962 Cover: 0.12 **NM** value: **20.00**

85 ❑ Sep 1962 Cover: 0.12 **NM** value: **18.00**
• Gold Key imprints begin

86 ❑ Nov 1962 Cover: 0.12 **NM** value: **18.00**

87 ❑ Jan 1963 Cover: 0.12 **NM** value: **18.00**
Circ: Statement: **293,800**

88 ❑ Mar 1963 Cover: 0.12 **NM** value: **18.00**
Circ: Statement: **293,800**

89 ❑ May 1963 Cover: 0.12 **NM** value: **18.00**
Circ: Statement: **293,800**

90 ❑ Jul 1963 Cover: 0.12 **NM** value: **18.00**
Circ: Statement: **293,800**

91 ❑ Sep 1963 Cover: 0.12 **NM** value: **18.00**
Circ: Statement: **293,800**

92 ❑ Nov 1963 Cover: 0.12 **NM** value: **18.00**
Circ: Statement: **293,800**

93 ❑ Jan 1964 Cover: 0.12 **NM** value: **18.00**
Circ: Statement: **316,657**

94 ❑ Mar 1964 Cover: 0.12 **NM** value: **18.00**
Circ: Statement: **316,657**

95 ❑ May 1964 Cover: 0.12 **NM** value: **18.00**
Circ: Statement: **316,657**

96 ❑ Jul 1964 Cover: 0.12 **NM** value: **18.00**
Circ: Statement: **316,657**

97 ❑ Sep 1964 Cover: 0.12 **NM** value: **18.00**
Circ: Statement: **316,657**

98 ❑ Nov 1964 Cover: 0.12 **NM** value: **18.00**
Circ: Statement: **316,657**

99 ❑ Jan 1965 Cover: 0.12 **NM** value: **18.00**
Circ: Statement: **298,144**
📖 Secret of Hondorica • Reprints story from Donald Duck #46

100 ❑ Mar 1965 Cover: 0.12 **NM** value: **18.00**
Circ: Statement: **298,144**

101 ❑ May 1965 Cover: 0.12 **NM** value: **16.00**
Circ: Statement: **298,144**
📖 The Incredible Golden Iceberg

102 ❑ Jul 1965 Cover: 0.12 **NM** value: **16.00**
Circ: Statement: **298,144**

103 ❑ Sep 1965 Cover: 0.12 **NM** value: **16.00**
Circ: Statement: **298,144**

104 ❑ Nov 1965 Cover: 0.12 **NM** value: **16.00**
Circ: Statement: **298,144**

105 ❑ Jan 1966 Cover: 0.12 **NM** value: **16.00**
Circ: Statement: **265,932**

106 ❑ Mar 1966 Cover: 0.12 **NM** value: **16.00**
Circ: Statement: **265,932**

107 ❑ May 1966 Cover: 0.12 **NM** value: **16.00**
Circ: Statement: **265,932**

108 ❑ Jul 1966 Cover: 0.12 **NM** value: **16.00**
Circ: Statement: **265,932**

109 ❑ Sep 1966 Cover: 0.12 **NM** value: **16.00**
Circ: Statement: **265,932**

110 ❑ Nov 1966 Cover: 0.12 **NM** value: **16.00**
Circ: Statement: **265,932**

111 ❑ Jan 1967 Cover: 0.12 **NM** value: **16.00**
Circ: Statement: **255,470**

112 ❑ Mar 1967 Cover: 0.12 **NM** value: **16.00**
Circ: Statement: **255,470**

113 ❑ May 1967 Cover: 0.12 **NM** value: **16.00**
Circ: Statement: **255,470**

114 ❑ Jul 1967 Cover: 0.12 **NM** value: **16.00**
Circ: Statement: **255,470**

115 ❑ Sep 1967 Cover: 0.12 **NM** value: **16.00**
Circ: Statement: **255,470**

116 ❑ Nov 1967 Cover: 0.12 **NM** value: **16.00**
Circ: Statement: **255,470**

117 ❑ Jan 1968 Cover: 0.12 **NM** value: **16.00**
Circ: Statement: **262,249**
📖 Pawns of the Loup Garou

118 ❑ Mar 1968 Cover: 0.12 **NM** value: **16.00**
Circ: Statement: **262,249**
• Has 1967 Statement, filed 9/28/67; avg print run 456,965; avg sales 253,585; avg subs 1,885; avg total paid 255,470; samples 561; max existent 256,031; 44% of run returned

119 ❑ May 1968 Cover: 0.12 **NM** value: **16.00**
Circ: Statement: **262,249**

120 ❑ Jul 1968 Cover: 0.12 **NM** value: **16.00**
Circ: Statement: **262,249**

121 ❑ Sep 1968 Cover: 0.15 **NM** value: **12.00**
Circ: Statement: **262,249**

122 ❑ Nov 1968 Cover: 0.15 **NM** value: **12.00**
Circ: Statement: **262,249**

123 ❑ Jan 1969 Cover: 0.15 **NM** value: **12.00**

124 ❑ Mar 1969 Cover: 0.15 **NM** value: **12.00**
• Has 1968 Statement, filed 9/27/68; avg print run 407,881; avg sales 260,166; avg subs 2,083; avg total paid 262,249; samples 498; max existent 262,747; 36% of run returned

125 ❑ May 1969 Cover: 0.15 **NM** value: **12.00**

126 ❑ Jul 1969 Cover: 0.15 **NM** value: **12.00**
📖 Officer of the Day

127 ❑ Sep 1969 Cover: 0.15 **NM** value: **12.00**

128 ❑ Nov 1969 Cover: 0.15 **NM** value: **12.00**
📖 Captives of the Sky Wizard

129 ❑ Jan 1970 Cover: 0.15 **NM** value: **12.00**

130 ❑ Mar 1970 Cover: 0.15 **NM** value: **12.00**

131 ❑ May 1970 Cover: 0.15 **NM** value: **12.00**
• **CGC:** 1 graded, best 7.0

132 ❑ Jul 1970 Cover: 0.15 **NM** value: **12.00**
• **CGC:** 1 graded, best 8.5

133 ❑ Sep 1970 Cover: 0.15 **NM** value: **12.00**
• **CGC:** 1 graded, best 7.0

134 ❑ Nov 1970 Cover: 0.15 **NM** value: **12.00**
• **CGC:** 1 graded, best 7.5
📖 Donald Duck and the Lost Peg Leg Mine; Donald Duck (Untitled) • Reprints stories from Donald Duck #52 and Walt Disney's Comics #194

135 ❑ Jan 1971 Cover: 0.15 **NM** value: **12.00**
Circ: Statement: **229,933** • **CGC:** 1 graded, best 6.0
📖 Knight in Shining Armor; The Firefly Tracker; Uncle Scrooge and His Handy Andy • Reprints stories from Uncle Scrooge #27 and Walt Disney's Comics #198

136 ❑ Mar 1971 Cover: 0.15 **NM** value: **10.00**
Circ: Statement: **229,933** • **CGC:** 1 graded, best 8.5

137 ❑ May 1971 Cover: 0.15 **NM** value: **10.00**
Circ: Statement: **229,933** • **CGC:** 1 graded, best 6.5

138 ❑ Jul 1971 Cover: 0.15 **NM** value: **10.00**
Circ: Statement: **229,933** • **CGC:** 1 graded, best 5.0
📖 A Day in a Duck's Life

139 ❑ Sep 1971 Cover: 0.15 **NM** value: **10.00**
Circ: Statement: **229,933** • **CGC:** 1 graded, best 7.0

140 ❑ Nov 1971 Cover: 0.15 **NM** value: **10.00**
Circ: Statement: **229,933** • **CGC:** 1 graded, best 7.0

141 ❑ Jan 1972 Cover: 0.15 **NM** value: **10.00**
• **CGC:** 1 graded, best 7.0

142 ❑ Mar 1972 Cover: 0.15 **NM** value: **10.00**
• **CGC:** 1 graded, best 8.5
• Has 1971 Statement; avg total paid circ 229,933

143 ❑ May 1972 Cover: 0.15 **NM** value: **10.00**
• **CGC:** 1 graded, best 7.0

144 ❑ Jul 1972 Cover: 0.15 **NM** value: **10.00**
• **CGC:** 1 graded, best 7.0

145 ❑ Sep 1972 Cover: 0.15 **NM** value: **10.00**
• **CGC:** 1 graded, best 8.0

146 ❑ Nov 1972 Cover: 0.15 **NM** value: **10.00**
• **CGC:** 1 graded, best 8.0

147 ❑ Jan 1973 Cover: 0.15 **NM** value: **10.00**
• **CGC:** 1 graded, best 7.5

148 ❑ Mar 1973 Cover: 0.15 **NM** value: **10.00**
• **CGC:** 1 graded, best 6.5

149 ❑ May 1973 Cover: 0.20 **NM** value: **10.00**
• **CGC:** 1 graded, best 8.0

150 ❑ Jul 1973 Cover: 0.20 **NM** value: **10.00**
• **CGC:** 1 graded, best 7.0

151 ❑ Sep 1973 Cover: 0.20 **NM** value: **9.00**
• **CGC:** 1 graded, best 7.5

152 ❑ Oct 1973 Cover: 0.20 **NM** value: **9.00**

153 ❑ Nov 1973 Cover: 0.20 **NM** value: **9.00**
• **CGC:** 1 graded, best 8.5

154 ❑ Jan 1974 Cover: 0.20 **NM** value: **9.00**
• **CGC:** 1 graded, best 9.0
📖 Secret of Hondorica • Reprints story from Donald Duck #46

155 ❑ Mar 1974 Cover: 0.20 **NM** value: **9.00**

156 ❑ May 1974 Cover: 0.20 **NM** value: **9.00**

157 ❑ Jul 1974 Cover: 0.25 **NM** value: **9.00**
• Reprints story from Donald Duck #45

158 ❑ Sep 1974 Cover: 0.25 **NM** value: **9.00**

159 ❑ Oct 1974 Cover: 0.25 **NM** value: **9.00**
• Reprints story from Walt Disney's Comics #192

160 ❑ Nov 1974 Cover: 0.25 **NM** value: **9.00**
📖 Hobblin' Goblins • Reprints story from Donald Duck #26

161 ❑ Jan 1975 Cover: 0.25 **NM** value: **8.00**

162 ❑ Mar 1975 Cover: 0.25 **NM** value: **8.00**

163 ❑ May 1975 Cover: 0.25 **NM** value: **8.00**

164 ❑ Jul 1975 Cover: 0.25 **NM** value: **8.00**

165 ❑ Sep 1975 Cover: 0.25 **NM** value: **8.00**

166 ❑ Oct 1975 Cover: 0.25 **NM** value: **8.00**

167 ❑ Nov 1975 Cover: 0.25 **NM** value: **8.00**

168 ❑ Jan 1976 Cover: 0.25 **NM** value: **8.00**

169 ❑ Mar 1976 Cover: 0.25 **NM** value: **8.00**

170 ❑ Apr 1976 Cover: 0.25 **NM** value: **8.00**

171 ❑ May 1976 Cover: 0.25 **NM** value: **6.00**

172 ❑ Jun 1976 Cover: 0.25 **NM** value: **6.00**

173 ❑ Jul 1976 Cover: 0.25 **NM** value: **6.00**

174 ❑ Aug 1976 Cover: 0.25 **NM** value: **6.00**
• **CGC:** 1 graded, best 9.6

175 ❑ Sep 1976 Cover: 0.30 **NM** value: **6.00**

176 ❑ Oct 1976 Cover: 0.30 **NM** value: **6.00**

177 ❑ Nov 1976 Cover: 0.30 **NM** value: **6.00**

178 ❑ Dec 1976 Cover: 0.30 **NM** value: **6.00**

179 ❑ Jan 1977 Cover: 0.30 **NM** value: **6.00**

180 ❑ Feb 1977 Cover: 0.30 **NM** value: **6.00**

181 ❑ Mar 1977 Cover: 0.30 **NM** value: **6.00**

182 ❑ Apr 1977 Cover: 0.30 **NM** value: **6.00**

183 ❑ May 1977 Cover: 0.30 **NM** value: **6.00**
📖 A Day in a Duck's Life • Reprints story from Donald Duck #138

184 ❑ Jun 1977 Cover: 0.30 **NM** value: **6.00**

185 ❑ Jul 1977 Cover: 0.30 **NM** value: **6.00**

186 ❑ Aug 1977 Cover: 0.30 **NM** value: **6.00**

187 ❑ Sep 1977 Cover: 0.30 **NM** value: **6.00**

188 ❑ Oct 1977 Cover: 0.30 **NM** value: **6.00**
📖 The Master Glasser • Reprints story from Donald Duck #68

189 ❑ Nov 1977 Cover: 0.30 **NM** value: **6.00**

190 ❑ Dec 1977 Cover: 0.35 **NM** value: **6.00**

191 ❑ Jan 1978 Cover: 0.35 **NM** value: **4.00**

192 ❑ Feb 1978 Cover: 0.35 **NM** value: **4.00**
📖 Donald Duck and the Titanic Ants!; Riding the Pony Express; Donald Duck (Untitled) • Reprints stories from Donald Duck #60 and Walt Disney's Comics #226 and 234

193 ❑ Mar 1978 Cover: 0.35 **NM** value: **4.00**

194 ❑ Apr 1978 Cover: 0.35 **NM** value: **4.00**

195 ❑ May 1978 Cover: 0.35 **NM** value: **4.00**

196 ❑ Jun 1978 Cover: 0.35 **NM** value: **4.00**

197 ❑ Jul 1978 Cover: 0.35 **NM** value: **4.00**

198 ❑ Aug 1978 Cover: 0.35 **NM** value: **4.00**

199 ❑ Sep 1978 Cover: 0.35 **NM** value: **4.00**

200 ❑ Oct 1978 Cover: 0.35 **NM** value: **4.00**

201 ❑ Nov 1978 Cover: 0.35 **NM** value: **4.00**
📖 The Christmas Cha Cha • Reprints story from Christmas Parade (Dell) #26

202 ❑ Dec 1978 Cover: 0.35 **NM** value: **4.00**

203 ❑ Jan 1979 Cover: 0.35 **NM** value: **4.00**

204 ❑ Feb 1979 Cover: 0.35 **NM** value: **4.00**

205 ❑ Mar 1979 Cover: 0.35 **NM** value: **4.00**

206 ❑ Apr 1979 Cover: 0.40 **NM** value: **4.00**

207 ❑ May 1979 Cover: 0.40 **NM** value: **4.00**

208 ❑ Jun 1979 Cover: 0.40 **NM** value: **4.00**

209 ❑ Jul 1979 Cover: 0.40 **NM** value: **4.00**

210 ❑ Aug 1979 Cover: 0.40 **NM** value: **4.00**

211 ❑ Sep 1979 Cover: 0.40 **NM** value: **3.00**

212 ❑ Oct 1979 Cover: 0.40 **NM** value: **3.00**

213 ❑ Nov 1979 Cover: 0.40 **NM** value: **3.00**

CGC-graded: Multiply prices above by **33 for 9.9 M • 16 for 9.8 NM/M • 7 for 9.6 NM+ • 5 for 9.4 NM • 2.5 for 9.2 NM- • 1.5 for 9.0 VF/NM**

214 ❑ Dec 1979 Cover: 0.40 **NM** value: **3.00**
215 ❑ Jan 1980 Cover: 0.40 **NM** value: **3.00**
216 ❑ Feb 1980 Cover: 0.40 **NM** value: **3.00**
217 ❑ Mar 1980 Cover: 0.40 **NM** value: **3.00**
• Whitman begins as publisher
218 ❑ Apr 1980 Cover: 0.40 **NM** value: **3.00**
219 ❑ May 1980 Cover: 0.40 **NM** value: **3.00**
220 ❑ Jun 1980 Cover: 0.40 **NM** value: **3.00**
• **CGC:** 1 graded, best 9.0
221 ❑ Aug 1980 Cover: 0.40 **NM** value: **3.00**
• **CGC:** 1 graded, best 9.4
222 ❑ Oct 1980 Cover: 0.40 **NM** value: **3.00**
• **CGC:** 2 graded, best 9.4
223 ❑ Dec 1980 Cover: 0.40 **NM** value: **3.00**
• **CGC:** 1 graded, best 9.4
224 ❑ Jan 1981 Cover: 0.40 **NM** value: **3.00**
• **CGC:** 1 graded, best 9.2
225 ❑ Feb 1981 Cover: 0.50 **NM** value: **3.00**
226 ❑ Mar 1981 Cover: 0.50 **NM** value: **3.00**
227 ❑ Apr 1981 Cover: 0.50 **NM** value: **3.00**
228 ❑ May 1981 Cover: 0.50 **NM** value: **3.00**
229 ❑ Jun 1981 Cover: 0.50 **NM** value: **3.00**
230 ❑ Jul 1981 Cover: 0.50 **NM** value: **3.00**
231 ❑ Aug 1981 Cover: 0.50 **NM** value: **3.00**
232 ❑ Sep 1981 Cover: 0.50 **NM** value: **3.00**
233 ❑ Oct 1981 Cover: 0.50 **NM** value: **3.00**
234 ❑ Nov 1981 Cover: 0.50 **NM** value: **3.00**
235 ❑ Dec 1981 Cover: 0.50 **NM** value: **3.00**
236 ❑ Jan 1982 Cover: 0.50 **NM** value: **3.00**
237 ❑ Feb 1982 Cover: 0.60 **NM** value: **3.00**
238 ❑ Mar 1982 Cover: 0.60 **NM** value: **3.00**
239 ❑ Apr 1983 Cover: 0.60 **NM** value: **3.00**
240 ❑ May 1982 Cover: 0.60 **NM** value: **3.00**
241 ❑ Apr 1982 Cover: 0.60 **NM** value: **3.00**
242 ❑ May 1983 Cover: 0.60 **NM** value: **3.00**
243 ❑ Mar 1984 Cover: 0.60 **NM** value: **3.00**
244 ❑ Apr 1984 Cover: 0.60 **NM** value: **3.00**
245 ❑ Jul 1984 Cover: 0.60 **NM** value: **3.00**
• Last issue of original run

DONALD DUCK (WALT DISNEY'S...) Gladstone

246 ❑ Oct 1986 Cover: 0.75 **NM** value: **8.00**
Circ: CapCity orders: **4,250** • **CGC:** 1 graded, best 9.2
• Series begins again (1986);Gladstone publishes **A:** Carl Barks
247 ❑ Nov 1986 Cover: 0.75 **NM** value: **5.00**
Circ: CapCity orders: **3,950**
A: Carl Barks
248 ❑ Dec 1986 Cover: 0.75 **NM** value: **5.00**
Circ: CapCity orders: **4,100**
A: Carl Barks
249 ❑ Jan 1987 Cover: 0.75 **NM** value: **5.00**
Circ: CapCity orders: **5,900**
A: Carl Barks
250 ❑ Feb 1987 Cover: 0.75 **NM** value: **8.00**
Circ: CapCity orders: **6,975**
• reprints 1st Barks comic **A:** Carl Barks
251 ❑ Mar 1987 Cover: 0.75 **NM** value: **4.00**
Circ: CapCity orders: **6,050**
A: Carl Barks
252 ❑ Apr 1987 Cover: 0.75 **NM** value: **4.00**
Circ: CapCity orders: **5,750**
A: Carl Barks
253 ❑ May 1987 Cover: 0.75 **NM** value: **4.00**
Circ: CapCity orders: **4,625**
A: Carl Barks
254 ❑ Jun 1987 Cover: 0.75 **NM** value: **4.00**
Circ: CapCity orders: **4,925**
255 ❑ Jul 1987 Cover: 0.95 **NM** value: **4.00**
Circ: CapCity orders: **4,575**
256 ❑ Aug 1987 Cover: 0.95 **NM** value: **4.00**
Circ: CapCity orders: **5,025**
257 ❑ Sep 1987 Cover: 0.95 **NM** value: **4.00**
Circ: CapCity orders: **5,275**
• forest fire **A:** Carl Barks
258 ❑ Oct 1987 Cover: 0.95 **NM** value: **4.00**
Circ: CapCity orders: **5,050**
A: Carl Barks
259 ❑ Nov 1987 Cover: 0.95 **NM** value: **4.00**
Circ: CapCity orders: **5,150**
A: Carl Barks
260 ❑ Dec 1987 Cover: 0.95 **NM** value: **4.00**
Circ: CapCity orders: **5,025**
A: Carl Barks
261 ❑ Jan 1988 Cover: 0.95 **NM** value: **3.00**
Circ: CapCity orders: **5,325**
A: Carl Barks
262 ❑ Mar 1988 Cover: 0.95 **NM** value: **3.00**
Circ: CapCity orders: **5,350**
A: Carl Barks
263 ❑ Jun 1988 Cover: 0.95 **NM** value: **3.00**
Circ: CapCity orders: **5,200**
A: Carl Barks
264 ❑ Jul 1988 Cover: 0.95 **NM** value: **3.00**
Circ: CapCity orders: **5,600**
A: Carl Barks
265 ❑ Aug 1988 Cover: 0.95 **NM** value: **3.00**
Circ: CapCity orders: **5,550**
266 ❑ Sep 1988 Cover: 0.95 **NM** value: **3.00**
Circ: CapCity orders: **5,550**
267 ❑ Oct 1988 Cover: 0.95 **NM** value: **3.00**
Circ: CapCity orders: **5,750**
268 ❑ Nov 1988 Cover: 0.95 **NM** value: **3.00**
Circ: CapCity orders: **5,700**
269 ❑ Jan 1989 Cover: 0.95 **NM** value: **3.00**
Circ: CapCity orders: **5,600**
270 ❑ Mar 1989 Cover: 0.95 **NM** value: **3.00**
Circ: CapCity orders: **5,800**
271 ❑ Apr 1989 Cover: 0.95 **NM** value: **2.50**
Circ: CapCity orders: **6,100**
says Jun on cover, Apr in indicia.
272 ❑ Jul 1989 Cover: 0.95 **NM** value: **2.50**
Circ: CapCity orders: **6,550**
273 ❑ Aug 1989 Cover: 0.95 **NM** value: **2.50**
Circ: CapCity orders: **6,350**
274 ❑ Sep 1989 Cover: 0.95 **NM** value: **2.50**
Circ: CapCity orders: **6,300**
275 ❑ Oct 1989 Cover: 0.95 **NM** value: **2.50**
Circ: CapCity orders: **6,700**
• Donocchio **A:** Carl Barks; Walt Kelly
276 ❑ Nov 1989 Cover: 0.95 **NM** value: **2.50**
Circ: CapCity orders: **6,500**
A: Carl Barks
277 ❑ Jan 1990 Cover: 0.95 **NM** value: **2.50**
Circ: CapCity orders: **6,550**
A: Carl Barks
278 ❑ Mar 1990 Cover: 0.95 **NM** value: **2.50**
Circ: CapCity orders: **6,450**
A: Carl Barks; Don Rosa
279 ❑ May 1990 Cover: 0.95 **NM** value: **2.50**
Circ: CapCity orders: **6,650**
• Series ends again (1990) **A:** Carl Barks
280 ❑ Sep 1993 Cover: 1.50 **NM** value: **Cover or less**
Circ: CapCity orders: **5,225**
• Series begins again (1993)
281 ❑ Nov 1993 Cover: 1.50 **NM** value: **Cover or less**
Circ: CapCity orders: **5,100**
282 ❑ Jan 1994 Cover: 1.50 **NM** value: **Cover or less**
Circ: CapCity orders: **5,000**
A: Carl Barks
283 ❑ Mar 1994 Cover: 1.50 **NM** value: **Cover or less**
Circ: CapCity orders: **4,875**
A: Don Rosa
284 ❑ May 1994 Cover: 1.50 **NM** value: **Cover or less**
Circ: CapCity orders: **4,275**
A: Carl Barks; Al Taliaferro
285 ❑ Jul 1994 Cover: 1.50 **NM** value: **Cover or less**
A: Carl Barks; Al Taliaferro
286 ❑ Sep 1994 Cover: 2.95 **NM** value: **3.00**
Circ: CapCity orders: **5,100**
• Giant-size. • Donald Duck's 60th
287 ❑ Nov 1994 Cover: 1.50 **NM** value: **Cover or less**
Circ: CapCity orders: **4,225**
288 ❑ Jan 1995 Cover: 1.50 **NM** value: **Cover or less**
Circ: CapCity orders: **4,100**
289 ❑ Mar 1995 Cover: 1.50 **NM** value: **Cover or less**
Circ: CapCity orders: **4,000**
290 ❑ May 1995 Cover: 1.50 **NM** value: **Cover or less**
Circ: CapCity orders: **3,775**
291 ❑ Jul 1995 Cover: 1.50 **NM** value: **Cover or less**
Circ: CapCity orders: **3,750**
292 ❑ Sep 1995 Cover: 1.95 **NM** value: **Cover or less**
Circ: CapCity orders: **3,725**
293 ❑ Nov 1995 Cover: 1.95 **NM** value: **Cover or less**
Circ: CapCity orders: **3,575**
294 ❑ Jan 1996 Cover: 1.95 **NM** value: **Cover or less**
📖 The Persistent Postman **A:** Carl Barks
295 ❑ Mar 1996 Cover: 1.50 **NM** value: **Cover or less**
newsprint covers begin.
296 ❑ May 1996 Cover: 1.50 **NM** value: **Cover or less**
297 ❑ Jul 1996 Cover: 1.50 **NM** value: **Cover or less**
298 ❑ Sep 1996 Cover: 1.50 **NM** value: **Cover or less**
299 ❑ Nov 1996 Cover: 1.50 **NM** value: **Cover or less**
300 ❑ Jan 1997 Cover: 2.25 **NM** value: **Cover or less**
Circ: Diamd. preorders: **9,465**
301 ❑ Mar 1997 Cover: 1.95 **NM** value: **Cover or less**
Circ: Diamd. preorders: **7,205**
newsprint covers end.
302 ❑ May 1997 Cover: 1.95 **NM** value: **Cover or less**
Circ: Diamd. preorders: **6,669**
📖 The Gold Finder **A:** Carl Barks **C:** Carl Barks
303 ❑ Jul 1997 Cover: 1.95 **NM** value: **Cover or less**
Circ: Diamd. preorders: **6,420**
304 ❑ Sep 1997 Cover: 1.95 **NM** value: **Cover or less**
Circ: Diamd. preorders: **6,790**
📖 Bubbleweight Champ **A:** Carl Barks
305 ❑ Nov 1997 Cover: 1.95 **NM** value: **Cover or less**
Circ: Diamd. preorders: **6,498**
📖 Mocking Bird Ridge; The Autograph; Beach Bombardment; Ping-Pong **A:** Carl Barks **W:** Carl Barks
306 ❑ Jan 1998 Cover: 1.95 **NM** value: **Cover or less**
Circ: Diamd. preorders: **6,460**
307 ❑ Mar 1998 Cover: 1.95 **NM** value: **Cover or less**
Circ: Diamd. preorders: **5,274**
final issue.

DONATELLO TEENAGE MUTANT NINJA TURTLE Mirage

1 ❑ Aug 1986, b&w Cover: 1.50 **NM** value: **2.00**
• **CGC:** 1 graded, best 8.5

DON FORTUNE MAGAZINE Don Fortune Publications

1 ❑ Aug 1946 Cover: 0.10 **NM** value: **120.00**
• **CGC:** 2 graded, best 8.0
2 ❑ Sep 1946 Cover: 0.10 **NM** value: **100.00**
3 ❑ Oct 1946 Cover: 0.10 **NM** value: **80.00**
4 ❑ Nov 1946 Cover: 0.10 **NM** value: **80.00**
5 ❑ Dec 1946 Cover: 0.10 **NM** value: **80.00**
6 ❑ Jan 1947 Cover: 0.10 **NM** value: **80.00**

DONIELLE: ENSLAVED AT SEA Raging Rhino

All issues are adults only.
1 ❑ b&w Cover: 2.95 **NM** value: **Cover or less**
2 ❑ b&w Cover: 2.95 **NM** value: **Cover or less**
3 ❑ b&w Cover: 2.95 **NM** value: **Cover or less**
4 ❑ b&w Cover: 2.95 **NM** value: **Cover or less**

DON MARTIN MAGAZINE Welsh

1 ❑ Cover: 2.50 **NM** value: **Cover or less**
Circ: CapCity orders: **4,400**
• poster
2 ❑ Cover: 2.50 **NM** value: **Cover or less**
Circ: CapCity orders: **3,800**
• poster
3 ❑ Cover: 2.50 **NM** value: **Cover or less**
Circ: CapCity orders: **3,397**

DONNA MATRIX Reactor

In the brave new world of 21st century Chicago, pleasure can be programmed. One unlucky guy stopped at Gorgeous Gadgets and bought himself a XTC-69 model for his "personal enjoyment." However, this guy had some rather special needs for his new purchase — needs like physical abuse and domination, long since outlawed by the Deviate Robot Sex Act. Undaunted, he traded with some shadowy characters for the special code (used in Cyber-SEAL military units) that would let his creation give him the domination he desired. He reprogrammed the XTC-69 and dubbed it Donna Matrix. Little did he guess that his reprogramming would work so well, transforming this "pleasure droid" into an engine of mass destruction — with him as the first victim!

Donna Matrix was created by Mike Saenz, better-known for his early computer-comic work on titles such as Shatter. This comic book was rendered entirely by computer in 3-D.

1 ❑ Aug 1993 Cover: 2.95 **NM** value: **3.50**
Circ: CapCity orders: **18,160**
• computer-generated ★ Origin of Donna Matrix. ★ 1st Appearance of Donna Matrix.

DONNA MIA Avatar

1 ❑ Dec 1996 Cover: 3.00 **NM** value: **Cover or less**
Circ: Direct Market orders: **5,116**
2 ❑ Jan 1997 Cover: 3.00 **NM** value: **Cover or less**
Circ: Diamd. preorders: **4,349**
3 ❑ Feb 1997 Cover: 3.00 **NM** value: **Cover or less**
Circ: Diamd. preorders: **4,236**

DONNA'S DAY Slab-O-Concrete

1 ❑ **NM** value: **1.00**
• Postcard comic book **A:** Peter Bagge; Donna Mathes **W:** Peter Bagge; Donna Mathes

DON NEWCOMBE Fawcett

1 ❑ ca. 1950 Cover: 0.10 **NM** value: **200.00**
• **CGC:** 1 graded, best 5.0

DON WINSLOW OF THE NAVY (1ST SERIES) Merwil

1 ❑ ca. 1937 Cover: 0.10 **NM** value: **2500.00**

DON WINSLOW OF THE NAVY (2ND SERIES) Fawcett

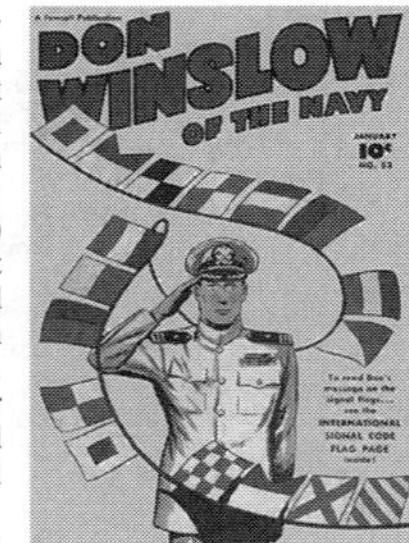

The character Don Winslow began as a newspaper-strip feature in 1934, created by Frank V. Martinek and drawn by Leon Beroth and Carl Hammond. There were two Don Winslow serials from Universal: Don Winslow of the Navy (1942) and Don Winslow of the Coast Guard (1943), with Winslow played by Don Terry. The radio serial ran from 1937 to 1939 and 1942-1943. Stories involved Lt. Commander Winslow and his sidekick, Lt. Red Pennington, working with Naval Intelligence.

The newspaper strip came to an end in 1955; reprints ran in Crackajack and Popular. But the material in the Fawcett version was new, created for the comic-book format. — Maggie

1 ❑ Feb 1943 Cover: 0.10 **NM** value: **650.00**
2 ❑ Mar 1943 Cover: 0.10 **NM** value: **325.00**
3 ❑ Apr 1943 Cover: 0.10 **NM** value: **200.00**
4 ❑ Jun 1943 Cover: 0.10 **NM** value: **165.00**
5 ❑ Jul 1943 Cover: 0.10 **NM** value: **165.00**
• **CGC:** 1 graded, best 9.6
6 ❑ Aug 1943 Cover: 0.10 **NM** value: **165.00**
• **CGC:** 1 graded, best 5.5
7 ❑ Sep 1943 Cover: 0.10 **NM** value: **125.00**
8 ❑ Oct 1943 Cover: 0.10 **NM** value: **125.00**
• **CGC:** 1 graded, best 9.6
9 ❑ Nov 1943 Cover: 0.10 **NM** value: **125.00**
10 ❑ Dec 1943 Cover: 0.10 **NM** value: **125.00**
11 ❑ Jan 1944 Cover: 0.10 **NM** value: **90.00**
12 ❑ Feb 1944 Cover: 0.10 **NM** value: **90.00**
13 ❑ Mar 1944 Cover: 0.10 **NM** value: **90.00**
14 ❑ Apr 1944 Cover: 0.10 **NM** value: **90.00**
15 ❑ May 1944 Cover: 0.10 **NM** value: **90.00**
16 ❑ Jun 1944 Cover: 0.10 **NM** value: **90.00**

Other grades: Multiply prices above by **1.5 for Mint • 2/3 for Very Fine • 1/3 for Fine • 1/5 for Very Good • 1/8 for Good**

17 ❑ Jul 1944 Cover: 0.10 **NM** value: **90.00**
18 ❑ Aug 1944 Cover: 0.10 **NM** value: **90.00**
• **CGC:** 1 graded, best 5.0
19 ❑ Sep 1944 Cover: 0.10 **NM** value: **90.00**
20 ❑ Oct 1944 Cover: 0.10 **NM** value: **90.00**
21 ❑ Nov 1944 Cover: 0.10 **NM** value: **65.00**
22 ❑ Jan 1945 Cover: 0.10 **NM** value: **65.00**
• **CGC:** 1 graded, best 9.6
23 ❑ Feb 1945 Cover: 0.10 **NM** value: **65.00**
• **CGC:** 1 graded, best 9.4
24 ❑ Mar 1945 Cover: 0.10 **NM** value: **65.00**
• **CGC:** 1 graded, best 9.2
25 ❑ Apr 1945 Cover: 0.10 **NM** value: **65.00**
26 ❑ May 1945 Cover: 0.10 **NM** value: **65.00**
27 ❑ Jul 1945 Cover: 0.10 **NM** value: **65.00**
28 ❑ Aug 1945 Cover: 0.10 **NM** value: **65.00**
29 ❑ Oct 1945 Cover: 0.10 **NM** value: **65.00**
30 ❑ Dec 1945 Cover: 0.10 **NM** value: **65.00**
• **CGC:** 1 graded, best 5.5
31 ❑ Feb 1946 Cover: 0.10 **NM** value: **55.00**
32 ❑ Mar 1946 Cover: 0.10 **NM** value: **55.00**
• **CGC:** 1 graded, best 9.4
33 ❑ Apr 1946 Cover: 0.10 **NM** value: **55.00**
34 ❑ May 1946 Cover: 0.10 **NM** value: **55.00**
35 ❑ Jun 1946 Cover: 0.10 **NM** value: **55.00**
• **CGC:** 1 graded, best 8.0
36 ❑ Jul 1946 Cover: 0.10 **NM** value: **55.00**
37 ❑ Aug 1946 Cover: 0.10 **NM** value: **55.00**
• **CGC:** 1 graded, best 9.2
38 ❑ Sep 1946 Cover: 0.10 **NM** value: **55.00**
39 ❑ Oct 1946 Cover: 0.10 **NM** value: **55.00**
40 ❑ Nov 1946 Cover: 0.10 **NM** value: **55.00**
41 ❑ Dec 1946 Cover: 0.10 **NM** value: **42.00**
42 ❑ Feb 1947 Cover: 0.10 **NM** value: **42.00**
43 ❑ Mar 1947 Cover: 0.10 **NM** value: **42.00**
44 ❑ Apr 1947 Cover: 0.10 **NM** value: **42.00**
45 ❑ May 1947 Cover: 0.10 **NM** value: **42.00**
46 ❑ Jun 1947 Cover: 0.10 **NM** value: **42.00**
47 ❑ Jul 1947 Cover: 0.10 **NM** value: **42.00**
48 ❑ Aug 1947 Cover: 0.10 **NM** value: **42.00**
Signal flags on cover read "Salute to the U.S. Navy". 📖 On Target; International Signal Code Flags; His Reign Is Over; The Snapshot that Didn't Snap; Ring of Death (text); Eaglebeak Spruder; Don Winslow of the Navy and the Doomed Atoll **W:** Richard G. Kraus ★ Appearance of Eaglebeak Spruder, Singapore Sal, Don Winslow, Jetsam Joe.
49 ❑ Sep 1947 Cover: 0.10 **NM** value: **42.00**
50 ❑ Oct 1947 Cover: 0.10 **NM** value: **42.00**
51 ❑ Nov 1947 Cover: 0.10 **NM** value: **42.00**
• **CGC:** 1 graded, best 6.5
52 ❑ Dec 1947 Cover: 0.10 **NM** value: **42.00**
53 ❑ Jan 1948 Cover: 0.10 **NM** value: **42.00**
54 ❑ Feb 1948 Cover: 0.10 **NM** value: **42.00**
• **CGC:** 1 graded, best 7.0
55 ❑ Mar 1948 Cover: 0.10 **NM** value: **42.00**
• **CGC:** 1 graded, best 2.5
56 ❑ Apr 1948 Cover: 0.10 **NM** value: **42.00**
57 ❑ May 1948 Cover: 0.10 **NM** value: **42.00**
• **CGC:** 1 graded, best 9.6
58 ❑ Jun 1948 Cover: 0.10 **NM** value: **42.00**
59 ❑ Jul 1948 Cover: 0.10 **NM** value: **42.00**
• **CGC:** 1 graded, best 9.2
60 ❑ Aug 1948 Cover: 0.10 **NM** value: **42.00**
61 ❑ Sep 1948 Cover: 0.10 **NM** value: **35.00**
62 ❑ Oct 1948 Cover: 0.10 **NM** value: **35.00**
63 ❑ Nov 1948 Cover: 0.10 **NM** value: **35.00**
64 ❑ Dec 1948 Cover: 0.10 **NM** value: **35.00**
65 ❑ Jan 1951 Cover: 0.10 **NM** value: **35.00**
66 ❑ Mar 1951 Cover: 0.10 **NM** value: **35.00**
67 ❑ May 1951 Cover: 0.10 **NM** value: **35.00**
68 ❑ Jul 1951 Cover: 0.10 **NM** value: **35.00**
Painted cover. 📖 Tugboat Tucker…Backward Fellow; The Atta
69 ❑ Sep 1951 Cover: 0.10 **NM** value: **35.00**
70 ❑ Mar 1955 Cover: 0.10 **NM** value: **35.00**
71 ❑ May 1955 Cover: 0.10 **NM** value: **35.00**
72 ❑ Jul 1955 Cover: 0.10 **NM** value: **35.00**
73 ❑ Sep 1955 Cover: 0.10 **NM** value: **35.00**

DON WINSLOW TROUBLE SHOOTER — AC

1 ❑ b&w Cover: 2.75 **NM** value: **Cover or less**

DOOFER — Fantagraphics

1 ❑ b&w Cover: 2.75 **NM** value: **Cover or less**

DOOFUS — Fantagraphics

1 ❑ Dec 1994, b&w Cover: 2.75 **NM** value: **Cover or less**
📖 What Color is Your Parachute?; Team America; Flower Town USA; Baby's Shitty Diaper **A:** Rick Altergott **W:** Rick Altergott
2 ❑ Spr 1997, b&w Cover: 2.75 **NM** value: **Cover or less**

DOOM — Marvel

1 ❑ Oct 2000 Cover: 2.99 **NM** value: **Cover or less**
Circ: Diamd. preorders: **39,317**
A: Leonardo Manco **W:** Chuck Dixon
2 ❑ Nov 2000 Cover: 2.99 **NM** value: **Cover or less**
Circ: Diamd. preorders: **32,703**
📖 Slaves **A:** Leonardo Manco **W:** Chuck Dixon
3 ❑ Dec 2000 Cover: 2.99 **NM** value: **Cover or less**
Circ: Diamd. preorders: **32,515**
📖 Fight Back to Baxter **A:** Leonardo Manco **W:** Chuck Dixon

DOOM FORCE SPECIAL — DC

1 ❑ Jul 1992 Cover: 2.95 **NM** value: **Cover or less**
Circ: CapCity orders: **13,750**
📖 Judgment Day • X-Force parody **A:** Steve Pugh; Paris Cullins; Mark McKenna; Richard Case; Ken Steacy; Walt Simonson; Duke Mighten; Brad Vancata; Ian Montgomery; Ray Kryssing **W:** Grant Morrison ★ 1st Appearance of Doom Force.

DOOM PATROL, THE (1ST SERIES) — DC

Appearing for the first time in My Greatest Adventure #80, the Doom Patrol proved a hit and that title was renamed The Doom Patrol beginning with issue #86. The Doom Patrol consists of Cliff Steele, a race car driver whose brain was saved in a robotic body after a crash and renamed Robotman; Rita Farr, the size-changing Elasti-Girl; Larry Trainor, the bandaged Negative Man; and their wheelchair-bound leader Niles Caulder, "The Chief."

This unlikely team fought some of the strangest foes of the DC universe, until their apparent death in 1968's Doom Patrol #120. 1973 saw two final, reprint issues of this series, then things fell silent. It was not until 1987 that The Doom Patrol would be resurrected in a new series. That series, which featured the writing of Grant Morrison, took an already offbeat team, and turned them into something undreamed of.

86 ❑ Mar 1964 Cover: 0.12 **NM** value: **75.00**
• **CGC:** 1 graded, best 9.8
📖 The Brotherhood of Evil; The Trail of the Terrible Titan; A Medal for 'Go-Buggy 3'! • Series continued from My Greatest Adventure #85 **A:** Bruno Premiani ★ 1st Appearance of Monsieur Mallah, The Brain, Madame Rouge.
87 ❑ May 1964 Cover: 0.12 **NM** value: **50.00**
• **CGC:** 1 graded, best 9.6
📖 The Terrible Secret of Negative Man; The Toys of Terror; Robotman Fights Alone **A:** Bruno Premiani
88 ❑ Jun 1964 Cover: 0.12 **NM** value: **40.00**
• **CGC:** 4 graded, best 9.4
📖 The Incredible Origin of the Chief; The Man Who Lived Twice; Showdown for the Chief! ★ Origin of The Chief.
89 ❑ Aug 1964 Cover: 0.12 **NM** value: **40.00**
• **CGC:** 3 graded, best 9.6
📖 The Animal-Vegetable-Mineral Menace; Lure of the Changing Nightmare; The Private War of Elasti-Girl
90 ❑ Sep 1964 Cover: 0.12 **NM** value: **40.00**
• **CGC:** 1 graded, best 9.6
📖 The Enemy Within the Doom Patrol; The Deadly Replacements; One of You Must Die!
91 ❑ Nov 1964 Cover: 0.12 **NM** value: **38.00**
• **CGC:** 2 graded, best 9.6
📖 Mento – The Man Who Split the Doom Patrol; Terror of the Android Master; Fortress in the Stratosphere ★ 1st Appearance of Mento.
92 ❑ Dec 1964 Cover: 0.12 **NM** value: **38.00**
• **CGC:** 3 graded, best 9.4
📖 The Sinister Secret of Dr. Tyme; The Terrifying Dr. Tyme; The Clocks of Death
93 ❑ Feb 1965 Cover: 0.12 **NM** value: **38.00**
Circ: Statement: **200,188** • **CGC:** 4 graded, best 9.6
📖 Showdown on Nightmare Road; Who Is Doctor Wilder?; The Beast of the Doom Patrol
94 ❑ Mar 1965 Cover: 0.12 **NM** value: **38.00**
Circ: Statement: **200,188** • **CGC:** 3 graded, best 9.4
📖 The Nightmare Fighters; The Chief 'Stands' Alone; Master of the Killer Birds • Has 1964 Statement, filed 10/1/64; no circ figures published
95 ❑ May 1965 Cover: 0.12 **NM** value: **38.00**
Circ: Statement: **200,188** • **CGC:** 4 graded, best 9.6
📖 Menace of the Turnabout Heroes; Return of the Animal-Vegetable-Mineral Man; Deadline for the Doom Patrol
96 ❑ Jun 1965 Cover: 0.12 **NM** value: **38.00**
Circ: Statement: **200,188** • **CGC:** 1 graded, best 9.6
📖 The Day the World Went Mad!; The Three Families of Fear; Whom the Gods Would Destroy
97 ❑ Aug 1965 Cover: 0.12 **NM** value: **38.00**
Circ: Statement: **200,188** • **CGC:** 4 graded, best 9.6
📖 The War Against the Mind Slaves; Three Trails to Terror; Prisoners of the Moon ★ 1st Appearance of Garguax.
98 ❑ Sep 1965 Cover: 0.12 **NM** value: **38.00**
Circ: Statement: **200,188** • **CGC:** 4 graded, best 9.4
📖 The Death of the Doom Patrol; It Takes a Chief to Kill a Chief; 60 Sinister Seconds
99 ❑ Nov 1965 Cover: 0.12 **NM** value: **45.00**
Circ: Statement: **200,188** • **CGC:** 3 graded, best 9.6
📖 The Deadly Sting of the Bug Man; In the Spider's Parlor; The Beast-Boy; That Kid's Not So Green! ★ 1st Appearance of Changeling.
100 ❑ Dec 1965 Cover: 0.12 **NM** value: **50.00**
Circ: Statement: **200,188** • **CGC:** 2 graded, best 9.4
📖 The Fantastic Origin of Beast-Boy; The Origin of Beast-Boy; Robotman – Wanted Dead or Alive **A:** Bruno Premiani ★ Origin of Changeling.
101 ❑ Feb 1966 Cover: 0.12 **NM** value: **25.00**
Circ: Statement: **191,420** • **CGC:** 1 graded, best 9.4
📖 I, Kranus, Robot Emperor; What Makes Kranus Run?; The Lonely Giant **A:** Bruno Premiani
102 ❑ Mar 1966 Cover: 0.12 **NM** value: **25.00**
Circ: Statement: **191,420** • **CGC:** 1 graded, best 9.4
📖 8 Against Eternity; The Zombies of Atlantis; The King Who Could Not Die **A:** Bruno Premiani ★ Appearance of Challengers of the Unknown.
103 ❑ May 1966 Cover: 0.12 **NM** value: **25.00**
Circ: Statement: **191,420** • **CGC:** 1 graded, best 4.0
📖 The Meteor Man; The Blazing Behemoth; No Home for a Robot **A:** Bruno Premiani
104 ❑ Jun 1966 Cover: 0.12 **NM** value: **25.00**
Circ: Statement: **191,420** • **CGC:** 1 graded, best 8.0
📖 The Bride of the Doom Patrol **A:** Bruno Premiani
105 ❑ Aug 1966 Cover: 0.12 **NM** value: **25.00**
Circ: Statement: **191,420**
📖 Honeymoon of Terror; The Robot-Maker Must Die • Has 1965 Statement, filed 10/1/65; avg print run 336,000; avg sales 199,000; avg subs 1,188; avg total paid 200,188; samples 142; max existent 200,330; 40% of run returned **A:** Bruno Premiani
106 ❑ Sep 1966 Cover: 0.12 **NM** value: **25.00**
Circ: Statement: **191,420** • **CGC:** 1 graded, best 9.0
📖 Blood Brothers; Mento Meets the Atom Masher; The Private World of Negative Man **A:** Bruno Premiani ★ Origin of Negative Man.
107 ❑ Nov 1966 Cover: 0.12 **NM** value: **25.00**
Circ: Statement: **191,420**
📖 The War Over Beast Boy; The Race Against Dr. Death **A:** Bruno Premiani
108 ❑ Dec 1966 Cover: 0.12 **NM** value: **25.00**
Circ: Statement: **191,420** • **CGC:** 1 graded, best 9.2
📖 Kid Disaster **A:** Bruno Premiani
109 ❑ Feb 1967 Cover: 0.12 **NM** value: **25.00**
Circ: Statement: **157,900** • **CGC:** 1 graded, best 9.2
📖 Mandred the Executioner; Flight into Fear • Has 1966 Statement, filed 10/1/66; avg print run 330,000; avg sales 190,000; avg subs 1,420; avg total paid 191,420; samples 265; max existent 191,685; 43% of run returned **A:** Bruno Premiani
110 ❑ Mar 1967 Cover: 0.12 **NM** value: **25.00**
Circ: Statement: **157,900** • **CGC:** 1 graded, best 3.5
📖 Trial By Terror **A:** Bruno Premiani
111 ❑ May 1967 Cover: 0.12 **NM** value: **25.00**
Circ: Statement: **157,900** • **CGC:** 1 graded, best 9.2
📖 Zarox-13, Emperor of the Cosmos; Neg Man's Last Road **A:** Bruno Premiani
112 ❑ Jun 1967 Cover: 0.12 **NM** value: **25.00**
Circ: Statement: **157,900**
📖 Brothers in Blood; Waif of the Wilderness **A:** Bruno Premiani
113 ❑ Aug 1967 Cover: 0.12 **NM** value: **25.00**
Circ: Statement: **157,900**
📖 Who Dares to Challenge the Arsenal?; The Diamonds of Destiny **A:** Bruno Premiani
114 ❑ Sep 1967 Cover: 0.12 **NM** value: **25.00**
Circ: Statement: **157,900**
📖 Kor – The Conquerer; The Kid Who Was King of Crooks **A:** Bruno Premiani
115 ❑ Nov 1967 Cover: 0.12 **NM** value: **25.00**
Circ: Statement: **157,900**
📖 The Mutant Master; General Beast Boy – of the Ape Brigade! **A:** Bruno Premiani
116 ❑ Dec 1967 Cover: 0.12 **NM** value: **25.00**
Circ: Statement: **157,900**
📖 Two to Get Ready… and Three to Die! **A:** Bruno Premiani
117 ❑ Feb 1968 Cover: 0.12 **NM** value: **25.00**
• **CGC:** 1 graded, best 9.2
📖 The Black Vulture; The Man with 100 Wigs • reprints story from Tales of the Unexpected #3 **A:** Bruno Premiani
118 ❑ Mar 1968 Cover: 0.12 **NM** value: **25.00**
• **CGC:** 2 graded, best 9.4
📖 Videx, Monarch of Light • Has 1967 Statement, filed 10/1/67; avg print run 315,000; avg sales 157,000; avg subs 900; avg total paid 157,900; samples 340; max existent 158,240; 50% of run returned **A:** Bruno Premiani
119 ❑ May 1968 Cover: 0.12 **NM** value: **25.00**
📖 In the Shadow of the Great Guru **A:** Bruno Premiani
120 ❑ Jun 1968 Cover: 0.12 **NM** value: **25.00**
• **CGC:** 1 graded, best 9.4
📖 The Rage of the Wrecker **A:** Bruno Premiani
121 ❑ Aug 1968 Cover: 0.12 **NM** value: **50.00**
• **CGC:** 5 graded, best 9.0
📖 The Death of the Doom Patrol **A:** Joe Orlando ★ Death of The Doom Patrol.
122 ❑ Feb 1973 Cover: 0.12 **NM** value: **2.00**
📖 The Animal-Vegetable-Mineral Menace; We Battle the Micro-Monster • Reprints begin (1973); From DP #76 and 89
123 ❑ Apr 1973 Cover: 0.12 **NM** value: **2.00**
📖 Menace of the Turnabout Heroes • From DP #95
124 ❑ Jun 1973 Cover: 0.12 **NM** value: **2.00**
• **CGC:** 1 graded, best 9.6
📖 The Enemy Within the Doom Patrol • From DP #90

DOOM PATROL (2ND SERIES) — DC

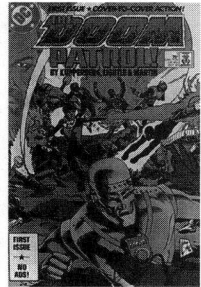

Arani Caulder, widow of original Doom Patrol founder Niles Caulder, pulled the current force together after the original Doom Patrol perished. The new force includes original member Cliff Steele — Robotman, a cyborg with the mind of a race car driver and a body of steel; Arani, who as Celsius can throw extreme heat or cold; Tempest, a doctor who can toss off power blasts; and Negative Woman, the latest repository of the Negative Man energy. Caulder was convinced that her hudband had not perished in the explosion that had killed most of the original team and used her new team to help her investigation.

Over time the cast of characters became steadily stranger, featuring Scissormen, monkey-faced girls, and a sentient boulevard named Danny the Street.

Much more than a super-hero series, Doom Patrol combines Dadaism, psychedelia, and adult themes into a compelling mix that makes it unique among comics.

1 ❑ Oct 1987 Cover: 0.75 **NM** value: **2.00**
Circ: CapCity orders: **41,050** • **CGC:** 2 graded, best 9.2
📖 The Doom Patrol • The Doom Patrol returns from their supposed deaths **A:** Steve Lightle **W:** Paul Kupperberg
2 ❑ Nov 1987 Cover: 0.75 **NM** value: **1.00**
Circ: CapCity orders: **34,350**
📖 Satellite Of Doom **A:** Steve Lightle **W:** Paul Kupperberg
3 ❑ Dec 1987 Cover: 0.75 **NM** value: **1.00**
Circ: CapCity orders: **29,000**
★ 1st Appearance of Rhea Jones, Lodestone.

CGC-graded: Multiply prices above by **33 for 9.9 M** • **16 for 9.8 NM/M** • **7 for 9.6 NM+** • **5 for 9.4 NM** • **2.5 for 9.2 NM-** • **1.5 for 9.0 VF/NM**

4 ❑ Jan 1988 Cover: 0.75 **NM** value: **1.00**
Circ: CapCity orders: **27,250**
🕮 Trouble In Kansas City **A:** Steve Lightle **W:** Paul Kupperberg ★ Origin of Lodestone.
5 ❑ Feb 1988 Cover: 0.75 **NM** value: **1.00**
Circ: CapCity orders: **25,800**
6 ❑ Mar 1988 Cover: 0.75 **NM** value: **1.00**
Circ: CapCity orders: **23,650**
🕮 Heroes And Villains **A:** Erik Larsen **W:** Paul Kupperberg
7 ❑ Apr 1988 Cover: 0.75 **NM** value: **1.00**
Circ: CapCity orders: **21,550**
★ 1st Appearance of Shrapnel.
8 ❑ May 1988 Cover: 0.75 **NM** value: **1.00**
Circ: CapCity orders: **19,500**
🕮 The Morning After **A:** Erik Larsen **C:** Arthur Adams **W:** Paul Kupperberg
9 ❑ Jun 1988 Cover: 0.75 **NM** value: **1.00**
Circ: CapCity orders: **17,650**
• Bonus Book
10 ❑ Jul 1988 Cover: 0.75 **NM** value: **1.00**
Circ: CapCity orders: **17,200**
★ Appearance of Superman.
11 ❑ Aug 1988 Cover: 1.00 **NM** value: **Cover or less**
Circ: CapCity orders: **14,400**
12 ❑ Sep 1988 Cover: 1.00 **NM** value: **Cover or less**
Circ: CapCity orders: **13,900**
13 ❑ Oct 1988 Cover: 1.00 **NM** value: **Cover or less**
Circ: CapCity orders: **14,050**
14 ❑ Nov 1988 Cover: 1.00 **NM** value: **Cover or less**
Circ: CapCity orders: **12,600**
★ 1st Appearance of Dorothy Spinner. ★ Appearance of Power Girl.
15 ❑ Dec 1988 Cover: 1.00 **NM** value: **Cover or less**
Circ: CapCity orders: **12,250**
★ Versus Animal-Vegetable-Mineral Man.
16 ❑ Dec 1988 Cover: 1.00 **NM** value: **Cover or less**
Circ: CapCity orders: **12,500**
17 ❑ Jan 1989 Cover: 1.00 **NM** value: **Cover or less**
Circ: CapCity orders: **14,000**
• Invasion! ★ Death of Celsius.
18 ❑ Jan 1989 Cover: 1.00 **NM** value: **Cover or less**
Circ: CapCity orders: **11,025**
🕮 Invasion • Invasion!
19 ❑ Feb 1989 Cover: 1.50 **NM** value: **3.00**
Circ: CapCity orders: **11,750** • **CGC:** 2 graded, best 9.6
🕮 Crawling From the Wreckage, Part 1 • 1st Grant Morrison;New, very strange direction for The Doom Patrol **W:** Grant Morrison ★ 1st Appearance of Crazy Jane.
20 ❑ Mar 1989 Cover: 1.50 **NM** value: **2.00**
Circ: CapCity orders: **10,900** • **CGC:** 1 graded, best 9.0
W: Grant Morrison ★ 1st Appearance of The Scissormen.
21 ❑ Apr 1989 Cover: 1.50 **NM** value: **2.00**
Circ: CapCity orders: **10,850**
W: Grant Morrison
22 ❑ May 1989 Cover: 1.50 **NM** value: **2.00**
Circ: CapCity orders: **11,250**
W: Grant Morrison
23 ❑ Jun 1989 Cover: 1.50 **NM** value: **2.00**
Circ: CapCity orders: **11,500**
W: Grant Morrison
24 ❑ Jul 1989 Cover: 1.50 **NM** value: **2.00**
Circ: CapCity orders: **11,450**
W: Grant Morrison
25 ❑ Aug 1989 Cover: 1.50 **NM** value: **2.00**
Circ: CapCity orders: **11,550**
W: Grant Morrison
26 ❑ Sep 1989 Cover: 1.50 **NM** value: **2.00**
Circ: CapCity orders: **11,350**
W: Grant Morrison ★ 1st Appearance of The Brotherhood of Dada.
27 ❑ Nov 1989 Cover: 1.50 **NM** value: **2.00**
Circ: CapCity orders: **10,950**
W: Grant Morrison
28 ❑ Dec 1989 Cover: 1.50 **NM** value: **2.00**
Circ: CapCity orders: **10,800**
W: Grant Morrison
29 ❑ Jan 1990 Cover: 1.50 **NM** value: **2.00**
Circ: CapCity orders: **10,550**
Superman cover. **A:** José Luis Garcia-Lopez **W:** Grant Morrison
30 ❑ Feb 1990 Cover: 1.50 **NM** value: **2.00**
Circ: CapCity orders: **10,550**
W: Grant Morrison
31 ❑ Apr 1990 Cover: 1.50 **NM** value: **2.00**
Circ: CapCity orders: **10,550**
W: Grant Morrison
32 ❑ May 1990 Cover: 1.50 **NM** value: **2.00**
Circ: CapCity orders: **10,450**
W: Grant Morrison
33 ❑ Jun 1990 Cover: 1.50 **NM** value: **2.00**
Circ: CapCity orders: **10,650**
W: Grant Morrison
34 ❑ Jul 1990 Cover: 1.50 **NM** value: **2.00**
Circ: CapCity orders: **11,050**
🕮 The Soul Of A New Machine **A:** Richard Case **W:** Grant Morrison
35 ❑ Aug 1990 Cover: 1.50 **NM** value: **2.00**
Circ: CapCity orders: **11,400**
W: Grant Morrison ★ 1st Appearance of Danny the Street, Flex Mentallo.
36 ❑ Sep 1990 Cover: 1.50 **NM** value: **2.00**
Circ: CapCity orders: **11,350**
W: Grant Morrison
37 ❑ Oct 1990 Cover: 1.50 **NM** value: **2.00**
🕮 Persephone **A:** Richard Case **W:** Grant Morrison
38 ❑ Nov 1990 Cover: 1.50 **NM** value: **2.00**
Circ: CapCity orders: **12,500**
W: Grant Morrison
39 ❑ Dec 1990 Cover: 1.50 **NM** value: **2.00**
Circ: CapCity orders: **12,950**
W: Grant Morrison
40 ❑ Jan 1991 Cover: 1.50 **NM** value: **2.00**
Circ: CapCity orders: **13,400**
🕮 Battlefield Of Dreams **A:** Richard Case **W:** Grant Morrison
41 ❑ Feb 1991 Cover: 1.50 **NM** value: **2.00**
Circ: CapCity orders: **13,550**
🕮 Fallen Angel **A:** Richard Case **W:** Grant Morrison
42 ❑ Mar 1991 Cover: 1.50 **NM** value: **2.00**
Circ: CapCity orders: **13,250**
W: Grant Morrison ★ Origin of Flex Mentallo. ★ 1st Appearance of The Fact.
43 ❑ Apr 1991 Cover: 1.50 **NM** value: **2.00**
Circ: CapCity orders: **13,000**
W: Grant Morrison
44 ❑ May 1991 Cover: 1.50 **NM** value: **2.00**
Circ: CapCity orders: **12,750**
W: Grant Morrison ★ 1st Appearance of The Candlemaker.
45 ❑ Jul 1991 Cover: 1.50 **NM** value: **2.00**
Circ: CapCity orders: **12,250**
W: Grant Morrison
46 ❑ Aug 1991 Cover: 1.50 **NM** value: **2.00**
Circ: CapCity orders: **12,300**
W: Grant Morrison
47 ❑ Sep 1991 Cover: 1.50 **NM** value: **2.00**
Circ: CapCity orders: **12,100**
W: Grant Morrison
48 ❑ Oct 1991 Cover: 1.50 **NM** value: **2.00**
Circ: CapCity orders: **12,400**
W: Grant Morrison
49 ❑ Nov 1991 Cover: 1.50 **NM** value: **2.00**
Circ: CapCity orders: **11,800**
W: Grant Morrison
50 ❑ Dec 1991 Cover: 2.50 **NM** value: **Cover or less**
Circ: CapCity orders: **14,150**
• Giant-size. 🕮 Tales Of Hoffman **W:** Grant Morrison
51 ❑ Jan 1992 Cover: 1.50 **NM** value: **2.00**
Circ: CapCity orders: **12,050**
W: Grant Morrison ★ 1st Appearance of Yankee Doodle Dandy.
52 ❑ Feb 1992 Cover: 1.50 **NM** value: **1.75**
Circ: CapCity orders: **11,300**
🕮 After The Cabaret **A:** Richard Case **W:** Grant Morrison
53 ❑ Mar 1992 Cover: 1.50 **NM** value: **1.75**
Circ: CapCity orders: **11,500**
🕮 And Men Shall Call Him Hero! • Fantastic Four parody **A:** Ken Steacy **W:** Grant Morrison
54 ❑ Apr 1992 Cover: 1.50 **NM** value: **1.75**
Circ: CapCity orders: **10,950**
Photo cover. 🕮 Aenigma Regis **A:** Richard Case **W:** Grant Morrison
55 ❑ May 1992 Cover: 1.50 **NM** value: **1.75**
Circ: CapCity orders: **10,700**
🕮 The Blood Of The Lamb **A:** Richard Case **W:** Grant Morrison
56 ❑ Jun 1992 Cover: 1.50 **NM** value: **1.75**
A: Richard Case **W:** Grant Morrison
57 ❑ Jul 1992 Cover: 1.50 **NM** value: **2.50**
• Giant-size. 🕮 The Nature Of The Catastrophe **A:** Richard Case **W:** Grant Morrison
58 ❑ Aug 1992 Cover: 1.50 **NM** value: **1.75**
🕮 In the Wonderful Land of Clockwork **A:** Sean Phillips **W:** Grant Morrison
59 ❑ Sep 1992 Cover: 1.50 **NM** value: **1.75**
🕮 Dying Inside **A:** Richard Case **W:** Grant Morrison
60 ❑ Oct 1992 Cover: 1.50 **NM** value: **1.75**
🕮 Brief Candles **A:** Richard Case **W:** Grant Morrison
61 ❑ Nov 1992 Cover: 1.75 **NM** value: **Cover or less**
A: Richard Case **W:** Grant Morrison
62 ❑ Dec 1992 Cover: 1.75 **NM** value: **Cover or less**
🕮 Planet Love **A:** Richard Case **W:** Grant Morrison
63 ❑ Jan 1993 Cover: 1.75 **NM** value: **Cover or less**
🕮 The Empire of Chairs **A:** Richard Case **W:** Grant Morrison
64 ❑ Mar 1993 Cover: 1.75 **NM** value: **Cover or less**
🕮 Sliding in the Wreckage, Part 1 • Begins Vertigo line **A:** Richard Case **W:** Rachel Pollack
65 ❑ Apr 1993 Cover: 1.75 **NM** value: **Cover or less**
Circ: CapCity orders: **13,850**
🕮 Sliding in the Wreckage, Part 2 **A:** Richard Case **W:** Rachel Pollack
66 ❑ May 1993 Cover: 1.75 **NM** value: **1.95**
Circ: CapCity orders: **13,750**
🕮 Sliding in the Wreckage, Part 3 **A:** Richard Case **W:** Rachel Pollack
67 ❑ Jun 1993 Cover: 1.95 **NM** value: **Cover or less**
Circ: CapCity orders: **14,000**
🕮 E Rose In The Autos **A:** Linda Medley **W:** Rachel Pollack
68 ❑ Jul 1993 Cover: 1.95 **NM** value: **Cover or less**
Circ: CapCity orders: **12,700**
A: Linda Medley **W:** Rachel Pollack
69 ❑ Aug 1993 Cover: 1.95 **NM** value: **Cover or less**
Circ: CapCity orders: **12,300**
🕮 Down Among The Underpinnings **A:** Linda Medley **W:** Rachel Pollack
70 ❑ Sep 1993 Cover: 1.95 **NM** value: **Cover or less**
Circ: CapCity orders: **11,150**
🕮 The Laughing Game **W:** Rachel Pollack
71 ❑ Oct 1993 Cover: 1.95 **NM** value: **Cover or less**
Circ: CapCity orders: **9,950**
🕮 The Fox And The Crow **A:** Linda Medley **W:** Rachel Pollack
72 ❑ Nov 1993 Cover: 1.95 **NM** value: **Cover or less**
Circ: CapCity orders: **9,300**
A: Linda Medley **W:** Rachel Pollack
73 ❑ Dec 1993 Cover: 1.95 **NM** value: **Cover or less**
Circ: CapCity orders: **8,750**
🕮 The Dream Patrol: Return Of The Widowmen **A:** Linda Medley **W:** Rachel Pollack
74 ❑ Jan 1994 Cover: 1.95 **NM** value: **Cover or less**
Circ: CapCity orders: **7,100**
A: Linda Medley **W:** Rachel Pollack
75 ❑ Feb 1994 Cover: 1.95 **NM** value: **Cover or less**
Circ: CapCity orders: **8,550**
🕮 The Teireseias Wars, Part 1 **A:** Ted McKeever **W:** Rachel Pollack
76 ❑ Mar 1994 Cover: 1.95 **NM** value: **Cover or less**
Circ: CapCity orders: **7,600**
🕮 The Teireseias Wars, Part 2 **A:** Ted McKeever **W:** Rachel Pollack
77 ❑ Apr 1994 Cover: 1.95 **NM** value: **Cover or less**
Circ: CapCity orders: **7,250**
🕮 The Teireseias Wars, Part 3 **A:** Ted McKeever **W:** Rachel Pollack
78 ❑ May 1994 Cover: 1.95 **NM** value: **Cover or less**
Circ: CapCity orders: **6,950**
🕮 The Teireseias Wars, Part 4 **A:** Ted McKeever **W:** Rachel Pollack
79 ❑ Jun 1994 Cover: 1.95 **NM** value: **Cover or less**
Circ: CapCity orders: **6,600**
🕮 The Teireseias Wars, Part 5 **A:** Ted McKeever **W:** Rachel Pollack
80 ❑ Jul 1994 Cover: 1.95 **NM** value: **Cover or less**
Circ: CapCity orders: **6,600**
🕮 The Dogs of Soul **A:** Arnold Pander; Jacob Pander **W:** Rachel Pollack
81 ❑ Aug 1994 Cover: 1.95 **NM** value: **Cover or less**
Circ: CapCity orders: **6,500**
🕮 Masquerade, Part 1
82 ❑ Sep 1994 Cover: 1.95 **NM** value: **Cover or less**
Circ: CapCity orders: **6,300**
🕮 Masquerade, Part 2
83 ❑ Oct 1994 Cover: 1.95 **NM** value: **Cover or less**
Circ: CapCity orders: **5,950**
84 ❑ Nov 1994 Cover: 1.95 **NM** value: **Cover or less**
Circ: CapCity orders: **5,650**
🕮 Imagine Ari's Friends, Part 1
85 ❑ Dec 1994 Cover: 1.95 **NM** value: **Cover or less**
Circ: CapCity orders: **5,500**
🕮 Imagine Ari's Friends, Part 2
86 ❑ Jan 1995 Cover: 1.95 **NM** value: **Cover or less**
Circ: CapCity orders: **5,100**
🕮 Imagine Ari's Friends, Part 3
87 ❑ Feb 1995 Cover: 1.95 **NM** value: **Cover or less**
Circ: CapCity orders: **4,925**
🕮 Imagine Ari's Friends, Part 4 final issue.
Anl 1❑ca. 1988 Cover: 1.50 **NM** value: **Cover or less**
Circ: CapCity orders: **13,400**
Anl 2❑ca. 1994 Cover: 3.95 **NM** value: **Cover or less**
Circ: CapCity orders: **11,050**
🕮 The Children's Crusade, Part 5 • Children's Crusade
Bk 1❑ Cover: 19.95 **NM** value: **Cover or less**
🕮 Crawling From the Wreckage • Collects Doom Patrol #19-25 **W:** Grant Morrison

DOOM PATROL AND SUICIDE SQUAD SPECIAL — DC

1 ❑ Feb 1988 Cover: 1.50 **NM** value: **2.00**
Circ: CapCity orders: **25,550**
🕮 Red Pawn **A:** Erik Larsen **W:** John Ostrander; Paul Kupperberg

DOOMSDAY + 1 — Charlton

1 ❑ Jul 1975 Cover: 0.25 **NM** value: **8.00**
A: John Byrne
2 ❑ Sep 1975 Cover: 0.25 **NM** value: **5.00**
A: John Byrne **W:** Joe Gill
3 ❑ Nov 1975 Cover: 0.25 **NM** value: **4.00**
🕮 Peace Keepers **A:** John Byrne **W:** Joe Gill
4 ❑ Jan 1976 Cover: 0.25 **NM** value: **4.00**
• **CGC:** 1 graded, best 9.4
A: John Byrne
5 ❑ Mar 1976 Cover: 0.25 **NM** value: **4.00**
A: John Byrne
6 ❑ May 1976 Cover: 0.25 **NM** value: **4.00**
• **CGC:** 2 graded, best 9.6
A: John Byrne
7 ❑ Jun 1978 Cover: 0.35 **NM** value: **3.00**
• Reprints Doomsday + 1 #1 **A:** John Byrne
8 ❑ 1978 Cover: 0.35 **NM** value: **3.00**
• Reprints Doomsday + 1 #2 **A:** John Byrne
9 ❑ 1978 Cover: 0.35 **NM** value: **3.00**
🕮 Peace Keepers • Reprints Doomsday + 1 #3 **A:** John Byrne **W:** Joe Gill
10 ❑ 1979 **NM** value: **3.00**
• **CGC:** 1 graded, best 9.6
• Reprints Doomsday + 1 #4 **A:** John Byrne
11 ❑ 1979 **NM** value: **3.00**
• Reprints Doomsday + 1 #5 **A:** John Byrne
12 ❑ 1979 **NM** value: **3.00**
• Reprints Doomsday + 1 #6 **A:** John Byrne

DOOMSDAY + 1 (AVALON) — Avalon

1 ❑ Cover: 2.95 **NM** value: **Cover or less**
A: John Byrne
2 ❑ Cover: 2.95 **NM** value: **Cover or less**
A: John Byrne

DOOMSDAY ANNUAL — DC

1 ❑ ca. 1995 Cover: 3.95 **NM** value: **Cover or less**
🕮 Communion **A:** Dennis Janke **W:** Jerry Ordway

DOOMSDAY SQUAD, THE — Fantagraphics

1 ❑ Aug 1986 Cover: 2.00 **NM** value: **Cover or less**
Circ: CapCity orders: **11,700**
🕮 Doomsday: Minus Two **A:** John Byrne **W:** Joe Gill
2 ❑ Cover: 2.00 **NM** value: **Cover or less**
Circ: CapCity orders: **8,225**
A: John Byrne
3 ❑ Cover: 2.00 **NM** value: **3.00**
Circ: CapCity orders: **7,475**
🕮 The Peace Keepers; Village of Fear **A:** John Byrne **W:** Joe Gill ★ Appearance of Usagi Yojimbo.
4 ❑ Cover: 2.00 **NM** value: **Cover or less**
Circ: CapCity orders: **6,825**
A: John Byrne
5 ❑ Cover: 2.00 **NM** value: **Cover or less**
Circ: CapCity orders: **5,925**
A: John Byrne
6 ❑ Cover: 2.00 **NM** value: **Cover or less**
Circ: CapCity orders: **5,200**
A: John Byrne
7 ❑ Cover: 2.00 **NM** value: **Cover or less**
Circ: CapCity orders: **5,050**
A: John Byrne

Other grades: Multiply prices above by **1.5 for Mint • 2/3 for Very Fine • 1/3 for Fine • 1/5 for Very Good • 1/8 for Good**

DOOM'S IV — Image

0.5 ❑ Dec 1994 — **NM** value: **2.50**
• Preview promotional edition.

1 ❑ Jul 1994 — Cover: 2.50 — **NM** value: **Cover or less**
Circ: CapCity orders: **43,625** • **CGC:** 1 graded, best 9.4
A: Mark Pacella **W:** Rob Liefeld

1/A ❑ Jul 1994 — Cover: 2.50 — **NM** value: **Cover or less**
Alternate cover with left half of yellow two-part picture. **A:** Mark Pacella **W:** Rob Liefeld

1/B ❑ Jul 1994 — Cover: 2.50 — **NM** value: **Cover or less**
Alternate cover with right half of yellow two-part picture. **A:** Mark Pacella **W:** Rob Liefeld

2 ❑ Aug 1994 — Cover: 2.50 — **NM** value: **Cover or less**
Circ: CapCity orders: **33,000**

2/A ❑ Aug 1994 — Cover: 2.50 — **NM** value: **Cover or less**

3 ❑ Sep 1994 — Cover: 2.50 — **NM** value: **Cover or less**
Circ: CapCity orders: **28,900**

4 ❑ Oct 1994 — Cover: 2.50 — **NM** value: **Cover or less**
Circ: CapCity orders: **27,600**

DOOM 2099 — Marvel

In the year 2099, the world is driven by the interests of corrupt corporations. Closed in by over-crowding and decay, even idyllic Latveria has become spoiled, its population frequenting the black market for synth-foods and designer drugs.

Into this dark future-world comes the most famous figure from Latveria's past. In a flash of energy, a man claiming to be Doctor Doom appears. A man out of time, he has come to take back the land that he once ruled with an iron fist. To do so, he must first dethrone the powerful Tiger Wylde, cyborg ruler of Latveria. Defeated in their initial confrontation, Doom is forced to turn to Latveria's gypsies and undesirables for help in reclaiming his heritage.

Doom 2099 joined Marvel's other 2099 titles, including Spider-Man 2099, Ravage 2099, and Punisher 2099.

1 ❑ Jan 1993 — Cover: 1.75 — **NM** value: **2.50**
Circ: Statement: **296,900** CapCity orders: **172,100**
Metallic ink cover. Muses of Fire! **A:** Pat Broderick **W:** John Francis Moore ★ 1st Appearance of Doom 2099.

2 ❑ Feb 1993 — Cover: 1.25 — **NM** value: **1.75**
Circ: Statement: **296,900** CapCity orders: **103,800**
A: Pat Broderick **W:** John Francis Moore

3 ❑ Mar 1993 — Cover: 1.25 — **NM** value: **1.75**
Circ: Statement: **296,900** CapCity orders: **83,700**
A: Pat Broderick **W:** John Francis Moore

4 ❑ Apr 1993 — Cover: 1.25 — **NM** value: **1.75**
Circ: Statement: **296,900** CapCity orders: **73,600**

5 ❑ May 1993 — Cover: 1.25 — **NM** value: **1.75**
Circ: Statement: **296,900** CapCity orders: **63,700**
★ 1st Appearance of Fever.

6 ❑ Jun 1993 — Cover: 1.25 — **NM** value: **1.50**
Circ: Statement: **296,900** CapCity orders: **58,600**

7 ❑ Jul 1993 — Cover: 1.25 — **NM** value: **1.50**
Circ: Statement: **296,900** CapCity orders: **54,200**

8 ❑ Aug 1993 — Cover: 1.25 — **NM** value: **1.50**
Circ: Statement: **296,900** CapCity orders: **49,900**

9 ❑ Sep 1993 — Cover: 1.25 — **NM** value: **1.50**
Circ: Statement: **296,900** CapCity orders: **43,200**

10 ❑ Oct 1993 — Cover: 1.25 — **NM** value: **1.50**
Circ: Statement: **296,900** CapCity orders: **39,800**
Covers of Doom 2099 10-12 combine to form triptych. **A:** Pat Broderick **W:** John Francis Moore ★ Appearance of Xandra.

11 ❑ Nov 1993 — Cover: 1.25 — **NM** value: **Cover or less**
Circ: Statement: **172,300** CapCity orders: **36,900**
Covers of Doom 2099 10-12 combine to form triptych.

12 ❑ Dec 1993 — Cover: 1.25 — **NM** value: **Cover or less**
Circ: Statement: **172,300** CapCity orders: **32,800**
Covers of Doom 2099 10-12 combine to form triptych.

13 ❑ Jan 1994 — Cover: 1.25 — **NM** value: **Cover or less**
Circ: Statement: **172,300** CapCity orders: **29,500**
• Has 1993 Statement, filed 10/1/93; avg print run 385,433; avg sales 294,808; avg subs 2,792; avg total paid 296,900; samples 125; office use 500; max existent 298,225; 23% of run returned

14 ❑ Feb 1994 — Cover: 1.25 — **NM** value: **Cover or less**
Circ: Statement: **172,300** CapCity orders: **40,600**
Fall of the Hammer, Part 4

15 ❑ Mar 1994 — Cover: 1.25 — **NM** value: **Cover or less**
Circ: Statement: **172,300** CapCity orders: **25,700**

16 ❑ Apr 1994 — Cover: 1.25 — **NM** value: **Cover or less**
Circ: Statement: **172,300** CapCity orders: **23,600**

17 ❑ May 1994 — Cover: 1.50 — **NM** value: **Cover or less**
Circ: Statement: **172,300** CapCity orders: **23,200**

18 ❑ May 1994 — Cover: 1.50 — **NM** value: **Cover or less**
Circ: Statement: **172,300** CapCity orders: **22,250**
• poster

19 ❑ Jul 1994 — Cover: 1.50 — **NM** value: **Cover or less**
Circ: Statement: **172,300** CapCity orders: **20,900**

20 ❑ Aug 1994 — Cover: 1.50 — **NM** value: **Cover or less**
Circ: Statement: **172,300** CapCity orders: **19,100**
Strangers in the Jungle **A:** John Nyberg **W:** John Francis Moore

21 ❑ Sep 1994 — Cover: 1.50 — **NM** value: **Cover or less**
Circ: Statement: **172,300** CapCity orders: **18,000**

22 ❑ Oct 1994 — Cover: 1.50 — **NM** value: **Cover or less**
Circ: Statement: **172,300** CapCity orders: **16,550**

23 ❑ Nov 1994 — Cover: 1.50 — **NM** value: **Cover or less**
Circ: Statement: **39,983** CapCity orders: **15,300**

24 ❑ Dec 1994 — Cover: 1.50 — **NM** value: **Cover or less**
Circ: Statement: **39,983** CapCity orders: **14,900**

25 ❑ Jan 1995 — Cover: 2.25 — **NM** value: **Cover or less**
Fables of the Deconstruction **A:** Pat Broderick **W:** Warren Ellis; John Francis Moore

25/SC❑ Jan 1995 — Cover: 2.95 — **NM** value: **Cover or less**
Circ: Statement: **39,983**
• Giant-size. **A:** Pat Broderick **W:** Warren Ellis; John Francis Moore

26 ❑ Feb 1995 — Cover: 1.50 — **NM** value: **Cover or less**
Circ: Statement: **39,983** CapCity orders: **13,225**

27 ❑ Mar 1995 — Cover: 1.50 — **NM** value: **Cover or less**
Circ: Statement: **39,983** CapCity orders: **12,075**
• Has 1994 Statement, filed 10/1/94; avg print run 172,975; avg sales 170,242; avg subs 2,058; avg total paid 172,300; samples 125; office use 500; max existent 172,925; 0% of run returned

28 ❑ Apr 1995 — Cover: 1.50 — **NM** value: **1.95**
Circ: Statement: **39,983** CapCity orders: **11,500**

29 ❑ May 1995 — Cover: 1.95 — **NM** value: **Cover or less**

29/SC❑ May 1995 — Cover: 3.50 — **NM** value: **Cover or less**
Circ: Statement: **39,983** CapCity orders: **17,650**
enhanced acetate overlay cover.

30 ❑ Jun 1995 — Cover: 1.95 — **NM** value: **Cover or less**
Circ: Statement: **39,983** CapCity orders: **13,425**

31 ❑ Jul 1995 — Cover: 1.95 — **NM** value: **Cover or less**
Circ: Statement: **39,983** CapCity orders: **12,100**

32 ❑ Aug 1995 — Cover: 1.95 — **NM** value: **Cover or less**
Circ: Statement: **39,983** CapCity orders: **11,850**

33 ❑ Sep 1995 — Cover: 1.95 — **NM** value: **Cover or less**
Circ: Statement: **39,983**

34 ❑ Oct 1995 — Cover: 1.95 — **NM** value: **Cover or less**
Circ: Statement: **39,983**

35 ❑ Nov 1995 — Cover: 1.95 — **NM** value: **Cover or less**

36 ❑ Dec 1995 — Cover: 1.95 — **NM** value: **Cover or less**

37 ❑ Jan 1996 — Cover: 1.95 — **NM** value: **Cover or less**
• Has 1995 Statement, filed 10/1/95; avg print run 42,420; avg sales 38,733; avg subs 1,250; avg total paid 39,983; samples 750; office use 500; max existent 41,233; 3% of run returned

38 ❑ Feb 1996 — Cover: 1.95 — **NM** value: **Cover or less**
X-Nation

39 ❑ Mar 1996 — Cover: 1.95 — **NM** value: **Cover or less**
May the Circle by Unbroken **A:** John Buscema **W:** Warren Ellis

39/SC❑ Mar 1996 — Cover: 3.50 — **NM** value: **Cover or less**
Special cover.

40 ❑ Apr 1996 — Cover: 1.95 — **NM** value: **Cover or less**
The Rage Against Time, Part 1 • Doom 2099 comes to present **A:** John Buscema **W:** Tom Peyer

41 ❑ May 1996 — Cover: 1.95 — **NM** value: **Cover or less**
★ Versus Namor. ★ Versus Daredevil.

42 ❑ Jun 1996 — Cover: 1.95 — **NM** value: **Cover or less**
★ Versus Fantastic Four.

43 ❑ Jul 1996 — Cover: 1.95 — **NM** value: **Cover or less**
• story continues in Fantastic Four 2099 #7

44 ❑ Aug 1996 — Cover: 1.95 — **NM** value: **Cover or less**
final issue. • continues in 2099: World of Tomorrow

DOORMAN (CALIBER) — Caliber

1 ❑ — Cover: 2.95 — **NM** value: **Cover or less**

DOORMAN (CULT) — Cult Press

1 ❑ b&w — Cover: 2.95 — **NM** value: **Cover or less**
Double-cover. My Brother's Keeper **A:** James Lyle **W:** Mike Leonard

2 ❑ b&w — Cover: 2.95 — **NM** value: **Cover or less**
Identical..., Part 1

3 ❑ b&w — Cover: 2.95 — **NM** value: **Cover or less**
Identical..., Part 2

4 ❑ b&w — Cover: 2.95 — **NM** value: **Cover or less**

Ash 1❑ — **NM** value: **1.00**
• ashcan

DOORMAN: FAMILY SECRETS — Caliber

1 ❑ — Cover: 2.95 — **NM** value: **Cover or less**
Brothers and Sisters **A:** James Lyle **W:** Mike Leonard

DOORWAY TO NIGHTMARE — DC

This supernatural series had a unique advantage over other titles in the same genre: a compelling main character, Madame Xanadu, who pulled all the other characters into a vortex of her own design. The Gypsy fortune teller has set up her own shop in New York City, and she does a lot more on the other characters' behalf than simply reading their tarot cards. In her own way, she acts as a guardian against the mystical forces which imperil her clients' lives.

An interesting, if short-lived title, this 1978 series lasted just five issues.

1 ❑ Feb 1978 — Cover: 0.35 — **NM** value: **2.50**
• **CGC:** 2 graded, best 9.0
A: Val Mayerik **W:** David Michelinie

2 ❑ Apr 1978 — Cover: 0.35 — **NM** value: **2.00**
• **CGC:** 1 graded, best 9.6
A: Vincente Alcazar **W:** Gerry Conway

3 ❑ Jun 1978 — Cover: 0.35 — **NM** value: **2.00**

4 ❑ Aug 1978 — Cover: 0.35 — **NM** value: **2.00**

5 ❑ Oct 1978 — Cover: 0.50 — **NM** value: **2.00**
• **CGC:** 1 graded, best 9.6
final issue.

DOPE COMIX — Kitchen Sink

1 ❑ — Cover: 1.50 — **NM** value: **4.00**

2 ❑ — Cover: 1.50 — **NM** value: **3.00**
Wam Bong Hai; Li'l Nirvana Sees God; Lulu and the G-Men; Trippin' Trouble; Tony Target in Trapped in a Pocket Watch; Saturday Night at Ranco Futura; A Typical Hippie Dope; High There!; Teenage Drug Addictee; This is The Life! **A:** Steve Stiles; Trina Robbins; J. Michael Leonard; Howard Cruse; Dan Steffan; Doug Hansen; Gary Whitney; Lee Marrs; Leonard Rifas; Joe Coleman; Sharon Dudahl **W:** Steve Stiles; Trina Robbins; J. Michael Leonard; Howard Cruse; Dan Steffan; Doug Hansen; Gary Whitney; Lee Marrs; Leonard Rifas; Joe Coleman; Sharon Dudahl

3 ❑ — Cover: 1.50 — **NM** value: **3.00**
The Guide; The Old Son of a Bitch; LSD; On Something; Smoker Scoffs; Dog Due; I Scream; Marijuana Detective; A Night in a Shop **A:** Steve Stiles; Howard Cruse; Dan Steffan; Gary Whitney; Joe Schwind; Larry Rippie; Doug Hanson **W:** Steve Stiles; Howard Cruse; Dan Steffan; Gary Whitney; Joe Schwind; Larry Rippie; Doug Hanson

4 ❑ — Cover: 1.50 — **NM** value: **3.00**
Mark Was There!; Tea For Two; By the Time I Get to Phoebus...; Feb. 21, 1965; Hey Dig it; Neato Fun With; Dope Trauma Tales; Th' Kid does Belladonna; Cold Turkey **A:** Tim Boxell; Steve Stiles; Jim Valentino; Michael T. Gilbert; Aline Kominsky-Crumb; Greg Irons; Jay Kinney **W:** Tim Boxell; Steve Stiles; Jim Valentino; Michael T. Gilbert; Aline Kominsky-Crumb; Greg Irons; Jay Kinney

5 ❑ — Cover: 1.50 — **NM** value: **3.00**
My First Marijuana Experience!; Dancing Water Voles; I can See It Now; New Wave Numbskull; White Boy's Burden; Vamp Dance; Here Come the Sun; Hydraulic Hash; Endangered Species; Them Flatulent Fuggheaded Fiend; The Adventures of Omaha; Peter Pressure **A:** William Wray; Steve Stiles; Mike Kazaleh; Reed Waller; Chris Browne; Dan Steffan; Gary Whitney; Joe Schwind; Monte Wolverton; Sharon Dahl **W:** William Wray; Steve Stiles; Mike Kazaleh; Reed Waller; Chris Browne; Dan Steffan; Gary Whitney; Joe Schwind; Monte Wolverton; Sharon Dahl

DOPEY DUCK — Timely

1 ❑ ca. 1945 — Cover: 0.10 — **NM** value: **100.00**

2 ❑ Apr 1946 — Cover: 0.10 — **NM** value: **100.00**

DOPIN' DAN — Last Gasp

1 ❑ — Cover: 0.75 — **NM** value: **5.00**
A: Ted Richards **W:** Ted Richards

2 ❑ — Cover: 0.75 — **NM** value: **3.00**
Heads or Tails; The Four Thousand Three Hundred and Twenty Four Hour **A:** Ted Richards **W:** Ted Richards

3 ❑ — Cover: 0.75 — **NM** value: **3.00**
Pay Day; I Ride the Vomit Comet; Alert; G.I. Rights and Army Justice; Dope Smoke; No More Draft; How SGT. Turdy Captured Che Guevara; **A:** Ted Richards **W:** Ted Richards

DORIS NELSON: ATOMIC HOUSEWIFE — Jake Comics

1 ❑ Dec 1995, b&w — Cover: 2.75 — **NM** value: **Cover or less**

DORK — Slave Labor

Without a doubt, Evan Dorkin is one of the funniest alternative cartoonists working in comics today. This series is a showcase for his hilarious work.

Leading off the pack is the Murder Family, a devilishly black situation comedy starring a family of serial killers. While slicing up a meter reader, they remark, "Damn! The knife snapped. Must've hit the breastbone...Aw Matt, your mother gave us that knife. I loved that knife!" Next is a collection of rock review comics Dorkin did with Kyle Baker for a defunct music magazine. Their comments on the crowds at alternative shows were dead-on funny. (A huge person is seen thinking, "I am much taller than Kyle, so I must stand directly in front of him at all times!") Rounding out the bunch are musings on Fisher-Price peg people, the infamous "Baby in the Microwave" story, and episodes from his hilarious Milk & Cheese series ("Dairy Products Gone Bad!").

1 ❑ Jun 1993, b&w — Cover: 2.50 — **NM** value: **3.00**
Murrrr-derrr Fa-mi-leeee!!!; Comic Industry Trading Cards; Fisher-Price Theatre Presents Shirley Jackson's "The Lottery"; Fisher-Price Theatre Presents "The Catcher in the Rye"; A Day of Change; Fun!; Great Ketchup Incidents 1989 **A:** Evan Dorkin **W:** Evan Dorkin

1-2 ❑ Aug 1995, b&w — Cover: 2.75 — **NM** value: **Cover or less**

1-3 ❑ Mar 1997, b&w — Cover: 2.75 — **NM** value: **Cover or less**

2 ❑ May 1994, b&w — Cover: 2.50 — **NM** value: **Cover or less**
The Murder Family: A Date With Death; Kyle and Evan: Critics at Large; Evan: Small Critic at Home; Where Have all the Ska-Zines Gone?; Baby...In the Microwave?; Fisher Price Theater: Of Mice and Men; Milk and Cheese: Tenement Cook-Out; Live Sex; Fun! **A:** Evan Dorkin **W:** Evan Dorkin

2-2 ❑ Jan 1996, b&w — Cover: 2.75 — **NM** value: **Cover or less**

3 ❑ Aug 1995, b&w — Cover: 2.75 — **NM** value: **Cover or less**
Generation Ecch!; Fun!; Milk & Cheese: There's No Business!; The Eltingville Club: Bread and Suck-Asses!; Mystery Date **A:** Evan Dorkin **W:** Evan Dorkin

3-2 ❑ Sep 1996, b&w — Cover: 2.75 — **NM** value: **Cover or less**

4 ❑ Mar 1997, b&w — Cover: 2.75 — **NM** value: **Cover or less**
Circ: Diamd. preorders: **5,635**
The Murder Family: Death and Taxidermists; They Make Me Sick; Fun for All; Fun in Your Time!; Even More Fun!; The Eltingville Club: The Marathon Men **A:** Evan Dorkin **W:** Evan Dorkin

5 ❑ Jan 1998, b&w — Cover: 2.95 — **NM** value: **Cover or less**
Circ: Diamd. preorders: **6,521**
Let the Fun Begin; It Came From the Pit; Life's Great Rewards; Welcome to the Invisible College **A:** Evan Dorkin **W:** Evan Dorkin

CGC-graded: Multiply prices above by **33 for 9.9 M** • **16 for 9.8 NM/M** • **7 for 9.6 NM+** • **5 for 9.4 NM** • **2.5 for 9.2 NM-** • **1.5 for 9.0 VF/NM**

6 ❑ May 1998, b&w Cover: 2.95 **NM** value: **Cover or less**
Circ: Diamd. preorders: **6,490**
A: Evan Dorkin **W:** Evan Dorkin

7 ❑ Aug 1999, b&w Cover: 2.95 **NM** value: **Cover or less**
Circ: Diamd. preorders: **6,761**
📖 What Does it Look Like I'm Doing!; Cluttered, Like My Head; Christzilla, King of the Messiahs; What Does it Look Like U'm Doing!
A: Evan Dorkin **W:** Evan Dorkin

8 ❑ Sep 2000, b&w Cover: 3.50 **NM** value: **Cover or less**
Circ: Diamd. preorders: **6,402**
A: Evan Dorkin **W:** Evan Dorkin

9 ❑ 2001 Cover: 2.95 **NM** value: **Cover or less**
Circ: Diamd. preorders: **7,225**
A: Evan Dorkin **W:** Evan Dorkin

DORK HOUSE COMICS — Parody Press

1 ❑ Cover: 2.50 **NM** value: **Cover or less**

DORKIER IMAGES — Parody Press

1 ❑ Mar 1993 Cover: 2.50 **NM** value: **Cover or less**
• Standard edition. 📖 Bloodwoof; The Faxx; Def Bro **A:** Bill Maus **W:** Bill Maus

1/SC❑ Cover: 2.95 **NM** value: **3.00**
• gold, silver, blue edition.

DORK TOWER — Corsair Publishing

Known for his popular (and very funny) "Wild Life" comic strip, John Kovalic took on the strange world of gamers with this, his first foray into comic-book publishing. Dork Tower, which began as a series of strips in various gaming magazine, follows Matt, Igor, Ken, and Carson the Muskrat (the latter from the Wild Life strip) as they barge through preposterous imaginary dungeons, launch into Talmudic discussions of gaming rules, and slowly come to realize that telling a woman you're a gamer is about as enticing as copping to a venereal disease.

OK, perhaps that overstates the point, but the characters and situations of Dork Tower will seem frighteningly (and hilariously) familiar to many a gamer.

1 ❑ Jul 1998 Cover: 2.95 **NM** value: **4.00**
A: John Kovalic **W:** John Kovalic

2 ❑ Oct 1998 Cover: 2.95 **NM** value: **3.00**
📖 Night in the City **A:** John Kovalic **W:** John Kovalic

3 ❑ Jan 1999 Cover: 2.95 **NM** value: **3.00**
📖 Global Village Idiot **A:** John Kovalic **W:** John Kovalic

4 ❑ May 1999 Cover: 2.95 **NM** value: **3.00**
📖 The Fandom Menace • Star Wars **A:** John Kovalic **W:** John Kovalic

5 ❑ Jul 1999 Cover: 2.95 **NM** value: **Cover or less**
• Babylon 5 **A:** John Kovalic **W:** John Kovalic

6 ❑ 1999 Cover: 2.95 **NM** value: **Cover or less**
A: John Kovalic **W:** John Kovalic

7 ❑ Jan 2000 Cover: 2.95 **NM** value: **Cover or less**
Circ: Diamd. preorders: **2,125**
A: John Kovalic **W:** John Kovalic

8 ❑ Mar 2000 Cover: 2.95 **NM** value: **Cover or less**
Circ: Diamd. preorders: **2,218**
📖 High Sobriety **A:** John Kovalic **W:** John Kovalic

DORK TOWER — Dork Storm

9 ❑ Aug 2000, b&w Cover: 2.95 **NM** value: **Cover or less**
Circ: Diamd. preorders: **2,414**
• switches to Dork Storm **A:** John Kovalic **W:** John Kovalic

10 ❑ Aug 2000 Cover: 2.95 **NM** value: **Cover or less**
Circ: Diamd. preorders: **2,350**
📖 Road Rules **A:** John Kovalic **W:** John Kovalic

11 ❑ Sep 2000 Cover: 2.95 **NM** value: **Cover or less**
Circ: Diamd. preorders: **2,344**
📖 World of Dorkness **A:** John Kovalic **W:** John Kovalic

12 ❑ Nov 2000 Cover: 2.95 **NM** value: **Cover or less**
Circ: Diamd. preorders: **2,629**
📖 Warhamster **A:** John Kovalic **W:** John Kovalic

13 ❑ 2001 Cover: 2.95 **NM** value: **Cover or less**
Circ: Diamd. preorders: **2,697**
A: John Kovalic **W:** John Kovalic

14 ❑ 2001 Cover: 2.95 **NM** value: **Cover or less**
Circ: Diamd. preorders: **2,847**
A: John Kovalic **W:** John Kovalic

15 ❑ 2001 Cover: 2.95 **NM** value: **Cover or less**
Circ: Diamd. preorders: **2,942**
A: John Kovalic **W:** John Kovalic

16 ❑ 2001 Cover: 2.95 **NM** value: **Cover or less**
Circ: Diamd. preorders: **3,592**
A: John Kovalic **W:** John Kovalic

Bk 1❑ Sep 2000 Cover: 15.95 **NM** value: **Cover or less**
• Trade Paperback. 📖 Dork Covenant: The Collected Dork Tower Vol. 1 • collects #1-6 **A:** John Kovalic **W:** John Kovalic

DOTHENRIDGE: TALES OF THE VAMPIRE MONARCHY — Dothenridge

0.5 ❑ Cover: 1.75 **NM** value: **Cover or less**
A: Eleazar Del Rosario **W:** Sean Glumace

DOTTY DRIPPLE COMICS — Harvey

Dotty Dripple was a domestic comedy strip from the mid-1940s, credited to "Buford Tune." It was, to say the least, strongly inspired in both art and writing by the more famous and long-lived Blondie and Dagwood. Horace Dripple is a put-upon family man who just wants to be left alone to nap on the couch. His bubble-brained, blond wife, Dotty, always has a project in the works to disrupt his tranquil life, and, of course, his irritable boss never leaves him alone either. Then there's the troublesome kids, teenaged son Wilbur and young daughter L'il Taffy. Even the family dog Pepper gets into the act. By the last pages of Dotty Dripple, it's very easy to wonder if the Blondie strips that Buford Tune traced aren't still attached somewhere underneath.

#	Date	Cover	NM value
1	❑ 1946	Cover: 0.10	**NM** value: **20.00**
2	❑ 1947	Cover: 0.10	**NM** value: **12.00**
3	❑ 1947	Cover: 0.10	**NM** value: **8.00**
4	❑ 1947	Cover: 0.10	**NM** value: **8.00**
5	❑ 1948	Cover: 0.10	**NM** value: **8.00**
6	❑ 1948	Cover: 0.10	**NM** value: **7.00**
7	❑ 1948	Cover: 0.10	**NM** value: **7.00**
8	❑ 1949	Cover: 0.10	**NM** value: **7.00**
9	❑ 1949	Cover: 0.10	**NM** value: **7.00**
10	❑ 1950	Cover: 0.10	**NM** value: **7.00**
11	❑ 1950	Cover: 0.10	**NM** value: **5.00**
12	❑ Jun 1950	Cover: 0.10	**NM** value: **5.00**
13	❑ Aug 1950	Cover: 0.10	**NM** value: **5.00**
14	❑ Oct 1950	Cover: 0.10	**NM** value: **5.00**
15	❑ Dec 1950	Cover: 0.10	**NM** value: **5.00**
16	❑ Feb 1951	Cover: 0.10	**NM** value: **5.00**
17	❑ Apr 1951	Cover: 0.10	**NM** value: **5.00**
18	❑ Jun 1951	Cover: 0.10	**NM** value: **5.00**
19	❑ Aug 1951	Cover: 0.10	**NM** value: **5.00**
20	❑ Oct 1951	Cover: 0.10	**NM** value: **5.00**
21	❑ Dec 1951	Cover: 0.10	**NM** value: **5.00**
22	❑ Feb 1952	Cover: 0.10	**NM** value: **5.00**

📖 Handy Man; Growing Pains; Dog Daze; On The Job; Loan Wolf; Lights Out; Home Sweet Home;

23 ❑ Apr 1952 Cover: 0.10 **NM** value: **5.00**

24 ❑ Jun 1952 Cover: 0.10 **NM** value: **5.00**
final issue.

DOUBLE ACTION COMICS — DC

2 ❑ Jan 1940 Cover: 0.10 **NM** value: **10000.00**
• **CGC:** 2 graded, best 9.2

DOUBLE-DARE ADVENTURES — Harvey

1 ❑ ca. 1966 Cover: 0.25 **NM** value: **20.00**
• **CGC:** 1 graded, best 9.0

2 ❑ ca. 1967 Cover: 0.25 **NM** value: **16.00**
📖 B-Man: The Revolt of the Queen Bee; B-Man: B-Day for B-Man; The Glowing Gladiator: The Two Deadly Faces of Destiny; The Glowing Gladiator: The Land of No Return; Sunken Treasure; The Secret Mountain; Magicmaster: Sorcery at the Circus ★ Origin of B-Man.

DOUBLE DRAGON — Marvel

1 ❑ Jul 1991 Cover: 1.00 **NM** value: **Cover or less**
Circ: CapCity orders: **27,600**
A: Tom Raney **W:** Dwayne McDuffie ★ Origin of Double Dragon (Billy & Jimmy Lee). ★ 1st Appearance of Double Dragon (Billy & Jimmy Lee).

2 ❑ Aug 1991 Cover: 1.00 **NM** value: **Cover or less**
Circ: CapCity orders: **17,800**

3 ❑ Sep 1991 Cover: 1.00 **NM** value: **Cover or less**
Circ: CapCity orders: **14,400**

4 ❑ Oct 1991 Cover: 1.00 **NM** value: **Cover or less**
Circ: CapCity orders: **14,100**

5 ❑ Nov 1991 Cover: 1.00 **NM** value: **Cover or less**
Circ: CapCity orders: **13,400**

6 ❑ Dec 1991 Cover: 1.00 **NM** value: **Cover or less**
Circ: CapCity orders: **12,500**
final issue.

DOUBLE EDGE: ALPHA — Marvel

1 ❑ Aug 1995 Cover: 4.95 **NM** value: **Cover or less**
• **CGC:** 2 graded, best 10.0
chromium cover. 📖 Reset • Punisher **A:** Tom Morgan; Kerry Gammill **W:** Larry Hama

DOUBLE EDGE: OMEGA — Marvel

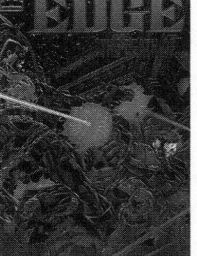

Frank Castle watched helplessly, himself critically injured, as his family was brutally murdered by mobsters. Vowing vengeance, he now spends his life dispensing lethal justice as the Punisher.

But the Punisher's memories have been altered, and he mistakenly believes Nick Fury to be the man who killed his family. With the apparent object of his crusade alive and well, not even the combined forces of S.H.I.E.L.D., Ghost Rider, and Daredevil can keep The Punisher from his sworn mission.

Fury has long been a mainstay of the Marvel universe, first as a soldier fighting alongside the Howling Commandos, and later as an agent of S.H.I.E.L.D. His death had repercussions that affected several other titles, including The Incredible Hulk and a new Punisher series, as well as being the launching point for the new Marvel Edge logo.

1 ❑ Oct 1995 Cover: 4.95 **NM** value: **Cover or less**
• **CGC:** 4 graded, best 9.8
enhanced wraparound cover. 📖 Glory Days • Punisher **A:** Douglas T. Wheatly **W:** Kim Yale; John Ostrander ★ Death of Nick Fury.

DOUBLE IMAGE — Image

1 ❑ Feb 2001 Cover: 2.95 **NM** value: **Cover or less**
Circ: Diamd. preorders: **12,268**
• Flip-book. 📖 Codeflesh; The Bod **A:** Joe Casey; Charles Adlard; John Heebink **W:** Joe Casey; Charles Adlard; Larry Young

2 ❑ Feb 2001 Cover: 2.95 **NM** value: **Cover or less**
Circ: Diamd. preorders: **8,650**
• Flip-book. 📖 Codeflesh; The Bod **A:** Joe Casey; Charles Adlard; John Heebink **W:** Joe Casey; Charles Adlard; Larry Young

3 ❑ Apr 2001 Cover: 2.95 **NM** value: **Cover or less**
Circ: Diamd. preorders: **7,498**
• Flip-book. 📖 The Bod; Codeflesh **A:** Joe Casey; Charles Adlard; John Heebink **W:** Joe Casey; Charles Adlard; Larry Young

DOUBLE IMPACT — High Impact

The vicious drug lord, Ernesto Castillos is threatening to expand his empire and take over the world. To that end he blew up the radio station on which he made that announcement. This called for desperate measures so the government sent rogue agent Mordred to find China and Jazz, the two covert agents betrayed by the government agency they worked for.

Mordred wastes no time tracking down his former partners in the strip bar where they've been keeping a low profile. Apparently China and Jazz are crucial to defeating Castillos because of their ability to stand up with their impossibly huge...guns.

This title epitomized the "bad girl" genre, relying on lascivious drawings of incredibly built women in place of a plot or reasonable dialogue. The men are represented no more realistically; depicted with one of two possible expressions: stoic or grim. And as if to utilize every possible ploy, this title also sported chromium covers, bagged editions, and, to irritate indexers and collectors alike, limited or incorrect indicia.

1 ❑ Mar 1995 Cover: 3.95 **NM** value: **Cover or less**
Circ: CapCity orders: **8,810**
No issue number. no cover price. • no indicia;gray polybag;preview of Double Impact #3 and 4;San Diego Comic-Con ed. **A:** Mo; Ramon Garcia; Rick Carralero **W:** Enrique Carralero

1/LE❑ Mar 1995 Cover: 3.95 **NM** value: **Cover or less**
No issue number. no cover price. • no indicia;black polybag;letters pages and pin-ups;limited to 5000

2 ❑ May 1995 Cover: 3.95 **NM** value: **Cover or less**
Circ: CapCity orders: **6,945**

3 ❑ Jul 1995 Cover: 3.95 **NM** value: **Cover or less**
Circ: CapCity orders: **5,810**

4 ❑ Sep 1995 Cover: 3.95 **NM** value: **Cover or less**
Circ: CapCity orders: **7,270**

DOUBLE IMPACT: ART ATTACK — ABC Studios

1 ❑ Cover: 3.00 **NM** value: **Cover or less**

1/A ❑ Cover: 6.00 **NM** value: **Cover or less**
• China & Jazz Nude Edition.

1/B ❑ Cover: 6.00 **NM** value: **Cover or less**
• Nude Jazz Edition.

DOUBLE IMPACT: ASSASSINS FOR HIRE — High Impact

All issues are adults only.

1 ❑ Apr 1997, b&w Cover: 2.95 **NM** value: **Cover or less**
Circ: Diamd. preorders: **5,648**
cardstock cover. • Hard Core! Edition.

DOUBLE IMPACT BIKINI SPECIAL — High Impact

1 ❑ Sep 1998, b&w Cover: 3.00 **NM** value: **Cover or less**
Circ: Diamd. preorders: **2,011**
• pin-ups

DOUBLE IMPACT: FROM THE ASHES — High Impact

All issues are adults only.

1 ❑ b&w Cover: 3.00 **NM** value: **Cover or less**

2 ❑ b&w Cover: 5.95 **NM** value: **Cover or less**

DOUBLE IMPACT/HELLINA — ABC Studios

1 ❑ Jan 1998, b&w Cover: 3.00 **NM** value: **Cover or less**
• crossover with Lightning **A:** David Germain **W:** John Ulloa

1/Aut❑ Mar 1996 **NM** value: **5.00**
A: David Germain **W:** John Ulloa

1/GO❑ Mar 1996 **NM** value: **5.00**
Gold nude cover. **A:** David Germain **W:** John Ulloa

1/Nude❑ Jan 1998 Cover: 3.00 **NM** value: **4.00**
Nude cover.

1/SC❑ Mar 1996 **NM** value: **4.00**
Nude cover. **A:** David Germain **W:** John Ulloa

DOUBLE IMPACT: ONE STEP BEYOND — High Impact

1 ❑ Sep 1998 Cover: 3.00 **NM** value: **Cover or less**
Circ: Diamd. preorders: **2,006**

Other grades: Multiply prices above by **1.5 for Mint • 2/3 for Very Fine • 1/3 for Fine • 1/5 for Very Good • 1/8 for Good**

1/SC❑ Cover: 20.00 **NM** value: **Cover or less**
Leather cover.

DOUBLE IMPACT: RAISING HELL — ABC Studios
All issues are adults only.
1 ❑ Sep 1997, b&w Cover: 2.95 **NM** value: **Cover or less**
Circ: Diamd. preorders: **3,678**
1/Nude❑Sep 1997, b&w Cover: 2.95 **NM** value: **4.00**
nude photo cover.

DOUBLE IMPACT: RAW — ABC Studios
1 ❑ Nov 1997 Cover: 2.95 **NM** value: **Cover or less**
cardstock cover.
1/A ❑ Nov 1997 **NM** value: **4.00**
no cover price. • Eurotika Edition.
1/Nude❑Nov 1997 **NM** value: **4.00**
nude photo cover. • Eurotika Edition.
1-2 ❑ Cover: 3.50 **NM** value: **Cover or less**
2 ❑ ca. 1998 Cover: 2.95 **NM** value: **Cover or less**
2/Nude❑ca. 1998 Cover: 2.95 **NM** value: **4.00**
nude photo cover.
3 ❑ ca. 1998 Cover: 2.95 **NM** value: **Cover or less**

DOUBLE IMPACT: RAW (VOL. 2) — ABC Studios
1/Nude❑Sep 1998 Cover: 3.00 **NM** value: **4.00**
Nude cover.

DOUBLE IMPACT: SUICIDE RUN — High Impact
1 ❑ Jun 1997 Cover: 3.00 **NM** value: **Cover or less**
Circ: Diamd. preorders: **4,720**
1/A ❑ Jun 1997 Cover: 8.00 **NM** value: **Cover or less**
1/Leather❑Jun 1997 **NM** value: **4.00**
no cover price.
1/Nude❑Jun 1997 Cover: 6.00 **NM** value: **Cover or less**

DOUBLE IMPACT: TRIGGER HAPPY — High Impact
1 ❑ ca. 1997 Cover: 3.00 **NM** value: **Cover or less**
1/B ❑ ca. 1997 Cover: 3.00 **NM** value: **Cover or less**
• Jazz Edition.
1/LE❑ ca. 1997 **NM** value: **4.00**
no cover price. • Gold edition. • limited to 300 copies

DOUBLE IMPACT (VOL. 2) — High Impact
0 ❑ Dec 1996 Cover: 2.95 **NM** value: **Cover or less**
Circ: Direct Market orders: **8,878**
A: Jude Millien; David Jermain **W:** Ricky Carralero; Jude Millien
1 ❑ 1997 Cover: 4.00 **NM** value: **Cover or less**
• **CGC:** 2 graded, best 9.8
Chronium Cover. **A:** Mo; Ramon Garcia; Rick Carralero **W:** Ricky Carralero; Enrique Carralero
2 ❑ 1997 Cover: 3.00 **NM** value: **Cover or less**
Circ: Diamd. preorders: **6,587**
A: Ricky Carralero **W:** Ricky Carralero
3 ❑ 1997 Cover: 3.00 **NM** value: **Cover or less**
A: Ricky Carralero **W:** Ricky Carralero
4 ❑ 1997 Cover: 3.00 **NM** value: **Cover or less**
A: Ricky Carralero **W:** Ricky Carralero
5 ❑ 1997 Cover: 3.00 **NM** value: **Cover or less**
A: Ricky Carralero **W:** Ricky Carralero
6 ❑ 1997 Cover: 3.00 **NM** value: **Cover or less**
A: Ricky Carralero **W:** Ricky Carralero
7 ❑ May 1996 Cover: 3.00 **NM** value: **Cover or less**
A: Ricky Carralero **W:** Ricky Carralero

DOUBLE LIFE OF PRIVATE STRONG — Archie
1 ❑ Jun 1959 Cover: 0.10 **NM** value: **500.00**
• **CGC:** 6 graded, best 9.4
📖 The Double Life of Captain Strong; Spawn of the X-World; The Hide-Out; Mystery of the Vanished Wreckage; The Menace of the Micro-Men
2 ❑ Aug 1959 Cover: 0.10 **NM** value: **250.00**
• **CGC:** 3 graded, best 9.4

DOUBLE TALK — Feature
1 ❑ 1962 **NM** value: **50.00**
No issue number. • giveaway; anti-Communism comic book

DOUBLE TROUBLE — St. John
1 ❑ Nov 1957 Cover: 0.10 **NM** value: **20.00**

DOUBLE UP — Eliot
1 ❑ ca. 1941 Cover: 0.10 **NM** value: **400.00**

DOVER THE BIRD — Famous Funnies
1 ❑ Spr 1955 Cover: 0.10 **NM** value: **30.00**

DOWNTIME — Forbidden Fruit
Bk 1❑ b&w Cover: 8.98 **NM** value: **Cover or less**
A: J. Zanotto **W:** E. Balcarce

DOWN WITH CRIME — Fawcett
1 ❑ Nov 1951 Cover: 0.10 **NM** value: **175.00**
2 ❑ Jan 1952 Cover: 0.10 **NM** value: **80.00**
3 ❑ Mar 1952 Cover: 0.10 **NM** value: **80.00**
4 ❑ May 1952 Cover: 0.10 **NM** value: **80.00**
5 ❑ Jul 1952 Cover: 0.10 **NM** value: **80.00**
6 ❑ Sep 1952 Cover: 0.10 **NM** value: **80.00**
7 ❑ Nov 1952 Cover: 0.10 **NM** value: **80.00**

DO YOU BELIEVE IN NIGHTMARES — St. John
1 ❑ Nov 1957 Cover: 0.10 **NM** value: **300.00**
2 ❑ Jan 1958 Cover: 0.10 **NM** value: **200.00**

D.P.7 — Marvel
Randy O'Brian is working in the emergency room when David Landers, a normal guy who had gained two hundred pounds of muscle in a week, is rushed in. When the wild Landers breaks his restraints, O'Brian is shocked to find a ghostly form rising from his own body.

Seeking help, O'Brian and Landers go to the Institute for Paranormal Research, where they meet other people with unusual powers. The Institute is a front for an agency that wants to use them as operatives, though, and the group flees, becoming known as D.P.7, or "seven displaced paranormals."

One of the better New Universe titles from Marvel (which isn't saying much), this X-Men analog lasted a little longer than the rest.

1 ❑ Nov 1986 Cover: 0.75 **NM** value: **1.00**
Circ: CapCity orders: **33,800**
📖 The Clinic **A:** Paul Ryan **W:** Mark Gruenwald ★ Origin of D.P.7.
2 ❑ Dec 1986 Cover: 0.75 **NM** value: **1.00**
Circ: CapCity orders: **24,900**
3 ❑ Jan 1987 Cover: 0.75 **NM** value: **1.00**
Circ: CapCity orders: **20,300**
4 ❑ Feb 1987 Cover: 0.75 **NM** value: **1.00**
Circ: CapCity orders: **21,100**
5 ❑ Mar 1987 Cover: 0.75 **NM** value: **1.00**
Circ: CapCity orders: **20,600**
📖 Exorcism **A:** Paul Ryan **W:** Mark Gruenwald
6 ❑ Apr 1987 Cover: 0.75 **NM** value: **1.00**
Circ: CapCity orders: **19,600**
7 ❑ May 1987 Cover: 0.75 **NM** value: **1.00**
Circ: CapCity orders: **18,100**
8 ❑ Jun 1987 Cover: 0.75 **NM** value: **1.00**
Circ: CapCity orders: **16,900**
9 ❑ Jul 1987 Cover: 0.75 **NM** value: **1.00**
Circ: CapCity orders: **15,600**
10 ❑ Aug 1987 Cover: 0.75 **NM** value: **1.00**
Circ: CapCity orders: **15,000**
11 ❑ Sep 1987 Cover: 0.75 **NM** value: **1.00**
Circ: CapCity orders: **14,900**
12 ❑ Oct 1987 Cover: 0.75 **NM** value: **1.00**
Circ: CapCity orders: **14,900**
13 ❑ Nov 1987 Cover: 0.75 **NM** value: **1.00**
Circ: CapCity orders: **14,300**
14 ❑ Dec 1987 Cover: 0.75 **NM** value: **1.00**
Circ: CapCity orders: **13,500**
15 ❑ Jan 1988 Cover: 0.75 **NM** value: **1.00**
Circ: CapCity orders: **13,600**
16 ❑ Feb 1988 Cover: 0.75 **NM** value: **1.00**
Circ: CapCity orders: **13,900**
17 ❑ Mar 1988 Cover: 0.75 **NM** value: **1.00**
Circ: CapCity orders: **13,600**
18 ❑ Apr 1988 Cover: 0.75 **NM** value: **1.00**
Circ: CapCity orders: **14,750**
19 ❑ May 1988 Cover: 1.25 **NM** value: **Cover or less**
Circ: CapCity orders: **13,700**
20 ❑ Jun 1988 Cover: 1.25 **NM** value: **Cover or less**
Circ: CapCity orders: **13,100**
21 ❑ Jul 1988 Cover: 1.25 **NM** value: **Cover or less**
Circ: CapCity orders: **13,500**
22 ❑ Aug 1988 Cover: 1.25 **NM** value: **Cover or less**
Circ: CapCity orders: **14,400**
23 ❑ Sep 1988 Cover: 1.25 **NM** value: **Cover or less**
Circ: CapCity orders: **13,700**
★ Appearance of Psi-Force.
24 ❑ Oct 1988 Cover: 1.25 **NM** value: **Cover or less**
Circ: CapCity orders: **13,300**
25 ❑ Nov 1988 Cover: 1.25 **NM** value: **Cover or less**
Circ: CapCity orders: **12,800**
★ Appearance of Nightmask.
26 ❑ Dec 1988 Cover: 1.50 **NM** value: **Cover or less**
Circ: CapCity orders: **12,100**
27 ❑ Jan 1989 Cover: 1.50 **NM** value: **Cover or less**
Circ: CapCity orders: **11,400**
28 ❑ Feb 1989 Cover: 1.50 **NM** value: **Cover or less**
Circ: CapCity orders: **10,500**
29 ❑ Mar 1989 Cover: 1.50 **NM** value: **Cover or less**
Circ: CapCity orders: **10,300**
30 ❑ Apr 1989 Cover: 1.50 **NM** value: **Cover or less**
Circ: CapCity orders: **10,500**
★ 1st Appearance of Captain Manhattan.
31 ❑ May 1989 Cover: 1.50 **NM** value: **Cover or less**
Circ: CapCity orders: **9,600**
32 ❑ Jun 1989 Cover: 1.50 **NM** value: **Cover or less**
Circ: CapCity orders: **9,700**
final issue.
Anl 1❑Nov 1987 Cover: 1.25 **NM** value: **Cover or less**
Circ: CapCity orders: **14,100**
★ Origin of D.P.7. ★ 1st Appearance of the Witness.

DRACULA 3-D — 3-D Zone
1 ❑ Cover: 3.95 **NM** value: **Cover or less**
No issue number.

DRACULA: A SYMPHONY IN MOONLIGHT AND NIGHTMARES — Marvel
Bk 1❑ Cover: 7.95 **NM** value: **Cover or less**

DRACULA (BRAM STOKER'S...) — Topps
1 ❑ Oct 1992 Cover: 2.95 **NM** value: **Cover or less**
Circ: CapCity orders: **45,725**
A: Mike Mignola **W:** Roy Thomas
1/SC❑Oct 1992 **NM** value: **3.50**
• **CGC:** 1 graded, best 9.4
no cover price.
2 ❑ Nov 1992 Cover: 2.95 **NM** value: **Cover or less**
Circ: CapCity orders: **24,950**
A: Mike Mignola **W:** Roy Thomas
3 ❑ Dec 1992 Cover: 2.95 **NM** value: **Cover or less**
Circ: CapCity orders: **34,400**
A: Mike Mignola **W:** Roy Thomas
4 ❑ Jan 1993 Cover: 2.95 **NM** value: **Cover or less**
Circ: CapCity orders: **40,925**
A: Mike Mignola **W:** Roy Thomas
Bk 1❑ Cover: 13.95 **NM** value: **Cover or less**

DRACULA CHRONICLES, THE — Topps
1 ❑ Cover: 2.50 **NM** value: **Cover or less**
Circ: CapCity orders: **2,775**
📖 I Am Dracula **A:** Esteban Maroto **W:** Roy Thomas
2 ❑ Cover: 2.50 **NM** value: **Cover or less**
Circ: CapCity orders: **2,175**
A: Esteban Maroto **W:** Roy Thomas
3 ❑ Cover: 2.50 **NM** value: **Cover or less**
Circ: CapCity orders: **2,250**
A: Esteban Maroto **W:** Roy Thomas

DRACULA (DELL) — Dell
Dell reinvented the most famous Transylvanian villain as a super-hero in this imaginative series. In short, after years of living down his family name's ill-deserved infamy, Al Dracula discovers a serum that can cure brain disease. Unfortunately, since the serum is derived from bats, it has a side effect: those who take it can turn into a bat at will as well as have the phenomenal radar sense of bats. When Dracula accidentally drinks some of his own serum, he decides to use his new super-powers to combat evil as it appears, especially in America, where he is introducing his miracle cure.

2 ❑ Nov 1966 Cover: 0.12 **NM** value: **20.00**
• **CGC:** 1 graded, best 8.0
★ Origin of Dracula (Super-Hero).
3 ❑ Feb 1967 Cover: 0.12 **NM** value: **12.00**
4 ❑ Mar 1967 Cover: 0.12 **NM** value: **12.00**
6 ❑ Jul 1972 Cover: 0.15 **NM** value: **7.00**
• Reprint (1972);Follows #4 (there was no #5)
7 ❑ Cover: 0.15 **NM** value: **7.00**
8 ❑ Jul 1973 Cover: 0.20 **NM** value: **7.00**
final issue.

DRACULA (ETERNITY) — Eternity
1 ❑ Cover: 3.50 **NM** value: **Cover or less**
A: Robert Schnieders **W:** Steve Jones
1-2 ❑ Cover: 2.50 **NM** value: **Cover or less**
2 ❑ b&w Cover: 2.50 **NM** value: **Cover or less**
A: Robert Schnieders **W:** Steve Jones
3 ❑ b&w Cover: 2.50 **NM** value: **Cover or less**
A: Robert Schnieders **W:** Steve Jones
4 ❑ b&w Cover: 2.50 **NM** value: **Cover or less**
A: Robert Schnieders **W:** Steve Jones
Bk 1❑ Cover: 9.95 **NM** value: **Cover or less**

DRACULA IN HELL — Apple
All issues are adults only.
1 ❑ b&w Cover: 2.50 **NM** value: **Cover or less**
2 ❑ b&w Cover: 2.50 **NM** value: **Cover or less**

DRACULA LIVES (MAGAZINE) — Marvel
1 ❑ Jun 1973 Cover: 0.75 **NM** value: **4.00**
2 ❑ Aug 1973 Cover: 0.75 **NM** value: **3.00**
★ Origin of Dracula.
3 ❑ Oct 1973 Cover: 0.75 **NM** value: **3.00**
★ Appearance of Soloman Kane.
4 ❑ Jan 1974 Cover: 0.75 **NM** value: **3.00**
• title changes to Dracula Lives!
5 ❑ Mar 1974 Cover: 0.75 **NM** value: **3.00**
• adapts Bram Stoker novel
6 ❑ May 1974 Cover: 0.75 **NM** value: **3.00**
7 ❑ Jul 1974 Cover: 0.75 **NM** value: **3.00**
📖 Master Of The Sky
8 ❑ Sep 1974 Cover: 0.75 **NM** value: **3.00**
9 ❑ Nov 1974 Cover: 0.75 **NM** value: **3.00**
10 ❑ Jan 1975 Cover: 0.75 **NM** value: **3.00**
11 ❑ Mar 1975 Cover: 0.75 **NM** value: **2.50**
12 ❑ May 1975 Cover: 0.75 **NM** value: **2.50**
13 ❑ Jul 1975 Cover: 0.75 **NM** value: **2.50**
final issue.
Anl 1❑ca. 1975, b&w Cover: 1.25 **NM** value: **Cover or less**
• magazine.

DRACULA: LORD OF THE UNDEAD — Marvel
1 ❑ Dec 1998 Cover: 2.99 **NM** value: **Cover or less**
Circ: Diamd. preorders: **15,381**
• gatefold summary. 📖 When Darkness Returns **A:** Patrick Olliffe **W:** Glenn Greenberg
2 ❑ Dec 1998 Cover: 2.99 **NM** value: **Cover or less**
Circ: Diamd. preorders: **14,072**
• gatefold summary.
3 ❑ Dec 1998 Cover: 2.99 **NM** value: **Cover or less**
Circ: Diamd. preorders: **13,642**
• gatefold summary.

DRACULA: RETURN OF THE IMPALER — Slave Labor
1 ❑ Jul 1993 Cover: 2.95 **NM** value: **Cover or less**
2 ❑ Jan 1994 Cover: 2.95 **NM** value: **Cover or less**
3 ❑ Mar 1994 Cover: 2.95 **NM** value: **Cover or less**
4 ❑ Oct 1994 Cover: 2.95 **NM** value: **Cover or less**

CGC-graded: Multiply prices above by **33 for 9.9 M • 16 for 9.8 NM/M • 7 for 9.6 NM+ • 5 for 9.4 NM • 2.5 for 9.2 NM- • 1.5 for 9.0 VF/NM**

DRACULA'S DAUGHTER — Fantagraphics / Eros

All issues are adults only.

1 ❑ b&w Cover: 2.50 **NM** value: **Cover or less**

DRACULA: THE LADY IN THE TOMB — Eternity

1 ❑ b&w Cover: 2.50 **NM** value: **Cover or less**

DRACULA: THE SUICIDE CLUB — Adventure

1 ❑ Aug 1992 Cover: 2.50 **NM** value: **Cover or less**
2 ❑ Sep 1992 Cover: 2.50 **NM** value: **Cover or less**
3 ❑ Oct 1992 Cover: 2.50 **NM** value: **Cover or less**
4 ❑ Nov 1992 Cover: 2.50 **NM** value: **Cover or less**

DRACULA VERSUS ZORRO — Topps

1 ❑ Oct 1993 Cover: 2.95 **NM** value: **4.00**
Circ: CapCity orders: **12,995**
A: Tom Yeates **W:** Don McGregor
2 ❑ Nov 1993 Cover: 2.95 **NM** value: **3.50**
Circ: CapCity orders: **10,300**
A: Tom Yeates **W:** Don McGregor

DRACULA VERSUS ZORRO (VOL. 2) — Topps

1 ❑ Apr 1994 Cover: 5.95 **NM** value: **Cover or less**

DRACULA VERSUS ZORRO (VOL. 3) — Image

Don Diego, better known as the vigilante Zorro, is on a journey from Spain to France. While securing his ship's passage, he is attracted to the beautiful Carmelita Rodriquez, a woman grief-stricken by the death of her father. There is another passenger, however, who is also drawn to the sad beauty: the mysterious and dangerous Count Dracula. At first, neither Carmelita nor Diego realize the true threat posed by this strange nobleman, and the vulnerable young woman begins to fall under his evil spell. When the vampire's true nature is at last revealed, it may already be too late for even the sword of Zorro to save the girl's soul. For all his skill, Zorro is still only human, and what mere mortal can hope to stand against the centuries-old Lord of Vampires?

1 ❑ Sep 1998 Cover: 2.95 **NM** value: **Cover or less**
A: Tom Yeates **W:** Don McGregor
2 ❑ Oct 1998 Cover: 2.95 **NM** value: **Cover or less**
A: Tom Yeates **W:** Don McGregor

DRACULA: VLAD THE IMPALER — Topps

1 ❑ Cover: 2.95 **NM** value: **Cover or less**
Circ: CapCity orders: **42,500**
I Am Dracula! • trading cards **A:** Estebán Maroto **W:** Roy Thomas
2 ❑ Cover: 2.95 **NM** value: **Cover or less**
Circ: CapCity orders: **31,050**
Dark Legend A-Borning • trading cards **A:** Estebán Maroto **W:** Roy Thomas
3 ❑ Cover: 2.95 **NM** value: **Cover or less**
Circ: CapCity orders: **22,575**
To Rise Again! • trading cards **A:** Estebán Maroto **W:** Roy Thomas

DRACULINA (2ND SERIES) — Draculina

1 ❑ Cover: 2.50 **NM** value: **Cover or less**
Blood Of The Bride ★ Origin of Draculina.

DRACULINA'S COZY COFFIN — Draculina

1 ❑ b&w Cover: 2.50 **NM** value: **Cover or less**
• no indicia
2 ❑ b&w Cover: 2.50 **NM** value: **Cover or less**
• no indicia

DRAFT, THE — Marvel

1 ❑ Jul 1988 Cover: 3.50 **NM** value: **Cover or less**
Circ: CapCity orders: **22,550**
• D.P.7, Nightmask **A:** Herb Trimpe **W:** Fabian Nicieza; Mark Gruenwald

DRAG COMICS (PETE MILLAR'S...) — Sham

1 ❑ Cover: 0.10 **NM** value: **5.00**
A: Pete Millar **W:** Pete Millar
2 ❑ Cover: 0.10 **NM** value: **4.00**
There's one in Every Crowd; The Gawfathers **A:** Pete Millar **W:** Pete Millar
3 ❑ Cover: 0.10 **NM** value: **4.00**
A: Pete Millar **W:** Pete Millar
4 ❑ Cover: 0.10 **NM** value: **4.00**
Aigas; The Mutha's Day Hustle '76; Hy Winder; Those Were **A:** Pete Millar **W:** Pete Millar

DRAGON — Comics Interview

1 ❑ Aug 1987 Cover: 1.75 **NM** value: **Cover or less**
• weekly
2 ❑ Aug 1987 Cover: 1.75 **NM** value: **Cover or less**
• weekly
3 ❑ Aug 1987 Cover: 1.75 **NM** value: **Cover or less**
• weekly
4 ❑ Aug 1987 Cover: 1.75 **NM** value: **Cover or less**
• weekly
Bk 1❑ Cover: 9.95 **NM** value: **Cover or less**

DRAGON (2ND SERIES) — Image

1 ❑ Mar 1996 Cover: 0.99 **NM** value: **2.00**
2 ❑ Apr 1996 Cover: 0.99 **NM** value: **2.00**
3 ❑ May 1996 Cover: 0.99 **NM** value: **2.00**
4 ❑ Jun 1996 Cover: 0.99 **NM** value: **2.00**
5 ❑ Jul 1996 Cover: 0.99 **NM** value: **2.00**
final issue. ★ Appearance of Badrock.

DRAGONBALL — Viz

1 ❑ Mar 1998 Cover: 2.95 **NM** value: **6.00**
Circ: Diamd. preorders: **24,688**
• 'Manga Style ' Edition. Bloomers and the Monkey King **A:** Akira Toriyama **W:** Akira Toriyama
2 ❑ Apr 1998 Cover: 2.95 **NM** value: **4.00**
Circ: Diamd. preorders: **19,393**
• 'Manga Style ' Edition. **A:** Akira Toriyama **W:** Akira Toriyama
3 ❑ May 1998 Cover: 2.95 **NM** value: **4.00**
Circ: Diamd. preorders: **18,141**
• 'Manga Style ' Edition. **A:** Akira Toriyama **W:** Akira Toriyama
4 ❑ Jun 1998 Cover: 2.95 **NM** value: **4.00**
Circ: Diamd. preorders: **15,005**
• 'Manga Style ' Edition. **A:** Akira Toriyama **W:** Akira Toriyama
5 ❑ Jul 1998 Cover: 2.95 **NM** value: **4.00**
Circ: Diamd. preorders: **12,097**
• 'Manga Style ' Edition. **A:** Akira Toriyama **W:** Akira Toriyama
6 ❑ Aug 1998 Cover: 2.95 **NM** value: **4.00**
Circ: Diamd. preorders: **12,563**
• 'Manga Style ' Edition. **A:** Akira Toriyama **W:** Akira Toriyama
7 ❑ Sep 1998 Cover: 2.95 **NM** value: **4.00**
Circ: Diamd. preorders: **12,243**
• 'Manga Style ' Edition. **A:** Akira Toriyama **W:** Akira Toriyama
8 ❑ Oct 1998 Cover: 2.95 **NM** value: **3.00**
Circ: Diamd. preorders: **9,991**
A: Akira Toriyama **W:** Akira Toriyama
9 ❑ Nov 1998 Cover: 2.95 **NM** value: **3.00**
Circ: Diamd. preorders: **9,784**
A: Akira Toriyama **W:** Akira Toriyama
10 ❑ Dec 1998 Cover: 2.95 **NM** value: **3.00**
Circ: Diamd. preorders: **10,243**
A: Akira Toriyama **W:** Akira Toriyama
11 ❑ Jan 1999 Cover: 2.95 **NM** value: **3.00**
Circ: Diamd. preorders: **11,166**
A: Akira Toriyama **W:** Akira Toriyama
12 ❑ Feb 1999 Cover: 2.95 **NM** value: **3.00**
Circ: Diamd. preorders: **10,767**
A: Akira Toriyama **W:** Akira Toriyama

DRAGONBALL PART TWO — Viz

1 ❑ Mar 1999 Cover: 2.95 **NM** value: **4.00**
Circ: Diamd. preorders: **11,894**
2 ❑ Apr 1999 Cover: 2.95 **NM** value: **3.00**
Circ: Diamd. preorders: **12,059**
3 ❑ May 1999 Cover: 2.95 **NM** value: **3.00**
Circ: Diamd. preorders: **12,288**
4 ❑ Jun 1999 Cover: 2.95 **NM** value: **3.00**
Circ: Diamd. preorders: **12,492**
5 ❑ Jul 1999 Cover: 2.95 **NM** value: **3.00**
Circ: Diamd. preorders: **12,865**
6 ❑ Aug 1999 Cover: 2.95 **NM** value: **3.00**
Circ: Diamd. preorders: **12,684**
7 ❑ Sep 1999 Cover: 2.95 **NM** value: **3.00**
Circ: Diamd. preorders: **12,970**
8 ❑ Oct 1999 Cover: 2.95 **NM** value: **3.00**
Circ: Diamd. preorders: **13,133**

DRAGONBALL Z — Viz

1 ❑ Mar 1998 Cover: 2.95 **NM** value: **6.00**
Circ: Diamd. preorders: **25,203** • **CGC:** 1 graded, best 7.5
2 ❑ Apr 1998 Cover: 2.95 **NM** value: **4.00**
Circ: Diamd. preorders: **19,309**
3 ❑ May 1998 Cover: 2.95 **NM** value: **4.00**
Circ: Diamd. preorders: **17,898**
4 ❑ Jun 1998 Cover: 2.95 **NM** value: **4.00**
Circ: Diamd. preorders: **16,550**
5 ❑ Jul 1998 Cover: 2.95 **NM** value: **4.00**
Circ: Diamd. preorders: **13,135**
6 ❑ Aug 1998 Cover: 2.95 **NM** value: **Cover or less**
Circ: Diamd. preorders: **13,516**
7 ❑ Sep 1998 Cover: 2.95 **NM** value: **Cover or less**
Circ: Diamd. preorders: **13,252**
8 ❑ Oct 1998 Cover: 2.95 **NM** value: **Cover or less**
Circ: Diamd. preorders: **10,856**
9 ❑ Nov 1998 Cover: 2.95 **NM** value: **Cover or less**
Circ: Diamd. preorders: **10,633**
10 ❑ **NM** value: **2.95**

DRAGONBALL Z PART 2 — Viz

The alien race, Saiyan, in pursuit of the wish-fullfilling Dragonballs, have arrived on Earth. Goku, who first appeared in Dragonball, has grown to become Earth's mightiest warrior and now he and his allies prepare for a battle which will determine the fate of the cosmos.

Rather than employing lasers or other high-tech weaponry, as would be the case in an American comic, this fight will be a martial arts showdown. As a product of Japanese culture, manga comics' confrontations invariably result in a hands-on denouement.

Akira Toriyama's Japanese manga series is translated for American readers in this series from Viz Comics. Unlike other manga series that are photographically reversed to allow readers in Western countries to read the book in the familiar left-to-right method, this series maintains the Japanese right-to-left direction. Aside from the chance of a logo or letterform appearing as a mirror image, flopping the artwork sometimes revealed flaws in perspective. Maintaining the traditional Japanese layout avoids these concerns.

1 ❑ Dec 1998 Cover: 2.95 **NM** value: **3.50**
Circ: Diamd. preorders: **12,258**
• 'Manga Style ' Edition. Here They Come…in Time to Kill!; Let the Games Begin! **A:** Akira Toriyama **W:** Akira Toriyama
2 ❑ Jan 1999 Cover: 2.95 **NM** value: **3.00**
Circ: Diamd. preorders: **12,463**
• 'Manga Style ' Edition. **A:** Akira Toriyama **W:** Akira Toriyama
3 ❑ Feb 1999 Cover: 2.95 **NM** value: **3.00**
Circ: Diamd. preorders: **12,185**
• 'Manga Style ' Edition. **A:** Akira Toriyama **W:** Akira Toriyama
4 ❑ Mar 1999 Cover: 2.95 **NM** value: **3.00**
Circ: Diamd. preorders: **12,814**
• 'Manga Style ' Edition. **A:** Akira Toriyama **W:** Akira Toriyama
5 ❑ Apr 1999 Cover: 2.95 **NM** value: **3.00**
Circ: Diamd. preorders: **13,601**
• 'Manga Style ' Edition. **A:** Akira Toriyama **W:** Akira Toriyama
6 ❑ May 1999 Cover: 2.95 **NM** value: **Cover or less**
Circ: Diamd. preorders: **14,045**
• 'Manga Style ' Edition. **A:** Akira Toriyama **W:** Akira Toriyama
7 ❑ Jun 1999 Cover: 2.95 **NM** value: **Cover or less**
Circ: Diamd. preorders: **14,167**
• 'Manga Style ' Edition. **A:** Akira Toriyama **W:** Akira Toriyama
8 ❑ Jul 1999 Cover: 2.95 **NM** value: **Cover or less**
Circ: Diamd. preorders: **14,840**
9 ❑ Aug 1999 Cover: 2.95 **NM** value: **Cover or less**
Circ: Diamd. preorders: **14,724**
10 ❑ Sep 1999 Cover: 2.95 **NM** value: **Cover or less**
Circ: Diamd. preorders: **15,194** • **CGC:** 1 graded, best 4.0
11 ❑ Oct 1999 Cover: 2.95 **NM** value: **Cover or less**
Circ: Diamd. preorders: **15,252** • **CGC:** 1 graded, best 5.5

DRAGON, THE: BLOOD & GUTS — Image

1 ❑ Mar 1995 Cover: 2.50 **NM** value: **Cover or less**
Circ: CapCity orders: **19,625**
2 ❑ Apr 1995 Cover: 2.50 **NM** value: **Cover or less**
Circ: CapCity orders: **16,200**
3 ❑ May 1995 Cover: 2.50 **NM** value: **Cover or less**
Circ: CapCity orders: **14,525**
Bk 1❑ Cover: 7.95 **NM** value: **Cover or less**
• Trade Paperback. • collects mini-series

DRAGON CHIANG — Eclipse

1 ❑ Cover: 3.95 **NM** value: **Cover or less**
• nn, b&w **A:** Tim Truman **W:** Tim Truman

DRAGONFIRE: THE CLASSIFIED FILES — Nightwynd

1 ❑ b&w Cover: 2.50 **NM** value: **Cover or less**
2 ❑ b&w Cover: 2.50 **NM** value: **Cover or less**
3 ❑ b&w Cover: 2.50 **NM** value: **Cover or less**
4 ❑ b&w Cover: 2.50 **NM** value: **Cover or less**

DRAGONFIRE: THE EARLY YEARS — Nightwynd

1 ❑ b&w Cover: 2.50 **NM** value: **Cover or less**
A: Dale Keown **W:** Barry Blair
2 ❑ b&w Cover: 2.50 **NM** value: **Cover or less**
A: Dale Keown **W:** Barry Blair
3 ❑ b&w Cover: 2.50 **NM** value: **Cover or less**
4 ❑ b&w Cover: 2.50 **NM** value: **Cover or less**
5 ❑ b&w Cover: 2.50 **NM** value: **Cover or less**
6 ❑ b&w Cover: 2.50 **NM** value: **Cover or less**
7 ❑ b&w Cover: 2.50 **NM** value: **Cover or less**
8 ❑ b&w Cover: 2.50 **NM** value: **Cover or less**

DRAGONFIRE: UFO WARS — Nightwynd

1 ❑ b&w Cover: 2.50 **NM** value: **Cover or less**
2 ❑ b&w Cover: 2.50 **NM** value: **Cover or less**
3 ❑ b&w Cover: 2.50 **NM** value: **Cover or less**

DRAGONFIRE (VOL. 1) — Nightwynd

Combining elements of super-hero, supernatural, science-fiction, and manga-style comics, this black-and-white limited series established a superteam of previous Nightwynd Enterprises creations — Kohl Drake, Maire Siddons, Mark Quay, and Kamakazi — to fight "something evil abroad in the land." A fairly noble mission, to be sure. Although the editorial text assures readers that they can "jump on to our story with no lengthy explanations," little effort is made to actually introduce the characters to the audience. While a first-issue backstory can be cumbersome and awkward, a complete lack of explanation starts things off on uncertain footing and makes luring readers a difficult task. Dragonfire's action sequences are compelling enough, but those who enjoy the characterization that is a staple of most superteam comics may find this series a bit empty.

1 ❑ b&w Cover: 2.50 **NM** value: **Cover or less**
A: Barry Blair **W:** Barry Blair
2 ❑ b&w Cover: 2.50 **NM** value: **Cover or less**
A: Barry Blair **W:** Barry Blair
3 ❑ b&w Cover: 2.50 **NM** value: **Cover or less**
A: Barry Blair **W:** Barry Blair
4 ❑ b&w Cover: 2.50 **NM** value: **Cover or less**
A: Barry Blair **W:** Barry Blair

DRAGONFIRE (VOL. 2) — Nightwynd

1 ❑ b&w Cover: 2.50 **NM** value: **Cover or less**
2 ❑ b&w Cover: 2.50 **NM** value: **Cover or less**
3 ❑ b&w Cover: 2.50 **NM** value: **Cover or less**
4 ❑ b&w Cover: 2.50 **NM** value: **Cover or less**

DRAGONFLIGHT — Eclipse

1 ❑ Feb 1991 Cover: 4.95 **NM** value: **Cover or less**
Circ: CapCity orders: **10,075**
• Anne McCaffrey **A:** Lela Dowling; Cynthia Martin **W:** Anne McCaffrey; Brynne Stephens

Other grades: Multiply prices above by **1.5 for Mint • 2/3 for Very Fine • 1/3 for Fine • 1/5 for Very Good • 1/8 for Good**

2 ❑ 1991 Cover: 4.95 **NM** value: **Cover or less**
Circ: CapCity orders: **7,875**
• Anne McCaffrey **A:** Lela Dowling; Cynthia Martin **W:** Anne McCaffrey; Brynne Stephens

3 ❑ 1991 Cover: 4.95 **NM** value: **Cover or less**
Circ: CapCity orders: **7,475**
• Anne McCaffrey **A:** Lela Dowling; Cynthia Martin **W:** Anne McCaffrey; Brynne Stephens

DRAGON FLUX — Antarctic

2 ❑ Jun 1996, b&w Cover: 2.95 **NM** value: **Cover or less**
3 ❑ Nov 1996, b&w Cover: 2.95 **NM** value: **Cover or less**

DRAGONFLY — AC

1 ❑ Aug 1985 Cover: 1.75 **NM** value: **Cover or less**
Circ: CapCity orders: **2,975**
2 ❑ Cover: 1.75 **NM** value: **Cover or less**
3 ❑ Cover: 1.75 **NM** value: **Cover or less**
Circ: CapCity orders: **2,475**
4 ❑ Cover: 1.75 **NM** value: **Cover or less**
Circ: CapCity orders: **2,575**
5 ❑ Cover: 1.75 **NM** value: **Cover or less**
Circ: CapCity orders: **2,775**
6 ❑ Feb 1987 Cover: 1.75 **NM** value: **Cover or less**
Circ: CapCity orders: **2,275**
7 ❑ Jul 1987 Cover: 1.75 **NM** value: **Cover or less**
Circ: CapCity orders: **2,200**
8 ❑ Cover: 1.95 **NM** value: **Cover or less**
Circ: CapCity orders: **1,850**
Bk 1❑ Cover: 9.95 **NM** value: **Cover or less**
• Cycle of Fire;collects Dragonfly #1 and 2

DRAGONFORCE — Aircel

1 ❑ ca. 1988, b&w Cover: 1.95 **NM** value: **2.00**
Circ: CapCity orders: **3,775**
A: Dale Keown ★ Origin of Dragonforce, Alloy. ★ 1st Appearance of Kohl, Maire, Dragonforce, Alloy, Kamikaze, Sental.
2 ❑ ca. 1988, b&w Cover: 1.95 **NM** value: **2.00**
Circ: CapCity orders: **2,625**
A: Dale Keown
3 ❑ ca. 1988, b&w Cover: 1.95 **NM** value: **2.00**
Circ: CapCity orders: **2,675**
A: Dale Keown
4 ❑ ca. 1988, b&w Cover: 1.95 **NM** value: **2.00**
Circ: CapCity orders: **2,800**
A: Dale Keown
5 ❑ ca. 1988, b&w Cover: 1.95 **NM** value: **2.00**
Circ: CapCity orders: **2,875**
A: Dale Keown
6 ❑ ca. 1988, b&w Cover: 1.95 **NM** value: **2.00**
Circ: CapCity orders: **2,775**
A: Dale Keown
7 ❑ ca. 1989, b&w Cover: 1.95 **NM** value: **2.00**
Circ: CapCity orders: **2,600**
A: Dale Keown
8 ❑ ca. 1989, b&w Cover: 1.95 **NM** value: **2.00**
A: Dale Keown
9 ❑ ca. 1989, b&w Cover: 1.95 **NM** value: **2.00**
A: Dale Keown
10 ❑ ca. 1989, b&w Cover: 1.95 **NM** value: **2.00**
A: Dale Keown
11 ❑ ca. 1989, b&w Cover: 1.95 **NM** value: **2.00**
A: Dale Keown
12 ❑ ca. 1989, b&w Cover: 1.95 **NM** value: **2.00**
A: Dale Keown
13 ❑ ca. 1989, b&w Cover: 1.95 **NM** value: **2.00**

DRAGONFORCE CHRONICLES — Aircel

1 ❑ ca. 1989, b&w Cover: 2.95 **NM** value: **Cover or less**
📖 Change **A:** Dale Keown **W:** Barry Blair
2 ❑ ca. 1989, b&w Cover: 2.95 **NM** value: **Cover or less**
3 ❑ ca. 1989, b&w Cover: 2.95 **NM** value: **Cover or less**
4 ❑ ca. 1989, b&w Cover: 2.95 **NM** value: **Cover or less**
5 ❑ ca. 1989, b&w Cover: 2.95 **NM** value: **Cover or less**
A: Dale Keown **W:** Dale Keown

DRAGONHEART — Topps

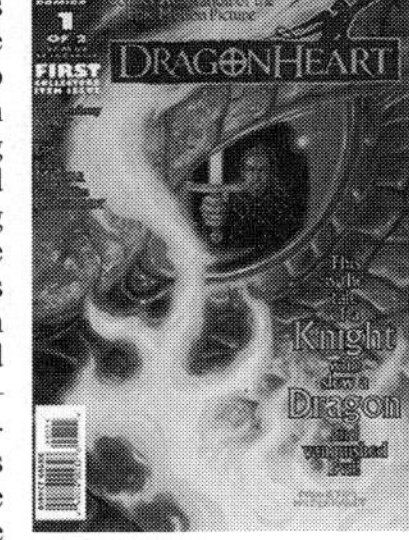

Camelot has fallen into legend and the Ancient Code of Honor has faded into obscurity. Only one knight, Sir Bowen, strives to keep "The Code" remembered. Though he hopes to pass it onto the young Prince Einon, the newly anointed king is only interested in expanding his kingdom. As Einon grows more concerned with power and less guided by "The Code," Sir Bowen comes to believe that an ancient and possibly evil force infects Einon — that of a Dragon's heart. Years prior, one of the Earth's last Dragons offered a part of his heart to save Einon's life in an attempt to make peace with those who had hunted his brethren into extinction. But is it the Dragon's heart that changed Einon? Or was it simply human greed and lust for power? Bowen is determined to discover the truth. But in doing so, help may come from an unlikely, fire-breathing source. This two-issue mini-series is the official adaptation of the motion picture starring Sean Connery and Dennis Quaid.

1 ❑ May 1996 Cover: 2.95 **NM** value: **Cover or less**
A: Ron Lim **C:** Greg Hildebrandt; Tim Hildebrandt **W:** David Anthony Kraft
2 ❑ Jun 1996 Cover: 4.95 **NM** value: **Cover or less**
A: Ron Lim **C:** Greg Hildebrandt; Tim Hildebrandt **W:** David Anthony Kraft

DRAGON KNIGHTS — Slave Labor

1 ❑ Aug 1998, b&w Cover: 1.75 **NM** value: **Cover or less**
A: Paul H. Way **W:** Jeremy Tinker
2 ❑ Cover: 1.75 **NM** value: **Cover or less**
3 ❑ Cover: 1.75 **NM** value: **Cover or less**

DRAGON LADY — Dragon Lady Press

1 ❑ Cover: 6.95 **NM** value: **Cover or less**
• King of Mounted
2 ❑ Cover: 6.95 **NM** value: **Cover or less**
• Red Ryder
3 ❑ Cover: 5.95 **NM** value: **Cover or less**
• Captain Easy
4 ❑ Cover: 5.95 **NM** value: **Cover or less**
• Secret Agent X-9 **A:** Al Williamson
5 ❑ Cover: 5.95 **NM** value: **Cover or less**
• Brick Bradford
6 ❑ Cover: 5.95 **NM** value: **Cover or less**
• Secret Agent X-9 **C:** Alex Toth
7 ❑ Cover: 5.95 **NM** value: **Cover or less**
• Captain Easy
8 ❑ Cover: 5.95 **NM** value: **Cover or less**
• Terry **C:** Alex Toth

DRAGONLANCE — DC

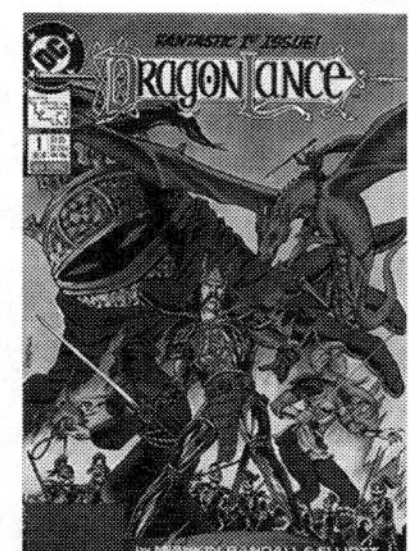

The Dragonlance world was developed by TSR for its role-playing game, Dungeons & Dragons, in the 1980s to provide gamers with an element they'd never really had: an official storyline with characters from the game manufacturer. It was very popular, leading to a revival not simply in the game, but in instilling an emphasis on storytelling in other role-playing games.

Dragonlance prose novels were very popular, and it's not surprising that comic books came along as well. The DC series, running side-by-side with its Advanced Dungeons & Dragons series, follows the surviving Solamnic Knights in their struggle against the Lord Soth and his Deathknights.

While comics about gamers would grow in popularity in the late 1990s, comics about gaming worlds tended to struggle, and DC ended this series after three years. — JJM

1 ❑ Dec 1988 Cover: 1.25 **NM** value: **2.00**
Circ: CapCity orders: **18,150**
📖 Fire & Light **A:** Ron Randall **W:** Dan Mishkin
2 ❑ Win 1988 Cover: 1.25 **NM** value: **1.50**
Circ: CapCity orders: **13,500**
3 ❑ Hol 1988 Cover: 1.25 **NM** value: **Cover or less**
Circ: CapCity orders: **12,450**
4 ❑ Jan 1989 Cover: 1.25 **NM** value: **Cover or less**
Circ: CapCity orders: **13,300**
5 ❑ Feb 1989 Cover: 1.25 **NM** value: **Cover or less**
Circ: CapCity orders: **12,900**
6 ❑ Mar 1989 Cover: 1.50 **NM** value: **Cover or less**
Circ: CapCity orders: **13,400**
7 ❑ Apr 1989 Cover: 1.50 **NM** value: **Cover or less**
Circ: CapCity orders: **13,900**
8 ❑ Jun 1989 Cover: 1.50 **NM** value: **Cover or less**
Circ: CapCity orders: **14,300**
9 ❑ Jul 1989 Cover: 1.50 **NM** value: **Cover or less**
Circ: CapCity orders: **14,350**
10 ❑ Aug 1989 Cover: 1.50 **NM** value: **Cover or less**
Circ: CapCity orders: **13,650**
11 ❑ Sep 1989 Cover: 1.50 **NM** value: **Cover or less**
Circ: CapCity orders: **12,450**
12 ❑ Oct 1989 Cover: 1.50 **NM** value: **Cover or less**
Circ: CapCity orders: **12,000**
13 ❑ Nov 1989 Cover: 1.50 **NM** value: **Cover or less**
Circ: CapCity orders: **11,300**
14 ❑ Dec 1989 Cover: 1.50 **NM** value: **Cover or less**
Circ: CapCity orders: **10,450**
15 ❑ Jan 1990 Cover: 1.50 **NM** value: **Cover or less**
Circ: CapCity orders: **10,650**
16 ❑ Feb 1990 Cover: 1.50 **NM** value: **Cover or less**
Circ: CapCity orders: **10,950**
17 ❑ Mar 1990 Cover: 1.50 **NM** value: **Cover or less**
Circ: CapCity orders: **10,750**
18 ❑ Apr 1990 Cover: 1.50 **NM** value: **Cover or less**
Circ: CapCity orders: **10,300**
19 ❑ May 1990 Cover: 1.50 **NM** value: **Cover or less**
Circ: CapCity orders: **10,550**
20 ❑ Jun 1990 Cover: 1.50 **NM** value: **Cover or less**
Circ: CapCity orders: **10,400**
21 ❑ Jul 1990 Cover: 1.50 **NM** value: **Cover or less**
Circ: CapCity orders: **10,400**
22 ❑ Aug 1990 Cover: 1.50 **NM** value: **Cover or less**
Circ: CapCity orders: **10,150**
23 ❑ Oct 1990 Cover: 1.50 **NM** value: **Cover or less**
Circ: CapCity orders: **10,150**
24 ❑ Nov 1990 Cover: 1.50 **NM** value: **1.75**
Circ: CapCity orders: **9,900**
25 ❑ Dec 1990 Cover: 1.75 **NM** value: **Cover or less**
Circ: CapCity orders: **10,050**
26 ❑ Jan 1991 Cover: 1.75 **NM** value: **Cover or less**
Circ: CapCity orders: **9,850**
27 ❑ Feb 1991 Cover: 1.75 **NM** value: **Cover or less**
Circ: CapCity orders: **9,800**
28 ❑ Mar 1991 Cover: 1.75 **NM** value: **Cover or less**
Circ: CapCity orders: **9,300**
29 ❑ Apr 1991 Cover: 1.75 **NM** value: **Cover or less**
Circ: CapCity orders: **8,800**
30 ❑ May 1991 Cover: 1.75 **NM** value: **Cover or less**
Circ: CapCity orders: **8,800**
31 ❑ Jun 1991 Cover: 1.75 **NM** value: **Cover or less**
Circ: CapCity orders: **8,700**
32 ❑ Jul 1991 Cover: 1.75 **NM** value: **Cover or less**
Circ: CapCity orders: **8,650**
33 ❑ Aug 1991 Cover: 1.75 **NM** value: **Cover or less**
Circ: CapCity orders: **8,850**
34 ❑ Sep 1991 Cover: 1.75 **NM** value: **Cover or less**
Circ: CapCity orders: **8,900**
final issue.
Anl 1❑Jan 1990 Cover: 2.95 **NM** value: **Cover or less**
Circ: CapCity orders: **9,900**

DRAGONLANCE COMIC BOOK — TSR

1 ❑ **NM** value: **1.00**
A: Artie Swekel **W:** Tom and Mary Bierbaum

DRAGONLANCE SAGA — TSR

1 ❑ Cover: 9.95 **NM** value: **Cover or less**
Circ: CapCity orders: **2,300**
A: Tom Yeates
2 ❑ Cover: 9.95 **NM** value: **Cover or less**
Circ: CapCity orders: **1,925**
A: Tom Yeates
3 ❑ Cover: 9.95 **NM** value: **Cover or less**
Circ: CapCity orders: **1,550**
A: Tom Yeates
4 ❑ Cover: 9.95 **NM** value: **Cover or less**
Circ: CapCity orders: **6,050**
5 ❑ Cover: 9.95 **NM** value: **Cover or less**
Circ: CapCity orders: **2,250**

DRAGON LINES — Marvel / Epic

1 ❑ May 1993 Cover: 2.50 **NM** value: **Cover or less**
Circ: CapCity orders: **37,500**
Embossed cover. 📖 The Year Of The Monkey **A:** Ron Lim **W:** Peter Quinones
2 ❑ Jun 1993 Cover: 1.95 **NM** value: **Cover or less**
Circ: CapCity orders: **14,500**
📖 Snapping The Dragon's Spine **A:** Ron Lim **W:** Peter Quinones
3 ❑ Jul 1993 Cover: 1.95 **NM** value: **Cover or less**
Circ: CapCity orders: **10,700**
A: Ron Lim **W:** Peter Quinones
4 ❑ Aug 1993 Cover: 1.95 **NM** value: **Cover or less**
Circ: CapCity orders: **9,800**
A: Ron Lim **W:** Peter Quinones

DRAGON LINES: WAY OF THE WARRIOR — Marvel / Epic

1 ❑ Nov 1993 Cover: 2.25 **NM** value: **Cover or less**
Circ: CapCity orders: **6,200**
2 ❑ Jan 1994 Cover: 2.25 **NM** value: **Cover or less**
Circ: CapCity orders: **4,600**

DRAGON OF THE VALKYR — Rak

1 ❑ b&w Cover: 1.75 **NM** value: **Cover or less**
2 ❑ Cover: 1.75 **NM** value: **Cover or less**
3 ❑ Cover: 1.75 **NM** value: **Cover or less**

DRAGON QUEST — Silverwolf

1 ❑ b&w **NM** value: **2.00**
A: Tim Vigil
2 ❑ **NM** value: **2.00**
A: Tim Vigil

DRAGONRING — Aircel

1 ❑ 1986b&w Cover: 2.00 **NM** value: **Cover or less**
📖 Demon Hunter **A:** Guang Yap **W:** Guang Yap
2 ❑ 1986b&w Cover: 2.00 **NM** value: **Cover or less**
A: Guang Yap **W:** Guang Yap
3 ❑ 1986b&w Cover: 2.00 **NM** value: **Cover or less**
A: Guang Yap **W:** Guang Yap
4 ❑ 1986b&w Cover: 2.00 **NM** value: **Cover or less**
📖 The King of Rock and Roll **A:** Guang Yap; Barry Blair; Dave Cooper **W:** Guang Yap; Dave Cooper
5 ❑ 1986b&w Cover: 2.00 **NM** value: **Cover or less**
A: Guang Yap **W:** Guang Yap
6 ❑ 1986b&w Cover: 2.00 **NM** value: **Cover or less**
📖 In the Box **A:** Guang Yap; Dave Cooper **W:** Guang Yap. Gordon Derry

DRAGONRING (VOL. 2) — Aircel

1 ❑ 1986 Cover: 2.00 **NM** value: **Cover or less**
Circ: CapCity orders: **10,000**
2 ❑ 1987 Cover: 2.00 **NM** value: **Cover or less**
Circ: CapCity orders: **5,375**
3 ❑ 1987 Cover: 2.00 **NM** value: **Cover or less**
Circ: CapCity orders: **4,800**
📖 Homecoming… **A:** Guang Yap **W:** Guang Yap; Don Lanouette
4 ❑ 1987 Cover: 2.00 **NM** value: **Cover or less**
Circ: CapCity orders: **4,250**
📖 Culmination **A:** Guang Yap **W:** Guang Yap; Don Lanouette
5 ❑ 1987 Cover: 2.00 **NM** value: **Cover or less**
Circ: CapCity orders: **4,000**
📖 Tiger's Teeth **A:** Guang Yap **W:** Guang Yap; Don Lanouette
6 ❑ 1987 Cover: 2.00 **NM** value: **Cover or less**
Circ: CapCity orders: **3,825**
A: Barry Blair; Patrick McEown **W:** Guang Yap; Barry Blair; Patrick McEown
7 ❑ 1987 Cover: 2.00 **NM** value: **Cover or less**
Circ: CapCity orders: **3,825**
A: Barry Blair; Patrick McEown **W:** Guang Yap; Barry Blair; Patrick McEown
8 ❑ 1987 Cover: 2.00 **NM** value: **Cover or less**

CGC-graded: Multiply prices above by **33 for 9.9 M • 16 for 9.8 NM/M • 7 for 9.6 NM+ • 5 for 9.4 NM • 2.5 for 9.2 NM- • 1.5 for 9.0 VF/NM**

A: Barry Blair; Patrick McEown W: Guang Yap; Barry Blair; Patrick McEown
9 ❑ 1987 Cover: 2.00 NM value: Cover or less
Circ: CapCity orders: 3,400
Edge of the Pit A: Dale Keown W: Barry Blair
10 ❑ 1987 Cover: 2.00 NM value: Cover or less
Circ: CapCity orders: 3,400
A: Dale Keown W: Barry Blair
11 ❑ 1987 Cover: 2.00 NM value: Cover or less
Circ: CapCity orders: 2,975
A: Dale Keown W: Barry Blair
12 ❑ 1987 Cover: 2.00 NM value: Cover or less
Circ: CapCity orders: 2,950
A: Dale Keown W: Barry Blair
13 ❑ 1987 Cover: 2.00 NM value: Cover or less
Circ: CapCity orders: 2,725
The Gathering Storm A: Barry Blair; Dale Keown W: Barry Blair
14 ❑ 1988 Cover: 2.00 NM value: Cover or less
Circ: CapCity orders: 2,450
Tiger's Tale A: Dale Keown W: Dale Keown
15 ❑ 1988 Cover: 2.00 NM value: Cover or less
Circ: CapCity orders: 2,200
A: Dale Keown

DRAGONROK SAGA, THE — Hanthercraft

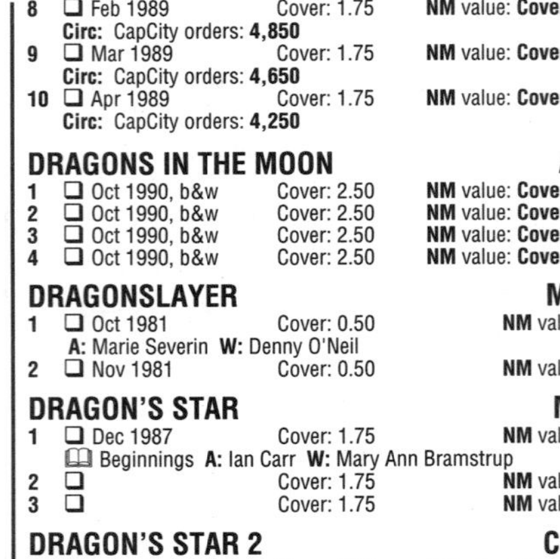

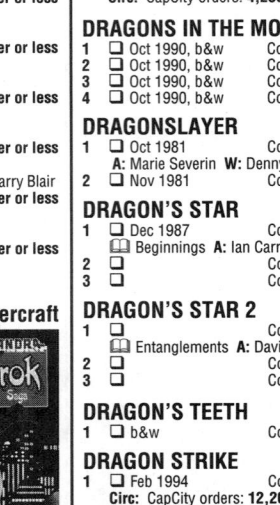

The Dragonrok Saga is a science-fiction comic about an alien female named Tremaine Chandler, who resides on Earth, posing as an incredibly wealthy and desirable human female. Curious about Chandler, a reporter named Trace Stanton digs around and tries to find the real story about the reclusive woman. He eventually discovers not only her secret identity, but that her race is involved in an interstellar war. Even when briefed by one of Tremaine's crew, Stanton still has a hard time trying to believe what he is hearing.

The Dragonrok Saga was created, written, and illustrated by Joe Hanther, generally known only by his last name. The Mississippi-based creator has been active in comics for decades, known also for his work on the fantasy series Tandra.

1 ❑ Cover: 2.50 NM value: Cover or less
2 ❑ Cover: 2.50 NM value: Cover or less
3 ❑ Cover: 2.50 NM value: Cover or less
4 ❑ Cover: 2.50 NM value: Cover or less
A: Tremaine Hanther W: Tremaine Hanther
5 ❑ Cover: 2.50 NM value: Cover or less
6 ❑ Cover: 2.50 NM value: Cover or less
7 ❑ Cover: 2.50 NM value: Cover or less
8 ❑ Cover: 2.50 NM value: Cover or less
9 ❑ Cover: 2.50 NM value: Cover or less
10 ❑ Cover: 2.50 NM value: Cover or less

DRAGON'S BANE — Hall of Heroes

1 ❑ Cover: 2.50 NM value: Cover or less
Rebirth A: Sean Murray W: Harry Bauer
Ash 1❑ Cover: 4.95 NM value: Cover or less
• Chicago Comic Con Ashcan limited to 100 copies A: Sean Murray W: Harry Bauer

DRAGON'S CLAWS — Marvel

Six thousand years in the future, the world is nearing destruction. The Earth has moved closer to the sun, causing the seas to dry up and threatening life everywhere. Unable to solve the problems, the World Development Council came up with a brilliant distraction: a contest known simply as "the Game."

Dragon's Claws — Mercy, Digit, Steel, Scavenger, and their leader Dragon — were the premier players of the Game. But when the Game turned deadly, the team dropped out.

Inevitably, the growing crisis draws the team back together. Only this time, they're playing a game of their own!

In addition to the non-stop action of the Dragon's Claws, this title is notable as the birthplace of the cyborg Death's Head (later Death's Head II).

1 ❑ Jul 1988 Cover: 1.25 NM value: 1.50
Circ: CapCity orders: 15,500
The Game! A: Geoff Senior W: Simon Furman ★ 1st Appearance of Dragon's Claws.
2 ❑ Aug 1988 Cover: 1.50 NM value: Cover or less
Circ: CapCity orders: 10,950
A: Geoff Senior W: Simon Furman
3 ❑ Sep 1988 Cover: 1.50 NM value: Cover or less
Circ: CapCity orders: 9,400
Heroes' Welcome A: Geoff Senior W: Simon Furman
4 ❑ Oct 1988 Cover: 1.50 NM value: Cover or less
Circ: CapCity orders: 7,150
5 ❑ Nov 1988 Cover: 1.75 NM value: 2.00
Circ: CapCity orders: 5,950
★ 1st Appearance of Death's Head I.
6 ❑ Dec 1988 Cover: 1.75 NM value: Cover or less
Circ: CapCity orders: 5,850
7 ❑ Jan 1989 Cover: 1.75 NM value: Cover or less
Circ: CapCity orders: 5,400
8 ❑ Feb 1989 Cover: 1.75 NM value: Cover or less
Circ: CapCity orders: 4,850
9 ❑ Mar 1989 Cover: 1.75 NM value: Cover or less
Circ: CapCity orders: 4,650
10 ❑ Apr 1989 Cover: 1.75 NM value: Cover or less
Circ: CapCity orders: 4,250

DRAGONS IN THE MOON — Aircel

1 ❑ Oct 1990, b&w Cover: 2.50 NM value: Cover or less
2 ❑ Oct 1990, b&w Cover: 2.50 NM value: Cover or less
3 ❑ Oct 1990, b&w Cover: 2.50 NM value: Cover or less
4 ❑ Oct 1990, b&w Cover: 2.50 NM value: Cover or less

DRAGONSLAYER — Marvel

1 ❑ Oct 1981 Cover: 0.50 NM value: 1.50
A: Marie Severin W: Denny O'Neil
2 ❑ Nov 1981 Cover: 0.50 NM value: 1.50

DRAGON'S STAR — Matrix

1 ❑ Dec 1987 Cover: 1.75 NM value: 2.00
Beginnings A: Ian Carr W: Mary Ann Bramstrup
2 ❑ Cover: 1.75 NM value: 2.00
3 ❑ Cover: 1.75 NM value: 2.00

DRAGON'S STAR 2 — Caliber

1 ❑ Cover: 2.95 NM value: Cover or less
Entanglements A: David Cullen W: Mary Ann Bramstrup
2 ❑ Cover: 2.95 NM value: Cover or less
3 ❑ Cover: 2.95 NM value: Cover or less

DRAGON'S TEETH — Dragon's Teeth

1 ❑ b&w Cover: 2.95 NM value: Cover or less

DRAGON STRIKE — Marvel

1 ❑ Feb 1994 Cover: 1.25 NM value: 1.50
Circ: CapCity orders: 12,200
Before The Strike! A: Mike Harris W: Jeff Grubb

DRAGONSTRIKE PRIME — Illusion Studios

2 ❑ Dec 1996, b&w Cover: 1.95 NM value: Cover or less

DRAGON WARS, THE — Ironcat

1 ❑ Apr 1998 Cover: 2.95 NM value: Cover or less
2 ❑ May 1998 Cover: 2.95 NM value: Cover or less
Circ: Diamd. preorders: 3,392
3 ❑ Jun 1998 Cover: 2.95 NM value: Cover or less
Circ: Diamd. preorders: 3,128
4 ❑ Jul 1998 Cover: 2.95 NM value: Cover or less
Circ: Diamd. preorders: 2,999
5 ❑ Aug 1998 Cover: 2.95 NM value: Cover or less
Circ: Diamd. preorders: 2,722
6 ❑ Sep 1998 Cover: 2.95 NM value: Cover or less
Circ: Diamd. preorders: 2,551

DRAKKON WARS, THE — Realm

0 ❑ Jul 1997 Cover: 2.99 NM value: Cover or less
• Battlestar Galactica story written by Richard Hatch A: Chris Scalf W: Richard Hatch

DRAKUUN — Dark Horse / Manga

The king of Ledomiam and Princess Rosalia have been captured by the emperor of Romunilia, and Princess Karula goes on a quest to rescue them. Along the way, she is assisted and has romantic entanglements with Dard, the commander of the Royal Border Guard, and Arl, a retainer.

Written and drawn by Johji Manabe (Outlanders), this Dark Horse series juxtaposes heavy action sequences with stylish humor, while playing loose with fantasy and science fiction conventions.

At press time, two collections of the regular Drakuun series had been released.

1 ❑ Feb 1997 Cover: 2.95 NM value: Cover or less
Circ: Diamd. preorders: 13,549
Rise of the Dragon Princess, Part 1 A: Johji Manabe W: Johji Manabe
2 ❑ Mar 1997 Cover: 2.95 NM value: Cover or less
Circ: Diamd. preorders: 10,547
Rise of the Dragon Princess, Part 2 A: Johji Manabe W: Johji Manabe
3 ❑ Apr 1997 Cover: 2.95 NM value: Cover or less
Circ: Diamd. preorders: 10,281
Rise of the Dragon Princess, Part 3 A: Johji Manabe W: Johji Manabe
4 ❑ May 1997 Cover: 2.95 NM value: Cover or less
Circ: Diamd. preorders: 9,463
Rise of the Dragon Princess, Part 4 A: Johji Manabe W: Johji Manabe
5 ❑ Jun 1997 Cover: 2.95 NM value: Cover or less
Circ: Diamd. preorders: 9,372
Rise of the Dragon Princess, Part 5 A: Johji Manabe W: Johji Manabe
6 ❑ Jul 1997 Cover: 2.95 NM value: Cover or less
Circ: Diamd. preorders: 8,926
Rise of the Dragon Princess, Part 6 A: Johji Manabe W: Johji Manabe
7 ❑ Aug 1997 Cover: 2.95 NM value: Cover or less
Circ: Diamd. preorders: 9,742
The Revenge of Gustav, Part 1 A: Johji Manabe W: Johji Manabe
8 ❑ Sep 1997 Cover: 2.95 NM value: Cover or less
Circ: Diamd. preorders: 9,060
The Revenge of Gustav, Part 2 A: Johji Manabe W: Johji Manabe
9 ❑ Oct 1997 Cover: 2.95 NM value: Cover or less
Circ: Diamd. preorders: 8,778
The Revenge of Gustav, Part 3 A: Johji Manabe W: Johji Manabe
10 ❑ Nov 1997 Cover: 2.95 NM value: Cover or less
Circ: Diamd. preorders: 8,552
The Revenge of Gustav, Part 4 A: Johji Manabe W: Johji Manabe
11 ❑ Dec 1997 Cover: 2.95 NM value: Cover or less
Circ: Diamd. preorders: 8,401
The Revenge of Gustav, Part 5 A: Johji Manabe W: Johji Manabe
12 ❑ Jan 1998 Cover: 2.95 NM value: Cover or less
Circ: Diamd. preorders: 7,971
The Revenge of Gustav, Part 6 A: Johji Manabe W: Johji Manabe
13 ❑ Feb 1998 Cover: 2.95 NM value: Cover or less
Circ: Diamd. preorders: 8,278
Shadow of the Warlock, Part 1 A: Johji Manabe W: Johji Manabe
14 ❑ Mar 1998 Cover: 2.95 NM value: Cover or less
Circ: Diamd. preorders: 7,678
Shadow of the Warlock, Part 2 A: Johji Manabe W: Johji Manabe
15 ❑ Apr 1998 Cover: 2.95 NM value: Cover or less
Circ: Diamd. preorders: 7,464
Shadow of the Warlock, Part 3 A: Johji Manabe W: Johji Manabe
16 ❑ May 1998 Cover: 2.95 NM value: Cover or less
Circ: Diamd. preorders: 9,463
Shadow of the Warlock, Part 4 A: Johji Manabe W: Johji Manabe
17 ❑ Jun 1998 Cover: 2.95 NM value: Cover or less
Circ: Diamd. preorders: 7,287
Shadow of the Warlock, Part 5 A: Johji Manabe W: Johji Manabe
18 ❑ Jul 1998 Cover: 2.95 NM value: Cover or less
Circ: Diamd. preorders: 6,941
Shadow of the Warlock, Part 6 A: Johji Manabe W: Johji Manabe
19 ❑ Oct 1998 Cover: 2.95 NM value: Cover or less
Circ: Diamd. preorders: 7,844
The Hidden War, Part 1 A: Johji Manabe W: Johji Manabe
20 ❑ Nov 1998 Cover: 2.95 NM value: Cover or less
Circ: Diamd. preorders: 6,915
The Hidden War, Part 2 A: Johji Manabe W: Johji Manabe
21 ❑ Dec 1998 Cover: 2.95 NM value: Cover or less
Circ: Diamd. preorders: 6,652
The Hidden War, Part 3
22 ❑ Jan 1999 Cover: 2.95 NM value: Cover or less
Circ: Diamd. preorders: 6,673
The Hidden War, Part 4
23 ❑ Feb 1999 Cover: 2.95 NM value: Cover or less
Circ: Diamd. preorders: 6,321
The Hidden War, Part 5
24 ❑ Mar 1999 Cover: 2.95 NM value: Cover or less
Circ: Diamd. preorders: 6,357
The Hidden War, Part 6
Bk 1❑ Apr 1998 Cover: 12.95 NM value: Cover or less
Rise of the Dragon Princess • Rise of the Dragon Princess;Collects Drakuun #1-6 A: Johji Manabe W: Johji Manabe
Bk 2❑ May 1999 Cover: 14.95 NM value: Cover or less
• The Revenge of Gustav;collects issues #7-12

DRAMA — Sirius Entertainment

1 ❑ Jun 1994 Cover: 2.95 NM value: 8.00
Circ: CapCity orders: 14,500 • CGC: 20 graded, best 9.8
No issue number. One-shot. The Fall of the Goddess; Psychobabble; Angry Christ A: Joseph Michael Linsner W: Joseph Michael Linsner
1/LE❑ Cover: 15.00 NM value: 20.00
• limited to 1400 copies

DRAWN & QUARTERLY — Drawn & Quarterly

1 ❑ b&w NM value: 3.00
2 ❑ NM value: 3.00
3 ❑ NM value: 3.00
4 ❑ NM value: 3.00
5 ❑ NM value: 3.00
6 ❑ NM value: 3.00
7 ❑ NM value: 3.00
8 ❑ Apr 1992, b&w Cover: 3.75 NM value: Cover or less

DREADLANDS — Marvel / Epic

1 ❑ ca. 1992 Cover: 3.95 NM value: Cover or less
Circ: CapCity orders: 6,400
2 ❑ ca. 1992 Cover: 3.95 NM value: Cover or less
Circ: CapCity orders: 4,050
3 ❑ ca. 1992 Cover: 3.95 NM value: Cover or less
Circ: CapCity orders: 3,250
4 ❑ ca. 1992 Cover: 3.95 NM value: Cover or less
Circ: CapCity orders: 2,900
Winter and Spring

DREAD OF NIGHT — Hamilton

1 ❑ b&w Cover: 3.95 NM value: Cover or less
2 ❑ b&w Cover: 3.95 NM value: Cover or less

DREADSTAR — Marvel / Epic

The first — and, most would agree, the best — series to come from Marvel's Epic line, Dreadstar follows Vanth Dreadstar as he leads an interstellar rebellion against the Instrumentality, a powerful religious order in service of the Twelve Gods.

First appearing in Epic Magazine, Jim Starlin's Dreadstar is joined by Syzygy Darklock (from the Eclipse graphic album "The Price"), Oedi the catman, Willow the psychic, and others as he works to stay one step ahead of his enemies. It's some of the best original space fantasy work to come from comics.

Other grades: Multiply prices above by **1.5 for Mint • 2/3 for Very Fine • 1/3 for Fine • 1/5 for Very Good • 1/8 for Good**

Starlin moved Dreadstar from Epic to First right at the culmination of the Instrumentality War, and he left the series at #40. Peter David took over the writing reins until the series' end. — JJM

1 ❑ Nov 1982 Cover: 1.50 **NM** value: **2.50**
📖 The Quest • Story continued from Epic Illustrated #15 **A:** Jim Starlin **W:** Jim Starlin
2 ❑ Jan 1983 Cover: 1.50 **NM** value: **2.00**
• Willow ★ Origin of Willow.
3 ❑ Mar 1983 Cover: 1.50 **NM** value: **2.00**
• Lord Papal
4 ❑ May 1983 Cover: 1.50 **NM** value: **2.00**
5 ❑ Jul 1983 Cover: 1.50 **NM** value: **2.00**
6 ❑ Sep 1983 Cover: 1.50 **NM** value: **1.75**
7 ❑ Nov 1983 Cover: 1.50 **NM** value: **1.75**
8 ❑ Jan 1984 Cover: 1.50 **NM** value: **1.75**
9 ❑ Mar 1984 Cover: 1.50 **NM** value: **1.75**
10 ❑ Apr 1984 Cover: 1.50 **NM** value: **1.75**
11 ❑ Jun 1984 Cover: 1.50 **NM** value: **1.75**
12 ❑ Jul 1984 Cover: 1.50 **NM** value: **1.75**
• New costume
13 ❑ Aug 1984 Cover: 1.50 **NM** value: **1.75**
14 ❑ Oct 1984 Cover: 1.50 **NM** value: **1.75**
• Fights Lord Papal
15 ❑ Nov 1984 Cover: 1.50 **NM** value: **1.75**
16 ❑ Dec 1984 Cover: 1.50 **NM** value: **Cover or less**
17 ❑ Feb 1985 Cover: 1.50 **NM** value: **Cover or less**
18 ❑ Apr 1985 Cover: 1.50 **NM** value: **Cover or less**
Circ: CapCity orders: **12,050**
19 ❑ Jun 1985 Cover: 1.50 **NM** value: **Cover or less**
Circ: CapCity orders: **12,100**
20 ❑ Aug 1985 Cover: 1.50 **NM** value: **Cover or less**
Circ: CapCity orders: **10,200**
21 ❑ Oct 1985 Cover: 1.50 **NM** value: **Cover or less**
Circ: CapCity orders: **11,100**
22 ❑ Dec 1985 Cover: 1.50 **NM** value: **Cover or less**
Circ: CapCity orders: **10,600**
23 ❑ Feb 1986 Cover: 1.50 **NM** value: **Cover or less**
Circ: CapCity orders: **10,250**
24 ❑ Apr 1986 Cover: 1.50 **NM** value: **Cover or less**
Circ: CapCity orders: **10,250**
25 ❑ Jun 1986 Cover: 1.50 **NM** value: **Cover or less**
Circ: CapCity orders: **10,150**
26 ❑ Aug 1986 Cover: 1.50 **NM** value: **Cover or less**
Circ: CapCity orders: **10,750**

DREADSTAR — First

27❑Nov 1986Cover: 1.75 **NM** value: **Cover or less**
Circ: CapCity orders: **11,050**
• First Comics begins publishing
28 ❑ Jan 1987 Cover: 1.75 **NM** value: **Cover or less**
Circ: CapCity orders: **9,875**
29 ❑ Mar 1987 Cover: 1.75 **NM** value: **Cover or less**
Circ: CapCity orders: **9,175**
30 ❑ May 1987 Cover: 1.75 **NM** value: **Cover or less**
Circ: CapCity orders: **9,750**
31 ❑ Jul 1987 Cover: 1.75 **NM** value: **Cover or less**
Circ: CapCity orders: **9,875**
32 ❑ Sep 1987 Cover: 1.75 **NM** value: **Cover or less**
Circ: CapCity orders: **10,675**
33 ❑ Nov 1987 Cover: 1.75 **NM** value: **Cover or less**
Circ: CapCity orders: **10,325**
34 ❑ Jan 1988 Cover: 1.75 **NM** value: **Cover or less**
Circ: CapCity orders: **9,650**
35 ❑ Mar 1988 Cover: 1.75 **NM** value: **Cover or less**
Circ: CapCity orders: **9,400**
36 ❑ May 1988 Cover: 1.75 **NM** value: **Cover or less**
Circ: CapCity orders: **8,700**
37 ❑ Jul 1988 Cover: 1.75 **NM** value: **Cover or less**
Circ: CapCity orders: **8,000**
38 ❑ Sep 1988 Cover: 1.75 **NM** value: **Cover or less**
Circ: CapCity orders: **7,350**
39 ❑ Nov 1988 Cover: 1.95 **NM** value: **Cover or less**
Circ: CapCity orders: **6,950**
📖 Crossroads
40 ❑ Jan 1989 Cover: 1.95 **NM** value: **Cover or less**
Circ: CapCity orders: **6,700**
41 ❑ Mar 1989 Cover: 1.95 **NM** value: **Cover or less**
Circ: CapCity orders: **6,725**
• Peter David writing starts **W:** Peter David
42 ❑ May 1989 Cover: 1.95 **NM** value: **Cover or less**
Circ: CapCity orders: **6,750**
43 ❑ Jun 1989 Cover: 1.95 **NM** value: **Cover or less**
Circ: CapCity orders: **6,750**
44 ❑ Jul 1989 Cover: 1.95 **NM** value: **Cover or less**
Circ: CapCity orders: **6,750**
45 ❑ Aug 1989 Cover: 1.95 **NM** value: **Cover or less**
Circ: CapCity orders: **6,750**
46 ❑ Sep 1989 Cover: 1.95 **NM** value: **Cover or less**
Circ: CapCity orders: **6,700**
47 ❑ Oct 1989 Cover: 1.95 **NM** value: **Cover or less**
Circ: CapCity orders: **6,875**
48 ❑ Nov 1989 Cover: 1.95 **NM** value: **Cover or less**
Circ: CapCity orders: **6,775**
49 ❑ Dec 1989 Cover: 1.95 **NM** value: **Cover or less**
Circ: CapCity orders: **6,825**
50 ❑ Jan 1990 Cover: 3.95 **NM** value: **Cover or less**
Circ: CapCity orders: **7,050**
Embossed cover. • Double-size.
51 ❑ Feb 1990 Cover: 1.95 **NM** value: **Cover or less**
Circ: CapCity orders: **6,625**
52 ❑ Mar 1990 Cover: 1.95 **NM** value: **Cover or less**
Circ: CapCity orders: **6,875**
53 ❑ Apr 1990 Cover: 1.95 **NM** value: **Cover or less**
Circ: CapCity orders: **6,725**
54 ❑ May 1990 Cover: 1.95 **NM** value: **Cover or less**
Circ: CapCity orders: **6,650**
55 ❑ Jun 1990 Cover: 1.95 **NM** value: **2.25**
Circ: CapCity orders: **6,425**
56 ❑ Jul 1990 Cover: 1.95 **NM** value: **2.25**
Circ: CapCity orders: **6,450**
57 ❑ Aug 1990 Cover: 1.95 **NM** value: **2.25**
Circ: CapCity orders: **6,425**
58 ❑ Sep 1990 Cover: 1.95 **NM** value: **2.25**
Circ: CapCity orders: **6,575**
59 ❑ Oct 1990 Cover: 2.25 **NM** value: **Cover or less**
Circ: CapCity orders: **6,425**
60 ❑ Nov 1990 Cover: 2.25 **NM** value: **Cover or less**
Circ: CapCity orders: **6,650**
61 ❑ Dec 1990 Cover: 2.25 **NM** value: **Cover or less**
Circ: CapCity orders: **6,675**
62 ❑ Jan 1991 Cover: 2.25 **NM** value: **Cover or less**
Circ: CapCity orders: **6,425**
63 ❑ Feb 1991 Cover: 2.25 **NM** value: **Cover or less**
Circ: CapCity orders: **6,650**
64 ❑ Mar 1991 Cover: 2.25 **NM** value: **Cover or less**
Circ: CapCity orders: **6,600**
final issue.
Anl 1❑Apr 1991 Cover: 2.00 **NM** value: **Cover or less**
📖 The Price **A:** Jim Starlin
Bk 1❑ Cover: 25.00 **NM** value: **Cover or less**
📖 The Price • Saddle-stitched paperback

DREADSTAR & CO. — Marvel / Epic

1 ❑ Jul 1985 Cover: 0.75 **NM** value: **1.00**
Circ: CapCity orders: **10,600**
📖 The Hand Of Darkness **A:** Jim Starlin **W:** Jim Starlin
2 ❑ Aug 1985 Cover: 0.75 **NM** value: **1.25**
Circ: CapCity orders: **8,400**
📖 Willow's Story **A:** Jim Starlin **W:** Jim Starlin
3 ❑ Sep 1985 Cover: 0.75 **NM** value: **1.25**
Circ: CapCity orders: **6,800**
📖 Holocaust **A:** Jim Starlin **W:** Jim Starlin
4 ❑ Oct 1985 Cover: 0.75 **NM** value: **1.25**
Circ: CapCity orders: **8,700**
5 ❑ Nov 1985 Cover: 0.75 **NM** value: **1.25**
Circ: CapCity orders: **5,600**
6 ❑ Dec 1985 Cover: 0.75 **NM** value: **1.25**
Circ: CapCity orders: **5,500**

DREADSTAR (MALIBU) — Malibu / Bravura

After a hiatus, 1994 saw the return of Jim Starlin's Dreadstar. To be honest, it's not Vanth Dreadstar, the peaceful man who raised a rebellion against the oppressive dictatorship of the galactic Papacy. This series from Malibu's Bravura line begins twenty years after the end of the old Dreadstar title and stars Kalla Dreadstar, Vanth's daughter.

Featuring writing by Peter David and art by comics great Ernie Colon, this new title places Kalla squarely against the invading might of the Papacy. Theirs is the power to destroy whole worlds, while she is armed only with her father's sword. If she and her people are to have any hope, she'll have to find Vanth, the father who left her so long ago. Fans of the old Dreadstar series will be glad to know that as Kalla begins her struggle, the old characters from the former series begin making reappearances.

0.5 ❑ Mar 1994 **NM** value: **2.00**
• Promotional edition included in Hero Illustrated.
1 ❑ Apr 1994 Cover: 2.50 **NM** value: **Cover or less**
Circ: CapCity orders: **28,050**
A: Ernie Colon **W:** Peter David
2 ❑ May 1994 Cover: 2.50 **NM** value: **Cover or less**
Circ: CapCity orders: **19,700**
📖 Contradiction **A:** Ernie Colon **W:** Peter David
3 ❑ Jun 1994 Cover: 2.50 **NM** value: **Cover or less**
Circ: CapCity orders: **16,400**
📖 Backstory **A:** Ernie Colon **W:** Peter David
4 ❑ Sep 1994 Cover: 2.50 **NM** value: **Cover or less**
Circ: CapCity orders: **15,125**
A: Ernie Colon **W:** Peter David
5 ❑ Oct 1994 Cover: 2.50 **NM** value: **Cover or less**
Circ: CapCity orders: **12,900**
📖 Convergence **A:** Ernie Colon **W:** Peter David ★ Death of Dreadstar (Vanth).
6 ❑ Jan 1995 Cover: 2.50 **NM** value: **Cover or less**
Circ: CapCity orders: **12,100**
final issue. **A:** Ernie Colon **W:** Peter David

DREAM ANGEL — Angel Entertainment

0 ❑ Fal 1996, b&w Cover: 2.95 **NM** value: **Cover or less**

DREAM ANGEL AND ANGEL GIRL — Angel

1 ❑ Cover: 3.00 **NM** value: **Cover or less**
A: Dan Lauer **W:** Lloyd Chasseur

DREAM ANGEL: THE QUANTUM DREAMER — Angel

0 ❑ Cover: 2.95 **NM** value: **Cover or less**
📖 I Saw It in a Dream…! **A:** Andriana Melo **W:** David Campiti
1 ❑ Cover: 2.95 **NM** value: **Cover or less**
2 ❑ Cover: 2.95 **NM** value: **Cover or less**

The prices seen above do not represent the highest possible prices seen in online auctions, but rather the prices we have seen these issues reliably fetch in a variety of environments (storefront retail, mail order, auction and convention).

DREAM CORRIDOR (HARLAN ELLISON'S...) — Dark Horse

Harlan Ellison is one of the most acclaimed fiction writers of all time, with credits ranging from film to books to, yes, comics. After far too many years, Dark Horse's Dream Corridor gave Ellison a series to call his own, featuring comic adaptations of some of his best short stories. It began with a top-selling special, and was followed by regular issues.

Each issue of this critically acclaimed series features an introduction by Ellison in comic form. Among the series' highlights is John Byrne's four-part adaptation of "I Have No Mouth and I Must Scream," one of the 10 most reprinted stories in the English language. The comic adaptation of this is presented along with the original text story, making for an enlightening comparison. Ellison also contributes a new story for each issue, inspired by the cover art of each issue.

1 ❑ Mar 1995 Cover: 2.95 **NM** value: **3.50**
Circ: CapCity orders: **9,500**
📖 I Have No Mouth and I Must Scream, Part 1; Midnight in the Sunken Cathedral (text story); Knox; Turnpike **A:** John Byrne **W:** Harlan Ellison
2 ❑ Apr 1995 Cover: 2.95 **NM** value: **3.25**
Circ: CapCity orders: **7,600**
📖 I Have No Mouth and I Must Scream, Part 2; S.R.O.; Enter the Fanatic, Stage Center; Anywhere but Here, With Anyone but You (text story) **A:** John Byrne **W:** Harlan Ellison
3 ❑ May 1995 Cover: 2.95 **NM** value: **3.00**
Circ: CapCity orders: **7,400**
📖 I Have No Mouth and I Must Scream, Part 3 **A:** John Byrne **W:** Harlan Ellison
4 ❑ Jun 1995 Cover: 2.95 **NM** value: **3.00**
Circ: CapCity orders: **7,675**
📖 I Have No Mouth and I Must Scream, Part 4; Catman, Part 1 **A:** John Byrne **W:** Harlan Ellison
5 ❑ Aug 1995 Cover: 2.95 **NM** value: **3.00**
Circ: CapCity orders: **7,425**
📖 Catman, Part 2; How's the Night Life on Cissalda? **W:** Harlan Ellison
6 ❑ Sep 1995 Cover: 2.95 **NM** value: **3.00**
Circ: CapCity orders: **5,600**
📖 Opposites Attract; One Life, Furnished in Early Poverty **W:** Harlan Ellison
Bk 1❑ Cover: 18.95 **NM** value: **Cover or less**
• collects Harlan Ellison's Dream Corridor #1-5 and Special **W:** Harlan Ellison
SE 1❑Jan 1995 Cover: 4.95 **NM** value: **5.00**
Circ: CapCity orders: **7,000**
• prestige format. 📖 On The Slab; Quicktime; Rat Hater; If This Be Utopia **W:** Harlan Ellison
SE 1-2❑Sep 1995 Cover: 4.95 **NM** value: **Cover or less**

DREAM CORRIDOR QUARTERLY (HARLAN ELLISON'S...) — Dark Horse

1 ❑ Aug 1996 Cover: 5.95 **NM** value: **Cover or less**
• prestige format. 📖 Opposites Attract; Rock God; The Voice in the Garden; One Life, Furnished in Early Poverty; Gnomebody **W:** Harlan Ellison

DREAMERY, THE — Eclipse

1 ❑ Dec 1986, b&w Cover: 2.00 **NM** value: **Cover or less**
📖 Andri's Christmas Shoes; Jabberwocky **A:** Lela Dowling; Donna Barr **W:** Donna Barr; Lewis Carroll ★ Appearance of Bruna Lowhard, Frau Wassergarn, Stinz Lowhard, Berdach Feuerbach, Veit Wassergarn, Andri Lowhard, Chicken.
2 ❑ Feb 1987, b&w Cover: 2.00 **NM** value: **Cover or less**
📖 Alice, Part I • Lela Dowling bio **A:** Lela Dowling **W:** Chris Weiman; Lewis Carroll ★ 1st Appearance of Alice, White Rabbit.
3 ❑ Apr 1987, b&w Cover: 2.00 **NM** value: **Cover or less**
📖 The Carp of Easter; Alice, Part II • Councilman Stinz story; Donna Barr bio **A:** Lela Dowling; Donna Barr **W:** Donna Barr; Chris Weiman; Lewis Carroll ★ 2nd Appearance of Alice. ★ Appearance of Bruna Lowhard, Stinz Lowhard, Odo, Ede, Andri Lowhard.
4 ❑ Jun 1987, b&w Cover: 2.00 **NM** value: **Cover or less**
📖 Alice, Part III; The Dreamery Gallery **A:** Lela Dowling; Ken Macklin **W:** Chris Weiman; Lewis Carroll ★ 1st Appearance of Cheshire Cat. ★ Appearance of Alice.
5 ❑ Aug 1987, b&w Cover: 2.00 **NM** value: **Cover or less**
📖 Alice, Part IV; Nothing Like Gone; Time Release **A:** Lela Dowling; Donna Barr; Phil Foglio **W:** Donna Barr; Phil Foglio; Chris Weiman; Lewis Carroll ★ Appearance of Quidam, Alice, Stinz Lowhard, Loch Ness Monster, Doctor Foon, Andri Lowhard.
6 ❑ Oct 1987, b&w Cover: 2.00 **NM** value: **Cover or less**
📖 Alice, Part V; Chicken **A:** Lela Dowling; Donna Barr **W:** Donna Barr; Chris Weiman; Lewis Carroll ★ Origin of Feuerbach family, Chicken. ★ 2nd Appearance of White Rabbit. ★ 2nd Appearance of Cheshire Cat. ★ Appearance of Alice, The Devil, Stinz Lowhard, Berdach Feuerbach, Chicken.
7 ❑ Dec 1987, b&w Cover: 2.00 **NM** value: **Cover or less**
📖 Alice, Part VI; The Last Horselaugh; The Lord of the Forest **A:** Monika Livingston; Lela Dowling; Donna Barr **W:** Donna Barr; Chris Weiman; Lewis Carroll; Lydia Marano ★ Appearance of Hans Bruchteil, Alice, Stinz Lowhard, Albert Dammling, White Rabbit, Margl Dammling, Uwe Wassergarn.
8 ❑ Feb 1988, b&w Cover: 2.00 **NM** value: **Cover or less**
📖 The Adventures of Prince Ivan: On the Birth of Prince Ivan; A Breathing Spill **A:** Donna Barr; Sherlock **W:** Donna Barr; Diane Duane ★ 1st Appearance of Prince Iv.

CGC-graded: Multiply prices above by **33 for 9.9 M • 16 for 9.8 NM/M • 7 for 9.6 NM+ • 5 for 9.4 NM • 2.5 for 9.2 NM- • 1.5 for 9.0 VF/NM**

9 ❑ Apr 1988, b&w Cover: 2.00 **NM value: Cover or less**
Animal Attraction; The Tale of Prince Ivan the Not-So-Experienced, Part the Second; The Natural History of Raccoons • Young Stinz story **A:** Donna Barr; Cathy Hill; Sherlock **W:** Donna Barr; Cathy Hill; Diane Duane

10 ❑ Jun 1988, b&w Cover: 2.00 **NM value: Cover or less**
The Proving Ground; The Raccoon Platoon Tune (song); The Raccoon Rhapsody (song); The Tale of Prince Ivan the Not-too-Experienced, Part the Third • Young Stinz story **A:** Donna Barr; Cathy Hill; Sherlock **W:** Donna Barr; Cathy Hill; Diane Duane ★ Appearance of Paul Lowhard, Stinz Lowhard.

11 ❑ Aug 1988, b&w Cover: 2.00 **NM value: Cover or less**
Smoked Out; Prince Ivan, Part IV; Raccoons and Music • Young Stinz story **A:** Donna Barr; Cathy Hill; Sherlock **W:** Donna Barr; Cathy Hill; Diane Duane ★ Appearance of Rauchl Schorsche.

12 ❑ Oct 1988, b&w Cover: 2.00 **NM value: Cover or less**
Sprunghack Hans; Next: How Prince Ivan Meets Various Insects and Critters, and What They Do for His Credit Rating, Part Five; Raccoons in Literature; The Order • Councilman Stinz story **A:** Tim Sale; Donna Barr; Cathy Hill; Sherlock **W:** Tim Sale; Donna Barr; Cathy Hill; Diane Duane ★ Origin of Sprunghack Han. ★ Appearance of Stinz Lowhard, Andri Lowhard.

13 ❑ Dec 1988, b&w Cover: 2.00 **NM value: Cover or less**
Not My Problem; The Tale of Prince Ivan the Slightly Experienced, Part VI; Raccoons in Art • Councilman Stinz story **A:** Donna Barr; Cathy Hill; Sherlock **W:** Donna Barr; Cathy Hill; Diane Duane ★ 1st Appearance of Little Humpback Horse (full). ★ Appearance of Raoul, Bruna Lowhard, Prince Ivan, Stinz Lowhard, Rolf, Baron von Geisel.

14 ❑ Feb 1989, b&w Cover: 2.00 **NM value: Cover or less**
Cover reads "The Ninjery". Hooves of Death; The Philosophy of Raccoons; The Owl and the Pussy-Cat final issue. **A:** Lela Dowling; Donna Barr; Cathy Hill **W:** Donna Barr; Cathy Hill; Edward Lear

DREAMING, THE — DC / Vertigo

When writer Neil Gaiman decided to end Sandman, the highly praised flagship title of the Vertigo line, DC Comics hoped to retain his readership with a new title that, although not about Morpheus or his successor Daniel, does include such supporting characters as Cain and Abel, Matthew, Eve, and Lucius.

The Dreaming is the name of the mystical realm everyone visits each night and is thus capable of telling as many kinds of stories as there are dreams. Much like Sandman, this book is essentially an anthology title with the universe established by Neil Gaiman as the foundation on which new writers and artists can build. It features a variety of stories, with new characters as well as old favorites.

1 ❑ Jun 1996 Cover: 2.50 **NM value: 4.00**
• **CGC:** 1 graded, best 9.6
The Goldie Factor, Part 1 **A:** Peter Snejbjerg **W:** Terry Laban

2 ❑ Jul 1996 Cover: 2.50 **NM value: 3.00**
The Goldie Factor, Part 2 **A:** Peter Snejbjerg **W:** Terry Laban

3 ❑ Aug 1996 Cover: 2.50 **NM value: 3.00**
The Goldie Factor, Part 3 **A:** Peter Snejbjerg **W:** Terry Laban

4 ❑ Sep 1996 Cover: 2.50 **NM value: 3.00**
The Lost Boy, Part 1 **A:** Steve Parkhouse **W:** Peter Hogan

5 ❑ Oct 1996 Cover: 2.50 **NM value: 3.00**
Photo cover. The Lost Boy, Part 2 **A:** Steve Parkhouse **W:** Peter Hogan

6 ❑ Nov 1996 Cover: 2.50 **NM value: 3.00**
Circ: Direct Market orders: **46,286**
The Lost Boy, Part 3 **A:** Steve Parkhouse; Dave McKean(cover) **W:** Peter Hogan

7 ❑ Dec 1996 Cover: 2.50 **NM value: 3.00**
Circ: Direct Market orders: **43,892**
The Lost Boy, Part 4 **A:** Steve Parkhouse **W:** Peter Hogan

8 ❑ Jan 1997 Cover: 2.50 **NM value: 3.00**
Circ: Diamd. preorders: **40,930**
cover says Nov 96, indicia says Jan 97. His Brother's Keeper • self-contained story **A:** Michael Zulli **W:** Alisa Kwitney

9 ❑ Feb 1997 Cover: 2.50 **NM value: 3.00**
Circ: Diamd. preorders: **38,020**
Weird Romance, Part 1 **A:** David Taylor **W:** Bryan Talbot

10 ❑ Mar 1997 Cover: 2.50 **NM value: 3.00**
Circ: Diamd. preorders: **36,769**
Weird Romance, Part 2 **A:** Peter Doherty **W:** Bryan Talbot

11 ❑ Apr 1997 Cover: 2.50 **NM value: Cover or less**
Circ: Diamd. preorders: **35,223**
Weird Romance, Part 3 **A:** Peter Doherty **W:** Bryan Talbot

12 ❑ May 1997 Cover: 2.50 **NM value: Cover or less**
Circ: Diamd. preorders: **34,515**
Weird Romance, Part 4 **A:** Peter Doherty **W:** Bryan Talbot

13 ❑ Jun 1997 Cover: 2.50 **NM value: Cover or less**
Circ: Diamd. preorders: **33,512**
Coyote's Kiss, Part 1

14 ❑ Jul 1997 Cover: 2.50 **NM value: Cover or less**
Circ: Diamd. preorders: **30,517**
Coyote's Kiss, Part 2

15 ❑ Aug 1997 Cover: 2.50 **NM value: Cover or less**
Circ: Diamd. preorders: **29,298**
Day's Work Night's Rest

16 ❑ Sep 1997 Cover: 2.50 **NM value: Cover or less**
Circ: Diamd. preorders: **27,784**
Ice

17 ❑ Oct 1997 Cover: 2.50 **NM value: Cover or less**
Circ: Diamd. preorders: **27,243**
Souvenirs, Part 1

18 ❑ Nov 1997 Cover: 2.50 **NM value: Cover or less**
Circ: Diamd. preorders: **26,338**
Souvenirs, Part 2 **A:** Peter Doherty **W:** Caitlin R. Kiernan

19 ❑ Dec 1997 Cover: 2.50 **NM value: Cover or less**
Circ: Diamd. preorders: **25,733**
Souvenirs, Part 3 **A:** Peter Doherty **W:** Caitlin R. Kiernan ★ Appearance of The Corinthian.

20 ❑ Jan 1998 Cover: 2.50 **NM value: Cover or less**
Circ: Diamd. preorders: **25,002**
The Dark Rose, Part 1

21 ❑ Feb 1998 Cover: 2.50 **NM value: Cover or less**
Circ: Diamd. preorders: **24,276**
The Dark Rose, Part 2

22 ❑ Mar 1998 Cover: 2.50 **NM value: Cover or less**
Circ: Diamd. preorders: **23,970**
The Unkindness of One, Part 1; Unkindness of One, Part 1

23 ❑ Apr 1998 Cover: 2.50 **NM value: Cover or less**
Circ: Diamd. preorders: **22,473**
The Unkindness of One, Part 2; Unkindness of One, Part 2

24 ❑ May 1998 Cover: 2.50 **NM value: Cover or less**
Circ: Diamd. preorders: **22,158**
The Unkindness of One, Part 3; Unkindness of One, Part 1

25 ❑ Jun 1998 Cover: 2.50 **NM value: Cover or less**
Circ: Diamd. preorders: **22,190**
My Year As A Man

26 ❑ Jul 1998 Cover: 2.50 **NM value: Cover or less**
Circ: Diamd. preorders: **21,200**
Restitution

27 ❑ Aug 1998 Cover: 2.50 **NM value: Cover or less**
Circ: Diamd. preorders: **21,040**
Many Mansions: Stormy Weather

28 ❑ Sep 1998 Cover: 2.50 **NM value: Cover or less**
Circ: Diamd. preorders: **20,028**
Many Mansions: Dreams the Burning Dream • House of Mystery burns down

29 ❑ Oct 1998 Cover: 2.50 **NM value: Cover or less**
Circ: Diamd. preorders: **19,504**
Many Mansions: Ashes

30 ❑ Nov 1998 Cover: 2.50 **NM value: Cover or less**
Circ: Diamd. preorders: **19,303**
Many Mansions: Temporary Overflow ★ Appearance of Lucien.

31 ❑ Dec 1998 Cover: 3.95 **NM value: Cover or less**
Circ: Diamd. preorders: **19,041**
Many Mansions: November Eve

32 ❑ Jan 1999 Cover: 2.50 **NM value: Cover or less**
Circ: Diamd. preorders: **18,448**
London Pride **A:** Steve Parkhouse; Dave McKean(cover) **W:** Paul Hogan ★ Appearance of Hob Gadling, Mad Hettie, Peggy Gadling.

33 ❑ Feb 1999 Cover: 2.50 **NM value: Cover or less**
Circ: Diamd. preorders: **18,438**
The Little Mermaid **A:** Dave McKean(cover); John Totleben **W:** Caitlan R. Kiernan

34 ❑ Mar 1999 Cover: 2.50 **NM value: Cover or less**
Circ: Diamd. preorders: **17,830**
Many Mansions: Ruin **A:** Marc Hempel; Dave McKean(cover) **W:** Caitlan R. Kiernan ★ Appearance of Abel, Cain, Eve.

35 ❑ Apr 1999 Cover: 2.50 **NM value: Cover or less**
Circ: Diamd. preorders: **16,938**
Kaleidoscope **A:** Rebecca Guay; Dave McKean(cover) **W:** Caitlan R. Kiernan

36 ❑ May 1999 Cover: 2.50 **NM value: Cover or less**
Circ: Diamd. preorders: **16,792**
Slow Dying; The Gyres, Part 1 **A:** Christian Højgaard; Dave McKean(cover) **W:** Caitlan R. Kiernan

37 ❑ Jun 1999 Cover: 2.50 **NM value: Cover or less**
Circ: Diamd. preorders: **16,775**
Pariah; The Gyres, Part 2 **A:** Christian Højgaard **W:** Caitlan R. Kiernan

38 ❑ Jul 1999 Cover: 2.50 **NM value: Cover or less**
Circ: Diamd. preorders: **16,525**
Apostate; The Gyres, Part 3 **A:** Christian Højgaard **W:** Caitlan R. Kiernan

39 ❑ Aug 1999 Cover: 2.50 **NM value: Cover or less**
Circ: Diamd. preorders: **16,438**
The Lost Language of Flowers **A:** Shawn McManus; Christian Højgaard **W:** Caitlan R. Kiernan

40 ❑ Sep 1999 Cover: 2.50 **NM value: Cover or less**
Circ: Diamd. preorders: **16,014**
Fox and Hounds, Part 1 **A:** Christian Højgaard; Dave McKean(cover) **W:** Caitlan R. Kiernan

41 ❑ Oct 1999 Cover: 2.50 **NM value: Cover or less**
Circ: Diamd. preorders: **15,648**
Fox and Hounds, Part 2 **A:** Christian Højgaard; Dave McKean(cover) **W:** Caitlan R. Kiernan

42 ❑ Nov 1999 Cover: 2.50 **NM value: Cover or less**
Circ: Diamd. preorders: **15,380**
Fox and Hounds, Part 3 **A:** Christian Højgaard; Dave McKean(cover) **W:** Caitlan R. Kiernan

43 ❑ Dec 1999 Cover: 2.50 **NM value: Cover or less**
Circ: Diamd. preorders: **15,843**
Fox and Hounds, Part 4 **A:** Christian Højgaard; Dave McKean(cover) **W:** Caitlan R. Kiernan

44 ❑ Jan 2000 Cover: 2.50 **NM value: Cover or less**
Circ: Diamd. preorders: **15,002**
Homesick **A:** Christian Højgaard; Dave McKean(cover) **W:** Caitlan R. Kiernan

45 ❑ Feb 2000 Cover: 2.50 **NM value: Cover or less**
Circ: Diamd. preorders: **16,581**
A: Christian Højgaard; Dave McKean(cover) **W:** Caitlan R. Kiernan

46 ❑ Mar 2000 Cover: 2.50 **NM value: Cover or less**
Circ: Diamd. preorders: **14,457**
A: Christian Højgaard; Dave McKean(cover) **W:** Caitlan R. Kiernan

47 ❑ Apr 2000 Cover: 2.50 **NM value: Cover or less**
Circ: Diamd. preorders: **13,809**
Ttrinket **A:** Christian Højgaard; Dave McKean(cover) **W:** Caitlan R. Kiernan

48 ❑ May 2000 Cover: 2.50 **NM value: Cover or less**
Circ: Diamd. preorders: **13,984**
Scary Monsters **A:** Christian Højgaard; Dave McKean(cover) **W:** Caitlan R. Kiernan

49 ❑ Jun 2000 Cover: 2.50 **NM value: Cover or less**
Circ: Diamd. preorders: **13,843**
A: Christian Højgaard; Dave McKean(cover) **W:** Caitlan R. Kiernan

50 ❑ Jul 2000 Cover: 2.50 **NM value: Cover or less**
Circ: Diamd. preorders: **15,334**
A: Christian Højgaard; Dave McKean(cover) **W:** Caitlan R. Kiernan

51 ❑ Aug 2000 Cover: 2.50 **NM value: Cover or less**
Circ: Diamd. preorders: **14,092**
A: Christian Højgaard; Dave McKean(cover) **W:** Caitlan R. Kiernan

52 ❑ Sep 2000 Cover: 2.50 **NM value: Cover or less**
Circ: Diamd. preorders: **14,141**
Exiles, Part 1 **A:** Ron Randall; Christian Højgaard; Dave McKean(cover) **W:** Caitlan R. Kiernan

53 ❑ Oct 2000 Cover: 2.50 **NM value: Cover or less**
Circ: Diamd. preorders: **13,395**
Exiles, Part 2 **A:** Ron Randall; Christian Højgaard; Dave McKean(cover) **W:** Caitlan R. Kiernan

54 ❑ Nov 2000 Cover: 2.50 **NM value: Cover or less**
Circ: Diamd. preorders: **13,427**
Exiles, Part 3 **A:** Ron Randall; Christian Højgaard; Dave McKean(cover) **W:** Caitlan R. Kiernan

55 ❑ Dec 2000 Cover: 2.50 **NM value: Cover or less**
Circ: Diamd. preorders: **13,666**
The Further Adventures of Danny Nod, Heroic Library Assistant **A:** Marc Laming; Paul Pope; Phil Jimenez; Bill Willingham; Linda Medley; Peter Gross; Michael W. Kaluta; Zander Cannon; John Stokes; Daniel Torres; Adam Highes; Albert Monteys **W:** Bill Willingham

56 ❑ Jan 2001 Cover: 2.50 **NM value: Cover or less**
Circ: Diamd. preorders: **13,109**
The First Adventure of Miss Catterina Poe **A:** Steve Leialoha **W:** Caitlan R. Kiernan

57 ❑ Feb 2001 Cover: 2.50 **NM value: Cover or less**
Circ: Diamd. preorders: **13,082**
Rise, Part 1 **A:** Ron Randall; Christian Højgaard; Dave McKean(cover) **W:** Caitlan R. Kiernan

58 ❑ Mar 2001 Cover: 2.50 **NM value: Cover or less**
Circ: Diamd. preorders: **12,603**
Rise, Part 2 **A:** Ron Randall; Christian Højgaard; Dave McKean(cover) **W:** Caitlan R. Kiernan

59 ❑ Apr 2001 Cover: 2.50 **NM value: Cover or less**
Circ: Diamd. preorders: **12,572**
Rise, Part 3 **A:** Ron Randall; Christian Højgaard; Dave McKean(cover) **W:** Caitlan R. Kiernan

60 ❑ May 2001 Cover: 2.50 **NM value: Cover or less**
Circ: Diamd. preorders: **12,646**
Rise, Part 4 **A:** Ron Randall; Christian Højgaard; Dave McKean(cover) **W:** Caitlan R. Kiernan

Bk 1❑ Cover: 19.95 **NM value: Cover or less**
• Beyond the Shores of Night;collects issues #1-8 with new introduction

Bk 3❑ Cover: 19.95 **NM value: Cover or less**
• Through the Gates of Horn and Ivory;collects #15-19, 22-25

SE 1❑ Jul 1998 Cover: 5.95 **NM value: Cover or less**
Circ: Diamd. preorders: **16,914**
wraparound cover. Trial and Error

DREAM-QUEST OF UNKNOWN KADATH, THE (H.P. LOVECRAFT'S...) — Mock Man

Randolph Carter escapes his squalid existence through dreams. Three times he dreamt of the opulent city named Kadath, and each time was denied entry by the Gods of Dream. Spurred by an unrelenting desire, Carter descended the "Seven-Hundred Steps to the Gate of Deeper Slumber," embarking on a metaphysical quest for the idyllic city.

This five-issue series is an ambitious attempt by writer-artist Jason Thompson to adapt one of H. P. Lovecraft's more atypical works. Not rife with slavering monstrosities like many of Lovecraft's other novels, this series is closer to the mythic fantasies of Tolkien. Although the characters and creatures of the dream world are drawn realistically, Randolph Carter is depicted as a generic iconic figure to impart the protagonist's "everyman" status.

1 ❑ Cover: 2.95 **NM value: Cover or less**
A: Jason B. Thompson **W:** Jason B. Thompson; H.P. Lovecraft

1-2 ❑ Mar 1998 Cover: 2.95 **NM value: Cover or less**
A: Jason B. Thompson **W:** Jason B. Thompson; H.P. Lovecraft

2 ❑ Cover: 2.95 **NM value: Cover or less**
A: Jason B. Thompson **W:** Jason B. Thompson; H.P. Lovecraft

3 ❑ Cover: 2.95 **NM value: Cover or less**
A: Jason B. Thompson **W:** Jason B. Thompson; H.P. Lovecraft

4 ❑ Cover: 2.95 **NM value: Cover or less**
A: Jason B. Thompson **W:** Jason B. Thompson; H.P. Lovecraft

5 ❑ Cover: 2.95 **NM value: Cover or less**
final issue. **A:** Jason B. Thompson **W:** Jason B. Thompson; H.P. Lovecraft

DREAMS CANNOT DIE! — Mark's Giant Economy Size

1 ❑ Jun 1996 Cover: 17.95 **NM value: Cover or less**
• Trade Paperback.

DREAMS 'N' SCHEMES OF COL. KILGORE — Special Studio

1 ❑ Mar 1991, b&w Cover: 2.50 **NM value: Cover or less**
2 ❑ May 1991, b&w Cover: 2.50 **NM value: Cover or less**

DREAMS OF A DOG — Rip Off

1 ❑ May 1990, b&w Cover: 2.00 **NM value: Cover or less**
2 ❑ Jun 1992, b&w Cover: 2.50 **NM value: Cover or less**

DREAMS OF EVERYMAN — Rip Off

1 ❑ Jun 1992 Cover: 2.50 **NM value: Cover or less**
No issue number.

Other grades: Multiply prices above by **1.5 for Mint • 2/3 for Very Fine • 1/3 for Fine • 1/5 for Very Good • 1/8 for Good**

DREAMS OF THE DARKCHYLDE — Darkchylde

This series, which takes place outside of the regular Darkchylde continuity, kicks off with gorgeous artwork from Brandon Peterson, whose work had appeared in Mystic, Uncanny X-Men. It continues with the equally gorgeous artwork of newcomer Ron Adrian, whose few previous credits had included Lady Pendragon.

The opening story by Darkchylde creator Randy Queen finds Ariel Chylde — a barely dressed runaway gal with demonic powers — reflecting on the loss of her childhood friend Kiley. The tale sets up Ariel as a young woman who has always been fighting demons, both figuratively and literally.

1 ❑ Oct 2000 Cover: 2.95 **NM** value: **Cover or less**
Circ: Diamd. preorders: **25,484**
🕮 No Possible Harm **A:** Brandon Peterson; Richard Bennet **W:** Randy Queen

DREAM TEAM — Malibu

1 ❑ Jul 1995 Cover: 4.95 **NM** value: **Cover or less**
• Malibu/Marvel Pin-ups

DREAMTIME — Blind Bat Press

1 ❑ May 1995, b&w Cover: 2.50 **NM** value: **Cover or less**
2 ❑ b&w Cover: 2.50 **NM** value: **Cover or less**
• no indicia

DREAMWALKER: AUTUMN LEAVES — Avatar

1 ❑ Sep 1999, b&w Cover: 3.00 **NM** value: **Cover or less**
2 ❑ Oct 1999, b&w Cover: 3.00 **NM** value: **Cover or less**

DREAMWALKER (AVATAR) — Avatar

0 ❑ Nov 1998, b&w Cover: 3.00 **NM** value: **Cover or less**
One-shot.

DREAMWALKER (CALIBER) — Caliber / Tapestry

1 ❑ Dec 1996, b&w Cover: 2.95 **NM** value: **Cover or less**
Circ: Direct Market orders: **2,694**
2 ❑ Feb 1997, b&w Cover: 2.95 **NM** value: **Cover or less**
Circ: Diamd. preorders: **1,670**
3 ❑ 1997b&w Cover: 2.95 **NM** value: **Cover or less**
4 ❑ Jul 1997, b&w Cover: 2.95 **NM** value: **Cover or less**
5 ❑ Sep 1997, b&w Cover: 2.95 **NM** value: **Cover or less**
6 ❑ Jul 1998, b&w Cover: 2.95 **NM** value: **Cover or less**

DREAMWALKER: CAROUSEL — Avatar

1 ❑ Mar 1999, b&w Cover: 3.00 **NM** value: **Cover or less**
2 ❑ Apr 1999, b&w Cover: 3.00 **NM** value: **Cover or less**

DREAMWALKER (DREAMWALKER) — Dreamwalker

1 ❑ ca. 1996, b&w Cover: 2.95 **NM** value: **Cover or less**
2 ❑ ca. 1996, b&w Cover: 2.95 **NM** value: **Cover or less**
3 ❑ ca. 1996, b&w Cover: 2.95 **NM** value: **Cover or less**
4 ❑ ca. 1996, b&w Cover: 2.95 **NM** value: **Cover or less**
5 ❑ ca. 1996, b&w Cover: 2.95 **NM** value: **Cover or less**

DREAMWALKER (MARVEL) — Marvel

1 ❑ Cover: 6.95 **NM** value: **Cover or less**
Circ: CapCity orders: **3,050**

DREAMWALKER: SUMMER RAIN — Avatar

1 ❑ Jul 1999, b&w Cover: 3.00 **NM** value: **Cover or less**
One-shot.

DREAM WEAVER — Robert Lankford

1 ❑ Aug 1987 Cover: 1.95 **NM** value: **Cover or less**
A: Bob Lankford **W:** Bob Lankford

DREAM WEAVERS — Golden Realm Unlimited

1 ❑ Cover: 2.50 **NM** value: **Cover or less**
2 ❑ Cover: 1.50 **NM** value: **Cover or less**

DREAM WOLVES — Dramenon Studios

1 ❑ b&w Cover: 3.00 **NM** value: **Cover or less**
2 ❑ Dec 1994, b&w Cover: 3.00 **NM** value: **Cover or less**
cardstock cover.
3 ❑ Jan 1995, b&w Cover: 3.00 **NM** value: **Cover or less**
cardstock cover.
4 ❑ Feb 1995, b&w Cover: 3.00 **NM** value: **Cover or less**

DREAM WOLVES SWIMSUIT BIZARRE — Gothic

0 ❑ Dec 1995 Cover: 3.00 **NM** value: **Cover or less**
A: Fauve; Tim Vigil; Michael Bair; Mike Harris; Daniel Presedo; Sandra Chang; BigDog; Brian Monroe; Daniel Shaw; JackHammer; Paul Way; Peter Lopez; Winston

DREDD BY BISLEY — Fleetway-Quality

1 ❑ Cover: 5.95 **NM** value: **Cover or less**
No issue number. 🕮 Judge Dredd: A Mega-City Primer; Heavy Metal Dredd: The Legend of Johnny Biker; Judge Dredd: Rock On, Tommy Who?!; Judge Dredd: Iron Fist: Live at the Mega-Dome; Heavy Metal Dredd: Chicken Run; Judge Dredd: A Santa Affair; Judge Dredd: Bimba **A:** Simon Bisley **W:** Alan Grant; John Wagner

Creator Key
W = Writer • A = Artist • C = Cover Artist

DREDD RULES! — Fleetway-Quality

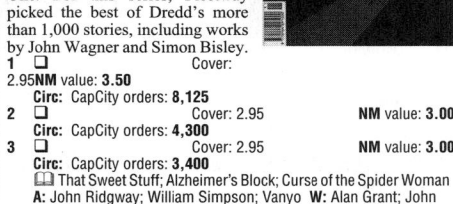

Dredd Rules! appeared as part of a revival of the Fleetway/Quality line in America in the early 1990s. It recolored and repackaged stories which originally ran in Britain's 2000 AD, and presented them in a glossy format which was miles better than 2000 AD's low-budget newsprint.

The stories all featured Judge Dredd, a tough future cop who worked to keep society under control in the sprawling Mega-City One. For this series, Fleetway picked the best of Dredd's more than 1,000 stories, including works by John Wagner and Simon Bisley.

1 ❑ Cover: 2.95**NM** value: **3.50**
Circ: CapCity orders: **8,125**
2 ❑ Cover: 2.95 **NM** value: **3.00**
Circ: CapCity orders: **4,300**
3 ❑ Cover: 2.95 **NM** value: **3.00**
Circ: CapCity orders: **3,400**
🕮 That Sweet Stuff; Alzheimer's Block; Curse of the Spider Woman **A:** John Ridgway; William Simpson; Vanyo **W:** Alan Grant; John Wagner
4 ❑ Cover: 2.95 **NM** value: **3.00**
Circ: CapCity orders: **2,975**
5 ❑ Cover: 2.95 **NM** value: **3.00**
Circ: CapCity orders: **2,800**
6 ❑ Cover: 2.95 **NM** value: **Cover or less**
Circ: CapCity orders: **3,275**
🕮 Breakdown on 9th St.; On Meeting Your Enemy; The Further Adventures of P.J. Maybe, Age 14; Locking Up the House **A:** John Higgins; Liam Sharp; Barry Kitson; Dougie Braithwaite; Boutell **W:** Alan Grant; John Wagner
7 ❑ Cover: 2.95 **NM** value: **Cover or less**
Circ: CapCity orders: **3,075**
8 ❑ Cover: 2.95 **NM** value: **Cover or less**
9 ❑ Cover: 2.95 **NM** value: **Cover or less**
Circ: CapCity orders: **2,850**
10 ❑ Cover: 2.95 **NM** value: **Cover or less**
Circ: CapCity orders: **5,700**
🕮 Judge Dredd: A Mega-City Primer; Judge Dredd: Bill Bailey, Won't You Please Come Home **A:** Simon Bisley; Vanyo **W:** John Wagner
11 ❑ Cover: 2.95 **NM** value: **Cover or less**
Circ: CapCity orders: **5,475**
12 ❑ Cover: 2.95 **NM** value: **Cover or less**
Circ: CapCity orders: **5,250**
13 ❑ Cover: 2.95 **NM** value: **Cover or less**
Circ: CapCity orders: **2,950**
14 ❑ Cover: 2.95 **NM** value: **Cover or less**
Circ: CapCity orders: **3,725**
★ Versus Santa.
15 ❑ Cover: 2.95 **NM** value: **Cover or less**
Circ: CapCity orders: **3,875**
16 ❑ Cover: 2.95 **NM** value: **Cover or less**
Circ: CapCity orders: **2,625**
17 ❑ Cover: 2.95 **NM** value: **Cover or less**
Circ: CapCity orders: **2,575**
18 ❑ Cover: 2.95 **NM** value: **Cover or less**
19 ❑ Cover: 2.95 **NM** value: **Cover or less**
20 ❑ Cover: 2.95 **NM** value: **Cover or less**
Circ: CapCity orders: **2,150**

DRESSED FOR SUCCESS: THE DIRTY BAKER'S DOZEN — Egesta

Bk 1❑ Feb 1995, b&w Cover: 12.00 **NM** value: **Cover or less**
• Collects first 13 issues of series

DRIFTER — Brainstorm

1 ❑ b&w Cover: 2.95 **NM** value: **Cover or less**

DRIFTERS — Infinity

1 ❑ Cover: 1.70 **NM** value: **2.00**

DRIFTERS, THE — Cornerstone

1 ❑ b&w Cover: 2.00 **NM** value: **Cover or less**

DROIDS — Marvel / Star

1 ❑ Apr 1986 Cover: 0.75 **NM** value: **4.00**
Circ: CapCity orders: **7,150** • **CGC:** 3 graded, best 9.6
2 ❑ Jun 1986 Cover: 0.75 **NM** value: **2.50**
Circ: CapCity orders: **5,100**
🕮 The Ultimate Weapon **A:** John Romita **W:** Dave Manak
3 ❑ Aug 1986 Cover: 0.75 **NM** value: **2.50**
Circ: CapCity orders: **3,450**
4 ❑ Oct 1986 Cover: 0.75 **NM** value: **2.50**
Circ: CapCity orders: **3,300**
5 ❑ Dec 1986 Cover: 0.75 **NM** value: **2.50**
Circ: CapCity orders: **2,550**
6 ❑ Feb 1987 Cover: 0.75 **NM** value: **2.50**
Circ: CapCity orders: **2,500**
• A New Hope told from droids' p.o.v.
7 ❑ Apr 1987 Cover: 0.75 **NM** value: **2.50**
Circ: CapCity orders: **2,300**
• A New Hope told from droids' p.o.v.
8 ❑ Jun 1987 Cover: 1.00 **NM** value: **2.50**
Circ: CapCity orders: **1,850**
final issue. • A New Hope told from droids' p.o.v.

DROOL MAGAZINE — Co. & Sons

1 ❑ Cover: 0.50 **NM** value: **3.00**

🕮 Survival of the Fittest; Shockwork Lemon; Nixon's Trip to Harlem; ABC Presents Art Wimpletter as The Patient; Liberated SistersRock'n'Role Forecast 1984; 15 Fingers of Doom **A:** Bill Skurski; Gail Burwen; Jay Finney; Joey Epstein; Peter Bramley; Ralph Reese; Tom Hactman; Ned Sontag **W:** Bill Skurski; Gail Burwen; Jay Finney; Joey Epstein; Peter Bramley; Ralph Reese; Tom Hactman; Ned Sontag

DROOPY — Dark Horse

Created by Tex Avery, Droopy Dog has become one of America's most beloved comics characters. Low-key to the extreme, he makes the perfect straight man to the outlandish comic situations Avery placed him in. Droopy's other trademark is the voice he was given in animated features — something which sadly, comics can't communicate.

Still, this three-issue series from Dark Horse does a terrific job of showing Droopy at his hilarious best. In the story "Doctor Droopenstein," Droopy needs a brain to complete his creation. So, when a wolf visitor drops by the castle, the little dog quietly launches scheme after scheme to hack his visitor to pieces in order to obtain the needed brain. What makes the story so funny is the good humor and courtesy Droopy shows his "guest" when his schemes fail. As an added bonus, the series also features backup stories starring Screwball Squirrel.

1 ❑ Oct 1995 Cover: 2.50 **NM** value: **Cover or less**
🕮 Droopy: Dr. Droopenstein; Screwball Squirrel: The Violent Zone • Screwball Squirrel back-up **A:** Greg Hyland; Brian Lemay; Scott Shaw(inks) **W:** Bob Fingerman; Brian Lemay
2 ❑ Nov 1995 Cover: 2.50 **NM** value: **Cover or less**
• Wolf and Red back-up
3 ❑ Dec 1995 Cover: 2.50 **NM** value: **Cover or less**
🕮 Droopy: Satan's Little Helpers final issue. • Screwball Squirrel back-up **A:** Brian Lemay; Greg Hyland(inks) **W:** Brian Lemay

DROPSIE AVENUE: THE NEIGHBORHOOD — Kitchen Sink Press

1 ❑ Jun 1995, b&w Cover: 15.95 **NM** value: **Cover or less**
A: Will Eisner

DRUG WARS — Pioneer

1 ❑ Cover: 1.95 **NM** value: **Cover or less**
Circ: CapCity orders: **1,675**
🕮 Just Say No **A:** Mike Clark **C:** Mike Grell **W:** Hal Schuster

DRUID — Marvel

1 ❑ May 1995 Cover: 2.50 **NM** value: **Cover or less**
Circ: CapCity orders: **12,875**
🕮 Sick Of This **A:** Leonardo Manco **W:** Warren Ellis ★ Origin of Doctor Druid.
2 ❑ Jun 1995 Cover: 1.95 **NM** value: **Cover or less**
Circ: CapCity orders: **9,025**
3 ❑ Jul 1995 Cover: 1.95 **NM** value: **Cover or less**
Circ: CapCity orders: **7,225**
4 ❑ Aug 1995 Cover: 1.95 **NM** value: **Cover or less**
Circ: CapCity orders: **6,400**
final issue.

DRUNKEN FIST — Jademan

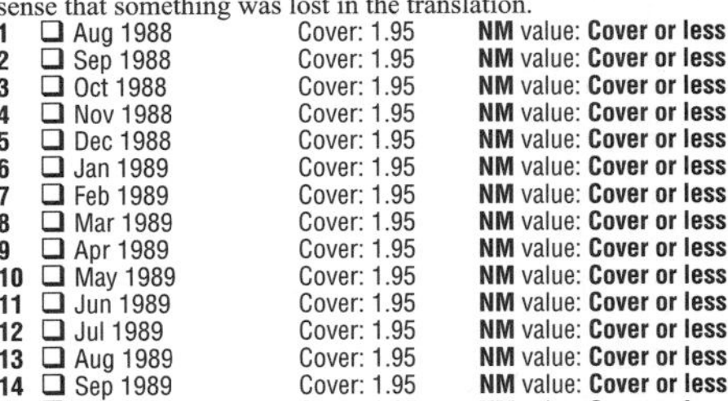

The Drunken Fist is a gentle form of Chinese martial arts capable of overcoming other harder styles. Mike Baron and Tony Wong introduce the form to an American audience in this series.

In the first issue, the living reincarnation of the Buddha Dalai Lama is born and, after being hunted by several villains, taken captive by the evil Indian Lama. Wong Mo Gei, Chek Fai and Drunken Kid fail in their mission to protect the Spiritual Child and set out to redeem themselves. Six years later, the child runs away from his captor, but seems to find greater trouble-he stumbles across the ruthless soldiers of the Eternal Clan. Luckily, Chek Fai appears to challenge the would-be kidnappers.

Attempting to capitalize on what was then a red-hot martial arts market, Drunken Fist misses the mark. While the fight sequences are illustrated so as to accentuate the action, flow through the story's panels is illogical and confusing, leaving readers with the sense that something was lost in the translation.

1 ❑ Aug 1988 Cover: 1.95 **NM** value: **Cover or less**
2 ❑ Sep 1988 Cover: 1.95 **NM** value: **Cover or less**
3 ❑ Oct 1988 Cover: 1.95 **NM** value: **Cover or less**
4 ❑ Nov 1988 Cover: 1.95 **NM** value: **Cover or less**
5 ❑ Dec 1988 Cover: 1.95 **NM** value: **Cover or less**
6 ❑ Jan 1989 Cover: 1.95 **NM** value: **Cover or less**
7 ❑ Feb 1989 Cover: 1.95 **NM** value: **Cover or less**
8 ❑ Mar 1989 Cover: 1.95 **NM** value: **Cover or less**
9 ❑ Apr 1989 Cover: 1.95 **NM** value: **Cover or less**
10 ❑ May 1989 Cover: 1.95 **NM** value: **Cover or less**
11 ❑ Jun 1989 Cover: 1.95 **NM** value: **Cover or less**
12 ❑ Jul 1989 Cover: 1.95 **NM** value: **Cover or less**
13 ❑ Aug 1989 Cover: 1.95 **NM** value: **Cover or less**
14 ❑ Sep 1989 Cover: 1.95 **NM** value: **Cover or less**
15 ❑ Oct 1989 Cover: 1.95 **NM** value: **Cover or less**

CGC-graded: Multiply prices above by **33 for 9.9 M** • **16 for 9.8 NM/M** • **7 for 9.6 NM+** • **5 for 9.4 NM** • **2.5 for 9.2 NM-** • **1.5 for 9.0 VF/NM**

16 ❑ Nov 1989 Cover: 1.95 **NM** value: **Cover or less**
17 ❑ Dec 1989 Cover: 1.95 **NM** value: **Cover or less**
18 ❑ Jan 1990 Cover: 1.95 **NM** value: **Cover or less**
19 ❑ Feb 1990 Cover: 1.95 **NM** value: **Cover or less**
20 ❑ Mar 1990 Cover: 1.95 **NM** value: **Cover or less**
21 ❑ Apr 1990 Cover: 1.95 **NM** value: **Cover or less**
22 ❑ May 1990 Cover: 1.95 **NM** value: **Cover or less**
23 ❑ Jun 1990 Cover: 1.95 **NM** value: **Cover or less**
24 ❑ Jul 1990 Cover: 1.95 **NM** value: **Cover or less**
25 ❑ Aug 1990 Cover: 1.95 **NM** value: **Cover or less**
26 ❑ Sep 1990 Cover: 1.95 **NM** value: **Cover or less**
27 ❑ Oct 1990 Cover: 1.95 **NM** value: **Cover or less**
28 ❑ Nov 1990 Cover: 1.95 **NM** value: **Cover or less**
29 ❑ Dec 1990 Cover: 1.95 **NM** value: **Cover or less**
30 ❑ Jan 1991 Cover: 1.95 **NM** value: **Cover or less**
31 ❑ Feb 1991 Cover: 1.95 **NM** value: **Cover or less**
32 ❑ Mar 1991 Cover: 1.95 **NM** value: **Cover or less**
33 ❑ Apr 1991 Cover: 1.95 **NM** value: **Cover or less**
34 ❑ May 1991 Cover: 1.95 **NM** value: **Cover or less**
35 ❑ Jun 1991 Cover: 1.95 **NM** value: **Cover or less**
36 ❑ Jul 1991 Cover: 1.95 **NM** value: **Cover or less**
37 ❑ Aug 1991 Cover: 1.95 **NM** value: **Cover or less**
38 ❑ Sep 1991 Cover: 1.95 **NM** value: **Cover or less**
39 ❑ Oct 1991 Cover: 1.95 **NM** value: **Cover or less**
40 ❑ Nov 1991 Cover: 1.95 **NM** value: **Cover or less**
41 ❑ Dec 1991 Cover: 1.95 **NM** value: **Cover or less**
42 ❑ Jan 1992 Cover: 1.95 **NM** value: **Cover or less**

DRY ROT — Zolton
1 ❑ b&w Cover: 2.95 **NM** value: **Cover or less**

DUCK AND COVER — Cat-Head
1 ❑ b&w Cover: 2.00 **NM** value: **Cover or less**
2 ❑ b&w Cover: 2.00 **NM** value: **Cover or less**

DUCKBOTS — Blackthorne
1 ❑ Cover: 1.75 **NM** value: **2.00**
2 ❑ Cover: 1.75 **NM** value: **2.00**

DUCKMAN — Dark Horse
1 ❑ Sep 1990, b&w Cover: 1.95 **NM** value: **2.00**
★ 1st Appearance of Duckman.
2 ❑ b&w Cover: 1.95 **NM** value: **2.00**
SE 1❑ Apr 1990, b&w Cover: 1.95 **NM** value: **2.00**
No issue number. One-shot.

DUCKMAN: THE MOB FROG SAGA — Topps
1 ❑ Nov 1994 Cover: 2.50 **NM** value: **Cover or less**
Circ: CapCity orders: **7,250**
A: Jay Lynch; Gary Whitney; Jim Siergey **W:** Stefan Petrucha
2 ❑ Dec 1994 Cover: 2.50 **NM** value: **Cover or less**
Circ: CapCity orders: **5,225**
A: Jay Lynch; Gary Whitney; Jim Siergey **W:** Stefan Petrucha
3 ❑ Feb 1995 Cover: 2.50 **NM** value: **Cover or less**
Circ: CapCity orders: **4,225**
A: Jay Lynch; Gary Fields; Scott Shaw(cover) **W:** Stefan Petrucha

DUCKMAN (TOPPS) — Topps
1 ❑ Nov 1994 Cover: 2.50 **NM** value: **Cover or less**
Circ: CapCity orders: **8,900**
Naked Duck; The Sewer People **A:** Craig Yoe **W:** Stefan Petrucha
2 ❑ Dec 1994 Cover: 2.50 **NM** value: **Cover or less**
Circ: CapCity orders: **6,175**
Where's Grandma-ma? **A:** Jay Lynch; Gary Whitney; Jim Siergey **W:** Stefan Petrucha ★ 1st Appearance of King Chicken. ★ Versus King Chicken.
3 ❑ Mar 1995 Cover: 2.50 **NM** value: **Cover or less**
Circ: CapCity orders: **4,700**
Night of the Living Duck **A:** Craig Yoe **W:** Stefan Petrucha
4 ❑ Mar 1995 Cover: 2.50 **NM** value: **Cover or less**
Circ: CapCity orders: **3,700**
W: Stefan Petrucha
5 ❑ May 1995 Cover: 2.50 **NM** value: **Cover or less**
Circ: CapCity orders: **3,250**
W: Stefan Petrucha
6 ❑ Cover: 2.50 **NM** value: **Cover or less**
Circ: CapCity orders: **2,825**
Star Trek: Abducckshuns **W:** Stefan Petrucha

DUCKTALES (DISNEY'S...) — Disney
1 ❑ Jun 1990 Cover: 1.50 **NM** value: **2.00**
Circ: CapCity orders: **10,150**
The Ice Demon **A:** Robert Bat; C. Quartieri **W:** Marv Wolfman
2 ❑ Jul 1990 Cover: 1.50 **NM** value: **Cover or less**
Circ: CapCity orders: **7,050**
A: Robert Bat; C. Quartieri **W:** Marv Wolfman
3 ❑ Aug 1990 Cover: 1.50 **NM** value: **Cover or less**
Circ: CapCity orders: **7,700**
The Fall of New Atlantis! **A:** Robert Bat; C. Quartieri **W:** Marv Wolfman ★ Versus Magica de Spell.
4 ❑ Sep 1990 Cover: 1.50 **NM** value: **Cover or less**
Circ: CapCity orders: **7,700**
5 ❑ Oct 1990 Cover: 1.50 **NM** value: **Cover or less**
Circ: CapCity orders: **7,650**
6 ❑ Nov 1990 Cover: 1.50 **NM** value: **Cover or less**
Circ: CapCity orders: **7,050**
7 ❑ Dec 1990 Cover: 1.50 **NM** value: **Cover or less**
Circ: CapCity orders: **6,650**
8 ❑ Jan 1991 Cover: 1.50 **NM** value: **Cover or less**
Circ: CapCity orders: **6,650**
Of Badges 'n' Beagles!
9 ❑ Feb 1991 Cover: 1.50 **NM** value: **Cover or less**
Circ: CapCity orders: **6,450**
The Gold Odyssey, Part 1; Terror at the Top of the World
10 ❑ Mar 1991 Cover: 1.50 **NM** value: **Cover or less**
Circ: CapCity orders: **6,200**
The Gold Odyssey, Part 2; Moon of Gold
11 ❑ Apr 1991 Cover: 1.50 **NM** value: **Cover or less**
Circ: CapCity orders: **5,700**
The Gold Odyssey, Part 3; The Once and Future Warlock
12 ❑ May 1991 Cover: 1.50 **NM** value: **Cover or less**
Circ: CapCity orders: **5,400**
The Gold Odyssey, Part 4; Lost Beyond the Milky Way
13 ❑ Jun 1991 Cover: 1.50 **NM** value: **Cover or less**
Circ: CapCity orders: **5,250**
The Gold Odyssey, Part 5
14 ❑ Jul 1991 Cover: 1.50 **NM** value: **Cover or less**
Circ: CapCity orders: **5,250**
The Gold Odyssey, Part 6; Planet Blue
15 ❑ Aug 1991 Cover: 1.50 **NM** value: **Cover or less**
Circ: CapCity orders: **5,200**
The Gold Odyssey, Part 7; Gold Odyssey, Part 7
16 ❑ Sep 1991 Cover: 1.50 **NM** value: **Cover or less**
Circ: CapCity orders: **5,100**
The Great Chase
17 ❑ Oct 1991 Cover: 1.50 **NM** value: **Cover or less**
Circ: CapCity orders: **5,150**
Time Tetrad, Part 4
18 ❑ Nov 1991 Cover: 1.50 **NM** value: **Cover or less**
Circ: CapCity orders: **4,900**
Dime in Time, Part 2

DUCKTALES (GLADSTONE) — Gladstone
1 ❑ Oct 1988 Cover: 1.50 **NM** value: **2.00**
Circ: CapCity orders: **7,375**
A: Carl Barks
2 ❑ Nov 1988 Cover: 1.50 **NM** value: **Cover or less**
Circ: CapCity orders: **5,400**
3 ❑ Jan 1989 Cover: 0.95 **NM** value: **1.50**
Circ: CapCity orders: **5,375**
4 ❑ Feb 1989 Cover: 0.95 **NM** value: **1.50**
Circ: CapCity orders: **6,175**
5 ❑ Apr 1989 Cover: 0.95 **NM** value: **1.50**
Circ: CapCity orders: **6,450**
6 ❑ May 1989 Cover: 0.95 **NM** value: **1.50**
Circ: CapCity orders: **6,400**
7 ❑ Jul 1989 Cover: 0.95 **NM** value: **1.50**
Circ: CapCity orders: **6,250**
8 ❑ Aug 1989 Cover: 0.95 **NM** value: **1.50**
Circ: CapCity orders: **6,300**
9 ❑ Oct 1989 Cover: 1.50 **NM** value: **Cover or less**
Circ: CapCity orders: **6,300**
A: Carl Barks
10 ❑ Nov 1989 Cover: 1.50 **NM** value: **Cover or less**
Circ: CapCity orders: **6,300**
A: Carl Barks
11 ❑ Jan 1990 Cover: 1.50 **NM** value: **Cover or less**
Circ: CapCity orders: **6,250**
A: Carl Barks
12 ❑ Mar 1990 Cover: 1.95 **NM** value: **Cover or less**
Circ: CapCity orders: **5,750**
The City Under The Ice; Mythtic Mystery **A:** Carl Barks
13 ❑ May 1990 Cover: 1.95 **NM** value: **Cover or less**
Circ: CapCity orders: **5,800**
A: Carl Barks

DUCKTALES: THE MOVIE — Disney
1 ❑ Cover: 5.95 **NM** value: **Cover or less**
Treasure of the Lost Lamp • adaptation **A:** Cosme Quartieri; Carlos Valenti; Robert Bat; Run Torreiro **W:** John Lustig

DUDLEY — Prize
1 ❑ Nov 1949 Cover: 0.10 **NM** value: **90.00**
2 ❑ Jan 1950 Cover: 0.10 **NM** value: **50.00**
3 ❑ Mar 1950 Cover: 0.10 **NM** value: **50.00**

DUDLEY DO-RIGHT — Charlton
Rocky and Bullwinkle TV appearances, courtesy of Jay Ward (1920-1989) and Bill Scott (1920-1985), in the early 1960s were accompanied by other features. The moronic Dudley (voiced by Scott) was a Canadian Mountie ever on the trail of the villainous Snidely Whiplash, who was often after Inspector Fenwick's daughter Nell (who yearned, in turn, for Dudley). Even Dudley's horse, Horse, was smarter than the bumbling Mountie. Eventually, Dudley got a show with his name in the title (1969-1970), The Dudley Do-Right Show. The comic book's run in 1970 and 1971 is a testimonial to the character. — Maggie

1 ❑ Aug 1970 Cover: 0.15 **NM** value: **20.00**
• **CGC:** 1 graded, best 9.0
2 ❑ Oct 1970 Cover: 0.15 **NM** value: **12.00**
3 ❑ Dec 1970 Cover: 0.15 **NM** value: **10.00**
4 ❑ Feb 1971 Cover: 0.15 **NM** value: **8.00**
5 ❑ Apr 1971 Cover: 0.15 **NM** value: **8.00**
6 ❑ Jun 1971 Cover: 0.15 **NM** value: **8.00**
7 ❑ Aug 1971 Cover: 0.15 **NM** value: **8.00**

DUMB-ASS EXPRESS — McMann & Tate
1 ❑ Cover: 2.95 **NM** value: **Cover or less**
• slightly oversized. Assie: Yo Assie's Mine!; Interior Decorator Man; Little Blot and Little Larda 1998; The Carneys: Fatal Ape-Traction!; Kisses from Uranus; Touched by an A**hole; Rich Retard: No Sense!; Hot Pants, Cold Sores **A:** Bill Golliher; Dan Parent **W:** Bill Golliher; Dan Parent ★ Appearance of Carneys.

DUMM $2099 — Parody Press
1 ❑ Cover: 2.95 **NM** value: **Cover or less**
Cover forms triptych with Rummage $2099, Pummeler $2099. **A:** Russ Sever **W:** Ross Turner

DUNC AND LOO — Dell
1 ❑ Oct 1961 Cover: 0.10 **NM** value: **80.00**
2 ❑ Jan 1962 Cover: 0.10 **NM** value: **60.00**
3 ❑ 1962 Cover: 0.10 **NM** value: **50.00**
4 ❑ 1962 Cover: 0.12 **NM** value: **40.00**
5 ❑ 1963 Cover: 0.12 **NM** value: **40.00**
6 ❑ Apr 1963 Cover: 0.12 **NM** value: **0.40**
7 ❑ Jul 1963 Cover: 0.12 **NM** value: **0.40**
8 ❑ Oct 1963 Cover: 0.12 **NM** value: **0.40**
• **CGC:** 2 graded, best 9.2

DUNCAN'S KINGDOM — Image
Bk 2❑ ca. 1999 Cover: 2.95 **NM** value: **Cover or less**
Circ: Diamd. preorders: **3,286**
A: Derek Kirk **W:** Gene Yang
Bk 1❑ ca. 1999 Cover: 2.95 **NM** value: **Cover or less**
Circ: Diamd. preorders: **5,580**
A: Derek Kirk **W:** Gene Yang

DUNE — Marvel
Director David Lynch brought Dune, the classic SF novel by Frank Herbert, to movie-going audiences in 1984. The film starred rock star Sting, Kyle MacLachlan, and Patrick Stewart ("Captain Picard" on Star Trek: The Next Generation). While a colossal critical and commercial failure, the film did manage to get a comics adaptation from Marvel.

Dune is set on the desert planet Arrakis, the only producer of the spice "melange" in the galaxy. Melange extends life, expands consciousness, and can be used to fold space and time in order to travel to any location without actually moving. Which is more than enough to make for a darn good maguffin in this story: As the saying goes, "He who controls the spice controls the universe!"

1 ❑ Apr 1985 Cover: 0.75 **NM** value: **1.50**
A: Bill Sienkiewicz **W:** Ralph Macchio
2 ❑ May 1985 Cover: 0.75 **NM** value: **1.50**
A: Bill Sienkiewicz **W:** Ralph Macchio
3 ❑ Jun 1985 Cover: 0.75 **NM** value: **1.50**
A: Bill Sienkiewicz **W:** Ralph Macchio
Bk 1❑ Cover: 3.95 **NM** value: **Cover or less**

DUNG BOYS, THE — Kitchen Sink
1 ❑ Apr 1996, b&w Cover: 2.95 **NM** value: **Cover or less**
2 ❑ May 1996 Cover: 2.95 **NM** value: **Cover or less**
nude cover with black bars.
3 ❑ Jun 1996 Cover: 2.95 **NM** value: **Cover or less**
final issue.

DUNGEONEERS, THE — Silverwolf
1 ❑ Cover: 1.50 **NM** value: **Cover or less**
2 ❑ Oct 1986 Cover: 1.50 **NM** value: **Cover or less**
Into the Ogres' Lair **A:** Tim Foster **W:** Kris Silver
3 ❑ Cover: 1.50 **NM** value: **Cover or less**
4 ❑ Cover: 1.50 **NM** value: **Cover or less**

DUPLEX PLANET ILLUSTRATED — Fantagraphics
1 ❑ Jan 1993, b&w Cover: 2.95 **NM** value: **Cover or less**
My First Funeral; What's the Wildest Party You Were At?; Ken Eglin's Wildest Party; A Visit to Larry Green; Shut Up; Larry Green & His Uncle; Abe and the Witches; Big Ideas **A:** Rick Altergott; Dan Clowes; Roberta Gregory; Doug Allen; Terry Laban; Dean Rohrer; Gary Leib; Mike Schafer; Tim Hensley; Wayno **W:** David Greenberger
2 ❑ 1993 Cover: 2.50 **NM** value: **Cover or less**
3 ❑ 1993 Cover: 2.50 **NM** value: **Cover or less**
4 ❑ 1993 Cover: 2.50 **NM** value: **Cover or less**
5 ❑ 1993 Cover: 2.95 **NM** value: **Cover or less**
6 ❑ 1994 **NM** value: **2.95**
7 ❑ 1994b&w Cover: 2.50 **NM** value: **Cover or less**
8 ❑ May 1994, b&w Cover: 2.50 **NM** value: **Cover or less**
9 ❑ Jul 1994, b&w Cover: 2.50 **NM** value: **Cover or less**
10 ❑ Sep 1994, b&w Cover: 2.50 **NM** value: **Cover or less**
11 ❑ Dec 1994 Cover: 2.75 **NM** value: **Cover or less**
Bern & Edwina; The King of Love; did you ever have a Broken Heart; Obstacles of Life; Cross over in the Brain; Bedtime; The Prettiest Girl in the World; Punching Ham Gravy; Thivierge; **A:** Michael Aushenker; Pat Moriarty; Ellen Forney; Dean Rohrer; Jim Blanchard; Jim Siergey; Mike Schafer; Pete Sickman-Garner; Wayno; Adam Godamnowics; Ben Prisk; C. Cilla; Paul Bryan **W:** David Greenberger
12 ❑ 1995 **NM** value: **2.50**
13 ❑ 1995 **NM** value: **2.50**
14 ❑ 1995 **NM** value: **2.50**
15 ❑ Apr 1996, b&w Cover: 4.95 **NM** value: **Cover or less**
C: Chris Ware

DURANGO KID, THE — AC
1 ❑ Cover: 2.50 **NM** value: **Cover or less**
• some color
2 ❑ b&w Cover: 2.75 **NM** value: **Cover or less**
A: Frank Frazetta
3 ❑ Cover: 4.95 **NM** value: **Cover or less**

Other grades: Multiply prices above by **1.5 for Mint • 2/3 for Very Fine • 1/3 for Fine • 1/5 for Very Good • 1/8 for Good**

DURANGO KID — Magazine Enterprises

The Durango Kid was the focal character of a string of Western movies in the 1940s starring Charles Starrett (1903-1986). The first installment featured him as Jim Lowery, also known as The Durango Kid. Soon, there was a series of films featuring Starrett as The Durango Kid, with a string of alter egos (Kip Allen, Steve Williams, Jeff Waring, Steve Ranson, Steve Buckner, etc.) through 1952.

The comic-book version ran from 1949 to 1955, and early issues featured photo covers of Starrett. Among notable features of the comic-book series was the Frank Frazetta art on the back-up starring Dan Brand and Tipi.

Reprints of this series would come decades later from Avalon.
— Maggie

1 ❑ Oct 1949 Cover: 0.10 **NM** value: **300.00**
• **CGC:** 1 graded, best 2.0
2 ❑ Dec 1949 Cover: 0.10 **NM** value: **200.00**
3 ❑ Feb 1950 Cover: 0.10 **NM** value: **200.00**
4 ❑ Apr 1950 Cover: 0.10 **NM** value: **100.00**
5 ❑ Jun 1950 Cover: 0.10 **NM** value: **100.00**
6 ❑ Aug 1950 Cover: 0.10 **NM** value: **50.00**
7 ❑ Oct 1950 Cover: 0.10 **NM** value: **50.00**
• **CGC:** 2 graded, best 9.0
8 ❑ Dec 1950 Cover: 0.10 **NM** value: **50.00**
9 ❑ 1951 Cover: 0.10 **NM** value: **50.00**
10 ❑ 1951 Cover: 0.10 **NM** value: **50.00**
11 ❑ 1951 Cover: 0.10 **NM** value: **50.00**
12 ❑ 1951 Cover: 0.10 **NM** value: **50.00**
13 ❑ 1951 Cover: 0.10 **NM** value: **50.00**
14 ❑ 1951 Cover: 0.10 **NM** value: **50.00**
15 ❑ 1952 Cover: 0.10 **NM** value: **50.00**
16 ❑ 1952 Cover: 0.10 **NM** value: **50.00**
17 ❑ 1952 Cover: 0.10 **NM** value: **50.00**
18 ❑ 1952 Cover: 0.10 **NM** value: **50.00**
19 ❑ 1952 Cover: 0.10 **NM** value: **50.00**
20 ❑ 1952 Cover: 0.10 **NM** value: **50.00**
21 ❑ Cover: 0.10 **NM** value: **50.00**
22 ❑ Cover: 0.10 **NM** value: **50.00**
23 ❑ 1953 Cover: 0.10 **NM** value: **50.00**
24 ❑ 1953 Cover: 0.10 **NM** value: **60.00**
25 ❑ 1953 Cover: 0.10 **NM** value: **50.00**
26 ❑ 1953 Cover: 0.10 **NM** value: **50.00**
27 ❑ Cover: 0.10 **NM** value: **50.00**
28 ❑ Cover: 0.10 **NM** value: **50.00**
29 ❑ 1954 Cover: 0.10 **NM** value: **50.00**
30 ❑ 1954 Cover: 0.10 **NM** value: **50.00**
31 ❑ 1954 Cover: 0.10 **NM** value: **50.00**
32 ❑ 1954 Cover: 0.10 **NM** value: **50.00**
33 ❑ 1954 Cover: 0.10 **NM** value: **50.00**
34 ❑ Cover: 0.10 **NM** value: **50.00**
35 ❑ Cover: 0.10 **NM** value: **50.00**
36 ❑ Cover: 0.10 **NM** value: **50.00**
37 ❑ Cover: 0.10 **NM** value: **50.00**
38 ❑ 1955 Cover: 0.10 **NM** value: **50.00**
39 ❑ 1955 Cover: 0.10 **NM** value: **50.00**
40 ❑ 1955 Cover: 0.10 **NM** value: **50.00**
41 ❑ 1955 Cover: 0.10 **NM** value: **50.00**

DUSK — Deadwood Press

1 ❑ b&w Cover: 3.00 **NM** value: **Cover or less**
cardstock cover.

DUSTCOVERS – THE COLLECTED SANDMAN COVERS — DC / Vertigo

Bk 1/HC❑ Cover: 39.95 **NM** value: **Cover or less**
hardcover. • contains new Sandman story

DUSTY STAR — Image

0 ❑ Apr 1997, b&w Cover: 2.95 **NM** value: **Cover or less**
Circ: Diamd. preorders: **10,889**
• collects stories from Negative Burn #28 and #37
1 ❑ Jun 1997, b&w Cover: 2.95 **NM** value: **Cover or less**
Circ: Diamd. preorders: **10,796**
📖 Aeroplane **A:** Andrew Robinson **W:** Joe Pruett

DUTCH DECKER AND THE VOODOO QUEEN — Caliber

1 ❑ b&w Cover: 2.50 **NM** value: **Cover or less**

DV8 — DC / Wildstorm

0 ❑ Dec 1998 Cover: 2.50 **NM** value: **3.00**
Circ: Diamd. preorders: **20,885**
0.5 ❑ Jan 1997 Cover: 5.00 **NM** value: **Cover or less**
• Wizard 1/2 Promotional edition.
0.5/A❑Jan 1997 **NM** value: **5.00**
variant cover. • Wizard 1/2 Promotional edition.
0.5/GO❑Jan 1997 Cover: 10.00 **NM** value: **Cover or less**
• Wizard 1/2 "Authentic Gold" promotional edition.
0.5/PI❑Jan 1997 Cover: 5.00 **NM** value: **Cover or less**
• Wizard 1/2 Platinum promotional edition. • Wizard promotional item;platinum version
1/A ❑ Aug 1996 Cover: 2.50 **NM** value: **3.00**
cover says Sep, indicia says Aug. 📖 Lust for Life **W:** Warren Ellis
1/B ❑ Aug 1996 Cover: 2.50 **NM** value: **3.00**
cover says Sep, indicia says Aug. 📖 Lust for Life **W:** Warren Ellis
1/C ❑ Aug 1996 Cover: 2.50 **NM** value: **4.00**
cover says Sep, indicia says Aug. 📖 Lust for Life **A:** Humberto Ramos; Jim Lee(cover) **W:** Warren Ellis
1/D ❑ Aug 1996 Cover: 2.50 **NM** value: **3.00**
cover says Sep, indicia says Aug. 📖 Lust for Life **W:** Warren Ellis
1/E ❑ Aug 1996 Cover: 2.50 **NM** value: **3.00**
cover says Sep, indicia says Aug. 📖 Lust for Life **C:** Jim Lee **W:** Warren Ellis
1/F ❑ Aug 1996 Cover: 2.50 **NM** value: **3.00**
cover says Sep, indicia says Aug. 📖 Lust for Life **W:** Warren Ellis
1/G ❑ Aug 1996 Cover: 2.50 **NM** value: **3.00**
cover says Sep, indicia says Aug. 📖 Lust for Life **W:** Warren Ellis
1/H ❑ Aug 1996 Cover: 2.50 **NM** value: **3.00**
cover says Sep, indicia says Aug. 📖 Lust for Life **W:** Warren Ellis
2 ❑ Nov 1996 Cover: 2.50 **NM** value: **Cover or less**
Circ: Direct Market orders: **74,323**
📖 Some Weird Sin **A:** Humberto Ramos **W:** Warren Ellis
3 ❑ Dec 1996 Cover: 2.50 **NM** value: **Cover or less**
Circ: Direct Market orders: **66,605**
📖 Neighborhood Threat **A:** Lopez **W:** Warren Ellis
4 ❑ Jan 1997 Cover: 2.50 **NM** value: **Cover or less**
Circ: Diamd. preorders: **53,636**
📖 Miss Drugstore **A:** Humberto Ramos **W:** Warren Ellis
5 ❑ Feb 1997 Cover: 2.50 **NM** value: **Cover or less**
Circ: Diamd. preorders: **48,051**
6 ❑ Mar 1997 Cover: 2.50 **NM** value: **Cover or less**
Circ: Diamd. preorders: **46,516**
7 ❑ Apr 1997 Cover: 2.50 **NM** value: **Cover or less**
Circ: Diamd. preorders: **42,006**
cover says May, indicia says Apr.
8 ❑ May 1997 Cover: 2.50 **NM** value: **Cover or less**
Circ: Diamd. preorders: **42,832**
cover says Jun, indicia says May.
9 ❑ Jun 1997 Cover: 2.50 **NM** value: **Cover or less**
Circ: Diamd. preorders: **42,060**
10 ❑ Jul 1997 Cover: 2.50 **NM** value: **Cover or less**
Circ: Diamd. preorders: **39,744**
11 ❑ Sep 1997 Cover: 2.50 **NM** value: **Cover or less**
Circ: Diamd. preorders: **35,142**
📖 Facets **A:** Juvaun Kirby **W:** Mike Heisler
12 ❑ Oct 1997 Cover: 2.50 **NM** value: **Cover or less**
Circ: Diamd. preorders: **33,943**
📖 Marriage Of Convenience **A:** Juvaun Kirby **W:** Mike Heisler
13 ❑ Nov 1997 Cover: 2.50 **NM** value: **Cover or less**
Circ: Diamd. preorders: **31,905**
📖 The Sad Tale of Senator Killory **A:** Juvaun Kirby **W:** Mike Heisler
14/A❑Dec 1997 Cover: 2.50 **NM** value: **Cover or less**
Circ: Diamd. preorders: **28,235**
Has woman on cover. 📖 Barely Legal **A:** Tom Raney **W:** Mike Heisler
14/B❑Dec 1997 Cover: 2.50 **NM** value: **Cover or less**
Whole group on cover. 📖 Barely Legal • white background **A:** Tom Raney **W:** Mike Heisler
14/C❑Dec 1997 Cover: 2.50 **NM** value: **6.00**
• Voyager pack with preview of Danger Girl
15 ❑ Jan 1998 Cover: 2.50 **NM** value: **Cover or less**
Circ: Diamd. preorders: **28,752**
📖 Settling Accounts **A:** Tom Raney **W:** Mike Heisler
16 ❑ Feb 1998 Cover: 2.50 **NM** value: **Cover or less**
Circ: Diamd. preorders: **26,581**
📖 Intersection **A:** Tom Raney **W:** Mike Heisler
17 ❑ Apr 1998 Cover: 2.50 **NM** value: **Cover or less**
Circ: Diamd. preorders: **26,034**
📖 Gen-Passive **A:** Jason Johnson **W:** Mike Heisler
18 ❑ May 1998 Cover: 2.50 **NM** value: **Cover or less**
Circ: Diamd. preorders: **24,126**
📖 Same as it Ever Was **A:** Jason Johnson **W:** Mike Heisler ★ Appearance of Grifter.
19 ❑ Jun 1998 Cover: 2.50 **NM** value: **Cover or less**
Circ: Diamd. preorders: **23,956**
📖 Larger Concerns **A:** Al Rio **W:** Mike Heisler
20 ❑ Jul 1998 Cover: 2.50 **NM** value: **Cover or less**
Circ: Diamd. preorders: **22,180**
📖 Lounging in the Ammo Dump **A:** Al Rio **W:** Mike Heisler
21 ❑ Aug 1998 Cover: 2.50 **NM** value: **Cover or less**
Circ: Diamd. preorders: **20,826**
📖 Anthrax! **A:** Al Rio **W:** Mike Heisler
22 ❑ Sep 1998 Cover: 2.50 **NM** value: **Cover or less**
Circ: Diamd. preorders: **22,688**
📖 Choices **A:** Al Rio **W:** Mike Heisler
22/A❑Sep 1998 Cover: 2.50 **NM** value: **Cover or less**
alternate cover (white background).
23 ❑ Oct 1998 Cover: 2.50 **NM** value: **Cover or less**
Circ: Diamd. preorders: **19,992**
📖 Gone to Ground **A:** Al Rio **W:** Mike Heisler
24 ❑ Nov 1998 Cover: 2.50 **NM** value: **Cover or less**
Circ: Diamd. preorders: **19,204**
📖 Slipstream Prologue; Slipstream **A:** Al Rio **W:** Mike Heisler
25 ❑ Dec 1998 Cover: 2.50 **NM** value: **Cover or less**
Circ: Diamd. preorders: **19,471**
📖 Slipstream **A:** Al Rio **W:** Mike Heisler
26 ❑ May 1999 Cover: 2.50 **NM** value: **Cover or less**
Circ: Diamd. preorders: **18,920**
📖 Lost and Found **A:** Al Rio **W:** Mike Heisler
27 ❑ Jun 1999 Cover: 2.50 **NM** value: **Cover or less**
Circ: Diamd. preorders: **19,241**
📖 Family **A:** Al Rio **W:** Mike Heisler
28 ❑ Jul 1999 Cover: 2.50 **NM** value: **Cover or less**
Circ: Diamd. preorders: **18,620**
A: Al Rio **W:** Mike Heisler
29 ❑ Aug 1999 Cover: 2.50 **NM** value: **Cover or less**
Circ: Diamd. preorders: **17,638**
📖 An Affront of Liberty **A:** Al Rio **W:** Mike Heisler
30 ❑ Sep 1999 Cover: 2.50 **NM** value: **Cover or less**
Circ: Diamd. preorders: **17,198**
📖 Things Fall Apart, Part 1 **A:** Al Rio **W:** Mike Heisler
31 ❑ Oct 1999 Cover: 2.50 **NM** value: **Cover or less**
Circ: Diamd. preorders: **16,240**
📖 Things Fall Apart, Part 2 **A:** Al Rio **W:** Mike Heisler
32 ❑ Nov 1999 Cover: 2.50 **NM** value: **Cover or less**
Circ: Diamd. preorders: **15,323**
Anl 1❑Jan 1998 Cover: 2.95 **NM** value: **Cover or less**
Circ: Diamd. preorders: **23,029**
📖 Head Trips **A:** Ale Garza **W:** Mike Heisler; Ruben Diaz
Anl 1999❑Mar 1999 Cover: 3.50 **NM** value: **Cover or less**
Circ: Diamd. preorders: **17,032**
No issue number. wraparound cover. • continued from Gen13 Annual 1999

DV8 RAVE — Image

1 ❑ Jul 1996 Cover: 1.75 **NM** value: **2.00**

DV8 VS. BLACK OPS — Image

The members of Black Ops were once the elite tactical unit for International Operations, until they were falsely branded as outlaws. Meanwhile, DV8 is a group of misfit powerhouses created by the same experiments that produced Gen13. They are led by the enigmatic Ivana Baiul, who uses their talents for her own dark ambitions.

Now begins the crossover. Ivana is chasing a nanovirus capable of rewriting human DNA. With it, she hopes to be able to control not just DV8, but eventually all of the world's superbeings. Meanwhile, Colonel Crane and his Black Ops team are determined to destroy the nanovirus before it falls into the wrong hands.

1 ❑ Oct 1997 Cover: 2.50 **NM** value: **Cover or less**
Circ: Diamd. preorders: **29,627**
📖 The Techtromis Design, Part 1 **A:** Dan Norton **W:** Shon Bury
2 ❑ Nov 1997 Cover: 2.50 **NM** value: **Cover or less**
Circ: Diamd. preorders: **26,273**
📖 The Techtromis Design, Part 2 **A:** Dan Norton **W:** Shon Bury
3 ❑ Dec 1997 Cover: 2.50 **NM** value: **Cover or less**
Circ: Diamd. preorders: **23,860**
📖 The Techtromis Design, Part 3 **A:** Dan Norton; Juvaun Kirby **W:** Shon Bury

DYKE'S DELIGHT — Fanny

1 ❑ **NM** value: **2.95**
📖 Auntie Studs: The Early Years **A:** Roberta Gregory **W:** Roberta Gregory
2 ❑ **NM** value: **2.95**
📖 Auntie Studs: Rebel Without A Cat! **A:** Karen Platt; Roberta Gregory **W:** Karen Platt; Roberta Gregory

DYLAN DOG — Dark Horse

1 ❑ Mar 1999 Cover: 4.95 **NM** value: **Cover or less**
Circ: Diamd. preorders: **7,109**
A: Angelo Stano **W:** Tiziano Sclavi
2 ❑ Apr 1999 Cover: 4.95 **NM** value: **Cover or less**
Circ: Diamd. preorders: **5,738**
A: Angelo Stano **W:** Tiziano Sclavi
3 ❑ May 1999 Cover: 4.95 **NM** value: **Cover or less**
Circ: Diamd. preorders: **4,693**
A: Angelo Stano **W:** Tiziano Sclavi
4 ❑ Jun 1999 Cover: 4.95 **NM** value: **Cover or less**
Circ: Diamd. preorders: **4,370**
A: Angelo Stano **W:** Tiziano Sclavi
5 ❑ Jul 1999 Cover: 4.95 **NM** value: **Cover or less**
Circ: Diamd. preorders: **4,306**
A: Angelo Stano **W:** Tiziano Sclavi
6 ❑ Aug 1999 Cover: 4.95 **NM** value: **Cover or less**
Circ: Diamd. preorders: **4,130**
A: Angelo Stano **W:** Tiziano Sclavi

DYNAMIC CLASSICS — DC

1 ❑ Sep 1978 Cover: 0.50 **NM** value: **2.50**
• **CGC:** 1 graded, best 9.6
📖 Batman:The Secret of the Waiting Graves; Manhunter: The Himalaya Incident

DYNAMIC COMICS — Harry A. Chesler

11 ❑ Sep 1944 Cover: 0.10 **NM** value: **900.00**
• **CGC:** 2 graded, best 9.2
12 ❑ Nov 1944 Cover: 0.10 **NM** value: **400.00**
• **CGC:** 1 graded, best 8.0
13 ❑ Jan 1945 Cover: 0.10 **NM** value: **400.00**
14 ❑ Apr 1945 Cover: 0.10 **NM** value: **300.00**
15 ❑ Jul 1945 Cover: 0.10 **NM** value: **300.00**
16 ❑ Oct 1945 Cover: 0.10 **NM** value: **300.00**
• **CGC:** 1 graded, best 7.5
17 ❑ Jan 1946 Cover: 0.10 **NM** value: **300.00**
• **CGC:** 1 graded, best 9.2
18 ❑ Apr 1946 Cover: 0.10 **NM** value: **200.00**
• **CGC:** 3 graded, best 8.0
19 ❑ Jul 1946 Cover: 0.10 **NM** value: **200.00**
• **CGC:** 1 graded, best 7.0
20 ❑ Oct 1946 Cover: 0.10 **NM** value: **200.00**
• **CGC:** 1 graded, best 7.5
21 ❑ Jul 1947 Cover: 0.10 **NM** value: **200.00**
22 ❑ Sep 1947 Cover: 0.10 **NM** value: **200.00**
23 ❑ Nov 1947 Cover: 0.10 **NM** value: **200.00**
24 ❑ Mar 1948 Cover: 0.10 **NM** value: **200.00**

DYNAMITE — Comic Media

1 ❑ May 1953 Cover: 0.10 **NM** value: **80.00**
• **CGC:** 1 graded, best 7.0
2 ❑ Jul 1953 Cover: 0.10 **NM** value: **60.00**
3 ❑ Sep 1953 Cover: 0.10 **NM** value: **60.00**
4 ❑ Nov 1953 Cover: 0.10 **NM** value: **60.00**
5 ❑ Jan 1954 Cover: 0.10 **NM** value: **60.00**
6 ❑ Mar 1954 Cover: 0.10 **NM** value: **60.00**

CGC-graded: Multiply prices above by **33 for 9.9 M • 16 for 9.8 NM/M • 7 for 9.6 NM+ • 5 for 9.4 NM • 2.5 for 9.2 NM- • 1.5 for 9.0 VF/NM**

7 ❑ May 1954 Cover: 0.10 **NM** value: **60.00**
8 ❑ Jul 1954 Cover: 0.10 **NM** value: **60.00**
9 ❑ Sep 1954 Cover: 0.10 **NM** value: **60.00**

DYNAMO — Tower

The Tower line of comics is ideal for collectors: there aren't that many of them to find, and they're generally very good. The line is primarily populated by charming, well-drawn, wittily written superheroes allied with the crime-fighting team called T.H.U.N.D.E.R. Agents.

Dynamo is one of the T.H.U.N.D.E.R. Agents, a powerful (but not too bright) foe of evil who gets his powers from a superbelt.

The four issues feature classic work by artist Wally Wood; other artists involved in the series include Spider-Man co-creator Steve Ditko and Reed Crandall. — Maggie

1 ❑ Aug 1966 Cover: 0.25 **NM** value: **40.00**
• **CGC:** 3 graded, best 9.2
A: Wally Wood
2 ❑ Oct 1966 Cover: 0.25 **NM** value: **30.00**
• **CGC:** 2 graded, best 9.0
A: Wally Wood
3 ❑ Mar 1967 Cover: 0.25 **NM** value: **30.00**
• **CGC:** 3 graded, best 9.4
A: Wally Wood
4 ❑ Jun 1967 Cover: 0.25 **NM** value: **30.00**
• **CGC:** 3 graded, best 9.4
A: Wally Wood

DYNAMO JOE — First

1 ❑ May 1986 Cover: 1.25 **NM** value: **1.50**
Circ: CapCity orders: **8,825**
2 ❑ Jun 1986 Cover: 1.25 **NM** value: **Cover or less**
Circ: CapCity orders: **6,900**
📖 Boldshot Brimfire! **A:** Brian Thomas; John Nyberg **W:** John Ostrander
3 ❑ Jul 1986 Cover: 1.25 **NM** value: **Cover or less**
Circ: CapCity orders: **7,025**
4 ❑ Feb 1987 Cover: 1.25 **NM** value: **Cover or less**
Circ: CapCity orders: **5,750**
5 ❑ Mar 1987 Cover: 1.25 **NM** value: **Cover or less**
Circ: CapCity orders: **5,625**
6 ❑ Apr 1987 Cover: 1.25 **NM** value: **Cover or less**
Circ: CapCity orders: **5,300**
7 ❑ May 1987 Cover: 1.25 **NM** value: **Cover or less**
Circ: CapCity orders: **4,825**
8 ❑ Jun 1987 Cover: 1.25 **NM** value: **Cover or less**
Circ: CapCity orders: **4,650**
9 ❑ Jul 1987 Cover: 1.25 **NM** value: **Cover or less**
Circ: CapCity orders: **4,500**
10 ❑ Aug 1987 Cover: 1.25 **NM** value: **Cover or less**
Circ: CapCity orders: **4,625**
11 ❑ Sep 1987 Cover: 1.25 **NM** value: **Cover or less**
Circ: CapCity orders: **4,750**
12 ❑ Oct 1987 Cover: 1.75 **NM** value: **Cover or less**
Circ: CapCity orders: **4,750**
13 ❑ Nov 1987 Cover: 1.75 **NM** value: **Cover or less**
Circ: CapCity orders: **4,725**
14 ❑ Dec 1987 Cover: 1.75 **NM** value: **Cover or less**
Circ: CapCity orders: **4,550**
15 ❑ Jan 1988 Cover: 1.75 **NM** value: **Cover or less**
Circ: CapCity orders: **4,575**
SE 1❑ Jan 1987 Cover: 1.25 **NM** value: **Cover or less**
Circ: CapCity orders: **6,325**

DYNOMUTT — Marvel

1 ❑ Nov 1977 Cover: 0.35 **NM** value: **6.00**
• **CGC:** 2 graded, best 9.6
• Scooby Doo
2 ❑ Jan 1978 Cover: 0.35 **NM** value: **4.00**
• Scooby Doo
3 ❑ Mar 1978 Cover: 0.35 **NM** value: **3.00**
• Scooby Doo
4 ❑ May 1978 Cover: 0.35 **NM** value: **3.00**
• Scooby Doo
5 ❑ Jul 1978 Cover: 0.35 **NM** value: **3.00**
• Scooby Doo
6 ❑ Sep 1978 Cover: 0.35 **NM** value: **3.00**
• Scooby Doo

DYSTOPIK SNOMEN — Slave Labor

1 ❑ Oct 1994 Cover: 4.95 **NM** value: **Cover or less**
• was college newspaper strip

DYSTOPIK SNOMEN (VOL. 2) — Slave Labor

1 ❑ Sep 1995 Cover: 1.50 **NM** value: **Cover or less**
📖 Purple Angst Kafe **A:** Don M. Haring Jr. **W:** Don M. Haring Jr.
2 ❑ Dec 1995 Cover: 1.75 **NM** value: **Cover or less**
📖 The Anxiety Engine **A:** Don M. Haring Jr. **W:** Don M. Haring Jr.

EAGLE (COMIC ZONE) — Comic Zone

1 ❑ b&w Cover: 2.75 **NM** value: **Cover or less**
2 ❑ b&w Cover: 2.75 **NM** value: **Cover or less**
3 ❑ b&w Cover: 2.75 **NM** value: **Cover or less**

EAGLE (CRYSTAL) — Crystal

1 ❑ Sep 1986 Cover: 1.50 **NM** value: **Cover or less**
📖 Night of 1000 Ninjas **A:** Gary Fields **W:** Jack Herman
1/LE❑ Sep 1986 **NM** value: **1.50**
• limited edition.

2 ❑ Cover: 1.50 **NM** value: **Cover or less**
3 ❑ 1987 Cover: 1.50 **NM** value: **Cover or less**
4 ❑ Apr 1987 Cover: 1.50 **NM** value: **Cover or less**
5 ❑ May 1987 Cover: 1.50 **NM** value: **Cover or less**
6 ❑ Jun 1987 Cover: 1.50 **NM** value: **Cover or less**
7 ❑ Jul 1987 Cover: 1.75 **NM** value: **Cover or less**
8 ❑ Aug 1987 Cover: 1.75 **NM** value: **Cover or less**
9 ❑ Sep 1987 Cover: 1.75 **NM** value: **Cover or less**
10 ❑ Oct 1987 Cover: 1.75 **NM** value: **Cover or less**
11 ❑ Nov 1987 Cover: 1.75 **NM** value: **Cover or less**
12 ❑ Dec 1987 Cover: 2.50 **NM** value: **Cover or less**
13 ❑ Jan 1988 Cover: 1.95 **NM** value: **Cover or less**
14 ❑ Feb 1988 Cover: 1.95 **NM** value: **Cover or less**
15 ❑ Mar 1988 Cover: 1.95 **NM** value: **Cover or less**
16 ❑ May 1988 Cover: 1.95 **NM** value: **Cover or less**
17 ❑ 1988b&w Cover: 1.95 **NM** value: **Cover or less**
18 ❑ Sep 1988, b&w Cover: 1.95 **NM** value: **Cover or less**
19 ❑ Oct 1988, b&w Cover: 1.95 **NM** value: **Cover or less**
20 ❑ b&w Cover: 1.95 **NM** value: **Cover or less**
21 ❑ 1989b&w Cover: 1.95 **NM** value: **Cover or less**
22 ❑ 1989b&w Cover: 1.95 **NM** value: **Cover or less**
23 ❑ 1989 Cover: 2.25 **NM** value: **Cover or less**

EAGLE (FOX) — Fox

1 ❑ Jul 1941 Cover: 0.10 **NM** value: **1500.00**
• **CGC:** 1 graded, best 9.6
2 ❑ Sep 1941 Cover: 0.10 **NM** value: **600.00**
3 ❑ Nov 1941 Cover: 0.10 **NM** value: **450.00**
4 ❑ Jan 1942 Cover: 0.10 **NM** value: **450.00**

EAGLE (RURAL HOME) — Rural Home

1 ❑ Feb 1945 Cover: 0.10 **NM** value: **300.00**
• **CGC:** 1 graded, best 9.0
2 ❑ Apr 1945 Cover: 0.10 **NM** value: **150.00**

EAGLES DARE — Aager

1 ❑ Cover: 1.95 **NM** value: **Cover or less**
2 ❑ Sep 1994 Cover: 1.95 **NM** value: **Cover or less**

EAGLE: THE DARK MIRROR SAGA — Comic Zone

1 ❑ Jan 1992 Cover: 2.75 **NM** value: **Cover or less**
📖 Reflections in a Dark Mirror **A:** Neil Vokes **W:** Jack Herman; Neil Vokes
2 ❑ Cover: 2.75 **NM** value: **Cover or less**
3 ❑ Cover: 2.75 **NM** value: **Cover or less**

EARLY DAYS OF THE SOUTHERN KNIGHTS — Comics Interview

1 ❑ 1986 Cover: 4.95 **NM** value: **Cover or less**
1-2 ❑ Cover: 4.95 **NM** value: **Cover or less**
2 ❑ Feb 1987 Cover: 4.95 **NM** value: **Cover or less**
3 ❑ Jul 1987 Cover: 4.95 **NM** value: **Cover or less**
4 ❑ 1987 Cover: 4.95 **NM** value: **Cover or less**
5 ❑ 1988 Cover: 5.95 **NM** value: **Cover or less**
6 ❑ Nov 1988 Cover: 6.50 **NM** value: **Cover or less**
7 ❑ Jan 1989 Cover: 6.95 **NM** value: **Cover or less**
8 ❑ Mar 1989 Cover: 6.95 **NM** value: **Cover or less**

EARTH 4 — Continuity

1 ❑ Cover: 2.50 **NM** value: **Cover or less**
Circ: CapCity orders: **12,175**
2 ❑ Dec 1993 Cover: 2.50 **NM** value: **Cover or less**
Circ: CapCity orders: **9,550**
3 ❑ Cover: 2.50 **NM** value: **Cover or less**
Circ: CapCity orders: **7,500**
4 ❑ Jan 1994 Cover: 2.50 **NM** value: **Cover or less**
Circ: CapCity orders: **6,600**

EARTH 4 DEATHWATCH 2000 — Continuity

0 ❑ Apr 1993 Cover: 2.50 **NM** value: **Cover or less**
• Trading Cards **A:** Aron Weisenfeld; Walter McDaniel **W:** Peter Stone
1 ❑ Apr 1993 Cover: 2.50 **NM** value: **Cover or less**
Circ: CapCity orders: **30,350**
• trading cards; indicia says #0, a misprint
2 ❑ May 1993 Cover: 2.50 **NM** value: **Cover or less**
Circ: CapCity orders: **22,700**
• trading card **A:** Aron Weisenfeld **W:** Peter Stone
3 ❑ Aug 1993 Cover: 2.50 **NM** value: **Cover or less**
Circ: CapCity orders: **28,900**
• trading card; Deathwatch 2000 dropped from indicia

EARTH 4 (VOL. 2) — Continuity

1 ❑ Dec 1993 Cover: 2.50 **NM** value: **Cover or less**
Circ: CapCity orders: **6,325**
2 ❑ Dec 1993 Cover: 2.50 **NM** value: **Cover or less**
Circ: CapCity orders: **3,285**
3 ❑ Dec 1993 Cover: 2.50 **NM** value: **Cover or less**
Circ: CapCity orders: **3,300**
4 ❑ Jan 1994 Cover: 2.50 **NM** value: **Cover or less**
Circ: CapCity orders: **2,350**

EARTH C.O.R.E. — Independent

1 ❑ Cover: 1.95 **NM** value: **Cover or less**

EARTHLORE — Eternity

1 ❑ Cover: 1.80 **NM** value: **2.00**
2 ❑ Cover: 1.80 **NM** value: **2.00**

Statement of Ownership figures are the average number of copies originally sold, as cited by the publisher to the U.S. Postal Service. These estimate **all** sales, in comics shops and on newsstands.

EARTH MAN ON VENUS, AN — Avon

This science-fiction one-shot was a showcase for the work of artist Wally Wood. The adaptation of a classic novel by Ralph Milne Farley (which appeared originally in Argosy magazine in 1924 as The Radio Man, the kick-off for a Radio Man series set on Venus, "The Radio Planet") was published in paperback form by Avon in 1950. (Avon may be best known in the comics field for its publication of the anti-Communist science-fiction one-shot Is This Tomorrow?) Perhaps looking for suitable properties to adapt to comic-book form, the publisher hit on this and Otis Adelbert Kline's Maza of the Moon (1930) (released in Avon's comics line as Rocket to the Moon). An Earth Man on Venus is highly collectible (and appeared in the I.W. series of reprints). — Maggie

1 ❑ 1951 Cover: 0.10 **NM** value: **1300.00**
• **CGC:** 8 graded, best 9.2
No issue number.

EARTHWORM JIM — Marvel

1 ❑ Dec 1995 Cover: 2.25 **NM** value: **Cover or less**
• based on video game
2 ❑ Jan 1996 Cover: 2.25 **NM** value: **Cover or less**
3 ❑ Feb 1996 Cover: 2.25 **NM** value: **Cover or less**

EARTH X — Marvel

In the near future, an experiment performed by Reed Richards will go horribly wrong. Richards manipulates the unstable substance vibranium and accidentally creates a virus. This virus now infects nearly all of humanity (Except Tony Stark, who is now a recluse: the likes of Howard Hughes). This virus gives super powers to the entire populace of Earth X.

Old heroes are twisted, new heroes have only the barest resemblance to their former namesakes, sort of a Marvel version of Kingdom Come. This is a world created by Alex Ross (Superman: Peace on Earth, Astro City). Though Earth X is a fully painted story by Ross, the first glimpse of this strange world was seen in a small comics insert to Wizard magazine. It merely contained the basic premise and some of Alex's concept sketches. These were later reprinted in a special edition to this series with a more complete set of sketches.

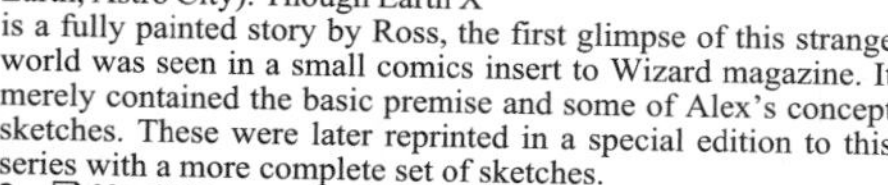

0 ❑ Mar 1999 Cover: 3.99 **NM** value: **4.00**
Circ: Diamd. preorders: **96,719** • **CGC:** 1 graded, best 9.6
0/A ❑ Mar 1999 **NM** value: **6.00**
Covers of series form giant picture. **A:** John Paul Leon; Alex Ross(cover) **W:** Alex Ross; Jim Krueger ★ Appearance of X-51, Watcher.
0/B ❑ Mar 1999 **NM** value: **4.00**
Covers of series form giant picture. **A:** John Paul Leon; Alex Ross(cover) **W:** Alex Ross; Jim Krueger ★ Appearance of X-51, Watcher.
0/C ❑ Mar 1999 **NM** value: **6.00**
DFE alternate cover by Alex Ross. **A:** John Paul Leon; Alex Ross(cover) **W:** Alex Ross; Jim Krueger ★ Appearance of X-51, Watcher.
1 ❑ Apr 1999 Cover: 2.99 **NM** value: **3.00**
Circ: Diamd. preorders: **98,971** • **CGC:** 8 graded, best 9.8
Covers of series form giant picture. **A:** John Paul Leon; Alex Ross(cover) **W:** Alex Ross; Jim Krueger ★ Appearance of Inhumans, Hydra.
1/A ❑ Apr 1999 **NM** value: **6.00**
Covers of series form giant picture. **A:** John Paul Leon; Alex Ross(cover) **W:** Alex Ross; Jim Krueger ★ Appearance of Inhumans, Hydra.
1/B ❑ Apr 1999 **NM** value: **3.50**
DFE alternate cover. **A:** John Paul Leon **W:** Alex Ross; Jim Krueger ★ Appearance of Inhumans, Hydra.
1/C ❑ Apr 1999 **NM** value: **6.00**
DFE alternate cover. **A:** John Paul Leon **W:** Alex Ross; Jim Krueger ★ Appearance of Inhumans, Hydra.
2 ❑ May 1999 Cover: 2.99 **NM** value: **Cover or less**
Circ: Diamd. preorders: **87,655** • **CGC:** 1 graded, best 9.6
3 ❑ Jun 1999 Cover: 2.99 **NM** value: **Cover or less**
Circ: Diamd. preorders: **86,233**
4 ❑ Jul 1999 Cover: 2.99 **NM** value: **Cover or less**
Circ: Diamd. preorders: **83,966**
5 ❑ Aug 1999 Cover: 2.99 **NM** value: **Cover or less**
Circ: Diamd. preorders: **81,966**
6 ❑ Sep 1999 Cover: 2.99 **NM** value: **Cover or less**
Circ: Diamd. preorders: **79,133**
7 ❑ Oct 1999 Cover: 2.99 **NM** value: **Cover or less**
Circ: Diamd. preorders: **74,986**
8 ❑ Nov 1999 Cover: 2.99 **NM** value: **Cover or less**
Circ: Diamd. preorders: **71,835**
9 ❑ Dec 1999 Cover: 2.99 **NM** value: **Cover or less**
Circ: Diamd. preorders: **70,976**
10 ❑ 2000 Cover: 2.99 **NM** value: **Cover or less**
Circ: Diamd. preorders: **67,559**
11 ❑ 2000 Cover: 2.99 **NM** value: **Cover or less**
Circ: Diamd. preorders: **64,789**
12 ❑ Apr 2000 Cover: 2.99 **NM** value: **Cover or less**
Circ: Diamd. preorders: **62,341**

Other grades: Multiply prices above by **1.5 for Mint • 2/3 for Very Fine • 1/3 for Fine • 1/5 for Very Good • 1/8 for Good**

13 ❑ Jun 2000 Cover: 3.99 **NM** value: **Cover or less**
Circ: Diamd. preorders: **63,701**
• "X" issue **A:** John Paul Leon; Alex Ross(cover) **W:** Alex Ross; Jim Krueger

EARTH X SKETCHBOOK — Marvel
1 ❑ Mar 1999 Cover: 3.99 **NM** value: **6.00**
Circ: Diamd. preorders: **36,129**

EAST MEETS WEST — Innovation
1 ❑ Apr 1990 Cover: 2.50 **NM** value: **Cover or less**
Circ: CapCity orders: **3,600**

EAT-MAN — Viz
1 ❑ Aug 1997, b&w Cover: 2.95 **NM** value: **Cover or less**
Circ: Diamd. preorders: **6,920**
📖 Aperitif **A:** Akihito Yoshitomi **W:** Akihito Yoshitomi
2 ❑ Sep 1997, b&w Cover: 2.95 **NM** value: **Cover or less**
Circ: Diamd. preorders: **5,321**
3 ❑ Oct 1997, b&w Cover: 2.95 **NM** value: **Cover or less**
Circ: Diamd. preorders: **4,974**
4 ❑ Nov 1997, b&w Cover: 2.95 **NM** value: **Cover or less**
Circ: Diamd. preorders: **5,144**
5 ❑ Dec 1997, b&w Cover: 2.95 **NM** value: **Cover or less**
Circ: Diamd. preorders: **4,995**
6 ❑ Jan 1997, b&w Cover: 2.95 **NM** value: **Cover or less**
Circ: Diamd. preorders: **4,757**
Bk 1❑ b&w Cover: 15.95 **NM** value: **Cover or less**
• collects first series

EAT-MAN SECOND COURSE — Viz
1 ❑ Feb 1998, b&w Cover: 2.95 **NM** value: **Cover or less**
Circ: Diamd. preorders: **4,710**
2 ❑ Mar 1998, b&w Cover: 3.50 **NM** value: **Cover or less**
3 ❑ Apr 1998, b&w Cover: 3.50 **NM** value: **Cover or less**
4 ❑ May 1998, b&w Cover: 3.25 **NM** value: **Cover or less**
5 ❑ b&w Cover: 2.95 **NM** value: **Cover or less**
Bk 1❑ Nov 1998 Cover: 15.95 **NM** value: **Cover or less**

EB'NN — Now
3 ❑ Jun 1986 Cover: 1.50 **NM** value: **Cover or less**
4 ❑ Aug 1986 Cover: 1.50 **NM** value: **Cover or less**
5 ❑ Nov 1986 Cover: 1.50 **NM** value: **Cover or less**
6 ❑ Jan 1987 Cover: 1.50 **NM** value: **Cover or less**

EB'NN THE RAVEN — Crowquill
1 ❑ **NM** value: **4.00**
2 ❑ **NM** value: **3.00**

EBONY WARRIOR — Africa Rising
1 ❑ Apr 1993 Cover: 1.95 **NM** value: **Cover or less**
Circ: CapCity orders: **8,200**

E.C. CLASSIC REPRINTS — East Coast Comix
The "other" E.C. — East Coast Comix — reprinted some of the greatest works of the William Gaines' E.C. comics in this 1970s series. Exceptionally faithful to the originals, this series reprinted, in their entirety, issues of Two-Fisted Tales, Haunt of Fear, Weird Science, Crime SuspenStories, and other great E.C. comics from the 1950s.

These comics represent the greatest moments in "comics noir," dark tales of fantasy and suspense which thrilled readers in the days before the Comics Code.

Covers carried the original issue's numbering, leaving the indicia as the only source of this reprint series chronology.

1 ❑ Cover: 1.00 **NM** value: **3.00**
📖 Upon Reflection; Blind Alleys; Success Story; Tatter Up! • Reprints Crypt of Terror #1 (a series meant to have been launched when EC ceased publishing horror) **A:** George Evans; Joe Orlando; Jack Davis; Graham Ingels **W:** Al Feldstein
2 ❑ Cover: 1.00 **NM** value: **3.00**
📖 The Martians!; Captivity; Miscalculation; Bum Steer • Reprints Weird Science #15 **A:** Al Williamson; Joe Orlando; Wally Wood; Jack Kamen **W:** Al Feldstein; William Gaines
3 ❑ Cover: 1.00 **NM** value: **2.50**
• Reprints Shock SuspenStories #12
4 ❑ Cover: 1.00 **NM** value: **2.50**
• Reprints Haunt of Fear #12
5 ❑ Cover: 1.00 **NM** value: **2.50**
📖 The End!; The Trip!; Home to Stay!; Don't Count Your Chickens… • Reprints Weird Fantasy #13
6 ❑ Cover: 1.00 **NM** value: **2.50**
📖 Three for the Money; Dog Food; Key Chain; The Squealer • Reprints Crime SuspenStories #25 **A:** George Evans; Bernie Krigstein; Reed Crandall
7 ❑ Cover: 1.00 **NM** value: **2.50**
📖 Two of a Kind!; Graft in Concrete!; Half-Way Horrible!; Hook, Line, and Stinker! • Reprints Vault of Horror #26
8 ❑ Cover: 1.00 **NM** value: **2.50**
📖 Under Cover!; Sugar 'n Spice 'n …; Not So Tough!; Dead Right! • Reprints Shock SuspenStories #6
9 ❑ Cover: 1.00 **NM** value: **2.50**
📖 Betsy!; Trial by Arms!; En Crapaudine!; Guynemer! • Reprints Two-Fisted Tales #34
10 ❑ Cover: 1.25 **NM** value: **2.50**
📖 Creep Course; No Silver Atoll; Hansel and Gretal; Country Clubbing • Reprints Haunt of Fear #23
11 ❑ Cover: 1.25 **NM** value: **2.50**
📖 Lost in the Microcosm; Dream of Doom; Murder in the 21st Century (text story); Experiment…In Death; "Things" From Outer Space • Reprints Weird Science #12
12 ❑ Cover: 1.25 **NM** value: **2.50**
📖 Kickback; Ge, Dad, It's a Daisy; The Patriots; Halloween • Reprints Shock SuspenStories #2

EC CLASSICS — Cochran
1 ❑ Cover: 4.95 **NM** value: **5.00**
2 ❑ Cover: 4.95 **NM** value: **5.00**
3 ❑ Cover: 4.95 **NM** value: **5.00**
4 ❑ Cover: 4.95 **NM** value: **5.00**
5 ❑ Cover: 4.95 **NM** value: **5.00**
📖 The Exile!; Mad Journey!; He Who Waits!; Ahead of the Game!; Revulsion!; By George!!; What He Saw!; There Will Come Soft Rains… • Reprints from Weird Fantasy #14, 15, 16, 17 **A:** Al Williamson
6 ❑ Cover: 4.95 **NM** value: **5.00**

ECHO — Image
0 ❑ Jul 2000 Cover: 2.50 **NM** value: **Cover or less**
Circ: Diamd. preorders: **16,125**
📖 Thick as Thieves **A:** Long Vo **W:** Ken Siu-Chong
1 ❑ Mar 2000 Cover: 2.95 **NM** value: **Cover or less**
Circ: Diamd. preorders: **16,456**
2 ❑ Apr 2000 Cover: 2.50 **NM** value: **Cover or less**
Circ: Diamd. preorders: **11,920**
3 ❑ May 2000 Cover: 2.50 **NM** value: **Cover or less**
Circ: Diamd. preorders: **14,276**
4 ❑ Jun 2000 Cover: 2.50 **NM** value: **Cover or less**
Circ: Diamd. preorders: **14,969**
📖 Desperate Times **A:** Long Vo **W:** Ken Siu-Chong
5 ❑ Sep 2000 Cover: 2.50 **NM** value: **Cover or less**
Circ: Diamd. preorders: **13,857**
📖 Welcoming Party **A:** Long Vo **W:** Ken Siu-Chong

ECHO OF FUTUREPAST — Continuity
1 ❑ May 1984 Cover: 2.95 **NM** value: **Cover or less**
📖 Bucky O'Hare; Tippie Toe Jones; Frankenstein; Virus; Mudwogs **A:** Michael Golden; Neal Adams; Arthur Suydam; Jean Teulé; Carlos Giménez **W:** Larry Hama; Neal Adams; Arthur Suydam; Jean Teulé; Carlos Giménez
2 ❑ 1984 Cover: 2.95 **NM** value: **Cover or less**
📖 Frankenstein; Virus; Mudwogs; Bucky O'Hare; Hom **A:** Michael Golden; Neal Adams; Arthur Suydam; Jean Teulé; Louis Mitchell **W:** Larry Hama; Neal Adams; Arthur Suydam; Jean Teulé; Lindley Farley
3 ❑ Nov 1984 Cover: 2.95 **NM** value: **Cover or less**
4 ❑ Feb 1985 Cover: 2.95 **NM** value: **Cover or less**
Circ: CapCity orders: **4,765**
5 ❑ Apr 1985 Cover: 2.95 **NM** value: **Cover or less**
Circ: CapCity orders: **4,235**
6 ❑ Jul 1985 Cover: 2.95 **NM** value: **Cover or less**
Circ: CapCity orders: **3,450**
📖 Tiipie Toe Jones; Virus; Bucky O'Hare; AE-35; Torpedo **A:** Alex Toth; Michael Golden; Neal Adams; Jean Teulé; Louis Mitchell; William Jungkuntz **W:** Larry Hama; Jean Teulé; E. Sanchéz Abuli; Lindley Farley; Tim Ryan
7 ❑ Aug 1985 Cover: 2.95 **NM** value: **Cover or less**
Circ: CapCity orders: **3,400**
8 ❑ Dec 1985 Cover: 2.95 **NM** value: **Cover or less**
Circ: CapCity orders: **3,125**
📖 AE-35; Star rat; Torpedo; Tippie Toe Jones; The Damned City **A:** Neal Adams; Goran Delic; Juan Gimenez; Jordi Bernet; Louis Mitchell; William Jungkuntz **W:** Goran Delic; E. Sanchéz Abuli; Lindley Farley; Ricardo Barriero; Tim Ryan
9 ❑ Jan 1986 Cover: 2.95 **NM** value: **Cover or less**
Circ: CapCity orders: **3,050**
📖 The Damned City; Tippie Toe Jones; Torpedo; AE-35 **A:** Neal Adams; Juan Gimenez; Jordi Bernet; Louis Mitchell; William Jungkuntz **W:** E. Sanchéz Abuli; Lindley Farley; Ricardo Barriero; Tim Ryan

ECLIPSE GRAPHIC ALBUM SERIES — Eclipse
1 ❑ Oct 1978 **NM** value: **8.00**
• Sabre **A:** Paul Gulacy **W:** Don McGregor
1-2 ❑ **NM** value: **6.00**
1-3 ❑ Cover: 5.95 **NM** value: **Cover or less**
2 ❑ Nov 1979 **NM** value: **5.00**
• Night Music **A:** P. Craig Russell **W:** P. Craig Russell
3 ❑ May 1980 Cover: 6.95 **NM** value: **7.00**
• Detectives, Inc. **A:** Marshall Rogers **W:** Don McGregor
4 ❑ Cover: 5.95 **NM** value: **6.00**
• Stewart the Rat **A:** Gene Colan **W:** Steve Gerber
5 ❑ **NM** value: **12.00**
• The Price **A:** Jim Starlin **W:** Jim Starlin
6 ❑ **NM** value: **6.00**
• I am Coyote **A:** Marshall Rogers **W:** Steve Englehart
7 ❑ **NM** value: **8.00**
• The Rocketeer **A:** Dave Stevens **W:** Dave Stevens
7/HC❑ Cover: 19.95 **NM** value: **Cover or less**
• Hardcover edition. • The Rocketeer **A:** Dave Stevens **W:** Dave Stevens
7-2 ❑ Cover: 7.95 **NM** value: **8.00**
7-3 ❑ Cover: 8.95 **NM** value: **9.00**
8 ❑ **NM** value: **6.00**
• Zorro **A:** Marcello **W:** Nedaud
9 ❑ Feb 1987 **NM** value: **14.00**
• Somerset Holmes; The Sacred and the Profane **A:** Dean Motter **W:** Ken Steacy
10 ❑ Mar 1987 **NM** value: **14.00**
• Sacred & Profane; Somerset Holmes **A:** Brent Anderson; April Campbell **W:** Bruce Jones
10/HC❑Mar 1987 Cover: 24.95 **NM** value: **Cover or less**
• Hardcover edition. • Somerset Holmes **A:** Brent Anderson; April Campbell **W:** Bruce Jones
11 ❑ 1987 Cover: 3.95 **NM** value: **4.00**
• Floyd Farland **A:** Chris Ware **W:** Chris Ware
12 ❑ Jul 1987 Cover: 7.95 **NM** value: **9.00**
• Silverheels **A:** Scott Hampton; April Campbell **W:** Bruce Jones
12/HC❑Jul 1987 Cover: 14.95 **NM** value: **Cover or less**
• Hardcover edition. • Silverheels **A:** Scott Hampton; April Campbell **W:** Bruce Jones
12/LE❑Jul 1987 Cover: 24.95 **NM** value: **Cover or less**
• Silverheels **A:** Scott Hampton; April Campbell **W:** Bruce Jones
13 ❑ Cover: 8.95 **NM** value: **10.00**
• The Sisterhood of Steel **A:** Peter Ledger **W:** Christy Marx
14 ❑ **NM** value: **5.00**
• Samurai, Son of Death **A:** Hiroshi Hirata **W:** Sharman DiVono
15 ❑ Cover: 3.95 **NM** value: **Cover or less**
📖 Termites From Mars; Fraternity; Night Dive • Twisted Tales **A:** Scott Saavedra; Henry Mayo; Rick Stasi **W:** Bruce Jones
16 ❑ **NM** value: **4.50**
• Air Fighters Classics #1
17 ❑ Cover: 6.95 **NM** value: **Cover or less**
📖 Valkyrie: Prisoner of the Past • Valkyrie: Prisoner of the Past **A:** Paul Gulacy **W:** Chuck Dixon
18 ❑ **NM** value: **4.50**
• Air Fighters Classics #2
19 ❑ Cover: 14.95 **NM** value: **Cover or less**
📖 Scout: The Four Monsters • Scout: Four Monsters; Collects Scout #1-7
20 ❑ **NM** value: **4.50**
• Air Fighters Classics #3
21 ❑ Cover: 3.95 **NM** value: **Cover or less**
• XYR "choose your own adventure" game
22 ❑ **NM** value: **5.00**
• Alien Worlds
23 ❑ **NM** value: **4.50**
• Air Fighters Classics #4
24 ❑ **NM** value: **5.00**
• Heartbreak Comics; Heartbreak
25 ❑ **NM** value: **9.00**
• Alex Toth's Zorro #1 **A:** Alex Toth **W:** Alex Toth
26 ❑ **NM** value: **9.00**
• Alex Toth's Zorro #2 **A:** Alex Toth **W:** Alex Toth
27 ❑ **NM** value: **6.00**
• She; Fast Fiction
28 ❑ **NM** value: **9.00**
📖 A Dream of Flying • Brought to Light **A:** Dave Gibbons; Bill Sienkiewicz; Tom Yeates **W:** Alan Moore
29 ❑ **NM** value: **13.00**
• Miracleman Book One **A:** Joe Simon; Jack Kirby **W:** Joe Simon; Jack Kirby
30 ❑ **NM** value: **9.00**
📖 Brought to Light • Real Love: The Best of Simon & Kirby Romance Comics **A:** Joe Simon; Bill Sienkiewicz; Jack Kirby **W:** Alan Moore
30/HC❑ **NM** value: **30.00**
• Hardcover edition. 📖 Brought to Light **A:** Bill Sienkiewicz **W:** Alan Moore
31 ❑ **NM** value: **7.00**
📖 Pigeons From Hell • Pigeons from Hell
31/LE❑ **NM** value: **30.00**
• Limited hardcover edition. 📖 Pigeons From Hell
32 ❑ Cover: 9.95 **NM** value: **Cover or less**
📖 Reform School Girl; Trapped!; The Bobby Sox Bandit Queen; Lucky Fights it Through; Gun Happy; I Worked for the Fence; Teen-Aged Dope Slaves; The Deadly Needle • Teenaged Dope Slaves & Reform School Girls **A:** Joe Simon; Harvey Kurtzman; Jack Kirby; Frank Edgington; Louis Zansky; Martin Bradley **W:** Joe Simon; Harvey Kurtzman; Jack Kirby; Frank Edgington; Louis Zansky; Martin Bradley
33 ❑ Cover: 9.95 **NM** value: **Cover or less**
• Bogie
34 ❑ Cover: 3.95 **NM** value: **Cover or less**
• Air Fighters Classics #5
35 ❑ Cover: 7.95 **NM** value: **Cover or less**
• Into the Shadow of the Sun, Rael
36 ❑ Cover: 4.95 **NM** value: **Cover or less**
• Ariane & Bluebeard **A:** P. Craig Russell
37 ❑ Cover: 3.95 **NM** value: **Cover or less**
• Air Fighters Classics #6
38 ❑ Cover: 8.95 **NM** value: **Cover or less**
• Doctor Watchstop; Dr. Watchstop
39 ❑ Cover: 4.95 **NM** value: **Cover or less**
• James Bond 007: Permission to Die 1 **A:** Mike Grell
40 ❑ Cover: 4.95 **NM** value: **Cover or less**
• James Bond 007: Permission to Die 2 **A:** Mike Grell
41 ❑ Cover: 4.95 **NM** value: **Cover or less**
• James Bond 007: Permission to Die 3 **A:** Mike Grell
42 ❑ Cover: 8.95 **NM** value: **Cover or less**
• James Bond 007: Licence to Kill **A:** Mike Grell
43 ❑ Cover: 7.95 **NM** value: **Cover or less**
• Tapping the Vein #1
44 ❑ Cover: 5.95 **NM** value: **Cover or less**
• Hobbit #1
45 ❑ Cover: 10.95 **NM** value: **Cover or less**
• Toadswart
46 ❑ Cover: 7.95 **NM** value: **Cover or less**
• Tapping the Vein #2
47 ❑ Cover: 14.95 **NM** value: **Cover or less**
• Scout: Mount Fire
48 ❑ Cover: 9.95 **NM** value: **Cover or less**
• Moderne Man Comics
49 ❑ Cover: 6.95 **NM** value: **Cover or less**
• Tapping the Vein #3
50 ❑ Cover: 12.95 **NM** value: **Cover or less**
• Miracleman Book Two
51 ❑ Cover: 7.95 **NM** value: **Cover or less**
• Tapping the Vein 4
52 ❑ Cover: 4.95 **NM** value: **Cover or less**
• James Bond 007: Permission to Die #3

CGC-graded: Multiply prices above by **33 for 9.9 M • 16 for 9.8 NM/M • 7 for 9.6 NM+ • 5 for 9.4 NM • 2.5 for 9.2 NM- • 1.5 for 9.0 VF/NM**

ECLIPSE MAGAZINE — Eclipse

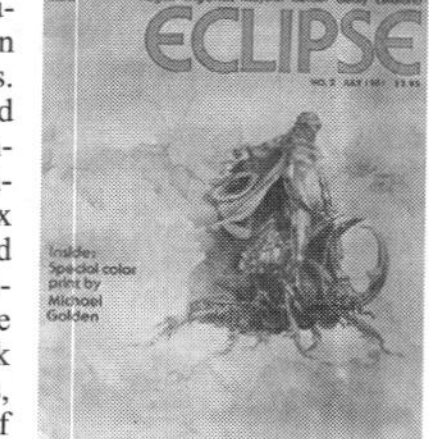

This black-and-white magazine from the early 1980s featured a couple of strips that earned their own color titles from Eclipse Comics. Steve Englehart (Avengers) and Marshall Rogers (Detective Comics) offered up Coyote, a dimension-hopping mystic, while Max Collins and Terry Beatty delivered another installment in the adventures of P.I. supreme Ms. Tree. The magazine also showcased work from Don McGregor (Detectives, Inc.) and Gene Colan (Tomb of Dracula), Steve Gerber (Howard the Duck) and Val Mayerick (Savage Sword of Conan), Charles Vess (Stardust), and Trina Robbins (Go Girl!).

1 ❑ May 1981, b&w Cover: 2.95 **NM** value: **Cover or less**
2 ❑ Jul 1981 Cover: 2.95 **NM** value: **Cover or less**
3 ❑ Nov 1981 Cover: 2.95 **NM** value: **Cover or less**
📖 Coyote, Part 2; Vamp Dance; Ragamuffins: Kingergarten Run; A Bag Full of Dreams; Large Cow Comix; Dope: The Fatal Cigarette; Role Model: Conclusion; Because; Ms. Tree: Death is a Little Black Book **A:** Gene Colan; Val Mayerik; Terry Beatty; Charles Vess; Trina Robbins; Kent Williams; Marshall Rogers; Hunt Emerson; Kaz **W:** George Pratt; Charles Vess; Trina Robbins; Hunt Emerson; Kaz; Max Allan Collins; Don McGregor; Steve Englehart; Steve Gerber ★ 1st Appearance of Ragamuffins.
4 ❑ Jan 1982 Cover: 2.95 **NM** value: **Cover or less**
5 ❑ Mar 1982 Cover: 2.95 **NM** value: **Cover or less**
6 ❑ Jul 1982 Cover: 2.95 **NM** value: **Cover or less**
7 ❑ Nov 1982 Cover: 2.95 **NM** value: **Cover or less**
8 ❑ Jan 1983 Cover: 2.95 **NM** value: **Cover or less**

ECLIPSE MONTHLY — Eclipse

1 ❑ Aug 1983 Cover: 2.00 **NM** value: **Cover or less**
📖 Cap'n Quick and a Foozie; The Bank Robbery; The Hide Butchers; A Visit to The Sin; The Beginning **A:** Steve Ditko; Doug Wildey; Klaus Janson; Trina Robbins; Marshall Rogers; B.C. Boyer **W:** Steve Ditko; Doug Wildey; Trina Robbins; Marshall Rogers; B.C. Boyer
2 ❑ Sep 1983 Cover: 2.00 **NM** value: **Cover or less**
3 ❑ Oct 1983 Cover: 2.00 **NM** value: **Cover or less**
4 ❑ Jan 1984 Cover: 1.50 **NM** value: **Cover or less**
5 ❑ Feb 1984 Cover: 1.50 **NM** value: **Cover or less**
6 ❑ Mar 1984 Cover: 1.50 **NM** value: **Cover or less**
7 ❑ Apr 1984 Cover: 1.50 **NM** value: **Cover or less**
8 ❑ May 1984 Cover: 1.50 **NM** value: **Cover or less**
9 ❑ Jun 1984 Cover: 1.75 **NM** value: **Cover or less**
10 ❑ Jul 1984 Cover: 1.75 **NM** value: **Cover or less**
📖 Flying Too High With Some Guy In The Sky; Robber's Roost; Frank Capra Memorial Hospital **A:** Doug Wildey; B.C. Boyer; Wayne Truman **W:** Doug Wildey; B.C. Boyer; Wayne Truman

ECLIPSO — DC

Eclipso, a vengeful demon, can — and does — possess any body at will, any body that has a soul thirsting for vengeance, that is. The result is often bloody and completely devastating.

Although born from the Eclipso crossover series in the DC superhero annuals, DC hoped to give this title a more supernatural leaning, along the same lines as other successes it has had with the genre, such as The House of Mystery and House of Secrets. Unfortunately, such was not the case, and the series was canceled after 18 unmemorable issues.

1 ❑ Nov 1992 Cover: 1.25 **NM** value: **2.00**
Circ: CapCity orders: **41,050**
2 ❑ Dec 1992 Cover: 1.25 **NM** value: **1.75**
Circ: CapCity orders: **25,850**
3 ❑ Jan 1993 Cover: 1.25 **NM** value: **1.75**
Circ: CapCity orders: **23,450**
4 ❑ Feb 1993 Cover: 1.25 **NM** value: **1.50**
Circ: CapCity orders: **18,900**
5 ❑ Mar 1993 Cover: 1.25 **NM** value: **1.50**
Circ: CapCity orders: **16,650**
6 ❑ Apr 1993 Cover: 1.25 **NM** value: **Cover or less**
Circ: CapCity orders: **15,850**
7 ❑ May 1993 Cover: 1.25 **NM** value: **Cover or less**
Circ: CapCity orders: **14,100**
8 ❑ Jun 1993 Cover: 1.25 **NM** value: **Cover or less**
Circ: CapCity orders: **12,400**
📖 Good Night Mr. Holmes **A:** Ted McKeever **W:** Robert Loren Fleming
9 ❑ Jul 1993 Cover: 1.25 **NM** value: **Cover or less**
Circ: CapCity orders: **10,700**
10 ❑ Aug 1993 Cover: 1.75 **NM** value: **Cover or less**
Circ: CapCity orders: **10,250**
11 ❑ Sep 1993 Cover: 1.25 **NM** value: **Cover or less**
Circ: CapCity orders: **10,100**
12 ❑ Oct 1993 Cover: 1.25 **NM** value: **Cover or less**
Circ: CapCity orders: **8,200**
13 ❑ Nov 1993 Cover: 1.25 **NM** value: **Cover or less**
Circ: CapCity orders: **8,400**
📖 Hour of Darkness **A:** Audwynn Jermaine Newman **W:** Robert Loren Fleming
14 ❑ Dec 1993 Cover: 1.25 **NM** value: **Cover or less**
Circ: CapCity orders: **7,100**
15 ❑ Jan 1994 Cover: 1.25 **NM** value: **1.50**
Circ: CapCity orders: **6,600**
16 ❑ Feb 1994 Cover: 1.50 **NM** value: **Cover or less**
Circ: CapCity orders: **6,250**
📖 Fallout **A:** Audwynn Jermaine Newman **W:** Robert Loren Fleming
17 ❑ Mar 1994 Cover: 1.50 **NM** value: **Cover or less**
Circ: CapCity orders: **5,600**
18 ❑ Apr 1994 Cover: 1.50 **NM** value: **Cover or less**
Circ: CapCity orders: **5,550**
final issue.
Anl 1❑ca. 1993 Cover: 2.50 **NM** value: **Cover or less**
Circ: CapCity orders: **16,500**
📖 Bloodlines • Bloodlines ★ 1st Appearance of Prism.

ECLIPSO: THE DARKNESS WITHIN — DC

1 ❑ Jul 1992 Cover: 2.50 **NM** value: **Cover or less**
Circ: CapCity orders: **12,850**
📖 Eclipso: The Darkness Within, Part 1 • Without plastic gem (newsstand version) **A:** Keith Giffen; Bart Sears **W:** Keith Giffen; Robert Loren Flemming
1/DM❑Jul 1992 Cover: 2.50 **NM** value: **3.00**
Circ: CapCity orders: **54,800**
plastic diamond glued to cover. • Direct Market edition. 📖 Eclipso: The Darkness Within, Part 1 **A:** Keith Giffen; Bart Sears **W:** Keith Giffen; Robert Loren Flemming
2 ❑ Jul 1992 Cover: 2.50 **NM** value: **Cover or less**
Circ: CapCity orders: **37,900**
📖 Eclipso: The Darkness Within, Part 20

ECTOKID — Marvel

1 ❑ Sep 1993 Cover: 2.50 **NM** value: **Cover or less**
Circ: CapCity orders: **30,200**
Foil embossed cover.
2 ❑ Oct 1993 Cover: 1.75 **NM** value: **Cover or less**
Circ: CapCity orders: **11,900**
3 ❑ Nov 1993 Cover: 1.75 **NM** value: **Cover or less**
Circ: CapCity orders: **10,800**
4 ❑ Dec 1993 Cover: 1.75 **NM** value: **Cover or less**
Circ: CapCity orders: **9,600**
📖 An Innocent Abroad **A:** Steve Skroce; Bob Dvorak **W:** James Robinson; Larry Wachowski
5 ❑ Jan 1994 Cover: 1.75 **NM** value: **Cover or less**
Circ: CapCity orders: **8,100**
6 ❑ Feb 1994 Cover: 1.75 **NM** value: **Cover or less**
Circ: CapCity orders: **6,350**
7 ❑ Mar 1994 Cover: 1.75 **NM** value: **Cover or less**
Circ: CapCity orders: **5,270**
8 ❑ Apr 1994 Cover: 1.75 **NM** value: **Cover or less**
Circ: CapCity orders: **4,400**
9 ❑ May 1994 Cover: 1.75 **NM** value: **Cover or less**
Circ: CapCity orders: **3,850**

ECTOKID UNLEASHED! — Marvel

1 ❑ Oct 1994 Cover: 2.95 **NM** value: **Cover or less**
Circ: CapCity orders: **5,250**
📖 Unnatural Causes! **A:** Hector Gomez **W:** Andy Lanning; Dan Abnett

ED — 3CG Comics

1 ❑ Mar 1997, b&w Cover: 2.95 **NM** value: **Cover or less**

EDDIE STANKY BASEBALL HERO — Fawcett

1 ❑ ca. 1951 Cover: 0.10 **NM** value: **250.00**
• **CGC:** 2 graded, best 8.0

EDDY CURRENT — Mad Dog

1 ❑ Jul 1987 Cover: 2.00 **NM** value: **Cover or less**
2 ❑ Sep 1987 Cover: 2.00 **NM** value: **Cover or less**
3 ❑ Oct 1987 Cover: 2.00 **NM** value: **Cover or less**
4 ❑ Nov 1987 Cover: 2.00 **NM** value: **Cover or less**
5 ❑ Jan 1988 Cover: 2.00 **NM** value: **Cover or less**
6 ❑ Feb 1988 Cover: 2.00 **NM** value: **Cover or less**
7 ❑ Apr 1988 Cover: 2.00 **NM** value: **Cover or less**
8 ❑ Jun 1988 Cover: 2.00 **NM** value: **Cover or less**
9 ❑ Jul 1988 Cover: 2.00 **NM** value: **Cover or less**
10 ❑ Sep 1988 Cover: 2.00 **NM** value: **Cover or less**
11 ❑ Nov 1988 Cover: 2.00 **NM** value: **Cover or less**
12 ❑ Dec 1988 Cover: 2.00 **NM** value: **Cover or less**

EDEN DESCENDANTS, THE — Quester Entertainment

1 ❑ b&w Cover: 3.95 **NM** value: **Cover or less**
cardstock cover.

EDEN MATRIX, THE — Adhesive

1/A ❑ Cover: 2.95 **NM** value: **Cover or less**
1/B ❑ Cover: 2.95 **NM** value: **Cover or less**

EDGAR ALLAN POE — Eternity

1 ❑ 1988b&w Cover: 1.95 **NM** value: **Cover or less**
• Black Cat
2 ❑ 1988b&w Cover: 1.95 **NM** value: **Cover or less**
• Pit & Pendulum
3 ❑ Dec 1988, b&w Cover: 1.95 **NM** value: **Cover or less**
• Red Death
4 ❑ 1989b&w Cover: 1.95 **NM** value: **Cover or less**
• Rue Morgue
5 ❑ 1989b&w Cover: 1.95 **NM** value: **Cover or less**
• Tell-Tale Heart

The prices seen above do not represent the highest possible prices seen in online auctions, but rather the prices we have seen these issues reliably fetch in a variety of environments (storefront retail, mail order, auction and convention).

EDGE — Bravura / Malibu

Edge is the story of a genetic engineer and his son who attempt to harness the powers of science to benefit mankind, only to unleash a fearsome wave of unintended consequences on the world. The Ultimates, a band of morally ambiguous costumed adventurers: Will Power, Barricade, Winged Victory, Free Agent, Intruder, and Phase Shifter — try to impose their vision of justice on an unwilling society, and only the genetic engineer's other son, Edge, can stop them and make his father and brother face up to their responsibility for their creations.

Edge was solicited as a four-issue mini-series written by Steven Grant and illustrated by veteran artist Gil Kane, but Malibu only managed to publish three issues before cancellation.

1 ❑ Jul 1994 Cover: 2.50 **NM** value: **Cover or less**
Circ: CapCity orders: **19,450**
2 ❑ Aug 1994 Cover: 2.50 **NM** value: **Cover or less**
Circ: CapCity orders: **13,200**
3 ❑ Apr 1995 Cover: 2.95 **NM** value: **Cover or less**
Circ: CapCity orders: **10,975**

EDGE OF CHAOS — Pacific

1 ❑ Jul 1983 Cover: 1.00 **NM** value: **Cover or less**
2 ❑ Oct 1984 **NM** value: **1.00**
3 ❑ Jan 1983 **NM** value: **1.00**

EEK! THE CAT — Hamilton

1 ❑ Feb 1994 Cover: 1.95 **NM** value: **Cover or less**
• TV show
2 ❑ Mar 1994 Cover: 1.95 **NM** value: **Cover or less**
• TV show
3 ❑ Apr 1994 Cover: 1.95 **NM** value: **Cover or less**
• TV show

EERIE ADVENTURES — Ziff-Davis

1 ❑ Win 1951 Cover: 0.10 **NM** value: **300.00**
• **CGC:** 1 graded, best 7.5

EERIE (AVON) — Avon

1 ❑ Jan 1947 Cover: 0.10 **NM** value: **2500.00**
• **CGC:** 13 graded, best 9.0
1-2 ❑ May 1951 Cover: 0.10 **NM** value: **500.00**
• reprints 1947 #1
2 ❑ Aug 1951 Cover: 0.10 **NM** value: **600.00**
• **CGC:** 2 graded, best 8.0
3 ❑ Oct 1951 Cover: 0.10 **NM** value: **600.00**
• **CGC:** 2 graded, best 5.0
4 ❑ Dec 1951 Cover: 0.10 **NM** value: **500.00**
• **CGC:** 3 graded, best 9.2
5 ❑ Feb 1952 Cover: 0.10 **NM** value: **500.00**
• **CGC:** 3 graded, best 7.5
6 ❑ Apr 1952 Cover: 0.10 **NM** value: **500.00**
• **CGC:** 1 graded, best 8.0
7 ❑ Jun 1952 Cover: 0.10 **NM** value: **450.00**
• **CGC:** 2 graded, best 8.0
8 ❑ Aug 1952 Cover: 0.10 **NM** value: **450.00**
• **CGC:** 2 graded, best 8.0
9 ❑ Oct 1952 Cover: 0.10 **NM** value: **400.00**
10 ❑ Dec 1952 Cover: 0.10 **NM** value: **400.00**
• **CGC:** 1 graded, best 6.0
11 ❑ Jun 1953 Cover: 0.10 **NM** value: **300.00**
• **CGC:** 1 graded, best 8.5
12 ❑ Aug 1953 Cover: 0.10 **NM** value: **300.00**
• **CGC:** 2 graded, best 8.0
13 ❑ Oct 1953 Cover: 0.10 **NM** value: **300.00**
• **CGC:** 1 graded, best 7.5
14 ❑ Jan 1954 Cover: 0.10 **NM** value: **250.00**
• **CGC:** 1 graded, best 5.5
15 ❑ Apr 1954 Cover: 0.10 **NM** value: **250.00**
• **CGC:** 1 graded, best 7.5
16 ❑ Jun 1954 Cover: 0.10 **NM** value: **250.00**
• **CGC:** 1 graded, best 8.5
17 ❑ Aug 1954 Cover: 0.10 **NM** value: **250.00**
• **CGC:** 2 graded, best 7.0

EERIE GREATEST HITS — Harris

Bk 1❑ Dec 1994 Cover: 12.95 **NM** value: **Cover or less**
• reprints Warren material

EERIE (I.W.) — I.W.

1 ❑ Cover: 0.10 **NM** value: **20.00**
📖 Mister Lucifer: Up Pops the Devil!; Gregory the Ghost; Cheap Skate; Dr. Paul Barer; The Obi Makes Jumbee
2 ❑ Cover: 0.10 **NM** value: **15.00**

Capital City orders are the actual sales of comic books by Capital City Distribution, once one of the largest U.S. sellers of comics to comics shops. Capital City's share of comics shop sales, while not known exactly, increases from around 10-20% in the mid-1980s to 30-35% in the mid-1990s. Capital City's share of comic books sold on newsstands (most Marvels and DCs) will be less.

Other grades: Multiply prices above by **1.5 for Mint • 2/3 for Very Fine • 1/3 for Fine • 1/5 for Very Good • 1/8 for Good**

EERIE TALES — Super

Eerie Tales appeared in the early 1960s and reprinted pre-Code horror and mystery stories from Star Publications titles like Blue Bolt, Spook, and Purple Claw. A bit more literary and pulp magazine-oriented than the buckets of blood style of most pre-Code horror books, these stories stand up fairly well despite the often crude illustration and cheaper-than-cheap printing process. Eerie Tales featured classic monsters like ghouls, werewolves, and vampires alongside contemporary shock-thrillers of psycho killers and sadists. Eerie Tales appeared without the nearly ubiquitous seal of the Comics Code Authority (and for good reason!), and was probably unable to get decent distribution as a result. Only a handful of (apparently randomly numbered) issues are known to have been printed.

12 ❑ Cover: 0.12 **NM** value: **15.00**
📖 The Werewolf of Warsham Manor!; King of the Living Dead; The Subway Horror!; The Monster from the Pit • Reprints(?)

EERIE (WARREN) — Warren

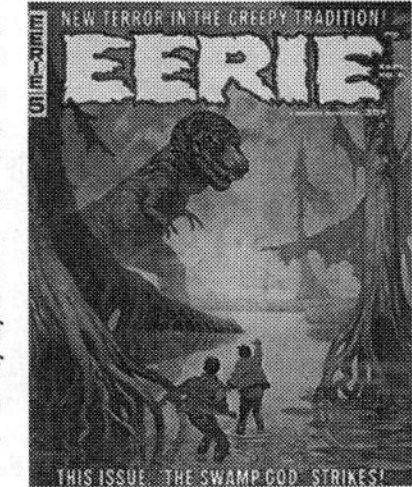

One of the true oddities of comics collecting is the first issue of Jim Warren's Eerie. Released in haste to protect the title trademark of the black-and-white horror magazine series that continued successfully for years, #1 was a black-and-white offset press print job with page dimensions of less than 6 by 8 inches (and poor printing). It reprinted stories from Warren's existing stock of material, and the primitive nature of its production led to attempts to counterfeit the issue. It takes an expert to discern the difference between a true first edition and later copies, though the limited printing of real copies and the success of the title make them valuable.

The series featured excellent art in what began as an anthology horror title; later issues carried some stories of ongoing characters, as well, including Dax, Vampirella, Exterminator One, Darklon the Mystic, and the like. — Maggie

1 ❑ Sep 1965 **NM** value: **75.00**
1-2 ❑ **NM** value: **40.00**
2 ❑ Mar 1966 Cover: 0.35 **NM** value: **40.00**
3 ❑ May 1966 Cover: 0.35 **NM** value: **25.00**
4 ❑ Jul 1966 Cover: 0.35 **NM** value: **18.00**
5 ❑ Sep 1966 Cover: 0.35 **NM** value: **18.00**
6 ❑ Nov 1966 Cover: 0.35 **NM** value: **12.00**
7 ❑ Jan 1967 Cover: 0.35 **NM** value: **12.00**
8 ❑ Mar 1967 Cover: 0.35 **NM** value: **12.00**
9 ❑ May 1967 Cover: 0.35 **NM** value: **12.00**
10 ❑ Jul 1967 Cover: 0.40 **NM** value: **12.00**
11 ❑ Sep 1967 Cover: 0.40 **NM** value: **10.00**
12 ❑ Nov 1967 Cover: 0.40 **NM** value: **10.00**
13 ❑ Feb 1968 Cover: 0.40 **NM** value: **10.00**
14 ❑ Apr 1968 Cover: 0.40 **NM** value: **10.00**
15 ❑ Jun 1968 Cover: 0.40 **NM** value: **10.00**
16 ❑ Jul 1968 Cover: 0.40 **NM** value: **10.00**
17 ❑ Sep 1968 Cover: 0.40 **NM** value: **30.00**
• Scarcer
18 ❑ Nov 1968 Cover: 0.40 **NM** value: **10.00**
19 ❑ Dec 1968 Cover: 0.40 **NM** value: **10.00**
20 ❑ Mar 1969 Cover: 0.40 **NM** value: **10.00**
21 ❑ May 1969 Cover: 0.40 **NM** value: **8.00**
22 ❑ Jul 1969 Cover: 0.40 **NM** value: **8.00**
23 ❑ Sep 1969 Cover: 0.50 **NM** value: **9.00**
24 ❑ Nov 1969 Cover: 0.50 **NM** value: **8.00**
25 ❑ Jan 1970 Cover: 0.50 **NM** value: **8.00**
26 ❑ Mar 1970 Cover: 0.50 **NM** value: **8.00**
27 ❑ May 1970 Cover: 0.50 **NM** value: **8.00**
28 ❑ Jul 1970 Cover: 0.50 **NM** value: **8.00**
29 ❑ Sep 1970 Cover: 0.50 **NM** value: **8.00**
30 ❑ Nov 1970 Cover: 0.60 **NM** value: **8.00**
31 ❑ Jan 1971 Cover: 0.60 **NM** value: **6.00**
32 ❑ Mar 1971 Cover: 0.60 **NM** value: **6.00**
33 ❑ May 1971 Cover: 0.60 **NM** value: **6.00**
34 ❑ Jul 1971 Cover: 0.60 **NM** value: **6.00**
35 ❑ Aug 1971 Cover: 0.60 **NM** value: **6.00**
36 ❑ Sep 1971 Cover: 0.60 **NM** value: **6.00**
37 ❑ Jan 1972 Cover: 0.60 **NM** value: **6.00**
38 ❑ Feb 1972 Cover: 0.60 **NM** value: **6.00**
39 ❑ Apr 1972 Cover: 0.60 **NM** value: **6.00**
40 ❑ Jun 1972 Cover: 0.75 **NM** value: **6.00**
41 ❑ Aug 1972 Cover: 0.75 **NM** value: **5.00**
42 ❑ Oct 1972 Cover: 1.00 **NM** value: **5.00**
43 ❑ Nov 1972 Cover: 0.75 **NM** value: **5.00**
44 ❑ Dec 1972 Cover: 0.75 **NM** value: **5.00**
45 ❑ Feb 1973 Cover: 0.75 **NM** value: **5.00**
46 ❑ Mar 1973 Cover: 0.75 **NM** value: **5.00**
47 ❑ Apr 1973 Cover: 0.75 **NM** value: **5.00**
48 ❑ Jun 1973 Cover: 0.75 **NM** value: **5.00**
49 ❑ Jul 1973 Cover: 0.75 **NM** value: **5.00**
50 ❑ Aug 1973 Cover: 0.75 **NM** value: **5.00**
51 ❑ Sep 1973 Cover: 0.75 **NM** value: **5.00**
52 ❑ Nov 1973 Cover: 0.75 **NM** value: **5.00**
53 ❑ Jan 1974 Cover: 0.75 **NM** value: **5.00**
Circ: Statement: **90,595**
54 ❑ Feb 1974 Cover: 1.00 **NM** value: **5.00**
Circ: Statement: **90,595**
55 ❑ Mar 1974 Cover: 1.00 **NM** value: **5.00**
Circ: Statement: **90,595**
56 ❑ Apr 1974 Cover: 1.00 **NM** value: **5.00**
Circ: Statement: **90,595**
57 ❑ Jun 1974 Cover: 1.00 **NM** value: **5.00**
Circ: Statement: **90,595**
58 ❑ Jul 1974 Cover: 1.00 **NM** value: **5.00**
Circ: Statement: **90,595**
59 ❑ Aug 1974 Cover: 1.25 **NM** value: **5.00**
Circ: Statement: **90,595**
60 ❑ Sep 1974 Cover: 1.25 **NM** value: **5.00**
Circ: Statement: **90,595**
61 ❑ Nov 1974 Cover: 1.00 **NM** value: **4.00**
Circ: Statement: **90,595**
62 ❑ Jan 1975 Cover: 1.00 **NM** value: **4.00**
Circ: Statement: **95,655**
63 ❑ Feb 1975 Cover: 1.25 **NM** value: **4.00**
Circ: Statement: **95,655**
64 ❑ Mar 1975 Cover: 1.00 **NM** value: **4.00**
Circ: Statement: **95,655**
65 ❑ Apr 1975 Cover: 1.00 **NM** value: **4.00**
Circ: Statement: **95,655**
• Has 1974 Statement, filed 10/1/74; avg print run 163,780; avg sales 90,080; avg subs 515; avg total paid 90,595; samples 100; office use 40,329; max existent 131,024; 20% of run returned
66 ❑ Jun 1975 Cover: 1.00 **NM** value: **4.00**
Circ: Statement: **95,655**
67 ❑ Aug 1975 Cover: 1.00 **NM** value: **4.00**
Circ: Statement: **95,655**
68 ❑ Sep 1975 Cover: 1.25 **NM** value: **4.00**
Circ: Statement: **95,655**
69 ❑ Oct 1975 Cover: 1.25 **NM** value: **4.00**
Circ: Statement: **95,655**
70 ❑ Nov 1975 Cover: 1.00 **NM** value: **4.00**
Circ: Statement: **95,655**
71 ❑ Jan 1976 Cover: 1.00 **NM** value: **4.00**
Circ: Statement: **86,100**
72 ❑ Feb 1976 Cover: 1.25 **NM** value: **4.00**
Circ: Statement: **86,100**
• Has 1975 Statement, filed 10/1/75; avg print run 173,100; avg sales 95,200; avg subs 455; avg total paid 95,655; samples 90; office use 42,735; max existent 138,480; 20% of run returned
73 ❑ Mar 1976 Cover: 1.00 **NM** value: **4.00**
Circ: Statement: **86,100**
74 ❑ May 1976 Cover: 1.00 **NM** value: **4.00**
Circ: Statement: **86,100**
75 ❑ Jun 1976 Cover: 1.00 **NM** value: **4.00**
Circ: Statement: **86,100**
76 ❑ Aug 1976 Cover: 1.00 **NM** value: **4.00**
Circ: Statement: **86,100**
77 ❑ Sep 1976 Cover: 1.25 **NM** value: **4.00**
Circ: Statement: **86,100**
78 ❑ Oct 1976 Cover: 1.25 **NM** value: **4.00**
Circ: Statement: **86,100**
79 ❑ Nov 1976 Cover: 1.25 **NM** value: **4.00**
Circ: Statement: **86,100**
80 ❑ Jan 1977 Cover: 1.25 **NM** value: **4.00**
Circ: Statement: **90,355**
81 ❑ Feb 1977 Cover: 1.50 **NM** value: **4.00**
Circ: Statement: **90,355**
• Has 1976 Statement, filed 10/1/76; avg print run 155,675; avg sales 85,620; avg subs 480; avg total paid 86,100; samples 72; office use 38,368; max existent 124,540; 20% of run returned
82 ❑ Mar 1977 Cover: 1.50 **NM** value: **4.00**
Circ: Statement: **90,355**
• 1st apperance of The Rook
83 ❑ May 1977 Cover: 1.50 **NM** value: **4.00**
Circ: Statement: **90,355**
84 ❑ Jun 1977 Cover: 1.50 **NM** value: **4.00**
Circ: Statement: **90,355**
85 ❑ Aug 1977 Cover: 1.50 **NM** value: **4.00**
Circ: Statement: **90,355**
86 ❑ Sep 1977 Cover: 1.50 **NM** value: **4.00**
Circ: Statement: **90,355**
87 ❑ Oct 1977 Cover: 2.00 **NM** value: **4.00**
Circ: Statement: **90,355**
88 ❑ Nov 1977 Cover: 1.25 **NM** value: **4.00**
Circ: Statement: **90,355**
89 ❑ Jan 1978 Cover: 1.25 **NM** value: **4.00**
Circ: Statement: **89,360**
90 ❑ Feb 1978 Cover: 1.50 **NM** value: **4.00**
Circ: Statement: **89,360**
• Has 1977 Statement, filed 11/30/77; avg print run 163,500; avg sales 89,925; avg subs 430; avg total paid 90,355; samples 85; office use 40,360; max existent 130,800; 20% of run returned
91 ❑ Mar 1978 Cover: 1.25 **NM** value: **4.00**
Circ: Statement: **89,360**
92 ❑ May 1978 Cover: 1.25 **NM** value: **4.00**
Circ: Statement: **89,360**
93 ❑ Jun 1978 Cover: 1.25 **NM** value: **4.00**
Circ: Statement: **89,360**
94 ❑ Aug 1978 Cover: 1.25 **NM** value: **4.00**
Circ: Statement: **89,360**
95 ❑ Sep 1978 Cover: 1.50 **NM** value: **4.00**
Circ: Statement: **89,360**
96 ❑ Oct 1978 Cover: 1.75 **NM** value: **4.00**
Circ: Statement: **89,360**
97 ❑ Nov 1978 Cover: 1.25 **NM** value: **4.00**
Circ: Statement: **89,360**
98 ❑ Jan 1979 Cover: 1.50 **NM** value: **4.00**
99 ❑ Feb 1979 Cover: 1.50 **NM** value: **4.00**
• Has 1978 Statement, filed 9/30/78; avg print run 161,560; avg sales 88,860; avg subs 500; avg total paid 89,360; samples 96; office use 39,794; max existent 129,250; 20% of run returned
100 ❑ Apr 1979 Cover: 2.00 **NM** value: **4.00**
101 ❑ Jun 1979 Cover: 1.50 **NM** value: **3.00**
102 ❑ Jul 1979 Cover: 1.50 **NM** value: **3.00**
103 ❑ Aug 1979 Cover: 1.75 **NM** value: **3.00**
104 ❑ Sep 1979 Cover: 1.75 **NM** value: **3.00**
105 ❑ Oct 1979 Cover: 1.75 **NM** value: **3.00**
106 ❑ Nov 1979 Cover: 1.50 **NM** value: **3.00**
📖 An Angel Shy of Hell; Kansas City Bomber; Brass Monkey; Gonna Nuke Mankind Right Outta My Hair; The Super-Abnormal Phenomena Survival Kit! **A:** Richard Corben; Juan Ortiz; John Severin **W:** Jim Stenstrum
107 ❑ Dec 1980 Cover: 1.50 **NM** value: **3.00**
108 ❑ Jan 1980 Cover: 1.50 **NM** value: **3.00**
109 ❑ Feb 1980 Cover: 1.75 **NM** value: **3.00**
110 ❑ Apr 1980 Cover: 1.75 **NM** value: **3.00**
111 ❑ Jun 1980 Cover: 1.75 **NM** value: **3.00**
112 ❑ Jul 1980 Cover: 1.75 **NM** value: **3.00**
113 ❑ Aug 1980 Cover: 1.75 **NM** value: **3.00**
114 ❑ Sep 1980 Cover: 1.75 **NM** value: **3.00**
115 ❑ Oct 1980 Cover: 1.75 **NM** value: **3.00**
116 ❑ Nov 1980 Cover: 1.75 **NM** value: **3.00**
117 ❑ Dec 1980 Cover: 1.75 **NM** value: **3.00**
118 ❑ Jan 1981 Cover: 1.75 **NM** value: **3.00**
119 ❑ Feb 1981 Cover: 1.95 **NM** value: **3.00**
120 ❑ Apr 1981 Cover: 2.50 **NM** value: **3.00**
121 ❑ Jun 1981 Cover: 2.00 **NM** value: **3.00**
122 ❑ Jul 1981 Cover: 2.00 **NM** value: **3.00**
123 ❑ Aug 1981 Cover: 2.00 **NM** value: **3.00**
124 ❑ Sep 1981 Cover: 2.00 **NM** value: **3.00**
125 ❑ Oct 1981 Cover: 2.00 **NM** value: **3.00**
126 ❑ Nov 1981 Cover: 2.00 **NM** value: **3.00**
127 ❑ Dec 1981 Cover: 2.00 **NM** value: **3.00**
128 ❑ Jan 1982 Cover: 2.00 **NM** value: **3.00**
Circ: Statement: **67,793**
129 ❑ Feb 1982 Cover: 2.00 **NM** value: **3.00**
Circ: Statement: **67,793**
130 ❑ Apr 1982 Cover: 2.00 **NM** value: **3.00**
Circ: Statement: **67,793**
131 ❑ Jun 1982 Cover: 2.00 **NM** value: **3.00**
Circ: Statement: **67,793**
132 ❑ Jul 1982 Cover: 2.00 **NM** value: **3.00**
Circ: Statement: **67,793**
133 ❑ Aug 1982 Cover: 2.00 **NM** value: **3.00**
Circ: Statement: **67,793**
134 ❑ Sep 1982 Cover: 2.25 **NM** value: **3.00**
Circ: Statement: **67,793**
135 ❑ Oct 1982 Cover: 2.50 **NM** value: **3.00**
Circ: Statement: **67,793**
136 ❑ Nov 1982 Cover: 2.25 **NM** value: **3.00**
Circ: Statement: **67,793**
137 ❑ Dec 1982 Cover: 2.25 **NM** value: **3.00**
Circ: Statement: **67,793**
138 ❑ Jan 1983 Cover: 2.25 **NM** value: **3.00**
139 ❑ Feb 1983 Cover: 2.25 **NM** value: **3.00**
• Has 1982 Statement, filed 10/1/82; avg print run 122,483; avg sales 67,365; avg subs 428; avg total paid 67,793; samples 258; office use 1,225; max existent 69,276; 43% of run returned
YB 1970 ❑ ca. 1970 **NM** value: **8.00**
YB 1971 ❑ ca. 1971 Cover: 0.60 **NM** value: **6.00**
YB 1972 ❑ ca. 1972 **NM** value: **6.00**

EGON — Dark Horse

1 ❑ Jan 1998 Cover: 2.95 **NM** value: **Cover or less**
Circ: Diamd. preorders: **6,029**

EGYPT — DC / Vertigo

1 ❑ Aug 1995 Cover: 2.50 **NM** value: **Cover or less**
Circ: CapCity orders: **12,025**
📖 The Book of the Remains **A:** Glyn Dillon **W:** Peter Milligan
2 ❑ Sep 1995 Cover: 2.50 **NM** value: **Cover or less**
Circ: CapCity orders: **9,375**
📖 The Book of the Shadows **A:** Glyn Dillon **W:** Peter Milligan
3 ❑ Oct 1995 Cover: 2.50 **NM** value: **Cover or less**
Circ: CapCity orders: **7,625**
📖 The Book of the Double **A:** Roberto Corona **W:** Peter Milligan
4 ❑ Nov 1995 Cover: 2.50 **NM** value: **Cover or less**
📖 The Book of the Heart **A:** Roberto Corona **W:** Peter Milligan
5 ❑ Dec 1995 Cover: 2.50 **NM** value: **Cover or less**
📖 The Book of the Angel **A:** Roberto Corona **W:** Peter Milligan
6 ❑ Jan 1996 Cover: 2.50 **NM** value: **Cover or less**
📖 The Book of the Power **A:** Roberto Corona **W:** Peter Milligan
7 ❑ Feb 1996 Cover: 2.50 **NM** value: **Cover or less**
📖 The Book of the Name final issue. **A:** Roberto Corona **W:** Peter Milligan

EH! — Charlton

Mad set the style for successful comic-book parody, and a year later Charlton produced this effort, which ran for only a year. Cluttering the panels with lots of sight gags wasn't sufficient by itself to draw an audience devoted to Harvey Kurtzman's creation. In addition to Kurtzman, the series featured art by Dick Ayers and Dick Giordano.

Subtitled "Dig This Crazy Magazine!," the series changed to From Here to Insanity with #7. It should also be noted that all the women in the series had strange shoulder-blades that made them look almost humpbacked. — Maggie

1 ❑ Dec 1953 Cover: 0.10 **NM** value: **250.00**
2 ❑ 1954 Cover: 0.10 **NM** value: **150.00**
3 ❑ 1954 Cover: 0.10 **NM** value: **125.00**
4 ❑ 1954 Cover: 0.10 **NM** value: **125.00**
5 ❑ 1954 Cover: 0.10 **NM** value: **125.00**
6 ❑ Aug 1954 Cover: 0.10 **NM** value: **100.00**
• **CGC:** 6 graded, best 9.0
7 ❑ Nov 1954 Cover: 0.10 **NM** value: **100.00**
• **CGC:** 1 graded, best 7.0

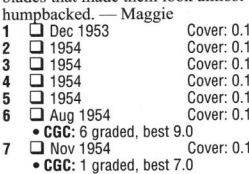

CGC-graded: Multiply prices above by **33 for 9.9 M • 16 for 9.8 NM/M • 7 for 9.6 NM+ • 5 for 9.4 NM • 2.5 for 9.2 NM- • 1.5 for 9.0 VF/NM**

EHLISSA — Highland Graphics

1 ❑ Nov 1992 Cover: 2.00 **NM** value: **Cover or less**
Color on cover. 📖 Strange New World **A:** Angus MacLeod **W:** Angus MacLeod
1-2 ❑ Cover: 2.00 **NM** value: **Cover or less**
1-3 ❑ Cover: 2.00 **NM** value: **Cover or less**
2 ❑ Dec 1992 Cover: 2.00 **NM** value: **Cover or less**
Color on cover. **A:** Angus MacLeod **W:** Angus MacLeod ★ 1st Appearance of Kalendes.
2-2 ❑ Cover: 2.00 **NM** value: **Cover or less**
3 ❑ Jan 1993 Cover: 2.00 **NM** value: **Cover or less**
Color on cover. **A:** Angus MacLeod **W:** Angus MacLeod
3-2 ❑ Cover: 2.00 **NM** value: **Cover or less**
4 ❑ Mar 1993 Cover: 2.00 **NM** value: **Cover or less**
Color on cover. **A:** Angus MacLeod **W:** Angus MacLeod
4-2 ❑ Cover: 2.00 **NM** value: **Cover or less**
5 ❑ Mar 1993 Cover: 2.00 **NM** value: **Cover or less**
Color on cover. **A:** Angus MacLeod **W:** Angus MacLeod
5-2 ❑ Cover: 2.00 **NM** value: **Cover or less**
6 ❑ Cover: 2.00 **NM** value: **Cover or less**
Color on cover. **A:** Angus MacLeod **W:** Angus MacLeod
6-2 ❑ Cover: 2.00 **NM** value: **Cover or less**
7 ❑ Cover: 2.00 **NM** value: **Cover or less**
Color on cover. **A:** Angus MacLeod **W:** Angus MacLeod
7-2 ❑ Cover: 2.00 **NM** value: **Cover or less**
8 ❑ May 1993 Cover: 2.00 **NM** value: **Cover or less**
Color on cover. **A:** Angus MacLeod **W:** Angus MacLeod
8-2 ❑ Cover: 2.00 **NM** value: **Cover or less**
9 ❑ Jul 1993 Cover: 2.00 **NM** value: **Cover or less**
Color on cover. **A:** Angus MacLeod **W:** Angus MacLeod
9-2 ❑ Cover: 2.00 **NM** value: **Cover or less**
10 ❑ 1993 Cover: 2.00 **NM** value: **Cover or less**
Color on cover. **A:** Angus MacLeod **W:** Angus MacLeod
10-2❑ Cover: 2.00 **NM** value: **Cover or less**
11 ❑ 1993 Cover: 2.00 **NM** value: **Cover or less**
Color on cover. 📖 Yesterme, Yesteryou **A:** Angus MacLeod **W:** Angus MacLeod
11-2❑ Cover: 2.00 **NM** value: **Cover or less**
12 ❑ 1993 Cover: 2.00 **NM** value: **Cover or less**
Color on cover. **A:** Angus MacLeod **W:** Angus MacLeod
12-2❑ Cover: 2.00 **NM** value: **Cover or less**
13 ❑ 1993 Cover: 2.00 **NM** value: **Cover or less**
Color on cover. **A:** Angus MacLeod **W:** Angus MacLeod
13-2❑ Cover: 2.00 **NM** value: **Cover or less**
14 ❑ Jan 1994 Cover: 2.00 **NM** value: **Cover or less**
Color on cover. **A:** Angus MacLeod **W:** Angus MacLeod
14-2❑ Cover: 2.00 **NM** value: **Cover or less**
15 ❑ Feb 1994 Cover: 2.00 **NM** value: **Cover or less**
Color cover. 📖 One Step Ahead of the Sheet **A:** Angus MacLeod; Ben Oliari **W:** Angus MacLeod ★ 1st Appearance of Ransard Maclin.
15-2❑ Cover: 2.00 **NM** value: **Cover or less**
Black & white cover. 📖 One Step Ahead of the Sheet **A:** Angus MacLeod; Ben Oliari **W:** Angus MacLeod ★ 1st Appearance of Ransard Maclin.
16 ❑ Mar 1994 Cover: 2.00 **NM** value: **Cover or less**
Color on cover. **A:** Angus MacLeod **W:** Angus MacLeod
16-2❑ Cover: 2.00 **NM** value: **Cover or less**
17 ❑ Apr 1994 Cover: 2.00 **NM** value: **Cover or less**
Color on cover. **A:** Angus MacLeod **W:** Angus MacLeod
17-2❑ Cover: 2.00 **NM** value: **Cover or less**
18 ❑ May 1994 Cover: 2.00 **NM** value: **Cover or less**
Color on cover. **A:** Angus MacLeod **W:** Angus MacLeod
18-2❑ Cover: 2.00 **NM** value: **Cover or less**
19 ❑ Jun 1994 Cover: 2.00 **NM** value: **Cover or less**
Color on cover. **A:** Angus MacLeod **W:** Angus MacLeod
19-2❑ Cover: 2.00 **NM** value: **Cover or less**
20 ❑ Jul 1994 Cover: 2.00 **NM** value: **Cover or less**
Color on cover. **A:** Angus MacLeod **W:** Angus MacLeod
20-2❑ Cover: 2.00 **NM** value: **Cover or less**
21 ❑ Aug 1994 Cover: 2.00 **NM** value: **Cover or less**
22 ❑ Sep 1994 Cover: 2.00 **NM** value: **Cover or less**
📖 Welcome to Zhuruk **A:** Angus MacLeod **W:** Angus MacLeod
23 ❑ Oct 1994 Cover: 2.00 **NM** value: **Cover or less**
24 ❑ Nov 1994 Cover: 2.00 **NM** value: **Cover or less**
25 ❑ Dec 1994 Cover: 2.00 **NM** value: **Cover or less**
26 ❑ Jan 1995 Cover: 2.00 **NM** value: **Cover or less**
27 ❑ Feb 1995 Cover: 2.00 **NM** value: **Cover or less**
28 ❑ Mar 1995 Cover: 2.00 **NM** value: **Cover or less**
29 ❑ Apr 1995 Cover: 2.00 **NM** value: **Cover or less**
30 ❑ May 1995 Cover: 2.00 **NM** value: **Cover or less**
📖 Stanzas From the Edge **A:** Angus MacLeod **W:** Angus MacLeod ★ 1st Appearance of Nathan.
31 ❑ Jun 1995 Cover: 2.00 **NM** value: **Cover or less**
• has #27's indicia **A:** Angus MacLeod **W:** Angus MacLeod
32 ❑ Cover: 2.00 **NM** value: **Cover or less**
📖 Interlude in Pre-Historia **A:** Angus MacLeod **W:** Angus MacLeod ★ 1st Appearance of Lanith.
33 ❑ Cover: 2.00 **NM** value: **Cover or less**

EIGHTBALL — Fantagraphics

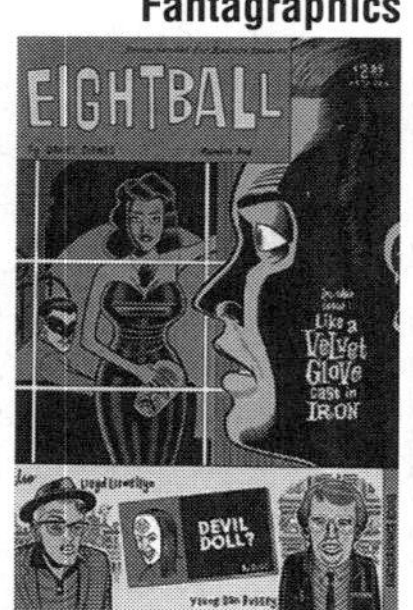

Eightball is perhaps the most famous work by alternative comics guru Dan Clowes. Clowes brings a shaky, claustrophobic feel to each of these stories, a mood that is reflected in everything from the perpetually furrowed brows of the characters to the surreal nature of situations they find themselves in. A good example of this is the series' lead story, "Like a Velvet Glove Cast in Iron." Here a man finds an all-knowing oracle in the bathroom of a movie theater and all he can think to ask is whether or not the oracle knew anything about the strange film he just watched. The images from that film reappear again when the man meets a person with fish in his eye sockets, an insane street bum, and a three-eyed prostitute.

Eightball is reminiscent of William S. Burroughs' "Naked Lunch," particularly in how the painfully dull lives of the characters are transformed to take on nightmarish dimensions.

1 ❑ **NM** value: **12.00**
• **CGC:** 1 graded, best 9.0
1-2 ❑ **NM** value: **5.00**
1-3 ❑ **NM** value: **3.50**
1-4 ❑ Cover: 2.95 **NM** value: **3.00**
2 ❑ Cover: 2.00 **NM** value: **7.00**
3 ❑ Cover: 2.00 **NM** value: **6.00**
4 ❑ Cover: 2.75 **NM** value: **6.00**
5 ❑ Cover: 2.75 **NM** value: **5.00**
📖 Like a Velvet Glove Cast in Iron; Just Another Day...; Playful Obsession; Paranoid **A:** Dan Clowes **W:** Dan Clowes
6 ❑ Cover: 2.75 **NM** value: **5.00**
7 ❑ Cover: 2.50 **NM** value: **4.00**
8 ❑ Cover: 2.95 **NM** value: **4.00**
Circ: CapCity orders: **2,665**
9 ❑ Cover: 2.75 **NM** value: **3.00**
10 ❑ Cover: 2.75 **NM** value: **3.00**
Circ: CapCity orders: **3,110**
11 ❑ Cover: 2.95 **NM** value: **3.00**
Circ: CapCity orders: **3,825**
12 ❑ Nov 1993 Cover: 2.75 **NM** value: **3.00**
Circ: CapCity orders: **3,515**
13 ❑ Cover: 2.95 **NM** value: **3.00**
Circ: CapCity orders: **80**
14 ❑ Cover: 2.95 **NM** value: **3.00**
Circ: CapCity orders: **3,725**
15 ❑ Cover: 2.95 **NM** value: **3.00**
Circ: CapCity orders: **3,787**
16 ❑ Nov 1995 Cover: 3.95 **NM** value: **4.00**
cardstock cover. **A:** Dan Clowes **W:** Dan Clowes
17 ❑ Cover: 3.95 **NM** value: **Cover or less**
18 ❑ Mar 1997 Cover: 3.95 **NM** value: **Cover or less**
Circ: Diamd. preorders: **9,886**
19 ❑ May 1998 Cover: 3.95 **NM** value: **Cover or less**
Circ: Diamd. preorders: **9,230**
20 ❑ Feb 1999 Cover: 4.50 **NM** value: **Cover or less**
Circ: Diamd. preorders: **8,416**
cardstock cover. **A:** Dan Clowes **W:** Dan Clowes
21 ❑ Feb 2000 Cover: 4.95 **NM** value: **Cover or less**
Circ: Diamd. preorders: **7,853**
22 ❑ Cover: 2.95 **NM** value: **Cover or less**
Circ: Diamd. preorders: **8,855**
23 ❑ Cover: 2.95 **NM** value: **Cover or less**

EIGHTH WONDER, THE — Dark Horse

1 ❑ Nov 1997, b&w Cover: 2.95 **NM** value: **Cover or less**
Circ: Diamd. preorders: **3,573**
No issue number. One-shot. cover says The 8th Wonder, indicia says The Eighth Wonder.

80 PAGE GIANT MAGAZINE — DC

1 ❑ Aug 1964 Cover: 0.25 **NM** value: **260.00**
• Superman; Imaginary stories
2 ❑ Sep 1964 Cover: 0.25 **NM** value: **80.00**
• Jimmy Olsen
3 ❑ Sep 1964 Cover: 0.25 **NM** value: **70.00**
• Lois Lane
4 ❑ Oct 1964 Cover: 0.25 **NM** value: **70.00**
• Flash
5 ❑ Nov 1964 Cover: 0.25 **NM** value: **70.00**
• Batman
6 ❑ Jan 1965 Cover: 0.25 **NM** value: **60.00**
• Superman
7 ❑ Feb 1965 Cover: 0.25 **NM** value: **60.00**
• Sgt. Rock
8 ❑ Mar 1965 Cover: 0.25 **NM** value: **100.00**
• Secret Origins
9 ❑ Apr 1965 Cover: 0.25 **NM** value: **60.00**
• Flash; reprints "Flash of Two Worlds"
10 ❑ May 1965 Cover: 0.25 **NM** value: **50.00**
• Superboy
11 ❑ Jun 1965 Cover: 0.25 **NM** value: **50.00**
• Superman
12 ❑ Jul 1965 Cover: 0.25 **NM** value: **50.00**
• Batman
13 ❑ Aug 1965 Cover: 0.25 **NM** value: **50.00**
• Jimmy Olsen
14 ❑ Sep 1965 Cover: 0.25 **NM** value: **50.00**
• Lois Lane
15 ❑ Oct 1965 Cover: 0.25 **NM** value: **50.00**
• Batman/Superman

EL DIABLO — DC

1 ❑ Aug 1989 Cover: 2.50 **NM** value: **Cover or less**
Circ: CapCity orders: **15,250**
• Double-size. ★ 1st Appearance of El Diablo.
2 ❑ Sep 1989 Cover: 1.50 **NM** value: **Cover or less**
Circ: CapCity orders: **11,600**
3 ❑ Oct 1989 Cover: 1.50 **NM** value: **Cover or less**
Circ: CapCity orders: **10,050**
4 ❑ Dec 1989 Cover: 1.50 **NM** value: **Cover or less**
Circ: CapCity orders: **9,050**
5 ❑ Jan 1990 Cover: 1.50 **NM** value: **Cover or less**
Circ: CapCity orders: **7,850**
6 ❑ Feb 1990 Cover: 1.50 **NM** value: **Cover or less**
Circ: CapCity orders: **7,400**
7 ❑ Mar 1990 Cover: 1.75 **NM** value: **Cover or less**
Circ: CapCity orders: **6,650**
8 ❑ Apr 1990 Cover: 1.75 **NM** value: **Cover or less**
Circ: CapCity orders: **6,050**
9 ❑ May 1990 Cover: 1.75 **NM** value: **Cover or less**
Circ: CapCity orders: **5,100**
10 ❑ Jun 1990 Cover: 1.75 **NM** value: **Cover or less**
Circ: CapCity orders: **4,850**
11 ❑ Jul 1990 Cover: 1.75 **NM** value: **Cover or less**
Circ: CapCity orders: **4,600**
12 ❑ Aug 1990 Cover: 2.00 **NM** value: **Cover or less**
Circ: CapCity orders: **4,300**
• Golden Age Vigilante
13 ❑ Sep 1990 Cover: 2.00 **NM** value: **Cover or less**
Circ: CapCity orders: **4,100**
14 ❑ Oct 1990 Cover: 2.00 **NM** value: **Cover or less**
Circ: CapCity orders: **3,850**
15 ❑ Dec 1990 Cover: 2.00 **NM** value: **Cover or less**
Circ: CapCity orders: **3,850**
16 ❑ Jan 1991 Cover: 2.00 **NM** value: **Cover or less**
Circ: CapCity orders: **3,900**
final issue.

EL DIABLO (MINI-SERIES) — Vertigo

Moses Stone is a man of few words. He used to make his living as a bounty hunter. But when he was looking for a place to hide, he decided to become the sheriff of a small town.

Things went smoothly for Moses, until the Monkey Joe Cash gang rode into town, followed by a mysterious stranger. Suddenly, nearly the whole gang ended up dead, and Moses has found himself searching for vengeance on the trail of a Wild West ghost.

Resurrecting the frontier phantom from the pages of Weird Western Tales, the killer of legend known only as El Diablo is going to raise Hell in this four-issue mini-series.

1 ❑ Mar 2001 Cover: 2.50 **NM** value: **Cover or less**
Circ: Diamd. preorders: **15,466**
2 ❑ Apr 2001 Cover: 2.50 **NM** value: **Cover or less**
Circ: Diamd. preorders: **12,590**
3 ❑ May 2001 Cover: 2.50 **NM** value: **Cover or less**
Circ: Diamd. preorders: **12,117**
4 ❑ Jun 2001 Cover: 2.50 **NM** value: **Cover or less**
Circ: Diamd. preorders: **13,135**

ELECTRIC FEAR — Sparks

1 ❑ Win 1984 Cover: 1.25 **NM** value: **1.50**
2 ❑ Spr 1986 Cover: 1.25 **NM** value: **1.50**

ELECTRIC GIRL — Mighty Gremlin

1 ❑ May 1998 Cover: 3.50 **NM** value: **Cover or less**
2 ❑ Spr 1999 Cover: 2.95 **NM** value: **Cover or less**
3 ❑ Sum 1999 Cover: 2.95 **NM** value: **Cover or less**

ELECTRIC WARRIOR — DC

1 ❑ May 1986 Cover: 2.00 **NM** value: **Cover or less**
Circ: CapCity orders: **13,400**
📖 The Whole Nasty Night **A:** Jim Baikie **W:** Doug Moench
2 ❑ Jun 1986 Cover: 1.50 **NM** value: **Cover or less**
Circ: CapCity orders: **10,350**
📖 Gene Tricks Berserk! **A:** Jim Baikie **W:** Doug Moench
3 ❑ Jul 1986 Cover: 1.50 **NM** value: **Cover or less**
Circ: CapCity orders: **9,750**
4 ❑ Aug 1986 Cover: 1.50 **NM** value: **Cover or less**
Circ: CapCity orders: **9,950**
5 ❑ Sep 1986 Cover: 1.50 **NM** value: **Cover or less**
Circ: CapCity orders: **10,450**
6 ❑ Oct 1986 Cover: 1.50 **NM** value: **Cover or less**
Circ: CapCity orders: **10,100**
7 ❑ Nov 1986 Cover: 1.50 **NM** value: **Cover or less**
Circ: CapCity orders: **9,000**
8 ❑ Dec 1986 Cover: 1.50 **NM** value: **Cover or less**
Circ: CapCity orders: **8,050**
9 ❑ Jan 1987 Cover: 1.50 **NM** value: **Cover or less**
Circ: CapCity orders: **7,650**
10 ❑ Feb 1987 Cover: 1.50 **NM** value: **Cover or less**
Circ: CapCity orders: **7,100**
11 ❑ Mar 1987 Cover: 1.50 **NM** value: **Cover or less**
Circ: CapCity orders: **7,300**
12 ❑ Apr 1987 Cover: 1.50 **NM** value: **Cover or less**
Circ: CapCity orders: **6,700**
13 ❑ May 1987 Cover: 1.50 **NM** value: **Cover or less**
Circ: CapCity orders: **6,050**
14 ❑ Jun 1987 Cover: 1.50 **NM** value: **Cover or less**
Circ: CapCity orders: **5,800**
15 ❑ Jul 1987 Cover: 1.50 **NM** value: **Cover or less**
Circ: CapCity orders: **5,750**
16 ❑ Aug 1987 Cover: 1.50 **NM** value: **Cover or less**
Circ: CapCity orders: **6,100**
17 ❑ Sep 1987 Cover: 1.50 **NM** value: **Cover or less**
Circ: CapCity orders: **6,000**
18 ❑ Oct 1987 Cover: 1.50 **NM** value: **Cover or less**
Circ: CapCity orders: **6,200**

ELEKTRA (1ST SERIES) — Marvel

1 ❑ Mar 1995 Cover: 2.95 **NM** value: **3.00**
Circ: CapCity orders: **28,300** • **CGC:** 3 graded, best 9.8
enhanced cover. 📖 The Force of The Killer **A:** Scott McDaniel **W:** D.G. Chichester
2 ❑ Apr 1995 Cover: 2.95 **NM** value: **3.00**
Circ: CapCity orders: **21,425**
enhanced cover.

Other grades: Multiply prices above by **1.5 for Mint • 2/3 for Very Fine • 1/3 for Fine • 1/5 for Very Good • 1/8 for Good**

3 ❑ May 1995 Cover: 2.95 **NM** value: **3.00**
Circ: CapCity orders: **19,825** • **CGC:** 2 graded, best 9.9
enhanced cover.

4 ❑ Jun 1995 Cover: 2.95 **NM** value: **3.00**
Circ: CapCity orders: **19,575**
enhanced cover.

ELEKTRA (2ND SERIES) Marvel

-1 ❑ Jul 1997 Cover: 1.95 **NM** value: **2.00**
• Flashback ★ Appearance of Daredevil.

1 ❑ Nov 1996 Cover: 1.95 **NM** value: **2.50**
Circ: Direct Market orders: **155,250** • **CGC:** 44 graded, best 9.8
📖 Afraid of the Dark **A:** Mike Deodato Jr. **W:** Peter Milligan

1/A ❑ Nov 1996 Cover: 1.95 **NM** value: **2.50**
variant cover. 📖 Afraid of the Dark **A:** Mike Deodato Jr. **W:** Peter Milligan

2 ❑ Dec 1996 Cover: 1.95 **NM** value: **2.50**
Circ: Direct Market orders: **71,500** • **CGC:** 7 graded, best 9.8
📖 Fathers Day **A:** Mike Deodato Jr. **W:** Peter Milligan ★ Versus Bullseye.

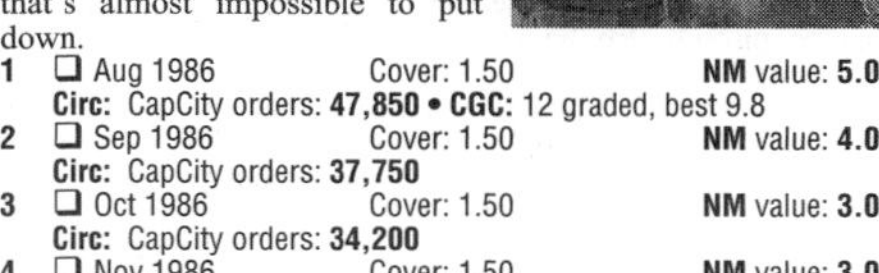

3 ❑ Jan 1997 Cover: 1.95 **NM** value: **2.50**
Circ: Statement: **70,671** Direct Market orders: **66,250** • **CGC:** 2 graded, best 9.6
📖 I Know How You Feel **A:** Mike Deodato Jr. **W:** Peter Milligan

4 ❑ Feb 1997 Cover: 1.95 **NM** value: **2.00**
Circ: Statement: **70,671** Direct Market orders: **60,500**
📖 A Little Piece of Paradise **A:** Mike Deodato Jr. **W:** Peter Milligan

5 ❑ Mar 1997 Cover: 1.95 **NM** value: **2.00**
Circ: Statement: **70,671** Direct Market orders: **54,500**
📖 Fourteen Days **A:** Mike Deodato Jr. **W:** Peter Milligan

6 ❑ Apr 1997 Cover: 1.95 **NM** value: **2.00**
Circ: Statement: **70,671** Direct Market orders: **51,500**
📖 Fury **A:** Mike Deodato Jr. **W:** Peter Milligan ★ Versus Razorfist.

7 ❑ May 1997 Cover: 1.95 **NM** value: **2.00**
Circ: Statement: **70,671** Diamd. preorders: **48,552**
📖 Out of the Night **A:** Mike Deodato Jr. **W:** Peter Milligan

8 ❑ Jun 1997 Cover: 1.95 **NM** value: **2.00**
Circ: Statement: **70,671** Diamd. preorders: **46,597**

9 ❑ Aug 1997 Cover: 1.99 **NM** value: **2.00**
Circ: Statement: **70,671**
• gatefold summary.

10 ❑ Sep 1997 Cover: 1.99 **NM** value: **2.00**
Circ: Statement: **70,671** Diamd. preorders: **39,812**
• gatefold summary.

11 ❑ Oct 1997 Cover: 1.99 **NM** value: **2.00**
Circ: Diamd. preorders: **36,270**
• gatefold summary. 📖 American Samurai, Part 1 ★ Appearance of Daredevil.

12 ❑ Nov 1997 Cover: 1.99 **NM** value: **2.00**
Circ: Diamd. preorders: **34,958**
• gatefold summary. 📖 American Samurai, Part 2 ★ Appearance of Daredevil.

13 ❑ Dec 1997 Cover: 1.99 **NM** value: **2.00**
Circ: Diamd. preorders: **33,988**
• gatefold summary. 📖 American Samurai, Part 3 • Has 1997 Statement; avg total paid circ 70,671 ★ Appearance of Daredevil.

14 ❑ Jan 1998 Cover: 1.99 **NM** value: **2.00**
Circ: Diamd. preorders: **33,883**
• gatefold summary.

15 ❑ Feb 1998 Cover: 1.99 **NM** value: **2.00**
Circ: Diamd. preorders: **31,714**
• gatefold summary.

16 ❑ Mar 1998 Cover: 1.99 **NM** value: **2.00**
Circ: Diamd. preorders: **30,020**
• gatefold summary.

17 ❑ Apr 1998 Cover: 1.99 **NM** value: **2.00**
Circ: Diamd. preorders: **27,818**
• gatefold summary.

18 ❑ May 1998 Cover: 1.99 **NM** value: **2.00**
Circ: Diamd. preorders: **26,983**
• gatefold summary.

19 ❑ Jun 1998 Cover: 1.99 **NM** value: **2.00**
Circ: Diamd. preorders: **27,019**
• gatefold summary. final issue.

ELEKTRA (3RD SERIES) Marvel / MAX

1 ❑ Sep 2001 Cover: 3.50 **NM** value: **Cover or less**
Circ: Diamd. preorders: **86,694**

2 ❑ 2001 Cover: 2.99 **NM** value: **Cover or less**
Circ: Diamd. preorders: **80,987**

3 ❑ 2001 Cover: 2.99 **NM** value: **Cover or less**
Circ: Diamd. preorders: **63,381**

3/A ❑ 2001 Cover: 2.99 **NM** value: **20.00**
• edition recalled because of nudity.

4 ❑ Dec 2001 Cover: 2.99 **NM** value: **Cover or less**
Circ: Diamd. preorders: **58,792**

5 ❑ 2001 Cover: 2.99 **NM** value: **Cover or less**
Circ: Diamd. preorders: **55,958**

6 ❑ 2002 Cover: 2.99 **NM** value: **Cover or less**
Circ: Diamd. preorders: **52,716**

ELEKTRA & WOLVERINE: THE REDEEMER Marvel

1 ❑ 2001 Cover: 5.95 **NM** value: **Cover or less**
2 ❑ 2001 Cover: 5.95 **NM** value: **Cover or less**
3 ❑ 2001 Cover: 5.95 **NM** value: **Cover or less**

The prices seen above do not represent the highest possible prices seen in online auctions, but rather the prices we have seen these issues reliably fetch in a variety of environments (storefront retail, mail order, auction and convention).

ELEKTRA: ASSASSIN Marvel / Epic

Elektra was easily one of Marvel's greatest characters, a female assassin that lit up the pages of Daredevil from her first appearance in issue #168 to her death in issue #181. Although her origin was sketched out in Daredevil, this series goes far deeper, delving into her own psyche to show how an innocent girl became transformed into an instrument of death.

Elektra: Assassin was written by Elektra's creator, Frank Miller, and painted by Bill Sienkiewicz. The result is a comic-book tour de force that's almost impossible to put down.

1 ❑ Aug 1986 Cover: 1.50 **NM** value: **5.00**
Circ: CapCity orders: **47,850** • **CGC:** 12 graded, best 9.8

2 ❑ Sep 1986 Cover: 1.50 **NM** value: **4.00**
Circ: CapCity orders: **37,750**

3 ❑ Oct 1986 Cover: 1.50 **NM** value: **3.00**
Circ: CapCity orders: **34,200**

4 ❑ Nov 1986 Cover: 1.50 **NM** value: **3.00**
Circ: CapCity orders: **28,400**
📖 Young Love **A:** Bill Sienkiewicz; Frank Miller **W:** Frank Miller

5 ❑ Dec 1986 Cover: 1.50 **NM** value: **3.00**
Circ: CapCity orders: **26,150**

6 ❑ Jan 1987 Cover: 1.50 **NM** value: **2.50**
Circ: CapCity orders: **24,900**

7 ❑ Feb 1987 Cover: 1.75 **NM** value: **2.50**
Circ: CapCity orders: **22,450**

8 ❑ Mar 1987 Cover: 1.75 **NM** value: **3.00**
Circ: CapCity orders: **21,200**
• Relatively scarce **A:** Bill Sienkiewicz; Frank Miller **W:** Frank Miller

Bk 1 ❑ Apr 1988 Cover: 12.95 **NM** value: **Cover or less**
• Trade Paperback. • Collects series **A:** Bill Sienkiewicz **W:** Frank Miller

ELEKTRA BATTLEBOOK Marvel

1 ❑ Cover: 3.99 **NM** value: **Cover or less**

ELEKTRA/CYBLADE Image

1 ❑ Mar 1997 Cover: 2.95 **NM** value: **3.50**
Circ: Diamd. preorders: **68,486**
📖 Devil's Reign, Part 7 • crossover with Marvel; concludes in Silver Surfer/Weapon Zero **A:** David Finch; Anthony Chun; Kirk Van Wormer; Billy Tan **W:** Brian Holguin; Howard Mackie

1/A ❑ Mar 1997 Cover: 2.95 **NM** value: **Cover or less**
alternate cover. 📖 Devil's Reign, Part 7 • crossover with Marvel; concludes in Silver Surfer/Weapon Zero

ELEKTRA LIVES AGAIN Marvel / Epic

1 ❑ Mar 1991 Cover: 24.95 **NM** value: **Cover or less**
Circ: CapCity orders: **16,300**
hardcover. **W:** Neil Gaiman

ELEKTRA MEGAZINE Marvel

1 ❑ Nov 1996 Cover: 3.95 **NM** value: **Cover or less**
• Reprints Elektra stories from Daredevil **A:** Frank Miller **W:** Frank Miller

2 ❑ Nov 1996 Cover: 3.95 **NM** value: **Cover or less**
• Reprints Elektra stories from Daredevil **A:** Frank Miller **W:** Frank Miller ★ Appearance of Punisher. ★ Death of Elektra.

ELEKTRA SAGA, THE Marvel

She was the deadly chief assassin for the band of evil Ninja known as "the Hand." She was also the great love of Matt Murdock (Daredevil)'s life. They had fallen in love long ago when their lives had been much different. Now they found themselves deadly enemies, playing an endgame from which only one would emerge alive.

Created by Frank Miller, this series tells her whole story from Daredevil Vol. 1, #168-181 (with all the non-Elektra material cut out). It traces Elektra from her first meeting with Matt Murdock to her brutal demise at the hands of Bullseye. Perhaps not the best way to read these stories, but it remains a thrilling, tragic tale, starring one of the best female characters Miller has ever created.

1 ❑ Feb 1984 Cover: 2.00 **NM** value: **4.00**
• Daredevil reprint **A:** Frank Miller **W:** Frank Miller

2 ❑ Mar 1984 Cover: 2.00 **NM** value: **3.50**
• Daredevil reprint **A:** Frank Miller **W:** Frank Miller

3 ❑ Apr 1984 Cover: 2.00 **NM** value: **3.50**
• Daredevil reprint **A:** Frank Miller **W:** Frank Miller

4 ❑ May 1984 Cover: 2.00 **NM** value: **3.50**
• Daredevil reprint **A:** Frank Miller **W:** Frank Miller

Bk 1 ❑ Cover: 16.95 **NM** value: **Cover or less**

ELEMENTALS: HOW THE WAR WAS WON Comico

1 ❑ Jun 1996 Cover: 2.95 **NM** value: **Cover or less**

ELEMENTALS LINGERIE Comico

1 ❑ May 1996 Cover: 2.95 **NM** value: **Cover or less**
Circ: CapCity orders: **5,150**
• pin-ups

ELEMENTALS SEX SPECIAL Comico

1 ❑ Oct 1991 Cover: 2.95 **NM** value: **Cover or less**
Circ: CapCity orders: **6,175**

2 ❑ Jun 1992 Cover: 2.95 **NM** value: **Cover or less**
Circ: CapCity orders: **5,100**

3 ❑ Sep 1992 Cover: 2.95 **NM** value: **Cover or less**
Circ: CapCity orders: **5,550**

4 ❑ Feb 1993 Cover: 2.95 **NM** value: **Cover or less**
Circ: CapCity orders: **5,275**

ELEMENTAL'S SEXY LINGERIE SPECIAL Comico

1/A ❑ Jan 1993 Cover: 2.95 **NM** value: **Cover or less**
• without poster

1/B ❑ Jan 1993 Cover: 5.95 **NM** value: **Cover or less**

ELEMENTALS SWIMSUIT SPECTACULAR 1996 Comico

1 ❑ Jun 1996 Cover: 2.95 **NM** value: **Cover or less**
• pin-ups

ELEMENTALS: THE VAMPIRES' REVENGE Comico

1 ❑ Jun 1996 Cover: 2.95 **NM** value: **Cover or less**

ELEMENTALS (VOL. 1) Comico

The Elementals are a loose band of super-heroes from the Comico world. Created by Bill Willingham, they first appeared in the Justice Machine Annual. In that story, four regular people were chosen to become super-powered heroes, modeled on the four elder forces of nature. The green-skinned Fathom represents water; Vortex represents air; Monolith draws powers from the earth; and Morningstar has powers based on fire. Although this first series treads through many standard super-hero plots, Willingham always gave the Elementals an extra dimension of reality and characterization which made the series special.

1 ❑ 1984 Cover: 1.50 **NM** value: **2.50**
• **CGC:** 1 graded, best 9.4

2 ❑ 1985 Cover: 1.50 **NM** value: **2.00**
📖 The Natural Order, Part 1 **A:** Bill Willingham **W:** Bill Willingham

3 ❑ 1985 Cover: 1.50 **NM** value: **2.00**

4 ❑ Jun 1985 Cover: 1.50 **NM** value: **2.00**
Circ: CapCity orders: **14,400**

5 ❑ Dec 1985 Cover: 1.50 **NM** value: **2.00**
Circ: CapCity orders: **14,925**

6 ❑ Feb 1986 Cover: 1.50 **NM** value: **Cover or less**
Circ: CapCity orders: **12,150**

7 ❑ Apr 1986 Cover: 1.50 **NM** value: **Cover or less**
Circ: CapCity orders: **11,825**

8 ❑ Jun 1986 Cover: 1.50 **NM** value: **Cover or less**
Circ: CapCity orders: **11,750**

9 ❑ Aug 1986 Cover: 1.50 **NM** value: **Cover or less**
Circ: CapCity orders: **9,825**

10 ❑ Oct 1986 Cover: 1.50 **NM** value: **Cover or less**
Circ: CapCity orders: **11,525**

11 ❑ Dec 1986 Cover: 1.50 **NM** value: **Cover or less**
Circ: CapCity orders: **10,650**

12 ❑ Feb 1987 Cover: 1.50 **NM** value: **Cover or less**
Circ: CapCity orders: **9,800**

13 ❑ Apr 1987 Cover: 1.50 **NM** value: **Cover or less**
Circ: CapCity orders: **9,650**

14 ❑ Jun 1987 Cover: 1.50 **NM** value: **Cover or less**
Circ: CapCity orders: **10,225**

15 ❑ Jul 1987 Cover: 1.50 **NM** value: **Cover or less**
Circ: CapCity orders: **10,275**

16 ❑ Aug 1987 Cover: 1.50 **NM** value: **Cover or less**
Circ: CapCity orders: **9,750**

17 ❑ Sep 1987 Cover: 1.50 **NM** value: **Cover or less**
Circ: CapCity orders: **9,825**

18 ❑ Oct 1987 Cover: 1.50 **NM** value: **Cover or less**
Circ: CapCity orders: **9,350**

19 ❑ Nov 1987 Cover: 1.50 **NM** value: **Cover or less**
Circ: CapCity orders: **9,225**

20 ❑ Dec 1987 Cover: 1.50 **NM** value: **Cover or less**
Circ: CapCity orders: **9,200**

21 ❑ Jan 1988 Cover: 1.50 **NM** value: **Cover or less**
Circ: CapCity orders: **8,350**

22 ❑ Feb 1988 Cover: 1.50 **NM** value: **Cover or less**
Circ: CapCity orders: **8,100**

23 ❑ Mar 1988 Cover: 1.75 **NM** value: **Cover or less**
Circ: CapCity orders: **8,050**

24 ❑ Apr 1988 Cover: 1.75 **NM** value: **Cover or less**
Circ: CapCity orders: **7,900**

25 ❑ May 1988 Cover: 1.75 **NM** value: **Cover or less**
Circ: CapCity orders: **7,950**

26 ❑ Jun 1988 Cover: 1.75 **NM** value: **Cover or less**
Circ: CapCity orders: **7,600**

27 ❑ Jul 1988 Cover: 1.75 **NM** value: **Cover or less**
Circ: CapCity orders: **7,000**

28 ❑ Aug 1988 Cover: 1.75 **NM** value: **Cover or less**
Circ: CapCity orders: **6,875**

29 ❑ Sep 1988 Cover: 1.75 **NM** value: **Cover or less**
Circ: CapCity orders: **6,500**
final issue.

Bk 1 ❑ Nov 1988 Cover: 10.95 **NM** value: **Cover or less**
Circ: CapCity orders: **1,375**
• The Natural Order

SE 1 ❑ Mar 1986 Cover: 1.75 **NM** value: **2.00**
📖 Episodes • Child abuse special **A:** Jack Herman **W:** Bill Willingham

CGC-graded: Multiply prices above by **33 for 9.9 M** • **16 for 9.8 NM/M** • **7 for 9.6 NM+** • **5 for 9.4 NM** • **2.5 for 9.2 NM-** • **1.5 for 9.0 VF/NM**

SE 2❑ Jan 1989 Cover: 1.95 **NM** value: **Cover or less**
Circ: CapCity orders: **5,900**

ELEMENTALS (VOL. 2) — Comico

1 ❑ Mar 1989 Cover: 1.95 **NM** value: **2.50**
Circ: CapCity orders: **9,100**
2 ❑ Apr 1989 Cover: 1.95 **NM** value: **2.00**
Circ: CapCity orders: **7,550**
3 ❑ May 1989 Cover: 1.95 **NM** value: **2.00**
Circ: CapCity orders: **7,050**
4 ❑ Jun 1989 Cover: 2.50 **NM** value: **Cover or less**
Circ: CapCity orders: **7,400**
5 ❑ Jul 1989 Cover: 2.50 **NM** value: **Cover or less**
Circ: CapCity orders: **7,700**
6 ❑ Aug 1989 Cover: 2.50 **NM** value: **Cover or less**
Circ: CapCity orders: **10,250**
7 ❑ Sep 1989 Cover: 2.50 **NM** value: **Cover or less**
Circ: CapCity orders: **7,950**
8 ❑ Oct 1989 Cover: 2.50 **NM** value: **Cover or less**
Circ: CapCity orders: **8,150**
9 ❑ Nov 1989 Cover: 2.50 **NM** value: **Cover or less**
Circ: CapCity orders: **7,950**
10 ❑ Dec 1989 Cover: 2.50 **NM** value: **Cover or less**
Circ: CapCity orders: **7,700**
📖 Oblivion War
11 ❑ Jan 1990 Cover: 2.50 **NM** value: **Cover or less**
Circ: CapCity orders: **7,350**
📖 Oblivion War
12 ❑ Feb 1990 Cover: 2.50 **NM** value: **Cover or less**
Circ: CapCity orders: **7,300**
📖 Oblivion War
13 ❑ Mar 1990 Cover: 2.50 **NM** value: **Cover or less**
Circ: CapCity orders: **7,450**
📖 Oblivion War
14 ❑ May 1990 Cover: 2.50 **NM** value: **Cover or less**
Circ: CapCity orders: **7,350**
15 ❑ Jul 1990 Cover: 2.50 **NM** value: **Cover or less**
Circ: CapCity orders: **7,400**
16 ❑ May 1991 Cover: 2.50 **NM** value: **Cover or less**
Circ: CapCity orders: **7,450**
17 ❑ May 1991 Cover: 2.50 **NM** value: **Cover or less**
Circ: CapCity orders: **7,500**
18 ❑ Jun 1991 Cover: 2.50 **NM** value: **Cover or less**
Circ: CapCity orders: **8,600**
19 ❑ Aug 1991 Cover: 2.50 **NM** value: **Cover or less**
Circ: CapCity orders: **7,600**
20 ❑ Oct 1991 Cover: 2.50 **NM** value: **Cover or less**
Circ: CapCity orders: **6,800**
21 ❑ Nov 1991 Cover: 2.50 **NM** value: **Cover or less**
Circ: CapCity orders: **6,700**
📖 Demon Massacre
22 ❑ Mar 1992 Cover: 2.50 **NM** value: **Cover or less**
Circ: CapCity orders: **6,375**
📖 Forever in this Halflife **A:** Mike Leeke **W:** Bill Willingham
23 ❑ May 1992 Cover: 2.50 **NM** value: **Cover or less**
Circ: CapCity orders: **6,325**
24 ❑ 1992 Cover: 2.50 **NM** value: **Cover or less**
Circ: CapCity orders: **6,300**
25 ❑ Nov 1992 Cover: 2.50 **NM** value: **Cover or less**
Circ: CapCity orders: **6,050**
26 ❑ Apr 1993 Cover: 2.50 **NM** value: **Cover or less**
Circ: CapCity orders: **6,050**
27 ❑ Cover: 2.50 **NM** value: **Cover or less**
Circ: CapCity orders: **6,175**
28 ❑ Cover: 2.50 **NM** value: **Cover or less**
Circ: CapCity orders: **6,100**
29 ❑ Cover: 2.50 **NM** value: **Cover or less**
Circ: CapCity orders: **6,375**
30 ❑ Cover: 2.50 **NM** value: **Cover or less**
31 ❑ Cover: 2.50 **NM** value: **Cover or less**
Circ: CapCity orders: **4,330**
32 ❑ Cover: 2.50 **NM** value: **Cover or less**
Circ: CapCity orders: **3,695**
📖 Birth of a Nation, Part 1
33 ❑ Cover: 2.50 **NM** value: **Cover or less**
Circ: CapCity orders: **3,295**
📖 Birth of a Nation, Part 2
34 ❑ Cover: 2.50 **NM** value: **Cover or less**
35 ❑ Cover: 2.50 **NM** value: **Cover or less**
• Never published?
36 ❑ Cover: 2.50 **NM** value: **Cover or less**
• Never published?
37 ❑ Cover: 2.50 **NM** value: **Cover or less**
• Never published?
38 ❑ Cover: 2.50 **NM** value: **Cover or less**
• Never published?
39 ❑ Cover: 2.50 **NM** value: **Cover or less**
• Never published?
40 ❑ Cover: 2.50 **NM** value: **Cover or less**
• Never published?
41 ❑ Cover: 2.50 **NM** value: **Cover or less**
• Never published?

ELEMENTALS (VOL. 3) — Comico

1 ❑ ca. 1995 Cover: 2.95 **NM** value: **Cover or less**
2 ❑ ca. 1996 Cover: 2.95 **NM** value: **Cover or less**
3 ❑ May 1996 Cover: 2.95 **NM** value: **Cover or less**

The prices seen above do not represent the highest possible prices seen in online auctions, but rather the prices we have seen these issues reliably fetch in a variety of environments (storefront retail, mail order, auction and convention).

ELEVEN OR ONE — Sirius Entertainment

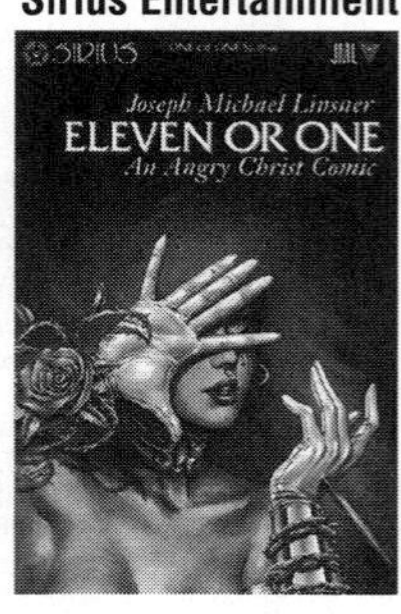

Joseph Michael Linsner, best known for his work on Dawn, here tells the story of Laddie Lopez, a New York City artist with a unique talent: he actually gets paid for his work. Laddie received countless telephone calls from agents who wanted to represent him, including his ex-wife. Of course, he turned them all down and decided to represent himself.

The stress of taking the lone route seems to have taken its toll on the young artist. Then one morning, Laddie woke with a second middle finger on his right hand. After convincing himself that he was not dreaming, he talked with all of his friends, one by one. None of them noticed his abnormality, even when he flashed his hand right in front of them. Laddie was inspired by this bizarre turn of events and decided to paint a series of paintings which he titled, Eleven or One. It asked the question: "Eleven parts or one whole?" It became a metaphor for Laddie's own search for meaning in his life.

1 ❑ Apr 1995 Cover: 2.95 **NM** value: **4.00**
• **CGC:** 2 graded, best 9.2
No issue number. • reprints new story from Angry Christ Comics tpb **A:** Joseph Michael Linsner **W:** Joseph Michael Linsner
1-2 ❑ Cover: 2.95 **NM** value: **3.00**

ELFHEIM — Nightwynd

1 ❑ 1991b&w Cover: 2.50 **NM** value: **Cover or less**
2 ❑ b&w Cover: 2.50 **NM** value: **Cover or less**
3 ❑ b&w Cover: 2.50 **NM** value: **Cover or less**
4 ❑ b&w Cover: 2.50 **NM** value: **Cover or less**

ELFHEIM: DRAGON DREAM (VOL. 5) — Nightwynd

1 ❑ Cover: 2.50 **NM** value: **Cover or less**
2 ❑ Cover: 2.50 **NM** value: **Cover or less**
3 ❑ Cover: 2.50 **NM** value: **Cover or less**
4 ❑ Cover: 2.50 **NM** value: **Cover or less**

ELFHEIM (VOL. 2) — Nightwynd

1 ❑ b&w Cover: 2.50 **NM** value: **Cover or less**
2 ❑ b&w Cover: 2.50 **NM** value: **Cover or less**
3 ❑ b&w Cover: 2.50 **NM** value: **Cover or less**
4 ❑ b&w Cover: 2.50 **NM** value: **Cover or less**

ELFHEIM (VOL. 3) — Nightwynd

1 ❑ b&w Cover: 2.50 **NM** value: **Cover or less**
2 ❑ b&w Cover: 2.50 **NM** value: **Cover or less**
3 ❑ b&w Cover: 2.50 **NM** value: **Cover or less**
4 ❑ b&w Cover: 2.50 **NM** value: **Cover or less**

ELFHEIM (VOL. 4) — Nightwynd

1 ❑ b&w Cover: 2.50 **NM** value: **Cover or less**
2 ❑ b&w Cover: 2.50 **NM** value: **Cover or less**

ELFIN ROMANCE — Mt. Wilson

1 ❑ Feb 1994, b&w Cover: 1.25 **NM** value: **1.50**
2 ❑ Apr 1994, b&w Cover: 1.25 **NM** value: **1.50**
3 ❑ Apr 1994, b&w Cover: 1.25 **NM** value: **1.50**
4 ❑ Jun 1994, b&w Cover: 2.00 **NM** value: **Cover or less**
5 ❑ Aug 1994, b&w Cover: 1.70 **NM** value: **2.00**
6 ❑ Oct 1994, b&w Cover: 1.75 **NM** value: **Cover or less**
7 ❑ Dec 1996, b&w Cover: 3.25 **NM** value: **Cover or less**

ELFLORD — Aircel

1 ❑ Feb 1986, b&w Cover: 2.00 **NM** value: **Cover or less**
1-2 ❑ Cover: 2.00 **NM** value: **Cover or less**
2 ❑ Mar 1986 Cover: 2.00 **NM** value: **Cover or less**
2-2 ❑ Cover: 2.00 **NM** value: **Cover or less**
3 ❑ Apr 1986 Cover: 2.00 **NM** value: **Cover or less**
4 ❑ May 1986 Cover: 2.00 **NM** value: **Cover or less**
5 ❑ Jun 1986 Cover: 2.00 **NM** value: **Cover or less**
6 ❑ Jul 1986 Cover: 2.00 **NM** value: **Cover or less**
7 ❑ Aug 1986 Cover: 2.00 **NM** value: **Cover or less**
• Never published?
8 ❑ Sep 1986 Cover: 2.00 **NM** value: **Cover or less**
• Never published?

ELFLORD (2ND SERIES) — Aircel

1 ❑ Oct 1986 Cover: 2.00 **NM** value: **Cover or less**
Circ: CapCity orders: **13,275**
2 ❑ Nov 1986 Cover: 2.00 **NM** value: **Cover or less**
Circ: CapCity orders: **10,250**
3 ❑ Dec 1986 Cover: 2.00 **NM** value: **Cover or less**
Circ: CapCity orders: **8,750**
4 ❑ Jan 1987 Cover: 2.00 **NM** value: **Cover or less**
Circ: CapCity orders: **8,650**
5 ❑ Feb 1987 Cover: 2.00 **NM** value: **Cover or less**
Circ: CapCity orders: **6,450**
6 ❑ Mar 1987 Cover: 2.00 **NM** value: **Cover or less**
Circ: CapCity orders: **5,900**
7 ❑ Apr 1987 Cover: 2.00 **NM** value: **Cover or less**
Circ: CapCity orders: **5,625**
8 ❑ May 1987 Cover: 2.00 **NM** value: **Cover or less**
Circ: CapCity orders: **5,600**
9 ❑ Jun 1987 Cover: 2.00 **NM** value: **Cover or less**
Circ: CapCity orders: **5,300**
10 ❑ Jul 1987 Cover: 2.00 **NM** value: **Cover or less**
Circ: CapCity orders: **5,000**
11 ❑ Aug 1987 Cover: 2.00 **NM** value: **Cover or less**
Circ: CapCity orders: **4,675**
12 ❑ Sep 1987 Cover: 2.00 **NM** value: **Cover or less**
Circ: CapCity orders: **4,675**
13 ❑ Oct 1987 Cover: 2.00 **NM** value: **Cover or less**
Circ: CapCity orders: **4,475**
14 ❑ Nov 1987 Cover: 2.00 **NM** value: **Cover or less**
15 ❑ Dec 1987 Cover: 2.00 **NM** value: **Cover or less**
Circ: CapCity orders: **4,525**
15.5❑ 1988 Cover: 2.00 **NM** value: **Cover or less**
Circ: CapCity orders: **3,750**
16 ❑ Jan 1988 Cover: 2.00 **NM** value: **Cover or less**
Circ: CapCity orders: **4,000**
17 ❑ Feb 1988 Cover: 2.00 **NM** value: **Cover or less**
Circ: CapCity orders: **3,675**
18 ❑ Mar 1988 Cover: 2.00 **NM** value: **Cover or less**
Circ: CapCity orders: **3,300**
19 ❑ 1988 Cover: 2.00 **NM** value: **Cover or less**
Circ: CapCity orders: **3,150**
20 ❑ 1988 Cover: 2.00 **NM** value: **Cover or less**
Circ: CapCity orders: **3,125**
21 ❑ 1988 Cover: 4.95 **NM** value: **Cover or less**
Circ: CapCity orders: **2,825**
• double-sized. 📖 Finale and DTnoument **A:** Barry Blair **W:** Barry Blair
22 ❑ 1988 Cover: 2.00 **NM** value: **Cover or less**
Circ: CapCity orders: **2,850**
📖 Red Sails in the Sunset **A:** Barry Blair **W:** Barry Blair
23 ❑ 1988 Cover: 1.95 **NM** value: **Cover or less**
Circ: CapCity orders: **2,850**
24 ❑ 1988 Cover: 1.95 **NM** value: **Cover or less**
Circ: CapCity orders: **2,600**
25 ❑ 1988 Cover: 1.95 **NM** value: **Cover or less**
Circ: CapCity orders: **2,425**
26 ❑ Dec 1988 Cover: 1.95 **NM** value: **Cover or less**
27 ❑ Jan 1989 Cover: 1.95 **NM** value: **Cover or less**
28 ❑ 1989 Cover: 1.95 **NM** value: **Cover or less**
29 ❑ 1989 Cover: 1.95 **NM** value: **Cover or less**
30 ❑ 1989 Cover: 1.95 **NM** value: **Cover or less**
31 ❑ 1989 Cover: 1.95 **NM** value: **Cover or less**

ELFLORD (3RD SERIES) — Nightwynd

This is a difficult title to comprehend when one is not familiar with the characters or universe. One could imagine a bad rock music video transposed into comic-book format complete with threadbare story, outrageous hair styles, and scantily clad effeminate adolescent elves skipping through the village. Lady Cloudshadow and the demon Ravenclaw have kidnapped the demon Borgamul's son for their own selfish purposes. It's King Hawk Erickson's responsibility to prevent them from usurping his rule. Frankly, this universe of elves is not for the more conservative-minded readership. Some readers could interpret the material to be sexually suggestive.

1 ❑ b&w Cover: 2.50 **NM** value: **Cover or less**
2 ❑ b&w Cover: 2.50 **NM** value: **Cover or less**
3 ❑ b&w Cover: 2.50 **NM** value: **Cover or less**
4 ❑ b&w Cover: 2.50 **NM** value: **Cover or less**

ELFLORD (4TH SERIES) — Warp

1 ❑ Jan 1997, b&w Cover: 2.95 **NM** value: **Cover or less**
Circ: Diamd. preorders: **6,195**
2 ❑ Feb 1997, b&w Cover: 2.95 **NM** value: **Cover or less**
Circ: Diamd. preorders: **4,861**
3 ❑ Mar 1997, b&w Cover: 2.95 **NM** value: **Cover or less**
Circ: Diamd. preorders: **4,517**
4 ❑ Apr 1997, b&w Cover: 2.95 **NM** value: **Cover or less**
Circ: Diamd. preorders: **4,286**

ELFLORD (5TH SERIES) — Warp

1 ❑ Sep 1997, b&w Cover: 2.95 **NM** value: **Cover or less**
📖 Cuts Loose **A:** Barry Blair; Colin Chan **W:** Barry Blair; Colin Chan
2 ❑ Oct 1997, b&w Cover: 2.95 **NM** value: **Cover or less**
📖 Only Human **A:** Barry Blair; Colin Chan **W:** Barry Blair; Colin Chan
3 ❑ Nov 1997, b&w Cover: 2.95 **NM** value: **Cover or less**
📖 See No See **A:** Barry Blair; Colin Chan **W:** Barry Blair; Colin Chan
4 ❑ Dec 1997, b&w Cover: 2.95 **NM** value: **Cover or less**
📖 Armageddon Outta Here **A:** Barry Blair; Colin Chan **W:** Barry Blair; Colin Chan
5 ❑ Jan 1997 Cover: 2.95 **NM** value: **Cover or less**
📖 Got Those Old Need to Get Outta Here Right Now Blues **A:** Barry Blair; Colin Chan **W:** Barry Blair; Colin Chan
6 ❑ Feb 1997 Cover: 2.95 **NM** value: **Cover or less**
📖 The long March **A:** Barry Blair; Colin Chan **W:** Barry Blair; Colin Chan
7 ❑ Mar 1997 Cover: 2.95 **NM** value: **Cover or less**
📖 The Best Ate Plans **A:** Barry Blair; Colin Chan **W:** Barry Blair; Colin Chan

ELFLORD CHRONICLES, THE — Aircel

1 ❑ Oct 1990, b&w Cover: 2.50 **NM** value: **Cover or less**
2 ❑ Oct 1990, b&w Cover: 2.50 **NM** value: **Cover or less**
3 ❑ Nov 1990, b&w Cover: 2.50 **NM** value: **Cover or less**
📖 War of Shadows **A:** Barry Blair **W:** Barry Blair
4 ❑ Dec 1990, b&w Cover: 2.50 **NM** value: **Cover or less**
📖 Dreams in the Mist **A:** Barry Blair **W:** Barry Blair
5 ❑ Jan 1991, b&w Cover: 2.50 **NM** value: **Cover or less**
📖 Light of Darkness **A:** Barry Blair **W:** Barry Blair
6 ❑ Feb 1991, b&w Cover: 2.50 **NM** value: **Cover or less**
7 ❑ Mar 1991, b&w Cover: 2.75 **NM** value: **Cover or less**
8 ❑ Apr 1991 Cover: 2.75 **NM** value: **Cover or less**

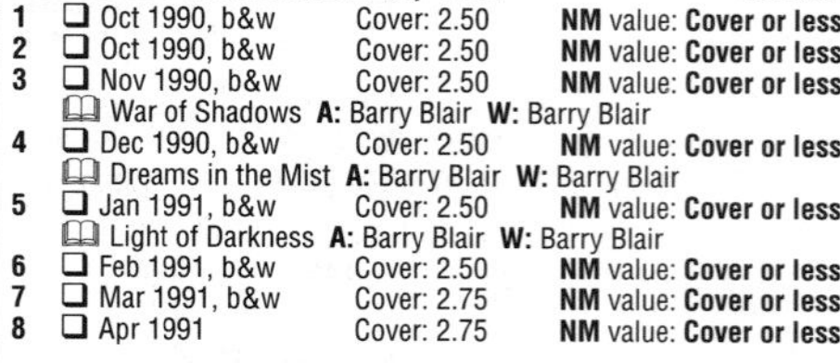

Other grades: Multiply prices above by **1.5 for Mint • 2/3 for Very Fine • 1/3 for Fine • 1/5 for Very Good • 1/8 for Good**

9 ❑ Cover: 2.75 **NM** value: **Cover or less**
10 ❑ Cover: 2.75 **NM** value: **Cover or less**
11 ❑ Cover: 2.75 **NM** value: **Cover or less**
12 ❑ Cover: 2.75 **NM** value: **Cover or less**

ELFLORD: DRAGON'S EYE — Nightwynd

1 ❑ ca. 1993 Cover: 2.50 **NM** value: **Cover or less**
2 ❑ ca. 1993 Cover: 2.50 **NM** value: **Cover or less**
3 ❑ ca. 1993 Cover: 2.50 **NM** value: **Cover or less**

ELFLORD: THE BLACK AND WHITE COMPILATION — Aircel

Bk 1❑ Cover: 4.95 **NM** value: **Cover or less**

ELFLORD THE RETURN — Mad Monkey

1 ❑ ca. 1996 Cover: 6.96 **NM** value: **Cover or less**

ELFLORD: THE RETURN OF THE KING — Nightwynd

1 ❑ Cover: 2.50 **NM** value: **Cover or less**
2 ❑ Cover: 2.50 **NM** value: **Cover or less**
3 ❑ Cover: 2.50 **NM** value: **Cover or less**
4 ❑ Cover: 2.50 **NM** value: **Cover or less**

ELFLORE — Nightwynd

1 ❑ b&w **NM** value: **2.50**
2 ❑ b&w **NM** value: **2.50**
3 ❑ b&w **NM** value: **2.50**
4 ❑ b&w **NM** value: **2.50**

ELFLORE: HIGH SEAS — Nightwynd

1 ❑ Cover: 2.50 **NM** value: **Cover or less**
2 ❑ Cover: 2.50 **NM** value: **Cover or less**
3 ❑ Cover: 2.50 **NM** value: **Cover or less**

ELFLORE (VOL. 2) — Nightwynd

1 ❑ b&w **NM** value: **2.50**
📖 Foxfire **A:** Barry Blair; Angel de Moiche **W:** Barry Blair; Angel de Moiche
2 ❑ b&w **NM** value: **2.50**
📖 Foxfire **A:** Barry Blair **W:** Barry Blair
3 ❑ b&w **NM** value: **2.50**
📖 Foxfire **A:** Barry Blair **W:** Barry Blair
4 ❑ b&w **NM** value: **2.50**
📖 Foxfire **A:** Barry Blair **W:** Barry Blair

ELFLORE (VOL. 3) — Nightwynd

1 ❑ b&w Cover: 2.50 **NM** value: **Cover or less**
2 ❑ b&w Cover: 2.50 **NM** value: **Cover or less**
3 ❑ b&w Cover: 2.50 **NM** value: **Cover or less**
4 ❑ b&w Cover: 2.50 **NM** value: **Cover or less**

ELFQUEST — Warp

Elfquest is a labor of love by husband-and-wife team, Wendy and Richard Pini. They described themselves as "two people who share a too-crowded apartment with elves, wolves, trolls, and lots of drawing paper!" From that environment, they wrote, drew, published, and distributed the comic magazine that would become a cult phenomenon.

Elfquest is the story of Cutter, a young elf, and his Wolfriders as they are driven from their forest home by humans and must travel far in search of a new one. With courage and steadfastness, Cutter leads his clan through all manner of danger and adversity, in an epic tale of fantasy.

1 ❑ Apr 1979 Cover: 1.00 **NM** value: **28.00**
1-2 ❑ Cover: 1.25 **NM** value: **10.00**
1-3 ❑ Cover: 1.50 **NM** value: **6.00**
1-4 ❑ Cover: 1.50 **NM** value: **4.00**
2 ❑ Aug 1978 Cover: 1.00 **NM** value: **16.00**
📖 Raid at Sorrow's End **A:** Wendy Pini **W:** Wendy Pini; Richard Pini
2-2 ❑ Cover: 1.25 **NM** value: **5.00**
2-3 ❑ Cover: 1.50 **NM** value: **3.00**
2-4 ❑ Cover: 1.50 **NM** value: **2.00**
3 ❑ Dec 1978 Cover: 1.00 **NM** value: **16.00**
📖 The Challenge **A:** Wendy Pini **W:** Wendy Pini; Richard Pini
3-2 ❑ Cover: 1.25 **NM** value: **2.00**
3-3 ❑ Cover: 1.50 **NM** value: **3.00**
3-4 ❑ Cover: 1.50 **NM** value: **2.00**
4 ❑ Apr 1979 Cover: 1.00 **NM** value: **16.00**
📖 Wolfsong **A:** Wendy Pini **W:** Wendy Pini; Richard Pini
4-2 ❑ Cover: 1.25 **NM** value: **5.00**
4-3 ❑ Cover: 1.50 **NM** value: **3.00**
4-4 ❑ Cover: 1.50 **NM** value: **Cover or less**
5 ❑ Aug 1979 Cover: 1.00 **NM** value: **16.00**
📖 Voice of the Sun **A:** Wendy Pini **W:** Wendy Pini; Richard Pini
5-2 ❑ Cover: 1.25 **NM** value: **2.00**
5-3 ❑ Cover: 1.50 **NM** value: **3.00**
6 ❑ Jan 1980 Cover: 1.25 **NM** value: **12.00**
📖 The Quest Begins **A:** Wendy Pini **W:** Wendy Pini; Richard Pini
6-2 ❑ Cover: 1.50 **NM** value: **4.00**
6-3 ❑ Cover: 1.50 **NM** value: **2.00**
7 ❑ May 1980 Cover: 1.25 **NM** value: **10.00**
📖 The Dreamberry Tales **A:** Wendy Pini **W:** Wendy Pini; Richard Pini
7-2 ❑ Cover: 1.50 **NM** value: **4.00**
7-3 ❑ Cover: 1.50 **NM** value: **2.00**
8 ❑ Sep 1980 Cover: 1.25 **NM** value: **10.00**
📖 Hands of the Symbol Maker **A:** Wendy Pini **W:** Wendy Pini; Richard Pini
8-2 ❑ Cover: 1.50 **NM** value: **4.00**
8-3 ❑ Cover: 1.50 **NM** value: **2.00**
9 ❑ Feb 1981 Cover: 1.25 **NM** value: **10.00**
📖 The Lodestone **A:** Wendy Pini **W:** Wendy Pini; Richard Pini
9-2 ❑ Cover: 1.50 **NM** value: **4.00**
9-3 ❑ Cover: 1.50 **NM** value: **2.00**
10 ❑ Jun 1981 Cover: 1.50 **NM** value: **7.50**
📖 The Forbidden Grove **A:** Wendy Pini **W:** Wendy Pini; Richard Pini
11 ❑ Oct 1981 Cover: 1.50 **NM** value: **7.50**
📖 Lair of the Bird Spirits **A:** Wendy Pini **W:** Wendy Pini; Richard Pini
12 ❑ Feb 1982 Cover: 1.50 **NM** value: **7.50**
📖 What is the Way? **A:** Wendy Pini **W:** Wendy Pini; Richard Pini
13 ❑ Jun 1982 Cover: 1.50 **NM** value: **7.50**
📖 The Secret of the Wolfriders **A:** Wendy Pini **W:** Wendy Pini; Richard Pini
14 ❑ Oct 1982 Cover: 1.50 **NM** value: **7.50**
📖 The Fall **A:** Wendy Pini **W:** Wendy Pini; Richard Pini
15 ❑ Feb 1983 Cover: 1.50 **NM** value: **7.50**
📖 The Quest Usurped **A:** Wendy Pini **W:** Wendy Pini; Richard Pini
16 ❑ Jun 1983 Cover: 1.50 **NM** value: **10.00**
📖 The Go-Backs; A Distant Soil **A:** Wendy Pini; Colleen Doran **W:** Wendy Pini; Colleen Doran; Richard Pini
17 ❑ Oct 1983 Cover: 1.50 **NM** value: **7.00**
📖 The First War • Elf orgy **A:** Wendy Pini **W:** Wendy Pini; Richard Pini
18 ❑ Feb 1984 Cover: 1.50 **NM** value: **7.00**
📖 The Treasure **A:** Wendy Pini **W:** Wendy Pini; Richard Pini
19 ❑ Jun 1984 Cover: 1.50 **NM** value: **7.00**
📖 Quest's End, Part 1 **A:** Wendy Pini **W:** Wendy Pini; Richard Pini
20 ❑ Oct 1984 Cover: 1.50 **NM** value: **7.00**
📖 Quest's End, Part 2 **A:** Wendy Pini **W:** Wendy Pini; Richard Pini
21 ❑ Feb 1985 Cover: 1.50 **NM** value: **7.00**
final issue. • all letters issue **A:** Wendy Pini **W:** Wendy Pini; Richard Pini
Bk 1❑ Cover: 15.95 **NM** value: **20.00**
• Reprints Elfquest #1-5 **A:** Wendy Pini **W:** Wendy Pini; Richard Pini
Bk 1/HC❑ Cover: 22.00 **NM** value: **35.00**
📖 Fire and Flight • Reprints Elfquest #1-5 **A:** Wendy Pini **W:** Wendy Pini; Richard Pini
Bk 1/HC-2❑ Cover: 22.00 **NM** value: **25.00**
📖 Fire and Flight • Reprints Elfquest #1-5 **A:** Wendy Pini **W:** Wendy Pini; Richard Pini
Bk 2❑ Cover: 15.95 **NM** value: **Cover or less**
• Reprints Elfquest #6-10 **A:** Wendy Pini **W:** Wendy Pini; Richard Pini
Bk 2/HC❑ Cover: 22.00 **NM** value: **28.00**
📖 The Forbidden Grove • Reprints Elfquest #6-10 **A:** Wendy Pini **W:** Wendy Pini; Richard Pini
Bk 2/HC-2❑ Cover: 22.00 **NM** value: **25.00**
📖 The Forbidden Grove • Reprints Elfquest #6-10 **A:** Wendy Pini **W:** Wendy Pini; Richard Pini
Bk 3❑ Cover: 15.95 **NM** value: **Cover or less**
• Reprints Elfquest #11-15 **A:** Wendy Pini **W:** Wendy Pini; Richard Pini
Bk 3/HC❑ Cover: 22.00 **NM** value: **25.00**
📖 Captives of the Blue Mountain • Reprints Elfquest #11-15 **A:** Wendy Pini **W:** Wendy Pini; Richard Pini
Bk 3/HC-2❑ Cover: 22.00 **NM** value: **Cover or less**
📖 Captives of the Blue Mountain • Reprints Elfquest #11-15 **A:** Wendy Pini **W:** Wendy Pini; Richard Pini
Bk 4❑ Cover: 15.95 **NM** value: **Cover or less**
• Reprints Elfquest #16-21 **A:** Wendy Pini **W:** Wendy Pini; Richard Pini
Bk 4/HC❑ Cover: 22.00 **NM** value: **25.00**
📖 Quest's End • Reprints Elfquest #16-21 **A:** Wendy Pini **W:** Wendy Pini; Richard Pini
Bk 4/HC-2❑ Cover: 22.00 **NM** value: **Cover or less**
📖 Quest's End • Reprints Elfquest #16-21 **A:** Wendy Pini **W:** Wendy Pini; Richard Pini
Bk 5❑ Cover: 15.95 **NM** value: **Cover or less**
Bk 5/HC❑ Cover: 22.00 **NM** value: **Cover or less**
📖 Siege at Blue Mountain **A:** Wendy Pini **W:** Wendy Pini; Richard Pini
Bk 6❑ Cover: 15.95 **NM** value: **Cover or less**
Bk 6/HC❑ Cover: 22.00 **NM** value: **Cover or less**
📖 The Secret of Two-Edge **A:** Wendy Pini **W:** Wendy Pini; Richard Pini
Bk 7/HC❑ Cover: 22.00 **NM** value: **Cover or less**
📖 The Cry From Beyond **A:** Wendy Pini **W:** Wendy Pini; Richard Pini

ELFQUEST: BLOOD OF TEN CHIEFS — Warp

Blood of Ten Chiefs goes off the beaten path to tell tales "from the wild side of Elfquest." These are stories that concentrate not on Cutter and the old Elfquest favorites, but on 10 chiefs of old. We follow Timmorn, whose blood is half-wolf, half-elf as he strives to find which world he belongs to. In another tale, Bearclaw tracks down a thief in the Holt in the tale, "The Phantom of the Berry Patch." History marches on through peace and struggle, leading up to the "current day" adventures that Elfquest fans are more familiar with.

Rotating creative teams bring their own touch to each story, making the stories in Blood of Ten Chiefs a varied and interesting title.

1 ❑ Aug 1993 Cover: 2.00 **NM** value: **2.50**
Circ: CapCity orders: **11,600**
2 ❑ Sep 1993 Cover: 2.00 **NM** value: **2.50**
Circ: CapCity orders: **8,650**
3 ❑ Nov 1993 Cover: 2.00 **NM** value: **2.50**
4 ❑ Jan 1994 Cover: 2.00 **NM** value: **2.50**
5 ❑ Mar 1994 Cover: 2.25 **NM** value: **2.50**
6 ❑ May 1994 Cover: 2.25 **NM** value: **2.50**
Circ: CapCity orders: **7,425**
7 ❑ Jun 1994 Cover: 2.25 **NM** value: **2.50**
Circ: CapCity orders: **7,350**
8 ❑ Jul 1994 Cover: 2.25 **NM** value: **2.50**
Circ: CapCity orders: **7,275**
9 ❑ Aug 1994 Cover: 2.25 **NM** value: **2.50**
Circ: CapCity orders: **7,075**
10 ❑ Sep 1994 Cover: 2.25 **NM** value: **2.50**
Circ: CapCity orders: **6,850**
11 ❑ Oct 1994 Cover: 2.25 **NM** value: **2.50**
Circ: CapCity orders: **6,775**
12 ❑ Nov 1994 Cover: 2.25 **NM** value: **2.50**
13 ❑ Dec 1994 Cover: 2.25 **NM** value: **2.50**
14 ❑ Jan 1995 Cover: 2.25 **NM** value: **2.50**
15 ❑ Feb 1995 Cover: 2.25 **NM** value: **2.50**
16 ❑ Apr 1995 Cover: 2.25 **NM** value: **2.50**
17 ❑ May 1995 Cover: 2.50 **NM** value: **Cover or less**
18 ❑ Jun 1995 Cover: 2.50 **NM** value: **Cover or less**
Circ: CapCity orders: **5,050**
19 ❑ Aug 1995 Cover: 2.50 **NM** value: **Cover or less**
Circ: CapCity orders: **4,525**
• contains Elfquest timeline
20 ❑ Sep 1995 Cover: 2.50 **NM** value: **Cover or less**
Circ: CapCity orders: **4,200**
final issue.
Bk 1❑ Cover: 8.00 **NM** value: **Cover or less**
Bk 2❑ Cover: 9.00 **NM** value: **Cover or less**
📖 Wolfsong
Bk 3❑ Cover: 9.00 **NM** value: **Cover or less**
📖 Winds of Change
Bk 4❑ Cover: 9.00 **NM** value: **Cover or less**
📖 Against the Wind
Bk 5❑ Cover: 9.00 **NM** value: **Cover or less**
📖 Dark Hours

ELFQUEST (EPIC) — Epic / Marvel

1 ❑ Aug 1985 Cover: 0.75 **NM** value: **3.25**
Circ: CapCity orders: **23,600** • **CGC:** 3 graded, best 9.6
2 ❑ Sep 1985 Cover: 0.75 **NM** value: **2.50**
Circ: CapCity orders: **19,600**
3 ❑ Oct 1985 Cover: 0.75 **NM** value: **2.50**
Circ: CapCity orders: **16,400**
4 ❑ Nov 1985 Cover: 0.75 **NM** value: **2.50**
Circ: CapCity orders: **15,800**
5 ❑ Dec 1985 Cover: 0.75 **NM** value: **2.50**
Circ: CapCity orders: **13,900**
6 ❑ Jan 1986 Cover: 0.75 **NM** value: **2.25**
Circ: Statement: **131,725** CapCity orders: **13,100**
7 ❑ Feb 1986 Cover: 0.75 **NM** value: **2.25**
Circ: Statement: **131,725** CapCity orders: **13,500**
8 ❑ Mar 1986 Cover: 0.75 **NM** value: **2.25**
Circ: Statement: **131,725** CapCity orders: **12,600**
9 ❑ Apr 1986 Cover: 0.75 **NM** value: **2.25**
Circ: Statement: **131,725** CapCity orders: **12,500**
10 ❑ May 1986 Cover: 0.75 **NM** value: **2.25**
Circ: Statement: **131,725** CapCity orders: **12,500**
11 ❑ Jun 1986 Cover: 0.75 **NM** value: **2.00**
Circ: Statement: **131,725** CapCity orders: **11,900**
12 ❑ Jul 1986 Cover: 0.75 **NM** value: **2.00**
Circ: Statement: **131,725** CapCity orders: **11,900**
13 ❑ Aug 1986 Cover: 0.75 **NM** value: **2.00**
Circ: Statement: **131,725** CapCity orders: **11,450**
14 ❑ Sep 1986 Cover: 0.75 **NM** value: **2.00**
Circ: Statement: **131,725** CapCity orders: **11,500**
15 ❑ Oct 1986 Cover: 0.75 **NM** value: **2.00**
Circ: Statement: **131,725** CapCity orders: **11,600**
16 ❑ Nov 1986 Cover: 0.75 **NM** value: **2.00**
Circ: Statement: **131,725** CapCity orders: **11,300**
17 ❑ Dec 1986 Cover: 0.75 **NM** value: **2.00**
Circ: Statement: **131,725** CapCity orders: **11,300**
18 ❑ Jan 1987 Cover: 0.75 **NM** value: **2.00**
Circ: CapCity orders: **11,950**
19 ❑ Feb 1987 Cover: 0.75 **NM** value: **2.00**
Circ: CapCity orders: **12,000**
20 ❑ Mar 1987 Cover: 0.75 **NM** value: **2.00**
Circ: CapCity orders: **11,700**
21 ❑ Apr 1987 Cover: 0.75 **NM** value: **1.50**
Circ: CapCity orders: **11,700**
22 ❑ May 1987 Cover: 1.00 **NM** value: **1.50**
Circ: CapCity orders: **11,100**
23 ❑ Jun 1987 Cover: 1.00 **NM** value: **1.50**
Circ: CapCity orders: **10,900**
24 ❑ Jul 1987 Cover: 1.00 **NM** value: **1.50**
Circ: CapCity orders: **10,700**
25 ❑ Aug 1987 Cover: 1.00 **NM** value: **1.50**
Circ: CapCity orders: **10,800**
26 ❑ Sep 1987 Cover: 1.00 **NM** value: **1.50**
Circ: CapCity orders: **11,600**
27 ❑ Oct 1987 Cover: 1.00 **NM** value: **1.50**
Circ: CapCity orders: **11,650**
28 ❑ Nov 1987 Cover: 1.00 **NM** value: **1.50**
Circ: CapCity orders: **11,600**
29 ❑ Dec 1987 Cover: 1.00 **NM** value: **1.50**
Circ: CapCity orders: **11,300**
30 ❑ Jan 1988 Cover: 1.00 **NM** value: **1.50**
Circ: CapCity orders: **11,300**
31 ❑ Feb 1988 Cover: 1.00 **NM** value: **1.50**
Circ: CapCity orders: **11,500**
32 ❑ Mar 1988 Cover: 1.00 **NM** value: **1.50**
Circ: CapCity orders: **11,600**
final issue. **A:** Wendy Pini **W:** Wendy Pini; Richard Pini

ELFQUEST GATHERUM — Father Tree

Bk 1❑ Cover: 8.95 **NM** value: **20.00**
Bk 2❑ Cover: 8.95 **NM** value: **16.00**
Dlx 1❑ **NM** value: **50.00**
• The Big Elquest Gatherum

CGC-graded: Multiply prices above by **33 for 9.9 M** • **16 for 9.8 NM/M** • **7 for 9.6 NM+** • **5 for 9.4 NM** • **2.5 for 9.2 NM-** • **1.5 for 9.0 VF/NM**

ELFQUEST: HIDDEN YEARS — Warp

This title follows on the heels of Elfquest: Kings of the Broken Wheel. That series served as a climax to the story of Cutter and his Wolfriders which began in the original Elfquest series. Now Elfquest: Hidden Years tells stories from the times in between.

In a departure for the Elfquest creative team, this title features fully colored artwork, instead of the black-and-white panels which had worked so well in the past. The first few issues of The Hidden Years feature painted artwork by Elfquest creator Wendy Pini. Afterward, she stepped into a managing role, handing over the writing and pencilling jobs to a new team. However, as the story and art director, she took care to make sure that The Hidden Years lived up to the high standards set by the original Elfquest. In a special crossover, Harbinger #11, by Valiant, featured a character reading a comic book which was actually a preview of Elfquest: The Hidden Years #3.

1 ❑ May 1992 Cover: 2.00 **NM** value: **3.00**
Circ: CapCity orders: **12,350**
2 ❑ Jul 1992 Cover: 2.00 **NM** value: **2.50**
Circ: CapCity orders: **10,450**
3 ❑ Sep 1992 Cover: 2.00 **NM** value: **2.50**
• This story was previewed in Harbinger #11 (character reads it as in a comic book)
4 ❑ Nov 1992 Cover: 2.00 **NM** value: **2.50**
Circ: CapCity orders: **10,875**
5 ❑ Jan 1993 Cover: 2.00 **NM** value: **2.50**
Circ: CapCity orders: **10,875**
6 ❑ Mar 1993 Cover: 2.00 **NM** value: **2.50**
Circ: CapCity orders: **11,100**
7 ❑ May 1993 Cover: 2.00 **NM** value: **2.50**
Circ: CapCity orders: **10,225**
8 ❑ Jul 1993 Cover: 2.00 **NM** value: **2.50**
Circ: CapCity orders: **9,550**
9 ❑ Sep 1993 Cover: 2.00 **NM** value: **2.50**
Circ: CapCity orders: **8,900**
9.5 ❑ Nov 1993 Cover: 2.95 **NM** value: **Cover or less**
Circ: CapCity orders: **8,950**
• double-sized.
10 ❑ Jan 1994 Cover: 2.00 **NM** value: **2.50**
Circ: CapCity orders: **7,850**
11 ❑ Mar 1994 Cover: 2.25 **NM** value: **2.50**
Circ: CapCity orders: **7,525**
12 ❑ Apr 1994 Cover: 2.25 **NM** value: **2.50**
Circ: CapCity orders: **7,825**
13 ❑ May 1994 Cover: 2.25 **NM** value: **2.50**
Circ: CapCity orders: **7,925**
14 ❑ Jun 1994 Cover: 2.25 **NM** value: **2.50**
Circ: CapCity orders: **7,850**
📖 Shards, Part 5 **A:** Brandon McKinney **W:** Wendy Pini; Richard Pini
15 ❑ Jul 1994 Cover: 3.50 **NM** value: **Cover or less**
Circ: CapCity orders: **7,875**
16 ❑ Aug 1994 Cover: 2.25 **NM** value: **2.50**
Circ: CapCity orders: **7,675**
17 ❑ Oct 1994 Cover: 2.25 **NM** value: **2.50**
Circ: CapCity orders: **7,500**
18 ❑ Dec 1994 Cover: 2.25 **NM** value: **2.50**
Circ: CapCity orders: **6,850**
19 ❑ Jan 1995 Cover: 2.25 **NM** value: **2.50**
Circ: CapCity orders: **6,325**
20 ❑ Apr 1995 Cover: 2.50 **NM** value: **Cover or less**
Circ: CapCity orders: **6,200**
21 ❑ May 1995 Cover: 2.50 **NM** value: **Cover or less**
Circ: CapCity orders: **5,750**
22 ❑ Jul 1995 Cover: 2.50 **NM** value: **Cover or less**
Circ: CapCity orders: **5,700**
23 ❑ Aug 1995 Cover: 2.50 **NM** value: **Cover or less**
Circ: CapCity orders: **5,275**
• contains Elfquest timeline
24 ❑ Sep 1995 Cover: 2.50 **NM** value: **Cover or less**
Circ: CapCity orders: **4,750**
25 ❑ Oct 1995, b&w Cover: 2.25 **NM** value: **2.50**
26 ❑ Dec 1995, b&w Cover: 2.25 **NM** value: **2.50**
27 ❑ Jan 1996, b&w Cover: 2.25 **NM** value: **2.50**
28 ❑ Feb 1996, b&w Cover: 2.25 **NM** value: **2.50**
29 ❑ Mar 1996, b&w Cover: 2.25 **NM** value: **2.50**
Bk 1❑ Cover: 19.95 **NM** value: **Cover or less**
Bk 2❑ Cover: 19.95 **NM** value: **Cover or less**
• gatefold summary. • "Rogue's Challenge"; Reprints Elfquest: Hidden Years #6-9, 9.5 (Holiday special)

ELFQUEST: JINK — Warp

1 ❑ Nov 1994 Cover: 2.25 **NM** value: **2.50**
Circ: CapCity orders: **14,325**
2 ❑ Dec 1994 Cover: 2.25 **NM** value: **2.50**
Circ: CapCity orders: **7,000**
3 ❑ Jan 1995 Cover: 2.25 **NM** value: **2.50**
Circ: CapCity orders: **6,100**
📖 Neverending Story **A:** David Boller **W:** Wendy Pini; John Ostrander
4 ❑ Apr 1995 Cover: 2.50 **NM** value: **Cover or less**
Circ: CapCity orders: **5,825**
5 ❑ May 1995 Cover: 2.50 **NM** value: **Cover or less**
Circ: CapCity orders: **5,000**
6 ❑ Jul 1995 Cover: 2.50 **NM** value: **Cover or less**
Circ: CapCity orders: **5,075**
• contains Elfquest world map
7 ❑ Aug 1995 Cover: 2.50 **NM** value: **Cover or less**
Circ: CapCity orders: **4,375**
• contains Elfquest timeline
8 ❑ Oct 1995 Cover: 2.25 **NM** value: **2.50**
• b&w for remainder of series
9 ❑ Nov 1995 Cover: 2.25 **NM** value: **2.50**
10 ❑ Dec 1995 Cover: 2.25 **NM** value: **2.50**
11 ❑ Jan 1996 Cover: 2.25 **NM** value: **2.50**
12 ❑ Feb 1996 Cover: 2.25 **NM** value: **2.50**

ELFQUEST: KAHVI — Warp

1 ❑ Oct 1995 Cover: 2.25 **NM** value: **Cover or less**
2 ❑ Nov 1995 Cover: 2.25 **NM** value: **Cover or less**
3 ❑ Dec 1995 Cover: 2.25 **NM** value: **Cover or less**
4 ❑ Jan 1996 Cover: 2.25 **NM** value: **Cover or less**
5 ❑ Feb 1996 Cover: 2.25 **NM** value: **Cover or less**
6 ❑ Mar 1996 Cover: 2.25 **NM** value: **Cover or less**

ELFQUEST: KINGS CROSS — Warp

1 ❑ Nov 1997, b&w Cover: 2.95 **NM** value: **Cover or less**
2 ❑ Dec 1997, b&w Cover: 2.95 **NM** value: **Cover or less**

ELFQUEST: KINGS OF THE BROKEN WHEEL — Warp

The elves' story began with an accident. The High Ones had been traveling through time from the medieval age and had missed their mark, ending up in an age where men were still basically savages. Instead of being welcomed with open arms, the High Ones found themselves subject to brutal attack by the humans. Disoriented, the High Ones fled their palace and sought refuge in this new world. They and their children eventually became the ancestors of the Cutter and the rest of the Elfquest elves.

Then Rayek, one of Cutter's kinsmen took it into his head to play god. He kidnapped Cutter's family and invaded the palace of the High Ones. Rayek was determined to travel back to the point of the original accident and "correct" it. He sought power, but it's doubtful that he understood the full implications of correcting a mistake that gave birth to his entire species. The elves' history was a broken wheel in time — and by repairing it, Rayek could destroy them all!

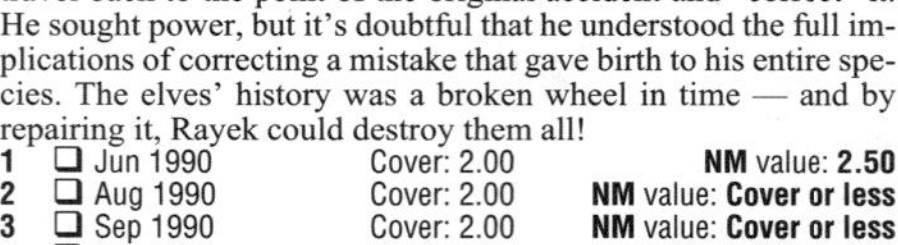

1 ❑ Jun 1990 Cover: 2.00 **NM** value: **2.50**
2 ❑ Aug 1990 Cover: 2.00 **NM** value: **Cover or less**
3 ❑ Sep 1990 Cover: 2.00 **NM** value: **Cover or less**
4 ❑ Dec 1990 Cover: 2.00 **NM** value: **Cover or less**
5 ❑ Feb 1991 Cover: 2.00 **NM** value: **Cover or less**
6 ❑ May 1991 Cover: 2.00 **NM** value: **Cover or less**
7 ❑ Aug 1991 Cover: 2.00 **NM** value: **Cover or less**
8 ❑ Nov 1991 Cover: 2.00 **NM** value: **Cover or less**
9 ❑ Feb 1992 Cover: 2.00 **NM** value: **Cover or less**
Circ: CapCity orders: **10,295**
Bk 1❑ Cover: 22.00 **NM** value: **Cover or less**
📖 Kings of the Broken Wheel **A:** Wendy Pini **W:** Wendy Pini; Richard Pini

ELFQUEST: METAMORPHOSIS — Warp

1 ❑ Apr 1996 Cover: 2.95 **NM** value: **Cover or less**
📖 The Wild Hunt; Rogue's Curse; Futurequest; Fire-Eye; Wave Dancers **A:** Wendy Pini; Barry Blair; Delfin Barral; Steve Blevins **W:** Barry Blair; Kathryn Bolinger; Bern Harkins; Joellyn Auklandus; Richard Pini

ELFQUEST: NEW BLOOD — Warp

1 ❑ Aug 1992, full color Cover: 2.00 **NM** value: **5.00**
Circ: CapCity orders: **11,375**
• gatefold summary. • "Elfquest Summer Special" **A:** John Byrne
2 ❑ Oct 1992 Cover: 2.00 **NM** value: **2.50**
3 ❑ Dec 1992 Cover: 2.00 **NM** value: **2.50**
4 ❑ Feb 1993 Cover: 2.00 **NM** value: **2.50**
Circ: CapCity orders: **10,150**
5 ❑ Apr 1993 Cover: 2.00 **NM** value: **2.50**
📖 Windkin **A:** Paul Abrams **W:** Vickie Murphy
6 ❑ Jun 1993 Cover: 2.00 **NM** value: **2.50**
Circ: CapCity orders: **9,275**
7 ❑ Jul 1993 Cover: 2.00 **NM** value: **2.50**
Circ: CapCity orders: **8,525**
8 ❑ Aug 1993 Cover: 2.00 **NM** value: **2.50**
Circ: CapCity orders: **8,775**
9 ❑ Sep 1993 Cover: 2.00 **NM** value: **2.50**
Circ: CapCity orders: **8,375**
10 ❑ Oct 1993 Cover: 2.00 **NM** value: **2.50**
Circ: CapCity orders: **7,875**
11 ❑ Nov 1993 Cover: 2.00 **NM** value: **2.25**
Circ: CapCity orders: **7,525**
12 ❑ Dec 1993 Cover: 2.00 **NM** value: **2.25**
Circ: CapCity orders: **7,550**
13 ❑ Jan 1994 Cover: 2.00 **NM** value: **2.25**
Circ: CapCity orders: **6,875**
14 ❑ Feb 1994 Cover: 2.25 **NM** value: **Cover or less**
Circ: CapCity orders: **7,050**
15 ❑ Mar 1994 Cover: 2.25 **NM** value: **Cover or less**
Circ: CapCity orders: **7,000**
16 ❑ Apr 1994 Cover: 2.25 **NM** value: **Cover or less**
Circ: CapCity orders: **7,275**
17 ❑ May 1994 Cover: 2.25 **NM** value: **Cover or less**
Circ: CapCity orders: **7,375**
18 ❑ Jun 1994 Cover: 2.25 **NM** value: **Cover or less**
Circ: CapCity orders: **7,600**
📖 Forevergreen, Part 6
19 ❑ Jul 1994 Cover: 2.25 **NM** value: **Cover or less**
Circ: CapCity orders: **7,375**
20 ❑ Aug 1994 Cover: 2.25 **NM** value: **Cover or less**
Circ: CapCity orders: **7,225**
21 ❑ Sep 1994 Cover: 2.25 **NM** value: **Cover or less**
Circ: CapCity orders: **7,025**
22 ❑ Oct 1994 Cover: 2.25 **NM** value: **Cover or less**
Circ: CapCity orders: **7,000**
23 ❑ Nov 1994 Cover: 2.25 **NM** value: **Cover or less**
Circ: CapCity orders: **10,925**
24 ❑ Dec 1994 Cover: 2.25 **NM** value: **Cover or less**
Circ: CapCity orders: **6,325**
25 ❑ Jan 1995 Cover: 2.25 **NM** value: **Cover or less**
Circ: CapCity orders: **5,925**
26 ❑ Feb 1995 Cover: 2.25 **NM** value: **Cover or less**
Circ: CapCity orders: **5,725**
27 ❑ Apr 1995 Cover: 2.50 **NM** value: **Cover or less**
Circ: CapCity orders: **5,575**
28 ❑ May 1995 Cover: 2.50 **NM** value: **Cover or less**
Circ: CapCity orders: **5,125**
29 ❑ Jul 1995 Cover: 2.50 **NM** value: **Cover or less**
Circ: CapCity orders: **5,125**
30 ❑ Aug 1995 Cover: 2.50 **NM** value: **Cover or less**
Circ: CapCity orders: **4,600**
• contains Elfquest timeline
31 ❑ Sep 1995 Cover: 2.50 **NM** value: **Cover or less**
Circ: CapCity orders: **4,225**
32 ❑ Oct 1995 Cover: 2.25 **NM** value: **2.50**
33 ❑ Nov 1995 Cover: 2.25 **NM** value: **2.50**
34 ❑ Dec 1995 Cover: 2.25 **NM** value: **Cover or less**
35 ❑ Jan 1996 Cover: 2.25 **NM** value: **Cover or less**
Bk 1❑ Cover: 22.00 **NM** value: **25.00**
SE 1❑ Jul 1993 Cover: 3.95 **NM** value: **Cover or less**

ELFQUEST: SHARDS — Warp

1 ❑ Aug 1994 Cover: 2.25 **NM** value: **2.50**
Circ: CapCity orders: **9,375**
2 ❑ Sep 1994 Cover: 2.25 **NM** value: **2.50**
Circ: CapCity orders: **7,900**
3 ❑ Oct 1994 Cover: 2.25 **NM** value: **2.50**
Circ: CapCity orders: **7,500**
4 ❑ Nov 1994 Cover: 2.25 **NM** value: **2.50**
Circ: CapCity orders: **11,625**
5 ❑ Dec 1994 Cover: 2.25 **NM** value: **2.50**
Circ: CapCity orders: **6,675**
6 ❑ Jan 1995 Cover: 2.25 **NM** value: **Cover or less**
Circ: CapCity orders: **6,175**
7 ❑ Mar 1995 Cover: 2.50 **NM** value: **Cover or less**
Circ: CapCity orders: **6,000**
8 ❑ May 1995 Cover: 2.50 **NM** value: **Cover or less**
Circ: CapCity orders: **5,475**
9 ❑ Jun 1995 Cover: 2.50 **NM** value: **Cover or less**
Circ: CapCity orders: **5,500**
10 ❑ Aug 1995 Cover: 2.50 **NM** value: **Cover or less**
Circ: CapCity orders: **4,975**
• contains Elfquest timeline **W:** Wendy Pini; Richard Pini
11 ❑ Sep 1995 Cover: 2.50 **NM** value: **Cover or less**
Circ: CapCity orders: **4,625**
12 ❑ Oct 1995 Cover: 2.25 **NM** value: **2.50**
13 ❑ Dec 1995 Cover: 2.25 **NM** value: **Cover or less**
14 ❑ Feb 1996 Cover: 2.25 **NM** value: **Cover or less**
15 ❑ Apr 1996 Cover: 2.25 **NM** value: **Cover or less**
16 ❑ Jun 1996 Cover: 2.25 **NM** value: **Cover or less**
Ash 1❑ Cover: 0.50 **NM** value: **1.00**
• ashcan preview/ San Diego Comic-Con premium

ELFQUEST: SIEGE AT BLUE MOUNTAIN — Warp / Apple

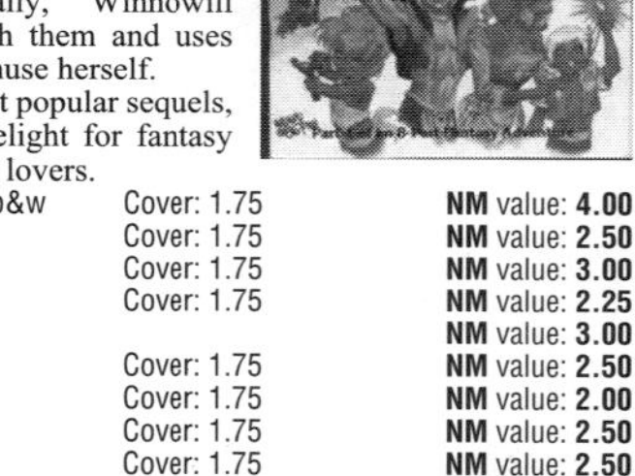

After a two-year hiatus, Elfquest returned in this eight-part series published by Apple Comics. This time, Cutter and the other Wolfriders were out to stop the evil Winnowill. Winnowill, one of the gliders, had convinced the local humans that they are "bird spirits," and that they should willingly come to her cave atop Blue Mountain. Once there, they become Winnowill's slaves. Eventually, Winnowill grows bored with them and uses their deaths to amuse herself.

One of the most popular sequels, the series is a delight for fantasy fans and Elfquest lovers.

1 ❑ Mar 1987, b&w Cover: 1.75 **NM** value: **4.00**
1-2 ❑ Cover: 1.75 **NM** value: **2.50**
2 ❑ May 1987 Cover: 1.75 **NM** value: **3.00**
2-2 ❑ Cover: 1.75 **NM** value: **2.25**
2-3 ❑ **NM** value: **3.00**
3 ❑ Jul 1987 Cover: 1.75 **NM** value: **2.50**
3-2 ❑ Cover: 1.75 **NM** value: **2.00**
4 ❑ Sep 1987 Cover: 1.75 **NM** value: **2.50**
5 ❑ Nov 1987 Cover: 1.75 **NM** value: **2.50**
6 ❑ Aug 1988 Cover: 1.95 **NM** value: **2.50**
7 ❑ Oct 1988 Cover: 1.95 **NM** value: **2.50**
8 ❑ Dec 1988 Cover: 1.95 **NM** value: **2.50**

ELFQUEST: THE REBELS — Warp

1 ❑ Nov 1994 Cover: 2.25 **NM** value: **Cover or less**
Circ: CapCity orders: **12,875**
📖 To Colder Seas **A:** Delfin Barral **W:** Bern Harkins
2 ❑ Dec 1994 Cover: 2.25 **NM** value: **Cover or less**
Circ: CapCity orders: **6,525**
3 ❑ Jan 1995 Cover: 2.25 **NM** value: **Cover or less**
Circ: CapCity orders: **5,750**
4 ❑ Mar 1995 Cover: 2.50 **NM** value: **Cover or less**
Circ: CapCity orders: **5,425**
5 ❑ Apr 1995 Cover: 2.50 **NM** value: **Cover or less**
Circ: CapCity orders: **5,000**
6 ❑ Jun 1995 Cover: 2.50 **NM** value: **Cover or less**
Circ: CapCity orders: **4,425**
7 ❑ Jul 1995 Cover: 2.50 **NM** value: **Cover or less**
Circ: CapCity orders: **4,300**
• contains Elfquest world map
8 ❑ Sep 1995 Cover: 2.50 **NM** value: **Cover or less**
Circ: CapCity orders: **3,575**
9 ❑ Oct 1995 Cover: 2.25 **NM** value: **Cover or less**

10 ❑ Nov 1995 Cover: 2.25 **NM** value: **Cover or less**
11 ❑ Jan 1996 Cover: 2.25 **NM** value: **Cover or less**
12 ❑ Feb 1996 Cover: 2.25 **NM** value: **Cover or less**

ELFQUEST: TWO-SPEAR — Warp

1 ❑ Oct 1995 Cover: 2.25 **NM** value: **Cover or less**
📖 Discoveries **A:** Barry Blair; Delfin Barral **W:** Terry Collins
2 ❑ Nov 1995 Cover: 2.25 **NM** value: **Cover or less**
3 ❑ Dec 1995 Cover: 2.25 **NM** value: **Cover or less**
4 ❑ Jan 1996 Cover: 2.25 **NM** value: **Cover or less**
5 ❑ Feb 1996 Cover: 2.25 **NM** value: **Cover or less**

ELFQUEST (VOL. 2) — Warp

1 ❑ May 1996 Cover: 4.95 **NM** value: **6.00**
2 ❑ Jun 1996 Cover: 4.95 **NM** value: **5.00**
3 ❑ Jul 1996 Cover: 4.95 **NM** value: **5.00**
4 ❑ Aug 1996 Cover: 4.95 **NM** value: **5.00**
5 ❑ Sep 1996 Cover: 4.95 **NM** value: **5.00**
Circ: Diamd. preorders: **15,109**
6 ❑ Nov 1996 Cover: 4.95 **NM** value: **5.00**
Circ: Diamd. preorders: **14,191**
7 ❑ Dec 1996 Cover: 4.95 **NM** value: **5.00**
8 ❑ Jan 1997 Cover: 4.95 **NM** value: **5.00**
Circ: Diamd. preorders: **12,340**
9 ❑ Feb 1997 Cover: 4.95 **NM** value: **5.00**
Circ: Diamd. preorders: **12,137**
10 ❑ Mar 1997 Cover: 4.95 **NM** value: **5.00**
Circ: Diamd. preorders: **11,822**
11 ❑ Apr 1997 Cover: 4.95 **NM** value: **Cover or less**
Circ: Diamd. preorders: **11,479**
12 ❑ May 1997 Cover: 4.95 **NM** value: **Cover or less**
Circ: Diamd. preorders: **11,701**
13 ❑ Jun 1997 Cover: 4.95 **NM** value: **Cover or less**
Circ: Diamd. preorders: **11,776**
14 ❑ Jul 1997 Cover: 4.95 **NM** value: **Cover or less**
Circ: Diamd. preorders: **11,158**
15 ❑ Aug 1997 Cover: 4.95 **NM** value: **Cover or less**
Circ: Diamd. preorders: **11,255**
16 ❑ Sep 1997 Cover: 4.95 **NM** value: **Cover or less**
Circ: Diamd. preorders: **11,000**
17 ❑ Oct 1997 Cover: 4.95 **NM** value: **Cover or less**
Circ: Diamd. preorders: **10,900**
18 ❑ Nov 1997 Cover: 4.95 **NM** value: **Cover or less**
Circ: Diamd. preorders: **10,726**
19 ❑ Dec 1997 Cover: 4.95 **NM** value: **Cover or less**
Circ: Diamd. preorders: **10,617**
20 ❑ Jan 1998 Cover: 4.95 **NM** value: **Cover or less**
Circ: Diamd. preorders: **10,480**
21 ❑ Feb 1998 Cover: 4.95 **NM** value: **Cover or less**
Circ: Diamd. preorders: **9,986**
22 ❑ Mar 1998 Cover: 4.95 **NM** value: **Cover or less**
Circ: Diamd. preorders: **9,979**
23 ❑ Apr 1998 Cover: 4.95 **NM** value: **Cover or less**
Circ: Diamd. preorders: **10,043**
24 ❑ May 1998 Cover: 4.95 **NM** value: **Cover or less**
Circ: Diamd. preorders: **9,586**
25 ❑ Jun 1998 Cover: 4.95 **NM** value: **Cover or less**
Circ: Diamd. preorders: **9,787**
needlepoint style cover.
26 ❑ Jul 1998 Cover: 4.95 **NM** value: **Cover or less**
Circ: Diamd. preorders: **9,121**
27 ❑ Aug 1998 Cover: 4.95 **NM** value: **Cover or less**
Circ: Diamd. preorders: **8,714**
28 ❑ Sep 1998 Cover: 4.95 **NM** value: **Cover or less**
Circ: Diamd. preorders: **8,700**
29 ❑ Oct 1998 Cover: 4.95 **NM** value: **Cover or less**
Circ: Diamd. preorders: **8,678**
30 ❑ Nov 1998 Cover: 4.95 **NM** value: **Cover or less**
Circ: Diamd. preorders: **8,516**
31 ❑ Dec 1998 Cover: 4.95 **NM** value: **Cover or less**
Circ: Diamd. preorders: **8,146**
Christmas cover.
32 ❑ Jan 1999 Cover: 2.95 **NM** value: **Cover or less**
Circ: Diamd. preorders: **8,273**
33 ❑ Feb 1999 Cover: 2.95 **NM** value: **Cover or less**
Circ: Diamd. preorders: **8,059**
final issue.

ELFQUEST (WARP REPRINTS) — Warp

1 ❑ May 1989 Cover: 1.50 **NM** value: **Cover or less**
2 ❑ Jun 1989 Cover: 1.50 **NM** value: **Cover or less**
3 ❑ Jul 1989 Cover: 1.50 **NM** value: **Cover or less**
4 ❑ Aug 1989 Cover: 1.50 **NM** value: **Cover or less**

ELFQUEST: WAVEDANCERS — Warp

1 ❑ Dec 1993 Cover: 2.00 **NM** value: **Cover or less**
Circ: CapCity orders: **9,050**
📖 Search for the True Crown, Part 1 ★ Origin of The Wavedancers.
2 ❑ Feb 1994 Cover: 2.25 **NM** value: **Cover or less**
Circ: CapCity orders: **7,150**
📖 Search for the True Crown, Part 2
3 ❑ Apr 1994 Cover: 2.25 **NM** value: **Cover or less**
Circ: CapCity orders: **7,725**
📖 Search for the True Crown, Part 3
4 ❑ Jun 1994 Cover: 2.25 **NM** value: **Cover or less**
Circ: CapCity orders: **7,850**
📖 Search for the True Crown, Part 4
5 ❑ Aug 1994 Cover: 2.25 **NM** value: **Cover or less**
Circ: CapCity orders: **7,550**
📖 Search for the True Crown, Part 5
6 ❑ Oct 1994 Cover: 2.25 **NM** value: **Cover or less**
Circ: CapCity orders: **7,275**
SE 1❑ Cover: 2.25 **NM** value: **Cover or less**

ELFQUEST: WORLDPOOL — Warp

1 ❑ Jul 1997, b&w Cover: 2.95 **NM** value: **Cover or less**
Circ: Diamd. preorders: **9,695**
📖 The Perception of Doors **A:** Barry Blair **W:** Richard Pini

ELF-THING — Eclipse

1 ❑ Mar 1987, b&w Cover: 1.50 **NM** value: **Cover or less**
📖 This Elf... This Monster **A:** James J. Friel **W:** Frank P. Marino

ELFTREK — Dimension

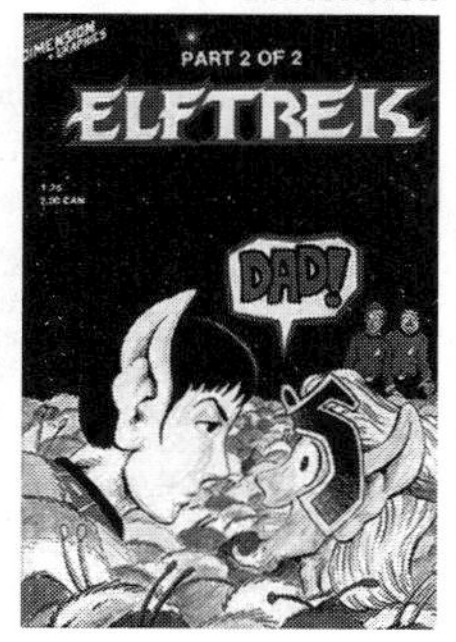

Marcus Lusk and Mark Poe have brought us the ultimate black-and-white fantasy/sci-fi parody: What if you mixed Star Trek with Elfquest? The answer is Elftrek!

Captain Jirk of the Corporation ship Big Surprise beams down to the Oasis Motel, a little place out on the edge of reality, to investigate unusual phenomena and party down. Meanwhile, on an uncharted jungle world, the Woofriders are running along when they encounter a mysterious hole in space that transports them to the bar where Jirk is getting totally smashed. Many questions of importance are answered, such as "does Mister Spark have children he's not aware of" and "what happens when you let a triblett touch alcohol". Only the mule knows for sure!

Each issue also continues the on-going saga of the uncanny Assmen!

1 ❑ Jul 1986 Cover: 1.75 **NM** value: **Cover or less**
• parody of Star Trek, Elfquest **A:** Mark Poe **W:** Marcus Lusk
2 ❑ Oct 1986 Cover: 1.75 **NM** value: **Cover or less**
📖 The Hassle with Troublets • parody of Star Trek, Elfquest **A:** Mark Poe **W:** Marcus Lusk

ELF WARRIOR — Adventure

1 ❑ Feb 1987 Cover: 1.95 **NM** value: **Cover or less**
2 ❑ Cover: 1.95 **NM** value: **Cover or less**
3 ❑ Cover: 1.95 **NM** value: **Cover or less**
4 ❑ Cover: 1.95 **NM** value: **Cover or less**

EL GATO NEGRO — Azteca

1 ❑ Oct 1993, b&w Cover: 2.00 **NM** value: **Cover or less**
📖 The Burning, Part 1; Unknown Passing, Unforgettable Return **A:** Richard Dominguez **W:** Richard Dominguez
2 ❑ Sum 1994, b&w Cover: 2.00 **NM** value: **Cover or less**
📖 The Burning, Part 2 **A:** Richard Dominguez **W:** Richard Dominguez
3 ❑ Fal 1995, b&w Cover: 2.00 **NM** value: **Cover or less**
4 ❑ Cover: 2.50 **NM** value: **Cover or less**

EL-HAZARD — Viz

El Hazard: The Magnificent World is a beautiful fantasy tale. Three students and a teacher are transported to a magical world from a modern Japanese high school. In the realm of El-Hazard, they become entangled in a giant war between the human inhabitants of Roshtaria, the insect drones of Bugrom, and the mysterious Shadow People, all of which are struggling to obtain the immense power of a weapon — the Eye of God. This is the realm of El-Hazard, the land of never-ending adventures. As long as there is a challenging spirit and a readiness to fly into infinity, its gate shall be forever open. The events of the series are loosely based on the El-Hazard, the Magnificent World OAV (Original Animated Video) series.

1 ❑ Apr 1997 Cover: 2.95 **NM** value: **Cover or less**
Circ: Diamd. preorders: **4,158**

ELIMINATOR, THE — Malibu / Ultraverse

0 ❑ Apr 1995 Cover: 2.95 **NM** value: **Cover or less**
Circ: CapCity orders: **5,975**
1 ❑ May 1995 Cover: 2.50 **NM** value: **Cover or less**
• 7th Infinity Gem revealed **A:** Mike Zeck **W:** Hank Kanalz; Roland Mann ★ 1st Appearance of Siren, Mannequin.
1/SC❑ May 1995 Cover: 3.95 **NM** value: **Cover or less**
Circ: CapCity orders: **6,225**
• Black cover edition. • 7th Infinity Gem revealed **A:** Mike Zeck **W:** Hank Kanalz; Roland Mann ★ 1st Appearance of Siren, Mannequin.
2 ❑ Jun 1995 Cover: 2.50 **NM** value: **Cover or less**
Circ: CapCity orders: **5,050**
3 ❑ Jul 1995 Cover: 2.50 **NM** value: **Cover or less**

ELIMINATOR (ETERNITY) — Eternity

1 ❑ b&w Cover: 2.50 **NM** value: **Cover or less**
2 ❑ b&w Cover: 2.50 **NM** value: **Cover or less**

ELIMINATOR FULL COLOR SPECIAL — Eternity

1 ❑ ca. 1991 Cover: 2.95 **NM** value: **Cover or less**
Circ: CapCity orders: **2,700**
📖 Lowell Cunningham **A:** Oct-91 **W:** Leonard Kirk; Mike Matthews

ELITE MR. BEAT — Moordam

Bk 1❑ Cover: 19.95 **NM** value: **Cover or less**

ELLERY QUEEN — Ziff-Davis

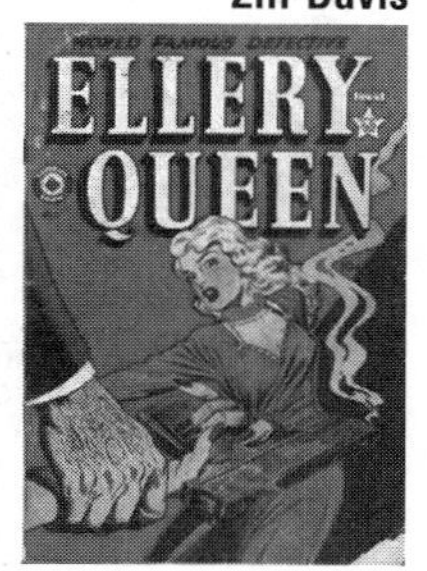

Ellery Queen was both the detective in a classic series of fiction and the pseudonym of the creator. "Ellery Queen" was actually cousins Frederic Dannay (1905-1982) and Manfred Lee (1905-1971), and they not only contributed the stories, but they also gave the name to an ongoing mystery magazine. The first appearance of the character was in The Roman Hat Mystery (1929), and he achieved popularity as a problem-solver. At the time of the two issues of the Ziff Davis comic book, the publisher (which was releasing such pulp magazines of the day as Amazing Stories and Fantastic Adventures), Ellery Queen's Mystery Magazine was being released by the publisher Mercury Press. The Adventures of Ellery Queen appeared on radio from 1939 to 1948 and in four different TV series airing between 1950 and 1976.

Queen is a detective working in conjunction with law-enforcement officials, and his usual plots are traditional in the "whodunit" mode. — Maggie

1 ❑ Jan 1952 Cover: 0.10 **NM** value: **500.00**
• **CGC:** 1 graded, best 8.5
2 ❑ Sum 1952 Cover: 0.10 **NM** value: **450.00**
• **CGC:** 1 graded, best 8.0

ELMO COMICS — St. John

1 ❑ Jan 1948 Cover: 0.10 **NM** value: **50.00**
• **CGC:** 1 graded, best 7.5

ELONGATED MAN — DC

1 ❑ Jan 1992 Cover: 1.00 **NM** value: **1.25**
Circ: CapCity orders: **29,350**
2 ❑ Feb 1992 Cover: 1.00 **NM** value: **Cover or less**
Circ: CapCity orders: **18,100**
3 ❑ Mar 1992 Cover: 1.00 **NM** value: **Cover or less**
Circ: CapCity orders: **12,850**
4 ❑ Apr 1992 Cover: 1.00 **NM** value: **Cover or less**
Circ: CapCity orders: **9,800**

EL PERFECTO COMICS — Print Mint

1 ❑ Cover: 0.50 **NM** value: **4.00**
• **CGC:** 1 graded, best 9.0
📖 My First LSD Trip; Rowdy Noody; Back Home in Pasadena on Acid; Illumination!; Annie Danow Takes a Trip; Duck Weevil; Louie Burns His Burger; I Am The Pontiac; Come Where in...the Future; El Dopo; The Happy **A:** Justin Green; Ted Richards; Trina; R.Crumb; Diane Noomin; Bill Griffith; Jay Kinney; Kim Deitch; Shelby; Bobwell Armstrong; Gary Hallren; Gary King; London; Terry Balawejder; Tim Mancusi; Willy Murray **W:** Justin Green; Ted Richards; Trina; R.Crumb; Diane Noomin; Bill Griffith; Jay Kinney; Kim Deitch; Shelby; Bobwell Armstrong; Gary Hallren; Gary King; London; Terry Balawejder; Tim Mancusi; Willy Murray

ELRIC — Pacific

1 ❑ Apr 1983 Cover: 1.50 **NM** value: **2.00**
• **CGC:** 1 graded, best 9.2
2 ❑ Aug 1983 Cover: 1.50 **NM** value: **1.75**
3 ❑ Oct 1983 Cover: 2.50 **NM** value: **Cover or less**
4 ❑ Dec 1983 Cover: 1.50 **NM** value: **1.75**
5 ❑ Feb 1984 Cover: 1.50 **NM** value: **1.75**
6 ❑ Apr 1984 Cover: 1.50 **NM** value: **1.75**

ELRIC: SAILOR ON THE SEAS OF FATE — First

1 ❑ Jun 1985 Cover: 1.75 **NM** value: **2.00**
Circ: CapCity orders: **8,375**
2 ❑ Aug 1985 Cover: 1.75 **NM** value: **Cover or less**
Circ: CapCity orders: **8,075**
3 ❑ Oct 1985 Cover: 1.75 **NM** value: **Cover or less**
Circ: CapCity orders: **8,125**
4 ❑ Dec 1985 Cover: 1.75 **NM** value: **Cover or less**
Circ: CapCity orders: **7,600**
5 ❑ Feb 1986 Cover: 1.75 **NM** value: **Cover or less**
Circ: CapCity orders: **7,200**
6 ❑ Apr 1986 Cover: 1.75 **NM** value: **Cover or less**
Circ: CapCity orders: **6,450**
7 ❑ Jun 1986 Cover: 1.75 **NM** value: **Cover or less**
Circ: CapCity orders: **6,375**

ELRIC: STORMBRINGER — Dark Horse / Topps

1 ❑ ca. 1997 Cover: 2.95 **NM** value: **Cover or less**
Circ: Diamd. preorders: **20,533**
2 ❑ ca. 1997 Cover: 2.95 **NM** value: **Cover or less**
Circ: Diamd. preorders: **15,238**
3 ❑ ca. 1997 Cover: 2.95 **NM** value: **Cover or less**
Circ: Diamd. preorders: **17,084**
4 ❑ ca. 1997 Cover: 2.95 **NM** value: **Cover or less**
Circ: Diamd. preorders: **13,977**
5 ❑ ca. 1997 Cover: 2.95 **NM** value: **Cover or less**
Circ: Diamd. preorders: **13,104**
6 ❑ ca. 1997 Cover: 2.95 **NM** value: **Cover or less**
Circ: Diamd. preorders: **12,205**
7 ❑ ca. 1997 Cover: 2.95 **NM** value: **Cover or less**
Circ: Diamd. preorders: **12,057**
Bk 1❑ Jun 1998 Cover: 17.95 **NM** value: **Cover or less**
• collects series **A:** P. Craig Russell

ELRIC: THE BANE OF THE BLACK SWORD — First

1 ❑ Aug 1988 Cover: 1.75 **NM** value: **2.00**
Circ: CapCity orders: **5,975**
2 ❑ Oct 1988 Cover: 1.95 **NM** value: **2.00**
Circ: CapCity orders: **5,050**

CGC-graded: Multiply prices above by **33 for 9.9 M • 16 for 9.8 NM/M • 7 for 9.6 NM+ • 5 for 9.4 NM • 2.5 for 9.2 NM- • 1.5 for 9.0 VF/NM**

3 ❑ Dec 1988 Cover: 1.95 **NM** value: **2.00**
Circ: CapCity orders: **4,875**
4 ❑ Feb 1989 Cover: 1.95 **NM** value: **2.00**
Circ: CapCity orders: **4,425**
5 ❑ Apr 1989 Cover: 1.95 **NM** value: **2.00**
Circ: CapCity orders: **4,550**
6 ❑ Jun 1989 Cover: 1.95 **NM** value: **2.00**
Circ: CapCity orders: **4,275**

ELRIC: THE VANISHING TOWER — First

1 ❑ Aug 1987 Cover: 1.75 **NM** value: **Cover or less**
Circ: CapCity orders: **8,100**
2 ❑ Oct 1987 Cover: 1.75 **NM** value: **Cover or less**
Circ: CapCity orders: **6,900**
3 ❑ Dec 1987 Cover: 1.75 **NM** value: **Cover or less**
Circ: CapCity orders: **6,375**
4 ❑ Feb 1988 Cover: 1.75 **NM** value: **Cover or less**
Circ: CapCity orders: **6,250**
5 ❑ Apr 1988 Cover: 1.75 **NM** value: **Cover or less**
Circ: CapCity orders: **5,525**
6 ❑ Jun 1988 Cover: 1.75 **NM** value: **Cover or less**
Circ: CapCity orders: **5,175**
📖 Tall Tower Vanishing **A:** Jan Duursema **W:** Roy Thomas

ELRIC (TOPPS) — Topps

P. Craig Russell adapts Neil Gaiman's 1994 prose story "One Life — Furnished in Early Moorcock" into comics form in this Elric special.

Twelve-year-old British student Richard Grey is obsessed with the works of Michael Moorcock. The Elric books provide Richard with a rich and rewarding fantasy world that he cannot find in his real life. The Elric books define Richard's existence, and inform Richard's developing imagination, and his spiritual and sexual life.

P. Craig Russell's adaptation is beautiful and Gaiman's prose eloquently relates the emotional attachment science fiction and fantasy has on us. This is a heartfelt story, a perfect tribute to the quality of Moorcock's creations, and it may have been overlooked next to higher-profile Gaiman material. (The title is a takeoff of Harlan Ellison's 1970 story, "One Life, Furnished in Early Poverty.")

0 ❑ ca. 1996 Cover: 2.95 **NM** value: **3.50**
• **CGC:** 1 graded, best 9.6
📖 One Life **A:** P. Craig Russell **W:** Neil Gaiman
1 ❑ ca. 1996 Cover: 2.95 **NM** value: **Cover or less**
2 ❑ ca. 1996 Cover: 2.95 **NM** value: **Cover or less**
3 ❑ ca. 1996 Cover: 2.95 **NM** value: **Cover or less**
4 ❑ ca. 1996 Cover: 2.95 **NM** value: **Cover or less**
📖 Chaos Wars **A:** P. Craig Russell **W:** P. Craig Russell; Michael Moorcock

ELRIC: WEIRD OF THE WHITE WOLF — First

1 ❑ Oct 1986 Cover: 1.75 **NM** value: **Cover or less**
Circ: CapCity orders: **9,650**
2 ❑ Dec 1986 Cover: 1.75 **NM** value: **Cover or less**
Circ: CapCity orders: **8,250**
3 ❑ Feb 1987 Cover: 1.75 **NM** value: **Cover or less**
Circ: CapCity orders: **7,225**
4 ❑ Apr 1987 Cover: 1.75 **NM** value: **Cover or less**
Circ: CapCity orders: **7,075**
5 ❑ Jun 1987 Cover: 1.75 **NM** value: **Cover or less**
Circ: CapCity orders: **6,475**

EL SALVADOR-A HOUSE DIVIDED — Eclipse

1 ❑ b&w Cover: 2.50 **NM** value: **Cover or less**

ELSEWHERE PRINCE, THE — Marvel / Epic

1 ❑ May 1990 Cover: 1.95 **NM** value: **Cover or less**
Circ: CapCity orders: **12,900**
2 ❑ Jun 1990 Cover: 1.95 **NM** value: **Cover or less**
Circ: CapCity orders: **10,000**
3 ❑ Jul 1990 Cover: 1.95 **NM** value: **Cover or less**
Circ: CapCity orders: **9,300**
4 ❑ Aug 1990 Cover: 1.95 **NM** value: **Cover or less**
Circ: CapCity orders: **7,950**
5 ❑ Sep 1990 Cover: 1.95 **NM** value: **Cover or less**
Circ: CapCity orders: **7,650**
6 ❑ Oct 1990 Cover: 1.95 **NM** value: **Cover or less**
Circ: CapCity orders: **7,700**

ELSEWORLDS 80-PAGE GIANT — DC

1 ❑ Aug 1999 Cover: 4.95 **NM** value: **240.00**
• **CGC:** 18 graded, best 9.8
• U.S. copies destroyed, only released in England; less than 700 copies estimated to exist

There are two different pricing tiers in the modern comic-book hobby. **The prices seen above** are the prices we have seen **loose copies** of these issues reliably fetch in a variety of environments. Condition alters the price by the fractions seen on the bar on the bottom of left-hand pages of this book. **Comics graded by CGC** usually sell for more. Use the guide on the bottom of right-hand pages of this book to estimate what copies have brought on eBay.

ELSEWORLD'S FINEST — DC

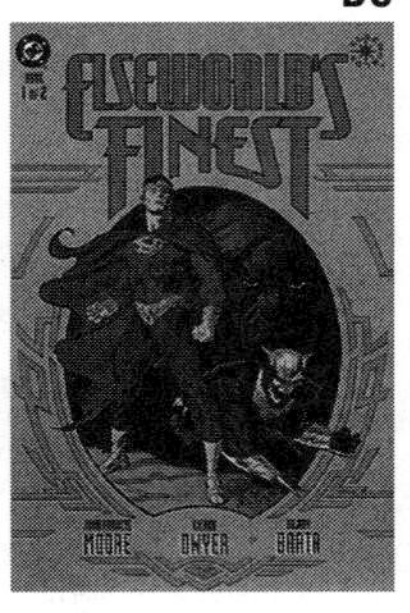

Imagine Clark Kent performing Superman-like feats but unaware of his alien heritage. Here Bruce Wayne portrays a penniless soldier of fortune with a rogue's heart. Welcome to Elseworld, where heroes are removed from familiar surroundings and placed into strange eras and locations. Some exist that could have existed, some don't exist, others can't, shouldn't, and won't.

Desperately seeking her father's whereabouts, Lana Lang enlists the aid of her high school sweetheart, Clark Kent, and an amoral Bruce Wayne. After the men form a shaky partnership, the real adventure begins in the Egyptian desert. Along with a young Jimmy Olsen, the group witnesses an unbelievable event: Prince Ra's Al-Ghul's corpse is restored to life! Solid writing, bold ideas, and interesting characters combined with no-nonsense artwork adds up to great reading.

1 ❑ ca. 1997 Cover: 4.95 **NM** value: **Cover or less**
Circ: Diamd. preorders: **38,598**
• prestige format. • Superman and Batman in the 1920s; Elseworlds story **A:** Kieron Dwyer **W:** John Francis Moore ★ Appearance of Jimmy Olsen, Bruce Wayne, Lex Luthor, Captain Marvel, Clark Kent, Lana Lang.
2 ❑ ca. 1997 Cover: 4.95 **NM** value: **Cover or less**
Circ: Diamd. preorders: **34,035**
• prestige format. • Superman and Batman in the 1920s **A:** Kieron Dwyer **W:** John Francis Moore

ELSEWORLD'S FINEST: SUPERGIRL & BATGIRL — DC

1 ❑ ca. 1998 Cover: 5.95 **NM** value: **Cover or less**
Circ: Diamd. preorders: **35,603**
No issue number. One-shot. • prestige format.
1/LE❑ ca. 1998 Cover: 18.95 **NM** value: **Cover or less**

ELVEN — Malibu / Ultraverse

0 ❑ Oct 1994 Cover: 2.95 **NM** value: **Cover or less**
Circ: CapCity orders: **11,525**
📖 Gimme Shelter; Prime-Itive Attraction **A:** Aaron Lopresti; Greg Luzniak **W:** Len Strazewski ★ 1st Appearance of Elven.
1 ❑ Feb 1995 Cover: 2.50 **NM** value: **Cover or less**
Circ: CapCity orders: **8,300**
📖 Eye for an Eye…Pain for Pain **A:** Aaron Lopresti **W:** Len Strazewski ★ Appearance of Prime.
1/LE❑ Feb 1995 **NM** value: **2.50**
• Limited foil edition. 📖 Eye for an Eye…Pain for Pain ★ Appearance of Prime.
2 ❑ Mar 1995 Cover: 2.50 **NM** value: **Cover or less**
Circ: CapCity orders: **6,600**
3 ❑ Apr 1995 Cover: 2.50 **NM** value: **Cover or less**
Circ: CapCity orders: **5,875**
4 ❑ May 1995 Cover: 2.50 **NM** value: **Cover or less**
Circ: CapCity orders: **5,450**

ELVIRA, MISTRESS OF THE DARK — Claypool

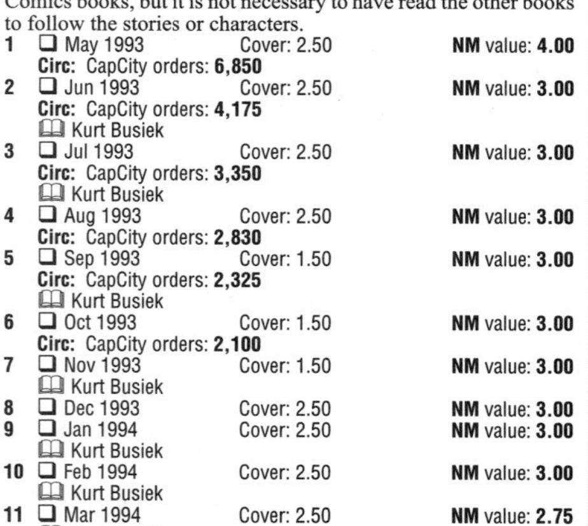

Based on the schlock horror movie hostess character created and portrayed by Cassandra Pederson, this comic features photo covers of Elvira, parody plots, and, in keeping with Elvira's persona, lots of bad jokes and puns. It has had a number of writers and artists, including Paul Dini and Kurt Busiek. The plots often launch from Elvira's job as a sexy horror movie hostess for station K-WHA? and her conflicts with her bosses and sponsors. It's intended to be a "funny book" in the truest sense of the word, and succeeds more often than not. There are occasional appearances by characters appearing in other Claypool Comics books, but it is not necessary to have read the other books to follow the stories or characters.

1 ❑ May 1993 Cover: 2.50 **NM** value: **4.00**
Circ: CapCity orders: **6,850**
2 ❑ Jun 1993 Cover: 2.50 **NM** value: **3.00**
Circ: CapCity orders: **4,175**
📖 Kurt Busiek
3 ❑ Jul 1993 Cover: 2.50 **NM** value: **3.00**
Circ: CapCity orders: **3,350**
📖 Kurt Busiek
4 ❑ Aug 1993 Cover: 2.50 **NM** value: **3.00**
Circ: CapCity orders: **2,830**
5 ❑ Sep 1993 Cover: 1.50 **NM** value: **3.00**
Circ: CapCity orders: **2,325**
📖 Kurt Busiek
6 ❑ Oct 1993 Cover: 1.50 **NM** value: **3.00**
Circ: CapCity orders: **2,100**
7 ❑ Nov 1993 Cover: 1.50 **NM** value: **3.00**
📖 Kurt Busiek
8 ❑ Dec 1993 Cover: 2.50 **NM** value: **3.00**
9 ❑ Jan 1994 Cover: 2.50 **NM** value: **3.00**
📖 Kurt Busiek
10 ❑ Feb 1994 Cover: 2.50 **NM** value: **3.00**
📖 Kurt Busiek
11 ❑ Mar 1994 Cover: 2.50 **NM** value: **2.75**
📖 Kurt Busiek
12 ❑ Apr 1994 Cover: 2.50 **NM** value: **2.75**
• **CGC:** 1 graded, best 8.5
13 ❑ May 1994 Cover: 2.50 **NM** value: **2.75**
14 ❑ Jun 1994 Cover: 2.50 **NM** value: **2.75**
15 ❑ Jul 1994 Cover: 2.50 **NM** value: **2.75**
16 ❑ Aug 1994 Cover: 2.50 **NM** value: **2.75**
17 ❑ Sep 1994 Cover: 2.50 **NM** value: **2.75**
18 ❑ Oct 1994 Cover: 2.50 **NM** value: **2.75**
19 ❑ Nov 1994 Cover: 2.50 **NM** value: **2.75**
20 ❑ Dec 1994 Cover: 2.50 **NM** value: **2.75**
• **CGC:** 1 graded, best 8.5
21 ❑ Jan 1995 Cover: 2.50 **NM** value: **Cover or less**
22 ❑ Feb 1995 Cover: 2.50 **NM** value: **Cover or less**
23 ❑ Mar 1995 Cover: 2.50 **NM** value: **Cover or less**
24 ❑ Apr 1995 Cover: 2.50 **NM** value: **Cover or less**
25 ❑ May 1995 Cover: 2.50 **NM** value: **Cover or less**
📖 Kurt Busiek
26 ❑ Jun 1995 Cover: 2.50 **NM** value: **Cover or less**
27 ❑ Jul 1995 Cover: 2.50 **NM** value: **Cover or less**
28 ❑ Aug 1995 Cover: 2.50 **NM** value: **Cover or less**
29 ❑ Sep 1995 Cover: 2.50 **NM** value: **Cover or less**
30 ❑ Oct 1995 Cover: 2.50 **NM** value: **Cover or less**
31 ❑ Nov 1995 Cover: 2.50 **NM** value: **Cover or less**
32 ❑ Dec 1995 Cover: 2.50 **NM** value: **Cover or less**
33 ❑ Jan 1996 Cover: 2.50 **NM** value: **Cover or less**
34 ❑ Feb 1996 Cover: 2.50 **NM** value: **Cover or less**
35 ❑ Mar 1996 Cover: 2.50 **NM** value: **Cover or less**
36 ❑ Apr 1996 Cover: 2.50 **NM** value: **Cover or less**
37 ❑ May 1996 Cover: 2.50 **NM** value: **Cover or less**
38 ❑ Jun 1996 Cover: 2.50 **NM** value: **Cover or less**
39 ❑ Jul 1996 Cover: 2.50 **NM** value: **Cover or less**
40 ❑ Aug 1996 Cover: 2.50 **NM** value: **Cover or less**
41 ❑ Sep 1996 Cover: 2.50 **NM** value: **Cover or less**
42 ❑ Oct 1996 Cover: 2.50 **NM** value: **Cover or less**
43 ❑ Nov 1996 Cover: 2.50 **NM** value: **Cover or less**
44 ❑ Dec 1996 Cover: 2.50 **NM** value: **Cover or less**
45 ❑ Jan 1997 Cover: 2.50 **NM** value: **Cover or less**
46 ❑ Feb 1997 Cover: 2.50 **NM** value: **Cover or less**
Circ: Diamd. preorders: **1,904**
47 ❑ Mar 1997 Cover: 2.50 **NM** value: **Cover or less**
48 ❑ Apr 1997 Cover: 2.50 **NM** value: **Cover or less**
49 ❑ May 1997 Cover: 2.50 **NM** value: **Cover or less**
50 ❑ Jun 1997 Cover: 2.50 **NM** value: **Cover or less**
51 ❑ Jul 1997 Cover: 2.50 **NM** value: **Cover or less**
52 ❑ Aug 1997 Cover: 2.50 **NM** value: **Cover or less**
53 ❑ Sep 1997 Cover: 2.50 **NM** value: **Cover or less**
54 ❑ Oct 1997 Cover: 2.50 **NM** value: **Cover or less**
55 ❑ Nov 1997 Cover: 2.50 **NM** value: **Cover or less**
56 ❑ Dec 1997 Cover: 2.50 **NM** value: **Cover or less**
57 ❑ Jan 1998 Cover: 2.50 **NM** value: **Cover or less**
58 ❑ Feb 1998 Cover: 2.50 **NM** value: **Cover or less**
59 ❑ Mar 1998 Cover: 2.50 **NM** value: **Cover or less**
60 ❑ Apr 1998 Cover: 2.50 **NM** value: **Cover or less**
61 ❑ May 1998 Cover: 2.50 **NM** value: **Cover or less**
62 ❑ Jun 1998 Cover: 2.50 **NM** value: **Cover or less**
63 ❑ Jul 1998 Cover: 2.50 **NM** value: **Cover or less**
64 ❑ Aug 1998 Cover: 2.50 **NM** value: **Cover or less**
65 ❑ Sep 1998 Cover: 2.50 **NM** value: **Cover or less**
66 ❑ Oct 1998 Cover: 2.50 **NM** value: **Cover or less**
67 ❑ Nov 1998 Cover: 2.50 **NM** value: **Cover or less**
📖 The Search for Schlock **A:** Ronn Sutton **W:** Frank Strom
68 ❑ Dec 1998 Cover: 2.50 **NM** value: **Cover or less**
69 ❑ Jan 1999 Cover: 2.50 **NM** value: **Cover or less**
Circ: Diamd. preorders: **1,350**
70 ❑ Feb 1999 Cover: 2.50 **NM** value: **Cover or less**
Circ: Diamd. preorders: **1,303**
71 ❑ Mar 1999 Cover: 2.50 **NM** value: **Cover or less**
72 ❑ Apr 1999 Cover: 2.50 **NM** value: **Cover or less**
Circ: Diamd. preorders: **1,303**
73 ❑ May 1999 Cover: 2.50 **NM** value: **Cover or less**
74 ❑ Jun 1999 Cover: 2.50 **NM** value: **Cover or less**
75 ❑ Jul 1999 Cover: 2.50 **NM** value: **Cover or less**
76 ❑ Aug 1999 Cover: 2.50 **NM** value: **Cover or less**
77 ❑ Sep 1999 Cover: 2.50 **NM** value: **Cover or less**
78 ❑ Oct 1999 Cover: 2.50 **NM** value: **Cover or less**
79 ❑ Nov 1999 Cover: 2.50 **NM** value: **Cover or less**
80 ❑ Dec 1999 Cover: 2.50 **NM** value: **Cover or less**
📖 Christmas on the Prowl
81 ❑ Jan 2000 Cover: 2.50 **NM** value: **Cover or less**
82 ❑ Feb 2000 Cover: 2.50 **NM** value: **Cover or less**
83 ❑ Mar 2000 Cover: 2.50 **NM** value: **Cover or less**
84 ❑ Apr 2000 Cover: 2.50 **NM** value: **Cover or less**
85 ❑ May 2000 Cover: 2.50 **NM** value: **Cover or less**
📖 Telechubby Alien Autopsy
86 ❑ Jun 2000 Cover: 2.50 **NM** value: **Cover or less**
📖 Snoop Troop
87 ❑ Jul 2000 Cover: 2.50 **NM** value: **Cover or less**
📖 Picture Perfect, Part 1: Portrait of the Artist as a B-Movie Bimbo!
88 ❑ Aug 2000 Cover: 2.50 **NM** value: **Cover or less**
📖 Picture Perfect, Part 2: A Brush with Disaster!; … That Old Get-up and Glow! **A:** Dan Day; Tod Smith **W:** Frank Strom; Richard Howell
89 ❑ Sep 2000 Cover: 2.50 **NM** value: **Cover or less**
📖 Picture Perfect, Part 3: S'Mource of My Discontent!; Web-Mistress of the Dark! **A:** Tod Smith; Ronn Sutton **W:** Frank Strom; Janet Hetherington
90 ❑ Oct 2000 Cover: 2.50 **NM** value: **Cover or less**
📖 Creepy Hollow; Boys on the Slide! **A:** Anna-Maria Cool; Ronn Sutton **W:** Frank Strom; Richard Howell
91 ❑ Nov 2000 Cover: 2.50 **NM** value: **Cover or less**
92 ❑ Dec 2000 Cover: 2.50 **NM** value: **Cover or less**
93 ❑ Jan 2001 Cover: 2.50 **NM** value: **Cover or less**
Circ: Diamd. preorders: **1,112**
94 ❑ Feb 2001 Cover: 2.50 **NM** value: **Cover or less**
95 ❑ Mar 2001 Cover: 2.50 **NM** value: **Cover or less**
Circ: Diamd. preorders: **1,066**
96 ❑ Apr 2001 Cover: 2.50 **NM** value: **Cover or less**
Circ: Diamd. preorders: **1,119**
97 ❑ May 2001 Cover: 2.50 **NM** value: **Cover or less**

Other grades: Multiply prices above by **1.5 for Mint • 2/3 for Very Fine • 1/3 for Fine • 1/5 for Very Good • 1/8 for Good**

Circ: Diamd. preorders: **1,061**
98 ❑ Jun 2001 Cover: 2.50 **NM** value: **Cover or less**
Circ: Diamd. preorders: **1,124 • CGC:** 1 graded, best 8.5
99 ❑ Jul 2001 Cover: 2.50 **NM** value: **Cover or less**
Bk 1❑ Cover: 12.95 **NM** value: **Cover or less**
📖 Comic Milestones – Comics Format!! • Comic Milestones – Comics Format!!
Bk 2❑ Cover: 12.95 **NM** value: **Cover or less**
📖 Double Delights

ELVIRA, MISTRESS OF THE DARK (MAGAZINE) — Marvel

1 ❑ ca. 1988 Cover: 2.00 **NM** value: **4.00**
Circ: CapCity orders: **6,100**

ELVIRA'S HOUSE OF MYSTERY — DC

Elvira has long been a cult favorite on the small screen. As host of her own late-night TV show, she would show truly terrible horror movies, using the time around commercial breaks to ridicule the movie with a series of awful jokes. And then there was the dress...

Naturally, when DC wanted a host for its new House of Mystery series, it chose her. So, for a brief, 11-issue run, the Mistress of the Dark had a new career. Instead of hosting terrible horror movies, she hosted some rather nice horror comic-book stories. Fans of the older House of Mystery series will be cheered to note that their old host, the ghoulish Cain, returned in issue #10 to stage a palace revolt. He got his comeuppance soon after, however, when his brother Abel, the old House of Secrets host, pushed Cain aside to host the 11th and final issue.

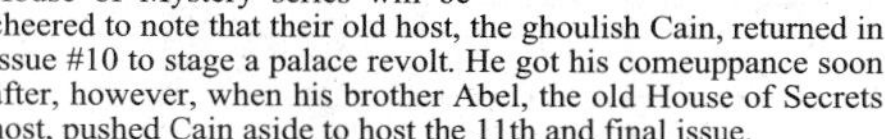

1 ❑ Jan 1986 Cover: 1.50 **NM** value: **3.00**
Photo cover. • Double-size. 📖 Play or Pay! **A:** James W. Fry III **W:** Paul Dini
2 ❑ Apr 1986 Cover: 0.75 **NM** value: **2.00**
Circ: CapCity orders: **6,600**
3 ❑ May 1986 Cover: 0.75 **NM** value: **2.00**
Circ: CapCity orders: **5,700**
4 ❑ Jun 1986 Cover: 0.75 **NM** value: **1.50**
Circ: CapCity orders: **5,050 • CGC:** 1 graded, best 9.4
5 ❑ Jul 1986 Cover: 0.75 **NM** value: **1.50**
Circ: CapCity orders: **4,550 • CGC:** 1 graded, best 9.6
6 ❑ Aug 1986 Cover: 0.75 **NM** value: **1.50**
Circ: CapCity orders: **4,350**
• sideways issue
7 ❑ Sep 1986 Cover: 0.75 **NM** value: **1.50**
Circ: CapCity orders: **4,100**
• science-fiction issue
8 ❑ Oct 1986 Cover: 0.75 **NM** value: **1.50**
Circ: CapCity orders: **4,300**
9 ❑ Nov 1986 Cover: 0.75 **NM** value: **1.50**
Circ: CapCity orders: **4,600**
10 ❑ Dec 1986 Cover: 0.75 **NM** value: **1.50**
Circ: CapCity orders: **4,200**
11 ❑ Jan 1987 Cover: 1.25 **NM** value: **1.50**
Circ: CapCity orders: **4,350**
• Double-size. final issue. **C:** Dave Stevens
SE 1❑ ca. 1987 Cover: 1.25 **NM** value: **2.00**
Circ: CapCity orders: **5,000**
• Christmas stories

ELVIS MANDIBLE, THE — DC / Piranha

1 ❑ ca. 1991, b&w Cover: 3.50 **NM** value: **Cover or less**
No issue number. One-shot. **A:** Douglas Michael **W:** Douglas Michael

ELVIS PRESLEY EXPERIENCE, THE — Revolutionary

1 ❑ Aug 1992, b&w Cover: 2.50 **NM** value: **Cover or less**
2 ❑ Oct 1992, b&w Cover: 2.50 **NM** value: **Cover or less**
3 ❑ Jan 1993, b&w Cover: 2.50 **NM** value: **Cover or less**
4 ❑ Feb 1993, b&w Cover: 2.50 **NM** value: **Cover or less**
5 ❑ Jul 1993, b&w Cover: 2.50 **NM** value: **Cover or less**
6 ❑ Aug 1993, b&w Cover: 2.50 **NM** value: **Cover or less**
7 ❑ Apr 1994, b&w Cover: 2.50 **NM** value: **Cover or less**

ELVIS SHRUGGED — Revolutionary

1 ❑ Feb 1992, b&w Cover: 2.50 **NM** value: **Cover or less**
2 ❑ Aug 1992, b&w Cover: 2.50 **NM** value: **Cover or less**
3 ❑ Apr 1992, b&w Cover: 3.95 **NM** value: **Cover or less**
Bk 1❑ Dec 1993, b&w Cover: 9.95 **NM** value: **Cover or less**

E-MAN (1ST SERIES) — Charlton

The star of Joe Staton's cheerful, goofy title was originally little more than a glob of energy floating about in space. Then, a passing spaceship caught the energy's fancy, and it hitched a ride. As luck would have it, the ship was bound for Pluto where it was supposed to destroy the planet in a test of its alien superweapon. However, when the energy took form while on the ship, the additional mass forced the ship off course, sending it crashing into Earth. The energy jumped ship before the crash, got tangled in some high tension lines, and eventually wound up trapped in a light bulb in exotic dancer Nova Kane's dressing room. Happens all the time!

When she freed him, he took on the form of a man. As E-Man, he's able to switch from energy to matter at will, taking on any form. He is also able to convert part of his mass into energy bolts which he can fire at enemies. He uses these powers to save our world from a variety of earthly and unearthly menaces.

1 ❑ Oct 1973 Cover: 0.20 **NM** value: **8.00**
2 ❑ Dec 1973 Cover: 0.20 **NM** value: **5.00**
3 ❑ Jun 1974 Cover: 0.25 **NM** value: **5.00**
4 ❑ Aug 1974 Cover: 0.25 **NM** value: **5.00**
5 ❑ Nov 1974 Cover: 0.25 **NM** value: **3.50**
6 ❑ Jan 1975 Cover: 0.25 **NM** value: **3.50**
7 ❑ Mar 1975 Cover: 0.25 **NM** value: **3.50**
8 ❑ May 1975 Cover: 0.25 **NM** value: **3.50**
• Nova becomes E-Man's partner **A:** John Byrne
9 ❑ Jul 1975 Cover: 0.25 **NM** value: **3.50**
10 ❑ Sep 1975 Cover: 0.25 **NM** value: **3.50**

E-MAN (2ND SERIES) — First

1 ❑ Apr 1983 Cover: 1.00 **NM** value: **1.50**
2 ❑ Jun 1983 Cover: 1.00 **NM** value: **1.25**
• X-Men parody **A:** Joe Staton ★ Appearance of F-Men.
3 ❑ Jun 1983 Cover: 1.00 **NM** value: **1.25**
4 ❑ Jul 1983 Cover: 1.00 **NM** value: **1.25**
5 ❑ Aug 1983 Cover: 1.00 **NM** value: **1.25**
6 ❑ Sep 1983 Cover: 1.00 **NM** value: **1.25**
7 ❑ Oct 1983 Cover: 1.00 **NM** value: **1.25**
8 ❑ Nov 1983 Cover: 1.00 **NM** value: **1.25**
9 ❑ Dec 1983 Cover: 1.00 **NM** value: **1.25**
10 ❑ Jan 1984 Cover: 1.00 **NM** value: **1.25**
11 ❑ Feb 1984 Cover: 1.00 **NM** value: **1.25**
12 ❑ Mar 1984 Cover: 1.00 **NM** value: **1.25**
13 ❑ Apr 1984 Cover: 1.00 **NM** value: **1.25**
14 ❑ May 1984 Cover: 1.00 **NM** value: **1.25**
15 ❑ Jun 1984 Cover: 1.00 **NM** value: **1.25**
16 ❑ Jul 1984 Cover: 1.00 **NM** value: **1.25**
17 ❑ Aug 1984 Cover: 1.00 **NM** value: **1.25**
18 ❑ Sep 1984 Cover: 1.00 **NM** value: **1.25**
19 ❑ Oct 1984 Cover: 1.00 **NM** value: **1.25**
20 ❑ Nov 1984 Cover: 1.25 **NM** value: **Cover or less**
21 ❑ Dec 1984 Cover: 1.25 **NM** value: **Cover or less**
22 ❑ Feb 1985 Cover: 1.25 **NM** value: **Cover or less**
23 ❑ Apr 1985 Cover: 1.25 **NM** value: **Cover or less**
24 ❑ Jun 1985 Cover: 1.25 **NM** value: **Cover or less**
25 ❑ Aug 1985 Cover: 1.25 **NM** value: **Cover or less**
final issue. **A:** Joe Staton

E-MAN (3RD SERIES) — Comico

1 ❑ Sep 1989 Cover: 2.75 **NM** value: **Cover or less**
Circ: CapCity orders: **4,700**
📖 E-Man: Quark and the Real World; Michael Mauser, Private Eye: Into Thin Air **A:** Joe Staton **W:** Nicola Cutii ★ Origin of Nova Kane, E-Man, Vamfire.

E-MAN (4TH SERIES) — Comico

1 ❑ Jan 1990 Cover: 2.50 **NM** value: **Cover or less**
Circ: CapCity orders: **4,500**
2 ❑ Feb 1990 Cover: 2.50 **NM** value: **Cover or less**
Circ: CapCity orders: **3,550**
📖 The Price of Paradise **A:** Joe Staton **W:** Nicola Cutii
3 ❑ Mar 1990 Cover: 2.50 **NM** value: **Cover or less**
Circ: CapCity orders: **3,350**

E-MAN (5TH SERIES) — Alpha

1 ❑ Oct 1993, full color Cover: 3.25 **NM** value: **Cover or less**
📖 E-Man Meets 'e'-Man; Mr. Jigsaw: A Day in the Park **A:** Joe Staton; Gary Kato **W:** Nicola Cutii; Ron Fortier ★ Origin of Eco-Man. ★ 1st Appearance of Eco-Man.

E-MAN RETURNS — Alpha Productions

1 ❑ Mar 1994, b&w Cover: 2.75 **NM** value: **Cover or less**

EMBLEM — Antarctic / Venus

All issues are adults only.
1 ❑ May 1994, b&w Cover: 3.50 **NM** value: **Cover or less**
2 ❑ Jun 1994, b&w Cover: 2.95 **NM** value: **Cover or less**
3 ❑ Jul 1994, b&w Cover: 2.95 **NM** value: **Cover or less**
5 ❑ Oct 1994, b&w Cover: 2.95 **NM** value: **Cover or less**
6 ❑ Nov 1994, b&w Cover: 2.95 **NM** value: **Cover or less**
7 ❑ Dec 1994, b&w Cover: 2.95 **NM** value: **Cover or less**
8 ❑ Feb 1995, b&w Cover: 2.95 **NM** value: **Cover or less**

EMBRACE — London Night

1 ❑ Jun 1997 Cover: 3.00 **NM** value: **Cover or less**
Circ: Diamd. preorders: **5,412**
Carmen Electra cover.
1/LE❑ Cover: 9.95 **NM** value: **Cover or less**

EMERALDAS — Eternity

1 ❑ b&w Cover: 2.25 **NM** value: **Cover or less**
2 ❑ b&w Cover: 2.25 **NM** value: **Cover or less**
📖 The Children of Eden, Part 2 **A:** Ben Dunn **W:** Robert W. Gibson
3 ❑ b&w Cover: 2.25 **NM** value: **Cover or less**
4 ❑ b&w Cover: 2.25 **NM** value: **Cover or less**

EMERGENCY! — Charlton

1 ❑ Jun 1976 Cover: 0.30 **NM** value: **22.00**
• **CGC:** 7 graded, best 9.6
2 ❑ Aug 1976 Cover: 0.30 **NM** value: **18.00**
• **CGC:** 2 graded, best 9.6
3 ❑ Oct 1976 Cover: 0.30 **NM** value: **15.00**
4 ❑ Dec 1976 Cover: 0.30 **NM** value: **15.00**
final issue. • Scarce

EMERGENCY! (MAGAZINE) — Charlton

1 ❑ Jun 1976 Cover: 1.00 **NM** value: **32.00**
2 ❑ Aug 1976 Cover: 1.00 **NM** value: **28.00**
3 ❑ Oct 1976 Cover: 1.00 **NM** value: **24.00**
4 ❑ Dec 1976 Cover: 1.00 **NM** value: **26.00**

EMISSARY — Strateia Studios

1 ❑ Jul 1998 Cover: 2.95 **NM** value: **Cover or less**

EMMA DAVENPORT — Lohman Hills

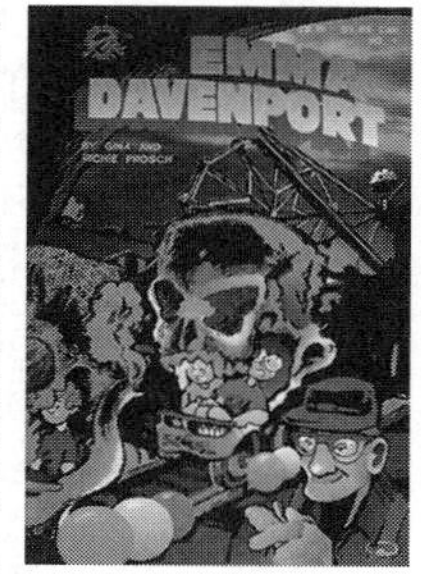

Richie and Gina Prosch's Emma Davenport made its debut as a strip in Comics Buyer's Guide. It became a comic in its own right with the premiere of this monthly series in 1995.

Emma, the title character, is a young girl who lives outside the town of Ashfall in the Midwest. She has a rich imagination, fueled by a love of pop culture, which leads her to spend large parts of her life lost in fantasy about comics, films, and an imaginary friend named Lyle. In large part, this is what makes this comic book so lovable. Emma represents the kid in all of us who is not above worrying whether or not Captain America could beat Batman in a fight, and who would never dream of getting on the scariest ride in the fairgrounds without daring fate by stuffing herself with a ton of French fries first.

1 ❑ Apr 1995, b&w Cover: 2.75 **NM** value: **3.00**
2 ❑ Jun 1995, b&w Cover: 2.75 **NM** value: **Cover or less**
3 ❑ Aug 1995, b&w Cover: 2.75 **NM** value: **Cover or less**
4 ❑ Oct 1995, b&w Cover: 2.75 **NM** value: **Cover or less**
5 ❑ Dec 1995, b&w Cover: 2.75 **NM** value: **Cover or less**
6 ❑ Feb 1996, b&w Cover: 2.75 **NM** value: **Cover or less**
7 ❑ Apr 1996, b&w Cover: 2.75 **NM** value: **Cover or less**
8 ❑ Feb 1996, b&w Cover: 2.75 **NM** value: **Cover or less**
• crossover with Femforce

EMPIRE — Eternity

1 ❑ Mar 1988 Cover: 1.95 **NM** value: **Cover or less**
Circ: Diamd. preorders: **33,766**
📖 The Uncrowned Lion **A:** John Gallagher **W:** Paul O'Connor
2 ❑ Apr 1988 Cover: 1.95 **NM** value: **Cover or less**
Circ: Diamd. preorders: **24,397**
3 ❑ May 1988 Cover: 1.95 **NM** value: **Cover or less**
Circ: Diamd. preorders: **19,440**
4 ❑ Jun 1988 Cover: 1.95 **NM** value: **Cover or less**
Circ: Diamd. preorders: **18,485**

EMPIRE (IMAGE) — Image

Ten years ago, the mysterious Golgoth, a super-being bent on world domination, did what so few super villains manage to do: He actually succeeded. Now, as absolute ruler of a great and terrible empire, Golgoth keeps order through his super-powered minions, who in turn are kept in check by means of a mysterious drug known as the Eucharist. One of his minions discovers the drug's secret, and now Golgoth must tighten his tyrannical grip even further, or risk losing control of the world. So why do we get the feeling that would be a bad thing?

Under the wise hand of writer Mark Waid, nothing is what it seems in this darkly familiar empire, which is rendered by artist Barry Kitson. In the end, readers are left feeling almost sympathetic for a despot who is on the verge of losing the world he holds in thrall.

1 ❑ May 2000 Cover: 2.50 **NM** value: **Cover or less**
2 ❑ Sep 2000 Cover: 2.50 **NM** value: **Cover or less**

EMPIRE LANES (KEYLINE) — Keyline

1 ❑ Cover: 1.75 **NM** value: **Cover or less**

EMPIRE LANES (NORTHERN LIGHTS) — Northern Lights

1 ❑ Cover: 1.75 **NM** value: **Cover or less**
2 ❑ Cover: 1.75 **NM** value: **Cover or less**
3 ❑ Cover: 1.75 **NM** value: **Cover or less**
4 ❑ Cover: 1.75 **NM** value: **Cover or less**

EMPIRE LANES (VOL. 2) — Keyline

1 ❑ Cover: 2.95 **NM** value: **Cover or less**
📖 The Innocent **A:** Peter Gross **W:** Peter Gross
Bk 1❑ Cover: 2.95 **NM** value: **Cover or less**
📖 The Blues **A:** Peter Gross **W:** Peter Gross

EMPIRES OF NIGHT — Rebel Studios

1 ❑ Dec 1993, b&w Cover: 2.25 **NM** value: **Cover or less**
2 ❑ Cover: 2.25 **NM** value: **Cover or less**
3 ❑ Cover: 2.25 **NM** value: **Cover or less**
4 ❑ Cover: 2.25 **NM** value: **Cover or less**

EMPTY LOVE STORIES — Slave Labor

1 ❑ Nov 1994, b&w Cover: 2.95 **NM** value: **Cover or less**
📖 White Trash Romance!; One of the Walking Dead; My Target! **A:** Lenin Delsol; Scott Beaderstadt; Hilary Barta; Alex Ross(cover); Paul Fricke **C:** Alex Ross **W:** Steve Darnall
2 ❑ Aug 1996, b&w Cover: 2.95 **NM** value: **Cover or less**

CGC-graded: Multiply prices above by **33 for 9.9 M • 16 for 9.8 NM/M • 7 for 9.6 NM+ • 5 for 9.4 NM • 2.5 for 9.2 NM- • 1.5 for 9.0 VF/NM**

EMPTY LOVE STORIES (2ND SERIES) — Funny Valentine

1 ❑ Jul 1998, b&w Cover: 2.95 **NM** value: **Cover or less**
• reprints Slave Labor issue **C:** Alex Ross
SE 1❑ Jan 1998, b&w Cover: 2.95 **NM** value: **Cover or less**
No issue number.

EMPTY SKULL COMICS — Fantagraphics

1 ❑ Apr 1996, b&w Cover: 4.95 **NM** value: **Cover or less**
No issue number. cardstock cover. • Oversized.

EMPTY ZONE — Sirius

1 ❑ Cover: 2.50 **NM** value: **Cover or less**
Circ: Diamd. preorders: **6,735**
2 ❑ Cover: 2.50 **NM** value: **Cover or less**
3 ❑ Cover: 2.50 **NM** value: **Cover or less**
4 ❑ Cover: 2.50 **NM** value: **Cover or less**
Bk 1❑ Cover: 11.95 **NM** value: **Cover or less**
• Under Dead Television Skies

EMPTY ZONE (2ND SERIES) — Sirius

1 ❑ ca. 1998 Cover: 2.95 **NM** value: **Cover or less**
2 ❑ ca. 1998 Cover: 2.95 **NM** value: **Cover or less**
Circ: Diamd. preorders: **2,006**
3 ❑ ca. 1998 Cover: 2.95 **NM** value: **Cover or less**
4 ❑ ca. 1998 Cover: 2.95 **NM** value: **Cover or less**
5 ❑ ca. 1998 Cover: 2.95 **NM** value: **Cover or less**
6 ❑ ca. 1998 Cover: 2.95 **NM** value: **Cover or less**
7 ❑ ca. 1998 Cover: 2.95 **NM** value: **Cover or less**
8 ❑ ca. 1998 Cover: 2.95 **NM** value: **Cover or less**

EMPTY ZONE: TRANCEMISSIONS — Sirius

1 ❑ Cover: 2.95 **NM** value: **Cover or less**
Circ: Diamd. preorders: **2,266**

ENCHANTED — Sirius

1 ❑ ca. 1997 Cover: 2.50 **NM** value: **2.95**
Circ: Diamd. preorders: **8,979**
2 ❑ ca. 1997 Cover: 2.50 **NM** value: **2.95**
Circ: Diamd. preorders: **5,517**
3 ❑ ca. 1997 Cover: 2.50 **NM** value: **2.95**
Circ: Diamd. preorders: **4,361**

ENCHANTED VALLEY — Blackthorne

1 ❑ Cover: 1.75 **NM** value: **Cover or less**
2 ❑ Cover: 1.75 **NM** value: **Cover or less**

ENCHANTED WORLDS — Blackmore

1 ❑ b&w Cover: 2.75 **NM** value: **Cover or less**

ENCHANTER — Eclipse

1 ❑ Oct 1985 Cover: 2.00 **NM** value: **Cover or less**
2 ❑ Nov 1985 Cover: 2.00 **NM** value: **Cover or less**
3 ❑ Dec 1985 Cover: 2.00 **NM** value: **Cover or less**
4 ❑ Jan 1986 Cover: 2.00 **NM** value: **Cover or less**
5 ❑ Feb 1986 Cover: 2.00 **NM** value: **Cover or less**
6 ❑ Mar 1986 Cover: 2.00 **NM** value: **Cover or less**
7 ❑ Apr 1986 Cover: 2.00 **NM** value: **Cover or less**
8 ❑ May 1986 Cover: 2.00 **NM** value: **Cover or less**

ENCHANTER: APOCALYPSE MOON — Express / Entity

1 ❑ b&w Cover: 2.95 **NM** value: **Cover or less**
• illustrated novella **A:** Tatsuya Ishida **W:** Don Chin

ENCHANTER: PRELUDE TO APOCALYPSE — Express

1 ❑ b&w Cover: 2.50 **NM** value: **Cover or less**
2 ❑ b&w Cover: 2.50 **NM** value: **Cover or less**
3 ❑ b&w Cover: 2.50 **NM** value: **Cover or less**

ENCHANTERS, THE — Hidden Poet

1 ❑ Jun 1996 Cover: 2.50 **NM** value: **Cover or less**
📖 School Daze **A:** Steven Gellman **W:** Steven Gellman

ENCYCLOPÆDIA DEADPOOLICA, THE — Marvel

1 ❑ Dec 1998 Cover: 2.99 **NM** value: **Cover or less**
Circ: Diamd. preorders: **19,725**
• Deadpool reference **W:** Frank Dunkerley; Julio Soto; Matt Brady; Michael Doran

END, THE: IN THE BEGINNING — AFC Studio

1 ❑ Jun 2000, b&w Cover: 2.95 **NM** value: **Cover or less**

ENDLESS GALLERY, THE — DC / Vertigo

1 ❑ Cover: 3.50 **NM** value: **Cover or less**
Circ: CapCity orders: **15,325**
• pin-ups; Introduction by Neil Gaiman **A:** Dave McKean; Bill Sienkiewicz; Rebecca Guay; Ted McKeever; Howard Chaykin; George Pratt; Richard Case; Mike Allred; Michael T. Gilbert; Christian Alamy; Peter Kuper; Al Davison; Greg Capullo; Mark Chiarello; Shary Flenniken; Rick Berry; Thom Ang

ENEMY — Dark Horse

1 ❑ May 1994 Cover: 2.50 **NM** value: **Cover or less**
Circ: CapCity orders: **6,725**
2 ❑ Jun 1994 Cover: 2.50 **NM** value: **Cover or less**
Circ: CapCity orders: **3,525**
3 ❑ Jul 1994 Cover: 2.50 **NM** value: **Cover or less**
Circ: CapCity orders: **3,125**
4 ❑ Aug 1994 Cover: 2.50 **NM** value: **Cover or less**
Circ: CapCity orders: **3,125**
5 ❑ Sep 1994 Cover: 2.50 **NM** value: **Cover or less**
Circ: CapCity orders: **2,700**

ENEMY ACE SPECIAL — DC

Rittmeister Hans Von Hammer, "The Hammer of Hell," first appeared in Our Army At War #151. After follow-ups in later issues of that title and in Showcase #57 and 58, he began his run as a regular feature in Star Spangled War Stories with #138. Aside from being a remarkably popular character, Enemy Ace was unique in that he showed the war from the enemy's point of view — a first for an American war series.

Enemy Ace Special reprints Von Hammer's first appearances from Our Army At War #151 and #153. It shows him not only as a brilliant warrior, but also as a man of great honor. For him, the sky is the real enemy — one that eventually will claim both him and his foes.

1 ❑ Oct 1990 Cover: 1.00 **NM** value: **3.00**
Circ: CapCity orders: **8,600**
• reprints Showcase and Our Army at War **A:** Joe Kubert

ENEMY ACE: WAR IDYLL — DC

1 ❑ ca. 1990 Cover: 4.95 **NM** value: **Cover or less**
No issue number. • prestige format. **A:** George Pratt
Bk 1❑ Cover: 14.95 **NM** value: **Cover or less**
Circ: CapCity orders: **2,000**
Bk 1/HC❑ Sep 1990 Cover: 24.95 **NM** value: **Cover or less**
Circ: CapCity orders: **7,060**
hardcover. **A:** George Pratt

ENEMY ACE: WAR IN HEAVEN — DC

1 ❑ Cover: 5.95 **NM** value: **Cover or less**
Circ: Diamd. preorders: **21,421**
2 ❑ Cover: 5.95 **NM** value: **Cover or less**
Circ: Diamd. preorders: **19,992**

ENFORCE — Reoccurring Images

1 ❑ Cover: 2.95 **NM** value: **Cover or less**

ENIGMA — DC / Vertigo

1 ❑ Mar 1993 Cover: 2.50 **NM** value: **Cover or less**
Circ: CapCity orders: **39,200**
2 ❑ Apr 1993 Cover: 2.50 **NM** value: **Cover or less**
Circ: CapCity orders: **23,350**
3 ❑ May 1993 Cover: 2.50 **NM** value: **Cover or less**
Circ: CapCity orders: **20,450**
4 ❑ Jun 1993 Cover: 2.50 **NM** value: **Cover or less**
Circ: CapCity orders: **18,000**
5 ❑ Jul 1993 Cover: 2.50 **NM** value: **Cover or less**
Circ: CapCity orders: **17,100**
6 ❑ Aug 1993 Cover: 2.50 **NM** value: **Cover or less**
Circ: CapCity orders: **16,950**
7 ❑ Sep 1993 Cover: 2.50 **NM** value: **Cover or less**
Circ: CapCity orders: **13,900**
📖 Sex in Arizona **A:** Duncan Fegredo **W:** Peter Milligan
8 ❑ Oct 1993 Cover: 2.50 **NM** value: **Cover or less**
Circ: CapCity orders: **12,900**
Bk 1❑ Cover: 19.95 **NM** value: **Cover or less**
• collects mini-series; Collects Enigma #1-8 **A:** Duncan Fegredo **W:** Peter Milligan

ENIGMA! (HECTOR TELLEZ) — Hector Tellez

1 ❑ Cover: 0.50 **NM** value: **3.00**
📖 The Garden of Zarg!; The Big Sleep; Metamorph; The Most Secret Origin of the Seasons; Crypts of the Moon **A:** Hector Tellez; Larry Todd; R. T. Reece; Tom Gasparotti **W:** Hector Tellez; Larry Todd; R. T. Reece; Tom Gasparotti

ENO & PLUM — Oni Press

1 ❑ Mar 1998, b&w Cover: 2.95 **NM** value: **Cover or less**

ENTROPY TALES — Entropy

1 ❑ Cover: 1.50 **NM** value: **Cover or less**
📖 Star Fox: Sweet Sixteen; Night Wolf: IntroductionMighty Slug; **A:** Peter Krause; Timothy Fay **W:** Peter Krause; Timothy Fay
2 ❑ Cover: 1.50 **NM** value: **Cover or less**
3 ❑ Cover: 1.50 **NM** value: **Cover or less**
4 ❑ Cover: 1.50 **NM** value: **Cover or less**

ENTS — Manic Press

1 ❑ b&w Cover: 2.50 **NM** value: **Cover or less**
2 ❑ b&w Cover: 2.50 **NM** value: **Cover or less**
3 ❑ b&w Cover: 2.50 **NM** value: **Cover or less**

EO — Rebel

1 ❑ Cover: 3.00 **NM** value: **Cover or less**
1/LE❑ Cover: 5.00 **NM** value: **Cover or less**
• Limited "Premier" edition,.
2 ❑ Cover: 3.00 **NM** value: **Cover or less**
2/LE❑ Cover: 3.00 **NM** value: **Cover or less**
• limited edition.
3 ❑ Cover: 3.00 **NM** value: **Cover or less**
4 ❑ Cover: 3.00 **NM** value: **Cover or less**

EPIC — Marvel / Epic

1 ❑ Cover: 4.95 **NM** value: **5.00**
Circ: CapCity orders: **6,750**

For up-to-the-week CGC ratios, consult the current issue of **Comics Buyer's Guide.**

📖 Hellraiser: Birth Rite; Stalkers: The Terrorist, Part 1; Dreadlands; Wild Cards: Masks of the Red Death **A:** Mike Collins; William Simpson; Kev Hopgood; Andy Lanning; Phil Gascoine; D'Israeli **W:** Andy Lanning; Mark Verheiden; Steve White; D.G. Chichester; Lewis Shiner; Walter John Williams
2 ❑ Cover: 4.95 **NM** value: **5.00**
Circ: CapCity orders: **5,050**
3 ❑ Cover: 4.95 **NM** value: **5.00**
Circ: CapCity orders: **4,750**
4 ❑ Cover: 4.95 **NM** value: **5.00**
Circ: CapCity orders: **4,150**

EPIC GRAPHIC NOVEL: SOMEPLACE STRANGE — Marvel / Epic

1 ❑ Cover: 6.95 **NM** value: **Cover or less**

EPIC GRAPHIC NOVEL: THE DEATH OF GROO — Marvel / Epic

1 ❑ Cover: 9.95 **NM** value: **Cover or less**
Circ: CapCity orders: **9,250**
1-2 ❑ Cover: 9.95 **NM** value: **Cover or less**
1-3 ❑ Cover: 9.95 **NM** value: **Cover or less**

EPIC ILLUSTRATED — Marvel / Epic

By the late 1970s, Marvel had begun to adventure into alternate types of publications and comics. It began by introducing a number of more adult-oriented comics in magazine format, including Marvel Preview and Savage Sword of Conan. They were followed, in 1980, by Epic Illustrated, a beautifully drawn magazine of fantasy and science-fiction stories. The success of Epic Illustrated led Marvel to pursue the adult comics idea in Epic, a new line of comics which included Dreadstar, Six From Sirius, The Sisterhood of Steel, and countless others.

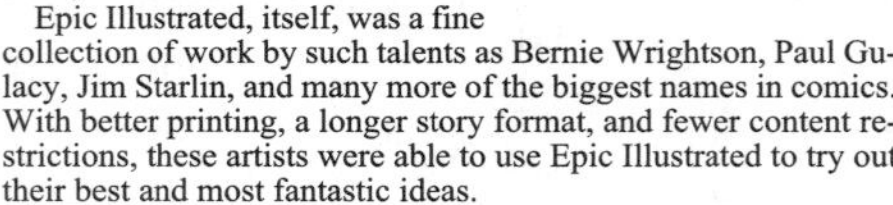

Epic Illustrated, itself, was a fine collection of work by such talents as Bernie Wrightson, Paul Gulacy, Jim Starlin, and many more of the biggest names in comics. With better printing, a longer story format, and fewer content restrictions, these artists were able to use Epic Illustrated to try out their best and most fantastic ideas.

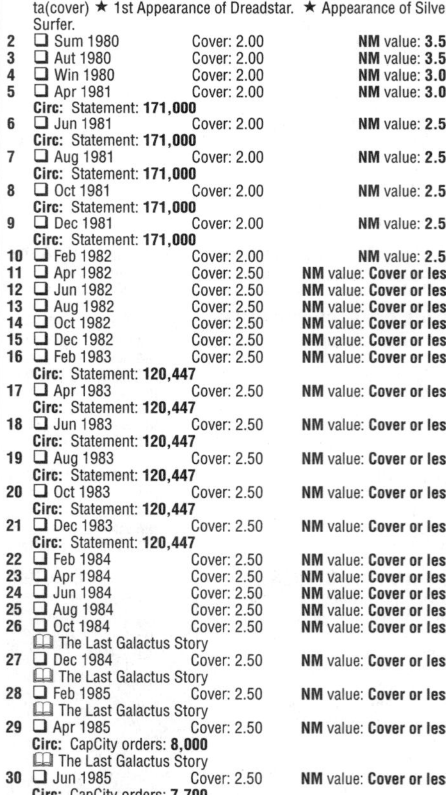

1 ❑ Spr 1980 Cover: 2.00 **NM** value: **5.00**
📖 The Answer; Home Spun; Aware; For the Next Sixty Seconds; Metamorphosis Odyssey: Aknaton; Lullaby of Bedlam; Elfspire; Fantasies; Convert; Heads; Za; Juliet; Detour; Topaz; Endgame **A:** Carl Potts; Wendy Pini; Jim Starlin; Rick Veitch; Ernie Colon; Frank Frazetta(cover) ★ 1st Appearance of Dreadstar. ★ Appearance of Silver Surfer.
2 ❑ Sum 1980 Cover: 2.00 **NM** value: **3.50**
3 ❑ Aut 1980 Cover: 2.00 **NM** value: **3.50**
4 ❑ Win 1980 Cover: 2.00 **NM** value: **3.00**
5 ❑ Apr 1981 Cover: 2.00 **NM** value: **3.00**
Circ: Statement: **171,000**
6 ❑ Jun 1981 Cover: 2.00 **NM** value: **2.50**
Circ: Statement: **171,000**
7 ❑ Aug 1981 Cover: 2.00 **NM** value: **2.50**
Circ: Statement: **171,000**
8 ❑ Oct 1981 Cover: 2.00 **NM** value: **2.50**
Circ: Statement: **171,000**
9 ❑ Dec 1981 Cover: 2.00 **NM** value: **2.50**
Circ: Statement: **171,000**
10 ❑ Feb 1982 Cover: 2.00 **NM** value: **2.50**
11 ❑ Apr 1982 Cover: 2.50 **NM** value: **Cover or less**
12 ❑ Jun 1982 Cover: 2.50 **NM** value: **Cover or less**
13 ❑ Aug 1982 Cover: 2.50 **NM** value: **Cover or less**
14 ❑ Oct 1982 Cover: 2.50 **NM** value: **Cover or less**
15 ❑ Dec 1982 Cover: 2.50 **NM** value: **Cover or less**
16 ❑ Feb 1983 Cover: 2.50 **NM** value: **Cover or less**
Circ: Statement: **120,447**
17 ❑ Apr 1983 Cover: 2.50 **NM** value: **Cover or less**
Circ: Statement: **120,447**
18 ❑ Jun 1983 Cover: 2.50 **NM** value: **Cover or less**
Circ: Statement: **120,447**
19 ❑ Aug 1983 Cover: 2.50 **NM** value: **Cover or less**
Circ: Statement: **120,447**
20 ❑ Oct 1983 Cover: 2.50 **NM** value: **Cover or less**
Circ: Statement: **120,447**
21 ❑ Dec 1983 Cover: 2.50 **NM** value: **Cover or less**
Circ: Statement: **120,447**
22 ❑ Feb 1984 Cover: 2.50 **NM** value: **Cover or less**
23 ❑ Apr 1984 Cover: 2.50 **NM** value: **Cover or less**
24 ❑ Jun 1984 Cover: 2.50 **NM** value: **Cover or less**
25 ❑ Aug 1984 Cover: 2.50 **NM** value: **Cover or less**
26 ❑ Oct 1984 Cover: 2.50 **NM** value: **Cover or less**
📖 The Last Galactus Story
27 ❑ Dec 1984 Cover: 2.50 **NM** value: **Cover or less**
📖 The Last Galactus Story
28 ❑ Feb 1985 Cover: 2.50 **NM** value: **Cover or less**
📖 The Last Galactus Story
29 ❑ Apr 1985 Cover: 2.50 **NM** value: **Cover or less**
Circ: CapCity orders: **8,000**
📖 The Last Galactus Story
30 ❑ Jun 1985 Cover: 2.50 **NM** value: **Cover or less**
Circ: CapCity orders: **7,700**
📖 The Last Galactus Story
31 ❑ Aug 1985 Cover: 2.50 **NM** value: **Cover or less**
Circ: CapCity orders: **6,900**
📖 The Last Galactus Story
32 ❑ Oct 1985 Cover: 2.50 **NM** value: **Cover or less**
Circ: CapCity orders: **6,450**
📖 The Last Galactus Story

Other grades: Multiply prices above by **1.5 for Mint • 2/3 for Very Fine • 1/3 for Fine • 1/5 for Very Good • 1/8 for Good**

33 ❑ Dec 1985 Cover: 2.50 **NM** value: **Cover or less**
Circ: CapCity orders: **5,750**
📖 The Last Galactus Story

34 ❑ Feb 1986 Cover: 2.50 **NM** value: **Cover or less**
Circ: CapCity orders: **5,750**
📖 The Last Galactus Story final issue.

EPIC LITE — Marvel / Epic

1 ❑ Sep 1991 Cover: 3.95 **NM** value: **4.00**
Circ: CapCity orders: **3,100**

EPICURUS THE SAGE — DC / Piranha

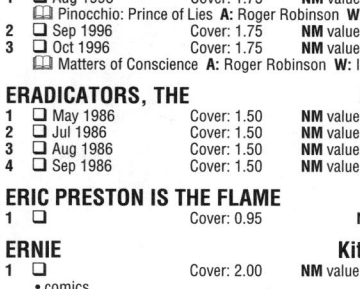

This wonderful title featured the writing of Journey writer-artist William Messner-Loebs and art of Sam Keith and starred the Greek philosopher (c. 340-c.270 B.C.) who really was tutor to Alexander the Great (356-323 B.C.), in addition to founding the Epicurean School of thought. Little survives of Epicurus' work (three letters and 40 maxims), but he basically taught that freedom from pain is the highest good and that it was most simple to get harmony of mind and body by virtue and simple living.

Messner-Loebs took those facts and constructed intellectual comedy. Alexander is a spoiled, hostile brat and Epicurus is depicted faithfully, insofar as anything is known of the philosopher: an incredible comics achievement. — Maggie

1 ❑ ca. 1991, full color Cover: 9.95 **NM** value: **Cover or less**
Circ: CapCity orders: **2,650**
📖 Visiting Hades **A:** Sam Keith **W:** William Messner-Loebs

2 ❑ ca. 1991, full color Cover: 9.95 **NM** value: **Cover or less**
Circ: CapCity orders: **2,750**
📖 The Many Loves of Zeus **A:** Sam Keith **W:** William Messner-Loebs

EPILEPTIC ENGINE — Epileptic Engine

1 ❑ **NM** value: **2.95**
2 ❑ **NM** value: **2.95**

EPISODE GUIDES, THE — Celebrity

1 ❑ Cover: 5.95 **NM** value: **Cover or less**
• index to Star Trek

EPSILON WAVE, THE — Independent

1 ❑ Oct 1985 Cover: 1.50 **NM** value: **Cover or less**
Circ: CapCity orders: **2,475**
• Independent Comics publishes★ Origin of Nightmare (super-hero). ★ 1st Appearance of Nightmare (super-hero).

2 ❑ Dec 1985 Cover: 1.50 **NM** value: **Cover or less**
Circ: CapCity orders: **1,977**

3 ❑ Feb 1986 Cover: 1.50 **NM** value: **Cover or less**
Circ: CapCity orders: **1,775**
📖 One Step Closer Toward Darkness

4 ❑ Apr 1986 Cover: 1.50 **NM** value: **Cover or less**
Circ: CapCity orders: **1,475**

5 ❑ May 1986 Cover: 1.75 **NM** value: **Cover or less**
Circ: CapCity orders: **1,410**
• Elite begins as publisher

6 ❑ Jun 1986 Cover: 1.75 **NM** value: **Cover or less**
Circ: CapCity orders: **1,550**

7 ❑ Aug 1986 Cover: 1.75 **NM** value: **Cover or less**
Circ: CapCity orders: **1,650**

8 ❑ 1986 Cover: 1.75 **NM** value: **Cover or less**
Circ: CapCity orders: **1,700**

EQUINE THE UNCIVILIZED — Graphxpress

1 ❑ b&w Cover: 2.00 **NM** value: **Cover or less**
2 ❑ Cover: 2.00 **NM** value: **Cover or less**
3 ❑ Cover: 2.00 **NM** value: **Cover or less**
4 ❑ Cover: 2.00 **NM** value: **Cover or less**
5 ❑ Cover: 2.00 **NM** value: **Cover or less**
6 ❑ Cover: 2.00 **NM** value: **Cover or less**

EQUINOX CHRONICLES — Innovation

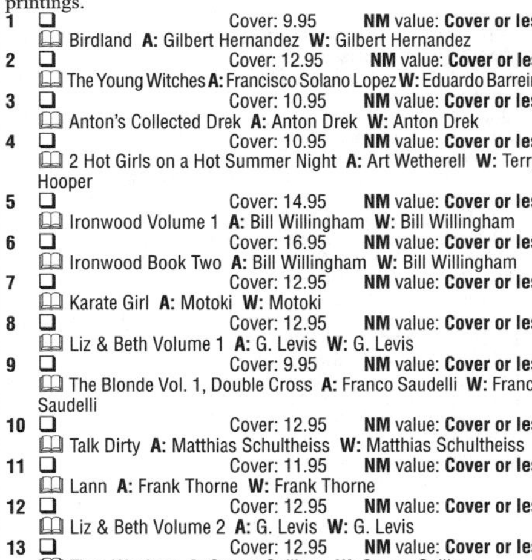

When Shannon Mallory, an employee of the influential corporation the Equinox Research Group (ERG), is kidnapped by the terrorist Black Avatar and her invention the Electron Laser Accelerator is stolen, the very fate of the world hangs in the balance. Now, Mallory's fellow members of Team Equinox must risk their lives to save Mallory and recapture the Accelerator, which was never meant to be used as a weapon. Meanwhile, Black Avatar hopes to use his new acquisition to bring about world peace by destroying the nuclear capabilities of various super-power nations, thereby bringing freedom to the people. But can true peace be achieved at the hands of a madman?

This story is written by Jeff Hendricks with art by Mark Jones, who also drew Quantum Leap and Lost in Space for Innovation.

1 ❑ b&w Cover: 2.25 **NM** value: **Cover or less**
2 ❑ b&w Cover: 2.25 **NM** value: **Cover or less**
📖 The Road to Apocalypse **A:** Mark Jones **W:** Jeff Hendricks

ERADICATOR — DC

1 ❑ Aug 1996 Cover: 1.75 **NM** value: **Cover or less**
📖 Pinocchio: Prince of Lies **A:** Roger Robinson **W:** Ivan Velez Jr.
2 ❑ Sep 1996 Cover: 1.75 **NM** value: **Cover or less**
3 ❑ Oct 1996 Cover: 1.75 **NM** value: **Cover or less**
📖 Matters of Conscience **A:** Roger Robinson **W:** Ivan Velez Jr.

ERADICATORS, THE — Silverwolf

1 ❑ May 1986 Cover: 1.50 **NM** value: **Cover or less**
2 ❑ Jul 1986 Cover: 1.50 **NM** value: **Cover or less**
3 ❑ Aug 1986 Cover: 1.50 **NM** value: **Cover or less**
4 ❑ Sep 1986 Cover: 1.50 **NM** value: **Cover or less**

ERIC PRESTON IS THE FLAME — B-Movie

1 ❑ Cover: 0.95 **NM** value: **1.00**

ERNIE — Kitchen Sink

1 ❑ Cover: 2.00 **NM** value: **Cover or less**
• comics

ERNIE COMICS — Current

22 ❑ Sep 1948 Cover: 0.10 **NM** value: **40.00**
23 ❑ Nov 1948 Cover: 0.10 **NM** value: **40.00**
24 ❑ Jan 1949 Cover: 0.10 **NM** value: **25.00**
25 ❑ Mar 1949 Cover: 0.10 **NM** value: **25.00**

EROS FORUM — Fantagraphics / Eros

All issues are adults only.

1 ❑ b&w Cover: 2.50 **NM** value: **Cover or less**
3 ❑ b&w Cover: 2.95 **NM** value: **Cover or less**

EROS GRAPHIC ALBUM — Fantagraphics / Eros

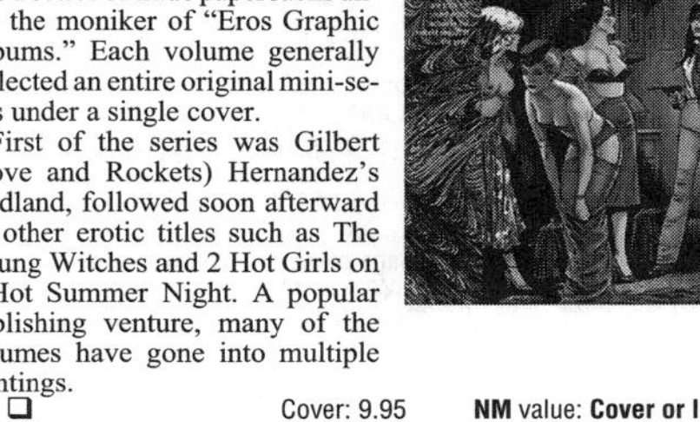

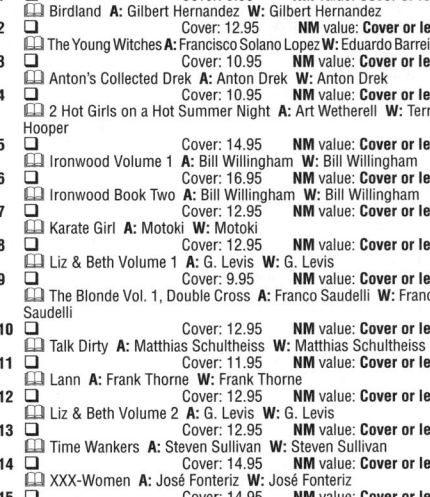

Fantagraphics' Eros division is one of the most prolific and varied publishers of adult comics. In 1993, it began to collect its "greatest hits" into a series of trade paperbacks under the moniker of "Eros Graphic Albums." Each volume generally collected an entire original mini-series under a single cover.

First of the series was Gilbert (Love and Rockets) Hernandez's Birdland, followed soon afterward by other erotic titles such as The Young Witches and 2 Hot Girls on a Hot Summer Night. A popular publishing venture, many of the volumes have gone into multiple printings.

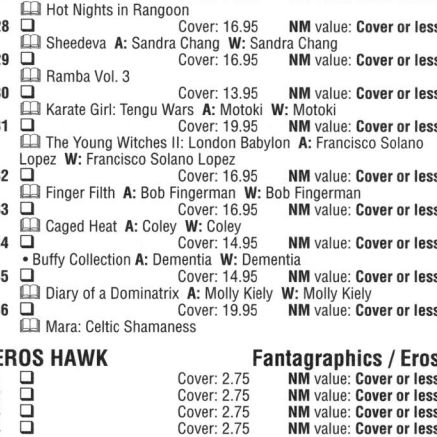

1 ❑ Cover: 9.95 **NM** value: **Cover or less**
📖 Birdland **A:** Gilbert Hernandez **W:** Gilbert Hernandez
2 ❑ Cover: 12.95 **NM** value: **Cover or less**
📖 The Young Witches **A:** Francisco Solano Lopez **W:** Eduardo Barreiro
3 ❑ Cover: 10.95 **NM** value: **Cover or less**
📖 Anton's Collected Drek **A:** Anton Drek **W:** Anton Drek
4 ❑ Cover: 10.95 **NM** value: **Cover or less**
📖 2 Hot Girls on a Hot Summer Night **A:** Art Wetherell **W:** Terry Hooper
5 ❑ Cover: 14.95 **NM** value: **Cover or less**
📖 Ironwood Volume 1 **A:** Bill Willingham **W:** Bill Willingham
6 ❑ Cover: 16.95 **NM** value: **Cover or less**
📖 Ironwood Book Two **A:** Bill Willingham **W:** Bill Willingham
7 ❑ Cover: 12.95 **NM** value: **Cover or less**
📖 Karate Girl **A:** Motoki **W:** Motoki
8 ❑ Cover: 12.95 **NM** value: **Cover or less**
📖 Liz & Beth Volume 1 **A:** G. Levis **W:** G. Levis
9 ❑ Cover: 9.95 **NM** value: **Cover or less**
📖 The Blonde Vol. 1, Double Cross **A:** Franco Saudelli **W:** Franco Saudelli
10 ❑ Cover: 12.95 **NM** value: **Cover or less**
📖 Talk Dirty **A:** Matthias Schultheiss **W:** Matthias Schultheiss
11 ❑ Cover: 11.95 **NM** value: **Cover or less**
📖 Lann **A:** Frank Thorne **W:** Frank Thorne
12 ❑ Cover: 12.95 **NM** value: **Cover or less**
📖 Liz & Beth Volume 2 **A:** G. Levis **W:** G. Levis
13 ❑ Cover: 12.95 **NM** value: **Cover or less**
📖 Time Wankers **A:** Steven Sullivan **W:** Steven Sullivan
14 ❑ Cover: 14.95 **NM** value: **Cover or less**
📖 XXX-Women **A:** José Fonteriz **W:** José Fonteriz
15 ❑ Cover: 14.95 **NM** value: **Cover or less**
📖 Ramba
16 ❑ Cover: 14.95 **NM** value: **Cover or less**
📖 Coley Running Wild **A:** Coley **W:** Coley
17 ❑ Cover: 15.95 **NM** value: **Cover or less**
📖 Mara of the Celts **A:** Val Mayerik; Frank Thorne; Dennis Cramer; P. Craig Russell; John Workman **W:** Dennis Cramer
18 ❑ Cover: 12.95 **NM** value: **Cover or less**
📖 The Blonde Vol. 2, Bondage Palace **A:** Franco Saudelli **W:** Franco Saudelli
19 ❑ Cover: 14.95 **NM** value: **Cover or less**
📖 Domino Lady **A:** Ron Wilber **W:** Ron Wilber
20 ❑ Cover: 12.95 **NM** value: **Cover or less**
📖 Liz & Beth Vol. 3 **A:** G. Levis **W:** G. Levis
21 ❑ Cover: 14.95 **NM** value: **Cover or less**
📖 The Iron Devil **A:** Frank Thorne **W:** Frank Thorne
22 ❑ Cover: 14.95 **NM** value: **Cover or less**
📖 Ramba Vol. 2
23 ❑ Cover: 12.95 **NM** value: **Cover or less**
📖 City of Dreams **A:** Brian Tarsis **W:** Brian Tarsis
24 ❑ Cover: 12.95 **NM** value: **Cover or less**
📖 The Blonde: Phoebus III **A:** Franco Saudelli **W:** Franco Saudelli
25 ❑ Cover: 16.95 **NM** value: **Cover or less**
📖 I Want to be your Dog **A:** Ho Che Anderson **W:** Ho Che Anderson
26 ❑ Cover: 13.95 **NM** value: **Cover or less**
📖 Beta Sexus
27 ❑ Cover: 11.95 **NM** value: **Cover or less**
📖 Hot Nights in Rangoon
28 ❑ Cover: 16.95 **NM** value: **Cover or less**
📖 Sheedeva **A:** Sandra Chang **W:** Sandra Chang
29 ❑ Cover: 16.95 **NM** value: **Cover or less**
📖 Ramba Vol. 3
30 ❑ Cover: 13.95 **NM** value: **Cover or less**
📖 Karate Girl: Tengu Wars **A:** Motoki **W:** Motoki
31 ❑ Cover: 19.95 **NM** value: **Cover or less**
📖 The Young Witches II: London Babylon **A:** Francisco Solano Lopez **W:** Francisco Solano Lopez
32 ❑ Cover: 16.95 **NM** value: **Cover or less**
📖 Finger Filth **A:** Bob Fingerman **W:** Bob Fingerman
33 ❑ Cover: 16.95 **NM** value: **Cover or less**
📖 Caged Heat **A:** Coley **W:** Coley
34 ❑ Cover: 14.95 **NM** value: **Cover or less**
• Buffy Collection **A:** Dementia **W:** Dementia
35 ❑ Cover: 14.95 **NM** value: **Cover or less**
📖 Diary of a Dominatrix **A:** Molly Kiely **W:** Molly Kiely
36 ❑ Cover: 19.95 **NM** value: **Cover or less**
📖 Mara: Celtic Shamaness

EROS HAWK — Fantagraphics / Eros

1 ❑ Cover: 2.75 **NM** value: **Cover or less**
2 ❑ Cover: 2.75 **NM** value: **Cover or less**
3 ❑ Cover: 2.75 **NM** value: **Cover or less**
4 ❑ Cover: 2.75 **NM** value: **Cover or less**

EROS HAWK III — Fantagraphics / Eros

1 ❑ Jul 1994, b&w Cover: 2.75 **NM** value: **Cover or less**

EROTICA (VAUGHN BODÉ'S...) — Fantagraphics

All issues are adults only.

Bk 1❑ Cover: 12.95 **NM** value: **Cover or less**
• reprints stories from Cavalier magazine.
Bk 2❑ May 1997 Cover: 12.95 **NM** value: **Cover or less**
• reprints stories from Cavalier magazine.
Bk 3❑ May 1997 Cover: 12.95 **NM** value: **Cover or less**
• reprints stories from Cavalier magazine.

EROTIC FABLES & FAERIE TALES — Fantagraphics / Eros

All issues are adults only.

1 ❑ b&w Cover: 2.50 **NM** value: **Cover or less**
2 ❑ b&w Cover: 2.50 **NM** value: **Cover or less**

EROTICOM — Caliber

1 ❑ Cover: 2.50 **NM** value: **Cover or less**

EROTICOM II — Caliber

1 ❑ ca. 1994, b&w Cover: 2.95 **NM** value: **Cover or less**
• pin-ups

EROTIC ORBITS — Comax

All issues are adults only.

1 ❑ b&w Cover: 2.95 **NM** value: **Cover or less**

EROTIC TALES — Aircel

All issues are adults only.

1 ❑ b&w Cover: 2.95 **NM** value: **Cover or less**
2 ❑ b&w Cover: 2.95 **NM** value: **Cover or less**
3 ❑ b&w Cover: 2.95 **NM** value: **Cover or less**

EROTIC WORLDS OF FRANK THORNE, THE — Fantagraphics / Eros

All issues are adults only.

1 ❑ Oct 1990 Cover: 2.95 **NM** value: **Cover or less**
sexy cover. 📖 The Deathman's Head; The Wizard and The Woman **A:** Frank Thorne **W:** Frank Thorne
1/A ❑ Oct 1990 Cover: 2.95 **NM** value: **Cover or less**
Violent cover. 📖 The Deathman's Head; The Wizard and The Woman **A:** Frank Thorne **W:** Frank Thorne
2 ❑ Cover: 2.50 **NM** value: **2.95**
3 ❑ Cover: 2.50 **NM** value: **2.95**
4 ❑ Cover: 2.50 **NM** value: **2.95**
5 ❑ Cover: 2.50 **NM** value: **2.95**
6 ❑ Cover: 2.50 **NM** value: **2.95**

EROTIQUE — Aircel

All issues are adults only.

1 ❑ b&w Cover: 2.50 **NM** value: **Cover or less**

ERSATZ PEACH, THE — Aeon

1 ❑ Jul 1995 Cover: 7.95 **NM** value: **Cover or less**
No issue number. • see also The Desert Peach; Charity fund-raiser; Desert Peach stories by various artists and writers

ERT! — Caliber

Matt Feazell's minimalist cartoon masterpiece Cynicalman returns in this diminutive compilation of mini-comics. Ert! (the sound of a vehicle stopping suddenly) collects many of Feazell's one-page sketchbook comics, as well as the previously published adventures of Cynicalman, Antisocialman, Cute Girl, Captain Videotape, and even the dreaded Stupid Boy.

Feazell draws most of the episodes in a deliberate, stick figure style. This is not a reflection of his artistic abilities (Ert! also features pages drawn in a more conventional style from time to time). Instead, the

CGC-graded: Multiply prices above by **33 for 9.9 M • 16 for 9.8 NM/M • 7 for 9.6 NM+ • 5 for 9.4 NM • 2.5 for 9.2 NM- • 1.5 for 9.0 VF/NM**

stick figure renderings get right to the heart of the stories-and the stories can be terribly funny, reflecting Feazell's alternately manic and blase outlook on life. Wonderful stuff.

1 ❑ Cover: 12.95 **NM** value: **Cover or less**

ESC — Comico

1 ❑ 1996 Cover: 2.95 **NM** value: **Cover or less**
🕮 Zaminidar, Part 1 **A:** Marc Caribé **W:** Stefan Petrucha

2 ❑ Sep 1996 Cover: 2.95 **NM** value: **Cover or less**
🕮 Zaminidar, Part 2 **A:** Marc Caribé **W:** Stefan Petrucha

3 ❑ 1996 Cover: 2.95 **NM** value: **Cover or less**
Circ: Diamd. preorders: **3,027**
🕮 Zaminidar, Part 3 **A:** Marc Caribé **W:** Stefan Petrucha

4 ❑ 1997 Cover: 2.95 **NM** value: **Cover or less**
🕮 Zaminidar, Part 4 **A:** Marc Caribé **W:** Stefan Petrucha

Bk 1 ❑ 1997 Cover: 14.95 **NM** value: **Cover or less**
🕮 Zaminidar • Collects Esc 1-4 **A:** Marc Caribé **W:** Stefan Petrucha

ESCAPADE IN FLORENCE — Gold Key

1 ❑ Jan 1963 **NM** value: **75.00**
• **CGC:** 2 graded, best 9.4

ESCAPE FROM FEAR — Planned Parenthood

1 ❑ ca. 1962 **NM** value: **75.00**
• **CGC:** 1 graded, best 9.6

ESCAPE FROM THE PLANET OF THE APES — Adventure

Bk 1 ❑ Cover: 9.95 **NM** value: **10.00**

ESCAPE TO THE STARS — Solson

1 ❑ Cover: 1.75 **NM** value: **Cover or less**
🕮 Cul-de-Sac **A:** Rich Buckler; Chuck Wojtkiewicz

ESCAPE VELOCITY — Escape Velocity

1 ❑ Cover: 1.50 **NM** value: **Cover or less**

2 ❑ Cover: 1.50 **NM** value: **Cover or less**

ESPERS — Eclipse

1 ❑ Jul 1986 Cover: 1.25 **NM** value: **2.50**
Circ: CapCity orders: **9,725**

2 ❑ Sep 1986 Cover: 1.25 **NM** value: **2.00**
Circ: CapCity orders: **7,150**

3 ❑ Nov 1986 Cover: 1.25 **NM** value: **2.00**
Circ: CapCity orders: **6,450**
🕮 Thunderhead **A:** David Lloyd; Brian Bolland(cover) **W:** James D. Hudnall

4 ❑ Feb 1987 Cover: 1.25 **NM** value: **2.00**
Circ: CapCity orders: **4,800**

5 ❑ Apr 1987 Cover: 1.75 **NM** value: **2.00**
Circ: CapCity orders: **4,800**
🕮 The Liquidators • Story continued in Interface #1 **A:** John Burns **W:** James D. Hudnall

Bk 1 ❑ Cover: 16.95 **NM** value: **Cover or less**
🕮 Interface • Interface, b&w

Bk 2 ❑ Oct 1990 Cover: 9.95 **NM** value: **Cover or less**

ESPERS (VOL. 2) — Halloween

1 ❑ 1996b&w Cover: 2.95 **NM** value: **3.00**

2 ❑ 1996b&w Cover: 2.95 **NM** value: **3.00**
🕮 Paradigm Shift **A:** Greg Horn **W:** James D. Hudnall

3 ❑ 1997b&w Cover: 2.95 **NM** value: **3.00**
Circ: Diamd. preorders: **8,140**

4 ❑ 1997b&w Cover: 2.95 **NM** value: **3.00**
Circ: Diamd. preorders: **6,432**

5 ❑ 1997b&w Cover: 2.95 **NM** value: **3.00**
Circ: Diamd. preorders: **5,384**

6 ❑ 1997 Cover: 2.95 **NM** value: **3.00**
🕮 Revelations **A:** Greg Horn **W:** James D. Hudnall

ESPERS (VOL. 3) — Image

1 ❑ 1997b&w Cover: 2.95 **NM** value: **3.50**
Circ: Diamd. preorders: **15,783**
🕮 Black Magic, Part 1 **A:** Greg Horn **W:** James D. Hudnall

2 ❑ 1997b&w Cover: 2.95 **NM** value: **3.00**
Circ: Diamd. preorders: **9,481**
🕮 Black Magic, Part 2 **A:** Greg Horn **W:** James D. Hudnall

3 ❑ Aug 1997, b&w Cover: 2.95 **NM** value: **3.00**
🕮 Black Magic, Part 3 **A:** Greg Horn **W:** James D. Hudnall

4 ❑ 1997b&w Cover: 2.95 **NM** value: **3.00**
🕮 Black Magic, Part 4 **A:** Greg Horn **W:** James D. Hudnall

5 ❑ 1997b&w Cover: 2.95 **NM** value: **3.00**
🕮 The Bad Joe **A:** Greg Horn **W:** James D. Hudnall

6 ❑ 1997b&w Cover: 2.95 **NM** value: **3.00**
Circ: Diamd. preorders: **4,504**
🕮 Cold Comforts **A:** Greg Horn **W:** James D. Hudnall

7 ❑ 1998b&w Cover: 2.95 **NM** value: **3.00**
Circ: Diamd. preorders: **3,678**
🕮 Down Rio Way **A:** Gene Gonzales **W:** James D. Hudnall

8 ❑ 1998 Cover: 2.95 **NM** value: **3.00**
Circ: Diamd. preorders: **3,238**

9 ❑ Cover: 2.95 **NM** value: **3.00**
Circ: Diamd. preorders: **3,099**

Bk 1 ❑ b&w Cover: 14.95 **NM** value: **Cover or less**
🕮 Black Magic • Black Magic; Collects issues #1-4 **A:** Greg Horn **W:** James D. Hudnall

The prices seen above do not represent the highest possible prices seen in online auctions, but rather the prices we have seen these issues reliably fetch in a variety of environments (storefront retail, mail order, auction and convention).

ESPIONAGE — Dell

Based on a popular early 1960s spy television show, Espionage depicts the adventures of operatives who worked behind the lines during World War II.

Stories feature such characters as the Chameleon, a British master of disguise who helped the French resistance by impersonating a Gestapo Colonel; a Japanese-American who bravely worked against the Japanese as a secret agent in the Pacific; and a Lawrence-of-Arabia-type partisan who helped turn the tide in North Africa.

The exciting adventures in Espionage are tightly written and rendered in a lean, minimalist style by the anonymous Dell creators.

1 ❑ Cover: 0.12 **NM** value: **16.50**
• **CGC:** 1 graded, best 9.6
🕮 The Chameleon; Small Spy-Big Explosion; Cloak and Kris

2 ❑ Cover: 0.12 **NM** value: **14.00**

ESSENTIAL ELFQUEST, THE — Warp

1 ❑ Apr 1995 **NM** value: **1.50**
No issue number. • giveaway. 🕮 Blood of Ten Chiefs; Shard; Hidden Years; New Blood; Jink; The Rebels • Free Preview **A:** Barry Blair; Delfin Barral; Dennis Fujitake; Al Nickerson; Steve Blevins; Brandon Mc Kinney; Charles Barnett **W:** Wendy Pini; Barry Blair; Bern Harkins; Joellyn Auklandus; John Ostrander; Richard Pini; Terry Collin

ESSENTIAL INCREDIBLE HULK — Marvel

Bk 1 ❑ Cover: 14.95 **NM** value: **Cover or less**
• Reprints Tales to Astonish #60-91 and Hulk #1-6 **A:** Steve Ditko; John Buscema; Jack Kirby; Gil Kane; John Romita Sr. **W:** Stan Lee

ESSENTIAL VERTIGO: SWAMP THING — DC / Vertigo

1 ❑ Nov 1996 Cover: 1.95 **NM** value: **2.50**
Circ: Diamd. preorders: **14,438**
• Reprints Saga of the Swamp Thing #21 **A:** John Totleben; Stephen Bissette **W:** Alan Moore

2 ❑ Dec 1996 Cover: 1.95 **NM** value: **2.00**
Circ: Diamd. preorders: **11,608**
🕮 Swamped • Reprints Saga of the Swamp Thing #22 **A:** John Totleben; Stephen Bissette **W:** Alan Moore

3 ❑ Jan 1997 Cover: 1.95 **NM** value: **2.00**
Circ: Diamd. preorders: **10,593**
• Reprints Saga of the Swamp Thing #23 **A:** John Totleben; Stephen Bissette **W:** Alan Moore

4 ❑ Feb 1997 Cover: 1.95 **NM** value: **2.00**
Circ: Diamd. preorders: **9,894**
• Reprints Saga of the Swamp Thing #24 **A:** John Totleben; Stephen Bissette **W:** Alan Moore

5 ❑ Mar 1997 Cover: 1.95 **NM** value: **2.00**
Circ: Diamd. preorders: **9,508**
🕮 The Sleep of Reason... • Reprints Saga of the Swamp Thing #25 **A:** John Totleben; Stephen Bissette **W:** Alan Moore

6 ❑ Apr 1997 Cover: 1.95 **NM** value: **2.00**
Circ: Diamd. preorders: **9,127**
• Reprints Saga of the Swamp Thing #26

7 ❑ May 1997 Cover: 1.95 **NM** value: **2.00**
Circ: Diamd. preorders: **8,794**
• Reprints Saga of the Swamp Thing #27

8 ❑ Jun 1997 Cover: 1.95 **NM** value: **2.00**
Circ: Diamd. preorders: **8,852**
• Reprints Saga of the Swamp Thing #28

9 ❑ Jul 1997 Cover: 1.95 **NM** value: **2.00**
Circ: Diamd. preorders: **7,768**
• Reprints Saga of the Swamp Thing #29

10 ❑ Aug 1997 Cover: 1.95 **NM** value: **2.00**
Circ: Diamd. preorders: **7,383**
• Reprints Saga of the Swamp Thing #30

11 ❑ Sep 1997 Cover: 1.95 **NM** value: **2.00**
Circ: Diamd. preorders: **6,964**
• Reprints Saga of the Swamp Thing #31

12 ❑ Oct 1997 Cover: 1.95 **NM** value: **2.00**
Circ: Diamd. preorders: **6,768**
• Reprints Saga of the Swamp Thing #32

13 ❑ Nov 1997 Cover: 1.95 **NM** value: **2.00**
Circ: Diamd. preorders: **6,763**
🕮 Pog • Reprints Saga of the Swamp Thing #33 **A:** Shawn McManus **W:** Alan Moore

14 ❑ Dec 1997 Cover: 1.95 **NM** value: **2.00**
Circ: Diamd. preorders: **6,465**
🕮 Abandoned Houses • Reprints Saga of the Swamp Thing #34 **A:** Ron Randall **W:** Alan Moore

15 ❑ Jan 1998 Cover: 1.95 **NM** value: **2.00**
Circ: Diamd. preorders: **6,384**
• Reprints Saga of the Swamp Thing #35

16 ❑ Feb 1998 Cover: 1.95 **NM** value: **2.00**
Circ: Diamd. preorders: **6,174**
• Reprints Saga of the Swamp Thing #36

17 ❑ Mar 1998 Cover: 1.95 **NM** value: **2.00**
Circ: Diamd. preorders: **5,927**
• Reprints Saga of the Swamp Thing #37

18 ❑ Apr 1998 Cover: 1.95 **NM** value: **2.00**
Circ: Diamd. preorders: **6,026**
• Reprints Saga of the Swamp Thing #38

19 ❑ May 1998 Cover: 1.95 **NM** value: **2.00**
Circ: Diamd. preorders: **5,855**
• Reprints Saga of the Swamp Thing #39

20 ❑ Jun 1998 Cover: 1.95 **NM** value: **2.00**
Circ: Diamd. preorders: **5,891**
• Reprints Saga of the Swamp Thing #40

21 ❑ Jul 1998 Cover: 1.95 **NM** value: **2.00**
Circ: Diamd. preorders: **5,621**
• Reprints Saga of the Swamp Thing #41

22 ❑ Aug 1998 Cover: 1.95 **NM** value: **2.00**
Circ: Diamd. preorders: **5,127**
• Reprints Saga of the Swamp Thing #42

23 ❑ Sep 1998 Cover: 2.25 **NM** value: **Cover or less**
Circ: Diamd. preorders: **5,116**
• Reprints Saga of the Swamp Thing #43

24 ❑ Oct 1998 Cover: 2.25 **NM** value: **Cover or less**
final issue.

ESSENTIAL VERTIGO: THE SANDMAN — DC / Vertigo

Reprinting the groundbreaking Sandman series from Neil Gaiman, Essential Vertigo: The Sandman provides readers unfamiliar with the award winning series an opportunity to catch it a second time around — much like a re-release of a famous movie.

The Sandman tells the story of the Lord of Dreams' return to power after being held captive by a human sorcerer for over half a century. After freeing himself from a 72-year imprisonment and discovering the deterioration of his realm, the Dreaming, Morpheus sets about recovering his tools of power-a pouch of sand, a sacred amulet and his helm of office. Not only does his quest take him to the seedy streets of mortal men, but it also drops him within the deepest recesses of hell itself.

1 ❑ Aug 1996 Cover: 1.95 **NM** value: **3.00**
🕮 Preludes & Nocturnes • Reprints Sandman #1 **A:** Sam Kieth; Mike Dringenberg **W:** Neil Gaiman

2 ❑ Sep 1996 Cover: 1.95 **NM** value: **2.50**
🕮 Preludes & Nocturnes • Reprints Sandman #2 **A:** Sam Kieth; Mike Dringenberg **W:** Neil Gaiman

3 ❑ Oct 1996 Cover: 1.95 **NM** value: **2.50**
🕮 Preludes & Nocturnes • Reprints Sandman #3 **A:** Sam Kieth; Mike Dringenberg **W:** Neil Gaiman

4 ❑ Oct 1996 Cover: 1.95 **NM** value: **2.50**
Circ: Diamd. preorders: **21,713**
🕮 Preludes & Nocturnes • Reprints Sandman #4 **A:** Sam Kieth; Mike Dringenberg **W:** Neil Gaiman

5 ❑ Dec 1996 Cover: 1.95 **NM** value: **2.50**
Circ: Diamd. preorders: **20,626**
🕮 Preludes & Nocturnes • Reprints Sandman #5 **A:** Sam Kieth; Malcolm Jones III **W:** Neil Gaiman

6 ❑ Jan 1997 Cover: 1.95 **NM** value: **2.00**
Circ: Diamd. preorders: **18,415**
🕮 Preludes & Nocturnes • Reprints Sandman #6 **A:** Malcolm Jones III; Mike Dringenberg **W:** Neil Gaiman

7 ❑ Feb 1997 Cover: 1.95 **NM** value: **2.00**
Circ: Diamd. preorders: **16,989**
• Reprints Sandman #7 **W:** Neil Gaiman

8 ❑ Mar 1997 Cover: 1.95 **NM** value: **2.00**
Circ: Diamd. preorders: **17,120**
🕮 The Sound of her Wings • Reprints Sandman #8 **A:** Malcolm Jones III; Mike Dringenberg **W:** Neil Gaiman ★ 1st Appearance of Death (Sandman).

9 ❑ Apr 1997 Cover: 1.95 **NM** value: **2.00**
Circ: Diamd. preorders: **14,901**
• Reprints Sandman #9 **W:** Neil Gaiman

10 ❑ May 1997 Cover: 1.95 **NM** value: **2.00**
Circ: Diamd. preorders: **14,514**
🕮 A Doll's House, Part 1 • Reprints Sandman #10 **W:** Neil Gaiman

11 ❑ Jun 1997 Cover: 1.95 **NM** value: **2.00**
Circ: Diamd. preorders: **14,069**
🕮 A Doll's House, Part 2 • Reprints Sandman #11 **W:** Neil Gaiman

12 ❑ Jul 1997 Cover: 1.95 **NM** value: **2.00**
Circ: Diamd. preorders: **12,613**
🕮 A Doll's House, Part 3 • Reprints Sandman #12 **W:** Neil Gaiman

13 ❑ Aug 1997 Cover: 1.95 **NM** value: **2.00**
Circ: Diamd. preorders: **11,966**
🕮 A Doll's House, Part 4 • Reprints Sandman #13 **W:** Neil Gaiman

14 ❑ Sep 1997 Cover: 1.95 **NM** value: **2.00**
Circ: Diamd. preorders: **11,231**
🕮 A Doll's House, Part 5 • Reprints Sandman #14 **W:** Neil Gaiman

15 ❑ Oct 1997 Cover: 1.95 **NM** value: **2.00**
Circ: Diamd. preorders: **10,797**
🕮 A Doll's House, Part 6 • Reprints Sandman #15 **W:** Neil Gaiman

16 ❑ Nov 1997 Cover: 1.95 **NM** value: **2.00**
Circ: Diamd. preorders: **10,413**
🕮 A Doll's House, Part 7 • Reprints Sandman #16 **A:** Malcolm Jones III; Mike Dringenberg **W:** Neil Gaiman

17 ❑ Dec 1997 Cover: 1.95 **NM** value: **2.00**
Circ: Diamd. preorders: **10,297**
🕮 Calliope • Reprints Sandman #17 **A:** Kelley Jones; Malcolm Jones III **W:** Neil Gaiman

18 ❑ Jan 1998 Cover: 1.95 **NM** value: **2.00**
Circ: Diamd. preorders: **9,898**
🕮 A Dream of a Thousand Cats • Reprints Sandman #18 **A:** Kelley Jones; Malcolm Jones III **W:** Neil Gaiman

19 ❑ Feb 1998 Cover: 1.95 **NM** value: **2.00**
Circ: Diamd. preorders: **9,906**
• Reprints Sandman #19 **W:** Neil Gaiman

20 ❑ Mar 1998 Cover: 1.95 **NM** value: **2.00**
Circ: Diamd. preorders: **9,080**
• Reprints Sandman #20 **W:** Neil Gaiman

21 ❑ Apr 1998 Cover: 1.95 **NM** value: **Cover or less**
Circ: Diamd. preorders: **8,506**

Other grades: Multiply prices above by **1.5 for Mint • 2/3 for Very Fine • 1/3 for Fine • 1/5 for Very Good • 1/8 for Good**

📖 Season of Mists, Part 0 • Reprints Sandman #21 **A:** Malcolm Jones III; Mike Dringenberg **W:** Neil Gaiman
22 ❑ May 1998 Cover: 1.95 **NM** value: **Cover or less**
Circ: Diamd. preorders: **8,310**
• Reprints Sandman #22 **W:** Neil Gaiman
23 ❑ Jun 1998 Cover: 1.95 **NM** value: **Cover or less**
Circ: Diamd. preorders: **8,245**
• Reprints Sandman #23 **W:** Neil Gaiman
24 ❑ Jul 1998 Cover: 1.95 **NM** value: **Cover or less**
Circ: Diamd. preorders: **7,769**
• Reprints Sandman #24 **W:** Neil Gaiman
25 ❑ Aug 1998 Cover: 1.95 **NM** value: **Cover or less**
Circ: Diamd. preorders: **7,520**
• Reprints Sandman #25 **W:** Neil Gaiman
26 ❑ Sep 1998 Cover: 2.25 **NM** value: **Cover or less**
Circ: Diamd. preorders: **7,126**
• Reprints Sandman #26 **W:** Neil Gaiman
27 ❑ Oct 1998 Cover: 2.25 **NM** value: **Cover or less**
Circ: Diamd. preorders: **6,986**
• Reprints Sandman #27 **W:** Neil Gaiman
28 ❑ Nov 1998 Cover: 2.25 **NM** value: **Cover or less**
Circ: Diamd. preorders: **6,765**
• Reprints Sandman #28 **W:** Neil Gaiman
29 ❑ Dec 1998 Cover: 2.25 **NM** value: **Cover or less**
Circ: Diamd. preorders: **6,726**
• Reprints Sandman #29 **W:** Neil Gaiman
30 ❑ Jan 1999 Cover: 2.25 **NM** value: **Cover or less**
Circ: Diamd. preorders: **6,520**
• Reprints Sandman #30 **W:** Neil Gaiman
31 ❑ Feb 1999 Cover: 2.25 **NM** value: **Cover or less**
Circ: Diamd. preorders: **6,222**
📖 Three Septembers and a January • Reprints Sandman #31 **A:** Shawn McManus; Dave McKean(cover) **W:** Neil Gaiman
32 ❑ Mar 1999 Cover: 4.50 **NM** value: **Cover or less**
Circ: Diamd. preorders: **5,962**
📖 Song of Orpheus final issue. • Reprints Sandman Special #1 **A:** Bryan Talbot; Dave McKean(cover) **W:** Neil Gaiman

ETC — DC / Piranha

1 ❑ full color Cover: 2.50 **NM** value: **Cover or less**
Circ: CapCity orders: **9,600**
2 ❑ full color Cover: 2.50 **NM** value: **Cover or less**
Circ: CapCity orders: **8,500**
3 ❑ full color Cover: 2.50 **NM** value: **Cover or less**
Circ: CapCity orders: **6,650**
4 ❑ full color Cover: 2.50 **NM** value: **Cover or less**
Circ: CapCity orders: **6,050**
5 ❑ full color Cover: 2.50 **NM** value: **Cover or less**
Circ: CapCity orders: **5,450**

ETERNAL ROMANCE — Best Destiny

1 ❑ Feb 1997, b&w Cover: 2.50 **NM** value: **3.00**
📖 Till Death Do Us Part; The Night Student; Togetherness; Blood Song **A:** Janet L. Hetherington **W:** Janet L. Hetherington
2 ❑ May 1997, b&w Cover: 2.50 **NM** value: **Cover or less**
📖 My Phantom Lover!; Once Bitten, Twice Shy!; The Mummy's Boy **A:** Janet L. Hetherington **W:** Janet L. Hetherington
3 ❑ Dec 1997 Cover: 2.50 **NM** value: **Cover or less**
📖 Kiss of Death!; Angel or Alien; **A:** Janet L. Hetherington **W:** Janet L. Hetherington
4 ❑ Jul 1998 Cover: 2.50 **NM** value: **Cover or less**
📖 Destine's Scream Date; The Green Eyed Monster!; The Masked Hurricane **A:** Janet L. Hetherington **W:** Janet L. Hetherington
Bk 1 ❑ Cover: 9.95 **NM** value: **Cover or less**
📖 The Mummy's Boy; The Ghost of New Year's Past; Destine's Scream Date!; Too Much at Stake!; Kiss of Death!; Till Death do us Part!; The Green-Eyed Monster!; Once Bitten, Twice Shy; My Phantom Lover!; The Night Student; My Love is Like a Pepperoni Pizza • Eternally Yours **A:** Janet L. Hetherington **W:** Janet L. Hetherington

ETERNAL ROMANCE LABOR OF LOVE SKETCHBOOK — Best Destiny

1 ❑ Cover: 2.50 **NM** value: **Cover or less**
• Labor of Love sketchbook. 250 printed **A:** Janet L. Hetherington **W:** Janet L. Hetherington

ETERNALS, THE — Marvel

Through a strange series of events, man comes to learn that, while though the old Greek legends may have been distorted by time, they were not entirely untrue. The truth is that man is not alone in the evolutionary chain, but is merely part of an experiment by a race known as the Celestials. The highest life forms are the Eternals — immortal beings whose names have become the stuff of legends. Led by Zuras (Zeus), their number includes Ikaris (Icarus), Sersi (Circe), Ajak (Ajax), and others.

Along with the discovery of the Eternals, man also learns of the Deviants, the embodiment of all that is base and evil. Once living beneath the surface, they have come forth to wreak havoc on earth. Now it seems that these age-old foes are destined to fight an epic battle, with mankind caught in the middle.

Far-flung fantasy by Jack Kirby in the late 1970s, The Eternals themselves never really reached legendary status with most Marvel readers.

1 ❑ Jul 1976 Cover: 0.25 **NM** value: **2.50**
• **CGC:** 26 graded, best 9.6
📖 The Day of the Gods **A:** Jack Kirby **W:** Jack Kirby ★ Origin of Eternals. ★ 1st Appearance of Kro, Margo Damian, Margo Damian, Brother Tode, Brother Tode, Ikaris, Ikaris.
2 ❑ Aug 1976 Cover: 0.25 **NM** value: **2.00**
📖 The Celestials **A:** Jack Kirby ★ 1st Appearance of Ajak, Arishem the Judge.
3 ❑ Sep 1976 Cover: 0.30 **NM** value: **2.00**
📖 The Devil inNew York **A:** Jack Kirby ★ 1st Appearance of Sersi.
4 ❑ Oct 1976 Cover: 0.30 **NM** value: **2.00**
📖 Night of the Demons **A:** Jack Kirby ★ 1st Appearance of Gammenon the Gatherer.
5 ❑ Nov 1976 Cover: 0.30 **NM** value: **2.00**
📖 Olympia **A:** Jack Kirby ★ 1st Appearance of Makkari, Zuras (Thena).
6 ❑ Dec 1976 Cover: 0.30 **NM** value: **1.50**
📖 Gods and Men at City College **A:** Jack Kirby
7 ❑ Jan 1977 Cover: 0.30 **NM** value: **1.50**
📖 The Fourth Host **A:** Jack Kirby ★ 1st Appearance of Nezarr.
8 ❑ Feb 1977 Cover: 0.30 **NM** value: **1.50**
📖 The City of Toads **A:** Jack Kirby ★ 1st Appearance of Karkas.
9 ❑ Mar 1977 Cover: 0.30 **NM** value: **1.50**
📖 The Killing Machine **A:** Jack Kirby ★ 1st Appearance of Sprite I.
10 ❑ Apr 1977 Cover: 0.30 **NM** value: **1.50**
📖 Mother **A:** Jack Kirby
11 ❑ May 1977 Cover: 0.30 **NM** value: **1.50**
📖 The Russians are Coming **A:** Jack Kirby ★ 1st Appearance of Aginar.
12 ❑ Jun 1977 Cover: 0.30 **NM** value: **1.50**
📖 Uni-Mind **A:** Jack Kirby ★ 1st Appearance of Uni-Mind.
13 ❑ Jul 1977 Cover: 0.30 **NM** value: **1.50**
• **CGC:** 1 graded, best 8.5
📖 Astronauts **A:** Jack Kirby ★ 1st Appearance of Gilgamesh, One Above All.
14 ❑ Aug 1977 Cover: 0.30 **NM** value: **1.50**
• **CGC:** 1 graded, best 9.2
📖 Ikaris and the Cosmic-Powered Hulk **A:** Jack Kirby ★ Appearance of Hulk.
15 ❑ Sep 1977 Cover: 0.30 **NM** value: **1.50**
📖 Disaster Area **A:** Jack Kirby ★ Appearance of Hulk.
16 ❑ Oct 1977 Cover: 0.30 **NM** value: **1.50**
📖 Big City Crypt **A:** Jack Kirby
17 ❑ Nov 1977 Cover: 0.35 **NM** value: **1.50**
📖 Sersi the Terrible **A:** Jack Kirby
18 ❑ Dec 1977 Cover: 0.35 **NM** value: **1.50**
📖 To Kill a Space God **A:** Jack Kirby
19 ❑ Jan 1978 Cover: 0.35 **NM** value: **1.50**
📖 The Pyramid **A:** Jack Kirby ★ 1st Appearance of Ziran.
Anl 1 ❑ Oct 1977 Cover: 0.50 **NM** value: **1.50**
📖 The Time Killers **A:** Jack Kirby

ETERNALS, THE (LTD. SERIES) — Marvel

1 ❑ Oct 1985 Cover: 1.25 **NM** value: **Cover or less**
Circ: CapCity orders: **17,900**
• Giant-size. ★ 1st Appearance of Khoryphos.
2 ❑ Nov 1985 Cover: 0.75 **NM** value: **1.00**
Circ: CapCity orders: **14,800**
3 ❑ Dec 1985 Cover: 0.75 **NM** value: **1.00**
Circ: CapCity orders: **13,700**
4 ❑ Jan 1986 Cover: 0.75 **NM** value: **1.00**
Circ: CapCity orders: **13,100**
5 ❑ Feb 1986 Cover: 0.75 **NM** value: **1.00**
Circ: CapCity orders: **12,400**
6 ❑ Mar 1986 Cover: 0.75 **NM** value: **1.00**
Circ: CapCity orders: **11,800**
7 ❑ Apr 1986 Cover: 0.75 **NM** value: **1.00**
Circ: CapCity orders: **10,900**
8 ❑ May 1986 Cover: 0.75 **NM** value: **1.00**
Circ: CapCity orders: **10,700**
9 ❑ Jun 1986 Cover: 0.75 **NM** value: **1.00**
Circ: CapCity orders: **10,100**
10 ❑ Jul 1986 Cover: 0.75 **NM** value: **1.00**
Circ: CapCity orders: **10,300**
11 ❑ Aug 1986 Cover: 0.75 **NM** value: **1.00**
Circ: CapCity orders: **9,700**
12 ❑ Sep 1986 Cover: 1.25 **NM** value: **Cover or less**
Circ: CapCity orders: **10,000**
• Giant-size.

ETERNALS: THE HEROD FACTOR — Marvel

1 ❑ Nov 1991 Cover: 2.50 **NM** value: **Cover or less**
Circ: CapCity orders: **18,100**

ETERNAL THIRST — Alpha Productions

3 ❑ b&w Cover: 1.95 **NM** value: **Cover or less**
📖 Treachery **A:** Hector Diaz **W:** Jim McNaughton
4 ❑ b&w Cover: 1.95 **NM** value: **Cover or less**
5 ❑ b&w Cover: 1.95 **NM** value: **Cover or less**

ETERNAL WARRIOR — Valiant

In a time before history, two brothers, Aram and Gilad, were fierce warriors of a nomadic tribe. As the years passed, they began to realize that they were not like others. It was next to impossible to seriously wound them, and they never seemed to grow old. In time, the brothers had to adopt different names and move from place to place to prevent others from discovering their true nature.

Occasionally, the brothers would come into contact with geomancers: mystics to whom the Earth itself told its secrets. "The end of all things is coming," they were warned, and those whose lives burned strong would be called on to save the world. Now Aram is known as "Armstrong" (of Archer & Armstrong fame), and Gilad — often accompanied by a young geomancer named Geoff — is the Eternal Warrior. Each must work, in his own way, to save the world from the evils that imperil it.

1 ❑ Aug 1992 Cover: 2.25 **NM** value: **3.00**
Circ: CapCity orders: **32,300** • **CGC:** 2 graded, best 9.6
📖 Unity, Part 2 • Unity **A:** John Dixon; Frank Miller(cover) **C:** Frank Miller **W:** Jim Shooter
1/GF ❑ Aug 1992 Cover: 2.25 **NM** value: **5.00**
📖 Unity, Part 2 • Gold foil logo (dealer promotion) **A:** John Dixon; Frank Miller(cover) **W:** Jim Shooter
1/GO ❑ Aug 1992 Cover: 2.25 **NM** value: **4.00**
📖 Unity, Part 2 • Gold logo (dealer promotion) **A:** John Dixon; Frank Miller(cover) **W:** Jim Shooter
2 ❑ Sep 1992 Cover: 2.25 **NM** value: **2.50**
Circ: CapCity orders: **30,700**
📖 Unity, Part 10 • Unity **A:** John Dixon **C:** Walt Simonson **W:** Jim Shooter
3 ❑ Oct 1992 Cover: 2.25 **NM** value: **2.50**
Circ: CapCity orders: **21,500**
4 ❑ Nov 1992 Cover: 2.25 **NM** value: **2.50**
Circ: CapCity orders: **21,950**
5 ❑ Dec 1992 Cover: 2.25 **NM** value: **2.50**
Circ: CapCity orders: **20,400**
6 ❑ Jan 1993 Cover: 2.25 **NM** value: **Cover or less**
Circ: CapCity orders: **21,600**
7 ❑ Feb 1993 Cover: 2.25 **NM** value: **Cover or less**
Circ: CapCity orders: **25,400**
8 ❑ Mar 1993 Cover: 4.50 **NM** value: **Cover or less**
Circ: CapCity orders: **51,800**
• Double-size. • combined with Archer & Armstrong #8
9 ❑ Apr 1993 Cover: 2.25 **NM** value: **Cover or less**
Circ: CapCity orders: **48,900**
📖 Book of the Geomancer, Part 1
10 ❑ May 1993 Cover: 2.25 **NM** value: **Cover or less**
Circ: CapCity orders: **60,400**
📖 Book of the Geomancer, Part 2 **A:** Mark Moretti **W:** Mark Moretti
11 ❑ Jun 1993 Cover: 2.25 **NM** value: **Cover or less**
Circ: CapCity orders: **65,500**
📖 A Gift Before Dying **A:** Mark Moretti **W:** Mark Moretti; Kevin VanHook
12 ❑ Jul 1993 Cover: 2.25 **NM** value: **Cover or less**
Circ: CapCity orders: **83,100**
📖 Return of the Immortal Enemy, Part 1
13 ❑ Aug 1993 Cover: 2.25 **NM** value: **Cover or less**
Circ: CapCity orders: **69,500**
📖 Return of the Immortal Enemy, Part 2 ★ Versus Eternal Enemy.
14 ❑ Sep 1993 Cover: 2.25 **NM** value: **Cover or less**
Circ: CapCity orders: **59,200**
15 ❑ Oct 1993 Cover: 2.25 **NM** value: **Cover or less**
Circ: CapCity orders: **47,900**
16 ❑ Nov 1993 Cover: 2.25 **NM** value: **Cover or less**
Circ: CapCity orders: **43,700**
17 ❑ Dec 1993 Cover: 2.25 **NM** value: **Cover or less**
Circ: CapCity orders: **38,100**
18 ❑ Jan 1994 Cover: 2.25 **NM** value: **Cover or less**
Circ: CapCity orders: **34,325**
19 ❑ Feb 1994 Cover: 2.25 **NM** value: **Cover or less**
Circ: CapCity orders: **29,700**
20 ❑ Mar 1994 Cover: 2.25 **NM** value: **Cover or less**
Circ: CapCity orders: **25,150**
21 ❑ Apr 1994 Cover: 2.25 **NM** value: **Cover or less**
Circ: CapCity orders: **2,100**
22 ❑ May 1994 Cover: 2.25 **NM** value: **Cover or less**
Circ: CapCity orders: **25,700**
• trading card
23 ❑ Jun 1994 Cover: 2.25 **NM** value: **Cover or less**
Circ: CapCity orders: **17,425**
24 ❑ Aug 1994 Cover: 2.25 **NM** value: **Cover or less**
Circ: CapCity orders: **16,200**
25 ❑ Sep 1994 Cover: 2.25 **NM** value: **Cover or less**
Circ: CapCity orders: **15,975**
26 ❑ Oct 1994 Cover: 2.75 **NM** value: **Cover or less**
Circ: CapCity orders: **21,950**
📖 The Chaos Effect: Gamma, Part 4 • indicia says August; Flip-book with Archer & Armstrong #26
27 ❑ Nov 1994 Cover: 2.25 **NM** value: **Cover or less**
Circ: CapCity orders: **15,700**
28 ❑ Dec 1994 Cover: 2.25 **NM** value: **Cover or less**
Circ: CapCity orders: **12,450**
29 ❑ Jan 1995 Cover: 2.25 **NM** value: **Cover or less**
Circ: CapCity orders: **11,300**
30 ❑ Feb 1995 Cover: 2.25 **NM** value: **Cover or less**
Circ: CapCity orders: **10,475**
31 ❑ Mar 1995 Cover: 2.25 **NM** value: **Cover or less**
Circ: CapCity orders: **9,175**
32 ❑ Apr 1995 Cover: 2.25 **NM** value: **Cover or less**
Circ: CapCity orders: **8,400**
33 ❑ May 1995 Cover: 1.95 **NM** value: **2.25**
Circ: CapCity orders: **7,500**
📖 Mortal Kin, Part 1
34 ❑ Jun 1995 Cover: 2.25 **NM** value: **Cover or less**
Circ: CapCity orders: **6,650**
35 ❑ Jul 1995 Cover: 2.50 **NM** value: **Cover or less**
Circ: CapCity orders: **7,250**
outer white cover with warning. • Birthquake
36 ❑ Jul 1995 Cover: 2.50 **NM** value: **Cover or less**
Circ: CapCity orders: **7,100**
• Birthquake
37 ❑ Aug 1995 Cover: 2.50 **NM** value: **Cover or less**
Circ: CapCity orders: **6,275**
38 ❑ Aug 1995 Cover: 2.50 **NM** value: **Cover or less**
Circ: CapCity orders: **6,275**
39 ❑ Sep 1995 Cover: 2.50 **NM** value: **Cover or less**
Circ: CapCity orders: **6,550**

CGC-graded: Multiply prices above by **33 for 9.9 M • 16 for 9.8 NM/M • 7 for 9.6 NM+ • 5 for 9.4 NM • 2.5 for 9.2 NM- • 1.5 for 9.0 VF/NM**

40 ❑ Sep 1995 Cover: 2.50 **NM** value: **Cover or less**
Circ: CapCity orders: **6,550**

41 ❑ Oct 1995 Cover: 2.50 **NM** value: **Cover or less**
Circ: CapCity orders: **6,200**

42 ❑ Oct 1995 Cover: 2.50 **NM** value: **Cover or less**
Circ: CapCity orders: **6,200**

43 ❑ Nov 1995 Cover: 2.50 **NM** value: **Cover or less**
Circ: CapCity orders: **5,975**

44 ❑ Nov 1995 Cover: 2.50 **NM** value: **Cover or less**
Circ: CapCity orders: **5,975**

45 ❑ Dec 1995 Cover: 2.50 **NM** value: **Cover or less**
Circ: CapCity orders: **5,125**

46 ❑ Dec 1995 Cover: 2.50 **NM** value: **Cover or less**
Circ: CapCity orders: **5,125**

47 ❑ Jan 1996 Cover: 2.50 **NM** value: **Cover or less**
Circ: CapCity orders: **4,550**

48 ❑ Jan 1996 Cover: 2.50 **NM** value: **Cover or less**
Circ: CapCity orders: **4,500**

49 ❑ Feb 1996 Cover: 2.50 **NM** value: **Cover or less**

50 ❑ Mar 1996 Cover: 2.50 **NM** value: **Cover or less**
final issue.★ Appearance of Geomancer.

SE 1❑ Feb 1996 Cover: 2.50 **NM** value: **Cover or less**
📖 The Wings of Justice **A:** John Dixon **W:** Art Comb

YB 1❑ ca. 1993 Cover: 3.95 **NM** value: **Cover or less**
Circ: CapCity orders: **38,125**
cardstock cover. • Yearbook 1.

YB 2❑ ca. 1994 Cover: 3.95 **NM** value: **Cover or less**
Circ: CapCity orders: **7,600**
cardstock cover. • Yearbook 2.

ETERNAL WARRIOR: FIST AND STEEL — Acclaim / Valiant

It is the year 1180 and Gilad is the Eternal Warrior, the protector of group of Tibetan monks pledged to guard the Earth from an ancient evil. But when time grows short for the last monk, Tashi Khatan, and no suitable replacement can be found, he resorts to a ritual to create a tulpa, a duplicate fashioned to train a successor. This effort goes awry however and the tulpa is loosed on the earth.

Eight hundred years later a blind man named Clay McHenry has followed the ley lines of geomantic energy in the earth to a graveyard where he is attacked by a skeletal apparition that he fends off with his silver cane. The struggle leaves McHenry with a vision of Tashi and a promise of enlightenment if he will but pass through the doorway. The skeletal apparition reappears and prevents his passage and as McHenry returns from the vision he is confronted by the Eternal Warrior.

1 ❑ May 1996 Cover: 2.50 **NM** value: **Cover or less**

2 ❑ Jun 1996 Cover: 2.50 **NM** value: **Cover or less**

ETERNAL WARRIORS — Acclaim / Valiant

1 ❑ Jun 1997 Cover: 3.95 **NM** value: **Cover or less**
Circ: Diamd. preorders: **18,921**
One-shot. 📖 Time and Treachery **A:** Doug Tropea-Wheatley **W:** Art Holcomb

1/SC❑ Jun 1997 Cover: 3.95 **NM** value: **Cover or less**
alternate painted cover.

Ash 1❑ Feb 1997, b&w **NM** value: **1.00**
no cover price. • preview of Time and Treachery one-shot

ETERNAL WARRIORS: ARCHER & ARMSTRONG — Acclaim / Valiant

1 ❑ Dec 1997 Cover: 3.95 **NM** value: **Cover or less**
Circ: Diamd. preorders: **11,484**
price stickered on cover. **A:** Robert Teranishi **W:** Art Holcomb; Jeff Gomez

ETERNAL WARRIORS BLACKWORKS — Acclaim / Valiant

1 ❑ Mar 1998 Cover: 3.95 **NM** value: **Cover or less**
Circ: Diamd. preorders: **8,801**

ETERNAL WARRIORS: DIGITAL ALCHEMY — Acclaim / Valiant

1 ❑ Sep 1997 Cover: 3.95 **NM** value: **Cover or less**
One-shot.

ETERNAL WARRIORS: MOG — Acclaim / Valiant

1 ❑ Mar 1998 Cover: 3.95 **NM** value: **Cover or less**
Circ: Diamd. preorders: **7,152**
One-shot.

ETERNAL WARRIOR SPECIAL — Acclaim / Valiant

1 ❑ Feb 1996 Cover: 2.50 **NM** value: **Cover or less**
• Eternal Warrior in WW II

ETERNAL WARRIORS: THE IMMORTAL ENEMY — Acclaim / Valiant

1 ❑ Cover: 3.95 **NM** value: **Cover or less**
Circ: Diamd. preorders: **6,574**
• Final issue of VH-2 universe **A:** Oscar Jimenez; Eduardo Alpuente; John Floyd **W:** Art Holcomb

ETERNAL WARRIORS: TIME AND TREACHERY — Acclaim / Valiant

1 ❑ ca. 1997 Cover: 3.95 **NM** value: **Cover or less**

ETERNITY SMITH (VOL. 1) — Renegade

1 ❑ Sep 1986, full color Cover: 1.25 **NM** value: **1.50**
Circ: CapCity orders: **6,750**

2 ❑ Nov 1986 Cover: 1.50 **NM** value: **Cover or less**
Circ: CapCity orders: **3,825**

3 ❑ Jan 1987 Cover: 1.50 **NM** value: **Cover or less**
Circ: CapCity orders: **4,025**

4 ❑ Mar 1987 Cover: 1.50 **NM** value: **Cover or less**
Circ: CapCity orders: **2,850**
📖 And Death Comes Softly Knocking **A:** Rick Hoberg **W:** Dennis Mallonee

5 ❑ May 1987 Cover: 1.50 **NM** value: **Cover or less**
Circ: CapCity orders: **2,325**

ETERNITY SMITH (VOL. 2) — Hero

1 ❑ Sep 1987 Cover: 1.95 **NM** value: **Cover or less**
📖 Final Ashowdown **A:** Rick Hoberg **W:** Dennis Mallonee

2 ❑ Oct 1987 Cover: 1.95 **NM** value: **Cover or less**

3 ❑ Nov 1987 Cover: 1.95 **NM** value: **Cover or less**

4 ❑ Dec 1987 Cover: 1.95 **NM** value: **Cover or less**

5 ❑ Jan 1988 Cover: 1.95 **NM** value: **Cover or less**
Circ: CapCity orders: **1,625**

6 ❑ Feb 1988 Cover: 1.95 **NM** value: **Cover or less**
Circ: CapCity orders: **1,800**

7 ❑ Apr 1988 Cover: 1.95 **NM** value: **Cover or less**
Circ: CapCity orders: **1,450**

8 ❑ Jun 1988 Cover: 1.95 **NM** value: **Cover or less**
Circ: CapCity orders: **1,400**

9 ❑ Aug 1988 Cover: 1.95 **NM** value: **Cover or less**
Circ: CapCity orders: **1,375**
final issue. **A:** Rick Hoberg **W:** Dennis Mallonee ★ Appearance of Walter Koenig.

ETERNITY TRIPLE ACTION — Eternity

1 ❑ b&w Cover: 2.50 **NM** value: **Cover or less**
Circ: CapCity orders: **4,580**
📖 Amazon Gazonga, Part 1; Gigantor, Part 1; Armored Road Police, Part 1

2 ❑ b&w Cover: 2.50 **NM** value: **Cover or less**
📖 Amazon Gazonga, Part 2; Gigantor, Part 2; Armored Road Police, Part 2

3 ❑ b&w Cover: 2.50 **NM** value: **Cover or less**
📖 Amazon Gazonga, Part 3; Gigantor, Part 3; Armored Road Police, Part 3

EUDAEMON, THE — Dark Horse

1 ❑ Aug 1993 Cover: 2.50 **NM** value: **Cover or less**
Circ: CapCity orders: **10,250**

2 ❑ Cover: 2.50 **NM** value: **Cover or less**
Circ: CapCity orders: **6,125**

3 ❑ Cover: 2.50 **NM** value: **Cover or less**

EUGENUS — Eugenus

1 ❑ b&w Cover: 3.50 **NM** value: **Cover or less**

2 ❑ b&w Cover: 3.50 **NM** value: **Cover or less**

3 ❑ Cover: 2.50 **NM** value: **Cover or less**

EUREKA — Radio Comix

1 ❑ Apr 2000, b&w Cover: 2.95 **NM** value: **Cover or less**

2 ❑ Jul 2000, b&w Cover: 2.95 **NM** value: **Cover or less**

3 ❑ Sep 2000, b&w Cover: 2.95 **NM** value: **Cover or less**

EUROPA AND THE PIRATE TWINS — Powder Monkey Productions

1 ❑ Oct 1996, b&w Cover: 2.95 **NM** value: **Cover or less**

1/A ❑ Oct 1996, b&w Cover: 2.95 **NM** value: **Cover or less**
no cover price.

Ash 1❑ Mar 1996, b&w **NM** value: **1.00**
No issue number. no cover price. • smaller than normal comic

EVANGELINE SPECIAL — Lodestone

1 ❑ Cover: 2.00 **NM** value: **Cover or less**

EVANGELINE (VOL. 1) — Comico

Evangeline is a science-fiction series about a pistol-packing nun (and this may be the first one of those in comics) who's out to avenge the loss of a Mars-based mission.

Evangeline's mission had been burned to the ground by raiders, and all her sister nuns were murdered. Behind it all was a company called UNetCo, which was willing slaughter nuns in order to claim their land. When Evangeline discovered what had happened, she traded in her nun's habit for adventurer's garb and a trio of custom-made guns. The series follows Evangeline as she tracks down those responsible for the attack, and exacts her own earthly retribution.

The series was the first independent title created by Chuck Dixon, who would later become known as one of the finest action writers in the business. He achieved special acclaim for his work on the Batman family of titles for DC.

1 ❑ ca. 1984 Cover: 1.50 **NM** value: **2.50**

2 ❑ ca. 1984 Cover: 1.50 **NM** value: **2.00**

EVANGELINE (VOL. 2) — First

1 ❑ May 1987 Cover: 1.75 **NM** value: **2.50**
Circ: CapCity orders: **9,575**

2 ❑ Jul 1987 Cover: 1.75 **NM** value: **2.00**
Circ: CapCity orders: **7,625**

3 ❑ Sep 1987 Cover: 1.75 **NM** value: **2.00**
Circ: CapCity orders: **7,325**

4 ❑ Nov 1987 Cover: 1.75 **NM** value: **2.00**
Circ: CapCity orders: **6,400**

5 ❑ Jan 1988 Cover: 1.75 **NM** value: **2.00**
Circ: CapCity orders: **5,750**

6 ❑ Mar 1988 Cover: 1.75 **NM** value: **2.00**
Circ: CapCity orders: **5,725**

7 ❑ May 1988 Cover: 1.75 **NM** value: **2.00**
Circ: CapCity orders: **5,050**

8 ❑ Jul 1988 Cover: 1.75 **NM** value: **2.00**
Circ: CapCity orders: **4,850**

9 ❑ Sep 1988 Cover: 1.75 **NM** value: **2.00**
Circ: CapCity orders: **4,550**

10 ❑ Nov 1988 Cover: 1.95 **NM** value: **2.00**
Circ: CapCity orders: **4,225**

11 ❑ Jan 1989 Cover: 1.95 **NM** value: **2.00**
Circ: CapCity orders: **4,050**

12 ❑ Mar 1989 Cover: 1.95 **NM** value: **2.00**
Circ: CapCity orders: **3,975**

EVEL KNIEVEL — Marvel

The motorcycle rider (1938-) got national publicity — and his own one-shot Marvel comic book. His stunting career was best known for his attempts to jump an assortment of hurdles — trucks, cars, rattlesnakes, the Caesar's Palace fountains, buses, the Snake River, and the Grand Canyon — on his motorcycle. There was an Evel Knievel movie in 1971 and Viva Knievel in 1976. The Marvel comic book was done in conjunction with toymaker Ideal, which had the toy license in 1974. Strangely enough, all the action in the story was performed using equipment that was also available as part of the toy line. In the late 1990s, Playing Mantis reissued the Evel Knievel stunt cycle, but not the other toys.

— Maggie

1 ❑ **NM** value: **3.50**
• giveaway.

E.V.E. PROTOMECHA — Image

1 ❑ Cover: 2.50 **NM** value: **Cover or less**
• **CGC:** 2 graded, best 9.8

2 ❑ Cover: 2.50 **NM** value: **Cover or less**

3 ❑ Cover: 2.50 **NM** value: **Cover or less**

4 ❑ Nov 2000 Cover: 2.50 **NM** value: **Cover or less**

5 ❑ Cover: 2.50 **NM** value: **Cover or less**

6 ❑ Sep 2000 Cover: 2.50 **NM** value: **Cover or less**

EVERWINDS — Slave Labor / Amaze Ink

1 ❑ Aug 1997, b&w Cover: 2.95 **NM** value: **Cover or less**
📖 Everwinds **A:** Steve Peters **W:** Steve Peters ★ Appearance of Lethargic Lad.

2 ❑ Oct 1997, b&w Cover: 2.95 **NM** value: **Cover or less**
📖 'Shrooms **A:** Steve Peters **W:** Steve Peters

3 ❑ Dec 1997, b&w Cover: 2.95 **NM** value: **Cover or less**

4 ❑ Mar 1998 Cover: 2.95 **NM** value: **Cover or less**
📖 A Woman's Touch; Genesis; Mouster U.S....CrTme-Filled Conspiracy; Avici; Awesome Girl...Bahama Mama; Mouster U.S....Cr-Fme-Filled Conspiracy **A:** Steve Peters; James Kochalka; Samantha Rosania; C.D. Regan **W:** Steve Peters; Nat Gertler

EVERYMAN, THE — Marvel / Epic

1 ❑ Nov 1991 Cover: 4.50 **NM** value: **Cover or less**
Circ: CapCity orders: **6,400**
No issue number. **W:** Mike Allred

EVERYTHING'S ARCHIE — Archie

This series began in 1969, when lots of things were certainly "Archie"-hit records, TV cartoons, and Post cereals, just to name a few.

Archie Andrews is probably the world's most recognizable teenager, and his decades-long quandary is legendary: Who will he choose, bubbly blonde Betty Cooper or snarky brunette Veronica Lodge? The answer changes in every story, but the fun is consistent.

The entire Archie gang is here, too: Jughead, Reggie, Moose, Big Ethel, Dilton, Midge, Miss Grundy, and Mr. Weatherbee; and a good bit of entertainment comes from following their adventures through the various phases of American pop culture. From bell-bottoms to disco from moonwalking to rap, Archie comics are a course in American cultural history.

1 ❑ May 1969 Cover: 0.25 **NM** value: **45.00**
• **CGC:** 1 graded, best 9.6
• Giant-size.

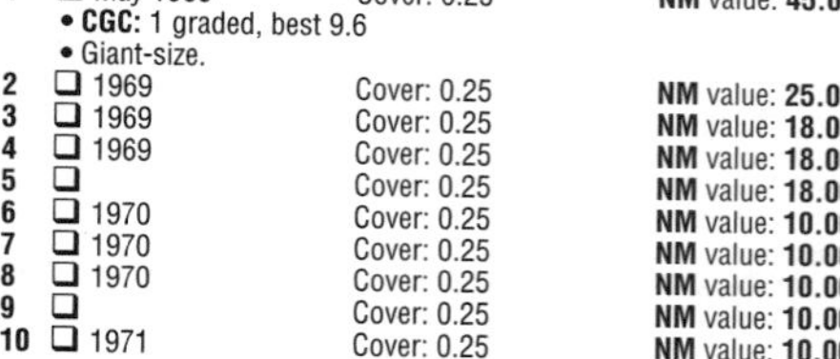

2 ❑ 1969 Cover: 0.25 **NM** value: **25.00**

3 ❑ 1969 Cover: 0.25 **NM** value: **18.00**

4 ❑ 1969 Cover: 0.25 **NM** value: **18.00**

5 ❑ Cover: 0.25 **NM** value: **18.00**

6 ❑ 1970 Cover: 0.25 **NM** value: **10.00**

7 ❑ 1970 Cover: 0.25 **NM** value: **10.00**

8 ❑ 1970 Cover: 0.25 **NM** value: **10.00**

9 ❑ Cover: 0.25 **NM** value: **10.00**

10 ❑ 1971 Cover: 0.25 **NM** value: **10.00**

Other grades: Multiply prices above by **1.5 for Mint • 2/3 for Very Fine • 1/3 for Fine • 1/5 for Very Good • 1/8 for Good**

11 ❑ 1971 Cover: 0.25 **NM** value: **6.00**
12 ❑ 1971 Cover: 0.25 **NM** value: **6.00**
13 ❑ 1971 Cover: 0.25 **NM** value: **6.00**
14 ❑ 1971 Cover: 0.25 **NM** value: **6.00**
15 ❑ 1971 Cover: 0.25 **NM** value: **6.00**
16 ❑ Cover: 0.25 **NM** value: **6.00**
17 ❑ 1972 Cover: 0.25 **NM** value: **6.00**
18 ❑ 1972 Cover: 0.25 **NM** value: **6.00**
19 ❑ 1972 Cover: 0.25 **NM** value: **6.00**
20 ❑ 1972 Cover: 0.25 **NM** value: **6.00**
21 ❑ Aug 1972 Cover: 0.25 **NM** value: **4.00**
22 ❑ Oct 1972 Cover: 0.25 **NM** value: **4.00**
23 ❑ Dec 1972 Cover: 0.25 **NM** value: **4.00**
24 ❑ Feb 1973 Cover: 0.25 **NM** value: **4.00**
25 ❑ Apr 1973 Cover: 0.25 **NM** value: **4.00**
26 ❑ Jun 1973 Cover: 0.25 **NM** value: **4.00**
27 ❑ Aug 1973 Cover: 0.25 **NM** value: **4.00**
28 ❑ Sep 1973 Cover: 0.25 **NM** value: **4.00**
29 ❑ Oct 1973 Cover: 0.25 **NM** value: **4.00**
30 ❑ Dec 1973 Cover: 0.25 **NM** value: **4.00**
31 ❑ Feb 1974 Cover: 0.25 **NM** value: **4.00**
Circ: Statement: **188,842**
32 ❑ Apr 1974 Cover: 0.25 **NM** value: **4.00**
Circ: Statement: **188,842**
33 ❑ Jun 1974 Cover: 0.25 **NM** value: **4.00**
Circ: Statement: **188,842**
34 ❑ Aug 1974 Cover: 0.25 **NM** value: **4.00**
Circ: Statement: **188,842**
35 ❑ Sep 1974 Cover: 0.25 **NM** value: **4.00**
Circ: Statement: **188,842**
36 ❑ Oct 1974 Cover: 0.25 **NM** value: **4.00**
Circ: Statement: **188,842**
37 ❑ Dec 1974 Cover: 0.25 **NM** value: **4.00**
Circ: Statement: **188,842**
38 ❑ Feb 1975 Cover: 0.25 **NM** value: **4.00**
Circ: Statement: **150,190**
39 ❑ Apr 1975 Cover: 0.25 **NM** value: **4.00**
Circ: Statement: **150,190**
40 ❑ Jun 1975 Cover: 0.25 **NM** value: **4.00**
Circ: Statement: **150,190**
41 ❑ Aug 1975 Cover: 0.25 **NM** value: **3.00**
Circ: Statement: **150,190**
42 ❑ Sep 1975 Cover: 0.25 **NM** value: **3.00**
Circ: Statement: **150,190**
43 ❑ Oct 1975 Cover: 0.25 **NM** value: **3.00**
Circ: Statement: **150,190**
44 ❑ Dec 1975 Cover: 0.25 **NM** value: **3.00**
Circ: Statement: **150,190**
45 ❑ Feb 1976 Cover: 0.30 **NM** value: **3.00**
Circ: Statement: **130,998**
46 ❑ Apr 1976 Cover: 0.30 **NM** value: **3.00**
Circ: Statement: **130,998**
47 ❑ May 1976 Cover: 0.30 **NM** value: **3.00**
Circ: Statement: **130,998**
48 ❑ Jun 1976 Cover: 0.30 **NM** value: **3.00**
Circ: Statement: **130,998**
49 ❑ Jul 1976 Cover: 0.30 **NM** value: **3.00**
Circ: Statement: **130,998**
50 ❑ Aug 1976 Cover: 0.30 **NM** value: **3.00**
Circ: Statement: **130,998**
51 ❑ Sep 1976 Cover: 0.30 **NM** value: **3.00**
Circ: Statement: **130,998**
52 ❑ Oct 1976 Cover: 0.30 **NM** value: **3.00**
Circ: Statement: **130,998**
53 ❑ Dec 1976 Cover: 0.30 **NM** value: **3.00**
Circ: Statement: **130,998**
54 ❑ Feb 1977 Cover: 0.30 **NM** value: **3.00**
Circ: Statement: **127,269**
55 ❑ Apr 1977 Cover: 0.30 **NM** value: **3.00**
Circ: Statement: **127,269**
56 ❑ May 1977 Cover: 0.30 **NM** value: **3.00**
Circ: Statement: **127,269**
57 ❑ Jun 1977 Cover: 0.35 **NM** value: **3.00**
Circ: Statement: **127,269**
58 ❑ Jul 1977 Cover: 0.35 **NM** value: **3.00**
Circ: Statement: **127,269**
59 ❑ Aug 1977 Cover: 0.35 **NM** value: **3.00**
Circ: Statement: **127,269**
60 ❑ Sep 1977 Cover: 0.35 **NM** value: **3.00**
Circ: Statement: **127,269**
61 ❑ Oct 1977 Cover: 0.35 **NM** value: **2.00**
Circ: Statement: **127,269**
62 ❑ Dec 1977 Cover: 0.35 **NM** value: **2.00**
Circ: Statement: **127,269**
63 ❑ Feb 1978 Cover: 0.35 **NM** value: **2.00**
Circ: Statement: **111,141**
64 ❑ Apr 1978 Cover: 0.35 **NM** value: **2.00**
Circ: Statement: **111,141**
65 ❑ May 1978 Cover: 0.35 **NM** value: **2.00**
Circ: Statement: **111,141**
66 ❑ Jun 1978 Cover: 0.35 **NM** value: **2.00**
Circ: Statement: **111,141**
67 ❑ Jul 1978 Cover: 0.35 **NM** value: **2.00**
Circ: Statement: **111,141**
68 ❑ Aug 1978 Cover: 0.35 **NM** value: **2.00**
Circ: Statement: **111,141**
69 ❑ Sep 1978 Cover: 0.35 **NM** value: **2.00**
Circ: Statement: **111,141**
70 ❑ Oct 1978 Cover: 0.35 **NM** value: **2.00**
Circ: Statement: **111,141**
71 ❑ Dec 1978 Cover: 0.35 **NM** value: **2.00**
Circ: Statement: **111,141**
72 ❑ Feb 1979 Cover: 0.35 **NM** value: **2.00**
73 ❑ Apr 1979 Cover: 0.40 **NM** value: **2.00**
74 ❑ May 1979 Cover: 0.40 **NM** value: **2.00**
75 ❑ Jun 1979 Cover: 0.40 **NM** value: **2.00**
76 ❑ Jul 1979 Cover: 0.40 **NM** value: **2.00**
77 ❑ Aug 1979 Cover: 0.40 **NM** value: **2.00**
78 ❑ Sep 1979 Cover: 0.40 **NM** value: **2.00**
79 ❑ Oct 1979 Cover: 0.40 **NM** value: **2.00**
80 ❑ Dec 1979 Cover: 0.40 **NM** value: **2.00**
81 ❑ Feb 1980 Cover: 0.40 **NM** value: **2.00**
82 ❑ Apr 1980 Cover: 0.40 **NM** value: **2.00**
83 ❑ May 1980 Cover: 0.40 **NM** value: **2.00**
84 ❑ Jun 1980 Cover: 0.40 **NM** value: **2.00**
85 ❑ Jul 1980 Cover: 0.40 **NM** value: **2.00**
86 ❑ Aug 1980 Cover: 0.50 **NM** value: **2.00**
87 ❑ Sep 1980 Cover: 0.50 **NM** value: **2.00**
88 ❑ Oct 1980 Cover: 0.50 **NM** value: **2.00**
89 ❑ Dec 1980 Cover: 0.50 **NM** value: **2.00**
90 ❑ Feb 1981 Cover: 0.50 **NM** value: **2.00**
91 ❑ Apr 1981 Cover: 0.50 **NM** value: **2.00**
92 ❑ May 1981 Cover: 0.50 **NM** value: **2.00**
93 ❑ Jun 1981 Cover: 0.50 **NM** value: **2.00**
94 ❑ Jul 1981 Cover: 0.50 **NM** value: **2.00**
95 ❑ Aug 1981 Cover: 0.50 **NM** value: **2.00**
96 ❑ Sep 1981 Cover: 0.50 **NM** value: **2.00**
97 ❑ Oct 1981 Cover: 0.50 **NM** value: **2.00**
98 ❑ Dec 1981 Cover: 0.60 **NM** value: **2.00**
99 ❑ Feb 1982 Cover: 0.60 **NM** value: **2.00**
100 ❑ Apr 1982 Cover: 0.60 **NM** value: **2.00**
101 ❑ Jun 1982 Cover: 0.60 **NM** value: **1.50**
102 ❑ Aug 1982 Cover: 0.60 **NM** value: **1.50**
103 ❑ Oct 1982 Cover: 0.60 **NM** value: **1.50**
104 ❑ Dec 1982 Cover: 0.60 **NM** value: **1.50**
105 ❑ Mar 1983 Cover: 0.60 **NM** value: **1.50**
106 ❑ Jun 1983 Cover: 0.60 **NM** value: **1.50**
107 ❑ Sep 1983 Cover: 0.60 **NM** value: **1.50**
108 ❑ Nov 1983 Cover: 0.60 **NM** value: **1.50**
109 ❑ Jan 1984 Cover: 0.60 **NM** value: **1.50**
110 ❑ Mar 1984 Cover: 0.60 **NM** value: **1.50**
111 ❑ May 1984 Cover: 0.60 **NM** value: **1.50**
112 ❑ Jul 1984 Cover: 0.60 **NM** value: **1.50**
113 ❑ Sep 1984 Cover: 0.60 **NM** value: **1.50**
114 ❑ Nov 1984 Cover: 0.60 **NM** value: **1.50**
📖 Archie the Barbarian: Feudin' Around; The Archies: Down Home Horror; Archie's Heavy Metal Fashions (pinup); Archie's Puzzle page; Reggie: Self Diagnosis; Archie: Cute Suit; Moose: Mighty Good Friend; Little Archie: The Ol' Swimmin' Hole • Veronica **A:** Stan Goldberg; Dexter Taylor **W:** Dexter Taylor; John Albano; Frank Doyle ★ Appearance of Reggie the Ruthless, Archie the Barbarian, Betty, Jughead.
115 ❑ Jan 1985 Cover: 0.60 **NM** value: **1.50**
116 ❑ Mar 1985 Cover: 0.65 **NM** value: **1.50**
117 ❑ May 1985 Cover: 0.65 **NM** value: **1.50**
118 ❑ Jul 1985 Cover: 0.65 **NM** value: **1.50**
119 ❑ Sep 1985 Cover: 0.65 **NM** value: **1.50**
120 ❑ Nov 1985 Cover: 0.65 **NM** value: **1.50**
121 ❑ Jan 1986 Cover: 0.65 **NM** value: **1.50**
122 ❑ Mar 1986 Cover: 0.65 **NM** value: **1.50**
123 ❑ May 1986 Cover: 0.65 **NM** value: **1.50**
124 ❑ Jul 1986 Cover: 0.75 **NM** value: **1.50**
125 ❑ Sep 1986 Cover: 0.75 **NM** value: **1.50**
126 ❑ Nov 1986 Cover: 0.75 **NM** value: **1.50**
127 ❑ Jan 1987 Cover: 0.75 **NM** value: **1.50**
128 ❑ Mar 1987 Cover: 0.75 **NM** value: **1.50**
129 ❑ May 1987 Cover: 0.75 **NM** value: **1.50**
130 ❑ Jul 1987 Cover: 0.75 **NM** value: **1.50**
131 ❑ Sep 1987 Cover: 0.75 **NM** value: **1.50**
132 ❑ Nov 1987 Cover: 0.75 **NM** value: **1.50**
133 ❑ Jan 1988 Cover: 0.75 **NM** value: **1.50**
134 ❑ Mar 1988 Cover: 0.75 **NM** value: **1.50**
135 ❑ May 1988 Cover: 0.75 **NM** value: **1.50**
136 ❑ Jul 1988 Cover: 0.75 **NM** value: **1.50**
137 ❑ Aug 1988 Cover: 0.75 **NM** value: **1.50**
138 ❑ Oct 1988 Cover: 0.75 **NM** value: **1.50**
139 ❑ Nov 1988 Cover: 0.75 **NM** value: **1.50**
140 ❑ Jan 1989 Cover: 0.75 **NM** value: **1.50**
141 ❑ Mar 1989 Cover: 0.75 **NM** value: **1.50**
142 ❑ May 1989 Cover: 0.75 **NM** value: **1.50**
143 ❑ Jul 1989 Cover: 0.95 **NM** value: **1.50**
144 ❑ Aug 1989 Cover: 0.95 **NM** value: **1.50**
145 ❑ Oct 1989 Cover: 0.95 **NM** value: **1.50**
146 ❑ Nov 1989 Cover: 0.95 **NM** value: **1.50**
147 ❑ Jan 1990 Cover: 1.00 **NM** value: **1.50**
148 ❑ Mar 1990 Cover: 1.00 **NM** value: **1.50**
149 ❑ May 1990 Cover: 1.00 **NM** value: **1.50**
150 ❑ Jul 1990 Cover: 1.00 **NM** value: **1.50**
151 ❑ Sep 1990 Cover: 1.00 **NM** value: **1.50**
152 ❑ Nov 1990 Cover: 1.00 **NM** value: **1.50**
153 ❑ Jan 1991 Cover: 1.00 **NM** value: **1.50**
154 ❑ Mar 1991 Cover: 1.00 **NM** value: **1.50**
155 ❑ May 1991 Cover: 1.00 **NM** value: **1.50**
156 ❑ Jul 1991 Cover: 1.00 **NM** value: **1.50**
157 ❑ Sep 1991 Cover: 1.00 **NM** value: **1.50**

EVIL ERNIE: BADDEST BATTLES — Chaos

1 ❑ Jan 1997 Cover: 1.50 **NM** value: **Cover or less**
1/SC ❑ Jan 1997 **NM** value: **1.50**
• Splatterfest Premium Edition cover. **A:** Steven Hughes; Georges Jeanty; Brian Denham; Jack Gray; Jason Jenson(cover); Jim Balent(cover)

EVIL ERNIE (CHAOS!) — Chaos

0 ❑ **NM** value: **3.00**
• **CGC:** 2 graded, best 9.4
0/PL ❑ **NM** value: **5.00**
• Platinum edition.
1 ❑ Jul 1998 Cover: 2.95 **NM** value: **3.00**
Circ: Diamd. preorders: **24,995**
📖 Vampire Vengeance, Part 1 **A:** David Brewer **W:** Brian Pulido; Phil Nutman
2 ❑ Aug 1998 Cover: 2.95 **NM** value: **3.00**
Circ: Diamd. preorders: **18,824**
📖 Vampire Vengeance, Part 2 **A:** David Brewer **W:** Brian Pulido; Phil Nutman
3 ❑ Sep 1998 Cover: 2.95 **NM** value: **3.00**
Circ: Diamd. preorders: **17,598**
📖 Vampire Vengeance, Part 3
4 ❑ Oct 1998 Cover: 2.95 **NM** value: **3.00**
Circ: Diamd. preorders: **17,351**
📖 Fear Itself
5 ❑ Nov 1998 Cover: 2.95 **NM** value: **Cover or less**
Circ: Diamd. preorders: **16,794**
📖 Fear Itself
6 ❑ Dec 1998 Cover: 2.95 **NM** value: **Cover or less**
Circ: Diamd. preorders: **16,197**
📖 Fear Itself
7 ❑ Jan 1999 Cover: 2.95 **NM** value: **Cover or less**
Circ: Diamd. preorders: **15,802**
📖 Christmas Evil
8 ❑ Feb 1999 Cover: 2.95 **NM** value: **Cover or less**
Circ: Diamd. preorders: **15,615**
📖 Trauma
9 ❑ Mar 1999 Cover: 2.95 **NM** value: **Cover or less**
Circ: Diamd. preorders: **13,887**
📖 Trauma
10 ❑ Apr 1999 Cover: 2.95 **NM** value: **Cover or less**
Circ: Diamd. preorders: **13,616**
📖 Trauma

EVIL ERNIE: DEPRAVED — Chaos

1 ❑ Jul 1999 Cover: 2.95 **NM** value: **Cover or less**
Circ: Diamd. preorders: **14,969**
2 ❑ Aug 1999 Cover: 2.95 **NM** value: **Cover or less**
Circ: Diamd. preorders: **13,101**
3 ❑ Sep 1999 Cover: 2.95 **NM** value: **Cover or less**
Circ: Diamd. preorders: **12,616**

EVIL ERNIE: DESTROYER — Chaos

This title puts Evil Ernie on the loose again in another cross-country rampage of mayhem and destruction.

With the ghoulish Chastity by his side, Evil Ernie's out to start World War III —and he will, if he can make it to the nuclear access codes in Atlanta, Georgia.

All that can stop him is the American Restoration Alliance, armed with alien technology from the mysterious Area 51, as well as hordes of reanimated dead along his route./P>Created by Brian Pulido, Evil Ernie continues to deliver a gory, violent free-for-all, for those who like that sort of thing.

1 ❑ Oct 1997 Cover: 2.95 **NM** value: **Cover or less**
Circ: Diamd. preorders: **31,230**
2 ❑ Nov 1997 Cover: 2.95 **NM** value: **Cover or less**
Circ: Diamd. preorders: **22,599**
3 ❑ Dec 1997 Cover: 2.95 **NM** value: **Cover or less**
Circ: Diamd. preorders: **21,546**
4 ❑ Jan 1998 Cover: 2.95 **NM** value: **Cover or less**
Circ: Diamd. preorders: **20,860**
5 ❑ Feb 1998 Cover: 2.95 **NM** value: **Cover or less**
Circ: Diamd. preorders: **18,277**
6 ❑ Mar 1998 Cover: 2.95 **NM** value: **Cover or less**
Circ: Diamd. preorders: **17,551**
7 ❑ Apr 1998 Cover: 2.95 **NM** value: **Cover or less**
Circ: Diamd. preorders: **17,721**
8 ❑ May 1998 Cover: 2.95 **NM** value: **Cover or less**
Circ: Diamd. preorders: **18,127**
9 ❑ Jun 1998 Cover: 2.95 **NM** value: **Cover or less**
Circ: Diamd. preorders: **17,120**
Ash 1 ❑ Sep 1997 Cover: 2.50 **NM** value: **Cover or less**

EVIL ERNIE (ETERNITY) — Eternity

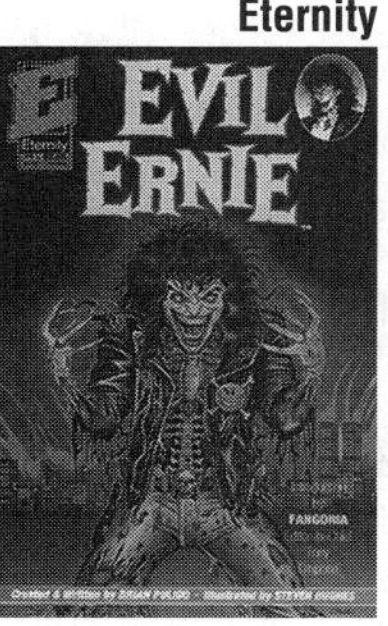

Ernie Fairchild was born with low-level telepathic abilities, able to read the thoughts of those around him. He felt different from the other kids, and became shy as a result. This frustrated his domineering father, who took to abusing him horribly.

Eventually, his parents take him to see Dr. Leonard Price, who tries an experimental "dream probe" to modify his behavior. Instead, it connects Ernie to the Endless Graveyard, home of the beautiful Lady Death. She promises to love Ernie if he takes up a quest to destroy all life on Earth. Ernie goes on a rampage, killing 35 people, including his parents, and is incarcerated in an institution where yet another experimental cure is tried — only this one kills him and turns him into an all-powerful zombie!

The first issue is notable for having the first appearance of Brian Pulido's Lady Death, who would become the flagship character for the "hard rock" comics company, Chaos.

1 ❑ ca. 1991, b&w Cover: 2.50 **NM** value: **28.00**
Circ: CapCity orders: **2,540** • **CGC:** 18 graded, best 9.4
1/LE ❑ **NM** value: **15.00**
• **CGC:** 2 graded, best 9.4
• Limited edition reprint (1992). **A:** Steven Hughes **W:** Brian Pulido; Phil Nutman ★ Origin of Evil Ernie. ★ 1st Appearance of Evil Ernie, Lady Death.

CGC-graded: Multiply prices above by **33 for 9.9 M • 16 for 9.8 NM/M • 7 for 9.6 NM+ • 5 for 9.4 NM • 2.5 for 9.2 NM- • 1.5 for 9.0 VF/NM**

2 ❑ ca. 1992, b&w Cover: 2.50 **NM** value: **20.00**
• **CGC:** 4 graded, best 9.4
3 ❑ ca. 1992, b&w Cover: 2.50 **NM** value: **16.00**
• **CGC:** 3 graded, best 9.6
4 ❑ ca. 1992, b&w Cover: 2.50 **NM** value: **15.00**
• **CGC:** 1 graded, best 9.6
5 ❑ ca. 1992, b&w Cover: 2.50 **NM** value: **15.00**
• **CGC:** 1 graded, best 9.2

EVIL ERNIE: NEW YEAR'S EVIL — Chaos

1 ❑ **NM** value: **5.00**
No issue number.

EVIL ERNIE: PIECES OF ME — Chaos

1 ❑ Nov 2000, b&w Cover: 2.95 **NM** value: **Cover or less**

EVIL ERNIE: REVENGE — Chaos

0 ❑ **NM** value: **2.50**
1 ❑ Oct 1994 Cover: 2.50 **NM** value: **3.00**
Circ: CapCity orders: **31,400**
1/Dlx❑Oct 1994 **NM** value: **4.50**
• **CGC:** 2 graded, best 9.8
• Master of Annihilation premium edition.
1/LE❑ Oct 1994 **NM** value: **4.50**
• Glow-in-the-dark limited edition. **W:** Brian Pulido
2 ❑ 1994 Cover: 2.50 **NM** value: **3.00**
Circ: CapCity orders: **20,725**
3 ❑ Jan 1995 Cover: 2.50 **NM** value: **Cover or less**
Circ: CapCity orders: **18,425**
4 ❑ Feb 1995 Cover: 2.50 **NM** value: **Cover or less**
Circ: CapCity orders: **18,775**

EVIL ERNIE: STRAIGHT TO HELL — Chaos

1 ❑ Oct 1995 Cover: 2.95 **NM** value: **3.00**
Circ: CapCity orders: **21,250** • **CGC:** 1 graded, best 9.6
Coffin fold-out cover. 📖 Beyond the Black **A:** Justiniano **W:** Brian Pulido
1/A ❑ Oct 1995 **NM** value: **5.00**
chromium cover. 📖 Beyond the Black **A:** Justiniano **W:** Brian Pulido
2 ❑ Dec 1995 Cover: 2.95 **NM** value: **3.00**
3 ❑ Feb 1996 Cover: 2.95 **NM** value: **3.00**
4 ❑ Apr 1996 Cover: 2.95 **NM** value: **3.00**
5 ❑ Jun 1996 Cover: 2.95 **NM** value: **3.00**
final issue. **A:** Justiniano **W:** Brian Pulido

EVIL ERNIE: THE RESURRECTION — Chaos

1 ❑ ca. 1993 Cover: 2.95 **NM** value: **4.00**
Circ: CapCity orders: **15,500** • **CGC:** 1 graded, best 9.6
1/GO❑ca. 1993 **NM** value: **10.00**
• Gold promotional edition. **A:** Joe Quesada(cover) **W:** Brian Pulido
★ Origin of Evil Ernie.
2 ❑ ca. 1994 Cover: 2.95 **NM** value: **3.50**
Circ: CapCity orders: **9,425**
3 ❑ ca. 1994 Cover: 2.95 **NM** value: **3.50**
Circ: CapCity orders: **7,025**
4 ❑ ca. 1994 Cover: 2.95 **NM** value: **3.00**
Circ: CapCity orders: **7,275**
Ash 1❑ca. 1993 **NM** value: **5.00**
Circ: CapCity orders: **13,475**
Bk 1❑ Cover: 14.95 **NM** value: **Cover or less**
• Collects Evil Ernie: The Resurrection #1-4 **W:** Brian Pulido

EVIL ERNIE VS. THE MOVIE MONSTERS — Chaos

1 ❑ ca. 1997 Cover: 2.95 **NM** value: **Cover or less**
One-shot.

EVIL ERNIE VS. THE SUPER HEROES — Chaos

1 ❑ Aug 1995 Cover: 2.95 **NM** value: **Cover or less**
Circ: CapCity orders: **28,975**
1/SC❑Aug 1995 **NM** value: **4.00**
no cover price. • premium edition (10, 000 copies). **W:** Brian Pulido
★ Origin of Evil Ernie.
2 ❑ Sep 1998 Cover: 2.95 **NM** value: **Cover or less**

EVIL ERNIE: WAR OF THE DEAD — Chaos

1 ❑ Nov 1999 Cover: 2.95 **NM** value: **Cover or less**
Circ: Diamd. preorders: **13,518**
2 ❑ Dec 1999 Cover: 2.95 **NM** value: **Cover or less**
Circ: Diamd. preorders: **11,852**
3 ❑ Jan 2000 Cover: 2.95 **NM** value: **Cover or less**
Circ: Diamd. preorders: **12,493**

EVIL ERNIE: YOUTH GONE WILD — Chaos

1 ❑ Nov 1996, b&w Cover: 1.95 **NM** value: **Cover or less**
• **CGC:** 1 graded, best 9.6
• reprints Eternity's Evil Ernie **W:** Brian Pulido
2 ❑ Dec 1996, b&w Cover: 1.95 **NM** value: **Cover or less**
• reprints Eternity's Evil Ernie **W:** Brian Pulido
3 ❑ Jan 1997, b&w Cover: 1.95 **NM** value: **Cover or less**
• reprints Eternity's Evil Ernie **W:** Brian Pulido
4 ❑ Feb 1997, b&w Cover: 1.95 **NM** value: **Cover or less**
• reprints Eternity's Evil Ernie **W:** Brian Pulido
5 ❑ Mar 1997, b&w Cover: 1.95 **NM** value: **Cover or less**
• reprints Eternity's Evil Ernie **W:** Brian Pulido
SE 1❑ Cover: 4.95 **NM** value: **Cover or less**
Circ: CapCity orders: **7,200**
• "Director's Cut" #1 **W:** Brian Pulido

EVIL EYE — Fantagraphics

1 ❑ Jun 1998 Cover: 2.95 **NM** value: **Cover or less**
2 ❑ Oct 1998 Cover: 2.95 **NM** value: **Cover or less**
3 ❑ Apr 1999 Cover: 2.95 **NM** value: **Cover or less**

EVILMAN SAVES THE WORLD — Moonstone

1 ❑ Jul 1996, b&w Cover: 2.95 **NM** value: **Cover or less**
No issue number.

EWOKS — Marvel / Star

1 ❑ May 1985 Cover: 0.65 **NM** value: **2.00**
Circ: CapCity orders: **7,300** • **CGC:** 2 graded, best 9.6
📖 The Rainbow Bridge **A:** Warren Kremer **W:** Dave Manak
2 ❑ Jul 1985 Cover: 0.65 **NM** value: **1.50**
Circ: CapCity orders: **4,100** • **CGC:** 1 graded, best 9.4
3 ❑ Sep 1985 Cover: 0.65 **NM** value: **1.50**
Circ: CapCity orders: **3,400**
📖 Flight to Danger **A:** Warren Kremer **W:** Dave Manak
4 ❑ Nov 1985 Cover: 0.65 **NM** value: **1.25**
Circ: CapCity orders: **2,700** • **CGC:** 1 graded, best 9.4
5 ❑ Jan 1986 Cover: 0.65 **NM** value: **1.25**
Circ: CapCity orders: **2,200**
6 ❑ Mar 1986 Cover: 0.75 **NM** value: **1.25**
Circ: CapCity orders: **2,150**
7 ❑ May 1986 Cover: 0.75 **NM** value: **1.25**
Circ: CapCity orders: **2,150**
8 ❑ Jul 1986 Cover: 0.75 **NM** value: **1.25**
Circ: CapCity orders: **2,350** • **CGC:** 1 graded, best 9.2
9 ❑ Sep 1986 Cover: 0.75 **NM** value: **1.25**
Circ: CapCity orders: **2,050** • **CGC:** 2 graded, best 9.6
10 ❑ Nov 1986 Cover: 0.75 **NM** value: **1.25**
Circ: CapCity orders: **2,150** • **CGC:** 1 graded, best 8.0
11 ❑ Jan 1987 Cover: 0.75 **NM** value: **1.25**
Circ: CapCity orders: **2,150**
12 ❑ Mar 1987 Cover: 0.75 **NM** value: **1.25**
Circ: CapCity orders: **2,100** • **CGC:** 2 graded, best 9.6
13 ❑ May 1987 Cover: 0.75 **NM** value: **1.25**
Circ: CapCity orders: **1,550**
14 ❑ Jul 1987 Cover: 1.00 **NM** value: **1.25**
Circ: CapCity orders: **1,450**

EXCALIBUR — Marvel

Drawn together by a common menace in the heart of England, the former X-Men Kitty Pryde, Nightcrawler, and Rachel Summers as Phoenix join forces with Captain Britain, shapeshifter Meggan, dragon Lockheed, and a robotic thing called Widget to become Excalibur.

Making its home in a haunted lighthouse, the team is called upon to battle everything from evil wraiths to necromancers bent on destroying the world. The members also travel been back and forth to Limbo enough times to merit frequent-teleport discounts.

Sort of X-Men writer Chris Claremont's pet series, Excalibur is distinguished from some of the other X-titles by its often whimsical bent. The series survived long past Claremont's departure, running exactly 10 years.

-1 ❑ Jul 1997 Cover: 1.99 **NM** value: **2.00**
• Flashback
1 ❑ Oct 1988 Cover: 1.50 **NM** value: **2.50**
Circ: CapCity orders: **93,800** • **CGC:** 6 graded, best 9.6
📖 Warwolves of London! **A:** Alan Davis **W:** Chris Claremont
2 ❑ Nov 1988 Cover: 1.50 **NM** value: **2.00**
Circ: CapCity orders: **68,200**
3 ❑ Dec 1988 Cover: 1.50 **NM** value: **2.00**
Circ: CapCity orders: **62,200**
4 ❑ Jan 1989 Cover: 1.50 **NM** value: **2.00**
Circ: Statement: **317,320** CapCity orders: **57,500**
★ 1st Appearance of Jester (in America), Red Queen (in America), The Crazy Gang (in America), Executioner (in America), Knave (in America).
5 ❑ Feb 1989 Cover: 1.50 **NM** value: **2.00**
Circ: Statement: **317,320** CapCity orders: **57,900**
6 ❑ Mar 1989 Cover: 1.50 **NM** value: **1.75**
Circ: Statement: **317,320** CapCity orders: **60,700**
📖 Inferno • Inferno
7 ❑ Apr 1989 Cover: 1.50 **NM** value: **1.75**
Circ: Statement: **317,320** CapCity orders: **63,100**
📖 Inferno • Inferno
8 ❑ May 1989 Cover: 1.50 **NM** value: **1.75**
Circ: Statement: **317,320** CapCity orders: **56,900**
9 ❑ Jun 1989 Cover: 1.50 **NM** value: **1.75**
Circ: Statement: **317,320** CapCity orders: **57,400**
10 ❑ Jul 1989 Cover: 1.50 **NM** value: **1.75**
Circ: Statement: **317,320** CapCity orders: **58,500**
11 ❑ Aug 1989 Cover: 1.50 **NM** value: **1.75**
Circ: Statement: **317,320** CapCity orders: **60,300**
12 ❑ Sep 1989 Cover: 1.50 **NM** value: **1.75**
Circ: Statement: **317,320** CapCity orders: **59,400**
13 ❑ Oct 1989 Cover: 1.50 **NM** value: **1.75**
Circ: Statement: **317,320** CapCity orders: **59,400**
📖 Cross-Time Caper
14 ❑ Nov 1989 Cover: 1.50 **NM** value: **1.75**
Circ: Statement: **317,320** CapCity orders: **58,200**
📖 Cross-Time Caper
15 ❑ Nov 1989 Cover: 1.50 **NM** value: **1.75**
Circ: Statement: **317,320** CapCity orders: **58,200**
📖 Cross-Time Caper
16 ❑ Dec 1989 Cover: 1.50 **NM** value: **1.75**
Circ: Statement: **317,320** CapCity orders: **57,900**
📖 Cross-Time Caper
17 ❑ Dec 1989 Cover: 1.50 **NM** value: **1.75**
Circ: Statement: **317,320** CapCity orders: **57,000**
📖 Cross-Time Caper
18 ❑ Jan 1990 Cover: 1.50 **NM** value: **1.75**
Circ: Statement: **264,991** CapCity orders: **56,100**
📖 Cross-Time Caper
19 ❑ Feb 1990 Cover: 1.50 **NM** value: **1.75**
Circ: Statement: **264,991** CapCity orders: **54,000**
20 ❑ Mar 1990 Cover: 1.50 **NM** value: **1.75**
Circ: Statement: **264,991** CapCity orders: **53,200**
21 ❑ Apr 1990 Cover: 1.50 **NM** value: **1.75**
Circ: Statement: **264,991** CapCity orders: **48,000**
📖 Cross-Time Caper
22 ❑ May 1990 Cover: 1.50 **NM** value: **1.75**
Circ: Statement: **264,991** CapCity orders: **47,600**
📖 Cross-Time Caper
23 ❑ Jun 1990 Cover: 1.50 **NM** value: **1.75**
Circ: Statement: **264,991** CapCity orders: **47,400**
📖 Cross-Time Caper
24 ❑ Jul 1990 Cover: 1.75 **NM** value: **Cover or less**
Circ: Statement: **264,991** CapCity orders: **46,600**
📖 Cross-Time Caper
25 ❑ Aug 1990 Cover: 1.75 **NM** value: **Cover or less**
Circ: Statement: **264,991** CapCity orders: **43,600**
26 ❑ Aug 1990 Cover: 1.75 **NM** value: **Cover or less**
Circ: Statement: **264,991** CapCity orders: **43,400**
27 ❑ Aug 1990 Cover: 1.75 **NM** value: **Cover or less**
Circ: Statement: **264,991** CapCity orders: **42,400**
28 ❑ Sep 1990 Cover: 1.75 **NM** value: **Cover or less**
Circ: Statement: **264,991** CapCity orders: **41,800**
29 ❑ Sep 1990 Cover: 1.75 **NM** value: **Cover or less**
Circ: Statement: **264,991** CapCity orders: **41,400**
30 ❑ Oct 1990 Cover: 1.75 **NM** value: **Cover or less**
Circ: Statement: **264,991** CapCity orders: **41,400**
31 ❑ Nov 1990 Cover: 1.75 **NM** value: **Cover or less**
Circ: Statement: **264,991** CapCity orders: **40,000**
32 ❑ Dec 1990 Cover: 1.75 **NM** value: **Cover or less**
Circ: Statement: **264,991** CapCity orders: **39,800**
📖 Girl's School Heck, Part 1 • with $1.75 price
32/A❑Dec 1990 Cover: 1.50 **NM** value: **1.75**
📖 Girl's School Heck, Part 1 • with $1.50 price
32/B❑Dec 1990 Cover: 1.75 **NM** value: **Cover or less**
• with $1.75 price
33 ❑ Jan 1991 Cover: 1.75 **NM** value: **Cover or less**
Circ: Statement: **164,188** CapCity orders: **38,600**
📖 Girl's School Heck, Part 2
34 ❑ Feb 1991 Cover: 1.75 **NM** value: **Cover or less**
Circ: Statement: **164,188** CapCity orders: **37,800**
📖 Girl's School Heck, Part 3
35 ❑ Mar 1991 Cover: 1.75 **NM** value: **Cover or less**
Circ: Statement: **164,188** CapCity orders: **35,400**
36 ❑ Apr 1991 Cover: 1.75 **NM** value: **Cover or less**
Circ: Statement: **164,188** CapCity orders: **34,500**
• Outlaws
37 ❑ May 1991 Cover: 1.75 **NM** value: **Cover or less**
Circ: Statement: **164,188** CapCity orders: **34,800** • **CGC:** 1 graded, best 9.6
📖 The Promethean Exchange, Part 1
38 ❑ Jun 1991 Cover: 1.75 **NM** value: **Cover or less**
Circ: Statement: **164,188** CapCity orders: **34,200**
📖 The Promethean Exchange, Part 2
39 ❑ Jul 1991 Cover: 1.75 **NM** value: **Cover or less**
Circ: Statement: **164,188** CapCity orders: **33,300**
📖 The Promethean Exchange, Part 3
40 ❑ Aug 1991 Cover: 1.75 **NM** value: **Cover or less**
Circ: Statement: **164,188** CapCity orders: **37,200**
41 ❑ Sep 1991 Cover: 1.75 **NM** value: **Cover or less**
Circ: Statement: **164,188** CapCity orders: **36,600**
42 ❑ Oct 1991 Cover: 1.75 **NM** value: **Cover or less**
Circ: Statement: **164,188** CapCity orders: **48,900**
43 ❑ Nov 1991 Cover: 1.75 **NM** value: **Cover or less**
Circ: Statement: **164,188** CapCity orders: **37,200**
44 ❑ Nov 1991 Cover: 1.75 **NM** value: **Cover or less**
Circ: Statement: **164,188** CapCity orders: **36,900**
45 ❑ Dec 1991 Cover: 1.75 **NM** value: **Cover or less**
Circ: Statement: **164,188** CapCity orders: **39,300**
46 ❑ Jan 1992 Cover: 1.75 **NM** value: **Cover or less**
Circ: Statement: **170,825** CapCity orders: **38,700**
47 ❑ Feb 1992 Cover: 1.75 **NM** value: **Cover or less**
Circ: Statement: **170,825** CapCity orders: **38,400**
48 ❑ Mar 1992 Cover: 1.75 **NM** value: **Cover or less**
Circ: Statement: **170,825** CapCity orders: **37,200**
49 ❑ Apr 1992 Cover: 1.75 **NM** value: **Cover or less**
Circ: Statement: **170,825** CapCity orders: **34,700**
50 ❑ May 1992 Cover: 2.75 **NM** value: **Cover or less**
Circ: Statement: **170,825** CapCity orders: **44,600**
glow in the dark cover. • Double-size. ★ Origin of Feron.
51 ❑ Jun 1992 Cover: 1.75 **NM** value: **Cover or less**
Circ: Statement: **170,825** CapCity orders: **35,000** • **CGC:** 1 graded, best 9.8
52 ❑ Jul 1992 Cover: 1.75 **NM** value: **Cover or less**
Circ: Statement: **170,825** CapCity orders: **37,100**
53 ❑ Aug 1992 Cover: 1.75 **NM** value: **Cover or less**
Circ: Statement: **170,825** CapCity orders: **36,900**
54 ❑ Sep 1992 Cover: 1.75 **NM** value: **Cover or less**
Circ: Statement: **170,825** CapCity orders: **34,600**
55 ❑ Oct 1992 Cover: 1.75 **NM** value: **Cover or less**
Circ: Statement: **170,825** CapCity orders: **34,800** • **CGC:** 1 graded, best 9.8
56 ❑ Nov 1992 Cover: 1.75 **NM** value: **Cover or less**
Circ: Statement: **170,825** CapCity orders: **34,900**
57 ❑ Nov 1992 Cover: 1.75 **NM** value: **Cover or less**
Circ: Statement: **170,825** CapCity orders: **34,100**
58 ❑ Dec 1992 Cover: 1.75 **NM** value: **Cover or less**
Circ: Statement: **170,825** CapCity orders: **34,000**
59 ❑ Dec 1992 Cover: 1.75 **NM** value: **Cover or less**
Circ: Statement: **170,825** CapCity orders: **33,600**
60 ❑ Jan 1993 Cover: 1.75 **NM** value: **Cover or less**
Circ: Statement: **123,792** CapCity orders: **32,800**
61 ❑ Jan 1993 Cover: 1.75 **NM** value: **Cover or less**
Circ: Statement: **123,792** CapCity orders: **32,700**
62 ❑ Feb 1993 Cover: 1.75 **NM** value: **Cover or less**
Circ: Statement: **123,792** CapCity orders: **33,800**
63 ❑ Mar 1993 Cover: 1.75 **NM** value: **Cover or less**
Circ: Statement: **123,792** CapCity orders: **32,100** • **CGC:** 1 graded, best 9.4

Other grades: Multiply prices above by **1.5 for Mint • 2/3 for Very Fine • 1/3 for Fine • 1/5 for Very Good • 1/8 for Good**

64 ❑ Apr 1993 Cover: 1.75 **NM** value: **Cover or less**
Circ: Statement: **123,792** CapCity orders: **34,200**

65 ❑ May 1993 Cover: 1.75 **NM** value: **Cover or less**
Circ: Statement: **123,792** CapCity orders: **32,100**

66 ❑ Jun 1993 Cover: 1.75 **NM** value: **Cover or less**
Circ: Statement: **123,792** CapCity orders: **32,700** • **CGC:** 1 graded, best 9.8

67 ❑ Jul 1993 Cover: 1.75 **NM** value: **Cover or less**
Circ: Statement: **123,792** CapCity orders: **33,800**

68 ❑ Aug 1993 Cover: 1.75 **NM** value: **Cover or less**
Circ: Statement: **123,792** CapCity orders: **30,400**

69 ❑ Sep 1993 Cover: 1.75 **NM** value: **Cover or less**
Circ: Statement: **123,792** CapCity orders: **29,500**

70 ❑ Oct 1993 Cover: 1.75 **NM** value: **Cover or less**
Circ: Statement: **123,792** CapCity orders: **29,000** • **CGC:** 1 graded, best 9.6

71 ❑ Nov 1993 Cover: 3.95 **NM** value: **4.00**
Circ: Statement: **123,792** CapCity orders: **62,400** • **CGC:** 1 graded, best 9.6
Hologram cover.

72 ❑ Dec 1993 Cover: 1.75 **NM** value: **Cover or less**
Circ: Statement: **123,792** CapCity orders: **30,200** • **CGC:** 1 graded, best 9.6

73 ❑ Jan 1994 Cover: 1.75 **NM** value: **Cover or less**
Circ: Statement: **137,800** CapCity orders: **28,700**

74 ❑ Feb 1994 Cover: 1.75 **NM** value: **Cover or less**
Circ: Statement: **137,800** CapCity orders: **29,850**
• Has 1993 Statement, filed 10/1/93; avg print run 129,344; avg sales 121,642; avg subs 2,150; avg total paid 123,792; samples 125; office use 500; max existent 124,417; 4% of run returned

75 ❑ Mar 1994 Cover: 2.25 **NM** value: **Cover or less**
Circ: Statement: **137,800** CapCity orders: **49,000** • **CGC:** 1 graded, best 9.8
• Giant-size. ★ 1st Appearance of Britannic.

75/SC❑Mar 1994 Cover: 3.50 **NM** value: **Cover or less**
Holo-grafix cover. • Giant-size. ★ 1st Appearance of Britannic..

76 ❑ Apr 1994 Cover: 2.25 **NM** value: **Cover or less**
Circ: Statement: **137,800** CapCity orders: **31,350**

77 ❑ May 1994 Cover: 1.95 **NM** value: **Cover or less**
Circ: Statement: **137,800** CapCity orders: **31,900**

78 ❑ Jun 1994 Cover: 1.95 **NM** value: **Cover or less**
Circ: Statement: **137,800** CapCity orders: **33,250**
📖 The Douglock Chronicles, Part 1

79 ❑ Jul 1994 Cover: 1.95 **NM** value: **Cover or less**
Circ: Statement: **137,800** CapCity orders: **31,900**
📖 The Douglock Chronicles, Part 2

80 ❑ Aug 1994 Cover: 1.95 **NM** value: **Cover or less**
Circ: Statement: **137,800** CapCity orders: **32,100**

81 ❑ Sep 1994 Cover: 1.95 **NM** value: **Cover or less**
Circ: Statement: **137,800** CapCity orders: **33,250**

82 ❑ Oct 1994 Cover: 2.50 **NM** value: **Cover or less**
• Giant-size. 📖 Life Signs, Part 3

82/SC❑Oct 1994 Cover: 3.50 **NM** value: **Cover or less**
Circ: Statement: **137,800**
foil cover. • Giant-size. 📖 Life Signs, Part 3

83 ❑ Nov 1994 Cover: 1.50 **NM** value: **Cover or less**
📖 Soul Sword Trilogy, Part 1

83/Dlx❑Nov 1994 Cover: 1.95 **NM** value: **Cover or less**
Circ: Statement: **137,800** CapCity orders: **32,650**
• Deluxe edition. 📖 Soul Sword Trilogy, Part 1

84 ❑ Dec 1994 Cover: 1.50 **NM** value: **Cover or less**
📖 Soul Sword Trilogy, Part 2

84/Dlx❑Dec 1994 Cover: 1.95 **NM** value: **Cover or less**
Circ: Statement: **137,800** CapCity orders: **33,700**
• Deluxe edition. 📖 Soul Sword Trilogy, Part 2

85 ❑ Jan 1995 Cover: 1.50 **NM** value: **Cover or less**
📖 Soul Sword Trilogy, Part 3

85/Dlx❑Jan 1995 Cover: 1.95 **NM** value: **Cover or less**
Circ: Statement: **167,243** CapCity orders: **33,650**
• Deluxe edition. 📖 Soul Sword Trilogy, Part 3

86 ❑ Feb 1995 Cover: 1.50 **NM** value: **1.95**

86/Dlx❑Feb 1995 Cover: 1.95 **NM** value: **Cover or less**
Circ: Statement: **167,243** CapCity orders: **43,775**
• Deluxe edition.

87 ❑ Jul 1995 Cover: 1.95 **NM** value: **Cover or less**
Circ: Statement: **167,243** CapCity orders: **51,400**
• Has 1994 Statement, filed 10/1/94; avg print run 230,933; avg sales 135,933; avg subs 1,867; avg total paid 137,800; samples 125; office use 500; max existent 138,425; 40% of run returned

88 ❑ Aug 1995 Cover: 1.95 **NM** value: **Cover or less**
Circ: Statement: **167,243** CapCity orders: **48,250**

89 ❑ Sep 1995 Cover: 1.95 **NM** value: **Cover or less**
Circ: Statement: **167,243**

90 ❑ Oct 1995 Cover: 1.95 **NM** value: **Cover or less**
Circ: Statement: **167,243**
• OverPower cards inserted

91 ❑ Nov 1995 Cover: 1.95 **NM** value: **Cover or less**
Circ: Statement: **167,243**

92 ❑ Dec 1995 Cover: 1.95 **NM** value: **Cover or less**
Circ: Statement: **160,838**
📖 Colossus Is Here! **A:** David Williams; Carlos Pacheco **W:** Warren Ellis ★ Appearance of Colossus, Pete Wisdom.

93 ❑ Jan 1996 Cover: 1.95 **NM** value: **Cover or less**
Circ: Statement: **160,838**
• Rahne's past

94 ❑ Feb 1996 Cover: 1.95 **NM** value: **Cover or less**
Circ: Statement: **160,838**
📖 Days of Future Tense • Has 1995 Statement, filed 10/1/95; avg print run 230,417; avg sales 165,082; avg subs 2,161; avg total paid 167,243; samples 750; office use 500; max existent 168,493; 27% of run returned

95 ❑ Mar 1996 Cover: 1.95 **NM** value: **Cover or less**
Circ: Statement: **160,838**

96 ❑ Apr 1996 Cover: 1.95 **NM** value: **Cover or less**
Circ: Statement: **160,838**

97 ❑ May 1996 Cover: 1.95 **NM** value: **Cover or less**
Circ: Statement: **160,838**

98 ❑ Jun 1996 Cover: 1.95 **NM** value: **Cover or less**
Circ: Statement: **160,838**

99 ❑ Jul 1996 Cover: 1.95 **NM** value: **Cover or less**
Circ: Statement: **160,838**

100❑ Aug 1996 Cover: 2.95 **NM** value: **Cover or less**
Circ: Statement: **160,838**
wraparound cover. • Giant-size. 📖 Onslaught: Impact 1

101❑ Sep 1996 Cover: 1.95 **NM** value: **Cover or less**
Circ: Statement: **160,838**

102❑ Oct 1996 Cover: 1.95 **NM** value: **Cover or less**
Circ: Statement: **112,177** Direct Market orders: **102,250**
• bound-in trading cards

103❑ Nov 1996 Cover: 1.95 **NM** value: **Cover or less**
Circ: Statement: **112,177**

104❑ Dec 1996 Cover: 1.95 **NM** value: **Cover or less**
Circ: Statement: **112,177** Direct Market orders: **100,750**

105❑ Jan 1997 Cover: 1.95 **NM** value: **Cover or less**
Circ: Statement: **112,177** Direct Market orders: **96,000**
📖 Hard Truths **A:** Bryan Hitch **W:** Keith Giffen

106❑ Feb 1997 Cover: 1.95 **NM** value: **Cover or less**
Circ: Statement: **112,177** Direct Market orders: **90,750**
📖 A Portrait of the Artist **A:** Aaron Lopresti; Randy Green; Rob Haynes; Casey Jones **W:** Ben Raab

107❑ Mar 1997 Cover: 1.95 **NM** value: **Cover or less**
Circ: Statement: **112,177** Direct Market orders: **85,250**
📖 Focus **A:** Salvador Larroca **W:** Ben Raab

108❑ Apr 1997 Cover: 1.95 **NM** value: **Cover or less**
Circ: Statement: **112,177** Direct Market orders: **81,250**
📖 The Old Ways **A:** Salvador Larroca **W:** Ben Raab

109❑ May 1997 Cover: 1.95 **NM** value: **Cover or less**
Circ: Statement: **112,177** Diamd. preorders: **80,026**
📖 Dragon Moon Rising **A:** Salvador Larroca **W:** Ben Raab ★ Versus Spiral.

110❑ Jun 1997 Cover: 1.95 **NM** value: **1.99**
Circ: Statement: **112,177** Diamd. preorders: **80,073**
📖 Hearts Bled Crimson **A:** Salvador Larroca **W:** Ben Raab

111❑ Aug 1997 Cover: 1.99 **NM** value: **Cover or less**
Circ: Statement: **112,177** Diamd. preorders: **73,365**
• gatefold summary.

112❑ Sep 1997 Cover: 1.99 **NM** value: **Cover or less**
Circ: Statement: **112,177** Diamd. preorders: **70,406**
• gatefold summary.

113❑ Oct 1997 Cover: 1.99 **NM** value: **Cover or less**
Circ: Diamd. preorders: **69,379**
• gatefold summary. ★ Appearance of High Evolutionary.

114❑ Nov 1997 Cover: 1.99 **NM** value: **Cover or less**
Circ: Diamd. preorders: **67,920**
• gatefold summary.

115❑ Dec 1997 Cover: 1.99 **NM** value: **Cover or less**
Circ: Diamd. preorders: **66,182**
• gatefold summary. • Has 1997 Statement, filed 10/1/97; avg print run 156,083; avg sales 110,127; avg subs 2,050; avg total paid 112,177; 28% of run returned

116❑ Jan 1998 Cover: 1.99 **NM** value: **Cover or less**
Circ: Diamd. preorders: **63,287**
• gatefold summary.

117❑ Feb 1998 Cover: 1.99 **NM** value: **Cover or less**
Circ: Diamd. preorders: **60,344**
• gatefold summary.

118❑ Mar 1998 Cover: 1.99 **NM** value: **Cover or less**
Circ: Diamd. preorders: **57,612**
• gatefold summary.

119❑ Apr 1998 Cover: 1.99 **NM** value: **Cover or less**
Circ: Diamd. preorders: **54,077**
• gatefold summary. ★ Versus Nightmare.

120❑ May 1998 Cover: 1.99 **NM** value: **Cover or less**
Circ: Diamd. preorders: **53,015**
• gatefold summary.

121❑ Jun 1998 Cover: 1.99 **NM** value: **Cover or less**
Circ: Diamd. preorders: **52,855**
• gatefold summary.

122❑ Jul 1998 Cover: 1.99 **NM** value: **Cover or less**
Circ: Diamd. preorders: **49,297**
• gatefold summary. ★ Versus Prime Sentinels.

123❑ Aug 1998 Cover: 1.99 **NM** value: **Cover or less**
Circ: Diamd. preorders: **49,164**
• gatefold summary. ★ Versus Mimic.

124❑ Sep 1998 Cover: 1.99 **NM** value: **Cover or less**
Circ: Diamd. preorders: **46,827**
• gatefold summary. • Captain Britain's bachelor party

125❑ Oct 1998 Cover: 2.99 **NM** value: **3.00**
Circ: Diamd. preorders: **50,336**
• Giant-size. final issue. • Wedding of Captain Britain, Meggan

Anl 1❑ca. 1993 Cover: 2.95 **NM** value: **Cover or less**
Circ: CapCity orders: **31,900**
📖 Soul Sword Trilogy, Part 3 • trading card ★ 1st Appearance of Ghath.

Anl 2❑ca. 1994 Cover: 2.95 **NM** value: **Cover or less**
Circ: CapCity orders: **22,950**

EXCALIBUR: AIR APPARENT — Marvel

1 ❑ Dec 1991 Cover: 4.95 **NM** value: **5.00**
No issue number. • Air Apparent Special Edition.

EXCALIBUR (MINI-SERIES) — Marvel

1 ❑ Feb 2001 Cover: 2.99 **NM** value: **Cover or less**
📖 Camelot Lost **A:** Pablo Raimondi **W:** Ben Raab

2 ❑ Mar 2001 Cover: 2.99 **NM** value: **Cover or less**
📖 The Ruined Land **A:** Pablo Raimondi **W:** Ben Raab

3 ❑ Apr 2001 Cover: 2.99 **NM** value: **Cover or less**
📖 Destiny's Children **A:** Pablo Raimondi **W:** Ben Raab

EXCALIBUR: MOJO MAYHEM — Marvel

1 ❑ Dec 1989 Cover: 4.50 **NM** value: **Cover or less**
No issue number.

EXCALIBUR: SWORD OF POWER — Marvel

1 ❑ 2002 Cover: 2.99 **NM** value: **Cover or less**
2 ❑ 2002 Cover: 2.99 **NM** value: **Cover or less**
3 ❑ 2002 Cover: 2.99 **NM** value: **Cover or less**
4 ❑ 2002 Cover: 2.99 **NM** value: **Cover or less**

EXCALIBUR: THE POSSESSION — Marvel

1 ❑ Jul 1991 Cover: 2.95 **NM** value: **Cover or less**
• **CGC:** 2 graded, best 9.6

EXCALIBUR: THE SWORD IS DRAWN — Marvel

1 ❑ ca. 1988 Cover: 3.25 **NM** value: **5.00**
Circ: CapCity orders: **73,400**
• prestige format. 📖 Sword is Drawn ★ Origin of Excalibur. ★ 1st Appearance of Excalibur.

1-2 ❑ Cover: 3.50 **NM** value: **Cover or less**
Circ: CapCity orders: **8,350**

1-3 ❑ Cover: 3.50 **NM** value: **Cover or less**

EXCALIBUR: WEIRD WAR III — Marvel

During the multi-issue Cross-Time Caper, Excalibur encountered an alternate dimension where the Nazis had won World War II and their counterparts acted as Hitler's personal guards.

Now, dimensional barriers have been breached again, causing the two worlds and all their citizens to merge, with only the members of Excalibur aware of the change. Unfortunately, the "evil" personas are most dominant, and the heroes find themselves fighting Professor Xavier, founder of the Uncanny X-Men. In service to Hitler, but also pursuing his own twisted goals, he is slaughtering mutants by the dozens, using the vast psychic energies released in their death throes to create the ultimate super-being.

The one hope for victory rests with Rachel Summers, the Phoenix, a unique being with no counterparts in either world or the rest of the multiverse.

1 ❑ Dec 1990 Cover: 9.95 **NM** value: **Cover or less**
Circ: CapCity orders: **8,850**

EXCALIBUR: XX CROSSING — Marvel

1 ❑ May 1992 Cover: 2.50 **NM** value: **Cover or less**
indicia says May, cover says Jul. ★ Appearance of X-Men.

EXCITING COMICS — Nedor

The anthology title featured a mix of stories, but the costumed hero The Black Terror (and sidekick Tim) was not only a focal character but also the cover feature for much of his run (#9 until the end of the series). Jungle-dwelling damsels Kara (the Jungle Empress) and Judy (of the Jungle) showed a bit of leg and provided a counterpoint to the Terror, but other features ranged from teen humor to detective to military stories.

The Terror and Tim, along with other characters from their universe, returned for an adventure in Alan Moore's Tom Strong in 2001. — Maggie

1 ❑ Apr 1940 Cover: 0.10 **NM** value: **3000.00**
• **CGC:** 1 graded, best 7.5
2 ❑ May 1940 Cover: 0.10 **NM** value: **1500.00**
• **CGC:** 2 graded, best 8.0
3 ❑ Jun 1940 Cover: 0.10 **NM** value: **1000.00**
• **CGC:** 1 graded, best 7.0
4 ❑ Jul 1940 Cover: 0.10 **NM** value: **650.00**
• **CGC:** 1 graded, best 7.5
5 ❑ Sep 1940 Cover: 0.10 **NM** value: **650.00**
• **CGC:** 1 graded, best 9.0
6 ❑ Nov 1940 Cover: 0.10 **NM** value: **650.00**
• **CGC:** 1 graded, best .5
7 ❑ Jan 1941 Cover: 0.10 **NM** value: **600.00**
• **CGC:** 2 graded, best 7.0
8 ❑ Mar 1941 Cover: 0.10 **NM** value: **600.00**
• **CGC:** 2 graded, best 7.0
9 ❑ May 1941 Cover: 0.10 **NM** value: **600.00**
10 ❑ Jun 1941 Cover: 0.10 **NM** value: **600.00**
11 ❑ Jul 1941 Cover: 0.10 **NM** value: **550.00**
• **CGC:** 1 graded, best 5.5
12 ❑ Aug 1941 Cover: 0.10 **NM** value: **550.00**
13 ❑ Oct 1941 Cover: 0.10 **NM** value: **550.00**
• **CGC:** 1 graded, best 5.0
14 ❑ Nov 1941 Cover: 0.10 **NM** value: **550.00**
15 ❑ Dec 1941 Cover: 0.10 **NM** value: **550.00**
16 ❑ Jan 1942 Cover: 0.10 **NM** value: **550.00**
17 ❑ Mar 1942 Cover: 0.10 **NM** value: **550.00**
18 ❑ Apr 1942 Cover: 0.10 **NM** value: **550.00**
19 ❑ May 1942 Cover: 0.10 **NM** value: **550.00**
20 ❑ Jul 1942 Cover: 0.10 **NM** value: **500.00**
21 ❑ Aug 1942 Cover: 0.10 **NM** value: **500.00**
• **CGC:** 1 graded, best 5.0
22 ❑ Oct 1942 Cover: 0.10 **NM** value: **500.00**
23 ❑ Dec 1942 Cover: 0.10 **NM** value: **500.00**
24 ❑ Jan 1943 Cover: 0.10 **NM** value: **500.00**
• **CGC:** 1 graded, best 9.0
25 ❑ Feb 1943 Cover: 0.10 **NM** value: **500.00**
26 ❑ Apr 1943 Cover: 0.10 **NM** value: **500.00**
• **CGC:** 2 graded, best 9.6
27 ❑ Jun 1943 Cover: 0.10 **NM** value: **500.00**

CGC-graded: Multiply prices above by **33 for 9.9 M** • **16 for 9.8 NM/M** • **7 for 9.6 NM+** • **5 for 9.4 NM** • **2.5 for 9.2 NM-** • **1.5 for 9.0 VF/NM**

28 ❑ Aug 1943 Cover: 0.10 **NM** value: **500.00**
• **CGC:** 1 graded, best 4.0
29 ❑ Oct 1943 Cover: 0.10 **NM** value: **500.00**
• **CGC:** 2 graded, best 6.0
30 ❑ Dec 1943 Cover: 0.10 **NM** value: **450.00**
• **CGC:** 1 graded, best 9.0
31 ❑ Feb 1944 Cover: 0.10 **NM** value: **450.00**
• **CGC:** 3 graded, best 9.6
32 ❑ Apr 1944 Cover: 0.10 **NM** value: **450.00**
• **CGC:** 1 graded, best 7.0
33 ❑ Jun 1944 Cover: 0.10 **NM** value: **450.00**
• **CGC:** 2 graded, best 9.0
34 ❑ Aug 1944 Cover: 0.10 **NM** value: **450.00**
• **CGC:** 2 graded, best 9.2
35 ❑ Oct 1944 Cover: 0.10 **NM** value: **450.00**
• **CGC:** 1 graded, best 9.0
36 ❑ Dec 1944 Cover: 0.10 **NM** value: **450.00**
37 ❑ Feb 1945 Cover: 0.10 **NM** value: **450.00**
• **CGC:** 1 graded, best 7.0
38 ❑ Apr 1945 Cover: 0.10 **NM** value: **450.00**
• **CGC:** 1 graded, best 9.2
39 ❑ Jun 1945 Cover: 0.10 **NM** value: **450.00**
• **CGC:** 4 graded, best 9.2
40 ❑ Aug 1945 Cover: 0.10 **NM** value: **450.00**
• **CGC:** 1 graded, best 7.5
41 ❑ Oct 1945 Cover: 0.10 **NM** value: **400.00**
• **CGC:** 2 graded, best 7.0
42 ❑ Dec 1945 Cover: 0.10 **NM** value: **400.00**
• **CGC:** 2 graded, best 7.5
43 ❑ Jan 1946 Cover: 0.10 **NM** value: **400.00**
• **CGC:** 1 graded, best 6.5
44 ❑ Feb 1946 Cover: 0.10 **NM** value: **400.00**
• **CGC:** 2 graded, best 7.5
45 ❑ Mar 1946 Cover: 0.10 **NM** value: **400.00**
46 ❑ Apr 1946 Cover: 0.10 **NM** value: **400.00**
47 ❑ May 1946 Cover: 0.10 **NM** value: **400.00**
48 ❑ Jun 1946 Cover: 0.10 **NM** value: **400.00**
• **CGC:** 1 graded, best 7.0
49 ❑ Jul 1946 Cover: 0.10 **NM** value: **400.00**
50 ❑ Aug 1946 Cover: 0.10 **NM** value: **400.00**
51 ❑ Sep 1946 Cover: 0.10 **NM** value: **350.00**
• **CGC:** 1 graded, best 9.4
52 ❑ Nov 1946 Cover: 0.10 **NM** value: **350.00**
• **CGC:** 3 graded, best 9.0
53 ❑ Jan 1947 Cover: 0.10 **NM** value: **350.00**
• **CGC:** 1 graded, best 2.5
54 ❑ Mar 1947 Cover: 0.10 **NM** value: **350.00**
55 ❑ May 1947 Cover: 0.10 **NM** value: **350.00**
• **CGC:** 1 graded, best 9.0
56 ❑ Jul 1947 Cover: 0.10 **NM** value: **350.00**
• **CGC:** 1 graded, best 9.4
57 ❑ Sep 1947 Cover: 0.10 **NM** value: **350.00**
• **CGC:** 7 graded, best 9.4
58 ❑ Nov 1947 Cover: 0.10 **NM** value: **350.00**
• **CGC:** 3 graded, best 9.4
59 ❑ Jan 1948 Cover: 0.10 **NM** value: **350.00**
• **CGC:** 6 graded, best 9.2
60 ❑ Mar 1948 Cover: 0.10 **NM** value: **350.00**
• **CGC:** 2 graded, best 9.0
61 ❑ May 1948 Cover: 0.10 **NM** value: **325.00**
• **CGC:** 1 graded, best 9.2
62 ❑ Jul 1948 Cover: 0.10 **NM** value: **325.00**
• **CGC:** 3 graded, best 9.2
63 ❑ Sep 1948 Cover: 0.10 **NM** value: **325.00**
64 ❑ Nov 1948 Cover: 0.10 **NM** value: **325.00**
• **CGC:** 3 graded, best 8.5
65 ❑ Jan 1949 Cover: 0.10 **NM** value: **325.00**
• **CGC:** 3 graded, best 9.4
66 ❑ Mar 1949 Cover: 0.10 **NM** value: **325.00**
• **CGC:** 2 graded, best 8.0
67 ❑ May 1949 Cover: 0.10 **NM** value: **325.00**
• **CGC:** 1 graded, best 9.8
68 ❑ Jul 1949 Cover: 0.10 **NM** value: **325.00**
• **CGC:** 1 graded, best 9.4
69 ❑ Sep 1949 Cover: 0.10 **NM** value: **325.00**

EXCITING WAR — Standard
5 ❑ Sep 1952 Cover: 0.10 **NM** value: **40.00**
• Series continued from.. (?)
6 ❑ Dec 1952 Cover: 0.10 **NM** value: **30.00**
• **CGC:** 1 graded, best 6.5
📖 Stand…or Die; Mop-Up Operation; G.I. General; Trojan Horse Korean Style (text story) **W:** Charles Strong
7 ❑ ca. 1953 Cover: 0.10 **NM** value: **30.00**
8 ❑ May 1953 Cover: 0.10 **NM** value: **30.00**
9 ❑ Nov 1953 Cover: 0.10 **NM** value: **30.00**
final issue.

EXCITING X-PATROL — Marvel / Amalgam
1 ❑ Jun 1997 Cover: 1.95 **NM** value: **Cover or less**
Circ: Diamd. preorders: **135,340**
📖 The Curse of Brother Brood! **A:** Bryan Hitch **W:** Barbara Kesel

EXECUTIONER, THE: DEATH SQUAD (DON PENDLETON'S...) — Vivid
1 ❑ b&w Cover: 12.95 **NM** value: **Cover or less**
• adapts prose novel

EXHIBITIONIST, THE — Eros
1 ❑ Cover: 2.75 **NM** value: **Cover or less**
2 ❑ Aug 1994 Cover: 2.75 **NM** value: **Cover or less**

EXILE — Eyeball Soup Designs
1 ❑ May 1996, b&w Cover: 2.95 **NM** value: **Cover or less**
cardstock cover.
2 ❑ Jul 1996, b&w Cover: 2.95 **NM** value: **Cover or less**
cardstock cover.

EXILED, THE — Exiled Studios
1 ❑ Jan 1998 Cover: 2.75 **NM** value: **Cover or less**
Circ: Diamd. preorders: **5,472**
📖 Cry Baby **A:** Greg LaRocque **W:** Greg LaRocque
2 ❑ Apr 1998 Cover: 2.75 **NM** value: **Cover or less**
3 ❑ Jun 1998 Cover: 2.75 **NM** value: **Cover or less**
cover says 98, indicia says 97.

EXILE EARTH — River City
1 ❑ ca. 1994 Cover: 1.95 **NM** value: **Cover or less**
2 ❑ ca. 1994 Cover: 1.95 **NM** value: **Cover or less**

EXILES — Malibu
Nobody seems to know where the Theta Virus comes from, but many know what it does. It radically affects the human DNA structure, causing strange mutations. Left to run its course, it is uniformly fatal. Nevertheless, the people infected with it are known as "potentials" — for if the mutations were somehow harnessed, it might be possible to turn the Theta victims into something more than human.

The Exiles are a super-powered group led by Dr. Rachel Deming. Their task is to find youngsters who have been infected by the Theta virus and try to save them. As it turns out, these victims need saving from more than the virus, for there are powerful forces in the world that rather like the idea of raising an army of super-powered soldiers — and they won't let a little bloodshed get in the way of achieving that goal.

Another attempt to go after X-Men's audience, Exiles would later cross over with that series once Marvel bought Malibu.

1 ❑ Aug 1993, b&w Cover: 1.95 **NM** value: **2.00**
Circ: CapCity orders: **33,150**
1/SC❑Aug 1993 **NM** value: **5.00**
Hologram cover. • hologram★ 1st Appearance of The Exiles.
2 ❑ Sep 1993 Cover: 1.95 **NM** value: **2.00**
3 ❑ Oct 1993 Cover: 2.50 **NM** value: **Cover or less**
Circ: CapCity orders: **28,950** Diamd. preorders: **45,771**
📖 Rune, Part E • Rune **A:** Barry Windsor-Smith
4 ❑ Nov 1993 Cover: 1.95 **NM** value: **2.00**
Circ: CapCity orders: **22,025** Diamd. preorders: **45,313**
final issue.★ Death of Exiles.

EXILES (ALPHA) — Alpha Productions
1 ❑ b&w Cover: 1.95 **NM** value: **Cover or less**

EXILES (MARVEL) — Marvel
1 ❑ 2001 Cover: 2.99 **NM** value: **Cover or less**
Circ: Diamd. preorders: **59,785** • **CGC:** 3 graded, best 9.6
2 ❑ 2001 Cover: 2.25 **NM** value: **Cover or less**
Circ: Diamd. preorders: **59,139**
3 ❑ 2001 Cover: 2.25 **NM** value: **Cover or less**
Circ: Diamd. preorders: **54,873**
4 ❑ 2001 Cover: 2.25 **NM** value: **Cover or less**
Circ: Diamd. preorders: **47,866**
5 ❑ 2001 Cover: 2.25 **NM** value: **Cover or less**
Circ: Diamd. preorders: **43,071**
6 ❑ 2002 Cover: 2.25 **NM** value: **Cover or less**
Circ: Diamd. preorders: **42,271**
7 ❑ 2002 Cover: 2.25 **NM** value: **Cover or less**
Circ: Diamd. preorders: **40,361**
8 ❑ 2002 Cover: 2.25 **NM** value: **Cover or less**
9 ❑ 2002 Cover: 2.25 **NM** value: **Cover or less**

EXIT 6 — Plastic Spoon Press
1 ❑ Aug 1998, b&w Cover: 2.95 **NM** value: **Cover or less**
2/Ash❑Aug 1998 Cover: 2.95 **NM** value: **Cover or less**
• preview of upcoming issue **A:** Sean Tiffany **W:** Sean Tiffany
3 ❑ Jan 1999 Cover: 2.95 **NM** value: **Cover or less**
3/Ash❑Aug 1998 Cover: 2.95 **NM** value: **Cover or less**
• preview of upcoming issue **A:** Sean Tiffany **W:** Sean Tiffany

EXIT FROM SHADOW — Bronze Man
4 ❑ Cover: 2.95 **NM** value: **Cover or less**
indicia has name change, cover doesn't. • was Secret Killers

EXIT (VOL. 2) — Caliber
1 ❑ Cover: 2.95 **NM** value: **Cover or less**
Circ: CapCity orders: **1,935**
📖 Traitors, Part 1 **A:** Nabiel Kanan **W:** Nabiel Kanan
2 ❑ Cover: 2.95 **NM** value: **Cover or less**
📖 Traitors, Part 2 **A:** Nabiel Kanan **W:** Nabiel Kanan
3 ❑ Cover: 2.95 **NM** value: **Cover or less**
📖 Traitors, Part 3 **A:** Nabiel Kanan **W:** Nabiel Kanan
4 ❑ Cover: 2.95 **NM** value: **Cover or less**
📖 Traitors, Part 4 **A:** Nabiel Kanan **W:** Nabiel Kanan
5 ❑ Cover: 2.95 **NM** value: **Cover or less**
📖 Traitors, Part 5 **A:** Nabiel Kanan **W:** Nabiel Kanan
Bk 1❑ Cover: 14.95 **NM** value: **Cover or less**

EX-MUTANTS (AMAZING) — Pied Piper / Amazing
1 ❑ Cover: 1.80 **NM** value: **2.00**
2 ❑ Cover: 1.80 **NM** value: **2.00**
3 ❑ Cover: 1.80 **NM** value: **2.00**
4 ❑ Cover: 1.95 **NM** value: **2.00**
5 ❑ Cover: 1.95 **NM** value: **2.00**
📖 Enter the New Humans **A:** Ron Lim; Tim Dzon **W:** David Lawrence
★ Appearance of New Humans.
6 ❑ Jul 1987 Cover: 1.95 **NM** value: **2.00**
7 ❑ Cover: 1.95 **NM** value: **2.00**
8 ❑ Cover: 1.95 **NM** value: **2.00**
SE 1❑ Spr 1987, b&w Cover: 1.80 **NM** value: **2.00**
Circ: CapCity orders: **1,585**

EX-MUTANTS (ETERNITY) — Eternity
Ex-Mutants tackles a familiar concept in fantasy fiction: the aftermath. On a world ravaged by atomic war, the landscape is peopled entirely of hideously mutated monsters who were once human. In this savage world, Dr. Emmanuel Cugat, a relatively mildly deformed professor, undertakes an experiment to create five normal humans who can rebuild the human race. Erin, Belushi, Vikki, Angela, and Lorelei soon find themselves hunted by the mutated creatures around them. To survive, they need both their wits and advanced skills in the martial arts.

If you didn't already know this was one more "mutant" title playing off the success of Marvel's X-Men, check out the leader's name again. Cugat. Xavier. Subtle, huh?

1 ❑ Cover: 1.80 **NM** value: **2.00**
• **CGC:** 1 graded, best 9.2
📖 A Breed Apart **A:** Ron Lim; Mike Witherby **W:** Anthony Pereira; David Lawrence
2 ❑ Cover: 1.95 **NM** value: **2.00**
3 ❑ Cover: 1.95 **NM** value: **2.00**
4 ❑ Oct 1988 Cover: 1.95 **NM** value: **2.00**
5 ❑ 1988 Cover: 1.95 **NM** value: **2.00**
6 ❑ 1988 Cover: 1.95 **NM** value: **2.00**
7 ❑ 1988 Cover: 1.95 **NM** value: **2.00**
Circ: CapCity orders: **5,550**
8 ❑ Jan 1989 Cover: 1.95 **NM** value: **2.00**
9 ❑ Feb 1989 Cover: 1.95 **NM** value: **2.00**
10 ❑ Cover: 1.95 **NM** value: **2.00**
11 ❑ Cover: 1.95 **NM** value: **2.00**
12 ❑ Cover: 1.95 **NM** value: **2.00**
13 ❑ Cover: 1.95 **NM** value: **2.00**
14 ❑ Cover: 1.95 **NM** value: **2.00**
15 ❑ Cover: 1.95 **NM** value: **Cover or less**
Anl 1❑Mar 1998 Cover: 1.95 **NM** value: **Cover or less**
Bk 1❑ b&w Cover: 6.95 **NM** value: **Cover or less**
Bk 2❑ Cover: 7.95 **NM** value: **Cover or less**
📖 Gods or Men

EX-MUTANTS (MALIBU) — Malibu
1 ❑ Nov 1992 Cover: 1.95 **NM** value: **2.00**
Circ: CapCity orders: **29,650**
1/SC❑Nov 1992 **NM** value: **2.50**
shiny cover. ★ Origin of Ex-Mutants.
2 ❑ Dec 1992 Cover: 1.95 **NM** value: **Cover or less**
Circ: CapCity orders: **14,350**
3 ❑ Jan 1993 Cover: 1.95 **NM** value: **Cover or less**
Circ: CapCity orders: **10,575**
4 ❑ Feb 1993 Cover: 1.95 **NM** value: **Cover or less**
Circ: CapCity orders: **9,775**
5 ❑ Mar 1993 Cover: 1.95 **NM** value: **Cover or less**
Circ: CapCity orders: **8,225**
6 ❑ Apr 1993 Cover: 1.95 **NM** value: **Cover or less**
Circ: CapCity orders: **7,300**
7 ❑ May 1993 Cover: 1.95 **NM** value: **Cover or less**
Circ: CapCity orders: **6,900**
8 ❑ Jun 1993 Cover: 1.95 **NM** value: **Cover or less**
Circ: CapCity orders: **6,525**
9 ❑ Jul 1993 Cover: 1.95 **NM** value: **Cover or less**
Circ: CapCity orders: **5,700**
10 ❑ Aug 1993 Cover: 1.95 **NM** value: **Cover or less**
Circ: CapCity orders: **5,275**
11 ❑ Sep 1993 Cover: 2.25 **NM** value: **Cover or less**
Circ: CapCity orders: **8,075**
12 ❑ Oct 1993 Cover: 2.25 **NM** value: **Cover or less**
Circ: CapCity orders: **7,375**
13 ❑ Nov 1993 Cover: 2.25 **NM** value: **Cover or less**
Circ: CapCity orders: **5,525**
• Genesis begins publishing
14 ❑ Dec 1993 Cover: 2.25 **NM** value: **Cover or less**
Circ: CapCity orders: **4,375**
• Genesis
15 ❑ Jan 1994 Cover: 2.50 **NM** value: **Cover or less**
Circ: CapCity orders: **3,775**
• Genesis
16 ❑ Feb 1994 Cover: 2.50 **NM** value: **Cover or less**
Circ: CapCity orders: **3,275**
• Genesis
17 ❑ Mar 1994 Cover: 2.50 **NM** value: **Cover or less**
Circ: CapCity orders: **2,975**
• Genesis
18 ❑ Apr 1994 Cover: 2.50 **NM** value: **Cover or less**
Circ: CapCity orders: **2,700**
final issue. • Genesis

EX-MUTANTS MICROSERIES: ERIN (LAWRENCE & LIM'S...) — Pied Piper
1 ❑ b&w Cover: 1.95 **NM** value: **Cover or less**

EX-MUTANTS PIN-UP BOOK — Eternity
1 ❑ Cover: 1.95 **NM** value: **Cover or less**
Circ: CapCity orders: **3,800**

EXODUS REVELATION — Exodus
1 ❑ Nov 1994, b&w **NM** value: **1.00**
no cover price.

EXOSQUAD — Topps
At the end of the 21st century, mankind began to settle Mars and Venus. To survive in these alien environments, it created Neo-Sapiens, genetically engineered to thrive under harsh conditions. The Neo-Sapiens staged a rebellion against the human rulers of Mars and Venus, and only the advanced "exo" technology employed by the humans allowed them to put down the rebellion.

Other grades: Multiply prices above by **1.5 for Mint • 2/3 for Very Fine • 1/3 for Fine • 1/5 for Very Good • 1/8 for Good**

These exo-skeletons of robotic armor and weaponry became the basis for the formation of "exo-squads"-daring troubleshooters who kept the peace. But now, 50 years after the original Neo-Sapien uprisings, the exo-squads are being called upon to stop a new threat by the still-resentful Neo-Sapiens.

It's techie adventure, based on a 1990s animated series, produced and created by Will Meugniot.

0 ❑ Jan 1994 Cover: 1.00 **NM** value: **Cover or less**
Circ: CapCity orders: **6,475**
cardstock cover. **A:** Joe Staton **W:** Len Wein ★ 1st Appearance of Exosquad.

EXOTICA — Cry for Dawn
All issues are adults only.
1 ❑ b&w **NM** value: **4.00**

EXOTIC FANTASY — Fantagraphics / Eros
All issues are adults only.
1 ❑ b&w Cover: 4.95 **NM** value: **Cover or less**
• sketches
2 ❑ b&w Cover: 4.95 **NM** value: **Cover or less**
• sketches
3 ❑ b&w Cover: 4.95 **NM** value: **Cover or less**
• sketches

EXOTIC ROMANCES — Comic Magazines
22 ❑ ca. 1955 Cover: 0.10 **NM** value: **28.00**
• Series continued from True War Romances #21
23 ❑ ca. 1955 Cover: 0.10 **NM** value: **28.00**
📖 The Man for Me; The Girl who was Left Behind!; My Heart was in the Ring; Gilded Love (text piece); One Life to Live
24 ❑ ca. 1956 Cover: 0.10 **NM** value: **28.00**
25 ❑ ca. 1956 Cover: 0.10 **NM** value: **28.00**
26 ❑ ca. 1956 Cover: 0.10 **NM** value: **28.00**
27 ❑ ca. 1956 Cover: 0.10 **NM** value: **28.00**
28 ❑ ca. 1956 Cover: 0.10 **NM** value: **28.00**
29 ❑ ca. 1956 Cover: 0.10 **NM** value: **28.00**
30 ❑ ca. 1956 Cover: 0.10 **NM** value: **24.00**
31 ❑ ca. 1956 Cover: 0.10 **NM** value: **24.00**
final issue.

EXPERIENCE, THE — Aircel
All issues are adults only.
1 ❑ b&w **NM** value: **3.25**

EXPLOITS OF DANIEL BOONE — Quality
1 ❑ Nov 1955 Cover: 0.10 **NM** value: **200.00**
• **CGC:** 1 graded, best 3.5
2 ❑ Jan 1956 Cover: 0.10 **NM** value: **125.00**
3 ❑ Mar 1956 Cover: 0.10 **NM** value: **100.00**
• **CGC:** 1 graded, best 4.5
4 ❑ May 1956 Cover: 0.10 **NM** value: **100.00**
5 ❑ Jul 1956 Cover: 0.10 **NM** value: **100.00**
6 ❑ Sep 1956 Cover: 0.10 **NM** value: **100.00**

EXPLORERS — Explorer
1 ❑ ca. 1996, b&w Cover: 2.95 **NM** value: **Cover or less**
2 ❑ ca. 1996, b&w Cover: 2.95 **NM** value: **Cover or less**
3 ❑ ca. 1996, b&w Cover: 2.95 **NM** value: **Cover or less**

EXPLORERS (VOL. 2) — Caliber / Tapestry
1 ❑ ca. 1996, b&w Cover: 2.95 **NM** value: **Cover or less**
2 ❑ ca. 1996, b&w Cover: 2.95 **NM** value: **Cover or less**

EXPLORERS OF THE UNKNOWN — Archie
1 ❑ Jun 1990 Cover: 1.00 **NM** value: **Cover or less**
2 ❑ Aug 1990 Cover: 1.00 **NM** value: **Cover or less**
3 ❑ Oct 1990 Cover: 1.00 **NM** value: **Cover or less**
4 ❑ Dec 1990 Cover: 1.00 **NM** value: **Cover or less**
5 ❑ Feb 1991 Cover: 1.00 **NM** value: **Cover or less**
6 ❑ Apr 1991 Cover: 1.00 **NM** value: **Cover or less**

EXPOSE — Cracked Pepper
1 ❑ Dec 1993, b&w Cover: 2.50 **NM** value: **Cover or less**

EXPOSED — D.S.
1 ❑ Mar 1948 Cover: 0.10 **NM** value: **150.00**
2 ❑ May 1948 Cover: 0.10 **NM** value: **150.00**
3 ❑ Jul 1948 Cover: 0.10 **NM** value: **100.00**
4 ❑ Sep 1948 Cover: 0.10 **NM** value: **100.00**
5 ❑ Nov 1948 Cover: 0.10 **NM** value: **100.00**
6 ❑ Jan 1949 Cover: 0.10 **NM** value: **75.00**
• **CGC:** 1 graded, best 8.5
7 ❑ Mar 1949 Cover: 0.10 **NM** value: **75.00**
8 ❑ May 1949 Cover: 0.10 **NM** value: **75.00**
9 ❑ Jul 1949 Cover: 0.10 **NM** value: **75.00**

EXPOSURE — Image

The hunt for a collection of ancient coins, roaming bands of vicious vampires, and tight, short clothing are just some of the irritants a female police officer and a psychic female coroner must deal with in this title.

Filled with good girl pinups, a very busy story, and lots of action, this offering from writers David Campiti and Al Rio offers a unique twist on the vampire legend. While the connection between the coins, a series of brutal Catholic murders in Old Town San Diego, and Judas Iscariot is more contrivance than explanation, it's still there. And for those who find even that too much plot to deal with, there's plenty of distraction offered by the skintight, rip-away outfits that fall off the heroines every other page.

1 ❑ Nov 1999 Cover: 2.50 **NM** value: **Cover or less**
Circ: Diamd. preorders: **21,676**
📖 Black Sabbath **A:** Al Rio; David Campiti **W:** Al Rio; David Campiti
2 ❑ Dec 1999 Cover: 2.50 **NM** value: **Cover or less**
Circ: Diamd. preorders: **14,992**
📖 The Strange Case of Mrs. Christenson!, Part 1 **A:** Al Rio; David Campiti **W:** Al Rio; David Campiti
2/A ❑ Dec 1999 Cover: 2.50 **NM** value: **Cover or less**
Photo cover. 📖 The Strange Case of Mrs. Christenson!, Part 1 **A:** Al Rio; David Campiti **W:** Al Rio; David Campiti
3 ❑ Jan 2000 Cover: 2.50 **NM** value: **Cover or less**
Circ: Diamd. preorders: **14,075**
📖 The Strange Case of Mrs. Christenson!, Part 2 **A:** Al Rio; David Campiti **W:** Al Rio; David Campiti
4 ❑ Feb 2000 Cover: 2.50 **NM** value: **Cover or less**
Circ: Diamd. preorders: **13,445**
5 ❑ Mar 2000 Cover: 3.50 **NM** value: **Cover or less**
📖 Second Coming **A:** Al Rio; David Campiti **W:** Al Rio; David Campiti
6 ❑ Apr 2000 Cover: 3.50 **NM** value: **Cover or less**
📖 Second Coming **A:** Al Rio; David Campiti **W:** Al Rio; David Campiti

EXQUISITE CORPSE — Dark Horse
1 ❑ Cover: 2.50 **NM** value: **Cover or less**
• Yellow issue **A:** Arnold & Jacob Pander **W:** Jerry Prosser
2 ❑ Cover: 2.50 **NM** value: **Cover or less**
• Red Issue **A:** Arnold & Jacob Pander **W:** Jerry Prosser
3 ❑ Cover: 2.50 **NM** value: **Cover or less**
• Green Issue **A:** Arnold & Jacob Pander **W:** Jerry Prosser

EXTINCT! — New England
1 ❑ b&w Cover: 3.50 **NM** value: **Cover or less**
2 ❑ b&w Cover: 3.50 **NM** value: **Cover or less**

EXTINCTIONERS — Shanda Fantasy Arts
1 ❑ Apr 1999, b&w Cover: 2.95 **NM** value: **Cover or less**
2 ❑ Cover: 2.95 **NM** value: **Cover or less**

EXTRA! — E.C.

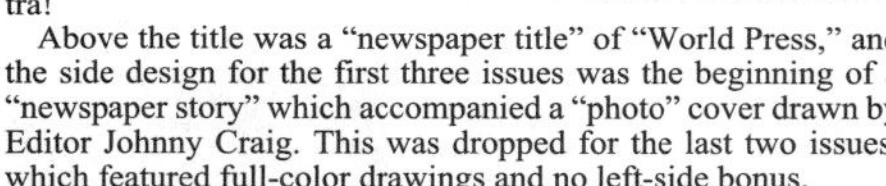

There were six E.C. titles in its "New Direction," cover-bannered as "an entirely novel and unique reading experience." The cover of each had a frame with the title on top and an identifying icon down the left side. The "New Direction" was one designed to accommodate the Comics Magazine Association of America's new Comics Code, though the first issue of each did not carry the Code stamp, and all but one lasted for five issues. The six titles were: Aces High, Impact, MD, Psychoanalysis, Valor — and Extra!

Above the title was a "newspaper title" of "World Press," and the side design for the first three issues was the beginning of a "newspaper story" which accompanied a "photo" cover drawn by Editor Johnny Craig. This was dropped for the last two issues, which featured full-color drawings and no left-side bonus.

The stories involved reporters investigating stories, and the three artists were Craig, John Severin, and Reed Crandall. "Dateline: Algiers" in #3 was an experiment later tried again in EC's short-lived magazine-format "Picto-Fiction" style of captioned illustrations. — Maggie

1 ❑ Mar 1955 Cover: 0.10 **NM** value: **150.00**
• **CGC:** 6 graded, best 9.4
📖 Dateline: Cayo Romano, Cuba!; Camera!; Holiday for Macduff; Dateline: Key West!
2 ❑ May 1955 Cover: 0.10 **NM** value: **100.00**
• **CGC:** 3 graded, best 9.4
📖 Dateline: Oslo; Stromboli!; Hong Kong!; Dateline: New York City
3 ❑ Jul 1955 Cover: 0.10 **NM** value: **100.00**
• **CGC:** 4 graded, best 9.4
📖 Steve Rampart; Geri Hamilton; Dateline: Paris
4 ❑ Sep 1955 Cover: 0.10 **NM** value: **10.00**
• **CGC:** 3 graded, best 9.6
📖 Dateline: New York City; Steve Rampart; Geri Hamilton; Dateline: Rio Para
5 ❑ Nov 1955 Cover: 0.10 **NM** value: **100.00**
• **CGC:** 3 graded, best 9.2
📖 Dateline: Long Island Sound; Steve Rampart; Geri Hamilton; Dateline: Germersheim

EXTRA! (GEMSTONE) — Gemstone
1 ❑ Jan 2000 Cover: 2.50 **NM** value: **Cover or less**
📖 Dateline: Cayo Romano, Cuba!; Camera!; Holiday for MacDuff; Dateline: Key West! **A:** Johnny Craig; John Severin; Reed Crandall **W:** Johnny Craig; John Severin; Reed Crandall
2 ❑ Feb 2000 Cover: 2.50 **NM** value: **Cover or less**
📖 Dateline: Oslo; Stromboli; Hong Kong!; Dateline: New York City **A:** Johnny Craig; John Severin; Reed Crandall **W:** Johnny Craig; John Severin; Reed Crandall
3 ❑ Mar 2000 Cover: 2.50 **NM** value: **Cover or less**
📖 Dateline: Algiers; Steve Rampart; Geri Hamilton; Dateline: Paris **A:** Johnny Craig; John Severin; Reed Crandall **W:** Johnny Craig; John Severin; Reed Crandall
4 ❑ Apr 2000 Cover: 2.50 **NM** value: **Cover or less**
📖 Dateline: New York City; Steve Rampart; Geri Hamilton; Dateline: Rio Para **A:** Johnny Craig; John Severin; Reed Crandall **W:** Johnny Craig; John Severin; Reed Crandall
5 ❑ May 2000 Cover: 2.50 **NM** value: **Cover or less**
📖 Dateline: Long Island Sound; Steve Rampart; Geri Hamilton; Dateline: Germersheim **A:** Johnny Craig; John Severin; Reed Crandall **W:** Johnny Craig; John Severin; Reed Crandall
Anl 1 ❑ Cover: 13.50 **NM** value: **Cover or less**

EXTRA TERRESTRIAL TRIO, THE — Smiling Face
1 ❑ Cover: 2.95 **NM** value: **Cover or less**

EXTREME — Image
0 ❑ Aug 1993 Cover: 2.50 **NM** value: **Cover or less**
📖 Cybrid; Law & Order; Risk; Code 9; Lancers; Black Flag **A:** Rob Liefeld; Dan Fraga; Marat Mychaels; Richard Horie; Chap Yaep; Chuck Jones **W:** Rob Liefeld; Dan Fraga; Marat Mychaels; Richard Horie; Chap Yaep; Chuck Jones
0/A ❑ Aug 1993 Cover: 2.50 **NM** value: **Cover or less**
📖 Cybrid; Law & Order; Risk; Code 9; Lancers; Black Flag **A:** Rob Liefeld; Dan Fraga; Marat Mychaels; Richard Horie; Chap Yaep; Chuck Jones **W:** Rob Liefeld; Dan Fraga; Marat Mychaels; Richard Horie; Chap Yaep; Chuck Jones
0/B ❑ Aug 1993 Cover: 2.50 **NM** value: **Cover or less**
• San Diego Con edition. 📖 Cybrid; Law & Order; Risk; Code 9; Lancers; Black Flag **A:** Rob Liefeld; Dan Fraga; Marat Mychaels; Richard Horie; Chap Yaep; Chuck Jones **W:** Rob Liefeld; Dan Fraga; Marat Mychaels; Richard Horie; Chap Yaep; Chuck Jones
0/GO ❑ Aug 1993 **NM** value: **3.00**
• Gold edition. 📖 Cybrid; Law & Order; Risk; Code 9; Lancers; Black Flag **A:** Rob Liefeld; Dan Fraga; Marat Mychaels; Richard Horie; Chap Yaep; Chuck Jones **W:** Rob Liefeld; Dan Fraga; Marat Mychaels; Richard Horie; Chap Yaep; Chuck Jones
HS 1 ❑ **NM** value: **1.00**
Circ: CapCity orders: **14,400**
No issue number. no cover price. • "Extreme Hero" promotional edition from Hero Magazine. 📖 Cybrid; Law & Order; Risk; Code 9; Lancers; Black Flag **A:** Rob Liefeld; Dan Fraga; Marat Mychaels; Richard Horie; Chap Yaep; Chuck Jones **W:** Rob Liefeld; Dan Fraga; Marat Mychaels; Richard Horie; Chap Yaep; Chuck Jones

EXTREME DESTROYER EPILOGUE — Image
1 ❑ Jan 1996 Cover: 2.50 **NM** value: **Cover or less**

EXTREME DESTROYER PROLOGUE — Image
1 ❑ Jan 1996 Cover: 2.50 **NM** value: **Cover or less**
• bagged with card **A:** Roger Cruz; Mark Pajarillo; Rob Liefeld; Dan Fraga; Logan Lubera; Richard Horie; Chap Yaep **W:** Rob Liefeld; Eric Stephenson

EXTREME JUSTICE — DC
0 ❑ Jan 1995 Cover: 1.50 **NM** value: **2.00**
Circ: CapCity orders: **25,950**
1 ❑ Feb 1995 Cover: 1.50 **NM** value: **1.75**
Circ: CapCity orders: **16,625**
📖 Mad Dogs and Super-Heroes **A:** Marc Campos **W:** Dan Vado
2 ❑ Mar 1995 Cover: 1.50 **NM** value: **1.75**
Circ: CapCity orders: **12,175**
3 ❑ Apr 1995 Cover: 1.50 **NM** value: **1.75**
Circ: CapCity orders: **10,375**
4 ❑ May 1995 Cover: 1.50 **NM** value: **1.75**
Circ: CapCity orders: **10,125**
5 ❑ Jun 1995 Cover: 1.75 **NM** value: **Cover or less**
Circ: CapCity orders: **9,300**
6 ❑ Jul 1995 Cover: 1.75 **NM** value: **Cover or less**
Circ: CapCity orders: **8,725**
7 ❑ Aug 1995 Cover: 1.75 **NM** value: **Cover or less**
Circ: CapCity orders: **9,050**
8 ❑ Sep 1995 Cover: 1.75 **NM** value: **Cover or less**
Circ: CapCity orders: **8,475**
9 ❑ Oct 1995 Cover: 1.75 **NM** value: **Cover or less**
Circ: CapCity orders: **7,125**
10 ❑ Nov 1995 Cover: 1.75 **NM** value: **Cover or less**
11 ❑ Dec 1995 Cover: 1.75 **NM** value: **Cover or less**
12 ❑ Jan 1996 Cover: 1.75 **NM** value: **Cover or less**
13 ❑ Feb 1996 Cover: 1.75 **NM** value: **Cover or less**
📖 King's Heeling **A:** Tom Morgan **W:** Robert L. Washington III ★ Versus Monarch.
14 ❑ Mar 1996 Cover: 1.75 **NM** value: **Cover or less**
📖 Kings Revealed and Kings Revealing **A:** Tom Morgan **W:** Robert L. Washington III
15 ❑ Apr 1996 Cover: 1.75 **NM** value: **Cover or less**
📖 Duel of Duals **A:** Tom Morgan **W:** Robert L. Washington III
16 ❑ May 1996 Cover: 1.75 **NM** value: **Cover or less**
17 ❑ Jun 1996 Cover: 1.75 **NM** value: **Cover or less**
18 ❑ Jul 1996 Cover: 1.75 **NM** value: **Cover or less**
final issue.

EXTREMELY SILLY — Antarctic
1 ❑ **NM** value: **3.00**

EXTREMELY SILLY (VOL. 2) — Antarctic
1 ❑ Nov 1996, b&w Cover: 1.25 **NM** value: **Cover or less**
• Star Trek parody

EXTREMELY YOUNGBLOOD — Image
1 ❑ Sep 1996 Cover: 3.50 **NM** value: **Cover or less**
Circ: Diamd. preorders: **17,991**
One-shot.

EXTREME PREJUDICE — Image
0 ❑ Nov 1994 Cover: 2.50 **NM** value: **Cover or less**

EXTREME PREVIEWS — Image
1 ❑ Mar 1996 **NM** value: **1.00**

EXTREME PREVIEWS 1997 — Image
1 ❑ **NM** value: **1.00**
No issue number. no cover price. • pin-ups

CGC-graded: Multiply prices above by **33 for 9.9 M • 16 for 9.8 NM/M • 7 for 9.6 NM+ • 5 for 9.4 NM • 2.5 for 9.2 NM- • 1.5 for 9.0 VF/NM**

EXTREME SACRIFICE — Image

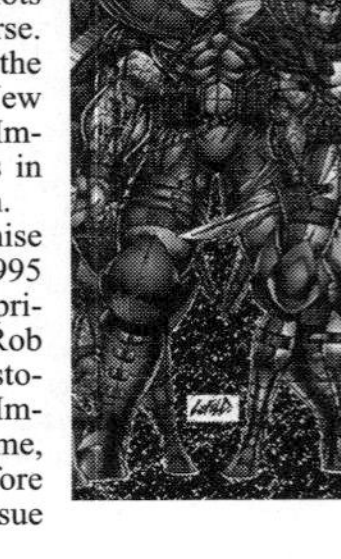

A battle rages in Hell as a dead renegade of the super-team Youngblood overthrows Satan and plots dominion of the entire universe. Only the mysterious Order of the Knight (with the aid of the New Men, Prophet, and the rest of the Image Universe of heroes) stands in the way of absolute annihilation.

Such is the over-the-top premise of this kick-off to Image's 1995 crossover event, with plot and primary art by Image founder Rob Liefeld. The Extreme Sacrifice storyline continued in most of the Image titles, including Supreme, Bloodstrike, and Brigade, before concluding in the "Epilogue" issue of this series.

1 ❑ Jan 1995 Cover: 2.50 **NM** value: **Cover or less**
Circ: CapCity orders: **26,550**
• Prelude, polybagged with trading card **A:** Rob Liefeld; Stephen Platt; Patrick Lee; Cedreic Nocon **W:** Rob Liefeld; Eric Stephenson

2 ❑ Jan 1995 Cover: 2.50 **NM** value: **Cover or less**
Circ: CapCity orders: **25,350**
• Epilogue **A:** Rob Liefeld; Cedric Nocon; Stephen Platt; Karl Altstaetter; Patrick Lee; Todd Nauck **W:** Rob Liefeld; Eric Stephenson

Bk 1❑ Aug 1995 Cover: 16.95 **NM** value: **Cover or less**
No issue number. • Trade Paperback. • collects crossover

EXTREMES OF VIOLET — Blackout

0 ❑ Cover: 2.95 **NM** value: **Cover or less**
Circ: CapCity orders: **6,260**

1 ❑ Cover: 2.95 **NM** value: **Cover or less**
Circ: CapCity orders: **5,975**

2 ❑ Cover: 2.95 **NM** value: **Cover or less**
Circ: CapCity orders: **3,280**

EXTREME SUPER CHRISTMAS SPECIAL — Image

1 ❑ Dec 1994 Cover: 2.95 **NM** value: **Cover or less**
Circ: CapCity orders: **14,400**

EXTREME SUPER TOUR BOOK — Image

1 ❑ **NM** value: **1.00**

1/GO❑ **NM** value: **2.00**
• Gold edition.

EXTREME TOUR BOOK — Image

1 ❑ **NM** value: **2.50**
no cover price.

1/GO❑ **NM** value: **2.50**
• Gold edition.

EXTREMIST, THE — DC / Vertigo

1 ❑ Sep 1993 Cover: 1.95 **NM** value: **2.50**
Circ: CapCity orders: **24,700**

1/PL❑ Sep 1993 **NM** value: **4.00**
• Platinum edition. **A:** Ted McKeever ★ 1st Appearance of The Extremist.

2 ❑ Oct 1993 Cover: 1.95 **NM** value: **2.50**
Circ: CapCity orders: **12,550**

3 ❑ Nov 1993 Cover: 1.95 **NM** value: **2.50**
Circ: CapCity orders: **10,950**

4 ❑ Dec 1993 Cover: 1.95 **NM** value: **2.50**
Circ: CapCity orders: **12,600**

EYE, THE — Hamster

"The return of the world's weirdest hero!" reads the tag line, and one look at this caped figure whose headgear resembles a gigantic, menacing eyeball makes it seem accurate. Eric Drake was an undercover cop who found he could best combat crime as The Eye, an "underworld executioner" who, in fact, merely hypnotizes his victims and hides them in a rest home. Thus he eliminates criminals without harming them, while maintaining his reputation as a feared assassin. But to one criminal organization, the Van Horn Syndicate, The Eye's interference must end. Enter Myopia, a woman whose chameleon-like costume can counter the hero's mysterious powers.

Written and drawn by Bill Schelly, this title came with the blessing of Biljo White, the man who first created The Eye for a small-press comic in the '60s. Though his art is simple, Schelly's story is richly textured.

SE 1❑ Jun 1999 Cover: 2.95 **NM** value: **Cover or less**
• Special edition. 📖 Face to Face with Myopia! **A:** Bill Schelly **W:** Bill Schelly

EYEBALL KID, THE — Dark Horse

1 ❑ b&w Cover: 2.25 **NM** value: **2.50**

2 ❑ b&w Cover: 2.25 **NM** value: **2.50**

3 ❑ b&w Cover: 2.25 **NM** value: **2.50**
final issue.

EYEBEAM — Adhesive

1 ❑ b&w Cover: 2.50 **NM** value: **Cover or less**
• strip reprints

2 ❑ ca. 1994, b&w Cover: 2.50 **NM** value: **Cover or less**
• strip reprints

3 ❑ ca. 1994, b&w Cover: 2.50 **NM** value: **Cover or less**
• strip reprints

4 ❑ b&w Cover: 2.50 **NM** value: **Cover or less**
• strip reprints

5 ❑ b&w Cover: 2.50 **NM** value: **Cover or less**
• strip reprints

EYE OF MONGOMBO — Fantagraphics

1 ❑ b&w Cover: 2.00 **NM** value: **Cover or less**

2 ❑ b&w Cover: 2.00 **NM** value: **Cover or less**

3 ❑ b&w Cover: 2.00 **NM** value: **Cover or less**

4 ❑ b&w Cover: 2.00 **NM** value: **Cover or less**

5 ❑ b&w Cover: 2.00 **NM** value: **Cover or less**

6 ❑ 1991b&w Cover: 2.00 **NM** value: **Cover or less**

7 ❑ Dec 1991, b&w Cover: 2.25 **NM** value: **Cover or less**

EYE OF THE STORM — Rival

1 ❑ Dec 1994 Cover: 2.95 **NM** value: **Cover or less**

F-3 BANDIT — Antarctic

1 ❑ Jan 1995 Cover: 2.95 **NM** value: **Cover or less**
Circ: CapCity orders: **2,295**
• mini-poster **A:** Bang Ippongi **W:** Bang Ippongi

2 ❑ Mar 1995 Cover: 2.95 **NM** value: **Cover or less**
📖 American Werewoman • trading card **A:** Bang Ippongi **W:** Bang Ippongi

3 ❑ May 1995 Cover: 2.95 **NM** value: **Cover or less**
📖 Alto Through the Looking-glass • trading card **A:** Bang Ippongi **W:** Bang Ippongi

4 ❑ Jul 1995 Cover: 2.95 **NM** value: **Cover or less**
• trading card **A:** Bang Ippongi **W:** Bang Ippongi

5 ❑ Sep 1995 Cover: 2.95 **NM** value: **Cover or less**
• trading card

6 ❑ Nov 1995 Cover: 2.95 **NM** value: **Cover or less**

7 ❑ Jan 1996 Cover: 2.95 **NM** value: **Cover or less**

8 ❑ Mar 1996 Cover: 2.95 **NM** value: **Cover or less**

9 ❑ May 1996, b&w Cover: 2.95 **NM** value: **Cover or less**

10 ❑ Jul 1996, b&w Cover: 2.95 **NM** value: **Cover or less**
final issue. • trading card

F5 — Image

1 ❑ Apr 2000 Cover: 2.50 **NM** value: **2.95**
Circ: Diamd. preorders: **38,803**

2 ❑ Jun 2000 Cover: 2.50 **NM** value: **Cover or less**
Circ: Diamd. preorders: **27,524**

3 ❑ Aug 2000 Cover: 2.50 **NM** value: **Cover or less**
Circ: Diamd. preorders: **26,501**

4 ❑ Oct 2000 Cover: 2.50 **NM** value: **Cover or less**
Circ: Diamd. preorders: **24,532**

Ash 1❑Jan 2000 Cover: 2.50 **NM** value: **Cover or less**
• Preview issue **W:** Tony Daniel

FAANS — Six Handed Press

1 ❑ b&w Cover: 2.95 **NM** value: **Cover or less**

FABLES BY THE BROTHERS DIMM — Dimm

1 ❑ Apr 1995, b&w Cover: 1.50 **NM** value: **Cover or less**
📖 The Electric Forest; Ragnarok!; Apartment; Corporate Enterprise **A:** Joe Brown; Ron Cornett; Rush Kress **W:** Ron Cornett; grunge; Lucas Guthrie; Tone Gardaux

FABULOUS FURRY FREAK BROTHERS, THE — Rip Off

Gilbert Shelton created the Fabulous Furry Freak Brothers as an underground newspaper strip in the late Sixties. The stars were brothers Fat Freddy, Phineas, and Freewheelin' Frank Freak. These lovable druggies were always broke and they seemingly spent nearly all their waking time looking for drugs. "After all," they held, "dope will get you through times with no money better than money will get you through times with no dope!"

Even read out of context from the San Francisco drug culture they reflected, the Furry Freak Brothers were truly funny. The strips were eventually collected in a series of regular comic books and became one of the most widely read underground comics ever published. They, along with titles like Fat Freddy's Cat, became the mainstay of longtime underground publisher Rip Off Press.

0 ❑ Cover: 2.95 **NM** value: **Cover or less**
• 1985 Compilation **A:** Gilbert Shelton **W:** Gilbert Shelton

1 ❑ b&w Cover: 0.70 **NM** value: **55.00**
📖 The Freaks Pull A Heist; Freak Brothers Go To College!; The Legendary Dope Famine Of '69; Little Orphan Amphetamine; Tricky Prickears • Collected Adventures of the...; 1971 **A:** Gilbert Shelton **W:** Gilbert Shelton

1-2 ❑ Cover: 2.95 **NM** value: **Cover or less**

2 ❑ b&w Cover: 0.50 **NM** value: **35.00**
📖 Shootout at the County Slammer; Buster Foyt Esq.; Dopin' Dan • Further Adventures of the... **A:** Ted Richards; Gilbert Shelton **W:** Ted Richards; Gilbert Shelton

2-2 ❑ Cover: 2.95 **NM** value: **Cover or less**

3 ❑ b&w Cover: 0.50 **NM** value: **15.00**
📖 The Adventures of Freewheelin' Franklin; Government Spies; I Led Nine Lives!; A Nice Polka-Dot Demon Gets the Royal Shaft • A Year Passes Like Nothing With... **A:** Gilbert Shelton; F. Cluck Wilverton **W:** Gilbert Shelton; F. Cluck Wilverton

4 ❑ b&w Cover: 0.75 **NM** value: **13.00**
📖 The 7th Voyage of the Fabulous Furry Freak Brothers: A Mexican Odyssey • Brother Can You Spare 75¢ For... **A:** Gilbert Shelton; Dave Sheridan **W:** Gilbert Shelton

5 ❑ b&w **NM** value: **10.00**
• Fabulous Furry Freak Brothers **A:** Gilbert Shelton; Dave Sheridan **W:** Gilbert Shelton

6 ❑ b&w **NM** value: **4.00**
• Six Snappy Sockeroos From the Archives Of... **A:** Gilbert Shelton; Paul Mavrides **W:** Gilbert Shelton

7 ❑ b&w Cover: 2.50 **NM** value: **Cover or less**

8 ❑ full color Cover: 2.95 **NM** value: **Cover or less**

9 ❑ full color Cover: 2.95 **NM** value: **Cover or less**

10 ❑ full color Cover: 2.95 **NM** value: **Cover or less**
Circ: CapCity orders: **2,875**

11 ❑ full color Cover: 2.50 **NM** value: **2.95**

12 ❑ b&w Cover: 2.95 **NM** value: **Cover or less**

13 ❑ b&w Cover: 2.95 **NM** value: **Cover or less**
• reprints stories from High Times **A:** Gilbert Shelton **W:** Gilbert Shelton

FABULOUS FURRY FREAK BROTHERS LIBRARY — Rip Off

Bk 1❑ b&w Cover: 7.95 **NM** value: **Cover or less**

Bk 1-2❑ Cover: 7.95 **NM** value: **Cover or less**

Bk 2❑ b&w Cover: 7.95 **NM** value: **Cover or less**

Bk 2-2❑ Cover: 7.95 **NM** value: **Cover or less**

Bk 3❑ b&w Cover: 7.95 **NM** value: **Cover or less**

Bk 3-2❑ Cover: 7.95 **NM** value: **Cover or less**

Bk 4❑ b&w Cover: 7.95 **NM** value: **Cover or less**

Bk 4-2❑ Cover: 7.95 **NM** value: **Cover or less**

FACE, THE — Columbia

1 ❑ ca. 1941 Cover: 0.10 **NM** value: **700.00**

2 ❑ ca. 1943 Cover: 0.10 **NM** value: **300.00**
• becomes Tony Trent, The Face

3 ❑ ca. 1948 Cover: 0.10 **NM** value: **100.00**

4 ❑ ca. 1949 Cover: 0.10 **NM** value: **100.00**

FACTOR, THE — About Comics

The media has dubbed New York's latest super-hero "the Factor." He's saving lives right and left and interfering with all sorts of illegal operations, but we don't really see him in this sharply written series from writer Nat Gertler and artists Jim Schumaker, Joe Staton, Alex Grecian, and Mike Vosburg. This series focuses on the effects of a super-hero on the lives of ordinary people-cops, kids, criminals, etc. — a premise not unlike that found in DC's Gotham Nights mini-series. Would cops suddenly feel inadequate in the shadow of a hero the public perceives as something more than human? Would kids become more violent? Would criminals beef up their efforts? Here, the super-hero is "the factor" that alters lives and destinies by simply doing what he thinks is right.

0 ❑ b&w Cover: 2.00 **NM** value: **Cover or less**
• continues from Negative Burn

1 ❑ b&w Cover: 2.95 **NM** value: **Cover or less**
📖 To Serve and Protect; Dubba-dubba-dum-dubba-dum-data; Escalation; Telephone for the 90's **A:** Jim Schumaker; Joe Staton; Alex Grecian **W:** Nat Gertler

2 ❑ Cover: 2.95 **NM** value: **Cover or less**

3 ❑ Cover: 2.95 **NM** value: **Cover or less**

FACTOR-X — Marvel

In 1995, Marvel put all the X-Men titles on hiatus and replaced them with titles that chronicled "the Age of Apocalypse," a reality where Apocalypse and his mutants rule the world. Factor X focuses on the Summers brothers, Cyclops and Havok. Together with Aurora, Northstar, and Cannonball, they work for Mr. Sinister as a strike force that captures renegade mutants and humans. Meanwhile a twisted, gray-furred version of the Beast performs genetic experiments on those mutants and humans to further Sinister's goal of creating hybrid supersoldiers for Apocalypse. Things get complicated when Sinister, weary of Apocalypse's shortsighted machinations, abandons the Summers brothers, and they-and particularly Cyclops-are forced to wrestle with the morality of Apocalypse's world order. All in all, it's fairly intriguing stuff which doesn't require much prior knowledge of convoluted X-Men lore.

1 ❑ Mar 1995 Cover: 1.95 **NM** value: **2.00**
Circ: CapCity orders: **67,075**
📖 Sinister Neglect **A:** Steve Epting **W:** John Francis Moore

2 ❑ Apr 1995 Cover: 1.95 **NM** value: **2.00**
Circ: CapCity orders: **66,175**

3 ❑ May 1995 Cover: 1.95 **NM** value: **2.00**
Circ: CapCity orders: **83,025**

4 ❑ Jun 1995 Cover: 1.95 **NM** value: **2.00**
Circ: CapCity orders: **90,425**

Bk 1❑ May 1995 Cover: 8.95 **NM** value: **Cover or less**
Gold foil cover. • Ultimate Factor-X; collects four-issue series

Statement of Ownership figures are the average number of copies originally sold, as cited by the publisher to the U.S. Postal Service. These estimate **all** sales, in comics shops and on newsstands.

Other grades: Multiply prices above by **1.5 for Mint • 2/3 for Very Fine • 1/3 for Fine • 1/5 for Very Good • 1/8 for Good**

FACTS O' LIFE FUNNIES — Rip Off

1 ❑ Cover: 0.50 **NM** value: **3.00**
Fat Freddy Gets the Claps; Fertile Fanny; Strawberry Fields; Bitsy the teenage Bunny; Trots and Bonnie; Dopin' Dan: Hold the Mashed Potatoes; Mute RockKnee; Man of the World Comes Clean; Sins of the Flesh **A:** Ted Richards; Gilbert Shelton; Gary Hallgren; Flenniken; Gary Frutkoff; Lora Fountain; Michele Brand; Bobby Crumb **W:** Ted Richards; Gilbert Shelton; Gary Hallgren; Flenniken; Gary Frutkoff; Lora Fountain; Michele Brand; Bobby Crumb

FACTUAL ILLUSION — Blackmore

1 ❑ b&w Cover: 2.50 **NM** value: **Cover or less**
No issue number. cover says Factual Illusions, indicia says Factual Illusion.

FACULTY FUNNIES — Archie

1 ❑ Jun 1989 Cover: 0.95 **NM** value: **3.00**
2 ❑ 1989 Cover: 0.95 **NM** value: **2.00**
3 ❑ Dec 1989 Cover: 0.95 **NM** value: **2.00**
4 ❑ Mar 1990 Cover: 1.00 **NM** value: **2.00**
5 ❑ May 1990 Cover: 1.00 **NM** value: **2.00**

FAERIE CODEX — Raven

1 ❑ b&w Cover: 2.95 **NM** value: **Cover or less**
2 ❑ b&w Cover: 2.95 **NM** value: **Cover or less**
3 ❑ Dec 1997, b&w Cover: 2.95 **NM** value: **Cover or less**

FAFHRD AND THE GRAY MOUSER — Marvel / Epic

1 ❑ Oct 1990 Cover: 4.50 **NM** value: **Cover or less**
Circ: CapCity orders: **12,900**
Ill Met in Lankhmar **A:** Mort Meskin; Al Williamson; Mike Mignola **W:** Howard Chaykin
2 ❑ Cover: 4.50 **NM** value: **Cover or less**
Circ: CapCity orders: **9,700**
The Circle Curse; The Howling Tower **A:** Mort Meskin; Al Williamson; Mike Mignola **W:** Howard Chaykin
3 ❑ Cover: 4.50 **NM** value: **Cover or less**
Circ: CapCity orders: **9,250**
The Price of Pain Ease; Bazaar of the Bizarre **A:** Mort Meskin; Al Williamson; Mike Mignola **W:** Howard Chaykin
4 ❑ Cover: 4.50 **NM** value: **Cover or less**
Circ: CapCity orders: **9,150**
Lean Times in Lankhmar; When The Sea King's Away **A:** Mort Meskin; Al Williamson; Mike Mignola **W:** Howard Chaykin

FAILED UNIVERSE — Blackthorne

1 ❑ Dec 1986 Cover: 1.75 **NM** value: **Cover or less**
Make Mine Mediocre **A:** David Cody Weiss **W:** Cliff Mac Gillivray

FAIRY TALE PARADE — Dell

Ordinarily, Dell used its Four Color title to test a series of one-shots before spinning them off into their own titles. Fairy Tale Parade is unusual in that it began as its own numbered series and then switched over to a sporadic release schedule as part of the Dell Four Color line.

The first issue looks very much as though it comprises samples from Walt Kelly, used to get work following a stint at the Disney animation studios — with elaborately decorated panels.

Stories included traditional fairy tales and original stories, and Kelly was soon joined by other artists including Dan Noonan. In recent years, Art Spiegelman has put together hardcover children's books inspired by this series, begun about 60 years earlier. — Maggie

1 ❑ Jun 1942 Cover: 0.10 **NM** value: **1000.00**
• **CGC:** 5 graded, best 9.2
2 ❑ Aug 1942 Cover: 0.10 **NM** value: **500.00**
3 ❑ Oct 1942 Cover: 0.10 **NM** value: **300.00**
4 ❑ Dec 1942 Cover: 0.10 **NM** value: **300.00**
• **CGC:** 1 graded, best 5.0
5 ❑ Feb 1943 Cover: 0.10 **NM** value: **300.00**
• **CGC:** 2 graded, best 9.0
6 ❑ May 1943 Cover: 0.10 **NM** value: **250.00**
7 ❑ Aug 1943 Cover: 0.10 **NM** value: **250.00**
8 ❑ ca. 1943 Cover: 0.10 **NM** value: **250.00**
9 ❑ Nov 1943 Cover: 0.10 **NM** value: **250.00**

FAIRY TALES OF OSCAR WILDE — NBM

Bk 1❑ Cover: 15.95 **NM** value: **Cover or less**
Bk 1/LE❑ Cover: 45.00 **NM** value: **Cover or less**
Bk 2❑ Cover: 15.95 **NM** value: **Cover or less**
Bk 2/LE❑ Cover: 45.00 **NM** value: **Cover or less**
Bk 3❑ Cover: 15.95 **NM** value: **Cover or less**
Bk 3/LE❑ Cover: 50.00 **NM** value: **Cover or less**

FAIRY TALES — Ziff-Davis

10 ❑ Apr 1951 Cover: 0.10 **NM** value: **250.00**
11 ❑ Jun 1951 Cover: 0.10 **NM** value: **250.00**

FAITH — DC / Vertigo

1 ❑ Nov 1999 Cover: 2.50 **NM** value: **Cover or less**
Circ: Diamd. preorders: **14,930**
An Act of Confession **A:** Ted McKeever **W:** Ted McKeever
2 ❑ Dec 1999 Cover: 2.50 **NM** value: **Cover or less**
Circ: Diamd. preorders: **12,621**
The Coverage of Sound **A:** Ted McKeever **W:** Ted McKeever
3 ❑ Jan 2000 Cover: 2.50 **NM** value: **Cover or less**
Circ: Diamd. preorders: **11,334**
Satanico Pandemonium **A:** Ted McKeever **W:** Ted McKeever
4 ❑ Feb 2000 Cover: 2.50 **NM** value: **Cover or less**
Circ: Diamd. preorders: **11,812**
5 ❑ Mar 2000 Cover: 2.50 **NM** value: **Cover or less**
Circ: Diamd. preorders: **9,415**
Coma Monkeys **A:** Ted McKeever **W:** Ted McKeever

FAITH: A FABLE — Carbon-Based Books

1 ❑ Jan 2000, b&w Cover: 8.95 **NM** value: **Cover or less**
No issue number. • Trade Paperback. • smaller than normal comic book **A:** Bill Knapp **W:** Bill Knapp

FAITHFUL — Marvel

1 ❑ Nov 1949 Cover: 0.10 **NM** value: **50.00**
2 ❑ Feb 1950 Cover: 0.10 **NM** value: **50.00**
• **CGC:** 1 graded, best 6.5

FAITH (LIGHTNING) — Lightning

1/A ❑ Jul 1997, b&w Cover: 2.95 **NM** value: **Cover or less**

FAITH OF THE FOE — Fandom House

1 ❑ b&w Cover: 4.50 **NM** value: **Cover or less**

FALCON — Marvel

Possessing no super-powers except the ability to fly through a set of advanced-technology wings, Sam Wilson fights crime as the Falcon. First appearing in Captain America #117, he became Cap's partner, and continued in that role until issue #223.

This mini-series finally gives the Falcon a chance to leave the nest and spread his wings, so to speak, as he fights to foil a plot against the President. Paul Smith, a little-known artist before taking on Uncanny X-Men in late 1982, drew the series, rendering the Falcon with his characteristic flair and attention to detail.

1 ❑ Nov 1983 Cover: 0.60 **NM** value: **1.50**
• **CGC:** 1 graded, best 9.4
2 ❑ Dec 1983 Cover: 0.60 **NM** value: **1.50**
3 ❑ Jan 1984 Cover: 0.60 **NM** value: **1.50**
4 ❑ Feb 1984 Cover: 0.60 **NM** value: **1.50**

FALL, THE (BIG BAD WORLD) — Big Bad World

1 ❑ b&w Cover: 3.00 **NM** value: **Cover or less**

FALL, THE (CALIBER) — Caliber

1 ❑ b&w Cover: 2.95 **NM** value: **Cover or less**

FALLEN ANGEL ON THE WORLD OF MAGIC: THE GATHERING — Acclaim / Armada

1 ❑ May 1996 Cover: 5.95 **NM** value: **Cover or less**
One-shot. • prestige format. • polybagged with Fallen Angel card **A:** Dennis Calero; Richard Kane-Ferguson **W:** Nancy Collins

FALLEN ANGELS — Marvel

A spinoff of a spin-off, this eight-issue limited series presents a chain of events which change the life of Sunspot, a member of the New Mutants.

Fourteen year-old Robert "Bobby" DaCosta is a hothead, both figuratively, and literally. As Sunspot, he is a mutant who can store and wield solar power. He joined the New Mutants to learn how best to use his powers, as well as to learn to control his temper.

But some lessons are not so easily learned. When he nearly kills one of his teammates in a fit of rage, Bobby runs away to New York. Far from escaping his troubles, he finds that the mean streets of the Big Apple present him with a different kind of danger.

1 ❑ Apr 1987 Cover: 0.75 **NM** value: **1.50**
Circ: CapCity orders: **37,000**
2 ❑ May 1987 Cover: 0.75 **NM** value: **1.25**
Circ: CapCity orders: **30,100**
3 ❑ Jun 1987 Cover: 0.75 **NM** value: **1.25**
Circ: CapCity orders: **29,700**
4 ❑ Jul 1987 Cover: 0.75 **NM** value: **1.25**
Circ: CapCity orders: **31,700**
5 ❑ Aug 1987 Cover: 0.75 **NM** value: **1.25**
Circ: CapCity orders: **32,700**
6 ❑ Sep 1987 Cover: 0.75 **NM** value: **1.25**
Circ: CapCity orders: **33,900**
7 ❑ Oct 1987 Cover: 0.75 **NM** value: **1.25**
Circ: CapCity orders: **33,700**
8 ❑ Nov 1987 Cover: 0.75 **NM** value: **1.25**
Circ: CapCity orders: **31,700**

FALLEN EMPIRES ON THE WORLD OF MAGIC: THE GATHERING — Acclaim / Armada

1 ❑ Sep 1995 Cover: 2.75 **NM** value: **Cover or less**
Circ: CapCity orders: **28,725**
Rumors of War • polybagged with pack of Fallen Empires cards **A:** Alex Maleev **W:** Jeff Gomez; Jeff G-mez; Kevin Maples
2 ❑ Oct 1995 Cover: 2.75 **NM** value: **Cover or less**
Circ: CapCity orders: **19,350**
• polybagged with sheet of creature tokens **A:** Alex Maleev **W:** Jeff Gomez; Jeff G-mez; Kevin Maples
Bk 1❑ Cover: 4.95 **NM** value: **Cover or less**
• prestige format. • collects mini-series; polybagged w/pack of Fallen Empires cards

FALLING IN LOVE — DC

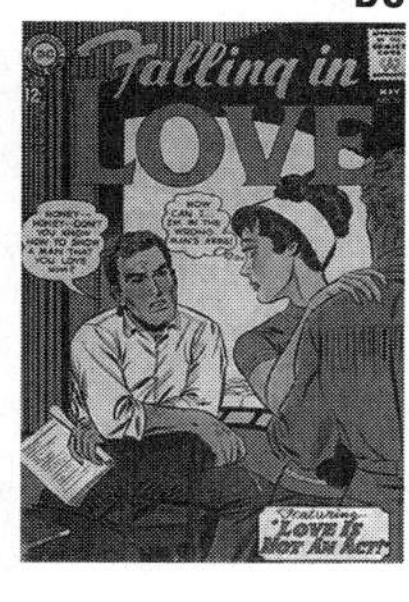

"Flight to Heartbreak!" "The Double Heart!" "Romantic New Stories for You!" These words can be read on covers of early issues of Falling in Love, a Code-approved romance series launched in 1955. The title began a long run which lasted until the early 1970s.

The stories in Falling in Love focus on the trials and tribulations befalling young lovers. True love inevitably wins out, but not before it has been tested by jealousy, parent trouble, distance, and so on.

Although many readers may have preferred more starry-eyed sagas, it's just such obstacles that put the romance in these love stories.

1 ❑ Nov 1955 Cover: 0.10 **NM** value: **265.00**
2 ❑ Dec 1955 Cover: 0.10 **NM** value: **140.00**
3 ❑ Feb 1956 Cover: 0.10 **NM** value: **90.00**
4 ❑ Cover: 0.10 **NM** value: **60.00**
5 ❑ Cover: 0.10 **NM** value: **60.00**
6 ❑ Cover: 0.10 **NM** value: **60.00**
7 ❑ Cover: 0.10 **NM** value: **60.00**
8 ❑ Cover: 0.10 **NM** value: **60.00**
9 ❑ Cover: 0.10 **NM** value: **60.00**
10 ❑ Cover: 0.10 **NM** value: **60.00**
11 ❑ Cover: 0.10 **NM** value: **35.00**
12 ❑ Cover: 0.10 **NM** value: **35.00**
13 ❑ Sep 1957 Cover: 0.10 **NM** value: **35.00**
14 ❑ Oct 1957 Cover: 0.10 **NM** value: **35.00**
15 ❑ 1957 Cover: 0.10 **NM** value: **35.00**
16 ❑ 1958 Cover: 0.10 **NM** value: **35.00**
17 ❑ Mar 1958 Cover: 0.10 **NM** value: **35.00**
18 ❑ ca. 1958 Cover: 0.10 **NM** value: **35.00**
19 ❑ ca. 1958 Cover: 0.10 **NM** value: **35.00**
20 ❑ Aug 1958 Cover: 0.10 **NM** value: **35.00**
21 ❑ Sep 1958 Cover: 0.10 **NM** value: **24.00**
22 ❑ Cover: 0.10 **NM** value: **24.00**
23 ❑ Cover: 0.10 **NM** value: **24.00**
24 ❑ 1959 Cover: 0.10 **NM** value: **24.00**
25 ❑ 1959 Cover: 0.10 **NM** value: **24.00**
26 ❑ 1959 Cover: 0.10 **NM** value: **24.00**
27 ❑ Jun 1959 Cover: 0.10 **NM** value: **24.00**
28 ❑ 1959 Cover: 0.10 **NM** value: **24.00**
29 ❑ 1959 Cover: 0.10 **NM** value: **24.00**
30 ❑ 1959 Cover: 0.10 **NM** value: **24.00**
31 ❑ 1959 Cover: 0.10 **NM** value: **24.00**
32 ❑ Cover: 0.10 **NM** value: **24.00**
33 ❑ 1960 Cover: 0.10 **NM** value: **24.00**
34 ❑ 1960 Cover: 0.10 **NM** value: **24.00**
35 ❑ 1960 Cover: 0.10 **NM** value: **24.00**
36 ❑ 1960 Cover: 0.10 **NM** value: **24.00**
37 ❑ 1960 Cover: 0.10 **NM** value: **24.00**
38 ❑ 1960 Cover: 0.10 **NM** value: **24.00**
39 ❑ Dec 1960 Cover: 0.10 **NM** value: **24.00**
40 ❑ ca. 1961 Cover: 0.10 **NM** value: **24.00**
41 ❑ ca. 1961 Cover: 0.10 **NM** value: **18.00**
42 ❑ May 1961 Cover: 0.10 **NM** value: **18.00**
43 ❑ ca. 1961 Cover: 0.10 **NM** value: **18.00**
44 ❑ ca. 1961 Cover: 0.10 **NM** value: **18.00**
45 ❑ Sep 1961 Cover: 0.10 **NM** value: **18.00**
46 ❑ ca. 1961 Cover: 0.10 **NM** value: **18.00**
47 ❑ Dec 1961 Cover: 0.10 **NM** value: **18.00**
48 ❑ 1962 Cover: 0.12 **NM** value: **18.00**
49 ❑ 1962 Cover: 0.12 **NM** value: **18.00**
50 ❑ 1962 Cover: 0.12 **NM** value: **18.00**
51 ❑ 1962 Cover: 0.12 **NM** value: **18.00**
52 ❑ 1962 Cover: 0.12 **NM** value: **18.00**
53 ❑ 1962 Cover: 0.12 **NM** value: **18.00**
54 ❑ 1962 Cover: 0.12 **NM** value: **18.00**
55 ❑ 1962 Cover: 0.12 **NM** value: **18.00**
56 ❑ Cover: 0.12 **NM** value: **18.00**
57 ❑ 1963 Cover: 0.12 **NM** value: **18.00**
58 ❑ 1963 Cover: 0.12 **NM** value: **18.00**
59 ❑ 1963 Cover: 0.12 **NM** value: **18.00**
60 ❑ 1963 Cover: 0.12 **NM** value: **14.00**
61 ❑ 1963 Cover: 0.12 **NM** value: **14.00**
62 ❑ 1963 Cover: 0.12 **NM** value: **14.00**
63 ❑ 1963 Cover: 0.12 **NM** value: **14.00**
64 ❑ Cover: 0.12 **NM** value: **14.00**
65 ❑ Cover: 0.12 **NM** value: **14.00**
66 ❑ 1964 Cover: 0.12 **NM** value: **14.00**
67 ❑ 1964 Cover: 0.12 **NM** value: **14.00**
68 ❑ 1964 Cover: 0.12 **NM** value: **14.00**
69 ❑ 1964 Cover: 0.12 **NM** value: **14.00**
70 ❑ 1964 Cover: 0.12 **NM** value: **14.00**
71 ❑ ca. 1964 Cover: 0.12 **NM** value: **14.00**
72 ❑ 1964 Cover: 0.12 **NM** value: **14.00**
73 ❑ Cover: 0.12 **NM** value: **14.00**
74 ❑ Cover: 0.12 **NM** value: **14.00**
75 ❑ May 1965 Cover: 0.12 **NM** value: **14.00**
76 ❑ Jul 1965 Cover: 0.12 **NM** value: **14.00**
77 ❑ Aug 1965 Cover: 0.12 **NM** value: **14.00**
78 ❑ Oct 1965 Cover: 0.12 **NM** value: **14.00**
79 ❑ Nov 1965 Cover: 0.12 **NM** value: **14.00**
80 ❑ Jan 1966 Cover: 0.12 **NM** value: **14.00**
81 ❑ Feb 1966 Cover: 0.12 **NM** value: **12.00**

CGC-graded: Multiply prices above by **33 for 9.9 M • 16 for 9.8 NM/M • 7 for 9.6 NM+ • 5 for 9.4 NM • 2.5 for 9.2 NM- • 1.5 for 9.0 VF/NM**

82 ☐ Apr 1966 Cover: 0.12 **NM** value: **12.00**
83 ☐ May 1966 Cover: 0.12 **NM** value: **12.00**
84 ☐ Jul 1966 Cover: 0.12 **NM** value: **12.00**
85 ☐ Aug 1966 Cover: 0.12 **NM** value: **12.00**
86 ☐ Oct 1966 Cover: 0.12 **NM** value: **12.00**
87 ☐ Nov 1966 Cover: 0.12 **NM** value: **12.00**
88 ☐ Jan 1967 Cover: 0.12 **NM** value: **12.00**
Circ: Statement: **170,400**
89 ☐ Feb 1967 Cover: 0.12 **NM** value: **12.00**
Circ: Statement: **170,400**
90 ☐ Apr 1967 Cover: 0.12 **NM** value: **12.00**
Circ: Statement: **170,400**
91 ☐ May 1967 Cover: 0.12 **NM** value: **12.00**
Circ: Statement: **170,400**
92 ☐ Jul 1967 Cover: 0.12 **NM** value: **12.00**
Circ: Statement: **170,400**
93 ☐ Aug 1967 Cover: 0.12 **NM** value: **12.00**
Circ: Statement: **170,400**
94 ☐ Oct 1967 Cover: 0.12 **NM** value: **Cover or less**
Circ: Statement: **170,400**
📖 I Want to Think It Over!; The Only One for Me!; Pledge for Love!; Her Last Chance for Romance!
95 ☐ Nov 1967 Cover: 0.12 **NM** value: **12.00**
Circ: Statement: **170,400**
96 ☐ Jan 1968 Cover: 0.12 **NM** value: **12.00**
97 ☐ Feb 1968 Cover: 0.12 **NM** value: **12.00**
98 ☐ Apr 1968 Cover: 0.12 **NM** value: **12.00**
99 ☐ May 1968 Cover: 0.12 **NM** value: **12.00**
100 ☐ Jul 1968 Cover: 0.12 **NM** value: **12.00**
101 ☐ Aug 1968 Cover: 0.12 **NM** value: **10.00**
102 ☐ Oct 1968 Cover: 0.12 **NM** value: **10.00**
103 ☐ Nov 1968 Cover: 0.12 **NM** value: **10.00**
104 ☐ Jan 1969 Cover: 0.12 **NM** value: **10.00**
105 ☐ Feb 1969 Cover: 0.12 **NM** value: **10.00**
106 ☐ Apr 1969 Cover: 0.12 **NM** value: **10.00**
107 ☐ May 1969 Cover: 0.12 **NM** value: **10.00**
108 ☐ Jul 1969 Cover: 0.15 **NM** value: **10.00**
109 ☐ Aug 1969 Cover: 0.15 **NM** value: **10.00**
110 ☐ Oct 1969 Cover: 0.15 **NM** value: **10.00**
111 ☐ Nov 1969 Cover: 0.15 **NM** value: **10.00**
112 ☐ Jan 1970 Cover: 0.15 **NM** value: **10.00**
113 ☐ Feb 1970 Cover: 0.15 **NM** value: **10.00**
114 ☐ Apr 1970 Cover: 0.15 **NM** value: **10.00**
115 ☐ May 1970 Cover: 0.15 **NM** value: **10.00**
116 ☐ Jul 1970 Cover: 0.15 **NM** value: **10.00**
117 ☐ ca. 1970 Cover: 0.15 **NM** value: **10.00**
118 ☐ ca. 1970 Cover: 0.15 **NM** value: **10.00**
119 ☐ ca. 1970 Cover: 0.15 **NM** value: **10.00**
120 ☐ ca. 1970 Cover: 0.15 **NM** value: **10.00**
121 ☐ Nov 1970 Cover: 0.15 **NM** value: **8.50**
122 ☐ Cover: 0.15 **NM** value: **8.50**
123 ☐ May 1971 Cover: 0.15 **NM** value: **8.50**
124 ☐ Jul 1971 Cover: 0.15 **NM** value: **8.50**
125 ☐ ca. 1971 Cover: 0.25 **NM** value: **8.50**
126 ☐ ca. 1971 Cover: 0.25 **NM** value: **8.50**
127 ☐ ca. 1971 Cover: 0.25 **NM** value: **8.50**
128 ☐ Jan 1972 Cover: 0.25 **NM** value: **8.50**
Circ: Statement: **125,959**
129 ☐ Feb 1972 Cover: 0.25 **NM** value: **8.50**
Circ: Statement: **125,959** • **CGC:** 1 graded, best 9.0
130 ☐ Mar 1972 Cover: 0.25 **NM** value: **8.50**
Circ: Statement: **125,959**
131 ☐ Apr 1972 Cover: 0.25 **NM** value: **8.50**
Circ: Statement: **125,959**
132 ☐ May 1972 Cover: 0.25 **NM** value: **8.50**
Circ: Statement: **125,959**
133 ☐ Jun 1972 Cover: 0.25 **NM** value: **8.50**
Circ: Statement: **125,959**
134 ☐ Jul 1972 Cover: 0.20 **NM** value: **8.50**
Circ: Statement: **125,959**
135 ☐ Aug 1972 Cover: 0.20 **NM** value: **8.50**
Circ: Statement: **125,959**
136 ☐ ca. 1972 Cover: 0.20 **NM** value: **8.50**
Circ: Statement: **125,959**
137 ☐ ca. 1972 Cover: 0.20 **NM** value: **8.50**
Circ: Statement: **125,959**
138 ☐ Dec 1972 Cover: 0.20 **NM** value: **8.50**
Circ: Statement: **125,959**
139 ☐ ca. 1973 Cover: 0.20 **NM** value: **8.50**
140 ☐ Apr 1973 Cover: 0.20 **NM** value: **8.50**
• Has 1972 Statement; avg total paid circ 125,959
141 ☐ ca. 1973 Cover: 0.20 **NM** value: **8.50**
142 ☐ Sep 1973 Cover: 0.20 **NM** value: **8.50**
143 ☐ Nov 1973 Cover: 0.20 **NM** value: **8.50**
final issue.

FALLING MAN, THE — Image

1 ☐ Feb 1998, b&w Cover: 2.95 **NM** value: **Cover or less**
Circ: Diamd. preorders: **3,843**

FALLOUT 3000 (MIKE DEODATO'S...) — Caliber

1 ☐ Cover: 2.95 **NM** value: **Cover or less**

FALLS THE GOTHAM RAIN — Comico

1 ☐ Cover: 4.95 **NM** value: **Cover or less**

Capital City orders are the actual sales of comic books by Capital City Distribution, once one of the largest U.S. sellers of comics to comics shops. Capital City's share of comics shop sales, while not known exactly, increases from around 10-20% in the mid-1980s to 30-35% in the mid-1990s. Capital City's share of comic books sold on newsstands (most Marvels and DCs) will be less.

FAMILY AFFAIR — Gold Key

Family Affair, a TV series starring Brian Keith (1921-1997) and Sebastian Cabot (1918-1977) as caretakers of three orphans, ran from 1966 to 1971. The show, featuring a bachelor who adopts his nephew and two nieces after the death of his brother, spawned a licensing phenomenon in which girls wanted their own Mrs. Beasley doll.

The comic book, one of Gold Key's many titles adapting 1960s situation comedies, met with less success and had a shorter run. The first issue is notable for the inclusion of a poster; copies without the poster today go for about half the value of copies with the poster. — Maggie

1 ☐ Jan 1970 Cover: 0.25 **NM** value: **30.00**
2 ☐ Apr 1970 Cover: 0.15 **NM** value: **18.00**
3 ☐ Jul 1970 Cover: 0.15 **NM** value: **12.00**
• **CGC:** 1 graded, best 6.5
4 ☐ Oct 1970 Cover: 0.15 **NM** value: **12.00**
final issue.

FAMILY FUNNIES — Harvey

1 ☐ Sep 1950 Cover: 0.10 **NM** value: **38.00**
📖 Blondie; Popeye; Katzenjammer Kids; Felix; Henry; Tippie; Buz Sawyer; Toots and Casper; Seein' Stars; Etta Kett; W **A:** Chic Young; Carl Anderson; Roy C **W:** Chic Young; Carl Anderson; Roy Crane; Jimmy
2 ☐ Oct 1950 Cover: 0.10 **NM** value: **30.00**
3 ☐ Nov 1950 Cover: 0.10 **NM** value: **25.00**
4 ☐ Dec 1950 Cover: 0.10 **NM** value: **25.00**
5 ☐ Jan 1951 Cover: 0.10 **NM** value: **25.00**
6 ☐ Feb 1951 Cover: 0.10 **NM** value: **21.00**
7 ☐ Mar 1951 Cover: 0.10 **NM** value: **21.00**
8 ☐ Apr 1951 Cover: 0.10 **NM** value: **21.00**
• Series continued in Tiny Tot Funnies #9 (?)

FAMILY MAN — DC / Paradox

1 ☐ b&w Cover: 4.95 **NM** value: **Cover or less**
Circ: CapCity orders: **2,800**
• digest. 📖 To Protect and Serve **A:** Joe Staton **W:** Jerome Charyn
2 ☐ b&w Cover: 4.95 **NM** value: **Cover or less**
Circ: CapCity orders: **2,200**
• digest.
3 ☐ b&w Cover: 4.95 **NM** value: **Cover or less**
• digest.

FAMOUS COMICS — Zain-Eppy

1 ☐ 1934 Cover: 0.10 **NM** value: **200.00**
2 ☐ Cover: 0.10 **NM** value: **200.00**
3 ☐ Cover: 0.10 **NM** value: **200.00**

FAMOUS CRIMES — Fox

1 ☐ Jun 1948 Cover: 0.10 **NM** value: **300.00**
• **CGC:** 4 graded, best 9.6
2 ☐ Aug 1948 Cover: 0.10 **NM** value: **250.00**
3 ☐ Oct 1948 Cover: 0.10 **NM** value: **125.00**
4 ☐ Dec 1948 Cover: 0.10 **NM** value: **75.00**
5 ☐ Jan 1949 Cover: 0.10 **NM** value: **75.00**
6 ☐ Feb 1949 Cover: 0.10 **NM** value: **75.00**
7 ☐ Mar 1949 Cover: 0.10 **NM** value: **75.00**
8 ☐ Apr 1949 Cover: 0.10 **NM** value: **75.00**
9 ☐ May 1949 Cover: 0.10 **NM** value: **75.00**
10 ☐ Jun 1949 Cover: 0.10 **NM** value: **60.00**
11 ☐ Jul 1949 Cover: 0.10 **NM** value: **60.00**
12 ☐ Aug 1949 Cover: 0.10 **NM** value: **60.00**
13 ☐ Sep 1949 Cover: 0.10 **NM** value: **60.00**
14 ☐ Nov 1949 Cover: 0.10 **NM** value: **60.00**
15 ☐ Jan 1950 Cover: 0.10 **NM** value: **60.00**
16 ☐ Mar 1950 Cover: 0.10 **NM** value: **50.00**
17 ☐ May 1950 Cover: 0.10 **NM** value: **50.00**
18 ☐ Jul 1950 Cover: 0.10 **NM** value: **50.00**
19 ☐ Sep 1950 Cover: 0.10 **NM** value: **50.00**
20 ☐ ca. 1951 Cover: 0.10 **NM** value: **50.00**

FAMOUS FAIRY TALES — K.K.

1 ☐ ca. 1942 Cover: 0.10 **NM** value: **350.00**
2 ☐ ca. 1943 Cover: 0.10 **NM** value: **250.00**
3 ☐ ca. 1944 Cover: 0.10 **NM** value: **200.00**

FAMOUS FEATURES (JERRY IGER'S ...) — Pacific

1 ☐ Jul 1984 Cover: 1.50 **NM** value: **2.00**
• Flamingo

FAMOUS FEATURE STORIES — Dell

1 ☐ ca. 1938 Cover: 0.10 **NM** value: **500.00**

There are two different pricing tiers in the modern comic-book hobby. **The prices seen above** are the prices we have seen **loose copies** of these issues reliably fetch in a variety of environments. Condition alters the price by the fractions seen on the bar on the bottom of left-hand pages of this book. **Comics graded by CGC** usually sell for more. Use the guide on the bottom of right-hand pages of this book to estimate what copies have brought on eBay.

FAMOUS FIRST EDITION — DC

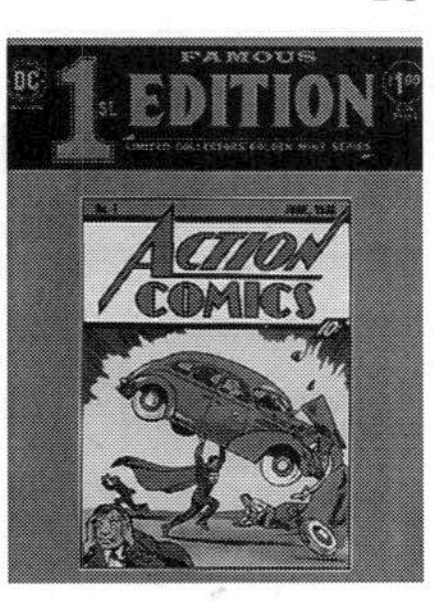

In 1974, DC began publishing these giant-sized reprints of its most important Golden Age comics. Double-covered, the reprints reproduced the originals exactly, including the ads for automatic mouth organs, crystal radios, blank cartridge pistols, and other great comic-book ephemera. Once you removed the outer covers, the only real difference between the originals and the reprints was the size — the reprints were printed in tabloid size. Still, some con artists have tried to pass off coverless versions of these reprints as the (much smaller) originals.

The series began with a bang with a reprinting of Action Comics #1, the first appearance of Superman. The original comic book would cost tens of thousands of dollars if it were purchased today, but the giant-sized reprint let you experience the wonder of reading it for just one dollar at the time. Other issues reprinted Detective Comics #27 (the first appearance of Batman), Flash Comics #1, and more.

4 ☐ Nov 1974 Cover: 1.00 **NM** value: **10.00**
• really F-4; reprints Whiz Comics #2
5 ☐ Jan 1975 Cover: 1.00 **NM** value: **8.00**
• really F-5; reprints Batman #1
6 ☐ May 1975 Cover: 1.00 **NM** value: **8.00**
• really F-6; reprints Wonder Woman #1
7 ☐ Jul 1975 Cover: 1.00 **NM** value: **10.00**
• really F-7; reprints All-Star #3
8 ☐ Sep 1975 Cover: 1.00 **NM** value: **8.00**
• really F-8; reprints Flash Comics #1
26 ☐ Cover: 1.00 **NM** value: **8.00**
📖 Superman • really C-26; reprints Action Comics #1 **A:** Joe Shuster **W:** Jerry Siegel ★ 1st Appearance of Superman.
28 ☐ Cover: 1.00 **NM** value: **8.00**
• really C-28; reprints Detective Comics #1; reprints Detective Comics #27
30 ☐ Cover: 1.00 **NM** value: **8.00**
• really C-30; reprints Sensation Comics #1 **W:** Charles Moulton ★ 1st Appearance of Wonder Woman.
61 ☐ Mar 1979 Cover: 1.00 **NM** value: **6.00**
• really C-61; reprints Superman #1

FAMOUS FUNNIES — Famous Funnies

Many consider this to be the first modern comic book. After all, it was circulated via newsstand sales. It was a four-color magazine of roughly the same size as the comics that followed it. It carried a cover price of a dime. And early issues kicked off a monthly publication schedule, which lasted for years and years for Famous Funnies and became the industry standard (though, of course, not all ongoing series are published monthly.

Created as a way to keep printing presses going at Eastern Color Printing in New York, its contents initially consisted of newspaper strip reprints. Such strips as Toonerville Folks, Mutt and Jeff, Connie, Tailspin Tommy, and The Nebbs provided content for the first issue, and later additions Buck Rogers and Invisible Scarlet O'Neil are among reasons it's collected today. — Maggie

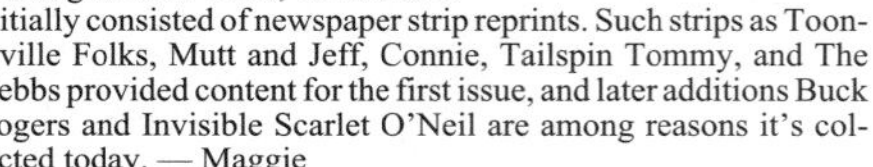

1 ☐ Jul 1934 Cover: 0.10 **NM** value: **15400.00**
• **CGC:** 1 graded, best 6.0
• First regular monthly comic book ever published
2 ☐ Sep 1934 Cover: 0.10 **NM** value: **3600.00**
3 ☐ Oct 1934 Cover: 0.10 **NM** value: **3900.00**
• Buck Rogers strips begin ★ 1st Appearance of Buck Rogers (in a comic book).
4 ☐ Nov 1934 Cover: 0.10 **NM** value: **1300.00**
5 ☐ Dec 1934 Cover: 0.10 **NM** value: **985.00**
6 ☐ Jan 1935 Cover: 0.10 **NM** value: **725.00**
7 ☐ Feb 1935 Cover: 0.10 **NM** value: **725.00**
8 ☐ Mar 1935 Cover: 0.10 **NM** value: **725.00**
9 ☐ Apr 1935 Cover: 0.10 **NM** value: **725.00**
10 ☐ May 1935 Cover: 0.10 **NM** value: **725.00**
11 ☐ Jun 1935 Cover: 0.10 **NM** value: **610.00**
12 ☐ Jul 1935 Cover: 0.10 **NM** value: **610.00**
• **CGC:** 1 graded, best 6.5
13 ☐ Aug 1935 Cover: 0.10 **NM** value: **385.00**
14 ☐ Sep 1935 Cover: 0.10 **NM** value: **385.00**
15 ☐ Oct 1935 Cover: 0.10 **NM** value: **385.00**
16 ☐ Nov 1935 Cover: 0.10 **NM** value: **385.00**
17 ☐ Dec 1935 Cover: 0.10 **NM** value: **385.00**
• **CGC:** 1 graded, best 7.5
18 ☐ Jan 1936 Cover: 0.10 **NM** value: **610.00**
19 ☐ Feb 1936 Cover: 0.10 **NM** value: **385.00**
• **CGC:** 1 graded, best 4.5
20 ☐ Mar 1936 Cover: 0.10 **NM** value: **385.00**
• **CGC:** 1 graded, best 7.0
21 ☐ Apr 1936 Cover: 0.10 **NM** value: **335.00**
• **CGC:** 1 graded, best 6.0
22 ☐ May 1936 Cover: 0.10 **NM** value: **325.00**
• **CGC:** 1 graded, best 5.0
23 ☐ Jun 1936 Cover: 0.10 **NM** value: **320.00**
• **CGC:** 1 graded, best 6.5
24 ☐ Jul 1936 Cover: 0.10 **NM** value: **320.00**

Other grades: Multiply prices above by **1.5 for Mint • 2/3 for Very Fine • 1/3 for Fine • 1/5 for Very Good • 1/8 for Good**

25 ❑ Aug 1936 Cover: 0.10 **NM** value: **320.00**
26 ❑ Sep 1936 Cover: 0.10 **NM** value: **320.00**
• **CGC:** 1 graded, best 4.0
27 ❑ Oct 1936 Cover: 0.10 **NM** value: **320.00**
• **CGC:** 3 graded, best 5.0
• War on Crime begins; 1st True-Crime in comics
28 ❑ Nov 1936 Cover: 0.10 **NM** value: **320.00**
• **CGC:** 1 graded, best 6.0
29 ❑ Dec 1936 Cover: 0.10 **NM** value: **320.00**
30 ❑ Jan 1937 Cover: 0.10 **NM** value: **320.00**
Circ: ABC: **485,136**
31 ❑ Feb 1937 Cover: 0.10 **NM** value: **215.00**
Circ: ABC: **460,468** • **CGC:** 1 graded, best 6.5
32 ❑ Mar 1937 Cover: 0.10 **NM** value: **215.00**
Circ: ABC: **380,427**
33 ❑ Apr 1937 Cover: 0.10 **NM** value: **215.00**
Circ: ABC: **396,371** • **CGC:** 1 graded, best 6.5
• Baby Face Nelson and John Dillinger stories
34 ❑ May 1937 Cover: 0.10 **NM** value: **215.00**
Circ: ABC: **351,913**
35 ❑ Jun 1937 Cover: 0.10 **NM** value: **215.00**
Circ: ABC: **371,202**
36 ❑ Jul 1937 Cover: 0.10 **NM** value: **215.00**
Circ: ABC: **438,824**
37 ❑ Aug 1937 Cover: 0.10 **NM** value: **215.00**
Circ: ABC: **485,151** • **CGC:** 1 graded, best 8.5
38 ❑ Sep 1937 Cover: 0.10 **NM** value: **225.00**
Circ: ABC: **530,824** • **CGC:** 1 graded, best 6.0
• Buck Rogers portrait
39 ❑ Oct 1937 Cover: 0.10 **NM** value: **200.00**
Circ: ABC: **440,837** • **CGC:** 1 graded, best 6.5
40 ❑ Nov 1937 Cover: 0.10 **NM** value: **200.00**
Circ: ABC: **429,298** • **CGC:** 1 graded, best 7.0
41 ❑ Dec 1937 Cover: 0.10 **NM** value: **165.00**
Circ: ABC: **456,050** • **CGC:** 1 graded, best 5.0
42 ❑ Jan 1938 Cover: 0.10 **NM** value: **165.00**
Circ: ABC: **438,937**
43 ❑ Feb 1938 Cover: 0.10 **NM** value: **165.00**
Circ: ABC: **420,162**
44 ❑ Mar 1938 Cover: 0.10 **NM** value: **165.00**
Circ: ABC: **401,002**
45 ❑ Apr 1938 Cover: 0.10 **NM** value: **165.00**
Circ: ABC: **349,070**
46 ❑ May 1938 Cover: 0.10 **NM** value: **165.00**
Circ: ABC: **324,098** • **CGC:** 1 graded, best 7.0
47 ❑ Jun 1938 Cover: 0.10 **NM** value: **165.00**
Circ: ABC: **323,795** • **CGC:** 1 graded, best 6.5
48 ❑ Jul 1938 Cover: 0.10 **NM** value: **165.00**
Circ: ABC: **378,122**
49 ❑ Aug 1938 Cover: 0.10 **NM** value: **165.00**
Circ: ABC: **373,295** • **CGC:** 1 graded, best 8.0
50 ❑ Sep 1938 Cover: 0.10 **NM** value: **165.00**
Circ: ABC: **425,970** • **CGC:** 1 graded, best 4.0
51 ❑ Oct 1938 Cover: 0.10 **NM** value: **150.00**
Circ: ABC: **343,233**
52 ❑ Nov 1938 Cover: 0.10 **NM** value: **150.00**
Circ: ABC: **312,589**
53 ❑ Dec 1938 Cover: 0.10 **NM** value: **150.00**
Circ: ABC: **331,827** • **CGC:** 1 graded, best 7.0
54 ❑ Jan 1939 Cover: 0.10 **NM** value: **150.00**
Circ: ABC: **357,386** • **CGC:** 1 graded, best 6.5
55 ❑ Feb 1939 Cover: 0.10 **NM** value: **150.00**
Circ: ABC: **356,893** • **CGC:** 1 graded, best 6.0
56 ❑ Mar 1939 Cover: 0.10 **NM** value: **150.00**
Circ: ABC: **348,914**
57 ❑ Apr 1939 Cover: 0.10 **NM** value: **150.00**
Circ: ABC: **334,377**
58 ❑ May 1939 Cover: 0.10 **NM** value: **150.00**
Circ: ABC: **280,350**
59 ❑ Jun 1939 Cover: 0.10 **NM** value: **150.00**
Circ: ABC: **328,153** • **CGC:** 1 graded, best 6.5
60 ❑ Jul 1939 Cover: 0.10 **NM** value: **150.00**
Circ: ABC: **367,736**
61 ❑ Aug 1939 Cover: 0.10 **NM** value: **130.00**
Circ: ABC: **389,005** • **CGC:** 1 graded, best 6.5
62 ❑ Sep 1939 Cover: 0.10 **NM** value: **130.00**
Circ: ABC: **408,545**
63 ❑ Oct 1939 Cover: 0.10 **NM** value: **130.00**
Circ: ABC: **311,541**
64 ❑ Nov 1939 Cover: 0.10 **NM** value: **130.00**
Circ: ABC: **310,173**
65 ❑ Dec 1939 Cover: 0.10 **NM** value: **130.00**
Circ: ABC: **327,685** • **CGC:** 1 graded, best 6.5
66 ❑ Jan 1940 Cover: 0.10 **NM** value: **130.00**
Circ: ABC: **329,629** • **CGC:** 1 graded, best 7.0
67 ❑ Feb 1940 Cover: 0.10 **NM** value: **130.00**
Circ: ABC: **319,277** • **CGC:** 1 graded, best 6.5
68 ❑ Mar 1940 Cover: 0.10 **NM** value: **130.00**
Circ: ABC: **266,483** • **CGC:** 1 graded, best 6.0
69 ❑ Apr 1940 Cover: 0.10 **NM** value: **130.00**
Circ: ABC: **241,918** • **CGC:** 1 graded, best 5.0
70 ❑ May 1940 Cover: 0.10 **NM** value: **130.00**
Circ: ABC: **218,009** • **CGC:** 1 graded, best 7.0
71 ❑ Jun 1940 Cover: 0.10 **NM** value: **90.00**
Circ: ABC: **203,608**
72 ❑ Jul 1940 Cover: 0.10 **NM** value: **90.00**
Circ: ABC: **239,716**
73 ❑ Aug 1940 Cover: 0.10 **NM** value: **90.00**
Circ: ABC: **249,258**
74 ❑ Sep 1940 Cover: 0.10 **NM** value: **90.00**
Circ: ABC: **281,761** • **CGC:** 1 graded, best 6.5
75 ❑ Oct 1940 Cover: 0.10 **NM** value: **90.00**
Circ: ABC: **225,236**
76 ❑ Nov 1940 Cover: 0.10 **NM** value: **90.00**
Circ: ABC: **198,228** • **CGC:** 1 graded, best 6.0
77 ❑ Dec 1940 Cover: 0.10 **NM** value: **90.00**
Circ: ABC: **214,825**
78 ❑ Jan 1941 Cover: 0.10 **NM** value: **90.00**
Circ: ABC: **251,900**
79 ❑ Feb 1941 Cover: 0.10 **NM** value: **90.00**
Circ: ABC: **224,942**
80 ❑ Mar 1941 Cover: 0.10 **NM** value: **90.00**
Circ: ABC: **219,904** • **CGC:** 1 graded, best 7.0
81 ❑ Apr 1941 Cover: 0.10 **NM** value: **75.00**
Circ: ABC: **227,062**
82 ❑ May 1941 Cover: 0.10 **NM** value: **90.00**
Circ: ABC: **165,922** • **CGC:** 1 graded, best 5.5
Buck Rogers cover.
83 ❑ Jun 1941 Cover: 0.10 **NM** value: **75.00**
Circ: ABC: **175,561**
84 ❑ Jul 1941 Cover: 0.10 **NM** value: **75.00**
85 ❑ Aug 1941 Cover: 0.10 **NM** value: **75.00**
86 ❑ Sep 1941 Cover: 0.10 **NM** value: **75.00**
87 ❑ Oct 1941 Cover: 0.10 **NM** value: **75.00**
88 ❑ Nov 1941 Cover: 0.10 **NM** value: **75.00**
• **CGC:** 1 graded, best 5.5
89 ❑ Dec 1941 Cover: 0.10 **NM** value: **75.00**
90 ❑ Jan 1942 Cover: 0.10 **NM** value: **75.00**
91 ❑ Feb 1942 Cover: 0.10 **NM** value: **65.00**
• **CGC:** 1 graded, best 7.5
92 ❑ Mar 1942 Cover: 0.10 **NM** value: **65.00**
93 ❑ Apr 1942 Cover: 0.10 **NM** value: **65.00**
94 ❑ May 1942 Cover: 0.10 **NM** value: **65.00**
• **CGC:** 1 graded, best 6.0
Buy war bonds cover. • New Buck Rogers story
95 ❑ Jun 1942 Cover: 0.10 **NM** value: **65.00**
96 ❑ Jul 1942 Cover: 0.10 **NM** value: **65.00**
97 ❑ Aug 1942 Cover: 0.10 **NM** value: **65.00**
• **CGC:** 1 graded, best 7.5
98 ❑ Sep 1942 Cover: 0.10 **NM** value: **65.00**
• **CGC:** 1 graded, best 9.2
99 ❑ Oct 1942 Cover: 0.10 **NM** value: **65.00**
• **CGC:** 1 graded, best 9.2
100 ❑ Nov 1942 Cover: 0.10 **NM** value: **70.00**
• 100th anniversary issue.
101 ❑ Dec 1942 Cover: 0.10 **NM** value: **55.00**
• **CGC:** 2 graded, best 9.2
102 ❑ Jan 1943 Cover: 0.10 **NM** value: **55.00**
• **CGC:** 2 graded, best 8.5
103 ❑ Feb 1943 Cover: 0.10 **NM** value: **55.00**
• **CGC:** 1 graded, best 7.0
104 ❑ Mar 1943 Cover: 0.10 **NM** value: **55.00**
• **CGC:** 1 graded, best 8.0
105 ❑ Apr 1943 Cover: 0.10 **NM** value: **55.00**
• **CGC:** 4 graded, best 9.4
106 ❑ May 1943 Cover: 0.10 **NM** value: **55.00**
107 ❑ Jun 1943 Cover: 0.10 **NM** value: **55.00**
108 ❑ Jul 1943 Cover: 0.10 **NM** value: **55.00**
• **CGC:** 1 graded, best 8.0
109 ❑ Aug 1943 Cover: 0.10 **NM** value: **55.00**
• **CGC:** 2 graded, best 9.0
110 ❑ Sep 1943 Cover: 0.10 **NM** value: **55.00**
• **CGC:** 2 graded, best 9.2
111 ❑ Oct 1943 Cover: 0.10 **NM** value: **45.00**
• **CGC:** 2 graded, best 9.6
112 ❑ Nov 1943 Cover: 0.10 **NM** value: **45.00**
• **CGC:** 2 graded, best 9.6
113 ❑ Dec 1943 Cover: 0.10 **NM** value: **45.00**
• **CGC:** 2 graded, best 7.0
114 ❑ Jan 1944 Cover: 0.10 **NM** value: **45.00**
• **CGC:** 2 graded, best 9.2
115 ❑ Feb 1944 Cover: 0.10 **NM** value: **45.00**
• **CGC:** 1 graded, best 7.0
116 ❑ Mar 1944 Cover: 0.10 **NM** value: **45.00**
• **CGC:** 2 graded, best 9.2
117 ❑ Apr 1944 Cover: 0.10 **NM** value: **45.00**
• **CGC:** 1 graded, best 9.0
118 ❑ May 1944 Cover: 0.10 **NM** value: **45.00**
• **CGC:** 2 graded, best 9.4
119 ❑ Jun 1944 Cover: 0.10 **NM** value: **45.00**
• **CGC:** 1 graded, best 8.5
120 ❑ Jul 1944 Cover: 0.10 **NM** value: **45.00**
• **CGC:** 1 graded, best 8.0
121 ❑ Aug 1944 Cover: 0.10 **NM** value: **45.00**
• **CGC:** 1 graded, best 9.2
122 ❑ Sep 1944 Cover: 0.10 **NM** value: **45.00**
• **CGC:** 1 graded, best 9.4
123 ❑ Oct 1944 Cover: 0.10 **NM** value: **45.00**
• **CGC:** 1 graded, best 8.5
124 ❑ Nov 1944 Cover: 0.10 **NM** value: **45.00**
• **CGC:** 2 graded, best 9.0
125 ❑ Dec 1944 Cover: 0.10 **NM** value: **45.00**
• **CGC:** 1 graded, best 8.0
126 ❑ Jan 1945 Cover: 0.10 **NM** value: **45.00**
• **CGC:** 1 graded, best 8.5
127 ❑ Feb 1945 Cover: 0.10 **NM** value: **45.00**
• **CGC:** 1 graded, best 9.2
128 ❑ Mar 1945 Cover: 0.10 **NM** value: **45.00**
• **CGC:** 1 graded, best 7.5
129 ❑ Apr 1945 Cover: 0.10 **NM** value: **45.00**
• **CGC:** 1 graded, best 7.5
130 ❑ May 1945 Cover: 0.10 **NM** value: **45.00**
• **CGC:** 1 graded, best 7.0
131 ❑ Jun 1945 Cover: 0.10 **NM** value: **35.00**
• **CGC:** 1 graded, best 6.0
132 ❑ Jul 1945 Cover: 0.10 **NM** value: **35.00**
• **CGC:** 1 graded, best 9.2
133 ❑ Aug 1945 Cover: 0.10 **NM** value: **35.00**
• **CGC:** 1 graded, best 9.4
134 ❑ Sep 1945 Cover: 0.10 **NM** value: **35.00**
• **CGC:** 1 graded, best 7.5
135 ❑ Oct 1945 Cover: 0.10 **NM** value: **35.00**
• **CGC:** 1 graded, best 8.5
136 ❑ Nov 1945 Cover: 0.10 **NM** value: **35.00**
• **CGC:** 1 graded, best 9.4
137 ❑ Dec 1945 Cover: 0.10 **NM** value: **35.00**
• **CGC:** 1 graded, best 9.4
138 ❑ Jan 1946 Cover: 0.10 **NM** value: **35.00**
• **CGC:** 2 graded, best 9.2
139 ❑ Feb 1946 Cover: 0.10 **NM** value: **35.00**
• **CGC:** 1 graded, best 9.2
140 ❑ Mar 1946 Cover: 0.10 **NM** value: **35.00**
• **CGC:** 2 graded, best 8.0
141 ❑ Apr 1946 Cover: 0.10 **NM** value: **35.00**
• **CGC:** 1 graded, best 9.4
142 ❑ May 1946 Cover: 0.10 **NM** value: **35.00**
• **CGC:** 1 graded, best 9.6
143 ❑ Jun 1946 Cover: 0.10 **NM** value: **35.00**
• **CGC:** 1 graded, best 9.0
144 ❑ Jul 1946 Cover: 0.10 **NM** value: **35.00**
• **CGC:** 1 graded, best 8.0
145 ❑ Aug 1946 Cover: 0.10 **NM** value: **35.00**
• **CGC:** 1 graded, best 9.0
146 ❑ Sep 1946 Cover: 0.10 **NM** value: **35.00**
• **CGC:** 1 graded, best 8.5
147 ❑ Oct 1946 Cover: 0.10 **NM** value: **35.00**
• **CGC:** 2 graded, best 9.2
148 ❑ Nov 1946 Cover: 0.10 **NM** value: **35.00**
• **CGC:** 1 graded, best 9.6
149 ❑ Dec 1946 Cover: 0.10 **NM** value: **35.00**
• **CGC:** 1 graded, best 9.4
150 ❑ Jan 1947 Cover: 0.10 **NM** value: **35.00**
• **CGC:** 1 graded, best 9.6
151 ❑ Feb 1947 Cover: 0.10 **NM** value: **26.00**
• **CGC:** 1 graded, best 9.6
152 ❑ Mar 1947 Cover: 0.10 **NM** value: **26.00**
• **CGC:** 1 graded, best 9.6
153 ❑ Apr 1947 Cover: 0.10 **NM** value: **26.00**
• **CGC:** 1 graded, best 9.6
154 ❑ May 1947 Cover: 0.10 **NM** value: **26.00**
155 ❑ Jun 1947 Cover: 0.10 **NM** value: **26.00**
• **CGC:** 1 graded, best 9.0
156 ❑ Jul 1947 Cover: 0.10 **NM** value: **26.00**
• **CGC:** 1 graded, best 9.0
157 ❑ Aug 1947 Cover: 0.10 **NM** value: **26.00**
• **CGC:** 1 graded, best 8.0
158 ❑ Sep 1947 Cover: 0.10 **NM** value: **26.00**
• **CGC:** 1 graded, best 9.2
159 ❑ Oct 1947 Cover: 0.10 **NM** value: **26.00**
• **CGC:** 1 graded, best 9.6
160 ❑ Nov 1947 Cover: 0.10 **NM** value: **26.00**
• **CGC:** 1 graded, best 9.2
161 ❑ Dec 1947 Cover: 0.10 **NM** value: **26.00**
• **CGC:** 1 graded, best 9.4
162 ❑ Jan 1948 Cover: 0.10 **NM** value: **26.00**
• **CGC:** 1 graded, best 9.4
163 ❑ Feb 1948 Cover: 0.10 **NM** value: **28.00**
• **CGC:** 1 graded, best 8.0
Valentine's Day cover.
164 ❑ Mar 1948 Cover: 0.10 **NM** value: **26.00**
• **CGC:** 1 graded, best 7.5
165 ❑ Apr 1948 Cover: 0.10 **NM** value: **26.00**
• **CGC:** 1 graded, best 9.2
166 ❑ May 1948 Cover: 0.10 **NM** value: **26.00**
• **CGC:** 1 graded, best 9.2
167 ❑ Jun 1948 Cover: 0.10 **NM** value: **26.00**
• **CGC:** 1 graded, best 9.2
168 ❑ Jul 1948 Cover: 0.10 **NM** value: **26.00**
• **CGC:** 1 graded, best 7.5
169 ❑ Aug 1948 Cover: 0.10 **NM** value: **65.00**
• **CGC:** 1 graded, best 9.0
• Al Williamson's first comic book work (illustrations for text piece)
A: Al Williamson(art on text piece)
170 ❑ Sep 1948 Cover: 0.10 **NM** value: **55.00**
• **CGC:** 1 graded, best 9.0
171 ❑ Oct 1948 Cover: 0.10 **NM** value: **26.00**
• **CGC:** 1 graded, best 9.0
172 ❑ Nov 1948 Cover: 0.10 **NM** value: **26.00**
173 ❑ Dec 1948 Cover: 0.10 **NM** value: **26.00**
• **CGC:** 1 graded, best 9.4
174 ❑ Jan 1949 Cover: 0.10 **NM** value: **26.00**
• **CGC:** 1 graded, best 9.4
175 ❑ Feb 1949 Cover: 0.10 **NM** value: **26.00**
• **CGC:** 1 graded, best 9.6
176 ❑ Mar 1949 Cover: 0.10 **NM** value: **26.00**
• **CGC:** 1 graded, best 9.4
177 ❑ Apr 1949 Cover: 0.10 **NM** value: **26.00**
• **CGC:** 1 graded, best 9.0
📖 Untitled stories; Blind Flight (text) • Buck Rogers, Steve Roper and Wahoo, Dickie Dare, Napoleon, Bobby Sox, Scorchy Smith, Oaky Doaks, Pen Pal Page
178 ❑ May 1949 Cover: 0.10 **NM** value: **26.00**
• **CGC:** 1 graded, best 9.0
179 ❑ Jun 1949 Cover: 0.10 **NM** value: **26.00**
• **CGC:** 1 graded, best 9.4
180 ❑ Jul 1949 Cover: 0.10 **NM** value: **26.00**
• **CGC:** 2 graded, best 9.4
181 ❑ Aug 1949 Cover: 0.10 **NM** value: **26.00**
• **CGC:** 1 graded, best 9.4
182 ❑ Sep 1949 Cover: 0.10 **NM** value: **26.00**
• **CGC:** 1 graded, best 9.4
183 ❑ Oct 1949 Cover: 0.10 **NM** value: **26.00**
• **CGC:** 1 graded, best 9.6
184 ❑ Nov 1949 Cover: 0.10 **NM** value: **26.00**
• **CGC:** 1 graded, best 9.2
185 ❑ Dec 1949 Cover: 0.10 **NM** value: **26.00**
• **CGC:** 1 graded, best 9.0
186 ❑ Jan 1950 Cover: 0.10 **NM** value: **26.00**
• **CGC:** 1 graded, best 9.2
187 ❑ Mar 1950 Cover: 0.10 **NM** value: **26.00**
• **CGC:** 1 graded, best 8.0
188 ❑ Jun 1950 Cover: 0.10 **NM** value: **26.00**
• **CGC:** 1 graded, best 8.5
189 ❑ Aug 1950 Cover: 0.10 **NM** value: **26.00**
• **CGC:** 1 graded, best 8.5

CGC-graded: Multiply prices above by **33 for 9.9 M • 16 for 9.8 NM/M • 7 for 9.6 NM+ • 5 for 9.4 NM • 2.5 for 9.2 NM- • 1.5 for 9.0 VF/NM**

190 ❑ Oct 1950 Cover: 0.10 **NM** value: **26.00**
• Buck Rogers strips end
191 ❑ Dec 1950 Cover: 0.10 **NM** value: **24.00**
• **CGC:** 1 graded, best 9.2
192 ❑ Feb 1951 Cover: 0.10 **NM** value: **24.00**
• **CGC:** 1 graded, best 9.0
193 ❑ Apr 1951 Cover: 0.10 **NM** value: **24.00**
• **CGC:** 1 graded, best 9.2
194 ❑ Jun 1951 Cover: 0.10 **NM** value: **24.00**
• **CGC:** 1 graded, best 8.5
195 ❑ Aug 1951 Cover: 0.10 **NM** value: **24.00**
• **CGC:** 1 graded, best 9.0
196 ❑ Oct 1951 Cover: 0.10 **NM** value: **24.00**
• **CGC:** 1 graded, best 8.0
197 ❑ Dec 1951 Cover: 0.10 **NM** value: **24.00**
• **CGC:** 2 graded, best 9.2
198 ❑ Feb 1952 Cover: 0.10 **NM** value: **24.00**
• **CGC:** 1 graded, best 9.4
199 ❑ Apr 1952 Cover: 0.10 **NM** value: **24.00**
• **CGC:** 1 graded, best 9.2
200 ❑ Jun 1952 Cover: 0.10 **NM** value: **24.00**
• **CGC:** 1 graded, best 8.5
201 ❑ Aug 1952 Cover: 0.10 **NM** value: **24.00**
• **CGC:** 1 graded, best 9.2
202 ❑ Oct 1952 Cover: 0.10 **NM** value: **24.00**
• **CGC:** 2 graded, best 9.0
203 ❑ Dec 1952 Cover: 0.10 **NM** value: **24.00**
• **CGC:** 1 graded, best 9.2
204 ❑ Feb 1953 Cover: 0.10 **NM** value: **24.00**
• **CGC:** 1 graded, best 9.6
205 ❑ Apr 1953 Cover: 0.10 **NM** value: **24.00**
• **CGC:** 1 graded, best 9.2
206 ❑ Jun 1953 Cover: 0.10 **NM** value: **24.00**
• **CGC:** 1 graded, best 9.0
207 ❑ Aug 1953 Cover: 0.10 **NM** value: **24.00**
• **CGC:** 1 graded, best 9.2
208 ❑ Oct 1953 Cover: 0.10 **NM** value: **24.00**
• **CGC:** 2 graded, best 9.0
209 ❑ Dec 1953 Cover: 0.10 **NM** value: **550.00**
• **CGC:** 20 graded, best 9.6
210 ❑ Feb 1954 Cover: 0.10 **NM** value: **550.00**
• **CGC:** 19 graded, best 9.6
211 ❑ May 1954 Cover: 0.10 **NM** value: **550.00**
• **CGC:** 17 graded, best 9.4
212 ❑ Jul 1954 Cover: 0.10 **NM** value: **550.00**
• **CGC:** 14 graded, best 9.0
213 ❑ Sep 1954 Cover: 0.10 **NM** value: **550.00**
• **CGC:** 6 graded, best 8.5
214 ❑ Nov 1954 Cover: 0.10 **NM** value: **550.00**
• **CGC:** 5 graded, best 9.0
• Buck Rogers **A:** Frank Frazetta(cover)
215 ❑ Jan 1955 Cover: 0.10 **NM** value: **550.00**
• **CGC:** 3 graded, best 8.0
216 ❑ Mar 1955 Cover: 0.10 **NM** value: **550.00**
• **CGC:** 4 graded, best 9.2
217 ❑ May 1955 Cover: 0.10 **NM** value: **25.00**
218 ❑ Jul 1955 Cover: 0.10 **NM** value: **25.00**
final issue.

FAMOUS FUNNIES: A CARNIVAL OF COMICS — Eastern Color
1 ❑ ca. 1933 **NM** value: **10000.00**
• **CGC:** 4 graded, best 7.5

FAMOUS FUNNIES SERIES 1 — Eastern Color
1 ❑ Feb 1934 Cover: 0.10 **NM** value: **20000.00**

FAMOUS GANGSTERS — Avon
1 ❑ Apr 1951 Cover: 0.10 **NM** value: **250.00**
2 ❑ Dec 1951 Cover: 0.10 **NM** value: **250.00**
• **CGC:** 1 graded, best 3.5
3 ❑ Aug 1952 Cover: 0.10 **NM** value: **250.00**

FAMOUS STARS — Ziff-Davis
1 ❑ Nov 1950 Cover: 0.10 **NM** value: **250.00**
• **CGC:** 1 graded, best 9.4
2 ❑ Jan 1951 Cover: 0.10 **NM** value: **150.00**
3 ❑ Mar 1951 Cover: 0.10 **NM** value: **150.00**
4 ❑ May 1951 Cover: 0.10 **NM** value: **150.00**
5 ❑ Win 1951 Cover: 0.10 **NM** value: **100.00**
6 ❑ Spr 1952 Cover: 0.10 **NM** value: **100.00**

FAMOUS STORIES — Dell
1 ❑ Cover: 0.10 **NM** value: **200.00**
2 ❑ Cover: 0.10 **NM** value: **200.00**

FAMOUS WESTERN BADMEN — Youthful
13 ❑ Cover: 0.10 **NM** value: **75.00**
14 ❑ Cover: 0.10 **NM** value: **50.00**
15 ❑ Cover: 0.10 **NM** value: **50.00**

FANA — Comax
All issues are adults only.
1 ❑ b&w Cover: 2.95 **NM** value: **Cover or less**

FANA THE JUNGLE GIRL — Comax
1 ❑ b&w Cover: 2.95 **NM** value: **Cover or less**

FANBOY — DC
"Fanboy" is a pejorative term describing a rabid comics fan who loves comics to the exclusion of anything resembling a normal life. In this six-issue mini-series Mark Evanier, (best known as Sergio Aragones' collaborator on Groo), uses that stereotypical image to depict a series of slice-of-life events as seen through the eyes of Finster, the quintessential fanboy. He works at a comics shop, lusts after a girl who will have nothing do with him while remaining oblivious to a girl who would, and most importantly, has a vivid imagination which places him in situations with Superman, Green Lantern, or the rest of the Justice League. The notable aspect of this series is that while Finster is living his normal life, Aragones draws him, but when he interacts with Green Lantern, for example, Gil Kane draws everything. Evanier procured some of the top artists in comics to depict Finster's daydreams, such as Jerry Ordway and Russ Heath.

Far from being a simple humor title, Fanboy uses the Walter Mitty-type reveries as a lighthearted approach to address important issues like self-worth and censorship.

1 ❑ Mar 1999 Cover: 2.50 **NM** value: **Cover or less**
Circ: Diamd. preorders: **19,550**
2 ❑ Apr 1999 Cover: 2.50 **NM** value: **Cover or less**
Circ: Diamd. preorders: **15,565**
3 ❑ May 1999 Cover: 2.50 **NM** value: **Cover or less**
Circ: Diamd. preorders: **14,823**
4 ❑ Jun 1999 Cover: 2.50 **NM** value: **Cover or less**
Circ: Diamd. preorders: **14,162**
📖 Our Fanboy at War • Our Army at War take-off **A:** Sergio Aragonés; Marie Severin; Russ Heath; Jordi Bernet **W:** Mark Evanier ★ Appearance of Sgt. Rock.
5 ❑ Jul 1999 Cover: 2.50 **NM** value: **Cover or less**
Circ: Diamd. preorders: **15,776**
6 ❑ Aug 1999 Cover: 2.50 **NM** value: **Cover or less**
Circ: Diamd. preorders: **13,542**
Bk 1 ❑ Cover: 12.95 **NM** value: **Cover or less**
• Collects series **A:** Sergio Aragonés; Phil Jimenez; Mike Grell; Steve Rude; Dan Spiegle **W:** Mark Evanier

FANG (CONQUEST) — Conquest
1 ❑ b&w Cover: 2.95 **NM** value: **Cover or less**

FANG (SIRIUS) — Sirius Entertainment
1 ❑ Feb 1995 Cover: 2.95 **NM** value: **Cover or less**
Circ: CapCity orders: **10,450**
2 ❑ Apr 1995 Cover: 2.95 **NM** value: **Cover or less**
Circ: CapCity orders: **6,680**
3 ❑ Jun 1995 Cover: 2.95 **NM** value: **Cover or less**
Circ: CapCity orders: **7,575**

FANGRAPHIX — Fangraphix
1 ❑ Cover: 1.95 **NM** value: **Cover or less**
2 ❑ Cover: 1.95 **NM** value: **Cover or less**
3 ❑ Cover: 1.95 **NM** value: **Cover or less**

FANG (TANGRAM) — Tangram
1 ❑ b&w Cover: 2.95 **NM** value: **Cover or less**
No issue number.

FANGS OF THE COBRA — Mythic
1 ❑ Win 1996 Cover: 2.95 **NM** value: **Cover or less**
• color and b&w

FANG: TESTAMENT — Sirius Entertainment
1 ❑ Cover: 2.50 **NM** value: **Cover or less**
Circ: Diamd. preorders: **11,719**
2 ❑ Cover: 2.50 **NM** value: **Cover or less**
Circ: Diamd. preorders: **8,891**
3 ❑ Cover: 2.50 **NM** value: **Cover or less**
Circ: Diamd. preorders: **7,618**
4 ❑ Cover: 2.50 **NM** value: **Cover or less**
Circ: Diamd. preorders: **4,872**
Bk 1 ❑ Cover: 11.95 **NM** value: **Cover or less**
• collects mini-series

FANNY — Fanny
1 ❑ **NM** value: **3.00**
2 ❑ **NM** value: **3.00**
3 ❑ b&w Cover: 3.95 **NM** value: **Cover or less**

FANNY HILL — Shunga
All issues are adults only.
1 ❑ b&w Cover: 2.50 **NM** value: **Cover or less**

FANTAESCAPE — Zinzinnati
1 ❑ Jun 1988 Cover: 1.75 **NM** value: **Cover or less**

FANTAGOR — Last Gasp
1 ❑ Cover: 0.50 **NM** value: **3.00**
📖 Twilight of The Dogs; Razar The Unhero; The Devil in the Well; Inn a Pit **A:** Richard Corben; Herb Arnold **W:** Richard Corben; Starr Armitage
2 ❑ Cover: 0.50 **NM** value: **3.00**
3 ❑ Cover: 0.50 **NM** value: **3.00**
📖 The Temple; Fugue; Kittens for Christian **A:** Richard Corben **W:** Richard Corben; Jan Strnad

FANTASCI — Apple
1 ❑ b&w Cover: 1.50 **NM** value: **2.00**
📖 Dull to Dynamic in One Difficult Lesson; A Hero Named Harold; Hunter XX: Games of Life and Death **A:** Don Lomax; Dave Hoover; Kevin Davies; Steve Stirlings **W:** Don Lomax; Kevin Davies; Steve Stirlings; Mark Stadler
2 ❑ b&w Cover: 1.50 **NM** value: **2.00**
📖 Hunter XX: Storm Patterns; The Elves of Awe San Tan; A Hero Named Harold; Stranger in a Strange Land **A:** Don Lomax; Dave Hoover; Kevin Davies; Steve Stirlings **W:** Don Lomax; Kevin Davies; Steve Stirlings; Mark Stadler
3 ❑ b&w Cover: 1.50 **NM** value: **2.00**
📖 Feelings, Wo-Wo-Wo Feelings; A Hero Named Harold; Bar Wars; Hunter XX: The Splendid Past, Shattered Present • Apple Comics publisher Begins **A:** Don Lomax; Dave Hoover; Kevin Davies; Steve Stirlings **W:** Don Lomax; Kevin Davies; Steve Stirlings; Mark Stadler
4 ❑ Cover: 1.75 **NM** value: **2.00**
📖 The Fatman Boogie; Swamp thingies, Questions Without Answers! **A:** Don Lomax; Dave Hoover; Kevin Davies; Steve Stirlings **W:** Don Lomax; Kevin Davies; Steve Stirlings; Mark Stadler
5 ❑ Cover: 1.75 **NM** value: **Cover or less**
6 ❑ Cover: 1.75 **NM** value: **Cover or less**
7 ❑ Cover: 1.75 **NM** value: **Cover or less**
8 ❑ Jul 1988 Cover: 1.75 **NM** value: **Cover or less**
9 ❑ Cover: 1.95 **NM** value: **Cover or less**

FANTASTIC — Youthful
8 ❑ Cover: 0.10 **NM** value: **300.00**
9 ❑ Apr 1952 Cover: 0.10 **NM** value: **200.00**
• **CGC:** 2 graded, best 7.5

FANTASTIC ADVENTURES — Super
10 ❑ ca. 1963 Cover: 0.12 **NM** value: **25.00**
11 ❑ Cover: 0.12 **NM** value: **20.00**
12 ❑ Cover: 0.12 **NM** value: **20.00**
13 ❑ Cover: 0.12 **NM** value: **20.00**
14 ❑ Cover: 0.12 **NM** value: **20.00**
15 ❑ Cover: 0.12 **NM** value: **20.00**
16 ❑ ca. 1964 Cover: 0.12 **NM** value: **20.00**
17 ❑ Cover: 0.12 **NM** value: **20.00**
18 ❑ Cover: 0.12 **NM** value: **20.00**

FANTASTIC ADVENTURES (ACE) — Ace
1 ❑ Mar 1987 Cover: 1.75 **NM** value: **Cover or less**
📖 Skool Yardley: ...Our man on the Corner; The Ace Killer From Outer Space; Mystery Woman of The Jungle Fantomah; Devil of the Deep; Seeds of Death; **A:** George Tuska; Barclay Flagg; Clarke; Defuccio; Rocke Masroserio **W:** George Tuska; Barclay Flagg; Clarke; Defuccio; Rocke Masroserio
2 ❑ Jun 1987 Cover: 1.75 **NM** value: **Cover or less**
3 ❑ Oct 1987 Cover: 1.75 **NM** value: **Cover or less**

FANTASTIC COMICS (FARRELL) — Farrell
10 ❑ Nov 1954 Cover: 0.10 **NM** value: **100.00**
• **CGC:** 1 graded, best 9.2
11 ❑ Jan 1955 Cover: 0.10 **NM** value: **100.00**

FANTASTIC COMICS (FOX) — Fox
1 ❑ Dec 1939 Cover: 0.10 **NM** value: **3000.00**
• **CGC:** 2 graded, best 5.5
2 ❑ Jan 1940 Cover: 0.10 **NM** value: **2000.00**
• **CGC:** 2 graded, best 7.5
3 ❑ Feb 1940 Cover: 0.10 **NM** value: **2000.00**
• **CGC:** 3 graded, best 5.5
4 ❑ Mar 1940 Cover: 0.10 **NM** value: **1500.00**
• **CGC:** 1 graded, best 8.5
5 ❑ Apr 1940 Cover: 0.10 **NM** value: **1500.00**
• **CGC:** 2 graded, best 2.5
6 ❑ May 1940 Cover: 0.10 **NM** value: **1000.00**
• **CGC:** 2 graded, best 5.5
7 ❑ Jun 1940 Cover: 0.10 **NM** value: **1000.00**
• **CGC:** 1 graded, best 5.0
8 ❑ Jul 1940 Cover: 0.10 **NM** value: **1000.00**
• **CGC:** 3 graded, best 7.5
9 ❑ Aug 1940 Cover: 0.10 **NM** value: **1000.00**
• **CGC:** 1 graded, best 8.5
10 ❑ Sep 1940 Cover: 0.10 **NM** value: **800.00**
• **CGC:** 2 graded, best 4.5
11 ❑ Oct 1940 Cover: 0.10 **NM** value: **800.00**
• **CGC:** 1 graded, best 2.0
12 ❑ Nov 1940 Cover: 0.10 **NM** value: **800.00**
13 ❑ Dec 1940 Cover: 0.10 **NM** value: **800.00**
14 ❑ Jan 1941 Cover: 0.10 **NM** value: **800.00**
15 ❑ Feb 1941 Cover: 0.10 **NM** value: **800.00**
• **CGC:** 1 graded, best 6.0
16 ❑ Mar 1941 Cover: 0.10 **NM** value: **750.00**
17 ❑ Apr 1941 Cover: 0.10 **NM** value: **750.00**
18 ❑ May 1941 Cover: 0.10 **NM** value: **750.00**
19 ❑ Jun 1941 Cover: 0.10 **NM** value: **750.00**
20 ❑ Jul 1941 Cover: 0.10 **NM** value: **750.00**
21 ❑ Aug 1941 Cover: 0.10 **NM** value: **750.00**
• **CGC:** 1 graded, best 9.0
22 ❑ Sep 1941 Cover: 0.10 **NM** value: **750.00**
23 ❑ Nov 1941 Cover: 0.10 **NM** value: **750.00**

FANTASTIC FABLES (BASIL WOLVERTON'S...) — Dark Horse
1 ❑ Oct 1993, b&w Cover: 2.50 **NM** value: **Cover or less**
📖 Meteor Morgan; Spacehawk; Biographically Basil; Jumpin' Jupiter; Rocket Rider and his Interplanetary Ferry **A:** Basil Wolverton **W:** Basil Wolverton
2 ❑ Cover: 2.50 **NM** value: **Cover or less**

FANTASTIC FANZINE — Arrow
1 ❑ Cover: 1.50 **NM** value: **Cover or less**
2 ❑ Cover: 1.50 **NM** value: **Cover or less**
3 ❑ Cover: 1.50 **NM** value: **Cover or less**

Other grades: Multiply prices above by **1.5 for Mint • 2/3 for Very Fine • 1/3 for Fine • 1/5 for Very Good • 1/8 for Good**

FANTASTIC FEARS — Farrell

1 ❑ May 1953 Cover: 0.10 **NM** value: **350.00**
• **CGC:** 4 graded, best 9.2
2 ❑ Jul 1953 Cover: 0.10 **NM** value: **250.00**
3 ❑ Sep 1953 Cover: 0.10 **NM** value: **175.00**
• **CGC:** 1 graded, best 8.5
4 ❑ Nov 1953 Cover: 0.10 **NM** value: **175.00**
• **CGC:** 1 graded, best 7.5
5 ❑ Jan 1954 Cover: 0.10 **NM** value: **150.00**
• **CGC:** 1 graded, best 3.0
6 ❑ Mar 1954 Cover: 0.10 **NM** value: **150.00**
• **CGC:** 2 graded, best 8.0
7 ❑ May 1954 Cover: 0.10 **NM** value: **150.00**
8 ❑ Jul 1954 Cover: 0.10 **NM** value: **100.00**
9 ❑ Sep 1954 Cover: 0.10 **NM** value: **100.00**

FANTASTIC FIVE — Marvel

1 ❑ Oct 1999 Cover: 1.99 **NM** value: **Cover or less**
Circ: Diamd. preorders: **45,503**
2 ❑ Nov 1999 Cover: 1.99 **NM** value: **Cover or less**
Circ: Diamd. preorders: **39,785**
2/A ❑ Nov 1999 Cover: 1.99 **NM** value: **Cover or less**
variant cover. **A:** Paul Ryan **W:** Tom DeFalco
3 ❑ Dec 1999 Cover: 1.99 **NM** value: **Cover or less**
Circ: Diamd. preorders: **32,567**
📖 Side by Side with Spider-Girl! **A:** Paul Ryan **W:** Tom DeFalco

FANTASTIC FORCE — Marvel

After the apparent death of Reed Richards, the Fantastic Four has disbanded. In their place stands a new group of heroes, led by the son of Mr. Fantastic and the Invisible Woman. Franklin Richards, a young adult displaced in time, is finally in control of his powerful psionic powers. Along with his aunt, a warrior from the future called Huntara, he struggles to form a team that can live up to the legend of its predecessors. Vibraxas, an arrogant Wakandan noble, only stays at the behest of his mentor, the Black Panther. The final member, Devlor is one of the outcast Inhumans, not quite in control of his powers.

Marvel launched Fantastic Force in November 1994 as a spin-off from Fantastic Four near the end of Marvel's aggressive expansion of its line, and the first issue appeared about the time that "Marvelution," a major reorganization of the publisher's editorial structure, began. Appearing almost a year into the industry recession of the early 1990s, the series attempted to bolster its dwindling parent title, which crossed over frequently with Force in its first year.

1 ❑ Nov 1994 Cover: 2.50 **NM** value: **Cover or less**
Circ: CapCity orders: **44,050**
foil cover. 📖 Legacy **A:** Dante Bastianoni **W:** Mike Kanterovich; Tom Brevoort ★ Origin of Fantastic Force. ★ 1st Appearance of Fantastic Force.
2 ❑ Dec 1994 Cover: 1.75 **NM** value: **2.00**
Circ: Statement: **33,675** CapCity orders: **28,000**
3 ❑ Jan 1995 Cover: 1.75 **NM** value: **2.00**
Circ: Statement: **33,675** CapCity orders: **20,600**
4 ❑ Feb 1995 Cover: 1.75 **NM** value: **Cover or less**
Circ: Statement: **33,675** CapCity orders: **15,550**
5 ❑ Mar 1995 Cover: 1.75 **NM** value: **Cover or less**
Circ: Statement: **33,675** CapCity orders: **12,625**
6 ❑ Apr 1995 Cover: 1.75 **NM** value: **Cover or less**
Circ: Statement: **33,675** CapCity orders: **10,600**
7 ❑ May 1995 Cover: 1.75 **NM** value: **Cover or less**
Circ: Statement: **33,675** CapCity orders: **10,500**
8 ❑ Jun 1995 Cover: 1.75 **NM** value: **Cover or less**
Circ: Statement: **33,675** CapCity orders: **10,625**
9 ❑ Jul 1995 Cover: 1.75 **NM** value: **Cover or less**
Circ: Statement: **33,675** CapCity orders: **9,450**
10 ❑ Aug 1995 Cover: 1.75 **NM** value: **Cover or less**
Circ: Statement: **33,675** CapCity orders: **8,575**
11 ❑ Sep 1995 Cover: 1.75 **NM** value: **Cover or less**
Circ: Statement: **33,675**
12 ❑ Oct 1995 Cover: 1.75 **NM** value: **Cover or less**
📖 Moments of Truth **A:** Dante Bastianoni; Pino Rinaldi **W:** Mike Kanterovich; Tom Brevoort
13 ❑ Nov 1995 Cover: 1.75 **NM** value: **Cover or less**
• She-Hulk joins team **W:** Mike Kanterovich; Tom Brevoort
14 ❑ Dec 1995 Cover: 1.75 **NM** value: **Cover or less**
15 ❑ Jan 1996 Cover: 1.75 **NM** value: **Cover or less**
cover says Jan 95, indicia says Jan 96. • Team disbands; Has 1995 Statement, filed 10/1/95; avg print run 36,057; avg sales 32,675; avg subs 1,000; avg total paid 33,675; samples 750; office use 500; max existent 34,925; 3% of run returned (title was direct-only at this point) **W:** Mike Kanterovich; Tom Brevoort
16 ❑ Feb 1996 Cover: 1.75 **NM** value: **Cover or less**
17 ❑ Mar 1996 Cover: 1.75 **NM** value: **Cover or less**
📖 Agendas Diabolik! **A:** Dante Bastianoni; Pino Rinaldi **W:** Mike Kanterovich; Tom Brevoort
18 ❑ Apr 1996 Cover: 1.75 **NM** value: **Cover or less**
📖 A Force of One final issue. **A:** Ralph Cabrera **W:** Mike Kanterovich; Tom Brevoort

> 📖 indicates **Story Title** or **Storyline** information.
> ★ indicates **Character Appearance** information.
> **W = Writer • A = Artist • C = Cover Artist**

FANTASTIC FOUR (VOL. 1) — Marvel

The 1961 premiere of this self-proclaimed "World's Greatest Comic Magazine" ushered in the Marvel Age of Comics. It all starts when Reed Richards, Susan Storm, Johnny Storm, and Ben Grimm take part in a space shot. Everything goes perfectly until they are bombarded with cosmic rays. Their inadequately shielded spaceship does not protect them, and suddenly the four find themselves altered by the radiation. Reed's body becomes elastic; Susan finds herself able to turn invisible at will; Ben becomes mutated into The Thing; and Johnny becomes a Human Torch. Together, they become The Fantastic Four.

In the decades that followed, The FF has saved the world more times than can be counted and introduced readers to such legendary characters as The Inhumans, The Silver Surfer, Galactus, and Doctor Doom. They're Marvel's longest-running team and a pivotal force in the Marvel universe.

1 ❑ Nov 1961 Cover: 0.10 **NM** value: **16500.00**
• **CGC:** 102 graded, best 9.6
📖 The Fantastic Four; The Fantastic Four Meet the Moleman; The Moleman's Secret • 1st appearance/origin **A:** Jack Kirby **W:** Jack Kirby; Stan Lee ★ Origin of Fantastic Four, Mole Man. ★ 1st Appearance of Fantastic Four, Mole Man.
1/GR❑ **NM** value: **180.00**
📖 The Fantastic Four • Golden Record reprint **A:** Jack Kirby **W:** Jack Kirby; Stan Lee
2 ❑ Jan 1962 Cover: 0.10 **NM** value: **3200.00**
• **CGC:** 60 graded, best 9.4
📖 The Fantastic Four Meet the Skrulls from Outer Space; Prisoner of the Skrulls; The Fantastic Four Fight Back; The Fantastic Four Captured **A:** Jack Kirby **W:** Jack Kirby; Stan Lee ★ Origin of The Fantastic Four. ★ 1st Appearance of The Skrulls.
3 ❑ Mar 1962 Cover: 0.12 **NM** value: **2200.00**
• **CGC:** 54 graded, best 9.4
📖 The Menace of the Miracle Man; The Monster Lives; The Flame that Died; In the Shadow of Defeat; The Final Challenge • Fantastic Four wear uniforms for first time **A:** Jack Kirby **W:** Jack Kirby; Stan Lee ★ 1st Appearance of Fantasti-Copter, The Miracle Man (Marvel), Fantasti-Car, Pogo Plane, Baxter Building.
4 ❑ May 1962 Cover: 0.12 **NM** value: **2400.00**
• **CGC:** 66 graded, best 9.4
📖 The Coming of the Sub-Mariner; On the Trail of the Torch; Enter the Sub-Mariner; Let the World Beware; Sub-Mariner's Revenge; Return to the Deep **A:** Jack Kirby **W:** Jack Kirby; Stan Lee ★ 1st Appearance of Sub-Mariner (in Silver Age), Giganto. ★ Death of Giganto.
5 ❑ Jul 1962 Cover: 0.12 **NM** value: **2700.00**
• **CGC:** 68 graded, best 9.4
📖 Prisoners of Doctor Doom; Back to the Past; On the Trail of Blackbeard; Battle!; The Vengeance of Doctor Doom **A:** Jack Kirby **W:** Jack Kirby; Stan Lee ★ Origin of Doctor Doom. ★ 1st Appearance of Doctor Doom.
6 ❑ Sep 1962 Cover: 0.12 **NM** value: **1200.00**
• **CGC:** 57 graded, best 9.6
📖 Captives of the Deadly Duo; When Super-Menaces Unite; When Friends Fall Out; Trapped!; The End…or the Beginning? • Doctor Doom & Sub-Mariner vs. Fantastic Four **A:** Jack Kirby **W:** Jack Kirby; Stan Lee ★ 1st Appearance of The Yancy Street Gang (name only). ★ Appearance of Doctor Doom.
7 ❑ Oct 1962 Cover: 0.12 **NM** value: **725.00**
• **CGC:** 33 graded, best 9.4
📖 Prisoners of Kurrgo, Master of Planet X; It Came from the Skies; Outlawed!; Bound for Planet X; Twenty Four Hours till Zero; The End of Planet X **A:** Jack Kirby **W:** Jack Kirby; Stan Lee ★ 1st Appearance of Kurrgo, The Xantha.
8 ❑ Nov 1962 Cover: 0.12 **NM** value: **700.00**
• **CGC:** 31 graded, best 9.4
📖 Prisoners of the Puppet Master; The Hands of the Puppet Master; The Lady and the Monster; Face-to-Face with the Puppet Master; Death of a Puppet **A:** Jack Kirby **W:** Jack Kirby; Stan Lee ★ 1st Appearance of Puppet Master, Alicia Masters.
9 ❑ Dec 1962 Cover: 0.12 **NM** value: **700.00**
• **CGC:** 42 graded, best 9.6
📖 The End of the Fantastic Four; Sub-Mariner Gives the Orders; The Fury of Mr. Fantastic; The Flame of Battle; Vengeance Is Ours **A:** Jack Kirby **W:** Jack Kirby; Stan Lee ★ Appearance of Sub-Mariner.
10 ❑ Jan 1963 Cover: 0.12 **NM** value: **700.00**
• **CGC:** 45 graded, best 9.4
📖 The Return of Doctor Doom; Back from the Dread; The End of Mr. Fantastic?; No Place to Turn; The Real Doctor Doom **A:** Jack Kirby **W:** Jack Kirby; Stan Lee ★ 1st Appearance of The Ovoids, Jack Kirby (as character in story), Stan Lee (as character in story). ★ Appearance of Doctor Doom. ★ Versus Doctor Doom.
11 ❑ Feb 1963 Cover: 0.12 **NM** value: **550.00**
• **CGC:** 28 graded, best 9.4
📖 A Visit with the Fantastic Four; The Impossible Man **A:** Jack Kirby **W:** Jack Kirby; Stan Lee ★ Origin of Fantastic Four, Impossible Man. ★ 1st Appearance of Willie Lumpkin (Fantastic Four's mailman)-Silver Age, Impossible Man, The Popuppians.
12 ❑ Mar 1963 Cover: 0.12 **NM** value: **1100.00**
• **CGC:** 63 graded, best 9.4
📖 The Incredible Hulk; Mission: Stop the Hulk; Who Is the Wrecker?; The Hulk at Last • Thing fights Hulk for 1st time **A:** Jack Kirby **W:** Jack Kirby; Stan Lee ★ 1st Appearance of The Wrecker I (Dr. Karl Kort). ★ Versus Hulk.
13 ❑ Apr 1963 Cover: 0.12 **NM** value: **450.00**
• **CGC:** 25 graded, best 9.2
📖 The Fantastic Four, Versus the Red Ghost and His Indescribable Super-Apes; Menace on the Moon; The Watcher Appears; Duel in the Dead City **A:** Jack Kirby **W:** Jack Kirby; Stan Lee ★ Origin of Red Ghost. ★ 1st Appearance of Red Ghost, The Watcher.
14 ❑ May 1963 Cover: 0.12 **NM** value: **300.00**
• **CGC:** 48 graded, best 9.6
📖 The Merciless Puppet Master **A:** Jack Kirby **W:** Jack Kirby; Stan Lee ★ Appearance of Sub-Mariner. ★ Versus Puppet Master. ★ Versus Sub-Mariner.
15 ❑ Jun 1963 Cover: 0.12 **NM** value: **300.00**
• **CGC:** 27 graded, best 9.6
📖 The Fantastic Four Battle the Mad Thinker and His Awesome Android **A:** Jack Kirby **W:** Jack Kirby; Stan Lee ★ 1st Appearance of Awesome Android, Mad Thinker.
16 ❑ Jul 1963 Cover: 0.12 **NM** value: **300.00**
• **CGC:** 21 graded, best 9.4
📖 The Micro-World of Doctor Doom **A:** Jack Kirby ★ Appearance of Ant Man, Doctor Doom, The Wasp. ★ Versus Dr. Doom. ★ Versus Doctor Doom.
17 ❑ Aug 1963 Cover: 0.12 **NM** value: **300.00**
• **CGC:** 21 graded, best 9.4
📖 Defeated By Doctor Doom **A:** Jack Kirby ★ Appearance of Ant Man, Doctor Doom. ★ Versus Dr. Doom. ★ Versus Doctor Doom.
18 ❑ Sep 1963 Cover: 0.12 **NM** value: **300.00**
• **CGC:** 24 graded, best 9.6
📖 A Skrull Walks Among Us • 1st appearance/origin of Super-Skrull **A:** Jack Kirby ★ Origin of Super-Skrull. ★ 1st Appearance of Super-Skrull.
19 ❑ Oct 1963 Cover: 0.12 **NM** value: **300.00**
• **CGC:** 35 graded, best 9.6
📖 Prisoners of the Pharoh **A:** Jack Kirby ★ Origin of Rama-Tut. ★ 1st Appearance of Rama-Tut.
20 ❑ Nov 1963 Cover: 0.12 **NM** value: **325.00**
• **CGC:** 26 graded, best 9.4
📖 The Mysterious Molecule Man • 1st appearance/origin of Molecule Man **A:** Jack Kirby ★ Origin of Molecule Man. ★ 1st Appearance of Molecule Man. ★ Appearance of Watcher.
21 ❑ Dec 1963 Cover: 0.12 **NM** value: **200.00**
• **CGC:** 18 graded, best 9.6
📖 The Hate-Monger **A:** Jack Kirby ★ Origin of Hate-Monger. ★ 1st Appearance of Hate-Monger. ★ Appearance of Nick Fury.
22 ❑ Jan 1964 Cover: 0.12 **NM** value: **140.00**
• **CGC:** 22 graded, best 9.4
📖 The Return of the Mole Man **A:** Jack Kirby ★ Versus Mole Man.
23 ❑ Feb 1964 Cover: 0.12 **NM** value: **140.00**
• **CGC:** 22 graded, best 9.6
📖 The Master Plan of Doctor Doom **A:** Jack Kirby ★ Appearance of Doctor Doom. ★ Versus Doctor Doom.
24 ❑ Mar 1964 Cover: 0.12 **NM** value: **140.00**
• **CGC:** 33 graded, best 9.6
📖 The Infant Terrible **A:** Jack Kirby ★ 1st Appearance of Moloids.
25 ❑ Apr 1964 Cover: 0.12 **NM** value: **385.00**
• **CGC:** 54 graded, best 9.6
📖 The Hulk vs. the Thing • first mention of Thing's Aunt Petunia; Hulk Battles Thing **A:** Jack Kirby ★ Appearance of Rick Jones, Avengers, Rick Jones, Avengers. ★ Versus Hulk.
26 ❑ May 1964 Cover: 0.12 **NM** value: **385.00**
• **CGC:** 51 graded, best 9.6
📖 The Avengers Take Over **A:** Jack Kirby ★ Appearance of Rick Jones, Avengers. ★ Versus Hulk.
27 ❑ Jun 1964 Cover: 0.12 **NM** value: **140.00**
• **CGC:** 37 graded, best 9.6
📖 The Search for the Sub-Mariner **A:** Jack Kirby ★ Appearance of Doctor Strange. ★ Versus Sub-Mariner.
28 ❑ Jul 1964 Cover: 0.12 **NM** value: **210.00**
• **CGC:** 43 graded, best 9.6
📖 We Have to Fight the X-Men **A:** Jack Kirby ★ Appearance of X-Men. ★ Versus Puppet Master. ★ Versus Mad Thinker.
29 ❑ Aug 1964 Cover: 0.12 **NM** value: **110.00**
• **CGC:** 19 graded, best 9.6
📖 It Started on Yancy Street **A:** Jack Kirby ★ Appearance of Watcher. ★ Versus Red Ghost.
30 ❑ Sep 1964 Cover: 0.12 **NM** value: **110.00**
• **CGC:** 23 graded, best 9.6
📖 The Dreaded Diablo **A:** Jack Kirby ★ Origin of Diablo. ★ 1st Appearance of Diablo.
31 ❑ Oct 1964 Cover: 0.12 **NM** value: **85.00**
• **CGC:** 18 graded, best 9.4
📖 The Mad Menace of the Macabre Mole Man **A:** Jack Kirby ★ Appearance of Avengers. ★ Versus Mole Man.
32 ❑ Nov 1964 Cover: 0.12 **NM** value: **85.00**
• **CGC:** 18 graded, best 9.6
📖 Death of a Hero **A:** Jack Kirby ★ 1st Appearance of Sue and Johnny's parents (Franklin and Mary). ★ Versus Super-Skrull.
33 ❑ Dec 1964 Cover: 0.12 **NM** value: **85.00**
• **CGC:** 23 graded, best 9.6
📖 Side-By-Side with Sub-Mariner • 1st appearance of Attuma **A:** Jack Kirby ★ 1st Appearance of Attuma. ★ Appearance of Sub-Mariner.
34 ❑ Jan 1965 Cover: 0.12 **NM** value: **85.00**
• **CGC:** 18 graded, best 9.4
📖 A House Divided **A:** Jack Kirby ★ 1st Appearance of Thomas Gideon (later becomes Glorian).
35 ❑ Feb 1965 Cover: 0.12 **NM** value: **85.00**
• **CGC:** 35 graded, best 9.6
📖 Calamity on the Campus! **A:** Jack Kirby ★ Origin of Dragon Man. ★ 1st Appearance of Dragon Man. ★ Versus Diablo.
36 ❑ Mar 1965 Cover: 0.12 **NM** value: **85.00**
• **CGC:** 28 graded, best 9.6
📖 The Frightful Four • 1st appearance of Madame Medusa and the Frightful Four **A:** Jack Kirby ★ Origin of Frightful Four. ★ 1st Appearance of Frightful Four, Medusa.
37 ❑ Apr 1965 Cover: 0.12 **NM** value: **85.00**
• **CGC:** 31 graded, best 9.4
📖 Behold, A Distant Star **A:** Jack Kirby
38 ❑ May 1965 Cover: 0.12 **NM** value: **85.00**
• **CGC:** 22 graded, best 9.6

CGC-graded: Multiply prices above by **33 for 9.9 M • 16 for 9.8 NM/M • 7 for 9.6 NM+ • 5 for 9.4 NM • 2.5 for 9.2 NM- • 1.5 for 9.0 VF/NM**

🕮 Defeated By the Frightful Four • Paste-Pot Pete becomes Trapster I **A:** Jack Kirby ★ 1st Appearance of Trapster I (Peter Petruski). ★ Appearance of Frightful Four.

39 ❑ Jun 1965 Cover: 0.12 **NM** value: **85.00**
• **CGC:** 31 graded, best 9.6
🕮 A Blind Man Shall Lead Them • Daredevil **A:** Jack Kirby ★ Appearance of Daredevil, Doctor Doom. ★ Versus Doctor Doom.

40 ❑ Jul 1965 Cover: 0.12 **NM** value: **85.00**
• **CGC:** 21 graded, best 9.6
🕮 The Battle of the Baxter Building **A:** Jack Kirby ★ Appearance of Daredevil. ★ Versus Doctor Doom.

41 ❑ Aug 1965 Cover: 0.12 **NM** value: **45.00**
• **CGC:** 28 graded, best 9.8
🕮 The Brutal Betrayal of Ben Grimm **A:** Jack Kirby ★ Versus Frightful Four.

42 ❑ Sep 1965 Cover: 0.12 **NM** value: **45.00**
• **CGC:** 25 graded, best 9.6
🕮 To Save You, Why Must I Kill You? **A:** Jack Kirby ★ Versus Frightful Four.

43 ❑ Oct 1965 Cover: 0.12 **NM** value: **45.00**
• **CGC:** 19 graded, best 9.4
🕮 Lo, There Shall Be an Ending **A:** Jack Kirby ★ Versus Frightful Four. ★ Versus Dr. Doom. ★ Versus Doctor Doom.

44 ❑ Nov 1965 Cover: 0.12 **NM** value: **45.00**
• **CGC:** 83 graded, best 9.6
🕮 The Gentleman's Name is Gorgon! **A:** Jack Kirby **W:** Stan Lee ★ 1st Appearance of Gorgon. ★ Appearance of Dragon Man, Medusa.

45 ❑ Dec 1965 Cover: 0.12 **NM** value: **55.00**
• **CGC:** 32 graded, best 9.8
🕮 Among Us Hide the Inhumans **A:** Jack Kirby ★ 1st Appearance of Karnak. ★ 1st Appearance of Inhumans, Crystal, Triton, Lockjaw, Black Bolt. ★ Appearance of Trapster I, Sandman. ★ Versus Maximus. ★ Versus Dragon Man.

46 ❑ Jan 1966 Cover: 0.12 **NM** value: **50.00**
Circ: Statement: **329,379** • **CGC:** 41 graded, best 9.8
🕮 Those Who Would Destroy Us **A:** Jack Kirby **W:** Jack Kirby; Stan Lee ★ Appearance of Inhumans.

47 ❑ Feb 1966 Cover: 0.12 **NM** value: **45.00**
Circ: Statement: **329,379** • **CGC:** 28 graded, best 9.8
🕮 Beware the Hidden Land **A:** Jack Kirby **W:** Jack Kirby; Stan Lee ★ 1st Appearance of Maximus. ★ Appearance of Inhumans. ★ Versus Maximus.

48 ❑ Mar 1966 Cover: 0.12 **NM** value: **900.00**
Circ: Statement: **329,379** • **CGC:** 383 graded, best 9.8
🕮 The Coming of Galactus • Silver Surfer, Galactus **A:** Jack Kirby **W:** Jack Kirby; Stan Lee ★ 1st Appearance of Galactus, Silver Surfer. ★ Appearance of Inhumans.

49 ❑ Apr 1966 Cover: 0.12 **NM** value: **245.00**
Circ: Statement: **329,379** • **CGC:** 70 graded, best 9.6
🕮 If This Be Doomsday • Silver Surfer, Galactus **A:** Jack Kirby **W:** Jack Kirby; Stan Lee ★ Appearance of Galactus, Silver Surfer, Watcher. ★ Versus Galactus.

50 ❑ May 1966 Cover: 0.12 **NM** value: **265.00**
Circ: Statement: **329,379** • **CGC:** 64 graded, best 9.6
🕮 The Startling Saga of the Silver Surfer • Silver Surfer vs. Galactus **A:** Jack Kirby **W:** Jack Kirby; Stan Lee ★ 1st Appearance of Wyatt Wingfoot. ★ Appearance of Galactus, Silver Surfer, Watcher. ★ Versus Galactus.

51 ❑ Jun 1966 Cover: 0.12 **NM** value: **42.00**
Circ: Statement: **329,379** • **CGC:** 13 graded, best 9.4
🕮 This Man, This Monster **A:** Jack Kirby **W:** Jack Kirby; Stan Lee ★ 1st Appearance of Negative Zone.

52 ❑ Jul 1966 Cover: 0.12 **NM** value: **75.00**
Circ: Statement: **329,379** • **CGC:** 45 graded, best 9.6
🕮 The Black Panther • 1st appearance of the Black Panther (had costume with cape) **A:** Jack Kirby **W:** Jack Kirby; Stan Lee ★ 1st Appearance of Black Panther.

53 ❑ Aug 1966 Cover: 0.12 **NM** value: **50.00**
Circ: Statement: **329,379** • **CGC:** 32 graded, best 9.6
🕮 The Way It Began • origin of the Black Panther **A:** Jack Kirby **W:** Jack Kirby; Stan Lee ★ Origin of Black Panther, Klaw. ★ 1st Appearance of Klaw. ★ 2nd Appearance of Black Panther.

54 ❑ Sep 1966 Cover: 0.12 **NM** value: **40.00**
Circ: Statement: **329,379** • **CGC:** 20 graded, best 9.4
🕮 Whosoever Finds the Evil Eye **A:** Jack Kirby **W:** Jack Kirby; Stan Lee ★ Origin of Prester John. ★ 1st Appearance of Prester John. ★ Appearance of Inhumans, Black Panther.

55 ❑ Oct 1966 Cover: 0.12 **NM** value: **65.00**
Circ: Statement: **329,379** • **CGC:** 52 graded, best 9.9
🕮 When Strikes the Silver Surfer • Thing vs. Silver Surfer **A:** Jack Kirby **W:** Jack Kirby; Stan Lee ★ Appearance of Silver Surfer.

56 ❑ Nov 1966 Cover: 0.12 **NM** value: **45.00**
Circ: Statement: **329,379** • **CGC:** 22 graded, best 9.4
🕮 Klaw, the Murderous Master of Sound **A:** Jack Kirby **W:** Jack Kirby; Stan Lee ★ Origin of Klaw. ★ Versus Klaw.

57 ❑ Dec 1966 Cover: 0.12 **NM** value: **45.00**
Circ: Statement: **329,379** • **CGC:** 25 graded, best 9.6
🕮 Enter Doctor Doom **A:** Jack Kirby **W:** Jack Kirby; Stan Lee ★ Appearance of Inhumans, Doctor Doom. ★ Versus Doctor Doom. ★ Versus Wizard. ★ Versus Sandman.

58 ❑ Jan 1967 Cover: 0.12 **NM** value: **45.00**
Circ: Statement: **329,536** • **CGC:** 27 graded, best 9.6
🕮 The Dismal Dregs of Defeat **A:** Jack Kirby **W:** Jack Kirby; Stan Lee ★ Appearance of Doctor Doom, Lockjaw, Silver Surfer. ★ Versus Doctor Doom.

59 ❑ Feb 1967 Cover: 0.12 **NM** value: **45.00**
Circ: Statement: **329,536** • **CGC:** 75 graded, best 9.8
🕮 Doomsday **A:** Jack Kirby **W:** Jack Kirby; Stan Lee ★ Appearance of Inhumans, Silver Surfer. ★ Versus Doctor Doom.

60 ❑ Mar 1967 Cover: 0.12 **NM** value: **45.00**
Circ: Statement: **329,536** • **CGC:** 40 graded, best 9.8
🕮 The Peril and the Power **A:** Jack Kirby **W:** Jack Kirby; Stan Lee ★ Appearance of Inhumans, Black Panther, Doctor Doom, Silver Surfer, Watcher. ★ Versus Doctor Doom.

61 ❑ Apr 1967 Cover: 0.12 **NM** value: **38.00**
Circ: Statement: **329,536** • **CGC:** 24 graded, best 9.6
🕮 Where Stalks the Sandman? • Has 1966 Statement, filed 10/1/66; avg print run 538,152; avg sales 326,979; avg subs 2,400; avg total paid 329,379; samples 60; max existent 329,439; 39% of run returned **A:** Jack Kirby **W:** Jack Kirby; Stan Lee ★ Appearance of Inhumans, Silver Surfer. ★ Versus Sandman.

62 ❑ May 1967 Cover: 0.12 **NM** value: **38.00**
Circ: Statement: **329,536** • **CGC:** 22 graded, best 9.6
🕮 And One Shall Save Him **A:** Jack Kirby **W:** Jack Kirby; Stan Lee ★ 1st Appearance of Blastaar. ★ Appearance of Sandman.

63 ❑ Jun 1967 Cover: 0.12 **NM** value: **38.00**
Circ: Statement: **329,536** • **CGC:** 11 graded, best 9.6
🕮 Blastaar, The Living Bomb-Burst **A:** Jack Kirby **W:** Jack Kirby; Stan Lee ★ Versus Blastaar. ★ Versus Sandman.

64 ❑ Jul 1967 Cover: 0.12 **NM** value: **38.00**
Circ: Statement: **329,536** • **CGC:** 31 graded, best 9.8
🕮 The Sentry Sinister **A:** Jack Kirby **W:** Jack Kirby; Stan Lee ★ 1st Appearance of Supreme Intelligence.

65 ❑ Aug 1967 Cover: 0.12 **NM** value: **38.00**
Circ: Statement: **329,536** • **CGC:** 22 graded, best 9.6
🕮 From Beyond This Planet Earth **A:** Jack Kirby **W:** Jack Kirby; Stan Lee ★ 1st Appearance of Kree, Kree Supreme Intelligence, Ronan the Accuser.

66 ❑ Sep 1967 Cover: 0.12 **NM** value: **35.00**
Circ: Statement: **329,536** • **CGC:** 26 graded, best 9.6
🕮 What Lurks Behind the Beehive? • Origin of Him (Warlock) part 1 **A:** Jack Kirby **W:** Jack Kirby; Stan Lee ★ Origin of The Enclave, Him (later Warlock). ★ 1st Appearance of Him (later Warlock), The Enclave (unnamed). ★ Appearance of Crystal.

67 ❑ Oct 1967 Cover: 0.12 **NM** value: **40.00**
Circ: Statement: **329,536** • **CGC:** 43 graded, best 9.8
🕮 When Opens the Cocoon • Origin of Him (Warlock) part 2; 1st appearance of Him (Warlock) **A:** Jack Kirby **W:** Jack Kirby; Stan Lee ★ Origin of Him (later Warlock). ★ Appearance of Him (later Warlock).

68 ❑ Nov 1967 Cover: 0.12 **NM** value: **30.00**
Circ: Statement: **329,536** • **CGC:** 24 graded, best 9.6
🕮 His Mission: Destroy the Fantastic Four **A:** Jack Kirby **W:** Jack Kirby; Stan Lee ★ Versus Mad Thinker.

69 ❑ Dec 1967 Cover: 0.12 **NM** value: **30.00**
Circ: Statement: **329,536** • **CGC:** 19 graded, best 9.8
🕮 By Ben Betrayed! **A:** Jack Kirby **W:** Jack Kirby; Stan Lee ★ Versus Mad Thinker.

70 ❑ Jan 1968 Cover: 0.12 **NM** value: **30.00**
Circ: Statement: **344,865** • **CGC:** 20 graded, best 9.8
🕮 When Fall The Mighty **A:** Jack Kirby **W:** Jack Kirby; Stan Lee ★ Versus Mad Thinker.

71 ❑ Feb 1968 Cover: 0.12 **NM** value: **26.00**
Circ: Statement: **344,865** • **CGC:** 15 graded, best 9.4
🕮 And So It Ends **A:** Jack Kirby **W:** Jack Kirby; Stan Lee ★ Versus Mad Thinker.

72 ❑ Mar 1968 Cover: 0.12 **NM** value: **35.00**
Circ: Statement: **344,865** • **CGC:** 31 graded, best 9.6
🕮 Where Soars the Silver Surfer **A:** Jack Kirby **W:** Jack Kirby; Stan Lee ★ Appearance of Silver Surfer.

73 ❑ Apr 1968 Cover: 0.12 **NM** value: **28.00**
Circ: Statement: **344,865** • **CGC:** 46 graded, best 9.8
🕮 The Flames of Battle • Has 1967 Statement, filed 10/1/67; avg print run 538,152; avg sales 326,979; avg subs 2,400; avg total paid 329,536; samples 95; max existent 329,631; 44% of run returned **A:** Jack Kirby **W:** Jack Kirby; Stan Lee ★ Appearance of Daredevil, Spider-Man, Thor. ★ Versus Doctor Doom.

74 ❑ May 1968 Cover: 0.12 **NM** value: **30.00**
Circ: Statement: **344,865** • **CGC:** 19 graded, best 9.6
🕮 When Calls Galactus **A:** Jack Kirby **W:** Jack Kirby; Stan Lee ★ Appearance of Galactus, Silver Surfer. ★ Versus Galactus.

75 ❑ Jun 1968 Cover: 0.12 **NM** value: **30.00**
Circ: Statement: **344,865** • **CGC:** 25 graded, best 9.8
🕮 Worlds Within Worlds **A:** Jack Kirby **W:** Jack Kirby; Stan Lee ★ Appearance of Galactus, Silver Surfer. ★ Versus Galactus.

76 ❑ Jul 1968 Cover: 0.12 **NM** value: **28.00**
Circ: Statement: **344,865** • **CGC:** 43 graded, best 9.8
🕮 Stranded in Sub-Atomica **A:** Jack Kirby **W:** Jack Kirby; Stan Lee ★ Appearance of Silver Surfer. ★ Versus Galactus. ★ Versus Psycho-Man.

77 ❑ Aug 1968 Cover: 0.12 **NM** value: **28.00**
Circ: Statement: **344,865** • **CGC:** 26 graded, best 9.8
🕮 Shall Earth Endure? **A:** Jack Kirby **W:** Jack Kirby; Stan Lee ★ Appearance of Silver Surfer. ★ Versus Galactus. ★ Versus Psycho-Man.

78 ❑ Sep 1968 Cover: 0.12 **NM** value: **28.00**
Circ: Statement: **344,865** • **CGC:** 38 graded, best 9.6
🕮 The Thing No More! **A:** Jack Kirby **W:** Jack Kirby; Stan Lee ★ Versus Wizard.

79 ❑ Oct 1968 Cover: 0.12 **NM** value: **28.00**
Circ: Statement: **344,865** • **CGC:** 17 graded, best 9.4
🕮 A Monster Forever? **A:** Jack Kirby **W:** Jack Kirby; Stan Lee ★ Versus Mad Thinker.

80 ❑ Nov 1968 Cover: 0.12 **NM** value: **28.00**
Circ: Statement: **344,865** • **CGC:** 16 graded, best 9.8
🕮 Where Treads the Living Totem **A:** Jack Kirby **W:** Jack Kirby; Stan Lee

81 ❑ Dec 1968 Cover: 0.12 **NM** value: **22.00**
Circ: Statement: **344,865** • **CGC:** 18 graded, best 9.6
🕮 Enter-The Exquisite Elemental • Crystal joins Fantastic Four **A:** Jack Kirby **W:** Jack Kirby; Stan Lee ★ Versus Wizard.

82 ❑ Jan 1969 Cover: 0.12 **NM** value: **22.00**
Circ: Statement: **340,363** • **CGC:** 25 graded, best 9.6
🕮 The Mark of the Madman **A:** Jack Kirby **W:** Jack Kirby; Stan Lee ★ Appearance of Inhumans. ★ Versus Maximus.

83 ❑ Feb 1969 Cover: 0.12 **NM** value: **22.00**
Circ: Statement: **340,363** • **CGC:** 19 graded, best 9.6
🕮 Shall Man Survive? **A:** Jack Kirby **W:** Jack Kirby; Stan Lee ★ Appearance of Inhumans. ★ Versus Maximus.

84 ❑ Mar 1969 Cover: 0.12 **NM** value: **22.00**
Circ: Statement: **340,363** • **CGC:** 20 graded, best 9.6
🕮 The Name Is – Doom! **A:** Jack Kirby **W:** Jack Kirby; Stan Lee ★ Appearance of Doctor Doom. ★ Versus Doctor Doom.

85 ❑ Apr 1969 Cover: 0.12 **NM** value: **22.00**
Circ: Statement: **340,363** • **CGC:** 8 graded, best 9.6
🕮 Within This Tortured Land • Has 1968 Statement, filed 10/1/68; avg print run 531,325; avg sales 341,680; avg subs 3,185; avg total paid 344,865; samples 400; max existent 345,265; 35% of run returned **A:** Jack Kirby **W:** Jack Kirby; Stan Lee ★ Appearance of Doctor Doom. ★ Versus Doctor Doom.

86 ❑ May 1969 Cover: 0.12 **NM** value: **22.00**
Circ: Statement: **340,363** • **CGC:** 19 graded, best 9.8
🕮 The Victims **A:** Jack Kirby **W:** Jack Kirby; Stan Lee ★ Appearance of Doctor Doom. ★ Versus Doctor Doom.

87 ❑ Jun 1969 Cover: 0.12 **NM** value: **22.00**
Circ: Statement: **340,363** • **CGC:** 13 graded, best 9.6
🕮 The Power And The Pride! **A:** Jack Kirby **W:** Jack Kirby; Stan Lee ★ Appearance of Doctor Doom. ★ Versus Doctor Doom.

88 ❑ Jul 1969 Cover: 0.12 **NM** value: **22.00**
Circ: Statement: **340,363** • **CGC:** 18 graded, best 9.6
🕮 A House There Was! **A:** Jack Kirby **W:** Jack Kirby; Stan Lee ★ Versus Mole Man.

89 ❑ Aug 1969 Cover: 0.15 **NM** value: **18.00**
Circ: Statement: **340,363** • **CGC:** 12 graded, best 9.6
🕮 The Madness of the Mole Man **A:** Jack Kirby **W:** Jack Kirby; Stan Lee ★ Versus Mole Man.

90 ❑ Sep 1969 Cover: 0.15 **NM** value: **18.00**
Circ: Statement: **340,363** • **CGC:** 12 graded, best 9.8
🕮 The Skrull Takes a Slave **A:** Jack Kirby **W:** Jack Kirby; Stan Lee ★ Versus Mole Man.

91 ❑ Oct 1969 Cover: 0.15 **NM** value: **18.00**
Circ: Statement: **340,363** • **CGC:** 16 graded, best 9.8
🕮 The Thing Enslaved **A:** Jack Kirby **W:** Jack Kirby; Stan Lee ★ 1st Appearance of Torgo.

92 ❑ Nov 1969 Cover: 0.15 **NM** value: **18.00**
Circ: Statement: **340,363** • **CGC:** 17 graded, best 9.6
🕮 Ben Grimm, Killer! **A:** Jack Kirby **W:** Jack Kirby; Stan Lee ★ 2nd Appearance of Torgo. ★ Versus Torgo.

93 ❑ Dec 1969 Cover: 0.15 **NM** value: **18.00**
Circ: Statement: **340,363** • **CGC:** 16 graded, best 9.6
🕮 At the Mercy of Torgo **A:** Jack Kirby **W:** Jack Kirby; Stan Lee ★ Appearance of Torgo. ★ Versus Torgo.

94 ❑ Jan 1970 Cover: 0.15 **NM** value: **18.00**
Circ: Statement: **285,639** • **CGC:** 10 graded, best 9.6
🕮 The Return of the Frightful Four **A:** Jack Kirby **W:** Jack Kirby; Stan Lee ★ 1st Appearance of Agatha Harkness. ★ Versus Trapster. ★ Versus Wizard. ★ Versus Sandman.

95 ❑ Feb 1970 Cover: 0.15 **NM** value: **18.00**
Circ: Statement: **285,639** • **CGC:** 11 graded, best 9.6
🕮 Tomorrow, World War Three **A:** Jack Kirby **W:** Jack Kirby; Stan Lee ★ 1st Appearance of The Monocle.

96 ❑ Mar 1970 Cover: 0.15 **NM** value: **18.00**
Circ: Statement: **285,639** • **CGC:** 14 graded, best 9.6
🕮 The Mad Thinker and His Androids of Death **A:** Jack Kirby **W:** Jack Kirby; Stan Lee ★ Versus Mad Thinker.

97 ❑ Apr 1970 Cover: 0.15 **NM** value: **18.00**
Circ: Statement: **285,639** • **CGC:** 20 graded, best 9.8
🕮 The Monster from the Lost Lagoon • Has 1969 Statement, filed 10/1/69; avg print run 546,820; avg sales 338,421; avg subs 1,942; avg total paid 340,363; samples 110; max existent 340,473; 38% of run returned **A:** Jack Kirby **W:** Jack Kirby; Stan Lee

98 ❑ May 1970 Cover: 0.15 **NM** value: **18.00**
Circ: Statement: **285,639** • **CGC:** 18 graded, best 9.6
🕮 Mystery on the Moon **A:** Jack Kirby **W:** Jack Kirby; Stan Lee ★ Appearance of Neil Armstrong.

99 ❑ Jun 1970 Cover: 0.15 **NM** value: **18.00**
Circ: Statement: **285,639** • **CGC:** 11 graded, best 9.8
🕮 The Torch Goes Wild **A:** Jack Kirby **W:** Jack Kirby; Stan Lee ★ Appearance of Inhumans.

100 ❑ Jul 1970 Cover: 0.15 **NM** value: **60.00**
Circ: Statement: **285,639** • **CGC:** 70 graded, best 9.8
• anniversary. 🕮 The Long Journey Home • Doctor Doom, Sandman, Sub-Mariner, others appear **A:** Jack Kirby **W:** Jack Kirby; Stan Lee ★ Versus Lots of villains.

101 ❑ Aug 1970 Cover: 0.15 **NM** value: **16.00**
Circ: Statement: **285,639** • **CGC:** 3 graded, best 9.6
🕮 Bedlam In The Baxter Building! **A:** Jack Kirby **W:** Jack Kirby; Stan Lee ★ 1st Appearance of Gimlet, Top Man.

102 ❑ Sep 1970 Cover: 0.15 **NM** value: **16.00**
Circ: Statement: **285,639** • **CGC:** 10 graded, best 9.8
🕮 The Strength Of The Sub-Mariner **A:** Jack Kirby **C:** John Romita **W:** Jack Kirby; Stan Lee ★ Appearance of Magneto, Sub-Mariner. ★ Versus Magneto.

103 ❑ Oct 1970 Cover: 0.15 **NM** value: **13.00**
Circ: Statement: **285,639** • **CGC:** 8 graded, best 9.6
🕮 At War With Atlantis! **A:** John Romita **W:** John Romita; Stan Lee ★ 2nd Appearance of Agatha Harkness. ★ Appearance of Richard M. Nixon, Magneto, Sub-Mariner. ★ Versus Magneto.

104 ❑ Nov 1970 Cover: 0.15 **NM** value: **13.00**
Circ: Statement: **285,639** • **CGC:** 3 graded, best 9.6
🕮 Our World Enslaved! **A:** John Romita **W:** Stan Lee ★ Appearance of Richard M. Nixon, Magneto, Sub-Mariner. ★ Versus Magneto.

105 ❑ Dec 1970 Cover: 0.15 **NM** value: **13.00**
Circ: Statement: **285,639** • **CGC:** 8 graded, best 9.6
🕮 The Monster In The Streets! **A:** John Romita **W:** Stan Lee ★ 1st Appearance of The "monster" (Larry Rambow), Dr. Phillip Zolten Rambow.

106 ❑ Jan 1971 Cover: 0.15 **NM** value: **13.00**
Circ: Statement: **275,930** • **CGC:** 10 graded, best 9.6
🕮 The Monster's Secret! **A:** John Romita **W:** John Romita; Stan Lee ★ 2nd Appearance of The "monster" (Larry Rambow). ★ 2nd Appearance of Dr. Phillip Zolten Rambow.

107 ❑ Feb 1971 Cover: 0.15 **NM** value: **13.00**
Circ: Statement: **275,930** • **CGC:** 4 graded, best 9.6
🕮 And Now The Thing! **A:** John Buscema **W:** Stan Lee ★ 1st Appearance of Janus (the scientist).

108 ❑ Mar 1971 Cover: 0.15 **NM** value: **13.00**
Circ: Statement: **275,930** • **CGC:** 13 graded, best 9.8
🕮 The Monstrous Mystery of the Nega-Man **A:** John Buscema; Jack Kirby **W:** Jack Kirby; John Romita; Stan Lee ★ 2nd Appearance of Janus (the scientist).

109 ❑ Apr 1971 Cover: 0.15 **NM** value: **13.00**

Other grades: Multiply prices above by **1.5 for Mint • 2/3 for Very Fine • 1/3 for Fine • 1/5 for Very Good • 1/8 for Good**

Circ: Statement: **275,930 • CGC:** 7 graded, best 9.8
Death In The Negative Zone! • Has 1970 Statement, filed 10/1/70; avg pring run 518,737; avg sales 283,435; avg subs 2,204; avg total paid 285,639; office use 110; max existent 285,749; 45% of run returned **A:** John Buscema **W:** Stan Lee ★ Appearance of Captain Marvel. ★ Death of Janus (the scientist). ★ Versus Annihilus.

110 ❑ May 1971 Cover: 0.15 **NM** value: **13.00**
Circ: Statement: **275,930 • CGC:** 9 graded, best 9.6
One From Four Leaves Three! **A:** John Buscema **W:** Stan Lee ★ Appearance of Joe Robertson, J. Jonah Jameson. ★ Versus Annihilus.

111 ❑ Jun 1971 Cover: 0.15 **NM** value: **13.00**
Circ: Statement: **275,930 • CGC:** 8 graded, best 9.6
The Thing Amok **A:** John Buscema **W:** Stan Lee ★ 1st Appearance of Collins (landlord of Baxter building). ★ Appearance of Joe Robertson, Peter Parker, Hulk, J. Jonah Jameson.

112 ❑ Jul 1971 Cover: 0.15 **NM** value: **42.00**
Circ: Statement: **275,930 • CGC:** 36 graded, best 9.6
Battle of the Behemoths • Thing vs. Hulk **A:** John Buscema **W:** Stan Lee ★ 2nd Appearance of Collins. ★ Appearance of Bruce Banner, Hulk, J. Jonah Jameson.

113 ❑ Aug 1971 Cover: 0.15 **NM** value: **11.00**
Circ: Statement: **275,930 • CGC:** 3 graded, best 9.4
The Power of the Over-Mind **A:** John Buscema **W:** Stan Lee ★ 1st Appearance of Overmind. ★ Appearance of Bruce Banner, The Watcher.

114 ❑ Sep 1971 Cover: 0.15 **NM** value: **11.00**
Circ: Statement: **275,930 • CGC:** 8 graded, best 9.6
But Who Shall Stop The Over-Mind? **A:** John Buscema **W:** Stan Lee ★ 2nd Appearance of Overmind. ★ Appearance of The Watcher. ★ Versus Overmind.

115 ❑ Oct 1971 Cover: 0.15 **NM** value: **11.00**
Circ: Statement: **275,930 • CGC:** 4 graded, best 9.6
The Secret of the Eternals **A:** John Buscema **W:** Stan Lee; Archie Goodwin ★ Origin of Overmind. ★ 1st Appearance of The Eternals (a.k.a. Eternians), Eternals. ★ Appearance of The Watcher.

116 ❑ Nov 1971 Cover: 0.25 **NM** value: **9.00**
Circ: Statement: **275,930 • CGC:** 10 graded, best 9.8
• Giant-size. The Alien, the Ally, and Armageddon; Now Falls the Final Hour **A:** John Buscema **W:** Archie Goodwin ★ Origin of Stranger. ★ Appearance of The Stranger, The Watcher, Edwin Jarvis, Doctor Doom.

117 ❑ Dec 1971 Cover: 0.20 **NM** value: **9.00**
Circ: Statement: **275,930 • CGC:** 4 graded, best 9.6
The Flame and the Quest **A:** John Buscema **W:** Archie Goodwin ★ 1st Appearance of Chiron, Asmodeus. ★ Appearance of Crystal, Diablo, Kaliban. ★ Versus Diablo.

118 ❑ Jan 1972 Cover: 0.20 **NM** value: **9.00**
Circ: Statement: **245,695 • CGC:** 4 graded, best 9.6
Thunder in the Ruins; What Mad World **A:** John Buscema **W:** Archie Goodwin ★ 1st Appearance of Reed Richards of Earth-A, Ben Grimm of Earth-A, Sue Storm Grimm of Earth-A. ★ Appearance of Crystal, Diablo, Lockjaw. ★ Versus Diablo.

119 ❑ Feb 1972 Cover: 0.20 **NM** value: **9.00**
Circ: Statement: **245,695 • CGC:** 3 graded, best 9.8
Three Stood Together **A:** John Buscema **W:** Roy Thomas ★ Appearance of Black Panther, Klaw. ★ Versus Klaw.

120 ❑ Mar 1972 Cover: 0.20 **NM** value: **9.00**
Circ: Statement: **245,695 • CGC:** 1 graded, best 9.6
The Horror That Walks on Air **A:** John Buscema **W:** John Buscema; Stan Lee ★ 1st Appearance of Air-Walker (robot form). ★ Appearance of General T. E. "Thunderbolt" Ross. ★ Versus Air-Walker Automaton.

121 ❑ Apr 1972 Cover: 0.20 **NM** value: **15.00**
Circ: Statement: **245,695 • CGC:** 9 graded, best 9.8
The Mysterious Mind-Blowing Secret of Gabriel **A:** John Buscema **W:** John Buscema; Stan Lee ★ 2nd Appearance of Air-Walker (robot form). ★ Appearance of Galactus, Silver Surfer. ★ Versus Air-Walker Automaton.

122 ❑ May 1972 Cover: 0.20 **NM** value: **15.00**
Circ: Statement: **245,695 • CGC:** 7 graded, best 9.6
Galactus Unleashed • Has 1971 Statement, filed 9/23/71; avg print run 460,000; avg sales 273,895; avg subs 2,035; avg total paid 275,930; samples 110; office use 1,635; max existent 277,675; 40% of run returned **A:** John Buscema **W:** Stan Lee ★ Appearance of Galactus, Silver Surfer. ★ Versus Galactus.

123 ❑ Jun 1972 Cover: 0.20 **NM** value: **15.00**
Circ: Statement: **245,695 • CGC:** 5 graded, best 9.4
This World Enslaved **A:** John Buscema **W:** Stan Lee ★ Appearance of Galactus, Richard M. Nixon, General T. E. "Thunderbold" Ross, Silver Surfer. ★ Versus Galactus.

124 ❑ Jul 1972 Cover: 0.20 **NM** value: **8.00**
Circ: Statement: **245,695 • CGC:** 3 graded, best 9.8
The Return of the Monster **A:** John Buscema **W:** Stan Lee

125 ❑ Aug 1972 Cover: 0.20 **NM** value: **8.00**
Circ: Statement: **245,695 • CGC:** 2 graded, best 9.8
The Monster's Secret **A:** John Buscema **W:** Stan Lee

126 ❑ Sep 1972 Cover: 0.20 **NM** value: **8.00**
Circ: Statement: **245,695 • CGC:** 3 graded, best 9.8
The Way It Began **A:** John Buscema **W:** Roy Thomas ★ Origin of Fantastic Four.

127 ❑ Oct 1972 Cover: 0.20 **NM** value: **8.00**
Circ: Statement: **245,695 • CGC:** 2 graded, best 9.4
Where the Sun Dares Not Shine **A:** John Buscema **W:** Roy Thomas ★ Versus Mole Man.

128 ❑ Nov 1972 Cover: 0.20 **NM** value: **9.00**
Circ: Statement: **245,695 • CGC:** 2 graded, best 9.8
Death in a Dark and Lonely Place **A:** John Buscema **W:** Roy Thomas ★ Versus Tyrannus. ★ Versus Mole Man.

129 ❑ Dec 1972 Cover: 0.20 **NM** value: **8.00**
Circ: Statement: **245,695 • CGC:** 3 graded, best 9.6
The Frightful Four-Plus One **A:** John Buscema **W:** Roy Thomas ★ 1st Appearance of Thundra. ★ Appearance of Medusa.

130 ❑ Jan 1973 Cover: 0.20 **NM** value: **7.00**
Circ: Statement: **225,671 • CGC:** 1 graded, best 9.4
Battleground: The Baxter Building **A:** John Buscema **W:** Roy Thomas ★ 2nd Appearance of Thundra. ★ Appearance of Inhumans. ★ Versus Trapster. ★ Versus Thundra. ★ Versus Wizard. ★ Versus Sandman.

131 ❑ Feb 1973 Cover: 0.20 **NM** value: **7.00**
Circ: Statement: **225,671 • CGC:** 3 graded, best 9.8
Revolt in Paradise **A:** Ross Andru **C:** John Buscema **W:** Roy Thomas ★ 1st Appearance of Omega (the ultimate Alpha Primitive). ★ Appearance of Inhumans. ★ Versus Maximus.

132 ❑ Mar 1973 Cover: 0.20 **NM** value: **7.00**
Circ: Statement: **225,671 • CGC:** 4 graded, best 9.4
Omega! The Ultimate Enemy! • Medusa Joins; Has 1972 Statement, filed 9/21/72; avg print run 457,990; avg sales 243,577; avg subs 2,118; avg total paid 245,695; samples 110; office use 1,993; max existent 247,798, 46% of run returned **A:** John Buscema **W:** Roy Thomas ★ Versus Maximus.

133 ❑ Apr 1973 Cover: 0.20 **NM** value: **7.00**
Circ: Statement: **225,671 • CGC:** 2 graded, best 9.8
Thundra at Dawn **A:** Ramona Fradon **C:** John Buscema **W:** Roy Thomas; Gerry Conway ★ Versus Trapster. ★ Versus Thundra. ★ Versus Wizard. ★ Versus Sandman.

134 ❑ May 1973 Cover: 0.20 **NM** value: **7.00**
Circ: Statement: **225,671 • CGC:** 3 graded, best 9.4
A Dragon Stalks the Skies **A:** John Buscema **W:** Gerry Conway ★ Versus Dragon Man.

135 ❑ Jun 1973 Cover: 0.20 **NM** value: **7.00**
Circ: Statement: **225,671 • CGC:** 4 graded, best 9.6
The Eternity Machine **A:** John Buscema **W:** Gerry Conway ★ Versus Dragon Man.

136 ❑ Jul 1973 Cover: 0.20 **NM** value: **7.00**
Circ: Statement: **225,671 • CGC:** 2 graded, best 9.8
Rock Around the Cosmos **A:** John Buscema **W:** Roy Thomas; Gerry Conway ★ Versus Shaper of Worlds.

137 ❑ Aug 1973 Cover: 0.20 **NM** value: **7.00**
Circ: Statement: **225,671 • CGC:** 2 graded, best 9.6
Rumble on Planet 3 **A:** John Buscema **W:** Roy Thomas; Gerry Conway ★ Versus Shaper of Worlds.

138 ❑ Sep 1973 Cover: 0.20 **NM** value: **7.00**
Circ: Statement: **225,671 • CGC:** 3 graded, best 9.6
Madness Is the Miracle Man **A:** John Buscema **W:** Gerry Conway ★ Versus Miracle Man.

139 ❑ Oct 1973 Cover: 0.20 **NM** value: **7.00**
Circ: Statement: **225,671 • CGC:** 3 graded, best 9.6
Target: Tomorrow! **A:** John Buscema **W:** Gerry Conway ★ Versus Miracle Man.

140 ❑ Nov 1973 Cover: 0.20 **NM** value: **7.00**
Circ: Statement: **225,671 • CGC:** 4 graded, best 9.6
Annihilus Revealed **A:** John Buscema **C:** Rich Buckler **W:** Gerry Conway ★ Origin of Annihilus. ★ Versus Annihilus.

141 ❑ Dec 1973 Cover: 0.20 **NM** value: **7.00**
Circ: Statement: **225,671 • CGC:** 2 graded, best 9.6
The End of the Fantastic Four **A:** John Buscema **C:** John Romita **W:** Gerry Conway ★ Versus Annihilus.

142 ❑ Jan 1974 Cover: 0.20 **NM** value: **7.00**
Circ: Statement: **218,330 • CGC:** 4 graded, best 9.6
No Friend Beside Him **A:** Rich Buckler ★ 1st Appearance of Darkoth the Death-Demon. ★ Versus Doctor Doom.

143 ❑ Feb 1974 Cover: 0.20 **NM** value: **7.00**
Circ: Statement: **218,330 • CGC:** 4 graded, best 9.6
The Terrible Triumph of Doctor Doom! **A:** Rich Buckler **C:** Gil Kane ★ Versus Doctor Doom.

144 ❑ Mar 1974 Cover: 0.20 **NM** value: **7.00**
Circ: Statement: **218,330 • CGC:** 5 graded, best 9.6
Attack! **A:** Rich Buckler ★ Appearance of Doctor Doom. ★ Versus Doctor Doom.

145 ❑ Apr 1974 Cover: 0.20 **NM** value: **7.00**
Circ: Statement: **218,330 • CGC:** 5 graded, best 9.4
Nightmare in the Snow **A:** Ross Andru **C:** Gil Kane ★ Appearance of Doctor Doom.

146 ❑ May 1974 Cover: 0.25 **NM** value: **7.00**
Circ: Statement: **218,330 • CGC:** 3 graded, best 9.6
Doomsday at 200-Degrees Below! • Has 1973 Statement, filed 9/25/73; avg print run 463,315; avg sales 227,387; avg subs 1,716; avg total paid 225,671; samples 150; office use 161; max existent 229,414; 51% of run returned **A:** Ross Andru **C:** Gil Kane

147 ❑ Jun 1974 Cover: 0.25 **NM** value: **7.00**
Circ: Statement: **218,330 • CGC:** 3 graded, best 9.6
The Sub-Mariner Strikes! **A:** Rich Buckler ★ Appearance of Sub-Mariner.

148 ❑ Jul 1974 Cover: 0.25 **NM** value: **7.00**
Circ: Statement: **218,330 • CGC:** 7 graded, best 9.8
War on the Thirty-Sixth Floor **A:** Rich Buckler ★ Versus Frightful Four.

149 ❑ Aug 1974 Cover: 0.25 **NM** value: **7.00**
Circ: Statement: **218,330 • CGC:** 5 graded, best 9.8
To Love, Honor, and Destroy! **A:** Rich Buckler

150 ❑ Sep 1974 Cover: 0.25 **NM** value: **7.00**
Circ: Statement: **218,330 • CGC:** 2 graded, best 9.4
Ultron-7: He'll Rule the World!; The Wedding of Crystal and Quicksilver • Wedding of Crystal and Quicksilver **A:** Rich Buckler **C:** Gil Kane ★ Appearance of Inhumans, Avengers.

151 ❑ Oct 1974 Cover: 0.25 **NM** value: **6.00**
Circ: Statement: **218,330 • CGC:** 2 graded, best 9.8
Thundra and Lightning! • part 1 **A:** Rich Buckler ★ Origin of Thundra. ★ 1st Appearance of Mahkizmo.

152 ❑ Nov 1974 Cover: 0.25 **NM** value: **6.00**
Circ: Statement: **218,330 • CGC:** 1 graded, best 9.2
A World of Madness Made • part 2 **A:** Rich Buckler

153 ❑ Dec 1974 Cover: 0.25 **NM** value: **6.00**
Circ: Statement: **218,330 • CGC:** 1 graded, best 8.5
Worlds in Collision! • part 3 **A:** Rich Buckler **C:** Gil Kane ★ Versus Mahkizmo.

154 ❑ Jan 1975 Cover: 0.25 **NM** value: **6.00**
Circ: Statement: **216,260 • CGC:** 3 graded, best 9.4
The Man in the Mystery Mask! • partial reprint of Strange Tales #127 **C:** Gil Kane

155 ❑ Feb 1975 Cover: 0.25 **NM** value: **7.00**
Circ: Statement: **216,260 • CGC:** 2 graded, best 9.6
Battle Royal **A:** Rich Buckler ★ Appearance of Silver Surfer. ★ Versus Doctor Doom.

156 ❑ Mar 1975 Cover: 0.25 **NM** value: **7.00**
Circ: Statement: **216,260 • CGC:** 3 graded, best 9.6
Middle Game **A:** Rich Buckler ★ Appearance of Doctor Doom, Silver Surfer. ★ Versus Dr. Doom. ★ Versus Doctor Doom.

157 ❑ Apr 1975 Cover: 0.25 **NM** value: **7.00**
Circ: Statement: **216,260 • CGC:** 2 graded, best 9.6
And Now the Endgame Cometh **A:** Rich Buckler ★ Appearance of Doctor Doom, Silver Surfer. ★ Versus Dr. Doom. ★ Versus Doctor Doom.

158 ❑ May 1975 Cover: 0.25 **NM** value: **6.00**
Circ: Statement: **216,260 • CGC:** 2 graded, best 9.4
Invasion from the 5th (Count It 5th) Dimension! • Has 1974 Statement, filed 9/18/74; avg print run 428,583; avg sales 216,768; avg subs 1,562; avg total paid 218,330; office use 4,657; max existent 222,987; 48% of run returned **A:** Rich Buckler ★ Versus Xemu.

159 ❑ Jun 1975 Cover: 0.25 **NM** value: **6.00**
Circ: Statement: **216,260 • CGC:** 2 graded, best 9.4
Havok in the Hidden Land **A:** Rich Buckler ★ Appearance of Inhumans. ★ Versus Xemu.

160 ❑ Jul 1975 Cover: 0.25 **NM** value: **6.00**
Circ: Statement: **216,260 • CGC:** 1 graded, best 9.6
In One World and Out the Other **A:** John Buscema **C:** Gil Kane ★ Versus Arkon.

161 ❑ Aug 1975 Cover: 0.25 **NM** value: **4.00**
Circ: Statement: **216,260 • CGC:** 2 graded, best 9.4
All the World Wars at Once **A:** Rich Buckler **W:** Roy Thomas ★ Appearance of Valeria, Reed Richards of Earth-A, Sue Grimm of Earth-A, Ben Grimm of Earth-A, Lockjaw, Phineas.

162 ❑ Sep 1975 Cover: 0.25 **NM** value: **4.00**
Circ: Statement: **216,260 • CGC:** 2 graded, best 9.2
The Shape of Things to Come **A:** Rich Buckler **W:** Roy Thomas ★ Appearance of Albert E. DeVoor, The "Old One", Valeria, Reed Richards of Earth-A, Gaard (Johnny Storm of Earth-A, reconstructed), Arkon, Ben Grimm of Earth-A, Phineas.

163 ❑ Oct 1975 Cover: 0.25 **NM** value: **4.00**
Circ: Statement: **216,260 • CGC:** 1 graded, best 9.2
Finale; Arkon at Bay; Victory in Hyper-Space **A:** Rich Buckler **W:** Roy Thomas ★ Appearance of Albert E. DeVoor, Reed Richards of Earth-A, Gaard (Johnny Storm of Earth-A, reconstructed), Arkon.

164 ❑ Nov 1975 Cover: 0.25 **NM** value: **4.00**
Circ: Statement: **216,260 • CGC:** 5 graded, best 9.6
The Crusader Syndrome **A:** George Pérez **C:** Jack Kirby **W:** Roy Thomas ★ 1st Appearance of Crusader (a.k.a. Marvel Boy), Crusader (Marvel Boy), Frankie Raye.

165 ❑ Dec 1975 Cover: 0.25 **NM** value: **4.00**
Circ: Statement: **216,260 • CGC:** 1 graded, best 9.4
The Light of Other Worlds **A:** George Pérez **W:** Roy Thomas ★ Origin of Crusader (a.k.a. Marvel Boy). ★ Death of Crusader.

166 ❑ Jan 1976 Cover: 0.25 **NM** value: **4.00**
Circ: Statement: **199,734 • CGC:** 6 graded, best 9.8
If It's Tuesday, This Must Be the Hulk **A:** George Pérez **C:** Rich Buckler **W:** Roy Thomas ★ Appearance of Hulk, Puppet Master. ★ Versus Hulk.

167 ❑ Feb 1976 Cover: 0.25 **NM** value: **4.00**
Circ: Statement: **199,734 • CGC:** 4 graded, best 9.6
Titans Two **A:** George Pérez **C:** Jack Kirby **W:** Roy Thomas ★ Appearance of Hulk, Puppet Master. ★ Versus Hulk.

168 ❑ Mar 1976 Cover: 0.25 **NM** value: **4.00**
Circ: Statement: **199,734 • CGC:** 3 graded, best 9.6
Where Have All The Powers Gone? • Thing replaced by Luke Cage (Power Man); Has 1975 Statement, filed 9/22/75; avg print run 429,115; avg sales 213,480; avg subs 2,780; avg total paid 216,260; office use 3,250; max existent 219,510; 49% of run returned **A:** Rich Buckler **W:** Roy Thomas ★ Appearance of Wreaker.

169 ❑ Apr 1976 Cover: 0.25 **NM** value: **4.00**
Circ: Statement: **199,734 • CGC:** 2 graded, best 9.6
Five Characters in Search of a Madman **A:** Rich Buckler **W:** Roy Thomas ★ Appearance of Luke Cage.

170 ❑ May 1976 Cover: 0.25 **NM** value: **4.00**
Circ: Statement: **199,734 • CGC:** 1 graded, best 9.4
A Sky-Full Of Fear! **A:** George Pérez **W:** Roy Thomas ★ Appearance of Luke Cage.

171 ❑ Jun 1976 Cover: 0.25 **NM** value: **3.00**
Circ: Statement: **199,734 • CGC:** 2 graded, best 9.4
Death is a Golden Gorilla **A:** Rich Buckler; George Pérez **C:** Jack Kirby **W:** Roy Thomas; Carla Conway ★ 1st Appearance of Gorr. ★ Versus Galactus.

172 ❑ Jul 1976 Cover: 0.25 **NM** value: **3.00**
Circ: Statement: **199,734 • CGC:** 1 graded, best 9.2
Cry, the Bedeviled Planet **A:** George Pérez **C:** Jack Kirby **W:** Roy Thomas; Bill Mantlo ★ 2nd Appearance of Gorr. ★ Appearance of Galactus, The High Evolutionary, The Destroyer. ★ Versus Galactus.

173 ❑ Aug 1976 Cover: 0.25 **NM** value: **3.00**
Circ: Statement: **199,734 • CGC:** 4 graded, best 9.4
Counter-Earth Must Die-At the Hand of Galactus **A:** John Buscema **C:** Jack Kirby **W:** Roy Thomas ★ Appearance of Galactus, Gorr, The High Evolutionary, Torgo. ★ Versus Galactus.

174 ❑ Sep 1976 Cover: 0.30 **NM** value: **3.00**
Circ: Statement: **199,734 • CGC:** 2 graded, best 9.4
Starquest **A:** John Buscema **C:** Jack Kirby **W:** Roy Thomas ★ Appearance of Galactus, Gorr, The High Evolutionary, Torgo. ★ Versus Galactus.

175 ❑ Oct 1976 Cover: 0.30 **NM** value: **3.00**
Circ: Statement: **199,734 • CGC:** 4 graded, best 9.6
When Giants Walk The Sky! **A:** John Buscema **C:** Jack Kirby **W:** Roy Thomas ★ Appearance of Galactus, The Impossible Man, Gorr, The High Evolutionary. ★ Versus Galactus.

176 ❑ Nov 1976 Cover: 0.30 **NM** value: **3.00**
Circ: Statement: **199,734 • CGC:** 2 graded, best 9.6
Improbable As It May Seem, The Impossible Man Is Back In Town **A:** George Pérez **C:** Jack Kirby **W:** Roy Thomas ★ Appearance of The Impossible Man, Roy Thomas, Stan Lee, Jack Kirby. ★ Versus Trapster. ★ Versus Wizard. ★ Versus Sandman.

177 ❑ Dec 1976 Cover: 0.30 **NM** value: **3.00**
Circ: Statement: **199,734 • CGC:** 4 graded, best 9.6

CGC-graded: Multiply prices above by **33 for 9.9 M • 16 for 9.8 NM/M • 7 for 9.6 NM+ • 5 for 9.4 NM • 2.5 for 9.2 NM- • 1.5 for 9.0 VF/NM**

🕮 Look Out for the Frightful Four **A:** George Pérez **C:** Jack Kirby **W:** Roy Thomas; Bob Wayne; Mike Friedrich ★ Origin of Texas Twister. ★ 1st Appearance of Texas Twister, Captain Ultra. ★ Appearance of Tigra, Impossible Man. ★ Versus Trapster. ★ Versus Brute. ★ Versus Wizard. ★ Versus Sandman.

178 ❑ Jan 1977 Cover: 0.30 **NM** value: **3.00**
Circ: Statement: **194,661 • CGC:** 2 graded, best 9.6
🕮 Call My Killer the Brute **A:** George Pérez **C:** John Romita **W:** Roy Thomas ★ Appearance of The Impossible Man, Brute. ★ Versus Trapster. ★ Versus Brute. ★ Versus Wizard. ★ Versus Sandman.

179 ❑ Feb 1977 Cover: 0.30 **NM** value: **3.00**
Circ: Statement: **194,661 • CGC:** 1 graded, best 9.6
🕮 A Robinson Crusoe in the Negative Zone **A:** Ron Wilson **C:** Al Milgrom **W:** Roy Thomas; Gerry Conway ★ 1st Appearance of Metalloid. ★ Appearance of Tigra, Thundra, Reed Richards of Counter-Earth, Impossible Man, Annihilus, Mad Thinker. ★ Versus Annihilus. ★ Versus Mad Thinker.

180 ❑ Mar 1977 Cover: 0.30 **NM** value: **3.00**
Circ: Statement: **194,661 • CGC:** 4 graded, best 9.6
🕮 Bedlam in the Baxter Building • reprints FF #101; Has 1976 Statement, filed 9/20/76; avg print run 431,962; avg sales 197,668; avg subs 2,066; avg total paid 199,734; office use 2,950; max existent 202,684; 53% of run returned **A:** Jack Kirby **C:** Jack Kirby **W:** Jack Kirby; Stan Lee

181 ❑ Apr 1977 Cover: 0.30 **NM** value: **2.50**
Circ: Statement: **194,661 • CGC:** 3 graded, best 9.8
🕮 Side by Side With – Annihilus? **A:** Ron Wilson **C:** Jack Kirby **W:** Roy Thomas ★ Appearance of Reed Richards of Counter-Earth, Annihilus. ★ Versus Reed Richards of Counter-Earth. ★ Versus Annihilus. ★ Versus Mad Thinker.

182 ❑ May 1977 Cover: 0.30 **NM** value: **2.50**
Circ: Statement: **194,661 • CGC:** 4 graded, best 9.6
🕮 Enter: The Mad Thinker **A:** Sal Buscema **W:** Jim Shooter; Len Wein; Archie Goodwin; Bill Mantlo ★ Versus Reed Richards of Counter-Earth. ★ Versus Annihilus. ★ Versus Mad Thinker.

183 ❑ Jun 1977 Cover: 0.30 **NM** value: **2.50**
Circ: Statement: **194,661 • CGC:** 5 graded, best 9.6
🕮 Battleground: The Baxter Building! **A:** Sal Buscema **C:** George Pérez **W:** Ralph Macchio; Jim Shooter; Len Wein; Roger Stern; Bill Mantlo; Roger Slifer ★ Appearance of Tigra, Thundra, Impossible Man, Brute, Annihilus, Mad Thinker. ★ Versus Brute. ★ Versus Annihilus. ★ Versus Mad Thinker.

184 ❑ Jul 1977 Cover: 0.30 **NM** value: **2.50**
Circ: Statement: **194,661 • CGC:** 2 graded, best 9.8
🕮 Aftermath: The Eliminator **A:** George Pérez **W:** Len Wein ★ Appearance of Tigra, Thundra, Impossible Man.

185 ❑ Aug 1977 Cover: 0.30 **NM** value: **2.50**
Circ: Statement: **194,661 • CGC:** 2 graded, best 9.6
🕮 Here There Be Witches **A:** George Pérez **W:** Len Wein ★ 1st Appearance of Nicholas Scratch. ★ 2nd Appearance of New Salem's Witches. ★ Appearance of Impossible Man.

186 ❑ Sep 1977 Cover: 0.30 **NM** value: **2.50**
Circ: Statement: **194,661 • CGC:** 1 graded, best 9.6
🕮 Enter: Salem's Seven **A:** George Pérez **W:** Len Wein ★ Origin of New Salem's Witches. ★ 2nd Appearance of Nicholas Scratch. ★ Appearance of Impossible Man.

187 ❑ Oct 1977 Cover: 0.30 **NM** value: **2.50**
Circ: Statement: **194,661**
🕮 Trouble Times Two **A:** George Pérez **W:** Len Wein ★ Appearance of Molecule Man, Klaw, Impossible Man. ★ Versus Molecule Man. ★ Versus Klaw.

188 ❑ Nov 1977 Cover: 0.35 **NM** value: **2.50**
Circ: Statement: **194,661 • CGC:** 2 graded, best 9.6
🕮 The Rampage of Reed Richards **A:** George Pérez **W:** Len Wein ★ Appearance of The Watcher, Molecule Man, Impossible Man. ★ Versus Molecule Man. ★ Versus Klaw.

189 ❑ Dec 1977 Cover: 0.35 **NM** value: **2.50**
Circ: Statement: **194,661**
🕮 The Torch That Was • reprints FF Annual #4 **A:** Jack Kirby **C:** Keith Pollard **W:** Jack Kirby; Stan Lee

190 ❑ Jan 1978 Cover: 0.35 **NM** value: **2.50**
Circ: Statement: **177,802 • CGC:** 1 graded, best 9.4
🕮 The Way It Was • Thing recounts FF's career **A:** Sal Buscema **C:** Jack Kirby **W:** Marv Wolfman

191 ❑ Feb 1978 Cover: 0.35 **NM** value: **2.50**
Circ: Statement: **177,802 • CGC:** 3 graded, best 9.6
🕮 Four No More • Fantastic Four resign **A:** George Pérez **W:** Len Wein ★ Appearance of Plunderer, Thundra. ★ Versus Plunderer.

192 ❑ Mar 1978 Cover: 0.35 **NM** value: **2.50**
Circ: Statement: **177,802 • CGC:** 1 graded, best 9.4
🕮 He Who Soweth the Wind • Has 1977 Statement, filed 9/20/77; avg print run 419,544; avg sales 187,709; avg subs 6,952; avg total paid 194,661; samples 150; office use 2,750; max existent 197,561; 53% of run returned **A:** George Pérez **W:** Len Wein; Roger Slifer ★ Appearance of Texas Twister.

193 ❑ Apr 1978 Cover: 0.35 **NM** value: **2.50**
Circ: Statement: **177,802 • CGC:** 2 graded, best 9.6
🕮 Day Of The Death-Demon **A:** Keith Pollard **W:** Keith Pollard; Len Wein; Bill Mantlo ★ Origin of Darketh the Death-Demon. ★ 1st Appearance of Victor Von Doom II (not face). ★ Appearance of Diablo, Impossible Man. ★ Versus Diablo.

194 ❑ May 1978 Cover: 0.35 **NM** value: **2.50**
Circ: Statement: **177,802 • CGC:** 1 graded, best 9.6
🕮 Vengeance is Mine **A:** Keith Pollard **C:** George Pérez **W:** Keith Pollard; Len Wein; Bill Mantlo ★ Appearance of Darketh, Diablo, Impossible Man, Sub-Mariner. ★ Versus Diablo.

195 ❑ Jun 1978 Cover: 0.35 **NM** value: **2.50**
Circ: Statement: **177,802 • CGC:** 2 graded, best 9.6
🕮 Beware the Ravaging Retrievers **A:** Keith Pollard **C:** George Pérez **W:** Marv Wolfman ★ 2nd Appearance of Victor Von Doom II (not face). ★ Appearance of Lord Vashti, Impossible Man, Sub-Mariner.

196 ❑ Jul 1978 Cover: 0.35 **NM** value: **2.50**
Circ: Statement: **177,802**
🕮 Who in the World Is the Invincible Man? **A:** Keith Pollard **C:** George Pérez **W:** Marv Wolfman ★ Appearance of Victor Von Doom II, Doctor Doom.

197 ❑ Aug 1978 Cover: 0.35 **NM** value: **2.50**
Circ: Statement: **177,802 • CGC:** 1 graded, best 9.6
🕮 The Riotous Return of the Red Ghost • Reed Richards gets powers back **A:** Keith Pollard **C:** George Pérez **W:** Marv Wolfman ★ Appearance of Red Ghost, Victor Von Doom II, Dr. Doom, Nick Fury. ★ Versus Red Ghost. ★ Versus Doctor Doom.

198 ❑ Sep 1978 Cover: 0.35 **NM** value: **2.50**
Circ: Statement: **177,802 • CGC:** 2 graded, best 9.6
🕮 Invasion! • Team gets together to fight Doctor Doom **A:** Keith Pollard **C:** John Buscema **W:** Marv Wolfman ★ Appearance of Prince Zorba, Victor Von Doom II, Doctor Doom. ★ Versus Doctor Doom.

199 ❑ Oct 1978 Cover: 0.35 **NM** value: **2.50**
Circ: Statement: **177,802**
🕮 The Son of Doctor Doom **A:** Keith Pollard **W:** Marv Wolfman ★ Origin of Victor Von Doom II. ★ Appearance of Prince Zorba, Doctor Doom. ★ Death of Victor Von Doom II.

200 ❑ Nov 1978 Cover: 0.60 **NM** value: **3.00**
Circ: Statement: **177,802 • CGC:** 7 graded, best 9.6
🕮 When Titans Clash; Beginning of the End; At Long Last, Defeat! At Long Last, Victory!; Latveria, a Nation Anew • Prince Zorba **A:** Keith Pollard **W:** Marv Wolfman ★ Appearance of Doctor Doom. ★ Versus Doctor Doom.

201 ❑ Dec 1978 Cover: 0.35 **NM** value: **2.00**
Circ: Statement: **177,802 • CGC:** 1 graded, best 8.5
🕮 Home Deadly Home **A:** Keith Pollard **W:** Marv Wolfman ★ Appearance of Prince Zorba, Quasimodo.

202 ❑ Jan 1979 Cover: 0.35 **NM** value: **2.00**
Circ: Statement: **267,511 • CGC:** 1 graded, best 8.5
🕮 There's One Iron Man Too Many **A:** John Buscema; Keith Pollard **W:** Marv Wolfman ★ Appearance of Iron Man, Quasimodo, Tony Stark.

203 ❑ Feb 1979 Cover: 0.35 **NM** value: **2.00**
Circ: Statement: **267,511**
🕮 And a Child Shall Slay Them **A:** Keith Pollard **W:** Marv Wolfman

204 ❑ Mar 1979 Cover: 0.35 **NM** value: **2.00**
Circ: Statement: **267,511 • CGC:** 1 graded, best 9.4
🕮 The Andromeda Attack • Has 1978 Statement, filed 9/25/78; avg print run 416,161; avg sales 164,290; avg total paid 177,802; samples 250; office use 1,290; max existent 179,342; 57% of run returned **A:** Keith Pollard **W:** Marv Wolfman ★ 1st Appearance of Queen Adora (of Xandar), Skrull X. ★ Appearance of Man-Wolf, The Watcher, Monocle, Edwin Jarvis, Spider-Man.

205 ❑ Apr 1979 Cover: 0.35 **NM** value: **2.00**
Circ: Statement: **267,511 • CGC:** 2 graded, best 9.4
🕮 When Worlds Die **A:** Keith Pollard **W:** Marv Wolfman ★ 1st Appearance of Thoran Rul (Protector). ★ 2nd Appearance of Queen Adora (of Xandar). ★ Appearance of The Watcher, Monocle, Emperor Dorrek.

206 ❑ May 1979 Cover: 0.40 **NM** value: **2.00**
Circ: Statement: **267,511**
🕮 The Death of the Fantastic Four **A:** Keith Pollard **W:** Marv Wolfman

207 ❑ Jun 1979 Cover: 0.40 **NM** value: **2.00**
Circ: Statement: **267,511 • CGC:** 2 graded, best 9.4
🕮 Might of the Monocle **A:** Sal Buscema **W:** Marv Wolfman ★ 1st Appearance of The Enclave (identified). ★ Appearance of Barney Bushkin, Medusa, Monocle, Spider-Man.

208 ❑ Jul 1979 Cover: 0.40 **NM** value: **2.00**
Circ: Statement: **267,511 • CGC:** 1 graded, best 9.2
🕮 The Power of the Sphinx **A:** Sal Buscema **W:** Marv Wolfman ★ Origin of Protector. ★ Appearance of Nova, Sphinx, Queen Adora, Comet, Diamondhead, Thoran Rul (Protector), Crimebuster, Doctor Sun, Powerhouse.

209 ❑ Aug 1979 Cover: 0.40 **NM** value: **2.00**
Circ: Statement: **267,511 • CGC:** 2 graded, best 9.6
🕮 Trapped in the Sargasso of Space **A:** John Byrne **W:** Marv Wolfman ★ 1st Appearance of Herbie.

210 ❑ Sep 1979 Cover: 0.40 **NM** value: **2.00**
Circ: Statement: **267,511 • CGC:** 2 graded, best 9.6
🕮 In Search of Galactus **A:** John Byrne **W:** Marv Wolfman ★ 2nd Appearance of Herbie. ★ Appearance of Galactus.

211 ❑ Oct 1979 Cover: 0.40 **NM** value: **2.00**
Circ: Statement: **267,511 • CGC:** 2 graded, best 9.6
🕮 If This Be Terrax **A:** John Byrne **W:** Marv Wolfman ★ 1st Appearance of Terrax the Tamer. ★ Appearance of Galactus, The Watcher.

212 ❑ Nov 1979 Cover: 0.40 **NM** value: **2.00**
Circ: Statement: **267,511 • CGC:** 2 graded, best 9.6
🕮 The Battle of the Titans **A:** John Byrne **W:** Marv Wolfman ★ Appearance of Galactus, Sphinx, The Watcher, Sayge, Skrull X.

213 ❑ Dec 1979 Cover: 0.40 **NM** value: **2.00**
Circ: Statement: **267,511 • CGC:** 1 graded, best 9.6
🕮 In Final Battle **A:** John Byrne **W:** Marv Wolfman ★ Appearance of Galactus, Sphinx, The Watcher, Sayge.

214 ❑ Jan 1980 Cover: 0.40 **NM** value: **2.00**
Circ: Statement: **243,786 • CGC:** 1 graded, best 9.6
🕮 And Then There Was One **A:** John Byrne **W:** Marv Wolfman ★ Appearance of Queen Adora, Dum Dum Dugan. ★ Death of Skrull X.

215 ❑ Feb 1980 Cover: 0.40 **NM** value: **2.00**
Circ: Statement: **243,786 • CGC:** 1 graded, best 9.6
🕮 Blastaar **A:** John Byrne

216 ❑ Mar 1980 Cover: 0.40 **NM** value: **2.00**
Circ: Statement: **243,786 • CGC:** 2 graded, best 9.2
🕮 Where There Be Gods • Has 1979 Statement, filed 10/1/79; avg print run 463,916; avg sales 253,831; avg subs 13,860; avg total paid 267,511; 590 samples; office use 1,683; max existent 464,096; 42% of run returned
A: John Byrne

217 ❑ Apr 1980 Cover: 0.40 **NM** value: **2.00**
Circ: Statement: **243,786 • CGC:** 1 graded, best 9.4
🕮 Masquerade **A:** John Byrne ★ Appearance of Dazzler.

218 ❑ May 1980 Cover: 0.40 **NM** value: **2.00**
Circ: Statement: **243,786 • CGC:** 3 graded, best 9.6
🕮 When A Spider-Man Comes Calling • Continued from Peter Parker, the Spectacular Spider-Man #42 **A:** John Byrne; Joe Sinnott **W:** Bill Mantlo

219 ❑ Jun 1980 Cover: 0.40 **NM** value: **2.00**
Circ: Statement: **243,786**
🕮 Leviathans

220 ❑ Jul 1980 Cover: 0.40 **NM** value: **2.00**
Circ: Statement: **243,786 • CGC:** 1 graded, best 9.6
🕮 ...And The Lights Went Out All Ever The World **A:** John Byrne **W:** John Byrne ★ Origin of Fantastic Four.

221 ❑ Aug 1980 Cover: 0.40 **NM** value: **2.00**
Circ: Statement: **243,786**
🕮 Tower of Crystal, Dreams of Glass **A:** John Byrne

222 ❑ Sep 1980 Cover: 0.50 **NM** value: **2.00**
Circ: Statement: **243,786**
🕮 The Possession Of Franklin Richards! **A:** Barry Windsor-Smith

223 ❑ Oct 1980 Cover: 0.50 **NM** value: **2.00**
Circ: Statement: **243,786**
🕮 That a Child May Live **A:** Barry Windsor-Smith

224 ❑ Nov 1980 Cover: 0.50 **NM** value: **2.00**
Circ: Statement: **243,786**
🕮 The Darkfield Illumination **A:** Barry Windsor-Smith

225 ❑ Dec 1980 Cover: 0.50 **NM** value: **2.00**
Circ: Statement: **243,786**
🕮 The Blind God's Tears **A:** Bill Sienkiewicz; Barry Windsor-Smith; Pablo Marcos **W:** Doug Moench ★ Appearance of Thor.

226 ❑ Jan 1981 Cover: 0.50 **NM** value: **2.00**
Circ: Statement: **192,731**
🕮 The Samurai Destroyer **A:** Barry Windsor-Smith

227 ❑ Feb 1981 Cover: 0.50 **NM** value: **2.00**
Circ: Statement: **192,731 • CGC:** 1 graded, best 9.4
🕮 The Brain Parasites! **A:** Bill Sienkiewicz; Barry Windsor-Smith; Bruce Patterson **W:** Doug Moench

228 ❑ Mar 1981 Cover: 0.50 **NM** value: **2.00**
Circ: Statement: **192,731**
🕮 Ego-Spawn **A:** Bill Sienkiewicz; Barry Windsor-Smith; Joe Sinnott **W:** Doug Moench

229 ❑ Apr 1981 Cover: 0.50 **NM** value: **2.00**
Circ: Statement: **192,731**
🕮 The Thing From The Black Hole • Has 1980 Statement, filed 10/1/80; avg print run 456,547; avg sales 228,207; avg subs 15,579; avg total paid 243,786; samples 645; office use 3,718; max existent 248,149; 46% of run returned **A:** Bill Sienkiewicz; Barry Windsor-Smith; Joe Sinnott **W:** Doug Moench

230 ❑ May 1981 Cover: 0.50 **NM** value: **2.00**
Circ: Statement: **192,731**
🕮 Firefrost And The Ebon Seeker **A:** Bill Sienkiewicz; Barry Windsor-Smith; Joe Sinnott **W:** Doug Moench

231 ❑ Jun 1981 Cover: 0.50 **NM** value: **2.00**
Circ: Statement: **192,731**
🕮 In All The Gathered Gloom! **A:** Bill Sienkiewicz; Barry Windsor-Smith; Joe Sinnott **W:** Doug Moench; Gurland

232 ❑ Jul 1981 Cover: 0.50 **NM** value: **2.50**
Circ: Statement: **192,731 • CGC:** 11 graded, best 9.6
🕮 Back To The Basics! **A:** John Byrne **W:** John Byrne

233 ❑ Aug 1981 Cover: 0.50 **NM** value: **2.50**
Circ: Statement: **192,731 • CGC:** 2 graded, best 9.6
🕮 Mission For A Dead Man! **A:** John Byrne **W:** John Byrne

234 ❑ Sep 1981 Cover: 0.50 **NM** value: **2.50**
Circ: Statement: **192,731**
🕮 The Man With The Power! **A:** John Byrne **W:** John Byrne

235 ❑ Oct 1981 Cover: 0.50 **NM** value: **2.50**
Circ: Statement: **192,731 • CGC:** 2 graded, best 9.8
🕮 Four Against Ego! **A:** John Byrne **W:** John Byrne ★ Versus Ego.

236 ❑ Nov 1981 Cover: 1.00 **NM** value: **2.50**
Circ: Statement: **192,731 • CGC:** 2 graded, best 9.4
• 20th Anniversary Issue. 🕮 Terror In A Tiny Town **A:** John Byrne **W:** John Byrne ★ Origin of Fantastic Four. ★ Versus Doctor Doom.

237 ❑ Dec 1981 Cover: 0.50 **NM** value: **2.50**
Circ: Statement: **192,731 • CGC:** 2 graded, best 9.6
🕮 The Eyes Have It! **A:** John Byrne **W:** John Byrne ★ 1st Appearance of Julie Angel.

238 ❑ Jan 1982 Cover: 0.60 **NM** value: **2.50**
Circ: Statement: **234,043 • CGC:** 1 graded, best 9.4
🕮 The Lady Is For Burning! **A:** John Byrne **W:** John Byrne ★ Origin of Frankie Raye. ★ Appearance of Aunt Petunia.

239 ❑ Feb 1982 Cover: 0.60 **NM** value: **2.50**
Circ: Statement: **234,043 • CGC:** 3 graded, best 9.6
🕮 Wendy's Friends **A:** John Byrne **W:** John Byrne

240 ❑ Mar 1982 Cover: 0.60 **NM** value: **2.50**
Circ: Statement: **234,043 • CGC:** 3 graded, best 9.8
🕮 Exodus **A:** John Byrne **W:** John Byrne ★ 1st Appearance of Luna.

241 ❑ Apr 1982 Cover: 0.60 **NM** value: **2.50**
Circ: Statement: **234,043 • CGC:** 3 graded, best 9.8
🕮 Render Unto Caesar • Has 1981 Statement, filed 10/1/81; avg print run 436,750; avg sales 176,237; avg subs 16,494; avg total paid 192,731; samples 601; office use 5,255; max existent 198,587; 56% of run returned **A:** John Byrne **W:** John Byrne ★ Appearance of Black Panther.

242 ❑ May 1982 Cover: 0.60 **NM** value: **2.50**
Circ: Statement: **234,043 • CGC:** 1 graded, best 9.2
🕮 Terrax The Untamed **A:** John Byrne **W:** John Byrne ★ Appearance of Daredevil.

243 ❑ Jun 1982 Cover: 0.60 **NM** value: **2.50**
Circ: Statement: **234,043**

244 ❑ Jul 1982 Cover: 0.60 **NM** value: **2.50**
Circ: Statement: **234,043 • CGC:** 1 graded, best 9.4
🕮 Beginnings And Endings • Frankie Raye becomes herald of Galactus **A:** John Byrne **W:** John Byrne ★ 1st Appearance of Nova II (Frankie Raye).

245 ❑ Aug 1982 Cover: 0.60 **NM** value: **2.50**
Circ: Statement: **234,043 • CGC:** 2 graded, best 9.6
🕮 Childhood's End **A:** John Byrne **W:** John Byrne

246 ❑ Sep 1982 Cover: 0.60 **NM** value: **2.50**
Circ: Statement: **234,043 • CGC:** 1 graded, best 9.4
🕮 Too Many Dooms! **A:** John Byrne **W:** John Byrne

247 ❑ Oct 1982 Cover: 0.60 **NM** value: **2.50**
Circ: Statement: **234,043 • CGC:** 3 graded, best 9.6
🕮 This Land Is Mine! **A:** John Byrne **W:** John Byrne ★ 1st Appearance of Kristoff Vernard.

248 ❑ Nov 1982 Cover: 0.60 **NM** value: **2.50**
Circ: Statement: **234,043 • CGC:** 3 graded, best 9.6
🕮 Nightmare! **A:** John Byrne **W:** John Byrne

249 ❑ Dec 1982 Cover: 0.60 **NM** value: **2.50**

Other grades: Multiply prices above by **1.5 for Mint • 2/3 for Very Fine • 1/3 for Fine • 1/5 for Very Good • 1/8 for Good**

Circ: Statement: **234,043** • **CGC:** 2 graded, best 9.6
Man And Super-Man! **A:** John Byrne **W:** John Byrne ★ Versus Gladiator.

250 ❑ Jan 1983 Cover: 1.00 **NM** value: **3.00**
Circ: Statement: **257,298** • **CGC:** 6 graded, best 9.9
• Double-size. X-Factor **A:** John Byrne **W:** John Byrne ★ Appearance of X-Men, Captain America, Spider-Man.

251 ❑ Feb 1983 Cover: 0.60 **NM** value: **2.50**
Circ: Statement: **257,298**
Into The Negative Zone! • Negative Zone **A:** John Byrne **W:** John Byrne

252 ❑ Mar 1983 Cover: 0.60 **NM** value: **2.50**
Circ: Statement: **257,298** • **CGC:** 1 graded, best 9.4
Cityscape • sideways format **A:** John Byrne **W:** John Byrne

253 ❑ Apr 1983 Cover: 0.60 **NM** value: **2.50**
Circ: Statement: **257,298** • **CGC:** 1 graded, best 9.4
Quest • Has 1982 Statement, filed 10/11/82; avg print run 443,238; avg sales 218,139; avg subs 15,904; avg total paid 234,043; samples 713; office use 4,116; max existent 238,872; 47% of run returned **A:** John Byrne **W:** John Byrne

254 ❑ May 1983 Cover: 0.60 **NM** value: **2.50**
Circ: Statement: **257,298**
The Minds Of Mantracora **A:** John Byrne **W:** John Byrne ★ Appearance of She-Hulk.

255 ❑ Jun 1983 Cover: 0.60 **NM** value: **2.50**
Circ: Statement: **257,298** • **CGC:** 2 graded, best 9.8
Trapped! **A:** John Byrne **W:** John Byrne

256 ❑ Jul 1983 Cover: 0.60 **NM** value: **2.50**
Circ: Statement: **257,298** • **CGC:** 2 graded, best 9.8
The Annihilation Gambit **A:** John Byrne **W:** John Byrne

257 ❑ Aug 1983 Cover: 0.60 **NM** value: **2.50**
Circ: Statement: **257,298** • **CGC:** 2 graded, best 9.6
Fragments **A:** John Byrne **W:** John Byrne

258 ❑ Sep 1983 Cover: 0.60 **NM** value: **2.50**
Circ: Statement: **257,298** • **CGC:** 2 graded, best 9.8

259 ❑ Oct 1983 Cover: 0.60 **NM** value: **2.50**
Circ: Statement: **257,298** • **CGC:** 1 graded, best 9.4
Choices **A:** John Byrne **W:** John Byrne

260 ❑ Nov 1983 Cover: 0.60 **NM** value: **3.00**
Circ: Statement: **257,298** • **CGC:** 1 graded, best 9.6
When Titans Clash! • Silver Surfer, Doctor Doom **A:** John Byrne **W:** John Byrne ★ Appearance of Doctor Doom, Silver Surfer. ★ Death of Terrax.

261 ❑ Dec 1983 Cover: 0.60 **NM** value: **2.50**
Circ: Statement: **257,298** • **CGC:** 1 graded, best 8.5

262 ❑ Jan 1984 Cover: 0.60 **NM** value: **2.50**
Circ: Statement: **268,568** • **CGC:** 1 graded, best 8.5
The Trial Of Reed Richards • Trial of Reed Richards; John Byrne appears in story **A:** John Byrne **W:** John Byrne ★ Origin of Galactus.

263 ❑ Feb 1984 Cover: 0.60 **NM** value: **2.50**
Circ: Statement: **268,568** • **CGC:** 1 graded, best 9.6

264 ❑ Mar 1984 Cover: 0.60 **NM** value: **2.50**
Circ: Statement: **268,568**
Cover swipe of Fantastic Four #1. Inferno **A:** John Byrne **W:** John Byrne ★ Versus Karisma.

265 ❑ Apr 1984 Cover: 0.60 **NM** value: **2.50**
Circ: Statement: **268,568**
• She-Hulk joins Fantastic Four (replaces Thing, who left in Secret Wars) **A:** John Byrne ★ 1st Appearance of Lyja (as Alicia Masters), Roberta the Receptionist.

266 ❑ May 1984 Cover: 0.60 **NM** value: **2.50**
Circ: Statement: **268,568**
Call Her Karisma! **A:** John Byrne; Kerry Gammill **W:** John Byrne

267 ❑ Jun 1984 Cover: 0.60 **NM** value: **2.50**
Circ: Statement: **268,568**
• Sue has a miscarriage; Has 1983 Statement, filed 10/5/83; avg print run 444,699; avg sales 239,568; avg subs 17,730; avg total paid 257,298; samples 807; office use 4,870; max existent 262,975; 41% of run returned **A:** John Byrne

268 ❑ Jul 1984 Cover: 0.60 **NM** value: **2.50**
Circ: Statement: **268,568**

269 ❑ Aug 1984 Cover: 0.60 **NM** value: **2.50**
Circ: Statement: **268,568**
Skyfall **A:** John Byrne **W:** John Byrne ★ 1st Appearance of Terminus.

270 ❑ Sep 1984 Cover: 0.60 **NM** value: **2.50**
Circ: Statement: **268,568**
Planet-Fall **A:** John Byrne **W:** John Byrne ★ Versus Terminus.

271 ❑ Oct 1984 Cover: 0.60 **NM** value: **2.50**
Circ: Statement: **268,568**
Happy Birthday Darling! **A:** John Byrne **W:** John Byrne

272 ❑ Nov 1984 Cover: 0.60 **NM** value: **2.50**
Circ: Statement: **268,568**
Cowboys And Idioms! **A:** John Byrne **W:** John Byrne ★ 1st Appearance of Nathaniel Richards (Reed's father).

273 ❑ Dec 1984 Cover: 0.60 **NM** value: **2.50**
Circ: Statement: **268,568**
Fathers And Others **A:** John Byrne **W:** John Byrne ★ Origin of Kang.

274 ❑ Jan 1985 Cover: 0.60 **NM** value: **2.50**
Circ: Statement: **264,760**
Monster Mash • Thing solo story; alien costume freed **A:** John Byrne **W:** John Byrne

275 ❑ Feb 1985 Cover: 0.60 **NM** value: **2.50**
Circ: Statement: **264,760**
The Naked Truth **A:** John Byrne **W:** John Byrne

276 ❑ Mar 1985 Cover: 0.60 **NM** value: **2.50**
Circ: Statement: **264,760**

277 ❑ Apr 1985 Cover: 0.65 **NM** value: **2.50**
Circ: Statement: **264,760**
Back From Beyond **A:** John Byrne **W:** John Byrne

278 ❑ May 1985 Cover: 0.65 **NM** value: **2.50**
Circ: Statement: **264,760** CapCity orders: **27,100**
True Lies • Kristoff becomes second Doctor Doom; Has 1984 Statement, filed 9/28/84; avg print run 441,031; avg sales 252,091; avg subs 16,477; avg total paid 268,568; samples 140; office use 4,152; max existent 272,860; 38% of run returned **A:** John Byrne **W:** John Byrne ★ Origin of Doctor Doom.

279 ❑ Jun 1985 Cover: 0.65 **NM** value: **2.50**
Circ: Statement: **264,760** CapCity orders: **25,500**
Crack Of Doom! **A:** John Byrne **W:** John Byrne

280 ❑ Jul 1985 Cover: 0.65 **NM** value: **2.50**
Circ: Statement: **264,760** CapCity orders: **26,000**
• Sue becomes Malice **A:** John Byrne **W:** John Byrne ★ 1st Appearance of Hate-Monger III ("H.M. Unger").

281 ❑ Aug 1985 Cover: 0.65 **NM** value: **2.50**
Circ: Statement: **264,760** CapCity orders: **27,300**
With Malice Towards All! **A:** John Byrne **W:** John Byrne

282 ❑ Sep 1985 Cover: 0.65 **NM** value: **2.50**
Circ: Statement: **264,760** CapCity orders: **34,200**
Inwards To Infinity! • Secret Wars II **A:** John Byrne **W:** John Byrne

283 ❑ Oct 1985 Cover: 0.65 **NM** value: **2.50**
Circ: Statement: **264,760** CapCity orders: **26,800**
Torment **A:** John Byrne **W:** John Byrne

284 ❑ Nov 1985 Cover: 0.65 **NM** value: **2.50**
Circ: Statement: **264,760** CapCity orders: **28,300**
Revolution! • Invisible Girl becomes Invisible Woman **A:** John Byrne **W:** John Byrne

285 ❑ Dec 1985 Cover: 0.65 **NM** value: **2.50**
Circ: Statement: **264,760** CapCity orders: **33,700**
Secret Wars II • Secret Wars II **A:** John Byrne **W:** John Byrne

286 ❑ Jan 1986 Cover: 0.65 **NM** value: **3.00**
Circ: Statement: **251,083** CapCity orders: **39,200** • **CGC:** 1 graded, best 9.6
Like A Phoenix! • return of Jean Grey **A:** John Byrne **W:** John Byrne ★ 2nd Appearance of X-Factor. ★ Appearance of X-Men.

287 ❑ Feb 1986 Cover: 0.75 **NM** value: **2.00**
Circ: Statement: **251,083** CapCity orders: **29,400**
Prisoner Of The Flesh **A:** John Byrne **W:** John Byrne ★ Appearance of Doctor Doom.

288 ❑ Mar 1986 Cover: 0.75 **NM** value: **2.00**
Circ: Statement: **251,083** CapCity orders: **33,300**
Secret Wars II • Secret Wars II; Doom vs. Beyonder; Doctor Doom vs. Beyonder **A:** John Byrne ★ Appearance of Doctor Doom.

289 ❑ Apr 1986 Cover: 0.75 **NM** value: **2.00**
Circ: Statement: **251,083** CapCity orders: **29,700**

290 ❑ May 1986 Cover: 0.75 **NM** value: **2.00**
Circ: Statement: **251,083** CapCity orders: **29,300**
Risk **A:** John Byrne **W:** John Byrne

291 ❑ Jun 1986 Cover: 0.75 **NM** value: **2.00**
Circ: Statement: **251,083** CapCity orders: **29,800**
The Times They Are A' Changing! • Has 1985 Statement, filed 10/1/85; avg print run 431,493; avg sales 248,594; avg subs 16,166; avg total paid 264,760; samples 165; office use 715; max existent 265,640; 38% of run returned **A:** John Byrne **W:** John Byrne

292 ❑ Jul 1986 Cover: 0.75 **NM** value: **2.00**
Circ: Statement: **251,083** CapCity orders: **29,900**
The Man Who Dreamed The World! **A:** John Byrne **W:** John Byrne ★ Appearance of Nick Fury.

293 ❑ Aug 1986 Cover: 0.75 **NM** value: **2.00**
Circ: Statement: **251,083** CapCity orders: **30,000**
Central City Does Not Answer! **A:** John Byrne

294 ❑ Sep 1986 Cover: 0.75 **NM** value: **2.00**
Circ: Statement: **251,083** CapCity orders: **27,200**
Hero Worship **A:** Jerry Ordway **W:** Roger Stern

295 ❑ Nov 1986 Cover: 0.75 **NM** value: **2.00**
Circ: Statement: **251,083** CapCity orders: **27,500**
Welcome To The Future! **A:** Jerry Ordway **W:** Roger Stern

296 ❑ Nov 1986 Cover: 1.50 **NM** value: **2.50**
Circ: Statement: **251,083** CapCity orders: **43,600**
• Double-size. • Thing comes back

297 ❑ Dec 1986 Cover: 0.75 **NM** value: **2.00**
Circ: Statement: **251,083** CapCity orders: **27,200**
Heart Of The Sun! **A:** John Buscema; Sal Buscema **W:** Roger Stern

298 ❑ Jan 1987 Cover: 0.75 **NM** value: **2.00**
Circ: Statement: **216,108** CapCity orders: **26,400**
Closer Than Brothers! **A:** John Buscema; Sal Buscema **W:** Roger Stern

299 ❑ Feb 1987 Cover: 0.75 **NM** value: **2.00**
Circ: Statement: **216,108** CapCity orders: **24,100**

300 ❑ Mar 1987 Cover: 0.75 **NM** value: **2.50**
Circ: Statement: **216,108** CapCity orders: **36,500**
Dearly Beloved… • Wedding of Johnny Storm and Alicia; "Alicia" later revealed to be Lyja (a Skrull) **A:** John Buscema; Sal Buscema **W:** Roger Stern

301 ❑ Apr 1987 Cover: 0.75 **NM** value: **2.00**
Circ: Statement: **216,108** CapCity orders: **26,500**
Dark Dreams **A:** John Buscema **W:** Roger Stern; Tom DeFalco

302 ❑ May 1987 Cover: 0.75 **NM** value: **2.00**
Circ: Statement: **216,108** CapCity orders: **25,300**
And Who Shall Survive?! • Has 1986 Statement, filed 10/6/86; avg print run 419,735; avg sales 240,458; avg subs 10,625; avg total paid 251,083; samples 225; office use 5,655; max existent 256,963; 39% of run returned **A:** John Buscema; Sal Buscema **W:** Roger Stern; Tom DeFalco

303 ❑ Jun 1987 Cover: 0.75 **NM** value: **2.00**
Circ: Statement: **216,108** CapCity orders: **24,300**
Alternatives **A:** John Buscema **W:** Roy Thomas

304 ❑ Jul 1987 Cover: 0.75 **NM** value: **2.00**
Circ: Statement: **216,108** CapCity orders: **23,700**
Pressure Drop • Reed and Sue take leave of absence **A:** John Buscema; Joe Sinnott **W:** Steve Englehart

305 ❑ Aug 1987 Cover: 0.75 **NM** value: **2.00**
Circ: Statement: **216,108** CapCity orders: **24,300**
All In The Family! **A:** John Buscema; Joe Sinnott **W:** Steve Englehart

306 ❑ Sep 1987 Cover: 0.75 **NM** value: **2.00**
Circ: Statement: **216,108** CapCity orders: **25,300**

307 ❑ Oct 1987 Cover: 0.75 **NM** value: **2.00**
Circ: Statement: **216,108** CapCity orders: **25,600**
• Crystal and new Ms. Marvel joins team

308 ❑ Nov 1987 Cover: 0.75 **NM** value: **2.00**
Circ: Statement: **216,108** CapCity orders: **26,100**
Fasaud! **A:** John Buscema; Joe Sinnott **W:** Steve Englehart ★ 1st Appearance of Fasaud.

309 ❑ Dec 1987 Cover: 0.75 **NM** value: **2.00**
Circ: Statement: **216,108** CapCity orders: **26,900**
Danger On The Air! **A:** John Buscema; Joe Sinnott **W:** Steve Englehart

310 ❑ Jan 1988 Cover: 0.75 **NM** value: **2.00**
Circ: Statement: **188,305** CapCity orders: **26,475**
• Ms. Marvel becomes She-Thing

311 ❑ Feb 1988 Cover: 0.75 **NM** value: **2.00**
Circ: Statement: **188,305** CapCity orders: **26,600**

312 ❑ Mar 1988 Cover: 0.75 **NM** value: **2.00**
Circ: Statement: **188,305** CapCity orders: **29,400**
Fall of the Mutants • Fall of Mutants ★ Appearance of Doctor Doom.

313 ❑ Apr 1988 Cover: 0.75 **NM** value: **2.00**
Circ: Statement: **188,305** CapCity orders: **27,800**
• Has 1987 Statement, filed 10/1/87; avg print run 381,784; avg sales 206,708; avg subs 9,400; avg total paid 218,940; 43% of run returned

314 ❑ May 1988 Cover: 0.75 **NM** value: **2.00**
Circ: Statement: **188,305** CapCity orders: **26,600**
The Scenic Route! **A:** Keith Pollard; Joe Sinnott **W:** Steve Englehart ★ Versus Belasco.

315 ❑ Jun 1988 Cover: 0.75 **NM** value: **2.00**
Circ: Statement: **188,305** CapCity orders: **26,200**
No Way Out! **A:** Keith Pollard; Joe Sinnott **W:** Steve Englehart

316 ❑ Jul 1988 Cover: 0.75 **NM** value: **2.00**
Circ: Statement: **188,305** CapCity orders: **25,900**
Cold Storage! **A:** Keith Pollard; Joe Sinnott **W:** Steve Englehart

317 ❑ Aug 1988 Cover: 0.75 **NM** value: **2.00**
Circ: Statement: **188,305** CapCity orders: **25,700**

318 ❑ Sep 1988 Cover: 0.75 **NM** value: **2.00**
Circ: Statement: **188,305** CapCity orders: **25,400**
• Doctor Doom

319 ❑ Oct 1988 Cover: 1.50 **NM** value: **2.50**
Circ: Statement: **188,305** CapCity orders: **25,800**
• Giant-size. • Doctor Doom v. Beyonder; Doctor Doom vs. Beyonder; Beyonder returns, merges with Molecule Man

320 ❑ Nov 1988 Cover: 0.75 **NM** value: **2.00**
Circ: Statement: **188,305** CapCity orders: **26,050**
• Thing vs. Hulk

321 ❑ Dec 1988 Cover: 0.75 **NM** value: **1.50**
Circ: Statement: **188,305** CapCity orders: **25,300**
• Ms. Marvel vs. She-Hulk ★ 1st Appearance of Aron the Rogue Watcher.

322 ❑ Jan 1989 Cover: 0.75 **NM** value: **1.50**
Circ: Statement: **180,000** CapCity orders: **29,200**
• Inferno

323 ❑ Feb 1989 Cover: 0.75 **NM** value: **1.50**
Circ: Statement: **180,000** CapCity orders: **30,000**
• Inferno

324 ❑ Mar 1989 Cover: 0.75 **NM** value: **1.50**
Circ: Statement: **180,000** CapCity orders: **30,400**
I Die Like The Stars! • Inferno **A:** Keith Pollard **W:** Steve Englehart

325 ❑ Apr 1989 Cover: 0.75 **NM** value: **1.50**
Circ: Statement: **180,000** CapCity orders: **30,200**
A Christmas Tale **A:** Rich Buckler **W:** Steve Englehart

326 ❑ May 1989 Cover: 0.75 **NM** value: **1.50**
Circ: Statement: **180,000** CapCity orders: **26,300**
• Reed and Sue return to team

327 ❑ Jun 1989 Cover: 0.75 **NM** value: **1.50**
Circ: Statement: **180,000** CapCity orders: **27,200**
• Thing reverts to human form

328 ❑ Jul 1989 Cover: 0.75 **NM** value: **1.50**
Circ: Statement: **180,000** CapCity orders: **27,100**
Bad Dream! **A:** Keith Pollard

329 ❑ Aug 1989 Cover: 0.75 **NM** value: **1.50**
Circ: Statement: **180,000** CapCity orders: **26,500**
…And You Can't Wake Up! **A:** Rich Buckler

330 ❑ Sep 1989 Cover: 1.00 **NM** value: **1.50**
Circ: Statement: **180,000** CapCity orders: **26,100**
Good Dreams! **A:** Rich Buckler ★ Versus Doom.

331 ❑ Oct 1989 Cover: 1.00 **NM** value: **1.50**
Circ: Statement: **180,000** CapCity orders: **26,700**
Metal Man! **A:** Rich Buckler ★ Versus Ultron.

332 ❑ Nov 1989 Cover: 1.00 **NM** value: **1.50**
Circ: Statement: **180,000** CapCity orders: **26,700**
Love's Labour Lost! **A:** Rich Buckler

333 ❑ Nov 1989 Cover: 1.00 **NM** value: **1.50**
Circ: Statement: **180,000** CapCity orders: **26,700**
The Dream Is Death, Part 2 **A:** Rich Buckler

334 ❑ Dec 1989 Cover: 1.00 **NM** value: **1.50**
Circ: Statement: **180,000** CapCity orders: **31,900**
Acts of Vengeance, Part 5 • Acts of Vengeance **A:** Walt Simonson

335 ❑ Dec 1989 Cover: 1.00 **NM** value: **1.50**
Circ: Statement: **180,000** CapCity orders: **30,700**
Acts of Vengeance, Part 14 • Acts of Vengeance **A:** Walt Simonson

336 ❑ Jan 1990 Cover: 1.00 **NM** value: **1.50**
Circ: Statement: **187,008** CapCity orders: **31,700**
Acts of Vengeance, Part 22 • Acts of Vengeance **A:** Walt Simonson

337 ❑ Feb 1990 Cover: 1.00 **NM** value: **2.00**
Circ: Statement: **187,008** CapCity orders: **38,300**

338 ❑ Mar 1990 Cover: 1.00 **NM** value: **2.00**
Circ: Statement: **187,008** CapCity orders: **35,400**
Kangs For The Memories! **A:** Walt Simonson **W:** Walt Simonson

339 ❑ Apr 1990 Cover: 1.00 **NM** value: **2.00**
Circ: Statement: **187,008** CapCity orders: **33,000**

340 ❑ May 1990 Cover: 1.00 **NM** value: **2.00**
Circ: Statement: **187,008** CapCity orders: **33,900**

341 ❑ Jun 1990 Cover: 1.00 **NM** value: **2.00**
Circ: Statement: **187,008** CapCity orders: **33,900**
The Ultimate Solution • Has 1989 Statement, filed 11/1/89; avg print run 296,375; avg sales 173,700; avg subs 6,300; avg total paid 180,000; samples 150; office use 600; max existent 180,750; 39% of run returned **A:** Walt Simonson **W:** Walt Simonson

342 ❑ Jul 1990 Cover: 1.00 **NM** value: **2.00**
Circ: Statement: **187,008** CapCity orders: **34,800**
Burnout! **A:** Rex Valve **W:** Danny Fingeroth ★ Appearance of Spider-Man.

343 ❑ Aug 1990 Cover: 1.00 **NM** value: **2.00**

CGC-graded: Multiply prices above by **33 for 9.9 M • 16 for 9.8 NM/M • 7 for 9.6 NM+ • 5 for 9.4 NM • 2.5 for 9.2 NM- • 1.5 for 9.0 VF/NM**

Circ: Statement: **187,008** CapCity orders: **33,600**
Nukebusters! **A:** Walt Simonson **W:** Walt Simonson

344 ❑ Sep 1990 Cover: 1.00 **NM** value: **2.00**
Circ: Statement: **187,008** CapCity orders: **33,000**
Nukebusters II **A:** Walt Simonson **W:** Walt Simonson

345 ❑ Oct 1990 Cover: 1.00 **NM** value: **2.00**
Circ: Statement: **187,008** CapCity orders: **31,200**
The Mesozoic Mambo! **A:** Walt Simonson

346 ❑ Nov 1990 Cover: 1.00 **NM** value: **2.00**
Circ: Statement: **187,008** CapCity orders: **30,300**
70 Million Years BC...And Then Some! **A:** Walt Simonson **W:** Walt Simonson

347 ❑ Dec 1990 Cover: 1.00 **NM** value: **2.50**
Circ: Statement: **187,008** CapCity orders: **47,400** • **CGC:** 1 graded, best 9.4
Big Trouble On Little Earth! **A:** Arthur Adams; Walt Simonson **W:** Walt Simonson ★ Appearance of Hulk, Ghost Rider, Wolverine, Spider-Man.

347-2 ❑ Dec 1990 Cover: 1.00 **NM** value: **1.50**
• **CGC:** 1 graded, best 9.4

348 ❑ Jan 1991 Cover: 1.00 **NM** value: **2.50**
Circ: Statement: **221,792** CapCity orders: **73,000** • **CGC:** 2 graded, best 9.6
Where Monsters Dwell! **A:** Arthur Adams; Walt Simonson **W:** Walt Simonson ★ Appearance of Hulk, Ghost Rider, Wolverine, Spider-Man.

348-2 ❑ Jan 1991 Cover: 1.00 **NM** value: **1.50**
• **CGC:** 1 graded, best 9.6

349 ❑ Feb 1991 Cover: 1.00 **NM** value: **2.50**
Circ: Statement: **221,792** CapCity orders: **79,200** • **CGC:** 2 graded, best 9.6
Eggs Got Legs! **A:** Arthur Adams; Walt Simonson **W:** Walt Simonson ★ Appearance of Punisher, Hulk, Ghost Rider, Wolverine, Spider-Man.

350 ❑ Mar 1991 Cover: 1.50 **NM** value: **2.50**
Circ: Statement: **221,792** CapCity orders: **46,200**
• Giant-size. The More Things Change...! • Return of Thing; Has 1990 Statement, filed 10/1/90; avg print run 310,723; avg sales 181,450; avg subs 5,558; avg total paid 187,008; samples 150; office use 600; max existent 187,758; 40% of run returned **A:** Walt Simonson **W:** Walt Simonson ★ Appearance of Doctor Doom.

351 ❑ Apr 1991 Cover: 1.00 **NM** value: **2.00**
Circ: Statement: **221,792** CapCity orders: **30,600**
Strange Interlude **A:** Mark Bagley **W:** Len Kaminski

352 ❑ May 1991 Cover: 1.00 **NM** value: **2.00**
Circ: Statement: **221,792** CapCity orders: **33,900**
No Time Like The Present! • Reed and Doctor Doom battle through time **A:** Walt Simonson **W:** Walt Simonson

353 ❑ Jun 1991 Cover: 1.00 **NM** value: **2.00**
Circ: Statement: **221,792** CapCity orders: **34,500**
So Little Time, So Much To Do **A:** Walt Simonson **W:** Walt Simonson

354 ❑ Jul 1991 Cover: 1.00 **NM** value: **2.00**
Circ: Statement: **221,792** CapCity orders: **35,400**
The Cross Time Express! **A:** Walt Simonson **W:** Walt Simonson

355 ❑ Aug 1991 Cover: 1.00 **NM** value: **2.00**
Circ: Statement: **221,792** CapCity orders: **33,000**
Rage **A:** Al Milgrom **W:** Danny Fingeroth

356 ❑ Sep 1991 Cover: 1.00 **NM** value: **2.00**
Circ: Statement: **221,792** CapCity orders: **36,900**
War With The New Warriors! • Alicia is Skrull; Fantastic Four vs. New Warriors **A:** Paul Ryan **W:** Tom DeFalco

357 ❑ Oct 1991 Cover: 1.00 **NM** value: **2.00**
Circ: Statement: **221,792** CapCity orders: **33,900**
The Monster Among Us! • Skrull's identity revealed as Lyja **A:** Paul Ryan **W:** Tom DeFalco ★ 1st Appearance of Lyja (in true form).

358 ❑ Nov 1991 Cover: 2.50 **NM** value: **Cover or less**
Circ: Statement: **221,792** • **CGC:** 1 graded, best 9.2
Die-cut cover. • 30th Anniversary Issue. Whatever Happened To Alicia?! **A:** Paul Ryan **W:** Tom DeFalco ★ Origin of Paibok the Power Skrull. ★ 1st Appearance of Paibok the Power Skrull.

359 ❑ Dec 1991 Cover: 1.00 **NM** value: **1.50**
Circ: Statement: **221,792** CapCity orders: **33,900**
Devos The Devastator! • The real Alicia returns **A:** Paul Ryan **W:** Tom DeFalco ★ 1st Appearance of Devos the Devastator.

360 ❑ Jan 1992 Cover: 1.00 **NM** value: **1.50**
Circ: Statement: **205,542** CapCity orders: **32,700**
At The Mercy Of Dreadface! **A:** Paul Ryan **W:** Tom DeFalco

361 ❑ Feb 1992 Cover: 1.25 **NM** value: **1.50**
Circ: Statement: **205,542** CapCity orders: **30,900**
Miracle On Yancy Street • Doctor Doom **A:** Paul Ryan; Tom DeFalco **W:** Paul Ryan; Tom DeFalco

362 ❑ Mar 1992 Cover: 1.25 **NM** value: **1.50**
Circ: Statement: **205,542** CapCity orders: **34,800**
Here Comes The Wild Blood! • Has 1991 Statement, filed 10/1/91; avg print run 318,275; avg sales 217,200; avg subs 4,592; avg total paid 221,792; samples 125; office use 250; max existent 222,167; 30% of run returned **A:** Paul Ryan; Tom DeFalco **W:** Paul Ryan; Tom DeFalco

363 ❑ Apr 1992 Cover: 1.25 **NM** value: **1.50**
Circ: Statement: **205,542** CapCity orders: **28,200**
Innerverse **A:** Paul Ryan; Tom DeFalco **W:** Paul Ryan; Tom DeFalco ★ Origin of Occulus. ★ 1st Appearance of Occulus.

364 ❑ May 1992 Cover: 1.25 **NM** value: **1.50**
Circ: Statement: **205,542** CapCity orders: **27,900**
Omnipotent Is Occulus! **A:** Paul Ryan; Tom DeFalco **W:** Paul Ryan; Tom DeFalco

365 ❑ Jun 1992 Cover: 1.25 **NM** value: **1.50**
Circ: Statement: **205,542** CapCity orders: **28,800**
With Defeat Comes Death! **A:** Paul Ryan; Tom DeFalco **W:** Paul Ryan; Tom DeFalco

366 ❑ Jul 1992 Cover: 1.25 **NM** value: **1.50**
Circ: Statement: **205,542** CapCity orders: **43,100**
Infinity War **A:** Paul Ryan; Tom DeFalco **W:** Paul Ryan; Tom DeFalco

367 ❑ Aug 1992 Cover: 1.25 **NM** value: **1.50**
Circ: Statement: **205,542** CapCity orders: **40,500**
Infinity War

368 ❑ Sep 1992 Cover: 1.25 **NM** value: **1.50**
Circ: Statement: **205,542** CapCity orders: **43,200**
Infinity War **A:** Paul Ryan; Tom DeFalco **W:** Paul Ryan; Tom DeFalco

369 ❑ Oct 1992 Cover: 1.25 **NM** value: **1.50**
Circ: Statement: **205,542** CapCity orders: **37,200**
Infinity War **A:** Paul Ryan; Tom DeFalco **W:** Paul Ryan; Tom DeFalco

370 ❑ Nov 1992 Cover: 1.25 **NM** value: **1.50**
Circ: Statement: **205,542** CapCity orders: **34,200**
Infinity War **A:** Paul Ryan; Tom DeFalco **W:** Paul Ryan; Tom DeFalco ★ 1st Appearance of Lyja the Lazerfist.

371 ❑ Dec 1992 Cover: 2.00 **NM** value: **3.50**
Circ: Statement: **205,542** CapCity orders: **52,500** • **CGC:** 6 graded, best 9.8
All-white embossed cover. This Flame, This Fury **A:** Paul Ryan; Tom DeFalco **W:** Paul Ryan; Tom DeFalco

371-2 ❑ Dec 1992 Cover: 2.00 **NM** value: **2.50**
Circ: CapCity orders: **36,100** • **CGC:** 1 graded, best 9.6

372 ❑ Jan 1993 Cover: 1.25 **NM** value: **Cover or less**
Circ: Statement: **217,625** CapCity orders: **27,800**

373 ❑ Feb 1993 Cover: 1.25 **NM** value: **Cover or less**
Circ: Statement: **217,625** CapCity orders: **26,800**

374 ❑ Mar 1993 Cover: 1.25 **NM** value: **Cover or less**
Circ: Statement: **217,625** CapCity orders: **52,200**
• Spider-Man, Hulk, Ghost Rider, Wolverine team up again; Secret Defenders x-over

375 ❑ Apr 1993 Cover: 2.95 **NM** value: **3.00**
Circ: Statement: **217,625** CapCity orders: **84,400**
Prism cover. It Is Always Darkest Before The...Doom! **A:** Paul Ryan; Tom DeFalco **W:** Paul Ryan; Tom DeFalco

376 ❑ May 1993 Cover: 1.25 **NM** value: **Cover or less**
Circ: Statement: **217,625** CapCity orders: **26,200**
To A Future Darkly! • Franklin returns from future as a young man **A:** Paul Ryan; Tom DeFalco **W:** Paul Ryan; Tom DeFalco

377 ❑ Jun 1993 Cover: 1.25 **NM** value: **Cover or less**
Circ: Statement: **217,625** CapCity orders: **31,500**
If This Be War! • Secret Defenders x-over **A:** Paul Ryan; Tom DeFalco **W:** Paul Ryan; Tom DeFalco ★ 1st Appearance of Huntara.

378 ❑ Jul 1993 Cover: 1.25 **NM** value: **Cover or less**
Circ: Statement: **217,625** CapCity orders: **35,500**

379 ❑ Aug 1993 Cover: 1.25 **NM** value: **1.50**
Circ: Statement: **217,625** CapCity orders: **34,700**

380 ❑ Sep 1993 Cover: 1.25 **NM** value: **1.50**
Circ: Statement: **217,625** CapCity orders: **32,100**

381 ❑ Oct 1993 Cover: 1.25 **NM** value: **3.00**
Circ: Statement: **217,625** CapCity orders: **31,700** • **CGC:** 1 graded, best 9.6

382 ❑ Nov 1993 Cover: 1.25 **NM** value: **2.00**
Circ: Statement: **217,625** CapCity orders: **31,100**

383 ❑ Dec 1993 Cover: 1.25 **NM** value: **Cover or less**
Circ: Statement: **217,625** CapCity orders: **32,300**

384 ❑ Jan 1994 Cover: 1.25 **NM** value: **Cover or less**
Circ: Statement: **151,275** CapCity orders: **34,200**

385 ❑ Feb 1994 Cover: 1.25 **NM** value: **Cover or less**
Circ: Statement: **151,275** CapCity orders: **33,000**
Starblast, Part 7

386 ❑ Mar 1994 Cover: 1.25 **NM** value: **Cover or less**
Circ: Statement: **151,275** CapCity orders: **31,550**
Starblast, Part 11 • Birth of Lyja's baby ★ 1st Appearance of Egg (Lyja's baby).

387 ❑ Apr 1994 Cover: 1.25 **NM** value: **Cover or less**
Nobody Gets Out Alive! **A:** Paul Ryan; Tom DeFalco **W:** Paul Ryan; Tom DeFalco

387/SC ❑ Apr 1994 Cover: 2.95 **NM** value: **3.00**
Circ: Statement: **151,275** CapCity orders: **54,050**
diecut cover.

388 ❑ May 1994 Cover: 1.50 **NM** value: **Cover or less**
Circ: Statement: **151,275** CapCity orders: **34,350**
• cards ★ Appearance of Avengers.

389 ❑ Jun 1994 Cover: 1.50 **NM** value: **Cover or less**
Circ: Statement: **151,275** CapCity orders: **34,300**

390 ❑ Jun 1994 Cover: 1.50 **NM** value: **Cover or less**
Circ: Statement: **151,275** CapCity orders: **33,750**

391 ❑ Aug 1994 Cover: 1.50 **NM** value: **Cover or less**
Circ: Statement: **151,275** CapCity orders: **37,300**

392 ❑ Sep 1994 Cover: 1.50 **NM** value: **Cover or less**
Circ: Statement: **151,275** CapCity orders: **36,750**

393 ❑ Oct 1994 Cover: 1.50 **NM** value: **Cover or less**
Circ: Statement: **151,275** CapCity orders: **31,300**
• Nathaniel Richards takes over Latveria ★ Appearance of Puppet Master.

394 ❑ Nov 1994 Cover: 1.50 **NM** value: **Cover or less**

394/CS ❑ Nov 1994 Cover: 2.95 **NM** value: **Cover or less**
Circ: Statement: **103,573** CapCity orders: **30,350**
• polybagged with 16-page Marvel Action Hour preview, acetate print, and other items

395 ❑ Dec 1994 Cover: 1.50 **NM** value: **Cover or less**
Circ: Statement: **103,573** CapCity orders: **38,050**

396 ❑ Jan 1995 Cover: 1.50 **NM** value: **Cover or less**
Circ: Statement: **103,573** CapCity orders: **27,625**

397 ❑ Feb 1995 Cover: 1.50 **NM** value: **Cover or less**
Circ: Statement: **103,573** CapCity orders: **26,000**

398 ❑ Mar 1995 Cover: 1.50 **NM** value: **Cover or less**
Watcher's Lie, Part 1

398/SC ❑ Mar 1995 Cover: 2.50 **NM** value: **Cover or less**
Circ: Statement: **103,573** CapCity orders: **24,750**
foil cover. Watcher's Lie, Part 1

399 ❑ Apr 1995 Cover: 1.50 **NM** value: **Cover or less**
Watcher's Lie, Part 2

399/SC ❑ Apr 1995 Cover: 2.50 **NM** value: **Cover or less**
Circ: Statement: **103,573** CapCity orders: **23,875**
enhanced cardstock cover. Watcher's Lie, Part 2

400 ❑ May 1995 Cover: 3.95 **NM** value: **Cover or less**
Circ: Statement: **103,573** CapCity orders: **33,900** • **CGC:** 1 graded, best 8.5
foil cover. • Giant-size. Watcher's Lie, Part 3

401 ❑ Jun 1995 Cover: 1.50 **NM** value: **Cover or less**
Circ: Statement: **103,573** CapCity orders: **22,675**
Atlantis Rising, Part 4

402 ❑ Jul 1995 Cover: 1.50 **NM** value: **Cover or less**
Circ: Statement: **103,573** CapCity orders: **22,350**
• Atlantis Rising ★ Appearance of Thor.

403 ❑ Aug 1995 Cover: 1.50 **NM** value: **Cover or less**
Circ: Statement: **103,573**

404 ❑ Sep 1995 Cover: 1.50 **NM** value: **Cover or less**
Circ: Statement: **103,573**

405 ❑ Oct 1995 Cover: 1.50 **NM** value: **Cover or less**
Circ: Statement: **103,573**
• The Thing becomes human ★ Appearance of Iron Man 2020, Conan, Red Raven, Young Allies, Zarko, Green Goblin.

406 ❑ Nov 1995 Cover: 1.50 **NM** value: **Cover or less**
Circ: Statement: **105,506**
• Return of Doctor Doom ★ 1st Appearance of Hyperstorm.

407 ❑ Dec 1995 Cover: 1.50 **NM** value: **Cover or less**
Circ: Statement: **105,506**
Return of Reed Richards • Return of Reed Richards **A:** Paul Ryan **W:** Tom DeFalco

408 ❑ Jan 1996 Cover: 1.50 **NM** value: **Cover or less**
Circ: Statement: **105,506**
Strange Days • Has 1995 Statement, filed 10/1/95; avg pring run 168,905; avg sales 98,473; avg subs 5,100; avg total paid 103,573; samples 750; office use 500; max existent 104,823; 38% of run returned ★ Versus Hyperstorm.

409 ❑ Feb 1996 Cover: 1.50 **NM** value: **Cover or less**
Circ: Statement: **105,506**
• The Thing's face is healed

410 ❑ Mar 1996 Cover: 1.50 **NM** value: **Cover or less**
Circ: Statement: **105,506**
The Ties That Bind! **A:** Paul Ryan; Tom DeFalco **W:** Paul Ryan; Tom DeFalco ★ Origin of Kristoff.

411 ❑ Apr 1996 Cover: 1.50 **NM** value: **Cover or less**
Circ: Statement: **105,506**
Black Bolt...Berserk! **A:** Paul Ryan **W:** Tom DeFalco ★ Appearance of Inhumans. ★ Versus Black Bolt.

412 ❑ May 1996 Cover: 1.50 **NM** value: **Cover or less**
Circ: Statement: **105,506**

413 ❑ Jun 1996 Cover: 1.50 **NM** value: **Cover or less**
Circ: Statement: **105,506**
• Franklin Richards becomes a child again

414 ❑ Jul 1996 Cover: 1.50 **NM** value: **Cover or less**
Circ: Statement: **105,506**

415 ❑ Aug 1996 Cover: 1.50 **NM** value: **2.00**
Circ: Statement: **105,506**
Onslaught: Phase 1; Onslaught • Franklin captured by Onslaught

416 ❑ Sep 1996 Cover: 2.50 **NM** value: **3.50**
Circ: Statement: **105,506** • **CGC:** 2 graded, best 9.8
wraparound cover. • Giant-size. Onslaught: Phase 2; Onslaught final issue.

Anl 1 ❑ ca. 1963 Cover: 0.25 **NM** value: **500.00**
• **CGC:** 65 graded, best 9.6
Sub-Mariner Versus the Human Race; A Gallery of the Fantastic Four's Most Famous Foes; Questions and Answers About the Fantastic Four; Inside the Baxter Building; The Fabulous Fantastic Four Meet Spider-Man; The Origin of the Fantastic Four • Spider-Man; reprints FF #1 **A:** Jack Kirby ★ Origin of Fantastic Four, Sub-Mariner. ★ 1st Appearance of Krang. ★ Appearance of Spider-Man, Doctor Doom, Sub-Mariner. ★ Versus Sub-Mariner.

Anl 2 ❑ ca. 1964 Cover: 0.25 **NM** value: **275.00**
• **CGC:** 34 graded, best 9.6
The Origin of Doctor Doom; A Gallery of the Fantastic Four's Most Famous Foes; Prisoners of Doctor Doom; The Final Victory of Doctor Doom • reprints FF #5 ★ Origin of Doctor Doom. ★ 1st Appearance of Boris.

Anl 3 ❑ ca. 1965 Cover: 0.25 **NM** value: **110.00**
• **CGC:** 31 graded, best 9.6
Bedlam at the Baxter Building; Captives of the Deadly Duo; A Visit with the Fantastic Four; The Impossible Man • Wedding of Reed Richards and Susan Storm; Virtually all Marvel super-heroes appear; reprints FF #6 and 11

Anl 4 ❑ Nov 1966 Cover: 0.25 **NM** value: **55.00**
• **CGC:** 25 graded, best 9.8
The Torch That Was; The Hulk vs. the Thing; The Avengers Take Over • Return of Golden Age Human Torch; reprints FF #25 and 26 **A:** Jack Kirby **W:** Jack Kirby; Stan Lee ★ 1st Appearance of Quasimodo.

Anl 5 ❑ Nov 1967 Cover: 0.25 **NM** value: **70.00**
• **CGC:** 38 graded, best 9.6
Divide and Conquer; This Is a Plot?; The Incomparable Inhumans; The Greatest Array of Supporting Characters Ever Assembled in One Issue; (Untitled); The Peerless Power of the Silver Surfer **A:** Jack Kirby **W:** Jack Kirby; Stan Lee ★ 1st Appearance of Psycho-Man. ★ Appearance of Inhumans, Black Panther, Inhumans, Black Panther.

Anl 6 ❑ Nov 1968 Cover: 0.25 **NM** value: **45.00**
• **CGC:** 13 graded, best 9.6
Let There Be Life **A:** Jack Kirby **W:** Jack Kirby; Stan Lee ★ 1st Appearance of Franklin Richards, Annihilus.

Anl 7 ❑ Nov 1969 Cover: 0.25 **NM** value: **18.00**
• **CGC:** 7 graded, best 9.4
The Fantastic Four Meet the Mole Man; The Moleman's Secret; Origin of Doctor Doom; The Final Victory of Dr. Doom; Because You Demanded It • reprints FF #1, FF Annual #2 **A:** Jack Kirby **W:** Jack Kirby; Stan Lee

Anl 8 ❑ Dec 1970 Cover: 0.25 **NM** value: **12.00**
• **CGC:** 4 graded, best 9.6
Sub-Mariner Versus the Human Race; Inside the Baxter Bldg.; A Gallery of the Fantastic Four's Most Famous Foes; Questions and Answers About the Fantastic Four • reprints FF Annual #1 **A:** Jack Kirby

Anl 9 ❑ Dec 1971 Cover: 0.25 **NM** value: **10.00**
Lo, There Shall Be an Ending; The Bouncing Ball of Doom; Bedlam at the Baxter Building • reprints stories from FF #43, Annual #3, and Strange Tales #131 **A:** Jack Kirby **W:** Jack Kirby; Stan Lee

Anl 10 ❑ ca. 1973 Cover: 0.35 **NM** value: **8.00**
• **CGC:** 2 graded, best 9.4

Other grades: Multiply prices above by **1.5 for Mint • 2/3 for Very Fine • 1/3 for Fine • 1/5 for Very Good • 1/8 for Good**

🕮 Bedlam at the Baxter Building; The Torch That Was • reprints stories from FF Annual #3 and 4; Reprints wedding of Reed and Sue Richards **A:** Jack Kirby **W:** Jack Kirby; Stan Lee

Anl 11❑ca. 1976 Cover: 0.50 **NM value: 6.00**
• **CGC:** 1 graded, best 9.4
🕮 And Then the Invaders; Nine Against Destiny **A:** John Buscema **C:** Jack Kirby **W:** Roy Thomas ★ Appearance of The Watcher, Invaders. ★ Versus Invaders.

Anl 12❑ca. 1977 Cover: 0.60 **NM value: 5.00**
🕮 The End of the Inhumans and the Fantastic Four; Hither Comes Crystal; Hollywood, Here We Are; Battle for the Great Refuge; And into Space; The Sphinx **A:** Keith Pollard; Bob Hall **W:** Marv Wolfman ★ Appearance of Karnak, Sphinx, Medusa, Crystal, Triton, Quicksilver, Lockjaw, Gorgon, Black Bolt.

Anl 13❑ca. 1978 Cover: 0.60 **NM value: 5.00**
🕮 Nightlife; Encounter; Confrontation; Pursuit; Battle **A:** Sal Buscema **W:** Bill Mantlo ★ Appearance of Daredevil, Mole Man.

Anl 14❑ca. 1979 Cover: 0.75 **NM value: 5.00**
🕮 Cat's Paw **A:** George Pérez **W:** Marv Wolfman

Anl 15❑ca. 1980 Cover: 0.75 **NM value: 3.00**
• **CGC:** 1 graded, best 9.6
🕮 Time For The Prime Ten • Skrulls **A:** George Pérez; Chic Stone; Jon D'Agostino; Mike Esposito **W:** Doug Moench

Anl 16❑ca. 1982 Cover: 0.75 **NM value: 3.00**
🕮 The Coming Of Dragon Lord! **A:** Steve Ditko; John Byrne **W:** Ed Hannigan

Anl 17❑ca. 1983 Cover: 1.00 **NM value: 3.00**
🕮 Legacy **A:** John Byrne **W:** John Byrne

Anl 18❑ca. 1984 Cover: 1.00 **NM value: 3.00**
🕮 Something Old, Something New! • Kree-Skrull War **A:** Mark D. Bright **W:** John Byrne

Anl 19❑ca. 1985 Cover: 1.25 **NM value: 3.00**
Circ: CapCity orders: **23,900**

Anl 20❑ca. 1986 Cover: 1.25 **NM value: 3.00**
Circ: CapCity orders: **25,600**

Anl 21❑ca. 1988 Cover: 1.75 **NM value: 3.00**
Circ: CapCity orders: **28,500**
🕮 Evolutionary War, Part 6

Anl 22❑ca. 1989 Cover: 2.00 **NM value: 3.00**
Circ: CapCity orders: **39,400**
🕮 Atlantis Attacks, Part 14 • Atlantis Attacks **A:** Rich Buckler; Mark Bagley; Ron Lim; Tom Morgan; Hilary Barta **W:** Greg Wright; Roy Thomas; Mark Gruenwald; Peter Sanderson

Anl 23❑ca. 1990 Cover: 2.00 **NM value: 3.00**
Circ: CapCity orders: **48,400**
🕮 Future Present; Days of Future Present, Part 1 ★ 1st Appearance of Kosmos.

Anl 24❑ca. 1991 Cover: 2.00 **NM value: 2.50**
🕮 Korvac Quest, Part 1 • Korvac Quest **A:** James Brock **W:** James Brock ★ Origin of Fantastic Four. ★ Appearance of Guardians of Galaxy.

Anl 25❑ca. 1992 Cover: 2.25 **NM value: 2.50**
Circ: CapCity orders: **26,300**
🕮 Citizen Kang, Part 3 • Citizen Kang **A:** Kirk Jarvinen; Herb Trimpe; Rich Yanizeski; Karl Altstaetter; Larry Alexander **W:** George Caragonne; Tom DeFalco; Mark Gruenwald; Peter Sanderson; Sonja Ratcliffe ★ 1st Appearance of Temptress.

Anl 26❑ca. 1993 Cover: 2.95 **NM value: 3.00**
Circ: CapCity orders: **38,800**
• Polybagged with trading card★ 1st Appearance of Wildstreak.

Anl 27❑ca. 1994 Cover: 2.95 **NM value: 3.00**
Circ: CapCity orders: **19,500**

Ash 1❑ Cover: 0.75 **NM value: Cover or less**
• ashcan edition. ★ Origin of Fantastic Four.

Bk 1❑ Cover: 14.95 **NM value: Cover or less**
Circ: CapCity orders: **7,100**
🕮 Essential Fantastic Four • Collects issues #1-24

GS 1❑ca. 1974 Cover: 0.35 **NM value: 15.00**
🕮 The Mind of the Monster; Someone's Been Sleeping in My Head; And in This Corner: The Incredible Hulk; In the Beginning (text); Giant-Size Super-Stacks (text); Rogues' Gallery • Thing battles Hulk **A:** Rich Buckler; Jack Kirby **W:** Roy Thomas; Stan Lee; Gerry Conway

GS 2❑ca. 1974 Cover: 0.50 **NM value: 8.00**
🕮 Cataclysm!; George Washington Almost Slept Here; The Great Grimmsby; Time Enough for Death; The Fantastic Four vs. the Red Ghost and His Indescribable Super-Apes! • Reprints FF #13

GS 3❑ca. 1974 Cover: 0.50 **NM value: 7.00**
🕮 Where Lurks Death, Ride the Four Horsemen; There Shall Come Pestilence; And War Shall Take the Land; And the Children Shall Hunger; All In the Valley Of Death; The Hate-Monger • Reprints FF #21

GS 4❑ca. 1975 Cover: 0.50 **NM value: 8.00**
🕮 Madrox the Multiple Man; We Have to Fight the X-Men • reprints FF #28 **A:** John Buscema; Jack Kirby **W:** Jack Kirby; Len Wein; Stan Lee; Chris Claremont ★ Origin of Madrox the Multiple Man. ★ 1st Appearance of Madrox the Multiple Man. ★ Appearance of Professor X, Medusa.

GS 5❑ca. 1975 Cover: 0.50 **NM value: 6.00**
🕮 Divide and Conquer; The Fantastic Four Battle the Mad Thinker and His Awesome Android • Reprints FF #15 and Annual #5

GS 6❑ca. 1975 Cover: 0.50 **NM value: 6.00**
🕮 Let There Be Life • Reprints FF Annual #6

SE 1❑ Cover: 2.00 **NM value: 2.50**
🕮 Sub-Mariner Versus the Human Race • Reprints Sub-Mariner vs. Fantastic Four from Annual #1 with added material **A:** John Byrne

There are two different pricing tiers in the modern comic-book hobby. **The prices seen above** are the prices we have seen **loose copies** of these issues reliably fetch in a variety of environments. Condition alters the price by the fractions seen on the bar on the bottom of left-hand pages of this book. **Comics graded by CGC** usually sell for more. Use the guide on the bottom of right-hand pages of this book to estimate what copies have brought on eBay.

FANTASTIC FOUR (VOL. 2) Marvel

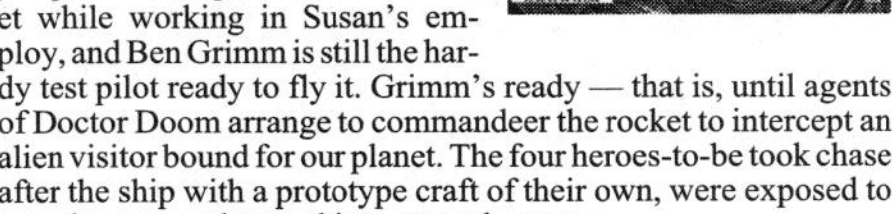

In 1996, Marvel's "Heroes Reborn" strategy turned control of its core titles over to Image, where Marvel alumni Jim Lee, Rob Liefeld, and others gave new origins to classic characters such as Iron Man, The Avengers, and The Fantastic Four.

In this revised version of the World's Greatest Comics Magazine, The Fantastic Four get their start in the mid-1990s. Here, Susan Storm is a powerful businesswoman, her brother Johnny is a hotshot casino manager, Reed Richards has just perfected a quantum drive rocket while working in Susan's employ, and Ben Grimm is still the hardy test pilot ready to fly it. Grimm's ready — that is, until agents of Doctor Doom arrange to commandeer the rocket to intercept an alien visitor bound for our planet. The four heroes-to-be took chase after the ship with a prototype craft of their own, were exposed to cosmic rays, and turned into super-heroes.

1 ❑ Nov 1996 Cover: 2.95 **NM value: 3.00**
Circ: Direct Market orders: **314,000** • **CGC:** 8 graded, best 9.8
🕮 Renaissance **A:** Jim Lee **W:** Jim Lee; Brandon Choi ★ Origin of Fantastic Four (new origin).

1/A ❑ Nov 1996 Cover: 2.95 **NM value: 4.00**
• **CGC:** 8 graded, best 9.8
alternate cover. 🕮 Renaissance **A:** Jim Lee **W:** Jim Lee; Brandon Choi ★ Origin of Fantastic Four (new origin).

1/B ❑ Nov 1996 **NM value: 5.00**
• **CGC:** 2 graded, best 9.8
🕮 Renaissance **A:** Jim Lee **W:** Jim Lee; Brandon Choi

2 ❑ Dec 1996 Cover: 1.95 **NM value: 2.00**
Circ: Statement: **212,554** Direct Market orders: **162,500**
🕮 Repercussions **A:** Jim Lee **W:** Jim Lee; Brandon Choi ★ Versus Namor.

3 ❑ Jan 1997 Cover: 1.95 **NM value: 2.00**
Circ: Statement: **212,554** Direct Market orders: **154,750**
🕮 Revelations **A:** Jim Lee **W:** Jim Lee; Brandon Choi ★ Appearance of Avengers. ★ Versus Namor.

4 ❑ Feb 1997 Cover: 1.95 **NM value: 2.00**
Circ: Statement: **212,554** Direct Market orders: **153,250**
🕮 The Heart Of Darkness **A:** Jim Lee **W:** Jim Lee; Brandon Choi ★ Appearance of Black Panther, Doctor Doom. ★ Versus Doctor Doom.

4/A ❑ Feb 1997 Cover: 1.95 **NM value: 2.00**
• **CGC:** 1 graded, best 9.4
🕮 The Heart Of Darkness **A:** Jim Lee **W:** Jim Lee; Brandon Choi

5 ❑ Mar 1997 Cover: 1.95 **NM value: 2.00**
Circ: Statement: **212,554** Direct Market orders: **152,750**
🕮 Auld Acquaintance **A:** Jim Lee **W:** Jim Lee; Brandon Choi ★ Versus Doctor Doom.

6 ❑ Apr 1997 Cover: 1.95 **NM value: 2.00**
Circ: Statement: **212,554** Direct Market orders: **155,750**
🕮 Industrial Revolution Prologue; Retribution; Industrial Revolution • continues in Avengers #6 **A:** Jim Lee **W:** Jim Lee; Brandon Choi ★ Appearance of Silver Surfer. ★ Versus Super Skrull.

7 ❑ May 1997 Cover: 1.95 **NM value: 2.00**
Circ: Statement: **212,554** Diamd. preorders: **153,457**
🕮 Into the Negative Zone **A:** Brett Booth **W:** Jim Lee; Brandon Choi ★ Appearance of Galactus, Wolverine, Blastaar.

8 ❑ Jun 1997 Cover: 1.95 **NM value: 2.00**
Circ: Statement: **212,554** Diamd. preorders: **154,912**
🕮 The Ties that Bind **A:** Brett Booth **W:** Jim Lee; Brandon Choi ★ Appearance of Inhumans.

9 ❑ Jul 1997 Cover: 1.99 **NM value: 2.00**
Circ: Statement: **212,554** Diamd. preorders: **142,321**

10 ❑ Aug 1997 Cover: 1.99 **NM value: 2.00**
Circ: Statement: **212,554** Diamd. preorders: **143,952**
• gatefold summary. ★ Appearance of Inhumans.

11 ❑ Sep 1997 Cover: 1.99 **NM value: 2.00**
Circ: Statement: **212,554** Diamd. preorders: **136,544**
• gatefold summary. ★ Versus Terrax.

12 ❑ Oct 1997 Cover: 1.99 **NM value: 2.99**
Circ: Statement: **212,554** Diamd. preorders: **137,192**
covers forms quadtych with Avengers #12, Iron Man #12, and Captain America #12. • gatefold summary. 🕮 Heroes Reunited, Part 1

13 ❑ Nov 1997 Cover: 1.99 **NM value: 2.00**
Circ: Statement: **212,554** Diamd. preorders: **130,089**
covers forms quadtych with Avengers #13, Iron Man #13, and Captain America #13. • gatefold summary. 🕮 World War 3, Part 1 final issue.★ Appearance of StormWatch, Wetworks, WildC.A.T.s.

FANTASTIC FOUR (VOL. 3) Marvel

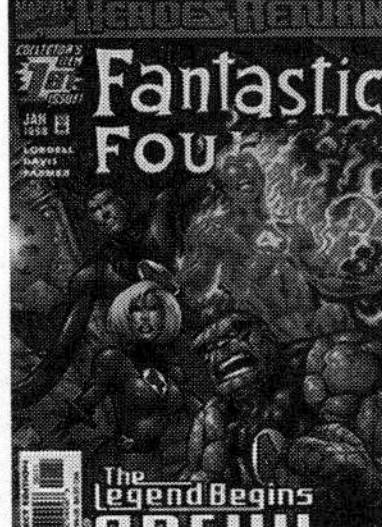

In 1998, after a year in a parallel universe under the "Heroes Reborn" banner, The Fantastic Four, The Avengers, and the other heroes who had been shunted to that dimension returned to the mainstream Marvel universe, where their respective series restarted with new first issues yet again.

Rather than giving the heroes new, updated origins, in "Heroes Return" as the event was appropriately called, the characters simply resumed their "normal" lives, although aspects of their time in that alternate dimension, created by the Richards' mutant son, Franklin, would come back to haunt them.

With this relaunch, Marvel's first super-team has once again faced dimensional invaders, Doctor Doom, The Puppet Master, and other foes familiar to fans of the original series. — Brent

1 ❑ Jan 1998 Cover: 2.99 **NM value: 3.50**
Circ: Statement: **170,649** Diamd. preorders: **209,793** • **CGC:** 12 graded, best 9.8
Cover has green background with team facing forward. • Giant-size. 🕮 Vive la Fantastique! **A:** Alan Davis **W:** Scott Lobdell

1/A ❑ Jan 1998 Cover: 2.99 **NM value: 4.00**
alternate cover. • gatefold summary. 🕮 Vive la Fantastique! **A:** Alan Davis **W:** Scott Lobdell

2 ❑ Feb 1998 Cover: 1.99 **NM value: 2.50**
Circ: Statement: **170,649** Diamd. preorders: **157,734**
• gatefold summary. • Has 1997 Statement, filed 10/1/97; avg print run 264,682; avg sales 207,965; avg subs 4,589; avg total paid 212,554; samples 459; office use 125; max existent 213,138; 20% of run returned **A:** Alan Davis **W:** Scott Lobdell

2/A ❑ Feb 1998 Cover: 1.99 **NM value: 2.50**
alternate cover. • gatefold summary. **A:** Alan Davis **W:** Scott Lobdell

3 ❑ Mar 1998 Cover: 1.99 **NM value: 2.50**
Circ: Statement: **170,649** Diamd. preorders: **121,664**
• gatefold summary. 🕮 Happy New Year, Reed Richards…Now Die! **A:** Alan Davis **W:** Scott Lobdell ★ 1st Appearance of Crucible.

4 ❑ Apr 1998 Cover: 2.99 **NM value: Cover or less**
Circ: Statement: **170,649** Diamd. preorders: **110,539**
• gatefold summary. ★ 1st Appearance of Billie the Postman. ★ Appearance of Silver Surfer. ★ Versus Terminus.

5 ❑ May 1998 Cover: 1.99 **NM value: 2.00**
Circ: Statement: **170,649** Diamd. preorders: **106,446**
• gatefold summary. ★ Versus Crucible.

6 ❑ Jun 1998 Cover: 1.99 **NM value: 2.00**
Circ: Statement: **170,649** Diamd. preorders: **108,066**
• gatefold summary. • Thing vs. Technet★ Appearance of Iron Fist.

7 ❑ Jul 1998 Cover: 1.99 **NM value: 2.00**
Circ: Statement: **170,649** Diamd. preorders: **102,259**
• gatefold summary. ★ Versus Warwolves.

8 ❑ Aug 1998 Cover: 1.99 **NM value: 2.00**
Circ: Statement: **170,649** Diamd. preorders: **100,666**
• gatefold summary.

9 ❑ Sep 1998 Cover: 1.99 **NM value: 2.00**
Circ: Statement: **104,941** Diamd. preorders: **94,277**
• gatefold summary. ★ Appearance of Spider-Man.

10 ❑ Oct 1998 Cover: 1.99 **NM value: 2.00**
Circ: Statement: **104,941** Diamd. preorders: **90,134**
• gatefold summary. ★ Versus Trapster.

11 ❑ Nov 1998 Cover: 1.99 **NM value: 2.00**
Circ: Statement: **104,941** Diamd. preorders: **87,990**
• gatefold summary. • Has 1998 Statement, filed 10/1/98; avg print run 243,145; avg sales 133,389; avg subs 3,487; avg total paid 170,649; samples 459; office use 125; max existent 137,460; 30% of run returned★ Appearance of Her.

12 ❑ Dec 1998 Cover: 2.99 **NM value: 3.00**
Circ: Statement: **104,941** Diamd. preorders: **86,202**
wraparound cover. • gatefold summary. ★ Versus Her. ★ Versus Crucible.

13 ❑ Jan 1999 Cover: 1.99 **NM value: 3.00**
Circ: Statement: **104,941** Diamd. preorders: **82,225**
• gatefold summary. ★ Versus Ronan.

14 ❑ Feb 1999 Cover: 1.99 **NM value: 2.00**
Circ: Statement: **104,941** Diamd. preorders: **78,654**
• gatefold summary. **A:** Salvador Larroca **W:** Chris Claremont ★ Appearance of Ronan the Accuser. ★ Versus Ronan.

15 ❑ Mar 1999 Cover: 1.99 **NM value: 2.00**
Circ: Statement: **104,941** Diamd. preorders: **76,986**
• Iron Man crossover, Part 1 **A:** Salvador Larroca **W:** Chris Claremont ★ Appearance of Kree, S.H.I.E.L.D., Shi'Ar, Iron Man, Ronan the Accuser, Watcher. ★ Versus Ronan.

16 ❑ Apr 1999 Cover: 1.99 **NM value: 2.00**
Circ: Statement: **104,941** Diamd. preorders: **72,194**
🕮 Unnatural Selection **A:** Salvador Larroca **W:** Chris Claremont ★ Appearance of Kree. ★ Versus Kree.

17 ❑ May 1999 Cover: 1.99 **NM value: Cover or less**
Circ: Statement: **104,941** Diamd. preorders: **70,857**

18 ❑ Jun 1999 Cover: 1.99 **NM value: Cover or less**
Circ: Statement: **104,941** Diamd. preorders: **71,545**

19 ❑ Jul 1999 Cover: 1.99 **NM value: Cover or less**
Circ: Statement: **104,941** Diamd. preorders: **68,720**

20 ❑ Aug 1999 Cover: 1.99 **NM value: Cover or less**
Circ: Statement: **104,941** Diamd. preorders: **67,353**

21 ❑ Sep 1999 Cover: 1.99 **NM value: Cover or less**
Circ: Statement: **104,941** Diamd. preorders: **65,692**

22 ❑ Oct 1999 Cover: 1.99 **NM value: Cover or less**
Circ: Diamd. preorders: **63,158**

23 ❑ Nov 1999 Cover: 1.99 **NM value: Cover or less**
Circ: Diamd. preorders: **60,157**

24 ❑ Dec 1999 Cover: 1.99 **NM value: Cover or less**
Circ: Diamd. preorders: **61,195**
• Has 1999 Statement, filed 10/1/99; avg print run 162,092; avg sales 133,300; avg subs 3,845; avg total paid 104,941; samples 2,575; office use 125; max existent 139,845; 35% of run returned

25 ❑ Jan 2000 Cover: 2.99 **NM value: Cover or less**
Circ: Diamd. preorders: **61,620**
• Giant-size.

26 ❑ Feb 2000 Cover: 1.99 **NM value: 2.25**
Circ: Diamd. preorders: **58,331**

27 ❑ Mar 2000 Cover: 1.99 **NM value: 2.25**
Circ: Diamd. preorders: **58,574**

28 ❑ Apr 2000 Cover: 1.99 **NM value: 2.25**
Circ: Diamd. preorders: **56,533**

29 ❑ May 2000 Cover: 1.99 **NM value: 2.25**
Circ: Diamd. preorders: **59,061**

30 ❑ Jun 2000 Cover: 2.25 **NM value: Cover or less**
Circ: Diamd. preorders: **58,212**

31 ❑ Jul 2000 Cover: 2.25 **NM value: Cover or less**
Circ: Diamd. preorders: **58,122**

32 ❑ Aug 2000 Cover: 2.25 **NM value: Cover or less**
Circ: Diamd. preorders: **59,211**

CGC-graded: Multiply prices above by **33 for 9.9 M • 16 for 9.8 NM/M • 7 for 9.6 NM+ • 5 for 9.4 NM • 2.5 for 9.2 NM- • 1.5 for 9.0 VF/NM**

33 ❑ Sep 2000 Cover: 2.25 **NM value: Cover or less**
Circ: Diamd. preorders: **57,932**
34 ❑ Oct 2000 Cover: 2.25 **NM value: Cover or less**
Circ: Statement: **69,645** Diamd. preorders: **54,898**
35 ❑ Nov 2000 Cover: 2.25 **NM value: Cover or less**
Circ: Statement: **69,645**
36 ❑ Dec 2000 Cover: 2.25 **NM value: Cover or less**
Circ: Statement: **69,645** Diamd. preorders: **53,244**
📖 Day of the Dark Sun **A:** Carlos Pacheco **W:** Carlos Pacheco; Rafael Marin ★ Appearance of Daredevil, Spider-Man, Diablo.
37 ❑ Jan 2001 Cover: 2.25 **NM value: Cover or less**
Circ: Statement: **69,645** Diamd. preorders: **52,516**
38 ❑ Feb 2001 Cover: 2.25 **NM value: Cover or less**
Circ: Statement: **69,645** Diamd. preorders: **52,393**
📖 Flesh and Stone **A:** Carlos Pacheco **W:** Carlos Pacheco; Rafael Marin
39 ❑ Mar 2001 Cover: 2.25 **NM value: Cover or less**
Circ: Statement: **69,645** Diamd. preorders: **51,594**
📖 Things Change • Thing can switch from rock form to human and back **A:** Carlos Pacheco **W:** Carlos Pacheco; Rafael Marin ★ Appearance of Grey Gargoyle, Avengers.
40 ❑ Apr 2001 Cover: 2.25 **NM value: Cover or less**
Circ: Statement: **69,645** Diamd. preorders: **51,788**
📖 Into the Breach • Baxter Building reopens **A:** Carlos Pacheco **W:** Carlos Pacheco; Rafael Marin
41 ❑ May 2001 Cover: 2.25 **NM value: Cover or less**
Circ: Statement: **69,645** Diamd. preorders: **51,617**
📖 Marooned **A:** Carlos Pacheco **W:** Jeph Loeb; Carlos Pacheco ★ Appearance of First.
42 ❑ Jun 2001 Cover: 2.25 **NM value: Cover or less**
Circ: Statement: **69,645** Diamd. preorders: **53,060**
43 ❑ Jul 2001 Cover: 2.25 **NM value: Cover or less**
Circ: Statement: **69,645** Diamd. preorders: **53,818**
44 ❑ Aug 2001 Cover: 2.25 **NM value: Cover or less**
Circ: Statement: **69,645** Diamd. preorders: **55,175**
45 ❑ Sep 2001 Cover: 2.25 **NM value: Cover or less**
Circ: Statement: **69,645** Diamd. preorders: **58,345**
46 ❑ Oct 2001 Cover: 2.25 **NM value: Cover or less**
Circ: Diamd. preorders: **57,731**
47 ❑ Nov 2001 Cover: 2.25 **NM value: Cover or less**
Circ: Diamd. preorders: **53,611**
48 ❑ Dec 2001 Cover: 2.25 **NM value: Cover or less**
Circ: Diamd. preorders: **52,164**
49 ❑ Jan 2002 Cover: 2.25 **NM value: Cover or less**
Circ: Diamd. preorders: **52,709**
50 ❑ Feb 2002 Cover: 3.99 **NM value: Cover or less**
Circ: Diamd. preorders: **56,394**
• Has 2001 Statement, filed 10/1/01; avg print run 96,408; avg sales 66,557; avg subs 3,088; avg total paid 69,645; samples 600; max existent 70,245; 27% of run returned
51 ❑ Mar 2002 Cover: 3.50 **NM value: Cover or less**
Circ: Diamd. preorders: **51,215**
52 ❑ Mar 2002 Cover: 2.25 **NM value: Cover or less**
Circ: Diamd. preorders: **49,808**
Anl 1998❑ca. 1998 Cover: 3.50 **NM value: Cover or less**
• Fantastic Four/Fantastic 4 '98; alternate universe FF **A:** Stuart Immonen **W:** Karl Kesel
Anl 1999❑ca. 1999 Cover: 3.50 **NM value: Cover or less**
• Fantastic Four/Fantastic 4 '99

FANTASTIC FOUR: 1234 — Marvel

1 ❑ 2001 Cover: 2.99 **NM value: Cover or less**
2 ❑ 2001 Cover: 2.99 **NM value: Cover or less**
3 ❑ 2001 Cover: 2.99 **NM value: Cover or less**
4 ❑ 2001 Cover: 2.99 **NM value: Cover or less**

FANTASTIC FOUR: ATLANTIS RISING — Marvel

1 ❑ Jun 1995 Cover: 3.95 **NM value: Cover or less**
Circ: CapCity orders: **19,350** • **CGC:** 2 graded, best 9.9
acetate outer cover. 📖 Atlantis Rising, Part 1 • Atlantis rises from sea
2 ❑ Jul 1995 Cover: 3.95 **NM value: Cover or less**
Circ: CapCity orders: **15,950**
acetate outer cover. 📖 Atlantis Rising
Ash 1❑May 1995 Cover: 2.25 **NM value: Cover or less**
• Collector's Preview ★ Origin of The Inhumans.

FANTASTIC FOUR (FIRESIDE BOOK) — Marvel

Bk 1❑ Cover: 3.95 **NM value: 5.00**
• Fireside

FANTASTIC FOUR: FIREWORKS — Marvel

1 ❑ Jan 1999 Cover: 2.99 **NM value: Cover or less**
• Marvel Remix **A:** Jeff Johnson **W:** Gerard Jones ★ Appearance of Inhumans.
2 ❑ Feb 1999 Cover: 2.99 **NM value: Cover or less**
• Marvel Remix **A:** Jeff Johnson **W:** Gerard Jones ★ Appearance of Inhumans.
3 ❑ Mar 1999 Cover: 2.99 **NM value: Cover or less**
• Marvel Remix **A:** Jeff Johnson **W:** Gerard Jones ★ Appearance of Inhumans.

FANTASTIC FOUR: FRANKLIN'S ADVENTURES — Marvel

1 ❑ Aug 1998 **NM value: 2.00**
No issue number. no cover price. • prototype for children's comic

FANTASTIC FOUR: MONSTERS UNLEASHED — Marvel

Bk 1❑ Cover: 5.95 **NM value: Cover or less**

FANTASTIC FOUR, THE (PAPERBACKS) — Marvel

Bk 1❑ Cover: 0.50 **NM value: 4.00**
• Lancer
Bk 2❑ Cover: 1.95 **NM value: 4.00**
• Pocket 1979
Bk 3❑ Cover: 1.75 **NM value: 4.00**

FANTASTIC FOUR RETURN, THE — Marvel

Bk 1❑ Cover: 0.50 **NM value: 3.00**
• Lancer

FANTASTIC FOUR ROAST — Marvel

One of the three or four funniest comic books ever to come from Marvel, Fantastic Four Roast celebrates the 20th anniversary of the super-team with an all-star comics banquet hosted by funnyman Fred Hembeck and drawn by many different Marvel artists.

It's a four-color Dean Martin Roast, as super-heroes truck to the stage and lob silly remarks at the foursome. Sight gags abound, with all of Marvel's bald characters seated at the same table. And, of course, some sinister agent is out to kill the Fantastic Four, by means of exploding soup and a living ice cream sundae.

Funny bits and trivia from one of the great satirists of comics, and still a wonderful value today. — JJM

1 ❑ May 1982 Cover: 1.00 **NM value: 2.00**
• **CGC:** 1 graded, best 9.6
• Celebrates 20th Anniversary of Fantastic Four. 📖 When Titans Chuckle! **A:** Murphy Anderson; Fred Hembeck; Michael Golden; John Buscema; Frank Miller; Tony DeZuniga **W:** Jim Shooter; Fred Hembeck

FANTASTIC FOUR SPECIAL — Marvel

1 ❑ May 1984 Cover: 2.00 **NM value: 3.00**
• reprints FF Annual #1 **C:** John Byrne

FANTASTIC FOUR: THE LEGEND — Marvel

1 ❑ Oct 1996 Cover: 3.95 **NM value: Cover or less**
• highlights of group's history ★ Origin of Fantastic Four and supporting cast.

FANTASTIC FOUR: THE SECRET STORY OF MARVEL'S COSMIC QUARTET — Marvel

Bk 1❑ Dec 1981 Cover: 2.95 **NM value: 3.50**
• Ideals

FANTASTIC FOUR: THE TRIAL OF GALACTUS — Marvel

Bk 1❑ Oct 1989 Cover: 12.95 **NM value: Cover or less**

FANTASTIC FOUR: THE WORLD'S GREATEST COMICS MAGAZINE — Marvel

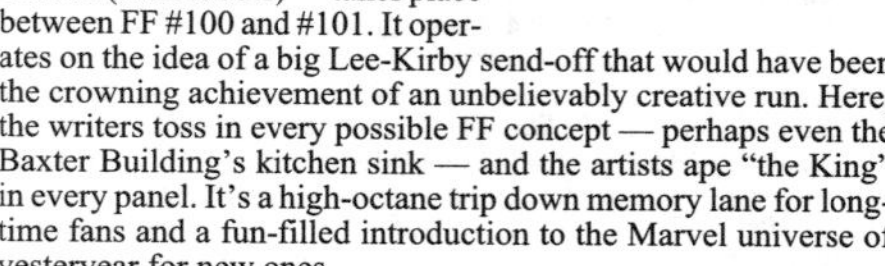

Stan Lee and Jack Kirby's legendary run on Fantastic Four (Vol. 1) is considered by many to be the best single run of a comic-book series — ever! But the end of that stellar run in 1970 was abrupt, coming seemingly out of nowhere. This 12-issue limited series by co-plotter artist Erik Larsen (Savage Dragon), co-plotter and scripter Eric Stephenson (Badrock), and a legion of others — including Bruce Timm (The Batman Adventures: Mad Love), Keith Giffen (The Heckler), Chuck Dixon (Nightwing), Jeph Loeb (Superman), and Michael Golden (Micronauts) — takes place between FF #100 and #101. It operates on the idea of a big Lee-Kirby send-off that would have been the crowning achievement of an unbelievably creative run. Here, the writers toss in every possible FF concept — perhaps even the Baxter Building's kitchen sink — and the artists ape "the King" in every panel. It's a high-octane trip down memory lane for long-time fans and a fun-filled introduction to the Marvel universe of yesteryear for new ones.

1 ❑ Feb 2001 Cover: 2.99 **NM value: Cover or less**
Circ: Diamd. preorders: **29,868**
📖 The Baxter Building Besieged! **A:** Keith Giffen; Erik Larsen; Bruce Timm; Jorge Lucas **C:** Erik Larsen; Bruce Timm **W:** Erik Larsen; Eric Stephenson
2 ❑ Mar 2001 Cover: 2.99 **NM value: Cover or less**
Circ: Diamd. preorders: **24,547**
📖 The Sinister Secret of the Sentry! **A:** Keith Giffen; Paul Ryan; Ron Frenz; Erik Larsen; Frank Fosco **C:** Michael Golden **W:** Erik Larsen; Chuck Dixon; Eric Stephenson
3 ❑ Apr 2001 Cover: 2.99 **NM value: Cover or less**
Circ: Diamd. preorders: **21,538**
📖 When Strike These Sentinels! **A:** Keith Giffen; Ron Frenz; Erik Larsen; Eric Shanower; Tom Scioli **C:** Jae Lee; Bruce Timm **W:** Erik Larsen; Tom DeFalco; Eric Stephenson
4 ❑ May 2001 Cover: 2.99 **NM value: Cover or less**
Circ: Diamd. preorders: **19,008**
5 ❑ Jun 2001 Cover: 2.99 **NM value: Cover or less**
Circ: Diamd. preorders: **18,161**
6 ❑ Jul 2001 Cover: 2.99 **NM value: Cover or less**
Circ: Diamd. preorders: **17,510**
7 ❑ Aug 2001 Cover: 2.99 **NM value: Cover or less**
Circ: Diamd. preorders: **17,261**
8 ❑ Sep 2001 Cover: 2.99 **NM value: Cover or less**
Circ: Diamd. preorders: **17,560**
9 ❑ Oct 2001 Cover: 2.99 **NM value: Cover or less**
Circ: Diamd. preorders: **17,164**
10 ❑ Nov 2001 Cover: 2.99 **NM value: Cover or less**
Circ: Diamd. preorders: **16,106**
11 ❑ Dec 2001 Cover: 2.99 **NM value: Cover or less**
Circ: Diamd. preorders: **15,555**
12 ❑ Jan 2002 Cover: 2.99 **NM value: Cover or less**
Circ: Diamd. preorders: **16,006**

FANTASTIC FOUR 2099 — Marvel

Marvel Comics introduced its line of 2099 comics in 1992 as a place where Marvel could reinvent some of its more famous characters. The Marvel universe of 2099 is a dystopia, where corporations battle for control of the world. Most of the characters in the 2099 line are new heroes inspired by their earlier counterparts, such as Spider-Man 2099, Ghost Rider 2099, and Punisher 2099.

In 1996, Marvel added this new series to the line. The Fantastic Four have been held prisoner in the neutral zone for 100 years. When they finally break free, they find a world of which they know nothing. Rumors abound that they are not the real Fantastic Four and that they are really test subjects or clones. Almost the entire planet is after them in some way or other. To make matters worse, Doctor Doom (Doom 2099) is the president. The series chronicles the team's adventures in this strange new world.

1 ❑ Jan 1996 Cover: 3.95 **NM value: Cover or less**
• **CGC:** 1 graded, best 9.8
enhanced wraparound cover.
2 ❑ Feb 1996 Cover: 1.95 **NM value: 2.00**
📖 Frightful 4 **A:** John Buscema **W:** Karl Kesel
3 ❑ Mar 1996 Cover: 1.95 **NM value: 2.00**
📖 Difficult to Recall **A:** Al Williamson(inks); Matt Ryan **W:** Karl Kesel
4 ❑ Apr 1996 Cover: 1.95 **NM value: 2.00**
📖 Negative Results **A:** Al Williamson(inks); Matt Ryan **W:** Karl Kesel ★ Appearance of Spider-Man 2099.
5 ❑ May 1996 Cover: 1.95 **NM value: 2.00**
6 ❑ Jun 1996 Cover: 1.95 **NM value: 2.00**
7 ❑ Jul 1996 Cover: 1.95 **NM value: 2.00**
8 ❑ Aug 1996 Cover: 1.95 **NM value: 2.00**

FANTASTIC FOUR UNLIMITED — Marvel

1 ❑ Mar 1993 Cover: 3.95 **NM value: 4.50**
Circ: CapCity orders: **43,500** • **CGC:** 1 graded, best 9.2
📖 Echoes! **A:** Herb Trimpe **W:** Roy Thomas
2 ❑ Jun 1993 Cover: 3.95 **NM value: 4.00**
Circ: CapCity orders: **27,300**
3 ❑ Sep 1993 Cover: 3.95 **NM value: 4.00**
Circ: CapCity orders: **24,700**
4 ❑ Dec 1993 Cover: 3.95 **NM value: Cover or less**
Circ: CapCity orders: **21,350**
• Thing vs. Hulk
5 ❑ Mar 1994 Cover: 3.95 **NM value: Cover or less**
Circ: CapCity orders: **17,100**
6 ❑ Jun 1994 Cover: 3.95 **NM value: Cover or less**
Circ: CapCity orders: **15,800**
7 ❑ Sep 1994 Cover: 3.95 **NM value: Cover or less**
Circ: CapCity orders: **15,150**
wraparound cover. ★ Versus early Marvel monsters.
8 ❑ Dec 1994 Cover: 3.95 **NM value: Cover or less**
Circ: CapCity orders: **13,700**
9 ❑ Mar 1995 Cover: 3.95 **NM value: Cover or less**
10 ❑ Jul 1995 Cover: 3.95 **NM value: Cover or less**
Circ: CapCity orders: **9,400**
11 ❑ Sep 1995 Cover: 3.95 **NM value: Cover or less**
12 ❑ Dec 1995 Cover: 3.95 **NM value: Cover or less**
wraparound cover. final issue. • how Reed and Doom vanished **A:** Herb Trimpe **W:** Roy Thomas; Tom DeFalco ★ Appearance of Hyperstorm, Doctor Doom.

FANTASTIC FOUR UNPLUGGED — Marvel

1 ❑ Sep 1995 Cover: 0.99 **NM value: 1.25**
📖 Adapt This! **A:** Hector Oliviera **W:** Mike Lackey
2 ❑ Nov 1995 Cover: 0.99 **NM value: 1.00**
• reading of Reed Richards' will **W:** Mike Lackey
3 ❑ Jan 1996 Cover: 0.99 **NM value: 1.00**
4 ❑ Mar 1996 Cover: 0.99 **NM value: 1.00**
5 ❑ May 1996 Cover: 0.99 **NM value: 1.00**
📖 Bomb Scared! **A:** Adriana Melo **W:** Mike Lackey ★ Versus Blastaar.
6 ❑ Jul 1996 Cover: 0.99 **NM value: 1.00**

FANTASTIC FOUR VS. X-MEN — Marvel

1 ❑ Feb 1987 Cover: 1.50 **NM value: 2.50**
Circ: CapCity orders: **54,300** • **CGC:** 1 graded, best 9.6
📖 Are You Sure?! **A:** Jon Bogdanove **W:** Chris Claremont
2 ❑ Mar 1987 Cover: 1.50 **NM value: 2.50**
Circ: CapCity orders: **46,600** • **CGC:** 1 graded, best 9.4
3 ❑ Apr 1987 Cover: 1.50 **NM value: 2.50**
Circ: CapCity orders: **43,800** • **CGC:** 1 graded, best 9.4
4 ❑ May 1987 Cover: 1.50 **NM value: 2.50**
Circ: CapCity orders: **40,400**
Bk 1❑ Nov 1990 Cover: 9.95 **NM value: Cover or less**
Circ: CapCity orders: **4,350**

FANTASTIC GIANTS VOL. 2 — Charlton

24 ❑ Sep 1966 Cover: 0.12 **NM value: 50.00**
• **CGC:** 3 graded, best 9.4

Other grades: Multiply prices above by **1.5 for Mint • 2/3 for Very Fine • 1/3 for Fine • 1/5 for Very Good • 1/8 for Good**

FANTASTIC PANIC — Antarctic

1 ❑ Aug 1993 Cover: 2.75 **NM** value: **Cover or less**
2 ❑ Oct 1993 Cover: 2.75 **NM** value: **Cover or less**
3 ❑ Dec 1993 Cover: 2.75 **NM** value: **Cover or less**
4 ❑ Feb 1994 Cover: 2.75 **NM** value: **Cover or less**
5 ❑ Apr 1994 Cover: 2.75 **NM** value: **Cover or less**
6 ❑ Jun 1994 Cover: 2.75 **NM** value: **Cover or less**
7 ❑ Aug 1994 Cover: 2.75 **NM** value: **Cover or less**
8 ❑ Oct 1994 Cover: 2.75 **NM** value: **Cover or less**
Bk 1❑ Jun 1996 Cover: 10.95 **NM** value: **Cover or less**

FANTASTIC PANIC (VOL. 2) — Antarctic

1 ❑ Nov 1995 Cover: 2.95 **NM** value: **Cover or less**
2 ❑ Jan 1996 Cover: 2.95 **NM** value: **Cover or less**
3 ❑ Mar 1996 Cover: 2.95 **NM** value: **Cover or less**
4 ❑ May 1996 Cover: 2.95 **NM** value: **Cover or less**
5 ❑ Jul 1996 Cover: 2.95 **NM** value: **Cover or less**
6 ❑ Sep 1996 Cover: 2.95 **NM** value: **Cover or less**
7 ❑ Nov 1996 Cover: 2.95 **NM** value: **Cover or less**
8 ❑ Dec 1996 Cover: 2.95 **NM** value: **Cover or less**
🕮 You Can't Do it **A:** Ganbear **W:** Ganbear

FANTASTIC TALES — I.W.

1 ❑ Cover: 0.10 **NM** value: **25.00**
🕮 City of the Living Dead!; The Glistening Death; Terror of the Skeleton Men (text story); The Witches Come at Midnight!; Death Has Many Tongues **A:** Nicholas Alascia; Harry Lazarus; Matt Hollingsworth; Norman Nodel **W:** Nicholas Alascia; Harry Lazarus; Matt Hollingsworth; Norman Nodel

FANTASTIC VOYAGE — Gold Key

1 ❑ Aug 1969 Cover: 0.15 **NM** value: **35.00**
• **CGC:** 1 graded, best 5.5
2 ❑ Dec 1969 Cover: 0.15 **NM** value: **25.00**
• **CGC:** 1 graded, best 7.0

FANTASTIC VOYAGES OF SINDBAD — Gold Key

1 ❑ Oct 1965 Cover: 0.12 **NM** value: **16.00**
• **CGC:** 2 graded, best 9.6
pin-up on back cover.
2 ❑ Jun 1967 Cover: 0.12 **NM** value: **10.00**
• **CGC:** 1 graded, best 6.5

FANTASTIC WORLDS — Flashback Comics

1 ❑ Sep 1995, b&w Cover: 2.95 **NM** value: **Cover or less**

FANTASTIC WORLDS — Standard

5 ❑ Sep 1952 Cover: 0.10 **NM** value: **250.00**
• **CGC:** 2 graded, best 6.5
6 ❑ Nov 1952 Cover: 0.10 **NM** value: **200.00**
• **CGC:** 1 graded, best 7.5
7 ❑ Jan 1953 Cover: 0.10 **NM** value: **125.00**

FANTASY FEATURES — AC

1 ❑ Cover: 1.75 **NM** value: **Cover or less**
Circ: CapCity orders: **2,800**
🕮 Eric the Dragon Slayer: Death Hunt; Back to Syros **A:** Mar T. Santana **W:** Frank W. Zenau(Xeno)
2 ❑ Cover: 1.95 **NM** value: **Cover or less**

FANTASY GIRLS — Comax

All issues are adults only.
1 ❑ b&w Cover: 2.50 **NM** value: **Cover or less**

FANTASY MASTERPIECES (VOL. 1) — Marvel

Fantasy Masterpieces reprinted some of the great stories from the Golden Age. Here readers could find some of the earliest appearances of Captain America, The Red Skull, The All-Winners Squad, The Human Torch, The Sub-Mariner, and other Golden Age greats. Thrown in with the super-hero stories are a number of monster and science-fiction thrillers from the same period. All of this came wrapped up in a giant-sized comic that sold for the princely price of 25 cents.

With issue #12, Fantasy Masterpieces changed names to become Marvel Super-Heroes (Vol. 1). That title followed much of the same format, but replaced the monster stories with new super-hero storylines.

1 ❑ Feb 1966 Cover: 0.12 **NM** value: **18.00**
• **CGC:** 66 graded, best 9.8
• Golden Age reprints **A:** Steve Ditko; Don Heck; Jack Kirby
2 ❑ Apr 1966 Cover: 0.12 **NM** value: **15.00**
• Golden Age reprints; Fin Fang Foom **A:** Steve Ditko; Don Heck; Jack Kirby
3 ❑ Jun 1966 Cover: 0.25 **NM** value: **14.00**
• **CGC:** 1 graded, best 9.4
🕮 The Hunchback Of Hollywood And The Movie Murder • Golden Age reprints; Captain America, other Golden Age super-heroes appear
4 ❑ Aug 1966 Cover: 0.25 **NM** value: **12.00**
• **CGC:** 1 graded, best 9.6
🕮 The Menace Of Dr. Grimm!; The Case Of The Fake Monkey Fiends; The Thing Called…It!; It Lives • Golden Age reprints; Captain America, other Golden Age super-heroes appear
5 ❑ Oct 1966 Cover: 0.25 **NM** value: **12.00**
🕮 Captain America And The Ringmaster Of Death; The Gruesome Secret Of The Dragon Of Doom; Mister Gregory And The Ghost!; The Things From Dimension X!; It Fell From The Flying Saucer!; Killers Of The Bund • Golden Age reprints; Captain America, other Golden Age super-heroes appear
6 ❑ Dec 1966 Cover: 0.25 **NM** value: **12.00**
• Golden Age reprints; Captain America, other Golden Age super-heroes appear
7 ❑ Feb 1967 Cover: 0.25 **NM** value: **12.00**
• **CGC:** 1 graded, best 9.6
• Golden Age reprints; Captain America, other Golden Age super-heroes appear
8 ❑ Apr 1967 Cover: 0.25 **NM** value: **13.00**
• **CGC:** 2 graded, best 9.2
• Golden Age reprints; Sub-Mariner vs. Human Torch (original)
9 ❑ Jun 1967 Cover: 0.25 **NM** value: **12.00**
• **CGC:** 1 graded, best 9.2
• Golden Age reprints; Reprinted from Marvel Comics #1 ★ Origin of Human Torch (original).
10 ❑ Aug 1967 Cover: 0.25 **NM** value: **10.00**
• **CGC:** 1 graded, best 9.0
🕮 The All Winners Squad!; The Whizzer; The Human Torch; Miss America; Sub-Mariner • Golden Age reprints; Reprinted from All Winners #19 ★ Origin of All Winners Squad. ★ 1st Appearance of All Winners Squad.
11 ❑ Oct 1967 Cover: 0.25 **NM** value: **10.00**
🕮 The Human Torch • Series continues as Marvel Super-Heroes; Reprinted from Human Torch #1 ★ Origin of Toro.

FANTASY MASTERPIECES (VOL. 2) — Marvel

1 ❑ Dec 1979 Cover: 0.75 **NM** value: **4.00**
• **CGC:** 3 graded, best 9.6
• Silver Surfer reprint **W:** Stan Lee
2 ❑ Jan 1980 Cover: 0.75 **NM** value: **2.50**
3 ❑ Feb 1980 Cover: 0.75 **NM** value: **2.50**
4 ❑ Mar 1980 Cover: 0.75 **NM** value: **2.50**
5 ❑ Apr 1980 Cover: 0.75 **NM** value: **2.50**
6 ❑ May 1980 Cover: 0.75 **NM** value: **2.00**
🕮 Worlds Without End! **A:** John Buscema **W:** Stan Lee
7 ❑ Jun 1980 Cover: 0.75 **NM** value: **2.00**
8 ❑ Jul 1980 Cover: 0.75 **NM** value: **2.00**
9 ❑ Aug 1980 Cover: 0.75 **NM** value: **2.00**
10 ❑ Sep 1980 Cover: 0.75 **NM** value: **2.00**
🕮 A World he Never Made **A:** John Buscema **W:** Stan Lee
11 ❑ Oct 1980 Cover: 0.75 **NM** value: **2.00**
12 ❑ Nov 1980 Cover: 0.75 **NM** value: **2.00**
13 ❑ Dec 1980 Cover: 0.75 **NM** value: **2.00**
14 ❑ Jan 1981 Cover: 0.50 **NM** value: **2.00**

FANTASY QUARTERLY — Independent Pub. Synd.

1 ❑ Spr 1978, b&w Cover: 1.00 **NM** value: **40.00**
• **CGC:** 12 graded, best 9.8
• back-up story with art by Sim **A:** Dave Sim ★ 1st Appearance of Elfquest.

FAREWELL, MOONSHADOW — DC / Vertigo

1 ❑ Jan 1997 Cover: 7.95 **NM** value: **Cover or less**
No issue number. One-shot. • prestige format. **A:** Jon J. Muth **W:** J.M. DeMatteis

FAREWELL TO WEAPONS — Marvel / Epic

1 ❑ Cover: 2.25 **NM** value: **Cover or less**
No issue number.

FARGO KID — Prize

3 ❑ Cover: 0.10 **NM** value: **125.00**
4 ❑ Cover: 0.10 **NM** value: **75.00**
5 ❑ Cover: 0.10 **NM** value: **75.00**

FARMER'S DAUGHTER — Stanhall

1 ❑ Feb 1954 Cover: 0.10 **NM** value: **150.00**
2 ❑ Apr 1954 Cover: 0.10 **NM** value: **100.00**
3 ❑ 1954 Cover: 0.10 **NM** value: **100.00**
4 ❑ 1954 Cover: 0.10 **NM** value: **100.00**

FAR WEST — Antarctic

1 ❑ Nov 1998 Cover: 2.95 **NM** value: **Cover or less**
2 ❑ Jan 1999 Cover: 2.95 **NM** value: **Cover or less**
Circ: Diamd. preorders: **1,527**
3 ❑ Mar 1999 Cover: 2.95 **NM** value: **Cover or less**
4 ❑ May 1999 Cover: 2.95 **NM** value: **Cover or less**
Circ: Diamd. preorders: **1,564**

FASHION IN ACTION — Eclipse

Smr 1❑ Aug 1986 Cover: 1.75 **NM** value: **2.00**
Circ: CapCity orders: **4,275**
• gatefold summary. 🕮 A Force of HabitThe RevenantThe Men in Black!; Luftmann's Move **A:** John K. Snyder III; Scott Hampton **W:** John K. Snyder III; Scott Hampton
WS 1❑ Cover: 2.00 **NM** value: **Cover or less**
Circ: CapCity orders: **2,800**
• anniversary.

FASHION POLICE, THE — Bryce Alan

1 ❑ **NM** value: **2.50**

The CGC numbers printed in individual listings above represent the **number of copies examined** and given a **Universal** grade by CGC and the **best such copy** graded at press time. For current populations, watch for special ***Comics Buyer's Guide*** issues or check **www.cgccomics.com.**

FAST FICTION — Seaboard

Fast Fiction, like the Classics Illustrated series, presents one-issue illustrated adaptations of famous works of literary fiction.

As an example of the series, #5 presents the story of "Beau Geste" by P.C. Wren. A major in the French Foreign Legion discovers a fort in North Africa manned by dead soldiers, propped up at their posts. Attacking Arabs would not have left the fort in such a state, so what is the story behind this mystery? And how is it related to the three Geste brothers and the theft of the Blue Water, the world's most priceless sapphire?

Other issues contain adaptations of such novels as the spy story The 39 Steps by John Buchan, the adventure-filled Scarlet Pimpernel by Baroness Orczy, and the exotic She by H. Rider Haggard. Fast Fiction offered famous stories "streamlined for action" and soon changed its logo to read "Stories by Famous Authors Illustrated."

1 ❑ Oct 1949 Cover: 0.10 **NM** value: **165.00**
• **CGC:** 1 graded, best 7.5
🕮 The Scarlet Pimpernel
2 ❑ Nov 1949 Cover: 0.10 **NM** value: **130.00**
🕮 Captain Blood
3 ❑ Dec 1949 Cover: 0.10 **NM** value: **130.00**
🕮 She **W:** H. Ryder Haggard
4 ❑ Jan 1950 Cover: 0.10 **NM** value: **130.00**
🕮 The 39 Steps
5 ❑ Mar 1950 Cover: 0.10 **NM** value: **130.00**
🕮 Beau Geste **A:** Henry C. Kiefer **W:** P.C. Wren

FAST FORWARD — DC / Piranha

1 ❑ Cover: 4.95 **NM** value: **Cover or less**
• phobias
2 ❑ Cover: 4.95 **NM** value: **Cover or less**
🕮 Lester Fenton & The Walking Dead; Brothers & Sisters; Hostage; The Last Wish Baby; Stockman; Sister From Around The Way • family **A:** Dean Motter; Brian Stelfreeze; Douglas Michael; Kyle Baker; Stephen DeStefano; Kirk Etienne **W:** Dean Motter; Douglas Michael; Kyle Baker; Mark Williams; Bob Rozakis; John Figueroa
3 ❑ Cover: 4.95 **NM** value: **Cover or less**
🕮 Riding The Sun; Toybox; Comic Nirvana; Windows On The World • Storytellers **A:** Steve Purcell; Sam Kieth; Duncan Eagleson; Max Siebel **W:** William Messner-Loebs; Steve Purcell; Damon Cardwell; Meg Wolitzer

FASTLANE ILLUSTRATED — Fastlane

0.5 ❑ **NM** value: **1.50**
• Giveaway at 1994 San Diego Comicon. 🕮 Fastlane Illustrated, Chapter 1; Sidewinder; Fastlocals; Fastlane Spotlight! **A:** Chris Tirri; Clay Sagun; Francisco Ramirez; Grant Miller **W:** Clay Sagun; Francisco Ramirez; Grant Miller
1 ❑ Sep 1994, b&w Cover: 2.50 **NM** value: **Cover or less**
2 ❑ Jun 1995, b&w Cover: 2.50 **NM** value: **Cover or less**
3 ❑ Jul 1996, b&w Cover: 2.50 **NM** value: **Cover or less**
wraparound cover.

FATAL BEAUTY — Illustration

ASH 1/A❑ Jun 1996 Cover: 3.95 **NM** value: **Cover or less**
Adult cover. **A:** Don Paresi; Steve Woron

FAT ALBERT — Gold Key

1 ❑ Mar 1974 Cover: 0.20 **NM** value: **8.00**
• **CGC:** 1 graded, best 8.5
2 ❑ Jun 1974 Cover: 0.20 **NM** value: **6.00**
• **CGC:** 1 graded, best 7.5
3 ❑ Sep 1974 Cover: 0.25 **NM** value: **5.00**
• **CGC:** 2 graded, best 9.2
4 ❑ Dec 1974 Cover: 0.25 **NM** value: **5.00**
• **CGC:** 1 graded, best 7.5
5 ❑ Feb 1975 Cover: 0.25 **NM** value: **5.00**
6 ❑ Apr 1975 Cover: 0.25 **NM** value: **5.00**
7 ❑ Jun 1975 Cover: 0.25 **NM** value: **4.00**
8 ❑ Aug 1975 Cover: 0.25 **NM** value: **4.00**
9 ❑ Oct 1975 Cover: 0.25 **NM** value: **4.00**
10 ❑ Dec 1975 Cover: 0.25 **NM** value: **4.00**
11 ❑ Feb 1976 Cover: 0.25 **NM** value: **4.00**
12 ❑ Apr 1976 Cover: 0.25 **NM** value: **4.00**
13 ❑ Jun 1976 Cover: 0.25 **NM** value: **4.00**
14 ❑ Aug 1976 Cover: 0.25 **NM** value: **4.00**
15 ❑ Oct 1976 Cover: 0.30 **NM** value: **4.00**
16 ❑ Dec 1976 Cover: 0.30 **NM** value: **4.00**
17 ❑ Feb 1977 Cover: 0.30 **NM** value: **4.00**
18 ❑ Apr 1977 Cover: 0.30 **NM** value: **4.00**
19 ❑ Jun 1977 Cover: 0.30 **NM** value: **4.00**
20 ❑ Aug 1977 Cover: 0.30 **NM** value: **4.00**
21 ❑ Oct 1977 Cover: 0.30 **NM** value: **4.00**
22 ❑ Dec 1977 Cover: 0.35 **NM** value: **4.00**
23 ❑ Feb 1978 Cover: 0.35 **NM** value: **4.00**
24 ❑ Apr 1978 Cover: 0.35 **NM** value: **4.00**
25 ❑ Jun 1978 Cover: 0.35 **NM** value: **4.00**
26 ❑ Aug 1978 Cover: 0.35 **NM** value: **4.00**
27 ❑ Oct 1978 Cover: 0.35 **NM** value: **4.00**
28 ❑ Dec 1978 Cover: 0.35 **NM** value: **4.00**
29 ❑ Feb 1979 Cover: 0.35 **NM** value: **4.00**

Do you have changes or corrections for the **Standard Catalog**? Send your original research to us at **allcomics@krause.com**

CGC-graded: Multiply prices above by **33 for 9.9 M • 16 for 9.8 NM/M • 7 for 9.6 NM+ • 5 for 9.4 NM • 2.5 for 9.2 NM- • 1.5 for 9.0 VF/NM**

FATALE — Broadway

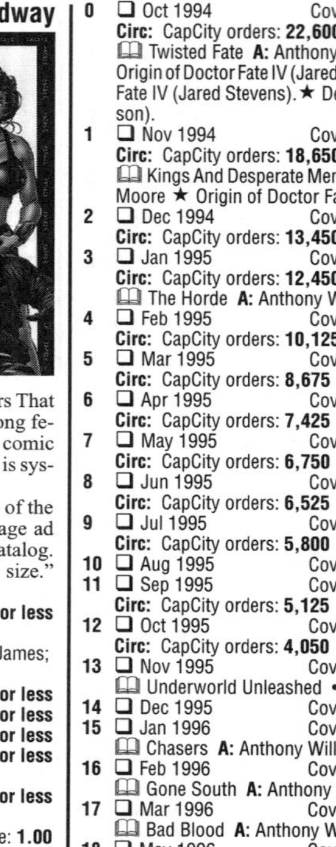

"Little bits of many heroic women became parts of Fatale," Jim Shooter, editor-in-chief of Broadway Comics and writer of this series, says on the text page that opens Fatale. Then he proceeds to tell the story of a very-well-endowed woman who can absorb energy and memories from others with a kiss, who is on the run (often in high heels) from a mysterious group called the Brotherhood, and who appears scantily clad (or unclad) in a number of cheesecake panels throughout the first issue and the remaining five issues of the short-lived series.

Ironic? Certainly! Entertaining? Somewhat. Fatale, who also appeared in Broadway's Powers That Be and Shadow State, represents an attempt to create a strong female lead character. Unfortunately, she quickly becomes a comic book cliche: The big-chested super-heroine whose costume is systematically ripped away over the course of a single issue.

Not to belabor the point, but Fatale was the focus of one of the biggest advertising missteps in recent memory: An full-page ad for an issue appeared in Diamond's Previews distributor catalog. The picture: Fatale's bust. The caption: "Shown actual size." Smooth...

1 ❑ Jan 1996 Cover: 2.50 **NM** value: **Cover or less**
• **CGC:** 2 graded, best 9.8
Embossed cover. 📖 Inherit the Earth **A:** J.G. Jones **W:** Joe James; Jim Shooter; Janet Jackson; Pauline Weiss
2 ❑ Feb 1996 Cover: 2.50 **NM** value: **Cover or less**
3 ❑ Mar 1996 Cover: 2.50 **NM** value: **Cover or less**
4 ❑ May 1996 Cover: 2.50 **NM** value: **Cover or less**
5 ❑ Jul 1996 Cover: 2.95 **NM** value: **Cover or less**
📖 The Word **A:** Jim Shooter **W:** Jim Shooter
6 ❑ Oct 1996 Cover: 2.95 **NM** value: **Cover or less**
final issue.
Ash 1❑ Sep 1995, b&w **NM** value: **1.00**
• giveaway preview edition.

FAT AND SLAT — E.C.

Fat and Slat were the "stage" names of two characters newspaper-comic-strip artist Ed Wheelan had created for his Minute Movies strip, which ran in the 1920s and 1930s — though the "actors" Fuller Phun and Archibald Clubb didn't appear as Fat and Slat until the Golden Age Flash comic book ran a Wheelan strip. The Minute Movies strip imitated movie types of the day, with feature films followed by short subjects, and its "cast" of actors (Hazel Dearie, Ralph McSneer, and the like) were cast in a variety of roles. The first issue Wheelan did for comic books appeared from DC's AA arm in 1944.

When the E.C. imprint was begun, Wheelan continued the comic book for that company, with the characters continuing in "bigfoot" comedy routines. In the morphing world that E.C. developed, the title turned into Gunfighter with the fifth issue. — Maggie

1 ❑ Sum 1947 Cover: 0.10 **NM** value: **250.00**
• **CGC:** 4 graded, best 7.5
2 ❑ Fal 1947 Cover: 0.10 **NM** value: **175.00**
• **CGC:** 2 graded, best 7.5
3 ❑ Win 1947 Cover: 0.10 **NM** value: **175.00**
• **CGC:** 4 graded, best 8.0
4 ❑ Spr 1948 Cover: 0.10 **NM** value: **175.00**
• **CGC:** 3 graded, best 8.5

FAT AND SLAT JOKE BOOK — Wise Publications

1 ❑ Sum 1944 Cover: 0.10 **NM** value: **200.00**
• **CGC:** 4 graded, best 6.5

FAT DOG MENDOZA — Dark Horse

1 ❑ Dec 1992, b&w Cover: 2.50 **NM** value: **Cover or less**

FATE — DC

Doctor Fate was one of the casualties of Zero Hour. That crisis in time results in the mystical trio, consisting of Doctor Fate and Kent and Inza Nelson, aging terribly as a result.

With their life forces ebbing away by the moment, they travel to the ruined temple in Egypt where the Doctor Fate arcana has returned. But a thief named Jared Stevens gets there first, stealing the artifacts, then heading back to the U.S., where he plans to fence them. Before he can cash in his ill-gotten gains, however, Fate catches up to him.

Kent and Inza use the last of their powers to locate Stevens and the arcana. They manage to subdue Stevens but are, in turn, killed by demons sent by arch-enemy Kingdom. Then, in a flash of light, the mystical relics of Doctor Fate choose a new champion. Stevens, a former thief, is literally branded — as the new Doctor Fate.

0 ❑ Oct 1994 Cover: 1.95 **NM** value: **2.50**
Circ: CapCity orders: **22,600**
📖 Twisted Fate **A:** Anthony Williams **W:** John Francis Moore ★ Origin of Doctor Fate IV (Jared Stevens). ★ 1st Appearance of Doctor Fate IV (Jared Stevens). ★ Death of Doctor Fate III (Kent & Inza Nelson).
1 ❑ Nov 1994 Cover: 1.95 **NM** value: **2.50**
Circ: CapCity orders: **18,650**
📖 Kings And Desperate Men **A:** Anthony Williams **W:** John Francis Moore ★ Origin of Doctor Fate IV (Jared Stevens).
2 ❑ Dec 1994 Cover: 1.95 **NM** value: **2.00**
Circ: CapCity orders: **13,450**
3 ❑ Jan 1995 Cover: 1.95 **NM** value: **2.00**
Circ: CapCity orders: **12,450**
📖 The Horde **A:** Anthony Williams **W:** John Francis Moore
4 ❑ Feb 1995 Cover: 1.95 **NM** value: **2.00**
Circ: CapCity orders: **10,125**
5 ❑ Mar 1995 Cover: 1.95 **NM** value: **2.00**
Circ: CapCity orders: **8,675**
6 ❑ Apr 1995 Cover: 1.95 **NM** value: **2.00**
Circ: CapCity orders: **7,425**
7 ❑ May 1995 Cover: 1.95 **NM** value: **2.00**
Circ: CapCity orders: **6,750**
8 ❑ Jun 1995 Cover: 2.25 **NM** value: **Cover or less**
Circ: CapCity orders: **6,525**
9 ❑ Jul 1995 Cover: 2.25 **NM** value: **Cover or less**
Circ: CapCity orders: **5,800**
10 ❑ Aug 1995 Cover: 2.25 **NM** value: **Cover or less**
11 ❑ Sep 1995 Cover: 2.25 **NM** value: **Cover or less**
Circ: CapCity orders: **5,125**
12 ❑ Oct 1995 Cover: 2.25 **NM** value: **Cover or less**
Circ: CapCity orders: **4,050**
13 ❑ Nov 1995 Cover: 2.25 **NM** value: **Cover or less**
📖 Underworld Unleashed • Underworld Unleashed
14 ❑ Dec 1995 Cover: 2.25 **NM** value: **Cover or less**
15 ❑ Jan 1996 Cover: 2.25 **NM** value: **Cover or less**
📖 Chasers **A:** Anthony Williams **W:** Len Kaminski
16 ❑ Feb 1996 Cover: 2.25 **NM** value: **Cover or less**
📖 Gone South **A:** Anthony Williams **W:** Len Kaminski
17 ❑ Mar 1996 Cover: 2.25 **NM** value: **Cover or less**
📖 Bad Blood **A:** Anthony Williams **W:** Len Kaminski
18 ❑ May 1996 Cover: 2.25 **NM** value: **Cover or less**
19 ❑ Jun 1996 Cover: 2.25 **NM** value: **Cover or less**
20 ❑ Jul 1996 Cover: 2.25 **NM** value: **Cover or less**
📖 The Hand of Fate, Part 1
21 ❑ Aug 1996 Cover: 2.25 **NM** value: **Cover or less**
📖 The Hand of Fate, Part 2
22 ❑ Sep 1996 Cover: 2.25 **NM** value: **Cover or less**
📖 The Hand of Fate, Part 3 final issue. • Kent and Inza Nelson go to heaven

FATE'S FIVE — Innervision

1 ❑ b&w Cover: 2.50 **NM** value: **Cover or less**
2 ❑ Cover: 2.50 **NM** value: **Cover or less**
3 ❑ Cover: 2.50 **NM** value: **Cover or less**
4 ❑ Cover: 2.50 **NM** value: **Cover or less**

FAT FREDDY'S CAT — Rip Off

All issues are adults only.

Fat Freddy is one of the Fabulous Furry Freak Brothers, a trio of lovable, comic druggies created by Gilbert Shelton. Since Fat Freddy and the gang are always either on drugs or looking for drugs, the cat is apt to feel neglected. As a result, Fat Freddy's Cat become something like a hilariously evil version of Garfield. FFC habitually gets into trouble, soils the apartment, and loves nothing more than sinking his claws into Fat Freddy's waterbed. At the same time, he has to contend with the cockroach militia that has organized in Fat Freddy's cupboards.

First appearing as a tiny second feature squeezed into the bottom of Fabulous Furry Freak Brothers newspaper strips, Fat Freddy's Cat was eventually enlarged and collected in this series. Although it was distributed primarily through head shops and other underground outlets, it nevertheless went on to become a remarkably popular comic book.

1 ❑ b&w Cover: 2.50 **NM** value: **18.00**
📖 I Led Nine Lives!
1-2 ❑ b&w Cover: 2.95 **NM** value: **4.00**
1-3 ❑ Cover: 2.95 **NM** value: **3.50**
📖 I Led Nine Lives! • 1988 printing
2 ❑ b&w Cover: 2.50 **NM** value: **9.00**
3 ❑ b&w Cover: 2.50 **NM** value: **8.00**
4 ❑ b&w Cover: 2.50 **NM** value: **4.00**
5 ❑ b&w Cover: 2.50 **NM** value: **4.00**
6 ❑ b&w Cover: 2.50 **NM** value: **3.00**
7 ❑ b&w Cover: 2.95 **NM** value: **3.00**
Bk 1❑ Jan 1990 Cover: 8.95 **NM** value: **Cover or less**
• Collected Fat Freddy's Cat
Bk 2❑ Feb 1990 Cover: 8.95 **NM** value: **Cover or less**
• Collected Fat Freddy's Cat; Collects Fat Freddy's Cat #4-8

FAT FREDDY'S COMICS & STORIES — Rip Off

1 ❑ Dec 1983 Cover: 2.50 **NM** value: **Cover or less**
2 ❑ Dec 1985 Cover: 2.50 **NM** value: **Cover or less**

FAT FURY SPECIAL — Avalon

1 ❑ b&w Cover: 2.95 **NM** value: **Cover or less**
• reprints Herbie stories

FATHER & SON — Kitchen Sink

1 ❑ Jul 1995, b&w Cover: 2.75 **NM** value: **Cover or less**
📖 The Seventies; Great Jobs; False; A Day in the Life of…; Richard Schultz's Complaint of The Month **A:** Jeff Nicholson **W:** Jeff Nicholson
2 ❑ Sep 1995, b&w Cover: 2.75 **NM** value: **Cover or less**
3 ❑ Dec 1995, b&w Cover: 2.75 **NM** value: **Cover or less**
4 ❑ Jan 1996, b&w Cover: 2.75 **NM** value: **Cover or less**
Ash 1❑ Jul 1995 **NM** value: **2.00**
• ashcan edition limited to 200, b&w.
SE 1❑ b&w Cover: 3.95 **NM** value: **Cover or less**
📖 Reality Soldiers; Road Trip; Honk If You Hate Cogdale; Studio Fool; Don't Tempt Fate; The Father and Son Story (text); 8 Great Reasons to Buy Ultra Klutz, Book One; Flying Colors • "Like, Special #1" **A:** Jeff Nicholson **W:** Jeff Nicholson

FATHOM (1ST SERIES) — Comico

1 ❑ May 1987 Cover: 1.50 **NM** value: **Cover or less**
Circ: CapCity orders: **10,550**
📖 Auld Lang Syne **A:** Jill Thompson **W:** Lawrence Schick
2 ❑ Jun 1987 Cover: 1.50 **NM** value: **Cover or less**
Circ: CapCity orders: **9,175**
3 ❑ Jul 1987 Cover: 1.50 **NM** value: **Cover or less**
Circ: CapCity orders: **8,300**
wraparound cover. **A:** Jill Thompson **W:** Lawrence Schick

FATHOM (2ND SERIES) — Comico

1 ❑ Cover: 2.50 **NM** value: **Cover or less**
Circ: CapCity orders: **4,925**
2 ❑ Cover: 2.50 **NM** value: **Cover or less**
Circ: CapCity orders: **4,425**
3 ❑ Cover: 2.50 **NM** value: **Cover or less**
Circ: CapCity orders: **4,050**
📖 Genie In A Bottle, Part 3 **A:** Tim Eldred **W:** Dave DeVries
Bk 1❑ Cover: 5.95 **NM** value: **Cover or less**

FATHOM (3RD SERIES) — Image

Aspen Matthews is a beautiful, unusual woman. She has the lung capacity of an Olympic swimmer and the bone flexibility and structure of a 14-year-old, even though she is in her 20s. But that is only the beginning of the mysteries surrounding Fathom and her newfound water powers.

Appearing on a boat thought long lost, with no memory of her childhood, Aspen later pursues a career as a marine biologist. While working in an underwater laboratory, she discovers an underwater race — and soon the underwater beings, the U.S. Military, and a Japanese organization are all embroiled in a complex mystery. Both the Japanese and the Americans are interested in a mysterious technology which may somehow involve Aspen and her forgotten past.

Fathom is created and illustrated by Michael Turner, the popular artist known for his work on Witchblade.

0 ❑ **NM** value: **3.00**
• Wizard Promotional Edition: Given away with subsrciption to Wizard. **A:** Michael Turner **W:** Michael Turner
0/A ❑ **NM** value: **6.00**
Green holografix cover. **A:** Michael Turner **W:** Michael Turner
0/B ❑ **NM** value: **8.00**
• Wizard authentic edition. **A:** Michael Turner **W:** Michael Turner
1/A ❑ Aug 1998 Cover: 2.50 **NM** value: **4.00**
Circ: Diamd. preorders: **257,087**
Variant covers, some pages. **A:** Michael Turner **W:** Michael Turner; Bill O'Neil
1/B ❑ Aug 1998 Cover: 2.50 **NM** value: **4.00**
Variant covers, some pages. • Fathom standing underwater **A:** Michael Turner **W:** Michael Turner; Bill O'Neil
1/C ❑ Aug 1998 Cover: 2.50 **NM** value: **4.00**
• **CGC:** 5 graded, best 9.8
Fathom, dolphins on cover w/inset close-up. **A:** Michael Turner **W:** Michael Turner; Bill O'Neil
1/D ❑ **NM** value: **150.00**
• Museum edition. • Limited to 50 copies. **A:** Michael Turner **W:** Michael Turner; Bill O'Neil
2 ❑ Sep 1998 Cover: 2.50 **NM** value: **3.00**
Circ: Diamd. preorders: **117,692** • **CGC:** 6 graded, best 9.8
3 ❑ Oct 1998 Cover: 2.50 **NM** value: **3.00**
Circ: Diamd. preorders: **122,451** • **CGC:** 4 graded, best 9.8
3/SC❑ **NM** value: **5.00**
• **CGC:** 2 graded, best 9.8
• Monster Edition: No cover price. **A:** Michael Turner **W:** Michael Turner; Bill O'Neil
4 ❑ Mar 1999 Cover: 2.50 **NM** value: **Cover or less**
Circ: Diamd. preorders: **106,388** • **CGC:** 4 graded, best 9.8
5 ❑ May 1999 Cover: 2.50 **NM** value: **Cover or less**
Circ: Diamd. preorders: **90,059** • **CGC:** 1 graded, best 9.6
6 ❑ Jun 1999 Cover: 2.50 **NM** value: **Cover or less**
Circ: Diamd. preorders: **78,640**
7 ❑ Aug 1999 Cover: 2.50 **NM** value: **Cover or less**
Circ: Diamd. preorders: **72,179**
8 ❑ Sep 1999 Cover: 2.50 **NM** value: **Cover or less**
Circ: Diamd. preorders: **69,643** • **CGC:** 1 graded, best 9.6
9 ❑ Oct 1999 Cover: 2.50 **NM** value: **Cover or less**
Circ: Diamd. preorders: **90,330** • **CGC:** 4 graded, best 9.8
9/A ❑ **NM** value: **12.00**
• **CGC:** 47 graded, best 10.0
• Holofoil edition. **A:** Michael Turner **W:** Michael Turner; Bill O'Neil
9/B ❑ **NM** value: **8.00**

Other grades: Multiply prices above by **1.5 for Mint • 2/3 for Very Fine • 1/3 for Fine • 1/5 for Very Good • 1/8 for Good**

• Platinum Holofoil edition. **A:** Michael Turner **W:** Michael Turner; Bill O'Neil
9/C ❑ **NM** value: **10.00**
• Aspen on outcropping **A:** Michael Turner **W:** Michael Turner; Bill O'Neil
9/D ❑ **NM** value: **15.00**
• Green logo variant w/Aspen on rock outcropping **A:** Michael Turner **W:** Michael Turner; Bill O'Neil
10 ❑ Jan 2000 Cover: 2.50 **NM** value: **Cover or less**
Circ: Diamd. preorders: **61,981**
10/A❑ **NM** value: **5.00**
• **CGC:** 1 graded, best 9.6
Perfect 10 DFE Alternate cover. **A:** Michael Turner **W:** Michael Turner; Bill O'Neil
10/B❑ **NM** value: **10.00**
• **CGC:** 1 graded, best 9.8
Perfect 10 DFE Alternate cover with Gold Stamp and certificate of authenticity. **A:** Michael Turner **W:** Michael Turner; Bill O'Neil
11 ❑ Apr 2000 Cover: 2.50 **NM** value: **Cover or less**
Circ: Diamd. preorders: **56,739**
12 ❑ Jul 2000 Cover: 2.50 **NM** value: **Cover or less**
Circ: Diamd. preorders: **124,504** • **CGC:** 1 graded, best 9.8
Witchblade in background, Fathom crawling on cover. **A:** Michael Turner **W:** Michael Turner; Bill O'Neil
12/A❑ **NM** value: **8.00**
12/B❑ **NM** value: **7.50**
• **CGC:** 43 graded, best 10.0
• Holofoil edition. **A:** Michael Turner **W:** Michael Turner; Bill O'Neil
12/C❑ **NM** value: **8.00**
• **CGC:** 1 graded, best 9.6
• DF Alternate edition. **A:** Michael Turner **W:** Michael Turner; Bill O'Neil
12/D❑ **NM** value: **10.00**
• **CGC:** 2 graded, best 9.8
• DF Alternate edition with certificate of authenticity. • Gold logo **A:** Michael Turner **W:** Michael Turner; Bill O'Neil
Bk 1❑ Mar 1999 Cover: 5.95 **NM** value: **Cover or less**
• Collects Fathom (3rd Series) #1-2 **A:** Michael Turner **W:** Michael Turner; Bill O'Neil
Bk 2❑ Mar 1999 Cover: 5.95 **NM** value: **Cover or less**
• Collects Fathom (3rd Series) #3-4 **A:** Michael Turner **W:** Michael Turner; Bill O'Neil
Bk 3❑ Nov 1999 Cover: 5.95 **NM** value: **Cover or less**
• Collects Fathom (3rd Series) #5-6 **A:** Michael Turner **W:** Michael Turner; Bill O'Neil
Bk 4❑ Cover: 5.95 **NM** value: **Cover or less**
• Collects Fathom (3rd Series) #7-8 **A:** Michael Turner **W:** Michael Turner; Bill O'Neil

FATHOM PREVIEW SPECIAL — Image

1 ❑ ca. 1998 **NM** value: **3.00**
• **CGC:** 16 graded, best 9.8

FATHOM SWIMSUIT SPECIAL — Image

1 ❑ May 1999 Cover: 2.95 **NM** value: **Cover or less**
2000❑ Dec 2000 Cover: 2.95 **NM** value: **Cover or less**

FATMAN, THE HUMAN FLYING SAUCER — Lightning

1 ❑ Apr 1967 Cover: 0.25 **NM** value: **50.00**
• **CGC:** 1 graded, best 9.4
2 ❑ Jun 1967 Cover: 0.25 **NM** value: **40.00**
3 ❑ Sep 1967 Cover: 0.25 **NM** value: **40.00**
• **CGC:** 1 graded, best 8.0

FAT NINJA, THE — Silverwolf

1 ❑ b&w Cover: 1.50 **NM** value: **Cover or less**
2 ❑ b&w Cover: 1.50 **NM** value: **Cover or less**
3 ❑ b&w Cover: 1.50 **NM** value: **Cover or less**
4 ❑ b&w Cover: 1.50 **NM** value: **Cover or less**
5 ❑ b&w Cover: 1.50 **NM** value: **Cover or less**

FATT FAMILY, THE — Side Show

1 ❑ b&w Cover: 2.95 **NM** value: **Cover or less**

FAULTLINES — DC / Vertigo

1 ❑ May 1997 Cover: 2.50 **NM** value: **Cover or less**
Circ: Diamd. preorders: **18,534**
📖 Fresh Meat, Old Lies **A:** Bill Koeb **W:** Lee Marrs
2 ❑ Jun 1997 Cover: 2.50 **NM** value: **Cover or less**
Circ: Diamd. preorders: **14,208**
3 ❑ Jul 1997 Cover: 2.50 **NM** value: **Cover or less**
Circ: Diamd. preorders: **11,807**
4 ❑ Aug 1997 Cover: 2.50 **NM** value: **Cover or less**
Circ: Diamd. preorders: **10,358**
5 ❑ Sep 1997 Cover: 2.50 **NM** value: **Cover or less**
Circ: Diamd. preorders: **9,420**
6 ❑ Oct 1997 Cover: 2.50 **NM** value: **Cover or less**
Circ: Diamd. preorders: **8,909**

FAUNA REBELLION, THE — Fantagraphics

1 ❑ Mar 1990, b&w Cover: 2.00 **NM** value: **Cover or less**
📖 Where There's Smoke **A:** R.L. Crabb **W:** R.L. Crabb
2 ❑ b&w Cover: 2.00 **NM** value: **Cover or less**
3 ❑ b&w Cover: 2.00 **NM** value: **Cover or less**

FAUNTLEROY COMICS — Archie

1 ❑ ca. 1950 Cover: 0.10 **NM** value: **50.00**
2 ❑ Cover: 0.10 **NM** value: **25.00**
3 ❑ Cover: 0.10 **NM** value: **25.00**

FAUST — Northstar

All issues are adults only.

Few comics have the nerve to balance as far out on the edge as Faust. Faust was created by David Quinn and artist Tim Vigil as a sort of Hell set in comic-book New York City. Its cast is a collection of nymphomaniacs, demons, serial killers, and warlocks. These form a potent mix of sex, blood, and utter depravity, as the players vie for power.

The stuff contained here is pure, high-octane horror. It's not suitable for many readers (and it's certainly not meant for children). Nevertheless, Faust found a devoted following and has had to be reprinted in its entirety to meet demand.

1 ❑ ca. 1989 Cover: 2.00**NM** value: **18.00**
• **CGC:** 7 graded, best 9.6
1-2 ❑ Cover: 2.00 **NM** value: **5.00**
1-3 ❑ Cover: 2.25 **NM** value: **3.00**
Circ: CapCity orders: **5,090**
2 ❑ ca. 1989 Cover: 2.00 **NM** value: **12.00**
• **CGC:** 2 graded, best 8.5
2-2 ❑ Cover: 2.00 **NM** value: **4.00**
2-3 ❑ Cover: 2.25 **NM** value: **3.00**
Circ: CapCity orders: **12,195**
3 ❑ ca. 1989 Cover: 2.25 **NM** value: **8.00**
• **CGC:** 2 graded, best 9.4
3-2 ❑ Cover: 2.25 **NM** value: **3.00**
4 ❑ Cover: 2.25 **NM** value: **5.00**
📖 Blues Wif' the Moon; Fritzwhitstle **A:** Tim Vigil **W:** David Quinn
4-2 ❑ Cover: 2.25 **NM** value: **3.00**
5 ❑ Aug 1989 Cover: 2.25 **NM** value: **5.00**
• **CGC:** 1 graded, best 9.4
5-2 ❑ Cover: 2.25 **NM** value: **3.00**
6 ❑ Nov 1989 Cover: 2.25 **NM** value: **4.00**
• **CGC:** 1 graded, best 9.6
• becomes Rebel title **A:** Tim Vigil **W:** David Quinn
6-2 ❑ Cover: 2.25 **NM** value: **3.00**
Circ: CapCity orders: **4,225**
7 ❑ Cover: 2.25 **NM** value: **4.00**
📖 Delicate Tone **A:** Tim Vigil **W:** David Quinn
7-2 ❑ Cover: 2.25 **NM** value: **2.50**
8 ❑ Cover: 2.25 **NM** value: **4.00**
📖 Jaded Love **A:** Tim Vigil **W:** David Quinn
8-2 ❑ Cover: 2.25 **NM** value: **2.50**
Circ: CapCity orders: **3,450**
9 ❑ Cover: 2.25 **NM** value: **3.50**
9-2 ❑ Cover: 2.25 **NM** value: **2.50**
10 ❑ Cover: 2.25 **NM** value: **3.50**
Circ: CapCity orders: **12,750**
10-2❑ Cover: 2.25 **NM** value: **2.50**
11 ❑ Cover: 2.25 **NM** value: **2.50**
📖 The Tantric Manifold **A:** Tim Vigil **W:** David Quinn
SE 1❑ ca. 1988 Cover: 2.50 **NM** value: **Cover or less**
• **CGC:** 1 graded, best 9.0

FAUST 777: THE WRATH — Avatar

0 ❑ Dec 1998 Cover: 3.00 **NM** value: **Cover or less**
Circ: Diamd. preorders: **7,204**
📖 Darkness in Collision, Part 1 **A:** Tim Vigil **W:** David Quinn
1 ❑ ca. 1998 Cover: 3.00 **NM** value: **Cover or less**
Circ: Diamd. preorders: **8,087**
1/A ❑ ca. 1998 Cover: 3.50 **NM** value: **Cover or less**
Circ: Diamd. preorders: **5,143**
wraparond cover.
2 ❑ ca. 1998 Cover: 3.00 **NM** value: **Cover or less**
Circ: Diamd. preorders: **8,079**
3 ❑ ca. 1998 Cover: 3.00 **NM** value: **Cover or less**
Circ: Diamd. preorders: **7,292**

FAUST: THE BOOK OF M — Avatar

1 ❑ **NM** value: **3.00**
Circ: Diamd. preorders: **7,164**

FAWCETT MINIATURES — Fawcett

In 1946, Fawcett Comics, the publishers of Captain Marvel (Shazam!) and other popular titles of the Golden Age, reprinted several of its stories in 3-3/4-by-5-inch 24-page booklets with newsprint covers and gave them away as promotions in packages of Wheaties Cereal. Issues featured a lead story with Captain Marvel or Captain Marvel Jr. and a backup with one of Fawcett's "second banana" characters such as Bulletman and Golden Arrow. Because of their unusual size, format, and distribution, it is hard to say how many issues were published (the Overstreet Price Guide lists four) or how many survived to the present day (Gerber's Photojournal does not list the promotional series at all).

1 ❑ **NM** value: **60.00**
• Captain Marvel: Horn of Plenty
2 ❑ **NM** value: **60.00**
• Captain Marvel: Raiders From Space
3 ❑ **NM** value: **60.00**
• Captain Marvel: Case of the Poison Press
4 ❑ **NM** value: **100.00**
• Delecta of the Planets **A:** C.C. Beck

FAWCETT MOVIE COMIC — Fawcett

nn ❑ ca. 1949 Cover: 0.10 **NM** value: **200.00**
1 ❑ Cover: 0.10 **NM** value: **275.00**
2 ❑ Cover: 0.10 **NM** value: **200.00**
3 ❑ Cover: 0.10 **NM** value: **200.00**
4 ❑ Cover: 0.10 **NM** value: **200.00**
5 ❑ ca. 1950 Cover: 0.10 **NM** value: **200.00**
6 ❑ 1950 Cover: 0.10 **NM** value: **200.00**
7 ❑ 1950 Cover: 0.10 **NM** value: **200.00**
8 ❑ 1950 Cover: 0.10 **NM** value: **200.00**
9 ❑ Feb 1951 Cover: 0.10 **NM** value: **200.00**
10 ❑ Apr 1951 Cover: 0.10 **NM** value: **200.00**
11 ❑ Jun 1951 Cover: 0.10 **NM** value: **200.00**
12 ❑ Aug 1951 Cover: 0.10 **NM** value: **200.00**
13 ❑ Oct 1951 Cover: 0.10 **NM** value: **200.00**
14 ❑ Dec 1951 Cover: 0.10 **NM** value: **200.00**
• **CGC:** 1 graded, best 5.0
15 ❑ Feb 1952 Cover: 0.10 **NM** value: **200.00**
16 ❑ Apr 1952 Cover: 0.10 **NM** value: **200.00**
17 ❑ Jun 1952 Cover: 0.10 **NM** value: **200.00**
18 ❑ Aug 1952 Cover: 0.10 **NM** value: **200.00**
19 ❑ Oct 1952 Cover: 0.10 **NM** value: **200.00**
20 ❑ Dec 1952 Cover: 0.10 **NM** value: **200.00**

FAWCETT'S FUNNY ANIMALS — Fawcett

Funny-animal strips have been a mainstay of comic books from the very beginning. The most popular were merely extensions of cartoon brand names-think Mickey Mouse and Looney Tunes — but lesser-known funny-animal comics were not any less well done. This Fawcett title is a perfect case in point. Featuring no major cartoonists and no Saturday matinee cartoon idols, it nevertheless offered cinematic-quality art and some truly funny stories. Its most popular and noteworthy character was Hoppy, the Captain Marvel Bunny. By shouting the same magic word ("Shazam!") as his human counterpart Captain Marvel, mild-mannered Hoppy Bunny could transform into a l'il Big Red Cheese, fighting the four-color good fight for truth, justice, and the animal way. Long before Underdog, Super Goof, or Captain Carrot, Hoppy was one of comicdom's first cross-genre characters (introduced in the 1940s, roughly the same time as Mighty Mouse), blending equal parts humor and action in his adventures.

1 ❑ Dec 1942 Cover: 0.10 **NM** value: **240.00**
• **CGC:** 2 graded, best 9.2
2 ❑ Jan 1942 Cover: 0.10 **NM** value: **125.00**
• **CGC:** 1 graded, best 9.4
3 ❑ Feb 1942 Cover: 0.10 **NM** value: **90.00**
4 ❑ Mar 1942 Cover: 0.10 **NM** value: **65.00**
5 ❑ Apr 1942 Cover: 0.10 **NM** value: **65.00**
6 ❑ May 1942 Cover: 0.10 **NM** value: **52.00**
7 ❑ Jun 1942 Cover: 0.10 **NM** value: **52.00**
8 ❑ Jul 1943 Cover: 0.10 **NM** value: **52.00**
9 ❑ Aug 1943 Cover: 0.10 **NM** value: **52.00**
10 ❑ Sep 1943 Cover: 0.10 **NM** value: **52.00**
11 ❑ Oct 1943 Cover: 0.10 **NM** value: **40.00**
12 ❑ Nov 1943 Cover: 0.10 **NM** value: **40.00**
13 ❑ Dec 1943 Cover: 0.10 **NM** value: **40.00**
14 ❑ Jan 1944 Cover: 0.10 **NM** value: **40.00**
15 ❑ Feb 1944 Cover: 0.10 **NM** value: **40.00**
16 ❑ Mar 1944 Cover: 0.10 **NM** value: **40.00**
17 ❑ Cover: 0.10 **NM** value: **40.00**
18 ❑ Cover: 0.10 **NM** value: **40.00**
19 ❑ Cover: 0.10 **NM** value: **40.00**
20 ❑ Cover: 0.10 **NM** value: **40.00**
21 ❑ Cover: 0.10 **NM** value: **30.00**
22 ❑ Cover: 0.10 **NM** value: **30.00**
23 ❑ Cover: 0.10 **NM** value: **30.00**
24 ❑ Cover: 0.10 **NM** value: **30.00**
25 ❑ Cover: 0.10 **NM** value: **30.00**
26 ❑ ca. 1945 Cover: 0.10 **NM** value: **30.00**
27 ❑ ca. 1945 Cover: 0.10 **NM** value: **30.00**
28 ❑ ca. 1945 Cover: 0.10 **NM** value: **30.00**
29 ❑ ca. 1945 Cover: 0.10 **NM** value: **30.00**
30 ❑ ca. 1945 Cover: 0.10 **NM** value: **30.00**
31 ❑ ca. 1945 Cover: 0.10 **NM** value: **30.00**
32 ❑ ca. 1945 Cover: 0.10 **NM** value: **30.00**
33 ❑ ca. 1945 Cover: 0.10 **NM** value: **30.00**
34 ❑ Cover: 0.10 **NM** value: **30.00**
35 ❑ Cover: 0.10 **NM** value: **30.00**
36 ❑ Mar 1946 Cover: 0.10 **NM** value: **30.00**
📖 Hoppy the Marvel Bunny: Candy Planet; Chuck the Duck: Gets a Check Up; B **A:** Chad
37 ❑ Cover: 0.10 **NM** value: **30.00**
38 ❑ Cover: 0.10 **NM** value: **30.00**
39 ❑ Cover: 0.10 **NM** value: **30.00**
40 ❑ Cover: 0.10 **NM** value: **30.00**
41 ❑ Cover: 0.10 **NM** value: **22.00**
42 ❑ Cover: 0.10 **NM** value: **22.00**
43 ❑ Cover: 0.10 **NM** value: **22.00**
44 ❑ Cover: 0.10 **NM** value: **22.00**
45 ❑ Cover: 0.10 **NM** value: **22.00**
46 ❑ Cover: 0.10 **NM** value: **22.00**
47 ❑ Cover: 0.10 **NM** value: **22.00**
48 ❑ Cover: 0.10 **NM** value: **22.00**
49 ❑ Cover: 0.10 **NM** value: **22.00**
50 ❑ Cover: 0.10 **NM** value: **22.00**
51 ❑ Cover: 0.10 **NM** value: **22.00**
52 ❑ Cover: 0.10 **NM** value: **22.00**
53 ❑ Cover: 0.10 **NM** value: **22.00**

CGC-graded: Multiply prices above by **33 for 9.9 M • 16 for 9.8 NM/M • 7 for 9.6 NM+ • 5 for 9.4 NM • 2.5 for 9.2 NM- • 1.5 for 9.0 VF/NM**

54 ❑ Cover: 0.10 **NM** value: **22.00**
55 ❑ Cover: 0.10 **NM** value: **22.00**
56 ❑ Cover: 0.10 **NM** value: **22.00**
57 ❑ Cover: 0.10 **NM** value: **22.00**
58 ❑ Cover: 0.10 **NM** value: **22.00**
59 ❑ Cover: 0.10 **NM** value: **22.00**
60 ❑ Cover: 0.10 **NM** value: **22.00**
61 ❑ Cover: 0.10 **NM** value: **18.00**
62 ❑ Cover: 0.10 **NM** value: **18.00**
63 ❑ Cover: 0.10 **NM** value: **18.00**
64 ❑ Cover: 0.10 **NM** value: **18.00**
65 ❑ Cover: 0.10 **NM** value: **18.00**
66 ❑ Cover: 0.10 **NM** value: **18.00**
67 ❑ Cover: 0.10 **NM** value: **18.00**
68 ❑ Cover: 0.10 **NM** value: **18.00**
69 ❑ Cover: 0.10 **NM** value: **18.00**
70 ❑ Cover: 0.10 **NM** value: **18.00**
71 ❑ Cover: 0.10 **NM** value: **18.00**
72 ❑ Cover: 0.10 **NM** value: **18.00**
73 ❑ Cover: 0.10 **NM** value: **18.00**
74 ❑ Cover: 0.10 **NM** value: **18.00**
75 ❑ Cover: 0.10 **NM** value: **18.00**
76 ❑ Cover: 0.10 **NM** value: **18.00**
77 ❑ Cover: 0.10 **NM** value: **18.00**
78 ❑ Cover: 0.10 **NM** value: **18.00**
79 ❑ Cover: 0.10 **NM** value: **18.00**
80 ❑ Cover: 0.10 **NM** value: **18.00**
81 ❑ Cover: 0.10 **NM** value: **18.00**
82 ❑ Cover: 0.10 **NM** value: **18.00**
83 ❑ Cover: 0.10 **NM** value: **18.00**
84 ❑ Cover: 0.10 **NM** value: **18.00**
85 ❑ Cover: 0.10 **NM** value: **18.00**
86 ❑ Cover: 0.10 **NM** value: **18.00**
87 ❑ Cover: 0.10 **NM** value: **18.00**
88 ❑ Cover: 0.10 **NM** value: **18.00**
89 ❑ Cover: 0.10 **NM** value: **18.00**
90 ❑ Cover: 0.10 **NM** value: **18.00**
91 ❑ Feb 1956 Cover: 0.10 **NM** value: **18.00**

FAX FROM SARAJEVO — Dark Horse

1 ❑ Oct 1996 Cover: 16.95 **NM** value: **Cover or less**
1/HC❑ Oct 1998 Cover: 24.95 **NM** value: **Cover or less**
hardcover. **A:** Joe Kubert

FAZE ONE FAZERS — AC

1 ❑ Cover: 1.75 **NM** value: **Cover or less**
Circ: CapCity orders: **3,400**
📖 Journey Part 1 **A:** Vic Bridges **W:** Vic Bridges
2 ❑ Cover: 1.75 **NM** value: **Cover or less**
Circ: CapCity orders: **2,725**
📖 Journey Part 2 **A:** Vic Bridges **W:** Vic Bridges
3 ❑ Cover: 1.75 **NM** value: **Cover or less**
Circ: CapCity orders: **2,425**
4 ❑ Cover: 1.75 **NM** value: **Cover or less**
Circ: CapCity orders: **3,775**
📖 Nightmare's End! **A:** Erik Larsen **W:** Vic Bridges; Leo Laney

FAZERS SKETCHBOOK (VIC BRIDGES'...) — AC

1 ❑ Cover: 1.75 **NM** value: **Cover or less**

FEAR — Marvel

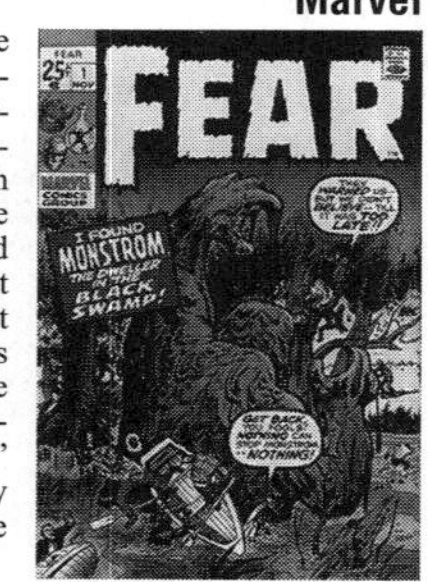

This quarterly series from the 1970s featured tales of horror involving both science and the supernatural. These short stories specialized in horrifying monster tales with ironic endings. Whether it was the cruel butterfly collector who found himself stranded on a world of giant butterflies or the brilliant scientist whose time-travel experiments were, literally, all in his mind, the moral of the story was often the saying, "Be careful what you wish for." The characters learn the hard way that expectations are not always the same as reality.

Like so many 1970s Marvel monster comics, Fear had its origin in a loosening of the boundaries of the Comics Code. Formerly, it had banned depictions of "the walking dead, torture, vampires, cannibalism, and werewolfism." When that stricture was loosened, Marvel was free to reprint stories from its inventory of horror tales from the 1950s and 1960s.

1 ❑ Nov 1970 Cover: 0.25 **NM** value: **10.00**
• **CGC:** 6 graded, best 9.6
2 ❑ Jan 1971 Cover: 0.25 **NM** value: **6.00**
• **CGC:** 3 graded, best 9.2
3 ❑ Mar 1971 Cover: 0.25 **NM** value: **4.00**
• **CGC:** 3 graded, best 9.2
4 ❑ Jul 1971 Cover: 0.25 **NM** value: **4.00**
• **CGC:** 3 graded, best 9.6
📖 Lo-Karr, Bringer of Doom!; Mister Gregory and the Ghost!; I Spent a Night in the Haunted Lighthouse!; My Nightmare Has No End!; The Boy Who Vanished!; He Walked Through Walls!; I Turned Into a Martian!; I Created Krang! **A:** Steve Ditko; Jack Kirby; Dick Ayers; Joe Sinnott
5 ❑ Nov 1971 Cover: 0.25 **NM** value: **4.00**
• **CGC:** 1 graded, best 9.2
📖 I Am the Gorilla-Man; One Look Means Doom!; Rocket Ship X-200; What Lurks on Channel X?; Menace From Mars!; The Return of the Gorilla-Man **A:** Steve Ditko
6 ❑ Feb 1972 Cover: 0.25 **NM** value: **4.00**
• **CGC:** 1 graded, best 9.4
📖 Midnight Monster; There is a Brain Behind the Fangs!; I Took a Journey into Fear!; Wings of the Butterfly!; The Last Laugh!; The Black Ray; The Voice of Fate! **A:** Steve Ditko; Don Heck **W:** Stan Lee
7 ❑ May 1972 Cover: 0.20 **NM** value: **4.00**
8 ❑ Jun 1972 Cover: 0.20 **NM** value: **4.00**
9 ❑ Aug 1972 Cover: 0.20 **NM** value: **4.00**
10 ❑ Oct 1972 Cover: 0.20 **NM** value: **12.00**
• **CGC:** 6 graded, best 9.8
• Man-Thing stories begin ("Adventures into Fear") **A:** Howard Chaykin
11 ❑ Dec 1972 Cover: 0.20 **NM** value: **6.00**
• Man-Thing
12 ❑ Feb 1973 Cover: 0.20 **NM** value: **4.00**
• Man-Thing
13 ❑ Apr 1973 Cover: 0.20 **NM** value: **4.00**
• Man-Thing
14 ❑ Jun 1973 Cover: 0.20 **NM** value: **4.00**
• Man-Thing
15 ❑ Aug 1973 Cover: 0.20 **NM** value: **4.00**
• Man-Thing
16 ❑ Sep 1973 Cover: 0.20 **NM** value: **4.00**
• Man-Thing
17 ❑ Oct 1973 Cover: 0.20 **NM** value: **4.00**
• Man-Thing★ Versus Wundarr.
18 ❑ Nov 1973 Cover: 0.20 **NM** value: **4.00**
• **CGC:** 1 graded, best 9.6
• Man-Thing
19 ❑ Dec 1973 Cover: 0.20 **NM** value: **14.00**
• **CGC:** 4 graded, best 9.6
• Man-Thing★ 1st Appearance of Howard the Duck.
20 ❑ Feb 1974 Cover: 0.20 **NM** value: **10.00**
• **CGC:** 12 graded, best 9.6
📖 Morbius the Living Vampire!; Midnight in the Wax Museum! • Morbius stories begin **A:** Paul Gulacy **W:** Mike Friedrich; Richard Doksee
21 ❑ Apr 1974 Cover: 0.20 **NM** value: **4.00**
• Morbius
22 ❑ Jun 1974 Cover: 0.25 **NM** value: **4.00**
• Morbius
23 ❑ Aug 1974 Cover: 0.25 **NM** value: **4.00**
• 1st Russell art **A:** P. Craig Russell ★ Appearance of Morbius.
24 ❑ Oct 1974 Cover: 0.25 **NM** value: **6.00**
• Morbius★ Appearance of Blade the Vampire Slayer. ★ Versus Blade.
25 ❑ Dec 1974 Cover: 0.25 **NM** value: **3.00**
• Morbius
26 ❑ Feb 1975 Cover: 0.25 **NM** value: **3.00**
• Morbius
27 ❑ Apr 1975 Cover: 0.25 **NM** value: **3.00**
• **CGC:** 1 graded, best 9.2
• Morbius★ Versus Simon Stroud.
28 ❑ Jun 1975 Cover: 0.25 **NM** value: **3.00**
📖 The Doorway Screaming Into Hell! • Morbius **A:** Frank Robbins **W:** Doug Moench
29 ❑ Aug 1975 Cover: 0.25 **NM** value: **3.00**
• **CGC:** 1 graded, best 9.6
📖 Through A Helleyes Darkly! **A:** Don Heck **W:** Bill Mantlo ★ Appearance of Helleyes, Simon Stroud, Morbius.
30 ❑ Oct 1975 Cover: 0.25 **NM** value: **3.00**
• **CGC:** 1 graded, best 9.6
• Morbius
31 ❑ Dec 1975 Cover: 0.25 **NM** value: **3.00**
final issue. • Morbius

FEAR BOOK — Eclipse

1 ❑ Cover: 1.75 **NM** value: **Cover or less**
Circ: CapCity orders: **3,775**

FEAR EFFECT SPECIAL — Image

1 ❑ May 2000 Cover: 2.95 **NM** value: **Cover or less**
Circ: Diamd. preorders: **13,611**

FEAR IS HELL — C&T

1 ❑ b&w Cover: 1.50 **NM** value: **Cover or less**

FEARLESS FOSDICK — Kitchen Sink

1 ❑ **NM** value: **12.00**
1-2 ❑ **NM** value: **10.00**
1-3 ❑ **NM** value: **10.00**

FEATURE BOOK — David McKay

Early issues of the series, sometimes calling itself "Feature Books" and sometimes "Feature Book" on the cover, were oversized, with heavy covers and black-and-white interiors, almost looking as though they were aimed at children looking for coloring books. They often featured adaptations of material that had appeared elsewhere, primarily strip reprints. (Gangbusters, #17, for example, was "adapted from the popular radio program.") Characters like Dick Tracy, Little Orphan Annie, Popeye, The Phantom, and Mandrake were featured; many of the covers featured new art, obviously not drawn by the popular artists of the strips inside. These command high prices for their age, their historical importance, and the popularity of the strips. Color was introduced with #26, featuring Hal Foster's Prince Valiant. — Maggie

1 ❑ Cover: 0.10 **NM** value: **6000.00**
2 ❑ Cover: 0.10 **NM** value: **1000.00**
3 ❑ Cover: 0.10 **NM** value: **800.00**
4 ❑ Cover: 0.10 **NM** value: **600.00**
5 ❑ ca. 1936 Cover: 0.10 **NM** value: **400.00**
6 ❑ Cover: 0.10 **NM** value: **400.00**
7 ❑ Cover: 0.10 **NM** value: **400.00**
8 ❑ Cover: 0.10 **NM** value: **400.00**
9 ❑ Cover: 0.10 **NM** value: **400.00**
10 ❑ Cover: 0.10 **NM** value: **350.00**
11 ❑ Cover: 0.10 **NM** value: **350.00**
12 ❑ Cover: 0.10 **NM** value: **350.00**
13 ❑ ca. 1934 Cover: 0.10 **NM** value: **350.00**
14 ❑ Cover: 0.10 **NM** value: **350.00**
15 ❑ ca. 1938 Cover: 0.10 **NM** value: **350.00**
16 ❑ Cover: 0.10 **NM** value: **350.00**
17 ❑ Cover: 0.10 **NM** value: **350.00**
18 ❑ Cover: 0.10 **NM** value: **350.00**
19 ❑ ca. 1938 Cover: 0.10 **NM** value: **350.00**
20 ❑ Cover: 0.10 **NM** value: **300.00**
21 ❑ Cover: 0.10 **NM** value: **300.00**
22 ❑ ca. 1936 Cover: 0.10 **NM** value: **300.00**
23 ❑ ca. 1938 Cover: 0.10 **NM** value: **300.00**
24 ❑ Cover: 0.10 **NM** value: **300.00**
25 ❑ Cover: 0.10 **NM** value: **300.00**
26 ❑ ca. 1941 Cover: 0.10 **NM** value: **300.00**
27 ❑ Cover: 0.10 **NM** value: **300.00**
28 ❑ ca. 1940 Cover: 0.10 **NM** value: **300.00**
• **CGC:** 1 graded, best 8.0
29 ❑ ca. 1939 Cover: 0.10 **NM** value: **300.00**
30 ❑ Cover: 0.10 **NM** value: **250.00**
31 ❑ Cover: 0.10 **NM** value: **250.00**
32 ❑ Cover: 0.10 **NM** value: **250.00**
33 ❑ Cover: 0.10 **NM** value: **250.00**
34 ❑ Cover: 0.10 **NM** value: **250.00**
35 ❑ ca. 1945 Cover: 0.10 **NM** value: **250.00**
36 ❑ Cover: 0.10 **NM** value: **250.00**
37 ❑ Cover: 0.10 **NM** value: **250.00**
38 ❑ Cover: 0.10 **NM** value: **250.00**
39 ❑ ca. 1943 Cover: 0.10 **NM** value: **250.00**
• **CGC:** 2 graded, best 9.2
40 ❑ ca. 1944 Cover: 0.10 **NM** value: **200.00**
41 ❑ Cover: 0.10 **NM** value: **200.00**
42 ❑ ca. 1945 Cover: 0.10 **NM** value: **200.00**
43 ❑ Cover: 0.10 **NM** value: **200.00**
44 ❑ Cover: 0.10 **NM** value: **200.00**
45 ❑ ca. 1945 Cover: 0.10 **NM** value: **200.00**
46 ❑ ca. 1945 Cover: 0.10 **NM** value: **200.00**
• **CGC:** 1 graded, best 7.0
47 ❑ Cover: 0.10 **NM** value: **200.00**
48 ❑ Cover: 0.10 **NM** value: **200.00**
49 ❑ ca. 1946 Cover: 0.10 **NM** value: **200.00**
50 ❑ Cover: 0.10 **NM** value: **150.00**
51 ❑ ca. 1948 Cover: 0.10 **NM** value: **150.00**
52 ❑ Cover: 0.10 **NM** value: **150.00**
53 ❑ Cover: 0.10 **NM** value: **150.00**
54 ❑ Cover: 0.10 **NM** value: **150.00**
55 ❑ Cover: 0.10 **NM** value: **150.00**
56 ❑ Cover: 0.10 **NM** value: **150.00**
57 ❑ Cover: 0.10 **NM** value: **150.00**

FEATURE COMICS — Quality

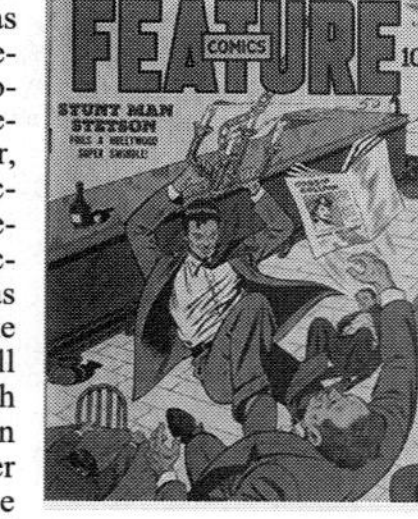

Feature Comics was the continuation of Feature Funnies. Starting as primarily a compilation of strip reprints of such features as Joe Palooka and Mickey Finn, the series began to add features. Moreover, those features tended toward the action-adventure strip that was becoming so popular with comic-book readership. Charlie Chan was introduced in #23 (Aug 39), and the Will Eisner-Lou Fine creation Doll Man began in #27 (Dec 39). Though there were still many gag covers in the series, Doll Man took the cover as often as not, and covers became more and more action-packed and appealing. — Maggie

21 ❑ Jun 1939 Cover: 0.10 **NM** value: **400.00**
Circ: ABC: **280,169**
22 ❑ Jul 1939 Cover: 0.10 **NM** value: **325.00**
Circ: ABC: **310,910**
23 ❑ Aug 1939 Cover: 0.10 **NM** value: **325.00**
Circ: ABC: **327,483**
24 ❑ Sep 1939 Cover: 0.10 **NM** value: **325.00**
Circ: ABC: **387,914**
25 ❑ Oct 1939 Cover: 0.10 **NM** value: **325.00**
Circ: ABC: **355,660**
26 ❑ Nov 1939 Cover: 0.10 **NM** value: **325.00**
Circ: ABC: **305,721**
27 ❑ Dec 1939 Cover: 0.10 **NM** value: **2600.00**
Circ: ABC: **320,961** • **CGC:** 2 graded, best 9.0
28 ❑ Jan 1940 Cover: 0.10 **NM** value: **1250.00**
Circ: ABC: **312,567**
29 ❑ Feb 1940 Cover: 0.10 **NM** value: **800.00**
Circ: ABC: **339,588** • **CGC:** 1 graded, best 5.0
30 ❑ Mar 1940 Cover: 0.10 **NM** value: **850.00**
Circ: ABC: **284,220**
31 ❑ Apr 1940 Cover: 0.10 **NM** value: **60.00**
Circ: ABC: **258,072**
32 ❑ May 1940 Cover: 0.10 **NM** value: **450.00**
Circ: ABC: **227,463**
33 ❑ Jun 1940 Cover: 0.10 **NM** value: **450.00**
Circ: ABC: **184,045**
34 ❑ Jul 1940 Cover: 0.10 **NM** value: **450.00**
35 ❑ Aug 1940 Cover: 0.10 **NM** value: **450.00**
36 ❑ Sep 1940 Cover: 0.10 **NM** value: **450.00**
37 ❑ Oct 1940 Cover: 0.10 **NM** value: **450.00**
38 ❑ Nov 1940 Cover: 0.10 **NM** value: **325.00**
• **CGC:** 2 graded, best 9.4
39 ❑ Dec 1940 Cover: 0.10 **NM** value: **325.00**
• **CGC:** 1 graded, best 4.5

Other grades: Multiply prices above by **1.5 for Mint • 2/3 for Very Fine • 1/3 for Fine • 1/5 for Very Good • 1/8 for Good**

40 ❑ Jan 1941 Cover: 0.10 **NM** value: **250.00**
41 ❑ Feb 1941 Cover: 0.10 **NM** value: **250.00**
• **CGC:** 1 graded, best 3.5
42 ❑ Mar 1941 Cover: 0.10 **NM** value: **250.00**
43 ❑ Apr 1941 Cover: 0.10 **NM** value: **250.00**
44 ❑ May 1941 Cover: 0.10 **NM** value: **250.00**
• **CGC:** 1 graded, best 7.0
45 ❑ Jun 1941 Cover: 0.10 **NM** value: **250.00**
46 ❑ Jul 1941 Cover: 0.10 **NM** value: **250.00**
• **CGC:** 1 graded, best 7.5
47 ❑ Aug 1941 Cover: 0.10 **NM** value: **250.00**
48 ❑ Sep 1941 Cover: 0.10 **NM** value: **250.00**
49 ❑ Oct 1941 Cover: 0.10 **NM** value: **250.00**
50 ❑ Nov 1941 Cover: 0.10 **NM** value: **250.00**
51 ❑ Dec 1941 Cover: 0.10 **NM** value: **175.00**
52 ❑ Jan 1942 Cover: 0.10 **NM** value: **175.00**
53 ❑ Feb 1942 Cover: 0.10 **NM** value: **175.00**
54 ❑ Mar 1942 Cover: 0.10 **NM** value: **175.00**
55 ❑ Apr 1942 Cover: 0.10 **NM** value: **175.00**
56 ❑ May 1942 Cover: 0.10 **NM** value: **175.00**
57 ❑ Jun 1942 Cover: 0.10 **NM** value: **175.00**
58 ❑ Jul 1942 Cover: 0.10 **NM** value: **175.00**
59 ❑ Aug 1942 Cover: 0.10 **NM** value: **175.00**
60 ❑ Sep 1942 Cover: 0.10 **NM** value: **125.00**
• **CGC:** 1 graded, best 3.0
61 ❑ Oct 1942 Cover: 0.10 **NM** value: **125.00**
• **CGC:** 1 graded, best 9.6
62 ❑ Nov 1942 Cover: 0.10 **NM** value: **125.00**
63 ❑ Dec 1942 Cover: 0.10 **NM** value: **125.00**
64 ❑ Jan 1943 Cover: 0.10 **NM** value: **125.00**
65 ❑ Feb 1943 Cover: 0.10 **NM** value: **125.00**
66 ❑ Mar 1943 Cover: 0.10 **NM** value: **125.00**
67 ❑ Apr 1943 Cover: 0.10 **NM** value: **125.00**
68 ❑ Jun 1943 Cover: 0.10 **NM** value: **125.00**
69 ❑ Jul 1943 Cover: 0.10 **NM** value: **125.00**
70 ❑ Aug 1943 Cover: 0.10 **NM** value: **125.00**
71 ❑ Sep 1943 Cover: 0.10 **NM** value: **90.00**
72 ❑ Oct 1943 Cover: 0.10 **NM** value: **90.00**
73 ❑ Nov 1943 Cover: 0.10 **NM** value: **90.00**
74 ❑ Jan 1944 Cover: 0.10 **NM** value: **90.00**
75 ❑ Feb 1944 Cover: 0.10 **NM** value: **90.00**
76 ❑ Mar 1944 Cover: 0.10 **NM** value: **90.00**
77 ❑ Apr 1944 Cover: 0.10 **NM** value: **90.00**
78 ❑ May 1944 Cover: 0.10 **NM** value: **90.00**
79 ❑ Jul 1944 Cover: 0.10 **NM** value: **90.00**
80 ❑ Aug 1944 Cover: 0.10 **NM** value: **90.00**
• **CGC:** 1 graded, best 9.2
81 ❑ Sep 1944 Cover: 0.10 **NM** value: **75.00**
82 ❑ Oct 1944 Cover: 0.10 **NM** value: **75.00**
83 ❑ Nov 1944 Cover: 0.10 **NM** value: **75.00**
84 ❑ Jan 1945 Cover: 0.10 **NM** value: **75.00**
85 ❑ Feb 1945 Cover: 0.10 **NM** value: **75.00**
86 ❑ Mar 1945 Cover: 0.10 **NM** value: **75.00**
87 ❑ Apr 1945 Cover: 0.10 **NM** value: **75.00**
88 ❑ May 1945 Cover: 0.10 **NM** value: **75.00**
89 ❑ Jul 1945 Cover: 0.10 **NM** value: **75.00**
90 ❑ Aug 1945 Cover: 0.10 **NM** value: **75.00**
91 ❑ Sep 1945 Cover: 0.10 **NM** value: **75.00**
92 ❑ Oct 1945 Cover: 0.10 **NM** value: **75.00**
93 ❑ Nov 1945 Cover: 0.10 **NM** value: **75.00**
94 ❑ Jan 1946 Cover: 0.10 **NM** value: **75.00**
95 ❑ Feb 1946 Cover: 0.10 **NM** value: **75.00**
96 ❑ Mar 1946 Cover: 0.10 **NM** value: **75.00**
97 ❑ Apr 1946 Cover: 0.10 **NM** value: **75.00**
98 ❑ May 1946 Cover: 0.10 **NM** value: **75.00**
99 ❑ Jun 1946 Cover: 0.10 **NM** value: **75.00**
100 ❑ Jul 1946 Cover: 0.10 **NM** value: **85.00**
101 ❑ Aug 1946 Cover: 0.10 **NM** value: **50.00**
102 ❑ Sep 1946 Cover: 0.10 **NM** value: **50.00**
103 ❑ Oct 1946 Cover: 0.10 **NM** value: **50.00**
104 ❑ Nov 1946 Cover: 0.10 **NM** value: **50.00**
105 ❑ Dec 1946 Cover: 0.10 **NM** value: **50.00**
106 ❑ Jan 1947 Cover: 0.10 **NM** value: **50.00**
107 ❑ Feb 1947 Cover: 0.10 **NM** value: **50.00**
108 ❑ Mar 1947 Cover: 0.10 **NM** value: **50.00**
109 ❑ Apr 1947 Cover: 0.10 **NM** value: **50.00**
110 ❑ May 1947 Cover: 0.10 **NM** value: **50.00**
111 ❑ Jun 1947 Cover: 0.10 **NM** value: **50.00**
112 ❑ Jul 1947 Cover: 0.10 **NM** value: **50.00**
113 ❑ Aug 1947 Cover: 0.10 **NM** value: **50.00**
114 ❑ Sep 1947 Cover: 0.10 **NM** value: **50.00**
115 ❑ Oct 1947 Cover: 0.10 **NM** value: **50.00**
116 ❑ Nov 1947 Cover: 0.10 **NM** value: **50.00**
117 ❑ Dec 1947 Cover: 0.10 **NM** value: **50.00**
118 ❑ Jan 1948 Cover: 0.10 **NM** value: **50.00**
📖 The Doll Man; Lala Palooza; Swing Sisson; Roscoe; Rusty Ryan; Track Fix (Text Story); Big Top; Perky; Officer Shenenigan ★ Appearance of Doll Man.
119 ❑ Feb 1948 Cover: 0.10 **NM** value: **50.00**
120 ❑ Mar 1948 Cover: 0.10 **NM** value: **50.00**
121 ❑ Apr 1948 Cover: 0.10 **NM** value: **50.00**
122 ❑ May 1948 Cover: 0.10 **NM** value: **50.00**
123 ❑ Jun 1948 Cover: 0.10 **NM** value: **50.00**
124 ❑ Jul 1948 Cover: 0.10 **NM** value: **50.00**
125 ❑ Aug 1948 Cover: 0.10 **NM** value: **50.00**
126 ❑ Sep 1948 Cover: 0.10 **NM** value: **50.00**
127 ❑ Oct 1948 Cover: 0.10 **NM** value: **50.00**
128 ❑ Nov 1948 Cover: 0.10 **NM** value: **50.00**
129 ❑ Dec 1948 Cover: 0.10 **NM** value: **50.00**
130 ❑ Jan 1949 Cover: 0.10 **NM** value: **50.00**
131 ❑ Feb 1949 Cover: 0.10 **NM** value: **50.00**
132 ❑ Mar 1949 Cover: 0.10 **NM** value: **50.00**
133 ❑ Apr 1949 Cover: 0.10 **NM** value: **50.00**
134 ❑ May 1949 Cover: 0.10 **NM** value: **50.00**
135 ❑ Jun 1949 Cover: 0.10 **NM** value: **50.00**
136 ❑ Jul 1949 Cover: 0.10 **NM** value: **50.00**
137 ❑ Aug 1949 Cover: 0.10 **NM** value: **50.00**
138 ❑ Sep 1949 Cover: 0.10 **NM** value: **50.00**
139 ❑ Oct 1949 Cover: 0.10 **NM** value: **50.00**
140 ❑ Nov 1949 Cover: 0.10 **NM** value: **50.00**
141 ❑ Dec 1949 Cover: 0.10 **NM** value: **50.00**
142 ❑ Jan 1950 Cover: 0.10 **NM** value: **50.00**
143 ❑ Mar 1950 Cover: 0.10 **NM** value: **50.00**
144 ❑ May 1950 Cover: 0.10 **NM** value: **50.00**
final issue.

FEATURE FILMS — DC

1 ❑ Mar 1950 Cover: 0.10 **NM** value: **500.00**
• **CGC:** 1 graded, best 9.2
2 ❑ May 1950 Cover: 0.10 **NM** value: **500.00**
• **CGC:** 2 graded, best 7.5
3 ❑ Jul 1950 Cover: 0.10 **NM** value: **500.00**
• **CGC:** 2 graded, best 9.4
4 ❑ Sep 1950 Cover: 0.10 **NM** value: **500.00**

FEATURE FUNNIES — Harry A. Chesler

It was only known for the first 20 issues as Feature Funnies, though it continued without a break as the almost-identical-looking Feature Comics with #21. In both cases, it was another early comic-book series that featured comic-strip reprints for the bulk of its content. (Feature Comics, of course, introduced Doll Man, but that came later.)

Among the features in Feature Funnies are Mickey Finn, Joe Palooka, The Bungle Family, Jane Arden, Dixie Dugan, Lala Palooza, and The Clock. Joe Palooka and Mickey Finn tended to be the focus of the gag covers, with borders embellished with images indicating the other contents. — Maggie

1 ❑ Oct 1937 Cover: 0.10 **NM** value: **2000.00**
• **CGC:** 1 graded, best 9.6
2 ❑ Nov 1937 Cover: 0.10 **NM** value: **1000.00**
3 ❑ Dec 1937 Cover: 0.10 **NM** value: **750.00**
4 ❑ Jan 1938 Cover: 0.10 **NM** value: **500.00**
Circ: ABC: **240,014**
5 ❑ Feb 1938 Cover: 0.10 **NM** value: **500.00**
Circ: ABC: **250,432**
6 ❑ Mar 1938 Cover: 0.10 **NM** value: **400.00**
Circ: ABC: **231,555**
7 ❑ Apr 1938 Cover: 0.10 **NM** value: **400.00**
Circ: ABC: **227,622**
8 ❑ May 1938 Cover: 0.10 **NM** value: **400.00**
Circ: ABC: **221,928**
9 ❑ Jun 1938 Cover: 0.10 **NM** value: **400.00**
Circ: ABC: **245,757**
10 ❑ Jul 1938 Cover: 0.10 **NM** value: **400.00**
Circ: ABC: **248,622**
11 ❑ Aug 1938 Cover: 0.10 **NM** value: **400.00**
Circ: ABC: **272,131**
12 ❑ Sep 1938 Cover: 0.10 **NM** value: **400.00**
Circ: ABC: **324,134**
13 ❑ Oct 1938 Cover: 0.10 **NM** value: **400.00**
Circ: ABC: **299,688**
14 ❑ Nov 1938 Cover: 0.10 **NM** value: **350.00**
Circ: ABC: **253,757**
15 ❑ Dec 1938 Cover: 0.10 **NM** value: **350.00**
Circ: ABC: **302,106**
16 ❑ Jan 1939 Cover: 0.10 **NM** value: **350.00**
Circ: ABC: **304,798**
17 ❑ Feb 1939 Cover: 0.10 **NM** value: **350.00**
Circ: ABC: **323,532**
18 ❑ Mar 1939 Cover: 0.10 **NM** value: **350.00**
Circ: ABC: **316,196**
19 ❑ Apr 1939 Cover: 0.10 **NM** value: **350.00**
Circ: ABC: **282,337**
20 ❑ May 1939 Cover: 0.10 **NM** value: **350.00**
Circ: ABC: **284,645**

FEATURE PRESENTATION — Fox

5 ❑ Apr 1950 Cover: 0.10 **NM** value: **300.00**

FEDERAL MEN COMICS — Gerard

2 ❑ ca. 1945 Cover: 0.10 **NM** value: **300.00**
• **CGC:** 1 graded, best 6.5

FEDS 'N' HEADS — Print Mint

1 ❑ Cover: 0.50 **NM** value: **4.00**
📖 Wonder Wart-Hog Meets The Elusive, Chimerical Chameleon!; 0 **A:** Gilbert Shelton **W:** Gilbert Shelton

FEEDERS — Dark Horse

1 ❑ Oct 1999 Cover: 2.95 **NM** value: **Cover or less**
Circ: Diamd. preorders: **10,238**
📖 After Prohibition; The Case of Doctor Feelgood: The TV Freak; A True Story or A Paranoid Fantasy; Will Hatcher Adventure; The Doctor Gets a Fat Lip **A:** Foolbert Sturgeon **W:** Foolbert Sturgeon

FEELGOOD FUNNIES — Rip Off

1 ❑ Cover: 0.50 **NM** value: **3.00**
📖 After Prohibition; The Case of Doctor Feelgood: The TV Freak; A True Story or A Paranoid Fantasy; Will Hatcher Adventure; The Doctor Gets a Fat Lip **A:** Foolbert Sturgeon **W:** Foolbert Sturgeon

FELICIA HARDY: THE BLACK CAT — Marvel

1 ❑ Jul 1994 Cover: 1.50 **NM** value: **Cover or less**
Circ: CapCity orders: **30,500**
📖 Chimera Lost, Part 1 **A:** Andrew Wildman **W:** Terry Kavanagh; Joey Cavalieri
2 ❑ Aug 1994 Cover: 1.50 **NM** value: **Cover or less**
Circ: CapCity orders: **21,000**
📖 Chimera Lost, Part 2
3 ❑ Sep 1994 Cover: 1.50 **NM** value: **Cover or less**
Circ: CapCity orders: **18,500**
📖 Chimera Lost, Part 3
4 ❑ Oct 1994 Cover: 1.50 **NM** value: **Cover or less**
Circ: CapCity orders: **16,450**
📖 Chimera Lost, Part 4 final issue.

FELICIA: MELARI'S WISH — Mu Press

Bk 1 ❑ Jan 1995, b&w Cover: 14.95 **NM** value: **Cover or less**
• collects material from Rowbrazzle APA, mailings 16-37; collects material from Rowbrazzle APA, mailings 16-37

FELIX AND HIS FRIENDS — Toby

1 ❑ Cover: 0.10 **NM** value: **250.00**
2 ❑ ca. 1954 Cover: 0.10 **NM** value: **125.00**
3 ❑ Cover: 0.10 **NM** value: **125.00**

FELIX'S NEPHEWS INKY AND DINKY — Harvey

1 ❑ ca. 1957 Cover: 0.10 **NM** value: **50.00**
• **CGC:** 1 graded, best 7.5
2 ❑ ca. 1957 Cover: 0.10 **NM** value: **25.00**
3 ❑ ca. 1958 Cover: 0.10 **NM** value: **25.00**
4 ❑ ca. 1958 Cover: 0.10 **NM** value: **25.00**
5 ❑ ca. 1958 Cover: 0.10 **NM** value: **25.00**
6 ❑ ca. 1958 Cover: 0.10 **NM** value: **25.00**
7 ❑ ca. 1958 Cover: 0.10 **NM** value: **25.00**

FELIX THE CAT (PAT SULLIVAN'S...) — Dell

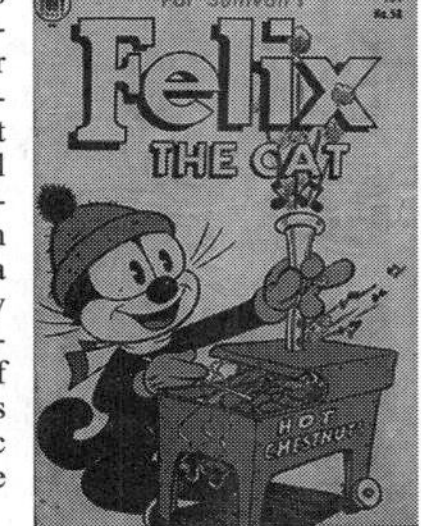

The inventive Felix the Cat has had many more than nine lives. Created by animator Otto Messmer for Pat Sullivan's animation studio, Felix first appeared (unnamed) in silent shorts "Feline Follies" and "Musical Mews" in 1919, with the first one-reeler, "Felix Saves the Day," in 1922. In 1923, the cat expanded to a Sunday newspaper strip, with a daily added four years later. His early adventures, featuring his handy "bag of tricks," won many fans and he was rarely out of print in either comic strips or comic books through the 1940s, '50s, and '60s.

In 19 issues at Dell and another 42 at Toby, the black feline cavorts with human and animal pals in a 1940s style. The inspired primitivism of the art gives those adventures the look of an illustrated children's book.

By comparison, the more familiar Harvey issues, which begin with #62, are something of a departure. They have a smoother, slicker look. Second-banana humor strips like Donny Boy and Flub fill out the remaining pages.

1 ❑ Feb 1948 Cover: 0.10 **NM** value: **225.00**
• **CGC:** 2 graded, best 9.4
2 ❑ Apr 1948 Cover: 0.10 **NM** value: **125.00**
• **CGC:** 1 graded, best 9.4
3 ❑ Jun 1948 Cover: 0.10 **NM** value: **90.00**
4 ❑ Aug 1948 Cover: 0.10 **NM** value: **90.00**
• **CGC:** 1 graded, best 9.4
5 ❑ Oct 1948 Cover: 0.10 **NM** value: **90.00**
6 ❑ Dec 1948 Cover: 0.10 **NM** value: **70.00**
7 ❑ Feb 1949 Cover: 0.10 **NM** value: **70.00**
• **CGC:** 1 graded, best 8.5
8 ❑ Apr 1949 Cover: 0.10 **NM** value: **70.00**
9 ❑ Jun 1949 Cover: 0.10 **NM** value: **70.00**
10 ❑ Aug 1949 Cover: 0.10 **NM** value: **70.00**
11 ❑ Oct 1949 Cover: 0.10 **NM** value: **60.00**
• **CGC:** 1 graded, best 7.5
12 ❑ Dec 1949 Cover: 0.10 **NM** value: **60.00**
13 ❑ Feb 1950 Cover: 0.10 **NM** value: **60.00**
14 ❑ Apr 1950 Cover: 0.10 **NM** value: **60.00**
15 ❑ Jun 1950 Cover: 0.10 **NM** value: **60.00**
16 ❑ Aug 1950 Cover: 0.10 **NM** value: **60.00**
• **CGC:** 1 graded, best 9.4
17 ❑ Oct 1950 Cover: 0.10 **NM** value: **60.00**
• **CGC:** 1 graded, best 9.4
18 ❑ Dec 1950 Cover: 0.10 **NM** value: **60.00**
• **CGC:** 1 graded, best 9.4
19 ❑ Feb 1951 Cover: 0.10 **NM** value: **60.00**
• Last Dell issue

FELIX THE CAT (PAT SULLIVAN) — Toby

20 ❑ ca. 1951 Cover: 0.10 **NM** value: **60.00**
• First Toby issue
21 ❑ ca. 1951 Cover: 0.10 **NM** value: **150.00**
22 ❑ ca. 1951 Cover: 0.10 **NM** value: **150.00**
23 ❑ ca. 1951 Cover: 0.10 **NM** value: **150.00**
24 ❑ Oct 1951 Cover: 0.10 **NM** value: **150.00**
• **CGC:** 1 graded, best 9.0
25 ❑ Nov 1951 Cover: 0.10 **NM** value: **150.00**
• **CGC:** 1 graded, best 8.5
26 ❑ Dec 1951 Cover: 0.10 **NM** value: **150.00**
• **CGC:** 1 graded, best 9.2
27 ❑ Jan 1952 Cover: 0.10 **NM** value: **150.00**
• **CGC:** 1 graded, best 8.5
28 ❑ Feb 1952 Cover: 0.10 **NM** value: **150.00**
29 ❑ Mar 1952 Cover: 0.10 **NM** value: **150.00**
30 ❑ ca. 1952 Cover: 0.10 **NM** value: **150.00**
31 ❑ ca. 1952 Cover: 0.10 **NM** value: **50.00**
32 ❑ ca. 1952 Cover: 0.10 **NM** value: **125.00**
33 ❑ ca. 1952 Cover: 0.10 **NM** value: **125.00**
34 ❑ ca. 1952 Cover: 0.10 **NM** value: **50.00**
35 ❑ Dec 1952 Cover: 0.10 **NM** value: **50.00**
36 ❑ 1953 Cover: 0.10 **NM** value: **125.00**
37 ❑ 1953 Cover: 0.10 **NM** value: **330.00**

CGC-graded: Multiply prices above by **33 for 9.9 M • 16 for 9.8 NM/M • 7 for 9.6 NM+ • 5 for 9.4 NM • 2.5 for 9.2 NM- • 1.5 for 9.0 VF/NM**

• Scarce
38 ❑ 1953 Cover: 0.10 **NM** value: **125.00**
39 ❑ 1953 Cover: 0.10 **NM** value: **125.00**
40 ❑ ca. 1953 Cover: 0.10 **NM** value: **125.00**
41 ❑ ca. 1953 Cover: 0.10 **NM** value: **100.00**
42 ❑ Jun 1953 Cover: 0.10 **NM** value: **100.00**
📖 Felix; Service with a Smile; Donny Boy; Fiber Fox(text story(; Oliver's Twist;
43 ❑ ca. 1953 Cover: 0.10 **NM** value: **100.00**
44 ❑ ca. 1953 Cover: 0.10 **NM** value: **100.00**
45 ❑ ca. 1953 Cover: 0.10 **NM** value: **100.00**
46 ❑ ca. 1953 Cover: 0.10 **NM** value: **100.00**
47 ❑ Cover: 0.10 **NM** value: **100.00**
48 ❑ Cover: 0.10 **NM** value: **100.00**
49 ❑ ca. 1954 Cover: 0.10 **NM** value: **100.00**
50 ❑ ca. 1954 Cover: 0.10 **NM** value: **100.00**
51 ❑ ca. 1954 Cover: 0.10 **NM** value: **100.00**
52 ❑ Jun 1954 Cover: 0.10 **NM** value: **90.00**
• **CGC:** 1 graded, best 8.0
53 ❑ ca. 1954 Cover: 0.10 **NM** value: **90.00**
54 ❑ ca. 1954 Cover: 0.10 **NM** value: **90.00**
55 ❑ 1954 Cover: 0.10 **NM** value: **90.00**
56 ❑ 1954 Cover: 0.10 **NM** value: **90.00**
57 ❑ 1955 Cover: 0.10 **NM** value: **90.00**
58 ❑ 1955 Cover: 0.10 **NM** value: **90.00**
59 ❑ ca. 1955 Cover: 0.10 **NM** value: **90.00**
60 ❑ ca. 1955 Cover: 0.10 **NM** value: **90.00**
61 ❑ ca. 1955 Cover: 0.10 **NM** value: **90.00**
• Last Toby issue; series moves to Harvey
Anl 1❑Sum 1953 Cover: 0.25 **NM** value: **250.00**
• Summer annual 1953
Anl 2❑ Cover: 0.25 **NM** value: **225.00**
• Winter annual 1954

FELIX THE CAT (HARVEY, 1ST SERIES) Harvey

62 ❑ Aug 1955 Cover: 0.10 **NM** value: **40.00**
63 ❑ Sep 1955 Cover: 0.10 **NM** value: **40.00**
64 ❑ Oct 1955 Cover: 0.10 **NM** value: **40.00**
65 ❑ Nov 1955 Cover: 0.10 **NM** value: **40.00**
66 ❑ Dec 1955 Cover: 0.10 **NM** value: **40.00**
67 ❑ Jan 1956 Cover: 0.10 **NM** value: **40.00**
68 ❑ Feb 1956 Cover: 0.10 **NM** value: **40.00**
69 ❑ Mar 1956 Cover: 0.10 **NM** value: **40.00**
70 ❑ Apr 1956 Cover: 0.10 **NM** value: **40.00**
71 ❑ May 1956 Cover: 0.10 **NM** value: **35.00**
72 ❑ Jun 1956 Cover: 0.10 **NM** value: **35.00**
73 ❑ Jul 1956 Cover: 0.10 **NM** value: **35.00**
74 ❑ Aug 1956 Cover: 0.10 **NM** value: **35.00**
75 ❑ Sep 1956 Cover: 0.10 **NM** value: **35.00**
76 ❑ Oct 1956 Cover: 0.10 **NM** value: **35.00**
77 ❑ Nov 1956 Cover: 0.10 **NM** value: **35.00**
78 ❑ Dec 1956 Cover: 0.10 **NM** value: **35.00**
79 ❑ Jan 1957 Cover: 0.10 **NM** value: **35.00**
80 ❑ Feb 1957 Cover: 0.10 **NM** value: **35.00**
81 ❑ Mar 1957 Cover: 0.10 **NM** value: **30.00**
82 ❑ Apr 1957 Cover: 0.10 **NM** value: **30.00**
83 ❑ May 1957 Cover: 0.10 **NM** value: **30.00**
84 ❑ Jun 1957 Cover: 0.10 **NM** value: **30.00**
85 ❑ Jul 1957 Cover: 0.10 **NM** value: **30.00**
86 ❑ Aug 1957 Cover: 0.10 **NM** value: **30.00**
87 ❑ Sep 1957 Cover: 0.10 **NM** value: **30.00**
88 ❑ Oct 1957 Cover: 0.10 **NM** value: **30.00**
89 ❑ Nov 1957 Cover: 0.10 **NM** value: **30.00**
90 ❑ Dec 1957 Cover: 0.10 **NM** value: **30.00**
91 ❑ Jan 1958 Cover: 0.10 **NM** value: **24.00**
92 ❑ Feb 1958 Cover: 0.10 **NM** value: **24.00**
93 ❑ Mar 1958 Cover: 0.10 **NM** value: **24.00**
94 ❑ Apr 1958 Cover: 0.10 **NM** value: **24.00**
95 ❑ May 1958 Cover: 0.10 **NM** value: **24.00**
96 ❑ Jun 1958 Cover: 0.10 **NM** value: **24.00**
97 ❑ Jul 1958 Cover: 0.10 **NM** value: **24.00**
98 ❑ Aug 1958 Cover: 0.10 **NM** value: **24.00**
99 ❑ Sep 1958 Cover: 0.10 **NM** value: **24.00**
100 ❑ Nov 1958 Cover: 0.10 **NM** value: **24.00**
101 ❑ Jan 1959 Cover: 0.10 **NM** value: **20.00**
102 ❑ Mar 1959 Cover: 0.10 **NM** value: **20.00**
103 ❑ May 1959 Cover: 0.10 **NM** value: **20.00**
104 ❑ Jul 1959 Cover: 0.10 **NM** value: **20.00**
105 ❑ Sep 1959 Cover: 0.10 **NM** value: **20.00**
106 ❑ Nov 1959 Cover: 0.10 **NM** value: **20.00**
107 ❑ Jan 1960 Cover: 0.10 **NM** value: **20.00**
Circ: Statement: **138,191**
108 ❑ Mar 1960 Cover: 0.10 **NM** value: **20.00**
Circ: Statement: **138,191**
109 ❑ May 1960 Cover: 0.10 **NM** value: **20.00**
Circ: Statement: **138,191**
110 ❑ Jul 1960 Cover: 0.10 **NM** value: **20.00**
Circ: Statement: **138,191**
111 ❑ Sep 1960 Cover: 0.10 **NM** value: **20.00**
Circ: Statement: **138,191**
112 ❑ Nov 1960 Cover: 0.10 **NM** value: **20.00**
Circ: Statement: **138,191**
113 ❑ Jan 1961 Cover: 0.10 **NM** value: **20.00**
114 ❑ Mar 1961 Cover: 0.10 **NM** value: **20.00**
115 ❑ May 1961 Cover: 0.10 **NM** value: **20.00**
• Has 1960 Statement, filed 10/1/60; avg total paid circ 138,191
116 ❑ Jul 1961 Cover: 0.10 **NM** value: **20.00**
117 ❑ Sep 1961 Cover: 0.10 **NM** value: **20.00**
118 ❑ Nov 1961 Cover: 0.10 **NM** value: **20.00**

FELIX THE CAT (DELL, 2ND SERIES) Dell

1 ❑ ca. 1962 Cover: 0.12 **NM** value: **35.00**
2 ❑ Jan 1963 Cover: 0.12 **NM** value: **25.00**
3 ❑ Apr 1963 Cover: 0.12 **NM** value: **25.00**
4 ❑ Jul 1963 Cover: 0.12 **NM** value: **25.00**
• **CGC:** 2 graded, best 9.4
5 ❑ Oct 1963 Cover: 0.12 **NM** value: **25.00**
• **CGC:** 1 graded, best 9.4
6 ❑ Jan 1964 Cover: 0.12 **NM** value: **25.00**
Circ: Statement: **199,443**
7 ❑ Apr 1964 Cover: 0.12 **NM** value: **25.00**
Circ: Statement: **199,443**
8 ❑ Jul 1964 Cover: 0.12 **NM** value: **25.00**
Circ: Statement: **199,443**
9 ❑ Oct 1964 Cover: 0.12 **NM** value: **25.00**
Circ: Statement: **199,443**
10 ❑ Jan 1965 Cover: 0.12 **NM** value: **25.00**
11 ❑ Apr 1965 Cover: 0.12 **NM** value: **25.00**
• Has 1964 Statement, filed 10/1/64; avg print run 337,500; avg sales 199,388; avg subs 55; avg total paid circ 199,443; samples 307; max existent 199,750; 42% of run returned
12 ❑ Jul 1965 Cover: 0.12 **NM** value: **25.00**

FELIX THE CAT (HARVEY, 2ND SERIES) Harvey

2 ❑ Nov 1991 Cover: 1.25 **NM** value: **Cover or less**
Circ: CapCity orders: **3,475**
3 ❑ Jan 1992 Cover: 1.25 **NM** value: **Cover or less**
Circ: CapCity orders: **3,075**
4 ❑ Mar 1992 Cover: 1.25 **NM** value: **Cover or less**
5 ❑ Jun 1992 Cover: 1.25 **NM** value: **Cover or less**
6 ❑ Sep 1992 Cover: 1.25 **NM** value: **Cover or less**
7 ❑ Jan 1993 Cover: 1.25 **NM** value: **Cover or less**
Bk 1❑ Cover: 15.95 **NM** value: **Cover or less**
• Keeps on Walkin'

FELIX THE CAT AND FRIENDS Felix

1 ❑ ca. 1994 Cover: 1.95 **NM** value: **Cover or less**
2 ❑ ca. 1994 Cover: 1.95 **NM** value: **Cover or less**
3 ❑ ca. 1994 Cover: 1.95 **NM** value: **Cover or less**
4 ❑ ca. 1994 Cover: 1.95 **NM** value: **Cover or less**
5 ❑ ca. 1994 Cover: 1.95 **NM** value: **Cover or less**

FELIX THE CAT BIG BOOK (VOL. 2) Harvey

1 ❑ Sep 1992 Cover: 1.95 **NM** value: **Cover or less**
📖 The Rainmaker; Bolts in the Blue; Heavenly Daze; Shore Enough; The Sure Thing; How Shocking **A:** Otto Messmer; Don Oriolo **W:** Otto Messmer; Don Oriolo

FELIX THE CAT BLACK & WHITE Felix

1 ❑ Cover: 1.95 **NM** value: **Cover or less**
📖 The Felix Cat; Magic Bag Mishap; Hello Out There; I'm Baby Felix
2 ❑ Cover: 1.95 **NM** value: **Cover or less**
3 ❑ Cover: 1.95 **NM** value: **Cover or less**
4 ❑ Cover: 1.95 **NM** value: **Cover or less**
5 ❑ Cover: 1.95 **NM** value: **Cover or less**
6 ❑ Cover: 1.95 **NM** value: **Cover or less**
7 ❑ Cover: 2.25 **NM** value: **Cover or less**
8 ❑ Cover: 2.25 **NM** value: **Cover or less**

FELIX THE CAT DIGEST MAGAZINE Harvey

1 ❑ Cover: 1.75 **NM** value: **Cover or less**

FEM 5 Express / Parody

1/A ❑ Cover: 2.95 **NM** value: **Cover or less**
variant cover. 📖 Breakthrough **A:** Shelby Robertson **W:** Shelby Robertson; Steven Mateo; Thomas Roan
1/B ❑ Cover: 2.95 **NM** value: **Cover or less**
variant cover. 📖 Breakthrough
1/C ❑ Cover: 2.95 **NM** value: **Cover or less**
variant cover. 📖 Breakthrough
1/D ❑ Cover: 2.95 **NM** value: **Cover or less**
variant cover. 📖 Breakthrough
2 ❑ Cover: 2.95 **NM** value: **Cover or less**

FEMALE SEX PIRATES Friendly

1 ❑ Cover: 2.95 **NM** value: **Cover or less**
📖 Scourge of the Seas **A:** Bavanier **W:** Buddy Perot

FEM FANTASTIQUE AC

1 ❑ Jul 1988, b&w Cover: 1.95 **NM** value: **Cover or less**
📖 Rad; Dragonfly **A:** Rik Levins; Bill Black; Victor Bridges **W:** Rik Levins; Bill Black

FEMFORCE AC

The American government has decided it wants an all-woman team of super-heroes, and that team is Femforce

Led by Ms. Victory, the team's key members include Nightveil, Dragonfly, She-Cat, Synn, and Stardust, with frequent additions of other super-characters. Many of the cast have origins in the 1940s and occasionally end up facing modernized foes from that era; fans of the Golden Age will find many tributes to its characters.

The stories are often more meaningful than usual super-hero bash-em-ups, with insights into the different characters' personalities, their families, and their pasts.

1 ❑ ca. 1985, full color Cover: 1.75 **NM** value: **5.00**
📖 Trek for the Time Twister! **A:** Mark Heike **W:** Bill Black ★ Origin of Femforce.
2 ❑ 1986full color Cover: 1.75 **NM** value: **3.50**
Circ: CapCity orders: **3,125**
3 ❑ 1986full color Cover: 1.75 **NM** value: **3.00**
Circ: CapCity orders: **2,625**
4 ❑ 1986full color Cover: 1.75 **NM** value: **3.00**
Circ: CapCity orders: **2,850**
📖 The Hypnotic Eye
5 ❑ 1986full color Cover: 1.75 **NM** value: **3.00**
Circ: CapCity orders: **2,775**
6 ❑ Feb 1987, full color Cover: 1.75 **NM** value: **2.50**
Circ: CapCity orders: **2,775**
7 ❑ May 1987, full color Cover: 1.75 **NM** value: **2.50**
Circ: CapCity orders: **3,125**
8 ❑ Jul 1987, full color Cover: 1.75 **NM** value: **2.50**
9 ❑ Aug 1987, full color Cover: 1.95 **NM** value: **2.50**
10 ❑ full color Cover: 1.95 **NM** value: **2.50**
Circ: CapCity orders: **2,200**
11 ❑ Mar 1988, full color Cover: 1.95 **NM** value: **2.50**
Circ: CapCity orders: **2,250**
12 ❑ May 1988, full color Cover: 1.95 **NM** value: **2.50**
Circ: CapCity orders: **2,100**
13 ❑ May 1988, full color Cover: 1.95 **NM** value: **2.50**
Circ: CapCity orders: **2,025**
14 ❑ 1988full color Cover: 1.95 **NM** value: **2.50**
Circ: CapCity orders: **2,125**
15 ❑ Aug 1988, full color Cover: 1.95 **NM** value: **2.50**
Circ: CapCity orders: **2,050**
16 ❑ 1988 Cover: 2.25 **NM** value: **2.50**
17 ❑ Jan 1989 Cover: 2.25 **NM** value: **2.50**
18 ❑ 1989 Cover: 2.25 **NM** value: **2.50**
19 ❑ Apr 1989 Cover: 2.25 **NM** value: **2.50**
20 ❑ 1989b&w Cover: 2.50 **NM** value: **Cover or less**
21 ❑ 1989b&w Cover: 2.50 **NM** value: **Cover or less**
22 ❑ 1989b&w Cover: 2.50 **NM** value: **Cover or less**
23 ❑ 1990b&w Cover: 2.50 **NM** value: **Cover or less**
24 ❑ Apr 1990, b&w Cover: 2.50 **NM** value: **Cover or less**
25 ❑ May 1990, b&w Cover: 2.50 **NM** value: **Cover or less**
26 ❑ Jun 1990, b&w Cover: 2.50 **NM** value: **Cover or less**
27 ❑ Jul 1990, b&w Cover: 2.50 **NM** value: **Cover or less**
28 ❑ Aug 1990, b&w Cover: 2.50 **NM** value: **Cover or less**
29 ❑ Sep 1990, b&w Cover: 2.50 **NM** value: **Cover or less**
30 ❑ Oct 1990, b&w Cover: 2.50 **NM** value: **Cover or less**
31 ❑ Nov 1990 Cover: 2.75 **NM** value: **Cover or less**
32 ❑ Dec 1990 Cover: 2.75 **NM** value: **Cover or less**
33 ❑ Jan 1991 Cover: 2.75 **NM** value: **Cover or less**
34 ❑ Feb 1991 Cover: 2.75 **NM** value: **Cover or less**
35 ❑ Mar 1991 Cover: 2.75 **NM** value: **Cover or less**
36 ❑ Apr 1991 Cover: 2.75 **NM** value: **Cover or less**
37 ❑ May 1991 Cover: 2.75 **NM** value: **Cover or less**
38 ❑ Jun 1991 Cover: 2.75 **NM** value: **Cover or less**
39 ❑ Jul 1991 Cover: 2.75 **NM** value: **Cover or less**
40 ❑ Aug 1991 Cover: 2.75 **NM** value: **Cover or less**
41 ❑ Sep 1991 Cover: 2.75 **NM** value: **Cover or less**
42 ❑ Oct 1991 Cover: 2.75 **NM** value: **Cover or less**
43 ❑ Nov 1991 Cover: 2.75 **NM** value: **Cover or less**
44 ❑ Dec 1991 Cover: 2.75 **NM** value: **Cover or less**
45 ❑ Jan 1992 Cover: 2.75 **NM** value: **Cover or less**
46 ❑ Feb 1992 Cover: 2.75 **NM** value: **Cover or less**
47 ❑ Mar 1992 Cover: 2.75 **NM** value: **Cover or less**
48 ❑ Apr 1992 Cover: 2.75 **NM** value: **Cover or less**
49 ❑ May 1992 Cover: 2.75 **NM** value: **Cover or less**
50 ❑ Jun 1992 Cover: 2.95 **NM** value: **Cover or less**
Circ: CapCity orders: **3,925**
• contains flexidisccolor
51 ❑ Jul 1992 Cover: 2.75 **NM** value: **Cover or less**
Photo cover.
52 ❑ Aug 1992 Cover: 2.75 **NM** value: **Cover or less**
📖 In the Clutches of the Claw!, Part 3 **A:** Dick Ayers **W:** Bill Black
53 ❑ Cover: 2.75 **NM** value: **Cover or less**
54 ❑ Cover: 2.75 **NM** value: **Cover or less**
Circ: CapCity orders: **2,050**
55 ❑ Cover: 2.75 **NM** value: **Cover or less**
Circ: CapCity orders: **2,000**
56 ❑ Cover: 2.75 **NM** value: **Cover or less**
Circ: CapCity orders: **2,175**
57 ❑ full color Cover: 2.75 **NM** value: **Cover or less**
Circ: CapCity orders: **3,750**
📖 The Capricorn Chronicles, Part 3
58 ❑ Cover: 2.75 **NM** value: **Cover or less**
Circ: CapCity orders: **2,225**
59 ❑ Cover: 2.75 **NM** value: **Cover or less**
60 ❑ Cover: 2.75 **NM** value: **Cover or less**
Circ: CapCity orders: **2,675**
61 ❑ Cover: 2.75 **NM** value: **Cover or less**
Circ: CapCity orders: **2,125**
62 ❑ Cover: 2.75 **NM** value: **Cover or less**
63 ❑ Cover: 2.95 **NM** value: **Cover or less**
📖 Assault of the 60 Foot Woman, Chapter 1 **A:** Bill Black **W:** Bill Black
64 ❑ Cover: 2.95 **NM** value: **Cover or less**
65 ❑ Cover: 2.95 **NM** value: **Cover or less**
66 ❑ Cover: 2.95 **NM** value: **Cover or less**
67 ❑ Cover: 2.95 **NM** value: **Cover or less**
68 ❑ Cover: 2.95 **NM** value: **Cover or less**
69 ❑ Cover: 2.95 **NM** value: **Cover or less**
70 ❑ Cover: 2.95 **NM** value: **Cover or less**
71 ❑ Cover: 2.95 **NM** value: **Cover or less**
72 ❑ Cover: 2.95 **NM** value: **Cover or less**
73 ❑ Cover: 2.95 **NM** value: **Cover or less**
74 ❑ Cover: 2.95 **NM** value: **Cover or less**
75 ❑ Cover: 2.95 **NM** value: **Cover or less**
76 ❑ Cover: 2.95 **NM** value: **Cover or less**
77 ❑ Cover: 2.95 **NM** value: **Cover or less**
78 ❑ Cover: 2.95 **NM** value: **Cover or less**
79 ❑ Cover: 2.95 **NM** value: **Cover or less**
80 ❑ Cover: 2.95 **NM** value: **Cover or less**
81 ❑ Cover: 2.95 **NM** value: **Cover or less**
82 ❑ Cover: 2.95 **NM** value: **Cover or less**
📖 Twilight's Last Gleaming, Part 1
83 ❑ Cover: 2.95 **NM** value: **Cover or less**
84 ❑ Cover: 2.95 **NM** value: **Cover or less**
📖 The Death of Joan Wayne
85 ❑ Cover: 2.95 **NM** value: **Cover or less**
86 ❑ Cover: 2.95 **NM** value: **Cover or less**
87 ❑ Cover: 3.50 **NM** value: **Cover or less**
• 10th anniversary issue. ★ Appearance of AC staff.

Other grades: Multiply prices above by **1.5 for Mint • 2/3 for Very Fine • 1/3 for Fine • 1/5 for Very Good • 1/8 for Good**

88 ❑ Cover: 2.95 **NM** value: **Cover or less**
89 ❑ Cover: 2.95 **NM** value: **Cover or less**
90 ❑ Cover: 2.95 **NM** value: **Cover or less**
91 ❑ Cover: 2.95 **NM** value: **Cover or less**
92 ❑ Cover: 2.95 **NM** value: **Cover or less**
93 ❑ Cover: 2.95 **NM** value: **Cover or less**
94 ❑ Cover: 2.95 **NM** value: **Cover or less**
95 ❑ Cover: 2.95 **NM** value: **Cover or less**
96 ❑ Cover: 2.95 **NM** value: **Cover or less**
97 ❑ b&w Cover: 2.95 **NM** value: **Cover or less**
98 ❑ b&w Cover: 2.95 **NM** value: **Cover or less**
• subtitled in Spanish
99 ❑ b&w Cover: 2.95 **NM** value: **Cover or less**
100 ❑ b&w Cover: 3.95 **NM** value: **Cover or less**
photo back cover.
100/CS❑ Cover: 6.90 **NM** value: **Cover or less**
101 ❑ b&w Cover: 4.95 **NM** value: **Cover or less**
📖 The Yesterday Syndrome, Part 1
102 ❑ b&w Cover: 4.95 **NM** value: **Cover or less**
📖 The Yesterday Syndrome, Part 2
103 ❑ b&w Cover: 4.95 **NM** value: **Cover or less**
104 ❑ b&w Cover: 4.95 **NM** value: **Cover or less**
📖 Return from the Ashes, Part 1; Prelude to Darkness **A:** Rik Levins; Brad Gorby **W:** Bill Black
105 ❑ b&w Cover: 4.95 **NM** value: **Cover or less**
📖 Return from the Ashes, Part 2
106 ❑ b&w Cover: 4.95 **NM** value: **Cover or less**
📖 Return from the Ashes, Part 3
107 ❑ Cover: 4.95 **NM** value: **Cover or less**
📖 Rampage; Old Flames **A:** Mark Heike; Brad Gorby **W:** Bill Black
108 ❑ Cover: 4.95 **NM** value: **Cover or less**
109 ❑ Cover: 4.95 **NM** value: **Cover or less**
110/A❑ Cover: 2.95 **NM** value: **Cover or less**
Rayda on cover.
110/B❑ Cover: 2.95 **NM** value: **Cover or less**
Femforce on cover.
111 ❑ Cover: 2.95 **NM** value: **Cover or less**
112 ❑ Cover: 2.95 **NM** value: **Cover or less**
113 ❑ Cover: 2.95 **NM** value: **Cover or less**
114 ❑ Cover: 2.95 **NM** value: **Cover or less**
Bk 1❑ Cover: 12.95 **NM** value: **Cover or less**
• Origins; collects origins of members and reprints Femforce #1
Bk 2❑ Cover: 24.95 **NM** value: **Cover or less**
• limited to 1000; color and b&w; Capricorn Chronicles
SE 1❑ Nov 1984 Cover: 1.50 **NM** value: **Cover or less**

FEMFORCE FRIGHTBOOK — AC
1 ❑ b&w Cover: 2.95 **NM** value: **Cover or less**

FEMFORCE IN THE HOUSE OF HORROR — AC
1 ❑ b&w Cover: 2.50 **NM** value: **Cover or less**

FEMFORCE: NIGHT OF THE DEMON — AC
1 ❑ b&w Cover: 2.75 **NM** value: **Cover or less**
No issue number.

FEMFORCE: OUT OF THE ASYLUM SPECIAL — AC
1 ❑ Aug 1987, b&w Cover: 2.50 **NM** value: **Cover or less**

FEMFORCE PIN UP PORTFOLIO — AC
1 ❑ Cover: 2.50 **NM** value: **Cover or less**
2 ❑ Cover: 2.50 **NM** value: **Cover or less**
3 ❑ Cover: 2.50 **NM** value: **Cover or less**
4 ❑ Dec 1991 Cover: 2.50 **NM** value: **Cover or less**
5 ❑ Cover: 5.00 **NM** value: **Cover or less**

FEMFORCE UP CLOSE — AC
1 ❑ Apr 1992, full color Cover: 2.75 **NM** value: **3.00**
• Nightveil
2 ❑ Jul 1992 Cover: 2.75 **NM** value: **3.00**
• Stardust
3 ❑ Cover: 2.75 **NM** value: **3.00**
• Dragonfly
4 ❑ Cover: 2.95 **NM** value: **Cover or less**
5 ❑ Cover: 2.95 **NM** value: **Cover or less**
• Blue Bulleteer
6 ❑ Cover: 2.95 **NM** value: **Cover or less**
• Ms. Victory
7 ❑ Cover: 2.95 **NM** value: **Cover or less**
• Ms. Victory
8 ❑ Cover: 2.95 **NM** value: **Cover or less**
• Tara, Garganta
9 ❑ Cover: 2.95 **NM** value: **Cover or less**
• Synn
10 ❑ b&w Cover: 2.95 **NM** value: **Cover or less**
• Yankee Girl
11 ❑ b&w Cover: 2.95 **NM** value: **Cover or less**
• Nightveil

FEMME MACABRE — London Night
1 ❑ Cover: 2.95 **NM** value: **Cover or less**

FEMME NOIRE — Cat-Head
1 ❑ Cover: 1.75 **NM** value: **Cover or less**
📖 The Shamness; Wimp Rock Babylon **A:** Steve Lafler; Dave Cherry; Shirin Tolle **W:** Steve Lafler; Dave Cherry; Shirin Tolle
2 ❑ Cover: 1.75 **NM** value: **Cover or less**
📖 Love Triangle; Yarhooty! **A:** Steve Lafler; Spenchy Racer **W:** Steve Lafler; Spenchy Racer

FENRY — Raven
1 ❑ Cover: 6.95 **NM** value: **Cover or less**
📖 Yesterday's Spirit **A:** Nathan Nassengill **W:** Sonny Nardone

FERRET (1ST SERIES) — Malibu
This 1992 one-shot marked the start of a general expansion of the Malibu super-hero line. The cornerstone of Malibu's super-heroes at the time was a group known as The Protectors, a group of interesting, but largely dysfunctional, super-heroes. The Ferret was among the worst of the bunch: a part-time rock singer whose super-powers consisted of the proportional speed and agility of a ferret, along with a fittingly crazed attitude.

In this one-shot, the Ferret takes on the Purple Dragons, a Chinese ninja-gangster organization responsible for the murder one of Ferret's closest friends. In doing battle with them, he's in for the fight of his life — as well as a huge surprise in the form of a legendary figure from the past, returning with murder on his mind.

1 ❑ ca. 1992 Cover: 1.95 **NM** value: **Cover or less**
📖 Flesh and Steel **A:** Thomas Derenick **W:** R.A. Jones

FERRET, THE (2ND SERIES) — Malibu
1 ❑ May 1993 Cover: 1.95 **NM** value: **Cover or less**
📖 In The Midnight Hour **A:** Dean Zachary **W:** R.A. Jones
1/SC❑ May 1993 Cover: 2.50 **NM** value: **Cover or less**
Circ: CapCity orders: **21,150**
📖 In The Midnight Hour • die-cut **A:** Dean Zachary **W:** R.A. Jones
2 ❑ Jun 1993 Cover: 2.50 **NM** value: **Cover or less**
Circ: CapCity orders: **8,375**
📖 Deadline Medix **A:** Dean Zachary **W:** R.A. Jones
3 ❑ Jul 1993 Cover: 2.50 **NM** value: **Cover or less**
Circ: CapCity orders: **6,275**
📖 Countdown To Oblivion **A:** Dean Zachary **W:** R.A. Jones
4 ❑ Aug 1993 Cover: 2.25 **NM** value: **2.50**
Circ: CapCity orders: **5,600**
5 ❑ Sep 1993 Cover: 2.25 **NM** value: **Cover or less**
📖 Thicker Than Water **A:** Dean Zachary **W:** R.A. Jones
6 ❑ Oct 1993 Cover: 2.25 **NM** value: **Cover or less**
Circ: CapCity orders: **6,350**
7 ❑ Nov 1993 Cover: 2.25 **NM** value: **Cover or less**
Circ: CapCity orders: **5,200**
8 ❑ Dec 1993 Cover: 2.25 **NM** value: **Cover or less**
Circ: CapCity orders: **4,175**
9 ❑ Jan 1994 Cover: 2.50 **NM** value: **Cover or less**
Circ: CapCity orders: **3,650**
10 ❑ Feb 1994 Cover: 2.50 **NM** value: **Cover or less**
Circ: CapCity orders: **3,150**

FEUD — Marvel / Epic
1 ❑ Jul 1993 Cover: 2.50 **NM** value: **Cover or less**
Circ: CapCity orders: **20,300**
embossed cardstock cover. **A:** Mark A. Nelson **W:** Mike Baron
2 ❑ Aug 1993 Cover: 1.95 **NM** value: **Cover or less**
Circ: CapCity orders: **8,900**
3 ❑ Sep 1993 Cover: 1.95 **NM** value: **Cover or less**
Circ: CapCity orders: **6,300**
4 ❑ Oct 1993 Cover: 1.95 **NM** value: **Cover or less**
Circ: CapCity orders: **5,100**

FEVER — Wonder Comix
1 ❑ b&w Cover: 1.95 **NM** value: **Cover or less**
📖 Fear (Text Story); I Suspect the Sea (Poem); The Portal; Small Suicide (Text Story); The Cosmos in November (Poem); Fugue State (Poem); Like Mother **A:** Nils Osmar; Joel McVey; Robin Walker **W:** Nils Osmar; Jerome Gold; Judith Skillman; Simon Drax

FEVER DREAMS — Kitchen Sink
1 ❑ Cover: 0.50 **NM** value: **3.00**
📖 The Unicorn Quest; To Meet the Faces You Meet **A:** Richard Corben; Jan Strnad; John Richardson **W:** Richard Corben; Jan Strnad; John Richardson

FIFTH FORCE FEATURING HAWK AND ANIMAL, THE — Antarctic
1 ❑ Apr 1999 Cover: 1.99 **NM** value: **Cover or less**
2 ❑ Jul 1999 Cover: 2.50 **NM** value: **Cover or less**

FIFTIES TERROR — Eternity
1 ❑ Oct 1988, b&w Cover: 1.95 **NM** value: **Cover or less**
2 ❑ Nov 1988, b&w Cover: 1.95 **NM** value: **Cover or less**
3 ❑ Dec 1988, b&w Cover: 1.95 **NM** value: **Cover or less**
4 ❑ Jan 1989, b&w Cover: 1.95 **NM** value: **Cover or less**
5 ❑ Feb 1989, b&w Cover: 1.95 **NM** value: **Cover or less**
6 ❑ Mar 1989, b&w Cover: 1.95 **NM** value: **Cover or less**

FIGHT AGAINST CRIME — Story
1 ❑ May 1951 Cover: 0.10 **NM** value: **300.00**
2 ❑ Jul 1951 Cover: 0.10 **NM** value: **150.00**
3 ❑ Sep 1951 Cover: 0.10 **NM** value: **125.00**
4 ❑ Nov 1951 Cover: 0.10 **NM** value: **125.00**
5 ❑ Jan 1952 Cover: 0.10 **NM** value: **125.00**
6 ❑ Mar 1952 Cover: 0.10 **NM** value: **100.00**
7 ❑ May 1952 Cover: 0.10 **NM** value: **100.00**
• **CGC:** 1 graded, best 6.0
8 ❑ Jul 1952 Cover: 0.10 **NM** value: **100.00**
9 ❑ Sep 1952 Cover: 0.10 **NM** value: **100.00**
10 ❑ Nov 1952 Cover: 0.10 **NM** value: **275.00**
• **CGC:** 1 graded, best 8.0
11 ❑ Jan 1953 Cover: 0.10 **NM** value: **275.00**
12 ❑ Mar 1953 Cover: 0.10 **NM** value: **275.00**
13 ❑ May 1953 Cover: 0.10 **NM** value: **275.00**
14 ❑ Jul 1953 Cover: 0.10 **NM** value: **275.00**
15 ❑ Sep 1953 Cover: 0.10 **NM** value: **275.00**
16 ❑ Nov 1953 Cover: 0.10 **NM** value: **300.00**
17 ❑ Jan 1954 Cover: 0.10 **NM** value: **300.00**
18 ❑ Mar 1954 Cover: 0.10 **NM** value: **250.00**
19 ❑ May 1954 Cover: 0.10 **NM** value: **250.00**
• **CGC:** 1 graded, best 8.0
20 ❑ Jul 1954 Cover: 0.10 **NM** value: **250.00**
• **CGC:** 5 graded, best 7.5
21 ❑ Sep 1954 Cover: 0.10 **NM** value: **250.00**
• **CGC:** 1 graded, best 4.0

FIGHT AGAINST THE GUILTY — Story
22 ❑ Dec 1954 Cover: 0.10 **NM** value: **200.00**
23 ❑ Mar 1955 Cover: 0.10 **NM** value: **150.00**

FIGHT COMICS — Fiction House
1 ❑ Jan 1940 Cover: 0.10 **NM** value: **2000.00**
• **CGC:** 3 graded, best 7.0
2 ❑ Feb 1940 Cover: 0.10 **NM** value: **1000.00**
• **CGC:** 1 graded, best 7.0
3 ❑ Mar 1940 Cover: 0.10 **NM** value: **750.00**
4 ❑ Apr 1940 Cover: 0.10 **NM** value: **500.00**
5 ❑ May 1940 Cover: 0.10 **NM** value: **500.00**
6 ❑ Jun 1940 Cover: 0.10 **NM** value: **500.00**
7 ❑ Jul 1940 Cover: 0.10 **NM** value: **400.00**
8 ❑ Aug 1940 Cover: 0.10 **NM** value: **400.00**
9 ❑ Oct 1940 Cover: 0.10 **NM** value: **400.00**
10 ❑ Dec 1940 Cover: 0.10 **NM** value: **400.00**
11 ❑ Feb 1941 Cover: 0.10 **NM** value: **350.00**
• **CGC:** 1 graded, best 8.0
12 ❑ Apr 1941 Cover: 0.10 **NM** value: **350.00**
13 ❑ Jun 1941 Cover: 0.10 **NM** value: **350.00**
14 ❑ Aug 1941 Cover: 0.10 **NM** value: **350.00**
15 ❑ Oct 1941 Cover: 0.10 **NM** value: **350.00**
16 ❑ Dec 1941 Cover: 0.10 **NM** value: **350.00**
17 ❑ Feb 1942 Cover: 0.10 **NM** value: **350.00**
18 ❑ Apr 1942 Cover: 0.10 **NM** value: **350.00**
19 ❑ Jun 1942 Cover: 0.10 **NM** value: **350.00**
• **CGC:** 1 graded, best 7.5
20 ❑ Aug 1942 Cover: 0.10 **NM** value: **300.00**
21 ❑ Oct 1942 Cover: 0.10 **NM** value: **300.00**
22 ❑ Dec 1942 Cover: 0.10 **NM** value: **300.00**
23 ❑ Jan 1943 Cover: 0.10 **NM** value: **300.00**
• **CGC:** 1 graded, best 7.0
24 ❑ Feb 1943 Cover: 0.10 **NM** value: **300.00**
25 ❑ Mar 1943 Cover: 0.10 **NM** value: **300.00**
26 ❑ Jun 1943 Cover: 0.10 **NM** value: **300.00**
27 ❑ Aug 1943 Cover: 0.10 **NM** value: **300.00**
28 ❑ Oct 1943 Cover: 0.10 **NM** value: **300.00**
29 ❑ Dec 1943 Cover: 0.10 **NM** value: **300.00**
• **CGC:** 1 graded, best 9.2
30 ❑ Feb 1944 Cover: 0.10 **NM** value: **250.00**
31 ❑ Apr 1944 Cover: 0.10 **NM** value: **250.00**
• **CGC:** 2 graded, best 7.5
32 ❑ Jun 1944 Cover: 0.10 **NM** value: **250.00**
• **CGC:** 1 graded, best 8.0
33 ❑ Aug 1944 Cover: 0.10 **NM** value: **250.00**
34 ❑ Oct 1944 Cover: 0.10 **NM** value: **250.00**
35 ❑ Dec 1944 Cover: 0.10 **NM** value: **250.00**
36 ❑ Feb 1945 Cover: 0.10 **NM** value: **250.00**
37 ❑ Apr 1945 Cover: 0.10 **NM** value: **250.00**
38 ❑ Jun 1945 Cover: 0.10 **NM** value: **250.00**
39 ❑ Aug 1945 Cover: 0.10 **NM** value: **250.00**
• **CGC:** 1 graded, best 9.0
40 ❑ Oct 1945 Cover: 0.10 **NM** value: **250.00**
41 ❑ Dec 1945 Cover: 0.10 **NM** value: **250.00**
42 ❑ Feb 1946 Cover: 0.10 **NM** value: **250.00**
• **CGC:** 1 graded, best 9.2
43 ❑ Apr 1946 Cover: 0.10 **NM** value: **250.00**
• **CGC:** 1 graded, best 9.6
44 ❑ Jun 1946 Cover: 0.10 **NM** value: **250.00**
• **CGC:** 2 graded, best 9.4
45 ❑ Aug 1946 Cover: 0.10 **NM** value: **175.00**
• **CGC:** 1 graded, best 9.0
46 ❑ Oct 1946 Cover: 0.10 **NM** value: **175.00**
• **CGC:** 1 graded, best 8.0
47 ❑ Dec 1946 Cover: 0.10 **NM** value: **175.00**
• **CGC:** 1 graded, best 8.5
48 ❑ Feb 1947 Cover: 0.10 **NM** value: **175.00**
49 ❑ Apr 1947 Cover: 0.10 **NM** value: **175.00**
• **CGC:** 1 graded, best 9.0
50 ❑ Jun 1947 Cover: 0.10 **NM** value: **150.00**
• **CGC:** 1 graded, best 7.0
51 ❑ Aug 1947 Cover: 0.10 **NM** value: **150.00**
• **CGC:** 3 graded, best 9.4
52 ❑ Oct 1947 Cover: 0.10 **NM** value: **150.00**
• **CGC:** 1 graded, best 8.0
53 ❑ Dec 1947 Cover: 0.10 **NM** value: **150.00**
54 ❑ Feb 1948 Cover: 0.10 **NM** value: **150.00**
• **CGC:** 1 graded, best 9.2
55 ❑ Apr 1948 Cover: 0.10 **NM** value: **150.00**
56 ❑ Jun 1948 Cover: 0.10 **NM** value: **150.00**
• **CGC:** 2 graded, best 9.4
57 ❑ Aug 1948 Cover: 0.10 **NM** value: **150.00**
• **CGC:** 2 graded, best 9.4
58 ❑ Oct 1948 Cover: 0.10 **NM** value: **150.00**
• **CGC:** 2 graded, best 9.0
59 ❑ Dec 1948 Cover: 0.10 **NM** value: **150.00**
60 ❑ Feb 1949 Cover: 0.10 **NM** value: **100.00**
• **CGC:** 2 graded, best 9.0
61 ❑ Apr 1949 Cover: 0.10 **NM** value: **150.00**
• **CGC:** 2 graded, best 9.4
62 ❑ Jun 1949 Cover: 0.10 **NM** value: **150.00**
• **CGC:** 2 graded, best 8.5
63 ❑ Aug 1949 Cover: 0.10 **NM** value: **150.00**
• **CGC:** 1 graded, best 9.2
64 ❑ Oct 1949 Cover: 0.10 **NM** value: **150.00**
• **CGC:** 1 graded, best 8.5

CGC-graded: Multiply prices above by **33 for 9.9 M • 16 for 9.8 NM/M • 7 for 9.6 NM+ • 5 for 9.4 NM • 2.5 for 9.2 NM- • 1.5 for 9.0 VF/NM**

65 ❑ Dec 1949 Cover: 0.10 **NM** value: **150.00**
66 ❑ Jan 1950 Cover: 0.10 **NM** value: **150.00**
67 ❑ Mar 1950 Cover: 0.10 **NM** value: **150.00**
68 ❑ May 1950 Cover: 0.10 **NM** value: **150.00**
69 ❑ Jul 1950 Cover: 0.10 **NM** value: **150.00**
• **CGC:** 1 graded, best 6.5
70 ❑ Sep 1950 Cover: 0.10 **NM** value: **125.00**
71 ❑ Nov 1950 Cover: 0.10 **NM** value: **125.00**
72 ❑ Jan 1951 Cover: 0.10 **NM** value: **125.00**
73 ❑ Mar 1951 Cover: 0.10 **NM** value: **125.00**
74 ❑ May 1951 Cover: 0.10 **NM** value: **125.00**
75 ❑ Jul 1951 Cover: 0.10 **NM** value: **125.00**
76 ❑ Sep 1951 Cover: 0.10 **NM** value: **125.00**
77 ❑ Nov 1951 Cover: 0.10 **NM** value: **125.00**
78 ❑ Jan 1952 Cover: 0.10 **NM** value: **125.00**
79 ❑ Mar 1952 Cover: 0.10 **NM** value: **125.00**
80 ❑ May 1952 Cover: 0.10 **NM** value: **125.00**
81 ❑ Jul 1952 Cover: 0.10 **NM** value: **125.00**
82 ❑ Sep 1952 Cover: 0.10 **NM** value: **125.00**
83 ❑ Nov 1952 Cover: 0.10 **NM** value: **125.00**
84 ❑ Win 1952 Cover: 0.10 **NM** value: **125.00**
85 ❑ Spr 1953 Cover: 0.10 **NM** value: **125.00**
86 ❑ Jan 1954 Cover: 0.10 **NM** value: **125.00**

FIGHT FOR LOVE — United Feature

1 ❑ ca. 1952 Cover: 0.10 **NM** value: **50.00**

FIGHTIN' 5 — Charlton

The Fightin' Five consisted of Hank Hennessey, a captain from the special forces and the unofficial leader of the Five; Granite Gallero, his right-hand man, and an expert in weaponry; Frenchy the Fox, a specialist in demolitions and underwater work; Irv the Nerve, a highly resourceful former investigator; and Tom Tom, an Olympic wrestler. They pool their skills to combat crime and such fanciful villains as D.E.A.T.H. (Dedicated Enemies of And Traitors to Humanity — also the first initials of each member's names). Despite the agents' high-tech schemes, the Fightin' Five always win out with their wits.

This series is also notable for issue #40's introduction of Peacemaker in a backup story. Peacemaker was Chris Smith, a man who deplored violence but would strap on a special battle suit and confront evil directly when there was no other option. Eventually Peacemaker moved to DC where he became a much darker character.

28 ❑ Jul 1964 Cover: 0.12 **NM** value: **20.00**
• **CGC:** 2 graded, best 9.2
29 ❑ Oct 1964 Cover: 0.12 **NM** value: **10.00**
• **CGC:** 1 graded, best 9.6
30 ❑ Dec 1964 Cover: 0.12 **NM** value: **10.00**
31 ❑ Feb 1965 Cover: 0.12 **NM** value: **9.00**
32 ❑ May 1965 Cover: 0.12 **NM** value: **9.00**
33 ❑ Jul 1965 Cover: 0.12 **NM** value: **9.00**
34 ❑ Sep 1965 Cover: 0.12 **NM** value: **9.00**
35 ❑ Nov 1965 Cover: 0.12 **NM** value: **9.00**
36 ❑ Jan 1966 Cover: 0.12 **NM** value: **9.00**
37 ❑ May 1966 Cover: 0.12 **NM** value: **9.00**
38 ❑ Jul 1966 Cover: 0.12 **NM** value: **9.00**
39 ❑ Sep 1966 Cover: 0.12 **NM** value: **9.00**
40 ❑ Nov 1966 Cover: 0.12 **NM** value: **18.00**
📖 The Agents Of D.E.A.T.H. **A:** Montes O Bache; Bache; Montes **W:** Joe Gill ★ 1st Appearance of The Peacemaker. ★ Appearance of Peacemaker.
41 ❑ Jan 1967 Cover: 0.12 **NM** value: **10.00**
42 ❑ Oct 1981 Cover: 0.50 **NM** value: **3.00**
43 ❑ Dec 1981 Cover: 0.50 **NM** value: **3.00**
44 ❑ Feb 1982 Cover: 0.60 **NM** value: **3.00**
45 ❑ Apr 1982 Cover: 0.60 **NM** value: **3.00**
46 ❑ Jun 1982 Cover: 0.60 **NM** value: **3.00**
47 ❑ Aug 1982 Cover: 0.60 **NM** value: **3.00**
48 ❑ Oct 1982 Cover: 0.60 **NM** value: **3.00**
49 ❑ Dec 1982 Cover: 0.60 **NM** value: **3.00**
final issue.

FIGHTIN' AIR FORCE — Charlton

3 ❑ Feb 1956 Cover: 0.10 **NM** value: **40.00**
• **CGC:** 1 graded, best 8.0
4 ❑ ca. 1956 Cover: 0.10 **NM** value: **25.00**
5 ❑ ca. 1956 Cover: 0.10 **NM** value: **25.00**
6 ❑ Cover: 0.10 **NM** value: **25.00**
7 ❑ Cover: 0.10 **NM** value: **25.00**
8 ❑ Cover: 0.10 **NM** value: **25.00**
9 ❑ Cover: 0.10 **NM** value: **25.00**
10 ❑ Cover: 0.10 **NM** value: **25.00**
11 ❑ Cover: 0.10 **NM** value: **20.00**
12 ❑ ca. 1957 Cover: 0.10 **NM** value: **20.00**
13 ❑ Dec 1958 Cover: 0.10 **NM** value: **20.00**
• **CGC:** 1 graded, best 7.5
14 ❑ ca. 1959 Cover: 0.10 **NM** value: **20.00**
15 ❑ ca. 1959 Cover: 0.10 **NM** value: **20.00**
16 ❑ ca. 1959 Cover: 0.10 **NM** value: **20.00**
17 ❑ ca. 1959 Cover: 0.10 **NM** value: **20.00**
18 ❑ ca. 1959 Cover: 0.10 **NM** value: **20.00**
19 ❑ Cover: 0.10 **NM** value: **20.00**
20 ❑ Cover: 0.10 **NM** value: **20.00**
21 ❑ Cover: 0.10 **NM** value: **20.00**
22 ❑ Cover: 0.10 **NM** value: **20.00**
23 ❑ Cover: 0.10 **NM** value: **20.00**
24 ❑ Dec 1960 Cover: 0.10 **NM** value: **20.00**
25 ❑ Feb 1961 Cover: 0.10 **NM** value: **20.00**
26 ❑ Apr 1961 Cover: 0.10 **NM** value: **20.00**
27 ❑ Jun 1961 Cover: 0.10 **NM** value: **20.00**
28 ❑ Aug 1961 Cover: 0.10 **NM** value: **20.00**
29 ❑ ca. 1961 Cover: 0.10 **NM** value: **20.00**
30 ❑ Dec 1961 Cover: 0.10 **NM** value: **20.00**
• **CGC:** 1 graded, best 9.0
31 ❑ Mar 1962 Cover: 0.12 **NM** value: **15.00**
• **CGC:** 2 graded, best 9.2
32 ❑ May 1962 Cover: 0.12 **NM** value: **15.00**
33 ❑ Jul 1962 Cover: 0.12 **NM** value: **15.00**
34 ❑ Sep 1962 Cover: 0.12 **NM** value: **15.00**
35 ❑ Nov 1962 Cover: 0.12 **NM** value: **15.00**
36 ❑ Jan 1963 Cover: 0.12 **NM** value: **15.00**
37 ❑ Mar 1963 Cover: 0.12 **NM** value: **15.00**
38 ❑ May 1963 Cover: 0.12 **NM** value: **15.00**
39 ❑ ca. 1963 Cover: 0.12 **NM** value: **15.00**
40 ❑ Cover: 0.12 **NM** value: **15.00**
41 ❑ Cover: 0.12 **NM** value: **15.00**
42 ❑ 1964 Cover: 0.12 **NM** value: **15.00**
43 ❑ 1964 Cover: 0.12 **NM** value: **15.00**
44 ❑ Jun 1964 Cover: 0.12 **NM** value: **15.00**
45 ❑ Sep 1964 Cover: 0.12 **NM** value: **15.00**
46 ❑ ca. 1964 Cover: 0.12 **NM** value: **15.00**
47 ❑ Jan 1965 Cover: 0.12 **NM** value: **15.00**
48 ❑ ca. 1965 Cover: 0.12 **NM** value: **15.00**
49 ❑ Jul 1965 Cover: 0.12 **NM** value: **15.00**
50 ❑ Aug 1965 Cover: 0.12 **NM** value: **15.00**
51 ❑ Oct 1965 Cover: 0.12 **NM** value: **15.00**
52 ❑ Dec 1965 Cover: 0.12 **NM** value: **15.00**
53 ❑ Mar 1966 Cover: 0.12 **NM** value: **15.00**

FIGHTIN' ARMY — Charlton

Charlton's war comics, while inferior to Marvel and DC's, did have a charm all their own.

Most memorable among the titles was the line of Fightin' ... titles, which focused on each branch of the service, from the Army to the Navy to the Air Force and the Marines. It's a wonder there wasn't a Fightin' Coast Guard or Fightin' WACs.

Among these, the best-known was probably Fightin' Army which began "The Lonely War of Willy Schultz" in #76, a series of stories focusing on a single soldier's battles with both the enemy and his own morale. — Brent

16 ❑ Jan 1956 Cover: 0.10 **NM** value: **20.00**
17 ❑ 1956 Cover: 0.10 **NM** value: **15.00**
18 ❑ 1956 Cover: 0.10 **NM** value: **15.00**
19 ❑ 1957 Cover: 0.10 **NM** value: **15.00**
20 ❑ 1957 Cover: 0.10 **NM** value: **15.00**
21 ❑ Jul 1957 Cover: 0.10 **NM** value: **12.00**
22 ❑ Oct 1957 Cover: 0.10 **NM** value: **12.00**
23 ❑ 1958 Cover: 0.10 **NM** value: **12.00**
24 ❑ 1958 Cover: 0.10 **NM** value: **12.00**
25 ❑ Feb 1959 Cover: 0.10 **NM** value: **12.00**
26 ❑ Apr 1959 Cover: 0.10 **NM** value: **12.00**
27 ❑ Jun 1959 Cover: 0.10 **NM** value: **12.00**
28 ❑ Aug 1959 Cover: 0.10 **NM** value: **12.00**
29 ❑ Oct 1959 Cover: 0.10 **NM** value: **12.00**
30 ❑ Dec 1959 Cover: 0.10 **NM** value: **12.00**
📖 The Liberators; Corregidor; Day of Shame; Water is War (text story); The Long Road Back
31 ❑ Jan 1960 Cover: 0.10 **NM** value: **9.00**
32 ❑ Feb 1960 Cover: 0.10 **NM** value: **9.00**
33 ❑ Mar 1960 Cover: 0.10 **NM** value: **9.00**
34 ❑ Apr 1960 Cover: 0.10 **NM** value: **9.00**
35 ❑ May 1960 Cover: 0.10 **NM** value: **9.00**
36 ❑ Jul 1960 Cover: 0.10 **NM** value: **9.00**
37 ❑ Sep 1960 Cover: 0.10 **NM** value: **9.00**
38 ❑ Nov 1960 Cover: 0.10 **NM** value: **9.00**
39 ❑ Jan 1961 Cover: 0.10 **NM** value: **9.00**
40 ❑ Mar 1961 Cover: 0.10 **NM** value: **9.00**
41 ❑ May 1961 Cover: 0.10 **NM** value: **9.00**
42 ❑ ca. 1961 Cover: 0.10 **NM** value: **9.00**
43 ❑ ca. 1961 Cover: 0.10 **NM** value: **9.00**
44 ❑ Dec 1961 Cover: 0.10 **NM** value: **9.00**
45 ❑ ca. 1962 **NM** value: **9.00**
46 ❑ ca. 1962 **NM** value: **9.00**
47 ❑ ca. 1962 **NM** value: **9.00**
48 ❑ ca. 1962 Cover: 0.12 **NM** value: **9.00**
49 ❑ Nov 1962 Cover: 0.12 **NM** value: **9.00**
50 ❑ Jan 1963 Cover: 0.12 **NM** value: **9.00**
51 ❑ ca. 1963 Cover: 0.12 **NM** value: **6.00**
52 ❑ ca. 1963 Cover: 0.12 **NM** value: **6.00**
53 ❑ Jul 1963 Cover: 0.12 **NM** value: **6.00**
54 ❑ Sep 1963 Cover: 0.12 **NM** value: **6.00**
55 ❑ Nov 1963 Cover: 0.12 **NM** value: **6.00**
56 ❑ 1964 Cover: 0.12 **NM** value: **6.00**
Circ: Statement: **157,240**
57 ❑ ca. 1964 Cover: 0.12 **NM** value: **6.00**
Circ: Statement: **157,240**
58 ❑ Jun 1964 Cover: 0.12 **NM** value: **6.00**
Circ: Statement: **157,240**
59 ❑ ca. 1964 Cover: 0.12 **NM** value: **6.00**
Circ: Statement: **157,240**
60 ❑ 1964 Cover: 0.12 **NM** value: **6.00**
Circ: Statement: **157,240**
61 ❑ 1965 Cover: 0.12 **NM** value: **6.00**
Circ: Statement: **144,865**
62 ❑ Mar 1965 Cover: 0.12 **NM** value: **6.00**
Circ: Statement: **144,865**
63 ❑ Jun 1965 Cover: 0.12 **NM** value: **6.00**
Circ: Statement: **144,865**
64 ❑ Aug 1965 Cover: 0.12 **NM** value: **6.00**
Circ: Statement: **144,865**
65 ❑ Oct 1965 Cover: 0.12 **NM** value: **6.00**
Circ: Statement: **144,865**
66 ❑ 1965 Cover: 0.12 **NM** value: **6.00**
Circ: Statement: **144,865**
67 ❑ Mar 1966 Cover: 0.12 **NM** value: **6.00**
Circ: Statement: **129,514**
68 ❑ May 1966 Cover: 0.12 **NM** value: **6.00**
Circ: Statement: **129,514**
69 ❑ Jul 1966 Cover: 0.12 **NM** value: **6.00**
Circ: Statement: **129,514**
70 ❑ ca. 1966 Cover: 0.12 **NM** value: **6.00**
Circ: Statement: **129,514**
71 ❑ 1966 Cover: 0.12 **NM** value: **6.00**
Circ: Statement: **129,514**
72 ❑ 1966 Cover: 0.12 **NM** value: **6.00**
Circ: Statement: **129,514**
73 ❑ Mar 1967 Cover: 0.12 **NM** value: **6.00**
Circ: Statement: **117,513**
74 ❑ ca. 1967 Cover: 0.12 **NM** value: **6.00**
Circ: Statement: **117,513**
75 ❑ Aug 1967 Cover: 0.12 **NM** value: **6.00**
Circ: Statement: **117,513**
76 ❑ Oct 1967 Cover: 0.12 **NM** value: **7.00**
Circ: Statement: **117,513**
• Lonely War of Capt. Willy Schultz begins
77 ❑ Dec 1967 Cover: 0.12 **NM** value: **5.00**
Circ: Statement: **117,513**
78 ❑ Feb 1968 Cover: 0.12 **NM** value: **5.00**
Circ: Statement: **111,820**
79 ❑ May 1968 Cover: 0.12 **NM** value: **5.00**
Circ: Statement: **111,820**
80 ❑ Jul 1968 Cover: 0.12 **NM** value: **5.00**
Circ: Statement: **111,820**
81 ❑ Sep 1968 Cover: 0.12 **NM** value: **5.00**
Circ: Statement: **111,820**
82 ❑ Nov 1968 Cover: 0.12 **NM** value: **5.00**
Circ: Statement: **111,820**
83 ❑ Jan 1969 Cover: 0.12 **NM** value: **5.00**
Circ: Statement: **141,335**
84 ❑ Mar 1969 Cover: 0.12 **NM** value: **5.00**
Circ: Statement: **141,335**
85 ❑ May 1969 Cover: 0.12 **NM** value: **5.00**
Circ: Statement: **141,335**
86 ❑ Jul 1969 Cover: 0.12 **NM** value: **5.00**
Circ: Statement: **141,335**
📖 The Lonely War of Capt. Willy Schultz; Escape
87 ❑ Sep 1969 Cover: 0.15 **NM** value: **5.00**
Circ: Statement: **141,335**
88 ❑ Nov 1969 Cover: 0.15 **NM** value: **5.00**
Circ: Statement: **141,335**
89 ❑ Jan 1970 Cover: 0.15 **NM** value: **5.00**
Circ: Statement: **142,430**
📖 The Lonely War of Capt. Willy Schultz; The Cross of Iron
90 ❑ Mar 1970 Cover: 0.15 **NM** value: **5.00**
Circ: Statement: **142,430**
91 ❑ May 1970 Cover: 0.15 **NM** value: **5.00**
Circ: Statement: **142,430**
92 ❑ Jul 1970 Cover: 0.15 **NM** value: **5.00**
Circ: Statement: **142,430**
93 ❑ Sep 1970 Cover: 0.15 **NM** value: **5.00**
Circ: Statement: **142,430**
94 ❑ Nov 1970 Cover: 0.15 **NM** value: **5.00**
Circ: Statement: **142,430**
95 ❑ Jan 1971 Cover: 0.15 **NM** value: **5.00**
96 ❑ Mar 1971 Cover: 0.15 **NM** value: **5.00**
97 ❑ May 1971 Cover: 0.15 **NM** value: **5.00**
98 ❑ Jul 1971 Cover: 0.15 **NM** value: **5.00**
99 ❑ Sep 1971 Cover: 0.20 **NM** value: **5.00**
100 ❑ Nov 1971 Cover: 0.20 **NM** value: **5.00**
101 ❑ Jan 1972 Cover: 0.20 **NM** value: **4.00**
Circ: Statement: **133,058**
102 ❑ Mar 1972 Cover: 0.20 **NM** value: **4.00**
Circ: Statement: **133,058**
103 ❑ May 1972 Cover: 0.20 **NM** value: **4.00**
Circ: Statement: **133,058**
104 ❑ Jul 1972 Cover: 0.20 **NM** value: **4.00**
Circ: Statement: **133,058**
105 ❑ Sep 1972 Cover: 0.20 **NM** value: **4.00**
Circ: Statement: **133,058**
106 ❑ Nov 1972 Cover: 0.20 **NM** value: **4.00**
Circ: Statement: **133,058**
107 ❑ Jan 1973 Cover: 0.20 **NM** value: **4.00**
Circ: Statement: **114,877**
108 ❑ Mar 1973 Cover: 0.20 **NM** value: **4.00**
Circ: Statement: **114,877**
109 ❑ May 1973 Cover: 0.20 **NM** value: **4.00**
Circ: Statement: **114,877**
110 ❑ Jul 1973 Cover: 0.20 **NM** value: **4.00**
Circ: Statement: **114,877**
111 ❑ Sep 1973 Cover: 0.20 **NM** value: **4.00**
Circ: Statement: **114,877**
112 ❑ Nov 1973 Cover: 0.20 **NM** value: **4.00**
Circ: Statement: **114,877**
113 ❑ May 1974 Cover: 0.25 **NM** value: **4.00**
Circ: Statement: **129,170**
114 ❑ Jul 1974 Cover: 0.25 **NM** value: **4.00**
Circ: Statement: **129,170**
115 ❑ Sep 1974 Cover: 0.25 **NM** value: **4.00**
Circ: Statement: **129,170**
📖 The Enemy; In Memoriam; No Way Back; The Scar (text)
116 ❑ Nov 1974 Cover: 0.25 **NM** value: **4.00**
Circ: Statement: **129,170**
117 ❑ Feb 1975 Cover: 0.25 **NM** value: **4.00**
Circ: Statement: **97,765**

Other grades: Multiply prices above by **1.5 for Mint • 2/3 for Very Fine • 1/3 for Fine • 1/5 for Very Good • 1/8 for Good**

118 ❑ ca. 1975 Cover: 0.25 **NM** value: **4.00**
Circ: Statement: **97,765**
119 ❑ Jun 1975 Cover: 0.25 **NM** value: **4.00**
Circ: Statement: **97,765**
120 ❑ Sep 1975 Cover: 0.25 **NM** value: **4.00**
Circ: Statement: **97,765**
121 ❑ Nov 1975 Cover: 0.25 **NM** value: **3.00**
Circ: Statement: **97,765**
122 ❑ 1976 Cover: 0.25 **NM** value: **3.00**
123 ❑ ca. 1976 Cover: 0.25 **NM** value: **3.00**
124 ❑ May 1976 Cover: 0.30 **NM** value: **3.00**
125 ❑ ca. 1976 Cover: 0.30 **NM** value: **3.00**
126 ❑ Oct 1976 Cover: 0.30 **NM** value: **3.00**
127 ❑ Dec 1976 Cover: 0.30 **NM** value: **3.00**
128 ❑ Sep 1977 Cover: 0.35 **NM** value: **3.00**
Circ: Statement: **108,930**
129 ❑ Nov 1977 Cover: 0.35 **NM** value: **3.00**
Circ: Statement: **108,930**
130 ❑ Feb 1978 Cover: 0.35 **NM** value: **3.00**
131 ❑ Mar 1978 Cover: 0.35 **NM** value: **3.00**
132 ❑ Apr 1978 Cover: 0.35 **NM** value: **3.00**
📖 The Outsider; Sniper; Operation Wait-and-Hope (text)
133 ❑ Jun 1978 Cover: 0.35 **NM** value: **3.00**
134 ❑ Sep 1978 Cover: 0.35 **NM** value: **3.00**
📖 A Walk Down Main Street; Alias Death; The Hit and Run War • has Iron Corporal story
135 ❑ Nov 1978 Cover: 0.35 **NM** value: **3.00**
136 ❑ **NM** value: **3.00**
137 ❑ ca. 1979 Cover: 0.40 **NM** value: **3.00**
138 ❑ May 1979 Cover: 0.40 **NM** value: **3.00**
139 ❑ Jul 1979 Cover: 0.40 **NM** value: **3.00**
140 ❑ Aug 1979 Cover: 0.40 **NM** value: **3.00**
141 ❑ ca. 1979 Cover: 0.40 **NM** value: **3.00**
142 ❑ Nov 1979 Cover: 0.40 **NM** value: **3.00**
143 ❑ Cover: 0.40 **NM** value: **3.00**
144 ❑ Feb 1980 Cover: 0.40 **NM** value: **3.00**
145 ❑ Apr 1980 Cover: 0.40 **NM** value: **3.00**
146 ❑ Jul 1980 Cover: 0.40 **NM** value: **3.00**
147 ❑ Sep 1980 Cover: 0.50 **NM** value: **3.00**
148 ❑ Nov 1980 Cover: 0.50 **NM** value: **3.00**
149 ❑ Jan 1981 Cover: 0.50 **NM** value: **3.00**
150 ❑ Mar 1981 Cover: 0.50 **NM** value: **3.00**
151 ❑ Apr 1981 Cover: 0.50 **NM** value: **2.00**
152 ❑ Jun 1981 Cover: 0.50 **NM** value: **2.00**
153 ❑ Aug 1981 Cover: 0.50 **NM** value: **2.00**
154 ❑ Oct 1981 Cover: 0.50 **NM** value: **2.00**
155 ❑ Dec 1981 Cover: 0.50 **NM** value: **2.00**
156 ❑ Feb 1982 Cover: 0.60 **NM** value: **2.00**
157 ❑ Apr 1982 Cover: 0.60 **NM** value: **2.00**
158 ❑ Jun 1982 Cover: 0.60 **NM** value: **2.00**
159 ❑ Aug 1982 Cover: 0.60 **NM** value: **2.00**
160 ❑ Oct 1982 Cover: 0.60 **NM** value: **2.00**
161 ❑ Dec 1982 Cover: 0.60 **NM** value: **2.00**
162 ❑ Feb 1983 Cover: 0.60 **NM** value: **2.00**
163 ❑ Apr 1983 Cover: 0.60 **NM** value: **2.00**
164 ❑ Jun 1983 Cover: 0.60 **NM** value: **2.00**
165 ❑ Aug 1983 Cover: 0.60 **NM** value: **2.00**
166 ❑ Oct 1983 Cover: 0.60 **NM** value: **2.00**
167 ❑ Cover: 0.60 **NM** value: **2.00**
168 ❑ Cover: 0.60 **NM** value: **2.00**
169 ❑ May 1984 Cover: 0.60 **NM** value: **2.00**
170 ❑ Jul 1984 Cover: 0.60 **NM** value: **2.00**
171 ❑ Sep 1984 Cover: 0.60 **NM** value: **2.00**
172 ❑ Nov 1984 Cover: 0.75 **NM** value: **2.00**

FIGHTING AMERICAN (AWESOME) Awesome

Fighting American was originally created in the 1950s by the team of Joe Simon and Jack Kirby as a humorous send-up of their more famous star-spangled creation, Captain America. In the original series, John Flagg and his crew battled such Cold War baddies as "Hotsky Trotsky" and "Poison Ivan."

In 1997, Fighting American fell into the hands of Rob Liefeld, who had departed early from his engagement as artist on Captain America (Vol. 2), and was left with a stack of unused pages depicting a shield-slinging do-gooder. When Marvel threatened legal action over Liefeld's "creation" Agent America, he licensed Fighting American from Joe Simon and relaunched the forgotten title. Fans of Liefeld's big artwork and unsubtle approach to storytelling (or anyone who was sorry to see him leave Captain America) will get what they came for.

1/A ❑ Aug 1997 Cover: 2.50 **NM** value: **Cover or less**
Diving at guns, bayonets on cover. 📖 Back in the Ring **A:** Rob Liefeld **W:** Jeph Loeb; Rob Liefeld
1/B ❑ Aug 1997 Cover: 2.50 **NM** value: **Cover or less**
Holding flag on cover. 📖 Back in the Ring **A:** Rob Liefeld **W:** Jeph Loeb; Rob Liefeld
1/C ❑ Aug 1997 Cover: 2.50 **NM** value: **Cover or less**
• Comics Cavalcade regular edition (two heroes diving toward a gun at lower left corner). 📖 Back in the Ring **A:** Rob Liefeld **W:** Jeph Loeb; Rob Liefeld
1/D ❑ Aug 1997 Cover: 15.95 **NM** value: **Cover or less**
• Comics Cavalcade Liberty Gold Foil Edition. 📖 Back in the Ring **A:** Rob Liefeld **W:** Jeph Loeb; Rob Liefeld
2 ❑ Oct 1997 Cover: 2.50 **NM** value: **Cover or less**
3 ❑ Dec 1997 Cover: 2.50 **NM** value: **Cover or less**

FIGHTING AMERICAN: DOGS OF WAR Awesome

1 ❑ Sep 1998 Cover: 2.50 **NM** value: **Cover or less**
Circ: Diamd. preorders: **20,638**
📖 Dogs of War! **A:** Stephen Platt **W:** Jim Starlin
1/A ❑ Sep 1998 **NM** value: **3.00**
• 98 Tour Edition cover. 📖 Dogs of War! **A:** Stephen Platt **W:** Jim Starlin

FIGHTING AMERICAN (HARVEY) Harvey

1 ❑ Oct 1966 Cover: 0.25 **NM** value: **22.00**
• **CGC:** 6 graded, best 9.6
📖 Round Robin; Peter Piper's Red Vipers; Roman Scoundrels; Duel To The Finish Line; • Reprints stories from 1950 series ★ Origin of Fighting American, Speedboy.

FIGHTING AMERICAN (HEADLINE) Headline

FIGHTING AMERICAN (MARVEL) Marvel

Bk 1/HC ❑ Jan 1990 Cover: 35.95 **NM** value: **Cover or less**
Circ: CapCity orders: **1,430**
hardcover. • Reprints **A:** Joe Simon; Jack Kirby

FIGHTING AMERICAN (MINI-SERIES) DC

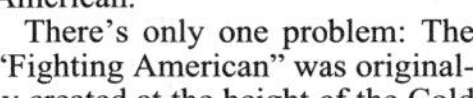

This six-issue mini-series resurrects Simon and Kirby's cold war super-hero for a new struggle in the confusing '90s. As this series tells it, the original Fighting American, Johnny Flagg, was gunned down in 1984. In a desperate bid to avenge him, his brother Nelson agreed to take part in a strange experiment. Nelson was placed in a tank of fluid for nine years, during which his consciousness was transformed into his brother's super-powered body. Now he is the new Fighting American.

There's only one problem: The "Fighting American" was originally created at the height of the Cold War to battle the "red menace". This new Fighting American was created at the very end of that conflict. Now when Nelson emerges from his transformation, he finds that the war for which he was created to fight, is long since over. Whatever is he to do now?

1 ❑ Feb 1994 Cover: 1.50 **NM** value: **Cover or less**
Circ: CapCity orders: **12,250**
📖 Brothers' Keepers Losers Weepers **A:** Greg LaRocque **W:** David Rawson; Pat McGreal ★ Origin of Fighting American.
2 ❑ Mar 1994 Cover: 1.50 **NM** value: **Cover or less**
Circ: CapCity orders: **6,950**
📖 Here Comes the Media Circus **A:** Greg LaRocque **W:** David Rawson; Pat McGreal
3 ❑ Apr 1994 Cover: 1.50 **NM** value: **Cover or less**
Circ: CapCity orders: **5,750**
4 ❑ May 1994 Cover: 1.50 **NM** value: **Cover or less**
Circ: CapCity orders: **5,200**
5 ❑ Jun 1994 Cover: 1.50 **NM** value: **Cover or less**
Circ: CapCity orders: **4,350**
6 ❑ Jul 1994 Cover: 1.50 **NM** value: **Cover or less**
Circ: CapCity orders: **4,050**
📖 The Fighting Ugly American **A:** Greg LaRocque **W:** David Rawson; Pat McGreal

FIGHTING AMERICAN: RULES OF THE GAME Awesome

1 ❑ Nov 1997 Cover: 2.50 **NM** value: **Cover or less**
Circ: Diamd. preorders: **30,861** • **CGC:** 1 graded, best 9.6
1/A ❑ Nov 1997 Cover: 2.50 **NM** value: **Cover or less**
Fighting American standing on cover. 📖 Do Not Pass "Go" **A:** Ed McGuinness **W:** Jeph Loeb
1/B ❑ Nov 1997 Cover: 2.50 **NM** value: **Cover or less**
Woman pointing gun on cover. 📖 Do Not Pass "Go" **A:** Ed McGuinness **W:** Jeph Loeb

FIGHTING AMERICAN SPECIAL COMICON EDITION Awesome

1 ❑ ca. 1997 **NM** value: **1.00**
No issue number. no cover price. • b&w preview of upcoming series given out at Comic-Con International: San Diego 1997

FIGHTING DANIEL BOONE Avon

1 ❑ ca. 1953 **NM** value: **100.00**

FIGHTING FEM CLASSICS Forbidden Fruit

All issues are adults only.
1 ❑ b&w Cover: 3.50 **NM** value: **Cover or less**

FIGHTING FEMS Forbidden Fruit

All issues are adults only.
1 ❑ b&w Cover: 3.50 **NM** value: **Cover or less**
2 ❑ b&w Cover: 3.50 **NM** value: **Cover or less**

FIGHTING FRONTS Harvey

1 ❑ Aug 1952 Cover: 0.10 **NM** value: **50.00**
• **CGC:** 1 graded, best 8.5
2 ❑ 1952 Cover: 0.10 **NM** value: **50.00**
3 ❑ 1952 Cover: 0.10 **NM** value: **45.00**
• **CGC:** 1 graded, best 9.2
4 ❑ 1952 Cover: 0.10 **NM** value: **45.00**
5 ❑ Jan 1953 Cover: 0.10 **NM** value: **45.00**

FIGHTING INHDIANS OF THE WILD WEST Avon

1 ❑ Mar 1952 Cover: 0.10 **NM** value: **100.00**
2 ❑ Nov 1952 Cover: 0.10 **NM** value: **75.00**

FIGHTING LEATHERNECKS Toby

1 ❑ Feb 1952 Cover: 0.10 **NM** value: **100.00**
2 ❑ Apr 1952 Cover: 0.10 **NM** value: **50.00**
3 ❑ Jun 1952 Cover: 0.10 **NM** value: **50.00**
4 ❑ Aug 1952 Cover: 0.10 **NM** value: **50.00**
5 ❑ Oct 1952 Cover: 0.10 **NM** value: **50.00**
6 ❑ Dec 1952 Cover: 0.10 **NM** value: **50.00**

FIGHTING MAN, THE Ajax

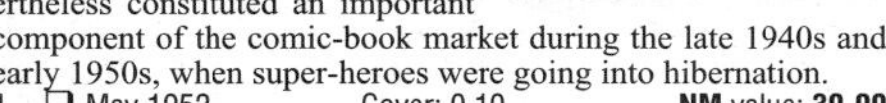

The Fighting Man was one of the anonymous recruits into the swelling ranks of war comics during the early 1950s, when publisher added titles to the genre, as America became involved in the United Nations action in Korea. An undercurrent of anticommunist propaganda, undistinguished art, and uninspired rehashes of tired war-comics cliches pervade the pages of Fighting Man.

Lacking the innocence of the first generation of war comics and the insight of later contributions to the genre, titles like Fighting Man nevertheless constituted an important component of the comic-book market during the late 1940s and early 1950s, when super-heroes were going into hibernation.

1 ❑ May 1952 Cover: 0.10 **NM** value: **30.00**
2 ❑ Jul 1952 Cover: 0.10 **NM** value: **20.00**
📖 Hay Seed!; A Question of Guts!; Red Fights Red (text story); The Kid from Detroit; Pick them off First!
3 ❑ Sep 1952 Cover: 0.10 **NM** value: **16.00**
4 ❑ Nov 1952 Cover: 0.10 **NM** value: **13.00**
5 ❑ Jan 1953 Cover: 0.10 **NM** value: **13.00**
6 ❑ Mar 1953 Cover: 0.10 **NM** value: **13.00**
7 ❑ May 1953 Cover: 0.10 **NM** value: **13.00**
8 ❑ Jul 1953 Cover: 0.10 **NM** value: **13.00**

FIGHTING UNDERSEA COMMANDOS Avon

1 ❑ May 1952 Cover: 0.10 **NM** value: **75.00**
2 ❑ Aug 1952 Cover: 0.10 **NM** value: **50.00**
3 ❑ Cover: 0.10 **NM** value: **50.00**
4 ❑ Cover: 0.10 **NM** value: **50.00**
5 ❑ Apr 1953 Cover: 0.10 **NM** value: **50.00**
• **CGC:** 1 graded, best 8.0

FIGHTING YANK Nedor

1 ❑ Sep 1942 Cover: 0.10 **NM** value: **2000.00**
• **CGC:** 2 graded, best 9.0
2 ❑ Nov 1942 Cover: 0.10 **NM** value: **900.00**
• **CGC:** 2 graded, best 9.2
3 ❑ Feb 1943 Cover: 0.10 **NM** value: **600.00**
• **CGC:** 1 graded, best 9.2
4 ❑ Jun 1943 Cover: 0.10 **NM** value: **600.00**
• **CGC:** 1 graded, best 9.4
5 ❑ Sep 1943 Cover: 0.10 **NM** value: **500.00**
• **CGC:** 1 graded, best 9.4
6 ❑ Dec 1943 Cover: 0.10 **NM** value: **500.00**
• **CGC:** 1 graded, best 9.0
7 ❑ Feb 1944 Cover: 0.10 **NM** value: **500.00**
• **CGC:** 1 graded, best 9.6
8 ❑ Jun 1944 Cover: 0.10 **NM** value: **500.00**
• **CGC:** 2 graded, best 9.4
9 ❑ Aug 1944 Cover: 0.10 **NM** value: **500.00**
• **CGC:** 3 graded, best 9.6
10 ❑ Dec 1944 Cover: 0.10 **NM** value: **500.00**
• **CGC:** 4 graded, best 9.4
11 ❑ Mar 1945 Cover: 0.10 **NM** value: **400.00**
12 ❑ Jun 1945 Cover: 0.10 **NM** value: **400.00**
• **CGC:** 2 graded, best 9.2
13 ❑ Sep 1945 Cover: 0.10 **NM** value: **400.00**
• **CGC:** 1 graded, best 9.4
14 ❑ Dec 1945 Cover: 0.10 **NM** value: **400.00**
• **CGC:** 1 graded, best 9.0
15 ❑ Feb 1946 Cover: 0.10 **NM** value: **400.00**
• **CGC:** 1 graded, best 9.4
16 ❑ May 1946 Cover: 0.10 **NM** value: **350.00**
• **CGC:** 1 graded, best 9.4
17 ❑ Aug 1946 Cover: 0.10 **NM** value: **350.00**
• **CGC:** 5 graded, best 9.0
18 ❑ Nov 1946 Cover: 0.10 **NM** value: **350.00**
• **CGC:** 2 graded, best 9.0
19 ❑ Feb 1947 Cover: 0.10 **NM** value: **350.00**
• **CGC:** 4 graded, best 9.6
20 ❑ May 1947 Cover: 0.10 **NM** value: **350.00**
• **CGC:** 2 graded, best 9.4
21 ❑ Aug 1947 Cover: 0.10 **NM** value: **300.00**
• **CGC:** 1 graded, best 9.0
22 ❑ Nov 1947 Cover: 0.10 **NM** value: **300.00**
23 ❑ Jan 1948 Cover: 0.10 **NM** value: **300.00**
• **CGC:** 5 graded, best 9.2
24 ❑ Apr 1948 Cover: 0.10 **NM** value: **300.00**
25 ❑ Jul 1948 Cover: 0.10 **NM** value: **300.00**
26 ❑ Oct 1948 Cover: 0.10 **NM** value: **300.00**
• **CGC:** 1 graded, best 8.0
27 ❑ Jan 1949 Cover: 0.10 **NM** value: **250.00**
• **CGC:** 1 graded, best 9.0
28 ❑ Apr 1949 Cover: 0.10 **NM** value: **250.00**
• **CGC:** 2 graded, best 7.0
29 ❑ Aug 1949 Cover: 0.10 **NM** value: **250.00**

Capital City orders are the actual sales of comic books by Capital City Distribution, once one of the largest U.S. sellers of comics to comics shops. Capital City's share of comics shop sales, while not known exactly, increases from around 10-20% in the mid-1980s to 30-35% in the mid-1990s. Capital City's share of comic books sold on newsstands (most Marvels and DCs) will be less.

CGC-graded: Multiply prices above by **33 for 9.9 M • 16 for 9.8 NM/M • 7 for 9.6 NM+ • 5 for 9.4 NM • 2.5 for 9.2 NM- • 1.5 for 9.0 VF/NM**

FIGHTIN' MARINES — Charlton

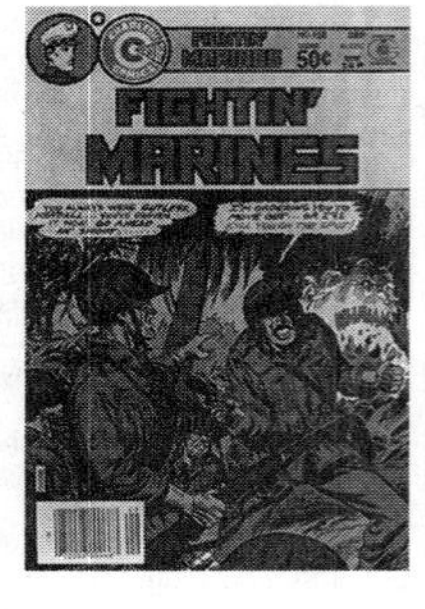

Fightin' Marines grew out of an earlier series known as The Texan. In 1951, that series changed its focus to bring us the combat exploits of the U.S. Marine Corps. As Fightin' Marines, it ran for more than 30 years, albeit with lengthy hiatuses in the later years, when Charlton was sputtering along. During its run, it brought readers countless profiles in courage, from the high seas to the jungles of Viet Nam.

Well-known artist Don Perlin provided some covers for the series. Among the stranger characters introduced were Shotgun Harker and The Chicken, while early issues featured the exploits of Canteen Kate.

1 ❑ Aug 1951 Cover: 0.10 **NM** value: **180.00**
#15 on cover. • Numbering continued from The Texan
2 ❑ Oct 1951 Cover: 0.10 **NM** value: **140.00**
3 ❑ Dec 1951 Cover: 0.10 **NM** value: **130.00**
• **CGC:** 1 graded, best 4.0
4 ❑ Cover: 0.10 **NM** value: **100.00**
5 ❑ Cover: 0.10 **NM** value: **100.00**
6 ❑ Cover: 0.10 **NM** value: **100.00**
7 ❑ Cover: 0.10 **NM** value: **85.00**
8 ❑ Cover: 0.10 **NM** value: **85.00**
9 ❑ Cover: 0.10 **NM** value: **85.00**
10 ❑ Cover: 0.10 **NM** value: **30.00**
11 ❑ Cover: 0.10 **NM** value: **20.00**
• No Canteen Kate
12 ❑ Cover: 0.10 **NM** value: **20.00**
13 ❑ Cover: 0.10 **NM** value: **20.00**
14 ❑ May 1955 Cover: 0.10 **NM** value: **75.00**
• Rare; Charlton begins publishing
15 ❑ Cover: 0.10 **NM** value: **28.00**
16 ❑ Cover: 0.10 **NM** value: **20.00**
17 ❑ Cover: 0.10 **NM** value: **55.00**
• Canteen Kate by Baker
18 ❑ Cover: 0.10 **NM** value: **15.00**
19 ❑ Cover: 0.10 **NM** value: **15.00**
20 ❑ Cover: 0.10 **NM** value: **15.00**
21 ❑ Cover: 0.10 **NM** value: **14.00**
22 ❑ Cover: 0.10 **NM** value: **14.00**
23 ❑ Cover: 0.10 **NM** value: **14.00**
24 ❑ ca. 1957 Cover: 0.10 **NM** value: **14.00**
25 ❑ Mar 1958 Cover: 0.10 **NM** value: **35.00**
• Giant-size.
26 ❑ ca. 1958 Cover: 0.25 **NM** value: **40.00**
• Giant-size.
27 ❑ ca. 1958 Cover: 0.10 **NM** value: **14.00**
28 ❑ Cover: 0.10 **NM** value: **14.00**
29 ❑ Cover: 0.10 **NM** value: **14.00**
30 ❑ Jun 1959 Cover: 0.10 **NM** value: **10.00**
31 ❑ Aug 1959 Cover: 0.10 **NM** value: **10.00**
32 ❑ ca. 1959 Cover: 0.10 **NM** value: **10.00**
33 ❑ Jan 1960 Cover: 0.10 **NM** value: **10.00**
34 ❑ Mar 1960 Cover: 0.10 **NM** value: **10.00**
35 ❑ May 1960 Cover: 0.10 **NM** value: **10.00**
36 ❑ Jul 1960 Cover: 0.10 **NM** value: **10.00**
37 ❑ Sep 1960 Cover: 0.10 **NM** value: **10.00**
38 ❑ Nov 1960 Cover: 0.10 **NM** value: **10.00**
39 ❑ Jan 1961 Cover: 0.10 **NM** value: **10.00**
40 ❑ Mar 1961 Cover: 0.10 **NM** value: **9.00**
41 ❑ May 1961 Cover: 0.10 **NM** value: **9.00**
42 ❑ Jul 1961 Cover: 0.10 **NM** value: **9.00**
43 ❑ Sep 1961 Cover: 0.10 **NM** value: **9.00**
44 ❑ Nov 1961 Cover: 0.10 **NM** value: **9.00**
• **CGC:** 2 graded, best 9.4
45 ❑ Feb 1962 Cover: 0.10 **NM** value: **9.00**
46 ❑ Apr 1962 Cover: 0.10 **NM** value: **9.00**
• **CGC:** 1 graded, best 9.4
47 ❑ Jun 1962 Cover: 0.12 **NM** value: **9.00**
48 ❑ Aug 1962 Cover: 0.12 **NM** value: **9.00**
49 ❑ Oct 1962 Cover: 0.12 **NM** value: **9.00**
50 ❑ Dec 1962 Cover: 0.12 **NM** value: **9.00**
51 ❑ Feb 1963 Cover: 0.12 **NM** value: **6.00**
Circ: Statement: **154,369**
52 ❑ Apr 1963 Cover: 0.12 **NM** value: **6.00**
Circ: Statement: **154,369**
53 ❑ Jun 1963 Cover: 0.12 **NM** value: **6.00**
Circ: Statement: **154,369**
54 ❑ Aug 1963 Cover: 0.12 **NM** value: **6.00**
Circ: Statement: **154,369**
55 ❑ 1963 Cover: 0.12 **NM** value: **6.00**
Circ: Statement: **154,369**
56 ❑ 1963 Cover: 0.12 **NM** value: **6.00**
Circ: Statement: **154,369**
57 ❑ 1964 Cover: 0.12 **NM** value: **6.00**
Circ: Statement: **158,912**
58 ❑ May 1964 Cover: 0.12 **NM** value: **6.00**
Circ: Statement: **158,912**
• Has 1963 Statement, filed 9/30/63; avg print run 236,658; avg sales 154,353; avg subs 16; avg total paid 154,369; samples 25; max existent 154,394; 35% of run returned
59 ❑ Jul 1964 Cover: 0.12 **NM** value: **6.00**
Circ: Statement: **158,912**
60 ❑ Oct 1964 Cover: 0.12 **NM** value: **6.00**
Circ: Statement: **158,912**
61 ❑ 1964 Cover: 0.12 **NM** value: **6.00**
Circ: Statement: **158,912**
62 ❑ 1965 Cover: 0.12 **NM** value: **6.00**
Circ: Statement: **144,487**
63 ❑ May 1965 Cover: 0.12 **NM** value: **6.00**
Circ: Statement: **144,487**
• Has 1964 Statement; avg total paid circ 158,912
64 ❑ Jul 1965 Cover: 0.12 **NM** value: **6.00**
Circ: Statement: **144,487**
65 ❑ Sep 1965 Cover: 0.12 **NM** value: **6.00**
Circ: Statement: **144,487**
66 ❑ Nov 1965 Cover: 0.12 **NM** value: **6.00**
Circ: Statement: **144,487**
67 ❑ Jan 1966 Cover: 0.12 **NM** value: **6.00**
68 ❑ Mar 1966 Cover: 0.12 **NM** value: **6.00**
• Has 1965 Statement, filed 9/30/65; avg print run 256,841; avg sales 144,471; avg subs 16; avg total paid 144,487; samples 25; max existent 144,512; 44% of run returned
69 ❑ ca. 1966 Cover: 0.12 **NM** value: **6.00**
70 ❑ Aug 1966 Cover: 0.12 **NM** value: **6.00**
71 ❑ 1966 Cover: 0.12 **NM** value: **6.00**
72 ❑ 1966 Cover: 0.12 **NM** value: **6.00**
73 ❑ 1967 Cover: 0.12 **NM** value: **6.00**
Circ: Statement: **123,517**
74 ❑ 1967 Cover: 0.12 **NM** value: **6.00**
Circ: Statement: **123,517**
75 ❑ Jul 1967 Cover: 0.12 **NM** value: **4.00**
Circ: Statement: **123,517**
76 ❑ Sep 1967 Cover: 0.12 **NM** value: **4.00**
Circ: Statement: **123,517**
77 ❑ Nov 1967 Cover: 0.12 **NM** value: **4.00**
Circ: Statement: **123,517**
78 ❑ Jan 1968 Cover: 0.12 **NM** value: **4.00**
Circ: Statement: **116,125**
📖 Major Haydock's Last War; The Leaners; The Second Time; The Tokyo Express; Introducing Shotgun Harker and the Chicken ★ 1st Appearance of Shotgun Harker, The Chicken.
79 ❑ ca. 1968 Cover: 0.12 **NM** value: **4.00**
Circ: Statement: **116,125**
80 ❑ Jul 1968 Cover: 0.12 **NM** value: **4.00**
Circ: Statement: **116,125**
• Has 1967 Statement, filed 9/30/67; avg print run 225,000; avg sales 123,500; avg subs 17; avg total paid 123,517; samples 25; max existent 116,250; 46% of run returned
81 ❑ Sep 1968 Cover: 0.12 **NM** value: **4.00**
Circ: Statement: **116,125**
82 ❑ Nov 1968 Cover: 0.12 **NM** value: **6.00**
Circ: Statement: **116,125**
• Giant-size.
83 ❑ Jan 1969 Cover: 0.12 **NM** value: **4.00**
84 ❑ Mar 1969 Cover: 0.12 **NM** value: **4.00**
85 ❑ May 1969 Cover: 0.12 **NM** value: **4.00**
📖 Trouble in the Night; Meet the Champ; Always Alert (text piece); A Question of Honor
86 ❑ Jul 1969 Cover: 0.12 **NM** value: **4.00**
87 ❑ Sep 1969 Cover: 0.15 **NM** value: **4.00**
88 ❑ Nov 1969 Cover: 0.15 **NM** value: **4.00**
89 ❑ Jan 1970 Cover: 0.15 **NM** value: **4.00**
90 ❑ Mar 1970 Cover: 0.15 **NM** value: **4.00**
📖 They Must Love U.S. Chicken; The Most Hated C.O. on Iwo Jima; The Unwilling Hero (text piece); His Mother's Son
91 ❑ May 1970 Cover: 0.15 **NM** value: **3.50**
92 ❑ Jul 1970 Cover: 0.15 **NM** value: **3.50**
93 ❑ Sep 1970 Cover: 0.15 **NM** value: **3.50**
94 ❑ Nov 1970 Cover: 0.15 **NM** value: **3.50**
📖 The Hunter; I Had the Japs Surrounded; Sam Spolo: Tape Trap (text); Village of Fear
95 ❑ Jan 1971 Cover: 0.15 **NM** value: **3.50**
Circ: Statement: **135,050**
96 ❑ Mar 1971 Cover: 0.15 **NM** value: **3.50**
Circ: Statement: **135,050**
97 ❑ May 1971 Cover: 0.15 **NM** value: **3.50**
Circ: Statement: **135,050**
98 ❑ Jul 1971 Cover: 0.15 **NM** value: **3.50**
Circ: Statement: **135,050**
99 ❑ Sep 1971 Cover: 0.15 **NM** value: **3.50**
Circ: Statement: **135,050**
100 ❑ Nov 1971 Cover: 0.20 **NM** value: **3.50**
Circ: Statement: **135,050**
101 ❑ Jan 1972 Cover: 0.20 **NM** value: **3.00**
102 ❑ Mar 1972 Cover: 0.20 **NM** value: **3.00**
103 ❑ Apr 1972 Cover: 0.20 **NM** value: **3.00**
• Has 1971 Statement, filed 9/30/71; avg print run 205,000; avg sales 135,000; avg subs 50; avg total paid 135,050; samples 200; office use 100; max existent 135,350; 34% of run returned
104 ❑ Jun 1972 Cover: 0.20 **NM** value: **3.00**
105 ❑ Aug 1972 Cover: 0.20 **NM** value: **3.00**
📖 The Voice of the Enemy; One Crummy Marine!; Kamikaze; I Cannot Kill! • Don Perlin cover
106 ❑ Oct 1972 Cover: 0.20 **NM** value: **3.00**
107 ❑ Dec 1972 Cover: 0.20 **NM** value: **3.00**
📖 The Hero!; The Victims!; Trouble and Treason (text); The Toughest Marine in Combat Zone 'C' • Nicolas A. Lascia cover
108 ❑ Jan 1973 Cover: 0.20 **NM** value: **3.00**
109 ❑ Mar 1973 Cover: 0.20 **NM** value: **3.00**
110 ❑ Apr 1973 Cover: 0.20 **NM** value: **3.00**
111 ❑ Jun 1973 Cover: 0.20 **NM** value: **3.00**
112 ❑ ca. 1973 Cover: 0.20 **NM** value: **3.00**
113 ❑ ca. 1973 Cover: 0.20 **NM** value: **3.00**
114 ❑ Oct 1973 Cover: 0.20 **NM** value: **3.00**
115 ❑ 1973 Cover: 0.20 **NM** value: **3.00**
116 ❑ Jan 1974 Cover: 0.20 **NM** value: **3.00**
Circ: Statement: **110,140**
117 ❑ Jun 1974 Cover: 0.25 **NM** value: **3.00**
Circ: Statement: **110,140**
118 ❑ ca. 1974 Cover: 0.25 **NM** value: **3.00**
Circ: Statement: **110,140**
119 ❑ Nov 1974 Cover: 0.25 **NM** value: **3.00**
Circ: Statement: **110,140**
120 ❑ Jan 1975 Cover: 0.25 **NM** value: **3.00**
Circ: Statement: **112,800**
120-2 ❑ ca. 1975 Cover: 0.35 **NM** value: **1.50**
• reprints Charlton #120
121 ❑ Mar 1975 Cover: 0.25 **NM** value: **3.00**
Circ: Statement: **112,800**
122 ❑ ca. 1975 Cover: 0.25 **NM** value: **3.00**
Circ: Statement: **112,800**
123 ❑ May 1975 Cover: 0.25 **NM** value: **3.00**
Circ: Statement: **112,800**
• Has 1974 Statement; avg total paid circ 110,140
124 ❑ ca. 1975 Cover: 0.25 **NM** value: **3.00**
Circ: Statement: **112,800**
125 ❑ ca. 1975 Cover: 0.25 **NM** value: **3.00**
Circ: Statement: **112,800**
126 ❑ ca. 1975 Cover: 0.25 **NM** value: **2.50**
Circ: Statement: **112,800**
127 ❑ Jan 1976 Cover: 0.25 **NM** value: **2.50**
128 ❑ Mar 1976 Cover: 0.25 **NM** value: **2.50**
129 ❑ May 1976 Cover: 0.30 **NM** value: **2.50**
130 ❑ Jul 1976 Cover: 0.30 **NM** value: **2.50**
131 ❑ Sep 1976 Cover: 0.30 **NM** value: **2.50**
132 ❑ Nov 1976 Cover: 0.30 **NM** value: **2.50**
133 ❑ Oct 1977 Cover: 0.35 **NM** value: **2.50**
134 ❑ Dec 1977 Cover: 0.35 **NM** value: **2.50**
135 ❑ Feb 1978 Cover: 0.35 **NM** value: **2.50**
136 ❑ Apr 1978 Cover: 0.35 **NM** value: **2.50**
137 ❑ Jun 1978 Cover: 0.35 **NM** value: **2.50**
138 ❑ Aug 1978 Cover: 0.35 **NM** value: **2.50**
139 ❑ Oct 1978 Cover: 0.35 **NM** value: **2.50**
140 ❑ **NM** value: **2.50**
141 ❑ **NM** value: **2.50**
142 ❑ ca. 1979 Cover: 0.40 **NM** value: **2.50**
143 ❑ ca. 1979 Cover: 0.40 **NM** value: **2.50**
144 ❑ Jul 1979 Cover: 0.40 **NM** value: **2.50**
145 ❑ ca. 1979 Cover: 0.40 **NM** value: **2.50**
146 ❑ ca. 1979 Cover: 0.40 **NM** value: **2.50**
147 ❑ Dec 1979 Cover: 0.40 **NM** value: **2.50**
148 ❑ Jan 1980 Cover: 0.40 **NM** value: **2.50**
149 ❑ Mar 1980 Cover: 0.40 **NM** value: **2.50**
150 ❑ May 1980 Cover: 0.40 **NM** value: **2.50**
151 ❑ ca. 1980 Cover: 0.40 **NM** value: **2.00**
152 ❑ Oct 1980 Cover: 0.50 **NM** value: **2.00**
153 ❑ Dec 1980 Cover: 0.50 **NM** value: **2.00**
154 ❑ Jan 1981 Cover: 0.50 **NM** value: **2.00**
155 ❑ Mar 1981 Cover: 0.50 **NM** value: **2.00**
156 ❑ May 1981 Cover: 0.50 **NM** value: **2.00**
157 ❑ Jul 1981 Cover: 0.50 **NM** value: **2.00**
158 ❑ Sep 1981 Cover: 0.50 **NM** value: **2.00**
📖 Clay Pigeon; Private War; The Little Fink; Okinawa the Last Island; The Sniper (text story) **A:** Nicholas Alascia; William Molno **W:** Joe Gill
159 ❑ Oct 1981 Cover: 0.50 **NM** value: **2.00**
160 ❑ Dec 1981 Cover: 0.50 **NM** value: **2.00**
161 ❑ Feb 1982 Cover: 0.60 **NM** value: **2.00**
162 ❑ Apr 1982 Cover: 0.60 **NM** value: **2.00**
163 ❑ Jul 1982 Cover: 0.60 **NM** value: **2.00**
164 ❑ Sep 1982 Cover: 0.60 **NM** value: **2.00**
165 ❑ Nov 1982 Cover: 0.60 **NM** value: **2.00**
166 ❑ Jan 1983 Cover: 0.60 **NM** value: **2.00**
167 ❑ Mar 1983 Cover: 0.60 **NM** value: **2.00**
168 ❑ May 1983 Cover: 0.60 **NM** value: **2.00**
169 ❑ Jul 1983 Cover: 0.60 **NM** value: **2.00**
170 ❑ Sep 1983 Cover: 0.60 **NM** value: **2.00**
171 ❑ Nov 1983 Cover: 0.60 **NM** value: **2.00**
172 ❑ Jan 1984 Cover: 0.60 **NM** value: **2.00**
173 ❑ Mar 1984 Cover: 0.60 **NM** value: **2.00**
174 ❑ May 1984 Cover: 0.60 **NM** value: **2.00**
175 ❑ Jul 1984 Cover: 0.75 **NM** value: **2.00**
176 ❑ Sep 1984 Cover: 0.75 **NM** value: **2.00**
final issue.

FIGHTIN' NAVY — Charlton

It only took five years to fight the battles of World War II, but they've been providing fodder for war comics for nearly half a century. Fightin' Navy, as the title indicates, focuses on the exploits of sea-borne forces during the "last good war," featuring the usual assortment of PT boat adventures, frogmen, tense submarine duels, and epic battleship slugfests in both the Atlantic and Pacific theatres.

Fightin' Navy was previously Don Winslow of the Navy, changing over in the mid-Fifties presumably to add some versatility to the range of stories (or perhaps because Charlton's license on Winslow, a newspaper strip, had expired). Fightin' Navy went down in 1966, but resurfaced for a few perfunctory issues in the mid-80s.

74 ❑ ca. 1956 Cover: 0.10 **NM** value: **20.00**
75 ❑ Cover: 0.10 **NM** value: **15.00**
76 ❑ Cover: 0.10 **NM** value: **15.00**
77 ❑ Cover: 0.10 **NM** value: **15.00**
78 ❑ Cover: 0.10 **NM** value: **15.00**
79 ❑ Cover: 0.10 **NM** value: **15.00**
80 ❑ Cover: 0.10 **NM** value: **15.00**
81 ❑ **NM** value: **12.00**
82 ❑ Cover: 0.15 **NM** value: **12.00**
83 ❑ **NM** value: **15.00**
84 ❑ **NM** value: **12.00**
85 ❑ **NM** value: **12.00**
86 ❑ **NM** value: **12.00**
87 ❑ **NM** value: **12.00**
88 ❑ **NM** value: **12.00**
89 ❑ **NM** value: **12.00**
90 ❑ **NM** value: **12.00**
91 ❑ **NM** value: **9.00**
92 ❑ **NM** value: **9.00**
93 ❑ **NM** value: **9.00**
94 ❑ **NM** value: **9.00**

Other grades: Multiply prices above by **1.5 for Mint • 2/3 for Very Fine • 1/3 for Fine • 1/5 for Very Good • 1/8 for Good**

95 ❑ 1959 NM value: **9.00**
96 ❑ Jan 1960 Cover: 0.10 NM value: **9.00**
97 ❑ Cover: 0.10 NM value: **9.00**
98 ❑ Cover: 0.10 NM value: **9.00**
99 ❑ Jul 1961 Cover: 0.10 NM value: **9.00**
100 ❑ Sep 1961 Cover: 0.10 NM value: **9.00**
101 ❑ Nov 1961 Cover: 0.10 NM value: **10.00**
102 ❑ Jan 1962 Cover: 0.10 NM value: **6.00**
103 ❑ Apr 1962 Cover: 0.10 NM value: **6.00**
104 ❑ ca. 1962 NM value: **6.00**
105 ❑ Aug 1962 Cover: 0.12 NM value: **6.00**
106 ❑ 1962 Cover: 0.12 NM value: **6.00**
107 ❑ 1962 Cover: 0.12 NM value: **6.00**
108 ❑ 1963 Cover: 0.12 NM value: **6.00**
Circ: Statement: **136,526**
109 ❑ 1963 Cover: 0.12 NM value: **6.00**
Circ: Statement: **136,526**
110 ❑ ca. 1963 Cover: 0.12 NM value: **6.00**
Circ: Statement: **136,526**
111 ❑ Aug 1963 Cover: 0.12 NM value: **6.00**
Circ: Statement: **136,526**
112 ❑ ca. 1963 Cover: 0.12 NM value: **6.00**
Circ: Statement: **136,526**
113 ❑ 1963 Cover: 0.12 NM value: **6.00**
Circ: Statement: **136,526**
114 ❑ Feb 1964 Cover: 0.12 NM value: **6.00**
115 ❑ May 1964 Cover: 0.12 NM value: **6.00**
• Has 1963 Statement; avg total paid circ 136,526
116 ❑ ca. 1964 Cover: 0.12 NM value: **6.00**
117 ❑ ca. 1964 Cover: 0.12 NM value: **6.00**
118 ❑ 1964 Cover: 0.12 NM value: **6.00**
119 ❑ Feb 1965 Cover: 0.12 NM value: **6.00**
120 ❑ May 1965 Cover: 0.12 NM value: **6.00**
📖 Operation Rat Hole; Masquerade; Paratrooper; Our Nuclear Navy (Text Story); The Pirates of Kiel; **A:** Montes O Bache **W:** Montes O Bache
121 ❑ ca. 1965 Cover: 0.12 NM value: **4.00**
122 ❑ ca. 1965 Cover: 0.12 NM value: **4.00**
123 ❑ Dec 1965 Cover: 0.12 NM value: **4.00**
124 ❑ Jan 1966 Cover: 0.12 NM value: **4.00**
125 ❑ 1966 Cover: 0.12 NM value: **4.00**
• Last issue of original run
126 ❑ Aug 1983 Cover: 0.60 NM value: **2.00**
• Series begins again
127 ❑ Oct 1983 Cover: 0.60 NM value: **2.00**
128 ❑ Dec 1983 Cover: 0.60 NM value: **2.00**
129 ❑ Feb 1984 Cover: 0.60 NM value: **2.00**
130 ❑ Apr 1984 Cover: 0.60 NM value: **2.00**
131 ❑ Jun 1984 Cover: 0.60 NM value: **2.00**
132 ❑ Aug 1984 Cover: 0.60 NM value: **2.00**
133 ❑ Oct 1984 Cover: 0.75 NM value: **2.00**
final issue.

FIGHTIN' TEXAN — St. John
16 ❑ ca. 1952 Cover: 0.10 NM value: **50.00**
17 ❑ ca. 1952 Cover: 0.10 NM value: **50.00**

FIGHT MAN — Marvel
1 ❑ Jun 1993 Cover: 2.00 NM value: **Cover or less**
Circ: CapCity orders: **12,700**
📖 The Big Fight! **A:** Evan Dorkin **W:** Evan Dorkin

FIGHT THE ENEMY — Tower
1 ❑ Aug 1966 Cover: 0.25 NM value: **21.00**
2 ❑ Oct 1966 Cover: 0.25 NM value: **16.00**
📖 Saga of the Lucky 7, Michel's Revenge; K.P. McGoof; The Ace; The Silent Service; Dead Wrong; Mike Manley Secret Agent; Green Berets **A:** Al Williams; Russ Jones **W:** Al Williams; Russ Jones
3 ❑ Cover: 0.25 NM value: **16.00**

FIGMENTS — Blackthorne
1 ❑ Cover: 1.75 NM value: **Cover or less**
2 ❑ Cover: 1.75 NM value: **Cover or less**

FIGMENTS UNLIMITED — Graphik
1 ❑ Cover: 1.25 NM value: **Cover or less**
2 ❑ Cover: 1.25 NM value: **Cover or less**
3 ❑ Cover: 1.25 NM value: **Cover or less**
📖 Vengeance is Mine **A:** Frank Turner **W:** Cliff Van Meter

FILES OF MS. TREE, THE — Renegade
1 ❑ Jun 1984, b&w NM value: **3.00**
2 ❑ Sep 1985, b&w NM value: **3.00**
3 ❑ b&w NM value: **3.00**

FILIBUSTING COMICS — Fantagraphics
1 ❑ Jan 1995, b&w Cover: 2.75 NM value: **Cover or less**

FILM FUNNIES — Marvel
1 ❑ Nov 1949 Cover: 0.10 NM value: **125.00**
2 ❑ Feb 1950 Cover: 0.10 NM value: **75.00**

FILM STARS ROMANCES — Star Publications
1 ❑ Jan 1950 Cover: 0.10 NM value: **300.00**
2 ❑ Mar 1950 Cover: 0.10 NM value: **250.00**
3 ❑ May 1950 Cover: 0.10 NM value: **175.00**

FILTHY — Fantagraphics
Bk 1 ❑ Cover: 9.95 NM value: **Cover or less**

FILTHY ANIMALS — Radio
1 ❑ Aug 1997 Cover: 2.95 NM value: **Cover or less**
📖 Of Toons & Poons... **A:** Cindy Crowell; Stan Jinx **W:** Stan Jinx
2 ❑ 1998 Cover: 2.95 NM value: **Cover or less**
3 ❑ Aug 1998 Cover: 2.95 NM value: **Cover or less**
4 ❑ Cover: 2.95 NM value: **Cover or less**

FILTHY HABITS — Aeon
1 ❑ Jul 1996, b&w Cover: 2.95 NM value: **Cover or less**
2 ❑ Nov 1996, b&w Cover: 2.95 NM value: **Cover or less**
📖 Lobsters Away!; Man Was She Fine **A:** Eric Jones **W:** Dylan Williams; Landry Walker
3 ❑ Feb 1997, b&w Cover: 2.95 NM value: **Cover or less**
📖 An Incidental Death; Really Small Hitler **A:** Eric Jones **W:** Landry Walker; Mario DeGovia

FINAL CYCLE, THE — Dragon's Teeth
1 ❑ b&w Cover: 1.75 NM value: **Cover or less**
2 ❑ b&w Cover: 1.75 NM value: **Cover or less**
3 ❑ b&w Cover: 1.75 NM value: **Cover or less**
4 ❑ b&w Cover: 1.75 NM value: **Cover or less**

FINAL MAN, THE — C&T
1 ❑ b&w Cover: 1.50 NM value: **Cover or less**

FINAL NIGHT, THE — DC
So, what would happen if a swirling black void called The Sun-Eater swept into our solar system and threatened to snuff out the sun? Every super-hero in the DC universe would swing into action, that's what! The Final Night finds The Justice League, The New Gods, The Marvel Family, and several time-lost members of the Legion of Super-Heroes, among others, trying to find a way to stop just such a sun-sapping menace in this four-issue mini-series which crossed over into several DC titles. Even villains like Lex Luthor and Doctor Polaris join the fight. Superman's role in the story is particularly interesting: he continues fighting his never-ending battle even as his solar energy-derived strength and abilities drastically and quickly diminish in the wake of the Sun-Eater's journey across the sky. The Final Night also features significant developments in the story of Parallax, formerly Silver Age Green Lantern, Hal Jordan.
1 ❑ Nov 1996 Cover: 1.95 NM value: **2.50**
Circ: Diamd. preorders: **91,401** • **CGC:** 1 graded, best 9.6
📖 Dusk **A:** Stuart Immonen **W:** Karl Kesel
2 ❑ Nov 1996 Cover: 1.95 NM value: **2.00**
Circ: Diamd. preorders: **84,635**
📖 Darker Grows the Night **A:** Stuart Immonen **W:** Karl Kesel
3 ❑ Nov 1996 Cover: 1.95 NM value: **2.00**
Circ: Diamd. preorders: **83,058**
📖 Keeping Hope Alive **A:** Stuart Immonen **W:** Karl Kesel
4 ❑ Cover: 1.95 NM value: **2.00**
Circ: Diamd. preorders: **82,402** • **CGC:** 16 graded, best 9.8
📖 The Final Knight **A:** Stuart Immonen **W:** Karl Kesel ★ Death of Hal Jordan.
Bk 1 ❑ Cover: 12.95 NM value: **Cover or less**
• collects Final Night Preview/ Final Night #1-4, and Parallax: Emerald Night #1 **A:** Stuart Immonen **W:** Karl Kesel ★ Death of Parallax.

FINALS — DC / Vertigo
At Knox State University, aka "Kaos U," students can form a cult, genetically tinker with the athletes, or build a time machine. They've got to do something extraordinary to graduate.

This four-issue series from writer Will Pfeifer and artist Jill Thompson explores how trying to meet the demands of such an unusual curriculum affects the relationship of a group of roommates and friends. Really, what do you do when your girlfriend has turned herself into a goddess as her senior project, and you can't even come up with an idea? And how bad is it to kill someone who just stepped out of a time machine?

Published in 1999, slight changes to the first issue's background action in the wake of the Columbine High School killings touched off a minor bit of controversy among fandom, though the creators insisted no act of censorship had been imposed on them from above.
1 ❑ Sep 1999 Cover: 2.95 NM value: **Cover or less**
Circ: Diamd. preorders: **15,007**
📖 Back to School **A:** Jill Thompson **W:** Will Pfeifer
2 ❑ Oct 1999 Cover: 2.95 NM value: **Cover or less**
Circ: Diamd. preorders: **12,087**
📖 All-Nighters **A:** Jill Thompson **W:** Will Pfeifer
3 ❑ Nov 1999 Cover: 2.95 NM value: **Cover or less**
Circ: Diamd. preorders: **10,891**
📖 Hell Week **A:** Jill Thompson **W:** Will Pfeifer
4 ❑ Dec 1999 Cover: 2.95 NM value: **Cover or less**
Circ: Diamd. preorders: **10,750**
📖 Pomp & Circumstance Beyond Our Control **A:** Jill Thompson **W:** Will Pfeifer

FINAL TABOO — Aircel
All issues are adults only.
1 ❑ b&w Cover: 2.50 NM value: **Cover or less**
2 ❑ b&w Cover: 2.50 NM value: **Cover or less**

FINDER — Lightspeed Press
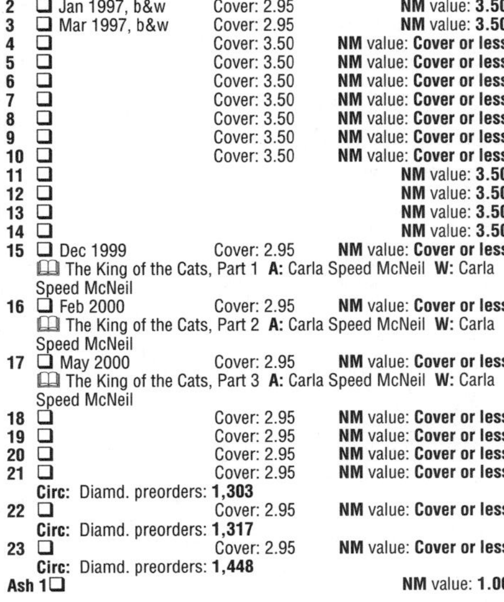

Jaeger Ayers is a Finder, a person talented in tracking people and things. He's a free spirit, a member of a native tribe more at home in the badlands or desert than in the city. Yet Jaeger is periodically drawn to the mega-city of Anvard and his friends who reside there.

The characters in Finder live in a setting that meshes science fiction and fantasy — lion creatures guard bookstores, museums of pain pay for memories, virtual-reality personalities run households and vie for favors, and the crumbling dome covering the crowded city is a mystery even to its residents.

Finder is a complex, mature story which follows Jaeger and the many lives he touches. It delivers an intense and compelling character study set in a strange and imaginative setting. In the issues, creator Carla Speed McNeil has provided extensive notes on the world she has created.
1 ❑ Nov 1996, b&w Cover: 2.95 NM value: **3.50**
wraparound cover. 📖 Salutation **A:** Carla Speed McNeil **W:** Carla Speed McNeil
2 ❑ Jan 1997, b&w Cover: 2.95 NM value: **3.50**
3 ❑ Mar 1997, b&w Cover: 2.95 NM value: **3.50**
4 ❑ Cover: 3.50 NM value: **Cover or less**
5 ❑ Cover: 3.50 NM value: **Cover or less**
6 ❑ Cover: 3.50 NM value: **Cover or less**
7 ❑ Cover: 3.50 NM value: **Cover or less**
8 ❑ Cover: 3.50 NM value: **Cover or less**
9 ❑ Cover: 3.50 NM value: **Cover or less**
10 ❑ Cover: 3.50 NM value: **Cover or less**
11 ❑ NM value: **3.50**
12 ❑ NM value: **3.50**
13 ❑ NM value: **3.50**
14 ❑ NM value: **3.50**
15 ❑ Dec 1999 Cover: 2.95 NM value: **Cover or less**
📖 The King of the Cats, Part 1 **A:** Carla Speed McNeil **W:** Carla Speed McNeil
16 ❑ Feb 2000 Cover: 2.95 NM value: **Cover or less**
📖 The King of the Cats, Part 2 **A:** Carla Speed McNeil **W:** Carla Speed McNeil
17 ❑ May 2000 Cover: 2.95 NM value: **Cover or less**
📖 The King of the Cats, Part 3 **A:** Carla Speed McNeil **W:** Carla Speed McNeil
18 ❑ Cover: 2.95 NM value: **Cover or less**
19 ❑ Cover: 2.95 NM value: **Cover or less**
20 ❑ Cover: 2.95 NM value: **Cover or less**
21 ❑ Cover: 2.95 NM value: **Cover or less**
Circ: Diamd. preorders: **1,303**
22 ❑ Cover: 2.95 NM value: **Cover or less**
Circ: Diamd. preorders: **1,317**
23 ❑ Cover: 2.95 NM value: **Cover or less**
Circ: Diamd. preorders: **1,448**
Ash 1 ❑ NM value: **1.00**

FINDER FOOTNOTES — Lightspeed
1 ❑ Cover: 6.00 NM value: **Cover or less**

FINIEOUS TREASURY, THE — TSR
1 ❑ Cover: 3.00 NM value: **Cover or less**
No issue number. • magazine-sized.

FINK, INC. — Fink, Inc.
1 ❑ Cover: 3.50 NM value: **Cover or less**

FINN — Fleetway-Quality
1 ❑ Cover: 2.95 NM value: **Cover or less**
2 ❑ Cover: 2.95 NM value: **Cover or less**
3 ❑ Cover: 2.95 NM value: **Cover or less**
4 ❑ Cover: 2.95 NM value: **Cover or less**

FIRE — Caliber
1 ❑ b&w Cover: 2.95 NM value: **Cover or less**
2 ❑ b&w Cover: 2.95 NM value: **Cover or less**
Bk 1 ❑ Cover: 9.95 NM value: **Cover or less**
No issue number. • Trade Paperback. • collects Caliber series **A:** Brian Michael Bendis **W:** Brian Michael Bendis

FIREARM — Malibu / Ultraverse
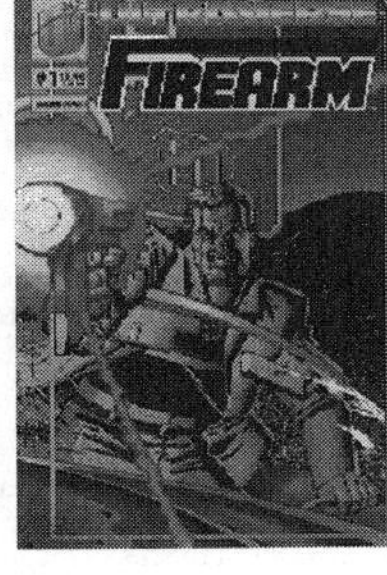

Alec Swan is the hardboiled star of the series. He's a former secret agent from England, now living in Southern California. While in England, he was a member of a covert bureau of the government called "The Lodge." They were the ones who gave him the nickname "Firearm," with reference to his expertise with a custom gun which fires everything from bullets to explosive charges.

Nowadays, he makes his living as a private detective. Swan charges $2,000 per day plus expenses, but for that he's willing to take on all manner of bad guys — including not a few ultra-powered criminals — in order to solve his case. He's not pretty, but he's very good at what he does.
0 ❑ Aug 1993 Cover: 14.95 NM value: **15.00**
• with videotape

CGC-graded: Multiply prices above by **33 for 9.9 M • 16 for 9.8 NM/M • 7 for 9.6 NM+ • 5 for 9.4 NM • 2.5 for 9.2 NM- • 1.5 for 9.0 VF/NM**

1 ❑ Sep 1993 Cover: 1.95 **NM** value: **2.25**
Circ: CapCity orders: **29,100**
American Pastimes, Part 1 **A:** Cully Hamner **W:** James Robinson ★ 1st Appearance of Firearm.

1/LE❑ Cover: 25.00 **NM** value: **Cover or less**
foil cover. • limited promotional edition. American Pastimes, Part 1 **A:** Cully Hamner **W:** James Robinson ★ 1st Appearance of Firearm.

2 ❑ Oct 1993 Cover: 2.50 **NM** value: **Cover or less**
Circ: CapCity orders: **29,050**
Rune, Part I; American Pastimes, Part 2 • Rune **A:** Cully Hamner; Barry Windsor-Smith **W:** James Robinson ★ 1st Appearance of Mosely.

3 ❑ Nov 1993 Cover: 1.95 **NM** value: **Cover or less**
Circ: CapCity orders: **21,150**
American Pastimes, Part 3 **A:** Cully Hamner **W:** James Robinson ★ 1st Appearance of The Sportsmen.

4 ❑ Dec 1993 Cover: 1.95 **NM** value: **Cover or less**
Circ: CapCity orders: **20,285**
American Pastimes, Part 4; Break-Thru • Break-Thru **A:** Cully Hamner **W:** James Robinson

5 ❑ Jan 1994 Cover: 1.95 **NM** value: **Cover or less**
Circ: CapCity orders: **16,775**
Said T.E. Lawrence, Picking Up His Fork... **A:** Kirk Van Wormer **W:** James Robinson

6 ❑ Feb 1994 Cover: 1.95 **NM** value: **Cover or less**
Circ: CapCity orders: **14,425**
Missing Child **A:** Cully Hamner **W:** James Robinson ★ Appearance of Prime.

7 ❑ Mar 1994 Cover: 1.95 **NM** value: **Cover or less**
Circ: CapCity orders: **12,475**
Mystery Tour **A:** Kirk Van Wormer **W:** James Robinson

8 ❑ May 1994 Cover: 1.95 **NM** value: **Cover or less**
Circ: CapCity orders: **11,700**
Kirby **A:** Bill Knapp **W:** James Robinson

9 ❑ Jun 1994 Cover: 1.95 **NM** value: **Cover or less**
Circ: CapCity orders: **10,900**
Idle Thoughts **A:** Cully Hamner **W:** James Robinson ★ 1st Appearance of Ms. Rule, Willy Manila.

10 ❑ Jul 1994 Cover: 3.50 **NM** value: **Cover or less**
Circ: CapCity orders: **10,350**
South of Watford, then Way, Way North, Part 1; Hang Time; Prime-itive Attraction; Remember Last Spring? • Flip book with Ultraverse Premiere #5 **A:** Sam Liu; Gary Erskine; Greg Luzniak; Brian O'Connell **W:** James Robinson; Mark Paniccia; Andy Mangels; Len Strazewski ★ 1st Appearance of Aeon, Iron Clad, Faulkner.

11 ❑ Jul 1994 Cover: 1.95 **NM** value: **Cover or less**
Circ: CapCity orders: **10,700**
South of Watford, then Way, Way North, Part 2 • flipbook with Ultraverse Premiere #5 **A:** Gary Erskine **W:** James Robinson ★ 1st Appearance of Doctor Z, Right Man.

12 ❑ Aug 1994 Cover: 1.95 **NM** value: **Cover or less**
Circ: CapCity orders: **8,625**
Rafferty Saga Prologue; The Rafferty Saga **A:** Steve Carr; Ben Herrera(cover) **W:** James Robinson ★ 1st Appearance of Rafferty. ★ Death of Lukasz. ★ Death of Doctor Z. ★ Death of Last.

13 ❑ Sep 1994 Cover: 1.95 **NM** value: **Cover or less**
Circ: CapCity orders: **7,575**
Rafferty Saga, Part 1; The Rafferty Saga, Part 1 **A:** Steve Carr; Ben Herrera(cover) **W:** James Robinson

14 ❑ Oct 1994 Cover: 1.95 **NM** value: **Cover or less**
Circ: CapCity orders: **7,100**
Rafferty Saga, Part 2; The Rafferty Saga, Part 2 **A:** Brian O'Connell; Howard Chaykin(cover) **W:** James Robinson ★ Death of Organism 0.9B. ★ Death of Vinaigrette.

15 ❑ Nov 1994 Cover: 1.95 **NM** value: **Cover or less**
Circ: CapCity orders: **6,400**
Rafferty Saga, Part 3; The Rafferty Saga, Part 3 **A:** Mike Edsey; Scott Kolins(cover) **W:** James Robinson

16 ❑ Dec 1994 Cover: 1.95 **NM** value: **Cover or less**
Circ: CapCity orders: **6,050**
Rafferty Saga, Part 4; The Rafferty Saga, Part 4 **A:** Arnie Jorgensen; Howard Chaykin(cover) **W:** James Robinson ★ 1st Appearance of Sigma. ★ Death of Sigma.

17 ❑ Jan 1995 Cover: 1.95 **NM** value: **Cover or less**
Circ: CapCity orders: **5,425**
Rafferty Saga, Part 5; The Rafferty Saga, Part 5 **A:** Keith Conroy **W:** James Robinson ★ 1st Appearance of The Silence. ★ Appearance of Elvis Presley (impersonator). ★ Death of The Silence.

18 ❑ Feb 1995 Cover: 2.50 **NM** value: **Cover or less**
Circ: CapCity orders: **5,225**
Rafferty Saga Finale; The Rafferty Saga **A:** Arnie Jorgensen; Keith Conroy; Howard Chaykin(cover) **W:** James Robinson ★ Death of Rafferty.

FIREBRAND — DC

Alex Sanchez lost his own family years ago in a fire. Perhaps it was his empathy for lost families that fueled his obsession with finding missing children. After months of work, he came to the conclusion that a rash of missing children cases was the result of an organized group. He returned home one night to hear a message from that group on his answering machine, moments before a bomb went off, sending his apartment up in flames.

Sanchez suffered massive damage to 70% of his body and would never have walked again if Noah Hightower (a rich man who had lost his own child mysteriously, 25 years ago) hadn't subjected him to a raft of experimental and costly treatments. Hightower developed a special suit for Sanchez, along with a satellite technology which could power the suit with a blast of energy from the sky. Hightower was looking for a hero to act as a force for good in the world, and Alex Sanchez was his man.

1 ❑ Feb 1996 Cover: 1.75 **NM** value: **2.00**
Ashes To Ashes **A:** Sal Velluto **W:** Brian Augustyn ★ Origin of Firebrand III (Alex Sanchez). ★ 1st Appearance of Firebrand III (Alex Sanchez).

2 ❑ Mar 1996 Cover: 1.75 **NM** value: **Cover or less**
Burning Bright **A:** Sal Velluto **W:** Brian Augustyn

3 ❑ Apr 1996 Cover: 1.75 **NM** value: **Cover or less**
The Best of Families **A:** Sal Velluto **W:** Brian Augustyn

4 ❑ May 1996 Cover: 1.75 **NM** value: **Cover or less**
5 ❑ Jun 1996 Cover: 1.75 **NM** value: **Cover or less**
6 ❑ Jul 1996 Cover: 1.75 **NM** value: **Cover or less**
7 ❑ Aug 1996 Cover: 1.75 **NM** value: **Cover or less**
8 ❑ Sep 1996 Cover: 1.75 **NM** value: **Cover or less**
9 ❑ Oct 1996 Cover: 1.75 **NM** value: **Cover or less**
Final Notice final issue. **A:** Sal Velluto **W:** Brian Augustyn

FIRE FROM HEAVEN — Image

0.5 ❑ **NM** value: **2.00**
1 ❑ Mar 1996 Cover: 2.50 **NM** value: **Cover or less**
wraparound cover.
2 ❑ Jul 1996 Cover: 2.50 **NM** value: **Cover or less**
Finale 2

FIREHAIR — Fiction House

1 ❑ Win 1948 Cover: 0.10 **NM** value: **400.00**
• **CGC:** 4 graded, best 9.4
2 ❑ Win 1949 Cover: 0.10 **NM** value: **200.00**
7 ❑ Spr 1951 Cover: 0.10 **NM** value: **125.00**
• **CGC:** 1 graded, best 9.2
8 ❑ Sum 1951 Cover: 0.10 **NM** value: **125.00**
• **CGC:** 3 graded, best 9.0
9 ❑ Fal 1951 Cover: 0.10 **NM** value: **125.00**
10 ❑ Win 1951 Cover: 0.10 **NM** value: **125.00**
• **CGC:** 2 graded, best 9.0
11 ❑ Dec 1952 Cover: 0.10 **NM** value: **125.00**
• **CGC:** 1 graded, best 7.0

FIRES — Catalan

1 ❑ Cover: 12.95 **NM** value: **Cover or less**
1/HC❑ Cover: 35.00 **NM** value: **Cover or less**
• Hardcover edition. • Limited to 500 copies **A:** Lorenzo Mattotti **W:** Lorenzo Mattotti

FIRE SALE — Rip Off

1 ❑ Dec 1989, b&w Cover: 2.50 **NM** value: **Cover or less**
• benefit

FIRESTAR — Marvel

1 ❑ Mar 1986 Cover: 0.75 **NM** value: **1.50**
Circ: CapCity orders: **36,200**
2 ❑ Apr 1986 Cover: 0.75 **NM** value: **1.50**
Circ: CapCity orders: **30,400**
3 ❑ May 1986 Cover: 0.75 **NM** value: **1.00**
Circ: CapCity orders: **27,200**
4 ❑ Jun 1986 Cover: 0.75 **NM** value: **1.00**
Circ: CapCity orders: **25,600**

FIRESTORM — DC

1 ❑ Mar 1978 Cover: 0.35 **NM** value: **3.00**
• **CGC:** 5 graded, best 9.8
Make Way for Firestorm! **A:** Al Milgrom; John Romita **W:** Gerry Conway ★ Origin of Firestorm. ★ 1st Appearance of Firestorm.
2 ❑ Apr 1978 Cover: 0.35 **NM** value: **1.75**
3 ❑ Jun 1978 Cover: 0.35 **NM** value: **1.75**
4 ❑ Aug 1978 Cover: 0.35 **NM** value: **1.75**
5 ❑ Oct 1978 Cover: 0.35 **NM** value: **1.75**

FIRESTORM, THE NUCLEAR MAN — DC

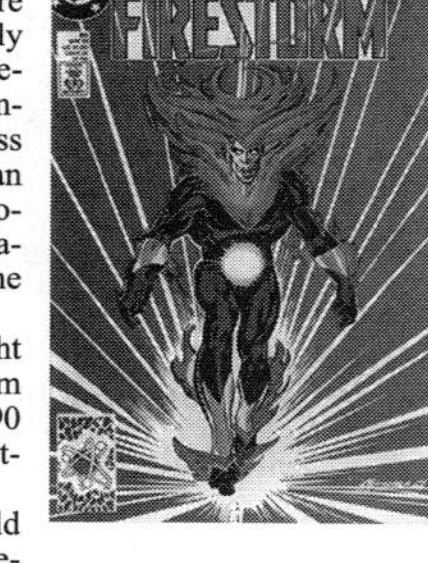

In nuclear physics, fusion is the process by which two molecules are forced together to form an entirely new one, while at the same time releasing an enormous amount of energy. This is the same sort of process that takes place when American teen Ron Raymond and Soviet professor Mikhail Denisovitch Arkadin combine to form Firestorm, the Nuclear Man.

This series picks up after a slight renaming from Fury of Firestorm #64. It ran from 1987 until 1990 when it concluded with the giant-sized issue #100.

In later years, Firestorm would return again, this time as a fire elemental.

65 ❑ Nov 1987 Cover: 0.75 **NM** value: **1.00**
Circ: CapCity orders: **10,550**
• Series continued from Fury of Firestorm #64 ★ Appearance of Green Lantern. ★ Appearance of new Firestorm.
66 ❑ Dec 1987 Cover: 0.75 **NM** value: **1.00**
Circ: CapCity orders: **10,900**
67 ❑ Jan 1988 Cover: 0.75 **NM** value: **1.00**
Circ: CapCity orders: **117,600**
Millennium • Millennium
68 ❑ Feb 1988 Cover: 0.75 **NM** value: **1.00**
Circ: CapCity orders: **18,450**
Millennium • Millennium
69 ❑ Mar 1988 Cover: 0.75 **NM** value: **1.00**
Circ: CapCity orders: **14,600**
70 ❑ Apr 1988 Cover: 0.75 **NM** value: **1.00**
Circ: CapCity orders: **14,850**
71 ❑ May 1988 Cover: 0.75 **NM** value: **1.00**
Circ: CapCity orders: **13,950**
Hammer and Tong **A:** Joe Brozowski **W:** John Ostrander
72 ❑ Jun 1988 Cover: 0.75 **NM** value: **1.00**
Circ: CapCity orders: **12,700**
73 ❑ Jul 1988 Cover: 0.75 **NM** value: **1.00**
Circ: CapCity orders: **12,150**
74 ❑ Aug 1988 Cover: 0.75 **NM** value: **1.00**
Circ: CapCity orders: **11,750**
75 ❑ Sep 1988 Cover: 1.00 **NM** value: **Cover or less**
Circ: CapCity orders: **11,500**
76 ❑ Oct 1988 Cover: 1.00 **NM** value: **Cover or less**
Circ: CapCity orders: **11,200**
77 ❑ Nov 1988 Cover: 1.00 **NM** value: **Cover or less**
Circ: CapCity orders: **10,350**
78 ❑ Dec 1988 Cover: 1.00 **NM** value: **Cover or less**
Circ: CapCity orders: **10,450**
79 ❑ Cover: 1.00 **NM** value: **Cover or less**
Circ: CapCity orders: **10,100**
no cover date.
80 ❑ Cover: 1.00 **NM** value: **Cover or less**
Circ: CapCity orders: **12,600**
no cover date. Invasion! • Invasion! ★ Appearance of Firehawk, Power Girl.
81 ❑ Jan 1989 Cover: 1.00 **NM** value: **Cover or less**
Circ: CapCity orders: **11,400**
Invasion! • Invasion! Aftermath **A:** Tom Grindberg; Arne Starr; Sam De La Rosa **W:** John Ostrander ★ Appearance of Soyuz.
82 ❑ Feb 1989 Cover: 1.00 **NM** value: **Cover or less**
Circ: CapCity orders: **10,200**
83 ❑ Mar 1989 Cover: 1.00 **NM** value: **Cover or less**
Circ: CapCity orders: **10,150**
84 ❑ Apr 1989 Cover: 1.00 **NM** value: **Cover or less**
Circ: CapCity orders: **10,000**
85 ❑ May 1989 Cover: 1.00 **NM** value: **Cover or less**
Circ: CapCity orders: **11,050**
• new Firestorm
86 ❑ Jun 1989 Cover: 1.00 **NM** value: **Cover or less**
Circ: CapCity orders: **11,350**
Janus Directive
87 ❑ Jul 1989 Cover: 1.00 **NM** value: **Cover or less**
Circ: CapCity orders: **10,800**
88 ❑ Aug 1989 Cover: 1.00 **NM** value: **Cover or less**
Circ: CapCity orders: **11,450**
89 ❑ Sep 1989 Cover: 1.00 **NM** value: **Cover or less**
Circ: CapCity orders: **11,450**
90 ❑ Oct 1989 Cover: 1.00 **NM** value: **Cover or less**
Circ: CapCity orders: **12,850**
The Elemental War, Part 1 ★ 1st Appearance of Naiad.
91 ❑ Nov 1989 Cover: 1.00 **NM** value: **Cover or less**
Circ: CapCity orders: **12,350**
92 ❑ Dec 1989 Cover: 1.00 **NM** value: **Cover or less**
Circ: CapCity orders: **12,200**
93 ❑ Jan 1990 Cover: 1.00 **NM** value: **Cover or less**
Circ: CapCity orders: **11,950**
94 ❑ Feb 1990 Cover: 1.00 **NM** value: **Cover or less**
Circ: CapCity orders: **11,450**
95 ❑ Mar 1990 Cover: 1.00 **NM** value: **Cover or less**
Circ: CapCity orders: **11,350**
96 ❑ Apr 1990 Cover: 1.00 **NM** value: **Cover or less**
Circ: CapCity orders: **11,000**
97 ❑ May 1990 Cover: 1.00 **NM** value: **Cover or less**
Circ: CapCity orders: **10,550**
98 ❑ Jun 1990 Cover: 1.00 **NM** value: **Cover or less**
Circ: CapCity orders: **10,300**
99 ❑ Jul 1990 Cover: 1.00 **NM** value: **Cover or less**
Circ: CapCity orders: **10,600**
100 ❑ Aug 1990 Cover: 2.95 **NM** value: **Cover or less**
Circ: CapCity orders: **10,850**
• Giant-size. final issue.

FIRE TEAM — Aircel

1 ❑ b&w Cover: 2.50 **NM** value: **Cover or less**
2 ❑ Jan 1991, b&w Cover: 2.50 **NM** value: **Cover or less**
Retribution **A:** Don Lomax **W:** Don Lomax
3 ❑ Feb 1991, b&w Cover: 2.50 **NM** value: **Cover or less**
Showdown **A:** Don Lomax **W:** Don Lomax
4 ❑ b&w Cover: 2.50 **NM** value: **Cover or less**
5 ❑ b&w Cover: 2.50 **NM** value: **Cover or less**
River of Shame **A:** Don Lomax **W:** Don Lomax
6 ❑ b&w Cover: 2.50 **NM** value: **Cover or less**

FIRKIN — Knockabout

All issues are adults only.

1 ❑ Cover: 2.50 **NM** value: **Cover or less**
2 ❑ Cover: 2.50 **NM** value: **Cover or less**
gentlemen; Ladies; Keep Fit With Firkin; Class; The Firkin Report on Sex and Class; Oral Sex; Sexual Anxiety; Once Upon a Time; It's Your Line to Doctor Stupid; How to Shoot Your Wife; Computer Dating; The Christmas Present **A:** Hunt Emerson; Tym Manley **W:** Hunt Emerson; Tym Manley
6 ❑ b&w **NM** value: **2.50**

To find prices for other grades for comic books not graded by CGC, multiply the above prices by:

Mint: 150%	VF-: 55%	VG-: 17%
NM/M:125%	F/VF: 48%	G+: 14%
NM+: 110%	F+: 40%	**Good: 12.5%**
NM-: 90%	**Fine: 33.3%**	G-: 11%
VF/NM: 83%	F-: 30%	FR/G: 10%
VF+: 75%	VG/F: 25%	**Fair: 8%**
Very Fine: 66.6%	VG+: 23%	**Poor: 2%**
	Very Good: 20%	

Other grades: Multiply prices above by **1.5 for Mint • 2/3 for Very Fine • 1/3 for Fine • 1/5 for Very Good • 1/8 for Good**

FIRST, THE — CrossGen

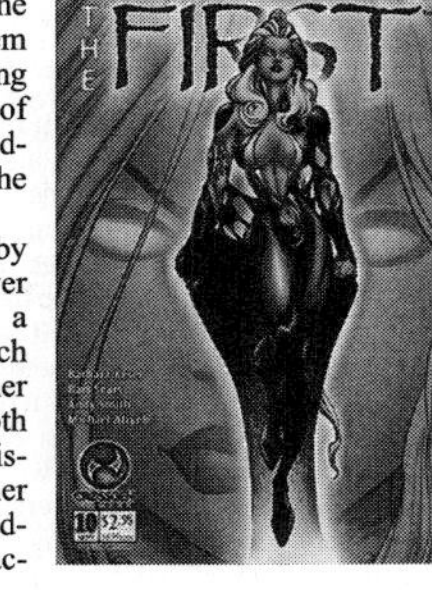

In the interwoven worlds of the CrossGen universe, The First seem like gods, split into two opposing forces. When they become aware of Sigil-Bearers and the powers wielded by those who carry the Sigil, The First set out to investigate.

Written by Barb Kesel with art by Bart Sears, the mythological power of these beings is tempered by a weakening force that affects each side when it crosses over to the other group's territory. Members of both factions make disguised and undisguised appearances in most other CrossGen titles, often acting as advisors to the other principal characters. — Maggie

1 ❑ Dec 2000 Cover: 2.95 **NM** value: **Cover or less**
• **CGC:** 24 graded, best 9.9
2 ❑ Jan 2001 Cover: 2.95 **NM** value: **Cover or less**
• **CGC:** 13 graded, best 9.8
3 ❑ Feb 2001 Cover: 2.95 **NM** value: **Cover or less**
4 ❑ Mar 2001 Cover: 2.95 **NM** value: **Cover or less**
5 ❑ Apr 2001 Cover: 2.95 **NM** value: **Cover or less**
6 ❑ May 2001 Cover: 2.95 **NM** value: **Cover or less**
7 ❑ Jun 2001 Cover: 2.95 **NM** value: **Cover or less**
8 ❑ Jul 2001 Cover: 2.95 **NM** value: **Cover or less**
9 ❑ Aug 2001 Cover: 2.95 **NM** value: **Cover or less**
10 ❑ Sep 2001 Cover: 2.95 **NM** value: **Cover or less**
11 ❑ Oct 2001 Cover: 2.95 **NM** value: **Cover or less**
12 ❑ Nov 2001 Cover: 2.95 **NM** value: **Cover or less**
13 ❑ Dec 2001 Cover: 2.95 **NM** value: **Cover or less**
14 ❑ Jan 2002 Cover: 2.95 **NM** value: **Cover or less**
15 ❑ Feb 2002 Cover: 2.95 **NM** value: **Cover or less**
16 ❑ Mar 2002 Cover: 2.95 **NM** value: **Cover or less**

FIRST ADVENTURES — First

1 ❑ Dec 1985 Cover: 1.25 **NM** value: **Cover or less**
Circ: CapCity orders: **8,950**
📖 Whisper: The Terminal Zone, Part 1; Blaze Barlow: Guns and Butter; Dynamo Hoe: Li'l Orphan Army **A:** Kelley Jones; Rich Larson; Doug Rice **W:** Steven Grant; John Ostrander; Peter B. Gillis
2 ❑ Jan 1986 Cover: 1.25 **NM** value: **Cover or less**
Circ: CapCity orders: **7,250**
📖 Whisper: The Terminal Zone, Part 2; Blaze Barlow: When Titans Party; Dynamo Joe: Destination: DMZ **A:** Rich Larson **W:** Steven Grant
3 ❑ Feb 1986 Cover: 1.25 **NM** value: **Cover or less**
Circ: CapCity orders: **6,725**
📖 Whisper: The Terminal Zone, Part 3
4 ❑ Mar 1986 Cover: 1.25 **NM** value: **Cover or less**
Circ: CapCity orders: **6,750**
📖 Whisper: The Terminal Zone, Part 4
5 ❑ Apr 1986 Cover: 1.25 **NM** value: **Cover or less**
Circ: CapCity orders: **6,175**
📖 Dynamo Joe: Call of Duty; Whisper: The Terminal Zone, Part 5; Whisper: The Terminal Zone, Part 6 **A:** Rich Larson; Doug Rice **W:** Steven Grant; John Ostrander

1ST FOLIO — Pacific

1 ❑ Mar 1984 Cover: 1.50 **NM** value: **Cover or less**
• Joe Kubert School

FIRST GRAPHIC NOVEL — First

Bk 1❑ Jan 1984 Cover: 5.95 **NM** value: **6.00**
• Beowulf
Bk 2❑ **NM** value: **6.00**
• Time Beavers
Bk 3❑ Jun 1985 Cover: 11.95 **NM** value: **Cover or less**
📖 Hard Times • American Flagg: Hard Times **A:** Howard Chaykin **W:** Howard Chaykin; Michael Moorcock
Bk 4❑ **NM** value: **6.00**
• Original Nexus
Bk 5❑ **NM** value: **6.00**
📖 Enchanted Apples of Oz
Bk 6❑ **NM** value: **14.95**
• Elric of Melnibone
Bk 7❑ **NM** value: **7.95**
• Secret Island of Oz
Bk 8❑ **NM** value: **7.95**
• Time2
Bk 9❑ **NM** value: **9.95**
• Teenage Mutant Ninja Turtles
Bk 10❑ **NM** value: **9.95**
• Turtles Book II
Bk 11❑ **NM** value: **14.95**
• Elric: Sailor on the Seas of Fate
Bk 12❑ **NM** value: **7.95**
• Time2 Satisfaction of Black Mariah **A:** Howard Chaykin
Bk 13❑ Cover: 11.95 **NM** value: **Cover or less**
• American Flagg: Southern Comfort **A:** Howard Chaykin
Bk 14❑ **NM** value: **7.95**
• Ice King of Oz
Bk 15❑ **NM** value: **9.95**
Circ: CapCity orders: **3,650**
• Turtles Book III
Bk 16❑ **NM** value: **8.95**
Circ: CapCity orders: **1,425**
• Badger: Hexbreaker
Bk 17❑ **NM** value: **8.95**
Circ: CapCity orders: **1,950**
📖 Forgotten Forest of Oz
Bk 18❑ **NM** value: **9.95**
• Turtles Book III
Bk 19❑ **NM** value: **8.95**
Circ: CapCity orders: **925**
• Mazinger
Bk 20❑ **NM** value: **12.95**
• Team Yankee
Bk 21❑ **NM** value: **9.95**
• Turtles Book IV
Bk 22❑ **NM** value: **19.95**
• Lone Wolf and Cub
Bk 23❑ Cover: 11.95 **NM** value: **Cover or less**
• American Flagg: State of the Union
Bk 24❑ **NM** value: **8.95**
• Grimjack: Demon Knight
Bk 25❑ **NM** value: **14.95**
• Elric: Weird of the White Wolf

FIRST ISSUE SPECIAL — DC

DC used this series as a springboard for introducing and testing new characters on its readers. In addition to introducing such little-known characters as the Green Team and Lady Cop, this series featured introductions of Jack Kirby's Atlas, special features on Doctor Fate and the Creeper, and spotlighted the return of the New Gods.

The most famous character introduced here? Warlord, who would soon have his own series, and several spinoffs, including Arak, Son of Thunder and Claw the Unconquered.

Infamous? That'd be The Dingbats of Danger Street, a Kirby send-up of some of his own teen-team devices, which had long been cliches by this time. They can't be described — they have to be seen first-hand!

1 ❑ Apr 1975 Cover: 0.25 **NM** value: **2.00**
📖 Atlas The Great! • Atlas **A:** Jack Kirby **W:** Jack Kirby ★ 1st Appearance of Atlas.
2 ❑ May 1975 Cover: 0.25 **NM** value: **2.00**
• Green Team
3 ❑ Jun 1975 Cover: 0.25 **NM** value: **2.00**
• Metamorpho
4 ❑ Jul 1975 Cover: 0.25 **NM** value: **2.00**
📖 Lady Cop • Lady Cop **A:** John Rosenberger; Vince Colletta **W:** Robert Kanigher
5 ❑ Aug 1975 Cover: 0.25 **NM** value: **2.00**
📖 The Electric Head • Manhunter **A:** Jack Kirby **W:** Jack Kirby ★ 1st Appearance of Manhunters ★ 1st Appearance of Manhunter II (Mark Shaw).
6 ❑ Sep 1975 Cover: 0.25 **NM** value: **2.00**
📖 Dingbats Of Danger Street; Meet the Gasser • Dingbats **A:** Jack Kirby **W:** Jack Kirby
7 ❑ Oct 1975 Cover: 0.25 **NM** value: **2.00**
8 ❑ Nov 1975 Cover: 0.25 **NM** value: **4.00**
📖 Land of Fear! **A:** Mike Grell **W:** Mike Grell ★ Origin of Warlord. ★ 1st Appearance of Deimos, Skartaris, Warlord.
9 ❑ Dec 1975 Cover: 0.25 **NM** value: **2.00**
10 ❑ Jan 1976 Cover: 0.25 **NM** value: **2.00**
• Outsiders
11 ❑ Feb 1976 Cover: 0.25 **NM** value: **2.00**
📖 Codename: Assassin • Code Name: Assassin **A:** Redondo Studio **W:** Steve Skeates; Gerry Conway
12 ❑ Mar 1976 Cover: 0.30 **NM** value: **2.00**
📖 Starman **A:** Mike Vosburg; Mike Rover **W:** Gerry Conway ★ Origin of Starman II (Mikaal Tomas). ★ 1st Appearance of Starman II (Mikaal Tomas).
13 ❑ Apr 1976 Cover: 0.30 **NM** value: **3.00**
📖 Lest Night Fall Forever! • Return of the New Gods **A:** Mike Vosburg **W:** Denny O'Neil; Gerry Conway

FIRST KINGDOM, THE — Bud Plant

1 ❑ Cover: 0.75 **NM** value: **3.00**
2 ❑ Cover: 1.00 **NM** value: **2.50**
3 ❑ Cover: 1.00 **NM** value: **2.50**
4 ❑ Cover: 1.00 **NM** value: **2.50**
5 ❑ Cover: 1.00 **NM** value: **2.50**
6 ❑ Cover: 1.00 **NM** value: **2.00**
7 ❑ Cover: 1.00 **NM** value: **2.00**
8 ❑ Cover: 1.00 **NM** value: **2.00**
9 ❑ Cover: 1.00 **NM** value: **2.00**
10 ❑ Cover: 1.00 **NM** value: **2.00**
11 ❑ Cover: 1.25 **NM** value: **2.00**
12 ❑ Cover: 1.25 **NM** value: **2.00**
13 ❑ Cover: 1.25 **NM** value: **2.00**
14 ❑ Cover: 1.50 **NM** value: **2.00**
15 ❑ Cover: 1.50 **NM** value: **2.00**
16 ❑ Cover: 1.50 **NM** value: **2.00**
17 ❑ Cover: 1.75 **NM** value: **2.00**
18 ❑ Cover: 1.75 **NM** value: **2.00**
19 ❑ Cover: 1.75 **NM** value: **2.00**
20 ❑ Cover: 1.75 **NM** value: **2.00**
21 ❑ Cover: 1.75 **NM** value: **2.00**
22 ❑ Cover: 1.75 **NM** value: **2.00**
23 ❑ Cover: 1.75 **NM** value: **2.00**
24 ❑ Cover: 1.75 **NM** value: **2.00**
final issue. **A:** Jack Katz **W:** Jack Katz

FIRST KISS — Charlton

Another of Charlton's romance titles, First Kiss ran from 1957 to 1965 and featured work by Dick Giordano, Charles Nicholas, Vince Alascia, the Vince Colletta Studio, Luis Dominguez, and Sal Trapani.

The stories ran to typical romance fare, from jilted brides to heart-broken lovers to the inevitable summer romance to the girl who spent her entire life caring for a sick relative only to find love when that relative finally kicked the bucket. No deep literary content here, just some fun cliches of a simpler era.

In the 1990s, artist and writer John Lustig acquired the original art to the series and began tinkering with the panels and covers, creating his own "Last Kiss" feature which appears in Comics Buyer's Guide and as its own comic-book series with longer stories. — Brent

1 ❑ Dec 1957 Cover: 0.10 **NM** value: **20.00**
📖 Campus Crush; One Stolen Kiss; No Kiss Tonight; Love's Crucible; Good Ole Joe; Boom Goes the Bachelor (text)
2 ❑ Feb 1958 Cover: 0.10 **NM** value: **10.00**
📖 Love Him, Love What He Does; Detour to Love; A Rich Man's Love; Solid Gold Heart; Pauline and Peter (text)
3 ❑ May 1958 Cover: 0.10 **NM** value: **10.00**
📖 To Stella with Love; The Girl Next Door; He Loves Me Not; Who Hooked Who?; Plain Jane; The Maharajah Marriage Maker (text)
4 ❑ ca. 1958 Cover: 0.10 **NM** value: **10.00**
📖 Party Girl; Made for Romance; Gay Farewell; Elopement; Infatuation; Maiden Must Meet Man (text)
5 ❑ ca. 1958 Cover: 0.10 **NM** value: **10.00**
📖 The Magic Perfume; Infatuation; My Confidence Man; He's Not Good Enough; The Sea Green Eyes
6 ❑ ca. 1958 Cover: 0.10 **NM** value: **10.00**
📖 Letter from Long Ago; Janice Has a Date; Plain Jane; The Boy From the City; Forced Meeting!; Castle for Corrine (text)
7 ❑ ca. 1959 Cover: 0.10 **NM** value: **10.00**
📖 Make Believe; Fooling with Love; Kiss Me Tonight; Sweethearts; Bachelor's Farewell; Darling Doll (text)
8 ❑ ca. 1959 Cover: 0.10 **NM** value: **10.00**
📖 The Gay Deception; Daring Young Man; Coffee and a Kiss, Darling!
9 ❑ ca. 1959 Cover: 0.10 **NM** value: **10.00**
📖 A Childish Dream; The Reason?; Irreseistable; Lucky Liz; The Arms of the Law; And So They Were Married (text)
10 ❑ Sep 1959 Cover: 0.10 **NM** value: **10.00**
📖 You Can Never Tell; The Masked Lover; He Came Back; Castle on the Hill; The Glass Ring (text)
11 ❑ Nov 1959 Cover: 0.10 **NM** value: **10.00**
📖 Girl Meets Boy; Don't Lie to a Loved One; A Kiss in the Dark; My Man; Love is the Cure (text)
12 ❑ Jan 1960 Cover: 0.10 **NM** value: **10.00**
📖 Playing it Cool; The Necklace; Heartbreaker; Lovers Quarrel; Hello Beautiful; Love Call; A Good Life; Too Young to Marry? (text)
13 ❑ Mar 1960 Cover: 0.10 **NM** value: **10.00**
📖 The Serious Type; Summer Always Passes; The Betraying Kiss; The Troublemaker; Tension Tennis and Love (text)
14 ❑ May 1960 Cover: 0.10 **NM** value: **10.00**
📖 Jealousy; My Ben; A Lonely Love; Love Will Point the Way; Diane and Dave (text)
15 ❑ Jul 1960 Cover: 0.10 **NM** value: **10.00**
📖 From Out of the Past; Love Among the Stars; Love Comes Later; Whose Broken Heart?; Really Ready For Romance (text)
16 ❑ ca. 1960 Cover: 0.10 **NM** value: **10.00**
📖 To Find My Love; Beloved Enemy; Too Young for Heartbreak; Magic in the Moon; Office Party; Is Romance Necessary? (text)
17 ❑ ca. 1960 Cover: 0.10 **NM** value: **10.00**
📖 The Sands of Fate; Be Sure, My Heart; My Heart Had Wings; Conflict; Two Cents Deposit (text)
18 ❑ ca. 1961 Cover: 0.10 **NM** value: **10.00**
📖 Take My Heart; Forever and a Day; Man Hater; Summers End; Marry the Man? (text)
19 ❑ ca. 1961 Cover: 0.10 **NM** value: **10.00**
📖 Love Can Hurt; The Face of Love; Suddenly, It's Love; My Lost Love; Ex-Girl Friday (text)
20 ❑ ca. 1961 **NM** value: **10.00**
📖 A Bouquet of Roses; Danger Heart-Break; Two Loves Had I; My Outlaw Lover; Love on the Lumerker Line (text)
21 ❑ ca. 1961 **NM** value: **10.00**
📖 A Moment to Remember; Take My Number; My Silent Love; How He Came to Kiss Me; My Foolish Heart; Love Leaps a Land (text)
22 ❑ ca. 1961 **NM** value: **10.00**
📖 Does He Love Me?; Return; Her Engagement Ring; Rebound; You and the Group (text)
23 ❑ ca. 1961 **NM** value: **10.00**
📖 Love Glows Forever; The Ugly One; I Gave My Heart; Tragic Love (text)
24 ❑ ca. 1962 Cover: 0.12 **NM** value: **10.00**
📖 Old Enough to Marry; No More Waiting; Honeymoon Continued; Change of Titles (text)
25 ❑ ca. 1962 Cover: 0.12 **NM** value: **10.00**
📖 The Love that Failed; Florence Nightingale; Don't Ever Love a Fool; Listen Girls; Deception; Teen Age Trouble (text)
26 ❑ ca. 1962 Cover: 0.12 **NM** value: **10.00**
📖 Hidden Love; You Love Her, Darling; Wait For Me, Sweetheart; With All My Heart; Talk of Love (text)
27 ❑ ca. 1962 Cover: 0.12 **NM** value: **10.00**
📖 My Secret; A Glow from the Hearth; Spinster at 21; No Dates, No Kisses; Lest We Forget; Mild Mannered Man (text)
28 ❑ ca. 1962 Cover: 0.12 **NM** value: **10.00**

CGC-graded: Multiply prices above by **33 for 9.9 M • 16 for 9.8 NM/M • 7 for 9.6 NM+ • 5 for 9.4 NM • 2.5 for 9.2 NM- • 1.5 for 9.0 VF/NM**

Strike-Out Queen; My Heart Soared; Year of the Tiger; Lucky Girl; Your Role in the Cold War: God is Never Out of Style; Fay Fades Away (text)

29 ❑ Dec 1962 Cover: 0.12 **NM** value: **10.00**
Hope Never Dies; Teach Me, My Love; Spanish Phantasy; For Better, Not Worse; Danner vs. Danner (text)

30 ❑ Feb 1963 Cover: 0.12 **NM** value: **10.00**
No Road to Romance; A Girl's Best Friend; Reckless Romance; Your Role in the Cold War: What You Do IN Your Spare Time; Through Other People's Eyes (text)

31 ❑ Apr 1963 Cover: 0.12 **NM** value: **10.00**
The Proposal; Meant for Each Other; A Winsome Smile; Kidnapped Kisses; Kid Sister Blues; Jealousy; The American Way; The Secret of Love (text)

32 ❑ Jun 1963 Cover: 0.12 **NM** value: **10.00**
Dream Along With Me; Our Love Was Forbidden; The Barren Years; The Big Mistake (Text)

33 ❑ Aug 1963 Cover: 0.12 **NM** value: **10.00**
Fallen Idol; Man vs. Diary; Second Time Around; Surrender (text)

34 ❑ Oct 1963 Cover: 0.12 **NM** value: **10.00**
The Ruling Clique; The Right Love; The End fo Summer; Symbol of Freedom; In Search of a Wedding (text)

35 ❑ Dec 1963 Cover: 0.12 **NM** value: **10.00**
Beware of Simon; In Love with Love; Meant for Each Other; Reborn (text)

36 ❑ ca. 1964 Cover: 0.12 **NM** value: **10.00**
Loves Lonely Marriage; That Lonely Sound; Belated Love; The Emperor and the Empress (text)

37 ❑ ca. 1964 Cover: 0.12 **NM** value: **10.00**
I Chose Heartbreak; Change of Heart; The Love Thief; Sanwo Likes a Sandwich (text)

38 ❑ ca. 1964 Cover: 0.12 **NM** value: **10.00**
A Grown-Up's Love; Perplexed; Take Me Back; Make No Mistake (text)

39 ❑ ca. 1964 Cover: 0.12 **NM** value: **10.00**
One Too Many Heartbreaks; Jealousy; Symphony of Love; Lover's Spat; My Sister My Enemy; Dear Diary; Look for Love (text)

40 ❑ ca. 1965 Cover: 0.12 **NM** value: **10.00**
Surprise Party; Bad Advice; Condemned; Passing Strangers; Something Special; Involuntary Bride; Clumsy; Martha Marsden Meditates (text)

FIRST LOVE ILLUSTRATED — Harvey

1 ❑ Feb 1949 Cover: 0.10 **NM** value: **125.00**
2 ❑ Apr 1949 Cover: 0.10 **NM** value: **75.00**
3 ❑ Jun 1949 Cover: 0.10 **NM** value: **75.00**
• **CGC:** 1 graded, best 9.2
4 ❑ Aug 1949 Cover: 0.10 **NM** value: **45.00**
5 ❑ Oct 1949 Cover: 0.10 **NM** value: **45.00**
6 ❑ Dec 1949 Cover: 0.10 **NM** value: **45.00**
7 ❑ Feb 1950 Cover: 0.10 **NM** value: **45.00**
8 ❑ Cover: 0.10 **NM** value: **45.00**
9 ❑ Cover: 0.10 **NM** value: **45.00**
10 ❑ Apr 1951 Cover: 0.10 **NM** value: **45.00**
11 ❑ ca. 1951 Cover: 0.10 **NM** value: **40.00**
12 ❑ ca. 1951 Cover: 0.10 **NM** value: **40.00**
13 ❑ ca. 1951 Cover: 0.10 **NM** value: **40.00**
14 ❑ Cover: 0.10 **NM** value: **40.00**
15 ❑ Cover: 0.10 **NM** value: **40.00**
16 ❑ Cover: 0.10 **NM** value: **40.00**
17 ❑ Cover: 0.10 **NM** value: **40.00**
18 ❑ Cover: 0.10 **NM** value: **40.00**
19 ❑ ca. 1952 Cover: 0.10 **NM** value: **40.00**
20 ❑ ca. 1952 Cover: 0.10 **NM** value: **40.00**
21 ❑ ca. 1952 Cover: 0.10 **NM** value: **40.00**
22 ❑ ca. 1952 Cover: 0.10 **NM** value: **40.00**
23 ❑ Nov 1952 Cover: 0.10 **NM** value: **40.00**
I Was a Japanese War Bride; Too Fast For Me; Strange Passion; I Didn't Believe in Love
24 ❑ Jan 1953 Cover: 0.10 **NM** value: **40.00**
25 ❑ Feb 1953 Cover: 0.10 **NM** value: **40.00**
26 ❑ Mar 1953 Cover: 0.10 **NM** value: **40.00**
27 ❑ Apr 1953 Cover: 0.10 **NM** value: **40.00**
28 ❑ May 1953 Cover: 0.10 **NM** value: **40.00**
29 ❑ Jun 1953 Cover: 0.10 **NM** value: **40.00**
30 ❑ Jul 1953 Cover: 0.10 **NM** value: **40.00**
31 ❑ Aug 1953 Cover: 0.10 **NM** value: **40.00**
32 ❑ Sep 1953 Cover: 0.10 **NM** value: **40.00**
33 ❑ Oct 1953 Cover: 0.10 **NM** value: **40.00**
34 ❑ Nov 1953 Cover: 0.10 **NM** value: **40.00**
35 ❑ Dec 1953 Cover: 0.10 **NM** value: **40.00**
36 ❑ Jan 1954 Cover: 0.10 **NM** value: **40.00**
37 ❑ Feb 1954 Cover: 0.10 **NM** value: **40.00**
38 ❑ Mar 1954 Cover: 0.10 **NM** value: **40.00**
39 ❑ Apr 1954 Cover: 0.10 **NM** value: **40.00**
40 ❑ May 1954 Cover: 0.10 **NM** value: **40.00**
41 ❑ Jun 1954 Cover: 0.10 **NM** value: **40.00**
42 ❑ Jul 1954 Cover: 0.10 **NM** value: **40.00**
• **CGC:** 1 graded, best 4.0
43 ❑ Cover: 0.10 **NM** value: **40.00**
44 ❑ Cover: 0.10 **NM** value: **40.00**
45 ❑ Cover: 0.10 **NM** value: **40.00**
46 ❑ Cover: 0.10 **NM** value: **40.00**
47 ❑ Cover: 0.10 **NM** value: **40.00**
48 ❑ Cover: 0.10 **NM** value: **40.00**
49 ❑ Cover: 0.10 **NM** value: **40.00**
50 ❑ Cover: 0.10 **NM** value: **35.00**
51 ❑ Cover: 0.10 **NM** value: **35.00**
52 ❑ Cover: 0.10 **NM** value: **35.00**
53 ❑ Cover: 0.10 **NM** value: **35.00**
54 ❑ Cover: 0.10 **NM** value: **35.00**
55 ❑ Cover: 0.10 **NM** value: **35.00**
56 ❑ Cover: 0.10 **NM** value: **35.00**
57 ❑ Cover: 0.10 **NM** value: **35.00**
58 ❑ Cover: 0.10 **NM** value: **35.00**
59 ❑ Cover: 0.10 **NM** value: **35.00**
60 ❑ Cover: 0.10 **NM** value: **35.00**
61 ❑ Cover: 0.10 **NM** value: **35.00**
62 ❑ Cover: 0.10 **NM** value: **35.00**
63 ❑ Cover: 0.10 **NM** value: **35.00**
64 ❑ Cover: 0.10 **NM** value: **35.00**
65 ❑ Cover: 0.10 **NM** value: **35.00**
66 ❑ Cover: 0.10 **NM** value: **35.00**
67 ❑ Cover: 0.10 **NM** value: **35.00**
68 ❑ Cover: 0.10 **NM** value: **35.00**
69 ❑ Cover: 0.10 **NM** value: **35.00**
70 ❑ Cover: 0.10 **NM** value: **35.00**

FIRST MAN — Image

1 ❑ Jun 1997 Cover: 2.50 **NM** value: **Cover or less**
cover says 1st Man, indicia says First Man. **A:** Andy Smith **W:** Andy Smith; Robert Snyder

FIRST ROMANCE MAGAZINE — Harvey

1 ❑ Aug 1949 Cover: 0.10 **NM** value: **100.00**
2 ❑ Oct 1949 Cover: 0.10 **NM** value: **60.00**
3 ❑ 1949 Cover: 0.10 **NM** value: **50.00**
4 ❑ 1950 Cover: 0.10 **NM** value: **50.00**
5 ❑ 1950 Cover: 0.10 **NM** value: **50.00**
6 ❑ 1950 Cover: 0.10 **NM** value: **40.00**
7 ❑ 1951 Cover: 0.10 **NM** value: **40.00**
8 ❑ 1951 Cover: 0.10 **NM** value: **40.00**
9 ❑ 1951 Cover: 0.10 **NM** value: **40.00**
10 ❑ Dec 1951 Cover: 0.10 **NM** value: **40.00**
11 ❑ 1952 Cover: 0.10 **NM** value: **35.00**
12 ❑ 1952 Cover: 0.10 **NM** value: **35.00**
13 ❑ 1952 Cover: 0.10 **NM** value: **35.00**
14 ❑ 1952 Cover: 0.10 **NM** value: **35.00**
15 ❑ 1952 Cover: 0.10 **NM** value: **35.00**
16 ❑ 1952 Cover: 0.10 **NM** value: **35.00**
17 ❑ 1953 Cover: 0.10 **NM** value: **35.00**
18 ❑ 1953 Cover: 0.10 **NM** value: **35.00**
19 ❑ 1953 Cover: 0.10 **NM** value: **35.00**
20 ❑ 1953 Cover: 0.10 **NM** value: **30.00**
21 ❑ 1953 Cover: 0.10 **NM** value: **30.00**
22 ❑ 1953 Cover: 0.10 **NM** value: **30.00**
23 ❑ 1954 Cover: 0.10 **NM** value: **30.00**
24 ❑ 1954 Cover: 0.10 **NM** value: **30.00**
25 ❑ 1954 Cover: 0.10 **NM** value: **30.00**
26 ❑ 1954 Cover: 0.10 **NM** value: **30.00**
27 ❑ 1954 Cover: 0.10 **NM** value: **30.00**
28 ❑ 1954 Cover: 0.10 **NM** value: **30.00**
29 ❑ 1954 Cover: 0.10 **NM** value: **30.00**
30 ❑ 1955 Cover: 0.10 **NM** value: **25.00**
31 ❑ 1955 Cover: 0.10 **NM** value: **25.00**
32 ❑ 1955 Cover: 0.10 **NM** value: **25.00**
33 ❑ 1955 Cover: 0.10 **NM** value: **25.00**
34 ❑ 1955 Cover: 0.10 **NM** value: **25.00**
35 ❑ 1955 Cover: 0.10 **NM** value: **25.00**
36 ❑ 1955 Cover: 0.10 **NM** value: **25.00**
37 ❑ 1956 Cover: 0.10 **NM** value: **25.00**
38 ❑ 1956 Cover: 0.10 **NM** value: **25.00**
39 ❑ 1956 Cover: 0.10 **NM** value: **25.00**
40 ❑ 1956 Cover: 0.10 **NM** value: **20.00**
41 ❑ Aug 1956 Cover: 0.10 **NM** value: **20.00**
42 ❑ Oct 1956 Cover: 0.10 **NM** value: **20.00**
43 ❑ Dec 1956 Cover: 0.10 **NM** value: **20.00**
44 ❑ Feb 1957 Cover: 0.10 **NM** value: **20.00**
45 ❑ 1957 Cover: 0.10 **NM** value: **20.00**
46 ❑ 1957 Cover: 0.10 **NM** value: **20.00**
47 ❑ 1957 Cover: 0.10 **NM** value: **20.00**
48 ❑ 1957 Cover: 0.10 **NM** value: **20.00**
49 ❑ 1958 Cover: 0.10 **NM** value: **20.00**
50 ❑ 1958 Cover: 0.10 **NM** value: **20.00**
51 ❑ 1958 Cover: 0.10 **NM** value: **20.00**
52 ❑ 1958 Cover: 0.10 **NM** value: **20.00**

FIRST SIX PACK — First

1 ❑ Jul 1987 Cover: 0.50 **NM** value: **1.00**
Circ: CapCity orders: **7,825**
Nexus, Badger, Jon, etc.
2 ❑ Cover: 0.50 **NM** value: **1.00**
Psychoblast, Shatter, American Flagg, Jon Sable, Dreadstar, Whisper **A:** Norm Breyfogle; Robb Phipps; Paul Smith; Luke McDonnell; Tony Salmons; Charlie Athanas **W:** Jim Starlin; Howard Chaykin; Mike Grell; Steven Grant; Mindy Newell; Peter B. Gillis

FIRST TRIP TO THE MOON — Avalon

1 ❑ b&w Cover: 2.50 **NM** value: **Cover or less**
• reprints Charlton story

FIRST WAVE — Andromeda

1 ❑ Dec 2000 Cover: 2.99 **NM** value: **Cover or less**
Circ: Diamd. preorders: **7,423**
Photo cover. **A:** Dan Parsons **W:** James Anthony Kuhoric

FISHMASTERS — Slave Labor

1 ❑ May 1994 Cover: 2.95 **NM** value: **Cover or less**
• adapts TV show **A:** Troy Nixey **W:** Dan Vado; Carl Edge; Kevin Graves ★ Origin of The Fishmasters. ★ 1st Appearance of The Fishmasters.

FISH POLICE (MARVEL) — Marvel

1 ❑ Oct 1992 Cover: 1.25 **NM** value: **Cover or less**
Circ: CapCity orders: **6,500**
Hairballs, Part 1 **A:** Steve Moncuse **W:** Steve Moncuse
2 ❑ Nov 1992 Cover: 1.25 **NM** value: **Cover or less**
Circ: CapCity orders: **4,000**
Hairballs, Part 2 **A:** Steve Moncuse **W:** Steve Moncuse
3 ❑ Dec 1992 Cover: 1.25 **NM** value: **Cover or less**
Circ: CapCity orders: **3,300**
Hairballs, Part 3 **A:** Steve Moncuse **W:** Steve Moncuse
4 ❑ Jan 1993 Cover: 1.25 **NM** value: **Cover or less**
Circ: CapCity orders: **2,500**
Hairballs, Part 4 **A:** Steve Moncuse **W:** Steve Moncuse
5 ❑ Feb 1993 Cover: 1.25 **NM** value: **Cover or less**
6 ❑ Mar 1993 Cover: 1.25 **NM** value: **Cover or less**
S.H.A.R.K. Bait **A:** Steve Moncuse **W:** Steve Moncuse

FISH POLICE (VOL. 1) — Fishwrap

Imagine an ill-tempered police detective who lives alone. Imagine a woman waiting for him when he comes home. Imagine that woman needing the detective's help. This scenario may seem like a scene from a film noir hardboiled detective story, except for one small difference. Every character in this book is a fish of some sort. This mid-1980s, self-published, black-and-white comic book tells the story of an alternate dimension in which fish function like people. They have the same problems — crime, love, and mean bosses — but these characters also have a hard time walking up stairs.

The first issue begins the "Hairball Saga," a tale about a drug that can supposedly send fish into another realm, where things called humans walk up stairs using legs. The title was later picked up by Marvel Comics for the Fish Police (Marvel) series in 1992, and it also received a short-lived TV adaptation.

1 ❑ Dec 1985 Cover: 1.25 **NM** value: **Cover or less**
Hairballs • Indicia title: Inspector Gill of the Fish Police **A:** Steve Moncuse **W:** Steve Moncuse
1-2 ❑ Cover: 1.25 **NM** value: **Cover or less**
2 ❑ Feb 1986 Cover: 1.25 **NM** value: **Cover or less**
3 ❑ Apr 1986 Cover: 1.25 **NM** value: **Cover or less**
4 ❑ Jun 1986 Cover: 1.50 **NM** value: **Cover or less**
5 ❑ Aug 1986 Cover: 1.50 **NM** value: **Cover or less**
6 ❑ 1986 Cover: 1.50 **NM** value: **Cover or less**
7 ❑ Feb 1987 Cover: 1.50 **NM** value: **Cover or less**
• indicia says Feb 86 **A:** Steve Moncuse **W:** Steve Moncuse
8 ❑ 1987 Cover: 1.50 **NM** value: **Cover or less**
9 ❑ 1987 Cover: 1.50 **NM** value: **Cover or less**
10 ❑ 1987 Cover: 1.50 **NM** value: **Cover or less**
11 ❑ 1987 Cover: 1.50 **NM** value: **Cover or less**
Bk 1 ❑ Cover: 9.95 **NM** value: **Cover or less**
• Hairballs trade paperback **A:** Steve Moncuse **W:** Steve Moncuse

FISH POLICE, THE (VOL. 2) — Comico

5 ❑ 1987 Cover: 1.75 **NM** value: **Cover or less**
Circ: CapCity orders: **3,150**
6 ❑ 1987 Cover: 1.75 **NM** value: **Cover or less**
Circ: CapCity orders: **2,925**
7 ❑ Cover: 1.75 **NM** value: **Cover or less**
Circ: CapCity orders: **2,925**
8 ❑ Cover: 1.75 **NM** value: **Cover or less**
Circ: CapCity orders: **3,025**
9 ❑ Cover: 1.75 **NM** value: **Cover or less**
Circ: CapCity orders: **2,975**
10 ❑ 1988 Cover: 1.75 **NM** value: **Cover or less**
Circ: CapCity orders: **2,600**
11 ❑ 1988 Cover: 1.75 **NM** value: **Cover or less**
Circ: CapCity orders: **2,625**
12 ❑ 1988 Cover: 1.75 **NM** value: **Cover or less**
Circ: CapCity orders: **3,300**
13 ❑ 1988 Cover: 1.75 **NM** value: **Cover or less**
Circ: CapCity orders: **2,900**
14 ❑ Dec 1988 Cover: 1.75 **NM** value: **Cover or less**
Circ: CapCity orders: **2,950**
15 ❑ Cover: 1.75 **NM** value: **Cover or less**
Circ: CapCity orders: **2,750**
16 ❑ Cover: 1.75 **NM** value: **Cover or less**
Circ: CapCity orders: **2,700**
17 ❑ Jun 1989 Cover: 2.50 **NM** value: **Cover or less**
Circ: CapCity orders: **2,600**
18 ❑ Aug 1989, b&w Cover: 2.25 **NM** value: **Cover or less**
• Black & white format begins, Apple Comics **A:** Steve Moncuse **W:** Steve Moncuse
19 ❑ Oct 1989, b&w Cover: 2.25 **NM** value: **Cover or less**
20 ❑ Mar 1990, b&w Cover: 2.25 **NM** value: **Cover or less**
21 ❑ 1990b&w Cover: 2.25 **NM** value: **Cover or less**
22 ❑ 1990b&w Cover: 2.25 **NM** value: **Cover or less**
23 ❑ 1990b&w Cover: 2.25 **NM** value: **Cover or less**
24 ❑ 1990b&w Cover: 2.25 **NM** value: **Cover or less**
25 ❑ Nov 1990, b&w Cover: 2.25 **NM** value: **Cover or less**
26 ❑ b&w Cover: 2.25 **NM** value: **Cover or less**
SE 1 ❑ ca. 1987 Cover: 2.50 **NM** value: **Cover or less**

FISH SHTICKS — Apple

1 ❑ Nov 1991, b&w Cover: 2.75 **NM** value: **Cover or less**
2 ❑ b&w Cover: 2.75 **NM** value: **Cover or less**
3 ❑ May 1992, b&w Cover: 2.75 **NM** value: **Cover or less**
4 ❑ b&w Cover: 2.75 **NM** value: **Cover or less**
5 ❑ b&w Cover: 2.75 **NM** value: **Cover or less**
6 ❑ b&w Cover: 2.75 **NM** value: **Cover or less**

FISSION CHICKEN — Fantagraphics

1 ❑ ca. 1990, b&w Cover: 2.00 **NM** value: **Cover or less**
2 ❑ b&w Cover: 2.00 **NM** value: **Cover or less**
3 ❑ b&w Cover: 2.00 **NM** value: **Cover or less**
4 ❑ b&w Cover: 2.00 **NM** value: **Cover or less**

FISSION CHICKEN: PLAN NINE FROM VORTOX — Mu Press

1 ❑ Jul 1994 Cover: 3.95 **NM** value: **Cover or less**

FIST OF GOD, THE — Eternity

1 ❑ May 1988 Cover: 1.95 **NM** value: **2.25**
2 ❑ Jul 1988 Cover: 1.95 **NM** value: **Cover or less**

Other grades: Multiply prices above by **1.5 for Mint • 2/3 for Very Fine • 1/3 for Fine • 1/5 for Very Good • 1/8 for Good**

3 ❑ Sep 1988 Cover: 1.95 **NM** value: **Cover or less**
4 ❑ Nov 1988 Cover: 1.95 **NM** value: **Cover or less**

FIST OF THE NORTH STAR — Viz
1 ❑ Cover: 2.95 **NM** value: **Cover or less**
📖 A Cry From the Heart, Part 1 **A:** Tetsuo Hara **W:** Buronson
2 ❑ Cover: 2.95 **NM** value: **Cover or less**
3 ❑ Cover: 2.95 **NM** value: **Cover or less**
4 ❑ Cover: 2.95 **NM** value: **Cover or less**
5 ❑ Cover: 2.95 **NM** value: **Cover or less**
6 ❑ Cover: 2.95 **NM** value: **Cover or less**
7 ❑ Cover: 2.95 **NM** value: **Cover or less**
8 ❑ Cover: 2.95 **NM** value: **Cover or less**
Bk 1❑ Apr 1995 Cover: 19.95 **NM** value: **Cover or less**
• Collects 16 chapters **A:** Tetsuo Hara **W:** Buronson

FIST OF THE NORTH STAR PART 2 — Viz
1 ❑ Cover: 2.75 **NM** value: **Cover or less**
2 ❑ Cover: 2.75 **NM** value: **Cover or less**
3 ❑ Cover: 2.95 **NM** value: **Cover or less**
4 ❑ Cover: 2.95 **NM** value: **Cover or less**
5 ❑ Cover: 2.95 **NM** value: **Cover or less**
6 ❑ Cover: 2.95 **NM** value: **Cover or less**
7 ❑ Cover: 2.95 **NM** value: **Cover or less**
8 ❑ Cover: 2.95 **NM** value: **Cover or less**
Bk 2❑ Cover: 16.95 **NM** value: **Cover or less**
📖 Night of the Jackal **A:** Tetsuo Hara **W:** Buronson

FIST OF THE NORTH STAR PART 3 — Viz
1 ❑ Cover: 2.95 **NM** value: **Cover or less**
📖 The Wolf Pack of Death **A:** Tetsuo Hara **W:** Buronson
2 ❑ Cover: 2.95 **NM** value: **Cover or less**
3 ❑ Sep 1996 Cover: 2.95 **NM** value: **Cover or less**
Circ: Diamd. preorders: **4,547**
4 ❑ Oct 1996 Cover: 2.95 **NM** value: **Cover or less**
Circ: Diamd. preorders: **4,354**
5 ❑ Nov 1996 Cover: 2.95 **NM** value: **Cover or less**
Circ: Diamd. preorders: **4,100**
Bk 3❑ Cover: 15.95 **NM** value: **Cover or less**
• Southern Cross **A:** Tetsuo Hara **W:** Buronson

FIST OF THE NORTH STAR PART 4 — Viz
1 ❑ Dec 1996 Cover: 2.95 **NM** value: **Cover or less**
Circ: Diamd. preorders: **4,582**
2 ❑ Jan 1997 Cover: 2.95 **NM** value: **Cover or less**
Circ: Diamd. preorders: **3,957**
3 ❑ Feb 1997 Cover: 2.95 **NM** value: **Cover or less**
Circ: Diamd. preorders: **3,467**
4 ❑ Mar 1997 Cover: 2.95 **NM** value: **Cover or less**
Circ: Diamd. preorders: **3,434**
5 ❑ Cover: 2.95 **NM** value: **Cover or less**
6 ❑ Cover: 2.95 **NM** value: **Cover or less**
7 ❑ Cover: 2.95 **NM** value: **Cover or less**
Bk 4❑ Jan 1998 Cover: 15.95 **NM** value: **Cover or less**
📖 Blood Brothers **A:** Tetsuo Hara **W:** Buronson

5-CENT COMICS — Fawcett
1 ❑ Jan 1940 Cover: 0.05 **NM** value: **8000.00**

FIVE LITTLE COMICS — Scott McCloud
1 ❑ Cover: 4.00 **NM** value: **Cover or less**
📖 Another Little Epic; Some Words Albert Likes; Fifteen Faces In Charcoal; Birth Of A Nation; Fun With Phonics! **A:** Scott McCloud **W:** Scott McCloud

FIVE YEARS OF PAIN — Boneyard
1 ❑ Jan 1997 Cover: 3.95 **NM** value: **Cover or less**
Circ: Diamd. preorders: **2,675**

FLAG FIGHTERS — Ironcat
1 ❑ Sep 1997, b&w Cover: 2.95 **NM** value: **Cover or less**
Circ: Diamd. preorders: **3,773**
📖 Flag Fight **A:** Masaomi Kanzaki **W:** Masaomi Kanzaki
2 ❑ 1997b&w Cover: 2.95 **NM** value: **Cover or less**
3 ❑ Nov 1997, b&w Cover: 2.95 **NM** value: **Cover or less**
4 ❑ Cover: 2.95 **NM** value: **Cover or less**
5 ❑ Cover: 2.95 **NM** value: **Cover or less**

FLAME — Fox
1 ❑ Sum 1940 Cover: 0.10 **NM** value: **3000.00**
• **CGC:** 3 graded, best 9.2
2 ❑ Fal 1940 Cover: 0.10 **NM** value: **1500.00**
3 ❑ Win 1940 Cover: 0.10 **NM** value: **800.00**

FLAME TWISTERS — Brown Study
1 ❑ Oct 1994, b&w Cover: 2.50 **NM** value: **Cover or less**
📖 Oppressions of the Bleak **A:** Erik Enervold **W:** M.E. Brown
2 ❑ Mar 1995, b&w Cover: 2.50 **NM** value: **Cover or less**

FLAMING CARROT COMICS — Aardvark-Vanaheim
Bob Burden's Flaming Carrot is a mix of super-hero action and surreal comedy. Its star is a man who decides to dress up as a vegetable on fire. Thus clad, he is ready to take on evildoers in his native Iron City as "the super-hero of last resort." Among the villains he faces are such nefarious characters as the dour Clown-9; lobster-handed Aunt Clau; the Puppet Monster Man; and a flying dead dog. And that's not even mentioning the really crazy people he runs into.

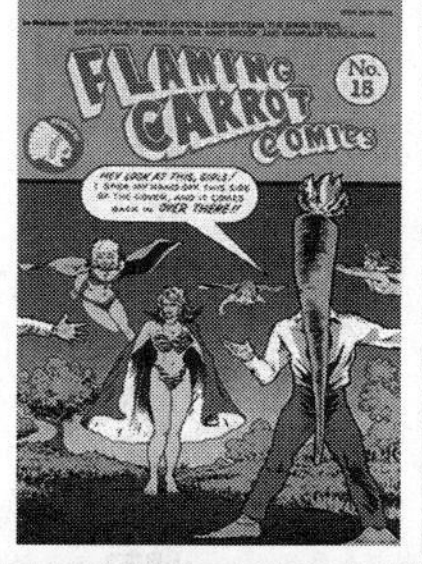

Either alone, or with his fellow super-heroes, the Mysterymen, Flaming Carrot takes on all comers and usually comes out on top — if only by outweirding the other guy.
1 ❑ May 1984 Cover: 2.00 **NM** value: **30.00**
• **CGC:** 7 graded, best 9.6
• Aardvark-Vanaheim publishes **A:** Bob Burden **W:** Bob Burden ★ 1st Appearance of Flaming Carrot.
2 ❑ Jul 1984 Cover: 2.00 **NM** value: **15.00**
• **CGC:** 1 graded, best 8.5
3 ❑ Sep 1984 Cover: 2.00 **NM** value: **12.00**
4 ❑ Nov 1984 Cover: 2.00 **NM** value: **10.00**
• **CGC:** 1 graded, best 9.2
5 ❑ Jan 1985 Cover: 2.00 **NM** value: **8.00**
6 ❑ Mar 1985 Cover: 1.70 **NM** value: **8.00**
• becomes Flaming Carrot Comics **A:** Bob Burden **W:** Bob Burden
7 ❑ May 1985 Cover: 2.00 **NM** value: **7.00**
• **CGC:** 1 graded, best 9.0
• Renegade begins publishing **A:** Bob Burden **W:** Bob Burden
8 ❑ Aug 1985 Cover: 2.00 **NM** value: **5.00**
9 ❑ Oct 1985 Cover: 2.00 **NM** value: **5.00**
10 ❑ Dec 1985 Cover: 2.00 **NM** value: **4.00**
11 ❑ Mar 1986 Cover: 1.70 **NM** value: **4.00**
12 ❑ May 1986 Cover: 1.70 **NM** value: **4.00**
13 ❑ Jul 1986 Cover: 1.70 **NM** value: **3.00**
14 ❑ Oct 1986 Cover: 2.00 **NM** value: **3.00**
15 ❑ Jan 1987 Cover: 2.00 **NM** value: **3.00**
📖 Monster Fighter **A:** Bob Burden **W:** Bob Burden
15/A❑ Jan 1987 **NM** value: **4.00**
no cover price. 📖 Monster Fighter **A:** Bob Burden **W:** Bob Burden
16 ❑ Jun 1987 Cover: 2.00 **NM** value: **4.00**
17 ❑ Jul 1987 Cover: 2.00 **NM** value: **3.00**
18 ❑ Jun 2001 Cover: 2.00 **NM** value: **3.00**
• Dark Horse begins publishing **A:** Bob Burden **W:** Bob Burden
19 ❑ Jun 2001 Cover: 2.00 **NM** value: **3.00**
📖 Hills Like Pink Elephants **A:** Bob Burden **W:** Bob Burden
20 ❑ Nov 1988 Cover: 2.00 **NM** value: **3.00**
21 ❑ Spr 1989 Cover: 2.00 **NM** value: **3.00**
22 ❑ Jun 1989 Cover: 2.00 **NM** value: **3.00**
23 ❑ Nov 1989 Cover: 2.00 **NM** value: **3.00**
24 ❑ Apr 1990 Cover: 2.95 **NM** value: **3.00**
📖 A Beautiful Day in the Neighborhood **A:** Bob Burden **W:** Bob Burden
25 ❑ Apr 1991 Cover: 2.00 **NM** value: **3.50**
📖 Dark City… **A:** Bob Burden **W:** Bob Burden ★ Appearance of Teenage Mutant Ninja Turtles.
26 ❑ Jun 1991 Cover: 2.25 **NM** value: **2.50**
27 ❑ Cover: 2.25 **NM** value: **2.50**
• no indicia **A:** Bob Burden **C:** Todd McFarlane **W:** Bob Burden ★ Appearance of Mystery Men, Teenage Mutant Ninja Turtles.
28 ❑ Aug 1992 Cover: 2.25 **NM** value: **2.50**
29 ❑ Oct 1992 Cover: 2.50 **NM** value: **Cover or less**
Circ: CapCity orders: **4,600**
📖 Night Of The Hunted **A:** Bob Burden **W:** Bob Burden
30 ❑ Dec 1992 Cover: 2.50 **NM** value: **Cover or less**
Circ: CapCity orders: **4,325**
• brown background **A:** Bob Burden **W:** Bob Burden
30/A❑ Dec 1992 Cover: 2.50 **NM** value: **Cover or less**
• blue background **A:** Bob Burden **W:** Bob Burden
31 ❑ Oct 1994 Cover: 2.50 **NM** value: **Cover or less**
Circ: CapCity orders: **4,250**
📖 Alas Poor Carrot! final issue. • Story originally scheduled for Herbie (Dark Horse) #3 **A:** Bob Burden **W:** Bob Burden ★ Appearance of Herbie.
Anl 1❑ Jan 1997, b&w Cover: 5.00 **NM** value: **Cover or less**
cardstock cover. • 1997 Annual **A:** Bob Burden **W:** Bob Burden ★ Appearance of Mystery Men.
Bk 1❑ Jul 1997, b&w Cover: 12.95 **NM** value: **Cover or less**
• Man of Mystery; collects issues #1-3 plus short stories and other material **A:** Bob Burden **W:** Bob Burden
Bk 2❑ Nov 1997, b&w Cover: 17.95 **NM** value: **Cover or less**
• The Wild Shall Wild Remain; collects issues #4-11 plus other material and new five-page story **A:** Bob Burden **W:** Bob Burden
Bk 3❑ Apr 1998 Cover: 17.95 **NM** value: **Cover or less**
• Greatest Hits; collects issues #12-18 plus new material **A:** Bob Burden **W:** Bob Burden
Bk 4❑ Nov 1998 Cover: 16.95 **NM** value: **Cover or less**
• Fortune Favors the Bold; collects issues #19-24 **A:** Bob Burden **W:** Bob Burden

FLAMING CARROT (KILLIAN) — Kilian
1 ❑ Sum 1981 Cover: 1.95 **NM** value: **40.00**
One-shot. • magazine.

FLAMING CARROT STORIES — Dark Horse
1 ❑ Cover: 5.00 **NM** value: **Cover or less**
📖 Green Bones Dancing • "Version A" **A:** Bob Burden **W:** Bob Burden

FLAMING LOVE — Quality
1 ❑ Dec 1949 Cover: 0.10 **NM** value: **250.00**
2 ❑ Feb 1950 Cover: 0.10 **NM** value: **125.00**
3 ❑ Apr 1950 Cover: 0.10 **NM** value: **100.00**
4 ❑ Jun 1950 Cover: 0.10 **NM** value: **100.00**
5 ❑ Aug 1950 Cover: 0.10 **NM** value: **100.00**
6 ❑ Oct 1950 Cover: 0.10 **NM** value: **100.00**

FLAMING WESTERN ROMANCES — Star Publications
3 ❑ Mar 1950 Cover: 0.10 **NM** value: **300.00**

FLARE — Hero
1 ❑ Cover: 2.75 **NM** value: **Cover or less**
2 ❑ Cover: 2.75 **NM** value: **Cover or less**
3 ❑ Jan 1989 Cover: 2.75 **NM** value: **Cover or less**

FLARE ADVENTURES — Hero
Teresa Gottman, or Flare, is gifted with the power of light. Like her namesake, Flare is able to project bright bursts of light capable of blinding people. She can also fly, has enhanced strength, and shows a considerable expanse of skin. Flare is a powerful member of The League of Champions as well as being the sister of Sparkplug, who possesses the power of lightning.

This series reprints issues of the Flare series. Although Flare is powerful, she is also emotional and falls in love easily. This flaw in her character seems to cause her problems.

This series is published as a flip-book with Champions Classics, which reprints classic issues of The League of Champions. That group consists of Icestar, Icicle, Rose, Flare, and others. As a super-group, they are remarkable, not only for their high-powered battles with bad guys, but also for their human battles with life.
1 ❑ Cover: 0.90 **NM** value: **1.00**
Circ: CapCity orders: **3,225**
2 ❑ Cover: 2.95 **NM** value: **Cover or less**
• Flip-book format with Champions Classics #2
3 ❑ Cover: 2.95 **NM** value: **Cover or less**
📖 Betrayal By Design; Dolf and the Formal Dance; The Curse of the Hellfire Crown, Part 3 • Flip-book format with Champions Classics #3 **A:** Chris Marrinan; Stan Sakai; Tim Burgard **W:** Dennis Mallonee
4 ❑ b&w **NM** value: **3.95**
• Flip-book format with Champions Classics #4
5 ❑ b&w **NM** value: **3.95**
• Flip-book format with Champions Classics #5
6 ❑ b&w **NM** value: **3.95**
• Flip-book format with Champions Classics #6
7 ❑ b&w **NM** value: **3.95**
• Flip-book format with Champions Classics #7
8 ❑ b&w Cover: 3.95 **NM** value: **Cover or less**
📖 Turnabout • Flip-book format with Champions Classics #8 **A:** Mark Beachum; Albert Deschesne; Habagat **W:** Dennis Mallonee
9 ❑ b&w Cover: 3.95 **NM** value: **Cover or less**
• Flip-book format
10 ❑ b&w Cover: 3.95 **NM** value: **Cover or less**
• Flip-book format
11 ❑ b&w Cover: 3.95 **NM** value: **Cover or less**
• Flip-book format
12 ❑ b&w Cover: 3.95 **NM** value: **Cover or less**
• Flip-book format
13 ❑ b&w Cover: 3.95 **NM** value: **Cover or less**
• Flip-book format

FLARE FIRST EDITION — Hero
1 ❑ **NM** value: **3.50**
• contents will vary
2 ❑ **NM** value: **3.50**
• contents will vary
3 ❑ b&w **NM** value: **3.50**
4 ❑ b&w **NM** value: **4.50**
5 ❑ b&w **NM** value: **4.50**
6 ❑ b&w Cover: 3.95 **NM** value: **Cover or less**
7 ❑ b&w Cover: 3.95 **NM** value: **Cover or less**
8 ❑ b&w Cover: 3.95 **NM** value: **Cover or less**
9 ❑ Cover: 3.95 **NM** value: **Cover or less**
• Sparkplug
10 ❑ Cover: 3.95 **NM** value: **Cover or less**
11 ❑ Oct 1993, b&w Cover: 3.95 **NM** value: **Cover or less**

FLARE (VOL. 2) — Hero
1 ❑ Cover: 2.75 **NM** value: **3.00**
Circ: CapCity orders: **2,175**
2 ❑ Cover: 2.75 **NM** value: **3.00**
Circ: CapCity orders: **1,700**
3 ❑ Jan 1989 Cover: 2.75 **NM** value: **3.00**
Circ: CapCity orders: **1,900**
📖 The Adventures of Sky Marshal; Freedom's Just another Word; Retribution **A:** Mark Beachum; Dell Barras; Carlos Baldorado **W:** Dennis Mallonee; David Berge ★ 1st Appearance of Britannia.
4 ❑ Cover: 2.75 **NM** value: **Cover or less**
Circ: CapCity orders: **2,525**
5 ❑ Cover: 2.75 **NM** value: **Cover or less**
Circ: CapCity orders: **3,650**
• Eternity Smith
6 ❑ Cover: 2.75 **NM** value: **Cover or less**
Circ: CapCity orders: **3,725**
7 ❑ Cover: 2.75 **NM** value: **Cover or less**
Circ: CapCity orders: **2,550**
8 ❑ b&w Cover: 3.50 **NM** value: **Cover or less**
Circ: CapCity orders: **2,250**
9 ❑ b&w Cover: 3.50 **NM** value: **Cover or less**
10 ❑ b&w Cover: 3.50 **NM** value: **Cover or less**
11 ❑ Apr 1993, b&w Cover: 2.95 **NM** value: **Cover or less**
12 ❑ Jun 1993, b&w Cover: 3.95 **NM** value: **Cover or less**
13 ❑ Aug 1993, b&w Cover: 3.95 **NM** value: **Cover or less**
14 ❑ Oct 1993, b&w Cover: 3.95 **NM** value: **Cover or less**
15 ❑ Jan 1994 Cover: 3.95 **NM** value: **Cover or less**
16 ❑ Cover: 2.95 **NM** value: **Cover or less**
Anl 1❑ b&w **NM** value: **4.50**
Circ: CapCity orders: **3,525**

📖 indicates **Story Title** or **Storyline** information.
★ indicates **Character Appearance** information.
W = Writer • A = Artist • C = Cover Artist

CGC-graded: Multiply prices above by **33 for 9.9 M • 16 for 9.8 NM/M • 7 for 9.6 NM+ • 5 for 9.4 NM • 2.5 for 9.2 NM- • 1.5 for 9.0 VF/NM**

FLASH, THE (1ST SERIES) DC

Picking up the numbering from Flash Comics, this series featured Barry Allen as the red-garbed speedster and Justice League member. Allen was the second person to take on the role of Flash, replacing Jay Garrick, the Flash of the Golden Age.

During the run of this series, Allen squared off against countless colorful villains, including Professor Zoom, Gorilla Grodd, and the Trickster. The series is also notable for the introduction of the hero, Elongated Man, as well as later witnessing EM's marriage to Sue Dearborn.

As can be expected by adventures of The Fastest Man Alive, most of the plots revolved around super-speed antics, including time travel, running across water, vibrating through walls, and creating mini-tornadoes by The Flash whirling his arms at super-speed.

The series ended in the early 1980s when Allen was put on trial for the murder of Zoom, and Allen later gave his life to save the universe in Crisis on Infinite Earths.

105 ❑ Feb 1959 Cover: 0.10 **NM** value: **4800.00**
• **CGC:** 34 graded, best 9.2
Conqueror from 8 Million B.C.!; The Master of Mirrors! • numbering continued from Flash Comics **A:** Carmine Infantino ★ Origin of Flash II (Barry Allen). ★ 1st Appearance of Mirror Master.

106 ❑ May 1959 Cover: 0.10 **NM** value: **1350.00**
• **CGC:** 12 graded, best 9.0
Menace of the Super-Gorilla!; The Pied Piper of Peril! **A:** Carmine Infantino ★ Origin of Pied Piper, Gorilla Grodd. ★ 1st Appearance of Gorilla City, Gorilla Grodd, The Pied Piper.

107 ❑ Jul 1959 Cover: 0.10 **NM** value: **685.00**
• **CGC:** 4 graded, best 9.0
Return of the Super-Gorilla!; The Amazing Race Against Time! **A:** Carmine Infantino ★ 2nd Appearance of Gorilla Grodd.

108 ❑ Sep 1959 Cover: 0.10 **NM** value: **650.00**
• **CGC:** 5 graded, best 9.0
The Speed of Doom!; The Super-Gorilla's Secret Identity! **A:** Carmine Infantino ★ Appearance of Gorilla Grodd.

109 ❑ Nov 1959 Cover: 0.10 **NM** value: **500.00**
• **CGC:** 9 graded, best 9.0
Return of the Mirror Master!; Secret of the Sunken Satellite! **A:** Carmine Infantino **W:** John Broome

110 ❑ Jan 1960 Cover: 0.10 **NM** value: **1250.00**
Circ: Statement: **298,000** • **CGC:** 13 graded, best 8.0
The Challenge of the Weathe Wizard!; Meet Kid Flash! **A:** Murphy Anderson; Carmine Infantino **W:** John Broome ★ Origin of Kid Flash. ★ 1st Appearance of Weather Wizard, Kid Flash.

111 ❑ Mar 1960 Cover: 0.10 **NM** value: **325.00**
Circ: Statement: **298,000** • **CGC:** 2 graded, best 9.4
The Invasion of the Cloud Creatures!; Kid Flash: The Challenge of the Crimson Crows! **A:** Carmine Infantino **W:** John Broome ★ 2nd Appearance of Kid Flash. ★ 2nd Appearance of Kid Flash.

112 ❑ May 1960 Cover: 0.10 **NM** value: **365.00**
Circ: Statement: **298,000** • **CGC:** 1 graded, best 9.0
The Mystery of the Elongated Man!; Kid Flash: Danger on Wheels! **A:** Carmine Infantino **W:** John Broome ★ Origin of Elongated Man. ★ 1st Appearance of Elongated Man.

113 ❑ Jul 1960 Cover: 0.10 **NM** value: **325.00**
Circ: Statement: **298,000** • **CGC:** 1 graded, best 6.5
Danger in the Air!; The Man Who Claimed the Earth! **A:** Carmine Infantino **W:** John Broome ★ Origin of Trickster. ★ 1st Appearance of Trickster.

114 ❑ Aug 1960 Cover: 0.10 **NM** value: **240.00**
Circ: Statement: **298,000** • **CGC:** 5 graded, best 9.0
The Big Freeze!; Kid Flash: King of the Beatniks! **A:** Carmine Infantino **W:** John Broome ★ Origin of Captain Cold.

115 ❑ Sep 1960 Cover: 0.10 **NM** value: **200.00**
Circ: Statement: **298,000** • **CGC:** 1 graded, best 5.0
The Day Flash Weighed 1000 Pounds!; The Elongated Man's Secret Weapon! **A:** Murphy Anderson; Carmine Infantino **W:** John Broome

116 ❑ Nov 1960 Cover: 0.10 **NM** value: **200.00**
Circ: Statement: **298,000** • **CGC:** 4 graded, best 9.4
The Man Who Stole Central City!; Kid Flash: The Race to Thunder Hill! **A:** Carmine Infantino **W:** John Broome

117 ❑ Dec 1960 Cover: 0.10 **NM** value: **240.00**
Circ: Statement: **298,000** • **CGC:** 6 graded, best 9.4
Here Comes Captain Boomerang!; The Madcap Inventors of Central City! **A:** Carmine Infantino ★ Origin of Captain Boomerang. ★ 1st Appearance of Captain Boomerang.

118 ❑ Feb 1961 Cover: 0.10 **NM** value: **200.00**
Circ: Statement: **305,000** • **CGC:** 2 graded, best 7.5
The Doomed Scarecrow!; The Midnight Peril! • Has 1960 Statement; avg total paid circ 298,000 **A:** Carmine Infantino

119 ❑ Mar 1961 Cover: 0.10 **NM** value: **200.00**
Circ: Statement: **305,000** • **CGC:** 5 graded, best 8.5
The Mirror Master's Magic Bullet!; The Elongated Man's Undersea Trap! • Wedding of Elongated Man and Sue Dearborn **A:** Carmine Infantino

120 ❑ May 1961 Cover: 0.10 **NM** value: **200.00**
Circ: Statement: **305,000** • **CGC:** 8 graded, best 9.4
Land of Golden Giants! **A:** Carmine Infantino

121 ❑ Jun 1961 Cover: 0.10 **NM** value: **150.00**
Circ: Statement: **305,000** • **CGC:** 5 graded, best 8.0
The Trickster Strikes Back!; The Secret of the Stolen Blueprint! **A:** Carmine Infantino

122 ❑ Aug 1961 Cover: 0.10 **NM** value: **150.00**
Circ: Statement: **305,000** • **CGC:** 4 graded, best 9.0
Beware the Atomic Grenade!; The Face Behind the Mask! **A:** Carmine Infantino ★ Origin of Top, The. ★ 1st Appearance of Top, The.

123 ❑ Sep 1961 Cover: 0.10 **NM** value: **950.00**
Circ: Statement: **305,000** • **CGC:** 48 graded, best 9.4
Flash of Two Worlds! • 1st meeting between Golden and Silver Age Flashes; First Alley Award winner: Best Cover, Best Single Issue of a Comic Book, Best Story ★ Origin of Flash I (Jay Garrick), Flash II (Barry Allen). ★ 1st Appearance of Earth-2 (as an alternate Earth). ★ Appearance of Flash I (Jay Garrick).

124 ❑ Nov 1961 Cover: 0.10 **NM** value: **110.00**
Circ: Statement: **305,000** • **CGC:** 4 graded, best 9.2
Space Boomerang Trap!; Vengeance Via Television! **A:** Carmine Infantino

125 ❑ Dec 1961 Cover: 0.12 **NM** value: **90.00**
Circ: Statement: **305,000** • **CGC:** 3 graded, best 9.2

126 ❑ Feb 1962 Cover: 0.12 **NM** value: **90.00**
Circ: Statement: **270,000** • **CGC:** 2 graded, best 9.4
• Has 1961 Statement, filed 10/1/61; avg total paid circ 305,000 **A:** Carmine Infantino

127 ❑ Mar 1962 Cover: 0.12 **NM** value: **90.00**
Circ: Statement: **270,000** • **CGC:** 2 graded, best 9.4

128 ❑ May 1962 Cover: 0.12 **NM** value: **90.00**
Circ: Statement: **270,000** • **CGC:** 2 graded, best 9.0

129 ❑ Jun 1962 Cover: 0.12 **NM** value: **250.00**
Circ: Statement: **270,000** • **CGC:** 24 graded, best 9.4

130 ❑ Aug 1962 Cover: 0.12 **NM** value: **90.00**
Circ: Statement: **270,000** • **CGC:** 2 graded, best 9.0

131 ❑ Sep 1962 Cover: 0.12 **NM** value: **90.00**
Circ: Statement: **270,000** • **CGC:** 6 graded, best 9.4

132 ❑ Nov 1962 Cover: 0.12 **NM** value: **90.00**
Circ: Statement: **270,000** • **CGC:** 4 graded, best 9.2

133 ❑ Dec 1962 Cover: 0.12 **NM** value: **90.00**
Circ: Statement: **270,000** • **CGC:** 3 graded, best 9.4

134 ❑ Feb 1963 Cover: 0.12 **NM** value: **90.00**
Circ: Statement: **270,000** • **CGC:** 3 graded, best 9.4
• Has 1962 Statement; avg total paid circ 270,000 **A:** Carmine Infantino

135 ❑ Mar 1963 Cover: 0.12 **NM** value: **90.00**
• **CGC:** 2 graded, best 9.2

136 ❑ May 1963 Cover: 0.12 **NM** value: **90.00**
• **CGC:** 3 graded, best 9.4

137 ❑ Jun 1963 Cover: 0.12 **NM** value: **250.00**
• **CGC:** 27 graded, best 9.6
• Vandal Savage **A:** Carmine Infantino ★ Appearance of Flash I (Jay Garrick).

138 ❑ Sep 1963 Cover: 0.12 **NM** value: **80.00**
• **CGC:** 4 graded, best 9.6

139 ❑ Sep 1963 Cover: 0.12 **NM** value: **115.00**
• **CGC:** 6 graded, best 9.6

140 ❑ Nov 1963 Cover: 0.12 **NM** value: **80.00**
• **CGC:** 4 graded, best 9.6

141 ❑ Dec 1963 Cover: 0.12 **NM** value: **60.00**
• **CGC:** 1 graded, best 9.6

142 ❑ Feb 1964 Cover: 0.12 **NM** value: **60.00**
• **CGC:** 1 graded, best 9.6
• Has 1963 Statement, filed 10/1/63; no circ figures published **A:** Carmine Infantino

143 ❑ Mar 1964 Cover: 0.12 **NM** value: **60.00**
• **CGC:** 3 graded, best 9.2

144 ❑ May 1964 Cover: 0.12 **NM** value: **60.00**
• **CGC:** 5 graded, best 9.4

145 ❑ Jun 1964 Cover: 0.12 **NM** value: **60.00**
• **CGC:** 12 graded, best 9.8

146 ❑ Aug 1964 Cover: 0.12 **NM** value: **60.00**
• **CGC:** 6 graded, best 9.4

147 ❑ Sep 1964 Cover: 0.12 **NM** value: **60.00**
• **CGC:** 2 graded, best 9.6

148 ❑ Nov 1964 Cover: 0.12 **NM** value: **60.00**
• **CGC:** 7 graded, best 9.8

149 ❑ Dec 1964 Cover: 0.12 **NM** value: **60.00**
• **CGC:** 11 graded, best 9.8

150 ❑ Feb 1965 Cover: 0.12 **NM** value: **60.00**
Circ: Statement: **298,151** • **CGC:** 3 graded, best 9.6
• Has 1964 Statement, filed 10/1/64; no circ figures published **A:** Carmine Infantino

151 ❑ Mar 1965 Cover: 0.12 **NM** value: **75.00**
Circ: Statement: **298,151** • **CGC:** 8 graded, best 9.6

152 ❑ May 1965 Cover: 0.12 **NM** value: **45.00**
Circ: Statement: **298,151** • **CGC:** 4 graded, best 9.6

153 ❑ Jun 1965 Cover: 0.12 **NM** value: **45.00**
Circ: Statement: **298,151** • **CGC:** 6 graded, best 9.6

154 ❑ Aug 1965 Cover: 0.12 **NM** value: **45.00**
Circ: Statement: **298,151** • **CGC:** 3 graded, best 9.2

155 ❑ Sep 1965 Cover: 0.12 **NM** value: **45.00**
Circ: Statement: **298,151** • **CGC:** 8 graded, best 9.6

156 ❑ Nov 1965 Cover: 0.12 **NM** value: **45.00**
Circ: Statement: **298,151** • **CGC:** 5 graded, best 9.6

157 ❑ Dec 1965 Cover: 0.12 **NM** value: **45.00**
Circ: Statement: **298,151** • **CGC:** 9 graded, best 9.6

158 ❑ Feb 1966 Cover: 0.12 **NM** value: **45.00**
Circ: Statement: **325,404** • **CGC:** 7 graded, best 9.6

159 ❑ Mar 1966 Cover: 0.12 **NM** value: **45.00**
Circ: Statement: **325,404** • **CGC:** 5 graded, best 9.6

160 ❑ Apr 1966 Cover: 0.25 **NM** value: **60.00**
Circ: Statement: **325,404** • **CGC:** 7 graded, best 9.6
• Giant-size. **A:** Carmine Infantino

161 ❑ May 1966 Cover: 0.12 **NM** value: **35.00**
Circ: Statement: **325,404** • **CGC:** 5 graded, best 9.4

162 ❑ Jun 1966 Cover: 0.12 **NM** value: **35.00**
Circ: Statement: **325,404** • **CGC:** 4 graded, best 9.4

163 ❑ Aug 1966 Cover: 0.12 **NM** value: **35.00**
Circ: Statement: **325,404** • **CGC:** 2 graded, best 8.5

164 ❑ Sep 1966 Cover: 0.12 **NM** value: **35.00**
Circ: Statement: **325,404** • **CGC:** 5 graded, best 9.6

165 ❑ Nov 1966 Cover: 0.12 **NM** value: **40.00**
Circ: Statement: **325,404** • **CGC:** 5 graded, best 9.4
• Wedding of Flash II (Barry Allen) and Iris West **A:** Carmine Infantino

166 ❑ Dec 1966 Cover: 0.12 **NM** value: **35.00**
Circ: Statement: **325,404** • **CGC:** 5 graded, best 9.4

167 ❑ Feb 1967 Cover: 0.12 **NM** value: **35.00**
Circ: Statement: **267,000** • **CGC:** 12 graded, best 9.6

168 ❑ Mar 1967 Cover: 0.12 **NM** value: **35.00**
Circ: Statement: **267,000** • **CGC:** 7 graded, best 9.6

169 ❑ May 1967 Cover: 0.25 **NM** value: **55.00**
Circ: Statement: **267,000** • **CGC:** 7 graded, best 9.4
• Giant-size. ★ Origin of Flash II (Barry Allen).

170 ❑ Jun 1967 Cover: 0.12 **NM** value: **35.00**
Circ: Statement: **267,000** • **CGC:** 2 graded, best 9.4

171 ❑ Jun 1967 Cover: 0.12 **NM** value: **32.00**
Circ: Statement: **267,000** • **CGC:** 1 graded, best 9.4

172 ❑ Aug 1967 Cover: 0.12 **NM** value: **32.00**
Circ: Statement: **267,000**

173 ❑ Sep 1967 Cover: 0.12 **NM** value: **32.00**
Circ: Statement: **267,000** • **CGC:** 2 graded, best 9.2

174 ❑ Nov 1967 Cover: 0.12 **NM** value: **32.00**
Circ: Statement: **267,000** • **CGC:** 2 graded, best 7.5
• Flash II reveals identity to wife ★ Versus Rogue's Gallery.

175 ❑ Dec 1967 Cover: 0.12 **NM** value: **100.00**
Circ: Statement: **267,000** • **CGC:** 31 graded, best 9.4
• Flash II races Superman

176 ❑ Feb 1968 Cover: 0.12 **NM** value: **32.00**
Circ: Statement: **268,025** • **CGC:** 9 graded, best 9.8

177 ❑ Mar 1968 Cover: 0.12 **NM** value: **32.00**
Circ: Statement: **268,025** • **CGC:** 7 graded, best 9.4

178 ❑ May 1968 Cover: 0.25 **NM** value: **40.00**
Circ: Statement: **268,025** • **CGC:** 4 graded, best 9.0
• Giant-size.

179 ❑ May 1968 Cover: 0.12 **NM** value: **32.00**
Circ: Statement: **268,025** • **CGC:** 3 graded, best 9.2
• Flash visits DC Comics

180 ❑ Jun 1968 Cover: 0.12 **NM** value: **32.00**
Circ: Statement: **268,025** • **CGC:** 5 graded, best 9.6

181 ❑ Aug 1968 Cover: 0.12 **NM** value: **20.00**
Circ: Statement: **268,025** • **CGC:** 6 graded, best 9.4

182 ❑ Sep 1968 Cover: 0.12 **NM** value: **20.00**
Circ: Statement: **268,025** • **CGC:** 3 graded, best 9.6

183 ❑ Nov 1968 Cover: 0.12 **NM** value: **20.00**
Circ: Statement: **268,025** • **CGC:** 3 graded, best 9.2

184 ❑ Dec 1968 Cover: 0.12 **NM** value: **20.00**
Circ: Statement: **268,025** • **CGC:** 8 graded, best 9.4

185 ❑ Feb 1969 Cover: 0.12 **NM** value: **20.00**
Circ: Statement: **221,470** • **CGC:** 7 graded, best 9.4

186 ❑ Mar 1969 Cover: 0.12 **NM** value: **20.00**
Circ: Statement: **221,470** • **CGC:** 2 graded, best 9.4

187 ❑ May 1969 Cover: 0.25 **NM** value: **30.00**
Circ: Statement: **221,470** • **CGC:** 7 graded, best 9.6
• Giant-size.

188 ❑ May 1969 Cover: 0.12 **NM** value: **18.00**
Circ: Statement: **221,470** • **CGC:** 4 graded, best 9.4

189 ❑ Jun 1969 Cover: 0.12 **NM** value: **18.00**
Circ: Statement: **221,470** • **CGC:** 2 graded, best 9.4

190 ❑ Aug 1969 Cover: 0.15 **NM** value: **18.00**
Circ: Statement: **221,470** • **CGC:** 1 graded, best 9.0

191 ❑ Sep 1969 Cover: 0.15 **NM** value: **15.00**
Circ: Statement: **221,470** • **CGC:** 1 graded, best 9.6

192 ❑ Nov 1969 Cover: 0.15 **NM** value: **15.00**
Circ: Statement: **221,470** • **CGC:** 3 graded, best 9.2

193 ❑ Dec 1969 Cover: 0.15 **NM** value: **15.00**
Circ: Statement: **221,470** • **CGC:** 2 graded, best 9.2

194 ❑ Feb 1970 Cover: 0.15 **NM** value: **15.00**
Circ: Statement: **184,479**

195 ❑ Mar 1970 Cover: 0.15 **NM** value: **15.00**
Circ: Statement: **184,479** • **CGC:** 1 graded, best 9.0

196 ❑ May 1970 Cover: 0.25 **NM** value: **30.00**
Circ: Statement: **184,479** • **CGC:** 3 graded, best 9.2
• Giant-size.

197 ❑ May 1970 Cover: 0.15 **NM** value: **15.00**
Circ: Statement: **184,479** • **CGC:** 1 graded, best 6.0

198 ❑ Jun 1970 Cover: 0.15 **NM** value: **15.00**
Circ: Statement: **184,479** • **CGC:** 2 graded, best 9.4

199 ❑ Aug 1970 Cover: 0.15 **NM** value: **15.00**
Circ: Statement: **184,479** • **CGC:** 3 graded, best 9.0

200 ❑ Sep 1970 Cover: 0.15 **NM** value: **15.00**
Circ: Statement: **184,479** • **CGC:** 3 graded, best 9.2

201 ❑ Nov 1970 Cover: 0.15 **NM** value: **10.00**
Circ: Statement: **184,479** • **CGC:** 2 graded, best 9.4

202 ❑ Dec 1970 Cover: 0.15 **NM** value: **10.00**
Circ: Statement: **184,479**

203 ❑ Feb 1971 Cover: 0.15 **NM** value: **10.00**
Circ: Statement: **181,380** • **CGC:** 2 graded, best 9.4

204 ❑ Mar 1971 Cover: 0.15 **NM** value: **10.00**
Circ: Statement: **181,380** • **CGC:** 1 graded, best 9.6

205 ❑ May 1971 Cover: 0.25 **NM** value: **10.00**
Circ: Statement: **181,380** • **CGC:** 2 graded, best 9.6
• Giant-size.

206 ❑ May 1971 Cover: 0.15 **NM** value: **10.00**
Circ: Statement: **181,380**

207 ❑ Jun 1971 Cover: 0.15 **NM** value: **10.00**
Circ: Statement: **181,380** • **CGC:** 1 graded, best 9.2

208 ❑ Aug 1971 Cover: 0.25 **NM** value: **10.00**
Circ: Statement: **181,380** • **CGC:** 4 graded, best 9.2
• Giant-size. • Elongated Man back-up

209 ❑ Sep 1971 Cover: 0.25 **NM** value: **10.00**
Circ: Statement: **181,380**
• Giant-size. ★ Versus Captain Boomerang. ★ Versus Trickster.

210 ❑ Dec 1971 Cover: 0.25 **NM** value: **10.00**
Circ: Statement: **181,380** • **CGC:** 3 graded, best 9.6
• Giant-size. • in future

211 ❑ Dec 1971 Cover: 0.25 **NM** value: **10.00**
Circ: Statement: **181,380** • **CGC:** 1 graded, best 8.5
• Giant-size. • Golden Age Flash back-up

212 ❑ Feb 1972 Cover: 0.25 **NM** value: **10.00**
Circ: Statement: **152,221** • **CGC:** 3 graded, best 9.6

213 ❑ Mar 1972 Cover: 0.25 **NM** value: **10.00**
Circ: Statement: **152,221** • **CGC:** 2 graded, best 9.4

214 ❑ Apr 1972 Cover: 0.50 **NM** value: **16.00**
Circ: Statement: **152,221** • **CGC:** 9 graded, best 9.6

Other grades: Multiply prices above by **1.5 for Mint • 2/3 for Very Fine • 1/3 for Fine • 1/5 for Very Good • 1/8 for Good**

wraparound cover. • a.k.a. DC 100-Page Super Spectacular #DC-11; reprints O: Metal Men; Reprints Showcase #37 **A:** Carmine Infantino ★ Origin of Metal Men.

215 ❑ May 1972 Cover: 0.25 **NM** value: **15.00**
Circ: Statement: **152,221** • **CGC:** 5 graded, best 9.4
• giant ★ Appearance of Golden Age Flash. ★ Versus Vandal Savage.

216 ❑ Jun 1972 Cover: 0.25 **NM** value: **10.00**
Circ: Statement: **152,221** • **CGC:** 1 graded, best 9.0

217 ❑ Sep 1972 Cover: 0.20 **NM** value: **10.00**
Circ: Statement: **152,221** • **CGC:** 3 graded, best 9.2
📖 The Flash Times Five is Fatal; The Killing of an Archer!, Part 1 • Green Lantern/Green Arrow back-up; Green Arrow back-up **A:** Frank McLaughlin; Dick Giordano; Neal Adams; Irv Novick **W:** Len Wein; Denny O'Neil

218 ❑ Nov 1972 Cover: 0.20 **NM** value: **10.00**
Circ: Statement: **152,221** • **CGC:** 1 graded, best 9.2

219 ❑ Jan 1973 Cover: 0.20 **NM** value: **10.00**
Circ: Statement: **163,604** • **CGC:** 4 graded, best 9.6
• last Green Arrow back-up **A:** Neal Adams

220 ❑ Mar 1973 Cover: 0.20 **NM** value: **7.00**
Circ: Statement: **163,604**

221 ❑ May 1973 Cover: 0.20 **NM** value: **7.00**
Circ: Statement: **163,604** • **CGC:** 1 graded, best 8.5
• Has 1972 Statement; avg total paid circ 152,221

222 ❑ Aug 1973 Cover: 0.20 **NM** value: **7.00**
Circ: Statement: **163,604**

223 ❑ Oct 1973 Cover: 0.20 **NM** value: **7.00**
Circ: Statement: **163,604**
• Green Lantern back-up **A:** Neal Adams

224 ❑ Dec 1973 Cover: 0.20 **NM** value: **7.00**
Circ: Statement: **163,604**

225 ❑ Feb 1974 Cover: 0.20 **NM** value: **7.00**
Circ: Statement: **184,749**

226 ❑ Apr 1974 Cover: 0.20 **NM** value: **10.00**
Circ: Statement: **184,749**

227 ❑ Jun 1974 Cover: 0.20 **NM** value: **7.00**
Circ: Statement: **184,749** • **CGC:** 1 graded, best 4.0
• Has 1973 Statement; avg total paid circ 163,604

228 ❑ Aug 1974 Cover: 0.20 **NM** value: **7.00**
Circ: Statement: **184,749**

229 ❑ Oct 1974 Cover: 0.60 **NM** value: **12.00**
Circ: Statement: **184,749** • **CGC:** 3 graded, best 9.4

230 ❑ Dec 1974 Cover: 0.20 **NM** value: **7.00**
Circ: Statement: **184,749**

231 ❑ Feb 1975 Cover: 0.25 **NM** value: **7.00**
Circ: Statement: **169,000**

232 ❑ Apr 1975 Cover: 0.60 **NM** value: **12.00**
Circ: Statement: **169,000** • **CGC:** 4 graded, best 9.6

233 ❑ May 1975 Cover: 0.25 **NM** value: **4.00**
Circ: Statement: **169,000**

234 ❑ Jun 1975 Cover: 0.25 **NM** value: **4.00**
Circ: Statement: **169,000**

235 ❑ Aug 1975 Cover: 0.25 **NM** value: **4.00**
Circ: Statement: **169,000** • **CGC:** 2 graded, best 9.2

236 ❑ Sep 1975 Cover: 0.25 **NM** value: **4.00**
Circ: Statement: **169,000**

237 ❑ Nov 1975 Cover: 0.25 **NM** value: **4.00**
Circ: Statement: **169,000**

238 ❑ Dec 1975 Cover: 0.25 **NM** value: **4.00**
Circ: Statement: **169,000**

239 ❑ Feb 1976 Cover: 0.25 **NM** value: **4.00**
Circ: Statement: **163,000**

240 ❑ Mar 1976 Cover: 0.30 **NM** value: **4.00**
Circ: Statement: **163,000**

241 ❑ May 1976 Cover: 0.30 **NM** value: **4.00**
Circ: Statement: **163,000**
• Has 1975 Statement, filed 10/1/75; avg print run 365,000; avg sales 168,000; avg subs 1,000; avg total paid 169,000; samples 1,000; office use 3,000; max existent 173,000; 53% of run returned

242 ❑ Jun 1976 Cover: 0.30 **NM** value: **4.00**
Circ: Statement: **163,000**

243 ❑ Aug 1976 Cover: 0.30 **NM** value: **4.00**
Circ: Statement: **163,000**

244 ❑ Sep 1976 Cover: 0.30 **NM** value: **4.00**
Circ: Statement: **163,000**

245 ❑ Nov 1976 Cover: 0.30 **NM** value: **4.00**
Circ: Statement: **163,000**

246 ❑ Jan 1977 Cover: 0.30 **NM** value: **4.00**
Circ: Statement: **153,299**

247 ❑ Mar 1977 Cover: 0.30 **NM** value: **4.00**
Circ: Statement: **153,299**

248 ❑ Apr 1977 Cover: 0.30 **NM** value: **4.00**
Circ: Statement: **153,299**

249 ❑ May 1977 Cover: 0.30 **NM** value: **4.00**
Circ: Statement: **153,299**
• Has 1976 Statement; avg total paid circ 163,000

250 ❑ Jun 1977 Cover: 0.35 **NM** value: **4.00**
Circ: Statement: **153,299**

251 ❑ Aug 1977 Cover: 0.35 **NM** value: **4.00**
Circ: Statement: **153,299**

252 ❑ Sep 1977 Cover: 0.35 **NM** value: **4.00**
Circ: Statement: **153,299**

253 ❑ Sep 1977 Cover: 0.35 **NM** value: **4.00**
Circ: Statement: **153,299**

254 ❑ Oct 1977 Cover: 0.35 **NM** value: **4.00**
Circ: Statement: **153,299**

255 ❑ Nov 1977 Cover: 0.35 **NM** value: **4.00**
Circ: Statement: **153,299**

256 ❑ Dec 1977 Cover: 0.35 **NM** value: **4.00**
Circ: Statement: **153,299**

257 ❑ Jan 1978 Cover: 0.35 **NM** value: **4.00**
Circ: Statement: **115,716**

258 ❑ Feb 1978 Cover: 0.35 **NM** value: **4.00**
Circ: Statement: **115,716**

259 ❑ Mar 1978 Cover: 0.35 **NM** value: **4.00**
Circ: Statement: **115,716**

260 ❑ Apr 1978 Cover: 0.35 **NM** value: **4.00**
Circ: Statement: **115,716**

261 ❑ May 1978 Cover: 0.35 **NM** value: **4.00**
Circ: Statement: **115,716**
• Has 1977 Statement; avg total paid circ 153,299

262 ❑ Jun 1978 Cover: 0.35 **NM** value: **4.00**
Circ: Statement: **115,716**

263 ❑ Jul 1978 Cover: 0.35 **NM** value: **4.00**
Circ: Statement: **115,716**

264 ❑ Aug 1978 Cover: 0.35 **NM** value: **4.00**
Circ: Statement: **115,716**

265 ❑ Sep 1978 Cover: 0.50 **NM** value: **4.00**
Circ: Statement: **115,716** • **CGC:** 1 graded, best 9.4

266 ❑ Oct 1978 Cover: 0.50 **NM** value: **4.00**
Circ: Statement: **115,716**

267 ❑ Nov 1978 Cover: 0.50 **NM** value: **4.00**
Circ: Statement: **115,716**

268 ❑ Dec 1978 Cover: 0.40 **NM** value: **4.00**
Circ: Statement: **115,716**

269 ❑ Jan 1979 Cover: 0.40 **NM** value: **4.00**
Circ: Statement: **102,297**

270 ❑ Mar 1979 Cover: 0.40 **NM** value: **4.00**
Circ: Statement: **102,297**

271 ❑ Mar 1979 Cover: 0.40 **NM** value: **3.50**
Circ: Statement: **102,297**

272 ❑ Apr 1979 Cover: 0.40 **NM** value: **3.50**
Circ: Statement: **102,297**

273 ❑ May 1979 Cover: 0.40 **NM** value: **3.50**
Circ: Statement: **102,297**

274 ❑ Jun 1979 Cover: 0.40 **NM** value: **3.50**
Circ: Statement: **102,297**

275 ❑ Jul 1979 Cover: 0.40 **NM** value: **3.50**
Circ: Statement: **102,297**

276 ❑ Aug 1979 Cover: 0.40 **NM** value: **3.50**
Circ: Statement: **102,297**

277 ❑ Sep 1979 Cover: 0.40 **NM** value: **3.50**
Circ: Statement: **102,297**

278 ❑ Oct 1979 Cover: 0.40 **NM** value: **3.50**
Circ: Statement: **102,297**

279 ❑ Nov 1979 Cover: 0.40 **NM** value: **3.50**
Circ: Statement: **102,297**

280 ❑ Dec 1979 Cover: 0.40 **NM** value: **3.50**
Circ: Statement: **102,297** • **CGC:** 1 graded, best 9.6

281 ❑ Jan 1980 Cover: 0.40 **NM** value: **3.50**
Circ: Statement: **109,756**

282 ❑ Feb 1980 Cover: 0.40 **NM** value: **3.50**
Circ: Statement: **109,756**

283 ❑ Mar 1980 Cover: 0.40 **NM** value: **3.50**
Circ: Statement: **109,756**

284 ❑ Apr 1980 Cover: 0.40 **NM** value: **3.50**
Circ: Statement: **109,756**
• Has 1979 Statement, filed 10/1/79; avg print run 254,324; avg sales 101,390; avg subs 907; avg total paid 102,297; office use 121; max existent 102,418; 60% of run returned

285 ❑ May 1980 Cover: 0.40 **NM** value: **3.50**
Circ: Statement: **109,756**

286 ❑ Jun 1980 Cover: 0.40 **NM** value: **3.50**
Circ: Statement: **109,756**

287 ❑ Jul 1980 Cover: 0.40 **NM** value: **3.50**
Circ: Statement: **109,756**

288 ❑ Aug 1980 Cover: 0.40 **NM** value: **3.50**
Circ: Statement: **109,756**

289 ❑ Sep 1980 Cover: 0.50 **NM** value: **5.00**
Circ: Statement: **109,756**
• George PTrez's first work at DC **A:** George Pérez; Don Heck

290 ❑ Oct 1980 Cover: 0.50 **NM** value: **3.00**
Circ: Statement: **109,756**

291 ❑ Nov 1980 Cover: 0.50 **NM** value: **3.00**
Circ: Statement: **109,756**

292 ❑ Dec 1980 Cover: 0.50 **NM** value: **3.00**
Circ: Statement: **109,756**

293 ❑ Jan 1981 Cover: 0.50 **NM** value: **3.00**
Circ: Statement: **92,024**

294 ❑ Feb 1981 Cover: 0.50 **NM** value: **3.00**
Circ: Statement: **92,024**

295 ❑ Mar 1981 Cover: 0.50 **NM** value: **3.00**
Circ: Statement: **92,024**

296 ❑ Apr 1981 Cover: 0.50 **NM** value: **3.00**
Circ: Statement: **92,024**

297 ❑ May 1981 Cover: 0.50 **NM** value: **3.00**
Circ: Statement: **92,024**
• Has 1980 Statement, filed 10/1/80; avg print run 286,886; avg sales 107,418; avg subs 2,338; avg total paid 109,756; samples 127; office use 2,866; max existent 112,749; 61% of run returned

298 ❑ Jun 1981 Cover: 0.50 **NM** value: **3.00**
Circ: Statement: **92,024**

299 ❑ Jul 1981 Cover: 0.50 **NM** value: **3.00**
Circ: Statement: **92,024**

300 ❑ Aug 1981 Cover: 1.00 **NM** value: **5.00**
Circ: Statement: **92,024** • **CGC:** 2 graded, best 9.8
wraparound cover. • Giant-size. **A:** Carmine Infantino ★ Origin of Flash. ★ Appearance of New Teen Titans.

301 ❑ Sep 1981 Cover: 0.50 **NM** value: **3.00**
Circ: Statement: **92,024**

302 ❑ Oct 1981 Cover: 0.60 **NM** value: **3.00**
Circ: Statement: **92,024**

303 ❑ Nov 1981 Cover: 0.60 **NM** value: **3.00**
Circ: Statement: **92,024**

304 ❑ Dec 1981 Cover: 0.60 **NM** value: **3.00**
Circ: Statement: **92,024**

305 ❑ Jan 1982 Cover: 0.60 **NM** value: **3.50**
Circ: Statement: **87,562**

306 ❑ Feb 1982 Cover: 0.60 **NM** value: **3.50**
Circ: Statement: **87,562**

307 ❑ Mar 1982 Cover: 0.60 **NM** value: **2.50**
Circ: Statement: **87,562**
• Doctor Fate back-up; Dr. Fate back-up **A:** Carmine Infantino; Keith Giffen

308 ❑ Apr 1982 Cover: 0.60 **NM** value: **2.50**
Circ: Statement: **87,562**

309 ❑ May 1982 Cover: 0.60 **NM** value: **2.50**
Circ: Statement: **87,562**

310 ❑ Jun 1982 Cover: 0.60 **NM** value: **2.50**
Circ: Statement: **87,562**

311 ❑ Jul 1982 Cover: 0.60 **NM** value: **2.50**
Circ: Statement: **87,562** • **CGC:** 1 graded, best 9.6

312 ❑ Aug 1982 Cover: 0.60 **NM** value: **2.50**
Circ: Statement: **87,562**

313 ❑ Sep 1982 Cover: 0.60 **NM** value: **2.50**
Circ: Statement: **87,562**

314 ❑ Oct 1982 Cover: 0.60 **NM** value: **2.50**
Circ: Statement: **87,562**

315 ❑ Nov 1982 Cover: 0.60 **NM** value: **2.50**
Circ: Statement: **87,562**

316 ❑ Dec 1982 Cover: 0.60 **NM** value: **2.50**
Circ: Statement: **87,562**

317 ❑ Jan 1983 Cover: 0.60 **NM** value: **2.50**
Circ: Statement: **72,771**

318 ❑ Feb 1983 Cover: 0.60 **NM** value: **2.50**
Circ: Statement: **72,771**

319 ❑ Mar 1983 Cover: 0.60 **NM** value: **2.50**
Circ: Statement: **72,771**

320 ❑ Apr 1983 Cover: 0.60 **NM** value: **2.50**
Circ: Statement: **72,771**

321 ❑ May 1983 Cover: 0.60 **NM** value: **2.50**
Circ: Statement: **72,771**
• Has 1982 Statement, filed 10/1/82; avg print run 241,330; avg sales 85,477; avg subs 2,085; avg total paid 87,562; samples 677; office use 1,424; max existent 89,663; 63% of run returned

322 ❑ Jun 1983 Cover: 0.60 **NM** value: **2.50**
Circ: Statement: **72,771**
• Flash Vs. Reverse Flash

323 ❑ Jul 1983 Cover: 0.60 **NM** value: **2.50**
Circ: Statement: **72,771**
• Flash Vs. Reverse Flash

324 ❑ Aug 1983 Cover: 0.60 **NM** value: **2.50**
Circ: Statement: **72,771**

325 ❑ Sep 1983 Cover: 0.60 **NM** value: **2.50**
Circ: Statement: **72,771**

326 ❑ Oct 1983 Cover: 0.60 **NM** value: **2.50**
Circ: Statement: **72,771**

327 ❑ Nov 1983 Cover: 0.60 **NM** value: **2.50**
Circ: Statement: **72,771**

328 ❑ Dec 1983 Cover: 0.75 **NM** value: **2.50**
Circ: Statement: **72,771**

329 ❑ Jan 1984 Cover: 0.75 **NM** value: **2.50**
Circ: Statement: **69,881**

330 ❑ Feb 1984 Cover: 0.75 **NM** value: **2.50**
Circ: Statement: **69,881**

331 ❑ Mar 1984 Cover: 0.75 **NM** value: **2.50**
Circ: Statement: **69,881**

332 ❑ Apr 1984 Cover: 0.75 **NM** value: **2.50**
Circ: Statement: **69,881**

333 ❑ May 1984 Cover: 0.75 **NM** value: **2.50**
Circ: Statement: **69,881**

334 ❑ Jun 1984 Cover: 0.75 **NM** value: **2.50**
Circ: Statement: **69,881**

335 ❑ Jul 1984 Cover: 0.75 **NM** value: **2.50**
Circ: Statement: **69,881**

336 ❑ Aug 1984 Cover: 0.75 **NM** value: **2.50**
Circ: Statement: **69,881**

337 ❑ Sep 1984 Cover: 0.75 **NM** value: **2.50**
Circ: Statement: **69,881**

338 ❑ Oct 1984 Cover: 0.75 **NM** value: **2.50**
Circ: Statement: **69,881**

339 ❑ Nov 1984 Cover: 0.75 **NM** value: **2.50**
Circ: Statement: **69,881**

340 ❑ Dec 1984 Cover: 0.75 **NM** value: **2.50**
Circ: Statement: **69,881**
• Trial begins

341 ❑ Jan 1985 Cover: 0.75 **NM** value: **2.50**
342 ❑ Feb 1985 Cover: 0.75 **NM** value: **2.50**
343 ❑ Mar 1985 Cover: 0.75 **NM** value: **2.50**
344 ❑ Apr 1985 Cover: 0.75 **NM** value: **2.50**
345 ❑ May 1985 Cover: 0.75 **NM** value: **2.50**
Circ: CapCity orders: **4,750**

346 ❑ Jun 1985 Cover: 0.75 **NM** value: **2.50**
Circ: CapCity orders: **4,900** • **CGC:** 1 graded, best 9.4

347 ❑ Jul 1985 Cover: 0.75 **NM** value: **2.50**
Circ: CapCity orders: **5,300**

348 ❑ Aug 1985 Cover: 0.75 **NM** value: **2.50**
Circ: CapCity orders: **5,600**

349 ❑ Sep 1985 Cover: 0.75 **NM** value: **2.50**
Circ: CapCity orders: **5,950** • **CGC:** 1 graded, best 9.2

350 ❑ Oct 1985 Cover: 1.25 **NM** value: **6.50**
Circ: CapCity orders: **13,300** • **CGC:** 2 graded, best 9.6
• Double-size. final issue.

Anl 1 ❑ Dec 1963 Cover: 0.25 **NM** value: **350.00**
• **CGC:** 26 graded, best 9.6
📖 Conqueror From 8 Million B.C.; Master of the Elements; Mystery of the Elongated Man; The Amazing Star Sapphire; Menace of the Super-Gorilla; Meet Kid Flash; How I Draw the Flash; Famous Flash Cover Firsts; Complete Flash Index • Golden-Age Flash story ★ Origin of Elongated Man, Kid Flash.

There are two different pricing tiers in the modern comic-book hobby. **The prices seen above** are the prices we have seen **loose copies** of these issues reliably fetch in a variety of environments. Condition alters the price by the fractions seen on the bar on the bottom of left-hand pages of this book. **Comics graded by CGC** usually sell for more. Use the guide on the bottom of right-hand pages of this book to estimate what copies have brought on eBay.

CGC-graded: Multiply prices above by **33 for 9.9 M • 16 for 9.8 NM/M • 7 for 9.6 NM+ • 5 for 9.4 NM • 2.5 for 9.2 NM- • 1.5 for 9.0 VF/NM**

FLASH (2ND SERIES) DC

In 1987, DC launched its second modern Flash series with a new face behind the red mask. The contemporary Flash, Wally West (formerly Kid Flash), was more cynical and not quite as fast as his Flash mentor, Barry Allen. In the early issues, Wally had a top speed of 705 miles an hour, which he could sustain for only a couple of hours before collapsing from exhaustion. The old Flash, by comparison, could travel faster than the speed of light, a power which Wally had shared only to lose it through a mental block.

Eventually, Wally overcame his psychological speed limit and regained all of his former speed, even surpassing it by tapping into The Speed Force, a mysterious dimension that grants all DC's super-speedsters their powers.

0 ❑ Oct 1994 Cover: 1.50 **NM** value: **2.50**
Circ: CapCity orders: **22,700**
1 ❑ Jun 1987 Cover: 0.75 **NM** value: **4.00**
Circ: CapCity orders: **31,550** • **CGC:** 18 graded, best 9.6
• Wally West as Flash **A:** Jackson Guice **W:** Mike Baron
2 ❑ Jul 1987 Cover: 0.75 **NM** value: **3.00**
Circ: CapCity orders: **22,350** • **CGC:** 1 graded, best 9.8
3 ❑ Aug 1987 Cover: 0.75 **NM** value: **2.50**
Circ: CapCity orders: **28,800**
4 ❑ Sep 1987 Cover: 0.75 **NM** value: **2.50**
Circ: CapCity orders: **31,000**
5 ❑ Oct 1987 Cover: 0.75 **NM** value: **2.50**
Circ: CapCity orders: **31,750**
6 ❑ Nov 1987 Cover: 0.75 **NM** value: **2.50**
Circ: CapCity orders: **31,350**
7 ❑ Dec 1987 Cover: 0.75 **NM** value: **2.50**
Circ: CapCity orders: **28,750**
8 ❑ Jan 1988 Cover: 0.75 **NM** value: **2.50**
Circ: CapCity orders: **33,650**
• Millennium
9 ❑ Feb 1988 Cover: 0.75 **NM** value: **2.50**
Circ: CapCity orders: **33,100**
• Millennium ★ 1st Appearance of Chunk.
10 ❑ Mar 1988 Cover: 0.75 **NM** value: **2.50**
Circ: CapCity orders: **29,150**
11 ❑ Apr 1988 Cover: 0.75 **NM** value: **2.50**
Circ: CapCity orders: **28,500**
12 ❑ May 1988 Cover: 0.75 **NM** value: **2.50**
Circ: CapCity orders: **27,850**
• Bonus Book #2
13 ❑ Jun 1988 Cover: 0.75 **NM** value: **2.50**
Circ: CapCity orders: **24,650**
14 ❑ Jul 1988 Cover: 0.75 **NM** value: **2.50**
Circ: CapCity orders: **24,550**
15 ❑ Aug 1988 Cover: 0.75 **NM** value: **2.50**
Circ: CapCity orders: **23,750**
16 ❑ Sep 1988 Cover: 0.75 **NM** value: **2.50**
Circ: CapCity orders: **22,900**
17 ❑ Oct 1988 Cover: 1.00 **NM** value: **2.50**
Circ: CapCity orders: **22,050**
18 ❑ Nov 1988 Cover: 1.00 **NM** value: **2.50**
Circ: CapCity orders: **20,850**
19 ❑ Dec 1988 Cover: 1.00 **NM** value: **2.50**
Circ: CapCity orders: **20,750**
• Bonus Book #9
20 ❑ Cover: 1.00 **NM** value: **2.50**
Circ: CapCity orders: **20,450**
21 ❑ Cover: 1.00 **NM** value: **2.00**
Circ: CapCity orders: **22,300**
• Invasion!
22 ❑ Jan 1989 Cover: 1.00 **NM** value: **2.00**
Circ: CapCity orders: **20,750**
• Invasion! ★ Appearance of Manhunter.
23 ❑ Feb 1989 Cover: 1.00 **NM** value: **2.00**
Circ: CapCity orders: **18,800**
24 ❑ Mar 1989 Cover: 1.00 **NM** value: **2.00**
Circ: CapCity orders: **18,350**
25 ❑ Apr 1989 Cover: 1.00 **NM** value: **2.00**
Circ: CapCity orders: **17,750**
26 ❑ May 1989 Cover: 1.00 **NM** value: **2.00**
Circ: CapCity orders: **17,450**
27 ❑ Jun 1989 Cover: 1.00 **NM** value: **2.00**
Circ: CapCity orders: **17,600**
28 ❑ Jul 1989 Cover: 1.00 **NM** value: **2.00**
Circ: CapCity orders: **17,950**
29 ❑ Aug 1989 Cover: 1.00 **NM** value: **2.00**
Circ: CapCity orders: **18,450**
30 ❑ Sep 1989 Cover: 1.00 **NM** value: **2.00**
Circ: CapCity orders: **18,000**
31 ❑ Oct 1989 Cover: 1.00 **NM** value: **1.50**
Circ: CapCity orders: **18,100**
32 ❑ Nov 1989 Cover: 1.00 **NM** value: **1.50**
Circ: CapCity orders: **18,100**
33 ❑ Dec 1989 Cover: 1.00 **NM** value: **1.50**
Circ: CapCity orders: **17,750**
34 ❑ Jan 1990 Cover: 1.00 **NM** value: **1.50**
Circ: CapCity orders: **17,300**
35 ❑ Feb 1990 Cover: 1.00 **NM** value: **1.50**
Circ: CapCity orders: **16,800**
36 ❑ Mar 1990 Cover: 1.00 **NM** value: **1.50**
Circ: CapCity orders: **16,350**
37 ❑ Apr 1990 Cover: 1.00 **NM** value: **1.50**
Circ: CapCity orders: **15,850**
38 ❑ May 1990 Cover: 1.00 **NM** value: **1.50**
Circ: CapCity orders: **16,050**
39 ❑ Jun 1990 Cover: 1.00 **NM** value: **1.50**
Circ: CapCity orders: **15,850**
40 ❑ Jul 1990 Cover: 1.00 **NM** value: **1.50**
Circ: CapCity orders: **15,550**
41 ❑ Aug 1990 Cover: 1.00 **NM** value: **1.50**
Circ: CapCity orders: **15,100**
42 ❑ Sep 1990 Cover: 1.00 **NM** value: **1.50**
Circ: CapCity orders: **15,000**
43 ❑ Oct 1990 Cover: 1.00 **NM** value: **1.50**
Circ: CapCity orders: **14,800**
44 ❑ Nov 1990 Cover: 1.00 **NM** value: **1.50**
Circ: CapCity orders: **15,100**
45 ❑ Dec 1990 Cover: 1.00 **NM** value: **1.50**
Circ: CapCity orders: **15,650**
46 ❑ Jan 1991 Cover: 1.00 **NM** value: **1.50**
Circ: CapCity orders: **16,550**
47 ❑ Feb 1991 Cover: 1.00 **NM** value: **1.50**
Circ: CapCity orders: **17,150**
48 ❑ Mar 1991 Cover: 1.00 **NM** value: **1.50**
Circ: CapCity orders: **18,200**
49 ❑ Apr 1991 Cover: 1.00 **NM** value: **1.50**
Circ: CapCity orders: **17,650**
50 ❑ May 1991 Cover: 1.75 **NM** value: **2.50**
Circ: CapCity orders: **25,300**
• Giant size.
51 ❑ Jun 1991 Cover: 1.00 **NM** value: **1.50**
Circ: CapCity orders: **18,000**
52 ❑ Jul 1991 Cover: 1.00 **NM** value: **1.50**
Circ: CapCity orders: **20,700**
53 ❑ Aug 1991 Cover: 1.00 **NM** value: **1.50**
Circ: CapCity orders: **25,400**
• Superman
54 ❑ Sep 1991 Cover: 1.00 **NM** value: **1.50**
Circ: CapCity orders: **23,500**
55 ❑ Oct 1991 Cover: 1.00 **NM** value: **1.50**
Circ: CapCity orders: **22,900**
📖 War of the Gods, Part 10 • War of the Gods
56 ❑ Nov 1991 Cover: 1.00 **NM** value: **1.50**
Circ: CapCity orders: **22,350**
• Icicle
57 ❑ Dec 1991 Cover: 1.00 **NM** value: **1.50**
Circ: CapCity orders: **21,400**
• Icicle
58 ❑ Jan 1992 Cover: 1.00 **NM** value: **1.50**
Circ: CapCity orders: **20,700**
59 ❑ Feb 1992 Cover: 1.00 **NM** value: **1.50**
Circ: CapCity orders: **18,700**
60 ❑ Mar 1992 Cover: 1.00 **NM** value: **1.50**
Circ: CapCity orders: **17,550**
61 ❑ Apr 1992 Cover: 1.00 **NM** value: **1.50**
Circ: CapCity orders: **16,150**
62 ❑ May 1992 Cover: 1.00 **NM** value: **2.00**
Circ: CapCity orders: **17,400**
📖 Flash: Year One, Part 1 **W:** Mark Waid ★ Origin of Flash.
63 ❑ May 1992 Cover: 1.00 **NM** value: **2.00**
Circ: CapCity orders: **17,250**
📖 Flash: Year One, Part 2 ★ Origin of Flash.
64 ❑ Jun 1992 Cover: 1.00 **NM** value: **1.50**
Circ: CapCity orders: **17,200**
📖 Flash: Year One, Part 3 ★ Origin of Flash.
65 ❑ Jun 1992 Cover: 1.00 **NM** value: **1.50**
Circ: CapCity orders: **17,050**
📖 Flash: Year One, Part 4 ★ Origin of Flash.
66 ❑ Jul 1992 Cover: 1.25 **NM** value: **1.50**
Circ: CapCity orders: **16,550**
• Aquaman
67 ❑ Aug 1992 Cover: 1.25 **NM** value: **1.50**
Circ: CapCity orders: **16,850**
68 ❑ Sep 1992 Cover: 1.25 **NM** value: **1.50**
Circ: CapCity orders: **15,150**
69 ❑ Oct 1992 Cover: 1.25 **NM** value: **1.50**
Circ: CapCity orders: **16,450**
70 ❑ Nov 1992 Cover: 1.25 **NM** value: **1.50**
Circ: CapCity orders: **15,400**
📖 Gorilla Warfare (conclusion) ★ Appearance of Green Lantern. ★ Versus Hector Hammond. ★ Versus Grodd, Hector Hammond. ★ Versus Grodd.
71 ❑ Dec 1992 Cover: 1.25 **NM** value: **1.50**
Circ: CapCity orders: **13,900**
72 ❑ Jan 1993 Cover: 1.25 **NM** value: **1.50**
Circ: CapCity orders: **13,900**
73 ❑ Feb 1993 Cover: 1.25 **NM** value: **1.50**
Circ: CapCity orders: **14,100**
74 ❑ Mar 1993 Cover: 1.25 **NM** value: **1.50**
Circ: CapCity orders: **13,450**
75 ❑ Apr 1993 Cover: 1.25 **NM** value: **1.50**
Circ: CapCity orders: **15,050**
76 ❑ May 1993 Cover: 1.25 **NM** value: **1.50**
Circ: CapCity orders: **16,250**
77 ❑ Jun 1993 Cover: 1.25 **NM** value: **1.50**
Circ: CapCity orders: **16,600**
78 ❑ Jul 1993 Cover: 1.25 **NM** value: **1.50**
Circ: CapCity orders: **17,550**
79 ❑ Jul 1993 Cover: 2.50 **NM** value: **Cover or less**
Circ: CapCity orders: **21,150**
📖 The Once and Future Flash **W:** Mark Waid
80 ❑ Aug 1993 Cover: 1.25 **NM** value: **1.50**
regular cover.
80/SC ❑ Aug 1993 Cover: 2.50 **NM** value: **Cover or less**
foil cover.
81 ❑ Sep 1993 Cover: 1.25 **NM** value: **1.50**
82 ❑ Oct 1993 Cover: 1.25 **NM** value: **1.50**
Circ: CapCity orders: **17,750**
83 ❑ Oct 1993 Cover: 1.25 **NM** value: **1.50**
Circ: CapCity orders: **17,700**
84 ❑ Nov 1993 Cover: 1.25 **NM** value: **1.50**
Circ: CapCity orders: **17,700**
85 ❑ Dec 1993 Cover: 1.50 **NM** value: **Cover or less**
Circ: CapCity orders: **16,800**
86 ❑ Jan 1994 Cover: 1.50 **NM** value: **Cover or less**
Circ: CapCity orders: **15,850**
87 ❑ Feb 1994 Cover: 1.50 **NM** value: **Cover or less**
Circ: CapCity orders: **14,750**
88 ❑ Mar 1994 Cover: 1.50 **NM** value: **2.00**
Circ: CapCity orders: **13,900**
89 ❑ Apr 1994 Cover: 1.50 **NM** value: **2.00**
Circ: CapCity orders: **13,000**
90 ❑ May 1994 Cover: 1.50 **NM** value: **2.00**
Circ: CapCity orders: **12,700**
91 ❑ Jun 1994 Cover: 1.50 **NM** value: **4.00**
Circ: CapCity orders: **12,550**
92 ❑ Jul 1994 Cover: 1.50 **NM** value: **9.00**
Circ: CapCity orders: **13,850** • **CGC:** 8 graded, best 9.6
📖 Reckless Youth, Part 1 **A:** Mike Wieringo **W:** Mark Waid ★ 1st Appearance of Impulse.
93 ❑ Aug 1994 Cover: 1.50 **NM** value: **4.50**
Circ: CapCity orders: **13,900**
📖 Reckless Youth, Part 2 **A:** Carlos Pacheco **W:** Mark Waid ★ 2nd Appearance of Impulse.
94 ❑ Sep 1994 Cover: 1.50 **NM** value: **4.00**
Circ: CapCity orders: **16,200**
📖 Reckless Youth, Part 3 • Zero Hour **A:** Carlos Pacheco **W:** Mark Waid
95 ❑ Nov 1994 Cover: 1.50 **NM** value: **3.00**
Circ: CapCity orders: **22,700**
📖 Terminal Velocity, Part 1
96 ❑ Dec 1994 Cover: 1.50 **NM** value: **2.00**
Circ: CapCity orders: **18,250**
📖 Terminal Velocity, Part 2
97 ❑ Jan 1995 Cover: 1.50 **NM** value: **2.00**
Circ: CapCity orders: **20,150**
📖 Terminal Velocity, Part 3 **A:** Salvador Larocca **W:** Mark Waid
98 ❑ Feb 1995 Cover: 1.50 **NM** value: **2.00**
Circ: CapCity orders: **21,150**
📖 Terminal Velocity, Part 4
99 ❑ Mar 1995 Cover: 1.50 **NM** value: **2.00**
Circ: CapCity orders: **21,000**
📖 Terminal Velocity, Part 5
100 ❑ Apr 1995 Cover: 2.50 **NM** value: **3.00**
• Giant-size. 📖 Terminal Velocity, Part 6
100/SC ❑ Apr 1995 Cover: 3.50 **NM** value: **4.00**
Circ: CapCity orders: **30,025**
Holo-grafix cover. • Giant-size. 📖 Terminal Velocity, Part 6
101 ❑ May 1995 Cover: 1.75 **NM** value: **Cover or less**
Circ: CapCity orders: **21,350**
102 ❑ Jun 1995 Cover: 1.75 **NM** value: **Cover or less**
Circ: CapCity orders: **20,850**
103 ❑ Jul 1995 Cover: 1.75 **NM** value: **Cover or less**
Circ: CapCity orders: **20,000**
104 ❑ Aug 1995 Cover: 1.75 **NM** value: **Cover or less**
Circ: CapCity orders: **19,825**
105 ❑ Sep 1995 Cover: 1.75 **NM** value: **Cover or less**
Circ: CapCity orders: **18,300**
106 ❑ Oct 1995 Cover: 1.75 **NM** value: **Cover or less**
Circ: CapCity orders: **15,075**
• return of Frances Kane
107 ❑ Nov 1995 Cover: 1.75 **NM** value: **Cover or less**
📖 Underworld Unleashed • Underworld Unleashed ★ Appearance of Captain Marvel.
108 ❑ Dec 1995 Cover: 1.75 **NM** value: **Cover or less**
📖 Dead Heat, Part 1
109 ❑ Jan 1996 Cover: 1.75 **NM** value: **Cover or less**
📖 Dead Heat, Part 2 • continues in Impulse #10
110 ❑ Feb 1996 Cover: 1.75 **NM** value: **Cover or less**
📖 Dead Heat, Part 4 • continues in Impulse #11 **A:** Oscar Jimenez **W:** Mark Waid
111 ❑ Mar 1996 Cover: 1.75 **NM** value: **Cover or less**
📖 Dead Heat Finale **A:** Oscar Jimenez **W:** Mark Waid
112 ❑ Apr 1996 Cover: 1.75 **NM** value: **Cover or less**
📖 Future Perfect **A:** Anthony Castrillo **W:** Mark Waid ★ Appearance of John Fox.
113 ❑ May 1996 Cover: 1.75 **NM** value: **Cover or less**
📖 Race Against Time, Part 1
114 ❑ Jun 1996 Cover: 1.75 **NM** value: **Cover or less**
📖 Race Against Time, Part 2 ★ Appearance of Don and Dawn Allen.
115 ❑ Jul 1996 Cover: 1.75 **NM** value: **Cover or less**
📖 Race Against Time, Part 3
116 ❑ Aug 1996 Cover: 1.75 **NM** value: **Cover or less**
📖 Race Against Time, Part 4
117 ❑ Sep 1996 Cover: 1.75 **NM** value: **Cover or less**
📖 Race Against Time, Part 5 • Flash returns to present
118 ❑ Oct 1996 Cover: 1.75 **NM** value: **Cover or less**
📖 Race Against Time **A:** Sergio Cariello **W:** Brian Augustyn; Mark Waid
119 ❑ Nov 1996 Cover: 1.75 **NM** value: **Cover or less**
Circ: Diamd. preorders: **53,708**
📖 Pray for the Dawn • Final Night **A:** Paul Ryan **W:** Brian Augustyn; Mark Waid
120 ❑ Dec 1996 Cover: 1.75 **NM** value: **Cover or less**
Circ: Diamd. preorders: **49,136**
📖 Presidential Race, Part 1 • Wally West asked to leave Keystone **A:** Paul Ryan **W:** Brian Augustyn; Mark Waid ★ Appearance of Trickster.
121 ❑ Jan 1997 Cover: 1.75 **NM** value: **Cover or less**
Circ: Diamd. preorders: **47,586**
📖 Presidential Race, Part 2 **A:** Paul Ryan **W:** Brian Augustyn; Mark Waid ★ Versus Top.
122 ❑ Feb 1997 Cover: 1.75 **NM** value: **Cover or less**
Circ: Diamd. preorders: **45,981**
📖 Running Away From Home • Flash becomes a commuting superhero **A:** Paul Ryan **W:** Brian Augustyn; Mark Waid
123 ❑ Mar 1997 Cover: 1.75 **NM** value: **Cover or less**
Circ: Diamd. preorders: **43,894**
📖 The Flash of Two Cities **A:** Paul Ryan **W:** Brian Augustyn; Mark Waid
124 ❑ Apr 1997 Cover: 1.75 **NM** value: **Cover or less**
Circ: Diamd. preorders: **41,171**

Other grades: Multiply prices above by **1.5 for Mint • 2/3 for Very Fine • 1/3 for Fine • 1/5 for Very Good • 1/8 for Good**

Quicker than the Eye **A:** Paul Ryan **W:** Brian Augustyn; Mark Waid ★ Versus Major Disaster.
125 ❑ May 1997 Cover: 1.75 **NM** value: **Cover or less**
Circ: Diamd. preorders: **40,516**
126 ❑ Jun 1997 Cover: 1.75 **NM** value: **Cover or less**
Circ: Diamd. preorders: **41,204**
• return of Rogues Gallery ★ Versus Major Disaster.
127 ❑ Jul 1997 Cover: 1.75 **NM** value: **Cover or less**
Circ: Diamd. preorders: **40,026**
128 ❑ Aug 1997 Cover: 1.75 **NM** value: **Cover or less**
Circ: Diamd. preorders: **41,017**
129 ❑ Sep 1997 Cover: 1.75 **NM** value: **Cover or less**
Circ: Diamd. preorders: **38,948**
130 ❑ Oct 1997 Cover: 1.75 **NM** value: **Cover or less**
Circ: Diamd. preorders: **46,232**
Emergency Stop, Part 1 • Wally has his legs broken **A:** Paul Ryan **W:** Gramt Morrison; Mark Millar
131 ❑ Nov 1997 Cover: 1.75 **NM** value: **Cover or less**
Circ: Diamd. preorders: **43,918**
Emergency Stop, Part 2 • Wally gets new costume **A:** Paul Ryan **W:** Gramt Morrison; Mark Millar
132 ❑ Dec 1997 Cover: 1.95 **NM** value: **Cover or less**
Circ: Diamd. preorders: **42,125**
Face cover. Emergency Stop, Part 3 **A:** Paul Ryan **W:** Gramt Morrison; Mark Millar ★ Appearance of Mirror Master.
133 ❑ Jan 1998 Cover: 1.95 **NM** value: **Cover or less**
Circ: Diamd. preorders: **42,615**
134 ❑ Feb 1998 Cover: 1.95 **NM** value: **Cover or less**
Circ: Diamd. preorders: **42,668**
135 ❑ Mar 1998 Cover: 1.95 **NM** value: **Cover or less**
Circ: Diamd. preorders: **46,846**
cover forms triptych with Green Arrow #130 and Green Lantern #96. Three of a Kind, Part 3 **A:** Paul Ryan **W:** Grant Morrison; Mark Millar
136 ❑ Apr 1998 Cover: 1.95 **NM** value: **Cover or less**
Circ: Diamd. preorders: **41,125**
The Human Race, Part 1 ★ Appearance of Krakkl.
137 ❑ May 1998 Cover: 1.95 **NM** value: **Cover or less**
Circ: Diamd. preorders: **41,277**
The Human Race, Part 2
138 ❑ Jun 1998 Cover: 1.95 **NM** value: **Cover or less**
Circ: Diamd. preorders: **42,682**
The Human Race, Part 3
139 ❑ Jul 1998 Cover: 1.95 **NM** value: **Cover or less**
Circ: Diamd. preorders: **40,378**
The Black Flash, Part 1 ★ Death of Linda Park.
140 ❑ Aug 1998 Cover: 1.99 **NM** value: **Cover or less**
Circ: Diamd. preorders: **40,659**
The Black Flash, Part 2 • Linda's funeral
141 ❑ Sep 1998 Cover: 1.99 **NM** value: **Cover or less**
Circ: Diamd. preorders: **39,395**
The Black Flash, Part 3 ★ Versus Black Flash.
142 ❑ Oct 1998 Cover: 1.99 **NM** value: **Cover or less**
Circ: Diamd. preorders: **40,906**
• Wedding of Wally and Linda
143 ❑ Dec 1998 Cover: 1.99 **NM** value: **Cover or less**
Circ: Diamd. preorders: **40,044**
144 ❑ Jan 1999 Cover: 1.99 **NM** value: **Cover or less**
Circ: Diamd. preorders: **40,085**
145 ❑ Feb 1999 Cover: 1.99 **NM** value: **Cover or less**
Circ: Diamd. preorders: **41,604**
Chain Lightning, Part 1 **A:** Paul Pelletier **W:** Brian Augustyn; Mark Waid ★ Appearance of Cobalt Blue.
146 ❑ Mar 1999 Cover: 1.99 **NM** value: **Cover or less**
Circ: Diamd. preorders: **39,432**
Chain Lightning, Part 2 **A:** Paul Pelletier **W:** Brian Augustyn; Mark Waid ★ Appearance of Cobalt Blue.
147 ❑ Apr 1999 Cover: 1.99 **NM** value: **Cover or less**
Circ: Diamd. preorders: **37,760**
Chain Lightning, Part 3 **A:** Paul Pelletier **W:** Brian Augustyn; Mark Waid ★ Appearance of Reverse Flash, Cobalt Blue.
148 ❑ May 1999 Cover: 1.99 **NM** value: **Cover or less**
Circ: Diamd. preorders: **38,637**
Chain Lightning, Part 4 **A:** Paul Pelletier **W:** Brian Augustyn; Mark Waid ★ Appearance of Barry Allen.
149 ❑ Jun 1999 Cover: 1.99 **NM** value: **Cover or less**
Circ: Diamd. preorders: **39,823**
Chain Lightning, Part 5 • Crisis ending changed **A:** Paul Pelletier **W:** Brian Augustyn; Mark Waid
150 ❑ Jul 1999 Cover: 2.95 **NM** value: **Cover or less**
Circ: Diamd. preorders: **41,850**
Chain Lightning, Part 6 • Wally vs. Anti-Monitor **A:** Paul Pelletier **W:** Brian Augustyn; Mark Waid
151 ❑ Aug 1999 Cover: 1.99 **NM** value: **Cover or less**
Circ: Diamd. preorders: **38,443**
Territorealis • Teen Titans adventure **A:** Paul Pelletier; Duncan Rouleau **W:** Joe Casey; Brian Augustyn; Mark Waid
152 ❑ Sep 1999 Cover: 1.99 **NM** value: **Cover or less**
Circ: Diamd. preorders: **44,118**
New Kid in Town **A:** Paul Pelletier **W:** Brian Augustyn; Mark Waid
153 ❑ Oct 1999 Cover: 1.99 **NM** value: **Cover or less**
Circ: Diamd. preorders: **40,634**
The Folded Man **A:** Paul Pelletier **W:** Brian Augustyn; Mark Waid ★ Versus Folded Man.
154 ❑ Nov 1999 Cover: 1.99 **NM** value: **Cover or less**
Circ: Diamd. preorders: **39,444**
• new Flash reveals identity
155 ❑ Dec 1999 Cover: 1.99 **NM** value: **Cover or less**
Circ: Diamd. preorders: **42,194**
Payback Unlimited **A:** Paul Pelletier **W:** Brian Augustyn; Mark Waid
156 ❑ Jan 2000 Cover: 1.99 **NM** value: **Cover or less**
Circ: Diamd. preorders: **41,374**
157 ❑ Feb 2000 Cover: 1.99 **NM** value: **Cover or less**
Circ: Diamd. preorders: **44,341**
158 ❑ Mar 2000 Cover: 1.99 **NM** value: **Cover or less**
Circ: Diamd. preorders: **40,930**
159 ❑ Apr 2000 Cover: 1.99 **NM** value: **Cover or less**
Circ: Diamd. preorders: **39,038**
Whirlwind Ceremony **A:** Paul Pelletier **W:** Brian Augustyn; Mark Waid
160 ❑ May 2000 Cover: 1.99 **NM** value: **Cover or less**
Circ: Diamd. preorders: **38,953**
Honeymoon on the Run **A:** Scott Kolins **W:** Brian Augustyn
161 ❑ Jun 2000 Cover: 1.99 **NM** value: **Cover or less**
Circ: Diamd. preorders: **38,742**
162 ❑ Jul 2000 Cover: 1.99 **NM** value: **Cover or less**
Circ: Diamd. preorders: **38,113**
163 ❑ Aug 2000 Cover: 1.99 **NM** value: **Cover or less**
Circ: Diamd. preorders: **36,902**
164 ❑ Sep 2000 Cover: 2.25 **NM** value: **Cover or less**
Circ: Diamd. preorders: **36,252**
Lightning in a Bottle; Joining the Tea Party, Part 1 **A:** Angel Unzueta **W:** Geoff Johns
165 ❑ Oct 2000 Cover: 2.25 **NM** value: **Cover or less**
Circ: Diamd. preorders: **34,076**
Joining the Tea Party, Part 2 **A:** Angel Unzueta **W:** Geoff Johns
166 ❑ Nov 2000 Cover: 2.25 **NM** value: **Cover or less**
Circ: Diamd. preorders: **33,775**
Joining the Tea Party, Part 3 **A:** Angel Unzueta **W:** Geoff Johns
167 ❑ Dec 2000 Cover: 2.25 **NM** value: **Cover or less**
Circ: Diamd. preorders: **32,407**
Joining the Tea Party, Part 4 **A:** Angel Unzueta **W:** Geoff Johns
168 ❑ Jan 2001 Cover: 2.25 **NM** value: **Cover or less**
Circ: Diamd. preorders: **32,077**
Joining the Tea Party, Part 5 **A:** Angel Unzueta **W:** Geoff Johns
169 ❑ Feb 2001 Cover: 2.25 **NM** value: **Cover or less**
Circ: Diamd. preorders: **31,456**
Joining the Tea Party, Part 6 **A:** Angel Unzueta **W:** Geoff Johns
170 ❑ Mar 2001 Cover: 2.25 **NM** value: **Cover or less**
Circ: Diamd. preorders: **30,342**
Blood Will Run, Part 1 **A:** Scott Kolins **W:** Geoff Johns
171 ❑ Apr 2001 Cover: 2.25 **NM** value: **Cover or less**
Circ: Diamd. preorders: **29,662**
Blood Will Run, Part 2 **A:** Scott Kolins **W:** Geoff Johns
172 ❑ May 2001 Cover: 2.25 **NM** value: **Cover or less**
Circ: Diamd. preorders: **28,884**
Blood Will Run, Part 3 **A:** Scott Kolins **W:** Geoff Johns
173 ❑ Jun 2001 Cover: 2.25 **NM** value: **Cover or less**
Circ: Diamd. preorders: **29,053**
174 ❑ Jul 2001 Cover: 2.25 **NM** value: **Cover or less**
Circ: Diamd. preorders: **28,712**
175 ❑ Aug 2001 Cover: 2.25 **NM** value: **Cover or less**
Circ: Diamd. preorders: **28,932**
176 ❑ Sep 2001 Cover: 2.25 **NM** value: **Cover or less**
Circ: Diamd. preorders: **30,204**
1000000 ❑ Nov 1998 Cover: 1.99 **NM** value: **Cover or less**
Circ: Diamd. preorders: **46,958**
Fast Forward **A:** Michael Jan Friedman **W:** Mark Waid
Anl 1 ❑ ca. 1987 Cover: 1.25 **NM** value: **3.00**
Circ: CapCity orders: **30,350**
Death Touch **A:** Jackson Guice **W:** Mike Baron
Anl 2 ❑ Cover: 1.50 **NM** value: **2.00**
Circ: CapCity orders: **21,900**
• Private Lives
Anl 3 ❑ Cover: 1.75 **NM** value: **2.25**
Circ: CapCity orders: **17,650**
• Who's Who entries
Anl 4 ❑ Cover: 2.00 **NM** value: **2.25**
Circ: CapCity orders: **34,200**
Armageddon 2001, Part 7 • Armageddon 2001
Anl 5 ❑ Cover: 2.50 **NM** value: **2.75**
Circ: CapCity orders: **22,050**
Eclipso: The Darkness Within, Part 9 • Eclipso
Anl 6 ❑ Cover: 2.50 **NM** value: **Cover or less**
Circ: CapCity orders: **31,750**
Bloodlines • Bloodlines ★ 1st Appearance of Argus. ★ 1st Appearance of Argus.
Anl 7 ❑ Cover: 2.95 **NM** value: **Cover or less**
Circ: CapCity orders: **13,050**
• Elseworlds
Anl 8 ❑ ca. 1995 Cover: 3.50 **NM** value: **Cover or less**
Circ: CapCity orders: **16,700**
• Year One
Anl 9 ❑ ca. 1996 Cover: 2.95 **NM** value: **Cover or less**
• Legends of the Dead Earth
Anl 10 ❑ ca. 1997 Cover: 3.95 **NM** value: **Cover or less**
• Pulp Heroes; 1997 Annual
Anl 11 ❑ ca. 1998 Cover: 2.95 **NM** value: **3.95**
• Ghosts; 1998 Annual ★ Appearance of Johnny Quick.
Anl 12 ❑ Oct 1999 Cover: 2.95 **NM** value: **Cover or less**
The Apes of Wrath • JLApe; 1999 Annual **A:** Dougie Braithwaite **W:** Brian Augustyn
Bk 1 ❑ Cover: 12.95 **NM** value: **Cover or less**
• collectsFlash #62-65, Flash Annual #8, Speed Force #1, andFlash 80-Page Giant #1. Terminal Velocity; Born to Run • Born to Run **A:** Humberto Ramos; Greg LaRocque; Pop Mhan; Jim Aparo **W:** Mark Waid; Tom Peyer
Bk 2 ❑ Cover: 12.95 **NM** value: **Cover or less**
• collects Flash #0, 95-100 ★ Origin of Max Mercury.
Bk 3 ❑ Cover: 12.95 **NM** value: **Cover or less**
• The Return of Barry Allen; Collects Flash (2nd Series) #74-79 **A:** Greg LaRocque; Sal Velluto **W:** Mark Waid
GS 1 ❑ Aug 1998 Cover: 4.95 **NM** value: **Cover or less**
A Celebration of the Heroic Legacy; The Speed of Life; Dark of the Sun; The 5,000 Rats of Bartholomew Allen; The Professional; Thunder and Lightning; Split-Seconds; Your Life Is My Business **A:** Mike Collins; Craig Rousseau; Ethan Van Sciver; John Byrne; Oscar Jimenez; Ariel Olivetti; Pop Mhan **W:** Michael Jan Friedman; Brian Augustyn; John Byrne; Christopher Priest; Mark Millar; Mark Waid; Todd Dezago ★ Appearance of Lightning, Flash III (Wally West), Jesse Quick, Impulse, Flash I (Jay Garrick), Captain Boomerang, Flash IV (John Fox).
GS 2 ❑ Apr 1999 Cover: 4.95 **NM** value: **Cover or less**
SE 1 ❑ Cover: 2.95 **NM** value: **3.50**
• 50th anniversary issue. • 3 Flashes **A:** Carmine Infantino **C:** Joe Kubert ★ 1st Appearance of John Fox.
TV 1 ❑ 1991 Cover: 3.95 **NM** value: **Cover or less**
Circ: CapCity orders: **23,400**
Photo cover. • TV Special; Stories about TV show Flash ★ Appearance of Kid Flash.

FLASH & GREEN LANTERN: THE BRAVE AND THE BOLD — DC

1 ❑ Oct 1999 Cover: 2.50 **NM** value: **Cover or less**
Circ: Diamd. preorders: **47,357**
Those Who Worship Evil's Might **A:** Barry Kitson **W:** Mark Waid; Tom Peyer
2 ❑ Nov 1999 Cover: 2.50 **NM** value: **Cover or less**
3 ❑ Dec 1999 Cover: 2.50 **NM** value: **Cover or less**
Circ: Diamd. preorders: **40,301**
A World of Hurt **A:** Barry Kitson **W:** Mark Waid; Tom Peyer
4 ❑ Jan 2000 Cover: 2.50 **NM** value: **Cover or less**
Circ: Diamd. preorders: **37,241**
How Many Times Can a Man Turn His Head? **A:** Tom Grindberg **W:** Mark Waid; Tom Peyer
5 ❑ Feb 2000 Cover: 2.50 **NM** value: **Cover or less**
The Man Without Fearlessness! **A:** Barry Kitson **W:** Mark Waid; Tom Peyer
6 ❑ Mar 2000 Cover: 2.50 **NM** value: **Cover or less**
Running on Empty **A:** Barry Kitson **W:** Mark Waid; Tom Peyer
Bk 1 ❑ Cover: 12.95 **NM** value: **Cover or less**
• Collects series **A:** Barry Kitson; Tom Grindberg **W:** Mark Waid; Tom Peyer

FLASH ARCHIVES, THE — DC

1 ❑ Cover: 49.95 **NM** value: **Cover or less**
• Collects Flash Comics #104, Showcase #4, 8, 13, and 14, and The Flash #105-108
2 ❑ Cover: 49.95 **NM** value: **Cover or less**
Return of the Mirror Master!; Secret of the Sunken Satellite!; The Challenge of the Weather Wizard!; The Invasion of the Cloud Creatures!; Kid Flash: The Challenge of the Crimson Crows!; The Mystery of the Elongated Man!; Kid Flash: Danger • Collects The Flash (1st Series) #109-116 **A:** Carmine Infantino; Joe Giella **W:** John Broome

FLASH COMICS — DC

Flash Comics began in 1939 and soon became a mainstay of DC's super-hero line. In issue #1, the world met Jay Garrick, a chemistry student who accidentally broke a container filled with hard (or heavy) water gases he had been experimenting on. The room filled with the strange vapors and Garrick barely managed to escape before losing consciousness. When he awoke, however, he found his body chemistry altered by the gas he had inhaled, and became transformed into The Flash, the fastest man alive.

In addition to its title character, Flash Comics introduced the world to Hawkman, Black Canary, and Johnny Thunder (a boy who could summon a "pet thunderbolt" by calling out the magic words "Cei-U" ["Say you!"]). The series ran successfully until 1949 when it fell, a victim of the declining sales of super-hero titles. The Golden Age Flash appeared as a Justice Society member in All-Star Comics for a few more years, then vanished for more than a decade.

1 ❑ Jan 1940 Cover: 0.10 **NM** value: **60000.00**
• **CGC:** 8 graded, best 9.4
The Flash • Or **A:** Harry Lampert; Shelly Moldoff(cover) **W:** Gardner Fox ★ Origin of Johnny Thunder, Flash I (Jay Garrick). ★ 1st Appearance of Johnny Thunder, Hawkgirl (as Shiera Sanders), The Whip, Flash I (Jay Garrick), Hawkman I (Carter Hall).
2 ❑ Feb 1940 Cover: 0.10 **NM** value: **6400.00**
• **CGC:** 1 graded, best 7.5
3 ❑ Mar 1940 Cover: 0.10 **NM** value: **4750.00**
4 ❑ Apr 1940 Cover: 0.10 **NM** value: **3650.00**
• **CGC:** 4 graded, best 8.0
5 ❑ May 1940 Cover: 0.10 **NM** value: **3250.00**
• **CGC:** 2 graded, best 9.0
6 ❑ Jun 1940 Cover: 0.10 **NM** value: **4200.00**
• **CGC:** 2 graded, best 4.5
Flash cover. **A:** E.E. Hibbard **W:** Gardner Fox
7 ❑ Jul 1940 Cover: 0.10 **NM** value: **2650.00**
• **CGC:** 1 graded, best 3.0
8 ❑ Aug 1940 Cover: 0.10 **NM** value: **2250.00**
• **CGC:** 4 graded, best 8.0
9 ❑ Sep 1940 Cover: 0.10 **NM** value: **2250.00**
• **CGC:** 1 graded, best 5.5
10 ❑ Oct 1940 Cover: 0.10 **NM** value: **2250.00**
• **CGC:** 4 graded, best 7.5
11 ❑ Nov 1940 Cover: 0.10 **NM** value: **1500.00**
• **CGC:** 3 graded, best 9.0
12 ❑ Dec 1940 Cover: 0.10 **NM** value: **1500.00**
• **CGC:** 2 graded, best 7.0
13 ❑ Jan 1941 Cover: 0.10 **NM** value: **1500.00**
• **CGC:** 2 graded, best 8.0
14 ❑ Feb 1941 Cover: 0.10 **NM** value: **1400.00**
• **CGC:** 3 graded, best 8.0
15 ❑ Mar 1941 Cover: 0.10 **NM** value: **1350.00**
• **CGC:** 2 graded, best 9.0
16 ❑ Apr 1941 Cover: 0.10 **NM** value: **1350.00**
• **CGC:** 1 graded, best 7.5
17 ❑ May 1941 Cover: 0.10 **NM** value: **1250.00**
• **CGC:** 1 graded, best 6.5
18 ❑ Jun 1941 Cover: 0.10 **NM** value: **1250.00**
• **CGC:** 1 graded, best 3.0
19 ❑ Jul 1941 Cover: 0.10 **NM** value: **1250.00**
• **CGC:** 1 graded, best 6.5

CGC-graded: Multiply prices above by **33 for 9.9 M • 16 for 9.8 NM/M • 7 for 9.6 NM+ • 5 for 9.4 NM • 2.5 for 9.2 NM- • 1.5 for 9.0 VF/NM**

20 ❑ Aug 1941 Cover: 0.10 **NM** value: **1250.00**
21 ❑ Sep 1941 Cover: 0.10 **NM** value: **1050.00**
• **CGC:** 3 graded, best 9.0
22 ❑ Oct 1941 Cover: 0.10 **NM** value: **1050.00**
23 ❑ Nov 1941 Cover: 0.10 **NM** value: **1050.00**
• **CGC:** 2 graded, best 5.0
24 ❑ Dec 1941 Cover: 0.10 **NM** value: **1600.00**
• **CGC:** 3 graded, best 7.0
25 ❑ Jan 1942 Cover: 0.10 **NM** value: **885.00**
• **CGC:** 1 graded, best 7.0
26 ❑ Feb 1942 Cover: 0.10 **NM** value: **885.00**
27 ❑ Mar 1942 Cover: 0.10 **NM** value: **885.00**
• **CGC:** 2 graded, best 6.0
28 ❑ Apr 1942 Cover: 0.10 **NM** value: **885.00**
• **CGC:** 1 graded, best 5.5
29 ❑ May 1942 Cover: 0.10 **NM** value: **885.00**
30 ❑ Jun 1942 Cover: 0.10 **NM** value: **885.00**
• **CGC:** 1 graded, best 9.4
31 ❑ Jul 1942 Cover: 0.10 **NM** value: **825.00**
32 ❑ Aug 1942 Cover: 0.10 **NM** value: **825.00**
33 ❑ Sep 1942 Cover: 0.10 **NM** value: **825.00**
• **CGC:** 1 graded, best 9.2
34 ❑ Oct 1942 Cover: 0.10 **NM** value: **825.00**
• **CGC:** 2 graded, best 9.2
35 ❑ Nov 1942 Cover: 0.10 **NM** value: **825.00**
• **CGC:** 1 graded, best 6.5
36 ❑ Dec 1942 Cover: 0.10 **NM** value: **825.00**
37 ❑ Jan 1943 Cover: 0.10 **NM** value: **825.00**
38 ❑ Feb 1943 Cover: 0.10 **NM** value: **825.00**
• **CGC:** 1 graded, best 7.5
39 ❑ Mar 1943 Cover: 0.10 **NM** value: **825.00**
40 ❑ Apr 1943 Cover: 0.10 **NM** value: **825.00**
• **CGC:** 2 graded, best 7.5
41 ❑ May 1943 Cover: 0.10 **NM** value: **725.00**
• **CGC:** 2 graded, best 6.5
42 ❑ Jun 1943 Cover: 0.10 **NM** value: **725.00**
43 ❑ Jul 1943 Cover: 0.10 **NM** value: **725.00**
• **CGC:** 2 graded, best 9.0
44 ❑ Aug 1943 Cover: 0.10 **NM** value: **725.00**
• **CGC:** 1 graded, best 8.0
45 ❑ Sep 1943 Cover: 0.10 **NM** value: **725.00**
• **CGC:** 1 graded, best 7.0
46 ❑ Oct 1943 Cover: 0.10 **NM** value: **725.00**
47 ❑ Nov 1943 Cover: 0.10 **NM** value: **725.00**
• **CGC:** 1 graded, best 7.5
48 ❑ Dec 1943 Cover: 0.10 **NM** value: **725.00**
49 ❑ Jan 1944 Cover: 0.10 **NM** value: **725.00**
• **CGC:** 1 graded, best 6.5
50 ❑ Feb 1944 Cover: 0.10 **NM** value: **725.00**
51 ❑ Mar 1944 Cover: 0.10 **NM** value: **600.00**
• **CGC:** 1 graded, best 9.2
52 ❑ Apr 1944 Cover: 0.10 **NM** value: **600.00**
• **CGC:** 1 graded, best 4.0
53 ❑ May 1944 Cover: 0.10 **NM** value: **600.00**
• **CGC:** 1 graded, best 9.0
54 ❑ Jun 1944 Cover: 0.10 **NM** value: **600.00**
• **CGC:** 2 graded, best 9.2
55 ❑ Jul 1944 Cover: 0.10 **NM** value: **600.00**
• **CGC:** 2 graded, best 8.5
56 ❑ Aug 1944 Cover: 0.10 **NM** value: **600.00**
• **CGC:** 7 graded, best 9.2
57 ❑ Sep 1944 Cover: 0.10 **NM** value: **600.00**
• **CGC:** 1 graded, best 6.5
58 ❑ Oct 1944 Cover: 0.10 **NM** value: **600.00**
59 ❑ Nov 1944 Cover: 0.10 **NM** value: **600.00**
• **CGC:** 1 graded, best 5.0
60 ❑ Dec 1944 Cover: 0.10 **NM** value: **600.00**
• **CGC:** 3 graded, best 9.2
61 ❑ Jan 1945 Cover: 0.10 **NM** value: **600.00**
62 ❑ Feb 1945 Cover: 0.10 **NM** value: **750.00**
• **CGC:** 1 graded, best 7.0
63 ❑ Mar 1945 Cover: 0.10 **NM** value: **600.00**
• **CGC:** 1 graded, best 8.0
64 ❑ Apr 1945 Cover: 0.10 **NM** value: **600.00**
• **CGC:** 1 graded, best 7.5
65 ❑ Jun 1945 Cover: 0.10 **NM** value: **600.00**
• **CGC:** 2 graded, best 9.0
66 ❑ Aug 1945 Cover: 0.10 **NM** value: **600.00**
• **CGC:** 2 graded, best 9.0
67 ❑ Oct 1945 Cover: 0.10 **NM** value: **600.00**
• **CGC:** 1 graded, best 8.0
68 ❑ Dec 1945 Cover: 0.10 **NM** value: **600.00**
• **CGC:** 1 graded, best 8.5
69 ❑ Feb 1946 Cover: 0.10 **NM** value: **600.00**
• **CGC:** 1 graded, best 9.4
70 ❑ Apr 1946 Cover: 0.10 **NM** value: **600.00**
• **CGC:** 1 graded, best 7.5
71 ❑ May 1946 Cover: 0.10 **NM** value: **600.00**
• **CGC:** 1 graded, best 9.0
72 ❑ Jun 1946 Cover: 0.10 **NM** value: **600.00**
• **CGC:** 1 graded, best 8.0
73 ❑ Jul 1946 Cover: 0.10 **NM** value: **600.00**
74 ❑ Aug 1946 Cover: 0.10 **NM** value: **600.00**
75 ❑ Sep 1946 Cover: 0.10 **NM** value: **600.00**
• **CGC:** 1 graded, best 9.2
76 ❑ Oct 1946 Cover: 0.10 **NM** value: **600.00**
77 ❑ Nov 1946 Cover: 0.10 **NM** value: **600.00**
78 ❑ Dec 1946 Cover: 0.10 **NM** value: **600.00**
• **CGC:** 2 graded, best 7.0
79 ❑ Jan 1947 Cover: 0.10 **NM** value: **600.00**
80 ❑ Feb 1947 Cover: 0.10 **NM** value: **600.00**
• **CGC:** 1 graded, best 7.0
81 ❑ Mar 1947 Cover: 0.10 **NM** value: **600.00**
• **CGC:** 3 graded, best 6.5
82 ❑ Apr 1947 Cover: 0.10 **NM** value: **600.00**
• **CGC:** 2 graded, best 7.5
83 ❑ May 1947 Cover: 0.10 **NM** value: **600.00**
• **CGC:** 1 graded, best 8.5
84 ❑ Jun 1947 Cover: 0.10 **NM** value: **600.00**
• **CGC:** 1 graded, best 6.5
85 ❑ Jul 1947 Cover: 0.10 **NM** value: **600.00**
86 ❑ Aug 1947 Cover: 0.10 **NM** value: **2000.00**
• **CGC:** 2 graded, best 8.0
📖 The Black Canary • Johnny Thunder/Black Canary backup ★ 1st Appearance of Black Canary I (Dinah Lance).
87 ❑ Sep 1947 Cover: 0.10 **NM** value: **900.00**
• **CGC:** 1 graded, best 6.5
📖 The Package of Peril! • Johnny Thunder/Black Canary backup
88 ❑ Oct 1947 Cover: 0.10 **NM** value: **900.00**
• **CGC:** 1 graded, best 4.5
📖 The Map That Wasn't There! • Johnny Thunder/Black Canary backup
89 ❑ Nov 1947 Cover: 0.10 **NM** value: **900.00**
📖 Produce the Crime! • Johnny Thunder/Black Canary backup ★ 1st Appearance of The Thorn.
90 ❑ Dec 1947 Cover: 0.10 **NM** value: **900.00**
• **CGC:** 1 graded, best 6.0
📖 Triple Exposure! • Johnny Thunder/Black Canary backup
91 ❑ Jan 1948 Cover: 0.10 **NM** value: **900.00**
• **CGC:** 2 graded, best 8.0
📖 The Tumbling Trees! • Johnny Thunder/Black Canary backup
92 ❑ Feb 1948 Cover: 0.10 **NM** value: **2350.00**
• **CGC:** 9 graded, best 9.4
📖 The Huntress of the Highway! • Solo Black Canary story; Difficult to find in NM
93 ❑ Mar 1948 Cover: 0.10 **NM** value: **950.00**
• **CGC:** 1 graded, best 6.5
📖 Mystery of the Crimson Crystal! • Solo Black Canary story
94 ❑ Apr 1948 Cover: 0.10 **NM** value: **950.00**
• **CGC:** 3 graded, best 9.4
📖 Corsage of Death! • Solo Black Canary story
95 ❑ May 1948 Cover: 0.10 **NM** value: **950.00**
• **CGC:** 1 graded, best 9.0
📖 An Orchid for the Deceased! • Solo Black Canary story
96 ❑ Jun 1948 Cover: 0.10 **NM** value: **950.00**
📖 The Riddle of the Topaz Brooch! • Solo Black Canary story
97 ❑ Jul 1948 Cover: 0.10 **NM** value: **950.00**
• **CGC:** 2 graded, best 9.0
📖 The Mystery of the Stolen Cloth! • Solo Black Canary story
98 ❑ Aug 1948 Cover: 0.10 **NM** value: **950.00**
• **CGC:** 1 graded, best 8.0
📖 The Byzantine Black! • Solo Black Canary story
99 ❑ Sep 1948 Cover: 0.10 **NM** value: **950.00**
• **CGC:** 1 graded, best 6.5
📖 Time Runs Out! • Solo Black Canary story
100 ❑ Oct 1948 Cover: 0.10 **NM** value: **2450.00**
• **CGC:** 2 graded, best 7.5
📖 The Circle of Terror! • Scarce; Solo Black Canary story
101 ❑ Nov 1948 Cover: 0.10 **NM** value: **1950.00**
• **CGC:** 1 graded, best 7.0
📖 The Day That Wouldn't End! • Scarce; Solo Black Canary story
102 ❑ Dec 1948 Cover: 0.10 **NM** value: **1950.00**
• **CGC:** 4 graded, best 9.2
📖 The Riddle of the Roses! • Scarce; Solo Black Canary story
103 ❑ Jan 1949 Cover: 0.10 **NM** value: **2250.00**
• **CGC:** 1 graded, best 5.5
📖 Mystery on Ice! • Scarce; Solo Black Canary story
104 ❑ Feb 1949 Cover: 0.10 **NM** value: **5800.00**
• **CGC:** 3 graded, best 7.0
📖 The Rival Flash!; Crime on Her Hands! • Scarce; Solo Black Canary story; Series numbering continued in Flash (1st Series) #105 ★ Origin of Flash I (Jay Garrick).

FLASH GORDON COMICS — Harvey

1 ❑ Oct 1950 Cover: 0.10 **NM** value: **250.00**
• **CGC:** 1 graded, best 8.0
2 ❑ Dec 1950 Cover: 0.10 **NM** value: **150.00**
• **CGC:** 1 graded, best 7.0
3 ❑ Feb 1951 Cover: 0.10 **NM** value: **150.00**
• **CGC:** 1 graded, best 3.5
4 ❑ Apr 1951 Cover: 0.10 **NM** value: **150.00**
5 ❑ Cover: 0.10 **NM** value: **150.00**

FLASH GORDON (DC) — DC

1 ❑ Jun 1988 Cover: 1.25 **NM** value: **2.00**
Circ: CapCity orders: **22,350**
📖 Into The Maelstrom **A:** Dan Jurgens **W:** Dan Jurgens
2 ❑ Jul 1988 Cover: 1.25 **NM** value: **1.50**
Circ: CapCity orders: **17,000**
3 ❑ Aug 1988 Cover: 1.25 **NM** value: **1.50**
Circ: CapCity orders: **15,000**
4 ❑ Sep 1988 Cover: 1.25 **NM** value: **1.50**
Circ: CapCity orders: **15,000**
5 ❑ Oct 1988 Cover: 1.25 **NM** value: **1.50**
Circ: CapCity orders: **14,000**
6 ❑ Nov 1988 Cover: 1.25 **NM** value: **1.50**
Circ: CapCity orders: **13,300**
7 ❑ Dec 1988 Cover: 1.25 **NM** value: **1.50**
Circ: CapCity orders: **12,650**
8 ❑ Win 1988 Cover: 1.25 **NM** value: **1.50**
Circ: CapCity orders: **12,000**
9 ❑ Hol 1988 Cover: 1.25 **NM** value: **1.50**
Circ: CapCity orders: **11,600**

FLASH GORDON (GOLD KEY ONE-SHOT) — Gold Key

1 ❑ Jun 1965 Cover: 0.12 **NM** value: **50.00**
• **CGC:** 2 graded, best 9.4

FLASH GORDON (KING/CHARLTON/GOLD KEY/WHITMAN) — King

Flash Gordon was created by Alex Raymond (1909-1956), one of the most famous comic-strip creators. The strip began in 1934, with a mysterious planet appearing on a collision course with the Earth. Star athlete Flash Gordon joins with the lovely Dale Arden and scientist Dr. Hans Zarkov to investigate. Taking Zarkov's rocketship, they fly to the planet, Mongo, ruled by the tyrant Ming the Merciless. Although they soon stopped Ming's plans to conquer the Earth, Flash, Dale, and Zarkov still had countless adventures in Mongo's many locales.

Flash Gordon has long been one of the best-loved science-fiction heroes, appearing in novels, movie serials — and in comic books published by half a dozen publishers. This title is no exception, beginning its run under the King label, moving on to Charlton, then to Western Publishing, which published Gordon under its Gold Key and Whitman imprints.

1 ❑ Sep 1966 Cover: 0.12 **NM** value: **45.00**
• **CGC:** 2 graded, best 9.4
• King begins publishing
2 ❑ Nov 1966 Cover: 0.12 **NM** value: **25.00**
📖 The Death Trap Of Mongo
3 ❑ Jan 1967 Cover: 0.12 **NM** value: **20.00**
4 ❑ Mar 1967 Cover: 0.12 **NM** value: **22.00**
5 ❑ May 1967 Cover: 0.12 **NM** value: **22.00**
• **CGC:** 4 graded, best 9.4
6 ❑ Jul 1967 Cover: 0.12 **NM** value: **22.00**
7 ❑ Aug 1967 Cover: 0.12 **NM** value: **22.00**
8 ❑ Sep 1967 Cover: 0.12 **NM** value: **22.00**
• **CGC:** 10 graded, best 9.4
9 ❑ Oct 1967 Cover: 0.12 **NM** value: **30.00**
10 ❑ Nov 1967 Cover: 0.12 **NM** value: **30.00**
11 ❑ Dec 1967 Cover: 0.15 **NM** value: **18.00**
12 ❑ Feb 1969 Cover: 0.12 **NM** value: **20.00**
• Charlton begins publishing
13 ❑ Apr 1969 Cover: 0.12 **NM** value: **16.00**
14 ❑ Jun 1969 Cover: 0.12 **NM** value: **12.00**
15 ❑ Aug 1969 Cover: 0.12 **NM** value: **12.00**
16 ❑ Oct 1969 Cover: 0.15 **NM** value: **12.00**
17 ❑ Nov 1969 Cover: 0.15 **NM** value: **12.00**
18 ❑ Jan 1969 Cover: 0.15 **NM** value: **12.00**
19 ❑ Sep 1978 Cover: 0.35 **NM** value: **8.00**
• Gold Key begins publishing
20 ❑ Nov 1978 Cover: 0.35 **NM** value: **5.00**
21 ❑ Jan 1979 Cover: 0.35 **NM** value: **5.00**
📖 Wolf in the Fold **A:** Frank Bolle **W:** John Warner
22 ❑ Mar 1979 Cover: 0.35 **NM** value: **5.00**
23 ❑ May 1979 Cover: 0.40 **NM** value: **5.00**
24 ❑ Jul 1979 Cover: 0.40 **NM** value: **4.00**
• Whitman begins publishing
25 ❑ Sep 1979 Cover: 0.40 **NM** value: **4.00**
26 ❑ Nov 1979 Cover: 0.40 **NM** value: **4.00**
27 ❑ Jan 1980 Cover: 0.40 **NM** value: **4.00**
28 ❑ Mar 1980 Cover: 0.40 **NM** value: **4.00**
📖 Into the Cave Kingdom
29 ❑ May 1980 Cover: 0.40 **NM** value: **4.00**
📖 The Deadly Depths
30 ❑ Oct 1980 Cover: 0.40 **NM** value: **4.00**
• **CGC:** 1 graded, best 9.4
31 ❑ Mar 1981 Cover: 0.40 **NM** value: **3.00**
• The Movie Adaptation **A:** Al Williamson
32 ❑ Apr 1981 Cover: 0.40 **NM** value: **3.00**
• The Movie Adaptation **A:** Al Williamson
33 ❑ May 1981 Cover: 0.40 **NM** value: **3.00**
• The Movie Adaptation **A:** Al Williamson
34 ❑ Oct 1981 Cover: 0.50 **NM** value: **3.00**
35 ❑ Dec 1981 Cover: 0.50 **NM** value: **3.00**
36 ❑ Feb 1982 Cover: 0.60 **NM** value: **3.00**
37 ❑ ca. 1982 Cover: 0.60 **NM** value: **3.00**

FLASH GORDON (MARVEL) — Marvel

1 ❑ Jun 1995 Cover: 2.95 **NM** value: **Cover or less**
Circ: CapCity orders: **9,150**
cardstock wraparound cover. 📖 Treachery in Torneo **A:** Al Williamson **W:** Mark Schultz
2 ❑ Jul 1995 Cover: 2.95 **NM** value: **Cover or less**
Circ: CapCity orders: **6,100**
wraparound cardstock cover. final issue.

FLASH GORDON: THE MOVIE — Golden Press

1 ❑ Cover: 1.95 **NM** value: **2.50**

FLASH/GREEN LANTERN: FASTER FRIENDS — DC

1 ❑ Cover: 4.95 **NM** value: **Cover or less**
• prestige format. • continued from Green Lantern/Flash: Faster Friends

FLASHMARKS — Fantagraphics

1 ❑ b&w Cover: 2.95 **NM** value: **Cover or less**

FLASH PLUS — DC

1 ❑ Jan 1997 Cover: 2.95 **NM** value: **Cover or less**
📖 Doorway to Nightmare **A:** Eduardo Barreto **W:** Brian Augustyn; Mark Waid ★ Appearance of Nightwing.

FLASHPOINT — DC

1 ❑ Dec 1999 Cover: 2.95 **NM** value: **Cover or less**
Circ: Diamd. preorders: **28,739**
• Elseworlds **A:** Norm Breyfogle **W:** Pat McGreal

2 ❑ Jan 2000 Cover: 2.95 **NM** value: **Cover or less**
Circ: Diamd. preorders: **24,520**
3 ❑ Feb 2000 Cover: 2.95 **NM** value: **Cover or less**
Circ: Diamd. preorders: **22,866**

FLASH SECRET FILES, THE — DC

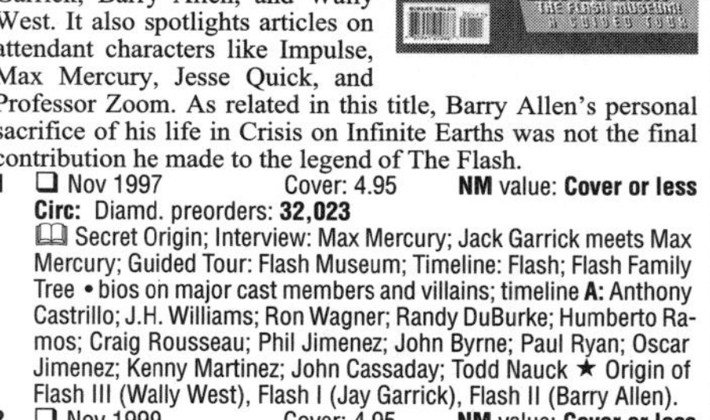

In 1997 the editors at DC Comics realized what complicated and elaborate histories some of their more venerable titles had accumulated. One of the characters most in need of this treatment was The Flash, who has existed in one form or another since the 1940s, and whose existence is the lynch pin on which much of the history of the DC universe turns.

The Flash Secrets Files relates the definitive origins of the three men who were known as The Flash: Jay Garrick, Barry Allen, and Wally West. It also spotlights articles on attendant characters like Impulse, Max Mercury, Jesse Quick, and Professor Zoom. As related in this title, Barry Allen's personal sacrifice of his life in Crisis on Infinite Earths was not the final contribution he made to the legend of The Flash.

1 ❑ Nov 1997 Cover: 4.95 **NM** value: **Cover or less**
Circ: Diamd. preorders: **32,023**
📖 Secret Origin; Interview: Max Mercury; Jack Garrick meets Max Mercury; Guided Tour: Flash Museum; Timeline: Flash; Flash Family Tree • bios on major cast members and villains; timeline **A:** Anthony Castrillo; J.H. Williams; Ron Wagner; Randy DuBurke; Humberto Ramos; Craig Rousseau; Phil Jimenez; John Byrne; Paul Ryan; Oscar Jimenez; Kenny Martinez; John Cassaday; Todd Nauck ★ Origin of Flash III (Wally West), Flash I (Jay Garrick), Flash II (Barry Allen).
2 ❑ Nov 1999 Cover: 4.95 **NM** value: **Cover or less**
Circ: Diamd. preorders: **23,557**
• updates on cast

FLAT TOP — Harvey

1 ❑ Nov 1953 Cover: 0.10 **NM** value: **40.00**
2 ❑ Feb 1954 Cover: 0.10 **NM** value: **25.00**
3 ❑ May 1954 Cover: 0.10 **NM** value: **20.00**
4 ❑ Mar 1955 Cover: 0.10 **NM** value: **20.00**
5 ❑ May 1955 Cover: 0.10 **NM** value: **20.00**
6 ❑ Jul 1955 Cover: 0.10 **NM** value: **20.00**
7 ❑ Sep 1955 Cover: 0.10 **NM** value: **20.00**

FLAXEN — Dark Horse

1 ❑ Cover: 2.95 **NM** value: **Cover or less**
Circ: CapCity orders: **4,025**
photo back cover. **A:** Richard Howell; Steve Rude(cover) **W:** Mark Evanier

FLAXEN: ALTER EGO — Caliber

1 ❑ Mar 1995 Cover: 2.95 **NM** value: **Cover or less**
Circ: CapCity orders: **2,380**
📖 Shakedown **A:** Brian Michael Bendis **W:** James D. Hudnall

FLEENER — Zongo

1 ❑ b&w Cover: 2.95 **NM** value: **Cover or less**
2 ❑ Dec 1996, b&w Cover: 2.95 **NM** value: **Cover or less**
Circ: Diamd. preorders: **2,610**
3 ❑ b&w Cover: 2.95 **NM** value: **Cover or less**

FLESH — Fleetway-Quality

1 ❑ Cover: 2.95 **NM** value: **Cover or less**
📖 Flesh: The Legend Of Shamana **A:** Carl Critchlow **W:** Pat Mills; Tony Skinner
2 ❑ Cover: 2.95 **NM** value: **Cover or less**
📖 Flesh: The Legend Of Shamana
3 ❑ Cover: 2.95 **NM** value: **Cover or less**
📖 Flesh: The Legend Of Shamana **A:** Carl Critchlow **W:** Pat Mills; Tony Skinner
4 ❑ Cover: 2.95 **NM** value: **Cover or less**
📖 Flesh: The Legend Of Shamana

FLESH & BLOOD — Brainstorm

1 ❑ Cover: 2.95 **NM** value: **Cover or less**
Partial foil cover. 📖 The Storm Is Rising **A:** Franco Aureliani **W:** Franco Aureliani
1/Ash❑ **NM** value: **1.00**
• Ashcan preview from 1995 Philadelphia Comic Con

FLESH & BLOOD: PRE-EXISTING CONDITIONS — Blindwolf

1 ❑ Cover: 2.95 **NM** value: **Cover or less**
📖 Flesh & Blood: Pre-Existing Conditions; The Angel; Blood Infatuation; Tears **A:** Franco Aureliani; Joseph Tomasini; Bud Larosa **W:** Franco Aureliani; Gary Brown; Wayne A. Harold

FLESH AND BONES — Upshot

1 ❑ full color Cover: 2.00 **NM** value: **Cover or less**
Circ: CapCity orders: **6,400**
📖 The Bojeffries Saga **A:** Dennis Fujitake **W:** Jan Strnad
2 ❑ full color Cover: 2.00 **NM** value: **Cover or less**
Circ: CapCity orders: **4,900**
3 ❑ full color Cover: 2.00 **NM** value: **Cover or less**
Circ: CapCity orders: **4,925**
4 ❑ full color Cover: 2.00 **NM** value: **Cover or less**
Circ: CapCity orders: **4,300**

FLESH CRAWLERS — Kitchen Sink

1 ❑ Cover: 2.50 **NM** value: **Cover or less**
2 ❑ Cover: 2.50 **NM** value: **Cover or less**
3 ❑ Cover: 2.50 **NM** value: **Cover or less**

FLESH GORDON — Aircel

1 ❑ Mar 1992 Cover: 2.95 **NM** value: **Cover or less**
2 ❑ Apr 1992 Cover: 2.95 **NM** value: **Cover or less**
3 ❑ May 1992 Cover: 2.95 **NM** value: **Cover or less**
4 ❑ Jun 1992 Cover: 2.95 **NM** value: **Cover or less**

FLESHPOT — Eros

1 ❑ Oct 1997 Cover: 2.95 **NM** value: **Cover or less**

FLEX MENTALLO — DC / Vertigo

1 ❑ Jun 1996 Cover: 2.50 **NM** value: **8.50**
📖 After the Fact, Part 1 **A:** Frank Quitely **W:** Grant Morrison
2 ❑ Jul 1996 Cover: 2.50 **NM** value: **5.50**
EC parody cover. 📖 After the Fact, Part 2 **A:** Frank Quitely **W:** Grant Morrison
3 ❑ Aug 1996 Cover: 2.50 **NM** value: **5.50**
Dark Knight parody cover. 📖 After the Fact, Part 3 **A:** Frank Quitely **W:** Grant Morrison
4 ❑ Sep 1996 Cover: 2.50 **NM** value: **5.50**
📖 After the Fact, Part 4 **A:** Frank Quitely **W:** Grant Morrison

FLICKERING FLESH — Boneyard

1 ❑ Mar 1993 Cover: 2.50 **NM** value: **Cover or less**

FLICKER'S FLEAS — Fifth Wheel

1 ❑ Cover: 3.00 **NM** value: **Cover or less**

FLINCH — DC / Vertigo

1 ❑ Jun 1999 Cover: 2.50 **NM** value: **Cover or less**
Circ: Diamd. preorders: **31,675**
📖 Rocket-Man; Nice Neighborhood; Wolf Girl Eats **A:** Richard Corben; Frank Quitely; Jim Lee **W:** Bruce Jones; Jen Van Meter; Richard Bruning
2 ❑ Jul 1999 Cover: 2.50 **NM** value: **Cover or less**
Circ: Diamd. preorders: **21,796**
📖 Maggie and Her Microscope; Found Object; Food Chain **A:** Pat McEown; Bill Sienkiewicz; Eduardo Risso **W:** Dean Motter; Bob Fingerman; Brian Azzarello
3 ❑ Aug 1999 Cover: 2.50 **NM** value: **Cover or less**
Circ: Diamd. preorders: **20,271**
📖 Night Terrors; A Walk in The Park; Satanic **A:** Kieron Dwyer; Kelley Jones; Marcelo Frusin **W:** Scott Cunningham; Garth Ennis; John Rozum
4 ❑ Sep 1999 Cover: 2.50 **NM** value: **Cover or less**
Circ: Diamd. preorders: **20,212**
📖 A Gift of Friendship; Fair Trade; Playing Dead **A:** Paul Gulacy; Ty Templeton; Kent Williams **W:** Ty Templeton; Bruce Jones; Kent Williams
5 ❑ Oct 1999 Cover: 2.50 **NM** value: **Cover or less**
Circ: Diamd. preorders: **17,947**
📖 Betrothed; Peeping Bob; Fumes **A:** Marc Hempel; Rick Burchett; James Romberger **W:** Mark Wheatley; Colin Raff; Joe R. Lansdale
6 ❑ Nov 1999 Cover: 2.50 **NM** value: **Cover or less**
Circ: Diamd. preorders: **16,544**
7 ❑ Dec 1999 Cover: 2.50 **NM** value: **Cover or less**
Circ: Diamd. preorders: **15,758**
📖 Parade; It Takes a Village; The Toy **A:** Randy DuBurke; Phil Jimenez; Bill Willingham **W:** Bill Willingham; Jim Woodring; Devin Grayson
8 ❑ Jan 2000 Cover: 2.50 **NM** value: **Cover or less**
Circ: Diamd. preorders: **14,604**
📖 Guts; You've Got Hate Mail; The Lots **A:** Jon J. Muth; Marcelo Frusin; James Romberger **W:** Greg Rucka; John Kuramoto; Robert Rodi
9 ❑ Feb 2000 Cover: 2.50 **NM** value: **Cover or less**
Circ: Diamd. preorders: **15,837**
10 ❑ Mar 2000 Cover: 2.50 **NM** value: **Cover or less**
Circ: Diamd. preorders: **12,719**
11 ❑ Apr 2000 Cover: 2.50 **NM** value: **Cover or less**
Circ: Diamd. preorders: **11,792**
📖 Red Romance; Emergent **A:** Bruce Timm; Cliff Wu Chiang; Dave Taylor **W:** Ian Carney; Joe R. Lansdale; John Rozum
12 ❑ May 2000 Cover: 2.50 **NM** value: **Cover or less**
Circ: Diamd. preorders: **11,601**
📖 Waching You; Mondays; Tin God **A:** Frank Quitely; Ryan Sook; Essad Ribic **W:** Bruce Jones; Scott Cunningham; John Arcudi
13 ❑ 2000 Cover: 2.50 **NM** value: **Cover or less**
Circ: Diamd. preorders: **11,243**
14 ❑ Sep 2000 Cover: 2.50 **NM** value: **Cover or less**
Circ: Diamd. preorders: **11,128**
📖 Resolve; Grave Wisdom, If Wishes Had Wings **A:** Berni Wrightson; Ted McKeever; Tim Levins **W:** Ted McKeever; Bruce Jones; Darko Macan
15 ❑ Nov 2000 Cover: 2.50 **NM** value: **Cover or less**
Circ: Diamd. preorders: **10,231**
📖 A Night to Forget; Watchful; The Future's So Bright **A:** Chris Weston; Arnold Pander; Jacob Pander; Robert Valley **W:** Lucius Shepard; Paul Jenkins; Will Pfeifer
16 ❑ Jan 2001 Cover: 2.50 **NM** value: **Cover or less**
Circ: Diamd. preorders: **9,817**
📖 The Wedding Breakfast; A Temporary Life; Descent **A:** Danijel Zezelj; Philip Bond; Craig Hamilton **W:** Charlie Boatner; Guy Gonzalez; Mike Carey

FLINT ARMBUSTER JR. SPECIAL — Alchemy

1 ❑ b&w Cover: 2.95 **NM** value: **Cover or less**
No issue number.

FLINTSTONE KIDS, THE — Marvel / Star

1 ❑ Aug 1987 Cover: 1.00 **NM** value: **Cover or less**
Circ: CapCity orders: **3,200**
2 ❑ Oct 1987 Cover: 1.00 **NM** value: **Cover or less**
3 ❑ Dec 1987 Cover: 1.00 **NM** value: **Cover or less**
4 ❑ Feb 1988 Cover: 1.00 **NM** value: **Cover or less**
Circ: CapCity orders: **1,650**
5 ❑ Apr 1988 Cover: 1.00 **NM** value: **Cover or less**
Circ: CapCity orders: **1,600**
6 ❑ Jun 1988 Cover: 1.00 **NM** value: **Cover or less**
Circ: CapCity orders: **1,250**
7 ❑ Aug 1988 Cover: 1.00 **NM** value: **Cover or less**
Circ: CapCity orders: **1,200**
📖 Get Lost, Freddy!; 3 Cheers 4 Betty! **A:** Warren Kremer **W:** Angelo Decesare
8 ❑ Oct 1988 Cover: 1.00 **NM** value: **Cover or less**
Circ: CapCity orders: **1,200**
9 ❑ Dec 1988 Cover: 1.00 **NM** value: **Cover or less**
Circ: CapCity orders: **1,100**
10 ❑ Feb 1989 Cover: 1.00 **NM** value: **Cover or less**
Circ: CapCity orders: **1,000**
11 ❑ Apr 1989 Cover: 1.00 **NM** value: **Cover or less**
Circ: CapCity orders: **1,100**

FLINTSTONES 3-D — Blackthorne

1 ❑ Apr 1987 Cover: 2.50 **NM** value: **Cover or less**
Circ: CapCity orders: **3,200**
📖 A-Weigh We Go! • a.k.a. Blackthorne 3-D #19 **A:** Jorge Pacheco **W:** John Stephenson
2 ❑ Fal 1987 Cover: 2.50 **NM** value: **Cover or less**
📖 Sheriff for a Day • a.k.a. Blackthorne 3-D #22 **A:** Jorge Pacheco **W:** John Stephenson
3 ❑ Cover: 2.50 **NM** value: **Cover or less**
Circ: CapCity orders: **1,550**
4 ❑ Cover: 2.50 **NM** value: **Cover or less**
Circ: CapCity orders: **1,150**

FLINTSTONES AND THE JETSONS, THE — DC

1 ❑ Aug 1997 Cover: 1.75 **NM** value: **2.00**
Circ: Diamd. preorders: **3,172**
📖 The Flintstones: Fired!; The Jetsons: Fired! **A:** Glen Hanson **W:** Mike Carlin
2 ❑ Sep 1997 Cover: 1.75 **NM** value: **2.00**
Circ: Diamd. preorders: **9,925**
📖 The Flintstones: The First Purple Dinosaur on TV; The Jetsons: Garbage in, Garbage Out **A:** Glen Hanson; Ivan Brunetti; Thad Doria **W:** Mike Carlin; Sam Henderson
3 ❑ Oct 1997 Cover: 1.75 **NM** value: **2.00**
Circ: Diamd. preorders: **6,835**
• Spacely turned into baby
4 ❑ Nov 1997 Cover: 1.75 **NM** value: **2.00**
Circ: Diamd. preorders: **5,824**
• Gazoo turns Fred and Barney into women
5 ❑ Dec 1997 Cover: 1.75 **NM** value: **2.00**
Circ: Diamd. preorders: **5,025**
📖 Wild Weekend; The Groovy Gruesomes • Judy and Elroy throw a party **A:** Bill Wray; Glen Hanson **W:** Robbie Busch; Matt Wayne
6 ❑ Jan 1998 Cover: 1.95 **NM** value: **2.00**
Circ: Diamd. preorders: **4,766**
📖 Dodo a-Go-Go; The Jetsons: Morphin' Than a Barrel of Monkeys **A:** Glen Hanson; Bill Alger **W:** Robbie Busch; Michael Kupperman
7 ❑ Feb 1998 Cover: 1.95 **NM** value: **2.00**
Circ: Diamd. preorders: **4,415**
• Spies issue
8 ❑ Mar 1998 Cover: 1.95 **NM** value: **2.00**
Circ: Diamd. preorders: **3,719**
• Kung Fu issue
9 ❑ Apr 1998 Cover: 1.95 **NM** value: **2.00**
Circ: Diamd. preorders: **3,351**
📖 I, Rosey!
10 ❑ May 1998 Cover: 1.95 **NM** value: **2.00**
Circ: Diamd. preorders: **3,368**
11 ❑ Jun 1998 Cover: 1.95 **NM** value: **2.00**
Circ: Diamd. preorders: **3,401**
• Time travel
12 ❑ Jul 1998 Cover: 1.95 **NM** value: **2.00**
13 ❑ Aug 1998 Cover: 1.95 **NM** value: **2.00**
Circ: Diamd. preorders: **3,331**
14 ❑ Oct 1998 Cover: 1.99 **NM** value: **2.00**
Circ: Diamd. preorders: **3,165**
15 ❑ Nov 1998 Cover: 1.99 **NM** value: **2.00**
Circ: Diamd. preorders: **2,883**
📖 The Return of Superstone; Cybersox • Super-Fred
16 ❑ Dec 1998 Cover: 1.99 **NM** value: **2.00**
Circ: Diamd. preorders: **2,894**
17 ❑ Jan 1999 Cover: 1.99 **NM** value: **2.00**
Circ: Diamd. preorders: **2,886**
18 ❑ Feb 1999 Cover: 1.99 **NM** value: **2.00**
Circ: Diamd. preorders: **2,809**
📖 It's a Wonderful Prehistoric Life • It's A Wonderful Life homage ★ Appearance of Great Gazoo.
19 ❑ Mar 1999 Cover: 1.99 **NM** value: **2.00**
Circ: Diamd. preorders: **2,608**
• Jetsons Bizarro story
20 ❑ Apr 1999 Cover: 1.99 **NM** value: **2.00**
Circ: Diamd. preorders: **2,566**
21 ❑ May 1999 Cover: 1.99 **NM** value: **Cover or less**
Circ: Diamd. preorders: **2,513**
📖 It's About Time! • Fred and George switch places **A:** Fernando Yache **W:** Allan Neuwirth

FLINTSTONES, THE (ARCHIE) — Archie

1 ❑ Sep 1995 Cover: 1.50 **NM** value: **Cover or less**
Circ: CapCity orders: **3,350** • **CGC:** 1 graded, best 9.6
2 ❑ Oct 1995 Cover: 1.50 **NM** value: **Cover or less**
Circ: CapCity orders: **2,200**
3 ❑ Nov 1995 Cover: 1.50 **NM** value: **Cover or less**

CGC-graded: Multiply prices above by **33 for 9.9 M • 16 for 9.8 NM/M • 7 for 9.6 NM+ • 5 for 9.4 NM • 2.5 for 9.2 NM- • 1.5 for 9.0 VF/NM**

4 ❑ Dec 1995 Cover: 1.50 **NM** value: **Cover or less**
5 ❑ Jan 1996 Cover: 1.50 **NM** value: **Cover or less**
6 ❑ Feb 1996 Cover: 1.50 **NM** value: **Cover or less**
7 ❑ Mar 1996 Cover: 1.50 **NM** value: **Cover or less**
8 ❑ Apr 1996 Cover: 1.50 **NM** value: **Cover or less**
9 ❑ May 1996 Cover: 1.50 **NM** value: **Cover or less**
10 ❑ Jun 1996 Cover: 1.50 **NM** value: **Cover or less**
12 ❑ Aug 1996 Cover: 1.50 **NM** value: **Cover or less**
13 ❑ Sep 1996 Cover: 1.50 **NM** value: **Cover or less**
14 ❑ Oct 1996 Cover: 1.50 **NM** value: **Cover or less**
15 ❑ Nov 1996 Cover: 1.50 **NM** value: **Cover or less**
16 ❑ Dec 1996 Cover: 1.50 **NM** value: **Cover or less**
17 ❑ Jan 1997 Cover: 1.50 **NM** value: **Cover or less**
18 ❑ Feb 1997 Cover: 1.50 **NM** value: **Cover or less**
• Fred becomes a cartoonist
19 ❑ Mar 1997 Cover: 1.50 **NM** value: **Cover or less**
20 ❑ Apr 1997 Cover: 1.50 **NM** value: **Cover or less**
Circ: Diamd. preorders: **2,339**
21 ❑ May 1997 Cover: 1.50 **NM** value: **Cover or less**
Circ: Diamd. preorders: **2,223**
22 ❑ Jun 1997 Cover: 1.50 **NM** value: **Cover or less**
Circ: Diamd. preorders: **2,321**

FLINTSTONES AT THE NEW YORK WORLD'S FAIR — Dell
1 ❑ ca. 1964 Cover: 0.25 **NM** value: **50.00**

FLINTSTONES BIG BOOK, THE — Harvey
1 ❑ Cover: 1.95 **NM** value: **Cover or less**
2 ❑ Cover: 1.95 **NM** value: **Cover or less**

FLINTSTONES BIGGER AND BOULDER — Gold Key
1 ❑ Nov 1962 Cover: 0.25 **NM** value: **75.00**
• **CGC:** 3 graded, best 9.4
2 ❑ Jun 1966 Cover: 0.25 **NM** value: **50.00**
• **CGC:** 2 graded, best 9.0

FLINTSTONES, THE (CHARLTON) — Charlton
With the original TV show on in reruns and its characters turning up in a variety of other animated programs, Charlton obtained the rights to adapt The Flintstones to comics in the early 1970s.

The characters were the "classic" versions, with Pebbles and Bamm-Bamm as infants. (They also appeared as teen-agers in a simultaneously published series from Charlton based on the CBS Saturday morning cartoon.)

Unlike some of Charlton's other humor titles which consisted of short gags, Flintstones mixed in a number of six-to-eight page stories. Art in the series is generally functional but rarely inspired, and Charlton's lackluster printing doesn't help. — JJM

1 ❑ Nov 1970 Cover: 0.15 **NM** value: **35.00**
2 ❑ Jan 1971 Cover: 0.15 **NM** value: **20.00**
3 ❑ Mar 1971 Cover: 0.15 **NM** value: **12.00**
4 ❑ May 1971 Cover: 0.15 **NM** value: **12.00**
5 ❑ Jul 1971 Cover: 0.15 **NM** value: **12.00**
6 ❑ Sep 1971 Cover: 0.15 **NM** value: **8.00**
7 ❑ Oct 1971 Cover: 0.20 **NM** value: **8.00**
8 ❑ Nov 1971 Cover: 0.20 **NM** value: **8.00**
9 ❑ Dec 1971 Cover: 0.20 **NM** value: **8.00**
10 ❑ Jan 1972 Cover: 0.20 **NM** value: **8.00**
Circ: Statement: **188,065**
11 ❑ Feb 1972 Cover: 0.20 **NM** value: **6.00**
Circ: Statement: **188,065**
12 ❑ Mar 1972 Cover: 0.20 **NM** value: **6.00**
Circ: Statement: **188,065**
13 ❑ May 1972 Cover: 0.20 **NM** value: **6.00**
Circ: Statement: **188,065**
14 ❑ Jun 1972 Cover: 0.20 **NM** value: **6.00**
Circ: Statement: **188,065**
15 ❑ Jul 1972 Cover: 0.20 **NM** value: **6.00**
Circ: Statement: **188,065**
16 ❑ Aug 1972 Cover: 0.20 **NM** value: **6.00**
Circ: Statement: **188,065**
17 ❑ Sep 1972 Cover: 0.20 **NM** value: **6.00**
Circ: Statement: **188,065**
18 ❑ Nov 1972 Cover: 0.20 **NM** value: **6.00**
Circ: Statement: **188,065**
19 ❑ Dec 1972 Cover: 0.20 **NM** value: **6.00**
Circ: Statement: **188,065**
20 ❑ Jan 1973 Cover: 0.20 **NM** value: **6.00**
Circ: Statement: **210,090**
21 ❑ Mar 1973 Cover: 0.20 **NM** value: **5.00**
Circ: Statement: **210,090**
22 ❑ Apr 1973 Cover: 0.20 **NM** value: **5.00**
Circ: Statement: **210,090**
• Has 1972 Statement, filed 9/30/72; avg print run 300,000; avg sales 188,000; avg subs 65; avg total paid 188,065; samples 250; office use 300; max existent 188,615; 37% of run returned
23 ❑ ca. 1973 Cover: 0.20 **NM** value: **5.00**
Circ: Statement: **210,090**
24 ❑ ca. 1973 Cover: 0.20 **NM** value: **5.00**
Circ: Statement: **210,090**
25 ❑ ca. 1973 Cover: 0.20 **NM** value: **5.00**
Circ: Statement: **210,090**
26 ❑ Oct 1973 Cover: 0.20 **NM** value: **5.00**
Circ: Statement: **210,090**
27 ❑ 1973 Cover: 0.20 **NM** value: **5.00**
Circ: Statement: **210,090**
28 ❑ 1974 **NM** value: **5.00**
Circ: Statement: **154,200**
29 ❑ May 1974 **NM** value: **5.00**
Circ: Statement: **154,200**
• Has 1973 Statement, filed 9/30/73; avg print run 375,000; avg sales 210,000; avg subs 90; avg total paid 210,090; samples 250; office use 1,000; max existent 211,340; 44% of run returned
30 ❑ ca. 1974 **NM** value: **5.00**
Circ: Statement: **154,200**
31 ❑ ca. 1974 **NM** value: **4.00**
Circ: Statement: **154,200**
32 ❑ ca. 1974 **NM** value: **4.00**
Circ: Statement: **154,200**
33 ❑ Oct 1974 Cover: 0.25 **NM** value: **4.00**
Circ: Statement: **154,200**
34 ❑ Nov 1974 Cover: 0.25 **NM** value: **4.00**
Circ: Statement: **154,200**
35 ❑ Feb 1975 Cover: 0.25 **NM** value: **4.00**
Circ: Statement: **127,750**
36 ❑ Mar 1975 Cover: 0.25 **NM** value: **4.00**
Circ: Statement: **127,750**
37 ❑ May 1975 Cover: 0.25 **NM** value: **4.00**
Circ: Statement: **127,750**
38 ❑ Jun 1975 Cover: 0.25 **NM** value: **4.00**
Circ: Statement: **127,750**
• Has 1974 Statement, filed 9/30/1974; avg print run 310,000; avg sales 154,000; avg subs 200; avg total paid 154,200; samples 200; office use 2,000; max existent 156,400; 50% of run returned
39 ❑ ca. 1975 Cover: 0.25 **NM** value: **4.00**
Circ: Statement: **127,750**
40 ❑ ca. 1975 Cover: 0.25 **NM** value: **4.00**
Circ: Statement: **127,750**
41 ❑ ca. 1975 Cover: 0.25 **NM** value: **4.00**
Circ: Statement: **127,750**
42 ❑ 1975 Cover: 0.25 **NM** value: **4.00**
Circ: Statement: **127,750**
43 ❑ Feb 1976 Cover: 0.25 **NM** value: **4.00**
44 ❑ Mar 1976 Cover: 0.25 **NM** value: **4.00**
📖 King of the Hill; Off to the Races; Bowl Me Down (text); Paper Caper; Only One Cavity, Mom; The Magician • Ray Dirgo, Jay Gill credits
45 ❑ ca. 1976 **NM** value: **4.00**
• Has 1975 Statement, filed 9/30/75; avg print run 325,000; avg sales 127,500; avg subs 250; avg total paid 127,750; samples 200; office use 9,782; max existent 137,732; 58% of run returned
46 ❑ ca. 1976 **NM** value: **4.00**
47 ❑ Aug 1976 Cover: 0.30 **NM** value: **4.00**
📖 Fidners Keepers; Mutiny on the Bedrock Bounty; Strike Out; Don't Bet on It (text) • Ray Dirgo, Jay Gill credits
48 ❑ Oct 1976 Cover: 0.30 **NM** value: **4.00**
📖 A Real Oil-O-Sauus; The Hot Rock; A Good Deal-er (text); Friends to the End • Ray Dirgo credits
49 ❑ Dec 1976 Cover: 0.30 **NM** value: **4.00**
50 ❑ Feb 1977 Cover: 0.30 **NM** value: **4.00**

FLINTSTONES, THE (DELL/GOLD KEY) — Dell / Gold Key
1 ❑ Cover: 0.25 **NM** value: **75.00**
• a.k.a. Dell Giant #48
2 ❑ Dec 1961 Cover: 0.15 **NM** value: **60.00**
3 ❑ Jan 1962 Cover: 0.15 **NM** value: **38.00**
• **CGC:** 1 graded, best 9.4
4 ❑ Mar 1962 Cover: 0.15 **NM** value: **38.00**
5 ❑ May 1962 Cover: 0.15 **NM** value: **38.00**
• **CGC:** 2 graded, best 9.6
6 ❑ Jul 1962 Cover: 0.12 **NM** value: **25.00**
• **CGC:** 1 graded, best 9.6
7 ❑ Oct 1962 Cover: 0.12 **NM** value: **28.00**
• First Gold Key issue
8 ❑ Cover: 0.12 **NM** value: **22.00**
9 ❑ Feb 1963 Cover: 0.12 **NM** value: **22.00**
Circ: Statement: **325,350** • **CGC:** 1 graded, best 8.5
10 ❑ Apr 1963 Cover: 0.12 **NM** value: **22.00**
Circ: Statement: **325,350** • **CGC:** 1 graded, best 9.4
11 ❑ Jun 1963 Cover: 0.12 **NM** value: **18.00**
Circ: Statement: **325,350**
12 ❑ Jul 1963 Cover: 0.12 **NM** value: **18.00**
Circ: Statement: **325,350**
13 ❑ Sep 1963 Cover: 0.12 **NM** value: **18.00**
Circ: Statement: **325,350**
14 ❑ Oct 1963, four-color Cover: 0.12 **NM** value: **18.00**
Circ: Statement: **325,350**
15 ❑ Nov 1963 Cover: 0.12 **NM** value: **18.00**
Circ: Statement: **325,350**
16 ❑ Jan 1964 Cover: 0.12 **NM** value: **18.00**
Circ: Statement: **379,792**
17 ❑ Mar 1964 Cover: 0.12 **NM** value: **18.00**
Circ: Statement: **379,792** • **CGC:** 1 graded, best 9.4
18 ❑ May 1964 Cover: 0.12 **NM** value: **18.00**
Circ: Statement: **379,792**
19 ❑ Jul 1964 Cover: 0.12 **NM** value: **18.00**
Circ: Statement: **379,792** • **CGC:** 1 graded, best 9.2
20 ❑ Aug 1964 Cover: 0.12 **NM** value: **18.00**
Circ: Statement: **379,792** • **CGC:** 1 graded, best 9.2
21 ❑ Sep 1964 Cover: 0.12 **NM** value: **15.00**
Circ: Statement: **379,792** • **CGC:** 1 graded, best 9.4
22 ❑ Oct 1964 Cover: 0.12 **NM** value: **15.00**
Circ: Statement: **379,792** • **CGC:** 1 graded, best 9.2
23 ❑ Nov 1964 Cover: 0.12 **NM** value: **15.00**
Circ: Statement: **379,792** • **CGC:** 1 graded, best 9.2
24 ❑ Jan 1965 Cover: 0.12 **NM** value: **15.00**
Circ: Statement: **374,332** • **CGC:** 1 graded, best 9.4
25 ❑ Mar 1965 Cover: 0.12 **NM** value: **15.00**
Circ: Statement: **374,332** • **CGC:** 1 graded, best 9.6
26 ❑ May 1965 Cover: 0.12 **NM** value: **15.00**
Circ: Statement: **374,332** • **CGC:** 1 graded, best 9.4
27 ❑ Jul 1965 Cover: 0.12 **NM** value: **15.00**
Circ: Statement: **374,332** • **CGC:** 1 graded, best 9.4
28 ❑ Aug 1965 Cover: 0.12 **NM** value: **15.00**
Circ: Statement: **374,332** • **CGC:** 1 graded, best 9.4
29 ❑ Sep 1965 Cover: 0.12 **NM** value: **15.00**
Circ: Statement: **374,332** • **CGC:** 1 graded, best 9.2
30 ❑ Oct 1965 Cover: 0.12 **NM** value: **15.00**
Circ: Statement: **374,332** • **CGC:** 1 graded, best 9.0
31 ❑ Dec 1965 Cover: 0.12 **NM** value: **12.00**
Circ: Statement: **374,332** • **CGC:** 1 graded, best 9.2
32 ❑ Feb 1966 Cover: 0.12 **NM** value: **12.00**
Circ: Statement: **332,362** • **CGC:** 1 graded, best 8.5
33 ❑ Apr 1966 Cover: 0.12 **NM** value: **12.00**
Circ: Statement: **332,362** • **CGC:** 1 graded, best 9.0
34 ❑ Jun 1966 Cover: 0.12 **NM** value: **12.00**
Circ: Statement: **332,362** • **CGC:** 2 graded, best 9.4
35 ❑ Aug 1966 Cover: 0.12 **NM** value: **12.00**
Circ: Statement: **332,362**
36 ❑ Oct 1966 Cover: 0.12 **NM** value: **12.00**
Circ: Statement: **332,362**
37 ❑ Dec 1966 Cover: 0.12 **NM** value: **12.00**
Circ: Statement: **332,362**
38 ❑ Feb 1967 Cover: 0.12 **NM** value: **12.00**
Circ: Statement: **279,885**
39 ❑ Apr 1967 Cover: 0.12 **NM** value: **12.00**
Circ: Statement: **279,885**
40 ❑ Jun 1967 Cover: 0.12 **NM** value: **12.00**
Circ: Statement: **279,885**
41 ❑ Aug 1967 Cover: 0.12 **NM** value: **10.00**
Circ: Statement: **279,885**
42 ❑ Oct 1967 Cover: 0.12 **NM** value: **10.00**
Circ: Statement: **279,885**
43 ❑ Dec 1967 Cover: 0.12 **NM** value: **10.00**
Circ: Statement: **279,885**
44 ❑ Feb 1968 Cover: 0.12 **NM** value: **10.00**
45 ❑ Apr 1968 Cover: 0.12 **NM** value: **10.00**
46 ❑ Jun 1968 Cover: 0.12 **NM** value: **10.00**
47 ❑ Aug 1968 Cover: 0.15 **NM** value: **10.00**
48 ❑ Oct 1968 Cover: 0.15 **NM** value: **10.00**
49 ❑ Dec 1968 Cover: 0.15 **NM** value: **10.00**
• **CGC:** 1 graded, best 9.2
50 ❑ Feb 1969 Cover: 0.15 **NM** value: **10.00**
• **CGC:** 1 graded, best 9.2
51 ❑ Apr 1969 Cover: 0.15 **NM** value: **10.00**
52 ❑ Jun 1969 Cover: 0.15 **NM** value: **10.00**
53 ❑ Aug 1969 Cover: 0.15 **NM** value: **10.00**
54 ❑ Oct 1969 Cover: 0.15 **NM** value: **10.00**
55 ❑ Dec 1969 Cover: 0.15 **NM** value: **10.00**
56 ❑ Feb 1970 Cover: 0.15 **NM** value: **10.00**
57 ❑ Apr 1970 Cover: 0.15 **NM** value: **10.00**
58 ❑ May 1970 Cover: 0.15 **NM** value: **10.00**
59 ❑ Jul 1970 Cover: 0.15 **NM** value: **10.00**
60 ❑ Sep 1970 Cover: 0.15 **NM** value: **10.00**

FLINTSTONES DOUBLEVISION, THE — Harvey
1 ❑ Sep 1994 Cover: 2.95 **NM** value: **Cover or less**
• polybagged with double vision glasses, adaptation of movie

FLINTSTONES GIANT SIZE — Harvey
2 ❑ ca. 1992 Cover: 2.25 **NM** value: **2.50**
3 ❑ ca. 1993 Cover: 2.25 **NM** value: **2.50**

FLINTSTONES, THE (HARVEY) — Harvey
1 ❑ Sep 1992 Cover: 1.25 **NM** value: **2.50**
2 ❑ Jan 1993 Cover: 1.25 **NM** value: **2.00**
3 ❑ ca. 1993 Cover: 1.25 **NM** value: **2.00**
4 ❑ Sep 1993 Cover: 1.25 **NM** value: **2.00**
5 ❑ Oct 1993 Cover: 1.25 **NM** value: **2.00**
6 ❑ Nov 1993 Cover: 1.50 **NM** value: **2.00**
7 ❑ Dec 1993 Cover: 1.50 **NM** value: **2.00**
📖 Derby Day; Little Supercaveman; Yaba-Daba-Do; Feedback; The Sleepwalker; Rich Man, Poor Man
8 ❑ Jan 1994 Cover: 1.50 **NM** value: **2.00**
9 ❑ Feb 1994 Cover: 1.50 **NM** value: **2.00**
📖 Fearless Fred; The Runaways; Fred the Floperoo; Bug Off; Pebbles and Bamm-Bamm in "The Cone"
10 ❑ Mar 1994 Cover: 1.50 **NM** value: **2.00**
📖 The Bedrock Grand Prix; A Puzzling Situation; Who's Who?: Fred Finds a Friend; Better Days are Comin'!
11 ❑ Apr 1994 Cover: 1.50 **NM** value: **2.00**
12 ❑ May 1994 Cover: 1.50 **NM** value: **2.00**
13 ❑ Jun 1994 Cover: 1.50 **NM** value: **2.00**

FLINTSTONES, THE (MARVEL) — Marvel
1 ❑ Oct 1977 Cover: 0.30 **NM** value: **5.00**
• **CGC:** 2 graded, best 9.0
2 ❑ Dec 1977 Cover: 0.35 **NM** value: **3.00**
3 ❑ Feb 1978 Cover: 0.35 **NM** value: **3.00**
4 ❑ Apr 1978 Cover: 0.35 **NM** value: **3.00**
5 ❑ Jun 1978 Cover: 0.35 **NM** value: **3.00**
6 ❑ Aug 1978 Cover: 0.35 **NM** value: **3.00**
7 ❑ Oct 1978 Cover: 0.35 **NM** value: **3.00**
8 ❑ Dec 1978 Cover: 0.35 **NM** value: **3.00**
9 ❑ Feb 1979 Cover: 0.35 **NM** value: **3.00**

FLINTSTONES WITH PEBBLES AND BAMM-BAMM, THE — Gold Key
1 ❑ Nov 1965 Cover: 0.25 **NM** value: **50.00**
• **CGC:** 1 graded, best 9.0
Regular paper (non-glossy) cover.

FLIP — Harvey
1 ❑ Apr 1954 Cover: 0.10 **NM** value: **150.00**
• **CGC:** 2 graded, best 7.5
2 ❑ Jun 1954 Cover: 0.10 **NM** value: **150.00**
• **CGC:** 2 graded, best 6.0

FLIPPER — Gold Key

1 ❑ Apr 1966 Cover: 0.12 **NM** value: **50.00**
• **CGC:** 1 graded, best 7.5
2 ❑ Nov 1966 Cover: 0.12 **NM** value: **40.00**
• **CGC:** 1 graded, best 9.0
3 ❑ Nov 1967 Cover: 0.12 **NM** value: **40.00**
• **CGC:** 1 graded, best 7.0

FLIPPITY AND FLOP — DC

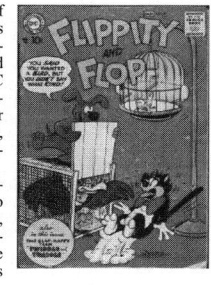

Following the decline of most of its super-hero titles in the late 1940s and early 1950s (only comics featuring Superman, Batman, and Wonder Woman survived), DC (then National Periodical Publications) experimented with other genres, including war, espionage, Westerns, crime, and funny animals.

While some series, such as Leading Comics, added funny animals to a previously super-hero title, others, such as Real Screen Comics, introduced new characters such as The Fox and the Crow, Tito and His Burrito, and Flippity and Flop.

This latter anthropomorphic duo was, respectively, a cat and a canary, who were joined in their misadventures by Sam, the dog. The stories proved popular enough to spin off into this long-running series that was published throughout the 1950s. — Brent

1 ❑ Dec 1951 Cover: 0.10 **NM** value: **200.00**
• **CGC:** 1 graded, best 6.0
2 ❑ Feb 1952 Cover: 0.10 **NM** value: **100.00**
3 ❑ Apr 1952 Cover: 0.10 **NM** value: **75.00**
4 ❑ Jun 1952 Cover: 0.10 **NM** value: **75.00**
5 ❑ Aug 1952 Cover: 0.10 **NM** value: **75.00**
6 ❑ Oct 1952 Cover: 0.10 **NM** value: **75.00**
7 ❑ Dec 1952 Cover: 0.10 **NM** value: **75.00**
8 ❑ Feb 1953 Cover: 0.10 **NM** value: **75.00**
9 ❑ Apr 1953 Cover: 0.10 **NM** value: **75.00**
10 ❑ Jun 1953 Cover: 0.10 **NM** value: **75.00**
11 ❑ Aug 1953 Cover: 0.10 **NM** value: **60.00**
12 ❑ Oct 1953 Cover: 0.10 **NM** value: **60.00**
13 ❑ Dec 1953 Cover: 0.10 **NM** value: **60.00**
14 ❑ Feb 1954 Cover: 0.10 **NM** value: **60.00**
15 ❑ Apr 1954 Cover: 0.10 **NM** value: **60.00**
16 ❑ Jun 1954 Cover: 0.10 **NM** value: **60.00**
17 ❑ Aug 1954 Cover: 0.10 **NM** value: **60.00**
18 ❑ Oct 1954 Cover: 0.10 **NM** value: **60.00**
19 ❑ Dec 1954 Cover: 0.10 **NM** value: **60.00**
20 ❑ Feb 1955 Cover: 0.10 **NM** value: **60.00**
21 ❑ Apr 1955 Cover: 0.10 **NM** value: **50.00**
22 ❑ Jun 1955 Cover: 0.10 **NM** value: **50.00**
23 ❑ Aug 1955 Cover: 0.10 **NM** value: **50.00**
24 ❑ Oct 1955 Cover: 0.10 **NM** value: **50.00**
25 ❑ Cover: 0.10 **NM** value: **50.00**
26 ❑ Cover: 0.10 **NM** value: **50.00**
27 ❑ ca. 1956 Cover: 0.10 **NM** value: **50.00**
28 ❑ ca. 1956 Cover: 0.10 **NM** value: **50.00**
29 ❑ ca. 1956 Cover: 0.10 **NM** value: **50.00**
30 ❑ ca. 1956 Cover: 0.10 **NM** value: **50.00**
31 ❑ Jan 1957 Cover: 0.10 **NM** value: **50.00**
32 ❑ Mar 1957 Cover: 0.10 **NM** value: **50.00**
33 ❑ May 1957 Cover: 0.10 **NM** value: **50.00**
34 ❑ Jul 1957 Cover: 0.10 **NM** value: **50.00**
35 ❑ Sep 1957 Cover: 0.10 **NM** value: **50.00**
36 ❑ Nov 1957 Cover: 0.10 **NM** value: **50.00**
37 ❑ Jan 1958 Cover: 0.10 **NM** value: **50.00**
38 ❑ Mar 1958 Cover: 0.10 **NM** value: **50.00**
39 ❑ May 1958 Cover: 0.10 **NM** value: **50.00**
40 ❑ Jul 1958 Cover: 0.10 **NM** value: **50.00**
41 ❑ Cover: 0.10 **NM** value: **50.00**
42 ❑ Cover: 0.10 **NM** value: **50.00**
43 ❑ Cover: 0.10 **NM** value: **50.00**
44 ❑ Cover: 0.10 **NM** value: **50.00**
45 ❑ Jul 1959 Cover: 0.10 **NM** value: **50.00**
46 ❑ Oct 1959 Cover: 0.10 **NM** value: **50.00**
47 ❑ Nov 1960 Cover: 0.10 **NM** value: **50.00**

FLOATERS — Dark Horse

1 ❑ b&w Cover: 2.50 **NM** value: **Cover or less**
Circ: CapCity orders: **9,400**
2 ❑ b&w Cover: 2.50 **NM** value: **Cover or less**
Circ: CapCity orders: **4,725**
3 ❑ b&w Cover: 2.50 **NM** value: **Cover or less**
Circ: CapCity orders: **3,575**
4 ❑ b&w Cover: 2.50 **NM** value: **Cover or less**
5 ❑ Cover: 2.50 **NM** value: **Cover or less**

FLOCK OF DREAMERS — Kitchen Sink Press

1 ❑ Nov 1997, b&w Cover: 12.95 **NM** value: **Cover or less**
No issue number.

FLOOD RELIEF — Malibu

1 ❑ **NM** value: **5.00**
• Ultraverse Red Cross giveaway.

FLOWERS — Drawn and Quarterly

1 ❑ Cover: 2.95 **NM** value: **Cover or less**

FLOWERS ON THE RAZORWIRE — Boneyard

1 ❑ b&w Cover: 2.95 **NM** value: **Cover or less**
📖 Crows; Silent Treatment; Blood Notes, Part 1; Necropedophile; Matchmaker; Identity Crisis
2 ❑ b&w Cover: 2.95 **NM** value: **Cover or less**
📖 Blood Notes, Part 2; Tears: The Crucifixion; Bumpy Face; Priests F*ck Little Boys **A:** David Badders; Michael Diana; Scott Tullis; Wayne Allen Sallee **W:** Michael Diana; Scott Tullis; Wayne Allen Sallee; William Harms
3 ❑ b&w Cover: 2.95 **NM** value: **Cover or less**
📖 Red Coats; Biffo's Blues; Jesus Crispies **A:** Nelson Danielson; Wayne Reid; Michael Diana **W:** Michael Diana; Pat Gehaty; William Harms
4 ❑ Nov 1994, b&w Cover: 2.95 **NM** value: **Cover or less**
📖 Poem #81 (text); I Wish I Were the Candyman; Poem #41 (text); Contagion; Remains; Blood Caulk
5 ❑ May 1995, b&w Cover: 2.95 **NM** value: **Cover or less**
📖 Dark Angel: The Quiet Demon; It Was Only a Dream; DMZ; The Hitman
6 ❑ May 1995, b&w Cover: 2.95 **NM** value: **Cover or less**
7 ❑ Oct 1995, b&w Cover: 2.95 **NM** value: **Cover or less**
8 ❑ b&w Cover: 2.95 **NM** value: **Cover or less**
9 ❑ b&w Cover: 2.95 **NM** value: **Cover or less**
10 ❑ Apr 1997, b&w Cover: 2.95 **NM** value: **Cover or less**

FLY, THE (ARCHIE) — Archie / Red Circle

1 ❑ May 1983 Cover: 1.00 **NM** value: **3.00**
• **CGC:** 1 graded, best 9.6
📖 The Return Of The Sinister Spider
2 ❑ Jul 1983 Cover: 1.00 **NM** value: **1.50**
3 ❑ Oct 1983 Cover: 1.00 **NM** value: **1.50**
4 ❑ Dec 1983 Cover: 1.00 **NM** value: **1.50**
5 ❑ Feb 1984 Cover: 0.75 **NM** value: **1.50**
6 ❑ Apr 1984 Cover: 0.75 **NM** value: **1.50**
7 ❑ Jun 1984 Cover: 0.75 **NM** value: **1.50**
8 ❑ Aug 1984 Cover: 0.75 **NM** value: **1.50**
9 ❑ Oct 1984 Cover: 0.75 **NM** value: **1.50**

FLY BOY — Ziff-Davis

1 ❑ Spr 1952 Cover: 0.10 **NM** value: **125.00**
2 ❑ Oct 1952 Cover: 0.10 **NM** value: **100.00**

FLY, THE (IMPACT) — DC / Impact

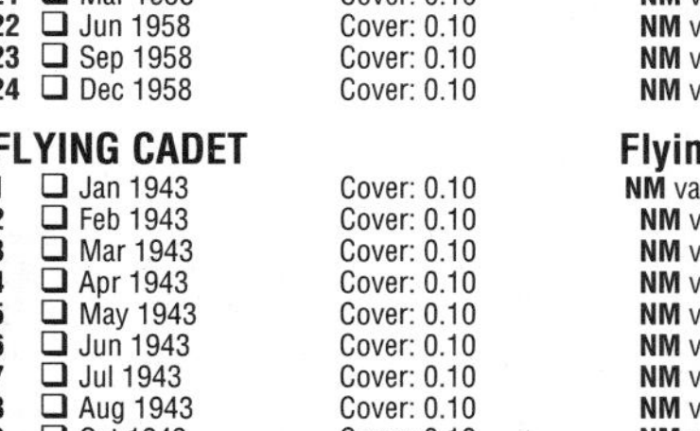

Originally created in the 1940s by Simon and Kirby (the same folks who brought fans Captain America and The Boy Commandos), the Fly has had an on-and-off comics run for almost half a century.

Impact's rendition is Jason Troy, a youngster with a bad habit of playing hand-held video games instead of paying attention in class. As a result, his substitute teacher gives him a special assignment: to create a new heroic character. Jason takes to the assignment, coming up with "The Flyster," a man with the ability of flight. Pleased with his progress, the teacher gives him a present: a fly encased in an amulet of amber. Later, when a villain called Burn-Out sets fire to a local mall, the amulet gives Jason the ability to turn into the character he has created. As The Fly, Jason battles against evil in all its forms — and, of course, the worst comes in spider form.

1 ❑ Aug 1991 Cover: 1.00 **NM** value: **1.25**
Circ: CapCity orders: **38,900**
📖 Forged In Fire **A:** Mike Parobeck **W:** Len Strazewski ★ Origin of The Fly.
2 ❑ Sep 1991 Cover: 1.00 **NM** value: **Cover or less**
Circ: CapCity orders: **21,700**
3 ❑ Oct 1991 Cover: 1.00 **NM** value: **Cover or less**
Circ: CapCity orders: **19,000**
4 ❑ Nov 1991 Cover: 1.00 **NM** value: **Cover or less**
Circ: CapCity orders: **17,150**
5 ❑ Dec 1991 Cover: 1.00 **NM** value: **Cover or less**
Circ: CapCity orders: **16,600**
6 ❑ Jan 1992 Cover: 1.00 **NM** value: **Cover or less**
Circ: CapCity orders: **13,950**
7 ❑ Feb 1992 Cover: 1.00 **NM** value: **Cover or less**
Circ: CapCity orders: **11,750**
8 ❑ Mar 1992 Cover: 1.00 **NM** value: **Cover or less**
Circ: CapCity orders: **10,050**
9 ❑ Apr 1992 Cover: 1.00 **NM** value: **Cover or less**
Circ: CapCity orders: **8,900**
📖 The Coming of The Crusaders, Part 3 ★ 1st Appearance of Fireball. ★ 1st Appearance of Fireball.
10 ❑ May 1992 Cover: 1.00 **NM** value: **Cover or less**
Circ: CapCity orders: **8,400**
11 ❑ Jun 1992 Cover: 1.25 **NM** value: **Cover or less**
Circ: CapCity orders: **8,000**
12 ❑ Jul 1992 Cover: 1.25 **NM** value: **Cover or less**
Circ: CapCity orders: **7,600**
13 ❑ Aug 1992 Cover: 1.25 **NM** value: **Cover or less**
Circ: CapCity orders: **7,700**
14 ❑ Sep 1992 Cover: 1.25 **NM** value: **Cover or less**
Circ: CapCity orders: **6,250**
15 ❑ Oct 1992 Cover: 1.25 **NM** value: **Cover or less**
Circ: CapCity orders: **6,000**
16 ❑ Nov 1992 Cover: 1.25 **NM** value: **Cover or less**
Circ: CapCity orders: **5,550**
📖 Curfew Violation **A:** Mike Parobeck
17 ❑ Dec 1992 Cover: 1.25 **NM** value: **Cover or less**
Circ: CapCity orders: **5,100**
final issue.
Anl 1❑ Cover: 2.50 **NM** value: **Cover or less**
Circ: CapCity orders: **9,300**
• trading card

FLYING ACES — Key

1 ❑ Jul 1955 Cover: 0.10 **NM** value: **35.00**
2 ❑ Sep 1955 Cover: 0.10 **NM** value: **20.00**
3 ❑ Nov 1955 Cover: 0.10 **NM** value: **20.00**
4 ❑ Jan 1956 Cover: 0.10 **NM** value: **20.00**
5 ❑ Mar 1956 Cover: 0.10 **NM** value: **20.00**

FLYING A'S RANGER RIDER — Dell

2 ❑ Jun 1953 Cover: 0.10 **NM** value: **75.00**
3 ❑ Sep 1953 Cover: 0.10 **NM** value: **50.00**
4 ❑ Dec 1953 Cover: 0.10 **NM** value: **50.00**
5 ❑ Mar 1954 Cover: 0.10 **NM** value: **50.00**
6 ❑ Jun 1954 Cover: 0.10 **NM** value: **50.00**
• **CGC:** 1 graded, best 9.2
7 ❑ Sep 1954 Cover: 0.10 **NM** value: **50.00**
8 ❑ Dec 1954 Cover: 0.10 **NM** value: **50.00**
9 ❑ Mar 1955 Cover: 0.10 **NM** value: **50.00**
10 ❑ Jun 1955 Cover: 0.10 **NM** value: **50.00**
• **CGC:** 1 graded, best 9.4
11 ❑ Sep 1955 Cover: 0.10 **NM** value: **40.00**
12 ❑ Dec 1955 Cover: 0.10 **NM** value: **40.00**
• **CGC:** 1 graded, best 9.8
13 ❑ Mar 1956 Cover: 0.10 **NM** value: **40.00**
14 ❑ Jun 1956 Cover: 0.10 **NM** value: **40.00**
15 ❑ Sep 1956 Cover: 0.10 **NM** value: **40.00**
• **CGC:** 1 graded, best 4.5
16 ❑ Dec 1956 Cover: 0.10 **NM** value: **40.00**
• **CGC:** 1 graded, best 5.5
17 ❑ Mar 1957 Cover: 0.10 **NM** value: **40.00**
18 ❑ Jun 1958 Cover: 0.10 **NM** value: **35.00**
19 ❑ Sep 1958 Cover: 0.10 **NM** value: **35.00**
20 ❑ Dec 1957 Cover: 0.10 **NM** value: **35.00**
21 ❑ Mar 1958 Cover: 0.10 **NM** value: **35.00**
22 ❑ Jun 1958 Cover: 0.10 **NM** value: **35.00**
23 ❑ Sep 1958 Cover: 0.10 **NM** value: **35.00**
24 ❑ Dec 1958 Cover: 0.10 **NM** value: **35.00**

FLYING CADET — Flying Cadet

1 ❑ Jan 1943 Cover: 0.10 **NM** value: **100.00**
2 ❑ Feb 1943 Cover: 0.10 **NM** value: **50.00**
3 ❑ Mar 1943 Cover: 0.10 **NM** value: **45.00**
4 ❑ Apr 1943 Cover: 0.10 **NM** value: **45.00**
5 ❑ May 1943 Cover: 0.10 **NM** value: **45.00**
6 ❑ Jun 1943 Cover: 0.10 **NM** value: **45.00**
7 ❑ Jul 1943 Cover: 0.10 **NM** value: **45.00**
8 ❑ Aug 1943 Cover: 0.10 **NM** value: **45.00**
9 ❑ Oct 1943 Cover: 0.10 **NM** value: **45.00**
10 ❑ Jan 1944 Cover: 0.10 **NM** value: **35.00**
11 ❑ Cover: 0.10 **NM** value: **35.00**
12 ❑ Cover: 0.10 **NM** value: **35.00**
13 ❑ Cover: 0.10 **NM** value: **35.00**
14 ❑ Cover: 0.10 **NM** value: **35.00**
15 ❑ Cover: 0.10 **NM** value: **35.00**
16 ❑ Cover: 0.10 **NM** value: **35.00**
17 ❑ Cover: 0.10 **NM** value: **35.00**

FLYING COLORS 10TH ANNIVERSARY SPECIAL — Flying Colors

Celebrating the 10th anniversary of Concord California's Flying Colors comic shop, this comic book collects artwork and editorials from comicdom's finest. Joe Field (listed as publisher/editor/retailer) brings together material from comics legends such as Marvel's Stan Lee, Daniel Bereton (World's Finest), Jeff Nicholson (Ultra Klutz), Andi Watson (Skeleton Key, Geisha), Jim Lee (Fantastic Four, X-Men), Jeff Johnson (Green Lantern), and others. They provide short stories or one-page salutes to the Flying Colors team, while the rest of the book has plenty of photos of some of the comic artists, writers, store staff, and fans who have visited the store over the years.

1 ❑ Sep 1998 Cover: 2.95 **NM** value: **Cover or less**
📖 Funboys: Raiders of the 1951 Chevy Fleetline (delux); Burrito: Godzilla Madness; Father & Son: History Lesson; Smith Brown Jones: Alien Accountant: Hey Kids, Comics!; The Fellowship: Breakfast! **A:** Jeff Bonivert; Ken Hooper; Jeff Johnson; Jim Lee; Andi Watson; Jeff Nicholson; Dan Brereton(cover art); Jon "Bean" Hastings; Carlos Salda±a **W:** Jeff Bonivert; Ken Hooper; Jeff Nicholson; Jon "Bean" Hastings; Carlos Salda±a

FLYING MODELS — Health

3 ❑ May 1954 Cover: 0.05 **NM** value: **50.00**

FLYING NUN — Dell

1 ❑ Feb 1968 Cover: 0.12 **NM** value: **50.00**
• **CGC:** 1 graded, best 8.0
2 ❑ May 1968 Cover: 0.12 **NM** value: **30.00**
• **CGC:** 1 graded, best 9.4
3 ❑ Aug 1968 Cover: 0.12 **NM** value: **30.00**
4 ❑ Cover: 0.12 **NM** value: **30.00**

FLYING SAUCERS — Avon

1 ❑ ca. 1950 Cover: 0.10 **NM** value: **700.00**
• **CGC:** 5 graded, best 8.0
2 ❑ ca. 1952 Cover: 0.10 **NM** value: **350.00**
• **CGC:** 2 graded, best 9.2
3 ❑ Cover: 0.10 **NM** value: **250.00**

FLYING SAUCERS (DELL) — Dell

1 ❑ Apr 1967 Cover: 0.12 **NM** value: **22.00**
• **CGC:** 2 graded, best 8.5
2 ❑ Jul 1967 Cover: 0.12 **NM** value: **12.50**

CGC-graded: Multiply prices above by **33 for 9.9 M • 16 for 9.8 NM/M • 7 for 9.6 NM+ • 5 for 9.4 NM • 2.5 for 9.2 NM- • 1.5 for 9.0 VF/NM**

3 ❑ Oct 1967 Cover: 0.12 **NM** value: **12.50**
4 ❑ Nov 1967 Cover: 0.12 **NM** value: **12.50**
📖 Race With a…?
5 ❑ Oct 1969 Cover: 0.15 **NM** value: **12.50**
final issue.

FLYIN' JENNY — Pentagon
1 ❑ ca. 1946 Cover: 0.10 **NM** value: **100.00**
2 ❑ Cover: 0.10 **NM** value: **100.00**

FLY MAN — Archie / Radio
When Tom Troy, attorney-at-law, rubs his Fly Man ring, he is transformed into The Fly, a being with insectlike powers. His amazing powers, weapons, and flying ability were granted to him by a mysterious alien named Turan, an inhabitant of the other-dimensional Fly World.

Passing back and forth through the dimensional passageway between the two worlds, Fly Man has adventures both on Earth and, at times, even on Fly World. He must survive encounters with such deadly villains as the insane Mighty Man, while maintaining his law practice and dating the gorgeous actress Kim Brand, also known as Fly Girl.

In addition to Fly Man tales, issues may contain short stories featuring other Mighty Comics Group heroes, such as the patriotic Shield, the henpecked Web, and the mysterious Black Hood, as well as additional members of the super-hero group the Mighty Crusaders — all presented in a familiar Silver Age style.

This series is continued from Adventures of the Fly #31 and is, itself, continued after issue #39 as Mighty Comics.

32 ❑ Jul 1965 Cover: 0.12 **NM** value: **18.00**
Circ: Statement: **160,235**
• Series continued from Adventures of the Fly #31
33 ❑ Sep 1965 Cover: 0.12 **NM** value: **16.00**
Circ: Statement: **160,235**
34 ❑ Nov 1965 Cover: 0.12 **NM** value: **16.00**
Circ: Statement: **160,235**
35 ❑ Jan 1966 Cover: 0.12 **NM** value: **16.00**
36 ❑ Mar 1966 Cover: 0.12 **NM** value: **16.00**
📖 Fly Man's Strangest Dilemma; The Shield: Sufer, Shield, Suffer!; The Origin of the Web **A:** Paul Are **W:** Jerry Ess ★ Origin of The Web.
37 ❑ May 1966 Cover: 0.12 **NM** value: **16.00**
• Has 1965 Statement, filed 10/1/65; avg print run 308,205; avg sales 160,235; avg subs 0; avg total paid 160,235; samples 0; max existent 160,235; 48% of run returned
38 ❑ Jul 1966 Cover: 0.12 **NM** value: **16.00**
39 ❑ Sep 1966 Cover: 0.12 **NM** value: **16.00**
• Series continued in Mighty Comics #40

FOCUS — DC
1 ❑ Sum 1987 **NM** value: **1.00**
no cover price. **A:** Bill Sienkiewicz; George Pérez

FOES — Ram
1 ❑ **NM** value: **1.95**

FOODANG — Continuüm
1 ❑ Jul 1994, b&w Cover: 1.95 **NM** value: **Cover or less**
foil cover. **A:** Michael Duggan **W:** Michael Duggan
Ash 1❑ **NM** value: **1.00**
• Ashcan promotional edition. • Previews Foodang #1; Flip Book with The Dark Ashcan #1 **A:** Michael Duggan **W:** Michael Duggan ★ 1st Appearance of Foodang.

FOODANG (2ND SERIES) — August House
1 ❑ Jan 1995 Cover: 2.50 **NM** value: **Cover or less**
enhanced cover. • oversized trading card.

FOODINI — Continental
1 ❑ Mar 1950 Cover: 0.10 **NM** value: **150.00**
2 ❑ Apr 1950 Cover: 0.10 **NM** value: **75.00**
3 ❑ May 1950 Cover: 0.10 **NM** value: **50.00**
4 ❑ Aug 1950 Cover: 0.10 **NM** value: **50.00**

FOOFUR — Marvel / Star
1 ❑ Aug 1987 Cover: 1.00 **NM** value: **Cover or less**
Circ: CapCity orders: **2,100**
2 ❑ Oct 1987 Cover: 1.00 **NM** value: **Cover or less**
3 ❑ Dec 1987 Cover: 1.00 **NM** value: **Cover or less**
4 ❑ Feb 1988 Cover: 1.00 **NM** value: **Cover or less**
📖 Fernando's Hideaway **A:** Ben Brown **W:** Tony Frango
5 ❑ Apr 1988 Cover: 1.00 **NM** value: **Cover or less**
Circ: CapCity orders: **1,150**
6 ❑ Jun 1988 Cover: 1.00 **NM** value: **Cover or less**
Circ: CapCity orders: **850**

FOOLKILLER — Marvel

Kurt Gerhardt's life was falling apart. His father had just been murdered by a gang of muggers who decided to kill him when they found he had only six dollars to steal. Still reeling from that loss, Kurt lost his job when his bank was declared insolvent. Then his wife left him. Kurt was forced to take a job at a fast-food restaurant, only to have the place robbed. And he got a crack on the head when he tried to stop the robbers.

Kurt is "born again" when he sees Greg Salinger, the Foolkiller (first seen in The Defenders), on a TV broadcast. Salinger inspires Kurt to stop the criminals, the thugs, the junkies — the "fools" of the world. Kurt soon takes on the costume, weapons, and mission of the FoolKiller. That mission was to eradicate fools, permanently.

FoolKiller is a haunting story of flawed justice and the penalties it exacts.

1 ❑ Oct 1990 Cover: 1.75 **NM** value: **2.00**
Circ: CapCity orders: **27,300**
2 ❑ Nov 1990 Cover: 1.75 **NM** value: **2.00**
Circ: CapCity orders: **20,800**
3 ❑ Dec 1990 Cover: 1.75 **NM** value: **2.00**
Circ: CapCity orders: **19,850**
cover says Nov, indicia says Dec.
4 ❑ Jan 1991 Cover: 1.75 **NM** value: **2.00**
Circ: CapCity orders: **19,700**
5 ❑ Feb 1991 Cover: 1.75 **NM** value: **2.00**
Circ: CapCity orders: **19,000**
📖 Body Count **A:** J.J. Birch; Tony DeZuniga **W:** Steve Gerber
6 ❑ Apr 1991 Cover: 1.75 **NM** value: **2.00**
Circ: CapCity orders: **16,700**
📖 Fool's Paradise **A:** J.J. Birch; Tony DeZuniga **W:** Steve Gerber
7 ❑ 1991 Cover: 1.75 **NM** value: **2.00**
Circ: CapCity orders: **15,000**
8 ❑ Jul 1991 Cover: 1.75 **NM** value: **2.00**
Circ: CapCity orders: **14,600**
• Spider-Man★ Appearance of Spider-Man.
9 ❑ 1991 Cover: 1.75 **NM** value: **2.00**
Circ: CapCity orders: **14,600**
10 ❑ 1991 Cover: 1.75 **NM** value: **2.00**
Circ: CapCity orders: **14,400**

FOOM MAGAZINE — Marvel
One of the hallmarks of Stan Lee's reign at Marvel Comics was the creation of fan clubs for loyal Marvel readers. These usually had crazy names, including M.M.M.S. (the Merry Marvel Marching Society) and FOOM (Friends of Ol' Marvel). Admission to the latter club was $4, for which the member would receive an official ID card, stick-ons, a poster, and a subscription to "Marveldom's favorite fan mag" — FOOM Magazine.

FOOM gave its readers the inside scoop on the goings on at madcap Marvel. Included were news on Marvel happenings around town, profiles on creators such as Ed Hannigan and John Romita, features on such then-new titles as The Defenders, and decidedly young-looking photos of legends like Gil Kane and Walt Simonson. By no stretch of the imagination was this the hard-hitting journalism the comics press strives for today, but FOOM was adorable in its silliness and self-promotion.

1 ❑ **NM** value: **16.00**
Circ: CapCity orders: **14,500**
2 ❑ **NM** value: **12.00**
3 ❑ **NM** value: **15.00**
• Spider-Man issue; Interview with Stan Lee
4 ❑ Win 1973 **NM** value: **10.00**
5 ❑ Spr 1974 **NM** value: **7.00**
6 ❑ **NM** value: **7.00**
7 ❑ **NM** value: **7.00**
8 ❑ **NM** value: **7.00**
9 ❑ **NM** value: **7.00**
10 ❑ **NM** value: **7.00**
11 ❑ **NM** value: **7.00**
12 ❑ **NM** value: **7.00**
13 ❑ **NM** value: **7.00**
14 ❑ **NM** value: **7.00**
15 ❑ **NM** value: **7.00**
16 ❑ **NM** value: **7.00**
17 ❑ **NM** value: **7.00**
18 ❑ **NM** value: **7.00**

FOOTBALL HEROES — Personality
1 ❑ b&w **NM** value: **2.95**
2 ❑ b&w **NM** value: **2.95**

FOOTBALL THRILLS — Ziff-Davis
1 ❑ Fal 1951 Cover: 0.10 **NM** value: **200.00**
2 ❑ Fal 1952 Cover: 0.10 **NM** value: **125.00**

FOOT SOLDIERS, THE — Dark Horse
This limited series from Jim Krueger and Michael Avon Oeming takes place in a dystopian future overrun by technological tyrants. All the old heroes are dead. Hope has been crushed by mechanical "beetles" that patrol the streets of the unnamed city in the unnamed country in which the story is set — until a mysterious hooded man encourages three kids (Story, Rags, and Johnny) to rob the heroes' graves, take their footgear, and become new heroes to the beleaguered citizenry. With that, The Second Story Kid, The Man of the Cloth, and Johnny Stomp burst onto the scene, inspiring faith in a promising future and turning the tide of oppression. As an added bonus, Foot Soldiers also sports cover and pinup art by the likes of Alex Ross, Mike Mignola, Paul Chadwick, and Mike Allred.

1 ❑ Jan 1996 Cover: 2.95 **NM** value: **Cover or less**
Circ: Diamd. preorders: **10,803**
2 ❑ Feb 1996 Cover: 2.95 **NM** value: **Cover or less**
Circ: Diamd. preorders: **8,032**
3 ❑ Mar 1996 Cover: 2.95 **NM** value: **Cover or less**
4 ❑ Apr 1996 Cover: 2.95 **NM** value: **Cover or less**
Bk 1❑ Cover: 14.95 **NM** value: **Cover or less**
• Collects Foot Soldiers #1-4 **A:** Michael Avon Oeming **W:** Jim Krueger

FOOT SOLDIERS (VOL. 2) — Image
1 ❑ Sep 1997, b&w Cover: 2.95 **NM** value: **Cover or less**
Circ: Diamd. preorders: **8,049**
📖 Walls; Arch Enemies, Part 1; First Steps **A:** Michael Avon Oeming **W:** Jim Krueger
2 ❑ Nov 1997, b&w Cover: 2.95 **NM** value: **Cover or less**
Circ: Diamd. preorders: **5,147**
📖 Arch Enemies, Part 2 **A:** Michael Avon Oeming **W:** Jim Krueger
3 ❑ Jan 1998, b&w Cover: 2.95 **NM** value: **Cover or less**
Circ: Diamd. preorders: **3,975**
📖 Arch Enemies, Part 3 **A:** Michael Avon Oeming **W:** Jim Krueger
4 ❑ Mar 1998, b&w Cover: 2.95 **NM** value: **Cover or less**
Circ: Diamd. preorders: **3,113**
📖 Arch Enemies, Part 4 **A:** Michael Avon Oeming **W:** Jim Krueger
5 ❑ May 1998, b&w Cover: 2.95 **NM** value: **Cover or less**
Circ: Diamd. preorders: **2,690**
📖 Arch Enemies, Part 5; The Battle of Old; Footsoldiers: The Spokesman **A:** Matt Smith; Steve Yeowell; Michael Avon Oeming; Phil Hester **W:** Jim Krueger

FORBIDDEN 3-D — 3-D Zone
1 ❑ Cover: 3.95 **NM** value: **Cover or less**
No issue number. • non 3-D version
1/3D❑ Cover: 3.95 **NM** value: **Cover or less**
No issue number. • 3-D version with glasses

FORBIDDEN FRANKENSTEIN — Fantagraphics / Eros
All issues are adults only.
1 ❑ b&w Cover: 2.25 **NM** value: **Cover or less**
2 ❑ b&w Cover: 2.50 **NM** value: **Cover or less**

FORBIDDEN KINGDOM, THE — Eastern
1 ❑ Nov 1987 Cover: 1.95 **NM** value: **Cover or less**

FORBIDDEN KNOWLEDGE — Last Gasp
1 ❑ Cover: 0.75 **NM** value: **4.00**
📖 The Notorious Hell-Fire-Club; Alcibiades The Phalos Smasher; Stars of The Roman Coliseum; Plague of Treponema Pallidum!; Blood Lust of The Tupinamba; A Most Unusual Way to… **A:** Art Vitello; Dennis Ellison; George Di Caprio; Jim Himes; Matt Golden; Milt Gray; Rich Chidlaw; Brent Boates; Chris Lane **W:** Art Vitello; Dennis Ellison; George Di Caprio; Jim Himes; Matt Golden; Milt Gray; Rich Chidlaw; Brent Boates; Chris Lane

FORBIDDEN KNOWLEDGE: ADVENTURE BEYOND THE DOORWAY TO SOULS WITH RADICAL DREAMER — Mark's Giant Economy Size
1 ❑ b&w Cover: 3.50 **NM** value: **Cover or less**
No issue number. One-shot. infinity cover.

FORBIDDEN LOVE — Quality
1 ❑ Mar 1950 Cover: 0.10 **NM** value: **400.00**
2 ❑ May 1950 Cover: 0.10 **NM** value: **250.00**
• **CGC:** 3 graded, best 8.5
3 ❑ Jul 1950 Cover: 0.10 **NM** value: **200.00**
4 ❑ Sep 1950 Cover: 0.10 **NM** value: **200.00**

FORBIDDEN PLANET — Innovation
1 ❑ Cover: 2.50 **NM** value: **Cover or less**
Circ: CapCity orders: **8,775**
📖 Relief Ship **A:** Daerick Gr÷ss **W:** David Campiti; Allen Adler; Cyril Hume; Irving Block
2 ❑ Cover: 2.50 **NM** value: **Cover or less**
Circ: CapCity orders: **5,415**
3 ❑ Sep 1992 Cover: 2.50 **NM** value: **Cover or less**
Circ: CapCity orders: **4,435**
4 ❑ Cover: 2.50 **NM** value: **Cover or less**
Circ: CapCity orders: **3,775**
Bk 1❑ **NM** value: **4.95**
📖 Saga of the Krell

FORBIDDEN SUBJECTS — Angel
0 ❑ Cover: 2.95 **NM** value: **Cover or less**
0/A ❑ Cover: 3.95 **NM** value: **Cover or less**
• Nude edition A. **A:** Kevin Townson
0/B ❑ Cover: 3.95 **NM** value: **Cover or less**
• Nude edition B. **A:** Kevin Townson

FORBIDDEN SUBJECTS: CANDY KISSES — Angel
1 ❑ Cover: 3.00 **NM** value: **Cover or less**
Censored cover. **A:** Kevin Townson
1/B ❑ Cover: 3.00 **NM** value: **Cover or less**
Adult cover. **A:** Kevin Townson

FORBIDDEN TALES OF DARK MANSION — DC
5 ❑ Jun 1972 Cover: 0.25 **NM** value: **8.00**
• **CGC:** 1 graded, best 9.0
• Series continued from The Dark Mansion of Forbidden Love #4
6 ❑ Aug 1972 Cover: 0.20 **NM** value: **8.00**
📖 The Psychic Blood-Hound; Mind-Bending Tales; Diary of a Dead Woman! **A:** José Delbo **W:** Mike Friedrich
7 ❑ Oct 1972 Cover: 0.20 **NM** value: **8.00**
📖 Eye of the Beholder; Realm of the Mystic; The Immortality Thieves!; The Royal Right **A:** Howard Chaykin; Fred Harper; Michael W. Kaluta; Tony DeZuniga; Bill Draut **W:** Joe Orlando; Robert Kanigher
8 ❑ Dec 1972 Cover: 0.20 **NM** value: **8.00**
9 ❑ Feb 1973 Cover: 0.20 **NM** value: **8.00**
10 ❑ Apr 1973 Cover: 0.20 **NM** value: **8.00**

Other grades: Multiply prices above by **1.5 for Mint • 2/3 for Very Fine • 1/3 for Fine • 1/5 for Very Good • 1/8 for Good**

11 ❑ Jul 1973 Cover: 0.20 **NM** value: **8.00**
12 ❑ Sep 1973 Cover: 0.20 **NM** value: **8.00**
📖 A Change Of Bodies; Death Laughed Last; Witch's Tails
13 ❑ Nov 1973 Cover: 0.20 **NM** value: **8.00**
14 ❑ Jan 1974 Cover: 0.20 **NM** value: **8.00**
15 ❑ Mar 1974 Cover: 0.20 **NM** value: **8.00**
final issue.

FORBIDDEN VAMPIRE — Angel

0 ❑ Cover: 2.95 **NM** value: **Cover or less**

FORBIDDEN WORLDS — ACG

ACG's Forbidden Worlds was another of the original science-fiction/horror titles of the early 1950s. The first several years of Forbidden Worlds featured stories with a horror theme. Toward the middle of the run, around the advent of the Comics Code, the focus shifted toward straight science fiction, with the usual space wars, giant robots, and dinosaur planets common to the stories of that time. In later issues, around the dawning of the Silver Age, Forbidden Worlds featured a science-fiction super-hero called Magicman. But the real hit was Ogden Whitney's kid-humor/super-hero spoof series, Herbie, the Fat Fury, which appeared several times in the unlikely pages of Forbidden Worlds before graduating to his own series.

ACG drew on some of the better comics talent of the day, with early issues featuring art by Al Williamson, Frank Frazetta, and Joe Orlando.

1 ❑ Jul 1951 Cover: 0.10 **NM** value: **1000.00**
• **CGC:** 8 graded, best 9.4
2 ❑ Sep 1951 Cover: 0.10 **NM** value: **540.00**
• **CGC:** 3 graded, best 9.0
3 ❑ Nov 1951 Cover: 0.10 **NM** value: **485.00**
• **CGC:** 1 graded, best 6.0
4 ❑ Jan 1952 Cover: 0.10 **NM** value: **270.00**
• **CGC:** 3 graded, best 9.2
5 ❑ Mar 1952 Cover: 0.10 **NM** value: **335.00**
• **CGC:** 1 graded, best 5.5
6 ❑ May 1952 Cover: 0.10 **NM** value: **335.00**
• **CGC:** 2 graded, best 9.2
7 ❑ Jul 1952 Cover: 0.10 **NM** value: **190.00**
• **CGC:** 1 graded, best 6.5
8 ❑ Aug 1952 Cover: 0.10 **NM** value: **190.00**
9 ❑ Sep 1952 Cover: 0.10 **NM** value: **190.00**
• **CGC:** 2 graded, best 9.4
10 ❑ Oct 1952 Cover: 0.10 **NM** value: **190.00**
11 ❑ Nov 1952 Cover: 0.10 **NM** value: **135.00**
12 ❑ Dec 1952 Cover: 0.10 **NM** value: **135.00**
• **CGC:** 3 graded, best 9.4
13 ❑ Jan 1953 Cover: 0.10 **NM** value: **135.00**
14 ❑ Feb 1953 Cover: 0.10 **NM** value: **135.00**
15 ❑ Mar 1953 Cover: 0.10 **NM** value: **135.00**
16 ❑ Apr 1953 Cover: 0.10 **NM** value: **100.00**
17 ❑ May 1953 Cover: 0.10 **NM** value: **100.00**
18 ❑ Jun 1953 Cover: 0.10 **NM** value: **100.00**
19 ❑ Jul 1953 Cover: 0.10 **NM** value: **100.00**
20 ❑ Aug 1953 Cover: 0.10 **NM** value: **100.00**
• **CGC:** 1 graded, best 9.0
21 ❑ Sep 1953 Cover: 0.10 **NM** value: **85.00**
22 ❑ Oct 1953 Cover: 0.10 **NM** value: **85.00**
• **CGC:** 1 graded, best 8.5
23 ❑ Nov 1953 Cover: 0.10 **NM** value: **85.00**
24 ❑ Dec 1953 Cover: 0.10 **NM** value: **85.00**
• **CGC:** 1 graded, best 8.5
25 ❑ Jan 1954 Cover: 0.10 **NM** value: **85.00**
• **CGC:** 1 graded, best 8.0
26 ❑ Feb 1954 Cover: 0.10 **NM** value: **85.00**
• **CGC:** 1 graded, best 8.0
27 ❑ Mar 1954 Cover: 0.10 **NM** value: **85.00**
28 ❑ Apr 1954 Cover: 0.10 **NM** value: **85.00**
• **CGC:** 1 graded, best 9.4
29 ❑ May 1954 Cover: 0.10 **NM** value: **85.00**
• **CGC:** 1 graded, best 9.0
30 ❑ Jun 1954 Cover: 0.10 **NM** value: **85.00**
• **CGC:** 1 graded, best 9.0
31 ❑ Jul 1954 Cover: 0.10 **NM** value: **75.00**
• **CGC:** 1 graded, best 8.5
32 ❑ Aug 1954 Cover: 0.10 **NM** value: **75.00**
• **CGC:** 1 graded, best 8.5
33 ❑ Sep 1954 Cover: 0.10 **NM** value: **75.00**
• **CGC:** 1 graded, best 9.4
34 ❑ Oct 1954 Cover: 0.10 **NM** value: **75.00**
35 ❑ Aug 1955 Cover: 0.10 **NM** value: **75.00**
36 ❑ Sep 1955 Cover: 0.10 **NM** value: **75.00**
37 ❑ Oct 1955 Cover: 0.10 **NM** value: **75.00**
38 ❑ Nov 1955 Cover: 0.10 **NM** value: **75.00**
39 ❑ Dec 1955 Cover: 0.10 **NM** value: **75.00**
40 ❑ Jan 1956 Cover: 0.10 **NM** value: **75.00**
41 ❑ Feb 1956 Cover: 0.10 **NM** value: **54.00**
• **CGC:** 1 graded, best 8.5
42 ❑ Mar 1956 Cover: 0.10 **NM** value: **54.00**
• **CGC:** 1 graded, best 9.0
43 ❑ May 1956 Cover: 0.10 **NM** value: **54.00**
44 ❑ Jul 1956 Cover: 0.10 **NM** value: **54.00**
45 ❑ Aug 1956 Cover: 0.10 **NM** value: **54.00**
46 ❑ Sep 1956 Cover: 0.10 **NM** value: **54.00**
47 ❑ Oct 1956 Cover: 0.10 **NM** value: **54.00**
48 ❑ Nov 1956 Cover: 0.10 **NM** value: **54.00**
49 ❑ Dec 1956 Cover: 0.10 **NM** value: **54.00**
50 ❑ Jan 1957 Cover: 0.10 **NM** value: **54.00**
51 ❑ Feb 1957 Cover: 0.10 **NM** value: **45.00**
52 ❑ Mar 1957 Cover: 0.10 **NM** value: **45.00**
53 ❑ Apr 1957 Cover: 0.10 **NM** value: **45.00**
54 ❑ May 1957 Cover: 0.10 **NM** value: **45.00**
• **CGC:** 1 graded, best 8.5
55 ❑ Jun 1957 Cover: 0.10 **NM** value: **45.00**
56 ❑ Jul 1957 Cover: 0.10 **NM** value: **45.00**
57 ❑ Aug 1957 Cover: 0.10 **NM** value: **45.00**
58 ❑ Sep 1957 Cover: 0.10 **NM** value: **45.00**
59 ❑ Oct 1957 Cover: 0.10 **NM** value: **45.00**
60 ❑ Nov 1957 Cover: 0.10 **NM** value: **45.00**
• **CGC:** 1 graded, best 9.0
61 ❑ Dec 1957 Cover: 0.10 **NM** value: **40.00**
62 ❑ Jan 1958 Cover: 0.10 **NM** value: **40.00**
63 ❑ Feb 1958 Cover: 0.10 **NM** value: **40.00**
64 ❑ Mar 1958 Cover: 0.10 **NM** value: **40.00**
65 ❑ Apr 1958 Cover: 0.10 **NM** value: **40.00**
66 ❑ May 1958 Cover: 0.10 **NM** value: **40.00**
67 ❑ Jun 1958 Cover: 0.10 **NM** value: **40.00**
68 ❑ Jul 1958 Cover: 0.10 **NM** value: **40.00**
69 ❑ Aug 1958 Cover: 0.10 **NM** value: **40.00**
70 ❑ Sep 1958 Cover: 0.10 **NM** value: **40.00**
71 ❑ Oct 1958 Cover: 0.10 **NM** value: **35.00**
72 ❑ Nov 1958 Cover: 0.10 **NM** value: **35.00**
73 ❑ Dec 1958 Cover: 0.10 **NM** value: **275.00**
74 ❑ Jan 1959 Cover: 0.10 **NM** value: **35.00**
75 ❑ Feb 1959 Cover: 0.10 **NM** value: **35.00**
76 ❑ Mar 1959 Cover: 0.10 **NM** value: **35.00**
77 ❑ Apr 1959 Cover: 0.10 **NM** value: **35.00**
78 ❑ May 1959 Cover: 0.10 **NM** value: **35.00**
79 ❑ Jun 1959 Cover: 0.10 **NM** value: **35.00**
80 ❑ Jul 1959 Cover: 0.10 **NM** value: **35.00**
81 ❑ Aug 1959 Cover: 0.10 **NM** value: **24.00**
82 ❑ Sep 1959 Cover: 0.10 **NM** value: **24.00**
83 ❑ Oct 1959 Cover: 0.10 **NM** value: **24.00**
84 ❑ Nov 1959 Cover: 0.10 **NM** value: **24.00**
85 ❑ Jan 1960 Cover: 0.10 **NM** value: **24.00**
Circ: Statement: **187,200**
86 ❑ Mar 1960 Cover: 0.10 **NM** value: **30.00**
Circ: Statement: **187,200** • **CGC:** 1 graded, best 9.2
Flying saucer cover. **A:** Ogden Whitney
87 ❑ May 1960 Cover: 0.10 **NM** value: **24.00**
Circ: Statement: **187,200**
88 ❑ Jul 1960 Cover: 0.10 **NM** value: **24.00**
Circ: Statement: **187,200**
89 ❑ Aug 1960 Cover: 0.10 **NM** value: **24.00**
Circ: Statement: **187,200** • **CGC:** 1 graded, best 9.4
90 ❑ Sep 1960 Cover: 0.10 **NM** value: **24.00**
Circ: Statement: **187,200**
91 ❑ Oct 1960 Cover: 0.10 **NM** value: **20.00**
Circ: Statement: **187,200**
92 ❑ Nov 1960 Cover: 0.10 **NM** value: **20.00**
Circ: Statement: **187,200**
93 ❑ Jan 1961 Cover: 0.10 **NM** value: **20.00**
Circ: Statement: **178,600**
94 ❑ Mar 1961 Cover: 0.10 **NM** value: **55.00**
Circ: Statement: **178,600**
95 ❑ May 1961 Cover: 0.10 **NM** value: **20.00**
Circ: Statement: **178,600**
96 ❑ Jul 1961 Cover: 0.10 **NM** value: **20.00**
Circ: Statement: **178,600**
97 ❑ Aug 1961 Cover: 0.10 **NM** value: **20.00**
Circ: Statement: **178,600**
98 ❑ Sep 1961 Cover: 0.10 **NM** value: **20.00**
Circ: Statement: **178,600**
99 ❑ Oct 1961 Cover: 0.10 **NM** value: **20.00**
Circ: Statement: **178,600**
100 ❑ Nov 1961 Cover: 0.10 **NM** value: **20.00**
Circ: Statement: **178,600**
101 ❑ Jan 1962 Cover: 0.12 **NM** value: **16.00**
Circ: Statement: **178,600**
102 ❑ Mar 1962 Cover: 0.12 **NM** value: **16.00**
Circ: Statement: **178,600** • **CGC:** 1 graded, best 9.4
103 ❑ May 1962 Cover: 0.12 **NM** value: **16.00**
Circ: Statement: **178,600**
104 ❑ Jul 1962 Cover: 0.12 **NM** value: **16.00**
Circ: Statement: **178,600**
105 ❑ Aug 1962 Cover: 0.12 **NM** value: **16.00**
Circ: Statement: **178,600**
106 ❑ Sep 1962 Cover: 0.12 **NM** value: **16.00**
Circ: Statement: **178,600**
107 ❑ Oct 1962 Cover: 0.12 **NM** value: **16.00**
Circ: Statement: **178,600**
📖 The Endless Rooms!; Mysterious Island; Child of Evil; The Ghost of the Museum! **A:** Ogden Whitney; Rudi Palais **W:** L'Afcadio Lee; Pierce Rand; Pierre Alonzo
108 ❑ Nov 1962 Cover: 0.12 **NM** value: **16.00**
Circ: Statement: **178,600**
109 ❑ Jan 1963 Cover: 0.12 **NM** value: **16.00**
Circ: Statement: **169,603**
110 ❑ Mar 1963 Cover: 0.12 **NM** value: **35.00**
Circ: Statement: **169,603**
111 ❑ May 1963 Cover: 0.12 **NM** value: **16.00**
Circ: Statement: **169,603**
112 ❑ Jul 1963 Cover: 0.12 **NM** value: **16.00**
Circ: Statement: **169,603**
📖 This Man is Dangerous!; The Case for E.S.P.; The Ghost of Lefty Shane; Land of Wonder **A:** Paul Reinman; Chic Stone; Gerald McCann **W:** Curt Carpenter; Greg Olivetti; Shane O'Shea
113 ❑ Aug 1963 Cover: 0.12 **NM** value: **16.00**
Circ: Statement: **169,603**
114 ❑ Sep 1963 Cover: 0.12 **NM** value: **35.00**
Circ: Statement: **169,603**
115 ❑ Oct 1963 Cover: 0.12 **NM** value: **16.00**
Circ: Statement: **169,603**
116 ❑ Nov 1963 Cover: 0.12 **NM** value: **30.00**
Circ: Statement: **169,603**
117 ❑ Jan 1964 Cover: 0.12 **NM** value: **16.00**
Circ: Statement: **179,330**
118 ❑ Mar 1964 Cover: 0.12 **NM** value: **16.00**
Circ: Statement: **179,330**
119 ❑ May 1964 Cover: 0.12 **NM** value: **16.00**
Circ: Statement: **179,330**
120 ❑ Jul 1964 Cover: 0.12 **NM** value: **16.00**
Circ: Statement: **179,330**
121 ❑ Aug 1964 Cover: 0.12 **NM** value: **12.00**
Circ: Statement: **179,330**
📖 The Man Without a Mind; Back to Yesterday!; Courier out of History; The Mild-Mannered Ghost **A:** Chic Stone; Edd Ashe; John Forte; Ogden Whitney(cover) **W:** Bob Standish; Kurato Osaki
122 ❑ Sep 1964 Cover: 0.12 **NM** value: **12.00**
Circ: Statement: **179,330**
123 ❑ Oct 1964 Cover: 0.12 **NM** value: **12.00**
Circ: Statement: **179,330**
124 ❑ Nov 1964 Cover: 0.12 **NM** value: **12.00**
Circ: Statement: **179,330**
125 ❑ Jan 1965 Cover: 0.12 **NM** value: **25.00**
Circ: Statement: **172,270**
126 ❑ Mar 1965 Cover: 0.12 **NM** value: **12.00**
Circ: Statement: **172,270**
127 ❑ May 1965 Cover: 0.12 **NM** value: **12.00**
Circ: Statement: **172,270**
• Has 1964 Statement, filed 10/1/64; avg print run 325,000; avg sales 179,250; avg subs 80; avg total paid circ and max existent 179,330; 45% of run returned
128 ❑ Jul 1965 Cover: 0.12 **NM** value: **14.00**
Circ: Statement: **172,270**
📖 Magicman Meets Merlin!; Only Tough Guys Get Places!; Loom of Fate! **A:** Paul Reinman; Pete Costanza; Edd Ashe **W:** Bob Standish; Pierre Alonzo; Zev Zimmer ★ Appearance of Magicman.
129 ❑ Aug 1965 Cover: 0.12 **NM** value: **12.00**
Circ: Statement: **172,270**
130 ❑ Sep 1965 Cover: 0.12 **NM** value: **14.00**
Circ: Statement: **172,270**
📖 Magicman vs. The Wizard of Science!; Stone Age Man; The Ghost That Died! **A:** Paul Reinman; Pete Costanza; Hy Eisman **W:** Kermit Lundgren; Kurato Osaki; Zev Zimmer ★ Appearance of Magicman.
131 ❑ Oct 1965 Cover: 0.12 **NM** value: **12.00**
Circ: Statement: **172,270**
132 ❑ Nov 1965 Cover: 0.12 **NM** value: **12.00**
Circ: Statement: **172,270**
133 ❑ Jan 1966 Cover: 0.12 **NM** value: **12.00**
Circ: Statement: **160,520** • **CGC:** 1 graded, best 7.0
134 ❑ Mar 1966 Cover: 0.12 **NM** value: **12.00**
Circ: Statement: **160,520**
135 ❑ May 1966 Cover: 0.12 **NM** value: **12.00**
Circ: Statement: **160,520**
136 ❑ Jul 1966 Cover: 0.12 **NM** value: **12.00**
Circ: Statement: **160,520**
137 ❑ Aug 1966 Cover: 0.12 **NM** value: **12.00**
Circ: Statement: **160,520**
138 ❑ Sep 1966 Cover: 0.12 **NM** value: **12.00**
Circ: Statement: **160,520**
139 ❑ Oct 1966 Cover: 0.12 **NM** value: **12.00**
Circ: Statement: **160,520**
140 ❑ Nov 1966 Cover: 0.12 **NM** value: **12.00**
Circ: Statement: **160,520** • **CGC:** 1 graded, best 8.5
141 ❑ Jan 1967 Cover: 0.12 **NM** value: **10.00**
142 ❑ Mar 1967 Cover: 0.12 **NM** value: **10.00**
143 ❑ May 1967 Cover: 0.12 **NM** value: **10.00**
144 ❑ Jul 1967 Cover: 0.12 **NM** value: **10.00**
145 ❑ Aug 1967 Cover: 0.12 **NM** value: **10.00**
final issue.

FORBIDDEN WORLDS (A+) — A-Plus

1 ❑ b&w Cover: 2.50 **NM** value: **Cover or less**
📖 An Old Man; Traveler; The Plague; The Secret of the Saucer; The Visitor; The Blue Men of Bantro; What Was It? **A:** Steve Ditko; Pat Boyette; Jim Aparo **W:** Pat Boyette; Jim Aparo

FORBIDDEN WORLDS (AVALON) — Avalon

1 ❑ Cover: 2.95 **NM** value: **Cover or less**
📖 His Own Little World; Lash Thunder Space Explorer

FORBIDDEN X ANGEL — Angel

1 ❑ Cover: 2.95 **NM** value: **Cover or less**

FORBIDDEN ZONE — Galaxy Entertainment

1 ❑ Cover: 5.95 **NM** value: **Cover or less**
📖 Motion: Tales of the Millennium; M80; Carmina; Sirens; Billy Bragg: Badge #373 NYC; That's Entertainment; Women are From Venus; Angel of Andromeda; Deadgirls in Purgatory; Spacetrash; Dreamdoll **A:** Maelo Cintron; Richard Corben; Mark Beachum; Randy DuBurke; Simon Bisley; John Cebollero; Joseph Michael Linsner; Arthur Suydam; Larry Stroman; Frank Cummings **W:** Bob Burden; Arthur Suydam; Chris Paper; Mike Lasko Gross

FORCE 10 — Crow

1 ❑ Cover: 2.50 **NM** value: **Cover or less**
📖 Children Of The Revolution, Part 1 **A:** Dave Morris **W:** Dave Morris; Jam Morris ★ 1st Appearance of Impel.
1/Ash❑ **NM** value: **3.00**
• Ashcan preview edition. 📖 Children Of The Revolution, Part 1 **A:** Dave Morris **W:** Dave Morris; Jam Morris ★ 1st Appearance of Flux, Armadillos, Spook, Rukh, Lodestar, Teknik, Leprechaun, Force 10.

FORCE OF BUDDHA'S PALM, THE — Jademan

1 ❑ ca. 1988 Cover: 1.95 **NM** value: **Cover or less**
2 ❑ ca. 1988 Cover: 1.95 **NM** value: **Cover or less**
3 ❑ ca. 1988 Cover: 1.95 **NM** value: **Cover or less**
4 ❑ ca. 1988 Cover: 1.95 **NM** value: **Cover or less**
5 ❑ ca. 1988 Cover: 1.95 **NM** value: **Cover or less**
6 ❑ ca. 1989 Cover: 1.95 **NM** value: **Cover or less**
7 ❑ ca. 1989 Cover: 1.95 **NM** value: **Cover or less**

CGC-graded: Multiply prices above by **33 for 9.9 M** • **16 for 9.8 NM/M** • **7 for 9.6 NM+** • **5 for 9.4 NM** • **2.5 for 9.2 NM-** • **1.5 for 9.0 VF/NM**

8 ❑ ca. 1989 Cover: 1.95 **NM** value: **Cover or less**
9 ❑ ca. 1989 Cover: 1.95 **NM** value: **Cover or less**
10 ❑ ca. 1989 Cover: 1.95 **NM** value: **Cover or less**
11 ❑ ca. 1989 Cover: 1.95 **NM** value: **Cover or less**
12 ❑ ca. 1989 Cover: 1.95 **NM** value: **Cover or less**
13 ❑ ca. 1989 Cover: 1.95 **NM** value: **Cover or less**
14 ❑ ca. 1989 Cover: 1.95 **NM** value: **Cover or less**
15 ❑ ca. 1989 Cover: 1.95 **NM** value: **Cover or less**
16 ❑ ca. 1989 Cover: 1.95 **NM** value: **Cover or less**
17 ❑ ca. 1989 Cover: 1.95 **NM** value: **Cover or less**
18 ❑ ca. 1990 Cover: 1.95 **NM** value: **Cover or less**
19 ❑ ca. 1990 Cover: 1.95 **NM** value: **Cover or less**
20 ❑ ca. 1990 Cover: 1.95 **NM** value: **Cover or less**
21 ❑ ca. 1990 Cover: 1.95 **NM** value: **Cover or less**
22 ❑ ca. 1990 Cover: 1.95 **NM** value: **Cover or less**
23 ❑ ca. 1990 Cover: 1.95 **NM** value: **Cover or less**
24 ❑ ca. 1990 Cover: 1.95 **NM** value: **Cover or less**
25 ❑ ca. 1990 Cover: 1.95 **NM** value: **Cover or less**
26 ❑ ca. 1990 Cover: 1.95 **NM** value: **Cover or less**
27 ❑ ca. 1990 Cover: 1.95 **NM** value: **Cover or less**
28 ❑ ca. 1990 Cover: 1.95 **NM** value: **Cover or less**
29 ❑ ca. 1990 Cover: 1.95 **NM** value: **Cover or less**
30 ❑ ca. 1991 Cover: 1.95 **NM** value: **Cover or less**
31 ❑ ca. 1991 Cover: 1.95 **NM** value: **Cover or less**
32 ❑ ca. 1991 Cover: 1.95 **NM** value: **Cover or less**
33 ❑ ca. 1991 Cover: 1.95 **NM** value: **Cover or less**
34 ❑ ca. 1991 Cover: 1.95 **NM** value: **Cover or less**
35 ❑ ca. 1991 Cover: 1.95 **NM** value: **Cover or less**
36 ❑ ca. 1991 Cover: 1.95 **NM** value: **Cover or less**
37 ❑ ca. 1991 Cover: 1.95 **NM** value: **Cover or less**
38 ❑ ca. 1991 Cover: 1.95 **NM** value: **Cover or less**
39 ❑ ca. 1991 Cover: 1.95 **NM** value: **Cover or less**
40 ❑ ca. 1991 Cover: 1.95 **NM** value: **Cover or less**
41 ❑ ca. 1991 Cover: 1.95 **NM** value: **Cover or less**
42 ❑ ca. 1992 Cover: 1.95 **NM** value: **Cover or less**

FORCE SEVEN — Lone Star

1 ❑ Aug 1999 Cover: 2.95 **NM** value: **Cover or less**
S.O.S. **A:** Kelsey Shannon **W:** Michael Wright
2 ❑ Sep 1999 Cover: 2.95 **NM** value: **Cover or less**
Fire in the Sky **A:** Brian Hagan **W:** Michael Wright
3 ❑ Mar 2000 Cover: 2.95 **NM** value: **Cover or less**
Extinction **A:** Brian Hagan **W:** Michael Wright

FORCE WORKS — Marvel

Force Works was formed by millionaire Tony Stark, who is best known as the alter ego of Iron Man. The group's membership changed over time, eventually including Scarlet Witch, Spider-Woman, U.S.Agent, Wonder Man, and the alien Century.

Running 22 issues in all from 1994 to 1996, it was primarily a team series featuring underused Marvel super-heroes, keeping their identities fresh in Marvel continuity. Sporting plots that were convoluted even by Marvel standards, involving such characters as The Avengers, Mantis, and Kang and even offering a flip book with #12 (Jun 95), the series was mostly overlooked during its run.

1 ❑ Jul 1994 Cover: 3.95 **NM** value: **Cover or less**
Circ: CapCity orders: **50,600**
Pop-up cover. • Giant-size. Daybreak **A:** Thomas Tenney **W:** Andy Lanning; Dan Abnett
2 ❑ Aug 1994 Cover: 1.50 **NM** value: **2.00**
Circ: CapCity orders: **33,450**
3 ❑ Sep 1994 Cover: 1.50 **NM** value: **2.00**
Circ: CapCity orders: **28,400**
4 ❑ Oct 1994 Cover: 1.50 **NM** value: **Cover or less**
Circ: CapCity orders: **25,250**
5 ❑ Nov 1994 Cover: 1.50 **NM** value: **Cover or less**
5/CS❑Nov 1994 Cover: 2.95 **NM** value: **Cover or less**
Circ: Statement: **59,881** CapCity orders: **24,950**
• with sericel
6 ❑ Dec 1994 Cover: 1.50 **NM** value: **Cover or less**
Circ: Statement: **59,881** CapCity orders: **24,150**
7 ❑ Jan 1995 Cover: 1.50 **NM** value: **Cover or less**
Circ: Statement: **59,881** CapCity orders: **20,750**
8 ❑ Feb 1995 Cover: 1.50 **NM** value: **Cover or less**
Circ: Statement: **59,881** CapCity orders: **18,275**
9 ❑ Mar 1995 Cover: 1.50 **NM** value: **Cover or less**
Circ: Statement: **59,881** CapCity orders: **16,650**
10 ❑ Apr 1995 Cover: 1.50 **NM** value: **Cover or less**
Circ: Statement: **59,881** CapCity orders: **15,325**
11 ❑ May 1995 Cover: 1.50 **NM** value: **Cover or less**
Circ: Statement: **59,881** CapCity orders: **13,975**
12 ❑ Jun 1995 Cover: 2.50 **NM** value: **Cover or less**
Circ: Statement: **59,881** CapCity orders: **13,275**
13 ❑ Jul 1995 Cover: 1.50 **NM** value: **Cover or less**
Circ: Statement: **59,881** CapCity orders: **12,325**
14 ❑ Aug 1995 Cover: 1.50 **NM** value: **Cover or less**
Circ: Statement: **59,881** CapCity orders: **11,675**
15 ❑ Sep 1995 Cover: 1.50 **NM** value: **Cover or less**
Circ: Statement: **59,881**
16 ❑ Oct 1995 Cover: 1.50 **NM** value: **Cover or less**
Circ: Statement: **59,881**
17 ❑ Nov 1995 Cover: 1.50 **NM** value: **Cover or less**
18 ❑ Dec 1995 Cover: 1.50 **NM** value: **Cover or less**
The Crossing **A:** Jimmy Cheung **W:** Andy Lanning; Dan Abnett ★ Appearance of War Machine, Avengers, Hawkeye.
19 ❑ Jan 1996 Cover: 1.50 **NM** value: **Cover or less**
• Has 1995 Statement, filed 10/1/95; avg print run 96,826; avg sales 58,031; avg subs 1,850; avg total paid 59,881; samples 750; office use 500; max existent 61,131; 37% of run returned ★ Appearance of Mantis, Kang.
20 ❑ Feb 1996 Cover: 1.50 **NM** value: **Cover or less**
21 ❑ Mar 1996 Cover: 1.50 **NM** value: **Cover or less**
Afterimage **A:** Yancey Labat; Andrew Wildman **W:** Andy Lanning; Dan Abnett
22 ❑ Apr 1996 Cover: 1.50 **NM** value: **Cover or less**
Pain Threshold final issue. **A:** Andrew Wildman **W:** Andy Lanning; Dan Abnett
Ash 1❑ Cover: 0.75 **NM** value: **Cover or less**
Circ: CapCity orders: **16,800**
• ashcan edition. • ashcan

FORE/PUNK — Parody Press

1/A ❑ Cover: 2.50 **NM** value: **Cover or less**
punk cover.
1/B ❑ Cover: 2.50 **NM** value: **Cover or less**
fore cover.

FORETERNITY — Antarctic

1 ❑ Jul 1997, b&w Cover: 2.95 **NM** value: **Cover or less**
Circ: Diamd. preorders: **4,525**
2 ❑ Sep 1997, b&w Cover: 2.95 **NM** value: **Cover or less**
3 ❑ Nov 1997, b&w Cover: 2.95 **NM** value: **Cover or less**
4 ❑ Jan 1998, b&w Cover: 2.95 **NM** value: **Cover or less**

FOREVER AMBER — Image

1/A ❑ Jul 1999 Cover: 2.95 **NM** value: **Cover or less**
Circ: Diamd. preorders: **11,029**
1/B ❑ Jul 1999 Cover: 2.95 **NM** value: **Cover or less**
alternate cover has white background. Welcome to My World **A:** Don Hudson **W:** Don Hudson
2 ❑ Aug 1999 Cover: 2.95 **NM** value: **Cover or less**
Circ: Diamd. preorders: **4,896**
The Center of Attention **A:** Don Hudson **W:** Don Hudson
3 ❑ Sep 1999 Cover: 2.95 **NM** value: **Cover or less**
Circ: Diamd. preorders: **4,437**
Let the Lawyers Sort it Out **A:** Don Hudson **W:** Don Hudson
4 ❑ Oct 1999 Cover: 2.95 **NM** value: **Cover or less**
Circ: Diamd. preorders: **3,669**

FOREVER NOW — Entertainment

1 ❑ Cover: 1.50 **NM** value: **Cover or less**
2 ❑ Cover: 1.50 **NM** value: **Cover or less**

FOREVER PEOPLE, THE — DC

When the old gods were gone, new gods appeared. They created two different worlds: the peaceful New Genesis, and the warlike Apokolips. The people of Apokolips seemed bent on destruction and, with their malevolent ruler Darkseid, they have made it their quest to destroy New Genesis.

The Forever People are a group of gods on New Genesis who strive to stop Darkseid and his machinations. Their mighty powers are aided by the Mother Box (a powerful computer and communications device) and the Super Cycle, which lets them teleport across vast spaces instantly.

This series was part of a grand vision by creator Jack Kirby. With The New Gods, Mister Miracle, The Forever People, and various other titles, he created a new mythology and a story that spanned the stars.

1 ❑ Mar 1971 Cover: 0.15 **NM** value: **26.00**
• **CGC:** 22 graded, best 9.6
In Search Of A Dream! • Darkseid **A:** Jack Kirby **W:** Jack Kirby ★ Origin of Forever People.
2 ❑ May 1971 Cover: 0.15 **NM** value: **18.00**
• **CGC:** 9 graded, best 9.6
Super War! • Darkseid **A:** Jack Kirby **W:** Jack Kirby ★ 1st Appearance of Desaad, Mantis (DC).
3 ❑ Jul 1971 Cover: 0.15 **NM** value: **15.00**
• **CGC:** 7 graded, best 9.8
Life vs. Anti-Life • Darkseid **A:** Jack Kirby **W:** Jack Kirby ★ 1st Appearance of Glorious Godfrey
4 ❑ Sep 1971 Cover: 0.25 **NM** value: **15.00**
• **CGC:** 9 graded, best 9.6
The Kingdom of the Damned • Darkseid **A:** Jack Kirby **W:** Jack Kirby
5 ❑ Nov 1971 Cover: 0.25 **NM** value: **15.00**
• **CGC:** 3 graded, best 9.6
• Giant-size. Sonny Sumo **A:** Jack Kirby **W:** Jack Kirby
6 ❑ Jan 1972 Cover: 0.25 **NM** value: **9.00**
• **CGC:** 3 graded, best 9.4
• Giant-size. The Omega Effect • Darkseid **A:** Jack Kirby **W:** Jack Kirby ★ Appearance of Sandy, Sandman.
7 ❑ Mar 1972 Cover: 0.25 **NM** value: **9.00**
• **CGC:** 1 graded, best 9.6
I'll Find You in Yesterday **A:** Jack Kirby **W:** Jack Kirby
8 ❑ May 1972 Cover: 0.25 **NM** value: **9.00**
• **CGC:** 5 graded, best 9.6
The Power • Darkseid **A:** Jack Kirby **W:** Jack Kirby
9 ❑ Jul 1972 Cover: 0.25 **NM** value: **9.00**
• **CGC:** 6 graded, best 9.6
Monster in the Morgue **A:** Jack Kirby **W:** Jack Kirby
10 ❑ Jul 1972 Cover: 0.20 **NM** value: **9.00**
• **CGC:** 2 graded, best 9.8
11 ❑ Nov 1972 Cover: 0.20 **NM** value: **9.00**
• **CGC:** 1 graded, best 9.6
Bk 1❑ Cover: 14.95 **NM** value: **Cover or less**
• Collects The Forever People #1-11 in black and white **A:** Jack Kirby **W:** Jack Kirby

FOREVER PEOPLE (MINI-SERIES) — DC

1 ❑ Feb 1988 Cover: 1.25 **NM** value: **2.00**
Circ: CapCity orders: **21,350**
The Day After Forever **A:** Karl Kesel; Paris Cullins **W:** J.M. DeMatteis
2 ❑ Mar 1988 Cover: 1.25 **NM** value: **1.50**
Circ: CapCity orders: **17,400**
From Earth to Forever **A:** Paris Cullins **W:** J.M. DeMatteis
3 ❑ Apr 1988 Cover: 1.25 **NM** value: **1.50**
Circ: CapCity orders: **15,750**
Forever's End? **A:** Paris Cullins **W:** J.M. DeMatteis
4 ❑ May 1988 Cover: 1.25 **NM** value: **1.50**
Circ: CapCity orders: **11,800**
5 ❑ Jun 1988 Cover: 1.25 **NM** value: **1.50**
Circ: CapCity orders: **10,200**
6 ❑ Jul 1988 Cover: 1.25 **NM** value: **1.50**
Circ: CapCity orders: **9,700**

FOREVER WARRIORS — CFD

1 ❑ May 1997 Cover: 2.95 **NM** value: **Cover or less**
The Wizard of Odd!; Trial by Holocaust! **A:** Rich Buckler; Jim Webb **W:** Rich Buckler; Roy Thomas; Matt Morello

FORGOTTEN REALMS (DC) — DC

Forgotten Realms is a lighthearted marriage of sword and sorcery, one of the several comics titles that DC Comics produced in conjunction with game manufacturer TSR, the makers of Advanced Dungeons & Dragons.

Forgotten Realms takes place in a sort of fantasy Middle Ages populated by elves, dwarves, humans, and assorted mystical creatures. This comic follows a group of explorers whose number includes a wizened old mage, a greedy dwarfish thief, an erstwhile paladin cursed with a drinking problem, and more. Bound together by a love of adventure, they take on evil and seek their fortune.

1 ❑ Sep 1989 Cover: 1.50 **NM** value: **Cover or less**
Circ: CapCity orders: **24,700**
The Hand of Vaprak, Part 1 **A:** Rags Morales **W:** Jeff Grubb
2 ❑ Oct 1989 Cover: 1.50 **NM** value: **Cover or less**
Circ: CapCity orders: **17,200**
The Hand of Vaprak, Part 2
3 ❑ Nov 1989 Cover: 1.50 **NM** value: **Cover or less**
Circ: CapCity orders: **15,650**
The Hand of Vaprak, Part 3
4 ❑ Dec 1989 Cover: 1.50 **NM** value: **Cover or less**
Circ: CapCity orders: **14,150**
The Hand of Vaprak, Part 4
5 ❑ Jan 1990 Cover: 1.50 **NM** value: **Cover or less**
Circ: CapCity orders: **12,700**
6 ❑ Feb 1990 Cover: 1.50 **NM** value: **Cover or less**
Circ: CapCity orders: **13,000**
7 ❑ Mar 1990 Cover: 1.50 **NM** value: **Cover or less**
Circ: CapCity orders: **13,000**
8 ❑ Apr 1990 Cover: 1.50 **NM** value: **Cover or less**
Circ: CapCity orders: **12,600**
9 ❑ May 1990 Cover: 1.50 **NM** value: **Cover or less**
Circ: CapCity orders: **12,000**
10 ❑ Jun 1990 Cover: 1.50 **NM** value: **Cover or less**
Circ: CapCity orders: **12,200**
11 ❑ Jul 1990 Cover: 1.50 **NM** value: **Cover or less**
Circ: CapCity orders: **12,050**
12 ❑ Aug 1990 Cover: 1.50 **NM** value: **Cover or less**
Circ: CapCity orders: **11,850**
13 ❑ Sep 1990 Cover: 1.50 **NM** value: **Cover or less**
Circ: CapCity orders: **11,650**
14 ❑ Oct 1990 Cover: 1.50 **NM** value: **Cover or less**
Circ: CapCity orders: **11,600**
15 ❑ Nov 1990 Cover: 1.50 **NM** value: **Cover or less**
Circ: CapCity orders: **11,000**
16 ❑ Dec 1990 Cover: 1.75 **NM** value: **Cover or less**
Circ: CapCity orders: **11,350**
17 ❑ Jan 1991 Cover: 1.75 **NM** value: **Cover or less**
Circ: CapCity orders: **10,800**
18 ❑ Feb 1991 Cover: 1.75 **NM** value: **Cover or less**
Circ: CapCity orders: **10,950**
19 ❑ Mar 1991 Cover: 1.75 **NM** value: **Cover or less**
Circ: CapCity orders: **10,500**
20 ❑ Apr 1991 Cover: 1.75 **NM** value: **Cover or less**
Circ: CapCity orders: **9,900**
21 ❑ May 1991 Cover: 1.75 **NM** value: **Cover or less**
Circ: CapCity orders: **10,000**
22 ❑ Jun 1991 Cover: 1.75 **NM** value: **Cover or less**
Circ: CapCity orders: **9,750**
23 ❑ Jul 1991 Cover: 1.75 **NM** value: **Cover or less**
Circ: CapCity orders: **9,650**
24 ❑ Aug 1991 Cover: 1.75 **NM** value: **Cover or less**
Circ: CapCity orders: **9,900**
25 ❑ Sep 1991 Cover: 1.75 **NM** value: **Cover or less**
Circ: CapCity orders: **10,750**
Wake OF The Realms Master final issue. **A:** Chas Truog **W:** Jeff Grubb
Anl 1❑ca. 1990 Cover: 2.95 **NM** value: **Cover or less**
Circ: CapCity orders: **10,300**

FORGOTTEN REALMS: THE GRAND TOUR — TSR

1 ❑ NM value: **1.00**
No issue number. no cover price. Grand Tour **A:** Todd Fox **W:** Jeff Grubb

FORTUNE AND GLORY — Oni

1 ❑ Dec 1999, b&w Cover: 4.95 **NM** value: **Cover or less**
Circ: Diamd. preorders: **3,422**
2 ❑ Feb 2000, b&w Cover: 4.95 **NM** value: **Cover or less**
Circ: Diamd. preorders: **2,395**
3 ❑ Apr 2000, b&w Cover: 4.95 **NM** value: **Cover or less**
Circ: Diamd. preorders: **2,798**
Bk 1❑ Cover: 14.95 **NM** value: **Cover or less**
• collects mini-series **A:** Marc Andreyko **W:** Brian Michael Bendis

FORTUNE'S FOOL, THE STORY OF JINXER — Cranium

0 ❑ Jul 1999 Cover: 2.95 **NM** value: **Cover or less**

FORTUNE'S FRIENDS: HELL WEEK — Aria

1 ❑ Cover: 6.95 **NM** value: **Cover or less**
• graphic novel

FORTY WINKS — Odd Jobs Limited

1 ❑ Nov 1997 Cover: 2.95 **NM** value: **Cover or less**
2 ❑ Dec 1997 Cover: 2.95 **NM** value: **Cover or less**
3 ❑ Mar 1998 Cover: 2.95 **NM** value: **Cover or less**
4 ❑ Jun 1998 Cover: 2.95 **NM** value: **Cover or less**

FORTY WINKS CHRISTMAS SPECIAL — Peregrine Entertainment

1 ❑ Aug 1998, b&w Cover: 2.95 **NM** value: **Cover or less**

FORTY WINKS SUPER SPECIAL EDITION: TV PARTY TONITE! — Peregrine Entertainment

1 ❑ Apr 1999, b&w Cover: 2.95 **NM** value: **Cover or less**

FOTON EFFECT, THE — Aced

1 ❑ Oct 1986 Cover: 1.50 **NM** value: **Cover or less**
2 ❑ Cover: 1.50 **NM** value: **Cover or less**
3 ❑ Cover: 1.50 **NM** value: **Cover or less**

FOUL! — Traitors Gait

1 ❑ Cover: 2.00 **NM** value: **3.00**
Scottish Manager; Freaky Formations; So...What's I Like to Be a Football Fan; Streaker Striker; The Fox Files; The Wages of Sin; Demon Defender; All in the Game; Are You and Your Club Compatible?; There's No Su **A:** Richard Johnson; Adam White; Dave Windett; Joe Martinez; Lee Farrell; Mutt; Paul Knight; Sami Lill; Simon Gurr; Simon Watson **W:** James Peaty; Simon Watson; Des Sawyer; Ferg Handley

4 — Marvel

1 ❑ Oct 2000 Cover: 3.99 **NM** value: **Cover or less**
• Universe X tie-in; Sue Richards restored to life **A:** Alex Ross; Brent Anderson **W:** Jim Krueger

FOUR CASES OF MURDER — Eternity

Bk 1❑ b&w Cover: 17.95 **NM** value: **Cover or less**
• Perry Mason strip reprints

FOUR COLOR COMICS (SERIES 1) — Dell

1 ❑ ca. 1939 Cover: 0.10 **NM** value: **7000.00**
• **CGC:** 1 graded, best 7.5
2 ❑ ca. 1939 Cover: 0.10 **NM** value: **1500.00**
3 ❑ ca. 1939 Cover: 0.10 **NM** value: **750.00**
4 ❑ ca. 1940 Cover: 0.10 **NM** value: **8000.00**
• **CGC:** 1 graded, best 3.0
5 ❑ ca. 1940 Cover: 0.10 **NM** value: **650.00**
6 ❑ ca. 1940 Cover: 0.10 **NM** value: **1000.00**
7 ❑ ca. 1940 Cover: 0.10 **NM** value: **400.00**
8 ❑ ca. 1940 Cover: 0.10 **NM** value: **800.00**
9 ❑ ca. 1940 Cover: 0.10 **NM** value: **600.00**
• **CGC:** 1 graded, best 6.0
10 ❑ ca. 1940 Cover: 0.10 **NM** value: **500.00**
11 ❑ ca. 1940 Cover: 0.10 **NM** value: **400.00**
12 ❑ ca. 1940 Cover: 0.10 **NM** value: **500.00**
13 ❑ ca. 1941 Cover: 0.10 **NM** value: **1000.00**
• **CGC:** 1 graded, best 7.5
14 ❑ ca. 1941 Cover: 0.10 **NM** value: **400.00**
15 ❑ ca. 1941 Cover: 0.10 **NM** value: **400.00**
16 ❑ ca. 1941 Cover: 0.10 **NM** value: **10000.00**
• **CGC:** 6 graded, best 7.5
17 ❑ ca. 1941 Cover: 0.10 **NM** value: **2000.00**
18 ❑ ca. 1941 Cover: 0.10 **NM** value: **400.00**
19 ❑ ca. 1941 Cover: 0.10 **NM** value: **400.00**
20 ❑ ca. 1942 Cover: 0.10 **NM** value: **300.00**
21 ❑ ca. 1942 Cover: 0.10 **NM** value: **700.00**
22 ❑ ca. 1942 Cover: 0.10 **NM** value: **300.00**
23 ❑ ca. 1942 Cover: 0.10 **NM** value: **300.00**
24 ❑ ca. 1942 Cover: 0.10 **NM** value: **400.00**
25 ❑ ca. 1942 Cover: 0.10 **NM** value: **800.00**
• **CGC:** 1 graded, best 1.0

Capital City orders are the actual sales of comic books by Capital City Distribution, once one of the largest U.S. sellers of comics to comics shops. Capital City's share of comics shop sales, while not known exactly, increases from around 10-20% in the mid-1980s to 30-35% in the mid-1990s. Capital City's share of comic books sold on newsstands (most Marvels and DCs) will be less.

FOUR COLOR COMICS — Dell

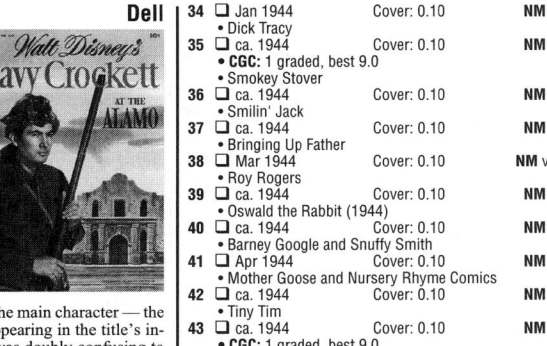

Published from 1941 until 1962, Dell's Four Color Comics series had more issues published than any other American comic, although not the full 1,354 its final number would indicate, since some numbers were not published. During its run of more than two decades, it featured dozens of comics icons including Uncle Scrooge, Prince Valiant, Bozo the Clown, Bugs Bunny, Tarzan, and Flash Gordon.

Despite its singular place in comics history, many comics readers have never heard the name "Four Color Comics." Why? Because virtually every issue ran under the name of the main character — the inscription "Four Color Comics" only appearing in the title's indicia and that only in some cases. This was doubly confusing to readers. A cover reading, say "Popeye" with an issue number of #145, naturally left readers wondering where Popeye #1-144 had gone.

The first complete list of Four Color Comics was compiled by Don and Maggie Thompson, solving a mystery that had puzzled fans for years.

1 ❑ Jun 1942 Cover: 0.10 **NM** value: **475.00**
• Little Joe
2 ❑ ca. 1942 Cover: 0.10 **NM** value: **250.00**
• Harold Teen
3 ❑ ca. 1942 Cover: 0.10 **NM** value: **475.00**
• **CGC:** 1 graded, best 9.2
• Alley Oop
4 ❑ ca. 1942 Cover: 0.10 **NM** value: **430.00**
• **CGC:** 1 graded, best 6.5
• Smilin' Jack
5 ❑ ca. 1942 Cover: 0.10 **NM** value: **450.00**
• Raggedy Ann and Andy
6 ❑ ca. 1942 Cover: 0.10 **NM** value: **220.00**
• Smitty **A:** Walter Berndt **W:** Walter Berndt
7 ❑ ca. 1942 Cover: 0.10 **NM** value: **315.00**
• Smokey Stover
8 ❑ ca. 1942 Cover: 0.10 **NM** value: **225.00**
• Tillie the Toiler
9 ❑ Aug 1942 Cover: 0.10 **NM** value: **7500.00**
• **CGC:** 13 graded, best 9.6
Donald Duck Finds Pirate Gold • Donald Duck **A:** Carl Barks
10 ❑ ca. 1942 Cover: 0.10 **NM** value: **785.00**
• **CGC:** 3 graded, best 9.2
• Flash Gordon **A:** Alex Raymond
11 ❑ ca. 1942 Cover: 0.10 **NM** value: **310.00**
• Wash Tubbs
12 ❑ ca. 1942 Cover: 0.10 **NM** value: **560.00**
• Bambi
13 ❑ ca. 1942 Cover: 0.10 **NM** value: **315.00**
• **CGC:** 1 graded, best 7.0
• Mr. District Attorney
14 ❑ ca. 1942 Cover: 0.10 **NM** value: **350.00**
• **CGC:** 2 graded, best 7.0
• Smilin' Jack
15 ❑ ca. 1942 Cover: 0.10 **NM** value: **700.00**
• **CGC:** 1 graded, best 8.5
• Felix the Cat
16 ❑ ca. 1942 Cover: 0.10 **NM** value: **750.00**
• Porky Pig in the Haunted House
17 ❑ Cover: 0.10 **NM** value: **550.00**
• Popeye and Wimpy
18 ❑ Cover: 0.10 **NM** value: **420.00**
• Little Orphan Annie
19 ❑ ca. 1943 Cover: 0.10 **NM** value: **620.00**
• Thumper Meets the Seven Dwarfs
20 ❑ ca. 1943 Cover: 0.10 **NM** value: **225.00**
• **CGC:** 1 graded, best 4.5
• Barney Baxter
21 ❑ ca. 1943 Cover: 0.10 **NM** value: **475.00**
• Oswald the Rabbit
22 ❑ ca. 1943 Cover: 0.10 **NM** value: **200.00**
• Tillie the Toiler
23 ❑ Jun 1943 Cover: 0.10 **NM** value: **375.00**
• Raggedy Ann and Andy
24 ❑ ca. 1943 Cover: 0.10 **NM** value: **525.00**
• Gang Busters
25 ❑ ca. 1943 Cover: 0.10 **NM** value: **500.00**
• Andy Panda
26 ❑ ca. 1943 Cover: 0.10 **NM** value: **500.00**
• Popeye
27 ❑ ca. 1943 Cover: 0.10 **NM** value: **890.00**
• **CGC:** 2 graded, best 9.2
• Mickey Mouse and the Seven-Colored Terror
28 ❑ ca. 1943 Cover: 0.10 **NM** value: **220.00**
• **CGC:** 1 graded, best 4.0
• Wash Tubbs
29 ❑ Sep 1943 Cover: 0.10 **NM** value: **6400.00**
• **CGC:** 6 graded, best 7.5
Donald Duck and the Mummy's Ring; The Hard Looser; Too Many Pets • Donald Duck
30 ❑ Oct 1943 Cover: 0.10 **NM** value: **550.00**
• **CGC:** 4 graded, best 8.5
• Bambi
31 ❑ ca. 1943 Cover: 0.10 **NM** value: **200.00**
• Moon Mullins
32 ❑ ca. 1943 Cover: 0.10 **NM** value: **170.00**
• Smitty **A:** Walter Berndt **W:** Walter Berndt
33 ❑ Dec 1943 Cover: 0.10 **NM** value: **775.00**
• **CGC:** 1 graded, best 5.0
• Bugs Bunny
34 ❑ Jan 1944 Cover: 0.10 **NM** value: **465.00**
• Dick Tracy
35 ❑ ca. 1944 Cover: 0.10 **NM** value: **165.00**
• **CGC:** 1 graded, best 9.0
• Smokey Stover
36 ❑ ca. 1944 Cover: 0.10 **NM** value: **210.00**
• Smilin' Jack
37 ❑ ca. 1944 Cover: 0.10 **NM** value: **185.00**
• Bringing Up Father
38 ❑ Mar 1944 Cover: 0.10 **NM** value: **1250.00**
• Roy Rogers
39 ❑ ca. 1944 Cover: 0.10 **NM** value: **350.00**
• Oswald the Rabbit (1944)
40 ❑ ca. 1944 Cover: 0.10 **NM** value: **230.00**
• Barney Google and Snuffy Smith
41 ❑ Apr 1944 Cover: 0.10 **NM** value: **230.00**
• Mother Goose and Nursery Rhyme Comics
42 ❑ ca. 1944 Cover: 0.10 **NM** value: **190.00**
• Tiny Tim
43 ❑ ca. 1944 Cover: 0.10 **NM** value: **360.00**
• **CGC:** 1 graded, best 9.0
• Popeye
44 ❑ May 1944 Cover: 0.10 **NM** value: **440.00**
• **CGC:** 1 graded, best 1.8
• Terry and the Pirates
45 ❑ ca. 1944 Cover: 0.10 **NM** value: **310.00**
• Raggedy Ann and Andy
46 ❑ Jun 1944 Cover: 0.10 **NM** value: **450.00**
• Felix the Cat and the Haunted Castle
47 ❑ Jul 1944 Cover: 0.10 **NM** value: **465.00**
• Gene Autry
48 ❑ Jul 1944 Cover: 0.10 **NM** value: **940.00**
• **CGC:** 1 graded, best 4.5
Porky of the Mounties • Porky Pig
49 ❑ ca. 1944 Cover: 0.10 **NM** value: **680.00**
• **CGC:** 1 graded, best 7.5
• Snow White and the Seven Dwarfs
50 ❑ ca. 1944 Cover: 0.10 **NM** value: **290.00**
• Fairy Tale Parade (1944) **A:** Walt Kelly
51 ❑ ca. 1944 Cover: 0.10 **NM** value: **385.00**
• Bugs Bunny
52 ❑ Sep 1944 Cover: 0.10 **NM** value: **300.00**
• Little Orphan Annie
53 ❑ ca. 1944 Cover: 0.10 **NM** value: **170.00**
• Wash Tubbs
54 ❑ ca. 1944 Cover: 0.10 **NM** value: **325.00**
• Andy Panda
55 ❑ ca. 1944 Cover: 0.10 **NM** value: **155.00**
• Tillie the Toiler
56 ❑ ca. 1944 Cover: 0.10 **NM** value: **375.00**
• **CGC:** 1 graded, best 3.0
• Dick Tracy
57 ❑ Nov 1944 Cover: 0.10 **NM** value: **420.00**
Raiders of the Range • Gene Autry
58 ❑ ca. 1944 Cover: 0.10 **NM** value: **210.00**
• Smilin' Jack
59 ❑ Nov 1944 Cover: 0.10 **NM** value: **215.00**
• Mother Goose and Nursery Rhyme Comics **A:** Walt Kelly
60 ❑ ca. 1944 Cover: 0.10 **NM** value: **150.00**
• Tiny Folks Funnies
61 ❑ Nov 1944 Cover: 0.10 **NM** value: **250.00**
• **CGC:** 1 graded, best 8.5
• Santa Claus Funnies **A:** Carl Barks
62 ❑ Jan 1945 Cover: 0.10 **NM** value: **2200.00**
• **CGC:** 4 graded, best 8.5
Frozed Gold; Mystery of the Swamp • Donald Duck
63 ❑ ca. 1945 Cover: 0.10 **NM** value: **525.00**
• Roy Rogers
64 ❑ Feb 1945 Cover: 0.10 **NM** value: **125.00**
• Smokey Stover
65 ❑ Mar 1945 Cover: 0.10 **NM** value: **125.00**
• Smitty **A:** Walter Berndt **W:** Walter Berndt
66 ❑ ca. 1945 Cover: 0.10 **NM** value: **375.00**
• **CGC:** 1 graded, best 9.0
Trail of Terror • Gene Autry
67 ❑ Apr 1945 Cover: 0.10 **NM** value: **190.00**
• Oswald the Rabbit
68 ❑ ca. 1945 Cover: 0.10 **NM** value: **200.00**
• Mother Goose and Nursery Rhyme Comics **A:** Walt Kelly
69 ❑ ca. 1945 Cover: 0.10 **NM** value: **255.00**
• **CGC:** 1 graded, best 9.0
• Fairy Tale Parade **A:** Walt Kelly
70 ❑ ca. 1945 Cover: 0.10 **NM** value: **300.00**
• Popeye and Wimpy
71 ❑ May 1945 Cover: 0.10 **NM** value: **800.00**
• **CGC:** 1 graded, best 9.0
• The Three Caballeros (Disney) **A:** Walt Kelly
72 ❑ ca. 1945 Cover: 0.10 **NM** value: **285.00**
• Raggedy Ann and Andy
73 ❑ ca. 1945 Cover: 0.10 **NM** value: **120.00**
• The Gumps
74 ❑ Jun 1945 Cover: 0.10 **NM** value: **1000.00**
• Little Lulu
75 ❑ Jun 1945 Cover: 0.10 **NM** value: **335.00**
• Gene Autry and the Wildcat
76 ❑ ca. 1945 Cover: 0.10 **NM** value: **275.00**
• Little Orphan Annie
77 ❑ Jul 1945 Cover: 0.10 **NM** value: **400.00**
• **CGC:** 1 graded, best 9.0
• Felix the Cat
78 ❑ Jul 1945 Cover: 0.10 **NM** value: **260.00**
• Porky Pig and the Bandit Twins
79 ❑ Aug 1945 Cover: 0.10 **NM** value: **1140.00**
• **CGC:** 2 graded, best 9.2
The Riddle of the Red Hat • Mickey Mouse **A:** Carl Barks
80 ❑ ca. 1945 Cover: 0.10 **NM** value: **160.00**
• Smilin' Jack
81 ❑ ca. 1945 Cover: 0.10 **NM** value: **100.00**
• Moon Mullins

CGC-graded: Multiply prices above by **33 for 9.9 M • 16 for 9.8 NM/M • 7 for 9.6 NM+ • 5 for 9.4 NM • 2.5 for 9.2 NM- • 1.5 for 9.0 VF/NM**

82 ❑ ca. 1945 Cover: 0.10 **NM** value: **485.00**
• **CGC:** 1 graded, best 5.5
• The Lone Ranger
83 ❑ Sep 1945 Cover: 0.10 **NM** value: **320.00**
• **CGC:** 1 graded, best 6.0
• Gene Autry
84 ❑ ca. 1945 Cover: 0.10 **NM** value: **425.00**
• **CGC:** 1 graded, best 9.2
• Flash Gordon **A:** Alex Raymond
85 ❑ Oct 1945 Cover: 0.10 **NM** value: **175.00**
The Mad Dog Mystery • Andy Panda
86 ❑ Oct 1945 Cover: 0.10 **NM** value: **380.00**
• Roy Rogers
87 ❑ Nov 1945 Cover: 0.10 **NM** value: **225.00**
• Fairy Tale Parade **A:** Walt Kelly
88 ❑ Sep 1945 Cover: 0.10 **NM** value: **225.00**
• Bugs Bunny's Great Adventure
89 ❑ Nov 1945 Cover: 0.10 **NM** value: **135.00**
• Tillie the Toiler
90 ❑ Dec 1945 Cover: 0.10 **NM** value: **200.00**
• Christmas with Mother Goose **A:** Walt Kelly
91 ❑ Dec 1945 Cover: 0.10 **NM** value: **200.00**
• Santa Claus Funnies **A:** Walt Kelly
92 ❑ Jan 1946 Cover: 0.10 **NM** value: **625.00**
• **CGC:** 1 graded, best 9.2
• Pinocchio (Disney) **A:** Walt Kelly
93 ❑ ca. 1946 Cover: 0.10 **NM** value: **285.00**
• **CGC:** 1 graded, best 8.5
The Bandit of Black Rock • Gene Autry
94 ❑ ca. 1946 Cover: 0.10 **NM** value: **110.00**
• Winnie Winkle
95 ❑ Feb 1946 Cover: 0.10 **NM** value: **375.00**
• Roy Rogers
96 ❑ ca. 1946 Cover: 0.10 **NM** value: **275.00**
• **CGC:** 2 graded, best 9.4
• Dick Tracy
97 ❑ ca. 1946 Cover: 0.10 **NM** value: **480.00**
• Little Lulu
98 ❑ ca. 1939 Cover: 0.10 **NM** value: **335.00**
• **CGC:** 1 graded, best 6.0
• The Lone Ranger
99 ❑ Mar 1946 Cover: 0.10 **NM** value: **100.00**
• Smitty **A:** Walter Berndt **W:** Walter Berndt
100 ❑ Mar 1946 Cover: 0.10 **NM** value: **275.00**
• **CGC:** 1 graded, best 6.0
• Gene Autry
101 ❑ ca. 1946 Cover: 0.10 **NM** value: **285.00**
• **CGC:** 1 graded, best 7.5
• Terry and the Pirates
102 ❑ Apr 1946 Cover: 0.10 **NM** value: **140.00**
• Oswald the Rabbit; Title becomes "Dell Color Comics"
103 ❑ Apr 1946 Cover: 0.10 **NM** value: **200.00**
• **CGC:** 1 graded, best 8.5
• Easter With Mother Goose **A:** Walt Kelly
104 ❑ Apr 1946 Cover: 0.10 **NM** value: **200.00**
• Fairy Tale Parade **A:** Walt Kelly
105 ❑ Apr 1946 Cover: 0.10 **NM** value: **720.00**
• Albert the Alligator and Pogo Possum **A:** Walt Kelly
106 ❑ May 1946 Cover: 0.10 **NM** value: **100.00**
• **CGC:** 2 graded, best 8.5
• Tillie the Toiler
107 ❑ May 1946 Cover: 0.10 **NM** value: **225.00**
• **CGC:** 1 graded, best 8.5
• Little Orphan Annie
108 ❑ ca. 1946 Cover: 0.10 **NM** value: **1585.00**
• **CGC:** 9 graded, best 9.4
The Terror of the River!; The Firebug; Sealss Are So Smart! • Donald Duck **A:** Carl Barks
109 ❑ Jun 1946 Cover: 0.10 **NM** value: **285.00**
• **CGC:** 2 graded, best 5.0
• Roy Rogers
110 ❑ Jun 1946 Cover: 0.10 **NM** value: **260.00**
• Little Lulu
111 ❑ Jun 1946 Cover: 0.10 **NM** value: **135.00**
• Captain Easy
112 ❑ Jul 1946 Cover: 0.10 **NM** value: **165.00**
• Porky Pig's Adventure in Gopher Gulch
113 ❑ Jul 1946 Cover: 0.10 **NM** value: **140.00**
• **CGC:** 3 graded, best 9.2
• Popeye
114 ❑ Jul 1946 Cover: 0.10 **NM** value: **190.00**
• **CGC:** 1 graded, best 8.5
• Fairy Tale Parade **A:** Walt Kelly
115 ❑ Aug 1946 Cover: 0.10 **NM** value: **360.00**
• Little Lulu
116 ❑ Aug 1946 Cover: 0.10 **NM** value: **250.00**
• Mickey Mouse
117 ❑ Sep 1946 Cover: 0.10 **NM** value: **220.00**
• Roy Rogers
118 ❑ Sep 1946 Cover: 0.10 **NM** value: **310.00**
• **CGC:** 1 graded, best 7.5
• The Lone Ranger
119 ❑ Sep 1946 Cover: 0.10 **NM** value: **325.00**
• **CGC:** 3 graded, best 9.0
• Felix the Cat
120 ❑ Oct 1946 Cover: 0.10 **NM** value: **310.00**
• Little Lulu
121 ❑ Oct 1946 Cover: 0.10 **NM** value: **115.00**
• Fairy Tale Parade
122 ❑ Oct 1946 Cover: 0.10 **NM** value: **125.00**
• Henry
123 ❑ Oct 1946 Cover: 0.10 **NM** value: **165.00**
• Bugs Bunny's Dangerous Venture
124 ❑ Nov 1946 Cover: 0.10 **NM** value: **205.00**
• Roy Rogers
125 ❑ Nov 1946 Cover: 0.10 **NM** value: **230.00**
• The Lone Ranger
126 ❑ Nov 1946 Cover: 0.10 **NM** value: **155.00**
• Christmas With Mother Goose **A:** Walt Kelly
127 ❑ Dec 1946 Cover: 0.10 **NM** value: **140.00**
• **CGC:** 2 graded, best 9.2
• Popeye
128 ❑ Dec 1946 Cover: 0.10 **NM** value: **150.00**
• Santa Claus Funnies **A:** Walt Kelly
129 ❑ ca. 1946 Cover: 0.10 **NM** value: **280.00**
• Uncle Remus and His Tales of Brer Rabbit (Disney)
130 ❑ Dec 1946 Cover: 0.10 **NM** value: **90.00**
• Andy Panda in the City of Ice
131 ❑ Jan 1947 Cover: 0.10 **NM** value: **290.00**
• **CGC:** 1 graded, best 6.5
• Little Lulu
132 ❑ Jan 1947 Cover: 0.10 **NM** value: **100.00**
• **CGC:** 1 graded, best 9.2
• Tillie the Toiler
133 ❑ Jan 1947 Cover: 0.10 **NM** value: **260.00**
• Dick Tracy
134 ❑ Feb 1947 Cover: 0.10 **NM** value: **640.00**
• **CGC:** 2 graded, best 9.0
• Tarzan and the Devil Ogre
135 ❑ Feb 1947 Cover: 0.10 **NM** value: **265.00**
• **CGC:** 2 graded, best 9.0
• Felix the Cat
136 ❑ Feb 1947 Cover: 0.10 **NM** value: **230.00**
• The Lone Ranger
137 ❑ Feb 1947 Cover: 0.10 **NM** value: **180.00**
• Roy Rogers
138 ❑ ca. 1947 Cover: 0.10 **NM** value: **90.00**
• Smitty **A:** Walter Berndt **W:** Walter Berndt
139 ❑ Mar 1947 Cover: 0.10 **NM** value: **275.00**
• Little Lulu
140 ❑ Mar 1947 Cover: 0.10 **NM** value: **160.00**
• **CGC:** 1 graded, best 7.0
• Easter With Mother Goose **A:** Walt Kelly
141 ❑ Mar 1947 Cover: 0.10 **NM** value: **215.00**
• Mickey Mouse
142 ❑ Apr 1947 Cover: 0.10 **NM** value: **145.00**
• **CGC:** 1 graded, best 9.2
• Bugs Bunny
143 ❑ Apr 1947 Cover: 0.10 **NM** value: **90.00**
• Oswald the Rabbit
144/A ❑ Apr 1947 Cover: 0.10 **NM** value: **160.00**
• Fairy Tale Parade; There were two #144's
144/B ❑ Apr 1947 Cover: 0.10 **NM** value: **205.00**
• Roy Rogers; There were two #144's
145 ❑ Feb 1947 Cover: 0.10 **NM** value: **130.00**
• Popeye
146 ❑ May 1947 Cover: 0.10 **NM** value: **165.00**
• Little Lulu
147 ❑ May 1947 Cover: 0.10 **NM** value: **1025.00**
• **CGC:** 11 graded, best 9.4
Volcano Valley • Donald Duck **A:** Carl Barks
148 ❑ May 1947 Cover: 0.10 **NM** value: **635.00**
• **CGC:** 2 graded, best 9.2
• Albert the Alligator and Pogo Possum **A:** Walt Kelly
149 ❑ ca. 1947 Cover: 0.10 **NM** value: **105.00**
• Smilin' Jack
150 ❑ Jun 1947 Cover: 0.10 **NM** value: **85.00**
• Tillie the Toiler
151 ❑ Jun 1947 Cover: 0.10 **NM** value: **205.00**
• **CGC:** 1 graded, best 7.5
• The Lone Ranger
152 ❑ ca. 1947 Cover: 0.10 **NM** value: **155.00**
• Little Orphan Annie
153 ❑ ca. 1947 Cover: 0.10 **NM** value: **170.00**
• Roy Rogers
154 ❑ Jul 1947 Cover: 0.10 **NM** value: **105.00**
• Andy Panda
155 ❑ Jul 1947 Cover: 0.10 **NM** value: **80.00**
• Henry
156 ❑ Jul 1947 Cover: 0.10 **NM** value: **115.00**
• **CGC:** 1 graded, best 9.0
• Porky Pig and the Phantom
157 ❑ Jul 1947 Cover: 0.10 **NM** value: **225.00**
• **CGC:** 3 graded, best 9.4
• Mickey Mouse and the Beanstalk
158 ❑ Aug 1947 Cover: 0.10 **NM** value: **250.00**
• Little Lulu
159 ❑ Aug 1947 Cover: 0.10 **NM** value: **785.00**
• **CGC:** 9 graded, best 9.6
Donald Duck and the Ghost of the Grotto; Adventure Down Under • Donald Duck **A:** Carl Barks
160 ❑ Aug 1947 Cover: 0.10 **NM** value: **170.00**
• Roy Rogers
161 ❑ Aug 1947 Cover: 0.10 **NM** value: **510.00**
• Tarzan and the Fields of Tohr
162 ❑ Sep 1947 Cover: 0.10 **NM** value: **215.00**
• **CGC:** 1 graded, best 9.2
• Felix the Cat
163 ❑ Sep 1947 Cover: 0.10 **NM** value: **190.00**
• **CGC:** 1 graded, best 3.5
• Dick Tracy
164 ❑ Sep 1947, four-color Cover: 0.10 **NM** value: **140.00**
• Bugs Bunny
165 ❑ Oct 1947 Cover: 0.10 **NM** value: **235.00**
• Little Lulu
166 ❑ Oct 1947 Cover: 0.10 **NM** value: **155.00**
• **CGC:** 2 graded, best 9.4
• Roy Rogers
167 ❑ Oct 1947 Cover: 0.10 **NM** value: **175.00**
• **CGC:** 3 graded, best 9.4
• The Lone Ranger
168 ❑ Oct 1947 Cover: 0.10 **NM** value: **145.00**
• Popeye
169 ❑ Oct 1947 Cover: 0.10 **NM** value: **145.00**
• **CGC:** 1 graded, best 9.6
• Woody Woodpecker
170 ❑ Nov 1947 Cover: 0.10 **NM** value: **175.00**
• Mickey Mouse on Spook's Island
171 ❑ Nov 1947 Cover: 0.10 **NM** value: **225.00**
• Charlie McCarthy and the 20 Thieves
172 ❑ Nov 1947 Cover: 0.10 **NM** value: **145.00**
• Christmas with Mother Goose **A:** Walt Kelly
173 ❑ Nov 1947 Cover: 0.10 **NM** value: **150.00**
• **CGC:** 1 graded, best 3.5
• Flash Gordon
174 ❑ ca. 1947 Cover: 0.10 **NM** value: **80.00**
• **CGC:** 1 graded, best 9.6
• Winnie Winkle
175 ❑ Dec 1947 Cover: 0.10 **NM** value: **135.00**
• **CGC:** 1 graded, best 6.0
• Santa Claus Funnies **A:** Walt Kelly
176 ❑ Dec 1947 Cover: 0.10 **NM** value: **85.00**
• Tillie the Toiler
177 ❑ Dec 1947 Cover: 0.10 **NM** value: **140.00**
• **CGC:** 1 graded, best 9.4
• Bugs Bunny
178 ❑ Dec 1947 Cover: 0.10 **NM** value: **2100.00**
• **CGC:** 8 graded, best 9.6
Christmas on Bear Mountain • Donald Duck **A:** Carl Barks ★ 1st Appearance of Uncle Scrooge.
179 ❑ Jan 1948 Cover: 0.10 **NM** value: **160.00**
• Uncle Wiggily
180 ❑ Feb 1948 Cover: 0.10 **NM** value: **90.00**
• Ozark Ike **A:** Ray Gotto **W:** Ray Gotto
181 ❑ Feb 1948 Cover: 0.10 **NM** value: **175.00**
• **CGC:** 2 graded, best 9.2
• Mickey Mouse
182 ❑ Feb 1948 Cover: 0.10 **NM** value: **110.00**
• Porky Pig in Ever-Never Land
183 ❑ Mar 1948 Cover: 0.10 **NM** value: **85.00**
• **CGC:** 1 graded, best 9.0
• Oswald the Rabbit
184 ❑ Mar 1948 Cover: 0.10 **NM** value: **80.00**
• Tillie the Toiler
185 ❑ ca. 1948 Cover: 0.10 **NM** value: **140.00**
• Easter with Mother Goose **A:** Walt Kelly
186 ❑ Apr 1948 Cover: 0.10 **NM** value: **175.00**
• Bambi
187 ❑ Apr 1948 Cover: 0.10 **NM** value: **120.00**
• Bugs Bunny and the Dreadful Dragon
188 ❑ May 1948 Cover: 0.10 **NM** value: **120.00**
• Woody Woodpecker
189 ❑ Jun 1948 Cover: 0.10 **NM** value: **790.00**
• **CGC:** 2 graded, best 7.5
The Old Castle's Secret • Donald Duck **A:** Carl Barks
190 ❑ Jun 1948 Cover: 0.10 **NM** value: **160.00**
• **CGC:** 2 graded, best 9.0
• Flash Gordon
191 ❑ Jun 1948 Cover: 0.10 **NM** value: **110.00**
• **CGC:** 1 graded, best 8.0
• Porky Pig to the Rescue
192 ❑ Jun 1948 Cover: 0.10 **NM** value: **130.00**
• The Brownies **A:** Walt Kelly
193 ❑ Jul 1948 Cover: 0.10 **NM** value: **150.00**
• **CGC:** 1 graded, best 8.0
• Tom and Jerry
194 ❑ Aug 1948 Cover: 0.10 **NM** value: **170.00**
• **CGC:** 1 graded, best 4.0
• Mickey Mouse in the World Under the Sea
195 ❑ Sep 1948 Cover: 0.10 **NM** value: **65.00**
• Tillie the Toiler
196 ❑ Sep 1948 Cover: 0.10 **NM** value: **175.00**
• Charlie McCarthy and the Haunted Hideout
197 ❑ Sep 1948 Cover: 0.10 **NM** value: **120.00**
• Spirit of the Border (Zane Grey)
198 ❑ Sep 1948 Cover: 0.10 **NM** value: **105.00**
• Andy Panda
199 ❑ Oct 1948 Cover: 0.10 **NM** value: **775.00**
• **CGC:** 3 graded, best 7.5
Sheriff of Bullet Valley • Donald Duck **A:** Carl Barks
200 ❑ Oct 1948 Cover: 0.10 **NM** value: **105.00**
• Bugs Bunny
201 ❑ Nov 1948 Cover: 0.10 **NM** value: **130.00**
• Christmas with Mother Goose **A:** Walt Kelly
202 ❑ ca. 1948 Cover: 0.10 **NM** value: **80.00**
• Woody Woodpecker
203 ❑ Dec 1948 Cover: 0.10 **NM** value: **640.00**
• **CGC:** 2 graded, best 8.5
The Golden Christmas Tree • Donald Duck **A:** Carl Barks
204 ❑ Dec 1948 Cover: 0.10 **NM** value: **135.00**
• **CGC:** 2 graded, best 8.5
• Flash Gordon
205 ❑ Dec 1948 Cover: 0.10 **NM** value: **130.00**
Ticky Tack, the Littlest Reindeer; Jingle Bells; The Three Kings; Santa's New Suits; Christmas in Many Lands; Petey Parrot's Christmas; The First Nowell; A Sled from Santa; Dear Santa; Santa's Sea Trip • Santa Claus Funnies **A:** Walt Kelly; Frank Jupo **W:** Frank Jupo; Henry Wadsworth Longfellow
206 ❑ Dec 1948 Cover: 0.10 **NM** value: **85.00**
• Little Orphan Annie
207 ❑ Dec 1948 Cover: 0.10 **NM** value: **170.00**
• King of the Royal Mounted
208 ❑ Jan 1949 Cover: 0.10 **NM** value: **130.00**
• Brer Rabbit Does it Again! (Disney)
209 ❑ Jan 1949 Cover: 0.10 **NM** value: **45.00**
• Harold Teen
210 ❑ Jan 1949 Cover: 0.10 **NM** value: **45.00**
• Tippie and Cap Stubbs
211 ❑ Jan 1949 Cover: 0.10 **NM** value: **75.00**
• Little Beaver
212 ❑ Jan 1949 Cover: 0.10 **NM** value: **45.00**
• Doctor Bobbs
213 ❑ Jan 1949 Cover: 0.10 **NM** value: **60.00**
• Tillie the Toiler
214 ❑ Feb 1949 Cover: 0.10 **NM** value: **160.00**
• Mickey Mouse and His Sky Adventure

Other grades: Multiply prices above by **1.5 for Mint • 2/3 for Very Fine • 1/3 for Fine • 1/5 for Very Good • 1/8 for Good**

215 ❑ Feb 1949 Cover: 0.10 **NM** value: **105.00**
• Dick Tracy
216 ❑ Feb 1949 Cover: 0.10 **NM** value: **70.00**
• Andy Panda
217 ❑ Feb 1949 Cover: 0.10 **NM** value: **100.00**
Court Jester • Bugs Bunny
218 ❑ Mar 1949 Cover: 0.10 **NM** value: **120.00**
• The Three Little Pigs and the Wonderful Magic Lamp (Disney)
219 ❑ Mar 1949 Cover: 0.10 **NM** value: **90.00**
• Swee'pea
220 ❑ Mar 1949 Cover: 0.10 **NM** value: **115.00**
• Easter with Mother Goose **A:** Walt Kelly
221 ❑ Mar 1949 Cover: 0.10 **NM** value: **105.00**
• Uncle Wiggily
222 ❑ Mar 1949 Cover: 0.10 **NM** value: **85.00**
• West of the Pecos (Zane Grey)
223 ❑ Apr 1949 Cover: 0.10 **NM** value: **860.00**
• **CGC:** 1 graded, best 9.2
Lost in the Andes! • Donald Duck; Famous "Square Eggs" story **A:** Carl Barks
224 ❑ Apr 1949 Cover: 0.10 **NM** value: **90.00**
• Little Iodine
225 ❑ Apr 1949 Cover: 0.10 **NM** value: **80.00**
• Oswald the Rabbit
226 ❑ Apr 1949 Cover: 0.10 **NM** value: **80.00**
• Porky Pig
227 ❑ May 1949 Cover: 0.10 **NM** value: **135.00**
• The Seven Dwarfs (Disney)
228 ❑ May 1949 Cover: 0.10 **NM** value: **235.00**
• Mark of Zorro
229 ❑ May 1949 Cover: 0.10 **NM** value: **50.00**
• Smokey Stover
230 ❑ May 1949 Cover: 0.10 **NM** value: **70.00**
• Sunset Pass (Zane Grey)
231 ❑ Jun 1949 Cover: 0.10 **NM** value: **140.00**
• Mickey Mouse
232 ❑ Jun 1949 Cover: 0.10 **NM** value: **70.00**
• Woody Woodpecker
233 ❑ Jun 1949 Cover: 0.10 **NM** value: **100.00**
• Bugs Bunny, Sleepwalking Sleuth
234 ❑ Jul 1949 Cover: 0.10 **NM** value: **95.00**
• **CGC:** 1 graded, best 6.5
Sky Voyage • Dumbo
235 ❑ Jul 1949 Cover: 0.10 **NM** value: **55.00**
• Tiny Tim
236 ❑ Jul 1949 Cover: 0.10 **NM** value: **75.00**
• Heritage of the Desert (Zane Grey)
237 ❑ Jul 1949 Cover: 0.10 **NM** value: **55.00**
• Tillie the Toiler
238 ❑ Aug 1949 Cover: 0.10 **NM** value: **675.00**
• **CGC:** 2 graded, best 7.5
Voodoo Hoodoo • Donald Duck **A:** Carl Barks
239 ❑ Aug 1949 Cover: 0.10 **NM** value: **50.00**
• Adventure Bound
240 ❑ Aug 1949 Cover: 0.10 **NM** value: **65.00**
• Andy Panda
241 ❑ Aug 1949 Cover: 0.10 **NM** value: **75.00**
• Porky Pig
242 ❑ Sep 1949 Cover: 0.10 **NM** value: **40.00**
• Tippie and Cap Stubbs
243 ❑ Sep 1949 Cover: 0.10 **NM** value: **110.00**
• Thumper Follows His Nose
244 ❑ Sep 1949 Cover: 0.10 **NM** value: **115.00**
• The Brownies **A:** Walt Kelly
245 ❑ Sep 1949 Cover: 0.10 **NM** value: **55.00**
• Dick's Adventures in Dreamland; Apparently last title to include strip reprints
246 ❑ Sep 1949 Cover: 0.10 **NM** value: **50.00**
• Thunder Mountain (Zane Grey)
247 ❑ Sep 1949 Cover: 0.10 **NM** value: **115.00**
• **CGC:** 3 graded, best 9.2
• Flash Gordon
248 ❑ Oct 1949 Cover: 0.10 **NM** value: **160.00**
• Mickey Mouse and the Black Sorcerer
249 ❑ Oct 1949 Cover: 0.10 **NM** value: **65.00**
The Globe Trotter • Woody Woodpecker
250 ❑ Oct 1949 Cover: 0.10 **NM** value: **100.00**
• **CGC:** 1 graded, best 8.5
• Bugs Bunny; "Diamonds thrown into the eyes" story cited in Seduction of the Innocent (p309)
251 ❑ Oct 1949 Cover: 0.10 **NM** value: **45.00**
• Hubert at Camp Moonbeam
252 ❑ Nov 1949 Cover: 0.10 **NM** value: **115.00**
• Pinocchio; Not by Kelly(?)
253 ❑ Nov 1949 Cover: 0.10 **NM** value: **115.00**
• Christmas with Mother Goose **A:** Walt Kelly
254 ❑ Nov 1949 Cover: 0.10 **NM** value: **115.00**
• Santa Claus Funnies **A:** Walt Kelly
255 ❑ Nov 1949 Cover: 0.10 **NM** value: **55.00**
• The Ranger (Zane Grey)
256 ❑ Dec 1949 Cover: 0.10 **NM** value: **475.00**
Luck of the North • Donald Duck
257 ❑ 1949 Cover: 0.10 **NM** value: **60.00**
• Little Iodine
258 ❑ Dec 1949 Cover: 0.10 **NM** value: **60.00**
• Andy Panda and the Balloon Race
259 ❑ Dec 1949 Cover: 0.10 **NM** value: **50.00**
• Santa and the Angel **A:** Moe Gollub
260 ❑ Dec 1949 Cover: 0.10 **NM** value: **70.00**
Hero of the Wild West • Porky Pig
261 ❑ Jan 1950 Cover: 0.10 **NM** value: **135.00**
• **CGC:** 1 graded, best 9.0
• Mickey Mouse
262 ❑ Jan 1950 Cover: 0.10 **NM** value: **75.00**
• **CGC:** 1 graded, best 7.5
• Raggedy Ann and Andy
263 ❑ Feb 1950 Cover: 0.10 **NM** value: **440.00**
• **CGC:** 1 graded, best 3.0
Land of the Totem Poles; Trail of the Unicorn • Donald Duck
264 ❑ Feb 1950 Cover: 0.10 **NM** value: **60.00**
The Magic Lantern • Woody Woodpecker
265 ❑ Feb 1950 Cover: 0.10 **NM** value: **80.00**
• King of the Royal Mounted
266 ❑ Feb 1950 Cover: 0.10 **NM** value: **95.00**
• Bugs Bunny on the Isle of Hercules
267 ❑ Feb 1950 Cover: 0.10 **NM** value: **40.00**
• Little Beaver
268 ❑ Mar 1950 Cover: 0.10 **NM** value: **135.00**
• Mickey Mouse's Surprise Visitor
269 ❑ Mar 1950 Cover: 0.10 **NM** value: **125.00**
• Bugs Bunny
270 ❑ Mar 1950 Cover: 0.10 **NM** value: **45.00**
• Drift Fence (Zane Grey)
271 ❑ Mar 1950 Cover: 0.10 **NM** value: **70.00**
Phantom of the Plains • Porky Pig
272 ❑ Apr 1950 Cover: 0.10 **NM** value: **110.00**
• Cinderella
273 ❑ Apr 1950 Cover: 0.10 **NM** value: **50.00**
• Oswald the Rabbit
274 ❑ Apr 1950 Cover: 0.10 **NM** value: **100.00**
• Bugs Bunny, Hare-Brained Reporter
275 ❑ May 1950 Cover: 0.10 **NM** value: **400.00**
Donald Dick in Ancient Persia • Donald Duck
276 ❑ May 1950 Cover: 0.10 **NM** value: **85.00**
• Uncle Wiggily
277 ❑ May 1950 Cover: 0.10 **NM** value: **70.00**
Desert Adventure • Porky Pig
278 ❑ May 1950 Cover: 0.10 **NM** value: **130.00**
• Wild Bill Elliott
279 ❑ Jun 1950 Cover: 0.10 **NM** value: **140.00**
• **CGC:** 2 graded, best 9.0
• Mickey Mouse and Pluto Battle the Giant Ants
280 ❑ Jun 1950 Cover: 0.10 **NM** value: **60.00**
The Isle of the Mechanical Men • Andy Panda
281 ❑ Jun 1950 Cover: 0.10 **NM** value: **95.00**
The Great Circus Mystery • Bugs Bunny
282 ❑ Jul 1950 Cover: 0.10 **NM** value: **400.00**
The Pixilated Parrot • Donald Duck
283 ❑ Jul 1950 Cover: 0.10 **NM** value: **80.00**
• King of the Royal Mounted
284 ❑ Jul 1950 Cover: 0.10 **NM** value: **70.00**
The Kingdom of Nowhere • Porky Pig
285 ❑ Jul 1950 Cover: 0.10 **NM** value: **210.00**
• Bozo the Clown and His Minkin Circus
286 ❑ Aug 1950 Cover: 0.10 **NM** value: **120.00**
• Mickey Mouse
287 ❑ Aug 1950 Cover: 0.10 **NM** value: **110.00**
• **CGC:** 1 graded, best 7.0
• Gene Autry
288 ❑ Aug 1950 Cover: 0.10 **NM** value: **60.00**
Klondike Gold • Woody Woodpecker
289 ❑ Aug 1950 Cover: 0.10 **NM** value: **95.00**
Indian Trouble • Bugs Bunny
290 ❑ Aug 1950 Cover: 0.10 **NM** value: **50.00**
• The Chief
291 ❑ Sep 1950 Cover: 0.10 **NM** value: **375.00**
• **CGC:** 2 graded, best 5.0
The Magic Hourglass • Donald Duck
292 ❑ Sep 1950 Cover: 0.10 **NM** value: **240.00**
• The Cisco Kid
293 ❑ Sep 1950 Cover: 0.10 **NM** value: **110.00**
• The Brownies
294 ❑ Sep 1950 Cover: 0.10 **NM** value: **40.00**
• Little Beaver
295 ❑ Sep 1950 Cover: 0.10 **NM** value: **70.00**
President Porky • Porky Pig
296 ❑ Oct 1950 Cover: 0.10 **NM** value: **120.00**
• **CGC:** 1 graded, best 7.5
• Mickey Mouse
297 ❑ Oct 1950 Cover: 0.10 **NM** value: **55.00**
• Andy Panda
298 ❑ Oct 1950 Cover: 0.10 **NM** value: **90.00**
Sheik for a Day • Bugs Bunny
299 ❑ Oct 1950 Cover: 0.10 **NM** value: **120.00**
• **CGC:** 1 graded, best 9.0
• Buck Jones
300 ❑ Nov 1950 Cover: 0.10 **NM** value: **375.00**
• **CGC:** 1 graded, best 7.0
Big-Top Bedlam • Donald Duck
301 ❑ Nov 1950 Cover: 0.10 **NM** value: **48.00**
• The Mysterious Rider (Zane Grey)
302 ❑ Nov 1950 Cover: 0.10 **NM** value: **45.00**
• Santa Claus Funnies
303 ❑ Nov 1950 Cover: 0.10 **NM** value: **55.00**
• Porky Pig in the Land of the Monstrous Flies
304 ❑ Dec 1950 Cover: 0.10 **NM** value: **95.00**
• Mickey Mouse
305 ❑ Dec 1950 Cover: 0.10 **NM** value: **45.00**
• Woody Woodpecker
306 ❑ Dec 1950 Cover: 0.10 **NM** value: **55.00**
• Raggedy Ann and Andy
307 ❑ Dec 1950 Cover: 0.10 **NM** value: **75.00**
Lumberjack Rabbit • Bugs Bunny
308 ❑ Jan 1951 Cover: 0.10 **NM** value: **335.00**
• **CGC:** 1 graded, best 6.5
Dangerous Disguise • Donald Duck
309 ❑ Jan 1951 Cover: 0.10 **NM** value: **55.00**
• Dollface and Her Gang (Betty Betz)
310 ❑ Jan 1951 Cover: 0.10 **NM** value: **70.00**
• King of the Royal Mounted
311 ❑ Jan 1951 Cover: 0.10 **NM** value: **50.00**
The Midget Horses of Hidden Valley • Porky Pig
312 ❑ Jan 1951 Cover: 0.10 **NM** value: **125.00**
• Tonto
313 ❑ Feb 1951 Cover: 0.10 **NM** value: **90.00**
• Mickey Mouse
314 ❑ Feb 1951 Cover: 0.10 **NM** value: **48.00**
• Ambush (Zane Grey)
315 ❑ Feb 1951 Cover: 0.10 **NM** value: **40.00**
• Oswald the Rabbit
316 ❑ Feb 1951 Cover: 0.10 **NM** value: **130.00**
• Rex Allen
317 ❑ Feb 1951 Cover: 0.10 **NM** value: **70.00**
• Bugs Bunny
318 ❑ Mar 1951 Cover: 0.10 **NM** value: **335.00**
• **CGC:** 4 graded, best 9.4
No Such Varmint • Donald Duck
319 ❑ Mar 1951 Cover: 0.10 **NM** value: **55.00**
• Gene Autry's Champion
320 ❑ Mar 1951 Cover: 0.10 **NM** value: **70.00**
• **CGC:** 1 graded, best 5.0
• Uncle Wiggily
321 ❑ Mar 1951 Cover: 0.10 **NM** value: **35.00**
• The Little Scouts
322 ❑ Mar 1951 Cover: 0.10 **NM** value: **45.00**
Roaring Rockets • Porky Pig
323 ❑ Mar 1951 Cover: 0.10 **NM** value: **40.00**
• Susie Q. Smith
324 ❑ Mar 1951 Cover: 0.10 **NM** value: **70.00**
• **CGC:** 1 graded, best 9.4
• I Met a Handsome Cowboy
325 ❑ Apr 1951 Cover: 0.10 **NM** value: **85.00**
• Mickey Mouse in the Haunted Castle
326 ❑ Apr 1951 Cover: 0.10 **NM** value: **40.00**
• Andy Panda
327 ❑ Apr 1951 Cover: 0.10 **NM** value: **65.00**
• Bugs Bunny
328 ❑ May 1951 Cover: 0.10 **NM** value: **335.00**
• **CGC:** 2 graded, best 9.2
Donald Duck in Old California • Donald Duck **A:** Carl Barks
329 ❑ May 1951 Cover: 0.10 **NM** value: **100.00**
• Trigger
330 ❑ May 1951 Cover: 0.10 **NM** value: **45.00**
• Porky Pig
331 ❑ May 1951 Cover: 0.10 **NM** value: **150.00**
• **CGC:** 1 graded, best 4.5
• Alice in Wonderland (Disney)
332 ❑ May 1951 Cover: 0.10 **NM** value: **40.00**
• Little Beaver
333 ❑ May 1951 Cover: 0.10 **NM** value: **40.00**
• Wilderness Trek (Zane Grey)
334 ❑ Jun 1951 Cover: 0.10 **NM** value: **85.00**
• Mickey Mouse and Yukon Gold
335 ❑ Jun 1951 Cover: 0.10 **NM** value: **80.00**
• Francis the Mule
336 ❑ Jun 1951 Cover: 0.10 **NM** value: **35.00**
• Woody Woodpecker
337 ❑ Jun 1951 Cover: 0.10 **NM** value: **40.00**
• The Brownies
338 ❑ Jun 1951 Cover: 0.10 **NM** value: **65.00**
• Bugs Bunny
339 ❑ Jul 1951 Cover: 0.10 **NM** value: **85.00**
• Donald Duck
340 ❑ Jul 1951 Cover: 0.10 **NM** value: **65.00**
• King of the Royal Mounted
341 ❑ Jul 1951 Cover: 0.10 **NM** value: **145.00**
• Unbirthday Party with Alice in Wonderland (Disney)
342 ❑ Jul 1951 Cover: 0.10 **NM** value: **40.00**
• Porky Pig
343 ❑ Aug 1951 Cover: 0.10 **NM** value: **75.00**
• Mickey Mouse
344 ❑ Aug 1951 Cover: 0.10 **NM** value: **130.00**
• Sgt. Preston of the Yukon
345 ❑ Aug 1951 Cover: 0.10 **NM** value: **35.00**
• Andy Panda
346 ❑ Aug 1951 Cover: 0.10 **NM** value: **48.00**
• Hideout (Zane Grey)
347 ❑ Aug 1951 Cover: 0.10 **NM** value: **65.00**
The Frigid Hare • Bugs Bunny
348 ❑ Sep 1951 Cover: 0.10 **NM** value: **140.00**
• **CGC:** 4 graded, best 8.5
The Crocodile Collector • Donald Duck
349 ❑ Sep 1951 Cover: 0.10 **NM** value: **65.00**
• Uncle Wiggily
350 ❑ Sep 1951 Cover: 0.10 **NM** value: **35.00**
• Woody Woodpecker
351 ❑ Sep 1951 Cover: 0.10 **NM** value: **40.00**
• Porky Pig
352 ❑ Oct 1951 Cover: 0.10 **NM** value: **70.00**
• Mickey Mouse
353 ❑ Oct 1951 Cover: 0.10 **NM** value: **80.00**
• Duck Album (Disney)
354 ❑ Oct 1951 Cover: 0.10 **NM** value: **50.00**
• Raggedy Ann and Andy
355 ❑ Oct 1951 Cover: 0.10 **NM** value: **65.00**
• Bugs Bunny
356 ❑ Nov 1951 Cover: 0.10 **NM** value: **135.00**
From Rags to Riches • Donald Duck
357 ❑ Nov 1951 Cover: 0.10 **NM** value: **42.00**
• Comeback (Zane Grey's Shepherd of Guadeloupe)
358 ❑ Nov 1951 Cover: 0.10 **NM** value: **35.00**
• Andy Panda
359 ❑ Nov 1951 Cover: 0.10 **NM** value: **80.00**
• Frosty the Snowman
360 ❑ Nov 1951 Cover: 0.10 **NM** value: **40.00**
• Porky Pig
361 ❑ Nov 1951 Cover: 0.10 **NM** value: **45.00**
• Santa Claus Funnies
362 ❑ Dec 1951 Cover: 0.10 **NM** value: **70.00**
• Mickey Mouse and the Smuggled Diamonds
363 ❑ Dec 1951 Cover: 0.10 **NM** value: **55.00**
• King of the Royal Mounted
364 ❑ Dec 1951 Cover: 0.10 **NM** value: **30.00**
• Woody Woodpecker
365 ❑ Dec 1951 Cover: 0.10 **NM** value: **40.00**
• The Brownies

CGC-graded: Multiply prices above by **33 for 9.9 M • 16 for 9.8 NM/M • 7 for 9.6 NM+ • 5 for 9.4 NM • 2.5 for 9.2 NM- • 1.5 for 9.0 VF/NM**

366 ❑ Dec 1951 Cover: 0.10 **NM** value: **65.00**
📖 Uncle Buckskin Comes to Town • Bugs Bunny
367 ❑ Jan 1952 Cover: 0.10 **NM** value: **330.00**
• **CGC:** 2 graded, best 7.0
📖 A Christmas for Shacktown • Donald Duck **A:** Carl Barks
368 ❑ Jan 1952 Cover: 0.10 **NM** value: **240.00**
• Beany and Cecil
369 ❑ Jan 1952 Cover: 0.10 **NM** value: **95.00**
• The Lone Ranger's Famous Horse Hi-Yo Silver
370 ❑ Jan 1952 Cover: 0.10 **NM** value: **35.00**
• Porky Pig
371 ❑ Feb 1952 Cover: 0.10 **NM** value: **65.00**
📖 The Inca Idol Case • Mickey Mouse
372 ❑ Feb 1952 Cover: 0.10 **NM** value: **40.00**
• Riders of the Purple Sage (Zane Grey)
373 ❑ Feb 1952 Cover: 0.10 **NM** value: **65.00**
• Sergeant Preston of the Yukon
374 ❑ Feb 1952 Cover: 0.10 **NM** value: **30.00**
• Woody Woodpecker
375 ❑ Feb 1952 Cover: 0.10 **NM** value: **250.00**
• **CGC:** 3 graded, best 9.0
• John Carter of Mars (Edgar Rice Burroughs) **A:** Jesse Marsh
376 ❑ Feb 1952 Cover: 0.10 **NM** value: **60.00**
• Bugs Bunny
377 ❑ Feb 1952 Cover: 0.10 **NM** value: **35.00**
• Suzie Q. Smith
378 ❑ Feb 1952 Cover: 0.10 **NM** value: **200.00**
• Tom Corbett, Space Cadet
379 ❑ Mar 1952 Cover: 0.10 **NM** value: **80.00**
• **CGC:** 1 graded, best 8.5
📖 Southern Hospitality • Donald Duck
380 ❑ Mar 1952 Cover: 0.10 **NM** value: **45.00**
• Raggedy Ann and Andy
381 ❑ Mar 1952 Cover: 0.10 **NM** value: **180.00**
• **CGC:** 1 graded, best 6.5
• Tubby
382 ❑ Mar 1952 Cover: 0.10 **NM** value: **130.00**
• **CGC:** 2 graded, best 7.5
• Snow White and the Seven Dwarfs (Disney)
383 ❑ Apr 1952 Cover: 0.10 **NM** value: **30.00**
• Andy Panda
384 ❑ Mar 1952 Cover: 0.10 **NM** value: **50.00**
• King of the Royal Mounted
385 ❑ Mar 1952 Cover: 0.10 **NM** value: **35.00**
• Porky Pig
386 ❑ Mar 1952 Cover: 0.10 **NM** value: **985.00**
• **CGC:** 16 graded, best 8.5
📖 Only a Poor Old Man • Uncle Scrooge (#1) **A:** Carl Barks
387 ❑ Apr 1952 Cover: 0.10 **NM** value: **65.00**
📖 High Tibet • Mickey Mouse
388 ❑ Apr 1952 Cover: 0.10 **NM** value: **40.00**
• Oswald the Rabbit
389 ❑ Apr 1952 Cover: 0.10 **NM** value: **35.00**
• Andy Hardy Comics
390 ❑ Apr 1952 Cover: 0.10 **NM** value: **30.00**
• Woody Woodpecker
391 ❑ Apr 1952 Cover: 0.10 **NM** value: **50.00**
• Uncle Wiggily
392 ❑ Apr 1952 Cover: 0.10 **NM** value: **60.00**
• Hi Yo Silver
393 ❑ Apr 1952 Cover: 0.10 **NM** value: **60.00**
• Bugs Bunny
394 ❑ May 1952 Cover: 0.10 **NM** value: **150.00**
• **CGC:** 1 graded, best 8.0
📖 Donald Duck in Malaysia • Donald Duck
395 ❑ May 1952 Cover: 0.10 **NM** value: **38.00**
• Forlorn River (Zane Grey)
396 ❑ May 1952 Cover: 0.10 **NM** value: **100.00**
• Tales of the Texas Rangers
397 ❑ May 1952 Cover: 0.10 **NM** value: **60.00**
• Sgt. Preston of the Yukon
398 ❑ May 1952 Cover: 0.10 **NM** value: **35.00**
• The Brownies
399 ❑ May 1952 Cover: 0.10 **NM** value: **35.00**
• Porky Pig
400 ❑ May 1952 Cover: 0.10 **NM** value: **145.00**
• Tom Corbett, Space Cadet
401 ❑ Jun 1952 Cover: 0.10 **NM** value: **50.00**
• Mickey Mouse
402 ❑ Jun 1952 Cover: 0.10 **NM** value: **80.00**
• Mary Jane and Sniffles
403 ❑ Jun 1952 Cover: 0.10 **NM** value: **65.00**
• Li'l Bad Wolf (Disney)
404 ❑ Jun 1952 Cover: 0.10 **NM** value: **100.00**
• Range Rider
405 ❑ Jun 1952 Cover: 0.10 **NM** value: **30.00**
• Woody Woodpecker
406 ❑ Jun 1952 Cover: 0.10 **NM** value: **65.00**
• **CGC:** 1 graded, best 9.0
• Tweety and Sylvester
407 ❑ Jun 1952 Cover: 0.10 **NM** value: **55.00**
• Bugs Bunny
408 ❑ Jul 1952 Cover: 0.10 **NM** value: **345.00**
• **CGC:** 4 graded, best 8.0
📖 The Golden Helmet • Donald Duck **A:** Carl Barks
409 ❑ Jul 1952 Cover: 0.10 **NM** value: **30.00**
• Andy Panda
410 ❑ Jul 1952 Cover: 0.10 **NM** value: **35.00**
• Porky Pig
411 ❑ Jul 1952 Cover: 0.10 **NM** value: **50.00**
• Mickey Mouse and the Old Sea Dog
412 ❑ ca. 1952 Cover: 0.10 **NM** value: **35.00**
• Nevada (Zane Grey)
413 ❑ ca. 1952 Cover: 0.10 **NM** value: **130.00**
• Robin Hood (Disney)
414 ❑ ca. 1952 Cover: 0.10 **NM** value: **170.00**
• Beany and Cecil
415 ❑ ca. 1952 Cover: 0.10 **NM** value: **120.00**
• Rootie Kazootie
416 ❑ Aug 1952 Cover: 0.10 **NM** value: **30.00**
• Woody Woodpecker
417 ❑ ca. 1952 Cover: 0.10 **NM** value: **30.00**
• Double Trouble with Goober
418 ❑ ca. 1952 Cover: 0.10 **NM** value: **45.00**
• Rusty Riley's Ruff and Ready
419 ❑ ca. 1952 Cover: 0.10 **NM** value: **65.00**
• Sgt. Preston of the Yukon
420 ❑ ca. 1952 Cover: 0.10 **NM** value: **50.00**
📖 Mysterious Buckaroo • Bugs Bunny
421 ❑ ca. 1952 Cover: 0.10 **NM** value: **125.00**
• **CGC:** 1 graded, best 8.0
• Tom Corbett, Space Cadet
422 ❑ Sep 1952 Cover: 0.10 **NM** value: **335.00**
• **CGC:** 1 graded, best 5.0
📖 The Gilded Man • Donald Duck **A:** Carl Barks
423 ❑ ca. 1952 Cover: 0.10 **NM** value: **40.00**
• Rhubarb, the Millionaire Cat
424 ❑ ca. 1952 Cover: 0.10 **NM** value: **110.00**
• Flash Gordon
425 ❑ ca. 1952 Cover: 0.10 **NM** value: **160.00**
• Return of Zorro
426 ❑ Sep 1952 Cover: 0.10 **NM** value: **35.00**
📖 The Scalawag Leprechaun • Porky Pig
427 ❑ ca. 1952 Cover: 0.10 **NM** value: **45.00**
• Mickey Mouse
428 ❑ ca. 1952 Cover: 0.10 **NM** value: **45.00**
• Uncle Wiggily
429 ❑ ca. 1952 Cover: 0.10 **NM** value: **75.00**
• **CGC:** 1 graded, best 7.0
📖 Why Dogs Leave Home • Pluto
430 ❑ ca. 1952 Cover: 0.10 **NM** value: **115.00**
• Tubby
431 ❑ ca. 1952 Cover: 0.10 **NM** value: **30.00**
• Woody Woodpecker
432 ❑ ca. 1952 Cover: 0.10 **NM** value: **45.00**
• Bugs Bunny
433 ❑ ca. 1952 Cover: 0.10 **NM** value: **35.00**
• Wildfire (Zane Grey)
434 ❑ Nov 1952 Cover: 0.10 **NM** value: **190.00**
📖 Dark Danger • Rin Tin Tin
435 ❑ ca. 1952 Cover: 0.10 **NM** value: **50.00**
• Frosty the Snowman
436 ❑ Nov 1952 Cover: 0.10 **NM** value: **35.00**
• The Brownies
437 ❑ ca. 1952 Cover: 0.10 **NM** value: **165.00**
• **CGC:** 1 graded, best 9.6
• John Carter of Mars (Edgar Rice Burroughs) **A:** Jesse Marsh
438 ❑ ca. 1952 Cover: 0.10 **NM** value: **135.00**
• Annie Oakley
439 ❑ ca. 1952 Cover: 0.10 **NM** value: **55.00**
• Little Hiawatha (Disney)
440 ❑ ca. 1952 Cover: 0.10 **NM** value: **35.00**
• Black Beauty
441 ❑ ca. 1952 Cover: 0.10 **NM** value: **35.00**
• **CGC:** 1 graded, best 8.5
• Fearless Fagan
442 ❑ ca. 1952 Cover: 0.10 **NM** value: **100.00**
• Peter Pan (Disney)
443 ❑ ca. 1953 Cover: 0.10 **NM** value: **60.00**
• Ben Bowie's Mountain Men
444 ❑ ca. 1953 Cover: 0.10 **NM** value: **110.00**
• Tubby
445 ❑ ca. 1953 Cover: 0.10 **NM** value: **55.00**
• Charlie McCarthy
446 ❑ ca. 1953 Cover: 0.10 **NM** value: **90.00**
• Captain Hook and Peter Pan (Disney)
447 ❑ ca. 1953 Cover: 0.10 **NM** value: **30.00**
• Andy Hardy
448 ❑ ca. 1953 Cover: 0.10 **NM** value: **160.00**
• Beany and Cecil
449 ❑ ca. 1953 Cover: 0.10 **NM** value: **35.00**
• Tappan's Burro (Zane Grey)
450 ❑ ca. 1953 Cover: 0.10 **NM** value: **65.00**
• Duck Album (Disney)
451 ❑ ca. 1953 Cover: 0.10 **NM** value: **40.00**
• Rusty Riley, A Boy, a Horse, and a Dog **A:** Frank Godwin **W:** Frank Godwin
452 ❑ ca. 1953 Cover: 0.10 **NM** value: **40.00**
• Raggedy Ann and Andy
453 ❑ Feb 1953 Cover: 0.10 **NM** value: **40.00**
• Susie Q. Smith
454 ❑ Feb 1953 Cover: 0.10 **NM** value: **40.00**
• Krazy Kat
455 ❑ Mar 1953 Cover: 0.10 **NM** value: **60.00**
• Johnny Mack Brown
456 ❑ ca. 1953 Cover: 0.10 **NM** value: **645.00**
• **CGC:** 3 graded, best 7.0
📖 Back to the Klondike; Somethin' Fishy Here • Uncle Scrooge (#2) **A:** Carl Barks
457 ❑ ca. 1953 Cover: 0.10 **NM** value: **90.00**
• Daffy
458 ❑ ca. 1953 Cover: 0.10 **NM** value: **30.00**
• Oswald the Rabbit
459 ❑ ca. 1953 Cover: 0.10 **NM** value: **85.00**
• Rootie Kazootie
460 ❑ Apr 1953 Cover: 0.10 **NM** value: **50.00**
• Buck Jones
461 ❑ ca. 1953 Cover: 0.10 **NM** value: **100.00**
• Tubby
462 ❑ ca. 1953 Cover: 0.10 **NM** value: **28.00**
• Little Scouts
463 ❑ ca. 1953 Cover: 0.10 **NM** value: **30.00**
• Petunia
464 ❑ Apr 1953 Cover: 0.10 **NM** value: **100.00**
• Bozo
465 ❑ ca. 1953 Cover: 0.10 **NM** value: **45.00**
• Francis the Mule
466 ❑ ca. 1953 Cover: 0.10 **NM** value: **32.00**
• Rhubarb, the Millionaire Cat
467 ❑ ca. 1953 Cover: 0.10 **NM** value: **32.00**
• Desert Gold (Zane Grey)
468 ❑ ca. 1953 Cover: 0.10 **NM** value: **125.00**
• Goofy (Disney)
469 ❑ ca. 1953 Cover: 0.10 **NM** value: **100.00**
• Beetle Bailey
470 ❑ ca. 1953 Cover: 0.10 **NM** value: **35.00**
• Elmer Fudd
471 ❑ ca. 1953 Cover: 0.10 **NM** value: **25.00**
• Double Trouble with Goober
472 ❑ Jun 1953 Cover: 0.10 **NM** value: **50.00**
• Wild Bill Elliott
473 ❑ ca. 1953 Cover: 0.10 **NM** value: **45.00**
• Li'l Bad Wolf (Disney)
474 ❑ ca. 1953 Cover: 0.10 **NM** value: **70.00**
• Mary Jane and Sniffles
475 ❑ ca. 1953 Cover: 0.10 **NM** value: **65.00**
• The Two Musketeers
476 ❑ ca. 1953 Cover: 0.10 **NM** value: **85.00**
• **CGC:** 1 graded, best 7.0
• Rin Tin Tin
477 ❑ ca. 1953 Cover: 0.10 **NM** value: **140.00**
• Beany and Cecil
478 ❑ ca. 1953 Cover: 0.10 **NM** value: **50.00**
• Charlie McCarthy
479 ❑ Jul 1953 Cover: 0.10 **NM** value: **200.00**
• **CGC:** 1 graded, best 9.0
• Queen of the West Dale Evans
480 ❑ ca. 1953 Cover: 0.10 **NM** value: **25.00**
• Andy Hardy
481 ❑ ca. 1953 Cover: 0.10 **NM** value: **85.00**
• Annie Oakley
482 ❑ ca. 1953 Cover: 0.10 **NM** value: **30.00**
• **CGC:** 1 graded, best 7.0
• The Brownies
483 ❑ ca. 1953 Cover: 0.10 **NM** value: **30.00**
• Little Beaver
484 ❑ Aug 1953 Cover: 0.10 **NM** value: **30.00**
• River Feud (Zane Grey)
485 ❑ Aug 1953 Cover: 0.10 **NM** value: **65.00**
• The Little People (Walt Scott) **A:** Walt Scott
486 ❑ ca. 1953 Cover: 0.10 **NM** value: **40.00**
• Rusty Riley
487 ❑ ca. 1953 Cover: 0.10 **NM** value: **60.00**
• Rudyard Kipling's Mowgli Jungle Book
488 ❑ ca. 1953 Cover: 0.10 **NM** value: **155.00**
• **CGC:** 1 graded, best 7.5
• John Carter of Mars (Edgar Rice Burroughs) **A:** Jesse Marsh
489 ❑ ca. 1953 Cover: 0.10 **NM** value: **35.00**
• Tweety and Sylvester
490 ❑ ca. 1953 Cover: 0.10 **NM** value: **75.00**
• **CGC:** 1 graded, best 8.0
• Jungle Jim
491 ❑ ca. 1953 Cover: 0.10 **NM** value: **80.00**
• Silvertip (Max Brand)
492 ❑ ca. 1953 Cover: 0.10 **NM** value: **55.00**
• Duck Album (Disney)
493 ❑ ca. 1953 Cover: 0.10 **NM** value: **55.00**
• Johnny Mack Brown
494 ❑ ca. 1953 Cover: 0.10 **NM** value: **90.00**
• The Little King
495 ❑ ca. 1953 Cover: 0.10 **NM** value: **495.00**
• **CGC:** 1 graded, best 5.5
📖 Untitled Uncle Scrooge Stories • Uncle Scrooge (#3); Next issue was #4, going into its own series; First 'Old Number One Dime' **A:** Carl Barks
496 ❑ ca. 1953 Cover: 0.10 **NM** value: **285.00**
• The Green Hornet
497 ❑ ca. 1953 Cover: 0.10 **NM** value: **170.00**
• The Sword of Zorro
498 ❑ Sep 1953 Cover: 0.10 **NM** value: **40.00**
• **CGC:** 1 graded, best 6.0
• Bugs Bunny's Album
499 ❑ ca. 1953 Cover: 0.10 **NM** value: **40.00**
• Spike and Tyke
500 ❑ ca. 1953 Cover: 0.10 **NM** value: **40.00**
• Buck Jones
501 ❑ ca. 1953 Cover: 0.10 **NM** value: **50.00**
• Francis the Mule
502 ❑ ca. 1953 Cover: 0.10 **NM** value: **75.00**
• Rootie Kazootie
503 ❑ Oct 1953 Cover: 0.10 **NM** value: **45.00**
• Uncle Wiggily
504 ❑ ca. 1953 Cover: 0.10 **NM** value: **40.00**
• Krazy Kat
505 ❑ Oct 1953 Cover: 0.10 **NM** value: **80.00**
• The Sword and the Rose (Disney's "When Knighthood was in Flower")
506 ❑ Oct 1953 Cover: 0.10 **NM** value: **22.00**
• The Little Scouts
507 ❑ ca. 1953 Cover: 0.10 **NM** value: **30.00**
• Oswald the Rabbit
508 ❑ ca. 1953 Cover: 0.10 **NM** value: **90.00**
• Bozo
509 ❑ Oct 1953 Cover: 0.10 **NM** value: **60.00**
• Pluto
510 ❑ ca. 1953 Cover: 0.10 **NM** value: **35.00**
• Son of Black Beauty
511 ❑ ca. 1953 Cover: 0.10 **NM** value: **30.00**
• Outlaw Trail (Zane Grey's Border Legion)
512 ❑ ca. 1953 Cover: 0.10 **NM** value: **60.00**
• **CGC:** 1 graded, best 3.5
• Flash Gordon
513 ❑ ca. 1953 Cover: 0.10 **NM** value: **35.00**
• Ben Bowie's Mountain Men
514 ❑ ca. 1953 Cover: 0.10 **NM** value: **40.00**
• Frosty the Snowman

Other grades: Multiply prices above by **1.5 for Mint • 2/3 for Very Fine • 1/3 for Fine • 1/5 for Very Good • 1/8 for Good**

515 ❑ ca. 1953 Cover: 0.10 **NM** value: **25.00**
• Andy Panda
516 ❑ Nov 1953 Cover: 0.10 **NM** value: **25.00**
• Double Trouble with Goober
517 ❑ ca. 1953 Cover: 0.10 **NM** value: **70.00**
• Chip 'n' Dale (Disney)
518 ❑ ca. 1953 Cover: 0.10 **NM** value: **30.00**
• Rivets
519 ❑ ca. 1953 Cover: 0.10 **NM** value: **85.00**
• Steve Canyon
520 ❑ ca. 1953 Cover: 0.10 **NM** value: **45.00**
• Wild Bill Elliott
521 ❑ ca. 1953 Cover: 0.10 **NM** value: **50.00**
• **CGC:** 1 graded, best 7.0
• Beetle Bailey
522 ❑ ca. 1953 Cover: 0.10 **NM** value: **30.00**
• The Brownies
523 ❑ Dec 1953 Cover: 0.10 **NM** value: **80.00**
• Rin Tin Tin
524 ❑ ca. 1953 Cover: 0.10 **NM** value: **30.00**
• Tweety and Sylvester
525 ❑ ca. 1953 Cover: 0.10 **NM** value: **40.00**
• Santa Claus Funnies
526 ❑ ca. 1954 Cover: 0.10 **NM** value: **25.00**
• Napoleon (and Uncle Elby)
527 ❑ ca. 1954 Cover: 0.10 **NM** value: **45.00**
• Charlie McCarthy
528 ❑ ca. 1954 Cover: 0.10 **NM** value: **100.00**
• Dale Evans
529 ❑ Jan 1954 Cover: 0.10 **NM** value: **30.00**
• **CGC:** 1 graded, best 9.4
• Little Beaver
530 ❑ ca. 1954 Cover: 0.10 **NM** value: **140.00**
• Beany and Cecil
531 ❑ ca. 1954 Cover: 0.10 **NM** value: **45.00**
• Duck Album (Disney)
532 ❑ Feb 1954 Cover: 0.10 **NM** value: **30.00**
• The Rustlers (adapts Zane Grey's "Raiders of Spanish Peak")
533 ❑ ca. 1954 Cover: 0.10 **NM** value: **35.00**
• Raggedy Ann and Andy
534 ❑ ca. 1954 Cover: 0.10 **NM** value: **50.00**
• Western Marshal
535 ❑ ca. 1954 Cover: 0.10 **NM** value: **500.00**
• **CGC:** 17 graded, best 9.4
• I Love Lucy
536 ❑ ca. 1954 Cover: 0.10 **NM** value: **45.00**
• Daffy
537 ❑ ca. 1954 Cover: 0.10 **NM** value: **40.00**
Stormy; Pluto: Uninvited • Stormy (Disney)
538 ❑ ca. 1954 Cover: 0.10 **NM** value: **155.00**
• Mask of Zorro
539 ❑ ca. 1954 Cover: 0.10 **NM** value: **35.00**
• Ben and Me (Disney)
540 ❑ Mar 1954 Cover: 0.10 **NM** value: **70.00**
• Knights of the Round Table
541 ❑ May 1954 Cover: 0.10 **NM** value: **50.00**
• Johnny Mack Brown
542 ❑ Mar 1954 Cover: 0.10 **NM** value: **60.00**
• Super Circus Featuring Mary Hartline
543 ❑ ca. 1954 Cover: 0.10 **NM** value: **40.00**
• Uncle Wiggily
544 ❑ ca. 1954 Cover: 0.10 **NM** value: **90.00**
• **CGC:** 1 graded, best 6.0
• Rob Roy (Disney)
545 ❑ ca. 1954 Cover: 0.10 **NM** value: **75.00**
• The Wonderful Adventures of Pinocchio (Disney) **A:** Walt Kelly
546 ❑ ca. 1954 Cover: 0.10 **NM** value: **45.00**
• Buck Jones
547 ❑ ca. 1954 Cover: 0.10 **NM** value: **45.00**
• Francis, the Talking Mule
548 ❑ ca. 1954 Cover: 0.10 **NM** value: **30.00**
• **CGC:** 1 graded, best 6.5
• Krazy Kat
549 ❑ ca. 1954 Cover: 0.10 **NM** value: **30.00**
• Oswald the Rabbit
550 ❑ ca. 1954 Cover: 0.10 **NM** value: **20.00**
• The Little Scouts
551 ❑ ca. 1954 Cover: 0.10 **NM** value: **85.00**
• Bozo the Clown
552 ❑ ca. 1954 Cover: 0.10 **NM** value: **45.00**
• Beetle Bailey
553 ❑ ca. 1954 Cover: 0.10 **NM** value: **25.00**
• Susie Q. Smith
554 ❑ ca. 1954 Cover: 0.10 **NM** value: **30.00**
• Rusty Riley
555 ❑ ca. 1954 Cover: 0.10 **NM** value: **30.00**
• Range War (adapts Zane Grey's "Hash Knife Outfit")
556 ❑ May 1954 Cover: 0.10 **NM** value: **20.00**
• Double Trouble with Goober
557 ❑ ca. 1954 Cover: 0.10 **NM** value: **40.00**
• Ben Bowie and His Mountain Men
558 ❑ ca. 1954 Cover: 0.10 **NM** value: **30.00**
• Elmer Fudd
559 ❑ ca. 1954 Cover: 0.10 **NM** value: **375.00**
• **CGC:** 5 graded, best 6.5
• I Love Lucy
560 ❑ May 1954 Cover: 0.10 **NM** value: **45.00**
• Duck Album (Disney)
561 ❑ ca. 1954 Cover: 0.10 **NM** value: **120.00**
• The Nearsighted Mr. Magoo
562 ❑ ca. 1954 Cover: 0.10 **NM** value: **70.00**
• Goofy (Disney)
563 ❑ ca. 1954 Cover: 0.10 **NM** value: **35.00**
• Rhubarb, the Millionaire Cat
564 ❑ ca. 1954 Cover: 0.10 **NM** value: **40.00**
• Li'l Bad Wolf (Disney)
565 ❑ ca. 1954 Cover: 0.10 **NM** value: **45.00**
• **CGC:** 1 graded, best 6.5
• Jungle Jim
566 ❑ ca. 1954 Cover: 0.10 **NM** value: **35.00**
• Son of Black Beauty
567 ❑ ca. 1954 Cover: 0.10 **NM** value: **115.00**
• **CGC:** 1 graded, best 6.5
• Prince Valiant
568 ❑ ca. 1954 Cover: 0.10 **NM** value: **45.00**
• Gypsy Colt
569 ❑ ca. 1954 Cover: 0.10 **NM** value: **28.00**
• Priscilla's Pop
570 ❑ ca. 1954 Cover: 0.10 **NM** value: **140.00**
• Beany and Cecil
571 ❑ ca. 1954 Cover: 0.10 **NM** value: **45.00**
• Charlie McCarthy
572 ❑ ca. 1954 Cover: 0.10 **NM** value: **40.00**
• Silvertip's Search (Max Brand)
573 ❑ ca. 1954 Cover: 0.10 **NM** value: **30.00**
• The Little People (Walt Scott) **A:** Walt Scott
574 ❑ ca. 1954 Cover: 0.10 **NM** value: **155.00**
• The Hand of Zorro
575 ❑ ca. 1954 Cover: 0.10 **NM** value: **85.00**
• **CGC:** 1 graded, best 9.2
• Annie Oakley and Tagg
576 ❑ ca. 1954 Cover: 0.10 **NM** value: **30.00**
• Angel
577 ❑ ca. 1954 Cover: 0.10 **NM** value: **25.00**
• Spike and Tyke
578 ❑ Aug 1954 Cover: 0.10 **NM** value: **55.00**
• Steve Canyon
579 ❑ ca. 1954 Cover: 0.10 **NM** value: **40.00**
• Francis, the Talking Mule
580 ❑ Aug 1954 Cover: 0.10 **NM** value: **35.00**
• Six Gun Ranch (Luke Short)
581 ❑ ca. 1954 Cover: 0.10 **NM** value: **50.00**
• Chip 'n' Dale (Disney)
582 ❑ ca. 1954 Cover: 0.10 **NM** value: **45.00**
• Mowgli-Jungle Book
583 ❑ ca. 1954 Cover: 0.10 **NM** value: **30.00**
• The Lost Wagon Train (Zane Grey)
584 ❑ ca. 1954 Cover: 0.10 **NM** value: **50.00**
• Johnny Mack Brown
585 ❑ ca. 1954 Cover: 0.10 **NM** value: **35.00**
• Bugs Bunny's Album
586 ❑ ca. 1954 Cover: 0.10 **NM** value: **45.00**
• Duck Album (Disney)
587 ❑ ca. 1954 Cover: 0.10 **NM** value: **20.00**
• The Little Scouts
588 ❑ ca. 1954 Cover: 0.10 **NM** value: **100.00**
• **CGC:** 1 graded, best 5.0
• King Richard and the Crusaders
589 ❑ ca. 1954 Cover: 0.10 **NM** value: **45.00**
• Buck Jones
590 ❑ ca. 1954 Cover: 0.10 **NM** value: **60.00**
• Hansel and Gretel
591 ❑ ca. 1954 Cover: 0.10 **NM** value: **60.00**
• Western Marshal (Ernest Haycox)
592 ❑ ca. 1954 Cover: 0.10 **NM** value: **50.00**
• Super Circus
593 ❑ ca. 1954 Cover: 0.10 **NM** value: **30.00**
• Oswald the Rabbit
594 ❑ Oct 1954 Cover: 0.10 **NM** value: **85.00**
• Bozo
595 ❑ ca. 1954 Cover: 0.10 **NM** value: **40.00**
• Pluto
596 ❑ ca. 1954 Cover: 0.10 **NM** value: **550.00**
• **CGC:** 7 graded, best 8.5
• Turok, Son of Stone ★ Origin of Turok. ★ 1st Appearance of Andar, Turok.
597 ❑ ca. 1954 Cover: 0.10 **NM** value: **55.00**
• The Little King
598 ❑ ca. 1954 Cover: 0.10 **NM** value: **40.00**
• Captain Davy Jones
599 ❑ ca. 1954 Cover: 0.10 **NM** value: **35.00**
• Ben Bowie and His Mountain Men
600 ❑ ca. 1954 Cover: 0.10 **NM** value: **65.00**
• Daisy Duck's Diary (Disney)
601 ❑ ca. 1954 Cover: 0.10 **NM** value: **35.00**
• Frosty the Snowman
602 ❑ ca. 1954 Cover: 0.10 **NM** value: **125.00**
• The Nearsighted Mr. Magoo and Gerald McBoing Boing
603 ❑ ca. 1954 Cover: 0.10 **NM** value: **45.00**
• The Two Musketeers
604 ❑ ca. 1954 Cover: 0.10 **NM** value: **45.00**
• Super Circus
605 ❑ Dec 1954 Cover: 0.10 **NM** value: **30.00**
• The Brownies
606 ❑ Dec 1954 Cover: 0.10 **NM** value: **85.00**
• Sir Lancelot
607 ❑ ca. 1954 Cover: 0.10 **NM** value: **35.00**
• Santa Claus Funnies
608 ❑ ca. 1954 Cover: 0.10 **NM** value: **45.00**
• Silvertip and the Valley of Vanishing Men (Max Brand)
609 ❑ Nov 1954 Cover: 0.10 **NM** value: **60.00**
• The Littlest Outlaw (Disney)
610 ❑ Jan 1955 Cover: 0.10 **NM** value: **95.00**
• Drum Beat
611 ❑ Jan 1955 Cover: 0.10 **NM** value: **50.00**
• Duck Album (Disney)
612 ❑ ca. 1955 Cover: 0.10 **NM** value: **30.00**
• Little Beaver
613 ❑ Feb 1955 Cover: 0.10 **NM** value: **50.00**
• Western Marshal (Ernest Haycox)
614 ❑ ca. 1955 Cover: 0.10 **NM** value: **95.00**
• 20,000 Leagues Under the Sea (Disney)
615 ❑ ca. 1955 Cover: 0.10 **NM** value: **45.00**
• Daffy
616 ❑ ca. 1955 Cover: 0.10 **NM** value: **30.00**
• To the Last Man (Zane Grey)
617 ❑ ca. 1955 Cover: 0.10 **NM** value: **145.00**
• Quest of Zorro
618 ❑ ca. 1955 Cover: 0.10 **NM** value: **50.00**
• Johnny Mack Brown
619 ❑ ca. 1955 Cover: 0.10 **NM** value: **40.00**
• Krazy Kat
620 ❑ ca. 1955 Cover: 0.10 **NM** value: **45.00**
• Mowgli-Jungle Book
621 ❑ ca. 1955 Cover: 0.10 **NM** value: **35.00**
• Francis, the Talking Mule
622 ❑ ca. 1955 Cover: 0.10 **NM** value: **35.00**
• Beetle Bailey
623 ❑ ca. 1955 Cover: 0.10 **NM** value: **25.00**
• Oswald the Rabbit
624 ❑ Apr 1955 Cover: 0.10 **NM** value: **75.00**
• **CGC:** 1 graded, best 7.5
• Treasure Island (Disney)
625 ❑ ca. 1955 Cover: 0.10 **NM** value: **50.00**
• Beaver Valley (Disney)
626 ❑ ca. 1955 Cover: 0.10 **NM** value: **35.00**
• Ben Bowie and His Mountain Men
627 ❑ ca. 1955 Cover: 0.10 **NM** value: **65.00**
• **CGC:** 1 graded, best 8.0
• Goofy (Disney)
628 ❑ May 1955 Cover: 0.10 **NM** value: **28.00**
• Elmer Fudd
629 ❑ May 1955 Cover: 0.10 **NM** value: **70.00**
• Lady and the Tramp (Disney)
630 ❑ ca. 1955 Cover: 0.10 **NM** value: **30.00**
• Priscilla's Pop
631 ❑ May 1955 Cover: 0.10 **NM** value: **155.00**
• **CGC:** 3 graded, best 8.0
• Davy Crockett, Indian Fighter (Disney)
632 ❑ ca. 1955 Cover: 0.10 **NM** value: **32.00**
• Fighting Caravans (Zane Grey)
633 ❑ ca. 1955 Cover: 0.10 **NM** value: **30.00**
• The Little People (Walt Scott) **A:** Walt Scott
634 ❑ ca. 1955 Cover: 0.10 **NM** value: **50.00**
• Lady and the Tramp Album (Disney)
635 ❑ ca. 1955 Cover: 0.10 **NM** value: **140.00**
• Beany and Cecil
636 ❑ ca. 1955 Cover: 0.10 **NM** value: **40.00**
• Chip 'n' Dale (Disney)
637 ❑ ca. 1955 Cover: 0.10 **NM** value: **40.00**
• Silvertip (Max Brand)
638 ❑ ca. 1955 Cover: 0.10 **NM** value: **25.00**
• Spike and Tyke
639 ❑ Jul 1955 Cover: 0.10 **NM** value: **135.00**
• **CGC:** 1 graded, best 9.2
• Davy Crockett at the Alamo (Disney)
640 ❑ ca. 1955 Cover: 0.10 **NM** value: **45.00**
• Western Marshal (Ernest Haycox)
641 ❑ ca. 1955 Cover: 0.10 **NM** value: **50.00**
• **CGC:** 1 graded, best 9.0
• Steve Canyon **A:** Milton Caniff
642 ❑ ca. 1955 Cover: 0.10 **NM** value: **45.00**
• The Two Musketeers
643 ❑ Jul 1955 Cover: 0.10 **NM** value: **35.00**
• Wild Bill Elliott
644 ❑ ca. 1955 Cover: 0.10 **NM** value: **70.00**
• Sir Walter Raleigh; 5/55; Based on movie, "The Virgin Queen"
645 ❑ ca. 1955 Cover: 0.10 **NM** value: **50.00**
• Johnny Mack Brown
646 ❑ Aug 1955 Cover: 0.10 **NM** value: **35.00**
• Dotty Dripple and Taffy
647 ❑ ca. 1955 Cover: 0.10 **NM** value: **40.00**
• Bugs Bunny Album
648 ❑ ca. 1955 Cover: 0.10 **NM** value: **55.00**
• Jace Pearson's Tales of the Texas Rangers
649 ❑ ca. 1955 Cover: 0.10 **NM** value: **50.00**
• Duck Album (Disney)
650 ❑ ca. 1955 Cover: 0.10 **NM** value: **70.00**
• **CGC:** 1 graded, best 7.5
• Prince Valiant
651 ❑ Sep 1955 Cover: 0.10 **NM** value: **35.00**
• King Colt (Luke Short)
652 ❑ ca. 1955 Cover: 0.10 **NM** value: **30.00**
• Buck Jones
653 ❑ ca. 1955 Cover: 0.10 **NM** value: **95.00**
• Smokey the Bear
654 ❑ ca. 1955 Cover: 0.10 **NM** value: **35.00**
• **CGC:** 1 graded, best 9.4
• Pluto
655 ❑ ca. 1955 Cover: 0.10 **NM** value: **30.00**
• Francis, the Talking Mule
656 ❑ ca. 1955 Cover: 0.10 **NM** value: **300.00**
• **CGC:** 2 graded, best 8.0
• Turok, Son of Stone ★ 2nd Appearance of Turok.
657 ❑ ca. 1955 Cover: 0.10 **NM** value: **35.00**
• Ben Bowie and His Mountain Men
658 ❑ ca. 1955 Cover: 0.10 **NM** value: **65.00**
• Goofy (Disney)
659 ❑ ca. 1955 Cover: 0.10 **NM** value: **45.00**
• Daisy Duck's Diary
660 ❑ ca. 1955 Cover: 0.10 **NM** value: **30.00**
• Little Beaver
661 ❑ ca. 1955 Cover: 0.10 **NM** value: **35.00**
• Frosty the Snowman
662 ❑ ca. 1955 Cover: 0.10 **NM** value: **50.00**
• Zoo Parade
663 ❑ ca. 1955 Cover: 0.10 **NM** value: **60.00**
• Winky Dink
664 ❑ ca. 1955 Cover: 0.10 **NM** value: **135.00**
• Davy Crockett and the Great Keelboat Race (Disney)
665 ❑ ca. 1955 Cover: 0.10 **NM** value: **50.00**
• **CGC:** 1 graded, best 3.0
• The African Lion (Disney)
666 ❑ ca. 1955 Cover: 0.10 **NM** value: **40.00**
• Santa Claus Funnies
667 ❑ Dec 1955 Cover: 0.10 **NM** value: **40.00**
• Silvertip and the Stolen Stallion (Max Brand)
668 ❑ ca. 1955 Cover: 0.10 **NM** value: **75.00**

CGC-graded: Multiply prices above by **33 for 9.9 M • 16 for 9.8 NM/M • 7 for 9.6 NM+ • 5 for 9.4 NM • 2.5 for 9.2 NM- • 1.5 for 9.0 VF/NM**

• **CGC:** 2 graded, best 9.2
• Dumbo (Disney)
669 ❑ Dec 1955 Cover: 0.10 **NM** value: **65.00**
• Robin Hood (Disney)
670 ❑ Jan 1956 Cover: 0.10 **NM** value: **35.00**
• Mouse Musketeers; Formerly "The Two Mouseketeers"
671 ❑ ca. 1955 Cover: 0.10 **NM** value: **135.00**
• **CGC:** 1 graded, best 9.6
• Davy Crockett and the River Pirates (Disney)
672 ❑ ca. 1956 Cover: 0.10 **NM** value: **65.00**
• Quentin Durward
673 ❑ ca. 1956 Cover: 0.10 **NM** value: **60.00**
• Buffalo Bill Jr.
674 ❑ ca. 1956 Cover: 0.10 **NM** value: **65.00**
• **CGC:** 1 graded, best 9.2
• The Little Rascals; 1/56
675 ❑ ca. 1956 Cover: 0.10 **NM** value: **65.00**
• Steve Donovan, Western Marshal
676 ❑ ca. 1956 Cover: 0.10 **NM** value: **25.00**
• Will-yum!
677 ❑ ca. 1956 Cover: 0.10 **NM** value: **60.00**
• The Little King
678 ❑ ca. 1956 Cover: 0.10 **NM** value: **65.00**
• The Last Hunt
679 ❑ ca. 1956 Cover: 0.10 **NM** value: **165.00**
• **CGC:** 2 graded, best 9.0
• Gunsmoke
680 ❑ Feb 1956 Cover: 0.10 **NM** value: **30.00**
• **CGC:** 1 graded, best 5.5
• Out Our Way with the Worry Wart
681 ❑ ca. 1956 Cover: 0.10 **NM** value: **105.00**
• Forever, Darling
682 ❑ ca. 1956 Cover: 0.10 **NM** value: **75.00**
• When Knighthood Was in Flower (Disney's "The Sword and the Rose")
683 ❑ ca. 1956 Cover: 0.10 **NM** value: **28.00**
• Hi and Lois
684 ❑ Mar 1956 Cover: 0.10 **NM** value: **120.00**
• **CGC:** 1 graded, best 6.5
• Helen of Troy
685 ❑ ca. 1956 Cover: 0.10 **NM** value: **50.00**
• Johnny Mack Brown
686 ❑ ca. 1956 Cover: 0.10 **NM** value: **50.00**
• Duck Album (Disney)
687 ❑ ca. 1956 Cover: 0.10 **NM** value: **60.00**
• The Indian Fighter
688 ❑ May 1956 Cover: 0.10 **NM** value: **75.00**
• **CGC:** 1 graded, best 5.5
• Alexander the Great
689 ❑ Mar 1956 Cover: 0.10 **NM** value: **30.00**
• Elmer Fudd
690 ❑ ca. 1956 Cover: 0.10 **NM** value: **165.00**
• **CGC:** 1 graded, best 7.0
• The Conqueror
691 ❑ ca. 1956 Cover: 0.10 **NM** value: **25.00**
• Dotty Dripple and Taffy
692 ❑ ca. 1956 Cover: 0.10 **NM** value: **30.00**
• The Little People in the Land of the Sky (Walt Scott) **A:** Walt Scott
693 ❑ ca. 1956 Cover: 0.10 **NM** value: **85.00**
• **CGC:** 1 graded, best 7.0
• Song of the South Featuring Brer Rabbit (Disney)
694 ❑ ca. 1956 Cover: 0.10 **NM** value: **55.00**
• Super Circus Featuring Mary Hartline
695 ❑ Apr 1956 Cover: 0.10 **NM** value: **30.00**
• Little Beaver
696 ❑ ca. 1956 Cover: 0.10 **NM** value: **35.00**
• **CGC:** 2 graded, best 7.0
• Krazy Kat
697 ❑ ca. 1956 Cover: 0.10 **NM** value: **25.00**
• Oswald the Rabbit
698 ❑ ca. 1956 Cover: 0.10 **NM** value: **30.00**
• Francis, the Talking Mule
699 ❑ ca. 1956 Cover: 0.10 **NM** value: **65.00**
• **CGC:** 1 graded, best 6.0
• Prince Valiant
700 ❑ ca. 1956 Cover: 0.10 **NM** value: **55.00**
• **CGC:** 1 graded, best 6.5
• Water Birds and the Olympic Elk (Disney)
701 ❑ May 1956 Cover: 0.10 **NM** value: **90.00**
• Jiminy Cricket (Disney)
702 ❑ ca. 1956 Cover: 0.10 **NM** value: **75.00**
• **CGC:** 1 graded, best 9.0
• The Goofy Success Story (Disney)
703 ❑ May 1956 Cover: 0.10 **NM** value: **85.00**
• Scamp (Disney)
704 ❑ May 1956 Cover: 0.10 **NM** value: **30.00**
• Priscilla's Pop
705 ❑ May 1956 Cover: 0.10 **NM** value: **55.00**
• Brave Eagle
706 ❑ ca. 1956 Cover: 0.10 **NM** value: **45.00**
• Bongo and Lumpjaw (Disney)
707 ❑ May 1956 Cover: 0.10 **NM** value: **70.00**
• Corky and White Shadow (Disney)
708 ❑ ca. 1956 Cover: 0.10 **NM** value: **55.00**
• **CGC:** 1 graded, best 7.5
• Smokey the Bear
709 ❑ Jun 1956 Cover: 0.10 **NM** value: **275.00**
• The Searchers
710 ❑ ca. 1956 Cover: 0.10 **NM** value: **30.00**
• Francis the Mule
711 ❑ ca. 1956 Cover: 0.10 **NM** value: **25.00**
• MGM's Mouse Musketeers
712 ❑ Jul 1956 Cover: 0.10 **NM** value: **60.00**
• The Great Locomotive Chase (Disney)
713 ❑ Aug 1956 Cover: 0.10 **NM** value: **55.00**
• The Animal World
714 ❑ ca. 1956 Cover: 0.10 **NM** value: **90.00**
• Spin and Marty (Disney)
715 ❑ Aug 1956 Cover: 0.10 **NM** value: **35.00**
• Timmy
716 ❑ ca. 1956 Cover: 0.10 **NM** value: **85.00**
• **CGC:** 1 graded, best 7.0
• Man in Space (Disney)
717 ❑ ca. 1956 Cover: 0.10 **NM** value: **85.00**
• Moby Dick
718 ❑ ca. 1956 Cover: 0.10 **NM** value: **25.00**
• Dotty Dripple and Taffy
719 ❑ ca. 1956 Cover: 0.10 **NM** value: **65.00**
• **CGC:** 1 graded, best 7.5
• Prince Valiant
720 ❑ ca. 1956 Cover: 0.10 **NM** value: **75.00**
• Gunsmoke
721 ❑ Aug 1956 Cover: 0.10 **NM** value: **160.00**
• Captain Kangaroo
722 ❑ ca. 1956 Cover: 0.10 **NM** value: **50.00**
• Johnny Mack Brown
723 ❑ ca. 1956 Cover: 0.10 **NM** value: **110.00**
• **CGC:** 1 graded, best 7.0
• Santiago
724 ❑ ca. 1956 Cover: 0.10 **NM** value: **40.00**
• Bugs Bunny's Album
725 ❑ Sep 1956 Cover: 0.10 **NM** value: **25.00**
• Elmer Fudd
726 ❑ ca. 1956 Cover: 0.10 **NM** value: **40.00**
• Duck Album
727 ❑ ca. 1956 Cover: 0.10 **NM** value: **25.00**
• Oswald the Rabbit
728 ❑ ca. 1956 Cover: 0.10 **NM** value: **25.00**
• Mouse Musketeers; 9/56
729 ❑ Nov 1956 Cover: 0.10 **NM** value: **35.00**
• **CGC:** 1 graded, best 9.0
• Jeb, Son of Battle
730 ❑ ca. 1956 Cover: 0.10 **NM** value: **30.00**
• **CGC:** 1 graded, best 7.0
• Smokey Stover
731 ❑ ca. 1956 Cover: 0.10 **NM** value: **40.00**
• Silvertip and the Fighting Four (Max Brand)
732 ❑ Oct 1956 Cover: 0.10 **NM** value: **145.00**
• **CGC:** 2 graded, best 9.0
• Challenge of Zorro
733 ❑ ca. 1956 Cover: 0.10 **NM** value: **35.00**
• Buck Jones; 10/56
734 ❑ ca. 1956 Cover: 0.10 **NM** value: **135.00**
• **CGC:** 1 graded, best 9.4
• Cheyenne
735 ❑ ca. 1956 Cover: 0.10 **NM** value: **250.00**
• **CGC:** 2 graded, best 9.0
• Crusader Rabbit
736 ❑ ca. 1956 Cover: 0.10 **NM** value: **40.00**
• Pluto; 10/56
737 ❑ ca. 1956 Cover: 0.10 **NM** value: **55.00**
• Steve Canyon **A:** Milton Caniff
738 ❑ ca. 1956 Cover: 0.10 **NM** value: **75.00**
• **CGC:** 5 graded, best 9.6
• Westward Ho, the Wagons (Disney)
739 ❑ ca. 1956 Cover: 0.10 **NM** value: **40.00**
• Bounty Guns (Luke Short)
740 ❑ ca. 1956 Cover: 0.10 **NM** value: **45.00**
• Chilly Willy (Walter Lantz)
741 ❑ ca. 1956 Cover: 0.10 **NM** value: **75.00**
• The Fastest Gun Alive; 9/56
742 ❑ ca. 1956 Cover: 0.10 **NM** value: **40.00**
• Buffalo Bill Jr.; 9/56
743 ❑ ca. 1956 Cover: 0.10 **NM** value: **40.00**
• Daisy Duck's Diary (Disney)
744 ❑ ca. 1956 Cover: 0.10 **NM** value: **30.00**
• Little Beaver
745 ❑ ca. 1956 Cover: 0.10 **NM** value: **30.00**
• Francis, the Famous Talking Mule
746 ❑ ca. 1956 Cover: 0.10 **NM** value: **25.00**
• Dotty Dripple and Taffy
747 ❑ ca. 1956 Cover: 0.10 **NM** value: **60.00**
• **CGC:** 1 graded, best 8.5
• Goofy (Disney)
748 ❑ ca. 1956 Cover: 0.10 **NM** value: **35.00**
• Frosty the Snowman; 11/56
749 ❑ ca. 1956 Cover: 0.10 **NM** value: **60.00**
• Secrets of Life (Disney); 11/56
750 ❑ ca. 1956 Cover: 0.10 **NM** value: **65.00**
• The Great Cat Family (Disney)
751 ❑ ca. 1956 Cover: 0.10 **NM** value: **80.00**
• Our Miss Brooks
752 ❑ ca. 1956 Cover: 0.10 **NM** value: **110.00**
• **CGC:** 1 graded, best 7.0
• Mandrake the Magician
753 ❑ ca. 1956 Cover: 0.10 **NM** value: **30.00**
• Walt Scott's Little People: Happy Holidays; 11/56
754 ❑ ca. 1956 Cover: 0.10 **NM** value: **50.00**
• Smokey the Bear
755 ❑ ca. 1956 Cover: 0.10 **NM** value: **40.00**
• The Littlest Snowman
756 ❑ ca. 1956 Cover: 0.10 **NM** value: **30.00**
• **CGC:** 1 graded, best 9.6
• Santa Claus Funnies; 12/56
757 ❑ ca. 1957 Cover: 0.10 **NM** value: **90.00**
• The True Story of Jesse James
758 ❑ ca. 1956 Cover: 0.10 **NM** value: **65.00**
• Bear Country (Disney)
759 ❑ ca. 1956 Cover: 0.10 **NM** value: **100.00**
• Circus Boy
760 ❑ ca. 1956 Cover: 0.10 **NM** value: **125.00**
• **CGC:** 1 graded, best 5.0
• The Hardy Boys (Disney)
761 ❑ ca. 1957 Cover: 0.10 **NM** value: **105.00**
• Howdy Doody
762 ❑ ca. 1957 Cover: 0.10 **NM** value: **90.00**
• The Sharkfighters
763 ❑ ca. 1957 Cover: 0.10 **NM** value: **60.00**
• Grandma Duck's Farm Friends (Disney); 1/57
764 ❑ ca. 1957 Cover: 0.10 **NM** value: **25.00**
• MGM's Mouse Musketeers
765 ❑ ca. 1957 Cover: 0.10 **NM** value: **25.00**
• Will-yum!
766 ❑ ca. 1957 Cover: 0.10 **NM** value: **40.00**
• Buffalo Bill Jr.; 2/57
767 ❑ ca. 1957 Cover: 0.10 **NM** value: **75.00**
• Spin and Marty (Disney)
768 ❑ ca. 1957 Cover: 0.10 **NM** value: **50.00**
• Steve Donovan, Western Marshal
769 ❑ ca. 1957 Cover: 0.10 **NM** value: **75.00**
• Gunsmoke
770 ❑ ca. 1957 Cover: 0.10 **NM** value: **35.00**
• Brave Eagle
771 ❑ ca. 1957 Cover: 0.10 **NM** value: **35.00**
• Brand of Empire (Luke Short); 3/57
772 ❑ Feb 1957 Cover: 0.10 **NM** value: **65.00**
• Cheyenne
773 ❑ ca. 1957 Cover: 0.10 **NM** value: **50.00**
• The Brave One
774 ❑ ca. 1957 Cover: 0.10 **NM** value: **25.00**
• Hi and Lois
775 ❑ ca. 1957 Cover: 0.10 **NM** value: **95.00**
• **CGC:** 5 graded, best 9.6
• Sir Lancelot and Brian
776 ❑ ca. 1957 Cover: 0.10 **NM** value: **50.00**
• Johnny Mack Brown
777 ❑ ca. 1957 Cover: 0.10 **NM** value: **65.00**
• Scamp (Disney)
778 ❑ ca. 1957 Cover: 0.10 **NM** value: **45.00**
• **CGC:** 1 graded, best 9.4
• The Little Rascals
779 ❑ ca. 1957 Cover: 0.10 **NM** value: **45.00**
• Lee Hunter, Indian Fighter; 3/57
780 ❑ ca. 1957 Cover: 0.10 **NM** value: **135.00**
• Captain Kangaroo
781 ❑ Aug 1957 Cover: 0.10 **NM** value: **90.00**
• Fury
782 ❑ ca. 1957 Cover: 0.10 **NM** value: **45.00**
• Duck Album (Disney)
783 ❑ Aug 1957 Cover: 0.10 **NM** value: **25.00**
• Elmer Fudd
784 ❑ ca. 1957 Cover: 0.10 **NM** value: **70.00**
• Around the World in 80 Days
785 ❑ Apr 1957 Cover: 0.10 **NM** value: **95.00**
• Circus Boy
786 ❑ ca. 1957 Cover: 0.10 **NM** value: **60.00**
• Cinderella (Disney)
787 ❑ ca. 1957 Cover: 0.10 **NM** value: **40.00**
• Little Hiawatha (Disney)
788 ❑ ca. 1957 Cover: 0.10 **NM** value: **65.00**
• **CGC:** 1 graded, best 7.0
• Prince Valiant
789 ❑ ca. 1957 Cover: 0.10 **NM** value: **45.00**
📖 Valley Thieves • Silvertip (Max Brand); 4/57
790 ❑ ca. 1957 Cover: 0.10 **NM** value: **175.00**
• **CGC:** 1 graded, best 9.2
• The Wings of Eagles
791 ❑ ca. 1957 Cover: 0.10 **NM** value: **75.00**
• **CGC:** 1 graded, best 7.0
• The 77th Bengal Lancers; 4/57
792 ❑ ca. 1957 Cover: 0.10 **NM** value: **25.00**
• Oswald the Rabbit; 4/57
793 ❑ ca. 1957 Cover: 0.10 **NM** value: **30.00**
• Morty Meekle
794 ❑ ca. 1957 Cover: 0.10 **NM** value: **100.00**
• **CGC:** 1 graded, best 6.5
• The Count of Monte Cristo; 9/57
795 ❑ ca. 1957 Cover: 0.10 **NM** value: **70.00**
• Jiminy Cricket (Disney)
796 ❑ ca. 1957 Cover: 0.10 **NM** value: **40.00**
• Ludwig Bemelman's Madeleine and Genevieve
797 ❑ ca. 1957 Cover: 0.10 **NM** value: **65.00**
• Gunsmoke
798 ❑ ca. 1957 Cover: 0.10 **NM** value: **45.00**
• Buffalo Bill Jr.
799 ❑ ca. 1957 Cover: 0.10 **NM** value: **30.00**
• Priscilla's Pop
800 ❑ ca. 1957 Cover: 0.10 **NM** value: **65.00**
• **CGC:** 1 graded, best 8.0
• The Buccaneers
801 ❑ ca. 1957 Cover: 0.10 **NM** value: **25.00**
• Dotty Dripple and Taffy
802 ❑ ca. 1957 Cover: 0.10 **NM** value: **70.00**
• Goofy (Disney)
803 ❑ ca. 1957 Cover: 0.10 **NM** value: **55.00**
• Cheyenne
804 ❑ ca. 1957 Cover: 0.10 **NM** value: **55.00**
• **CGC:** 1 graded, best 6.0
• Steve Canyon; 5/57 **A:** Milton Caniff
805 ❑ ca. 1957 Cover: 0.10 **NM** value: **185.00**
• Crusader Rabbit
806 ❑ ca. 1957 Cover: 0.10 **NM** value: **60.00**
• Scamp (Disney)
807 ❑ ca. 1957 Cover: 0.10 **NM** value: **35.00**
• Savage Range (Luke Short)
808 ❑ ca. 1957 Cover: 0.10 **NM** value: **80.00**
• Spin and Marty (Disney)
809 ❑ ca. 1957 Cover: 0.10 **NM** value: **30.00**
• The Little People in the Days of Knights (Walt Scott)
810 ❑ ca. 1957 Cover: 0.10 **NM** value: **30.00**
• Francis the Mule
811 ❑ ca. 1957 Cover: 0.10 **NM** value: **110.00**
• Howdy Doody
812 ❑ ca. 1957 Cover: 0.10 **NM** value: **85.00**
• **CGC:** 1 graded, best 8.5
• The Big Land

Other grades: Multiply prices above by **1.5 for Mint • 2/3 for Very Fine • 1/3 for Fine • 1/5 for Very Good • 1/8 for Good**

813 ❑ ca. 1957 Cover: 0.10 **NM** value: **95.00**
• **CGC:** 1 graded, best 9.0
• Circus Boy
814 ❑ ca. 1957 Cover: 0.10 **NM** value: **55.00**
Covered Wagons, Ho! (Disney).
815 ❑ ca. 1957 Cover: 0.10 **NM** value: **75.00**
• Dragoon Wells Massacre
816 ❑ ca. 1957 Cover: 0.10 **NM** value: **35.00**
• Brave Eagle; 7/57
817 ❑ ca. 1957 Cover: 0.10 **NM** value: **25.00**
• Little Beaver
818 ❑ ca. 1957 Cover: 0.10 **NM** value: **50.00**
• Smokey the Bear; 6/57
819 ❑ ca. 1957 Cover: 0.10 **NM** value: **40.00**
• Mickey Mouse in Magic Land
820 ❑ ca. 1957 Cover: 0.10 **NM** value: **70.00**
• The Oklahoman
821 ❑ ca. 1957 Cover: 0.10 **NM** value: **80.00**
• **CGC:** 1 graded, best 9.0
• Wringle Wrangle (Disney)
822 ❑ Aug 1957 Cover: 0.10 **NM** value: **110.00**
• Paul Revere's Ride with Johnny Tremaine (Disney)
823 ❑ ca. 1957 Cover: 0.10 **NM** value: **25.00**
• Timmy
824 ❑ ca. 1957 Cover: 0.10 **NM** value: **95.00**
• **CGC:** 1 graded, best 6.0
• The Pride and the Passion; 8/57
825 ❑ ca. 1957 Cover: 0.10 **NM** value: **45.00**
• **CGC:** 1 graded, best 9.0
• The Little Rascals
826 ❑ ca. 1957 Cover: 0.10 **NM** value: **225.00**
• **CGC:** 1 graded, best 9.2
• Spin and Marty and Annette (Disney)
827 ❑ ca. 1957 Cover: 0.10 **NM** value: **30.00**
• **CGC:** 1 graded, best 7.5
• Smokey Stover
828 ❑ ca. 1957 Cover: 0.10 **NM** value: **35.00**
• Buffalo Bill Jr.
829 ❑ ca. 1957 Cover: 0.10 **NM** value: **45.00**
• Tales of the Pony Express; 8/57
830 ❑ ca. 1957 Cover: 0.10 **NM** value: **90.00**
📖 Secret of the Old Mine • The Hardy Boys (Disney)
831 ❑ Sep 1957 Cover: 0.10 **NM** value: **60.00**
• No Sleep 'Til Dawn
832 ❑ ca. 1957 Cover: 0.10 **NM** value: **40.00**
• Lolly and Pepper
833 ❑ ca. 1957 Cover: 0.10 **NM** value: **60.00**
• Scamp (Disney); 9/57
834 ❑ ca. 1957 Cover: 0.10 **NM** value: **45.00**
• Johnny Mack Brown
835 ❑ ca. 1957 Cover: 0.10 **NM** value: **40.00**
• Silvertip and the False Rider (Max Brand)
836 ❑ ca. 1957 Cover: 0.10 **NM** value: **65.00**
• Man in Flight (Disney); 9/57
837 ❑ ca. 1957 Cover: 0.10 **NM** value: **55.00**
• All-American Athlete Cotton Woods
838 ❑ Sep 1957 Cover: 0.10 **NM** value: **50.00**
• Bugs Bunny's Life Story Album
839 ❑ ca. 1957 Cover: 0.10 **NM** value: **75.00**
• **CGC:** 1 graded, best 7.5
• The Vigilantes
840 ❑ ca. 1957 Cover: 0.10 **NM** value: **45.00**
• Duck Album (Disney)
841 ❑ ca. 1957 Cover: 0.10 **NM** value: **25.00**
• Elmer Fudd
842 ❑ ca. 1957 Cover: 0.10 **NM** value: **60.00**
• **CGC:** 1 graded, best 6.5
• The Nature of Things (Disney)
843 ❑ ca. 1957 Cover: 0.10 **NM** value: **75.00**
• **CGC:** 1 graded, best 6.0
• The First Americans (Disney)
844 ❑ ca. 1957 Cover: 0.10 **NM** value: **65.00**
• Gunsmoke
845 ❑ ca. 1957 Cover: 0.10 **NM** value: **130.00**
• The Land Unknown
846 ❑ Oct 1957 Cover: 0.10 **NM** value: **115.00**
• **CGC:** 1 graded, best 8.0
• Gun Glory
847 ❑ ca. 1957 Cover: 0.10 **NM** value: **45.00**
• Perri (Disney)
848 ❑ ca. 1957 Cover: 0.10 **NM** value: **35.00**
• Marauder's Moon
849 ❑ ca. 1957 Cover: 0.10 **NM** value: **60.00**
• **CGC:** 1 graded, best 8.0
• Prince Valiant
850 ❑ ca. 1957 Cover: 0.10 **NM** value: **35.00**
• Buck Jones
851 ❑ ca. 1958 Cover: 0.10 **NM** value: **70.00**
• **CGC:** 1 graded, best 6.5
• The Story of Mankind
852 ❑ ca. 1958 Cover: 0.10 **NM** value: **25.00**
• Chilly Willy
853 ❑ ca. 1957 Cover: 0.10 **NM** value: **45.00**
• Pluto
854 ❑ ca. 1957 Cover: 0.10 **NM** value: **125.00**
• **CGC:** 1 graded, best 7.0
• The Hunchback of Notre Dame
855 ❑ Nov 1957 Cover: 0.10 **NM** value: **45.00**
• Broken Arrow
856 ❑ ca. 1957 Cover: 0.10 **NM** value: **40.00**
• Buffalo Bill Jr.
857 ❑ ca. 1957 Cover: 0.10 **NM** value: **65.00**
• The Goofy Adventure Story (Disney)
858 ❑ ca. 1957 Cover: 0.10 **NM** value: **45.00**
• **CGC:** 1 graded, best 8.0
• Daisy Duck's Diary (Disney)
859 ❑ Nov 1957 Cover: 0.10 **NM** value: **45.00**
• Topper and Neil
860 ❑ ca. 1957 Cover: 0.10 **NM** value: **115.00**
• Wyatt Earp
861 ❑ ca. 1957 Cover: 0.10 **NM** value: **35.00**
• Frosty the Snowman; 11/56
862 ❑ ca. 1957 Cover: 0.10 **NM** value: **75.00**
• **CGC:** 1 graded, best 7.0
• The Truth About Mother Goose (Disney)
863 ❑ ca. 1957 Cover: 0.10 **NM** value: **30.00**
• Francis
864 ❑ ca. 1957 Cover: 0.10 **NM** value: **40.00**
• The Littlest Snowman Rescues Christmas
865 ❑ ca. 1957 Cover: 0.10 **NM** value: **85.00**
• Andy Burnett (Disney)
866 ❑ ca. 1957 Cover: 0.10 **NM** value: **85.00**
• **CGC:** 1 graded, best 6.5
• Mars and Beyond (Disney)
867 ❑ ca. 1957 Cover: 0.10 **NM** value: **40.00**
• Santa Claus Funnies
868 ❑ ca. 1957 Cover: 0.10 **NM** value: **30.00**
📖 Topsy-Turvy Christmas • Walt Scott's Little People; 12/57
869 ❑ ca. 1958 Cover: 0.10 **NM** value: **70.00**
• Old Yeller (Disney)
870 ❑ ca. 1958 Cover: 0.10 **NM** value: **30.00**
• Little Beaver
871 ❑ ca. 1958 Cover: 0.10 **NM** value: **30.00**
• Curly Kayoe vs. the Barefoot Blockbuster
872 ❑ Jan 1958, four-color Cover: 0.10 **NM** value: **130.00**
• **CGC:** 1 graded, best 7.5
📖 A Most Unhappy Burro; The Unhappiest Knight; The Gentle Giant; Midnight Mystery • Captain Kangaroo
873 ❑ Jan 1958 Cover: 0.10 **NM** value: **45.00**
• Grandma Duck's Farm Friends
874 ❑ ca. 1958 Cover: 0.10 **NM** value: **80.00**
• **CGC:** 1 graded, best 6.5
• Old Ironsides with Johnny Tremaine (Disney); 1/58
875 ❑ ca. 1958 Cover: 0.10 **NM** value: **30.00**
• Trumpets West (Luke Short); 2/58
876 ❑ ca. 1958 Cover: 0.10 **NM** value: **95.00**
• Tales of Wells Fargo; 2/58
877 ❑ ca. 1958 Cover: 0.10 **NM** value: **100.00**
• Frontier Doctor Featuring Rex Allen; 2/58
878 ❑ ca. 1958 Cover: 0.10 **NM** value: **200.00**
• **CGC:** 3 graded, best 8.0
• Peanuts; 2/58 **A:** Charles Schulz(cover)
879 ❑ ca. 1958 Cover: 0.10 **NM** value: **35.00**
• Brave Eagle
880 ❑ ca. 1958 Cover: 0.10 **NM** value: **40.00**
• Steve Donovan, Western Marshal
881 ❑ Feb 1958 Cover: 0.10 **NM** value: **35.00**
• **CGC:** 2 graded, best 7.5
• The Captain and the Kids
882 ❑ ca. 1958 Cover: 0.10 **NM** value: **165.00**
• **CGC:** 2 graded, best 9.2
• Zorro (Disney); First Disney issue of Zorro
883 ❑ ca. 1958 Cover: 0.10 **NM** value: **40.00**
• **CGC:** 1 graded, best 9.2
• The Little Rascals
884 ❑ ca. 1958 Cover: 0.10 **NM** value: **80.00**
• Hawkeye and the Last of the Mohicans
885 ❑ ca. 1958 Cover: 0.10 **NM** value: **85.00**
• Fury
886 ❑ ca. 1958 Cover: 0.10 **NM** value: **35.00**
• Bongo and Lumpjaw (Disney)
887 ❑ ca. 1958 Cover: 0.10 **NM** value: **100.00**
📖 Mystery of Ghost Farm • The Hardy Boys (Disney)
888 ❑ ca. 1958 Cover: 0.10 **NM** value: **25.00**
• Elmer Fudd
889 ❑ ca. 1958 Cover: 0.10 **NM** value: **110.00**
• Clint and Mac (Disney)
890 ❑ ca. 1958 Cover: 0.10 **NM** value: **70.00**
• Wyatt Earp
891 ❑ ca. 1958 Cover: 0.10 **NM** value: **75.00**
• **CGC:** 2 graded, best 8.0
• Light in the Forest (Disney); 3/58
892 ❑ ca. 1958 Cover: 0.10 **NM** value: **200.00**
• **CGC:** 2 graded, best 8.5
• Maverick
893 ❑ ca. 1958 Cover: 0.10 **NM** value: **55.00**
• The Adventures of Jim Bowie
894 ❑ ca. 1958 Cover: 0.10 **NM** value: **25.00**
• Oswald the Rabbit
895 ❑ ca. 1958 Cover: 0.10 **NM** value: **105.00**
• Wagon Train
896 ❑ ca. 1958 Cover: 0.10 **NM** value: **75.00**
• **CGC:** 1 graded, best 9.4
• The Adventures of Tinker Bell (Disney)
897 ❑ ca. 1958 Cover: 0.10 **NM** value: **65.00**
• Jiminy Cricket (Disney)
898 ❑ ca. 1958 Cover: 0.10 **NM** value: **40.00**
• Silvertip's Trap (Max Brand)
899 ❑ ca. 1958 Cover: 0.10 **NM** value: **45.00**
• Goofy (Disney)
900 ❑ ca. 1958 Cover: 0.10 **NM** value: **60.00**
• **CGC:** 1 graded, best 7.5
• Prince Valiant
901 ❑ ca. 1958 Cover: 0.10 **NM** value: **45.00**
• Little Hiawatha (Disney)
902 ❑ May 1958 Cover: 0.10 **NM** value: **26.00**
• Will-yum!
903 ❑ ca. 1958 Cover: 0.10 **NM** value: **25.00**
• Dotty Dripple and Taffy
904 ❑ ca. 1958 Cover: 0.10 **NM** value: **30.00**
• Lee Hunter, Indian Fighter
905 ❑ ca. 1958 Cover: 0.10 **NM** value: **250.00**
• Annette (Disney)
906 ❑ ca. 1958 Cover: 0.10 **NM** value: **30.00**
• Francis the Mule
907 ❑ ca. 1958 Cover: 0.10 **NM** value: **125.00**
• **CGC:** 2 graded, best 9.6
• Sugarfoot
908 ❑ ca. 1958 Cover: 0.10 **NM** value: **30.00**
• The Little People and the Giant (Walt Scott)
909 ❑ ca. 1958 Cover: 0.10 **NM** value: **25.00**
• Smitty and Herby
910 ❑ Jun 1958 Cover: 0.10 **NM** value: **95.00**
• **CGC:** 1 graded, best 6.5
• The Vikings
911 ❑ ca. 1958 Cover: 0.10 **NM** value: **85.00**
• The Gray Ghost
912 ❑ ca. 1958 Cover: 0.10 **NM** value: **185.00**
• **CGC:** 2 graded, best 8.5
• Leave It to Beaver
913 ❑ ca. 1958 Cover: 0.10 **NM** value: **100.00**
• The Left-Handed Gun; 7/58
914 ❑ ca. 1958 Cover: 0.10 **NM** value: **95.00**
• **CGC:** 2 graded, best 9.0
• No Time for Sergeants; 7/58
915 ❑ ca. 1958 Cover: 0.10 **NM** value: **65.00**
• Casey Jones
916 ❑ ca. 1958 Cover: 0.10 **NM** value: **40.00**
• Red Ryder Ranch Comics
917 ❑ ca. 1958 Cover: 0.10 **NM** value: **125.00**
• The Life of Riley
918 ❑ Jul 1958 Cover: 0.10 **NM** value: **85.00**
• Beep Beep the Roadrunner
919 ❑ ca. 1958 Cover: 0.10 **NM** value: **75.00**
• Boots and Saddles
920 ❑ Jun 1958 Cover: 0.10 **NM** value: **160.00**
• **CGC:** 2 graded, best 8.0
• Zorro (Disney)
921 ❑ ca. 1958 Cover: 0.10 **NM** value: **65.00**
• Wyatt Earp
922 ❑ ca. 1958 Cover: 0.10 **NM** value: **50.00**
• Johnny Mack Brown
923 ❑ ca. 1958 Cover: 0.10 **NM** value: **25.00**
• Timmy
924 ❑ ca. 1958 Cover: 0.10 **NM** value: **90.00**
• Colt.45
925 ❑ Aug 1958 Cover: 0.10 **NM** value: **65.00**
• Last of the Fast Guns
926 ❑ ca. 1958 Cover: 0.10 **NM** value: **55.00**
• Peter Pan (Disney)
927 ❑ ca. 1958 Cover: 0.10 **NM** value: **35.00**
• Top Gun (Luke Short)
928 ❑ ca. 1958 Cover: 0.10 **NM** value: **125.00**
• **CGC:** 1 graded, best 5.0
• Sea Hunt
929 ❑ ca. 1958 Cover: 0.10 **NM** value: **30.00**
• Brave Eagle
930 ❑ ca. 1958 Cover: 0.10 **NM** value: **115.00**
• **CGC:** 1 graded, best 8.0
• Maverick
931 ❑ ca. 1958 Cover: 0.10 **NM** value: **115.00**
• **CGC:** 1 graded, best 9.4
• Have Gun, Will Travel
932 ❑ ca. 1958 Cover: 0.10 **NM** value: **55.00**
• Smokey the Bear: His Life Story
933 ❑ ca. 1958 Cover: 0.10 **NM** value: **145.00**
• **CGC:** 4 graded, best 9.2
• Zorro (Disney)
934 ❑ ca. 1958 Cover: 0.10 **NM** value: **95.00**
• The Restless Gun
935 ❑ ca. 1958 Cover: 0.10 **NM** value: **40.00**
• King of the Royal Mounted
936 ❑ ca. 1958 Cover: 0.10 **NM** value: **40.00**
• **CGC:** 1 graded, best 9.4
• The Little Rascals
937 ❑ ca. 1958 Cover: 0.10 **NM** value: **115.00**
• **CGC:** 1 graded, best 7.0
• Ruff and Reddy
938 ❑ Sep 1958 Cover: 0.10 **NM** value: **25.00**
• Elmer Fudd
939 ❑ ca. 1958 Cover: 0.10 **NM** value: **45.00**
• **CGC:** 1 graded, best 6.0
• Steve Canyon
940 ❑ ca. 1958 Cover: 0.10 **NM** value: **35.00**
• Lolly and Pepper
941 ❑ Oct 1958 Cover: 0.10 **NM** value: **35.00**
• Pluto (Disney)
942 ❑ ca. 1958 Cover: 0.10 **NM** value: **50.00**
• Tales of the Pony Express
943 ❑ ca. 1958 Cover: 0.10 **NM** value: **60.00**
• **CGC:** 1 graded, best 6.5
• White Wilderness (Disney)
944 ❑ Sep 1958 Cover: 0.10 **NM** value: **160.00**
• **CGC:** 3 graded, best 9.0
• The 7th Voyage of Sinbad
945 ❑ Oct 1958 Cover: 0.10 **NM** value: **95.00**
• Maverick
946 ❑ ca. 1958 Cover: 0.10 **NM** value: **75.00**
• The Big Country
947 ❑ ca. 1958 Cover: 0.10 **NM** value: **45.00**
• Broken Arrow
948 ❑ ca. 1958 Cover: 0.10 **NM** value: **45.00**
• Daisy Duck's Diary (Disney)
949 ❑ ca. 1958 Cover: 0.10 **NM** value: **50.00**
• **CGC:** 1 graded, best 5.0
• Lowell Thomas' High Adventure
950 ❑ Dec 1958 Cover: 0.10 **NM** value: **40.00**
• Frosty the Snowman
951 ❑ ca. 1958 Cover: 0.10 **NM** value: **125.00**
• **CGC:** 1 graded, best 8.0
• The Lennon Sisters Life Story
952 ❑ ca. 1958 Cover: 0.10 **NM** value: **40.00**
• Goofy (Disney)
953 ❑ ca. 1958 Cover: 0.10 **NM** value: **35.00**
• Francis the Mule
954 ❑ ca. 1959 Cover: 0.10 **NM** value: **75.00**
• Man in Space-Satellites (Disney)

CGC-graded: Multiply prices above by **33 for 9.9 M • 16 for 9.8 NM/M • 7 for 9.6 NM+ • 5 for 9.4 NM • 2.5 for 9.2 NM- • 1.5 for 9.0 VF/NM**

955❑ ca. 1958 Cover: 0.10 **NM** value: **25.00**
• Hi and Lois

956❑ ca. 1958 Cover: 0.10 **NM** value: **180.00**
• Ricky Nelson

957❑ ca. 1958 Cover: 0.10 **NM** value: **90.00**
• Buffalo Bee

958❑ ca. 1958 Cover: 0.10 **NM** value: **40.00**
• Santa Claus Funnies

959❑ Dec 1958 Cover: 0.10 **NM** value: **40.00**
• Walt Scott's Christmas Stories

960❑ Dec 1958 Cover: 0.10 **NM** value: **140.00**
• **CGC:** 1 graded, best 7.5
• Zorro (Disney)

961❑ ca. 1959 Cover: 0.10 **NM** value: **55.00**
• Jace Pearson's Tales of the Texas Rangers

962❑ ca. 1959 Cover: 0.10 **NM** value: **95.00**
• **CGC:** 1 graded, best 8.0
• Maverick

963❑ Jan 1959 Cover: 0.10 **NM** value: **45.00**
• Johnny Mack Brown

964❑ ca. 1959 Cover: 0.10 **NM** value: **100.00**
📖 The Mystery of the Caves • The Hardy Boys (Disney)

965❑ ca. 1959 Cover: 0.10 **NM** value: **50.00**
• Grandma Duck's Farm Friends (Disney)

966❑ Jan 1959 Cover: 0.10 **NM** value: **70.00**
• Tonka (Disney)

967❑ ca. 1959 Cover: 0.10 **NM** value: **35.00**
• Chilly Willy

968❑ Feb 1959 Cover: 0.10 **NM** value: **80.00**
• **CGC:** 1 graded, best 7.5
• Tales of Wells Fargo

969❑ Feb 1959 Cover: 0.10 **NM** value: **160.00**
• **CGC:** 1 graded, best 8.5
• Peanuts **A:** Charles Schulz(cover)

970❑ Dec 1958 Cover: 0.10 **NM** value: **90.00**
• Lawman

971❑ Feb 1959 Cover: 0.10 **NM** value: **55.00**
• Wagon Train

972❑ Jan 1959 Cover: 0.10 **NM** value: **110.00**
• Tom Thumb (George Pal)

973❑ ca. 1959 Cover: 0.10 **NM** value: **100.00**
• Sleeping Beauty and the Prince (Disney)

974❑ ca. 1959 Cover: 0.10 **NM** value: **40.00**
• Spanky and Alfalfa, the Little Rascals

975❑ Mar 1959 Cover: 0.10 **NM** value: **65.00**
• Fury

976❑ Mar 1959 Cover: 0.10 **NM** value: **140.00**
• **CGC:** 1 graded, best 8.5
• Zorro (Disney)

977❑ Feb 1959 Cover: 0.10 **NM** value: **25.00**
• Elmer Fudd

978❑ Feb 1959 Cover: 0.10 **NM** value: **25.00**
• Lolly and Pepper

979❑ Apr 1959 Cover: 0.10 **NM** value: **25.00**
• Oswald the Rabbit

980❑ Feb 1959 Cover: 0.10 **NM** value: **95.00**
• **CGC:** 1 graded, best 8.5
• Maverick

981❑ ca. 1959 Cover: 0.10 **NM** value: **70.00**
• Ruff and Reddy; Possibly also Wyatt Earp

982❑ ca. 1959 Cover: 0.10 **NM** value: **70.00**
• The New Adventures of Tinker Bell (Disney)

983❑ ca. 1959 Cover: 0.10 **NM** value: **70.00**
• **CGC:** 1 graded, best 9.2
• Have Gun, Will Travel

984❑ ca. 1959 Cover: 0.10 **NM** value: **100.00**
• Sleeping Beauty's Fairy Godmothers (Disney)

985❑ May 1959 Cover: 0.10 **NM** value: **65.00**
• Shaggy Dog (Disney)

986❑ Apr 1959 Cover: 0.10 **NM** value: **70.00**
• Restless Gun

987❑ ca. 1959 Cover: 0.10 **NM** value: **45.00**
• Goofy (Disney)

988❑ ca. 1959 Cover: 0.10 **NM** value: **40.00**
• Little Hiawatha (Disney)

989❑ May 1959 Cover: 0.10 **NM** value: **60.00**
• Jiminy Cricket (Disney)

990❑ ca. 1959 Cover: 0.10 **NM** value: **100.00**
• Huckleberry Hound

991❑ May 1959, four-color Cover: 0.10 **NM** value: **30.00**
📖 Follow that Chariot+D9339 • Francis the Mule

992❑ May 1959 Cover: 0.10 **NM** value: **100.00**
• **CGC:** 1 graded, best 7.0
• Sugarfoot

993❑ ca. 1959 Cover: 0.10 **NM** value: **55.00**
• Jim Bowie

994❑ May 1959 Cover: 0.10 **NM** value: **105.00**
• **CGC:** 1 graded, best 9.4
• Sea Hunt

995❑ May 1959 Cover: 0.10 **NM** value: **45.00**
• Duck Album (Disney)

996❑ ca. 1959 Cover: 0.10 **NM** value: **30.00**
• Nevada (Zane Grey)

997❑ ca. 1959 Cover: 0.10 **NM** value: **70.00**
📖 The 9 Lives of Elfrego Baca • Walt Disney Presents: Tales of Texas John Slaughter; 6-8/59

998❑ ca. 1959 Cover: 0.10 **NM** value: **185.00**
• **CGC:** 1 graded, best 7.5
• Ricky Nelson

999❑ ca. 1959 Cover: 0.10 **NM** value: **160.00**
• **CGC:** 1 graded, best 9.0
• Leave It to Beaver

1000❑Jun 1959 Cover: 0.10 **NM** value: **85.00**
• The Gray Ghost

1001❑Aug 1959 Cover: 0.10 **NM** value: **48.00**
• Lowell Thomas' High Adventure

1002❑ca. 1959 Cover: 0.10 **NM** value: **60.00**
• Buffalo Bee

1003❑ca. 1959 Cover: 0.10 **NM** value: **145.00**
• **CGC:** 1 graded, best 9.4
• Zorro (Disney)

1004❑Jun 1959 Cover: 0.10 **NM** value: **70.00**
• Colt.45

1005❑ca. 1959 Cover: 0.10 **NM** value: **90.00**
• **CGC:** 1 graded, best 9.4
• Maverick

1006❑ca. 1959 Cover: 0.10 **NM** value: **100.00**
• **CGC:** 1 graded, best 7.5
• Hercules

1007❑Aug 1959 Cover: 0.10 **NM** value: **65.00**
• John Paul Jones

1008❑ca. 1959 Cover: 0.10 **NM** value: **75.00**
• Rocky and His Friends **A:** Jay Ward

1009❑Jul 1959 Cover: 0.10 **NM** value: **175.00**
• **CGC:** 1 graded, best 6.5
• The Rifleman

1010❑Jul 1959 Cover: 0.10 **NM** value: **100.00**
📖 The Flying Farm Hand; A Honey of a Hen; The Weather Watchers; The Sheepish Cowboys • Grandma Duck's Farm Friends (Disney) **A:** Carl Barks

1011❑Jul 1959 Cover: 0.10 **NM** value: **80.00**
• Buckskin

1012❑ca. 1959 Cover: 0.10 **NM** value: **70.00**
• Last Train from Gun Hill

1013❑Aug 1959 Cover: 0.10 **NM** value: **95.00**
• Bat Masterson

1014❑Jul 1959 Cover: 0.10 **NM** value: **110.00**
• **CGC:** 2 graded, best 9.4
• The Lennon Sisters

1015❑Aug 1959 Cover: 0.10 **NM** value: **150.00**
• Peanuts **A:** Charles Schulz(cover)

1016❑ca. 1959 Cover: 0.10 **NM** value: **40.00**
• Smokey the Bear Nature Stories

1017❑ca. 1959 Cover: 0.10 **NM** value: **30.00**
• Chilly Willy

1018❑Jun 1959 Cover: 0.10 **NM** value: **200.00**
• **CGC:** 1 graded, best 9.0
• Rio Bravo

1019❑Aug 1959 Cover: 0.10 **NM** value: **55.00**
• **CGC:** 1 graded, best 9.2
• Wagon Train

1020❑Aug 1959 Cover: 0.10 **NM** value: **38.00**
• Jungle Jim

1021❑Aug 1959 Cover: 0.10 **NM** value: **55.00**
• Jace Pearson's Tales of the Texas Rangers

1022❑ca. 1959 Cover: 0.10 **NM** value: **25.00**
• Timmy

1023❑ca. 1959 Cover: 0.10 **NM** value: **85.00**
• **CGC:** 3 graded, best 9.2
• Tales of Wells Fargo

1024❑ca. 1959 Cover: 0.10 **NM** value: **100.00**
• **CGC:** 1 graded, best 8.5
• Darby O'Gill and the Little People (Disney)

1025❑ca. 1959 Cover: 0.10 **NM** value: **210.00**
• **CGC:** 2 graded, best 8.5
📖 Mastering the Matterhorn; Trail Tycoon; The Dream Planet • Vacation in Disneyland **A:** Carl Barks

1026❑ca. 1959 Cover: 0.10 **NM** value: **85.00**
• Spin and Marty (Disney)

1027❑ca. 1959 Cover: 0.10 **NM** value: **75.00**
• **CGC:** 2 graded, best 9.2
• The Texan

1028❑ca. 1959 Cover: 0.10 **NM** value: **230.00**
• **CGC:** 3 graded, best 9.4
• Rawhide

1029❑ca. 1959 Cover: 0.10 **NM** value: **50.00**
• Boots and Saddles

1030❑ca. 1959 Cover: 0.10 **NM** value: **40.00**
• **CGC:** 1 graded, best 8.5
• Spanky and Alfalfa The Little Rascals

1031❑ca. 1959 Cover: 0.10 **NM** value: **60.00**
• Fury

1032❑ca. 1959 Cover: 0.10 **NM** value: **25.00**
• Elmer Fudd

1033❑Sep 1959 Cover: 0.10 **NM** value: **45.00**
• **CGC:** 1 graded, best 9.0
• Steve Canyon

1034❑Sep 1959 Cover: 0.10 **NM** value: **35.00**
• Nancy and Sluggo: Summer Camp

1035❑ca. 1959 Cover: 0.10 **NM** value: **55.00**
• Lawman

1036❑Aug 1959 Cover: 0.10 **NM** value: **55.00**
• The Big Circus

1037❑ca. 1959 Cover: 0.10 **NM** value: **145.00**
• **CGC:** 2 graded, best 9.2
• Zorro (Disney)

1038❑Oct 1959 Cover: 0.10 **NM** value: **60.00**
• Ruff and Reddy

1039❑Nov 1959 Cover: 0.10 **NM** value: **40.00**
• Pluto (Disney)

1040❑ca. 1959 Cover: 0.10 **NM** value: **120.00**
• **CGC:** 1 graded, best 7.0
• Quick Draw McGraw

1041❑Oct 1959 Cover: 0.10 **NM** value: **100.00**
• Sea Hunt

1042❑ca. 1959 Cover: 0.10 **NM** value: **45.00**
• The Three Chipmunks

1043❑Oct 1959 Cover: 0.10 **NM** value: **120.00**
• **CGC:** 1 graded, best 9.4
• The Three Stooges

1044❑Oct 1959 Cover: 0.10 **NM** value: **70.00**
• **CGC:** 2 graded, best 9.2
• Have Gun-Will Travel

1045❑ca. 1959 Cover: 0.10 **NM** value: **60.00**
• The Restless Gun

1046❑ca. 1959 Cover: 0.10 **NM** value: **45.00**
• Beep Beep the Road Runner; 11/59-1/60

1047❑Nov 1959 Cover: 0.10 **NM** value: **200.00**
• **CGC:** 1 graded, best 9.2
📖 The Gab-Muffer; The Stubborn Stork; Milktime Melodies; The Lost Rabbit Foot; The Bird Camera; The Odd Order • Gyro Gearloose (Disney) **A:** Carl Barks

1048❑ca. 1959 Cover: 0.10 **NM** value: **160.00**
• **CGC:** 1 graded, best 9.2
• The Horse Soldiers

1049❑ca. 1959 Cover: 0.10 **NM** value: **65.00**
• Don't Give Up the Ship

1050❑Oct 1959 Cover: 0.10 **NM** value: **65.00**
• Huckleberry Hound

1051❑ca. 1959 Cover: 0.10 **NM** value: **110.00**
• Donald in Mathmagic Land (Disney)

1052❑ca. 1959 Cover: 0.10 **NM** value: **110.00**
• Ben Hur **A:** Russ Manning

1053❑ca. 1959 Cover: 0.10 **NM** value: **45.00**
• Goofy (Disney)

1054❑Dec 1959 Cover: 0.10 **NM** value: **65.00**
• Huckleberry Hound Winter Fun

1055❑Nov 1959 Cover: 0.10 **NM** value: **100.00**
📖 Daisy's Dazed Days; The Librarian; The Double Date; The TV Babysitter; Donald's Party; The Beauty Queen; Tight Shoes; The Framed Mirror; The New Girl • Daisy Duck's Diary (Disney) **A:** Carl Barks

1056❑ca. 1959 Cover: 0.10 **NM** value: **50.00**
• **CGC:** 1 graded, best 9.0
• Yellowstone Kelly

1057❑Nov 1959 Cover: 0.10 **NM** value: **45.00**
• Mickey Mouse Album (Disney)

1058❑ca. 1959 Cover: 0.10 **NM** value: **70.00**
• **CGC:** 1 graded, best 8.5
• Colt.45

1059❑ca. 1959 Cover: 0.10 **NM** value: **75.00**
• **CGC:** 1 graded, best 9.0
• Sugarfoot

1060❑Nov 1959 Cover: 0.10 **NM** value: **130.00**
• **CGC:** 2 graded, best 9.0
• Journey to the Center of the Earth

1061❑ca. 1959 Cover: 0.10 **NM** value: **55.00**
• Buffalo Bee

1062❑Dec 1959 Cover: 0.10 **NM** value: **40.00**
• Walt Scott's Christmas Stories

1063❑ca. 1959 Cover: 0.10 **NM** value: **40.00**
• Santa Claus Funnies

1064❑Dec 1959 Cover: 0.10 **NM** value: **45.00**
• Bugs Bunny's Merry Christmas

1065❑ca. 1959 Cover: 0.10 **NM** value: **40.00**
• Frosty the Snowman

1066❑ca. 1960 Cover: 0.10 **NM** value: **125.00**
• **CGC:** 3 graded, best 9.4
• 77 Sunset Strip

1067❑Dec 1959 Cover: 0.10 **NM** value: **115.00**
• **CGC:** 1 graded, best 6.5
• Yogi Bear

1068❑ca. 1959 Cover: 0.10 **NM** value: **30.00**
• Francis the Talking Mule in Africa

1069❑Nov 1959 Cover: 0.10 **NM** value: **110.00**
• The FBI Story

1070❑Dec 1959 Cover: 0.10 **NM** value: **110.00**
• **CGC:** 1 graded, best 8.5
• Solomon and Sheba

1071❑Jan 1960 Cover: 0.10 **NM** value: **100.00**
• **CGC:** 1 graded, best 9.4
• The Real McCoys

1072❑Feb 1960 Cover: 0.10 **NM** value: **45.00**
• Blythe

1073❑Jan 1960 Cover: 0.10 **NM** value: **125.00**
📖 Mopping Up; Touche' Toupee'; The Snow Chaser; Free Ski Spree • Grandma Duck's Farm Friends (Disney) **A:** Carl Barks

1074❑ca. 1960 Cover: 0.10 **NM** value: **30.00**
• Chilly Willy

1075❑ca. 1960 Cover: 0.10 **NM** value: **75.00**
• **CGC:** 2 graded, best 9.4
• Tales of Wells Fargo

1076❑ca. 1960 Cover: 0.10 **NM** value: **90.00**
• **CGC:** 2 graded, best 9.6
• The Rebel

1077❑ca. 1960 Cover: 0.10 **NM** value: **110.00**
• **CGC:** 4 graded, best 9.4
• The Deputy

1078❑ca. 1960 Cover: 0.10 **NM** value: **90.00**
• **CGC:** 2 graded, best 9.4
• The Three Stooges

1079❑Feb 1960 Cover: 0.10 **NM** value: **40.00**
• **CGC:** 1 graded, best 8.5
• Spanky and Alfalfa, The Little Rascals

1080❑ca. 1960 Cover: 0.10 **NM** value: **60.00**
• Fury

1081❑Feb 1960 Cover: 0.10 **NM** value: **25.00**
• Elmer Fudd

1082❑ca. 1960 Cover: 0.10 **NM** value: **75.00**
• Spin and Marty (Disney)

1083❑ca. 1960 Cover: 0.10 **NM** value: **60.00**
• **CGC:** 1 graded, best 9.2
• Men Into Space

1084❑ca. 1960 Cover: 0.10 **NM** value: **35.00**
• Speedy Gonzales

1085❑ca. 1960 Cover: 0.10 **NM** value: **165.00**
• **CGC:** 2 graded, best 9.2
• The Time Machine

1086❑ca. 1960 Cover: 0.10 **NM** value: **25.00**
• Lolly and Pepper

1087❑ca. 1960 Cover: 0.10 **NM** value: **110.00**
• **CGC:** 3 graded, best 9.6
• Peter Gunn

1088❑ca. 1960 Cover: 0.10 **NM** value: **45.00**
• A Dog of Flanders

1089❑ca. 1960 Cover: 0.10 **NM** value: **65.00**
• **CGC:** 1 graded, best 9.6
• Restless Gun
1090❑ca. 1960 Cover: 0.10 **NM** value: **25.00**
• Francis, the Famous Talking Mule
1091❑ca. 1960 Cover: 0.10 **NM** value: **50.00**
• Jacky's Diary
1092❑ca. 1960 Cover: 0.10 **NM** value: **70.00**
• Toby Tyler (Disney)
1093❑ca. 1960 Cover: 0.10 **NM** value: **65.00**
• Mackenzie's Raiders
1094❑ca. 1960 Cover: 0.10 **NM** value: **40.00**
• Goofy (Disney)
1095❑Apr 1960 Cover: 0.10 **NM** value: **120.00**
• **CGC:** 1 graded, best 9.0
📖 The Call of the Wild; Cave of the Winds; Mixed-Up Mixer; The Madball Pitcher; The Bear Tamer; Tale of the Tape; His Shining Hour • Gyro Gearloose (Disney) **A:** Carl Barks
1096❑ca. 1960 Cover: 0.10 **NM** value: **65.00**
• The Texan
1097❑ca. 1960 Cover: 0.10 **NM** value: **160.00**
• **CGC:** 3 graded, best 9.2
• Rawhide
1098❑ca. 1960 Cover: 0.10 **NM** value: **70.00**
• **CGC:** 1 graded, best 9.4
• Sugarfoot
1099❑ca. 1960 Cover: 0.10 **NM** value: **45.00**
• Donald Duck Album (Disney)
1100❑May 1960 Cover: 0.10 **NM** value: **220.00**
• **CGC:** 1 graded, best 8.5
• Annette's Life Story (Disney)
1101❑ca. 1960 Cover: 0.10 **NM** value: **65.00**
• Kidnapped (Disney)
1102❑ca. 1960 Cover: 0.10 **NM** value: **95.00**
• **CGC:** 1 graded, best 9.4
• Wanted: Dead or Alive
1103❑Jun 1960 Cover: 0.10 **NM** value: **160.00**
• **CGC:** 4 graded, best 9.4
• Leave It to Beaver
1104❑ca. 1960 Cover: 0.10 **NM** value: **70.00**
• Yogi Bear Goes to College
1105❑ca. 1960 Cover: 0.10 **NM** value: **95.00**
• **CGC:** 1 graded, best 9.0
• Oh, Susanna-Gale Storm
1106❑ca. 1960 Cover: 0.10 **NM** value: **100.00**
• **CGC:** 1 graded, best 9.2
• 77 Sunset Strip
1107❑ca. 1960 Cover: 0.10 **NM** value: **65.00**
• Buckskin
1108❑ca. 1960 Cover: 0.10 **NM** value: **65.00**
• The Troubleshooters
1109❑ca. 1960 Cover: 0.10 **NM** value: **210.00**
• **CGC:** 1 graded, best 9.0
• This Is Your Life, Donald Duck (Disney) ★ Origin of Donald Duck.
1110❑ca. 1960 Cover: 0.10 **NM** value: **295.00**
• **CGC:** 3 graded, best 7.5
• Bonanza
1111❑ca. 1960 Cover: 0.10 **NM** value: **55.00**
• Shotgun Slade
1112❑ca. 1960 Cover: 0.10 **NM** value: **55.00**
• Pixie and Dixie and Mr. Jinks
1113❑ca. 1960 Cover: 0.10 **NM** value: **80.00**
• Tales of Wells Fargo
1114❑ca. 1960 Cover: 0.10 **NM** value: **60.00**
• Huck Finn
1115❑ca. 1960 Cover: 0.10 **NM** value: **165.00**
• **CGC:** 2 graded, best 8.5
• Ricky Nelson
1116❑ca. 1960 Cover: 0.10 **NM** value: **55.00**
• Boots and Saddles
1117❑ca. 1960 Cover: 0.10 **NM** value: **65.00**
• The Boy and the Pirates
1118❑ca. 1960 Cover: 0.10 **NM** value: **85.00**
• The Sword and the Dragon
1119❑ca. 1960 Cover: 0.10 **NM** value: **40.00**
• Smokey the Bear Nature Stories; 8/60
1120❑ca. 1960 Cover: 0.10 **NM** value: **70.00**
• Dinosaurus!; 8/60
1121❑ca. 1960 Cover: 0.10 **NM** value: **100.00**
• **CGC:** 1 graded, best 9.4
• Hercules Unchained
1122❑ca. 1960 Cover: 0.10 **NM** value: **30.00**
• Chilly Willy
1123❑ca. 1960 Cover: 0.10 **NM** value: **85.00**
• **CGC:** 2 graded, best 9.6
• Tombstone Territory
1124❑Aug 1960 Cover: 0.10 **NM** value: **85.00**
• **CGC:** 1 graded, best 9.4
• Whirlybirds
1125❑Aug 1960 Cover: 0.10 **NM** value: **80.00**
• **CGC:** 1 graded, best 9.4
• Laramie
1126❑Aug 1960 Cover: 0.10 **NM** value: **65.00**
• **CGC:** 1 graded, best 9.4
• Sundance
1127❑ca. 1960 Cover: 0.10 **NM** value: **85.00**
• The Three Stooges
1128❑Aug 1960 Cover: 0.10 **NM** value: **400.00**
• **CGC:** 1 graded, best 9.4
• Rocky and His Friends **A:** Jay Ward
1129❑Aug 1960 Cover: 0.10 **NM** value: **90.00**
• **CGC:** 2 graded, best 9.0
• Pollyanna (Disney)
1130❑Sep 1960 Cover: 0.10 **NM** value: **85.00**
• The Deputy
1131❑Sep 1960 Cover: 0.10 **NM** value: **25.00**
• Elmer Fudd
1132❑ca. 1960 Cover: 0.10 **NM** value: **45.00**
• Space Mouse
1133❑ca. 1960 Cover: 0.10 **NM** value: **60.00**
• Fury
1134❑ca. 1960 Cover: 0.10 **NM** value: **100.00**
• **CGC:** 1 graded, best 8.0
• The Real McCoys
1135❑Sep 1960 Cover: 0.10 **NM** value: **30.00**
• Mouse Musketeers
1136❑Sep 1960 Cover: 0.10 **NM** value: **60.00**
• **CGC:** 1 graded, best 6.0
• Jungle Cat (Disney)
1137❑ca. 1960 Cover: 0.10 **NM** value: **40.00**
• **CGC:** 1 graded, best 8.0
• The Little Rascals
1138❑ca. 1960 Cover: 0.10 **NM** value: **75.00**
• **CGC:** 1 graded, best 9.6
• The Rebel
1139❑ca. 1960 Cover: 0.10 **NM** value: **160.00**
• **CGC:** 2 graded, best 9.2
• Spartacus
1140❑ca. 1960 Cover: 0.10 **NM** value: **45.00**
• **CGC:** 1 graded, best 9.0
• Donald Duck Album (Disney)
1141❑ca. 1960 Cover: 0.10 **NM** value: **70.00**
• Huckleberry Hound for President
1142❑ca. 1960 Cover: 0.10 **NM** value: **70.00**
• **CGC:** 1 graded, best 9.0
• Johnny Ringo
1143❑Nov 1960 Cover: 0.10 **NM** value: **40.00**
• Pluto (Disney)
1144❑ca. 1960 Cover: 0.10 **NM** value: **85.00**
• The Story of Ruth
1145❑ca. 1960 Cover: 0.10 **NM** value: **120.00**
• The Lost World
1146❑Nov 1960 Cover: 0.10 **NM** value: **65.00**
• **CGC:** 2 graded, best 9.4
• The Restless Gun
1147❑Nov 1960 Cover: 0.10 **NM** value: **65.00**
• Sugarfoot
1148❑ca. 1960 Cover: 0.10 **NM** value: **85.00**
• I Aim at the Stars; the Werner von Braun Story
1149❑ca. 1960 Cover: 0.10 **NM** value: **40.00**
• Goofy (Disney)
1150❑Dec 1960 Cover: 0.10 **NM** value: **100.00**
• **CGC:** 1 graded, best 9.0
📖 Small Fryers; A Sticky Situation; Ring Leader Roundup; Too Much Help; Ruling the Roost; Daringly Different; False Flattery; Friendly Enemy; Undercover Girl; The Inventive Gentleman • Daisy Duck's Diary (Disney) **A:** Carl Barks
1151❑ca. 1960 Cover: 0.10 **NM** value: **40.00**
• Mickey Mouse Album
1152❑ca. 1960 Cover: 0.10 **NM** value: **265.00**
• Rocky and His Friends **A:** Jay Ward
1153❑ca. 1960 Cover: 0.10 **NM** value: **40.00**
• Frosty the Snowman
1154❑ca. 1960 Cover: 0.10 **NM** value: **40.00**
• Santa Claus Funnies
1155❑ca. 1960 Cover: 0.10 **NM** value: **160.00**
• North to Alaska
1156❑ca. 1960 Cover: 0.10 **NM** value: **90.00**
• Swiss Family Robinson (Disney)
1157❑ca. 1961 Cover: 0.15 **NM** value: **60.00**
• Master of the World
1158❑ca. 1961 Cover: 0.15 **NM** value: **75.00**
• The 3 Worlds of Gulliver
1159❑Feb 1961 Cover: 0.15 **NM** value: **90.00**
• **CGC:** 1 graded, best 9.4
• 77 Sunset Strip
1160❑Feb 1961 Cover: 0.15 **NM** value: **165.00**
• **CGC:** 2 graded, best 8.5
• Rawhide
1161❑ca. 1961 Cover: 0.15 **NM** value: **95.00**
• **CGC:** 1 graded, best 8.0
📖 The Whole Herd of Help; The Day the Farm Stood Still; The Training Farm Fuss; The Reversed Rescue • Grandma Duck's Farm Friends (Disney) **A:** Carl Barks
1162❑ca. 1961 Cover: 0.15 **NM** value: **70.00**
• **CGC:** 1 graded, best 8.5
• Yogi Bear Joins the Marines
1163❑ca. 1961 Cover: 0.15 **NM** value: **60.00**
• **CGC:** 1 graded, best 9.2
• Daniel Boone
1164❑ca. 1961 Cover: 0.15 **NM** value: **75.00**
• **CGC:** 1 graded, best 9.4
• Wanted: Dead or Alive!
1165❑ca. 1961 Cover: 0.15 **NM** value: **110.00**
• **CGC:** 3 graded, best 9.4
• Ellery Queen, Detective
1166❑ca. 1961 Cover: 0.15 **NM** value: **235.00**
• **CGC:** 3 graded, best 9.6
• Rocky and His Friends **A:** Jay Ward
1167❑ca. 1961 Cover: 0.15 **NM** value: **75.00**
• **CGC:** 1 graded, best 9.6
• Tales of Wells Fargo
1168❑ca. 1961 Cover: 0.15 **NM** value: **90.00**
• **CGC:** 2 graded, best 8.5
• The Detectives
1169❑ca. 1961 Cover: 0.15 **NM** value: **150.00**
• **CGC:** 1 graded, best 9.2
• The New Adventures of Sherlock Holmes
1170❑ca. 1961 Cover: 0.15 **NM** value: **80.00**
• **CGC:** 1 graded, best 8.0
• The Three Stooges
1171❑ca. 1961 Cover: 0.15 **NM** value: **25.00**
• Elmer Fudd
1172❑ca. 1961 Cover: 0.15 **NM** value: **55.00**
• Fury
1173❑May 1961 Cover: 0.15 **NM** value: **220.00**
📖 Specter of Youth; The Phantom Lighthouse; Doom by Prediction • The Twilight Zone **A:** Reed Crandall
1174❑ca. 1961 Cover: 0.15 **NM** value: **35.00**
• **CGC:** 2 graded, best 9.4
• The Little Rascals
1175❑ca. 1961 Cover: 0.15 **NM** value: **25.00**
• MGM's Mouse Musketeers
1176❑ca. 1961 Cover: 0.15 **NM** value: **40.00**
• Dondi
1177❑ca. 1961 Cover: 0.15 **NM** value: **30.00**
• Chilly Willy
1178❑ca. 1960 Cover: 0.15 **NM** value: **60.00**
• Ten Who Dared (Disney)
1179❑ca. 1961 Cover: 0.15 **NM** value: **70.00**
• **CGC:** 2 graded, best 9.8
• The Swamp Fox (Disney)
1180❑ca. 1961 Cover: 0.15 **NM** value: **160.00**
• **CGC:** 3 graded, best 9.6
• The Danny Thomas Show
1181❑ca. 1961 Cover: 0.15 **NM** value: **55.00**
• Texas John Slaughter (Disney)
1182❑ca. 1961 Cover: 0.15 **NM** value: **45.00**
• Donald Duck Album (Disney)
1183❑ca. 1961 Cover: 0.15 **NM** value: **105.00**
• **CGC:** 1 graded, best 9.0
• 101 Dalmatians (Disney)
1184❑ca. 1961 Cover: 0.15 **NM** value: **125.00**
📖 The Nose Knows; Monsterville; The Cube; Mighty But Miserable; Brain-Strain; The Old Timer; Mechanized Mess • Gyro Gearloose (Disney) **A:** Carl Barks
1185❑ca. 1961 Cover: 0.15 **NM** value: **35.00**
• Sweetie Pie
1186❑ca. 1961 Cover: 0.15 **NM** value: **75.00**
📖 The Touchables, How To Bat 400; Human Gumbo; Yak Yak Prediction; How To Win Friends; Drama vs. Realism; Hysterical History Quiz; Yak Yak Nursery Rhymes • Yak Yak: A Pathology of Humor **A:** Jack Davis
1187❑ca. 1961 Cover: 0.15 **NM** value: **80.00**
• The Three Stooges
1188❑ca. 1961 Cover: 0.15 **NM** value: **110.00**
• **CGC:** 1 graded, best 9.4
• Atlantis: The Lost Continent
1189❑ca. 1961 Cover: 0.15 **NM** value: **65.00**
• Greyfriars Bobby (Disney)
1190❑ca. 1961 Cover: 0.15 **NM** value: **70.00**
• **CGC:** 1 graded, best 8.0
• Donald and the Wheel (Disney)
1191❑ca. 1961 Cover: 0.15 **NM** value: **165.00**
• **CGC:** 1 graded, best 9.0
• Leave It to Beaver
1192❑ca. 1961 Cover: 0.15 **NM** value: **150.00**
• **CGC:** 1 graded, best 9.4
• Ricky Nelson
1193❑ca. 1961 Cover: 0.15 **NM** value: **85.00**
• The Real McCoys
1194❑ca. 1961 Cover: 0.15 **NM** value: **40.00**
• Pepe
1195❑ca. 1961 Cover: 0.15 **NM** value: **70.00**
• National Velvet
1196❑ca. 1961 Cover: 0.15 **NM** value: **45.00**
• Pixie and Dixie and Mr. Jinks
1197❑ca. 1961 Cover: 0.15 **NM** value: **65.00**
• **CGC:** 1 graded, best 9.2
• The Aquanauts; 5-7/61
1198❑ca. 1961 Cover: 0.15 **NM** value: **70.00**
• Donald in Mathmagic Land (Disney)
1199❑ca. 1961 Cover: 0.15 **NM** value: **75.00**
• The Absent-Minded Professor (Disney)
1200❑ca. 1961 Cover: 0.15 **NM** value: **60.00**
• Hennessey
1201❑ca. 1962 Cover: 0.15 **NM** value: **40.00**
• Goofy and His Goof-Kart (Disney)
1202❑ca. 1961 Cover: 0.15 **NM** value: **150.00**
• **CGC:** 1 graded, best 8.5
• Rawhide
1203❑ca. 1962 Cover: 0.15 **NM** value: **55.00**
• The Wonderful Adventures of Pinocchio (Disney)
1204❑ca. 1961 Cover: 0.15 **NM** value: **40.00**
• Scamp (Disney)
1205❑ca. 1961 Cover: 0.15 **NM** value: **60.00**
• David and Goliath
1206❑ca. 1961 Cover: 0.15 **NM** value: **25.00**
• Lolly and Pepper
1207❑ca. 1961 Cover: 0.15 **NM** value: **80.00**
• **CGC:** 1 graded, best 8.5
• The Rebel
1208❑ca. 1961 Cover: 0.15 **NM** value: **225.00**
• **CGC:** 2 graded, best 9.4
• Rocky and His Friends **A:** Jay Ward
1209❑ca. 1961 Cover: 0.15 **NM** value: **65.00**
• Sugarfoot
1210❑ca. 1961 Cover: 0.15 **NM** value: **85.00**
• The Parent Trap (Disney)
1211❑ca. 1961 Cover: 0.15 **NM** value: **80.00**
• **CGC:** 1 graded, best 9.2
• 77 Sunset Strip
1212❑ca. 1961 Cover: 0.15 **NM** value: **30.00**
• Chilly Willy (#8)
1213❑ca. 1962 Cover: 0.15 **NM** value: **90.00**
• **CGC:** 1 graded, best 9.2
• Mysterious Island
1214❑ca. 1961 Cover: 0.15 **NM** value: **40.00**
• Smokey the Bear Nature Stories
1215❑ca. 1961 Cover: 0.15 **NM** value: **70.00**
• Tales of Wells Fargo
1216❑ca. 1961 Cover: 0.15 **NM** value: **80.00**
• Whirlybirds
1218❑ca. 1961 Cover: 0.15 **NM** value: **55.00**
• Fury

CGC-graded: Multiply prices above by **33 for 9.9 M • 16 for 9.8 NM/M • 7 for 9.6 NM+ • 5 for 9.4 NM • 2.5 for 9.2 NM- • 1.5 for 9.0 VF/NM**

1219❑ca. 1962 Cover: 0.15 **NM** value: **75.00**
• The Detectives
1220❑ca. 1961 Cover: 0.15 **NM** value: **75.00**
• **CGC:** 1 graded, best 8.0
• Gunslinger
1221❑ca. 1961 Cover: 0.15 **NM** value: **190.00**
• Bonanza
1222❑ca. 1961 Cover: 0.15 **NM** value: **25.00**
• Elmer Fudd
1223❑ca. 1961 Cover: 0.15 **NM** value: **55.00**
• Laramie
1224❑ca. 1961 Cover: 0.15 **NM** value: **35.00**
• **CGC:** 1 graded, best 9.0
• The Little Rascals; 10-12/61
1225❑ca. 1961 Cover: 0.15 **NM** value: **85.00**
The Renegade Rustler; Hide-Out Town • The Deputy
1226❑ca. 1961 Cover: 0.15 **NM** value: **55.00**
• Nikki, Wild Dog of the North (Disney)
1227❑ca. 1961 Cover: 0.15 **NM** value: **80.00**
• Morgan the Pirate
1229❑ca. 1961 Cover: 0.15 **NM** value: **105.00**
• Thief of Baghdad
1230❑ca. 1961 Cover: 0.15 **NM** value: **110.00**
• **CGC:** 1 graded, best 7.5
• Voyage to the Bottom of the Sea
1231❑ca. 1961 Cover: 0.15 **NM** value: **110.00**
• Danger Man
1232❑ca. 1961 Cover: 0.15 **NM** value: **50.00**
• On the Double
1233❑ca. 1961 Cover: 0.15 **NM** value: **60.00**
• Tammy, Tell Me True
1234❑ca. 1961 Cover: 0.15 **NM** value: **60.00**
• The Phantom Planet
1235❑ca. 1961 Cover: 0.15 **NM** value: **95.00**
• Mister Magoo
1236❑ca. 1961 Cover: 0.15 **NM** value: **80.00**
• King of Kings
1237❑ca. 1961 Cover: 0.15 **NM** value: **185.00**
• **CGC:** 1 graded, best 7.5
• The Untouchables
1238❑ca. 1961 Cover: 0.15 **NM** value: **90.00**
• Deputy Dawg
1239❑ca. 1961 Cover: 0.15 **NM** value: **45.00**
• Donald Duck Album
1240❑ca. 1961 Cover: 0.15 **NM** value: **75.00**
• **CGC:** 1 graded, best 7.0
• The Detectives
1241❑ca. 1961 Cover: 0.15 **NM** value: **30.00**
• Sweetie Pie
1242❑ca. 1961 Cover: 0.15 **NM** value: **110.00**
• King Leonardo and His Short Subjects
1243❑ca. 1961 Cover: 0.15 **NM** value: **95.00**
• Ellery Queen, Detective
1244❑ca. 1961 Cover: 0.15 **NM** value: **42.00**
• Space Mouse
1245❑ca. 1961 Cover: 0.15 **NM** value: **145.00**
• **CGC:** 1 graded, best 9.4
• The New Adventures of Sherlock Holmes
1246❑ca. 1961 Cover: 0.15 **NM** value: **35.00**
• Mickey Mouse Album
1247❑ca. 1961 Cover: 0.15 **NM** value: **40.00**
• Daisy Duck's Diary (Disney)
1248❑ca. 1961 Cover: 0.15 **NM** value: **40.00**
• Pluto Joins the Circus (Disney)
1249❑ca. 1961 Cover: 0.15 **NM** value: **145.00**
• **CGC:** 1 graded, best 9.4
• The Danny Thomas Show
1250❑ca. 1962 Cover: 0.15 **NM** value: **80.00**
• The Four Horsemen of the Apocalypse
1251❑ca. 1962 Cover: 0.15 **NM** value: **48.00**
• Everything's Ducky
1252❑ca. 1962 Cover: 0.15 **NM** value: **265.00**
• **CGC:** 2 graded, best 9.4
• Andy Griffith
1253❑ca. 1962 Cover: 0.15 **NM** value: **80.00**
• Space Man
1254❑ca. 1962 Cover: 0.15 **NM** value: **60.00**
• Diver Dan
1255❑ca. 1962 Cover: 0.15 **NM** value: **70.00**
• The Wonders of Aladdin
1256❑ca. 1962 Cover: 0.15 **NM** value: **65.00**
• Kona, Monarch of Monster Isle ★ 1st Appearance of Kona.
1257❑ca. 1962 Cover: 0.15 **NM** value: **75.00**
• **CGC:** 1 graded, best 5.0
• Car 54, Where Are You?
1258❑ca. 1962 Cover: 0.15 **NM** value: **75.00**
• The Frogmen
1259❑ Cover: 0.15 **NM** value: **70.00**
• El Cid
1260❑ca. 1961 Cover: 0.15 **NM** value: **100.00**
• The Horsemasters (Disney)
1261❑ca. 1961 Cover: 0.15 **NM** value: **140.00**
• **CGC:** 3 graded, best 9.0
• Rawhide
1262❑ca. 1961 Cover: 0.15 **NM** value: **70.00**
• The Rebel
1263❑ca. 1961 Cover: 0.15 **NM** value: **80.00**
• 77 Sunset Strip
1264❑ca. 1961 Cover: 0.15 **NM** value: **40.00**
• Pixie and Dixie and Mr. Jinks
1265❑ca. 1961 Cover: 0.15 **NM** value: **75.00**
• **CGC:** 1 graded, best 9.2
• The Real McCoys
1266❑ca. 1961 Cover: 0.15 **NM** value: **26.00**
• Spike and Tyke
1267❑ca. 1961 Cover: 0.15 **NM** value: **85.00**
• **CGC:** 1 graded, best 6.5
Buffaloed By Buffaloes • Gyro Gearloose (Disney) **A:** Carl Barks
1268❑ca. 1961 Cover: 0.15 **NM** value: **25.00**
• Oswald the Rabbit
1269❑ca. 1962 Cover: 0.15 **NM** value: **140.00**
• **CGC:** 1 graded, best 8.0
• Rawhide
1270❑ca. 1962 Cover: 0.15 **NM** value: **200.00**
• **CGC:** 3 graded, best 9.4
• Bullwinkle and Rocky **A:** Jay Ward
1271❑ca. 1961 Cover: 0.15 **NM** value: **60.00**
• Yogi Bear's Birthday Party
1272❑Dec 1961 Cover: 0.15 **NM** value: **35.00**
• Frosty the Snowman
1273❑ca. 1962 Cover: 0.15 **NM** value: **65.00**
• Hans Brinker (Disney)
1274❑ca. 1961 Cover: 0.15 **NM** value: **35.00**
• Santa Claus Funnies
1275❑ca. 1961 Cover: 0.15 **NM** value: **200.00**
• **CGC:** 3 graded, best 9.4
• Rocky and His Friends **A:** Jay Ward
1276❑ca. 1961 Cover: 0.15 **NM** value: **30.00**
• Dondi
1278❑ca. 1962 Cover: 0.15 **NM** value: **110.00**
• King Leonardo and His Short Subjects
1279❑ca. 1962 Cover: 0.15 **NM** value: **45.00**
• Grandma Duck's Farm Friends (Disney)
1280❑ca. 1962 Cover: 0.15 **NM** value: **55.00**
• Hennessey
1281❑ca. 1962 Cover: 0.15 **NM** value: **28.00**
• Chilly Willy
1282❑ca. 1962 Cover: 0.15 **NM** value: **125.00**
• Babes in Toyland (Disney)
1283❑ca. 1962 Cover: 0.15 **NM** value: **175.00**
• Bonanza
1284❑ca. 1962 Cover: 0.15 **NM** value: **55.00**
• Laramie
1285❑ca. 1962 Cover: 0.15 **NM** value: **140.00**
• **CGC:** 1 graded, best 8.0
• Leave It to Beaver
1286❑ca. 1962 Cover: 0.15 **NM** value: **165.00**
• The Untouchables
1287❑ca. 1962 Cover: 0.15 **NM** value: **55.00**
• Man from Wells Fargo
1288❑Apr 1962 Cover: 0.15 **NM** value: **135.00**
• The Twilight Zone
1289❑Mar 1962 Cover: 0.15 **NM** value: **85.00**
• Ellery Queen, Detective
1290❑ca. 1962 Cover: 0.15 **NM** value: **25.00**
• Mouse Musketeers
1291❑ca. 1962 Cover: 0.15 **NM** value: **70.00**
• 77 Sunset Strip
1293❑ca. 1962 Cover: 0.15 **NM** value: **25.00**
• Elmer Fudd
1294❑ca. 1962 Cover: 0.15 **NM** value: **65.00**
• Ripcord
1295❑ca. 1962 Cover: 0.15 **NM** value: **140.00**
• **CGC:** 4 graded, best 9.4
• Mister Ed the Talking Horse
1296❑ca. 1962 Cover: 0.15 **NM** value: **50.00**
• Fury
1297❑ca. 1962 Cover: 0.15 **NM** value: **35.00**
• **CGC:** 1 graded, best 9.2
• Spanky and Alfalfa, the Little Rascals
1298❑ca. 1962 Cover: 0.15 **NM** value: **48.00**
• The Hathaways
1299❑ca. 1962 Cover: 0.15 **NM** value: **110.00**
• **CGC:** 1 graded, best 9.4
• Deputy Dawg
1300❑ca. 1962 Cover: 0.15 **NM** value: **150.00**
• The Comancheros
1301❑ca. 1962 Cover: 0.15 **NM** value: **45.00**
• Adventures in Paradise
1302❑ca. 1962 Cover: 0.15 **NM** value: **35.00**
• Johnny Jason, Teen Reporter
1303❑ca. 1962 Cover: 0.15 **NM** value: **40.00**
• Lad: A Dog
1304❑ca. 1962 Cover: 0.15 **NM** value: **75.00**
• Nellie the Nurse **A:** John Stanley
1305❑ca. 1962 Cover: 0.15 **NM** value: **90.00**
• Mister Magoo
1306❑ca. 1962 Cover: 0.15 **NM** value: **60.00**
• Target: The Corrupters
1307❑ca. 1962 Cover: 0.15 **NM** value: **40.00**
• Margie
1308❑ca. 1962 Cover: 0.15 **NM** value: **110.00**
• Tales of the Wizard of Oz
1309❑ca. 1962 Cover: 0.15 **NM** value: **90.00**
• 87th Precinct **A:** Bernie Krigstein
1310❑ca. 1962 Cover: 0.15 **NM** value: **60.00**
• Huck and Yogi Winter Sports
1311❑ca. 1962 Cover: 0.15 **NM** value: **200.00**
• **CGC:** 2 graded, best 9.4
• Rocky and His Friends **A:** Jay Ward
1312❑ca. 1962 Cover: 0.15 **NM** value: **50.00**
• National Velvet
1313❑ca. 1962 Cover: 0.15 **NM** value: **70.00**
• Moon Pilot (Disney)
1328❑ca. 1962 Cover: 0.15 **NM** value: **75.00**
• The Underwater City
1330❑ca. 1962 Cover: 0.15 **NM** value: **125.00**
• Brain Boy (Frank Springer) **A:** Gil Kane; Al Jaffee **W:** Herb Castle
★ 1st Appearance of Brain Boy.
1332❑ca. 1962 Cover: 0.15 **NM** value: **75.00**
• Bachelor Father
1333❑ca. 1962 Cover: 0.15 **NM** value: **55.00**
• Short Ribs
1335❑ca. 1962 Cover: 0.15 **NM** value: **35.00**
• Aggie Mack
1336❑ca. 1962 Cover: 0.15 **NM** value: **45.00**
• On Stage
1337❑ca. 1962 Cover: 0.15 **NM** value: **80.00**
• Doctor Kildare
1341❑ca. 1962 Cover: 0.15 **NM** value: **225.00**
• **CGC:** 2 graded, best 9.2
• Andy Griffith
1348❑ca. 1962 Cover: 0.15 **NM** value: **75.00**
• Yak Yak **A:** Jack Davis
1349❑ca. 1962 Cover: 0.15 **NM** value: **100.00**
• Yogi Bear Visits the UN
1350❑ca. 1962 Cover: 0.15 **NM** value: **55.00**
• Comanche (Disney)
1354❑ca. 1962 Cover: 0.15 **NM** value: **70.00**
final issue. • Calvin and the Colonel

4-D MONKEY, THE — Dr. Leung's

1 ❑ 1988 Cover: 1.80 **NM** value: **2.00**
2 ❑ 1988 Cover: 1.80 **NM** value: **2.00**
3 ❑ 1988 Cover: 1.80 **NM** value: **2.00**
4 ❑ 1989 Cover: 1.80 **NM** value: **2.00**
5 ❑ 1989 Cover: 1.80 **NM** value: **2.00**
6 ❑ 1989 Cover: 2.00 **NM** value: **Cover or less**
7 ❑ 1989 Cover: 2.00 **NM** value: **Cover or less**
8 ❑ 1989 Cover: 2.00 **NM** value: **Cover or less**
9 ❑ 1990 Cover: 2.00 **NM** value: **Cover or less**
10 ❑ 1990 Cover: 2.00 **NM** value: **Cover or less**
11 ❑ 1990 Cover: 2.00 **NM** value: **Cover or less**
12 ❑ 1990 Cover: 2.00 **NM** value: **Cover or less**

FOUR FAVORITES — Ace

1 ❑ Sep 1941 Cover: 0.10 **NM** value: **1000.00**
• **CGC:** 1 graded, best 6.5
2 ❑ Nov 1941 Cover: 0.10 **NM** value: **500.00**
3 ❑ Jan 1942 Cover: 0.10 **NM** value: **400.00**
4 ❑ Mar 1942 Cover: 0.10 **NM** value: **300.00**
5 ❑ May 1942 Cover: 0.10 **NM** value: **300.00**
6 ❑ Jul 1942 Cover: 0.10 **NM** value: **300.00**
7 ❑ Oct 1942 Cover: 0.10 **NM** value: **300.00**
8 ❑ Dec 1942 Cover: 0.10 **NM** value: **300.00**
9 ❑ Feb 1943 Cover: 0.10 **NM** value: **300.00**
10 ❑ May 1943 Cover: 0.10 **NM** value: **300.00**
11 ❑ Aug 1943 Cover: 0.10 **NM** value: **300.00**
12 ❑ Nov 1943 Cover: 0.10 **NM** value: **250.00**
13 ❑ Feb 1944 Cover: 0.10 **NM** value: **250.00**
• **CGC:** 1 graded, best 6.5
14 ❑ May 1944 Cover: 0.10 **NM** value: **250.00**
15 ❑ Aug 1944 Cover: 0.10 **NM** value: **250.00**
16 ❑ Nov 1944 Cover: 0.10 **NM** value: **250.00**
17 ❑ Feb 1945 Cover: 0.10 **NM** value: **250.00**
18 ❑ May 1945 Cover: 0.10 **NM** value: **250.00**
19 ❑ Aug 1945 Cover: 0.10 **NM** value: **250.00**
20 ❑ Nov 1945 Cover: 0.10 **NM** value: **250.00**
21 ❑ Jan 1946 Cover: 0.10 **NM** value: **200.00**
22 ❑ Mar 1946 Cover: 0.10 **NM** value: **200.00**
23 ❑ May 1946 Cover: 0.10 **NM** value: **200.00**
24 ❑ Jul 1946 Cover: 0.10 **NM** value: **200.00**
25 ❑ Sep 1946 Cover: 0.10 **NM** value: **200.00**
26 ❑ Nov 1946 Cover: 0.10 **NM** value: **200.00**
27 ❑ Jan 1947 Cover: 0.10 **NM** value: **200.00**
28 ❑ Mar 1947 Cover: 0.10 **NM** value: **125.00**
29 ❑ Jun 1947 Cover: 0.10 **NM** value: **200.00**
30 ❑ Aug 1947 Cover: 0.10 **NM** value: **200.00**
31 ❑ Oct 1947 Cover: 0.10 **NM** value: **200.00**
32 ❑ Dec 1947 Cover: 0.10 **NM** value: **200.00**

FOUR HORSEMEN — Vertigo

The legendary Four Horsemen of the Apocalypse have landed in New York City's equally legendary Times Square at midnight Jan. 1, 2000. Let the mayhem that marks the beginning of the end of time commence, right?

Wrong.

The fabled chaos-bringers are actually welcomed by a crowd that feels that the world is rotten: full of dangers and evils far worse than any the Horsemen can unleash upon it. After taking refuge in a bar to mull this turn of events, Famine learns of the political and personal minefield that is reproductive rights; War hears of the bloody battles that take place in corporate boardrooms; Pestilence is exposed to constant invasions of privacy that plague contemporary society; and Death — well, that would be telling. This intriguing four-parter gives readers much to consider; it was released as a part of Vertigo's "Y2K" event.

1 ❑ Feb 2000 Cover: 2.50 **NM** value: **Cover or less**
Circ: Diamd. preorders: **15,785**
Famine **A:** Essad Ribic **W:** Robert Rodi
2 ❑ Mar 2000 Cover: 2.50 **NM** value: **Cover or less**
Circ: Diamd. preorders: **11,699**
3 ❑ Apr 2000 Cover: 2.50 **NM** value: **Cover or less**
Circ: Diamd. preorders: **11,088**
Pestilence **A:** Essad Ribic **W:** Robert Rodi
4 ❑ May 2000 Cover: 2.50 **NM** value: **Cover or less**
Circ: Diamd. preorders: **10,636**
Death **A:** Essad Ribic **W:** Robert Rodi

FOUR KUNOICHI, THE: BLOODLUST — Lightning

1 ❑ Dec 1996, b&w Cover: 2.75 **NM** value: **Cover or less**
Circ: Diamd. preorders: **3,632**
• Standard edition. **A:** John Cleary **W:** John Cleary
1/Nude❑ Cover: 9.95 **NM** value: **Cover or less**
Nude cover. **A:** John Cleary **W:** John Cleary

Other grades: Multiply prices above by **1.5 for Mint • 2/3 for Very Fine • 1/3 for Fine • 1/5 for Very Good • 1/8 for Good**

1/PL❑ Cover: 9.95 **NM** value: **Cover or less**
• Platinum edition. **A:** John Cleary **W:** John Cleary
1/PLND❑ Cover: 29.95 **NM** value: **Cover or less**
• Platinum Nude edition. **A:** John Cleary **W:** John Cleary

FOUR KUNOICHI: ENTER THE SINJA — Lightning

1 ❑ Feb 1997, b&w Cover: 2.95 **NM** value: **Cover or less**

4MOST — Premium

1 ❑ Win 1942 Cover: 0.10 **NM** value: **750.00**
2 ❑ Spr 1942 Cover: 0.10 **NM** value: **340.00**
3 ❑ Sum 1942 Cover: 0.10 **NM** value: **260.00**
Flag cover.
4 ❑ Aut 1942 Cover: 0.10 **NM** value: **250.00**
5 ❑ Win 1943 Cover: 0.10 **NM** value: **100.00**
6 ❑ Spr 1943 Cover: 0.10 **NM** value: **80.00**
7 ❑ Sum 1943 Cover: 0.10 **NM** value: **80.00**
8 ❑ Fal 1943 Cover: 0.10 **NM** value: **100.00**
Pumpkins carved in shape of Axis rulers on cover (being shot with slingshots).
9 ❑ Win 1944 Cover: 0.10 **NM** value: **60.00**
10 ❑ Spr 1944 Cover: 0.10 **NM** value: **45.00**
11 ❑ Sum 1944 Cover: 0.10 **NM** value: **45.00**
12 ❑ Fal 1944 Cover: 0.10 **NM** value: **45.00**
13 ❑ Win 1944 Cover: 0.10 **NM** value: **45.00**
14 ❑ Spr 1945 Cover: 0.10 **NM** value: **30.00**
15 ❑ Sum 1945 Cover: 0.10 **NM** value: **30.00**
16 ❑ Fal 1945 Cover: 0.10 **NM** value: **30.00**
17 ❑ Win 1945 Cover: 0.10 **NM** value: **35.00**
18 ❑ Spr 1946 Cover: 0.10 **NM** value: **28.00**
19 ❑ Sum 1946 Cover: 0.10 **NM** value: **28.00**
20 ❑ Fal 1946 Cover: 0.10 **NM** value: **28.00**
21 ❑ Win 1946 Cover: 0.10 **NM** value: **35.00**
22 ❑ Spr 1947 Cover: 0.10 **NM** value: **28.00**
23 ❑ Sum 1947 Cover: 0.10 **NM** value: **28.00**
24 ❑ Sep 1947 Cover: 0.10 **NM** value: **28.00**
25 ❑ Nov 1947 Cover: 0.10 **NM** value: **40.00**
26 ❑ Jan 1948 Cover: 0.10 **NM** value: **30.00**
27 ❑ Mar 1948 Cover: 0.10 **NM** value: **24.00**
28 ❑ May 1948 Cover: 0.10 **NM** value: **24.00**
29 ❑ Jul 1948 Cover: 0.10 **NM** value: **24.00**
30 ❑ Sep 1948 Cover: 0.10 **NM** value: **24.00**
31 ❑ Nov 1948 Cover: 0.10 **NM** value: **24.00**
📖 Dick Cole; Lem the Grem; The Devil's House (text story); Boitram the Boiglar; Edison Bell; The Cadet **A:** Art Helfant; Nina Albright **W:** Art Helfant; Nina Albright; Lindley Mann
32 ❑ Jan 1949 Cover: 0.10 **NM** value: **28.00**
33 ❑ Mar 1949 Cover: 0.10 **NM** value: **22.00**
34 ❑ May 1949 Cover: 0.10 **NM** value: **22.00**
35 ❑ Jul 1949 Cover: 0.10 **NM** value: **22.00**
36 ❑ Sep 1949 Cover: 0.10 **NM** value: **22.00**
37 ❑ Nov 1949 Cover: 0.10 **NM** value: **22.00**
38 ❑ Jan 1950 Cover: 0.10 **NM** value: **35.00**
• The True Life Story of Johnny Weissmuler
39 ❑ Mar 1950 Cover: 0.10 **NM** value: **22.00**
40 ❑ Apr 1950 Cover: 0.10 **NM** value: **22.00**
• Series continued in Thrilling Crime Cases #41

FOUR-STAR BATTLE TALES — DC

1 ❑ Feb 1973 Cover: 0.20 **NM** value: **6.50**
• **CGC:** 2 graded, best 9.4
📖 The Last Target; Indians Don't Fight By The Book!
2 ❑ May 1973 Cover: 0.20 **NM** value: **4.00**
3 ❑ Aug 1973 Cover: 0.20 **NM** value: **4.00**
4 ❑ Oct 1973 Cover: 0.20 **NM** value: **4.00**
5 ❑ Nov 1973 Cover: 0.20 **NM** value: **4.00**
final issue.

FOUR STAR SPECTACULAR — DC

1 ❑ Apr 1976 Cover: 0.50 **NM** value: **5.00**
• Giant-size.
2 ❑ Jun 1976 Cover: 0.50 **NM** value: **4.00**
• Giant-size.
3 ❑ Aug 1976 Cover: 0.50 **NM** value: **4.00**
• Giant-size. • Bicentennial #15
4 ❑ Oct 1976 Cover: 0.50 **NM** value: **4.00**
• Giant-size.
5 ❑ Dec 1976 Cover: 0.50 **NM** value: **4.00**
• Giant-size. 📖 Superboy: The Man Who Hunted Superboy; Vigilante: The Unlucky Horseshoe; The Green Arrow: The Rainbow Archer; Wonder Woman **A:** Howard Sherman; George Papp; Charles Moulton **W:** Charles Moulton
6 ❑ Feb 1977 Cover: 0.50 **NM** value: **4.00**
• Giant-size. final issue.

FOUR TEENERS — A.A. Wyn

34 ❑ Apr 1948 **NM** value: **25.00**
• **CGC:** 1 graded, best 7.0

FOURTH WORLD GALLERY, THE — DC

1 ❑ Cover: 3.50 **NM** value: **Cover or less**
No issue number. • pin-ups based on Jack Kirby creations **A:** Norm Breyfogle; Mark Badger; Brett Breeding; John Byrne; Mike McKone; Dan Jurgens; Jim Calafiore; Eduardo Barreto; Walt Simonson; Steve Crespo; Gene Ha; David Roach; Bob Wiacek; Lee Loughbridge

The CGC numbers printed in individual listings above represent the **number of copies examined** and given a **Universal** grade by CGC and the **best such copy** graded at press time. For current populations, watch for special ***Comics Buyer's Guide*** issues or check **www.cgccomics.com.**

FOURTH WORLD (JACK KIRBY'S...) — DC

When Jack Kirby left Marvel to go to DC in 1970, he set up a super-character universe of his own, one in which the good super-beings of New Genesis are in constant conflict with the nasty super-beings of Apokolips, led by the evil Darkseid. Among the characters involved in the complex storyline are Orion (Darkseid's son, raised in New Genesis), Big Barda, Scott Free, Oberon, Black Racer, Desaad, Granny Goodness, and so on and so forth. Titles involved in the universe included New Gods, Forever People, and Mister Miracle.

Though this title is Jack Kirby's Fourth World, it is, in fact, not stories by Kirby but new material created by John Byrne and Walter Simonson, playing with the toys Kirby created for the playground he planned as his major work. — Maggie

1 ❑ Mar 1997 Cover: 1.95 **NM** value: **2.50**
📖 Born of Thunder, Born of Flame **A:** John Byrne **C:** Walt Simonson **W:** John Byrne
2 ❑ Apr 1997 Cover: 1.95 **NM** value: **2.00**
3 ❑ May 1997 Cover: 1.95 **NM** value: **2.00**
4 ❑ Jun 1997 Cover: 1.95 **NM** value: **2.00**
📖 Back from the Source **A:** John Byrne **C:** Walt Simonson **W:** John Byrne
5 ❑ Jul 1997 Cover: 1.95 **NM** value: **2.00**
6 ❑ Aug 1997 Cover: 1.95 **NM** value: **2.00**
7 ❑ Sep 1997 Cover: 1.95 **NM** value: **2.00**
8 ❑ Oct 1997 Cover: 1.95 **NM** value: **2.00**
• Genesis **A:** John Byrne **C:** Walt Simonson **W:** John Byrne
9 ❑ Nov 1997 Cover: 1.95 **NM** value: **2.00**
📖 Sons of the Father **A:** John Byrne **C:** Walt Simonson **W:** John Byrne
10 ❑ Dec 1997 Cover: 1.95 **NM** value: **2.00**
Face cover. 📖 Aftermath **A:** John Byrne **C:** Walt Simonson **W:** John Byrne
11 ❑ Jan 1998 Cover: 1.95 **NM** value: **2.00**
12 ❑ Feb 1998 Cover: 1.95 **NM** value: **2.00**
13 ❑ Mar 1998 Cover: 1.95 **NM** value: **2.00**
14 ❑ Apr 1998 Cover: 1.95 **NM** value: **2.00**
• Darkseid and Ares escape Source Wall **A:** John Byrne **C:** Walt Simonson **W:** John Byrne
15 ❑ May 1998 Cover: 1.95 **NM** value: **2.00**
16 ❑ Jun 1998 Cover: 1.95 **NM** value: **2.00**
17 ❑ Jul 1998 Cover: 1.95 **NM** value: **2.00**
18 ❑ Aug 1998 Cover: 1.95 **NM** value: **2.00**
19 ❑ Sep 1998 Cover: 2.25 **NM** value: **Cover or less**
• Return of Supertown **A:** John Byrne **C:** Walt Simonson **W:** John Byrne
20 ❑ Oct 1998 Cover: 2.25 **NM** value: **Cover or less**

FOX AND THE CROW — DC

Creator James F. Davis produced many, many short stories in which the crow works to outwit the relatively simple fox. As Crow says in Real Screen Comics #42, "If dey gave da Nobel Prize for bein' a great chiseler, I'd win every year!" This series from the late 1950s and 1960s pits the crow against the fox in stories reminiscent of Aesop's fables. However, in this series, the clever crow is also sometimes too clever for his own good. Moreover, he's unabashedly nasty. As a result, the simple fox comes off as more lovable than foolish.

Fox and the Crow also featured a series of backup stories such as Hare and Hound. These were eventually usurped by Stanley and His Monster, a feature which proved so popular that Fox and the Crow later changed its name to Stanley and His Monster.

1 ❑ Dec 1951 Cover: 0.10 **NM** value: **760.00**
• **CGC:** 3 graded, best 7.5
2 ❑ Feb 1952 Cover: 0.10 **NM** value: **385.00**
3 ❑ Apr 1952 Cover: 0.10 **NM** value: **275.00**
4 ❑ Jun 1952 Cover: 0.10 **NM** value: **275.00**
• **CGC:** 1 graded, best 6.5
5 ❑ Aug 1952 Cover: 0.10 **NM** value: **275.00**
• **CGC:** 1 graded, best 4.5
6 ❑ Oct 1952 Cover: 0.10 **NM** value: **185.00**
7 ❑ Dec 1952 Cover: 0.10 **NM** value: **185.00**
8 ❑ Feb 1953 Cover: 0.10 **NM** value: **185.00**
• **CGC:** 1 graded, best 5.0
9 ❑ Apr 1953 Cover: 0.10 **NM** value: **185.00**
10 ❑ Jun 1953 Cover: 0.10 **NM** value: **185.00**
• **CGC:** 1 graded, best 6.5
11 ❑ Aug 1953 Cover: 0.10 **NM** value: **130.00**
• **CGC:** 1 graded, best 6.0
12 ❑ Oct 1953 Cover: 0.10 **NM** value: **130.00**
• **CGC:** 1 graded, best 4.0
13 ❑ Dec 1953 Cover: 0.10 **NM** value: **130.00**
• **CGC:** 2 graded, best 8.0
14 ❑ Feb 1954 Cover: 0.10 **NM** value: **130.00**
15 ❑ Mar 1954 Cover: 0.10 **NM** value: **130.00**
16 ❑ Apr 1954 Cover: 0.10 **NM** value: **115.00**
17 ❑ Jun 1954 Cover: 0.10 **NM** value: **115.00**
18 ❑ Aug 1954 Cover: 0.10 **NM** value: **115.00**
19 ❑ Sep 1954 Cover: 0.10 **NM** value: **115.00**
20 ❑ Oct 1954 Cover: 0.10 **NM** value: **115.00**
21 ❑ Dec 1954 Cover: 0.10 **NM** value: **85.00**
22 ❑ Feb 1955 Cover: 0.10 **NM** value: **85.00**
23 ❑ Mar 1955 Cover: 0.10 **NM** value: **85.00**
24 ❑ Apr 1955 Cover: 0.10 **NM** value: **85.00**
25 ❑ Jun 1955 Cover: 0.10 **NM** value: **85.00**
26 ❑ Aug 1955 Cover: 0.10 **NM** value: **85.00**
27 ❑ Sep 1955 Cover: 0.10 **NM** value: **85.00**
28 ❑ Oct 1955 Cover: 0.10 **NM** value: **85.00**
29 ❑ Dec 1955 Cover: 0.10 **NM** value: **85.00**
30 ❑ Feb 1956 Cover: 0.10 **NM** value: **85.00**
31 ❑ Mar 1956 Cover: 0.10 **NM** value: **80.00**
32 ❑ Apr 1956 Cover: 0.10 **NM** value: **80.00**
33 ❑ Jun 1956 Cover: 0.10 **NM** value: **80.00**
34 ❑ Aug 1956 Cover: 0.10 **NM** value: **80.00**
35 ❑ Sep 1956 Cover: 0.10 **NM** value: **80.00**
36 ❑ Oct 1956 Cover: 0.10 **NM** value: **80.00**
37 ❑ Dec 1956 Cover: 0.10 **NM** value: **80.00**
38 ❑ Feb 1957 Cover: 0.10 **NM** value: **80.00**
• **CGC:** 1 graded, best 7.0
39 ❑ Mar 1957 Cover: 0.10 **NM** value: **80.00**
40 ❑ Apr 1957 Cover: 0.10 **NM** value: **80.00**
41 ❑ Jun 1957 Cover: 0.10 **NM** value: **58.00**
42 ❑ Aug 1957 Cover: 0.10 **NM** value: **58.00**
43 ❑ Sep 1957 Cover: 0.10 **NM** value: **58.00**
44 ❑ Oct 1957 Cover: 0.10 **NM** value: **58.00**
45 ❑ Dec 1957 Cover: 0.10 **NM** value: **58.00**
46 ❑ Feb 1958 Cover: 0.10 **NM** value: **58.00**
47 ❑ Mar 1958 Cover: 0.10 **NM** value: **58.00**
48 ❑ Apr 1958 Cover: 0.10 **NM** value: **58.00**
49 ❑ Jun 1958 Cover: 0.10 **NM** value: **58.00**
50 ❑ Aug 1958 Cover: 0.10 **NM** value: **58.00**
51 ❑ Sep 1958 Cover: 0.10 **NM** value: **58.00**
52 ❑ Oct 1958 Cover: 0.10 **NM** value: **58.00**
53 ❑ Cover: 0.10 **NM** value: **58.00**
54 ❑ Mar 1959 Cover: 0.10 **NM** value: **58.00**
55 ❑ May 1959 Cover: 0.10 **NM** value: **58.00**
56 ❑ Jul 1959 Cover: 0.10 **NM** value: **58.00**
57 ❑ Sep 1959 Cover: 0.10 **NM** value: **58.00**
58 ❑ Nov 1959 Cover: 0.10 **NM** value: **58.00**
59 ❑ Jan 1960 Cover: 0.10 **NM** value: **58.00**
Circ: Statement: **193,000**
60 ❑ Mar 1960 Cover: 0.10 **NM** value: **58.00**
Circ: Statement: **193,000**
61 ❑ May 1960 Cover: 0.10 **NM** value: **58.00**
Circ: Statement: **193,000**
62 ❑ Jul 1960 Cover: 0.10 **NM** value: **40.00**
Circ: Statement: **193,000**
63 ❑ Sep 1960 Cover: 0.10 **NM** value: **40.00**
Circ: Statement: **193,000**
64 ❑ Nov 1960 Cover: 0.10 **NM** value: **40.00**
Circ: Statement: **193,000**
65 ❑ Jan 1961 Cover: 0.10 **NM** value: **40.00**
Circ: Statement: **165,000**
66 ❑ Mar 1961 Cover: 0.10 **NM** value: **40.00**
Circ: Statement: **165,000**
67 ❑ May 1961 Cover: 0.10 **NM** value: **40.00**
Circ: Statement: **165,000**
68 ❑ Jul 1961 Cover: 0.10 **NM** value: **40.00**
Circ: Statement: **165,000**
69 ❑ Sep 1961 Cover: 0.10 **NM** value: **40.00**
Circ: Statement: **165,000**
70 ❑ Nov 1961 Cover: 0.10 **NM** value: **40.00**
Circ: Statement: **165,000**
71 ❑ Jan 1962 Cover: 0.10 **NM** value: **40.00**
Circ: Statement: **145,000**
72 ❑ Mar 1962 Cover: 0.10 **NM** value: **40.00**
Circ: Statement: **145,000**
• Has 1961 Statement, filed 10/1/61; avg total paid circ 165,000
73 ❑ May 1962 Cover: 0.10 **NM** value: **40.00**
Circ: Statement: **145,000**
74 ❑ Jul 1962 **NM** value: **40.00**
Circ: Statement: **145,000**
75 ❑ Sep 1962 **NM** value: **40.00**
Circ: Statement: **145,000**
76 ❑ Nov 1962 Cover: 0.12 **NM** value: **40.00**
Circ: Statement: **145,000**
77 ❑ Jan 1963 Cover: 0.12 **NM** value: **40.00**
78 ❑ Mar 1963 Cover: 0.12 **NM** value: **40.00**
• Has 1962 Statement, filed 10/1/62; avg total paid circ 145,000
79 ❑ May 1963 Cover: 0.12 **NM** value: **40.00**
80 ❑ Jul 1963 Cover: 0.12 **NM** value: **40.00**
81 ❑ Sep 1963 Cover: 0.12 **NM** value: **25.00**
82 ❑ Nov 1963 Cover: 0.12 **NM** value: **25.00**
83 ❑ Jan 1964 Cover: 0.12 **NM** value: **25.00**
84 ❑ Mar 1964 Cover: 0.12 **NM** value: **25.00**
85 ❑ May 1964 Cover: 0.12 **NM** value: **25.00**
86 ❑ Jul 1964 Cover: 0.12 **NM** value: **25.00**
87 ❑ Sep 1964 Cover: 0.12 **NM** value: **25.00**
88 ❑ Nov 1964 Cover: 0.12 **NM** value: **25.00**
89 ❑ Jan 1965 Cover: 0.12 **NM** value: **25.00**
Circ: Statement: **160,515**
90 ❑ Feb 1965 Cover: 0.12 **NM** value: **25.00**
Circ: Statement: **160,515** • **CGC:** 1 graded, best 9.4
91 ❑ May 1965 Cover: 0.12 **NM** value: **25.00**
Circ: Statement: **160,515**
92 ❑ Jul 1965 Cover: 0.12 **NM** value: **25.00**
Circ: Statement: **160,515**
93 ❑ Sep 1965 Cover: 0.12 **NM** value: **25.00**
Circ: Statement: **160,515**
94 ❑ Nov 1965 Cover: 0.12 **NM** value: **25.00**
Circ: Statement: **160,515**
95 ❑ Dec 1965 Cover: 0.12 **NM** value: **45.00**
Circ: Statement: **160,515** • **CGC:** 1 graded, best 9.2
96 ❑ Mar 1966 Cover: 0.12 **NM** value: **20.00**
Circ: Statement: **142,720**
97 ❑ May 1966 Cover: 0.12 **NM** value: **20.00**
Circ: Statement: **142,720**
98 ❑ Jul 1966 Cover: 0.12 **NM** value: **20.00**
Circ: Statement: **142,720**

CGC-graded: Multiply prices above by **33 for 9.9 M • 16 for 9.8 NM/M • 7 for 9.6 NM+ • 5 for 9.4 NM • 2.5 for 9.2 NM- • 1.5 for 9.0 VF/NM**

99 ❑ Sep 1966 Cover: 0.12 **NM** value: **20.00**
Circ: Statement: **142,720**
• Has 1965 Statement, filed 10/1/65; avg print run 305,000; avg sales 160,000; avg subs 515; avg total paid 160,515; samples 142; max existent 160,657; 47% of run returned
100 ❑ Nov 1966 Cover: 0.12 **NM** value: **22.00**
Circ: Statement: **142,720**
101 ❑ Jan 1967 Cover: 0.12 **NM** value: **16.00**
Circ: Statement: **114,700**
102 ❑ Mar 1967 Cover: 0.12 **NM** value: **16.00**
Circ: Statement: **114,700**
• Has 1966 Statement, filed 10/1/66; avg print run 306,000; avg sales 142,000; avg subs 720; avg total paid 142,720; samples 265; max existent 142,985; 53% of run returned
103 ❑ May 1967 Cover: 0.12 **NM** value: **16.00**
Circ: Statement: **114,700**
104 ❑ Jul 1967 Cover: 0.12 **NM** value: **16.00**
Circ: Statement: **114,700**
105 ❑ Sep 1967 Cover: 0.12 **NM** value: **16.00**
Circ: Statement: **114,700**
106 ❑ Nov 1967 Cover: 0.12 **NM** value: **16.00**
Circ: Statement: **114,700**
107 ❑ Jan 1968 Cover: 0.12 **NM** value: **16.00**
108 ❑ Mar 1968 Cover: 0.12 **NM** value: **16.00**
final issue. • Series continued in Stanley and His Monster; Has 1967 Statement, filed 10/1/67; avg print run 287,000; avg sales 114,000; avg subs 700; avg total paid 114,700; samples 340; max existent 115,040; 60% of run returned

FOX COMICS — Fantagraphics

24 ❑ b&w Cover: 2.95 **NM** value: **Cover or less**
25 ❑ b&w Cover: 2.95 **NM** value: **Cover or less**
26 ❑ b&w Cover: 2.95 **NM** value: **Cover or less**
SE 1 ❑ b&w Cover: 2.95 **NM** value: **Cover or less**
• Australian; Special

FOX COMICS LEGENDS SERIES — Fantagraphics

1 ❑ Jul 1992, b&w Cover: 2.25 **NM** value: **2.50**
• Three Stooges
2 ❑ b&w Cover: 2.50 **NM** value: **Cover or less**
📖 The Unauthorized Biography of Elvis • Elvis **A:** Ian Eddy **W:** Ian Eddy

FOXFIRE (MALIBU) — Malibu / Ultraverse

1 ❑ Feb 1996 Cover: 1.50 **NM** value: **Cover or less**
📖 Interview with an Ultra **A:** Kevin West **W:** Dan Abnett; Ian Edgington
2 ❑ Mar 1996 Cover: 1.50 **NM** value: **Cover or less**
📖 Tunnel Vision **A:** Kevin West **W:** Dan Abnett; Ian Edgington ★ Versus UltraForce.

FOXFIRE (NIGHT WYND) — Nightwynd

1 ❑ b&w Cover: 2.50 **NM** value: **Cover or less**
2 ❑ b&w Cover: 2.50 **NM** value: **Cover or less**
3 ❑ b&w Cover: 2.50 **NM** value: **Cover or less**

FOXHOLE — Mainline

1 ❑ Sep 1954 Cover: 0.10 **NM** value: **300.00**
2 ❑ Dec 1954 Cover: 0.10 **NM** value: **200.00**
3 ❑ Feb 1955 Cover: 0.10 **NM** value: **125.00**
4 ❑ Apr 1955 Cover: 0.10 **NM** value: **125.00**
5 ❑ Jul 1955 Cover: 0.10 **NM** value: **125.00**
6 ❑ Oct 1955 Cover: 0.10 **NM** value: **100.00**
7 ❑ Mar 1956 Cover: 0.10 **NM** value: **100.00**

FOX KIDS FUNHOUSE — Acclaim

1 ❑ Cover: 4.50 **NM** value: **Cover or less**
• digest. • The Tick, Life with Louie, Bobby's World
2 ❑ Cover: 4.50 **NM** value: **Cover or less**
📖 Raw, Uncooked Justice!; Bobby's World: Nasty Neighbor; Life with Louie: A Cushy Way to Make a Buck **A:** Brandon Kruse; Michael Duggan; Mike Kazaleh; Rusty Haller **W:** Rurik Tyler; Dwayne McDuffie; Bill Matheny

FOXY FAGAN — Dearfield

1 ❑ Dec 1946 Cover: 0.10 **NM** value: **75.00**
2 ❑ Mar 1947 Cover: 0.10 **NM** value: **45.00**
3 ❑ Jun 1947 Cover: 0.10 **NM** value: **45.00**
4 ❑ Sep 1947 Cover: 0.10 **NM** value: **40.00**
5 ❑ Dec 1947 Cover: 0.10 **NM** value: **40.00**
6 ❑ 1948 Cover: 0.10 **NM** value: **40.00**
7 ❑ Sum 1948 Cover: 0.10 **NM** value: **40.00**

FRACTURED FAIRY TALES — Gold Key

1 ❑ Oct 1962 **NM** value: **100.00**
• **CGC:** 1 graded, best 9.6

FRAGGLE ROCK (MARVEL) — Marvel

1 ❑ Apr 1988 Cover: 1.00 **NM** value: **Cover or less**
Circ: CapCity orders: **1,250**
2 ❑ Jun 1988 Cover: 0.65 **NM** value: **1.00**
3 ❑ Jun 1988 Cover: 1.00 **NM** value: **Cover or less**
Circ: CapCity orders: **850**
4 ❑ Jul 1988 Cover: 1.00 **NM** value: **Cover or less**
Circ: CapCity orders: **800**
5 ❑ Aug 1988 Cover: 1.00 **NM** value: **Cover or less**
Circ: CapCity orders: **900**

The prices seen above do not represent the highest possible prices seen in online auctions, but rather the prices we have seen these issues reliably fetch in a variety of environments (storefront retail, mail order, auction and convention).

FRAGGLE ROCK (STAR) — Marvel / Star

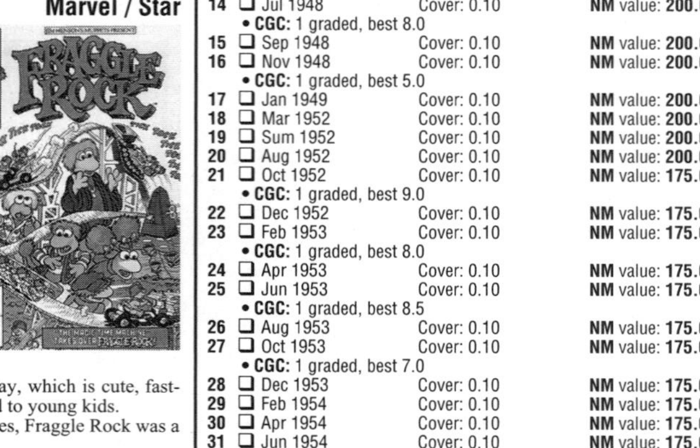

Jim Henson's Fraggle Rock lasted five seasons and 96 episodes starting in January 1983 and ending in March 1987. Stories in the series involved characters Doc and Sprocket who were oblivious until the last episode of The Fraggles.This fantasy series from the mid-1980s came out on Marvel's kid-oriented Star imprint, and featured characters from the zany world of Muppet creator Jim Henson. The Fraggles are cute, goofy, nonsense creatures who populate a magical subterranean world. Enjoyment of the series is greatly enhanced by imagining the voices of Muppeteers Henson and Frank Oz behind the dialogue and character interplay, which is cute, fast-moving, and great stuff for parents to read to young kids.

In addition to starring in this comic series, Fraggle Rock was a successful children's television series.

1 ❑ Apr 1985 Cover: 0.65 **NM** value: **1.00**
📖 The Magic Time Machine **A:** Marie Severin **W:** Stan Kay
2 ❑ Jun 1985 Cover: 0.65 **NM** value: **1.00**
Circ: CapCity orders: **3,800**
📖 #1! **A:** Marie Severin **W:** Stan Kay
3 ❑ Aug 1985 Cover: 0.65 **NM** value: **1.00**
Circ: CapCity orders: **2,900**
4 ❑ Oct 1985 Cover: 0.65 **NM** value: **1.00**
Circ: CapCity orders: **2,300**
5 ❑ Dec 1985 Cover: 0.65 **NM** value: **1.00**
Circ: CapCity orders: **1,900**
6 ❑ Feb 1986 Cover: 0.65 **NM** value: **1.00**
Circ: CapCity orders: **1,800**
7 ❑ Apr 1986 Cover: 0.75 **NM** value: **1.00**
Circ: CapCity orders: **1,650**
8 ❑ Jun 1986 Cover: 0.75 **NM** value: **1.00**
Circ: CapCity orders: **1,600**

FRAGMENTS — Screaming Cat

1 ❑ Cover: 2.50 **NM** value: **Cover or less**

FRANCIS, BROTHER OF THE UNIVERSE — Marvel

1 ❑ Cover: 0.75 **NM** value: **1.50**

FRANK BUCK — Fox

70 ❑ Jul 1950 Cover: 0.10 **NM** value: **250.00**
71 ❑ Sep 1950 Cover: 0.10 **NM** value: **125.00**
3 ❑ May 1950 Cover: 0.10 **NM** value: **100.00**

FRANKENSTEIN (DELL) — Dell

1 ❑ Mar 1963 Cover: 0.12 **NM** value: **40.00**
• **CGC:** 1 graded, best 9.0
2 ❑ Cover: 0.12 **NM** value: **25.00**
3 ❑ Dec 1966 Cover: 0.12 **NM** value: **15.00**
4 ❑ Mar 1967 Cover: 0.12 **NM** value: **15.00**
• **CGC:** 1 graded, best 9.2

FRANKENSTEIN/DRACULA WAR, THE — Topps

1 ❑ Feb 1995 Cover: 2.50 **NM** value: **Cover or less**
📖 The Gathering Storm **A:** Claude St. Aubin **W:** Roy Thomas
2 ❑ Cover: 2.50 **NM** value: **Cover or less**
3 ❑ Cover: 2.50 **NM** value: **Cover or less**

FRANKENSTEIN (ETERNITY) — Eternity

1 ❑ b&w Cover: 1.95 **NM** value: **Cover or less**
Circ: CapCity orders: **3,675**
2 ❑ b&w Cover: 1.95 **NM** value: **Cover or less**
Circ: CapCity orders: **3,500**
3 ❑ b&w Cover: 1.95 **NM** value: **Cover or less**
Circ: CapCity orders: **3,475**
Bk 1 ❑ Cover: 1.95 **NM** value: **Cover or less**

FRANKENSTEIN (MARY SHELLEY'S...) — Topps

1 ❑ Oct 1994 Cover: 2.95 **NM** value: **Cover or less**
Circ: CapCity orders: **9,700**
2 ❑ Cover: 2.95 **NM** value: **Cover or less**
Circ: CapCity orders: **7,000**
3 ❑ Cover: 2.95 **NM** value: **Cover or less**
Circ: CapCity orders: **6,000**
4 ❑ Cover: 2.95 **NM** value: **Cover or less**
Circ: CapCity orders: **5,625**

FRANKENSTEIN: OR THE MODERN PROMETHEUS — Caliber

1 ❑ Cover: 2.95 **NM** value: **Cover or less**

FRANKENSTEIN (PRIZE) — Prize

1 ❑ ca. 1945 Cover: 0.10 **NM** value: **900.00**
2 ❑ ca. 1945 Cover: 0.10 **NM** value: **450.00**
3 ❑ Jul 1946 Cover: 0.10 **NM** value: **300.00**
4 ❑ Sep 1946 Cover: 0.10 **NM** value: **300.00**
• **CGC:** 2 graded, best 7.5
5 ❑ Nov 1946 Cover: 0.10 **NM** value: **300.00**
• **CGC:** 2 graded, best 8.5
6 ❑ Jan 1947 Cover: 0.10 **NM** value: **250.00**
7 ❑ May 1947 Cover: 0.10 **NM** value: **250.00**
8 ❑ Jul 1947 Cover: 0.10 **NM** value: **250.00**
9 ❑ Sep 1947 Cover: 0.10 **NM** value: **250.00**
10 ❑ Nov 1947 Cover: 0.10 **NM** value: **250.00**
11 ❑ Jan 1948 Cover: 0.10 **NM** value: **200.00**
12 ❑ Mar 1948 Cover: 0.10 **NM** value: **200.00**
13 ❑ May 1948 Cover: 0.10 **NM** value: **200.00**
14 ❑ Jul 1948 Cover: 0.10 **NM** value: **200.00**
• **CGC:** 1 graded, best 8.0
15 ❑ Sep 1948 Cover: 0.10 **NM** value: **200.00**
16 ❑ Nov 1948 Cover: 0.10 **NM** value: **200.00**
• **CGC:** 1 graded, best 5.0
17 ❑ Jan 1949 Cover: 0.10 **NM** value: **200.00**
18 ❑ Mar 1952 Cover: 0.10 **NM** value: **200.00**
19 ❑ Sum 1952 Cover: 0.10 **NM** value: **200.00**
20 ❑ Aug 1952 Cover: 0.10 **NM** value: **200.00**
21 ❑ Oct 1952 Cover: 0.10 **NM** value: **175.00**
• **CGC:** 1 graded, best 9.0
22 ❑ Dec 1952 Cover: 0.10 **NM** value: **175.00**
23 ❑ Feb 1953 Cover: 0.10 **NM** value: **175.00**
• **CGC:** 1 graded, best 8.0
24 ❑ Apr 1953 Cover: 0.10 **NM** value: **175.00**
25 ❑ Jun 1953 Cover: 0.10 **NM** value: **175.00**
• **CGC:** 1 graded, best 8.5
26 ❑ Aug 1953 Cover: 0.10 **NM** value: **175.00**
27 ❑ Oct 1953 Cover: 0.10 **NM** value: **175.00**
• **CGC:** 1 graded, best 7.0
28 ❑ Dec 1953 Cover: 0.10 **NM** value: **175.00**
29 ❑ Feb 1954 Cover: 0.10 **NM** value: **175.00**
30 ❑ Apr 1954 Cover: 0.10 **NM** value: **175.00**
31 ❑ Jun 1954 Cover: 0.10 **NM** value: **175.00**
• **CGC:** 1 graded, best 8.0
32 ❑ Aug 1954 Cover: 0.10 **NM** value: **175.00**
33 ❑ Oct 1954 Cover: 0.10 **NM** value: **175.00**

FRANKENSTEIN (THE MONSTER OF...) — Marvel

As it did with Tomb of Dracula, Marvel made another hero out of a horror-movie staple — in this case, Frankenstein's monster. An effort was made in this series to pick things up from where Mary Shelley's 1818 novel left off. As the series starts, Frankenstein's monster has been encased in ice for nearly a century, when the great-grandson of the last person ever to see the monster finds him and brings him aboard ship. The monster escapes, when a fire on the ship melts his ice casing and walks among humanity again. As this series evolves, readers find out that the monster sometimes has more kindness and compassion in him than do many humans.

1 ❑ Jan 1973 Cover: 0.20 **NM** value: **24.00**
• **CGC:** 34 graded, best 9.6
2 ❑ Mar 1973 Cover: 0.20 **NM** value: **12.00**
• **CGC:** 6 graded, best 9.8
📖 Bride Of The Monster! **A:** Mike Ploog; Gary Friedrich **W:** Mike Ploog; Gary Friedrich ★ Origin of Bride of Frankenstein.
3 ❑ May 1973 Cover: 0.20 **NM** value: **9.00**
• **CGC:** 2 graded, best 9.2
4 ❑ Jul 1973 Cover: 0.20 **NM** value: **9.00**
• **CGC:** 1 graded, best 8.5
5 ❑ Sep 1973 Cover: 0.20 **NM** value: **9.00**
• **CGC:** 1 graded, best 9.0
6 ❑ Oct 1973 Cover: 0.20 **NM** value: **7.00**
• **CGC:** 1 graded, best 8.5
Cover changes titles to "The Frankenstein Monster".
7 ❑ Nov 1973 Cover: 0.20 **NM** value: **7.00**
• **CGC:** 1 graded, best 9.2
8 ❑ Jan 1974 Cover: 0.20 **NM** value: **10.00**
• **CGC:** 1 graded, best 9.6
9 ❑ Mar 1974 Cover: 0.20 **NM** value: **10.00**
• **CGC:** 1 graded, best 7.0
10 ❑ May 1974 Cover: 0.25 **NM** value: **6.00**
11 ❑ Jul 1974 Cover: 0.25 **NM** value: **5.00**
12 ❑ Sep 1974 Cover: 0.25 **NM** value: **5.00**
• **CGC:** 1 graded, best 9.4
• The monster comes to the modern day
13 ❑ Nov 1974 Cover: 0.25 **NM** value: **5.00**
• **CGC:** 1 graded, best 9.6
14 ❑ Jan 1975 Cover: 0.25 **NM** value: **5.00**
15 ❑ Mar 1975 Cover: 0.25 **NM** value: **5.00**
📖 Tactics of Death!; The Shadow • Back-up story reprinted from Tales of Suspense #10 **A:** Al Hartley; Val Mayerik; Klaus Janson(inks) **W:** Doug Moench
16 ❑ May 1975 Cover: 0.25 **NM** value: **5.00**
17 ❑ Jul 1975 Cover: 0.25 **NM** value: **5.00**
• Monster regains speech★ Versus Berserker.
18 ❑ Sep 1975 Cover: 0.25 **NM** value: **5.00**
final issue.

FRANK (FANTAGRAPHICS) — Fantagraphics

1 ❑ Sep 1996, b&w Cover: 2.95 **NM** value: **Cover or less**
2 ❑ Dec 1997, b&w Cover: 3.95 **NM** value: **Cover or less**

FRANK FRAZETTA FANTASY ILLUSTRATED — Frank Frazetta Fantasy Illustrated

1 ❑ Spr 1998 Cover: 5.99 **NM** value: **7.00**
1/SC ❑ Spr 1998 Cover: 5.99 **NM** value: **8.00**
alternate cover.
2 ❑ Sum 1998 Cover: 5.99 **NM** value: **10.00**
• Battle Chasers story
2/SC ❑ Sum 1998 Cover: 5.99 **NM** value: **6.00**
alternate cover. **C:** Joe Maduiera
3 ❑ Fal 1998 Cover: 5.99 **NM** value: **6.00**
3/SC ❑ Fal 1998 Cover: 5.99 **NM** value: **6.00**
alternate cover.
4 ❑ Win 1998 Cover: 5.99 **NM** value: **Cover or less**
4/SC ❑ Win 1998 Cover: 5.99 **NM** value: **6.00**
alternate cover.

Other grades: Multiply prices above by **1.5 for Mint • 2/3 for Very Fine • 1/3 for Fine • 1/5 for Very Good • 1/8 for Good**

5 ❑ Mar 1999 Cover: 5.99 **NM** value: **Cover or less**
5/SC❑Mar 1999 Cover: 5.99 **NM** value: **7.50**
alternate cover.
6 ❑ May 1999 Cover: 5.99 **NM** value: **6.00**
6/SC❑May 1999 Cover: 5.99 **NM** value: **7.00**
alternate cover.
7 ❑ Jul 1999 Cover: 5.99 **NM** value: **Cover or less**
7/SC❑Jul 1999 Cover: 5.99 **NM** value: **Cover or less**
alternate cover.

FRANKIE COMICS — Margood

Fishing around for a "hit" following the post-war collapse of superhero comics, Marvel (here aka Margood) Comics turned briefly to a staple theme from the 1920s, so-called college humor, with Frankie Comics. Frankie Fuddle, an irresponsible, somewhat witless, but always likeable college student in the standard uniform of hat, bow-tie, and sport coat, manages to get himself in every variety of girl trouble in the course of the three to five short stories in each issue. The formula usually features stock characters like the bullying football star, the nerdy "brain," and lots and lots of pretty girls.

The GI Bill and the realities of postwar America eroded the fundamental assumptions of 1920s-style college humor: that colleges are the preserve of spoiled rich kids with nothing better to do than pull pranks and chase skirts — and Frankie Comics withered away by 1949.

4 ❑ ca. 1946 Cover: 0.10 **NM** value: **35.00**
5 ❑ Cover: 0.10 **NM** value: **25.00**
6 ❑ Cover: 0.10 **NM** value: **22.00**
7 ❑ Cover: 0.10 **NM** value: **22.00**
8 ❑ Cover: 0.10 **NM** value: **22.00**
9 ❑ Cover: 0.10 **NM** value: **22.00**
10 ❑ Cover: 0.10 **NM** value: **22.00**
📖 Frankie: Double Trouble!; Cindy: School Daze!; The Masterpiece (text piece); Frankie: The Ghost!; Cindy: Fun at the Fountain!
11 ❑ Cover: 0.10 **NM** value: **18.00**
12 ❑ Cover: 0.10 **NM** value: **18.00**
13 ❑ Cover: 0.10 **NM** value: **18.00**
14 ❑ Cover: 0.10 **NM** value: **18.00**
15 ❑ Cover: 0.10 **NM** value: **18.00**

FRANK IN THE RIVER — Tundra

1 ❑ Cover: 2.95 **NM** value: **Cover or less**

FRANK LUTHER'S SILLY PILLY COMICS — Children Comics

1 ❑ ca. 1949 Cover: 0.10 **NM** value: **40.00**

FRANK MERRIWELL AT YALE — Charlton

1 ❑ Jun 1955 Cover: 0.10 **NM** value: **35.00**
2 ❑ 1955 Cover: 0.10 **NM** value: **25.00**
3 ❑ 1955 Cover: 0.10 **NM** value: **25.00**
4 ❑ 1955 Cover: 0.10 **NM** value: **25.00**

FRANK (NEMESIS) — Nemesis

1 ❑ Apr 1994 Cover: 1.75 **NM** value: **Cover or less**
📖 Tail-Bone Connects to the Elbow • newsstand **A:** Denys Cowan **W:** D.G. Chichester
1/DM❑Apr 1994 Cover: 2.50 **NM** value: **Cover or less**
Circ: CapCity orders: **6,750**
variant cover. 📖 Tail-Bone Connects to the Elbow • direct sale **A:** Denys Cowan **W:** D.G. Chichester
2 ❑ May 1994 Cover: 1.75 **NM** value: **Cover or less**
• newsstand **A:** Denys Cowan **W:** D.G. Chichester
2/DM❑May 1994 Cover: 2.50 **NM** value: **Cover or less**
Circ: CapCity orders: **3,700**
• direct sale **A:** Denys Cowan **W:** D.G. Chichester
3 ❑ Jun 1994 Cover: 1.75 **NM** value: **Cover or less**
• newsstand **A:** Denys Cowan **W:** D.G. Chichester
3/DM❑Jun 1994 Cover: 2.50 **NM** value: **Cover or less**
Circ: CapCity orders: **3,625**
• direct sale **A:** Denys Cowan **W:** D.G. Chichester
4 ❑ Jul 1994 Cover: 2.50 **NM** value: **Cover or less**
• newsstand **A:** Denys Cowan **W:** D.G. Chichester
4/DM❑Jul 1994 Cover: 2.50 **NM** value: **Cover or less**
Circ: CapCity orders: **3,450**
• direct sale **A:** Denys Cowan **W:** D.G. Chichester

FRANK THE UNICORN — Fragments West

1 ❑ Sep 1986 Cover: 2.00 **NM** value: **Cover or less**
2 ❑ Nov 1986 Cover: 2.00 **NM** value: **Cover or less**
3 ❑ Jan 1987 Cover: 2.00 **NM** value: **Cover or less**
4 ❑ Cover: 2.00 **NM** value: **Cover or less**
5 ❑ Cover: 2.00 **NM** value: **Cover or less**
6 ❑ Cover: 2.00 **NM** value: **Cover or less**
7 ❑ Cover: 2.00 **NM** value: **Cover or less**
8 ❑ Cover: 2.00 **NM** value: **Cover or less**
9 ❑ Cover: 2.00 **NM** value: **Cover or less**

FRANK ZAPPA: VIVA LA BIZARRE — Revolutionary

1 ❑ Feb 1994, b&w Cover: 2.50 **NM** value: **Cover or less**

FREAK FORCE — Image

The Freak Force is a group of super-beings formerly employed by the Chicago Police Department, now trying to set up on their own. The team consists of the massive Barbaric and the bouncing girl wonder Ricochet, both of whom were runaways with unknown backgrounds; super-soldier-turned-cyborg SuperPatriot; the reptilian Horridus; electricity-wielding knockout Rapture; the powerful Mighty Man (whose spirit now inhabits the body of an inexperienced new host); and team-leader and projectile-thrower, Dart.

Erik Larsen created these characters as part of Savage Dragon and SuperPatriot titles and now puts them together in their own team series. It's an odd collection of characters with which Larsen and co-plotter Keith Giffen are clearly having fun.

1 ❑ Dec 1993 Cover: 1.95 **NM** value: **Cover or less**
Circ: CapCity orders: **49,750**
2 ❑ Jan 1994 Cover: 1.95 **NM** value: **Cover or less**
Circ: CapCity orders: **32,450**
3 ❑ Feb 1994 Cover: 1.95 **NM** value: **Cover or less**
Circ: CapCity orders: **26,925**
4 ❑ Mar 1994 Cover: 1.95 **NM** value: **Cover or less**
Circ: CapCity orders: **24,250**
5 ❑ Apr 1994 Cover: 1.95 **NM** value: **Cover or less**
Circ: CapCity orders: **22,000**
6 ❑ Jun 1994 Cover: 1.95 **NM** value: **Cover or less**
Circ: CapCity orders: **21,850**
• Identity of Mighty Man revealed
7 ❑ Jul 1994 Cover: 1.95 **NM** value: **Cover or less**
Circ: CapCity orders: **20,475**
8 ❑ Aug 1994 Cover: 2.50 **NM** value: **Cover or less**
Circ: CapCity orders: **18,825**
9 ❑ Sep 1994 Cover: 2.50 **NM** value: **Cover or less**
Circ: CapCity orders: **17,900**
10 ❑ Oct 1994 Cover: 2.50 **NM** value: **Cover or less**
Circ: CapCity orders: **16,350**
11 ❑ Nov 1994 Cover: 2.50 **NM** value: **Cover or less**
Circ: CapCity orders: **14,400**
12 ❑ Dec 1994 Cover: 2.50 **NM** value: **Cover or less**
Circ: CapCity orders: **13,000**
13 ❑ Jan 1995 Cover: 2.50 **NM** value: **Cover or less**
Circ: CapCity orders: **11,450**
• Jerry Ordway pin-up
13/A❑Jan 1995 Cover: 2.50 **NM** value: **Cover or less**
alternate cover.
14 ❑ Feb 1995 Cover: 2.50 **NM** value: **Cover or less**
Circ: CapCity orders: **10,475**
15 ❑ Mar 1995 Cover: 2.50 **NM** value: **Cover or less**
Circ: CapCity orders: **10,050**
16 ❑ Apr 1995 Cover: 2.50 **NM** value: **Cover or less**
Circ: CapCity orders: **9,675**
17 ❑ Jun 1995 Cover: 2.50 **NM** value: **Cover or less**
Circ: CapCity orders: **9,550**
18 ❑ Jul 1995 Cover: 2.50 **NM** value: **Cover or less**
Circ: CapCity orders: **9,625**
final issue.

FREAK FORCE (MINI-SERIES) — Image

1 ❑ Apr 1997 Cover: 2.95 **NM** value: **Cover or less**
Circ: Diamd. preorders: **15,064**
2 ❑ May 1997 Cover: 2.95 **NM** value: **Cover or less**
Circ: Diamd. preorders: **12,384**
3 ❑ Jul 1997 Cover: 2.95 **NM** value: **Cover or less**
Circ: Diamd. preorders: **11,105**

FREAK OUT ON INFANT EARTHS — Blackthorne

1 ❑ Jan 1987 Cover: 2.00 **NM** value: **Cover or less**
2 ❑ Cover: 2.00 **NM** value: **Cover or less**

FREAKS — Fantagraphics / Monster

1 ❑ Cover: 2.25 **NM** value: **Cover or less**
2 ❑ Cover: 2.25 **NM** value: **Cover or less**
3 ❑ Cover: 2.25 **NM** value: **Cover or less**

FREAKS' AMOUR — Dark Horse

1 ❑ Cover: 3.95 **NM** value: **Cover or less**
📖 The Grinning Man **A:** Phil Hester **W:** Mark Burbey; Tom DeHaven
2 ❑ Cover: 3.95 **NM** value: **Cover or less**
3 ❑ Cover: 3.95 **NM** value: **Cover or less**

FRECKLES AND HIS FRIENDS — Standard

5 ❑ Nov 1947 Cover: 0.10 **NM** value: **20.00**
6 ❑ Feb 1948 Cover: 0.10 **NM** value: **20.00**
7 ❑ May 1948 Cover: 0.10 **NM** value: **20.00**
8 ❑ Aug 1948 Cover: 0.10 **NM** value: **20.00**
9 ❑ Nov 1948 Cover: 0.10 **NM** value: **20.00**
10 ❑ Feb 1949 Cover: 0.10 **NM** value: **20.00**
11 ❑ May 1949 Cover: 0.10 **NM** value: **20.00**
12 ❑ Aug 1949 Cover: 0.10 **NM** value: **20.00**
1 ❑ Nov 1955 Cover: 0.10 **NM** value: **30.00**
2 ❑ Cover: 0.10 **NM** value: **20.00**
3 ❑ ca. 1956 Cover: 0.10 **NM** value: **20.00**
4 ❑ Jun 1956 Cover: 0.10 **NM** value: **20.00**

FRED & BIANCA CENSORSHIP SUCKS SPECIAL — Comics Interview

1 ❑ b&w Cover: 2.25 **NM** value: **Cover or less**

FRED & BIANCA MOTHER'S DAY MASSACRE — Comics Interview

1 ❑ b&w Cover: 2.25 **NM** value: **Cover or less**

FRED & BIANCA VALENTINE'S DAY MASSACRE — Comics Interview

1 ❑ b&w Cover: 2.25 **NM** value: **Cover or less**

FREDDY KRUEGER'S NIGHTMARE ON ELM STREET — Marvel

1 ❑ Oct 1989, b&w Cover: 2.25 **NM** value: **Cover or less**
• magazine. 📖 Dreamstalkers, Part 1 **A:** Rich Buckler; Alfredo Alcala; Tony DeZuniga **W:** Steve Gerber ★ Origin of Freddy Krueger.
2 ❑ Nov 1989, b&w Cover: 2.25 **NM** value: **Cover or less**
• magazine. 📖 Dreamstalkers, Part 2 **A:** Alfredo Alcala; Tony DeZuniga **W:** Steve Gerber

FREDDY'S DEAD: THE FINAL NIGHTMARE — Innovation

1 ❑ Cover: 2.50 **NM** value: **Cover or less**
Circ: CapCity orders: **6,290**
📖 Little John In Slumberland **A:** Mike Witherby **W:** Andy Mangels
1/3D❑ **NM** value: **2.50**
• part 3-D
2 ❑ Cover: 2.50 **NM** value: **Cover or less**
Circ: CapCity orders: **5,095**
3 ❑ Cover: 2.50 **NM** value: **Cover or less**
📖 Memories...Like The Killings In My Mind **A:** Robb Phipps **W:** Andy Mangels
3/3D❑ Cover: 2.50 **NM** value: **Cover or less**
• 3-D version of #3; Requires glasses provided at movie showings **W:** Andy Mangels
Bk 1❑ Cover: 6.95 **NM** value: **Cover or less**
• Collects Freddy's Dead #1-3 **A:** Robb Phipps; Mike Witherby **W:** Andy Mangels

FREDERIC REMINGTON: THE MAN WHO PAINTED THE WEST — Tome Press

1 ❑ b&w Cover: 2.95 **NM** value: **Cover or less**

FRED HEMBECK DESTROYS THE MARVEL UNIVERSE — Marvel

Who could have been devious enough to give a case of black plague to Black Panther, Black Bolt, Black Widow, Black Knight, and Black Cat? Who did away with Captain Marvel (the second one) by trapping her in a perpetual rerun of Three's Company? Who could have done in Ant-Man by popping him in a microwave? Or staged a (Ragna-) rock concert for Asgard?

The answer, actually, is Crackers, Clown Prince of Death. We're talking about a cosmic force at work here.

Since Fred Hembeck drew the cartoons in which it happened, he's the one who's really responsible for destroying the Marvel Universe. In this one-shot special, the hilarious cartoonist who gave us Fantastic Four Roast returns to do in all of Marveldom's finest in the funniest manner possible.

1 ❑ Jul 1989 Cover: 1.50 **NM** value: **Cover or less**
Circ: CapCity orders: **26,500**
📖 When Titans Croak! **A:** Fred Hembeck **W:** Fred Hembeck ★ Death of Everyone.

FRED HEMBECK SELLS THE MARVEL UNIVERSE — Marvel

1 ❑ Oct 1990 Cover: 1.25 **NM** value: **1.50**
Circ: CapCity orders: **9,400**
📖 The New Adventures Of Brother Voodoo! **A:** Fred Hembeck **C:** Terry Austin **W:** Fred Hembeck

FRED THE POSSESSED FLOWER — Happy Predator

1 ❑ Cover: 2.95 **NM** value: **Cover or less**
📖 The Plant Behind the Scenes **A:** Happy **W:** Happy
2 ❑ Cover: 2.95 **NM** value: **Cover or less**
3 ❑ Cover: 2.95 **NM** value: **Cover or less**
4 ❑ Cover: 2.95 **NM** value: **Cover or less**
5 ❑ Cover: 2.95 **NM** value: **Cover or less**
6 ❑ Cover: 2.95 **NM** value: **Cover or less**

FREEBOOTERS/YOUNG GODS/PARADOXMAN PREVIEW — Dark Horse

1 ❑ Cover: 1.00 **NM** value: **Cover or less**

FREE CEREBUS — Aardvark-Vanaheim

1 ❑ **NM** value: **1.00**
No issue number. • giveaway. **A:** Dave Sim; Gerhard **W:** Dave Sim

The CGC numbers printed in individual listings above represent the **number of copies examined** and given a **Universal** grade by CGC and the **best such copy** graded at press time. For current populations, watch for special ***Comics Buyer's Guide*** issues or check **www.cgccomics.com.**

CGC-graded: Multiply prices above by **33 for 9.9 M • 16 for 9.8 NM/M • 7 for 9.6 NM+ • 5 for 9.4 NM • 2.5 for 9.2 NM- • 1.5 for 9.0 VF/NM**

FREEDOM FIGHTERS — DC

The Freedom Fighters first banded together in their own dimension, Earth-X, to fight the tyrants in a world where the Nazis had won World War II. The team includes Uncle Sam, who has super strength and can see for brief periods into the future; The Ray, a solar-powered being who can turn himself into pure light; The Human Bomb, who can blast through anything by simply removing his glove; Phantom Lady, who can turn everything into night with her blackout ray; Doll Man, who can shrink himself to a diminutive size; and Black Condor, who can fly like a bird. Eventually, the super team decimated the Nazi leadership with the help of the JLA and JSA and, later, teleported itself to Earth-1 where the Freedom Fighters' adventures continued.

The characters' Golden Age adventures were originally published by Quality, later acquired by DC.

1 ❑ Apr 1976 Cover: 0.25 **NM** value: **4.00**
• **CGC:** 15 graded, best 9.6
• Freedom Fighters arrive on Earth-1 **A:** Ric Estrada **W:** Martin Pasko ★ 1st Appearance of Silver Ghost ★ Versus Silver Ghost.
2 ❑ Jun 1976 Cover: 0.30 **NM** value: **3.00**
3 ❑ Aug 1976 Cover: 0.30 **NM** value: **3.00**
• Bicentennial #8 ★ Appearance of Wonder Woman.
4 ❑ Oct 1976 Cover: 0.30 **NM** value: **2.50**
• **CGC:** 2 graded, best 8.5
5 ❑ Dec 1976 Cover: 0.30 **NM** value: **2.50**
6 ❑ Feb 1977 Cover: 0.30 **NM** value: **2.00**
7 ❑ Apr 1977 Cover: 0.30 **NM** value: **2.00**
8 ❑ Jun 1977 Cover: 0.30 **NM** value: **2.00**
9 ❑ Aug 1977 Cover: 0.35 **NM** value: **2.00**
10 ❑ Oct 1977 Cover: 0.35 **NM** value: **2.00**
📖 Murder In Miniature **A:** Dick Ayers **W:** Bob Rozakis ★ Origin of Doll Man. ★ Versus Cat-Man.
11 ❑ Dec 1977 Cover: 0.35 **NM** value: **2.00**
12 ❑ Feb 1978 Cover: 0.35 **NM** value: **2.00**
13 ❑ Apr 1978 Cover: 0.35 **NM** value: **2.00**
14 ❑ Jun 1978 Cover: 0.35 **NM** value: **2.00**
15 ❑ Aug 1978 Cover: 0.35 **NM** value: **2.00**
final issue. • events continue in Secret Society of Super Villains #16 ★ Origin of Phantom Lady.

FREEDOM TRAIN — Street & Smith

1 ❑ ca. 1948 **NM** value: **150.00**

FREEFLIGHT — Thinkblots

1 ❑ Apr 1994 Cover: 2.95 **NM** value: **Cover or less**
📖 Void, Part 1; How Much Longer?; Good Clean Fun, Part 1; Meanwhile:; Rich Bitch at the Aquarium **A:** Gary Hudson; Mike Ritchie; Mike Rudyk; Poa Guerra **W:** Gary Hudson; Mike Ritchie; Mike Rudyk; Fraser Cain; Patrick Sauriol

FREEJACK — Now

1 ❑ Apr 1992 Cover: 1.95 **NM** value: **Cover or less**
• newsstand **A:** Ernie Stiner **W:** Chuck Dixon; Clint McElroy
1/DM❑ Apr 1992 Cover: 2.50 **NM** value: **Cover or less**
• direct-sale edition. **A:** Ernie Stiner **W:** Chuck Dixon; Clint McElroy
2 ❑ May 1992 Cover: 1.95 **NM** value: **Cover or less**
• newsstand **A:** Ernie Stiner **W:** Chuck Dixon; Clint McElroy
2/DM❑ May 1992 Cover: 2.50 **NM** value: **Cover or less**
• direct-sale **A:** Ernie Stiner **W:** Chuck Dixon; Clint McElroy
3 ❑ Jun 1992 Cover: 1.95 **NM** value: **Cover or less**
• newsstand **A:** Ernie Stiner **W:** Chuck Dixon; Clint McElroy
3/DM❑ Jun 1992 Cover: 2.50 **NM** value: **Cover or less**
• direct-sale **A:** Ernie Stiner **W:** Chuck Dixon; Clint McElroy

FREE LAUGHS — Deschaine

1 ❑ b&w Cover: 1.00 **NM** value: **Cover or less**

FREE SPEECHES — Oni

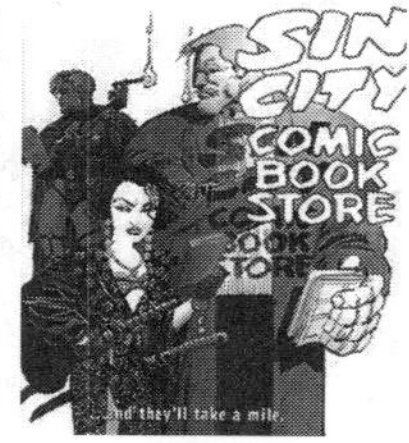

Created by comic-book industry notables and Oni Press, proceeds from Free Speeches helped support the Comic Book Legal Defense Fund. There were pieces of artwork by several artists and a forward by Denis Kitchen detailing the creation of the CBLDF. The bulk of the book is a group of enlightening essays concerning free speech and the comic-book industry (including a copy of the Comics Code Authority guidelines). The essays (speeches) are by Nadine Strossen of the ACLU, Dave Sim (Cerebus), Neil Gaiman (A Distant Soil, Miraclemen), and Frank Miller (Ronin, Sin City). In addition, throughout the book, the margins are filled with quotes from famous people, all on the subject of free speech.

1 ❑ Aug 1998 Cover: 2.95 **NM** value: **Cover or less**
No issue number. 📖 The Comic Book Legal Defense Fun • collects Nadine Strossen, Dave Sim, Neil Gaiman, and Frank Miller speeches; collects Nadine Strossen, Dave Sims, Neil Gaiman, and Frank Miller speeches; Fundraiser for Comic Book Legal Defense Fund **A:** Peter Bagge; Evan Dorkin; Bill Sienkiewicz; Will Eisner; Troy Nixey; Mike Allred; Bob Fingerman; Roberta Gregory; Dave Cooper; Judd Winick; Jeff Smith; Donna Barr; Shannon Wheele **W:** Denis Kitchen; Dave Sim; Frank Miller; Nadine Strossen; Neil Gaiman

FREE-VIEW — Acclaim

1 ❑ Mar 1993 **NM** value: **1.00**

FREEWAY NINJA HANZO — SleepyHouse

1 ❑ Cover: 3.50 **NM** value: **Cover or less**
📖 Lured from the Depths • Heavyweight premiere issue **A:** Michio Tsuzuki **W:** Michio Tsuzuki

FREEX — Malibu / Ultraverse

Super-powers are not always a blessing. Lewis was a high-school football star until he was hit so hard in a game that he temporarily lost consciousness and his body went into its ultra-powered, but liquid, state. Val's power to burn things led her to prison, where she was abused by the guards. And Ray's parents were so shocked by his rock-like appearance that they kept him locked in the basement for years. These are just some of the hapless teen-agers who become outcasts due to the same sorts of ultra-powers that made others (like The Strangers) into heroes.

Then, these "freaks" receive a reprieve of sorts in the form of a mysterious message that calls them together. In doing so, they discover that they are not alone. They become a gang of sorts, the Freex, leaning on each other in order to survive.

1 ❑ Jul 1993 Cover: 1.95 **NM** value: **2.00**
Circ: CapCity orders: **32,950**
📖 Freaked **A:** Ben Herrera **W:** Gerard Jones ★ 1st Appearance of Freex, Pressure.
1/Hol❑ Jul 1993 **NM** value: **5.00**
Hologram cover. 📖 Freaked • Ultra Limited **A:** Ben Herrera **W:** Gerard Jones ★ 1st Appearance of Freex, Pressure.
2 ❑ Aug 1993 Cover: 1.95 **NM** value: **2.00**
Circ: CapCity orders: **19,150**
📖 Blown Apart **A:** Ben Herrera **W:** Gerard Jones ★ 1st Appearance of Rush.
3 ❑ Sep 1993 Cover: 1.95 **NM** value: **2.00**
Circ: CapCity orders: **20,775**
4 ❑ Oct 1993 Cover: 2.50 **NM** value: **Cover or less**
Circ: CapCity orders: **29,200**
📖 Rune, Part E • Rune **A:** Barry Windsor-Smith; David Williams **W:** Gerard Jones
5 ❑ Nov 1993 Cover: 1.95 **NM** value: **Cover or less**
Circ: CapCity orders: **21,000**
6 ❑ Dec 1993 Cover: 1.95 **NM** value: **Cover or less**
Circ: CapCity orders: **20,375**
📖 Break-Thru • Break-Thru **W:** Gerard Jones
7 ❑ Jan 1994 Cover: 1.95 **NM** value: **Cover or less**
Circ: CapCity orders: **17,000**
📖 Too Much Pressure **A:** Ben Herrera **W:** Gerard Jones ★ Origin of Pressure, Hardcase.
8 ❑ Feb 1994 Cover: 1.95 **NM** value: **Cover or less**
Circ: CapCity orders: **14,400**
9 ❑ Mar 1994 Cover: 1.95 **NM** value: **Cover or less**
Circ: CapCity orders: **12,700**
10 ❑ Apr 1994 Cover: 1.95 **NM** value: **Cover or less**
Circ: CapCity orders: **12,050**
11 ❑ May 1994 Cover: 1.95 **NM** value: **Cover or less**
Circ: CapCity orders: **10,950**
📖 The Destiny Trail, Part 1 **W:** Gerard Jones ★ Origin of Plug.
12 ❑ Aug 1994 Cover: 1.95 **NM** value: **Cover or less**
Circ: CapCity orders: **8,350**
📖 The Destiny Trail, Part 2 **A:** Scott Kolins **W:** Gerard Jones ★ 1st Appearance of The Guardian.
13 ❑ Sep 1994 Cover: 1.95 **NM** value: **Cover or less**
Circ: CapCity orders: **7,300**
📖 The Destiny Trail, Part 3 **A:** Scott Kolins **W:** Gerard Jones ★ 1st Appearance of Prometheus.
14 ❑ Oct 1994 Cover: 1.95 **NM** value: **Cover or less**
Circ: CapCity orders: **6,800**
📖 The Destiny Trail, Part 4 **A:** Scott Kolins **W:** Gerard Jones ★ 1st Appearance of The Savior.
15 ❑ Jan 1995 Cover: 3.50 **NM** value: **Cover or less**
Circ: CapCity orders: **6,425**
📖 Death's Axis; Neverland Blues, Part 3; A New Game of Death, Part 1; Breakdown • Flip-book with Ultraverse Premiere #9 **A:** Scott Kolins; Steve Ellis; Ben Herrera(cover); Brian Kong; Mike Edsey **W:** Gerard Jones; James D. Hudnall; Len Strazewski ★ 1st Appearance of Eliminator, Manic, Oyabun.
16 ❑ Jan 1995 Cover: 1.95 **NM** value: **Cover or less**
Circ: CapCity orders: **5,550**
📖 Saying Goodbye **A:** Klebs de Moura e Silva; Scott Kolins(cover) **W:** Gerard Jones
17 ❑ Feb 1995 Cover: 2.50 **NM** value: **Cover or less**
Circ: CapCity orders: **4,425**
📖 Call Him Mr. Thebes **A:** Scott Kolins; Jon Holdredge **W:** Gerard Jones ★ Appearance of Rune.
18 ❑ Feb 1995 Cover: 2.50 **NM** value: **Cover or less**
Circ: CapCity orders: **4,275**
📖 Forever in Dreams final issue. **A:** Steve Ellis; Scott Kolins(cover) **W:** Gerard Jones ★ 1st Appearance of A.J. Analla, Tulath.
GS 1❑ Cover: 2.50 **NM** value: **Cover or less**
Circ: CapCity orders: **10,200**
• Giant-Size Freex #1. **A:** Scott Kolins; Jeff Parker **W:** Gerard Jones ★ 1st Appearance of Pixx.

FRENCH ICE — Renegade

1 ❑ b&w Cover: 2.00 **NM** value: **Cover or less**
📖 The Sanitation Department; The Visit; The Workman and the Old Lady; One Afternoon **A:** Odalaudie-Lelong **W:** Odalaudie-Lelong
2 ❑ Apr 1987, b&w Cover: 2.00 **NM** value: **Cover or less**
3 ❑ May 1987, b&w Cover: 2.00 **NM** value: **Cover or less**
4 ❑ Jun 1987, b&w Cover: 2.00 **NM** value: **Cover or less**
5 ❑ Jul 1987, b&w Cover: 2.00 **NM** value: **Cover or less**
6 ❑ Sep 1987, b&w Cover: 2.00 **NM** value: **Cover or less**
7 ❑ Oct 1987, b&w Cover: 2.00 **NM** value: **Cover or less**
8 ❑ Nov 1987, b&w Cover: 2.00 **NM** value: **Cover or less**
9 ❑ Dec 1987, b&w Cover: 2.00 **NM** value: **Cover or less**
10 ❑ Jan 1988, b&w Cover: 2.00 **NM** value: **Cover or less**
11 ❑ Feb 1988, b&w Cover: 2.00 **NM** value: **Cover or less**
12 ❑ Mar 1988, b&w Cover: 2.00 **NM** value: **Cover or less**
13 ❑ Apr 1988, b&w Cover: 2.00 **NM** value: **Cover or less**

FRENCH TICKLERS — Kitchen Sink

1 ❑ Oct 1989, b&w Cover: 2.00 **NM** value: **Cover or less**
2 ❑ Oct 1989, b&w Cover: 2.00 **NM** value: **Cover or less**
3 ❑ Oct 1989, b&w Cover: 2.00 **NM** value: **Cover or less**

FRENZY — Independent

1 ❑ Cover: 1.00 **NM** value: **Cover or less**
1/A ❑ Cover: 1.00 **NM** value: **Cover or less**

FRIDAY FOSTER — Dell

1 ❑ Oct 1972 Cover: 0.15 **NM** value: **25.00**
• **CGC:** 1 graded, best 6.5

FRIENDLY GHOST, CASPER, THE — Harvey

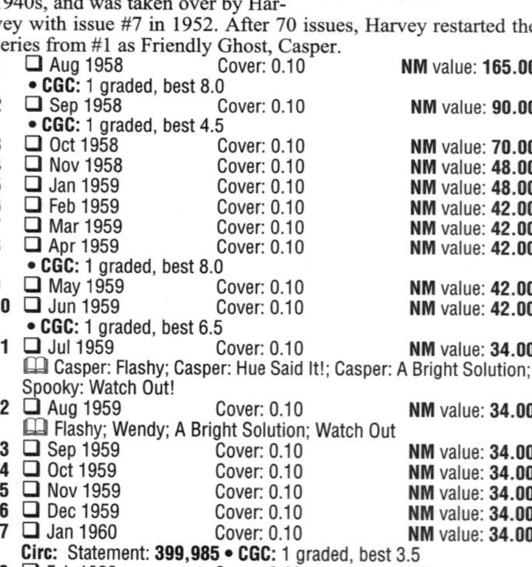

No, you won't find the longest-running Casper title filed under Casper. Harvey called it The Friendly Ghost, Casper. You can't fight City Hall.

Anyway, whatever his title is called, Casper is one of the more successful and memorable characters to spring from the pages of comics, starring in cartoons, games, and an effects-laden live action film in the 1990s. The goofy, good-natured ghost is also the signature character of the Harvey publishing enterprise.

Casper's original run in comics came from St. John in the late 1940s, and was taken over by Harvey with issue #7 in 1952. After 70 issues, Harvey restarted the series from #1 as Friendly Ghost, Casper.

1 ❑ Aug 1958 Cover: 0.10 **NM** value: **165.00**
• **CGC:** 1 graded, best 8.0
2 ❑ Sep 1958 Cover: 0.10 **NM** value: **90.00**
• **CGC:** 1 graded, best 4.5
3 ❑ Oct 1958 Cover: 0.10 **NM** value: **70.00**
4 ❑ Nov 1958 Cover: 0.10 **NM** value: **48.00**
5 ❑ Jan 1959 Cover: 0.10 **NM** value: **48.00**
6 ❑ Feb 1959 Cover: 0.10 **NM** value: **42.00**
7 ❑ Mar 1959 Cover: 0.10 **NM** value: **42.00**
8 ❑ Apr 1959 Cover: 0.10 **NM** value: **42.00**
• **CGC:** 1 graded, best 8.0
9 ❑ May 1959 Cover: 0.10 **NM** value: **42.00**
10 ❑ Jun 1959 Cover: 0.10 **NM** value: **42.00**
• **CGC:** 1 graded, best 6.5
11 ❑ Jul 1959 Cover: 0.10 **NM** value: **34.00**
📖 Casper: Flashy; Casper: Hue Said It!; Casper: A Bright Solution; Spooky: Watch Out!
12 ❑ Aug 1959 Cover: 0.10 **NM** value: **34.00**
📖 Flashy; Wendy; A Bright Solution; Watch Out
13 ❑ Sep 1959 Cover: 0.10 **NM** value: **34.00**
14 ❑ Oct 1959 Cover: 0.10 **NM** value: **34.00**
15 ❑ Nov 1959 Cover: 0.10 **NM** value: **34.00**
16 ❑ Dec 1959 Cover: 0.10 **NM** value: **34.00**
17 ❑ Jan 1960 Cover: 0.10 **NM** value: **34.00**
Circ: Statement: **399,985** • **CGC:** 1 graded, best 3.5
18 ❑ Feb 1960 Cover: 0.10 **NM** value: **34.00**
Circ: Statement: **399,985**
19 ❑ Mar 1960 Cover: 0.10 **NM** value: **34.00**
Circ: Statement: **399,985**
20 ❑ Apr 1960 Cover: 0.10 **NM** value: **34.00**
Circ: Statement: **399,985** • **CGC:** 1 graded, best 9.4
21 ❑ May 1960 Cover: 0.10 **NM** value: **22.00**
Circ: Statement: **399,985**
22 ❑ Jun 1960 Cover: 0.10 **NM** value: **22.00**
Circ: Statement: **399,985**
23 ❑ Jul 1960 Cover: 0.10 **NM** value: **22.00**
Circ: Statement: **399,985**
24 ❑ Aug 1960 Cover: 0.10 **NM** value: **22.00**
Circ: Statement: **399,985** • **CGC:** 1 graded, best 9.0
25 ❑ Sep 1960 Cover: 0.10 **NM** value: **22.00**
Circ: Statement: **399,985**
26 ❑ Oct 1960 Cover: 0.10 **NM** value: **22.00**
Circ: Statement: **399,985**
27 ❑ Nov 1960 Cover: 0.10 **NM** value: **22.00**
Circ: Statement: **399,985**
28 ❑ Dec 1960 Cover: 0.10 **NM** value: **22.00**
Circ: Statement: **399,985**
29 ❑ Jan 1961 Cover: 0.10 **NM** value: **22.00**
• **CGC:** 1 graded, best 9.4
30 ❑ Feb 1961 Cover: 0.10 **NM** value: **22.00**
31 ❑ Mar 1961 Cover: 0.10 **NM** value: **16.00**

📖 indicates **Story Title** or **Storyline** information.
★ indicates **Character Appearance** information.
W = Writer • A = Artist • C = Cover Artist

Other grades: Multiply prices above by **1.5 for Mint • 2/3 for Very Fine • 1/3 for Fine • 1/5 for Very Good • 1/8 for Good**

32 ❑ Apr 1961 Cover: 0.10 **NM** value: **16.00**
• Has 1960 Statement; avg total paid circ 399,985
33 ❑ May 1961 Cover: 0.10 **NM** value: **16.00**
34 ❑ Jun 1961 Cover: 0.10 **NM** value: **16.00**
35 ❑ Jul 1961 Cover: 0.10 **NM** value: **16.00**
36 ❑ Aug 1961 Cover: 0.10 **NM** value: **16.00**
• **CGC:** 1 graded, best 8.5
37 ❑ Sep 1961 Cover: 0.10 **NM** value: **16.00**
• **CGC:** 1 graded, best 9.0
38 ❑ Oct 1961 Cover: 0.10 **NM** value: **16.00**
39 ❑ Nov 1961 Cover: 0.10 **NM** value: **16.00**
40 ❑ Dec 1961 **NM** value: **16.00**
41 ❑ Jan 1962 **NM** value: **14.00**
Circ: Statement: **436,153**
42 ❑ Feb 1962 **NM** value: **14.00**
Circ: Statement: **436,153** • **CGC:** 1 graded, best 7.0
43 ❑ Mar 1962 **NM** value: **14.00**
Circ: Statement: **436,153**
44 ❑ Apr 1962 **NM** value: **14.00**
Circ: Statement: **436,153** • **CGC:** 1 graded, best 8.5
45 ❑ May 1962 **NM** value: **14.00**
Circ: Statement: **436,153** • **CGC:** 1 graded, best 8.0
46 ❑ Jun 1962 **NM** value: **14.00**
Circ: Statement: **436,153**
47 ❑ Jul 1962 **NM** value: **14.00**
Circ: Statement: **436,153**
48 ❑ Aug 1962 **NM** value: **14.00**
Circ: Statement: **436,153**
49 ❑ Sep 1962 **NM** value: **14.00**
Circ: Statement: **436,153**
50 ❑ Oct 1962 Cover: 0.12 **NM** value: **14.00**
Circ: Statement: **436,153**
51 ❑ Nov 1962 Cover: 0.12 **NM** value: **12.00**
Circ: Statement: **436,153**
52 ❑ Dec 1962 Cover: 0.12 **NM** value: **12.00**
Circ: Statement: **436,153**
53 ❑ Jan 1963 Cover: 0.12 **NM** value: **12.00**
54 ❑ Feb 1963 Cover: 0.12 **NM** value: **12.00**
55 ❑ Mar 1963 Cover: 0.12 **NM** value: **12.00**
56 ❑ Apr 1963 Cover: 0.12 **NM** value: **12.00**
• Has 1962 Statement; avg total paid circ 436,153
57 ❑ May 1963 Cover: 0.12 **NM** value: **12.00**
58 ❑ Jun 1963 Cover: 0.12 **NM** value: **12.00**
59 ❑ Jul 1963 Cover: 0.12 **NM** value: **12.00**
60 ❑ Aug 1963 Cover: 0.12 **NM** value: **12.00**
61 ❑ Sep 1963 Cover: 0.12 **NM** value: **10.00**
62 ❑ Oct 1963 Cover: 0.12 **NM** value: **10.00**
63 ❑ Nov 1963 Cover: 0.12 **NM** value: **10.00**
64 ❑ Dec 1963 Cover: 0.12 **NM** value: **10.00**
65 ❑ Jan 1964 Cover: 0.12 **NM** value: **10.00**
66 ❑ Feb 1964 Cover: 0.12 **NM** value: **10.00**
67 ❑ Mar 1964 Cover: 0.12 **NM** value: **10.00**
68 ❑ Apr 1964 Cover: 0.12 **NM** value: **10.00**
• Has 1964 Statement, filed 10/1/63; no figures published
69 ❑ May 1964 Cover: 0.12 **NM** value: **10.00**
70 ❑ Jun 1964 Cover: 0.12 **NM** value: **10.00**
71 ❑ Jul 1964 Cover: 0.12 **NM** value: **8.00**
72 ❑ Aug 1964 Cover: 0.12 **NM** value: **8.00**
73 ❑ Sep 1964 Cover: 0.12 **NM** value: **8.00**
74 ❑ Oct 1964 Cover: 0.12 **NM** value: **8.00**
75 ❑ Nov 1964 Cover: 0.12 **NM** value: **8.00**
76 ❑ Dec 1964 Cover: 0.12 **NM** value: **8.00**
77 ❑ Jan 1965 Cover: 0.12 **NM** value: **8.00**
78 ❑ Feb 1965 Cover: 0.12 **NM** value: **8.00**
79 ❑ Mar 1965 Cover: 0.12 **NM** value: **8.00**
80 ❑ Apr 1965 Cover: 0.12 **NM** value: **8.00**
81 ❑ May 1965 Cover: 0.12 **NM** value: **7.00**
82 ❑ Jun 1965 Cover: 0.12 **NM** value: **7.00**
83 ❑ Jul 1965 Cover: 0.12 **NM** value: **7.00**
84 ❑ Aug 1965 Cover: 0.12 **NM** value: **7.00**
85 ❑ Sep 1965 Cover: 0.12 **NM** value: **7.00**
86 ❑ Oct 1965 Cover: 0.12 **NM** value: **7.00**
87 ❑ Nov 1965 Cover: 0.12 **NM** value: **7.00**
88 ❑ Dec 1965 Cover: 0.12 **NM** value: **7.00**
89 ❑ Jan 1966 Cover: 0.12 **NM** value: **7.00**
90 ❑ Feb 1966 Cover: 0.12 **NM** value: **6.00**
91 ❑ Mar 1966 Cover: 0.12 **NM** value: **6.00**
92 ❑ Apr 1966 Cover: 0.12 **NM** value: **6.00**
93 ❑ May 1966 Cover: 0.12 **NM** value: **6.00**
94 ❑ Jun 1966 Cover: 0.12 **NM** value: **6.00**
95 ❑ Jul 1966 Cover: 0.12 **NM** value: **6.00**
96 ❑ Aug 1966 Cover: 0.12 **NM** value: **6.00**
97 ❑ Sep 1966 Cover: 0.12 **NM** value: **6.00**
98 ❑ Oct 1966 Cover: 0.12 **NM** value: **6.00**
99 ❑ Nov 1966 Cover: 0.12 **NM** value: **6.00**
100 ❑ Dec 1966 Cover: 0.12 **NM** value: **6.00**
101 ❑ Jan 1967 Cover: 0.12 **NM** value: **5.00**
102 ❑ Feb 1967 Cover: 0.12 **NM** value: **5.00**
103 ❑ Mar 1967 Cover: 0.12 **NM** value: **5.00**
104 ❑ Apr 1967 Cover: 0.12 **NM** value: **5.00**
105 ❑ May 1967 Cover: 0.12 **NM** value: **5.00**
106 ❑ Jun 1967 Cover: 0.12 **NM** value: **5.00**
107 ❑ Jul 1967 Cover: 0.12 **NM** value: **5.00**
108 ❑ Aug 1967 Cover: 0.12 **NM** value: **5.00**
109 ❑ Sep 1967 Cover: 0.12 **NM** value: **5.00**
110 ❑ Oct 1967 Cover: 0.12 **NM** value: **5.00**
111 ❑ Nov 1967 Cover: 0.12 **NM** value: **5.00**
112 ❑ Dec 1967 Cover: 0.12 **NM** value: **5.00**
113 ❑ Jan 1968 Cover: 0.12 **NM** value: **5.00**
114 ❑ Feb 1968 Cover: 0.12 **NM** value: **5.00**
115 ❑ Mar 1968 Cover: 0.12 **NM** value: **5.00**
116 ❑ Apr 1968 Cover: 0.12 **NM** value: **5.00**
117 ❑ May 1968 Cover: 0.12 **NM** value: **5.00**
118 ❑ Jun 1968 Cover: 0.12 **NM** value: **5.00**
119 ❑ Jul 1968 Cover: 0.12 **NM** value: **5.00**
120 ❑ Aug 1968 Cover: 0.12 **NM** value: **5.00**
121 ❑ Sep 1968 Cover: 0.12 **NM** value: **4.00**
122 ❑ Oct 1968 Cover: 0.12 **NM** value: **4.00**
123 ❑ Nov 1968 Cover: 0.12 **NM** value: **4.00**
124 ❑ Dec 1968 Cover: 0.12 **NM** value: **4.00**
125 ❑ Jan 1969 Cover: 0.12 **NM** value: **4.00**
126 ❑ Feb 1969 Cover: 0.12 **NM** value: **4.00**
127 ❑ Mar 1969 Cover: 0.12 **NM** value: **4.00**
128 ❑ Apr 1969 Cover: 0.12 **NM** value: **4.00**
129 ❑ May 1969 Cover: 0.12 **NM** value: **4.00**
• Has 1968 Statement; no figures published
130 ❑ Jun 1969 Cover: 0.12 **NM** value: **4.00**
131 ❑ Jul 1969 Cover: 0.12 **NM** value: **4.00**
132 ❑ Aug 1969 Cover: 0.15 **NM** value: **4.00**
133 ❑ Sep 1969 Cover: 0.15 **NM** value: **4.00**
134 ❑ Oct 1969 Cover: 0.15 **NM** value: **4.00**
135 ❑ Nov 1969 Cover: 0.15 **NM** value: **4.00**
136 ❑ Dec 1969 Cover: 0.15 **NM** value: **4.00**
137 ❑ Jan 1970 Cover: 0.15 **NM** value: **4.00**
138 ❑ Feb 1970 Cover: 0.15 **NM** value: **4.00**
139 ❑ Mar 1970 Cover: 0.15 **NM** value: **4.00**
140 ❑ Apr 1970 Cover: 0.15 **NM** value: **4.00**
141 ❑ May 1970 Cover: 0.15 **NM** value: **3.00**
142 ❑ Jun 1970 Cover: 0.15 **NM** value: **3.00**
143 ❑ Jul 1970 Cover: 0.15 **NM** value: **3.00**
144 ❑ Aug 1970 Cover: 0.15 **NM** value: **3.00**
145 ❑ Sep 1970 Cover: 0.15 **NM** value: **3.00**
146 ❑ Oct 1970 Cover: 0.15 **NM** value: **3.00**
147 ❑ Nov 1970 Cover: 0.15 **NM** value: **3.00**
148 ❑ Dec 1970 Cover: 0.15 **NM** value: **3.00**
149 ❑ Jan 1971 Cover: 0.15 **NM** value: **3.00**
150 ❑ Feb 1971 Cover: 0.15 **NM** value: **3.00**
151 ❑ Mar 1971 Cover: 0.15 **NM** value: **3.00**
152 ❑ Apr 1971 Cover: 0.15 **NM** value: **3.00**
153 ❑ May 1971 Cover: 0.15 **NM** value: **3.00**
154 ❑ Jun 1971 Cover: 0.15 **NM** value: **3.00**
155 ❑ Jul 1971 Cover: 0.15 **NM** value: **3.00**
156 ❑ Aug 1971 Cover: 0.15 **NM** value: **3.00**
157 ❑ Sep 1971 Cover: 0.15 **NM** value: **3.00**
158 ❑ Oct 1971 Cover: 0.15 **NM** value: **3.00**
159 ❑ Nov 1971 Cover: 0.15 **NM** value: **3.00**
160 ❑ Mar 1972 Cover: 0.25 **NM** value: **3.00**
161 ❑ May 1972 Cover: 0.25 **NM** value: **3.00**
162 ❑ Jul 1972 Cover: 0.25 **NM** value: **3.00**
163 ❑ Sep 1972 Cover: 0.25 **NM** value: **3.00**
164 ❑ Nov 1972 Cover: 0.20 **NM** value: **3.00**
165 ❑ Jan 1973 Cover: 0.20 **NM** value: **3.00**
Circ: Statement: **171,031**
166 ❑ Mar 1973 Cover: 0.20 **NM** value: **3.00**
Circ: Statement: **171,031**
167 ❑ May 1973 Cover: 0.20 **NM** value: **3.00**
Circ: Statement: **171,031**
168 ❑ Jul 1973 Cover: 0.20 **NM** value: **3.00**
Circ: Statement: **171,031**
169 ❑ Sep 1973 Cover: 0.20 **NM** value: **3.00**
Circ: Statement: **171,031**
170 ❑ Nov 1973 Cover: 0.20 **NM** value: **2.00**
Circ: Statement: **171,031**
171 ❑ Jan 1974 Cover: 0.20 **NM** value: **2.00**
Circ: Statement: **169,315**
172 ❑ Mar 1974 Cover: 0.20 **NM** value: **2.00**
Circ: Statement: **169,315**
173 ❑ May 1974 Cover: 0.25 **NM** value: **2.00**
Circ: Statement: **169,315**
174 ❑ Jul 1974 Cover: 0.25 **NM** value: **2.00**
Circ: Statement: **169,315**
• Has 1973 Statement; avg total paid circ 171,031
175 ❑ Sep 1974 Cover: 0.25 **NM** value: **2.00**
Circ: Statement: **169,315**
176 ❑ Nov 1974 Cover: 0.25 **NM** value: **2.00**
Circ: Statement: **169,315**
177 ❑ Jan 1975 Cover: 0.25 **NM** value: **2.00**
Circ: Statement: **131,235**
178 ❑ Mar 1975 Cover: 0.25 **NM** value: **2.00**
Circ: Statement: **131,235**
179 ❑ May 1975 Cover: 0.25 **NM** value: **2.00**
Circ: Statement: **131,235**
180 ❑ Jul 1975 Cover: 0.25 **NM** value: **2.00**
Circ: Statement: **131,235**
• Has 1974 Statement; avg print run 296,618; avg sales 169,000; avg subs 15; avg total paid 169,315; samples 345; max existent 169,360; 43% of run returned
181 ❑ Sep 1975 Cover: 0.25 **NM** value: **2.00**
Circ: Statement: **131,235**
182 ❑ Nov 1975 Cover: 0.25 **NM** value: **2.00**
Circ: Statement: **131,235**
183 ❑ Jan 1976 Cover: 0.25 **NM** value: **2.00**
184 ❑ Mar 1976 Cover: 0.25 **NM** value: **2.00**
185 ❑ Apr 1976 Cover: 0.25 **NM** value: **2.00**
186 ❑ Jun 1976 Cover: 0.25 **NM** value: **2.00**
187 ❑ Aug 1976 Cover: 0.25 **NM** value: **2.00**
188 ❑ Oct 1976, four-color Cover: 0.30 **NM** value: **2.00**
🕮 Take-a-Chance Tommy; The Witch's Curse; Dare to Be Good; Spooky: Destiny's Child
189 ❑ Dec 1976 Cover: 0.30 **NM** value: **2.00**
• Has 1975 Statement, filed 10/1/1975; avg print run 283,329; avg sales 131,220; avg subs 15; avg total paid 131,235; samples 345; max existent 131,580; 54% of run returned
190 ❑ Feb 1977 Cover: 0.30 **NM** value: **2.00**
191 ❑ Apr 1977 **NM** value: **2.00**
192 ❑ Jun 1977 **NM** value: **2.00**
193 ❑ Aug 1977 **NM** value: **2.00**
194 ❑ Oct 1977 Cover: 0.35 **NM** value: **2.00**
195 ❑ Dec 1977 Cover: 0.35 **NM** value: **2.00**
196 ❑ Feb 1978 Cover: 0.35 **NM** value: **2.00**
197 ❑ Apr 1978 Cover: 0.35 **NM** value: **2.00**
198 ❑ Jun 1978 Cover: 0.35 **NM** value: **2.00**
199 ❑ Aug 1978 Cover: 0.35 **NM** value: **2.00**
200 ❑ Oct 1978 Cover: 0.35 **NM** value: **2.00**
201 ❑ Dec 1978 Cover: 0.35 **NM** value: **2.00**
202 ❑ Feb 1979 Cover: 0.35 **NM** value: **2.00**
203 ❑ Apr 1979 Cover: 0.35 **NM** value: **2.00**
204 ❑ Jun 1979 Cover: 0.35 **NM** value: **2.00**
205 ❑ Aug 1979 Cover: 0.35 **NM** value: **2.00**
206 ❑ Oct 1979 Cover: 0.40 **NM** value: **2.00**
207 ❑ Dec 1979 Cover: 0.40 **NM** value: **2.00**
208 ❑ Feb 1980 Cover: 0.40 **NM** value: **2.00**
209 ❑ Apr 1980 Cover: 0.40 **NM** value: **2.00**
210 ❑ Jun 1980 Cover: 0.40 **NM** value: **2.00**
211 ❑ Aug 1980 Cover: 0.40 **NM** value: **2.00**
212 ❑ Oct 1980 Cover: 0.50 **NM** value: **2.00**
213 ❑ Dec 1980 Cover: 0.50 **NM** value: **2.00**
214 ❑ Feb 1981 Cover: 0.50 **NM** value: **2.00**
215 ❑ Apr 1981 Cover: 0.50 **NM** value: **2.00**
216 ❑ Jun 1981 Cover: 0.50 **NM** value: **2.00**
217 ❑ Aug 1981 Cover: 0.50 **NM** value: **2.00**
218 ❑ Oct 1981 Cover: 0.50 **NM** value: **2.00**
219 ❑ Dec 1981 Cover: 0.50 **NM** value: **2.00**
220 ❑ Feb 1982 Cover: 0.60 **NM** value: **2.00**
221 ❑ Apr 1982 Cover: 0.60 **NM** value: **2.00**
222 ❑ Jun 1982 Cover: 0.60 **NM** value: **2.00**
223 ❑ Aug 1982 Cover: 0.60 **NM** value: **2.00**
224 ❑ Oct 1982 Cover: 0.60 **NM** value: **2.00**
225 ❑ **NM** value: **2.00**
226 ❑ Nov 1983 Cover: 0.75 **NM** value: **2.00**
227 ❑ Dec 1983 Cover: 0.75 **NM** value: **2.00**
228 ❑ Jan 1984 Cover: 0.75 **NM** value: **2.00**
229 ❑ Feb 1984 Cover: 0.75 **NM** value: **2.00**
230 ❑ Mar 1984 Cover: 0.75 **NM** value: **2.00**
231 ❑ Apr 1984 Cover: 0.75 **NM** value: **2.00**
232 ❑ May 1984 Cover: 0.75 **NM** value: **2.00**
233 ❑ Jun 1984 Cover: 0.75 **NM** value: **2.00**
234 ❑ Jul 1984 Cover: 0.75 **NM** value: **2.00**
235 ❑ Aug 1984 Cover: 0.75 **NM** value: **2.00**
236 ❑ Sep 1984 Cover: 0.75 **NM** value: **2.00**
237 ❑ Oct 1984 Cover: 0.75 **NM** value: **2.00**
238 ❑ Jan 1985 Cover: 1.00 **NM** value: **2.00**
239 ❑ Mar 1985 Cover: 1.00 **NM** value: **2.00**
240 ❑ May 1985 Cover: 1.00 **NM** value: **2.00**
241 ❑ Jul 1985 Cover: 1.00 **NM** value: **2.00**
242 ❑ Sep 1985 Cover: 1.00 **NM** value: **2.00**
243 ❑ Nov 1985 Cover: 1.00 **NM** value: **2.00**
244 ❑ Jan 1986 Cover: 1.00 **NM** value: **2.00**
245 ❑ Mar 1986 Cover: 1.00 **NM** value: **2.00**
246 ❑ Jul 1986 Cover: 1.00 **NM** value: **2.00**
247 ❑ 1986 Cover: 1.00 **NM** value: **2.00**
248 ❑ Oct 1986 Cover: 1.00 **NM** value: **2.00**
249 ❑ Cover: 1.00 **NM** value: **2.00**
250 ❑ Mar 1987 Cover: 1.00 **NM** value: **2.00**
251 ❑ Apr 1987 Cover: 1.00 **NM** value: **2.00**
252 ❑ May 1987 Cover: 1.00 **NM** value: **2.00**
253 ❑ Jun 1987 Cover: 1.00 **NM** value: **2.00**
• Series continued in Casper the Friendly Ghost #254

FRIENDS — Renegade

1 ❑ May 1987, b&w Cover: 2.00 **NM** value: **Cover or less**
2 ❑ b&w Cover: 2.00 **NM** value: **Cover or less**
3 ❑ b&w Cover: 2.00 **NM** value: **Cover or less**

FRIENDS OF MAXX — Image

1 ❑ Apr 1996 Cover: 2.95 **NM** value: **Cover or less**
• Dude Japan **A:** Sam Keith **W:** Sam Keith
2 ❑ Nov 1996 Cover: 2.95 **NM** value: **Cover or less**
Circ: Diamd. preorders: **23,517**
🕮 Broadminded • Broadminded **A:** Sam Keith **W:** Sam Keith
3 ❑ Mar 1997 Cover: 2.95 **NM** value: **Cover or less**
Circ: Diamd. preorders: **23,198**

FRIGHT — Atlas-Seaboard

1 ❑ Jun 1975 Cover: 0.25 **NM** value: **2.00**
• **CGC:** 1 graded, best 8.5
🕮 And Unto Dracula Was Born A Son ★ Origin of Son of Dracula.

FRIGHT (ETERNITY) — Eternity

1 ❑ Cover: 1.95 **NM** value: **2.00**
2 ❑ Cover: 1.95 **NM** value: **2.00**
3 ❑ Cover: 1.95 **NM** value: **2.00**
🕮 The Claws of Death!; The Man With No Face; Maxwell's Bloody Hammer;
4 ❑ Cover: 1.95 **NM** value: **2.00**
🕮 Hickory Dickory Dock; The Day that Satan Died; Blind Fate; The Boutique Macabre
5 ❑ Cover: 1.95 **NM** value: **2.00**
🕮 The 13 Dead Things; Gothic Fairy Tales: I Never Heard of a Ghost Actually Killing Anyone!!; The House of Demons!
6 ❑ Cover: 1.95 **NM** value: **2.00**
7 ❑ Cover: 1.95 **NM** value: **2.00**
8 ❑ Cover: 1.95 **NM** value: **2.00**
🕮 The Night in the Horror Hotel; The Lunatic Mummy; Down to Hades…To Die!
9 ❑ Cover: 1.95 **NM** value: **2.00**
🕮 The Butchered at Earth's Core!!!; Messrs. Crypts and Graves: Undertakers; The Black Orchids; Snake Wizard
10 ❑ Cover: 1.95 **NM** value: **2.00**
🕮 Them, Part 1; A Tale of Horror; Now…Another Maniac! **A:** Maelo Cintron **W:** Howie Anderson
11 ❑ Cover: 1.95 **NM** value: **2.00**
🕮 Tomorrow the Snowman Will Kill You!; The Mummy Khafre; They Lived in Darkos Manse; A Garden of Hellish Delights **A:** Cesar Lopez; Collado; Maro Nava **W:** Alan Newetson; Augustine Funnell; Edward Farthing; John Dentyn
12 ❑ Cover: 1.95 **NM** value: **2.00**
🕮 The Fetid Belle of the Mississipi; Get Up and Die Again; Horror has a Thousand Faces

CGC-graded: Multiply prices above by **33 for 9.9 M • 16 for 9.8 NM/M • 7 for 9.6 NM+ • 5 for 9.4 NM • 2.5 for 9.2 NM- • 1.5 for 9.0 VF/NM**

FRIGHT NIGHT — Now

An adaptation of Tom Holland's 1985 film Fright Night runs through the first three issues of this 22-issue series from Now Comics. High-school student Charley Brewster discovers that his new next-door neighbor is a vampire, and he and his friends enlist the aid of B-grade horror movie actor and TV horror show host Peter Vincent, "the Great Vampire Killer," to expose the mysterious Jerry Dandrige and put an end to a series of brutal killings that happen to coincide with his arrival in town. After the movie adaptation concludes, the series continues with more typical horror fare. Like the film that inspired it, Fright Night operates on a campy, tongue-in-cheek level and manages to have fun with the horror genre. While it's certainly not of the quality of E.C.'s Tales from the Crypt and The Haunt of Fear — or even DC's House of Mystery and House of Secrets — Fright Night is an entertaining horror fix for fans of such things.

1 ❑ Oct 1988 Cover: 1.75 **NM** value: **2.00**
Circ: CapCity orders: **3,300** • **CGC:** 1 graded, best 9.4
• Adapts movie **A:** Lenin Delsol **W:** Joe Gentile
2 ❑ Nov 1988 Cover: 1.75 **NM** value: **2.00**
Circ: CapCity orders: **2,850**
• Adapts movie **A:** Lenin Delsol **W:** Joe Gentile
3 ❑ Dec 1988 Cover: 1.75 **NM** value: **2.00**
Circ: CapCity orders: **3,175**
📖 The Dead Remember **A:** Lenin Delsol **W:** Joe Gentile
4 ❑ Feb 1989 Cover: 1.75 **NM** value: **2.00**
Circ: CapCity orders: **3,200**
📖 Eight Arms to Hold You **A:** Doug Murphy **W:** James Van Hise
5 ❑ Mar 1989 Cover: 1.75 **NM** value: **2.00**
Circ: CapCity orders: **3,000**
📖 The Spider Boy **A:** Lenin Delsol **W:** James Van Hise
6 ❑ Apr 1989 Cover: 1.75 **NM** value: **2.00**
Circ: CapCity orders: **2,750**
📖 The Legion of Endless Night, Part 1 **A:** Doug Murphy **W:** James Van Hise
7 ❑ May 1989 Cover: 1.75 **NM** value: **2.00**
Circ: CapCity orders: **2,500**
📖 The Legion of Endless Night, Part 2 **A:** Doug Murphy **W:** James Van Hise
8 ❑ Jun 1989 Cover: 1.75 **NM** value: **2.00**
Circ: CapCity orders: **2,350**
📖 The Revenge of Evil Ed, Part 1 **A:** Neil Vokes **W:** Tony Caputo
9 ❑ Jul 1989 Cover: 1.75 **NM** value: **2.00**
Circ: CapCity orders: **2,425**
📖 The Revenge of Evil Ed, Part 2 **A:** Neil Vokes **W:** Tony Caputo
10 ❑ Aug 1989 Cover: 1.75 **NM** value: **2.00**
Circ: CapCity orders: **2,375**
📖 Psychedelic Death, Part 1 **A:** Neil Vokes **W:** Tony Caputo
11 ❑ Sep 1989 Cover: 1.75 **NM** value: **2.00**
Circ: CapCity orders: **2,225**
📖 Psychedelic Death, Part 2 **A:** Neil Vokes **W:** Tony Caputo
12 ❑ Oct 1989 Cover: 1.75 **NM** value: **2.00**
Circ: CapCity orders: **2,175**
📖 Bull Whipped **A:** Neil Vokes **W:** Tony Caputo
13 ❑ Nov 1989 Cover: 1.75 **NM** value: **2.00**
Circ: CapCity orders: **2,225**
📖 Pup Pet **A:** Neil Vokes **W:** Mark Wheatley
14 ❑ Dec 1989 Cover: 1.75 **NM** value: **2.00**
Circ: CapCity orders: **2,175**
📖 The Resurrection of Dracula, Part 1 **A:** Neil Vokes **W:** Tony Caputo
15 ❑ Jan 1990 Cover: 1.75 **NM** value: **2.00**
Circ: CapCity orders: **2,100**
📖 The Resurrection of Dracula, Part 2 **A:** Neil Vokes **W:** Tony Caputo
16 ❑ Feb 1990 Cover: 1.75 **NM** value: **2.00**
Circ: CapCity orders: **1,950**
📖 Potion Motion **A:** Neil Vokes **W:** Katherine Llewellyn
17 ❑ Mar 1990 Cover: 1.75 **NM** value: **2.00**
Circ: CapCity orders: **1,800**
📖 Blood Ball **A:** Kevin West **W:** Katherine Llewellyn
18 ❑ Apr 1990 Cover: 1.75 **NM** value: **2.00**
Circ: CapCity orders: **1,800**
19 ❑ May 1990 Cover: 1.75 **NM** value: **2.00**
Circ: CapCity orders: **1,800**
📖 Daddy's Girl **A:** Kevin West **W:** Katherine Llewellyn
20 ❑ Jun 1990 Cover: 1.75 **NM** value: **2.00**
Circ: CapCity orders: **1,650**
📖 The Charge of the Dead Brigade **A:** Kevin West **W:** Diane Piron
21 ❑ Jul 1990 Cover: 1.75 **NM** value: **2.00**
Circ: CapCity orders: **1,700**
22 ❑ Aug 1990 Cover: 1.75 **NM** value: **2.00**
Circ: CapCity orders: **1,575**

FRIGHT NIGHT 1993 HALLOWEEN ANNUAL — Now

1 ❑ Cover: 2.95 **NM** value: **Cover or less**
Circ: CapCity orders: **1,625**
No issue number. • 3-D.

FRIGHT NIGHT 3-D — Now

1 ❑ Jun 1992 Cover: 2.95 **NM** value: **Cover or less**
Circ: CapCity orders: **1,625**
• with glasses
2 ❑ Fal 1992 Cover: 2.95 **NM** value: **Cover or less**
Circ: CapCity orders: **1,425**
• Dracula

FRIGHT NIGHT 3-D WINTER SPECIAL — Now

1 ❑ Win 1993 Cover: 2.95 **NM** value: **Cover or less**
No issue number. • Brainbats

FRIGHT NIGHT II GRAPHIC NOVEL — Now

1 ❑ Cover: 3.95 **NM** value: **Cover or less**

FRINGE — Caliber

1 ❑ b&w Cover: 2.50 **NM** value: **Cover or less**
2 ❑ b&w Cover: 2.50 **NM** value: **Cover or less**
3 ❑ b&w Cover: 2.50 **NM** value: **Cover or less**
4 ❑ b&w Cover: 2.50 **NM** value: **Cover or less**
5 ❑ b&w Cover: 2.50 **NM** value: **Cover or less**
6 ❑ b&w Cover: 2.50 **NM** value: **Cover or less**
7 ❑ b&w Cover: 2.50 **NM** value: **Cover or less**
8 ❑ b&w Cover: 2.50 **NM** value: **Cover or less**

FRISKY ANIMALS — Star Publications

44 ❑ Jan 1951 Cover: 0.10 **NM** value: **150.00**
45 ❑ Apr 1951 Cover: 0.10 **NM** value: **150.00**
46 ❑ Jul 1951 Cover: 0.10 **NM** value: **150.00**
47 ❑ Oct 1951 Cover: 0.10 **NM** value: **150.00**
48 ❑ Jan 1952 Cover: 0.10 **NM** value: **150.00**
49 ❑ Apr 1952 Cover: 0.10 **NM** value: **150.00**
50 ❑ Jul 1952 Cover: 0.10 **NM** value: **150.00**
51 ❑ Oct 1952 Cover: 0.10 **NM** value: **150.00**
52 ❑ Jan 1953 Cover: 0.10 **NM** value: **150.00**
53 ❑ Apr 1953 Cover: 0.10 **NM** value: **150.00**
54 ❑ Jul 1953 Cover: 0.10 **NM** value: **150.00**
55 ❑ Oct 1953 Cover: 0.10 **NM** value: **150.00**

FRISKY ANIMALS ON PARADE — Ajax

1 ❑ Sep 1957 Cover: 0.10 **NM** value: **125.00**
2 ❑ Nov 1957 Cover: 0.10 **NM** value: **100.00**
3 ❑ Feb 1958 Cover: 0.10 **NM** value: **75.00**

FRISKY FABLES — Premium

1 ❑ Spr 1945 Cover: 0.10 **NM** value: **150.00**
2 ❑ Fal 1945 Cover: 0.10 **NM** value: **75.00**
3 ❑ Win 1945 Cover: 0.10 **NM** value: **75.00**
4 ❑ Apr 1946 Cover: 0.10 **NM** value: **75.00**
5 ❑ May 1946 Cover: 0.10 **NM** value: **50.00**
6 ❑ Jun 1946 Cover: 0.10 **NM** value: **50.00**
7 ❑ Jul 1946 Cover: 0.10 **NM** value: **50.00**
8 ❑ Aug 1946 Cover: 0.10 **NM** value: **50.00**
9 ❑ Sep 1946 Cover: 0.10 **NM** value: **50.00**
10 ❑ Oct 1946 Cover: 0.10 **NM** value: **50.00**
11 ❑ Nov 1946 Cover: 0.10 **NM** value: **50.00**
12 ❑ Dec 1946 Cover: 0.10 **NM** value: **50.00**
13 ❑ Jan 1947 Cover: 0.10 **NM** value: **50.00**
14 ❑ Feb 1947 Cover: 0.10 **NM** value: **50.00**
15 ❑ Mar 1947 Cover: 0.10 **NM** value: **50.00**
16 ❑ Apr 1947 Cover: 0.10 **NM** value: **40.00**
17 ❑ May 1947 Cover: 0.10 **NM** value: **40.00**
18 ❑ Jun 1947 Cover: 0.10 **NM** value: **40.00**
19 ❑ Jul 1947 Cover: 0.10 **NM** value: **40.00**
20 ❑ Aug 1947 Cover: 0.10 **NM** value: **40.00**
21 ❑ Sep 1947 Cover: 0.10 **NM** value: **40.00**
22 ❑ Oct 1947 Cover: 0.10 **NM** value: **40.00**
23 ❑ Nov 1947 Cover: 0.10 **NM** value: **40.00**
24 ❑ Dec 1947 Cover: 0.10 **NM** value: **40.00**
25 ❑ Jan 1948 Cover: 0.10 **NM** value: **40.00**
26 ❑ Feb 1948 Cover: 0.10 **NM** value: **40.00**
27 ❑ Mar 1948 Cover: 0.10 **NM** value: **40.00**
28 ❑ Apr 1948 Cover: 0.10 **NM** value: **40.00**
29 ❑ May 1948 Cover: 0.10 **NM** value: **40.00**
• **CGC:** 1 graded, best 9.4
30 ❑ Jun 1948 Cover: 0.10 **NM** value: **35.00**
31 ❑ Aug 1948 Cover: 0.10 **NM** value: **35.00**
32 ❑ Oct 1948 Cover: 0.10 **NM** value: **35.00**
33 ❑ Dec 1948 Cover: 0.10 **NM** value: **35.00**
34 ❑ Feb 1949 Cover: 0.10 **NM** value: **35.00**
35 ❑ Apr 1949 Cover: 0.10 **NM** value: **35.00**
36 ❑ Jun 1949 Cover: 0.10 **NM** value: **35.00**
37 ❑ Aug 1949 Cover: 0.10 **NM** value: **35.00**
38 ❑ Mar 1949 Cover: 0.10 **NM** value: **35.00**
39 ❑ Dec 1949 Cover: 0.10 **NM** value: **35.00**
40 ❑ Feb 1950 Cover: 0.10 **NM** value: **35.00**
41 ❑ Apr 1950 Cover: 0.10 **NM** value: **35.00**
42 ❑ Jul 1950 Cover: 0.10 **NM** value: **35.00**
43 ❑ Oct 1950 Cover: 0.10 **NM** value: **35.00**

FRITZI RITZ — St. John

Ernie Bushmiller (1905-1982) didn't create Fritzi Ritz. (That was a man named Larry Whittington, who began the comedy strip in 1922 about a gorgeous, high-class beauty. Whittington took the character to Hollywood, and the gag strip turned to showgirl punchlines.) Bushmiller eventually took on the strip and added her little niece, Nancy, in 1933; soon, much of the focus turned to Nancy and her boyfriend, tough-kid Sluggo Smith. Covers on the Fritzi Ritz title, though, focused primarily on Fritzi and her boyfriend, Phil Fumble.

A number of issues of Fritzi Ritz had been believed not to exist, although some of those have been coming to light, as eBay has extended the reach of collectors. One such is #38, seen here. — Maggie

3 ❑ Cover: 0.10 **NM** value: **50.00**
4 ❑ Cover: 0.10 **NM** value: **45.00**
5 ❑ Cover: 0.10 **NM** value: **45.00**
6 ❑ Cover: 0.10 **NM** value: **45.00**
7 ❑ Cover: 0.10 **NM** value: **45.00**
27 ❑ Cover: 0.10 **NM** value: **25.00**
28 ❑ May 1953 Cover: 0.10 **NM** value: **25.00**
29 ❑ ca. 1953 Cover: 0.10 **NM** value: **25.00**
30 ❑ ca. 1953 Cover: 0.10 **NM** value: **25.00**
31 ❑ ca. 1953 Cover: 0.10 **NM** value: **25.00**
32 ❑ ca. 1953 Cover: 0.10 **NM** value: **25.00**
33 ❑ ca. 1953 Cover: 0.10 **NM** value: **25.00**
34 ❑ Cover: 0.10 **NM** value: **25.00**
35 ❑ Cover: 0.10 **NM** value: **25.00**
36 ❑ Cover: 0.10 **NM** value: **25.00**
37 ❑ Apr 1955 Cover: 0.10 **NM** value: **25.00**
• **CGC:** 1 graded, best 4.0
38 ❑ Cover: 0.10 **NM** value: **30.00**
42 ❑ Cover: 0.10 **NM** value: **25.00**
43 ❑ Cover: 0.10 **NM** value: **25.00**
44 ❑ Cover: 0.10 **NM** value: **25.00**
45 ❑ Cover: 0.10 **NM** value: **25.00**
46 ❑ Cover: 0.10 **NM** value: **25.00**
47 ❑ Cover: 0.10 **NM** value: **25.00**
48 ❑ Nov 1956 Cover: 0.10 **NM** value: **25.00**
• **CGC:** 1 graded, best 8.5
49 ❑ Cover: 0.10 **NM** value: **25.00**
50 ❑ ca. 1957 Cover: 0.10 **NM** value: **20.00**
51 ❑ ca. 1957 Cover: 0.10 **NM** value: **20.00**
52 ❑ ca. 1957 Cover: 0.10 **NM** value: **20.00**
53 ❑ ca. 1957 Cover: 0.10 **NM** value: **20.00**
54 ❑ Jun 1957 Cover: 0.10 **NM** value: **20.00**
55 ❑ Cover: 0.10 **NM** value: **20.00**
56 ❑ Cover: 0.10 **NM** value: **20.00**
57 ❑ Cover: 0.10 **NM** value: **20.00**
58 ❑ Jun 1958 Cover: 0.10 **NM** value: **20.00**
59 ❑ Sep 1958 Cover: 0.10 **NM** value: **20.00**

FROGMAN COMICS — Hillman

1 ❑ Jan 1952 Cover: 0.10 **NM** value: **60.00**
2 ❑ May 1952 Cover: 0.10 **NM** value: **38.00**
• **CGC:** 1 graded, best 9.0
3 ❑ Jul 1952 Cover: 0.10 **NM** value: **28.00**
4 ❑ Sep 1952 Cover: 0.10 **NM** value: **28.00**
📖 Saturday Afternoon Frogman; Underwater Lighthouse; Objective Sam; The Twenty-First Cave (text story); Gulf Stream Riddle; The Pirate Frogman
5 ❑ Nov 1952 Cover: 0.10 **NM** value: **28.00**
6 ❑ Dec 1952 Cover: 0.10 **NM** value: **24.00**
• **CGC:** 1 graded, best 6.5
7 ❑ Jan 1953 Cover: 0.10 **NM** value: **24.00**
8 ❑ Feb 1953 Cover: 0.10 **NM** value: **24.00**
9 ❑ Mar 1953 Cover: 0.10 **NM** value: **24.00**
10 ❑ Apr 1953 Cover: 0.10 **NM** value: **24.00**
11 ❑ May 1953 Cover: 0.10 **NM** value: **24.00**
final issue.

FROGMEN, THE — Dell

2 ❑ May 1962 Cover: 0.15 **NM** value: **30.00**
• Continued from Four Color Comics #1258
3 ❑ Sep 1962 Cover: 0.12 **NM** value: **25.00**
4 ❑ Feb 1963 Cover: 0.12 **NM** value: **18.00**
5 ❑ May 1963 Cover: 0.12 **NM** value: **20.00**
6 ❑ Aug 1963 Cover: 0.12 **NM** value: **18.00**
7 ❑ Nov 1963 Cover: 0.12 **NM** value: **16.00**
8 ❑ Feb 1964 Cover: 0.12 **NM** value: **16.00**
9 ❑ May 1964 Cover: 0.12 **NM** value: **16.00**
10 ❑ Aug 1964 Cover: 0.12 **NM** value: **16.00**
📖 Strange Disappearance
11 ❑ Nov 1964 Cover: 0.12 **NM** value: **16.00**
final issue.

FROM BEYONDE — Studio Insidio

1 ❑ b&w Cover: 2.25 **NM** value: **Cover or less**

FROM BEYOND THE UNKNOWN — DC

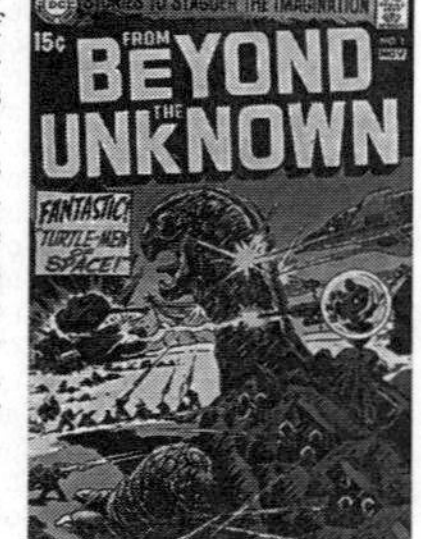

Supertitled "stories to stagger the imagination," this series was one of DC's most consistent science-fiction titles. Brilliant scientists doomed themselves with inventions that work all too well, such as the scientist who gained immortality but turned himself into marble in the process; gigantic monsters trampled major cities, either inadvertently or maliciously; and intrepid explorers found themselves on bizarre worlds, other dimensions, or trapped either in the past or the future.

Like many science-fiction magazines, this comic also included odd bits of scientific trivia, here called Scienti-Facts. For instance, one Scienti-Fact pointed out that if all the capillaries in the human blood stream were gathered together they would cover an entire acre.

1 ❑ Nov 1969 Cover: 0.15 **NM** value: **30.00**
• **CGC:** 3 graded, best 9.0
2 ❑ Jan 1970 Cover: 0.15 **NM** value: **16.00**
3 ❑ Mar 1970 Cover: 0.15 **NM** value: **12.00**
4 ❑ May 1970 Cover: 0.15 **NM** value: **12.00**
5 ❑ Jul 1970 Cover: 0.15 **NM** value: **12.00**
6 ❑ Sep 1970 Cover: 0.15 **NM** value: **10.00**
7 ❑ Nov 1970 Cover: 0.25 **NM** value: **10.00**
8 ❑ Jan 1971 Cover: 0.25 **NM** value: **10.00**
• **CGC:** 1 graded, best 9.4
9 ❑ Mar 1971 Cover: 0.25 **NM** value: **10.00**
10 ❑ May 1971 Cover: 0.25 **NM** value: **10.00**
11 ❑ Jul 1971 Cover: 0.25 **NM** value: **9.00**
12 ❑ Sep 1971 Cover: 0.25 **NM** value: **9.00**
13 ❑ Nov 1971 Cover: 0.25 **NM** value: **9.00**
14 ❑ Jan 1972 Cover: 0.25 **NM** value: **9.00**

Other grades: Multiply prices above by **1.5 for Mint • 2/3 for Very Fine • 1/3 for Fine • 1/5 for Very Good • 1/8 for Good**

15 ❑ Mar 1972 Cover: 0.25 **NM** value: **9.00**
16 ❑ May 1972 Cover: 0.25 **NM** value: **9.00**
📖 The World Wrecker; Doom From Station X; The Man Who Discovered the "Earth"; Captives Of The Eclipse; **A:** Murphy Anderson; Carmine Infantino; John Giunta; Manny Stallman; Sid Greene **W:** France Herron; John Broome; Otto Binder
17 ❑ Jul 1972 Cover: 0.25 **NM** value: **9.00**
18 ❑ Sep 1972 Cover: 0.20 **NM** value: **8.00**
19 ❑ Nov 1972 Cover: 0.20 **NM** value: **8.00**
20 ❑ Jan 1973 Cover: 0.20 **NM** value: **8.00**
21 ❑ Mar 1973 Cover: 0.20 **NM** value: **8.00**
22 ❑ May 1973 Cover: 0.20 **NM** value: **8.00**
23 ❑ Aug 1973 Cover: 0.20 **NM** value: **8.00**
24 ❑ Oct 1973 Cover: 0.20 **NM** value: **8.00**
25 ❑ Dec 1973 Cover: 0.20 **NM** value: **8.00**
final issue.

FROM HELL — Tundra

Artist Eddie Campbell and writer Alan Moore teamed to tell this ambitious story of the Whitechapel Murderer — better known as Jack the Ripper. "Jack" stalked London in the years just prior to the turn of the century, killing and then anatomizing a number of women with surgical precision.

Despite a massive police investigation, the murders were never solved. In the years that followed, countless theories have been offered, with suggestions being made concerning possible involvement of Freemasons and even of the royal family. Moore and Campbell's version draws from a variety of sources to offer a chilling, historical account of the most notorious serial killer of all time.

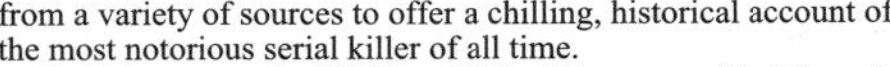

Alan Moore won the 1995 Best Writer Eisner award for his work on this series, and the film version was released in 2001, starring Johnny Depp, Heather Graham, Ian Holm, Robbie Coltrane, and Ian Richardson.

1 ❑ Mar 1991 Cover: 4.95 **NM** value: **8.00**
• **CGC:** 2 graded, best 9.8
1-2 ❑ Feb 1992 Cover: 4.95 **NM** value: **5.00**
1-3 ❑ Cover: 4.95 **NM** value: **5.00**
• 3rd printing (Kitchen Sink) **A:** Eddie Campbell **W:** Alan Moore
1-4 ❑ Cover: 4.95 **NM** value: **Cover or less**
• 4th printing (Kitchen Sink)
2 ❑ Cover: 4.95 **NM** value: **6.00**
• **CGC:** 1 graded, best 9.6
2-2 ❑ Cover: 4.95 **NM** value: **5.00**
• 2nd printing (Kitchen Sink) **A:** Eddie Campbell **W:** Alan Moore
2-3 ❑ Cover: 4.95 **NM** value: **5.00**
3 ❑ Dec 1993 Cover: 4.95 **NM** value: **6.00**
Circ: CapCity orders: **3,405**
3-2 ❑ Cover: 4.95 **NM** value: **5.00**
3-3 ❑ Cover: 4.95 **NM** value: **5.00**
4 ❑ Mar 1994 Cover: 4.95 **NM** value: **5.00**
Circ: CapCity orders: **4,230**
4-2 ❑ Cover: 4.95 **NM** value: **5.00**
4-3 ❑ Cover: 4.95 **NM** value: **5.00**
5 ❑ Jun 1994 Cover: 4.95 **NM** value: **Cover or less**
Circ: CapCity orders: **4,355**
6 ❑ Nov 1994 Cover: 4.95 **NM** value: **Cover or less**
Circ: CapCity orders: **4,125**
7 ❑ Apr 1995 Cover: 4.95 **NM** value: **Cover or less**
Circ: CapCity orders: **4,090** • **CGC:** 2 graded, best 9.8
8 ❑ Jul 1995 Cover: 4.95 **NM** value: **Cover or less**
Circ: CapCity orders: **4,170**
9 ❑ Apr 1996 Cover: 4.95 **NM** value: **Cover or less**
10 ❑ Aug 1996 Cover: 4.95 **NM** value: **Cover or less**
Circ: Diamd. preorders: **9,154**
final issue. **A:** Eddie Campbell **W:** Alan Moore
11 ❑ Sep 1998 Cover: 4.95 **NM** value: **Cover or less**
Bk 1/HC❑ **NM** value: **140.00**
• Limited edition hardcover. **A:** Eddie Campbell **W:** Alan Moore
Bk 1/LE❑ **NM** value: **29.99**
• Trade Paperback. **A:** Eddie Campbell **W:** Alan Moore

FROM HELL: DANCE OF THE GULL CATCHERS — Kitchen Sink

1 ❑ Cover: 4.95 **NM** value: **Cover or less**
Circ: Diamd. preorders: **7,784**
No issue number. • sequel to From Hell

FROM HERE TO INSANITY (VOL. 3) — Charlton

8 ❑ Feb 1955 Cover: 0.10 **NM** value: **100.00**
9 ❑ Apr 1955 Cover: 0.10 **NM** value: **100.00**
10 ❑ Jun 1955 Cover: 0.10 **NM** value: **100.00**
11 ❑ Aug 1955 Cover: 0.10 **NM** value: **100.00**
12 ❑ Oct 1955 Cover: 0.10 **NM** value: **100.00**
1 ❑ Apr 1957 Cover: 0.10 **NM** value: **125.00**
• **CGC:** 1 graded, best 6.0

FROM THE DARKNESS — Adventure

1 ❑ **NM** value: **6.00**
2 ❑ **NM** value: **5.00**
3 ❑ b&w **NM** value: **4.00**
4 ❑ b&w **NM** value: **4.00**

FROM THE DARKNESS BOOK II: BLOOD VOWS — Cry for Dawn

1 ❑ Cover: 2.50 **NM** value: **Cover or less**
2 ❑ Cover: 2.50 **NM** value: **Cover or less**
3 ❑ Cover: 2.50 **NM** value: **Cover or less**
Circ: CapCity orders: **2,475**

FRONTIER — Slave Labor

1 ❑ Jul 1994 Cover: 2.95 **NM** value: **Cover or less**

FRONTIER FIGHTERS — DC

1 ❑ Sep 1955 Cover: 0.10 **NM** value: **250.00**
• **CGC:** 2 graded, best 9.0
2 ❑ Nov 1955 Cover: 0.10 **NM** value: **175.00**
3 ❑ Jan 1956 Cover: 0.10 **NM** value: **175.00**
• **CGC:** 1 graded, best 4.5
4 ❑ Mar 1956 Cover: 0.10 **NM** value: **150.00**
5 ❑ May 1956 Cover: 0.10 **NM** value: **150.00**
6 ❑ Jul 1956 Cover: 0.10 **NM** value: **150.00**
7 ❑ Sep 1956 Cover: 0.10 **NM** value: **150.00**
8 ❑ Nov 1956 Cover: 0.10 **NM** value: **150.00**

FRONTIER ROMANCES — Avon

1 ❑ Nov 1949 Cover: 0.10 **NM** value: **400.00**
• **CGC:** 1 graded, best 7.5
2 ❑ Feb 1950 Cover: 0.10 **NM** value: **300.00**
• **CGC:** 1 graded, best 7.5

FRONTIERS '86 PRESENTS — Frontiers

1 ❑ Cover: 1.50 **NM** value: **Cover or less**
• Crusaders
2 ❑ Cover: 1.50 **NM** value: **Cover or less**
• Crusaders

FRONTIER WESTERN — Atlas

1 ❑ Feb 1956 Cover: 0.10 **NM** value: **125.00**
2 ❑ Apr 1956 Cover: 0.10 **NM** value: **100.00**
3 ❑ Jun 1956 Cover: 0.10 **NM** value: **100.00**
4 ❑ Aug 1956 Cover: 0.10 **NM** value: **50.00**
5 ❑ Oct 1956 Cover: 0.10 **NM** value: **50.00**
6 ❑ Dec 1956 Cover: 0.10 **NM** value: **50.00**
7 ❑ Feb 1957 Cover: 0.10 **NM** value: **50.00**
8 ❑ Apr 1957 Cover: 0.10 **NM** value: **50.00**
9 ❑ Jun 1957 Cover: 0.10 **NM** value: **50.00**
10 ❑ Aug 1957 Cover: 0.10 **NM** value: **50.00**

FRONTLINE COMBAT (E.C.) — E.C.

This E.C. title, carrying the spine-long message "War and Fighting Men," was one of two of Editor Harvey Kurtzman's major projects at E.C. (The other was Mad, which began as a comic book, shifted to magazine format with #24, and continues to this day.) Along with Two-Fisted Tales, Frontline Combat focused on war stories, ranging from Caesar's combats to a moving civilian story featuring the atom bomb. Kurtzman wrote many of the scripts, and the art included work by Jack Davis, Will Elder, George Evans, John Severin, Wally Wood, and Kurtzman himself. There were three special issues, one on Iwo Jima, one on the Civil War, and one on the Air Force. — Maggie

1 ❑ Jul 1951 Cover: 0.10 **NM** value: **520.00**
• **CGC:** 3 graded, best 9.6
📖 Unterseeboot 113; The Fatal Step (text story); Enemy Assault; O.P.!; Marines Retreat! **A:** Harvey Kurtzman; Wally Wood; Russ Heath; Jack Davis; Severin
2 ❑ Sep 1951 Cover: 0.10 **NM** value: **300.00**
• **CGC:** 4 graded, best 9.8
📖 Bouncing Bertha; Zero Hour!; Gettysburg!; Contact! **A:** Harvey Kurtzman; Bill Elder; Wally Wood; Jack Davis; Severin **W:** Harvey Kurtzman; John Severin; Bill Elder; Wally Wood; Jack Davis
3 ❑ Nov 1951 Cover: 0.10 **NM** value: **220.00**
• **CGC:** 4 graded, best 9.6
📖 Tin Can!; Desert Fox!; Prisoner of War!; How They Die!
4 ❑ Jan 1952 Cover: 0.10 **NM** value: **175.00**
• **CGC:** 4 graded, best 9.8
📖 Combat Medic!; Light Brigade!; Air Burst!; Bomb Run! **A:** Harvey Kurtzman **W:** Harvey Kurtzman
5 ❑ Mar 1952 Cover: 0.10 **NM** value: **175.00**
• **CGC:** 4 graded, best 9.8
📖 442nd Combat Team; Stonewall Jackson!; War Machines!; Big 'If'!
6 ❑ May 1952 Cover: 0.10 **NM** value: **130.00**
Circ: Diamd. preorders: **4,400** • **CGC:** 3 graded, best 9.6
📖 A Platoon!; Bellyrobber!; War of 1812!; Ace!; Fate (text story) **A:** John Severin; Bill Elder; Jack Davis; Harvey Kurtzman(cover) **W:** John Severin; Bill Elder; Jack Davis
7 ❑ Jul 1952 Cover: 0.10 **NM** value: **130.00**
Circ: Diamd. preorders: **4,439** • **CGC:** 5 graded, best 9.4
📖 Iwo Jima!; The Landing!; The Caves!; Mopping Up! **A:** John Severin; Bill Elder; Wally Wood; Jack Davis; Harvey Kurtzman(cover) **W:** John Severin; Bill Elder; Wally Wood; Jack Davis
8 ❑ Sep 1952, four-color Cover: 0.10 **NM** value: **130.00**
Circ: Diamd. preorders: **4,523** • **CGC:** 3 graded, best 9.6
📖 Thunderjet!; Caesar!; Chickamauga!; Night Patrol! **A:** Alex Toth; John Severin; Bill Elder; Wally Wood; Jack Davis; Harvey Kurtzman(cover) **W:** Alex Toth; John Severin; Bill Elder; Wally Wood; Jack Davis
9 ❑ Nov 1952 Cover: 0.10 **NM** value: **130.00**
Circ: Diamd. preorders: **4,703** • **CGC:** 4 graded, best 9.6
📖 Abe Lincoln!; First Shot!; Choose Sides!; Bull Run!; Speech (text story) **A:** John Severin; Bill Elder; Wally Wood; Jack Davis; Harvey Kurtzman(cover) **W:** John Severin; Bill Elder; Wally Wood; Jack Davis
10 ❑ Jan 1953 Cover: 0.10 **NM** value: **130.00**
Circ: Diamd. preorders: **4,382** • **CGC:** 3 graded, best 9.6
📖 A Baby!; Geronimo! Napoleon!; Anzio!; Bayonet Drill (text story) **A:** John Severin; Bill Elder; Wally Wood; Jack Davis; Harvey Kurtzman(cover) **W:** George Evans; John Severin; Bill Elder; Wally Wood; Jack Davis
11 ❑ Mar 1953 Cover: 0.10 **NM** value: **100.00**
Circ: Diamd. preorders: **4,179** • **CGC:** 3 graded, best 9.4
📖 Bird-Dogs!; Rough Riders!; Lufbery!; Sailor!
12 ❑ May 1953 Cover: 0.10 **NM** value: **100.00**
Circ: Diamd. preorders: **4,001** • **CGC:** 3 graded, best 9.2
📖 F-94!; F-86 Sabre Jet!; B-26 Invader!; H-5
13 ❑ Jul 1953 Cover: 0.10 **NM** value: **100.00**
Circ: Diamd. preorders: **4,084** • **CGC:** 2 graded, best 9.6
📖 Pantherjet!; War Dance!; Wolf!; Frank Luke!
14 ❑ Oct 1953 Cover: 0.10 **NM** value: **100.00**
Circ: Diamd. preorders: **3,717** • **CGC:** 2 graded, best 7.5
📖 Albatross!; Bonhomme Richard!; Immelman!; Whupped!
15 ❑ Jan 1954 Cover: 0.10 **NM** value: **100.00**
Circ: Diamd. preorders: **3,660** • **CGC:** 3 graded, best 9.6
📖 Perimeter!; McCudden!; Captain Teach (text story); Vengeful Sioux!; Belts n' Celts! final issue. **A:** George Evans; John Severin; Wally Wood **W:** George Evans; John Severin; Wally Wood; Fletcher Pratt

FRONTLINE COMBAT (RCP) — Gemstone

1 ❑ Aug 1995 Cover: 2.00 **NM** value: **Cover or less**
Circ: CapCity orders: **2,350**
📖 Unterseeboot 113; The Fatal Step (text story); Enemy Assault; O.P.!; Marines Retreat! • Reprints Frontline Combat (EC) #1 **A:** Harvey Kurtzman; Wally Wood; Russ Heath; Jack Davis; Severin
2 ❑ Nov 1995 Cover: 2.00 **NM** value: **Cover or less**
📖 Bouncing Bertha; Zero Hour!; Gettysburg!; Contact! • Reprints Frontline Combat (EC) #2 **A:** Harvey Kurtzman; Bill Elder; Wally Wood; Jack Davis; Severin **W:** Harvey Kurtzman; John Severin; Bill Elder; Wally Wood; Jack Davis
3 ❑ Feb 1996 Cover: 2.00 **NM** value: **Cover or less**
📖 Tin Can • Reprints Frontline Combat (EC) #3
4 ❑ May 1996 Cover: 2.00 **NM** value: **Cover or less**
📖 Air Burst! • Reprints Frontline Combat (EC) #4
5 ❑ Aug 1996 Cover: 2.50 **NM** value: **Cover or less**
• Reprints Frontline Combat (EC) #5
6 ❑ Nov 1996 Cover: 2.50 **NM** value: **Cover or less**
📖 A Platoon!; Bellyrobber!; War of 1812!; Ace!; Fate (text story) • Reprints Frontline Combat (EC) #6 **A:** John Severin; Bill Elder; Jack Davis; Harvey Kurtzman(cover) **W:** John Severin; Bill Elder; Jack Davis
7 ❑ Feb 1997 Cover: 2.50 **NM** value: **Cover or less**
Circ: Statement: **5,124**
📖 Iwo Jima!; The Landing!; The Caves!; Mopping Up! • Reprints Frontline Combat (EC) #7 **A:** John Severin; Bill Elder; Wally Wood; Jack Davis; Harvey Kurtzman(cover) **W:** John Severin; Bill Elder; Wally Wood; Jack Davis
8 ❑ May 1997 Cover: 2.50 **NM** value: **Cover or less**
Circ: Statement: **5,124**
📖 Thunderjet!; Caesar!; Chickamauga!; Night Patrol! • Reprints Frontline Combat (EC) #8 **A:** Alex Toth; John Severin; Bill Elder; Wally Wood; Jack Davis; Harvey Kurtzman(cover) **W:** Alex Toth; John Severin; Bill Elder; Wally Wood; Jack Davis
9 ❑ Aug 1997 Cover: 2.50 **NM** value: **Cover or less**
Circ: Statement: **5,124**
📖 Abe Lincoln!; First Shot!; Choose Sides!; Bull Run!; Speech (text story) • Reprints Frontline Combat (EC) #9 **A:** John Severin; Bill Elder; Wally Wood; Jack Davis; Harvey Kurtzman(cover) **W:** John Severin; Bill Elder; Wally Wood; Jack Davis
10 ❑ Nov 1997 Cover: 2.50 **NM** value: **Cover or less**
Circ: Statement: **5,124**
📖 A Baby!; Geronimo! Napoleon!; Anzio!; Bayonet Drill (text story) • Reprints Frontline Combat (EC) #10 **A:** John Severin; Bill Elder; Wally Wood; Jack Davis; Harvey Kurtzman(cover) **W:** George Evans; John Severin; Bill Elder; Wally Wood; Jack Davis
11 ❑ Feb 1998 Cover: 2.50 **NM** value: **Cover or less**
• Reprints Frontline Combat (EC) #11; Has 1997 Statement; avg total paid circ 5,124
12 ❑ May 1998 Cover: 2.50 **NM** value: **Cover or less**
• Reprints Frontline Combat (EC) #12
13 ❑ Aug 1998 Cover: 2.50 **NM** value: **Cover or less**
• Reprints Frontline Combat (EC) #13
14 ❑ Nov 1998 Cover: 2.50 **NM** value: **Cover or less**
• Reprints Frontline Combat (EC) #14
15 ❑ Feb 1999 Cover: 2.50 **NM** value: **Cover or less**
• Reprints Frontline Combat (EC) #15
Anl 1❑ Cover: 10.95 **NM** value: **Cover or less**
• Collects Frontline Combat #1-5 **A:** Harvey Kurtzman; Bill Elder; Wally Wood; Jack Davis; Severin **W:** Harvey Kurtzman; John Severin; Bill Elder; Wally Wood; Jack Davis
Anl 2❑ Cover: 12.95 **NM** value: **Cover or less**
• Collects Frontline Combat #6-10 **A:** Alex Toth; John Severin; Bill Elder; Wally Wood; Jack Davis; Harvey Kurtzman(cover) **W:** George Evans; Alex Toth; John Severin; Bill Elder; Wally Wood; Jack Davis

FRONT PAGE COMIC BOOK — Harvey

1 ❑ **NM** value: **300.00**

FROST — Caliber

1 ❑ b&w Cover: 1.95 **NM** value: **Cover or less**

FROSTBITER: WRATH OF THE WENDIGO — Caliber

1 ❑ Cover: 2.95 **NM** value: **Cover or less**
2 ❑ Cover: 2.95 **NM** value: **Cover or less**
3 ❑ Cover: 2.95 **NM** value: **Cover or less**

FROST: THE DYING BREED — Caliber

1 ❑ b&w Cover: 2.95 **NM** value: **Cover or less**
📖 Memorial **A:** Kevin VanHook **W:** Kevin VanHook
2 ❑ b&w Cover: 2.95 **NM** value: **Cover or less**
3 ❑ b&w Cover: 2.95 **NM** value: **Cover or less**
Bk 1❑ b&w Cover: 9.95 **NM** value: **Cover or less**
• Graphic Novel

CGC-graded: Multiply prices above by **33 for 9.9 M** • **16 for 9.8 NM/M** • **7 for 9.6 NM+** • **5 for 9.4 NM** • **2.5 for 9.2 NM-** • **1.5 for 9.0 VF/NM**

FROZEN EMBRYO — Slave Labor
1 ❑ Dec 1992 Cover: 2.95 **NM** value: **Cover or less**

F-TROOP — Gold Key
1 ❑ Aug 1966 Cover: 0.12 **NM** value: **50.00**
Photo cover. Don't Cross Your Bridges; The Buffalo Hunter; Indian Trader
2 ❑ Nov 1966 Cover: 0.12 **NM** value: **40.00**
3 ❑ Feb 1967 Cover: 0.12 **NM** value: **36.00**
4 ❑ Apr 1967 Cover: 0.12 **NM** value: **36.00**
• **CGC:** 1 graded, best 8.0
5 ❑ May 1967 Cover: 0.12 **NM** value: **36.00**
6 ❑ Jun 1967 Cover: 0.12 **NM** value: **32.00**
7 ❑ Aug 1967 Cover: 0.12 **NM** value: **32.00**
final issue.

FUGITIVE — Caliber
1 ❑ Cover: 2.50 **NM** value: **Cover or less**
Delaney's Heroes; Where No Madmad Has Gone Before; A Family Visit; Wild, Wild Western **A:** James Tucker; Roy Burdine; Mitch Foust; James O'Barr **W:** Charles Marshall

FUGITIVES FROM JUSTICE — St. John
1 ❑ Feb 1952 Cover: 0.10 **NM** value: **100.00**
2 ❑ Apr 1952 Cover: 0.10 **NM** value: **50.00**
3 ❑ Jun 1952 Cover: 0.10 **NM** value: **50.00**
4 ❑ Aug 1952 Cover: 0.10 **NM** value: **40.00**
5 ❑ Oct 1952 Cover: 0.10 **NM** value: **40.00**

FUGITOID — Mirage
1 ❑ Cover: 1.50 **NM** value: **3.00**
• Teenage Mutant Ninja Turtles tie-in; Continued from TMNT #4; continued in TMNT #5

FULL METAL FICTION — London Night
1 ❑ Mar 1997 Cover: 3.95 **NM** value: **Cover or less**
Razor: Year one; Arizona: The Wild; Killing Machine; Sade **A:** Shelby Robertson; Scott Pentzer; P.D. Peterson; Stephen Sandoval **W:** Everette Hartsoe; David Quinn; Kevin Hill; S.D. Lester

FULL OF FUN — Decker
1 ❑ Aug 1957 Cover: 0.10 **NM** value: **40.00**
2 ❑ Cover: 0.10 **NM** value: **25.00**

FULL THROTTLE — Aircel
1 ❑ b&w Cover: 2.95 **NM** value: **Cover or less**
Escape from Eden **A:** Glenn Lumsden; Dave de Vries **W:** Glenn Lumsden; Dave de Vries
2 ❑ b&w Cover: 2.95 **NM** value: **Cover or less**

FUN AND GAMES MAGAZINE — Marvel
1 ❑ Sep 1979 Cover: 0.50 **NM** value: **3.00**
• **CGC:** 1 graded, best 9.0
2 ❑ Oct 1979 Cover: 0.50 **NM** value: **2.00**
3 ❑ Nov 1979 Cover: 0.50 **NM** value: **2.00**
4 ❑ Dec 1979 Cover: 0.50 **NM** value: **2.00**
5 ❑ Jan 1980 Cover: 0.50 **NM** value: **2.00**
6 ❑ Feb 1980 Cover: 0.50 **NM** value: **2.00**
7 ❑ Mar 1980 Cover: 0.50 **NM** value: **2.00**
8 ❑ Apr 1980 Cover: 0.50 **NM** value: **2.00**
9 ❑ May 1980 Cover: 0.50 **NM** value: **2.00**
10 ❑ Jun 1980 Cover: 0.50 **NM** value: **2.00**
11 ❑ Jul 1980 Cover: 0.50 **NM** value: **2.00**
12 ❑ Aug 1980 Cover: 0.50 **NM** value: **2.00**
13 ❑ Sep 1980 Cover: 0.50 **NM** value: **2.00**

FUN BOYS SPRING SPECIAL — Tundra
1 ❑ b&w Cover: 1.95 **NM** value: **Cover or less**
No issue number. **A:** Jeff Bonivert **W:** Jeff Bonivert

FUN COMICS — Star Publications
The Star Comics line of the 1950s (as opposed to Marvel's Star Comics line of the 1980s) is generally remembered by collectors as the publisher of gruesome crime and horror comics luridly illustrated by L.B. Cole. Fun Comics showed that Cole and Star had their tender side, as well. Formerly Holiday Comics, Fun Comics featured the usual assortment of funny-animal antics popular in kids' comics of the time from Disney on down. Fun Comics #12 introduced Mighty Bear, a clownish black bear cub who took over the title with the next issue, and featured a wonderful cover in wild Day-Glo poster-paint style by Cole.

9 ❑ Jan 1953 Cover: 0.25 **NM** value: **110.00**
• Giant-size. • Series continued from Holiday Comics #8
10 ❑ Apr 1953 Cover: 0.10 **NM** value: **85.00**
11 ❑ Jul 1953 Cover: 0.10 **NM** value: **85.00**
12 ❑ Oct 1953 Cover: 0.10 **NM** value: **85.00**
• Series continued in Mighty Bear #13

FUN COMICS (BILL BLACK'S...) — AC
1 ❑ Cover: 2.00 **NM** value: **Cover or less**
2 ❑ Cover: 2.00 **NM** value: **Cover or less**
3 ❑ Cover: 2.00 **NM** value: **Cover or less**
4 ❑ Cover: 2.00 **NM** value: **Cover or less**
Stardust Descending; The Mystic Origin of Nightfall • Captain Paragon, Nightfall **A:** Mark Heike; Bill Black; III; Jim Sanders; Pat Boroderick; Roy Richardson **W:** Bill Black; Benjamin Smith; R.C. Harvey

FUN HOUSE — MN Design
1 ❑ full color Cover: 6.50 **NM** value: **Cover or less**
No issue number. • photos

FUN HOUSE (J.R. WILLIAMS'...) — Starhead
All issues are adults only.
1 ❑ Nov 1993, b&w Cover: 3.95 **NM** value: **Cover or less**
• Collections of Comics, Strips... **A:** J.R. Williams **W:** J.R. Williams

FUN-IN — Gold Key
1 ❑ Feb 1970 Cover: 0.15 **NM** value: **16.00**
• **CGC:** 1 graded, best 9.2
2 ❑ 1970 Cover: 0.15 **NM** value: **10.00**
3 ❑ 1970 Cover: 0.15 **NM** value: **9.00**
4 ❑ Nov 1970 Cover: 0.15 **NM** value: **9.00**
5 ❑ Jan 1971 Cover: 0.15 **NM** value: **8.00**
• Motormouse and Autocat, Dastardly and Muttley
6 ❑ Mar 1971 Cover: 0.15 **NM** value: **8.00**
• Dastardly and Muttley, It's the Wolf
7 ❑ May 1971 Cover: 0.15 **NM** value: **6.00**
• Motormouse and Autocat, Dastardly and Muttley, It's the Wolf
8 ❑ Jul 1971 Cover: 0.15 **NM** value: **6.00**
9 ❑ Oct 1971 Cover: 0.15 **NM** value: **6.00**
10 ❑ Jan 1972 Cover: 0.15 **NM** value: **6.00**
11 ❑ Apr 1974 Cover: 0.20 **NM** value: **4.00**
• **CGC:** 1 graded, best 9.4
12 ❑ Jun 1974 Cover: 0.20 **NM** value: **4.00**
13 ❑ Aug 1974 Cover: 0.25 **NM** value: **4.00**
• **CGC:** 1 graded, best 9.2
14 ❑ Oct 1974 Cover: 0.25 **NM** value: **4.00**
• **CGC:** 1 graded, best 9.2
15 ❑ **NM** value: **4.00**

FUNKY PHANTOM — Gold Key
The Funky Phantom cartoon may not be everyone's cup of tea, but the comic-book version — thankfully minus the Hanna-Barbera laugh track — is a lot more palatable. Muddles, a revolutionary war figure, helps a group of teen-agers fight crime along with his ghostly cat. (It's amazing anyone pays for a police force at all in the Funtastic World of Hanna-Barbera with all these kid detectives running around.)

Formulaic as the source material may be, some of the longer mystery stories from this series do show some imagination and invention on the part of the creators. If it's a choice between watching the cartoon and reading the comic book, though, take the comic book. — JJM

1 ❑ Mar 1972 Cover: 0.15 **NM** value: **26.00**
• **CGC:** 2 graded, best 8.5
2 ❑ Jun 1972 Cover: 0.15 **NM** value: **15.00**
3 ❑ Sep 1972 Cover: 0.15 **NM** value: **10.00**
• **CGC:** 7 graded, best 9.6
4 ❑ Dec 1972 Cover: 0.20 **NM** value: **10.00**
5 ❑ Mar 1973 Cover: 0.20 **NM** value: **10.00**
6 ❑ Jun 1973 Cover: 0.20 **NM** value: **8.00**
7 ❑ Sep 1973 Cover: 0.20 **NM** value: **8.00**
8 ❑ Dec 1973 Cover: 0.20 **NM** value: **8.00**
The Ben Franklin Bridge Plot; Ghost of the Lost City of Cibola ★ Appearance of April, Skip, Augie, Elmo, Prissy Atwater.
9 ❑ Mar 1974 Cover: 0.20 **NM** value: **8.00**
10 ❑ Jun 1974 Cover: 0.20 **NM** value: **8.00**
11 ❑ Sep 1974 Cover: 0.25 **NM** value: **6.00**
12 ❑ Dec 1974 Cover: 0.25 **NM** value: **6.00**
13 ❑ Mar 1975 Cover: 0.25 **NM** value: **6.00**

FUNLAND — Ziff-Davis
1 ❑ ca. 1949 Cover: 0.25 **NM** value: **125.00**

FUNLAND COMICS — Croyden
1 ❑ ca. 1945 Cover: 0.10 **NM** value: **100.00**

FUNNIES — Dell
Initially packed with strip reprints (several early covers boasted, "Over 100 comics"), Funnies carried such strips as Alley Oop, Boots, Captain Easy, Dan Dunn, Freckles, Henry, Major Hoople, Out Our Way, and Tailspin Tommy. Other features were eventually added (Sheldon Mayer's Scribbly, for example, was featured on the cover of #26), but the emphasis stayed on gag strips until #35. Suddenly, there was a sharp transition to action-adventure material, and characters like Edgar Rice Burroughs' John Carter of Mars took pre-eminent spots. Eventually, Phantasmo ("Master of the World") appeared, and then Captain Midnight took over on the cover.

Then Pearl Harbor was bombed, Andy Panda showed up on the cover of Funnies, and the next issue saw the series continuing its numbering as New Funnies with Andy Panda as its star. — Maggie

1 ❑ Oct 1936 Cover: 0.10 **NM** value: **2500.00**
2 ❑ Nov 1936 Cover: 0.10 **NM** value: **1000.00**
• **CGC:** 1 graded, best 7.0
3 ❑ Dec 1936 Cover: 0.10 **NM** value: **800.00**
4 ❑ Jan 1937 Cover: 0.10 **NM** value: **650.00**
5 ❑ Feb 1937 Cover: 0.10 **NM** value: **650.00**
6 ❑ Mar 1937 Cover: 0.10 **NM** value: **500.00**
7 ❑ Apr 1937 Cover: 0.10 **NM** value: **500.00**
8 ❑ May 1937 Cover: 0.10 **NM** value: **500.00**
9 ❑ Jun 1937 Cover: 0.10 **NM** value: **500.00**
10 ❑ Jul 1937 Cover: 0.10 **NM** value: **500.00**
11 ❑ Aug 1937 Cover: 0.10 **NM** value: **400.00**
12 ❑ Sep 1937 Cover: 0.10 **NM** value: **400.00**
13 ❑ Oct 1937 Cover: 0.10 **NM** value: **400.00**
14 ❑ Nov 1937 Cover: 0.10 **NM** value: **400.00**
15 ❑ Dec 1937 Cover: 0.10 **NM** value: **400.00**
16 ❑ Jan 1938 Cover: 0.10 **NM** value: **400.00**
17 ❑ Feb 1938 Cover: 0.10 **NM** value: **400.00**
18 ❑ Mar 1938 Cover: 0.10 **NM** value: **400.00**
19 ❑ Apr 1938 Cover: 0.10 **NM** value: **400.00**
20 ❑ May 1938 Cover: 0.10 **NM** value: **400.00**
21 ❑ Jun 1938 Cover: 0.10 **NM** value: **350.00**
22 ❑ Jul 1938 Cover: 0.10 **NM** value: **350.00**
23 ❑ Aug 1938 Cover: 0.10 **NM** value: **350.00**
24 ❑ Sep 1938 Cover: 0.10 **NM** value: **350.00**
25 ❑ Oct 1938 Cover: 0.10 **NM** value: **350.00**
• **CGC:** 3 graded, best 4.5
26 ❑ Nov 1938 Cover: 0.10 **NM** value: **350.00**
27 ❑ Dec 1938 Cover: 0.10 **NM** value: **350.00**
28 ❑ Jan 1939 Cover: 0.10 **NM** value: **350.00**
29 ❑ Feb 1939 Cover: 0.10 **NM** value: **350.00**
30 ❑ Apr 1939 Cover: 0.10 **NM** value: **350.00**
31 ❑ May 1939 Cover: 0.10 **NM** value: **300.00**
32 ❑ Jun 1939 Cover: 0.10 **NM** value: **300.00**
33 ❑ Jul 1939 Cover: 0.10 **NM** value: **300.00**
34 ❑ Aug 1939 Cover: 0.10 **NM** value: **300.00**
35 ❑ Sep 1939 Cover: 0.10 **NM** value: **300.00**
36 ❑ Oct 1939 Cover: 0.10 **NM** value: **300.00**
37 ❑ Nov 1939 Cover: 0.10 **NM** value: **300.00**
38 ❑ Dec 1939 Cover: 0.10 **NM** value: **300.00**
39 ❑ Jan 1940 Cover: 0.10 **NM** value: **300.00**
40 ❑ Feb 1940 Cover: 0.10 **NM** value: **300.00**
41 ❑ Mar 1940 Cover: 0.10 **NM** value: **250.00**
42 ❑ Apr 1940 Cover: 0.10 **NM** value: **250.00**
43 ❑ May 1940 Cover: 0.10 **NM** value: **250.00**
44 ❑ Jun 1940 Cover: 0.10 **NM** value: **250.00**
45 ❑ Jul 1940 Cover: 0.10 **NM** value: **250.00**
46 ❑ Aug 1940 Cover: 0.10 **NM** value: **250.00**
47 ❑ Sep 1940 Cover: 0.10 **NM** value: **250.00**
48 ❑ Oct 1940 Cover: 0.10 **NM** value: **250.00**
49 ❑ Nov 1940 Cover: 0.10 **NM** value: **250.00**
50 ❑ Dec 1940 Cover: 0.10 **NM** value: **200.00**
51 ❑ Jan 1941 Cover: 0.10 **NM** value: **200.00**
52 ❑ Feb 1941 Cover: 0.10 **NM** value: **200.00**
53 ❑ Mar 1941 Cover: 0.10 **NM** value: **200.00**
54 ❑ Apr 1941 Cover: 0.10 **NM** value: **200.00**
55 ❑ May 1941 Cover: 0.10 **NM** value: **200.00**
56 ❑ Jun 1941 Cover: 0.10 **NM** value: **200.00**
• **CGC:** 1 graded, best 8.5
57 ❑ Jul 1941 Cover: 0.10 **NM** value: **200.00**
• **CGC:** 1 graded, best 9.4
58 ❑ Aug 1941 Cover: 0.10 **NM** value: **200.00**
• **CGC:** 1 graded, best 7.0
59 ❑ Sep 1941 Cover: 0.10 **NM** value: **200.00**
• **CGC:** 2 graded, best 9.2
60 ❑ Oct 1941 Cover: 0.10 **NM** value: **200.00**
61 ❑ Nov 1941 Cover: 0.10 **NM** value: **200.00**
• **CGC:** 1 graded, best 4.0
62 ❑ Dec 1941 Cover: 0.10 **NM** value: **200.00**
63 ❑ Mar 1942 Cover: 0.10 **NM** value: **200.00**
64 ❑ May 1942 Cover: 0.10 **NM** value: **200.00**

FUNNIES ANNUAL — Avon
1 ❑ ca. 1959 Cover: 1.00 **NM** value: **350.00**

FUNNIES ON PARADE — Eastern Color
1 ❑ ca. 1933 **NM** value: **10000.00**
• **CGC:** 2 graded, best 7.5

FUNNY ANIMALS — Charlton
1 ❑ ca. 1984 Cover: 0.60 **NM** value: **4.00**
2 ❑ ca. 1985 Cover: 0.60 **NM** value: **2.50**

FUNNYBONE — LaSalle
1 ❑ ca. 1943 Cover: 0.25 **NM** value: **200.00**

FUNNY BOOK — Parents' Magazine Institute
1 ❑ Dec 1942 Cover: 0.10 **NM** value: **100.00**
• **CGC:** 1 graded, best 8.0
2 ❑ Feb 1943 Cover: 0.10 **NM** value: **50.00**
3 ❑ Mar 1943 Cover: 0.10 **NM** value: **40.00**
4 ❑ 1943 Cover: 0.10 **NM** value: **40.00**
5 ❑ Aut 1943 Cover: 0.10 **NM** value: **40.00**
6 ❑ Cover: 0.10 **NM** value: **40.00**
7 ❑ Cover: 0.10 **NM** value: **40.00**
8 ❑ Cover: 0.10 **NM** value: **40.00**

FUNNY FABLES — Decker
1 ❑ Aug 1957 Cover: 0.10 **NM** value: **25.00**
2 ❑ ca. 1957 Cover: 0.10 **NM** value: **20.00**

The CGC numbers printed in individual listings above represent the **number of copies examined** and given a **Universal** grade by CGC and the **best such copy** graded at press time. For current populations, watch for special ***Comics Buyer's Guide*** issues or check **www.cgccomics.com.**

Other grades: Multiply prices above by **1.5 for Mint • 2/3 for Very Fine • 1/3 for Fine • 1/5 for Very Good • 1/8 for Good**

FUNNY FILMS — ACG

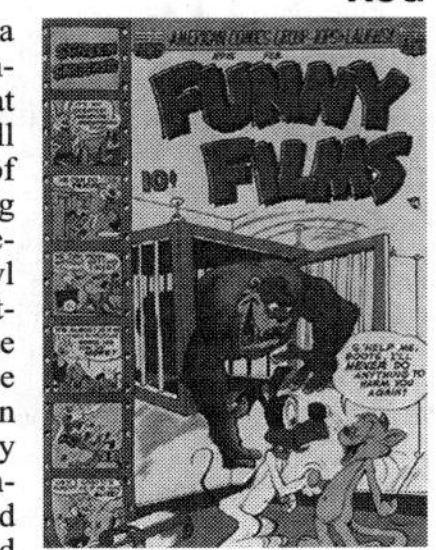
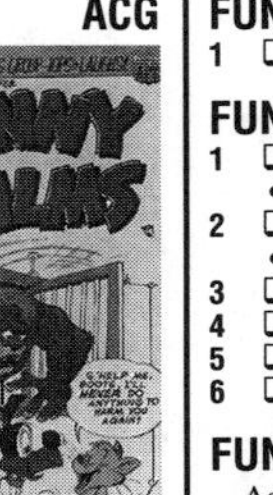

Funny Films from ACG was a late-1940s entry into the funny-animal field, already crowded by that time with classic material from Dell Comics. Characters in the pages of Funny Films included cat and dog comedy team Puss and Boots, wise-cracking rabbit Blunder Bunny, owl detective Whoo-Dunnit, and Western dog marshal Alaki Ike. The hook to Funny Films is that, because all of its characters are based on (forgotten) film cartoons, each story starts with a room full of kids watching the comics story being projected on a movie screen, and film-related elements such as "screen snapshots" are featured on the cover.

1 ❑ Sep 1949 Cover: 0.10 **NM** value: **70.00**
2 ❑ Nov 1949 Cover: 0.10 **NM** value: **40.00**
3 ❑ Jan 1950 Cover: 0.10 **NM** value: **32.00**
4 ❑ Mar 1950 Cover: 0.10 **NM** value: **32.00**
5 ❑ May 1950 Cover: 0.10 **NM** value: **32.00**
6 ❑ Jul 1950 Cover: 0.10 **NM** value: **26.00**
7 ❑ Sep 1950 Cover: 0.10 **NM** value: **26.00**
8 ❑ Nov 1950 Cover: 0.10 **NM** value: **26.00**
9 ❑ Jan 1951 Cover: 0.10 **NM** value: **26.00**
10 ❑ Mar 1951 Cover: 0.10 **NM** value: **26.00**
11 ❑ May 1951 Cover: 0.10 **NM** value: **20.00**
12 ❑ Jul 1951 Cover: 0.10 **NM** value: **20.00**
13 ❑ Sep 1951 Cover: 0.10 **NM** value: **20.00**
14 ❑ Nov 1951 Cover: 0.10 **NM** value: **20.00**
15 ❑ Jan 1952 Cover: 0.10 **NM** value: **20.00**
 Puss an' Boots; The Spotted Cat (text story); Blunderbunny; Whoo-Doodit; Haunted House (text story); Alkali Ike
16 ❑ Mar 1952 Cover: 0.10 **NM** value: **20.00**
17 ❑ May 1952 Cover: 0.10 **NM** value: **20.00**
18 ❑ Jul 1952 Cover: 0.10 **NM** value: **20.00**
19 ❑ Sep 1952 Cover: 0.10 **NM** value: **20.00**
20 ❑ Nov 1952 Cover: 0.10 **NM** value: **20.00**
21 ❑ Jan 1953 Cover: 0.10 **NM** value: **15.00**
22 ❑ Mar 1953 Cover: 0.10 **NM** value: **15.00**
23 ❑ May 1953 Cover: 0.10 **NM** value: **15.00**
24 ❑ Jul 1953 Cover: 0.10 **NM** value: **15.00**
25 ❑ Sep 1953 Cover: 0.10 **NM** value: **15.00**
26 ❑ Nov 1953 Cover: 0.10 **NM** value: **15.00**
27 ❑ Jan 1954 Cover: 0.10 **NM** value: **15.00**
28 ❑ Mar 1954 Cover: 0.10 **NM** value: **15.00**
29 ❑ May 1954 Cover: 0.10 **NM** value: **15.00**
 final issue.

FUNNY FOLKS — DC

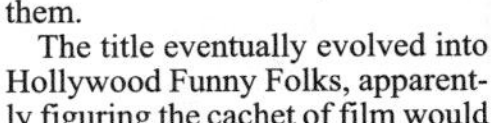
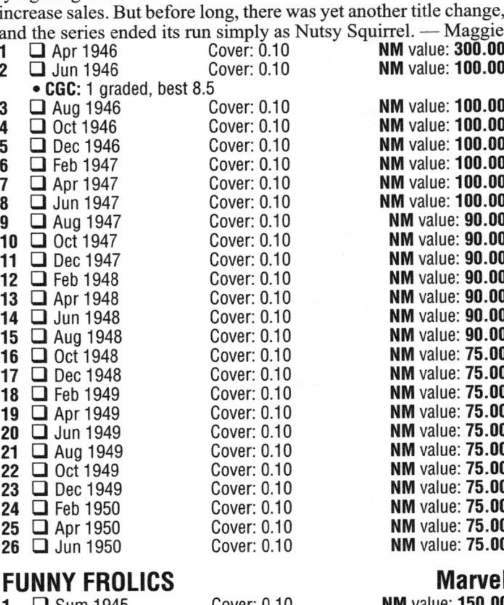

Funny Folks was a "funny animal" comic book with the primary focus of Nutsy Squirrel, introduced in the first issue and created by Rube Grossman. The zany character is chiefly distinguished by his red-and-white-striped long tie — admittedly, nutsy apparel for a squirrel. Occasionally, artists use the tie for comic effect, as in the cover for #13, in which he's preparing to eat a sandwich consisting of two pieces of bread with the tie looped between them.

The title eventually evolved into Hollywood Funny Folks, apparently figuring the cachet of film would increase sales. But before long, there was yet another title change, and the series ended its run simply as Nutsy Squirrel. — Maggie

1 ❑ Apr 1946 Cover: 0.10 **NM** value: **300.00**
2 ❑ Jun 1946 Cover: 0.10 **NM** value: **100.00**
 • **CGC:** 1 graded, best 8.5
3 ❑ Aug 1946 Cover: 0.10 **NM** value: **100.00**
4 ❑ Oct 1946 Cover: 0.10 **NM** value: **100.00**
5 ❑ Dec 1946 Cover: 0.10 **NM** value: **100.00**
6 ❑ Feb 1947 Cover: 0.10 **NM** value: **100.00**
7 ❑ Apr 1947 Cover: 0.10 **NM** value: **100.00**
8 ❑ Jun 1947 Cover: 0.10 **NM** value: **100.00**
9 ❑ Aug 1947 Cover: 0.10 **NM** value: **90.00**
10 ❑ Oct 1947 Cover: 0.10 **NM** value: **90.00**
11 ❑ Dec 1947 Cover: 0.10 **NM** value: **90.00**
12 ❑ Feb 1948 Cover: 0.10 **NM** value: **90.00**
13 ❑ Apr 1948 Cover: 0.10 **NM** value: **90.00**
14 ❑ Jun 1948 Cover: 0.10 **NM** value: **90.00**
15 ❑ Aug 1948 Cover: 0.10 **NM** value: **90.00**
16 ❑ Oct 1948 Cover: 0.10 **NM** value: **75.00**
17 ❑ Dec 1948 Cover: 0.10 **NM** value: **75.00**
18 ❑ Feb 1949 Cover: 0.10 **NM** value: **75.00**
19 ❑ Apr 1949 Cover: 0.10 **NM** value: **75.00**
20 ❑ Jun 1949 Cover: 0.10 **NM** value: **75.00**
21 ❑ Aug 1949 Cover: 0.10 **NM** value: **75.00**
22 ❑ Oct 1949 Cover: 0.10 **NM** value: **75.00**
23 ❑ Dec 1949 Cover: 0.10 **NM** value: **75.00**
24 ❑ Feb 1950 Cover: 0.10 **NM** value: **75.00**
25 ❑ Apr 1950 Cover: 0.10 **NM** value: **75.00**
26 ❑ Jun 1950 Cover: 0.10 **NM** value: **75.00**

FUNNY FROLICS — Marvel

1 ❑ Sum 1945 Cover: 0.10 **NM** value: **150.00**
2 ❑ Cover: 0.10 **NM** value: **90.00**
3 ❑ Spr 1948 Cover: 0.10 **NM** value: **60.00**
4 ❑ Cover: 0.10 **NM** value: **60.00**
5 ❑ Dec 1946 Cover: 0.10 **NM** value: **50.00**

FUNNY FUNNIES — Nedor

1 ❑ Cover: 0.10 **NM** value: **100.00**

FUNNYMAN — Magazine Enterprises

1 ❑ Jan 1948 Cover: 0.10 **NM** value: **350.00**
 • **CGC:** 2 graded, best 9.2
2 ❑ Mar 1948 Cover: 0.10 **NM** value: **200.00**
 • **CGC:** 1 graded, best 9.0
3 ❑ 1948 Cover: 0.10 **NM** value: **200.00**
4 ❑ 1948 Cover: 0.10 **NM** value: **175.00**
5 ❑ 1948 Cover: 0.10 **NM** value: **175.00**
6 ❑ 1948 Cover: 0.10 **NM** value: **175.00**

FUNNY PAGES (CENTAUR) — Centaur

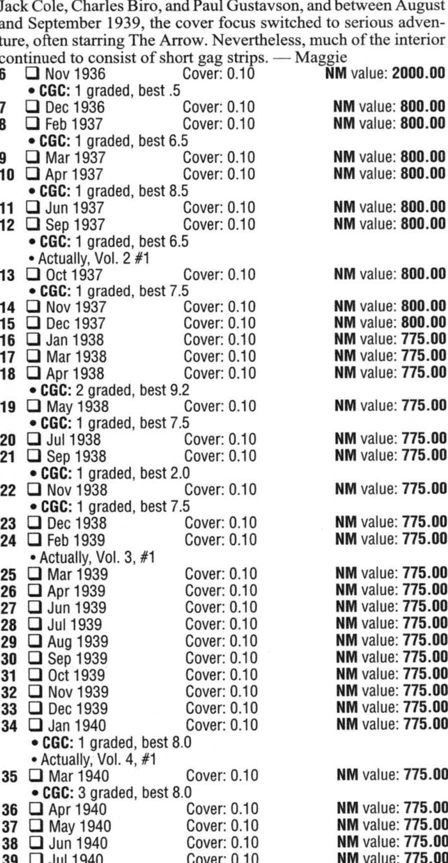

As was the case with DC's More Fun title, Centaur's Funny Pages kicked off its run with short funny animals bits, gag sequences, and the like, only to switch its emphasis later on to the adventures of costumed heroes. For some of its run in the 1930s, the cover carried the subhead "Fun for the entire family," and there was a focus on mischievous kids.

Issues #12-34 do not continue ordinal numbering; the 12th issue is the first issue of Volume 2; the 24th issue is the first of Volume 3, and the 34th issue is the start of Volume 4. With #35, continuous numbering appers on the cover.

. The series functioned as an early venue for such creators as Jack Cole, Charles Biro, and Paul Gustavson, and between August and September 1939, the cover focus switched to serious adventure, often starring The Arrow. Nevertheless, much of the interior continued to consist of short gag strips. — Maggie

6 ❑ Nov 1936 Cover: 0.10 **NM** value: **2000.00**
 • **CGC:** 1 graded, best .5
7 ❑ Dec 1936 Cover: 0.10 **NM** value: **800.00**
8 ❑ Feb 1937 Cover: 0.10 **NM** value: **800.00**
 • **CGC:** 1 graded, best 6.5
9 ❑ Mar 1937 Cover: 0.10 **NM** value: **800.00**
10 ❑ Apr 1937 Cover: 0.10 **NM** value: **800.00**
 • **CGC:** 1 graded, best 8.5
11 ❑ Jun 1937 Cover: 0.10 **NM** value: **800.00**
12 ❑ Sep 1937 Cover: 0.10 **NM** value: **800.00**
 • **CGC:** 1 graded, best 6.5
 • Actually, Vol. 2 #1
13 ❑ Oct 1937 Cover: 0.10 **NM** value: **800.00**
 • **CGC:** 1 graded, best 7.5
14 ❑ Nov 1937 Cover: 0.10 **NM** value: **800.00**
15 ❑ Dec 1937 Cover: 0.10 **NM** value: **800.00**
16 ❑ Jan 1938 Cover: 0.10 **NM** value: **775.00**
17 ❑ Mar 1938 Cover: 0.10 **NM** value: **775.00**
18 ❑ Apr 1938 Cover: 0.10 **NM** value: **775.00**
 • **CGC:** 2 graded, best 9.2
19 ❑ May 1938 Cover: 0.10 **NM** value: **775.00**
 • **CGC:** 1 graded, best 7.5
20 ❑ Jul 1938 Cover: 0.10 **NM** value: **775.00**
21 ❑ Sep 1938 Cover: 0.10 **NM** value: **775.00**
 • **CGC:** 1 graded, best 2.0
22 ❑ Nov 1938 Cover: 0.10 **NM** value: **775.00**
 • **CGC:** 1 graded, best 7.5
23 ❑ Dec 1938 Cover: 0.10 **NM** value: **775.00**
24 ❑ Feb 1939 Cover: 0.10 **NM** value: **775.00**
 • Actually, Vol. 3, #1
25 ❑ Mar 1939 Cover: 0.10 **NM** value: **775.00**
26 ❑ Apr 1939 Cover: 0.10 **NM** value: **775.00**
27 ❑ Jun 1939 Cover: 0.10 **NM** value: **775.00**
28 ❑ Jul 1939 Cover: 0.10 **NM** value: **775.00**
29 ❑ Aug 1939 Cover: 0.10 **NM** value: **775.00**
30 ❑ Sep 1939 Cover: 0.10 **NM** value: **775.00**
31 ❑ Oct 1939 Cover: 0.10 **NM** value: **775.00**
32 ❑ Nov 1939 Cover: 0.10 **NM** value: **775.00**
33 ❑ Dec 1939 Cover: 0.10 **NM** value: **775.00**
34 ❑ Jan 1940 Cover: 0.10 **NM** value: **775.00**
 • **CGC:** 1 graded, best 8.0
 • Actually, Vol. 4, #1
35 ❑ Mar 1940 Cover: 0.10 **NM** value: **775.00**
 • **CGC:** 3 graded, best 8.0
36 ❑ Apr 1940 Cover: 0.10 **NM** value: **775.00**
37 ❑ May 1940 Cover: 0.10 **NM** value: **775.00**
38 ❑ Jun 1940 Cover: 0.10 **NM** value: **775.00**
39 ❑ Jul 1940 Cover: 0.10 **NM** value: **775.00**
40 ❑ Aug 1940 Cover: 0.10 **NM** value: **775.00**
 • **CGC:** 1 graded, best 9.4
41 ❑ Sep 1940 Cover: 0.10 **NM** value: **775.00**
 • **CGC:** 1 graded, best 9.4
42 ❑ Oct 1940 Cover: 0.10 **NM** value: **775.00**
 • **CGC:** 1 graded, best 9.4

FUNNY PICTURE STORIES — Comics Magazine

1 ❑ Nov 1936 Cover: 0.10 **NM** value: **3000.00**
2 ❑ Dec 1936 Cover: 0.10 **NM** value: **1000.00**
3 ❑ Jan 1937 Cover: 0.10 **NM** value: **700.00**
4 ❑ Feb 1937 Cover: 0.10 **NM** value: **700.00**
5 ❑ Mar 1937 Cover: 0.10 **NM** value: **700.00**
6 ❑ Apr 1937 Cover: 0.10 **NM** value: **700.00**
7 ❑ Jun 1937 Cover: 0.10 **NM** value: **700.00**

FUNNY PICTURE STORIES (2ND SERIES) — Centaur

1 ❑ Sep 1937 Cover: 0.10 **NM** value: **400.00**
2 ❑ Oct 1937 Cover: 0.10 **NM** value: **400.00**
3 ❑ Nov 1937 Cover: 0.10 **NM** value: **400.00**
4 ❑ Dec 1937 Cover: 0.10 **NM** value: **400.00**
5 ❑ Jan 1938 Cover: 0.10 **NM** value: **400.00**
6 ❑ Mar 1938 Cover: 0.10 **NM** value: **400.00**
7 ❑ Apr 1938 Cover: 0.10 **NM** value: **400.00**
8 ❑ May 1938 Cover: 0.10 **NM** value: **400.00**
9 ❑ Jul 1938 Cover: 0.10 **NM** value: **400.00**
10 ❑ Sep 1938 Cover: 0.10 **NM** value: **400.00**
11 ❑ Nov 1938 Cover: 0.10 **NM** value: **400.00**

FUNNY PICTURE STORIES (3RD SERIES) — Centaur

1 ❑ Jan 1939 Cover: 0.10 **NM** value: **300.00**
2 ❑ Mar 1939 Cover: 0.10 **NM** value: **300.00**
3 ❑ May 1939 Cover: 0.10 **NM** value: **300.00**

FUNNY STUFF — DC

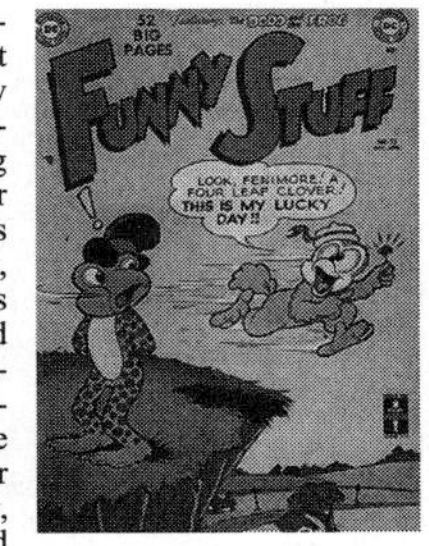

Though best known for practically every other genre of comics it published, DC did produce a few funny-animal titles aimed at beginning readers. Funny Stuff, along with The Fox and the Crow, later issues of Leading Comics, Comics Cavalcade, and Peter Porkchops, featured loony-style animal capers throughout the mid-1940s and 1950s. Funny Stuff offered a cornucopia of the animal kingdom, including the stars, The Dodo and the Frog, with backup from Blabber Mouse, J. Rufus Lion, Blackie Bear, and Bernard the Brave (a hound dog). Hard to imagine any kid passing up Uncle Scrooge or Animal Comics to grab a copy of Funny Stuff, but someone must have bought, it because it ran more than 80 issues before changing to Dodo and the Frog for the last year or so.

1 ❑ Sum 1944 Cover: 0.10 **NM** value: **550.00**
 • **CGC:** 2 graded, best 7.0
2 ❑ Fal 1944 Cover: 0.10 **NM** value: **275.00**
 • **CGC:** 1 graded, best 4.0
3 ❑ Win 1944 Cover: 0.10 **NM** value: **150.00**
4 ❑ Spr 1945 Cover: 0.10 **NM** value: **150.00**
 • **CGC:** 1 graded, best 9.4
5 ❑ Sum 1945 Cover: 0.10 **NM** value: **140.00**
6 ❑ Fal 1945 Cover: 0.10 **NM** value: **100.00**
7 ❑ Win 1945 Cover: 0.10 **NM** value: **100.00**
8 ❑ Apr 1946 Cover: 0.10 **NM** value: **100.00**
9 ❑ May 1946 Cover: 0.10 **NM** value: **100.00**
10 ❑ Jun 1946 Cover: 0.10 **NM** value: **100.00**
11 ❑ Jul 1946 Cover: 0.10 **NM** value: **80.00**
12 ❑ Aug 1946 Cover: 0.10 **NM** value: **80.00**
13 ❑ Sep 1946 Cover: 0.10 **NM** value: **80.00**
14 ❑ Oct 1946 Cover: 0.10 **NM** value: **80.00**
15 ❑ Nov 1946 Cover: 0.10 **NM** value: **80.00**
16 ❑ Dec 1946 Cover: 0.10 **NM** value: **80.00**
17 ❑ Jan 1947 Cover: 0.10 **NM** value: **80.00**
18 ❑ Feb 1947 Cover: 0.10 **NM** value: **80.00**
19 ❑ Mar 1947 Cover: 0.10 **NM** value: **80.00**
20 ❑ Apr 1947 Cover: 0.10 **NM** value: **80.00**
21 ❑ May 1947 Cover: 0.10 **NM** value: **60.00**
22 ❑ Jun 1947 Cover: 0.10 **NM** value: **100.00**
23 ❑ Jul 1947 Cover: 0.10 **NM** value: **60.00**
24 ❑ Aug 1947 Cover: 0.10 **NM** value: **60.00**
25 ❑ Sep 1947 Cover: 0.10 **NM** value: **60.00**
26 ❑ Oct 1947 Cover: 0.10 **NM** value: **60.00**
27 ❑ Nov 1947 Cover: 0.10 **NM** value: **60.00**
28 ❑ Dec 1947 Cover: 0.10 **NM** value: **60.00**
29 ❑ Jan 1948 Cover: 0.10 **NM** value: **60.00**
30 ❑ Feb 1948 Cover: 0.10 **NM** value: **60.00**
31 ❑ Mar 1948 Cover: 0.10 **NM** value: **40.00**
32 ❑ Apr 1948 Cover: 0.10 **NM** value: **40.00**
33 ❑ May 1948 Cover: 0.10 **NM** value: **40.00**
34 ❑ Jun 1948 Cover: 0.10 **NM** value: **40.00**
35 ❑ Jul 1948 Cover: 0.10 **NM** value: **40.00**
36 ❑ Aug 1948 Cover: 0.10 **NM** value: **40.00**
37 ❑ Sep 1948 Cover: 0.10 **NM** value: **40.00**
38 ❑ Oct 1948 Cover: 0.10 **NM** value: **40.00**
39 ❑ Nov 1948 Cover: 0.10 **NM** value: **40.00**
40 ❑ Dec 1948 Cover: 0.10 **NM** value: **40.00**
41 ❑ Jan 1949 Cover: 0.10 **NM** value: **32.00**
42 ❑ Feb 1949 Cover: 0.10 **NM** value: **32.00**
43 ❑ Mar 1949 Cover: 0.10 **NM** value: **32.00**
44 ❑ Apr 1949 Cover: 0.10 **NM** value: **32.00**
45 ❑ May 1949 Cover: 0.10 **NM** value: **32.00**
46 ❑ Jun 1949 Cover: 0.10 **NM** value: **32.00**
47 ❑ Jul 1949 Cover: 0.10 **NM** value: **32.00**
48 ❑ Aug 1949 Cover: 0.10 **NM** value: **32.00**
49 ❑ Sep 1949 Cover: 0.10 **NM** value: **32.00**
50 ❑ Oct 1949 Cover: 0.10 **NM** value: **32.00**
51 ❑ Nov 1949 Cover: 0.10 **NM** value: **26.00**
52 ❑ Jan 1950 Cover: 0.10 **NM** value: **26.00**
53 ❑ Mar 1950 Cover: 0.10 **NM** value: **26.00**
 Fenimore's Travel; Blabber Mouse; J. Rufus Lion; Blackie Bear; Bernard The Brave; The Foolish Owl (Text Story); The Dodo and The Frog
54 ❑ May 1950 Cover: 0.10 **NM** value: **26.00**
55 ❑ Jul 1950 Cover: 0.10 **NM** value: **26.00**
56 ❑ Sep 1950 Cover: 0.10 **NM** value: **26.00**
57 ❑ Nov 1950 Cover: 0.10 **NM** value: **26.00**
58 ❑ Jan 1951 Cover: 0.10 **NM** value: **26.00**
59 ❑ Mar 1951 Cover: 0.10 **NM** value: **26.00**
60 ❑ May 1951 Cover: 0.10 **NM** value: **20.00**
61 ❑ Jul 1951 Cover: 0.10 **NM** value: **20.00**
62 ❑ Sep 1951 Cover: 0.10 **NM** value: **20.00**
63 ❑ Nov 1951 Cover: 0.10 **NM** value: **20.00**
 • **CGC:** 1 graded, best 7.5
64 ❑ Jan 1952 Cover: 0.10 **NM** value: **20.00**
 • **CGC:** 1 graded, best 9.6
65 ❑ Mar 1952 Cover: 0.10 **NM** value: **20.00**

CGC-graded: Multiply prices above by **33 for 9.9 M • 16 for 9.8 NM/M • 7 for 9.6 NM+ • 5 for 9.4 NM • 2.5 for 9.2 NM- • 1.5 for 9.0 VF/NM**

66 ❑ May 1952 Cover: 0.10 **NM** value: **20.00**
67 ❑ Jul 1952 Cover: 0.10 **NM** value: **20.00**
68 ❑ Sep 1952 Cover: 0.10 **NM** value: **20.00**
69 ❑ Nov 1952 Cover: 0.10 **NM** value: **20.00**
70 ❑ Jan 1953 Cover: 0.10 **NM** value: **20.00**
71 ❑ Mar 1953 Cover: 0.10 **NM** value: **16.00**
72 ❑ May 1953 Cover: 0.10 **NM** value: **16.00**
73 ❑ Jul 1953 Cover: 0.10 **NM** value: **16.00**
74 ❑ Sep 1953 Cover: 0.10 **NM** value: **16.00**
75 ❑ Nov 1953 Cover: 0.10 **NM** value: **16.00**
76 ❑ Jan 1954 Cover: 0.10 **NM** value: **16.00**
77 ❑ Mar 1954 Cover: 0.10 **NM** value: **16.00**
78 ❑ May 1954 Cover: 0.10 **NM** value: **16.00**
79 ❑ Jul 1954 Cover: 0.10 **NM** value: **16.00**
final issue.

FUNNY STUFF STOCKING STUFFER — DC

1 ❑ Mar 1985 Cover: 1.25 **NM** value: **Cover or less**
📖 Christmas Comes but Once...Next Year!; See Ya Later Aviator!; Don't Toy with Me!; Here's Looking at You, Kids!; It's Beginning to Look a lot Like Groundhog's Day **A:** Jim Engel; Chuck Fiala; Mike Tiefenbacher **W:** Jim Engel; Chuck Fiala; Mike Tiefenbacher

FUNNY 3-D — Harvey

1 ❑ Dec 1953 Cover: 0.25 **NM** value: **75.00**
• **CGC:** 1 graded, best 9.0

FUNNYTIME FEATURES — Eenieweenie

1 ❑ Jul 1994, b&w Cover: 2.50 **NM** value: **Cover or less**
📖 Arachnid Kid: Our Country At War **A:** Derek Drymon **W:** Derek Drymon
1-2 ❑ b&w Cover: 2.50 **NM** value: **Cover or less**
2 ❑ ca. 1994, b&w Cover: 2.50 **NM** value: **Cover or less**
3 ❑ ca. 1994, b&w Cover: 2.50 **NM** value: **Cover or less**
4 ❑ ca. 1995, b&w Cover: 2.50 **NM** value: **Cover or less**
5 ❑ ca. 1995, b&w Cover: 2.50 **NM** value: **Cover or less**
6 ❑ ca. 1995, b&w Cover: 2.50 **NM** value: **Cover or less**
7 ❑ ca. 1995 Cover: 2.50 **NM** value: **Cover or less**
• **CGC:** 1 graded, best 9.2

FUNNY TUNES — U.S.A.

16 ❑ Sum 1944 Cover: 0.10 **NM** value: **100.00**
17 ❑ Fal 1944 Cover: 0.10 **NM** value: **85.00**
18 ❑ Win 1944 Cover: 0.10 **NM** value: **60.00**
19 ❑ Jul 1945 Cover: 0.10 **NM** value: **60.00**
20 ❑ Fal 1945 Cover: 0.10 **NM** value: **60.00**
21 ❑ Apr 1946 Cover: 0.10 **NM** value: **60.00**
22 ❑ Sum 1946 Cover: 0.10 **NM** value: **60.00**
23 ❑ Fal 1946 Cover: 0.10 **NM** value: **60.00**

FUNNY WORLD — Marbak Press

1 ❑ ca. 1947 Cover: 0.10 **NM** value: **50.00**
2 ❑ Cover: 0.10 **NM** value: **40.00**
3 ❑ Cover: 0.10 **NM** value: **40.00**

FUNTASTIC WORLD OF HANNA-BARBERA — Marvel

1 ❑ Dec 1977 Cover: 1.25 **NM** value: **13.00**
📖 Flintstone's Christmas Party
2 ❑ Mar 1978 Cover: 1.25 **NM** value: **9.00**
3 ❑ Jun 1978 Cover: 1.25 **NM** value: **6.00**

FUN TIME — Ace

1 ❑ Spr 1953 Cover: 0.25 **NM** value: **125.00**
2 ❑ Sum 1953 Cover: 0.25 **NM** value: **100.00**
3 ❑ Fal 1953 Cover: 0.25 **NM** value: **100.00**
4 ❑ Win 1953 Cover: 0.25 **NM** value: **100.00**

FUN WITH MILK & CHEESE — Slave Labor

1 ❑ Apr 1994, b&w Cover: 9.95 **NM** value: **Cover or less**
No issue number. • collects stories; has pages 59 and 62 switched
Bk 1-2❑ Oct 1994 Cover: 9.95 **NM** value: **Cover or less**
Bk 1-3❑ Nov 1995 Cover: 11.95 **NM** value: **Cover or less**
Bk 1-4❑ Aug 1994 Cover: 11.95 **NM** value: **Cover or less**

FURIES (AVATAR) — Avatar

0 ❑ Feb 1997 Cover: 3.00 **NM** value: **Cover or less**
Circ: Diamd. preorders: **2,613**
0/Nude❑ Cover: 5.00 **NM** value: **Cover or less**
Nude cover.

FURIES, THE (CARBON-BASED) — Carbon-Based

1 ❑ May 1996, b&w Cover: 2.75 **NM** value: **Cover or less**
2 ❑ Jul 1996, b&w Cover: 2.75 **NM** value: **Cover or less**
3 ❑ Sep 1996, b&w Cover: 2.75 **NM** value: **Cover or less**
4 ❑ Nov 1996, b&w Cover: 2.75 **NM** value: **Cover or less**
5 ❑ Jan 1997, b&w Cover: 2.75 **NM** value: **Cover or less**
6 ❑ Mar 1997, b&w Cover: 2.75 **NM** value: **Cover or less**

FURKINDRED, THE — Mu Press

1 ❑ Jan 1992, b&w Cover: 6.95 **NM** value: **Cover or less**
📖 Otter Madness
2 ❑ Nov 1992, b&w Cover: 7.95 **NM** value: **Cover or less**
📖 Renewal of Porpoise
Bk 1❑ Jul 1991 Cover: 14.95 **NM** value: **Cover or less**
• A Shared World

The prices seen above do not represent the highest possible prices seen in online auctions, but rather the prices we have seen these issues reliably fetch in a variety of environments (storefront retail, mail order, auction and convention).

FURRLOUGH — Antarctic

Furrlough is one of the the longest-running anthologies of anthropomorphic characters. (Anthropomorphics are animal characters with human attributes and attitudes. The genre is wide enough to range from talking cartoon mice to the decidedly adult antics of Omaha the Cat Dancer.) What distinguishes "furries" like the ones in Furrlough from the cartoons of old is the general willingness of their creators to cast the characters in complex roles and situations.

Furrlough is an military-and action-oriented anthology series with a surprising range of content. Stories like "Ninjara" star catlike Ninjas. "Viva la Revolution" is a space war story. Others, like Scotty Arsenault's "Heebas" with its mice swashbucklers, strike an almost Disney-like sword-and-sorcery note.

1 ❑ Nov 1991 Cover: 2.50 **NM** value: **3.50**
📖 Panzercorps: The Prototype; Empires: Thunderhead; Romanics: Ferae Bestiae; Stosstrupp, Part 1; Chet & Valentine; At the Mercy of Love **A:** Alex Tucker; Eric Elliot; Joe Rosales; John Riley; Lance Rund; M. Dutchman; Pete Stoller; Steve Blake; Ted Dhsppard **W:** Brian Sutton; Joe Rosales; John Riley; Noel Tominack; Ted Dhsppard; Chris Grant; Eric Gilreath
2 ❑ Feb 1992 Cover: 2.50 **NM** value: **3.00**
📖 Romanics: Res Futura; Why Desert Winds Howl; Stosstrupp, Part 2 **A:** Joe Rosales; John Riley; Ted Sheppard **W:** Joe Rosales; John Riley; Ted Sheppard
3 ❑ May 1992 Cover: 2.50 **NM** value: **3.00**
📖 Stosstrupp, Part 3; Panzercorps: Rainy Season; Why Desert Winds Howl, Part 2 **A:** Brian Sutton; John Riley; Ted Sheppard **W:** Brian Sutton; John Riley; Ted Sheppard
4 ❑ Jul 1992 Cover: 2.50 **NM** value: **2.75**
📖 Stosstrupp; Romanics: Gravia Avspicia; Doberman Thule Mk. 6 **A:** Jerry Collins; Joe Rosales; Ted Sheppard **W:** Jerry Collins; Joe Rosales; Ted Sheppard
5 ❑ Nov 1992 Cover: 2.50 **NM** value: **2.75**
📖 Final Cliche; Stosstrupp; True Enemy; Why Desert Winds Howl, Part 3 **A:** Chuck Dillon; John Riley; Mark Stanley; Pat Dolan; Ted Sheppard **W:** John Riley; Ted Sheppard; Dusty Rhoades; Genesis Cook
6 ❑ Jan 1993 Cover: 2.50 **NM** value: **2.75**
📖 Romanics: Viri Magni Momenti; Hairlift; The Last Step **A:** Charles Davies; Joe Rosales; Carol Monahan **W:** Joe Rosales; James Ernest; Todd Sutherland
7 ❑ Mar 1993 Cover: 2.50 **NM** value: **2.75**
📖 Stosstrupp, Part 6; Dog Starr, Part 1; Officer Talk, Part 1; Simple Extradition, Part 1 **A:** John Riley; Kyla Littlejohn; Pat Dolan; Ted Sheppard **W:** John Riley; Pat Dolan; Ted Sheppard; Keith Wood
8 ❑ May 1993 Cover: 2.50 **NM** value: **2.75**
📖 Germany, 1945; Dog Starr, Part 2; Simple Extradition, Part 2; Colonel Bogey; Stosstrupp, Part 7; Officer Talk, Part 2 **A:** John Riley; Kyla Littlejohn; Pat Dolan; Ted Sheppard; Mel. White **W:** John Riley; Pat Dolan; Ted Sheppard; Keith Wood; Mel. White
9 ❑ Jul 1993 Cover: 2.50 **NM** value: **2.75**
📖 Risuko, Part 1; Under Realm; Treasure Chest **A:** Fred Perry; Chris Tennaro; Pat Dolan **W:** Fred Perry; Pat Dolan; John DiGiorgio
10 ❑ Sep 1993 Cover: 2.50 **NM** value: **2.75**
📖 Walter Kitty, Part 1; Ice Cream Parlor; Star Magic; Know Your Anthropomorphics **A:** Mark Shaw; Christina Hanson; Jeff Wood; Kurt Wilcken **W:** Mark Shaw; Christina Hanson; Jeff Wood; Kurt Wilcken
11 ❑ Nov 1993 Cover: 2.75 **NM** value: **Cover or less**
📖 Stosstrupp, Part 8; Under Realm; The Walker; Desert Storm; Recoilless **A:** Fred Perry; Jim Groat; Jimmy Chin; Jordan Greywolf; Ted Sheppard; Toivo Rovainen **W:** Fred Perry; Jim Groat; Jimmy Chin; Jordan Greywolf; Ted Sheppard
12 ❑ Dec 1993 Cover: 2.75 **NM** value: **Cover or less**
📖 Walter Kitty, Part 2; Scud; Bomb Kitty; Conrad's Commandos **A:** Mark Shaw; Pat Kelley; Fred Perry; Andrew Hume; Charles Davies; Dan Seneres; Jim Groat; Scott Alston **W:** Mark Shaw; Andrew Hume; Bill Fitts; Jim Groat
13 ❑ Jan 1994 Cover: 2.75 **NM** value: **Cover or less**
📖 Watering Hole, Part 1; Bat Lancers; Game Over; Sex Kitten **A:** Pat Kelley; Fred Perry; Kurt Wilcken; Scott Alston; Stephan Peregrine; Toivo Rovainen **W:** Pat Kelley; Kurt Wilcken; Stephan Peregrine; Toivo Rovainen
14 ❑ Feb 1994 Cover: 2.75 **NM** value: **Cover or less**
📖 Watering Hole, Part 2; Walter Kitty, Part 3; The Sound & The Furry, Part 1 **A:** Mark Shaw; Pat Kelley; Cindy Crowell; Kurt Wilcken **W:** Mark Shaw; Pat Kelley; Cindy Crowell; Eric Oppen
15 ❑ Mar 1994 Cover: 2.75 **NM** value: **Cover or less**
📖 Stosstrupp, Part 9; Collars & Cuffs; Target Practice; The Sound & The Furry, Part 2 **A:** Dan Seneres; Dennis Clark; Kurt Wilcken; Ted Sheppard **W:** Bill Fitts; Ted Sheppard; Eric Oppen; Robin Lane
16 ❑ Apr 1994 Cover: 2.75 **NM** value: **Cover or less**
📖 Live by the Bulley, Die by the Blade; Watering Hole, Part 3; Coven A' My House **A:** Pat Kelley; Kurt Wilcken; Scott Brooks **W:** Pat Kelley; Randy Zimmerman; Kurt Wilcken
17 ❑ May 1994 Cover: 2.75 **NM** value: **Cover or less**
📖 Here Comes a Candle, Part 1; The Sound & The Furry, Part 3; Samurai Mice **A:** Kurt Wilcken; Mary Hanson-Roberts; Stephan Peregrine **W:** Mary Hanson-Roberts; Stephan Peregrine; Eric Oppen
18 ❑ Jun 1994 Cover: 2.75 **NM** value: **Cover or less**
📖 Stosstrupp, Part 10; Here Comes a Candle, Part 2; Girls' Night Out **A:** Dennis Clark; Jerry Collins; Mary Hanson-Roberts; Shon Howell; Ted Sheppard **W:** Mary Hanson-Roberts; Ted Sheppard; Robin Lane
19 ❑ Jul 1994 Cover: 2.75 **NM** value: **Cover or less**
📖 The Adventure; Here Comes a Candle, Part 4 **A:** Mary Hanson-Roberts; Scott Brooks **W:** Mary Hanson-Roberts; Mary Ann Lewis
20 ❑ Aug 1994 Cover: 2.75 **NM** value: **Cover or less**
📖 Jack, Part 1; Here Comes a Candle, Part 3; The Sounds & the Furry, Part 4 **A:** Kurt Wilcken; Mary Hanson-Roberts; Sonny Strait **W:** Mary Hanson-Roberts; Sonny Strait; Eric Oppen
21 ❑ Sep 1994 Cover: 2.75 **NM** value: **Cover or less**
📖 Zaibatsu Tears, Part 1; Here Comes a Candle Part 5; Mandala **A:** Richard Bartrop; Mary Hanson-Roberts; Stephan Peregrine **W:** Richard Bartrop; Mary Hanson-Roberts; Stephan Peregrine
22 ❑ Oct 1994 Cover: 2.75 **NM** value: **Cover or less**
📖 Here Comes a Candle, Part 6; Guardian Knights: The Renegar Affair, Part 1; Zaibatsu Tears, Part 2; One Rainy Night in a Foxhole **A:** Richard Bartrop; Carl Gafford; Chris Tennaro; Dean Graf; Mary Hanson-Roberts **W:** Richard Bartrop; Carl Gafford; Mary Hanson-Roberts; Tygger
23 ❑ Nov 1994 Cover: 3.50 **NM** value: **Cover or less**
• Giant-size. 📖 Here Comes a Candle, Part 7; Under Realm, Part 4; Blazin' Charlotte; Risuko, Part 2; Uni-Universe; Stosstrupp, Part 11; Legend **A:** Pat Kelley; Fred Perry; Bill Fitts; Chris Tennaro; Dean Lee Norton; Joseph Ny; Mary Hanson-Roberts; Shon Howell; Stephan Peregrine; Ted Sheppard **W:** Fred Perry; Bill Fitts; Dean Lee Norton; Mary Hanson-Roberts; Stephan Peregrine; Ted Sheppard; John DiGiorgio
24 ❑ Dec 1994 Cover: 2.75 **NM** value: **Cover or less**
📖 Zaibatsu Tears; Here Comes a Candle, Part 8; The Iron Panther, Part 1; Guardian Knights: The Renegade Affair, Part 2 **A:** Richard Bartrop; Dean Graf; Mary Hanson-Roberts; Milton Teruel **W:** Randy Zimmerman; Richard Bartrop; Mary Hanson-Roberts; Tygger
25 ❑ Jan 1995 Cover: 2.75 **NM** value: **Cover or less**
📖 Here Comes a Candle, Part 9; Bronze Fur **A:** Mark Shaw; Bill Fitts; Maggie de Alarcon; Mary Hanson-Roberts **W:** Mark Shaw; Mary Hanson-Roberts
26 ❑ Feb 1995 Cover: 2.75 **NM** value: **Cover or less**
📖 Here Comes a Candle, Part 10; Watering Hole, Part 4; The Iron Panther, Part 2 **A:** Pat Kelley; Mary Hanson-Roberts; Milton Teruel **W:** Pat Kelley; Randy Zimmerman; Mary Hanson-Roberts
27 ❑ Mar 1995 Cover: 2.75 **NM** value: **Cover or less**
📖 Here Comes a Candle, Part 11; Bronze Fur, Part 2 **A:** Mark Shaw; Jerry Collins; Mary Hanson-Roberts **W:** Mark Shaw; Mary Hanson-Roberts
28 ❑ Apr 1995 Cover: 2.75 **NM** value: **Cover or less**
📖 Here Comes a Candle, Part 12; Stellar Babe; Stosstrupp, Part 12; Risuko, Part 3 **A:** Chris Tennaro; Mary Hanson-Roberts; Phil Morrissey; Ted Sheppard **W:** Mary Hanson-Roberts; Phil Morrissey; Ted Sheppard; John DiGiorgio
29 ❑ May 1995 Cover: 2.75 **NM** value: **Cover or less**
📖 Here Comes a Candle, Part 13; Bronze Fur, Part 3 **A:** Mark Shaw; Mary Hanson-Roberts **W:** Mark Shaw; Mary Hanson-Roberts
30 ❑ Jun 1995 Cover: 2.75 **NM** value: **Cover or less**
📖 Here Comes a Candle, Part 14; Scavengers; Risuko, Part 4 **A:** Mark Moore; Chris Tennaro; Mary Hanson-Roberts **W:** Mark Moore; Mary Hanson-Roberts; John DiGiorgio
31 ❑ Jul 1995 Cover: 2.75 **NM** value: **Cover or less**
📖 Here Comes a Candle, Part 15; Bronze Fur, Part 4; The Ballad of Bill Hubbard **A:** Mark Shaw; Mary Hanson-Roberts; Scott A.H. Ruggels **W:** Mark Shaw; Mary Hanson-Roberts; Roz Gibson
32 ❑ Aug 1995 Cover: 2.75 **NM** value: **Cover or less**
📖 Here Comes a Candle, Part 16; Stinz: Bad Memories; Risuko, Part 5 **A:** Donna Barr; Chris Tennaro; Mary Hanson-Roberts **W:** Donna Barr; Mary Hanson-Roberts; John DiGiorgio
33 ❑ Sep 1995 Cover: 2.75 **NM** value: **Cover or less**
📖 Bronze Fur, Part 5; Massacre on Main Street; Here Comes a Candle, Part 17 **A:** Mark Shaw; Carl Gafford; Mary Hanson-Roberts **W:** Mark Shaw; Carl Gafford; Mary Hanson-Roberts
34 ❑ Oct 1995 Cover: 2.75 **NM** value: **Cover or less**
📖 Here Comes a Candle, Part 18; Weekend Wehrmacht; Stellar Babe; Risuko, Part 6 **A:** Chris Tennaro; Mary Hanson-Roberts; Phil Morrissey; Scott A.H.Ruggels **W:** Mary Hanson-Roberts; Phil Morrissey; John DiGiorgio; Scott A.H. Ruggels
35 ❑ Nov 1995 Cover: 3.50 **NM** value: **Cover or less**
• fourth anniversary special. 📖 Here Comes a Candle; Bronze Fur; Watering Hole, Part 5; Jeckyll & Hyde; Zaibatsu Tears: Puppet Warriors, Part 1; A Furwell to Arms, Part 1 **A:** Mark Shaw; Pat Kelley; Richard Bartrop; Chris Whalen; Kurt Wilcken; Mary Hanson-Roberts **W:** Mark Shaw; Pat Kelley; Richard Bartrop; Chris Whalen; Mary Hanson-Roberts; Eric Oppen
36 ❑ Dec 1995 Cover: 3.50 **NM** value: **Cover or less**
📖 Escape to New York, Part 1; Ultimate Weapon; A Furwell to Arms, Part 2; Uni-Universe; Stosstrupp, Part 13 **A:** Bill Fitts; Kurt Wilcken; Roz Gibson; Stephan Peregrine; Ted Sheppard **W:** Bill Fitts; Roz Gibson; Stephan Peregrine; Ted Sheppard; Eric Oppen
37 ❑ Jan 1996 Cover: 3.50 **NM** value: **Cover or less**
📖 Zaibatsu Tears: Puppet Warriors, Part 2; Stellar Babe; Chronob: Quantum Mechanic; Irene the Black; The Prize, Part 1 **A:** Richard Bartrop; Jerry Collins; Laura Pierson; Marc Manalli; Phil Morrissey **W:** Richard Bartrop; Brian Sutton; Laura Pierson; Marc Manalli; Phil Morrissey
38 ❑ Feb 1996 Cover: 3.50 **NM** value: **Cover or less**
📖 Escape to New York, Part 2; Luna; Die Panzerkinder; A Furwell to Arms **A:** Bryant Velez; Kurt Wilcken; Roz Gibson; Stephan Peregrine **W:** Bryant Velez; Roz Gibson; Stephan Peregrine; Eric Oppen
39 ❑ Mar 1996 Cover: 3.50 **NM** value: **Cover or less**
📖 The Adventures of Swimmer, Part 1; Stellar Babe; The Walker, Part 2; Uni-Universe; The Prize, Part 2; Internet Fun **A:** Ben Dunn; Chris Whalen; Jordan Greywolf; Laura Pierson; Phil Morrissey; Stephan Peregrine **W:** Ben Dunn; Chris Whalen; Jordan Greywolf; Laura Pierson; Phil Morrissey; Stephan Peregrine
40 ❑ Apr 1996 Cover: 3.50 **NM** value: **Cover or less**
📖 Escape to New York, Part 3; The Adventures of Swimmer, Part 2; Zaibatsu Tears: Puppet Warriors, Part 3; Not Too Sirius **W:** Ben Dunn; Richard Bartrop; Roz Gibson; Shon Howell
41 ❑ May 1996 Cover: 2.95 **NM** value: **Cover or less**
📖 Star Run, Part 1; Occupational Hazard; The Adventures of Swimmer, Part 3; Spring Thaw; Stellar Babe; The Idealist **A:** Ben Dunn; Jay Naylor; Bill Fitts; Chris Whalen; David Stein; Phil Morrissey; Robert Newell; Steve Fair **W:** Ben Dunn; Chris Whalen; Kjartan Arnorsson; Phil Morrissey; Diana Harlan Stein; Gordon Smuder
42 ❑ Jun 1996 Cover: 2.95 **NM** value: **Cover or less**

Other grades: Multiply prices above by **1.5 for Mint • 2/3 for Very Fine • 1/3 for Fine • 1/5 for Very Good • 1/8 for Good**

🕮 Escape to New York, Part 4; Star Run, Part 2; The Adventures of Swimmer, Part 4 **A:** Ben Dunn; Bill Fitts; Roz Gibson; Steve Fair **W:** Ben Dunn; Roz Gibson; Gordon Smuder

43 ❑ Jul 1996 Cover: 2.95 **NM** value: **Cover or less**
🕮 Fort Ord Follies; Star Run; The Adventures of Swimmer, Part 5 **A:** Ben Dunn; Scott A.H.Ruggels; Steve Fair **W:** Ben Dunn; Scott A.H.Ruggels; Gordon Smuder

44 ❑ Aug 1996 Cover: 2.95 **NM** value: **Cover or less**
🕮 Escape to New York, Part 5; Freedom, Part 1; Tex Peccary, Part 1 **A:** Malaki Keller; Roz Gibson; Brad Lesher **W:** Roz Gibson; Brad Lesher; Jeff Rogers

45 ❑ Sep 1996 Cover: 2.95 **NM** value: **Cover or less**
🕮 Star Run, Part 4; Freedom, Part 2; The Adventures of Swimmer; Cause & Effect **A:** Ben Dunn; Brian O'Connell; Malaki Keller; Stephan Peregrine; Steve Fair **W:** Ben Dunn; Stephan Peregrine; Gordon Smuder; Jeff Rogers

46 ❑ Oct 1996 Cover: 2.95 **NM** value: **Cover or less**
🕮 Freedom, Part 3; Escape to New York; The Adventures of Swimmer **A:** Ben Dunn; Malaki Keller; Roz Gibson **W:** Ben Dunn; Roz Gibson; Jeff Rogers

47 ❑ Nov 1996 Cover: 3.95 **NM** value: **Cover or less**
🕮 Ninjara, Part 1; The Adventures of Swimmer; Rig; Irene the Black; Stosstrupp, Part 14; Danger Bunnies, Part 1; Internet Fun II; Catty Town **A:** Ben Dunn; Chris Allan; Chris Whalen; Cindy Crowell; Elin Winkler; Jerry Collins; Shon Howell; Steve Fair; Ted Sheppard **W:** Ben Dunn; Brian Sutton; Chris Whalen; Cindy Crowell; Elin Winkler; Shon Howell; Ted Sheppard; Dean Clarrain; Gordon Smuder

48 ❑ Dec 1996 Cover: 2.95 **NM** value: **Cover or less**
🕮 Ninjara, Part 2; Heebas, Part 1; Viva La Revolution **A:** Phil Morrissey; Scott Arsenault **W:** Scott Arsenault; Craig Sheeley

49 ❑ Jan 1997 Cover: 2.95 **NM** value: **Cover or less**
🕮 Star Run, Part 6; Tiger Orange, Part 1; Irene the Black; Field Tripping **A:** Darin Brown; Jerry Collins; Kenichi Lowe; Canopy Productions **W:** Brian Sutton; Darin Brown; Kurt Wilcken; Canopy Productions

50 ❑ Feb 1997 Cover: 3.95 **NM** value: **Cover or less**
Circ: Diamd. preorders: **1,862**
• Giant-size. 🕮 Tobias Wah: Vampyre Hunter, Part 1; Distractions; Loverboy; Stosstrupp, Part 15; Heebas, Part 2; Danger Bunnies, Part 2 **A:** Chris Whalen; Joe Rosales; Kevin Muranaka; Scott Arsenault; Shon Howell; Ted Sheppard **C:** Stan Sakai **W:** Chris Whalen; Joe Rosales; Kevin Muranaka; Scott Arsenault; Shon Howell; Ted Sheppard

51 ❑ Mar 1997 Cover: 2.95 **NM** value: **Cover or less**
🕮 Star Run, Part 7; The Pranksters; Tiger Orange, Part 2; Danger Bunnies, Part 3 **A:** Kenichi Lowe; Louis Frank; Scott A.H.Ruggels **W:** Kurt Wilcken; Scott A.H.Ruggels; Clarke Stone; Gordon Smuder

52 ❑ Apr 1997 Cover: 2.95 **NM** value: **Cover or less**
53 ❑ May 1997 Cover: 2.95 **NM** value: **Cover or less**
54 ❑ Jun 1997 Cover: 2.95 **NM** value: **Cover or less**
55 ❑ Jul 1997 Cover: 2.95 **NM** value: **Cover or less**
56 ❑ Aug 1997 Cover: 2.95 **NM** value: **Cover or less**
57 ❑ Sep 1997 Cover: 2.95 **NM** value: **Cover or less**
58 ❑ Oct 1997 Cover: 2.95 **NM** value: **Cover or less**
59 ❑ Nov 1997 Cover: 2.95 **NM** value: **Cover or less**
60 ❑ Dec 1997 Cover: 2.95 **NM** value: **Cover or less**
61 ❑ Jan 1998 Cover: 2.95 **NM** value: **Cover or less**
62 ❑ Feb 1998 Cover: 2.95 **NM** value: **Cover or less**
63 ❑ Mar 1998 Cover: 2.95 **NM** value: **Cover or less**
64 ❑ Apr 1998 Cover: 2.95 **NM** value: **Cover or less**
65 ❑ May 1998 Cover: 2.95 **NM** value: **Cover or less**
66 ❑ Jun 1998 Cover: 2.95 **NM** value: **Cover or less**
67 ❑ Jul 1998 Cover: 2.95 **NM** value: **Cover or less**
68 ❑ Aug 1998 Cover: 2.95 **NM** value: **Cover or less**
69 ❑ Sep 1998 Cover: 2.95 **NM** value: **Cover or less**
70 ❑ Oct 1998 Cover: 2.95 **NM** value: **Cover or less**
71 ❑ Nov 1998 Cover: 2.95 **NM** value: **Cover or less**
72 ❑ Dec 1998 Cover: 2.95 **NM** value: **Cover or less**
Circ: Diamd. preorders: **1,776**
73 ❑ Jan 1999 Cover: 2.95 **NM** value: **Cover or less**
Circ: Diamd. preorders: **1,796**
79 ❑ Jul 1999 Cover: 2.95 **NM** value: **Cover or less**
Circ: Diamd. preorders: **1,724**
80 ❑ Aug 1999 Cover: 2.95 **NM** value: **Cover or less**
Circ: Diamd. preorders: **1,805**
81 ❑ Sep 1999 Cover: 2.95 **NM** value: **Cover or less**
82 ❑ Oct 1999 Cover: 2.95 **NM** value: **Cover or less**
83 ❑ Nov 1999 Cover: 2.95 **NM** value: **Cover or less**
84 ❑ Dec 1999 Cover: 2.95 **NM** value: **Cover or less**
85 ❑ Jan 2000 Cover: 2.95 **NM** value: **Cover or less**
Circ: Diamd. preorders: **1,840**
86 ❑ Feb 2000 Cover: 2.95 **NM** value: **Cover or less**
Circ: Diamd. preorders: **1,753**
87 ❑ Mar 2000 Cover: 2.95 **NM** value: **Cover or less**
88 ❑ Apr 2000 Cover: 2.95 **NM** value: **Cover or less**
89 ❑ May 2000 Cover: 2.95 **NM** value: **Cover or less**
Circ: Diamd. preorders: **1,773**
90 ❑ Jun 2000 Cover: 2.95 **NM** value: **Cover or less**
91 ❑ Jul 2000 Cover: 2.95 **NM** value: **Cover or less**
92 ❑ Aug 2000 Cover: 2.95 **NM** value: **Cover or less**
93 ❑ Sep 2000 Cover: 2.95 **NM** value: **Cover or less**
94 ❑ Oct 2000 Cover: 2.95 **NM** value: **Cover or less**
Circ: Diamd. preorders: **1,804**
95 ❑ Nov 2000 Cover: 2.95 **NM** value: **Cover or less**
Circ: Diamd. preorders: **1,816**
96 ❑ Dec 2000 Cover: 2.95 **NM** value: **Cover or less**
Circ: Diamd. preorders: **1,829**
97 ❑ Jan 2001 Cover: 2.95 **NM** value: **Cover or less**
Circ: Diamd. preorders: **1,763**
98 ❑ Feb 2001 Cover: 2.95 **NM** value: **Cover or less**
Circ: Diamd. preorders: **1,788**
99 ❑ Mar 2001 Cover: 2.95 **NM** value: **Cover or less**
Circ: Diamd. preorders: **1,729**
100 ❑ Apr 2001 Cover: 2.95 **NM** value: **Cover or less**
Circ: Diamd. preorders: **2,061**
101 ❑ May 2001 Cover: 2.95 **NM** value: **Cover or less**
Circ: Diamd. preorders: **1,759**
102 ❑ Jun 2001 Cover: 2.95 **NM** value: **Cover or less**
Circ: Diamd. preorders: **1,836**
103 ❑ Jul 2001 Cover: 2.99 **NM** value: **Cover or less**
Circ: Diamd. preorders: **1,862**

FURTHER ADVENTURES OF CYCLOPS AND PHOENIX, THE — Marvel

1 ❑ Jun 1996 Cover: 1.95 **NM** value: **Cover or less**
🕮 Digging Up the Past **A:** John Paul Leon **W:** Peter Milligan ★ Origin of Mr. Sinister.
2 ❑ Jul 1996 Cover: 1.95 **NM** value: **Cover or less**
3 ❑ Aug 1996 Cover: 1.95 **NM** value: **Cover or less**
4 ❑ Sep 1996 Cover: 1.95 **NM** value: **Cover or less**
Bk 1 ❑ Cover: 14.99 **NM** value: **Cover or less**

FURTHER ADVENTURES OF INDIANA JONES, THE — Marvel

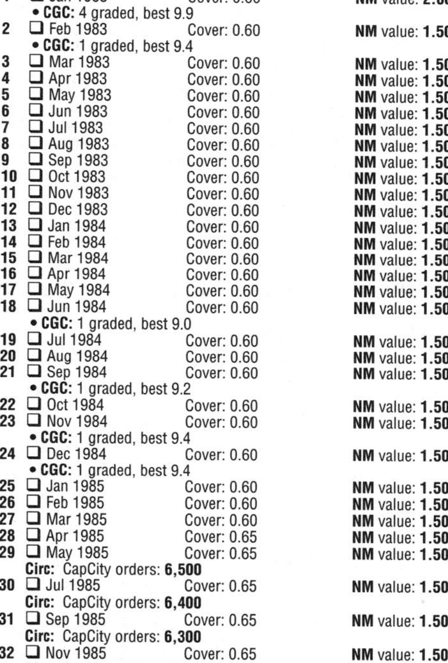

Less successful than Marvel's adaptation of Lucasfilm's Star Wars series, The Further Adventures of Indiana Jones nonetheless captures the spirit of Raiders of the Lost Ark's swashbuckling archaeologist hero.

The key is in the story structure, and in launching the series, John Byrne creates a good model for later creators to follow. Most stories in the series are two-parters, giving an introduction to the latest maguffin to be tracked down and then the action, separated by a cliffhanger.

Several characters from Raiders appear in adventures here, including Captain Katanga and Jock, the biplane pilot. — JJM

1 ❑ Jan 1983 Cover: 0.60 **NM** value: **2.00**
• **CGC:** 4 graded, best 9.9
2 ❑ Feb 1983 Cover: 0.60 **NM** value: **1.50**
• **CGC:** 1 graded, best 9.4
3 ❑ Mar 1983 Cover: 0.60 **NM** value: **1.50**
4 ❑ Apr 1983 Cover: 0.60 **NM** value: **1.50**
5 ❑ May 1983 Cover: 0.60 **NM** value: **1.50**
6 ❑ Jun 1983 Cover: 0.60 **NM** value: **1.50**
7 ❑ Jul 1983 Cover: 0.60 **NM** value: **1.50**
8 ❑ Aug 1983 Cover: 0.60 **NM** value: **1.50**
9 ❑ Sep 1983 Cover: 0.60 **NM** value: **1.50**
10 ❑ Oct 1983 Cover: 0.60 **NM** value: **1.50**
11 ❑ Nov 1983 Cover: 0.60 **NM** value: **1.50**
12 ❑ Dec 1983 Cover: 0.60 **NM** value: **1.50**
13 ❑ Jan 1984 Cover: 0.60 **NM** value: **1.50**
14 ❑ Feb 1984 Cover: 0.60 **NM** value: **1.50**
15 ❑ Mar 1984 Cover: 0.60 **NM** value: **1.50**
16 ❑ Apr 1984 Cover: 0.60 **NM** value: **1.50**
17 ❑ May 1984 Cover: 0.60 **NM** value: **1.50**
18 ❑ Jun 1984 Cover: 0.60 **NM** value: **1.50**
• **CGC:** 1 graded, best 9.0
19 ❑ Jul 1984 Cover: 0.60 **NM** value: **1.50**
20 ❑ Aug 1984 Cover: 0.60 **NM** value: **1.50**
21 ❑ Sep 1984 Cover: 0.60 **NM** value: **1.50**
• **CGC:** 1 graded, best 9.2
22 ❑ Oct 1984 Cover: 0.60 **NM** value: **1.50**
23 ❑ Nov 1984 Cover: 0.60 **NM** value: **1.50**
• **CGC:** 1 graded, best 9.4
24 ❑ Dec 1984 Cover: 0.60 **NM** value: **1.50**
• **CGC:** 1 graded, best 9.4
25 ❑ Jan 1985 Cover: 0.60 **NM** value: **1.50**
26 ❑ Feb 1985 Cover: 0.60 **NM** value: **1.50**
27 ❑ Mar 1985 Cover: 0.60 **NM** value: **1.50**
28 ❑ Apr 1985 Cover: 0.65 **NM** value: **1.50**
29 ❑ May 1985 Cover: 0.65 **NM** value: **1.50**
Circ: CapCity orders: **6,500**
30 ❑ Jul 1985 Cover: 0.65 **NM** value: **1.50**
Circ: CapCity orders: **6,400**
31 ❑ Sep 1985 Cover: 0.65 **NM** value: **1.50**
Circ: CapCity orders: **6,300**
32 ❑ Nov 1985 Cover: 0.65 **NM** value: **1.50**
Circ: CapCity orders: **6,100**
33 ❑ Jan 1986 Cover: 0.65 **NM** value: **1.50**
Circ: CapCity orders: **5,500**
34 ❑ Mar 1986 Cover: 0.75 **NM** value: **1.50**
Circ: CapCity orders: **5,300**
final issue.

FURTHER ADVENTURES OF NYOKA THE JUNGLE GIRL, THE — AC

1 ❑ Cover: 1.95 **NM** value: **2.25**
🕮 The Many Perils of Nyoka; The Serpent Strikes!; Tahiti Belle **A:** Mark Heike; Bill Black **W:** Bill Black
2 ❑ Cover: 1.95 **NM** value: **2.25**
Photo cover.
3 ❑ b&w Cover: 2.25 **NM** value: **Cover or less**
Photo cover. 🕮 The Skull Squad!; Jungle Jousts of Death; The Symbol of Danger!; The Ivory Pirates **A:** Bill Lux **W:** Bill Black
4 ❑ b&w Cover: 2.25 **NM** value: **Cover or less**
5 ❑ Cover: 2.50 **NM** value: **Cover or less**

FURTHER ADVENTURES OF YOUNG JEFFY DAHMER, THE — Boneyard

All issues are adults only.

1 ❑ b&w Cover: 2.75 **NM** value: **4.00**

FURTHER FATTENING ADVENTURES OF PUDGE, GIRL BLIMP, THE — Star*Reach

1 ❑ **NM** value: **3.00**
• Comic size.
1/A ❑ **NM** value: **3.00**
• large size.
2 ❑ Cover: 3.00 **NM** value: **Cover or less**
• Comic size.
3 ❑ Cover: 3.00 **NM** value: **Cover or less**
• Comic size.

FURY (1ST SERIES) — Marvel

1 ❑ May 1994 Cover: 2.95 **NM** value: **3.00**
Circ: CapCity orders: **21,300**

FURY (2ND SERIES) — Marvel / MAX

1 ❑ Cover: 2.99 **NM** value: **Cover or less**
Circ: Diamd. preorders: **56,308** • **CGC:** 12 graded, best 9.9
2 ❑ Cover: 2.99 **NM** value: **Cover or less**
Circ: Diamd. preorders: **44,578** • **CGC:** 2 graded, best 9.8
3 ❑ Cover: 2.99 **NM** value: **Cover or less**
Circ: Diamd. preorders: **45,051**
4 ❑ Cover: 2.99 **NM** value: **Cover or less**
Circ: Diamd. preorders: **42,884**
5 ❑ Cover: 2.99 **NM** value: **Cover or less**
Circ: Diamd. preorders: **40,386**
6 ❑ Cover: 2.99 **NM** value: **Cover or less**
Circ: Diamd. preorders: **38,494**

FURY/AGENT 13 — Marvel

1 ❑ Jun 1998 Cover: 2.99 **NM** value: **Cover or less**
Circ: Diamd. preorders: **24,549**
• gatefold summary. 🕮 ...And Destroy! **A:** Ramon Bernado **W:** Terry Kavanagh ★ Appearance of Howling Commandos.
2 ❑ Jul 1998 Cover: 2.99 **NM** value: **Cover or less**
Circ: Diamd. preorders: **20,869**
• gatefold summary. • Fury returns to Marvel universe

FURY/BLACK WIDOW: DEATH DUTY — Marvel

1 ❑ Feb 1995 Cover: 5.95 **NM** value: **Cover or less**
• prestige format.

FURY OF FIRESTORM, THE — DC

The moral of Firestorm seems to be to "watch out who you get into nuclear accidents with!" Physicist Martin Stein and high school basketball star Ronnie Raymond were caught in one, and they merged into one being, becoming Firestorm, the nuclear man.

Strange as the premise sounds, the split personality hero worked quite well as a character. Out of costume, the two alter-egos managed to bridge a generation gap and become friends. Super-villains had a tough time defeating a hero who was a team in and of itself, and they often went to great (and imaginative!) lengths in the attempt.

While Raymond provided the brawn, Stein provided the brain, advising Ron on how best to use his powers of transmutation to fight crime and save lives.

1 ❑ Jun 1982 Cover: 0.60 **NM** value: **2.50**
• **CGC:** 2 graded, best 9.8
🕮 Day of the Bison **A:** Pat Broderick **W:** Gerry Conway ★ Origin of Firestorm. ★ 1st Appearance of Lorraine Reilly, Black Bison.
2 ❑ Jul 1982 Cover: 0.60 **NM** value: **1.75**
3 ❑ Aug 1982 Cover: 0.60 **NM** value: **1.75**
🕮 A Cold Time in the Old Town Tonight ... **A:** Pat Broderick **W:** Gerry Conway ★ Appearance of Killer Frost.
4 ❑ Sep 1982 Cover: 0.60 **NM** value: **1.75**
🕮 The Icy Heart of Killer Frost! **A:** Pat Broderick **W:** Gerry Conway ★ Appearance of Justice League of America, Killer Frost.
5 ❑ Oct 1982 Cover: 0.60 **NM** value: **1.75**
🕮 The Pied Piper's Pipes of Peril **A:** Pat Broderick **W:** Gerry Conway ★ Appearance of Pied Piper.
6 ❑ Nov 1982 Cover: 0.60 **NM** value: **1.50**
🕮 The Pandrakos Plot • Master of the Universe preview insert **A:** Pat Broderick; Rodin Rodriguez **W:** Gerry Conway
7 ❑ Dec 1982 Cover: 0.60 **NM** value: **1.50**
🕮 Plastique is Another Word for Fear! **A:** Pat Broderick **W:** Gerry Conway ★ 1st Appearance of Plastique.
8 ❑ Jan 1983 Cover: 0.60 **NM** value: **1.50**
🕮 Typhoon Warning **A:** Jerome Moore **W:** Gerry Conway ★ Appearance of Typhoon.
9 ❑ Feb 1983 Cover: 0.60 **NM** value: **1.50**
🕮 Baby, the Rain Must Fall! **A:** Jerome Moore **W:** Gerry Conway ★ Appearance of Typhoon.
10 ❑ Mar 1983 Cover: 0.60 **NM** value: **1.50**
🕮 Prowl **A:** Pat Broderick **W:** Gerry Conway ★ Appearance of Hyena.
11 ❑ Apr 1983 Cover: 0.60 **NM** value: **1.25**
🕮 Waking Darkness **A:** Pat Broderick; Rodin Rodriguez **W:** Gerry Conway
12 ❑ May 1983 Cover: 0.60 **NM** value: **1.25**
🕮 Howl **A:** Pat Broderick; Rodin Rodriguez **W:** Gerry Conway
13 ❑ Jun 1983 Cover: 0.60 **NM** value: **1.25**
🕮 Split! **A:** Pat Broderick; Rodin Rodriguez **W:** Gerry Conway
14 ❑ Jul 1983 Cover: 0.60 **NM** value: **1.25**
🕮 Enforcer **A:** Pat Broderick; Rodin Rodriguez **W:** Gerry Conway ★ 1st Appearance of Mica (Enforcer II), Enforcer I (Leroy Merkyn).
15 ❑ Aug 1983 Cover: 0.60 **NM** value: **1.25**
🕮 Breakout **A:** Pat Broderick; Rodin Rodriguez **W:** Gerry Conway ★ Appearance of Multiplex.
16 ❑ Sep 1983 Cover: 0.60 **NM** value: **1.25**
🕮 Blackout! **A:** Pat Broderick; Rodin Rodriguez **W:** Gerry Conway
17 ❑ Oct 1983 Cover: 0.60 **NM** value: **1.25**
🕮 On Wings of Fire **A:** Pat Broderick; George Tuska; Rodin Rodriguez **W:** Gerry Conway ★ 1st Appearance of Firehawk.

CGC-graded: Multiply prices above by **33 for 9.9 M • 16 for 9.8 NM/M • 7 for 9.6 NM+ • 5 for 9.4 NM • 2.5 for 9.2 NM- • 1.5 for 9.0 VF/NM**

18 ❑ Nov 1983 Cover: 0.60 **NM** value: **1.25**
Squeeze Play **A:** George Tuska; Rodin Rodriguez **W:** Gerry Conway ★ 1st Appearance of Enforcer II (Mica).

19 ❑ Jan 1984 Cover: 0.75 **NM** value: **1.25**
Golden Boy! **A:** Gene Colan **W:** Gerry Conway ★ Versus Goldenrod.

20 ❑ Feb 1984 Cover: 0.75 **NM** value: **1.25**
Frostbite! **A:** Rafael Kayanan; Rodin Rodriguez **W:** Gerry Conway ★ 1st Appearance of Louise Lincoln. ★ Appearance of Firehawk. ★ Versus Killer Frost.

21 ❑ Mar 1984 Cover: 0.75 **NM** value: **1.00**
22 ❑ Apr 1984 Cover: 0.75 **NM** value: **1.00**
The Secret Origin of Firestorm **A:** Pat Broderick **W:** Gerry Conway ★ Origin of Firestorm.

23 ❑ May 1984 Cover: 0.75 **NM** value: **1.00**
24 ❑ Jun 1984 Cover: 0.75 **NM** value: **1.00**
25 ❑ Jul 1984 Cover: 0.75 **NM** value: **1.00**
26 ❑ Aug 1984 Cover: 0.75 **NM** value: **1.00**
27 ❑ Sep 1984 Cover: 0.75 **NM** value: **1.00**
28 ❑ Oct 1984 Cover: 0.75 **NM** value: **1.00**
29 ❑ Nov 1984 Cover: 0.75 **NM** value: **1.00**
30 ❑ Dec 1984 Cover: 0.75 **NM** value: **1.00**
31 ❑ Jan 1985 Cover: 0.75 **NM** value: **1.00**
32 ❑ Feb 1985 Cover: 0.75 **NM** value: **1.00**
33 ❑ Mar 1985 Cover: 0.75 **NM** value: **1.00**
34 ❑ Apr 1985 Cover: 0.75 **NM** value: **1.00**
35 ❑ May 1985 Cover: 0.75 **NM** value: **1.00**
Circ: CapCity orders: **7,200**

36 ❑ Jun 1985 Cover: 0.75 **NM** value: **1.00**
Circ: CapCity orders: **7,150**

37 ❑ Jul 1985 Cover: 0.75 **NM** value: **1.00**
Circ: CapCity orders: **7,100**

38 ❑ Aug 1985 Cover: 0.75 **NM** value: **1.00**
Circ: CapCity orders: **7,000**

39 ❑ Sep 1985 Cover: 0.75 **NM** value: **1.00**
Circ: CapCity orders: **7,250**

40 ❑ Oct 1985 Cover: 0.75 **NM** value: **1.00**
Circ: CapCity orders: **7,200**

41 ❑ Nov 1985 Cover: 0.75 **NM** value: **1.00**
Circ: CapCity orders: **10,400**
Crisis On Infinite Earths • Crisis

42 ❑ Dec 1985 Cover: 0.75 **NM** value: **1.00**
Circ: CapCity orders: **10,450**
Crisis On Infinite Earths • Crisis

43 ❑ Jan 1986 Cover: 0.75 **NM** value: **1.00**
Circ: CapCity orders: **6,900**

44 ❑ Feb 1986 Cover: 0.75 **NM** value: **1.00**
Circ: CapCity orders: **7,600**

45 ❑ Mar 1986 Cover: 0.75 **NM** value: **1.00**
Circ: CapCity orders: **7,650**

46 ❑ Apr 1986 Cover: 0.75 **NM** value: **1.00**
Circ: CapCity orders: **7,950**

47 ❑ May 1986 Cover: 0.75 **NM** value: **1.00**
Circ: CapCity orders: **7,650**

48 ❑ Jun 1986 Cover: 0.75 **NM** value: **1.00**
Circ: CapCity orders: **7,500**

49 ❑ Jul 1986 Cover: 0.75 **NM** value: **1.00**
Circ: CapCity orders: **7,550**

50 ❑ Aug 1986 Cover: 1.25 **NM** value: **Cover or less**
Circ: CapCity orders: **8,000**

51 ❑ Sep 1986 Cover: 0.75 **NM** value: **1.00**
Circ: CapCity orders: **7,900**

52 ❑ Oct 1986 Cover: 0.75 **NM** value: **1.00**
Circ: CapCity orders: **8,150**

53 ❑ Nov 1986 Cover: 0.75 **NM** value: **1.00**
Circ: CapCity orders: **8,300**

54 ❑ Dec 1986 Cover: 0.75 **NM** value: **1.00**
Circ: CapCity orders: **8,250**

55 ❑ Jan 1987 Cover: 0.75 **NM** value: **1.00**
Circ: CapCity orders: **12,950**
• Legends ★ Appearance of Cosmic Boy. ★ Versus Brimstone. ★ Versus Brimstone.

56 ❑ Feb 1987 Cover: 0.75 **NM** value: **1.00**
Circ: CapCity orders: **13,350**
• Legends ★ Appearance of Hawk.

57 ❑ Mar 1987 Cover: 0.75 **NM** value: **1.00**
Circ: CapCity orders: **7,450**

58 ❑ Apr 1987 Cover: 0.75 **NM** value: **1.00**
Circ: CapCity orders: **9,550**

59 ❑ May 1987 Cover: 0.75 **NM** value: **1.00**
Circ: CapCity orders: **8,450**

60 ❑ Jun 1987 Cover: 0.75 **NM** value: **1.00**
Circ: CapCity orders: **8,100**

61 ❑ Jul 1987 Cover: 0.75 **NM** value: **1.00**
Circ: CapCity orders: **8,150** • **CGC:** 4 graded, best 9.8
regular cover. ★ Versus Typhoon.

61/A ❑ Jul 1987 Cover: 0.75 **NM** value: **4.00**
• **CGC:** 22 graded, best 9.8
Alternate cover (test cover). ★ Versus Typhoon.

62 ❑ Aug 1987 Cover: 0.75 **NM** value: **1.00**
Circ: CapCity orders: **9,000**

63 ❑ Sep 1987 Cover: 0.75 **NM** value: **1.00**
Circ: CapCity orders: **10,550**

64 ❑ Oct 1987 Cover: 0.75 **NM** value: **1.00**
Circ: CapCity orders: **10,150**
final issue. • series continues as Firestorm, the Nuclear Man ★ Appearance of Suicide Squad.

Anl 1 ❑ ca. 1983 Cover: 1.25 **NM** value: **2.00**
All the Answers ... **A:** Rafael Kayanan; Rodin Rodriguez **W:** Gerry Conway

Anl 2 ❑ ca. 1984 Cover: 1.25 **NM** value: **1.50**
• text story

Anl 3 ❑ ca. 1985 Cover: 1.25 **NM** value: **1.50**
Circ: CapCity orders: **7,650**

Anl 4 ❑ ca. 1986 Cover: 1.25 **NM** value: **1.50**
Circ: CapCity orders: **8,350**

FURY OF HELLINA — Lightning

1 ❑ Jan 1995, b&w Cover: 2.75 **NM** value: **Cover or less**
Circ: CapCity orders: **4,005**

FURY OF S.H.I.E.L.D. — Marvel

1 ❑ Apr 1995 Cover: 2.50 **NM** value: **3.00**
Circ: CapCity orders: **15,550**
chromium cover. Hell Hath No Fury, Part 1 **A:** Corky C. Lehmkuhl **W:** Howard Chaykin

2 ❑ May 1995 Cover: 1.95 **NM** value: **2.00**
Circ: CapCity orders: **9,775**
Hell Hath No Fury, Part 2 **A:** Corky C. Lehmkuhl **W:** Howard Chaykin ★ Appearance of Iron Man.

3 ❑ Jun 1995 Cover: 1.95 **NM** value: **2.00**
Circ: CapCity orders: **8,275**
Hell Hath No Fury, Part 3 **A:** Corky C. Lehmkuhl **W:** Howard Chaykin ★ Appearance of Iron Man.

4 ❑ Jul 1995 Cover: 2.50 **NM** value: **Cover or less**
Circ: CapCity orders: **8,100**
Hell Hath No Fury, Part 4 • polybagged with decoder **A:** Corky C. Lehmkuhl **W:** Howard Chaykin

FUSION — Eclipse

1 ❑ Jan 1987, b&w Cover: 2.00 **NM** value: **Cover or less**
2 ❑ Mar 1987, b&w Cover: 2.00 **NM** value: **Cover or less**
3 ❑ May 1987, b&w Cover: 2.00 **NM** value: **Cover or less**
The Soulstar Commission Part 3 **A:** Lela Dowling; Steve Gallacci **W:** Steven Barnes

4 ❑ Jul 1987, b&w Cover: 2.00 **NM** value: **Cover or less**
5 ❑ Sep 1987, b&w Cover: 2.00 **NM** value: **Cover or less**
6 ❑ Nov 1987, b&w Cover: 2.00 **NM** value: **Cover or less**
7 ❑ Jan 1988, b&w Cover: 2.00 **NM** value: **Cover or less**
8 ❑ Mar 1988, b&w Cover: 2.00 **NM** value: **Cover or less**
9 ❑ May 1988, b&w Cover: 2.00 **NM** value: **Cover or less**
10 ❑ Jul 1988, b&w Cover: 2.00 **NM** value: **Cover or less**
11 ❑ Sep 1988, b&w Cover: 2.00 **NM** value: **Cover or less**
12 ❑ Nov 1988, b&w Cover: 2.00 **NM** value: **Cover or less**
13 ❑ Jan 1989, b&w Cover: 2.00 **NM** value: **Cover or less**
14 ❑ Mar 1989, b&w Cover: 2.00 **NM** value: **Cover or less**
15 ❑ May 1989, b&w Cover: 2.00 **NM** value: **Cover or less**
The Nestling Part 2 **A:** Lela Dowling; Judy Meadows; Larry Dixon; Steve Gallacci **W:** Axel Shaikman; Christy Marx

16 ❑ Jul 1989, b&w Cover: 2.00 **NM** value: **Cover or less**
Trouble with Babies

17 ❑ Sep 1989, b&w Cover: 2.00 **NM** value: **Cover or less**

FUTABA-KUN CHANGE — Ironcat

1 ❑ Cover: 2.95 **NM** value: **Cover or less**
Circ: Diamd. preorders: **2,442**

2 ❑ Cover: 2.95 **NM** value: **Cover or less**
3 ❑ Cover: 2.95 **NM** value: **Cover or less**
Circ: Diamd. preorders: **1,929**

FUTABA-KUN CHANGE (VOL. 3) — Ironcat

1 ❑ Jul 1999 Cover: 2.95 **NM** value: **Cover or less**
Circ: Diamd. preorders: **2,546**
Futaba-Kun Fights to Win

2 ❑ Cover: 2.95 **NM** value: **Cover or less**
Circ: Diamd. preorders: **2,501**

3 ❑ Cover: 2.95 **NM** value: **Cover or less**
Circ: Diamd. preorders: **2,404**

4 ❑ Cover: 2.95 **NM** value: **Cover or less**
Circ: Diamd. preorders: **2,462**

FUTURAMA — Slave Labor

1 ❑ Apr 1989, b&w Cover: 1.75 **NM** value: **2.00**
2 ❑ Jun 1989, b&w Cover: 1.75 **NM** value: **2.00**
3 ❑ Aug 1989, b&w Cover: 1.75 **NM** value: **2.00**

FUTURAMA (BONGO) — Bongo

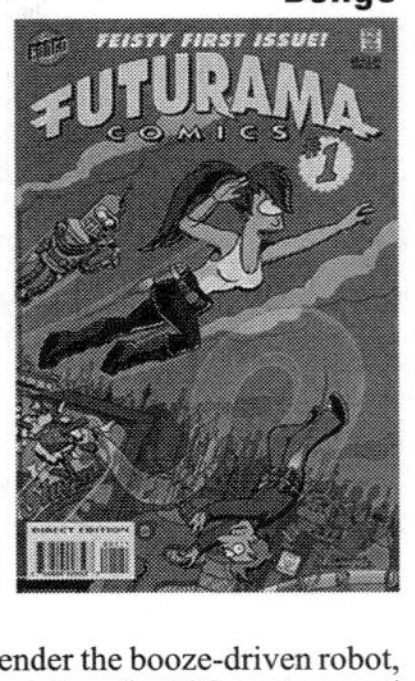

"Our humble aim," wrote Futurama Comics creator Matt Groening in the foreword to the series' first issue, "is to both honor science fiction and to make fun of the genre's built in absurdities..." Futurama Comics, based upon the animated Fox television show, is an outrageously funny and often strange world envisioned by Groening, the same man responsible for the wildly popular television series, The Simpsons.

Futurama Comics follows the adventures of seven very different employees of Planet Express Delivery Service as they try to make a living in the year 3000. Making up the three core members of the cast are Bender the booze-driven robot, Fry a cryogenically frozen delivery boy from the 20th century, and Leela the one-eyed captain of the delivery spaceship. Most of their adventures circle around the rather feeble-minded Fry's nostalgic reminisces of life in the 20th Century and his search to share his previous life with his new friends, often ending with disastrous results.

1 ❑ ca. 2000 Cover: 2.50 **NM** value: **Cover or less**
• **CGC:** 3 graded, best 9.8
Monkey Sea, Monkey Doom! **A:** James Lloyd **W:** Eric Rogers

2 ❑ Cover: 2.50 **NM** value: **Cover or less**
... But Deliver Us To Evil! **A:** Tom King **W:** Eric Rogers

FUTURE BEAT — Oasis

1 ❑ Jul 1986 Cover: 1.50 **NM** value: **Cover or less**
...It's Better This Way; The Exodus **A:** Richard Johnson **W:** Tracy Schell

2 ❑ Cover: 1.50 **NM** value: **Cover or less**

FUTURE COMICS — David McKay

1 ❑ Jun 1940 Cover: 0.10 **NM** value: **2000.00**
2 ❑ Jul 1940 Cover: 0.10 **NM** value: **1000.00**
3 ❑ Aug 1940 Cover: 0.10 **NM** value: **750.00**
4 ❑ Sep 1940 Cover: 0.10 **NM** value: **750.00**

FUTURE COP: L.A.P.D. — DC / Wildstorm

1 ❑ Jan 1999 Cover: 4.95 **NM** value: **Cover or less**
• magazine-sized.

Ash 1 ❑ **NM** value: **1.00**
Situation Critical **A:** Ron Lim **W:** Kris Oprisko

FUTURE COURSE — Reoccurring Images

1 ❑ Cover: 2.95 **NM** value: **Cover or less**
Circ: CapCity orders: **2,625**

FUTURETECH — Mushroom

1 ❑ Feb 1995, b&w Cover: 3.50 **NM** value: **Cover or less**
• 2nd Printing (first printing published by BlackLine Studios, Oct 94) **A:** Perry S. Yem **W:** Perry S. Yem

FUTURE WORLD COMICS — George W. Dougherty

1 ❑ Sum 1946 Cover: 0.10 **NM** value: **200.00**
• **CGC:** 1 graded, best 7.5

2 ❑ Fal 1946 Cover: 0.10 **NM** value: **200.00**
• **CGC:** 1 graded, best 9.2

FUTURIANS BY DAVE COCKRUM, THE — Lodestone

The first solo work from veteran X-Men artist Dave Cockrum, The Futurians first appeared in Marvel Graphic Novel #9. Their story continues here and takes place in a future where hope has gone black.

A shadowy group called the Inheritors claimed ownership of the world, and dropped meteor bombs onto most major cities in an attempt to frighten the world's governments into capitulation. A group of superhumans called the Futurians managed to stop them, but not before London, Paris, Moscow, New York, and other cities were leveled. As a result, millions died, and millions more became hapless refugees. In the wake of this catastrophe, civil strife has become epidemic. It's up to the Futurians to do something about it...

1 ❑ Oct 1985 Cover: 1.50 **NM** value: **2.00**
Circ: CapCity orders: **11,125**
Aftermath! • Story continued from Marvel Graphic Novel #9 **A:** Dave Cockrum **W:** Dave Cockrum ★ 1st Appearance of Doctor Zeus, Hammerhand. ★ 2nd Appearance of The Futurians.

2 ❑ Dec 1985 Cover: 1.50 **NM** value: **2.00**
Circ: CapCity orders: **8,500**

3 ❑ Apr 1986 Cover: 1.50 **NM** value: **2.00**
Circ: CapCity orders: **9,550**
final issue. **A:** Dave Cockrum **W:** Dave Cockrum

Bk 1 ❑ Cover: 9.95 **NM** value: **Cover or less**
• reprints Lodestone series with additional material

FUTURIANS (VOL. 2) — Aardwolf

1 ❑ Aug 1995 Cover: 2.95 **NM** value: **Cover or less**

FUZZY BUZZARD AND FRIENDS — Hall of Heroes

1 ❑ Apr 1995 Cover: 2.50 **NM** value: **Cover or less**
The Upside Down Cake; Tricky Answers; The White Fly; The Secret Mission **A:** Ethan Van Sciver **W:** Mister Tom

G-8 AND HIS BATTLE ACES — Blazing

1 ❑ Oct 1966, full color Cover: 1.50 **NM** value: **Cover or less**
Circ: CapCity orders: **3,000**
Grun--The Green Terror! **A:** Sam Glanzman **W:** Chuck Dixon

GABBY — Quality

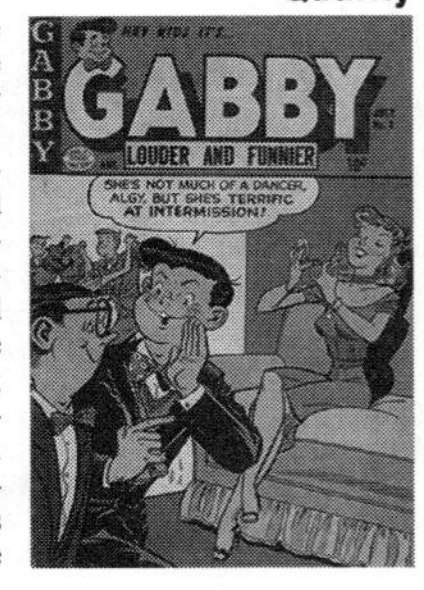

A teen humor offering from the mid-1950s, Gabby was one of the final titles released by the Quality Comics group.

Issues of Gabby provide the standard teen laughs, with the standard cast of characters: Gabby, the luckless "average teen;" his high-handed rival Smedley; fickle girlfriend Taffy; and the supporting cast of the "brain;" the dumb, buzz-cut jock; and a generous measure of hopelessly square authoritarian adults. Each issue features a variety of stories focusing on different members of the cast, plus a few single-page gag strips.

Gabby folded in 1954 when the Quality Comics line sputtered out.

1 ❑ Jul 1953 Cover: 0.10 **NM** value: **30.00**
2 ❑ Sep 1953 Cover: 0.10 **NM** value: **18.00**
3 ❑ Nov 1953 Cover: 0.10 **NM** value: **14.00**
4 ❑ 1954 Cover: 0.10 **NM** value: **10.00**
5 ❑ 1954 Cover: 0.10 **NM** value: **10.00**
6 ❑ 1954 Cover: 0.10 **NM** value: **10.00**
7 ❑ 1954 Cover: 0.10 **NM** value: **10.00**
8 ❑ Jul 1954 Cover: 0.10 **NM** value: **10.00**
The Play's the Thing; Candy; Psychological Warfare; Beauty Vs. Duty; Fair Exchange; Just for Spite (text); Dirty Politics

9 ❑ Sep 1954 Cover: 0.10 **NM** value: **10.00**

Other grades: Multiply prices above by **1.5 for Mint • 2/3 for Very Fine • 1/3 for Fine • 1/5 for Very Good • 1/8 for Good**

GABBY HAYES WESTERN — Fawcett

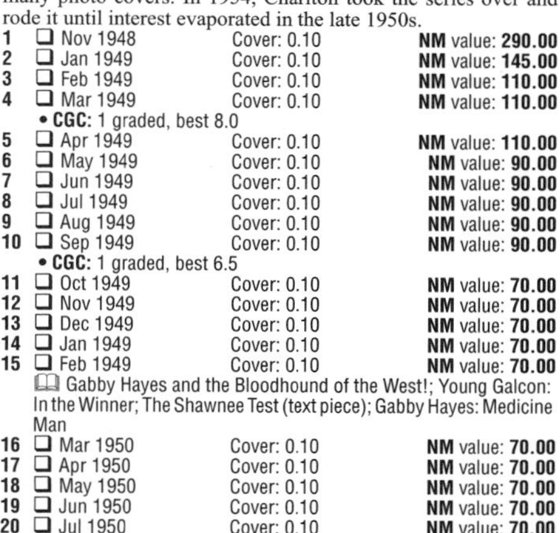

Gabby Hayes Western is based on the exploits of cantankerous old-timer Hayes, a star of movie westerns in the 1940s and 1950s. Together with his horse Corker, Gabby Hayes and his pals keep the old West safe from cattle rustlers and other desperados, all with a touch of good humor and wit.

Gabby's dialogue, delivered in a deadpan drawl, is especially memorable: "Keep a-comin' chump! One more step and I'll drop yuh!" "Dingbust it! I don't like these fool shenanigans!"

Fawcett published the title until 1953, attractively packaged with many photo covers. In 1954, Charlton took the series over and rode it until interest evaporated in the late 1950s.

1 ❑ Nov 1948 Cover: 0.10 **NM** value: **290.00**
2 ❑ Jan 1949 Cover: 0.10 **NM** value: **145.00**
3 ❑ Feb 1949 Cover: 0.10 **NM** value: **110.00**
4 ❑ Mar 1949 Cover: 0.10 **NM** value: **110.00**
• **CGC:** 1 graded, best 8.0
5 ❑ Apr 1949 Cover: 0.10 **NM** value: **110.00**
6 ❑ May 1949 Cover: 0.10 **NM** value: **90.00**
7 ❑ Jun 1949 Cover: 0.10 **NM** value: **90.00**
8 ❑ Jul 1949 Cover: 0.10 **NM** value: **90.00**
9 ❑ Aug 1949 Cover: 0.10 **NM** value: **90.00**
10 ❑ Sep 1949 Cover: 0.10 **NM** value: **90.00**
• **CGC:** 1 graded, best 6.5
11 ❑ Oct 1949 Cover: 0.10 **NM** value: **70.00**
12 ❑ Nov 1949 Cover: 0.10 **NM** value: **70.00**
13 ❑ Dec 1949 Cover: 0.10 **NM** value: **70.00**
14 ❑ Jan 1949 Cover: 0.10 **NM** value: **70.00**
15 ❑ Feb 1949 Cover: 0.10 **NM** value: **70.00**
📖 Gabby Hayes and the Bloodhound of the West!; Young Galcon: In the Winner; The Shawnee Test (text piece); Gabby Hayes: Medicine Man
16 ❑ Mar 1950 Cover: 0.10 **NM** value: **70.00**
17 ❑ Apr 1950 Cover: 0.10 **NM** value: **70.00**
18 ❑ May 1950 Cover: 0.10 **NM** value: **70.00**
19 ❑ Jun 1950 Cover: 0.10 **NM** value: **70.00**
20 ❑ Jul 1950 Cover: 0.10 **NM** value: **70.00**
21 ❑ Aug 1950 Cover: 0.10 **NM** value: **58.00**
22 ❑ Sep 1950 Cover: 0.10 **NM** value: **58.00**
23 ❑ Oct 1950 Cover: 0.10 **NM** value: **58.00**
24 ❑ Nov 1950 Cover: 0.10 **NM** value: **58.00**
25 ❑ Dec 1950 Cover: 0.10 **NM** value: **58.00**
26 ❑ Jan 1951 Cover: 0.10 **NM** value: **58.00**
27 ❑ Feb 1951 Cover: 0.10 **NM** value: **58.00**
28 ❑ Mar 1951 Cover: 0.10 **NM** value: **58.00**
29 ❑ Apr 1951 Cover: 0.10 **NM** value: **58.00**
30 ❑ May 1951 Cover: 0.10 **NM** value: **58.00**
31 ❑ Jun 1951 Cover: 0.10 **NM** value: **40.00**
32 ❑ Jul 1951 Cover: 0.10 **NM** value: **40.00**
33 ❑ Aug 1951 Cover: 0.10 **NM** value: **40.00**
34 ❑ Sep 1951 Cover: 0.10 **NM** value: **40.00**
35 ❑ Oct 1951 Cover: 0.10 **NM** value: **40.00**
36 ❑ Nov 1951 Cover: 0.10 **NM** value: **40.00**
37 ❑ Dec 1951 Cover: 0.10 **NM** value: **40.00**
38 ❑ Jan 1952 Cover: 0.10 **NM** value: **40.00**
39 ❑ Feb 1952 Cover: 0.10 **NM** value: **40.00**
40 ❑ Mar 1952 Cover: 0.10 **NM** value: **40.00**
41 ❑ Apr 1952 Cover: 0.10 **NM** value: **32.00**
42 ❑ May 1952 Cover: 0.10 **NM** value: **32.00**
43 ❑ Jun 1952 Cover: 0.10 **NM** value: **32.00**
44 ❑ Jul 1952 Cover: 0.10 **NM** value: **32.00**
45 ❑ Aug 1952 Cover: 0.10 **NM** value: **32.00**
46 ❑ Sep 1952 Cover: 0.10 **NM** value: **32.00**
47 ❑ Oct 1952 Cover: 0.10 **NM** value: **32.00**
48 ❑ Nov 1952 Cover: 0.10 **NM** value: **32.00**
49 ❑ Dec 1952 Cover: 0.10 **NM** value: **32.00**
50 ❑ Jan 1953 Cover: 0.10 **NM** value: **32.00**
51 ❑ Dec 1954 Cover: 0.10 **NM** value: **26.00**
52 ❑ 1955 Cover: 0.10 **NM** value: **26.00**
53 ❑ Cover: 0.10 **NM** value: **26.00**
54 ❑ Cover: 0.10 **NM** value: **26.00**
55 ❑ Cover: 0.10 **NM** value: **26.00**
56 ❑ Cover: 0.10 **NM** value: **26.00**
57 ❑ Cover: 0.10 **NM** value: **26.00**
58 ❑ Cover: 0.10 **NM** value: **26.00**
59 ❑ Cover: 0.10 **NM** value: **26.00**
final issue.

GABRIEL — Caliber

1 ❑ b&w Cover: 3.95 **NM** value: **Cover or less**
One-shot. • prestige format. **A:** David Hill **W:** Jim Alexander

!GAG! — Harrier

1 ❑ 1987 Cover: 1.95 **NM** value: **3.50**
📖 Dapper John; Stories of the Saints; It's Time to See Calico County; The 7 Faces of Manlyville; Paris the Man of Plaster; A True Story; Alex **A:** Eddie Campbell; Ed Pinsent; Phil Laskey; Steve Way; Trevs Phoenix; Chris Flewitt; John Bagnall **W:** Eddie Campbell; Glenn Dakin; Ed Pinsent; Phil Laskey; Trevs Phoenix; Chris Flewitt; John Bagnall
2 ❑ Jul 1987 Cover: 1.95 **NM** value: **3.00**
3 ❑ 1987 Cover: 1.95 **NM** value: **3.00**
4 ❑ 1987 Cover: 2.95 **NM** value: **3.00**
• magazine.
5 ❑ 1988 Cover: 2.95 **NM** value: **3.00**
• magazine.
6 ❑ 1988 Cover: 2.95 **NM** value: **3.00**
• magazine.
7 ❑ 1988 Cover: 2.95 **NM** value: **3.00**
• magazine. 📖 Burglar Bill **A:** Eddie Campbell; Paul Grist

GAG REFLEX (SKIP WILLIAMSON'S...) — Williamson

1 ❑ Jan 1994, b&w Cover: 2.95 **NM** value: **Cover or less**

GAIJIN (CALIBER) — Caliber

1 ❑ b&w Cover: 3.50 **NM** value: **Cover or less**
📖 The Dark Edge of Beauty **A:** Gabriel Morrissette **W:** Gabriel Morrissette

GAIJIN (MATRIX) — Matrix

1 ❑ Feb 1987 Cover: 1.75 **NM** value: **Cover or less**
📖 First Assault **A:** Gabriel Morrissette **W:** Gabriel Morrissette

GAJIT GANG, THE — Amazing

1 ❑ Cover: 1.95 **NM** value: **Cover or less**

GAKK, CHOKE, BLURG! — Slave Labor

Bk 1 ❑ Jun 1994 Cover: 9.95 **NM** value: **Cover or less**
• reprints Doctor Radium: Gizmos and Special; reprints Dr. Radium: Gizmos and Special

GALACTICA: THE NEW MILLENNIUM — Realm

1 ❑ Sep 1999 Cover: 2.99 **NM** value: **Cover or less**
Circ: Diamd. preorders: **6,904**
📖 Fear of Flying **A:** Dan Parsons **W:** Jim Shooter

GALACTIC GUARDIANS — Marvel

The Galactic Guardians live in an alternate timeline some 2,000 years from now. In their version of history, the world became the victim of anti-mutant hysteria in the late 20th century, leading to a mutant slaughter at the hands of the Sentinels. Magneto and his followers decided to flee to the stars, while others stayed behind. Those who stayed were wiped out by a Martian invasion. Others eventually arrived on a world they called Haven, humanity's new home.

Years later, on a world controlled by Mainframe, a latter-day incarnation of the Vision, something is wrong. Mainframe has been having mysterious power failures, threatening the entire world. At the same time, he has discovered clues that suggest the Martian invasion was sponsored by an outside force. In this 4-issue mini-series, the Galactic Guardians are reunited with age-old Avenger Wonder Man on a mission to solve this deadly mystery.

1 ❑ Jul 1994 Cover: 1.50 **NM** value: **Cover or less**
Circ: CapCity orders: **24,450**
📖 Amid The Encircling Gloom **A:** Kevin West **W:** Michael Gallagher
2 ❑ Aug 1994 Cover: 1.50 **NM** value: **Cover or less**
Circ: CapCity orders: **15,850**
📖 I Have Loved the Stars Too Fondly to be Fearful of the Night
3 ❑ Sep 1994 Cover: 1.50 **NM** value: **Cover or less**
Circ: CapCity orders: **14,350**
4 ❑ Oct 1994 Cover: 1.50 **NM** value: **Cover or less**
Circ: CapCity orders: **13,350**

GALACTIC PATROL — Eternity

1 ❑ Jul 1990, b&w Cover: 2.25 **NM** value: **Cover or less**
📖 A Lensman Side Story; Decoy **A:** Tim Eldred **W:** Tim Eldred
2 ❑ b&w Cover: 2.25 **NM** value: **Cover or less**
3 ❑ b&w Cover: 2.25 **NM** value: **Cover or less**
4 ❑ b&w Cover: 2.25 **NM** value: **Cover or less**
5 ❑ b&w Cover: 2.25 **NM** value: **Cover or less**
Bk 1 ❑ Cover: 12.95 **NM** value: **Cover or less**

GALACTUS THE DEVOURER — Marvel

1 ❑ Sep 1999 Cover: 3.50 **NM** value: **Cover or less**
Circ: Diamd. preorders: **47,988**
📖 Hunger! **A:** Jon J. Muth; Bill Sienkiewicz **W:** Louise Simonson
2 ❑ Oct 1999 Cover: 2.50 **NM** value: **3.50**
Circ: Diamd. preorders: **39,710**
3 ❑ Nov 1999 Cover: 2.50 **NM** value: **3.50**
Circ: Diamd. preorders: **37,024**
4 ❑ Dec 1999 Cover: 2.50 **NM** value: **3.50**
Circ: Diamd. preorders: **34,090**
📖 Truth or Consequences **A:** John Buscema **W:** Louise Simonson
5 ❑ Jan 2000 Cover: 3.50 **NM** value: **Cover or less**
Circ: Diamd. preorders: **31,275**
6 ❑ Feb 2000 Cover: 3.50 **NM** value: **Cover or less**
Circ: Diamd. preorders: **31,822**

GALAXINA — Aircel

All issues are adults only.

1 ❑ 1991b&w Cover: 2.95 **NM** value: **Cover or less**
Circ: CapCity orders: **3,390**
2 ❑ 1991b&w Cover: 2.95 **NM** value: **Cover or less**
3 ❑ 1991b&w Cover: 2.95 **NM** value: **Cover or less**
4 ❑ 1991 Cover: 2.95 **NM** value: **Cover or less**

GALAXION — Helikon

1 ❑ May 1997, b&w Cover: 2.75 **NM** value: **Cover or less**
📖 A Moment in Time **A:** Tara Jenkins **W:** Tara Jenkins
2 ❑ Jul 1997, b&w Cover: 2.75 **NM** value: **Cover or less**
3 ❑ Sep 1997, b&w Cover: 2.75 **NM** value: **Cover or less**
4 ❑ Nov 1997, b&w Cover: 2.75 **NM** value: **Cover or less**
5 ❑ Jan 1998, b&w Cover: 2.75 **NM** value: **Cover or less**
6 ❑ Mar 1998, b&w Cover: 2.75 **NM** value: **Cover or less**
7 ❑ 1998 Cover: 2.75 **NM** value: **Cover or less**
8 ❑ 1998 Cover: 2.75 **NM** value: **Cover or less**
9 ❑ 1999 Cover: 2.75 **NM** value: **Cover or less**
Circ: Diamd. preorders: **1,148**
10 ❑ 1999 Cover: 2.75 **NM** value: **Cover or less**
11 ❑ Nov 1999 Cover: 2.75 **NM** value: **Cover or less**
📖 Confined and Released **A:** Tara Tallan **W:** Tara Tallan
Bk 1 ❑ Cover: 15.95 **NM** value: **Cover or less**
• Collects issues #1-6, plus Prologue from "Thieves & Kings"
SE 1 ❑ May 1998, b&w Cover: 0.99 **NM** value: **1.00**

GALAXY EXPRESS 999 — Viz

Bk 1 ❑ Oct 1998, b&w Cover: 16.95 **NM** value: **Cover or less**

GALAXY GIRL — Dynamic

1 ❑ b&w Cover: 2.50 **NM** value: **Cover or less**

GALL FORCE: ETERNAL STORY — CPM

1 ❑ Mar 1995 Cover: 2.95 **NM** value: **Cover or less**
Circ: CapCity orders: **2,635**
2 ❑ May 1995 Cover: 2.95 **NM** value: **Cover or less**
3 ❑ Jul 1995 Cover: 2.95 **NM** value: **Cover or less**
4 ❑ Sep 1995 Cover: 2.95 **NM** value: **Cover or less**

GAMBIT (1ST SERIES) — Eternity

1 ❑ Sep 1988, b&w Cover: 1.95 **NM** value: **Cover or less**
📖 Trust Me **A:** Scott Bieser **W:** Scott Bieser

GAMBIT (2ND SERIES) — Oracle

1 ❑ Sep 1986 Cover: 1.50 **NM** value: **Cover or less**
2 ❑ Nov 1986 Cover: 1.50 **NM** value: **Cover or less**

GAMBIT (3RD SERIES) — Marvel

Gambit is Remy LeBeau, a Cajun thief with the mutant ability to "energize" objects he holds, turning them into deadly weapons. First appearing in Uncanny X-Men Annual #14, he later joins the team and beomes a key member.

Still, questions linger about his shadowy past. Moreover, he and fellow teammate Rogue have engaged in a long and stormy romance filled with unsolved problems.

This four-issue limited series gives readers a chance to explore Gambit's character and history. It begins as a war erupts between the Thieves Guild and the Assassins Guild in Gambit's native New Orleans. Leading the attack is Julien, the brother of Remy's long-lost wife, Bella Donna. Since Remy had personally killed Julien with his sword, their reunion comes as a great surprise to him!

1 ❑ Dec 1993 Cover: 2.50 **NM** value: **3.00**
Circ: CapCity orders: **136,700** • **CGC:** 6 graded, best 9.8
foil cover. 📖 Tithing **A:** Lee Weeks **W:** Howard Mackie
1/GO ❑ Dec 1993 **NM** value: **4.00**
• **CGC:** 6 graded, best 9.8
• Gold promotion edition.
2 ❑ Jan 1994 Cover: 2.00 **NM** value: **2.50**
Circ: CapCity orders: **80,200**
3 ❑ Feb 1994 Cover: 2.00 **NM** value: **2.50**
Circ: CapCity orders: **72,900**
4 ❑ Mar 1994 Cover: 2.00 **NM** value: **2.50**
Circ: CapCity orders: **69,000**

GAMBIT (4TH SERIES) — Marvel

1 ❑ Sep 1997 Cover: 2.50 **NM** value: **Cover or less**
Circ: Diamd. preorders: **83,706**
• gatefold summary.
2 ❑ Oct 1997 Cover: 2.50 **NM** value: **Cover or less**
Circ: Diamd. preorders: **69,420**
• gatefold summary.
3 ❑ Nov 1997 Cover: 2.50 **NM** value: **Cover or less**
Circ: Diamd. preorders: **68,356**
4 ❑ Dec 1997 Cover: 2.50 **NM** value: **Cover or less**
Circ: Diamd. preorders: **67,144**

GAMBIT (5TH SERIES) — Marvel

1 ❑ Feb 1999 Cover: 1.99 **NM** value: **3.00**
Circ: Diamd. preorders: **117,437**
📖 The Man of Steal **A:** Steve Skroce **W:** Fabian Nicieza ★ Appearance of X-Men, X-Cutioner.
1/A ❑ Feb 1999 Cover: 2.99 **NM** value: **5.00**
• **CGC:** 2 graded, best 9.4
DFE alternate cover. 📖 The Man of Steal **A:** Steve Skroce **W:** Fabian Nicieza ★ Appearance of X-Men, X-Cutioner.
1/B ❑ Feb 1999 Cover: 2.99 **NM** value: **10.00**
DFE alternate cover. 📖 The Man of Steal **A:** Steve Skroce **W:** Fabian Nicieza ★ Appearance of X-Men, X-Cutioner.
1/C ❑ Feb 1999 Cover: 2.99 **NM** value: **10.00**
Marvel Authentix printed sketch cover. 📖 The Man of Steal • 600 printed **A:** Steve Skroce **W:** Fabian Nicieza ★ Appearance of X-Men, X-Cutioner.
2 ❑ Mar 1999 Cover: 1.99 **NM** value: **2.50**
Circ: Diamd. preorders: **86,129**
3 ❑ Apr 1999 Cover: 1.99 **NM** value: **2.50**
Circ: Diamd. preorders: **66,559**
4 ❑ May 1999 Cover: 1.99 **NM** value: **2.50**
Circ: Diamd. preorders: **63,524**
📖 Old Wounds, Fresh Blood! **A:** Steve Skroce **W:** Fabian Nicieza
5 ❑ Jun 1999 Cover: 1.99 **NM** value: **Cover or less**
Circ: Diamd. preorders: **59,689**
6 ❑ Jul 1999 Cover: 1.99 **NM** value: **Cover or less**
Circ: Diamd. preorders: **54,004**
• early adventure
7 ❑ Aug 1999 Cover: 1.99 **NM** value: **Cover or less**
Circ: Diamd. preorders: **51,938**
8 ❑ Sep 1999 Cover: 1.99 **NM** value: **Cover or less**
Circ: Diamd. preorders: **49,285**
9 ❑ Oct 1999 Cover: 1.99 **NM** value: **Cover or less**
Circ: Diamd. preorders: **46,399**
10 ❑ Nov 1999 Cover: 1.99 **NM** value: **Cover or less**
Circ: Diamd. preorders: **43,235**
11 ❑ Dec 1999 Cover: 1.99 **NM** value: **Cover or less**
Circ: Diamd. preorders: **44,250**
12 ❑ Jan 2000 Cover: 1.99 **NM** value: **Cover or less**
Circ: Diamd. preorders: **41,479**
13 ❑ Feb 2000 Cover: 1.99 **NM** value: **Cover or less**
Circ: Diamd. preorders: **43,326**
14 ❑ Mar 2000 Cover: 1.99 **NM** value: **Cover or less**
Circ: Diamd. preorders: **38,978**
15 ❑ Apr 2000 Cover: 1.99 **NM** value: **Cover or less**
Circ: Diamd. preorders: **36,733**

CGC-graded: Multiply prices above by **33 for 9.9 M** • **16 for 9.8 NM/M** • **7 for 9.6 NM+** • **5 for 9.4 NM** • **2.5 for 9.2 NM-** • **1.5 for 9.0 VF/NM**

16 ❑ May 2000 Cover: 1.99 **NM** value: **Cover or less**
Circ: Diamd. preorders: **43,375**
17 ❑ Jun 2000 Cover: 2.25 **NM** value: **Cover or less**
Circ: Diamd. preorders: **36,946**
18 ❑ Jul 2000 Cover: 2.25 **NM** value: **Cover or less**
Circ: Diamd. preorders: **37,126**
19 ❑ Aug 2000 Cover: 2.25 **NM** value: **Cover or less**
Circ: Diamd. preorders: **38,159**
20 ❑ Sep 2000 Cover: 2.25 **NM** value: **Cover or less**
Circ: Diamd. preorders: **37,543**
21 ❑ Oct 2000 Cover: 2.25 **NM** value: **Cover or less**
Circ: Diamd. preorders: **35,155**
22 ❑ Nov 2000 Cover: 2.25 **NM** value: **Cover or less**
Circ: Diamd. preorders: **35,364**
📖 Follow the Leader **A:** Yanick Paquette **W:** Fabian Nicieza
23 ❑ Dec 2000 Cover: 2.25 **NM** value: **Cover or less**
Circ: Diamd. preorders: **36,605**
📖 Maximum Security; Shell Game **A:** Yanick Paquette **W:** Fabian Nicieza
24 ❑ Jan 2001 Cover: 2.25 **NM** value: **Cover or less**
Circ: Diamd. preorders: **35,351**
📖 Sunrise Sunset **A:** Yanick Paquette **W:** Fabian Nicieza
25 ❑ Feb 2001 Cover: 2.99 **NM** value: **Cover or less**
Circ: Diamd. preorders: **35,360**
• double-sized. 📖 Stop Draggin' My Heart Around **A:** Georges Jeanty **W:** Scott Lobdell; Joe Pruett
Anl 1999❑ Sep 1999 Cover: 3.50 **NM** value: **Cover or less**
GS 1❑ Feb 1998 Cover: 3.99 **NM** value: **Cover or less**
Circ: Diamd. preorders: **19,831**
• Giant sized. 📖 The Hearts of Thieves; Dreams Die; A Nation Rising; The Nature of Evil **A:** Ron Garney; Bryan Hitch; Andy Kubert; Joe Madureira **W:** Scott Lobdell; Fabian Nicieza

GAMBIT AND ASSOCIATES — Eclectic
1 ❑ Cover: 1.75 **NM** value: **Cover or less**
2 ❑ Cover: 1.75 **NM** value: **Cover or less**
3 ❑ Cover: 1.75 **NM** value: **Cover or less**
📖 Dead City Twist **A:** Alan Oldham **W:** Alan Oldham

GAMBIT AND BISHOP — Marvel
1 ❑ Mar 2001 Cover: 2.25 **NM** value: **Cover or less**
2 ❑ Apr 2001 Cover: 2.25 **NM** value: **Cover or less**
📖 Enter ... The Witness! **A:** Cary Nord **W:** Scott Lobdell; Joe Pruett
3 ❑ May 2001 Cover: 2.25 **NM** value: **Cover or less**
📖 That's Stryfe That's What People Say! **A:** Georges Jeanty **W:** Scott Lobdell; Joe Pruett
4 ❑ Jun 2001 Cover: 2.25 **NM** value: **Cover or less**
📖 My Brother, My Enemy! **A:** Thomas Derenick **W:** Scott Lobdell; Joe Pruett
5 ❑ May 2001 Cover: 2.25 **NM** value: **Cover or less**
📖 Are We Ourselves **A:** Cary Nord; Georges Jeanty **W:** Scott Lobdell; Joe Pruett

GAMBIT AND BISHOP ALPHA — Marvel
1 ❑ Feb 2001 Cover: 2.25 **NM** value: **Cover or less**
Circ: Diamd. preorders: **33,016**
📖 May Tomorrow Never Die! **A:** Cary Nord **W:** Scott Lobdell; Joe Pruett

GAMBIT AND BISHOP GENESIS — Marvel
1 ❑ Mar 2001 Cover: 3.50 **NM** value: **Cover or less**
📖 Gambit: Out of the Frying Pan; Bishop's Crossing; Tooth and Claw • reprints Uncanny X-Men #266, Uncanny X-Men #283, and X-Men (2nd series) #8 **A:** Whilce Portacio; Jim Lee; Michael Collins; Art Thibert **W:** Whilce Portacio; Jim Lee; Chris Claremont

GAMBIT & THE X-TERNALS — Marvel
1 ❑ Mar 1995 Cover: 1.95 **NM** value: **Cover or less**
Circ: CapCity orders: **72,175**
📖 Some of us Looking to the Stars **A:** Tony Daniel **W:** Fabian Nicieza
2 ❑ Apr 1995 Cover: 1.95 **NM** value: **Cover or less**
Circ: CapCity orders: **71,000**
3 ❑ May 1995 Cover: 1.95 **NM** value: **Cover or less**
Circ: CapCity orders: **86,900**
4 ❑ Jun 1995 Cover: 1.95 **NM** value: **Cover or less**
Circ: CapCity orders: **94,175**
Bk 1❑ May 1995 Cover: 8.95 **NM** value: **Cover or less**
Gold foil cover. • Ultimate Gambit & The X-Ternals; collects four-issue series

GAMBIT BATTLEBOOK — Marvel
1 ❑ Cover: 3.99 **NM** value: **Cover or less**

GAME BOY — Valiant
1 ❑ Cover: 1.95 **NM** value: **Cover or less**
Circ: CapCity orders: **2,500**
📖 In the Palm of Your Hand... **A:** Gray Morrow; Paul Creddick; Art Nichols; George Caragonne; Ken Lopez; The Gradations; Todd Haedrich **W:** Gray Morrow; Paul Creddick; Art Nichols; George Caragonne; Ken Lopez; The Gradations; Todd Haedrich
2 ❑ Cover: 1.95 **NM** value: **Cover or less**
Circ: CapCity orders: **1,600**
3 ❑ Cover: 1.95 **NM** value: **Cover or less**
Circ: CapCity orders: **1,400**
4 ❑ Cover: 1.95 **NM** value: **Cover or less**
📖 Pipes is Pipes **A:** Gray Morrow; Bill Vallely; Jade; Pocho Morrow; Mark McClellan **W:** Gray Morrow; Bill Vallely; Jade; Pocho Morrow; Mark McClellan

GAME GUYS! — Wonder
1 ❑ Cover: 2.50 **NM** value: **Cover or less**
📖 A Thousand Ways To Die **A:** Nils Osmar **W:** Nils Osmar

GAMERA — Dark Horse
1 ❑ Aug 1996 Cover: 2.95 **NM** value: **Cover or less**
📖 The Shadow of Evil-Gyaos! **A:** Mozart Couto; Mitsuaki Hashimoto(cover) **W:** Dave Chipps ★ Versus Gyaos.
2 ❑ Sep 1996 Cover: 2.95 **NM** value: **Cover or less**
Circ: Diamd. preorders: **11,844**
📖 Wreckoning **A:** Mozart Couto; Mitsuaki Hashimoto(cover) **W:** Dave Chipps
3 ❑ Oct 1996 Cover: 2.95 **NM** value: **Cover or less**
Circ: Diamd. preorders: **10,740**
4 ❑ Nov 1996 Cover: 2.95 **NM** value: **Cover or less**
Circ: Diamd. preorders: **9,590**
📖 The Last Hope final issue. **A:** Mozart Couto; Yuji Kaida(cover) **W:** Dave Chipps

GAMMARAUDERS — DC

A fun — but sometimes incomprehensible — series by Peter B. Gillis and Martin King, Gammarauders is based on the futuristic role-playing game from TSR. The series stars Jok Tasworth, a biodroid handler, who will be a key player in the Gamma Age's greatest war. Jok, meanwhile, seems totally clueless as to his destiny, and is easily fascinated by anything bright and shiny.

The biodroids account for a good deal of the series' weirdness. They appear to be cyborgs based on various animals-the odder the better. Thus we have kangaroids, triceri-ans, and something that looks like a robotic bear with space goggles. These biodroids are the friends, allies-and power tools of Jok and the other biodroid handlers.

Based as it is on one of TSR's less successful properties, the performance of the series was probably never in doubt.

1 ❑ Jan 1989 Cover: 1.25 **NM** value: **Cover or less**
Circ: CapCity orders: **14,600**
📖 Shut Down on the Big Nada! **A:** Martin King **W:** Peter B. Gillis
2 ❑ Mar 1989 Cover: 1.25 **NM** value: **Cover or less**
Circ: CapCity orders: **10,600**
3 ❑ Apr 1989 Cover: 1.25 **NM** value: **Cover or less**
Circ: CapCity orders: **9,550**
4 ❑ May 1989 Cover: 1.25 **NM** value: **Cover or less**
Circ: CapCity orders: **8,300**
5 ❑ Jul 1989 Cover: 1.25 **NM** value: **Cover or less**
Circ: CapCity orders: **6,750**
6 ❑ Aug 1989 Cover: 1.25 **NM** value: **Cover or less**
Circ: CapCity orders: **4,750**
7 ❑ Sep 1989 Cover: 2.00 **NM** value: **Cover or less**
Circ: CapCity orders: **3,800**
8 ❑ Oct 1989 Cover: 2.00 **NM** value: **Cover or less**
Circ: CapCity orders: **3,450**
9 ❑ Nov 1989 Cover: 2.00 **NM** value: **Cover or less**
Circ: CapCity orders: **3,550**
10 ❑ Dec 1989 Cover: 2.00 **NM** value: **Cover or less**
Circ: CapCity orders: **3,000**
final issue. **A:** Martin King **W:** Peter B. Gillis

GAMORRA SWIMSUIT SPECIAL — Image
1 ❑ Jun 1996 Cover: 2.50 **NM** value: **Cover or less**
• pin-ups

GANDY GOOSE — St. John
1 ❑ Mar 1953 Cover: 0.10 **NM** value: **38.00**
2 ❑ May 1953 Cover: 0.10 **NM** value: **25.00**
3 ❑ Jul 1953 Cover: 0.10 **NM** value: **18.00**
4 ❑ Sep 1953 Cover: 0.10 **NM** value: **15.00**
5 ❑ Nov 1953 Cover: 0.10 **NM** value: **12.00**
6 ❑ Sum 1958 Cover: 0.10 **NM** value: **12.00**

GANGBANG GIRLS: ALL WET — Angel
1 ❑ Cover: 3.00 **NM** value: **Cover or less**

GANGBUSTERS — DC

Although Westerns were big in comics in the 1950s, true-to-life crime dramas had their own successful niche. One of DC's better enrties in this genre is Gangbusters, based in part on the radio and TV series of the same name, which was a peer with such classics as Dragnet and Highway Patrol. While nowhere near as edgy or innovative as, say, EC's Crime SuspensStories or the seminal Crime Does Not Pay, Gangbusters has its own appeal, full of relatively nonviolent crime stories with clever twists.

Like many DC comics of the era, however, plots also tended to rely on unlikely gimmicks and premises, such as "Indian Detective," the tale of a plainclothes Native American cop who uses stereotypical devices like smoke signals, and bows and arrows to help stop the bad guys.

Many of the top comics artists of the era, including Frank Frazetta, Jack Kirby and even Mad's Mort Drucker, contributed to the short stories of this title, which enjoyed a modest run.

1 ❑ Dec 1947 Cover: 0.10 **NM** value: **550.00**
• **CGC:** 3 graded, best 9.4
2 ❑ Mar 1948 Cover: 0.10 **NM** value: **285.00**
• **CGC:** 1 graded, best 8.5
3 ❑ May 1948 Cover: 0.10 **NM** value: **185.00**
• **CGC:** 1 graded, best 8.0
4 ❑ Jul 1948 Cover: 0.10 **NM** value: **165.00**
5 ❑ Sep 1948 Cover: 0.10 **NM** value: **165.00**
6 ❑ Nov 1948 Cover: 0.10 **NM** value: **130.00**
• **CGC:** 2 graded, best 9.4
7 ❑ Jan 1948 Cover: 0.10 **NM** value: **130.00**
8 ❑ Mar 1949 Cover: 0.10 **NM** value: **130.00**
• **CGC:** 2 graded, best 9.2
9 ❑ May 1949 Cover: 0.10 **NM** value: **130.00**
• **CGC:** 1 graded, best 9.4
10 ❑ Jul 1949 Cover: 0.10 **NM** value: **130.00**
• **CGC:** 1 graded, best 9.0
11 ❑ Sep 1949 Cover: 0.10 **NM** value: **100.00**
• **CGC:** 2 graded, best 9.6
12 ❑ Nov 1949 Cover: 0.10 **NM** value: **100.00**
• **CGC:** 1 graded, best 8.5
Photo cover.
13 ❑ Jan 1950 Cover: 0.10 **NM** value: **100.00**
• **CGC:** 2 graded, best 9.4
14 ❑ Mar 1950 Cover: 0.10 **NM** value: **150.00**
15 ❑ May 1950 Cover: 0.10 **NM** value: **75.00**
• **CGC:** 1 graded, best 9.4
16 ❑ Jul 1950 Cover: 0.10 **NM** value: **75.00**
17 ❑ Sep 1950 Cover: 0.10 **NM** value: **140.00**
• **CGC:** 2 graded, best 9.2
18 ❑ Nov 1950 Cover: 0.10 **NM** value: **75.00**
• **CGC:** 1 graded, best 9.0
19 ❑ Jan 1951 Cover: 0.10 **NM** value: **75.00**
• **CGC:** 1 graded, best 9.4
20 ❑ Mar 1951 Cover: 0.10 **NM** value: **75.00**
• **CGC:** 1 graded, best 9.4
21 ❑ May 1951 Cover: 0.10 **NM** value: **60.00**
22 ❑ Jul 1951 Cover: 0.10 **NM** value: **60.00**
23 ❑ Sep 1951 Cover: 0.10 **NM** value: **60.00**
• **CGC:** 2 graded, best 9.6
24 ❑ Nov 1951 Cover: 0.10 **NM** value: **60.00**
• **CGC:** 1 graded, best 9.4
25 ❑ Jan 1952 Cover: 0.10 **NM** value: **60.00**
26 ❑ Mar 1952 Cover: 0.10 **NM** value: **60.00**
• **CGC:** 1 graded, best 9.4
27 ❑ May 1952 Cover: 0.10 **NM** value: **60.00**
• **CGC:** 1 graded, best 8.0
28 ❑ Jul 1952 Cover: 0.10 **NM** value: **60.00**
29 ❑ Sep 1952 Cover: 0.10 **NM** value: **60.00**
30 ❑ Nov 1952 Cover: 0.10 **NM** value: **60.00**
31 ❑ Jan 1953 Cover: 0.10 **NM** value: **46.00**
32 ❑ Mar 1953 Cover: 0.10 **NM** value: **46.00**
33 ❑ May 1953 Cover: 0.10 **NM** value: **46.00**
34 ❑ Jul 1953 Cover: 0.10 **NM** value: **46.00**
35 ❑ Sep 1953 Cover: 0.10 **NM** value: **46.00**
36 ❑ Nov 1953 Cover: 0.10 **NM** value: **46.00**
37 ❑ Jan 1954 Cover: 0.10 **NM** value: **46.00**
• **CGC:** 1 graded, best 9.0
38 ❑ Mar 1954 Cover: 0.10 **NM** value: **46.00**
39 ❑ May 1954 Cover: 0.10 **NM** value: **46.00**
40 ❑ Jul 1954 Cover: 0.10 **NM** value: **46.00**
41 ❑ Sep 1954 Cover: 0.10 **NM** value: **46.00**
42 ❑ Nov 1954 Cover: 0.10 **NM** value: **46.00**
43 ❑ Jan 1955 Cover: 0.10 **NM** value: **46.00**
44 ❑ Mar 1955 Cover: 0.10 **NM** value: **46.00**
45 ❑ May 1955 Cover: 0.10 **NM** value: **46.00**
46 ❑ Jul 1955 Cover: 0.10 **NM** value: **46.00**
47 ❑ Sep 1955 Cover: 0.10 **NM** value: **46.00**
48 ❑ Nov 1955 Cover: 0.10 **NM** value: **46.00**
49 ❑ Jan 1956 Cover: 0.10 **NM** value: **46.00**
50 ❑ Mar 1956 Cover: 0.10 **NM** value: **46.00**
51 ❑ May 1956 Cover: 0.10 **NM** value: **46.00**
52 ❑ Jul 1956 Cover: 0.10 **NM** value: **38.00**
53 ❑ Sep 1956 Cover: 0.10 **NM** value: **38.00**
54 ❑ Nov 1956 Cover: 0.10 **NM** value: **38.00**
55 ❑ Jan 1957 Cover: 0.10 **NM** value: **38.00**
56 ❑ Mar 1957 Cover: 0.10 **NM** value: **38.00**
57 ❑ May 1957 Cover: 0.10 **NM** value: **38.00**
58 ❑ Jul 1957 Cover: 0.10 **NM** value: **38.00**
59 ❑ Sep 1957 Cover: 0.10 **NM** value: **38.00**
📖 12 Desperate Hours; The Secret Life of Badge 22
60 ❑ Nov 1957 Cover: 0.10 **NM** value: **38.00**
61 ❑ Jan 1958 Cover: 0.10 **NM** value: **38.00**
62 ❑ Mar 1958 Cover: 0.10 **NM** value: **38.00**
63 ❑ May 1958 Cover: 0.10 **NM** value: **38.00**
64 ❑ Jul 1958 Cover: 0.10 **NM** value: **38.00**
65 ❑ Sep 1958 Cover: 0.10 **NM** value: **38.00**
66 ❑ Nov 1958 Cover: 0.10 **NM** value: **38.00**
67 ❑ Jan 1959 Cover: 0.10 **NM** value: **38.00**

GANGLAND — DC / Vertigo
1 ❑ Jun 1998 Cover: 2.95 **NM** value: **Cover or less**
Circ: Diamd. preorders: **23,727**
cover overlay. 📖 Clean House; Chains; Your Special Day; The Bear **A:** Dave Gibbons; Tim Bradstreet; Frank Quitely; Peter Kuper **W:** Dave Gibbons; Peter Kuper; Brian Azzarello; Doselle Young
2 ❑ Jul 1998 Cover: 2.95 **NM** value: **Cover or less**
Circ: Diamd. preorders: **18,159**
3 ❑ Aug 1998 Cover: 2.95 **NM** value: **Cover or less**
Circ: Diamd. preorders: **19,079**
📖 Gang Buff; Original Gangster; Small Time; Worldwide Gangster Robots **A:** Tayyar Ozkan; Kilian Plunkett; Eric Shanower; Daniel Zezelj **W:** Tayyar Ozkan; Ed Brubaker; Darko Macan; Scott Cunningham
4 ❑ Sep 1998 Cover: 2.95 **NM** value: **Cover or less**
Circ: Diamd. preorders: **17,971**
Bk 1❑ Cover: 12.95 **NM** value: **Cover or less**
• Collects series

GANGSTERS AND GUNMOLLS — Realistic Comics
1 ❑ Sep 1951 Cover: 0.10 **NM** value: **Cover or less**
• **CGC:** 1 graded, best 7.0
2 ❑ Dec 1951 Cover: 0.10 **NM** value: **Cover or less**
3 ❑ Mar 1952 Cover: 0.10 **NM** value: **Cover or less**
• **CGC:** 2 graded, best 7.5
4 ❑ Jun 1951 Cover: 0.10 **NM** value: **Cover or less**
• **CGC:** 1 graded, best 7.0

Other grades: Multiply prices above by **1.5 for Mint • 2/3 for Very Fine • 1/3 for Fine • 1/5 for Very Good • 1/8 for Good**

GANGSTERS CAN'T WIN — D.S.

Gangsters Can't Win, a late-1940s crime title from D.S. Publishing, specialized in dark, terse, brutal, and allegedly true tales of crime and punishment. The general tone of these stories is that fate or conscience will eventually bring down the guilty, even if they elude the machinery of justice.

Tightly told and well-illustrated, the stories in Gangsters Can't Win owe a lot to the hardboiled pulp writing popularized by Black Mask and other crime magazines, and to the visual look of postwar thrillers and suspense movies. Six eight-page features and the obligatory text-only story fill out each issue.

1 ❑ Feb 1948 Cover: 0.10 **NM** value: **125.00**
• **CGC:** 1 graded, best 8.0
2 ❑ Apr 1948 Cover: 0.10 **NM** value: **80.00**
3 ❑ Jun 1948 Cover: 0.10 **NM** value: **70.00**
4 ❑ Aug 1948 Cover: 0.10 **NM** value: **55.00**
5 ❑ Oct 1948 Cover: 0.10 **NM** value: **55.00**
6 ❑ Dec 1948 Cover: 0.10 **NM** value: **55.00**
7 ❑ Feb 1949 Cover: 0.10 **NM** value: **55.00**
📖 The Evil that Men Do; The Talisman Trail; Accidentally-It's Murder (text story); Bacteria X; The Impostor; Dying Men of Piranha **A:** Al McWilliams; Robert Jenney(cover)
8 ❑ Apr 1949 Cover: 0.10 **NM** value: **55.00**
9 ❑ Jun 1949 Cover: 0.10 **NM** value: **55.00**

GANTAR-THE LAST NABU — Target

1 ❑ Dec 1986 Cover: 1.75 **NM** value: **Cover or less**
📖 Cometh The Agonistes **A:** John A. Peck **W:** John A. Peck
2 ❑ Feb 1987 Cover: 1.75 **NM** value: **Cover or less**
3 ❑ 1987 Cover: 1.75 **NM** value: **Cover or less**
4 ❑ Cover: 1.75 **NM** value: **Cover or less**
5 ❑ Cover: 1.75 **NM** value: **Cover or less**
6 ❑ Cover: 1.75 **NM** value: **Cover or less**
7 ❑ Cover: 1.75 **NM** value: **Cover or less**

GARGOYLE — Marvel

Isaac Christians was an old man whose beloved town was headed into ruin. To save it, Isaac made a deal with a demon named Avarish, who agreed to help him ... under certain conditions. Avarish placed Isaac in the body of a stone gargoyle, which he imbued with sorcerous power. Needless to say, Isaac began having second thoughts about the deal, and when the Defenders battled Avarish, Isaac took their side. Avarish was defeated, but Isaac remained trapped in the stone body of the Gargoyle.

This series begins when Isaac decides to make a visit to his old town of Christiansboro. To his horror, he discovers that his old body is very much alive, but is inhabited by the evil spirit of the original Gargoyle. What follows is a supernatural conflict which changes the way readers view this star-crossed member of the Defenders.

1 ❑ Jun 1985 Cover: 0.75 **NM** value: **1.50**
Circ: CapCity orders: **20,600**
2 ❑ Jul 1985 Cover: 0.75 **NM** value: **1.50**
Circ: CapCity orders: **16,900**
3 ❑ Aug 1985 Cover: 0.75 **NM** value: **1.50**
Circ: CapCity orders: **16,300**
4 ❑ Sep 1985 Cover: 0.75 **NM** value: **1.50**
Circ: CapCity orders: **17,200**

GARGOYLES — Marvel

1 ❑ Feb 1995 Cover: 2.50 **NM** value: **Cover or less**
Circ: CapCity orders: **11,025**
enhanced cover.
2 ❑ Mar 1995 Cover: 1.50 **NM** value: **Cover or less**
Circ: CapCity orders: **6,525**
📖 Always Darkest Before the Dawn **A:** Amanda Conner **W:** Martin Pasko
3 ❑ Apr 1995 Cover: 1.50 **NM** value: **Cover or less**
Circ: CapCity orders: **5,675**
4 ❑ May 1995 Cover: 1.50 **NM** value: **Cover or less**
Circ: CapCity orders: **5,150**
5 ❑ Jun 1995 Cover: 1.50 **NM** value: **Cover or less**
Circ: CapCity orders: **4,800**
6 ❑ Jul 1995 Cover: 1.50 **NM** value: **Cover or less**
Circ: CapCity orders: **4,525**
7 ❑ Aug 1995 Cover: 1.50 **NM** value: **Cover or less**
8 ❑ Sep 1995 Cover: 1.50 **NM** value: **Cover or less**
9 ❑ Oct 1995 Cover: 1.50 **NM** value: **Cover or less**
📖 The Egg and I **A:** Amanda Conner **W:** Mort Todd
10 ❑ Nov 1995 Cover: 1.50 **NM** value: **Cover or less**
11 ❑ Dec 1995 Cover: 1.50 **NM** value: **Cover or less**
final issue. **A:** Amanda Conner **W:** Mort Todd ★ Appearance of Xanatos, Elisa.

GAROU: THE LONE WOLF — Bare Bones

1 ❑ Jul 1999 Cover: 2.00 **NM** value: **Cover or less**
📖 Fear No Evil **A:** Victor Moya **W:** Mike Purcell

GARRISON'S GORILLAS — Dell

1 ❑ Jan 1968 Cover: 0.12 **NM** value: **20.00**
• **CGC:** 1 graded, best 4.5
Photo cover. 📖 Break Out; The Gremlins; The Frame-Up
2 ❑ Apr 1968 Cover: 0.12 **NM** value: **12.00**
• **CGC:** 1 graded, best 7.0
Photo cover. 📖 There's a Rat in the Underground; Big Bertha;
3 ❑ Jul 1968 Cover: 0.12 **NM** value: **12.00**
4 ❑ Oct 1968 Cover: 0.12 **NM** value: **12.00**
5 ❑ Oct 1969 Cover: 0.12 **NM** value: **10.00**
📖 Break Out; The Gremlins; The Frame-Up • Reprints #1

G.A.S.P. — Quebecor

1 ❑ 1994 **NM** value: **1.00**
📖 Buckie Godot; Die • Previews Tyrant, Rare Bit Fiends, Wandering Star, and more. Contains new Buck Godot, Zap Gun for Hire story. **A:** Tremaine Hanther; Barry Blair; Paul Pope; Donald Simpson; Rick Veitch; Drew Hayes; Terry Moore; Stephen R. Bissette; Teri S. Wood; Batton Lash; Phil Foglio; Marcus Harwell; Mark Sherman; Brian Clifton; Eric Treadway; John Mitchell **W:** Tremaine Hanther; Barry Blair; Paul Pope; Donald Simpson; Rick Veitch; Drew Hayes; Terry Moore; Stephen R. Bissette; Teri S. Wood; Batton Lash; Phil Foglio; Adam Harwell; Jana Christy; Michael Cohen; John Holland; Rick Molchan

GATECRASHER: RING OF FIRE — Black Bull

1 ❑ Mar 2000 Cover: 2.50 **NM** value: **Cover or less**
Yellow cover with five figures. **A:** Amanda Conner **W:** Mark Waid
1/A ❑ Mar 2000 Cover: 2.50 **NM** value: **Cover or less**
Green cover with two figures. **A:** Amanda Conner **W:** Mark Waid
2 ❑ Apr 2000 Cover: 2.50 **NM** value: **Cover or less**
3 ❑ May 2000 Cover: 2.50 **NM** value: **Cover or less**
3/A ❑ May 2000 Cover: 2.50 **NM** value: **Cover or less**
variant cover. **A:** Amanda Conner **W:** Mark Waid
4 ❑ Jun 2000 Cover: 2.50 **NM** value: **Cover or less**
4/A ❑ Jun 2000 Cover: 2.50 **NM** value: **Cover or less**
• Variant (woman in lingerie, shipped 1:4) **A:** Amanda Conner **W:** Mark Waid

GATEKEEPER — Gatekeeper

1 ❑ b&w Cover: 2.50 **NM** value: **Cover or less**

GATES OF EDEN — Fantaco

1 ❑ Cover: 3.50 **NM** value: **Cover or less**

GATES OF PANDRAGON — Ianus

1 ❑ b&w Cover: 2.25 **NM** value: **Cover or less**

GATEWAY TO HORROR (BASIL WOLVERTON'S...) — Dark Horse

1 ❑ Aug 1987, b&w Cover: 1.75 **NM** value: **Cover or less**

GATHERING OF TRIBES — KC Arts

1 ❑ **NM** value: **1.00**
No issue number. no cover price. • giveaway.

GAUNTLET, THE — Aircel

1 ❑ Jul 1992 Cover: 2.95 **NM** value: **Cover or less**
2 ❑ Aug 1992 Cover: 2.95 **NM** value: **Cover or less**
3 ❑ Sep 1992 Cover: 2.95 **NM** value: **Cover or less**
4 ❑ Oct 1992 Cover: 2.95 **NM** value: **Cover or less**
5 ❑ Nov 1992 Cover: 2.95 **NM** value: **Cover or less**
6 ❑ Dec 1992 Cover: 2.95 **NM** value: **Cover or less**
7 ❑ Jan 1993 Cover: 2.95 **NM** value: **Cover or less**
8 ❑ Feb 1993 Cover: 2.95 **NM** value: **Cover or less**
Bk 1 ❑ Cover: 29.95 **NM** value: **Cover or less**
• Collects The Gauntlet #1-8 **A:** Peter Hsu **W:** Peter Hsu; Stephanie Boyd
Bk 1/HC ❑ Cover: 59.95 **NM** value: **Cover or less**
• Hardcover edition. • Collects The Gauntlet #1-8 **A:** Peter Hsu **W:** Peter Hsu; Stephanie Boyd

GAY COMICS — U.S.A.

A deceptively simple humor anthology title from the 1940s, Gay Comics didn't feature many regular strips and characters per se. Rather, it served as an outlet for the talents of two of the most wildly funny and creative cartoonists in comics history: Harvey Kurtzman (whose insane genius later helped spawn the groundbreaking Mad title for EC), and Basil Wolverton (the inspiration for an entire generation of underground comix artists in the 1960s).

Kurtzman was just beginning to explore his style and develop his early signature strip, "Hey Look!" but Wolverton's mastery of grotesque caricature and mind-numbing detail were at their full peak, producing some beautiful and hilarious three-to-four page gems. Issues were filled out with romantic, slapstick, and military-service comedy strips by other inspired lunatics.

1 ❑ May 1944 Cover: 0.10 **NM** value: **340.00**
18 ❑ Fal 1944 Cover: 0.10 **NM** value: **160.00**
19 ❑ Win 1944 Cover: 0.10 **NM** value: **160.00**
20 ❑ Jul 1945 Cover: 0.10 **NM** value: **130.00**
21 ❑ Fal 1945 Cover: 0.10 **NM** value: **130.00**
22 ❑ Win 1945 Cover: 0.10 **NM** value: **130.00**
📖 Snoopy And Dr. Nutzy; Poke In Nose; Squat Car Squad; Eustace Hayseed And Choo-Choo; Rolly & Solly; Star And Tar; Powerhouse Pepper **A:** Basil Wolverton
23 ❑ Spr 1946 Cover: 0.10 **NM** value: **130.00**
24 ❑ Aug 1946 Cover: 0.10 **NM** value: **130.00**
25 ❑ Nov 1946 Cover: 0.10 **NM** value: **130.00**
26 ❑ Feb 1947 Cover: 0.10 **NM** value: **115.00**
27 ❑ May 1947 Cover: 0.10 **NM** value: **115.00**
28 ❑ Aug 1947 Cover: 0.10 **NM** value: **115.00**
29 ❑ Nov 1947 Cover: 0.10 **NM** value: **115.00**
30 ❑ Feb 1948 Cover: 0.10 **NM** value: **58.00**
31 ❑ Apr 1948 Cover: 0.10 **NM** value: **58.00**
32 ❑ Jun 1948 Cover: 0.10 **NM** value: **40.00**
33 ❑ Aug 1948 Cover: 0.10 **NM** value: **58.00**
34 ❑ Oct 1948 Cover: 0.10 **NM** value: **58.00**
35 ❑ Dec 1948 Cover: 0.10 **NM** value: **40.00**
36 ❑ Feb 1949 Cover: 0.10 **NM** value: **58.00**
37 ❑ Apr 1949 Cover: 0.10 **NM** value: **58.00**
38 ❑ Jun 1949 Cover: 0.10 **NM** value: **40.00**
39 ❑ Aug 1949 Cover: 0.10 **NM** value: **40.00**
40 ❑ Oct 1949 Cover: 0.10 **NM** value: **40.00**
• Series continued in Honeymoon #41

GAY COMICS (BOB ROSS) — Bob Ross

Absolutely not to be confused with the series of the same name from the 1940s (and we doubt anyone has ever made the mistake), this series serves a forum for lesbian and gay comics artists. Creators contributing to this series range from well-known artists to cartoonists for local papers.

Included in various issues is "Servants to the Cause" by Alison Bechdel of "Dykes to Watch Out For" fame; Jerry Mills' Poppers; Roberta Gregory's Bitchy Butch; and Tim Barela's Leonard and Larry. Reed Waller, co-creator of the renowned adult series Omaha the Cat Dancer, also contributes a story focusing on gay members' of that series cast.

1 ❑ **NM** value: **12.50**
2 ❑ **NM** value: **8.00**
3 ❑ **NM** value: **6.00**
4 ❑ **NM** value: **6.00**
5 ❑ **NM** value: **6.00**
6 ❑ Cover: 2.00 **NM** value: **4.50**
7 ❑ Cover: 2.00 **NM** value: **4.50**
8 ❑ Cover: 2.00 **NM** value: **4.50**
9 ❑ Win 1986 Cover: 2.00 **NM** value: **4.50**
10 ❑ Cover: 2.00 **NM** value: **3.50**
11 ❑ Cover: 2.00 **NM** value: **3.50**
• Wee-Wee's Gayhouse **A:** Roberta Gregory **W:** Roberta Gregory
12 ❑ Spr 1988 Cover: 2.50 **NM** value: **3.50**
13 ❑ Sum 1991 Cover: 2.50 **NM** value: **3.50**
14 ❑ 1991 Cover: 2.00 **NM** value: **3.50**
15 ❑ Cover: 2.00 **NM** value: **3.50**
📖 Queer Fish **A:** Donna Barr **W:** Donna Barr
16 ❑ Sum 1992 Cover: 2.95 **NM** value: **3.50**
📖 Pigeonholed • Desert Peach story **A:** Donna Barr **W:** Donna Barr
17 ❑ 1992 Cover: 2.95 **NM** value: **3.00**
18 ❑ Cover: 2.95 **NM** value: **3.00**
19 ❑ Cover: 2.95 **NM** value: **3.00**
• Alison Bechdel Special **A:** Alison Bechdel **W:** Alison Bechdel
20 ❑ Cover: 2.95 **NM** value: **3.00**
• super-heroes
21 ❑ Cover: 2.95 **NM** value: **3.00**
22 ❑ Sum 1994 Cover: 2.95 **NM** value: **5.00**
• Funny Animals Special with Omaha the Cat Dancer story
23 ❑ Sum 1996 Cover: 3.50 **NM** value: **5.00**
• Funny Animals Special
24 ❑ Fal 1996 Cover: 3.50 **NM** value: **5.00**
25 ❑ ca. 1997 Cover: 3.50 **NM** value: **Cover or less**

GAZILLION — Image

1 ❑ Nov 1998 Cover: 2.50 **NM** value: **Cover or less**
1/SC ❑ Nov 1998 Cover: 2.50 **NM** value: **Cover or less**
alternate cover. • framed **A:** Keron Grant **W:** Howard M. Shum

GD MINUS 18 — Antarctic

1 ❑ Feb 1998, b&w Cover: 2.95 **NM** value: **Cover or less**
Circ: Diamd. preorders: **2,934**
• Gold Digger Special

GEAR — Fireman

1 ❑ Nov 1998 Cover: 2.95 **NM** value: **Cover or less**
Circ: Diamd. preorders: **2,352**
2 ❑ Dec 1998 Cover: 2.95 **NM** value: **Cover or less**
Circ: Diamd. preorders: **1,945**
3 ❑ Jan 1999 Cover: 2.95 **NM** value: **Cover or less**
Circ: Diamd. preorders: **1,499**
4 ❑ Feb 1999 Cover: 2.95 **NM** value: **Cover or less**
Circ: Diamd. preorders: **1,353**
5 ❑ ca. 1999 Cover: 2.95 **NM** value: **Cover or less**
6 ❑ Apr 1999 Cover: 2.95 **NM** value: **Cover or less**
Circ: Diamd. preorders: **1,360**

GEAR STATION, THE — Image

1 ❑ Mar 2000 Cover: 2.50 **NM** value: **Cover or less**
Circ: Diamd. preorders: **51,937** • **CGC:** 1 graded, best 9.6
📖 This Hero's Journey **A:** Dan Fraga **W:** Dan Fraga; Ford Lytle Gilmore; Janak Alford
2 ❑ Apr 2000 Cover: 2.50 **NM** value: **Cover or less**
Circ: Diamd. preorders: **30,338**
3 ❑ Jun 2000 Cover: 2.50 **NM** value: **Cover or less**
Circ: Diamd. preorders: **22,734**
📖 Crossing the Threshold **A:** Dan Fraga **W:** Ford Lytle Gilmore; Janak Alford
4 ❑ Jul 2000 Cover: 2.50 **NM** value: **Cover or less**
Circ: Diamd. preorders: **22,829**

CGC-graded: Multiply prices above by **33 for 9.9 M** • **16 for 9.8 NM/M** • **7 for 9.6 NM+** • **5 for 9.4 NM** • **2.5 for 9.2 NM-** • **1.5 for 9.0 VF/NM**

Final Destination **A:** Dan Fraga **W:** Dan Fraga; Ford Lytle Gilmore; Janak Alford
5 ❑ Nov 2000 Cover: 2.50 **NM** value: **Cover or less**
Circ: Diamd. preorders: **15,139**

GEEKSVILLE — 3 Finger Prints

Geeksville is a collaborative fusion of two pre-existing titles, Rich Koslowski's The 3 Geeks and Gary Sassaman's Innocent Bystander.

The 3 Geeks stories chronicle the misadventures of lovable comic book fanboys Allen, Keith, and Jim. One humorous outing finds the Geeks trick-or-treating well past the age limit for such activities and drooling over the Halloween offerings of an old man who's passing out comics in lieu of candy.

Geeksville also features "True Tales of the Comic Shop" by Koslowski (who, along with Craig Boldman, produces the Geeks' adventures), as well Sassaman's illustrated essay feature "Innocent Bystander."

An excellent series, it moved to Image before playing out.

1 ❑ Aug 1999, b&w Cover: 2.75 **NM** value: **3.00**
Circ: Diamd. preorders: **2,304** • **CGC:** 1 graded, best 9.6
The 3 Geeks: Factor M; Innocent Bystander; True Tales From the Comic Shop **A:** Sandy Koslowski; Rich Koslowski; Garry Sassaman **W:** Sandy Koslowski; Rich Koslowski; Garry Sassaman; Al Armstrong
2 ❑ Oct 1999, b&w Cover: 2.75 **NM** value: **3.00**
Circ: Diamd. preorders: **2,082** • **CGC:** 1 graded, best 9.6
True Tales From the Comic Shop; Innocent Bystander; The 3 Geeks Go a' Haunting **A:** Rich Koslowski; Craig Boldman; Garry Sassaman **W:** Rich Koslowski; Craig Boldman; Garry Sassaman
3 ❑ Dec 1999, b&w Cover: 2.75 **NM** value: **Cover or less**

GEEKSVILLE (VOL. 2) — Image

0 ❑ Mar 2000, b&w Cover: 2.75 **NM** value: **3.00**
• **CGC:** 2 graded, best 9.9
1 ❑ May 2000, b&w Cover: 2.75 **NM** value: **3.00**
Circ: Diamd. preorders: **4,276**
2 ❑ Jul 2000, b&w Cover: 2.95 **NM** value: **Cover or less**
Circ: Diamd. preorders: **3,628** • **CGC:** 1 graded, best 9.4
The 3 Geeks: Breaking into the Biz, Part Two: How Much?!?; Innocent Bystander: Drive West on Sunset; True Tales From the Comic Shop: Lost in Cyber-Space; The 3 Geeks: Breaking into the Biz, Part 2 **A:** Sandy Koslowski; Rich Koslowski; Gary Sassaman **W:** Sandy Koslowski; Rich Koslowski; Gary Sassaman
3 ❑ Sep 2000, b&w Cover: 2.95 **NM** value: **Cover or less**
Circ: Diamd. preorders: **3,338** • **CGC:** 1 graded, best 9.4
The 3 Geeks: Breaking into the Biz, Part 3; Babes and Blades; Dark Sky; Innocent Bystander: How I Survived My Parents (Is Beyond Me!), Part 1; True Tales From the Comic Shop **A:** Jeff Rebner; Sandy Koslowski; Rich Koslowski; Allen George; Craig Boldman; Gary Sassaman **W:** Sandy Koslowski; Rich Koslowski; Gary Sassaman; Caryn Gordon; Keith Pankowski; Tamphear; Tony Isabella
4 ❑ Nov 2000, b&w Cover: 2.95 **NM** value: **Cover or less**
Circ: Diamd. preorders: **3,256**
The 3 Geeks: Breaking into the Biz, Part 4; Dark Sky, Part 2; Innocent Bystander: How I Survived My Parents (Is Beyond Me!), Part 2 **A:** Sandy Koslowski; Rich Koslowski; Gary Sassaman **W:** Sandy Koslowski; Rich Koslowski; Gary Sassaman; Caryn Gordon
5 ❑ Jan 2001 Cover: 2.95 **NM** value: **Cover or less**
Circ: Diamd. preorders: **2,970**
The 3 Geeks: Divide and Conquer, Part 1; Innocent Bystander: Nighthawks **A:** Sandy Koslowski; Gary Sassaman; Justin Wasson **W:** Rich Koslowski; Gary Sassaman
6 ❑ Mar 2001 Cover: 2.95 **NM** value: **Cover or less**
Circ: Diamd. preorders: **3,109**
All Good Things… final issue. **A:** Sandy Koslowski **W:** Rich Koslowski

GEISHA — Oni Press

1 ❑ Sep 1998 Cover: 2.95 **NM** value: **Cover or less**
Circ: Diamd. preorders: **4,949**
2 ❑ Oct 1998 Cover: 2.95 **NM** value: **Cover or less**
Circ: Diamd. preorders: **3,772**
3 ❑ Nov 1998 Cover: 2.95 **NM** value: **Cover or less**
Circ: Diamd. preorders: **3,642**
4 ❑ Dec 1998 Cover: 2.95 **NM** value: **Cover or less**
Circ: Diamd. preorders: **3,912**
Bk 1❑ Cover: 9.95 **NM** value: **Cover or less**
• collects issues #1-4

GEM COMICS — Spotlight

GEMINAR — Image

SE 1❑ Jul 2000 Cover: 4.95 **NM** value: **Cover or less**

Diamond preorders are the estimated number of comics sold, prior to their release, to comics shops in North America by Diamond Comic Distributors, the largest distributor. These figures underreport the actual number of circulating copies by the amount of reorders Diamond took (usually 5-10% again of the preorders) and sales by publishers to newsstand and bookstore distributors. For many independent publishers, Diamond's preorders may be quite close to the actual number of copies in circulation.

GEMINI BLOOD — DC / Helix

It's 2094, the Age of Options. Thanks to advances in genetic technology coupled with good old fashioned greed, the world has gone to heck in a handbasket. The elite control most of the world's resources, amusing themselves with singing dogs and robotic courtesans. The poor, meanwhile, are starving, as usual.

Then there are the Paratwa: pairs of human fetuses genetically altered to hhave telepathic links. With the ability to act as one, these twins grow to become more than a match for any human. Unfortunately, these "beings of Gemini Blood" are bred from birth to hunt humans.

Part of DC's unsuccessful attempt at a science-fiction imprint, this nine-issue series explores this bleak future world, and the lives of four people who dared to go up against the Paratwa.

1 ❑ Sep 1996 Cover: 2.25 **NM** value: **Cover or less**
Species: Paratwa, Part 1 **A:** Tommy Lee Edwards **W:** Christopher Hinz
2 ❑ Oct 1996 Cover: 2.25 **NM** value: **Cover or less**
Species: Paratwa, Part 2 **A:** Tommy Lee Edwards **W:** Christopher Hinz
3 ❑ Nov 1996 Cover: 2.25 **NM** value: **Cover or less**
Circ: Diamd. preorders: **14,740**
Species: Paratwa, Part 3 **A:** Tommy Lee Edwards **W:** Christopher Hinz
4 ❑ Dec 1996 Cover: 2.25 **NM** value: **Cover or less**
Circ: Diamd. preorders: **12,553**
Species: Paratwa, Part 4 **A:** Tommy Lee Edwards **W:** Christopher Hinz
5 ❑ Jan 1997 Cover: 2.25 **NM** value: **Cover or less**
Circ: Diamd. preorders: **10,424**
Species: Paratwa, Part 5 **A:** Tommy Lee Edwards **W:** Christopher Hinz
6 ❑ Feb 1997 Cover: 2.25 **NM** value: **Cover or less**
Circ: Diamd. preorders: **8,833**
Species: Paratwa, Part 6 **A:** Tommy Lee Edwards **W:** Christopher Hinz
7 ❑ Mar 1997 Cover: 2.25 **NM** value: **Cover or less**
Circ: Diamd. preorders: **7,820**
Infrangibility **A:** Tommy Lee Edwards **W:** Christopher Hinz
8 ❑ Apr 1997 Cover: 2.25 **NM** value: **Cover or less**
Circ: Diamd. preorders: **6,952**
Loothka Bl-Modal, Part 1 **A:** Tommy Lee Edwards **W:** Christopher Hinz
9 ❑ May 1997 Cover: 2.25 **NM** value: **Cover or less**
Circ: Diamd. preorders: **6,258**
Loothka Bl-Modal, Part 2 **A:** Tommy Lee Edwards **W:** Christopher Hinz

GEN12 — Image

1 ❑ Feb 1998 Cover: 2.50 **NM** value: **Cover or less**
Circ: Diamd. preorders: **56,810**
The Legacy **A:** Michael Ryan **W:** Brandon Choi
2 ❑ Mar 1998 Cover: 2.50 **NM** value: **Cover or less**
Circ: Diamd. preorders: **45,459**
3 ❑ Apr 1998 Cover: 2.50 **NM** value: **Cover or less**
Circ: Diamd. preorders: **38,124**
4 ❑ May 1998 Cover: 2.50 **NM** value: **Cover or less**
Circ: Diamd. preorders: **32,839**
5 ❑ Jun 1998 Cover: 2.50 **NM** value: **Cover or less**
Circ: Diamd. preorders: **30,401**

GEN13 — Image

Gen13 owes its popularity to beautiful bodies sporting smart-aleck attitudes and a genuine enthusiasm for adventuring. Spurred by the wild success of the Gen13 mini-series, the group of super-powered 20-somethings received an ongoing title in March, 1995. To celebrate, Image kicked off issue #1 with an unprecedented (and, to many purists, appalling) 13 variant covers. (Plus yet another that appeared as part of a collection!).

The team consists of Burnout, a terse young man who has the ability to fire plasma blasts; Freefall, an independent woman who can control the forces of gravity; Rainmaker, a new addition to the team who controls the forces of nature; Grunge, the team's "class clown," who also has the ability to alter his genetic structure at will; and leader Fairchild, the gorgeous, smart, and super-strong leader of the team. They also get adult supervision of sorts in the form of John Lynch, their mentor.

Gen13 spawned umpteen specials and limited series, even before Jim Lee took the series to DC.

-1 ❑ Jan 1997 Cover: 2.50 **NM** value: **4.00**
• **CGC:** 2 graded, best 9.6
• American Entertainment exclusive
0 ❑ Sep 1994 Cover: 2.50 **NM** value: **3.00**
• **CGC:** 1 graded, best 9.4
Coming Home; Desert Bloom; Big Deal; Things Change **A:** J. Scott Campbell **W:** J. Scott Campbell; Brandon Choi
1/3D❑ Feb 1998 Cover: 4.95 **NM** value: **Cover or less**
• 3D Edition. Among Friends and Enemies • with glasses **A:** J. Scott Campbell **W:** J. Scott Campbell; Brandon Choi ★ 1st Appearance of Trance, The Bounty Hunters, Alex Fairchild.
1/A ❑ Mar 1995 Cover: 2.95 **NM** value: **4.00**
Circ: CapCity orders: **91,000** • **CGC:** 5 graded, best 9.9
Cover 1 of 13: Charge!. Among Friends and Enemies • Common **A:** J. Scott Campbell **W:** J. Scott Campbell; Brandon Choi ★ 1st Appearance of Trance, The Bounty Hunters, Alex Fairchild.
1/B ❑ Mar 1995 Cover: 2.95 **NM** value: **4.00**
• **CGC:** 4 graded, best 9.9
Cover 2 of 13: Thumbs Up. Among Friends and Enemies • Common **A:** J. Scott Campbell **W:** J. Scott Campbell; Brandon Choi ★ 1st Appearance of Trance, The Bounty Hunters, Alex Fairchild.
1/C ❑ Mar 1995 Cover: 2.95 **NM** value: **5.00**
• **CGC:** 2 graded, best 9.4
Cover 3 of 13: Li'l GEN13. Among Friends and Enemies **A:** J. Scott Campbell **W:** J. Scott Campbell; Brandon Choi ★ 1st Appearance of Trance, The Bounty Hunters, Alex Fairchild.
1/D ❑ Mar 1995 Cover: 2.95 **NM** value: **5.00**
• **CGC:** 1 graded, best 9.6
Cover 4 of 13: Barbari-GEN. Among Friends and Enemies **A:** J. Scott Campbell **W:** J. Scott Campbell; Brandon Choi ★ 1st Appearance of Trance, The Bounty Hunters, Alex Fairchild.
1/E ❑ Mar 1995 Cover: 2.95 **NM** value: **5.00**
• **CGC:** 4 graded, best 9.8
Cover 5 of 13: Your Friendly Neighborhood Grunge. Among Friends and Enemies **A:** J. Scott Campbell **W:** J. Scott Campbell; Brandon Choi ★ 1st Appearance of Trance, The Bounty Hunters, Alex Fairchild.
1/F ❑ Mar 1995 Cover: 2.95 **NM** value: **5.00**
Cover 6 of 13: Gen13 Goes Madison Avenue. Among Friends and Enemies **A:** J. Scott Campbell **W:** J. Scott Campbell; Brandon Choi ★ 1st Appearance of Trance, The Bounty Hunters, Alex Fairchild.
1/G ❑ Mar 1995 Cover: 2.95 **NM** value: **10.00**
• **CGC:** 10 graded, best 9.9
Cover 7 of 13: Lin-GEN-re. Among Friends and Enemies **A:** J. Scott Campbell **W:** J. Scott Campbell; Brandon Choi ★ 1st Appearance of Trance, The Bounty Hunters, Alex Fairchild.
1/H ❑ Mar 1995 Cover: 2.95 **NM** value: **10.00**
• **CGC:** 14 graded, best 9.9
Cover 8 of 13: GEN-et Jackson. Among Friends and Enemies **A:** J. Scott Campbell **W:** J. Scott Campbell; Brandon Choi ★ 1st Appearance of Trance, The Bounty Hunters, Alex Fairchild.
1/I ❑ Mar 1995 Cover: 2.95 **NM** value: **5.00**
Cover 9 of 13: That's the Way We Became the GEN13. Among Friends and Enemies **A:** J. Scott Campbell **W:** J. Scott Campbell; Brandon Choi ★ 1st Appearance of Trance, The Bounty Hunters, Alex Fairchild.
1/J ❑ Mar 1995 Cover: 2.95 **NM** value: **5.00**
• **CGC:** 1 graded, best 9.6
Cover 10 of 13: All Dolled Up. Among Friends and Enemies **A:** J. Scott Campbell **W:** J. Scott Campbell; Brandon Choi ★ 1st Appearance of Trance, The Bounty Hunters, Alex Fairchild.
1/K ❑ Mar 1995 Cover: 2.95 **NM** value: **5.00**
• **CGC:** 2 graded, best 9.6
Cover 11 of 13: Verti-GEN. Among Friends and Enemies **A:** J. Scott Campbell **W:** J. Scott Campbell; Brandon Choi ★ 1st Appearance of Trance, The Bounty Hunters, Alex Fairchild.
1/L ❑ Mar 1995 Cover: 2.95 **NM** value: **5.00**
• **CGC:** 2 graded, best 9.6
Cover 12 of 13: Picto-Fiction. Among Friends and Enemies **A:** J. Scott Campbell **W:** J. Scott Campbell; Brandon Choi ★ 1st Appearance of Trance, The Bounty Hunters, Alex Fairchild.
1/M❑ Mar 1995 Cover: 2.95 **NM** value: **5.00**
Cover 13 of 13: Do-It-Yourself-Cover. Among Friends and Enemies **A:** J. Scott Campbell **W:** J. Scott Campbell; Brandon Choi ★ 1st Appearance of Trance, The Bounty Hunters, Alex Fairchild.
1/N ❑ Cover: 39.95 **NM** value: **60.00**
Included all variant covers, plus new puzzle cover. Among Friends and Enemies **A:** J. Scott Campbell **W:** J. Scott Campbell; Brandon Choi ★ 1st Appearance of Trance, The Bounty Hunters, Alex Fairchild.
1-2 ❑ Cover: 2.50 **NM** value: **Cover or less**
Fairchild in French maid outfit on cover. • "Encore edition".
2 ❑ May 1995 Cover: 2.50 **NM** value: **Cover or less**
Circ: CapCity orders: **72,000**
Flip cover. Wildstorm Rising, Part 4 **A:** J. Scott Campbell **W:** J. Scott Campbell; Brandon Choi ★ 1st Appearance of Helmut.
3 ❑ Jul 1995 Cover: 2.50 **NM** value: **Cover or less**
Circ: CapCity orders: **81,875**
4 ❑ Jul 1995 Cover: 2.50 **NM** value: **Cover or less**
Circ: CapCity orders: **79,300**
indicia says Jul, cover says Aug. ★ 1st Appearance of Lucius.
5 ❑ Oct 1995 Cover: 2.50 **NM** value: **Cover or less**
Circ: CapCity orders: **62,850**
6 ❑ Nov 1995 Cover: 2.50 **NM** value: **Cover or less**
Circ: CapCity orders: **43,025**
7 ❑ Jan 1996 Cover: 2.50 **NM** value: **Cover or less**
indicia says Jan, cover says Dec. ★ 1st Appearance of Copycat, Evo.
8 ❑ Feb 1996 Cover: 2.50 **NM** value: **Cover or less**
9 ❑ Mar 1996 Cover: 2.50 **NM** value: **Cover or less**
10 ❑ Apr 1996 Cover: 2.50 **NM** value: **Cover or less**
Fire from Heaven, Part 3 ★ 1st Appearance of Sigma.
11 ❑ May 1996 Cover: 2.50 **NM** value: **Cover or less**
Fire from Heaven, Part 9
11/A❑ May 1996 Cover: 2.50 **NM** value: **3.00**
• **CGC:** 3 graded, best 10.0
• European Tour Edition. Fire from Heaven, Part 9
12 ❑ Aug 1996 Cover: 2.50 **NM** value: **Cover or less**
• **CGC:** 1 graded, best 9.4
13/A❑ Nov 1996 Cover: 1.30 **NM** value: **1.50**
13/B❑ Nov 1996 Cover: 1.30 **NM** value: **1.50**
cover says Oct, indicia says Sep. **A:** J. Scott Campbell **W:** Brandon Choi ★ Appearance of TMNTs, Bone, Beanworld, Spawn, Madman.
13/C❑ Nov 1996 Cover: 1.30 **NM** value: **1.50**
• **CGC:** 1 graded, best 9.6
13/CS❑ Nov 1996 Cover: 6.95 **NM** value: **Cover or less**

• Collected Edition of #13A, B, and C. **A:** J. Scott Campbell **W:** Brandon Choi ★ Appearance of Maxx, Madman, Hellboy, Bone, Shi, Teenage Mutant Ninja Turtles, Spawn.

13/D❑Nov 1996 Cover: 6.95 **NM** value: **Cover or less**
• Collected Edition of #13A, B, and C. **A:** J. Scott Campbell **W:** Brandon Choi ★ Appearance of Maxx, Madman, Hellboy, Bone, Shi, Teenage Mutant Ninja Turtles, Spawn.

14 ❑ Nov 1996 Cover: 2.50 **NM** value: **Cover or less**
Circ: Diamd. preorders: **121,937**

15 ❑ Dec 1996 Cover: 2.50 **NM** value: **Cover or less**
Circ: Diamd. preorders: **116,896**

16 ❑ Jan 1997 Cover: 2.50 **NM** value: **Cover or less**
Circ: Diamd. preorders: **111,548**
Babes in Toyland **A:** J. Scott Campbell **W:** J. Scott Campbell; Jim Lee; Brandon Choi

17 ❑ Feb 1997 Cover: 2.50 **NM** value: **Cover or less**
Circ: Diamd. preorders: **98,548**

18 ❑ Apr 1997 Cover: 2.50 **NM** value: **Cover or less**
Circ: Diamd. preorders: **98,295**

19 ❑ May 1997 Cover: 2.50 **NM** value: **Cover or less**
Circ: Diamd. preorders: **95,665**

20 ❑ Jun 1997 Cover: 2.50 **NM** value: **Cover or less**
Circ: Diamd. preorders: **93,885**

21 ❑ Aug 1997 Cover: 2.50 **NM** value: **Cover or less**
Circ: Diamd. preorders: **88,052**
• in space

22 ❑ Sep 1997 Cover: 2.50 **NM** value: **Cover or less**
Circ: Diamd. preorders: **86,135**
Homecoming **A:** Al Rio **W:** Brandon Choi

23 ❑ Oct 1997 Cover: 2.50 **NM** value: **Cover or less**
Circ: Diamd. preorders: **84,662**
Life in the Big City **A:** Al Rio **W:** Brandon Choi

24 ❑ Nov 1997 Cover: 2.50 **NM** value: **Cover or less**
Circ: Diamd. preorders: **82,158**
Judgment Day **A:** Al Rio; Tom Raney; Terry Shoemaker **W:** Brandon Choi; Peterson Choi

25 ❑ Dec 1997 Cover: 3.50 **NM** value: **Cover or less**
Circ: Diamd. preorders: **34,483** • **CGC:** 1 graded, best 7.0
...Where Angels Fear to Tread... **A:** Al Rio; J. Scott Campbell(cover) **W:** Brandon Choi

25/A❑Dec 1997 Cover: 3.50 **NM** value: **Cover or less**
alternate cover. ...Where Angels Fear to Tread... • white background **W:** Brandon Choi

25/B❑Dec 1997 Cover: 3.50 **NM** value: **Cover or less**
• **CGC:** 2 graded, best 9.8
chromium cover. ...Where Angels Fear to Tread... **W:** Brandon Choi

25/CS❑Dec 1997 Cover: 3.50 **NM** value: **4.00**
...Where Angels Fear to Tread... • Voyager pack **A:** Al Rio; J. Scott Campbell(cover) **W:** Brandon Choi

26 ❑ Feb 1998 Cover: 2.50 **NM** value: **Cover or less**
Circ: Diamd. preorders: **63,133**
When Worlds Collide **A:** Gary Frank **W:** John Arcudi

26/A❑Feb 1998 Cover: 2.50 **NM** value: **Cover or less**
alternate cover. • fight scene

27 ❑ Mar 1998 Cover: 2.50 **NM** value: **Cover or less**
Circ: Diamd. preorders: **61,108**
Search and Seizure **A:** Gary Frank **W:** John Arcudi

28 ❑ Apr 1998 Cover: 2.50 **NM** value: **Cover or less**
Circ: Diamd. preorders: **60,528**
Remote Control **A:** Gary Frank **W:** John Arcudi

29 ❑ May 1998 Cover: 2.50 **NM** value: **Cover or less**
Circ: Diamd. preorders: **55,079**
A Firm Grip on Reality! **A:** Gary Frank **W:** John Arcudi

30 ❑ Jun 1998 Cover: 2.50 **NM** value: **Cover or less**
Circ: Diamd. preorders: **53,630**
Stranger Than Fiction **A:** Gary Frank **W:** John Arcudi

30/A❑Jun 1998 Cover: 2.50 **NM** value: **Cover or less**
alternate swimsuit cover. **C:** Gary Frank

31 ❑ Jul 1998 Cover: 2.50 **NM** value: **Cover or less**
Circ: Diamd. preorders: **48,997**
Paradigm Shift **A:** Gary Frank **W:** John Arcudi

32 ❑ Aug 1998 Cover: 2.50 **NM** value: **Cover or less**
Circ: Diamd. preorders: **47,094**
Red Skies at Morning **A:** Gary Frank **W:** John Arcudi

33 ❑ Sep 1998 Cover: 2.50 **NM** value: **Cover or less**
Circ: Diamd. preorders: **45,143** • **CGC:** 2 graded, best 9.6
Burning the Candle at Both Ends • Planetary preview **A:** Gary Frank **W:** John Arcudi

34 ❑ Oct 1998 Cover: 2.50 **NM** value: **Cover or less**
Circ: Diamd. preorders: **46,199**
Overture **A:** Gary Frank **W:** John Arcudi

34/A❑Oct 1998 Cover: 2.50 **NM** value: **Cover or less**
Variant cover by Arthur Adams (Fairchild posing). • black background **A:** Gary Frank; Arthur Adams(cover) **W:** John Arcudi

35 ❑ Nov 1998 Cover: 2.50 **NM** value: **Cover or less**
Circ: Diamd. preorders: **40,605**
But You Can't Hide **A:** Gary Frank **W:** John Arcudi

36 ❑ Dec 1998 Cover: 2.50 **NM** value: **Cover or less**
Circ: Diamd. preorders: **42,186**
That Was Then **A:** Gary Frank **C:** Gary Frank **W:** John Arcudi

36/A❑Dec 1998 Cover: 2.50 **NM** value: **Cover or less**
Variant cover by Kevin Nowlan (corn dogs). That Was Then **A:** Gary Frank; Kevin Nowlan(cover) **C:** Kevin Nowlan **W:** John Arcudi

37 ❑ Mar 1999 Cover: 2.50 **NM** value: **Cover or less**
Circ: Diamd. preorders: **38,726**

38 ❑ Apr 1999 Cover: 2.50 **NM** value: **Cover or less**
Circ: Diamd. preorders: **37,965**

38/SC❑Apr 1999 Cover: 2.50 **NM** value: **Cover or less**
Variant cover by Doug Mahnke (Grunge w/popcorn). **A:** Doug Mahnke(cover)

39 ❑ May 1999 Cover: 2.50 **NM** value: **Cover or less**
Circ: Diamd. preorders: **36,331**
Death and the Broken Promise, Part 1 **A:** Gary Frank **W:** John Arcudi

40 ❑ Jun 1999 Cover: 2.50 **NM** value: **Cover or less**
Circ: Diamd. preorders: **37,653**
Death and the Broken Promise, Part 2 **A:** Gary Frank **W:** John Arcudi

40/SC❑Jun 1999 Cover: 2.50 **NM** value: **Cover or less**
Variant cover by Kyle Baker (Roxy in shower). Death and the Broken Promise, Part 2 **A:** Gary Frank; Kyle Baker(cover) **W:** John Arcudi

41 ❑ Jul 1999 Cover: 2.50 **NM** value: **Cover or less**
Circ: Diamd. preorders: **34,843**
Death and the Broken Promise, Part 3 **A:** Gary Frank

42 ❑ Aug 1999 Cover: 2.50 **NM** value: **Cover or less**
Circ: Diamd. preorders: **33,653**

43 ❑ Sep 1999 Cover: 2.50 **NM** value: **Cover or less**
Circ: Diamd. preorders: **34,014**
A Savage Breast, Part 1 **A:** Lee Bermejo **W:** Adam Warren

44 ❑ Oct 1999 Cover: 2.50 **NM** value: **Cover or less**
Circ: Diamd. preorders: **31,922**
A Savage Breast, Part 2 **A:** Lee Bermejo **W:** Adam Warren ★ Appearance of Mr. Majestic.

45 ❑ Nov 1999 Cover: 2.50 **NM** value: **Cover or less**
Circ: Diamd. preorders: **31,423**

46 ❑ Dec 2000 Cover: 2.50 **NM** value: **Cover or less**
Circ: Diamd. preorders: **29,825**
The Grunge that ate Manhattan **A:** Ed Benés **W:** Scott Lobdell

47 ❑ Jan 2000 Cover: 2.50 **NM** value: **Cover or less**
Circ: Diamd. preorders: **28,675**

48 ❑ Feb 2000 Cover: 2.50 **NM** value: **Cover or less**
Circ: Diamd. preorders: **29,718**

49 ❑ Mar 2000 Cover: 2.50 **NM** value: **Cover or less**
Circ: Diamd. preorders: **27,339**

50 ❑ Apr 2000 Cover: 3.95 **NM** value: **Cover or less**
Circ: Diamd. preorders: **29,210**
• Giant-size. Over my Dead Body **A:** Scott Benefiel; Steve Ellis; Pay Quinn; Ed Benés **W:** Scott Lobdell; John Layman

51 ❑ May 2000 Cover: 2.50 **NM** value: **Cover or less**
Circ: Diamd. preorders: **26,879**

52 ❑ Jun 2000 Cover: 2.50 **NM** value: **Cover or less**
Circ: Diamd. preorders: **26,932**

53 ❑ Jul 2000 Cover: 2.50 **NM** value: **Cover or less**
Circ: Diamd. preorders: **26,608**

54 ❑ Aug 2000 Cover: 2.50 **NM** value: **Cover or less**
Circ: Diamd. preorders: **27,017**
The Fairchild Trilogy, Part 1 **A:** Ed Benés **W:** Jeff Marriotte

55 ❑ Sep 2000 Cover: 2.50 **NM** value: **Cover or less**
Circ: Diamd. preorders: **26,536**
The Fairchild Trilogy, Part 2 **A:** Ed Benés **W:** Jeff Marriotte

56 ❑ Oct 2000 Cover: 2.50 **NM** value: **Cover or less**
Circ: Diamd. preorders: **24,933**
The Fairchild Trilogy, Part 3 **A:** Ed Benés **W:** Jeff Marriotte

57 ❑ Nov 2000 Cover: 2.50 **NM** value: **Cover or less**
Circ: Diamd. preorders: **25,041**
Priscilla, Queen of the Monsters **A:** Ed Benés **W:** Ben Raab

58 ❑ Dec 2000 Cover: 2.50 **NM** value: **Cover or less**
Circ: Diamd. preorders: **24,447**
Gotta Kill 'Em All! **A:** Ed Benés **W:** Ben Raab

59 ❑ Jan 2001 Cover: 2.50 **NM** value: **Cover or less**
Circ: Diamd. preorders: **24,361**
Ghost, No Shell, Over Easy **A:** Ed Benés **W:** Ben Raab

60 ❑ Feb 2001 Cover: 2.50 **NM** value: **Cover or less**
Circ: Diamd. preorders: **26,113**
Behind the Powers **A:** Adam Warren **W:** Adam Warren

61 ❑ Mar 2001 Cover: 2.50 **NM** value: **Cover or less**
Circ: Diamd. preorders: **23,269**
Goin' Back to Cali to Cali, to Cali **A:** Ed Benés **W:** Adam Warren

62 ❑ Apr 2001 Cover: 2.50 **NM** value: **Cover or less**
Circ: Diamd. preorders: **22,919**
Please Pull Ahead, or Would You Like Misogyny With That? **A:** Ed Benés **W:** Adam Warren

63 ❑ May 2001 Cover: 2.50 **NM** value: **Cover or less**
Circ: Diamd. preorders: **22,389**
Fire on High **A:** Ed Benés **W:** Adam Warren

64 ❑ Jun 2001 Cover: 2.50 **NM** value: **Cover or less**
Circ: Diamd. preorders: **21,767**

65 ❑ Jul 2001 Cover: 2.50 **NM** value: **Cover or less**
Circ: Diamd. preorders: **21,245**

66 ❑ Aug 2001 Cover: 2.50 **NM** value: **Cover or less**
Circ: Diamd. preorders: **21,787**

67 ❑ Sep 2001 Cover: 2.50 **NM** value: **Cover or less**
Circ: Diamd. preorders: **21,836**

3D 1❑ Cover: 4.95 **NM** value: **5.00**
• European Tour Edition. Mauling! **A:** Arthur Adams **W:** Arthur Adams

3D 1/A❑ Cover: 4.95 **NM** value: **5.00**
Fairchild holding open dinosaur mouth on cover. • double-sized. Mauling! **A:** Arthur Adams **W:** Arthur Adams

Anl 1❑May 1997 Cover: 2.95 **NM** value: **Cover or less**
• 1997 Annual

Anl 1999❑Mar 1999 Cover: 3.50 **NM** value: **Cover or less**
No issue number. wraparound cover. • continues in DV8 Annual 1999

Anl 2000❑Dec 2000 Cover: 3.50 **NM** value: **Cover or less**
Return of the Demon **A:** Kaare Andrews **W:** Ben Raab

Bk 1❑ Apr 1998, b&w Cover: 12.99 **NM** value: **Cover or less**
A Firm Grip on Reality! • Gen13 Archives; collects mini-series and issues #1, 2, 0-13C, and Sourcebook **A:** J. Scott Campbell **W:** J. Scott Campbell; Brandon Choi

Bk 2❑ Jun 1996 Cover: 6.95 **NM** value: **Cover or less**
• Lost in Paradise; collects three issues of ongoing series

Bk 3❑ Cover: 14.95 **NM** value: **Cover or less**
• Starting Over; collects #1-7

Bk 4❑ Cover: 9.95 **NM** value: **Cover or less**
• I Love New York; collects story from #25 and #26-29

Bk 5❑ Aug 1997 Cover: 6.95 **NM** value: **Cover or less**
• European Vacation; collects two issues of regular series

Bk 6❑ Cover: 14.95 **NM** value: **Cover or less**
• We'll Take Manhattan; Collects Gen13 #45-50 **A:** Ed Benés **W:** Scott Lobdell

GEN13: A CHRISTMAS CAPER — WildStorm

1 ❑ Jan 2000 Cover: 5.95 **NM** value: **Cover or less**

GEN13: BACKLIST — Image

1 ❑ Nov 1996 Cover: 2.50 **NM** value: **Cover or less**
• collects Gen13 #1/2, Gen13 #0, Gen13 #1, Gen13: The Unreal World, and WildStorm! #1

GEN13 BIKINI PIN-UP SPECIAL — Image

1 ❑ **NM** value: **5.00**
• **CGC:** 1 graded, best 9.4
• American Entertainment Exclusive

GEN13 BOOTLEG — Image

In this series, creators who don't usually work on the popular Gen13 series, such as Terry Moore, Adam Warren, and others, have a chance to craft original stories, and sometimes even new costumes, for the popular super-heroes Rainmaker, Freefall, Fairchild, Grunge, and Burnout. Though the relationships between the characters remains true, the creators' unique style inevitably surfaces.

In Mark Farmer's and Alan Davis' "Lindquist's Fault" for instance, Rainmaker sports a remarkable costume made of twigs and leaves and team members are suddenly faced with their worst fears, brought on by other-dimensional telepaths which need to feed off emotional extremes.

1/A ❑ Nov 1996 Cover: 2.50 **NM** value: **3.00**
Circ: Diamd. preorders: **108,471**
Team standing, Fairchild front on cover. **A:** Alan Davis **W:** Mark Farmer

1/B ❑ Cover: 2.50 **NM** value: **3.00**
• Team falling **A:** Alan Davis **W:** Mark Farmer

2 ❑ Dec 1996 Cover: 2.50 **NM** value: **Cover or less**
Circ: Diamd. preorders: **89,618**
Lindquist's Fault **A:** Alan Davis **W:** Mark Farmer

3 ❑ Jan 1997 Cover: 2.50 **NM** value: **Cover or less**
Circ: Diamd. preorders: **81,187**
A Gen13 Fairy Tale **A:** Dan Norton **W:** Dan Norton

4 ❑ Feb 1997 Cover: 2.50 **NM** value: **Cover or less**
Circ: Diamd. preorders: **68,523**
Little Girl Lost **A:** Walt Simonson; Louise Simonson **W:** Walt Simonson; Louise Simonson

5 ❑ Mar 1997 Cover: 2.50 **NM** value: **Cover or less**
Circ: Diamd. preorders: **64,495**

6 ❑ Apr 1997 Cover: 2.50 **NM** value: **Cover or less**
Circ: Diamd. preorders: **55,528**

7 ❑ May 1997 Cover: 2.50 **NM** value: **Cover or less**
Circ: Diamd. preorders: **54,896**

8 ❑ Jun 1997 Cover: 2.50 **NM** value: **Cover or less**
Circ: Diamd. preorders: **51,225**
• manga-style story **A:** Adam Warren **W:** Adam Warren

9 ❑ Jul 1997 Cover: 2.50 **NM** value: **Cover or less**
Circ: Diamd. preorders: **47,270**
• manga-style story; action movie references **A:** Adam Warren **W:** Adam Warren

10 ❑ Aug 1997 Cover: 2.50 **NM** value: **Cover or less**
Circ: Diamd. preorders: **49,983**
• manga-style story; video game references

11 ❑ Sep 1997 Cover: 2.50 **NM** value: **Cover or less**
Circ: Diamd. preorders: **46,489**
The Castle of Doctor Monstro, Part 1 **A:** Aaron Lopresti **W:** Aaron Lopresti; Walt Simonson

12 ❑ Oct 1997 Cover: 2.50 **NM** value: **Cover or less**
Circ: Diamd. preorders: **45,828**
The Castle of Doctor Monstro, Part 2 **A:** Aaron Lopresti **W:** Aaron Lopresti; Walt Simonson

13 ❑ Nov 1997 Cover: 2.50 **NM** value: **Cover or less**
Circ: Diamd. preorders: **44,178**
The Trickster **A:** Matt Wieringo **W:** Matt Wieringo

14 ❑ Dec 1997 Cover: 2.50 **NM** value: **Cover or less**
Circ: Diamd. preorders: **39,136**

15 ❑ Jan 1998 Cover: 2.50 **NM** value: **Cover or less**
Circ: Diamd. preorders: **36,361**
Hangin', Part 1 **A:** Sean Shaw **W:** Jan Strnad

16 ❑ Feb 1998 Cover: 2.50 **NM** value: **Cover or less**
Circ: Diamd. preorders: **32,407**
Hangin', Part 2 **A:** Sean Shaw **W:** Jan Strnad

17/A❑Mar 1998 Cover: 2.50 **NM** value: **Cover or less**
Circ: Diamd. preorders: **31,250**
alternate cover. Virgil Chu's Reality • videogame **A:** Juvaun Kirby **W:** Robert Loren Flemming

17/B❑Mar 1998 Cover: 2.50 **NM** value: **Cover or less**
alternate cover. Virgil Chu's Reality • videogame **A:** Juvaun Kirby **W:** Robert Loren Flemming

18/A❑May 1998 Cover: 2.50 **NM** value: **Cover or less**
Circ: Diamd. preorders: **28,132**
Surfing cover. • surfin'

18/B❑May 1998 Cover: 2.50 **NM** value: **Cover or less**
Beach cover. • surfin'

19 ❑ Jun 1998 Cover: 2.50 **NM** value: **Cover or less**
Circ: Diamd. preorders: **27,619**

20 ❑ Jul 1998 Cover: 2.50 **NM** value: **Cover or less**
Circ: Diamd. preorders: **25,574**
The Numbskulls final issue. **A:** Charles Adlard **W:** Christopher Golden

Anl 1❑Feb 1998 Cover: 2.95 **NM** value: **Cover or less**
New York Confidential **A:** Steve Dillon **W:** Warren Ellis

Bk 1❑ Oct 1998 Cover: 11.95 **NM** value: **Cover or less**

CGC-graded: Multiply prices above by **33 for 9.9 M • 16 for 9.8 NM/M • 7 for 9.6 NM+ • 5 for 9.4 NM • 2.5 for 9.2 NM- • 1.5 for 9.0 VF/NM**

• Trade Paperback. 📖 Lindquist's Fault; A Gen13 Fairy Tale; Little Girl Lost • Collects Gen13 Bootleg #1-4 **A:** Alan Davis **W:** Mark Farmer

Bk 2 ❑ Dec 1997 Cover: 9.95 **NM value: Cover or less**
📖 Grunge, the Movie • Grunge: The Movie; Collects Gen13 Bootleg #8-10 **A:** Adam Warren **W:** Adam Warren

GEN13: CARNY FOLK — WildStorm

1 ❑ Jan 2000 Cover: 3.50 **NM value: Cover or less**
📖 Scenes at an Exhibition; I Want my Mommaaaaa!!; No Good Deed; Greasepaint; Sideshow on the Edge of Forever; That was Now, This is Then **A:** Arthur Adams; Doug Mahnke; Kyle Baker; Kevin Nowlan; Lee Bermejo **W:** Jerry Prosser; John Arcudi

GEN13/FANTASTIC FOUR — WildStorm

1 ❑ Cover: 5.95 **NM value: Cover or less**
📖 Qeelock's Really Big New York Adventure **A:** Kevin Maguire **W:** Kevin Maguire

GEN13/GENERATION X — Image

1/A ❑ Jul 1997 Cover: 2.95 **NM value: Cover or less**
📖 Generation Gap • crossover with Marvel **A:** Arthur Adams; J. Scott Campbell(cover) **W:** Arthur Adams; Brandon Choi

1/B ❑ Jul 1997 Cover: 2.95 **NM value: Cover or less**
alternate cover. 📖 Generation Gap • crossover with Marvel **A:** Arthur Adams **C:** Arthur Adams **W:** Arthur Adams; Brandon Choi

1/C ❑ Jul 1997 Cover: 4.95 **NM value: 5.00**
Limited cover. • 3D Edition. 📖 Generation Gap **A:** Arthur Adams **W:** Brandon Choi

1/D ❑ Jul 1997 Cover: 4.95 **NM value: 5.00**
alternate cover. • 3D Edition. 📖 Generation Gap • crossover with Marvel; with glasses **A:** Arthur Adams **C:** Arthur Adams **W:** Brandon Choi

1/E ❑ Jul 1997 Cover: 2.95 **NM value: 4.00**
• San Diego Comic-Con edition. 📖 Generation Gap **A:** Arthur Adams **W:** Brandon Choi

GEN13: GOING WEST — DC / Wildstorm

1 ❑ Jun 1999 Cover: 2.50 **NM value: Cover or less**
No issue number. One-shot. 📖 Where the B uffalo Roam **A:** Andrew Robinson **W:** Joe Pruett

GEN13: GRUNGE SAVES THE WORLD — DC / Wildstorm

1 ❑ May 1999 Cover: 5.95 **NM value: Cover or less**
• prestige format. **A:** Kevin Altieri **W:** Kevin Altieri

GEN13 INTERACTIVE — Image

1 ❑ Oct 1997 Cover: 2.50 **NM value: Cover or less**
Circ: Diamd. preorders: **45,401**
📖 Any Color You Like **A:** Jason Johnson **W:** Mike Heisler

2 ❑ Nov 1997 Cover: 2.50 **NM value: Cover or less**
Circ: Diamd. preorders: **41,025**
📖 Up For Grabs **A:** Jason Johnson **W:** Mike Heisler

3 ❑ Jan 1998 Cover: 2.50 **NM value: Cover or less**
Circ: Diamd. preorders: **34,957**
cover says Dec, indicia says Jan. 📖 How to Start a Panic **A:** Jason Johnson **W:** Mike Heisler

Bk 1 ❑ Jan 1998 Cover: 2.50 **NM value: 11.95**
No issue number. • prestige format. • Collects Gen13 Interactive #1-3, 3-D Special, Gen13 Sports Gallery **A:** Jason Johnson **W:** Mike Heisler

GEN13: MAGICAL DRAMA QUEEN ROXY — Image

1 ❑ Oct 1998 Cover: 3.50 **NM value: Cover or less**
1/A ❑ Oct 1998 Cover: 3.50 **NM value: 6.00**
alternate cover. **A:** Adam Warren **W:** Adam Warren
1/B ❑ Oct 1998 Cover: 3.50 **NM value: 8.00**
DFE alternate cover. **A:** Adam Warren **W:** Adam Warren
2 ❑ Nov 1998 Cover: 3.50 **NM value: Cover or less**
2/A ❑ Nov 1998 Cover: 3.50 **NM value: Cover or less**
• **CGC:** 1 graded, best 9.6
alternate cover.
3 ❑ Dec 1998 Cover: 3.50 **NM value: Cover or less**
3/A ❑ Dec 1998 Cover: 3.50 **NM value: Cover or less**
alternate cover.

GEN13/MAXX — Image

1 ❑ Dec 1995 Cover: 3.50 **NM value: Cover or less**

GEN13: MEDICINE SONG — WildStorm

1 ❑ Cover: 5.95 **NM value: Cover or less**

GEN13 (MINI-SERIES) — Image

0 ❑ Sep 1994 Cover: 2.50 **NM value: 3.50**
Circ: CapCity orders: **65,725**
0.5 ❑ Mar 1994 **NM value: 2.00**
• **CGC:** 4 graded, best 9.4
• Wizard promotional edition.
0.5/A ❑ Mar 1994 **NM value: 10.00**
1 ❑ Feb 1994 Cover: 2.50 **NM value: 6.00**
Circ: CapCity orders: **45,625** • **CGC:** 46 graded, best 9.8
• first printing ★ 1st Appearance of Grunge (full appearance), Burnout (full appearance), Freefall (full appearance).
1/A ❑ Oct 1997 Cover: 4.95 **NM value: Cover or less**
alternate cover. • 3-D. • with glasses ★ 1st Appearance of Grunge (full appearance), Burnout (full appearance), Freefall (full appearance).
1/B ❑ Oct 1997 Cover: 4.95 **NM value: 5.00**
• 3-D. • with glasses ★ 1st Appearance of Grunge (full appearance), Burnout (full appearance), Freefall (full appearance).
1/C ❑ Cover: 2.50 **NM value: 6.00**
Fairchild flexing on cover. ★ 1st Appearance of Grunge (full appearance), Burnout (full appearance), Freefall (full appearance).
1-2 ❑ Jun 1994 Cover: 2.50 **NM value: 3.00**
2 ❑ Mar 1994 Cover: 2.50 **NM value: 3.00**
Circ: CapCity orders: **35,600** • **CGC:** 10 graded, best 9.8
📖 Species: Paratwa, Part 2 **A:** Tommy Lee Edwards **W:** Christopher Hinz
3 ❑ Apr 1994 Cover: 1.95 **NM value: 3.00**
Circ: CapCity orders: **38,925** • **CGC:** 7 graded, best 9.8
4 ❑ May 1994 Cover: 1.95 **NM value: 2.50**
Circ: CapCity orders: **52,000** • **CGC:** 2 graded, best 9.6
5 ❑ Jul 1994 Cover: 1.95 **NM value: 2.50**
Circ: CapCity orders: **57,575** • **CGC:** 3 graded, best 9.6
5/A ❑ Jul 1994 Cover: 1.95 **NM value: 2.50**
• **CGC:** 3 graded, best 9.6
alternate cover. **A:** Whilce Portacio(cover)
Ash 1 ❑ **NM value: 6.00**
• ashcan edition.
Bk 1 ❑ Dec 1994 Cover: 12.95 **NM value: Cover or less**
1st printing.
Bk 1/HC ❑ Cover: 39.95 **NM value: Cover or less**
• Hardcover edition.
Bk 1-2 ❑ Sep 1995 Cover: 12.95 **NM value: Cover or less**
Bk 1-3 ❑ Mar 1996 Cover: 12.95 **NM value: Cover or less**
Bk 1-4 ❑ Cover: 12.95 **NM value: Cover or less**

GEN13/MONKEYMAN & O'BRIEN — Image

1 ❑ Jun 1998 Cover: 2.50 **NM value: Cover or less**
Circ: Diamd. preorders: **17,302**
1/A ❑ Jun 1998 Cover: 2.50 **NM value: 4.00**
alternate cover. **A:** Arthur Adams **W:** Arthur Adams
1/B ❑ Jun 1998 Cover: 2.50 **NM value: 6.00**
• **CGC:** 2 graded, best 9.6
Variant chromium cover. **A:** Arthur Adams **W:** Arthur Adams
1/C ❑ Jun 1998 Cover: 2.50 **NM value: 6.00**
Monkeyman holding team on cover, blue/gold background. **A:** Arthur Adams **W:** Arthur Adams
2 ❑ Aug 1998 Cover: 2.50 **NM value: Cover or less**
Circ: Diamd. preorders: **38,700**
2/A ❑ Aug 1998 Cover: 2.50 **NM value: Cover or less**
alternate cover. **A:** Arthur Adams **W:** Arthur Adams

GEN13: ORDINARY HEROES — Image

1 ❑ Feb 1996 Cover: 2.50 **NM value: Cover or less**
📖 Desolation Row **A:** Adam Hughes **W:** Adam Hughes
2 ❑ Jul 1996 Cover: 2.50 **NM value: Cover or less**

GEN13 RAVE — Image

1 ❑ Mar 1995 Cover: 1.50 **NM value: 3.00**
Circ: CapCity orders: **31,050**
wraparound cover. **A:** Jeff Rebner; Paul Pelletier; Cam Smith; Michael Lopez; Matt Feazell; Jon Holdredge **W:** Matt Feazell; Jeff Mariotte; Tom Harrington

GEN13: SCIENCE FRICTION — WildStorm

1 ❑ Cover: 5.95 **NM value: Cover or less**

GEN13: THE UNREAL WORLD — Image

1 ❑ Jul 1996 Cover: 2.95 **NM value: Cover or less**
One-shot. ★ 1st Appearance of Cull.

GEN13: WIRED — DC / Wildstorm

1 ❑ Apr 1999 Cover: 2.50 **NM value: Cover or less**

GEN13 YEARBOOK '97 — Image

1 ❑ Jun 1997 Cover: 2.50 **NM value: Cover or less**
• Yearbook-style info on team.

GEN13 'ZINE — Image

1 ❑ Dec 1996, b&w Cover: 1.95 **NM value: 2.00**
• digest.

GEN-ACTIVE — WildStorm

1 ❑ May 2000 Cover: 3.95 **NM value: Cover or less**
Superchick Smackdown cover. 📖 Nature vs. Nurture **A:** Dan Norton **W:** Jay Faerber
1/A ❑ May 2000 Cover: 3.95 **NM value: Cover or less**
Woman with knife on cover. 📖 Nature vs. Nurture **A:** Dan Norton **W:** Jay Faerber
2 ❑ 2000 Cover: 3.95 **NM value: Cover or less**
Group cover.
2/A ❑ 2000 Cover: 3.95 **NM value: Cover or less**
Woman kicking on cover.
3 ❑ Nov 2000 Cover: 3.95 **NM value: Cover or less**
📖 Devil May Care **A:** Brian Stelfreeze **W:** Eric DeSantis
4 ❑ Feb 2001 Cover: 3.95 **NM value: Cover or less**
📖 Abandon All Hope… **A:** Michael O'Hare **W:** Ben Raab
5 ❑ May 2001 Cover: 3.95 **NM value: Cover or less**
📖 Father's Day **A:** Cully Hamner **W:** Jay Faerber

GENE AUTRY AND CHAMPION — Dell

102 ❑ Aug 1955 Cover: 0.10 **NM value: 18.00**
103 ❑ Sep 1955 Cover: 0.10 **NM value: 18.00**
104 ❑ Oct 1955 Cover: 0.10 **NM value: 18.00**
105 ❑ Nov 1955 Cover: 0.10 **NM value: 18.00**
106 ❑ Dec 1955 Cover: 0.10 **NM value: 18.00**
107 ❑ Jan 1956 Cover: 0.10 **NM value: 18.00**
108 ❑ Feb 1956 Cover: 0.10 **NM value: 18.00**
109 ❑ Mar 1956 Cover: 0.10 **NM value: 18.00**
110 ❑ Apr 1956 Cover: 0.10 **NM value: 18.00**
111 ❑ Jul 1956 Cover: 0.10 **NM value: 18.00**
112 ❑ Oct 1956 Cover: 0.10 **NM value: 18.00**
113 ❑ Jan 1957 Cover: 0.10 **NM value: 18.00**
114 ❑ Apr 1957 Cover: 0.10 **NM value: 18.00**
115 ❑ Jul 1957 Cover: 0.10 **NM value: 18.00**
116 ❑ Oct 1957 Cover: 0.10 **NM value: 18.00**
117 ❑ Jan 1958 Cover: 0.10 **NM value: 18.00**
118 ❑ Apr 1958 Cover: 0.10 **NM value: 18.00**
119 ❑ Jul 1958 Cover: 0.10 **NM value: 18.00**
120 ❑ Oct 1958 Cover: 0.10 **NM value: 18.00**
121 ❑ Jan 1959 Cover: 0.10 **NM value: 18.00**

GENE AUTRY COMICS — Dell

1 ❑ Jun 1946 Cover: 0.10 **NM value: 425.00**
• **CGC:** 1 graded, best 5.5
2 ❑ Aug 1946 Cover: 0.10 **NM value: 250.00**
3 ❑ Oct 1946 Cover: 0.10 **NM value: 185.00**
4 ❑ Dec 1946 Cover: 0.10 **NM value: 135.00**
5 ❑ Feb 1947 Cover: 0.10 **NM value: 135.00**
• **CGC:** 1 graded, best 9.4
6 ❑ Apr 1947 Cover: 0.10 **NM value: 100.00**
• **CGC:** 1 graded, best 9.0
7 ❑ Jun 1947 Cover: 0.10 **NM value: 100.00**
• **CGC:** 1 graded, best 9.2
8 ❑ Aug 1947 Cover: 0.10 **NM value: 100.00**
9 ❑ Oct 1947 Cover: 0.10 **NM value: 100.00**
10 ❑ Dec 1947 Cover: 0.10 **NM value: 100.00**
11 ❑ Jan 1948 Cover: 0.10 **NM value: 65.00**
• Dell Publication begins
12 ❑ Feb 1948 Cover: 0.10 **NM value: 65.00**
• **CGC:** 2 graded, best 9.6
13 ❑ Mar 1948 Cover: 0.10 **NM value: 65.00**
14 ❑ Apr 1948 Cover: 0.10 **NM value: 65.00**
• **CGC:** 1 graded, best 9.2
15 ❑ May 1948 Cover: 0.10 **NM value: 65.00**
• **CGC:** 1 graded, best 9.4
16 ❑ Jun 1948 Cover: 0.10 **NM value: 65.00**
• **CGC:** 1 graded, best 9.2
17 ❑ Jul 1948 Cover: 0.10 **NM value: 65.00**
• **CGC:** 1 graded, best 8.5
18 ❑ Aug 1948 Cover: 0.10 **NM value: 65.00**
19 ❑ Sep 1948 Cover: 0.10 **NM value: 65.00**
20 ❑ Oct 1948 Cover: 0.10 **NM value: 65.00**
• **CGC:** 1 graded, best 9.0
21 ❑ Nov 1948 Cover: 0.10 **NM value: 48.00**
22 ❑ Dec 1948 Cover: 0.10 **NM value: 48.00**
• **CGC:** 1 graded, best 9.2
23 ❑ Jan 1949 Cover: 0.10 **NM value: 48.00**
• **CGC:** 2 graded, best 9.2
24 ❑ Feb 1949 Cover: 0.10 **NM value: 48.00**
25 ❑ Mar 1949 Cover: 0.10 **NM value: 48.00**
26 ❑ Apr 1949 Cover: 0.10 **NM value: 48.00**
27 ❑ May 1949 Cover: 0.10 **NM value: 48.00**
28 ❑ Jun 1949 Cover: 0.10 **NM value: 48.00**
29 ❑ Jul 1949 Cover: 0.10 **NM value: 48.00**
30 ❑ Aug 1949 Cover: 0.10 **NM value: 48.00**
• **CGC:** 1 graded, best 9.4
31 ❑ Sep 1949 Cover: 0.10 **NM value: 48.00**
• **CGC:** 1 graded, best 9.4
32 ❑ Oct 1949 Cover: 0.10 **NM value: 48.00**
33 ❑ Nov 1949 Cover: 0.10 **NM value: 48.00**
34 ❑ Dec 1949 Cover: 0.10 **NM value: 48.00**
• **CGC:** 1 graded, best 7.5
35 ❑ Jan 1950 Cover: 0.10 **NM value: 48.00**
36 ❑ Feb 1950 Cover: 0.10 **NM value: 48.00**
• **CGC:** 3 graded, best 9.6
37 ❑ Mar 1950 Cover: 0.10 **NM value: 48.00**
38 ❑ Apr 1950 Cover: 0.10 **NM value: 48.00**
• **CGC:** 2 graded, best 9.4
39 ❑ May 1950 Cover: 0.10 **NM value: 48.00**
40 ❑ Jun 1950 Cover: 0.10 **NM value: 48.00**
41 ❑ Jul 1950 Cover: 0.10 **NM value: 38.00**
• **CGC:** 1 graded, best 9.0
42 ❑ Aug 1950 Cover: 0.10 **NM value: 38.00**
43 ❑ Sep 1950 Cover: 0.10 **NM value: 38.00**
44 ❑ Oct 1950 Cover: 0.10 **NM value: 38.00**
45 ❑ Nov 1950 Cover: 0.10 **NM value: 38.00**
46 ❑ Dec 1950 Cover: 0.10 **NM value: 38.00**
47 ❑ Jan 1951 Cover: 0.10 **NM value: 38.00**
48 ❑ Feb 1951 Cover: 0.10 **NM value: 38.00**
49 ❑ Mar 1951 Cover: 0.10 **NM value: 38.00**
50 ❑ Apr 1951 Cover: 0.10 **NM value: 38.00**
• **CGC:** 1 graded, best 9.2
51 ❑ May 1951 Cover: 0.10 **NM value: 38.00**
• **CGC:** 1 graded, best 9.6
52 ❑ Jun 1951 Cover: 0.10 **NM value: 38.00**
53 ❑ Jul 1951 Cover: 0.10 **NM value: 38.00**
54 ❑ Aug 1951 Cover: 0.10 **NM value: 38.00**
55 ❑ Sep 1951 Cover: 0.10 **NM value: 38.00**
56 ❑ Oct 1951 Cover: 0.10 **NM value: 38.00**
57 ❑ Nov 1951 Cover: 0.10 **NM value: 38.00**
58 ❑ Dec 1951 Cover: 0.10 **NM value: 38.00**
📖 Gene Autry and the Mysterious Arrows; The Slumbering Sheriff (Text Story); The Orneriest Crook
59 ❑ Jan 1952 Cover: 0.10 **NM value: 38.00**
60 ❑ Feb 1952 Cover: 0.10 **NM value: 38.00**
61 ❑ Mar 1952 Cover: 0.10 **NM value: 32.00**
62 ❑ Apr 1952 Cover: 0.10 **NM value: 32.00**
63 ❑ May 1952 Cover: 0.10 **NM value: 32.00**
64 ❑ Jun 1952 Cover: 0.10 **NM value: 32.00**
65 ❑ Jul 1952 Cover: 0.10 **NM value: 32.00**
66 ❑ Aug 1952 Cover: 0.10 **NM value: 32.00**
67 ❑ Sep 1952 Cover: 0.10 **NM value: 32.00**
68 ❑ Oct 1952 Cover: 0.10 **NM value: 32.00**
69 ❑ Nov 1952 Cover: 0.10 **NM value: 32.00**
70 ❑ Dec 1952 Cover: 0.10 **NM value: 32.00**
71 ❑ Jan 1953 Cover: 0.10 **NM value: 32.00**
72 ❑ Feb 1953 Cover: 0.10 **NM value: 32.00**
73 ❑ Mar 1953 Cover: 0.10 **NM value: 32.00**
74 ❑ Apr 1953 Cover: 0.10 **NM value: 32.00**
75 ❑ May 1953 Cover: 0.10 **NM value: 32.00**
76 ❑ Jun 1953 Cover: 0.10 **NM value: 32.00**
77 ❑ Jul 1953 Cover: 0.10 **NM value: 32.00**
78 ❑ Aug 1953 Cover: 0.10 **NM value: 32.00**
• **CGC:** 1 graded, best 8.0
79 ❑ Sep 1953 Cover: 0.10 **NM value: 32.00**
80 ❑ Oct 1953 Cover: 0.10 **NM value: 32.00**
• **CGC:** 1 graded, best 7.0
81 ❑ Nov 1953 Cover: 0.10 **NM value: 26.00**

Other grades: Multiply prices above by **1.5 for Mint • 2/3 for Very Fine • 1/3 for Fine • 1/5 for Very Good • 1/8 for Good**

82 ❑ Dec 1953 Cover: 0.10 **NM** value: **26.00**
83 ❑ Jan 1954 Cover: 0.10 **NM** value: **26.00**
84 ❑ Feb 1954 Cover: 0.10 **NM** value: **26.00**
85 ❑ Mar 1954 Cover: 0.10 **NM** value: **26.00**
86 ❑ Apr 1954 Cover: 0.10 **NM** value: **26.00**
87 ❑ May 1954 Cover: 0.10 **NM** value: **26.00**
88 ❑ Jun 1954 Cover: 0.10 **NM** value: **26.00**
89 ❑ Jul 1954 Cover: 0.10 **NM** value: **26.00**
90 ❑ Aug 1954 Cover: 0.10 **NM** value: **26.00**
91 ❑ Sep 1954 Cover: 0.10 **NM** value: **26.00**
92 ❑ Oct 1954 Cover: 0.10 **NM** value: **26.00**
93 ❑ Nov 1954 Cover: 0.10 **NM** value: **26.00**
• **CGC:** 1 graded, best 8.5
94 ❑ Dec 1954 Cover: 0.10 **NM** value: **26.00**
• **CGC:** 1 graded, best 9.0
95 ❑ Jan 1955 Cover: 0.10 **NM** value: **26.00**
• **CGC:** 1 graded, best 8.5
96 ❑ Feb 1955 Cover: 0.10 **NM** value: **26.00**
• **CGC:** 1 graded, best 9.4
97 ❑ Mar 1955 Cover: 0.10 **NM** value: **26.00**
• **CGC:** 1 graded, best 8.0
98 ❑ Apr 1955 Cover: 0.10 **NM** value: **26.00**
• **CGC:** 1 graded, best 8.5
99 ❑ May 1955 Cover: 0.10 **NM** value: **26.00**
• **CGC:** 1 graded, best 8.5
100 ❑ Jun 1955 Cover: 0.10 **NM** value: **26.00**
• **CGC:** 2 graded, best 9.2
101 ❑ Jul 1955 Cover: 0.10 **NM** value: **18.00**
• **CGC:** 1 graded, best 8.0
• Becomes Gene Autry and Champion

GENE DOGS — Marvel

1 ❑ Oct 1993 Cover: 2.75 **NM** value: **Cover or less**
Circ: CapCity orders: **14,400**
🕮 Storm Warning • four trading cards; Polybagged **A:** David Taylor **W:** John Freeman ★ Appearance of MyS-TECH.
2 ❑ Nov 1993 Cover: 1.75 **NM** value: **Cover or less**
Circ: CapCity orders: **6,900**
3 ❑ Dec 1993 Cover: 1.75 **NM** value: **Cover or less**
Circ: CapCity orders: **5,150**
🕮 Showdown in Siberia! **A:** David Taylor **W:** John Freeman
4 ❑ Jan 1994 Cover: 1.75 **NM** value: **Cover or less**
Circ: CapCity orders: **4,300**

GENERATION HEX — DC / Amalgam

1 ❑ Jun 1997 Cover: 1.95 **NM** value: **Cover or less**
🕮 Humanity's Last Stand **A:** Adam Pollina **W:** Peter Milligan

GENERATION NEXT — Marvel

1 ❑ Mar 1995 Cover: 1.95 **NM** value: **Cover or less**
Circ: CapCity orders: **79,625**
🕮 From the Top **A:** Scott Lobdell; Chris Bachalo **W:** Scott Lobdell; Chris Bachalo
2 ❑ Apr 1995 Cover: 1.95 **NM** value: **Cover or less**
Circ: CapCity orders: **77,800**
3 ❑ May 1995 Cover: 1.95 **NM** value: **Cover or less**
Circ: CapCity orders: **91,650**
4 ❑ Jun 1995 Cover: 1.95 **NM** value: **Cover or less**
Circ: CapCity orders: **97,100**
Bk 1 ❑ May 1995 Cover: 8.95 **NM** value: **Cover or less**
Gold foil cover. • Ultimate Generation Next; collects four-issue series

GENERATION X — Marvel

Taking as its own the title of a popular work of pop-culture nonfiction, Generation X can be considered sort of the "New" New Mutants. Another class of mutants arrives for training at Professor Xavier's School for Gifted Youngsters, and they're hipper and more diverse than the X-Men and the New Mutants who came before them. Among the most interesting are: Jubilation Lee, a pyrokinetic who was adopted by the X-Men and took part in their adventures before honing her talents formally at the school; ambitious Paige Guthrie, whose ability to shed her skin, damaged or not, has given her the super-hero name, Husk; British Jonathan Starsmore, who wants to be able to harness the powers of the bio-psionic field within him; and a Samoan called Mondo who can absorb others' physical mass, but has yet to develop a battle instinct.

Although guided by telekinetic Emma Frost and Sean Cassidy (Banshee), as well as a mysterious being known only as Gateway, these teenagers are see more live super-hero action than formal schooling.

-1 ❑ Jul 1997 Cover: 1.99 **NM** value: **2.00**
🕮 The Beginning of a Beautiful Friendship • Flashback **A:** Chris Bachalo **W:** James Robinson ★ Appearance of Stan Lee.
0.5 ❑ ca. 1998 **NM** value: **2.50**
• **CGC:** 3 graded, best 9.6
0.5/LE ❑ ca. 1998 **NM** value: **6.00**
1 ❑ Nov 1994 Cover: 3.95 **NM** value: **4.00**
Circ: CapCity orders: **124,200** • **CGC:** 19 graded, best 10.0
enhanced cover. 🕮 Third Genesis **A:** Chris Bachalo **W:** Scott Lobdell
2 ❑ Dec 1994 Cover: 1.50 **NM** value: **1.75**
2/Dlx ❑ Dec 1994 Cover: 1.95 **NM** value: **2.00**
Circ: CapCity orders: **91,800**
• Deluxe edition.
3 ❑ Jan 1995 Cover: 1.50 **NM** value: **1.75**
3/Dlx ❑ Jan 1995 Cover: 1.95 **NM** value: **2.00**
Circ: CapCity orders: **80,375**
• Deluxe edition.
4 ❑ Feb 1995 Cover: 1.50 **NM** value: **1.75**
4/Dlx ❑ Feb 1995 Cover: 1.95 **NM** value: **2.00**
Circ: CapCity orders: **79,750**
• Deluxe edition.
5 ❑ Jul 1995 Cover: 1.95 **NM** value: **2.00**
Circ: CapCity orders: **69,850**
6 ❑ Aug 1995 Cover: 1.95 **NM** value: **2.00**
Circ: CapCity orders: **71,975**
7 ❑ Sep 1995 Cover: 1.95 **NM** value: **2.00**
8 ❑ Oct 1995 Cover: 1.95 **NM** value: **2.00**
Circ: Statement: **247,828**
9 ❑ Nov 1995 Cover: 1.95 **NM** value: **2.00**
Circ: Statement: **247,828**
10 ❑ Dec 1995 Cover: 1.95 **NM** value: **2.00**
Circ: Statement: **247,828**
🕮 Banshee vs. Omega Red! **A:** Tom Grummettt **W:** Scott Lobdell ★ Appearance of Wolverine, Omega Red, Banshee. ★ Versus Omega Red.
11 ❑ Jan 1996 Cover: 1.95 **NM** value: **2.00**
Circ: Statement: **247,828**
12 ❑ Feb 1996 Cover: 1.95 **NM** value: **2.00**
Circ: Statement: **247,828**
13 ❑ Mar 1996 Cover: 1.95 **NM** value: **2.00**
Circ: Statement: **247,828**
14 ❑ Apr 1996 Cover: 1.95 **NM** value: **2.00**
Circ: Statement: **247,828**
15 ❑ May 1996 Cover: 1.95 **NM** value: **2.00**
Circ: Statement: **247,828**
16 ❑ Jun 1996 Cover: 1.95 **NM** value: **2.00**
Circ: Statement: **247,828**
17 ❑ Jul 1996 Cover: 1.95 **NM** value: **2.00**
Circ: Statement: **247,828**
18 ❑ Aug 1996 Cover: 1.95 **NM** value: **2.00**
Circ: Statement: **247,828**
🕮 Onslaught: Impact 1
19 ❑ Sep 1996 Cover: 1.95 **NM** value: **2.00**
Circ: Statement: **171,606**
🕮 Onslaught: Impact 2
20 ❑ Oct 1996 Cover: 1.95 **NM** value: **2.00**
Circ: Statement: **171,606**
21 ❑ Nov 1996 Cover: 1.95 **NM** value: **2.00**
Circ: Statement: **171,606** Direct Market orders: **141,000**
• Has 1996 Statement, filed 10/1/96 (Alert: Issue shipped before filing date); avg print run 296,414; avg sales 242,259; avg subs 5,569; avg total paid 247,828; samples 600; office use 125; max existent 248,553; 16% of run returned ★ Appearance of Howard the Duck.
22 ❑ Dec 1996 Cover: 1.95 **NM** value: **2.00**
Circ: Statement: **171,606** Direct Market orders: **137,250**
🕮 All Hallows Eve **A:** Mitch Byrd **W:** Scott Lobdell ★ Appearance of Nightmare.
23 ❑ Jan 1997 Cover: 1.95 **NM** value: **2.00**
Circ: Statement: **171,606** Direct Market orders: **131,750**
🕮 We Give Thanks **A:** Mitch Byrd **W:** Scott Lobdell
24 ❑ Feb 1997 Cover: 1.95 **NM** value: **2.00**
Circ: Statement: **171,606** Direct Market orders: **123,250**
🕮 Home for the Holidays **A:** Rick Leonardi **W:** Scott Lobdell
25 ❑ Mar 1997 Cover: 2.99 **NM** value: **3.00**
Circ: Statement: **171,606** Direct Market orders: **118,250**
wraparound cover. • Giant-size. **A:** Chris Bachalo **W:** Scott Lobdell
26 ❑ Apr 1997 Cover: 1.95 **NM** value: **2.00**
Circ: Statement: **171,606** Direct Market orders: **111,750**
🕮 Adrift **A:** Joe Bennett; Joe Pimentel **W:** Scott Lobdell
27 ❑ May 1997 Cover: 1.95 **NM** value: **2.00**
Circ: Statement: **171,606** Diamd. preorders: **111,830**
🕮 The Last X Man **A:** Pop Mhan; Chris Bachalo **W:** Scott Lobdell
28 ❑ Jun 1997 Cover: 1.95 **NM** value: **2.00**
Circ: Statement: **171,606** Diamd. preorders: **112,936**
🕮 Oh, Now I Get It… **A:** Chris Bachalo **W:** Scott Lobdell
29 ❑ Aug 1997 Cover: 1.99 **NM** value: **2.00**
Circ: Statement: **171,606** Diamd. preorders: **104,577**
• gatefold summary. • Operation Zero Tolerance
30 ❑ Sep 1997 Cover: 1.99 **NM** value: **2.00**
Circ: Diamd. preorders: **101,818**
• gatefold summary. • Operation Zero Tolerance
31 ❑ Oct 1997 Cover: 1.99 **NM** value: **2.00**
Circ: Diamd. preorders: **100,212**
• gatefold summary. • Operation Zero Tolerance
32 ❑ Nov 1997 Cover: 1.99 **NM** value: **2.00**
Circ: Diamd. preorders: **98,658**
• gatefold summary. ★ Versus Circus of Crime.
33 ❑ Dec 1997 Cover: 1.99 **NM** value: **2.00**
Circ: Diamd. preorders: **97,447**
• gatefold summary. • Has 1997 Statement, filed 10/1/97; avg print run 250,742; avg sales 166,156; avg subs 5,450; avg total paid 171,606; samples 545; office use 125; max existent 172,276; 31% of run returned
34 ❑ Jan 1998 Cover: 1.99 **NM** value: **2.00**
Circ: Diamd. preorders: **94,498**
• gatefold summary. ★ Versus White Queen.
35 ❑ Feb 1998 Cover: 1.99 **NM** value: **2.00**
Circ: Diamd. preorders: **88,552**
• gatefold summary.
36 ❑ Mar 1998 Cover: 1.99 **NM** value: **2.00**
Circ: Diamd. preorders: **83,688**
• gatefold summary.
37 ❑ Apr 1998 Cover: 1.99 **NM** value: **2.00**
Circ: Diamd. preorders: **77,190**
• gatefold summary.
38 ❑ May 1998 Cover: 1.99 **NM** value: **2.00**
Circ: Diamd. preorders: **75,620**
• gatefold summary. 🕮 Mystery Train **A:** Chris Bachalo **W:** Scott Lobdell
39 ❑ Jun 1998 Cover: 1.99 **NM** value: **2.00**
Circ: Diamd. preorders: **73,192**
• gatefold summary. 🕮 Return From Forever **A:** Chris Bachalo **W:** Scott Lobdell
40 ❑ Jul 1998 Cover: 1.99 **NM** value: **2.00**
Circ: Diamd. preorders: **67,938**
• gatefold summary.
41 ❑ Aug 1998 Cover: 1.99 **NM** value: **2.00**
Circ: Diamd. preorders: **65,729**
• gatefold summary.
42 ❑ Sep 1998 Cover: 1.99 **NM** value: **2.00**
Circ: Diamd. preorders: **62,409**
• gatefold summary.
43 ❑ Oct 1998 Cover: 1.99 **NM** value: **2.00**
Circ: Diamd. preorders: **59,726**
• gatefold summary. • White Queen powerless
44 ❑ Nov 1998 Cover: 1.99 **NM** value: **2.00**
Circ: Diamd. preorders: **58,351**
• gatefold summary.
45 ❑ Dec 1998 Cover: 1.99 **NM** value: **2.00**
Circ: Diamd. preorders: **57,223**
• gatefold summary. • White Queen regains powers
46 ❑ Dec 1998 Cover: 1.99 **NM** value: **2.00**
Circ: Diamd. preorders: **56,286**
• gatefold summary.
47 ❑ Jan 1999 Cover: 1.99 **NM** value: **2.00**
Circ: Diamd. preorders: **55,606**
• gatefold summary. ★ Appearance of Forge.
48 ❑ Feb 1999 Cover: 1.99 **NM** value: **2.00**
Circ: Diamd. preorders: **54,519**
49 ❑ Mar 1999 Cover: 1.99 **NM** value: **2.00**
Circ: Diamd. preorders: **52,895**
50 ❑ Apr 1999 Cover: 2.99 **NM** value: **3.00**
Circ: Diamd. preorders: **54,071**
🕮 War of the Mutants, part 1 **A:** Terry Dodson **W:** Jay Faerber ★ Appearance of Dark Beast.
50/Aut ❑ Apr 1999 Cover: 2.99 **NM** value: **8.00**
🕮 War of the Mutants, part 1 **A:** Terry Dodson **W:** Jay Faerber ★ Appearance of Dark Beast.
51 ❑ May 1999 Cover: 1.99 **NM** value: **2.00**
Circ: Diamd. preorders: **49,923**
52 ❑ Jun 1999 Cover: 1.99 **NM** value: **2.00**
Circ: Diamd. preorders: **51,026**
53 ❑ Jul 1999 Cover: 1.99 **NM** value: **2.00**
Circ: Diamd. preorders: **49,648**
54 ❑ Aug 1999 Cover: 1.99 **NM** value: **2.00**
Circ: Diamd. preorders: **48,799**
55 ❑ Sep 1999 Cover: 1.99 **NM** value: **2.00**
Circ: Diamd. preorders: **48,731**
56 ❑ Oct 1999 Cover: 1.99 **NM** value: **2.00**
Circ: Diamd. preorders: **47,086**
57 ❑ Nov 1999 Cover: 2.99 **NM** value: **Cover or less**
Circ: Diamd. preorders: **45,376**
58 ❑ Dec 1999 Cover: 2.99 **NM** value: **Cover or less**
Circ: Diamd. preorders: **45,516**
59 ❑ Jan 2000 Cover: 1.99 **NM** value: **Cover or less**
Circ: Diamd. preorders: **44,080**
60 ❑ Feb 2000 **NM** value: **2.25**
Circ: Diamd. preorders: **46,586**
61 ❑ Mar 2000 **NM** value: **2.25**
Circ: Diamd. preorders: **41,598**
62 ❑ Apr 2000 **NM** value: **2.25**
Circ: Diamd. preorders: **39,378**
63 ❑ May 2000 **NM** value: **2.25**
Circ: Diamd. preorders: **51,982**
64 ❑ Jun 2000 **NM** value: **2.25**
Circ: Diamd. preorders: **44,788**
65 ❑ Jul 2000 **NM** value: **2.25**
Circ: Diamd. preorders: **46,017**
66 ❑ Aug 2000 **NM** value: **2.25**
Circ: Diamd. preorders: **46,456**
67 ❑ Sep 2000 **NM** value: **2.25**
Circ: Diamd. preorders: **45,455**
68 ❑ Oct 2000 Cover: 2.25 **NM** value: **Cover or less**
Circ: Diamd. preorders: **41,855**
69 ❑ Nov 2000 Cover: 2.25 **NM** value: **Cover or less**
Circ: Diamd. preorders: **41,835**
🕮 Come On Die Young, Part 3 **A:** Alan Evans **W:** Brian Wood; Warren Ellis
70 ❑ Dec 2000 Cover: 2.25 **NM** value: **Cover or less**
Circ: Diamd. preorders: **41,539**
71 ❑ Jan 2001 Cover: 2.25 **NM** value: **Cover or less**
Circ: Diamd. preorders: **40,744**
🕮 Four Days, Part 1 **A:** Steve Pugh **W:** Brian Wood
72 ❑ Feb 2001 Cover: 2.25 **NM** value: **Cover or less**
Circ: Diamd. preorders: **39,292**
🕮 Four Days, Part 2 **A:** Steve Pugh **W:** Brian Wood
73 ❑ Mar 2001 Cover: 2.25 **NM** value: **Cover or less**
Circ: Diamd. preorders: **37,802**
🕮 Four Days, Part 3 **A:** Ron Lim **W:** Brian Wood
74 ❑ Apr 2001 Cover: 2.25 **NM** value: **Cover or less**
Circ: Diamd. preorders: **36,667**
🕮 Four Days, Part 4 **A:** Steve Pugh **W:** Brian Wood
75 ❑ Cover: 2.99 **NM** value: **Cover or less**
Circ: Diamd. preorders: **36,928** • **CGC:** 1 graded, best 9.4
Anl 1995 ❑ ca. 1995 Cover: 3.95 **NM** value: **Cover or less**
wraparound cover.
Anl 1996 ❑ ca. 1996 Cover: 2.99 **NM** value: **Cover or less**
wraparound cover. 🕮 Everyday People • Generation X '96 **A:** Jeff Johnson; Dan Panosian **W:** Michael Golden
Anl 1997 ❑ ca. 1997 Cover: 2.99 **NM** value: **Cover or less**
wraparound cover. • gatefold summary. • Generation X '97
Anl 1998 ❑ ca. 1998 Cover: 3.50 **NM** value: **Cover or less**
wraparound cover. • gatefold summary. • Generation X/Dracula '98
Anl 1999 ❑ ca. 1999 Cover: 3.50 **NM** value: **Cover or less**
Ash 1 ❑ Cover: 0.75 **NM** value: **Cover or less**
• ashcan edition.
HS 1 ❑ Feb 1998 Cover: 3.50 **NM** value: **Cover or less**
• Giant-size. 🕮 Yes, Jubilee-there is a Santa Clause • Holiday Special **A:** Adam Pollina **W:** Joseph Harris

GENERATION X/GEN13 — Marvel

1 ❑ ca. 1997 Cover: 3.99 **NM** value: **4.00**
• **CGC:** 1 graded, best 9.6

CGC-graded: Multiply prices above by **33 for 9.9 M • 16 for 9.8 NM/M • 7 for 9.6 NM+ • 5 for 9.4 NM • 2.5 for 9.2 NM- • 1.5 for 9.0 VF/NM**

No issue number. One-shot. wraparound cover. • crossover with Image
1/A ❑ ca. 1997 Cover: 2.95 **NM** value: **4.00**
variant cover.

GENERATION X UNDERGROUND — Marvel

1 ❑ May 1998, b&w Cover: 2.50 **NM** value: **Cover or less**
Circ: Diamd. preorders: **43,456**
cardstock cover. 📖 The Big Game; Jubilee's Scrapbook; Banshee's Angels; Gen X Bootleg Trading Cards; Half a Face **A:** Jim Mahfood **W:** Jim Mahfood

GENERATION ZERO — DC

Bk 1❑ Cover: 14.95 **NM** value: **Cover or less**
• reprint from Epic

GENERIC COMIC, THE — Marvel

Responding to the inflation of the late 1970s, grocers began stocking "generic" foods. They had long had their own "house" brands of canned goods and other foodstuffs, but, the theory went, eliminating all color and design altogether from packaging would make the items even more affordable. Thus, racks of bland-looking black-and-white packages appeared in grocery stores, making customers in this era wonder if they hadn't wondered into a shop in, say, Minsk.

The whole idea provides the springboard for one of Marvel's stranger one-shots. The Generic Comic Book comes with a Super-Hero complete with 2.65 Super-Powers, an Assortment of Neurotic Tendencies, and a Girlfriend.

It's done completely straight, and deserves a spot in comics history, if only for its truth in advertising. — JJM

1 ❑ Apr 1983 Cover: 0.60 **NM** value: **2.50**

GENESIS (DC) — DC

1 ❑ Oct 1997 Cover: 1.95 **NM** value: **Cover or less**
Circ: Diamd. preorders: **86,141**
📖 Resonance **A:** Ron Wagner **W:** John Byrne
2 ❑ Oct 1997 Cover: 1.95 **NM** value: **Cover or less**
Circ: Diamd. preorders: **80,276**
3 ❑ Oct 1997 Cover: 1.95 **NM** value: **Cover or less**
Circ: Diamd. preorders: **78,599**
4 ❑ Oct 1997 Cover: 1.95 **NM** value: **Cover or less**
Circ: Diamd. preorders: **77,936**

GENESIS (MALIBU) — Malibu

0 ❑ Oct 1993 Cover: 3.50 **NM** value: **Cover or less**
Circ: CapCity orders: **20,675**
foil cover. 📖 Rock in a Hard Place; Revelations; The Fantastic, Jurassic Four; Passing the Torch **A:** Rich Buckler; Curt Swan; Patrick Rolo; Jimmy Palmiotti **W:** Charles Marshall; R.A. Jones; Roland Mann; Tom Mason

GENESIS: THE #1 COLLECTION — Image

1 ❑ Cover: 9.99 **NM** value: **Cover or less**
• Reprints Backlash #1, DV8 #1, Deathblow #1, Gen13 #1, Grifter #1, StormWatch #1, Union #1, Wetworks #1, WildC.A.T.s #1, Urban Storm **A:** J. Scott Campbell; Mark Texeira; Humberto Ramos; Whilce Portacio; Ryan Benjamin; Brett Booth; Jim Lee; Scott Clark **W:** J. Scott Campbell; Whilce Portacio; Brett Booth; Warren Ellis; Jim Lee; Brandon Choi; Jeff Mariotte; Mike Heisler; Pat C.; Sean Huffner; Steven Seagle

GENETIX — Marvel

1 ❑ Oct 1993 Cover: 2.75 **NM** value: **Cover or less**
Circ: CapCity orders: **15,000**
wraparound cover. 📖 Deadly Harvest, Part 1 **A:** Andy Lanning; Phil Gascoine **W:** Andy Lanning; Graham Marks ★ Appearance of Genetix.
2 ❑ Nov 1993 Cover: 1.75 **NM** value: **Cover or less**
Circ: CapCity orders: **8,100**
📖 Deadly Harvest, Part 2 **A:** Phil Gascoine **W:** Graham Marks
3 ❑ Dec 1993 Cover: 1.75 **NM** value: **Cover or less**
Circ: CapCity orders: **5,700**
📖 Deadly Harvest, Part 3 **A:** Phil Gascoine **W:** Graham Marks
4 ❑ Jan 1994 Cover: 1.75 **NM** value: **Cover or less**
Circ: CapCity orders: **4,750**
📖 Deadly Harvest, Part 4 **A:** Phil Gascoine **W:** Graham Marks
5 ❑ Feb 1994 Cover: 1.75 **NM** value: **Cover or less**
Circ: CapCity orders: **3,850**
📖 Deadly Harvest, Part 5 **A:** Phil Gascoine **W:** Graham Marks
6 ❑ Mar 1994 Cover: 1.75 **NM** value: **Cover or less**
Circ: CapCity orders: **2,850**
📖 Deadly Harvest, Part 6 **A:** Phil Gascoine **W:** Graham Marks

GENOCIDE — Renegade Tribe

1 ❑ Aug 1994 Cover: 2.95 **NM** value: **Cover or less**
1-2 ❑ Aug 1994 Cover: 2.95 **NM** value: **Cover or less**

GENOCYBER — Viz

1 ❑ 1993b&w Cover: 2.75 **NM** value: **Cover or less**
Circ: CapCity orders: **5,375**
• Japanese **A:** Tony Takezaki **W:** Tony Takezaki
2 ❑ 1993b&w Cover: 2.75 **NM** value: **Cover or less**
Circ: CapCity orders: **3,250**
• Japanese **A:** Tony Takezaki **W:** Tony Takezaki
3 ❑ b&w Cover: 2.75 **NM** value: **Cover or less**
Circ: CapCity orders: **3,150**
📖 The Birth of Genocyber, Part 2 • Japanese **A:** Tony Takezaki **W:** Tony Takezaki
4 ❑ b&w Cover: 2.75 **NM** value: **Cover or less**
• Japanese **A:** Tony Takezaki **W:** Tony Takezaki
5 ❑ b&w Cover: 2.75 **NM** value: **Cover or less**
• Japanese **A:** Tony Takezaki **W:** Tony Takezaki

GEN OF HIROSHIMA — Educomics

1 ❑ Jan 1980 Cover: 1.50 **NM** value: **2.00**
2 ❑ Cover: 2.00 **NM** value: **Cover or less**

GENSAGA — Express / Entity

1 ❑ Cover: 2.50 **NM** value: **Cover or less**

GENUS — Antarctic / Venus

All issues are adults only.

Perhaps comics can be said to have arrived: They've added a new fetish to the library of sexual behavior.

Fans of funny animal, or "furry," comics have their own corner of comics fandom, and there's a niche of those folks who are into seeing those anthropomorhic characters in sexual situations. It doesn't seem that its fans find animals sexually appealing, so much as they find the notion of fantasy creatures with human bodies and animal faces appealing: a bit of transferance to keep the latter-day Freuds busy.

Anyway, Genus, as published by Antarctic and then Radio, has been the flagship adult furry title since the early 1990s, featuring humor and dramatic stories, usually sexual in nature, featuring a variety of funny animals. There have even been issues devoted to lesbian unicorns, which is about all the description you need. For adults only, of course. — JJM

1 ❑ May 1993 Cover: 2.95 **NM** value: **3.50**
• Antarctic publishes
2 ❑ Sep 1993 Cover: 2.95 **NM** value: **3.00**
3 ❑ Nov 1993 Cover: 2.95 **NM** value: **3.00**
4 ❑ Jan 1994 Cover: 2.95 **NM** value: **3.00**
5 ❑ Mar 1994 Cover: 2.95 **NM** value: **3.00**
6 ❑ May 1994 Cover: 2.95 **NM** value: **3.00**
7 ❑ Jul 1994 Cover: 2.95 **NM** value: **3.00**
8 ❑ Sep 1994 Cover: 2.95 **NM** value: **3.00**
9 ❑ Nov 1994 Cover: 2.95 **NM** value: **3.00**
10 ❑ Jan 1995 Cover: 3.50 **NM** value: **Cover or less**
11 ❑ Mar 1995 Cover: 2.95 **NM** value: **Cover or less**
12 ❑ May 1995 Cover: 2.95 **NM** value: **Cover or less**
📖 Terry Times Three; Rat & Ruin; Mink: Shell Game **A:** Fred Perry; Kjartan Arnorsson; Paul Kidd & Mitch Beiro **W:** Fred Perry; Kjartan Arnorsson; Paul Kidd & Mitch Beiro
13 ❑ Jul 1995 Cover: 2.95 **NM** value: **Cover or less**
📖 Mink: Hometown Blues; Gainful Enjoyment; Undercover **W:** Chris Tennaro; Kjartan Arnorsson; John DiGiorgio; Rueter
14 ❑ Sep 1995 Cover: 2.95 **NM** value: **Cover or less**
15 ❑ Nov 1995 Cover: 2.95 **NM** value: **Cover or less**
16 ❑ Jan 1996 Cover: 2.95 **NM** value: **Cover or less**
17 ❑ Mar 1996 Cover: 2.95 **NM** value: **Cover or less**
18 ❑ May 1996 Cover: 2.95 **NM** value: **Cover or less**
19 ❑ Jul 1996 Cover: 2.95 **NM** value: **Cover or less**
20 ❑ Sep 1996 Cover: 3.95 **NM** value: **Cover or less**
Circ: Diamd. preorders: **2,926**
21 ❑ Nov 1996 Cover: 2.95 **NM** value: **Cover or less**
Circ: Diamd. preorders: **2,690**
22 ❑ Jan 1997 Cover: 2.95 **NM** value: **Cover or less**
Circ: Diamd. preorders: **2,566**
📖 The Right Size; Savage Squirrels Dating Tips; Squeaky Clean; Centerfold Mink; Toy Boy; Behind The Squeals **A:** Jay Naylor; Barnet; Dutch; Karno; Kjartan Arnorsson; Walko; Brian O'Connor **W:** Jay Naylor; Barnet; Dutch; Karno; Kjartan Arnorsson; Walko; Brian O'Connor

GENUS — Radio

23 ❑ Apr 1997 Cover: 2.95 **NM** value: **Cover or less**
• all-skunk issue; Radio Comix publishes
24 ❑ Jun 1997 Cover: 2.95 **NM** value: **Cover or less**
25 ❑ Aug 1997 Cover: 2.95 **NM** value: **Cover or less**
26 ❑ Oct 1997 Cover: 2.95 **NM** value: **Cover or less**
27 ❑ Dec 1997 Cover: 2.95 **NM** value: **Cover or less**
28 ❑ Feb 1998 Cover: 2.95 **NM** value: **Cover or less**
29 ❑ Apr 1998 Cover: 2.95 **NM** value: **Cover or less**
30 ❑ Jun 1998 Cover: 2.95 **NM** value: **Cover or less**
31 ❑ Aug 1998 Cover: 2.95 **NM** value: **Cover or less**
Circ: Diamd. preorders: **2,225**
32 ❑ Oct 1998 Cover: 2.95 **NM** value: **Cover or less**
Circ: Diamd. preorders: **2,205**
33 ❑ Dec 1998 Cover: 2.95 **NM** value: **Cover or less**
Circ: Diamd. preorders: **2,327**
34 ❑ Feb 1999 Cover: 2.95 **NM** value: **Cover or less**
Circ: Diamd. preorders: **2,209**
35 ❑ Apr 1999 Cover: 2.95 **NM** value: **Cover or less**
Circ: Diamd. preorders: **2,279**
36 ❑ Jun 1999 Cover: 2.95 **NM** value: **Cover or less**
Circ: Diamd. preorders: **2,343**
37 ❑ Aug 1999 Cover: 2.95 **NM** value: **Cover or less**
Circ: Diamd. preorders: **2,378**
38 ❑ Oct 1999 Cover: 2.95 **NM** value: **Cover or less**
Circ: Diamd. preorders: **2,330**
39 ❑ Dec 1999 Cover: 2.95 **NM** value: **Cover or less**
40 ❑ Feb 2000 Cover: 2.95 **NM** value: **Cover or less**
Circ: Diamd. preorders: **2,165**
41 ❑ Apr 2000 Cover: 2.95 **NM** value: **Cover or less**
Circ: Diamd. preorders: **2,221**
📖 Rat Maze; Crammin'; Mink: You Can't Save Them All
42 ❑ Jun 2000 Cover: 2.95 **NM** value: **Cover or less**
Circ: Diamd. preorders: **2,244**
📖 Anthony; Big Little Brother; Do-It-Yourself Porno Home Video; Centerfold; Kanata & Mistress Renge
43 ❑ Aug 2000 Cover: 2.95 **NM** value: **Cover or less**
Circ: Diamd. preorders: **2,199**
📖 Anthony; Collars & Cuffs; Don & Kat: Dream On; Demon Hunter Ernest

GENUS GREATEST HITS — Antarctic

1 ❑ Apr 1996 Cover: 4.50 **NM** value: **Cover or less**
2 ❑ May 1997 Cover: 4.95 **NM** value: **Cover or less**

GENUS SPOTLIGHT — Radio

1 ❑ Jul 1998 Cover: 2.95 **NM** value: **Cover or less**
• Skunkworks
2 ❑ Nov 1998 Cover: 2.95 **NM** value: **Cover or less**
• Skunkworks

GEOBREEDERS — CPM Manga

1 ❑ Mar 1999 Cover: 2.95 **NM** value: **Cover or less**
Circ: Diamd. preorders: **4,660**
2 ❑ Apr 1999 Cover: 2.95 **NM** value: **Cover or less**
Circ: Diamd. preorders: **3,780**
3 ❑ May 1999 Cover: 2.95 **NM** value: **Cover or less**
Circ: Diamd. preorders: **3,768**
4 ❑ Jun 1999 Cover: 2.95 **NM** value: **Cover or less**
Circ: Diamd. preorders: **3,677**
5 ❑ Jul 1999 Cover: 2.95 **NM** value: **Cover or less**
Circ: Diamd. preorders: **3,493**
6 ❑ Aug 1999 Cover: 2.95 **NM** value: **Cover or less**
Circ: Diamd. preorders: **3,273**
7 ❑ Sep 1999 Cover: 2.95 **NM** value: **Cover or less**
Circ: Diamd. preorders: **3,103**
8 ❑ Oct 1999 Cover: 2.95 **NM** value: **Cover or less**
Circ: Diamd. preorders: **3,184**
9 ❑ Nov 1999 Cover: 2.95 **NM** value: **Cover or less**
Circ: Diamd. preorders: **2,966**
10 ❑ Dec 1999 Cover: 2.95 **NM** value: **Cover or less**
11 ❑ Jan 2000 Cover: 2.95 **NM** value: **Cover or less**
Circ: Diamd. preorders: **2,819**
12 ❑ Feb 2000 Cover: 2.95 **NM** value: **Cover or less**
Circ: Diamd. preorders: **2,721**
13 ❑ Mar 2000 Cover: 2.95 **NM** value: **Cover or less**
Circ: Diamd. preorders: **2,706**
14 ❑ Apr 2000 Cover: 2.95 **NM** value: **Cover or less**
Circ: Diamd. preorders: **2,656**
15 ❑ May 2000 Cover: 2.95 **NM** value: **Cover or less**
Circ: Diamd. preorders: **2,700**
16 ❑ Jun 2000 Cover: 2.95 **NM** value: **Cover or less**
Circ: Diamd. preorders: **2,740**
17 ❑ Jul 2000 Cover: 2.95 **NM** value: **Cover or less**
Circ: Diamd. preorders: **2,740**
18 ❑ Aug 2000 Cover: 2.95 **NM** value: **Cover or less**
Circ: Diamd. preorders: **2,579**
19 ❑ Sep 2000 Cover: 2.95 **NM** value: **Cover or less**
Circ: Diamd. preorders: **2,582**
20 ❑ Oct 2000 Cover: 2.95 **NM** value: **Cover or less**
Circ: Diamd. preorders: **2,613**
21 ❑ Nov 2000 Cover: 2.95 **NM** value: **Cover or less**
Circ: Diamd. preorders: **2,483**
22 ❑ Dec 2000 Cover: 2.95 **NM** value: **Cover or less**
Circ: Diamd. preorders: **2,423**
23 ❑ Jan 2001 Cover: 2.95 **NM** value: **Cover or less**
Circ: Diamd. preorders: **2,305**
24 ❑ Feb 2001 Cover: 2.95 **NM** value: **Cover or less**
Circ: Diamd. preorders: **2,264**
25 ❑ Mar 2001 Cover: 2.95 **NM** value: **Cover or less**
Circ: Diamd. preorders: **2,266**
26 ❑ Apr 2001 Cover: 2.95 **NM** value: **Cover or less**
Circ: Diamd. preorders: **2,221**
27 ❑ May 2001 Cover: 2.95 **NM** value: **Cover or less**
Circ: Diamd. preorders: **2,136**
28 ❑ Jun 2001 Cover: 2.95 **NM** value: **Cover or less**
Circ: Diamd. preorders: **2,166**
29 ❑ Jul 2001 Cover: 2.95 **NM** value: **Cover or less**
Circ: Diamd. preorders: **2,229**
30 ❑ Aug 2001 Cover: 2.95 **NM** value: **Cover or less**
Circ: Diamd. preorders: **2,174**
31 ❑ Sep 2001 Cover: 2.95 **NM** value: **Cover or less**
Circ: Diamd. preorders: **2,047**
Bk 1❑ b&w Cover: 15.95 **NM** value: **Cover or less**
Bk 2❑ Sep 2000, b&w Cover: 15.95 **NM** value: **Cover or less**
📖 They Work Hard for Their Money **A:** Akihiro Ito **W:** Akihiro Ito

GEOMANCER — Valiant

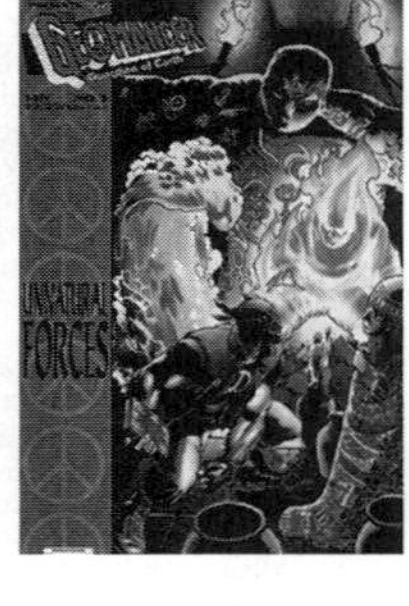

Throughout history, certain people have been called to represent the earth itself. The earth spoke to these people, whispered its secrets to them. And in turn, these Geomancers spoke for the earth. Protected both by their magic and their champion, Gilad Anni-Padda (the Eternal Warrior), their line has continued throughout history.

The most recent Geomancer was Geoff McHenry, a young boy who helped protect Earth during the Unity crisis, and also served as a catalyst to usher in such heroes as Bloodshot. In the end, he apparently sacrificed himself during the Chaos Effect crisis.

Earth needed a new Geomancer and the Eternal Warrior chose Clay McHenry, a crooked cop who lost his vision during an illegal "transaction." Now he has the chance to become a hero...if he lives that long!

Other grades: Multiply prices above by **1.5 for Mint • 2/3 for Very Fine • 1/3 for Fine • 1/5 for Very Good • 1/8 for Good**

1 ❑ Nov 1994 Cover: 3.75 **NM** value: **Cover or less**
Circ: CapCity orders: **29,600**
Chromium wraparound cover. Awakenings **A:** Rags Morales **W:** Maurice Fontenot ★ 1st Appearance of Clay McHenry. ★ Appearance of Eternal Warrior.
2 ❑ Dec 1994 Cover: 2.25 **NM** value: **Cover or less**
Circ: CapCity orders: **16,250**
3 ❑ Jan 1995 Cover: 2.25 **NM** value: **Cover or less**
Circ: CapCity orders: **13,100**
Challenge **A:** Rags Morales **W:** Maurice Fontenot
4 ❑ Feb 1995 Cover: 2.25 **NM** value: **Cover or less**
Circ: CapCity orders: **12,000**
5 ❑ Mar 1995 Cover: 2.25 **NM** value: **Cover or less**
Circ: CapCity orders: **10,025**
Riot Gear, Part 1 ★ Appearance of Turok.
6 ❑ Apr 1995 Cover: 2.25 **NM** value: **Cover or less**
Circ: CapCity orders: **8,950**
Riot Gear, Part 2 ★ Appearance of Turok.
7 ❑ May 1995 Cover: 2.25 **NM** value: **Cover or less**
Circ: CapCity orders: **7,650**
8 ❑ Jun 1995 Cover: 2.25 **NM** value: **Cover or less**
Circ: CapCity orders: **6,600**
final issue.

GEORGE OF THE JUNGLE — Gold Key

1 ❑ Feb 1969 Cover: 0.15 **NM** value: **40.00**
• George, Tom Slick, and Super Chicken stories
2 ❑ Oct 1969 Cover: 0.15 **NM** value: **25.00**
• George, Tom Slick, and Super Chicken stories

GEORGIE COMICS — Timely

Sometimes described on covers as "America's Laff-Wit," Georgie is another of those teen guys who are perpetually panting after "Good Girl Art" women. In this case, the focus of the title character's affections is a spectacular brunette named Judy, and the very first issue makes George's obsession clear, as he accidentally drenches a policeman with his hose while distracted by Judy walking by.

In some issues, Georgie is wearing a distinctive checkered top (in one case, a checkered T-shirt); in some issues, he seems old enough to vote; in others he's in a school environment. In almost all cases, he's head-over-heels infatuated with gorgeous gals. — Maggie

GEPETTO FILES, THE — Quick to Fly

1 ❑ Sep 1998 Cover: 3.00 **NM** value: **Cover or less**
Santa; Cold Timmy; Bunny and The Klaus in The Men's Room **A:** Aaron M. Bordner **W:** C.T. Talvitie; Chris Wesley; Evan Derian; Ted Talvitie

GERALD MCBOING BOING AND THE NEARSIGHTED MR. MAGOO — Dell

Gerald McBoing Boing was not like other kids. Instead of speaking in words, he spoke in sound effects, usually "Boing! Boing!" or some variation thereof.

Little Gerald's antics were entertaining in his animated adventures, but necessarily difficult to translate to the comic book page, where the sound effects had to be represented as graphic icons: a fire-bell or a foghorn, for example.

Much more adaptable to print was Gerald's partner in comedy, the bumbling, nearsighted Mr. Magoo. Magoo's premise was just as thin: He would continually mistake objects for other things because he couldn't see them, and he was too stubborn to admit it. Much of Magoo's humor depends on the reader imagining the dialogue delivered with the impeccable inflections and comic timing of Jim Backus (Mr. Howell from Gilligan's Island), who provided the memorable voice work for the cartoon series.

1 ❑ Aug 1952 Cover: 0.10 **NM** value: **80.00**
2 ❑ Nov 1952 Cover: 0.10 **NM** value: **50.00**
3 ❑ Feb 1953 Cover: 0.10 **NM** value: **50.00**
4 ❑ May 1953 Cover: 0.10 **NM** value: **50.00**
5 ❑ Aug 1953 Cover: 0.10 **NM** value: **50.00**
final issue.

GERIATRIC GANGRENE JUJITSU GERBILS — Planet-X

1 ❑ b&w Cover: 1.50 **NM** value: **Cover or less**
2 ❑ Cover: 1.50 **NM** value: **Cover or less**

GERIATRICMAN — C&T

1 ❑ b&w Cover: 1.75 **NM** value: **Cover or less**

GE ROUGE — Verotik

All issues are adults only.

0.5 ❑ Oct 1998 Cover: 2.95 **NM** value: **Cover or less**
1 ❑ Feb 1997 Cover: 2.95 **NM** value: **Cover or less**
Circ: Diamd. preorders: **8,922**
Glenn Danzig **A:** Feb-97 **W:** Calvin Irving
2 ❑ Apr 1997 Cover: 2.95 **NM** value: **Cover or less**
Circ: Diamd. preorders: **7,460**
Glenn Danzig **W:** Calvin Irving
3 ❑ Jul 1997 Cover: 2.95 **NM** value: **Cover or less**
Circ: Diamd. preorders: **6,117**
Glenn Danzig **W:** Calvin Irving

GERTIE THE DINOSAUR COMICS — Gertie the Dinosaur

1 ❑ Jul 2000 Cover: 2.95 **NM** value: **Cover or less**

GESTALT (CALIBER) — Caliber

0 ❑ Cover: 2.95 **NM** value: **Cover or less**
From the Pages of Seeker **A:** Adam J. Walters **W:** Gary Reed

GESTALT (NEC) — New England

1 ❑ Apr 1993, b&w Cover: 1.95 **NM** value: **Cover or less**
The Voices of Delirium **A:** Andrew Hite; Bill Devine; George Suarez; Larry Boyd; Bob Polio **W:** Andrew Hite
2 ❑ Cover: 1.95 **NM** value: **Cover or less**

GET ALONG GANG — Marvel / Star

1 ❑ May 1985 Cover: 0.65 **NM** value: **1.00**
Circ: CapCity orders: **4,600**
The Ice Cold Mystery; Getting Ready; Get Ready, Get Set **A:** Carlos Garzon **W:** Dave Manak
2 ❑ Jul 1985 Cover: 0.65 **NM** value: **1.00**
Circ: CapCity orders: **3,100**
3 ❑ Sep 1985 Cover: 0.65 **NM** value: **1.00**
Circ: CapCity orders: **2,500**
4 ❑ Nov 1985 Cover: 0.65 **NM** value: **1.00**
Circ: CapCity orders: **1,900**
5 ❑ Jan 1986 Cover: 0.65 **NM** value: **1.00**
Circ: CapCity orders: **1,700**
6 ❑ Mar 1986 Cover: 0.65 **NM** value: **1.00**
Circ: CapCity orders: **1,650**

GET LOST — Mikeross Publications

GET LOST (VOL. 2) — New Comics

1 ❑ Oct 1987, b&w Cover: 1.95 **NM** value: **Cover or less**
2 ❑ ca. 1988, b&w Cover: 1.95 **NM** value: **Cover or less**
• **CGC:** 1 graded, best 8.0
The Invincible Mr. Mann; I Killed Cock Robin; The Sewer Keeper; Don't Miss S.S. Gigantic; The Robin Hood **A:** Ross Andru; Mike Esposito; Paul Hodge **W:** Ross Andru; Mike Esposito; Paul Hodge; Sickley
3 ❑ ca. 1988, b&w Cover: 1.95 **NM** value: **Cover or less**
They Called Him Sam; Der Spider Und Der Fly; The Something; Ride in the Subway; Know Your Enemy; Gunga Dean **A:** Andru Ross; Robsjon Gluck; Z. Von Fraud **C:** Brian Bolland **W:** Andru Ross; Robsjon Gluck; Z. Von Fraud

GET REAL COMICS — Tides Center

1 ❑ Cover: 1.95 **NM** value: **Cover or less**

GET SMART — Dell

1 ❑ Jun 1966 Cover: 0.12 **NM** value: **40.00**
• **CGC:** 1 graded, best 7.0
2 ❑ Sep 1966 Cover: 0.12 **NM** value: **28.00**
3 ❑ Nov 1966 Cover: 0.12 **NM** value: **20.00**
4 ❑ Jan 1967 Cover: 0.12 **NM** value: **20.00**
5 ❑ Mar 1967 Cover: 0.12 **NM** value: **20.00**
6 ❑ Apr 1967 Cover: 0.12 **NM** value: **18.00**
• **CGC:** 1 graded, best 9.0
7 ❑ Jun 1967, four-color Cover: 0.12 **NM** value: **18.00**
• **CGC:** 1 graded, best 7.0
8 ❑ Sep 1967 Cover: 0.12 **NM** value: **18.00**

GHETTO BITCH — Eros

All issues are adults only.

1 ❑ b&w Cover: 2.75 **NM** value: **Cover or less**

GHETTO BLASTERS, THE — Whiplash

1 ❑ Sep 1997, b&w Cover: 2.50 **NM** value: **Cover or less**

GHOST — Dark Horse

Corrupted by organized crime, corporate robber barons, and dishonest leaders, Arcadia is a film-noir-style city with an eclectic cast of characters, including men in fedora hats and extraterrestrials with psionic powers. And inn Arcadia, reporter Elisa Cameron follows her leads to uncover an amazing news story — and pays for it with her life.

She becomes Ghost, a vigilante spectre who spares Arcadia's criminals no kindness, as she tries to figure out why, how, and by whom she was killed. Ironically, this ghost is herself haunted, though not by the dead, but by the living: her alcoholic parents, who are addled by years of alcohol abuse, and her emotionally unstable sister, who has slipped into Arcadia's sleazy underground.

One of Dark Horse's more durable original characters, Ghost has appeared in several other titles.

1 ❑ Apr 1995 Cover: 2.50 **NM** value: **3.00**
Circ: CapCity orders: **16,825** • **CGC:** 1 graded, best 9.4
Arcadia Nocturne, Part 1 **A:** Adam Hughes **W:** Eric Luke
2 ❑ May 1995 Cover: 2.50 **NM** value: **Cover or less**
Circ: CapCity orders: **12,900**
Arcadia Nocturne, Part 2 **A:** Adam Hughes **W:** Eric Luke
3 ❑ Jun 1995 Cover: 2.50 **NM** value: **Cover or less**
Circ: CapCity orders: **15,950**
Arcadia Nocturne, Part 3 **A:** Adam Hughes **W:** Eric Luke
4 ❑ Jul 1995 Cover: 2.50 **NM** value: **Cover or less**
Circ: CapCity orders: **16,900**
5 ❑ Aug 1995 Cover: 2.50 **NM** value: **Cover or less**
Circ: CapCity orders: **16,125**
6 ❑ Sep 1995 Cover: 2.50 **NM** value: **Cover or less**
Circ: CapCity orders: **13,300**
7 ❑ Oct 1995 Cover: 2.50 **NM** value: **Cover or less**
Circ: CapCity orders: **9,425**
8 ❑ Nov 1995 Cover: 2.50 **NM** value: **Cover or less**
9 ❑ Dec 1995 Cover: 2.50 **NM** value: **Cover or less**
10 ❑ Jan 1996 Cover: 2.50 **NM** value: **Cover or less**
11 ❑ Feb 1996 Cover: 2.50 **NM** value: **Cover or less**
Crack in the Wall **A:** David Bullock **W:** Eric Luke
12 ❑ Mar 1996 Cover: 2.50 **NM** value: **Cover or less**
• preview of Ghost/Hellboy crossover **A:** David Bullock **W:** Eric Luke
13 ❑ Apr 1996 Cover: 2.50 **NM** value: **Cover or less**
14 ❑ May 1996 Cover: 2.50 **NM** value: **Cover or less**
15 ❑ Jun 1996 Cover: 2.50 **NM** value: **Cover or less**
16 ❑ Jul 1996 Cover: 2.50 **NM** value: **Cover or less**
Hell and Back **A:** Dougie Braithwaite **W:** Eric Luke
17 ❑ Aug 1996 Cover: 2.50 **NM** value: **Cover or less**
Dead City **A:** Ivan Reis **W:** Eric Luke
18 ❑ Sep 1996 Cover: 2.50 **NM** value: **Cover or less**
Circ: Diamd. preorders: **22,538**
Black Heart, Part 1 **A:** Ivan Reis **W:** Eric Luke ★ Appearance of Barb Wire.
19 ❑ Nov 1996 Cover: 2.50 **NM** value: **Cover or less**
Circ: Diamd. preorders: **20,123**
Black Heart, Part 2 **A:** Ivan Reis **W:** Eric Luke ★ Appearance of Barb Wire.
20 ❑ Dec 1996 Cover: 2.50 **NM** value: **Cover or less**
Circ: Diamd. preorders: **18,954**
Exhuming Elisa, Part 1 **A:** Ivan Reis **W:** Eric Luke
21 ❑ Jan 1997 Cover: 2.50 **NM** value: **Cover or less**
Circ: Diamd. preorders: **18,055**
Exhuming Elisa, Part 2 **A:** Ivan Reis **W:** Eric Luke ★ Appearance of X.
22 ❑ Feb 1997 Cover: 2.50 **NM** value: **Cover or less**
Circ: Diamd. preorders: **17,076**
Exhuming Elisa, Part 3 **A:** Ivan Reis **W:** Eric Luke
23 ❑ Mar 1997 Cover: 2.50 **NM** value: **Cover or less**
Circ: Diamd. preorders: **16,584**
Exhuming Elisa, Part 4 **A:** Ivan Reis **W:** Eric Luke
24 ❑ Apr 1997 Cover: 2.50 **NM** value: **Cover or less**
Circ: Diamd. preorders: **16,701**
Exhuming Elisa, Part 5 **A:** Ivan Reis **W:** Eric Luke
25 ❑ May 1997 Cover: 3.50 **NM** value: **3.95**
Circ: Diamd. preorders: **16,886**
photo front and back covers. • Giant-size. Elisa Exhumed **A:** Ivan Reis **W:** Eric Luke ★ Origin of Ghost. ★ Appearance of King Tiger, X. ★ Death of Crux.
26 ❑ Jun 1997 Cover: 2.95 **NM** value: **Cover or less**
Circ: Diamd. preorders: **15,799**
October Knight **A:** Scott Benefiel **W:** Eric Luke
27 ❑ Jul 1997 Cover: 2.95 **NM** value: **Cover or less**
Circ: Diamd. preorders: **15,207**
October Day **A:** John Cassaday **W:** Eric Luke
28 ❑ Aug 1997 Cover: 2.95 **NM** value: **Cover or less**
Circ: Diamd. preorders: **15,372**
Painful Music, Part 1 **A:** Ivan Reis **W:** Eric Luke
29 ❑ Sep 1997 Cover: 2.95 **NM** value: **Cover or less**
Circ: Diamd. preorders: **14,784**
Painful Music, Part 2 • flip-book with Timecop story **A:** Ivan Reis **W:** Eric Luke
30 ❑ Oct 1997 Cover: 2.95 **NM** value: **Cover or less**
Circ: Diamd. preorders: **14,726**
Painful Music, Part 3 **A:** Ivan Reis **W:** Eric Luke
31 ❑ Nov 1997 Cover: 2.95 **NM** value: **Cover or less**
Circ: Diamd. preorders: **14,560**
Painful Music, Part 4 **A:** Ivan Reis **W:** Eric Luke
32 ❑ Dec 1997 Cover: 2.95 **NM** value: **Cover or less**
Circ: Diamd. preorders: **14,470**
A Pathless Land **A:** H.M. Baker **W:** Eric Luke
33 ❑ Jan 1998 Cover: 2.95 **NM** value: **Cover or less**
Circ: Diamd. preorders: **14,169**
Jade Cathedral, Part 1 **A:** Ivan Reis **W:** Eric Luke
34 ❑ Feb 1998 Cover: 2.95 **NM** value: **Cover or less**
Circ: Diamd. preorders: **13,301**
Jade Cathedral, Part 2 **A:** Ivan Reis **W:** Eric Luke
35 ❑ Mar 1998 Cover: 2.95 **NM** value: **Cover or less**
Circ: Diamd. preorders: **13,305**
Jade Cathedral, Part 3 **A:** Ivan Reis **W:** Eric Luke
36 ❑ Apr 1998 Cover: 2.95 **NM** value: **Cover or less**
Circ: Diamd. preorders: **13,465**
Jade Cathedral, Part 4 **A:** Ivan Reis **W:** Eric Luke
Bk 1 ❑ May 1996 Cover: 9.95 **NM** value: **Cover or less**
• Nocturnes; collects Ghost #1-3 and 5 **W:** Eric Luke
Bk 2 ❑ Jan 1999 Cover: 14.95 **NM** value: **Cover or less**
• Black October; collects #6-9, #26, and #27 **W:** Eric Luke
Bk 3 ❑ Oct 1997 Cover: 17.95 **NM** value: **Cover or less**
• Exhuming Elisa; collects issues #20-25
Bk 4 ❑ Jun 1999 Cover: 9.95 **NM** value: **Cover or less**
• Painful Music; collects #28-32
SE 1 ❑ Jul 1994 Cover: 3.95 **NM** value: **Cover or less**
Circ: CapCity orders: **12,850** • **CGC:** 1 graded, best 9.6
• Ghost Special **W:** Eric Luke
SE 2 ❑ Jun 1998 Cover: 3.95 **NM** value: **Cover or less**
Photo cover. • Immortal Coil
SE 3 ❑ Dec 1998 Cover: 3.95 **NM** value: **Cover or less**
• Scary Monsters

GHOST AND THE SHADOW — Dark Horse

1 ❑ Dec 1995 Cover: 2.95 **NM** value: **Cover or less**
No issue number. One-shot. **A:** H.M. Baker **W:** Doug Moench

GHOST/BATGIRL — Dark Horse

1 ❑ Sep 2000 Cover: 2.95 **NM** value: **Cover or less**

CGC-graded: Multiply prices above by **33 for 9.9 M • 16 for 9.8 NM/M • 7 for 9.6 NM+ • 5 for 9.4 NM • 2.5 for 9.2 NM- • 1.5 for 9.0 VF/NM**

📖 The Resurrection Engine, Part 1 **A:** Ryan Benjamin **W:** Mike Kennedy
2 ❑ Oct 2000 Cover: 2.99 **NM** value: **Cover or less**
📖 The Resurrection Engine, Part 2 **A:** Ryan Benjamin **W:** Mike Kennedy
3 ❑ Nov 2000 Cover: 2.95 **NM** value: **Cover or less**
📖 The Resurrection Engine, Part 3 **A:** Ryan Benjamin **W:** Mike Kennedy
4 ❑ Dec 2000 Cover: 2.95 **NM** value: **Cover or less**
📖 The Resurrection Engine, Part 4 **A:** Ryan Benjamin **W:** Mike Kennedy

GHOSTBUSTERS — First

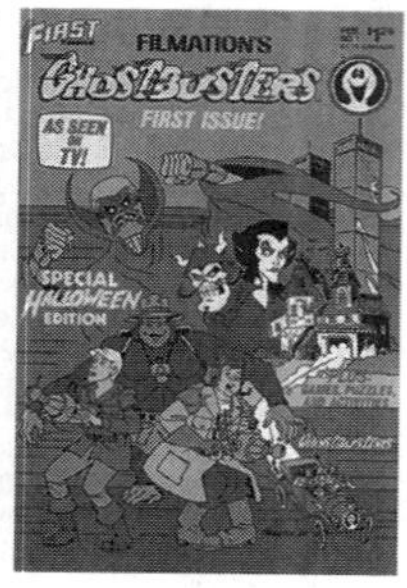

These Ghostbusters are a gaggle of misfits who stop ghosts, wherever they may be haunting. The team comprises dashing leader Jake, Eddie, who is gawky but humorous; talking ape Tracy; Futura, a space woman from the future, and the team's pet bat Belfry. By hopping in their Ghost Buggy, they are able to travel across time and space to save people who are being terrorized by ghosts. Once the ghosts are found, the usual tactic is to zap them with a dematerializer to wipe them out. In addition to relating their adventures, this series contained numerous puzzle pages, games, and other activities.

Following the hit movie, Filmation Associates succeeded in grabbing use of the trademark "Ghostbusters" for their animated kids' show, from which this series is adapted.

Shortly after, Columbia Pictures released a more direct (and successful) adaptation of the movie under the pointed name "The Real Ghostbusters."

1 ❑ Feb 1986 Cover: 1.25 **NM** value: **1.50**
Circ: CapCity orders: **7,825**
📖 A Halloween Haunting **A:** Howard Bender **W:** Hilarie Staton
2 ❑ Mar 1986 Cover: 1.25 **NM** value: **1.50**
Circ: CapCity orders: **4,700**
3 ❑ May 1986 Cover: 1.25 **NM** value: **1.50**
Circ: CapCity orders: **3,500**
4 ❑ Jun 1986 Cover: 1.25 **NM** value: **1.50**
Circ: CapCity orders: **1,825**
5 ❑ Aug 1986 Cover: 1.25 **NM** value: **1.50**
6 ❑ Sep 1986 Cover: 1.25 **NM** value: **1.50**
Circ: CapCity orders: **1,275**

GHOSTBUSTERS II — Now

1 ❑ Oct 1989 Cover: 1.95 **NM** value: **2.00**
Circ: CapCity orders: **4,425**
📖 Together Again For The First Time, Part 2 **A:** John Tobias **W:** James Van Hise
2 ❑ Nov 1989 Cover: 1.95 **NM** value: **2.00**
📖 The Slime of their Lives **A:** John Tobias **W:** James Van Hise
3 ❑ Dec 1989 Cover: 1.95 **NM** value: **2.00**
Bk 1❑ Cover: 8.95 **NM** value: **Cover or less**
• Trade Paperback.

GHOST COMICS — Fiction House

GHOSTDANCING — DC / Vertigo

1 ❑ Mar 1995 Cover: 1.95 **NM** value: **Cover or less**
Circ: CapCity orders: **11,975**
📖 First Tremor **A:** Richard Case **W:** Jamie Delano
2 ❑ Apr 1995 Cover: 1.95 **NM** value: **Cover or less**
Circ: CapCity orders: **8,675**
📖 Second Tremor **A:** Richard Case **W:** Jamie Delano
3 ❑ Jun 1995 Cover: 2.50 **NM** value: **Cover or less**
Circ: CapCity orders: **7,625**
📖 Third Tremor **A:** Richard Case **W:** Jamie Delano
4 ❑ Jul 1995 Cover: 2.50 **NM** value: **Cover or less**
Circ: CapCity orders: **7,225**
5 ❑ Aug 1995 Cover: 2.50 **NM** value: **Cover or less**
Circ: CapCity orders: **7,100**
📖 Fifth Tremor **A:** Richard Case **W:** Jamie Delano
6 ❑ Sep 1995 Cover: 2.50 **NM** value: **Cover or less**
Circ: CapCity orders: **6,475**
📖 The Big One **A:** Richard Case **W:** Jamie Delano

GHOST HANDBOOK — Dark Horse

1 ❑ Aug 1999 Cover: 2.95 **NM** value: **Cover or less**
Circ: Diamd. preorders: **10,661**
No issue number. • background on characters **A:** Adam Hughes

GHOST/HELLBOY SPECIAL — Dark Horse

1 ❑ May 1996 Cover: 2.50 **NM** value: **Cover or less**
2 ❑ Jun 1996 Cover: 2.50 **NM** value: **Cover or less**
final issue. **A:** Scott Benefiel **W:** Mike Mignola
Bk 1❑ Jun 1997 Cover: 4.95 **NM** value: **Cover or less**
• Collects series **A:** Scott Benefiel **W:** Mike Mignola

Capital City orders are the actual sales of comic books by Capital City Distribution, once one of the largest U.S. sellers of comics to comics shops. Capital City's share of comics shop sales, while not known exactly, increases from around 10-20% in the mid-1980s to 30-35% in the mid-1990s. Capital City's share of comic books sold on newsstands (most Marvels and DCs) will be less.

GHOST IN THE SHELL — Dark Horse / Manga

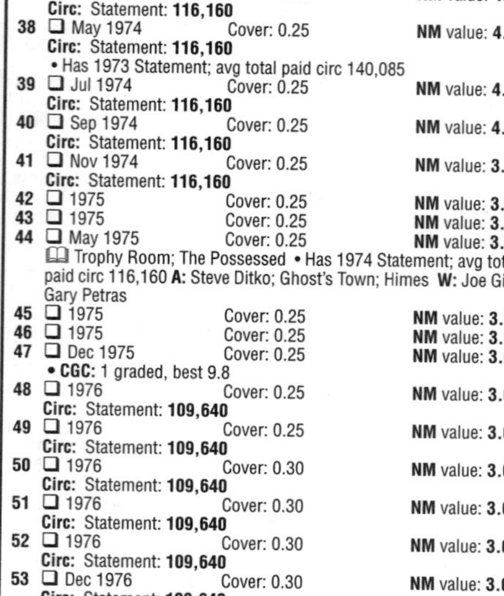

In the future, technology and information access has become ever more important. Perhaps it was inevitable that human beings would find their own bodies wedded to cybertechnology. Ultimately, "cyberbrain" technology allows for the transplanting of human consciousness into mechanical bodies. Such beings became little more than human minds — "ghosts" — in mechanical shells.

Creator Matsamunu Shirow created a startling vision of the future with his movie Ghost in the Shell, on which this comics series is based. Nominally, it's a crime drama wherein a futuristic cyborg police officer searches for the killer of a prominent businessman. Below the surface, however, it's a story of alienation and the search for identity in a world where technology strips the individual of the very things which make them human.

1 ❑ Mar 1995 Cover: 3.95 **NM** value: **15.00**
Circ: CapCity orders: **8,900** • **CGC:** 10 graded, best 9.8
2 ❑ Apr 1995 Cover: 3.95 **NM** value: **10.00**
Circ: CapCity orders: **6,550** • **CGC:** 2 graded, best 9.6
3 ❑ Apr 1995 Cover: 3.95 **NM** value: **8.00**
Circ: CapCity orders: **6,675** • **CGC:** 2 graded, best 9.8
4 ❑ Jun 1995 Cover: 3.95 **NM** value: **8.00**
Circ: CapCity orders: **8,650**
5 ❑ Jul 1995 Cover: 3.95 **NM** value: **6.00**
Circ: CapCity orders: **9,375**
6 ❑ Aug 1995 Cover: 3.95 **NM** value: **6.00**
Circ: CapCity orders: **9,675**
7 ❑ Sep 1995 Cover: 3.95 **NM** value: **5.00**
8 ❑ Oct 1995 Cover: 3.95 **NM** value: **5.00**
final issue. **A:** Masamune Shirow **W:** Masamune Shirow
Bk 1❑ Cover: 24.95 **NM** value: **Cover or less**
• Collects Ghost In the Shell #1-8 **A:** Masamune Shirow **W:** Masamune Shirow

GHOSTLY HAUNTS — Charlton

By the mid-1970s, DC and Marvel were spending most of their energy and resources on super-hero titles, which gave perennial also-ran Charlton an opening to compete in the low-rent district of horror-mystery comics. Titles like Ghostly Haunts and its spinoffs, including The Many Ghosts of Dr. Graves, featured the tried-and-true formula of the horror "host" introducing three short stories per issue, all offering chilling and generally predictable tales of zombies, vampires, trolls, witches, and demons.

The best efforts of the artists and writers to imitate the spooky and atmospheric work in DC and Marvel comics like The House of Mystery and Tower of Shadows were usually undone by Charlton's packaging and cheap production. Ghostly Haunts folded for good in 1978.

20 ❑ Sep 1971 Cover: 0.20 **NM** value: **5.00**
Circ: Statement: **165,060**
📖 I'll Love You Forever and Ever!; A report on UFO's; The Visitor; Self Portrait! • Series continued from Ghost Manor (1st Series) #19 **A:** Steve Ditko; Hewton; Sanko Kim **W:** Joe Gill; Nicola Cutii; Tom Peterson
21 ❑ 1971 Cover: 0.20 **NM** value: **5.00**
Circ: Statement: **165,060**
22 ❑ 1972 Cover: 0.20 **NM** value: **5.00**
Circ: Statement: **115,055**
23 ❑ 1972 Cover: 0.20 **NM** value: **5.00**
Circ: Statement: **115,055**
24 ❑ Apr 1972 Cover: 0.20 **NM** value: **5.00**
Circ: Statement: **115,055**
• Has 1971 Statement; avg total paid circ 165,060
25 ❑ 1972 Cover: 0.20 **NM** value: **5.00**
Circ: Statement: **115,055**
26 ❑ 1972 Cover: 0.20 **NM** value: **5.00**
Circ: Statement: **115,055**
27 ❑ 1972 Cover: 0.20 **NM** value: **5.00**
Circ: Statement: **115,055**
28 ❑ 1972 Cover: 0.20 **NM** value: **5.00**
Circ: Statement: **115,055**
29 ❑ 1972 Cover: 0.20 **NM** value: **5.00**
Circ: Statement: **115,055**
30 ❑ 1973 Cover: 0.20 **NM** value: **5.00**
Circ: Statement: **140,085**
31 ❑ 1973 Cover: 0.20 **NM** value: **4.00**
Circ: Statement: **140,085**
32 ❑ May 1973 Cover: 0.20 **NM** value: **4.00**
Circ: Statement: **140,085**
• Has 1972 Statement; avg total paid circ 115,055
33 ❑ 1973 Cover: 0.20 **NM** value: **4.00**
Circ: Statement: **140,085**
34 ❑ 1973 Cover: 0.20 **NM** value: **4.00**
Circ: Statement: **140,085**
35 ❑ Oct 1973 Cover: 0.20 **NM** value: **4.00**
Circ: Statement: **140,085** • **CGC:** 1 graded, best 7.5
36 ❑ Nov 1973 Cover: 0.20 **NM** value: **4.00**
Circ: Statement: **140,085**
37 ❑ 1974 Cover: 0.20 **NM** value: **4.00**
Circ: Statement: **116,160**
38 ❑ May 1974 Cover: 0.25 **NM** value: **4.00**
Circ: Statement: **116,160**
• Has 1973 Statement; avg total paid circ 140,085
39 ❑ Jul 1974 Cover: 0.25 **NM** value: **4.00**
Circ: Statement: **116,160**
40 ❑ Sep 1974 Cover: 0.25 **NM** value: **4.00**
Circ: Statement: **116,160**
41 ❑ Nov 1974 Cover: 0.25 **NM** value: **3.00**
Circ: Statement: **116,160**
42 ❑ 1975 Cover: 0.25 **NM** value: **3.00**
43 ❑ 1975 Cover: 0.25 **NM** value: **3.00**
44 ❑ May 1975 Cover: 0.25 **NM** value: **3.00**
📖 Trophy Room; The Possessed • Has 1974 Statement; avg total paid circ 116,160 **A:** Steve Ditko; Ghost's Town; Himes **W:** Joe Gill; Gary Petras
45 ❑ 1975 Cover: 0.25 **NM** value: **3.00**
46 ❑ 1975 Cover: 0.25 **NM** value: **3.00**
47 ❑ Dec 1975 Cover: 0.25 **NM** value: **3.00**
• **CGC:** 1 graded, best 9.8
48 ❑ 1976 Cover: 0.25 **NM** value: **3.00**
Circ: Statement: **109,640**
49 ❑ 1976 Cover: 0.25 **NM** value: **3.00**
Circ: Statement: **109,640**
50 ❑ 1976 Cover: 0.30 **NM** value: **3.00**
Circ: Statement: **109,640**
51 ❑ 1976 Cover: 0.30 **NM** value: **3.00**
Circ: Statement: **109,640**
52 ❑ 1976 Cover: 0.30 **NM** value: **3.00**
Circ: Statement: **109,640**
53 ❑ Dec 1976 Cover: 0.30 **NM** value: **3.00**
Circ: Statement: **109,640**
📖 The Bayou Devil Cat; The Happy Medium; Birthday Gift from Beyond (text story); The Creep!
54 ❑ 1977 Cover: 0.35 **NM** value: **3.00**
55 ❑ 1977 Cover: 0.35 **NM** value: **3.00**
56 ❑ 1978 Cover: 0.35 **NM** value: **3.00**
57 ❑ Mar 1978 Cover: 0.35 **NM** value: **3.00**
• Has 1977 Statement; avg total paid circ 109,640
58 ❑ Apr 1978 Cover: 0.35 **NM** value: **3.00**
final issue.

GHOSTLY TALES — Charlton

As with more than one other Charlton "spooky" title, this series had a host who introduced each story in the issue. The demonic Mr. Dedd presided over the earlier issues of this horror anthology, later to be replaced by the more ghoulish host Dr. Graves. In most respects, this was a standard Charlton ghost series, characterized by potboiler plots, O. Henry-style "surprise" endings, and lower-than-average production values. On the upside, artist Steve Ditko contributed to numerous issues of the series, where his off-kilter sensibility was a perfect match for its supernatural subject matter.

55 ❑ Apr 1966 Cover: 0.12 **NM** value: **16.00**
• **CGC:** 1 graded, best 9.4
56 ❑ Jul 1966 Cover: 0.12 **NM** value: **7.00**
57 ❑ 1966 Cover: 0.12 **NM** value: **7.00**
58 ❑ 1966 Cover: 0.12 **NM** value: **7.00**
59 ❑ 1967 Cover: 0.12 **NM** value: **7.00**
Circ: Statement: **135,266**
60 ❑ 1967 Cover: 0.12 **NM** value: **5.00**
Circ: Statement: **135,266**
61 ❑ 1967 Cover: 0.12 **NM** value: **5.00**
Circ: Statement: **135,266**
62 ❑ 1967 Cover: 0.12 **NM** value: **5.00**
Circ: Statement: **135,266**
63 ❑ 1967 Cover: 0.12 **NM** value: **5.00**
Circ: Statement: **135,266**
64 ❑ Dec 1967 Cover: 0.12 **NM** value: **5.00**
Circ: Statement: **135,266** • **CGC:** 1 graded, best 8.0
65 ❑ Feb 1968 Cover: 0.12 **NM** value: **5.00**
Circ: Statement: **142,635**
66 ❑ May 1968 Cover: 0.12 **NM** value: **5.00**
Circ: Statement: **142,635**
67 ❑ Jul 1968 Cover: 0.12 **NM** value: **5.00**
Circ: Statement: **142,635**
68 ❑ Sep 1968 Cover: 0.12 **NM** value: **5.00**
Circ: Statement: **142,635**
69 ❑ Oct 1968 Cover: 0.12 **NM** value: **5.00**
Circ: Statement: **142,635**
70 ❑ 1968 Cover: 0.12 **NM** value: **5.00**
Circ: Statement: **142,635**
71 ❑ Jan 1969 Cover: 0.12 **NM** value: **4.00**
Circ: Statement: **178,545**
72 ❑ 1969 Cover: 0.12 **NM** value: **4.00**
Circ: Statement: **178,545**
73 ❑ 1969 Cover: 0.12 **NM** value: **4.00**
Circ: Statement: **178,545**
74 ❑ Jul 1969 Cover: 0.12 **NM** value: **4.00**
Circ: Statement: **178,545**
• Has 1968 Statement, filed 9/30/68; avg print run 230,000; avg sales 142,600; avg subs 35; avg total paid 142,635; samples 125; max existent 42,760; 38% of run returned
75 ❑ 1969 Cover: 0.15 **NM** value: **4.00**
Circ: Statement: **178,545**
76 ❑ 1969 Cover: 0.15 **NM** value: **4.00**
Circ: Statement: **178,545**
77 ❑ 1970 Cover: 0.15 **NM** value: **4.00**

Circ: Statement: **140,040**
Don't Help Me!; The Copper Kettle; House Call; Spirit Justice (text story) **A:** George Lopez
78 ❑ 1970 Cover: 0.15 **NM** value: **4.00**
Circ: Statement: **140,040**
79 ❑ Apr 1970 Cover: 0.15 **NM** value: **4.00**
Circ: Statement: **140,040**
• Has 1969 Statement, filed 9/30/69; avg print run 270,000; avg sales 178,500; avg subs 45; avg total paid 178,545; samples 125; max existent 178,670; 34% of run returned
80 ❑ 1970 Cover: 0.15 **NM** value: **4.00**
Circ: Statement: **140,040**
81 ❑ 1970 Cover: 0.15 **NM** value: **4.00**
Circ: Statement: **140,040**
82 ❑ 1970 Cover: 0.15 **NM** value: **4.00**
Circ: Statement: **140,040**
83 ❑ Dec 1970 Cover: 0.15 **NM** value: **4.00**
Circ: Statement: **140,040**
84 ❑ 1971 Cover: 0.15 **NM** value: **4.00**
85 ❑ 1971 Cover: 0.15 **NM** value: **4.00**
86 ❑ Jun 1971 Cover: 0.15 **NM** value: **4.00**
• Has 1970 Statement; avg total paid circ 140,040
87 ❑ Aug 1971 Cover: 0.20 **NM** value: **4.00**
• **CGC:** 1 graded, best 7.5
88 ❑ 1971 Cover: 0.20 **NM** value: **4.00**
89 ❑ 1971 Cover: 0.20 **NM** value: **4.00**
90 ❑ 1971 Cover: 0.20 **NM** value: **4.00**
91 ❑ Jan 1972 Cover: 0.20 **NM** value: **3.00**
Circ: Statement: **172,061**
92 ❑ Feb 1972 Cover: 0.20 **NM** value: **3.00**
Circ: Statement: **172,061** • **CGC:** 1 graded, best 8.0
93 ❑ 1972 Cover: 0.20 **NM** value: **3.00**
Circ: Statement: **172,061**
94 ❑ 1972 Cover: 0.20 **NM** value: **3.00**
Circ: Statement: **172,061**
95 ❑ 1972 Cover: 0.20 **NM** value: **3.00**
Circ: Statement: **172,061**
96 ❑ 1972 Cover: 0.20 **NM** value: **3.00**
Circ: Statement: **172,061**
97 ❑ Aug 1972 Cover: 0.20 **NM** value: **3.00**
Circ: Statement: **172,061** • **CGC:** 1 graded, best 8.0
98 ❑ Oct 1972 Cover: 0.20 **NM** value: **3.00**
Circ: Statement: **172,061**
99 ❑ Nov 1972 Cover: 0.20 **NM** value: **3.00**
Circ: Statement: **172,061**
100 ❑ Dec 1972 Cover: 0.20 **NM** value: **3.00**
Circ: Statement: **172,061** • **CGC:** 1 graded, best 9.2
101 ❑ 1973 Cover: 0.20 **NM** value: **3.00**
Circ: Statement: **146,085**
102 ❑ 1973 Cover: 0.20 **NM** value: **3.00**
Circ: Statement: **146,085**
103 ❑ Apr 1973 Cover: 0.20 **NM** value: **3.00**
Circ: Statement: **146,085**
• Has 1972 Statement; avg total paid circ 172,061
104 ❑ 1973 Cover: 0.20 **NM** value: **3.00**
Circ: Statement: **146,085**
105 ❑ 1973 Cover: 0.20 **NM** value: **3.00**
Circ: Statement: **146,085**
106 ❑ 1973 Cover: 0.20 **NM** value: **3.00**
Circ: Statement: **146,085**
107 ❑ Oct 1973 Cover: 0.20 **NM** value: **3.00**
Circ: Statement: **146,085**
108 ❑ 1973 Cover: 0.20 **NM** value: **3.00**
Circ: Statement: **146,085**
109 ❑ Jan 1974 Cover: 0.20 **NM** value: **3.00**
Circ: Statement: **138,130**
110 ❑ 1974 Cover: 0.20 **NM** value: **3.00**
Circ: Statement: **138,130**
111 ❑ Sep 1974 Cover: 0.25 **NM** value: **2.50**
Circ: Statement: **138,130**
• Has 1973 Statement; avg total paid circ 146,085
112 ❑ 1974 Cover: 0.25 **NM** value: **2.50**
Circ: Statement: **138,130**
113 ❑ 1974 Cover: 0.25 **NM** value: **2.50**
Circ: Statement: **138,130**
114 ❑ 1975 Cover: 0.25 **NM** value: **2.50**
Circ: Statement: **103,785**
115 ❑ 1975 Cover: 0.25 **NM** value: **2.50**
Circ: Statement: **103,785**
The Not so Great Escape!; Wings of Death! • Has 1974 Statement; avg total paid circ 138,130 **W:** Randy Heaps
116 ❑ 1975 Cover: 0.25 **NM** value: **2.50**
Circ: Statement: **103,785**
117 ❑ 1975 Cover: 0.25 **NM** value: **2.50**
Circ: Statement: **103,785**
118 ❑ Nov 1975 Cover: 0.25 **NM** value: **2.50**
Circ: Statement: **103,785**
119 ❑ 1976 Cover: 0.25 **NM** value: **2.50**
120 ❑ 1976 Cover: 0.30 **NM** value: **2.50**
121 ❑ 1976 Cover: 0.30 **NM** value: **2.50**
• Has 1975 Statement; avg total paid circ 103,785
122 ❑ 1976 Cover: 0.30 **NM** value: **2.50**
123 ❑ 1976 Cover: 0.30 **NM** value: **2.50**
124 ❑ Dec 1976 Cover: 0.30 **NM** value: **2.50**
125 ❑ 1977 Cover: 0.30 **NM** value: **2.50**
Circ: Statement: **112,603**
126 ❑ Oct 1977 Cover: 0.35 **NM** value: **2.50**
Circ: Statement: **112,603**
127 ❑ ca. 1977 Cover: 0.35 **NM** value: **2.50**
Circ: Statement: **112,603**
128 ❑ ca. 1978 Cover: 0.35 **NM** value: **2.50**
• Has 1977 Statement; avg total paid circ 112,603
129 ❑ ca. 1978 Cover: 0.35 **NM** value: **2.50**
130 ❑ ca. 1978 Cover: 0.35 **NM** value: **2.50**
131 ❑ ca. 1978 Cover: 0.35 **NM** value: **2.50**
132 ❑ ca. 1978 Cover: 0.35 **NM** value: **2.50**
133 ❑ ca. 1978 Cover: 0.35 **NM** value: **2.50**
134 ❑ ca. 1979 Cover: 0.40 **NM** value: **2.50**
135 ❑ ca. 1979 Cover: 0.40 **NM** value: **2.50**
136 ❑ ca. 1979 Cover: 0.40 **NM** value: **2.50**
137 ❑ ca. 1979 Cover: 0.40 **NM** value: **2.50**
138 ❑ ca. 1979 Cover: 0.40 **NM** value: **2.50**
The Souvenir Hunter; The Crown of Isis!; The Spirit Speaks (text story); Triumph of Evil!; Gayle's Ghost (text story) **A:** Steve Ditko; Pat Boyette **W:** Joe Gill
139 ❑ ca. 1979 Cover: 0.40 **NM** value: **2.50**
140 ❑ ca. 1980 Cover: 0.40 **NM** value: **2.50**
141 ❑ ca. 1980 Cover: 0.40 **NM** value: **2.50**
142 ❑ ca. 1980 Cover: 0.40 **NM** value: **2.50**
143 ❑ ca. 1980 Cover: 0.50 **NM** value: **2.50**
144 ❑ ca. 1980 Cover: 0.50 **NM** value: **2.50**
145 ❑ Oct 1980 Cover: 0.50 **NM** value: **2.50**
146 ❑ Dec 1980 Cover: 0.50 **NM** value: **2.50**
147 ❑ Feb 1981 Cover: 0.50 **NM** value: **2.50**
148 ❑ Apr 1981 Cover: 0.50 **NM** value: **2.50**
149 ❑ Jun 1981 Cover: 0.50 **NM** value: **2.50**
150 ❑ Aug 1981 Cover: 0.50 **NM** value: **2.50**
151 ❑ Oct 1981 Cover: 0.50 **NM** value: **2.50**
152 ❑ Dec 1981 Cover: 0.50 **NM** value: **2.50**
153 ❑ Feb 1982 Cover: 0.60 **NM** value: **2.50**
154 ❑ Apr 1982 Cover: 0.60 **NM** value: **2.50**
155 ❑ Jun 1982 Cover: 0.60 **NM** value: **2.50**
156 ❑ Aug 1982 Cover: 0.60 **NM** value: **2.50**
157 ❑ Oct 1982 Cover: 0.60 **NM** value: **2.50**
158 ❑ Dec 1982 Cover: 0.60 **NM** value: **2.50**
159 ❑ Feb 1983 Cover: 0.60 **NM** value: **2.50**
160 ❑ 1983 Cover: 0.60 **NM** value: **2.50**
161 ❑ May 1983 Cover: 0.60 **NM** value: **2.50**
162 ❑ 1983 Cover: 0.60 **NM** value: **2.50**
163 ❑ Oct 1983 Cover: 0.60 **NM** value: **2.50**
164 ❑ Cover: 0.60 **NM** value: **2.50**
165 ❑ 1984 Cover: 0.60 **NM** value: **2.50**
166 ❑ 1984 Cover: 0.60 **NM** value: **2.50**
167 ❑ Jun 1984 Cover: 0.60 **NM** value: **2.50**
168 ❑ **NM** value: **2.50**
169 ❑ Oct 1984 Cover: 0.75 **NM** value: **2.50**
final issue.

GHOSTLY WEIRD STORIES — Star Publications

120 ❑ Sep 1953 Cover: 0.10 **NM** value: **Cover or less**
• **CGC:** 1 graded, best 8.0
121 ❑ Dec 1953 Cover: 0.10 **NM** value: **Cover or less**
122 ❑ Mar 1954 Cover: 0.10 **NM** value: **Cover or less**
• **CGC:** 1 graded, best 8.0
123 ❑ Jun 1954 Cover: 0.10 **NM** value: **Cover or less**
124 ❑ Sep 1954 Cover: 0.10 **NM** value: **Cover or less**
• **CGC:** 1 graded, best 8.0

GHOST MANOR (1ST SERIES) — Charlton

1 ❑ Jul 1968 Cover: 0.12 **NM** value: **10.00**
• **CGC:** 1 graded, best 8.5
A Matter of Grave Concern!; Death Defying (text story); Mr. Henshaw's Friend;
2 ❑ Sep 1968 Cover: 0.12 **NM** value: **6.00**
3 ❑ Nov 1968 Cover: 0.12 **NM** value: **6.00**
4 ❑ Jan 1969 Cover: 0.12 **NM** value: **6.00**
5 ❑ Mar 1969 Cover: 0.12 **NM** value: **6.00**
6 ❑ May 1969 Cover: 0.12 **NM** value: **5.00**
Nobody's Home; The Deepest Grave; The Old Man's Cat **A:** Sanho Kim **W:** Joe Gill
7 ❑ Jul 1969 Cover: 0.15 **NM** value: **5.00**
8 ❑ Sep 1969 Cover: 0.15 **NM** value: **5.00**
9 ❑ Nov 1969 Cover: 0.15 **NM** value: **5.00**
10 ❑ Jan 1970 Cover: 0.15 **NM** value: **5.00**
Circ: Statement: **180,050**
11 ❑ Mar 1970 Cover: 0.15 **NM** value: **4.00**
Circ: Statement: **180,050**
12 ❑ May 1970 Cover: 0.15 **NM** value: **4.00**
Circ: Statement: **180,050**
13 ❑ Jul 1970 Cover: 0.15 **NM** value: **4.00**
Circ: Statement: **180,050**
14 ❑ Sep 1970 Cover: 0.15 **NM** value: **4.00**
Circ: Statement: **180,050**
15 ❑ Nov 1970 Cover: 0.15 **NM** value: **4.00**
Circ: Statement: **180,050**
16 ❑ Jan 1971 Cover: 0.15 **NM** value: **4.00**
Circ: Statement: **165,060**
17 ❑ Mar 1971 Cover: 0.15 **NM** value: **4.00**
Circ: Statement: **165,060**
18 ❑ May 1971 Cover: 0.15 **NM** value: **4.00**
Circ: Statement: **165,060**
19 ❑ Jul 1971 Cover: 0.15 **NM** value: **4.00**
Circ: Statement: **165,060**
• Series continued in Ghostly Haunts #20; Has 1970 Statement, filed 9/30/70; avg print run 280,000; avg sales 180,000; avg subs 50; avg total paid 180,050; samples 300; max existent 180,350; 36% of run returned

GHOST MANOR (2ND SERIES) — Charlton

Mr. Bones is your host in this second volume of Charlton's chilling series.

Ghost Manor itself was built in 1833, at the orders of a ruthless aristocrat. At its heart was a secret, soundproof room which the aristocrat had specially constructed. He stored his most important papers there, and within that room he felt he could do whatever he pleased. Only he knew of its existence. He even murdered the carpenter who had built.

He desired a woman named Agatha Brown and forced her to marry him, lest he drive her father into bankruptcy. She demanded, however, that he rip up her father's promissory note before the ceremony. But as he went to the room to retrieve the papers, the ghost of the carpenter closed the door behind him, trapping him forever.

In this series, he's just one of many ghosts who haunt the manor as Mr. Bones spins tales of terror.

1 ❑ Oct 1971 Cover: 0.20 **NM** value: **10.00**
2 ❑ Dec 1971 Cover: 0.20 **NM** value: **6.00**
3 ❑ Feb 1972 Cover: 0.20 **NM** value: **6.00**
4 ❑ Apr 1972 Cover: 0.20 **NM** value: **6.00**
5 ❑ Jun 1972 Cover: 0.20 **NM** value: **6.00**
6 ❑ Aug 1972 Cover: 0.20 **NM** value: **6.00**
7 ❑ Oct 1972 Cover: 0.20 **NM** value: **6.00**
8 ❑ Nov 1972 Cover: 0.20 **NM** value: **7.50**
9 ❑ Feb 1973 Cover: 0.20 **NM** value: **5.00**
Circ: Statement: **130,055**
10 ❑ Mar 1973 Cover: 0.20 **NM** value: **5.00**
Circ: Statement: **130,055**
11 ❑ Apr 1973 Cover: 0.20 **NM** value: **4.00**
Circ: Statement: **130,055**
12 ❑ Jun 1973 Cover: 0.20 **NM** value: **4.00**
Circ: Statement: **130,055**
13 ❑ Jul 1973 Cover: 0.20 **NM** value: **4.00**
Circ: Statement: **130,055**
14 ❑ Sep 1973 Cover: 0.20 **NM** value: **4.00**
Circ: Statement: **130,055**
15 ❑ Oct 1973 Cover: 0.20 **NM** value: **4.00**
Circ: Statement: **130,055**
16 ❑ Dec 1973 Cover: 0.20 **NM** value: **4.00**
Circ: Statement: **130,055**
17 ❑ Jan 1974 Cover: 0.20 **NM** value: **4.00**
Circ: Statement: **116,140**
18 ❑ May 1974 Cover: 0.25 **NM** value: **4.00**
Circ: Statement: **116,140**
• Has 1973 Statement; avg total paid circ 130,055
19 ❑ Jul 1974 Cover: 0.25 **NM** value: **4.00**
Circ: Statement: **116,140**
20 ❑ Sep 1974 Cover: 0.25 **NM** value: **4.00**
Circ: Statement: **116,140**
21 ❑ Nov 1974 Cover: 0.25 **NM** value: **4.00**
Circ: Statement: **116,140**
22 ❑ Mar 1975 Cover: 0.25 **NM** value: **4.00**
Circ: Statement: **101,166**
23 ❑ May 1975 Cover: 0.25 **NM** value: **4.00**
Circ: Statement: **101,166** • **CGC:** 1 graded, best 7.0
• Has 1974 Statement; avg total paid circ 116,140
24 ❑ Jul 1975 Cover: 0.25 **NM** value: **4.00**
Circ: Statement: **101,166** • **CGC:** 1 graded, best 9.0
25 ❑ Sep 1975 Cover: 0.25 **NM** value: **4.00**
Circ: Statement: **101,166**
26 ❑ Nov 1975 Cover: 0.25 **NM** value: **4.00**
Circ: Statement: **101,166**
27 ❑ Jan 1976 Cover: 0.25 **NM** value: **4.00**
Circ: Statement: **98,465**
28 ❑ Mar 1976 Cover: 0.25 **NM** value: **4.00**
Circ: Statement: **98,465**
29 ❑ Jun 1976 Cover: 0.30 **NM** value: **4.00**
Circ: Statement: **98,465**
30 ❑ Aug 1976 Cover: 0.30 **NM** value: **4.00**
Circ: Statement: **98,465**
31 ❑ Oct 1976 Cover: 0.30 **NM** value: **3.00**
Circ: Statement: **98,465**
32 ❑ Dec 1976 Cover: 0.30 **NM** value: **3.00**
Circ: Statement: **98,465**
33 ❑ Sep 1977 Cover: 0.35 **NM** value: **3.00**
Circ: Statement: **109,640**
34 ❑ Nov 1977 Cover: 0.35 **NM** value: **3.00**
Circ: Statement: **109,640**
35 ❑ Feb 1978 Cover: 0.35 **NM** value: **3.00**
36 ❑ Mar 1978 Cover: 0.35 **NM** value: **3.00**
37 ❑ May 1978 Cover: 0.35 **NM** value: **3.00**
38 ❑ Jun 1978 Cover: 0.35 **NM** value: **3.00**
39 ❑ Oct 1978 Cover: 0.35 **NM** value: **3.00**
The Noblest Work of Man; The Curse fo Prince Dmitri; When Witches Walk; Who Am I? (text)
40 ❑ Dec 1978 Cover: 0.35 **NM** value: **3.00**
An Ancient Crime; Flight into Oblivion; Fearless Frank Fairless (text); Step Forward, Brother • Warren Sattler credits
41 ❑ Feb 1979 Cover: 0.40 **NM** value: **3.00**
42 ❑ Mar 1979 Cover: 0.40 **NM** value: **3.00**
• Has 1976 Statement; avg total paid circ 98,465
43 ❑ Jun 1979 Cover: 0.40 **NM** value: **3.00**
44 ❑ Jul 1979 Cover: 0.40 **NM** value: **3.00**
45 ❑ Sep 1979 Cover: 0.40 **NM** value: **3.00**
46 ❑ Oct 1979 Cover: 0.40 **NM** value: **3.00**
47 ❑ Nov 1979 Cover: 0.40 **NM** value: **3.00**
48 ❑ Jan 1979 Cover: 0.40 **NM** value: **3.00**
49 ❑ Mar 1980 Cover: 0.40 **NM** value: **3.00**
50 ❑ May 1980 Cover: 0.40 **NM** value: **3.00**
51 ❑ Jul 1980 Cover: 0.40 **NM** value: **3.00**
52 ❑ Sep 1980 Cover: 0.50 **NM** value: **3.00**
53 ❑ Nov 1980 Cover: 0.50 **NM** value: **3.00**
54 ❑ Jan 1981 Cover: 0.50 **NM** value: **3.00**
55 ❑ Mar 1981 Cover: 0.50 **NM** value: **3.00**
56 ❑ May 1981 Cover: 0.50 **NM** value: **3.00**
57 ❑ Jul 1981 Cover: 0.50 **NM** value: **3.00**
• Has 1977 Statement; avg total paid circ 109,640
58 ❑ Aug 1981 Cover: 0.50 **NM** value: **3.00**
59 ❑ Oct 1981 Cover: 0.50 **NM** value: **3.00**
60 ❑ Dec 1981 Cover: 0.50 **NM** value: **3.00**
61 ❑ Feb 1982 Cover: 0.60 **NM** value: **3.00**
62 ❑ Apr 1982 Cover: 0.60 **NM** value: **3.00**
63 ❑ Jun 1982 Cover: 0.60 **NM** value: **3.00**
64 ❑ Aug 1982 Cover: 0.60 **NM** value: **3.00**
65 ❑ Oct 1982 Cover: 0.60 **NM** value: **3.00**
66 ❑ Dec 1982 Cover: 0.60 **NM** value: **3.00**
67 ❑ Feb 1983 Cover: 0.60 **NM** value: **3.00**

CGC-graded: Multiply prices above by **33 for 9.9 M • 16 for 9.8 NM/M • 7 for 9.6 NM+ • 5 for 9.4 NM • 2.5 for 9.2 NM- • 1.5 for 9.0 VF/NM**

68 ❑ Apr 1983 Cover: 0.60 **NM** value: **3.00**
69 ❑ Jul 1983 Cover: 0.60 **NM** value: **3.00**
70 ❑ Sep 1983 Cover: 0.60 **NM** value: **3.00**
71 ❑ Nov 1983 Cover: 0.60 **NM** value: **3.00**
72 ❑ Jan 1984 Cover: 0.60 **NM** value: **3.00**
73 ❑ Mar 1984 Cover: 0.60 **NM** value: **3.00**
74 ❑ May 1984 Cover: 0.60 **NM** value: **3.00**
75 ❑ Jul 1984 Cover: 0.60 **NM** value: **3.00**
76 ❑ Sep 1984 Cover: 0.75 **NM** value: **3.00**
77 ❑ Nov 1984 Cover: 0.75 **NM** value: **3.00**

GHOST RIDER, THE — Marvel

In the Old West of the 1870s, school teacher Carter Slade was ambushed by desperados and left for dead. He was discovered by a friendly Indian tribe, which bestowed him with gifts to help him bring his attackers to justice: a bolt of white, glow-in-the-dark material made with the dust of a phosphorescent meteorite, and a white stallion named Banshee. Armed with these and a pair of six-guns, Slade rides by night to strike fear in the heart of evildoers as the Ghost Rider.

Created by longtime Marvel hand Dick Ayers, the Ghost Rider bears resemblance to a similarly-named character from the 1950s, published by Magazine Enterprises. The Marvel western Ghost Rider was renamed Night Rider in the 1970s to avoid confusion with the blazing-skulled, motorcycle-riding Ghost Rider of the present day. There are a few comics readers who really wish the cowboy would take his name back.

1 ❑ Feb 1967 Cover: 0.12 **NM** value: **24.00**
• **CGC:** 10 graded, best 9.4
📖 The Origin of The Ghost Rider; Kid Colt Outlaw: The Menace of the Mask Maker • Western; back-up reprints story from Kid Colt Outlaw #105 **A:** Dick Ayers **W:** Gary Friedrich; Roy Thomas ★ Origin of Ghost Rider. ★ 1st Appearance of Ghost Rider.

2 ❑ Apr 1967 Cover: 0.12 **NM** value: **15.00**
• **CGC:** 4 graded, best 9.8
• Western; back-up reprints story from Kid Colt Outlaw #99 **A:** Dick Ayers ★ Versus Tarantula.

3 ❑ Jun 1967 Cover: 0.12 **NM** value: **15.00**
• **CGC:** 1 graded, best 9.4
• Western; back-up reprints story from Kid Colt Outlaw #116 **A:** Dick Ayers

4 ❑ Aug 1967 Cover: 0.12 **NM** value: **10.00**
• **CGC:** 1 graded, best 9.0
• Western; back-up reprints story from Two-Gun Kid #69 **A:** Dick Ayers ★ Appearance of Tarantula. ★ Versus Sting-Ray a.k.a. Scorpion.

5 ❑ Sep 1967 Cover: 0.12 **NM** value: **10.00**
• **CGC:** 1 graded, best 9.2
• Western **A:** Dick Ayers ★ Versus Tarantula.

6 ❑ Oct 1967 Cover: 0.12 **NM** value: **10.00**
• **CGC:** 2 graded, best 9.6
• Western **A:** Dick Ayers ★ Versus Towering Oak.

7 ❑ Nov 1967 Cover: 0.12 **NM** value: **10.00**
• **CGC:** 1 graded, best 9.4
final issue. • Western **A:** Dick Ayers

GHOST RIDER & CABLE: SERVANTS OF THE DEAD — Marvel

1 ❑ Sep 1991 Cover: 3.95 **NM** value: **Cover or less**
Circ: CapCity orders: **15,700**
cardstock cover. • no indicia; Reprints Ghost Rider/Cable series from Marvel Comics Presents

GHOST RIDER AND THE MIDNIGHT SONS MAGAZINE — Marvel

1 ❑ Cover: 3.95 **NM** value: **Cover or less**
Circ: CapCity orders: **8,400**

GHOST RIDER/BALLISTIC — Marvel

1 ❑ Feb 1997 Cover: 2.95 **NM** value: **Cover or less**
📖 Devil's Reign, Part 3; Devil's Reign • crossover with Top Cow; continues in Ballistic/Wolverine **A:** Billy Tan Mung Khoy **W:** Warren Ellis

GHOST RIDER/BLAZE: SPIRITS OF VENGEANCE — Marvel

1 ❑ Aug 1992 Cover: 2.75 **NM** value: **Cover or less**
📖 Rise of the Midnight Sons, Part 2 • without poster **W:** Howard Mackie

1/CS❑ Aug 1992 Cover: 2.75 **NM** value: **Cover or less**
Circ: CapCity orders: **150,600**
📖 Rise of the Midnight Sons, Part 2 **W:** Howard Mackie

2 ❑ Sep 1992 Cover: 1.75 **NM** value: **Cover or less**
Circ: CapCity orders: **93,600**
📖 Steel Vengeance **A:** Adam Kubert **W:** Howard Mackie

3 ❑ Oct 1992 Cover: 1.75 **NM** value: **Cover or less**
Circ: CapCity orders: **80,700**
📖 Fathers **A:** Adam Kubert **W:** Howard Mackie

4 ❑ Nov 1992 Cover: 1.75 **NM** value: **Cover or less**
Circ: CapCity orders: **76,800**

5 ❑ Dec 1992 Cover: 1.75 **NM** value: **Cover or less**
Circ: CapCity orders: **75,900**
📖 Spirits of Venom, Part 2 • Venom **A:** Adam Kubert **W:** Howard Mackie

6 ❑ Jan 1993 Cover: 1.75 **NM** value: **Cover or less**
Circ: CapCity orders: **61,200**
📖 Spirits of Venom, Part 4 **W:** Howard Mackie

7 ❑ Feb 1993 Cover: 1.75 **NM** value: **Cover or less**
Circ: CapCity orders: **46,800**

8 ❑ Mar 1993 Cover: 1.75 **NM** value: **Cover or less**
Circ: CapCity orders: **45,000**
📖 Devil Dance **A:** Adam Kubert **W:** Howard Mackie

9 ❑ Apr 1993 Cover: 1.75 **NM** value: **Cover or less**
Circ: CapCity orders: **44,400**
📖 Carnival of Death, Part 1 **W:** Howard Mackie

10 ❑ May 1993 Cover: 1.75 **NM** value: **Cover or less**
Circ: CapCity orders: **38,900**
📖 Carnival of Death, Part 2 **W:** Howard Mackie

11 ❑ Jun 1993 Cover: 1.75 **NM** value: **Cover or less**
Circ: CapCity orders: **35,300**

12 ❑ Jul 1993 Cover: 2.75 **NM** value: **Cover or less**
Circ: CapCity orders: **58,500**
Glow-in-the-dark cover. 📖 Obligations **A:** Adam Kubert **W:** Howard Mackie

13 ❑ Aug 1993 Cover: 2.50 **NM** value: **Cover or less**
Circ: CapCity orders: **52,500**
black cover. 📖 Midnight Massacre, Part 5 **W:** Howard Mackie

14 ❑ Sep 1993 Cover: 1.75 **NM** value: **Cover or less**
Circ: CapCity orders: **33,600**
📖 Truth is Only Skin Deep **A:** Mike Manley **W:** Howard Mackie

15 ❑ Oct 1993 Cover: 1.75 **NM** value: **Cover or less**
Circ: CapCity orders: **30,700**
Neon ink cover. 📖 Road to Vengeance, Part 4 • Blaze's new costume and powers **A:** Mike Manley **W:** Howard Mackie ★ Appearance of Lilith, Centurious, Vengeance.

16 ❑ Nov 1993 Cover: 1.75 **NM** value: **Cover or less**
Circ: CapCity orders: **30,000**

17 ❑ Dec 1993 Cover: 1.75 **NM** value: **Cover or less**
Circ: CapCity orders: **31,350**
Neon inks on cover. 📖 Siege of Darkness, Part 8 **W:** Howard Mackie

18 ❑ Jan 1994 Cover: 1.75 **NM** value: **Cover or less**
Circ: CapCity orders: **26,300**
Spot-varnished cover. 📖 Siege of Darkness, Part 16 **W:** Howard Mackie

19 ❑ Feb 1994 Cover: 1.75 **NM** value: **Cover or less**
Circ: CapCity orders: **23,000**
📖 Alone! **A:** Henry Martinez **W:** Howard Mackie; David Quinn

20 ❑ Mar 1994 Cover: 1.75 **NM** value: **Cover or less**
Circ: CapCity orders: **21,000**

21 ❑ Apr 1994 Cover: 1.75 **NM** value: **Cover or less**
Circ: CapCity orders: **19,100**

22 ❑ May 1994 Cover: 1.95 **NM** value: **Cover or less**
Circ: CapCity orders: **18,000**

23 ❑ Jun 1994 Cover: 1.95 **NM** value: **Cover or less**
Circ: CapCity orders: **16,800**
📖 An Ending final issue. **A:** Henry Martinez **W:** Howard Mackie

GHOST RIDER/CAPTAIN AMERICA: FEAR — Marvel

1 ❑ Oct 1992 Cover: 5.95 **NM** value: **Cover or less**
Circ: CapCity orders: **26,500**
No issue number. Fold-out cover. **A:** Lee Weeks **W:** Howard Mackie

GHOST RIDER: CROSSROADS — Marvel

1 ❑ Dec 1995 Cover: 3.95 **NM** value: **Cover or less**
One-shot. enhanced wraparound cardstock cover. ★ Appearance of Ghost Rider II (Dan Ketch), Ghost Rider I (Johnny Blaze).

GHOST RIDER: HIGHWAY TO HELL — Marvel

1 ❑ Cover: 3.50 **NM** value: **Cover or less**

GHOST RIDER (MAGAZINE ENTERPRISES) — Magazine Enterprises

1 ❑ ca. 1950 Cover: 0.10 **NM** value: **500.00**
• **CGC:** 9 graded, best 8.5
2 ❑ Cover: 0.10 **NM** value: **400.00**
3 ❑ ca. 1951 Cover: 0.10 **NM** value: **400.00**
• **CGC:** 2 graded, best 8.0
4 ❑ ca. 1951 Cover: 0.10 **NM** value: **400.00**
• **CGC:** 2 graded, best 9.0
5 ❑ Cover: 0.10 **NM** value: **300.00**
6 ❑ Cover: 0.10 **NM** value: **300.00**
7 ❑ Cover: 0.10 **NM** value: **200.00**
8 ❑ Cover: 0.10 **NM** value: **200.00**
9 ❑ Cover: 0.10 **NM** value: **200.00**
10 ❑ Cover: 0.10 **NM** value: **200.00**
• **CGC:** 1 graded, best 7.0
11 ❑ Cover: 0.10 **NM** value: **200.00**
12 ❑ Cover: 0.10 **NM** value: **200.00**
13 ❑ Cover: 0.10 **NM** value: **200.00**
14 ❑ Cover: 0.10 **NM** value: **200.00**

GHOST RIDER POSTER MAGAZINE — Marvel

1 ❑ Cover: 4.95 **NM** value: **Cover or less**

GHOST RIDER: THE HAMMER LANE — Marvel

1 ❑ Cover: 2.99 **NM** value: **Cover or less**
Circ: Diamd. preorders: **53,211**
2 ❑ Cover: 2.99 **NM** value: **Cover or less**
Circ: Diamd. preorders: **48,231**
3 ❑ Cover: 2.99 **NM** value: **Cover or less**
Circ: Diamd. preorders: **47,287**
4 ❑ Cover: 2.99 **NM** value: **Cover or less**
Circ: Diamd. preorders: **42,925**
5 ❑ Cover: 2.99 **NM** value: **Cover or less**
Circ: Diamd. preorders: **38,664**
6 ❑ Cover: 2.99 **NM** value: **Cover or less**
Circ: Diamd. preorders: **35,930**

Looking for further information about a specific comic book or line of comics? Write a letter to ***Comics Buyer's Guide*** at ohso@krause.com — if we don't know, one of our readers always does!

GHOST RIDER 2099 — Marvel

Marvel's Ghost Rider had grown inexplicably popular in the early 1990s — strange, since he had never really been popular the first time around — and Marvel regarded the downbeat demon as a good candidate for inclusion in its line of comics set in a dystopic future. Hence, Ghost Rider 2099. It sounds like an idea Max Bialystock would have had.

Anyway, this future-era Ghost Rider was once Kenshiro Cochrane, a member of a gang of technological criminal. While trying to escape with stolen information, Cochrane is killed — but not before sending his consciousness into a computer realm, where he's recast into a robot body similar to Marvel's original fiery-skull cyclist. People get beat up after that.— JJM

1 ❑ May 1994 Cover: 1.50 **NM** value: **2.00**
Circ: Statement: **104,850** CapCity orders: **12,300** • **CGC:** 2 graded, best 9.6
📖 Burning Chrome **A:** Mark Buckingham; Chris Bachalo **W:** Len Kaminski ★ Origin of Ghost Rider 2099. ★ 1st Appearance of Ghost Rider 2099.

1/CS❑ May 1994 Cover: 2.25 **NM** value: **2.50**
Circ: CapCity orders: **60,400**
📖 Burning Chrome • Polybagged with trading card **A:** Mark Buckingham; Chris Bachalo **W:** Len Kaminski

2 ❑ Jun 1994 Cover: 1.50 **NM** value: **Cover or less**
Circ: Statement: **104,850** CapCity orders: **34,200**
📖 Detonation Boulevard • Polybagged with poster **A:** Mark Buckingham; Chris Bachalo **W:** Len Kaminski

3 ❑ Jul 1994 Cover: 1.50 **NM** value: **Cover or less**
Circ: Statement: **104,850** CapCity orders: **31,350**
4 ❑ Aug 1994 Cover: 1.50 **NM** value: **Cover or less**
Circ: Statement: **104,850** CapCity orders: **26,750**
5 ❑ Sep 1994 Cover: 1.50 **NM** value: **Cover or less**
Circ: Statement: **104,850** CapCity orders: **24,100**
6 ❑ Oct 1994 Cover: 1.50 **NM** value: **Cover or less**
Circ: Statement: **104,850** CapCity orders: **21,400**
7 ❑ Nov 1994 Cover: 1.50 **NM** value: **Cover or less**
Circ: Statement: **104,850** CapCity orders: **19,350**
8 ❑ Dec 1994 Cover: 1.50 **NM** value: **Cover or less**
Circ: Statement: **38,325** CapCity orders: **17,950**
9 ❑ Jan 1995 Cover: 1.50 **NM** value: **Cover or less**
Circ: Statement: **38,325** CapCity orders: **16,425**
10 ❑ Feb 1995 Cover: 1.50 **NM** value: **Cover or less**
Circ: Statement: **38,325** CapCity orders: **15,775**
11 ❑ Mar 1995 Cover: 1.50 **NM** value: **Cover or less**
Circ: Statement: **38,325** CapCity orders: **13,750**
12 ❑ Apr 1995 Cover: 1.50 **NM** value: **Cover or less**
Circ: Statement: **38,325** CapCity orders: **12,900**
• Has 1994 Statement, filed 10/1/94; avg print run 166,618; avg sales 104,608; avg subs 242; avg total paid 104,850; samples 125; office use 500; max existent 105,475; 37% of run returned
13 ❑ May 1995 Cover: 1.95 **NM** value: **Cover or less**
Circ: Statement: **38,325** CapCity orders: **15,175**
14 ❑ Jun 1995 Cover: 1.95 **NM** value: **Cover or less**
Circ: Statement: **38,325** CapCity orders: **12,775**
15 ❑ Jul 1995 Cover: 1.95 **NM** value: **Cover or less**
Circ: Statement: **38,325** CapCity orders: **11,600**
16 ❑ Aug 1995 Cover: 1.95 **NM** value: **Cover or less**
Circ: Statement: **38,325** CapCity orders: **10,725**
17 ❑ Sep 1995 Cover: 1.95 **NM** value: **Cover or less**
Circ: Statement: **38,325**
18 ❑ Oct 1995 Cover: 1.95 **NM** value: **Cover or less**
Circ: Statement: **38,325**
19 ❑ Nov 1995 Cover: 1.95 **NM** value: **Cover or less**
20 ❑ Dec 1995 Cover: 1.95 **NM** value: **Cover or less**
21 ❑ Jan 1996 Cover: 1.95 **NM** value: **Cover or less**
• Has 1995 Statement, filed 10/1/95; avg print run 40,972; avg sales 37,325; avg subs 1,000; avg total paid 38,325; samples 750; office use 500; max existent 39,575; 3% of run returned
22 ❑ Feb 1996 Cover: 1.95 **NM** value: **Cover or less**
23 ❑ Mar 1996 Cover: 1.95 **NM** value: **Cover or less**
📖 Bad Craziness **A:** Ashley Wood **W:** Len Kaminski
24 ❑ Apr 1996 Cover: 1.95 **NM** value: **Cover or less**
📖 Road To Ruin **A:** Ashley Wood **W:** Len Kaminski
25 ❑ May 1996 Cover: 2.95 **NM** value: **Cover or less**
wraparound cover. • double-sized. final issue.

GHOST RIDER (VOL. 1) — Marvel

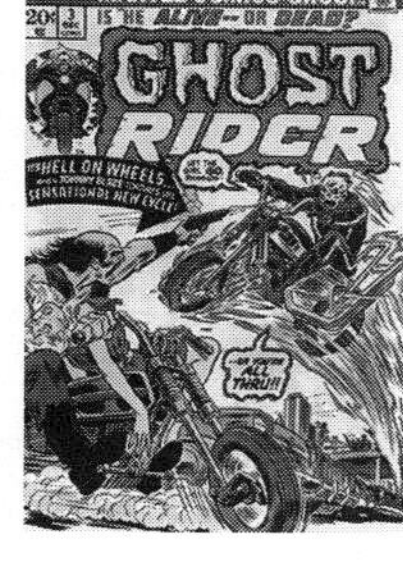

His surrogate father dying from an incurable disease, stunt-rider Johnny Blaze summoned the demon Mephisto and offered to trade his soul to save him. The spell was interrupted before the deal could be completed, but Mephisto still managed to get the better of Johnny. His guardian was cured, but was killed the next night in a failed stunt. Mephisto also bonded Zarathos, the flaming spirit of vengeance, to Johnny. Whenever Zarathos was in control, Johnny became a fiery skeleton, riding a bike made of hellfire. As this Ghost Rider, he became a force of vengeance against evildoers.

An attempt to marry cycle action with the occult, Ghost Rider found some converts in the 1970s but felt dated by the 1980s, never really making it to the A-list of Marvel super-heroes.

Other grades: Multiply prices above by **1.5 for Mint • 2/3 for Very Fine • 1/3 for Fine • 1/5 for Very Good • 1/8 for Good**

1 ❑ Aug 1973 Cover: 0.20 **NM** value: **30.00**
• **CGC:** 55 graded, best 9.6
📖 A Woman Possessed **A:** Gil Kane ★ 1st Appearance of Son of Satan (partially shown).

2 ❑ Oct 1973 Cover: 0.20 **NM** value: **14.00**
• **CGC:** 6 graded, best 9.6
📖 Shake Hands with Satan!

3 ❑ Dec 1973 Cover: 0.20 **NM** value: **9.00**
• **CGC:** 2 graded, best 8.5
📖 Wheels On Fire **A:** Jim Mooney **W:** Gary Friedrich

4 ❑ Feb 1974 Cover: 0.20 **NM** value: **9.00**
📖 Death Stalks Demolition Derby! **A:** Jim Mooney **W:** Gary Friedrich

5 ❑ Apr 1974 Cover: 0.20 **NM** value: **9.00**
• **CGC:** 1 graded, best 9.4
📖 And Vegas Writhes in Flames

6 ❑ Jun 1974 Cover: 0.25 **NM** value: **7.00**
📖 Zodiac II

7 ❑ Aug 1974 Cover: 0.20 **NM** value: **7.00**
📖 And Loose His Own Soul!

8 ❑ Oct 1974 Cover: 0.20 **NM** value: **6.00**
• **CGC:** 2 graded, best 9.6
📖 Satan Himself! **A:** Jim Mooney **W:** Tony Isabella ★ 1st Appearance of Inferno. ★ Appearance of Roxanne.

9 ❑ Dec 1974 Cover: 0.20 **NM** value: **6.00**
📖 The Hell-Bound Hero!

10 ❑ Feb 1975 Cover: 0.20 **NM** value: **6.00**
📖 Ghost Rider • Reprints Marvel Spotlight #5★ Appearance of Hulk.

11 ❑ Apr 1975 Cover: 0.25 **NM** value: **4.50**
📖 The Desolation Run **A:** Sal Buscema; Gil Kane; Klaus Janson ★ Appearance of Hulk.

12 ❑ Jun 1975 Cover: 0.25 **NM** value: **4.50**
📖 Phantom of the Killer Skies ★ Death of Phantom Eagle.

13 ❑ Aug 1975 Cover: 0.25 **NM** value: **4.50**
📖 You've Got a Second Chance, Johnny Blaze

14 ❑ Oct 1975 Cover: 0.25 **NM** value: **4.50**
📖 A Spectre Stalks the Soundstage

15 ❑ Dec 1975 Cover: 0.25 **NM** value: **4.50**
📖 Vengeance on the Ventura Freeway!

16 ❑ Feb 1976 Cover: 0.25 **NM** value: **4.50**
📖 Blood in the Water!

17 ❑ Apr 1976 Cover: 0.25 **NM** value: **4.50**
📖 Prelude to a Private Armageddon

18 ❑ Jun 1976 Cover: 0.25 **NM** value: **4.50**
• **CGC:** 1 graded, best 6.0
📖 The Salvation Run! ★ Appearance of Spider-Man.

19 ❑ Aug 1976 Cover: 0.25 **NM** value: **4.50**
📖 Resurrection

20 ❑ Oct 1976 Cover: 0.30 **NM** value: **6.00**
📖 Two Against Death! **A:** John Byrne; Gil Kane; Klaus Janson ★ Appearance of Daredevil.

21 ❑ Dec 1976 Cover: 0.30 **NM** value: **3.50**
📖 Deathplay! ★ Death of Eel I (Leopold Stryke).

22 ❑ Feb 1977 Cover: 0.30 **NM** value: **3.50**
📖 Nobody Beats the Enforcer! ★ 1st Appearance of Enforcer (Marvel).

23 ❑ Apr 1977 Cover: 0.30 **NM** value: **3.50**
📖 Wrath of the Water Wizard! ★ Origin of Water Wizard. ★ 1st Appearance of Water Wizard.

24 ❑ Jun 1977 Cover: 0.30 **NM** value: **3.50**
📖 I, the Enforcer!

25 ❑ Aug 1977 Cover: 0.30 **NM** value: **3.50**
📖 Menace is a Man Called Malice!

26 ❑ Oct 1977 Cover: 0.30 **NM** value: **3.50**
📖 A Doom Named Dr. Druid!

27 ❑ Dec 1977 Cover: 0.35 **NM** value: **3.50**
📖 At the Mercy of the Manticore

28 ❑ Feb 1978 Cover: 0.35 **NM** value: **3.50**
📖 Evil is the Orb!

29 ❑ Apr 1978 Cover: 0.35 **NM** value: **3.50**
📖 Deadly Pawn

30 ❑ Jun 1978 Cover: 0.35 **NM** value: **3.50**
📖 The Mage and the Monster

31 ❑ Aug 1978 Cover: 0.35 **NM** value: **2.50**
📖 Demon's Rage

32 ❑ Oct 1978 Cover: 0.35 **NM** value: **2.50**
📖 The Price

33 ❑ Dec 1978 Cover: 0.35 **NM** value: **2.50**
📖 Whom a Child Would Destroy

34 ❑ Feb 1979 Cover: 0.35 **NM** value: **2.50**
Circ: Statement: **135,107**
📖 The Boy Who Lived Forever

35 ❑ Apr 1979 Cover: 0.35 **NM** value: **2.50**
Circ: Statement: **135,107**
📖 Death Race!

36 ❑ Jun 1979 Cover: 0.40 **NM** value: **2.50**
Circ: Statement: **135,107**
📖 A Demon in Denver

37 ❑ Aug 1979 Cover: 0.40 **NM** value: **2.50**
Circ: Statement: **135,107**
📖 Night of the Flame Cycles

38 ❑ Oct 1979 Cover: 0.40 **NM** value: **2.50**
Circ: Statement: **135,107**
📖 The Cult of Doom!

39 ❑ Dec 1979 Cover: 0.40 **NM** value: **2.50**
Circ: Statement: **135,107** • **CGC:** 1 graded, best 9.6
📖 Into the Abyss!

40 ❑ Jan 1980 Cover: 0.40 **NM** value: **2.50**
Circ: Statement: **132,129**
📖 The Menace of the Nuclear Man!

41 ❑ Feb 1980 Cover: 0.40 **NM** value: **2.50**
Circ: Statement: **132,129**
📖 The Freight Train to Oblivion

42 ❑ Mar 1980 Cover: 0.40 **NM** value: **2.50**
Circ: Statement: **132,129**
📖 The Lonesome Death of Johnny Blaze! • Has 1979 Statement; avg print run 277,030; avg sales 134,549; avg subs 558; avg total paid 135,107; max existent 135,107; 51% of run returned

43 ❑ Apr 1980 Cover: 0.40 **NM** value: **2.50**
Circ: Statement: **132,129**
📖 Night of the Crimson Mage

44 ❑ May 1980 Cover: 0.40 **NM** value: **2.50**
Circ: Statement: **132,129**
📖 Cloak of Crimson, Soul of Dust

45 ❑ Jun 1980 Cover: 0.40 **NM** value: **2.50**
Circ: Statement: **132,129**
📖 To Banish a Ghost!

46 ❑ Jul 1980 Cover: 0.40 **NM** value: **2.50**
Circ: Statement: **132,129**
📖 The End of a Champion

47 ❑ Aug 1980 Cover: 0.40 **NM** value: **2.50**
Circ: Statement: **132,129**
📖 The Demon Within

48 ❑ Sep 1980 Cover: 0.50 **NM** value: **2.50**
Circ: Statement: **132,129**
📖 Wind of the Undead

49 ❑ Oct 1980 Cover: 0.50 **NM** value: **2.50**
Circ: Statement: **132,129**
📖 The Wrath of the Manitou

50 ❑ Nov 1980 Cover: 0.75 **NM** value: **4.00**
Circ: Statement: **132,129** • **CGC:** 1 graded, best 9.6
• Giant-size. 📖 Manitou's Anger, Tarantula's Sting **A:** Don Perlin ★ Appearance of Night Rider.

51 ❑ Dec 1980 Cover: 0.50 **NM** value: **2.50**
Circ: Statement: **132,129**
📖 The Diesel of Doom!

52 ❑ Jan 1981 Cover: 0.50 **NM** value: **2.50**
Circ: Statement: **121,227**
📖 The Sirens of Kronos

53 ❑ Feb 1981 Cover: 0.50 **NM** value: **2.50**
Circ: Statement: **121,227**

54 ❑ Mar 1981 Cover: 0.50 **NM** value: **2.50**
Circ: Statement: **121,227**

55 ❑ Apr 1981 Cover: 0.50 **NM** value: **2.50**
Circ: Statement: **121,227**
📖 Touch of Terror • Has 1980 Statement; avg print run 279,576; avg sales 131,014; avg subs 1,115; avg total paid 132,129; max existent 132,129; 52% of run returned

56 ❑ May 1981 Cover: 0.50 **NM** value: **2.50**
Circ: Statement: **121,227**

57 ❑ Jun 1981 Cover: 0.50 **NM** value: **2.50**
Circ: Statement: **121,227**

58 ❑ Jul 1981 Cover: 0.50 **NM** value: **2.50**
Circ: Statement: **121,227**

59 ❑ Aug 1981 Cover: 0.50 **NM** value: **2.50**
Circ: Statement: **121,227**
📖 Moon Over Dark Water

60 ❑ Sep 1981 Cover: 0.50 **NM** value: **2.50**
Circ: Statement: **121,227**

61 ❑ Oct 1981 Cover: 0.50 **NM** value: **2.50**
Circ: Statement: **121,227**

62 ❑ Nov 1981 Cover: 0.50 **NM** value: **2.50**
Circ: Statement: **121,227**

63 ❑ Dec 1981 Cover: 0.50 **NM** value: **2.50**
Circ: Statement: **121,227**

64 ❑ Jan 1982 Cover: 0.60 **NM** value: **2.50**
Circ: Statement: **117,769**

65 ❑ Feb 1982 Cover: 0.60 **NM** value: **2.50**
Circ: Statement: **117,769**

66 ❑ Mar 1982 Cover: 0.60 **NM** value: **2.50**
Circ: Statement: **117,769**

67 ❑ Apr 1982 Cover: 0.60 **NM** value: **2.50**
Circ: Statement: **117,769**
• Has 1981 Statement; avg print run 273,048; avg sales 119,266; avg subs 1,961; avg total paid 121,227; max existent 121,227; 56% of run returned

68 ❑ May 1982 Cover: 0.60 **NM** value: **3.00**
Circ: Statement: **117,769**

69 ❑ Jun 1982 Cover: 0.60 **NM** value: **2.50**
Circ: Statement: **117,769**

70 ❑ Jul 1982 Cover: 0.60 **NM** value: **2.50**
Circ: Statement: **117,769**

71 ❑ Aug 1982 Cover: 0.60 **NM** value: **2.50**
Circ: Statement: **117,769**

72 ❑ Sep 1982 Cover: 0.60 **NM** value: **2.50**
Circ: Statement: **117,769**

73 ❑ Oct 1982 Cover: 0.60 **NM** value: **2.50**
Circ: Statement: **117,769**

74 ❑ Nov 1982 Cover: 0.60 **NM** value: **2.50**
Circ: Statement: **117,769** • **CGC:** 1 graded, best 8.0

75 ❑ Dec 1982 Cover: 0.60 **NM** value: **2.50**
Circ: Statement: **117,769**

76 ❑ Jan 1983 Cover: 0.60 **NM** value: **2.50**

77 ❑ Feb 1983 Cover: 0.60 **NM** value: **2.50**

78 ❑ Mar 1983 Cover: 0.60 **NM** value: **2.50**

79 ❑ Apr 1983 Cover: 0.60 **NM** value: **2.50**

80 ❑ May 1983 Cover: 0.60 **NM** value: **2.50**

81 ❑ Jun 1983 Cover: 0.60 **NM** value: **3.50**
• **CGC:** 1 graded, best 9.6
• Zarathos leaves Johnny Blaze-end of Ghost Rider I★ Death of Ghost Rider.

There are two different pricing tiers in the modern comic-book hobby. **The prices seen above** are the prices we have seen **loose copies** of these issues reliably fetch in a variety of environments. Condition alters the price by the fractions seen on the bar on the bottom of left-hand pages of this book. **Comics graded by CGC** usually sell for more. Use the guide on the bottom of right-hand pages of this book to estimate what copies have brought on eBay.

GHOST RIDER (VOL. 2) — Marvel

Johnny Blaze having been relieved of his curse at the end of Volume 1, Volume 2 found another victim.

Dan Ketch and his sister Barb were in a graveyard on Halloween night, where they encountered mobsters fighting over a mysterious suitcase. Barb was killed by a villain named Deathwatch. Covered with his sister's blood, Dan searched desperately for a way out, only to stumble across an abandoned motorcycle. When his blood-stained hands touched the gas cap, Dan found himself transformed into the fiery spirit of vengeance known as Ghost Rider.

With the boom of the early 1990s in full swing, Marvel relaunched dozens of characters from past series into new vehicles, and Ghost Rider was one. This version, however, seemed more focused on sheer violence and mayhem than the previous, moodier title, becoming, in the eyes of some Marvelites at that time, an example of what had gone wrong with comics in general and Marvel in particular.

-1 ❑ Jul 1997 Cover: 1.95 **NM** value: **Cover or less**
• Flashback **W:** Howard Mackie

1 ❑ May 1990 Cover: 1.95 **NM** value: **3.00**
Circ: CapCity orders: **44,700** • **CGC:** 35 graded, best 9.8
📖 Life's Blood **A:** Javier Saltares **W:** Howard Mackie ★ Origin of Ghost Rider II (Dan Ketch). ★ 1st Appearance of Ghost Rider II (Dan Ketch), Deathwatch.

1-2 ❑ Sep 1990 Cover: 1.95 **NM** value: **Cover or less**
📖 Life's Blood • 2nd Printing (gold) **W:** Howard Mackie ★ Origin of Ghost Rider II (Dan Ketch). ★ 1st Appearance of Ghost Rider II (Dan Ketch), Deathwatch.

2 ❑ Jun 1990 Cover: 1.50 **NM** value: **2.00**
Circ: CapCity orders: **33,500** • **CGC:** 2 graded, best 9.9
📖 Do Be Afraid Of The Dark! **A:** Javier Saltares **W:** Howard Mackie ★ 1st Appearance of Blackout II.

3 ❑ Jul 1990 Cover: 1.50 **NM** value: **2.00**
Circ: CapCity orders: **37,100** • **CGC:** 1 graded, best 9.6
📖 Death Watch **A:** Javier Saltares **W:** Howard Mackie ★ Versus Blackout. ★ Versus Kingpin. ★ Versus Deathwatch.

4 ❑ Aug 1990 Cover: 1.50 **NM** value: **2.00**
Circ: CapCity orders: **39,900**
• Scarcer **W:** Howard Mackie ★ Versus Mr. Hyde.

5 ❑ Sep 1990 Cover: 1.50 **NM** value: **2.00**
Circ: CapCity orders: **52,800**
📖 Getting Paid! **A:** Jim Lee(cover) **W:** Howard Mackie ★ Appearance of Punisher.

5/SC❑ Jun 1994 Cover: 2.95 **NM** value: **Cover or less**
Die-cut cover. 📖 Getting Paid! **A:** Jim Lee(cover) **W:** Howard Mackie ★ Appearance of Punisher.

5-2 ❑ Sep 1990 Cover: 1.50 **NM** value: **Cover or less**
📖 Getting Paid! • 2nd printing (gold) **A:** Jim Lee(cover) **W:** Howard Mackie ★ Appearance of Punisher.

6 ❑ Oct 1990 Cover: 1.50 **NM** value: **2.00**
Circ: CapCity orders: **49,600** • **CGC:** 2 graded, best 9.6

7 ❑ Nov 1990 Cover: 1.50 **NM** value: **2.00**
Circ: CapCity orders: **44,600**

8 ❑ Dec 1990 Cover: 1.50 **NM** value: **2.00**
Circ: CapCity orders: **50,100**

9 ❑ Jan 1991 Cover: 1.50 **NM** value: **2.00**
Circ: CapCity orders: **58,700**

10 ❑ Feb 1991 Cover: 1.50 **NM** value: **2.00**
Circ: CapCity orders: **56,700**
📖 Stars Of Blood **A:** Javier Saltares **W:** Howard Mackie

11 ❑ Mar 1991 Cover: 1.50 **NM** value: **Cover or less**
Circ: CapCity orders: **56,400**

12 ❑ Apr 1991 Cover: 1.50 **NM** value: **Cover or less**
Circ: CapCity orders: **56,100**

13 ❑ May 1991 Cover: 1.50 **NM** value: **Cover or less**
Circ: CapCity orders: **61,500**

14 ❑ Jun 1991 Cover: 1.50 **NM** value: **Cover or less**
Circ: CapCity orders: **60,300**
• Johnny Blaze; Ghost Rider vs. Johnny Blaze

15 ❑ Jul 1991 Cover: 1.75 **NM** value: **2.00**
Circ: CapCity orders: **100,500** • **CGC:** 3 graded, best 9.6
glow in the dark cover. 📖 Last Hope **A:** Mark Texeira **W:** Howard Mackie

15-2❑ Cover: 1.75 **NM** value: **2.00**
glow in the dark cover. 📖 Last Hope • 2nd Printing (gold) **A:** Mark Texeira **W:** Howard Mackie

16 ❑ Aug 1991 Cover: 1.75 **NM** value: **Cover or less**
Circ: CapCity orders: **69,600**

17 ❑ Sep 1991 Cover: 1.75 **NM** value: **Cover or less**
Circ: CapCity orders: **83,400**
📖 You've Got to Have Faith **A:** Mark Texeira **W:** Howard Mackie ★ Appearance of Hobgoblin, Spider-Man.

18 ❑ Oct 1991 Cover: 1.75 **NM** value: **Cover or less**
Circ: CapCity orders: **75,600**
Painted cover. 📖 Lost Souls! **A:** Mark Texeira **W:** Howard Mackie

19 ❑ Nov 1991 Cover: 1.75 **NM** value: **Cover or less**
Circ: CapCity orders: **75,600**
📖 The Deal **A:** Mark Texeira **W:** Howard Mackie

20 ❑ Dec 1991 Cover: 1.75 **NM** value: **Cover or less**
Circ: CapCity orders: **80,700**
📖 Sign Of Death **A:** Ron Wagner **W:** Howard Mackie

21 ❑ Jan 1992 Cover: 1.75 **NM** value: **Cover or less**
Circ: Statement: **357,200** CapCity orders: **76,500**
📖 Bad To The Bone! **A:** Ron Wagner **W:** Howard Mackie

22 ❑ Feb 1992 Cover: 1.75 **NM** value: **Cover or less**
Circ: Statement: **357,200** CapCity orders: **69,900**
📖 Death's Eyes **A:** Mark Texeira **W:** Howard Mackie

CGC-graded: Multiply prices above by **33 for 9.9 M • 16 for 9.8 NM/M • 7 for 9.6 NM+ • 5 for 9.4 NM • 2.5 for 9.2 NM- • 1.5 for 9.0 VF/NM**

23 ❑ Mar 1992 Cover: 1.75 **NM** value: **Cover or less**
Circ: Statement: **357,200** CapCity orders: **62,100**
📖 Death Drive **A:** Mark Texeira **W:** Howard Mackie ★ Versus Deathwatch.
24 ❑ Apr 1992 Cover: 1.75 **NM** value: **Cover or less**
Circ: Statement: **357,200** CapCity orders: **60,000**
📖 Death Duel **A:** Mark Texeira; Andy Kubert **W:** Howard Mackie ★ Death of Snowblind. ★ Versus Deathwatch.
25 ❑ May 1992 Cover: 2.75 **NM** value: **Cover or less**
Circ: Statement: **357,200** CapCity orders: **117,000**
• Pop-up centerfold, double-sized. 📖 You Can't Go Home Again **A:** Ron Wagner **W:** Howard Mackie
26 ❑ Jun 1992 Cover: 1.75 **NM** value: **Cover or less**
Circ: Statement: **357,200** CapCity orders: **99,000**
📖 ...Blood Feud! **A:** Ron Wagner **W:** Howard Mackie ★ Appearance of X-Men.
27 ❑ Jul 1992 Cover: 1.75 **NM** value: **Cover or less**
Circ: Statement: **357,200** CapCity orders: **88,500**
📖 Vengeance. Pure And Simple. **A:** Ron Wagner **W:** Howard Mackie ★ Appearance of X-Men.
28 ❑ Aug 1992 Cover: 2.50 **NM** value: **Cover or less**
Circ: Statement: **357,200** CapCity orders: **132,300**
📖 Rise of the Midnight Sons, Part 1 **A:** Andy Kubert **W:** Howard Mackie ★ 1st Appearance of Lilith II.
29 ❑ Sep 1992 Cover: 1.75 **NM** value: **Cover or less**
Circ: Statement: **357,200** CapCity orders: **97,500**
📖 Biting the Hand that Feeds You! **A:** Andy Kubert; Joe Kubert(inks) **W:** Howard Mackie ★ Appearance of Wolverine, Beast.
30 ❑ Oct 1992 Cover: 1.75 **NM** value: **Cover or less**
Circ: Statement: **357,200** CapCity orders: **83,100**
📖 Nightmares of Truth **A:** Andy Kubert; Joe Kubert(inks) **W:** Howard Mackie ★ Versus Nightmare.
31 ❑ Nov 1992 Cover: 2.50 **NM** value: **Cover or less**
Circ: Statement: **357,200** CapCity orders: **123,000**
📖 Rise of the Midnight Sons, Part 6 **A:** Andy Kubert; Joe Kubert(inks) **W:** Howard Mackie
32 ❑ Dec 1992 Cover: 1.75 **NM** value: **Cover or less**
Circ: Statement: **357,200** CapCity orders: **69,000**
📖 Fight For Life **A:** Bret Blevins **W:** Howard Mackie
33 ❑ Jan 1993 Cover: 1.75 **NM** value: **Cover or less**
Circ: Statement: **322,642** CapCity orders: **64,500**
📖 What Does it Matter? **A:** Bret Blevins; Al Williamson(inks) **W:** Howard Mackie
34 ❑ Feb 1993 Cover: 1.75 **NM** value: **Cover or less**
Circ: Statement: **322,642** CapCity orders: **59,700**
📖 Victims Of Our Past **A:** Bret Blevins **W:** Howard Mackie
35 ❑ Mar 1993 Cover: 1.75 **NM** value: **Cover or less**
Circ: Statement: **322,642** CapCity orders: **52,500**
📖 You Can't Always Get What You Want **A:** Bret Blevins; Al Williamson(inks) **W:** Howard Mackie
36 ❑ Apr 1993 Cover: 1.75 **NM** value: **Cover or less**
Circ: Statement: **322,642** CapCity orders: **48,600**
📖 Transformations In Pain • Has 1992 Statement, filed 10/1/92; avg print run 475,183; avg sales 353,083; avg subs 4,117; avg total paid 357,200; samples 250; office use 500; max existent 357,950; 25% of run returned **A:** Bret Blevins **W:** Howard Mackie
37 ❑ May 1993 Cover: 1.75 **NM** value: **Cover or less**
Circ: Statement: **322,642** CapCity orders: **46,200**
📖 Forward to the Shadows **A:** Bret Blevins **W:** Howard Mackie
38 ❑ Jun 1993 Cover: 1.75 **NM** value: **Cover or less**
Circ: Statement: **322,642** CapCity orders: **42,500**
📖 Blood Obligations **A:** Mike Manley **W:** Howard Mackie
39 ❑ Jul 1993 Cover: 1.75 **NM** value: **Cover or less**
Circ: Statement: **322,642** CapCity orders: **41,100**
40 ❑ Aug 1993 Cover: 2.25 **NM** value: **Cover or less**
Circ: Statement: **322,642** • **CGC:** 1 graded, best 10.0
black cover.
41 ❑ Sep 1993 Cover: 1.75 **NM** value: **Cover or less**
Circ: Statement: **322,642** CapCity orders: **42,900**
42 ❑ Oct 1993 Cover: 1.75 **NM** value: **Cover or less**
Circ: Statement: **322,642** CapCity orders: **38,000**
Neon cover. 📖 Road to Vengeance: The Missing Link, Part 3 **A:** Ron Garney **W:** Howard Mackie ★ Appearance of Deathwatch, Centurius, Ghostie, John Blaze.
43 ❑ Nov 1993 Cover: 1.75 **NM** value: **Cover or less**
Circ: Statement: **322,642** CapCity orders: **25,500**
📖 Road to Vengeance: The Missing Link **A:** Ron Garney **W:** Howard Mackie
44 ❑ Dec 1993 Cover: 1.75 **NM** value: **Cover or less**
Circ: Statement: **158,275** CapCity orders: **37,200**
Neon cover. 📖 Siege of Darkness, Part 2 **A:** Ron Garney **W:** Howard Mackie
45 ❑ Jan 1994 Cover: 1.75 **NM** value: **Cover or less**
Circ: Statement: **158,275** CapCity orders: **31,300**
Spot-varnished cover. 📖 Siege of Darkness, Part 10 **A:** Ron Garney **W:** Howard Mackie
46 ❑ Feb 1994 Cover: 1.75 **NM** value: **Cover or less**
Circ: Statement: **158,275** CapCity orders: **27,400**
📖 If a Skull Could Weep... **A:** Ron Garney **W:** Howard Mackie
47 ❑ Mar 1994 Cover: 1.75 **NM** value: **Cover or less**
Circ: Statement: **158,275** CapCity orders: **25,950**
📖 Under Fire, Part 1 **A:** Ron Garney **W:** Howard Mackie
48 ❑ Apr 1994 Cover: 1.75 **NM** value: **Cover or less**
Circ: Statement: **158,275**
📖 Under Fire, Part 2 **A:** Ron Garney **W:** Howard Mackie ★ Appearance of Spider-Man.
49 ❑ May 1994 Cover: 1.75 **NM** value: **Cover or less**
Circ: Statement: **158,275** CapCity orders: **23,850**
📖 Under Fire, Part 3 **A:** Ron Garney **W:** Howard Mackie
50 ❑ Jun 1994 Cover: 2.50 **NM** value: **Cover or less**
foil cover. • Giant-size. 📖 Reborn Again **A:** Ron Garney **W:** Howard Mackie
50/SC❑Jun 1994 Cover: 2.95 **NM** value: **Cover or less**
Circ: Statement: **158,275** CapCity orders: **36,000**
Die-cut cover. • Giant-size. 📖 Reborn Again; A Lover's Eyes **A:** Ron Garney; Roger Cruz **W:** Howard Mackie
51 ❑ Jul 1994 Cover: 1.95 **NM** value: **Cover or less**
Circ: Statement: **158,275** CapCity orders: **22,950**
52 ❑ Aug 1994 Cover: 1.95 **NM** value: **Cover or less**
Circ: Statement: **158,275** CapCity orders: **21,200**
📖 A Trail of Flames **A:** Ron Garney **W:** Howard Mackie
53 ❑ Sep 1994 Cover: 1.95 **NM** value: **Cover or less**
Circ: Statement: **158,275** CapCity orders: **20,700**
📖 Reunions **A:** Salvador Larroca **W:** Howard Mackie
54 ❑ Oct 1994 Cover: 1.95 **NM** value: **Cover or less**
Circ: Statement: **158,275** CapCity orders: **18,850**
📖 A Thirst for Celebrity **A:** Salvador Larroca **W:** Howard Mackie
55 ❑ Nov 1994 Cover: 1.95 **NM** value: **Cover or less**
Circ: Statement: **77,339** CapCity orders: **17,850**
56 ❑ Dec 1994 Cover: 1.95 **NM** value: **Cover or less**
Circ: Statement: **77,339** CapCity orders: **17,050**
57 ❑ Jan 1995 Cover: 1.95 **NM** value: **Cover or less**
Circ: Statement: **77,339** CapCity orders: **21,650**
📖 Where to Life? **A:** Salvador Larroca **W:** Howard Mackie ★ Appearance of Wolverine.
58 ❑ Feb 1995 Cover: 1.95 **NM** value: **Cover or less**
Circ: Statement: **77,339** CapCity orders: **15,075**
📖 Betrayals, Part 1 **A:** Salvador Larroca **W:** Howard Mackie
59 ❑ Mar 1995 Cover: 1.95 **NM** value: **Cover or less**
Circ: Statement: **77,339** CapCity orders: **13,775**
📖 Betrayals, Part 1; Betrayals, Part 2 **A:** Salvador Larroca **W:** Howard Mackie
60 ❑ Apr 1995 Cover: 1.95 **NM** value: **Cover or less**
Circ: Statement: **77,339** CapCity orders: **13,075**
📖 Betrayals, Part 2; Betrayals, Part 3 **A:** Salvador Larroca **W:** Howard Mackie
61 ❑ May 1995 Cover: 2.50 **NM** value: **Cover or less**
Circ: Statement: **77,339** CapCity orders: **12,975**
• Giant-size. 📖 Betrayals, Part 3; Betrayals, Part 4
62 ❑ Jun 1995 Cover: 1.95 **NM** value: **Cover or less**
Circ: Statement: **77,339** CapCity orders: **12,650**
📖 In Chains, Part 1
63 ❑ Jul 1995 Cover: 1.95 **NM** value: **Cover or less**
Circ: Statement: **77,339** CapCity orders: **12,000**
📖 In Chains, Part 2
64 ❑ Aug 1995 Cover: 1.95 **NM** value: **Cover or less**
Circ: Statement: **77,339** CapCity orders: **11,625**
📖 In Chains, Part 3
65 ❑ Sep 1995 Cover: 1.95 **NM** value: **Cover or less**
Circ: Statement: **77,339**
📖 In Chains, Part 4 Over the Edge; In Chains, Part 4
66 ❑ Oct 1995 Cover: 1.95 **NM** value: **Cover or less**
Circ: Statement: **77,339**
67 ❑ Nov 1995 Cover: 1.95 **NM** value: **Cover or less**
Circ: Statement: **58,642**
68 ❑ Dec 1995 Cover: 1.95 **NM** value: **Cover or less**
Circ: Statement: **58,642**
69 ❑ Jan 1996 Cover: 1.95 **NM** value: **Cover or less**
Circ: Statement: **58,642**
• Has 1995 Statement, filed 10/1/95; avg print run 156,966; avg sales 76,224; avg subs 1,115; avg total paid 77,339; samples 750; office use 500; max existent 78,589; 50% of run returned
70 ❑ Feb 1996 Cover: 1.95 **NM** value: **Cover or less**
Circ: Statement: **58,642**
71 ❑ Mar 1996 Cover: 1.95 **NM** value: **Cover or less**
Circ: Statement: **58,642**
📖 Blue Shadows **A:** Salvador Larroca **W:** Ivan Velez Jr.
72 ❑ Apr 1996 Cover: 1.95 **NM** value: **Cover or less**
Circ: Statement: **58,642**
73 ❑ May 1996 Cover: 1.95 **NM** value: **Cover or less**
Circ: Statement: **58,642**
74 ❑ Jun 1996 Cover: 1.95 **NM** value: **Cover or less**
Circ: Statement: **58,642**
75 ❑ Jul 1996 Cover: 1.50 **NM** value: **Cover or less**
Circ: Statement: **58,642**
76 ❑ Aug 1996 Cover: 1.50 **NM** value: **Cover or less**
Circ: Statement: **58,642**
77 ❑ Sep 1996 Cover: 1.50 **NM** value: **Cover or less**
Circ: Statement: **32,566**
78 ❑ Oct 1996 Cover: 1.50 **NM** value: **Cover or less**
Circ: Statement: **32,566**
79 ❑ Nov 1996 Cover: 1.50 **NM** value: **Cover or less**
Circ: Statement: **32,566** Direct Market orders: **29,250**
• Has 1996 Statement, filed 10/1/96; avg print run 85,698; avg sales 57,607; avg subs 1,035; avg total paid 58,642; samples 600; office use 125; max existent 59,367; 31% of run returned
80 ❑ Dec 1996 Cover: 1.50 **NM** value: **Cover or less**
Circ: Statement: **32,566** Direct Market orders: **28,250**
📖 Storm Of Blood **A:** Salvador Larroca **W:** Ivan Velez Jr.
81 ❑ Jan 1997 Cover: 1.50 **NM** value: **Cover or less**
Circ: Statement: **32,566** Direct Market orders: **32,750**
📖 Caught Between A Duck And A Hard Place **A:** Salvador Larroca **W:** Ivan Velez Jr. ★ Appearance of Howard the Duck.
82 ❑ Feb 1997 Cover: 1.50 **NM** value: **Cover or less**
Circ: Statement: **32,566** Direct Market orders: **27,750**
📖 The Duck and the Amok **A:** Pop Mhan **W:** Ivan Velez Jr. ★ Appearance of Devil Dinosaur, Howard the Duck, Moonboy.
83 ❑ Mar 1997 Cover: 1.95 **NM** value: **Cover or less**
Circ: Statement: **32,566** Direct Market orders: **26,000**
📖 House of Burning Souls **A:** Pop Mhan **W:** Ivan Velez Jr.
84 ❑ Apr 1997 Cover: 1.95 **NM** value: **Cover or less**
Circ: Statement: **32,566** Direct Market orders: **25,500**
📖 Loss of Blood **A:** Pop Mhan **W:** Ivan Velez Jr.
85 ❑ May 1997 Cover: 1.95 **NM** value: **Cover or less**
Circ: Statement: **32,566** Diamd. preorders: **24,366**
📖 Ashes of my Soul **A:** Gabe Alberola **W:** Ivan Velez Jr. ★ Appearance of Scarecrow.
86 ❑ Jun 1997 Cover: 1.95 **NM** value: **Cover or less**
Circ: Statement: **32,566** Diamd. preorders: **24,003**
📖 Faultlines **A:** Pop Mhan **W:** Ivan Velez Jr.
87 ❑ Aug 1997 Cover: 1.99 **NM** value: **Cover or less**
Circ: Statement: **32,566** Diamd. preorders: **21,528**
• gatefold summary. 📖 Wallow **A:** Karl Kesel **W:** Ivan Velez Jr.
88 ❑ Sep 1997 Cover: 1.99 **NM** value: **Cover or less**
Circ: Diamd. preorders: **20,478**
• gatefold summary. 📖 A Kind Face **A:** Josh Hood **W:** Ivan Velez Jr.
89 ❑ Oct 1997 Cover: 1.99 **NM** value: **Cover or less**
Circ: Diamd. preorders: **20,082**
• gatefold summary. 📖 Doghead & Spiked Tails **A:** Javier Saltares **W:** Ivan Velez Jr.
90 ❑ Nov 1997 Cover: 1.99 **NM** value: **Cover or less**
Circ: Diamd. preorders: **19,994**
• gatefold summary. 📖 The Last Temptation, Part 1 **A:** Javier Saltares **W:** Ivan Velez Jr.
91 ❑ Dec 1997 Cover: 1.99 **NM** value: **Cover or less**
Circ: Diamd. preorders: **19,121**
• gatefold summary. 📖 Down Among the Dead Men... **A:** Javier Saltares **W:** Ivan Velez Jr.
92 ❑ Jan 1998 Cover: 1.99 **NM** value: **Cover or less**
Circ: Diamd. preorders: **18,681**
• gatefold summary. • Has 1997 Statement, filed 10/1/97; avg print run 40,708; avg sales 31,636; avg subs 930; avg total paid 32,566; samples 93; office use 125; max existent 32,784; 20% of run returned
93 ❑ Feb 1998 Cover: 2.99 **NM** value: **Cover or less**
Circ: Diamd. preorders: **18,291**
• Giant-size. final issue.
Anl 1❑ca. 1993 Cover: 2.95 **NM** value: **Cover or less**
Circ: CapCity orders: **35,900**
• trading card
Anl 2❑ca. 1994 Cover: 2.95 **NM** value: **Cover or less**
Circ: CapCity orders: **15,150**
📖 Wish for Pain; Raising Cain; Truck Stop **A:** Javier Saltares; Kevin Kobasic; Reggie Jones **W:** Warren Ellis; Frank Lovece; Ian Edgington ★ Versus Scarecrow.
Bk 1❑ Cover: 12.95 **NM** value: **Cover or less**
Circ: CapCity orders: **5,350**
📖 Resurrected • Collects issues #1-7 **A:** Mark Texeira; Javier Saltares **W:** Howard Mackie ★ Origin of Ghost Rider II (Dan Ketch). ★ 1st Appearance of Ghost Rider II (Dan Ketch), Blackout II, Deathwatch. ★ Appearance of Punisher.

GHOST RIDER; WOLVERINE; PUNISHER: THE DARK DESIGN — Marvel

1 ❑ Dec 1991 Cover: 5.95 **NM** value: **Cover or less**
Circ: CapCity orders: **84,700**
Double fold-out cover. • squarebound **A:** Ron Garney **W:** Howard Mackie ★ Death of Mephisto.

GHOSTS — DC

Subtitled "True Tales of the Supernatural," Ghosts presented, each month, new and imaginative stories, each involving at least one ghost and a clever ending. No matter how strange or uncanny these tales seemed, Ghosts contended that each was absolutely true. "These eerie reports [were] startling testimony to the existence of a frightening world of the spectral and supernatural."

This series ran from 1971 into the early 1980s, when DC was publishing several titles with supernatural themes. Ordinary as these things go, Ghosts mixed short "Believe it or Not!"-style features with conventional supernatural genre stories.

1 ❑ Oct 1971 Cover: 0.25 **NM** value: **20.00**
• **CGC:** 16 graded, best 9.4
📖 Death's Bridegroom; Ghost in the Iron Coffin; The Tattooed Terror!; The Last Dream!; The Cadaver Comes Home (text story); The Spectral Coachman! **A:** Tony DeZuniga; Jim Aparo; David George **W:** Leo Dorfman; Sam Glanzman; Geoff Browne
2 ❑ Dec 1971 Cover: 0.25 **NM** value: **12.00**
• **CGC:** 4 graded, best 9.2
📖 No Grave Can Hold Me!; The Sorrow of the Spirits!; Enter the Ghost!; Galleon of Death **A:** Tony DeZuniga **W:** Leo Dorfman
3 ❑ Feb 1972 Cover: 0.25 **NM** value: **8.00**
• **CGC:** 1 graded, best 9.4
📖 Death is my Mother; The Magician who Haunted Hollywood; The Dark Goddess of Doom; Station G-H-O-S-T!; Legion of the Dead; The Screaming Skulls **A:** Leo Dorfman **W:** Tony DeZuniga
4 ❑ Apr 1972 Cover: 0.25 **NM** value: **8.00**
5 ❑ Jun 1972 Cover: 0.25 **NM** value: **8.00**
6 ❑ Aug 1972 Cover: 0.20 **NM** value: **6.00**
7 ❑ Sep 1972 Cover: 0.20 **NM** value: **6.00**
8 ❑ Oct 1972 Cover: 0.20 **NM** value: **6.00**
9 ❑ Nov 1972 Cover: 0.20 **NM** value: **6.00**
10 ❑ Jan 1973 Cover: 0.20 **NM** value: **6.00**
11 ❑ Feb 1973 Cover: 0.20 **NM** value: **6.00**
12 ❑ Mar 1973 Cover: 0.20 **NM** value: **6.00**
13 ❑ Apr 1973 Cover: 0.20 **NM** value: **6.00**
14 ❑ May 1973 Cover: 0.20 **NM** value: **6.00**
15 ❑ Jun 1973 Cover: 0.20 **NM** value: **6.00**
16 ❑ Jul 1973 Cover: 0.20 **NM** value: **6.00**
17 ❑ Aug 1973 Cover: 0.20 **NM** value: **6.00**
18 ❑ Sep 1973 Cover: 0.20 **NM** value: **6.00**
19 ❑ Oct 1973 Cover: 0.20 **NM** value: **6.00**
20 ❑ Nov 1973 Cover: 0.20 **NM** value: **6.00**
• **CGC:** 1 graded, best 9.4
21 ❑ Dec 1973 Cover: 0.20 **NM** value: **5.00**
22 ❑ Jan 1974 Cover: 0.20 **NM** value: **5.00**
• **CGC:** 1 graded, best 9.4
23 ❑ Feb 1974 Cover: 0.20 **NM** value: **5.00**
24 ❑ Mar 1974 Cover: 0.20 **NM** value: **5.00**
25 ❑ Apr 1974 Cover: 0.20 **NM** value: **5.00**
26 ❑ May 1974 Cover: 0.20 **NM** value: **5.00**
27 ❑ Jun 1974 Cover: 0.20 **NM** value: **5.00**
• **CGC:** 1 graded, best 9.8
28 ❑ Jul 1974 Cover: 0.20 **NM** value: **5.00**
29 ❑ Aug 1974 Cover: 0.20 **NM** value: **5.00**
30 ❑ Sep 1974 Cover: 0.20 **NM** value: **5.00**

Other grades: Multiply prices above by **1.5 for Mint • 2/3 for Very Fine • 1/3 for Fine • 1/5 for Very Good • 1/8 for Good**

31 ❑ Oct 1974 Cover: 0.20 **NM** value: **4.00**
32 ❑ Nov 1974 Cover: 0.20 **NM** value: **4.00**
33 ❑ Dec 1974 Cover: 0.20 **NM** value: **4.00**
34 ❑ Jan 1975 Cover: 0.20 **NM** value: **4.00**
Circ: Statement: **186,000**
35 ❑ Feb 1975 Cover: 0.25 **NM** value: **4.00**
Circ: Statement: **186,000**
36 ❑ Mar 1975 Cover: 0.25 **NM** value: **4.00**
Circ: Statement: **186,000**
37 ❑ Apr 1975 Cover: 0.25 **NM** value: **4.00**
Circ: Statement: **186,000**
38 ❑ May 1975 Cover: 0.25 **NM** value: **4.00**
Circ: Statement: **186,000**
39 ❑ Jun 1975 Cover: 0.25 **NM** value: **4.00**
Circ: Statement: **186,000** • **CGC:** 1 graded, best 9.4
40 ❑ Jul 1975 Cover: 0.25 **NM** value: **4.00**
Circ: Statement: **186,000** • **CGC:** 2 graded, best 9.6
• giant
41 ❑ Aug 1975 Cover: 0.25 **NM** value: **4.00**
Circ: Statement: **186,000** • **CGC:** 1 graded, best 9.4
42 ❑ Sep 1975 Cover: 0.25 **NM** value: **4.00**
Circ: Statement: **186,000** • **CGC:** 1 graded, best 9.4
43 ❑ Oct 1975 Cover: 0.25 **NM** value: **4.00**
Circ: Statement: **186,000** • **CGC:** 1 graded, best 9.4
44 ❑ Nov 1975 Cover: 0.25 **NM** value: **4.00**
Circ: Statement: **186,000**
45 ❑ Jan 1976 Cover: 0.25 **NM** value: **4.00**
Circ: Statement: **135,000** • **CGC:** 1 graded, best 9.4
46 ❑ Mar 1976 Cover: 0.30 **NM** value: **4.00**
Circ: Statement: **135,000**
47 ❑ Jun 1976 Cover: 0.30 **NM** value: **4.00**
Circ: Statement: **135,000**
48 ❑ 1976 Cover: 0.30 **NM** value: **4.00**
Circ: Statement: **135,000**
• Bicentennial #2
49 ❑ 1976 Cover: 0.30 **NM** value: **4.00**
Circ: Statement: **135,000** • **CGC:** 1 graded, best 9.4
50 ❑ Nov 1976 Cover: 0.30 **NM** value: **4.00**
Circ: Statement: **135,000** • **CGC:** 1 graded, best 9.0
🕮 Home Is Where The Grave Is!; The Trapped Phantom; Most Fearful Villain Of The Supernatural
51 ❑ Jan 1977 Cover: 0.30 **NM** value: **4.00**
Circ: Statement: **114,734**
52 ❑ 1977 Cover: 0.30 **NM** value: **4.00**
Circ: Statement: **114,734**
53 ❑ 1977 Cover: 0.30 **NM** value: **4.00**
Circ: Statement: **114,734**
54 ❑ May 1977 Cover: 0.30 **NM** value: **4.00**
Circ: Statement: **114,734** • **CGC:** 1 graded, best 9.0
55 ❑ 1977 Cover: 0.35 **NM** value: **4.00**
Circ: Statement: **114,734**
56 ❑ Sep 1977 Cover: 0.35 **NM** value: **4.00**
Circ: Statement: **114,734**
57 ❑ Oct 1977 Cover: 0.35 **NM** value: **4.00**
Circ: Statement: **114,734** • **CGC:** 1 graded, best 9.0
58 ❑ Nov 1977 Cover: 0.35 **NM** value: **4.00**
Circ: Statement: **114,734** • **CGC:** 2 graded, best 9.0
59 ❑ Dec 1977 Cover: 0.35 **NM** value: **4.00**
Circ: Statement: **114,734** • **CGC:** 1 graded, best 9.2
60 ❑ Jan 1978 Cover: 0.35 **NM** value: **4.00**
• **CGC:** 1 graded, best 9.4
61 ❑ Feb 1978 Cover: 0.35 **NM** value: **4.00**
62 ❑ Mar 1978 Cover: 0.35 **NM** value: **4.00**
63 ❑ Apr 1978 Cover: 0.35 **NM** value: **4.00**
64 ❑ May 1978 Cover: 0.35 **NM** value: **4.00**
65 ❑ Jun 1978 Cover: 0.35 **NM** value: **4.00**
66 ❑ Jul 1978 Cover: 0.35 **NM** value: **4.00**
67 ❑ Aug 1978 Cover: 0.35 **NM** value: **4.00**
68 ❑ Sep 1978 Cover: 0.50 **NM** value: **4.00**
69 ❑ Oct 1978 Cover: 0.50 **NM** value: **4.00**
70 ❑ Nov 1978 Cover: 0.50 **NM** value: **4.00**
71 ❑ Dec 1978 Cover: 0.40 **NM** value: **3.00**
72 ❑ Jan 1979 Cover: 0.40 **NM** value: **3.00**
73 ❑ Feb 1979 Cover: 0.40 **NM** value: **3.00**
74 ❑ Mar 1979 Cover: 0.40 **NM** value: **3.00**
75 ❑ Apr 1979 Cover: 0.40 **NM** value: **3.00**
76 ❑ May 1979 Cover: 0.40 **NM** value: **3.00**
77 ❑ Jun 1979 Cover: 0.40 **NM** value: **3.00**
78 ❑ Jul 1979 Cover: 0.40 **NM** value: **3.00**
79 ❑ Aug 1979 Cover: 0.40 **NM** value: **3.00**
80 ❑ Sep 1979 Cover: 0.40 **NM** value: **3.00**
81 ❑ Oct 1979 Cover: 0.40 **NM** value: **3.00**
82 ❑ Nov 1979 Cover: 0.40 **NM** value: **3.00**
83 ❑ Dec 1979 Cover: 0.40 **NM** value: **3.00**
84 ❑ Jan 1980 Cover: 0.40 **NM** value: **3.00**
Circ: Statement: **95,317**
85 ❑ Feb 1980 Cover: 0.40 **NM** value: **3.00**
Circ: Statement: **95,317**
86 ❑ Mar 1980 Cover: 0.40 **NM** value: **3.00**
Circ: Statement: **95,317**
87 ❑ Apr 1980 Cover: 0.40 **NM** value: **3.00**
Circ: Statement: **95,317**
88 ❑ May 1980 Cover: 0.40 **NM** value: **3.00**
Circ: Statement: **95,317**
89 ❑ Jun 1980 Cover: 0.40 **NM** value: **3.00**
Circ: Statement: **95,317**
90 ❑ Jul 1980 Cover: 0.40 **NM** value: **3.00**
Circ: Statement: **95,317**
91 ❑ Aug 1980 Cover: 0.40 **NM** value: **3.00**
Circ: Statement: **95,317**
92 ❑ Sep 1980 Cover: 0.50 **NM** value: **3.00**
Circ: Statement: **95,317**
93 ❑ Oct 1980 Cover: 0.50 **NM** value: **3.00**
Circ: Statement: **95,317**
94 ❑ Nov 1980 Cover: 0.50 **NM** value: **3.00**
Circ: Statement: **95,317**
95 ❑ Dec 1980 Cover: 0.50 **NM** value: **3.00**
Circ: Statement: **95,317**
96 ❑ Jan 1981 Cover: 0.50 **NM** value: **3.00**
Circ: Statement: **87,537** • **CGC:** 1 graded, best 9.4
97 ❑ Feb 1981 Cover: 0.50 **NM** value: **3.00**
Circ: Statement: **87,537**
98 ❑ Mar 1981 Cover: 0.50 **NM** value: **3.00**
Circ: Statement: **87,537**
99 ❑ Apr 1981 Cover: 0.50 **NM** value: **3.00**
Circ: Statement: **87,537**
100 ❑ May 1981 Cover: 0.50 **NM** value: **3.00**
Circ: Statement: **87,537**
101 ❑ Jun 1981 Cover: 0.50 **NM** value: **3.00**
Circ: Statement: **87,537**
102 ❑ Jul 1981 Cover: 0.50 **NM** value: **3.00**
Circ: Statement: **87,537**
103 ❑ Aug 1981 Cover: 0.60 **NM** value: **3.00**
Circ: Statement: **87,537**
104 ❑ Sep 1981 Cover: 0.60 **NM** value: **3.00**
Circ: Statement: **87,537**
105 ❑ Oct 1981 Cover: 0.60 **NM** value: **3.00**
Circ: Statement: **87,537**
106 ❑ Nov 1981 Cover: 0.60 **NM** value: **3.00**
Circ: Statement: **87,537**
107 ❑ Dec 1981 Cover: 0.60 **NM** value: **3.00**
Circ: Statement: **87,537**
108 ❑ Jan 1982 Cover: 0.60 **NM** value: **3.00**
109 ❑ Feb 1982 Cover: 0.60 **NM** value: **3.00**
• **CGC:** 1 graded, best 9.2
110 ❑ Mar 1982 Cover: 0.60 **NM** value: **3.00**
111 ❑ Apr 1982 Cover: 0.60 **NM** value: **3.00**
112 ❑ May 1982 Cover: 0.60 **NM** value: **3.00**
final issue.

GHOST SHIP — Slave Labor

1 ❑ Mar 1996, b&w Cover: 3.50 **NM** value: **Cover or less**
cardstock cover. 🕮 Scurvy; Nikolas Leads to Harder Things; **A:** Jon Lewis **W:** Jon Lewis
2 ❑ Jun 1996, b&w Cover: 2.95 **NM** value: **Cover or less**
cardstock cover. 🕮 Crucial Beast; I Just Want One Real Friend in This World **A:** Jon Lewis **W:** Jon Lewis
3 ❑ Oct 1996, b&w Cover: 2.95 **NM** value: **Cover or less**
cardstock cover. 🕮 Father's Day; How Eynops Fell in Love **A:** Jon Lewis **W:** Jon Lewis

GHOSTS OF DRACULA — Eternity

1 ❑ b&w Cover: 2.50 **NM** value: **Cover or less**
2 ❑ b&w Cover: 2.50 **NM** value: **Cover or less**
3 ❑ b&w Cover: 2.50 **NM** value: **Cover or less**
4 ❑ b&w Cover: 2.50 **NM** value: **Cover or less**
5 ❑ b&w Cover: 2.50 **NM** value: **Cover or less**

GHOST STORIES — Dell

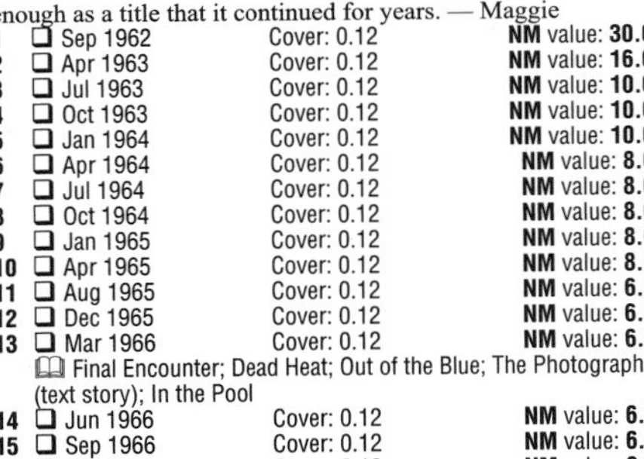

The horror-story anthology title is an oddity, introduced (with a few others) into a line that for years had carried as its slogan, "Dell Comics are good comics!" accompanying a pledge to parents that there the contents would contain nothing inappropriate for young readers. However, while other ongoing comics titles of its day had carried the Comics Magazine Association of America stamp for six years and were subjected to careful content control, the Codeless Ghost Stories offered at least one memorably horrifying tale.

The first issue carried the cover text "Stories to shock you! Ghostly tales of suspense and terror!" And many of those who read it as children remember it to this day. Written by John Stanley, the opening story — "The Monster of Dread End ..." — gave many young readers nightmares. It featured a monstrous hand on the end of a tentacle — a hand that sucked out the contents of a person's body, leaving behind only the skin. Brrr. Not all the stories were that memorable, but it was successful enough as a title that it continued for years. — Maggie

1 ❑ Sep 1962 Cover: 0.12 **NM** value: **30.00**
2 ❑ Apr 1963 Cover: 0.12 **NM** value: **16.00**
3 ❑ Jul 1963 Cover: 0.12 **NM** value: **10.00**
4 ❑ Oct 1963 Cover: 0.12 **NM** value: **10.00**
5 ❑ Jan 1964 Cover: 0.12 **NM** value: **10.00**
6 ❑ Apr 1964 Cover: 0.12 **NM** value: **8.00**
7 ❑ Jul 1964 Cover: 0.12 **NM** value: **8.00**
8 ❑ Oct 1964 Cover: 0.12 **NM** value: **8.00**
9 ❑ Jan 1965 Cover: 0.12 **NM** value: **8.00**
10 ❑ Apr 1965 Cover: 0.12 **NM** value: **8.00**
11 ❑ Aug 1965 Cover: 0.12 **NM** value: **6.00**
12 ❑ Dec 1965 Cover: 0.12 **NM** value: **6.00**
13 ❑ Mar 1966 Cover: 0.12 **NM** value: **6.00**
🕮 Final Encounter; Dead Heat; Out of the Blue; The Photographer (text story); In the Pool
14 ❑ Jun 1966 Cover: 0.12 **NM** value: **6.00**
15 ❑ Sep 1966 Cover: 0.12 **NM** value: **6.00**
16 ❑ Dec 1966 Cover: 0.12 **NM** value: **6.00**
17 ❑ Mar 1967 Cover: 0.12 **NM** value: **6.00**
18 ❑ May 1967 Cover: 0.12 **NM** value: **6.00**
19 ❑ Aug 1967 Cover: 0.12 **NM** value: **6.00**
20 ❑ Nov 1967 Cover: 0.12 **NM** value: **6.00**
21 ❑ Oct 1968 Cover: 0.12 **NM** value: **5.00**
22 ❑ Oct 1969 Cover: 0.15 **NM** value: **5.00**
23 ❑ Jan 1970 Cover: 0.15 **NM** value: **5.00**
24 ❑ May 1970 Cover: 0.15 **NM** value: **5.00**
🕮 To My Killer with Affection; Have I Been Here Before?; The Face in the Picture; The Watchful Eye! (text story); Appointment with Sam Mara
25 ❑ Jul 1970 Cover: 0.15 **NM** value: **5.00**
26 ❑ Oct 1970 Cover: 0.15 **NM** value: **5.00**
27 ❑ Jan 1971 Cover: 0.15 **NM** value: **5.00**
🕮 Larger than Life; Blood Will Tell; The Magic Box; The Death Room; Who Ever Heard of a Spooked Pen? (text story);
28 ❑ Apr 1971 Cover: 0.15 **NM** value: **5.00**
🕮 Piece of the Past!; Needed: One Miracle!; A Fistfull of Evil; Auto-Suggestion (text story); Death and Beyond
29 ❑ Jul 1971 Cover: 0.15 **NM** value: **5.00**
30 ❑ Oct 1971 Cover: 0.15 **NM** value: **5.00**
31 ❑ Jan 1972 Cover: 0.15 **NM** value: **5.00**
32 ❑ Apr 1972 Cover: 0.15 **NM** value: **5.00**
33 ❑ Jul 1972 Cover: 0.15 **NM** value: **5.00**
34 ❑ Oct 1972 Cover: 0.15 **NM** value: **5.00**
35 ❑ Jan 1973 Cover: 0.20 **NM** value: **5.00**
36 ❑ Jul 1973 Cover: 0.20 **NM** value: **5.00**
37 ❑ Oct 1973 Cover: 0.20 **NM** value: **5.00**
final issue.

GHOST (VOL. 2) — Dark Horse

1 ❑ Sep 1998 Cover: 2.95 **NM** value: **3.50**
Circ: Diamd. preorders: **17,030**
🕮 No World So Dark **A:** Christian Zanier **W:** Chris Warner
2 ❑ Oct 1998 Cover: 2.95 **NM** value: **3.00**
Circ: Diamd. preorders: **14,285**
3 ❑ Nov 1998 Cover: 2.95 **NM** value: **3.00**
Circ: Diamd. preorders: **14,365**
4 ❑ Dec 1998 Cover: 2.95 **NM** value: **3.00**
🕮 Stare at the Sun, Part 1 **A:** Christian Zanier **W:** Chris Warner
5 ❑ Jan 1999 Cover: 2.95 **NM** value: **3.00**
🕮 Stare at the Sun, Part 2 **A:** Christian Zanier **W:** Chris Warner
6 ❑ Feb 1999 Cover: 2.95 **NM** value: **Cover or less**
🕮 Stare at the Sun, Part 3 **A:** Christian Zanier **W:** Chris Warner
7 ❑ Mar 1999 Cover: 2.95 **NM** value: **Cover or less**
Circ: Diamd. preorders: **12,933**
🕮 Shifter, Part 1 **A:** Christian Zanier **W:** Chris Warner; Mike Kennedy
8 ❑ Apr 1999 Cover: 2.95 **NM** value: **Cover or less**
Circ: Diamd. preorders: **13,072**
🕮 Shifter, Part 2 **A:** Christian Zanier **W:** Chris Warner; Mike Kennedy
9 ❑ May 1999 Cover: 2.95 **NM** value: **Cover or less**
Circ: Diamd. preorders: **12,683**
🕮 Shifter, Part 3 **A:** Christian Zanier **W:** Chris Warner; Mike Kennedy
10 ❑ Jun 1999 Cover: 2.95 **NM** value: **Cover or less**
Circ: Diamd. preorders: **12,610**
🕮 Shifter, Part 4 **A:** Christian Zanier **W:** Chris Warner; Mike Kennedy
★ Appearance of Vortex.
11 ❑ Jul 1999 Cover: 2.95 **NM** value: **Cover or less**
Circ: Diamd. preorders: **12,461**
🕮 Blood & Roses **A:** Ryan Benjamin **W:** Chris Warner
12 ❑ Sep 1999 Cover: 2.95 **NM** value: **Cover or less**
Circ: Diamd. preorders: **11,662**
🕮 Red Shadows, Part 1 **A:** Ryan Benjamin **W:** Chris Warner
13 ❑ Oct 1999 Cover: 2.95 **NM** value: **Cover or less**
Circ: Diamd. preorders: **11,672**
🕮 Red Shadows, Part 2 **A:** Ryan Benjamin **W:** Chris Warner
14 ❑ Nov 1999 Cover: 2.95 **NM** value: **Cover or less**
Circ: Diamd. preorders: **11,140**
🕮 Red Shadows, Part 3 **A:** Ryan Benjamin **W:** Chris Warner
15 ❑ Dec 1999 Cover: 2.95 **NM** value: **Cover or less**
Circ: Diamd. preorders: **11,833**
🕮 Red Shadows, Part 4 **A:** Ryan Benjamin **W:** Chris Warner
16 ❑ Jan 2000 Cover: 2.95 **NM** value: **Cover or less**
Circ: Diamd. preorders: **10,868**
🕮 When the Devil Daydreams, Part 1 **A:** Ryan Benjamin **W:** Mike Kennedy
17 ❑ Feb 2000 Cover: 2.95 **NM** value: **Cover or less**
Circ: Diamd. preorders: **10,297**
18 ❑ Mar 2000 Cover: 2.95 **NM** value: **Cover or less**
Circ: Diamd. preorders: **10,402**
19 ❑ Apr 2000 Cover: 2.95 **NM** value: **Cover or less**
Circ: Diamd. preorders: **10,402**
🕮 Wish in One Hand... **A:** Ryan Benjamin **W:** Mike Kennedy
20 ❑ Jun 2000 Cover: 2.95 **NM** value: **Cover or less**
Circ: Diamd. preorders: **10,326**
21 ❑ Jul 2000 Cover: 2.95 **NM** value: **Cover or less**
Circ: Diamd. preorders: **10,290**
22 ❑ Aug 2000 Cover: 2.95 **NM** value: **Cover or less**
Circ: Diamd. preorders: **10,163**
🕮 Caesura **A:** Ryan Benjamin; Lucas Marancan **W:** Mike Kennedy

GHOULS — Eternity

1 ❑ b&w Cover: 2.25 **NM** value: **Cover or less**

GIANT COMICS EDITIONS — St. John

1 ❑ ca. 1948 Cover: 0.25 **NM** value: **Cover or less**
2 ❑ Jul 1948 Cover: 0.25 **NM** value: **Cover or less**
3 ❑ Oct 1948 Cover: 0.25 **NM** value: **Cover or less**
4 ❑ Jan 1949 Cover: 0.25 **NM** value: **Cover or less**
5 ❑ Apr 1949 Cover: 0.25 **NM** value: **Cover or less**
6 ❑ Jul 1949 Cover: 0.25 **NM** value: **Cover or less**
7 ❑ ca. 1949 Cover: 0.25 **NM** value: **Cover or less**
8 ❑ Oct 1949 Cover: 0.25 **NM** value: **Cover or less**
9 ❑ Cover: 0.25 **NM** value: **Cover or less**
10 ❑ Cover: 0.25 **NM** value: **Cover or less**
11 ❑ ca. 1950 Cover: 0.25 **NM** value: **Cover or less**
12 ❑ ca. 1950 Cover: 0.25 **NM** value: **Cover or less**
• **CGC:** 1 graded, best 4.0
13 ❑ ca. 1950 Cover: 0.25 **NM** value: **Cover or less**
14 ❑ ca. 1950 Cover: 0.25 **NM** value: **Cover or less**
15 ❑ ca. 1950 Cover: 0.25 **NM** value: **Cover or less**
• **CGC:** 2 graded, best 4.5
16 ❑ ca. 1950 Cover: 0.25 **NM** value: **Cover or less**
17 ❑ Nov 1950 Cover: 0.25 **NM** value: **Cover or less**
• **CGC:** 1 graded, best 9.4

GIANTKILLER — DC

1 ❑ Aug 1999 Cover: 2.50 **NM** value: **Cover or less**
Circ: Diamd. preorders: **23,670**

CGC-graded: Multiply prices above by **33 for 9.9 M** • **16 for 9.8 NM/M** • **7 for 9.6 NM+** • **5 for 9.4 NM** • **2.5 for 9.2 NM-** • **1.5 for 9.0 VF/NM**

2 ❑ Sep 1999 Cover: 2.50 **NM** value: **Cover or less**
Circ: Diamd. preorders: **18,915**
3 ❑ Oct 1999 Cover: 2.50 **NM** value: **Cover or less**
Circ: Diamd. preorders: **17,119**
4 ❑ Nov 1999 Cover: 2.50 **NM** value: **Cover or less**
Circ: Diamd. preorders: **15,954**
5 ❑ Dec 1999 Cover: 2.50 **NM** value: **Cover or less**
Circ: Diamd. preorders: **15,073**
6 ❑ Jan 2000 Cover: 2.50 **NM** value: **Cover or less**
Circ: Diamd. preorders: **14,327**

GIANTKILLER A TO Z — DC

1 ❑ Aug 1999 Cover: 2.50 **NM** value: **Cover or less**
Circ: Diamd. preorders: **16,335**
No issue number. • no indicia; biographical monster information **A:** Dan Brereton **W:** Dan Brereton

GIANT-SIZE AMAZING SPIDER-MAN — Marvel

1 ❑ Aug 1999 Cover: 4.50 **NM** value: **Cover or less**
cardstock cover. • reprints stories from Spider-Man Adventures #6, #11, #12, and Marvel Tales #205

GIANT-SIZE AVENGERS — Marvel

1 ❑ Aug 1974 Cover: 0.50 **NM** value: **12.00**
• **CGC:** 4 graded, best 9.6
2 ❑ Nov 1974 Cover: 0.50 **NM** value: **6.00**
📖 A Blast From the Past • reprints Fantastic Four #19 (Rama-Tut) **A:** Dave Cockrum **W:** Steve Englehart ★ Origin of Rama-Tut. ★ Death of Swordsman.
3 ❑ Feb 1975 Cover: 0.50 **NM** value: **6.00**
• **CGC:** 1 graded, best 9.4
📖 What Time Hath Put Asunder • continued from Avengers #132; reprints Avengers #2 **A:** Dave Cockrum **W:** Roy Thomas ★ Origin of Immortus, Kang. ★ Appearance of Wonder Man, Zemo, Human Torch, Frankenstein's Monster.
4 ❑ Cover: 0.50 **NM** value: **6.00**
📖 Let All Men Bring Together • Wedding of Vision and Scarlet Witch; Wedding of Vision & Scarlet Witch **A:** Don Heck **W:** Steve Englehart
5 ❑ Dec 1975 Cover: 0.50 **NM** value: **5.00**
• **CGC:** 3 graded, best 9.6
📖 The Monstrous Master Plan of the Mandarin

GIANT-SIZE CAPTAIN AMERICA — Marvel

1 ❑ Cover: 0.50 **NM** value: **14.00**
• **CGC:** 3 graded, best 9.4

GIANT-SIZE CAPTAIN MARVEL — Marvel

In the 1970s, Marvel produced a series of giant-size specials titled — appropriately enough — Giant-Size Avengers, Giant-Size Spider-Man, Giant-Size Defenders, etc. Some of these extra-thick titles featured new stories, while others were composed of reprints.

The first and only issue of Giant-Size Captain Marvel reprints #17, #20, and #21 of the Kree warrior's title, which features scripts by Roy Thomas (All-Star Squadron) and Gil Kane (Green Lantern). Here, Marvel's space-born super-hero bonds with perennial sidekick Rick Jones — the stereotypical teen-ager who palled around with Captain America and the Avengers — and frees himself from the Negative Zone. This bond allows the Captain and Rick to switch places, when one or the other is needed, making their relationship similar to the one between a certain Billy Batson and another Captain Marvel. This reprint collection also features a battle royal between Captain Marvel and The Hulk, another of Rick Jones' former partners.

1 ❑ Cover: 0.50 **NM** value: **10.00**
• **CGC:** 6 graded, best 9.4

GIANT-SIZE CHILLERS (1ST SERIES) — Marvel

1 ❑ Jun 1974 Cover: 0.35 **NM** value: **13.00**
• **CGC:** 13 graded, best 9.6
• Dracula **A:** Gene Colan ★ 1st Appearance of Lilith.

GIANT-SIZE CHILLERS (2ND SERIES) — Marvel

1 ❑ Cover: 0.50 **NM** value: **9.00**
• **CGC:** 3 graded, best 9.4
2 ❑ Aug 1975 Cover: 0.50 **NM** value: **6.00**
• **CGC:** 1 graded, best 9.6
3 ❑ Cover: 0.50 **NM** value: **6.00**

GIANT-SIZE CONAN — Marvel

1 ❑ Sep 1974 Cover: 0.50 **NM** value: **5.00**
• **CGC:** 5 graded, best 9.6
2 ❑ Dec 1974 Cover: 0.50 **NM** value: **4.00**
📖 Conan Bound! **A:** Tom Sutton; Barry Windsor-Smith; Gil Kane **W:** Roy Thomas
3 ❑ Apr 1975 Cover: 0.50 **NM** value: **4.00**
• **CGC:** 3 graded, best 9.4
📖 To Tarantia-And The Tower **A:** Gil Kane **W:** Roy Thomas
4 ❑ Jun 1975 Cover: 0.50 **NM** value: **4.00**
• **CGC:** 2 graded, best 9.6
📖 Swords Of The South **A:** Gil Kane **W:** Roy Thomas
5 ❑ Jun 1975 Cover: 0.50 **NM** value: **4.00**
• **CGC:** 4 graded, best 9.4
📖 A Sword Called Stormbringer **A:** Barry Windsor-Smith **W:** Roy Thomas

GIANT-SIZE CREATURES — Marvel

1 ❑ Jul 1974 Cover: 0.35 **NM** value: **10.00**
• **CGC:** 3 graded, best 9.0
📖 Tigra the Were-Woman!; Where Walks the Werewolf! • Marvel Value Stamp A-34 (Mr. Fantastic) **A:** Don Perlin; Reed Crandall **W:** Len Wein; Tony Isabella ★ Origin of Tigra. ★ 1st Appearance of Tigra.

GIANT-SIZE DAREDEVIL — Marvel

1 ❑ ca. 1975 Cover: 0.50 **NM** value: **8.00**
• **CGC:** 3 graded, best 9.4

GIANT-SIZE DEFENDERS — Marvel

1 ❑ Jul 1974 Cover: 0.50 **NM** value: **6.00**
• **CGC:** 9 graded, best 9.6
📖 The Way They Were!; Banished To Outer Space; • Silver Surfer **A:** Jim Starlin **W:** Tony Isabella ★ Appearance of Silver Surfer.
2 ❑ Oct 1974 Cover: 0.50 **NM** value: **4.00**
• **CGC:** 1 graded, best 9.2
• Son of Satan **A:** Gil Kane; Klaus Janson
3 ❑ Jan 1975 Cover: 0.50 **NM** value: **4.00**
• **CGC:** 1 graded, best 9.4
📖 Games Godlings Play!; **A:** Don Newton; Jim Starlin; Jim Mooney; Dan Adkins **W:** Steve Gerber ★ 1st Appearance of Korvac.
4 ❑ Apr 1975 Cover: 0.50 **NM** value: **4.00**
📖 Too Cold A Night For Dying! **A:** Don Heck **W:** Steve Gerber
5 ❑ Jul 1975 Cover: 0.50 **NM** value: **4.00**
• **CGC:** 5 graded, best 9.6
📖 Eelar Moves Mysterious Ways! **A:** Don Heck **W:** Steve Gerber ★ Appearance of Guardians of the Galaxy.

GIANT-SIZE DOC SAVAGE — Marvel

1 ❑ Jan 1975 Cover: 0.50 **NM** value: **6.00**
• **CGC:** 4 graded, best 9.6
📖 The Man of Bronze! • reprints Doc Savage (Marvel) #1 and 2; adapts Man of Bronze **A:** Ross Andru **W:** Roy Thomas; Steve Englehart

GIANT-SIZE DOCTOR STRANGE — Marvel

1 ❑ ca. 1975 Cover: 0.50 **NM** value: **5.00**
• **CGC:** 3 graded, best 9.6
📖 Nightmare!; The Mystic and the Machine!; Nothing can Halt Voltorg!; This Dream...This Doom!; Exile! • Reprints stories from Strange Tales #164, 165, 166, 167, 168 **A:** George Tuska; Dan Adkins **W:** Denny O'Neil; Jim Lawrence

GIANT-SIZE DRACULA — Marvel

2 ❑ Sep 1974 Cover: 0.50 **NM** value: **6.00**
• Series continued from Giant-Size Chillers (1st Series) #1. 📖 Call them Triad...Call them Death!; The Girl in the Black Hood!; On With the Dance!; Sweet Old Ladies **A:** Don Heck **W:** Larry Lieber; Stan Lee; Chris Claremont
3 ❑ Dec 1974 Cover: 0.50 **NM** value: **5.00**
• **CGC:** 1 graded, best 9.0
4 ❑ Mar 1975 Cover: 0.50 **NM** value: **5.00**
5 ❑ Jun 1975 Cover: 0.50 **NM** value: **5.00**

GIANT-SIZE FANTASTIC FOUR — Marvel

1 ❑ May 1974 Cover: 0.35 **NM** value: **15.00**
• published as Giant-Size Super-Stars. 📖 The Mind of the Monster; Someone's Been Sleeping in My Head; And in This Corner: The Incredible Hulk; In the Beginning (text); Giant-Size Super-Stacks (text); Rogues' Gallery • Thing battles Hulk **A:** Rich Buckler; Jack Kirby **W:** Roy Thomas; Stan Lee; Gerry Conway ★ Appearance of Fantastic Four, Hulk.
2 ❑ Aug 1974 Cover: 0.50 **NM** value: **8.00**
• **CGC:** 1 graded, best 9.8
• Title changes to Giant-Size Fantastic Four. • also reprints Fantastic Four #13 **A:** John Buscema **C:** Gil Kane ★ Appearance of Willie Lumpkin. ★ Versus Tempus.
3 ❑ Nov 1974 Cover: 0.50 **NM** value: **7.00**
• also reprints Fantastic Four #21 **A:** Rich Buckler
4 ❑ Feb 1975 Cover: 0.50 **NM** value: **8.00**
📖 Madrox the Multiple Man; We Have to Fight the X-Men **A:** John Buscema; Jack Kirby **C:** Rich Buckler **W:** Jack Kirby; Len Wein; Stan Lee; Chris Claremont ★ Origin of Madrox the Multiple Man. ★ 1st Appearance of Madrox the Multiple Man. ★ Appearance of Professor X, Medusa.
5 ❑ May 1975 Cover: 0.50 **NM** value: **6.00**
• reprints Fantastic Four Annual #5 and Fantastic Four #15
6 ❑ Oct 1975 Cover: 0.50 **NM** value: **6.00**
• **CGC:** 1 graded, best 9.4
final issue. • reprints Fantastic Four Annual #6

GIANT-SIZE HULK — Marvel

1 ❑ Jan 1975 Cover: 0.50 **NM** value: **8.00**
• **CGC:** 4 graded, best 9.4
• reprints Hulk Annual #1

GIANT-SIZE INVADERS — Marvel

1 ❑ Jun 1975 Cover: 0.50 **NM** value: **5.00**
• **CGC:** 13 graded, best 9.6
📖 The Coming of the Invaders • reprints O: Sub-Mariner ★ Origin of Invaders. ★ 1st Appearance of Invaders.

GIANT-SIZE IRON MAN — Marvel

1 ❑ ca. 1975 Cover: 0.50 **NM** value: **5.00**
• **CGC:** 5 graded, best 9.6

GIANT-SIZE KID COLT — Marvel

1 ❑ Cover: 0.50 **NM** value: **20.00**
2 ❑ Cover: 0.50 **NM** value: **15.00**
• **CGC:** 1 graded, best 9.4
3 ❑ Jul 1975 Cover: 0.50 **NM** value: **15.00**
• **CGC:** 1 graded, best 9.4

GIANT-SIZE MAN-THING — Marvel

1 ❑ Aug 1974 Cover: 0.50 **NM** value: **8.00**
• **CGC:** 1 graded, best 9.6
2 ❑ Cover: 0.50 **NM** value: **6.00**
3 ❑ Feb 1975 Cover: 0.50 **NM** value: **6.00**
• **CGC:** 2 graded, best 9.2
4 ❑ May 1975 Cover: 0.50 **NM** value: **10.00**
• **CGC:** 3 graded, best 9.6
• Howard the Duck **A:** Frank Brunner
5 ❑ Aug 1975 Cover: 0.50 **NM** value: **8.00**
• **CGC:** 1 graded, best 9.2
• Howard the Duck **A:** Frank Brunner

GIANT-SIZE MARVEL TRIPLE ACTION — Marvel

1 ❑ May 1975 Cover: 0.50 **NM** value: **4.00**
• **CGC:** 2 graded, best 9.4
2 ❑ Jul 1975 Cover: 0.50 **NM** value: **4.00**

GIANT-SIZE MASTER OF KUNG FU — Marvel

1 ❑ Sep 1974 Cover: 0.50 **NM** value: **8.00**
• **CGC:** 1 graded, best 9.2
2 ❑ Dec 1974 Cover: 0.50 **NM** value: **4.00**
3 ❑ Mar 1975 Cover: 0.50 **NM** value: **4.00**
4 ❑ Jun 1975 Cover: 0.50 **NM** value: **4.00**
• **CGC:** 2 graded, best 9.2
• Yellow Claw **A:** Jack Kirby

GIANT-SIZE MINI COMICS — Eclipse

1 ❑ Aug 1986, b&w Cover: 1.50 **NM** value: **Cover or less**
2 ❑ Oct 1986, b&w Cover: 1.50 **NM** value: **Cover or less**
📖 Mightyguy: The Big Break!; Danger is Fun!; Florida Vacation!; A Halloween I'd Just as Soon Forget!; Pert Herman; Origin of Fanboy; Tornado Alley; How we Travelled from Planet Plumpet to Planet Earth; Afterword **A:** Tim Corrigan; Jeff Nicholson; Matt Feazell; David Steinlicht; Dissmeyer; Mike Ernest; Ted Bolman **W:** Tim Corrigan; Jeff Nicholson; Matt Feazell; David Steinlicht; Dissmeyer; Mike Ernest; Ted Bolman
3 ❑ Dec 1986, b&w Cover: 1.50 **NM** value: **Cover or less**
4 ❑ Feb 1987, b&w Cover: 1.50 **NM** value: **Cover or less**

GIANT-SIZE MINI-MARVELS STARRING SPIDEY — Marvel

1 ❑ Cover: 3.50 **NM** value: **Cover or less**

GIANT SIZE OFFICIAL PRINCE VALIANT — Pioneer

1 ❑ b&w Cover: 3.95 **NM** value: **Cover or less**
• Hal Foster

GIANT-SIZE POWER MAN — Marvel

1 ❑ ca. 1975 Cover: 0.50 **NM** value: **4.00**
• **CGC:** 3 graded, best 9.4

GIANT-SIZE SPIDER-MAN — Marvel

1 ❑ Jul 1974 Cover: 0.50 **NM** value: **18.00**
• **CGC:** 6 graded, best 9.4
📖 Ship of Fiends; The Masque of the Black Death; On the Trail of the Amazing Spider-Man • reprints story from Strange Tales Annual #2 **A:** Ross Andru **C:** John Romita **W:** Len Wein ★ Appearance of Dracula.
2 ❑ Oct 1974 Cover: 0.50 **NM** value: **10.00**
• **CGC:** 12 graded, best 9.6
📖 Masterstroke; Cross and Double-Cross; Pinnacle of Doom; To Become an Avenger • reprints story from Amazing Spider-Man Annual #3 **A:** Gil Kane; Ross Andru **C:** John Romita **W:** Len Wein ★ Appearance of Shang-Chi.
3 ❑ Jan 1975 Cover: 0.50 **NM** value: **10.00**
• **CGC:** 4 graded, best 9.6
📖 The Yesterday Connection; The Secret Out of Time; Tomorrow Is too Late; Other People, Other Times; The Future is Now; Duel with Daredevil • also reprints story from Amazing Spider-Man #16 **A:** Ross Andru **C:** Gil Kane **W:** Gerry Conway ★ Appearance of Doc Savage.
4 ❑ Apr 1975 Cover: 0.50 **NM** value: **20.00**
• **CGC:** 40 graded, best 9.8
📖 To Sow the Seeds of Death's Day; Attack of the War Machine; Death-Camp at the Edge of the World; The Wondrous World of Dr. Strange **A:** Ross Andru **C:** Gil Kane **W:** Gerry Conway ★ 1st Appearance of Moses Magnum (Magnum Force). ★ Appearance of Punisher.
5 ❑ Jul 1975 Cover: 0.50 **NM** value: **7.00**
• **CGC:** 7 graded, best 9.6
📖 Beware the Path of the Monster; The Lurker in the Swamp; Bring Back My Man-Thing to Me; Where Flies the Beetle **A:** Ross Andru **C:** Gil Kane **W:** Gerry Conway ★ Appearance of Man-Thing. ★ Versus Lizard.
6 ❑ Sep 1975 Cover: 0.50 **NM** value: **7.00**
• **CGC:** 2 graded, best 9.4
📖 The Web and the Flame • reprints Amazing Spider-Man Annual #4

GIANT SIZE SPIDER-MAN (2ND SERIES) — Marvel

1 ❑ Dec 1998 Cover: 3.99 **NM** value: **Cover or less**
• reprints stories from Marvel Team-Up

GIANT-SIZE SUPER-HEROES — Marvel

1 ❑ Jun 1974 Cover: 0.35 **NM** value: **15.00**
• **CGC:** 11 graded, best 9.6
📖 Man-Wolf at Midnight; Duel of the Deadly Duo; When Strikes the Vampire; Rogue's Gallery; How Stan and Steve Create(d) Spider-Man (text) • "How Stan..." reprinted from Amazing Spider-Man Annual #1 **A:** Gil Kane **W:** Gerry Conway ★ Appearance of Man-Wolf, Spider-Man, Morbius.

GIANT-SIZE SUPER-STARS — Marvel

1 ❑ May 1974 **NM** value: **5.00**
• **CGC:** 16 graded, best 9.6

Other grades: Multiply prices above by **1.5 for Mint • 2/3 for Very Fine • 1/3 for Fine • 1/5 for Very Good • 1/8 for Good**

GIANT-SIZE SUPER-VILLAIN TEAM-UP — Marvel

1 ❑ Mar 1975 Cover: 0.50 **NM** value: **4.00**
• **CGC:** 1 graded, best 9.0
2 ❑ Jun 1975 Cover: 0.50 **NM** value: **4.00**
• **CGC:** 6 graded, best 9.4
• Doctor Doom, Sub-Mariner

GIANT-SIZE THOR — Marvel

1 ❑ Jul 1975 Cover: 0.50 **NM** value: **4.00**
• **CGC:** 1 graded, best 9.0

GIANT-SIZE WEREWOLF BY NIGHT — Marvel

2 ❑ Cover: 0.50 **NM** value: **3.00**
• Title changes to Giant Size Werewolf by Night. • Frankenstein reprint **A:** Steve Ditko
3 ❑ Cover: 0.50 **NM** value: **3.00**
• **CGC:** 3 graded, best 9.2
📖 Castle Curse! **A:** Gil Kane
4 ❑ Cover: 0.50 **NM** value: **3.00**
5 ❑ Cover: 0.50 **NM** value: **3.00**

GIANT-SIZE X-MEN — Marvel

1 ❑ Sum 1975 Cover: 0.50 **NM** value: **600.00**
• **CGC:** 643 graded, best 9.8
📖 Second Geesis! **A:** Gil Kane; Dave Cockrum **W:** Len Wein ★ Origin of Storm, Nightcrawler. ★ 1st Appearance of X-Men (new), Thunderbird, Colossus, Storm, Nightcrawler, Illyana Rasputin.
2 ❑ Nov 1975 Cover: 0.50 **NM** value: **60.00**
• **CGC:** 25 graded, best 9.6
• reprints X-Men #57-59 **A:** Gil Kane; Klaus Janson

GIANT THB PARADE — Horse

1 ❑ b&w Cover: 4.95 **NM** value: **5.00**
• over-sized.

G.I. COMBAT — DC

This action and adventure series ran for more than 30 years and is considered something of a classic in the war comics genre.

There's something for everyone, from soldiers in combat to soldiers to Allied spies in intrigues — and almost every story has a surprise twist.

One of G.I. Combat's most popular features is Jeb Stuart's Haunted Tank. This tank has a ghostly guardian who uses supernatural powers to aid the tank's crew in their fight against the Axis forces. Later, G.I. Combat went on to introduce The Losers, a team of hard-fighting heroes. They went on to become one of DC's more popular war features.

1 ❑ Oct 1952 Cover: 0.10 **NM** value: **385.00**
2 ❑ Dec 1952 Cover: 0.10 **NM** value: **175.00**
3 ❑ Feb 1953 Cover: 0.10 **NM** value: **125.00**
4 ❑ Mar 1953 Cover: 0.10 **NM** value: **125.00**
5 ❑ Apr 1953 Cover: 0.10 **NM** value: **125.00**
6 ❑ May 1953 Cover: 0.10 **NM** value: **100.00**
7 ❑ Jun 1953 Cover: 0.10 **NM** value: **100.00**
8 ❑ Jul 1953 Cover: 0.10 **NM** value: **100.00**
9 ❑ Sep 1953 Cover: 0.10 **NM** value: **100.00**
10 ❑ Oct 1953 Cover: 0.10 **NM** value: **110.00**
11 ❑ Nov 1953 Cover: 0.10 **NM** value: **75.00**
12 ❑ Dec 1953 Cover: 0.10 **NM** value: **75.00**
13 ❑ Feb 1954 Cover: 0.10 **NM** value: **75.00**
14 ❑ Apr 1954 Cover: 0.10 **NM** value: **75.00**
15 ❑ Jun 1954 Cover: 0.10 **NM** value: **75.00**
16 ❑ Aug 1954 Cover: 0.10 **NM** value: **75.00**
17 ❑ Oct 1954 Cover: 0.10 **NM** value: **75.00**
18 ❑ Nov 1954 Cover: 0.10 **NM** value: **75.00**
19 ❑ Dec 1954 Cover: 0.10 **NM** value: **75.00**
20 ❑ Jan 1955 Cover: 0.10 **NM** value: **75.00**
21 ❑ Feb 1955 Cover: 0.10 **NM** value: **60.00**
22 ❑ Mar 1955 Cover: 0.10 **NM** value: **60.00**
23 ❑ Apr 1955 Cover: 0.10 **NM** value: **60.00**
24 ❑ May 1955 Cover: 0.10 **NM** value: **60.00**
25 ❑ Jun 1955 Cover: 0.10 **NM** value: **60.00**
26 ❑ Jul 1955 Cover: 0.10 **NM** value: **60.00**
27 ❑ Aug 1955 Cover: 0.10 **NM** value: **60.00**
28 ❑ Sep 1955 Cover: 0.10 **NM** value: **60.00**
29 ❑ Oct 1955 Cover: 0.10 **NM** value: **60.00**
30 ❑ Nov 1955 Cover: 0.10 **NM** value: **60.00**
31 ❑ Dec 1955 Cover: 0.10 **NM** value: **60.00**
32 ❑ Jan 1956 Cover: 0.10 **NM** value: **90.00**
"Atomic Rocket Assault" (nuclear war) cover.
33 ❑ Feb 1956 Cover: 0.10 **NM** value: **60.00**
34 ❑ Mar 1956 Cover: 0.10 **NM** value: **60.00**
35 ❑ Apr 1956 Cover: 0.10 **NM** value: **60.00**
36 ❑ May 1956 Cover: 0.10 **NM** value: **60.00**
37 ❑ Jun 1956 Cover: 0.10 **NM** value: **60.00**
• **CGC:** 1 graded, best 7.0
38 ❑ Jul 1956 Cover: 0.10 **NM** value: **60.00**
39 ❑ Aug 1956 Cover: 0.10 **NM** value: **60.00**
40 ❑ Sep 1956 Cover: 0.10 **NM** value: **60.00**
41 ❑ Oct 1956 Cover: 0.10 **NM** value: **60.00**
42 ❑ Nov 1956 Cover: 0.10 **NM** value: **60.00**
43 ❑ Dec 1956 Cover: 0.10 **NM** value: **60.00**
44 ❑ Jan 1957 Cover: 0.10 **NM** value: **350.00**
• **CGC:** 1 graded, best 7.5
• DC begins publishing
45 ❑ Feb 1957 Cover: 0.10 **NM** value: **200.00**
46 ❑ Mar 1957 Cover: 0.10 **NM** value: **100.00**
47 ❑ Apr 1957 Cover: 0.10 **NM** value: **90.00**
48 ❑ May 1957 Cover: 0.10 **NM** value: **90.00**
49 ❑ Jun 1957 Cover: 0.10 **NM** value: **90.00**
50 ❑ Jul 1957 Cover: 0.10 **NM** value: **90.00**
51 ❑ Aug 1957 Cover: 0.10 **NM** value: **80.00**
52 ❑ Sep 1957 Cover: 0.10 **NM** value: **80.00**
53 ❑ Oct 1957 Cover: 0.10 **NM** value: **80.00**
54 ❑ Nov 1957 Cover: 0.10 **NM** value: **80.00**
55 ❑ Dec 1957 Cover: 0.10 **NM** value: **80.00**
56 ❑ Jan 1958 Cover: 0.10 **NM** value: **80.00**
• **CGC:** 1 graded, best 3.5
57 ❑ Feb 1958 Cover: 0.10 **NM** value: **80.00**
58 ❑ Mar 1958 Cover: 0.10 **NM** value: **80.00**
59 ❑ Apr 1958 Cover: 0.10 **NM** value: **80.00**
60 ❑ May 1958 Cover: 0.10 **NM** value: **80.00**
61 ❑ Jun 1958 Cover: 0.10 **NM** value: **65.00**
62 ❑ Jul 1958 Cover: 0.10 **NM** value: **65.00**
63 ❑ Aug 1958 Cover: 0.10 **NM** value: **65.00**
64 ❑ Sep 1958 Cover: 0.10 **NM** value: **65.00**
65 ❑ Oct 1958 Cover: 0.10 **NM** value: **65.00**
66 ❑ Nov 1958 Cover: 0.10 **NM** value: **65.00**
67 ❑ Dec 1958 Cover: 0.10 **NM** value: **100.00**
68 ❑ Jan 1959 Cover: 0.10 **NM** value: **65.00**
• **CGC:** 1 graded, best 3.5
69 ❑ Feb 1959 Cover: 0.10 **NM** value: **65.00**
70 ❑ Mar 1959 Cover: 0.10 **NM** value: **65.00**
71 ❑ Apr 1959 Cover: 0.10 **NM** value: **65.00**
72 ❑ May 1959 Cover: 0.10 **NM** value: **65.00**
73 ❑ Jun 1959 Cover: 0.10 **NM** value: **65.00**
74 ❑ Jul 1959 Cover: 0.10 **NM** value: **65.00**
• **CGC:** 1 graded, best 4.0
75 ❑ Aug 1959 Cover: 0.10 **NM** value: **65.00**
• **CGC:** 1 graded, best 4.0
76 ❑ Sep 1959 Cover: 0.10 **NM** value: **65.00**
77 ❑ Oct 1959 Cover: 0.10 **NM** value: **65.00**
• **CGC:** 1 graded, best 9.0
78 ❑ Nov 1959 Cover: 0.10 **NM** value: **65.00**
79 ❑ Dec 1959 Cover: 0.10 **NM** value: **65.00**
80 ❑ 1960 Cover: 0.10 **NM** value: **65.00**
81 ❑ 1960 Cover: 0.10 **NM** value: **65.00**
82 ❑ 1960 Cover: 0.10 **NM** value: **65.00**
83 ❑ 1960 Cover: 0.10 **NM** value: **65.00**
84 ❑ 1960 Cover: 0.10 **NM** value: **65.00**
85 ❑ Jan 1961 Cover: 0.10 **NM** value: **65.00**
86 ❑ Mar 1961 Cover: 0.10 **NM** value: **65.00**
87 ❑ May 1961 Cover: 0.10 **NM** value: **240.00**
• **CGC:** 2 graded, best 7.0
88 ❑ Jul 1961 Cover: 0.10 **NM** value: **50.00**
89 ❑ Sep 1961 Cover: 0.10 **NM** value: **50.00**
90 ❑ Nov 1961 Cover: 0.10 **NM** value: **50.00**
91 ❑ Jan 1962 Cover: 0.12 **NM** value: **50.00**
Circ: Statement: **240,000**
92 ❑ Mar 1962 Cover: 0.12 **NM** value: **50.00**
Circ: Statement: **240,000**
93 ❑ May 1962 Cover: 0.12 **NM** value: **50.00**
Circ: Statement: **240,000** • **CGC:** 1 graded, best 6.0
94 ❑ Jul 1962 Cover: 0.12 **NM** value: **50.00**
Circ: Statement: **240,000**
95 ❑ Sep 1962 Cover: 0.12 **NM** value: **50.00**
Circ: Statement: **240,000**
96 ❑ Nov 1962 Cover: 0.12 **NM** value: **50.00**
Circ: Statement: **240,000**
97 ❑ Jan 1963 Cover: 0.12 **NM** value: **50.00**
• **CGC:** 1 graded, best 7.0
98 ❑ Mar 1963 Cover: 0.12 **NM** value: **50.00**
99 ❑ May 1963 Cover: 0.12 **NM** value: **50.00**
100 ❑ Jul 1963 Cover: 0.12 **NM** value: **50.00**
• **CGC:** 2 graded, best 9.0
101 ❑ Sep 1963 Cover: 0.12 **NM** value: **40.00**
102 ❑ Nov 1963 Cover: 0.12 **NM** value: **40.00**
• **CGC:** 1 graded, best 4.0
103 ❑ Jan 1964 Cover: 0.12 **NM** value: **40.00**
Painted cover.
104 ❑ Mar 1964 Cover: 0.12 **NM** value: **40.00**
• Sgt. Mule back-up; Has 1963 Statement, filed 10/1/63; no figures published
105 ❑ May 1964 Cover: 0.12 **NM** value: **40.00**
106 ❑ Jul 1964 Cover: 0.12 **NM** value: **40.00**
107 ❑ Sep 1964 Cover: 0.12 **NM** value: **40.00**
• **CGC:** 1 graded, best 8.0
108 ❑ Nov 1964 Cover: 0.12 **NM** value: **40.00**
• **CGC:** 1 graded, best 9.0
109 ❑ Jan 1965 Cover: 0.12 **NM** value: **40.00**
Circ: Statement: **320,607**
110 ❑ Mar 1965 Cover: 0.12 **NM** value: **40.00**
Circ: Statement: **320,607**
📖 Choose Your War; Battle Exterminator!
111 ❑ May 1965 Cover: 0.12 **NM** value: **35.00**
Circ: Statement: **320,607** • **CGC:** 1 graded, best 4.0
112 ❑ Jul 1965 Cover: 0.12 **NM** value: **35.00**
Circ: Statement: **320,607**
113 ❑ Sep 1965 Cover: 0.12 **NM** value: **35.00**
Circ: Statement: **320,607**
114 ❑ Nov 1965 Cover: 0.12 **NM** value: **75.00**
Circ: Statement: **320,607** • **CGC:** 2 graded, best 9.0
115 ❑ Jan 1966 Cover: 0.12 **NM** value: **25.00**
Circ: Statement: **255,496**
116 ❑ Mar 1966 Cover: 0.12 **NM** value: **25.00**
Circ: Statement: **255,496**
117 ❑ May 1966 Cover: 0.12 **NM** value: **25.00**
Circ: Statement: **255,496**
118 ❑ Jul 1966 Cover: 0.12 **NM** value: **25.00**
Circ: Statement: **255,496**
119 ❑ Sep 1966 Cover: 0.12 **NM** value: **25.00**
Circ: Statement: **255,496** • **CGC:** 1 graded, best 3.5
120 ❑ Nov 1966 Cover: 0.12 **NM** value: **25.00**
Circ: Statement: **255,496**
121 ❑ Jan 1967 Cover: 0.12 **NM** value: **20.00**
Circ: Statement: **202,100** • **CGC:** 1 graded, best 3.0
122 ❑ Mar 1967 Cover: 0.12 **NM** value: **20.00**
Circ: Statement: **202,100** • **CGC:** 1 graded, best 3.5
123 ❑ May 1967 Cover: 0.12 **NM** value: **20.00**
Circ: Statement: **202,100**
124 ❑ Jul 1967 Cover: 0.12 **NM** value: **20.00**
Circ: Statement: **202,100** • **CGC:** 1 graded, best 9.2
125 ❑ Sep 1967 Cover: 0.12 **NM** value: **20.00**
Circ: Statement: **202,100**
126 ❑ Nov 1967 Cover: 0.12 **NM** value: **20.00**
Circ: Statement: **202,100**
127 ❑ Jan 1968 Cover: 0.12 **NM** value: **20.00**
Circ: Statement: **209,640**
128 ❑ Mar 1968 Cover: 0.12 **NM** value: **20.00**
Circ: Statement: **209,640**
129 ❑ May 1968 Cover: 0.12 **NM** value: **20.00**
Circ: Statement: **209,640**
📖 Hold That Town for a Dead Man!; Combat Nightmare
130 ❑ Jul 1968 Cover: 0.12 **NM** value: **20.00**
Circ: Statement: **209,640**
131 ❑ Sep 1968 Cover: 0.12 **NM** value: **20.00**
Circ: Statement: **209,640**
132 ❑ Nov 1968 Cover: 0.12 **NM** value: **20.00**
Circ: Statement: **209,640**
133 ❑ Jan 1969 Cover: 0.12 **NM** value: **20.00**
Circ: Statement: **186,264**
134 ❑ Mar 1969 Cover: 0.12 **NM** value: **20.00**
Circ: Statement: **186,264**
135 ❑ May 1969 Cover: 0.12 **NM** value: **20.00**
Circ: Statement: **186,264**
• Has 1968 Statement; avg print run 402,000; avg sales 209,000; avg subs 640; avg total paid 209,640; samples 386; max existent 210,026; 48% of run returned **C:** Joe Kubert
136 ❑ Jul 1969 Cover: 0.15 **NM** value: **20.00**
Circ: Statement: **186,264**
137 ❑ Sep 1969 Cover: 0.15 **NM** value: **20.00**
Circ: Statement: **186,264**
138 ❑ Nov 1969 Cover: 0.15 **NM** value: **38.00**
Circ: Statement: **186,264** • **CGC:** 4 graded, best 9.4
139 ❑ Jan 1970 Cover: 0.15 **NM** value: **20.00**
Circ: Statement: **178,363** • **CGC:** 1 graded, best 5.5
140 ❑ Mar 1970 Cover: 0.15 **NM** value: **20.00**
Circ: Statement: **178,363** • **CGC:** 1 graded, best 5.0
141 ❑ May 1970 Cover: 0.15 **NM** value: **7.50**
Circ: Statement: **178,363** • **CGC:** 1 graded, best 7.0
• Has 1969 Statement; avg total paid circ 186,264
142 ❑ Jul 1970 Cover: 0.15 **NM** value: **7.50**
Circ: Statement: **178,363**
143 ❑ Sep 1970 Cover: 0.15 **NM** value: **7.50**
Circ: Statement: **178,363** • **CGC:** 1 graded, best 9.8
144 ❑ Nov 1970 Cover: 0.25 **NM** value: **7.50**
Circ: Statement: **178,363**
145 ❑ Jan 1971 Cover: 0.25 **NM** value: **7.50**
Circ: Statement: **167,841** • **CGC:** 1 graded, best 9.2
146 ❑ Mar 1971 Cover: 0.25 **NM** value: **7.50**
Circ: Statement: **167,841**
• Giant-size.
147 ❑ May 1971 Cover: 0.25 **NM** value: **7.50**
Circ: Statement: **167,841**
• Giant-size. • Has 1970 Statement, filed 10/1/70; avg print run 360,509; avg sales 178,203; avg subs 160; avg total paid 178,363; samples 122; max existent 178,363; 51% of run returned
148 ❑ Jul 1971 Cover: 0.25 **NM** value: **7.50**
Circ: Statement: **167,841**
• Giant-size.
149 ❑ Sep 1971 Cover: 0.25 **NM** value: **7.50**
Circ: Statement: **167,841**
• Sgt. Rock back-up **C:** Joe Kubert
150 ❑ Nov 1971 Cover: 0.25 **NM** value: **7.50**
Circ: Statement: **167,841** • **CGC:** 1 graded, best 9.0
📖 Ice Cream Soldier • Reprints 1 **C:** Joe Kubert ★ 1st Appearance of New Haunted Tank.
151 ❑ Jan 1972 Cover: 0.25 **NM** value: **7.50**
Circ: Statement: **158,312**
152 ❑ Mar 1972 Cover: 0.25 **NM** value: **7.50**
Circ: Statement: **158,312**
153 ❑ May 1972 Cover: 0.25 **NM** value: **7.50**
Circ: Statement: **158,312**
• Has 1971 Statement, filed 10/1/1971; avg print run 343,333; avg sales 167,841; no subscriptions; total paid 167,841; office use 1,001; max existent 168,842; 51% of run returned
154 ❑ Jul 1972 Cover: 0.25 **NM** value: **7.50**
Circ: Statement: **158,312**
155 ❑ Sep 1972 Cover: 0.25 **NM** value: **7.50**
Circ: Statement: **158,312**
156 ❑ Nov 1972 Cover: 0.25 **NM** value: **7.50**
Circ: Statement: **158,312**
157 ❑ Jan 1973 Cover: 0.20 **NM** value: **7.50**
Circ: Statement: **161,702**
158 ❑ Feb 1973 Cover: 0.20 **NM** value: **7.50**
Circ: Statement: **161,702**
159 ❑ Mar 1973 Cover: 0.20 **NM** value: **7.50**
Circ: Statement: **161,702**
• Has 1972 Statement; avg total paid circ 158,312
160 ❑ May 1973 Cover: 0.20 **NM** value: **7.50**
Circ: Statement: **161,702**
161 ❑ Jun 1973 Cover: 0.20 **NM** value: **6.00**
Circ: Statement: **161,702**
162 ❑ Jul 1973 Cover: 0.20 **NM** value: **6.00**
Circ: Statement: **161,702**
163 ❑ Aug 1973 Cover: 0.20 **NM** value: **6.00**
Circ: Statement: **161,702**
164 ❑ Sep 1973 Cover: 0.20 **NM** value: **6.00**
Circ: Statement: **161,702**
165 ❑ Oct 1973 Cover: 0.20 **NM** value: **6.00**
Circ: Statement: **161,702**
166 ❑ Nov 1973 Cover: 0.20 **NM** value: **6.00**
Circ: Statement: **161,702**
167 ❑ Dec 1973 Cover: 0.20 **NM** value: **6.00**
Circ: Statement: **161,702**

CGC-graded: Multiply prices above by **33 for 9.9 M • 16 for 9.8 NM/M • 7 for 9.6 NM+ • 5 for 9.4 NM • 2.5 for 9.2 NM- • 1.5 for 9.0 VF/NM**

168 ❑ Jan 1974 Cover: 0.20 **NM** value: **6.00**
Circ: Statement: **168,042**
169 ❑ Feb 1974 Cover: 0.20 **NM** value: **6.00**
Circ: Statement: **168,042**
170 ❑ Mar 1974 Cover: 0.20 **NM** value: **6.00**
Circ: Statement: **168,042**
171 ❑ Jun 1974 Cover: 0.20 **NM** value: **6.00**
Circ: Statement: **168,042**
• Has 1973 Statement; avg total paid circ 161,702
172 ❑ Aug 1974 Cover: 0.20 **NM** value: **6.00**
Circ: Statement: **168,042**
173 ❑ Oct 1974 Cover: 0.20 **NM** value: **6.00**
Circ: Statement: **168,042**
174 ❑ Dec 1974 Cover: 0.20 **NM** value: **6.00**
Circ: Statement: **168,042**
175 ❑ Feb 1975 Cover: 0.25 **NM** value: **6.00**
176 ❑ Mar 1975 Cover: 0.25 **NM** value: **6.00**
177 ❑ Apr 1975 Cover: 0.25 **NM** value: **6.00**
178 ❑ May 1975 Cover: 0.25 **NM** value: **6.00**
179 ❑ Jun 1975 Cover: 0.25 **NM** value: **6.00**
180 ❑ Jul 1975 Cover: 0.25 **NM** value: **6.00**
181 ❑ Aug 1975 Cover: 0.25 **NM** value: **4.50**
182 ❑ Sep 1975 Cover: 0.25 **NM** value: **4.50**
183 ❑ Oct 1975 Cover: 0.25 **NM** value: **4.50**
184 ❑ Nov 1975 Cover: 0.25 **NM** value: **4.50**
185 ❑ Dec 1975 Cover: 0.25 **NM** value: **4.50**
186 ❑ Jan 1976 Cover: 0.25 **NM** value: **4.50**
Circ: Statement: **135,000**
187 ❑ Feb 1976 Cover: 0.25 **NM** value: **4.50**
Circ: Statement: **135,000**
188 ❑ Mar 1976 Cover: 0.30 **NM** value: **4.50**
Circ: Statement: **135,000**
189 ❑ Apr 1976 Cover: 0.30 **NM** value: **4.50**
Circ: Statement: **135,000**
190 ❑ May 1976 **NM** value: **4.50**
Circ: Statement: **135,000**
191 ❑ Jun 1976 **NM** value: **4.50**
Circ: Statement: **135,000**
192 ❑ Jul 1976 **NM** value: **4.50**
Circ: Statement: **135,000**
• Bicentennial #27
193 ❑ Aug 1976 **NM** value: **4.50**
Circ: Statement: **135,000**
194 ❑ Sep 1976 **NM** value: **4.50**
Circ: Statement: **135,000**
195 ❑ Oct 1976 **NM** value: **4.50**
Circ: Statement: **135,000**
196 ❑ Nov 1976 **NM** value: **4.50**
Circ: Statement: **135,000**
197 ❑ Dec 1976 **NM** value: **4.50**
Circ: Statement: **135,000**
198 ❑ Jan 1977 **NM** value: **4.50**
Circ: Statement: **124,996**
📖 The Haunted Tank: The Devil Rides a Panzer; The Ship that Wouldn't Die **A:** Sam Glanzman; E.R. Cruz **W:** E.R. Cruz; Robert Kanigher
199 ❑ Feb 1977 **NM** value: **4.50**
Circ: Statement: **124,996**
200 ❑ Mar 1977 **NM** value: **4.50**
Circ: Statement: **124,996**
201 ❑ Apr 1977 Cover: 1.00 **NM** value: **2.50**
Circ: Statement: **124,996**
202 ❑ Jun 1977 Cover: 1.00 **NM** value: **2.50**
Circ: Statement: **124,996**
• Has 1976 Statement, filed 10/1/76; avg print run 325,000; avg sales 134,000; avg subs 1,000; avg total paid 135,000; samples 1,000; office use 2,000; max existent 138,000; 58% of run returned
203 ❑ Aug 1977 Cover: 1.00 **NM** value: **2.50**
Circ: Statement: **124,996**
204 ❑ Oct 1977 Cover: 1.00 **NM** value: **2.50**
Circ: Statement: **124,996**
205 ❑ Dec 1977 Cover: 1.00 **NM** value: **2.50**
Circ: Statement: **124,996**
206 ❑ Feb 1978 Cover: 1.00 **NM** value: **2.50**
207 ❑ Apr 1978 Cover: 1.00 **NM** value: **2.50**
208 ❑ Jun 1978 Cover: 1.00 **NM** value: **2.50**
• Has 1977 Statement; avg total paid circ 124,996
209 ❑ Aug 1978 Cover: 1.00 **NM** value: **2.50**
210 ❑ Oct 1978 Cover: 1.00 **NM** value: **2.50**
211 ❑ Dec 1978 Cover: 1.00 **NM** value: **2.50**
212 ❑ Feb 1979 Cover: 1.00 **NM** value: **2.50**
213 ❑ Apr 1979 Cover: 1.00 **NM** value: **2.50**
214 ❑ Jun 1979 Cover: 1.00 **NM** value: **2.50**
215 ❑ Aug 1979 Cover: 1.00 **NM** value: **2.50**
216 ❑ Oct 1979 Cover: 1.00 **NM** value: **2.50**
217 ❑ Dec 1979 Cover: 1.00 **NM** value: **2.50**
218 ❑ Feb 1980 Cover: 1.00 **NM** value: **2.50**
219 ❑ Apr 1980 Cover: 1.00 **NM** value: **2.50**
220 ❑ Jun 1980 Cover: 1.00 **NM** value: **2.50**
221 ❑ Aug 1980 Cover: 1.00 **NM** value: **2.50**
222 ❑ Oct 1980 Cover: 1.00 **NM** value: **2.50**
223 ❑ Nov 1980 Cover: 1.00 **NM** value: **2.50**
224 ❑ Dec 1980 Cover: 1.00 **NM** value: **2.50**
225 ❑ Jan 1981 Cover: 1.00 **NM** value: **2.50**
Circ: Statement: **69,000**
226 ❑ Feb 1981 Cover: 1.00 **NM** value: **2.50**
Circ: Statement: **69,000**
227 ❑ Mar 1981 Cover: 1.00 **NM** value: **2.50**
Circ: Statement: **69,000**
📖 The Haunted Tank: I, Tank; The Spy Who Died Twice!; The Unknown War: Signal From a Dead Soldier **A:** Sam Glanzman; Dick Ayers; Jun Borillo **W:** George Kashdan; Robert Kanigher
228 ❑ Apr 1981 Cover: 1.00 **NM** value: **2.50**
Circ: Statement: **69,000**
229 ❑ May 1981 Cover: 1.00 **NM** value: **2.50**
Circ: Statement: **69,000**
230 ❑ Jun 1981 Cover: 1.00 **NM** value: **2.50**
Circ: Statement: **69,000**
231 ❑ Jul 1981 Cover: 1.00 **NM** value: **2.50**
Circ: Statement: **69,000**
232 ❑ Aug 1981 Cover: 1.00 **NM** value: **2.50**
Circ: Statement: **69,000**
233 ❑ Sep 1981 Cover: 1.00 **NM** value: **2.50**
Circ: Statement: **69,000**
234 ❑ Oct 1981 Cover: 1.00 **NM** value: **2.50**
Circ: Statement: **69,000**
235 ❑ Nov 1981 Cover: 1.00 **NM** value: **2.50**
Circ: Statement: **69,000**
236 ❑ Dec 1981 Cover: 1.00 **NM** value: **2.50**
Circ: Statement: **69,000**
237 ❑ Jan 1982 Cover: 1.00 **NM** value: **2.50**
238 ❑ Feb 1982 Cover: 1.00 **NM** value: **2.50**
239 ❑ Mar 1982 Cover: 1.00 **NM** value: **2.50**
240 ❑ Apr 1982 Cover: 1.00 **NM** value: **2.50**
241 ❑ May 1982 Cover: 1.00 **NM** value: **2.50**
242 ❑ Jun 1982 Cover: 1.00 **NM** value: **2.50**
243 ❑ Jul 1982 Cover: 1.00 **NM** value: **2.50**
244 ❑ Aug 1982 Cover: 1.00 **NM** value: **2.50**
245 ❑ Sep 1982 Cover: 1.00 **NM** value: **2.50**
246 ❑ Oct 1982 Cover: 1.50 **NM** value: **2.50**
• 30th anniversary. ★ Appearance of Ninja, Johnny Cloud, Gunner & Sarge, Sgt. Rock, Captain Storm, Falcon, Haunted Tank.
247 ❑ Nov 1982 Cover: 1.00 **NM** value: **2.50**
248 ❑ Dec 1982 Cover: 1.00 **NM** value: **2.50**
249 ❑ Jan 1983 Cover: 1.00 **NM** value: **2.50**
250 ❑ Feb 1983 Cover: 1.00 **NM** value: **2.50**
251 ❑ Mar 1983 Cover: 1.00 **NM** value: **2.00**
252 ❑ Apr 1983 Cover: 1.00 **NM** value: **2.00**
253 ❑ May 1983 Cover: 1.00 **NM** value: **2.00**
254 ❑ Jun 1983 Cover: 1.00 **NM** value: **2.00**
255 ❑ Jul 1983 Cover: 1.00 **NM** value: **2.00**
256 ❑ Aug 1983 Cover: 1.00 **NM** value: **2.00**
257 ❑ Sep 1983 Cover: 1.00 **NM** value: **2.00**
258 ❑ Oct 1983 Cover: 1.00 **NM** value: **2.00**
259 ❑ Nov 1983 **NM** value: **2.00**
📖 One Last Shot; Sweet Taste Of Death; A Trinket Of Time; Dead Heat Of Battle; Surprise Weapon **A:** Sam Glanzman; E.R. Cruz; Angel Trinidad Jr.; Tenny Henson **W:** George Kashdan; Robert Kanigher
260 ❑ Dec 1983 Cover: 1.25 **NM** value: **2.00**
261 ❑ Jan 1984 Cover: 1.25 **NM** value: **2.00**
262 ❑ Feb 1984 Cover: 1.25 **NM** value: **2.00**
263 ❑ Mar 1984 Cover: 1.25 **NM** value: **2.00**
264 ❑ Apr 1984 Cover: 1.25 **NM** value: **2.00**
265 ❑ May 1984 Cover: 1.25 **NM** value: **2.00**
266 ❑ Jun 1984 Cover: 1.25 **NM** value: **2.00**
267 ❑ Jul 1984 Cover: 1.25 **NM** value: **2.00**
268 ❑ Aug 1984 Cover: 1.25 **NM** value: **2.00**
269 ❑ Sep 1984 Cover: 1.25 **NM** value: **2.00**
270 ❑ Oct 1984 Cover: 1.25 **NM** value: **2.00**
271 ❑ Nov 1984 Cover: 1.25 **NM** value: **2.00**
272 ❑ Dec 1984 Cover: 1.25 **NM** value: **2.00**
273 ❑ Jan 1985 Cover: 1.25 **NM** value: **2.00**
Circ: Statement: **48,092**
274 ❑ Feb 1985 Cover: 1.25 **NM** value: **2.00**
Circ: Statement: **48,092**
275 ❑ Mar 1985 Cover: 1.25 **NM** value: **2.00**
Circ: Statement: **48,092**
276 ❑ Apr 1985 Cover: 1.25 **NM** value: **2.00**
Circ: Statement: **48,092**
277 ❑ May 1985 Cover: 1.25 **NM** value: **2.00**
Circ: Statement: **48,092** CapCity orders: **1,250**
278 ❑ Jul 1985 Cover: 1.25 **NM** value: **2.00**
Circ: Statement: **48,092** CapCity orders: **1,300**
279 ❑ Sep 1985 Cover: 1.25 **NM** value: **2.00**
Circ: Statement: **48,092** CapCity orders: **1,400**
280 ❑ Nov 1985 Cover: 1.25 **NM** value: **2.00**
Circ: Statement: **48,092** CapCity orders: **1,350**
281 ❑ Jan 1986 Cover: 1.25 **NM** value: **2.00**
Circ: CapCity orders: **1,450**
282 ❑ Mar 1986 Cover: 0.75 **NM** value: **2.00**
Circ: CapCity orders: **1,700**
• Mercenaries **C:** Joe Kubert
283 ❑ May 1986 Cover: 0.75 **NM** value: **2.00**
Circ: CapCity orders: **1,700**
• Mercenaries; Has 1985 Statement, filed 10/1/1985; avg print run 179,423; avg sales 47,545; avg subs 547; avg total paid 48,092; samples 137; office use 1,630; max existent 49,859; 72% of run returned
284 ❑ Jul 1986 Cover: 0.75 **NM** value: **2.00**
Circ: CapCity orders: **1,750**
• Mercenaries **C:** Joe Kubert
285 ❑ Sep 1986 Cover: 0.75 **NM** value: **2.00**
Circ: CapCity orders: **1,800**
• Mercenaries **C:** Joe Kubert
286 ❑ Nov 1986 Cover: 0.75 **NM** value: **2.00**
Circ: CapCity orders: **1,900**
• Mercenaries **C:** Joe Kubert
287 ❑ Jan 1987 Cover: 0.75 **NM** value: **2.00**
Circ: CapCity orders: **1,900**
• Haunted Tank **C:** Joe Kubert
288 ❑ Mar 1987 Cover: 0.75 **NM** value: **2.00**
Circ: CapCity orders: **1,950**
final issue. • Haunted Tank **C:** Joe Kubert

GIDEON HAWK — Big Shot

1 ❑ Jan 1995 Cover: 2.00 **NM** value: **Cover or less**
📖 The Jewel of Shambali **A:** Steve Brooks **W:** Steve Brooks
2 ❑ Mar 1995, b&w Cover: 2.00 **NM** value: **Cover or less**
3 ❑ Jun 1995, b&w Cover: 2.00 **NM** value: **Cover or less**

GIFT, THE: A FIRST PUBLISHING HOLIDAY SPECIAL — First

1 ❑ Nov 1990 Cover: 5.95 **NM** value: **Cover or less**
No issue number. **A:** Kim Yale; Scot Eaton; Tim Vigil; Tom Sutton; Steve Rude; Joe Staton; Steven Butler; Hugh Haynes; Matt Wagner(cover) **W:** Mike Baron; David Barbour; John Ostrander; Peter David; Stefan Petrucha ★ Appearance of Dreadstar, Nexus, Badger.

GIFTS OF THE NIGHT — DC / Vertigo

1 ❑ Feb 1999 Cover: 2.95 **NM** value: **Cover or less**
Circ: Diamd. preorders: **20,778**
2 ❑ Mar 1999 Cover: 2.95 **NM** value: **Cover or less**
Circ: Diamd. preorders: **16,537**
3 ❑ Apr 1999 Cover: 2.95 **NM** value: **Cover or less**
Circ: Diamd. preorders: **14,678**
4 ❑ May 1999 Cover: 2.95 **NM** value: **Cover or less**
Circ: Diamd. preorders: **14,081**

GIGANTOR — Antarctic / Vertigo

1 ❑ Jan 2000 Cover: 2.50 **NM** value: **Cover or less**
Circ: Diamd. preorders: **7,397**

GIGGLE COMICS — ACG

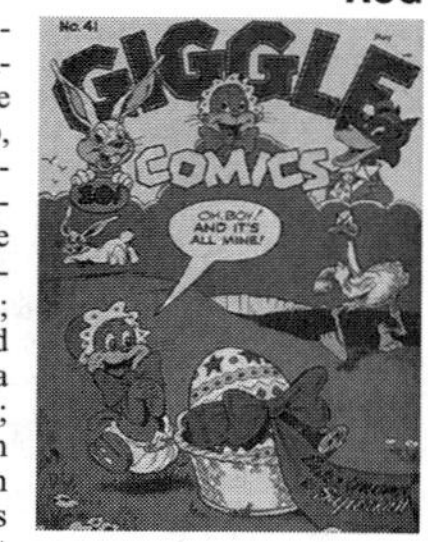

Giggle Comics was an occasionally amusing but generally undistinguished funny-animal title from the Golden Age, when talking sheep, rabbits, ducks, and dogs were everywhere on the comics racks. Giggle Comics featured a menagerie that included Superkatt (a diaper-clad feline) and his barnyard pals; the Duke and the Dope (a dog and pig police team); Spencer Spook (a work-a-day ghost in a bowler hat); and Binky (a cocker-spaniel pooch who actually interacts with human beings as the family pet). Issues were filled out with other one-shot stories, text-page features, and kid-oriented entertainment like search-a-word and connect-the-dots games.

1 ❑ Oct 1943 Cover: 0.10 **NM** value: **125.00**
2 ❑ Nov 1943 Cover: 0.10 **NM** value: **75.00**
3 ❑ Dec 1943 Cover: 0.10 **NM** value: **60.00**
4 ❑ Jan 1944 Cover: 0.10 **NM** value: **60.00**
5 ❑ Feb 1944 Cover: 0.10 **NM** value: **60.00**
6 ❑ Mar 1944 Cover: 0.10 **NM** value: **45.00**
7 ❑ Apr 1944 Cover: 0.10 **NM** value: **45.00**
8 ❑ May 1944 Cover: 0.10 **NM** value: **45.00**
9 ❑ Jun 1944 Cover: 0.10 **NM** value: **45.00**
10 ❑ Jul 1944 Cover: 0.10 **NM** value: **45.00**
11 ❑ Aug 1944 Cover: 0.10 **NM** value: **30.00**
12 ❑ Sep 1944 Cover: 0.10 **NM** value: **30.00**
13 ❑ Oct 1944 Cover: 0.10 **NM** value: **30.00**
14 ❑ Nov 1944 Cover: 0.10 **NM** value: **30.00**
15 ❑ Dec 1944 Cover: 0.10 **NM** value: **30.00**
16 ❑ Jan 1945 Cover: 0.10 **NM** value: **30.00**
17 ❑ Feb 1945 Cover: 0.10 **NM** value: **30.00**
18 ❑ Mar 1945 Cover: 0.10 **NM** value: **30.00**
19 ❑ Apr 1945 Cover: 0.10 **NM** value: **30.00**
20 ❑ May 1945 Cover: 0.10 **NM** value: **30.00**
21 ❑ Jun 1945 Cover: 0.10 **NM** value: **22.00**
22 ❑ Jul 1945 Cover: 0.10 **NM** value: **22.00**
23 ❑ Aug 1945 Cover: 0.10 **NM** value: **22.00**
24 ❑ Sep 1945 Cover: 0.10 **NM** value: **22.00**
25 ❑ Oct 1945 Cover: 0.10 **NM** value: **22.00**
26 ❑ Nov 1945 Cover: 0.10 **NM** value: **22.00**
27 ❑ Dec 1945 Cover: 0.10 **NM** value: **22.00**
28 ❑ Jan 1946 Cover: 0.10 **NM** value: **22.00**
29 ❑ Feb 1946 Cover: 0.10 **NM** value: **22.00**
30 ❑ Mar 1946 Cover: 0.10 **NM** value: **22.00**
31 ❑ Apr 1946 Cover: 0.10 **NM** value: **20.00**
32 ❑ May 1946 Cover: 0.10 **NM** value: **20.00**
33 ❑ Jun 1946 Cover: 0.10 **NM** value: **20.00**
34 ❑ Jul 1946 Cover: 0.10 **NM** value: **20.00**
35 ❑ Aug 1946 Cover: 0.10 **NM** value: **20.00**
36 ❑ Sep 1946 Cover: 0.10 **NM** value: **20.00**
37 ❑ Oct 1946 Cover: 0.10 **NM** value: **20.00**
38 ❑ Nov 1946 Cover: 0.10 **NM** value: **20.00**
39 ❑ Dec 1946 Cover: 0.10 **NM** value: **20.00**
40 ❑ Jan 1947 Cover: 0.10 **NM** value: **20.00**
41 ❑ Feb 1947 Cover: 0.10 **NM** value: **20.00**
📖 Superkatt; The Magic Nut (text story); The Duke and the Dope; Monty Monk; Spencer Spook; Stop, Thief! (text story); Binky; Wacky Wolf; Giles; Open and Shut (text story); Corky **A:** Ken Hultgren **W:** Ken Hultgren
42 ❑ Mar 1947 Cover: 0.10 **NM** value: **20.00**
43 ❑ Apr 1947 Cover: 0.10 **NM** value: **20.00**
44 ❑ May 1947 Cover: 0.10 **NM** value: **20.00**
45 ❑ Jun 1947 Cover: 0.10 **NM** value: **20.00**
46 ❑ Jul 1947 Cover: 0.10 **NM** value: **20.00**
47 ❑ Aug 1947 Cover: 0.10 **NM** value: **20.00**
48 ❑ Sep 1947 Cover: 0.10 **NM** value: **20.00**
49 ❑ Oct 1947 Cover: 0.10 **NM** value: **20.00**
50 ❑ Nov 1947 Cover: 0.10 **NM** value: **20.00**
51 ❑ Dec 1947 Cover: 0.10 **NM** value: **16.00**
52 ❑ Jan 1948 Cover: 0.10 **NM** value: **16.00**
53 ❑ Feb 1948 Cover: 0.10 **NM** value: **16.00**
54 ❑ Mar 1948 Cover: 0.10 **NM** value: **16.00**
55 ❑ Apr 1948 Cover: 0.10 **NM** value: **16.00**
56 ❑ May 1948 Cover: 0.10 **NM** value: **16.00**
57 ❑ Jun 1948 Cover: 0.10 **NM** value: **16.00**
58 ❑ Jul 1948 Cover: 0.10 **NM** value: **16.00**
59 ❑ Aug 1948 Cover: 0.10 **NM** value: **16.00**
60 ❑ Sep 1948 Cover: 0.10 **NM** value: **16.00**
61 ❑ Oct 1948 Cover: 0.10 **NM** value: **16.00**
62 ❑ Nov 1948 Cover: 0.10 **NM** value: **16.00**
63 ❑ Jan 1949 Cover: 0.10 **NM** value: **16.00**
64 ❑ Mar 1949 Cover: 0.10 **NM** value: **16.00**
65 ❑ May 1949 Cover: 0.10 **NM** value: **16.00**

Other grades: Multiply prices above by **1.5 for Mint • 2/3 for Very Fine • 1/3 for Fine • 1/5 for Very Good • 1/8 for Good**

66 ❑ Jul 1949 Cover: 0.10 **NM** value: **16.00**
67 ❑ Sep 1949 Cover: 0.10 **NM** value: **16.00**
68 ❑ Nov 1949 Cover: 0.10 **NM** value: **16.00**
69 ❑ Jan 1950 Cover: 0.10 **NM** value: **16.00**
70 ❑ Mar 1950 Cover: 0.10 **NM** value: **16.00**
71 ❑ May 1950 Cover: 0.10 **NM** value: **14.00**
72 ❑ Jul 1950 Cover: 0.10 **NM** value: **14.00**
73 ❑ Sep 1950 Cover: 0.10 **NM** value: **14.00**
74 ❑ Nov 1950 Cover: 0.10 **NM** value: **14.00**
75 ❑ Jan 1951 Cover: 0.10 **NM** value: **14.00**
76 ❑ Mar 1951 Cover: 0.10 **NM** value: **14.00**
77 ❑ May 1951 Cover: 0.10 **NM** value: **14.00**
📖 Spencer Spook **A:** Lynn Karp
78 ❑ Jul 1951 Cover: 0.10 **NM** value: **14.00**
79 ❑ Sep 1951 Cover: 0.10 **NM** value: **14.00**
80 ❑ Nov 1951 Cover: 0.10 **NM** value: **14.00**
81 ❑ Jan 1952 Cover: 0.10 **NM** value: **14.00**
82 ❑ Mar 1952 Cover: 0.10 **NM** value: **14.00**
83 ❑ May 1952 Cover: 0.10 **NM** value: **14.00**
84 ❑ Jul 1952 Cover: 0.10 **NM** value: **14.00**
85 ❑ Sep 1952 Cover: 0.10 **NM** value: **14.00**
86 ❑ Nov 1952 Cover: 0.10 **NM** value: **14.00**
87 ❑ Jan 1953 Cover: 0.10 **NM** value: **14.00**
88 ❑ Mar 1953 Cover: 0.10 **NM** value: **14.00**
89 ❑ May 1953 Cover: 0.10 **NM** value: **14.00**
90 ❑ Jul 1953 Cover: 0.10 **NM** value: **14.00**
91 ❑ Sep 1953 Cover: 0.10 **NM** value: **14.00**
92 ❑ Nov 1953 Cover: 0.10 **NM** value: **14.00**
93 ❑ Jan 1954 Cover: 0.10 **NM** value: **14.00**
94 ❑ Mar 1954 Cover: 0.10 **NM** value: **14.00**
95 ❑ May 1954 Cover: 0.10 **NM** value: **14.00**
96 ❑ Jul 1954 Cover: 0.10 **NM** value: **14.00**
97 ❑ Sep 1954 Cover: 0.10 **NM** value: **14.00**
98 ❑ Nov 1954 Cover: 0.10 **NM** value: **14.00**
99 ❑ Jan 1955 Cover: 0.10 **NM** value: **14.00**
final issue.

GIGOLO — Fantagraphics / Eros

1 ❑ Cover: 2.95 **NM** value: **Cover or less**
2 ❑ Nov 1995 Cover: 2.95 **NM** value: **Cover or less**
📖 W is for Wimmens Record **A:** Sit Koitus **W:** Sit Koitus

G.I. GOVERNMENT ISSUED — Paranoid

1 ❑ Cover: 2.00 **NM** value: **Cover or less**
2 ❑ Aug 1994 Cover: 2.00 **NM** value: **Cover or less**

G-I IN BATTLE — Four Star

1 ❑ Aug 1952 Cover: 0.10 **NM** value: **40.00**
• **CGC:** 1 graded, best 8.0
2 ❑ Cover: 0.10 **NM** value: **22.00**
3 ❑ Cover: 0.10 **NM** value: **18.00**
4 ❑ Cover: 0.10 **NM** value: **18.00**
5 ❑ Cover: 0.10 **NM** value: **18.00**
6 ❑ Cover: 0.10 **NM** value: **15.00**
📖 Lest We Forget; Iron Beast; Surprise Surrender (text); Battle Boy; Glory Guns
7 ❑ May 1953 Cover: 0.10 **NM** value: **15.00**
8 ❑ Jun 1953 Cover: 0.10 **NM** value: **15.00**
9 ❑ Jul 1953 Cover: 0.10 **NM** value: **15.00**
Anl 1❑ Cover: 0.25 **NM** value: **35.00**
• 1957 annual
Anl 1/A❑ **NM** value: **110.00**
• 1952 annual
Anl 2❑ Cover: 0.25 **NM** value: **20.00**
Anl 3❑ Cover: 0.25 **NM** value: **20.00**
Anl 4❑ Cover: 0.25 **NM** value: **18.00**
Anl 5❑ Cover: 0.25 **NM** value: **18.00**
Anl 6❑ Cover: 0.25 **NM** value: **18.00**

G.I. JACKRABBITS — Excalibur

1 ❑ Dec 1986 Cover: 1.50 **NM** value: **Cover or less**

G.I. JANE — Stanhall

1 ❑ May 1953 Cover: 0.10 **NM** value: **75.00**
2 ❑ Jul 1953 Cover: 0.10 **NM** value: **45.00**
3 ❑ Sep 1953 Cover: 0.10 **NM** value: **45.00**
4 ❑ Nov 1953 Cover: 0.10 **NM** value: **45.00**
5 ❑ Jan 1954 Cover: 0.10 **NM** value: **45.00**
6 ❑ Mar 1954 Cover: 0.10 **NM** value: **45.00**
7 ❑ May 1954 Cover: 0.10 **NM** value: **35.00**
8 ❑ Jul 1954 Cover: 0.10 **NM** value: **35.00**
9 ❑ Sep 1954 Cover: 0.10 **NM** value: **35.00**
10 ❑ Nov 1954 Cover: 0.10 **NM** value: **35.00**

G.I. JOE AND THE TRANSFORMERS — Marvel

1 ❑ Jan 1987 Cover: 0.75 **NM** value: **1.00**
Circ: CapCity orders: **39,600** • **CGC:** 2 graded, best 9.6
📖 Blood On The Tracks **A:** Herb Trimpe **W:** Michael Higgins
2 ❑ Feb 1987 Cover: 0.75 **NM** value: **1.00**
Circ: CapCity orders: **34,600**
3 ❑ Mar 1987 Cover: 0.75 **NM** value: **1.00**
Circ: CapCity orders: **32,800** • **CGC:** 1 graded, best 9.6
4 ❑ Apr 1987 Cover: 0.75 **NM** value: **1.00**
Circ: CapCity orders: **31,600**

G.I. JOE COMICS MAGAZINE — Marvel

1 ❑ Dec 1986 Cover: 1.50 **NM** value: **Cover or less**
Circ: CapCity orders: **12,300**
• digest.
2 ❑ Feb 1987 Cover: 1.50 **NM** value: **Cover or less**
Circ: CapCity orders: **7,900**
• digest.
3 ❑ Apr 1987 Cover: 1.50 **NM** value: **Cover or less**
• digest.
4 ❑ Jun 1987 Cover: 1.50 **NM** value: **Cover or less**
Circ: CapCity orders: **2,400**
• digest.
5 ❑ Aug 1987 Cover: 1.50 **NM** value: **Cover or less**
Circ: CapCity orders: **2,450**
• digest.
6 ❑ Oct 1987 Cover: 1.50 **NM** value: **Cover or less**
• digest.
7 ❑ Dec 1987 Cover: 1.50 **NM** value: **Cover or less**
• digest.
8 ❑ Feb 1988 Cover: 1.50 **NM** value: **Cover or less**
• digest.
9 ❑ Apr 1988 Cover: 1.50 **NM** value: **Cover or less**
Circ: CapCity orders: **1,200**
• digest.
10 ❑ Jun 1988 Cover: 1.50 **NM** value: **Cover or less**
Circ: CapCity orders: **950**
• digest.
11 ❑ Aug 1988 Cover: 1.50 **NM** value: **Cover or less**
• digest.
12 ❑ Oct 1988 Cover: 1.50 **NM** value: **Cover or less**
• digest.
13 ❑ Dec 1988 Cover: 1.50 **NM** value: **Cover or less**
Circ: CapCity orders: **600**
• digest.

G.I. JOE EUROPEAN MISSIONS — Marvel

G.I. Joe European Missions reprints the Action Force comic from the United Kingdom. In the U.S., Action Force is more commonly known as the "Joes" (featured in the American series G.I. Joe, a Real American Hero).

The Action Force is a group of elite strike teams located in London, New York, and various other cities around the world. Each member has a codename and a particular specialty. For instance, Sci-fi is an ace marksman who uses his laser rifle to bulls-eye targets from two miles off; Roadblock is a huge, 50-caliber machine gun-toting powerhouse. The Action Force's mission is to safeguard world peace-and to stop the terrorist Cobra Commander and his minions, the Crimson Guard.

The Transformers, that other great Hasbro toy line-turned-comic-book, are featured in backup stories throughout this series.

1 ❑ Jun 1988 Cover: 1.50 **NM** value: **Cover or less**
Circ: CapCity orders: **17,200**
2 ❑ Jul 1988 Cover: 1.50 **NM** value: **Cover or less**
Circ: CapCity orders: **13,000**
3 ❑ Aug 1988 Cover: 1.50 **NM** value: **Cover or less**
Circ: CapCity orders: **9,800**
4 ❑ Sep 1988 Cover: 1.50 **NM** value: **Cover or less**
Circ: CapCity orders: **8,300**
5 ❑ Oct 1988 Cover: 1.50 **NM** value: **Cover or less**
Circ: CapCity orders: **7,400**
6 ❑ Nov 1988 Cover: 1.50 **NM** value: **Cover or less**
Circ: CapCity orders: **7,100**
7 ❑ Dec 1988 Cover: 1.50 **NM** value: **Cover or less**
Circ: CapCity orders: **6,300**
8 ❑ Jan 1989 Cover: 1.50 **NM** value: **Cover or less**
Circ: CapCity orders: **5,950**
9 ❑ Feb 1989 Cover: 1.50 **NM** value: **Cover or less**
Circ: CapCity orders: **5,650**
10 ❑ Mar 1989 Cover: 1.50 **NM** value: **Cover or less**
Circ: CapCity orders: **5,550**
11 ❑ Apr 1989 Cover: 1.50 **NM** value: **Cover or less**
Circ: CapCity orders: **5,700**
12 ❑ May 1989 Cover: 1.75 **NM** value: **Cover or less**
Circ: CapCity orders: **5,400**
13 ❑ Jun 1989 Cover: 1.75 **NM** value: **Cover or less**
Circ: CapCity orders: **5,200**
14 ❑ Jul 1989 Cover: 1.75 **NM** value: **Cover or less**
Circ: CapCity orders: **5,100**
15 ❑ Aug 1989 Cover: 1.75 **NM** value: **Cover or less**
Circ: CapCity orders: **4,850**

G.I. JOE IN 3-D — Blackthorne

1 ❑ Jul 1987 Cover: 2.50 **NM** value: **Cover or less**
Circ: CapCity orders: **13,400**
📖 of Birds and Men **A:** E.R. Cruz **W:** John Stephenson
2 ❑ Oct 1987 Cover: 2.50 **NM** value: **Cover or less**
Circ: CapCity orders: **8,225**
3 ❑ Jan 1988 Cover: 2.50 **NM** value: **Cover or less**
Circ: CapCity orders: **5,475**
📖 The Quiet War **A:** E.R. Cruz **W:** John Stephenson
4 ❑ Apr 1988 Cover: 2.50 **NM** value: **Cover or less**
Circ: CapCity orders: **2,925**
5 ❑ Jul 1988 Cover: 2.50 **NM** value: **Cover or less**
Circ: CapCity orders: **2,250**
6 ❑ Oct 1988 Cover: 2.00 **NM** value: **2.50**
Circ: CapCity orders: **1,025**

G.I. JOE ORDER OF BATTLE — Marvel

1 ❑ Dec 1986 Cover: 1.25 **NM** value: **Cover or less**
• The Official G.I. Joe Handbook **A:** Herb Trimpe **W:** Larry Hama
2 ❑ Jan 1987 Cover: 1.25 **NM** value: **Cover or less**
• Rocky Balboa
3 ❑ Feb 1987 Cover: 1.25 **NM** value: **Cover or less**
4 ❑ Mar 1987 Cover: 1.25 **NM** value: **Cover or less**
Circ: CapCity orders: **30,000**

Do you have changes or corrections for the **Standard Catalog**? Send your original research to us at
allcomics@krause.com

G.I. JOE, A REAL AMERICAN HERO — Marvel

Marvel had done comic books about toys before, but this was the first to show what real, active support by a toy company could mean.

Hasbro relaunched G.I. Joe for the Reagan era, casting G.I. Joe as a team of special military operatives with such code names as Hawk, Snake-Eyes, and Scarlett. The "Joes" took on a colorful villain in Cobra, sort of an action-figure equivalent of Marvel's Hydra. The Marvel series gave personalities to these characters.

Not many remember that Marvel's G.I. Joe was not initially popular. A gag in a fanzine at the time depicts a comics shop with the plaintive poster, "Buy G.I. Joe... please?" All that changed when Hasbro, unable to use animation in its action figure ads due to U.S. advertising regulations, did an end run by airing $3 million in animated ads for Marvel's comic books. These, and the syndicated cartoon series that followed, turned the Joes into a back-issue hit for a time, with the low-distribution #2 becoming the Holy Grail.

The fever cooled after the series left the air, and the Joes faded away quietly. But as Generation X-ers got nostalgic, back-issue sales picked up dramatically — and Image found a hit in a relaunched G.I. Joe in late 2001. — JJM

1 ❑ Jun 1982 Cover: 1.50 **NM** value: **3.00**
• **CGC:** 84 graded, best 9.8
• Giant-size. 📖 Operation: Lady Doomsday **A:** Herb Trimpe **W:** Larry Hama
2 ❑ Aug 1982 Cover: 0.60 **NM** value: **2.50**
• **CGC:** 14 graded, best 9.8
2-2 ❑ Aug 1982 Cover: 0.75 **NM** value: **1.00**
3 ❑ Sep 1982 Cover: 0.60 **NM** value: **2.00**
• **CGC:** 10 graded, best 9.6
3-2 ❑ Sep 1982 Cover: 0.75 **NM** value: **1.00**
4 ❑ Oct 1982 Cover: 0.60 **NM** value: **2.00**
• **CGC:** 4 graded, best 9.6
4-2 ❑ Oct 1982 Cover: 0.75 **NM** value: **1.00**
5 ❑ Nov 1982 Cover: 0.60 **NM** value: **2.00**
• **CGC:** 7 graded, best 9.8
5-2 ❑ Nov 1982 Cover: 0.75 **NM** value: **1.00**
6 ❑ Dec 1982 Cover: 0.60 **NM** value: **2.00**
• **CGC:** 6 graded, best 9.8
6-2 ❑ Dec 1982 Cover: 0.75 **NM** value: **1.00**
7 ❑ Jan 1983 Cover: 0.60 **NM** value: **2.00**
Circ: Statement: **157,920** • **CGC:** 1 graded, best 9.8
7-2 ❑ Jan 1983 Cover: 0.75 **NM** value: **1.00**
8 ❑ Feb 1983 Cover: 0.60 **NM** value: **2.00**
Circ: Statement: **157,920** • **CGC:** 5 graded, best 9.6
8-2 ❑ Feb 1983 Cover: 0.75 **NM** value: **1.00**
9 ❑ Mar 1983 Cover: 0.60 **NM** value: **2.00**
Circ: Statement: **157,920** • **CGC:** 3 graded, best 9.6
9-2 ❑ Mar 1983 Cover: 0.75 **NM** value: **1.00**
10 ❑ Apr 1983 Cover: 0.60 **NM** value: **2.00**
Circ: Statement: **157,920** • **CGC:** 3 graded, best 9.6
10-2❑ Apr 1983 Cover: 0.75 **NM** value: **1.00**
11 ❑ May 1983 Cover: 0.60 **NM** value: **2.00**
Circ: Statement: **157,920** • **CGC:** 6 graded, best 9.8
11-2❑ May 1983 Cover: 0.75 **NM** value: **1.00**
12 ❑ Jun 1983 Cover: 0.60 **NM** value: **2.00**
Circ: Statement: **157,920** • **CGC:** 5 graded, best 9.8
12-2❑ Jun 1983 Cover: 0.75 **NM** value: **1.00**
13 ❑ Jul 1983 Cover: 0.60 **NM** value: **2.00**
Circ: Statement: **157,920** • **CGC:** 5 graded, best 9.8
13-2❑ Jul 1983 Cover: 0.75 **NM** value: **1.00**
14 ❑ Aug 1983 Cover: 0.60 **NM** value: **2.00**
Circ: Statement: **157,920** • **CGC:** 5 graded, best 9.8
14-2❑ Aug 1983 Cover: 0.75 **NM** value: **1.00**
15 ❑ Sep 1983 Cover: 0.60 **NM** value: **2.00**
Circ: Statement: **157,920** • **CGC:** 5 graded, best 9.6
15-2❑ Sep 1983 Cover: 0.75 **NM** value: **1.00**
16 ❑ Oct 1983 Cover: 0.60 **NM** value: **2.00**
Circ: Statement: **157,920** • **CGC:** 3 graded, best 9.8
16-2❑ Oct 1983 Cover: 0.75 **NM** value: **1.00**
17 ❑ Nov 1983 Cover: 0.60 **NM** value: **2.00**
Circ: Statement: **157,920** • **CGC:** 3 graded, best 9.6
17-2❑ Nov 1983 Cover: 0.75 **NM** value: **1.00**
18 ❑ Dec 1983 Cover: 0.60 **NM** value: **2.00**
Circ: Statement: **157,920** • **CGC:** 3 graded, best 9.8
18-2❑ Dec 1983 Cover: 0.75 **NM** value: **1.00**
19 ❑ Jan 1984 Cover: 0.60 **NM** value: **2.00**
Circ: Statement: **183,466** • **CGC:** 4 graded, best 9.8
19-2❑ Jan 1984 Cover: 0.75 **NM** value: **1.00**
20 ❑ Feb 1984 Cover: 0.60 **NM** value: **2.00**
Circ: Statement: **183,466** • **CGC:** 1 graded, best 9.4
20-2❑ Feb 1984 Cover: 0.75 **NM** value: **1.00**
21 ❑ Mar 1984 Cover: 0.60 **NM** value: **2.00**
Circ: Statement: **183,466** • **CGC:** 35 graded, best 9.6
• "silent" issue
21-2❑ Mar 1984 Cover: 0.75 **NM** value: **1.00**
22 ❑ Apr 1984 Cover: 0.60 **NM** value: **2.00**
Circ: Statement: **183,466** • **CGC:** 1 graded, best 9.6
22-2❑ Apr 1984 Cover: 0.75 **NM** value: **1.00**
23 ❑ May 1984 Cover: 0.60 **NM** value: **2.00**
Circ: Statement: **183,466** • **CGC:** 3 graded, best 9.6
23-2❑ May 1984 Cover: 0.75 **NM** value: **1.00**
24 ❑ Jun 1984 Cover: 0.60 **NM** value: **2.00**
Circ: Statement: **183,466**
24-2❑ Jun 1984 Cover: 0.75 **NM** value: **1.00**
25 ❑ Jul 1984 Cover: 0.60 **NM** value: **2.00**
Circ: Statement: **183,466** • **CGC:** 1 graded, best 9.8

CGC-graded: Multiply prices above by **33 for 9.9 M • 16 for 9.8 NM/M • 7 for 9.6 NM+ • 5 for 9.4 NM • 2.5 for 9.2 NM- • 1.5 for 9.0 VF/NM**

25-2 ❑ Jul 1984 Cover: 0.75 **NM** value: **1.00**

26 ❑ Aug 1984 Cover: 0.60 **NM** value: **2.00**
Circ: Statement: **183,466** • **CGC:** 2 graded, best 9.6

26-2 ❑ Aug 1984 Cover: 0.60 **NM** value: **1.00**

27 ❑ Sep 1984 Cover: 0.60 **NM** value: **2.00**
Circ: Statement: **183,466** • **CGC:** 4 graded, best 9.4

27-2 ❑ Sep 1984 Cover: 0.60 **NM** value: **1.00**

28 ❑ Oct 1984 Cover: 0.60 **NM** value: **2.00**
Circ: Statement: **183,466** • **CGC:** 1 graded, best 9.4

28-2 ❑ Oct 1984 Cover: 0.60 **NM** value: **1.00**

29 ❑ Nov 1984 Cover: 0.60 **NM** value: **2.00**
Circ: Statement: **183,466** • **CGC:** 1 graded, best 9.4

29-2 ❑ Nov 1984 Cover: 0.60 **NM** value: **1.00**

30 ❑ Dec 1984 Cover: 0.60 **NM** value: **2.00**
Circ: Statement: **183,466**

30-2 ❑ Dec 1984 Cover: 0.60 **NM** value: **1.00**

31 ❑ Jan 1985 Cover: 0.60 **NM** value: **1.50**
Circ: Statement: **290,080** • **CGC:** 3 graded, best 9.6

31-2 ❑ Jan 1985 Cover: 0.60 **NM** value: **1.00**

32 ❑ Feb 1985 Cover: 0.60 **NM** value: **1.50**
Circ: Statement: **290,080**

32-2 ❑ Feb 1985 Cover: 0.60 **NM** value: **1.00**

33 ❑ Mar 1985 Cover: 0.60 **NM** value: **1.50**
Circ: Statement: **290,080** • **CGC:** 1 graded, best .5

33-2 ❑ Mar 1985 Cover: 0.60 **NM** value: **1.00**

34 ❑ Apr 1985 Cover: 0.75 **NM** value: **1.50**
Circ: Statement: **290,080** • **CGC:** 1 graded, best 9.4

34-2 ❑ Apr 1985 Cover: 0.75 **NM** value: **1.00**

35 ❑ May 1985 Cover: 0.75 **NM** value: **1.50**
Circ: Statement: **290,080** CapCity orders: **18,100**

35-2 ❑ May 1985 Cover: 0.75 **NM** value: **1.00**

36 ❑ Jun 1985 Cover: 0.75 **NM** value: **1.50**
Circ: Statement: **290,080** CapCity orders: **16,100**

36-2 ❑ Jun 1985 Cover: 0.75 **NM** value: **1.00**

37 ❑ Jul 1985 Cover: 0.75 **NM** value: **1.50**
Circ: Statement: **290,080** CapCity orders: **16,000**

38 ❑ Aug 1985 Cover: 0.75 **NM** value: **1.50**
Circ: Statement: **290,080** CapCity orders: **15,000** • **CGC:** 2 graded, best 9.8

39 ❑ Sep 1985 Cover: 0.75 **NM** value: **1.50**
Circ: Statement: **290,080** CapCity orders: **15,200** • **CGC:** 1 graded, best 9.8

40 ❑ Oct 1985 Cover: 0.75 **NM** value: **1.50**
Circ: Statement: **290,080** CapCity orders: **15,000**

41 ❑ Nov 1985 Cover: 0.75 **NM** value: **1.50**
Circ: Statement: **290,080** CapCity orders: **14,700**

42 ❑ Dec 1985 Cover: 0.75 **NM** value: **1.50**
Circ: Statement: **290,080** CapCity orders: **15,300**

43 ❑ Jan 1986 Cover: 0.75 **NM** value: **1.50**
Circ: Statement: **331,475** CapCity orders: **15,700**

44 ❑ Feb 1986 Cover: 0.75 **NM** value: **1.50**
Circ: Statement: **331,475** CapCity orders: **16,500**

45 ❑ Mar 1986 Cover: 0.75 **NM** value: **1.50**
Circ: Statement: **331,475** CapCity orders: **17,000**

46 ❑ Apr 1986 Cover: 0.75 **NM** value: **1.50**
Circ: Statement: **331,475** CapCity orders: **18,400** • **CGC:** 3 graded, best 9.6

47 ❑ May 1986 Cover: 0.75 **NM** value: **1.50**
Circ: Statement: **331,475** CapCity orders: **20,700** • **CGC:** 1 graded, best 9.6

48 ❑ Jun 1986 Cover: 0.75 **NM** value: **1.50**
Circ: Statement: **331,475** CapCity orders: **20,500**

49 ❑ Jul 1986 Cover: 0.75 **NM** value: **1.50**
Circ: Statement: **331,475** CapCity orders: **23,600**

50 ❑ Aug 1986 Cover: 1.25 **NM** value: **1.75**
Circ: Statement: **331,475** CapCity orders: **28,500** • **CGC:** 1 graded, best 9.6
• Double-size. 📖 The Battle Of Springfield **A:** Rod Whigham **W:** Larry Hama

51 ❑ Sep 1986 Cover: 0.75 **NM** value: **1.25**
Circ: Statement: **331,475** CapCity orders: **28,600**

52 ❑ Oct 1986 Cover: 0.75 **NM** value: **1.25**
Circ: Statement: **331,475** CapCity orders: **30,800**

53 ❑ Nov 1986 Cover: 0.75 **NM** value: **1.25**
Circ: Statement: **331,475** CapCity orders: **35,800** • **CGC:** 2 graded, best 9.8

54 ❑ Dec 1986 Cover: 0.75 **NM** value: **1.25**
Circ: Statement: **331,475** CapCity orders: **36,400**

55 ❑ Jan 1987 Cover: 0.75 **NM** value: **1.25**
Circ: CapCity orders: **33,800** • **CGC:** 1 graded, best 9.6

56 ❑ Feb 1987 Cover: 0.75 **NM** value: **1.25**
Circ: CapCity orders: **33,000**

57 ❑ Mar 1987 Cover: 0.75 **NM** value: **1.25**
Circ: CapCity orders: **33,800**
• Has 1986 Statement, filed 10/6/86; avg print run 499,151; avg sales 291,375; avg subs 40,100; avg total paid 331,475; samples 675; office use 12,566; max existent 344,716; 32% of run returned

58 ❑ Apr 1987 Cover: 0.75 **NM** value: **1.25**
Circ: CapCity orders: **35,400**

59 ❑ May 1987 Cover: 1.00 **NM** value: **1.25**
Circ: CapCity orders: **32,000** • **CGC:** 2 graded, best 9.6

60 ❑ Jun 1987 Cover: 1.00 **NM** value: **1.50**
Circ: CapCity orders: **30,800** • **CGC:** 3 graded, best 9.8

61 ❑ Jul 1987 Cover: 1.00 **NM** value: **1.25**
Circ: CapCity orders: **32,300**

62 ❑ Aug 1987 Cover: 1.00 **NM** value: **1.25**
Circ: CapCity orders: **31,600**

63 ❑ Sep 1987 Cover: 1.00 **NM** value: **1.25**
Circ: CapCity orders: **33,800** • **CGC:** 1 graded, best 9.4

64 ❑ Oct 1987 Cover: 1.00 **NM** value: **1.25**
Circ: CapCity orders: **32,900**

65 ❑ Nov 1987 Cover: 1.00 **NM** value: **1.25**
Circ: CapCity orders: **32,400**

66 ❑ Dec 1987 Cover: 1.00 **NM** value: **1.25**
Circ: CapCity orders: **29,700**

67 ❑ Jan 1988 Cover: 1.00 **NM** value: **1.25**
Circ: Statement: **257,100** CapCity orders: **28,000**

68 ❑ Feb 1988 Cover: 1.00 **NM** value: **1.25**
Circ: Statement: **257,100** CapCity orders: **29,800**

69 ❑ Mar 1988 Cover: 1.00 **NM** value: **1.25**
Circ: Statement: **257,100** CapCity orders: **27,200**

70 ❑ Apr 1988 Cover: 1.00 **NM** value: **1.25**
Circ: Statement: **257,100** CapCity orders: **25,700**

71 ❑ May 1988 Cover: 1.00 **NM** value: **1.25**
Circ: Statement: **257,100** CapCity orders: **22,500**

72 ❑ Jun 1988 Cover: 1.00 **NM** value: **1.25**
Circ: Statement: **257,100** CapCity orders: **21,000**

73 ❑ Jul 1988 Cover: 1.00 **NM** value: **1.25**
Circ: Statement: **257,100** CapCity orders: **20,500**

74 ❑ Aug 1988 Cover: 1.00 **NM** value: **1.25**
Circ: Statement: **257,100** CapCity orders: **19,400**

75 ❑ Sep 1988 Cover: 1.00 **NM** value: **1.25**
Circ: Statement: **257,100** CapCity orders: **18,900**

76 ❑ Sep 1988 Cover: 1.00 **NM** value: **1.25**
Circ: Statement: **257,100** CapCity orders: **18,800**

77 ❑ Oct 1988 Cover: 1.00 **NM** value: **1.25**
Circ: Statement: **257,100** CapCity orders: **18,100**

78 ❑ Oct 1988 Cover: 1.00 **NM** value: **1.25**
Circ: Statement: **257,100** CapCity orders: **17,800**

79 ❑ Nov 1988 Cover: 1.00 **NM** value: **1.25**
Circ: Statement: **257,100** CapCity orders: **16,700**

80 ❑ Nov 1988 Cover: 1.00 **NM** value: **1.25**
Circ: Statement: **257,100** CapCity orders: **16,700**

81 ❑ Dec 1988 Cover: 1.00 **NM** value: **Cover or less**
Circ: Statement: **257,100** CapCity orders: **16,400**

82 ❑ Jan 1989 Cover: 1.00 **NM** value: **Cover or less**
Circ: Statement: **152,785** CapCity orders: **15,400**

83 ❑ Feb 1989 Cover: 1.00 **NM** value: **Cover or less**
Circ: Statement: **152,785** CapCity orders: **15,100**

84 ❑ Mar 1989 Cover: 1.00 **NM** value: **Cover or less**
Circ: Statement: **152,785** CapCity orders: **15,100**

85 ❑ Apr 1989 Cover: 1.00 **NM** value: **Cover or less**
Circ: Statement: **152,785** CapCity orders: **15,200**

86 ❑ May 1989 Cover: 1.00 **NM** value: **Cover or less**
Circ: Statement: **152,785** CapCity orders: **14,100**

87 ❑ Jun 1989 Cover: 1.00 **NM** value: **Cover or less**
Circ: Statement: **152,785** CapCity orders: **13,900**

88 ❑ Jul 1989 Cover: 1.00 **NM** value: **Cover or less**
Circ: Statement: **152,785** CapCity orders: **14,200**

89 ❑ Aug 1989 Cover: 1.00 **NM** value: **Cover or less**
Circ: Statement: **152,785** CapCity orders: **14,200**

90 ❑ Sep 1989 Cover: 1.00 **NM** value: **Cover or less**
Circ: Statement: **152,785** CapCity orders: **14,200**

91 ❑ Oct 1989 Cover: 1.00 **NM** value: **Cover or less**
Circ: Statement: **152,785** CapCity orders: **13,600**

92 ❑ Nov 1989 Cover: 1.00 **NM** value: **Cover or less**
Circ: Statement: **152,785** CapCity orders: **13,100**

93 ❑ Nov 1989 Cover: 1.00 **NM** value: **Cover or less**
Circ: Statement: **152,785** CapCity orders: **12,600** • **CGC:** 2 graded, best 9.4

94 ❑ Dec 1989 Cover: 1.00 **NM** value: **Cover or less**
Circ: Statement: **152,785** CapCity orders: **13,700**

95 ❑ Dec 1989 Cover: 1.00 **NM** value: **Cover or less**
Circ: Statement: **152,785** CapCity orders: **13,600**

96 ❑ Jan 1990 Cover: 1.00 **NM** value: **Cover or less**
Circ: Statement: **137,833** CapCity orders: **14,700**

97 ❑ Feb 1990 Cover: 1.00 **NM** value: **Cover or less**
Circ: Statement: **137,833** CapCity orders: **14,200**

98 ❑ Mar 1990 Cover: 1.00 **NM** value: **Cover or less**
Circ: Statement: **137,833** CapCity orders: **15,700**

99 ❑ Apr 1990 Cover: 1.00 **NM** value: **Cover or less**
Circ: Statement: **137,833** CapCity orders: **15,500**

100 ❑ May 1990 Cover: 1.50 **NM** value: **Cover or less**
Circ: Statement: **137,833** CapCity orders: **18,100** • **CGC:** 1 graded, best 9.4
• Giant size.

101 ❑ Jun 1990 Cover: 1.00 **NM** value: **Cover or less**
Circ: Statement: **137,833** CapCity orders: **14,600**

102 ❑ Jul 1990 Cover: 1.00 **NM** value: **Cover or less**
Circ: Statement: **137,833** CapCity orders: **14,000**

103 ❑ Aug 1990 Cover: 1.00 **NM** value: **Cover or less**
Circ: Statement: **137,833** CapCity orders: **13,700**

104 ❑ Sep 1990 Cover: 1.00 **NM** value: **Cover or less**
Circ: Statement: **137,833** CapCity orders: **13,000**

105 ❑ Oct 1990 Cover: 1.00 **NM** value: **Cover or less**
Circ: Statement: **137,833** CapCity orders: **11,900**

106 ❑ Nov 1990 Cover: 1.00 **NM** value: **Cover or less**
Circ: Statement: **137,833** CapCity orders: **11,500**

107 ❑ Dec 1990 Cover: 1.00 **NM** value: **Cover or less**
Circ: Statement: **137,833** CapCity orders: **11,800**

108 ❑ Jan 1991 Cover: 1.00 **NM** value: **Cover or less**
Circ: CapCity orders: **13,200**
• Dossiers begin

109 ❑ Feb 1991 Cover: 1.00 **NM** value: **Cover or less**
Circ: CapCity orders: **13,400**

110 ❑ Mar 1991 Cover: 1.00 **NM** value: **Cover or less**
Circ: CapCity orders: **12,000**

111 ❑ Apr 1991 Cover: 1.00 **NM** value: **Cover or less**
Circ: CapCity orders: **12,500**

112 ❑ May 1991 Cover: 1.00 **NM** value: **Cover or less**
Circ: CapCity orders: **12,500**

113 ❑ Jun 1991 Cover: 1.00 **NM** value: **Cover or less**
Circ: CapCity orders: **12,800**

114 ❑ Jul 1991 Cover: 1.00 **NM** value: **Cover or less**
Circ: CapCity orders: **12,900**

115 ❑ Aug 1991 Cover: 1.00 **NM** value: **Cover or less**
Circ: CapCity orders: **13,300**

116 ❑ Sep 1991 Cover: 1.00 **NM** value: **Cover or less**
Circ: CapCity orders: **13,200**

117 ❑ Oct 1991 Cover: 1.00 **NM** value: **Cover or less**
Circ: CapCity orders: **13,000**

118 ❑ Nov 1991 Cover: 1.00 **NM** value: **Cover or less**
Circ: CapCity orders: **17,200** • **CGC:** 1 graded, best 9.6

119 ❑ Dec 1991 Cover: 1.00 **NM** value: **Cover or less**
Circ: CapCity orders: **13,000**

120 ❑ Jan 1992 Cover: 1.00 **NM** value: **Cover or less**
Circ: CapCity orders: **13,000**

121 ❑ Feb 1992 Cover: 1.25 **NM** value: **Cover or less**
Circ: CapCity orders: **12,200**

122 ❑ Mar 1992 Cover: 1.25 **NM** value: **Cover or less**
Circ: CapCity orders: **11,700**

123 ❑ Apr 1992 Cover: 1.25 **NM** value: **Cover or less**
Circ: CapCity orders: **10,900**

124 ❑ May 1992 Cover: 1.25 **NM** value: **Cover or less**
Circ: CapCity orders: **11,100**

125 ❑ Jun 1992 Cover: 1.25 **NM** value: **Cover or less**
Circ: CapCity orders: **11,400**

126 ❑ Jul 1992 Cover: 1.25 **NM** value: **Cover or less**
Circ: CapCity orders: **11,100**

127 ❑ Sep 1992 Cover: 1.25 **NM** value: **Cover or less**
Circ: CapCity orders: **11,200**

128 ❑ Sep 1992 Cover: 1.25 **NM** value: **Cover or less**
Circ: CapCity orders: **10,200**

129 ❑ Oct 1992 Cover: 1.25 **NM** value: **Cover or less**
Circ: CapCity orders: **10,000**

130 ❑ Nov 1992 Cover: 1.25 **NM** value: **Cover or less**
Circ: CapCity orders: **9,600**

131 ❑ Dec 1992 Cover: 1.25 **NM** value: **Cover or less**
Circ: CapCity orders: **9,500**

132 ❑ Jan 1993 Cover: 1.25 **NM** value: **Cover or less**
Circ: CapCity orders: **8,700**

133 ❑ Feb 1993 Cover: 1.25 **NM** value: **Cover or less**
Circ: CapCity orders: **8,800**

134 ❑ Mar 1993 Cover: 1.25 **NM** value: **Cover or less**
Circ: CapCity orders: **8,600**

135 ❑ Apr 1993 Cover: 1.75 **NM** value: **Cover or less**
Circ: CapCity orders: **17,400**
• Polybagged with trading card; Team members are regrouped into three strike teams

136 ❑ May 1993 Cover: 1.75 **NM** value: **Cover or less**
Circ: CapCity orders: **17,100**
• trading card

137 ❑ Jun 1993 Cover: 1.75 **NM** value: **Cover or less**
Circ: CapCity orders: **16,100**
• trading card

138 ❑ Jul 1993 Cover: 1.75 **NM** value: **Cover or less**
Circ: CapCity orders: **15,500**
• trading card

139 ❑ Aug 1993 Cover: 1.25 **NM** value: **Cover or less**
Circ: CapCity orders: **14,700** • **CGC:** 1 graded, best 9.0
• Transformers

140 ❑ Sep 1993 Cover: 1.25 **NM** value: **Cover or less**
Circ: CapCity orders: **13,100** • **CGC:** 3 graded, best 9.6
• Transformers

141 ❑ Oct 1993 Cover: 1.25 **NM** value: **Cover or less**
Circ: CapCity orders: **12,200**
📖 Sucker Punch **W:** Larry Hama ★ Appearance of Transformers: Generation 2, Megatron, Cobra Commander.

142 ❑ Nov 1993 Cover: 1.25 **NM** value: **Cover or less**
Circ: CapCity orders: **11,750** • **CGC:** 2 graded, best 9.6
• Transformers

143 ❑ Dec 1993 Cover: 1.25 **NM** value: **Cover or less**
Circ: CapCity orders: **10,600**

144 ❑ Jan 1994 Cover: 1.25 **NM** value: **Cover or less**
Circ: CapCity orders: **9,450** • **CGC:** 1 graded, best 9.2

145 ❑ Feb 1994 Cover: 1.25 **NM** value: **Cover or less**
Circ: CapCity orders: **9,750**

146 ❑ Mar 1994 Cover: 1.25 **NM** value: **Cover or less**
Circ: CapCity orders: **8,700**

147 ❑ Apr 1994 Cover: 1.25 **NM** value: **Cover or less**
Circ: CapCity orders: **7,950**

148 ❑ May 1994 Cover: 1.25 **NM** value: **Cover or less**
Circ: CapCity orders: **7,700**

149 ❑ Jun 1994 Cover: 1.25 **NM** value: **Cover or less**
Circ: CapCity orders: **7,500** • **CGC:** 1 graded, best 9.6

150 ❑ Jul 1994 Cover: 2.00 **NM** value: **Cover or less**
Circ: CapCity orders: **9,300** • **CGC:** 1 graded, best 9.0
• Giant-size.

151 ❑ Aug 1994 Cover: 1.25 **NM** value: **Cover or less**
Circ: CapCity orders: **7,050** • **CGC:** 1 graded, best 9.4

152 ❑ Sep 1994 Cover: 1.25 **NM** value: **Cover or less**
Circ: CapCity orders: **6,750** • **CGC:** 4 graded, best 9.4

153 ❑ Oct 1994 Cover: 1.50 **NM** value: **Cover or less**
Circ: CapCity orders: **6,650** • **CGC:** 2 graded, best 9.6

154 ❑ Nov 1994 Cover: 1.50 **NM** value: **Cover or less**
Circ: CapCity orders: **6,450** • **CGC:** 2 graded, best 9.4

155 ❑ Dec 1994 Cover: 1.50 **NM** value: **Cover or less**
Circ: CapCity orders: **7,000** • **CGC:** 21 graded, best 9.6
final issue.

YB 1 ❑ Mar 1985 Cover: 1.50 **NM** value: **2.50**
• **CGC:** 1 graded, best 7.5
• Yearbook (annual) #1.

YB 2 ❑ Mar 1986 Cover: 1.50 **NM** value: **2.00**
Circ: CapCity orders: **2,300** • **CGC:** 2 graded, best 9.6
• Yearbook (annual) #2.

YB 3 ❑ Mar 1987 Cover: 1.50 **NM** value: **2.00**
Circ: CapCity orders: **36,500**
• Yearbook (annual) #3.

YB 4 ❑ Feb 1988 Cover: 1.50 **NM** value: **Cover or less**
• Yearbook (annual) #4.

G.I. JOE SPECIAL MISSIONS — Marvel

1 ❑ Oct 1986 Cover: 0.75 **NM** value: **1.00**
Circ: CapCity orders: **66,100**

2 ❑ Dec 1986 Cover: 0.75 **NM** value: **1.00**
Circ: CapCity orders: **48,500**

3 ❑ Feb 1987 Cover: 0.75 **NM** value: **1.00**
Circ: CapCity orders: **35,800**

4 ❑ Apr 1987 Cover: 0.75 **NM** value: **1.00**
Circ: CapCity orders: **31,300**

5 ❑ Jun 1987 Cover: 1.00 **NM** value: **Cover or less**
Circ: CapCity orders: **25,700**

6 ❑ Aug 1987 Cover: 1.00 **NM** value: **Cover or less**
Circ: CapCity orders: **28,400**

Other grades: Multiply prices above by **1.5 for Mint • 2/3 for Very Fine • 1/3 for Fine • 1/5 for Very Good • 1/8 for Good**

7 ❑ Oct 1987 Cover: 1.00 **NM** value: **Cover or less**
Circ: CapCity orders: **26,200**
8 ❑ Dec 1987 Cover: 1.00 **NM** value: **Cover or less**
Circ: CapCity orders: **23,200**
9 ❑ Feb 1988 Cover: 1.00 **NM** value: **Cover or less**
Circ: Statement: **189,200** CapCity orders: **21,900**
10 ❑ Apr 1988 Cover: 1.00 **NM** value: **Cover or less**
Circ: Statement: **189,200** CapCity orders: **20,000**
11 ❑ Jun 1988 Cover: 1.00 **NM** value: **Cover or less**
Circ: Statement: **189,200** CapCity orders: **16,200**
12 ❑ Aug 1988 Cover: 1.00 **NM** value: **Cover or less**
Circ: Statement: **189,200** CapCity orders: **14,600**
13 ❑ Sep 1988 Cover: 1.00 **NM** value: **Cover or less**
Circ: Statement: **189,200** CapCity orders: **14,200**
14 ❑ Oct 1988 Cover: 1.00 **NM** value: **Cover or less**
Circ: Statement: **189,200** CapCity orders: **14,400**
15 ❑ Nov 1988 Cover: 1.00 **NM** value: **Cover or less**
Circ: Statement: **189,200** CapCity orders: **12,550**
16 ❑ Dec 1988 Cover: 1.00 **NM** value: **Cover or less**
Circ: Statement: **189,200** CapCity orders: **12,000**
17 ❑ Jan 1989 Cover: 1.00 **NM** value: **Cover or less**
Circ: CapCity orders: **11,300**
18 ❑ Feb 1989 Cover: 1.00 **NM** value: **Cover or less**
Circ: CapCity orders: **10,500**
19 ❑ Mar 1989 Cover: 1.00 **NM** value: **Cover or less**
Circ: CapCity orders: **10,600**
20 ❑ Apr 1989 Cover: 1.00 **NM** value: **Cover or less**
Circ: CapCity orders: **10,500**
21 ❑ May 1989 Cover: 1.00 **NM** value: **Cover or less**
Circ: CapCity orders: **9,500**
22 ❑ Jun 1989 Cover: 1.00 **NM** value: **Cover or less**
Circ: CapCity orders: **9,300**
23 ❑ Jul 1989 Cover: 1.00 **NM** value: **Cover or less**
Circ: CapCity orders: **9,500**
24 ❑ Aug 1989 Cover: 1.00 **NM** value: **Cover or less**
Circ: CapCity orders: **9,600**
25 ❑ Sep 1989 Cover: 1.00 **NM** value: **Cover or less**
Circ: CapCity orders: **9,300**
26 ❑ Oct 1989 Cover: 1.00 **NM** value: **Cover or less**
Circ: CapCity orders: **9,000**
27 ❑ Nov 1989 Cover: 1.00 **NM** value: **Cover or less**
Circ: CapCity orders: **8,800**
28 ❑ Nov 1989 Cover: 1.00 **NM** value: **Cover or less**
Circ: CapCity orders: **8,600**
Bk 1 ❑ Feb 1989 Cover: 6.95 **NM** value: **Cover or less**
Circ: CapCity orders: **1,100**

GI JOE (VOL. 1) — Dark Horse

1 ❑ Dec 1995 Cover: 1.95 **NM** value: **2.00**
• **CGC:** 1 graded, best 9.6
📖 From the Ashes, Part 1 **A:** Jerry Bingham; Tatsuya Ishida; Frank Miller(cover) **W:** Mike Richardson; Mike W. Barr ★ 1st Appearance of Tall Sally, Short Fuse.
2 ❑ Jan 1996 Cover: 1.95 **NM** value: **2.00**
3 ❑ Mar 1996 Cover: 1.95 **NM** value: **2.00**
📖 Island Assault **A:** Tatsuya Ishida; Simon Morse(cover) **W:** Mike W. Barr
4 ❑ Apr 1996 Cover: 1.95 **NM** value: **2.00**
📖 All This and World War II; The Last, Wild Heart, Part 1 final issue. **A:** Frank Teran; Joel Napestek **W:** Mike W. Barr; Nathaniel Lachenmeyer

GI JOE (VOL. 2) — Dark Horse

1 ❑ Jun 1996 Cover: 2.50 **NM** value: **Cover or less**
📖 Red Scream, Part 1 **A:** Tatsuya Ishida **W:** Mike W. Barr
2 ❑ Jul 1996 Cover: 2.50 **NM** value: **Cover or less**
📖 Red Scream, Part 2 **W:** Mike W. Barr
3 ❑ Aug 1996 Cover: 2.50 **NM** value: **Cover or less**
4 ❑ Sep 1996 Cover: 2.50 **NM** value: **Cover or less**
Circ: Diamd. preorders: **9,419**
final issue. **W:** Mike W. Barr

G.I. JOE (ZIFF-DAVIS) — Ziff-Davis

Not at all the souped-up, techno-toy series that Marvel would launch decades later, the first G.I. Joe title is a straightforward collection of adventure stories, starring U.S. soldiers.

Many of the stories in G.I. Joe star servicemen living on bases in occupied Japan following World War II. There are many stories involving camp life and the Japanese townsfolk, and not quite so many featuring the out-and-out warfare that characterizes later war comics. There are stories here, for example, with G.I.s breaking up smuggling rings or solving murders.

A backup humor feature, The Yardbirds, is solidly in the Beetle Bailey and Sad Sack vein.

1 ❑ ca. 1950 Cover: 0.10 **NM** value: **90.00**
• #10 from 1950
2 ❑ Apr 1951 Cover: 0.10 **NM** value: **50.00**
• #11 from 1951
3 ❑ Jun 1951 Cover: 0.10 **NM** value: **50.00**
• #12 from 1951
4 ❑ Aug 1951 Cover: 0.10 **NM** value: **50.00**
• #13 from 1951
5 ❑ Oct 1951 Cover: 0.10 **NM** value: **50.00**
• #14 from 1951
6 ❑ Dec 1951 Cover: 0.10 **NM** value: **40.00**
7 ❑ Jan 1952 Cover: 0.10 **NM** value: **40.00**
8 ❑ Feb 1952 Cover: 0.10 **NM** value: **40.00**
9 ❑ Mar 1952 Cover: 0.10 **NM** value: **40.00**
10 ❑ Apr 1952 Cover: 0.10 **NM** value: **40.00**
• First issue of new run

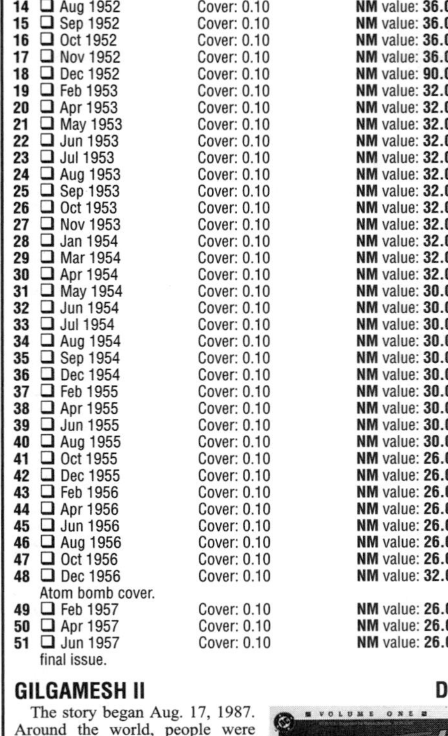

11 ❑ May 1952 Cover: 0.10 **NM** value: **36.00**
12 ❑ Jun 1952 Cover: 0.10 **NM** value: **36.00**
13 ❑ Jul 1952 Cover: 0.10 **NM** value: **36.00**
14 ❑ Aug 1952 Cover: 0.10 **NM** value: **36.00**
15 ❑ Sep 1952 Cover: 0.10 **NM** value: **36.00**
16 ❑ Oct 1952 Cover: 0.10 **NM** value: **36.00**
17 ❑ Nov 1952 Cover: 0.10 **NM** value: **36.00**
18 ❑ Dec 1952 Cover: 0.10 **NM** value: **90.00**
19 ❑ Feb 1953 Cover: 0.10 **NM** value: **32.00**
20 ❑ Apr 1953 Cover: 0.10 **NM** value: **32.00**
21 ❑ May 1953 Cover: 0.10 **NM** value: **32.00**
22 ❑ Jun 1953 Cover: 0.10 **NM** value: **32.00**
23 ❑ Jul 1953 Cover: 0.10 **NM** value: **32.00**
24 ❑ Aug 1953 Cover: 0.10 **NM** value: **32.00**
25 ❑ Sep 1953 Cover: 0.10 **NM** value: **32.00**
26 ❑ Oct 1953 Cover: 0.10 **NM** value: **32.00**
27 ❑ Nov 1953 Cover: 0.10 **NM** value: **32.00**
28 ❑ Jan 1954 Cover: 0.10 **NM** value: **32.00**
29 ❑ Mar 1954 Cover: 0.10 **NM** value: **32.00**
30 ❑ Apr 1954 Cover: 0.10 **NM** value: **32.00**
31 ❑ May 1954 Cover: 0.10 **NM** value: **30.00**
32 ❑ Jun 1954 Cover: 0.10 **NM** value: **30.00**
33 ❑ Jul 1954 Cover: 0.10 **NM** value: **30.00**
34 ❑ Aug 1954 Cover: 0.10 **NM** value: **30.00**
35 ❑ Sep 1954 Cover: 0.10 **NM** value: **30.00**
36 ❑ Dec 1954 Cover: 0.10 **NM** value: **30.00**
37 ❑ Feb 1955 Cover: 0.10 **NM** value: **30.00**
38 ❑ Apr 1955 Cover: 0.10 **NM** value: **30.00**
39 ❑ Jun 1955 Cover: 0.10 **NM** value: **30.00**
40 ❑ Aug 1955 Cover: 0.10 **NM** value: **30.00**
41 ❑ Oct 1955 Cover: 0.10 **NM** value: **26.00**
42 ❑ Dec 1955 Cover: 0.10 **NM** value: **26.00**
43 ❑ Feb 1956 Cover: 0.10 **NM** value: **26.00**
44 ❑ Apr 1956 Cover: 0.10 **NM** value: **26.00**
45 ❑ Jun 1956 Cover: 0.10 **NM** value: **26.00**
46 ❑ Aug 1956 Cover: 0.10 **NM** value: **26.00**
47 ❑ Oct 1956 Cover: 0.10 **NM** value: **26.00**
48 ❑ Dec 1956 Cover: 0.10 **NM** value: **32.00**
Atom bomb cover.
49 ❑ Feb 1957 Cover: 0.10 **NM** value: **26.00**
50 ❑ Apr 1957 Cover: 0.10 **NM** value: **26.00**
51 ❑ Jun 1957 Cover: 0.10 **NM** value: **26.00**
final issue.

GILGAMESH II — DC

The story began Aug. 17, 1987. Around the world, people were gearing up for the Harmonic Convergence, a rare astronomical event that is predicted to bring about cosmic changes on Earth. As things turn out, that's exactly what happens. Circling around its atmosphere is an alien craft carrying the last survivors of a race in search of a new home. Bad luck has brought it, badly damaged, to Earth. Only Earth is already inhabited.

The captain of the ship decides that there is no other choice but to land. The ship is picked up on U.S. radar and immediately shot down. Only the two infants escape, having been placed in escape pods earlier. Landing on Earth, one infant is found by a hippie couple and raised as their son. When Earth falls into cataclysmic wars, the infant, known as Gilgamesh, will become a hero and later become a world leader. Not until much later will the world learn of their leader's brother.

1 ❑ Cover: 3.95 **NM** value: **Cover or less**
Circ: CapCity orders: **21,300**
• prestige format. 📖 A Mad New World **A:** Jim Starlin **W:** Jim Starlin ★ Origin of Gilgamesh.
2 ❑ Cover: 3.95 **NM** value: **Cover or less**
Circ: CapCity orders: **17,450**
• prestige format. **A:** Jim Starlin
3 ❑ Cover: 3.95 **NM** value: **Cover or less**
Circ: CapCity orders: **17,400**
• prestige format. **A:** Jim Starlin
4 ❑ Cover: 3.95 **NM** value: **Cover or less**
Circ: CapCity orders: **18,900**
• prestige format. **A:** Jim Starlin

GIMME — Head Imports

1 ❑ Cover: 0.50 **NM** value: **3.00**
📖 Swine hog; Mr. Pencil; Quozimodo; Special Bonus! A Movie Wheel!! It Really Works; Donkey's Donut; Gag Man; Odds and Adds; The Adventures of Tommy the Carrot and Carl Tomato **A:** Leonard Rifas; Bob Garcia **W:** Leonard Rifas; Charly Price; Nick Ciampi; Phil Collins; Ripp

G.I.M.P.: THE MONKEY BOY AND THE SHORT ORDER DWARF — Wasteland

1 ❑ Cover: 2.95 **NM** value: **Cover or less**
📖 Conunction **A:** Scott Reed **W:** John Early; Matt Early

G.I. MUTANTS — Eternity

1 ❑ ca. 1987 Cover: 1.95 **NM** value: **Cover or less**
📖 Ruin and Robots **A:** Martin Berkenwald **W:** Martin Berkenwald
2 ❑ ca. 1987 Cover: 1.95 **NM** value: **Cover or less**
3 ❑ ca. 1987 Cover: 1.95 **NM** value: **Cover or less**
4 ❑ ca. 1987 Cover: 1.95 **NM** value: **Cover or less**

📖 indicates **Story Title** or **Storyline** information.
★ indicates **Character Appearance** information.
W = Writer • **A = Artist** • **C = Cover Artist**

GINGER — Archie

Ginger is a minor figure in the Archie pantheon of teen-humor characters. Ginger, "America's typical teen-age girl," is an air-headed flirt who is predictably clueless about the effects her girlish charms have on members of the (equally air-headed) opposite sex. Issues feature humor strips starring Ginger and her pals, running from one to eight pages and drawn in the recognizable Archie house style.

Ginger inhabits the insular Archie world of high-school classrooms, soda fountains, and suburban living rooms, the battlegrounds where carefree adolescents square off against witlessly authoritarian (and perpetually frustrated) adults. Wholesome, predictable, and charming, Ginger epitomizes the appeal and limitations of the Archie franchise.

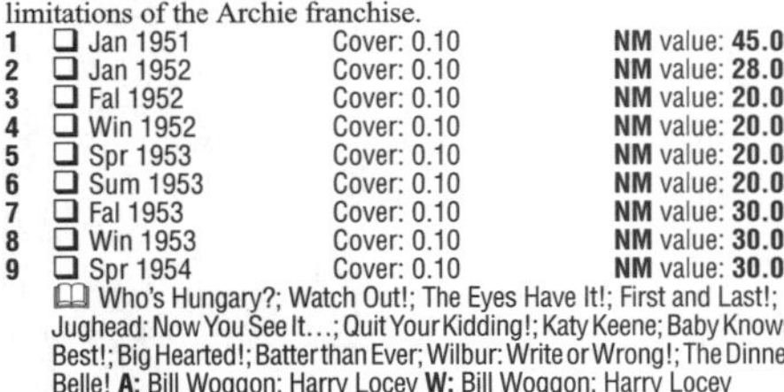

1 ❑ Jan 1951 Cover: 0.10 **NM** value: **45.00**
2 ❑ Jan 1952 Cover: 0.10 **NM** value: **28.00**
3 ❑ Fal 1952 Cover: 0.10 **NM** value: **20.00**
4 ❑ Win 1952 Cover: 0.10 **NM** value: **20.00**
5 ❑ Spr 1953 Cover: 0.10 **NM** value: **20.00**
6 ❑ Sum 1953 Cover: 0.10 **NM** value: **20.00**
7 ❑ Fal 1953 Cover: 0.10 **NM** value: **30.00**
8 ❑ Win 1953 Cover: 0.10 **NM** value: **30.00**
9 ❑ Spr 1954 Cover: 0.10 **NM** value: **30.00**
📖 Who's Hungary?; Watch Out!; The Eyes Have It!; First and Last!; Jughead: Now You See It…; Quit Your Kidding!; Katy Keene; Baby Knows Best!; Big Hearted!; Batter than Ever; Wilbur: Write or Wrong!; The Dinner Belle! **A:** Bill Woggon; Harry Lucey **W:** Bill Woggon; Harry Lucey
10 ❑ Sum 1954 Cover: 0.10 **NM** value: **30.00**

GINGER FOX — Comico

1 ❑ Sep 1988 Cover: 1.75 **NM** value: **Cover or less**
Circ: CapCity orders: **6,075**
• Yellow **A:** Arnold Pander; Jacob Pander **W:** Mike Baron
2 ❑ Oct 1988 Cover: 1.75 **NM** value: **Cover or less**
Circ: CapCity orders: **4,475**
3 ❑ Nov 1988 Cover: 1.75 **NM** value: **Cover or less**
Circ: CapCity orders: **4,200**
4 ❑ Dec 1988 Cover: 1.75 **NM** value: **Cover or less**
Circ: CapCity orders: **4,150**

GIN-RYU — Believe in Yourself

1 ❑ Mar 1995 Cover: 2.75 **NM** value: **Cover or less**
2 ❑ May 1995 Cover: 2.75 **NM** value: **Cover or less**
3 ❑ Cover: 2.75 **NM** value: **Cover or less**
3/Ash ❑ **NM** value: **1.00**

G.I. R.A.M.B.O.T. — Wonder Color

1 ❑ Apr 1987 Cover: 1.95 **NM** value: **Cover or less**
📖 Coming of Age **A:** Tom Lyle **W:** Kevin Juaire

GIRL — DC / Vertigo

1 ❑ Jul 1996 Cover: 2.50 **NM** value: **Cover or less**
📖 Terminal City **A:** Duncan Fegredo **W:** Peter Milligan
2 ❑ Aug 1996 Cover: 2.50 **NM** value: **Cover or less**
3 ❑ Sep 1996 Cover: 2.50 **NM** value: **Cover or less**

GIRL, THE — Rip Off

All issues are adults only.

1 ❑ Feb 1991, b&w Cover: 2.50 **NM** value: **Cover or less**
• **CGC:** 1 graded, best 8.5
1-2 ❑ Oct 1992, b&w Cover: 2.50 **NM** value: **Cover or less**
2 ❑ May 1991, b&w Cover: 2.50 **NM** value: **Cover or less**
3 ❑ Aug 1991, b&w Cover: 2.50 **NM** value: **Cover or less**
4 ❑ Dec 1991, b&w Cover: 2.50 **NM** value: **Cover or less**

GIRL CALLED...WILLOW!, A — Angel

1 ❑ Fal 1996, b&w Cover: 2.95 **NM** value: **Cover or less**

GIRL CALLED...WILLOW! SKETCHBOOK, A — Angel

1 ❑ b&w Cover: 2.95 **NM** value: **Cover or less**
wraparound cover. • pin-ups and rough pencil sketches

GIRL CRAZY — Dark Horse

1 ❑ May 1996, b&w Cover: 2.95 **NM** value: **Cover or less**
📖 What's Knittin' Kitten? **A:** Gilbert Hernandez **W:** Gilbert Hernandez
2 ❑ Jul 1996, b&w Cover: 2.95 **NM** value: **Cover or less**
3 ❑ Jul 1996, b&w Cover: 2.95 **NM** value: **Cover or less**
Bk 1 ❑ Aug 1997, b&w Cover: 9.95 **NM** value: **Cover or less**
• collects mini-series

GIRL FIGHT COMICS — Print Mint

1 ❑ Cover: 0.50 **NM** value: **3.00**
📖 Fox; She; Sacrifice in the Temple; Speed Demon Among the Freudians; Space Dykes **A:** Trina **W:** Trina

GIRL FROM U.N.C.L.E., THE — Gold Key

This spinoff from the popular Man From U.N.C.L.E. spy series featured the characters April Dancer (played by Stefanie Powers) and her swingin' British partner Mark Slate (played by Noel Harrison). It ran only one season, in which the pair of secret agents used their wits—and a huge assortment of exotic gadgets—to battle the evil plans of T.H.R.U.S.H., the Technological Hierarchy for the Removal of Undesirables and the Subjugation of Humanity. This short-lived series did a fine job of adapting the series and featured photo covers with the Powers and Harrison.

CGC-graded: Multiply prices above by **33 for 9.9 M** • **16 for 9.8 NM/M** • **7 for 9.6 NM+** • **5 for 9.4 NM** • **2.5 for 9.2 NM-** • **1.5 for 9.0 VF/NM**

1 ❑ Jan 1967 Cover: 0.12 **NM** value: **35.00**
• **CGC:** 2 graded, best 9.4
pin-up on back cover. 📖 The Fatal Accidents Affair • 10197-701
2 ❑ Apr 1967 Cover: 0.12 **NM** value: **22.00**
• **CGC:** 1 graded, best 9.4
Photo cover.
3 ❑ Jun 1967 Cover: 0.12 **NM** value: **18.00**
• **CGC:** 1 graded, best 9.4
Photo cover.
4 ❑ Aug 1967 Cover: 0.12 **NM** value: **14.00**
• **CGC:** 1 graded, best 9.2
Photo cover.
5 ❑ Oct 1967 Cover: 0.12 **NM** value: **14.00**
• **CGC:** 2 graded, best 9.4
Photo cover. 📖 The Harem-Scarem Affair; Leopold Swift-Courier: Bubble Trouble final issue.

GIRL GENIUS — Studio Foglio

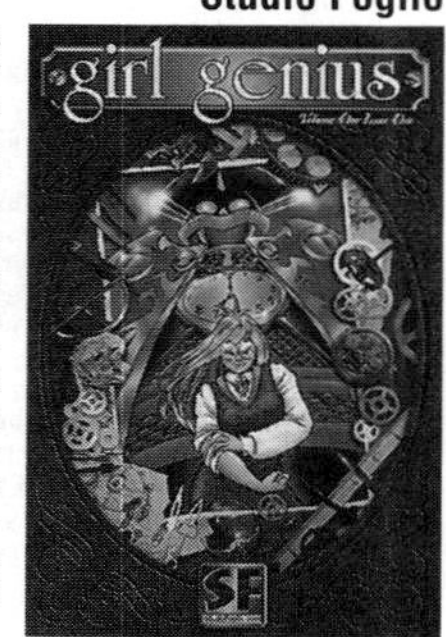

Written by Phil and Kaja Foglio and drawn by Phil (Funny Stuff Stocking Stuffer), Girl Genius is the story of Agatha Clay, a bespectacled student and lab assistant at Transylvania Polygnostic University in a world where the Industrial Revolution went out of control and left the world at the mercy of Mad Science. Agatha bumbles and fumbles, but her saga is just beginning, as this black-and-white series from StudioFoglio gets under way. She is destined for greatness in a universe rife with pneumatic robots, bizarre dirigibles, and scientists committed to discovery.

1 ❑ Feb 2001, b&w Cover: 2.95 **NM** value: **Cover or less**
Circ: Diamd. preorders: **5,525**
cardstock cover. **A:** Phil Foglio **W:** Phil Foglio; Kaja Foglio
Ash 1❑Oct 2000, b&w **NM** value: **1.00**
no cover price. • preview of upcoming series; smaller than normal comic book

GIRLHERO — High Drive

1 ❑ Aug 1993, b&w Cover: 3.00 **NM** value: **Cover or less**
2 ❑ Feb 1994, b&w Cover: 2.95 **NM** value: **3.00**
3 ❑ Jul 1994, b&w Cover: 2.95 **NM** value: **3.00**

GIRL ON GIRL COLLEGE KINK: NEW YEAR'S BABES — Angel

1 ❑ Cover: 3.00 **NM** value: **Cover or less**
📖 New Year's Babes **A:** Mark Kuettner

GIRL ON GIRL: FEEDIN' TIME — Angel

1 ❑ Cover: 3.00 **NM** value: **Cover or less**

GIRL ON GIRL: TICKLISH — Angel

1 ❑ Cover: 3.00 **NM** value: **Cover or less**
📖 Tickle Football **A:** C. Fouts **W:** Esperanza

GIRLS' LOVE STORIES — DC

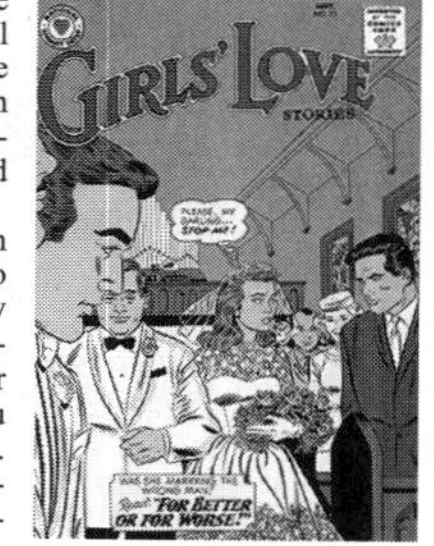

Like most other publishers in the late 1940s, National Periodical Publications (later DC) tested the burgeoning romance genre with several titles, including the similarly named Girls' Love Stories and Girls' Romances.

Girls' Love Stories began first in mid-1949 with a series of photo covers, usually featuring a happy couple engaged in a romantic activity, such as a visit to the beach or holding hands or the athletic beau showing his girl how to shoot a bow. The series eventually ran 180 issues, even more than Girls' Romances, which began in early 1950.
— Brent

1 ❑ Aug 1949 Cover: 0.10 **NM** value: **300.00**
2 ❑ Oct 1949 Cover: 0.10 **NM** value: **150.00**
3 ❑ Jul 1950 Cover: 0.10 **NM** value: **120.00**
4 ❑ Mar 1950 Cover: 0.10 **NM** value: **100.00**
5 ❑ May 1950 Cover: 0.10 **NM** value: **100.00**
6 ❑ Jul 1950 Cover: 0.10 **NM** value: **100.00**
7 ❑ Sep 1950 Cover: 0.10 **NM** value: **100.00**
8 ❑ Nov 1950 Cover: 0.10 **NM** value: **100.00**
9 ❑ Jan 1951 Cover: 0.10 **NM** value: **100.00**
10 ❑ Mar 1951 Cover: 0.10 **NM** value: **100.00**
11 ❑ May 1951 Cover: 0.10 **NM** value: **100.00**
12 ❑ Jul 1951 Cover: 0.10 **NM** value: **70.00**
13 ❑ Sep 1951 Cover: 0.10 **NM** value: **70.00**
14 ❑ Nov 1951 Cover: 0.10 **NM** value: **70.00**
15 ❑ Jan 1952 Cover: 0.10 **NM** value: **70.00**
16 ❑ Mar 1952 Cover: 0.10 **NM** value: **70.00**
17 ❑ May 1952 Cover: 0.10 **NM** value: **70.00**
18 ❑ Jul 1952 Cover: 0.10 **NM** value: **70.00**
19 ❑ Sep 1952 Cover: 0.10 **NM** value: **70.00**
• **CGC:** 1 graded, best 8.0
20 ❑ Nov 1952 Cover: 0.10 **NM** value: **70.00**
21 ❑ Jan 1953 Cover: 0.10 **NM** value: **70.00**
22 ❑ Mar 1953 Cover: 0.10 **NM** value: **70.00**
23 ❑ May 1953 Cover: 0.10 **NM** value: **45.00**
24 ❑ Jul 1953 Cover: 0.10 **NM** value: **45.00**
25 ❑ Sep 1953 Cover: 0.10 **NM** value: **45.00**
26 ❑ Nov 1953 Cover: 0.10 **NM** value: **45.00**
27 ❑ Jan 1954 Cover: 0.10 **NM** value: **45.00**
28 ❑ Mar 1954 Cover: 0.10 **NM** value: **45.00**
29 ❑ May 1954 Cover: 0.10 **NM** value: **45.00**
30 ❑ Jul 1954 Cover: 0.10 **NM** value: **45.00**
31 ❑ Sep 1954 Cover: 0.10 **NM** value: **45.00**
32 ❑ Nov 1954 Cover: 0.10 **NM** value: **45.00**
33 ❑ Jan 1955 Cover: 0.10 **NM** value: **36.00**
34 ❑ Mar 1955 Cover: 0.10 **NM** value: **36.00**
35 ❑ May 1955 Cover: 0.10 **NM** value: **36.00**
36 ❑ Jul 1955 Cover: 0.10 **NM** value: **36.00**
37 ❑ Sep 1955 Cover: 0.10 **NM** value: **36.00**
38 ❑ Nov 1955 Cover: 0.10 **NM** value: **36.00**
39 ❑ Jan 1956 Cover: 0.10 **NM** value: **36.00**
40 ❑ Mar 1956 Cover: 0.10 **NM** value: **36.00**
41 ❑ May 1956 Cover: 0.10 **NM** value: **36.00**
42 ❑ Jul 1956 Cover: 0.10 **NM** value: **36.00**
43 ❑ Sep 1956 Cover: 0.10 **NM** value: **36.00**
44 ❑ Nov 1956 Cover: 0.10 **NM** value: **36.00**
45 ❑ Jan 1957 Cover: 0.10 **NM** value: **36.00**
46 ❑ Mar 1957 Cover: 0.10 **NM** value: **36.00**
47 ❑ May 1957 Cover: 0.10 **NM** value: **36.00**
48 ❑ Jul 1957 Cover: 0.10 **NM** value: **36.00**
49 ❑ Sep 1957 Cover: 0.10 **NM** value: **36.00**
50 ❑ Nov 1957 Cover: 0.10 **NM** value: **28.00**
51 ❑ Dec 1957 Cover: 0.10 **NM** value: **28.00**
52 ❑ Feb 1958 Cover: 0.10 **NM** value: **28.00**
53 ❑ Mar 1958 Cover: 0.10 **NM** value: **28.00**
54 ❑ May 1958 Cover: 0.10 **NM** value: **28.00**
55 ❑ Jun 1958 Cover: 0.10 **NM** value: **28.00**
56 ❑ Aug 1958 Cover: 0.10 **NM** value: **28.00**
57 ❑ Sep 1958 Cover: 0.10 **NM** value: **28.00**
58 ❑ Nov 1958 Cover: 0.10 **NM** value: **28.00**
59 ❑ Dec 1958 Cover: 0.10 **NM** value: **28.00**
60 ❑ Feb 1959 Cover: 0.10 **NM** value: **28.00**
61 ❑ Mar 1959 Cover: 0.10 **NM** value: **28.00**
62 ❑ May 1959 Cover: 0.10 **NM** value: **28.00**
63 ❑ Jun 1959 Cover: 0.10 **NM** value: **28.00**
64 ❑ Aug 1959 Cover: 0.10 **NM** value: **28.00**
65 ❑ Sep 1959 Cover: 0.10 **NM** value: **28.00**
66 ❑ Nov 1959 Cover: 0.10 **NM** value: **28.00**
67 ❑ Dec 1959 Cover: 0.10 **NM** value: **28.00**
68 ❑ Feb 1960 Cover: 0.10 **NM** value: **28.00**
69 ❑ Mar 1960 Cover: 0.10 **NM** value: **28.00**
70 ❑ May 1960 Cover: 0.10 **NM** value: **28.00**
71 ❑ Jun 1960 Cover: 0.10 **NM** value: **28.00**
72 ❑ Aug 1960 Cover: 0.10 **NM** value: **24.00**
• **CGC:** 1 graded, best 7.5
73 ❑ Sep 1960 Cover: 0.10 **NM** value: **24.00**
74 ❑ Oct 1960 Cover: 0.10 **NM** value: **24.00**
75 ❑ Nov 1960 Cover: 0.10 **NM** value: **24.00**
76 ❑ Feb 1961 Cover: 0.10 **NM** value: **24.00**
77 ❑ Mar 1961 Cover: 0.10 **NM** value: **24.00**
78 ❑ May 1961 Cover: 0.10 **NM** value: **24.00**
79 ❑ Jun 1961 Cover: 0.10 **NM** value: **24.00**
80 ❑ Jul 1961 Cover: 0.10 **NM** value: **24.00**
81 ❑ Sep 1961 Cover: 0.10 **NM** value: **24.00**
82 ❑ Oct 1961 Cover: 0.10 **NM** value: **24.00**
83 ❑ Nov 1961 Cover: 0.10 **NM** value: **24.00**
84 ❑ Jan 1962 Cover: 0.12 **NM** value: **24.00**
85 ❑ Feb 1962 Cover: 0.12 **NM** value: **24.00**
86 ❑ Apr 1962 Cover: 0.12 **NM** value: **24.00**
87 ❑ May 1962 Cover: 0.12 **NM** value: **24.00**
88 ❑ Jul 1962 Cover: 0.12 **NM** value: **24.00**
89 ❑ Sep 1962 Cover: 0.12 **NM** value: **24.00**
90 ❑ Oct 1962 Cover: 0.12 **NM** value: **24.00**
91 ❑ Nov 1962 Cover: 0.12 **NM** value: **24.00**
92 ❑ Jan 1963 Cover: 0.12 **NM** value: **24.00**
93 ❑ Feb 1963 Cover: 0.12 **NM** value: **24.00**
94 ❑ Apr 1963 Cover: 0.12 **NM** value: **24.00**
95 ❑ May 1963 Cover: 0.12 **NM** value: **18.00**
96 ❑ Jul 1963 Cover: 0.12 **NM** value: **18.00**
97 ❑ Sep 1963 Cover: 0.12 **NM** value: **18.00**
98 ❑ Oct 1963 Cover: 0.12 **NM** value: **18.00**
99 ❑ Nov 1963 Cover: 0.12 **NM** value: **18.00**
100 ❑ Jan 1964 Cover: 0.12 **NM** value: **18.00**
101 ❑ Feb 1964 Cover: 0.12 **NM** value: **18.00**
102 ❑ Apr 1964 Cover: 0.12 **NM** value: **18.00**
103 ❑ May 1964 Cover: 0.12 **NM** value: **18.00**
104 ❑ Jul 1964 Cover: 0.12 **NM** value: **18.00**
105 ❑ Sep 1964 Cover: 0.12 **NM** value: **18.00**
106 ❑ Oct 1964 Cover: 0.12 **NM** value: **16.00**
107 ❑ Nov 1964 Cover: 0.12 **NM** value: **16.00**
108 ❑ Jan 1965 Cover: 0.12 **NM** value: **16.00**
109 ❑ Feb 1965 Cover: 0.12 **NM** value: **16.00**
110 ❑ Apr 1965 Cover: 0.12 **NM** value: **16.00**
111 ❑ May 1965 Cover: 0.12 **NM** value: **16.00**
112 ❑ Jul 1965 Cover: 0.12 **NM** value: **14.00**
113 ❑ Sep 1965 Cover: 0.12 **NM** value: **14.00**
114 ❑ Oct 1965 Cover: 0.12 **NM** value: **14.00**
115 ❑ Nov 1965 Cover: 0.12 **NM** value: **14.00**
116 ❑ Jan 1966 Cover: 0.12 **NM** value: **14.00**
117 ❑ Feb 1966 Cover: 0.12 **NM** value: **14.00**
118 ❑ Apr 1966 Cover: 0.12 **NM** value: **14.00**
119 ❑ May 1966 Cover: 0.12 **NM** value: **14.00**
120 ❑ Jul 1966 Cover: 0.12 **NM** value: **14.00**
121 ❑ Sep 1966 Cover: 0.12 **NM** value: **14.00**
122 ❑ Oct 1966 Cover: 0.12 **NM** value: **14.00**
123 ❑ Nov 1966 Cover: 0.12 **NM** value: **14.00**
124 ❑ Jan 1967 Cover: 0.12 **NM** value: **12.00**
Circ: Statement: **178,300**
125 ❑ Feb 1967 Cover: 0.12 **NM** value: **12.00**
Circ: Statement: **178,300**
126 ❑ Apr 1967 Cover: 0.12 **NM** value: **12.00**
Circ: Statement: **178,300**
127 ❑ May 1967 Cover: 0.12 **NM** value: **12.00**
Circ: Statement: **178,300**
128 ❑ Jul 1967 Cover: 0.12 **NM** value: **12.00**
Circ: Statement: **178,300**
129 ❑ Sep 1967 Cover: 0.12 **NM** value: **12.00**
Circ: Statement: **178,300**
130 ❑ Oct 1967 Cover: 0.12 **NM** value: **12.00**
Circ: Statement: **178,300**
131 ❑ Nov 1967 Cover: 0.12 **NM** value: **12.00**
Circ: Statement: **178,300**
132 ❑ Jan 1968 Cover: 0.12 **NM** value: **12.00**
133 ❑ Feb 1968 Cover: 0.12 **NM** value: **12.00**
134 ❑ Apr 1968 Cover: 0.12 **NM** value: **12.00**
135 ❑ May 1968 Cover: 0.12 **NM** value: **12.00**
136 ❑ Jul 1968 Cover: 0.12 **NM** value: **12.00**
137 ❑ Sep 1968 Cover: 0.12 **NM** value: **12.00**
138 ❑ Oct 1968 Cover: 0.12 **NM** value: **12.00**
139 ❑ Nov 1968 Cover: 0.12 **NM** value: **12.00**
140 ❑ Jan 1969 Cover: 0.12 **NM** value: **12.00**
141 ❑ Feb 1969 Cover: 0.12 **NM** value: **12.00**
142 ❑ Apr 1969 Cover: 0.12 **NM** value: **12.00**
143 ❑ May 1969 Cover: 0.12 **NM** value: **12.00**
144 ❑ Jul 1969 Cover: 0.15 **NM** value: **8.00**
145 ❑ Sep 1969 Cover: 0.15 **NM** value: **8.00**
146 ❑ Oct 1969 Cover: 0.15 **NM** value: **8.00**
147 ❑ Nov 1969 Cover: 0.15 **NM** value: **8.00**
148 ❑ Jan 1970 Cover: 0.15 **NM** value: **8.00**
149 ❑ Feb 1970 Cover: 0.15 **NM** value: **8.00**
150 ❑ Apr 1970 Cover: 0.15 **NM** value: **8.00**
151 ❑ May 1970 Cover: 0.15 **NM** value: **8.00**
152 ❑ Jul 1970 Cover: 0.15 **NM** value: **8.00**
153 ❑ Sep 1970 Cover: 0.15 **NM** value: **8.00**
154 ❑ Oct 1970 Cover: 0.15 **NM** value: **8.00**
155 ❑ Nov 1970 Cover: 0.15 **NM** value: **8.00**
156 ❑ Jan 1971 Cover: 0.15 **NM** value: **8.00**
157 ❑ May 1971 Cover: 0.15 **NM** value: **8.00**
158 ❑ Jun 1971 Cover: 0.15 **NM** value: **8.00**
159 ❑ Jul 1971 Cover: 0.15 **NM** value: **8.00**
160 ❑ Aug 1971 Cover: 0.25 **NM** value: **8.00**
161 ❑ Sep 1971 Cover: 0.25 **NM** value: **8.00**
• **CGC:** 1 graded, best 9.0
162 ❑ Oct 1971 Cover: 0.25 **NM** value: **8.00**
163 ❑ Nov 1971 Cover: 0.25 **NM** value: **8.00**
164 ❑ Dec 1971 Cover: 0.25 **NM** value: **8.00**
165 ❑ Jan 1972 Cover: 0.25 **NM** value: **6.00**
Circ: Statement: **122,983**
166 ❑ Feb 1972 Cover: 0.25 **NM** value: **6.00**
Circ: Statement: **122,983**
167 ❑ Mar 1972 Cover: 0.25 **NM** value: **6.00**
Circ: Statement: **122,983**
168 ❑ Apr 1972 Cover: 0.25 **NM** value: **6.00**
Circ: Statement: **122,983** • **CGC:** 1 graded, best 7.5
169 ❑ May 1972 Cover: 0.25 **NM** value: **6.00**
Circ: Statement: **122,983**
170 ❑ Jun 1972 Cover: 0.25 **NM** value: **6.00**
Circ: Statement: **122,983**
171 ❑ Jul 1972 Cover: 0.20 **NM** value: **6.00**
Circ: Statement: **122,983**
172 ❑ Aug 1972 Cover: 0.20 **NM** value: **6.00**
Circ: Statement: **122,983**
173 ❑ Sep 1972 Cover: 0.20 **NM** value: **6.00**
Circ: Statement: **122,983**
174 ❑ Oct 1972 Cover: 0.20 **NM** value: **6.00**
Circ: Statement: **122,983**
175 ❑ Dec 1972 Cover: 0.20 **NM** value: **6.00**
Circ: Statement: **122,983**
176 ❑ Feb 1973 Cover: 0.20 **NM** value: **6.00**
177 ❑ May 1973 Cover: 0.20 **NM** value: **6.00**
• Has 1972 Statement; avg total paid circ 122,983
178 ❑ Aug 1973 Cover: 0.20 **NM** value: **6.00**
179 ❑ Oct 1973 Cover: 0.20 **NM** value: **6.00**
180 ❑ Dec 1973 Cover: 0.20 **NM** value: **6.00**

GIRLS OF '95: GOOD, BAD & DEADLY — Lost Cause

1 ❑ Feb 1996 Cover: 3.95 **NM** value: **Cover or less**
📖 Bad to the Bone!; **A:** Sky Owens **W:** Brian J.L. Glass

GIRLS OF NINJA HIGH SCHOOL — Antarctic

Everyone has fond memories of high school, right? The cliques of "cool" kids who never let you forget you weren't part of the gang, the bitter rivalries over boyfriends that could split up even the best of friends, the peer pressure that could turn even the calmest kid into a fight waiting to happen: Oh, yeah, those were the days.

Could it possibly get any worse? Well, when the student body comprises novice ninjas, neophyte sorceresses, and other characters befitting a manga-style Advanced Dungeons & Dragons, the daily routine seldom includes home room and pep rallies. These short, funny adventure stories are loosely linked to a central group of characters, who are just trying to grow up as normal in the completely whacked world of Ninja High School. Some issues are published with alternate covers satirizing popular comics and television shows, such as the Comedy Channel's South Park.

1 ❑ b&w Cover: 3.75 **NM** value: **Cover or less**
2 ❑ b&w Cover: 3.75 **NM** value: **Cover or less**
3 ❑ b&w Cover: 3.95 **NM** value: **Cover or less**
4 ❑ Apr 1994, b&w Cover: 3.95 **NM** value: **Cover or less**
• 1994 Annual
5 ❑ Apr 1995 Cover: 4.50 **NM** value: **Cover or less**

Other grades: Multiply prices above by **1.5 for Mint • 2/3 for Very Fine • 1/3 for Fine • 1/5 for Very Good • 1/8 for Good**

📖 The Test of Endurance; The N Files; Nightmare; Basket Bout; Happy Birthday, Sammi; Family Ties; Broops and Breeps; Ninja Highlander; Selina-nomaly; Quagmire Carwash; For Sister's Sake • 1995 Annual **A:** Matt Lunsford; Robert DeJesus; Tyrone Ford; David Matsuoka; Jim Eldridge; John Riley; Kenichi Lowe; Serapio Calm II; Steve Moore; Doug Gracey; Karen O'Donnell; Marian O'Donnell; Mike Smith **W:** Matt Lunsford; Robert DeJesus; Tyrone Ford; David Matsuoka; Jim Eldridge; John Riley; Kenichi Lowe; Serapio Calm II; Steve Moore; Doug Gracey; Karen O'Donnell; Marian O'Donnell; Mike Smith

6 ❑ Cover: 3.95 **NM** value: **Cover or less**
📖 Welcome Home • 1996 Annual **A:** David Hahn; Tyrone Ford; Michele Light; Danny Fahs; Leopoldo Pena; Steve Moore; Tim Ely; Terry Karvonen; Bill Grapes; David R. Son; Franco; Joel Prather; Mike Smith; Sean Macklin; Steven Gonzales; Thom Marrion **W:** David Hahn; Tyrone Ford; Michele Light; Danny Fahs; Leopoldo Pena; Steve Moore; Tim Ely; Terry Karvonen; Bill Grapes; David R. Son; Franco; Joel Prather; Mike Smith; Sean Macklin; Steven Gonzales; Thom Marrion

7 ❑ May 1997 Cover: 3.95 **NM** value: **Cover or less**
• 1997 Annual

8/A ❑ May 1998 Cover: 2.95 **NM** value: **3.95**
📖 Flights of Fantasy; Sprockets and Rockets; Ghost Writer; Price$; It's Fast or It's Free; Anna Ambush; Zetrapersons; The Oracle • 1998 Annual **A:** Rod Espinosa; Cody Pickrodt; Evan Hayden; James Schaad; Jim Eldridge; Pat Rea; Phuong-Mai Bui-Quang; San Gonzaga; Serapio Calm II **W:** Rod Espinosa; Cody Pickrodt; Evan Hayden; James Schaad; Pat Rea; Phuong-Mai Bui-Quang; San Gonzaga; Serapio Calm II

8/B ❑ May 1998 Cover: 2.95 **NM** value: **3.95**
alternate cover (manga-style). 📖 Ninja Tricks 3-1/2; Treasure Hunt; PenguinBall GT; Soft-Core Not Ninja High School • 1998 Annual **A:** Abraham Sterber; Amanjoku; Jimbo; John Prather; Lou; Thor Thorvaldson; Brain Fingers **W:** Abraham Sterber; Amanjoku; Jimbo; John Prather; Thor Thorvaldson; Brian Fingers

9 ❑ Apr 1999 Cover: 2.99 **NM** value: **Cover or less**
back cover pin-up. 📖 Women of Ninja High School Unite!, Derek Cheung, Kyle A. Carrozza • Nylon Menaces: Dandelion; Minerva: Blind Spot **A:** PmBQ **W:** PmBQ; Cody Pickrodt; Kyle A. Carrozza

GIRL SQUAD X — Fantaco

1 ❑ b&w Cover: 2.95 **NM** value: **Cover or less**

GIRLS' ROMANCES — DC

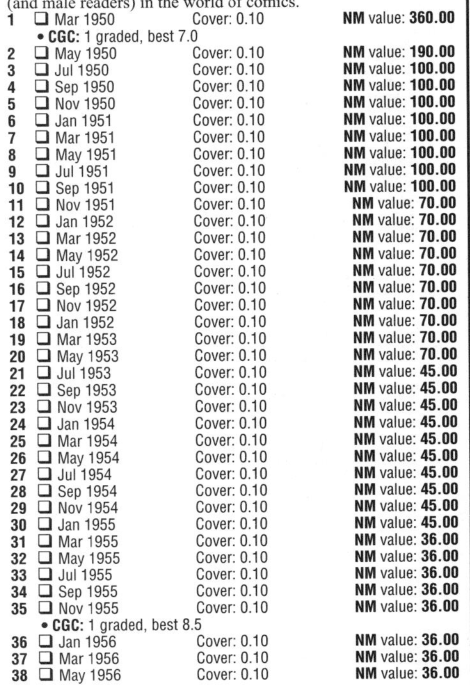

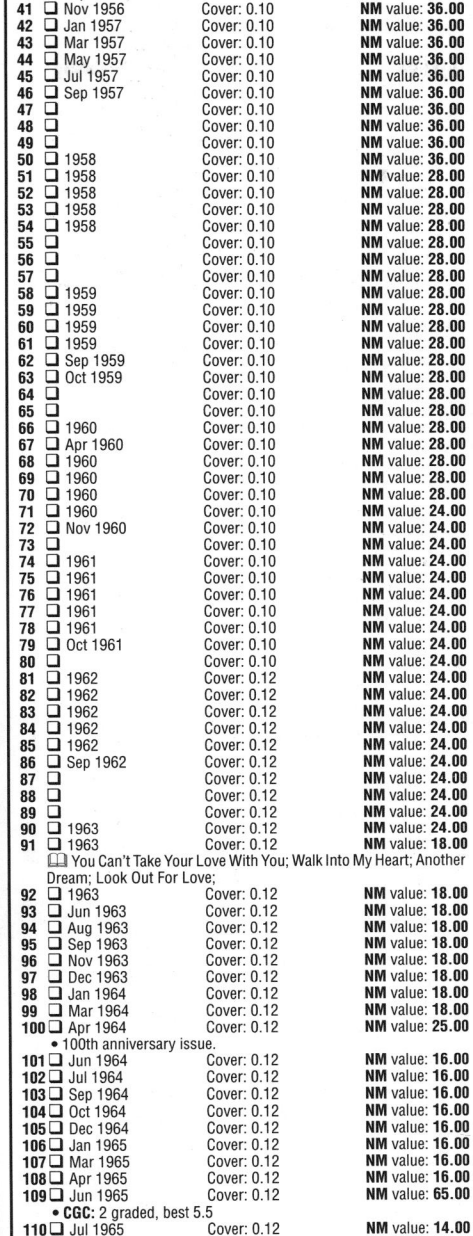

Girls' Romances was one of the many romance comics that sprang up in the 1950s and '60s. At that time, comics still attracted a fairly wide female readership, something the super-hero comics popular today often do not.

Stories contained in Girls' Romances were of the "girl meets boy, girl loses boy, girl gets boy back" (or a suitable replacement) variety. Typical of these was "You Can't Take Your Love with You," in which a young woman named Claudia becomes a camp counselor for a summer in hopes of making her longtime boyfriend (but never fiance) miss her enough to ask her to marry him. The slow-moving boyfriend eventually does, but only after Claudia has found true love with a fellow camp counselor.

After a run of some two decades, Girls' Romances finally ended in 1971, victim of the almost complete dominance of super-heroes (and male readers) in the world of comics.

1 ❑ Mar 1950 Cover: 0.10 **NM** value: **360.00**
• **CGC:** 1 graded, best 7.0
2 ❑ May 1950 Cover: 0.10 **NM** value: **190.00**
3 ❑ Jul 1950 Cover: 0.10 **NM** value: **100.00**
4 ❑ Sep 1950 Cover: 0.10 **NM** value: **100.00**
5 ❑ Nov 1950 Cover: 0.10 **NM** value: **100.00**
6 ❑ Jan 1951 Cover: 0.10 **NM** value: **100.00**
7 ❑ Mar 1951 Cover: 0.10 **NM** value: **100.00**
8 ❑ May 1951 Cover: 0.10 **NM** value: **100.00**
9 ❑ Jul 1951 Cover: 0.10 **NM** value: **100.00**
10 ❑ Sep 1951 Cover: 0.10 **NM** value: **100.00**
11 ❑ Nov 1951 Cover: 0.10 **NM** value: **70.00**
12 ❑ Jan 1952 Cover: 0.10 **NM** value: **70.00**
13 ❑ Mar 1952 Cover: 0.10 **NM** value: **70.00**
14 ❑ May 1952 Cover: 0.10 **NM** value: **70.00**
15 ❑ Jul 1952 Cover: 0.10 **NM** value: **70.00**
16 ❑ Sep 1952 Cover: 0.10 **NM** value: **70.00**
17 ❑ Nov 1952 Cover: 0.10 **NM** value: **70.00**
18 ❑ Jan 1952 Cover: 0.10 **NM** value: **70.00**
19 ❑ Mar 1953 Cover: 0.10 **NM** value: **70.00**
20 ❑ May 1953 Cover: 0.10 **NM** value: **70.00**
21 ❑ Jul 1953 Cover: 0.10 **NM** value: **45.00**
22 ❑ Sep 1953 Cover: 0.10 **NM** value: **45.00**
23 ❑ Nov 1953 Cover: 0.10 **NM** value: **45.00**
24 ❑ Jan 1954 Cover: 0.10 **NM** value: **45.00**
25 ❑ Mar 1954 Cover: 0.10 **NM** value: **45.00**
26 ❑ May 1954 Cover: 0.10 **NM** value: **45.00**
27 ❑ Jul 1954 Cover: 0.10 **NM** value: **45.00**
28 ❑ Sep 1954 Cover: 0.10 **NM** value: **45.00**
29 ❑ Nov 1954 Cover: 0.10 **NM** value: **45.00**
30 ❑ Jan 1955 Cover: 0.10 **NM** value: **45.00**
31 ❑ Mar 1955 Cover: 0.10 **NM** value: **36.00**
32 ❑ May 1955 Cover: 0.10 **NM** value: **36.00**
33 ❑ Jul 1955 Cover: 0.10 **NM** value: **36.00**
34 ❑ Sep 1955 Cover: 0.10 **NM** value: **36.00**
35 ❑ Nov 1955 Cover: 0.10 **NM** value: **36.00**
• **CGC:** 1 graded, best 8.5
36 ❑ Jan 1956 Cover: 0.10 **NM** value: **36.00**
37 ❑ Mar 1956 Cover: 0.10 **NM** value: **36.00**
38 ❑ May 1956 Cover: 0.10 **NM** value: **36.00**
39 ❑ Jul 1956 Cover: 0.10 **NM** value: **36.00**
40 ❑ Sep 1956 Cover: 0.10 **NM** value: **36.00**
41 ❑ Nov 1956 Cover: 0.10 **NM** value: **36.00**
42 ❑ Jan 1957 Cover: 0.10 **NM** value: **36.00**
43 ❑ Mar 1957 Cover: 0.10 **NM** value: **36.00**
44 ❑ May 1957 Cover: 0.10 **NM** value: **36.00**
45 ❑ Jul 1957 Cover: 0.10 **NM** value: **36.00**
46 ❑ Sep 1957 Cover: 0.10 **NM** value: **36.00**
47 ❑ Cover: 0.10 **NM** value: **36.00**
48 ❑ Cover: 0.10 **NM** value: **36.00**
49 ❑ Cover: 0.10 **NM** value: **36.00**
50 ❑ 1958 Cover: 0.10 **NM** value: **36.00**
51 ❑ 1958 Cover: 0.10 **NM** value: **28.00**
52 ❑ 1958 Cover: 0.10 **NM** value: **28.00**
53 ❑ 1958 Cover: 0.10 **NM** value: **28.00**
54 ❑ 1958 Cover: 0.10 **NM** value: **28.00**
55 ❑ Cover: 0.10 **NM** value: **28.00**
56 ❑ Cover: 0.10 **NM** value: **28.00**
57 ❑ Cover: 0.10 **NM** value: **28.00**
58 ❑ 1959 Cover: 0.10 **NM** value: **28.00**
59 ❑ 1959 Cover: 0.10 **NM** value: **28.00**
60 ❑ 1959 Cover: 0.10 **NM** value: **28.00**
61 ❑ 1959 Cover: 0.10 **NM** value: **28.00**
62 ❑ Sep 1959 Cover: 0.10 **NM** value: **28.00**
63 ❑ Oct 1959 Cover: 0.10 **NM** value: **28.00**
64 ❑ Cover: 0.10 **NM** value: **28.00**
65 ❑ Cover: 0.10 **NM** value: **28.00**
66 ❑ 1960 Cover: 0.10 **NM** value: **28.00**
67 ❑ Apr 1960 Cover: 0.10 **NM** value: **28.00**
68 ❑ 1960 Cover: 0.10 **NM** value: **28.00**
69 ❑ 1960 Cover: 0.10 **NM** value: **28.00**
70 ❑ 1960 Cover: 0.10 **NM** value: **28.00**
71 ❑ 1960 Cover: 0.10 **NM** value: **24.00**
72 ❑ Nov 1960 Cover: 0.10 **NM** value: **24.00**
73 ❑ Cover: 0.10 **NM** value: **24.00**
74 ❑ 1961 Cover: 0.10 **NM** value: **24.00**
75 ❑ 1961 Cover: 0.10 **NM** value: **24.00**
76 ❑ 1961 Cover: 0.10 **NM** value: **24.00**
77 ❑ 1961 Cover: 0.10 **NM** value: **24.00**
78 ❑ 1961 Cover: 0.10 **NM** value: **24.00**
79 ❑ Oct 1961 Cover: 0.10 **NM** value: **24.00**
80 ❑ Cover: 0.10 **NM** value: **24.00**
81 ❑ 1962 Cover: 0.12 **NM** value: **24.00**
82 ❑ 1962 Cover: 0.12 **NM** value: **24.00**
83 ❑ 1962 Cover: 0.12 **NM** value: **24.00**
84 ❑ 1962 Cover: 0.12 **NM** value: **24.00**
85 ❑ 1962 Cover: 0.12 **NM** value: **24.00**
86 ❑ Sep 1962 Cover: 0.12 **NM** value: **24.00**
87 ❑ Cover: 0.12 **NM** value: **24.00**
88 ❑ Cover: 0.12 **NM** value: **24.00**
89 ❑ Cover: 0.12 **NM** value: **24.00**
90 ❑ 1963 Cover: 0.12 **NM** value: **24.00**
91 ❑ 1963 Cover: 0.12 **NM** value: **18.00**
📖 You Can't Take Your Love With You; Walk Into My Heart; Another Dream; Look Out For Love;
92 ❑ 1963 Cover: 0.12 **NM** value: **18.00**
93 ❑ Jun 1963 Cover: 0.12 **NM** value: **18.00**
94 ❑ Aug 1963 Cover: 0.12 **NM** value: **18.00**
95 ❑ Sep 1963 Cover: 0.12 **NM** value: **18.00**
96 ❑ Nov 1963 Cover: 0.12 **NM** value: **18.00**
97 ❑ Dec 1963 Cover: 0.12 **NM** value: **18.00**
98 ❑ Jan 1964 Cover: 0.12 **NM** value: **18.00**
99 ❑ Mar 1964 Cover: 0.12 **NM** value: **18.00**
100 ❑ Apr 1964 Cover: 0.12 **NM** value: **25.00**
• 100th anniversary issue.
101 ❑ Jun 1964 Cover: 0.12 **NM** value: **16.00**
102 ❑ Jul 1964 Cover: 0.12 **NM** value: **16.00**
103 ❑ Sep 1964 Cover: 0.12 **NM** value: **16.00**
104 ❑ Oct 1964 Cover: 0.12 **NM** value: **16.00**
105 ❑ Dec 1964 Cover: 0.12 **NM** value: **16.00**
106 ❑ Jan 1965 Cover: 0.12 **NM** value: **16.00**
107 ❑ Mar 1965 Cover: 0.12 **NM** value: **16.00**
108 ❑ Apr 1965 Cover: 0.12 **NM** value: **16.00**
109 ❑ Jun 1965 Cover: 0.12 **NM** value: **65.00**
• **CGC:** 2 graded, best 5.5
110 ❑ Jul 1965 Cover: 0.12 **NM** value: **14.00**
111 ❑ Sep 1965 Cover: 0.12 **NM** value: **14.00**
112 ❑ Oct 1965 Cover: 0.12 **NM** value: **14.00**
113 ❑ Dec 1965 Cover: 0.12 **NM** value: **14.00**
114 ❑ Jan 1966 Cover: 0.12 **NM** value: **14.00**
115 ❑ Mar 1966 Cover: 0.12 **NM** value: **14.00**
116 ❑ Apr 1966 Cover: 0.12 **NM** value: **14.00**
117 ❑ Jun 1966 Cover: 0.12 **NM** value: **14.00**
118 ❑ Jul 1966 Cover: 0.12 **NM** value: **14.00**
119 ❑ Sep 1966 Cover: 0.12 **NM** value: **14.00**
120 ❑ Oct 1966 Cover: 0.12 **NM** value: **14.00**
121 ❑ Dec 1966 Cover: 0.12 **NM** value: **12.00**
122 ❑ Jan 1967 Cover: 0.12 **NM** value: **12.00**
Circ: Statement: **170,400**
123 ❑ Mar 1967 Cover: 0.12 **NM** value: **12.00**
Circ: Statement: **170,400**
124 ❑ Apr 1967 Cover: 0.12 **NM** value: **12.00**
Circ: Statement: **170,400**
125 ❑ Jun 1967 Cover: 0.12 **NM** value: **12.00**
Circ: Statement: **170,400**
126 ❑ Jul 1967 Cover: 0.12 **NM** value: **12.00**
Circ: Statement: **170,400**
127 ❑ Sep 1967 Cover: 0.12 **NM** value: **12.00**
Circ: Statement: **170,400**
128 ❑ Oct 1967, four-color Cover: 0.12 **NM** value: **12.00**
Circ: Statement: **170,400**
📖 I Wish I Could Love You, Don't Stop Loving Me!, We'll Never Meet Again Pt. II
129 ❑ Dec 1967, four-color Cover: 0.12 **NM** value: **12.00**
Circ: Statement: **170,400**
130 ❑ Jan 1968, four-color Cover: 0.12 **NM** value: **12.00**
131 ❑ Mar 1968, four-color Cover: 0.12 **NM** value: **12.00**
132 ❑ Apr 1968, four-color Cover: 0.12 **NM** value: **12.00**
133 ❑ Jun 1968, four-color Cover: 0.12 **NM** value: **12.00**
134 ❑ Jul 1968, four-color Cover: 0.12 **NM** value: **12.00**
135 ❑ Sep 1968, four-color Cover: 0.12 **NM** value: **12.00**
136 ❑ Oct 1968 Cover: 0.12 **NM** value: **12.00**
137 ❑ Dec 1968, four-color Cover: 0.12 **NM** value: **12.00**
138 ❑ Jan 1969, four-color Cover: 0.12 **NM** value: **12.00**
139 ❑ Mar 1969, four-color Cover: 0.12 **NM** value: **12.00**
140 ❑ Apr 1969, four-color Cover: 0.12 **NM** value: **12.00**
141 ❑ Jun 1969, four-color Cover: 0.12 **NM** value: **8.00**
142 ❑ Jul 1969, four-color Cover: 0.12 **NM** value: **8.00**
143 ❑ Sep 1969, four-color Cover: 0.12 **NM** value: **8.00**
144 ❑ Oct 1969 Cover: 0.12 **NM** value: **8.00**
145 ❑ Dec 1969, four-color Cover: 0.12 **NM** value: **8.00**
146 ❑ Jan 1970, four-color Cover: 0.12 **NM** value: **8.00**
147 ❑ Mar 1970, four-color Cover: 0.12 **NM** value: **8.00**
148 ❑ Apr 1970, four-color Cover: 0.12 **NM** value: **8.00**
• **CGC:** 1 graded, best 9.0
149 ❑ Jun 1970, four-color Cover: 0.12 **NM** value: **8.00**
150 ❑ Jul 1970, four-color Cover: 0.12 **NM** value: **8.00**
151 ❑ Sep 1970, four-color Cover: 0.12 **NM** value: **8.00**
152 ❑ Oct 1970 Cover: 0.12 **NM** value: **8.00**
153 ❑ Dec 1970 Cover: 0.12 **NM** value: **8.00**
154 ❑ Jan 1971, four-color Cover: 0.12 **NM** value: **8.00**
155 ❑ Mar 1971, four-color Cover: 0.12 **NM** value: **8.00**
156 ❑ Apr 1971, four-color Cover: 0.12 **NM** value: **8.00**
157 ❑ Jun 1971, four-color Cover: 0.12 **NM** value: **8.00**
158 ❑ Jul 1971, four-color Cover: 0.12 **NM** value: **8.00**
159 ❑ Sep 1971, four-color Cover: 0.12 **NM** value: **8.00**
160 ❑ Oct 1971, four-color Cover: 0.12 **NM** value: **8.00**
final issue.

GIRL TALK — Fantagraphics

4 ❑ Sum 1996, b&w Cover: 3.50 **NM** value: **Cover or less**

GIRL: THE RULE OF DARKNESS — Cry for Dawn

All issues are adults only.

1 ❑ b&w Cover: 2.50 **NM** value: **Cover or less**

GIRL WHO WOULD BE DEATH, THE — DC / Vertigo

1 ❑ Dec 1998 Cover: 2.50 **NM** value: **Cover or less**
Circ: Diamd. preorders: **24,906**
2 ❑ Jan 1999 Cover: 2.50 **NM** value: **Cover or less**
Circ: Diamd. preorders: **21,303**
📖 Warning: Impersonating Death May Be Hazardous to Your Health **A:** Dean Ormston **W:** Caitlan R. Kiernan
3 ❑ Feb 1999 Cover: 2.50 **NM** value: **Cover or less**
Circ: Diamd. preorders: **20,231**
4 ❑ Mar 1999 Cover: 2.50 **NM** value: **Cover or less**
Circ: Diamd. preorders: **19,122**

GIVE IT UP! AND OTHER SHORT STORIES — NBM

1 ❑ Jul 1995, b&w Cover: 14.95 **NM** value: **Cover or less**
hardcover. • Peter Kuper adaptations of Kafka stories

GIVE ME LIBERTY — Dark Horse

America has slipped into the abyss. With each election year, the skies grow more polluted, crime grows worse, and political unrest begins to give way to a police state. Sooner than anyone would dream, the country is controlled by the unholy marriage of corporate interests and executive abuse. Liberty, as we know it, becomes a sad joke.

Then someone blows up the White House, killing the president and almost all his cabinet; improbably, a drunken Secretary of Agriculture becomes the new president. Needless to say, things don't improve much.

Give Me Liberty is focused on a young black woman named Martha Washington. Born in housing projects that have become a restricted death zone, she has no real chance in life. But from the projects to the war in the rain forests of South America, Washington is ever the survivor. And in that survival lies an incredible story.

1 ❑ Jun 1990 Cover: 4.95 **NM** value: **5.00**
Circ: CapCity orders: **25,725** • **CGC:** 2 graded, best 9.8
• prestige format. 📖 Homes & Gardens **A:** Dave Gibbons; Dick Giordano **W:** Frank Miller ★ 1st Appearance of Martha Washington.
2 ❑ Sep 1990 Cover: 4.95 **NM** value: **5.00**
Circ: CapCity orders: **21,125**
• prestige format. **A:** Dave Gibbons; Dick Giordano **W:** Frank Miller
3 ❑ Dec 1990 Cover: 4.95 **NM** value: **5.00**
Circ: CapCity orders: **19,375**
• prestige format. 📖 Health & Welfare **A:** Dave Gibbons; Dick Giordano **W:** Frank Miller
4 ❑ Apr 1991 Cover: 4.95 **NM** value: **5.00**
Circ: CapCity orders: **17,425**
• prestige format. **A:** Dave Gibbons; Dick Giordano **W:** Frank Miller
Bk 1 ❑ Cover: 19.95 **NM** value: **Cover or less**
• Collects Give Me Liberty #1-4 **A:** Dave Gibbons **W:** Frank Miller
Bk 1/LE ❑ Cover: 114.95 **NM** value: **Cover or less**
• Limited edition hardcover. • Collects Give Me Liberty #1-4 **A:** Dave Gibbons **W:** Frank Miller

GIVE ME LIBERTY! (RIP OFF) — Rip Off

1 ❑ Jan 1976 Cover: 0.75 **NM** value: **4.00**

G.I. WAR TALES — DC

1 ❑ Mar 1973 Cover: 0.20 **NM** value: **8.00**
• **CGC:** 1 graded, best 8.0
2 ❑ Jun 1973 Cover: 0.20 **NM** value: **5.00**
• **CGC:** 1 graded, best 9.4

CGC-graded: Multiply prices above by **33 for 9.9 M • 16 for 9.8 NM/M • 7 for 9.6 NM+ • 5 for 9.4 NM • 2.5 for 9.2 NM- • 1.5 for 9.0 VF/NM**

📖 The Killing Ground!; Warrior (text story), Suicide Volunteer • Reprints stories from Star Spangled War Stories #134, G.I. Combat #133
3 ❑ Aug 1973 Cover: 0.20 **NM** value: **4.00**
📖 Split-Second Target; The G.I. Who Replaced Himself! • Reprints stories from All American Men of War #55, 38 **A:** Joe Kubert; Russ Heath **W:** Robert Kanigher
4 ❑ Oct 1973 Cover: 0.20 **NM** value: **4.00**

GIZMO AND THE FUGITOID — Mirage
1 ❑ Jun 1989, b&w Cover: 1.75 **NM** value: **2.00**
2 ❑ Jun 1989, b&w Cover: 1.75 **NM** value: **2.00**

GIZMO (CHANCE) — Chance
1 ❑ Cover: 1.50 **NM** value: **3.00**
📖 That Was No Teddy Bear That Was My...

GIZMO (MIRAGE) — Mirage
1 ❑ Feb 1987, b&w Cover: 1.50 **NM** value: **Cover or less**
2 ❑ Mar 1987, b&w Cover: 1.50 **NM** value: **Cover or less**
3 ❑ Apr 1987, b&w Cover: 1.50 **NM** value: **Cover or less**
4 ❑ May 1987, b&w Cover: 1.50 **NM** value: **Cover or less**
5 ❑ Jun 1987, b&w Cover: 1.50 **NM** value: **Cover or less**
6 ❑ Jul 1987, b&w Cover: 1.50 **NM** value: **Cover or less**
Bk 1❑ Dec 1988 Cover: 12.95 **NM** value: **Cover or less**
• The Collected Gizmo

GLADIATOR/SUPREME — Marvel
1 ❑ Mar 1997 Cover: 4.99 **NM** value: **Cover or less**
Circ: Direct Market orders: **22,750**

GLADSTONE COMIC ALBUM — Gladstone
Bk 1❑ Cover: 5.95 **NM** value: **Cover or less**
• Uncle Scrooge **A:** Carl Barks
Bk 2❑ Cover: 5.95 **NM** value: **Cover or less**
• Donald Duck **A:** Carl Barks
Bk 3❑ Cover: 5.95 **NM** value: **Cover or less**
Circ: CapCity orders: **2,100**
• Mickey Mouse **A:** Floyd Gottfredson
Bk 4❑ Cover: 5.95 **NM** value: **Cover or less**
Circ: CapCity orders: **2,550**
• Uncle Scrooge **A:** Carl Barks
Bk 5❑ Cover: 5.95 **NM** value: **Cover or less**
Circ: CapCity orders: **2,300**
• Donald Duck **A:** Carl Barks
Bk 6❑ Cover: 5.95 **NM** value: **Cover or less**
Circ: CapCity orders: **2,200**
• Uncle Scrooge **A:** Carl Barks
Bk 7❑ Cover: 5.95 **NM** value: **Cover or less**
Circ: CapCity orders: **1,900**
• Donald Duck **A:** Carl Barks
Bk 8❑ Cover: 5.95 **NM** value: **Cover or less**
• Mickey Mouse **A:** Floyd Gottfredson
Bk 9❑ Cover: 5.95 **NM** value: **Cover or less**
• Bambi
Bk 10❑ Cover: 5.95 **NM** value: **Cover or less**
• Donald Duck **A:** Carl Barks
Bk 11❑ Cover: 5.95 **NM** value: **Cover or less**
• Uncle Scrooge **A:** Carl Barks
Bk 12❑ Cover: 5.95 **NM** value: **Cover or less**
• Donald & Daisy **A:** Carl Barks
Bk 13❑ Cover: 5.95 **NM** value: **Cover or less**
• Donald Duck **A:** Carl Barks
Bk 14❑ Cover: 5.95 **NM** value: **Cover or less**
• Uncle Scrooge **A:** Carl Barks
Bk 15❑ Cover: 5.95 **NM** value: **Cover or less**
• Donald & Gladstone **A:** Carl Barks
Bk 16❑ Cover: 5.95 **NM** value: **Cover or less**
• Donald Duck **A:** Carl Barks
Bk 17❑ Cover: 5.95 **NM** value: **Cover or less**
• Mickey Mouse **A:** Floyd Gottfredson
Bk 18❑ Cover: 5.95 **NM** value: **Cover or less**
• Junior Woodchucks **A:** Carl Barks
Bk 19❑ Cover: 5.95 **NM** value: **Cover or less**
• Uncle Scrooge **A:** Carl Barks
Bk 20❑ Cover: 5.95 **NM** value: **Cover or less**
• Uncle Scrooge **A:** Carl Barks
Bk 21❑ Cover: 5.95 **NM** value: **Cover or less**
• Duck Family **A:** Carl Barks
Bk 22❑ Cover: 5.95 **NM** value: **Cover or less**
• Mickey Mouse **A:** Floyd Gottfredson
Bk 23❑ Cover: 5.95 **NM** value: **Cover or less**
• Donald Duck; Halloween **A:** Carl Barks
Bk 24❑ Cover: 5.95 **NM** value: **Cover or less**
• Uncle Scrooge **A:** Carl Barks
Bk 25❑ Cover: 5.95 **NM** value: **Cover or less**
• Donald Duck; Xmas **A:** Carl Barks
Bk 26❑ Cover: 9.95 **NM** value: **Cover or less**
• Mickey & Donald **A:** Floyd Gottfredson
Bk 27❑ Cover: 9.95 **NM** value: **Cover or less**
• early Donald Duck **A:** Carl Barks
Bk 28❑ Cover: 9.95 **NM** value: **Cover or less**
• Uncle Scrooge & Donald Duck **A:** Don Rosa

GLADSTONE COMIC ALBUM SPECIAL — Gladstone
Bk 1❑ Cover: 8.95 **NM** value: **Cover or less**
📖 Pirate Gold **A:** Carl Barks
Bk 2❑ Cover: 8.95 **NM** value: **Cover or less**
• Uncle Scrooge, Donald **A:** Carl Barks
Bk 3❑ Cover: 8.95 **NM** value: **Cover or less**
• Mickey Mouse **A:** Floyd Gottfredson
Bk 4❑ Cover: 11.95 **NM** value: **Cover or less**
• Uncle Scrooge **A:** Carl Barks; Don Rosa
Bk 5❑ Cover: 11.95 **NM** value: **Cover or less**
• Donald **A:** Carl Barks
Bk 6❑ Cover: 12.95 **NM** value: **Cover or less**
• Uncle Scrooge **A:** Carl Barks
Bk 7❑ Cover: 13.95 **NM** value: **Cover or less**
• Mickey Mouse **A:** Floyd Gottfredson

GLAMOROUS GRAPHIX PRESENTS — Glamorous Graphix
1 ❑ Jan 1996, b&w Cover: 3.95 **NM** value: **Cover or less**
• Becky Sunshine; pin-ups

GLASS JAW — Clay Heeled Press
1 ❑ Cover: 2.95 **NM** value: **Cover or less**
• no date

GLOBAL FORCE — Silverline
1 ❑ full color Cover: 1.95 **NM** value: **Cover or less**

GLORIANNA — Press This
1 ❑ b&w Cover: 3.95 **NM** value: **Cover or less**
No issue number. One-shot. 📖 The Conscience of King **A:** Daniel Nauenburg **W:** J. Kevin Carrier

GLORY — Image
Glory was created by comics industry legend and one of the founders of Image Comics Rob Liefeld. This four-issue mini-series began in 1995.

Like DC's Wonder Woman, Glory is an Amazon who traces her history back to World War II. Her real name is Gloriana, and she is the daughter of the legendary Lady Demeter. In this series, she teams up with friends named Vandal and Rumble. In a story called, "Who Wrote the Book Of Love?" Glory is framed for multiple murders, and the three friends have to find out who caused the frame-up and why. In doing so, they must also unravel the mystery behind a demonic "Book of Love" and a strange symbol that shows up at the murder scenes.

Mike Deodato handles the pencilling with scripts by Jo Duffy.

0 ❑ Feb 1996 Cover: 2.50 **NM** value: **Cover or less**
Circ: CapCity orders: **26,175**
1 ❑ Mar 1995 Cover: 2.50 **NM** value: **Cover or less**
Circ: CapCity orders: **34,050**
📖 Who Wrote the Book of Love?, Part 1 **A:** Mike Deodato Jr. **W:** Mary Jo Duffy
1/A ❑ Mar 1995 Cover: 2.50 **NM** value: **Cover or less**
alternate cover. 📖 Who Wrote the Book of Love?, Part 1 • Image publishes **A:** Mike Deodato Jr. **W:** Mary Jo Duffy
2 ❑ Apr 1995 Cover: 2.50 **NM** value: **Cover or less**
Circ: CapCity orders: **25,800**
📖 Who Wrote the Book of Love?, Part 2 **A:** Mike Deodato Jr. **W:** Mary Jo Duffy
3 ❑ May 1995 Cover: 2.50 **NM** value: **Cover or less**
Circ: CapCity orders: **26,325**
📖 Who Wrote the Book of Love?, Part 3 **A:** Mike Deodato Jr. **W:** Mary Jo Duffy
4 ❑ Jun 1995 Cover: 2.50 **NM** value: **Cover or less**
Circ: CapCity orders: **27,050**
📖 Who Wrote the Book of Love?, Part 4 **W:** Mary Jo Duffy
4/A ❑ Jun 1995 Cover: 2.50 **NM** value: **Cover or less**
Quesada/Palmiotti variant cover. 📖 Who Wrote the Book of Love?, Part 4 **A:** Jimmy Palmiotti(cover); Joe Quesada(cover) **W:** Mary Jo Duffy
5 ❑ Aug 1995 Cover: 2.50 **NM** value: **Cover or less**
Circ: CapCity orders: **25,075**
• polybagged with trading card **W:** Mary Jo Duffy
6 ❑ Sep 1995 Cover: 2.50 **NM** value: **Cover or less**
Circ: CapCity orders: **19,400**
7 ❑ Oct 1995 Cover: 2.50 **NM** value: **Cover or less**
Circ: CapCity orders: **12,750**
8 ❑ Nov 1995 Cover: 2.50 **NM** value: **Cover or less**
• Babewatch **W:** Mary Jo Duffy
9 ❑ Dec 1995 Cover: 2.50 **NM** value: **Cover or less**
📖 Extreme Destroyer, Part 5 • polybagged with Glory card **W:** Mary Jo Duffy
10 ❑ Mar 1996 Cover: 2.50 **NM** value: **Cover or less**
11 ❑ Apr 1996 Cover: 2.50 **NM** value: **Cover or less**
12 ❑ May 1996 Cover: 3.50 **NM** value: **Cover or less**
• double-sized anniversary issue. **W:** Mary Jo Duffy
12/A❑ May 1996 Cover: 3.50 **NM** value: **Cover or less**
alternate cover (photo). • double-sized anniversary issue.
13 ❑ Jun 1996 Cover: 2.50 **NM** value: **Cover or less**
14 ❑ Jul 1996 Cover: 2.50 **NM** value: **Cover or less**
15 ❑ Sep 1996 Cover: 2.50 **NM** value: **Cover or less**
Circ: Diamd. preorders: **29,599**
16 ❑ Oct 1996 Cover: 2.50 **NM** value: **Cover or less**
Circ: Diamd. preorders: **27,697**
• Maximum begins as publisher **W:** Mary Jo Duffy
17 ❑ Nov 1996 Cover: 2.50 **NM** value: **Cover or less**
Circ: Diamd. preorders: **23,783**
18 ❑ Dec 1996 Cover: 2.50 **NM** value: **Cover or less**
Circ: Diamd. preorders: **22,300**
19 ❑ Jan 1997 Cover: 2.50 **NM** value: **Cover or less**
Circ: Diamd. preorders: **20,654**
20 ❑ Feb 1997 Cover: 2.50 **NM** value: **Cover or less**
Circ: Diamd. preorders: **18,669**
21 ❑ ca. 1997 Cover: 2.50 **NM** value: **Cover or less**
Circ: Diamd. preorders: **17,607**
22 ❑ ca. 1997 Cover: 2.50 **NM** value: **Cover or less**
Circ: Diamd. preorders: **17,565**
23 ❑ ca. 1997 Cover: 2.50 **NM** value: **Cover or less**
Circ: Diamd. preorders: **16,880**
final issue.
Bk 1❑ Aug 1996 Cover: 9.95 **NM** value: **Cover or less**
📖 Who Wrote the Book of Love? • Collects Glory #1-4 **A:** Mike Deodato Jr. **W:** Mary Jo Duffy

GLORY & FRIENDS BIKINI FEST — Image
1 ❑ Sep 1995 Cover: 2.50 **NM** value: **Cover or less**
Circ: CapCity orders: **20,025**
• pin-ups
1/SC❑ Sep 1995 Cover: 2.50 **NM** value: **Cover or less**
alternate cover (photo). • pin-ups

GLORY & FRIENDS CHRISTMAS SPECIAL — Image
1 ❑ Dec 1995 Cover: 2.50 **NM** value: **Cover or less**
📖 Home For The Holidays?; Bloodpool; Riptide; Nightmare **A:** Brian Denham; Todd Nauck; J. Morrigan **W:** Robert Napton; Eric Stephenson

GLORY & FRIENDS LINGERIE SPECIAL — Image
1 ❑ Sep 1995 Cover: 2.95 **NM** value: **Cover or less**
• pin-ups
1/SC❑ Sep 1995 Cover: 2.95 **NM** value: **Cover or less**
alternate cover (photo). • pin-ups

GLORY/ANGELA: ANGELS IN HELL — Image
1 ❑ Apr 1996 Cover: 2.50 **NM** value: **Cover or less**
• **CGC:** 1 graded, best 9.8
One-shot. • flipbook with Darkchylde preview

GLORY/AVENGELYNE — Image
1/A ❑ Oct 1995 Cover: 3.95 **NM** value: **Cover or less**
no title information on cover.
1/B ❑ Oct 1995 Cover: 3.95 **NM** value: **Cover or less**
no title information on cover.

GLORY/CELESTINE: DARK ANGEL — Image
1 ❑ Sep 1996 Cover: 2.50 **NM** value: **Cover or less**
Circ: Diamd. preorders: **38,967**
📖 The Doomsday Talisman **A:** Patrick Lee **W:** Mary Jo Duffy
2 ❑ Oct 1996 Cover: 2.50 **NM** value: **Cover or less**
Circ: Diamd. preorders: **34,013**

GLYPH — Labor of Love
1 ❑ b&w Cover: 4.95 **NM** value: **Cover or less**
No issue number. • magazine.
2 ❑ b&w Cover: 4.95 **NM** value: **Cover or less**
• magazine.
3 ❑ b&w Cover: 4.95 **NM** value: **Cover or less**
• magazine.

G-MEN — Caliber
1 ❑ b&w Cover: 2.50 **NM** value: **Cover or less**

GNATRAT: THE DARK GNAT RETURNS — Prelude

Those who have read Frank Miller's landmark '80s series Batman: The Dark Knight — and who hasn't? — have a pretty good idea of the story in this witty, well-drawn spoof. It is 50 years after the retirement of the legendary vigilante crime-fighter the Gnatrat, but crime has not retired with him. In fact, thriving is the villainous Art Gang, determined to take control of the entire comic-book industry. To fight these evil, shadowy figures, billionaire play-rat Boo Swain takes up the cowl and Gnatmobile once more. Not content to merely spoof The Dark Knight, though, the Mark Martin also lampoons Miller's other well-known works, including Ronin and his Daredevil "Born Again" series.

Everything from the artistic style to the panel layout and the dialogue is a dead-on parody of Miller's work, with perfect moments scattered throughout. Written and drawn in an incredibly short time after the conclusion of the Miller series, it was published by Prelude Graphics.

1 ❑ b&w Cover: 1.95 **NM** value: **Cover or less**
• Batman parody; continues in Darerat/Tadpole **A:** Mark Martin **W:** Mark Martin

GNATRAT: THE MOVIE — Innovation
1 ❑ b&w Cover: 2.25 **NM** value: **Cover or less**
• Batman parody

G'N'R'S GREATEST HITS — Revolutionary
1 ❑ Oct 1993, b&w Cover: 2.50 **NM** value: **Cover or less**

GOBBLEDYGOOK (1ST SERIES) — Mirage
1 ❑ **NM** value: **125.00**
2 ❑ **NM** value: **80.00**

GOBBLEDYGOOK (2ND SERIES) — Mirage
1 ❑ Dec 1986 Cover: 6.00 **NM** value: **Cover or less**
• **CGC:** 1 graded, best 9.2
📖 Don't Sleep on Main Street; Technofear!; The Crossing; The Adventures of Splat & Beggar; You Had to be There; The Cosmic Crows-Before the Cola Wars; Pursuit; That old Sinking Feeling!; A Few Well Chosen Words; Shopping Spree; Crazy Man **A:** Kevin Eastman; Ryan Brown; Peter Laird; Michael Dooney; Steve Lavigne **W:** Kevin Eastman; Ryan Brown; Peter Laird; Michael Dooney; Steve Lavigne

GOBLIN LORD — Goblin Studios
1 ❑ Oct 1996 Cover: 2.50 **NM** value: **Cover or less**
Circ: Diamd. preorders: **7,643**
2 ❑ Cover: 2.50 **NM** value: **Cover or less**
Circ: Diamd. preorders: **4,829**
3 ❑ Feb 1997 Cover: 2.50 **NM** value: **Cover or less**
Circ: Diamd. preorders: **4,194**

GOBLIN MAGAZINE, THE — Warren
1 ❑ Cover: 2.25 **NM** value: **8.00**

Other grades: Multiply prices above by **1.5 for Mint • 2/3 for Very Fine • 1/3 for Fine • 1/5 for Very Good • 1/8 for Good**

2 ❑ Cover: 2.25 **NM** value: **5.00**
3 ❑ Nov 1982 Cover: 2.25 **NM** value: **5.00**
📖 The Goblin; The Tin Man; Troll Patrol; Buccaneers; Wormglow **A:** Rudy Nebres; Luis Bermejo; Abel Axamana; Lee Saile; Alex Ni±o **W:** Bill Dubay; Timothy Moriarty
4 ❑ Cover: 2.25 **NM** value: **5.00**

GOBLIN MARKET — Tome Press
1 ❑ b&w Cover: 2.50 **NM** value: **Cover or less**
• poem

GOBLIN STUDIOS — Goblin Studios
1 ❑ Cover: 2.25 **NM** value: **Cover or less**
2 ❑ Cover: 2.25 **NM** value: **Cover or less**
3 ❑ Cover: 2.25 **NM** value: **Cover or less**
4 ❑ Cover: 2.25 **NM** value: **Cover or less**
5 ❑ Aug 1995 Cover: 2.25 **NM** value: **Cover or less**

GODDESS — DC / Vertigo
1 ❑ Jun 1995 Cover: 2.95 **NM** value: **Cover or less**
Circ: CapCity orders: **13,300**
📖 Dangerous To Man **A:** Phil Winslade **W:** Garth Ennis
2 ❑ Jul 1995 Cover: 2.95 **NM** value: **Cover or less**
Circ: CapCity orders: **9,875**
3 ❑ Aug 1995 Cover: 2.95 **NM** value: **Cover or less**
Circ: CapCity orders: **10,225**
4 ❑ Sep 1995 Cover: 2.95 **NM** value: **Cover or less**
Circ: CapCity orders: **9,775**
5 ❑ Oct 1995 Cover: 2.95 **NM** value: **Cover or less**
Circ: CapCity orders: **8,600**
6 ❑ Nov 1995 Cover: 2.95 **NM** value: **Cover or less**
7 ❑ Dec 1995 Cover: 2.95 **NM** value: **Cover or less**
8 ❑ Jan 1996 Cover: 2.95 **NM** value: **Cover or less**
📖 Mine Eyes Have Seen the Glory final issue. **A:** Phil Winslade **W:** Garth Ennis

GODDESS (TWILIGHT TWINS) — Twilight Twins
1 ❑ b&w Cover: 2.00 **NM** value: **Cover or less**
• Zolastraya

GODHEAD — Anubis
1 ❑ Cover: 2.75 **NM** value: **15.00**
📖 Distortion **A:** John Bergerud
1/LE❑ Cover: 2.75 **NM** value: **25.00**
• limited edition. 📖 Distortion **A:** John Bergerud ★ 1st Appearance of Jhatori.
2 ❑ Cover: 2.75 **NM** value: **6.00**
2/LE❑ Cover: 2.75 **NM** value: **3.00**
3 ❑ Cover: 2.75 **NM** value: **4.00**

GODS & TULIPS — Westhampton
1 ❑ Cover: 3.00 **NM** value: **Cover or less**
📖 Good Comics and Why you should Sell Them; On Signings; Writing (the Pro/con speech) **A:** Michael W. Kaluta; Chester Brown; Chris Shadoian **W:** Neil Gaiman

GODS FOR HIRE — Hot
1 ❑ Dec 1986 Cover: 1.50 **NM** value: **2.00**
Circ: CapCity orders: **6,950**
2 ❑ Jan 1987 Cover: 1.75 **NM** value: **2.00**
Circ: CapCity orders: **4,250**

GOD'S HAMMER — Caliber
1 ❑ b&w Cover: 2.50 **NM** value: **Cover or less**
2 ❑ b&w Cover: 2.50 **NM** value: **Cover or less**
3 ❑ b&w Cover: 2.50 **NM** value: **Cover or less**

GOD'S SMUGGLER — Spire
1 ❑ Cover: 0.39 **NM** value: **5.00**
📖 God's Smuggler • Based on the book "God's Smuggler" by Brother Andrew **A:** Al Hartley **W:** Al Hartley; Brother Andrew

GODWHEEL — Malibu / Ultraverse
0 ❑ Jan 1995 Cover: 2.50 **NM** value: **Cover or less**
Circ: CapCity orders: **11,350**
Flip cover. 📖 The Crucible; Destiny **A:** Scott Benefiel; Keith Conroy; Mark Pacella **W:** Chris Ulm; Dan Danko ★ 1st Appearance of Primevil.
1 ❑ Jan 1995 Cover: 2.50 **NM** value: **Cover or less**
Circ: CapCity orders: **11,075**
Flip cover. 📖 The Decision; The Quest **A:** Aaron Lopresti; Gary Frank **W:** James D. Hudnall ★ 1st Appearance of Primevil. ★ Appearance of Thor.
2 ❑ Feb 1995 Cover: 2.50 **NM** value: **Cover or less**
Circ: CapCity orders: **10,800**
Flip cover. 📖 The Wheel; Pumpkin Trouble **A:** Mike Wieringo; Gabriel Gecko **W:** Gerard Jones
3 ❑ Feb 1995 Cover: 2.50 **NM** value: **Cover or less**
Circ: CapCity orders: **10,775**
Flip cover. 📖 Reinventing the Wheel; Thunder in Vahdala • Marvel, Malibu universes cross **A:** George Pérez; John Statema; Joe Madureira **W:** Mike W. Barr ★ Appearance of Thor.

Diamond preorders are the estimated number of comics sold, prior to their release, to comics shops in North America by Diamond Comic Distributors, the largest distributor. These figures underreport the actual number of circulating copies by the amount of reorders Diamond took (usually 5-10% again of the preorders) and sales by publishers to newsstand and bookstore distributors. For many independent publishers, Diamond's preorders may be quite close to the actual number of copies in circulation.

GODZILLA — Marvel
Gojira was released in Japan in 1954; with a name-change, cuts, and additional scenes, Godzilla, King of the Monsters stomped into U.S. theaters the same year. Marvel imported Japanese cinema's favorite grumpy lizard in this 1970s series.

Eons ago, Godzilla, a hybrid of land and sea reptiles, was trapped in a state of suspended animation. Awakened by an undersea nuclear test, he rose again. Now, with fiery breath and awesome, city-smashing strength, Godzilla shows the world how much he hates having his sleep interrupted.

Fearsome but not evil, Godzilla is befriended by a young man, Rob Takiguchi. Rob has his hands full, however, trying to keep this giant friend out of trouble and out of the hands of those who want to control him.

1 ❑ Aug 1977 Cover: 0.30 **NM** value: **6.00**
• **CGC:** 44 graded, best 9.9
📖 The Coming! **A:** Herb Trimpe; Jim Mooney **W:** Doug Moench
2 ❑ Sep 1977 Cover: 0.30 **NM** value: **3.50**
• **CGC:** 2 graded, best 9.0
3 ❑ Oct 1977 Cover: 0.30 **NM** value: **3.00**
• **CGC:** 1 graded, best 8.5
4 ❑ Nov 1977 Cover: 0.35 **NM** value: **3.00**
• **CGC:** 2 graded, best 9.2
5 ❑ Dec 1977 Cover: 0.35 **NM** value: **3.00**
• **CGC:** 1 graded, best 9.4
6 ❑ Jan 1978 Cover: 0.35 **NM** value: **3.00**
• **CGC:** 1 graded, best 9.2
7 ❑ Feb 1978 Cover: 0.35 **NM** value: **3.00**
8 ❑ Mar 1978 Cover: 0.35 **NM** value: **3.00**
9 ❑ Apr 1978 Cover: 0.35 **NM** value: **3.00**
10 ❑ May 1978 Cover: 0.35 **NM** value: **3.00**
11 ❑ Jun 1978 Cover: 0.35 **NM** value: **2.50**
12 ❑ Jul 1978 Cover: 0.35 **NM** value: **2.50**
13 ❑ Aug 1978 Cover: 0.35 **NM** value: **2.50**
14 ❑ Sep 1978 Cover: 0.35 **NM** value: **2.50**
15 ❑ Oct 1978 Cover: 0.35 **NM** value: **2.50**
16 ❑ Nov 1978 Cover: 0.35 **NM** value: **2.50**
17 ❑ Dec 1978 Cover: 0.35 **NM** value: **2.50**
• Godzilla shrunk by Henry Pym's gas
18 ❑ Jan 1979 Cover: 0.35 **NM** value: **2.50**
19 ❑ Feb 1979 Cover: 0.35 **NM** value: **2.50**
📖 With Dugan On The Docks! **A:** Herb Trimpe **W:** Doug Moench
20 ❑ Mar 1979 Cover: 0.35 **NM** value: **2.50**
21 ❑ Apr 1979 Cover: 0.35 **NM** value: **2.50**
• **CGC:** 1 graded, best 9.4
22 ❑ May 1979 Cover: 0.40 **NM** value: **2.50**
23 ❑ Jun 1979 Cover: 0.40 **NM** value: **2.50**
• **CGC:** 1 graded, best 9.8
24 ❑ Jul 1979 Cover: 0.40 **NM** value: **2.50**
final issue. ★ Appearance of Spider-Man. ★ Versus Fantastic Four. ★ Versus Avengers.

GODZILLA COLOR SPECIAL — Dark Horse
1 ❑ Aug 1992 **NM** value: **4.00**
Circ: CapCity orders: **11,100** • **CGC:** 1 graded, best 9.2

GODZILLA (DARK HORSE) — Dark Horse
0 ❑ May 1995 Cover: 2.50 **NM** value: **4.00**
Circ: CapCity orders: **10,550**
📖 Blast From the Past • reprints and expands story from Dark Horse Comics #10 and 11 **A:** Bobby Rubio; Rich Suchy **W:** Randy Stradley
1 ❑ Jun 1995 Cover: 2.50 **NM** value: **3.00**
Circ: CapCity orders: **11,250**
2 ❑ Jul 1995 Cover: 2.50 **NM** value: **3.00**
Circ: CapCity orders: **9,150**
3 ❑ Aug 1995 Cover: 2.50 **NM** value: **3.00**
Circ: CapCity orders: **8,075**
4 ❑ Sep 1995 Cover: 2.50 **NM** value: **3.00**
Circ: CapCity orders: **7,025**
5 ❑ Oct 1995 Cover: 2.50 **NM** value: **3.00**
📖 Target: Godzilla, Part 1
6 ❑ Nov 1995 Cover: 2.50 **NM** value: **2.95**
📖 Target: Godzilla, Part 2
7 ❑ Dec 1995 Cover: 2.50 **NM** value: **2.95**
📖 Target: Godzilla, Part 3
8 ❑ Jan 1996 Cover: 2.50 **NM** value: **2.95**
📖 Target: Godzilla, Part 4
9 ❑ Mar 1996 Cover: 2.50 **NM** value: **2.95**
📖 Lost in Time, Part 1
10 ❑ Apr 1996 Cover: 2.50 **NM** value: **2.95**
📖 Lost in Time, Part 2 • Godzilla vs. Spanish Armada
11 ❑ May 1996 Cover: 2.50 **NM** value: **2.95**
• Godzilla travels through time to sink the Titanic
12 ❑ Jun 1996 Cover: 2.95 **NM** value: **Cover or less**
13 ❑ Jun 1996 Cover: 2.95 **NM** value: **Cover or less**
14 ❑ Jul 1996 Cover: 2.95 **NM** value: **Cover or less**
📖 To Climb the Highest Monster! **A:** Gordon Purcell **W:** Eric Gein
15 ❑ Aug 1996 Cover: 2.95 **NM** value: **Cover or less**
📖 The Yamazaki Endowment **A:** Brandon McKinney; Chris Scalf(cover) **W:** Ryder Windham ★ Versus Lord Howe Monster.
16 ❑ Cover: 2.95 **NM** value: **Cover or less**
Circ: Diamd. preorders: **13,583**
final issue.
Bk 1❑ Mar 1998 Cover: 17.95 **NM** value: **Cover or less**
• Past Present Future; collects issues #5-15 and story from A Decade of Dark Horse

GODZILLA, KING OF THE MONSTERS SPECIAL — Dark Horse
1/A ❑ Aug 1987 Cover: 1.50 **NM** value: **3.00**
1/B ❑ **NM** value: **3.00**
misprinted cover. • fewer than 100 **A:** Ron Randall; Steve Bissette **W:** Steve Bissette; Randy Stradley

GODZILLA (MINI-SERIES) — Dark Horse
1 ❑ Jul 1987, b&w Cover: 1.95 **NM** value: **4.00**
• manga **A:** Kazuhira Iwashi **W:** Kazuhisa Iwashi
2 ❑ Aug 1987, b&w Cover: 1.95 **NM** value: **3.00**
• manga **A:** Kazuhira Iwashi **W:** Kazuhisa Iwashi
3 ❑ Sep 1987, b&w Cover: 1.95 **NM** value: **3.00**
• manga **A:** Kazuhira Iwashi **W:** Kazuhisa Iwashi
4 ❑ Oct 1987, b&w Cover: 1.95 **NM** value: **3.00**
• manga **A:** Kazuhira Iwashi **W:** Kazuhisa Iwashi
5 ❑ Nov 1987, b&w Cover: 1.95 **NM** value: **3.00**
• manga **A:** Kazuhira Iwashi **W:** Kazuhisa Iwashi
6 ❑ Dec 1987, b&w Cover: 1.95 **NM** value: **3.00**
• manga **A:** Kazuhira Iwashi **W:** Kazuhisa Iwashi
Bk 1❑ Cover: 10.95 **NM** value: **Cover or less**
• collects mini-series **A:** Kazuhira Iwashi **W:** Kazuhisa Iwashi
Bk 1-2❑ May 1995 Cover: 17.95 **NM** value: **Cover or less**

GODZILLA VS. BARKLEY — Dark Horse

Arguably one of the strangest ideas ever committed to paper, this one-shot gives the reader exactly what the title implies: a one-on-one showdown of immense proportions.

One day, Godzilla forsakes his Asian stomping grounds and comes ashore in sunny southern California, where basketball player Charles Barkley is shooting a commercial. Through the intervention of a small boy and a magic coin, Sir Charles is soon the tallest player in the NBA (by a few hundred feet) and is staring eye-to-eye with the big lizard. Before long, they're shooting hoops together at an abandoned missile base.

If the idea of this ultimate pick-up game isn't enough to hook you, consider that this is probably your only chance to see Godzilla wearing Nikes or to see Barkley lecture a radioactive monster on honor and sportsmanship.

Barkley also appears in another improbable comics release, Sir Charles Barkley and the Referee Murders.

1 ❑ Cover: 2.95 **NM** value: **3.00**
Circ: CapCity orders: **15,575**
No issue number. **A:** Jeff Butler **W:** Mike Baron

GODZILLA VERSUS HERO ZERO — Dark Horse
1 ❑ Jul 1995 Cover: 2.50 **NM** value: **Cover or less**
Circ: CapCity orders: **7,500**

GO GIRL! — Image
1 ❑ Aug 2000 Cover: 3.50 **NM** value: **Cover or less**
Circ: Diamd. preorders: **3,744**
2 ❑ Nov 2000 Cover: 3.50 **NM** value: **Cover or less**
Circ: Diamd. preorders: **2,660**
📖 A Day in the Wonderful Life **A:** Anne Timmons **W:** Trina Robbins
3 ❑ Nov 2001 Cover: 3.50 **NM** value: **Cover or less**
Circ: Diamd. preorders: **2,456**
📖 The Teacher From Hell! **A:** Anne Timmons **W:** Trina Robbins

GO-GO BOY ASHCAN — Mermaid
Ash 1❑ b&w **NM** value: **1.00**
no cover price.

GOG (VILLAINS) — DC
1 ❑ Feb 1998 Cover: 1.95 **NM** value: **Cover or less**
📖 The Road to Hell • New Year's Evil **A:** Jerry Ordway **W:** Mark Waid

GOING HOME — Aardvark-Vanaheim
1 ❑ **NM** value: **2.00**
• no date

GOJIN — Antarctic
1 ❑ Apr 1995 Cover: 3.50 **NM** value: **Cover or less**
Circ: CapCity orders: **1,750**
2 ❑ Jun 1995 Cover: 2.95 **NM** value: **Cover or less**
3 ❑ Aug 1995 Cover: 2.95 **NM** value: **Cover or less**
3/A ❑ Aug 1995 Cover: 2.95 **NM** value: **Cover or less**
alternate cover. **A:** Kazuho Takizawa; Yutaka Koudo **W:** Kazuho Takizawa; Yutaka Koudo
4 ❑ b&w Cover: 2.95 **NM** value: **Cover or less**
5 ❑ b&w Cover: 2.95 **NM** value: **Cover or less**
6 ❑ b&w Cover: 2.95 **NM** value: **Cover or less**
7 ❑ b&w Cover: 2.95 **NM** value: **Cover or less**
8 ❑ Jun 1996, b&w Cover: 2.95 **NM** value: **Cover or less**

GOLD DIGGER — Antarctic
1 ❑ Sep 1992 Cover: 2.50 **NM** value: **55.00**
• **CGC:** 1 graded, best 9.4
2 ❑ Nov 1992 Cover: 2.50 **NM** value: **35.00**
3 ❑ Jan 1993 Cover: 2.50 **NM** value: **25.00**
4 ❑ Mar 1993 Cover: 2.50 **NM** value: **20.00**
Bk 1❑ Oct 1994 Cover: 9.95 **NM** value: **15.00**
• collects mini-series **A:** Fred Perry **W:** Fred Perry
Bk 1-2❑ Mar 1995 Cover: 9.95 **NM** value: **10.00**

CGC-graded: Multiply prices above by **33 for 9.9 M • 16 for 9.8 NM/M • 7 for 9.6 NM+ • 5 for 9.4 NM • 2.5 for 9.2 NM- • 1.5 for 9.0 VF/NM**

GOLD DIGGER (2ND SERIES) — Antarctic

Gina Diggers and her adopted were-cheetah sister, Brittany, are archaeologists, a la Indiana Jones. Gina is the brains and Brittany is the brawn. They love finding treasure and ancient artifacts, receiving notoriety and rewards for their finds, meeting handsome men during their adventures, traveling the world, shopping, receiving research grants, finding lost civilizations, and earning bounties. Is it any wonder Gina is called Gold Digger?

The series has also spawned a computer videogame and several follow-up series.

1❑Jul 1993Cover: 2.50**NM** value: **15.00**
2 ❑ Aug 1993 Cover: 2.50 **NM** value: **10.00**
3 ❑ Sep 1993 Cover: 2.50 **NM** value: **8.00**
4 ❑ Oct 1993 Cover: 2.75 **NM** value: **8.00**
5 ❑ Nov 1993 Cover: 2.75 **NM** value: **8.00**
has issue #0 on cover. • production mistake **A:** Fred Perry **W:** Fred Perry
6 ❑ Dec 1993 Cover: 2.75 **NM** value: **6.00**
7 ❑ Jan 1994 Cover: 2.75 **NM** value: **6.00**
• **CGC:** 2 graded, best 9.6
8 ❑ Feb 1994 Cover: 2.75 **NM** value: **6.00**
9 ❑ Mar 1994 Cover: 2.75 **NM** value: **6.00**
• **CGC:** 1 graded, best 9.6
10 ❑ Apr 1994 Cover: 2.75 **NM** value: **6.00**
11 ❑ May 1994 Cover: 2.75 **NM** value: **4.00**
12 ❑ Jun 1994 Cover: 2.75 **NM** value: **4.00**
13 ❑ Jul 1994 Cover: 2.75 **NM** value: **4.00**
14 ❑ Aug 1994 Cover: 2.75 **NM** value: **4.00**
15 ❑ Sep 1994 Cover: 2.75 **NM** value: **4.00**
16 ❑ Oct 1994 Cover: 2.75 **NM** value: **4.00**
17 ❑ Nov 1994 Cover: 2.75 **NM** value: **4.00**
18 ❑ Dec 1994 Cover: 2.75 **NM** value: **4.00**
19 ❑ Feb 1995 Cover: 2.75 **NM** value: **4.00**
20 ❑ Apr 1995 Cover: 2.75 **NM** value: **4.00**
21 ❑ May 1995 Cover: 2.75 **NM** value: **3.50**
22 ❑ Jun 1995 Cover: 2.75 **NM** value: **3.50**
23 ❑ Jul 1995 Cover: 2.75 **NM** value: **3.50**
24 ❑ Aug 1995 Cover: 2.75 **NM** value: **3.50**
25 ❑ Oct 1995 Cover: 2.75 **NM** value: **3.50**
26 ❑ Nov 1995 Cover: 2.75 **NM** value: **3.50**
27 ❑ Dec 1995 Cover: 2.75 **NM** value: **3.50**
28 ❑ Feb 1996 Cover: 2.75 **NM** value: **3.50**
29 ❑ Apr 1996 Cover: 2.95 **NM** value: **3.50**
30 ❑ Jul 1996 Cover: 2.95 **NM** value: **3.50**
31 ❑ Aug 1996 Cover: 2.95 **NM** value: **3.50**
32 ❑ Oct 1996 Cover: 2.95 **NM** value: **3.50**
Circ: Diamd. preorders: **3,864**
Time Warp, Part 1 **A:** Fred Perry **W:** Fred Perry
33 ❑ Dec 1996 Cover: 2.95 **NM** value: **3.50**
Circ: Diamd. preorders: **3,872**
Time Warp, Part 3 **A:** Fred Perry **W:** Fred Perry
34 ❑ Feb 1997 Cover: 2.95 **NM** value: **3.50**
Circ: Diamd. preorders: **3,845**
Time Warp, Part 5 **A:** Fred Perry **W:** Fred Perry
35 ❑ Apr 1997 Cover: 2.95 **NM** value: **3.50**
Circ: Diamd. preorders: **3,879**
Time Warp, Part 7 **A:** Fred Perry **W:** Fred Perry
36 ❑ Jul 1997 Cover: 2.95 **NM** value: **3.50**
Circ: Diamd. preorders: **4,076**
37 ❑ Aug 1997 Cover: 2.95 **NM** value: **3.50**
Circ: Diamd. preorders: **4,097**
38 ❑ Jan 1998 Cover: 2.95 **NM** value: **3.50**
Circ: Diamd. preorders: **4,074**
cover says Nov 97, indicia says Jan 98. **A:** Fred Perry **W:** Fred Perry
39 ❑ Mar 1998 Cover: 2.95 **NM** value: **3.50**
Circ: Diamd. preorders: **4,081**
40 ❑ May 1998 Cover: 2.95 **NM** value: **3.50**
Circ: Diamd. preorders: **4,075**
41 ❑ Jun 1998 Cover: 2.95 **NM** value: **3.50**
Circ: Diamd. preorders: **4,267**
42 ❑ Jul 1998 Cover: 2.95 **NM** value: **3.50**
Circ: Diamd. preorders: **4,170**
43 ❑ Aug 1998 Cover: 2.95 **NM** value: **3.50**
Circ: Diamd. preorders: **4,172**
44 ❑ Sep 1998 Cover: 2.95 **NM** value: **3.50**
Circ: Diamd. preorders: **4,088**
45 ❑ Oct 1998 Cover: 2.95 **NM** value: **3.50**
Circ: Diamd. preorders: **4,194**
46 ❑ Dec 1998 Cover: 2.95 **NM** value: **3.50**
Circ: Diamd. preorders: **4,171**
47 ❑ Jan 1999 Cover: 2.95 **NM** value: **3.50**
Circ: Diamd. preorders: **4,184**
48 ❑ Feb 1999 Cover: 2.99 **NM** value: **3.50**
Circ: Diamd. preorders: **4,162**
49 ❑ Apr 1999 Cover: 2.99 **NM** value: **3.50**
Circ: Diamd. preorders: **4,404**
50 ❑ Jun 1999 Cover: 2.99 **NM** value: **3.50**
Circ: Diamd. preorders: **3,977**
50/CS❑Jun 1999 Cover: 2.99 **NM** value: **5.99**
• poster edition. **A:** Fred Perry **W:** Fred Perry
Anl 1❑Sep 1995 Cover: 3.95 **NM** value: **Cover or less**
Anl 2❑Sep 1996, b&w Cover: 3.95 **NM** value: **Cover or less**
Anl 3❑Sep 1997, b&w Cover: 3.95 **NM** value: **Cover or less**
Proving Ground; A Fishy Revenge; A Word From Our Sponsor; First Love; Temple of Dunn; A Gold Digger Quickie; Money Talks; Before Hours Bargain; Peace • 1997 Annual **A:** Jim Schumaker; Cody Pickrodt; Michael Vega; Anita Sengupta; Brandon Franklin; David Barrack; Ferdie Poblete; John Barrett; Ryan Burke; TAB; Phillip Shafer **W:** Jim Schumaker; Cody Pickrodt; Anita Sengupta; Brandon Franklin; David Barrack; Ferdie Poblete; John Barrett; Ryan Burke; TAB
Anl 4❑Sep 1998, b&w Cover: 3.95 **NM** value: **Cover or less**
Fatal Fury; Return of the Lich King; Romeo; Showdown in Aisle 7; Guest in the Machine; The Shun Goku Satsu of Love • 1998 Annual **A:** Bart Sandel; Christie Majors; Darin Brown; Jerzy Drozd; Mike Kelly; Ron Murphy; Thor Thorvaldson **W:** Christie Majors; Darin Brown; Mike Kelly; Ron Murphy; Thor Thorvaldson; Tom Root
Bk 1❑ Cover: 9.95 **NM** value: **10.95**
GD-18 Years • collects first four issues of ongoing series **A:** Fred Perry **W:** Fred Perry
Bk 2❑ Cover: 10.95 **NM** value: **Cover or less**
• Collects issue #1-4
Bk 3❑ Cover: 10.95 **NM** value: **Cover or less**
• Collects issue #5-8
Bk 4❑ Cover: 10.95 **NM** value: **Cover or less**
• Collects issue #9-12
Bk 5❑ Cover: 10.95 **NM** value: **Cover or less**
• Collects issue #13-16
Bk 6❑ Feb 1997, b&w Cover: 10.95 **NM** value: **Cover or less**
GD-18 The Peeper Controversy • Collects issue #17-20 **A:** Fred Perry **W:** Fred Perry
Bk 7❑ Feb 1998 Cover: 10.95 **NM** value: **Cover or less**
Bk 8❑ Dec 1998 Cover: 10.95 **NM** value: **Cover or less**
GN 1❑ Cover: 10.95 **NM** value: **Cover or less**
• Graphic Novel **A:** Fred Perry **W:** Fred Perry
SE 1❑ Cover: 2.75 **NM** value: **Cover or less**
• Special edition. **A:** Fred Perry **W:** Fred Perry

GOLD DIGGER (3RD SERIES) — Antarctic

1 ❑ Jul 1999 Cover: 2.50 **NM** value: **6.00**
Circ: Diamd. preorders: **3,843**
• new color series **A:** Fred Perry **W:** Fred Perry
2 ❑ Aug 1999 Cover: 2.50 **NM** value: **4.00**
Circ: Diamd. preorders: **5,319**
• new color series **A:** Fred Perry **W:** Fred Perry
3 ❑ Sep 1999 **NM** value: **3.00**
Circ: Diamd. preorders: **5,394**
4 ❑ Oct 1999 **NM** value: **3.00**
Circ: Diamd. preorders: **5,741**
5 ❑ Nov 1999 **NM** value: **3.00**
Circ: Diamd. preorders: **5,609**
6 ❑ Dec 1999 **NM** value: **3.00**
Circ: Diamd. preorders: **5,657**
7 ❑ Jan 2000 **NM** value: **3.00**
Circ: Diamd. preorders: **5,561**
8 ❑ Feb 2000 **NM** value: **3.00**
Circ: Diamd. preorders: **5,352**
9 ❑ Mar 2000 **NM** value: **3.00**
Circ: Diamd. preorders: **5,551**
10 ❑ Apr 2000 **NM** value: **3.00**
Circ: Diamd. preorders: **5,504**
11 ❑ May 2000 **NM** value: **3.00**
Circ: Diamd. preorders: **5,541**
12 ❑ Jun 2000 **NM** value: **3.00**
Circ: Diamd. preorders: **5,691**
13 ❑ Jul 2000 **NM** value: **3.00**
Circ: Diamd. preorders: **3,099**
14 ❑ Aug 2000 **NM** value: **3.00**
Circ: Diamd. preorders: **5,643**
15 ❑ Sep 2000 **NM** value: **3.00**
Circ: Diamd. preorders: **5,634**
16 ❑ Oct 2000 **NM** value: **3.00**
Circ: Diamd. preorders: **5,543**
17 ❑ Nov 2000 **NM** value: **3.00**
Circ: Diamd. preorders: **5,236**
18 ❑ Dec 2000 Cover: 2.95 **NM** value: **3.00**
Circ: Diamd. preorders: **5,295**
19 ❑ Jan 2001 Cover: 2.95 **NM** value: **3.00**
Circ: Diamd. preorders: **5,267**
20 ❑ Feb 2001 Cover: 2.95 **NM** value: **3.00**
Circ: Diamd. preorders: **5,131**
21 ❑ Mar 2001 Cover: 2.95 **NM** value: **Cover or less**
Circ: Diamd. preorders: **5,207**
22 ❑ Apr 2001 Cover: 2.95 **NM** value: **Cover or less**
Circ: Diamd. preorders: **5,126**
23 ❑ May 2001 Cover: 2.95 **NM** value: **Cover or less**
Circ: Diamd. preorders: **5,084**
24 ❑ Jun 2001 Cover: 2.95 **NM** value: **Cover or less**
Circ: Diamd. preorders: **5,252**

GOLD DIGGER: BETA — Antarctic

1 ❑ Feb 1998 Cover: 2.95 **NM** value: **Cover or less**
Circ: Diamd. preorders: **5,455**

GOLD DIGGER: EDGE GUARD — Radio Comix

1 ❑ Aug 2000 Cover: 2.95 **NM** value: **Cover or less**
Circ: Diamd. preorders: **4,303**

GOLD DIGGER MANGAZINE — Antarctic

1 ❑ Mar 1994 Cover: 2.75 **NM** value: **2.99**
1-2 ❑ Apr 1999 Cover: 2.99 **NM** value: **Cover or less**

GOLD DIGGER PERFECT MEMORY — Antarctic

1 ❑ Jul 1996, b&w Cover: 4.50 **NM** value: **Cover or less**
• story synopses, character profiles, and other material

The prices seen above do not represent the highest possible prices seen in online auctions, but rather the prices we have seen these issues reliably fetch in a variety of environments (storefront retail, mail order, auction and convention).

GOLDEN AGE, THE — DC

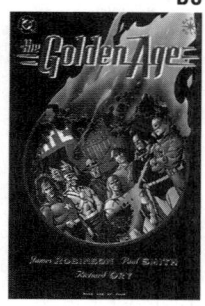

In the early 1940s, America was engulfed in the most widely fought war it had ever seen. But, for all the tragedy, it was also a time of wonder and heroes. On the home front, such legends as Hawkman, Green Lantern, Doctor Mid-Nite, Hourman, and countless others fought the good fight against crime and sabotage. They would have fought the war itself, had it not been for a German superman called Parsifal, whose power negated theirs. Parsifal was eventually defeated by Americommando, but by then the bomb had been developed. Soon, it was all over.

It was the beginning of a new age of hope for America but the end of the Golden Age for its heroes. Some retired, others went insane. Some did worse.

The Golden Age is a masterfully crafted Elseworlds series by James Robinson and Paul Smith. Because it's an Elseworlds story, it didn't happen — but it could have.

1 ❑ Cover: 4.95 **NM** value: **5.50**
Circ: CapCity orders: **26,850**
The World Was at Peace • Elseworlds **A:** Paul Smith **W:** James Robinson
2 ❑ Cover: 4.95 **NM** value: **5.50**
Circ: CapCity orders: **15,500**
We Had the Bomb • Elseworlds **A:** Paul Smith **W:** James Robinson ★ Origin of Dynaman.
3 ❑ Cover: 4.95 **NM** value: **5.50**
Circ: CapCity orders: **13,600**
We Had Prosperity • Elseworlds **A:** Paul Smith **W:** James Robinson
4 ❑ Apr 2001 Cover: 4.95 **NM** value: **5.50**
Circ: CapCity orders: **13,550**
We Had it All • Elseworlds **A:** Paul Smith **W:** James Robinson ★ Death of Dynaman. ★ Death of Ultra-Humanite. ★ Death of Hawkman. ★ Death of Doll Man. ★ Death of Miss America.
Bk 1❑ Cover: 19.95 **NM** value: **Cover or less**
• Elseworlds; collects series; Introduction by Howard Chaykin **A:** Paul Smith **W:** James Robinson; Howard Chaykin

GOLDEN AGE FLASH ARCHIVES — DC

1 ❑ Sep 1999 Cover: 49.95 **NM** value: **Cover or less**
Circ: Diamd. preorders: **3,347**
• Reprints Flash stories from Flash Comics #1-17 **A:** E.E. Hibbard; Dennis Neville(cover); George Storm(cover); Harry Lampert; Shelly Moldoff(cover) **W:** Gardner Fox

GOLDEN-AGE GREATS — AC / Paragon

Bk 1❑ Win 1994 Cover: 9.95 **NM** value: **Cover or less**
• Reprints Golden Age stories
Bk 2❑ Cover: 9.95 **NM** value: **Cover or less**
• Reprints Golden Age stories; Collects Phantom Lady #13-15, All-Top Comics #8 **A:** Matt Baker **W:** Matt Baker
Bk 3❑ b&w Cover: 9.95 **NM** value: **Cover or less**
• Reprints Golden Age stories with The Flame, Espionage – Black X, Black Terror, Fighting Yank
Bk 4❑ b&w Cover: 9.95 **NM** value: **Cover or less**
• reprints Golden Age stories
Bk 5❑ Cover: 11.95 **NM** value: **Cover or less**
• Reprints Golden Age stories
Bk 6❑ Cover: 9.95 **NM** value: **Cover or less**
Bk 7❑ Cover: 9.95 **NM** value: **Cover or less**
• Best of the West **A:** Frank Frazetta; Dick Ayers; Frank Bolle; Bob Powell; Craig Flessel; Fred Guardineer; Charles Quinlan **W:** Bill Black
Bk 8❑ Cover: 9.95 **NM** value: **Cover or less**
Bk 9❑ Cover: 9.95 **NM** value: **Cover or less**
Bk 10❑ Cover: 9.95 **NM** value: **Cover or less**
• Reprints Golden Age stories
Bk 11❑ Cover: 11.95 **NM** value: **Cover or less**
• Western reprints **W:** Bill Black
Bk 12❑ Cover: 9.95 **NM** value: **Cover or less**
Bk 13❑ Cover: 9.95 **NM** value: **Cover or less**
Bk 14❑ Cover: 11.95 **NM** value: **Cover or less**
Comic Book Jungle!

GOLDEN AGE GREEN LANTERN ARCHIVES — DC

1 ❑ Cover: 49.95 **NM** value: **Cover or less**
• Collects All-American Comics #16-30, Green Lantern (1st Series) #1 **A:** E.E. Hibbard; Irwin Hasen; Martin Nodell; Shelly Moldoff **W:** Bill Finger ★ Origin of Green Lantern I (Alan Scot). ★ 1st Appearance of Green Lantern I (Alan Scot).

GOLDEN AGE OF MARVEL — Marvel

Bk 1❑ Cover: 19.99 **NM** value: **Cover or less**
Bk 2❑ Cover: 19.95 **NM** value: **Cover or less**

GOLDEN AGE OF TRIPLE-X, THE — Revisionary

All issues are adults only.
1 ❑ b&w Cover: 3.50 **NM** value: **Cover or less**

GOLDEN AGE OF TRIPLE-X: JOHN HOLMES SPECIAL "JOHNNY DOES PARIS" — Re-Visionary

1 ❑ Cover: 2.95 **NM** value: **Cover or less**

GOLDEN AGE SECRET FILES — DC

1 ❑ Feb 2001 Cover: 4.95 **NM** value: **Cover or less**
Circ: Diamd. preorders: **20,054**

Other grades: Multiply prices above by **1.5 for Mint • 2/3 for Very Fine • 1/3 for Fine • 1/5 for Very Good • 1/8 for Good**

The Dawn of the Golden Age; The Crimson Avenger Speaks!; Scenes From the Class Struggle at JSA Mansion; The Sentinel; Show and Tell **A:** Mike Collins; Michael Lark; Peter Gross; Peter Grau; Jamal Igle; Cliff Chiang; Mark Propbst **W:** Peter Gross; Scott Beatty; Jason Hernandez-Rosenblatt; John Ostrander; Tom Peyer

GOLDEN AGE STARMAN ARCHIVES, THE — DC
1 ❑ Cover: 49.95 **NM** value: **Cover or less**

GOLDEN ARROW — Fawcett
1 ❑ ca. 1942 Cover: 0.10 **NM** value: **Cover or less**
• **CGC:** 2 graded, best 7.0
2 ❑ ca. 1943 Cover: 0.10 **NM** value: **Cover or less**
3 ❑ Win 1945 Cover: 0.10 **NM** value: **Cover or less**
4 ❑ Spr 1946 Cover: 0.10 **NM** value: **Cover or less**
5 ❑ Fal 1947 Cover: 0.10 **NM** value: **Cover or less**
6 ❑ Spr 1947 Cover: 0.10 **NM** value: **Cover or less**

GOLDEN DRAGON — Synchronicity
1 ❑ Cover: 1.50 **NM** value: **Cover or less**
Anything That Doesn't Kill You Makes You Stronger **A:** Michael Martin; Ted Hales **W:** Marc Haines

GOLDEN FEATURES (JERRY IGER'S...) — Blackthorne
1 ❑ Cover: 2.00 **NM** value: **Cover or less**
2 ❑ Cover: 2.00 **NM** value: **Cover or less**
3 ❑ Jun 1986 Cover: 2.00 **NM** value: **Cover or less**
4 ❑ Aug 1986 Cover: 2.00 **NM** value: **Cover or less**
5 ❑ Oct 1986 Cover: 2.00 **NM** value: **Cover or less**
6 ❑ Cover: 2.00 **NM** value: **Cover or less**

GOLDEN LAD — Fact and Fiction Publications
1 ❑ Jul 1945 Cover: 0.10 **NM** value: **Cover or less**
• **CGC:** 1 graded, best 5.5
2 ❑ Nov 1945 Cover: 0.10 **NM** value: **Cover or less**
3 ❑ Feb 1946 Cover: 0.10 **NM** value: **Cover or less**
4 ❑ Apr 1946 Cover: 0.10 **NM** value: **Cover or less**
• **CGC:** 1 graded, best 9.2
5 ❑ Jun 1946 Cover: 0.10 **NM** value: **Cover or less**

GOLDEN WARRIOR — Industrial Design
1 ❑ Mar 1997, b&w Cover: 2.95 **NM** value: **Cover or less**

GOLDEN WARRIOR ICZER ONE — Antarctic
1 ❑ Apr 1994, b&w Cover: 2.95 **NM** value: **Cover or less**
2 ❑ May 1994, b&w Cover: 2.95 **NM** value: **Cover or less**
Circ: CapCity orders: **2,655**
3 ❑ Jun 1994, b&w Cover: 2.95 **NM** value: **Cover or less**
Circ: CapCity orders: **2,615**
4 ❑ Jul 1994, b&w Cover: 2.95 **NM** value: **Cover or less**
5 ❑ Aug 1994, b&w Cover: 2.95 **NM** value: **Cover or less**
final issue.

GOLDEN WEST RODEO TREASURY — Dell
1 ❑ Oct 1957 **NM** value: **Cover or less**
• **CGC:** 1 graded, best 9.0

GOLDFISH — Image
1 ❑ Cover: 16.95 **NM** value: **Cover or less**
• Collects AKA Goldfish series plus new material **A:** Brian Michael Bendis **W:** Brian Michael Bendis

GOLD KEY SPOTLIGHT — Gold Key
Gold Key Spotlight was a showcase for a variety of Gold Key comics features. In its 11 issues that ran for nearly two years, it spanned the whole range of genres, from the lighthearted high school comedy of Tom, Dick and Harriet to the far-off science-fiction of Tragg and the Sky Gods. Other Gold Key features such as O.G. Whiz, Cracky, Dagar, Wacky Witch, and Dr. Spektor (the latter from Spine-Tingling Tales) also put in appearances in their own issues of this series.

The series provides another opportunity for fans to pick up stories of their favorite characters.

1 ❑ May 1976 Cover: 0.25**NM** value: **5.00**
Class Warfare; Mid-Term Mania; Cheesecake Photo • Tom, Dick, and Harriet
2 ❑ 1976 Cover: 0.25 **NM** value: **3.50**
3 ❑ 1976 Cover: 0.25 **NM** value: **3.50**
4 ❑ 1977 Cover: 0.30 **NM** value: **3.50**
5 ❑ 1977 Cover: 0.30 **NM** value: **3.50**
6 ❑ Jun 1977 Cover: 0.30 **NM** value: **3.50**
• Dagar
7 ❑ 1977 Cover: 0.30 **NM** value: **3.50**
8 ❑ 1977 Cover: 0.30 **NM** value: **3.50**
9 ❑ 1977 Cover: 0.30 **NM** value: **3.50**
10 ❑ 1977 Cover: 0.30 **NM** value: **3.50**
11 ❑ 1978 Cover: 0.30 **NM** value: **3.50**

GOLD MEDAL COMICS — Cambridge
1 ❑ ca. 1945 Cover: 0.25 **NM** value: **150.00**
• **CGC:** 1 graded, best 8.0

GOLDYN 3-D — Blackthorne
1 ❑ Cover: 2.00 **NM** value: **Cover or less**
Circ: CapCity orders: **3,575**

GOLGO 13 (2ND SERIES) — Viz
1 ❑ b&w Cover: 4.95 **NM** value: **Cover or less**
2 ❑ b&w Cover: 4.95 **NM** value: **Cover or less**
3 ❑ b&w Cover: 4.95 **NM** value: **Cover or less**

GOLGOTHIKA — Caliber
1 ❑ Nov 1996 Cover: 2.95 **NM** value: **Cover or less**
Circ: Diamd. preorders: **3,307**
Leviathan **A:** John Bergin **W:** John Bergin

GOLGO 13 — Lead Publishing Co.
1 ❑ b&w Cover: 1.00 **NM** value: **Cover or less**
The Impossible Hit **A:** Takao Saito **W:** Takao Saito
2 ❑ full color Cover: 1.50 **NM** value: **Cover or less**

GO-MAN! — Caliber
1 ❑ b&w Cover: 2.50 **NM** value: **Cover or less**
2 ❑ b&w Cover: 2.50 **NM** value: **Cover or less**
3 ❑ b&w Cover: 2.50 **NM** value: **Cover or less**
4 ❑ b&w Cover: 2.50 **NM** value: **Cover or less**
Bk 1❑ Cover: 9.95 **NM** value: **Cover or less**

GOMER PYLE — Gold Key
1 ❑ Jul 1966 Cover: 0.12 **NM** value: **50.00**
• **CGC:** 1 graded, best 7.5
2 ❑ Jan 1967 Cover: 0.12 **NM** value: **40.00**
3 ❑ Oct 1967 Cover: 0.12 **NM** value: **40.00**

GON — DC / Paradox Press
1 ❑ b&w Cover: 5.95 **NM** value: **Cover or less**
• digest. Gon Eats and Sleeps **A:** Masashi Tanaka **W:** Masashi Tanaka
2 ❑ b&w Cover: 5.95 **NM** value: **Cover or less**
• digest. Gon Again! **A:** Masashi Tanaka **W:** Masashi Tanaka
3 ❑ b&w Cover: 5.95 **NM** value: **Cover or less**
• digest. Here Today Gon Tomorrow! **A:** Masashi Tanaka **W:** Masashi Tanaka
4 ❑ b&w Cover: 5.95 **NM** value: **Cover or less**
Circ: Diamd. preorders: **7,134**
• digest. Going, Going...Gon **A:** Masashi Tanaka **W:** Masashi Tanaka
5 ❑ b&w Cover: 6.95 **NM** value: **Cover or less**
• digest. Gon Swimmin' **A:** Masashi Tanaka **W:** Masashi Tanaka
Bk 1❑ Cover: 9.95 **NM** value: **Cover or less**
• Collects Gon #1-2 **A:** Masashi Tanaka **W:** Masashi Tanaka

GONAD THE BARBARIAN — Eternity
1 ❑ Cover: 1.95 **NM** value: **2.25**
Circ: CapCity orders: **676**

GON COLOR SPECTACULAR — DC / Paradox Press
1 ❑ Cover: 5.95 **NM** value: **Cover or less**
No issue number. • prestige format.

GON ON SAFARI — DC / Paradox
1 ❑ Cover: 7.95 **NM** value: **Cover or less**

GON UNDERGROUND — DC / Paradox
1 ❑ Cover: 7.95 **NM** value: **Cover or less**

GOOD-BYE, CHUNKY RICE — Top Shelf
1 ❑ Oct 1999, b&w Cover: 14.95 **NM** value: **Cover or less**
No issue number. • graphic novel

GOOD GIRL ART QUARTERLY — AC
1 ❑ Jul 1990 Cover: 3.50 **NM** value: **3.95**
• new & reprints
2 ❑ Fal 1990 Cover: 3.95 **NM** value: **Cover or less**
3 ❑ Win 1991 Cover: 3.95 **NM** value: **Cover or less**
4 ❑ Spr 1991 Cover: 3.95 **NM** value: **Cover or less**
5 ❑ Sum 1991 Cover: 3.95 **NM** value: **Cover or less**
6 ❑ Fal 1991 Cover: 3.95 **NM** value: **Cover or less**
• Fall 1991
7 ❑ Win 1992 Cover: 3.95 **NM** value: **Cover or less**
8 ❑ Spr 1992 Cover: 3.95 **NM** value: **Cover or less**
9 ❑ Sum 1992 Cover: 3.95 **NM** value: **Cover or less**
10 ❑ Fal 1992 Cover: 3.95 **NM** value: **Cover or less**
11 ❑ Win 1993 Cover: 3.95 **NM** value: **Cover or less**
12 ❑ Spr 1993 Cover: 3.95 **NM** value: **Cover or less**
13 ❑ Sum 1993 Cover: 3.95 **NM** value: **Cover or less**
14 ❑ Fal 1993 Cover: 3.95 **NM** value: **Cover or less**
15 ❑ Win 1994 Cover: 3.95 **NM** value: **Cover or less**
16 ❑ Spr 1994 Cover: 3.95 **NM** value: **Cover or less**
17 ❑ Sum 1994 Cover: 3.95 **NM** value: **Cover or less**
18 ❑ Fal 1994 Cover: 3.95 **NM** value: **Cover or less**
19 ❑ Win 1995 Cover: 6.95 **NM** value: **Cover or less**

GOOD GIRLS — Fantagraphics
1 ❑ Apr 1987, b&w Cover: 2.00 **NM** value: **Cover or less**
Ms. Lonelyhearts **A:** Carol Lay **W:** Carol Lay
2 ❑ Oct 1987 Cover: 2.00 **NM** value: **Cover or less**
Number 23 **A:** Carol Lay **W:** Carol Lay
3 ❑ 1988 Cover: 2.00 **NM** value: **Cover or less**
4 ❑ Feb 1989 Cover: 2.00 **NM** value: **Cover or less**
Dreamland **A:** Carol Lay **W:** Carol Lay
6 ❑ Jun 1991, b&w Cover: 2.00 **NM** value: **Cover or less**

The CGC numbers printed in individual listings above represent the **number of copies examined** and given a **Universal** grade by CGC and the **best such copy** graded at press time. For current populations, watch for special ***Comics Buyer's Guide*** issues or check **www.cgccomics.com.**

GOOD GUYS, THE — Defiant
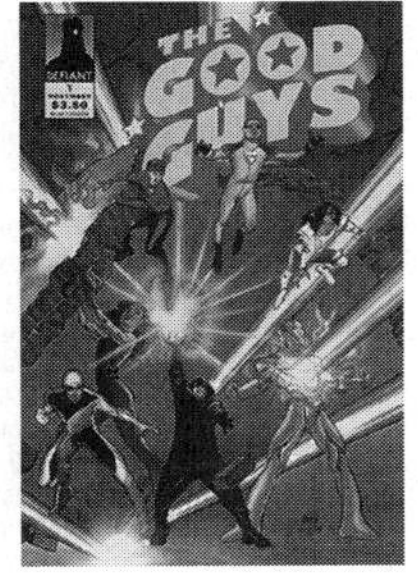

This series may be the ultimate exercise in comic-book wish-fulfillment. The Good Guys are a group of super-powered youngsters, based on actual people who won Defiant's "casting call" contest.

It all begins when Matt and his younger brother Zack set off for a Rob Liefeld signing at the new Mile High Comics shop. To scrape up spending money, Matt does the collecting for his paper route — but, at house after house, he comes up with nothing. In desperation, he goes to the spooky Simpson house. There, instead of finding the usual envelope under the mat, the door opens and a woman invites Matt inside. She tells him a strange tale, hands him what she says is a magic box, and asks him to bury it for her. Instead, Matt takes it with him to the comics shop, where the box acts as the impetus for seven strangers to gain powers which reflect their fondest dreams — and gives another youth the power for incredible destruction.

1 ❑ Nov 1993 Cover: 3.50 **NM** value: **Cover or less**
Circ: CapCity orders: **40,550**
• Giant-size. To Wish A Mile High **A:** Grey **W:** Jim Mooney; Jan Childress ★ Origin of The Good Guys. ★ 1st Appearance of The Good Guys, Master Ridgely Gatesman.
2 ❑ Dec 1993 Cover: 2.50 **NM** value: **Cover or less**
Circ: CapCity orders: **24,275**
Steppin' Out! **A:** Grey; Greg Boone; Robert Laquinta **W:** Jan Childress
3 ❑ Jan 1994 Cover: 2.50 **NM** value: **Cover or less**
Circ: CapCity orders: **17,150**
And From The Darkness...Chasm **A:** Charles Adlard **W:** Jim Shooter; Jan Childress; Janet Jackson
4 ❑ Feb 1994 Cover: 3.25 **NM** value: **Cover or less**
Circ: CapCity orders: **12,725**
5 ❑ Mar 1994 Cover: 2.50 **NM** value: **Cover or less**
Circ: CapCity orders: **10,575**
Monster Truck **A:** Greg Boone **W:** Jim Shooter; D.G. Chichester; Janet Jackson
6 ❑ Apr 1994 Cover: 2.50 **NM** value: **Cover or less**
Circ: CapCity orders: **9,225**
Assault On Scourge Island **A:** Alan Kupperberg; Greg Boone **W:** Jim Shooter; Ed Polgardy; Janet Jackson
7 ❑ May 1994 Cover: 2.50 **NM** value: **Cover or less**
Circ: CapCity orders: **8,200**
Master Of The World **A:** Greg Boone **W:** Jim Shooter; Ed Polgardy; Janet Jackson; Ken Gale; Winston Fowlkes ★ Appearance of Charlemagne.
8 ❑ Jun 1994 Cover: 2.50 **NM** value: **Cover or less**
Circ: CapCity orders: **7,000**
9 ❑ Jul 1994 Cover: 2.50 **NM** value: **Cover or less**
Circ: CapCity orders: **6,125**
10 ❑ Aug 1994 Cover: 2.50 **NM** value: **Cover or less**
Circ: CapCity orders: **5,300**
11 ❑ Sep 1994 Cover: 2.50 **NM** value: **Cover or less**
Circ: CapCity orders: **4,350**
12 ❑ Oct 1994 Cover: 2.50 **NM** value: **Cover or less**

GOODY GOOD COMICS — Fantagraphics
1 ❑ Jun 2000 Cover: 2.95 **NM** value: **Cover or less**
Circ: Diamd. preorders: **3,258**
Extend the Hand of Love to All Who Can Use It, Doofus, Greaseball, Mike Hayes **A:** Rick Altergott; Gilbert Hernandez; Jaime Hernandez; Johnny Ryan **W:** Rick Altergott; Gilbert Hernandez; Jaime Hernandez; Johnny Ryan

GOOFY ADVENTURES — Disney
1 ❑ Jun 1990 Cover: 1.50 **NM** value: **2.50**
Circ: CapCity orders: **8,800**
Balboa de Goofy; Goofy Frankenstein, Part 1; Goofy Frankenstein **A:** Rick Hoover; De Urtiaga; Torreiro **W:** Mike Kazaleh; Greg Crosby
2 ❑ Jul 1990 Cover: 1.50 **NM** value: **Cover or less**
Circ: CapCity orders: **6,150**
Goofy Frankenstein, Part 2; Goofy Peary & the North Pole; The Goof Brothers at Kitty Hawk **A:** Rick Hoover; Hector Saavedra; De Urtiaga; Robert Bat; Torreiro **W:** Joshua Quagmire; Cal Howard; Greg Crosby
3 ❑ Aug 1990 Cover: 1.50 **NM** value: **Cover or less**
Circ: CapCity orders: **6,600**
Covered Wagons, Ho!; Alexander the Goof **A:** Hector Saavedra; Tony Strobl **C:** Rick Hoover **W:** Carl Fallberg; Floyd Norman; Lee Nordling; Pete Hansen
4 ❑ Sep 1990 Cover: 1.50 **NM** value: **Cover or less**
Circ: CapCity orders: **6,500**
The Great Goofdini; The Goofy Goalie; Once Upon a Time in the Neolithic; Goofy Mozart; Hunter Goofy's African Diary; Captain Goofy and Pirate Pete **A:** Rick Hoover; Lou Scarborough; Tony Strobl **C:** Rick Hoover **W:** Joshua Quagmire; Doug Rice; Don Ferguson; Vic Lockman
5 ❑ Oct 1990 Cover: 1.50 **NM** value: **Cover or less**
Circ: CapCity orders: **6,650**
6 ❑ Nov 1990 Cover: 1.50 **NM** value: **Cover or less**
Circ: CapCity orders: **6,050**
7 ❑ Dec 1990 Cover: 1.50 **NM** value: **Cover or less**
Circ: CapCity orders: **5,400**
• Three Musketeers
8 ❑ Jan 1991 Cover: 1.50 **NM** value: **Cover or less**
Circ: CapCity orders: **5,250**
Goofy Washington; A Goofy Look at Movies; Star Goof **A:** Hector Saavedra **C:** Rick Hoover **W:** Greg Crosby; William Rotsler
9 ❑ Feb 1991 Cover: 1.50 **NM** value: **Cover or less**

CGC-graded: Multiply prices above by **33 for 9.9 M • 16 for 9.8 NM/M • 7 for 9.6 NM+ • 5 for 9.4 NM • 2.5 for 9.2 NM- • 1.5 for 9.0 VF/NM**

Circ: CapCity orders: **5,000**
James Goof – Master Spy; Goofy Caruso; Goofy Wolfman; Goof Street Blues; The Goofy Crooner • James Bond parody **A:** Miguel Pujol; Hector Saavedra; Floyd Gottfredson **C:** Patrice Croci **W:** Bill Walsh; Don Ferguson; Philippe Gasc

10 ❑ Mar 1991 Cover: 1.50 **NM** value: **Cover or less**
Circ: CapCity orders: **5,000**
Samurai Goofy; A Goofy Look at Doors; Agent Goofy, the G-Man **A:** Rick Hoover **C:** Rick Hoover **W:** Scott Saavedra; Carl Fallberg

11 ❑ Apr 1991 Cover: 1.50 **NM** value: **Cover or less**
Circ: CapCity orders: **4,400**
Goofis Kahn; A Goofy Look at Weather; The Return of Goofy Da Vinci **A:** Al Hubbard; John Costanza; Hector Urtiaga **C:** Jukka Murtosaari **W:** John Blair Moore; Cal Howard

12 ❑ May 1991 Cover: 1.50 **NM** value: **Cover or less**
Circ: CapCity orders: **4,250**
Arizona Goof and the Lost Temple, Part 1 **A:** Maria Luisa Uggetti **C:** Jukka Murtosaari **W:** Dwight Decker; Bruno Sarda

13 ❑ Jun 1991 Cover: 1.50 **NM** value: **Cover or less**
Circ: CapCity orders: **4,150**
Arizona Goof and the Lost Temple, Part 2 **A:** Maria Luisa Uggetti **C:** Jukka Murtosaari **W:** Dwight Decker; Bruno Sarda

14 ❑ Jul 1991 Cover: 1.50 **NM** value: **Cover or less**
Circ: CapCity orders: **4,050**
Alexander the Goof: The Early Years; Goofylution; The Time Thefts **A:** Rick Hoover; Bill Fugate **C:** Keith Tucker **W:** John Blair Moore; Marc Hansen

15 ❑ Aug 1991 Cover: 1.50 **NM** value: **Cover or less**
Circ: CapCity orders: **4,050**
Super Goof vs. the Cold Ray; A Goofy Look at Sleep • Super-Goof **C:** Jim Mitchell

16 ❑ Sep 1991 Cover: 1.50 **NM** value: **Cover or less**
Circ: CapCity orders: **4,000**
Sheerluck Goof and the Giggling Ghost of Nottenny Moor • Sherlock Holmes parody **A:** Bill Fugate **C:** Keith Tucker **W:** John Blair Moore

17 ❑ Oct 1991 Cover: 1.50 **NM** value: **Cover or less**
Circ: CapCity orders: **3,950**
Back in Time; Goofy Thuh Kid; Tomb of Goofula final issue. **A:** Gene Colan **C:** Jim Mitchell **W:** John Blair Moore; Marv Wolfman

GOOFY COMICS — Nedor

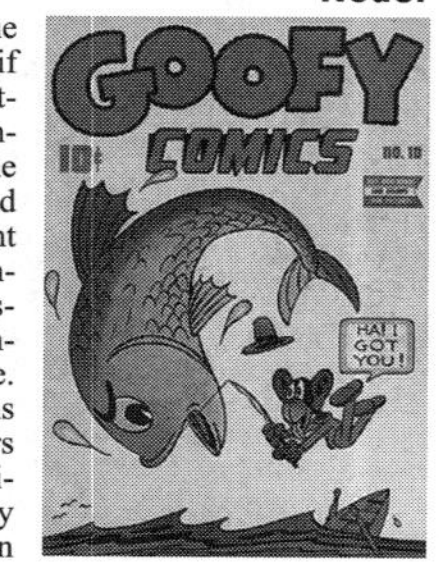

At the great funny animals of the 1940s reunion (an event which, if fully attended, would require renting the San Diego Convention Center), Uncle Pigly, Charley the Paracub, Doc Owleye, Zomby and Bomby, and Alley Bob-Cat might be found over by the punchbowl under the Goofy Comics banner, pestered by the occasional fan but generally ignored by everyone else. This cast provided what laughs were to be found between the covers of Goofy Comics, the companion title to the equally obscure Happy Comics, through its 10-year run from 1943 to 1953. In later issues, some text illustrations were provided by the young Frank Frazetta, who did a lot of funny-animal art before launching his career as a fantasy painter.

1 ❑ Jun 1943 Cover: 0.10 **NM** value: **125.00**
• **CGC:** 1 graded, best 4.5
2 ❑ Cover: 0.10 **NM** value: **60.00**
3 ❑ Cover: 0.10 **NM** value: **45.00**
4 ❑ Cover: 0.10 **NM** value: **45.00**
5 ❑ Cover: 0.10 **NM** value: **45.00**
6 ❑ Cover: 0.10 **NM** value: **38.00**
7 ❑ Cover: 0.10 **NM** value: **38.00**
8 ❑ Cover: 0.10 **NM** value: **38.00**
9 ❑ Cover: 0.10 **NM** value: **38.00**
10 ❑ Cover: 0.10 **NM** value: **38.00**
Uncle Pigly; Charley the Paracub; The New Fireman (text story); Zomby and Bomby; Alley Bob-Cat and the Naughty Thieves...; **A:** Ken Hultgren; Lynn Karp; Dressler **W:** Ken Hultgren; Lynn Karp; Dressler; Mickey Marks
11 ❑ Cover: 0.10 **NM** value: **32.00**
12 ❑ Cover: 0.10 **NM** value: **32.00**
13 ❑ Cover: 0.10 **NM** value: **32.00**
14 ❑ Cover: 0.10 **NM** value: **32.00**
15 ❑ Cover: 0.10 **NM** value: **32.00**
16 ❑ Cover: 0.10 **NM** value: **32.00**
17 ❑ Cover: 0.10 **NM** value: **32.00**
18 ❑ Cover: 0.10 **NM** value: **32.00**
19 ❑ Cover: 0.10 **NM** value: **32.00**
20 ❑ Cover: 0.10 **NM** value: **45.00**
21 ❑ Cover: 0.10 **NM** value: **45.00**
22 ❑ Cover: 0.10 **NM** value: **45.00**
23 ❑ 1947 Cover: 0.10 **NM** value: **45.00**
24 ❑ 1948 Cover: 0.10 **NM** value: **45.00**
25 ❑ Cover: 0.10 **NM** value: **45.00**
26 ❑ Cover: 0.10 **NM** value: **45.00**
27 ❑ Cover: 0.10 **NM** value: **45.00**
28 ❑ Cover: 0.10 **NM** value: **45.00**
29 ❑ Cover: 0.10 **NM** value: **45.00**
30 ❑ Cover: 0.10 **NM** value: **38.00**
31 ❑ Cover: 0.10 **NM** value: **38.00**
32 ❑ Cover: 0.10 **NM** value: **38.00**
33 ❑ Cover: 0.10 **NM** value: **38.00**
34 ❑ Cover: 0.10 **NM** value: **38.00**
35 ❑ Cover: 0.10 **NM** value: **38.00**
36 ❑ Cover: 0.10 **NM** value: **24.00**
37 ❑ Cover: 0.10 **NM** value: **24.00**
38 ❑ Cover: 0.10 **NM** value: **24.00**
39 ❑ Sep 1950 Cover: 0.10 **NM** value: **24.00**
40 ❑ Cover: 0.10 **NM** value: **24.00**
41 ❑ Cover: 0.10 **NM** value: **24.00**
42 ❑ Cover: 0.10 **NM** value: **24.00**
43 ❑ Cover: 0.10 **NM** value: **24.00**
44 ❑ Cover: 0.10 **NM** value: **24.00**
45 ❑ Cover: 0.10 **NM** value: **24.00**
46 ❑ Cover: 0.10 **NM** value: **24.00**
47 ❑ Cover: 0.10 **NM** value: **24.00**
48 ❑ 1952 Cover: 0.10 **NM** value: **24.00**
final issue.

GOON PATROL — Pinnacle

1 ❑ Cover: 1.75 **NM** value: **Cover or less**
A Transylvanian Affair; The Origin of the Beanman **A:** Alan Larsen; Bill Mitchell **W:** Alan Larsen; Bill Mitchell

GORDON YAMAMOTO AND THE KING OF THE GEEKS — Humble

1 ❑ Oct 1997, b&w Cover: 2.95 **NM** value: **Cover or less**

GORE SHRIEK — Fantaco

1 ❑ b&w Cover: 1.50 **NM** value: **3.00**
• 1st Greg Capullo story **W:** Greg Capullo
2 ❑ b&w Cover: 1.50 **NM** value: **3.00**
3 ❑ b&w Cover: 2.95 **NM** value: **3.00**
4 ❑ b&w Cover: 2.95 **NM** value: **3.00**
Circ: CapCity orders: **1,700**
5 ❑ Cover: 3.50 **NM** value: **Cover or less**
Fallen Leaves; Mal Occhio; Zombie Buzzsaw Apocalypse 2000AD; Intruder at the Gates of the Mind; The Bleeding Mirror, The Lost "Ghoul" **A:** Rick McCollum; Chas Balun; Chris Pelletiere; David Marshall; Stan Wiater; Tom Veitch **W:** Rick McCollum; Chas Balun; Chris Pelletiere; David Marshall
6 ❑ Cover: 3.50 **NM** value: **Cover or less**
Anl 1 ❑ b&w Cover: 4.95 **NM** value: **Cover or less**

GORE SHRIEK DELECTUS — Fantaco

1 ❑ Cover: 8.95 **NM** value: **Cover or less**
No issue number.

GORE SHRIEK (VOL. 2) — Fantaco

1 ❑ b&w Cover: 2.50 **NM** value: **Cover or less**
2 ❑ b&w Cover: 2.50 **NM** value: **Cover or less**
3 ❑ b&w Cover: 2.50 **NM** value: **Cover or less**

GORGANA'S GHOUL GALLERY — AC

1 ❑ b&w Cover: 2.95 **NM** value: **Cover or less**
2 ❑ Cover: 2.95 **NM** value: **Cover or less**
I Released the Muck Man!; Deadtime Story; The Haunted Corpse!; Mortal Combat!

GORGO — Charlton

1 ❑ May 1961 Cover: 0.10 **NM** value: **115.00**
• **CGC:** 1 graded, best 2.0
2 ❑ Aug 1961 Cover: 0.10 **NM** value: **75.00**
• **CGC:** 1 graded, best 9.4
3 ❑ Sep 1961 Cover: 0.10 **NM** value: **50.00**
• **CGC:** 1 graded, best 7.0
The Return of Gorgo; Tall Tree (text); Men and Monsters **A:** Steve Ditko
4 ❑ Nov 1961 Cover: 0.10 **NM** value: **40.00**
• **CGC:** 1 graded, best 8.0
5 ❑ Jan 1962 Cover: 0.10 **NM** value: **40.00**
• **CGC:** 1 graded, best 8.5
6 ❑ Apr 1962 **NM** value: **35.00**
• **CGC:** 7 graded, best 9.2
7 ❑ Jun 1962 **NM** value: **35.00**
8 ❑ Aug 1962 Cover: 0.12 **NM** value: **35.00**
9 ❑ Oct 1962 Cover: 0.12 **NM** value: **35.00**
10 ❑ Dec 1962 Cover: 0.12 **NM** value: **35.00**
11 ❑ Feb 1963 Cover: 0.12 **NM** value: **25.00**
12 ❑ Apr 1963 Cover: 0.12 **NM** value: **25.00**
13 ❑ Jun 1963 Cover: 0.12 **NM** value: **35.00**
14 ❑ Aug 1963 Cover: 0.12 **NM** value: **35.00**
15 ❑ Oct 1963 Cover: 0.12 **NM** value: **35.00**
• **CGC:** 1 graded, best 8.0
16 ❑ Dec 1963 Cover: 0.12 **NM** value: **35.00**
17 ❑ Feb 1964 Cover: 0.12 **NM** value: **16.00**
18 ❑ May 1964 Cover: 0.12 **NM** value: **16.00**
19 ❑ Jul 1964 Cover: 0.12 **NM** value: **16.00**
• **CGC:** 1 graded, best 9.4
The World Shaker! **A:** Montes O Bache
20 ❑ 1965 Cover: 0.12 **NM** value: **16.00**
21 ❑ Dec 1964 Cover: 0.12 **NM** value: **16.00**
22 ❑ 1965 Cover: 0.12 **NM** value: **16.00**
23 ❑ Sep 1965 Cover: 0.12 **NM** value: **16.00**

GORGON — Venus

1 ❑ Jun 1996 Cover: 2.95 **NM** value: **Cover or less**
Dark Bandit **A:** Chouji Maboroshi **W:** Chouji Maboroshi
2 ❑ Jun 1996 Cover: 2.95 **NM** value: **Cover or less**
3 ❑ Jun 1996 Cover: 2.95 **NM** value: **Cover or less**
4 ❑ Jun 1996 Cover: 2.95 **NM** value: **Cover or less**
5 ❑ Aug 1996 Cover: 2.95 **NM** value: **Cover or less**

GORILLA GUNSLINGER — Mojo

0 ❑ Cover: 0.50 **NM** value: **1.00**
The Good, The Bad...and The Gorilla • Sampler **A:** Marc Erickson **W:** Norman Partridge

GOTCHA! — Rip Off

All issues are adults only.
1 ❑ Sep 1991, b&w Cover: 2.50 **NM** value: **Cover or less**

G.O.T.H. — Verotik

1 ❑ **NM** value: **3.00**
2 ❑ **NM** value: **3.00**
3 ❑ **NM** value: **3.00**
Bk 1 ❑ Oct 1996 Cover: 9.95 **NM** value: **Cover or less**
• collects mini-series

GOTHAM NIGHTS — DC

A desperate man who turns to crime to support his family becomes convinced that his wife is cheating on him.

An attractive woman who has her heart broken going from bed to bed ignores the longtime friend who could give her the love she needs.

An old man, loved by his wife, but dying of disease and high medical bills, looks for a way out for both of them.

A train-station doughnut-seller is bored with life. She's convinced that the man who comes by for breakfast every day is really Batman and is sure that he secretly loves her. One day, she climbs to a rooftop with a hunting rifle in order to force his hand.

In a city built for giants, the streets are filled with regular people. Gotham Nights is their story.

1 ❑ Mar 1992 Cover: 1.25 **NM** value: **1.50**
Circ: CapCity orders: **77,950**
Giants **A:** Mary Mitchell **W:** John Ostrander
2 ❑ Apr 1992 Cover: 1.25 **NM** value: **1.50**
Circ: CapCity orders: **47,700**
The Lessons Of Life **A:** Mary Mitchell **W:** John Ostrander
3 ❑ May 1992 Cover: 1.25 **NM** value: **1.50**
Circ: CapCity orders: **40,850**
Organisms **A:** Mary Mitchell **W:** John Ostrander
4 ❑ Jun 1992 Cover: 1.25 **NM** value: **1.50**
Circ: CapCity orders: **37,000**

GOTHAM NIGHTS II — DC

1 ❑ Mar 1995 Cover: 1.95 **NM** value: **2.00**
Circ: CapCity orders: **26,700**
2 ❑ Apr 1995 Cover: 1.95 **NM** value: **2.00**
Circ: CapCity orders: **21,625**
3 ❑ May 1995 Cover: 1.95 **NM** value: **2.00**
Circ: CapCity orders: **20,800**
Final Blows **A:** Mary Mitchell; Bret Blevins **W:** John Ostrander
4 ❑ Jun 1995 Cover: 1.95 **NM** value: **2.00**
Circ: CapCity orders: **18,800**
Ashes to Ashes **A:** Mary Mitchell; Bret Blevins **W:** John Ostrander

GOTHIC — 5th Panel

1 ❑ Apr 1997, b&w Cover: 1.95 **NM** value: **2.50**
Foundation **A:** Kevin Leen **W:** Marc Reichardt
2 ❑ Cover: 2.50 **NM** value: **Cover or less**

GOTHIC MOON — Anarchy Bridgeworks

1 ❑ Cover: 5.95 **NM** value: **Cover or less**

GOTHIC NIGHTS — Rebel

1 ❑ b&w Cover: 2.00 **NM** value: **Cover or less**
Circ: CapCity orders: **4,275**
2 ❑ Cover: 2.00 **NM** value: **Cover or less**

GOTHIC RED — Boneyard

1 ❑ Cover: 2.95 **NM** value: **Cover or less**
3 ❑ Mar 1997, b&w Cover: 2.95 **NM** value: **Cover or less**

GOTHIC SCROLLS, THE: DRAYVEN — Davdez

1 ❑ Dec 1997 Cover: 2.95 **NM** value: **Cover or less**
The Beginning **A:** David Hernandez **W:** David Hernandez
2 ❑ Feb 1998 Cover: 2.50 **NM** value: **Cover or less**
3 ❑ Mar 1998 Cover: 2.50 **NM** value: **Cover or less**
Ash 1 ❑ Aug 1997 Cover: 1.50 **NM** value: **Cover or less**
cover says Sep, indicia says Aug. • Preview edition.

GRACKLE, THE — Acclaim

Cross is an ex-cop, working security for an illegal gambling casino run by a Chinese drug lord. When the mayor's chief aide, Ryan Rozum, self-combusts due to a new designer drug during a rival gang's invasion, Cross finds himself hip-deep in city politics and intrigue. The death of his assistant in an illegal gambling den is an embarrassment for the mayor but a boon to his opponent, Derek Mancini, whose daughter Cross just happens to be dating.

Fans of hardboiled crime stories will appreciate this title from prolific writer Mike Baron (Batman, Punisher, Nexus) and veteran artist Paul Gulacy (Master of Kung Fu). Gulacy's distinctive figures and expressive faces convey a sense of hard-edged realism that complements Baron's down-to earth script.

1 ❑ Jan 1997, b&w Cover: 2.95 **NM** value: **Cover or less**
Doublecross, Part 1 **A:** Paul Gulacy **W:** Mike Baron
2 ❑ Feb 1997, b&w Cover: 2.95 **NM** value: **Cover or less**
Doublecross, Part 2 **A:** Paul Gulacy **W:** Mike Baron
3 ❑ Mar 1997, b&w Cover: 2.95 **NM** value: **Cover or less**
Doublecross, Part 3 **A:** Paul Gulacy **W:** Mike Baron
4 ❑ Apr 1997, b&w Cover: 2.95 **NM** value: **Cover or less**
Circ: Diamd. preorders: **8,097**
Doublecross, Part 4 **A:** Paul Gulacy **W:** Mike Baron

GRAFFITI KITCHEN — Tundra

1 ❑ Cover: 2.95 **NM value: Cover or less**
No issue number. **A:** Eddie Campbell **W:** Eddie Campbell

GRAFIK MUZIK — Caliber

1 ❑ b&w Cover: 3.50 **NM value: 20.00**
Circ: CapCity orders: **3,775**
2 ❑ ca. 1991 Cover: 2.50 **NM value: 12.00**
Circ: CapCity orders: **2,175** • **CGC:** 1 graded, best 9.2
3 ❑ Cover: 2.50 **NM value: 8.00**
Circ: CapCity orders: **1,695**
4 ❑ Cover: 2.50 **NM value: 8.00**
Circ: CapCity orders: **1,175**

GRAMMAR PATROL, THE — Castel Publications

1 ❑ Cover: 2.00 **NM value: Cover or less**

GRAND PRIX — Charlton

Porsches, Lotuses, Ferraris, and other formula cars are the real stars of this series, which features the European style of cross-country auto racing. Although the cars are the hook, for plot purposes, the stories pivot on the drivers, who race for reasons ranging from familial duty to proving self-worth to greed. Artists like Don Perlin (who drew The Defenders) and Jack Keller (who filled in on Kid Colt Outlaw for Marvel) contributed art.

Like romance comics and military titles, comics for racing enthusiasts are a branch of the industry that has withered and died for lack of enthusiasm. This title from Charlton was one of a stable of four comics relating to auto sports. Hot Rods and Racing Cars, Worlds of Wheels, and Drag n' Wheels populated the comics racks along side Grand Prix in the late 1960s.

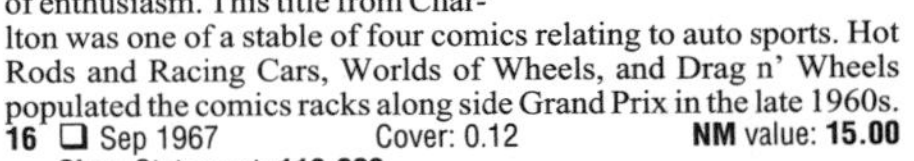

16 ❑ Sep 1967 Cover: 0.12 **NM value: 15.00**
Circ: Statement: **118,002**
17 ❑ 1967 Cover: 0.12 **NM value: 9.00**
Circ: Statement: **118,002**
18 ❑ 1968 Cover: 0.12 **NM value: 9.00**
Circ: Statement: **119,400**
19 ❑ May 1968 Cover: 0.12 **NM value: 9.00**
Circ: Statement: **119,400**
20 ❑ Jul 1968 Cover: 0.12 **NM value: 9.00**
Circ: Statement: **119,400**
21 ❑ Sep 1968 Cover: 0.12 **NM value: 6.00**
Circ: Statement: **119,400**
22 ❑ Nov 1968 Cover: 0.12 **NM value: 6.00**
Circ: Statement: **119,400**
23 ❑ Jan 1969 Cover: 0.12 **NM value: 6.00**
24 ❑ Mar 1969 Cover: 0.12 **NM value: 6.00**
25 ❑ May 1969 Cover: 0.12 **NM value: 6.00**
📖 Dead Man's Hands!; Fear Takes the Wheel; Rick Roberts: Smash-up **A:** Don Perlin; Jack Keller **W:** Jack Keller; Joe Gill
26 ❑ Jul 1969 Cover: 0.12 **NM value: 6.00**
27 ❑ Sep 1969 Cover: 0.15 **NM value: 6.00**
28 ❑ Nov 1969 Cover: 0.15 **NM value: 6.00**
29 ❑ Jan 1970 Cover: 0.15 **NM value: 6.00**
30 ❑ Mar 1970 Cover: 0.15 **NM value: 6.00**
31 ❑ May 1970 Cover: 0.15 **NM value: 6.00**

GRAND SLAM COMICS — Double A Comics

51 ❑ Feb 1946 Cover: 0.10 **NM value: Cover or less**
52 ❑ 1946 Cover: 0.10 **NM value: Cover or less**
53 ❑ Jul 1946 Cover: 0.10 **NM value: Cover or less**

GRANDSON OF ORIGINS OF MARVEL COMICS — Marvel

1 ❑ Cover: 24.99 **NM value: Cover or less**

GRAPHIC — Fantaco

1 ❑ Cover: 3.95 **NM value: Cover or less**

GRAPHIC HEROES IN HOUSE OF CARDS — Graphic Staffing

1 ❑ **NM value: 0.50**
No issue number. • personalized promotional piece for temporary graphics employees

GRAPHIC STORY MONTHLY — Fantagraphics

1 ❑ b&w Cover: 2.95 **NM value: 4.00**
2 ❑ b&w Cover: 2.95 **NM value: 3.50**
3 ❑ b&w Cover: 2.95 **NM value: 3.50**
4 ❑ b&w Cover: 2.95 **NM value: 3.50**
5 ❑ b&w Cover: 2.95 **NM value: 3.50**
6 ❑ b&w Cover: 2.95 **NM value: 3.50**
7 ❑ Cover: 3.50 **NM value: Cover or less**

GRAPHIQUE MUSIQUE — Slave Labor

1 ❑ Dec 1989, b&w Cover: 2.95 **NM value: 8.00**
2 ❑ Mar 1990, b&w Cover: 2.95 **NM value: 8.00**
3 ❑ May 1990, b&w Cover: 2.95 **NM value: 8.00**

GRASA DEL SOL — Estatua

1 ❑ Sep 1998 Cover: 3.00 **NM value: Cover or less**
📖 Espeso Seis **A:** Alejandro Fuentes **W:** Alejandro Fuentes

GRATEFUL DEAD COMIX — Kitchen Sink

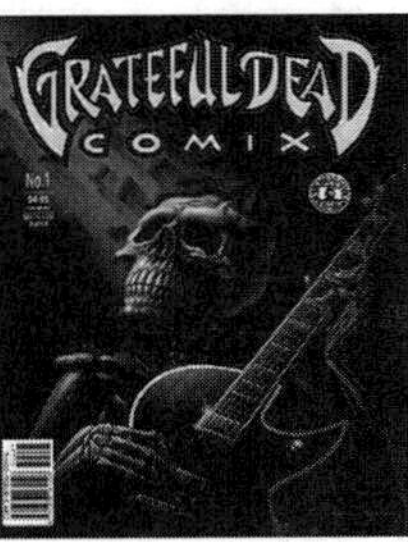

Grateful Dead Comix takes lyrics from the legendary rock band and adapts those stories to comic-book form. Although this is of obvious appeal to fans of The Grateful Dead, comics lovers should also take note of the wide variety of inspired art from the likes of Timothy Truman and Nina Paley.

In a nice touch, the comic book is printed on recycled paper with soy-based inks. The credits also note, "...with its high fiber content and soybean ink, this is probably a very tasty product if stir-fried with a little tarragon and basil. Maybe some hot sauce, too."

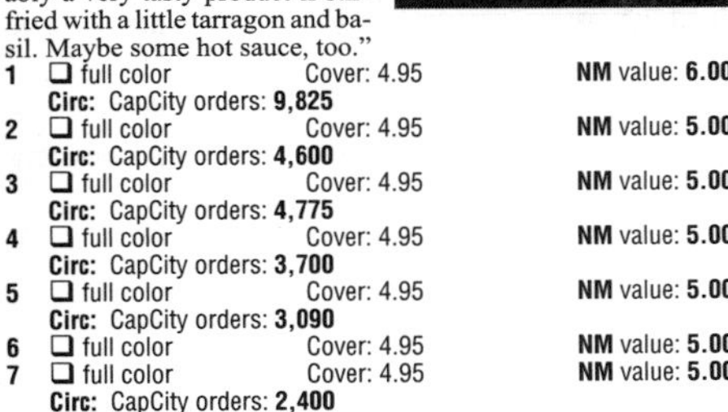

1 ❑ full color Cover: 4.95 **NM value: 6.00**
Circ: CapCity orders: **9,825**
2 ❑ full color Cover: 4.95 **NM value: 5.00**
Circ: CapCity orders: **4,600**
3 ❑ full color Cover: 4.95 **NM value: 5.00**
Circ: CapCity orders: **4,775**
4 ❑ full color Cover: 4.95 **NM value: 5.00**
Circ: CapCity orders: **3,700**
5 ❑ full color Cover: 4.95 **NM value: 5.00**
Circ: CapCity orders: **3,090**
6 ❑ full color Cover: 4.95 **NM value: 5.00**
7 ❑ full color Cover: 4.95 **NM value: 5.00**
Circ: CapCity orders: **2,400**

GRATEFUL DEAD COMIX (VOL. 2) — Kitchen Sink

1 ❑ Cover: 3.95 **NM value: Cover or less**
Circ: CapCity orders: **2,990**
• comic-book size.
2 ❑ Apr 1994 Cover: 3.95 **NM value: Cover or less**

GRAVEDIGGERS — Acclaim

1 ❑ Nov 1996, b&w Cover: 2.95 **NM value: Cover or less**
📖 Magic Bullet **A:** Mark Moretti **W:** Mark Moretti
2 ❑ Dec 1996, b&w Cover: 2.95 **NM value: Cover or less**
📖 The Wrong Man **A:** Mark Moretti **W:** Mark Moretti
3 ❑ Jan 1997, b&w Cover: 2.95 **NM value: Cover or less**
📖 Losses Unknown **A:** Mark Moretti **W:** Mark Moretti
4 ❑ Feb 1997, b&w Cover: 2.95 **NM value: Cover or less**
final issue.

GRAVEDIGGER TALES — Avalon

1 ❑ b&w Cover: 2.95 **NM value: Cover or less**

GRAVESTONE — Malibu

1 ❑ Cover: 2.25 **NM value: Cover or less**
Circ: CapCity orders: **10,475**
📖 Orpheus Descending **A:** Thomas Derenick **W:** Martin Powell
2 ❑ Cover: 2.25 **NM value: Cover or less**
Circ: CapCity orders: **5,200**
3 ❑ Sep 1993 Cover: 2.25 **NM value: Cover or less**
📖 Near Death Experience • Genesis **A:** Thomas Derenick **W:** Martin Powell
4 ❑ Cover: 2.25 **NM value: Cover or less**
Circ: CapCity orders: **6,125**
5 ❑ Cover: 2.25 **NM value: Cover or less**
Circ: CapCity orders: **4,975**
• Genesis **A:** Thomas Derenick **W:** Martin Powell
6 ❑ Cover: 2.25 **NM value: Cover or less**
Circ: CapCity orders: **3,925**
• Genesis **A:** Thomas Derenick **W:** Martin Powell
7 ❑ Feb 1994 Cover: 2.25 **NM value: Cover or less**
Circ: CapCity orders: **3,350**
• Genesis; last issue **A:** Thomas Derenick **W:** Martin Powell

GRAVESTOWN — Ariel

1 ❑ Oct 1997 Cover: 2.95 **NM value: Cover or less**

GRAVE TALES — Hamilton

1 ❑ Oct 1991, b&w Cover: 3.95 **NM value: Cover or less**
2 ❑ b&w Cover: 3.95 **NM value: Cover or less**
3 ❑ b&w Cover: 3.95 **NM value: Cover or less**

GREASE MONKEY — Kitchen Sink

1 ❑ Oct 1995 Cover: 3.50 **NM value: Cover or less**
📖 Art Lovers **A:** Tim Eldred **W:** Tim Eldred
2 ❑ Oct 1995 Cover: 3.50 **NM value: Cover or less**
📖 The Gift **A:** Tim Eldred **W:** Tim Eldred

GREASE MONKEY (IMAGE) — Image

1 ❑ Jan 1998 Cover: 2.95 **NM value: Cover or less**
Circ: Diamd. preorders: **3,106**
2 ❑ Mar 1998 Cover: 2.95 **NM value: Cover or less**
📖 Gorilla Tactics **A:** Tim Eldred **W:** Tim Eldred

GREAT AMERICAN WESTERN — AC

1 ❑ Cover: 1.75 **NM value: 2.00**
Circ: CapCity orders: **2,225**
📖 Dark Rider; Santee; The Missourian: Murder in Marlboro **A:** Rich Burchett; Dan Secrese **W:** Rich Burchett; Dan Secrese
2 ❑ Cover: 2.95 **NM value: Cover or less**
Circ: CapCity orders: **1,300**
3 ❑ Cover: 2.95 **NM value: Cover or less**
4 ❑ Cover: 3.50 **NM value: Cover or less**
5 ❑ Cover: 5.00 **NM value: Cover or less**

GREAT BIG BEEF — ERR

97 ❑ Jun 1996, b&w Cover: 1.97 **NM value: 2.00**
98 ❑ Jan 1997, b&w Cover: 1.98 **NM value: 2.00**
cover says Apr, indicia says Jan.
99 ❑ Sep 1997, b&w Cover: 1.99 **NM value: 2.00**

GREAT COMICS (GREAT COMICS) — Great Comics

1 ❑ Nov 1941 Cover: 0.10 **NM value: 500.00**
2 ❑ Dec 1941 Cover: 0.10 **NM value: 500.00**
3 ❑ Jan 1942 Cover: 0.10 **NM value: 800.00**
• **CGC:** 2 graded, best 8.0

GREAT COMICS (NOVACK) — Novack

1 ❑ ca. 1945 **NM value: 200.00**
• **CGC:** 11 graded, best 9.4

GREAT DETECTIVE, THE — Avalon

Avalon presents the adventures of Sir Arthur Conan Doyle's legendary detective in this collection of classic black-and-white newspaper-strip reprints from the 1950s. Sherlock Holmes and Doctor Watson tackle some of their toughest cases and battle some of their cleverest foes. Highlights include a tale of wits, as Holmes battles his arch-enemy Professor Moriarty, who intends to release a plague on the unsuspecting inhabitants of the city of Edinburgh. The stories are written by Edith Meiser (who also wrote the Holmes radio show) and drawn by Frank Giacoia (who worked on The Avengers and Marvel Saga and also inked the first appearance of The Punisher in Amazing Spider-Man #129). It should be noted that, from 1988 to 1990, Eternity released a collection of these same strips.

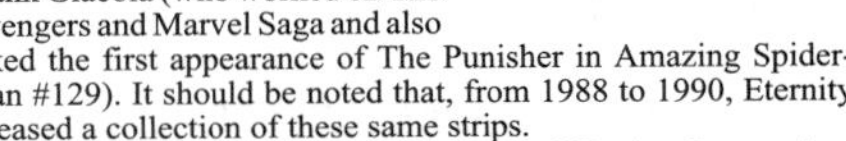

1 ❑ Cover: 2.95 **NM value: Cover or less**
2 ❑ Cover: 2.95 **NM value: Cover or less**
📖 Welcome Home,. Darling **A:** Frank Giacoia; Joe Gill **W:** George Wildman; Edith Meiser
3 ❑ Cover: 2.95 **NM value: Cover or less**
4 ❑ Cover: 2.95 **NM value: Cover or less**
5 ❑ Cover: 2.95 **NM value: Cover or less**
📖 A Direct Order **A:** Frank Giacoia **W:** Edith Meiser
6 ❑ Cover: 2.95 **NM value: Cover or less**
📖 The Tunnel Scheme; The Deadly Inheritance
7 ❑ Cover: 2.95 **NM value: Cover or less**
📖 Two Fisted Fix **A:** Nicholas Alascia; Frank Giacoia **W:** Edith Meiser

GREATEST 1950S STORIES EVER TOLD — DC

Bk 1❑ ca. 1991 Cover: 14.95 **NM value: Cover or less**
Bk 1/HC❑ Nov 1991 Cover: 29.95 **NM value: Cover or less**
Circ: CapCity orders: **2,350**
hardcover.

GREATEST AMERICAN COMIC BOOK — Ocean

1 ❑ Cover: 2.55 **NM value: Cover or less**
• Spider-Man parody; Batman

GREATEST BATMAN STORIES EVER TOLD, THE — DC

Bk 1❑ Cover: 15.95 **NM value: Cover or less**
Circ: CapCity orders: **11,700**
Bk 1/HC❑ Jan 1989 Cover: 29.95 **NM value: Cover or less**
Circ: CapCity orders: **5,050**
hardcover.
Bk 2❑ Cover: 15.95 **NM value: Cover or less**

GREATEST BATTLES OF THE AVENGERS — Marvel

Bk 1❑ Cover: 15.95 **NM value: Cover or less**
• Reprints Avengers #54, 55, 79, 160, and Avengers Annual # 7, 10 **A:** Michael Golden **W:** Jim Starlin; Chris Claremont ★ 1st Appearance of Rogue, Destiny. ★ Appearance of X-Men, Black Panther, Warlock. ★ Death of Gamora. ★ Death of Warlock.

GREATEST DIGGS OF ALL TIME! — Rip Off

1 ❑ Feb 1991, b&w Cover: 2.00 **NM value: Cover or less**
No issue number.

GREATEST FLASH STORIES EVER TOLD — DC

Bk 1❑ Cover: 14.95 **NM value: Cover or less**
Circ: CapCity orders: **3,250**
Bk 1/HC❑ Jan 1991 Cover: 29.95 **NM value: Cover or less**
hardcover.

GREATEST GOLDEN AGE STORIES EVER TOLD — DC

Bk 1/HC❑ Feb 1990 Cover: 24.95 **NM value: Cover or less**
Circ: CapCity orders: **4,650**
hardcover.

GREATEST JOKER STORIES EVER TOLD — DC

Bk 1❑ Aug 1989 Cover: 15.95 **NM value: Cover or less**
Circ: CapCity orders: **8,400**
Bk 1/HC❑ Feb 1989 Cover: 29.95 **NM value: Cover or less**
Circ: CapCity orders: **5,700**
hardcover.

GREATEST SUPERMAN STORIES EVER TOLD — DC

Bk 1❑ May 1989 Cover: 15.95 **NM value: Cover or less**
Circ: CapCity orders: **5,000**
Bk 1/HC❑ Mar 1988 Cover: 24.95 **NM value: Cover or less**
Circ: CapCity orders: **2,100**
hardcover.

CGC-graded: Multiply prices above by **33 for 9.9 M • 16 for 9.8 NM/M • 7 for 9.6 NM+ • 5 for 9.4 NM • 2.5 for 9.2 NM- • 1.5 for 9.0 VF/NM**

GREATEST TEAM-UP STORIES EVER TOLD — DC

Bk 1 ❑ Jul 1990 Cover: 14.95 **NM** value: **Cover or less**
Bk 1/HC ❑ Jan 1990 Cover: 24.95 **NM** value: **Cover or less**
Circ: CapCity orders: **5,200**
hardcover.

GREAT EXPLOITS — Decker

1 ❑ Oct 1957 Cover: 0.10 **NM** value: **24.00**
📖 Frog Men Against Belzar; Explorer Joe: Murder in the Himilayas; The Son of Robin Hood; The Terrorist

GREAT GALAXIES — Zub

0 ❑ b&w Cover: 2.95 **NM** value: **Cover or less**
📖 The Glory; Nal Ralone, Interstellar Archeologist; Work-a-Day World; The Warp Patrol in "Tourist Trap"; Andrew Cleese & The Alien **A:** Sam Salas **W:** Torger ★ 1st Appearance of The Warp Patrol.
1 ❑ b&w Cover: 2.50 **NM** value: **Cover or less**
📖 News Maker; Antique Death; The Conquered People **A:** Sam Salas **W:** Torger ★ Origin of Captain Dean.
2 ❑ b&w Cover: 2.50 **NM** value: **Cover or less**
📖 Final Objective; Death Stealer; The Warp Patrol: Night Shift **A:** Sam Salas **W:** Torger
3 ❑ b&w Cover: 2.50 **NM** value: **Cover or less**
📖 A Real Thrill; Stolen Kisses; The Warp Patrol: Payday **A:** Sam Salas **W:** Torger
4 ❑ b&w Cover: 2.50 **NM** value: **Cover or less**
📖 Funeral; Hacker!; Nal Ralone, Interstellar Archaeologist: Just Another Dragon Story; **A:** Sam Salas **W:** Torger
5 ❑ b&w Cover: 2.50 **NM** value: **Cover or less**
📖 The Warp Wars Saga **A:** Sam Salas **W:** Dave Beers
6/Ash ❑ **NM** value: **0.50**
📖 Glass Coffin • Flip book with Telluria Ashcan #6 **A:** Sam Salas **W:** Dave Beers

GREAT MORONS IN HISTORY — Revolutionary

1 ❑ Oct 1993, b&w Cover: 2.50 **NM** value: **Cover or less**
• Dan Quayle

GREAT SOCIETY COMIC BOOK, THE — Parallax

A bizarre political satire by D.J. Arneson and Tony Tallarico, The Great Society Comic Book casts the chief political figures of 1966 as a band of hapless super-heroes and villains. In the first issue, SuperLBJ (President Lyndon Johnson) is missing, and it's up to the Group Resigned to End All Threats, commonly known as the G.R.E.A.T Society, to find him.

In fairness, the satire is oblique at best, and the comics moments fall flat more often than not. Still, political wonks and history buffs can have royal sport playing "name that politician," as Fidel Castro, Nikita Khrushchev, Richard Nixon, Lady Bird Johnson, Hubert Humphrey, Barry Goldwater, and numerous others do battle in super-hero guises.

1 ❑ Cover: 1.00 **NM** value: **14.00**
📖 Super LBJ is Missing **A:** Tony Tallarico **W:** D.J. Arneson
2 ❑ Cover: 1.00 **NM** value: **10.00**

GREEENLOCK — Aircel

1 ❑ b&w Cover: 2.50 **NM** value: **Cover or less**

GREEN ARROW — DC

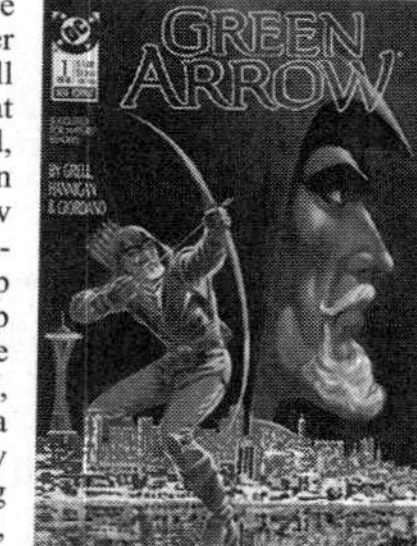

Originally introduced in More Fun Comics #73 (Nov 1941), Oliver Queen was a millionaire, who fell overboard off a yacht one night at sea. Washed up on a deserted island, Queen found himself with tiime on his hands and learned to wield a bow and arrow to survive with. He eventually devised trick arrows to help catch small game and, when a group of criminal invaded the island, he captured them and returned home, turning his new-found skills into a crime-fighting career that closely paralleled Batman's with a young sidekick (Speedy), an Arrowcave, Arrowcar, and Arrowplane.

After losing his fortune and fancier gadgets due to an unscrupulous partner's dealings, Queen took a more simplistic approach to crimefighting in Green Arrow: The Longbow Hunters by Mike Grell, eschewing the trick arrows for more traditional ones.

This series continued the adventures from that prestige format mini-series, with Queen's illegitimate son, Connor, taking on the title role near the series' end. — Brent

0 ❑ Oct 1994 Cover: 1.95 **NM** value: **2.50**
Circ: CapCity orders: **16,150**
1 ❑ Feb 1988 Cover: 1.00 **NM** value: **3.00**
Circ: CapCity orders: **56,850** • **CGC:** 4 graded, best 9.6
Painted cover. 📖 Hunters Moon, Part 1 **A:** Dick Giordano; Ed Hannigan **C:** Mike Grell **W:** Mike Grell
2 ❑ Mar 1988 Cover: 1.00 **NM** value: **2.50**
Circ: CapCity orders: **47,400** • **CGC:** 1 graded, best 9.6
Painted cover. 📖 Hunters Moon, Part 2 **A:** Dick Giordano; Ed Hannigan **C:** Mike Grell **W:** Mike Grell
3 ❑ Apr 1988 Cover: 1.00 **NM** value: **2.00**
Circ: CapCity orders: **42,300**
Painted cover. 📖 The Champions, Part 1 **A:** Frank McLaughlin; Dick Giordano; Ed Hannigan **C:** Mike Grell **W:** Mike Grell
4 ❑ May 1988 Cover: 1.00 **NM** value: **2.00**
Circ: CapCity orders: **37,800**
📖 The Champions, Part 2 **A:** Ed Hannigan **C:** Mike Grell **W:** Mike Grell
5 ❑ Jun 1988 Cover: 1.00 **NM** value: **2.00**
Circ: CapCity orders: **33,650**
📖 Gauntlet, Part 1
6 ❑ Jul 1988 Cover: 1.00 **NM** value: **2.00**
Circ: CapCity orders: **32,550**
📖 Gauntlet, Part 2
7 ❑ Aug 1988 Cover: 1.00 **NM** value: **2.00**
Circ: CapCity orders: **31,450**
8 ❑ Sep 1988 Cover: 1.00 **NM** value: **2.00**
Circ: CapCity orders: **30,150**
9 ❑ Oct 1988 Cover: 1.00 **NM** value: **2.00**
Circ: CapCity orders: **29,700**
📖 Here There Be Dragons, Part 1
10 ❑ Nov 1988 Cover: 1.00 **NM** value: **2.00**
Circ: CapCity orders: **27,900**
📖 Here There Be Dragons, Part 2 **C:** Mike Grell
11 ❑ Dec 1988 Cover: 1.00 **NM** value: **1.50**
📖 Here There Be Dragons, Part 3 **C:** Mike Grell
12 ❑ Dec 1988 Cover: 1.00 **NM** value: **1.50**
Circ: CapCity orders: **26,750**
📖 Here There Be Dragons, Part 4 **C:** Mike Grell
13 ❑ Jan 1989 Cover: 1.25 **NM** value: **1.50**
Circ: CapCity orders: **25,850**
📖 Moving Target, Part 1
14 ❑ Jan 1989 Cover: 1.25 **NM** value: **1.50**
Circ: CapCity orders: **25,800**
📖 Moving Target, Part 2
15 ❑ Feb 1989 Cover: 1.25 **NM** value: **1.50**
Circ: CapCity orders: **26,100**
📖 Seattle & Die, Part 1
16 ❑ Mar 1989 Cover: 1.25 **NM** value: **1.50**
Circ: CapCity orders: **24,550**
📖 Seattle & Die, Part 2
17 ❑ Apr 1989 Cover: 1.25 **NM** value: **1.50**
Circ: CapCity orders: **23,700**
📖 The Horseman, Part 1
18 ❑ May 1989 Cover: 1.25 **NM** value: **1.50**
Circ: CapCity orders: **23,250**
📖 The Horseman, Part 2
19 ❑ Jun 1989 Cover: 1.25 **NM** value: **1.50**
Circ: CapCity orders: **23,200**
📖 The Trial of Oliver Queen, Part 1
20 ❑ Jul 1989 Cover: 1.25 **NM** value: **1.50**
Circ: CapCity orders: **23,000**
📖 The Trial of Oliver Queen, Part 2
21 ❑ Aug 1989 Cover: 1.25 **NM** value: **2.50**
Circ: CapCity orders: **23,450**
📖 Blood of the Dragon, Part 1 ★ 1st Appearance of Connor Hawke (baby).
22 ❑ Aug 1989 Cover: 1.25 **NM** value: **1.50**
Circ: CapCity orders: **23,250**
📖 Blood of the Dragon, Part 2
23 ❑ Sep 1989 Cover: 1.25 **NM** value: **1.50**
Circ: CapCity orders: **23,150**
📖 Blood of the Dragon, Part 3
24 ❑ Sep 1989 Cover: 1.25 **NM** value: **1.50**
Circ: CapCity orders: **23,100**
📖 Blood of the Dragon, Part 4
25 ❑ Oct 1989 Cover: 1.25 **NM** value: **1.50**
Circ: CapCity orders: **23,250**
📖 Witch Hunt, Part 1
26 ❑ Nov 1989 Cover: 1.25 **NM** value: **1.50**
Circ: CapCity orders: **22,750**
📖 Witch Hunt, Part 2
27 ❑ Dec 1989 Cover: 1.25 **NM** value: **1.50**
Circ: CapCity orders: **23,950**
28 ❑ Jan 1990 Cover: 1.25 **NM** value: **1.50**
Circ: CapCity orders: **23,900**
29 ❑ Feb 1990 Cover: 1.25 **NM** value: **1.50**
Circ: CapCity orders: **22,800**
📖 Coyote Tears, Part 1
30 ❑ Mar 1990 Cover: 1.20 **NM** value: **1.50**
Circ: CapCity orders: **22,050**
📖 Coyote Tears, Part 2
31 ❑ Apr 1990 Cover: 1.20 **NM** value: **1.50**
Circ: CapCity orders: **22,100**
📖 The Canary is a Bird of Prey, Part 1
32 ❑ May 1990 Cover: 1.20 **NM** value: **1.50**
Circ: CapCity orders: **22,400**
📖 The Canary is a Bird of Prey, Part 2
33 ❑ Jun 1990 Cover: 1.20 **NM** value: **1.50**
Circ: CapCity orders: **21,750**
34 ❑ Jul 1990 Cover: 1.20 **NM** value: **1.50**
Circ: CapCity orders: **21,200**
35 ❑ Aug 1990 Cover: 1.25 **NM** value: **1.50**
Circ: CapCity orders: **20,750**
📖 The Black Arrow Saga, Part 1 • Black Arrow
36 ❑ Sep 1990 Cover: 1.25 **NM** value: **1.50**
Circ: CapCity orders: **20,500**
📖 The Black Arrow Saga, Part 2 • Black Arrow
37 ❑ Sep 1990 Cover: 1.25 **NM** value: **1.50**
Circ: CapCity orders: **20,400**
📖 The Black Arrow Saga, Part 3 • Black Arrow
38 ❑ Oct 1990 Cover: 1.25 **NM** value: **1.50**
Circ: CapCity orders: **19,800**
📖 The Black Arrow Saga, Part 4 • Black Arrow
39 ❑ Nov 1990 Cover: 1.25 **NM** value: **1.50**
Circ: CapCity orders: **19,500**
40 ❑ Dec 1990 Cover: 1.25 **NM** value: **1.50**
Circ: CapCity orders: **20,000**
41 ❑ Dec 1990 Cover: 1.25 **NM** value: **1.50**
42 ❑ Jan 1991 Cover: 1.25 **NM** value: **1.50**
Circ: CapCity orders: **20,000**
43 ❑ Feb 1991 Cover: 1.25 **NM** value: **1.50**
Circ: CapCity orders: **20,000**
44 ❑ Mar 1991 Cover: 1.25 **NM** value: **1.50**
Circ: CapCity orders: **19,400**
📖 Rock and Runes, Part 1
45 ❑ Apr 1991 Cover: 1.25 **NM** value: **1.50**
Circ: CapCity orders: **18,450**
📖 Rock and Runes, Part 2
46 ❑ May 1991 Cover: 1.25 **NM** value: **1.50**
Circ: CapCity orders: **17,800**
📖 Round the Horn, Part 1
47 ❑ Jun 1991 Cover: 1.50 **NM** value: **Cover or less**
Circ: CapCity orders: **17,250**
📖 Round the Horn, Part 2
48 ❑ Jun 1991 Cover: 1.50 **NM** value: **Cover or less**
Circ: CapCity orders: **17,100**
📖 Round the Horn, Part 3
49 ❑ Jul 1991 Cover: 1.50 **NM** value: **Cover or less**
Circ: CapCity orders: **17,000**
50 ❑ Aug 1991 Cover: 2.50 **NM** value: **Cover or less**
Circ: CapCity orders: **18,400**
• Giant-size.
51 ❑ Aug 1991 Cover: 1.50 **NM** value: **Cover or less**
52 ❑ Sep 1991 Cover: 1.50 **NM** value: **Cover or less**
Circ: CapCity orders: **17,350**
53 ❑ Oct 1991 Cover: 1.50 **NM** value: **Cover or less**
Circ: CapCity orders: **17,200**
54 ❑ Nov 1991 Cover: 1.50 **NM** value: **Cover or less**
Circ: CapCity orders: **16,800**
55 ❑ Dec 1991 Cover: 1.50 **NM** value: **Cover or less**
Circ: CapCity orders: **16,950**
📖 Justice is Mine, Part 1 **A:** Rick Hoberg **W:** Mike Grell
56 ❑ Jan 1992 Cover: 1.50 **NM** value: **Cover or less**
Circ: CapCity orders: **15,950**
📖 Justice is Mine, Part 2
57 ❑ Feb 1992 Cover: 1.25 **NM** value: **1.50**
Circ: CapCity orders: **15,600**
📖 ...And Not a Drop to Drink, Part 1
58 ❑ Mar 1992 Cover: 1.25 **NM** value: **1.50**
Circ: CapCity orders: **14,700**
📖 ...And Not a Drop to Drink, Part 2
59 ❑ Apr 1992 Cover: 1.25 **NM** value: **1.50**
Circ: CapCity orders: **13,950**
📖 Predator, Part 1
60 ❑ May 1992 Cover: 1.25 **NM** value: **1.50**
Circ: CapCity orders: **13,550**
📖 Predator, Part 2
61 ❑ May 1992 Cover: 1.50 **NM** value: **Cover or less**
Circ: CapCity orders: **13,500**
62 ❑ Jun 1992 Cover: 1.50 **NM** value: **Cover or less**
Circ: CapCity orders: **13,800**
63 ❑ Jun 1992 Cover: 1.50 **NM** value: **Cover or less**
Circ: CapCity orders: **13,950**
📖 The Hunt for the Red Dragon, Part 1
64 ❑ Jul 1992 Cover: 1.50 **NM** value: **Cover or less**
Circ: CapCity orders: **13,550**
📖 The Hunt for the Red Dragon, Part 2
65 ❑ Aug 1992 Cover: 1.50 **NM** value: **Cover or less**
Circ: CapCity orders: **14,050**
📖 The Hunt for the Red Dragon, Part 3
66 ❑ Sep 1992 Cover: 1.50 **NM** value: **Cover or less**
Circ: CapCity orders: **12,850**
📖 The Hunt for the Red Dragon, Part 4
67 ❑ Oct 1992 Cover: 1.50 **NM** value: **Cover or less**
Circ: CapCity orders: **12,550**
📖 Bum Rap, Part 1
68 ❑ Nov 1992 Cover: 1.50 **NM** value: **Cover or less**
Circ: CapCity orders: **12,550**
📖 Bum Rap, Part 2
69 ❑ Dec 1992 Cover: 1.75 **NM** value: **Cover or less**
Circ: CapCity orders: **12,250**
📖 Reunion Tour, Part 1 **A:** Rick Hoberg **W:** Mike Grell
70 ❑ Jan 1993 Cover: 1.75 **NM** value: **Cover or less**
Circ: CapCity orders: **11,900**
📖 Reunion Tour, Part 2
71 ❑ Feb 1993 Cover: 1.75 **NM** value: **Cover or less**
Circ: CapCity orders: **12,050**
📖 Wild in the Streets, Part 1
72 ❑ Mar 1993 Cover: 1.75 **NM** value: **Cover or less**
Circ: CapCity orders: **11,750**
📖 Wild in the Streets, Part 2
73 ❑ Apr 1993 Cover: 1.75 **NM** value: **Cover or less**
Circ: CapCity orders: **11,950**
📖 Trigger, Part 1
74 ❑ May 1993 Cover: 1.75 **NM** value: **Cover or less**
Circ: CapCity orders: **11,950**
📖 Trigger, Part 2
75 ❑ Jun 1993 Cover: 2.50 **NM** value: **Cover or less**
Circ: CapCity orders: **15,550**
• Giant-size.
76 ❑ Jul 1993 Cover: 1.75 **NM** value: **Cover or less**
Circ: CapCity orders: **11,700**
📖 Killing Camp, Part 1 ★ Origin of Green Lantern and Green Arrow.
77 ❑ Aug 1993 Cover: 1.75 **NM** value: **Cover or less**
Circ: CapCity orders: **11,700**
📖 Killing Camp, Part 2
78 ❑ Sep 1993 Cover: 1.75 **NM** value: **Cover or less**
Circ: CapCity orders: **11,000**
📖 Killing Camp, Part 3
79 ❑ Oct 1993 Cover: 1.75 **NM** value: **Cover or less**
Circ: CapCity orders: **11,000**
📖 New Dogs, Old Tricks, Part 1
80 ❑ Nov 1993 Cover: 1.75 **NM** value: **Cover or less**
Circ: CapCity orders: **10,500**
📖 New Dogs, Old Tricks, Part 2 **A:** Rick Hoberg **W:** Mike Grell
81 ❑ Dec 1993 Cover: 1.75 **NM** value: **Cover or less**
Circ: CapCity orders: **10,500**
82 ❑ Jan 1994 Cover: 1.75 **NM** value: **Cover or less**
Circ: CapCity orders: **10,300**
📖 Night of the Bow **A:** Jim Aparo **W:** Kevin Dooley

Other grades: Multiply prices above by **1.5 for Mint • 2/3 for Very Fine • 1/3 for Fine • 1/5 for Very Good • 1/8 for Good**

83 ❑ Feb 1994 Cover: 1.75 **NM** value: **Cover or less**
Circ: CapCity orders: **10,050**

84 ❑ Mar 1994 Cover: 1.75 **NM** value: **Cover or less**
Circ: CapCity orders: **9,600**

85 ❑ Apr 1994 Cover: 1.75 **NM** value: **Cover or less**
Circ: CapCity orders: **9,250**

86 ❑ May 1994 Cover: 1.75 **NM** value: **Cover or less**
Circ: CapCity orders: **11,650**
• Catwoman

87 ❑ Jun 1994 Cover: 1.75 **NM** value: **1.95**
Circ: CapCity orders: **9,350**

88 ❑ Jul 1994 Cover: 1.95 **NM** value: **Cover or less**
Circ: CapCity orders: **9,550**
📖 The Hero Descending **A:** Jim Aparo **W:** Kevin Dooley ★ Appearance of JLA.

89 ❑ Aug 1994 Cover: 1.95 **NM** value: **Cover or less**
Circ: CapCity orders: **9,500**

90 ❑ Sep 1994 Cover: 1.95 **NM** value: **2.25**
Circ: CapCity orders: **11,800**
📖 Crossroads Conclusion; Zero Hour • Zero Hour

91 ❑ Nov 1994 Cover: 1.95 **NM** value: **Cover or less**
Circ: CapCity orders: **9,550**

92 ❑ Dec 1994 Cover: 1.95 **NM** value: **Cover or less**
Circ: CapCity orders: **10,050**

93 ❑ Jan 1995 Cover: 1.95 **NM** value: **Cover or less**
Circ: CapCity orders: **10,000**

94 ❑ Feb 1995 Cover: 1.95 **NM** value: **Cover or less**
Circ: CapCity orders: **10,025**

95 ❑ Mar 1995 Cover: 1.95 **NM** value: **Cover or less**
Circ: CapCity orders: **9,450**

96 ❑ Apr 1995 Cover: 1.95 **NM** value: **3.00**
Circ: CapCity orders: **9,850**
📖 Where Angels Fear to Tread, Part 1

97 ❑ Jun 1995 Cover: 2.25 **NM** value: **3.00**
Circ: CapCity orders: **8,950**
📖 Where Angels Fear to Tread, Part 2

98 ❑ Jul 1995 Cover: 2.25 **NM** value: **3.00**
Circ: CapCity orders: **9,500**
📖 Where Angels Fear to Tread, Part 3

99 ❑ Aug 1995 Cover: 2.25 **NM** value: **3.00**
Circ: CapCity orders: **9,900**
📖 Where Angels Fear to Tread, Part 4

100 ❑ Sep 1995 Cover: 3.95 **NM** value: **7.00**
Circ: CapCity orders: **15,600** • **CGC:** 4 graded, best 9.8
enhanced cover. • Giant-size. 📖 Where Angels Fear to Tread, Part 5

101 ❑ Oct 1995 Cover: 2.25 **NM** value: **26.00**
Circ: CapCity orders: **8,750** • **CGC:** 15 graded, best 9.8
📖 Where Angels Fear to Tread, Part 6 ★ Death of Green Arrow I (Oliver Queen). ★ Death of Oliver Queen.

102 ❑ Nov 1995 Cover: 2.25 **NM** value: **Cover or less**
📖 Underworld Unleashed • Underworld Unleashed

103 ❑ Dec 1995 Cover: 2.25 **NM** value: **Cover or less**

104 ❑ Jan 1996 Cover: 2.25 **NM** value: **Cover or less**

105 ❑ Feb 1996 Cover: 2.25 **NM** value: **Cover or less**
📖 Open Season **A:** Rodolfo DaMaggio **W:** Chuck Dixon ★ Appearance of Robin.

106 ❑ Mar 1996 Cover: 2.25 **NM** value: **Cover or less**
📖 Enter the Roustabout **A:** Rodolfo DaMaggio **W:** Chuck Dixon

107 ❑ Apr 1996 Cover: 2.25 **NM** value: **Cover or less**
📖 Viva Los Dragons! **A:** Rodolfo DaMaggio **W:** Chuck Dixon

108 ❑ May 1996 Cover: 2.25 **NM** value: **Cover or less**

109 ❑ Jun 1996 Cover: 2.25 **NM** value: **Cover or less**

110 ❑ Jul 1996 Cover: 2.25 **NM** value: **Cover or less**
📖 Hard-Traveling Heroes: The Next Generation, Part 2

111 ❑ Aug 1996 Cover: 2.25 **NM** value: **Cover or less**
📖 Hard-Traveling Heroes: The Next Generation, Part 4

112 ❑ Sep 1996 Cover: 2.25 **NM** value: **Cover or less**
📖 The Lotus Seed, Part 1

113 ❑ Oct 1996 Cover: 2.25 **NM** value: **Cover or less**
📖 The Lotus Seed, Part 2 **A:** Will Rosado **W:** Chuck Dixon

114 ❑ Nov 1996 Cover: 2.25 **NM** value: **Cover or less**
Circ: Diamd. preorders: **29,017**
📖 The Thousand Year Night • Final Night **A:** Will Rosado **W:** Chuck Dixon

115 ❑ Dec 1996 Cover: 2.25 **NM** value: **Cover or less**
Circ: Diamd. preorders: **21,872**
📖 The Iron Death, Part 1 **A:** Will Rosado **W:** Chuck Dixon ★ Appearance of Shado, Black Canary.

116 ❑ Jan 1997 Cover: 2.25 **NM** value: **Cover or less**
Circ: Diamd. preorders: **21,119**
📖 The Iron Death, Part 2 **A:** Will Rosado **W:** Chuck Dixon ★ Appearance of Black Canary, Oracle, Shado.

117 ❑ Feb 1997 Cover: 2.25 **NM** value: **Cover or less**
Circ: Diamd. preorders: **20,230**
📖 The Iron Death, Part 3; The Death that Walks **A:** Will Rosado **W:** Chuck Dixon ★ Appearance of Black Canary.

118 ❑ Mar 1997 Cover: 2.25 **NM** value: **Cover or less**
Circ: Diamd. preorders: **19,421**
📖 Endangered Species, Part 1 **A:** Dougie Braithwaite **W:** Chuck Dixon

119 ❑ Apr 1997 Cover: 2.25 **NM** value: **Cover or less**
Circ: Diamd. preorders: **18,957**
📖 Endangered Species, Part 2 **A:** Dougie Braithwaite **W:** Chuck Dixon ★ Appearance of Warlord.

120 ❑ May 1997 Cover: 2.25 **NM** value: **Cover or less**
Circ: Diamd. preorders: **18,684**

121 ❑ Jun 1997 Cover: 2.25 **NM** value: **Cover or less**
Circ: Diamd. preorders: **19,486**

122 ❑ Jul 1997 Cover: 2.25 **NM** value: **Cover or less**
Circ: Diamd. preorders: **18,879**
📖 Stormbringers, Part 1

123 ❑ Aug 1997 Cover: 2.25 **NM** value: **Cover or less**
Circ: Diamd. preorders: **18,721**
📖 Stormbringers, Part 2

124 ❑ Sep 1997 Cover: 2.25 **NM** value: **Cover or less**
Circ: Diamd. preorders: **18,022**

125 ❑ Oct 1997 Cover: 3.50 **NM** value: **Cover or less**
Circ: Diamd. preorders: **27,513**
• Giant-size. 📖 Hate Crimes, Part 1 • continues in Green Lantern #92

126 ❑ Nov 1997 Cover: 2.50 **NM** value: **Cover or less**
Circ: Diamd. preorders: **27,646**
📖 Hate Crimes, Part 3 **A:** Dougie Braithwaite **W:** Chuck Dixon

127 ❑ Dec 1997 Cover: 2.50 **NM** value: **Cover or less**
Circ: Diamd. preorders: **19,718**
Face cover. 📖 Doubleback **A:** Dougie Braithwaite **W:** Chuck Dixon

128 ❑ Jan 1998 Cover: 2.50 **NM** value: **Cover or less**
Circ: Diamd. preorders: **20,182**
📖 Deadly Comrades, Part 1

129 ❑ Feb 1998 Cover: 2.50 **NM** value: **Cover or less**
Circ: Diamd. preorders: **19,391**
📖 Deadly Comrades, Part 2

130 ❑ Mar 1998 Cover: 2.50 **NM** value: **Cover or less**
Circ: Diamd. preorders: **33,499**
cover forms triptych with Flash #135 and Green Lantern #96. 📖 Three of a Kind, Part 2

131 ❑ Apr 1998 Cover: 2.50 **NM** value: **Cover or less**
Circ: Diamd. preorders: **18,873**

132 ❑ May 1998 Cover: 2.50 **NM** value: **Cover or less**
Circ: Diamd. preorders: **20,569**
📖 Like A God, Part 1

133 ❑ Jun 1998 Cover: 2.50 **NM** value: **Cover or less**
Circ: Diamd. preorders: **26,076**
📖 Like A God, Part 2 ★ Appearance of JLA.

134 ❑ Jul 1998 Cover: 2.50 **NM** value: **Cover or less**
Circ: Diamd. preorders: **31,806**
📖 Brotherhood of the Fist, Part 1 • continues in Detective Comics #723 ★ Appearance of Batman.

135 ❑ Aug 1998 Cover: 2.50 **NM** value: **Cover or less**
Circ: Diamd. preorders: **29,877**
📖 Brotherhood of the Fist, Part 5 ★ Versus Lady Shiva.

136 ❑ Sep 1998 Cover: 2.50 **NM** value: **Cover or less**
Circ: Diamd. preorders: **34,525**
📖 Greener Pastures, Part 1 ★ Appearance of Hal Jordan.

137 ❑ Oct 1998 Cover: 2.50 **NM** value: **Cover or less**
Circ: Diamd. preorders: **26,686** • **CGC:** 23 graded, best 9.6
📖 Full Circle final issue. ★ Appearance of Superman.

1000000 ❑ Nov 1998 Cover: 2.50 **NM** value: **Cover or less**
Circ: Diamd. preorders: **34,343**
📖 All Down the Years final issue. **A:** Frank Teran **W:** Chuck Dixon

Anl 1 ❑ Sep 1988 Cover: 2.00 **NM** value: **3.50**
Circ: CapCity orders: **30,750**

Anl 2 ❑ Aug 1989 Cover: 2.50 **NM** value: **3.00**
Circ: CapCity orders: **23,400**

Anl 3 ❑ Dec 1990 Cover: 2.50 **NM** value: **3.00**
Circ: CapCity orders: **23,350**

Anl 4 ❑ Jun 1991 Cover: 2.95 **NM** value: **3.00**
Circ: CapCity orders: **16,350**
• 50th Anniversary. • Robin Hood

Anl 5 ❑ ca. 1994 Cover: 3.00 **NM** value: **Cover or less**
Circ: CapCity orders: **19,950**
📖 Eclipso: The Darkness Within, Part 8 • Eclipso, Batman

Anl 6 ❑ ca. 1994 Cover: 3.50 **NM** value: **Cover or less**
Circ: CapCity orders: **19,100**
📖 Bloodlines • Bloodlines ★ 1st Appearance of Hook.

Anl 7 ❑ ca. 1994 Cover: 3.95 **NM** value: **Cover or less**
📖 Year One • Year One

GREEN ARROW (2ND SERIES) DC

1 ❑ Apr 2001 Cover: 2.50 **NM** value: **6.00**
Circ: Diamd. preorders: **85,046** • **CGC:** 318 graded, best 9.9
📖 Quiver, Part 1 • Return of Oliver Queen **A:** Phil Hester **W:** Kevin Smith

2 ❑ May 2001 Cover: 2.50 **NM** value: **Cover or less**
Circ: Diamd. preorders: **70,862** • **CGC:** 74 graded, best 10.0
📖 Quiver, Part 2 **A:** Phil Hester **W:** Kevin Smith

3 ❑ Jun 2001 Cover: 2.50 **NM** value: **Cover or less**
Circ: Diamd. preorders: **69,693** • **CGC:** 15 graded, best 9.8

4 ❑ Jul 2001 Cover: 2.50 **NM** value: **Cover or less**
Circ: Diamd. preorders: **85,317** • **CGC:** 6 graded, best 9.9

5 ❑ Aug 2001 Cover: 2.50 **NM** value: **Cover or less**
Circ: Diamd. preorders: **88,063** • **CGC:** 5 graded, best 9.8

6 ❑ Sep 2001 Cover: 2.50 **NM** value: **Cover or less**
Circ: Diamd. preorders: **90,703** • **CGC:** 4 graded, best 9.9

GREEN ARROW (MINI-SERIES) DC

1 ❑ May 1983 Cover: 0.60 **NM** value: **3.00**

2 ❑ Jun 1983 Cover: 0.60 **NM** value: **2.50**
📖 A Slight Case Of Vertigo..! **A:** Dick Giordano; Trevor Von Eeden **W:** Mike W. Barr

3 ❑ Jul 1983 Cover: 0.60 **NM** value: **2.00**

4 ❑ Aug 1983 Cover: 0.60 **NM** value: **2.00**

GREEN ARROW: THE LONGBOW HUNTERS DC

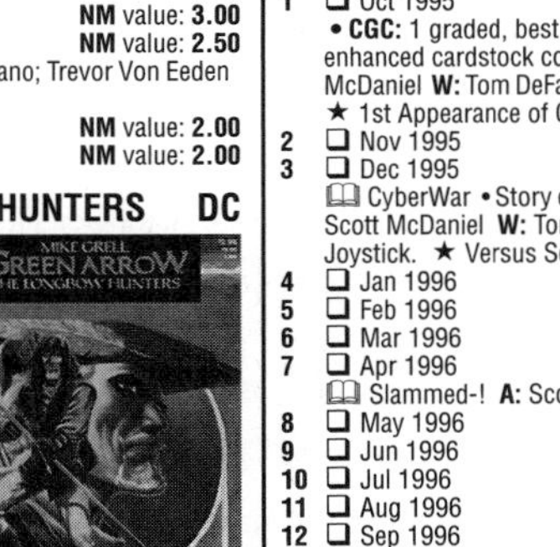

Created by writer and artist Mike Grell, The Longbow Hunters is widely recognized as one of the finest Green Arrow stories. It begins with Green Arrow stalking a slasher who preyed on prostitutes. But when Arrow finally found his quarry, he was in for a surprise: the slasher had been killed by a single, black arrow. Apparently, there was a new archer in town.

But the slasher was not the only victim. A growing list of middle-aged men were being found dead, killed by similar arrows. The only common factor seemed to be that the victims were middle-aged men with no military records.

Arrow followed the trail, eventually coming face-to-face with a beautiful young woman named Shado who wielded a very deadly bow. Inevitably, their lives would intertwine, and Arrow would find himself drawn into her personal quest for revenge.

1 ❑ Aug 1987 Cover: 2.95 **NM** value: **4.00**
Circ: CapCity orders: **25,400** • **CGC:** 7 graded, best 9.8
📖 The Hunters **A:** Mike Grell **W:** Mike Grell ★ 1st Appearance of Shado.

1-2 ❑ Aug 1987 Cover: 2.95 **NM** value: **3.00**

1-3 ❑ Aug 1987 Cover: 2.95 **NM** value: **3.00**

2 ❑ Sep 1987 Cover: 2.95 **NM** value: **3.00**
Circ: CapCity orders: **24,875**
📖 Dragon Hunt **A:** Mike Grell **W:** Mike Grell

3 ❑ Oct 1987 Cover: 2.95 **NM** value: **3.00**
Circ: CapCity orders: **30,050**
📖 Tracking Snow **A:** Mike Grell **W:** Mike Grell

Bk 1 ❑ Jun 1989 Cover: 12.95 **NM** value: **Cover or less**
Circ: CapCity orders: **4,600**
📖 The Hunters; Dragon Hunt; Tracking Snow • Collects Green Arrow: The Longbow Hunters #1-3 **A:** Mike Grell **W:** Mike Grell

GREEN ARROW: THE WONDER YEAR DC

1 ❑ Feb 1993 Cover: 1.75 **NM** value: **2.00**
Circ: CapCity orders: **17,650**

2 ❑ Mar 1993 Cover: 1.75 **NM** value: **2.00**
Circ: CapCity orders: **13,900**

3 ❑ Apr 1993 Cover: 1.75 **NM** value: **2.00**
Circ: CapCity orders: **13,300**

4 ❑ May 1993 Cover: 1.75 **NM** value: **2.00**
Circ: CapCity orders: **13,000**

GREEN CANDLES DC / Paradox

1 ❑ ca. 1995, b&w Cover: 5.95 **NM** value: **Cover or less**
• digest. **A:** Robin Smith **W:** Tom De Haven

2 ❑ ca. 1995, b&w Cover: 5.95 **NM** value: **Cover or less**
• digest. **A:** Robin Smith **W:** Tom De Haven

3 ❑ ca. 1995, b&w Cover: 5.95 **NM** value: **Cover or less**
• digest. **A:** Robin Smith **W:** Tom De Haven

Bk 1 ❑ Cover: 9.95 **NM** value: **Cover or less**
• collects mini-series

GREENER PASTURES Kronos

1 ❑ Cover: 2.50 **NM** value: **Cover or less**

1-2 ❑ Jan 1997 Cover: 2.50 **NM** value: **Cover or less**

2 ❑ Oct 1994 Cover: 2.50 **NM** value: **Cover or less**

3 ❑ Feb 1995 Cover: 2.50 **NM** value: **Cover or less**

4 ❑ Dec 1995 Cover: 2.50 **NM** value: **Cover or less**

4.5 ❑ Feb 1996 Cover: 1.95 **NM** value: **Cover or less**

5 ❑ Aug 1996 Cover: 2.95 **NM** value: **Cover or less**

6 ❑ Nov 1996 Cover: 2.95 **NM** value: **Cover or less**

7 ❑ Feb 1997 Cover: 2.95 **NM** value: **Cover or less**

GREEN GIANT COMICS Pelican Publications

1 ❑ Jan 1940 **NM** value: **Cover or less**
• **CGC:** 1 graded, best 1.5

GREEN GOBLIN Marvel

Long-time readers of Marvel comics will recognize the Green Goblin as the arch-nemesis of Spider-Man. In this series, the Green Goblin's mantle has passed to Philip Urich, nephew of veteran Daily Bugle reporter Ben Urich. Even more interestingly, this Green Goblin was not a villain.

This series portrays a young man who has acquired an assortment of weapons and paraphernalia and who tries to do the right thing without placing himself in danger. The tried-and-true Marvel tactic of depicting ordinary people dealing with extraordinary situations is much in evidence here, and evokes the feel of early Spider-Man stories. But can the super-villain legacy of Green Goblin be overcome? Though Philip Urich revels in the excitement, he may not have the devotion necessary to be accepted as a hero.

1 ❑ Oct 1995 Cover: 2.95 **NM** value: **Cover or less**
• **CGC:** 1 graded, best 9.8
enhanced cardstock cover. 📖 Enter the Green Goblin **A:** Scott McDaniel **W:** Tom DeFalco ★ Origin of Green Goblin IV (Phil Urich). ★ 1st Appearance of Green Goblin IV (Phil Urich).

2 ❑ Nov 1995 Cover: 1.95 **NM** value: **Cover or less**

3 ❑ Dec 1995 Cover: 1.95 **NM** value: **Cover or less**
📖 CyberWar • Story continued from Amazing Scarlet Spider #2 **A:** Scott McDaniel **W:** Tom DeFalco ★ Appearance of Scarlet Spider, Joystick. ★ Versus Scarlet Spider.

4 ❑ Jan 1996 Cover: 1.95 **NM** value: **Cover or less**

5 ❑ Feb 1996 Cover: 1.95 **NM** value: **Cover or less**

6 ❑ Mar 1996 Cover: 1.95 **NM** value: **Cover or less**

7 ❑ Apr 1996 Cover: 1.95 **NM** value: **Cover or less**
📖 Slammed-! **A:** Scott McDaniel **W:** Tom DeFalco

8 ❑ May 1996 Cover: 1.95 **NM** value: **Cover or less**

9 ❑ Jun 1996 Cover: 1.95 **NM** value: **Cover or less**

10 ❑ Jul 1996 Cover: 1.95 **NM** value: **Cover or less**

11 ❑ Aug 1996 Cover: 1.95 **NM** value: **Cover or less**

12 ❑ Sep 1996 Cover: 1.95 **NM** value: **Cover or less**
📖 Onslaught: Impact 2

13 ❑ Oct 1996 Cover: 1.95 **NM** value: **Cover or less**
final issue.

GREEN-GREY SPONGE-SUIT SUSHI TURTLES Mirage

1 ❑ full color Cover: 3.33 **NM** value: **3.50**
Circ: CapCity orders: **10,900**
cardstock cover. • parody **A:** Mark Martin **C:** Mark Martin **W:** Mark Martin

CGC-graded: Multiply prices above by **33 for 9.9 M** • **16 for 9.8 NM/M** • **7 for 9.6 NM+** • **5 for 9.4 NM** • **2.5 for 9.2 NM-** • **1.5 for 9.0 VF/NM**

GREENHAVEN — Aircel

1 ❑ full color Cover: 2.00 **NM** value: **Cover or less**
Circ: CapCity orders: **2,950**
2 ❑ full color Cover: 2.00 **NM** value: **Cover or less**
Circ: CapCity orders: **2,250**
3 ❑ full color Cover: 2.00 **NM** value: **Cover or less**
Circ: CapCity orders: **2,150**
• Continued in Elfford #21 **A:** Barry Blair; David Cooper **W:** Barry Blair

GREEN HORNET ANNIVERSARY SPECIAL — Now

1 ❑ Aug 1992 Cover: 2.50 **NM** value: **Cover or less**
Circ: CapCity orders: **16,100**
• bagged; with button
2 ❑ Sep 1992 Cover: 1.95 **NM** value: **Cover or less**
Circ: CapCity orders: **14,275**
3 ❑ Oct 1992 Cover: 1.95 **NM** value: **Cover or less**

GREEN HORNET COMICS — Harvey

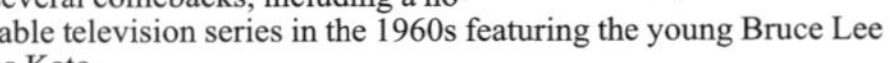

Frustrated with the slow speed of justice and the corruption of the police, newspaper publisher Brit Reid donned a green hat, coat, and mask to fight denizens of the underworld as the Green Hornet. Alongside his Asian servant Kato, the Green Hornet made life tough for racketeers and crooks on his famous radio show during the 1930s and 40s, and inevitably made the jump to comics early in the Golden Age. First published by Holyoke, The Green Hornet was taken over by Harvey, which continued the run through the late 1940s. The Hornet has made several comebacks, including a notable television series in the 1960s featuring the young Bruce Lee as Kato.

1 ❑ Dec 1940, four-color Cover: 0.10 **NM** value: **3600.00**
• **CGC:** 3 graded, best 4.0
2 ❑ Mar 1941 Cover: 0.10 **NM** value: **1200.00**
• **CGC:** 2 graded, best 9.2
3 ❑ Apr 1941 Cover: 0.10 **NM** value: **950.00**
• **CGC:** 1 graded, best 6.0
4 ❑ May 1941 Cover: 0.10 **NM** value: **700.00**
5 ❑ Jun 1941 Cover: 0.10 **NM** value: **700.00**
6 ❑ Aug 1941 Cover: 0.10 **NM** value: **650.00**
• **CGC:** 1 graded, best 3.0
7 ❑ Jun 1942 Cover: 0.10 **NM** value: **575.00**
8 ❑ Aug 1942 Cover: 0.10 **NM** value: **575.00**
9 ❑ Oct 1942, four-color Cover: 0.10 **NM** value: **625.00**
• **CGC:** 2 graded, best 9.8
10 ❑ Dec 1942 Cover: 0.10 **NM** value: **575.00**
• **CGC:** 2 graded, best 7.5
11 ❑ Feb 1943 Cover: 0.10 **NM** value: **450.00**
12 ❑ Apr 1943 Cover: 0.10 **NM** value: **450.00**
• **CGC:** 1 graded, best 9.6
13 ❑ Jul 1943 Cover: 0.10 **NM** value: **450.00**
14 ❑ Sep 1943 Cover: 0.10 **NM** value: **450.00**
• **CGC:** 1 graded, best 7.0
15 ❑ Nov 1943 Cover: 0.10 **NM** value: **450.00**
16 ❑ Jan 1944 Cover: 0.10 **NM** value: **450.00**
17 ❑ Mar 1944 Cover: 0.10 **NM** value: **450.00**
18 ❑ May 1944 Cover: 0.10 **NM** value: **450.00**
19 ❑ Jul 1944 Cover: 0.10 **NM** value: **450.00**
20 ❑ Sep 1944 Cover: 0.10 **NM** value: **450.00**
• **CGC:** 1 graded, best 9.4
21 ❑ Nov 1944 Cover: 0.10 **NM** value: **325.00**
22 ❑ Jan 1945 Cover: 0.10 **NM** value: **325.00**
23 ❑ Mar 1945 Cover: 0.10 **NM** value: **325.00**
24 ❑ Apr 1945 Cover: 0.10 **NM** value: **325.00**
• **CGC:** 1 graded, best 9.4
25 ❑ Jul 1945 Cover: 0.10 **NM** value: **325.00**
• **CGC:** 2 graded, best 9.6
26 ❑ Jun 1945 Cover: 0.10 **NM** value: **325.00**
• **CGC:** 1 graded, best 6.5
27 ❑ Nov 1945 Cover: 0.10 **NM** value: **325.00**
• **CGC:** 3 graded, best 9.2
28 ❑ Jan 1946 Cover: 0.10 **NM** value: **325.00**
• **CGC:** 1 graded, best 8.0
29 ❑ Mar 1946 Cover: 0.10 **NM** value: **325.00**
• **CGC:** 4 graded, best 8.5
30 ❑ May 1946 Cover: 0.10 **NM** value: **325.00**
• **CGC:** 3 graded, best 9.2
31 ❑ Nov 1946 Cover: 0.10 **NM** value: **300.00**
32 ❑ Feb 1947 Cover: 0.10 **NM** value: **265.00**
• **CGC:** 2 graded, best 7.0
33 ❑ May 1947 Cover: 0.10 **NM** value: **265.00**
34 ❑ Jul 1947 Cover: 0.10 **NM** value: **265.00**
35 ❑ Sep 1947 Cover: 0.10 **NM** value: **265.00**
• **CGC:** 2 graded, best 7.0
36 ❑ Nov 1947 Cover: 0.10 **NM** value: **265.00**
• **CGC:** 3 graded, best 9.2
37 ❑ Jan 1948 Cover: 0.10 **NM** value: **265.00**
• **CGC:** 4 graded, best 9.4
📖 Green Hornet in The Case of Maker of Madness; Spirit of '76 in Kidnap Kaper
38 ❑ Mar 1948 Cover: 0.10 **NM** value: **265.00**
• **CGC:** 1 graded, best 5.0
39 ❑ May 1948 Cover: 0.10 **NM** value: **325.00**
• **CGC:** 3 graded, best 8.5
40 ❑ Jul 1948 Cover: 0.10 **NM** value: **265.00**
• **CGC:** 3 graded, best 9.2
41 ❑ Sep 1948 Cover: 0.10 **NM** value: **185.00**
• **CGC:** 5 graded, best 9.6
42 ❑ Nov 1948 Cover: 0.10 **NM** value: **185.00**
• **CGC:** 4 graded, best 9.4
43 ❑ Jan 1949 Cover: 0.10 **NM** value: **185.00**
• **CGC:** 1 graded, best 9.4
44 ❑ Mar 1949 Cover: 0.10 **NM** value: **185.00**
• **CGC:** 3 graded, best 9.4
45 ❑ May 1949 Cover: 0.10 **NM** value: **185.00**
• **CGC:** 2 graded, best 9.2
46 ❑ Jul 1949 Cover: 0.10 **NM** value: **185.00**
47 ❑ Sep 1949 Cover: 0.10 **NM** value: **185.00**
• **CGC:** 3 graded, best 9.4
final issue.

GREEN HORNET, THE: DARK TOMORROW — Now

1 ❑ Jun 1993 Cover: 2.50 **NM** value: **Cover or less**
Circ: CapCity orders: **4,500**
📖 A Blacker Shade of Green **A:** Dave Simons **W:** Clint McElroy
2 ❑ Jul 1993 Cover: 2.50 **NM** value: **Cover or less**
Circ: CapCity orders: **3,800**
3 ❑ Aug 1993 Cover: 2.50 **NM** value: **Cover or less**
Circ: CapCity orders: **3,675**

GREEN HORNET (GOLD KEY) — Gold Key

1 ❑ Feb 1967 Cover: 0.12 **NM** value: **150.00**
• **CGC:** 10 graded, best 9.4
2 ❑ May 1967 Cover: 0.12 **NM** value: **150.00**
• **CGC:** 6 graded, best 9.4
3 ❑ Aug 1967 Cover: 0.12 **NM** value: **150.00**
• **CGC:** 5 graded, best 9.6

GREEN HORNET, THE: SOLITARY SENTINEL — Now

1 ❑ Dec 1992 Cover: 2.50 **NM** value: **Cover or less**
Circ: CapCity orders: **5,725**
📖 Strike Force **A:** Ken Penders **W:** James Van Hise
2 ❑ Jan 1993 Cover: 2.50 **NM** value: **Cover or less**
Circ: CapCity orders: **4,825**
📖 Black Marauders **A:** Ken Penders **W:** James Van Hise
3 ❑ Feb 1993 Cover: 2.50 **NM** value: **Cover or less**
Circ: CapCity orders: **4,475**
📖 Crime Vs. Crime **A:** Ken Penders **W:** James Van Hise

GREEN HORNET, THE (VOL. 1) — Now

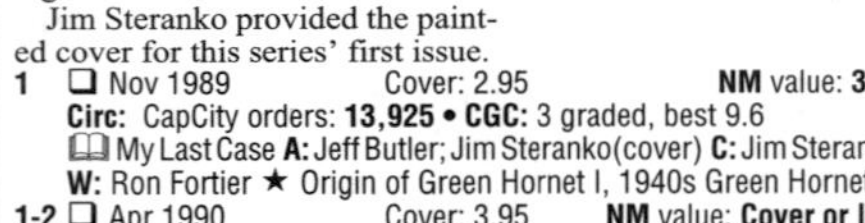

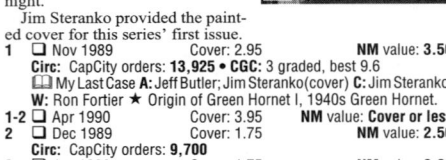

A star of old-time radio and TV, the Green Hornet returned in this stylish comic series by Now Comics. In it, the mantle of the Green Hornet moved to the shoulders of Paul Reid, nephew of Brit Reid, the original Green Hornet. Accompanied by his chauffeur and companion Kato (himself a descendent of the original Kato), The Hornet takes on crime in his city.

The Green Hornet bears a remarkable resemblance to the Crimson Avenger, DC's Golden Age hero who was also a publisher by day and masked crimefighter by night.

Jim Steranko provided the painted cover for this series' first issue.

1 ❑ Nov 1989 Cover: 2.95 **NM** value: **3.50**
Circ: CapCity orders: **13,925** • **CGC:** 3 graded, best 9.6
📖 My Last Case **A:** Jeff Butler; Jim Steranko(cover) **C:** Jim Steranko **W:** Ron Fortier ★ Origin of Green Hornet I, 1940s Green Hornet.
1-2 ❑ Apr 1990 Cover: 3.95 **NM** value: **Cover or less**
2 ❑ Dec 1989 Cover: 1.75 **NM** value: **2.50**
Circ: CapCity orders: **9,700**
3 ❑ Jan 1990 Cover: 1.75 **NM** value: **2.00**
Circ: CapCity orders: **9,575**
4 ❑ Feb 1990 Cover: 1.75 **NM** value: **2.00**
Circ: CapCity orders: **11,175**
5 ❑ Mar 1990 Cover: 1.75 **NM** value: **2.00**
Circ: CapCity orders: **14,675**
6 ❑ Apr 1990 Cover: 1.75 **NM** value: **2.00**
Circ: CapCity orders: **14,450**
7 ❑ May 1990 Cover: 1.75 **NM** value: **2.00**
Circ: CapCity orders: **15,900**
📖 Bloodlines • Mishi becomes new Kato **A:** Jeff Butler **C:** Bill Sienkiewicz **W:** Ron Fortier ★ 1st Appearance of new Kato.
8 ❑ Jun 1990 Cover: 1.75 **NM** value: **2.00**
Circ: CapCity orders: **15,150**
9 ❑ Jul 1990 Cover: 1.75 **NM** value: **2.00**
Circ: CapCity orders: **15,825**
10 ❑ Aug 1990 Cover: 1.75 **NM** value: **2.00**
Circ: CapCity orders: **15,750**
11 ❑ Sep 1990 Cover: 1.75 **NM** value: **2.00**
Circ: CapCity orders: **15,025**
12 ❑ Oct 1990 Cover: 1.75 **NM** value: **2.00**
Circ: CapCity orders: **14,350**
13 ❑ Nov 1990 Cover: 1.75 **NM** value: **2.00**
Circ: CapCity orders: **13,500**
14 ❑ Feb 1991 Cover: 1.75 **NM** value: **2.00**
Circ: CapCity orders: **12,500**
final issue.

GREEN HORNET, THE (VOL. 2) — Now

1 ❑ Sep 1991 Cover: 1.95 **NM** value: **2.00**
Circ: CapCity orders: **16,900**
📖 Money Talks **A:** Tod Smith **W:** Chuck Dixon
2 ❑ Oct 1991 Cover: 1.95 **NM** value: **2.00**
Circ: CapCity orders: **12,200**
3 ❑ Nov 1991 Cover: 1.95 **NM** value: **2.00**
Circ: CapCity orders: **11,450**
4 ❑ Dec 1991 Cover: 1.95 **NM** value: **2.00**
Circ: CapCity orders: **11,100**
5 ❑ Jan 1992 Cover: 1.95 **NM** value: **2.00**
Circ: CapCity orders: **10,300**
6 ❑ Feb 1992 Cover: 1.95 **NM** value: **2.00**
Circ: CapCity orders: **9,350**
7 ❑ Mar 1992 Cover: 1.95 **NM** value: **2.00**
Circ: CapCity orders: **8,400**
8 ❑ Apr 1992 Cover: 1.95 **NM** value: **2.00**
Circ: CapCity orders: **7,625**
9 ❑ May 1992 Cover: 1.95 **NM** value: **2.00**
Circ: CapCity orders: **7,025**
10 ❑ Jun 1992 Cover: 1.95 **NM** value: **2.00**
Circ: CapCity orders: **7,150**
11 ❑ Jul 1992 Cover: 1.95 **NM** value: **2.00**
Circ: CapCity orders: **6,875**
12 ❑ Aug 1992 Cover: 2.50 **NM** value: **Cover or less**
Circ: CapCity orders: **7,275**
📖 The Odyssey of the Crimson Wasp, Part 1 • bagged; with button **A:** Tod Smith **W:** Ron Fortier ★ Versus Crimson Wasp.
13 ❑ Sep 1992 Cover: 1.95 **NM** value: **Cover or less**
Circ: CapCity orders: **6,075**
📖 The Odyssey of the Crimson Wasp, Part 2
14 ❑ Oct 1992 Cover: 1.95 **NM** value: **Cover or less**
Circ: CapCity orders: **5,850**
📖 The Odyssey of the Crimson Wasp, Part 3
15 ❑ Nov 1992 Cover: 1.95 **NM** value: **Cover or less**
Circ: CapCity orders: **5,700**
16 ❑ Dec 1992 Cover: 1.95 **NM** value: **Cover or less**
Circ: CapCity orders: **5,200**
17 ❑ Jan 1993 Cover: 1.95 **NM** value: **Cover or less**
Circ: CapCity orders: **5,050**
18 ❑ Feb 1993 Cover: 1.95 **NM** value: **Cover or less**
Circ: CapCity orders: **4,825**
19 ❑ Mar 1993 Cover: 1.95 **NM** value: **Cover or less**
Circ: CapCity orders: **4,525**
20 ❑ Apr 1993 Cover: 1.95 **NM** value: **Cover or less**
Circ: CapCity orders: **4,500**
21 ❑ May 1993 Cover: 1.95 **NM** value: **Cover or less**
Circ: CapCity orders: **4,375**
22 ❑ Jun 1993 Cover: 2.95 **NM** value: **Cover or less**
• newsstand, trading card; newsstand; Has UPC, Comics Code seal
22/DM ❑ Jun 1993 Cover: 2.95 **NM** value: **Cover or less**
Circ: CapCity orders: **5,550**
alternate cover. • direct sale; trading card; No Comics Code seal
23 ❑ Jul 1993 Cover: 2.95 **NM** value: **Cover or less**
Circ: CapCity orders: **5,575**
24 ❑ Aug 1993 Cover: 1.95 **NM** value: **Cover or less**
Circ: CapCity orders: **4,100**
25 ❑ Sep 1993 Cover: 1.95 **NM** value: **Cover or less**
Circ: CapCity orders: **3,875**
26 ❑ Oct 1993 Cover: 2.95 **NM** value: **Cover or less**
Circ: CapCity orders: **3,700**
27 ❑ Nov 1993 Cover: 2.95 **NM** value: **Cover or less**
Circ: CapCity orders: **4,100**
28 ❑ Dec 1993 Cover: 1.95 **NM** value: **Cover or less**
Circ: CapCity orders: **3,725**
29 ❑ Jan 1994 Cover: 1.95 **NM** value: **Cover or less**
Circ: CapCity orders: **3,500**
30 ❑ Feb 1994 Cover: 1.95 **NM** value: **Cover or less**
Circ: CapCity orders: **3,300**
31 ❑ Mar 1994 Cover: 2.50 **NM** value: **Cover or less**
Circ: CapCity orders: **3,275**
32 ❑ Apr 1994 Cover: 1.95 **NM** value: **Cover or less**
Circ: CapCity orders: **3,095**
33 ❑ May 1994 Cover: 1.95 **NM** value: **Cover or less**
Circ: CapCity orders: **3,035**
34 ❑ Jun 1994 Cover: 1.95 **NM** value: **Cover or less**
Circ: CapCity orders: **2,940**
35 ❑ Jul 1994 Cover: 1.95 **NM** value: **Cover or less**
Circ: CapCity orders: **3,000**
36 ❑ Aug 1994 Cover: 1.95 **NM** value: **Cover or less**
Circ: CapCity orders: **2,850**
37 ❑ Sep 1994 Cover: 1.95 **NM** value: **Cover or less**
38 ❑ Nov 1994 Cover: 2.50 **NM** value: **Cover or less**
39 ❑ Dec 1994 Cover: 1.95 **NM** value: **Cover or less**
40 ❑ Jan 1995 Cover: 2.50 **NM** value: **Cover or less**
Anl 1 ❑ Dec 1992 Cover: 2.50 **NM** value: **Cover or less**
Anl 1994 ❑ Oct 1994 Cover: 2.95 **NM** value: **Cover or less**

GREEN LAMA — Spark Publications

1 ❑ Dec 1944 Cover: 0.10 **NM** value: **Cover or less**
• **CGC:** 3 graded, best 7.5
2 ❑ Feb 1945 Cover: 0.10 **NM** value: **Cover or less**
• **CGC:** 2 graded, best 9.4
3 ❑ Mar 1945 Cover: 0.10 **NM** value: **Cover or less**
• **CGC:** 1 graded, best 7.0
4 ❑ Apr 1945 Cover: 0.10 **NM** value: **Cover or less**
• **CGC:** 2 graded, best 8.0
5 ❑ May 1945 Cover: 0.10 **NM** value: **Cover or less**
• **CGC:** 1 graded, best 9.0
6 ❑ Aug 1945 Cover: 0.10 **NM** value: **Cover or less**
• **CGC:** 9 graded, best 9.4
7 ❑ Jan 1946 Cover: 0.10 **NM** value: **Cover or less**
8 ❑ May 1946 Cover: 0.10 **NM** value: **Cover or less**

GREEN LANTERN (1ST SERIES) — DC

Engineer Alan Scott was working on a railroad bridge when rivals decided to get even by blowing it up. Scott survived, and the antique lantern he carried for good luck turned out to be an ancient artifact capable of bestowing him with the power to seek justice against evildoers. Scott fashioned a ring from the lantern as a portable rechargeable power source, and began his career as the Golden Age super-hero Green Lantern.

Green Lantern first appeared in All-American Comics #16 in July, 1940 and won his own title in 1941. He also appeared in All Star Comics

Other grades: Multiply prices above by **1.5 for Mint • 2/3 for Very Fine • 1/3 for Fine • 1/5 for Very Good • 1/8 for Good**

as a member of the Justice Society of America, and in Comic Cavalcade alongside the Flash and Wonder Woman. He was revived in the 1960s as the "Earth-2" counterpart to the Silver Age Green Lantern (originally Hal Jordan) and continues (as Sentinel) to appear in DC comics to the present day.

1 ❑ Sep 1941 Cover: 0.10 **NM** value: **27500.00**
• **CGC:** 16 graded, best 8.0
📖 Green Lantern-His Personal History; The Masquerading Mare; Will Power; Disease; Arson in the Slums; Hop Harrigan: Trailers of Treachery; Green Lantern • Very rare **A:** Howard Purcell(cover); Martin Nodell **W:** Bill Finger; Dr. William Moulton Marston ★ Origin of Green Lantern I (Alan Scott).

2 ❑ Win 1941 Cover: 0.10 **NM** value: **6000.00**
• **CGC:** 2 graded, best 8.0

3 ❑ Spr 1942 Cover: 0.10 **NM** value: **4200.00**
• **CGC:** 4 graded, best 8.0

4 ❑ Sum 1942 Cover: 0.10 **NM** value: **3250.00**
• **CGC:** 7 graded, best 9.0

5 ❑ Fal 1942 Cover: 0.10 **NM** value: **2200.00**
• **CGC:** 1 graded, best 2.5

6 ❑ Win 1942 Cover: 0.10 **NM** value: **1700.00**
• **CGC:** 2 graded, best 7.0

7 ❑ Spr 1943 Cover: 0.10 **NM** value: **1700.00**
• **CGC:** 5 graded, best 8.5

8 ❑ Fal 1943 Cover: 0.10 **NM** value: **1450.00**
• **CGC:** 3 graded, best 8.0

9 ❑ Fal 1943 Cover: 0.10 **NM** value: **1450.00**
• **CGC:** 2 graded, best 9.4

10 ❑ Win 1943 Cover: 0.10 **NM** value: **1450.00**
• **CGC:** 2 graded, best 8.5

11 ❑ Spr 1944 Cover: 0.10 **NM** value: **1150.00**
• **CGC:** 2 graded, best 9.4

12 ❑ Sum 1944 Cover: 0.10 **NM** value: **1150.00**
• **CGC:** 3 graded, best 9.0

13 ❑ Fal 1944 Cover: 0.10 **NM** value: **1150.00**
• **CGC:** 4 graded, best 8.0

14 ❑ Win 1944 Cover: 0.10 **NM** value: **1150.00**
• **CGC:** 2 graded, best 8.0

15 ❑ Spr 1945 Cover: 0.10 **NM** value: **1150.00**
• **CGC:** 2 graded, best 9.0

16 ❑ Sum 1945 Cover: 0.10 **NM** value: **1150.00**

17 ❑ Fal 1945 Cover: 0.10 **NM** value: **1150.00**

18 ❑ Win 1945 Cover: 0.10 **NM** value: **1150.00**
• **CGC:** 3 graded, best 9.4

19 ❑ Apr 1946 Cover: 0.10 **NM** value: **1150.00**
• **CGC:** 2 graded, best 7.0

20 ❑ Jun 1946 Cover: 0.10 **NM** value: **1150.00**
• **CGC:** 4 graded, best 9.4

21 ❑ Aug 1946 Cover: 0.10 **NM** value: **1025.00**
• **CGC:** 1 graded, best 9.6

22 ❑ Oct 1946 Cover: 0.10 **NM** value: **1025.00**
• **CGC:** 1 graded, best 4.0

23 ❑ Dec 1946 Cover: 0.10 **NM** value: **1025.00**
• **CGC:** 2 graded, best 8.5

24 ❑ Feb 1947 Cover: 0.10 **NM** value: **1025.00**
• **CGC:** 2 graded, best 8.0

25 ❑ Apr 1947 Cover: 0.10 **NM** value: **1025.00**
• **CGC:** 3 graded, best 8.5

26 ❑ Jun 1947 Cover: 0.10 **NM** value: **1025.00**
• **CGC:** 3 graded, best 9.2

27 ❑ Aug 1947 Cover: 0.10 **NM** value: **1025.00**
• **CGC:** 1 graded, best 7.5

28 ❑ Oct 1947 Cover: 0.10 **NM** value: **1025.00**
• **CGC:** 2 graded, best 6.5

29 ❑ Dec 1947 Cover: 0.10 **NM** value: **1025.00**
• **CGC:** 2 graded, best 8.0
📖 The Challenge of the Harlequin; The Harlequin Haunts Green Lantern; Quiet, Please • All-Harlequin issue **W:** Charles King ★ Appearance of The Harlequin.

30 ❑ Feb 1948 Cover: 0.10 **NM** value: **1025.00**
• **CGC:** 1 graded, best 7.0

31 ❑ Mar 1948 Cover: 0.10 **NM** value: **885.00**
• **CGC:** 1 graded, best 5.5

32 ❑ May 1948 Cover: 0.10 **NM** value: **885.00**
• **CGC:** 2 graded, best 9.2

33 ❑ Jul 1948 Cover: 0.10 **NM** value: **885.00**

34 ❑ Sep 1948 Cover: 0.10 **NM** value: **885.00**
• **CGC:** 1 graded, best 8.5

35 ❑ Nov 1948 Cover: 0.10 **NM** value: **1100.00**

36 ❑ Jan 1949 Cover: 0.10 **NM** value: **1100.00**

37 ❑ Mar 1949 Cover: 0.10 **NM** value: **1100.00**

38 ❑ May 1949 Cover: 0.10 **NM** value: **1100.00**
final issue.

GREEN LANTERN (2ND SERIES) DC

In Showcase #22, test pilot Hal Jordan encountered a dying alien who gave Hal his power ring. Upon wearing that ring, Hal became Earth's new Green Lantern (the Golden Age version, Alan Scott, operated on an alternate Earth). Hal's power ring gave him almost unlimited powers, but the ring needed to be recharged from a special battery every 24 hours. He also had a weakness to anything yellow. For instance, bullets would bounce off the energy field created by his ring, but Hal could still be knocked out by a club painted yellow.

Green Lantern was one of DC's key super-heroes and a longtime member of the Justice League of America. Although later Green Lantern series would put Hal through a great deal of spiritual and emotional turmoil, this 1960-1986 title was primarily focused on high-flying adventure.

1 ❑ Aug 1960 Cover: 0.10 **NM** value: **2800.00**
• **CGC:** 51 graded, best 9.2
📖 The Planet of Doomed Men!; The Menace of the Giant Puppet! **A:** Gil Kane ★ Origin of Green Lantern II (Hal Jordan). ★ 1st Appearance of the Guardians.

2 ❑ Oct 1960 Cover: 0.10 **NM** value: **750.00**
• **CGC:** 16 graded, best 9.2
📖 The Secret of the Golden Thunderbolts!; Riddle of the Frozen Ghost Town **A:** Gil Kane ★ 1st Appearance of Qward, Pieface.

3 ❑ Dec 1960 Cover: 0.10 **NM** value: **450.00**
• **CGC:** 8 graded, best 9.0
📖 The Amazing Theft of the Power Lamp!; The Leap Year Menace! **A:** Gil Kane

4 ❑ Feb 1961 Cover: 0.10 **NM** value: **340.00**
Circ: Statement: **255,000** • **CGC:** 10 graded, best 9.0
📖 The Diabolical Missile from Qward!; Secret of Green Lantern's Mask! **A:** Gil Kane

5 ❑ Apr 1961 Cover: 0.10 **NM** value: **340.00**
Circ: Statement: **255,000** • **CGC:** 10 graded, best 9.4
📖 The Power Ring That Vanished! **A:** Gil Kane ★ 1st Appearance of Hector Hammond.

6 ❑ Jun 1961 Cover: 0.10 **NM** value: **275.00**
Circ: Statement: **255,000** • **CGC:** 9 graded, best 9.2
📖 The World of Living Phantoms! **A:** Gil Kane ★ 1st Appearance of Tomar.

7 ❑ Aug 1961 Cover: 0.10 **NM** value: **250.00**
Circ: Statement: **255,000** • **CGC:** 6 graded, best 9.6
📖 The Day 100,000 People Vanished!; Wings of Destiny! **A:** Gil Kane ★ Origin of Sinestro. ★ 1st Appearance of Sinestro.

8 ❑ Oct 1961 Cover: 0.10 **NM** value: **250.00**
Circ: Statement: **255,000** • **CGC:** 6 graded, best 8.5
📖 The Challenge from 5700 A.D.! **A:** Gil Kane

9 ❑ Dec 1961 Cover: 0.10 **NM** value: **250.00**
Circ: Statement: **255,000** • **CGC:** 6 graded, best 8.0
📖 The Battle of the Power Rings!; Green Lantern's Brother Act! **A:** Gil Kane

10 ❑ Jan 1962 Cover: 0.12 **NM** value: **250.00**
Circ: Statement: **240,000** • **CGC:** 5 graded, best 9.2
📖 Prisoner of the Power Ring!; The Origin of Green Lantern's Oath! **A:** Gil Kane

11 ❑ Mar 1962 Cover: 0.12 **NM** value: **175.00**
Circ: Statement: **240,000** • **CGC:** 8 graded, best 9.4
📖 The Strange Trial of Green Lantern!; The Trail of the Missing Power Ring! • Has 1961 Statement, filed 10/1/61; avg total paid circ 255,000 **A:** Gil Kane ★ 1st Appearance of The Green Lantern Corps.

12 ❑ Apr 1962 Cover: 0.12 **NM** value: **175.00**
Circ: Statement: **240,000** • **CGC:** 12 graded, best 9.0
📖 Green Lantern's Statue Goes to War!; Zero Hour in the Silent City! **A:** Gil Kane ★ 1st Appearance of Doctor Polaris.

13 ❑ Jun 1962 Cover: 0.12 **NM** value: **200.00**
Circ: Statement: **240,000** • **CGC:** 7 graded, best 9.0
📖 The Dual of the Super-Heroes! **A:** Gil Kane ★ Appearance of Flash II (Barry Allen).

14 ❑ Jul 1962 Cover: 0.12 **NM** value: **150.00**
Circ: Statement: **240,000** • **CGC:** 3 graded, best 9.4
📖 The Man Who Conquered Sound!; My Brother, Green Lantern! **A:** Gil Kane ★ 1st Appearance of Sonar.

15 ❑ Sep 1962 Cover: 0.12 **NM** value: **145.00**
Circ: Statement: **240,000** • **CGC:** 5 graded, best 9.4
📖 Peril of the Yellow World!; Zero Hour in Rocket City! **A:** Gil Kane

16 ❑ Oct 1962 Cover: 0.12 **NM** value: **145.00**
Circ: Statement: **240,000** • **CGC:** 7 graded, best 9.2
📖 The Secret Life of Star Sapphire!; Earth's First Green Lantern! **A:** Gil Kane ★ Origin of Star Sapphire. ★ 1st Appearance of Star Sapphire, Zamarons.

17 ❑ Dec 1962 Cover: 0.12 **NM** value: **135.00**
Circ: Statement: **240,000** • **CGC:** 7 graded, best 9.6
📖 The Spy-Eye That Doomed Green Lantern! **A:** Gil Kane

18 ❑ Jan 1963 Cover: 0.12 **NM** value: **135.00**
• **CGC:** 8 graded, best 9.6
📖 The World of Perilous Traps!; Green Lantern vs. Power Ring! **A:** Gil Kane

19 ❑ Mar 1963 Cover: 0.12 **NM** value: **135.00**
• **CGC:** 5 graded, best 9.6
📖 The Defeat of Green Lantern; The Trail of the Horse-and-Buggy Bandits! • Has 1962 Statement, filed 10/1/62; avg total paid circ 240,000 **A:** Gil Kane

20 ❑ Apr 1963 Cover: 0.12 **NM** value: **135.00**
• **CGC:** 7 graded, best 9.4
📖 Parasite Planet Peril! **A:** Gil Kane ★ Appearance of Flash II (Barry Allen).

21 ❑ Jun 1963 Cover: 0.12 **NM** value: **120.00**
• **CGC:** 7 graded, best 9.4
📖 The Man Who Mastered Magnetism!; Hal Jordan Betrays Green Lantern! **A:** Gil Kane ★ Origin of Dr. Polaris, Doctor Polaris.

22 ❑ Jul 1963 Cover: 0.12 **NM** value: **120.00**
• **CGC:** 3 graded, best 9.0

23 ❑ Sep 1963 Cover: 0.12 **NM** value: **120.00**
• **CGC:** 4 graded, best 9.6

24 ❑ Oct 1963 Cover: 0.12 **NM** value: **120.00**
• **CGC:** 4 graded, best 9.0

25 ❑ Dec 1963 Cover: 0.12 **NM** value: **120.00**
• **CGC:** 3 graded, best 9.2

26 ❑ Jan 1964 Cover: 0.12 **NM** value: **120.00**
• **CGC:** 2 graded, best 7.5

27 ❑ Mar 1964 Cover: 0.12 **NM** value: **120.00**
• **CGC:** 4 graded, best 9.6
• Has 1963 Statement, filed 10/1/63; no circ figures published **A:** Gil Kane

28 ❑ Apr 1964 Cover: 0.12 **NM** value: **120.00**
• **CGC:** 4 graded, best 9.4

29 ❑ Jun 1964 Cover: 0.12 **NM** value: **130.00**
• **CGC:** 4 graded, best 9.4

30 ❑ Jul 1964 Cover: 0.12 **NM** value: **120.00**
• **CGC:** 6 graded, best 9.6

31 ❑ Sep 1964 Cover: 0.12 **NM** value: **100.00**
• **CGC:** 6 graded, best 9.2

32 ❑ Oct 1964 Cover: 0.12 **NM** value: **100.00**
• **CGC:** 2 graded, best 8.0

33 ❑ Dec 1964 Cover: 0.12 **NM** value: **100.00**
• **CGC:** 7 graded, best 9.2

34 ❑ Jan 1965 Cover: 0.12 **NM** value: **100.00**
Circ: Statement: **273,527** • **CGC:** 5 graded, best 9.2

35 ❑ Mar 1965 Cover: 0.12 **NM** value: **100.00**
Circ: Statement: **273,527** • **CGC:** 4 graded, best 9.2
• Has 1964 Statement, filed 10/1/64; no circ figures published **A:** Gil Kane

36 ❑ Apr 1965 Cover: 0.12 **NM** value: **100.00**
Circ: Statement: **273,527** • **CGC:** 2 graded, best 8.0

37 ❑ Jun 1965 Cover: 0.12 **NM** value: **100.00**
Circ: Statement: **273,527** • **CGC:** 1 graded, best 6.0

38 ❑ Jul 1965 Cover: 0.12 **NM** value: **100.00**
Circ: Statement: **273,527** • **CGC:** 7 graded, best 9.4

39 ❑ Sep 1965 Cover: 0.12 **NM** value: **100.00**
Circ: Statement: **273,527** • **CGC:** 4 graded, best 9.0

40 ❑ Oct 1965 Cover: 0.12 **NM** value: **465.00**
Circ: Statement: **273,527** • **CGC:** 63 graded, best 9.6

41 ❑ Dec 1965 Cover: 0.12 **NM** value: **60.00**
Circ: Statement: **273,527** • **CGC:** 10 graded, best 9.8

42 ❑ Jan 1966 Cover: 0.12 **NM** value: **60.00**
Circ: Statement: **245,699** • **CGC:** 2 graded, best 9.4

43 ❑ Mar 1966 Cover: 0.12 **NM** value: **60.00**
Circ: Statement: **245,699** • **CGC:** 4 graded, best 9.4
• Has 1965 Statement, filed 10/1/64; avg total paid circ 273,527 **A:** Gil Kane ★ 1st Appearance of Major Disaster. ★ Appearance of Flash II (Barry Allen).

44 ❑ Apr 1966 Cover: 0.12 **NM** value: **60.00**
Circ: Statement: **245,699** • **CGC:** 5 graded, best 9.4

45 ❑ Jun 1966 Cover: 0.12 **NM** value: **90.00**
Circ: Statement: **245,699** • **CGC:** 16 graded, best 9.4

46 ❑ Jul 1966 Cover: 0.12 **NM** value: **60.00**
Circ: Statement: **245,699** • **CGC:** 1 graded, best 9.4

47 ❑ Sep 1966 Cover: 0.12 **NM** value: **60.00**
Circ: Statement: **245,699** • **CGC:** 4 graded, best 9.0

48 ❑ Oct 1966 Cover: 0.12 **NM** value: **60.00**
Circ: Statement: **245,699** • **CGC:** 4 graded, best 9.2

49 ❑ Dec 1966 Cover: 0.12 **NM** value: **60.00**
Circ: Statement: **245,699** • **CGC:** 5 graded, best 9.2

50 ❑ Jan 1967 Cover: 0.12 **NM** value: **60.00**
Circ: Statement: **201,700** • **CGC:** 2 graded, best 9.6

51 ❑ Mar 1967 Cover: 0.12 **NM** value: **40.00**
Circ: Statement: **201,700** • **CGC:** 4 graded, best 9.4
• Has 1966 Statement, filed 10/1/66; avg print run 414,000; avg sales 242,000; avg subs 3,699; avg total paid 245,699; samples 265; max existent 245,964; 41% of run returned

52 ❑ Apr 1967 Cover: 0.12 **NM** value: **45.00**
Circ: Statement: **201,700** • **CGC:** 4 graded, best 9.2

53 ❑ Jun 1967 Cover: 0.12 **NM** value: **40.00**
Circ: Statement: **201,700** • **CGC:** 6 graded, best 9.6

54 ❑ Jul 1967 Cover: 0.12 **NM** value: **40.00**
Circ: Statement: **201,700** • **CGC:** 6 graded, best 9.4

55 ❑ Sep 1967 Cover: 0.12 **NM** value: **40.00**
Circ: Statement: **201,700** • **CGC:** 5 graded, best 9.4

56 ❑ Oct 1967 Cover: 0.12 **NM** value: **40.00**
Circ: Statement: **201,700** • **CGC:** 2 graded, best 9.4

57 ❑ Dec 1967 Cover: 0.12 **NM** value: **40.00**
Circ: Statement: **201,700** • **CGC:** 2 graded, best 9.2

58 ❑ Jan 1968 Cover: 0.12 **NM** value: **40.00**
Circ: Statement: **211,750** • **CGC:** 4 graded, best 9.6

59 ❑ Mar 1968 Cover: 0.12 **NM** value: **200.00**
Circ: Statement: **211,750** • **CGC:** 39 graded, best 9.8
• Has 1967 Statement, filed 10/1/67; avg print run 366,000; avg sales 199,000; avg subs 2,700; avg total paid 201,700; samples 340; max existent 202,040; 45% of run returned ★ 1st Appearance of Guy Gardner.

60 ❑ Apr 1968 Cover: 0.12 **NM** value: **26.00**
Circ: Statement: **211,750** • **CGC:** 3 graded, best 9.6

61 ❑ Jun 1968 Cover: 0.12 **NM** value: **40.00**
Circ: Statement: **211,750** • **CGC:** 7 graded, best 9.4

62 ❑ Jul 1968 Cover: 0.12 **NM** value: **26.00**
Circ: Statement: **211,750** • **CGC:** 2 graded, best 9.4

63 ❑ Sep 1968 Cover: 0.12 **NM** value: **26.00**
Circ: Statement: **211,750** • **CGC:** 6 graded, best 9.4

64 ❑ Oct 1968 Cover: 0.12 **NM** value: **26.00**
Circ: Statement: **211,750** • **CGC:** 3 graded, best 9.2

65 ❑ Dec 1968 Cover: 0.12 **NM** value: **26.00**
Circ: Statement: **211,750** • **CGC:** 8 graded, best 9.2

66 ❑ Jan 1969 Cover: 0.12 **NM** value: **26.00**
Circ: Statement: **160,423** • **CGC:** 7 graded, best 9.4

67 ❑ Mar 1969 Cover: 0.12 **NM** value: **26.00**
Circ: Statement: **160,423**
• Has 1968 Statement, filed 10/1/68; avg print run 364,000; avg sales 211,000; avg subs 750; avg total paid 211,750; samples 386; max existent 212,136; 42% of run returned

68 ❑ Apr 1969 Cover: 0.12 **NM** value: **26.00**
Circ: Statement: **160,423** • **CGC:** 4 graded, best 9.4

69 ❑ Jun 1969 Cover: 0.12 **NM** value: **26.00**
Circ: Statement: **160,423** • **CGC:** 1 graded, best 9.4

70 ❑ Jul 1969 Cover: 0.15 **NM** value: **26.00**
Circ: Statement: **160,423** • **CGC:** 1 graded, best 9.4

71 ❑ Sep 1969 Cover: 0.15 **NM** value: **20.00**
Circ: Statement: **160,423** • **CGC:** 2 graded, best 9.0

72 ❑ Oct 1969 Cover: 0.15 **NM** value: **20.00**
Circ: Statement: **160,423** • **CGC:** 3 graded, best 9.4

73 ❑ Dec 1969 Cover: 0.15 **NM** value: **20.00**
Circ: Statement: **160,423** • **CGC:** 1 graded, best 9.0

74 ❑ Jan 1970 Cover: 0.15 **NM** value: **20.00**
Circ: Statement: **134,150** • **CGC:** 2 graded, best 9.2

75 ❑ Mar 1970 Cover: 0.15 **NM** value: **20.00**
Circ: Statement: **134,150** • **CGC:** 3 graded, best 9.4
• Has 1969 Statement, filed 10/1/69; avg print run 333,000; avg sales 160,000; avg subs 346; avg total paid 160,423; samples 346; max existent 160,769; 52% of run returned **A:** Gil Kane

76 ❑ Apr 1970 Cover: 0.15 **NM** value: **135.00**

CGC-graded: Multiply prices above by **33 for 9.9 M** • **16 for 9.8 NM/M** • **7 for 9.6 NM+** • **5 for 9.4 NM** • **2.5 for 9.2 NM-** • **1.5 for 9.0 VF/NM**

Circ: Statement: **134,150** • **CGC:** 37 graded, best 9.2
• Green Lantern/Green Arrow series **A:** Neal Adams ★ Appearance of Green Arrow.

77 ❑ Jun 1970 Cover: 0.15 **NM** value: **65.00**
Circ: Statement: **134,150** • **CGC:** 5 graded, best 9.6
• Green Lantern/Green Arrow series **A:** Neal Adams ★ Appearance of Green Arrow.

78 ❑ Jul 1970 Cover: 0.15 **NM** value: **65.00**
Circ: Statement: **134,150** • **CGC:** 5 graded, best 9.4
• Green Lantern/Green Arrow series **A:** Neal Adams ★ Appearance of Green Arrow.

79 ❑ Sep 1970 Cover: 0.15 **NM** value: **50.00**
Circ: Statement: **134,150** • **CGC:** 6 graded, best 9.2
• Green Lantern/Green Arrow series **A:** Neal Adams ★ Appearance of Green Arrow.

80 ❑ Oct 1970 Cover: 0.15 **NM** value: **50.00**
Circ: Statement: **134,150** • **CGC:** 11 graded, best 9.4
• Green Lantern/Green Arrow series **A:** Neal Adams ★ Appearance of Green Arrow.

81 ❑ Dec 1970 Cover: 0.15 **NM** value: **35.00**
Circ: Statement: **134,150** • **CGC:** 11 graded, best 9.4
• Green Lantern/Green Arrow series **A:** Neal Adams ★ Appearance of Green Arrow.

82 ❑ Mar 1971 Cover: 0.15 **NM** value: **35.00**
Circ: Statement: **142,657** • **CGC:** 9 graded, best 9.4
• Green Lantern/Green Arrow series **A:** Neal Adams ★ Appearance of Green Arrow.

83 ❑ May 1971 Cover: 0.15 **NM** value: **35.00**
Circ: Statement: **142,657** • **CGC:** 9 graded, best 9.8
• Green Lantern/Green Arrow series; Green Arrow; Anti-drug issue; Has 1970 Statement, filed 10/1/70; avg print run 282,122; avg sales 133,836; avg subs 314; avg total paid 134,150; samples 122; max existent 134,272; 53% of run returned **A:** Neal Adams ★ Appearance of Green Arrow.

84 ❑ Jul 1971 Cover: 0.15 **NM** value: **35.00**
Circ: Statement: **142,657** • **CGC:** 8 graded, best 9.6
• Green Arrow; Green Lantern/Green Arrow series **A:** Bernie Wrightson; Neal Adams

85 ❑ Sep 1971 Cover: 0.25 **NM** value: **50.00**
Circ: Statement: **142,657** • **CGC:** 29 graded, best 9.8
• Green Arrow; Anti-drug issue; Green Lantern/Green Arrow series **A:** Neal Adams

86 ❑ Nov 1971 Cover: 0.25 **NM** value: **50.00**
Circ: Statement: **142,657** • **CGC:** 27 graded, best 9.6
• Green Lantern/Green Arrow series; Green Arrow; Anti-drug issue **A:** Neal Adams

87 ❑ Jan 1972 Cover: 0.25 **NM** value: **40.00**
• **CGC:** 12 graded, best 9.2
• Guy Gardner cameo; Green Lantern/Green Arrow series **A:** Neal Adams; Gil Kane ★ 1st Appearance of John Stewart. ★ Appearance of Green Arrow.

88 ❑ Mar 1972 Cover: 0.25 **NM** value: **9.00**
• **CGC:** 4 graded, best 9.6

89 ❑ May 1972 Cover: 0.25 **NM** value: **15.00**
• **CGC:** 12 graded, best 9.8
• Green Lantern/Green Arrow series; Has 1971 Statement, filed 10/1/71; avg print run 280,000; avg sales 142,657; avg total paid 142,657; office use 573; max existent 142,230; 49% of run returned **A:** Neal Adams ★ Appearance of Green Arrow.

90 ❑ Sep 1976 Cover: 0.30 **NM** value: **5.00**
• **CGC:** 8 graded, best 9.6
• Green Lantern/Green Arrow series **A:** Mike Grell **W:** Mike Grell ★ Appearance of Green Arrow.

91 ❑ Nov 1976 Cover: 0.30 **NM** value: **5.00**
92 ❑ Dec 1976 Cover: 0.30 **NM** value: **5.00**
• **CGC:** 1 graded, best 9.4

93 ❑ Feb 1977 Cover: 0.30 **NM** value: **4.00**
• **CGC:** 1 graded, best 9.6

94 ❑ Apr 1977 Cover: 0.30 **NM** value: **4.00**
95 ❑ Jun 1977 Cover: 0.35 **NM** value: **4.00**
96 ❑ Aug 1977 Cover: 0.35 **NM** value: **4.00**
97 ❑ Oct 1977 Cover: 0.35 **NM** value: **4.00**
• **CGC:** 1 graded, best 9.4

98 ❑ Nov 1977 Cover: 0.35 **NM** value: **4.00**
99 ❑ Dec 1977 Cover: 0.35 **NM** value: **4.00**
100 ❑ Jan 1978 Cover: 0.35 **NM** value: **6.00**
• **CGC:** 1 graded, best 7.0
• 100th anniversary issue. **A:** Mike Grell ★ 1st Appearance of Air Wave II (Harry "Hal" Jordan), Air Wave.

101 ❑ Feb 1978 Cover: 0.35 **NM** value: **4.00**
• McGinty

102 ❑ Mar 1978 Cover: 0.35 **NM** value: **4.00**
103 ❑ Apr 1978 Cover: 0.35 **NM** value: **4.00**
104 ❑ May 1978 Cover: 0.35 **NM** value: **4.00**
105 ❑ Jun 1978 Cover: 0.35 **NM** value: **4.00**
106 ❑ Jul 1978 Cover: 0.35 **NM** value: **4.00**
107 ❑ Aug 1978 Cover: 0.35 **NM** value: **4.00**
108 ❑ Sep 1978 Cover: 0.50 **NM** value: **4.00**
• Golden Age Green Lantern back-up **A:** Mike Grell ★ Appearance of Green Arrow.

109 ❑ Oct 1978 Cover: 0.50 **NM** value: **4.00**
• Golden Age Green Lantern back-up **A:** Mike Grell ★ Appearance of Green Arrow.

110 ❑ Nov 1978 Cover: 0.50 **NM** value: **4.00**
111 ❑ Dec 1978 Cover: 0.40 **NM** value: **4.00**
112 ❑ Jan 1979 Cover: 0.40 **NM** value: **8.00**
Circ: Statement: **97,249** • **CGC:** 1 graded, best 9.4

113 ❑ Feb 1979 Cover: 0.40 **NM** value: **3.00**
Circ: Statement: **97,249**

114 ❑ Mar 1979 Cover: 0.40 **NM** value: **3.00**
Circ: Statement: **97,249**

115 ❑ Apr 1979 Cover: 0.40 **NM** value: **3.00**
Circ: Statement: **97,249**

116 ❑ May 1979 Cover: 0.40 **NM** value: **12.00**
Circ: Statement: **97,249** • **CGC:** 8 graded, best 9.6
• Guy Gardner becomes a Green Lantern

117 ❑ Jun 1979 Cover: 0.40 **NM** value: **3.00**
Circ: Statement: **97,249**

118 ❑ Jul 1979 Cover: 0.40 **NM** value: **3.00**
Circ: Statement: **97,249**

119 ❑ Aug 1979 Cover: 0.40 **NM** value: **2.50**
Circ: Statement: **97,249**

120 ❑ Sep 1979 Cover: 0.40 **NM** value: **2.50**
Circ: Statement: **97,249**

121 ❑ Oct 1979 Cover: 0.40 **NM** value: **2.50**
Circ: Statement: **97,249**

122 ❑ Nov 1979 Cover: 0.40 **NM** value: **3.50**
Circ: Statement: **97,249**

123 ❑ Dec 1979 Cover: 0.40 **NM** value: **6.00**
Circ: Statement: **97,249**
• Guy Gardner as Green Lantern

124 ❑ Jan 1980 Cover: 0.40 **NM** value: **2.50**
Circ: Statement: **99,915**

125 ❑ Feb 1980 Cover: 0.40 **NM** value: **2.50**
Circ: Statement: **99,915**

126 ❑ Mar 1980 Cover: 0.40 **NM** value: **2.50**
Circ: Statement: **99,915**

127 ❑ Apr 1980 Cover: 0.40 **NM** value: **2.50**
Circ: Statement: **99,915**
• Has 1979 Statement; avg print run 233,393; avg sales 96,302; avg subs 948; avg total paid 97,249; office use 121; max existent 97,371; 58% of run returned **A:** Joe Staton

128 ❑ May 1980 Cover: 0.40 **NM** value: **2.50**
Circ: Statement: **99,915**

129 ❑ Jun 1980 Cover: 0.40 **NM** value: **2.50**
Circ: Statement: **99,915** • **CGC:** 1 graded, best 9.6

130 ❑ Jun 1980 Cover: 0.40 **NM** value: **2.50**
Circ: Statement: **99,915**

131 ❑ Aug 1980 Cover: 0.40 **NM** value: **2.25**
Circ: Statement: **99,915**

132 ❑ Sep 1980 Cover: 0.50 **NM** value: **2.25**
Circ: Statement: **99,915**

133 ❑ Oct 1980 Cover: 0.50 **NM** value: **2.25**
Circ: Statement: **99,915**

134 ❑ Nov 1980 Cover: 0.50 **NM** value: **2.25**
Circ: Statement: **99,915**

135 ❑ Dec 1980 Cover: 0.50 **NM** value: **2.25**
Circ: Statement: **99,915**

136 ❑ Jan 1981 Cover: 0.50 **NM** value: **2.50**
Circ: Statement: **91,104**

137 ❑ Feb 1981 Cover: 0.50 **NM** value: **2.50**
Circ: Statement: **91,104**

138 ❑ Mar 1981 Cover: 0.50 **NM** value: **2.50**
Circ: Statement: **91,104**

139 ❑ Apr 1981 Cover: 0.50 **NM** value: **2.50**
Circ: Statement: **91,104**

140 ❑ May 1981 Cover: 0.50 **NM** value: **2.00**
Circ: Statement: **91,104**
• Has 1980 Statement; avg print run 268,869; avg sales 97,643; avg subs 2,272; avg total paid 99,915; samples 127; office use 1,920; max existent 101,835; 62% of run returned **A:** Joe Staton

141 ❑ Jun 1981 Cover: 0.50 **NM** value: **3.00**
Circ: Statement: **91,104**

142 ❑ Jul 1981 Cover: 0.50 **NM** value: **2.50**
Circ: Statement: **91,104**

143 ❑ Aug 1981 Cover: 0.50 **NM** value: **2.50**
Circ: Statement: **91,104**

144 ❑ Sep 1981 Cover: 0.50 **NM** value: **2.50**
Circ: Statement: **91,104**

145 ❑ Oct 1981 Cover: 0.60 **NM** value: **2.00**
Circ: Statement: **91,104**

146 ❑ Nov 1981 Cover: 0.60 **NM** value: **2.00**
Circ: Statement: **91,104**

147 ❑ Dec 1981 Cover: 0.60 **NM** value: **2.00**
Circ: Statement: **91,104**

148 ❑ Jan 1982 Cover: 0.60 **NM** value: **2.00**
Circ: Statement: **89,657**

149 ❑ Feb 1982 Cover: 0.60 **NM** value: **2.00**
Circ: Statement: **89,657**

150 ❑ Mar 1982 Cover: 1.00 **NM** value: **3.00**
Circ: Statement: **89,657**
• 150th anniversary issue. **A:** Joe Staton

151 ❑ Apr 1982 Cover: 0.60 **NM** value: **2.00**
Circ: Statement: **89,657**

152 ❑ May 1982 Cover: 0.60 **NM** value: **2.00**
Circ: Statement: **89,657**
• Has 1981 Statement; avg print run 252,301; avg sales 88,865; avg subs 2,239; avg total paid 91,104; samples 127; office use 4,052; max existent 95,156; 62% of run returned

153 ❑ Jun 1982 Cover: 0.60 **NM** value: **2.00**
Circ: Statement: **89,657**

154 ❑ Jul 1982 Cover: 0.60 **NM** value: **2.00**
Circ: Statement: **89,657**

155 ❑ Aug 1982 Cover: 0.60 **NM** value: **2.00**
Circ: Statement: **89,657**

156 ❑ Sep 1982 Cover: 0.60 **NM** value: **2.00**
Circ: Statement: **89,657**

157 ❑ Oct 1982 Cover: 0.60 **NM** value: **2.00**
Circ: Statement: **89,657**

158 ❑ Nov 1982 Cover: 0.60 **NM** value: **2.00**
Circ: Statement: **89,657**
📖 A Loop in Time

159 ❑ Dec 1982 Cover: 0.60 **NM** value: **2.00**
Circ: Statement: **89,657**

160 ❑ Jan 1983 Cover: 0.60 **NM** value: **2.00**
Circ: Statement: **89,795**
• Omega Men

161 ❑ Feb 1983 Cover: 0.60 **NM** value: **1.50**
Circ: Statement: **89,795**
• Omega Men

162 ❑ Mar 1983 Cover: 0.60 **NM** value: **1.50**
Circ: Statement: **89,795**

163 ❑ Apr 1983 Cover: 0.60 **NM** value: **1.50**
Circ: Statement: **89,795**

164 ❑ May 1983 Cover: 0.60 **NM** value: **1.50**
Circ: Statement: **89,795**
• Has 1982 Statement; avg print run 235,877; avg sales 87,504; avg subs 2,153; avg total paid 89,657; samples 677; office use 2,398; max existent 92,055; 61% of run returned **A:** Keith Pollard ★ 1st Appearance of The Green Man.

165 ❑ Jun 1983 Cover: 0.60 **NM** value: **1.50**
Circ: Statement: **89,795**

166 ❑ Jul 1983 Cover: 0.60 **NM** value: **1.50**
Circ: Statement: **89,795**

167 ❑ Aug 1983 Cover: 0.60 **NM** value: **1.50**
Circ: Statement: **89,795**

168 ❑ Sep 1983 Cover: 0.60 **NM** value: **1.50**
Circ: Statement: **89,795**

169 ❑ Oct 1983 Cover: 0.60 **NM** value: **1.50**
Circ: Statement: **89,795**

170 ❑ Nov 1983 Cover: 0.60 **NM** value: **1.50**
Circ: Statement: **89,795**

171 ❑ Dec 1983 Cover: 0.75 **NM** value: **1.50**
Circ: Statement: **89,795**

172 ❑ Jan 1984 Cover: 0.75 **NM** value: **1.50**
Circ: Statement: **87,050**

173 ❑ Feb 1984 Cover: 0.75 **NM** value: **1.50**
Circ: Statement: **87,050**

174 ❑ Mar 1984 Cover: 0.75 **NM** value: **1.50**
Circ: Statement: **87,050**

175 ❑ Apr 1984 Cover: 0.75 **NM** value: **1.50**
Circ: Statement: **87,050**
• Has 1983 Statement; avg print run 218,593; avg sales 88,532; avg subs 1,263; avg total paid 89,795; samples 750; office use 2,315; max existent 92,110; 58% of run returned **A:** Dick Giordano ★ Appearance of Flash. ★ Versus Shark.

176 ❑ May 1984 Cover: 0.75 **NM** value: **1.50**
Circ: Statement: **87,050**

177 ❑ Jun 1984 Cover: 0.75 **NM** value: **1.50**
Circ: Statement: **87,050**

178 ❑ Jul 1984 Cover: 0.75 **NM** value: **1.50**
Circ: Statement: **87,050**

179 ❑ Aug 1984 Cover: 0.75 **NM** value: **1.50**
Circ: Statement: **87,050**

180 ❑ Sep 1984 Cover: 0.75 **NM** value: **1.50**
Circ: Statement: **87,050**

181 ❑ Oct 1984 Cover: 0.75 **NM** value: **1.50**
Circ: Statement: **87,050**
• Hal Jordan quits as Green Lantern; Hal Jordan resigns as Green Lantern **A:** Dick Giordano

182 ❑ Nov 1984 Cover: 0.75 **NM** value: **1.50**
Circ: Statement: **87,050**
• John Stewart becomes new Green Lantern; retells origin **A:** Dick Giordano

183 ❑ Dec 1984 Cover: 0.75 **NM** value: **1.50**
Circ: Statement: **87,050**

184 ❑ Jan 1985 Cover: 0.75 **NM** value: **1.50**
Circ: Statement: **80,765**
• reprints origin of Guy Gardner **A:** Gil Kane

185 ❑ Feb 1985 Cover: 0.75 **NM** value: **1.50**
Circ: Statement: **80,765**

186 ❑ Mar 1985 Cover: 0.75 **NM** value: **1.50**
Circ: Statement: **80,765**

187 ❑ Apr 1985 Cover: 0.75 **NM** value: **1.50**
Circ: Statement: **80,765**

188 ❑ May 1985 Cover: 0.75 **NM** value: **1.50**
Circ: Statement: **80,765** CapCity orders: **7,250**
• John Stewart reveals ID to public; Has 1984 Statement; avg print run 204,113; avg sales 85,863; avg subs 1,187; avg total paid 87,050; samples 272; office use 2,816; max existent 89,866; 56% of run returned

189 ❑ Jun 1985 Cover: 0.75 **NM** value: **1.50**
Circ: Statement: **80,765** CapCity orders: **7,100**

190 ❑ Jul 1985 Cover: 0.75 **NM** value: **1.50**
Circ: Statement: **80,765** CapCity orders: **6,850**

191 ❑ Aug 1985 Cover: 0.75 **NM** value: **1.50**
Circ: Statement: **80,765** CapCity orders: **7,000**

192 ❑ Sep 1985 Cover: 0.75 **NM** value: **1.50**
Circ: Statement: **80,765** CapCity orders: **7,150**

193 ❑ Oct 1985 Cover: 0.75 **NM** value: **1.50**
Circ: Statement: **80,765** CapCity orders: **6,600**

194 ❑ Nov 1985 Cover: 0.75 **NM** value: **2.50**
Circ: Statement: **80,765** CapCity orders: **10,100**
• Crisis; Guy Gardner returns; Guy Gardner vs. Hal Jordan

195 ❑ Dec 1985 Cover: 0.75 **NM** value: **3.00**
Circ: Statement: **80,765** CapCity orders: **10,000** • **CGC:** 1 graded, best 9.4
• Crisis; Guy Gardner becomes new Green Lantern of Earth

196 ❑ Jan 1986 Cover: 0.75 **NM** value: **1.50**
Circ: Statement: **96,488** CapCity orders: **7,200**
• Crisis

197 ❑ Feb 1986 Cover: 0.75 **NM** value: **1.50**
Circ: Statement: **96,488** CapCity orders: **7,800**
• Crisis; Guy Gardner vs. John Stewart

198 ❑ Mar 1986 Cover: 1.25 **NM** value: **1.50**
Circ: Statement: **96,488** CapCity orders: **11,000**
• Crisis; giant; Hal Jordan returns as Green Lantern

199 ❑ Apr 1986 Cover: 0.75 **NM** value: **1.50**
Circ: Statement: **96,488** CapCity orders: **9,350**
📖 Ignition • Crisis; Hal Jordan returns as GL; Has 1985 Statement; avg print run 198,173; avg sales 79,294; avg subs 1,471; avg total paid 80,765; samples 132; office use 1,445; max existent 82,210; 53% of run returned

200 ❑ May 1986 Cover: 1.25 **NM** value: **2.00**
Circ: Statement: **96,488** CapCity orders: **13,050**
• Crisis; Guardians join Zamarons

201 ❑ Jun 1986 Cover: 0.75 **NM** value: **1.50**
Circ: Statement: **96,488** CapCity orders: **11,800**
• Crisis aftermath

202 ❑ Jul 1986 Cover: 0.75 **NM** value: **1.50**
Circ: Statement: **96,488** CapCity orders: **10,550**

203 ❑ Aug 1986 Cover: 0.75 **NM** value: **1.50**
Circ: Statement: **96,488** CapCity orders: **10,700**

204 ❑ Sep 1986 Cover: 0.75 **NM** value: **1.50**
Circ: Statement: **96,488** CapCity orders: **12,000**

Other grades: Multiply prices above by **1.5 for Mint • 2/3 for Very Fine • 1/3 for Fine • 1/5 for Very Good • 1/8 for Good**

205 ❑ Oct 1986 Cover: 0.75 **NM** value: **1.50**
Circ: Statement: **96,488** CapCity orders: **12,150**
• Series continues as Green Lantern Corps

SE 1 ❑ Dec 1988 Cover: 1.50 **NM** value: **2.50**
Circ: CapCity orders: **18,300**
📖 With This Ring…! **A:** Tod Smith **W:** James Owsley

SE 2 ❑ ca. 1989 Cover: 1.50 **NM** value: **2.50**
Circ: CapCity orders: **16,850**

GREEN LANTERN (3RD SERIES) DC

This third Green Lantern series initially featured Hal Jordan, Guy Gardner, and John Stewart sharing Green Lantern duties on Earth and its immediate space. Jordan would become increasingly cynical as the series progressed and, in 1993, was pushed over the edge of insanity by the destruction of his hometown of Coast City. Destroying the rest of the Green Lantern Corps in an attempt to force The Guardians of the Universe to restore the town, Jordan became Parallax, a time-altering maniac who was eventually destroyed by the events of Final Night.

The one remaining Guardian gave the one remaining power ring to Kyle Rayner, a New York City artist, who now serves as Earth's sole Green Lantern. — Brent

0 ❑ Oct 1994 Cover: 1.50 **NM** value: **3.00**
Circ: CapCity orders: **43,650**
📖 Second Chances • Oa destroyed **A:** Darryl Banks **W:** Ron Marz ★ Origin of Green Lantern (Kyle Rayner). ★ Versus Hal Jordan.

1 ❑ Jun 1990 Cover: 1.00 **NM** value: **3.00**
Circ: CapCity orders: **54,500** • **CGC:** 8 graded, best 9.8
📖 Down to Earth **A:** Pat Broderick **W:** Gerard Jones

2 ❑ Jul 1990 Cover: 1.00 **NM** value: **2.50**
Circ: CapCity orders: **38,900**
📖 Pursuit Of Happiness! **A:** Pat Broderick **W:** Gerard Jones

3 ❑ Aug 1990 Cover: 1.00 **NM** value: **2.00**
Circ: CapCity orders: **37,350**
• Hal vs. Guy

4 ❑ Sep 1990 Cover: 1.00 **NM** value: **2.00**
Circ: CapCity orders: **36,950**

5 ❑ Oct 1990 Cover: 1.00 **NM** value: **2.00**
Circ: CapCity orders: **34,900**

6 ❑ Nov 1990 Cover: 1.00 **NM** value: **1.50**
Circ: CapCity orders: **33,750**

7 ❑ Dec 1990 Cover: 1.00 **NM** value: **1.50**
Circ: CapCity orders: **33,550**

8 ❑ Jan 1991 Cover: 1.00 **NM** value: **1.50**
Circ: CapCity orders: **33,600**

9 ❑ Feb 1991 Cover: 1.00 **NM** value: **1.50**
Circ: CapCity orders: **33,800**

10 ❑ Mar 1991 Cover: 1.00 **NM** value: **1.50**
Circ: CapCity orders: **32,550** • **CGC:** 2 graded, best 9.4

11 ❑ Apr 1991 Cover: 1.00 **NM** value: **1.50**
Circ: CapCity orders: **31,300**

12 ❑ May 1991 Cover: 1.00 **NM** value: **1.50**
Circ: CapCity orders: **31,250**

13 ❑ Jun 1991 Cover: 1.75 **NM** value: **2.25**
Circ: CapCity orders: **30,700**
• Giant-size.

14 ❑ Jul 1991 Cover: 1.00 **NM** value: **1.50**
Circ: CapCity orders: **30,550**

15 ❑ Aug 1991 Cover: 1.00 **NM** value: **1.50**
Circ: CapCity orders: **30,600**

16 ❑ Sep 1991 Cover: 1.00 **NM** value: **1.50**
Circ: CapCity orders: **30,700**

17 ❑ Oct 1991 Cover: 1.00 **NM** value: **1.50**
Circ: CapCity orders: **29,900**

18 ❑ Nov 1991 Cover: 1.00 **NM** value: **1.50**
Circ: CapCity orders: **28,850**

19 ❑ Dec 1991 Cover: 1.75 **NM** value: **2.00**
Circ: CapCity orders: **33,650**
• Giant-size. **C:** Gil Kane

20 ❑ Jan 1992 Cover: 1.00 **NM** value: **1.50**
Circ: CapCity orders: **26,250**

21 ❑ Feb 1992 Cover: 1.00 **NM** value: **1.50**
Circ: CapCity orders: **24,400**

22 ❑ Mar 1992 Cover: 1.00 **NM** value: **1.50**
Circ: CapCity orders: **23,250**

23 ❑ Apr 1992 Cover: 1.00 **NM** value: **1.50**
Circ: CapCity orders: **21,850**

24 ❑ May 1992 Cover: 1.00 **NM** value: **1.50**
Circ: CapCity orders: **21,200**

25 ❑ Jun 1992 Cover: 1.75 **NM** value: **2.25**
Circ: CapCity orders: **30,850**
• Giant size. • Hal Jordan vs. Guy Gardner

26 ❑ Jul 1992 Cover: 1.00 **NM** value: **1.50**
Circ: CapCity orders: **22,700**
📖 Evil Star Rising, Part 1

27 ❑ Aug 1992 Cover: 1.25 **NM** value: **Cover or less**
Circ: CapCity orders: **22,300**
📖 Evil Star Rising, Part 2

28 ❑ Sep 1992 Cover: 1.25 **NM** value: **Cover or less**
📖 Evil Star Rising, Part 3

29 ❑ Sep 1992 Cover: 1.25 **NM** value: **Cover or less**
Circ: CapCity orders: **20,950**

30 ❑ Oct 1992 Cover: 1.25 **NM** value: **Cover or less**
Circ: CapCity orders: **21,400**

31 ❑ Oct 1992 Cover: 1.25 **NM** value: **Cover or less**

32 ❑ Nov 1992 Cover: 1.25 **NM** value: **Cover or less**
Circ: CapCity orders: **19,600**

33 ❑ Nov 1992 Cover: 1.25 **NM** value: **Cover or less**
Circ: CapCity orders: **19,550**

34 ❑ Dec 1992 Cover: 1.25 **NM** value: **Cover or less**
Circ: CapCity orders: **18,000**

35 ❑ Jan 1993 Cover: 1.25 **NM** value: **Cover or less**
Circ: CapCity orders: **17,350**

36 ❑ Feb 1993 Cover: 1.25 **NM** value: **Cover or less**
Circ: CapCity orders: **17,350**

37 ❑ Mar 1993 Cover: 1.25 **NM** value: **Cover or less**
Circ: CapCity orders: **16,800**

38 ❑ Apr 1993 Cover: 1.25 **NM** value: **Cover or less**
Circ: CapCity orders: **16,700**
• Adam Strange

39 ❑ May 1993 Cover: 1.25 **NM** value: **Cover or less**
Circ: CapCity orders: **16,700**

40 ❑ May 1993 Cover: 1.25 **NM** value: **Cover or less**
Circ: CapCity orders: **17,050**

41 ❑ Jun 1993 Cover: 1.25 **NM** value: **Cover or less**
Circ: CapCity orders: **16,650**

42 ❑ Jun 1993 Cover: 1.25 **NM** value: **Cover or less**
Circ: CapCity orders: **16,750**

43 ❑ Jul 1993 Cover: 1.25 **NM** value: **Cover or less**
Circ: CapCity orders: **15,350**

44 ❑ Aug 1993 Cover: 1.25 **NM** value: **Cover or less**
Circ: CapCity orders: **20,800**

45 ❑ Sep 1993 Cover: 1.25 **NM** value: **Cover or less**
Circ: CapCity orders: **17,850**

46 ❑ Oct 1993 Cover: 1.25 **NM** value: **4.00**
Circ: CapCity orders: **69,850** • **CGC:** 3 graded, best 9.6
📖 Reign of The Supermen ★ Appearance of Superman. ★ Versus Mongul.

47 ❑ Nov 1993 Cover: 1.25 **NM** value: **2.00**
Circ: CapCity orders: **15,850**

48 ❑ Jan 1994 Cover: 1.50 **NM** value: **6.00**
Circ: CapCity orders: **35,200** • **CGC:** 10 graded, best 9.8
📖 Emerald Twilight; Emerald Twilight, Part 1 **A:** Bill Willingham **W:** Ron Marz

49 ❑ Feb 1994 Cover: 1.50 **NM** value: **6.00**
Circ: CapCity orders: **34,850** • **CGC:** 5 graded, best 9.6
📖 Emerald Twilight; Emerald Twilight, Part 2 **A:** Fred Haynes **W:** Ron Marz

50 ❑ Mar 1994 Cover: 2.95 **NM** value: **6.00**
Circ: CapCity orders: **54,550** • **CGC:** 37 graded, best 9.9
Glow-in-the-dark cover. • Double-size. 📖 Emerald Twilight; Emerald Twilight, Part 3 **A:** Darryl Banks **W:** Ron Marz ★ 1st Appearance of Green Lantern IV (Kyle Rayner). ★ Death of Sinestro. ★ Death of Kilowog.

51 ❑ May 1994 Cover: 1.50 **NM** value: **3.00**
Circ: CapCity orders: **41,700** • **CGC:** 1 graded, best 9.2
📖 Changing The Guard • New costume **A:** Darryl Banks **W:** Ron Marz

52 ❑ Jun 1994 Cover: 1.50 **NM** value: **2.00**
Circ: CapCity orders: **36,600**

53 ❑ Jul 1994 Cover: 1.50 **NM** value: **2.00**
Circ: CapCity orders: **37,900**

54 ❑ Aug 1994 Cover: 1.50 **NM** value: **2.00**
Circ: CapCity orders: **35,450**

55 ❑ Sep 1994 Cover: 1.50 **NM** value: **2.00**
Circ: CapCity orders: **35,700**
📖 Zero Hour • Zero Hour **A:** Darryl Banks; Derec Aucoin; Craig Hamilton **W:** Ron Marz ★ Appearance of Green Lantern I, Alan Scott.

56 ❑ Nov 1994 Cover: 1.50 **NM** value: **2.00**
Circ: CapCity orders: **31,100**

57 ❑ Dec 1994 Cover: 1.50 **NM** value: **2.00**
Circ: CapCity orders: **31,000**
• continues in New Titans #116 **W:** Ron Marz ★ Appearance of New Titans.

58 ❑ Jan 1995 Cover: 1.50 **NM** value: **2.00**
Circ: CapCity orders: **29,650**
📖 Conjuring **A:** Cully Hamner **W:** Ron Marz

59 ❑ Feb 1995 Cover: 1.50 **NM** value: **2.00**
Circ: CapCity orders: **28,100**

60 ❑ Mar 1995 Cover: 1.50 **NM** value: **2.00**
Circ: CapCity orders: **25,800**
📖 Capital Punishment, Part 3 **W:** Ron Marz ★ Appearance of Guy Gardner. ★ Versus Major Force.

61 ❑ Apr 1995 Cover: 1.50 **NM** value: **2.00**
Circ: CapCity orders: **23,650**

62 ❑ May 1995 Cover: 1.50 **NM** value: **2.00**
Circ: CapCity orders: **22,800**

63 ❑ Jun 1995 Cover: 1.75 **NM** value: **2.00**
Circ: CapCity orders: **26,200**
📖 Parallax View, Part 1 **W:** Ron Marz

64 ❑ Jul 1995 Cover: 1.75 **NM** value: **2.00**
Circ: CapCity orders: **24,050**
📖 Parallax View, Part 2 **W:** Ron Marz

65 ❑ Aug 1995 Cover: 1.75 **NM** value: **2.00**
Circ: CapCity orders: **23,300**
📖 The Siege of The Zi Charam, Part 2 • continues in Darkstars #34 **W:** Ron Marz

66 ❑ Sep 1995 Cover: 1.75 **NM** value: **2.00**
Circ: CapCity orders: **22,425**
• teams with Flash **W:** Ron Marz

67 ❑ Oct 1995 Cover: 1.75 **NM** value: **2.00**
Circ: CapCity orders: **19,450**

68 ❑ Nov 1995 Cover: 1.75 **NM** value: **2.00**
• Underworld Unleashed **W:** Ron Marz ★ Appearance of Donna Troy.

69 ❑ Dec 1995 Cover: 1.75 **NM** value: **2.00**
📖 Underworld Unleashed • Underworld Unleashed **W:** Ron Marz

70 ❑ Jan 1996 Cover: 1.75 **NM** value: **2.00**

71 ❑ Feb 1996 Cover: 1.75 **NM** value: **2.00**
📖 Hero Quest, Part 1 **A:** Paul Pelletier **W:** Ron Marz ★ Appearance of Robin, Sentinel, Batman.

72 ❑ Mar 1996 Cover: 1.75 **NM** value: **2.00**
📖 Hero Quest, Part 2 **A:** Paul Pelletier **W:** Ron Marz ★ Appearance of Captain Marvel.

73 ❑ Apr 1996 Cover: 1.75 **NM** value: **2.00**
📖 Hero Quest, Part 3 **A:** Paul Pelletier **W:** Ron Marz ★ Appearance of Wonder Woman.

74 ❑ Jun 1996 Cover: 1.75 **NM** value: **2.00**

75 ❑ Jul 1996 Cover: 1.75 **NM** value: **2.00**

76 ❑ Jul 1996 Cover: 1.75 **NM** value: **2.00**
📖 Hard-Traveling Heroes: The Next Generation, Part 1 **W:** Ron Marz

77 ❑ Aug 1996 Cover: 1.75 **NM** value: **2.00**
📖 Hard-Traveling Heroes: The Next Generation, Part 3 **W:** Ron Marz

78 ❑ Sep 1996 Cover: 1.75 **NM** value: **2.00**

79 ❑ Oct 1996 Cover: 1.75 **NM** value: **2.00**
📖 Hard Time **A:** Darryl Banks **W:** Ron Marz ★ Versus Sonar.

80 ❑ Nov 1996 Cover: 1.75 **NM** value: **2.00**
Circ: Diamd. preorders: **55,499**
📖 Light in Darkness • Final Night **A:** J.H. Williams **W:** Ron Marz ★ Versus Doctor Light. ★ Versus Dr. Light.

81 ❑ Dec 1996 Cover: 1.75 **NM** value: **3.00**
• **CGC:** 4 graded, best 9.8
📖 Funeral for a Hero • Funeral of Hal Jordan; Memorial for Hal Jordan **A:** Darryl Banks **W:** Ron Marz

81/SC ❑ Dec 1996 Cover: 3.95 **NM** value: **4.00**
Embossed cover. 📖 Funeral for a Hero • Funeral of Hal Jordan; Kane back-up story; reprints origin; Memorial for Hal Jordan **A:** Darryl Banks **W:** Ron Marz

82 ❑ Jan 1997 Cover: 1.75 **NM** value: **Cover or less**
Circ: Diamd. preorders: **51,558**
📖 Adventures in Babysitting **A:** Tom Grindberg **W:** Ron Marz

83 ❑ Feb 1997 Cover: 1.75 **NM** value: **Cover or less**
Circ: Diamd. preorders: **50,075**
📖 Retribution, Part 1 **W:** Ron Marz

84 ❑ Mar 1997 Cover: 1.75 **NM** value: **Cover or less**
Circ: Diamd. preorders: **47,902**
📖 Retribution, Part 2 **A:** Darryl Banks **W:** Ron Marz

85 ❑ Apr 1997 Cover: 1.75 **NM** value: **Cover or less**
Circ: Diamd. preorders: **45,828**
📖 Retribution, Part 3 **W:** Ron Marz

86 ❑ May 1997 Cover: 1.75 **NM** value: **Cover or less**
Circ: Diamd. preorders: **45,757**

87 ❑ Jun 1997 Cover: 1.75 **NM** value: **Cover or less**
Circ: Diamd. preorders: **47,138**

88 ❑ Jul 1997 Cover: 1.75 **NM** value: **Cover or less**
Circ: Diamd. preorders: **47,152**

89 ❑ Aug 1997 Cover: 1.75 **NM** value: **Cover or less**
Circ: Diamd. preorders: **47,455**

90 ❑ Sep 1997 Cover: 1.75 **NM** value: **Cover or less**
Circ: Diamd. preorders: **46,412**

91 ❑ Oct 1997 Cover: 1.75 **NM** value: **Cover or less**
Circ: Diamd. preorders: **48,798**
📖 Torture • Genesis **A:** Darryl Banks; Georges Jeanty **W:** Ron Marz ★ Versus Desaad.

92 ❑ Nov 1997 Cover: 1.75 **NM** value: **Cover or less**
Circ: Diamd. preorders: **46,730**
📖 Hate Crimes, Part 2 • concludes in Green Arrow #126 **W:** Ron Marz

93 ❑ Dec 1997 Cover: 1.75 **NM** value: **1.95**
Circ: Diamd. preorders: **46,487**
Face cover. 📖 All Hallow's Eve **A:** Darryl Banks; Tom Grindberg **W:** Ron Marz ★ Appearance of Deadman.

94 ❑ Jan 1998 Cover: 1.95 **NM** value: **Cover or less**
Circ: Diamd. preorders: **45,805**
📖 Idol Worship, Part 1 **A:** Paul Pelletier **W:** Ron Marz ★ Appearance of Superboy.

95 ❑ Feb 1998 Cover: 1.95 **NM** value: **Cover or less**
Circ: Diamd. preorders: **45,594**

96 ❑ Mar 1998 Cover: 1.95 **NM** value: **Cover or less**
Circ: Diamd. preorders: **47,449**
cover forms triptych with Flash #135 and Green Arrow #130. 📖 Three of a Kind, Part 1 **W:** Ron Marz

97 ❑ Apr 1998 Cover: 1.95 **NM** value: **Cover or less**
Circ: Diamd. preorders: **41,447**
📖 Loose Ends **A:** Mike McKone **W:** Ron Marz ★ Versus Grayven.

98 ❑ May 1998 Cover: 1.95 **NM** value: **Cover or less**
Circ: Diamd. preorders: **43,222**
📖 Future Shock, Part 1 **W:** Ron Marz ★ 1st Appearance of Cary Wren as Green Lantern. ★ Appearance of Legion of Super-Heroes.

99 ❑ Jun 1998 Cover: 1.95 **NM** value: **Cover or less**
Circ: Diamd. preorders: **49,371**
📖 Future Shock, Part 2 **W:** Ron Marz

100/A ❑ Jul 1998 Cover: 2.95 **NM** value: **Cover or less**
Hal Jordan cover (Kyle Rayner cover inside).

100/Aut ❑ Jul 1998 Cover: 2.95 **NM** value: **8.00**
📖 Emerald Knights **W:** Ron Marz

100/B ❑ Jul 1998 Cover: 2.95 **NM** value: **Cover or less**
Kyle Rayner cover (Hal Jordan cover inside).

101 ❑ Aug 1998 Cover: 1.95 **NM** value: **Cover or less**
Circ: Diamd. preorders: **54,268**
📖 Emerald Knights, Part 1; Emerald Knights **W:** Ron Marz

102 ❑ Aug 1998 Cover: 1.95 **NM** value: **Cover or less**
Circ: Diamd. preorders: **54,026**
📖 Emerald Knights, Part 2; Emerald Knights **W:** Ron Marz ★ Versus Kalibak.

103 ❑ Sep 1998 Cover: 1.99 **NM** value: **Cover or less**
Circ: Diamd. preorders: **52,901**
📖 Emerald Knights, Part 3; Emerald Knights **W:** Ron Marz ★ Appearance of JLA.

104 ❑ Sep 1998 Cover: 1.99 **NM** value: **Cover or less**
Circ: Diamd. preorders: **52,878**
📖 Emerald Knights, Part 4; Emerald Knights **W:** Ron Marz ★ Appearance of Green Arrow.

105 ❑ Oct 1998 Cover: 1.99 **NM** value: **Cover or less**
Circ: Diamd. preorders: **58,782**
📖 Emerald Knights, Part 5; Emerald Knights **W:** Ron Marz ★ Versus Parallax.

106 ❑ Oct 1998 Cover: 1.99 **NM** value: **Cover or less**
Circ: Diamd. preorders: **58,782**
📖 Emerald Knights, Part 6; Emerald Knights • Hal returned to past **W:** Ron Marz

107 ❑ Dec 1998 Cover: 1.99 **NM** value: **Cover or less**
Circ: Diamd. preorders: **56,530**
• Kyle gives a ring to Jade **W:** Ron Marz

108 ❑ Jan 1999 Cover: 1.99 **NM** value: **Cover or less**
Circ: Diamd. preorders: **54,926**
• Wonder Woman **W:** Ron Marz

CGC-graded: Multiply prices above by **33 for 9.9 M • 16 for 9.8 NM/M • 7 for 9.6 NM+ • 5 for 9.4 NM • 2.5 for 9.2 NM- • 1.5 for 9.0 VF/NM**

109❑ Feb 1999 Cover: 1.99 **NM** value: **Cover or less**
Circ: Diamd. preorders: **52,078**
• Green Lantern IV (Jade) **A:** Brian Pelletier **W:** Ron Marz
110❑ Mar 1999 Cover: 1.99 **NM** value: **Cover or less**
Circ: Diamd. preorders: **51,453**
111❑ Apr 1999 Cover: 1.99 **NM** value: **Cover or less**
Circ: Diamd. preorders: **48,061**
112❑ May 1999 Cover: 1.99 **NM** value: **Cover or less**
Circ: Diamd. preorders: **47,983**
• Kyle returns **A:** Darryl Banks **W:** Ron Marz
113❑ Jun 1999 Cover: 1.99 **NM** value: **Cover or less**
Circ: Diamd. preorders: **49,161**
🕮 Burning in Effigy, Part 1 **A:** Darryl Banks **W:** Ron Marz
114❑ Jul 1999 Cover: 1.99 **NM** value: **Cover or less**
Circ: Diamd. preorders: **47,345**
🕮 Burning in Effigy, Part 2 **A:** Ron Lim; Georges Jeanty **W:** Ron Marz
115❑ Aug 1999 Cover: 1.99 **NM** value: **Cover or less**
Circ: Diamd. preorders: **46,590**
🕮 The Package **A:** Mike S. Miller **W:** Dan Jurgens ★ Appearance of Plastic Man, Booster Gold.
116❑ Sep 1999 Cover: 1.99 **NM** value: **Cover or less**
Circ: Diamd. preorders: **46,045**
🕮 Machinations, Misconceptions and, Revelations! **A:** Tom Lyle **W:** Dan Jurgens ★ Appearance of Plastic Man, Booster Gold.
117❑ Oct 1999 Cover: 1.99 **NM** value: **Cover or less**
Circ: Diamd. preorders: **44,556**
🕮 Found Art **A:** Darryl Banks **W:** Ron Marz ★ Versus Manhunter.
118❑ Nov 1999 Cover: 1.99 **NM** value: **Cover or less**
Circ: Diamd. preorders: **46,110**
🕮 Women • Day of Judgment **A:** Darryl Banks **W:** Ron Marz ★ Appearance of Enchantress.
119❑ Dec 1999 Cover: 1.99 **NM** value: **Cover or less**
Circ: Diamd. preorders: **44,308**
120❑ Jan 2000 Cover: 1.99 **NM** value: **Cover or less**
Circ: Diamd. preorders: **42,515**
🕮 Target **A:** Darryl Banks **W:** Ron Marz
121❑ Feb 2000 Cover: 1.99 **NM** value: **Cover or less**
Circ: Diamd. preorders: **42,562**
🕮 New World **A:** Darryl Banks **W:** Ron Marz
122❑ Mar 2000 Cover: 1.99 **NM** value: **Cover or less**
Circ: Diamd. preorders: **41,032**
123❑ Apr 2000 Cover: 1.99 **NM** value: **Cover or less**
Circ: Diamd. preorders: **39,345**
124❑ May 2000 Cover: 1.99 **NM** value: **Cover or less**
Circ: Diamd. preorders: **39,858**
🕮 Control Freak **A:** Darryl Banks **W:** Ron Marz
125❑ Jun 2000 Cover: 1.99 **NM** value: **Cover or less**
Circ: Diamd. preorders: **39,774**
🕮 Tomb Raider **A:** Jeff Johnson **W:** Ron Marz
126❑ Jul 2000 Cover: 1.99 **NM** value: **Cover or less**
Circ: Diamd. preorders: **39,091**
127❑ Aug 2000 Cover: 1.99 **NM** value: **Cover or less**
Circ: Diamd. preorders: **38,941**
128❑ Sep 2000 Cover: 1.99 **NM** value: **Cover or less**
Circ: Diamd. preorders: **37,882**
129❑ Oct 2000 Cover: 2.25 **NM** value: **Cover or less**
Circ: Diamd. preorders: **37,647**
🕮 Something Old, Something New **A:** Darryl Banks **W:** Judd Winick
130❑ Nov 2000 Cover: 2.25 **NM** value: **Cover or less**
Circ: Diamd. preorders: **36,784**
🕮 Prodigal Son **A:** Darryl Banks **W:** Judd Winick
131❑ Dec 2000 Cover: 2.25 **NM** value: **Cover or less**
Circ: Diamd. preorders: **36,605**
132❑ Jan 2001 Cover: 2.25 **NM** value: **Cover or less**
Circ: Diamd. preorders: **36,870**
🕮 While Rome Burned, Part 1 **A:** Mark Bright; Daryl Banks **W:** Judd Winick
133❑ Feb 2001 Cover: 2.25 **NM** value: **Cover or less**
Circ: Diamd. preorders: **36,516**
🕮 While Rome Burned, Part 2 **A:** Mark Bright **W:** Judd Winick
134❑ Mar 2001 Cover: 2.25 **NM** value: **Cover or less**
Circ: Diamd. preorders: **35,940**
🕮 While Rome Burned, Part 3 **A:** Darryl Banks **W:** Judd Winick
135❑ Apr 2001 Cover: 2.25 **NM** value: **Cover or less**
Circ: Diamd. preorders: **36,122**
🕮 While Rome Burned, Part 4 **A:** Darryl Banks **W:** Judd Winick
136❑ May 2001 Cover: 2.25 **NM** value: **Cover or less**
Circ: Diamd. preorders: **35,052**
🕮 While Rome Burned, Part 5 **A:** Dale Eaglesham **W:** Judd Winick
137❑ Jun 2001 Cover: 2.25 **NM** value: **Cover or less**
Circ: Diamd. preorders: **36,087**
🕮 The Bonds of Friends and Lovers **A:** Darryl Banks **W:** Judd Winick
138❑ Jul 2001 Cover: 2.25 **NM** value: **Cover or less**
Circ: Diamd. preorders: **35,822**
139❑ Aug 2001 Cover: 2.25 **NM** value: **Cover or less**
Circ: Diamd. preorders: **36,552**
140❑ Sep 2001 Cover: 2.25 **NM** value: **Cover or less**
Circ: Diamd. preorders: **38,637**
1000000❑Nov 1998 Cover: 1.99 **NM** value: **Cover or less**
Circ: Diamd. preorders: **59,921**
• One Million
3D 1❑Dec 1998 Cover: 3.95 **NM** value: **Cover or less**
3D 1/LE❑Dec 1998 Cover: 16.95 **NM** value: **Cover or less**
Anl 1❑ca. 1992 Cover: 2.50 **NM** value: **3.00**
Circ: CapCity orders: **27,900**
🕮 Eclipso: the Darkness Within, Part 3 • Eclipso: The Darkness Within **A:** Andy Smith **W:** Gerard Jones
Anl 2❑ca. 1993 Cover: 2.50 **NM** value: **Cover or less**
Circ: CapCity orders: **20,750**
🕮 Bloodlines • Bloodlines: Outbreak★ Origin of Nightblade. ★ 1st Appearance of Nightblade.
Anl 3❑ca. 1994 Cover: 2.95 **NM** value: **3.00**
Circ: CapCity orders: **23,450**
• Elseworlds
Anl 4❑ca. 1995 Cover: 3.50 **NM** value: **Cover or less**
Circ: CapCity orders: **15,550**
• Year One; Kyle and Hal switch places
Anl 5❑ca. 1996 Cover: 2.95 **NM** value: **Cover or less**
• Legends of the Dead Earth
Anl 6❑Oct 1997 Cover: 3.95 **NM** value: **Cover or less**
Circ: Diamd. preorders: **35,484**
• Pulp Heroes; John Carter of Mars theme
Anl 7❑Oct 1998 Cover: 2.95 **NM** value: **Cover or less**
Circ: Diamd. preorders: **37,627**
• Ghosts
Anl 8❑Oct 1999 Cover: 2.95 **NM** value: **Cover or less**
Circ: Diamd. preorders: **35,185**
🕮 Grunts • JLApe **A:** Octavio Cariello **W:** Keith Giffen
Anl 9❑Oct 2000 Cover: 3.50 **NM** value: **Cover or less**
Circ: Diamd. preorders: **28,820**
🕮 Mother of Heaven • Planet DC★ 1st Appearance of Sala.
Anl 1963❑ Cover: 4.95 **NM** value: **Cover or less**
• **CGC:** 1 graded, best 9.8
cardstock cover. • published in 1998 in style of 1963 annuals
Bk 1❑ Cover: 5.95 **NM** value: **Cover or less**
• Emerald Twilight
Bk 2❑ Cover: 9.95 **NM** value: **Cover or less**
🕮 A New Dawn • A New Dawn; collects Green Lantern #50-55 **A:** Darryl Banks **W:** Ron Marz
Bk 3❑ Cover: 12.95 **NM** value: **Cover or less**
• Emerald Knights; collects #99-106 and Green Arrow #136 **A:** Paul Pelletier; Darryl Banks **W:** Ron Marz
Bk 4❑ Cover: 12.95 **NM** value: **Cover or less**
• Baptism of Fire; collects #59, #66, #67, and #70-75
GS 1❑Dec 1998 Cover: 4.95 **NM** value: **Cover or less**
Circ: Diamd. preorders: **35,677**
GS 2❑Jun 1999 Cover: 4.95 **NM** value: **Cover or less**
Circ: Diamd. preorders: **30,475**
🕮 Team-Ups from A to Z; Phases; Art Attack; Fallen Idols; Everybody Goes to Guy's; The Lantern's Apprentice; Anything You Can Do; Crosscut **A:** Matt Smith; Mark D. Bright; Kevin West; George Freeman; Oscar Jimenez; Mike McKone; Andy Kuhn **W:** Andy Lanning; Chuck Dixon; Steven Grant; Christopher Priest; Dan Abnett; Hank Kanalz; Mark Waid; Marv Wolfman ★ Appearance of Plastic Man, Guy Gardner, Deadman, Impulse, Zatanna, Big Barda, Aquaman.

GREEN LANTERN/ADAM STRANGE — DC

1 ❑ Oct 2000 Cover: 2.50 **NM** value: **Cover or less**
🕮 We Rann All Night **A:** Cary Nord **W:** Brian K. Vaughan

GREEN LANTERN ARCHIVES — DC

1 ❑ Cover: 39.95 **NM** value: **Cover or less**
• Reprints Showcase #22-24, Green Lantern (2nd Series) #1-5
2 ❑ Cover: 49.95 **NM** value: **Cover or less**
• Collects Green Lantern (2nd Series) #6-13

GREEN LANTERN/ATOM — DC

1 ❑ Oct 2000 Cover: 2.50 **NM** value: **Cover or less**
🕮 Unusual Suspects **A:** Trevor McCarthy **W:** Brian K. Vaughan

GREEN LANTERN: CIRCLE OF FIRE — DC

1 ❑ Oct 2000 Cover: 4.95 **NM** value: **Cover or less**
🕮 Darkness Visible **A:** Norm Breyfogle **W:** Brian K. Vaughan
2 ❑ Oct 2000 Cover: 4.95 **NM** value: **Cover or less**
🕮 Full Circle **A:** Robert Teranishi **W:** Brian K. Vaughan

GREEN LANTERN CORPS, THE — DC

Unlike other super-heroes, the various people who have wielded the awesome power of Green Lantern are not solo adventurers. They are actually intergalactic policemen, assigned to their own "beats" (Hal Jordan's was sector 2814: the area around Earth). At the same time, they are part of a larger force known as the Green Lantern Corps. The Corps was set up by the Guardians of the Universe, an advanced race from the planet Oa, and is responsible for maintaining order throughout the universe. When extraordinary danger threatens, however, the Corps members may be called to handle it together.

This series was continued from Green Lantern (2nd Series) #204. It marked a shift in focus away from the solo Green Lantern heroes (notably Hal Jordan) and toward a cast of less distinguished Green Lanterns. The series later concluded with issue #224.

205❑ **NM** value: **1.50**
• Series continued from Green Lantern (2nd Series) #204
206❑ Nov 1986 Cover: 0.75 **NM** value: **1.50**
Circ: Statement: **96,488** CapCity orders: **11,550**
207❑ Dec 1986 Cover: 0.75 **NM** value: **1.50**
Circ: Statement: **96,488** CapCity orders: **14,950**
• Legends
208❑ Jan 1987 Cover: 0.75 **NM** value: **1.50**
Circ: Statement: **85,739** CapCity orders: **10,250**
209❑ Feb 1987 Cover: 0.75 **NM** value: **1.50**
Circ: Statement: **85,739** CapCity orders: **10,150**
210❑ Mar 1987 Cover: 0.75 **NM** value: **1.50**
Circ: Statement: **85,739** CapCity orders: **10,000**
211❑ Apr 1987 Cover: 0.75 **NM** value: **1.50**
Circ: Statement: **85,739** CapCity orders: **10,450**
• Has 1986 Statement; avg print run 193,241; avg sales 94,779; avg subs 1,709; avg total paid 96,488; samples 181; office use 2,108; max existent 98,596; 49% of run returned
212❑ May 1987 Cover: 0.75 **NM** value: **1.50**
Circ: Statement: **85,739** CapCity orders: **10,300**
213❑ Jun 1987 Cover: 0.75 **NM** value: **1.50**
Circ: Statement: **85,739** CapCity orders: **10,600**
214❑ Jul 1987 Cover: 0.75 **NM** value: **1.50**
Circ: Statement: **85,739** CapCity orders: **10,550**
215❑ Aug 1987 Cover: 0.75 **NM** value: **1.50**
Circ: Statement: **85,739** CapCity orders: **11,800**
216❑ Sep 1987 Cover: 0.75 **NM** value: **1.50**
Circ: Statement: **85,739** CapCity orders: **12,550**
217❑ Oct 1987 Cover: 0.75 **NM** value: **1.50**
Circ: Statement: **85,739** CapCity orders: **12,500**
218❑ Nov 1987 Cover: 0.75 **NM** value: **1.50**
Circ: Statement: **85,739** CapCity orders: **13,800**
219❑ Dec 1987 Cover: 0.75 **NM** value: **1.50**
Circ: Statement: **85,739** CapCity orders: **12,550**
220❑ Jan 1988 Cover: 0.75 **NM** value: **1.50**
Circ: CapCity orders: **17,650**
• Millennium
221❑ Feb 1988 Cover: 0.75 **NM** value: **1.50**
Circ: CapCity orders: **18,450**
• Millennium
222❑ Mar 1988 Cover: 0.75 **NM** value: **1.50**
Circ: CapCity orders: **13,700**
223❑ Apr 1988 Cover: 0.75 **NM** value: **1.50**
Circ: CapCity orders: **14,050**
• Has 1987 Statement; avg print run 184,052; avg sales 84,449; avg subs 1,290; avg total paid 85,739; samples 979; office use 14,851; max existent 100,590; 45% of run returned
224❑ May 1988 Cover: 1.50 **NM** value: **Cover or less**
Circ: CapCity orders: **16,800**
• Giant-size. final issue. **A:** Gil Kane
Anl 1❑ **NM** value: **2.50**
Circ: CapCity orders: **12,200**
Anl 2❑ **NM** value: **2.25**
Anl 3❑ **NM** value: **2.00**

GREEN LANTERN CORPS QUARTERLY — DC

1 ❑ Sum 1992 Cover: 2.50 **NM** value: **Cover or less**
Circ: CapCity orders: **27,000**
🕮 The Book of Everything **A:** Mark D. Bright **W:** Gerard Jones
2 ❑ Aut 1992 Cover: 2.50 **NM** value: **Cover or less**
Circ: CapCity orders: **16,500**
• Hector Hammond vs. Alan Scott **A:** Mark D. Bright **W:** Gerard Jones
3 ❑ Win 1992 Cover: 2.50 **NM** value: **Cover or less**
Circ: CapCity orders: **13,250**
🕮 The Book of Stories **A:** Mark D. Bright **W:** Gerard Jones ★ Death of Black Canary I.
4 ❑ Spr 1993 Cover: 2.50 **NM** value: **Cover or less**
• Alan Scott vs. Solomon Grundy
5 ❑ Sum 1993 Cover: 2.50 **NM** value: **Cover or less**
6 ❑ Aut 1993 Cover: 2.95 **NM** value: **Cover or less**
Circ: CapCity orders: **10,650**
• Alan Scott vs. New Harlequin
7 ❑ Win 1993 Cover: 2.95 **NM** value: **Cover or less**
Circ: CapCity orders: **10,500**
🕮 Horrors **A:** Tim Vigil **W:** Ron Marz
8 ❑ Spr 1994 Cover: 2.95 **NM** value: **Cover or less**
Circ: CapCity orders: **11,200**
🕮 The Book of Endings • Jack Chance vs. Lobo **A:** Howard Porter; Carlos Franco **W:** Mike Carlin; Darwin McPherson

GREEN LANTERN: EMERALD ALLIES — DC

1 ❑ Cover: 14.95 **NM** value: **Cover or less**
• Collects Green Lantern #76, 77, 92 and Green Arrow #104, 110, 111, 125, 126 **A:** Paul Pelletier; Darryl Banks; Will Rosado; Rodolfo DaMaggio; Dougie Braithwaite **W:** Chuck Dixon; Ron Marz

GREEN LANTERN: EMERALD DAWN — DC

1 ❑ Dec 1989 Cover: 1.00 **NM** value: **2.00**
Circ: CapCity orders: **84,200** • **CGC:** 6 graded, best 9.8
🕮 The Sign **A:** Mark D. Bright **W:** James Owsley ★ Origin of Green Lantern II (Hal Jordan), Green Lantern.
2 ❑ Jan 1990 Cover: 1.00 **NM** value: **1.50**
Circ: CapCity orders: **59,100**
3 ❑ Feb 1990 Cover: 1.00 **NM** value: **1.50**
Circ: CapCity orders: **51,950**
4 ❑ Mar 1990 Cover: 1.00 **NM** value: **1.50**
Circ: CapCity orders: **53,550**
🕮 The Corps **A:** Mark D. Bright **W:** Keith Giffen; Gerard Jones; James Owsley
5 ❑ Apr 1990 Cover: 1.00 **NM** value: **1.50**
Circ: CapCity orders: **53,000**
6 ❑ May 1990 Cover: 1.00 **NM** value: **1.50**
Circ: CapCity orders: **49,900**
Bk 1❑ Apr 1991 Cover: 4.95 **NM** value: **Cover or less**
Circ: CapCity orders: **7,900**
• collects mini-series

GREEN LANTERN: EMERALD DAWN II — DC

1 ❑ Apr 1991 Cover: 1.00 **NM** value: **1.50**
Circ: CapCity orders: **26,350** • **CGC:** 1 graded, best 9.4
🕮 The Powers That Be **A:** Mark D. Bright **W:** Keith Giffen; Gerard Jones
2 ❑ May 1991 Cover: 1.00 **NM** value: **Cover or less**
Circ: CapCity orders: **21,950**
3 ❑ Jun 1991 Cover: 1.00 **NM** value: **Cover or less**
Circ: CapCity orders: **21,400**
4 ❑ Jul 1991 Cover: 1.00 **NM** value: **Cover or less**
Circ: CapCity orders: **26,600**
5 ❑ Aug 1991 Cover: 1.00 **NM** value: **Cover or less**
Circ: CapCity orders: **26,850**
6 ❑ Sep 1991 Cover: 1.00 **NM** value: **Cover or less**
Circ: CapCity orders: **28,200**

GREEN LANTERN: FEAR ITSELF — DC

Bk 1❑ Cover: 14.95 **NM** value: **Cover or less**
softcover. **A:** Brad Parker **W:** Ron Marz
Bk 1/HC❑ Cover: 24.95 **NM** value: **Cover or less**
hardcover. **A:** Brad Parker **W:** Ron Marz

GREEN LANTERN/FIRESTORM — DC

1 ❑ Oct 2000 Cover: 2.50 **NM** value: **Cover or less**
Circ: Diamd. preorders: **29,978**
🕮 Missing Pieces **A:** Ron Randall **W:** Jay Faerber

Other grades: Multiply prices above by **1.5 for Mint • 2/3 for Very Fine • 1/3 for Fine • 1/5 for Very Good • 1/8 for Good**

GREEN LANTERN/FLASH: FASTER FRIENDS — DC

1 ❑ Cover: 4.95 **NM value: Cover or less**
No issue number. • prestige format. • concludes in Flash/Green Lantern: Faster Friends **A:** Bart Sears; Ron Lim; Jeff Johnson; Tom Grindberg; Andy Smith **W:** Ron Marz

GREEN LANTERN GALLERY — DC

1 ❑ Dec 1996 Cover: 3.50 **NM value: Cover or less**
• pin-ups **C:** Gil Kane **W:** Adam Warren; Cully Hamner; Jim Starlin; Joe Phillips; Bernie Wrightson; Gil Kane; Mike Zeck; Marty Nodell

GREEN LANTERN: GANTHET'S TALE — DC

1 ❑ Cover: 5.95 **NM value: Cover or less**
Circ: CapCity orders: **22,100**
No issue number. One-shot. enhanced cover. • prestige format. • Larry Niven **A:** John Byrne **W:** Larry Niven

GREEN LANTERN/GREEN ARROW — DC

1 ❑ Oct 1983 Cover: 2.00 **NM value: 3.50**
No Evil Shall Escape My Sight! **A:** Dick Giordano; Neal Adams **W:** Denny O'Neil

2 ❑ Nov 1983 Cover: 2.00 **NM value: 3.00**
Journey to Desolation **A:** Dick Giordano; Neal Adams **W:** Denny O'Neil

3 ❑ Dec 1983 Cover: 2.00 **NM value: 3.00**
A Kind of Loving, A Way of Death **A:** Dick Giordano; Neal Adams **W:** Denny O'Neil

4 ❑ Jan 1984 Cover: 2.00 **NM value: 3.00**
Ulysses Star is Still Alive! **A:** Dick Giordano; Neal Adams **W:** Denny O'Neil

5 ❑ Feb 1984 Cover: 2.00 **NM value: 3.00**
Peril In Plastic; Even an Immortal can Die! **A:** Bernie Wrightson; Dick Giordano; Neal Adams **W:** Denny O'Neil

6 ❑ Mar 1984 Cover: 2.00 **NM value: 3.00**
Death be My Destiny! **A:** Dick Giordano; Neal Adams **W:** Denny O'Neil

7 ❑ Apr 1984 Cover: 2.50 **NM value: 3.00**
...And a Child Shall Destroy Them! **A:** Dick Giordano; Neal Adams **W:** Denny O'Neil

Bk 1❑ Cover: 12.95 **NM value: Cover or less**
• Trade Paperback. Hard Travelling Heroes • Collects series **A:** Dick Giordano; Neal Adams **W:** Denny O'Neil

GREEN LANTERN/GREEN LANTERN — DC

1 ❑ Oct 2000 Cover: 2.50 **NM value: Cover or less**
Circ: Diamd. preorders: **30,787**
Against the Dying of the Light **A:** Randy Green **W:** Judd Winick

GREEN LANTERN: MOSAIC — DC

1 ❑ Jun 1992 Cover: 1.25 **NM value: Cover or less**
Circ: CapCity orders: **46,150**
Do You Want To See? **A:** Cully Hamner **W:** Gerard Jones

2 ❑ Jul 1992 Cover: 1.25 **NM value: Cover or less**
Circ: CapCity orders: **27,300**
Nuts **A:** Cully Hamner **W:** Gerard Jones ★ Death of Ch'p (Green Lantern squirrel).

3 ❑ Aug 1992 Cover: 1.25 **NM value: Cover or less**
Circ: CapCity orders: **25,600**
Something Red **A:** Cully Hamner **W:** Gerard Jones

4 ❑ Sep 1992 Cover: 1.25 **NM value: Cover or less**
Circ: CapCity orders: **19,300**
Not Yet **A:** Cully Hamner **W:** Gerard Jones

5 ❑ Oct 1992 Cover: 1.25 **NM value: Cover or less**
Circ: CapCity orders: **17,400**
The Child-Man And The Great White Hero **A:** Cully Hamner **W:** Gerard Jones

6 ❑ Nov 1992 Cover: 1.25 **NM value: Cover or less**
Circ: CapCity orders: **14,850**

7 ❑ Dec 1992 Cover: 1.25 **NM value: Cover or less**
Circ: CapCity orders: **13,550**

8 ❑ Jan 1993 Cover: 1.25 **NM value: Cover or less**
Circ: CapCity orders: **12,300**

9 ❑ Feb 1993 Cover: 1.25 **NM value: Cover or less**
Circ: CapCity orders: **12,150**

10 ❑ Mar 1993 Cover: 1.25 **NM value: Cover or less**
Circ: CapCity orders: **11,350**

11 ❑ Apr 1993 Cover: 1.25 **NM value: Cover or less**
Circ: CapCity orders: **10,950**
I Am Myself Mosaic **A:** Mitch Byrd **W:** Gerard Jones

12 ❑ May 1993 Cover: 1.25 **NM value: Cover or less**
Circ: CapCity orders: **10,400**
Any Means Necessary **A:** Cully Hamner **W:** Gerard Jones

13 ❑ Jun 1993 Cover: 1.25 **NM value: Cover or less**
Circ: CapCity orders: **10,250**
What Xenophobia Means To Me **A:** Cully Hamner **W:** Gerard Jones

14 ❑ Jul 1993 Cover: 1.25 **NM value: Cover or less**
Circ: CapCity orders: **9,600**
The Sleep of Monsters Produces Reason **A:** Luke McDonnell **W:** Gerard Jones

15 ❑ Aug 1993 Cover: 1.25 **NM value: Cover or less**
Circ: CapCity orders: **9,550**
What Dis Be **A:** Cully Hamner; Chris Hunter **W:** Gerard Jones

16 ❑ Sep 1993 Cover: 1.25 **NM value: Cover or less**
Circ: CapCity orders: **8,650**
Great Speckled Bird **A:** Luke McDonnell **W:** Gerard Jones

17 ❑ Oct 1993 Cover: 1.25 **NM value: Cover or less**
Circ: CapCity orders: **8,500**

18 ❑ Nov 1993 Cover: 1.25 **NM value: Cover or less**
Circ: CapCity orders: **8,500**
final issue.

GREEN LANTERN: 1001 EMERALD NIGHTS — DC

1 ❑ Cover: 6.95 **NM value: Cover or less**
• **CGC:** 1 graded, best 9.6
• Elseworlds **A:** Rebecca Guay **W:** Terry Laban

GREEN LANTERN PLUS — DC

1 ❑ Dec 1996 Cover: 2.95 **NM value: Cover or less**

GREEN LANTERN/POWER GIRL — DC

1 ❑ Oct 2000 Cover: 2.50 **NM value: Cover or less**
Deep Down Below the Surface **A:** Pete Woods **W:** Scott Beatty

GREEN LANTERN SECRET FILES — DC

1 ❑ Jul 1998 Cover: 4.95 **NM value: Cover or less**
• background on all Green Lanterns

2 ❑ Sep 1999 Cover: 4.95 **NM value: Cover or less**
Keeping Secrets; Jade in Hidden Thorns; Green Laatern & Flash Team-up • background on all Green Lanterns **A:** Gil Kane; Joe Staton; Ken Lashley; Shawn Martinbrough; Cully Hammer **W:** Dana Kurtin; Geoff Johns; Mark Waid; Ron Marz

GREEN LANTERN/SENTINEL: HEART OF DARKNESS — DC

1 ❑ Mar 1998 Cover: 1.95 **NM value: Cover or less**
covers form triptych. Fathers & Sons **A:** Paul Pelletier **W:** Ron Marz

2 ❑ Apr 1998 Cover: 1.95 **NM value: Cover or less**
covers form triptych. **A:** Paul Pelletier **W:** Ron Marz

3 ❑ May 1998 Cover: 1.95 **NM value: Cover or less**
covers form triptych. **A:** Paul Pelletier **W:** Ron Marz

GREEN LANTERN/SILVER SURFER: UNHOLY ALLIANCES — DC

1 ❑ Cover: 4.95 **NM value: Cover or less**
No issue number. One-shot. • prestige format. • crossover with Marvel **A:** Darryl Banks **W:** Ron Marz ★ Appearance of Parallax, Terrax, Thanos, Cyborg Superman.

GREEN LANTERN/SUPERMAN: LEGEND OF THE GREEN FLAME — DC

1 ❑ Cover: 5.95 **NM value: Cover or less**
• **CGC:** 2 graded, best 9.8

GREEN LANTERN: THE NEW CORPS — DC

1 ❑ ca. 1999 Cover: 4.95 **NM value: Cover or less**
• prestige format. **A:** Scot Eaton **W:** Chuck Dixon

1/Aut❑ca. 1999 **NM value: 8.00**

2 ❑ ca. 1999 Cover: 4.95 **NM value: Cover or less**
• prestige format. **A:** Scot Eaton **W:** Chuck Dixon

GREEN LANTERN: THE ROAD BACK — DC

Bk 1❑ Cover: 8.95 **NM value: Cover or less**

GREEN LANTERN VS. ALIENS — DC

1 ❑ Sep 2000 Cover: 2.95 **NM value: Cover or less**
2 ❑ Oct 2000 Cover: 2.95 **NM value: Cover or less**
3 ❑ Nov 2000 Cover: 2.95 **NM value: Cover or less**
4 ❑ Dec 2000 Cover: 2.95 **NM value: Cover or less**

GREENLEAF IN EXILE — Cat's Paw

1 ❑ Cover: 2.95 **NM value: Cover or less**
2 ❑ Cover: 2.95 **NM value: Cover or less**
3 ❑ Cover: 2.95 **NM value: Cover or less**
4 ❑ Cover: 2.95 **NM value: Cover or less**
5 ❑ Cover: 2.95 **NM value: Cover or less**
6 ❑ Cover: 2.95 **NM value: Cover or less**

GREENLOCK — Aircel

1 ❑ Mar 1991, b&w Cover: 2.50 **NM value: Cover or less**
One-shot.

GREEN MASK — Fox

In the spirit of many other superhero adventures of the Golden Age, The Green Mask featured a non-super-powered hero who donned, what else, a Green Mask. Additionally attired in blue tights and a green cape, The Green Mask was accompanied by a young sidekick, Domino (a name taken from the boy's type of mask, although he did occasionally wear a cowl similar to his mentor's).

With Lou Fine covers and art by George Tuska and Bob Powell, the series ran 17 issues from 1940 to 1946. Other features in the series included Rick Evans, Adventurer; Dick Transom, Detective; and One Round Hogan. — Brent

1 ❑ Sum 1940 Cover: 0.10 **NM value: 2000.00**
• **CGC:** 5 graded, best 8.5
2 ❑ Fal 1940 Cover: 0.10 **NM value: 600.00**
3 ❑ Win 1940 Cover: 0.10 **NM value: 450.00**
• **CGC:** 1 graded, best 9.0
4 ❑ Spr 1941 Cover: 0.10 **NM value: 350.00**
5 ❑ Jun 1941 Cover: 0.10 **NM value: 350.00**
6 ❑ Aug 1941 Cover: 0.10 **NM value: 300.00**
7 ❑ Oct 1941 Cover: 0.10 **NM value: 200.00**
8 ❑ Dec 1941 Cover: 0.10 **NM value: 200.00**
9 ❑ Feb 1942 Cover: 0.10 **NM value: 200.00**
10 ❑ Aug 1944 Cover: 0.10 **NM value: 100.00**
• **CGC:** 2 graded, best 9.6
11 ❑ Nov 1944 Cover: 0.10 **NM value: 100.00**
• **CGC:** 1 graded, best 6.5
12 ❑ Spr 1945 Cover: 0.10 **NM value: 100.00**
13 ❑ Sum 1945 Cover: 0.10 **NM value: 100.00**
• **CGC:** 1 graded, best 9.4

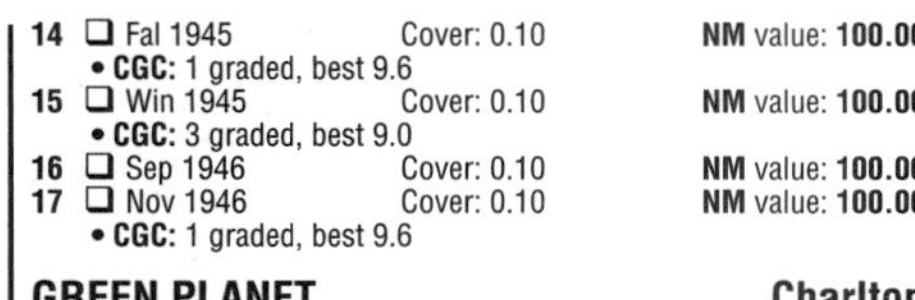

14 ❑ Fal 1945 Cover: 0.10 **NM value: 100.00**
• **CGC:** 1 graded, best 9.6
15 ❑ Win 1945 Cover: 0.10 **NM value: 100.00**
• **CGC:** 3 graded, best 9.0
16 ❑ Sep 1946 Cover: 0.10 **NM value: 100.00**
17 ❑ Nov 1946 Cover: 0.10 **NM value: 100.00**
• **CGC:** 1 graded, best 9.6

GREEN PLANET — Charlton

1 ❑ ca. 1962 Cover: 0.12 **NM value: Cover or less**

GREEN SKULL, THE — Known Associates

1 ❑ Cover: 2.50 **NM value: Cover or less**
No issue number. One-shot.

GREGORY — DC / Piranha

Marc Hempel's Gregory is a delightful little neurotic who is never so happy as when locked up in a small room wearing a straitjacket. Gregory burbles away cheerfully most of the time, speaking primarily in vowels. The only thing that really troubles him is when do-gooders decide to take him away from his familiar, dank cell and put him someplace soft, padded, and thoroughly disturbing. Of course, Gregory's cheerful nature always gets him ahead in the end, and madness triumphs over altruism.

Gregory's blissful existence as a baby-like lunatic is enlivened by visits from his rat friend Herman Vermin. The rascally Herman is constantly getting squashed by some catastrophe or other, only to reappear as an equally obnoxious reincarnation of himself.

1 ❑ b&w Cover: 7.95 **NM value: Cover or less**
The Thing From Outside!; The Incredibly Odd And Mystifying Spectacle Of Herman Vermin; The Face That Launched A Thousand Ships; It's Spring; The Therapist; Muffin, The Cat Thing; A Hello To Arms; A Ro **A:** Marc Hempel **W:** Marc Hempel

1-2 ❑ Cover: 7.95 **NM value: Cover or less**

2 ❑ Cover: 4.95 **NM value: Cover or less**
• Herman Vermin's Very Own Best-selling & Critically Acclaimed Book with Gregory **A:** Marc Hempel **W:** Marc Hempel

3 ❑ Cover: 4.95 **NM value: 7.95**
It's The Terwilliger Show; I Gregory; Pants The Night Away; Out **A:** Marc Hempel **W:** Marc Hempel

3/GO❑ Cover: 7.95 **NM value: 10.00**
• Gold logo edition (limited printing). It's The Terwilliger Show; I Gregory; Pants The Night Away; Out **A:** Marc Hempel **W:** Marc Hempel

4 ❑ b&w Cover: 4.95 **NM value: Cover or less**
• Fat Boy **A:** Marc Hempel **W:** Marc Hempel

GREMLIN TROUBLE — Anti-Ballistic

When the stormfairy, Cypher, runs afoul of the chief imp, he sadistically rips off her wings and leaves her for dead in a vat of toxic waste. Normally, of course, stormfairies slowly pine and die without their wings. But Cypher is astonished when the toxic waste changes her from a stormfairy to a gremlin.

This twist of fate supplies her with the will to live. She forgets her woes by immersing herself in the tools and gadgetry of gremlin society. Unfortunately, Cypher's technological prowess is noticed by the human government and she is mistaken for a terrorist. Can Cypher convince humanity that she is harmless before they blow her away?

E.T and Elizabeth Bryan have hung in there for a long time with this self-published fantasy series, developing a small but devoted following.

1 ❑ Cover: 2.95 **NM value: 3.50**
Circ: CapCity orders: **2,290**
Unfortunate Encounters **A:** E.T. Bryan **W:** E.T. Bryan; Elizabeth Bryan ★ 1st Appearance of Remi-el, Xynophylyen, The Chief Imp, Cypher.

2 ❑ Cover: 2.95 **NM value: 3.00**
Working within the System **A:** E.T. Bryan **W:** E.T. Bryan; Elizabeth Bryan ★ 2nd Appearance of Cypher. ★ 2nd Appearance of High Commi.

3 ❑ Cover: 2.95 **NM value: 3.00**
Rude Awakenings **A:** E.T. Bryan **W:** E.T. Bryan; Elizabeth Bryan

4 ❑ Cover: 2.95 **NM value: 3.00**
Fun with Electricity, Part 1 **A:** E.T. Bryan **W:** E.T. Bryan; Elizabeth Bryan ★ 1st Appearance of Prince Frothbar of the Mountain Fairies. ★ 2nd Appearance of Dr. Candy Tsai. ★ 2nd Appearance of Grommet. ★ Appearance of High Commissioner Del Delage, Cam, Murt.

5 ❑ Cover: 2.95 **NM value: 3.00**
Fun with Electricity, Part 2 **A:** E.T. Bryan **W:** E.T. Bryan; Elizabeth Bryan ★ 2nd Appearance of Prince.

6 ❑ Cover: 2.95 **NM value: Cover or less**
Fun with Electricity, Part 3 **A:** E.T. Bryan **W:** E.T. Bryan; Elizabeth Bryan ★ Appearance of High Commissioner Del Delage, Sorcerer General, Dr. Candy Tsai, Cam, Xynophylyen, The Chief Imp, Prince Hex.

7 ❑ Cover: 2.95 **NM value: Cover or less**

CGC-graded: Multiply prices above by **33 for 9.9 M • 16 for 9.8 NM/M • 7 for 9.6 NM+ • 5 for 9.4 NM • 2.5 for 9.2 NM- • 1.5 for 9.0 VF/NM**

📖 Cypher in Fairyland **A:** E.T. Bryan **W:** E.T. Bryan; Elizabeth Bryan ★ 2nd Appearance of King of the Mountain Fai.
8 ❑ Cover: 2.95 **NM** value: **Cover or less**
📖 Candy's Picnic Adventure **A:** E.T. Bryan **W:** E.T. Bryan; Elizabeth Bryan ★ 1st Appearance of Goblin General Grafsnout, Tuberian Nebulian Cruiser ship. ★ Appearance of Prince Frothbar, Dr. Candy Tsai, Cam, Prince Hex, Grommet.
9 ❑ Cover: 2.95 **NM** value: **Cover or less**
📖 The Technolution Is Not a Tea Party **A:** E.T. Bryan **W:** E.T. Bryan; Elizabeth Bryan ★ 1st Appearance of Dr. Brandy Schwarzchild, Candy Tsai and the Moist Towelettes, Dr. Pi Yukawa. ★ Appearance of Dr. Candy Tsai, High Commissioner Ragweed.
10 ❑ Cover: 2.95 **NM** value: **Cover or less**
📖 The Tuberians Are Coming **A:** E.T. Bryan **W:** E.T. Bryan; Elizabeth Bryan
11 ❑ Cover: 2.95 **NM** value: **Cover or less**
📖 Cypher Gets a Job **A:** E.T. Bryan **W:** E.T. Bryan; Elizabeth Bryan ★ 2nd Appearance of X the Unmentionable. ★ Appearance of Annette, Sorcerer General, Dr. Candy Tsai.
12 ❑ Cover: 2.95 **NM** value: **Cover or less**
📖 The Battle at Site Z **A:** E.T. Bryan **W:** E.T. Bryan; Elizabeth Bryan ★ 1st Appearance of Ballpoint P. Greml.
13 ❑ Cover: 2.95 **NM** value: **Cover or less**
📖 The Battle at Forest Meadows, Part 1 **A:** E.T. Bryan **W:** E.T. Bryan; Elizabeth Bryan ★ 2nd Appearance of General Grafsnout. ★ 2nd Appearance of Ballpoint P. Gremlin. ★ Appearance of Annette, Dr. Candy Tsai, Cam, Grommet.
14 ❑ Cover: 2.95 **NM** value: **Cover or less**
📖 The Battle at Forest Meadows, Part 2 **A:** E.T. Bryan **W:** E.T. Bryan; Elizabeth Bryan ★ 2nd Appearance of The Moist Towel. ★ 2nd Appearance of Tuberians. ★ Appearance of Annette, General Grafsnout, Princess Pentangle.
15 ❑ Cover: 2.95 **NM** value: **Cover or less**
16 ❑ Cover: 2.95 **NM** value: **Cover or less**
Circ: Diamd. preorders: **1,303**
17 ❑ Cover: 2.95 **NM** value: **Cover or less**
Circ: Diamd. preorders: **1,371**
19 ❑ Cover: 2.95 **NM** value: **Cover or less**
18 ❑ Cover: 2.95 **NM** value: **Cover or less**
Bk 1❑ Cover: 14.95 **NM** value: **Cover or less**

GRENDEL (1ST SERIES) Comico

In the ancient story of Beowulf, Grendel was a monster in human form who would sneak inside in the dead of night to slaughter Beowulf's men. He was said to be a descendent of Cain-and the very personification of evil.

Matt Wagner borrows from that ancient story in creating his own Grendel for the modern age. To those who oppose him, Grendel is the devil himself: mysterious, deadly, and cunning beyond words. The mere mention of his name is enough to cause the faces of men to turn pale. If not evil personified, Wagner's Grendel is the very spirit of vengeance. Cross him at your peril.

1 ❑ Mar 1983, b&w Cover: 1.50 **NM** value: **65.00**
• **CGC:** 19 graded, best 9.6
2 ❑ ca. 1983, b&w Cover: 1.50 **NM** value: **45.00**
• **CGC:** 6 graded, best 9.2
3 ❑ Feb 1984, b&w Cover: 1.50 **NM** value: **40.00**
• **CGC:** 9 graded, best 9.4

GRENDEL (2ND SERIES) Comico

1 ❑ Oct 1986 Cover: 1.50 **NM** value: **7.00**
Circ: CapCity orders: **15,400** • **CGC:** 17 graded, best 9.8
1-2 ❑ Cover: 1.50 **NM** value: **2.50**
2 ❑ Nov 1986 Cover: 1.50 **NM** value: **5.00**
Circ: CapCity orders: **11,300**
3 ❑ Dec 1986 Cover: 1.50 **NM** value: **4.00**
Circ: CapCity orders: **10,200**
4 ❑ Jan 1987 Cover: 1.50 **NM** value: **4.00**
Circ: CapCity orders: **10,225**
📖 Touch Not the Devil **A:** Pander Bros. **C:** Dave Stevens **W:** Matt Wagner
5 ❑ Feb 1987 Cover: 1.50 **NM** value: **4.00**
Circ: CapCity orders: **10,325**
6 ❑ Mar 1987 Cover: 1.50 **NM** value: **3.00**
Circ: CapCity orders: **10,925**
7 ❑ Apr 1987 Cover: 1.50 **NM** value: **3.00**
Circ: CapCity orders: **10,250**
8 ❑ May 1987 Cover: 1.50 **NM** value: **3.00**
Circ: CapCity orders: **10,650**
9 ❑ Jun 1987 Cover: 1.50 **NM** value: **3.00**
Circ: CapCity orders: **11,525**
10 ❑ Jul 1987 Cover: 1.50 **NM** value: **3.00**
Circ: CapCity orders: **11,325**
11 ❑ Aug 1987 Cover: 1.50 **NM** value: **3.00**
Circ: CapCity orders: **10,575**
12 ❑ Sep 1987 Cover: 1.50 **NM** value: **3.00**
Circ: CapCity orders: **10,900**
13 ❑ Oct 1987 Cover: 1.50 **NM** value: **3.00**
Circ: CapCity orders: **10,600**
• new Grendel **A:** Matt Wagner **W:** Matt Wagner
14 ❑ Nov 1987 Cover: 1.50 **NM** value: **3.00**
Circ: CapCity orders: **10,650**
• new Grendel **A:** Matt Wagner **W:** Matt Wagner
15 ❑ Dec 1987 Cover: 1.50 **NM** value: **3.00**
Circ: CapCity orders: **10,700**
• new Grendel **A:** Matt Wagner **W:** Matt Wagner
16 ❑ Jan 1988 Cover: 1.50 **NM** value: **4.00**
Circ: CapCity orders: **13,300**
• Mage begins **A:** Matt Wagner **W:** Matt Wagner
17 ❑ Feb 1988 Cover: 1.50 **NM** value: **2.50**
Circ: CapCity orders: **13,450**
18 ❑ Apr 1988 Cover: 1.75 **NM** value: **3.00**
Circ: CapCity orders: **12,100**
19 ❑ May 1988 Cover: 1.75 **NM** value: **2.50**
Circ: CapCity orders: **10,550**
20 ❑ Jun 1988 Cover: 1.75 **NM** value: **2.50**
Circ: CapCity orders: **9,900**
21 ❑ Jul 1988 Cover: 1.75 **NM** value: **2.50**
Circ: CapCity orders: **8,950**
22 ❑ Aug 1988 Cover: 1.75 **NM** value: **2.50**
Circ: CapCity orders: **8,275**
23 ❑ Sep 1988 Cover: 1.75 **NM** value: **2.50**
Circ: CapCity orders: **8,175**
24 ❑ Oct 1988 Cover: 1.75 **NM** value: **2.50**
Circ: CapCity orders: **8,425**
25 ❑ Nov 1988 Cover: 1.75 **NM** value: **2.50**
Circ: CapCity orders: **7,675**
26 ❑ Dec 1988 Cover: 1.75 **NM** value: **2.50**
Circ: CapCity orders: **7,700**
27 ❑ Jan 1989 Cover: 1.95 **NM** value: **2.50**
Circ: CapCity orders: **7,550**
28 ❑ Feb 1989 Cover: 1.95 **NM** value: **2.50**
Circ: CapCity orders: **7,500**
29 ❑ Mar 1989 Cover: 1.95 **NM** value: **2.50**
Circ: CapCity orders: **7,450**
30 ❑ Apr 1989 Cover: 1.95 **NM** value: **2.50**
Circ: CapCity orders: **7,500**
31 ❑ May 1989 Cover: 1.95 **NM** value: **2.50**
Circ: CapCity orders: **7,400**
32 ❑ Jun 1989 Cover: 1.95 **NM** value: **2.50**
Circ: CapCity orders: **7,100**
33 ❑ Jul 1989 Cover: 2.75 **NM** value: **3.75**
Circ: CapCity orders: **7,100**
• Giant-size. **A:** Matt Wagner **W:** Matt Wagner
34 ❑ Aug 1989 Cover: 2.50 **NM** value: **Cover or less**
Circ: CapCity orders: **7,250**
35 ❑ Sep 1989 Cover: 2.50 **NM** value: **Cover or less**
Circ: CapCity orders: **7,050**
36 ❑ Oct 1989 Cover: 2.50 **NM** value: **Cover or less**
Circ: CapCity orders: **7,050**
37 ❑ Nov 1989 Cover: 2.50 **NM** value: **Cover or less**
Circ: CapCity orders: **6,850**
38 ❑ Dec 1989 Cover: 2.50 **NM** value: **Cover or less**
Circ: CapCity orders: **7,975**
39 ❑ Jan 1990 Cover: 2.50 **NM** value: **Cover or less**
Circ: CapCity orders: **6,550** • **CGC:** 1 graded, best 9.6
40 ❑ Feb 1990 Cover: 3.50 **NM** value: **Cover or less**
Circ: CapCity orders: **6,900**
final issue. • flip book with Grendel Tales Special Preview **A:** Matt Wagner **W:** Matt Wagner

GRENDEL: BLACK, WHITE, & RED Dark Horse

1 ❑ Nov 1998 Cover: 3.95 **NM** value: **4.00**
2 ❑ Dec 1998 Cover: 3.95 **NM** value: **4.00**
📖 Devil's Cue; Devil's Requiem; Devil's Coup; Devil's Blessing; Devil's Garden **A:** Tim Bradstreet; Bernie Mireault; David Mack; C. Scott Morse; Paul Chadwick **W:** Matt Wagner
3 ❑ Jan 1999 Cover: 3.95 **NM** value: **4.00**
📖 Devil's Apogee; Devil's Curse; The Devil's in the Punctuation; Devil on My Back; Devil's Ladyrinth **A:** Teddy Kristiansen; Mike Allred; Guy Davis; Arnold Pander; Jacob Pander; Stan Shaw **W:** Matt Wagner
4 ❑ Feb 1999 Cover: 3.95 **NM** value: **4.00**
📖 Devil's Cage; Devil's Witness; Devil's Domain; Devil's Stigma; Devil's Mark **A:** Jason Pearson; Chris Sprouse; Troy Nixey; Woodrow Phoenix; Jay Geldhof **W:** Matt Wagner

GRENDEL CLASSICS Dark Horse

1 ❑ Jul 1995 Cover: 3.95 **NM** value: **Cover or less**
Circ: CapCity orders: **5,900**
cardstock cover. 📖 Devil Tracks **A:** Matt Wagner **W:** Matt Wanger
2 ❑ Aug 1995 Cover: 3.95 **NM** value: **Cover or less**
cardstock cover. 📖 Devil Eyes final issue. **A:** Matt Wagner **W:** Matt Wanger

GRENDEL CYCLE Dark Horse

1 ❑ Oct 1995 Cover: 5.95 **NM** value: **Cover or less**
No issue number. • prestige format. • background information on the various series including a timeline

GRENDEL: DEVIL BY THE DEED Comico

1 ❑ Cover: 10.00 **NM** value: **Cover or less**
No issue number. cardstock cover. • graphic novel; reprints Comico one-shot **A:** Matt Wagner
1/LE❑ **NM** value: **17.50**
• Limited to 2000 **A:** Matt Wagner
1-2 ❑ Jul 1993 Cover: 3.95 **NM** value: **Cover or less**
No issue number. cardstock cover. • reprints Comico one-shot **A:** Matt Wagner

GRENDEL: DEVIL CHILD Dark Horse

1 ❑ Jun 1999 Cover: 2.95 **NM** value: **Cover or less**
cardstock cover. **A:** Tim Sale **W:** Diane Schultz
2 ❑ Aug 1999 Cover: 2.95 **NM** value: **Cover or less**
cardstock cover. **A:** Tim Sale **W:** Diane Schultz

GRENDEL: DEVIL QUEST Dark Horse

1 ❑ Nov 1995 Cover: 4.95 **NM** value: **Cover or less**
No issue number. One-shot. • prestige format. **A:** Matt Wagner **W:** Matt Wagner

GRENDEL: DEVIL'S LEGACY Comico

1 ❑ Jan 2000 Cover: 2.95 **NM** value: **Cover or less**
Circ: Diamd. preorders: **13,521**
2 ❑ Feb 2000 Cover: 2.95 **NM** value: **Cover or less**
Circ: Diamd. preorders: **12,507**
3 ❑ Apr 2000 Cover: 2.95 **NM** value: **Cover or less**
Circ: Diamd. preorders: **12,215**
4 ❑ Jun 2000 Cover: 2.95 **NM** value: **Cover or less**
Circ: Diamd. preorders: **11,853**
📖 Touch not the Devil **A:** Arnold Pander; Jacob Pander **W:** Matt Wagner
5 ❑ Jul 2000 Cover: 2.95 **NM** value: **Cover or less**
Circ: Diamd. preorders: **11,181**
📖 Devil in Despair **A:** Arnold Pander; Jacob Pander **W:** Matt Wagner
6 ❑ Aug 2000 Cover: 2.95 **NM** value: **Cover or less**
Circ: Diamd. preorders: **9,280**
📖 Challenge the Devil **A:** Arnold Pander; Jacob Pander **W:** Matt Wagner
7 ❑ Sep 2000 Cover: 2.95 **NM** value: **Cover or less**
Circ: Diamd. preorders: **10,175**
📖 Devil's Dance **A:** Arnold Pander; Jacob Pander **W:** Matt Wagner
8 ❑ Oct 2000 Cover: 2.95 **NM** value: **Cover or less**
Circ: Diamd. preorders: **9,759**
📖 After the Devil **A:** Arnold Pander; Jacob Pander **W:** Matt Wagner
9 ❑ Nov 2000 Cover: 2.95 **NM** value: **Cover or less**
Circ: Diamd. preorders: **9,013**
📖 Devil's Revenge **A:** Arnold Pander; Jacob Pander **W:** Matt Wagner
10 ❑ Dec 2000 Cover: 2.95 **NM** value: **Cover or less**
Circ: Diamd. preorders: **8,695**
📖 Devil on Edge **A:** Arnold Pander; Jacob Pander **W:** Matt Wagner
11 ❑ Jan 2001 Cover: 2.95 **NM** value: **Cover or less**
Circ: Diamd. preorders: **8,209**
📖 Devil"s Rampage **A:** Arnold Pander; Jacob Pander **W:** Matt Wagner
12 ❑ Feb 2001 Cover: 2.95 **NM** value: **Cover or less**
Circ: Diamd. preorders: **8,051**
📖 Devil's Ends **A:** Arnold Pander; Jacob Pander **W:** Matt Wagner
Bk 1❑ Cover: 14.95 **NM** value: **Cover or less**
Circ: CapCity orders: **850**
• graphic novel

GRENDEL: DEVIL'S VAGARY Comico

1 ❑ b&w and red Cover: 5.00 **NM** value: **8.00**

GRENDEL: DEVIL TALES Dark Horse

Bk 1❑ Aug 1999 Cover: 9.95 **NM** value: **Cover or less**
• Reprints Grendel Classics #1-2 **A:** Matt Wagner **W:** Matt Wagner

GRENDEL TALES: DEVILS AND DEATHS Dark Horse

1 ❑ Oct 1994 Cover: 2.95 **NM** value: **Cover or less**
Circ: CapCity orders: **11,625**
📖 Devil's Lot; Meat Machine, Part 1 **A:** Matt Wagner; Edvin Biukovic **W:** Matt Wagner; Darko Macan
2 ❑ Nov 1994 Cover: 2.95 **NM** value: **Cover or less**
Circ: CapCity orders: **9,625**
📖 Meat Machine, Part 2 **A:** Matt Wagner **W:** Matt Wagner
Bk 1❑ Cover: 16.95 **NM** value: **Cover or less**
• collects Devils and Deaths #1 and 2 and Devil's Choices #1-4

GRENDEL TALES: DEVIL'S CHOICES Dark Horse

1 ❑ Mar 1995 Cover: 2.95 **NM** value: **Cover or less**
Circ: CapCity orders: **8,975**
2 ❑ Apr 1995 Cover: 2.95 **NM** value: **Cover or less**
Circ: CapCity orders: **8,250**
3 ❑ May 1995 Cover: 2.95 **NM** value: **Cover or less**
Circ: CapCity orders: **8,325**
4 ❑ Jun 1995 Cover: 2.95 **NM** value: **Cover or less**
Circ: CapCity orders: **8,375**

GRENDEL TALES: DEVIL'S HAMMER Dark Horse

1 ❑ Feb 1994 Cover: 2.95 **NM** value: **Cover or less**
Circ: CapCity orders: **14,225**
📖 Black Blood; Devil Quest, Part 1 **A:** Matt Wagner; Bernie Mireault; Kathryn Delaney **W:** Matt Wagner; Rob Walton
2 ❑ Mar 1994 Cover: 2.95 **NM** value: **Cover or less**
Circ: CapCity orders: **12,975**
3 ❑ Apr 1994 Cover: 2.95 **NM** value: **Cover or less**
Circ: CapCity orders: **12,600**

GRENDEL TALES: FOUR DEVILS, ONE HELL Dark Horse

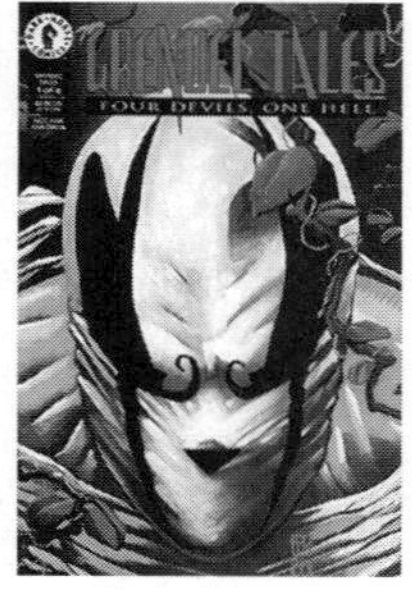

For Josef Mantovani, it all began when he was hired to find the killer of a Cajun restaurant owner. His question was, "Why Hire a P.I. when there are so many Grendels running around willing to do the job for free?"

Readers might ask the same question, but will have to read beyond the first issue for the answer. In this post-apocalyptic world, there are numerous people who have taken on the mask of vengeance and become a Grendel. They range from the deluded Bixby to the nefarious gambler Calhoun. They all have their own agendas, but ultimately are destined to come together.

Creator Matt Wagner uses this series to explore their various lives and to extend the concept of the Grendel. He has also indicated his plans to let other writers explore the character in future episodes of Grendel Tales.

1 ❑ Aug 1993 Cover: 2.95 **NM** value: **3.00**
Circ: CapCity orders: **22,425**
cardstock cover. 📖 Four Beginnings, One Case **A:** Teddy Kristiansen **W:** James Robinson
2 ❑ Sep 1993 Cover: 2.95 **NM** value: **3.00**
Circ: CapCity orders: **17,975**
cardstock cover. 📖 Three searchers, One Lucky Streak **A:** Teddy Kristiansen **W:** James Robinson

Other grades: Multiply prices above by **1.5 for Mint • 2/3 for Very Fine • 1/3 for Fine • 1/5 for Very Good • 1/8 for Good**

3 ❑ Oct 1993 Cover: 2.95 **NM** value: **3.00**
Circ: CapCity orders: **18,200**
cardstock cover. **A:** Teddy Kristiansen **W:** James Robinson

4 ❑ Oct 1993 Cover: 2.95 **NM** value: **3.00**
Circ: CapCity orders: **16,525**
cardstock cover. 📖 One Rite, Three Wrongs **A:** Teddy Kristiansen **W:** James Robinson

5 ❑ Dec 1993 Cover: 2.95 **NM** value: **3.00**
Circ: CapCity orders: **15,075**
cardstock cover. 📖 One Carnival, Three Captives **A:** Teddy Kristiansen **W:** James Robinson

6 ❑ Jan 1994 Cover: 2.95 **NM** value: **3.00**
Circ: CapCity orders: **14,100**
cardstock cover. 📖 Four Fates, One Finale • Grendel-Prime returns **A:** Teddy Kristiansen **W:** James Robinson

Bk 1❑ Cover: 17.95 **NM** value: **Cover or less**
• Collects Grendel Tales: Four Devils, One Hell #1-6 **A:** Teddy Kristiansen **W:** James Robinson

GRENDEL TALES: HOMECOMING — Dark Horse

1 ❑ Dec 1994 Cover: 2.95 **NM** value: **Cover or less**
Circ: CapCity orders: **10,500**
cardstock cover. 📖 Part 1; Babylon Crash, Part 1 **A:** Matt Wagner; Dave Cooper **W:** Matt Wagner; Pat McEown

2 ❑ Jan 1995 Cover: 2.95 **NM** value: **Cover or less**
Circ: CapCity orders: **8,825**
cardstock cover. 📖 Part 2; Babylon Crash, Part 2 **A:** Matt Wagner; Pat McEown **W:** Matt Wagner; Pat McEown

3 ❑ Feb 1995 Cover: 2.95 **NM** value: **Cover or less**
Circ: CapCity orders: **8,450**
cardstock cover. 📖 Part 3; Devil Quest **A:** Pat McEown; Matt Wagner(cover) **W:** Matt Wagner; Pat McEown

GRENDEL TALES: THE DEVIL IN OUR MIDST — Dark Horse

1 ❑ May 1994 Cover: 2.95 **NM** value: **Cover or less**
Circ: CapCity orders: **13,725**
📖 Devil Quest, Part 2 **A:** Paul Grist **W:** Steven Seagle

2 ❑ Jun 1994 Cover: 2.95 **NM** value: **Cover or less**
Circ: CapCity orders: **12,200**
📖 Devil Quest, Part 3

3 ❑ Jul 1994 Cover: 2.95 **NM** value: **Cover or less**
Circ: CapCity orders: **11,325**

4 ❑ Aug 1994 Cover: 2.95 **NM** value: **Cover or less**
Circ: CapCity orders: **10,600**

5 ❑ Sep 1994 Cover: 2.95 **NM** value: **Cover or less**
Circ: CapCity orders: **10,100**

Bk 1❑ Apr 1998 Cover: 15.95 **NM** value: **Cover or less**
• collects mini-series

GRENDEL TALES: THE DEVIL MAY CARE — Dark Horse

1 ❑ Dec 1995 Cover: 2.95 **NM** value: **Cover or less**
cardstock cover. **A:** Peter Doherty **W:** Terry Laban

2 ❑ Jan 1996 Cover: 2.95 **NM** value: **Cover or less**
cardstock cover. **A:** Peter Doherty **W:** Terry Laban

3 ❑ Feb 1996 Cover: 2.95 **NM** value: **Cover or less**
cardstock cover. **A:** Peter Doherty **W:** Terry Laban

4 ❑ Mar 1996 Cover: 2.95 **NM** value: **Cover or less**
cardstock cover. **A:** Peter Doherty **W:** Terry Laban

5 ❑ Apr 1996 Cover: 2.95 **NM** value: **Cover or less**
cardstock cover. **A:** Peter Doherty **W:** Terry Laban

6 ❑ May 1996 Cover: 2.95 **NM** value: **Cover or less**
cardstock cover. final issue. **A:** Peter Doherty **W:** Terry Laban

GRENDEL TALES: THE DEVIL'S APPRENTICE — Dark Horse

1 ❑ Sep 1997 Cover: 2.95 **NM** value: **Cover or less**
2 ❑ Oct 1997 Cover: 2.95 **NM** value: **Cover or less**
3 ❑ Nov 1997 Cover: 2.95 **NM** value: **Cover or less**

GRENDEL: THE DEVIL INSIDE — Comico

Bk 1❑ Cover: 11.95 **NM** value: **Cover or less**

GRENDEL: WAR CHILD — Dark Horse

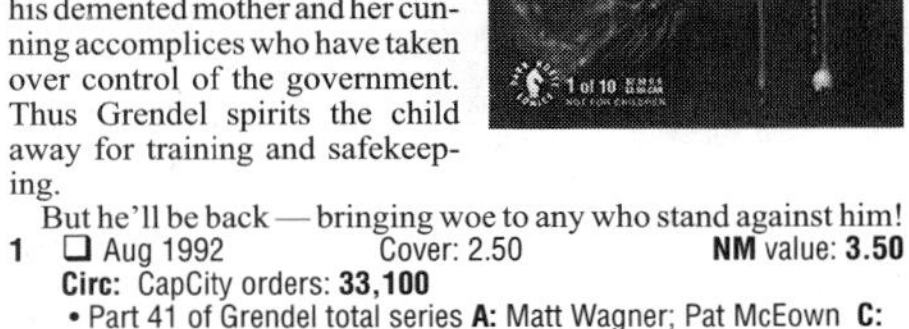

This series takes place in the post-cataclysmic future, several years after Grendel #40, and the death of ruler Orion Assante. Those trouble-filled times become even more chaotic when the child heir to the throne, Jupiter Assante, is kidnapped. As it turns out, the kidnapper is none other than Grendel Prime.

Grendel is a fierce warrior who will stop at nothing to fulfill his duty to the dead ruler. This time that means saving the child from his demented mother and her cunning accomplices who have taken over control of the government. Thus Grendel spirits the child away for training and safekeeping.

But he'll be back — bringing woe to any who stand against him!

1 ❑ Aug 1992 Cover: 2.50 **NM** value: **3.50**
Circ: CapCity orders: **33,100**
• Part 41 of Grendel total series **A:** Matt Wagner; Pat McEown **C:** Simon Bisley **W:** Matt Wagner

2 ❑ Sep 1992 Cover: 2.50 **NM** value: **3.00**
Circ: CapCity orders: **19,375**
• Part 42 of Grendel total series **A:** Pat McEown **W:** Matt Wagner

3 ❑ Oct 1992 Cover: 2.50 **NM** value: **3.00**
Circ: CapCity orders: **2,000**
• Part 43 of Grendel total series **A:** Pat McEown **W:** Matt Wagner

4 ❑ Nov 1992 Cover: 2.50 **NM** value: **3.00**
Circ: CapCity orders: **20,850**
• Part 44 of Grendel total series **A:** Pat McEown **W:** Matt Wagner

5 ❑ Dec 1992 Cover: 2.50 **NM** value: **3.00**
Circ: CapCity orders: **21,475**
• Part 45 of Grendel total series **A:** Pat McEown **W:** Matt Wagner

6 ❑ Jan 1993 Cover: 2.50 **NM** value: **Cover or less**
Circ: CapCity orders: **22,150**
• Part 46 of Grendel total series **A:** Pat McEown **W:** Matt Wagner

7 ❑ Jan 1993 Cover: 2.50 **NM** value: **Cover or less**
Circ: CapCity orders: **22,525**
• Part 47 of Grendel total series **A:** Pat McEown **W:** Matt Wagner

8 ❑ Mar 1993 Cover: 2.50 **NM** value: **Cover or less**
Circ: CapCity orders: **21,175**
• Part 48 of Grendel total series **A:** Pat McEown **W:** Matt Wagner

9 ❑ Apr 1993 Cover: 2.50 **NM** value: **Cover or less**
Circ: CapCity orders: **20,275**
• Part 49 of Grendel total series **A:** Pat McEown **W:** Matt Wagner

10 ❑ Jun 1993 Cover: 3.50 **NM** value: **3.75**
Circ: CapCity orders: **20,075**
• Double-size. final issue. • Part 50 of Grendel total series **A:** Pat McEown **W:** Matt Wagner

Bk 1❑ Cover: 18.95 **NM** value: **Cover or less**
• Trade Paperback. • Collects Grendel: War Child #1-10 **A:** Pat McEown **W:** Matt Wagner

Bk 1/LE❑ Cover: 99.95 **NM** value: **Cover or less**
• Limited edition hardcover. • Collects Grendel: War Child #1-10 **A:** Pat McEown **W:** Matt Wagner

GREY — Viz

1 ❑ Oct 1989 Cover: 2.95 **NM** value: **5.00**
2 ❑ Nov 1989 Cover: 2.95 **NM** value: **4.00**
3 ❑ Dec 1989 Cover: 2.95 **NM** value: **3.50**
4 ❑ Jan 1989 Cover: 2.95 **NM** value: **3.50**
5 ❑ Feb 1989 Cover: 2.95 **NM** value: **3.50**
6 ❑ Mar 1989 Cover: 2.95 **NM** value: **3.25**
7 ❑ Apr 1989 Cover: 3.25 **NM** value: **Cover or less**
8 ❑ May 1989 Cover: 3.25 **NM** value: **Cover or less**
9 ❑ Jun 1989 Cover: 3.25 **NM** value: **Cover or less**
Bk 1❑ Cover: 17.95 **NM** value: **Cover or less**
Bk 2❑ Cover: 17.95 **NM** value: **Cover or less**

GREY LEGACY — Fragile Elite

1 ❑ b&w Cover: 2.75 **NM** value: **Cover or less**

GREYLORE — Sirius Comics

1 ❑ Dec 1985 Cover: 1.50 **NM** value: **Cover or less**
Circ: CapCity orders: **5,250**
📖 A Pox Upon Him **A:** Bo Hampton **W:** David Campiti; Kevin Juaire; Pteter Palmer

2 ❑ Jan 1986 Cover: 1.50 **NM** value: **Cover or less**
Circ: CapCity orders: **3,325**

3 ❑ Jan 1986 Cover: 1.50 **NM** value: **Cover or less**
Circ: CapCity orders: **3,675**
📖 Natural Affinity

4 ❑ Jan 1986 Cover: 1.50 **NM** value: **Cover or less**
Circ: CapCity orders: **3,275**
📖 The Sins of the Father

5 ❑ Jan 1986 Cover: 1.50 **NM** value: **Cover or less**
Circ: CapCity orders: **2,975**

GREYMATTER — Alaffinity

1 ❑ Oct 1993 Cover: 2.95 **NM** value: **Cover or less**

2 ❑ Nov 1993 Cover: 2.95 **NM** value: **Cover or less**
📖 Show & Tell **A:** Adam Harwell; Marcus Harwell

3 ❑ Dec 1993 Cover: 2.95 **NM** value: **Cover or less**
📖 Revolution Less Revelation **A:** Adam Harwell; Marcus Harwell

4 ❑ Jan 1994 Cover: 2.95 **NM** value: **Cover or less**
📖 No Time To Say Hello Goodbye **A:** Adam Harwell; Marcus Harwell

5 ❑ Apr 1994 Cover: 2.95 **NM** value: **Cover or less**

6 ❑ Sep 1994 Cover: 2.95 **NM** value: **Cover or less**
cover forms diptych with #7.

7 ❑ Oct 1994 Cover: 2.95 **NM** value: **Cover or less**
cover forms diptych with #6.

8 ❑ Mar 1995 Cover: 2.95 **NM** value: **Cover or less**
9 ❑ Dec 1995 Cover: 2.95 **NM** value: **Cover or less**
10 ❑ Mar 1996 Cover: 2.95 **NM** value: **Cover or less**
11 ❑ Jun 1996 Cover: 2.95 **NM** value: **Cover or less**

GRIFFIN, THE (AMAZE INK) — Slave Labor

1 ❑ May 1997 Cover: 2.95 **NM** value: **Cover or less**
Circ: Diamd. preorders: **4,155**

GRIFFIN, THE (DC) — DC

1 ❑ Nov 1991 Cover: 4.95 **NM** value: **Cover or less**
Circ: CapCity orders: **12,100**
📖 The Griffin Returns; Friendly Fire **A:** Norman Felchle **W:** Dan Vado ★ Origin of The Griffin.

2 ❑ Dec 1991 Cover: 4.95 **NM** value: **Cover or less**
Circ: CapCity orders: **8,600**

3 ❑ Jan 1992 Cover: 4.95 **NM** value: **Cover or less**
Circ: CapCity orders: **7,950**

4 ❑ Feb 1992 Cover: 4.95 **NM** value: **Cover or less**
Circ: CapCity orders: **7,300**

5 ❑ Mar 1992 Cover: 4.95 **NM** value: **Cover or less**
Circ: CapCity orders: **6,950**
📖 Run Like Hell; Against The Wall **A:** Norman Felchle **W:** Dan Vado

6 ❑ Apr 1992 Cover: 4.95 **NM** value: **Cover or less**
Circ: CapCity orders: **6,500**

Creator Key
W = Writer • A = Artist • C = Cover Artist

GRIFFIN, THE (SLAVE LABOR) — Slave Labor

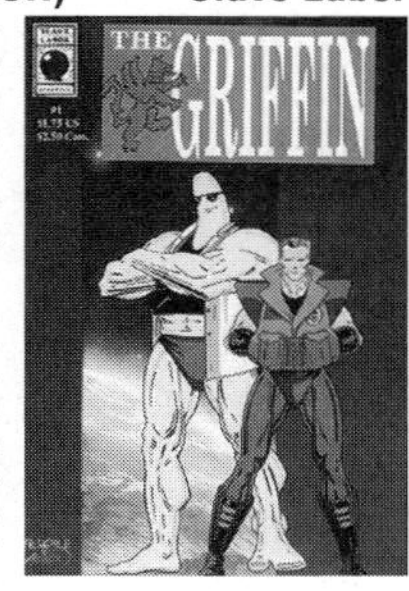

Matt Williams, a typical American teen-ager, was picked up one night by recruiters of the Acacian Imperiacy Star Fleet looking for a human subject who would be willing to undergo a procedure to make him invincible and one of their best weapons in interplanetary conflicts. Matt said yes. Twenty years later, tired and just wanting to go home, he deserted with his friend Lt. Stomu, stole a starship, and went back to Earth. Unfortunately, the empire wants one more job done — capture an insane super renegade they've managed to dump on Earth and only The Griffin can stop.

The Griffin began as a black-and-white comic at Slave Labor Graphics, spent time as a six-issue mini-series at DC in 1991, and then returned to Slave Labor Graphics.

1 ❑ Jul 1988, b&w Cover: 1.75 **NM** value: **Cover or less**
1-2 ❑ Apr 1989, b&w Cover: 1.75 **NM** value: **Cover or less**
2 ❑ Dec 1988 Cover: 1.75 **NM** value: **Cover or less**
3 ❑ Apr 1989 Cover: 1.75 **NM** value: **Cover or less**

GRIFFITH OBSERVATORY — Fantagraphics

1 ❑ Cover: 4.95 **NM** value: **Cover or less**
No issue number.

GRIFTER AND THE MASK — Dark Horse

1 ❑ Sep 1996 Cover: 2.50 **NM** value: **Cover or less**
Circ: Diamd. preorders: **27,469**
📖 Cleaving Las Vegas, Part 1 • crossover with Image **A:** Luciano Lima **W:** Steven Seagle

2 ❑ Oct 1996 Cover: 2.50 **NM** value: **Cover or less**
Circ: Diamd. preorders: **21,690**
📖 Cleaving Las Vegas, Part 2 • crossover with Image **A:** Luciano Lima **W:** Steven Seagle

GRIFTER/BADROCK — Image

1/A ❑ Oct 1995 Cover: 2.50 **NM** value: **Cover or less**
Circ: CapCity orders: **13,375**

1/B ❑ Oct 1995 Cover: 2.50 **NM** value: **Cover or less**
alternate cover.

2/A ❑ Nov 1995 Cover: 2.50 **NM** value: **Cover or less**
• flipbook with Badrock #2A

2/B ❑ Nov 1995 Cover: 2.50 **NM** value: **Cover or less**
• flipbook with Badrock #2A

GRIFTER: ONE SHOT — Image

1 ❑ Jan 1995 Cover: 4.95 **NM** value: **Cover or less**
Circ: CapCity orders: **25,300**

GRIFTER/SHI — Image

1 ❑ Apr 1996 Cover: 2.95 **NM** value: **Cover or less**
cover says Mar, indicia says Apr. • crossover with Crusade

2 ❑ May 1996 Cover: 2.95 **NM** value: **Cover or less**
• crossover with Crusade

GRIFTER (VOL. 1) — Image

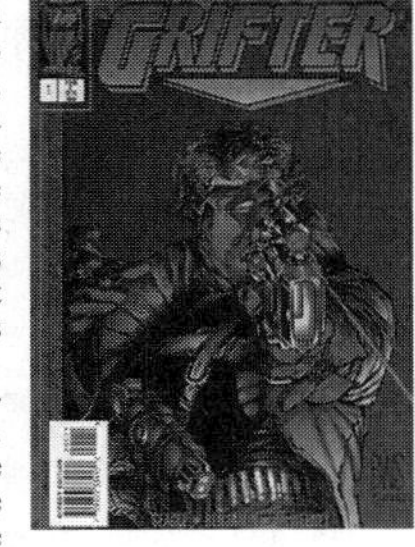

Grifter was the first of the WildC.A.T.S gang to get his own series. Cole Cash, aka Grifter, was a one-time member of Team 7, fighting alongside Deathblow in a series of covert actions across the world. Later, he would join the struggle against the Daemonites as part of WildC.A.T.S, although this series begins just after he had quit that group, feeling that his skills were getting stale.

Grifter's main power is his unerring ability with firearms of all sorts. Dressed like a Western badman, he specializes in cracking jokes while pulling off shots that would make Annie Oakley gape in astonishment. This series, by writer Steven Seagle and an assortment of pencillers, is consistently entertaining, and a good primer on the larger conflicts in the Image universe.

1 ❑ May 1995 Cover: 1.95 **NM** value: **2.50**
📖 WildStorm Rising, Part 5 • bound-in trading cards **A:** Ryan Benjamin **W:** Steven Seagle

1/DM❑ May 1995 Cover: 2.50 **NM** value: **3.00**
Circ: CapCity orders: **41,675**
• Direct Market edition. 📖 Wildstorm Rising, Part 5 **A:** Ryan Benjamin **W:** Steven Seagle

2 ❑ Jun 1995 Cover: 1.95 **NM** value: **2.00**
Circ: CapCity orders: **32,325**

3 ❑ Jul 1995 Cover: 1.95 **NM** value: **2.00**
Circ: CapCity orders: **29,675**
indicia says Jul, cover says Aug. **W:** Steven Seagle

4 ❑ Aug 1995 Cover: 1.95 **NM** value: **2.00**
Circ: CapCity orders: **24,700**

5 ❑ Oct 1995 Cover: 1.95 **NM** value: **2.00**
Circ: CapCity orders: **20,900**
indicia says Oct, cover says Jun. **W:** Steven Seagle

6 ❑ Nov 1995 Cover: 1.95 **NM** value: **2.00**
Circ: CapCity orders: **13,950**

7 ❑ Dec 1995 Cover: 1.95 **NM** value: **2.00**
8 ❑ Jan 1996 Cover: 1.95 **NM** value: **2.00**

9 ❑ Feb 1996 Cover: 1.95 **NM** value: **2.00**
📖 City of Angels, Part 3 **W:** Steven Seagle

10 ❑ Mar 1996 Cover: 1.95 **NM** value: **2.00**
📖 City of Angels, Part 4 final issue. **W:** Steven Seagle

CGC-graded: Multiply prices above by **33 for 9.9 M • 16 for 9.8 NM/M • 7 for 9.6 NM+ • 5 for 9.4 NM • 2.5 for 9.2 NM- • 1.5 for 9.0 VF/NM**

GRIFTER (VOL. 2) — Image

1 ❑ Jul 1996 Cover: 2.50 **NM** value: **Cover or less**
2 ❑ Aug 1996 Cover: 2.50 **NM** value: **Cover or less**
3 ❑ Sep 1996 Cover: 2.50 **NM** value: **Cover or less**
Circ: Diamd. preorders: **34,670**
4 ❑ Oct 1996 Cover: 2.50 **NM** value: **Cover or less**
Circ: Diamd. preorders: **32,941**
5 ❑ Nov 1996 Cover: 2.50 **NM** value: **Cover or less**
Circ: Diamd. preorders: **30,188**
6 ❑ Dec 1996 Cover: 2.50 **NM** value: **Cover or less**
Circ: Diamd. preorders: **28,178**
cover says Nov, indicia says Dec. **A:** Michael Ryan **W:** Steven Grant
7 ❑ Jan 1997 Cover: 2.50 **NM** value: **Cover or less**
Circ: Diamd. preorders: **27,387**
8 ❑ Feb 1997 Cover: 2.50 **NM** value: **Cover or less**
Circ: Diamd. preorders: **25,615**
9 ❑ Mar 1997 Cover: 2.50 **NM** value: **Cover or less**
Circ: Diamd. preorders: **25,762**
10 ❑ Apr 1997 Cover: 2.50 **NM** value: **Cover or less**
Circ: Diamd. preorders: **24,715**
11 ❑ May 1997 Cover: 2.50 **NM** value: **Cover or less**
Circ: Diamd. preorders: **23,754**
12 ❑ Jun 1997 Cover: 2.50 **NM** value: **Cover or less**
Circ: Diamd. preorders: **23,021**
13 ❑ Jul 1997 Cover: 2.50 **NM** value: **Cover or less**
Circ: Diamd. preorders: **21,588**
14 ❑ Aug 1997 Cover: 2.50 **NM** value: **Cover or less**
Circ: Diamd. preorders: **20,874**
final issue.

GRIM GHOST, THE — Atlas-Seaboard

1 ❑ Jan 1975 Cover: 0.25 **NM** value: **2.00**
• **CGC:** 8 graded, best 9.4
📖 Enter The Grim Ghost ★ Origin of Grim Ghost. ★ 1st Appearance of Grim Ghost.
2 ❑ Mar 1975 Cover: 0.25 **NM** value: **2.00**
3 ❑ Jul 1975 Cover: 0.25 **NM** value: **2.00**

GRIMJACK — First

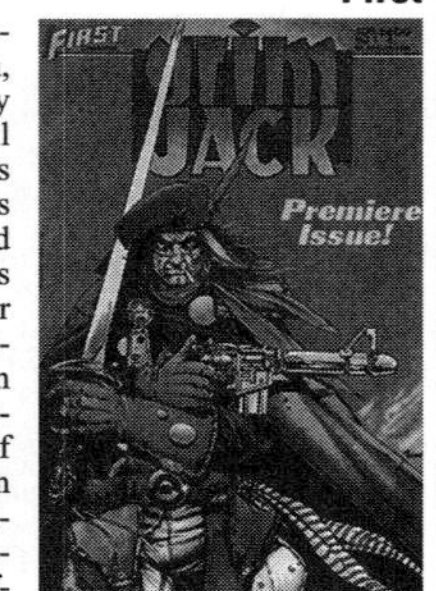

Grimjack, together with BlackJacMac, Jericho, Chris Heyman, and others fight to protect their city from murdering cyborgs, evil gangs, and all the other social ills that plague the world after a series of trade wars has nearly decimated the population. Grimjack works closely with BlackJacMac; together they're almost like a team of contemporary detectives. Jericho is in charge of letting them know the local action. Chris Heyman is one of the few remaining Free Marines in the world, a militaristic band of vigilantes. Each episode has more suspense than action and the cliffhangers really leave you breathless for more.

Issue #26 of the series was backed with a much less serious story, as the Teenage Mutant Ninja Turtles made one of their first color appearances, visiting a transdimensional bar where they fight sailors, drink illegally (they're underage, after all!), and win a dance contest.

1 ❑ Aug 1984 Cover: 1.25 **NM** value: **2.00**
📖 A Shade Of Truth **A:** Tim Truman **W:** John Ostrander
2 ❑ Sep 1984 Cover: 1.25 **NM** value: **1.75**
3 ❑ Oct 1984 Cover: 1.25 **NM** value: **1.75**
4 ❑ Nov 1984 Cover: 1.25 **NM** value: **1.75**
5 ❑ Dec 1984 Cover: 1.25 **NM** value: **1.75**
6 ❑ Jan 1985 Cover: 1.25 **NM** value: **1.75**
7 ❑ Feb 1985 Cover: 1.25 **NM** value: **1.75**
8 ❑ Mar 1985 Cover: 1.25 **NM** value: **1.75**
9 ❑ Apr 1985 Cover: 1.25 **NM** value: **1.75**
10 ❑ May 1985 Cover: 1.25 **NM** value: **1.75**
Circ: CapCity orders: **7,800**
11 ❑ Jun 1985 Cover: 1.25 **NM** value: **1.75**
Circ: CapCity orders: **8,150**
12 ❑ Jul 1985 Cover: 1.25 **NM** value: **1.75**
Circ: CapCity orders: **7,650**
13 ❑ Aug 1985 Cover: 1.25 **NM** value: **1.75**
Circ: CapCity orders: **8,575**
14 ❑ Sep 1985 Cover: 1.25 **NM** value: **1.75**
Circ: CapCity orders: **7,875**
15 ❑ Oct 1985 Cover: 1.25 **NM** value: **1.75**
Circ: CapCity orders: **7,475**
16 ❑ Nov 1985 Cover: 1.25 **NM** value: **1.75**
Circ: CapCity orders: **6,975**
17 ❑ Dec 1985 Cover: 1.25 **NM** value: **1.75**
Circ: CapCity orders: **6,625**
18 ❑ Jan 1986 Cover: 1.25 **NM** value: **1.75**
Circ: CapCity orders: **6,625**
19 ❑ Feb 1986 Cover: 1.25 **NM** value: **1.75**
Circ: CapCity orders: **6,650**
20 ❑ Mar 1986 Cover: 1.25 **NM** value: **1.75**
Circ: CapCity orders: **6,075**
21 ❑ Apr 1986 Cover: 1.25 **NM** value: **1.50**
Circ: CapCity orders: **6,175**
22 ❑ May 1986 Cover: 1.25 **NM** value: **1.50**
Circ: CapCity orders: **6,325**
📖 Demon Blood, Part One; Mother's Calling
23 ❑ Jun 1986 Cover: 1.25 **NM** value: **1.50**
Circ: CapCity orders: **6,050**
24 ❑ Jul 1986 Cover: 1.25 **NM** value: **1.50**
Circ: CapCity orders: **6,575**
25 ❑ Aug 1986 Cover: 1.25 **NM** value: **1.50**
Circ: CapCity orders: **6,250**
26 ❑ Sep 1986 Cover: 1.25 **NM** value: **3.00**
Circ: CapCity orders: **15,875**
📖 Twisted Metal **A:** Tom Sutton **W:** John Ostrander ★ Appearance of Teenage Mutant Ninja Turtles.
27 ❑ Oct 1986 Cover: 1.25 **NM** value: **1.50**
Circ: CapCity orders: **6,600**
28 ❑ Nov 1986 Cover: 1.25 **NM** value: **1.50**
Circ: CapCity orders: **6,700**
29 ❑ Dec 1986 Cover: 1.25 **NM** value: **1.50**
Circ: CapCity orders: **7,100**
30 ❑ Jan 1987 Cover: 1.25 **NM** value: **1.50**
Circ: CapCity orders: **6,275**
• Dynamo Joe
31 ❑ Feb 1987 Cover: 1.25 **NM** value: **1.50**
Circ: CapCity orders: **6,150**
32 ❑ Mar 1987 Cover: 1.25 **NM** value: **1.50**
Circ: CapCity orders: **5,725**
33 ❑ Apr 1987 Cover: 1.25 **NM** value: **1.50**
Circ: CapCity orders: **5,950**
34 ❑ May 1987 Cover: 1.25 **NM** value: **1.50**
Circ: CapCity orders: **5,700**
35 ❑ Jun 1987 Cover: 1.25 **NM** value: **1.50**
Circ: CapCity orders: **5,750**
36 ❑ Jul 1987 Cover: 1.25 **NM** value: **1.50**
Circ: CapCity orders: **5,650**
37 ❑ Aug 1987 Cover: 1.25 **NM** value: **1.50**
Circ: CapCity orders: **5,700**
38 ❑ Sep 1987 Cover: 1.25 **NM** value: **1.50**
Circ: CapCity orders: **5,975**
39 ❑ Oct 1987 Cover: 1.75 **NM** value: **Cover or less**
Circ: CapCity orders: **5,850**
40 ❑ Nov 1987 Cover: 1.75 **NM** value: **1.95**
Circ: CapCity orders: **5,825**
41 ❑ Dec 1987 Cover: 1.75 **NM** value: **1.95**
Circ: CapCity orders: **5,750**
42 ❑ Jan 1988 Cover: 1.75 **NM** value: **1.95**
Circ: CapCity orders: **5,575**
43 ❑ Feb 1988 Cover: 1.75 **NM** value: **1.95**
Circ: CapCity orders: **5,800**
44 ❑ Mar 1988 Cover: 1.75 **NM** value: **1.95**
Circ: CapCity orders: **5,775**
45 ❑ Apr 1988 Cover: 1.75 **NM** value: **1.95**
Circ: CapCity orders: **4,925**
46 ❑ May 1988 Cover: 1.75 **NM** value: **1.95**
Circ: CapCity orders: **5,525**
47 ❑ Jun 1988 Cover: 1.75 **NM** value: **1.95**
Circ: CapCity orders: **5,150**
48 ❑ Jul 1988 Cover: 1.75 **NM** value: **1.95**
Circ: CapCity orders: **5,200**
49 ❑ Aug 1988 Cover: 1.75 **NM** value: **1.95**
Circ: CapCity orders: **5,075**
📖 Hellbent **A:** Tom Mandrake **W:** John Ostrander
50 ❑ Sep 1988 Cover: 1.75 **NM** value: **1.95**
Circ: CapCity orders: **5,125**
📖 Blood Bath **A:** Tom Mandrake **W:** John Ostrander
51 ❑ Oct 1988 Cover: 1.75 **NM** value: **1.95**
Circ: CapCity orders: **4,825**
52 ❑ Nov 1988 Cover: 1.95 **NM** value: **Cover or less**
Circ: CapCity orders: **4,800**
📖 Crossroads
53 ❑ Dec 1988 Cover: 1.95 **NM** value: **Cover or less**
Circ: CapCity orders: **4,775**
54 ❑ Jan 1989 Cover: 1.95 **NM** value: **Cover or less**
Circ: CapCity orders: **4,625**
55 ❑ Feb 1989 Cover: 1.95 **NM** value: **Cover or less**
Circ: CapCity orders: **4,975**
• new Grimjack
56 ❑ Mar 1989 Cover: 1.95 **NM** value: **Cover or less**
Circ: CapCity orders: **4,725**
57 ❑ Apr 1989 Cover: 1.95 **NM** value: **Cover or less**
Circ: CapCity orders: **5,000**
58 ❑ May 1989 Cover: 1.95 **NM** value: **Cover or less**
Circ: CapCity orders: **5,100**
59 ❑ Jun 1989 Cover: 1.95 **NM** value: **Cover or less**
Circ: CapCity orders: **5,050**
60 ❑ Jul 1989 Cover: 1.95 **NM** value: **Cover or less**
Circ: CapCity orders: **5,150**
61 ❑ Aug 1989 Cover: 1.95 **NM** value: **Cover or less**
Circ: CapCity orders: **5,200**
62 ❑ Sep 1989 Cover: 1.95 **NM** value: **Cover or less**
Circ: CapCity orders: **5,300**
📖 Reunion, Bloody Lies **A:** Flint Henry **W:** John Ostrander
63 ❑ Oct 1989 Cover: 1.95 **NM** value: **Cover or less**
Circ: CapCity orders: **5,475**
64 ❑ Nov 1989 Cover: 1.95 **NM** value: **Cover or less**
Circ: CapCity orders: **5,575**
65 ❑ Dec 1989 Cover: 1.95 **NM** value: **Cover or less**
Circ: CapCity orders: **5,725**
66 ❑ Jan 1990 Cover: 1.95 **NM** value: **Cover or less**
Circ: CapCity orders: **5,625**
📖 Demon Wars
67 ❑ Feb 1990 Cover: 1.95 **NM** value: **Cover or less**
Circ: CapCity orders: **5,375**
📖 Demon Wars
68 ❑ Mar 1990 Cover: 1.95 **NM** value: **Cover or less**
Circ: CapCity orders: **5,500**
📖 Demon Wars
69 ❑ Apr 1990 Cover: 1.95 **NM** value: **Cover or less**
Circ: CapCity orders: **5,525**
📖 Demon Wars
70 ❑ May 1990 Cover: 1.95 **NM** value: **Cover or less**
Circ: CapCity orders: **5,450**
71 ❑ Jun 1990 Cover: 1.95 **NM** value: **2.00**
72 ❑ Jul 1990 Cover: 1.95 **NM** value: **2.00**
Circ: CapCity orders: **5,425**
73 ❑ Aug 1990 Cover: 1.95 **NM** value: **2.00**
Circ: CapCity orders: **5,475**
74 ❑ Sep 1990 Cover: 1.95 **NM** value: **2.00**
Circ: CapCity orders: **5,500**
75 ❑ Oct 1990 Cover: 5.95 **NM** value: **Cover or less**
Circ: CapCity orders: **5,225**
• Giant 75th issue
76 ❑ Nov 1990 Cover: 2.25 **NM** value: **Cover or less**
Circ: CapCity orders: **5,300**
77 ❑ Dec 1990 Cover: 2.25 **NM** value: **Cover or less**
Circ: CapCity orders: **5,350**
78 ❑ Jan 1991 Cover: 2.25 **NM** value: **Cover or less**
Circ: CapCity orders: **5,450**
79 ❑ Feb 1991 Cover: 2.25 **NM** value: **Cover or less**
Circ: CapCity orders: **5,575**
80 ❑ Mar 1991 Cover: 2.25 **NM** value: **Cover or less**
Circ: CapCity orders: **5,450**
81 ❑ Apr 1991 Cover: 2.25 **NM** value: **Cover or less**
Circ: CapCity orders: **5,500**
final issue.

GRIMJACK CASEFILES — First

1 ❑ Nov 1990 Cover: 1.95 **NM** value: **Cover or less**
Circ: CapCity orders: **3,425**
• Truman **A:** Tim Truman
2 ❑ Dec 1990 Cover: 1.95 **NM** value: **Cover or less**
Circ: CapCity orders: **2,300**
• Truman **A:** Tim Truman
3 ❑ Jan 1991 Cover: 1.95 **NM** value: **Cover or less**
Circ: CapCity orders: **2,375**
• Truman **A:** Tim Truman
4 ❑ Feb 1991 Cover: 1.95 **NM** value: **Cover or less**
Circ: CapCity orders: **2,250**
• Truman **A:** Tim Truman
5 ❑ Mar 1991 Cover: 1.95 **NM** value: **Cover or less**
Circ: CapCity orders: **2,175**
• Truman **A:** Tim Truman

GRIMLOCK — Empyre

1 ❑ Jan 1996, b&w Cover: 2.95 **NM** value: **Cover or less**
2 ❑ b&w Cover: 2.95 **NM** value: **Cover or less**
no cover date.

GRIMMAX — Defiant

0 ❑ Aug 1994 **NM** value: **1.00**
no cover price.

GRIMM'S GHOST STORIES — Gold Key

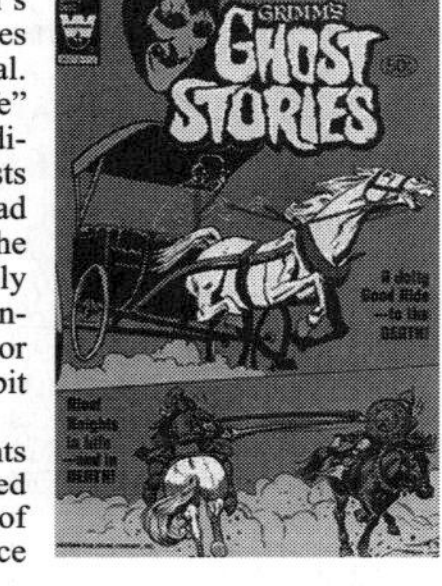

From 1972 to 1982, Grimm's Ghost Stories brought readers tales of ghosts and the supernatural. While some claimed to be "real life" hauntings, most were more traditional horror stories whereby ghosts gained revenge on people who had wronged them in life. Although the material consisted almost entirely of straight ghost stories, it did manage to give some tales a romantic or humorous twist in order to lend a bit of variety to the series.

As the series advanced, reprints of earlier stories were interspersed under the assumption that readers of those early issues had long since moved on to other pursuits.

1 ❑ Jan 1972 Cover: 0.15 **NM** value: **12.00**
2 ❑ Mar 1972 Cover: 0.15 **NM** value: **7.00**
3 ❑ May 1972 Cover: 0.15 **NM** value: **7.00**
4 ❑ Jul 1972 Cover: 0.15 **NM** value: **7.00**
5 ❑ Sep 1972 Cover: 0.15 **NM** value: **8.00**
6 ❑ Nov 1972 Cover: 0.15 **NM** value: **6.00**
• Misprinted editions duplicated stories. 📖 I Haunted My Killer; The Witch Watch: Trick or Treat (text story); The Evicted Ghost; Vendetta; Motive Unknown
7 ❑ Jan 1973 Cover: 0.15 **NM** value: **6.00**
8 ❑ Mar 1973 Cover: 0.15 **NM** value: **6.00**
📖 The Genius Touch; The Perfect Butler; You Bet Your Life!; The Locket **A:** Al Williamson
9 ❑ May 1973 Cover: 0.20 **NM** value: **6.00**
10 ❑ Jul 1973 Cover: 0.20 **NM** value: **6.00**
11 ❑ Aug 1973 Cover: 0.20 **NM** value: **4.00**
📖 The Golden Eyes; Old Trees Never Die; The Trouble With Emma; On Canvas
12 ❑ Sep 1973 Cover: 0.20 **NM** value: **4.00**
13 ❑ Nov 1973 Cover: 0.20 **NM** value: **4.00**
14 ❑ Jan 1974 Cover: 0.20 **NM** value: **4.00**
15 ❑ Mar 1974 Cover: 0.20 **NM** value: **4.00**
16 ❑ May 1974 Cover: 0.20 **NM** value: **4.00**
17 ❑ Jul 1974 Cover: 0.25 **NM** value: **4.00**
18 ❑ Aug 1974 Cover: 0.25 **NM** value: **3.50**
19 ❑ Sep 1974 Cover: 0.25 **NM** value: **3.50**
20 ❑ Nov 1974 Cover: 0.25 **NM** value: **3.50**
21 ❑ Jan 1975 Cover: 0.25 **NM** value: **3.50**
22 ❑ Mar 1975 Cover: 0.25 **NM** value: **3.50**
23 ❑ May 1975 Cover: 0.25 **NM** value: **3.50**
24 ❑ Jul 1975 Cover: 0.25 **NM** value: **3.50**
25 ❑ Aug 1975 Cover: 0.25 **NM** value: **3.50**
26 ❑ Sep 1975 Cover: 0.25 **NM** value: **3.50**
27 ❑ Nov 1975 Cover: 0.25 **NM** value: **3.50**
28 ❑ Jan 1976 Cover: 0.25 **NM** value: **3.50**
29 ❑ Mar 1976 Cover: 0.25 **NM** value: **3.50**
30 ❑ May 1976 Cover: 0.25 **NM** value: **3.50**
📖 A Sudden Loss of Appetite; Where's The Body?; The First Ghost; It Takes One to Catch One **A:** Jack Sparling; Ed Robbins; George Roussos; John Celardo **W:** Arnold Drake; Paul S. Newman
31 ❑ Jul 1976 Cover: 0.25 **NM** value: **3.00**
32 ❑ Aug 1976 Cover: 0.25 **NM** value: **3.00**
33 ❑ Sep 1976 Cover: 0.30 **NM** value: **3.00**
34 ❑ Oct 1976 Cover: 0.30 **NM** value: **3.00**

Other grades: Multiply prices above by **1.5 for Mint • 2/3 for Very Fine • 1/3 for Fine • 1/5 for Very Good • 1/8 for Good**

35 ❑ Nov 1976 Cover: 0.30 **NM** value: **3.00**
36 ❑ 1977 Cover: 0.30 **NM** value: **2.50**
37 ❑ May 1977 Cover: 0.30 **NM** value: **2.50**
38 ❑ 1977 Cover: 0.30 **NM** value: **2.50**
39 ❑ 1977 Cover: 0.30 **NM** value: **2.50**
40 ❑ 1977 Cover: 0.30 **NM** value: **2.50**
🕮 What Waits There?; Appointment From Beyond; Ghost of Honor **A:** Jack Sparling; Adolfo Buylla **W:** Arnold Drake
41 ❑ Oct 1977 Cover: 0.30 **NM** value: **2.50**
🕮 The Gambling Fool; Experiment Perilous; Now You See It...; Happy Hunting Grounds **A:** Bob McLeod; Frank Bolle; Jack Sparling; George Gamma **W:** George Kashdan; Mark Lasky; Paul S. Newman
42 ❑ Nov 1977 Cover: 0.30 **NM** value: **2.50**
43 ❑ 1978 Cover: 0.35 **NM** value: **2.50**
🕮 The Blue Cavalier; The Method Actor; The Walking Bones; Split Personality; Old Ghosts Home; The Business of Living; Sam, The Skeleton Man **A:** Joe Brozowski; Frank Bolle; Jack Sparling; Joe Certa; John Celardo; Luis Dominguez **W:** Arnold Drake; D.J. Arneson; George Kashdan; Mark Lasky; Paul S. Newman
44 ❑ May 1978 Cover: 0.50 **NM** value: **2.50**
45 ❑ Jul 1978 Cover: 0.35 **NM** value: **2.50**
46 ❑ Sep 1978 Cover: 0.35 **NM** value: **2.50**
47 ❑ Oct 1978 Cover: 0.35 **NM** value: **2.50**
48 ❑ Nov 1978 Cover: 0.35 **NM** value: **2.50**
49 ❑ Mar 1979 Cover: 0.35 **NM** value: **2.50**
🕮 Funeral Pyre; Daddy Told Me So!; Patient Spirit; The Joker **A:** Win Mortimer; Luis Dominguez; Oscar Novelle; José Delbo **W:** Arnold Drake; George Kashdan; Paul S. Newman
50 ❑ May 1979 Cover: 0.40 **NM** value: **2.50**
51 ❑ Jul 1979 Cover: 0.40 **NM** value: **2.50**
52 ❑ Sep 1979 Cover: 0.40 **NM** value: **2.50**
53 ❑ Oct 1979 Cover: 0.40 **NM** value: **2.50**
54 ❑ Nov 1979 Cover: 0.40 **NM** value: **2.50**
🕮 How much Longer Can We Wait?; Sparks Fly; The Fire Phantom; The Punishing Stick; The Falcon's Quarry
55 ❑ Apr 1981 Cover: 0.50 **NM** value: **2.50**
56 ❑ Oct 1981 Cover: 0.50 **NM** value: **2.50**
57 ❑ Dec 1981 Cover: 0.50 **NM** value: **2.50**
🕮 Duel to the Death; Face the Music!; Never Say Die!; A Jolly Good Ride; A Goodly Crew; A Grave Romance **A:** Frank Bolle; Jack Sparling; John Celardo **W:** Mark Lasky; Paul Kuhn; Paul S. Newman
58 ❑ Feb 1982 Cover: 0.60 **NM** value: **2.50**
🕮 Uncle Bert's Children; The Haunting of December Hill; Grandma's House; The Ghost Watch; Childhood Ghost **A:** Win Mortimer; Jack Sparling **W:** Freff; Arnold Drake
59 ❑ May 1982 Cover: 0.60 **NM** value: **2.50**
🕮 The Perfect Mark; King of the Court!; Tower of Vengeance; The Perfect Butler; The Locket **A:** Win Mortimer; Jack Sparling **W:** Mark Laskey; Roger McKenzie; Winston Blakely
60 ❑ Cover: 0.60 **NM** value: **2.50**
🕮 Valhalla; The Spirit's Not for Hanging; Retribution!; Walk the Plank!; The Little Red Schoolhouse final issue. **A:** Win Mortimer; Jack Sparling; José Delbo **W:** George Kashdan; Robin Snyder; Roger McKenzie

GRINGO — Caliber
1 ❑ b&w Cover: 1.95 **NM** value: **Cover or less**

GRIPS — Silverwolf
1 ❑ Sep 1986 Cover: 1.50 **NM** value: **4.00**
• **CGC:** 3 graded, best 9.4
1/LE❑ Cover: 9.95 **NM** value: **50.00**
2 ❑ Oct 1986 Cover: 1.50 **NM** value: **3.00**
3 ❑ Nov 1986 Cover: 1.50 **NM** value: **3.00**
4 ❑ Dec 1986 **NM** value: **3.00**

GRIPS (VOL. 2) — Greater Mercury
1 ❑ **NM** value: **4.00**

GRIT BATH — Fantagraphics
1 ❑ b&w Cover: 2.50 **NM** value: **Cover or less**
2 ❑ **NM** value: **2.50**
no cover price.
3 ❑ Aug 1994 **NM** value: **2.50**
no cover price.

GROO AND RUFFERTO (SERGIO ARAGONÉS'...) — Dark Horse
1 ❑ Dec 1998 Cover: 2.95 **NM** value: **Cover or less**
• Rufferto sent through time **A:** Sergio Aragonés **W:** Sergio Aragonés; Mark Evanier
2 ❑ Jan 1999 Cover: 2.95 **NM** value: **Cover or less**
3 ❑ Feb 1999 Cover: 2.95 **NM** value: **Cover or less**
4 ❑ Mar 1999 Cover: 2.95 **NM** value: **Cover or less**

GROO CARNIVAL, THE — Marvel / Epic
Groo is strong as an ox and definitely not in charge of his faculties. Arcadio, the Minstrel and the Sage all lend a helping hand and vague guidance to the big guy in this trade paperback. The level of violence and destruction that ensues when the wrong word is spoken into the wrong ear wired into the wrong brain is hilarious. Although the unfortunate souls who are "saved" by Groo's misguided deeds do not consider mayhem hilarious. There is nothing more dangerous than a sword-wielding barbarian with an unnatural obsession for cheese dip. Let's face it folks, he does the wrong thing at the right time and does the right thing at the right time-most of the time. Okay, okay-some of the time.
This trade paperback reprinted Groo the Wanderer #9-12
1 ❑ Cover: 8.95 **NM** value: **Cover or less**

GROO CHRONICLES, THE — Marvel / Epic
1 ❑ Jun 1989 Cover: 3.50 **NM** value: **Cover or less**
Circ: CapCity orders: **12,600**
🕮 Friends and Enemies; The Missive! • squarebound **A:** Sergio Aragonés **W:** Mark Evanier
2 ❑ 1989 Cover: 3.50 **NM** value: **Cover or less**
Circ: CapCity orders: **11,150**
🕮 The Caravan • squarebound **A:** Sergio Aragonés **W:** Mark Evanier
3 ❑ 1989 Cover: 3.50 **NM** value: **Cover or less**
Circ: CapCity orders: **10,250**
🕮 The Turn of the Wheel!; Shanghaied! • squarebound **A:** Sergio Aragonés **W:** Mark Evanier
4 ❑ Cover: 3.50 **NM** value: **Cover or less**
Circ: CapCity orders: **10,250**
🕮 The Wizard War; The Music of Murkos! • squarebound **A:** Sergio Aragonés **W:** Mark Evanier
5 ❑ Cover: 3.50 **NM** value: **Cover or less**
Circ: CapCity orders: **9,750**
🕮 Chakaal; Groo and the Poachers • squarebound **A:** Sergio Aragonés **W:** Mark Evanier
6 ❑ Feb 1990 Cover: 3.50 **NM** value: **Cover or less**
Circ: CapCity orders: **8,800**
🕮 Warriors Two; The Swords of Groo • squarebound **A:** Sergio Aragonés **W:** Mark Evanier

GROO (DARK HORSE) — Dark Horse
1 ❑ Jan 1998 Cover: 2.95 **NM** value: **Cover or less**
2 ❑ Feb 1998 Cover: 2.95 **NM** value: **Cover or less**
3 ❑ Mar 1998 Cover: 2.95 **NM** value: **Cover or less**
4 ❑ Apr 1998 Cover: 2.95 **NM** value: **Cover or less**
Bk 1❑ Nov 1998 Cover: 9.95 **NM** value: **Cover or less**
wraparound cover. • The Most Intelligent Man in the World

GROO HOUNDBOOK, THE (SERGIO ARAGONÉS'...) — Dark Horse
Bk 1❑ May 1999 Cover: 9.95 **NM** value: **Cover or less**
No issue number. • Trade Paperback. • collects Epic issues #29-#32

GROO (IMAGE) — Image
1 ❑ Dec 1994 Cover: 1.95 **NM** value: **2.50**
Circ: CapCity orders: **18,300**
🕮 The Promised Land **A:** Sergio Aragonés **W:** Mark Evanier
2 ❑ Jan 1995 Cover: 1.95 **NM** value: **2.50**
Circ: CapCity orders: **12,625**
🕮 The Aqualarre • indicia says issue #1 **A:** Sergio Aragonés **W:** Mark Evanier
3 ❑ Feb 1995 Cover: 1.95 **NM** value: **2.50**
Circ: CapCity orders: **11,450**
4 ❑ Mar 1995 Cover: 1.95 **NM** value: **2.00**
Circ: CapCity orders: **11,225**
🕮 A Drink of Water **A:** Sergio Aragonés **W:** Mark Evanier
5 ❑ Apr 1995 Cover: 1.95 **NM** value: **2.00**
Circ: CapCity orders: **10,750**
6 ❑ May 1995 Cover: 1.95 **NM** value: **2.00**
Circ: CapCity orders: **10,650**
7 ❑ Jun 1995 Cover: 1.95 **NM** value: **2.00**
Circ: CapCity orders: **10,625**
8 ❑ Jul 1995 Cover: 1.95 **NM** value: **2.00**
Circ: CapCity orders: **10,525**
9 ❑ Aug 1995 Cover: 2.25 **NM** value: **Cover or less**
Circ: CapCity orders: **9,525**
10 ❑ Sep 1995 Cover: 2.25 **NM** value: **Cover or less**
Circ: CapCity orders: **8,700**
11 ❑ Oct 1995 Cover: 2.25 **NM** value: **Cover or less**
Circ: CapCity orders: **6,450**
🕮 The Gamblers **A:** Sergio Aragonés **W:** Mark Evanier
12 ❑ Nov 1995 Cover: 2.25 **NM** value: **Cover or less**
final issue. **A:** Sergio Aragonés **W:** Mark Evanier

GROO: MIGHTIER THAN THE SWORD (SERGIO ARAGONÉS...) — Dark Horse
1 ❑ Jan 2000 Cover: 2.95 **NM** value: **Cover or less**
2 ❑ Feb 2000 Cover: 2.95 **NM** value: **Cover or less**
3 ❑ Mar 2000 Cover: 2.95 **NM** value: **Cover or less**
4 ❑ Apr 2000 Cover: 2.95 **NM** value: **Cover or less**

GROO THE WANDERER — Marvel / Epic
1 ❑ Mar 1985 Cover: 0.75 **NM** value: **7.00**
• **CGC:** 6 graded, best 9.8
🕮 The Song of Groo **A:** Sergio Aragonés **W:** Mark Evanier ★ 1st Appearance of Minstrel.
2 ❑ Apr 1985 Cover: 0.75 **NM** value: **5.00**
🕮 Dragon Killer! **A:** Sergio Aragonés **W:** Mark Evanier
3 ❑ May 1985 Cover: 0.75 **NM** value: **4.00**
Circ: CapCity orders: **13,700**
🕮 The Medallion **A:** Sergio Aragonés **W:** Mark Evanier
4 ❑ Jun 1985 Cover: 0.75 **NM** value: **4.00**
Circ: CapCity orders: **12,600**
🕮 World Without Women **A:** Sergio Aragonés **W:** Mark Evanier
5 ❑ Jul 1985 Cover: 0.75 **NM** value: **3.50**
Circ: CapCity orders: **12,800**
🕮 Slavers **A:** Sergio Aragonés **W:** Mark Evanier
6 ❑ Aug 1985 Cover: 0.75 **NM** value: **3.50**
Circ: CapCity orders: **12,900**
🕮 Eye of the Kabula **A:** Sergio Aragonés **W:** Mark Evanier
7 ❑ Sep 1985 Cover: 0.75 **NM** value: **3.50**
Circ: CapCity orders: **13,800**
🕮 The Ivory Graveyard **A:** Sergio Aragonés **W:** Mark Evanier
8 ❑ Oct 1985 Cover: 0.75 **NM** value: **3.50**
Circ: CapCity orders: **13,100**
🕮 The Treasure Of Kantor **A:** Sergio Aragonés **W:** Mark Evanier
9 ❑ Nov 1985 Cover: 0.75 **NM** value: **3.50**
Circ: CapCity orders: **11,900**
🕮 Pigs And Apples **A:** Sergio Aragonés **W:** Mark Evanier
10 ❑ Dec 1985 Cover: 0.75 **NM** value: **3.50**
Circ: CapCity orders: **11,800**
🕮 Groo Meets The Hero **A:** Sergio Aragonés **W:** Mark Evanier
11 ❑ Jan 1986 Cover: 0.75 **NM** value: **3.00**
Circ: Statement: **109,675** CapCity orders: **11,200**
🕮 A Hero's Task **A:** Sergio Aragonés **W:** Mark Evanier
12 ❑ Feb 1986 Cover: 0.75 **NM** value: **3.00**
Circ: Statement: **109,675** CapCity orders: **11,400**
🕮 Groo Meets The Thespians **A:** Sergio Aragonés **W:** Mark Evanier
13 ❑ Mar 1986 Cover: 0.75 **NM** value: **3.00**
Circ: Statement: **109,675** CapCity orders: **11,800**
🕮 Groo And The Tale Of King Sage **A:** Sergio Aragonés **W:** Mark Evanier
14 ❑ Apr 1986 Cover: 0.75 **NM** value: **3.00**
Circ: Statement: **109,675** CapCity orders: **10,700**
🕮 The Quarry **A:** Sergio Aragonés **W:** Mark Evanier
15 ❑ May 1986 Cover: 0.75 **NM** value: **3.00**
Circ: Statement: **109,675** CapCity orders: **10,800**
🕮 Groo And The Monks **A:** Sergio Aragonés **W:** Mark Evanier
16 ❑ Jun 1986 Cover: 0.75 **NM** value: **3.00**
Circ: Statement: **109,675** CapCity orders: **10,700**
🕮 Groo and the Shipyard **A:** Sergio Aragonés **W:** Mark Evanier
17 ❑ Jul 1986 Cover: 0.75 **NM** value: **3.00**
Circ: Statement: **109,675** CapCity orders: **10,700**
🕮 Pescatel (The Hatchery) **A:** Sergio Aragonés **W:** Mark Evanier
18 ❑ Aug 1986 Cover: 0.75 **NM** value: **3.00**
Circ: Statement: **109,675** CapCity orders: **11,100**
🕮 Groo Sister's City! **A:** Sergio Aragonés **W:** Mark Evanier
19 ❑ Sep 1986 Cover: 0.75 **NM** value: **3.00**
Circ: Statement: **109,675** CapCity orders: **11,100**
🕮 Groo And The Siege! **A:** Sergio Aragonés **W:** Mark Evanier
20 ❑ Oct 1986 Cover: 0.75 **NM** value: **3.00**
Circ: Statement: **109,675** CapCity orders: **11,900**
🕮 Groo And The Siege (Second Try) **A:** Sergio Aragonés **W:** Mark Evanier
21 ❑ Nov 1986 Cover: 0.75 **NM** value: **2.50**
Circ: Statement: **109,675** CapCity orders: **12,000**
🕮 Groo And The Witches Of Brujas **A:** Sergio Aragonés **W:** Mark Evanier
22 ❑ Dec 1986 Cover: 0.75 **NM** value: **2.50**
Circ: Statement: **109,675** CapCity orders: **12,100**
🕮 Groo and the Ambassador **A:** Sergio Aragonés **W:** Mark Evanier
23 ❑ Jan 1987 Cover: 0.75 **NM** value: **2.50**
Circ: Statement: **108,158** CapCity orders: **12,000**
🕮 Groo Meets Pal n Drumm **A:** Sergio Aragonés **W:** Mark Evanier
24 ❑ Feb 1987 Cover: 0.75 **NM** value: **2.50**
Circ: Statement: **108,158** CapCity orders: **12,500**
🕮 Arcadio's Quest **A:** Sergio Aragonés **W:** Mark Evanier
25 ❑ Mar 1987 Cover: 0.75 **NM** value: **2.50**
Circ: Statement: **108,158** CapCity orders: **12,600**
🕮 Divide and Conquer! **A:** Sergio Aragonés **W:** Mark Evanier
26 ❑ Apr 1987 Cover: 0.75 **NM** value: **2.50**
Circ: Statement: **108,158** CapCity orders: **12,700**
🕮 Arba Dakarba **A:** Sergio Aragonés **W:** Mark Evanier
27 ❑ May 1987 Cover: 1.00 **NM** value: **2.50**
Circ: Statement: **108,158** CapCity orders: **11,200**
🕮 Spies! **A:** Sergio Aragonés **W:** Mark Evanier
28 ❑ Jun 1987 Cover: 1.00 **NM** value: **2.50**
Circ: Statement: **108,158** CapCity orders: **11,800**
🕮 Gourmet Kings **A:** Sergio Aragonés **W:** Mark Evanier
29 ❑ Jul 1987 Cover: 1.00 **NM** value: **2.50**
Circ: Statement: **108,158** CapCity orders: **11,700**
🕮 Rufferto **A:** Sergio Aragonés **W:** Mark Evanier
30 ❑ Aug 1987 Cover: 1.00 **NM** value: **2.50**
Circ: Statement: **108,158** CapCity orders: **12,400**
🕮 Rufferto II **A:** Sergio Aragonés **W:** Mark Evanier
31 ❑ Sep 1987 Cover: 1.00 **NM** value: **2.00**
Circ: Statement: **108,158** CapCity orders: **12,800**
🕮 The Arms Deal **A:** Sergio Aragonés **W:** Mark Evanier
32 ❑ Oct 1987 Cover: 1.00 **NM** value: **2.00**
Circ: Statement: **108,158** CapCity orders: **13,200**
🕮 The Bankers of Avara **A:** Sergio Aragonés **W:** Mark Evanier
33 ❑ Nov 1987 Cover: 1.00 **NM** value: **2.00**
Circ: Statement: **108,158** CapCity orders: **13,100**
🕮 The Pirates of Salgari **A:** Sergio Aragonés **W:** Mark Evanier
34 ❑ Dec 1987 Cover: 1.00 **NM** value: **2.00**
Circ: Statement: **108,158** CapCity orders: **12,700**
🕮 The Amulet **A:** Sergio Aragonés **W:** Mark Evanier
35 ❑ Jan 1988 Cover: 1.00 **NM** value: **2.00**
Circ: Statement: **96,205** CapCity orders: **13,100**
🕮 Wishes **A:** Sergio Aragonés **W:** Mark Evanier
36 ❑ Feb 1988 Cover: 1.00 **NM** value: **2.00**
Circ: Statement: **96,205** CapCity orders: **13,600**
🕮 Rhyme Nor Reason **A:** Sergio Aragonés **W:** Mark Evanier
37 ❑ Mar 1988 Cover: 1.00 **NM** value: **2.00**
Circ: Statement: **96,205** CapCity orders: **13,600**
🕮 The Village of Miggledy **A:** Sergio Aragonés **W:** Mark Evanier
38 ❑ Apr 1988 Cover: 1.00 **NM** value: **2.00**
Circ: Statement: **96,205** CapCity orders: **13,900**
🕮 Mealtime **A:** Sergio Aragonés **W:** Mark Evanier
39 ❑ May 1988 Cover: 1.00 **NM** value: **2.00**
Circ: Statement: **96,205** CapCity orders: **13,700**
🕮 A Groo's Best Friend **A:** Sergio Aragonés **W:** Mark Evanier
40 ❑ Jun 1988 Cover: 1.00 **NM** value: **2.00**
Circ: Statement: **96,205** CapCity orders: **12,900**
🕮 The Glass Carafe **A:** Sergio Aragonés **W:** Mark Evanier
41 ❑ Jul 1988 Cover: 1.00 **NM** value: **2.00**
Circ: Statement: **96,205** CapCity orders: **13,100**
🕮 Granny Groo **A:** Sergio Aragonés **W:** Mark Evanier
42 ❑ Aug 1988 Cover: 1.00 **NM** value: **2.00**
Circ: Statement: **96,205** CapCity orders: **13,100**
🕮 The Weddings of Groo **A:** Sergio Aragonés **W:** Mark Evanier
43 ❑ Sep 1988 Cover: 1.00 **NM** value: **2.00**
Circ: Statement: **96,205** CapCity orders: **13,000**
🕮 Slave! **A:** Sergio Aragonés **W:** Mark Evanier
44 ❑ Oct 1988 Cover: 1.00 **NM** value: **2.00**
Circ: Statement: **96,205** CapCity orders: **13,500**
🕮 Ruffeto Reverie **A:** Sergio Aragonés **W:** Mark Evanier
45 ❑ Nov 1988 Cover: 1.00 **NM** value: **2.00**
Circ: Statement: **96,205** CapCity orders: **12,900**
🕮 Rufferto Reality! **A:** Sergio Aragonés **W:** Mark Evanier
46 ❑ Dec 1988 Cover: 1.00 **NM** value: **2.00**
Circ: Statement: **96,205** CapCity orders: **13,100**
🕮 Groo's Clothes **A:** Sergio Aragonés **W:** Mark Evanier
47 ❑ Jan 1989 Cover: 1.00 **NM** value: **2.00**
Circ: Statement: **90,830** CapCity orders: **12,800**
🕮 The 300% Solution **A:** Sergio Aragonés **W:** Mark Evanier

CGC-graded: Multiply prices above by **33 for 9.9 M • 16 for 9.8 NM/M • 7 for 9.6 NM+ • 5 for 9.4 NM • 2.5 for 9.2 NM- • 1.5 for 9.0 VF/NM**

48 ❑ Feb 1989 Cover: 1.00 **NM** value: **2.00**
Circ: Statement: **90,830** CapCity orders: **12,200**
📖 The Wanderer! **A:** Sergio Aragonés **W:** Mark Evanier
49 ❑ Mar 1989 Cover: 1.00 **NM** value: **2.00**
Circ: Statement: **90,830** CapCity orders: **12,500**
📖 The Protector **A:** Sergio Aragonés **W:** Mark Evanier ★ Appearance of Chakaal.
50 ❑ Apr 1989 Cover: 1.50 **NM** value: **3.00**
Circ: Statement: **90,830** CapCity orders: **13,400**
• Giant-size. 📖 Chakaal Again! **A:** Sergio Aragonés **W:** Mark Evanier ★ Appearance of Chakaal.
51 ❑ May 1989 Cover: 1.00 **NM** value: **2.00**
Circ: Statement: **90,830** CapCity orders: **12,600**
📖 The Valley of Mas and Menos **A:** Sergio Aragonés **W:** Mark Evanier ★ Appearance of Chakaal.
52 ❑ Jun 1989 Cover: 1.00 **NM** value: **2.00**
Circ: Statement: **90,830** CapCity orders: **12,700**
📖 The Arana **A:** Sergio Aragonés **W:** Mark Evanier ★ Appearance of Chakaal.
53 ❑ Jul 1989 Cover: 1.00 **NM** value: **2.00**
Circ: Statement: **90,830** CapCity orders: **13,200**
📖 Dragons for Sale **A:** Sergio Aragonés **W:** Mark Evanier ★ Appearance of Chakaal.
54 ❑ Aug 1989 Cover: 1.00 **NM** value: **2.00**
Circ: Statement: **90,830** CapCity orders: **13,400**
📖 The Armadas **A:** Sergio Aragonés **W:** Mark Evanier
55 ❑ Sep 1989 Cover: 1.00 **NM** value: **2.00**
Circ: Statement: **90,830** CapCity orders: **14,000**
📖 The Island of Felicidad **A:** Sergio Aragonés **W:** Mark Evanier
56 ❑ Oct 1989 Cover: 1.00 **NM** value: **2.00**
Circ: Statement: **90,830** CapCity orders: **13,500**
📖 A Minstrel's Tale **A:** Sergio Aragonés **W:** Mark Evanier
57 ❑ Nov 1989 Cover: 1.00 **NM** value: **2.00**
Circ: Statement: **90,830** CapCity orders: **13,400**
📖 The Captain of Chinampa **A:** Sergio Aragonés **W:** Mark Evanier
58 ❑ Nov 1989 Cover: 1.00 **NM** value: **2.00**
Circ: Statement: **90,830** CapCity orders: **13,600**
📖 The Idol **A:** Sergio Aragonés **W:** Mark Evanier
59 ❑ Dec 1989 Cover: 1.00 **NM** value: **2.00**
Circ: Statement: **90,830** CapCity orders: **13,600**
📖 One Fine Day **A:** Sergio Aragonés **W:** Mark Evanier
60 ❑ Dec 1989 Cover: 1.00 **NM** value: **2.00**
Circ: Statement: **90,830** CapCity orders: **13,400**
📖 The Mendicants **A:** Sergio Aragonés **W:** Mark Evanier
61 ❑ Jan 1990 Cover: 1.00 **NM** value: **2.00**
Circ: Statement: **88,883** CapCity orders: **13,800**
📖 The Horses of Caballo! **A:** Sergio Aragonés **W:** Mark Evanier
62 ❑ Feb 1990 Cover: 1.00 **NM** value: **2.00**
Circ: Statement: **88,883** CapCity orders: **13,700**
📖 Horse Sense **A:** Sergio Aragonés **W:** Mark Evanier
63 ❑ Mar 1990 Cover: 1.00 **NM** value: **2.00**
Circ: Statement: **88,883** CapCity orders: **13,600**
📖 Real Estate **A:** Sergio Aragonés **W:** Mark Evanier
64 ❑ Apr 1990 Cover: 1.00 **NM** value: **2.00**
Circ: Statement: **88,883** CapCity orders: **12,900**
📖 The Painter **A:** Sergio Aragonés **W:** Mark Evanier
65 ❑ May 1990 Cover: 1.00 **NM** value: **2.00**
Circ: Statement: **88,883** CapCity orders: **13,000**
📖 The Garbage Issue **A:** Sergio Aragonés **W:** Mark Evanier
66 ❑ Jun 1990 Cover: 1.00 **NM** value: **2.00**
Circ: Statement: **88,883** CapCity orders: **13,100**
📖 The Gurus **A:** Sergio Aragonés **W:** Mark Evanier
67 ❑ Jul 1990 Cover: 1.00 **NM** value: **2.00**
Circ: Statement: **88,883** CapCity orders: **13,400**
📖 Dragon Quest **A:** Sergio Aragonés **W:** Mark Evanier
68 ❑ Aug 1990 Cover: 1.00 **NM** value: **2.00**
Circ: Statement: **88,883** CapCity orders: **13,400**
📖 The Hero of Lerolero **A:** Sergio Aragonés **W:** Mark Evanier
69 ❑ Sep 1990 Cover: 1.00 **NM** value: **2.00**
Circ: Statement: **88,883** CapCity orders: **13,400**
📖 One if By Land, Two if By Sea! **A:** Sergio Aragonés **W:** Mark Evanier
70 ❑ Oct 1990 Cover: 1.00 **NM** value: **2.00**
Circ: Statement: **88,883** CapCity orders: **13,500**
📖 The Greatest Hero **A:** Sergio Aragonés **W:** Mark Evanier
71 ❑ Nov 1990 Cover: 1.00 **NM** value: **1.50**
Circ: Statement: **88,883** CapCity orders: **12,400**
📖 Laughingstock **A:** Sergio Aragonés **W:** Mark Evanier
72 ❑ Dec 1990 Cover: 1.00 **NM** value: **1.50**
Circ: Statement: **88,883** CapCity orders: **13,000**
📖 Shaman **A:** Sergio Aragonés **W:** Mark Evanier
73 ❑ Jan 1991 Cover: 1.00 **NM** value: **1.50**
Circ: Statement: **69,525** CapCity orders: **12,900**
📖 The Scepter of King Cetro, Part 1 **A:** Sergio Aragonés **W:** Mark Evanier
74 ❑ Feb 1991 Cover: 1.00 **NM** value: **1.50**
Circ: Statement: **69,525** CapCity orders: **12,700**
📖 The Scepter of King Cetro, Part 2 **A:** Sergio Aragonés **W:** Mark Evanier
75 ❑ Mar 1991 Cover: 1.00 **NM** value: **1.50**
Circ: Statement: **69,525** CapCity orders: **12,300**
📖 The Scepter of King Cetro, Part 3 **A:** Sergio Aragonés **W:** Mark Evanier
76 ❑ Apr 1991 Cover: 1.00 **NM** value: **1.50**
Circ: Statement: **69,525** CapCity orders: **11,900**
📖 The Mines of Minas **A:** Sergio Aragonés **W:** Mark Evanier
77 ❑ May 1991 Cover: 1.00 **NM** value: **1.50**
Circ: Statement: **69,525** CapCity orders: **12,300**
📖 Rufferto's Magic Wish **A:** Sergio Aragonés **W:** Mark Evanier
78 ❑ Jun 1991 Cover: 1.00 **NM** value: **1.50**
Circ: Statement: **69,525** CapCity orders: **11,900**
📖 The Book Burners • bookburners **A:** Sergio Aragonés **W:** Mark Evanier
79 ❑ Jul 1991 Cover: 1.00 **NM** value: **1.50**
Circ: Statement: **69,525** CapCity orders: **11,900**
📖 The Monks of Monjes **A:** Sergio Aragonés **W:** Mark Evanier
80 ❑ Aug 1991 Cover: 1.00 **NM** value: **1.50**
Circ: Statement: **69,525** CapCity orders: **12,400**
📖 Legend of Thaais, Part 1; The Legend of Thaais, Part 1 **A:** Sergio Aragonés **W:** Mark Evanier
81 ❑ Sep 1991 Cover: 1.00 **NM** value: **1.50**
Circ: Statement: **69,525**
📖 Legend of Thaais, Part 2; The Legend of Thaais, Part 2 **A:** Sergio Aragonés **W:** Mark Evanier
82 ❑ Oct 1991 Cover: 1.00 **NM** value: **1.50**
Circ: Statement: **69,525** CapCity orders: **12,100**
📖 Legend of Thaais, Part 3; The Legend of Thaais, Part 3 **A:** Sergio Aragonés **W:** Mark Evanier
83 ❑ Nov 1991 Cover: 1.00 **NM** value: **1.50**
Circ: Statement: **69,525** CapCity orders: **11,800**
📖 Legend of Thaais, Part 4; The Legend of Thaais, Part 4 **A:** Sergio Aragonés **W:** Mark Evanier
84 ❑ Dec 1991 Cover: 1.00 **NM** value: **1.50**
Circ: Statement: **69,525** CapCity orders: **12,400**
85 ❑ Jan 1992 Cover: 1.00 **NM** value: **1.50**
Circ: Statement: **47,165** CapCity orders: **12,200**
86 ❑ Feb 1992 Cover: 1.00 **NM** value: **1.50**
Circ: Statement: **47,165** CapCity orders: **11,900**
📖 The Two Doors **A:** Sergio Aragonés **W:** Mark Evanier
87 ❑ Mar 1992 Cover: 2.25 **NM** value: **Cover or less**
Circ: Statement: **47,165** CapCity orders: **11,100**
📖 The Supreme General **A:** Sergio Aragonés **W:** Mark Evanier
88 ❑ Apr 1992 Cover: 2.25 **NM** value: **Cover or less**
Circ: Statement: **47,165** CapCity orders: **10,700**
📖 Prairie War **A:** Sergio Aragonés **W:** Mark Evanier
89 ❑ May 1992 Cover: 2.25 **NM** value: **Cover or less**
Circ: Statement: **47,165** CapCity orders: **10,600**
90 ❑ Jun 1992 Cover: 2.25 **NM** value: **Cover or less**
Circ: Statement: **47,165** CapCity orders: **10,400**
91 ❑ Jul 1992 Cover: 2.25 **NM** value: **Cover or less**
Circ: Statement: **47,165** CapCity orders: **10,000**
92 ❑ Aug 1992 Cover: 2.25 **NM** value: **Cover or less**
Circ: Statement: **47,165** CapCity orders: **9,900**
• Groo finds fountain of youth **A:** Sergio Aragonés **W:** Mark Evanier
93 ❑ Sep 1992 Cover: 2.25 **NM** value: **Cover or less**
Circ: Statement: **47,165** CapCity orders: **9,400**
• Groo finds fountain of youth **A:** Sergio Aragonés **W:** Mark Evanier
94 ❑ Oct 1992 Cover: 2.25 **NM** value: **Cover or less**
Circ: Statement: **47,165** CapCity orders: **9,000**
📖 Water **A:** Sergio Aragonés **W:** Mark Evanier
95 ❑ Nov 1992 Cover: 2.25 **NM** value: **Cover or less**
Circ: Statement: **47,165** CapCity orders: **8,800**
📖 The Menagerie **A:** Sergio Aragonés **W:** Mark Evanier
96 ❑ Dec 1992 Cover: 2.25 **NM** value: **Cover or less**
Circ: Statement: **47,165** CapCity orders: **8,700**
📖 Wager of the Gods, Part 1; The Wager of the Gods, Part 1 **A:** Sergio Aragonés **W:** Mark Evanier
97 ❑ Jan 1993 Cover: 2.25 **NM** value: **Cover or less**
Circ: Statement: **34,277** CapCity orders: **8,900**
📖 Wager of the Gods, Part 2; The Wager of the Gods, Part 2 **A:** Sergio Aragonés **W:** Mark Evanier
98 ❑ Feb 1993 Cover: 2.25 **NM** value: **Cover or less**
Circ: Statement: **34,277** CapCity orders: **9,500**
📖 Wager of the Gods, Part 3; The Wager of the Gods, Part 3 **A:** Sergio Aragonés **W:** Mark Evanier
99 ❑ Mar 1993 Cover: 2.25 **NM** value: **Cover or less**
Circ: Statement: **34,277** CapCity orders: **9,500**
📖 Wager of the Gods, Part 4 **A:** Sergio Aragonés **W:** Mark Evanier
100 ❑ Apr 1993 Cover: 2.95 **NM** value: **Cover or less**
Circ: Statement: **34,277** CapCity orders: **13,600**
• 100th anniversary issue. • Groo learns to read **A:** Sergio Aragonés **W:** Mark Evanier
101 ❑ May 1993 Cover: 2.25 **NM** value: **Cover or less**
Circ: Statement: **34,277** CapCity orders: **10,400**
102 ❑ Jun 1993 Cover: 2.25 **NM** value: **Cover or less**
Circ: Statement: **34,277** CapCity orders: **10,100**
103 ❑ Aug 1993 Cover: 2.25 **NM** value: **Cover or less**
Circ: Statement: **34,277** CapCity orders: **10,500**
104 ❑ Sep 1993 Cover: 2.25 **NM** value: **Cover or less**
Circ: Statement: **34,277** CapCity orders: **9,600**
📖 A Home for Oso **A:** Sergio Aragonés **W:** Mark Evanier ★ Origin of Rufferto (Groo's Dog).
105 ❑ Oct 1993 Cover: 2.25 **NM** value: **Cover or less**
Circ: Statement: **34,277** CapCity orders: **9,450**
📖 The Curse of Criaturas **A:** Sergio Aragonés **W:** Mark Evanier
106 ❑ Nov 1993 Cover: 2.25 **NM** value: **Cover or less**
Circ: Statement: **34,277** CapCity orders: **9,050**
📖 Man of the People, Part 1 **A:** Sergio Aragonés **W:** Mark Evanier
107 ❑ Dec 1993 Cover: 2.25 **NM** value: **Cover or less**
Circ: Statement: **34,277** CapCity orders: **8,850**
📖 Man of the People, Part 2 **A:** Sergio Aragonés **W:** Mark Evanier
108 ❑ Jan 1994 Cover: 2.25 **NM** value: **Cover or less**
Circ: CapCity orders: **8,450**
📖 Man of the People, Part 3 **A:** Sergio Aragonés **W:** Mark Evanier
109 ❑ Feb 1994 Cover: 2.25 **NM** value: **Cover or less**
Circ: CapCity orders: **8,400**
📖 Man of the People, Part 4 **A:** Sergio Aragonés **W:** Mark Evanier
110 ❑ Mar 1994 Cover: 2.25 **NM** value: **Cover or less**
Circ: CapCity orders: **8,000**
111 ❑ Apr 1994 Cover: 2.25 **NM** value: **Cover or less**
Circ: CapCity orders: **7,750**
112 ❑ May 1994 Cover: 2.25 **NM** value: **Cover or less**
Circ: CapCity orders: **7,900**
113 ❑ Jun 1994 Cover: 2.25 **NM** value: **Cover or less**
Circ: CapCity orders: **7,700**
114 ❑ Jul 1994 Cover: 2.25 **NM** value: **Cover or less**
Circ: CapCity orders: **7,850**
115 ❑ Aug 1994 Cover: 2.25 **NM** value: **Cover or less**
Circ: CapCity orders: **7,800**
116 ❑ Sep 1994 Cover: 2.25 **NM** value: **Cover or less**
Circ: CapCity orders: **7,750**
117 ❑ Oct 1994 Cover: 2.25 **NM** value: **Cover or less**
Circ: CapCity orders: **7,450**
118 ❑ Nov 1994 Cover: 2.25 **NM** value: **Cover or less**
Circ: CapCity orders: **7,200**
119 ❑ Dec 1994 Cover: 2.25 **NM** value: **Cover or less**
Circ: CapCity orders: **7,150**
120 ❑ Jan 1995 Cover: 2.25 **NM** value: **Cover or less**
Circ: CapCity orders: **7,625**
final issue. **A:** Sergio Aragonés **W:** Mark Evanier
Bk 1 ❑ Cover: 8.95 **NM** value: **Cover or less**
Circ: CapCity orders: **2,300**
Bk 2 ❑ Cover: 9.95 **NM** value: **Cover or less**
Bk 3 ❑ Cover: 10.95 **NM** value: **Cover or less**
Bk 4 ❑ Cover: 10.95 **NM** value: **Cover or less**
📖 Festival • Reprints issues #21-24 **A:** Sergio Aragonés **W:** Mark Evanier
Bk 5 ❑ Cover: 10.95 **NM** value: **Cover or less**
📖 Garden **A:** Sergio Aragonés **W:** Mark Evanier
SE 1 ❑ Oct 1984 Cover: 2.00 **NM** value: **3.00**
• **CGC:** 3 graded, best 9.8
📖 The Swords of Groo; The Music of Murkos; Groo the Wanderer • Eclipse publishes **A:** Sergio Aragonés **W:** Mark Evanier ★ 1st Appearance of Groo.

GROO THE WANDERER (SERGIO ARAGONÉS'...) Pacific

He's fierce! He's strong! He's a sword-wielding barbarian! He's...really, really stupid!

He's Groo — a cheese dip-addicted barbarian who poses a great danger to friends and foe alike. When he wanders from town to town, he is easily tracked because of the impressive destruction he leaves in his path. Searching for someone who will hire him as a mercenary, Groo's fondest dream is to earn enough kopins to buy himself a lifetime supply of cheese dip.

Created by Mad Magazine's Sergio Aragones with embellishments by Mark Evanier, Groo the Wanderer is a supremely funny spoof on such sword-and-sorcery heroes as Conan the Barbarian.

The series originally started at Pacific Comics in 1982, then moved to Marvel's Epic imprint for more than 120 issues, before wandering to Image for a short while, and then moving on to Dark Horse where it became a series of mini-series. Even with Groo's influence, most of these companies are still in business.

1 ❑ Dec 1982 Cover: 1.00 **NM** value: **11.00**
• **CGC:** 13 graded, best 9.8
📖 Friends and Enemies **A:** Sergio Aragonés **W:** Mark Evanier ★ 1st Appearance of Sage.
2 ❑ Feb 1983 Cover: 1.00 **NM** value: **7.00**
• **CGC:** 3 graded, best 9.6
📖 The Missive! **A:** Sergio Aragonés **W:** Mark Evanier
3 ❑ Apr 1983 Cover: 1.00 **NM** value: **6.00**
• **CGC:** 1 graded, best 9.8
📖 The Caravan **A:** Sergio Aragonés **W:** Mark Evanier
4 ❑ Sep 1983 Cover: 1.00 **NM** value: **6.00**
• **CGC:** 1 graded, best 9.8
📖 The Turn of the Wheel **A:** Sergio Aragonés **W:** Mark Evanier
5 ❑ Oct 1983 Cover: 1.00 **NM** value: **6.00**
• **CGC:** 1 graded, best 9.8
📖 Shanghaied! **A:** Sergio Aragonés **W:** Mark Evanier
6 ❑ Dec 1983 Cover: 1.00 **NM** value: **5.00**
• **CGC:** 2 graded, best 9.8
📖 The Wizard War **A:** Sergio Aragonés **W:** Mark Evanier
7 ❑ Feb 1984 Cover: 1.00 **NM** value: **5.00**
• **CGC:** 1 graded, best 9.8
📖 Chakaal **A:** Sergio Aragonés **W:** Mark Evanier
8 ❑ Apr 1984 Cover: 1.00 **NM** value: **5.00**
• **CGC:** 1 graded, best 9.6
📖 Groo The Wanderer Warriors Two **A:** Sergio Aragonés **W:** Mark Evanier

GROOTLORE Fantagraphics

1 ❑ b&w Cover: 2.00 **NM** value: **Cover or less**
2 ❑ b&w Cover: 2.00 **NM** value: **Cover or less**

GROOTLORE (VOL. 2) Fantagraphics

1 ❑ b&w Cover: 2.00 **NM** value: **Cover or less**
2 ❑ b&w Cover: 2.00 **NM** value: **Cover or less**
3 ❑ Cover: 2.25 **NM** value: **Cover or less**

GROOVY Marvel

1 ❑ Mar 1968 Cover: 0.12 **NM** value: **35.00**
• **CGC:** 3 graded, best 8.5
2 ❑ May 1968 Cover: 0.12 **NM** value: **22.00**
📖 Misery Loves Company **A:** Suzanne Heller **W:** Suzanne Heller
3 ❑ Jul 1968 Cover: 0.12 **NM** value: **22.00**
• Marvel Comics Group Publisher

GROSS POINT DC

1 ❑ Aug 1997 Cover: 2.50 **NM** value: **3.00**
Circ: Diamd. preorders: **12,930**
📖 Welcome to Gross Point **A:** Brian Augustyn **W:** Mark Waid
2 ❑ Sep 1997 Cover: 2.50 **NM** value: **Cover or less**
Circ: Diamd. preorders: **10,154**
3 ❑ Oct 1997 Cover: 2.50 **NM** value: **Cover or less**
Circ: Diamd. preorders: **8,140**
4 ❑ Nov 1997 Cover: 2.50 **NM** value: **Cover or less**
Circ: Diamd. preorders: **6,853**
📖 Mourning Becomes Elective **A:** Roger Langridge **W:** Matt Wayne
5 ❑ Dec 1997 Cover: 2.50 **NM** value: **Cover or less**
Circ: Diamd. preorders: **5,565**
📖 The Duck of Mystery **A:** Roger Langridge **W:** Dan Slott
6 ❑ Dec 1997 Cover: 2.50 **NM** value: **Cover or less**
Circ: Diamd. preorders: **4,685**

Other grades: Multiply prices above by **1.5 for Mint • 2/3 for Very Fine • 1/3 for Fine • 1/5 for Very Good • 1/8 for Good**

📖 You Can't Get There From Here **A:** Roger Langridge; Joe Staton **W:** Paul Kupperberg
7 ❑ Jan 1998 Cover: 2.50 **NM** value: **Cover or less**
Circ: Diamd. preorders: **4,673**
8 ❑ Feb 1998 Cover: 2.50 **NM** value: **Cover or less**
Circ: Diamd. preorders: **3,571**
9 ❑ Mar 1998 Cover: 2.50 **NM** value: **Cover or less**
Circ: Diamd. preorders: **3,092**
📖 Possession is Nine-Tenths of the Flaw **A:** Roger Langridge; Joe Staton **W:** Matt Wayne
10 ❑ Apr 1998 Cover: 2.50 **NM** value: **Cover or less**
Circ: Diamd. preorders: **2,859**
11 ❑ May 1998 Cover: 2.50 **NM** value: **Cover or less**
12 ❑ Jun 1998 Cover: 2.50 **NM** value: **Cover or less**
13 ❑ Jul 1998 Cover: 2.50 **NM** value: **Cover or less**
14 ❑ Aug 1998 Cover: 2.50 **NM** value: **Cover or less**
final issue.

GROUND POUND! COMIX — Blackthorne

1 ❑ Jan 1987 Cover: 2.00 **NM** value: **Cover or less**
📖 Ronald's Surprise Birthday; Ronald The Barbarian; The Wishing World; A Boy and His Dorrg!; Flip the Bird; Dr. Flip; Macho Motor; **A:** John Pound; Peter Max **W:** John Pound; Mark Evanier; Peter Max

GROUND ZERO — Eternity

1 ❑ b&w Cover: 2.50 **NM** value: **Cover or less**
2 ❑ b&w Cover: 2.50 **NM** value: **Cover or less**

GROUP LARUE, THE (MIKE BARON'S...) — Innovation

1 ❑ Aug 1989 Cover: 1.95 **NM** value: **Cover or less**
Circ: CapCity orders: **3,675**
📖 Enter The Group LaRue! **A:** Andy Khun **W:** Mike Baron
2 ❑ Cover: 1.95 **NM** value: **Cover or less**
Circ: CapCity orders: **2,650**
3 ❑ Cover: 1.95 **NM** value: **Cover or less**
Circ: CapCity orders: **2,500**
4 ❑ Cover: 1.95 **NM** value: **Cover or less**
Bk 1 ❑ Cover: 8.95 **NM** value: **Cover or less**
• graphic album

GRRL SCOUTS (JIM MAHFOOD'S...) — Oni Press

1 ❑ Mar 1999, b&w Cover: 2.95 **NM** value: **Cover or less**
Circ: Diamd. preorders: **7,144**
2 ❑ Jun 1999, b&w Cover: 2.95 **NM** value: **Cover or less**
Circ: Diamd. preorders: **4,902**
3 ❑ Sep 1999, b&w Cover: 2.95 **NM** value: **Cover or less**
Circ: Diamd. preorders: **4,758**
Bk 1 ❑ Jun 2000, b&w Cover: 11.95 **NM** value: **Cover or less**
• Trade Paperback. • collects mini-series

GRRRL SQUAD — Amazing Aaron

1 ❑ Mar 1999, b&w Cover: 2.95 **NM** value: **Cover or less**
Circ: Diamd. preorders: **1,303**
One-shot. **A:** Aaron Warner **W:** Aaron Warner; Robert Brewer

GRUN — Harrier

1 ❑ Jun 1987 Cover: 1.95 **NM** value: **Cover or less**
2 ❑ Aug 1987 Cover: 1.95 **NM** value: **Cover or less**
3 ❑ Oct 1987 Cover: 1.95 **NM** value: **Cover or less**
4 ❑ Cover: 1.95 **NM** value: **Cover or less**

GRUNTS — Mirage

1 ❑ Nov 1987, b&w Cover: 2.00 **NM** value: **Cover or less**

GUANO COMIX — Print Mint

4 ❑ Cover: 0.50 **NM** value: **3.00**
📖 Everyday and Welcome Home; Deja Vu; Not for Certain; Yowkers!; My Ball; Ya Gotta Keep on truckin'; Dinner Spring; • #1-3 never published

GUARDIAN, THE — Spectrum

1 ❑ Mar 1984 Cover: 1.00 **NM** value: **Cover or less**
2 ❑ Jun 1984 Cover: 1.00 **NM** value: **Cover or less**

GUARDIAN KNIGHTS: DEMON'S KNIGHT — Limelight

1 ❑ b&w Cover: 2.95 **NM** value: **Cover or less**
• no indicia **A:** Tygger Graf **W:** Tygger Graf; D.A. Graf
2 ❑ b&w Cover: 2.95 **NM** value: **Cover or less**
• no indicia **A:** Tygger Graf **W:** Tygger Graf; D.A. Graf

GUARDIANS OF METROPOLIS, THE — DC

1 ❑ Nov 1994 Cover: 1.50 **NM** value: **Cover or less**
Circ: CapCity orders: **18,350**
📖 No One Can Stop... Trevorr! **A:** Kieron Dwyer **W:** Karl Kesel
2 ❑ Dec 1994 Cover: 1.50 **NM** value: **Cover or less**
Circ: CapCity orders: **13,750**
📖 Donovan's Circus! **A:** Kieron Dwyer **W:** Karl Kesel
3 ❑ Jan 1995 Cover: 1.50 **NM** value: **Cover or less**
Circ: CapCity orders: **11,600**
📖 All this and World War II **A:** Kieron Dwyer **W:** Karl Kesel
4 ❑ Feb 1995 Cover: 1.50 **NM** value: **Cover or less**
Circ: CapCity orders: **8,750**
📖 Race the Devil! **A:** Kieron Dwyer **W:** Karl Kesel ★ Versus Female Furies.

The prices seen above do not represent the highest possible prices seen in online auctions, but rather the prices we have seen these issues reliably fetch in a variety of environments (storefront retail, mail order, auction and convention).

GUARDIANS OF THE GALAXY — Marvel

One of Marvel's few series set in the future to gain much traction, Guardians of the Galaxy follows a group of 31st Century refugees from the Badoon invasion of the solar system in their adventures in the cosmos.

Marvel had published appearances of Vance Astro, Charlie-27, Martinex, Yondu, and the others in various titles since the 1970s — in fact, they probably spent more time visiting the 20th Century than they spent in their own. The team never really caught on until this title, in which writer Jim Valentino sent the Guardians off in search of the artifacts of the Marvel universe. Where did Captain America's shield wind up? Where did all the mutants go? Could there be a civilization based on Iron Man's armor? Great, imaginative stories were the rule for Valentino's tenure — but the title faded after his departure. — JJM

1 ❑ Jun 1990 Cover: 1.00 **NM** value: **2.00**
Circ: CapCity orders: **41,500**
📖 Taserface! **A:** Jim Valentino **W:** Jim Valentino
2 ❑ Jul 1990 Cover: 1.00 **NM** value: **1.75**
Circ: CapCity orders: **29,600**
3 ❑ Aug 1990 Cover: 1.00 **NM** value: **1.75**
Circ: CapCity orders: **27,000**
4 ❑ Sep 1990 Cover: 1.00 **NM** value: **1.75**
Circ: CapCity orders: **26,200**
5 ❑ Oct 1990 Cover: 1.00 **NM** value: **1.75**
Circ: CapCity orders: **26,400**
6 ❑ Nov 1990 Cover: 1.00 **NM** value: **1.50**
Circ: CapCity orders: **25,600**
7 ❑ Dec 1990 Cover: 1.00 **NM** value: **1.50**
Circ: CapCity orders: **25,400**
8 ❑ Jan 1991 Cover: 1.00 **NM** value: **1.50**
Circ: Statement: **142,767** CapCity orders: **26,200**
9 ❑ Feb 1991 Cover: 1.00 **NM** value: **1.50**
Circ: Statement: **142,767** CapCity orders: **29,600**
10 ❑ Mar 1991 Cover: 1.00 **NM** value: **1.50**
Circ: Statement: **142,767** CapCity orders: **31,000**
11 ❑ Apr 1991 Cover: 1.00 **NM** value: **1.50**
Circ: Statement: **142,767** CapCity orders: **29,600**
12 ❑ May 1991 Cover: 1.00 **NM** value: **1.50**
Circ: Statement: **142,767** CapCity orders: **27,400**
13 ❑ Jun 1991 Cover: 1.00 **NM** value: **2.00**
Circ: Statement: **142,767** CapCity orders: **39,600**
14 ❑ Jul 1991 Cover: 1.00 **NM** value: **2.00**
Circ: Statement: **142,767** CapCity orders: **48,000**
15 ❑ Aug 1991 Cover: 1.00 **NM** value: **1.50**
Circ: Statement: **142,767** CapCity orders: **35,100**
16 ❑ Sep 1991 Cover: 1.50 **NM** value: **1.75**
Circ: Statement: **142,767** CapCity orders: **35,200**
• Giant-size.
17 ❑ Oct 1991 Cover: 1.00 **NM** value: **1.50**
Circ: Statement: **142,767** CapCity orders: **38,800**
📖 Homecoming **A:** Jim Valentino **W:** Jim Valentino
18 ❑ Nov 1991 Cover: 1.00 **NM** value: **1.50**
Circ: Statement: **142,767** CapCity orders: **39,600**
📖 Punished **A:** Jim Valentino **W:** Jim Valentino
19 ❑ Dec 1991 Cover: 1.00 **NM** value: **1.50**
Circ: Statement: **142,767** CapCity orders: **36,300**
20 ❑ Jan 1992 Cover: 1.00 **NM** value: **1.50**
Circ: Statement: **211,008** CapCity orders: **38,700**
• Vance Astro becomes Major Victory★ Appearance of Captain America's shield.
21 ❑ Feb 1992 Cover: 1.25 **NM** value: **1.50**
Circ: Statement: **211,008** CapCity orders: **37,500**
22 ❑ Mar 1992 Cover: 1.25 **NM** value: **1.50**
Circ: Statement: **211,008** CapCity orders: **34,500**
• Has 1991 Statement, filed 10/1/91; avg print run 233,925; avg sales 141,008; avg subs 1,758; avg total paid 142,767; samples 125; office use 250; max existent 143,141; 39% of run returned
23 ❑ Apr 1992 Cover: 1.25 **NM** value: **1.50**
Circ: Statement: **211,008** CapCity orders: **31,300**
24 ❑ May 1992 Cover: 1.25 **NM** value: **1.50**
Circ: Statement: **211,008** CapCity orders: **34,500**
25 ❑ Jun 1992 Cover: 2.50 **NM** value: **Cover or less**
regular cover. ★ Versus Galactus.
25/SC ❑ Jun 1992 Cover: 2.50 **NM** value: **Cover or less**
Circ: Statement: **211,008** CapCity orders: **49,900**
foil cover. ★ Versus Galactus.
26 ❑ Jul 1992 Cover: 1.25 **NM** value: **1.50**
Circ: Statement: **211,008** CapCity orders: **35,300**
27 ❑ Aug 1992 Cover: 1.25 **NM** value: **1.50**
Circ: Statement: **211,008** CapCity orders: **44,500**
📖 Infinity War ★ Origin of Talon.
28 ❑ Sep 1992 Cover: 1.25 **NM** value: **1.50**
Circ: Statement: **211,008** CapCity orders: **43,800**
📖 Infinity War • Infinity War★ Versus Doctor Octopus.
29 ❑ Oct 1992 Cover: 1.25 **NM** value: **1.50**
Circ: Statement: **211,008** CapCity orders: **43,500**
📖 Infinity War • Infinity War
30 ❑ Nov 1992 Cover: 1.25 **NM** value: **Cover or less**
Circ: Statement: **211,008** CapCity orders: **30,600**
31 ❑ Dec 1992 Cover: 1.25 **NM** value: **Cover or less**
Circ: Statement: **211,008** CapCity orders: **27,900**
32 ❑ Jan 1993 Cover: 1.25 **NM** value: **Cover or less**
Circ: Statement: **120,509** CapCity orders: **26,200**
33 ❑ Feb 1993 Cover: 1.25 **NM** value: **Cover or less**
Circ: Statement: **120,509** CapCity orders: **25,000**
34 ❑ Mar 1993 Cover: 1.25 **NM** value: **Cover or less**
Circ: Statement: **120,509** CapCity orders: **23,400**
• Yellowjacket joins team; Has 1992 Statement, filed 10/1/92; avg print run 289,842; avg sales 208,317; avg subs 2,692; avg total paid 211,008; samples 250; office use 683; max existent 211,942; 27% of run returned
35 ❑ Apr 1993 Cover: 1.25 **NM** value: **Cover or less**
regular cover. ★ 1st Appearance of Galactic Guardians.
35/SC ❑ Apr 1993 Cover: 2.95 **NM** value: **Cover or less**
Circ: Statement: **120,509** CapCity orders: **24,400**
sculpted cover. ★ 1st Appearance of Galactic Guardians.
36 ❑ May 1993 Cover: 1.25 **NM** value: **Cover or less**
Circ: Statement: **120,509** CapCity orders: **24,100**
37 ❑ Jun 1993 Cover: 1.25 **NM** value: **Cover or less**
Circ: Statement: **120,509** CapCity orders: **23,300**
38 ❑ Jul 1993 Cover: 1.25 **NM** value: **Cover or less**
Circ: Statement: **120,509** CapCity orders: **22,900**
39 ❑ Aug 1993 Cover: 2.95 **NM** value: **Cover or less**
Circ: Statement: **120,509** CapCity orders: **35,900**
Holo-grafix cover. • Rancor vs. Doom
40 ❑ Sep 1993 Cover: 1.25 **NM** value: **Cover or less**
Circ: Statement: **120,509** CapCity orders: **21,800**
41 ❑ Oct 1993 Cover: 1.25 **NM** value: **Cover or less**
Circ: Statement: **120,509** CapCity orders: **21,400**
42 ❑ Nov 1993 Cover: 1.25 **NM** value: **Cover or less**
Circ: Statement: **120,509** CapCity orders: **22,200**
43 ❑ Dec 1993 Cover: 1.25 **NM** value: **Cover or less**
Circ: Statement: **120,509** CapCity orders: **19,800**
44 ❑ Jan 1994 Cover: 1.25 **NM** value: **Cover or less**
Circ: Statement: **52,354** CapCity orders: **18,000**
45 ❑ Feb 1994 Cover: 1.25 **NM** value: **Cover or less**
Circ: Statement: **52,354** CapCity orders: **18,100**
46 ❑ Mar 1994 Cover: 1.25 **NM** value: **Cover or less**
Circ: Statement: **52,354** CapCity orders: **16,500**
47 ❑ Apr 1994 Cover: 1.25 **NM** value: **Cover or less**
Circ: Statement: **52,354** CapCity orders: **15,450**
• Protege vs. Beyonder
48 ❑ May 1994 Cover: 1.50 **NM** value: **Cover or less**
Circ: Statement: **52,354** CapCity orders: **14,900**
49 ❑ Jun 1994 Cover: 1.50 **NM** value: **Cover or less**
Circ: Statement: **52,354** CapCity orders: **14,750**
50 ❑ Jul 1994 Cover: 2.00 **NM** value: **Cover or less**
• Giant-size. 📖 Future History, Part 1
50/SC ❑ Jul 1994 Cover: 2.95 **NM** value: **Cover or less**
Circ: Statement: **52,354** CapCity orders: **24,250**
foil cover. • Giant-size. 📖 Future History, Part 1
51 ❑ Aug 1994 Cover: 1.50 **NM** value: **Cover or less**
Circ: Statement: **52,354** CapCity orders: **15,150**
52 ❑ Sep 1994 Cover: 1.50 **NM** value: **Cover or less**
Circ: Statement: **52,354** CapCity orders: **14,800**
53 ❑ Oct 1994 Cover: 1.50 **NM** value: **Cover or less**
Circ: Statement: **52,354** CapCity orders: **13,950**
• Drax vs. Wolfhound
54 ❑ Nov 1994 Cover: 1.50 **NM** value: **Cover or less**
Circ: Statement: **52,354** CapCity orders: **13,750**
• final fate of Spider-Man
55 ❑ Dec 1994 Cover: 1.50 **NM** value: **Cover or less**
Circ: Statement: **52,354** CapCity orders: **12,700**
56 ❑ Jan 1995 Cover: 1.50 **NM** value: **Cover or less**
Circ: CapCity orders: **11,775**
57 ❑ Feb 1995 Cover: 1.50 **NM** value: **Cover or less**
Circ: CapCity orders: **11,325**
58 ❑ Mar 1995 Cover: 1.50 **NM** value: **Cover or less**
Circ: CapCity orders: **10,450**
• Has 1994 Statement, filed 10/1/94; avg print run 56,743; avg sales 51,363; avg subs 992; avg total paid 52,354; samples 125; office use 500; max existent 52,980; 7% of run returned
59 ❑ Apr 1995 Cover: 1.50 **NM** value: **Cover or less**
Circ: CapCity orders: **10,025**
60 ❑ May 1995 Cover: 1.50 **NM** value: **Cover or less**
Circ: CapCity orders: **9,950**
61 ❑ Jun 1995 Cover: 1.50 **NM** value: **Cover or less**
Circ: CapCity orders: **9,675**
62 ❑ Jul 1995 Cover: 2.50 **NM** value: **Cover or less**
Circ: CapCity orders: **9,900**
• Giant-size. final issue.
Anl 1 ❑ Jul 1991 Cover: 2.00 **NM** value: **3.00**
Circ: CapCity orders: **28,500**
📖 Korvac Quest, Part 4 • Korvac Quest **A:** Jim Valentino **W:** Jim Valentino
Anl 2 ❑ ca. 1992 Cover: 2.25 **NM** value: **2.50**
Circ: CapCity orders: **32,200**
📖 The System Bytes, Part 4
Anl 3 ❑ ca. 1993 Cover: 2.95 **NM** value: **Cover or less**
Circ: CapCity orders: **26,500**
• trading card
Anl 4 ❑ ca. 1994 Cover: 2.95 **NM** value: **Cover or less**
Circ: CapCity orders: **11,750**
📖 Future History, Part 3

GUERRILLA GROUNDHOG — Eclipse

1 ❑ Jan 1987 Cover: 1.50 **NM** value: **Cover or less**
2 ❑ Mar 1987 Cover: 1.50 **NM** value: **Cover or less**
📖 Guerrilla Groundhog Goes to Washington **A:** Andy Ice **W:** Chuck Wagner

GUERRILLA WAR — Dell

12 ❑ Cover: 0.12 **NM** value: **8.00**
• Series continued from Jungle War Stories #11
13 ❑ Cover: 0.12 **NM** value: **8.00**
14 ❑ Mar 1966 Cover: 0.12 **NM** value: **8.00**
📖 Death From Below!; End of the Rope!; First Mission (text story); The Brainless Ones! final issue.

GUFF! — Dark Horse

1 ❑ Apr 1998, b&w Cover: 1.95 **NM** value: **Cover or less**
Circ: Diamd. preorders: **9,209**

CGC-graded: Multiply prices above by **33 for 9.9 M • 16 for 9.8 NM/M • 7 for 9.6 NM+ • 5 for 9.4 NM • 2.5 for 9.2 NM- • 1.5 for 9.0 VF/NM**

No issue number. One-shot. Timoteo; Zombie Girl; Icky Animal; Sour Milks • bound-in Meanie Babies card **A:** Pat McEown; Sergio Aragonés; Jay Stephens; Dave Cooper; Gavin McInnes **W:** Pat McEown; Sergio Aragonés; Jay Stephens; Dave Cooper; Gavin McInnes

GUMBY 3-D — Blackthorne

1 ❑ Cover: 2.50 **NM** value: **Cover or less**
Circ: CapCity orders: **4,575**
2 ❑ Cover: 2.50 **NM** value: **Cover or less**
Circ: CapCity orders: **3,900**
The Eggs And Trixie **A:** David Cody Weiss **W:** David Cody Weiss; Art Clokey
3 ❑ Cover: 2.50 **NM** value: **Cover or less**
Circ: CapCity orders: **2,387**
4 ❑ Cover: 2.50 **NM** value: **Cover or less**
5 ❑ Cover: 2.50 **NM** value: **Cover or less**
Circ: CapCity orders: **1,825**
6 ❑ Cover: 2.50 **NM** value: **Cover or less**
Circ: CapCity orders: **1,650**
7 ❑ Cover: 2.50 **NM** value: **Cover or less**
Circ: CapCity orders: **1,075**

GUMBY'S SUMMER FUN SPECIAL — Comico

1 ❑ Jul 1987 Cover: 4.00 **NM** value: **Cover or less**
Circ: CapCity orders: **7,675**
Gumby's Summer Fun Adventure **A:** Arthur Adams **W:** Bob Burden

GUMBY'S WINTER FUN SPECIAL — Comico

1 ❑ Cover: 2.50 **NM** value: **Cover or less**
Circ: CapCity orders: **8,800**
Gumby's Winter Fun Adventure **A:** Arthur Adams **W:** Steve Purcell

GUMPS, THE — Bridgeport Herald

1 ❑ Mar 1947 Cover: 0.10 **NM** value: **80.00**
2 ❑ May 1947 Cover: 0.10 **NM** value: **48.00**
3 ❑ Jul 1947 Cover: 0.10 **NM** value: **38.00**
Valley of the Dinosaurs; Adventure in the Caves; The Mysterious Wildman **A:** Gus Edson
4 ❑ Sep 1947 Cover: 0.10 **NM** value: **32.00**
5 ❑ Nov 1947 Cover: 0.10 **NM** value: **32.00**

GUNFIGHTER — E.C.

The E.C. Western title was one of the first to evolve from an earlier title. The first four issues were something completely different: Ed Wheelan's Fat and Slat.

The lead character in Gunfighter is The Buckskin Kid, and three of the artists most associated with the classic era of E.C. did work for the series: Graham Ingels, Al Feldstein, and Johnny Craig.

As the E.C. line shifted to find its niche in the marketplace, it kept its series numbering but radically changed title and contents of its later-designated "Pre-Trend" titles. So, at the end of its run, Gunfighter morphed again: into the E.C. horror title The Haunt of Fear with #15. — Maggie

5 ❑ Sum 1948 Cover: 0.10 **NM** value: **Cover or less**
• **CGC:** 3 graded, best 8.5
The Dead Man's Hand!; A Wagon Train to Trouble!; The Apache Assassin!; Moon Girl Meets-The Hangman!
6 ❑ Fal 1948 Cover: 0.10 **NM** value: **Cover or less**
• **CGC:** 3 graded, best 9.0
The Sandyville Slasher!; The Medicine Man of Buffalo Flats!; I'll go out in Smoke An' Fire!; The Cave of the 1000 Winds
7 ❑ Win 1948 Cover: 0.10 **NM** value: **Cover or less**
• **CGC:** 4 graded, best 8.0
The Pool in Coulee Canyon; Smokin' Six-Guns!; The Stool Pigeon's Nest!; Raid of the Renegades; Big Shot
8 ❑ Apr 1949 Cover: 0.10 **NM** value: **Cover or less**
• **CGC:** 4 graded, best 8.0
The Trouble in the Territory!; The Story of the Black Phantom; The Buckskin Kid!
9 ❑ Jun 1949 Cover: 0.10 **NM** value: **Cover or less**
• **CGC:** 4 graded, best 8.5
The Skeleton of the Skyline Gap!; Blood and the Law; Your Newsdealer--He is your Friend!; Blackfoot Butcher!
10 ❑ Aug 1949 Cover: 0.10 **NM** value: **Cover or less**
• **CGC:** 5 graded, best 6.0
Sixguns and the Sisters!; The Curse of the Jessie James Treasure; Your Newsdealer--He is your friend!; The End of the Trail
11 ❑ Oct 1949 Cover: 0.10 **NM** value: **Cover or less**
• **CGC:** 3 graded, best 8.0
The Corpse Who Came Back!; Substitute Sheriff!; The Dealers in Death!
12 ❑ Dec 1949 Cover: 0.10 **NM** value: **Cover or less**
• **CGC:** 5 graded, best 9.2
The Bandits of Eagle Rock!; Bert Sutton...Texas Ranger; The Eyes have it!
13 ❑ Feb 1950 Cover: 0.10 **NM** value: **Cover or less**
• **CGC:** 3 graded, best 8.0
The Ghost from the Wagontrain!; Terror on the Trail!; The Day of Death; The Salivated Stetson!
14 ❑ Apr 1950 Cover: 0.10 **NM** value: **Cover or less**
• **CGC:** 3 graded, best 8.5
The Dead Man's Trail!; ....The Secret Strangler!; Ramsey's Revenge!; The Golden Killer!

For up-to-the-week CGC ratios, consult the current issue of **Comics Buyer's Guide.**

GUNFIGHTERS (CHARLTON) — Charlton

Under its former title, Kid Montana, this series focused on an innocent fugitive trying to avoid the trouble that always seems to come his way. Renamed Gunfighters in 1966, the series continued to feature Kid Montana, but also added other characters, including Wild Bill Hickok and his sidekick, Jingles, who keep and sometimes even make the law in the old West; a good-looking Lone Ranger type called the Masked Raider; and a noble gunfighter named the Cheyenne Kid.

The final issue of this series is notable for reprinting a Jack Kirby and Joe Simon story from the 1950s — and, given Charlton's poor circulation by 1984, colectors might think it as hard to find as the version from 30 years earlier. Not quite; it only seems that way!

51 ❑ **NM** value: **6.00**
• Continued from Kid Montana #50
52 ❑ Oct 1966 Cover: 0.12 **NM** value: **6.00**
• Final issue of original run (1967)
53 ❑ **NM** value: **4.00**
• Series begins again (1977)
54 ❑ 1979 **NM** value: **2.50**
55 ❑ 1979 **NM** value: **2.50**
56 ❑ 1979 **NM** value: **2.50**
57 ❑ Nov 1979 Cover: 0.40 **NM** value: **2.50**
58 ❑ Jan 1980 Cover: 0.40 **NM** value: **2.50**
59 ❑ Mar 1980 Cover: 0.40 **NM** value: **2.50**
60 ❑ May 1980 Cover: 0.40 **NM** value: **2.50**
61 ❑ Jul 1980 Cover: 0.40 **NM** value: **2.50**
62 ❑ Sep 1980 **NM** value: **2.50**
63 ❑ Nov 1980 Cover: 0.50 **NM** value: **2.50**
64 ❑ Jan 1981 Cover: 0.50 **NM** value: **2.50**
65 ❑ Mar 1981 Cover: 0.50 **NM** value: **2.50**
66 ❑ May 1981 Cover: 0.50 **NM** value: **2.50**
Kid Montana; Wild Bill Hickok And Jingles; Masked Raider A Hard Way!; Cheyenne Kid
67 ❑ Jul 1981 Cover: 0.50 **NM** value: **2.50**
68 ❑ Aug 1981 Cover: 0.50 **NM** value: **2.50**
69 ❑ Oct 1981 Cover: 0.50 **NM** value: **2.50**
70 ❑ Dec 1981 Cover: 0.50 **NM** value: **2.50**
71 ❑ Feb 1982 **NM** value: **2.50**
72 ❑ Apr 1982 **NM** value: **2.50**
73 ❑ Jun 1982 Cover: 0.60 **NM** value: **2.50**
74 ❑ Sep 1982 Cover: 0.60 **NM** value: **2.50**
75 ❑ Oct 1982 Cover: 0.60 **NM** value: **2.50**
76 ❑ Dec 1982 Cover: 0.60 **NM** value: **2.50**
77 ❑ 1983 **NM** value: **2.50**
78 ❑ 1983 **NM** value: **2.50**
79 ❑ 1983 **NM** value: **2.50**
80 ❑ 1983 **NM** value: **2.50**
81 ❑ 1983 **NM** value: **2.50**
82 ❑ **NM** value: **2.50**
83 ❑ **NM** value: **2.50**
84 ❑ **NM** value: **2.50**
85 ❑ Jul 1984 **NM** value: **2.50**
final issue.

GUN FIGHTERS IN HELL — Rebel

1 ❑ Cover: 2.25 **NM** value: **Cover or less**
2 ❑ Cover: 2.25 **NM** value: **Cover or less**
3 ❑ b&w Cover: 2.25 **NM** value: **Cover or less**
4 ❑ Cover: 2.25 **NM** value: **Cover or less**
5 ❑ Cover: 2.25 **NM** value: **Cover or less**

GUNFIGHTERS (SUPER COMICS) — Super

15 ❑ Cover: 0.12 **NM** value: **6.00**

GUNFIRE — DC

Gunfire made his debut in Deathstroke the Terminator Annual #2, one of many heroes that appeared as part of DC's "New Blood" crossover series. Gunfire is Andrew Van Horn, heir to his despised father's munitions empire, and a veritable living weapon himself. Andrew has the power of "molecular agitation" which he can use to "fire" the atoms of any object at a target.

But Andrew is more than some human arsenal. He's a thoughtful (dare we say sensitive?) young man who is struggling to manage his father's legacy while dealing with his own power. Luckily, he has the aid of Benjamin, a close friend and technical wizard, and Yvette Dubois, a beauty who can take care of herself.

0 ❑ Oct 1994 Cover: 1.95 **NM** value: **2.00**
Circ: CapCity orders: **10,500**
Forward Thrust! • Continued in Gunfire #6 **A:** Ed Benés **W:** Len Wein
1 ❑ May 1994 Cover: 1.75 **NM** value: **2.00**
Circ: CapCity orders: **13,850**
Deadly Homecoming **A:** Steve Erwin **W:** Len Wein
2 ❑ Jun 1994 Cover: 1.75 **NM** value: **2.00**
Circ: CapCity orders: **7,600**
On The Rebound **A:** Steve Erwin **W:** Len Wein
3 ❑ Jul 1994 Cover: 1.75 **NM** value: **2.00**
Circ: CapCity orders: **6,450**
Enter: Purge **A:** Steve Erwin **W:** Len Wein
4 ❑ Aug 1994 Cover: 1.75 **NM** value: **2.00**
Circ: CapCity orders: **5,700**
Squeeze Play **A:** Steve Erwin **W:** Len Wein
5 ❑ Sep 1994 Cover: 1.75 **NM** value: **2.00**
Circ: CapCity orders: **4,950**
The Day of the Exomorphic Man • Continued in Gunfire #0 **A:** Steve Erwin **W:** Len Wein
6 ❑ Nov 1994 Cover: 1.95 **NM** value: **2.00**
Circ: CapCity orders: **4,600**
It's All Done With Mirrors! **A:** Ed Benés **W:** Len Wein
7 ❑ Dec 1994 Cover: 1.95 **NM** value: **2.00**
Circ: CapCity orders: **4,500**
The Big Blow-Out! **A:** Ed Benés **W:** Len Wein
8 ❑ Jan 1995 Cover: 1.95 **NM** value: **2.00**
Circ: CapCity orders: **4,300**
The Trail of the Dragon! **A:** Chris Wozniak **W:** Len Wein
9 ❑ Feb 1995 Cover: 1.95 **NM** value: **2.00**
Circ: CapCity orders: **3,725**
Hard News **A:** Chris Wozniak **W:** Paul Kupperberg
10 ❑ Mar 1995 Cover: 1.95 **NM** value: **2.00**
Circ: CapCity orders: **3,175**
The Hong Kong Shuffle **A:** Ed Benés **W:** Len Wein
11 ❑ Apr 1995 Cover: 1.95 **NM** value: **2.00**
Circ: CapCity orders: **2,825**
12 ❑ May 1995 Cover: 1.95 **NM** value: **2.00**
Circ: CapCity orders: **2,650**
13 ❑ Jun 1995 Cover: 2.25 **NM** value: **Cover or less**
Circ: CapCity orders: **2,575**
final issue.

GUN FURY — Aircel

1 ❑ Jan 1989, b&w Cover: 1.95 **NM** value: **Cover or less**
2 ❑ Feb 1989, b&w Cover: 1.95 **NM** value: **Cover or less**
3 ❑ Mar 1989, b&w Cover: 1.95 **NM** value: **Cover or less**
4 ❑ Apr 1989, b&w Cover: 1.95 **NM** value: **Cover or less**
5 ❑ May 1989, b&w Cover: 1.95 **NM** value: **Cover or less**
6 ❑ Jun 1989, b&w Cover: 1.95 **NM** value: **Cover or less**
7 ❑ Jul 1989, b&w Cover: 1.95 **NM** value: **Cover or less**
Patrol **A:** Barry Blair **W:** Barry Blair
8 ❑ Aug 1989, b&w Cover: 1.95 **NM** value: **Cover or less**
In God We Trust **A:** Barry Blair **W:** Barry Blair
9 ❑ Sep 1989, b&w Cover: 1.95 **NM** value: **Cover or less**
10 ❑ Oct 1989, b&w Cover: 1.95 **NM** value: **Cover or less**

GUN FURY RETURNS — Aircel

1 ❑ Sep 1990, b&w Cover: 2.25 **NM** value: **Cover or less**
2 ❑ Oct 1990, b&w Cover: 2.25 **NM** value: **Cover or less**
Enter the Yesmen
3 ❑ Nov 1990, b&w Cover: 2.25 **NM** value: **Cover or less**
4 ❑ Dec 1990, b&w Cover: 2.25 **NM** value: **Cover or less**

GUNG HO — Avalon

1 ❑ b&w Cover: 2.95 **NM** value: **Cover or less**

GUNHAWK — Atlas

12 ❑ Nov 1950 Cover: 0.10 **NM** value: **Cover or less**
13 ❑ Feb 1951 Cover: 0.10 **NM** value: **Cover or less**
14 ❑ Apr 1951 Cover: 0.10 **NM** value: **Cover or less**
• **CGC:** 1 graded, best 8.0
15 ❑ Jun 1951 Cover: 0.10 **NM** value: **Cover or less**
16 ❑ Aug 1951 Cover: 0.10 **NM** value: **Cover or less**
17 ❑ Oct 1951 Cover: 0.10 **NM** value: **Cover or less**
18 ❑ Dec 1951 Cover: 0.10 **NM** value: **Cover or less**

GUNHAWKS — Marvel

Westerns can be filled with cliches. Marvel was particularly guilty of this, having produced numerous titles (such as Rawhide Kid and Two-Gun Kid) whose star was a good-hearted fugitive who had either been framed or had shot a man in self-defense. And, of course, a number of Western comics were hardly adroit at handling racial issues.

Gunhawks was a valiant 1972 attempt by Marvel to tell fast-paced Western tales and make some worthy moral points, and avoid the curse of the cliche. Its stars are two ex-Georgians, the white Kid Cassidy and the black Reno Jones. Loyal friends who have saved each other's lives countless times, they both aid and battle men of all races in this series. In all cases, the point is clear that it's the content of a man's heart — not his skin color — that decides his worth.

1 ❑ Oct 1972 Cover: 0.20 **NM** value: **7.00**
2 ❑ Dec 1972 Cover: 0.20 **NM** value: **5.00**
3 ❑ Feb 1973 Cover: 0.20 **NM** value: **5.00**
4 ❑ Apr 1973 Cover: 0.20 **NM** value: **4.00**
Trial By Ordeal **A:** Syd Shores **W:** Gary Friedrich
5 ❑ Jun 1973 Cover: 0.20 **NM** value: **4.00**
6 ❑ Aug 1973 Cover: 0.20 **NM** value: **4.00**
7 ❑ Oct 1973 Cover: 0.20 **NM** value: **4.00**
final issue. • Title changes to Gunhawk

GUNHED — Viz

1 ❑ full color Cover: 4.95 **NM** value: **7.00**
Circ: CapCity orders: **6,400**
• Japanese
2 ❑ full color Cover: 4.95 **NM** value: **7.00**

Other grades: Multiply prices above by **1.5 for Mint • 2/3 for Very Fine • 1/3 for Fine • 1/5 for Very Good • 1/8 for Good**

Circ: CapCity orders: **4,675**
• Japanese
3 ❑ full color Cover: 4.95 **NM** value: **7.00**
Circ: CapCity orders: **4,800**
• Japanese
Bk 1❑ Cover: 14.95 **NM** value: **Cover or less**

GUNNER — Gun Dog

1 ❑ Mar 1999 Cover: 2.95 **NM** value: **Cover or less**

GUN RUNNER — Marvel

1 ❑ Oct 1993 Cover: 2.75 **NM** value: **Cover or less**
Circ: CapCity orders: **14,400**
wraparound cover. • four cards; Polybagged **A:** Terry Clarke **W:** Andy Lanning; Dan Abnett
2 ❑ Nov 1993 Cover: 1.75 **NM** value: **Cover or less**
Circ: CapCity orders: **8,600**
Desert Storm **A:** Terry Clarke; Anthony Williams **W:** Andy Lanning; Dan Abnett
3 ❑ Dec 1993 Cover: 1.75 **NM** value: **Cover or less**
Circ: CapCity orders: **5,100**
Heaven Can't Wait! **A:** Terry Clarke; Anthony Williams **W:** Andy Lanning; Dan Abnett
4 ❑ Jan 1994 Cover: 1.75 **NM** value: **Cover or less**
Circ: CapCity orders: **3,900**
Thicker than Water! **A:** Terry Clarke; Anthony Williams **W:** Andy Lanning; Dan Abnett
5 ❑ Feb 1994 Cover: 1.75 **NM** value: **Cover or less**
Circ: CapCity orders: **2,900**
You Can't Go Home Again! **A:** Terry Clarke; Anthony Williams **W:** Andy Lanning; Dan Abnett
6 ❑ Mar 1994 Cover: 1.75 **NM** value: **Cover or less**
Circ: CapCity orders: **2,200**
Showdown on a Dying World **A:** Terry Clarke; Anthony Williams **W:** Andy Lanning; Dan Abnett

GUNS AGAINST GANGSTERS — Novelty Press

1 ❑ Oct 1948 Cover: 0.10 **NM** value: **Cover or less**
• **CGC:** 2 graded, best 9.2
2 ❑ Dec 1948 Cover: 0.10 **NM** value: **Cover or less**
3 ❑ Feb 1949 Cover: 0.10 **NM** value: **Cover or less**
4 ❑ Apr 1949 Cover: 0.10 **NM** value: **Cover or less**
• **CGC:** 2 graded, best 8.0
5 ❑ Jun 1949 Cover: 0.10 **NM** value: **Cover or less**
• **CGC:** 1 graded, best 8.5
6 ❑ Aug 1949 Cover: 0.10 **NM** value: **Cover or less**
• **CGC:** 3 graded, best 8.5
7 ❑ Oct 1949 Cover: 0.10 **NM** value: **Cover or less**

GUNSMITH CATS — Dark Horse / Manga

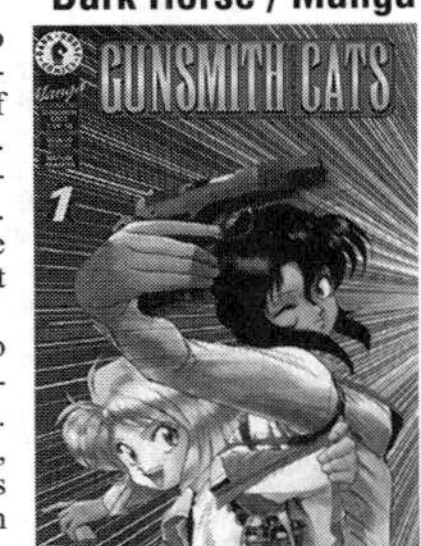

Gunsmith Cats follows two women who work in the traditionally male-dominated professions of bounty-hunting and demolition. Rally Vincent is the brunette gunsmith and sometime bounty hunter. "Minnie" May Hawkins is an ace demolitions expert when she's not busy driving Rally crazy.

An attorney contracts the duo to capture and deliver Dodge, Chicago's most notorious drug dealer. Dodge has more than one enemy, however. John Harper, Dodge's boss is afraid that Dodge will turn stool pigeon if caught by the police, and wants to "whack" him. The series is loaded with action as the two girls go from one problem to another in this black-and-white series.

Created by Kenichi Sonoda, with English translations provided by Studio Proteus and Dark Horse Comics, this was the first of a string of Gunsmith Cats limited series.

1 ❑ Sep 1995 Cover: 2.95 **NM** value: **3.00**
Circ: CapCity orders: **4,900**
2 ❑ Sep 1995 Cover: 2.95 **NM** value: **Cover or less**
3 ❑ Sep 1995 Cover: 2.95 **NM** value: **Cover or less**
Circ: CapCity orders: **4,425**
Bonnie and Clyde **A:** Kenichi Sonoda **W:** Kenichi Sonoda
4 ❑ Sep 1995 Cover: 2.95 **NM** value: **3.00**
Circ: CapCity orders: **4,350**
5 ❑ Sep 1995 Cover: 2.95 **NM** value: **3.00**
Circ: CapCity orders: **4,225**
6 ❑ Oct 1995 Cover: 2.95 **NM** value: **3.00**
7 ❑ Nov 1995 Cover: 2.95 **NM** value: **3.00**
8 ❑ Dec 1995 Cover: 2.95 **NM** value: **3.00**
9 ❑ Jan 1996 Cover: 2.95 **NM** value: **3.00**
10 ❑ Feb 1996 Cover: 2.95 **NM** value: **3.00**
Bk 1❑ Oct 1996 Cover: 12.95 **NM** value: **Cover or less**
Bonnie and Clyde • Bonnie and Clyde; collects Gunsmith Cats #1-6 **A:** Kenichi Sonoda **W:** Kenichi Sonoda
Bk 2❑ Oct 1996 Cover: 12.95 **NM** value: **Cover or less**
• Misfire; collects Gunsmith Cats #7-10 and Gunsmith Cats: The Return of Gray #1-3

GUNSMITH CATS: BAD TRIP — Dark Horse / Manga

1 ❑ Jun 1998 Cover: 2.95 **NM** value: **Cover or less**
Psychedelic **A:** Kenichi Sonoda **W:** Kenichi Sonoda
2 ❑ Jun 1998 Cover: 2.95 **NM** value: **Cover or less**
Circ: Diamd. preorders: **11,621**
3 ❑ Aug 1998 Cover: 2.95 **NM** value: **Cover or less**
Circ: Diamd. preorders: **11,273**
Hammer Release **A:** Kenichi Sonoda **W:** Kenichi Sonoda
4 ❑ Sep 1998 Cover: 2.95 **NM** value: **Cover or less**
Circ: Diamd. preorders: **11,300**
Poison of the Scorpion **A:** Kenichi Sonoda **W:** Kenichi Sonoda
5 ❑ Oct 1998 Cover: 2.95 **NM** value: **Cover or less**
Circ: Diamd. preorders: **11,169**
Lost Game **A:** Kenichi Sonoda **W:** Kenichi Sonoda
6 ❑ Nov 1998 Cover: 2.95 **NM** value: **Cover or less**
Circ: Diamd. preorders: **10,954**
Cool Down **A:** Kenichi Sonoda **W:** Kenichi Sonoda

GUNSMITH CATS: BEAN BANDIT — Dark Horse / Manga

1 ❑ Jan 1999 Cover: 2.95 **NM** value: **Cover or less**
Circ: Diamd. preorders: **11,540**
Rolling Bean **A:** Kenichi Sonoda **W:** Kenichi Sonoda
2 ❑ Feb 1999 Cover: 2.95 **NM** value: **Cover or less**
Circ: Diamd. preorders: **10,493**
Sleeper **A:** Kenichi Sonoda **W:** Kenichi Sonoda
3 ❑ Mar 1999 Cover: 2.95 **NM** value: **Cover or less**
Circ: Diamd. preorders: **10,523**
V26 **A:** Kenichi Sonoda **W:** Kenichi Sonoda
4 ❑ Apr 1999 Cover: 2.95 **NM** value: **Cover or less**
Circ: Diamd. preorders: **10,890**
Hot Motor **A:** Kenichi Sonoda **W:** Kenichi Sonoda
5 ❑ May 1999 Cover: 2.95 **NM** value: **Cover or less**
Circ: Diamd. preorders: **10,235**
6 ❑ Jun 1999 Cover: 2.95 **NM** value: **Cover or less**
Circ: Diamd. preorders: **10,733**
7 ❑ Jul 1999 Cover: 2.95 **NM** value: **Cover or less**
Circ: Diamd. preorders: **10,760**
8 ❑ Aug 1999 Cover: 2.95 **NM** value: **Cover or less**
Circ: Diamd. preorders: **10,548**
Crossfire **A:** Kenichi Sonoda **W:** Kenichi Sonoda
9 ❑ Sep 1999 Cover: 2.95 **NM** value: **Cover or less**
Circ: Diamd. preorders: **10,286**
Game, Set... **A:** Kenichi Sonoda **W:** Kenichi Sonoda

GUNSMITH CATS: GOLDIE VS. MISTY — Dark Horse / Manga

1 ❑ Nov 1997 Cover: 2.95 **NM** value: **Cover or less**
Circ: Diamd. preorders: **14,061**
Misty Brown... **A:** Kenichi Sonoda **W:** Kenichi Sonoda
2 ❑ Dec 1997 Cover: 2.95 **NM** value: **Cover or less**
Circ: Diamd. preorders: **13,033**
...Decoy **A:** Kenichi Sonoda **W:** Kenichi Sonoda
3 ❑ Jan 1998 Cover: 2.95 **NM** value: **Cover or less**
Circ: Diamd. preorders: **12,595**
...Handicap **A:** Kenichi Sonoda **W:** Kenichi Sonoda
4 ❑ Feb 1998 Cover: 2.95 **NM** value: **Cover or less**
Circ: Diamd. preorders: **11,969**
...Fast Burning **A:** Kenichi Sonoda **W:** Kenichi Sonoda
5 ❑ Mar 1998 Cover: 2.95 **NM** value: **Cover or less**
Circ: Diamd. preorders: **12,142**
...Minnie May **A:** Kenichi Sonoda **W:** Kenichi Sonoda
6 ❑ Apr 1998 Cover: 2.95 **NM** value: **Cover or less**
Circ: Diamd. preorders: **13,392**
...Injection **A:** Kenichi Sonoda **W:** Kenichi Sonoda
7 ❑ May 1998 Cover: 2.95 **NM** value: **Cover or less**
Circ: Diamd. preorders: **11,865**
...Bad Trip **A:** Kenichi Sonoda **W:** Kenichi Sonoda

GUNSMITH CATS: KIDNAPPED — Dark Horse / Manga

1 ❑ Nov 1999 Cover: 2.95 **NM** value: **Cover or less**
Circ: Diamd. preorders: **10,863**
2 ❑ Dec 1999 Cover: 2.95 **NM** value: **Cover or less**
Circ: Diamd. preorders: **11,064**
3 ❑ Jan 2000 Cover: 2.95 **NM** value: **Cover or less**
Circ: Diamd. preorders: **10,053**
Long Night **A:** Kenichi Sonoda **W:** Kenichi Sonoda
4 ❑ Feb 2000 Cover: 2.95 **NM** value: **Cover or less**
Circ: Diamd. preorders: **9,473**
5 ❑ Mar 2000 Cover: 2.95 **NM** value: **Cover or less**
Circ: Diamd. preorders: **9,646**
6 ❑ Apr 2000 Cover: 2.95 **NM** value: **Cover or less**
Circ: Diamd. preorders: **9,486**
7 ❑ May 2000 Cover: 2.95 **NM** value: **Cover or less**
Circ: Diamd. preorders: **9,606**
Bloody Rally **A:** Kenichi Sonoda **W:** Kenichi Sonoda
8 ❑ Jun 2000 Cover: 2.95 **NM** value: **Cover or less**
Circ: Diamd. preorders: **9,658**
9mm vs. 40mm **A:** Kenichi Sonoda **W:** Kenichi Sonoda
9 ❑ Jul 2000 Cover: 2.95 **NM** value: **Cover or less**
Circ: Diamd. preorders: **9,590**
Family **A:** Kenichi Sonoda **W:** Kenichi Sonoda
10 ❑ Aug 2000 Cover: 2.95 **NM** value: **Cover or less**
Circ: Diamd. preorders: **9,046**
Home Sweet Home **A:** Kenichi Sonoda **W:** Kenichi Sonoda

GUNSMITH CATS: MISTER V — Dark Horse / Manga

1 ❑ Oct 2000 Cover: 3.50 **NM** value: **Cover or less**
Circ: Diamd. preorders: **9,549**
Goldie...Again **A:** Kenichi Sonoda **W:** Kenichi Sonoda
2 ❑ Nov 2000 Cover: 3.50 **NM** value: **Cover or less**
Circ: Diamd. preorders: **9,013**
Breakthrough **A:** Kenichi Sonoda **W:** Kenichi Sonoda
3 ❑ Dec 2000 Cover: 3.50 **NM** value: **Cover or less**
Circ: Diamd. preorders: **8,797**
Father **A:** Kenichi Sonoda **W:** Kenichi Sonoda
4 ❑ Jan 2001 Cover: 3.50 **NM** value: **Cover or less**
Circ: Diamd. preorders: **8,487**
Last Night **A:** Kenichi Sonoda **W:** Kenichi Sonoda
5 ❑ Feb 2001 Cover: 3.50 **NM** value: **Cover or less**
Circ: Diamd. preorders: **8,360**
Daddy's 12-Gauge **A:** Kenichi Sonoda **W:** Kenichi Sonoda
6 ❑ Mar 2001 Cover: 3.50 **NM** value: **Cover or less**
Circ: Diamd. preorders: **8,263**
Smokin' High **A:** Kenichi Sonoda **W:** Kenichi Sonoda
7 ❑ Apr 2001 Cover: 3.50 **NM** value: **Cover or less**
Circ: Diamd. preorders: **8,258**
Guns n' Doses **A:** Kenichi Sonoda **W:** Kenichi Sonoda
8 ❑ May 2001 Cover: 3.50 **NM** value: **Cover or less**
Circ: Diamd. preorders: **8,116**
9 ❑ Jun 2001 Cover: 3.50 **NM** value: **Cover or less**
Circ: Diamd. preorders: **8,199**
10 ❑ Jul 2001 Cover: 3.50 **NM** value: **Cover or less**
Circ: Diamd. preorders: **8,442**
11 ❑ Aug 2001 Cover: 3.50 **NM** value: **Cover or less**
Circ: Diamd. preorders: **8,555**

GUNSMITH CATS: SHADES OF GRAY — Dark Horse / Manga

1 ❑ May 1997 Cover: 2.95 **NM** value: **Cover or less**
Circ: Diamd. preorders: **15,354**
Hammerless **A:** Kenichi Sonoda **W:** Kenichi Sonoda
2 ❑ Jun 1997 Cover: 2.95 **NM** value: **Cover or less**
Circ: Diamd. preorders: **13,343**
Big Game **A:** Kenichi Sonoda **W:** Kenichi Sonoda
3 ❑ Jul 1997 Cover: 2.95 **NM** value: **Cover or less**
Circ: Diamd. preorders: **13,261**
SIG-SG550 **A:** Kenichi Sonoda **W:** Kenichi Sonoda
4 ❑ Aug 1997 Cover: 2.95 **NM** value: **Cover or less**
Circ: Diamd. preorders: **13,026**
Lost **A:** Kenichi Sonoda **W:** Kenichi Sonoda
5 ❑ Sep 1997 Cover: 2.95 **NM** value: **Cover or less**
Circ: Diamd. preorders: **13,398**
Slide Stop **A:** Kenichi Sonoda **W:** Kenichi Sonoda
Bk 1❑ Cover: 12.95 **NM** value: **Cover or less**
• Misfire trade paperback **A:** Kenichi Sonoda **W:** Kenichi Sonoda

GUNSMITH CATS: THE RETURN OF GRAY — Dark Horse / Manga

1 ❑ Aug 1996 Cover: 2.95 **NM** value: **Cover or less**
Magnum Primer **A:** Kenichi Sonoda **W:** Kenichi Sonoda
2 ❑ Sep 1996 Cover: 2.95 **NM** value: **Cover or less**
Circ: Diamd. preorders: **12,839**
Sight-In, Part 1 **A:** Kenichi Sonoda **W:** Kenichi Sonoda
3 ❑ Oct 1996 Cover: 2.95 **NM** value: **Cover or less**
Circ: Diamd. preorders: **12,693**
Sight-In, Part 2 **A:** Kenichi Sonoda **W:** Kenichi Sonoda
4 ❑ Nov 1996 Cover: 2.95 **NM** value: **Cover or less**
Circ: Diamd. preorders: **12,382**
Hard Touch **A:** Kenichi Sonoda **W:** Kenichi Sonoda
5 ❑ Dec 1996 Cover: 2.95 **NM** value: **Cover or less**
Circ: Diamd. preorders: **12,074**
Wood Bullet **A:** Kenichi Sonoda **W:** Kenichi Sonoda
6 ❑ Jan 1997 Cover: 2.95 **NM** value: **Cover or less**
Circ: Diamd. preorders: **11,961**
7 ❑ Feb 1997 Cover: 2.95 **NM** value: **Cover or less**
Circ: Diamd. preorders: **12,137**
Bean Bandit **A:** Kenichi Sonoda **W:** Kenichi Sonoda
Bk 1❑ Apr 1998, b&w Cover: 17.95 **NM** value: **Cover or less**
• Collects Gunsmith Cats: The Return of Gray **A:** Kenichi Sonoda **W:** Kenichi Sonoda

GUNSMOKE WESTERN — Marvel

75 ❑ Mar 1963 Cover: 0.12 **NM** value: **20.00**
• Has 1962 Statement, filed 10/1/1962; avg total paid circ 126,475

GUNSMOKE (DELL) — Dell

Dell was famous for its licensed comics based on movie and TV properties from the 1940s through the 1960s, a practice continued by Gold Key.

Gunsmoke began its run as a radio series in 1952 starring William Conrad as Matt Dillon. That series ran until 1961, while the TV series began in 1955 and ran 20 years on CBS, making it the longest-running prime-time television show. While John Wayne had been approached to play the role, he turned it down and tall, lanky James Arness took on the part of U.S. Marshal Dillon ahead of the cameras.

The Western adventures were set in and around Dodge City, Kansas, in the late 1800s and often involved Dillon bringing some lawbreaker to justice or righting a wrong that was a veiled reference to a social ill of the modern-day. The comics series began in Dell's Four Color run for five tryout issues before being rewarded its own series that ran another 22 in the late 1950s. Gold Key published a shorter run in 1969 and 1970. — Brent

GUNSMOKE (GOLD KEY) — Gold Key

1 ❑ Feb 1969 Cover: 0.15 **NM** value: **Cover or less**
2 ❑ Apr 1969 Cover: 0.15 **NM** value: **Cover or less**
3 ❑ Jun 1969 Cover: 0.15 **NM** value: **Cover or less**
4 ❑ Aug 1969 Cover: 0.15 **NM** value: **Cover or less**
5 ❑ Nov 1969 Cover: 0.15 **NM** value: **Cover or less**
6 ❑ Feb 1970 Cover: 0.15 **NM** value: **Cover or less**

GUNS OF SHAR-PEI — Caliber

1 ❑ b&w Cover: 2.95 **NM** value: **Cover or less**
2 ❑ b&w Cover: 2.95 **NM** value: **Cover or less**
3 ❑ b&w Cover: 2.95 **NM** value: **Cover or less**

GUNS OF THE DRAGON — DC

1 ❑ Oct 1998 Cover: 2.50 **NM** value: **Cover or less**
Circ: Diamd. preorders: **15,687**
Dragon Island **A:** Tim Truman **W:** Tim Truman
2 ❑ Nov 1998 Cover: 2.50 **NM** value: **Cover or less**
Circ: Diamd. preorders: **12,521**

CGC-graded: Multiply prices above by **33 for 9.9 M • 16 for 9.8 NM/M • 7 for 9.6 NM+ • 5 for 9.4 NM • 2.5 for 9.2 NM- • 1.5 for 9.0 VF/NM**

3 ❑ Dec 1998 Cover: 2.50 **NM** value: **Cover or less**
Circ: Diamd. preorders: **10,548**
4 ❑ Jan 1999 Cover: 2.50 **NM** value: **Cover or less**
Circ: Diamd. preorders: **10,153**

GUN THAT WON THE WEST, THE — Winchester

1 ❑ **NM** value: **22.00**
• giveaway.

GUSTAV P.I. — NBM

1 ❑ Cover: 9.95 **NM** value: **Cover or less**
cardstock cover. • Oversized. **A:** Ken Meyer Jr. **W:** Malcolm Bourne

GUTWALLOW — Numbskull

1 ❑ Feb 1998, b&w Cover: 2.95 **NM** value: **Cover or less**

GUY GARDNER — DC

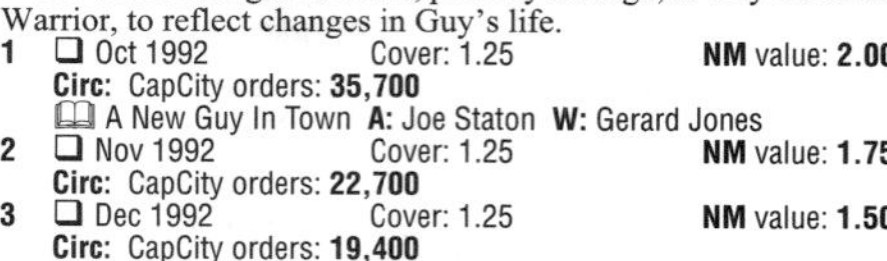

This is one crass, brash, annoying Guy.

Guy Gardner first appeared in 1968's Green Lantern #59. Even then, it seemed unbelievable that this despicable, self-serving opportunist could ever have been chosen by the Green Lantern Corps to become a Green Lantern. But of course, that's exactly what happened.

Although he was a founding member of the new Justice League, Guy retains a habit of rubbing his compatriots the wrong way. Perhaps it's all for the best that he now stars in a series of his own. Armed with Sinestro's power ring, he's got all of Green Lantern's power, but without the weakness to the color yellow that had traditionally plagued his emerald counterpart.

The series changes its name, partway through, to Guy Gardner, Warrior, to reflect changes in Guy's life.

1 ❑ Oct 1992 Cover: 1.25 **NM** value: **2.00**
Circ: CapCity orders: **35,700**
A New Guy In Town **A:** Joe Staton **W:** Gerard Jones
2 ❑ Nov 1992 Cover: 1.25 **NM** value: **1.75**
Circ: CapCity orders: **22,700**
3 ❑ Dec 1992 Cover: 1.25 **NM** value: **1.50**
Circ: CapCity orders: **19,400**
4 ❑ Jan 1993 Cover: 1.25 **NM** value: **1.50**
Circ: CapCity orders: **17,800**
5 ❑ Feb 1993 Cover: 1.25 **NM** value: **1.50**
Circ: CapCity orders: **16,950**
6 ❑ Mar 1993 Cover: 1.25 **NM** value: **Cover or less**
Circ: CapCity orders: **14,800**
Two for the Seesaw **A:** Joe Staton **W:** Will Jacobs; Gerard Jones
7 ❑ Apr 1993 Cover: 1.25 **NM** value: **Cover or less**
Circ: CapCity orders: **14,600**
Mexicali Gold **A:** Joe Staton **W:** Will Jacobs; Gerard Jones
8 ❑ May 1993 Cover: 1.25 **NM** value: **Cover or less**
Circ: CapCity orders: **15,350**
The Lord of the Ring **A:** Joe Staton **W:** Will Jacobs; Gerard Jones
9 ❑ Jun 1993 Cover: 1.25 **NM** value: **Cover or less**
Circ: CapCity orders: **12,650**
The Medusa Plague **A:** Joe Staton **W:** Will Jacobs
10 ❑ Jul 1993 Cover: 1.25 **NM** value: **Cover or less**
Circ: CapCity orders: **11,600**
Manifest Destiny **A:** Joe Staton **W:** Will Jacobs
11 ❑ Aug 1993 Cover: 1.25 **NM** value: **Cover or less**
Circ: CapCity orders: **12,150**
Yesterday's Sins, Part 1 **A:** Joe Staton **W:** Chuck Dixon
12 ❑ Sep 1993 Cover: 1.25 **NM** value: **Cover or less**
Circ: CapCity orders: **10,650**
Dream a Deadly Dream **A:** Joe Staton **W:** Chuck Dixon
13 ❑ Oct 1993 Cover: 1.25 **NM** value: **Cover or less**
Circ: CapCity orders: **10,050**
14 ❑ Nov 1993 Cover: 1.25 **NM** value: **Cover or less**
Circ: CapCity orders: **10,150**
15 ❑ Dec 1993 Cover: 1.50 **NM** value: **Cover or less**
Circ: CapCity orders: **9,650**
Collateral Damage **A:** Chris Hunter **W:** Chuck Dixon
16 ❑ Jan 1994 Cover: 1.50 **NM** value: **Cover or less**
Circ: CapCity orders: **8,950**
Total Warfare • Series continued in Guy Gardner: Warrior #17 **A:** Mark Tenney **W:** Chuck Dixon

GUY GARDNER REBORN — DC

1 ❑ ca. 1992 Cover: 4.95 **NM** value: **Cover or less**
Circ: CapCity orders: **25,050**
2 ❑ ca. 1992 Cover: 4.95 **NM** value: **Cover or less**
Circ: CapCity orders: **21,850**
3 ❑ ca. 1992 Cover: 4.95 **NM** value: **Cover or less**
Circ: CapCity orders: **17,000**

GUY GARDNER: WARRIOR — DC

0 ❑ Oct 1994 Cover: 1.50 **NM** value: **1.75**
Circ: CapCity orders: **19,850**
17 ❑ Feb 1994 Cover: 1.50 **NM** value: **Cover or less**
Circ: CapCity orders: **9,100**
Warrior Road • Title changes to Guy Gardner: Warrior; Series continued from Guy Gardner #16 **A:** Mitch Byrd **W:** Chuck Dixon
18 ❑ Mar 1994 Cover: 1.50 **NM** value: **Cover or less**
Circ: CapCity orders: **8,850** • **CGC:** 1 graded, best 9.2
19 ❑ Apr 1994 Cover: 1.50 **NM** value: **Cover or less**
Circ: CapCity orders: **8,300**
20 ❑ May 1994 Cover: 1.50 **NM** value: **Cover or less**
Circ: CapCity orders: **11,350**
21 ❑ Jun 1994 Cover: 1.50 **NM** value: **Cover or less**
Circ: CapCity orders: **15,150**
Emerald Fallout, Part 4 ★ Versus Parallax.
22 ❑ Jul 1994 Cover: 1.50 **NM** value: **Cover or less**
Circ: CapCity orders: **11,650**
23 ❑ Aug 1994 Cover: 1.50 **NM** value: **Cover or less**
Circ: CapCity orders: **11,550**
24 ❑ Sep 1994 Cover: 1.50 **NM** value: **Cover or less**
Circ: CapCity orders: **17,250**
• Zero Hour
25 ❑ Nov 1994 Cover: 2.50 **NM** value: **Cover or less**
Circ: CapCity orders: **12,400**
• Giant-size.
26 ❑ Dec 1994 Cover: 1.50 **NM** value: **Cover or less**
Circ: CapCity orders: **12,400**
27 ❑ Jan 1995 Cover: 1.50 **NM** value: **Cover or less**
Circ: CapCity orders: **12,100**
28 ❑ Feb 1995 Cover: 1.50 **NM** value: **Cover or less**
Circ: CapCity orders: **12,200**
Capital Punishment, Part 2
29 ❑ Mar 1995 Cover: 1.50 **NM** value: **Cover or less**
• Giant-size.
29/SC❑ May 1995 Cover: 2.95 **NM** value: **Cover or less**
Circ: CapCity orders: **11,850**
enhanced foldout cover. • Giant-size.
30 ❑ Apr 1995 Cover: 1.50 **NM** value: **Cover or less**
Circ: CapCity orders: **11,175**
31 ❑ Jun 1995 Cover: 1.75 **NM** value: **Cover or less**
Circ: CapCity orders: **10,025**
32 ❑ Jul 1995 Cover: 1.75 **NM** value: **Cover or less**
Circ: CapCity orders: **10,825**
33 ❑ Aug 1995 Cover: 1.75 **NM** value: **Cover or less**
Circ: CapCity orders: **10,525**
34 ❑ Sep 1995 Cover: 1.75 **NM** value: **Cover or less**
Circ: CapCity orders: **9,925**
The Way of The Warrior, Part 7
35 ❑ Oct 1995 Cover: 1.75 **NM** value: **Cover or less**
Circ: CapCity orders: **7,975**
36 ❑ Nov 1995 Cover: 1.75 **NM** value: **Cover or less**
Underworld Unleashed • Underworld Unleashed
37 ❑ Dec 1995 Cover: 1.75 **NM** value: **Cover or less**
• Underworld Unleashed
38 ❑ Jan 1996 Cover: 1.75 **NM** value: **Cover or less**
39 ❑ Feb 1996 Cover: 1.75 **NM** value: **Cover or less**
Merriment, Mistletoe, and Mayhem! • Christmas party at Warriors **A:** Marc Campos **W:** Beau Smith
40 ❑ Mar 1996 Cover: 1.75 **NM** value: **Cover or less**
Good Things Ain't Been Comin' in The Packages I've Been Getting' **A:** Aaron Lopresti **W:** Beau Smith
41 ❑ Apr 1996 Cover: 1.75 **NM** value: **Cover or less**
Guys & Babes in Toyland **A:** Marc Campos **W:** Beau Smith
42 ❑ May 1996 Cover: 1.75 **NM** value: **Cover or less**
• Guy becomes a woman
43 ❑ Jun 1996 Cover: 1.75 **NM** value: **Cover or less**
44 ❑ Jul 1996 Cover: 1.75 **NM** value: **Cover or less**
A Warrior's Passing, Part 2 final issue. ★ Versus Major Force.
Anl 1❑ ca. 1995 Cover: 3.50 **NM** value: **Cover or less**
Circ: CapCity orders: **8,800**
• Year One; 1995 Annual
Anl 2❑ ca. 1996 Cover: 2.95 **NM** value: **Cover or less**
• Legends of the Dead Earth; 1996 Annual

GUY PUMPKINHEAD — Saint Gray

1 ❑ Cover: 2.50 **NM** value: **Cover or less**

GUZZI LEMANS — Antarctic

1 ❑ Aug 1996, b&w Cover: 2.95 **NM** value: **Cover or less**
2 ❑ Oct 1996, b&w Cover: 2.95 **NM** value: **Cover or less**
final issue. **A:** Jim Lawson **W:** Jim Lawson

GYRE — Abaculus

1 ❑ Dec 1997, b&w Cover: 2.95 **NM** value: **3.50**
Soul Keeper, Part 1 **A:** Marc Laming **W:** Martin Shipp
2 ❑ Feb 1998, b&w Cover: 2.95 **NM** value: **Cover or less**
Soul Keeper, Part 2; Six Degrees: The Five Giants, Part 6 **A:** Marc Laming; John Welding **W:** Martin Shipp
3 ❑ Apr 1998 Cover: 2.95 **NM** value: **Cover or less**
Soul Keeper, Part 3; Six Degrees: The Five Giants, Part 7 **A:** Marc Laming **W:** Martin Shipp
Ash 1❑ **NM** value: **0.50**
• Preview of Gyre #1 **A:** Marc Laming **W:** Martin Shipp
SE 1❑ Cover: 4.50 **NM** value: **Cover or less**
Head Count; Dead Babies; Traditions & Interruptions **A:** Marc Laming **W:** Martin Shipp

GYRE: TRADITIONS & INTERRUPTIONS — Abaculus

1 ❑ b&w Cover: 0.99 **NM** value: **1.00**
No issue number. • Promotional book for series **A:** Marc Laming **W:** Martin Shipp

GYRO COMICS — Rip Off

1 ❑ ca. 1988, b&w Cover: 2.00 **NM** value: **Cover or less**
2 ❑ ca. 1988, b&w Cover: 2.00 **NM** value: **Cover or less**
3 ❑ ca. 1988, b&w Cover: 2.00 **NM** value: **Cover or less**

Diamond preorders are the estimated number of comics sold, prior to their release, to comics shops in North America by Diamond Comic Distributors, the largest distributor. These figures underreport the actual number of circulating copies by the amount of reorders Diamond took (usually 5-10% again of the preorders) and sales by publishers to newsstand and bookstore distributors. For many independent publishers, Diamond's preorders may be quite close to the actual number of copies in circulation.

HACKER FILES, THE — DC

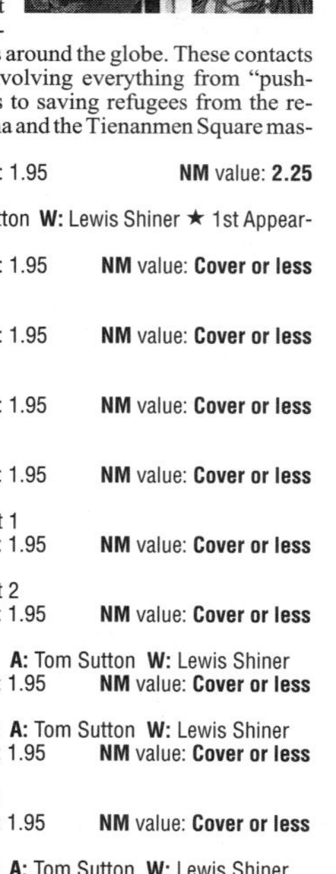

Computers brought with them the prospect for revolution — revolution in information, that most important of all sources of power. Business, the military, and governments sought to use computers for their own ends. But for "hackers" like Jack Marshall, the only true safety lay in distributing their power as widely as possible.

Marshall is an anarchist — or at least someone who doesn't trust those in power to use it for the best. His own way of rebelling is to break into computer systems. This has made him some powerful enemies, but it has also put him in contact with a sort of "digital underground" of freethinkers around the globe. These contacts have led Jack on adventures involving everything from "push-button war" among the generals to saving refugees from the repressive government of Red China and the Tienanmen Square massacre of 1989.

1 ❑ Aug 1992 Cover: 1.95 **NM** value: **2.25**
Circ: CapCity orders: **9,550**
Soft War, Part 1 **A:** Tom Sutton **W:** Lewis Shiner ★ 1st Appearance of Jack Marshall.
2 ❑ Sep 1992 Cover: 1.95 **NM** value: **Cover or less**
Circ: CapCity orders: **7,000**
Soft War, Part 2
3 ❑ Oct 1992 Cover: 1.95 **NM** value: **Cover or less**
Circ: CapCity orders: **6,500**
Soft War, Part 3
4 ❑ Nov 1992 Cover: 1.95 **NM** value: **Cover or less**
Circ: CapCity orders: **6,250**
Soft War, Part 4
5 ❑ Dec 1992 Cover: 1.95 **NM** value: **Cover or less**
Circ: CapCity orders: **5,800**
Operation: Moonwitch, Part 1
6 ❑ Jan 1993 Cover: 1.95 **NM** value: **Cover or less**
Circ: CapCity orders: **5,750**
Operation: Moonwitch, Part 2
7 ❑ Feb 1993 Cover: 1.95 **NM** value: **Cover or less**
Circ: CapCity orders: **5,900**
Working Class Hero, Part 1 **A:** Tom Sutton **W:** Lewis Shiner
8 ❑ Mar 1993 Cover: 1.95 **NM** value: **Cover or less**
Circ: CapCity orders: **5,600**
Working Class Hero, Part 2 **A:** Tom Sutton **W:** Lewis Shiner
9 ❑ Apr 1993 Cover: 1.95 **NM** value: **Cover or less**
Circ: CapCity orders: **5,650**
Working Class Hero, Part 3
10 ❑ May 1993 Cover: 1.95 **NM** value: **Cover or less**
Circ: CapCity orders: **5,450**
Working Class Hero, Part 4 **A:** Tom Sutton **W:** Lewis Shiner
11 ❑ Jun 1993 Cover: 1.95 **NM** value: **Cover or less**
Circ: CapCity orders: **5,550**
12 ❑ Jul 1993 Cover: 1.95 **NM** value: **Cover or less**
Circ: CapCity orders: **5,050**

HACKMASTERS OF EVERKNIGHT — Kenzer and Company

1 ❑ May 2000 Cover: 2.95 **NM** value: **Cover or less**
2 ❑ Jul 2000 Cover: 2.95 **NM** value: **Cover or less**
3 ❑ Sep 2000 Cover: 2.95 **NM** value: **Cover or less**
4 ❑ Nov 2000 Cover: 2.95 **NM** value: **Cover or less**
5 ❑ Jan 2001 Cover: 2.95 **NM** value: **Cover or less**
6 ❑ Mar 2001 Cover: 2.95 **NM** value: **Cover or less**
7 ❑ May 2001 Cover: 2.95 **NM** value: **Cover or less**
8 ❑ Jul 2001 Cover: 2.95 **NM** value: **Cover or less**

HÄGAR THE HORRIBLE — Avalon

0 ❑ Cover: 2.00 **NM** value: **Cover or less**
A change of Luck; Too Pooped to Plunder (Text Story); Home isThe Hero; The Impulsive Imps

HA HA COMICS — ACG

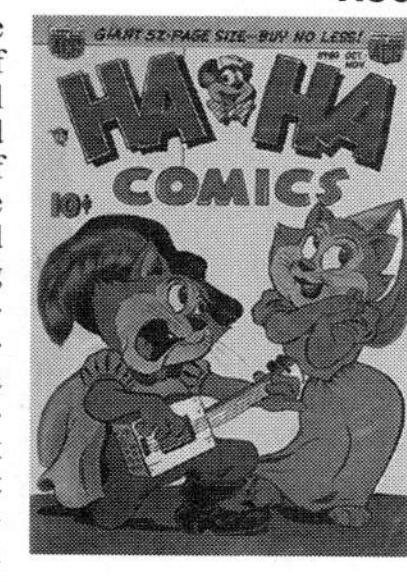

Ha Ha Comics is another in the seemingly endless assortment of undistinguished funny-animal comics that brought cheer and good-natured gags to the lives of kids during the Golden Age. The mainstays in Ha Ha were: Izzy and Dizzy, a pair of twin troublemaking mice; the Impulsive Imps, who cavort around an Alice-in-Wonderland fantasy world; Robespier, a scrappy alley cat; and Daniel Spaniel, who leads a dog's life in the back pages of the comic book. The cast provides satisfactory laughs and entertainment in typical funny-animal style, benefiting from competent drawing and big, bold colorful layouts.

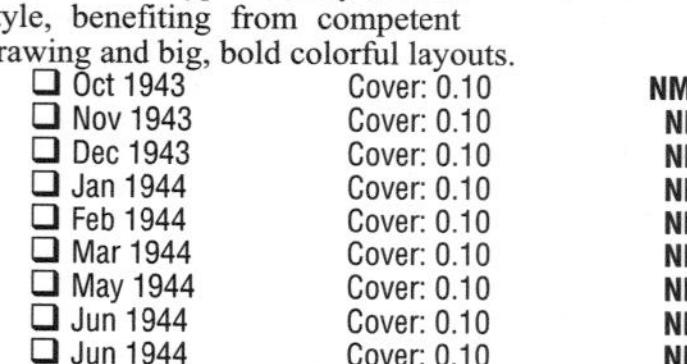

1 ❑ Oct 1943 Cover: 0.10 **NM** value: **150.00**
2 ❑ Nov 1943 Cover: 0.10 **NM** value: **85.00**
3 ❑ Dec 1943 Cover: 0.10 **NM** value: **65.00**
4 ❑ Jan 1944 Cover: 0.10 **NM** value: **60.00**
5 ❑ Feb 1944 Cover: 0.10 **NM** value: **60.00**
6 ❑ Mar 1944 Cover: 0.10 **NM** value: **45.00**
7 ❑ May 1944 Cover: 0.10 **NM** value: **45.00**
8 ❑ Jun 1944 Cover: 0.10 **NM** value: **45.00**
9 ❑ Jun 1944 Cover: 0.10 **NM** value: **45.00**

Other grades: Multiply prices above by **1.5 for Mint • 2/3 for Very Fine • 1/3 for Fine • 1/5 for Very Good • 1/8 for Good**

10 ❑ Jul 1944 Cover: 0.10 **NM** value: **45.00**
11 ❑ Aug 1944 Cover: 0.10 **NM** value: **35.00**
12 ❑ Sep 1944 Cover: 0.10 **NM** value: **35.00**
13 ❑ Oct 1944 Cover: 0.10 **NM** value: **35.00**
14 ❑ Nov 1944 Cover: 0.10 **NM** value: **35.00**
15 ❑ Dec 1944 Cover: 0.10 **NM** value: **35.00**
16 ❑ Jan 1945 Cover: 0.10 **NM** value: **35.00**
17 ❑ Feb 1945 Cover: 0.10 **NM** value: **35.00**
18 ❑ 1945 Cover: 0.10 **NM** value: **35.00**
19 ❑ 1945 Cover: 0.10 **NM** value: **35.00**
20 ❑ 1945 Cover: 0.10 **NM** value: **35.00**
21 ❑ 1945 Cover: 0.10 **NM** value: **28.00**
22 ❑ 1945 Cover: 0.10 **NM** value: **28.00**
23 ❑ Nov 1945 Cover: 0.10 **NM** value: **28.00**
24 ❑ Dec 1945 Cover: 0.10 **NM** value: **28.00**
25 ❑ Jan 1946 Cover: 0.10 **NM** value: **28.00**
26 ❑ Feb 1946 Cover: 0.10 **NM** value: **28.00**
27 ❑ Mar 1946 Cover: 0.10 **NM** value: **28.00**
28 ❑ Apr 1946 Cover: 0.10 **NM** value: **28.00**
29 ❑ May 1946 Cover: 0.10 **NM** value: **28.00**
30 ❑ Jun 1946 Cover: 0.10 **NM** value: **28.00**
31 ❑ Jul 1946 Cover: 0.10 **NM** value: **24.00**
32 ❑ Aug 1946 Cover: 0.10 **NM** value: **24.00**
33 ❑ Sep 1946 Cover: 0.10 **NM** value: **24.00**
34 ❑ Oct 1946 Cover: 0.10 **NM** value: **24.00**
35 ❑ Nov 1946 Cover: 0.10 **NM** value: **24.00**
36 ❑ Dec 1946 Cover: 0.10 **NM** value: **24.00**
📖 Izzy and Dizzy; The Old Top (text story); Hortense; Robespier; The Gobbler's Story (text story); Grabbit O'Rabbit vs. Homer Hound; The Little Burro (text story); Daniel Spaniel; Eek and Zeek; Punch **A:** Ken Hultgren; Bob Wick **W:** Ken Hultgren; Bob Wick
37 ❑ Jan 1947 Cover: 0.10 **NM** value: **24.00**
38 ❑ Feb 1947 Cover: 0.10 **NM** value: **24.00**
39 ❑ Mar 1947 Cover: 0.10 **NM** value: **24.00**
40 ❑ Apr 1947 Cover: 0.10 **NM** value: **24.00**
41 ❑ May 1947 Cover: 0.10 **NM** value: **20.00**
42 ❑ Jun 1947 Cover: 0.10 **NM** value: **20.00**
43 ❑ Jul 1947 Cover: 0.10 **NM** value: **20.00**
44 ❑ Aug 1947 Cover: 0.10 **NM** value: **20.00**
45 ❑ Sep 1947 Cover: 0.10 **NM** value: **20.00**
46 ❑ Oct 1947 Cover: 0.10 **NM** value: **20.00**
47 ❑ Nov 1947 Cover: 0.10 **NM** value: **20.00**
48 ❑ Dec 1947 Cover: 0.10 **NM** value: **20.00**
49 ❑ Jan 1948 Cover: 0.10 **NM** value: **20.00**
50 ❑ Feb 1948 Cover: 0.10 **NM** value: **20.00**
51 ❑ Mar 1948 Cover: 0.10 **NM** value: **18.00**
52 ❑ Apr 1948 Cover: 0.10 **NM** value: **18.00**
53 ❑ May 1948 Cover: 0.10 **NM** value: **18.00**
54 ❑ Jun 1948 Cover: 0.10 **NM** value: **18.00**
55 ❑ Jul 1948 Cover: 0.10 **NM** value: **18.00**
56 ❑ Aug 1948 Cover: 0.10 **NM** value: **18.00**
57 ❑ Sep 1948 Cover: 0.10 **NM** value: **18.00**
58 ❑ Oct 1948 Cover: 0.10 **NM** value: **18.00**
59 ❑ Nov 1948 Cover: 0.10 **NM** value: **18.00**
60 ❑ Dec 1948 Cover: 0.10 **NM** value: **18.00**
61 ❑ Jan 1949 Cover: 0.10 **NM** value: **18.00**
62 ❑ Feb 1949 Cover: 0.10 **NM** value: **18.00**
63 ❑ Mar 1949 Cover: 0.10 **NM** value: **18.00**
64 ❑ Apr 1949 Cover: 0.10 **NM** value: **18.00**
65 ❑ May 1949 Cover: 0.10 **NM** value: **18.00**
66 ❑ Jun 1949 Cover: 0.10 **NM** value: **18.00**
67 ❑ Aug 1949 Cover: 0.10 **NM** value: **18.00**
68 ❑ Oct 1949 Cover: 0.10 **NM** value: **18.00**
69 ❑ Dec 1949 Cover: 0.10 **NM** value: **18.00**
70 ❑ Feb 1950 Cover: 0.10 **NM** value: **18.00**
71 ❑ Apr 1950 Cover: 0.10 **NM** value: **16.00**
72 ❑ Jun 1950 Cover: 0.10 **NM** value: **16.00**
73 ❑ Aug 1950 Cover: 0.10 **NM** value: **16.00**
74 ❑ Oct 1950 Cover: 0.10 **NM** value: **16.00**
75 ❑ Dec 1950 Cover: 0.10 **NM** value: **16.00**
76 ❑ Feb 1951 Cover: 0.10 **NM** value: **16.00**
77 ❑ Apr 1951 Cover: 0.10 **NM** value: **16.00**
78 ❑ Jun 1951 Cover: 0.10 **NM** value: **16.00**
79 ❑ Aug 1951 Cover: 0.10 **NM** value: **16.00**
80 ❑ Oct 1951 Cover: 0.10 **NM** value: **16.00**
📖 The Rocking Horse That Ran Away
81 ❑ Dec 1951 Cover: 0.10 **NM** value: **16.00**
82 ❑ Feb 1952 Cover: 0.10 **NM** value: **16.00**
83 ❑ Apr 1952 Cover: 0.10 **NM** value: **16.00**
84 ❑ Jul 1952 Cover: 0.10 **NM** value: **16.00**
85 ❑ Sep 1952 Cover: 0.10 **NM** value: **16.00**
86 ❑ Nov 1952 Cover: 0.10 **NM** value: **16.00**
87 ❑ Jan 1953 Cover: 0.10 **NM** value: **16.00**
88 ❑ Mar 1953 Cover: 0.10 **NM** value: **16.00**
89 ❑ May 1953 Cover: 0.10 **NM** value: **16.00**
90 ❑ Jul 1953 Cover: 0.10 **NM** value: **16.00**
91 ❑ Sep 1953 Cover: 0.10 **NM** value: **13.00**
92 ❑ Nov 1953 Cover: 0.10 **NM** value: **13.00**
93 ❑ Jan 1954 Cover: 0.10 **NM** value: **13.00**
94 ❑ Mar 1954 Cover: 0.10 **NM** value: **13.00**
95 ❑ May 1954 Cover: 0.10 **NM** value: **13.00**
96 ❑ Jul 1954 Cover: 0.10 **NM** value: **13.00**
97 ❑ Sep 1954 Cover: 0.10 **NM** value: **13.00**
98 ❑ Nov 1954 Cover: 0.10 **NM** value: **13.00**
99 ❑ Jan 1955 Cover: 0.10 **NM** value: **55.00**
3D cover.

HAIRBAT — Screaming Rice

1 ❑ b&w Cover: 2.50 **NM** value: **Cover or less**
2 ❑ b&w Cover: 2.50 **NM** value: **Cover or less**
3 ❑ b&w Cover: 2.50 **NM** value: **Cover or less**

HAIRBAT (VOL. 2) — Slave Labor

1 ❑ Jul 1995 Cover: 2.95 **NM** value: **Cover or less**

HAIR BEAR BUNCH, THE — Gold Key

Visualize, if you will, Yogi and Boo-Boo. Now make them hippies.

If you're still here, you may be able to wrap your brain around one of the odder funny-animal cartoon series from Hanna-Barbera, which Gold Key adapted in a short-running series. Hair Bair and his buddies live in the zoo, have frizzy hair, and dress like slobs — and escape into the outside world every so often to have hip adventures.

Incredibly dated when it was on the air, Hair Bear is a little more palatable in comics form, even if his adventures do seem to be interchangeable with those of several other ongoing Gold Key adaptations at the time. — JJM

1 ❑ Feb 1972 Cover: 0.15 **NM** value: **12.00**
• **CGC:** 1 graded, best 9.4
2 ❑ May 1972 Cover: 0.15 **NM** value: **7.00**
3 ❑ Aug 1972 Cover: 0.15 **NM** value: **7.00**
4 ❑ Nov 1972 Cover: 0.15 **NM** value: **7.00**
5 ❑ Feb 1973 Cover: 0.15 **NM** value: **7.00**
6 ❑ May 1973 Cover: 0.15 **NM** value: **5.00**
7 ❑ Aug 1973 Cover: 0.15 **NM** value: **5.00**
8 ❑ Nov 1973 Cover: 0.15 **NM** value: **5.00**
9 ❑ Feb 1974 Cover: 0.15 **NM** value: **5.00**
• **CGC:** 1 graded, best 9.0

HAIRBUTT THE HIPPO — Ratrace

1 ❑ Spr 1997, b&w Cover: 2.95 **NM** value: **Cover or less**
• no indicia
2 ❑ Sum 1997, b&w Cover: 2.95 **NM** value: **Cover or less**
• no indicia

HAIRBUTT THE HIPPO CRIME FILES — Rat Race

1 ❑ Dec 1995 Cover: 3.50 **NM** value: **Cover or less**
📖 Sadly Ever Thus; Sins of My Father; Arny Dillo in Who Cares? Just Read it! **A:** Jason Paulos; Nick Pill **W:** Nick Pill; Bodine Amerikah; Simon Brown
2 ❑ Cover: 3.50 **NM** value: **Cover or less**
• Exists?
3 ❑ Cover: 3.50 **NM** value: **Cover or less**
• Exists?
4 ❑ Cover: 3.50 **NM** value: **Cover or less**
• Exists?
5 ❑ Cover: 3.50 **NM** value: **Cover or less**
• Exists?
6 ❑ Cover: 3.50 **NM** value: **Cover or less**
• Exists?

HALIFAX EXPLOSION — Halifax

1 ❑ Apr 1997, b&w Cover: 2.50 **NM** value: **Cover or less**

HALLELUJAH TRAIL — Dell

1 ❑ Feb 1966 Cover: 0.12 **NM** value: **40.00**
• **CGC:** 1 graded, best 9.6

HALL OF FAME — J.C.

1 ❑ Cover: 1.00 **NM** value: **1.50**
2 ❑ Cover: 1.00 **NM** value: **1.50**
3 ❑ Cover: 1.00 **NM** value: **1.50**

HALL OF HEROES — Hall of Heroes

1 ❑ May 1997, b&w Cover: 2.50 **NM** value: **Cover or less**
• **CGC:** 1 graded, best 9.0

HALL OF HEROES HALLOWEEN SPECIAL — Hall of Heroes

1 ❑ Oct 1997, b&w Cover: 2.50 **NM** value: **Cover or less**
No issue number. One-shot.

HALL OF HEROES PRESENTS (1ST SERIES) — Hall of Heroes

1 ❑ Aug 1993 Cover: 2.50 **NM** value: **Cover or less**
📖 Wrath of Fire **A:** Trent Kaniuga **W:** Trent Kaniuga
2 ❑ Sep 1993 Cover: 2.50 **NM** value: **Cover or less**
📖 The World of Nadir **A:** Bob Burns **W:** Bob Burns
3 ❑ Nov 1993 Cover: 2.50 **NM** value: **Cover or less**
📖 Silent Wind **A:** Cameron Enders **W:** Cameron Enders

HALL OF HEROES PRESENTS (2ND SERIES) — Hall of Heroes

0/A ❑ Mar 1997, b&w Cover: 2.50 **NM** value: **Cover or less**
Circ: Diamd. preorders: **4,080**
Slingers cover.
0/B ❑ Mar 1997, b&w Cover: 2.50 **NM** value: **Cover or less**
Salamandroid cover.
0/C ❑ Mar 1997, b&w Cover: 2.50 **NM** value: **Cover or less**
The Fuzz cover.
1 ❑ Jul 1996, b&w Cover: 2.50 **NM** value: **Cover or less**
📖 Sinister **A:** Dennis Anderson **W:** Dennis Anderson
2 ❑ Sep 1996, b&w Cover: 2.50 **NM** value: **Cover or less**
📖 Elijah's Fury in the Last Days; Elijah's Fury in Last Day
3/A ❑ b&w Cover: 2.50 **NM** value: **Cover or less**
📖 Power of the Golem • no indicia
3/B ❑ Cover: 2.50 **NM** value: **Cover or less**
alternate b cover with Nazi swastika in background.
4 ❑ May 1997 Cover: 2.50 **NM** value: **Cover or less**
• Turaxx
5 ❑ Sep 1997 Cover: 2.50 **NM** value: **Cover or less**
• The Becoming; extra-wide

HALLOWED KNIGHT — Shea

1 ❑ Apr 1997, b&w Cover: 2.95 **NM** value: **Cover or less**
2 ❑ Sep 1997, b&w Cover: 2.95 **NM** value: **Cover or less**

HALLOWEEN — Chaos

1 ❑ Nov 2000 Cover: 2.95 **NM** value: **Cover or less**
Photo cover. • based on movie **A:** David Brewer **W:** Daniel Farrands; Phil Nutman

HALLOWEEN HORROR — Eclipse

1 ❑ Oct 1987 Cover: 1.75 **NM** value: **2.00**
Circ: CapCity orders: **3,775**
📖 Mother Hubbard; The Secret of Thurman Renauld; Ultimate Destiny; the Monster of Frankenstein and The Plant; • a.k.a. Seduction of the Innocent #7 **A:** Jay Disbrow; Dick Briefer; Lou Cameron **W:** Jay Disbrow; Dick Briefer; Lou Cameron

HALLOWEEN MEGAZINE — Marvel

1 ❑ Dec 1996 Cover: 3.95 **NM** value: **Cover or less**
📖 Night of the Screaming House; To Kill a Vampire!; Dracula is Dead!; Fear is the Name of the Game! • reprints stories from Tomb of Dracula **A:** Gene Colan **W:** Marv Wolfman ★ Origin of Blade, the Vampire Hunter.

HALLOWEEN TERROR — Eternity

1 ❑ b&w Cover: 2.50 **NM** value: **Cover or less**
📖 The Long Way Home; Kin; The Fearless Vampire Killer; Willie & Phil vs. The Mummy; On Hold **A:** John Ross; Bruce McCorkindale; Marvin Perry Mann; Michael Rydwell **W:** Bruce McCorkindale; Bill Spangler; Lowell Cunningham; S.A. Bennett; Steve Jones

HALLS OF HORROR (JOHN BOLTON'S...) — Eclipse

1 ❑ Jun 1985 Cover: 1.75 **NM** value: **Cover or less**
Circ: CapCity orders: **6,200**
📖 The Monster Cabaret; The Werewolf **A:** John Bolton **W:** Dez Skinn
2 ❑ Jun 1985 Cover: 1.75 **NM** value: **Cover or less**
Circ: CapCity orders: **4,975**
📖 Where Monsters Roamed; Father Shandor **A:** John Bolton **W:** Steve Moore
3 ❑ Cover: 1.75 **NM** value: **Cover or less**

HALO, AN ANGEL'S STORY — Sirius

1 ❑ Apr 1996 Cover: 2.95 **NM** value: **Cover or less**
2 ❑ May 1996 Cover: 2.95 **NM** value: **Cover or less**
Bk 1❑ Cover: 12.95 **NM** value: **Cover or less**
• collects mini-series

HALSTED STREET — Kitchen Sink

Bk 1❑ Cover: 8.95 **NM** value: **Cover or less**
• Skip Williamson **A:** Skip Williamson
Bk 1/HC❑ Cover: 17.95 **NM** value: **Cover or less**
hardcover. **A:** Skip Williamson

HAMMER, THE — Dark Horse

Fans of Kelley Jones' dark, moody art on Batman will appreciate the four-issue mini-series from Dark Horse that Jones also wrote. Jones' style is especially appropriate for this tale of evil monstrosities with a decidedly Lovecraftian design.

Professor Malleus has been possessed by The Hammer, the spirit of an alien warrior who lived 1,500 years ago. He uses methods as mysterious as the occult and as overt as a huge sword to defeat the evil that seeks to devour the innocent. The horror of the stories is mitigated somewhat by the presence of Professor Malleus' friends Carl and Alex, whose primary function is to take The Hammer to a Denny's restaurant, because his body requires a high-fat, high-cholesterol diet.

1 ❑ Oct 1997 Cover: 2.95 **NM** value: **Cover or less**
2 ❑ Nov 1997 Cover: 2.95 **NM** value: **Cover or less**
3 ❑ Dec 1997 Cover: 2.95 **NM** value: **Cover or less**
4 ❑ Jan 1998 Cover: 2.95 **NM** value: **Cover or less**
Bk 1❑ Nov 1998 Cover: 12.95 **NM** value: **Cover or less**
📖 The Opener of the Way • collects mini-series **A:** Kelley Jones **W:** Kelley Jones

HAMMERLOCKE — DC

Archer Locke was the greatest scientist of his generation. His was the mind behind the Olympus Starbridge, a tower that stretched 72,000 kilometers into space. Cargo could be affordably transported up the starbridge into space, solving a crucial problem for man as he makes his journey toward the stars. Tragically, in 2025, Locke was caught in an accident during construction of the starbridge, and was critically injured. He survived thanks to an organization called UNICORN: The United Nations Covert Operations and Research Network. They rebuilt him using cyberprosthetics, but Locke put himself in self-imposed exile for seven years rather than be beholden to UNICORN and its director Jacob Kingman Rhee.

CGC-graded: Multiply prices above by **33 for 9.9 M** • **16 for 9.8 NM/M** • **7 for 9.6 NM+** • **5 for 9.4 NM** • **2.5 for 9.2 NM-** • **1.5 for 9.0 VF/NM**

After Locke's daughter was kidnapped by a group of post-Luddites led by a lunatic named Tharn, Locke returned to save her, even it if meant playing into the hands of the ambitious Rhee and selling out his dream.

1 ❑ Sep 1992 Cover: 2.50 **NM** value: **Cover or less**
Circ: CapCity orders: **11,650**
📖 Now These Her Princes **A:** Chris Sprouse **W:** Tom Joyner ★ 1st Appearance of Hammerlocke.
2 ❑ Oct 1992 Cover: 1.75 **NM** value: **Cover or less**
Circ: CapCity orders: **7,900**
3 ❑ Nov 1992 Cover: 1.75 **NM** value: **Cover or less**
4 ❑ Dec 1992 Cover: 1.75 **NM** value: **Cover or less**
Circ: CapCity orders: **6,100**
5 ❑ Jan 1993 Cover: 1.75 **NM** value: **Cover or less**
Circ: CapCity orders: **5,000**
6 ❑ Feb 1993 Cover: 1.75 **NM** value: **Cover or less**
Circ: CapCity orders: **4,800**
7 ❑ Mar 1993 Cover: 1.75 **NM** value: **Cover or less**
Circ: CapCity orders: **4,550**
8 ❑ Apr 1993 Cover: 1.75 **NM** value: **Cover or less**
Circ: CapCity orders: **4,550**
9 ❑ May 1993 Cover: 1.75 **NM** value: **Cover or less**
Circ: CapCity orders: **4,350**
final issue.

HAMMER OF GOD — First
1 ❑ Cover: 1.95 **NM** value: **Cover or less**
Circ: CapCity orders: **7,500**
📖 Red Carnation **A:** Steve Rude; Mike Baron **W:** Steve Rude; Mike Baron
2 ❑ Cover: 1.95 **NM** value: **Cover or less**
Circ: CapCity orders: **5,850**
3 ❑ Cover: 1.95 **NM** value: **Cover or less**
Circ: CapCity orders: **5,175**
4 ❑ Cover: 1.95 **NM** value: **Cover or less**
Circ: CapCity orders: **4,900**

HAMMER OF GOD: BUTCH — Dark Horse
1 ❑ May 1994 Cover: 2.50 **NM** value: **Cover or less**
Circ: CapCity orders: **4,375**
📖 Butch **A:** Shea Anton Pensa **W:** Mike Baron
2 ❑ Jul 1994 Cover: 2.50 **NM** value: **Cover or less**
Circ: CapCity orders: **3,200**
3 ❑ Aug 1994 Cover: 2.50 **NM** value: **Cover or less**
final issue.

HAMMER OF GOD: PENTATHLON — Dark Horse
1 ❑ Cover: 2.50 **NM** value: **Cover or less**
Circ: CapCity orders: **5,475**
No issue number. **A:** Neil Vokes **W:** Mike Baron

HAMMER OF GOD: SWORD OF JUSTICE — First
1 ❑ Cover: 4.95 **NM** value: **Cover or less**
Circ: CapCity orders: **3,225**
2 ❑ Cover: 4.95 **NM** value: **Cover or less**
Circ: CapCity orders: **2,750**

HAMMER, THE: THE OUTSIDER — Dark Horse
1 ❑ Feb 1999 Cover: 2.95 **NM** value: **Cover or less**
2 ❑ Mar 1999 Cover: 2.95 **NM** value: **Cover or less**
3 ❑ Apr 1999 Cover: 2.95 **NM** value: **Cover or less**

HAMMER, THE: UNCLE ALEX — Dark Horse
1 ❑ Aug 1998 Cover: 2.95 **NM** value: **Cover or less**
Circ: Diamd. preorders: **6,293**

HAMSTER VICE (BLACKTHORNE) — Blackthorne
1 ❑ Cover: 1.50 **NM** value: **Cover or less**
📖 Rumble Roach **A:** Dwayne Ferguson **W:** Dwayne Ferguson
2 ❑ Cover: 2.00 **NM** value: **Cover or less**
3 ❑ Cover: 2.00 **NM** value: **Cover or less**
4 ❑ Cover: 2.00 **NM** value: **Cover or less**
5 ❑ Cover: 2.00 **NM** value: **Cover or less**
6 ❑ Cover: 2.00 **NM** value: **Cover or less**
7 ❑ Cover: 2.00 **NM** value: **Cover or less**
8 ❑ Jul 1987 Cover: 2.00 **NM** value: **Cover or less**
9 ❑ Cover: 1.50 **NM** value: **Cover or less**
3D 1❑ Nov 1986 Cover: 2.50 **NM** value: **Cover or less**
Circ: CapCity orders: **2,510**
📖 Zombie Quest 3D **A:** Dwayne Ferguson **W:** Dwayne Ferguson
3D 2❑ Feb 1987 Cover: 2.50 **NM** value: **Cover or less**
• a.k.a. Blackthorne 3-D #15 **A:** Dwayne Ferguson **W:** Dwayne Ferguson

HAMSTER VICE (ETERNITY) — Eternity
1 ❑ Apr 1989, b&w Cover: 1.95 **NM** value: **Cover or less**
2 ❑ b&w Cover: 1.95 **NM** value: **Cover or less**

HAND OF FATE — Eclipse
1 ❑ Feb 1988, full color Cover: 1.75 **NM** value: **Cover or less**
Circ: CapCity orders: **4,900**
📖 Night of the Siren **A:** Gerald Forton **W:** Bruce Jones
8 ❑ Dec 1951 Cover: 0.10 **NM** value: **200.00**
9 ❑ Feb 1952 Cover: 0.10 **NM** value: **150.00**
• **CGC:** 2 graded, best 7.0
2 ❑ Mar 1988, full color Cover: 1.75 **NM** value: **Cover or less**
Circ: CapCity orders: **3,650**
📖 Night of the Widow **A:** Gerald Forton **W:** Bruce Jones
3 ❑ Apr 1988, b&w Cover: 2.00 **NM** value: **Cover or less**
10 ❑ Apr 1952 Cover: 0.10 **NM** value: **150.00**
11 ❑ Jun 1952 Cover: 0.10 **NM** value: **150.00**
12 ❑ Aug 1952 Cover: 0.10 **NM** value: **150.00**
13 ❑ Oct 1952 Cover: 0.10 **NM** value: **150.00**
14 ❑ Nov 1952 Cover: 0.10 **NM** value: **150.00**
15 ❑ Dec 1952 Cover: 0.10 **NM** value: **150.00**
• **CGC:** 1 graded, best 9.4
16 ❑ Feb 1953 Cover: 0.10 **NM** value: **125.00**
• **CGC:** 1 graded, best 7.5
17 ❑ Apr 1953 Cover: 0.10 **NM** value: **125.00**
18 ❑ Jun 1953 Cover: 0.10 **NM** value: **125.00**
19 ❑ Aug 1953 Cover: 0.10 **NM** value: **125.00**
• **CGC:** 1 graded, best 7.5
20 ❑ Oct 1953 Cover: 0.10 **NM** value: **125.00**
• **CGC:** 1 graded, best 9.2
21 ❑ Dec 1953 Cover: 0.10 **NM** value: **100.00**
22 ❑ Mar 1954 Cover: 0.10 **NM** value: **100.00**
• **CGC:** 1 graded, best 6.5
23 ❑ Jun 1954 Cover: 0.10 **NM** value: **100.00**
24 ❑ Aug 1954 Cover: 0.10 **NM** value: **100.00**
• **CGC:** 2 graded, best 9.0
25 ❑ Nov 1954 Cover: 0.10 **NM** value: **100.00**

HAND SHADOWS — Doyan
1 ❑ Cover: 1.50 **NM** value: **Cover or less**
2 ❑ Nov 1986 Cover: 1.50 **NM** value: **Cover or less**
📖 Gone Fission; Christopher Q. Cosmos, Space Janitor; Eye, Part 2; Maxwell Hammer; Reach Out and Touch Someone; Uno **A:** Randy Post; S. Green; TS Hart **W:** Frank Bell; Jennifer Bowles; North

HANDS OFF! — Ward Sutton
1 ❑ b&w Cover: 2.95 **NM** value: **Cover or less**
One-shot.

HANDS OF THE DRAGON — Atlas-Seaboard
1 ❑ Jun 1975 Cover: 0.25 **NM** value: **3.00**
• **CGC:** 2 graded, best 8.5

HANGMAN COMICS — M.L.J.
2 ❑ Spr 1942 Cover: 0.10 **NM** value: **1500.00**
3 ❑ Sum 1942 Cover: 0.10 **NM** value: **1000.00**
• **CGC:** 4 graded, best 7.0
4 ❑ Fal 1942 Cover: 0.10 **NM** value: **750.00**
• **CGC:** 1 graded, best 3.5
5 ❑ Win 1942 Cover: 0.10 **NM** value: **750.00**
• **CGC:** 1 graded, best 9.0
6 ❑ Spr 1943 Cover: 0.10 **NM** value: **750.00**
• **CGC:** 2 graded, best 8.5
7 ❑ Sum 1943 Cover: 0.10 **NM** value: **750.00**
• **CGC:** 2 graded, best 8.0
8 ❑ Fal 1943 Cover: 0.10 **NM** value: **750.00**

HANNA-BARBERA ALL-STARS — Archie
1 ❑ Oct 1995 Cover: 1.50 **NM** value: **Cover or less**
Circ: CapCity orders: **2,050**
2 ❑ Dec 1995 Cover: 1.50 **NM** value: **Cover or less**
3 ❑ Feb 1996 Cover: 1.50 **NM** value: **Cover or less**
4 ❑ Apr 1996 Cover: 1.50 **NM** value: **Cover or less**

HANNA-BARBERA BANDWAGON — Gold Key
1 ❑ Oct 1962 Cover: 0.12 **NM** value: **70.00**
• **CGC:** 1 graded, best 8.0
2 ❑ Jan 1963 Cover: 0.12 **NM** value: **50.00**
• **CGC:** 1 graded, best 8.0
3 ❑ Apr 1963 Cover: 0.12 **NM** value: **50.00**

HANNA-BARBERA BIG BOOK — Harvey
1 ❑ Jun 1993 Cover: 1.95 **NM** value: **Cover or less**
📖 The Old Gray Bear; Bargain Day at Stonehill!; Tiger by the Tail; Pet Show; New Man; Figure Eight; Boxed; The Soda Jerk; Fibber Takes a Dive! **A:** Ray Dirgo; Gwen Krause **W:** Ray Dirgo; Gwen Krause
3 ❑ Cover: 2.50 **NM** value: **Cover or less**

HANNA-BARBERA GIANT SIZE — Harvey
2 ❑ Nov 1992 Cover: 2.25 **NM** value: **Cover or less**
📖 Rememger **A:** Ray Dirgo **W:** Ray Dirgo

HANNA-BARBERA PARADE — Charlton
William Hanna met Joseph Barbera at MGM studios in 1939 and began one of the most prolific partnerships in animation history.

Hanna-Barbera Parade takes some of the animated characters created by the duo and puts them into original stories full of fun and excitement. The Flintstones, Dixie & Pixie, Huckleberry Hound, Yakky Doodle, Fibber Fox & Chopper, Hokey Wolf, Yogi Bear and Boo Boo, Quickdraw McGraw, Snagglepuss, and most of the animal characters created by Hanna and Barbera make appearances in these short, fun stories. Sadly, this particular series only lasted 10 issues.

1 ❑ Sep 1971 Cover: 0.15 **NM** value: **30.00**
2 ❑ Cover: 0.15 **NM** value: **20.00**
3 ❑ Cover: 0.15 **NM** value: **16.00**
4 ❑ Cover: 0.15 **NM** value: **14.00**
5 ❑ 1972 Cover: 0.15 **NM** value: **14.00**
6 ❑ Apr 1972 Cover: 0.20 **NM** value: **12.00**
📖 The Flintstones: One Breakfast Comi • Dixie cameo; Pixie cameo **A:** Ray Dirgo **W:** Gwen Krause ★ Appearance of Wilma Flintstone, Fred Flintstone, Pebbles Flintstone.
7 ❑ May 1972 Cover: 0.20 **NM** value: **12.00**
8 ❑ Cover: 0.20 **NM** value: **12.00**
9 ❑ Cover: 0.20 **NM** value: **12.00**
10 ❑ Cover: 0.20 **NM** value: **12.00**

HANNA-BARBERA PRESENTS — Archie
1 ❑ Nov 1995 Cover: 1.50 **NM** value: **Cover or less**
• Atom Ant and Secret Squirrel
2 ❑ Jan 1996 Cover: 1.50 **NM** value: **Cover or less**
• Wacky Races
3 ❑ Mar 1996 Cover: 1.50 **NM** value: **Cover or less**
• Yogi Bear
4 ❑ May 1996 Cover: 1.50 **NM** value: **Cover or less**
• Quick Draw McGraw and Magilla Gorilla
5 ❑ Jul 1996 Cover: 1.50 **NM** value: **Cover or less**
📖 A Pup Named Scooby-Doo
6 ❑ Aug 1996 Cover: 1.50 **NM** value: **Cover or less**
• Superstar Olympics
8 ❑ Oct 1996 Cover: 1.50 **NM** value: **Cover or less**
• Frankenstein Jr. and the Impossibles

HANNA-BARBERA PRESENTS ALL-NEW COMICS — Harvey
1 ❑ **NM** value: **1.00**
• giveaway promo.

HANNA-BARBERA SUPER TV HEROES — Gold Key
1 ❑ Apr 1968 Cover: 0.15 **NM** value: **60.00**
• **CGC:** 4 graded, best 9.4
• Herculoids
2 ❑ Jul 1968 Cover: 0.15 **NM** value: **38.00**
• **CGC:** 3 graded, best 9.6
• Birdman
3 ❑ Oct 1968 Cover: 0.15 **NM** value: **35.00**
• **CGC:** 1 graded, best 9.2
📖 Terrors of Turaba; The Plague of Giants; Undersea Invasion; The Solar Scorpions; The Cosmic Werewolf • Shazzan, Space Ghost, Moby Dick, Birdman, Young Samson and Goliath
4 ❑ Jan 1969 Cover: 0.15 **NM** value: **30.00**
• **CGC:** 1 graded, best 9.4
• Herculoids, Birdman, Shazzan, Moby Dick, Mighty Mightor
5 ❑ Apr 1969 Cover: 0.15 **NM** value: **30.00**
• **CGC:** 1 graded, best 9.4
6 ❑ Jul 1969 Cover: 0.15 **NM** value: **36.00**
• **CGC:** 1 graded, best 9.0
• Space Ghost
7 ❑ Oct 1969 Cover: 0.15 **NM** value: **36.00**
• **CGC:** 1 graded, best 5.0
• Space Ghost

HANSI, THE GIRL WHO LOVED THE SWASTIKA — Spire
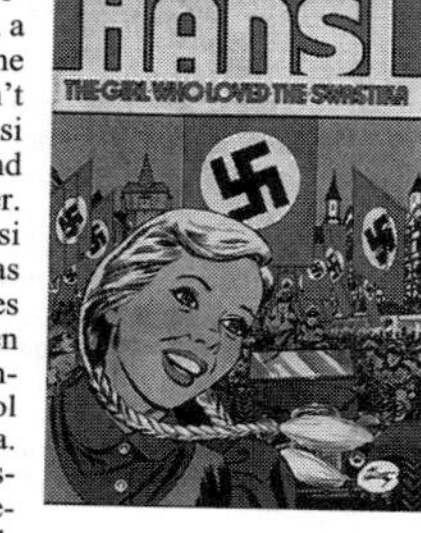

Hansi is a young German girl who becomes enamored with Nazi literature and soon wins a position in a youth training school. As she leaves, her mother tells her "don't ever forget Jesus"; however Hansi is soon swept up in the fervor and excitement of the training center. When the Third Reich falls, Hansi and her fellow students end up as Russian prisoners. Hansi manages to escape to West Germany, then under American occupation. Eventually, after marrying her school sweetheart, she moves to America. Nevertheless, Hansi and her husband, haunted by their former beliefs and actions, are unhappy until, one day, they turn to the Bible. Hansi now inspires her students to love America, where freedom reigns.

Spire Christian Comics presented many Christian-oriented comics like this one in the early 1970s, including God's Smuggler and My Brother's Keeper.

1 ❑ ca. 1973 Cover: 0.39 **NM** value: **5.00**
• **CGC:** 4 graded, best 9.8

HAP HAZARD — Fandom House
1 ❑ b&w Cover: 2.00 **NM** value: **Cover or less**

HAPPENSTANCE JACK, III — -Ism
1 ❑ May 1998 Cover: 2.98 **NM** value: **3.00**
📖 What the Hell Were We Thinking? **A:** Rich Koslowski; Michael Bianco **W:** Rich Koslowski; Kyle Dakota

HAPPY — Wonder Comics
1 ❑ b&w Cover: 2.00 **NM** value: **Cover or less**

HAPPY BIRTHDAY GNATRAT! — Dimension
1 ❑ Cover: 1.95 **NM** value: **Cover or less**

HAPPY BIRTHDAY MARTHA WASHINGTON — Dark Horse / Legend
1 ❑ Mar 1995 Cover: 2.95 **NM** value: **3.00**
Circ: CapCity orders: **12,300**
cardstock cover. 📖 Collateral Damage **A:** Dave Gibbons **W:** Frank Miller

There are two different pricing tiers in the modern comic-book hobby. **The prices seen above** are the prices we have seen **loose copies** of these issues reliably fetch in a variety of environments. Condition alters the price by the fractions seen on the bar on the bottom of left-hand pages of this book. **Comics graded by CGC** usually sell for more. Use the guide on the bottom of right-hand pages of this book to estimate what copies have brought on eBay.

Other grades: Multiply prices above by **1.5 for Mint • 2/3 for Very Fine • 1/3 for Fine • 1/5 for Very Good • 1/8 for Good**

HAPPY COMICS — Standard

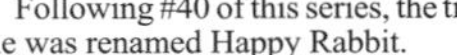

Like its sister publications Barnyard Comics and Coo Coo Comics, Happy Comics is an inoffensive humor title aimed at young readers. The most notable character is Happy Rabbit, an accident-prone bunny that comes off as a nicer version of the movie star Bugs Bunny. Unlike Bugs, Happy has a girlfriend (the hard-to-please Bonny Bunny) as well as an inventor uncle who can be counted on to provide him with an array of unworkable devices. Other characters featured in this series include Wally Wolf and Dizzy Duck: stock animal comedy characters.

Following #40 of this series, the title was renamed Happy Rabbit.

1 ❑ Aug 1943 Cover: 0.10 **NM** value: **125.00**
2 ❑ Cover: 0.10 **NM** value: **75.00**
3 ❑ 1944 Cover: 0.10 **NM** value: **45.00**
4 ❑ Cover: 0.10 **NM** value: **45.00**
5 ❑ Cover: 0.10 **NM** value: **45.00**
6 ❑ 1945 Cover: 0.10 **NM** value: **35.00**
7 ❑ 1945 Cover: 0.10 **NM** value: **35.00**
8 ❑ Jul 1945 Cover: 0.10 **NM** value: **35.00**
9 ❑ Sep 1945 Cover: 0.10 **NM** value: **35.00**
10 ❑ Nov 1945 Cover: 0.10 **NM** value: **35.00**
11 ❑ Jan 1946 Cover: 0.10 **NM** value: **28.00**
12 ❑ Mar 1946 Cover: 0.10 **NM** value: **28.00**
13 ❑ May 1946 Cover: 0.10 **NM** value: **28.00**
14 ❑ Jul 1946 Cover: 0.10 **NM** value: **28.00**
15 ❑ Sep 1946 Cover: 0.10 **NM** value: **28.00**
16 ❑ Nov 1946 Cover: 0.10 **NM** value: **28.00**
17 ❑ Jan 1947 Cover: 0.10 **NM** value: **28.00**
18 ❑ Mar 1947 Cover: 0.10 **NM** value: **28.00**
19 ❑ May 1947 Cover: 0.10 **NM** value: **28.00**
20 ❑ Jul 1947 Cover: 0.10 **NM** value: **28.00**
21 ❑ Sep 1947 Cover: 0.10 **NM** value: **35.00**
22 ❑ Nov 1947 Cover: 0.10 **NM** value: **35.00**
23 ❑ Jan 1948 Cover: 0.10 **NM** value: **35.00**
24 ❑ Mar 1948 Cover: 0.10 **NM** value: **35.00**
25 ❑ May 1948 Cover: 0.10 **NM** value: **35.00**
26 ❑ Jul 1948 Cover: 0.10 **NM** value: **35.00**
27 ❑ Sep 1948 Cover: 0.10 **NM** value: **35.00**
28 ❑ Nov 1948 Cover: 0.10 **NM** value: **35.00**
29 ❑ Jan 1949 Cover: 0.10 **NM** value: **35.00**
30 ❑ Mar 1949 Cover: 0.10 **NM** value: **35.00**
31 ❑ May 1949 Cover: 0.10 **NM** value: **35.00**
32 ❑ Jul 1949 Cover: 0.10 **NM** value: **90.00**
33 ❑ Sep 1949 Cover: 0.10 **NM** value: **125.00**
• Scarce **A:** Frank Frazetta
34 ❑ Nov 1949 Cover: 0.10 **NM** value: **35.00**
35 ❑ Jan 1950 Cover: 0.10 **NM** value: **35.00**
36 ❑ Mar 1950 Cover: 0.10 **NM** value: **35.00**
37 ❑ May 1950 Cover: 0.10 **NM** value: **35.00**
📖 Clean-Up Kid; No Sale; Trouble in the Wind; The Rose Colored Glasses **A:** Frank Frazetta
38 ❑ Jul 1950 Cover: 0.10 **NM** value: **18.00**
39 ❑ Sep 1950 Cover: 0.10 **NM** value: **18.00**
40 ❑ Nov 1950 Cover: 0.10 **NM** value: **18.00**
• Series continued in Happy Rabbit #41

HAPPYDALE: DEVILS IN THE DESERT — DC / Vertigo

1 ❑ Cover: 6.95 **NM** value: **Cover or less**
Circ: Diamd. preorders: **8,457**
• prestige format. **A:** Seth Fisher **W:** Andrew Dabb
2 ❑ Cover: 6.95 **NM** value: **Cover or less**
Circ: Diamd. preorders: **7,385**
• prestige format. **A:** Seth Fisher **W:** Andrew Dabb

HAPPY HOULIHANS — E.C.

"Introducing America's craziest and most lovable family!" the title cross-promoted Blackstone #1 and Moon Girl and the Prince: odd links. Art was mostly by Ed Wheelan and Don Cameron. The Happy Houlihans was bigfoot slapstick but quickly morphed into another, otherwise unconnected, E.C. series — Saddle Justice — with #3. — Maggie

1 ❑ Fal 1947 **NM** value: **300.00**
• **CGC:** 2 graded, best 9.0
📖 Introducing-The Happy Houlihans; Fat and Slat; The Mysterious Stranger!; Introducing Moon Girl and the Prince; Art for Arthur's Sake!
2 ❑ Win 1947 **NM** value: **200.00**
• **CGC:** 4 graded, best 7.5
📖 The Ruckus and the Rassler; Fat and Slat & Big Shot; Real Sand and Reel Stars; Corny Cobb; The Houlihan's Last Resort; Fat and Slat

To find the median price offered on eBay at press time for pre-1990 **CGC-graded comics**, multiply by:

9.9 (M): **33**	8.5 (VF+): **1.25**
9.8(NM/M): **16**	8.0 (VF): **0.85**
9.6 (NM+): **7**	7.5 (VF-): **0.6**
9.4 (NM): **5**	7.0 (F/VF): **0.5**
9.2 (NM-): **2.5**	6.5 (F+): **0.4**
9.0 (VF/NM): **1.5**	6.0 (F-): **0.33**

These are median prices of all CGC comics auctioned on eBay; prices for individual issues will vary.

HARBINGER — Valiant

Toyo Harada is the powerful head of the Harbinger Foundation. He named the Foundation as such because Harada, a mutant himself, believes other mutants to be the harbingers of a new era for humanity and he wants to gather such mutants to him and to train them as he sees fit.

Many Harbingers have grown to use their powers in Harada's personal service, becoming his "Eggbreakers." Others, fortunately, have rebelled — leaving the Foundation in order to lead lives of their own. This series focuses on these youths as they struggle to make it on their own and to use their powers for good.

0 ❑ Feb 1993 **NM** value: **2.50**
• **CGC:** 10 graded, best 9.6
• sendaway; Special issue given as a premium from coupons in Harbinger #1-6 ★ Origin of Sting.
0-2 ❑ **NM** value: **2.50**
1 ❑ Jan 1992 Cover: 1.95 **NM** value: **4.00**
Circ: CapCity orders: **10,900** • **CGC:** 4 graded, best 9.2
📖 Childred of the Eighth Day **A:** David Lapham **W:** Jim Shooter ★ Origin of Harbinger. ★ 1st Appearance of Flamingo, Zeppelin, Sting, Kris, Torque, Harbinger kids.
2 ❑ Feb 1992 Cover: 1.95 **NM** value: **2.50**
Circ: CapCity orders: **9,100** • **CGC:** 1 graded, best 9.8
3 ❑ Mar 1992 Cover: 1.95 **NM** value: **2.50**
Circ: CapCity orders: **8,900**
4 ❑ Apr 1992 Cover: 1.95 **NM** value: **2.50**
Circ: CapCity orders: **8,500**
• Scarce
5 ❑ May 1992 Cover: 2.50 **NM** value: **Cover or less**
Circ: CapCity orders: **8,600**
6 ❑ Jun 1992 Cover: 2.50 **NM** value: **Cover or less**
Circ: CapCity orders: **9,000**
7 ❑ Jul 1992 Cover: 2.25 **NM** value: **2.50**
Circ: CapCity orders: **10,500**
8 ❑ Aug 1992 Cover: 2.50 **NM** value: **Cover or less**
Circ: CapCity orders: **26,400**
📖 Unity, Part 8 • Unity **A:** Frank Miller(cover) **C:** Frank Miller
9 ❑ Sep 1992 Cover: 2.50 **NM** value: **Cover or less**
Circ: CapCity orders: **30,900**
📖 Unity, Part 16 • Unity; Birth of Magnus **C:** Walt Simonson
10 ❑ Oct 1992 Cover: 2.50 **NM** value: **Cover or less**
Circ: CapCity orders: **20,700**
11 ❑ Nov 1992 Cover: 2.50 **NM** value: **Cover or less**
Circ: CapCity orders: **19,600**
12 ❑ Dec 1992 Cover: 2.50 **NM** value: **Cover or less**
Circ: CapCity orders: **19,200**
📖 Twilight of the Eighth Day, Part 1
13 ❑ Jan 1993 Cover: 2.50 **NM** value: **Cover or less**
Circ: CapCity orders: **22,100**
Dark Knight cover. 📖 Twilight of the Eighth Day, Part 2
14 ❑ Feb 1993 Cover: 2.50 **NM** value: **Cover or less**
Circ: CapCity orders: **24,900**
📖 Twilight of the Eighth Day, Part 3
15 ❑ Mar 1993 Cover: 2.50 **NM** value: **Cover or less**
Circ: CapCity orders: **35,200**
16 ❑ Apr 1993 Cover: 2.50 **NM** value: **Cover or less**
Circ: CapCity orders: **42,700**
17 ❑ May 1993 Cover: 2.50 **NM** value: **Cover or less**
Circ: CapCity orders: **51,100**
18 ❑ Jun 1993 Cover: 2.50 **NM** value: **Cover or less**
Circ: CapCity orders: **64,800**
19 ❑ Jul 1993 Cover: 2.50 **NM** value: **Cover or less**
Circ: CapCity orders: **77,600**
📖 Enter Kaliph **A:** Howard Simpson **W:** Howard Simpson; Maurice Fontenot
20 ❑ Aug 1993 Cover: 2.50 **NM** value: **Cover or less**
Circ: CapCity orders: **68,500**
21 ❑ Sep 1993 Cover: 2.50 **NM** value: **Cover or less**
Circ: CapCity orders: **57,600**
22 ❑ Oct 1993 Cover: 2.50 **NM** value: **Cover or less**
Circ: CapCity orders: **47,100**
23 ❑ Nov 1993 Cover: 2.50 **NM** value: **Cover or less**
Circ: CapCity orders: **41,650**
24 ❑ Dec 1993 Cover: 2.50 **NM** value: **Cover or less**
Circ: CapCity orders: **37,525**
25 ❑ Jan 1994 Cover: 3.50 **NM** value: **Cover or less**
Circ: CapCity orders: **50,600**
• Giant-size. 📖 Armageddon • Sting vs. Harada; Harada put into coma; Sting loses powers **A:** Howard Simpson **W:** Maurice Fontenot ★ Death of Rock. ★ Versus Harada.
26 ❑ Feb 1994 Cover: 2.50 **NM** value: **Cover or less**
Circ: CapCity orders: **34,350**
• new team; Zephyr rejoins Harbinger foundation ★ 1st Appearance of Sonix, Anvil, Amazon, Microwave, Jolt.
27 ❑ Mar 1994 Cover: 2.50 **NM** value: **Cover or less**
Circ: CapCity orders: **23,800**
28 ❑ Apr 1994 Cover: 2.50 **NM** value: **Cover or less**
Circ: CapCity orders: **21,125**
29 ❑ May 1994 Cover: 2.50 **NM** value: **Cover or less**
Circ: CapCity orders: **25,525**
• trading card
30 ❑ Jun 1994 Cover: 2.50 **NM** value: **Cover or less**
Circ: CapCity orders: **17,300**
📖 Bad Omen, Part 1 **A:** Sean Chen **W:** Maurice Fontenot ★ Appearance of H.A.R.D.Corps.
31 ❑ Aug 1994 Cover: 2.50 **NM** value: **Cover or less**
Circ: CapCity orders: **15,875**
32 ❑ Sep 1994 Cover: 2.50 **NM** value: **Cover or less**
Circ: CapCity orders: **14,875**
33 ❑ Oct 1994 Cover: 2.50 **NM** value: **Cover or less**
Circ: CapCity orders: **14,925**
34 ❑ Nov 1994 Cover: 2.50 **NM** value: **Cover or less**
Circ: CapCity orders: **11,500**
📖 The Chaos Effect: Delta, Part 1 • Chaos Effect
35 ❑ Dec 1994 Cover: 2.50 **NM** value: **Cover or less**
36 ❑ Jan 1995 Cover: 2.50 **NM** value: **Cover or less**
Circ: CapCity orders: **11,275**
37 ❑ Feb 1995 Cover: 2.50 **NM** value: **Cover or less**
Circ: CapCity orders: **9,800**
Painted cover.
38 ❑ Mar 1995 Cover: 2.50 **NM** value: **Cover or less**
Circ: CapCity orders: **8,200**
39 ❑ Apr 1995 Cover: 2.50 **NM** value: **Cover or less**
Circ: CapCity orders: **7,600**
40 ❑ May 1995 Cover: 2.50 **NM** value: **Cover or less**
Circ: CapCity orders: **6,775**
41 ❑ Jun 1995 Cover: 2.50 **NM** value: **Cover or less**
Circ: CapCity orders: **5,925**
final issue.
Bk 1❑ Cover: 15.00 **NM** value: **Cover or less**
• Trade Paperback. • Collects Harbinger #1-4 and includes Harbinger #0
Bk 1/A❑ Cover: 15.00 **NM** value: **Cover or less**
• Blue edition.
Bk 2❑ Cover: 9.95 **NM** value: **Cover or less**
• Children Of The Eighth Day; bagged with Harbinger #0

HARBINGER: ACTS OF GOD — Acclaim

1 ❑ Cover: 3.95 **NM** value: **Cover or less**
Circ: Diamd. preorders: **11,609**

HARBINGER FILES — Valiant

1 ❑ Aug 1994 Cover: 2.50 **NM** value: **Cover or less**
Circ: CapCity orders: **20,425**
2 ❑ Feb 1995 Cover: 2.50 **NM** value: **Cover or less**
Circ: CapCity orders: **9,800**

HARDBALL — Aircel

1 ❑ 1991 Cover: 2.95 **NM** value: **Cover or less**
2 ❑ 1991 Cover: 2.95 **NM** value: **Cover or less**
3 ❑ Aug 1991 Cover: 2.95 **NM** value: **Cover or less**
4 ❑ 1991 Cover: 2.95 **NM** value: **Cover or less**

HARD BOILED — Dark Horse

This magazine-sized limited series from Dark Horse and creators Frank Miller and Geof Darrow tells the story of a cyborg tax collector — no, he's an insurance investigator — who rebels against his programming and his creators. It's an over-the-top, no-holds-barred violence-fest, but with Miller-noted for his taught, gritty writing style — and Darrow — noted for his painstakingly detailed illustrations — at the helm, you know you're in for a good ride.

The three-part series contains mature themes that may not be suitable for all readers.

1 ❑ Sep 1990 Cover: 4.95 **NM** value: **Cover or less**
Circ: CapCity orders: **22,850**
2 ❑ Dec 1990 Cover: 5.95 **NM** value: **Cover or less**
Circ: CapCity orders: **18,950**
3 ❑ Mar 1992 Cover: 5.95 **NM** value: **Cover or less**
Circ: CapCity orders: **16,550**
Bk 1❑ May 1993 Cover: 15.95 **NM** value: **Cover or less**
No issue number. • Trade Paperback. • collects series

HARDCASE — Malibu / Ultraverse

In 1992, Tom Hawke — Hardcase — is a member of the super-powered group known as The Squad. As "Ultras," they are used to overwhelming any foe easily. But on March 10, 1992, they fight their first really powerful enemy — another Ultra. That battle ends in disaster, leaving two Squad members dead and a third crippled. Hardcase is the only one to pull through.

Hardcase gives up crime-fighting after this and uses his abilities to become a famed action movie actor. Once he was a hero, but now he swears to avoid such danger. All that changes, when a super-powered being named Headknocker begins slaughtering innocents in a bank robbery, scarcely a mile from where Hardcase is shooting a movie. Hardcase steps in and stops the carnage, but it is too late for some of Headknocker's victims. This tragedy teaches Hardcase a powerful lesson, and he once again joins the fight against crime.

1 ❑ Jun 1993 Cover: 1.95 **NM** value: **2.50**
Circ: CapCity orders: **55,775**
📖 Winners Never Quit **A:** Jim Callahan **W:** James D. Hudnall ★ 1st Appearance of NM-E, Nicholas Lone (Solitaire), Hardcase.
1/Hol❑Jun 1993 **NM** value: **5.00**
• **CGC:** 1 graded, best 9.6
Holographic cover. **A:** Jim Callahan **W:** James D. Hudnall
1/LE❑ Jun 1993 Cover: 1.95 **NM** value: **3.00**
• Ultrafoil limited edition. **A:** Jim Callahan **W:** James D. Hudnall
2 ❑ Jul 1993 Cover: 1.95 **NM** value: **2.00**
Circ: CapCity orders: **20,225**

CGC-graded: Multiply prices above by **33 for 9.9 M • 16 for 9.8 NM/M • 7 for 9.6 NM+ • 5 for 9.4 NM • 2.5 for 9.2 NM- • 1.5 for 9.0 VF/NM**

📖 Hard Choices • trading card **A:** Cranial Implant Studio **W:** James D. Hudnall ★ 1st Appearance of Choice.

3 ❑ Aug 1993 Cover: 1.95 **NM** value: **2.00**
Circ: CapCity orders: **18,575**
📖 Hard Decisions **A:** Jim Callahan **W:** James D. Hudnall ★ 1st Appearance of The Needler, Gun Nut, Trouble.

4 ❑ Sep 1993 Cover: 1.95 **NM** value: **2.00**
Circ: CapCity orders: **21,850**
Fold-out cover. 📖 Strangers In The Night **A:** Roger Robinson **W:** James D. Hudnall ★ Origin of Hardcase.

5 ❑ Oct 1993 Cover: 2.50 **NM** value: **Cover or less**
Circ: CapCity orders: **29,725**
📖 Friends and Enemies, Part 1; Rune, Part D • Rune **A:** Barry Windsor-Smith **W:** James D. Hudnall

6 ❑ Nov 1993 Cover: 1.95 **NM** value: **Cover or less**
Circ: CapCity orders: **21,825**
📖 Friends and Enemies, Part 2 **A:** Scott Benefiel **W:** James D. Hudnall

7 ❑ Dec 1993 Cover: 1.95 **NM** value: **Cover or less**
Circ: CapCity orders: **22,350**
📖 Break-Thru: Sudden Surprises • Break-Thru **A:** Scott Benefiel **W:** James D. Hudnall

8 ❑ Jan 1994 Cover: 1.95 **NM** value: **Cover or less**
Circ: CapCity orders: **17,900**

9 ❑ Feb 1994 Cover: 1.95 **NM** value: **Cover or less**
Circ: CapCity orders: **15,200**

10 ❑ Mar 1994 Cover: 1.95 **NM** value: **Cover or less**
Circ: CapCity orders: **13,475**

11 ❑ Apr 1994 Cover: 1.95 **NM** value: **Cover or less**
Circ: CapCity orders: **12,700**

12 ❑ May 1994 Cover: 1.95 **NM** value: **Cover or less**
Circ: CapCity orders: **11,900**

13 ❑ Jun 1994 Cover: 1.95 **NM** value: **Cover or less**
Circ: CapCity orders: **11,025**
📖 The Turning Point **A:** Kelly Krantz; Scott Benefiel(cover) **W:** James D. Hudnall ★ 1st Appearance of Karr, Wynn.

14 ❑ Jul 1994 Cover: 1.95 **NM** value: **Cover or less**
Circ: CapCity orders: **9,775**
📖 Transition **A:** Steve Carr **W:** James D. Hudnall

15 ❑ Aug 1994 Cover: 1.95 **NM** value: **Cover or less**
Circ: CapCity orders: **8,800**
📖 Slash and Burn **A:** Tim Hamilton; Greg Luzniak **W:** James D. Hudnall

16 ❑ Oct 1994 Cover: 3.50 **NM** value: **Cover or less**
📖 Battle Royale, Part 1; Fall; Neverland Blues, Part 1; End of Story • Flip book with Ultraverse Premiere #7 **A:** Tim Hamilton; Keith Conroy; Brian Kong; Brian Murray(cover); Greg Luzniak(cover); Kris Renkewitz **W:** Kurt Busiek; Mark Paniccia; James D. Hudnall

17 ❑ Nov 1994 Cover: 1.95 **NM** value: **Cover or less**
Circ: CapCity orders: **7,325**
📖 Battle Royale, Part 2 **A:** Tim Hamilton; Greg Luzniak(cover) **W:** James D. Hudnall ★ 1st Appearance of The Genius.

18 ❑ Dec 1994 Cover: 1.95 **NM** value: **Cover or less**
Circ: CapCity orders: **6,400**
📖 Battle Royale, Part 3 **A:** Tim Hamilton **W:** James D. Hudnall

19 ❑ Jan 1995 Cover: 1.95 **NM** value: **Cover or less**
Circ: CapCity orders: **6,075**
📖 Here Today… **A:** Bill Knapp; Greg Horn; Keith Conroy(cover); Kenn Bivins **W:** James D. Hudnall ★ 1st Appearance of Trauma, Bismark.

20 ❑ Feb 1995 Cover: 2.50 **NM** value: **Cover or less**
Circ: CapCity orders: **5,000**
📖 Reversals **A:** Greg Luzniak(cover); Kenn Bivins **W:** James D. Hudnall

21 ❑ Mar 1995 Cover: 2.50 **NM** value: **Cover or less**
Circ: CapCity orders: **4,800**
📖 Hard Road **A:** Tim Hamilton; Greg Luzniak(cover) **W:** James D. Hudnall

22 ❑ Apr 1995 Cover: 2.50 **NM** value: **Cover or less**
Circ: CapCity orders: **4,525**
📖 Mundi Quest, Part 1 **A:** Tim Hamilton **W:** James D. Hudnall ★ Death of Trouble.

23 ❑ May 1995 Cover: 2.50 **NM** value: **Cover or less**
Circ: CapCity orders: **5,650**
📖 Mundi Quest, Part 2 **A:** Tim Hamilton **W:** James D. Hudnall

24 ❑ Jun 1995 Cover: 2.50 **NM** value: **Cover or less**
Circ: CapCity orders: **4,400**

25 ❑ Jul 1995 Cover: 2.50 **NM** value: **Cover or less**

26 ❑ Aug 1995 Cover: 2.95 **NM** value: **Cover or less**
final issue. **W:** James D. Hudnall

HARDCORE — DC / Piranha

Bk 1 ❑ full color Cover: 9.95 **NM** value: **Cover or less**
Circ: CapCity orders: **2,200**

HARDCORE STATION — DC

1 ❑ Jul 1998 Cover: 2.50 **NM** value: **Cover or less**
Circ: Diamd. preorders: **21,100**
📖 Genesis **A:** Jim Starlin **W:** Jim Starlin

2 ❑ Aug 1998 Cover: 2.50 **NM** value: **Cover or less**
Circ: Diamd. preorders: **15,104**

3 ❑ Sep 1998 Cover: 2.50 **NM** value: **Cover or less**
Circ: Diamd. preorders: **14,115**

4 ❑ Oct 1998 Cover: 2.50 **NM** value: **Cover or less**
Circ: Diamd. preorders: **11,843**

5 ❑ Nov 1998 Cover: 2.50 **NM** value: **Cover or less**
Circ: Diamd. preorders: **12,434**

6 ❑ Dec 1998 Cover: 2.50 **NM** value: **Cover or less**
Circ: Diamd. preorders: **11,622**

H.A.R.D. CORPS, THE — Valiant

Life after death doesn't get much better than this, if you ever wanted to see action. Omen Enterprises, in its ongoing effort to thwart Harada and the Harbinger Foundation, has brought the dead, or at least the comatose, back to life. They are revived as the H.A.R.D. Corps: The Harbinger Active Resistance Division. Each member has a brain implant that gives them super-powers, such as weightlessness, invulnerability, heat bursts, and force fields. The trick is, each team member can only use one power at a time and the powers need to be activated from a mainframe computer by another member of the team.

1 ❑ Dec 1992 Cover: 2.50 **NM** value: **Cover or less**
Circ: CapCity orders: **67,600**
Fold-out cover. **C:** José Luis Garcia-Lopez

1/GO ❑ Dec 1992 Cover: 2.50 **NM** value: **3.00**
Fold-out cover. • Gold (promotional) edition.

2 ❑ Jan 1993 Cover: 2.25 **NM** value: **Cover or less**
Circ: CapCity orders: **32,600**

3 ❑ Feb 1993 Cover: 2.25 **NM** value: **Cover or less**
Circ: CapCity orders: **34,300**
📖 Slaughter Street **A:** Mike Leeke **W:** Bob Layton; David Michelinie

4 ❑ Apr 1993 Cover: 2.25 **NM** value: **Cover or less**
Circ: CapCity orders: **48,200**

5 ❑ Apr 1993 Cover: 2.25 **NM** value: **Cover or less**
Circ: CapCity orders: **52,000**

6 ❑ May 1993 Cover: 2.25 **NM** value: **Cover or less**
Circ: CapCity orders: **53,400**

7 ❑ Jun 1993 Cover: 2.25 **NM** value: **Cover or less**
Circ: CapCity orders: **75,600**

8 ❑ Jul 1993 Cover: 2.25 **NM** value: **Cover or less**
Circ: CapCity orders: **73,500**
📖 The B-Team, or Some Like it Hot(Shot) **A:** Mike Leeke **W:** David Michelinie

9 ❑ Aug 1993 Cover: 2.25 **NM** value: **Cover or less**
Circ: CapCity orders: **64,900**

10 ❑ Sep 1993 Cover: 2.25 **NM** value: **Cover or less**
Circ: CapCity orders: **63,400**

11 ❑ Oct 1993 Cover: 2.25 **NM** value: **Cover or less**
Circ: CapCity orders: **46,800**

12 ❑ Nov 1993 Cover: 2.25 **NM** value: **Cover or less**
Circ: CapCity orders: **40,925**

13 ❑ Dec 1993 Cover: 2.25 **NM** value: **Cover or less**
Circ: CapCity orders: **36,850**

14 ❑ Jan 1994 Cover: 2.25 **NM** value: **Cover or less**
Circ: CapCity orders: **31,950**
📖 The Trouble With Midnight **A:** Yvel Guichet **W:** David Michelinie

15 ❑ Feb 1994 Cover: 2.25 **NM** value: **Cover or less**
Circ: CapCity orders: **27,875**

16 ❑ Mar 1994 Cover: 2.25 **NM** value: **Cover or less**
Circ: CapCity orders: **23,375**

17 ❑ Apr 1994 Cover: 2.25 **NM** value: **Cover or less**
Circ: CapCity orders: **21,375**

18 ❑ May 1994 Cover: 2.25 **NM** value: **Cover or less**
Circ: CapCity orders: **25,650**
• trading card

19 ❑ Jun 1994 Cover: 2.25 **NM** value: **Cover or less**
Circ: CapCity orders: **16,925**
📖 Bad Omen, Part 2 • Harada awakes from coma

20 ❑ Jul 1994 Cover: 2.25 **NM** value: **Cover or less**
Circ: CapCity orders: **15,575**

21 ❑ Sep 1994 Cover: 2.25 **NM** value: **Cover or less**
Circ: CapCity orders: **14,875**
📖 The Return of the Midnight Earl, Part 1

22 ❑ Oct 1994 Cover: 2.25 **NM** value: **Cover or less**
Circ: CapCity orders: **14,325**
📖 The Return of the Midnight Earl, Part 2

23 ❑ Nov 1994 Cover: 2.25 **NM** value: **Cover or less**
Circ: CapCity orders: **20,200**
📖 The Chaos Effect: Delta, Part 4 • Chaos Effect

24 ❑ Dec 1994 Cover: 2.50 **NM** value: **Cover or less**
Circ: CapCity orders: **11,500**

25 ❑ Jan 1995 Cover: 2.50 **NM** value: **Cover or less**
Circ: CapCity orders: **11,225**

26 ❑ Feb 1995 Cover: 2.50 **NM** value: **Cover or less**
Circ: CapCity orders: **9,625**

27 ❑ Mar 1995 Cover: 2.50 **NM** value: **Cover or less**
Circ: CapCity orders: **8,175**

28 ❑ Apr 1995 Cover: 2.50 **NM** value: **Cover or less**
Circ: CapCity orders: **7,250**

29 ❑ May 1995 Cover: 2.25 **NM** value: **Cover or less**
Circ: CapCity orders: **6,375**

30 ❑ Jun 1995 Cover: 2.25 **NM** value: **Cover or less**
Circ: CapCity orders: **5,675**
final issue.

HARDKORR — Aircel

All issues are adults only.

1 ❑ Jun 1991, b&w Cover: 2.50 **NM** value: **Cover or less**
2 ❑ Jul 1991, b&w Cover: 2.50 **NM** value: **Cover or less**
3 ❑ Aug 1991, b&w Cover: 2.50 **NM** value: **Cover or less**
4 ❑ Sep 1991, b&w Cover: 2.50 **NM** value: **Cover or less**

For up-to-the-week CGC ratios, consult the current issue of **Comics Buyer's Guide.**

HARD LOOKS — Dark Horse

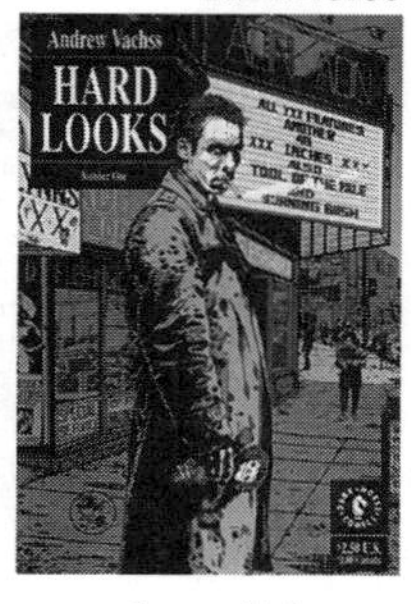

This black-and-white series is a showcase for the gritty fiction of Andrew Vachss. Hard Looks is an anthology series that focuses on the darker things in life: shady alleyways and pit-bull fights, secret deals, psychopaths, and cold-blooded murders.

The 10 issues of Hard Looks kick off with an adaptation of a story that first appeared in "A Matter Of Crime Vol. III." In "Dumping Ground," a pair of police officers who, it seems, are doing a routine check of a deserted area are, in fact, dumping the bodies of women whom they have sexually abused and murdered. The pair think they can never be caught, because the place where they dump the bodies is supposedly toxic, so nobody dares to explore. They assume the place is not truly dangerous because a pack of wild dogs lives there, apparently unaffected. The cops make a deadly mistake, however, in assuming that, because dogs live there, it will be safe for them.

1 ❑ 1992b&w Cover: 2.50 **NM** value: **Cover or less**
Circ: CapCity orders: **2,700**
📖 Dumping Ground; Statute of Limitations; Unwritten Law; Hostage **A:** Dave Gibbons; Tim Bradstreet; Gary Gianni; Rick Magyar **W:** Andrew Vachss

2 ❑ 1992b&w Cover: 2.50 **NM** value: **Cover or less**

3 ❑ 1992b&w Cover: 2.50 **NM** value: **Cover or less**
📖 Crippler; Step on a Crack; Anytime I Want **A:** James O'Barr **W:** Andrew Vachss

4 ❑ b&w Cover: 2.50 **NM** value: **Cover or less**

5 ❑ b&w Cover: 2.50 **NM** value: **Cover or less**
📖 Treatment; Crime Partner (text story); Drive By **A:** Gary Gianni; Christopher Moeller; Richard Olsen **W:** Andrew Vachss; Joe Lansdale

6 ❑ b&w Cover: 2.95 **NM** value: **Cover or less**
📖 Dead Game; Bandit; A Flash of White; Mad Dog **A:** John Bergin; David Lloyd; Tom Artis; Phil Hester **W:** Andrew Vachss; Neal Barrett Jr.; Rose Dawn Bedford

7 ❑ b&w Cover: 2.95 **NM** value: **Cover or less**
Circ: CapCity orders: **2,575**

8 ❑ b&w Cover: 2.95 **NM** value: **Cover or less**
Circ: CapCity orders: **2,200**

9 ❑ b&w Cover: 2.95 **NM** value: **Cover or less**
📖 Cain; Working Roots; Joy Ride; Placebo **A:** Klaus Janson; Bob Fingerman; John Watkiss; James O'Barr **W:** Andrew Vachss; Jerry Prosser; Neal Barrett Jr.

10 ❑ b&w Cover: 3.50 **NM** value: **Cover or less**
📖 Cain; Working Roots (text story); Joy Ride; Placebo **A:** Klaus Janson; Bob Fingerman; John Watkiss; Bob Fingerman(cover); James O'Barr **W:** Andrew Vachss

Bk 1 ❑ Sep 1996 Cover: 17.95 **NM** value: **Cover or less**
• collects adaptations of Andrew Vachss stories **W:** Andrew Vachss

HARD ROCK COMICS — Revolutionary

1 ❑ Mar 1992, b&w Cover: 2.50 **NM** value: **4.00**
• Metallica; early

2 ❑ Apr 1992, b&w Cover: 2.50 **NM** value: **3.00**
• Motley Crue

3 ❑ May 1992, b&w Cover: 2.50 **NM** value: **Cover or less**
• Jane's Addiction

4 ❑ Jun 1992, b&w Cover: 2.50 **NM** value: **Cover or less**
• Nirvana

5 ❑ Jul 1992, b&w Cover: 2.50 **NM** value: **8.00**
• Kiss: Tales From the Tours

5-2 ❑ Jul 1992 Cover: 2.50 **NM** value: **6.00**

6 ❑ Sep 1992, b&w Cover: 2.50 **NM** value: **Cover or less**
• Def Leppard II

7 ❑ Oct 1992, b&w Cover: 2.50 **NM** value: **Cover or less**
• Red Hot Chili Peppers

8 ❑ Nov 1992, b&w Cover: 2.50 **NM** value: **Cover or less**
• Soundgarden, Pearl Jam

9 ❑ Dec 1992, b&w Cover: 2.50 **NM** value: **Cover or less**
• Queen II

10 ❑ Jan 1993, b&w Cover: 2.50 **NM** value: **Cover or less**
• Birth of Punk

11 ❑ Feb 1993, b&w Cover: 2.50 **NM** value: **Cover or less**
• Pantera

12 ❑ Mar 1993, b&w Cover: 2.50 **NM** value: **Cover or less**
• Hendrix

13 ❑ Apr 1993, b&w Cover: 2.50 **NM** value: **Cover or less**
• Dead Kennedys

14 ❑ May 1993, b&w Cover: 2.50 **NM** value: **Cover or less**
• Van Halen II

15 ❑ Jun 1993 Cover: 2.50 **NM** value: **Cover or less**
• Megadeath, Motorhead, b&w

16 ❑ Jul 1993, b&w Cover: 2.50 **NM** value: **Cover or less**
• Joan Jett, Lita Ford

17 ❑ Cover: 2.50 **NM** value: **Cover or less**
• never published; British Metal

18 ❑ Sep 1993, b&w Cover: 2.50 **NM** value: **Cover or less**
• Queensryche II

19 ❑ Oct 1993, b&w Cover: 2.50 **NM** value: **Cover or less**
• Tesla, Spirit, UKJ

20 ❑ Nov 1993, b&w Cover: 2.50 **NM** value: **Cover or less**
📖 The Sweet; Ratt; Warrant L.A. Down Boys; The New Censorship; George Clinton; • Ratt, P-Funk, Sweet **A:** Stuart Immonen; Dave Garcia; Lyndal Funkson; Steve Goupil **W:** Dean Hsieh; Todd Loren

HARDWARE — DC / Milestone

1 ❑ Apr 1993 Cover: 1.50 **NM** value: **Cover or less**
📖 The Man In The Machine, Chapter 1 • newsstand **A:** Denys Cowan **W:** Dwayne McDuffie ★ Origin of Hardware. ★ 1st Appearance of Reprise, Edwin Alva, Hardware.

Other grades: Multiply prices above by **1.5 for Mint • 2/3 for Very Fine • 1/3 for Fine • 1/5 for Very Good • 1/8 for Good**

1/CS ❑ Apr 1993 Cover: 2.95 **NM** value: **3.00**
Circ: CapCity orders: **58,150**
📖 The Man In The Machine, Chapter 1 • bagged **A:** Denys Cowan **W:** Dwayne McDuffie ★ Origin of Hardware. ★ 1st Appearance of Reprise, Edwin Alva, Hardware.

1/PL ❑ Apr 1993 Cover: 2.95 **NM** value: **3.50**
no cover price. • Platinum (promotional) edition. 📖 The Man In The Machine, Chapter 1 • platinum **A:** Denys Cowan **W:** Dwayne McDuffie ★ Origin of Hardware. ★ 1st Appearance of Reprise, Edwin Alva, Hardware.

2 ❑ May 1993 Cover: 1.50 **NM** value: **Cover or less**
Circ: CapCity orders: **24,650**
📖 The Man In The Machine, Chapter 2 **A:** Denys Cowan **W:** Dwayne McDuffie ★ 1st Appearance of Barraki Young.

3 ❑ May 1993 Cover: 1.50 **NM** value: **Cover or less**
Circ: CapCity orders: **23,200**
📖 Confrontations **A:** Denys Cowan **W:** Dwayne McDuffie ★ 1st Appearance of Systematic.

4 ❑ Jun 1993 Cover: 1.50 **NM** value: **Cover or less**
Circ: CapCity orders: **18,350**
📖 Resolution **A:** Denys Cowan **W:** Dwayne McDuffie

5 ❑ Jul 1993 Cover: 1.50 **NM** value: **Cover or less**
Circ: CapCity orders: **18,150**

6 ❑ Aug 1993 Cover: 1.50 **NM** value: **Cover or less**
Circ: CapCity orders: **15,150**

7 ❑ Sep 1993 Cover: 1.50 **NM** value: **Cover or less**
Circ: CapCity orders: **13,050**

8 ❑ Oct 1993 Cover: 1.50 **NM** value: **Cover or less**
Circ: CapCity orders: **11,800**

9 ❑ Nov 1993 Cover: 1.50 **NM** value: **Cover or less**
Circ: CapCity orders: **9,950**

10 ❑ Dec 1993 Cover: 1.50 **NM** value: **Cover or less**
Circ: CapCity orders: **9,500**

11 ❑ Jan 1994 Cover: 1.50 **NM** value: **Cover or less**
Circ: CapCity orders: **12,450**
📖 Shadow War; Shadow War, Part 1 ★ 1st Appearance of Shadowspire, Dharma, The Star Chamber.

12 ❑ Feb 1994 Cover: 1.50 **NM** value: **Cover or less**
Circ: CapCity orders: **8,050**
📖 No Harm Done **A:** Rich Buckler **W:** Dwayne McDuffie

13 ❑ Mar 1994 Cover: 1.50 **NM** value: **Cover or less**
Circ: CapCity orders: **7,250**
📖 Weekend Getaway **A:** Denys Cowan **W:** Dwayne McDuffie

14 ❑ Apr 1994 Cover: 1.50 **NM** value: **Cover or less**
Circ: CapCity orders: **6,550**

15 ❑ May 1994 Cover: 1.50 **NM** value: **Cover or less**
Circ: CapCity orders: **6,100**

16 ❑ Jun 1994 Cover: 2.50 **NM** value: **Cover or less**

16/SC ❑ Jun 1994 Cover: 3.95 **NM** value: **Cover or less**
Circ: CapCity orders: **6,850**
Fold-out cover. ★ 1st Appearance of Hardware Version 2.0.

17 ❑ Jul 1994 Cover: 1.50 **NM** value: **Cover or less**
Circ: CapCity orders: **23,050**
📖 Worlds Collide; Worlds Collide, Part 2

18 ❑ Aug 1994 Cover: 1.75 **NM** value: **Cover or less**
Circ: CapCity orders: **19,300**
📖 Worlds Collide, Part 9

19 ❑ Sep 1994 Cover: 1.75 **NM** value: **Cover or less**
Circ: CapCity orders: **6,350**

20 ❑ Oct 1994 Cover: 1.75 **NM** value: **Cover or less**
Circ: CapCity orders: **6,650**

21 ❑ Nov 1994 Cover: 1.75 **NM** value: **Cover or less**
Circ: CapCity orders: **6,100**

22 ❑ Dec 1994 Cover: 1.75 **NM** value: **Cover or less**
Circ: CapCity orders: **5,550**

23 ❑ Jan 1995 Cover: 1.75 **NM** value: **Cover or less**
Circ: CapCity orders: **4,700**
📖 My Brother's Keeper? **A:** Humberto Ramos **W:** Denton Fixx Jr.; Otis Wesley Clay

24 ❑ Feb 1995 Cover: 1.75 **NM** value: **Cover or less**
Circ: CapCity orders: **4,125**

25 ❑ Mar 1995 Cover: 2.95 **NM** value: **Cover or less**
Circ: CapCity orders: **3,750**
• Giant-size.

26 ❑ Apr 1995 Cover: 1.75 **NM** value: **Cover or less**
Circ: CapCity orders: **3,425**

27 ❑ May 1995 Cover: 1.75 **NM** value: **Cover or less**
Circ: CapCity orders: **3,375**

28 ❑ Jun 1995 Cover: 1.75 **NM** value: **Cover or less**
Circ: CapCity orders: **3,275**

29 ❑ Jul 1995 Cover: 2.50 **NM** value: **Cover or less**
Circ: CapCity orders: **3,725**
cover has both.99 and 2.50 cover price.

30 ❑ Aug 1995 Cover: 2.50 **NM** value: **Cover or less**
Circ: CapCity orders: **3,350**
📖 Long Hot Summer

31 ❑ Sep 1995 Cover: 2.50 **NM** value: **Cover or less**
Circ: CapCity orders: **3,275**
📖 The Long Hot Summer ★ Death of Edwin Alva.

32 ❑ Oct 1995 Cover: 2.50 **NM** value: **Cover or less**
Circ: CapCity orders: **2,650**

33 ❑ Nov 1995 Cover: 2.50 **NM** value: **Cover or less**

34 ❑ Dec 1995 Cover: 2.50 **NM** value: **Cover or less**

35 ❑ Jan 1996 Cover: 2.50 **NM** value: **Cover or less**

36 ❑ Feb 1996 Cover: 2.50 **NM** value: **Cover or less**
📖 T-Minus **A:** Denys Cowan **W:** John Rozum

37 ❑ Mar 1996 Cover: 2.50 **NM** value: **Cover or less**
📖 Pressure Suit **A:** Eric Battle **W:** John Rozum

38 ❑ Apr 1996 Cover: 2.50 **NM** value: **Cover or less**
📖 Unsuited **A:** J.J. Birch **W:** John Rozum

39 ❑ May 1996 Cover: 2.50 **NM** value: **Cover or less**

40 ❑ Jun 1996 Cover: 2.50 **NM** value: **Cover or less**

41 ❑ Jul 1996 Cover: 2.50 **NM** value: **Cover or less**

42 ❑ Aug 1996 Cover: 2.50 **NM** value: **Cover or less**

43 ❑ Sep 1996 Cover: 2.50 **NM** value: **Cover or less**
📖 Doorway to Nightmares **A:** Prentis Rollins **W:** Joseph Illidge

44 ❑ Oct 1996 Cover: 2.50 **NM** value: **Cover or less**
📖 Closure **A:** Prentis Rollins **W:** Joseph Illidge

45 ❑ Nov 1996 Cover: 2.50 **NM** value: **Cover or less**
Circ: Diamd. preorders: **4,952**
📖 Sweating it Out • return of Edwin Alva **A:** Prentis Rollins **W:** D.G. Chichester

46 ❑ Dec 1996 Cover: 2.50 **NM** value: **Cover or less**
Circ: Diamd. preorders: **4,852**
📖 Give them the Works **A:** Prentis Rollins **W:** D.G. Chichester

47 ❑ Jan 1997 Cover: 2.50 **NM** value: **Cover or less**
Circ: Diamd. preorders: **4,710**

48 ❑ Feb 1997 Cover: 2.50 **NM** value: **Cover or less**
Circ: Diamd. preorders: **4,510**

49 ❑ Mar 1997 Cover: 2.50 **NM** value: **Cover or less**
Circ: Diamd. preorders: **4,355**

50 ❑ Apr 1997 Cover: 3.95 **NM** value: **Cover or less**
Circ: Diamd. preorders: **4,945**
• Giant-size. final issue.

HARDWIRED — Bangtro

1 ❑ May 1994 Cover: 2.25 **NM** value: **Cover or less**

HARDY BOYS — Gold Key

1 ❑ Apr 1970 Cover: 0.15 **NM** value: **30.00**

2 ❑ Jul 1970 Cover: 0.15 **NM** value: **20.00**

3 ❑ Oct 1970 Cover: 0.15 **NM** value: **20.00**
• **CGC:** 1 graded, best 9.4

4 ❑ Jan 1971 Cover: 0.15 **NM** value: **20.00**
• **CGC:** 1 graded, best 9.4

HAR*HAR — Fantagraphics

1 ❑ b&w Cover: 2.25 **NM** value: **Cover or less**

2 ❑ b&w Cover: 2.25 **NM** value: **Cover or less**

HARI KARI — Black Out

0 ❑ Cover: 2.95 **NM** value: **Cover or less**
Circ: CapCity orders: **6,705**
📖 Her Art is Death • indicia says "#0 #1" **A:** Guy Dorian **W:** Guy Dorian; Gilbert King

1 ❑ Cover: 2.95 **NM** value: **Cover or less**

HARI KARI: LIVE & UNTAMED — Blackout

0 ❑ Cover: 2.95 **NM** value: **Cover or less**
Circ: Diamd. preorders: **9,421**
📖 Moons Over My Hammy **A:** Tommy Castillo **W:** T. Virkaitis

0/SC ❑ Cover: 9.95 **NM** value: **Cover or less**
variant cover. 📖 Moons Over My Hammy **A:** Tommy Castillo **W:** T. Virkaitis

1 ❑ Cover: 2.95 **NM** value: **Cover or less**
Circ: Diamd. preorders: **7,238**

HARI KARI PRIVATE GALLERY — Blackout

0 ❑ Cover: 2.95 **NM** value: **Cover or less**
• Pin-Ups **A:** Brock L. Hor; Fauve; Tim Vigil; Gene Colan; Mark McKenna; Bill Maus; Bob Berry; Dan Day; David Day; Jake Jacobsen; Jonathan D. Smith; Joe Philip; Jr.; Chris Berkeley; Dave Guttierez; Eben Matthews; Fred Galpern; Jeff; Mike Lily; Mike Ocming

HARI KARI: REBIRTH — Black Out

1 ❑ Cover: 2.95 **NM** value: **Cover or less**
Circ: Diamd. preorders: **9,984**
📖 Picking Up The Pieces **A:** Tommy Castillo **W:** Virkaitis

HARI KARI RESURRECTION — Blackout

1 ❑ Cover: 2.95 **NM** value: **Cover or less**
Circ: Diamd. preorders: **6,139**

HARI KARI: THE BEGINNING — Black Out

1 ❑ Cover: 2.95 **NM** value: **Cover or less**

HARI KARI: THE DIARY OF KARI SUN — Blackout

1-2 ❑ Cover: 2.95 **NM** value: **Cover or less**
Circ: Diamd. preorders: **7,453**
• prose accompanied with pin-ups

HARI KARI: THE SILENCE OF EVIL — Black Out

0 ❑ Cover: 2.95 **NM** value: **Cover or less**

HARLEM BEAT — Pocket Mixx

Bk 1 ❑ Cover: 9.95 **NM** value: **Cover or less**
• no date

HARLEM GLOBETROTTERS — Gold Key

Based on the Hanna-Barbera animated series from the early 1970s, the Harlem Globetrotters comic book ran for a dozen issues between 1972 and 1975 and featured the Clown Princes of Basketball in a number of wild adventures, from being trapped in a haunted castle to being the prisoners of a race of abominable snowmen.

Of course, all of these situations can be remedied by a little friendly competition — namely, a game of hoops in which Meadowlark, Curly, Geese, and the gang can show what they've got.

As the comics feature the most recognizable Globetrotter personalities of all time (and the cartoon is responsible for some part of this), no Globetrotter memorabilia collection should be without them.

1 ❑ Apr 1972 Cover: 0.15 **NM** value: **12.00**

2 ❑ Jul 1972 Cover: 0.15 **NM** value: **8.00**

3 ❑ Oct 1972 Cover: 0.15 **NM** value: **7.00**
📖 Granny's Royal Ruckus ★ Appearance of Curly, Gip, Pabs, Geese, Granny, Dribbles, B.J., Meadowlark.

4 ❑ Jan 1973 Cover: 0.15 **NM** value: **7.00**

5 ❑ Apr 1973, four-color Cover: 0.15 **NM** value: **7.00**
📖 Westward Whoa!

6 ❑ Jul 1973 Cover: 0.20 **NM** value: **5.00**

7 ❑ Oct 1973 Cover: 0.20 **NM** value: **5.00**

8 ❑ Jan 1974 Cover: 0.20 **NM** value: **5.00**
• **CGC:** 1 graded, best 8.5

9 ❑ Apr 1974 Cover: 0.20 **NM** value: **5.00**

10 ❑ Jul 1974 Cover: 0.20 **NM** value: **5.00**

11 ❑ Oct 1974 Cover: 0.20 **NM** value: **5.00**

12 ❑ Jan 1975 Cover: 0.20 **NM** value: **5.00**

HARLEM HEROES — Fleetway-Quality

1 ❑ b&w Cover: 1.95 **NM** value: **Cover or less**
📖 The Harlem Heroes, Part 1 **A:** Kevin Walker; S. Pillon **W:** Michael Fleisher

2 ❑ b&w Cover: 1.95 **NM** value: **Cover or less**

3 ❑ b&w Cover: 1.95 **NM** value: **Cover or less**

4 ❑ b&w Cover: 1.95 **NM** value: **Cover or less**

5 ❑ b&w Cover: 1.95 **NM** value: **Cover or less**

6 ❑ b&w Cover: 1.95 **NM** value: **Cover or less**

HARLEQUIN — Caliber

1 ❑ b&w Cover: 2.95 **NM** value: **Cover or less**
No issue number.

HARLEY QUINN — DC

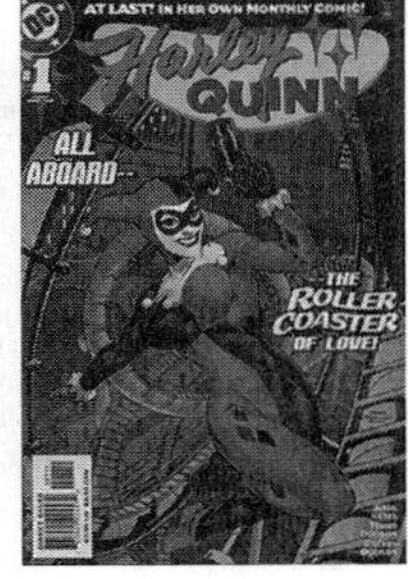

When psychiatrist Harleen Quinzel was assigned to the Joker's case, she never realized she would fall in love, go somewhat insane herself, and enter into a life of crime. But falling for the Clown Prince of Crime is a curse, and Harley soon finds herself out on her own in a one woman crime spree and loving every minute of her new found freedom.

DC finally brought the Harley Quinn character from the popular animated television series into its universe and discovered she was a character with staying power. Her series gives her a chance to interact with the rest of Gotham's best and worst.

1 ❑ Dec 2000 Cover: 2.95 **NM** value: **Cover or less**
Circ: Diamd. preorders: **62,682** • **CGC:** 73 graded, best 9.9
📖 Harley Quinn Romance **A:** Terry Dodson **W:** Karl Kesel

2 ❑ Jan 2001 Cover: 2.25 **NM** value: **Cover or less**
Circ: Diamd. preorders: **49,410** • **CGC:** 1 graded, best 9.8
📖 A Heart Broken in Two! **A:** Terry Dodson **W:** Karl Kesel

3 ❑ Feb 2001 Cover: 2.25 **NM** value: **Cover or less**
Circ: Diamd. preorders: **44,264**

4 ❑ Mar 2001 Cover: 2.25 **NM** value: **Cover or less**
Circ: Diamd. preorders: **38,212** • **CGC:** 1 graded, best 9.8
📖 The Wilde Life **A:** Terry Dodson **W:** Karl Kesel

5 ❑ Apr 2001 Cover: 2.25 **NM** value: **Cover or less**
Circ: Diamd. preorders: **35,500**
📖 Larger than Life **A:** Terry Dodson **W:** Karl Kesel

6 ❑ May 2001 Cover: 2.25 **NM** value: **Cover or less**
Circ: Diamd. preorders: **33,615**
📖 Who Wants to Rob a Millionaire? **A:** Terry Dodson **W:** Karl Kesel

7 ❑ Jun 2001 Cover: 2.25 **NM** value: **Cover or less**
Circ: Diamd. preorders: **32,256**
📖 Gods and Monsters **A:** Terry Dodson **W:** Karl Kesel

8 ❑ Jul 2001 Cover: 2.25 **NM** value: **Cover or less**
Circ: Diamd. preorders: **30,722**

9 ❑ Aug 2001 Cover: 2.25 **NM** value: **Cover or less**
Circ: Diamd. preorders: **30,268**

10 ❑ Sep 2001 Cover: 2.25 **NM** value: **Cover or less**
Circ: Diamd. preorders: **33,531**

HARLEY RIDER — Hungness

An astonishing hodgepodge of a comic celebrating the legend of the Harley-Davidson motorcycle. Fact and fiction alternate in a series of short pieces, all featuring at least one Harley-Davidson, but with as much as possible crammed into the issue, anything stretching to five pages is positively epic. Gray Morrow and Frank Springer deliver their usual professional work, but the remaining art is very poor, and the writing is clipped and sparse in the manner of 1940s comics. A story is told, often in captions, and there's no space for anything but plot. It's difficult to know who this was meant to appeal to. That it's officially licensed is heavily promoted, but it's difficult to imagine bikers or comics readers picking this up, each being alienated by the other's interest.

In fact, several thousand copies of the issue were still available in an automotive museum in southern Illinois in the early 1990s.

1 ❑ Cover: 2.00 **NM** value: **Cover or less**
Circ: CapCity orders: **1,150**
📖 History of the Harley Davidson; A Harley Davidson Legend in San Francisco; Heavenly Harley; The Eagle Lives; Jezebel Rides Again; The Freedom Fighter **A:** Gray Morrow; Frank Springer; Bill Overgard; Neal Cohan; Vince Waller **W:** Carl Hungness; Jim Lawrence

CGC-graded: Multiply prices above by **33 for 9.9 M** • **16 for 9.8 NM/M** • **7 for 9.6 NM+** • **5 for 9.4 NM** • **2.5 for 9.2 NM-** • **1.5 for 9.0 VF/NM**

HAROLD HEDD IN "HITLER'S COCAINE"
Kitchen Sink

1 ❑ Cover: 2.00 **NM** value: **3.00**
📖 Hitler's Cocaine **A:** Rand Holmes **W:** Rand Holmes
2 ❑ Cover: 2.00 **NM** value: **3.00**

HAROLD HEDD (LAST GASP)
Last Gasp Eco-Funnies

1 ❑ Cover: 0.50 **NM** value: **8.00**
2 ❑ Cover: 1.50 **NM** value: **4.00**
📖 Police Should Be Obscene and Not Absurd; Wings over Tijuana **A:** Rand Holme **W:** Rand Holme

HARPY PIN-UP SPECIAL
Peregrine Entertainment

1 ❑ May 1998, b&w Cover: 3.00 **NM** value: **Cover or less**

HARPY PREVIEW
Ground Zero

1 ❑ Oct 1996, b&w Cover: 3.00 **NM** value: **Cover or less**

HARPY: PRIZE OF THE OVERLORD
Ground Zero

1 ❑ Dec 1996, b&w Cover: 3.00 **NM** value: **Cover or less**
Circ: Diamd. preorders: **3,072**
2 ❑ Feb 1997, b&w Cover: 3.00 **NM** value: **Cover or less**
Circ: Diamd. preorders: **1,694**
3 ❑ Apr 1997, b&w Cover: 3.00 **NM** value: **Cover or less**
cover says Blood of the Demon.
Bk 1❑ May 1998 Cover: 14.95 **NM** value: **Cover or less**
No issue number. • Trade Paperback. • collects series

HARRIER PREVIEW
Harrier

1 ❑ Cover: 1.95 **NM** value: **Cover or less**
📖 Cuirass: The Fallen Star; Nightbird: Bird in Flight **A:** John Marshall; Cam Smith **W:** Alan Cowsill; Martin Lock ★ 1st Appearance of Cuirass, Night Bird.

HARRIERS
Express / Entity

1 ❑ Cover: 2.95 **NM** value: **Cover or less**
Foil stamped cover. **A:** Erren Jay Anacleto; Mark Vuycankiat **W:** Bailly Lim-It; Narcisco Roxas Jr.; Ronaldo Roxas
2 ❑ Cover: 2.50 **NM** value: **2.95**
3 ❑ Cover: 2.50 **NM** value: **2.95**

HARROWERS, THE (CLIVE BARKER'S...)
Marvel / Epic

1 ❑ Dec 1993 Cover: 2.95 **NM** value: **Cover or less**
Circ: CapCity orders: **11,000**
glow in the dark cover. 📖 First Strike! **A:** Gene Colan **W:** Malcolm Smith; McNally Sagal
2 ❑ Jan 1994 Cover: 2.50 **NM** value: **Cover or less**
Circ: CapCity orders: **5,300**
3 ❑ Feb 1994 Cover: 2.50 **NM** value: **Cover or less**
Circ: CapCity orders: **4,300**
4 ❑ Mar 1994 Cover: 2.50 **NM** value: **Cover or less**
Circ: CapCity orders: **3,400**
5 ❑ Apr 1994 Cover: 2.50 **NM** value: **Cover or less**
Circ: CapCity orders: **2,850**
6 ❑ May 1994 Cover: 2.50 **NM** value: **Cover or less**
Circ: CapCity orders: **2,550**

HARRY THE COP
Slave Labor

1 ❑ Apr 1992, b&w Cover: 2.95 **NM** value: **Cover or less**
1-2 ❑ Oct 1992, b&w Cover: 2.95 **NM** value: **Cover or less**

HARSH REALM
Harris

1 ❑ Feb 1994, full color Cover: 2.95 **NM** value: **Cover or less**
Circ: CapCity orders: **3,800**
📖 The Case **A:** Andrew Paquette **W:** James D. Hudnall
2 ❑ Mar 1994, full color Cover: 2.95 **NM** value: **Cover or less**
Circ: CapCity orders: **3,000**
📖 The City **A:** Andrew Paquette **W:** James D. Hudnall
3 ❑ Apr 1994, full color Cover: 2.95 **NM** value: **Cover or less**
Circ: CapCity orders: **2,400**
📖 The Hazards **A:** Andrew Paquette **W:** James D. Hudnall
4 ❑ May 1994, full color Cover: 2.95 **NM** value: **Cover or less**
Circ: CapCity orders: **2,325**
5 ❑ Jun 1994, full color Cover: 2.95 **NM** value: **Cover or less**
📖 The Crucible **A:** Andrew Paquette **W:** James D. Hudnall
6 ❑ Jul 1994 Cover: 2.95 **NM** value: **Cover or less**
📖 The End **A:** Andrew Paquette **W:** James D. Hudnall

HARTE OF DARKNESS
Eternity

1 ❑ b&w Cover: 2.50 **NM** value: **Cover or less**
2 ❑ b&w Cover: 2.50 **NM** value: **Cover or less**
3 ❑ b&w Cover: 2.50 **NM** value: **Cover or less**
4 ❑ b&w Cover: 2.50 **NM** value: **Cover or less**

HARVEY
Marvel

1 ❑ Oct 1970 Cover: 0.20 **NM** value: **18.00**
• **CGC:** 3 graded, best 9.0
• humor
2 ❑ Dec 1970 Cover: 0.20 **NM** value: **10.00**
• **CGC:** 1 graded, best 9.0
• humor
3 ❑ Jun 1972 Cover: 0.20 **NM** value: **8.00**
• humor
4 ❑ Aug 1972 Cover: 0.20 **NM** value: **6.00**
• humor
5 ❑ Oct 1972 Cover: 0.20 **NM** value: **6.00**
• humor
6 ❑ Dec 1972 Cover: 0.20 **NM** value: **6.00**
• humor

HARVEY COLLECTORS COMICS
Harvey

1 ❑ Cover: 0.35 **NM** value: **6.00**
2 ❑ Cover: 0.35 **NM** value: **3.00**
3 ❑ Jan 1976 Cover: 0.35 **NM** value: **2.50**
📖 Out West; From Richie to Rags; Pool of Fun; Oil's Well; Tree's a Crowd; Living it Up; Crime Doesn't Play; The Experiment • Reprints Richie Rich Millions #1
4 ❑ 1976 Cover: 0.35 **NM** value: **2.50**
5 ❑ 1976 Cover: 0.35 **NM** value: **2.50**
6 ❑ Jul 1976 Cover: 0.35 **NM** value: **2.50**
📖 Fully Protected; Careful With Money; Cadbury: Dapper Dave; Little Dot: She's a Big Girl Now; Perfect City; There's Be Some Changes Made; The Safety Pack; Take Me On a Hike • Reprints Richie Rich Success #1-2
7 ❑ Cover: 0.50 **NM** value: **2.50**
8 ❑ Cover: 0.50 **NM** value: **2.50**
9 ❑ Cover: 0.50 **NM** value: **2.50**
10 ❑ Cover: 0.50 **NM** value: **2.50**
11 ❑ Cover: 0.50 **NM** value: **2.00**
12 ❑ Cover: 0.50 **NM** value: **2.00**
13 ❑ Cover: 0.50 **NM** value: **2.00**
14 ❑ Cover: 0.50 **NM** value: **2.00**
15 ❑ Cover: 0.50 **NM** value: **2.00**
16 ❑ Cover: 0.50 **NM** value: **2.00**

HARVEY COMICS HITS
Harvey

51 ❑ Oct 1951 Cover: 0.10 **NM** value: **200.00**
52 ❑ Nov 1951 Cover: 0.10 **NM** value: **150.00**
53 ❑ Dec 1951 Cover: 0.10 **NM** value: **150.00**
• **CGC:** 2 graded, best 9.0
54 ❑ Feb 1952 Cover: 0.10 **NM** value: **150.00**
• **CGC:** 2 graded, best 9.6
55 ❑ Mar 1952 Cover: 0.10 **NM** value: **125.00**
56 ❑ Apr 1952 Cover: 0.10 **NM** value: **125.00**
• **CGC:** 1 graded, best 9.0
57 ❑ May 1952 Cover: 0.10 **NM** value: **125.00**
• **CGC:** 3 graded, best 9.4
58 ❑ Jun 1952 Cover: 0.10 **NM** value: **125.00**
59 ❑ Aug 1952 Cover: 0.10 **NM** value: **125.00**
• **CGC:** 3 graded, best 9.0
60 ❑ Sep 1952 Cover: 0.10 **NM** value: **100.00**
61 ❑ Oct 1952 Cover: 0.10 **NM** value: **100.00**
62 ❑ Apr 1953 Cover: 0.10 **NM** value: **100.00**

HARVEY COMICS LIBRARY
Harvey

1 ❑ Apr 1952 Cover: 0.10 **NM** value: **600.00**
• **CGC:** 4 graded, best 8.0
2 ❑ Jul 1952 Cover: 0.10 **NM** value: **200.00**

HARVEY HITS
Harvey

In its heyday from the mid-1950s to the late '70s, Harvey was a formidable comic-book presence, with a line-up that included The Friendly Ghost (Casper), Sad Sack, Wendy (the Good Little Witch), Little Dot, and Richie Rich, plus adventure stalwart The Phantom. Harvey Hits provides a rotating showcase for this cavalcade of kiddie faves, with the spotlight often on such backup characters as Casper's horse Nightmare (the Galloping Ghost), Sad Sack's dog (Muttsy), and, early in the run, Richie Rich himself, when the world's poorest little rich kid was second-fiddle to Little Dot. Harvey offered dependable entertainment by rarely straying from the formula of fun, wholesome stories, and simple, friendly-looking characters.

1 ❑ Sep 1957 Cover: 0.10 **NM** value: **150.00**
• **CGC:** 1 graded, best 8.5
• The Phantom
2 ❑ Oct 1957 Cover: 0.10 **NM** value: **20.00**
• **CGC:** 2 graded, best 7.5
• Rags Rabbit
3 ❑ Nov 1957 Cover: 0.10 **NM** value: **525.00**
• **CGC:** 2 graded, best 9.0
• Richie Rich; 1st full book of Richie Rich
4 ❑ Dec 1957 Cover: 0.10 **NM** value: **100.00**
• **CGC:** 1 graded, best 9.0
• Little Dot's Uncles
5 ❑ Jan 1958 Cover: 0.10 **NM** value: **15.00**
• Steve Mazie's Boy Friend
6 ❑ Feb 1958 Cover: 0.10 **NM** value: **110.00**
• The Phantom
7 ❑ Mar 1958 Cover: 0.10 **NM** value: **115.00**
• Wendy the Good Little Witch
8 ❑ Apr 1958 Cover: 0.10 **NM** value: **35.00**
• Sad Sack
9 ❑ May 1958 Cover: 0.10 **NM** value: **300.00**
• **CGC:** 1 graded, best 4.5
• Richie Rich
10 ❑ Jun 1958 Cover: 0.10 **NM** value: **80.00**
• Little Lotta's Lunch Box
11 ❑ Jul 1958 Cover: 0.10 **NM** value: **50.00**
• Little Audrey's Summer Fun
12 ❑ Aug 1958 Cover: 0.10 **NM** value: **95.00**
• **CGC:** 1 graded, best 5.0
• The Phantom **A:** Jack Kirby(cover)
13 ❑ Sep 1958 Cover: 0.10 **NM** value: **65.00**
• **CGC:** 1 graded, best 8.0
• Little Dot's Uncles
14 ❑ Oct 1958 Cover: 0.10 **NM** value: **14.00**
• Herman & Katnip
15 ❑ Dec 1958 Cover: 0.10 **NM** value: **95.00**
• The Phantom
16 ❑ Jan 1959 Cover: 0.10 **NM** value: **75.00**
• Wendy the Good Little Witch
17 ❑ Feb 1959 Cover: 0.10 **NM** value: **32.00**
• Sad Sack
18 ❑ Mar 1959 Cover: 0.10 **NM** value: **15.00**
• Buzzy & The Crow
19 ❑ Apr 1959 Cover: 0.10 **NM** value: **35.00**
• Little Audrey
20 ❑ May 1959 Cover: 0.10 **NM** value: **45.00**
• Casper & Spooky
21 ❑ Jun 1959 Cover: 0.10 **NM** value: **45.00**
• Wendy the Good Little Witch
22 ❑ Jul 1959 Cover: 0.10 **NM** value: **26.00**
• Sad Sack
23 ❑ Aug 1959 Cover: 0.10 **NM** value: **40.00**
• Wendy the Good Little Witch
24 ❑ Sep 1959 Cover: 0.10 **NM** value: **50.00**
• Little Dot's Uncles
25 ❑ Oct 1959 Cover: 0.10 **NM** value: **14.00**
• Herman & Katnip
26 ❑ Nov 1959 Cover: 0.10 **NM** value: **75.00**
• The Phantom
27 ❑ Dec 1959 Cover: 0.10 **NM** value: **40.00**
• Wendy the Good Little Witch
28 ❑ Jan 1960 Cover: 0.10 **NM** value: **20.00**
• Sad Sack
29 ❑ Feb 1960 Cover: 0.10 **NM** value: **24.00**
• Harvey-Toon #1
30 ❑ Mar 1960 Cover: 0.10 **NM** value: **40.00**
• Wendy the Good Little Witch
31 ❑ Apr 1960 Cover: 0.10 **NM** value: **12.00**
• Herman & Katnip
32 ❑ May 1960 Cover: 0.10 **NM** value: **15.00**
• Sad Sack
33 ❑ Jun 1960 Cover: 0.10 **NM** value: **32.00**
• Wendy the Good Little Witch
34 ❑ Jul 1960 Cover: 0.10 **NM** value: **18.00**
• Harvey-Toon
35 ❑ Aug 1960 Cover: 0.10 **NM** value: **12.00**
• Funday Funnies
36 ❑ Sep 1960 Cover: 0.10 **NM** value: **65.00**
• The Phantom
37 ❑ Oct 1960 Cover: 0.10 **NM** value: **30.00**
• Casper & Nightmare
38 ❑ Nov 1960 Cover: 0.10 **NM** value: **16.00**
📖 Casper; Let's Space it; Buzzy; Salesman's Luck! (Text Story); Camping Trip-Up; Drown and Out; The Noble Fox (Text Story); Food for Fought • Harvey-Toon
39 ❑ Dec 1960 Cover: 0.10 **NM** value: **12.00**
• Sad Sack
40 ❑ Jan 1961 Cover: 0.10 **NM** value: **8.00**
• Funday Funnies
41 ❑ Feb 1961 Cover: 0.10 **NM** value: **9.00**
• Herman & Katnip
42 ❑ Mar 1961 Cover: 0.10 **NM** value: **12.00**
• Harvey-Toon
43 ❑ Apr 1961 Cover: 0.10 **NM** value: **9.00**
• Sad Sack
44 ❑ May 1961 Cover: 0.10 **NM** value: **52.00**
• The Phantom
45 ❑ Jun 1961 Cover: 0.10 **NM** value: **22.00**
📖 Horse Laughs; Herman And Katnip; The Ghosts Go West; The Space Man; Eyes Right; The Baby Duck-tor; • Casper and Nightmare
46 ❑ Jul 1961 Cover: 0.10 **NM** value: **9.00**
• Harvey-Toon
47 ❑ Aug 1961 Cover: 0.10 **NM** value: **9.00**
• Sad Sack
48 ❑ Sep 1961 Cover: 0.10 **NM** value: **45.00**
• The Phantom
49 ❑ Oct 1961 Cover: 0.10 **NM** value: **55.00**
• Stumbo the Giant
50 ❑ Nov 1961 Cover: 0.10 **NM** value: **8.00**
• Harvey-Toon
51 ❑ Dec 1961 Cover: 0.10 **NM** value: **7.50**
• Sad Sack
52 ❑ Jan 1962 Cover: 0.12 **NM** value: **20.00**
• Casper & Nightmare
53 ❑ Feb 1962 Cover: 0.12 **NM** value: **7.50**
• Harvey-Toon
54 ❑ Mar 1962 Cover: 0.12 **NM** value: **40.00**
• Stumbo the Giant
55 ❑ Apr 1962 Cover: 0.12 **NM** value: **7.50**
• Sad Sack
56 ❑ May 1962 Cover: 0.12 **NM** value: **18.00**
• Casper & Nightmare
57 ❑ Jun 1962 Cover: 0.12 **NM** value: **30.00**
• Stumbo the Giant
58 ❑ Jul 1962 Cover: 0.12 **NM** value: **7.50**
• Sad Sack
59 ❑ Aug 1962 Cover: 0.12 **NM** value: **18.00**
• Casper & Nightmare
60 ❑ Sep 1962 Cover: 0.12 **NM** value: **26.00**
• Stumbo the Giant
61 ❑ Oct 1962 Cover: 0.12 **NM** value: **6.00**
• Sad Sack
62 ❑ Nov 1962 Cover: 0.12 **NM** value: **15.00**
• Casper & Nightmare
63 ❑ Dec 1962 Cover: 0.12 **NM** value: **24.00**
• Stumbo the Giant
64 ❑ Jan 1963 Cover: 0.12 **NM** value: **6.00**
• Sad Sack
65 ❑ Feb 1963 Cover: 0.12 **NM** value: **15.00**
• Casper & Nightmare
66 ❑ Mar 1963 Cover: 0.12 **NM** value: **24.00**
• Stumbo the Giant
67 ❑ Apr 1963 Cover: 0.12 **NM** value: **6.00**
• Sad Sack
68 ❑ May 1963 Cover: 0.12 **NM** value: **15.00**
• Casper & Nightmare
69 ❑ Jun 1963 Cover: 0.12 **NM** value: **24.00**
• Stumbo the Giant

Other grades: Multiply prices above by **1.5 for Mint • 2/3 for Very Fine • 1/3 for Fine • 1/5 for Very Good • 1/8 for Good**

70 ❑ Jul 1963 Cover: 0.12 **NM** value: **5.00**
• Sad Sack
71 ❑ Aug 1963 Cover: 0.12 **NM** value: **12.00**
• Casper & Nightmare
72 ❑ Sep 1963 Cover: 0.12 **NM** value: **20.00**
• Stumbo the Giant
73 ❑ Oct 1963 Cover: 0.12 **NM** value: **6.00**
• Little Sad Sack
74 ❑ Nov 1963 Cover: 0.12 **NM** value: **6.00**
• Sad Sack's Muttsy
75 ❑ Dec 1963 Cover: 0.12 **NM** value: **12.00**
• Casper & Nightmare
76 ❑ Jan 1964 Cover: 0.12 **NM** value: **6.00**
• Little Sad Sack
77 ❑ Feb 1964 Cover: 0.12 **NM** value: **6.00**
• Sad Sack's Muttsy
78 ❑ Mar 1964 Cover: 0.12 **NM** value: **24.00**
• Stumbo the Giant
79 ❑ Apr 1964 Cover: 0.12 **NM** value: **6.00**
• Little Sad Sack
80 ❑ May 1964 Cover: 0.12 **NM** value: **6.00**
• Sad Sack's Muttsy
81 ❑ Jun 1964 Cover: 0.12 **NM** value: **6.00**
• Little Sad Sack
82 ❑ Jul 1964 Cover: 0.12 **NM** value: **6.00**
• Sad Sack's Muttsy
83 ❑ Aug 1964 Cover: 0.12 **NM** value: **6.00**
• Little Sad Sack
84 ❑ Sep 1964 Cover: 0.12 **NM** value: **6.00**
• Sad Sack's Muttsy
85 ❑ Oct 1964 Cover: 0.12 **NM** value: **6.00**
• Gabby Gob
86 ❑ Nov 1964 Cover: 0.12 **NM** value: **6.00**
• G.I. Juniors
87 ❑ Dec 1964 Cover: 0.12 **NM** value: **6.00**
• Sad Sack's Muttsy
88 ❑ Jan 1965 Cover: 0.12 **NM** value: **15.00**
• Stumbo the Giant
89 ❑ Feb 1965 Cover: 0.12 **NM** value: **6.00**
• Sad Sack's Muttsy
90 ❑ Mar 1965 Cover: 0.12 **NM** value: **6.00**
• Gabby Gob
91 ❑ Apr 1965 Cover: 0.12 **NM** value: **5.00**
• G.I. Juniors
92 ❑ May 1965 Cover: 0.12 **NM** value: **5.00**
• Sad Sack's Muttsy
93 ❑ Jun 1965 Cover: 0.12 **NM** value: **5.00**
• Sadie Sack
94 ❑ Jul 1965 Cover: 0.12 **NM** value: **5.00**
• Gabby Gob
95 ❑ Aug 1965 Cover: 0.12 **NM** value: **5.00**
• G.I. Juniors
96 ❑ Sep 1965 Cover: 0.12 **NM** value: **5.00**
• Sad Sack's Muttsy
97 ❑ Oct 1965 Cover: 0.12 **NM** value: **5.00**
• Gabby Gob
98 ❑ Nov 1965 Cover: 0.12 **NM** value: **5.00**
📖 The Hero; Who's in Charge?; The Casualty; Quiet, Genius at Work; Only the Fit Shall Survive!; Follow Our Fearless Leader! (text story); And a Child Shall Lead Them! • G.I. Juniors
99 ❑ Dec 1965 Cover: 0.12 **NM** value: **5.00**
• Sad Sack's Muttsy
100 ❑ Jan 1966 Cover: 0.12 **NM** value: **5.00**
• Gabby Gob
101 ❑ Feb 1966 Cover: 0.12 **NM** value: **5.00**
• G.I. Juniors
102 ❑ Mar 1966 Cover: 0.12 **NM** value: **5.00**
• Sad Sack's Muttsy
103 ❑ Apr 1966 Cover: 0.12 **NM** value: **5.00**
• Gabby Gob
104 ❑ May 1966 Cover: 0.12 **NM** value: **5.00**
• G.I. Juniors
105 ❑ Jun 1966 Cover: 0.12 **NM** value: **5.00**
• Sad Sack's Muttsy
106 ❑ Jul 1966 Cover: 0.12 **NM** value: **5.00**
• Gabby Gob
107 ❑ Aug 1966 Cover: 0.12 **NM** value: **5.00**
• G.I. Juniors
108 ❑ Sep 1966 Cover: 0.12 **NM** value: **5.00**
• Sad Sack's Muttsy
109 ❑ Oct 1966 Cover: 0.12 **NM** value: **5.00**
• Gabby Gob
110 ❑ Nov 1966 Cover: 0.12 **NM** value: **5.00**
• G.I. Juniors
111 ❑ Dec 1966 Cover: 0.12 **NM** value: **5.00**
• Sad Sack's Muttsy
112 ❑ Jan 1967 Cover: 0.12 **NM** value: **5.00**
• G.I. Juniors
113 ❑ Feb 1967 Cover: 0.12 **NM** value: **5.00**
• Sad Sack's Muttsy
114 ❑ Mar 1967 Cover: 0.12 **NM** value: **5.00**
• G.I. Juniors
115 ❑ Apr 1967 Cover: 0.12 **NM** value: **5.00**
• Sad Sack's Muttsy
116 ❑ May 1967 Cover: 0.12 **NM** value: **5.00**
• G.I. Juniors
117 ❑ Jun 1967 Cover: 0.12 **NM** value: **5.00**
• Sad Sack's Muttsy
118 ❑ Jul 1967 Cover: 0.12 **NM** value: **5.00**
• G.I. Juniors
119 ❑ Aug 1967 Cover: 0.12 **NM** value: **5.00**
• Sad Sack's Muttsy
120 ❑ Sep 1967 Cover: 0.12 **NM** value: **5.00**
• G.I. Juniors
121 ❑ Oct 1967 Cover: 0.12 **NM** value: **5.00**
• Sad Sack's Muttsy
122 ❑ Nov 1967 Cover: 0.12 **NM** value: **5.00**
final issue. • G.I. Juniors

HARVEY SPOTLITE — Harvey

1 ❑ Cover: 0.75 **NM** value: **3.50**
📖 A Rose Is a Rose; Clean Player; Nap Sack and Muttsy: Bragging; Sad Sack and Skater Sack: Just Rolling Along; Harveyland Map (pinup); Sad Sack and Sunny Sack: Oh, Happy Day; Help; Sad Sack and Sunny Sack: On the Way; Nap Sack and Muttsy: Big Search • Spotlite on Sad Sack; Skater Sack★ Appearance of Nap Sack, Muttsy, Sunny Sack.
2 ❑ Cover: 0.75 **NM** value: **2.50**
• Spotlite on Baby Huey
3 ❑ Cover: 0.75 **NM** value: **2.50**
• Spotlite on Little Dot
4 ❑ Cover: 1.00 **NM** value: **2.50**
• Spotlite on Little Audrey

HATE — Fantagraphics

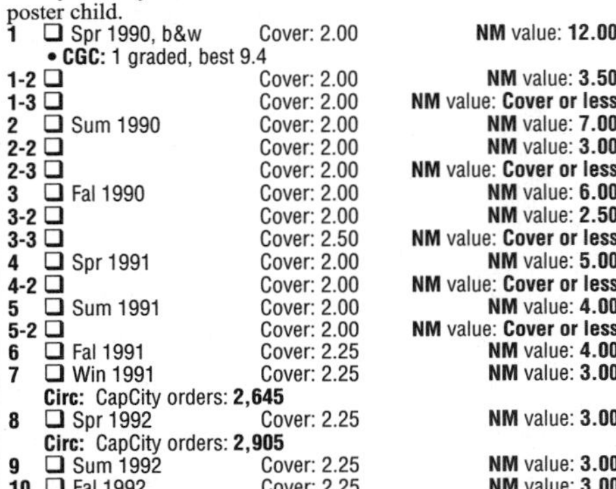

Hate is the Harvey Award-winning title from Peter Bagge, following up on characters introduced in his previous work, Neat Stuff. Hate is primarily the story of a loser named Buddy Bradley, a man living the slacker equivalent of the good life in a dumpy apartment in Seattle. Buddy works at crummy jobs, watches the neighbors for recreation, and his main cultural aspiration is to become a true beer connoisseur.

His life may be purposeless and depressing, but he's really just an Everyman for the Nineties. Some years after the start of this 1990 series, journalists would give the post-Baby Boom generation the moniker "Generation X." Supposedly, Gen X-ers lived in an era of diminished expectations, condemned to dreary "McJobs" and cynical about what the future holds. If so, Buddy Bradley would make a fine candidate as the Generation-X poster child.

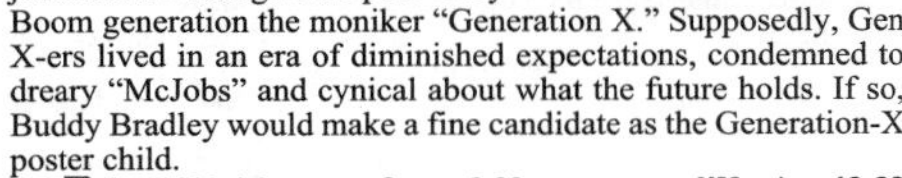

1 ❑ Spr 1990, b&w Cover: 2.00 **NM** value: **12.00**
• **CGC:** 1 graded, best 9.4
1-2 ❑ Cover: 2.00 **NM** value: **3.50**
1-3 ❑ Cover: 2.00 **NM** value: **Cover or less**
2 ❑ Sum 1990 Cover: 2.00 **NM** value: **7.00**
2-2 ❑ Cover: 2.00 **NM** value: **3.00**
2-3 ❑ Cover: 2.00 **NM** value: **Cover or less**
3 ❑ Fal 1990 Cover: 2.00 **NM** value: **6.00**
3-2 ❑ Cover: 2.00 **NM** value: **2.50**
3-3 ❑ Cover: 2.50 **NM** value: **Cover or less**
4 ❑ Spr 1991 Cover: 2.00 **NM** value: **5.00**
4-2 ❑ Cover: 2.00 **NM** value: **Cover or less**
5 ❑ Sum 1991 Cover: 2.00 **NM** value: **4.00**
5-2 ❑ Cover: 2.00 **NM** value: **Cover or less**
6 ❑ Fal 1991 Cover: 2.25 **NM** value: **4.00**
7 ❑ Win 1991 Cover: 2.25 **NM** value: **3.00**
Circ: CapCity orders: **2,645**
8 ❑ Spr 1992 Cover: 2.25 **NM** value: **3.00**
Circ: CapCity orders: **2,905**
9 ❑ Sum 1992 Cover: 2.25 **NM** value: **3.00**
10 ❑ Fal 1992 Cover: 2.25 **NM** value: **3.00**
Circ: CapCity orders: **3,025**
11 ❑ Win 1993 Cover: 2.50 **NM** value: **Cover or less**
Circ: CapCity orders: **3,650**
12 ❑ Spr 1993 Cover: 2.50 **NM** value: **Cover or less**
Circ: CapCity orders: **3,750**
13 ❑ Sum 1993 Cover: 2.50 **NM** value: **Cover or less**
Circ: CapCity orders: **4,075**
14 ❑ Fal 1993 Cover: 2.50 **NM** value: **Cover or less**
Circ: CapCity orders: **4,200**
15 ❑ Spr 1994 Cover: 2.50 **NM** value: **Cover or less**
Circ: CapCity orders: **4,575**
16 ❑ Fal 1994 Cover: 2.95 **NM** value: **Cover or less**
Circ: CapCity orders: **5,292**
• color story **A:** Peter Bagge **W:** Peter Bagge
17 ❑ Win 1995, full color Cover: 2.95 **NM** value: **Cover or less**
Circ: CapCity orders: **4,806**
📖 Let's Get Serious **A:** Peter Bagge **W:** Peter Bagge
18 ❑ Apr 1995, full color Cover: 2.95 **NM** value: **Cover or less**
Circ: CapCity orders: **4,975**
19 ❑ Jun 1995, full color Cover: 2.95 **NM** value: **Cover or less**
Circ: CapCity orders: **5,065**
20 ❑ Sep 1995 Cover: 2.95 **NM** value: **Cover or less**
Circ: CapCity orders: **4,860**
• color and b&w **A:** Peter Bagge **W:** Peter Bagge
21 ❑ Dec 1995 Cover: 2.95 **NM** value: **Cover or less**
22 ❑ Apr 1996 Cover: 2.95 **NM** value: **Cover or less**
23 ❑ Jun 1996, full color Cover: 2.95 **NM** value: **Cover or less**
24 ❑ Sep 1996, full color Cover: 2.95 **NM** value: **Cover or less**
25 ❑ Dec 1996, full color Cover: 2.95 **NM** value: **Cover or less**
Circ: Diamd. preorders: **13,246**
26 ❑ Mar 1997 Cover: 2.95 **NM** value: **Cover or less**
Circ: Diamd. preorders: **11,853**
27 ❑ May 1997 Cover: 2.95 **NM** value: **Cover or less**
Circ: Diamd. preorders: **12,968**
28 ❑ Jul 1997 Cover: 2.95 **NM** value: **Cover or less**
Circ: Diamd. preorders: **11,035**
29 ❑ Jan 1998 Cover: 2.95 **NM** value: **Cover or less**
Circ: Diamd. preorders: **11,222**
30 ❑ Jun 1998 Cover: 3.95 **NM** value: **Cover or less**
Circ: Diamd. preorders: **11,759**
final issue. • color and b&w **A:** Peter Bagge **W:** Peter Bagge

HATEBALL — Fantagraphics

1 ❑ **NM** value: **1.00**
No issue number. • giveaway.

HATE JAMBOREE! — Fantagraphics

1 ❑ Oct 1998, b&w and color Cover: 4.50 **NM** value: **Cover or less**
newsprint cover. **A:** Peter Bagge **W:** Peter Bagge

HAUNTED — Charlton

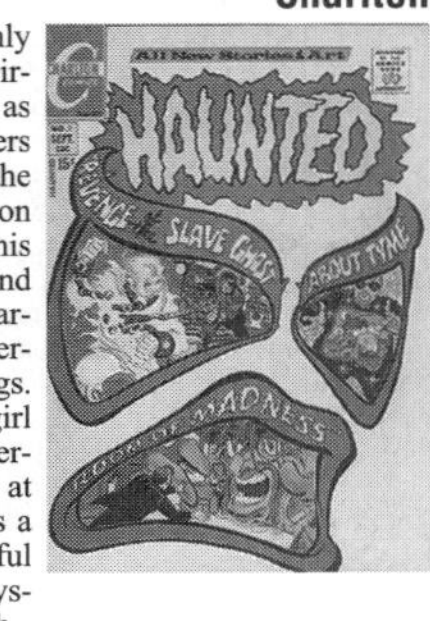

This series was more commonly known by its cover title, "Baron Weirwulf's Haunted Library." Just as DC's Cain and Abel gave readers tours of the House of Mystery and the House of Secrets, Charlton's Baron Weirwulf led readers through his Haunted Library. The mysterious and sinister Weirwulf's whole home, particularly his library, held many a terrifying tale, often with ironic endings. Stories included a peculiar little girl who has found a unique — and supernatural — way to be everywhere at once; a lifelike doll who becomes a cuckolded husband's only faithful companion; and a couple who is mysteriously brought together by death.

1 ❑ Sep 1971 Cover: 0.20 **NM** value: **9.00**
📖 The Room of Madness!; Revenge of the Slave Ghost; Transmutation Trouble (Text Story); It's About Time **A:** Steve Ditko **W:** Steve Ditko
2 ❑ Nov 1971 Cover: 0.20 **NM** value: **4.50**
3 ❑ Jan 1972 Cover: 0.20 **NM** value: **4.50**
4 ❑ Feb 1972 Cover: 0.20 **NM** value: **3.50**
5 ❑ Apr 1972 Cover: 0.20 **NM** value: **3.50**
📖 The Garden of 1,000 Delights; Let Us Work Together; This How It Is!; Spaceship to Freedom (Text Story)
6 ❑ Jun 1972 Cover: 0.20 **NM** value: **3.50**
7 ❑ Aug 1972 Cover: 0.20 **NM** value: **3.50**
8 ❑ Oct 1972 Cover: 0.20 **NM** value: **3.50**
9 ❑ Dec 1972 Cover: 0.20 **NM** value: **3.50**
10 ❑ Jan 1973 Cover: 0.20 **NM** value: **3.50**
11 ❑ Mar 1973 Cover: 0.20 **NM** value: **3.00**
12 ❑ May 1973 Cover: 0.20 **NM** value: **3.00**
13 ❑ Jul 1973 Cover: 0.20 **NM** value: **3.00**
14 ❑ Sep 1973 Cover: 0.20 **NM** value: **3.00**
• **CGC:** 1 graded, best 8.5
15 ❑ Nov 1973 Cover: 0.20 **NM** value: **3.00**
16 ❑ Jun 1974 Cover: 0.25 **NM** value: **3.00**
17 ❑ Jul 1974 Cover: 0.25 **NM** value: **3.00**
📖 Greed; The Voice From Beyond (Text Story); Sargasso Trap; A Budding Evil
18 ❑ Oct 1974 Cover: 0.25 **NM** value: **3.00**
19 ❑ Dec 1974 Cover: 0.25 **NM** value: **3.00**
• **CGC:** 1 graded, best 8.0
20 ❑ Feb 1975 Cover: 0.25 **NM** value: **3.00**
21 ❑ Apr 1975 Cover: 0.25 **NM** value: **3.00**
22 ❑ Jun 1975 Cover: 0.25 **NM** value: **3.00**
📖 I Can Sing Forever; The Plague; Manmade Monster; Fear Has a Name! **A:** Tom Sutton; Joe Staton **W:** Nicola Cutii; Britton Bloom; Gary Petras
23 ❑ Sep 1975 Cover: 0.25 **NM** value: **3.00**
24 ❑ Nov 1975 Cover: 0.25 **NM** value: **3.00**
25 ❑ Jan 1976 Cover: 0.25 **NM** value: **3.00**
26 ❑ Mar 1976 Cover: 0.25 **NM** value: **3.00**
27 ❑ May 1976 Cover: 0.30 **NM** value: **3.00**
28 ❑ Jul 1976 Cover: 0.30 **NM** value: **3.00**
29 ❑ Cover: 0.30 **NM** value: **3.00**
30 ❑ Cover: 0.30 **NM** value: **3.00**
31 ❑ Sep 1977 Cover: 0.35 **NM** value: **3.00**
32 ❑ Oct 1977 Cover: 0.35 **NM** value: **2.50**
33 ❑ Dec 1977 Cover: 0.35 **NM** value: **2.50**
34 ❑ Feb 1978 Cover: 0.35 **NM** value: **2.50**
35 ❑ Apr 1978 Cover: 0.35 **NM** value: **2.50**
36 ❑ May 1978 Cover: 0.35 **NM** value: **2.50**
37 ❑ Jul 1978 Cover: 0.35 **NM** value: **2.50**
📖 Quest For Linda; Everywhere There's Lisa-Anne; The Painted Smile
38 ❑ 1978 Cover: 0.35 **NM** value: **2.50**
39 ❑ Dec 1978 Cover: 0.35 **NM** value: **2.50**
40 ❑ Feb 1979 Cover: 0.40 **NM** value: **2.50**
41 ❑ Apr 1979 Cover: 0.40 **NM** value: **2.00**
42 ❑ Jun 1979 Cover: 0.40 **NM** value: **2.00**
43 ❑ Jul 1979 Cover: 0.40 **NM** value: **2.00**
44 ❑ Sep 1979 Cover: 0.40 **NM** value: **2.00**
45 ❑ Oct 1979 Cover: 0.40 **NM** value: **2.00**
46 ❑ 1979 Cover: 0.40 **NM** value: **2.00**
47 ❑ Jan 1980 Cover: 0.40 **NM** value: **2.00**
48 ❑ Mar 1980 Cover: 0.40 **NM** value: **2.00**
49 ❑ May 1980 Cover: 0.40 **NM** value: **2.00**
50 ❑ 1980 **NM** value: **2.00**
51 ❑ 1980 **NM** value: **2.00**
52 ❑ Dec 1980 Cover: 0.50 **NM** value: **2.00**
53 ❑ Jan 1981 Cover: 0.50 **NM** value: **2.00**
54 ❑ Mar 1981 Cover: 0.50 **NM** value: **2.00**
55 ❑ May 1981 Cover: 0.50 **NM** value: **2.00**
56 ❑ Jul 1981 Cover: 0.50 **NM** value: **2.00**
57 ❑ Sep 1981 Cover: 0.50 **NM** value: **2.00**
58 ❑ Oct 1981 Cover: 0.50 **NM** value: **2.00**
59 ❑ Jan 1982 Cover: 0.60 **NM** value: **2.00**
60 ❑ Mar 1982 Cover: 0.60 **NM** value: **2.00**
61 ❑ Apr 1982 Cover: 0.60 **NM** value: **2.00**
62 ❑ Jul 1982 Cover: 0.60 **NM** value: **2.00**
63 ❑ Sep 1982 Cover: 0.60 **NM** value: **2.00**
64 ❑ Nov 1982 Cover: 0.60 **NM** value: **2.00**
65 ❑ Jan 1983 Cover: 0.60 **NM** value: **2.00**
66 ❑ Mar 1983 Cover: 0.60 **NM** value: **2.00**
67 ❑ May 1983 Cover: 0.60 **NM** value: **2.00**
📖 Stranger on the Loose; Death Scene; Welcome Home, Darling **A:** Tom Sutton; Steve Ditko **W:** Joe Gill; John Walker; Steve Morris
68 ❑ Jul 1983 Cover: 0.60 **NM** value: **2.00**
69 ❑ Sep 1983 Cover: 0.60 **NM** value: **2.00**
70 ❑ Nov 1983 Cover: 0.75 **NM** value: **2.00**
71 ❑ Jan 1984 Cover: 0.75 **NM** value: **2.00**
72 ❑ Mar 1984 Cover: 0.75 **NM** value: **2.00**
73 ❑ May 1984 Cover: 0.75 **NM** value: **2.00**
74 ❑ Jul 1984 Cover: 0.75 **NM** value: **2.00**
75 ❑ Sep 1984 Cover: 0.75 **NM** value: **2.00**
final issue.

CGC-graded: Multiply prices above by **33 for 9.9 M • 16 for 9.8 NM/M • 7 for 9.6 NM+ • 5 for 9.4 NM • 2.5 for 9.2 NM- • 1.5 for 9.0 VF/NM**

HAUNTED LOVE — Charlton

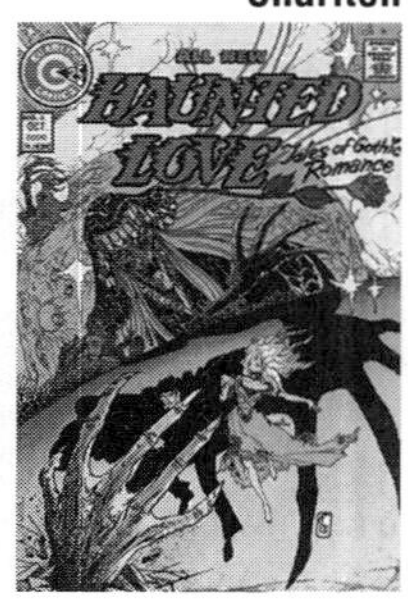

This title adeptly combined horror with romance, a classic combination, as lovers of Gothic romance are aware. Each story is a period piece set in the 19th or early 20th century. Typical of the stories is "The Vanishing Wreck," in which a fisherman has a premonition of a beautiful woman's drowning — leading him to save her from that fate when he meets her shortly afterward in real life. In another tale "Sleep, My Love" a young woman's fiance unwittingly helps her fiendish mistress possess her body.

1 ❑ Apr 1973 Cover: 0.20 **NM** value: **9.00**
2 ❑ Jun 1973 Cover: 0.20 **NM** value: **5.00**
3 ❑ **NM** value: **5.00**
4 ❑ **NM** value: **3.50**
5 ❑ **NM** value: **3.50**
6 ❑ Oct 1974 Cover: 0.25 **NM** value: **3.50**
The Vanishing Wreck; Sleep. My Love… **A:** Fred Himes **W:** Joe Gill
7 ❑ Jan 1975 Cover: 0.25 **NM** value: **3.50**
8 ❑ Mar 1975 Cover: 0.25 **NM** value: **3.50**
9 ❑ May 1975 Cover: 0.25 **NM** value: **3.50**
10 ❑ Jul 1975 Cover: 0.25 **NM** value: **3.50**
11 ❑ Sep 1975 Cover: 0.25 **NM** value: **3.50**
final issue.

HAUNTED MAN, THE — Dark Horse

1 ❑ Mar 2000 Cover: 2.95 **NM** value: **Cover or less**
Circ: Diamd. preorders: **5,139**
A Present of the Past **A:** Mark Badger **W:** Gerard Jones
2 ❑ Cover: 2.95 **NM** value: **Cover or less**
Circ: Diamd. preorders: **3,591**
3 ❑ Cover: 2.95 **NM** value: **Cover or less**

HAUNTED THRILLS — Farrell

One of the more horrific horror titles of the early 1950s, Haunted Thrills featured some very bizarre covers with zombies, corpses with dripping flesh, and mangy skeletons.

The interior stories were also bizarre, featuring drug use, an appearance by Adolf Hitler, a Nazi death camp story, and, late in the series, an appearance by Jesus Christ (perhaps an attempt to raise its reputation?).

Stories from Farrell's Ellery Queen #1 were reprinted in the first two issues and L.B. Cole provided art for at least one story in issue #2. — Brent

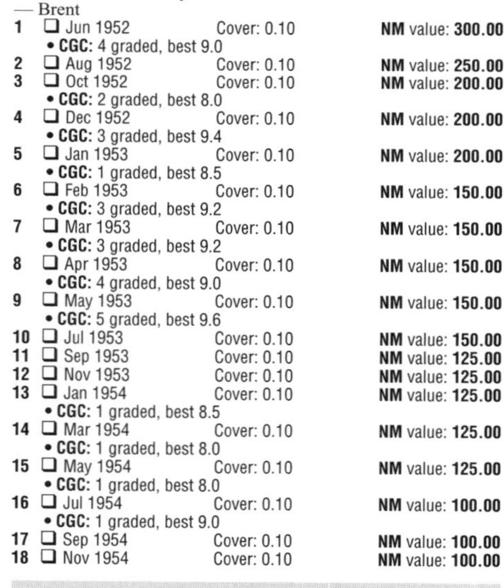

1 ❑ Jun 1952 Cover: 0.10 **NM** value: **300.00**
• **CGC:** 4 graded, best 9.0
2 ❑ Aug 1952 Cover: 0.10 **NM** value: **250.00**
3 ❑ Oct 1952 Cover: 0.10 **NM** value: **200.00**
• **CGC:** 2 graded, best 8.0
4 ❑ Dec 1952 Cover: 0.10 **NM** value: **200.00**
• **CGC:** 3 graded, best 9.4
5 ❑ Jan 1953 Cover: 0.10 **NM** value: **200.00**
• **CGC:** 1 graded, best 8.5
6 ❑ Feb 1953 Cover: 0.10 **NM** value: **150.00**
• **CGC:** 3 graded, best 9.2
7 ❑ Mar 1953 Cover: 0.10 **NM** value: **150.00**
• **CGC:** 3 graded, best 9.2
8 ❑ Apr 1953 Cover: 0.10 **NM** value: **150.00**
• **CGC:** 4 graded, best 9.0
9 ❑ May 1953 Cover: 0.10 **NM** value: **150.00**
• **CGC:** 5 graded, best 9.6
10 ❑ Jul 1953 Cover: 0.10 **NM** value: **150.00**
11 ❑ Sep 1953 Cover: 0.10 **NM** value: **125.00**
12 ❑ Nov 1953 Cover: 0.10 **NM** value: **125.00**
13 ❑ Jan 1954 Cover: 0.10 **NM** value: **125.00**
• **CGC:** 1 graded, best 8.5
14 ❑ Mar 1954 Cover: 0.10 **NM** value: **125.00**
• **CGC:** 1 graded, best 8.0
15 ❑ May 1954 Cover: 0.10 **NM** value: **125.00**
• **CGC:** 1 graded, best 8.0
16 ❑ Jul 1954 Cover: 0.10 **NM** value: **100.00**
• **CGC:** 1 graded, best 9.0
17 ❑ Sep 1954 Cover: 0.10 **NM** value: **100.00**
18 ❑ Nov 1954 Cover: 0.10 **NM** value: **100.00**

Capital City orders are the actual sales of comic books by Capital City Distribution, once one of the largest U.S. sellers of comics to comics shops. Capital City's share of comics shop sales, while not known exactly, increases from around 10-20% in the mid-1980s to 30-35% in the mid-1990s. Capital City's share of comic books sold on newsstands (most Marvels and DCs) will be less.

HAUNT OF FEAR, THE (E.C.) — E.C.

This title was the morphed form that Gunfighter took, when E.C. took its turn into horror storytelling. The numbering is a bit confusing, since #15-17 carried the logo "Introducing a New Trend in magazines … Illustrated SuspenStories we dare you to read!" and then ran three issues before morphing into the non-horror title Two-Fisted Tales to provide that series with a start at #18 — and then the Haunt of Fear continued the following month by quietly counting those three issues as if they'd been numbered #1-3 and starting up with #4. This meant there was a #15 that was May 50, a #16 that was Aug 50, and a #17 that was Oct 50 — and a #15 that was Sep 52, a #16 that was Nov 52, and a #17 that was Jan 53.

In the earlier #17, Bill Gaines and Al Feldstein appeared in a story about the way the E.C. horror line supposedly was created: "Horror beneath the Streets." "Host" of The Haunt of Fear was The Old Witch.

The title carried work of those thought of as the core artists that made E.C. the focus of fan attention: Johnny Craig, Harvey Kurtzman, Al Feldstein, Graham Ingels, Jack Davis, Will Elder, Jack Kamen, Reed Crandall, George Evans, Bernie Krigstein, Joe Orlando, and Wally Wood. Some of the stories were adaptations of stories by the likes of Bennett Cerf, John Collier, and Ray Bradbury — and two adaptations of W.W. Jacobs' "The Monkey's Paw." The series came to an end with the Comics Magazine Association of America's implementation of the Comics Code, which forbade "all scenes of horror" in newsstand comics. — Maggie

1 ❑ May 1950 Cover: 0.10 **NM** value: **2100.00**
• **CGC:** 5 graded, best 9.8
The Wall; House of Horror; The Mad Magician; The Thing in the Swamp • (Haunt of Fear #15) Numbering continued from Gunfighters
2 ❑ Jul 1950 Cover: 0.10 **NM** value: **865.00**
• **CGC:** 6 graded, best 9.6
Vampire!; Horror-Ahead!; The Killer in the Coffin!; The Mummy's Return! • (Haunt of Fear #16) Numbering continued from Gunfighters
3 ❑ Sep 1950 Cover: 0.10 **NM** value: **865.00**
• **CGC:** 6 graded, best 9.6
Nightmare!; Television Terror!; Monster Maker!; Horror Beneath the Streets! • (Haunt of Fear #17) Numbering continued from Gunfighters ★ Origin of The Crypt of Terror, The Vault of Horror, The Haunt of Fear.
4 ❑ Nov 1950 Cover: 0.10 **NM** value: **650.00**
• **CGC:** 5 graded, best 9.4
The Hunchback!; The Tunnel of Terror!; The Living Mummy; Man From the Grave!
5 ❑ Jan 1951 Cover: 0.10 **NM** value: **450.00**
• **CGC:** 4 graded, best 9.6
A Biting Finish!; Horror in the Freak Tent!; A Tasty Morsel!; Seeds of Death! • Graphic eye-injury panel
6 ❑ Mar 1951 Cover: 0.10 **NM** value: **350.00**
• **CGC:** 7 graded, best 9.6
A Strange Undertaking…; So They Finally Pinned You Down; A Grave Gag; Cheese, That's Horrible!
7 ❑ May 1951 Cover: 0.10 **NM** value: **350.00**
• **CGC:** 7 graded, best 9.8
Room For One More; The Basket; Horror in the School Room; The Howling Banshee
8 ❑ Jul 1951 Cover: 0.10 **NM** value: **350.00**
• **CGC:** 3 graded, best 9.6
Hounded to Death; The Very Strange Mummy; Diminishing Returns; The Irony of Death
9 ❑ Sep 1951 Cover: 0.10 **NM** value: **350.00**
• **CGC:** 6 graded, best 9.6
Warts so Horrible?; Forbidden Fruit; The Age-Old Story; The Gorilla's Paw
10 ❑ Nov 1951 Cover: 0.10 **NM** value: **325.00**
• **CGC:** 6 graded, best 9.8
Grave Business; The Vamp; My Uncle Ekar; Bum Steer
11 ❑ Jan 1952 Cover: 0.10 **NM** value: **240.00**
• **CGC:** 5 graded, best 9.8
Ooze in the Cellar?; The Acid Test!; Extermination; Ear Today…Gone Tomorrow!
12 ❑ Mar 1952 Cover: 0.10 **NM** value: **240.00**
• **CGC:** 8 graded, best 9.6
Poetic Justice!; …On a Dead Man's Chest!; Till Death do we Part!; What's Cookin'? **A:** Johnny Craig
13 ❑ May 1952 Cover: 0.10 **NM** value: **240.00**
• **CGC:** 3 graded, best 9.8
For the Love of Death!; Fed Up!; Minor Error!; Wolf Bait!
14 ❑ Jul 1952 Cover: 0.10 **NM** value: **300.00**
• **CGC:** 6 graded, best 9.8
A Little Stranger!; Take Your Pick!; Ship-Shape!; This Little Piggy… ★ Origin of The Old Witch.
15 ❑ Sep 1952 Cover: 0.10 **NM** value: **225.00**
• **CGC:** 8 graded, best 9.8
Chatter-Boxed!; All Washed Up!; Marriage Vows!; Death of Some Salesmen!
16 ❑ Nov 1952 Cover: 0.10 **NM** value: **225.00**
• **CGC:** 6 graded, best 9.8
Nobody There!; A Creep in the Deep!; …From Hunger!; The Coffin! • Ray Bradbury adaptation **A:** George Evans; Jack Kamen; Jack Davis; Graham Ingels; Ray Bradbury **W:** George Evans; Jack Kamen; Jack Davis; Graham Ingels
17 ❑ Jan 1953 Cover: 0.10 **NM** value: **225.00**
• **CGC:** 6 graded, best 9.6
Horror We? How's Bayou?; Gorilla My Dreams!; A Likely Story!; Garden Party!; Hiding Place (text story) **A:** George Evans; Jack Kamen; Jack Davis; Graham Ingels **W:** George Evans; Jack Kamen; Jack Davis; Graham Ingels
18 ❑ Mar 1953 Cover: 0.10 **NM** value: **240.00**
• **CGC:** 6 graded, best 9.8
Pipe Down; Bedtime Gory!; Pot-Shot!; The Black Ferris! • Ray Bradbury adaptation **A:** George Evans; Jack Kamen; Jack Davis; Graham Ingels; Ray Bradbury **W:** George Evans; Jack Kamen; Jack Davis; Graham Ingels
19 ❑ May 1953 Cover: 0.10 **NM** value: **275.00**
• **CGC:** 7 graded, best 9.8
Sucker Bait!; Lover, Come Hack to Me!; Double-Header!; Foul Play! • Mentioned in Seduction of the Innocent: "A comic book baseball game" **A:** George Evans; Jack Kamen; Jack Davis; Graham Ingels **W:** George Evans; Jack Kamen; Jack Davis; Graham Ingels
20 ❑ Jul 1953 Cover: 0.10 **NM** value: **200.00**
• **CGC:** 3 graded, best 9.6
Thump Fun!; Terror Train; Bloody Sure; Hyde and Go Shriek **A:** George Evans; Jack Kamen; Jack Davis; Graham Ingels; Ray Bradbury **W:** George Evans; Jack Kamen; Jack Davis; Graham Ingels
21 ❑ Sep 1953 Cover: 0.10 **NM** value: **165.00**
• **CGC:** 5 graded, best 9.6
An Off-Color Heir; Dig that Cat...He's Real Gone!; Corker!; The High Cost of Dying!
22 ❑ Nov 1953 Cover: 0.10 **NM** value: **165.00**
• **CGC:** 3 graded, best 9.2
Wish You Were Here; Chess-Mate; Snow White and the Seven Drawfs; Model Nephew
23 ❑ Jan 1954 Cover: 0.10 **NM** value: **165.00**
• **CGC:** 4 graded, best 9.0
Creep Course; No Silver Atoll; Hansel and Gretel!; Country Clubbing
24 ❑ Mar 1954 Cover: 0.10 **NM** value: **165.00**
• **CGC:** 6 graded, best 9.4
Drink to Me Only With Thine Eyes…; …Only Sin Deep; The Secret; Head-Room! • Mentioned in Seduction of the Innocent
25 ❑ May 1954 Cover: 0.10 **NM** value: **165.00**
• **CGC:** 3 graded, best 9.6
The New Arrival; Indisposed!; Out Cold; The Light in His Life!
26 ❑ Jul 1954 Cover: 0.10 **NM** value: **165.00**
• **CGC:** 5 graded, best 9.6
Marriage Vows; The Shadow Knows; Spoiled; Comes the Dawn! **A:** Reed Crandall; Jack Kamen; Jack Davis; Graham Ingels **W:** Reed Crandall; Jack Kamen; Jack Davis; Graham Ingels
27 ❑ Sep 1954 Cover: 0.10 **NM** value: **165.00**
• **CGC:** 6 graded, best 9.6
About Face; Game Washed Out; The Silent Treatment; Swamped • Cannibalism story **W:** George Evans; Jack Kamen; Jack Davis; Graham Ingels
28 ❑ Nov 1954 Cover: 0.10 **NM** value: **165.00**
• **CGC:** 5 graded, best 9.6
The Prude; Numbskull; Audition; A Work of Art **A:** Bernie Krigstein; Jack Kamen; Jack Davis; Graham Ingels **W:** Bernie Krigstein; Jack Kamen; Jack Davis; Graham Ingels

HAUNT OF FEAR, THE (GLADSTONE) — Gladstone

1 ❑ May 1991 Cover: 2.00 **NM** value: **Cover or less**
Circ: CapCity orders: **12,000**
2 ❑ Jul 1991 Cover: 2.00 **NM** value: **Cover or less**
Circ: CapCity orders: **8,850**

HAUNT OF FEAR, THE (RCP) — Gemstone

In 1993, Russ Cochran Presents began reprinting the entire E.C. "New Trend" line-up, including Vault of Horror, Weird Science, Crime SuspenStories, and Haunt of Fear. RCP published issues of each title in their original sequence, giving readers an idea of how each title progressed over its run.

In Haunt's case, it started out bloody and got worse. Eerie tales of vampires and shrunken heads eventually gave way to shocking tales of cannibalism and mutilation. If anything, this chilling series was even scarier than its more famous sister publication, Tales From the Crypt.

1 ❑ Nov 1992 Cover: 1.50 **NM** value: **2.00**
Circ: CapCity orders: **4,700**
• Reprints The Haunt of Fear (EC) #1
2 ❑ Feb 1993 Cover: 1.50 **NM** value: **2.00**
Circ: Statement: **22,088** CapCity orders: **4,500**
• Reprints The Haunt of Fear (EC) #2
3 ❑ May 1993 Cover: 1.50 **NM** value: **2.00**
Circ: Statement: **22,088** CapCity orders: **4,300**
• Reprints The Haunt of Fear (EC) #3
4 ❑ Aug 1993 Cover: 2.00 **NM** value: **Cover or less**
Circ: Statement: **22,088** CapCity orders: **4,100**
• Reprints The Haunt of Fear (EC) #4
5 ❑ Nov 1993 Cover: 2.00 **NM** value: **Cover or less**
Circ: Statement: **22,088** CapCity orders: **3,575**
• Reprints The Haunt of Fear (EC) #5
6 ❑ Feb 1994 Cover: 2.00 **NM** value: **Cover or less**
Circ: Statement: **15,119** CapCity orders: **3,275**
A Strange Undertaking…; So They Finally Pinned You Down; A Grave Gag • Reprints The Haunt of Fear (EC) #6
7 ❑ May 1994 Cover: 2.00 **NM** value: **Cover or less**
Circ: Statement: **15,119** CapCity orders: **3,000**
Room For One More; The Basket; Horror in the School Room; The Howling Banshee • Reprints The Haunt of Fear (EC) #7
8 ❑ Aug 1994 Cover: 2.00 **NM** value: **Cover or less**
Circ: Statement: **15,119** CapCity orders: **3,000**
Hounded to Death; The Very Strange Mummy; Diminishing Returns; The Irony of Death • Reprints The Haunt of Fear (EC) #8
9 ❑ Nov 1994 Cover: 2.00 **NM** value: **Cover or less**
Circ: Statement: **15,119** CapCity orders: **2,925**

Other grades: Multiply prices above by **1.5 for Mint • 2/3 for Very Fine • 1/3 for Fine • 1/5 for Very Good • 1/8 for Good**

📖 Warts so Horrible?; Forbidden Fruit; The Age-Old Story; The Gorilla's Paw • Reprints The Haunt of Fear (EC) #9

10 ❑ Feb 1995 Cover: 2.00 **NM** value: **Cover or less**
Circ: CapCity orders: **2,800**
📖 Grave Business; The Vamp; My Uncle Ekar; Bum Steer • Reprints The Haunt of Fear (EC) #10

11 ❑ May 1995 Cover: 2.00 **NM** value: **Cover or less**
Circ: CapCity orders: **2,650**
📖 Ooze in the Cellar?; The Acid Test!; Extermination; Ear Today...Gone Tomorrow! • Reprints The Haunt of Fear (EC) #11

12 ❑ Aug 1995 Cover: 2.00 **NM** value: **Cover or less**
Circ: CapCity orders: **2,625**
📖 Poetic Justice!; ...On a Dead Man's Chest!; Till Death do we Part!; What's Cookin'? • Reprints The Haunt of Fear (EC) #12

13 ❑ Nov 1995 Cover: 2.00 **NM** value: **Cover or less**
Circ: CapCity orders: **2,450**
📖 For the Love of Death!; Fed Up!; Minor Error!; Wolf Bait! • Reprints The Haunt of Fear (EC) #13

14 ❑ Feb 1996 Cover: 2.00 **NM** value: **Cover or less**
Circ: Statement: **6,692**
📖 A Little Stranger!; Take Your Pick!; Ship-Shape!; This Little Piggy... • Reprints The Haunt of Fear (EC) #14 ★ Origin of The Old Witch.

15 ❑ May 1996 Cover: 2.00 **NM** value: **Cover or less**
Circ: Statement: **6,692**
📖 Chatter-Boxed!; All Washed Up!; Marriage Vows!; Death of Some Salesmen! • Reprints The Haunt of Fear (EC) #15

16 ❑ Aug 1996 Cover: 2.50 **NM** value: **Cover or less**
Circ: Statement: **6,692**
📖 Nobody There!; A Creep in the Deep!; ...From Hunger!; The Coffin! • Ray Bradbury story; Reprints The Haunt of Fear (EC) #16; Ray Bradbury adaptation **A:** George Evans; Jack Kamen; Jack Davis; Graham Ingels; Ray Bradbury **W:** George Evans; Jack Kamen; Jack Davis; Graham Ingels

17 ❑ Nov 1996 Cover: 2.50 **NM** value: **Cover or less**
Circ: Statement: **6,692**
📖 Horror We? How's Bayou?; Gorilla My Dreams!; A Likely Story!; Garden Party!; Hiding Place (text story) • Reprints The Haunt of Fear (EC) #17 **A:** George Evans; Jack Kamen; Jack Davis; Graham Ingels **W:** George Evans; Jack Kamen; Jack Davis; Graham Ingels

18 ❑ Feb 1997 Cover: 2.50 **NM** value: **Cover or less**
Circ: Statement: **6,122**
📖 Pipe Down; Bedtime Gory!; Pot-Shot!; The Black Ferris! • Ray Bradbury story; Reprints The Haunt of Fear (EC) #18; Has 1996 Statement, filed 9/15/96; avg print run 8,204; avg sales 5,975; avg subs 717; avg total paid 6,692; office use 1,512; max existent 8,204; no newsstand sales **A:** George Evans; Jack Kamen; Jack Davis; Graham Ingels; Ray Bradbury **W:** George Evans; Jack Kamen; Jack Davis; Graham Ingels

19 ❑ May 1997 Cover: 2.50 **NM** value: **Cover or less**
Circ: Statement: **6,122**
📖 Sucker Bait!; Lover, Come Hack to Me!; Double-Header!; Foul Play! • Reprints The Haunt of Fear (EC) #19; Mentioned in Seduction of the Innocent "A comic book baseball game" **A:** George Evans; Jack Kamen; Jack Davis; Graham Ingels **W:** George Evans; Jack Kamen; Jack Davis; Graham Ingels

20 ❑ Aug 1997 Cover: 2.50 **NM** value: **Cover or less**
Circ: Statement: **6,122**
• Reprints The Haunt of Fear (EC) #20

21 ❑ Nov 1997 Cover: 2.50 **NM** value: **Cover or less**
Circ: Statement: **6,122**
• Reprints The Haunt of Fear (EC) #21

22 ❑ Feb 1998 Cover: 2.50 **NM** value: **Cover or less**
• Reprints The Haunt of Fear (EC) #22; Has 1997 Statement; avg total paid circ 6,122

23 ❑ May 1998 Cover: 2.50 **NM** value: **Cover or less**
• Reprints The Haunt of Fear (EC) #23

24 ❑ Aug 1998 Cover: 2.50 **NM** value: **Cover or less**
• Reprints The Haunt of Fear (EC) #24

25 ❑ Nov 1998 Cover: 2.50 **NM** value: **Cover or less**
• Reprints The Haunt of Fear (EC) #25

26 ❑ Feb 1999 Cover: 2.50 **NM** value: **Cover or less**
📖 Marriage Vows; The Shadow Knows; Spoiled; Comes the Dawn! • Reprints The Haunt of Fear (EC) #26 **A:** Reed Crandall; Jack Kamen; Jack Davis; Graham Ingels **W:** Reed Crandall; Jack Kamen; Jack Davis; Graham Ingels

27 ❑ May 1999 Cover: 2.50 **NM** value: **Cover or less**
📖 About Face; Game Washed Out; The Silent Treatment; Swamped • Reprints The Haunt of Fear (EC) #27 **W:** George Evans; Jack Kamen; Jack Davis; Graham Ingels

28 ❑ Aug 1999 Cover: 2.50 **NM** value: **Cover or less**
📖 Purge; Numbskull; Audition; A Work of Art! • Reprints The Haunt of Fear (EC) #28 **A:** Bernie Krigstein; Jack Kamen; Jack Davis; Graham Ingels **W:** Bernie Krigstein; Jack Kamen; Jack Davis; Graham Ingels

Anl 1❑ Cover: 8.95 **NM** value: **Cover or less**
• Reprints The Haunt of Fear #1-5

Anl 2❑ Cover: 9.95 **NM** value: **Cover or less**
📖 A Strange Undertaking; So They Finally Pinned You Down!; A Grave Gag!; Cheese, That's Horrible; Room For One More; The Basket!; Horror In T • Reprints The Haunt of Fear #6-10

Anl 3❑ Cover: 10.95 **NM** value: **Cover or less**
📖 Ooze In The Cellar?; The Acid Test!; Extermination; Ear Today...Gone Tomorrow; Poetic Justice; ...O • Reprints The Haunt of Fear #11-15

Anl 4❑ Cover: 10.50 **NM** value: **Cover or less**
• Reprints The Haunt of Fear #16-20

Anl 5❑ **NM** value: **11.95**
• Reprints The Haunt of Fear #21-25

Anl 6❑ Cover: 8.95 **NM** value: **Cover or less**
📖 Marriage Vows; The Shadow Knows; Spoiled; Comes the Dawn! • Reprints The Haunt of Fear #26-28 **A:** Reed Crandall; Jack Kamen; Jack Davis; Graham Ingels **W:** Reed Crandall; Jack Kamen; Jack Davis; Graham Ingels

HAUNT OF FEAR (RCP) — Cochran

1 ❑ Sep 1991 Cover: 2.00 **NM** value: **Cover or less**
Circ: CapCity orders: **5,000**
• Giant-size. 📖 A Little Stranger!; Take Your Pick!; Bee-Nip! (text story); Ship-Shape!; This Little Piggy...; The End!; The Trip!; Discovery!; Home to Stay!; Don't Count Your Chickens... • Reprints Haunt of Fear #14, Weird Fantasy #13 ★ Origin of Old Witch.

2 ❑ Nov 1991 Cover: 2.00 **NM** value: **Cover or less**
Circ: CapCity orders: **3,353**
• Giant-size.

3 ❑ Jan 1992 Cover: 2.00 **NM** value: **Cover or less**
Circ: CapCity orders: **5,325**
• Giant-size.

4 ❑ Mar 1992 Cover: 2.00 **NM** value: **Cover or less**
Circ: CapCity orders: **5,075**
• Giant-size.

5 ❑ May 1992 Cover: 2.00 **NM** value: **Cover or less**
Circ: CapCity orders: **4,700**
• Giant-size.

HAUNT OF HORROR — Marvel

1 ❑ May 1974 Cover: 0.75 **NM** value: **5.00**
2 ❑ Jul 1974 Cover: 0.75 **NM** value: **4.00**
3 ❑ Sep 1974 Cover: 0.75 **NM** value: **4.00**
4 ❑ Nov 1974 Cover: 0.75 **NM** value: **4.00**
5 ❑ Jan 1975 Cover: 0.75 **NM** value: **4.00**

HAVE GUN, WILL TRAVEL — Dell

4 ❑ Jan 1960 Cover: 0.10 **NM** value: **75.00**
5 ❑ Apr 1960 Cover: 0.10 **NM** value: **75.00**
• **CGC:** 2 graded, best 9.4
6 ❑ Jul 1960 Cover: 0.10 **NM** value: **75.00**
• **CGC:** 1 graded, best 9.2
7 ❑ Oct 1960 Cover: 0.10 **NM** value: **75.00**
8 ❑ Jan 1961 Cover: 0.10 **NM** value: **75.00**
9 ❑ Jun 1961 Cover: 0.15 **NM** value: **75.00**
10 ❑ Jul 1961 Cover: 0.12 **NM** value: **75.00**
11 ❑ Oct 1961 Cover: 0.12 **NM** value: **60.00**
12 ❑ Jan 1962 Cover: 0.12 **NM** value: **60.00**
13 ❑ Apr 1962 Cover: 0.12 **NM** value: **60.00**
• **CGC:** 1 graded, best 9.2
14 ❑ Jul 1962 Cover: 0.12 **NM** value: **60.00**

HAVOC, INC. — Radio Comix

1 ❑ Mar 1998 Cover: 2.95 **NM** value: **Cover or less**
2 ❑ Jun 1998 Cover: 2.95 **NM** value: **Cover or less**
3 ❑ Sep 1998 Cover: 2.95 **NM** value: **Cover or less**
4 ❑ Dec 1998 Cover: 2.95 **NM** value: **Cover or less**
5 ❑ 1999 Cover: 2.95 **NM** value: **Cover or less**
6 ❑ 1999 Cover: 2.95 **NM** value: **Cover or less**
7 ❑ Cover: 2.95 **NM** value: **Cover or less**
8 ❑ Jul 2000 Cover: 2.95 **NM** value: **Cover or less**

HAVOK & WOLVERINE: MELTDOWN — Marvel / Epic

1 ❑ Mar 1989 Cover: 3.50 **NM** value: **4.00**
Circ: CapCity orders: **61,450** • **CGC:** 1 graded, best 9.6

2 ❑ ca. 1989 Cover: 3.50 **NM** value: **4.00**
Circ: CapCity orders: **55,400** • **CGC:** 1 graded, best 9.2
📖 Tender Loving Lies! **A:** Jon J. Muth **W:** Walt Simonson; Louise Simonson

3 ❑ ca. 1989 Cover: 3.50 **NM** value: **4.00**
Circ: CapCity orders: **54,250** • **CGC:** 1 graded, best 9.2
📖 Duel **A:** Jon J. Muth **W:** Walt Simonson; Louise Simonson

4 ❑ Oct 1989 Cover: 3.50 **NM** value: **4.00**
Circ: CapCity orders: **50,050** • **CGC:** 1 graded, best 9.0

HAWK — Ziff-Davis

1 ❑ Win 1951 Cover: 0.10 **NM** value: **150.00**
• **CGC:** 1 graded, best 6.5
2 ❑ Sum 1952 Cover: 0.10 **NM** value: **75.00**
3 ❑ Nov 1952 Cover: 0.10 **NM** value: **75.00**
4 ❑ Jan 1953 Cover: 0.10 **NM** value: **75.00**
8 ❑ Sep 1954 Cover: 0.10 **NM** value: **60.00**
9 ❑ Nov 1954 Cover: 0.10 **NM** value: **60.00**
10 ❑ Jan 1955 Cover: 0.10 **NM** value: **60.00**
11 ❑ Mar 1955 Cover: 0.10 **NM** value: **60.00**
12 ❑ May 1955 Cover: 0.10 **NM** value: **60.00**
3D 1❑Nov 1953 Cover: 0.25 **NM** value: **250.00**

HAWK & THE DOVE, THE (1ST SERIES) — DC

1 ❑ Aug 1968 Cover: 0.12 **NM** value: **35.00**
• **CGC:** 13 graded, best 9.2
📖 The Dove is a Very Gentle Bird **A:** Steve Ditko **W:** Steve Skeates

2 ❑ Oct 1968 Cover: 0.12 **NM** value: **20.00**
• **CGC:** 2 graded, best 9.4
📖 Jailbreak! **A:** Steve Ditko **W:** Dick Giordano; Steve Skeates

3 ❑ Dec 1968 Cover: 0.12 **NM** value: **20.00**
• **CGC:** 2 graded, best 9.6
📖 After the Cat; Twice Burned! **A:** Gil Kane **W:** Dick Giordano; Steve Skeates

4 ❑ Feb 1969 Cover: 0.12 **NM** value: **20.00**
• **CGC:** 2 graded, best 9.4
📖 The Sell-Out! **A:** Gil Kane **W:** Dick Giordano; Steve Skeates

5 ❑ Mar 1969 Cover: 0.12 **NM** value: **20.00**
• **CGC:** 1 graded, best 9.4
📖 Walk With Me, O' Brother...Death Has Taken My Hand! **A:** Gil Kane **W:** Dick Giordano ★ Appearance of Teen Titans.

6 ❑ Jun 1969 Cover: 0.12 **NM** value: **20.00**
• **CGC:** 1 graded, best 9.2
📖 Judgment in a Small, Dark Place final issue. **A:** Gil Kane **W:** Dick Giordano; Gil Kane

HAWK AND DOVE (2ND SERIES) — DC

1 ❑ Oct 1988 Cover: 1.00 **NM** value: **3.00**
Circ: CapCity orders: **19,050**
📖 Ghosts And Demons **A:** Rob Liefeld **W:** Karl Kesel; Barbara Kesel ★ 1st Appearance of Dove II.

2 ❑ Nov 1988 Cover: 1.00 **NM** value: **2.50**
Circ: CapCity orders: **14,850**

3 ❑ Dec 1988 Cover: 1.00 **NM** value: **2.00**
Circ: CapCity orders: **14,900**

4 ❑ Win 1988 Cover: 1.00 **NM** value: **2.00**
Circ: CapCity orders: **15,150**

5 ❑ Hol 1989 Cover: 1.00 **NM** value: **2.00**
Circ: CapCity orders: **15,750**

Bk 1❑ Cover: 9.95 **NM** value: **Cover or less**
No issue number.

HAWK AND DOVE (3RD SERIES) — DC

1 ❑ Jun 1989 Cover: 1.00 **NM** value: **1.50**
Circ: CapCity orders: **31,250**
📖 Gauntlet! **A:** Greg Guler **W:** Karl Kesel; Barbara Kesel

2 ❑ Jul 1989 Cover: 1.00 **NM** value: **Cover or less**
Circ: CapCity orders: **23,650**

3 ❑ Aug 1989 Cover: 1.00 **NM** value: **Cover or less**
Circ: CapCity orders: **21,400**

4 ❑ Sep 1989 Cover: 1.00 **NM** value: **Cover or less**
Circ: CapCity orders: **19,200**

5 ❑ Oct 1989 Cover: 1.00 **NM** value: **Cover or less**
Circ: CapCity orders: **17,400**

6 ❑ Nov 1989 Cover: 1.00 **NM** value: **Cover or less**
Circ: CapCity orders: **15,650**

7 ❑ Dec 1989 Cover: 1.00 **NM** value: **Cover or less**
Circ: CapCity orders: **14,550**

8 ❑ Jan 1990 Cover: 1.00 **NM** value: **Cover or less**
Circ: CapCity orders: **14,200**

9 ❑ Feb 1990 Cover: 1.00 **NM** value: **Cover or less**
Circ: CapCity orders: **13,550**

10 ❑ Mar 1990 Cover: 1.00 **NM** value: **Cover or less**
Circ: CapCity orders: **13,300**

11 ❑ Apr 1990 Cover: 1.00 **NM** value: **Cover or less**
Circ: CapCity orders: **12,850**

12 ❑ May 1990 Cover: 1.00 **NM** value: **Cover or less**
Circ: CapCity orders: **13,000**

13 ❑ Jun 1990 Cover: 1.00 **NM** value: **Cover or less**
Circ: CapCity orders: **12,100**

14 ❑ Jul 1990 Cover: 1.00 **NM** value: **Cover or less**
Circ: CapCity orders: **11,900**

15 ❑ Aug 1990 Cover: 1.00 **NM** value: **Cover or less**
Circ: CapCity orders: **11,600**

16 ❑ Sep 1990 Cover: 1.00 **NM** value: **Cover or less**
Circ: CapCity orders: **11,400**

17 ❑ Oct 1990 Cover: 1.00 **NM** value: **Cover or less**
Circ: CapCity orders: **11,300**

18 ❑ Nov 1990 Cover: 1.00 **NM** value: **Cover or less**
Circ: CapCity orders: **11,850**

19 ❑ Dec 1990 Cover: 1.00 **NM** value: **Cover or less**
Circ: CapCity orders: **12,200**

20 ❑ Jan 1991 Cover: 1.00 **NM** value: **Cover or less**
Circ: CapCity orders: **11,950**

21 ❑ Feb 1991 Cover: 1.00 **NM** value: **Cover or less**
Circ: CapCity orders: **11,800**

22 ❑ Mar 1991 Cover: 1.00 **NM** value: **Cover or less**
Circ: CapCity orders: **11,650**

23 ❑ Apr 1991 Cover: 1.00 **NM** value: **Cover or less**
Circ: CapCity orders: **11,150**

24 ❑ May 1991 Cover: 1.00 **NM** value: **Cover or less**
Circ: CapCity orders: **10,750**

25 ❑ Jun 1991 Cover: 2.00 **NM** value: **Cover or less**
Circ: CapCity orders: **11,050**
• Giant-size.

26 ❑ Aug 1992 Cover: 1.25 **NM** value: **Cover or less**
Circ: CapCity orders: **10,550**

27 ❑ Sep 1991 Cover: 1.25 **NM** value: **Cover or less**
Circ: CapCity orders: **11,150**

28 ❑ Oct 1991 Cover: 2.00 **NM** value: **Cover or less**
Circ: CapCity orders: **12,000**
• Giant-size. 📖 War of the Gods • War of the Gods

Anl 1❑Oct 1990 Cover: 2.00 **NM** value: **Cover or less**
• Titans West

Anl 2❑Sep 1991 Cover: 2.00 **NM** value: **Cover or less**
Circ: CapCity orders: **25,000**
📖 Armageddon 2001, Part 5 • Armageddon 2001

HAWK AND DOVE (4TH SERIES) — DC

1 ❑ Nov 1997 Cover: 2.50 **NM** value: **Cover or less**
Circ: Diamd. preorders: **24,678**
📖 Feathers **A:** Dean Zachary **W:** Mike Baron ★ Origin of new team.

2 ❑ Dec 1997 Cover: 2.50 **NM** value: **Cover or less**
Circ: Diamd. preorders: **20,247**
📖 Flight Into Madness **A:** Dean Zachary **W:** Mike Baron ★ Appearance of Vixen.

3 ❑ Jan 1998 Cover: 2.50 **NM** value: **Cover or less**
Circ: Diamd. preorders: **17,145**
📖 Hellhound on my Trail! **A:** Dean Zachary **W:** Mike Baron

4 ❑ Feb 1998 Cover: 2.50 **NM** value: **Cover or less**
Circ: Diamd. preorders: **14,322**
📖 Road Rules! **A:** Dean Zachary **W:** Mike Baron ★ Appearance of Vixen. ★ Versus Count Vertigo.

5 ❑ Mar 1998 Cover: 2.50 **NM** value: **Cover or less**
Circ: Diamd. preorders: **12,309**
final issue. **A:** Dean Zachary **W:** Mike Baron

HAWK & WINDBLADE — Warp

1 ❑ Aug 1997 Cover: 2.95 **NM** value: **Cover or less**
📖 All the Lonely Places... **A:** Barry Blair; Colin Chan **W:** Barry Blair; Colin Chan

2 ❑ Sep 1997 Cover: 2.95 **NM** value: **Cover or less**

HAWKEYE: EARTH'S MIGHTIEST MARKSMAN — Marvel

1 ❑ Oct 1998 Cover: 2.99 **NM** value: **Cover or less**
Circ: Diamd. preorders: **26,691**
One-shot. 📖 Battered by Batroc!; Assaulted by Oddball!; Trounced by Taskmaster! **A:** Mark Bagley; Jeff Johnson; Dave Ross **W:** Tom DeFalco ★ Appearance of Firestar, Justice. ★ Versus Taskmaster, Oddball.

CGC-graded: Multiply prices above by **33 for 9.9 M • 16 for 9.8 NM/M • 7 for 9.6 NM+ • 5 for 9.4 NM • 2.5 for 9.2 NM- • 1.5 for 9.0 VF/NM**

HAWKEYE (VOL. 1) — Marvel

Originally appearing in Tales of Suspense #57 (where he was mistaken as a villain), the master archer Hawkeye soon cleared things up and joined the Avengers in Avengers #16. After 20 years of adventuring, in and out of the Avengers, he finally appeared in this, his own limited series.

This saga introduces him to Mockingbird, the woman he would eventually marry, and sets the stage for the founding of the West Coast Avengers. It also attempts to provide Hawkeye with his own rogue's gallery. The villain's plan to use Hawkeye in a plot to kill America's super-heroes is both clever and convincing.

1 ❑ Sep 1983 Cover: 0.60 **NM** value: **2.50**
• **CGC:** 1 graded, best 9.4
📖 Listen to the Mockingbird **A:** Brett Breeding **W:** Mark Gruenwald ★ Origin of Hawkeye.
2 ❑ Oct 1983 Cover: 0.60 **NM** value: **2.00**
3 ❑ Nov 1983 Cover: 0.60 **NM** value: **2.00**
4 ❑ Dec 1983 Cover: 0.60 **NM** value: **2.00**
Bk 1 ❑ Jul 1988 Cover: 5.95 **NM** value: **Cover or less**

HAWKEYE (VOL. 2) — Marvel

1 ❑ Jan 1994 Cover: 1.75 **NM** value: **Cover or less**
Circ: CapCity orders: **29,800**
📖 Shafted **A:** Scott Kolins **W:** Chuck Dixon
2 ❑ Feb 1994 Cover: 1.75 **NM** value: **Cover or less**
Circ: CapCity orders: **19,000**
3 ❑ Mar 1994 Cover: 1.75 **NM** value: **Cover or less**
Circ: CapCity orders: **15,950**
4 ❑ Apr 1994 Cover: 1.75 **NM** value: **Cover or less**
Circ: CapCity orders: **14,500**

HAWKMAN (1ST SERIES) — DC

Having first appeared in The Brave and the Bold #34, this title gave the Silver Age Hawkman a series of his own. The original Hawkman was Carter Hall, a native of Earth-2 (an alternate world which was used to explain away the differences between DC's Golden Age and Silver Age super-heroes). This Hawkman is Katar Hol, a native of the planet Thanagar, but who now patrols Earth-1 (the primary Earth where the modern super-heroes live).

Katar and his wife Shayera were police officers on Thanagar who came to Earth to pursue a felon from their world. Armed with flight belts and other gizmos from Thanagar, they caught the crook, then decided to stay on Earth to fight crime as super-heroes.

This first Hawkman series was notable not only for the adventures of its colorful lead characters, but also for introducing supermagician Zatanna, the daughter of Zatara, who originally appeared in Action Comics #1.

1 ❑ May 1964 Cover: 0.12 **NM** value: **500.00**
• **CGC:** 56 graded, best 9.8
📖 Rivalry of the Winged Wonders; Master of the Sky Weapons **A:** Murphy Anderson **W:** Gardner Fox
2 ❑ Jul 1964 Cover: 0.12 **NM** value: **190.00**
• **CGC:** 19 graded, best 9.4
📖 Secret of the Sizzling Sparklers; Wings Across Time **A:** Murphy Anderson **W:** Gardner Fox
3 ❑ Sep 1964 Cover: 0.12 **NM** value: **115.00**
• **CGC:** 8 graded, best 9.6
📖 The Fear That Haunted Hawkman; Birds in the Gilded Cage **A:** Murphy Anderson **W:** Gardner Fox
4 ❑ Nov 1964 Cover: 0.12 **NM** value: **150.00**
• **CGC:** 10 graded, best 9.6
📖 The Girl Who Split in Two; The Machine That Magnetized Men **A:** Murphy Anderson **W:** Gardner Fox ★ Origin of Zatanna. ★ 1st Appearance of Zatanna.
5 ❑ Jan 1965 Cover: 0.12 **NM** value: **115.00**
• **CGC:** 12 graded, best 9.8
📖 Steal, Shadow-Steal **A:** Murphy Anderson **W:** Gardner Fox
6 ❑ Mar 1965 Cover: 0.12 **NM** value: **85.00**
• **CGC:** 6 graded, best 9.6
📖 World Where Evolution Ran Wild **A:** Murphy Anderson **W:** Gardner Fox
7 ❑ May 1965 Cover: 0.12 **NM** value: **85.00**
• **CGC:** 6 graded, best 9.6
📖 Amazing Return of the I.Q. Gang; Attack of the Crocodile Man **A:** Murphy Anderson **W:** Gardner Fox
8 ❑ Jul 1965 Cover: 0.12 **NM** value: **85.00**
• **CGC:** 4 graded, best 9.4
📖 Giant in the Golden Mask; Battle of the Bird-Man Bandits **A:** Murphy Anderson **W:** Gardner Fox
9 ❑ Sep 1965 Cover: 0.12 **NM** value: **85.00**
• **CGC:** 4 graded, best 9.2
📖 Master Trap of the Matter Master **A:** Murphy Anderson **W:** Gardner Fox
10 ❑ Nov 1965 Cover: 0.12 **NM** value: **85.00**
• **CGC:** 6 graded, best 9.6
📖 Hawkman Clips the Claws of C.A.W.; The Magic Mirror Mystery **A:** Murphy Anderson **W:** Gardner Fox
11 ❑ Jan 1966 Cover: 0.12 **NM** value: **56.00**
• **CGC:** 4 graded, best 9.2
📖 The Shrike Strikes at Night **A:** Murphy Anderson **W:** Gardner Fox
12 ❑ Mar 1966 Cover: 0.12 **NM** value: **56.00**
• **CGC:** 5 graded, best 9.6
📖 The Million-Year-Long War **A:** Murphy Anderson **W:** Gardner Fox
13 ❑ May 1966 Cover: 0.12 **NM** value: **56.00**
• **CGC:** 8 graded, best 9.6
📖 Quest of the Immortal Queen **A:** Murphy Anderson **W:** Gardner Fox
14 ❑ Jul 1966 Cover: 0.12 **NM** value: **56.00**
• **CGC:** 5 graded, best 9.6
📖 The Treasure of the Talking Head **A:** Murphy Anderson **W:** Gardner Fox
15 ❑ Sep 1966 Cover: 0.12 **NM** value: **56.00**
• **CGC:** 6 graded, best 9.6
📖 Scourge of the Human Race **A:** Murphy Anderson **W:** Gardner Fox
16 ❑ Nov 1966 Cover: 0.12 **NM** value: **42.00**
• **CGC:** 4 graded, best 9.2
📖 Lord of the Flying Gorillas **A:** Murphy Anderson **W:** Gardner Fox
17 ❑ Jan 1967 Cover: 0.12 **NM** value: **42.00**
• **CGC:** 5 graded, best 9.2
📖 Ruse of the Robbing Raven; Enigma of the Escape-Happy Jewel Thieves **A:** Murphy Anderson **W:** Gardner Fox
18 ❑ Mar 1967 Cover: 0.12 **NM** value: **42.00**
• **CGC:** 8 graded, best 9.8
📖 World That Vanished **A:** Murphy Anderson **W:** Gardner Fox ★ Appearance of Adam Strange. ★ Versus Manhawks.
19 ❑ May 1967 Cover: 0.12 **NM** value: **42.00**
• **CGC:** 8 graded, best 9.4
📖 Parasite Planet Peril **A:** Murphy Anderson **W:** Gardner Fox
20 ❑ Jul 1967 Cover: 0.12 **NM** value: **38.00**
• **CGC:** 4 graded, best 9.4
📖 Death of the Living Flame; Lion-Mane-The Tabu Menace **A:** Murphy Anderson **W:** Gardner Fox
21 ❑ Sep 1967 Cover: 0.12 **NM** value: **38.00**
• **CGC:** 5 graded, best 9.2
📖 Attack of the Jungle Juggernaut **A:** Murphy Anderson **W:** Gardner Fox
22 ❑ Nov 1967 Cover: 0.12 **NM** value: **38.00**
• **CGC:** 2 graded, best 9.6
📖 Quoth the Falcon, "Hawkman Die" **A:** Dick Dillin **W:** Bob Haney
23 ❑ Jan 1968 Cover: 0.12 **NM** value: **38.00**
• **CGC:** 6 graded, best 9.4
📖 The Hawkman From 1,000,000 B.C. **A:** Dick Dillin **W:** Bob Haney
24 ❑ Mar 1968 Cover: 0.12 **NM** value: **38.00**
• **CGC:** 3 graded, best 9.4
📖 The Robot Raiders From Planet Midnight; The Man Who Grew Wings **A:** Dick Dillin **W:** Raymond Marais
25 ❑ May 1968 Cover: 0.12 **NM** value: **38.00**
• **CGC:** 4 graded, best 9.4
📖 Return of the Death Goddess **A:** Dick Dillin; Shelly Moldoff **W:** Raymond Marais
26 ❑ Jul 1968 Cover: 0.12 **NM** value: **38.00**
• **CGC:** 2 graded, best 9.4
📖 Last Stand on Thanagar **A:** Dick Dillin; Chuck Cuidera **W:** Raymond Marais
27 ❑ Sep 1968 Cover: 0.12 **NM** value: **38.00**
• **CGC:** 2 graded, best 9.4
📖 ... When the Snow-Fiend Strikes final issue. **A:** Dick Dillin **W:** Raymond Marais
Bk 1 ❑ Cover: 19.95 **NM** value: **Cover or less**
Circ: CapCity orders: **2,000**
• collects stories from Brave and the Bold **A:** Joe Kubert

HAWKMAN (2ND SERIES) — DC

Writer Tony Isabella gave Hawkman a much-needed reworking in the mini-series The Shadow War of Hawkman. In it, he stripped Katar and Shiera Hall of their Thanagarian technology (which tended to pop up in the middle of a fight as a weak story device to let the pair gain victory), removed Shiera's rival Mavis Trent, and told of Thanagar's quiet invasion of Earth.

That latter point constituted the real story of the Shadow War, a plot which is continued in this second Hawkman series. Thanagar, once a freedom-loving world has embraced totalitarianism, and now, through infiltration, intends to take over the governments of Earth. As this series begins, Thanagar is well on its way to controlling the next president of the United States—but only Katar and Shiera are even aware that the invasion is underway...

1 ❑ Aug 1986 Cover: 0.75 **NM** value: **2.00**
Circ: CapCity orders: **16,300**
📖 Shadow War; Secrets... **A:** Richard Howell **W:** Tony Isabella
2 ❑ Sep 1986 Cover: 0.75 **NM** value: **1.50**
Circ: CapCity orders: **13,000**
📖 Shadows... **A:** Richard Howell **W:** Tony Isabella ★ Versus Shadow Thief.
3 ❑ Oct 1986 Cover: 0.75 **NM** value: **1.50**
Circ: CapCity orders: **12,350**
📖 Secrets, Shadows and Sinners **A:** Richard Howell **W:** Tony Isabella ★ Versus Shadow Thief.
4 ❑ Nov 1986 Cover: 0.75 **NM** value: **1.25**
Circ: CapCity orders: **11,400**
📖 For the Benefit of Mr. Kite **A:** Richard Howell **W:** Tony Isabella ★ Appearance of Zatanna.
5 ❑ Dec 1986 Cover: 0.75 **NM** value: **1.25**
Circ: CapCity orders: **10,050**
📖 The Lionmane Diversion **A:** Richard Howell **W:** Tony Isabella ★ Versus Lionmane.
6 ❑ Jan 1987 Cover: 0.75 **NM** value: **1.25**
Circ: CapCity orders: **9,150**
📖 A Lion in the Streets **A:** Richard Howell **W:** Tony Isabella ★ Versus Lionmane.
7 ❑ Feb 1987 Cover: 0.75 **NM** value: **1.25**
Circ: CapCity orders: **8,900**
8 ❑ Mar 1987 Cover: 0.75 **NM** value: **1.25**
Circ: CapCity orders: **8,250**
9 ❑ Apr 1987 Cover: 0.75 **NM** value: **1.25**
Circ: CapCity orders: **8,300**
10 ❑ May 1987 Cover: 0.75 **NM** value: **1.25**
Circ: CapCity orders: **8,500**
11 ❑ Jun 1987 Cover: 0.75 **NM** value: **1.25**
Circ: CapCity orders: **7,600**
12 ❑ Jul 1987 Cover: 0.75 **NM** value: **1.25**
Circ: CapCity orders: **7,550**
13 ❑ Aug 1987 Cover: 0.75 **NM** value: **1.25**
Circ: CapCity orders: **8,400**
14 ❑ Sep 1987 Cover: 0.75 **NM** value: **1.25**
Circ: CapCity orders: **8,750**
15 ❑ Oct 1987 Cover: 0.75 **NM** value: **1.25**
Circ: CapCity orders: **8,550**
16 ❑ Nov 1987 Cover: 1.00 **NM** value: **1.25**
Circ: CapCity orders: **8,250**
17 ❑ Dec 1987 Cover: 1.00 **NM** value: **1.25**
Circ: CapCity orders: **7,750**
SE 1 ❑ Mar 1986 Cover: 1.25 **NM** value: **1.50**
Circ: CapCity orders: **12,300**
📖 Last Rights **A:** Richard Howell **W:** Richard Howell; Tony Isabella

HAWKMAN (3RD SERIES) — DC

The first Hawkman was Carter Hall, whose powers came from his discovery of a gravity-defying metal. His wife, Shiera Hall, became Hawkgirl and the two served long terms in the Justice Society of America.

The next Hawkman was an alien counterpart to the original, hailing from the planet Thanagar. That Hawkman, Katar Hol, was joined by Shayera Thal, who became known as Hawkwoman. The two came to this planet as intergalactic policemen, but decided to stay as super-heroes. Seven months after Hawkwoman was apparently killed (in the final issue of Hawkworld), Hawkman vanished rather than face return to Thanagar.

Now a new Hawkman has appeared, with a new costume and a darker aspect. Who is this new Hawkman, and what is he after?

0 ❑ Oct 1994 Cover: 1.95 **NM** value: **2.00**
Circ: CapCity orders: **16,300**
📖 Old Scores **A:** Steve Lieber **W:** William Messner-Loebs ★ Origin of Hawkman (new).
1 ❑ Sep 1993 Cover: 2.50 **NM** value: **Cover or less**
Circ: CapCity orders: **33,200** • **CGC:** 2 graded, best 9.8
foil cover. 📖 Winged Fury **A:** Jan Duursema **W:** John Ostrander
2 ❑ Oct 1993 Cover: 1.75 **NM** value: **Cover or less**
Circ: CapCity orders: **15,650**
📖 Dead End **A:** Jan Duursema **W:** John Ostrander
3 ❑ Nov 1993 Cover: 1.75 **NM** value: **Cover or less**
Circ: CapCity orders: **14,150**
4 ❑ Dec 1993 Cover: 1.75 **NM** value: **Cover or less**
Circ: CapCity orders: **15,200**
5 ❑ Jan 1994 Cover: 1.75 **NM** value: **Cover or less**
Circ: CapCity orders: **14,400**
📖 A Rage of Hawks **A:** Steve Lieber **W:** John Ostrander
6 ❑ Feb 1994 Cover: 1.75 **NM** value: **Cover or less**
Circ: CapCity orders: **14,200**
7 ❑ Mar 1994 Cover: 1.75 **NM** value: **Cover or less**
Circ: CapCity orders: **12,200**
📖 King of the Netherworld, Part 1 **A:** Luke McDonnell **W:** Paul Kupperberg
8 ❑ Apr 1994 Cover: 1.75 **NM** value: **Cover or less**
Circ: CapCity orders: **10,900**
📖 King of the Netherworld, Part 2 **A:** Luke McDonnell **W:** Paul Kupperberg
9 ❑ May 1994 Cover: 1.75 **NM** value: **Cover or less**
Circ: CapCity orders: **11,600**
10 ❑ Jun 1994 Cover: 1.75 **NM** value: **Cover or less**
Circ: CapCity orders: **10,250**
11 ❑ Jul 1994 Cover: 1.75 **NM** value: **Cover or less**
Circ: CapCity orders: **10,150**
12 ❑ Aug 1994 Cover: 1.95 **NM** value: **Cover or less**
Circ: CapCity orders: **9,900**
13 ❑ Sep 1994 Cover: 1.95 **NM** value: **Cover or less**
Circ: CapCity orders: **11,250**
📖 Godspawn, Part 5 **W:** William Messner-Loebs
14 ❑ Nov 1994 Cover: 1.95 **NM** value: **Cover or less**
Circ: CapCity orders: **10,800**
📖 Eyes of the Hawk, Part 1; Old Ephraim's Folly **A:** Steve Lieber **W:** William Messner-Loebs
15 ❑ Dec 1994 Cover: 1.95 **NM** value: **Cover or less**
Circ: CapCity orders: **10,650**
📖 Eyes of the Hawk, Part 2; Among the Minnows **A:** Steve Lieber **W:** William Messner-Loebs ★ Appearance of Aquaman.
16 ❑ Jan 1995 Cover: 1.95 **NM** value: **Cover or less**
Circ: CapCity orders: **10,750**
📖 Eyes of the Hawk, Part 3; The Roar of the Bull **A:** Steve Lieber **W:** William Messner-Loebs ★ Appearance of Wonder Woman.
17 ❑ Feb 1995 Cover: 1.95 **NM** value: **Cover or less**
Circ: CapCity orders: **10,000**
📖 Eyes of the Hawk, Part 4; Sting of the Viper **A:** Steve Lieber **W:** William Messner-Loebs
18 ❑ May 1995 Cover: 1.95 **NM** value: **Cover or less**
Circ: CapCity orders: **9,225**
📖 Identity **A:** Steve Ellis **W:** Steven T. Seagle

Other grades: Multiply prices above by **1.5 for Mint • 2/3 for Very Fine • 1/3 for Fine • 1/5 for Very Good • 1/8 for Good**

19 ❑ Apr 1995 Cover: 1.95 **NM** value: **Cover or less**
Circ: CapCity orders: **8,700**
Mayhem in Motion **A:** Steve Lieber
20 ❑ May 1995 Cover: 1.95 **NM** value: **Cover or less**
Circ: CapCity orders: **8,300**
Clash of Wings **A:** Steve Lieber
21 ❑ Jun 1995 Cover: 2.25 **NM** value: **Cover or less**
Circ: CapCity orders: **8,350**
Party Lines **A:** Steve Lieber(cover) ★ Versus Shadow Thief. ★ Versus Gentleman Ghost.
22 ❑ Jul 1995 Cover: 2.25 **NM** value: **Cover or less**
Circ: CapCity orders: **8,850**
The Way of The Warrior, Part 3; Storm Over Thanagar **A:** Steve Lieber
23 ❑ Aug 1995 Cover: 2.25 **NM** value: **Cover or less**
Circ: CapCity orders: **8,750**
The Way of The Warrior, Part 6; Essential Warfare **A:** Steve Lieber
24 ❑ Sep 1995 Cover: 2.25 **NM** value: **Cover or less**
Circ: CapCity orders: **7,300**
Lion Hunt, Part 1; Hunting the Lion, Part 1 **A:** Steve Lieber
25 ❑ Oct 1995 Cover: 2.25 **NM** value: **Cover or less**
Circ: CapCity orders: **7,250**
Lion Hunt, Part 2; Hunting the Lion, Part 2 **A:** Steve Lieber
26 ❑ Nov 1995 Cover: 2.25 **NM** value: **Cover or less**
Underworld Unleashed; Fear Visits • Underworld Unleashed **A:** Steve Lieber ★ Appearance of Scarecrow.
27 ❑ Dec 1995 Cover: 2.25 **NM** value: **Cover or less**
Underworld Unleashed; Hawkmad • Underworld Unleashed **A:** Steve Lieber ★ Appearance of Neuron, Neuron, Silent Knight.
28 ❑ Jan 1996 Cover: 2.25 **NM** value: **Cover or less**
Free Fall **A:** Steve Lieber(cover) ★ Versus Dr. Polaris. ★ Versus Doctor Polaris.
29 ❑ Feb 1996 Cover: 2.25 **NM** value: **Cover or less**
Voices of Descent, Part 1 **A:** Anthony Castrillo **W:** Pat McGreal ★ Appearance of Vandal Savage.
30 ❑ Mar 1996 Cover: 2.25 **NM** value: **Cover or less**
Voices of Descent, Part 2 **A:** Anthony Castrillo **W:** Pat McGreal
31 ❑ Apr 1996 Cover: 2.25 **NM** value: **Cover or less**
Hunter, Hunted, Prey!, Part 1 **A:** Mike Collins **W:** Christopher Priest
32 ❑ Jun 1996 Cover: 2.25 **NM** value: **Cover or less**
Hunter, Hunted, Prey!, Part 2 **A:** Mike Collins **W:** Christopher Priest
33 ❑ Jul 1996 Cover: 2.25 **NM** value: **Cover or less**
Hunter, Hunted, Prey!, Part 3 final issue. **A:** Mike Collins **W:** Christopher Priest ★ Appearance of Arion. ★ Death of Hawkman.
Anl 1❑ca. 1993 Cover: 3.50 **NM** value: **Cover or less**
Circ: CapCity orders: **19,450**
Bloodlines • Bloodlines ★ 1st Appearance of Mongrel.
Anl 2❑ca. 1995 Cover: 3.95 **NM** value: **Cover or less**
Circ: CapCity orders: **6,525**
• Year One

HAWKMAN ARCHIVES, THE — DC
1 ❑ Cover: 49.95 **NM** value: **Cover or less**

HAWKMOON: THE JEWEL IN THE SKULL — First
1 ❑ May 1986 Cover: 1.75 **NM** value: **Cover or less**
Circ: CapCity orders: **8,575**
2 ❑ Jul 1986 Cover: 1.75 **NM** value: **Cover or less**
Circ: CapCity orders: **7,075**
3 ❑ Sep 1986 Cover: 1.75 **NM** value: **Cover or less**
Circ: CapCity orders: **6,800**
4 ❑ Nov 1986 Cover: 1.75 **NM** value: **Cover or less**
Circ: CapCity orders: **6,875**
Bk 1❑ Cover: 9.95 **NM** value: **Cover or less**

HAWKMOON: THE MAD GOD'S AMULET — First
1 ❑ Jan 1987 Cover: 1.75 **NM** value: **Cover or less**
Circ: CapCity orders: **7,450**
2 ❑ Feb 1987 Cover: 1.75 **NM** value: **Cover or less**
Circ: CapCity orders: **6,200**
3 ❑ Mar 1987 Cover: 1.75 **NM** value: **Cover or less**
Circ: CapCity orders: **5,875**
4 ❑ Apr 1987 Cover: 1.75 **NM** value: **Cover or less**
Circ: CapCity orders: **5,975**

HAWKMOON: THE RUNESTAFF — First
1 ❑ ca. 1988 Cover: 1.75 **NM** value: **2.00**
Circ: CapCity orders: **5,375**
2 ❑ ca. 1988 Cover: 1.75 **NM** value: **2.00**
Circ: CapCity orders: **4,625**
3 ❑ ca. 1988 Cover: 1.95 **NM** value: **2.00**
Circ: CapCity orders: **4,375**
4 ❑ ca. 1988 Cover: 1.95 **NM** value: **2.00**
Circ: CapCity orders: **4,150**

HAWKMOON: THE SWORD OF THE DAWN — First
1 ❑ Sep 1987 Cover: 1.75 **NM** value: **Cover or less**
Circ: CapCity orders: **7,375**
2 ❑ Nov 1987 Cover: 1.75 **NM** value: **Cover or less**
Circ: CapCity orders: **5,925**
3 ❑ Jan 1988 Cover: 1.75 **NM** value: **Cover or less**
Circ: CapCity orders: **5,525**
4 ❑ Mar 1988 Cover: 1.75 **NM** value: **Cover or less**
Circ: CapCity orders: **5,725**

HAWKSHAWS — Image
1 ❑ Mar 2000, b&w Cover: 2.95 **NM** value: **Cover or less**
Circ: Diamd. preorders: **5,790**

HAWK, STREET AVENGER — Taurus Publishing
1 ❑ Jun 1996, b&w Cover: 2.50 **NM** value: **Cover or less**

HAWKWORLD — DC
Katar Hol is the grandson of Paran Katar, the scientist who made it possible for his world to conquer others. As such, Katar is practically aristocracy, but he's decided to take his first job as an ensign with the Wingmen, a police-like force that keeps the less fortunate in line. Problem is, Katar feels compassion for the conquered, who are treated as little more than slaves on his "civilized" world. That could make his job — and his role as one of his world's leaders — very difficult.

Hol is later sent to Earth as an ambassador and visiting super-hero. A clever P.R. person dubs him "Hawkman" — a moniker that sticks with him as he begins his terrestrial war on crime. In that unending struggle, at least, he finds his world and Earth to be remarkably similar.

This series is a regular monthly that followed the events of the Hawkworld mini-series.

1 ❑ Jun 1990 Cover: 1.50 **NM** value: **2.50**
Circ: CapCity orders: **39,550** • **CGC:** 1 graded, best 9.0
2 ❑ Jul 1990 Cover: 1.50 **NM** value: **1.75**
Circ: CapCity orders: **28,550**
3 ❑ Aug 1990 Cover: 1.50 **NM** value: **1.75**
Circ: CapCity orders: **26,650**
4 ❑ Sep 1990 Cover: 1.50 **NM** value: **1.75**
Circ: CapCity orders: **25,200**
5 ❑ Oct 1990 Cover: 1.50 **NM** value: **1.75**
Circ: CapCity orders: **23,500**
6 ❑ Dec 1990 Cover: 1.50 **NM** value: **1.75**
Circ: CapCity orders: **21,700**
7 ❑ Jan 1991 Cover: 1.50 **NM** value: **1.75**
Circ: CapCity orders: **20,850**
8 ❑ Feb 1991 Cover: 1.50 **NM** value: **1.75**
Circ: CapCity orders: **19,350**
9 ❑ Mar 1991 Cover: 1.50 **NM** value: **1.75**
Circ: CapCity orders: **16,850**
10 ❑ Apr 1991 Cover: 1.50 **NM** value: **1.75**
Circ: CapCity orders: **15,200**
11 ❑ May 1991 Cover: 1.50 **NM** value: **Cover or less**
Circ: CapCity orders: **14,650**
12 ❑ Jun 1991 Cover: 1.50 **NM** value: **Cover or less**
Circ: CapCity orders: **14,200**
13 ❑ Jul 1991 Cover: 1.50 **NM** value: **Cover or less**
Circ: CapCity orders: **13,750**
14 ❑ Aug 1991 Cover: 1.50 **NM** value: **Cover or less**
Circ: CapCity orders: **13,700**
15 ❑ Sep 1991 Cover: 1.50 **NM** value: **Cover or less**
Circ: CapCity orders: **20,350**
War of the Gods, Part 4 • War of the Gods
16 ❑ Oct 1991 Cover: 1.50 **NM** value: **Cover or less**
Circ: CapCity orders: **17,900**
War of the Gods, Part 12 • War of the Gods
17 ❑ Nov 1991 Cover: 1.50 **NM** value: **Cover or less**
Circ: CapCity orders: **13,550**
18 ❑ Dec 1991 Cover: 1.50 **NM** value: **Cover or less**
Circ: CapCity orders: **13,450**
19 ❑ Jan 1992 Cover: 1.50 **NM** value: **Cover or less**
Circ: CapCity orders: **13,000**
20 ❑ Feb 1992 Cover: 1.50 **NM** value: **Cover or less**
Circ: CapCity orders: **12,050**
21 ❑ Mar 1992 Cover: 1.25 **NM** value: **1.50**
Circ: CapCity orders: **11,400**
22 ❑ Apr 1992 Cover: 1.50 **NM** value: **Cover or less**
Circ: CapCity orders: **10,200**
23 ❑ May 1992 Cover: 1.50 **NM** value: **Cover or less**
Circ: CapCity orders: **10,650**
24 ❑ Jul 1992 Cover: 1.50 **NM** value: **Cover or less**
Circ: CapCity orders: **9,950**
25 ❑ Aug 1992 Cover: 1.50 **NM** value: **Cover or less**
Circ: CapCity orders: **10,050**
26 ❑ Sep 1992 Cover: 1.50 **NM** value: **Cover or less**
Circ: CapCity orders: **9,250**
27 ❑ Oct 1992 Cover: 1.75 **NM** value: **Cover or less**
Circ: CapCity orders: **9,650**
Flight's End, Part 1 ★ 1st Appearance of The White Dragon.
28 ❑ Nov 1992 Cover: 1.75 **NM** value: **Cover or less**
Circ: CapCity orders: **9,050**
Flight's End, Part 2
29 ❑ Dec 1992 Cover: 1.75 **NM** value: **Cover or less**
Circ: CapCity orders: **8,900**
Flight's End, Part 3
30 ❑ Jan 1993 Cover: 1.75 **NM** value: **Cover or less**
Circ: CapCity orders: **8,750**
Flight's End, Part 4 ★ 1st Appearance of Count Viper, The Netherworld.
31 ❑ Feb 1993 Cover: 1.75 **NM** value: **Cover or less**
Circ: CapCity orders: **9,000**
Flight's End, Part 5
32 ❑ Mar 1993 Cover: 1.75 **NM** value: **Cover or less**
Circ: CapCity orders: **11,600**
Flight's End, Part 6 final issue.
Anl 1❑Dec 1990 Cover: 2.95 **NM** value: **3.00**
Anl 2❑Aug 1991 Cover: 2.95 **NM** value: **Cover or less**
Circ: CapCity orders: **24,650**
Armageddon Factor; Armageddon 2001, Part 6
Anl 2-2❑Aug 1991 Cover: 2.95 **NM** value: **Cover or less**
Anl 3❑ca. 1992 Cover: 2.95 **NM** value: **Cover or less**
Circ: CapCity orders: **14,850**
Eclipso: The Darkness Within, Part 11 • Eclipso

HAWKWORLD (MINI-SERIES) — DC
1 ❑ Aug 1989 Cover: 3.95 **NM** value: **4.00**
Flashzone • New costume **A:** Tim Truman; Enrique Alcatena **W:** Tim Truman ★ Origin of Hawkman.
2 ❑ Sep 1989 Cover: 3.95 **NM** value: **4.00**
• Truman **A:** Tim Truman
3 ❑ Oct 1989 Cover: 3.95 **NM** value: **4.00**
• Truman **A:** Tim Truman
Bk 1❑ Cover: 16.95 **NM** value: **Cover or less**

HAYWIRE — DC
Deep in the heart of a secured facility, a very special armored suit has been developed. Capable of unbelievable, deadly force, the suit is driven by a psionic link with its wearer. Unfortunately that meant that the suit could only be driven to its full potential by a person with a rare kind of highly repressed personality.

Accordingly, "auditions" were held. But although the applicants were screened carefully, an outsider somehow managed to infiltrate the program and proved all too perfect a match for the armored suit. Driving the suit to its full power, he suddenly went "haywire" and began killing the technicians. This stranger managed to steal the suit and is using it to carry out a particularly nasty war against organized crime.

Nobody seems to know who Haywire is — including Haywire himself!

1 ❑ Oct 1988 Cover: 1.25 **NM** value: **Cover or less**
Circ: CapCity orders: **18,150**
Kaleidoscope **A:** Vince Giarrano **W:** Michael Fleisher ★ 1st Appearance of Haywire.
2 ❑ Nov 1988 Cover: 1.25 **NM** value: **Cover or less**
Circ: CapCity orders: **12,700**
Black Dragon **A:** Vince Giarrano **W:** Michael Fleisher
3 ❑ Dec 1988 Cover: 1.25 **NM** value: **Cover or less**
Circ: CapCity orders: **11,850**
4 ❑ Dec 1988 Cover: 1.25 **NM** value: **Cover or less**
Circ: CapCity orders: **10,500**
Recognitions **A:** Vince Giarrano **W:** Michael Fleisher
5 ❑ Jan 1989 Cover: 1.25 **NM** value: **Cover or less**
Circ: CapCity orders: **9,450**
6 ❑ Jan 1989 Cover: 1.25 **NM** value: **Cover or less**
Circ: CapCity orders: **9,050**
7 ❑ Mar 1989 Cover: 1.50 **NM** value: **Cover or less**
Circ: CapCity orders: **8,800**
8 ❑ Apr 1989 Cover: 1.50 **NM** value: **Cover or less**
Circ: CapCity orders: **8,200**
9 ❑ May 1989 Cover: 1.50 **NM** value: **Cover or less**
Circ: CapCity orders: **7,850**
10 ❑ Jun 1989 Cover: 1.50 **NM** value: **Cover or less**
Circ: CapCity orders: **7,750**
11 ❑ Jul 1989 Cover: 1.50 **NM** value: **Cover or less**
Circ: CapCity orders: **7,200**
12 ❑ Aug 1989 Cover: 1.50 **NM** value: **Cover or less**
Circ: CapCity orders: **7,200**
13 ❑ Sep 1989 Cover: 1.50 **NM** value: **Cover or less**
Circ: CapCity orders: **6,950**
final issue.

HAZARD — Image
1 ❑ Jun 1996 Cover: 1.75 **NM** value: **Cover or less**
2 ❑ Jul 1996 Cover: 1.75 **NM** value: **Cover or less**
cover says Jun, indicia says Jul.
3 ❑ Jul 1996 Cover: 1.75 **NM** value: **Cover or less**
4 ❑ Aug 1996 Cover: 1.75 **NM** value: **Cover or less**
5 ❑ Sep 1996 Cover: 1.75 **NM** value: **Cover or less**
Circ: Diamd. preorders: **14,431**
6 ❑ Oct 1996 Cover: 1.75 **NM** value: **2.25**
Circ: Diamd. preorders: **12,581**
cover says Sep, indicia says Oct.
7 ❑ Nov 1996 Cover: 2.25 **NM** value: **Cover or less**
Circ: Diamd. preorders: **10,519**
final issue.

HAZARD! (MOTION) — Motion
1 ❑ b&w Cover: 2.50 **NM** value: **Cover or less**
• Breakneck Blvd.

HAZARD! (RECKLESS VISION) — Reckless Vision
1 ❑ b&w Cover: 2.50 **NM** value: **Cover or less**
• first Breakneck Blvd. Story

H-BOMB — Antarctic
All issues are adults only.
1 ❑ Apr 1993, b&w Cover: 2.95 **NM** value: **Cover or less**

HEADBANGER — Parody Press
1 ❑ Cover: 2.50 **NM** value: **Cover or less**
A Different Drummer **A:** Thad Rhodes **W:** Nat Gertler

HEADBUSTER — Antarctic
1 ❑ Sep 1998, b&w Cover: 2.95 **NM** value: **Cover or less**

HEADHUNTERS — Image
1 ❑ Apr 1997, b&w Cover: 2.95 **NM** value: **Cover or less**
Circ: Diamd. preorders: **14,111**
cover says Mar, indicia says Apr. **A:** Chris Marrinan **W:** Chris Marrinan
2 ❑ May 1997, b&w Cover: 2.95 **NM** value: **Cover or less**
Circ: Diamd. preorders: **9,258**
3 ❑ Jun 1997, b&w Cover: 2.95 **NM** value: **Cover or less**
Circ: Diamd. preorders: **6,772**

HEADLESS HORSEMAN — Eternity
1 ❑ b&w Cover: 2.25 **NM** value: **Cover or less**
2 ❑ b&w Cover: 2.25 **NM** value: **Cover or less**

CGC-graded: Multiply prices above by **33 for 9.9 M • 16 for 9.8 NM/M • 7 for 9.6 NM+ • 5 for 9.4 NM • 2.5 for 9.2 NM- • 1.5 for 9.0 VF/NM**

HEADLINE COMICS — Headline

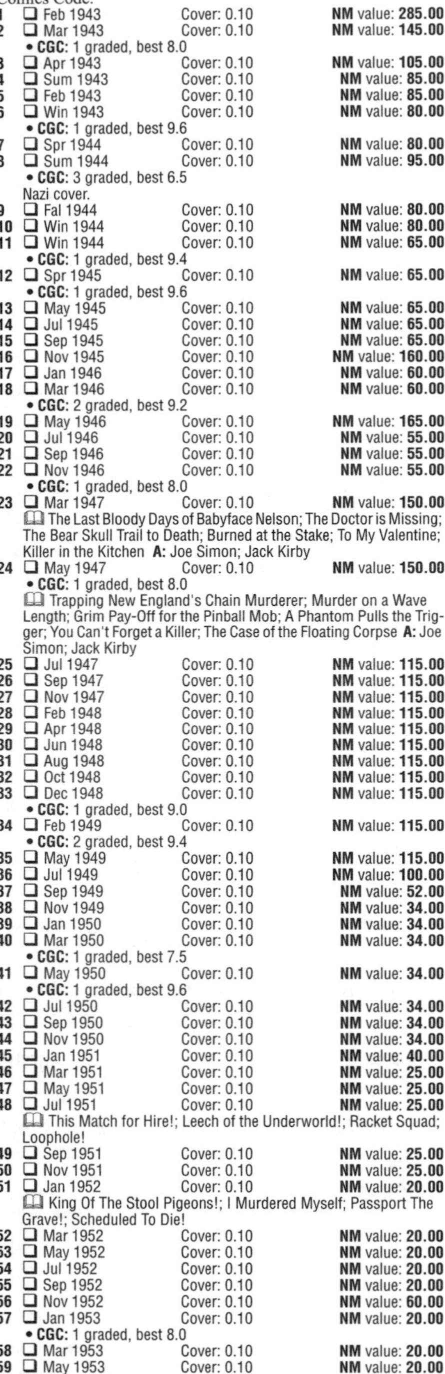

Headline Comics was a late, and not especially notable, entry into the World War II comic-book boom, featuring patriotic heroes such as Yank and Doodle, The Junior Rangers, and The Blue Streak. Following the atomic bombing of Japan in 1945, a super-hero named Atomic Man made a brief appearance in the pages of Headline, but soon faded away along with most of the other super-heroes of the late 1940s.

Headline changed direction with issue #23 in December 1947, when the creative team of Simon and Kirby introduced a hard-edged true crime format to the title. From then until its demise in 1956, Headline featured the typically brutal, morally ambiguous, and luridly sensational crime stories that eventually led to the formation of the Comics Code.

1 ❑ Feb 1943 Cover: 0.10 **NM** value: **285.00**
2 ❑ Mar 1943 Cover: 0.10 **NM** value: **145.00**
• **CGC:** 1 graded, best 8.0
3 ❑ Apr 1943 Cover: 0.10 **NM** value: **105.00**
4 ❑ Sum 1943 Cover: 0.10 **NM** value: **85.00**
5 ❑ Feb 1943 Cover: 0.10 **NM** value: **85.00**
6 ❑ Win 1943 Cover: 0.10 **NM** value: **80.00**
• **CGC:** 1 graded, best 9.6
7 ❑ Spr 1944 Cover: 0.10 **NM** value: **80.00**
8 ❑ Sum 1944 Cover: 0.10 **NM** value: **95.00**
• **CGC:** 3 graded, best 6.5
Nazi cover.
9 ❑ Fal 1944 Cover: 0.10 **NM** value: **80.00**
10 ❑ Win 1944 Cover: 0.10 **NM** value: **80.00**
11 ❑ Win 1944 Cover: 0.10 **NM** value: **65.00**
• **CGC:** 1 graded, best 9.4
12 ❑ Spr 1945 Cover: 0.10 **NM** value: **65.00**
• **CGC:** 1 graded, best 9.6
13 ❑ May 1945 Cover: 0.10 **NM** value: **65.00**
14 ❑ Jul 1945 Cover: 0.10 **NM** value: **65.00**
15 ❑ Sep 1945 Cover: 0.10 **NM** value: **65.00**
16 ❑ Nov 1945 Cover: 0.10 **NM** value: **160.00**
17 ❑ Jan 1946 Cover: 0.10 **NM** value: **60.00**
18 ❑ Mar 1946 Cover: 0.10 **NM** value: **60.00**
• **CGC:** 2 graded, best 9.2
19 ❑ May 1946 Cover: 0.10 **NM** value: **165.00**
20 ❑ Jul 1946 Cover: 0.10 **NM** value: **55.00**
21 ❑ Sep 1946 Cover: 0.10 **NM** value: **55.00**
22 ❑ Nov 1946 Cover: 0.10 **NM** value: **55.00**
• **CGC:** 1 graded, best 8.0
23 ❑ Mar 1947 Cover: 0.10 **NM** value: **150.00**
📖 The Last Bloody Days of Babyface Nelson; The Doctor is Missing; The Bear Skull Trail to Death; Burned at the Stake; To My Valentine; Killer in the Kitchen **A:** Joe Simon; Jack Kirby
24 ❑ May 1947 Cover: 0.10 **NM** value: **150.00**
• **CGC:** 1 graded, best 8.0
📖 Trapping New England's Chain Murderer; Murder on a Wave Length; Grim Pay-Off for the Pinball Mob; A Phantom Pulls the Trigger; You Can't Forget a Killer; The Case of the Floating Corpse **A:** Joe Simon; Jack Kirby
25 ❑ Jul 1947 Cover: 0.10 **NM** value: **115.00**
26 ❑ Sep 1947 Cover: 0.10 **NM** value: **115.00**
27 ❑ Nov 1947 Cover: 0.10 **NM** value: **115.00**
28 ❑ Feb 1948 Cover: 0.10 **NM** value: **115.00**
29 ❑ Apr 1948 Cover: 0.10 **NM** value: **115.00**
30 ❑ Jun 1948 Cover: 0.10 **NM** value: **115.00**
31 ❑ Aug 1948 Cover: 0.10 **NM** value: **115.00**
32 ❑ Oct 1948 Cover: 0.10 **NM** value: **115.00**
33 ❑ Dec 1948 Cover: 0.10 **NM** value: **115.00**
• **CGC:** 1 graded, best 9.0
34 ❑ Feb 1949 Cover: 0.10 **NM** value: **115.00**
• **CGC:** 2 graded, best 9.4
35 ❑ May 1949 Cover: 0.10 **NM** value: **115.00**
36 ❑ Jul 1949 Cover: 0.10 **NM** value: **100.00**
37 ❑ Sep 1949 Cover: 0.10 **NM** value: **52.00**
38 ❑ Nov 1949 Cover: 0.10 **NM** value: **34.00**
39 ❑ Jan 1950 Cover: 0.10 **NM** value: **34.00**
40 ❑ Mar 1950 Cover: 0.10 **NM** value: **34.00**
• **CGC:** 1 graded, best 7.5
41 ❑ May 1950 Cover: 0.10 **NM** value: **34.00**
• **CGC:** 1 graded, best 9.6
42 ❑ Jul 1950 Cover: 0.10 **NM** value: **34.00**
43 ❑ Sep 1950 Cover: 0.10 **NM** value: **34.00**
44 ❑ Nov 1950 Cover: 0.10 **NM** value: **34.00**
45 ❑ Jan 1951 Cover: 0.10 **NM** value: **40.00**
46 ❑ Mar 1951 Cover: 0.10 **NM** value: **25.00**
47 ❑ May 1951 Cover: 0.10 **NM** value: **25.00**
48 ❑ Jul 1951 Cover: 0.10 **NM** value: **25.00**
📖 This Match for Hire!; Leech of the Underworld!; Racket Squad; Loophole!
49 ❑ Sep 1951 Cover: 0.10 **NM** value: **25.00**
50 ❑ Nov 1951 Cover: 0.10 **NM** value: **25.00**
51 ❑ Jan 1952 Cover: 0.10 **NM** value: **20.00**
📖 King Of The Stool Pigeons!; I Murdered Myself; Passport The Grave!; Scheduled To Die!
52 ❑ Mar 1952 Cover: 0.10 **NM** value: **20.00**
53 ❑ May 1952 Cover: 0.10 **NM** value: **20.00**
54 ❑ Jul 1952 Cover: 0.10 **NM** value: **20.00**
55 ❑ Sep 1952 Cover: 0.10 **NM** value: **20.00**
56 ❑ Nov 1952 Cover: 0.10 **NM** value: **60.00**
57 ❑ Jan 1953 Cover: 0.10 **NM** value: **20.00**
• **CGC:** 1 graded, best 8.0
58 ❑ Mar 1953 Cover: 0.10 **NM** value: **20.00**
59 ❑ May 1953 Cover: 0.10 **NM** value: **20.00**
📖 Getaway Mob!; The Lines on the Map!; Killers are Never Alone!
60 ❑ Jul 1953 Cover: 0.10 **NM** value: **20.00**
📖 Finger Man!; F.B.I. Radio Broadcast; Circle of Death!
61 ❑ Sep 1953 Cover: 0.10 **NM** value: **16.00**
📖 Moonshine!; The Homicide That Wasn't; Brain of the Underworld; First Mistake
62 ❑ Nov 1954 Cover: 0.10 **NM** value: **16.00**
63 ❑ Jan 1954 Cover: 0.10 **NM** value: **16.00**
64 ❑ Mar 1954 Cover: 0.10 **NM** value: **16.00**
65 ❑ May 1954 Cover: 0.10 **NM** value: **16.00**
66 ❑ Jul 1954 Cover: 0.10 **NM** value: **16.00**
67 ❑ Sep 1954 Cover: 0.10 **NM** value: **16.00**
68 ❑ Nov 1954 Cover: 0.10 **NM** value: **16.00**
69 ❑ Jan 1955 Cover: 0.10 **NM** value: **16.00**
70 ❑ 1955 Cover: 0.10 **NM** value: **16.00**
71 ❑ 1955 Cover: 0.10 **NM** value: **13.00**
72 ❑ 1955 Cover: 0.10 **NM** value: **13.00**
73 ❑ Cover: 0.10 **NM** value: **13.00**
74 ❑ Cover: 0.10 **NM** value: **13.00**
75 ❑ Cover: 0.10 **NM** value: **13.00**
76 ❑ Cover: 0.10 **NM** value: **13.00**
77 ❑ Cover: 0.10 **NM** value: **13.00**
final issue.

HEADMAN — Innovation

1 ❑ Cover: 2.50 **NM** value: **Cover or less**
Circ: CapCity orders: **2,700**
📖 Head Games **A:** Matt Thompson **W:** Matt Thompson

HEAP — Skywald

1 ❑ Sep 1971 Cover: 0.25 **NM** value: **14.00**
📖 Shadows of Satan; When The Sea Goes Dry!; Death on the Earth-Mars Run!; Ballast of Gold **A:** Tom Sutton; Jack Abel **W:** Bob Kanigher

HEARTBREAK COMICS — Eclipse

1 ❑ b&w Cover: 3.95 **NM** value: **Cover or less**
• magazine.

HEARTBREAKERS — Dark Horse

1 ❑ Apr 1996 Cover: 2.95 **NM** value: **Cover or less**
2 ❑ May 1996 Cover: 2.95 **NM** value: **Cover or less**
3 ❑ Jun 1996 Cover: 2.95 **NM** value: **Cover or less**
4 ❑ Jul 1996 Cover: 2.95 **NM** value: **Cover or less**
final issue. **A:** Lenin Delsol; Paul Guinan; Anina Bennett **W:** Paul Guinan; Anina Bennett

HEARTBREAKERS BUST OUT! — Image

Bk 1❑ Jun 1997 Cover: 9.95 **NM** value: **Cover or less**
• reprints story from Dark Horse Presents

HEARTBREAKERS SUPERDIGEST: YEAR TEN — Image

1 ❑ Dec 1999 Cover: 13.95 **NM** value: **Cover or less**
📖 The Last Strand; Sailing Vessels of the Southwest Sands; Stork Spreads Wings; Shot 'Til you Dropkick; Home Again, Home Again; It's Science! **A:** Lenin Delsol; Paul Guinan; Steve Leialoha; Anina Bennett; Lee Marrs **W:** Paul Guinan; Anina Bennett; Lee Marrs

HEARTLAND — DC / Vertigo

1 ❑ Mar 1997 Cover: 4.95 **NM** value: **Cover or less**
Circ: Diamd. preorders: **29,151**
One-shot.

HEART OF DARKNESS — Hardline

1 ❑ Cover: 2.95 **NM** value: **Cover or less**

HEART OF EMPIRE — Dark Horse

This sequel to the epic Adventures of Luther Arkwright revolves around an alternate history of Britain, where the Empire never diminished, Queen Anne never died, and Oliver Cromwell's puritanical influence never faded. Unknown to the despotic Queen and her subjects, a catastrophic event is coming, and may focus on her daughter Victoria, who suffers from mysterious migraines and blackouts as well as the shadowy legacy of her missing father Luther Arkwright. There are rumors that the Pope has sent his best assassin to the Imperial Palace in London to commit a dreadful deed, and that Armageddon begins in seven days. Throw in healthy doses of historical reverence, political satire, eroticism, and fart jokes, and add celebrity cameos and you have the makings of a classic in a comic book. From the sublime to the profane, Bryan Talbot has once again woven a remarkably complex tale of politics, personalities, and perverse eccentricities.

1 ❑ Apr 1999 Cover: 2.95 **NM** value: **Cover or less**
Circ: Diamd. preorders: **10,070**
2 ❑ May 1999 Cover: 2.95 **NM** value: **Cover or less**
Circ: Diamd. preorders: **8,213**
3 ❑ Jun 1999 Cover: 2.95 **NM** value: **Cover or less**
Circ: Diamd. preorders: **8,255**
4 ❑ Jul 1999 Cover: 2.95 **NM** value: **Cover or less**
Circ: Diamd. preorders: **8,424**
5 ❑ Aug 1999 Cover: 2.95 **NM** value: **Cover or less**
Circ: Diamd. preorders: **8,790**
6 ❑ Sep 1999 Cover: 2.95 **NM** value: **Cover or less**
Circ: Diamd. preorders: **8,445**
7 ❑ Oct 1999 Cover: 2.95 **NM** value: **Cover or less**
Circ: Diamd. preorders: **8,794**
8 ❑ Nov 1999 Cover: 2.95 **NM** value: **Cover or less**
Circ: Diamd. preorders: **8,461**
9 ❑ Dec 1999 Cover: 2.95 **NM** value: **Cover or less**
Circ: Diamd. preorders: **11,608**

HEART OF THE BEAST, THE — DC / Vertigo

1 ❑ Cover: 19.95 **NM** value: **Cover or less**

HEARTS AND MINDS — Marvel / Epic

Bk 1❑ Cover: 8.95 **NM** value: **Cover or less**
Circ: CapCity orders: **2,450**

HEARTS OF AFRICA — Slave Labor

1 ❑ Cover: 10.95 **NM** value: **Cover or less**

HEARTS OF DARKNESS — Marvel

1 ❑ Dec 1991 Cover: 4.95 **NM** value: **Cover or less**
• Ghost Rider, Wolverine, and Punisher vs. Blackheart **A:** John Romita Jr. **W:** Howard Mackie

HEART THROBS — DC

DC inherited Heart Throbs from Quality Comics in the 1950s and continued to churn out issues until the market for love comics finally dried up in the early 1970s. The stories and art in Heart Throbs were as stiff and formulaic as the worst of the love comic genre could be, but were burnished with the cool professionalism of the DC house style and packaged as a slick and attractive product for the sisters of the readers of DC's harder-edged super-hero and war comics. The goofy stories and off-the-wall features, including some bizarre fashion tips and love poetry submitted by readers, make Heart Throbs a campy reading experience for modern audiences.

Stories from Heart Throbs and other DC love comics were collected in a "Heart Throbs" trade paperback edition in the late 1970s.

1 ❑ Aug 1949 Cover: 0.10 **NM** value: **200.00**
2 ❑ Oct 1949 Cover: 0.10 **NM** value: **110.00**
3 ❑ Dec 1949 Cover: 0.10 **NM** value: **50.00**
4 ❑ Feb 1950 Cover: 0.10 **NM** value: **75.00**
5 ❑ Apr 1950 Cover: 0.10 **NM** value: **42.00**
6 ❑ 1950 Cover: 0.10 **NM** value: **75.00**
7 ❑ Cover: 0.10 **NM** value: **42.00**
8 ❑ Cover: 0.10 **NM** value: **75.00**
9 ❑ Mar 1952 Cover: 0.10 **NM** value: **42.00**
10 ❑ Apr 1952 Cover: 0.10 **NM** value: **42.00**
11 ❑ 1952 Cover: 0.10 **NM** value: **25.00**
12 ❑ Jul 1952 Cover: 0.10 **NM** value: **25.00**
13 ❑ Aug 1952 Cover: 0.10 **NM** value: **25.00**
14 ❑ Sep 1952 Cover: 0.10 **NM** value: **25.00**
15 ❑ Oct 1952 Cover: 0.10 **NM** value: **25.00**
16 ❑ Nov 1952 Cover: 0.10 **NM** value: **22.00**
17 ❑ Cover: 0.10 **NM** value: **22.00**
18 ❑ 1953 Cover: 0.10 **NM** value: **22.00**
19 ❑ 1953 Cover: 0.10 **NM** value: **22.00**
20 ❑ 1953 Cover: 0.10 **NM** value: **22.00**
21 ❑ 1953 Cover: 0.10 **NM** value: **42.00**
22 ❑ 1953 Cover: 0.10 **NM** value: **30.00**
23 ❑ 1953 Cover: 0.10 **NM** value: **30.00**
24 ❑ Cover: 0.10 **NM** value: **19.00**
25 ❑ Cover: 0.10 **NM** value: **19.00**
26 ❑ Cover: 0.10 **NM** value: **19.00**
27 ❑ Cover: 0.10 **NM** value: **19.00**
28 ❑ Cover: 0.10 **NM** value: **19.00**
29 ❑ Cover: 0.10 **NM** value: **19.00**
30 ❑ Cover: 0.10 **NM** value: **19.00**
31 ❑ Nov 1955 Cover: 0.10 **NM** value: **19.00**
32 ❑ Jan 1955 Cover: 0.10 **NM** value: **19.00**
33 ❑ Mar 1955 Cover: 0.10 **NM** value: **19.00**
34 ❑ Cover: 0.10 **NM** value: **19.00**
35 ❑ Cover: 0.10 **NM** value: **19.00**
36 ❑ Cover: 0.10 **NM** value: **19.00**
37 ❑ Cover: 0.10 **NM** value: **19.00**
38 ❑ Cover: 0.10 **NM** value: **19.00**
📖 Tearful Dates; On the Rebound; Ring on my Finger; I Won't Be Hurt Again
39 ❑ Cover: 0.10 **NM** value: **19.00**
40 ❑ Cover: 0.10 **NM** value: **19.00**
41 ❑ Cover: 0.10 **NM** value: **17.00**
42 ❑ Cover: 0.10 **NM** value: **17.00**
43 ❑ 1956 Cover: 0.10 **NM** value: **17.00**
44 ❑ Cover: 0.10 **NM** value: **17.00**
45 ❑ Cover: 0.10 **NM** value: **17.00**
46 ❑ Cover: 0.10 **NM** value: **17.00**
47 ❑ May 1957 Cover: 0.10 **NM** value: **120.00**
• DC begins as publisher
48 ❑ Jul 1957 Cover: 0.10 **NM** value: **65.00**
49 ❑ Sep 1957 Cover: 0.10 **NM** value: **60.00**
50 ❑ Nov 1957 Cover: 0.10 **NM** value: **60.00**
51 ❑ Jan 1958 Cover: 0.10 **NM** value: **48.00**
52 ❑ Mar 1958 Cover: 0.10 **NM** value: **48.00**
53 ❑ May 1958 Cover: 0.10 **NM** value: **48.00**
54 ❑ Jul 1958 Cover: 0.10 **NM** value: **48.00**
55 ❑ Sep 1958 Cover: 0.10 **NM** value: **48.00**
56 ❑ Nov 1958 Cover: 0.10 **NM** value: **48.00**
57 ❑ Jan 1959 Cover: 0.10 **NM** value: **48.00**
58 ❑ Feb 1959 Cover: 0.10 **NM** value: **48.00**
59 ❑ May 1959 Cover: 0.10 **NM** value: **48.00**
60 ❑ Jul 1959 Cover: 0.10 **NM** value: **48.00**
61 ❑ Sep 1959 Cover: 0.10 **NM** value: **38.00**
62 ❑ Nov 1959 Cover: 0.10 **NM** value: **38.00**
63 ❑ Jan 1960 Cover: 0.10 **NM** value: **38.00**
64 ❑ Mar 1960 Cover: 0.10 **NM** value: **38.00**
65 ❑ May 1960 Cover: 0.10 **NM** value: **38.00**
66 ❑ Jul 1960 Cover: 0.10 **NM** value: **38.00**
67 ❑ Sep 1960 Cover: 0.10 **NM** value: **38.00**
68 ❑ Nov 1960 Cover: 0.10 **NM** value: **38.00**
69 ❑ Jan 1961 Cover: 0.10 **NM** value: **38.00**
• **CGC:** 1 graded, best 9.4
70 ❑ Mar 1961 Cover: 0.10 **NM** value: **38.00**

Other grades: Multiply prices above by **1.5 for Mint • 2/3 for Very Fine • 1/3 for Fine • 1/5 for Very Good • 1/8 for Good**

71 ❑ May 1961 Cover: 0.10 **NM** value: **27.00**
72 ❑ Jul 1961 Cover: 0.10 **NM** value: **27.00**
73 ❑ Sep 1961 Cover: 0.10 **NM** value: **27.00**
74 ❑ Nov 1961 Cover: 0.10 **NM** value: **27.00**
75 ❑ Jan 1962 Cover: 0.12 **NM** value: **27.00**
76 ❑ Mar 1962 Cover: 0.12 **NM** value: **27.00**
77 ❑ May 1962 Cover: 0.12 **NM** value: **27.00**
78 ❑ Jul 1962 Cover: 0.12 **NM** value: **27.00**
79 ❑ Sep 1962 Cover: 0.12 **NM** value: **27.00**
80 ❑ Nov 1962 Cover: 0.12 **NM** value: **27.00**
81 ❑ Jan 1963 Cover: 0.12 **NM** value: **20.00**
82 ❑ Mar 1963 Cover: 0.12 **NM** value: **20.00**
83 ❑ May 1963 Cover: 0.12 **NM** value: **20.00**
84 ❑ Jul 1963 Cover: 0.12 **NM** value: **20.00**
85 ❑ Sep 1963 Cover: 0.12 **NM** value: **20.00**
86 ❑ Nov 1963 Cover: 0.12 **NM** value: **20.00**
87 ❑ Jan 1964 Cover: 0.12 **NM** value: **20.00**
88 ❑ Mar 1964 Cover: 0.12 **NM** value: **20.00**
89 ❑ May 1964 Cover: 0.12 **NM** value: **20.00**
90 ❑ Jul 1964 Cover: 0.12 **NM** value: **20.00**
91 ❑ Sep 1964 Cover: 0.12 **NM** value: **16.00**
92 ❑ Nov 1964 Cover: 0.12 **NM** value: **16.00**
93 ❑ Jan 1965 Cover: 0.12 **NM** value: **16.00**
94 ❑ Mar 1965 Cover: 0.12 **NM** value: **16.00**
95 ❑ May 1965 Cover: 0.12 **NM** value: **16.00**
96 ❑ Jul 1965 Cover: 0.12 **NM** value: **16.00**
97 ❑ Sep 1965 Cover: 0.12 **NM** value: **16.00**
98 ❑ Nov 1965 Cover: 0.12 **NM** value: **16.00**
99 ❑ Jan 1966 Cover: 0.12 **NM** value: **16.00**
100 ❑ Mar 1966 Cover: 0.12 **NM** value: **16.00**
101 ❑ May 1966 Cover: 0.12 **NM** value: **60.00**
102 ❑ Jul 1966 Cover: 0.12 **NM** value: **13.00**
103 ❑ Sep 1966 Cover: 0.12 **NM** value: **13.00**
104 ❑ Nov 1966 Cover: 0.12 **NM** value: **13.00**
105 ❑ Jan 1967 Cover: 0.12 **NM** value: **13.00**
Circ: Statement: **174,500**
106 ❑ Mar 1967 Cover: 0.12 **NM** value: **13.00**
Circ: Statement: **174,500**
107 ❑ May 1967 Cover: 0.12 **NM** value: **13.00**
Circ: Statement: **174,500**
108 ❑ Jul 1967 Cover: 0.12 **NM** value: **13.00**
Circ: Statement: **174,500**
109 ❑ Sep 1967 Cover: 0.12 **NM** value: **13.00**
Circ: Statement: **174,500**
110 ❑ Nov 1967 Cover: 0.12 **NM** value: **13.00**
Circ: Statement: **174,500**
111 ❑ Jan 1968 Cover: 0.12 **NM** value: **10.00**
📖 Unlock My Yearning Heart!; Give Love a Chance; Their Lives-Their Loves
112 ❑ Mar 1968 Cover: 0.12 **NM** value: **10.00**
113 ❑ May 1968 Cover: 0.12 **NM** value: **10.00**
114 ❑ Jul 1968 Cover: 0.12 **NM** value: **10.00**
115 ❑ Sep 1968 Cover: 0.12 **NM** value: **10.00**
116 ❑ Nov 1968 Cover: 0.12 **NM** value: **10.00**
117 ❑ Jan 1969 Cover: 0.12 **NM** value: **10.00**
118 ❑ Mar 1969 Cover: 0.12 **NM** value: **10.00**
119 ❑ May 1969 Cover: 0.12 **NM** value: **10.00**
120 ❑ Jul 1969 Cover: 0.15 **NM** value: **10.00**
121 ❑ Sep 1969 Cover: 0.15 **NM** value: **10.00**
122 ❑ Nov 1969 Cover: 0.15 **NM** value: **10.00**
123 ❑ Jan 1970 Cover: 0.15 **NM** value: **10.00**
124 ❑ Mar 1970 Cover: 0.15 **NM** value: **10.00**
125 ❑ May 1970 Cover: 0.15 **NM** value: **10.00**
126 ❑ Jul 1970 Cover: 0.15 **NM** value: **10.00**
127 ❑ Sep 1970 Cover: 0.15 **NM** value: **10.00**
128 ❑ Nov 1970 Cover: 0.15 **NM** value: **10.00**
129 ❑ Jan 1971 Cover: 0.15 **NM** value: **10.00**
130 ❑ Mar 1971 Cover: 0.15 **NM** value: **10.00**
Circ: Statement: **157,182**
131 ❑ May 1971 Cover: 0.15 **NM** value: **9.00**
Circ: Statement: **157,182**
132 ❑ Jul 1971 Cover: 0.15 **NM** value: **9.00**
Circ: Statement: **157,182**
133 ❑ Sep 1971 Cover: 0.25 **NM** value: **9.00**
Circ: Statement: **157,182**
134 ❑ Oct 1971 Cover: 0.25 **NM** value: **9.00**
Circ: Statement: **157,182**
135 ❑ Nov 1971 Cover: 0.25 **NM** value: **9.00**
Circ: Statement: **157,182**
136 ❑ Dec 1971 Cover: 0.25 **NM** value: **9.00**
Circ: Statement: **157,182**
137 ❑ Jan 1972 Cover: 0.25 **NM** value: **9.00**
Circ: Statement: **118,749**
138 ❑ Feb 1972 Cover: 0.25 **NM** value: **9.00**
Circ: Statement: **118,749**
139 ❑ Mar 1972 Cover: 0.25 **NM** value: **9.00**
Circ: Statement: **118,749**
140 ❑ Apr 1972 Cover: 0.25 **NM** value: **9.00**
Circ: Statement: **118,749**
141 ❑ May 1972 Cover: 0.25 **NM** value: **9.00**
Circ: Statement: **118,749**
142 ❑ Jun 1972 Cover: 0.25 **NM** value: **9.00**
Circ: Statement: **118,749**
143 ❑ Jul 1972 Cover: 0.20 **NM** value: **9.00**
Circ: Statement: **118,749**
final issue.

HEARTTHROBS (VERTIGO) — DC / Vertigo

1 ❑ Jan 1999 Cover: 2.95 **NM** value: **Cover or less**
📖 The Princess and the Frog; The Prince and the Witch; Genes and a T-Shirt; Diagnosis **A:** Tim Sale; Phil Jimenez; Brian Bolland **W:** Brian Bolland; Robert Rodi; Steven Seagle
2 ❑ Feb 1999 Cover: 2.95 **NM** value: **Cover or less**
📖 The Other Side of Town; Romancing the Stone; Jericho **A:** Tim Bradstreet; Frank Quitely; Tony Salmons **W:** Ilya; Brian Azzarello; Doselle Young
3 ❑ Mar 1999 Cover: 2.95 **NM** value: **Cover or less**
📖 Apposites Attract; Mister Right; Sleeping Beauty **A:** Richard Corben; James Romberger; Eduardo Risso **W:** Simon Revelstroke; Peter Milligan; Marguerite van Cook
4 ❑ Apr 1999 Cover: 2.95 **NM** value: **Cover or less**
📖 Heartache 1.0; Love... with a Twist; Kissing Cousin **A:** Danijel Zezelj; Pat McEown; Miran Kim **W:** Bob Fingerman; Scott Cunningham; Steve Gerber

HEATHCLIFF — Marvel / Star

The star of this series is a rather mischievous cat named Heathcliff. Unlike his low-key cartoon contemporary, Garfield, Heathcliff is always up to something or other: usually, getting into trouble. His favorite pastimes include chasing birds and mice; annoying Spike, the huge neighborhood dog; and romancing Sonya, his girlfriend. All of it is done for laughs in high style.

Heathcliff enjoyed long-running popularity as a newspaper cartoon before making the transition to comics. This helps account for the relative longevity of Heathcliff as a comic book. Heathcliff ran for over 50 issues, outlasting the Marvel's Star line of children's comics itself. In contrast, the majority of Star titles ceased publication after less than a dozen issues.

1 ❑ Apr 1985 Cover: 0.65 **NM** value: **1.50**
2 ❑ Jun 1985 Cover: 0.65 **NM** value: **1.00**
Circ: CapCity orders: **3,900**
3 ❑ Aug 1985 Cover: 0.65 **NM** value: **1.00**
Circ: CapCity orders: **3,300**
4 ❑ Oct 1985 Cover: 0.65 **NM** value: **1.00**
Circ: CapCity orders: **2,800**
5 ❑ Dec 1985 Cover: 0.65 **NM** value: **1.00**
Circ: CapCity orders: **2,400**
📖 Computer Cat; Tale of Two Kitties; The Birthday Surprise **A:** Warren Kremer **W:** Michael Gallagher
6 ❑ Feb 1986 Cover: 0.65 **NM** value: **1.00**
Circ: CapCity orders: **2,200**
7 ❑ Apr 1986 Cover: 0.75 **NM** value: **1.00**
Circ: CapCity orders: **2,200**
8 ❑ Jun 1986 Cover: 0.75 **NM** value: **1.00**
Circ: CapCity orders: **2,000**
9 ❑ Aug 1986 Cover: 0.75 **NM** value: **1.00**
Circ: CapCity orders: **2,250**
10 ❑ Sep 1986 Cover: 0.75 **NM** value: **1.00**
Circ: CapCity orders: **2,000**
11 ❑ Oct 1986 Cover: 0.75 **NM** value: **1.00**
Circ: CapCity orders: **2,300**
12 ❑ Nov 1986 Cover: 0.75 **NM** value: **1.00**
Circ: CapCity orders: **2,200**
📖 Spaced-Out Cat; The Kitnap Kaper; Knight Life
13 ❑ Dec 1986 Cover: 0.75 **NM** value: **1.00**
Circ: CapCity orders: **2,150**
14 ❑ Feb 1987 Cover: 0.75 **NM** value: **1.00**
Circ: Statement: **79,400** CapCity orders: **2,250**
15 ❑ Apr 1987 Cover: 0.75 **NM** value: **1.00**
Circ: Statement: **79,400** CapCity orders: **2,100**
16 ❑ Jun 1987 Cover: 1.00 **NM** value: **Cover or less**
Circ: Statement: **79,400** CapCity orders: **1,500**
17 ❑ Aug 1987 Cover: 1.00 **NM** value: **Cover or less**
Circ: Statement: **79,400** CapCity orders: **1,450**
18 ❑ Sep 1987 Cover: 1.00 **NM** value: **Cover or less**
Circ: Statement: **79,400**
19 ❑ Oct 1987 Cover: 1.00 **NM** value: **Cover or less**
Circ: Statement: **79,400**
20 ❑ Nov 1987 Cover: 1.00 **NM** value: **Cover or less**
Circ: Statement: **79,400**
21 ❑ Dec 1987 Cover: 1.00 **NM** value: **Cover or less**
Circ: Statement: **79,400**
22 ❑ Feb 1988 Cover: 1.00 **NM** value: **Cover or less**
Circ: Statement: **64,225** CapCity orders: **1,500**
23 ❑ Apr 1988 Cover: 1.00 **NM** value: **Cover or less**
Circ: Statement: **64,225** CapCity orders: **1,600**
24 ❑ Jun 1988 Cover: 1.00 **NM** value: **Cover or less**
Circ: Statement: **64,225** CapCity orders: **1,400**
25 ❑ Aug 1988 Cover: 1.00 **NM** value: **Cover or less**
Circ: Statement: **64,225** CapCity orders: **1,400**
26 ❑ Sep 1988 Cover: 1.00 **NM** value: **Cover or less**
Circ: Statement: **64,225** CapCity orders: **1,300**
27 ❑ Oct 1988 Cover: 1.00 **NM** value: **Cover or less**
Circ: Statement: **64,225** CapCity orders: **13,100**
28 ❑ Nov 1988 Cover: 1.00 **NM** value: **Cover or less**
Circ: Statement: **64,225** CapCity orders: **1,200**
29 ❑ Dec 1988 Cover: 1.00 **NM** value: **Cover or less**
Circ: Statement: **64,225** CapCity orders: **1,200**
30 ❑ Feb 1989 Cover: 1.00 **NM** value: **Cover or less**
Circ: Statement: **38,090** CapCity orders: **1,200**
31 ❑ Mar 1989 Cover: 1.00 **NM** value: **Cover or less**
Circ: Statement: **38,090** CapCity orders: **1,200**
32 ❑ Apr 1989 Cover: 1.00 **NM** value: **Cover or less**
Circ: Statement: **38,090** CapCity orders: **1,300**
33 ❑ May 1989 Cover: 1.00 **NM** value: **Cover or less**
Circ: Statement: **38,090** CapCity orders: **1,300**
34 ❑ Jun 1989 Cover: 1.00 **NM** value: **Cover or less**
Circ: Statement: **38,090** CapCity orders: **1,200**
35 ❑ Jul 1989 Cover: 1.00 **NM** value: **Cover or less**
Circ: Statement: **38,090** CapCity orders: **1,200**
36 ❑ Aug 1989 Cover: 1.00 **NM** value: **Cover or less**
Circ: Statement: **38,090** CapCity orders: **1,200**
37 ❑ Sep 1989 Cover: 1.00 **NM** value: **Cover or less**
Circ: Statement: **38,090** CapCity orders: **1,350**
38 ❑ Oct 1989 Cover: 1.00 **NM** value: **Cover or less**
Circ: Statement: **38,090** CapCity orders: **1,250**
39 ❑ Nov 1989 Cover: 1.00 **NM** value: **Cover or less**
Circ: Statement: **38,090** CapCity orders: **1,300**
40 ❑ Nov 1989 Cover: 1.00 **NM** value: **Cover or less**
Circ: Statement: **38,090**
41 ❑ Dec 1989 Cover: 1.00 **NM** value: **Cover or less**
Circ: Statement: **38,090**
42 ❑ Dec 1989 Cover: 1.00 **NM** value: **Cover or less**
Circ: Statement: **38,090** CapCity orders: **1,200**
43 ❑ Jan 1990 Cover: 1.00 **NM** value: **Cover or less**
Circ: CapCity orders: **1,550**
44 ❑ Feb 1990 Cover: 1.00 **NM** value: **Cover or less**
45 ❑ Mar 1990 Cover: 1.00 **NM** value: **Cover or less**
Circ: CapCity orders: **1,200**
46 ❑ Apr 1990 Cover: 1.00 **NM** value: **Cover or less**
47 ❑ May 1990 Cover: 1.00 **NM** value: **Cover or less**
Circ: CapCity orders: **1,450**
• Batman parody; has 1989 Statement, filed 11/1/89; avg print run 123,110; avg sales 34,245; avg subs 3,845; avg total paid circ 38,090; samples 150; office use 600; max existent 38,840; 69% of run returned
48 ❑ Jun 1990 Cover: 1.00 **NM** value: **Cover or less**
Circ: CapCity orders: **1,150**
49 ❑ Jul 1990 Cover: 1.00 **NM** value: **Cover or less**
Circ: CapCity orders: **950**
50 ❑ Aug 1990 Cover: 1.50 **NM** value: **Cover or less**
• Giant-size. • giant
51 ❑ Sep 1990 Cover: 1.00 **NM** value: **Cover or less**
52 ❑ Oct 1990 Cover: 1.00 **NM** value: **Cover or less**
53 ❑ Nov 1990 Cover: 1.00 **NM** value: **Cover or less**
54 ❑ Dec 1990 Cover: 1.00 **NM** value: **Cover or less**
55 ❑ Jan 1991 Cover: 1.00 **NM** value: **Cover or less**
56 ❑ Feb 1991 Cover: 1.00 **NM** value: **Cover or less**
final issue.
Anl 1 ❑ ca. 1987 Cover: 1.25 **NM** value: **Cover or less**

HEATHCLIFF'S FUNHOUSE — Marvel / Star

1 ❑ May 1987 Cover: 1.00 **NM** value: **1.25**
Circ: CapCity orders: **2,700**
📖 Karate Kitty; Undercover Cat; He's a Card; The Bet; Burp; Heathcliff's Photo Album **A:** Warren Kremer; Howie Post **W:** Warren Kremer; George Gladir; Michael Gallagher
2 ❑ Jun 1987 Cover: 1.00 **NM** value: **Cover or less**
Circ: CapCity orders: **1,550**
3 ❑ Jul 1987 Cover: 1.00 **NM** value: **Cover or less**
Circ: CapCity orders: **1,550**
4 ❑ Aug 1987 Cover: 1.00 **NM** value: **Cover or less**
5 ❑ Sep 1987 Cover: 1.00 **NM** value: **Cover or less**
6 ❑ Oct 1987 Cover: 1.00 **NM** value: **Cover or less**
Circ: CapCity orders: **1,450**
7 ❑ Nov 1987 Cover: 1.00 **NM** value: **Cover or less**
Circ: CapCity orders: **1,250**
8 ❑ Dec 1987 Cover: 1.00 **NM** value: **Cover or less**
Circ: CapCity orders: **1,200**
9 ❑ Jan 1988 Cover: 1.00 **NM** value: **Cover or less**
Circ: CapCity orders: **1,200**
10 ❑ Feb 1988 Cover: 1.00 **NM** value: **Cover or less**
Circ: CapCity orders: **1,200**

HEATSEEKER — Fantaco

1 ❑ Cover: 5.95 **NM** value: **Cover or less**
No issue number.

HEAVY ARMOR — Fantasy General

1 ❑ Cover: 1.70 **NM** value: **Cover or less**
2 ❑ Cover: 1.70 **NM** value: **Cover or less**
3 ❑ Cover: 1.70 **NM** value: **Cover or less**

HEAVY HITTERS — Marvel / Epic

Anl 1 ❑ Cover: 3.75 **NM** value: **Cover or less**
Circ: CapCity orders: **5,000**
📖 Lawdog: Unrealed; Feud: A Movable Beast; Alien Legion: Altered State; The Trouble With Girls: Girls Just Want to Have Fun; Spyke: Blemish **A:** Flint Henry; Bill Reinhold; Bret Blevins; Mark A. Nelson **W:** Carl Potts; Will Jacobs; Chuck Dixon; Mike Baron; Gerard Jones

HEAVY LIQUID — DC / Vertigo

1 ❑ Oct 1999 Cover: 5.95 **NM** value: **Cover or less**
Circ: Diamd. preorders: **12,171**
2 ❑ Nov 1999 Cover: 5.95 **NM** value: **Cover or less**
Circ: Diamd. preorders: **10,234**
3 ❑ Dec 1999 Cover: 5.95 **NM** value: **Cover or less**
Circ: Diamd. preorders: **9,321**
4 ❑ Jan 2000 Cover: 5.95 **NM** value: **Cover or less**
Circ: Diamd. preorders: **8,576**
5 ❑ Feb 2000 Cover: 5.95 **NM** value: **Cover or less**
Circ: Diamd. preorders: **8,112**
Bk 1 ❑ Cover: 29.95 **NM** value: **Cover or less**
• Collects Series **A:** Paul Pope **W:** Paul Pope

HEAVY METAL — Metal Mammoth

Heavy Metal is one of the longest-running and most distinguished American comics magazines. From the magazine's inception in 1977, Heavy Metal has made great strides in bringing illustrated comics art to an adult audience. At the same time, it has refined its approach over the years, cutting back on pop culture filler pieces and interviews and adding in new showcases for alternative comic art. Today, it's one of the most accessible (and affordable) ways to see what's best in the world of illustrated fiction.

The list of creators who have contributed work to Heavy Metal is both long and impressive. Among them: Boris Vallejo, Howard Chaykin, Walt Simonson, Harlan Ellison, Moebius, Bernie Wrightson, and even Robert Crumb. Its masthead also reveals a pleasant surprise: the editor in chief (as of 1993) is Kevin Eastman, indie comics pioneer and co-creator of the Teenage Mutant Ninja Turtles.

The Heavy Metal staff provided the Standard Catalog indexers their complete Statement of Ownership files, making the process of compiling those figures considerably easier than what is normally the case.

1 ❑ Apr 1977 Cover: 1.50 **NM** value: **12.00**
Circ: Statement: **144,232**
🕮 1996, Part 1; The Adventures of Yriss; Age of Ages, Part 1; Conquering Armies, Part 1; Den, Part 1; Manipulation; Rut; Selenia; Space Punks; Sunspot, Part 1; Sword of Shannara; Traumwatch **A:** Richard Corben; Laura Pierson; Macedo; Philippe Druillet; Alexis; Chantal Montellier; Gal; Marre; Mezieres; Mouchel; Philippe Dionnet; Roy; Rubington; Terry Brooks; Vaughn Bode; Voss; Jean-Michel Nicollet(cover) **W:** Richard Corben; Laura Pierson; Macedo; Philippe Druillet; Alexis; Chantal Montellier; Gal; Marre; Mezieres; Mouchel; Philippe Dionnet; Roy; Rubington; Terry Brooks; Vaughn Bode; Voss

2 ❑ May 1977 Cover: 1.50 **NM** value: **8.00**
Circ: Statement: **144,232**
🕮 1996, Part 2; Adventures of Yriss; Age of Ages, Part 2; Conquering Armies, Part 2; Den, Part 2; Harzak, Part 1; Meaobbin Mecru; Sunspot; Conquering Armies, Part 2; Den, Part 2; Festival; Roger, Part 1; Star-Death of Margaret Omali; Sunspot, Part 2, Virgo **A:** Richard Corben; Jacques Tardi; Philippe Druillet; Alexis; Baret; Caza; Chantal Montellier; Gal; James Triptree Jr.; Locquet; Philippe Dionnet; Picaret; Rubington; Souchu; Vaughn Bode; Moebius(cover) **W:** Richard Corben; Jacques Tardi; Philippe Druillet; Alexis; Baret; Caza; Chantal Montellier; Gal; James Triptree Jr.; Locquet; Philippe Dionnet; Picaret; Rubington; Souchu; Vaughn Bode

3 ❑ Jun 1977 Cover: 1.50 **NM** value: **8.00**
Circ: Statement: **144,232**
🕮 1996, Part 3; Age of Ages, Part 3; Conquering Armies, Part 3; Den, Part 3; Gail, Part 1; Harzak, Part 2; Night Images; Rockblitz; Sloane; Sunspot, Part 3; Vengeance; Vessel; World Apart, Part 1 **A:** Richard Corben; Gary Davis; Jacques Tardi; Macedo; Philippe Druillet; Alexis; Chantal Montellier; Dominique He; Gal; Philippe Dionnet; Rubington; Vaughn Bode; Moebius(cover) **W:** Richard Corben; Gary Davis; Jacques Tardi; Macedo; Philippe Druillet; Alexis; Chantal Montellier; Dominique He; Gal; Philippe Dionnet; Robert E. Howard; Rubington; Vaughn Bode

4 ❑ Jul 1977 Cover: 1.50 **NM** value: **6.00**
Circ: Statement: **144,232**
🕮 1996, Part 4; Approaching Centauri; Conquering Armies, Part 4; Crossroads of the Universe; Den, Part 4; Golden Queen; Harzak, Part 3; The Long Tomorrow, Part 1; Nep Simo; Prince of Mist; Sunspot, Part 4; World Apart, Part 2 **A:** Richard Corben; Moebius; Gary Davis; Eniki Bilal; Philippe Druillet; Bihanic; Chantal Montellier; Gal; O'Bannon; Philippe Dionnet; Vaughn Bode; Voss; Walter Perry; Moebius(cover) **W:** Richard Corben; Moebius; Gary Davis; Eniki Bilal; Philippe Druillet; Bihanic; Chantal Montellier; Gal; O'Bannon; Philippe Dionnet; Vaughn Bode; Voss; Walter Perry

5 ❑ Aug 1977 Cover: 1.50 **NM** value: **6.00**
Circ: Statement: **144,232**
🕮 1996, Part 5; Age of Ages, Part 4; Black Queen; Coincidence; Den, Part 5; Fever; Green Hand; Hamilton Potemkine; The Long Tomorrow, Part 2; Our Own Little Mardis Gras; Package For You, Missus Jones; Polonius, Part 1; Roger, Part 2; World Apart, Part 3 **A:** Richard Corben; Moebius; Gary Davis; Jacques Tardi; Nicole Claveloux; Philippe Druillet; Zha; Alesc; Chantal Montellier; Gotlieb; Halmos; Locquet; O'Bannon; Picaret; Richard Lupoff; Rubington; Souchu; Voss; Berni Wrightson(cover) **W:** Richard Corben; Moebius; Gary Davis; Jacques Tardi; Nicole Claveloux; Philippe Druillet; Zha; Alesc; Chantal Montellier; Gotlieb; Halmos; Locquet; O'Bannon; Picaret; Richard Lupoff; Rubington; Souchu; Voss

6 ❑ Sep 1977 Cover: 1.50 **NM** value: **6.00**
Circ: Statement: **144,232**
🕮 1996, Part 6; AAARRRZZZ; Den, Part 6; Is There a Demon Lover in the House?; It's a Small Universe; Last Vodka on Smirnov; Major Fatal; Night Grass; Orcyb; Polonius, Part 2; Teonanactl Genese; World Apart, Part 4 **A:** Richard Corben; Moebius; Gary Davis; Jacques Tardi; Macedo; Nicole Claveloux; Philippe Druillet; Zha; Alain; Chantal Montellier; Cortman; Lesueur; Picaret **W:** Richard Corben; Moebius; Gary Davis; Jacques Tardi; Macedo; Nicole Claveloux; Philippe Druillet; Zha; Alain; Chantal Montellier; Cortman; Lesueur; Picaret; Roger Zelazny

7 ❑ Oct 1977 Cover: 1.50 **NM** value: **6.00**
Circ: Statement: **144,232**
🕮 1996, Part 7; Den, Part 7; The Garage, Part 1; How Good is Man?; In You I Am Reborn; Jet Man; Operation Omega; Polonius, Part 3; Singsong of Cecily Snow; Turod; The White Knight **A:** Berni Wrightson; Angus McKie; Brian LeBlanc; Richard Corben; Moebius; Jacques Tardi; Nicole Claveloux; Zha; Jean Sole; Lire; Philippe Dionnet; Rosilio; Jean-Michel Nicollet(cover) **W:** Berni Wrightson; Angus McKie; Brian LeBlanc; Richard Corben; Moebius; Jacques Tardi; Nicole Claveloux; Zha; Jean Sole; Lire; Philippe Dionnet; Rosilio; Theodore Sturgeon

8 ❑ Nov 1977 Cover: 1.50 **NM** value: **6.00**
Circ: Statement: **202,818**
🕮 1996, Part 8; A Visit to Jivaskilla Technexp; Airtight Garage of Jerry Corne, Part 2; Ballade; Bird of Dust; Blue Terror; Den, Part 8; Feet Upon the Stomach; How's the Nightlife on...; Master; Polonius, Part 4; World Apart, Part 5 **A:** Richard Corben; Moebius; Gary Davis; Jacques Tardi; Nicole Claveloux; Zha; Bazolli; Caza; F'Murr; Jean-Michel Nicollet; Lesueur; Picaret; Tom Barber; George Proctor(cover) **W:** Richard Corben; Moebius; Gary Davis; Jacques Tardi; Nicole Claveloux; Zha; Bazolli; Caza; F'Murr; Jean-Michel Nicollet; Lesueur; Picaret; Tom Barber

9 ❑ Dec 1977 Cover: 1.50 **NM** value: **6.00**
Circ: Statement: **202,818**
🕮 Close Encounters of the Third Kind; Den, Part 9; Fortune's Fool; Mauve Sideshow; Telefield, Part 1; Vuzz **A:** Richard Corben; Howard Chaykin; Jean Sole(cover); Len Wein; Macedo; Nicole Claveloux; Philippe Druillet; Steven Spielberg; Zha **W:** Richard Corben; Howard Chaykin; Len Wein; Macedo; Nicole Claveloux; Philippe Druillet; Steven Spielberg; Zha

10 ❑ Jan 1978 Cover: 1.50 **NM** value: **6.00**
Circ: Statement: **202,818**
🕮 1996, Part 9; A Rose for Ecclesiastes; Airtight Garage of Jerry Corne, Part 3; Conquering Armies, Part 5; Den, Part 10; Miss Heavy Metal 1978; Space Soap Opera; Talaplaca; Ulysses **A:** Richard Corben; Gray Morrow; Moebius; Pichard; Chantal Montellier; Dominique He; Gal; Helme; Homer; Lob; Meehan; Philippe Dionnet; Val Mayerik(cover) **W:** Richard Corben; Gray Morrow; Moebius; Pichard; Chantal Montellier; Dominique He; Gal; Helme; Homer; Lob; Meehan; Philippe Dionnet; Roger Zelazny

11 ❑ Feb 1978 Cover: 1.50 **NM** value: **6.00**
Circ: Statement: **202,818**
🕮 1996, Part 10; **A:** Richard Corben; Moebius; Denis Sire; Forest; Macedo; Philippe Druillet; Alain; Chantal Montellier; Jean-Claude; Lesueur; Luis Garcia; Mora; Richard Lupoff; Rubington; Alex Niño(cover) **W:** Richard Corben; Moebius; Denis Sire; Forest; Macedo; Philippe Druillet; Alain; Chantal Montellier; Jean-Claude; Lesueur; Luis Garcia; Mora; Richard Lupoff; Rubington

12 ❑ Mar 1978 Cover: 1.50 **NM** value: **5.00**
Circ: Statement: **202,818**
🕮 1996, Part 11; Abracax Effect; Airtight Garage of Jerry Corne; Barbarella, Part 2; Den, Part 12; Diabolical Planet; Galactic Geographic, Part 1; Hitchhike; Lost; Orion, Part 1; Paradise 9; Ruse; Self-Portrait; Underground Comic; Urm, Part 2 **A:** Richard Corben; Gray Morrow; Charles Vess; Moebius; Denis Sire; Forest; Jim Burns(cover); Karl Kofoed; Philippe Druillet; Chantal Montellier; Jean-Michel Nicollet; Sean Kelly; Stuart Nezin; Thomas Bridges; Trip; Voss **W:** Richard Corben; Gray Morrow; Charles Vess; Moebius; Denis Sire; Forest; Karl Kofoed; Philippe Druillet; Chantal Montellier; Jean-Michel Nicollet; Sean Kelly; Stuart Nezin; Thomas Bridges; Trip; Voss

13 ❑ Apr 1978 Cover: 1.50 **NM** value: **5.00**
Circ: Statement: **202,818**
🕮 Airtight Garage of Jerry Corne, Part 5; Barbarella, Part 3; City of Flowers; Galactic Geographic, Part 2; Orion, Part 2; Urm the Mad **A:** Gray Morrow; Moebius; Forest; Karl Kofoed; Philippe Druillet; Picotto; Robert Morello(cover) **W:** Gray Morrow; Moebius; Forest; Karl Kofoed; Philippe Druillet; Picotto

14 ❑ May 1978 Cover: 1.50 **NM** value: **5.00**
Circ: Statement: **202,818**
🕮 1996, Part 12; An Image; Barbarella, Part 4; Fed Up; Galactic Geographic, Part 3; Going to Pieces; Jungle Gym; Lost Time; Margerin; Orion, Part 3; Ozone Alley; Tap-Dancing on a Tender...; The Day; The Uptight Garbage of Jerry Corne; Urm, Part 3 **A:** Gray Morrow; Moebius; Forest; Karl Kofoed; Macedo; Schuiten; Alex Ni±o; Blanc; Chantal Montellier; Dominique He; Dumont; Fourgeaud; Norville; Richard Raxlen; Tendre; Voss; Philippe Druillet(cover) **W:** Gray Morrow; Moebius; Forest; Karl Kofoed; Macedo; Schuiten; Alex Ni±o; Blanc; Chantal Montellier; Dominique He; Dumont; Fourgeaud; Norville; Richard Raxlen; Tendre; Voss

15 ❑ Jun 1978 Cover: 1.50 **NM** value: **5.00**
Circ: Statement: **202,818**

16 ❑ Jul 1978 Cover: 1.50 **NM** value: **5.00**
Circ: Statement: **202,818**
🕮 1996, Part 14; Barbarella, Part 6; Death of Orlaon; Frontispiece; Gail, Part 2; Galactic Geographic, Part 5; Heilman, Part 2; Last Voyage of Sinbad; More Than Human, Part 2; Orion, Part 4; Q Claf 1; Story of the Acrylic Magus and... **A:** Richard Corben; Gray Morrow; Moebius; Eniki Bilal; Forest; Jan Strnad; Karl Kofoed; Philippe Druillet; Picotto; Alex Ni±o; Bihanic; Chantal Montellier; Doug Moench; Voss; Caza(cover) **W:** Richard Corben; Gray Morrow; Moebius; Eniki Bilal; Forest; Jan Strnad; Karl Kofoed; Philippe Druillet; Picotto; Alex Ni±o; Bihanic; Chantal Montellier; Doug Moench; Theodore Sturgeon; Voss

17 ❑ Aug 1978 Cover: 1.50 **NM** value: **5.00**
Circ: Statement: **202,818**
🕮 Age of Ages, Part 6; Airtight Garage of Jerry Corne, Part 7; Frontispiece; Gail, Part 3; Galactic Geographic, Part 6; Georg **A:** Rub **W:** del Piombo; Rubington

18 ❑ Sep 1978 Cover: 1.50 **NM** value: **5.00**
Circ: Statement: **202,818**
🕮 Airtight Garage of Jerry Corne, Part 8; At Play in Time and Space; Croatian; Gail, Part 4; **A:** Steve Oliff; Richard Corben; Gray Morrow; Moebius; Jan Strnad; Jay Kinney; Jim Burns(cover); John Workman; Karl Kofoed; Ned Sonntag; Nicole Claveloux; Philippe Druillet; Steve Bissette; Zha; Benoit; Brocal Remohi; Jacques Rochberny; Richard Lupoff; Voss **W:** Steve Oliff; Richard Corben; Gray Morrow; Moebius; Jan Strnad; Jay Kinney; John Workman; Karl Kofoed; Ned Sonntag; Nicole Claveloux; Philippe Druillet; Steve Bissette; Zha; Benoit; Brocal Remohi; Harlan Ellison; Jacques Rochberny; Richard Lupoff; Voss

19 ❑ Oct 1978 Cover: 1.50 **NM** value: **5.00**
Circ: Statement: **202,818**
🕮 Airtight Garage of Jerry Corne, Part 9; Blob; Cu **A:** Angus McKie; Richard Corben; Gray Morrow; Doug Wheatley; Moebius; Eniki Bilal; Jan Strnad; Philippe Druillet; Steve Bissette; Stout; Jacques Rochberny; Romero; Sparrow; Voss; Ron Walotsky(cover) **W:** Angus McKie; Richard Corben; Gray Morrow; Doug Wheatley; Moebius; Eniki Bilal; Jan Strnad; Philippe Druillet; Steve Bissette; Stout; Harlan Ellison; Jacques Rochberny; Romero; Sparrow; Voss

20 ❑ Nov 1978 Cover: 1.50 **NM** value: **5.00**
Circ: Statement: **204,015**
🕮 Empire; Exterminator **A:** Angus McKie; Richard Corben; Gray Morrow; Howard Chaykin; Moebius; Denis Sire; Eniki Bilal; Jan Strnad; Karl Kofoed; Nicole Claveloux; Philippe Druillet; Steve Bissette; Zha; Delany; Voss; Marcus Boas(cover) **W:** Angus McKie; Richard Corben; Gray Morrow; Howard Chaykin; Moebius; Denis Sire; Eniki Bilal; Jan Strnad; Karl Kofoed; Nicole Claveloux; Philippe Druillet; Steve Bissette; Zha; Delany; Voss

21 ❑ Dec 1978 Cover: 1.50 **NM** value: **5.00**
Circ: Statement: **204,015**
🕮 Colored Lights; De **A:** Angus McKie; Richard Corben; Gray Morrow; Alfredo Alcala; Moebius; Eniki Bilal; Jan Strnad; Nicole Claveloux; Paul Kirchner; Phil Trumbo; Philippe Druillet; Zha; Ben Katchor; Bob Aull; Shell; Peter A. Jones(cover) **W:** Angus McKie; Richard Corben; Gray Morrow; Alfredo Alcala; Moebius; Eniki Bilal; Jan Strnad; Nicole Claveloux; Paul Kirchner; Phil Trumbo; Philippe Druillet; Zha; Ben Katchor; Bob Aull; Shell

22 ❑ Jan 1979 Cover: 1.50 **NM** value: **5.00**
Circ: Statement: **204,015**
🕮 1996, Part 15; Airtight Garage of Jerry Corne, Part 10; The Bus, Part 1; Dreamland; Exercise in Gold; Exterminator 17, Part 4; Gail, Part **A:** Angus McKie; Richard Corben; Trina Robbins; Moebius; Mark Wheatley; Eniki Bilal; Jan Strnad; John Totleben; Macedo; Paul Kirchner; Philippe Druillet; Alias; Chantal Montellier; Lesueur; Rochenberny; Stuart Nezin; Jo Ellen Trilling(cover) **W:** Angus McKie; Richard Corben; Trina Robbins; Moebius; Mark Wheatley; Eniki Bilal; Jan Strnad; John Totleben; Macedo; Paul Kirchner; Philippe Druillet; Alias; Chantal Montellier; Lesueur; Rochenberny; Stuart Nezin

23 ❑ Feb 1979 Cover: 1.50 **NM** value: **4.00**
Circ: Statement: **204,015**
🕮 1996, Part 16; The Bus, Part 2; Exterminator 17, Part 5; **A:** Angus McKie; Richard Corben; Moebius; Arthur Suydam; Eniki Bilal; Jan Strnad; Karl Kofoed; Kenneth Smith; Macedo; Paul Kirchner; Yves Chaland; Caza; Chantal Montellier; Halmos; John Pocsik; Kane; Sabine; Derek Rigg(cover) **W:** Angus McKie; Richard Corben; Moebius; Arthur Suydam; Eniki Bilal; Jan Strnad; Karl Kofoed; Kenneth Smith; Macedo; Paul Kirchner; Yves Chaland; Caza; Chantal Montellier; Halmos; John Pocsik; Kane; Sabine

24 ❑ Mar 1979 Cover: 1.50 **NM** value: **4.00**
Circ: Statement: **204,015**
🕮 1996, Part 17; A Mass for the Dead; Airtight Garage of Jerry Corne, Pa **A:** Richard Corben; Moebius; Angus McKie(cover); Denis Sire; Eniki Bilal; Jan Strnad; Kenneth Smith; Alex Ni±o; Alfred Bester; Blanc; Chantal Montellier; Dumont; Jacques Rochberny; John Pocsik; Kane; Malaskoy; Preiss; Tom Barber **W:** Richard Corben; Moebius; Denis Sire; Eniki Bilal; Jan Strnad; Kenneth Smith; Alex Ni±o; Alfred Bester; Blanc; Chantal Montellier; Dumont; Harlan Ellison; Jacques Rochberny; John Pocsik; Kane; Malaskoy; Preiss; Tom Barber

25 ❑ Apr 1979 Cover: 1.50 **NM** value: **4.00**
Circ: Statement: **204,015**
🕮 Alien, Part 1; The Bus, Part 3; The Garage, Part 5; Gideon Faust **A:** Scanlon **W:** Angus McKie; Scanlon; Richard Corben; Val Mayerik; Howard Chaykin; Moebius; Arthur Cover; Eniki Bilal; Giroux; Jan Strnad; Len Wein; Michael Gross; Paul Kirchner; Picotto; Rodolphe; Rue; Yves Chaland; Alias; Curtis King; John Pocsik; Rouge

26 ❑ May 1979 Cover: 1.50 **NM** value: **4.00**
Circ: Statement: **204,015**
🕮 Ah! The Pierrot; Airtight Garage of Jerry Corne, Part 12; Alien, Part 2; Blast Bartleby; Dan **A:** Vincente Alcazar **W:** Vincente Alcazar; Richard Corben; Paul Abrams; Gray Morrow; Rick Veitch; Walt Simonson; Moebius; Goodwin; Jan Strnad; John Workman; Philippe Druillet; Alias; Arnold; Ben Katchor; David Manak; James Cherry; John Pocsik; Petillion; Rogers; Sarrantonio

27 ❑ Jun 1979 Cover: 1.50 **NM** value: **4.00**
Circ: Statement: **204,015**
🕮 Alien: The Illustrated Story; An East Wind Coming; Captain Future; New Tales of the Arabian Nights: Sinbad, Part 11; Pyloon; So Beautiful and So Dangerous, Part 8 **A:** Richard Corben; Walt Simonson; Arthur Cover; Angus McKie(cover); Giroux; Goodwin; Jan Strnad; Manoeuvre; Rue; Serge Clerc **W:** Richard Corben; Walt Simonson; Arthur Cover; Giroux; Goodwin; Jan Strnad; Manoeuvre; Rue; Serge Clerc

28 ❑ Jul 1979 Cover: 1.50 **NM** value: **4.00**
Circ: Statement: **204,015**
🕮 Rears Its Ugly Head; Airtight Garage of Jerry Corne, Part 13; Attila the Frog; T **A:** Don Lomax; Gray Morrow; Moebius; Adams; Denis Sire; Jan Strnad; Macedo; Paul Kirchner; Richard Corben(cover); Alias; Chantal Montellier; John Pocsik; Mark Fisher; Michael Hinge; Nicholas Yermakov; Stuart Nezin; Vaughn Bode; Courtney(cover) **W:** Don Lomax; Gray Morrow; Moebius; Adams; Denis Sire; Jan Strnad; Macedo; Paul Kirchner; Alias; Chantal Montellier; John Pocsik; Mark Fisher; Michael Hinge; Nicholas Yermakov; Stuart Nezin; Vaughn Bode

29 ❑ Aug 1979 Cover: 1.50 **NM** value: **4.00**
Circ: Statement: **204,015**
🕮 A Space Story; Airtight Garage of Jerry Corne, Part 14; Amber II; Th **A:** Peter Kuper; Moebiu **W:** Todd Klein; Jim Starlin; Val Mayerik; Moebius; Arthur Suydam; Peter Kuper; Denis Sire; Karl Kofoed; Kenneth Smith; Lee Marrs; Martin Springett; Paul Kirchner; Caza; Jacques Rochberny; Jagger; John Pocsik; Margerin; Preiss; Reaves; Richards; Vaughn Bode

30 ❑ Sep 1979 Cover: 1.50 **NM** value: **4.00**
Circ: Statement: **204,015**
🕮 A World Between; Airt **A:** Gray Morrow; Moebius; Francois Thomas; Kenneth Smith; Macedo; Paul Kirchner; Alias; Chantal Montellier; Dominique He; J.K. Potter; Lawrence; Norman Spinard; O'Bannon; Richard Monaco; Thomas Warkentin; James Cherry(cover) **W:** Gray Morrow; Moebius; Francois Thomas; Kenneth Smith; Macedo; Paul Kirchner; Alias; Chantal Montellier; Dominique He; J.K. Potter; Lawrence; Michael Moorcock; Norman Spinard; O'Bannon; Richard Monaco; Thomas Warkentin

31 ❑ Oct 1979 Cover: 1.50 **NM** value: **4.00**
Circ: Statement: **204,015**
🕮 The Agony Column; The Alchemist's Notebook; Bad Breath; The Beasts; Dewsbury's Masterpiece; The Dunwich Horror; Final Justice; H. P. L.: KTULU; The Language of Cats; Love's Craft; The Man From Blackhole; The Necronomicon; Pat and Vivian; The Thing **A:** Moebius; Arthur Suydam; Nicole Claveloux; Philippe Druillet; Serge Clerc; Yves Chaland; Alberto Breccia; Baetz; Ceppi; Chateau; Dank; Hurd; Jean-Michel Nicollet; Luc Cornillion; Margerin; Sean Kelly; Vepy; Voss; J.K. Potter(cover) **W:** Moebius; Arthur Suydam; Nicole Claveloux; Philippe Druillet; Serge Clerc; Yves Chaland; Alberto Breccia; Baetz; Ceppi; Chateau; Dank; Hurd; Jean-Michel Nicollet; Luc Cornillion; Margerin; Sean Kelly; Vepy; Voss

32 ❑ Nov 1979 Cover: 1.50 **NM** value: **4.00**
Circ: Statement: **183,886**
🕮 Airtight Garage of Jerry Corne, Part 16; Barlowe's Guidebook to Extrate; Egg-Stained Wine; Elric, Part 2; Galactic Geographic, Part 11; Homer's Idyll; Jim; Moon Flight; Rowlf, Part 1; Shelter, Part 4; The Stars My Destination; Zooks, Part 3 **A:** Richard Corben; Frank Brunner; Moebius; Joe Jusko(cover); Karl Kofoed; Phil Trumbo; Alfred Bester; Barlowe; Chantal Montellier; Charles Hess; Luc Cornillion; Summers; Vaughn Bode; Voss **W:** Richard Corben; Frank Brunner; Moebius; Karl Kofoed; Phil Trumbo; Alfred Bester; Barlowe; Chantal Montellier; Charles Hess; Luc Cornillion; Michael Moorcock; Summers; Vaughn Bode; Voss

33 ❑ Dec 1979 Cover: 1.50 **NM** value: **4.00**
Circ: Statement: **183,886**

Other grades: Multiply prices above by **1.5 for Mint • 2/3 for Very Fine • 1/3 for Fine • 1/5 for Very Good • 1/8 for Good**

📖 A Tale of Christmas; After the Fall; Christmas Carol; Combing Out The Kinks; December 24 **A:** Steve Stiles; Richard Corben; Trina Robbins; Moebius; Arthur Suydam; Karl Kofoed; Lon Cohen(cover); Serge Clerc; Townley(cover); Caza; Flaw; Harold; Heller; Luc Cornillion; Luck; Montxo Algora; Rebellion; Scarce; Voss; Wijngg **W:** Steve Stiles; Richard Corben; Trina Robbins; Moebius; Arthur Suydam; Karl Kofoed; Serge Clerc; Caza; Flaw; Harlan Ellison; Harold; Heller; Luc Cornillion; Luck; Montxo Algora; Rebellion; Scarce; Voss; Wijngg

34 ❑ Jan 1980 Cover: 1.50 **NM** value: **4.00**
Circ: Statement: **183,886**
📖 Alien Comix; The Bus, Part 7; Comix, Part 1; Exit/In **A:** Rick Veitch; Paul Kirchner **W:** R

35 ❑ Feb 1980 Cover: 2.00 **NM** value: **4.00**
Circ: Statement: **183,886**
📖 9 A.M.; The Airtight Garage, Part 1; The Beast of Wolfton, Part 1; Buried Music; The Child **A:** Dick Matena; Moebius; Ri **W:** Angus McKie; Steve Stiles; Dick Matena; Rod Kierkegaard; Richard Corben; Matt Howarth; Moebius; Howard Cruse; Eniki Bilal; Jay Kinney; Lou Stathis; Steve Bissette; Bhob Stewart; Caza; Ilic; Richard Lupoff; Steve Brown; Ted White; The Circus

36 ❑ Mar 1980 Cover: 2.00 **NM** value: **4.00**
Circ: Statement: **183,886**
📖 The Airtight Garage, Part 2; Am **A:** Steve Stiles; Dick Matena; Rod Kierkegaard; Richard Corben; Matt Howarth; Moebius; Jay Kinney; John Bolton(cover); Lee Marrs; Lou Stathis; Bhob Stewart; Gerry Capelle; Richard Lupoff; Shinobu Kaze; Steve Brown; Vaughn Bode; Brothers Schuiten(cover) **W:** Steve Stiles; Dick Matena; Rod Kierkegaard; Richard Corben; Matt Howarth; Moebius; Jay Kinney; Lee Marrs; Lou Stathis; Bhob Stewart; Gerry Capelle; Richard Lupoff; Shinobu Kaze; Steve Brown; Vaughn Bode

37 ❑ Apr 1980 Cover: 2.00 **NM** value: **4.00**
Circ: Statement: **183,886**
📖 The Airtight Garage, Part 3; The Beast of Wolfton, Part 3; Champakou; Changes, Part 2; Comix I **A:** Mo **W:** Steve Stiles; Rod Kierkegaard; Richard Corben; Matt Howarth; Moebius; Eniki Bilal; Lou Stathis; Bhob Stewart; Caza; Gerry Capelle; Jacques Rochberny; Jeronaton; Maurice Horn; Mee; Norman Spinard; Richard Lupoff; Steve Brown; Vaughn Bode

38 ❑ May 1980 Cover: 2.00 **NM** value: **4.00**
Circ: Statement: **183,886**
📖 The Alchemist Supreme, Part 1; the Bus part 8; Champakou; Changes, Pa **A:** Godard; Paul Ki; Ribera **W:** Steve Stiles; Carl Potts; Rod Kierkegaard; Richard Corben; Matt Howarth; Eniki Bilal; Godard; Jay Kinney; Lou Stathis; Paul Kirchner; Ribera; Steve Bissette; Barry Malzberg; Bhob Stewart; Caza; Gerry Capelle; Jeronaton; Perry; Richard Lupoff; Steve Brown

39 ❑ Jun 1980 Cover: 2.00 **NM** value: **4.00**
Circ: Statement: **183,886**
📖 The Alchemist Supreme, Part 2; The Bus, Part 9; Captain Sternn: Featuring Ha **W:** Berni Wrightson; Steve Stiles; Rod Kierkegaard; Matt Howarth; Godard; Jay Kinney; John Workman; Lou Stathis; Paul Kirchner; Ribera; Bhob Stewart; Bill Maher; Caza; Champakou; Gerry Capelle; Richard Lupoff; Schuiten Brothers; Steve Brown

40 ❑ Jul 1980 Cover: 2.00 **NM** value: **4.00**
Circ: Statement: **183,886**
📖 2005; A Message From the Shadows; A Seventies Retrospective; The Alchemist Supreme, Part 3; The Bus, Part **A:** Dick Matena **W:** Steve Stiles; Dick Matena; Rod Kierkegaard; Matt Howarth; Rick Veitch; Moebius; Howard Cruse; Eniki Bilal; Godard; Jay Kinney; Karl Kofoed; Paul Kirchner; Philippe Druillet; Ribera; Caza; Don Butler; Jim Farber; Richard Lupoff; Sokal; Steve Brown

41 ❑ Aug 1980 Cover: 2.00 **NM** value: **4.00**
Circ: Statement: **183,886**
📖 The Alchemist Supreme, Part 4; The Bus, P **A:** Larry Elmore; Steve Stiles; Rod Kierkegaard; Matt Howarth; Rick Veitch; Moebius; Eniki Bilal; Godard; Jay Kinney; Lou Stathis; Paul Kirchner; Philippe Druillet; Ribera; Bhob Stewart; Maurice Horn; Richard Lupoff; Steve Brown; James Cherry(cover) **W:** Larry Elmore; Steve Stiles; Rod Kierkegaard; Matt Howarth; Rick Veitch; Moebius; Eniki Bilal; Godard; Jay Kinney; Lou Stathis; Paul Kirchner; Philippe Druillet; Ribera; Bhob Stewart; Maurice Horn; Richard Lupoff; Steve Brown

42 ❑ Sep 1980 Cover: 2.00 **NM** value: **4.00**
Circ: Statement: **183,886**
📖 The Alchemist Supreme, Part 5; The Bus, Part 12; Changes, Part 7; Comix, Part 8 **A:** Pau **W:** Pau

43 ❑ Oct 1980 Cover: 2.00 **NM** value: **4.00**
Circ: Statement: **183,886**
📖 Changes, Part 8; Comix, Part 9; Flix, **A:** Angus McKie; Dick Matena; Rod Kierkegaard; Tom Yeates; Matt Howarth; Ernie Colon; Moebius; Jay Kinney; Jooste Swarte; Lou Stathis; Philippe Druillet; Spain Rodriguez; Bhob Stewart; Dominique He; Dr. Progresso; Steve Brown; Voss; White; Liz Bijl(cover) **W:** Angus McKie; Dick Matena; Rod Kierkegaard; Tom Yeates; Matt Howarth; Ernie Colon; Moebius; Jay Kinney; Jooste Swarte; Lou Stathis; Philippe Druillet; Spain Rodriguez; Bhob Stewart; Dominique He; Dr. Progresso; Steve Brown; Voss; White

44 ❑ Nov 1980 Cover: 2.00 **NM** value: **4.00**
Circ: Statement: **172,116**
📖 Awaken; Blind Citadel; The Bookshelf; The Bus, Part 13; Changes, Part 9; Comix, Part 10; Comix International; Flix, Part 10; Interference; Little Tiny Comics, Part 3; **A:** Matt Howarth; Michael W. Kaluta; Giraud; Jay Kinney; Martin Springett; Paul Kirchner **W:** M; Michael W. Kaluta; Giraud; Martin Springett; Paul Kirchner

45 ❑ Dec 1980 Cover: 2.00 **NM** value: **4.00**
Circ: Statement: **172,116**
📖 Bloodstar, Part 1; The Bus, Part 14; Changes, Part 10; Comix, Part 11; T **A:** Paul K **W:** Steve Stiles; Dick Matena; Rod Kierkegaard; Matt Howarth; Rick Veitch; Moebius; Guido Crepax; Jay Kinney; Lou Stathis; Paul Kirchner; Ribera; Derek Parks-Carter; Godar; Klee; Richard Lupoff; Robert E. Howard; Schuiten Brothers; Steve Brown; White Lindall

46 ❑ Jan 1981 Cover: 2.00 **NM** value: **4.00**
Circ: Statement: **172,116**
📖 Ambassador of the Shadows, Part 1; Bang, Hah; Bloodstar, Part 2; Gallery Section: Kingdom of the; Gallery Section: Secret Art; Rock Opera, Part 13; There Is a Prince Charming on…; Valentina, Part 2; What is Reality, Papa?, Part 2; Woman **A:** Rod Kierkegaard; Richard Corben; Moebius; Bill Walsh; Christin; Godard; Guido Crepax; Ribera; Don Wood; Ian Miller; Jeronaton; Mezieres; Wenzel; Robert Burger(cover) **W:** Rod Kierkegaard; Richard Corben; Moebius; Bill Walsh; Christin; Godard; Guido Crepax; Ribera; Don Wood; Ian Miller; Jeronaton; Mezieres; Robert E. Howard; Wenzel

47 ❑ Feb 1981 Cover: 2.00 **NM** value: **4.00**
Circ: Statement: **172,116**
📖 Ambassador of the Shadows, Part 2; Bloodstar, Part 3; The Bus, Part 15; Civilian Defense; The Horny Goof; K.O.; Rock Opera, Part 14; Salammbo; The Tip of the Iceberg at Lucca; What is Reality, Papa?, Part 3 **A:** Rod Kierkegaard; Richard Corben; Rick Veitch; Moebius; Christin; Godard; Jim Burns(cover); Paul Kirchner; Philippe Druillet; Ribera; Mezieres; Voss; William Burroughs **W:** Rod Kierkegaard; Richard Corben; Rick Veitch; Moebius; Christin; Godard; Paul Kirchner; Philippe Druillet; Ribera; Mezieres; Robert E. Howard; Voss; William Burroughs

48 ❑ Mar 1981 Cover: 2.00 **NM** value: **4.00**
Circ: Statement: **172,116**
📖 Ambassador of the Shadows, Part 3; Bloodstar, Part 4; Changes, Part 11; Edward in Love; The Empire Grows Back; Fear Not Your Enemies; The Man With the Suitcase; Milady 3000; Rock Opera, Part 15; Salammbo; Tex Arcana, Part 1; What is Reality, Papa?, Part 4 **A:** Rod Kierkegaard; Richard Corben; Matt Howarth; Christin; Godard; Jean Teule; John Findley; Philippe Druillet; Ribera; Dominique He; Don Butler; Magnus; Mezieres; Abdul Mati Klarwein(cover) **W:** Rod Kierkegaard; Richard Corben; Matt Howarth; Christin; Godard; Jean Teule; John Findley; Philippe Druillet; Ribera; Dominique He; Don Butler; Harlan Ellison; Magnus; Mezieres; Robert E. Howard

49 ❑ Apr 1981 Cover: 2.00 **NM** value: **4.00**
Circ: Statement: **172,116**
📖 Ambassador of the Shadows, Part 4; Art and the Nazis; Bloodstar, Part 5; Changes, Part 12; Dangerous Curves; Good-Bye, Soldier; Rock Opera, Part 16; Stories from London; Tex Arcana, Part 2; What is Reality, Papa?, Part 5 **A:** Rod Kierkegaard; Richard Corben; Matt Howarth; Juan Gimenez; Mike Barreiro; Christin; Godard; John Findley; Ribera; Brad Balfour; Caza; Harry North; Mezieres; Esteban Maroto(cover) **W:** Rod Kierkegaard; Richard Corben; Matt Howarth; Juan Gimenez; Mike Barreiro; Christin; Godard; John Findley; Ribera; Brad Balfour; Caza; Harry North; Mezieres; Robert E. Howard

50 ❑ May 1981 Cover: 2.00 **NM** value: **4.00**
Circ: Statement: **172,116**
📖 1:09:00 AM; Bloodstar, Part 6; The Bus, Part 16; Cody Starbuck, Part 1; Gallery; Immorality; The Immortals' Fete, Part 1; Pillars of P-11507; Rock Opera, Part 17; Tex Arcana, Part 3; The Toll Bridge; Valentina, Part 3 **A:** Rod Kierkegaard; Richard Corben; Howard Chaykin; Arthur Suydam; Eniki Bilal; Guido Crepax; John Findley; Paul Kirchner; Charles Waller; Dzintars MeZullis; Koch; William Burroughs; Enric Rebollo(cover) **W:** Rod Kierkegaard; Richard Corben; Howard Chaykin; Arthur Suydam; Eniki Bilal; Guido Crepax; John Findley; Paul Kirchner; Charles Waller; Dzintars MeZullis; Koch; Robert E. Howard; William Burroughs

51 ❑ Jun 1981 Cover: 2.00 **NM** value: **4.00**
Circ: Statement: **172,116**
📖 The Birdwoman of **A:** Rod Kierkegaard; Richard Corben; Howard Chaykin; Matt Howarth; Jim Steranko; Arthur Suydam; Eniki Bilal; Guido Crepax; John Findley; John Workman; Mark Harrison; Paul Kirchner; Caza; Mark Fisher **W:** Rod Kierkegaard; Richard Corben; Howard Chaykin; Matt Howarth; Jim Steranko; Arthur Suydam; Eniki Bilal; Guido Crepax; John Findley; John Workman; Mark Harrison; Paul Kirchner; Caza; Mark Fisher; Robert E. Howard

52 ❑ Jul 1981 Cover: 2.00 **NM** value: **4.00**
Circ: Statement: **172,116**
📖 Bloodstar, Part 8; The Blue Air Compressor; The Bus, Part 18; Cody Starbuck, Part 3; Firaz; The Immortals' Fete, Part 3; Outland, Part 2; Paradise; Ri-vyu-ed; Rock Opera, Part 19; Shore Leave; Tex Arcana, Part 5; Whoodoo the Voodoo? **A:** Don Lomax; Moebius; Adams; Denis Sire; Jan Strnad; Paul Kirchner; Richard Corben(cover); Alias; Caza; Mark Fisher; Michael Hinge; Nicholas Yermakov; Stuart Nezin; Tex Arcana; Courtney(cover) **W:** Don Lomax; Moebius; Adams; Denis Sire; Jan Strnad; Paul Kirchner; Alias; Caza; Mark Fisher; Michael Hinge; Nicholas Yermakov; Stuart Nezin; Tex Arcana

53 ❑ Aug 1981 Cover: 2.00 **NM** value: **4.00**
Circ: Statement: **172,116**
📖 5:00:00 AM; The Bus, Part 19; Cody Starbuck, Part 4; Bert; Homo Detritus; The Immoral Majority; The Immortals' Fete, Part 4; Martelaine; Outland, Part 3; Paradise Lost; Pigs on the Wing; Rock Opera, Part 20; Shore Leave; Yawn **A:** Rod Kierkegaard; Howard Chaykin; Tom Yeates; Jim Steranko; Juan Gimenez; Moebius; Eniki Bilal; John Workman; Paul Kirchner; Steve Bissette; Bert; Caza; Feduniewicz; Mark Fisher; Mora; Norman Spinard; Esteban Maroto(cover) **W:** Rod Kierkegaard; Howard Chaykin; Tom Yeates; Jim Steranko; Juan Gimenez; Moebius; Eniki Bilal; John Workman; Paul Kirchner; Steve Bissette; Bert; Caza; Feduniewicz; Mark Fisher; Mora; Norman Spinard

54 ❑ Sep 1981 Cover: 2.00 **NM** value: **4.00**
Circ: Statement: **172,116**
📖 Born Again; The Bus, Part 20; Cody Starbuck, P **A:** Dick Matena; Rod Kierkegaard; Richard Corben; Howard Chaykin; Jeff Jones; Jim Steranko; Juan Gimenez; Eniki Bilal; John Findley; Paul Kirchner; Brocal Remohi; Charles Platt; Neal McPheeters; Timothy Lucas; Chris Achilleos(cover) **W:** Dick Matena; Rod Kierkegaard; Richard Corben; Howard Chaykin; Jim Steranko; Juan Gimenez; Eniki Bilal; John Findley; Paul Kirchner; Brocal Remohi; Charles Platt; Neal McPheeters; Timothy Lucas

55 ❑ Oct 1981 Cover: 2.00 **NM** value: **4.00**
Circ: Statement: **172,116**
📖 B.J. Butterfly; The B **A:** Rod Kierkegaard; Richard Corben; Howard Chaykin; Jeff Jones; Jim Steranko; Walt Simonson; Gary Davis; Eniki Bilal; John Workman; Jose Bea Font; Paul Kirchner; Segrelles; Brad Balfour; Caza; Jean-Michel Nicollet; Thomas Warkentin(cover) **W:** Rod Kierkegaard; Richard Corben; Howard Chaykin; Jim Steranko; Walt Simonson; Gary Davis; Eniki Bilal; John Workman; Jose Bea Font; Paul Kirchner; Segrelles; Brad Balfour; Caza; Jean-Michel Nicollet

56 ❑ Sep 1993 Cover: 3.95 **NM** value: **4.00**
📖 The Crow; Little Ego; Little Bit Here; The Upturned Stone; The Mirror: Arabia 1902, Panic Under the Clothesline • The Crow feature

57 ❑ Nov 1981 Cover: 2.00 **NM** value: **4.00**
Circ: Statement: **234,106**
📖 At The Middle of Cymbiola, Part **A:** Paul Abrams; Howard Chaykin; Jeff Jones; Arthur Suydam; Eniki Bilal; John Findley; Michael Gross; Paul Kirchner; Renard; Schuiten; Altarriba; Caza; Jeronaton; Mick Farren; Rafael Estrada; Royo; Segrelles(cover) **W:** Paul Abrams; Howard Chaykin; Arthur Suydam; Eniki Bilal; John Findley; Michael Gross; Paul Kirchner; Renard; Schuiten; Altarriba; Caza; Jeronaton; Mick Farren; Rafael Estrada; Royo

58 ❑ Dec 1981 Cover: 2.00 **NM** value: **4.00**
Circ: Statement: **234,106**
📖 At The Middle of Cymbiola, Part 2; The Bus, Part 23; De **A:** Rod Kierkegaard; Richard Corben; Dan Barry; Howard Chaykin; Jeff Jones; Walt Simonson; Moebius; Eniki Bilal; John Findley; Paul Kirchner; Phil Trumbo; Renard; Schuiten; Segrelles; Caza; Chris Stein(cover) **W:** Rod Kierkegaard; Richard Corben; Dan Barry; Howard Chaykin; Walt Simonson; Moebius; Eniki Bilal; John Findley; Paul Kirchner; Phil Trumbo; Renard; Schuiten; Segrelles; Caza

59 ❑ Jan 1982 Cover: 2.00 **NM** value: **4.00**
Circ: Statement: **234,106**
📖 At The Middle of Cymbiola, Part 3; The Bus, Part 24; Den II, Part 4; Happy Future: The Autonomous…; I'm Ag **A:** Renar; Schuiten **W:** Steve Stiles; Richard Corben; Howard Chaykin; Jim Steranko; Walt Simonson; Gary Davis; Lou Stathis; Paul Kirchner; Philippe Druillet; Renard; Schuiten; Segrelles; Arno; Brad Balfour; Chudnow; Dominique He; Gillon; Loustal; Lovelace; Voss

60 ❑ Feb 1982 Cover: 2.00 **NM** value: **4.00**
Circ: Statement: **234,106**
📖 An Unmarried Machine; The Appointment; At The Middle of Cymbiola, Part 4; The Bus, Part 25; Den II, Part 5; Editorial: **A:** Marc Hempel

61 ❑ Mar 1982 Cover: 2.00 **NM** value: **4.00**
Circ: Statement: **234,106**
📖 Ahh, Earth…; Artificial Boundaries; At The Middle of Cymbiola, Part 5; The Bus, Par **A:** A; Hassell; John Workman **W:** John Workman

62 ❑ Apr 1982 Cover: 2.00 **NM** value: **4.00**
Circ: Statement: **234,106**
📖 At The Middle of Cymbiola, Part 6; Den II, Part 7; Gallery Section: She; I'm Age, Part 8; The Incal Light, Part 3; J.G. Ballard: Vi **A:** Jim Burns(cover); Renard; Richard Corbe; Schuiten **W:** Renard; Schuiten; R

63 ❑ May 1982 Cover: 2.00 **NM** value: **4.00**
Circ: Statement: **234,106**
📖 The Black Night; The Bus, Part 27; Den II, Part 8; Exiled; I'm Age, **A:** Eberoni; Lon Cohen(cover); Paul Kirchner; Ri; Townley(cover) **W:** Eberoni; Paul

64 ❑ Jun 1982 Cover: 2.00 **NM** value: **4.00**
Circ: Statement: **234,106**
📖 Back and Forth; At The Middle of Cymbiola, Part 7; Blade Runner: This is the City; The Bus, Part 28; The Concorde; Den II, Part 9; Futuropolis Section; The Gladiators; H. Fertig Inadvertent **A:** Rod Kierkegaard; Richard Corben; Robert Crumb; Jeff Jones; Moebius; Christin; Eniki Bilal; Jodorowsky; Lou Stathis; Paul Kirchner; Philippe Druillet; Anthony Scibelli; Ben Katchor; Caza; Ceesepe; Fernando Fernandez; Filippo Giansanti; Luis Garcia; Mead **W:** Rod Kierkegaard; Richard Corben; Robert Crumb; Moebius; Christin; Eniki Bilal; Jodorowsky; Lou Stathis; Paul Kirchner; Philippe Druillet; Anthony Scibelli; Ben Katchor; Caza; Ceesepe; Fernando Fernandez; Filippo Giansanti; Luis Garcia; Mead

65 ❑ Jul 1982 Cover: 2.00 **NM** value: **4.00**
Circ: Statement: **234,106**
📖 Ancient Innocence; At The Middle of Cymbiola, **A:** Rod Kierkegaard; Richard Corben; Jeff Jones; Moebius; Peter Kuper; Christin; Eniki Bilal; Hugo Pratt; Jodorowsky; Paul Kirchner; Philippe Druillet; David Black; Fernando Fernandez; Lacome; Luis Garcia; Marcelle; Thomas Warkentin(cover) **W:** Rod Kierkegaard; Richard Corben; Moebius; Peter Kuper; Christin; Eniki Bilal; Hugo Pratt; Jodorowsky; Paul Kirchner; Philippe Druillet; David Black; Fernando Fernandez; Lacome; Luis Garcia; Marcelle

66 ❑ Aug 1982 Cover: 2.00 **NM** value: **4.00**
Circ: Statement: **234,106**
📖 Amusing Stories; The Ape, Part 1; The Bulge; The Bus, Part 30; Classics from the Intergalactic; Day in the Log of the Cit **A:** Milo Manara; Pisu; Bill Plympton; Michael Gross; Paul Kirchner; Carlo Moggia **W:** Pisu; Carlo Moggia; Milo Man

67 ❑ Sep 1982 Cover: 2.00 **NM** value: **4.00**
Circ: Statement: **234,106**
📖 Ad **A:** Berni Wrightson; Milo Manara; Pisu; Rod Kierkegaard; Richard Corben; Jeff Jones; Walt Simonson; Christin; Eberoni; Eniki Bilal; Paul Kirchner; Philippe Druillet; Alan Hecht; Clyde Caldwell; Fernando Fernandez; Michael Hinge; Michael Gross(cover) **W:** Berni Wrightson; Milo Manara; Pisu; Rod Kierkegaard; Richard Corben; Walt Simonson; Christin; Eberoni; Eniki Bilal; Paul Kirchner; Philippe Druillet; Alan Hecht; Clyde Caldwell; Fernando Fernandez; Michael Hinge

68 ❑ Oct 1982 Cover: 2.00 **NM** value: **4.00**
Circ: Statement: **234,106**
📖 The Ape, Part 3; Birth; The Blind Flock; The Bus, Part 32; Color Line; Den II, Part 13; Exit; Freak Show; **A:** M **W:** Berni Wrightson; Milo Manara; Rod Kierkegaard; Richard Corben; Peter Kuper; Eniki Bilal; Paul Kirchner; Philippe Druillet; Trillo; Alberto Breccia; David Black; Fernando Fernandez; J.K. Potter; Jeff Goldberg; John Stevens; Paul McCusker; Stonier

69 ❑ Nov 1982 Cover: 2.00 **NM** value: **4.00**
Circ: Statement: **205,856**
📖 The Bus, Part 33; Den II, Part 14; Freak Shoe; I'm Age, Part 15; June 2050, Part 1; A Lot of Nothing; Rock Opera, Part 34; Starstruck, Part 1; Tex Arcana, Part 9; The Voyage of Those Forgotten, Part 7; Yragael, Part 8; Zora, Part 10 **A:** Berni Wrightson; Joe Orlando **W:** Berni Wrightson; Milo Manara; Pisu; Rod Kierkegaard; Richard Corben; Gray Morrow; Michael W. Kaluta; Kent Williams; Christin; Eniki Bilal; Harris; John Findley; John Workman; Paul Kirchner; Philippe Druillet; Fernando Fernandez; Lee

70 ❑ Dec 1982 Cover: 2.00 **NM** value: **4.00**
Circ: Statement: **205,856**

CGC-graded: Multiply prices above by **33 for 9.9 M • 16 for 9.8 NM/M • 7 for 9.6 NM+ • 5 for 9.4 NM • 2.5 for 9.2 NM- • 1.5 for 9.0 VF/NM**

Aemorraghe; Amino Men; The Ape, Part 5; The Bus, Part 34; Den II, Pa **A:** Berni Wrightson; Milo Manara; Rod Kierkegaard; Richard Corben; Jeff Jones; Michael W. Kaluta; Moebius; Arthur Suydam; Adal Maldonado; Nicole Claveloux; Paul Kirchner; Philippe Druillet; Jacques Rochberny; Lee; Mark Fischer; Nicola Cuti; Fernando Fernande **W:** Berni Wrightson; Milo Manara; Rod Kierkegaard; Richard Corben; Michael W. Kaluta; Moebius; Arthur Suydam; Adal Maldonado; Harris; Nicole Claveloux; Paul Kirchner; Philippe Druillet; Fernando Fernandez; Jacques Rochberny; Mark Fischer; Nicola Cuti

71 ❑ Jan 1983 Cover: 2.00 **NM** value: **4.00**
Circ: Statement: **205,856**
The Ape, Part 6; Burnout; The Bus, Part 35; Den II, Part 16; Freak Show; The Hunter; I'm Age, Part 17; June 2050, Part 3; The Man From Harlem, Part 1; Me and Space; Mudwog; Robot Love; Starstruck, Part 3; Yragael, Part 10; Zora, Part 12 **A:** Pisu **W:** Berni Wrightson; Milo Manara; Charles Burns; Pisu; Richard Corben; Michael W. Kaluta; Arthur Suydam; Howard Cruse; Guido Crepax; John Workman; Martin Springett; Paul Kirchner; Philippe Druillet; Fernando Fernandez; Keaton Sheffield; Lee

72 ❑ Feb 1983 Cover: 2.00 **NM** value: **4.00**
Circ: Statement: **205,856**
The Ape, Part 7; The Ark; **A:** Pisu; Milo Mana **W:** Milo Manara; Angus McKie; Pisu; Rod Kierkegaard; Richard Corben; Dick Giordano; Michael W. Kaluta; Guido Crepax; Harris; John Workman; Kim Deitch; Paul Kirchner; Arno; Caza; Fernando Fernandez; Julie Simmons-Lynch; Lee; Macek

73 ❑ Mar 1983 Cover: 2.00 **NM** value: **4.00**
Circ: Statement: **205,856**
*#^*&!; Adrenaline; The Ape, Part 8; The Bus, Part 37; Den II, Part 18; Escapee; Hellfire; I'm Age, Part 19; June 2050, Part 5; Lamar Killer of Fools; The Man From Harlem, Part 3; Rock Opera, Part 37; She; Starstruck, Part 5; The City That Didn't Exist **A:** George Metzger **W:** Milo Manara; Pisu; George Metzger; Rod Kierkegaard; Richard Corben; Michael W. Kaluta; Kent Williams; Christin; Eniki Bilal; Guido Crepax; Kenneth Smith; Paul Kirchner; Seth Tobocman; Anglefred; Lee; Nicola Cuti; Poirier; Setbon; Simmons; Voss

74 ❑ Apr 1983 Cover: 2.00 **NM** value: **4.00**
Circ: Statement: **205,856**
The Ape, Part 9; B.J. Butterfly, Part 2; The Bus, Part 38; The City That Didn't Exist, Part 1; Crisalida; The Dead Pi **A:** Joseph Grau; Milo Manara; Pisu; Rod Kierkegaard; Jeff Jones; Michael W. Kaluta; Moebius; Christin; Eniki Bilal; Guido Crepax; John Workman; Paul Kirchner; Antonio Navarro; Lee; Nicola Cuti; Chris Achilleos(cover); David Higgins; Mick Angel; Williams **W:** Pisu; Mil

75 ❑ May 1983 Cover: 2.00 **NM** value: **4.00**
Circ: Statement: **205,856**
The Ap **A:** Pisu **W:** Milo Manara; Dick Matena; Pisu; Gary Frank; Michael W. Kaluta; Christin; Eniki Bilal; Guido Crepax; Hugo Pratt; John Workman; Paul Kirchner; Pepe Moreno; Anne Kobaysashi; Bertotti; Buroni; Fernando Fernandez; Lee; Navarro; Sauri

76 ❑ Jun 1983 Cover: 2.00 **NM** value: **4.00**
Circ: Statement: **205,856**
The Bus, Part 40; Catharsis; The City That Didn't Exist, Part 3; Crunch!; Doomscult; Everyday Strangeness **A:** Barclay Shaw; Christin; Eniki Bilal; Hugo Pratt; Paul Kirchner **W:** Hugo Pratt; Paul Kirchner; Ch

77 ❑ Jul 1983 Cover: 2.00 **NM** value: **4.00**
Circ: Statement: **205,856**
The Bus, Part 41; The City That Didn't Exist, Part 4; Enoch; HM's Star Dissections, Part 1; I'm Age, Part 23; June 2050, Part 10; The Odyssey, Part 4; The Peace; RanXerox, Part 1; Rock Opera, Part 40; Shoe; Snow Whitish; Starstruck, Part 9; Zora, Part 16 **A:** Drew Friedman; Rod Kierkegaard; Jeff Jones; Michael W. Kaluta; Christin; Eniki Bilal; Nicole Claveloux; Paul Kirchner; Antonio Navarro; Bill Dubay; Caza; Don Wood; Fernando Fernandez; Gaetano Liberatore; Lee; Royo; Sauri; Tamburini **W:** Drew Friedman; Rod Kierkegaard; Michael W. Kaluta; Christin; Eniki Bilal; Nicole Claveloux; Paul Kirchner; Antonio Navarro; Bill Dubay; Caza; Don Wood; Fernando Fernandez; Gaetano Liberatore; Lee; Royo; Sauri; Tamburini

78 ❑ Aug 1983 Cover: 2.00 **NM** value: **4.00**
Circ: Statement: **205,856**
The Bus, Part 42; The City That Didn't Exist, Part 5; El Borbah **A:** Charles Burns; Drew Friedman; Rod Kierkegaard; Jeff Jones; Juan Gimenez; Peter Kuper; Christin; Eniki Bilal; Greg Hildebrandt(cover); Jodorowsky; Paul Kirchner; Antonio Navarro; Arno; Bertotti; Brian McCall; Buroni; Fernando Fernandez; Nicola Cuti; Sauri **W:** Charles Burns; Drew Friedman; Rod Kierkegaard; Juan Gimenez; Peter Kuper; Christin; Eniki Bilal; Jodorowsky; Paul Kirchner; Antonio Navarro; Arno; Bertotti; Brian McCall; Buroni; Fernando Fernandez; Nicola Cuti; Sauri

79 ❑ Sep 1983 Cover: 2.00 **NM** value: **4.00**
Circ: Statement: **205,856**
The Bus, Part 43; The City That Didn't Exist; The Hunt for Louth; I'm Age, Part 25; June 2050, Part 12; The Odyssey, Part 6; Professor Neutron; RanXerox, Part 2; Rock Opera, Part 42; Tex Arcana, Part 11; The Way of the Worlds; Zora, Part 18 **A:** Todd Klein; Rod Kierkegaard; Jeff Jones; Christin; Eniki Bilal; Jodorowsky; John Findley; Paul Kirchner; Anderson; Antonio Navarro; Arno; Chris Lincoln; Fernando Fernandez; Gaetano Liberatore; Nicola Cuti; Sauri; Tamburini; Enric Rebollo(cover) **W:** Todd Klein; Rod Kierkegaard; Christin; Eniki Bilal; Jodorowsky; John Findley; Paul Kirchner; Anderson; Antonio Navarro; Arno; Chris Lincoln; Fernando Fernandez; Gaetano Liberatore; Nicola Cuti; Sauri; Tamburini

80 ❑ Oct 1983 Cover: 2.00 **NM** value: **4.00**
Circ: Statement: **205,856**
The Bus, Part 44; The Elevator; HM's Star Dissections, Part 3; I'm Age, Part 26; June 2050, Part 13; Lolla, Part 1; Nimble Fingers; RanXerox, Part 3; Rock Opera, Part 43; Tex Arcana, Part 12; Third Song: God's Tower **A:** Drew Friedman; Rod Kierkegaard; Jerry Bingham; Jeff Jones; Eberoni; Jodorowsky; John Findley; Paul Kirchner; Pepe Moreno; Rodolphe; Royo(cover); Arno; Gaetano Liberatore; Lacome; Marcelle; Tamburini **W:** Drew Friedman; Rod Kierkegaard; Jerry Bingham; Eberoni; Jodorowsky; John Findley; Paul Kirchner; Pepe Moreno; Rodolphe; Arno; Gaetano Liberatore; Lacome; Marcelle; Tamburini

81 ❑ Nov 1983 Cover: 2.00 **NM** value: **4.00**
Circ: Statement: **171,970**
As in a Dream; Th **A:** Pau; Miltos Scouras **W:** Drew Friedman; Rod Kierkegaard; Will Eisner; Guido Crepax; Jodorowsky; John Findley; Miltos Scouras; Paul Kirchner; Antonio Navarro; Arno; Barson; Davy Berg; Gaetano Liberatore; Hampton; Lacome; Marcelle; Ringgenberg; Sauri; Tamburini; White

82 ❑ Dec 1983 Cover: 2.00 **NM** value: **4.00**
Circ: Statement: **171,970**
The Bus, Part 46; A Chance in a Million; Cycle of the Werewolf; Fi **A:** Jooste Swarte; Paul Kirchner; Chris Achilleos(co **W:** Paul Kirchne

83 ❑ Jan 1984 Cover: 2.00 **NM** value: **4.00**
Circ: Statement: **171,970**
1992; Alien in New York; Bird Dust; The Bus, Part 47; Er **A:** Prei; Segrelles **W:** Drew Friedman; Dick Matena; Rod Kierkegaard; Tom Yeates; Clarke; Guido Crepax; John Findley; Len Wein; Paul Kirchner; Segrelles; Alex Ni±o; Caza; David Black; Enos; Gaetano Liberatore; Murad Gumen; Preiss; Tamburini; Tom Barber; Woods

84 ❑ Feb 1984 **NM** value: **4.00**
Circ: Statement: **171,970**
An Unmarried Pillsbury Doughperson; The Bus, Part 48; Headcut 3000; HM's Star Dissections, Part 7; I'm Age, Part 30; June 2050, Part 17; My Vampires: A Memoir; **A:** Rod Kierkegaard **W:** Drew Friedman; Rod Kierkegaard; Richard Corben; Moebius; Chris Browne; Guido Crepax; Hugo Pratt; Jodorowsky; John Findley; Jose Bea Font; Paul Kirchner; Philippe Druillet; Angelwine; Caza; David Black; Enos; Gaetano Liberatore; Tamburini

85 ❑ Mar 1984 **NM** value: **4.00**
Circ: Statement: **171,970**
The Bus, Part 49; El Borbah, Part 2; Forbidden Passions; HM' **A:** Charles Burns; Angus McKie; Drew Friedman; Rod Kierkegaard; Jeff Jones; Moebius; Guido Crepax; Jodorowsky; John Findley; Paul Kirchner; Philippe Druillet; Gaetano Liberatore; Milton Knight; Mitch O'Connell; Nicola Cuti; Tamburini; Andy Lackow(cover) **W:** Charles Burns; Angus McKie; Drew Friedman; Rod Kierkegaard; Moebius; Guido Crepax; Jodorowsky; John Findley; Paul Kirchner; Philippe Druillet; Gaetano Liberatore; Milton Knight; Mitch O'Connell; Nicola Cuti; Tamburini

86 ❑ Apr 1984 **NM** value: **4.00**
Circ: Statement: **171,970**
The Bus, Part 50; CommuniquT; **A:** Charles Burns; Angus McKie; Drew Friedman; Rod Kierkegaard; Rick Geary; Jeff Jones; Howard Cruse; Boris Vallejo(cover); Guido Crepax; John Findley; Paul Kirchner; Pepe Moreno; Philippe Druillet; Gaetano Liberatore; Tamburini **W:** Charles Burns; Angus McKie; Drew Friedman; Rod Kierkegaard; Rick Geary; Howard Cruse; Guido Crepax; John Findley; Paul Kirchner; Pepe Moreno; Philippe Druillet; Gaetano Liberatore; Tamburini

87 ❑ May 1984 **NM** value: **4.00**
Circ: Statement: **171,970**
Alien, Part 3; Bunker 6A; The Bus, Part 51; El Borbah, Part 4; He Came Fro **A:** Rod Kierkegaard; Paul Ki; Pepe Moreno **W:** Rod Kierkeg

88 ❑ Jun 1984 **NM** value: **4.00**
Circ: Statement: **171,970**
The Bus, Part 52; Butterfly; El Borba **A:** Charles Burns; Drew Friedman; Rod Kierkegaard; Frank Thorne; Jeff Jones; Juan Gimenez; Moebius; Howard Cruse; Christin; Eniki Bilal; Herikberto; Jodorowsky; John Findley; Paul Kirchner; Philippe Druillet; Renard; Schuiten; Esteban Maroto(cover) **W:** Charles Burns; Drew Friedman; Rod Kierkegaard; Frank Thorne; Juan Gimenez; Moebius; Howard Cruse; Christin; Eniki Bilal; Herikberto; Jodorowsky; John Findley; Paul Kirchner; Philippe Druillet; Renard; Schuiten

89 ❑ Jul 1984 **NM** value: **4.00**
Circ: Statement: **171,970**
The Bus, Part 53; Captain Virgil; Cozmik Punk: A Program o **A:** Pau **W:** Drew Friedman; Frank Thorne; Alfonso Azpiri; Christin; Eniki Bilal; John Findley; Paul Kirchner; Philippe Druillet; Renard; Schuiten; Arnie Clapman; Jeronaton; Steve Sabella; Terry Brooks; Varyl Trivieri

90 ❑ Aug 1984 **NM** value: **4.00**
Circ: Statement: **171,970**
The Bus, Part 54; The Great Passage, Part 2; HM's Star Dissectio **A:** Paul Kirc **W:** Drew Friedman; Bill Wray; Jon J. Muth; Rod Kierkegaard; Frank Thorne; Peter Kuper; Christin; Eniki Bilal; Herikberto; John Findley; Paul Kirchner; Philippe Druillet; Renard; Schuiten; Seth Tobocman; Bjorn Ousland; Caza; Jeronaton; Nicola Cuti

91 ❑ Sep 1984 **NM** value: **4.00**
Circ: Statement: **171,970**
The Bus, Part 55 **A:** Drew Friedman; Rod Kierkegaard; Frank Thorne; Peter Kuper; Chris Browne; Christin; Eniki Bilal; J.D. King; John Findley; Paul Kirchner; Philippe Druillet; Renard; Royo(cover); Schuiten; Jeronaton; Nicola Cuti; Peterson McPheeter **W:** Drew Friedman; Rod Kierkegaard; Frank Thorne; Peter Kuper; Chris Browne; Christin; Eniki Bilal; J.D. King; John Findley; Paul Kirchner; Philippe Druillet; Renard; Schuiten; Jeronaton; Nicola Cuti; Peterson McPheeter

92 ❑ Oct 1984 **NM** value: **4.00**
Circ: Statement: **171,970**
Atomax; The Bus, Part 56; Cinders; The Great Pa **A:** Paul; Yves Chaland **W:** Drew Friedman; Juan Gimenez; Mark Wheatley; Juan Alcantara; Christin; Denis Sire; Eniki Bilal; John Findley; Paul Kirchner; Pepe Moreno; Yves Chaland; Beja; Caza; Fromental; Gauckler; Imbert; Jeronaton; Nicola Cuti; Patrick Saint Amour; Terrance Lindall

93 ❑ Nov 1984 **NM** value: **4.00**
Circ: Statement: **147,870**
The Bus, Part 57; Critical Mass of Cool; The Great Passage, Part 5; HM's Star Dissections, Part 16; The Hunting Party, Part 6; I'm in Love With and Economist; Lann, Part 5; A Second Babel; Tex Arcana, Part 25; Triton, Part 1; The Walls of Samaris, Part 1 **A:** Drew Friedman; Frank Thorne; Christin; Daniel Torres; Eniki Bilal; John Findley; Jooste Swarte; Nicole Claveloux; Olivia De Berardinis; Paul Kirchner; Schuiten; Jeronaton; Salamon **W:** Drew Friedman; Frank Thorne; Christin; Daniel Torres; Eniki Bilal; John Findley; Jooste Swarte; Nicole Claveloux; Paul Kirchner; Schuiten; Jeronaton; Salamon

94 ❑ Dec 1984 **NM** value: **4.00**
Circ: Statement: **147,870**
An Author in Search of Six Cha..., Part 1; The Bus, Part 58; Enslaved by the Needle; HM's Star Dissections, Part 17; The Hunting Party, Part 7; Rock Opera, Part 53; Tex Arcana, Part 26; Triton, Part 2; The Walls of Samaris, Part 2 **A:** Milo Manara; Drew Friedman; Rod Kierkegaard; Christin; Daniel Torres; Eniki Bilal; John Findley; Jooste Swarte; Paul Kirchner; Richard Corben(cover); Schuiten **W:** Milo Manara; Drew Friedman; Rod Kierkegaard; Christin; Daniel Torres; Eniki Bilal; John Findley; Jooste Swarte; Paul Kirchner; Schuiten

95 ❑ Jan 1985 **NM** value: **4.00**
Circ: Statement: **147,870**
An Author in Search of Six Cha..., Part 2; The Bus, Part **A:** Milo Manara; Charles Burns; Drew Friedman; Rod Kierkegaard; Christin; Daniel Torres; Eniki Bilal; John Findley; Kenneth Smith; Paul Kirchner; Schuiten; Beppe Madaudo; Bertotti; Buroni; Gaetano Liberatore; Lindahn **W:** Milo Manara; Charles Burns; Drew Friedman; Rod Kierkegaard; Christin; Daniel Torres; Eniki Bilal; John Findley; Kenneth Smith; Paul Kirchner; Schuiten; Beppe Madaudo; Bertotti; Buroni; Gaetano Liberatore; Lindahn

96 ❑ Feb 1985 **NM** value: **4.00**
Circ: Statement: **147,870**
Albinos; An Author in Search of Six Cha..., Part 3; The Bus, Part 60; El Borbah, Part 7; HM's Hollywood Hell, Part 2; The Hunting Party, Part 9; It's Not a Bad Life; Matter of Time: Chronology; Tex Arcana, Part 28; The Walls of Samaris, Part 4 **A:** Milo Manara; Charles Burns; Drew Friedman; Juan Gimenez; Christin; Eniki Bilal; J.D. King; John Findley; Paul Kirchner; Peeters; Schuiten; Beb Deum; Michael Kanarek(cover) **W:** Milo Manara; Charles Burns; Drew Friedman; Juan Gimenez; Christin; Eniki Bilal; J.D. King; John Findley; Paul Kirchner; Peeters; Schuiten; Beb Deum

97 ❑ Mar 1985 **NM** value: **4.00**
Circ: Statement: **147,870**
An Author in Search of Six Cha..., Part 4; Bourbon Threat; The Bus, Part 61; El Borbah, Part 8; HM's Hollywood Hell, Part 3; The Hunting Party, Part 10; Rebel, Part 1; Rock Opera, Part 55; The Stranger; Tex Arcana, Part 29; The Walls of Samaris, Part 5 **A:** Milo Manara; Charles Burns; Drew Friedman; Rod Kierkegaard; Christin; Eniki Bilal; Herikberto; John Findley; Paul Kirchner; Peeters; Royo(cover); Schuiten; Sylvester Hingley; Wong Stenstrum **W:** Milo Manara; Charles Burns; Drew Friedman; Rod Kierkegaard; Christin; Eniki Bilal; Herikberto; John Findley; Paul Kirchner; Peeters; Schuiten; Sylvester Hingley; Wong Stenstrum

98 ❑ Apr 1985 Cover: 2.50 **NM** value: **4.00**
Circ: Statement: **147,870**
An Author in Search of Six Cha..., Part 5; Bodyssey, Part 1; The Bus, Part 62; El Borbah, Part 9; The Fighter; Fragments; Goodbye; HM's Hollywood Hell, Part 4; Le Chat; Rebel, Part 2; Superflite **A:** Milo Manara; Charles Burns; Drew Friedman; Richard Corben; Boris Vallejo(cover); Jooste Swarte; Manoeuvre; Paul Kirchner; Beja; Gal; Heriberte; Philippe Dionnet; Revelstroke; Sylvester Hingley; Voss **W:** Milo Manara; Charles Burns; Drew Friedman; Richard Corben; Jooste Swarte; Manoeuvre; Paul Kirchner; Beja; Gal; Heriberte; Philippe Dionnet; Revelstroke; Sylvester Hingley; Voss

99 ❑ May 1985 **NM** value: **4.00**
Circ: Statement: **147,870**
An Author in Search of Six Cha..., Part 6; Autocracy; Bodyssey, Part 2; El Borbah, Part 10; HM's Hollywood Hell, Part 5; Rebel, Part 3; Rock Opera, Part 56; Skydancer; Tex Arcana, Part 30; The Whisper Mystery, Part 1 **A:** Milo Manara; Charles Burns; Drew Friedman; Rod Kierkegaard; Richard Corben; Daniel Torres; John Findley; Massimo Ghini; Pepe Moreno; Randy Jones; Revelstroke; Gaetano Liberatore(cover) **W:** Milo Manara; Charles Burns; Drew Friedman; Rod Kierkegaard; Richard Corben; Daniel Torres; John Findley; Massimo Ghini; Pepe Moreno; Randy Jones; Revelstroke

100 ❑ Jun 1985 **NM** value: **4.00**
Circ: Statement: **147,870**
An Author in Search of Six Cha..., Part 6; Bodyssey, Part 3; The Bus, Part 63; The Destroyer; El Borbah, Part 11; HM's Hollywood Hell, Part 6; Rebel, Part 4; Robots; Sillavango: Holiday; Skydancer; Tex Arcana, Part 31; The Whisper Mystery, Part 2 **A:** Milo Manara; Charles Burns; Drew Friedman; Richard Corben; Daniel Torres; Denis Sire; Herikberto; John Findley; Massimo Ghini; Olivia De Berardinis(Cover); Paul Kirchner; Pepe Moreno; Randy Jones; Revelstroke; James Cherry(cover) **W:** Milo Manara; Charles Burns; Drew Friedman; Richard Corben; Daniel Torres; Denis Sire; Herikberto; John Findley; Massimo Ghini; Paul Kirchner; Pepe Moreno; Randy Jones; Revelstroke

101 ❑ Jul 1985 **NM** value: **4.00**
Circ: Statement: **147,870**
Another Image; Bodyssey, Part 4; Elephant Cemetery, Part 1; HM's Hollywood Hell, Part 7; Metamorphosis; Metropolis; Rebel, Part 5; Rock Opera, Part 57; Sillavango, Part 1; Tex Arcana, Part 32; Trance-End; Trivial Metal, Part 1; The Whisper Mystery, Part 3 **A:** Drew Friedman; Rod Kierkegaard; Richard Corben; Daniel Torres; John Findley; Massimo Ghini; Pepe Moreno; Sesar; Yves Chaland; Dominicana; Lindahn; Revelstroke; Voss; Adam Kubert(cover) **W:** Drew Friedman; Rod Kierkegaard; Richard Corben; Daniel Torres; John Findley; Massimo Ghini; Pepe Moreno; Sesar; Yves Chaland; Dominicana; Lindahn; Revelstroke; Voss

102 ❑ Aug 1985 **NM** value: **4.00**
Circ: Statement: **147,870**
Body **A:** Drew Friedman; Richard Corben; Juan Gimenez; Daniel Torres; John Findley; Massimo Ghini; Nicole Claveloux; Paul Kirchner; Pepe Moreno; Toni Taylor(cover); Yves Chaland; Mitch O'Connell; Revelstroke **W:** Drew Friedman; Richard Corben; Juan Gimenez; Daniel Torres; John Findley; Massimo Ghini; Nicole Claveloux; Paul Kirchner; Pepe Moreno; Yves Chaland; Mitch O'Connell; Revelstroke

103 ❑ Sep 1985 **NM** value: **4.00**
Circ: Statement: **147,870**
Bodyssey, Part 6; E **A:** Drew Friedman; Rod Kierkegaard; Richard Corben; Juan Gimenez; Daniel Torres; Eniki Bilal; Greg Hildebrandt(cover); John Findley; Jose Ma Bea; Massimo Ghini; Yves Chaland; Nicola Cuti; Rebel; Revelstroke **W:** Drew Friedman; Rod Kierkegaard; Richard Corben; Juan Gimenez; Daniel Torres; Eniki Bilal; John Findley; Jose Ma Bea; Massimo Ghini; Yves Chaland; Nicola Cuti; Rebel; Revelstroke

104 ❑ Oct 1985 **NM** value: **4.00**
Circ: Statement: **147,870**
Elephant Cemetery, Part 4; HM's Hollywood Hell, Part 10; The Jealous God, Part 2; Mara's Edge; Rebel, Part 7; Slot Machine: Risks; Timescooter; Weird Soup **A:** Drew Friedman; Juan Gimenez; Horatio Altuna; Jodorowsky; Olivia De Berardinis; Pepe Moreno; Yves Chaland; Trillo; Cadelo; Milton Knight; Nicola Cuti; Riggenberg **W:** Drew Friedman; Juan Gimenez; Horatio Altuna; Jodorowsky; Olivia De Berardinis; Pepe Moreno; Yves Chaland; Trillo; Cadelo; Milton Knight; Nicola Cuti; Riggenberg

105 ❑ Nov 1985 **NM** value: **4.00**
Circ: Statement: **122,475**

Other grades: Multiply prices above by **1.5 for Mint • 2/3 for Very Fine • 1/3 for Fine • 1/5 for Very Good • 1/8 for Good**

🕮 The Bus, Part 65; Elephant Cemetery, Part 5; HM's Hollywood Hell, Part 11; The Jealous God, Part 3; Jessie, This is Sahamis Base...; Poe! Phooey!; Rock Opera, Part 59; Slot Machine; Tex Arcana, Part 35 **A:** Drew Friedman; Rod Kierkegaard; Boris Vallejo(cover); Carlos Gimenez; Horatio Altuna; Jodorowsky; John Findley; Paul Kirchner; Yves Chaland; Trillo; Alberto Breccia; Cadelo **W:** Drew Friedman; Rod Kierkegaard; Carlos Gimenez; Horatio Altuna; Jodorowsky; John Findley; Paul Kirchner; Yves Chaland; Trillo; Alberto Breccia; Cadelo

106 ❑ Dec 1985 **NM** value: **4.00**
Circ: Statement: **122,475**
🕮 The Bus, Part 66; The Duel; Foxxhole; HM's Hollywood Hell, Part 12; The Jealous God, Part 1; Jessie, This is Sahamis Base...; Modern Image; Papa Superstar; Rock Opera, Part 60; Tex Arcana, Part 36; The Trial of Marlon Malone **A:** Drew Friedman; Rod Kierkegaard; Matt Howarth; Carlos Gimenez; Jodorowsky; John Findley; Jooste Swarte; Paul Kirchner; Ribera; Cadelo; Caza; Voss; Ajin(cover) **W:** Drew Friedman; Rod Kierkegaard; Matt Howarth; Carlos Gimenez; Jodorowsky; John Findley; Jooste Swarte; Paul Kirchner; Ribera; Cadelo; Caza; Voss

107 ❑ Jan 1986 **NM** value: **4.00**
Circ: Statement: **122,475**
🕮 An Essay on the Essential Elem; Daughters of the Night; The Great Kong; The Mystery at Bray; Opium **A:** Daniel Torres; Hugo Pratt; Jean Teule; Massimo Ghini **W:** Daniel Torres; Hugo Pratt; Jean Teule; Massimo Ghini

108 ❑ Mar 1986 **NM** value: **4.00**
Circ: Statement: **122,475**
🕮 Celestial Venice; Cinderella; The Crazy Monk; Doctor! Doctor!; The Dream; The Experiment; Kamikazee Electrik; The Knockout **A:** Esteban Maroto; Moebius; Francisco Solano Lopez; Beb Duem; Buffink; Justo Jimeno; Nicole Claveloux; Rocarels(cover); Rodolphe; Vink **W:** Esteban Maroto; Moebius; Francisco Solano Lopez; Beb Duem; Buffink; Justo Jimeno; Nicole Claveloux; Rodolphe; Vink

109 ❑ Jun 1986 **NM** value: **4.00**
Circ: Statement: **122,475**
🕮 Berlin at Dawn; Lisa Bay; Morbus Gravis; Summer in the City; Sunrise **A:** Angel de la Calle; Das Pastoras; Denis Sire; Miguel Angel Prado; Paolo Eleuteri Serpieri(cover) **W:** Angel de la Calle; Das Pastoras; Denis Sire; Miguel Angel Prado

110 ❑ Sep 1986 **NM** value: **4.00**
Circ: Statement: **122,475**
🕮 Funkensien's Mon-Star; Le Petit Peintre; Please Don't Feed the Animals; Primabell; The Trapped Woman; Weekend Drive **A:** Rod Kierkegaard; Juan Gimenez; Berberian; Dupay; Eniki Bilal; J.D. King; Ortiz; Rocarels(cover) **W:** Rod Kierkegaard; Juan Gimenez; Berberian; Dupay; Eniki Bilal; J.D. King; Ortiz

111 ❑ Dec 1986 **NM** value: **4.00**
Circ: Statement: **112,457**
🕮 Level One **A:** Miguel Angel Prado; Paolo Eleuteri Serpieri(cover) **W:** Miguel Angel Prado

112 ❑ Mar 1987 **NM** value: **4.00**
Circ: Statement: **112,457**
🕮 Captain Tozudo; Garbage; Pilatorium; Sabotage; Twenty-Four Hours **A:** Juan Gimenez; Peter Kuper; Daniel Torres; Das Pastoras; Fernando Rubio; Jim Warren; Trillo **W:** Juan Gimenez; Peter Kuper; Daniel Torres; Das Pastoras; Fernando Rubio; Jim Warren; Trillo

113 ❑ Jun 1987 **NM** value: **4.00**
Circ: Statement: **112,457**
🕮 Country; Distant Star; Fmeh: The Monster From Outer Space; The Gold Digger; I'm Age, Part 37; Sillavengo, Part 4; So Beautiful So Dangerous, Part 9; Tex Arcana, Part 36 **A:** Angus McKie; Drew Friedman; Jeff Jones; Moebius; Daniel Torres; John Findley; Massimo Ghini; Rowena Morrill(cover); Stephen Hall **W:** Angus McKie; Drew Friedman; Moebius; Daniel Torres; John Findley; Massimo Ghini; Stephen Hall

114 ❑ Sep 1987 **NM** value: **4.00**
Circ: Statement: **112,457**
🕮 Adventures of Dieter Lumpen; The Creator; Crossed Destinies; Edison is Back; Freddy Lombard; Great Chief of the Seattle...; Man; Mercenary: The Sacrifice; No Respect; Tropicana **A:** Rick Geary; Moebius; Peter Kuper; Antonia Segura; Daniel Torres; Herikberto; Jorge Zentner; Miguel Angel Prado; Olivia De Berardinis; Ortiz; Segrelles; Yves Chaland; Gallardo; Pellejero **W:** Rick Geary; Moebius; Peter Kuper; Antonia Segura; Daniel Torres; Herikberto; Jorge Zentner; Miguel Angel Prado; Ortiz; Segrelles; Yves Chaland; Gallardo; Pellejero

115 ❑ Dec 1987 Cover: 3.95 **NM** value: **4.00**
Circ: Statement: **114,923**
🕮 Adventures of Dieter Lumpen; Cyberpunks Reinvent Science...; Incongruent Stories #2; The Red Shirt; Saxxon; Sensations **A:** Daniel Riche; Daniel Torres; Greg Hildebrandt; Jorge Zentner; Miguel Angel Prado; Ruben; Shepard; Theureau **W:** Daniel Riche; Daniel Torres; Greg Hildebrandt; Jorge Zentner; Miguel Angel Prado; Ruben; Shepard; Theureau

116 ❑ Mar 1988 Cover: 3.95 **NM** value: **4.00**
Circ: Statement: **114,923**
🕮 All Too Human; The Bullfighter; Hector; Manuel Montana; Morbus Gravis: Druuna; Nightmares of the Rich and Famous; One Dollar; to See Naples **A:** Moebius; Peter Kuper; Alan Craddock(cover); Daniel Torres; Fernando Rubio; Herikberto; Miguel Angel Prado; Paolo Eleuteri Serpieri **W:** Moebius; Peter Kuper; Daniel Torres; Fernando Rubio; Herikberto; Miguel Angel Prado; Paolo Eleuteri Serpieri

117 ❑ Jun 1988 Cover: 3.95 **NM** value: **4.00**
Circ: Statement: **114,923**
🕮 Adolphus Claa **A:** Milo Manara; Will Eisner; Juan Gimenez; Antonia Segura; Jorge Zentner; Miguel Angel Prado; Mike Dorey; Ortiz; Paolo Eleuteri Serpieri; Ruben; Yves Chaland; Alberto Breccia; Cava; Palacios; Sicomoro; Chichioni(cover) **W:** Milo Manara; Will Eisner; Juan Gimenez; Antonia Segura; Jorge Zentner; Miguel Angel Prado; Mike Dorey; Ortiz; Paolo Eleuteri Serpieri; Ruben; Yves Chaland; Alberto Breccia; Cava; Palacios; Sicomoro

118 ❑ Sep 1988 Cover: 3.95 **NM** value: **4.00**
Circ: Statement: **114,923**
🕮 Airhead; Frank Cappa: What the Hell Am I Doing?; H; Manuel Montana; Movie Posters; Red Tape; Stan Hoe; Stan the Alligator; The Stolen God; Valentina Rediscovered **A:** Drew Friedman; Peter Kuper; Fernando Rubio; Francois Thomas; Guido Crepax; Jose Ma Beroy; Lou Stathis; Miguel Angel Prado; Olivia De Berardinis(Cover); Stephen Hall; Trillo; Manfred Sommer **W:** Drew Friedman; Peter Kuper; Fernando Rubio; Francois Thomas; Guido Crepax; Jose Ma Beroy; Lou Stathis; Miguel Angel Prado; Stephen Hall; Trillo; Manfred Sommer

119 ❑ Dec 1988 Cover: 3.95 **NM** value: **4.00**
Circ: Statement: **111,479**
🕮 Adolphus Claar and the Polo...; Deadly Medley; Details; Earth vs. Saturn; Forgotten Films; Hey, Mister Can You Spare a Buck?; Lord of Eltingville; Nocturne; The Scarlet Mummy; Utopias **A:** Drew Friedman; Daniel Torres; Fernando Rubio; Miguel Angel Prado; Olivia De Berardinis(Cover); Peeters; Schuiten; Stephen Hall; Yves Chaland; Gaetano Liberatore; Sicomoro **W:** Drew Friedman; Daniel Torres; Fernando Rubio; Miguel Angel Prado; Peeters; Schuiten; Stephen Hall; Yves Chaland; Gaetano Liberatore; Sicomoro

120 ❑ Feb 1988 Cover: 3.95 **NM** value: **4.00**
Circ: Statement: **111,479**
🕮 Blindman's Bluff; Dieter Lumpen; Fragments; Hombre; The Shanghai Express Affair • Winter **A:** Antonia Segura; Bastille; Cabane; Jorge Zentner; Miguel Angel Prado; Ortiz; Royo(cover); Ruben; Sesar **W:** Antonia Segura; Bastille; Cabane; Jorge Zentner; Miguel Angel Prado; Ortiz; Ruben; Sesar

121 ❑ Mar 1988 Cover: 3.95 **NM** value: **4.00**
Circ: Statement: **111,479**
🕮 Alien, Part 4; The Artist; Burton & Cyb: The Next God Willing; Fragments: Arena; Leo Roa; Mask; Signals; The Specialists **A:** Juan Gimenez; James Fletcher; Jose Ma Beroy; Miguel Angel Prado; Pichard; Royo(cover) **W:** Juan Gimenez; James Fletcher; Jose Ma Beroy; Miguel Angel Prado; Pichard

122 ❑ May 1989 Cover: 3.95 **NM** value: **4.00**
Circ: Statement: **111,479**
🕮 Adventures of Glenn Dykstra; Burned; The Hollow Planet; July Butterfly; Manuel Montana; Mystery; Protoplasmid Zen-Master Sphinx; Wet Papier-MGchT **A:** Peter Kuper; Daniel Torres; Galliano; Herikberto; Kenneth Smith; Miguel Angel Prado; Olivia De Berardinis; Theureau; Antonio Navarro; Schuiten Brothers **W:** Peter Kuper; Daniel Torres; Galliano; Herikberto; Kenneth Smith; Miguel Angel Prado; Theureau; Antonio Navarro; Schuiten Brothers

123 ❑ Jul 1989 Cover: 3.95 **NM** value: **4.00**
Circ: Statement: **111,479**
🕮 Alien, Part 5; Alien, Too; The Blue Rock; Caribe: Dieter Lumpen; Editorial; The Jellyfish From Outer Space; The Rabbit's Paw; Tiger G-I **A:** Moebius; Antonia Segura; Galliano; Jorge Zentner; Jose Ma Beroy; Ortiz; Rowena(cover); Ruben; Rubio; Theureau; Zeljko Pahek **W:** Moebius; Antonia Segura; Galliano; Jorge Zentner; Jose Ma Beroy; Ortiz; Ruben; Rubio; Theureau; Zeljko Pahek

124 ❑ Sep 1989 Cover: 3.95 **NM** value: **4.00**
Circ: Statement: **111,479**
🕮 Double Uh-Oh; Firebrand; Manuel Montana and the Case of...; Microcosmos; Opium; Pillow Talk; Revenge; Ruins; Stratos; Voodoo Queen and Demon Boy **A:** Angus McKie; Bob Fingerman; Mark Pacella; Daniel Torres; Herikberto; Jose Ma Beroy; Kenneth Smith; Miguel Angel Prado; Hermann; Wayne Buford(cover) **W:** Angus McKie; Bob Fingerman; Mark Pacella; Daniel Torres; Herikberto; Jose Ma Beroy; Kenneth Smith; Miguel Angel Prado; Hermann

125 ❑ Nov 1989 Cover: 3.95 **NM** value: **4.00**
Circ: Statement: **115,883**
🕮 Dieter Lumpen: Istanbul; Metangible; No Imagination; Stan Croc Goes Back in Time; The Wall **A:** Francois Thomas; Horatio Altuna; Jorge Zentner; Kordej; Mikalacki; Royo(cover); Ruben; Valaquez **W:** Francois Thomas; Horatio Altuna; Jorge Zentner; Kordej; Mikalacki; Ruben; Valaquez

126 ❑ Jan 1990 Cover: 3.95 **NM** value: **4.00**
Circ: Statement: **115,883**
🕮 1881; The Fourth Quarter; Linen's Lipstick; The New Frontier; Return to the Sea **A:** Rick Geary; Juan Gimenez; Michael Cherkas; Galliano; Miguel Angel Prado; Ovi Hondru(cover); Sabljic; Theureau **W:** Rick Geary; Juan Gimenez; Michael Cherkas; Galliano; Miguel Angel Prado; Sabljic; Theureau

127 ❑ Mar 1990 Cover: 3.95 **NM** value: **4.00**
Circ: Statement: **115,883**
🕮 Girl Trouble; Gorillas; In the Heart of the Impregnable; Iron Wheel; Taxi; Vega-One **A:** Bob Fingerman; Moebius; Peter Kuper; Fernando Rubio; Jodorowsky; Jose Bea Font; Olivia De Berardinis; Zeljko Pahek **W:** Bob Fingerman; Moebius; Peter Kuper; Fernando Rubio; Jodorowsky; Zeljko Pahek; Alfonso Font

128 ❑ May 1990 Cover: 3.95 **NM** value: **4.00**
Circ: Statement: **115,883**
🕮 Burton and Cyb; Ciao, Jessica!; Comic Artist; Just One of Those Days; Prisoners of Our Lady of...; Rounds; The Waters of the Dead Moon; The Wish **A:** Angus McKie; Ovi Hondru; Adamov; Antonia Segura; Boris Vallejo(cover); Cothias; Galliano; Kenneth Smith; Miguel Angel Prado; Ortiz; Theureau; Milton Knight **W:** Angus McKie; Ovi Hondru; Adamov; Antonia Segura; Cothias; Galliano; Kenneth Smith; Miguel Angel Prado; Ortiz; Theureau; Milton Knight

129 ❑ Jul 1990 Cover: 3.95 **NM** value: **4.00**
Circ: Statement: **115,883**
🕮 Attila, Part 1; Brief Encounter; The Fallen Angel; General Store; Heroes; Home Sweet Home; Lorna; The Night; Towers of Bois-Maurys; The Wall **A:** Rick Geary; Peter Kuper; Alfonso Azpiri; Antonia Segura; Daniel Torres; Galliano; Miguel Angel Prado; Ortiz; Theureau; Hermann; Marillo; Montana; Joseph Zavilinski(cover) **W:** Rick Geary; Peter Kuper; Alfonso Azpiri; Daniel Torres; Galliano; Miguel Angel Prado; Ortiz; Theureau; Hermann; Marillo; Montana; Segura

130 ❑ Sep 1990 Cover: 3.95 **NM** value: **4.00**
Circ: Statement: **115,883**
🕮 New Frontier: The Queen of...; Opium in Barcelona; Shmegeggi of the Cave Men; Waters of Dead Moon **A:** Harvey Kurtzman; Michael Cherkas; Adamov; Cothias; Daniel Torres; Hernandez; Royo(cover); Sabljic; Stout; Marcos **W:** Harvey Kurtzman; Michael Cherkas; Adamov; Cothias; Daniel Torres; Hernandez; Sabljic; Stout; Marcos

131 ❑ Nov 1990 Cover: 3.95 **NM** value: **4.00**
Circ: Statement: **114,856**
🕮 Behind the Cursed Curtain; Bonnie and Clyde; Dieter Lumpen; Modern World, Part 1; Semel Insabivims Omnes AKA The...; The Time Zuck Company **A:** Angus McKie; Rick Geary; James Fletcher; Peter Kuper; Frank Frazetta(cover); Jorge Zentner; Rebecca Fletcher; Ruben; Zeljko Pahek **W:** Angus McKie; Rick Geary; James Fletcher; Peter Kuper; Jorge Zentner; Rebecca Fletcher; Ruben; Zeljko Pahek

132 ❑ Jan 1991 Cover: 3.95 **NM** value: **4.00**
Circ: Statement: **114,856**
🕮 Hello, Sylvania; Madness of Everyday Life, Modern World; The New Frontier; Onion; Slaine; Tizon **A:** Simon Bisley; Michael Cherkas; Peter Kuper; Alec Stevens; Galliano; Herikberto; Miguel Angel Prado; Sabljic; Theureau; Wayne Duford(cover) **W:** Michael Cherkas; Peter Kuper; Alec Stevens; Galliano; Herikberto; Miguel Angel Prado; Sabljic; Theureau; Pat Mills

133 ❑ Mar 1991 Cover: 3.95 **NM** value: **4.00**
Circ: Statement: **114,856**
🕮 Attila, Part 2; The Cat at the Window; For a Couple of Lousy Apples; Inkangaroous; L; Modern World, Part 2 **A:** Rick Geary; Peter Kuper; Antonia Segura; Dan Steffan; Eric Drooker; Lou Stathis; Nigel Prado; Ortiz; Sirvent(cover) **W:** Rick Geary; Peter Kuper; Dan Steffan; Eric Drooker; Lou Stathis; Nigel Prado; Ortiz; Segura

134 ❑ May 1991 Cover: 3.95 **NM** value: **4.00**
Circ: Statement: **114,856**
🕮 City in Flames; Modern World, Part 3; Shrinking Assets; Tragedy of 319 East 8th Street; Waters if Dead Moon, Part III **A:** Bruce Jones; Peter Kuper; Adamov; Cothias; Daniel Torres; Royo(cover); Seth Tobocman **W:** Bruce Jones; Peter Kuper; Adamov; Cothias; Daniel Torres; Seth Tobocman

135 ❑ Jul 1991 Cover: 3.95 **NM** value: **4.00**
Circ: Statement: **114,856**
🕮 Burton and Cyb: Brother Can You; Double V in All Dead Men Wear; Dreams of Reason; Modern World, Part 4; The New Frontieru; Nogegon; The Warrior's Repose **A:** Michael Cherkas; Peter Kuper; Antonia Segura; Boucq; Daniel Torres; Olivia De Berardinis(Cover); Ortiz; Sabljic; Brothers Schuiten **W:** Michael Cherkas; Peter Kuper; Boucq; Daniel Torres; Ortiz; Sabljic; Brothers Schuiten; Segura

136 ❑ Sep 1991 Cover: 3.95 **NM** value: **4.00**
Circ: Statement: **114,856**
🕮 Bombs Away; CA-RT-OON; The Dear Friend; Desert Bones; The Eskimo Song; The Little Tree; Modern World, Part 5; Tragedy in Orbit; Waters of Dead Moon: Eyes of... **A:** Rick Geary; Juan Gimenez; Peter Kuper; Adamov; Cothias; Daniel Torres; Eric Drooker; Mick Aarestrup; Miguel Angel Prado; Toni Taylor(cover) **W:** Rick Geary; Juan Gimenez; Peter Kuper; Adamov; Cothias; Daniel Torres; Eric Drooker; Mick Aarestrup; Miguel Angel Prado

137 ❑ Nov 1991 Cover: 3.95 **NM** value: **4.00**
Circ: Statement: **114,887**
🕮 Adventures of Tristan Karma; Buddy the Chicken; Burton and Cub: The Mine; Full Moon in the Carpathian; The Great Martian Scare of 1936; New Frontier: Rubi Fields Story **A:** Rick Geary; Michael Cherkas; Antonia Segura; Boucq; Jose Ma Beroy; Ortiz; Royo(cover); Sabljic; Zeljko Pahek **W:** Rick Geary; Michael Cherkas; Antonia Segura; Boucq; Jose Ma Beroy; Ortiz; Sabljic; Zeljko Pahek

138 ❑ Jan 1992 Cover: 3.95 **NM** value: **4.00**
Circ: Statement: **114,887**
🕮 Dreams of Reason; Eat at Ed's; Gun But Not Forgotten; 20 Nude Dancers 20!; Modern World, Part 6; Payne's Inferno; Planetoid; Raoul Fleetfoot and the Mystery... **A:** Mark Martin; Richard Corben; Bob Fingerman; Peter Kuper; Alvarez; Gelli; Greg Gallo; Price; Tronchet; Turner **W:** Mark Martin; Richard Corben; Bob Fingerman; Peter Kuper; Alvarez; Gelli; Greg Gallo; Price; Tronchet; Turner

139 ❑ Mar 1992 Cover: 3.95 **NM** value: **4.00**
Circ: Statement: **114,887**
🕮 Cypher; Foligatto; The Jungle; Modern World; Morocco **A:** Peter Kuper; de Crecy; Milan Trene; Royo(cover); Troyas; Brad Teare **W:** Peter Kuper; de Crecy; Milan Trene; Troyas; Brad Teare

140 ❑ May 1992 Cover: 3.95 **NM** value: **4.00**
Circ: Statement: **114,887**
🕮 The Eighth Day; Five Seasons: Autumn; Marius Dark: Purity; Modern World, Part 7; Mr. Nickelodeon; Persona **A:** Pascual Ferry; Rick Geary; Peter Kuper; Igor Kordey; Daniel Torres; Django; Guido Crepax; Pelaez(cover) **W:** Pascual Ferry; Rick Geary; Peter Kuper; Daniel Torres; Django; Guido Crepax; Kordey

141 ❑ Jul 1992 Cover: 3.95 **NM** value: **4.00**
Circ: Statement: **114,887**
🕮 Alien Metaphor, Part 1, Cypher; Dawson's Law; Flood; Modern World, Part 8; Mr. Monster; Siren of the Stars; Skintight Orbit **A:** Brian Bolland; Simon Bisley; Michael T. Gilbert; Phil Winslade; Henry Flint; Peter Kuper; Eric Drooker; Fernando Rubio; Guiral; Pelaez(cover); Scott Cunningham; Brad Teare; Lee **W:** Brian Bolland; Michael T. Gilbert; Phil Winslade; Peter Kuper; Eric Drooker; Fernando Rubio; Guiral; Scott Cunningham; Brad Teare; Henry; Lee

142 ❑ Sep 1992 Cover: 3.95 **NM** value: **4.00**
Circ: Statement: **114,887**
🕮 Alien Metaphor, Part 2; The Ceremony; Good-Bye, Sun; Mercenary: The Evidence; Modern World, Part 9; The Mounds; Randy the Skeleton; Tina Bloom: Hurricane; Waters of the Dead Moon **A:** Milo Manara; Carl Potts; Richard Corben; Tom Carney; Peter Kuper; Adamov; Cothias; Julie Bell(cover); Kaz; Scott Cunningham; Segrelles; Silvia **W:** Milo Manara; Carl Potts; Richard Corben; Tom Carney; Peter Kuper; Adamov; Cothias; Kaz; Scott Cunningham; Segrelles; Silvia

143 ❑ Nov 1992 Cover: 3.95 **NM** value: **4.00**
Circ: Statement: **130,263**
🕮 Alien Metaphor, Part 3; All-Girl Amazon Attack Battalion; Animation; The Atomic Garden; Bog's Deal; Druuna: Creature; Flood; Frank in the Wilderness; Flood; Inspector #23; Lives of Artists: Pablo Picasso; Modern Age; Mr. Pumpie's World; Randy the Skeleton **A:** Carl Potts; Mark Martin; Richard Corben; Jim Woodring; Rick Geary; Tom Carney; Gary Leach; Peter Kuper; Daniel Torres; Eric Drooker; Kaz; Paolo Eleuteri Serpieri; Scott Cunningham; Simon Bisley(cover); P. Revess **W:** Carl Potts; Mark Martin; Richard Corben; Jim Woodring; Rick Geary; Tom Carney; Gary Leach; Peter Kuper; Daniel Torres; Eric Drooker; Kaz; Paolo Eleuteri Serpieri; Scott Cunningham; P. Revess

144 ❑ Jan 1993 Cover: 3.95 **NM** value: **4.00**
Circ: Statement: **130,263**

CGC-graded: Multiply prices above by **33 for 9.9 M • 16 for 9.8 NM/M • 7 for 9.6 NM+ • 5 for 9.4 NM • 2.5 for 9.2 NM- • 1.5 for 9.0 VF/NM**

The Game; Palomita; The Hermit and the Fool; Striptease; TKO; Vit; White Trash; Incongruent Stories **A:** Mark Martin; Martin Emond; Matthias Schultheiss; Paul Mavrides; Peter Kuper; Denis Sire; Kaz; Miguel Angel Prado; Milan Trene; Paolo Eleuteri Serpieri; Fabrice Lamy; Gordon Rennie; Michael Kupperman **W:** Mark Martin; Martin Emond; Matthias Schultheiss; Paul Mavrides; Peter Kuper; Denis Sire; Kaz; Miguel Angel Prado; Milan Trene; Paolo Eleuteri Serpieri; Fabrice Lamy; Gordon Rennie; Michael Kupperman

145 ❑ Mar 1993 Cover: 3.95 **NM** value: **4.00**
Circ: Statement: **130,263**
Melting Pot; Hombre: A Useless Old Man; Ramparts of Spray; Pachyderm; A Cloudy Day; Striptease; The Next Best Thing **A:** Kevin Eastman; Simon Bisley; Michael W. Kaluta; Antonia Segura; Elaine Lee; Eric Talbot; Ortiz; Barron Storey; Bocq; Harry North; Joel Mouclier; Turf **W:** Kevin Eastman; Simon Bisley; Michael W. Kaluta; Antonia Segura; Elaine Lee; Eric Talbot; Ortiz; Barron Storey; Bocq; Harry North; Joel Mouclier; Turf

146 ❑ May 1993 Cover: 3.95 **NM** value: **4.00**
Circ: Statement: **130,263**
A New Form of Transport; Little Ego; Eva Medusa; Hibernation; Idle Gods; Time and Reflection; Mea Culpa; The Dream; Strip Tease **A:** Alfonso Azpiri; Ana Miralles; Antonia Segura; Boucq; De Blas; Massimo Frezzato; Miguel Angel Prado; Stefania Venturino; Vittorio Giardino **W:** Alfonso Azpiri; Ana Miralles; Antonia Segura; Boucq; De Blas; Massimo Frezzato; Miguel Angel Prado; Stefania Venturino; Vittorio Giardino

147 ❑ Jul 1993 Cover: 3.95 **NM** value: **4.00**
Circ: Statement: **130,263**

148 ❑ Sep 1993 Cover: 3.95 **NM** value: **4.00**
Circ: Statement: **130,263**
Little Ego; Little Bit Here; The Upturned Stone; The Mirror: Arabia 1902; Striptease; Panic Under the Clothesline **A:** Scott Hampton; Alfonso Azpiri; Clavé; De Blas; Hugo Pratt; Louis Rétif; Vittorio Giardino **W:** Scott Hampton; Alfonso Azpiri; Clavé; De Blas; Hugo Pratt; Louis Rétif; Vittorio Giardino

149 ❑ Nov 1993 Cover: 3.95 **NM** value: **4.00**
Circ: Statement: **142,958**
Network; Eden; Little Ego; Reflections; A Gift from Upstairs; Striptease; A Pleasant Walk; For Private Eyes **A:** Matthias Schultheiss; Asziri; De Blas; Horatio Altuna; Jose Bea Font; Martel; Vince; Vittorio Giardino **W:** Matthias Schultheiss; Asziri; De Blas; Horatio Altuna; Martel; Vince; Vittorio Giardino; Font

150 ❑ Jan 1994 Cover: 3.95 **NM** value: **4.00**
Circ: Statement: **142,958**

151 ❑ Mar 1994 Cover: 3.95 **NM** value: **4.00**
Circ: Statement: **142,958**

152 ❑ May 1994 Cover: 3.95 **NM** value: **4.00**
Circ: Statement: **142,958**

153 ❑ Jul 1994 Cover: 3.95 **NM** value: **4.00**
Circ: Statement: **142,958**

154 ❑ Sep 1994 Cover: 3.95 **NM** value: **4.00**
Circ: Statement: **142,958**

155 ❑ Nov 1994 Cover: 3.95 **NM** value: **4.00**
Circ: Statement: **141,827**

156 ❑ Jan 1995 Cover: 3.95 **NM** value: **4.00**
Circ: Statement: **141,827**

157 ❑ Mar 1995 Cover: 3.95 **NM** value: **4.00**
Circ: Statement: **141,827**
Zone C: In a Place of the Mind; Master Volume: Showtime; Hombre: Rabid; Kicking the Monolithic Habit; Striptease; The Diaries of Sandra F. **A:** Milo Manara; Henry Flint; Antonia Segura; Jose Ma Bea; Ortiz; Siro; John Tomlinson **W:** Milo Manara; Henry Flint; Antonia Segura; Jose Ma Bea; Ortiz; Siro; John Tomlinson

158 ❑ May 1995 Cover: 3.95 **NM** value: **4.00**
Circ: Statement: **141,827**

159 ❑ Jul 1995 Cover: 4.50 **NM** value: **Cover or less**
Circ: Statement: **141,827**

160 ❑ Sep 1995 Cover: 4.50 **NM** value: **Cover or less**
Circ: Statement: **141,827**

161 ❑ Nov 1995 Cover: 4.50 **NM** value: **Cover or less**
Circ: Statement: **127,917**
The Great Undart; Black Dekker: The River of Fire; Ringside; The Way of the Warrior; Heroes of the Stars; Machonismechs; Marie Claire; Bit Degeneration; Bull Digger **A:** Milo Manara; Richard Corben; Alfonso Azpiri; Boucq; Bruno Brindisi; Fernando de Felipe; Peiro; Stan; Vince **W:** Milo Manara; Richard Corben; Alfonso Azpiri; Boucq; Bruno Brindisi; Fernando de Felipe; Peiro; Stan; Vince

162 ❑ Jan 1996 Cover: 4.50 **NM** value: **Cover or less**
Circ: Statement: **127,917**
Burton & Cyb: The Conquest of the West; Dear Enemy; Macguffin; Geronimo Stew: Psychomotor Blockade; Museum; Caveman; Super Zero; Bronx II: The Actor **A:** Tayyar Ozkan; Alberto Saichann; Antonia Segura; Boucq; Fernando de Felipe; Guiral; Massimo Frezzato; Ortiz; Rubin; Stan Vince **W:** Tayyar Ozkan; Alberto Saichann; Boucq; Fernando de Felipe; Guiral; Massimo Frezzato; Ortiz; Rubin; Stan Vince; Segura

163 ❑ Mar 1996 Cover: 4.50 **NM** value: **Cover or less**
Circ: Statement: **127,917**

164 ❑ May 1996 Cover: 4.50 **NM** value: **Cover or less**
Circ: Statement: **127,917**

165 ❑ Jul 1996 Cover: 4.50 **NM** value: **Cover or less**
Circ: Statement: **127,917**

166 ❑ Sep 1996 Cover: 4.50 **NM** value: **Cover or less**
Circ: Statement: **127,917**

167 ❑ Nov 1996 Cover: 4.50 **NM** value: **Cover or less**
168 ❑ Jan 1997 Cover: 4.50 **NM** value: **Cover or less**
169 ❑ Mar 1997 Cover: 4.50 **NM** value: **Cover or less**
170 ❑ May 1997 Cover: 4.50 **NM** value: **Cover or less**
171 ❑ Jul 1997 Cover: 4.50 **NM** value: **Cover or less**
172 ❑ Sep 1997 Cover: 4.50 **NM** value: **Cover or less**
173 ❑ Nov 1997 Cover: 4.50 **NM** value: **Cover or less**
174 ❑ Jan 1998 Cover: 4.95 **NM** value: **Cover or less**
175 ❑ Mar 1998 Cover: 4.95 **NM** value: **Cover or less**
176 ❑ May 1998 Cover: 4.95 **NM** value: **Cover or less**
177 ❑ Jul 1998 Cover: 4.95 **NM** value: **Cover or less**
178 ❑ Sep 1998 Cover: 4.95 **NM** value: **Cover or less**
179 ❑ Nov 1998 Cover: 4.95 **NM** value: **Cover or less**
180 ❑ Jan 1999 Cover: 4.95 **NM** value: **Cover or less**
181 ❑ Mar 1999 Cover: 4.95 **NM** value: **Cover or less**
182 ❑ May 1999 Cover: 4.95 **NM** value: **Cover or less**
183 ❑ Jul 1999 Cover: 4.95 **NM** value: **Cover or less**
184 ❑ Sep 1999 Cover: 4.95 **NM** value: **Cover or less**
185 ❑ Nov 1999 Cover: 4.95 **NM** value: **Cover or less**
186 ❑ Jan 2000 Cover: 4.95 **NM** value: **Cover or less**
187 ❑ Mar 2000 Cover: 4.95 **NM** value: **Cover or less**
188 ❑ May 2000 Cover: 4.95 **NM** value: **Cover or less**
189 ❑ Jul 2000 Cover: 4.95 **NM** value: **Cover or less**
190 ❑ Sep 2000 Cover: 4.95 **NM** value: **Cover or less**
191 ❑ Nov 2000 Cover: 4.95 **NM** value: **Cover or less**
192 ❑ Jan 2001 Cover: 4.95 **NM** value: **Cover or less**
193 ❑ Mar 2001 Cover: 4.95 **NM** value: **Cover or less**
194 ❑ May 2001 Cover: 4.95 **NM** value: **Cover or less**
Dossier; Galactic Geographic; A Bit of Theory...; Why Have Sex?; The Trend; Angel Dust; War; The Forgotten Planet; Fistfull of Blood; The Pugilist; Star-Crossed **A:** Kevin Eastman; Simon Bisley; Philip Xavier; Jeff Jones; Langdon Foss; Karl Kofoed; Paolo Eleuteri Serpieri; Coupil; Greg Follender; Meredith Bogard; S.C. Ringgenberg; Walter **W:** Kevin Eastman; Simon Bisley; Philip Xavier; Langdon Foss; Karl Kofoed; Paolo Eleuteri Serpieri; Coupil; Greg Follender; Meredith Bogard; S.C. Ringgenberg; Walter

HEAVY METAL GREATEST HITS — HM Communications

1 ❑ Jan 1992 Cover: 4.95 **NM** value: **6.00**
The Gray Man; Sandra, the She Devil; Christmas Carol; Once Upon a Time; Time Out III: The Pause that Refreshes; Master; Erotica pa

HEAVY METAL HAVOC — HM Communications

1 ❑ Cover: 4.95 **NM** value: **6.00**
Burton & Cyb: Tourist Business; News at Five; Hanibal 5: Flesh of the Orchid for the Cyborg; Two Angels; Dreams of Armed Ants; Peos; Blue Chip; Dome Battle **A:** John Bolton; Richard Corben; Alfonso Azpiri; Félix Vega; Horacio Altuna; Koller; Ortiz **W:** Félix Vega; Horacio Altuna; Chris Claremont; Segura

HEAVY METAL MONSTERS — Revolutionary

1 ❑ Jan 1992, b&w Cover: 2.50 **NM** value: **3.00**
2 ❑ • 3-D. Cover: 3.95 **NM** value: **Cover or less**

HEAVY METAL WAR MACHINE — HM Communications

1 ❑ Cover: 3.95 **NM** value: **6.00**
Kyrn; Zirk: Marooned; War Machine: Rogue Trooper; Max Carnage **A:** Dave Gibbons; Simon Bisley; Gary Leach **W:** John Higgins; William Simpson; Simon Bisley; Dave Elliott; Pedro Harvey

HECK! — Rip Off

1 ❑ b&w Cover: 7.95 **NM** value: **Cover or less**
• Trade Paperback.

HECKLE AND JECKLE (GOLD KEY) — Gold Key

1 ❑ Nov 1962 Cover: 0.12 **NM** value: **50.00**
2 ❑ Jan 1963 Cover: 0.12 **NM** value: **25.00**
3 ❑ Dec 1962 Cover: 0.12 **NM** value: **25.00**
4 ❑ Feb 1963 Cover: 0.12 **NM** value: **25.00**

HECKLE AND JECKLE (DELL) — Dell

1 ❑ May 1966 Cover: 0.12 **NM** value: **35.00**
2 ❑ Oct 1966 Cover: 0.12 **NM** value: **25.00**
• **CGC:** 1 graded, best 8.0
3 ❑ Aug 1967 Cover: 0.12 **NM** value: **25.00**

HECKLER, THE — DC

1 ❑ Sep 1992 Cover: 1.25 **NM** value: **Cover or less**
2 ❑ Oct 1992 Cover: 1.25 **NM** value: **Cover or less**
3 ❑ Nov 1992 Cover: 1.25 **NM** value: **Cover or less**
4 ❑ Dec 1992 Cover: 1.25 **NM** value: **Cover or less**
5 ❑ Jan 1993 Cover: 1.25 **NM** value: **Cover or less**
Circ: CapCity orders: **8,900**
6 ❑ Feb 1993 Cover: 1.25 **NM** value: **Cover or less**
Circ: CapCity orders: **8,250**

HECTIC PLANET — Slave Labor

6 ❑ Nov 1993 Cover: 2.50 **NM** value: **Cover or less**
• previously titled Pirate Corp$! **A:** Evan Dorkin **W:** Evan Dorkin
6-2 ❑ Jan 1996 Cover: 2.75 **NM** value: **Cover or less**
Bk 1 ❑ Aug 1998, b&w Cover: 12.95 **NM** value: **Cover or less**
• Dim Future **A:** Evan Dorkin **W:** Evan Dorkin
Bk 2 ❑ Aug 1998, b&w Cover: 12.95 **NM** value: **Cover or less**
• Checkered Past **A:** Evan Dorkin **W:** Evan Dorkin

HEDY DE VINE COMICS — Red Circle

Curvaceous, empty-headed society girl and would-be actress Hedy Devine provides the slapstick laughs and goofy adventures in this light romantic title from the late 1940s. Teasing her boyfriends, infuriating her jealous girlfriends, spending money, and getting mixed up in spicy mishaps are Hedy's main occupations. Each story also presents a convenient opportunity for Hedy to shed her evening wear for a flattering swimsuit, ballet tutu, or lingerie.

The formulaic lead stories in Hedy Devine are often upstaged by one-or two-page gag strips like Harvey Kurtzman's "Hey Look," or pre-psychedelic fill-ins by the truly demented Basil Wolverton. Hedy also shared the spotlight with stories featuring Nellie the Nurse and Millie the Model.

22 ❑ Aug 1947 Cover: 0.10 **NM** value: **65.00**
23 ❑ Oct 1947 Cover: 0.10 **NM** value: **50.00**
24 ❑ Dec 1947 Cover: 0.10 **NM** value: **50.00**
25 ❑ Feb 1948 Cover: 0.10 **NM** value: **50.00**
26 ❑ Apr 1948 Cover: 0.10 **NM** value: **50.00**
27 ❑ Jun 1948 Cover: 0.10 **NM** value: **50.00**
28 ❑ Aug 1948 Cover: 0.10 **NM** value: **50.00**
Hedy De Vine: Hedy's Hosts of Ghosts; Millie the Model: Basket Beauties; Hedy De Vine: Hedy Flies High; Nellie the Nurse: Nellie Gets Her Man; Hedy De Vine: The Hedy Who Wasn't • C.C. Beck art on Captain Tootsie ad **A:** Harvey Kurtzman; C.C. Beck **W:** Harvey Kurtzman
29 ❑ Oct 1948 Cover: 0.10 **NM** value: **50.00**
30 ❑ Dec 1948 Cover: 0.10 **NM** value: **50.00**
31 ❑ Feb 1949 Cover: 0.10 **NM** value: **36.00**
32 ❑ Apr 1949 Cover: 0.10 **NM** value: **36.00**
33 ❑ Jun 1949 Cover: 0.10 **NM** value: **36.00**
34 ❑ Aug 1949 Cover: 0.10 **NM** value: **36.00**
35 ❑ Oct 1949 Cover: 0.10 **NM** value: **36.00**
36 ❑ Cover: 0.10 **NM** value: **36.00**
37 ❑ Cover: 0.10 **NM** value: **36.00**
38 ❑ Cover: 0.10 **NM** value: **36.00**
39 ❑ Cover: 0.10 **NM** value: **36.00**
40 ❑ Cover: 0.10 **NM** value: **30.00**
41 ❑ Cover: 0.10 **NM** value: **30.00**
42 ❑ Cover: 0.10 **NM** value: **30.00**
43 ❑ Cover: 0.10 **NM** value: **30.00**
44 ❑ Cover: 0.10 **NM** value: **30.00**
45 ❑ Cover: 0.10 **NM** value: **30.00**
46 ❑ Cover: 0.10 **NM** value: **30.00**
47 ❑ Cover: 0.10 **NM** value: **30.00**
48 ❑ Cover: 0.10 **NM** value: **30.00**
49 ❑ Cover: 0.10 **NM** value: **30.00**
50 ❑ Cover: 0.10 **NM** value: **30.00**
final issue.

HEE HAW — Charlton

1 ❑ Aug 1970 Cover: 0.15 **NM** value: **12.00**
2 ❑ Oct 1970 Cover: 0.15 **NM** value: **8.00**
3 ❑ Dec 1970 Cover: 0.15 **NM** value: **6.00**
4 ❑ Feb 1971 Cover: 0.15 **NM** value: **6.00**
5 ❑ Apr 1971 Cover: 0.15 **NM** value: **6.00**
6 ❑ Jun 1971 Cover: 0.15 **NM** value: **6.00**
7 ❑ Aug 1971 Cover: 0.15 **NM** value: **6.00**

HE IS JUST A RAT — Exclaim! Brand Comics

1 ❑ Spr 1995 Cover: 2.75 **NM** value: **Cover or less**
2 ❑ Fal 1995 Cover: 2.75 **NM** value: **Cover or less**
3 ❑ Spr 1996 Cover: 2.75 **NM** value: **Cover or less**
4 ❑ Fal 1996 Cover: 2.75 **NM** value: **Cover or less**
5 ❑ Spr 1997 Cover: 2.75 **NM** value: **Cover or less**

HELLBENDER — Eternity

1 ❑ b&w Cover: 2.25 **NM** value: **Cover or less**
• Shuriken **A:** Wes Abbott **W:** S.A. Bennett

HELLBLAZER — DC

Hellblazer is the dark story of demon-foiler John Constantine, who first appeared in Saga of the Swamp Thing. Dying of inoperable cancer, he thwarted three demons by selling each of them his soul. Then, he calmly slashed his own wrists. Each demon learned he was about to die, and showed up to claim his prize. Each was shocked, of course, to learn that they had been duped. To keep from sparking a war in Hell, the demons were forced not only to heal Constantine, but to cure his cancer as well. Constantine returned the favor by ever defying them, thumbing his nose at both heaven and hell, and meddling in all manner of celestial affairs.

1 ❑ Jan 1988 Cover: 1.25 **NM** value: **6.00**
Circ: CapCity orders: **20,750** • **CGC:** 15 graded, best 9.6
Hunger **A:** John Ridgway **W:** Jamie Delano
2 ❑ Feb 1988 Cover: 1.25 **NM** value: **4.00**
Circ: CapCity orders: **17,100** • **CGC:** 1 graded, best 8.0
A Feast For Friends **A:** John Ridgway **W:** Jamie Delano
3 ❑ Mar 1988 Cover: 1.25 **NM** value: **4.00**
Circ: CapCity orders: **16,900**
Going For It **A:** John Ridgway **W:** Jamie Delano
4 ❑ Apr 1988 Cover: 1.25 **NM** value: **4.00**
Circ: CapCity orders: **16,400**
Waiting For The Man **A:** John Ridgway **W:** Jamie Delano
5 ❑ May 1988 Cover: 1.25 **NM** value: **4.00**
Circ: CapCity orders: **14,950**
When Johhny Comes Marching Home **A:** John Ridgway **W:** Jamie Delano
6 ❑ Jun 1988 Cover: 1.25 **NM** value: **3.50**
Circ: CapCity orders: **13,300**
7 ❑ Jul 1988 Cover: 1.25 **NM** value: **3.50**
Circ: CapCity orders: **12,950**
Ghosts in the Machine **A:** John Ridgway **W:** Jamie Delano
8 ❑ Aug 1988 Cover: 1.25 **NM** value: **3.50**
Circ: CapCity orders: **12,350**
9 ❑ Sep 1988 Cover: 1.25 **NM** value: **3.50**
Circ: CapCity orders: **12,400**
Shot to Hell **A:** John Ridgway; Alfredo Alcala **W:** Jamie Delano
10 ❑ Oct 1988 Cover: 1.25 **NM** value: **3.50**
Circ: CapCity orders: **12,200**
Sex and Death **A:** Richard Piers Rayner **W:** Jamie Delano
11 ❑ Nov 1988 Cover: 1.25 **NM** value: **3.00**
Circ: CapCity orders: **11,550**
Newcastle: A Taste of Things to Come **W:** Jamie Delano
12 ❑ Dec 1988 Cover: 1.25 **NM** value: **3.00**
Circ: CapCity orders: **11,800**
The Devil You Know **A:** Richard Piers Rayner; Mark Buckingham **W:** Jamie Delano

Other grades: Multiply prices above by **1.5 for Mint • 2/3 for Very Fine • 1/3 for Fine • 1/5 for Very Good • 1/8 for Good**

13 ❑ Dec 1988 Cover: 1.25 **NM** value: **3.00**
Circ: CapCity orders: **11,750**
On the Beach **A:** Richard Piers Rayner; Mark Buckingham **W:** Jamie Delano

14 ❑ Jan 1989 Cover: 1.25 **NM** value: **3.00**
Circ: CapCity orders: **11,800**
The Fear Machine, Part 1 **A:** Richard Piers Rayner; Mark Buckingham **W:** Jamie Delano

15 ❑ Jan 1989 Cover: 1.25 **NM** value: **3.00**
Circ: CapCity orders: **11,800**
The Fear Machine, Part 2 **A:** Richard Piers Rayner; Mark Buckingham **W:** Jamie Delano

16 ❑ Feb 1989 Cover: 1.25 **NM** value: **3.00**
Circ: CapCity orders: **11,850**
The Fear Machine, Part 3 **A:** Richard Piers Rayner; Mark Buckingham **W:** Jamie Delano

17 ❑ Apr 1989 Cover: 1.25 **NM** value: **3.00**
Circ: CapCity orders: **11,450**
The Fear Machine, Part 4 **A:** Mike Hoffman **W:** Jamie Delano

18 ❑ May 1989 Cover: 1.50 **NM** value: **3.00**
Circ: CapCity orders: **11,050**
The Fear Machine, Part 5 **A:** Mark Buckingham; Alfredo Alcala **W:** Jamie Delano

19 ❑ Jun 1989 Cover: 1.50 **NM** value: **3.00**
Circ: CapCity orders: **11,450**
The Fear Machine, Part 6 **A:** Mark Buckingham; Alfredo Alcala **W:** Jamie Delano

20 ❑ Jul 1989 Cover: 1.50 **NM** value: **3.00**
Circ: CapCity orders: **11,100**
The Fear Machine, Part 7 **A:** Mark Buckingham; Alfredo Alcala **W:** Jamie Delano

21 ❑ Aug 1989 Cover: 1.50 **NM** value: **2.50**
Circ: CapCity orders: **11,150**
The Fear Machine, Part 8 **A:** Mark Buckingham; Alfredo Alcala **W:** Jamie Delano

22 ❑ Sep 1989 Cover: 1.50 **NM** value: **2.50**
Circ: CapCity orders: **11,150**
The Fear Machine, Part 9 **A:** Mark Buckingham; Alfredo Alcala **W:** Jamie Delano

23 ❑ Oct 1989 Cover: 1.50 **NM** value: **2.50**
Circ: CapCity orders: **10,950**
Larger than Life **A:** Dean Motter; Ron Tiner **W:** Jamie Delano

24 ❑ Nov 1989 Cover: 1.50 **NM** value: **2.50**
Circ: CapCity orders: **11,200**
The Family Man **A:** Ron Tiner **W:** Jamie Delano

25 ❑ Jan 1990 Cover: 1.50 **NM** value: **2.50**
Circ: CapCity orders: **11,150**
Early Warning **A:** David Lloyd **W:** Grant Morrison

26 ❑ Feb 1990 Cover: 1.50 **NM** value: **2.50**
Circ: CapCity orders: **11,650**
How I Learned to Love The Bomb **A:** David Lloyd **W:** Grant Morrison

27 ❑ Mar 1990 Cover: 1.50 **NM** value: **10.00**
Circ: CapCity orders: **11,400** • **CGC:** 4 graded, best 9.6
Hold Me **A:** Dave McKean **W:** Neil Gaiman

28 ❑ Apr 1990 Cover: 1.50 **NM** value: **3.00**
Circ: CapCity orders: **10,750**
Thicker than Water **A:** Ron Tiner; Kevin Walker **W:** Jamie Delano ★ Death of Thomas Constantine.

29 ❑ May 1990 Cover: 1.50 **NM** value: **3.00**
Circ: CapCity orders: **10,850**

30 ❑ Jun 1990 Cover: 1.50 **NM** value: **3.00**
Circ: CapCity orders: **10,950**
Fatality **A:** Ron Tiner; Mark Buckingham **W:** Jamie Delano

31 ❑ Jul 1990 Cover: 1.50 **NM** value: **3.00**
Circ: CapCity orders: **10,950**
Mourning of the Magician **A:** Sean Phillips **W:** Jamie Delano

32 ❑ Aug 1990 Cover: 1.50 **NM** value: **3.00**
Circ: CapCity orders: **10,900**
New Tricks **A:** Steve Pugh **W:** Jamie Delano

33 ❑ Sep 1990 Cover: 1.50 **NM** value: **3.00**
Circ: CapCity orders: **10,900**
Sundays are Different **A:** Dean Motter; Mark Pennington **W:** Jamie Delano

34 ❑ Oct 1990 Cover: 1.50 **NM** value: **3.00**
Circ: CapCity orders: **10,750**
The Bogeyman **A:** Sean Phillips **W:** Jamie Delano

35 ❑ Nov 1990 Cover: 1.50 **NM** value: **3.00**
Circ: CapCity orders: **10,950**
Dead-Boy's Heart **A:** Sean Phillips **W:** Jamie Delano

36 ❑ Dec 1990 Cover: 1.50 **NM** value: **3.00**
Circ: CapCity orders: **11,000**

37 ❑ Jan 1991 Cover: 1.50 **NM** value: **3.00**
Circ: CapCity orders: **11,050**
Man's Work **A:** Steve Pugh **W:** Jamie Delano

38 ❑ Feb 1991 Cover: 1.50 **NM** value: **3.00**
Circ: CapCity orders: **10,850**
Boy's Games **A:** Steve Pugh **W:** Jamie Delano

39 ❑ Mar 1991 Cover: 1.50 **NM** value: **3.00**
Circ: CapCity orders: **10,300**

40 ❑ Apr 1991 Cover: 2.25 **NM** value: **3.50**
Circ: CapCity orders: **10,400**
Magus **A:** Dave McKean **W:** Jamie Delano

41 ❑ May 1991 Cover: 1.50 **NM** value: **6.00**
Circ: CapCity orders: **10,200** • **CGC:** 2 graded, best 9.6
Dangerous Habits, Part 1 • 1st Garth Ennis story **A:** William Simpson **W:** Garth Ennis

42 ❑ Jun 1991 Cover: 1.50 **NM** value: **4.00**
Circ: CapCity orders: **9,900**
Dangerous Habits, Part 2 **A:** William Simpson **W:** Garth Ennis

43 ❑ Jul 1991 Cover: 1.50 **NM** value: **4.00**
Circ: CapCity orders: **10,450**
Dangerous Habits, Part 3 **A:** William Simpson **W:** Garth Ennis

44 ❑ Aug 1991 Cover: 1.75 **NM** value: **4.00**
Circ: CapCity orders: **10,950**
Dangerous Habits, Part 4 **A:** William Simpson **W:** Garth Ennis

45 ❑ Sep 1991 Cover: 1.75 **NM** value: **4.00**
Circ: CapCity orders: **11,150**
Dangerous Habits, Part 5 **A:** William Simpson **W:** Garth Ennis

46 ❑ Oct 1991 Cover: 1.75 **NM** value: **4.00**
Circ: CapCity orders: **11,100**
Dangerous Habits, Part 6 **A:** William Simpson **W:** Garth Ennis

47 ❑ Nov 1991 Cover: 1.75 **NM** value: **3.00**
Circ: CapCity orders: **10,800**
The Pub Where I Was Born **A:** William Simpson **W:** Garth Ennis

48 ❑ Dec 1991 Cover: 1.75 **NM** value: **3.00**
Circ: CapCity orders: **11,400**
Love Kills **A:** Mike Hoffman **W:** Garth Ennis

49 ❑ Jan 1992 Cover: 1.75 **NM** value: **3.00**
Circ: CapCity orders: **11,350**
Lord Of The Dance **A:** Steve Dillon **W:** Garth Ennis

50 ❑ Feb 1992 Cover: 3.00 **NM** value: **4.00**
Circ: CapCity orders: **12,350**
• Giant-size. Remarkable Lives **A:** William Simpson **W:** Garth Ennis

51 ❑ Mar 1992 Cover: 1.75 **NM** value: **2.50**
Circ: CapCity orders: **10,750**
Counting to Ten **A:** Sean Phillips **W:** John Smith

52 ❑ Apr 1992 Cover: 1.75 **NM** value: **2.50**
Circ: CapCity orders: **10,650** • **CGC:** 1 graded, best 9.4
Royal Blood, Part 1 **A:** William Simpson **W:** Garth Ennis

53 ❑ May 1992 Cover: 1.75 **NM** value: **2.50**
Circ: CapCity orders: **10,300**
Royal Blood, Part 2 **A:** William Simpson **W:** Garth Ennis

54 ❑ Jun 1992 Cover: 1.75 **NM** value: **2.50**
Circ: CapCity orders: **10,750**
Royal Blood, Part 3 **A:** William Simpson **W:** Garth Ennis

55 ❑ Jul 1992 Cover: 1.75 **NM** value: **2.50**
Circ: CapCity orders: **10,550**
Royal Blood, Part 4 **A:** William Simpson **W:** Garth Ennis

56 ❑ Aug 1992 Cover: 1.75 **NM** value: **2.50**
Circ: CapCity orders: **11,150**
This is the Diary of Danny Drake **A:** David Lloyd **W:** Garth Ennis

57 ❑ Sep 1992 Cover: 1.75 **NM** value: **2.50**
Circ: CapCity orders: **10,200**
Mortal Clay **A:** Steve Dillon **W:** Garth Ennis

58 ❑ Oct 1992 Cover: 1.75 **NM** value: **2.50**
Circ: CapCity orders: **10,500**
Body and Soul **A:** Steve Dillon **W:** Garth Ennis

59 ❑ Nov 1992 Cover: 1.75 **NM** value: **2.50**
Circ: CapCity orders: **10,650**
Guys and Dolls, Part 1 **A:** William Simpson **W:** Garth Ennis

60 ❑ Dec 1992 Cover: 1.75 **NM** value: **2.50**
Circ: CapCity orders: **10,850**
Guys and Dolls, Part 2 **A:** William Simpson **W:** Garth Ennis

61 ❑ Jan 1993 Cover: 1.75 **NM** value: **2.50**
Circ: CapCity orders: **11,000**
She's Buying a Stairway to Heaven **A:** William Simpson **W:** Garth Ennis

62 ❑ Feb 1993 Cover: 1.75 **NM** value: **2.50**
Circ: CapCity orders: **14,850**
End of the Line **A:** Steve Dillon **W:** Garth Ennis

63 ❑ Mar 1993 Cover: 1.75 **NM** value: **2.50**
Circ: CapCity orders: **26,550**
Forty **A:** Steve Dillon **W:** Garth Ennis

64 ❑ Apr 1993 Cover: 1.75 **NM** value: **2.50**
Circ: CapCity orders: **16,550**
Fear and Loathing, Part 1 **A:** Steve Dillon **W:** Garth Ennis

65 ❑ May 1993 Cover: 1.75 **NM** value: **2.50**
Circ: CapCity orders: **16,800**
Fear and Loathing, Part 2 **A:** Steve Dillon **W:** Garth Ennis

66 ❑ Jun 1993 Cover: 1.95 **NM** value: **2.50**
Circ: CapCity orders: **16,800**
Fear and Loathing, Part 3 **A:** Steve Dillon **W:** Garth Ennis

67 ❑ Jul 1993 Cover: 1.95 **NM** value: **2.50**
Circ: CapCity orders: **16,350**
End Of The Line **A:** Steve Dillon **W:** Garth Ennis

68 ❑ Aug 1993 Cover: 1.95 **NM** value: **2.50**
Circ: CapCity orders: **16,650**
Down all the Days **A:** Steve Dillon **W:** Garth Ennis

69 ❑ Sep 1993 Cover: 1.95 **NM** value: **2.50**
Circ: CapCity orders: **15,200**
Rough Trade **A:** Steve Dillon **W:** Garth Ennis

70 ❑ Oct 1993 Cover: 1.95 **NM** value: **2.50**
Circ: CapCity orders: **14,600**
Heartland **A:** Steve Dillon **W:** Garth Ennis

71 ❑ Nov 1993 Cover: 1.95 **NM** value: **2.50**
Circ: CapCity orders: **14,200**
Finest Hour **A:** Steve Dillon **W:** Garth Ennis

72 ❑ Dec 1993 Cover: 1.95 **NM** value: **2.50**
Circ: CapCity orders: **14,650**
Damnation's Flame, Part 1 **A:** Steve Dillon **W:** Garth Ennis

73 ❑ Jan 1994 Cover: 1.95 **NM** value: **2.50**
Circ: CapCity orders: **13,600**
Damnation's Flame, Part 2 **A:** Steve Dillon **W:** Garth Ennis

74 ❑ Feb 1994 Cover: 1.95 **NM** value: **2.50**
Circ: CapCity orders: **14,000**
Damnation's Flame, Part 3 **A:** Steve Dillon **W:** Garth Ennis

75 ❑ Mar 1994 Cover: 2.95 **NM** value: **Cover or less**
Circ: CapCity orders: **14,700**
• Double-size. Damnation's Flame, Part 4 **A:** Steve Dillon **W:** Garth Ennis

76 ❑ Apr 1994 Cover: 1.95 **NM** value: **2.50**
Circ: CapCity orders: **13,650**
Confessions Of An Irish Rebel **A:** Steve Dillon **W:** Garth Ennis

77 ❑ May 1994 Cover: 1.95 **NM** value: **2.50**
Circ: CapCity orders: **13,550**
And The Crowd Goes Wild **A:** Steve Dillon **W:** Garth Ennis

78 ❑ Jun 1994 Cover: 1.95 **NM** value: **2.50**
Circ: CapCity orders: **13,600**
Rake at the Gates of Hell, Part 1 **A:** Steve Dillon **W:** Garth Ennis

79 ❑ Jul 1994 Cover: 1.95 **NM** value: **2.50**
Circ: CapCity orders: **13,650**
Rake at the Gates of Hell, Part 2 **A:** Steve Dillon **W:** Garth Ennis

80 ❑ Aug 1994 Cover: 1.95 **NM** value: **2.50**
Circ: CapCity orders: **13,500**
Rake at the Gates of Hell, Part 3 **A:** Steve Dillon **W:** Garth Ennis

81 ❑ Sep 1994 Cover: 1.95 **NM** value: **2.50**
Circ: CapCity orders: **13,350**
Rake at the Gates of Hell, Part 4 **A:** Steve Dillon **W:** Garth Ennis

82 ❑ Oct 1994 Cover: 1.95 **NM** value: **2.50**
Circ: CapCity orders: **13,650**
Rake at the Gates of Hell, Part 5 **A:** Steve Dillon **W:** Garth Ennis

83 ❑ Nov 1994 Cover: 1.95 **NM** value: **2.50**
Circ: CapCity orders: **14,100**
Rake at the Gates of Hell, Part 6 **A:** Steve Dillon **W:** Garth Ennis

84 ❑ Dec 1994 Cover: 1.95 **NM** value: **2.50**
Circ: CapCity orders: **13,450**
In Another Part Of Hell **A:** Sean Phillips **W:** Jamie Delano

85 ❑ Jan 1995 Cover: 1.95 **NM** value: **2.50**
Circ: CapCity orders: **12,950**
Warped Notions, Part 1 **A:** Sean Phillips **W:** Eddie Campbell

86 ❑ Feb 1995 Cover: 1.95 **NM** value: **2.50**
Circ: CapCity orders: **12,500**
Warped Notions, Part 2 **A:** Sean Phillips **W:** Eddie Campbell

87 ❑ Mar 1995 Cover: 1.95 **NM** value: **2.50**
Circ: CapCity orders: **11,875**
Warped Notions, Part 3 **A:** Sean Phillips **W:** Eddie Campbell

88 ❑ Apr 1995 Cover: 1.95 **NM** value: **2.50**
Circ: CapCity orders: **11,475**
Warped Notions, Part 4 **A:** Sean Phillips **W:** Eddie Campbell

89 ❑ May 1995 Cover: 2.25 **NM** value: **2.50**
Circ: CapCity orders: **11,325**
Dreamtime **A:** Sean Phillips **W:** Paul Jenkins

90 ❑ Jun 1995 Cover: 2.25 **NM** value: **2.50**
Circ: CapCity orders: **11,075**
Dangerous Ground **A:** Sean Phillips **W:** Paul Jenkins

91 ❑ Jul 1995 Cover: 2.25 **NM** value: **2.50**
Circ: CapCity orders: **10,925**
Riding the Green Lanes **A:** Sean Phillips **W:** Paul Jenkins

92 ❑ Aug 1995 Cover: 2.25 **NM** value: **2.50**
Circ: CapCity orders: **11,000**
Critical Mass, Part 1 **A:** Sean Phillips **W:** Paul Jenkins

93 ❑ Sep 1995 Cover: 2.25 **NM** value: **2.50**
Circ: CapCity orders: **10,125**
Critical Mass, Part 2 **A:** Sean Phillips **W:** Paul Jenkins

94 ❑ Oct 1995 Cover: 2.25 **NM** value: **2.50**
Circ: CapCity orders: **8,875**
Critical Mass, Part 3 **A:** Sean Phillips **W:** Paul Jenkins

95 ❑ Nov 1995 Cover: 2.25 **NM** value: **2.50**
Critical Mass, Part 4 **A:** Sean Phillips **W:** Paul Jenkins

96 ❑ Dec 1995 Cover: 2.25 **NM** value: **2.50**
Critical Mass, Part 5 **A:** Sean Phillips **W:** Paul Jenkins

97 ❑ Jan 1996 Cover: 2.25 **NM** value: **2.50**
The Nature Of The Beast **A:** Sean Phillips **W:** Paul Jenkins

98 ❑ Feb 1996 Cover: 2.25 **NM** value: **2.50**
Walking the Dog **A:** Sean Phillips **W:** Paul Jenkins

99 ❑ Mar 1996 Cover: 2.25 **NM** value: **2.50**
Punkin' up the Great Outdoors **A:** Sean Phillips **W:** Paul Jenkins

100 ❑ Apr 1996 Cover: 3.50 **NM** value: **Cover or less**
Sins of the Father **A:** Sean Phillips **W:** Paul Jenkins

101 ❑ May 1996 Cover: 2.25 **NM** value: **2.50**
Football: It's a Funny Old Game **A:** Sean Phillips **W:** Paul Jenkins

102 ❑ Jun 1996 Cover: 2.25 **NM** value: **2.50**
Difficult Beginnings, Part 1 **A:** Sean Phillips **W:** Paul Jenkins

103 ❑ Jul 1996 Cover: 2.25 **NM** value: **2.50**
Difficult Beginnings, Part 2 **A:** Sean Phillips **W:** Paul Jenkins

104 ❑ Aug 1996 Cover: 2.25 **NM** value: **2.50**
Difficult Beginnings, Part 3 **A:** Sean Phillips **W:** Paul Jenkins

105 ❑ Sep 1996 Cover: 2.25 **NM** value: **2.50**
A Taste of Heaven **A:** Sean Phillips **W:** Paul Jenkins

106 ❑ Oct 1996 Cover: 2.25 **NM** value: **2.50**
In the Line of Fire, Part 1 **A:** Sean Phillips **W:** Paul Jenkins

107 ❑ Nov 1996 Cover: 2.25 **NM** value: **2.50**
Circ: Diamd. preorders: **24,823**
In the Line of Fire, Part 2 **A:** Sean Phillips **W:** Paul Jenkins

108 ❑ Dec 1996 Cover: 2.25 **NM** value: **2.50**
Circ: Diamd. preorders: **24,820**
In the Line of Fire, Part 2; Days of Wine and Roses **A:** Charles Adlard **W:** Paul Jenkins

109 ❑ Jan 1997 Cover: 2.25 **NM** value: **2.50**
Circ: Diamd. preorders: **23,830**
The Wild Hunt **A:** Sean Phillips **W:** Paul Jenkins

110 ❑ Feb 1997 Cover: 2.25 **NM** value: **2.50**
Circ: Diamd. preorders: **23,491**
Last Man Standing, Part 1 **A:** Sean Phillips **W:** Paul Jenkins

111 ❑ Mar 1997 Cover: 2.25 **NM** value: **2.50**
Circ: Diamd. preorders: **23,069**
Last Man Standing, Part 2 **A:** Sean Phillips **W:** Paul Jenkins

112 ❑ Apr 1997 Cover: 2.25 **NM** value: **2.50**
Circ: Diamd. preorders: **22,460**
Last Man Standing, Part 3 **A:** Sean Phillips **W:** Paul Jenkins

113 ❑ May 1997 Cover: 2.25 **NM** value: **2.50**
Circ: Diamd. preorders: **22,477**
Last Man Standing, Part 4 **A:** Sean Phillips **W:** Paul Jenkins

114 ❑ Jun 1997 Cover: 2.25 **NM** value: **2.50**
Circ: Diamd. preorders: **22,903**
Last Man Standing, Part 5 **A:** Sean Phillips **W:** Paul Jenkins

115 ❑ Jul 1997 Cover: 2.25 **NM** value: **2.50**
Circ: Diamd. preorders: **19,563**
In the Red Corner **A:** Warren Pleece **W:** Paul Jenkins

116 ❑ Aug 1997 Cover: 2.25 **NM** value: **2.50**
Circ: Diamd. preorders: **19,298**
Widdershins, Part 1 **A:** Sean Phillips **W:** Paul Jenkins

117 ❑ Sep 1997 Cover: 2.25 **NM** value: **2.50**
Circ: Diamd. preorders: **18,863**
Widdershins, Part 2 **A:** Sean Phillips **W:** Paul Jenkins

118 ❑ Oct 1997 Cover: 2.25 **NM** value: **2.50**
Circ: Diamd. preorders: **18,786**
Life and Death and Taxis **A:** Sean Phillips **W:** Paul Jenkins

119 ❑ Nov 1997 Cover: 2.25 **NM** value: **2.50**
Circ: Diamd. preorders: **18,317**
Undertow **A:** Sean Phillips **W:** Paul Jenkins

120 ❑ Dec 1997 Cover: 3.50 **NM** value: **Cover or less**
Circ: Diamd. preorders: **19,070**
• Giant-size. Desperately Seeking Something **A:** Sean Phillips **W:** Paul Jenkins ★ Appearance of Alan Moore.

121 ❑ Jan 1998 Cover: 2.25 **NM** value: **Cover or less**
Circ: Diamd. preorders: **17,965**
Up the Down Staircase, Part 1 **A:** Warren Pleece **W:** Paul Jenkins

CGC-graded: Multiply prices above by **33 for 9.9 M** • **16 for 9.8 NM/M** • **7 for 9.6 NM+** • **5 for 9.4 NM** • **2.5 for 9.2 NM-** • **1.5 for 9.0 VF/NM**

122 ❑ Feb 1998 Cover: 2.25 **NM** value: **Cover or less**
Circ: Diamd. preorders: **17,465**
Up the Down Staircase, Part 2 **A:** Warren Pleece **W:** Paul Jenkins
123 ❑ Mar 1998 Cover: 2.25 **NM** value: **Cover or less**
Circ: Diamd. preorders: **17,398**
Up the Down Staircase, Part 3 **A:** Warren Pleece **W:** Paul Jenkins
124 ❑ Apr 1998 Cover: 2.25 **NM** value: **Cover or less**
Circ: Diamd. preorders: **16,626**
Up the Down Staircase, Part 4 **A:** Warren Pleece **W:** Paul Jenkins
125 ❑ May 1998 Cover: 2.25 **NM** value: **Cover or less**
Circ: Diamd. preorders: **16,828**
How to Play With Fire, Part 1 **A:** Warren Pleece **W:** Paul Jenkins
126 ❑ Jun 1998 Cover: 2.25 **NM** value: **Cover or less**
Circ: Diamd. preorders: **16,752**
How to Play With Fire, Part 2 **A:** Warren Pleece **W:** Paul Jenkins
127 ❑ Jul 1998 Cover: 2.25 **NM** value: **Cover or less**
Circ: Diamd. preorders: **15,830**
How to Play With Fire, Part 3 **A:** Warren Pleece **W:** Paul Jenkins
128 ❑ Aug 1998 Cover: 2.25 **NM** value: **Cover or less**
Circ: Diamd. preorders: **15,767**
How to Play With Fire, Part 4 **A:** Warren Pleece **W:** Paul Jenkins
129 ❑ Sep 1998 Cover: 2.50 **NM** value: **Cover or less**
Circ: Diamd. preorders: **21,909**
Son of Man, Part 1 **A:** John Higgins **W:** Garth Ennis
130 ❑ Oct 1998 Cover: 2.50 **NM** value: **Cover or less**
Circ: Diamd. preorders: **20,772**
Son of Man, Part 2 **A:** John Higgins **W:** Garth Ennis
131 ❑ Nov 1998 Cover: 2.50 **NM** value: **Cover or less**
Circ: Diamd. preorders: **21,102**
Son of Man, Part 3 **A:** John Higgins **W:** Garth Ennis
132 ❑ Dec 1998 Cover: 2.50 **NM** value: **Cover or less**
Circ: Diamd. preorders: **21,514**
Son of Man, Part 4 **A:** John Higgins **W:** Garth Ennis
133 ❑ Jan 1999 Cover: 2.50 **NM** value: **Cover or less**
Circ: Diamd. preorders: **21,290**
Son of Man, Part 5 **A:** John Higgins **W:** Garth Ennis
134 ❑ Feb 1999 Cover: 2.50 **NM** value: **Cover or less**
Circ: Diamd. preorders: **20,309**
Haunted, Part 1 **A:** John Higgins **W:** Warren Ellis
135 ❑ Mar 1999 Cover: 2.50 **NM** value: **Cover or less**
Circ: Diamd. preorders: **19,723**
Haunted, Part 2 **A:** John Higgins **W:** Warren Ellis
136 ❑ Apr 1999 Cover: 2.50 **NM** value: **Cover or less**
Circ: Diamd. preorders: **19,028**
Haunted, Part 3 **A:** John Higgins **W:** Warren Ellis
137 ❑ May 1999 Cover: 2.50 **NM** value: **Cover or less**
Circ: Diamd. preorders: **19,474**
Haunted, Part 4 **A:** John Higgins **W:** Warren Ellis
138 ❑ Jun 1999 Cover: 2.50 **NM** value: **Cover or less**
Circ: Diamd. preorders: **20,052**
Haunted, Part 5 **A:** John Higgins **W:** Warren Ellis
139 ❑ Jul 1999 Cover: 2.50 **NM** value: **Cover or less**
Circ: Diamd. preorders: **19,800**
Haunted, Part 6 **A:** John Higgins **W:** Warren Ellis
140 ❑ Aug 1999 Cover: 2.50 **NM** value: **Cover or less**
Circ: Diamd. preorders: **19,407**
Locked **A:** Frank Teran **W:** Warren Ellis
141 ❑ Oct 1999 Cover: 2.50 **NM** value: **Cover or less**
Circ: Diamd. preorders: **19,706**
The Crib **A:** Tim Bradstreet **W:** Warren Ellis
142 ❑ Nov 1999 Cover: 2.50 **NM** value: **Cover or less**
Circ: Diamd. preorders: **19,277**
Setting Sun, One Last Love Song
143 ❑ Dec 1999 Cover: 2.50 **NM** value: **Cover or less**
Circ: Diamd. preorders: **18,825**
Telling Tales **A:** Marcelo Frusin **W:** Warren Ellis
144 ❑ Jan 2000 Cover: 2.50 **NM** value: **Cover or less**
Circ: Diamd. preorders: **19,091**
Ashes & Honey, Part 1 **A:** Gary Erskine; Glenn Fabry(cover) **W:** Darko Macan
145 ❑ Feb 2000 Cover: 2.50 **NM** value: **Cover or less**
Circ: Diamd. preorders: **21,663**
146 ❑ Mar 2000 Cover: 2.50 **NM** value: **Cover or less**
Circ: Diamd. preorders: **18,153**
Hard Time, Part 1 **A:** Richard Corben **W:** Brian Azzarello
147 ❑ Apr 2000 Cover: 2.50 **NM** value: **Cover or less**
Circ: Diamd. preorders: **16,876**
Hard Time, Part 2 **A:** Richard Corben **W:** Brian Azzarello
148 ❑ May 2000 Cover: 2.50 **NM** value: **Cover or less**
Circ: Diamd. preorders: **17,382**
Hard Time, Part 3 **A:** Richard Corben **W:** Brian Azzarello
149 ❑ Jun 2000 Cover: 2.50 **NM** value: **Cover or less**
Circ: Diamd. preorders: **17,967**
Hard Time, Part 4 **A:** Richard Corben **W:** Brian Azzarello
150 ❑ Jul 2000 Cover: 2.50 **NM** value: **Cover or less**
Circ: Diamd. preorders: **18,754**
151 ❑ Aug 2000 Cover: 2.50 **NM** value: **Cover or less**
Circ: Diamd. preorders: **18,811**
152 ❑ Sep 2000 Cover: 2.50 **NM** value: **Cover or less**
Circ: Diamd. preorders: **19,142**
Good Intentions, Part 2 **A:** Marcelo Frusin **W:** Brian Azzarello
153 ❑ Oct 2000 Cover: 2.50 **NM** value: **Cover or less**
Circ: Diamd. preorders: **18,403**
Good Intentions, Part 3 **A:** Marcelo Frusin **W:** Brian Azzarello
154 ❑ Nov 2000 Cover: 2.50 **NM** value: **Cover or less**
Circ: Diamd. preorders: **19,161**
Good Intentions, Part 4 **A:** Marcelo Frusin **W:** Brian Azzarello
155 ❑ Dec 2000 Cover: 2.50 **NM** value: **Cover or less**
Circ: Diamd. preorders: **19,413**
Good Intentions, Part 5 **A:** Marcelo Frusin **W:** Brian Azzarello
156 ❑ Jan 2001 Cover: 2.50 **NM** value: **Cover or less**
Circ: Diamd. preorders: **19,616**
Good Intentions, Part 6 **A:** Marcelo Frusin **W:** Brian Azzarello
157 ❑ Feb 2001 Cover: 2.50 **NM** value: **Cover or less**
Circ: Diamd. preorders: **19,767**
...And Buried **A:** Steve Dillon **W:** Brian Azzarello
158 ❑ Mar 2001 Cover: 2.50 **NM** value: **Cover or less**
Circ: Diamd. preorders: **19,167**
Freezes Over, Part 1 **A:** Marcelo Frusin **W:** Brian Azzarello
159 ❑ Apr 2001 Cover: 2.50 **NM** value: **Cover or less**
Circ: Diamd. preorders: **19,114**
Freezes Over, Part 2 **A:** Marcelo Frusin **W:** Brian Azzarello
160 ❑ May 2001 Cover: 2.50 **NM** value: **Cover or less**
Circ: Diamd. preorders: **18,960**
Freezes Over, Part 3 **A:** Marcelo Frusin **W:** Brian Azzarello
161 ❑ Jun 2001 Cover: 2.50 **NM** value: **Cover or less**
Circ: Diamd. preorders: **19,341**
Freezes Over, Part 4 **A:** Marcelo Frusin **W:** Brian Azzarello
162 ❑ Jul 2001 Cover: 2.50 **NM** value: **Cover or less**
Circ: Diamd. preorders: **19,213**
163 ❑ Aug 2001 Cover: 2.50 **NM** value: **Cover or less**
Circ: Diamd. preorders: **19,519**
164 ❑ Sep 2001 Cover: 2.50 **NM** value: **Cover or less**
Circ: Diamd. preorders: **20,574**
Anl 1 ❑ Oct 1989 Cover: 2.95 **NM** value: **6.00**
Circ: CapCity orders: **12,400**
The Bloody Saint **A:** Bryan Talbot **W:** Jamie Delano
Bk 1 ❑ Cover: 16.95 **NM** value: **Cover or less**
• Original Sins: Reprints Hellblazer #1-9
Bk 2 ❑ Cover: 14.95 **NM** value: **Cover or less**
• Dangerous Habits; collects issues #41-46 **W:** Garth Ennis
Bk 2-2 ❑ **NM** value: **14.95**
Bk 2-3 ❑ Cover: 14.95 **NM** value: **Cover or less**
Bk 3 ❑ Cover: 6.50 **NM** value: **10.00**
• British edition, collects Hellblazer/Swamp Thing issues (4 total) in black & white. **A:** Tom Mandrake; Richard Piers Rayner; John Ridgway; Rick Veitch **W:** Rick Veitch; Jamie Delano
Bk 4 ❑ Cover: 6.50 **NM** value: **10.00**
• British edition, collects Hellblazer#11-14. **A:** Richard Piers Rayner **W:** Jamie Delano
Bk 5 ❑ Cover: 14.95 **NM** value: **Cover or less**
• Fear And Loathing; collects #62-67 **A:** Steve Dillon **W:** Garth Ennis
Bk 6 ❑ Cover: 16.95 **NM** value: **Cover or less**
• Tainted Love; collects issues #68-71, Hellblazer Special #1, Vertigo Jam #1
Bk 7 ❑ Cover: 16.95 **NM** value: **Cover or less**
Damnation's Flame • Damnation's Flame; collects #72-77 **A:** William Simpson; Steve Dillon; Peter Snejbjerg **W:** Garth Ennis
Bk 8 ❑ Cover: 16.95 **NM** value: **Cover or less**
Hard Time • Hard Time; Collects Hellblazer #145-148 **A:** Richard Corben **W:** Brian Azzarello
SE 1 ❑ Jan 1993 Cover: 3.95 **NM** value: **5.00**
Circ: CapCity orders: **14,700**
Confessional **A:** Steve Dillon **W:** Garth Ennis

HELLBLAZER SPECIAL: BAD BLOOD DC / Vertigo

1 ❑ Sep 2000 Cover: 2.95 **NM** value: **Cover or less**
Circ: Diamd. preorders: **17,158**
2 ❑ Oct 2000 Cover: 2.95 **NM** value: **Cover or less**
Circ: Diamd. preorders: **15,316**
3 ❑ Nov 2000 Cover: 2.95 **NM** value: **Cover or less**
Circ: Diamd. preorders: **16,033**
4 ❑ Dec 2000 Cover: 2.95 **NM** value: **Cover or less**
Circ: Diamd. preorders: **15,911**

HELLBLAZER/THE BOOKS OF MAGIC DC / Vertigo

1 ❑ Dec 1997 Cover: 2.50 **NM** value: **3.00**
Circ: Diamd. preorders: **28,451**
Ascent **A:** Paul Lee **W:** John Ney Rieber; Paul Jenkins
2 ❑ Jan 1998 Cover: 2.50 **NM** value: **3.00**
Circ: Diamd. preorders: **25,338**

HELLBOY: ALMOST COLOSSUS Dark Horse / Legend

1 ❑ Jun 1997 Cover: 2.95 **NM** value: **Cover or less**
Circ: Diamd. preorders: **28,146**
Almost Colossus; Autopsy in B-Flat **A:** Mike Mignola **W:** Mike Mignola
2 ❑ Jul 1997 Cover: 2.95 **NM** value: **Cover or less**
Circ: Diamd. preorders: **26,797**
Almost Colossus; Autopsy in B-Flat **A:** Mike Mignola; Gary Gianni **W:** Mike Mignola; Gary Gianni

HELLBOY: BOX FULL OF EVIL Dark Horse / Maverick

1 ❑ Aug 1999 Cover: 2.95 **NM** value: **Cover or less**
Box Full of Evil, Part 1 **A:** Mike Mignola **W:** Mike Mignola
2 ❑ Sep 1999 Cover: 2.95 **NM** value: **Cover or less**
Box Full of Evil, Part 2; Abe Sapien vs. Science **A:** Matt Smith; Mike Mignola **W:** Mike Mignola

HELLBOY CHRISTMAS SPECIAL Dark Horse

1 ❑ Dec 1997 Cover: 3.95 **NM** value: **Cover or less**
No issue number. One-shot. A Christmas Underground; Ernie's Holiday Ditty; A Strange Story; Christmas; Toybox; Corpus Monstrum in a Gift for the Wicked; Further Reading **A:** Geof Darrow; Mike Mignola; Steve Purcell; Gary Gianni **W:** Geof Darrow; Mike Mignola; Steve Purcell; Gary Gianni

HELLBOY: CONQUEROR WORM Dark Horse / Maverick

1 ❑ May 2001 Cover: 2.99 **NM** value: **Cover or less**
• **CGC:** 1 graded, best 9.8
2 ❑ Cover: 2.99 **NM** value: **Cover or less**
3 ❑ Cover: 2.99 **NM** value: **Cover or less**
4 ❑ Cover: 2.99 **NM** value: **Cover or less**

HELLBOY, THE CORPSE AND THE IRON SHOES Dark Horse / Legend

1 ❑ Cover: 2.95 **NM** value: **3.50**
No issue number. The Corpse; The Iron Shoes • collects the story serialized in the distributor catalog Advance Comics #75-82 **A:** Mike Mignola **W:** Mike Mignola

HELLBOY JR. Dark Horse

1 ❑ Oct 1999 Cover: 2.95 **NM** value: **Cover or less**
Circ: Diamd. preorders: **16,860**
Hellbooy Jr.'s Magical Mushroom Trip; The Wolvertons; Squid of Man **A:** Pat McEown; Mike Mignola; Dave Cooper **W:** William Wray
2 ❑ Nov 1999 Cover: 2.95 **NM** value: **Cover or less**
Circ: Diamd. preorders: **15,143**
The House of Candy Pain; Sparky Bear; Huge Retarded Duck; Hellboy Jr. Gets a Car **A:** William Wray; Mike Mignola; Hilary Barta **W:** William Wray; Mike Mignola

HELLBOY JR. HALLOWEEN SPECIAL Dark Horse

1 ❑ Oct 1997 Cover: 3.95 **NM** value: **Cover or less**
Circ: Diamd. preorders: **20,106**
No issue number. One-shot. wraparound cover. Maggots, Maggots, Everywhere; Wheezy the Sick Little Witch; the Ginger-Beef Boy; The Creation of Hellboy Jr.; Somnambo the Sleeping Giant; The Devil Don't Smoke • Hellboy Jr. pinup **A:** William Wray; Mike Mignola; Stephen DeStefano; Hilary Barta; Dave Cooper **W:** William Wray

HELLBOY: SEED OF DESTRUCTION Dark Horse / Legend

First appearing in Dark Horse Presents (and as a comics character in Next Men), Hellboy now appears in his own multiple Eisner award-winning series. His story begins as the Third Reich began ticking down its final hours. The Nazis made a last, desperate attempt to turn the tide by summoning unearthly powers to come to their rescue. What they got was a strange red child — Hellboy.

Hellboy fell into the hands of the Allies and has now grown into adulthood. No stranger to weird phenomena, he now makes his living as a paranormal investigator. In "Seed of Destruction," he takes on his strangest case yet — the murder of his adoptive father. Joined by Elizabeth Sherman, a pyrokinetic, and Abraham Sapien, a genetically engineered man-fish, they'll take on all manner of danger in order to solve the case. And before it's all over, Hellboy will have come face-to-face with the sorcerer who summoned him into this world...

1 ❑ Mar 1994 Cover: 2.50 **NM** value: **4.00**
Circ: CapCity orders: **16,300** • **CGC:** 2 graded, best 9.6
2 ❑ Apr 1994 Cover: 2.50 **NM** value: **3.50**
Circ: CapCity orders: **12,850**
3 ❑ May 1994 Cover: 2.50 **NM** value: **3.50**
Circ: CapCity orders: **13,025**
4 ❑ Jun 1994 Cover: 2.50 **NM** value: **3.50**
Circ: CapCity orders: **14,375**
Bk 1 ❑ Oct 1994 Cover: 17.95 **NM** value: **Cover or less**
No issue number. • Trade Paperback. • collects mini-series; Collects Hellboy: Seed of Destruction #1-4 **A:** Mike Mignola **W:** Mike Mignola
Bk 1/LE ❑ Cover: 99.95 **NM** value: **Cover or less**
• Limited edition hardcover. • Collects Hellboy: Seed of Destruction #1-4 **A:** Mike Mignola **W:** Mike Mignola
Bk 1-2 ❑ Jun 1997 Cover: 17.95 **NM** value: **Cover or less**

HELLBOY: THE CHAINED COFFIN AND OTHERS Dark Horse

Bk 1 ❑ Aug 1998 Cover: 17.95 **NM** value: **Cover or less**
No issue number. • Trade Paperback. • collects several stories **A:** Mike Mignola **W:** Mike Mignola

HELLBOY: THE WOLVES OF SAINT AUGUST Dark Horse / Legend

1 ❑ Cover: 4.95 **NM** value: **Cover or less**
No issue number. One-shot. • prestige format. • collects the story from Dark Horse Presents #88-91

HELLBOY: WAKE THE DEVIL Dark Horse / Legend

1 ❑ Jun 1996 Cover: 2.95 **NM** value: **Cover or less**
• Silent as the Grave back-up **A:** Mike Mignola **W:** Mike Mignola
2 ❑ Jul 1996 Cover: 2.95 **NM** value: **Cover or less**
The MonsterMen: Silent as the Grave • Silent as the Grave back-up **A:** Mike Mignola; Gary Gianni **W:** Mike Mignola; Gary Gianni
3 ❑ Aug 1996 Cover: 2.95 **NM** value: **Cover or less**
The MonsterMen: Silent as the Grave • Silent as the Grave back-up **A:** Mike Mignola; Gary Gianni **W:** Mike Mignola; Gary Gianni
4 ❑ Sep 1996 Cover: 2.95 **NM** value: **Cover or less**
Circ: Diamd. preorders: **30,027**
The MonsterMen: Silent as the Grave • Silent as the Grave back-up **A:** Mike Mignola **W:** Mike Mignola
5 ❑ Oct 1996 Cover: 2.95 **NM** value: **Cover or less**
Circ: Diamd. preorders: **30,057**
The MonsterMen: Silent as the Grave • Silent as the Grave back-up **A:** Mike Mignola **W:** Mike Mignola
Bk 1 ❑ May 1997 Cover: 17.95 **NM** value: **Cover or less**
• collects mini-series

HELL CAR COMIX Alternating Crimes Publishing

1 ❑ Fal 1998 Cover: 2.95 **NM** value: **Cover or less**

HELLCAT Marvel

1 ❑ Sep 2000 Cover: 2.99 **NM** value: **Cover or less**
Circ: Diamd. preorders: **26,278**
One Life to Live **A:** Norm Breyfogle **W:** Steve Englehart

HELL CITY, HELL Diablo Musica

1 ❑ Cover: 2.25 **NM** value: **Cover or less**
• shrinkwrapped with CD-ROM

HELLCOP Image

1 ❑ Aug 1998 Cover: 2.50 **NM** value: **Cover or less**

Other grades: Multiply prices above by **1.5 for Mint • 2/3 for Very Fine • 1/3 for Fine • 1/5 for Very Good • 1/8 for Good**

Circ: Diamd. preorders: **37,697**
cover says Oct, indicia says Aug. 📖 ...Like of Woman Scorned **A:** Gilbert Monsanto **W:** Joe Casey; Brian Holguin; Brian Haberlin

1/A ❑ Aug 1998 Cover: 2.50 **NM** value: **Cover or less**
alternate cover. 📖 ...Like of Woman Scorned • Man kneeling with gun, woman, faces in background **A:** Gilbert Monsanto **W:** Joe Casey; Brian Holguin; Brian Haberlin

2 ❑ Nov 1998 Cover: 2.50 **NM** value: **Cover or less**
Circ: Diamd. preorders: **24,309**
📖 The Fates Roared **A:** Gilbert Monsanto **W:** Joe Casey; Brian Holguin; Brian Haberlin

2/A ❑ Nov 1998 Cover: 2.50 **NM** value: **Cover or less**
alternate cover. **A:** Gilbert Monsanto **W:** Joe Casey; Brian Holguin; Brian Haberlin

3 ❑ Jan 1999 Cover: 2.50 **NM** value: **Cover or less**
Circ: Diamd. preorders: **22,906**
📖 Into the Abyss of an Empty Heart **A:** Gilbert Monsanto **W:** Joe Casey; Brian Holguin; Brian Haberlin

4 ❑ Mar 1999 Cover: 2.50 **NM** value: **Cover or less**
Circ: Diamd. preorders: **19,954**
📖 Pandemonium Reigned **A:** Gilbert Monsanto **W:** Joe Casey; Brian Holguin; Brian Haberlin

HELL ETERNAL — DC / Vertigo

1 ❑ Cover: 6.95 **NM** value: **Cover or less**
No issue number. One-shot. • prestige format.

HELLGIRL: DEMONSEED — Knight

1 ❑ Mar 1995 Cover: 2.95 **NM** value: **Cover or less**

HELLHOLE — Image

1 ❑ Jul 1999 Cover: 2.50 **NM** value: **Cover or less**
2 ❑ Oct 1999 Cover: 2.50 **NM** value: **Cover or less**

HELLHOUNDS — Dark Horse

1 ❑ b&w Cover: 2.50 **NM** value: **Cover or less**
• Japanese

2 ❑ Cover: 2.95 **NM** value: **Cover or less**

HELLHOUNDS: PANZER CORPS — Dark Horse

1 ❑ b&w Cover: 2.50 **NM** value: **Cover or less**
Circ: CapCity orders: **3,450**

2 ❑ b&w Cover: 2.50 **NM** value: **Cover or less**
Circ: CapCity orders: **2,500**

3 ❑ Apr 1994, b&w Cover: 2.50 **NM** value: **Cover or less**
Circ: CapCity orders: **2,200**
📖 Stray Dog **A:** Kamui Fujiwara; Studio 2B **W:** Mamoru Oshii

4 ❑ May 1994, b&w Cover: 2.50 **NM** value: **Cover or less**
Circ: CapCity orders: **2,650**

5 ❑ Jun 1994, b&w Cover: 2.95 **NM** value: **Cover or less**
Circ: CapCity orders: **2,625**

6 ❑ Jul 1994, b&w Cover: 2.95 **NM** value: **Cover or less**

HELLHOUND: THE REDEMPTION QUEST — Marvel / Epic

1 ❑ Dec 1993 Cover: 2.25 **NM** value: **Cover or less**
Circ: CapCity orders: **7,900**
📖 Hellhound On My Trail **A:** Floyd Hughes **W:** John Miller

2 ❑ Jan 1994 Cover: 2.25 **NM** value: **Cover or less**
Circ: CapCity orders: **3,950**

3 ❑ Feb 1994 Cover: 2.25 **NM** value: **Cover or less**
Circ: CapCity orders: **3,250**

4 ❑ Mar 1994 Cover: 2.25 **NM** value: **Cover or less**
Circ: CapCity orders: **3,000**

HELLINA — Lightning

1 ❑ Sep 1994, b&w Cover: 2.75 **NM** value: **Cover or less**
Circ: CapCity orders: **6,375 • CGC:** 2 graded, best 9.6

HELLINA 1997 PIN-UP SPECIAL — Lightning

1 ❑ Feb 1997 Cover: 3.50 **NM** value: **Cover or less**
cover version A. • b&w pin-ups

HELLINA/CATFIGHT — Lightning

1 ❑ Oct 1995, b&w Cover: 2.75 **NM** value: **3.00**
1/A ❑ Oct 1995 **NM** value: **3.00**
• Olive metallic edition.

1-2 ❑ Aug 1997, b&w Cover: 2.95 **NM** value: **Cover or less**
• reprints Hellina, Catfight

HELLINA: CHRISTMAS IN HELL — Lightning

1 ❑ Dec 1996, b&w Cover: 2.95 **NM** value: **Cover or less**
1/A ❑ Dec 1996 Cover: 9.95 **NM** value: **Cover or less**
nude cover A.

1/B ❑ Dec 1996 Cover: 9.95 **NM** value: **Cover or less**
nude cover B.

HELLINA/CYNDER — Lightning

1 ❑ Sep 1997 Cover: 2.95 **NM** value: **Cover or less**

HELLINA/DOUBLE IMPACT — Lightning

1 ❑ Feb 1996 Cover: 2.75 **NM** value: **Cover or less**
1/A ❑ Feb 1996 Cover: 3.00 **NM** value: **Cover or less**
• crossover with High Impact

1/B ❑ Feb 1996 Cover: 3.00 **NM** value: **Cover or less**
alternate cover.

1/Nude❑Feb 1996 Cover: 9.95 **NM** value: **Cover or less**
polybagged nude cover. • Nude edition with certificate of authenticity. **A:** Paul Abrams **W:** Steven Zyskowski

1/PL❑ **NM** value: **3.00**
• Platinum edition. **A:** Paul Abrams **W:** Steven Zyskowski

HELLINA: GENESIS — Lightning

1 ❑ Apr 1996, b&w Cover: 3.50 **NM** value: **Cover or less**
• bagged with Hellina poster

HELLINA: HEART OF THORNS — Lightning

2 ❑ Sep 1996 Cover: 2.75 **NM** value: **Cover or less**
2/Nude❑Sep 1996 Cover: 9.95 **NM** value: **Cover or less**
• nude cover edition.

HELLINA: HELLBORN — Lightning

1 ❑ Dec 1997, b&w Cover: 2.95 **NM** value: **Cover or less**
Circ: Diamd. preorders: **8,616**

HELLINA: HELL'S ANGEL — Lightning

1 ❑ Nov 1996, b&w Cover: 2.75 **NM** value: **Cover or less**
2 ❑ Dec 1996, b&w Cover: 2.75 **NM** value: **Cover or less**
Circ: Diamd. preorders: **4,086**

HELLINA: IN THE FLESH — Lightning

1 ❑ Aug 1997, b&w Cover: 2.95 **NM** value: **Cover or less**

HELLINA: KISS OF DEATH — Lightning

1 ❑ Jul 1995, b&w Cover: 2.75 **NM** value: **Cover or less**
Circ: CapCity orders: **5,570**

1/GO❑ Cover: 2.75 **NM** value: **3.00**
• Gold edition. **A:** Paul Abrams **W:** Steven Zyskowski

1/Nude❑Jul 1995, b&w Cover: 9.95 **NM** value: **Cover or less**
• Nude edition. **A:** Paul Abrams **W:** Steven Zyskowski

1-2 ❑ Mar 1997 Cover: 2.95 **NM** value: **Cover or less**
alternate cover. • Encore edition.

HELLINA: NAKED DESIRE — Lightning

1 ❑ May 1997 Cover: 2.95 **NM** value: **Cover or less**

HELLINA/NIRA X — Lightning

1 ❑ Aug 1996 Cover: 3.00 **NM** value: **Cover or less**
• crossover with Entity

HELLINA: SKYBOLT TOYZ LIMITED EDITION — Lightning

1/A ❑ Aug 1997, b&w Cover: 1.50 **NM** value: **Cover or less**
• reprints Hellina #1

1/B ❑ Aug 1997 Cover: 1.50 **NM** value: **Cover or less**
alternate cover.

HELLINA: TAKING BACK THE NIGHT — Lightning

1 ❑ Cover: 4.50 **NM** value: **Cover or less**

HELLINA TRADE PAPERBACK — Lightning

Bk 1❑ Feb 1995, b&w Cover: 8.95 **NM** value: **Cover or less**
• collects material from Perg #4-7, Hellina #1, and Fury of Hellina #1

HELLINA: WICKED WAYS — Lightning

1/A ❑ Nov 1995, b&w Cover: 2.75 **NM** value: **Cover or less**
alternate cover. • polybagged

1/B ❑ Nov 1995 Cover: 3.00 **NM** value: **Cover or less**
• polybagged

1/Nude❑Nov 1995 Cover: 9.95 **NM** value: **Cover or less**
cover C. • polybagged

1/SI❑ **NM** value: **2.75**
• silver edition.

HELLRAISER (CLIVE BARKER'S...) — Marvel / Epic

Bk 1❑ Cover: 4.95 **NM** value: **Cover or less**
Circ: CapCity orders: **17,100**
• prestige format.

Bk 2❑ Cover: 4.95 **NM** value: **Cover or less**
Circ: CapCity orders: **17,800**
• prestige format. 📖 The Vault; Diver's Hands; Writer's Lament; The Threshold; The Pleasures of Deception **A:** Jon J. Muth; Mike Hoffman; Bill Sienkiewicz; Bill Koeb; Jorge Zaffino; Phil Felix; Kevin O'Neill **W:** Scott Hampton; Dwayne McDuffie; Marc McLaurin; James Robert Smith; Mark Kneece; Phil Nutman

Bk 3❑ Cover: 4.95 **NM** value: **Cover or less**
Circ: CapCity orders: **15,650**
• prestige format.

Bk 4❑ Cover: 4.95 **NM** value: **Cover or less**
Circ: CapCity orders: **12,600**
• prestige format. 📖 Cenobyte!; Like Flies to Wanton Boys; To Prepare a Face **A:** Bill Sienkiewicz; Kent Williams; Scott Hampton; John Van Fleet; Mark Chiarello **W:** Jan Strnad; Bunny Hampton-Mack; Nicholas Vince

Bk 5❑ Cover: 5.95 **NM** value: **Cover or less**
Circ: CapCity orders: **11,100**
• prestige format.

Bk 6❑ Cover: 5.95 **NM** value: **Cover or less**
Circ: CapCity orders: **9,250**
• prestige format. 📖 Original Sin; Lingerings; Tunnel of Love; The Trainer **A:** William Wray; Bill Koeb; Mark Bloodworth; Jamie Tolagson; John Van Fleet; Jorge Zaffino; Derek Yaniger; Joe Barruso; SMS; John Rheaume(cover); Steven Johnson; Timothy Georgerakis **W:** Bill Mumy; D.G. Chichester; Erik Saltzgaber; James Robert Smith; Miguel Ferrer; Ron Wolfe

Bk 7❑ Cover: 5.95 **NM** value: **Cover or less**
Circ: CapCity orders: **8,500**
• prestige format. 📖 I in the Pyramid; Under the Knife; Demons to Some, Angels to Others; Clowning Around; Devil's Brigade, Part 1 **A:** John Bolton; Bill Reinhold; Paris Cullins; Kyle Baker; Tom Palmer; John Rheaume **W:** Robert Washington III; Dwayne McDuffie; D.G. Chichester; Nicholas Vince; Ron Wolfe

Bk 8❑ Cover: 5.95 **NM** value: **Cover or less**
Circ: CapCity orders: **5,950**
• prestige format. 📖 Homecoming; Devil's Brigade, Part 2; Losing Herself in the Part; Devil's Brigade, Part 3 **A:** Mark Texeira; John Van Fleet; Dwayne McDuffie; Joe Barruso **W:** Dwayne McDuffie; Doug Murray; John Rozum; Larry Wachowski; Ron Wolfe

Bk 9❑ Cover: 5.95 **NM** value: **Cover or less**
Circ: CapCity orders: **6,150**
• prestige format. 📖 Closets; The Tontine; Devil's Brigade, Part 4; Devil's Brigade, Part 5 **A:** Miran Kim; Denys Cowan; Mark Bloodworth; John Van Fleet **W:** Scott Hampton; Dwayne McDuffie; D.G. Chichester; Erik Saltzgaber; Larry Wachowski

Bk 10❑ Cover: 4.50 **NM** value: **4.95**
Circ: CapCity orders: **7,750**
• prestige format.

Bk 11❑ Cover: 4.50 **NM** value: **4.95**
Circ: CapCity orders: **7,400**
• prestige format.

Bk 12❑ Cover: 4.50 **NM** value: **4.95**
Circ: CapCity orders: **7,150**
• prestige format.

Bk 13❑ Cover: 4.95 **NM** value: **Cover or less**
Circ: CapCity orders: **7,000**
• prestige format.

Bk 14❑ Cover: 4.95 **NM** value: **Cover or less**
Circ: CapCity orders: **6,800**
• prestige format.

Bk 15❑ Cover: 4.95 **NM** value: **Cover or less**
Circ: CapCity orders: **6,600**
• prestige format.

Bk 16❑ Cover: 4.95 **NM** value: **Cover or less**
Circ: CapCity orders: **6,000**

Bk 19❑ Cover: 4.95 **NM** value: **Cover or less**
Circ: CapCity orders: **5,600**

Bk 20❑ Cover: 4.95 **NM** value: **Cover or less**
Circ: CapCity orders: **6,650 • CGC:** 1 graded, best 9.6
final issue. **A:** Dave McKean **W:** Neil Gaiman

HS 1❑ Cover: 4.95 **NM** value: **Cover or less**
• Nude edition with certificate of authenticity. • Dark Holiday Special

Smr 1❑ Cover: 5.95 **NM** value: **Cover or less**
Circ: CapCity orders: **6,050**
• Giant-size.

Spr 1❑ Cover: 6.95 **NM** value: **Cover or less**
• Spring Special

HELLRAISER III: HELL ON EARTH — Marvel / Epic

1 ❑ Cover: 4.95 **NM** value: **5.00**
📖 Cruising The Ruins; Dark Star Rising **A:** Miran Kim **W:** Peter Atkins; Tony Randel

HELLRAISER NIGHTBREED-JIHAD — Marvel / Epic

Bk 1❑ Cover: 4.50 **NM** value: **Cover or less**
📖 As Above... **A:** Paul Johnson **W:** D.G. Chichester

Bk 2❑ Cover: 4.50 **NM** value: **Cover or less**

HELLRAISER POSTERBOOK (CLIVE BARKER'S...) — Marvel / Epic

1 ❑ Cover: 4.95 **NM** value: **Cover or less**

HELLRAISER: SPRING SLAUGHTER — Marvel / Epic

1 ❑ Cover: 6.95 **NM** value: **Cover or less**

HELLSAINT — Black Diamond

1 ❑ Mar 1998 Cover: 2.50 **NM** value: **Cover or less**
📖 Retribution **A:** William Jamison **W:** Gary Hannon

HELL'S ANGEL — Marvel

When Ranulph Haldane was suddenly (err...) removed from the board of MyS-TECH, his daughter, Shevaun, was ready to assume his place. Shevaun learned of the abuses and dark dealings that MyS-TECH had indulged in over the years, and now she makes it her mission to put things right. She is aided in this quest by a strange encounter with Darkangel, the Angel of Death. He cloaks her in a costume made from the very fabric of the universe, a costume which adds greatly to her own mystical powers. Shevaun Haldane thus became Hell's Angel — an otherworldly avenger and MyS-TECH's worst nightmare.

With issue #6, the series changed names to Dark Angel, in response to a lawsuit brought against Marvel by the Hell's Angels motorcycle club.

1 ❑ Jul 1993 Cover: 1.75 **NM** value: **Cover or less**
Circ: CapCity orders: **24,700**

2 ❑ Aug 1993 Cover: 1.75 **NM** value: **Cover or less**
Circ: CapCity orders: **19,700**

3 ❑ Sep 1993 Cover: 1.75 **NM** value: **Cover or less**
Circ: CapCity orders: **15,700**

4 ❑ Oct 1993 Cover: 1.75 **NM** value: **Cover or less**
Circ: CapCity orders: **23,300**

5 ❑ Nov 1993 Cover: 1.75 **NM** value: **Cover or less**
Circ: CapCity orders: **21,900**
• Series continued as Dark Angel #6★ Appearance of X-Men.

6 ❑ Dec 1993 Cover: 1.75 **NM** value: **Cover or less**
Circ: CapCity orders: **18,400**

HELLSHOCK — Image

1 ❑ Jan 1997 Cover: 2.95 **NM** value: **Cover or less**
Circ: Diamd. preorders: **55,962**
📖 A Kairos Moment **A:** Jose Villarubia **W:** Jae Lee

1/A ❑ Jan 1997 Cover: 2.95 **NM** value: **Cover or less**
📖 A Kairos Moment

2 ❑ Feb 1997 Cover: 2.50 **NM** value: **2.95**
Circ: Diamd. preorders: **35,138**
📖 The Milk of Paradise **A:** Jose Villarubia **W:** Jae Lee

3 ❑ Mar 1997 Cover: 2.50 **NM** value: **2.95**
Circ: Diamd. preorders: **33,145**
📖 The Science of Faith **A:** Jose Villarubia **W:** Jae Lee

CGC-graded: Multiply prices above by **33 for 9.9 M • 16 for 9.8 NM/M • 7 for 9.6 NM+ • 5 for 9.4 NM • 2.5 for 9.2 NM- • 1.5 for 9.0 VF/NM**

4 ❑ Cover: 2.95 NM value: Cover or less
Circ: Diamd. preorders: 32,363
• Never published?
5 ❑ Cover: 2.95 NM value: Cover or less
Circ: Diamd. preorders: 31,259
• Never published?
6 ❑ Cover: 2.95 NM value: Cover or less
Circ: Diamd. preorders: 30,370
• Never published?
7 ❑ Cover: 3.95 NM value: Cover or less
Circ: Diamd. preorders: 29,208
• Never published?

HELLSHOCK (MINI-SERIES) Image

1 ❑ Jul 1994 Cover: 1.95 NM value: 2.00
Circ: CapCity orders: 57,800
📖 The Sign Of The Cross, Part 1 A: Jose Villarubia; Jae Lee W: Jae Lee
2 ❑ Aug 1994 Cover: 1.95 NM value: 2.00
Circ: CapCity orders: 43,725
3 ❑ Oct 1994 Cover: 1.95 NM value: 2.00
Circ: CapCity orders: 41,700
📖 Falling Angel A: Jose Villarubia; Jae Lee W: Jae Lee ★ Origin of Hellshock.
4 ❑ Cover: 1.95 NM value: 2.00
Circ: CapCity orders: 40,250
4/A ❑ Nov 1994 Cover: 1.95 NM value: 2.00
variant cover. A: Jae Lee W: Jae Lee
4/B ❑ Nov 1994 Cover: 1.95 NM value: Cover or less
Ash 1❑ NM value: 1.00
• ashcan

HELLSPAWN Image

1 ❑ Aug 2000 Cover: 2.50 NM value: Cover or less
Circ: Diamd. preorders: 46,735 • CGC: 3 graded, best 9.6
📖 The Clown, Part 1 A: Ashley Wood W: Brian Michael Bendis
2 ❑ Sep 2000 Cover: 2.50 NM value: Cover or less
Circ: Diamd. preorders: 36,032
📖 The Clown, Part 2 A: Ashley Wood W: Brian Michael Bendis
3 ❑ Oct 2000 Cover: 2.50 NM value: Cover or less
Circ: Diamd. preorders: 33,610
📖 Hate Me A: Ashley Wood W: Brian Michael Bendis
4 ❑ Nov 2000 Cover: 2.50 NM value: Cover or less
Circ: Diamd. preorders: 31,428
📖 Hate You A: Ashley Wood W: Brian Michael Bendis
5 ❑ Jan 2001 Cover: 2.50 NM value: Cover or less
Circ: Diamd. preorders: 28,058
📖 Selling Fear A: Ashley Wood W: Brian Michael Bendis
6 ❑ Feb 2001 Cover: 2.50 NM value: Cover or less
Circ: Diamd. preorders: 25,589 • CGC: 6 graded, best 9.8
📖 The Big Leagues A: Ashley Wood W: Brian Michael Bendis
7 ❑ Apr 2001 Cover: 2.50 NM value: Cover or less
Circ: Diamd. preorders: 23,957
📖 Shed A: Ashley Wood; Todd McFarlane W: Steve Niles
8 ❑ May 2001 Cover: 2.50 NM value: Cover or less
Circ: Diamd. preorders: 21,189
9 ❑ Jun 2001 Cover: 2.50 NM value: Cover or less
Circ: Diamd. preorders: 19,992
10 ❑ Jul 2001 Cover: 2.50 NM value: Cover or less
Circ: Diamd. preorders: 18,931
11 ❑ Aug 2001 Cover: 2.50 NM value: Cover or less
Circ: Diamd. preorders: 18,482
12 ❑ Sep 2001 Cover: 2.50 NM value: Cover or less
Circ: Diamd. preorders: 18,825

HELLSPOCK Express / Parody

1 ❑ b&w Cover: 2.95 NM value: Cover or less
One-shot.

HELLSTALKER Rebel Creations

1 ❑ Cover: 2.25 NM value: Cover or less
2 ❑ Jul 1989 Cover: 2.25 NM value: Cover or less
📖 Tricks of The Trade A: Kevin Rasel W: Aheron

HELLSTORM: PRINCE OF LIES Marvel

Daimon Hellstrom, the Son of Satan, appeared for the first time in Ghost Rider (Vol. 1) #1. Born of the Devil himself, he eventually exorcised the source of blackness within him — his Darksoul — and became a member of the Defenders. In time he settled down, marrying fellow Defender Patsy Walker (Hellcat). However, without his Darksoul, his life began to fail him. In desperation Patsy called upon his dread father to restore it to him, for without his Darksoul, Daimon's good half could not survive. Although that decision saved Daimon's life, it cost Patsy dearly. Moreover, the person who rose from the pentagram that night was no longer her husband...he was now once more the Son of Satan.

It's in this grim form that Daimon appears in this title. Borrowing from a misspelling, he is now Hellstorm, an appropriate name for a force of such dark fury.

1 ❑ Apr 1993 Cover: 2.95 NM value: Cover or less
Circ: CapCity orders: 122,300 • CGC: 1 graded, best 9.8
parchment cover. 📖 Storm Clouds A: Michael Bair W: Rafael Nieves
2 ❑ May 1993 Cover: 2.00 NM value: Cover or less
Circ: CapCity orders: 49,300
3 ❑ Jun 1993 Cover: 2.00 NM value: Cover or less
Circ: CapCity orders: 38,600
📖 Paradise Lost A: Michael Bair W: Rafael Nieves
4 ❑ Jul 1993 Cover: 2.00 NM value: Cover or less
Circ: CapCity orders: 32,800
5 ❑ Aug 1993 Cover: 2.00 NM value: Cover or less
Circ: CapCity orders: 26,100
6 ❑ Sep 1993 Cover: 2.00 NM value: Cover or less
Circ: CapCity orders: 21,300
📖 Lisa A: Leonardo Manco; Michael Bair(cover) W: Rafael Nieves
7 ❑ Oct 1993 Cover: 2.00 NM value: Cover or less
Circ: CapCity orders: 18,400
8 ❑ Nov 1993 Cover: 2.00 NM value: Cover or less
Circ: CapCity orders: 16,600
9 ❑ Dec 1993 Cover: 2.00 NM value: Cover or less
Circ: CapCity orders: 14,500
10 ❑ Jan 1994 Cover: 2.00 NM value: Cover or less
Circ: CapCity orders: 13,300
11 ❑ Feb 1994 Cover: 2.00 NM value: Cover or less
Circ: CapCity orders: 11,400
12 ❑ Mar 1994 Cover: 2.00 NM value: Cover or less
Circ: CapCity orders: 10,250
13 ❑ Apr 1994 Cover: 2.00 NM value: Cover or less
Circ: CapCity orders: 9,300
14 ❑ May 1994 Cover: 2.00 NM value: Cover or less
Circ: CapCity orders: 8,900 • CGC: 1 graded, best 9.4
15 ❑ Jun 1994 Cover: 2.00 NM value: Cover or less
Circ: CapCity orders: 9,300
16 ❑ Jul 1994 Cover: 2.00 NM value: Cover or less
Circ: CapCity orders: 8,150
17 ❑ Aug 1994 Cover: 2.00 NM value: Cover or less
Circ: CapCity orders: 7,650
18 ❑ Sep 1994 Cover: 2.00 NM value: Cover or less
Circ: CapCity orders: 7,300
19 ❑ Oct 1994 Cover: 2.00 NM value: Cover or less
Circ: CapCity orders: 7,000
20 ❑ Nov 1994 Cover: 2.00 NM value: Cover or less
Circ: CapCity orders: 6,800
21 ❑ Dec 1994 Cover: 2.00 NM value: Cover or less
Circ: CapCity orders: 6,850
final issue.

HELM PREMIERE Helm

1 ❑ Mar 1995, b&w Cover: 2.95 NM value: Cover or less
• Preview edition.

HELSING Caliber

1 ❑ b&w Cover: 2.95 NM value: Cover or less
Circ: Diamd. preorders: 3,039
1/A ❑ Cover: 2.95 NM value: Cover or less
Cover has woman in black standing. A: Chris Wozniak
2 ❑ b&w Cover: 2.95 NM value: Cover or less

HELTER SKELTER Antarctic

0 ❑ May 1997, b&w Cover: 2.95 NM value: Cover or less
1 ❑ Jun 1997, b&w Cover: 2.95 NM value: Cover or less
2 ❑ Sep 1997, b&w Cover: 2.95 NM value: Cover or less
3 ❑ Nov 1997, b&w Cover: 2.95 NM value: Cover or less
4 ❑ Dec 1997, b&w Cover: 2.95 NM value: Cover or less
5 ❑ Jan 1998, b&w Cover: 2.95 NM value: Cover or less

HELYUN: BONES OF THE BACKWOODS Slave Labor

1 ❑ Nov 1991, b&w Cover: 2.95 NM value: Cover or less

HELYUN BOOK 1 Slave Labor

1 ❑ Aug 1990, b&w Cover: 6.95 NM value: Cover or less
No issue number.

HE-MAN Toby

1 ❑ May 1954 Cover: 0.10 NM value: 100.00
2 ❑ Jul 1954 Cover: 0.10 NM value: 75.00
• CGC: 1 graded, best 8.0

HEMBECK Fantaco

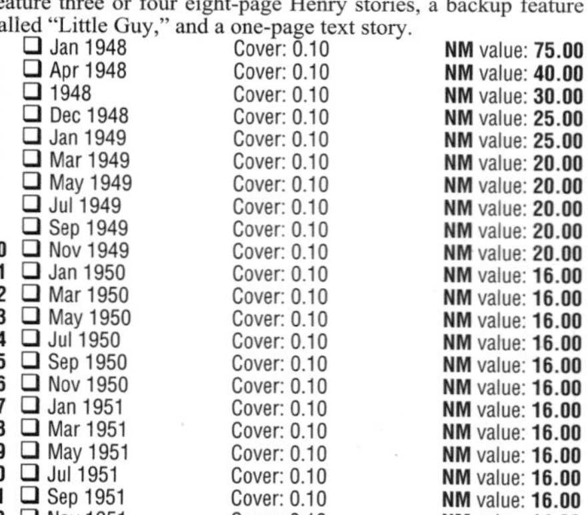

Fred Hembeck, whose Dateline @#&% cartoons had been seen in the precursor to Comics Buyer's Guide, The Buyer's Guide to Comic Fandom in the 1970s and early 1980s, collected them in Hembeck #1 for Fantaco. While harder to read at this smaller size, the zany interviews conducted by Cartoon Fred with Marvel, DC, and other companies' characters are knee-slappers for those in the know. Better still are the original extended stories written for this series taking place in a world where characters from different companies — as well as real-life figures — interact. (Doctor Octopus arrives on scene with eight pies in search of Soupy Sales, for example.

The attention from CBG and this series led to freelance work for Marvel. Hembeck restarted Dateline in Comics Buyer's Guide in the late 1990s, sending up a new generation of comic books. — JJM

1 ❑ Cover: 2.50 NM value: Cover or less
• Best of Dateline: @!!?#
2 ❑ Feb 1980 Cover: 2.50 NM value: Cover or less
📖 Hembeck 1980 or The Son of the Best of Dateline: @!!?# A: Fred Hembeck
3 ❑ Jun 1980 Cover: 1.25 NM value: 1.50
📖 Abbott & Costello Meet Bride of Hembeck
4 ❑ Nov 1980 Cover: 1.25 NM value: 1.50
📖 Bah Hembeck!
5 ❑ Feb 1981 Cover: 2.50 NM value: Cover or less
📖 Hembeck File A: Fred Hembeck
6 ❑ Sep 1981 Cover: 2.25 NM value: Cover or less
cardstock cover. • Jimmy Olsen's Pal
7 ❑ Jan 1983 Cover: 1.95 NM value: Cover or less
• Dial H for Hembeck

HEMP FOR VICTORY Starhead

1 ❑ Sep 1993, b&w Cover: 2.50 NM value: Cover or less
• based on 1943 USDA film A: Art Penn W: Art Penn

HENRY ALDRICH Dell

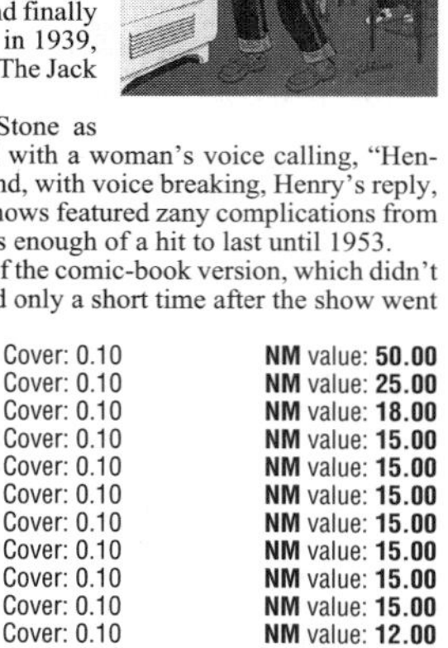

In Pep Comics #22 (Dec 41), Archie Andrews made his first appearance. The teen humor feature became a universe that eventually supported the entire comic-book company from which he came. However, such teen comedy did not begin with Archie Andrews. Andy Hardy was introduced in the 1937 feature film A Family Affair, and The Aldrich Family, initially a segment of The Rudy Vallee Show, introduced Henry Aldrich and finally got its own half-hour spot in 1939, a summer replacement for The Jack Benny Program.

Initially starring Ezra Stone as Henry, each show opened with a woman's voice calling, "Henreeeee! Henry Aldrich!" and, with voice breaking, Henry's reply, "Coming, Mother!" The shows featured zany complications from simple beginnings and was enough of a hit to last until 1953.

The same can't be said of the comic-book version, which didn't begin until 1950 and lasted only a short time after the show went off the air. — Maggie

1 ❑ Aug 1950 Cover: 0.10 NM value: 50.00
2 ❑ Sep 1950 Cover: 0.10 NM value: 25.00
3 ❑ Oct 1950 Cover: 0.10 NM value: 18.00
4 ❑ Jan 1951 Cover: 0.10 NM value: 15.00
5 ❑ 1951 Cover: 0.10 NM value: 15.00
6 ❑ Jun 1951 Cover: 0.10 NM value: 15.00
7 ❑ Aug 1951 Cover: 0.10 NM value: 15.00
8 ❑ Oct 1951 Cover: 0.10 NM value: 15.00
9 ❑ Dec 1951 Cover: 0.10 NM value: 15.00
10 ❑ Feb 1952 Cover: 0.10 NM value: 15.00
11 ❑ Apr 1952 Cover: 0.10 NM value: 12.00
12 ❑ Jun 1952 Cover: 0.10 NM value: 12.00
13 ❑ Aug 1952 Cover: 0.10 NM value: 12.00
14 ❑ Oct 1952 Cover: 0.10 NM value: 12.00
15 ❑ Dec 1952 Cover: 0.10 NM value: 12.00
16 ❑ Mar 1953 Cover: 0.10 NM value: 12.00
📖 The Card Party Catastrophe (Text Story); Henry Aldrich; Homer A: Bill Williams W: Bill Williams
17 ❑ Jun 1953 Cover: 0.10 NM value: 12.00
18 ❑ Sep 1953 Cover: 0.10 NM value: 12.00
19 ❑ Dec 1953 Cover: 0.10 NM value: 12.00
20 ❑ Mar 1954 Cover: 0.10 NM value: 12.00
21 ❑ Jun 1954 Cover: 0.10 NM value: 12.00
22 ❑ Sep 1954 Cover: 0.10 NM value: 12.00

HENRY (CARL ANDERSON'S...) Dell

Carl Anderson's Henry, familiar to Sunday newspaper readers the world over, enjoyed a run of comic-book popularity during the 1950s. After a few trial appearances in Dell's Four Color Comics, Henry got his own series which allowed longer, fuller stories than the simple half-page gag strips that ran in the newspapers.

Henry is a normal kid about 12 years old, with a distinctive bald, bulbous head, and a naive charm due to his simply drawn, blank features. He has a knack for getting in trouble with teachers, parents, neighbors, girlfriends, and the neighborhood bully, but always manages to get the best of the situation. Henry comics generally feature three or four eight-page Henry stories, a backup feature called "Little Guy," and a one-page text story.

1 ❑ Jan 1948 Cover: 0.10 NM value: 75.00
2 ❑ Apr 1948 Cover: 0.10 NM value: 40.00
3 ❑ 1948 Cover: 0.10 NM value: 30.00
4 ❑ Dec 1948 Cover: 0.10 NM value: 25.00
5 ❑ Jan 1949 Cover: 0.10 NM value: 25.00
6 ❑ Mar 1949 Cover: 0.10 NM value: 20.00
7 ❑ May 1949 Cover: 0.10 NM value: 20.00
8 ❑ Jul 1949 Cover: 0.10 NM value: 20.00
9 ❑ Sep 1949 Cover: 0.10 NM value: 20.00
10 ❑ Nov 1949 Cover: 0.10 NM value: 20.00
11 ❑ Jan 1950 Cover: 0.10 NM value: 16.00
12 ❑ Mar 1950 Cover: 0.10 NM value: 16.00
13 ❑ May 1950 Cover: 0.10 NM value: 16.00
14 ❑ Jul 1950 Cover: 0.10 NM value: 16.00
15 ❑ Sep 1950 Cover: 0.10 NM value: 16.00
16 ❑ Nov 1950 Cover: 0.10 NM value: 16.00
17 ❑ Jan 1951 Cover: 0.10 NM value: 16.00
18 ❑ Mar 1951 Cover: 0.10 NM value: 16.00
19 ❑ May 1951 Cover: 0.10 NM value: 16.00
20 ❑ Jul 1951 Cover: 0.10 NM value: 16.00
21 ❑ Sep 1951 Cover: 0.10 NM value: 16.00
22 ❑ Nov 1951 Cover: 0.10 NM value: 14.00
23 ❑ Jan 1952 Cover: 0.10 NM value: 14.00
24 ❑ Mar 1952 Cover: 0.10 NM value: 14.00
25 ❑ May 1952 Cover: 0.10 NM value: 14.00
26 ❑ Jul 1952 Cover: 0.10 NM value: 14.00
27 ❑ Sep 1952 Cover: 0.10 NM value: 14.00
28 ❑ Nov 1952 Cover: 0.10 NM value: 14.00
29 ❑ Jan 1953 Cover: 0.10 NM value: 14.00
30 ❑ Mar 1953 Cover: 0.10 NM value: 14.00
31 ❑ May 1953 Cover: 0.10 NM value: 10.00
32 ❑ Jul 1953 Cover: 0.10 NM value: 10.00
33 ❑ Sep 1953 Cover: 0.10 NM value: 10.00
34 ❑ Nov 1953 Cover: 0.10 NM value: 10.00

Other grades: Multiply prices above by **1.5 for Mint • 2/3 for Very Fine • 1/3 for Fine • 1/5 for Very Good • 1/8 for Good**

35 ❑ Jan 1954 Cover: 0.10 **NM** value: **10.00**
36 ❑ Mar 1954 Cover: 0.10 **NM** value: **10.00**
37 ❑ May 1954 Cover: 0.10 **NM** value: **10.00**
38 ❑ Jul 1954 Cover: 0.10 **NM** value: **10.00**
39 ❑ Sep 1954 Cover: 0.10 **NM** value: **10.00**
40 ❑ Nov 1954 Cover: 0.10 **NM** value: **10.00**
41 ❑ Jan 1955 Cover: 0.10 **NM** value: **9.00**
42 ❑ Apr 1955 Cover: 0.10 **NM** value: **9.00**
43 ❑ Jul 1955 Cover: 0.10 **NM** value: **9.00**
44 ❑ Oct 1955 Cover: 0.10 **NM** value: **9.00**
45 ❑ Jan 1956 Cover: 0.10 **NM** value: **9.00**
46 ❑ Apr 1956 Cover: 0.10 **NM** value: **9.00**
47 ❑ Jul 1956 Cover: 0.10 **NM** value: **9.00**
48 ❑ Oct 1956 Cover: 0.10 **NM** value: **9.00**
49 ❑ Jan 1957 Cover: 0.10 **NM** value: **9.00**
50 ❑ Apr 1957 Cover: 0.10 **NM** value: **9.00**
51 ❑ Jul 1957 Cover: 0.10 **NM** value: **7.00**
52 ❑ Oct 1957 Cover: 0.10 **NM** value: **7.00**
53 ❑ 1958 Cover: 0.10 **NM** value: **7.00**
54 ❑ 1958 Cover: 0.10 **NM** value: **7.00**
55 ❑ 1958 Cover: 0.10 **NM** value: **7.00**
56 ❑ Cover: 0.10 **NM** value: **7.00**
57 ❑ 1959 Cover: 0.10 **NM** value: **7.00**
58 ❑ 1959 Cover: 0.10 **NM** value: **7.00**
59 ❑ 1959 Cover: 0.10 **NM** value: **7.00**
60 ❑ Jan 1960 Cover: 0.10 **NM** value: **7.00**
61 ❑ Apr 1960 Cover: 0.10 **NM** value: **7.00**
62 ❑ Jul 1960 Cover: 0.10 **NM** value: **7.00**
🕮 The Bouncing Meat Ball!; The False Alarm; A Midsummer Day's Steam!; The Doghouse Gang **A:** Carl Anderson **W:** Carl Anderson
63 ❑ Oct 1960 Cover: 0.10 **NM** value: **7.00**
64 ❑ Jan 1961 Cover: 0.10 **NM** value: **7.00**
65 ❑ Apr 1961 Cover: 0.10 **NM** value: **7.00**

HENRY V — Caliber / Tome

1 ❑ b&w Cover: 2.95 **NM** value: **Cover or less**

HEPCATS — Double Diamond

Martin Wagner originally drew for his college newspaper, The Daily Texan. Started as a funny animals humor strip, the characters of Hepcats have grown and evolved into serious characters.

This later incarnation of Hepcats centered around Erika, an exotic dancer, and Arnie, her harried boyfriend and sometime club DJ. Through their cartoon world, Wagner confronted difficult issues such as domestic violence, child abuse, and the problems of modern relationships.

In the midst of the storyline, Wagner abruptly disappeared, leaving fans to wonder what would have happened next to the characters.

1 ❑ May 1989 Cover: 2.00 **NM** value: **10.00**
• **CGC:** 1 graded, best 9.6
🕮 Joey Gunther **A:** Martin Wagner **W:** Martin Wagner
1/LE❑ Cover: 2.00 **NM** value: **6.00**
• Special edition with new material. **A:** Martin Wagner **W:** Martin Wagner
2 ❑ Jul 1989 Cover: 2.00 **NM** value: **6.00**
2/LE❑ Cover: 2.00 **NM** value: **4.00**
• Special edition with new material. **A:** Martin Wagner **W:** Martin Wagner
3 ❑ Aug 1989 Cover: 2.00 **NM** value: **5.00**
🕮 Snowblind, Part 1 **A:** Martin Wagner **W:** Martin Wagner
4 ❑ Nov 1989 Cover: 2.00 **NM** value: **4.00**
🕮 Snowblind, Part 2 **A:** Martin Wagner **W:** Martin Wagner
5 ❑ Feb 1989 Cover: 2.00 **NM** value: **4.00**
🕮 Snowblind, Part 3 **A:** Martin Wagner **W:** Martin Wagner
6 ❑ Cover: 2.25 **NM** value: **4.00**
🕮 Snowblind, Part 4 **A:** Martin Wagner **W:** Martin Wagner
7 ❑ Cover: 2.25 **NM** value: **4.00**
🕮 Snowblind, Part 5 **A:** Martin Wagner **W:** Martin Wagner
8 ❑ Cover: 2.25 **NM** value: **4.00**
🕮 Snowblind, Part 6 **A:** Martin Wagner **W:** Martin Wagner
9 ❑ Cover: 2.25 **NM** value: **3.00**
🕮 Snowblind, Part 7 **A:** Martin Wagner **W:** Martin Wagner
10 ❑ Cover: 2.50 **NM** value: **3.00**
🕮 Snowblind, Part 8 **A:** Martin Wagner **W:** Martin Wagner
11 ❑ Jan 1994 Cover: 2.50 **NM** value: **3.00**
🕮 Snowblind, Part 9 **A:** Martin Wagner **W:** Martin Wagner
12 ❑ Jul 1994 Cover: 2.50 **NM** value: **3.00**
🕮 Snowblind, Part 10 **A:** Martin Wagner **W:** Martin Wagner
13 ❑ Cover: 2.50 **NM** value: **3.00**
14 ❑ Cover: 2.50 **NM** value: **Cover or less**
Bk 1❑ Cover: 9.95 **NM** value: **Cover or less**
• Collects college strips from Daily Texan, Cougar **A:** Martin Wagner **W:** Martin Wagner
Bk 1-2❑ Cover: 14.95 **NM** value: **Cover or less**
SE 1❑ Cover: 2.00 **NM** value: **4.00**
SE 2❑ Cover: 2.00 **NM** value: **4.00**

HEPCATS (ANTARCTIC) — Antarctic

0 ❑ Nov 1996 Cover: 2.95 **NM** value: **4.00**
🕮 Friday **A:** Martin Wagner **W:** Martin Wagner
0/A ❑ Cover: 5.95 **NM** value: **Cover or less**
• Comics Cavalcade Commemorative Edition. 🕮 Saturday **A:** Martin Wagner **W:** Martin Wagner
0/Dlx❑Nov 1996 Cover: 9.95 **NM** value: **Cover or less**
• Radio Hepcats edition. • polybagged with compact disc
1 ❑ Dec 1996 Cover: 2.95 **NM** value: **3.50**
Circ: Diamd. preorders: **5,389**
2 ❑ Jan 1997 Cover: 2.95 **NM** value: **3.50**
Circ: Diamd. preorders: **5,032**
🕮 Trial by Intimacy **A:** Martin Wagner **W:** Martin Wagner
3 ❑ Feb 1997 Cover: 2.95 **NM** value: **3.00**
Circ: Diamd. preorders: **4,764**
🕮 Snowblind, Part 1 **A:** Martin Wagner **W:** Martin Wagner
4 ❑ Mar 1997 Cover: 2.95 **NM** value: **3.00**
Circ: Diamd. preorders: **5,139**
🕮 Snowblind, Part 2 **A:** Martin Wagner **W:** Martin Wagner
5 ❑ Apr 1997 Cover: 2.95 **NM** value: **3.00**
Circ: Diamd. preorders: **5,259**
🕮 Snowblind, Part 3 **A:** Martin Wagner **W:** Martin Wagner
6 ❑ Jan 1998 Cover: 2.95 **NM** value: **Cover or less**
Circ: Diamd. preorders: **4,839**
🕮 Snowblind, Part 4 **A:** Martin Wagner **W:** Martin Wagner
7 ❑ Mar 1998 Cover: 2.95 **NM** value: **Cover or less**
Circ: Diamd. preorders: **4,778**
🕮 Snowblind, Part 5 **A:** Martin Wagner **W:** Martin Wagner
8 ❑ Cover: 2.95 **NM** value: **Cover or less**
Circ: Diamd. preorders: **4,328**
🕮 Snowblind, Part 6 **A:** Martin Wagner **W:** Martin Wagner
9 ❑ Apr 1998 Cover: 2.95 **NM** value: **Cover or less**
🕮 Snowblind, Part 7 **A:** Martin Wagner **W:** Martin Wagner
10 ❑ May 1998 Cover: 2.95 **NM** value: **Cover or less**
🕮 Snowblind, Part 8 **A:** Martin Wagner **W:** Martin Wagner
11 ❑ May 1998 Cover: 2.95 **NM** value: **Cover or less**
🕮 Snowblind, Part 9 **A:** Martin Wagner **W:** Martin Wagner
12 ❑ Jun 1998 Cover: 2.95 **NM** value: **Cover or less**
🕮 Snowblind, Part 10 **A:** Martin Wagner **W:** Martin Wagner

HERBIE (A+) — A-Plus

1 ❑ Cover: 2.50 **NM** value: **Cover or less**
🕮 Herbie And the Spirits!; Make Way For That Fat Fury; Da Shadano; I Saw It With My Own Eyes!; Christopher Columbus Popnecker!; • Reprints (including part of Herbie #8) **A:** Ogden Whitney **W:** Shane O'Shea ★ Origin of The Fat Fury.
2 ❑ Cover: 2.50 **NM** value: **Cover or less**
3 ❑ Cover: 2.50 **NM** value: **Cover or less**
🕮 Pirate Gold!; Herbie Claus is Coming to Town!; Cookie; Someone to Watch Over You! **A:** Ogden Whitney **W:** Shane O'Shea
4 ❑ Cover: 2.50 **NM** value: **Cover or less**
5 ❑ Cover: 2.50 **NM** value: **Cover or less**
6 ❑ Cover: 2.50 **NM** value: **Cover or less**

HERBIE (ACG) — American Comics Group

Herbie first appeared in Forbidden Worlds #73. Although he was a rotund boy with a strange way of speaking which omitted all prepositions, he also possessed incredible powers — some of which even he's unfamiliar with. Sitting around the house one day, he saw an ad for super-hero school and decided to start his challenging career as a Fully Licensed Super-Hero. Unfortunately, he was never really able to master the trick of swinging the bad guy around in mid-air, so he flunked out.

Undaunted, he decided to become a super-hero anyway, modified an oversized pair of pajamas, stuck a plunger on his head, and took on the identity of The Fat Fury. Armed with a collection of lollipops which impart special powers (including the "super bopper" for slugging villains and the "television-pop" for spying on them as if they were on TV), he was ready to take on evildoers.

Herbie's simplistic humor is part of its appeal, especially his catch-phrase, "You want I should bop you with this here lollipop?"

1 ❑ Apr 1964 Cover: 0.12 **NM** value: **100.00**
2 ❑ Jun 1964 Cover: 0.12 **NM** value: **65.00**
3 ❑ Aug 1964 Cover: 0.12 **NM** value: **50.00**
4 ❑ Sep 1964 Cover: 0.12 **NM** value: **50.00**
5 ❑ Oct 1964 Cover: 0.12 **NM** value: **50.00**
6 ❑ Dec 1964 Cover: 0.12 **NM** value: **38.00**
7 ❑ Feb 1965 Cover: 0.12 **NM** value: **38.00**
• **CGC:** 1 graded, best 6.5
8 ❑ Mar 1965 Cover: 0.12 **NM** value: **50.00**
• **CGC:** 1 graded, best 7.0
9 ❑ Apr 1965 Cover: 0.12 **NM** value: **38.00**
10 ❑ Jun 1965 Cover: 0.12 **NM** value: **38.00**
11 ❑ Aug 1965 Cover: 0.12 **NM** value: **30.00**
12 ❑ Sep 1965 Cover: 0.12 **NM** value: **30.00**
• Fat Fury story **A:** Ogden Whitney
13 ❑ Oct 1965 Cover: 0.12 **NM** value: **30.00**
🕮 Pirate Gold!; Mom's New Coat! **A:** Ogden Whitney **W:** Shane O'Shea
14 ❑ Dec 1965 Cover: 0.12 **NM** value: **30.00**
15 ❑ Feb 1966 Cover: 0.12 **NM** value: **30.00**
16 ❑ Mar 1966 Cover: 0.12 **NM** value: **30.00**
17 ❑ Apr 1966 Cover: 0.12 **NM** value: **30.00**
18 ❑ Jun 1966 Cover: 0.12 **NM** value: **30.00**
19 ❑ Aug 1966 Cover: 0.12 **NM** value: **30.00**
20 ❑ Sep 1966 Cover: 0.12 **NM** value: **30.00**
• Fat Fury vs. Dracula **A:** Ogden Whitney
21 ❑ Oct 1966 Cover: 0.12 **NM** value: **30.00**
22 ❑ Dec 1966 Cover: 0.12 **NM** value: **30.00**
• Fat Fury learns magic **A:** Ogden Whitney ★ Appearance of Charles de Gaulle, Queen Elizabeth, Ben Franklin.
23 ❑ Feb 1967 Cover: 0.12 **NM** value: **30.00**
final issue. **A:** Ogden Whitney

HERBIE (DARK HORSE) — Dark Horse

1 ❑ Oct 1992 Cover: 2.50 **NM** value: **Cover or less**
Circ: CapCity orders: **3,950**
🕮 The Most Beautiful Mom In The World; Make Way For That Fat Fury!; Professor Flipdome's Screwy Machine **A:** Ogden Whitney; John Byrne **W:** John Byrne
2 ❑ Nov 1992 Cover: 2.50 **NM** value: **Cover or less**
Circ: CapCity orders: **2,225**
final issue. • Series cancelled **A:** Ogden Whitney

HERCULES (CHARLTON) — Charlton

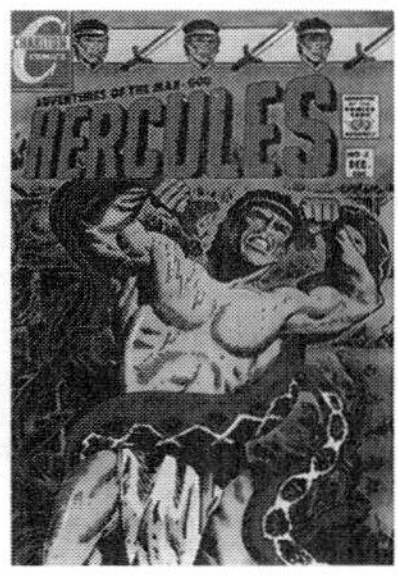

This Charlton title features the mythological Greek god Hercules and the 12 tasks he was commanded to perform to enter Olympus.

Hercules was the son of Zeus and a mortal woman, much to the resentment of Zeus' wife Hera. The art of the lead story was pencilled by Sam Glanzman, better known for his work on war comics.

A backup feature was Thane of Bagarth, a Prince Valiant/King Arthur-type story written by Steve Skeates and drawn by the up-and-coming Jim Aparo.

1 ❑ Oct 1967 Cover: 0.12 **NM** value: **12.00**
• **CGC:** 1 graded, best 9.4
🕮 Adventures of the Man-God; meeko the Microbe (text); Thane of Bagarth: The Feud • Thane of Bagarth by Steve Skeates and Jim Aparo
2 ❑ Dec 1967 Cover: 0.12 **NM** value: **7.00**
• **CGC:** 1 graded, best 9.6
🕮 When Man Meets Monster!; Thane of Bagarth: The Plot • Thane of Bagarth by Steve Skeates and Jim Aparo
3 ❑ Feb 1968 Cover: 0.12 **NM** value: **5.00**
• **CGC:** 1 graded, best 9.4
4 ❑ Jun 1968 Cover: 0.12 **NM** value: **5.00**
• **CGC:** 1 graded, best 9.2
5 ❑ Jul 1968 Cover: 0.12 **NM** value: **5.00**
• **CGC:** 1 graded, best 9.4
6 ❑ Sep 1968 Cover: 0.12 **NM** value: **4.00**
7 ❑ Nov 1968 Cover: 0.12 **NM** value: **4.00**
8 ❑ Dec 1968 Cover: 0.12 **NM** value: **4.00**
• **CGC:** 1 graded, best 8.5
🕮 The Boar; The Legend of Hercules; Thane of Bagarth • Thane of Bagarth by Steve Skeates and Jim Aparo **A:** Sam Glanzman; Jim Aparo **W:** Joe Gill; Steve Skeates
8/A ❑ Dec 1968 Cover: 0.35 **NM** value: **9.00**
• Magazine-sized issue. • Low distribution
9 ❑ Feb 1969 Cover: 0.12 **NM** value: **4.00**
10 ❑ Apr 1967 Cover: 0.12 **NM** value: **4.00**
11 ❑ 1967 Cover: 0.12 **NM** value: **4.00**
12 ❑ Jul 1967 Cover: 0.12 **NM** value: **4.00**
13 ❑ Oct 1967 Cover: 0.12 **NM** value: **4.00**
final issue.

HERCULES: HEART OF CHAOS — Marvel

1 ❑ Aug 1997 Cover: 2.50 **NM** value: **Cover or less**
Circ: Diamd. preorders: **24,249**
• gatefold summary. 🕮 Even an Immortal Can Die! **A:** Pat Oliffe **W:** Ron Frenz; Tom DeFalco
2 ❑ Sep 1997 Cover: 2.50 **NM** value: **Cover or less**
Circ: Diamd. preorders: **19,564**
• gatefold summary. **A:** Pat Oliffe **W:** Ron Frenz; Tom DeFalco
3 ❑ Oct 1997 Cover: 2.50 **NM** value: **Cover or less**
Circ: Diamd. preorders: **17,671**
• gatefold summary. **A:** Pat Oliffe **W:** Ron Frenz; Tom DeFalco

HERCULES: OFFICIAL COMICS MOVIE ADAPTATION — Acclaim

1 ❑ Cover: 4.50 **NM** value: **Cover or less**
No issue number. • digest. • adapts movie

HERCULES PRINCE OF POWER: FULL CIRCLE — Marvel

Bk 1❑ Cover: 6.95 **NM** value: **Cover or less**
Circ: CapCity orders: **6,900**

HERCULES PROJECT, THE — Monster

1 ❑ b&w Cover: 1.95 **NM** value: **Cover or less**
2 ❑ b&w Cover: 1.95 **NM** value: **Cover or less**
🕮 War **A:** Sean Wilkinson **W:** Sean Wilkinson

HERCULES: THE LEGENDARY JOURNEYS — Topps

1 ❑ Jun 1996 Cover: 2.95 **NM** value: **3.00**
wraparound cover. 🕮 The Trial of Hercules, Part 1 **A:** Jeff Butler **W:** Roy Thomas
2 ❑ Jul 1996 Cover: 2.95 **NM** value: **3.00**
🕮 The Trial of Hercules, Part 2 **A:** Jeff Butler **W:** Roy Thomas
3/A ❑ Aug 1996 Cover: 2.95 **NM** value: **4.00**
• **CGC:** 5 graded, best 9.8
art cover. ★ Appearance of Xena.
3/B ❑ Aug 1996 Cover: 2.95 **NM** value: **5.00**
• **CGC:** 3 graded, best 9.6
Photo cover. ★ Appearance of Xena.
3/GO❑Aug 1996 **NM** value: **5.00**
• **CGC:** 1 graded, best 9.0
Photo cover. • Gold logo variant **A:** Jeff Butler **W:** Roy Thomas ★ 1st Appearance of Xena.
4 ❑ Sep 1996 Cover: 2.95 **NM** value: **3.50**
Circ: Diamd. preorders: **13,952**
5 ❑ Oct 1996 Cover: 2.95 **NM** value: **3.50**
Circ: Diamd. preorders: **12,490**

HERCULES UNBOUND — DC

For a thousand years, Hercules has been bound by magic and chains on a hidden island off the coast of Greece. Then four weeks after World War III, he finds his spell suddenly broken. What new designs did Ares, who had bound him there, have planned for him now?

Within days, Hercules had his answer. The god of war was once again on the Earth, glorying in the destruction he has caused. Trapped by radioactive fallout, large numbers of men have become hideous monsters, and the only organized armies are being tricked into pointlessly slaughtering each other. Into this apocalyptic world steps Hercules, the greatest champion of mythology. But can even this legendary hero save a world gone mad?

The series is also notable for being one of Walter Simonson's early assignments.

1 ❑ Nov 1975 Cover: 0.25 **NM** value: **4.00**
• **CGC:** 5 graded, best 9.4
📖 Hercules Unbound! **A:** Wally Wood; Jose Luis Gacia **W:** Gerry Conway
2 ❑ Jan 1976 Cover: 0.25 **NM** value: **2.50**
3 ❑ Mar 1976 Cover: 0.25 **NM** value: **2.50**
4 ❑ May 1976 Cover: 0.30 **NM** value: **2.50**
5 ❑ Jul 1976 Cover: 0.30 **NM** value: **2.50**
6 ❑ Sep 1976 Cover: 0.30 **NM** value: **2.50**
7 ❑ Nov 1976 Cover: 0.30 **NM** value: **2.50**
8 ❑ Jan 1977 Cover: 0.30 **NM** value: **2.50**
9 ❑ Mar 1977 Cover: 0.30 **NM** value: **2.50**
10 ❑ May 1977 Cover: 0.30 **NM** value: **2.50**
11 ❑ Jul 1977 Cover: 0.35 **NM** value: **2.50**
12 ❑ Sep 1977 Cover: 0.35 **NM** value: **2.50**
final issue.

HERCULES (VOL. 1) — Marvel

Motivated by the popularity of Marvel Super-Heroes Contest of Champions, Marvel introduced several more in the summer of 1992. The first issue of Bob Layton's four-issue Hercules limited series released the same day as Chris Claremont and Frank Miller's acclaimed Wolverine limited series. Creatively, the two series couldn't be farther apart.

One major difference is that Hercules is laugh-out-loud funny. Layton takes the pompous mythological Avenger and banishes him from Olympus, sending him on a journey with a robot Recorder. The android proves a goofy foil for a godling who has never really been taken seriously since this series.

Layton would follow up Hercules with a much darker second series and a Marvel Graphic Novel inspired by events suggested in #2 of the first mini-series. — JJM

1 ❑ Sep 1982 Cover: 0.60 **NM** value: **1.50**
📖 What Fools These Immortals Be! **A:** Bob Layton **W:** Bob Layton
2 ❑ Oct 1982 Cover: 0.60 **NM** value: **1.50**
📖 For The Love Of Gods **A:** Bob Layton; Luke McDonnell **W:** Bob Layton
3 ❑ Nov 1982 Cover: 0.60 **NM** value: **1.50**
4 ❑ Dec 1982 Cover: 0.60 **NM** value: **1.50**
📖 -Not Just Another Galactus Story! **A:** Rick Parker; Bob Layton **W:** Bob Layton

HERCULES (VOL. 2) — Marvel

1 ❑ Mar 1984 Cover: 0.60 **NM** value: **1.50**
📖 My Love Is...Green? **A:** Bob Layton **W:** Bob Layton
2 ❑ Apr 1984 Cover: 0.60 **NM** value: **1.25**
📖 Red Wolf Stalks The Stars! **A:** Bob Layton **W:** Bob Layton
3 ❑ May 1984 Cover: 0.60 **NM** value: **1.25**
📖 Deadly Legacy **A:** Bob Layton **W:** Bob Layton
4 ❑ Jun 1984 Cover: 0.60 **NM** value: **1.25**
📖 A Pearl Of Great Price! **A:** Bob Layton **W:** Bob Layton

HERE COMES...DAREDEVIL — Marvel

Bk 1❑ Cover: 0.50 **NM** value: **3.00**
• Lancer

HERE COME THE BIG PEOPLE — Event

1 ❑ Sep 1997 Cover: 2.95 **NM** value: **Cover or less**
Circ: Diamd. preorders: **6,003**
1/A ❑ Sep 1997 Cover: 2.95 **NM** value: **Cover or less**
Alternate cover (large woman burping man). **A:** Amanda Conner; Jimmy Palmiotti(cover art) **W:** Trace Beaulieu

The CGC numbers printed in individual listings above represent the **number of copies examined** and given a **Universal** grade by CGC and the **best such copy** graded at press time. For current populations, watch for special ***Comics Buyer's Guide*** issues or check **www.cgccomics.com.**

HERE'S HOWIE — DC

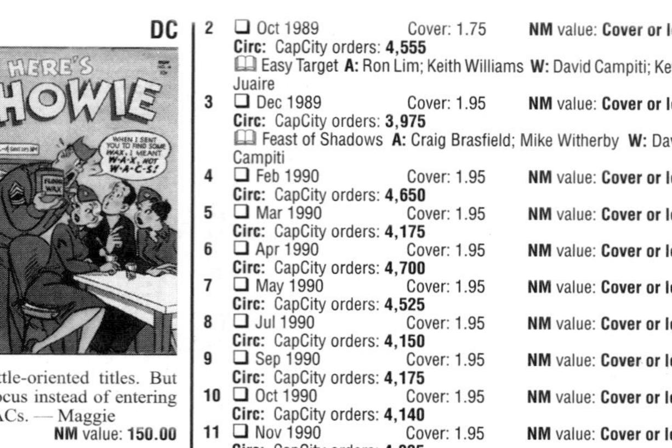

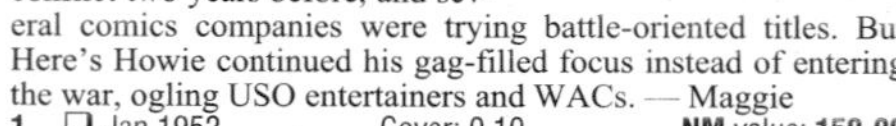

Here's Howie sounds like a typical teen gag comic book, with its focus on some version of the popular Andy Hardy, Henry Aldrich, Archie character. It certainly looks that way to begin with, the first issue featuring Howie in bed, counting pretty women (instead of sheep) jumping over a fence. He dated, he danced, he sported on the beach — all with gorgeous women. But with #5 (Sep 52), a line at the top of the cover reads, "He's in the Army now!" and, from that point on, the gag covers are Army-related. America had entered the Korean conflict two years before, and several comics companies were trying battle-oriented titles. But Here's Howie continued his gag-filled focus instead of entering the war, ogling USO entertainers and WACs. — Maggie

1 ❑ Jan 1952 Cover: 0.10 **NM** value: **150.00**
• **CGC:** 1 graded, best 8.0
2 ❑ Mar 1952 Cover: 0.10 **NM** value: **75.00**
3 ❑ May 1952 Cover: 0.10 **NM** value: **75.00**
4 ❑ Jul 1952 Cover: 0.10 **NM** value: **75.00**
5 ❑ Sep 1952 Cover: 0.10 **NM** value: **75.00**
6 ❑ Nov 1952 Cover: 0.10 **NM** value: **75.00**
7 ❑ Jan 1953 Cover: 0.10 **NM** value: **75.00**
8 ❑ Mar 1953 Cover: 0.10 **NM** value: **75.00**
9 ❑ May 1953 Cover: 0.10 **NM** value: **75.00**
10 ❑ Jul 1953 Cover: 0.10 **NM** value: **75.00**
11 ❑ Sep 1953 Cover: 0.10 **NM** value: **60.00**
12 ❑ Nov 1953 Cover: 0.10 **NM** value: **60.00**
13 ❑ Jan 1954 Cover: 0.10 **NM** value: **60.00**
14 ❑ Mar 1954 Cover: 0.10 **NM** value: **60.00**
15 ❑ May 1954 Cover: 0.10 **NM** value: **60.00**
16 ❑ Jul 1954 Cover: 0.10 **NM** value: **50.00**
17 ❑ Sep 1954 Cover: 0.10 **NM** value: **50.00**
18 ❑ Nov 1954 Cover: 0.10 **NM** value: **50.00**

HERETIC, THE — Dark Horse / Blanc Noir

1 ❑ Nov 1996 Cover: 2.95 **NM** value: **Cover or less**
Circ: Diamd. preorders: **12,959**
📖 Of Little Faith, Part 1 • Maximum Velocity back-up **A:** Joe Phillips **W:** Joe Phillips
2 ❑ Jan 1997 Cover: 2.95 **NM** value: **Cover or less**
Circ: Diamd. preorders: **9,431**
📖 Of Little Faith, Part 2; Maximum Velocity: Pursuit • Maximum Velocity back-up **A:** Brian Stelfreeze; Joe Phillips; Karl Story **W:** Brian Stelfreeze; Joe Phillips; Karl Story
3 ❑ Feb 1997 Cover: 2.95 **NM** value: **Cover or less**
Circ: Diamd. preorders: **8,136**
📖 Of Little Faith, Part 3; Maximum Velocity: Capture • Maximum Velocity back-up **A:** Brian Stelfreeze; Joe Phillips; Karl Story **W:** Brian Stelfreeze; Joe Phillips; Karl Story
4 ❑ Mar 1997 Cover: 2.95 **NM** value: **Cover or less**
Circ: Diamd. preorders: **7,871**
📖 Of Little Faith, Part 4 • Maximum Velocity back-up **A:** Joe Phillips **W:** Joe Phillips

HERETICS — Iguana / Blanc Noir

1 ❑ Nov 1993 Cover: 2.95 **NM** value: **Cover or less**
Circ: CapCity orders: **3,160**
• Foil-embossed logo **A:** Rosy Chun **W:** Thomas Herzen

HERMES VS. THE EYEBALL KID — Dark Horse

1 ❑ Dec 1994, b&w Cover: 2.95 **NM** value: **Cover or less**
2 ❑ Jan 1995, b&w Cover: 2.95 **NM** value: **Cover or less**
3 ❑ Feb 1995, b&w Cover: 2.95 **NM** value: **Cover or less**

HERO — Marvel

1 ❑ May 1990 Cover: 1.50 **NM** value: **Cover or less**
Circ: CapCity orders: **17,300**
📖 A Hero Is Born! **A:** Steve Purcell **W:** David Michelinie
2 ❑ Jun 1990 Cover: 1.50 **NM** value: **Cover or less**
Circ: CapCity orders: **11,800**
3 ❑ Jul 1990 Cover: 1.50 **NM** value: **Cover or less**
Circ: CapCity orders: **10,400**
📖 Essential Evil
4 ❑ Aug 1990 Cover: 1.50 **NM** value: **Cover or less**
Circ: CapCity orders: **8,100**
5 ❑ Sep 1990 Cover: 1.50 **NM** value: **Cover or less**
Circ: CapCity orders: **7,300**
6 ❑ Oct 1990 Cover: 1.50 **NM** value: **Cover or less**
Circ: CapCity orders: **6,900**

HERO ALLIANCE & JUSTICE MACHINE: IDENTITY CRISIS — Innovation

1 ❑ Oct 1990 Cover: 2.75 **NM** value: **Cover or less**
Circ: CapCity orders: **4,495**

HERO ALLIANCE: END OF THE GOLDEN AGE — Innovation

1 ❑ Jul 1989 Cover: 1.75 **NM** value: **Cover or less**
Circ: CapCity orders: **4,650**
2 ❑ Jul 1989 Cover: 1.75 **NM** value: **Cover or less**
3 ❑ Aug 1989 Cover: 1.75 **NM** value: **Cover or less**
Circ: CapCity orders: **1,975**

HERO ALLIANCE (INNOVATION) — Innovation

1 ❑ Sep 1989 Cover: 1.75 **NM** value: **Cover or less**
Circ: CapCity orders: **5,027**
📖 Easy Target **A:** Ron Lim; Keith Williams **W:** David Campiti; Kevin Juaire
2 ❑ Oct 1989 Cover: 1.75 **NM** value: **Cover or less**
Circ: CapCity orders: **4,555**
📖 Easy Target **A:** Ron Lim; Keith Williams **W:** David Campiti; Kevin Juaire
3 ❑ Dec 1989 Cover: 1.95 **NM** value: **Cover or less**
Circ: CapCity orders: **3,975**
📖 Feast of Shadows **A:** Craig Brasfield; Mike Witherby **W:** David Campiti
4 ❑ Feb 1990 Cover: 1.95 **NM** value: **Cover or less**
Circ: CapCity orders: **4,650**
5 ❑ Mar 1990 Cover: 1.95 **NM** value: **Cover or less**
Circ: CapCity orders: **4,175**
6 ❑ Apr 1990 Cover: 1.95 **NM** value: **Cover or less**
Circ: CapCity orders: **4,700**
7 ❑ May 1990 Cover: 1.95 **NM** value: **Cover or less**
Circ: CapCity orders: **4,525**
8 ❑ Jul 1990 Cover: 1.95 **NM** value: **Cover or less**
Circ: CapCity orders: **4,150**
9 ❑ Sep 1990 Cover: 1.95 **NM** value: **Cover or less**
Circ: CapCity orders: **4,175**
10 ❑ Oct 1990 Cover: 1.95 **NM** value: **Cover or less**
Circ: CapCity orders: **4,140**
11 ❑ Nov 1990 Cover: 1.95 **NM** value: **Cover or less**
Circ: CapCity orders: **4,335**
12 ❑ Dec 1990 Cover: 1.95 **NM** value: **Cover or less**
Circ: CapCity orders: **4,000**
13 ❑ Mar 1991 Cover: 1.95 **NM** value: **Cover or less**
Circ: CapCity orders: **3,705**
14 ❑ Apr 1991 Cover: 1.95 **NM** value: **Cover or less**
Circ: CapCity orders: **3,705**
15 ❑ May 1991 Cover: 1.95 **NM** value: **Cover or less**
Circ: CapCity orders: **3,480**
16 ❑ Jun 1991 Cover: 1.95 **NM** value: **Cover or less**
Circ: CapCity orders: **3,690**
17 ❑ Jul 1991 Cover: 2.50 **NM** value: **Cover or less**
Circ: CapCity orders: **3,650**
Anl 1❑Sep 1990 Cover: 2.75 **NM** value: **Cover or less**
Circ: CapCity orders: **4,460**
SE 1❑ Cover: 2.50 **NM** value: **Cover or less**
Circ: CapCity orders: **3,225**

HERO ALLIANCE QUARTERLY — Innovation

1 ❑ Sep 1991 Cover: 2.75 **NM** value: **Cover or less**
Circ: CapCity orders: **3,795**
2 ❑ Dec 1991 Cover: 2.75 **NM** value: **Cover or less**
Circ: CapCity orders: **3,370**
3 ❑ Mar 1992 Cover: 2.75 **NM** value: **Cover or less**
Circ: CapCity orders: **2,735**
📖 Child Endangerment **A:** J.H. Williams **W:** Robert Ingersoll
4 ❑ Cover: 2.75 **NM** value: **Cover or less**

HERO ALLIANCE (WONDER COLOR) — Wonder Color

Victor was a member of the Guardmen, a team of super-heroes who protected the land, and he was the favorite of the Golden Guardman, the team's leader. But when the group is wiped out in a terrible battle, Victor is the lone survivor struggling with remorse as he tries to rebuild the team. His passion for his leader's daughter only complicates matters, as does her brother, a murderer.

This series explores the aftermath of events in Hero Alliance: End of the Golden Age, and its stories connect with Hero Alliance Quarterly. It aims for a sophisticated approach to super-heroes, concentrating on their lives outside of the big battles. But its soap-opera feel and visuals may have turned off some readers, and the series — a rare color one in the black-and-white glut — ended after one issue.

Creator David Campiti went on to create Jade Warriors for Image, as well as establish Glass House Studios.

1 ❑ May 1987 Cover: 1.95 **NM** value: **Cover or less**
📖 But What Have You Done For Us Lately? **A:** Ron Lim **W:** David Campiti; Kevin Juaire

HERO BEAR AND THE KID — Astonish

1 ❑ 1999b&w and red Cover: 2.95 **NM** value: **Cover or less**
Circ: Diamd. preorders: **4,426**
📖 Small Beginnings
2 ❑ 2000b&w and red Cover: 2.95 **NM** value: **Cover or less**
Circ: Diamd. preorders: **5,148**
📖 Dreams

HEROES AGAINST HUNGER — DC

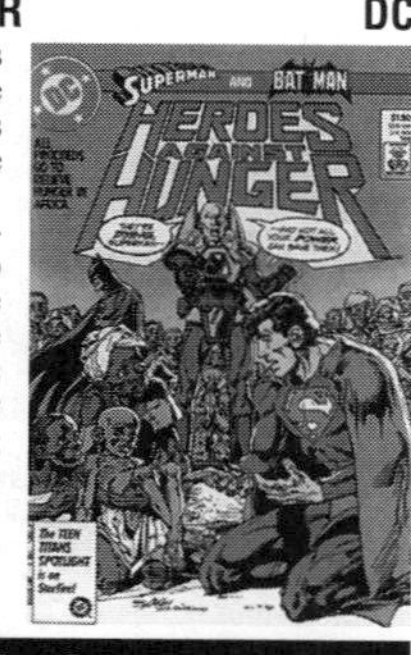

After Marvel released its Heroes for Hope, DC pulled together the best of its talent to put together its own benefit comic book to relieve hunger in Africa.

In the story, Superman and Batman are doing their best to help Ethiopia, but they're face-to-face with the allegorical Master. The Master finds his strength in places that once supported life but now have died. He would love nothing better than to play a tune and have Ethiopia turn to waste.

The two super-heroes have to turn to science in order to turn things

Other grades: Multiply prices above by **1.5 for Mint • 2/3 for Very Fine • 1/3 for Fine • 1/5 for Very Good • 1/8 for Good**

around, finding an unlikely, but excellent, ally in super-villain mastermind Lex Luthor. But even if they defeat the Master, can they save a country which has had its once-rich farmland destroyed by greed and neglect?

1 ❑ Aug 1986 Cover: 1.50 **NM** value: **3.00**
Circ: CapCity orders: **19,800** • **CGC:** 1 graded, best 9.6
📖 A Song Of Pain And Sorrow! • Charity benefit comic for Ethiopian famine victims **A:** Dave Gibbons; Carmine Infantino; Paris Cullins; Keith Giffen; Jan Duursema; George Pérez; Barry Windsor-Smith; Denys Cowan; Jack Kirby; Joe Kubert; Dan Jurgens; Ross Andru; Ernie Colon; Dave Ross; James Sherman; Marshall Rogers **W:** Jim Starlin; Paul Levitz; Len Wein; Roy Thomas; Bob Rozakis; Cary Bates; Doug Moench; Elliott S! Maggin; Gerry Conway; J.M. DeMatteis; Marv Wolfman; Michael Fleisher; Mike W. Barr; Robert Loren Fleming; Tony Isabella

HEROES (BLACKBIRD) Blackbird

1 ❑ **NM** value: **5.00**
2 ❑ Cover: 1.75 **NM** value: **Cover or less**
3 ❑ Cover: 1.75 **NM** value: **Cover or less**
4 ❑ Nov 1987 Cover: 2.00 **NM** value: **Cover or less**
5 ❑ Cover: 2.00 **NM** value: **Cover or less**
6 ❑ Cover: 2.00 **NM** value: **Cover or less**
Bk 1/LE❑ Cover: 4.95 **NM** value: **Cover or less**

HEROES FOR HIRE Marvel

1 ❑ Jul 1997 Cover: 2.99 **NM** value: **Cover or less**
Circ: Diamd. preorders: **50,466**
wraparound cover. 📖 Heroes and Villains • Hulk, Hercules, Iron Fist, Luke Cage, Black Knight, White Tiger **A:** Pascual Ferry **W:** Roger Stern; John Ostrander
2/A ❑ Aug 1997 Cover: 1.99 **NM** value: **Cover or less**
Circ: Diamd. preorders: **25,304**
• gatefold summary. • Jim Hammond (original Human Torch) joins team
2/B ❑ Aug 1997 Cover: 1.99 **NM** value: **Cover or less**
Circ: Diamd. preorders: **21,119**
alternate cover. • gatefold summary. • Jim Hammond (original Human Torch) joins team
3 ❑ Sep 1997 Cover: 1.99 **NM** value: **Cover or less**
Circ: Diamd. preorders: **35,780**
• gatefold summary.
4 ❑ Oct 1997 Cover: 1.99 **NM** value: **Cover or less**
Circ: Diamd. preorders: **37,994**
• gatefold summary. 📖 Controlled! **A:** Pascual Ferry **W:** John Ostrander ★ Versus Controller.
5 ❑ Nov 1997 Cover: 1.99 **NM** value: **Cover or less**
Circ: Diamd. preorders: **38,412**
• gatefold summary. ★ Appearance of Jane Foster, Sersi.
6 ❑ Dec 1997 Cover: 1.99 **NM** value: **Cover or less**
Circ: Diamd. preorders: **37,241**
• gatefold summary.
7 ❑ Jan 1998 Cover: 1.99 **NM** value: **Cover or less**
Circ: Diamd. preorders: **36,313**
• gatefold summary.
8 ❑ Feb 1998 Cover: 1.99 **NM** value: **Cover or less**
Circ: Diamd. preorders: **32,846**
• gatefold summary.
9 ❑ Mar 1998 Cover: 1.99 **NM** value: **Cover or less**
Circ: Diamd. preorders: **31,414**
• gatefold summary. ★ Appearance of Punisher.
10 ❑ Apr 1998 Cover: 1.99 **NM** value: **Cover or less**
Circ: Diamd. preorders: **30,197**
• gatefold summary.
11 ❑ May 1998 Cover: 1.99 **NM** value: **Cover or less**
Circ: Diamd. preorders: **30,209**
• gatefold summary. ★ Versus Wild Pack.
12 ❑ Jun 1998 Cover: 2.99 **NM** value: **Cover or less**
Circ: Diamd. preorders: **31,488**
• gatefold summary.
13 ❑ Jul 1998 Cover: 1.99 **NM** value: **Cover or less**
Circ: Diamd. preorders: **31,580**
• gatefold summary. • Ant-Man inside Hammond's body ★ Appearance of Brother Voodoo.
14 ❑ Aug 1998 Cover: 1.99 **NM** value: **Cover or less**
Circ: Diamd. preorders: **29,852**
• gatefold summary. • Black Knight vs. dragons
15 ❑ Sep 1998 Cover: 1.99 **NM** value: **Cover or less**
Circ: Diamd. preorders: **29,602**
• gatefold summary.
16 ❑ Oct 1998 Cover: 1.99 **NM** value: **Cover or less**
Circ: Diamd. preorders: **28,438**
• gatefold summary. 📖 The Siege of Wundagore, Part 3
17 ❑ Nov 1998 Cover: 1.99 **NM** value: **Cover or less**
Circ: Diamd. preorders: **27,055**
• gatefold summary. ★ Appearance of She-Hulk.
18 ❑ Dec 1998 Cover: 1.99 **NM** value: **Cover or less**
Circ: Diamd. preorders: **28,399**
• gatefold summary. ★ Appearance of Wolverine, Wolverine, Shang-Chi, Shang-Chi.
19 ❑ Jan 1999 Cover: 1.99 **NM** value: **Cover or less**
Circ: Diamd. preorders: **27,120**
• gatefold summary. final issue. ★ Appearance of Wolverine, Wolverine, Shang-Chi, Shang-Chi.
Anl 1998❑ Cover: 2.99 **NM** value: **Cover or less**
wraparound cover. • gatefold summary. 📖 The Siege of Wundagore, Part 5 • Heroes for Hire/Quicksilver '98

The prices seen above do not represent the highest possible prices seen in online auctions, but rather the prices we have seen these issues reliably fetch in a variety of environments (storefront retail, mail order, auction and convention).

HEROES FOR HOPE Marvel

The mid-1980s were a time of need for many, and the world responded with a number of benefit events, such as Live Aid and Farm Aid, and benefit recordings, such as "We Are the World." Eventually, benevolent intentions began to fade into the background of what became a fad of increasingly silly staged events. (Hands Across America, anyone?) But Marvel can be said to have reacted rather quickly in putting together its own charity edition for Ethiopian famine relief, well before such efforts began to appear driven by public relations rather than need.

Marvel brought in Steven King, Harlan Ellison, and many of its own top writers and artists to contribute portions of a story about the X-Men battling against the forces of disease and starvation on a fantasy plane. The issue is entertaining in its own right, as well as notable for its historical significance. — JJM

1 ❑ Dec 1985 Cover: 1.50 **NM** value: **5.00**
• **CGC:** 5 graded, best 9.6
• famine relief **A:** John Bolton; Richard Corben; Bernie Wrightson; Gray Morrow; John Buscema; John Byrne; Jackson Guice; John Romita Jr.; Steve Rude; Brian Bolland; Frank Miller; Brent Anderson; Bret Blevins; Michael W. Kaluta; Charles Vess **W:** Jim Shooter; Mike Grell; Bruce Jones; Louise Simonson; Mary Jo Duffy; Mike Baron; Stan Lee; Alan Moore; Archie Goodwin; Bill Mantlo; Chris Claremont; Denny O'Neil; George Martin; Harlan Ellison; Stephen King; Steve Englehart

HEROES FROM WORDSMITH Special Studio

1 ❑ b&w Cover: 2.50 **NM** value: **Cover or less**

HEROES INC. PRESENTS CANNON Wally Wood

1 ❑ ca. 1969 **NM** value: **10.00**
2 ❑ **NM** value: **10.00**

HEROES, INC. PRESENTS CANNON Armed Services

1 ❑ ca. 1969 Cover: 0.15 **NM** value: **12.00**
• **CGC:** 13 graded, best 9.8
No issue number. 📖 Cannon; The Misfits; Dragonella **A:** Wally Wood; Ralph Reese **W:** Wally Wood; Ralph Reese; Ron Whyte

HEROES (MILESTONE) DC / Milestone

1 ❑ May 1996 Cover: 2.50 **NM** value: **Cover or less**
2 ❑ Jun 1996 Cover: 2.50 **NM** value: **Cover or less**
📖 Home of the Heroes **A:** Chris Cross **W:** Matt Wayne ★ Versus Shadow Cabinet.
3 ❑ Jul 1996 Cover: 2.50 **NM** value: **Cover or less**
4 ❑ Aug 1996 Cover: 2.50 **NM** value: **Cover or less**
5 ❑ Sep 1996 Cover: 2.50 **NM** value: **Cover or less**
6 ❑ Nov 1996 Cover: 2.50 **NM** value: **Cover or less**
📖 All for Love or The World Well Lost **A:** Keith Pollard; Rodney Ramos; James Fry; Hector Collazo; Noelle C. Giddings; Rey Garcia; Rich Faber **W:** Matt Wayne
Bk 1/LE❑ Cover: 4.95 **NM** value: **Cover or less**

HEROES OF FAITH Coretoons

1 ❑ Jun 1992 Cover: 2.50 **NM** value: **Cover or less**

HEROES OF ROCK 'N FIRE Wonder Comix

1 ❑ Apr 1987 Cover: 1.95 **NM** value: **Cover or less**

HEROES REBORN Marvel

0.5 ❑ 1996 **NM** value: **3.00**
• **CGC:** 3 graded, best 9.8
📖 Faith • With certificate of authenticity **A:** Rob Liefeld; Dan Fraga **W:** Jeph Loeb

HEROES REBORN: ASHEMA Marvel

1 ❑ Jan 2000 Cover: 1.99 **NM** value: **Cover or less**

HEROES REBORN: DOOM Marvel

1 ❑ Jan 2000 Cover: 1.99 **NM** value: **Cover or less**

HEROES REBORN: DOOMSDAY Marvel

1 ❑ Jan 2000 Cover: 1.99 **NM** value: **Cover or less**
Circ: Diamd. preorders: **46,670**

HEROES REBORN: MASTERS OF EVIL Marvel

1 ❑ Feb 1999 Cover: 1.99 **NM** value: **Cover or less**
Circ: Diamd. preorders: **37,581**
📖 Battleship Downs **A:** Charles Adlard **W:** Joe Casey

HEROES REBORN MINI COMIC Marvel

1 ❑ **NM** value: **0.50**

HEROES REBORN: REBEL Marvel

1 ❑ Jan 2000 Cover: 1.99 **NM** value: **Cover or less**
Circ: Diamd. preorders: **36,628**
📖 Wild Blue **A:** Matt Haley **W:** Joe Kelly

HEROES REBORN: REMNANTS Marvel

1 ❑ Jan 2000 Cover: 1.99 **NM** value: **Cover or less**
Circ: Diamd. preorders: **37,120**
📖 The Day the Earth Got Ill! **A:** Ethan Van Sciver **W:** Joe Kelly

HEROES REBORN: THE RETURN Marvel

Faced with sagging sales on their core super-hero titles, Marvel Comics turned over the reins of Fantastic Four, The Avengers, Captain America, and Iron Man to Jim Lee, Rob Liefeld, and other one-time Marvel artists who had since left to form Image Comics. The result was "Heroes Reborn," a revamped Marvel universe that restarted the aforementioned titles at Vol. 2, #1, and updated origins for the characters to reflect modern-day sensibilities.

A little more than a year later (the length of the contracts with the new teams), Marvel undid the whole thing by "returning" the established heroes to their place in the mainstream Marvel universe. The other universe, it seems, was merely a pocket universe created by young Franklin Richards. Credit this series which gives us one of the great lines of dialogue: "Mom! Dad! They told me I gotta wipe out a universe...and I don't know which one...! Tell which one I should get ridda...and promise you won't be mad at me...?"

1 ❑ Dec 1997 Cover: 2.50 **NM** value: **Cover or less**
Circ: Diamd. preorders: **160,541**
1/SC❑ Dec 1997 Cover: 2.50 **NM** value: **4.00**
• **CGC:** 2 graded, best 9.6
Franklin Richards on cover. **A:** Salvador Larroca **W:** Peter David
2 ❑ Dec 1997 Cover: 2.50 **NM** value: **Cover or less**
Circ: Diamd. preorders: **145,583**
2/SC❑ Dec 1997 Cover: 2.50 **NM** value: **3.00**
Spider-Man/Hulk variant cover. **A:** Salvador Larroca **W:** Peter David
3 ❑ Dec 1997 Cover: 2.50 **NM** value: **Cover or less**
Circ: Diamd. preorders: **143,529**
3/SC❑ Dec 1997 Cover: 2.50 **NM** value: **3.00**
Iron Man variant cover. **A:** Salvador Larroca **W:** Peter David
4 ❑ Dec 1997 Cover: 2.50 **NM** value: **Cover or less**
Circ: Diamd. preorders: **144,137**
📖 Fourth & Goal **A:** Salvador Larroca **W:** Peter David
4/SC❑ Dec 1997 Cover: 2.50 **NM** value: **3.00**
Reed Richards variant cover. 📖 Fourth & Goal **A:** Salvador Larroca **W:** Peter David
Ash 1❑ Dec 1997 **NM** value: **1.00**
📖 Onslaught Update **A:** Rob Liefeld; Jim Lee **W:** Jim Krueger

HEROES REBORN: YOUNG ALLIES Marvel

1 ❑ Jan 2000 Cover: 1.99 **NM** value: **Cover or less**
Circ: Diamd. preorders: **37,450**

HERO FOR HIRE Marvel

Lucas is a small-time loser, sent to Seagate Prison for a crime he didn't commit. While there, a sadistic prison guard named Rackham makes it his business to make Lucas' life miserable. Lucas' one hope for salvation is to agree to take part in a risky cell-regeneration experiment conducted by Doc Burstein. The experiment proved fatal to all the previous subjects, but, if Lucas survives, he will be granted parole.

Lucas takes the gamble and is locked into a bio-bath full of strange chemicals. Rackham hates Lucas so much that he turns up the electricity flowing to the bio-bath, hoping to electrocute him. The power overloads, but, instead of killing Lucas, it gives him incredible power and steel-hard skin. He breaks out of his tank, then escapes to New York, where he sets up shop as Luke Cage, Hero for Hire. Later, he adopts the moniker Power Man and teams up with Iron Fist in a continuation of this, his first title.

1 ❑ Jun 1972 Cover: 0.20 **NM** value: **24.00**
• **CGC:** 19 graded, best 9.6
📖 Out of Hell...A Hero! **A:** George Tuska; John Romita **W:** Archie Goodwin ★ Origin of Power Man II (Luke Cage). ★ 1st Appearance of Diamondback, Power Man II (Luke Cage).
2 ❑ Aug 1972 Cover: 0.20 **NM** value: **12.00**
• **CGC:** 1 graded, best 9.8
3 ❑ Oct 1972 Cover: 0.20 **NM** value: **8.00**
4 ❑ Dec 1972 Cover: 0.20 **NM** value: **6.00**
5 ❑ Jan 1973 Cover: 0.20 **NM** value: **6.00**
6 ❑ Feb 1973 Cover: 0.20 **NM** value: **5.00**
7 ❑ Mar 1973 Cover: 0.20 **NM** value: **5.00**
8 ❑ Apr 1973 Cover: 0.20 **NM** value: **5.00**
• **CGC:** 1 graded, best 9.6
9 ❑ May 1973 Cover: 0.20 **NM** value: **5.00**
10 ❑ Jun 1973 Cover: 0.20 **NM** value: **5.00**
11 ❑ Jul 1973 Cover: 0.20 **NM** value: **4.00**
12 ❑ Aug 1973 Cover: 0.20 **NM** value: **4.00**
13 ❑ Sep 1973 Cover: 0.20 **NM** value: **4.00**
14 ❑ Oct 1973 Cover: 0.20 **NM** value: **4.00**
📖 Retribution! **A:** Billy Graham **W:** Billy Graham; Steve Englehart ★ Origin of Luke Cage. ★ Versus Big Ben.
15 ❑ Nov 1973 Cover: 0.20 **NM** value: **4.00**
• Sub-Mariner back-up
16 ❑ Dec 1973 Cover: 0.20 **NM** value: **4.00**
• series continues as Power Man ★ Origin of Stiletto. ★ Death of Rackham. ★ Versus Stiletto.

HERO GRAPHICS SUPER-SPECTACULAR Hero

1 ❑ Cover: 3.95 **NM** value: **Cover or less**

CGC-graded: Multiply prices above by **33 for 9.9 M** • **16 for 9.8 NM/M** • **7 for 9.6 NM+** • **5 for 9.4 NM** • **2.5 for 9.2 NM-** • **1.5 for 9.0 VF/NM**

front cover misprinted on back (front cover appeared on Southern Knights #35). • contents vary

HERO HOTLINE — DC

1 ❑ Apr 1989 Cover: 1.75 **NM** value: **2.00**
Circ: CapCity orders: **16,600**
2 ❑ May 1989 Cover: 1.75 **NM** value: **2.00**
Circ: CapCity orders: **12,300**
3 ❑ Jun 1989 Cover: 1.75 **NM** value: **2.00**
Circ: CapCity orders: **10,800**
4 ❑ Jul 1989 Cover: 1.75 **NM** value: **2.00**
Circ: CapCity orders: **8,850**
5 ❑ Aug 1989 Cover: 1.75 **NM** value: **2.00**
Circ: CapCity orders: **7,300**
6 ❑ Sep 1989 Cover: 1.75 **NM** value: **2.00**
Circ: CapCity orders: **6,550**

HEROIC — Lightning

1 ❑ Cover: 1.75 **NM** value: **Cover or less**

HEROIC 17 — Pennacle

1 ❑ Sep 1993 Cover: 2.95 **NM** value: **Cover or less**
📖 The Future Shock! **A:** Snook #85 **W:** Snook #85

HEROIC COMICS — Famous Funnies

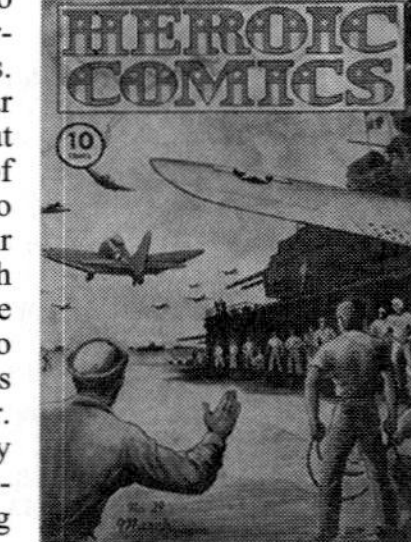

This title began as a super-hero comic book before switching formats to concentrate on war stories. Still, it was more than just a war comic book — this title was about real-life heroism. The majority of its stars were the actual soldiers who risked their lives in order save their comrades or who fought through hardships and injuries to win the day. Just as heroism isn't limited to combat, New Heroic Comics wasn't limited to covering the war. It also featured stories of everyday people who displayed extraordinary courage: running into burning buildings to save trapped people, car-crash victims who crawl up the sides of mountains in order to get help — even children who save their playmates' lives.

Covers carried the statement, "Herein are stories of truly heroic men and women chosen by this publication for their daring actions in hazardous tasks." This comic book was published during the 1950s, when many parents worried about the effect that comics might have on their children. Few parents would have quarreled with the timeless values that New Heroic Comics extolled.

1 ❑ Aug 1940 Cover: 0.10 **NM** value: **925.00**
• **CGC:** 4 graded, best 9.0
2 ❑ Oct 1940 Cover: 0.10 **NM** value: **475.00**
• **CGC:** 1 graded, best 7.5
3 ❑ Nov 1940 Cover: 0.10 **NM** value: **385.00**
4 ❑ Jan 1941 Cover: 0.10 **NM** value: **350.00**
5 ❑ Mar 1941 Cover: 0.10 **NM** value: **285.00**
• **CGC:** 1 graded, best 8.5
6 ❑ May 1941 Cover: 0.10 **NM** value: **285.00**
7 ❑ Jul 1941 Cover: 0.10 **NM** value: **300.00**
• **CGC:** 1 graded, best 9.0
8 ❑ Sep 1941 Cover: 0.10 **NM** value: **200.00**
• **CGC:** 1 graded, best 7.5
9 ❑ Nov 1941 Cover: 0.10 **NM** value: **200.00**
10 ❑ Jan 1942 Cover: 0.10 **NM** value: **200.00**
• **CGC:** 2 graded, best 9.4
11 ❑ Mar 1942 Cover: 0.10 **NM** value: **175.00**
12 ❑ May 1942 Cover: 0.10 **NM** value: **175.00**
13 ❑ Jul 1942 Cover: 0.10 **NM** value: **175.00**
• **CGC:** 1 graded, best 6.5
14 ❑ Sep 1942 Cover: 0.10 **NM** value: **200.00**
• **CGC:** 1 graded, best 9.4
15 ❑ Nov 1942 Cover: 0.10 **NM** value: **200.00**
• **CGC:** 2 graded, best 9.2
16 ❑ Jan 1943 Cover: 0.10 **NM** value: **120.00**
17 ❑ Mar 1943 Cover: 0.10 **NM** value: **120.00**
• **CGC:** 1 graded, best 9.2
18 ❑ May 1943 Cover: 0.10 **NM** value: **120.00**
• **CGC:** 1 graded, best 9.4
19 ❑ Jul 1943 Cover: 0.10 **NM** value: **120.00**
• **CGC:** 1 graded, best 7.0
20 ❑ Sep 1943 Cover: 0.10 **NM** value: **120.00**
• **CGC:** 2 graded, best 9.2
21 ❑ Nov 1943 Cover: 0.10 **NM** value: **85.00**
• **CGC:** 1 graded, best 8.5
22 ❑ Jan 1944 Cover: 0.10 **NM** value: **85.00**
23 ❑ Mar 1944 Cover: 0.10 **NM** value: **85.00**
• **CGC:** 1 graded, best 8.0
24 ❑ May 1944 Cover: 0.10 **NM** value: **85.00**
• **CGC:** 1 graded, best 8.5
25 ❑ Jul 1944 Cover: 0.10 **NM** value: **85.00**
• **CGC:** 1 graded, best 7.0
26 ❑ Sep 1944 Cover: 0.10 **NM** value: **85.00**
• **CGC:** 1 graded, best 7.0
27 ❑ Nov 1944 Cover: 0.10 **NM** value: **85.00**
• **CGC:** 1 graded, best 7.0
28 ❑ Jan 1945 Cover: 0.10 **NM** value: **85.00**
• **CGC:** 1 graded, best 7.0
29 ❑ Mar 1945 Cover: 0.10 **NM** value: **85.00**
• Hydroman stories end
30 ❑ May 1945 Cover: 0.10 **NM** value: **80.00**
• **CGC:** 2 graded, best 9.6
31 ❑ Jul 1945 Cover: 0.10 **NM** value: **38.00**
• **CGC:** 1 graded, best 9.2
32 ❑ Sep 1945 Cover: 0.10 **NM** value: **40.00**
• **CGC:** 1 graded, best 9.6
33 ❑ Nov 1945 Cover: 0.10 **NM** value: **40.00**
• **CGC:** 2 graded, best 9.0
34 ❑ Jan 1946 Cover: 0.10 **NM** value: **30.00**
• **CGC:** 2 graded, best 9.0
35 ❑ Mar 1946 Cover: 0.10 **NM** value: **40.00**
• **CGC:** 1 graded, best 6.5
36 ❑ May 1946 Cover: 0.10 **NM** value: **40.00**
• **CGC:** 1 graded, best 6.0
37 ❑ Jul 1946 Cover: 0.10 **NM** value: **40.00**
• **CGC:** 1 graded, best 4.5
38 ❑ Sep 1946 Cover: 0.10 **NM** value: **40.00**
• **CGC:** 1 graded, best 9.0
39 ❑ Nov 1946 Cover: 0.10 **NM** value: **40.00**
• **CGC:** 3 graded, best 9.0
40 ❑ Jan 1947 Cover: 0.10 **NM** value: **40.00**
• **CGC:** 2 graded, best 9.2
41 ❑ Mar 1947 Cover: 0.10 **NM** value: **40.00**
• **CGC:** 1 graded, best 7.5
42 ❑ May 1947 Cover: 0.10 **NM** value: **40.00**
• **CGC:** 1 graded, best 8.5
43 ❑ Jul 1947 Cover: 0.10 **NM** value: **36.00**
• **CGC:** 1 graded, best 9.4
44 ❑ Sep 1947 Cover: 0.10 **NM** value: **36.00**
• **CGC:** 1 graded, best 7.5
45 ❑ Nov 1947 Cover: 0.10 **NM** value: **36.00**
• **CGC:** 1 graded, best 7.0
46 ❑ Jan 1948 Cover: 0.10 **NM** value: **36.00**
• **CGC:** 2 graded, best 9.0
47 ❑ Mar 1948 Cover: 0.10 **NM** value: **36.00**
48 ❑ May 1948 Cover: 0.10 **NM** value: **28.00**
49 ❑ Jul 1948 Cover: 0.10 **NM** value: **36.00**
50 ❑ Sep 1948 Cover: 0.10 **NM** value: **36.00**
51 ❑ Nov 1948 Cover: 0.10 **NM** value: **40.00**
• **CGC:** 1 graded, best 6.0
52 ❑ Jan 1949 Cover: 0.10 **NM** value: **37.00**
• **CGC:** 1 graded, best 8.5
53 ❑ Mar 1949 Cover: 0.10 **NM** value: **30.00**
• **CGC:** 1 graded, best 8.0
54 ❑ May 1949 Cover: 0.10 **NM** value: **25.00**
• **CGC:** 1 graded, best 8.0
55 ❑ Jul 1949 Cover: 0.10 **NM** value: **25.00**
• **CGC:** 1 graded, best 8.0
📖 Her Baby's Life at Stake; Down for the Last Time **A:** Alex Toth
56 ❑ Sep 1949 Cover: 0.10 **NM** value: **37.00**
• **CGC:** 1 graded, best 9.0
57 ❑ Nov 1949 Cover: 0.10 **NM** value: **32.00**
• **CGC:** 1 graded, best 8.0
58 ❑ Jan 1950 Cover: 0.10 **NM** value: **32.00**
• **CGC:** 1 graded, best 9.0
59 ❑ Mar 1950 Cover: 0.10 **NM** value: **32.00**
• **CGC:** 1 graded, best 9.4
60 ❑ May 1950 Cover: 0.10 **NM** value: **32.00**
• **CGC:** 1 graded, best 8.5
61 ❑ Jul 1950 Cover: 0.10 **NM** value: **22.00**
• **CGC:** 2 graded, best 9.0
62 ❑ Sep 1950 Cover: 0.10 **NM** value: **22.00**
63 ❑ Nov 1950 Cover: 0.10 **NM** value: **22.00**
64 ❑ Jan 1951 Cover: 0.10 **NM** value: **22.00**
• **CGC:** 1 graded, best 8.0
65 ❑ Mar 1951 Cover: 0.10 **NM** value: **60.00**
• **CGC:** 1 graded, best 8.5
66 ❑ May 1951 Cover: 0.10 **NM** value: **35.00**
67 ❑ Jul 1951 Cover: 0.10 **NM** value: **35.00**
68 ❑ Sep 1951 Cover: 0.10 **NM** value: **24.00**
• **CGC:** 1 graded, best 9.0
69 ❑ Nov 1951 Cover: 0.10 **NM** value: **44.00**
• **CGC:** 1 graded, best 7.0
70 ❑ Jan 1952 Cover: 0.10 **NM** value: **35.00**
📖 Near Death in Ice Box; Death Was Up a Tree; The He **A:** Frank Frazetta
71 ❑ Mar 1952 Cover: 0.10 **NM** value: **35.00**
72 ❑ May 1952 Cover: 0.10 **NM** value: **44.00**
• **CGC:** 1 graded, best 6.5
73 ❑ Jul 1952 Cover: 0.10 **NM** value: **35.00**
• **CGC:** 1 graded, best 5.5
74 ❑ Aug 1952 Cover: 0.10 **NM** value: **25.00**
• **CGC:** 1 graded, best 7.0
75 ❑ Sep 1952 Cover: 0.10 **NM** value: **35.00**
76 ❑ Oct 1952 Cover: 0.10 **NM** value: **15.00**
• **CGC:** 1 graded, best 9.4
📖 My Story; The Medal Collector; Precipice Plunge; The Soldier Who Refused To Retreat; Evacuation Complete; He Came Back For More!; Man Of Action; The Fargo Express; Belting Beltran; She Lost Her Mittens
77 ❑ Nov 1952 Cover: 0.10 **NM** value: **15.00**
• **CGC:** 1 graded, best 9.2
78 ❑ Dec 1952 Cover: 0.10 **NM** value: **15.00**
• **CGC:** 1 graded, best 7.0
79 ❑ Jan 1953 Cover: 0.10 **NM** value: **15.00**
80 ❑ Feb 1953 Cover: 0.10 **NM** value: **15.00**
81 ❑ Mar 1953 Cover: 0.10 **NM** value: **18.00**
• **CGC:** 1 graded, best 9.0
82 ❑ Apr 1953 Cover: 0.10 **NM** value: **18.00**
83 ❑ May 1953 Cover: 0.10 **NM** value: **15.00**
• **CGC:** 1 graded, best 8.5
84 ❑ Jun 1953 Cover: 0.10 **NM** value: **15.00**
• **CGC:** 1 graded, best 8.5
85 ❑ Jul 1953 Cover: 0.10 **NM** value: **15.00**
86 ❑ Aug 1953 Cover: 0.10 **NM** value: **25.00**
87 ❑ Sep 1953 Cover: 0.10 **NM** value: **25.00**
88 ❑ Nov 1953 Cover: 0.10 **NM** value: **15.00**
• **CGC:** 2 graded, best 9.2
89 ❑ Jan 1954 Cover: 0.10 **NM** value: **15.00**
• **CGC:** 1 graded, best 8.0
90 ❑ Mar 1954 Cover: 0.10 **NM** value: **15.00**
91 ❑ May 1954 Cover: 0.10 **NM** value: **15.00**
92 ❑ Jul 1954 Cover: 0.10 **NM** value: **15.00**
93 ❑ Sep 1954 Cover: 0.10 **NM** value: **15.00**
• **CGC:** 1 graded, best 7.0
94 ❑ Nov 1954 Cover: 0.10 **NM** value: **15.00**
95 ❑ Feb 1955 Cover: 0.10 **NM** value: **15.00**
• **CGC:** 1 graded, best 8.0
96 ❑ Apr 1955 Cover: 0.10 **NM** value: **15.00**
• **CGC:** 1 graded, best 7.0
97 ❑ Jun 1955 Cover: 0.10 **NM** value: **15.00**
final issue.

HEROIC TALES — Lone Star

1 ❑ Jun 1997 Cover: 2.50 **NM** value: **Cover or less**
📖 Amazon: Steel of a Soldier's Heart, Part 1 • Amazon **A:** Robb Phipps **W:** Bill Williams; Mark Finn
2 ❑ Aug 1997 Cover: 2.50 **NM** value: **Cover or less**
📖 Amazon: Steel of a Soldier's Heart, Part 2; The Universal Monster's Guide to Men • Amazon **A:** Robb Phipps **W:** Bill Williams; Mark Finn
3 ❑ Oct 1997 Cover: 2.50 **NM** value: **Cover or less**
📖 Amazon: Steel of a Soldier's Heart, Part 3; Ace of Diamonds **A:** Robb Phipps **W:** Bill Williams; Glenn Porzig
4 ❑ Dec 1997 Cover: 2.50 **NM** value: **Cover or less**
📖 Amazon: Not Without Dust and Heart, Part 1; The B-Movie Grimoire of Lesser Monsters **A:** Robb Phipps; John Lucas **W:** Bill Williams; Mark Finn
5 ❑ Feb 1998 Cover: 2.50 **NM** value: **Cover or less**
📖 Amazon: Not Without Dust and Heart, Part 2; Ace of Diamonds Preview II **A:** Robb Phipps; Art Nichols **W:** Bill Williams; Glenn Porzig
6 ❑ May 1998 Cover: 2.50 **NM** value: **Cover or less**
📖 Blackheart: A Victim of Fate; Amazon Meets Mr. Muscles; The Seventh Raven • Amazon and Blackheart **A:** Matt Reynolds; Robb Phipps; Bobby Diaz **W:** Matt Reynolds; Bill Williams; Bill Willingham
7 ❑ Jul 1998 Cover: 2.50 **NM** value: **Cover or less**
📖 The Children of Atlas, Part 1; Single Combat • Amazon and Gunslinger **A:** Matt Reynolds; Robb Phipps **W:** Bill Williams; Bill Willingham
8 ❑ Aug 1998 Cover: 2.50 **NM** value: **Cover or less**
📖 Atlas: The Judgment of Atlas; The Children of Atlas, Part 2 • Atlas **A:** Robb Phipps; Jeff Parker **W:** Bill Williams
9 ❑ Apr 2000 Cover: 2.50 **NM** value: **Cover or less**
📖 Gunslinger: Claws & Effect **A:** Jeff Parker **W:** Bill Williams
10 ❑ May 2000 Cover: 2.50 **NM** value: **Cover or less**
📖 Blackheart: A Matter of the Heart; Ape Company; The Artist: The Self-Portrait **A:** Jeff Parker; Bobby Diaz **W:** Bill Williams; Jeff Parker; Bill Willingham

HEROINE — Axess

0/A ❑ Cover: 2.99 **NM** value: **Cover or less**
• Collector's edition. **A:** Mike Gerardo **W:** Mike Gerardo
0/B ❑ Cover: 2.99 **NM** value: **Cover or less**
• Icon edition. **A:** Mike Gerardo **W:** Mike Gerardo

HEROINES INC. — Avatar

1 ❑ b&w Cover: 1.75 **NM** value: **Cover or less**

HEROMAN — Dimension

1 ❑ Oct 1986 Cover: 1.75 **NM** value: **Cover or less**
📖 The Origin of Heroman **A:** John Cummins **W:** Ken Jones

HERO ON A STICK — Big-Baby

1 ❑ Cover: 2.95 **NM** value: **Cover or less**

HERO SANDWICH — Slave Labor

They're a team of super-hero detectives for hire to whom no case is too unusual — or too dangerous. If the money is attractive and there are plenty of opportunities to either beat people up or to meet beautiful women, it's bound to entrance at least one member of this irreverent, oft-bickering team.

In one story arc, the group — including an elastic man; a former spy with some dark secrets; a wise-cracking alien; two women who represent the brains, and the "kick-ass" attitude of the group — is hired by a vampire to capture a killer. In another, they're forced to confront a past that has a reach from beyond the grave. Wherever the case takes them, the adventurers keep their cool, making for a sharp-witted series with a focus on fun. Written by Dan Vado and illustrated by Chuck Austen, Pete Krause, and Aldin Baroza, this black-and-white series helped put Slave Labor Graphics on the map.

1 ❑ Feb 1987 Cover: 1.50 **NM** value: **2.00**
📖 They Say Nobody Lives Forever… **A:** Ed Savage **W:** Dan Vado
2 ❑ May 1987 Cover: 1.50 **NM** value: **Cover or less**
3 ❑ Aug 1987 Cover: 1.50 **NM** value: **Cover or less**
4 ❑ Jan 1988 Cover: 1.75 **NM** value: **Cover or less**
5 ❑ Oct 1988 Cover: 1.75 **NM** value: **Cover or less**
6 ❑ Feb 1989 Cover: 1.75 **NM** value: **Cover or less**
7 ❑ Mar 1990 Cover: 2.25 **NM** value: **Cover or less**
8 ❑ Jun 1991 Cover: 2.50 **NM** value: **Cover or less**
9 ❑ May 1992 Cover: 2.50 **NM** value: **Cover or less**
Bk 1 ❑ Aug 1989, b&w Cover: 7.95 **NM** value: **24.95**
📖 They Say Nobody Lives Forever…; Guns and Money • Nobody Lives Forever; "The Works"; Collects Hero Sandwich #1-9 **A:** Peter Krause; Aldin Baroza; Chuck Austen **W:** Dan Vado

HERO ZERO — Dark Horse

0 ❑ Sep 1994 Cover: 2.50 **NM** value: **Cover or less**
Circ: CapCity orders: **6,700**

HERU, SON OF AUSAR — Ania

1 ❑ Apr 1993 Cover: 1.95 **NM** value: **Cover or less**
Circ: CapCity orders: **7,300**
📖 The Coming Of Heru ★ 1st Appearance of Heru.

Other grades: Multiply prices above by **1.5 for Mint • 2/3 for Very Fine • 1/3 for Fine • 1/5 for Very Good • 1/8 for Good**

HE SAID/SHE SAID COMICS — First Amendment

1 ❑ Cover: 3.00 NM value: Cover or less
• Amy Fisher/Joey Buttafuoco

2 ❑ Cover: 3.00 NM value: Cover or less
• Woody Allen/Mia Farrow **A:** Phil Avelli **W:** Barney Dunn; Howard Prince

3 ❑ Cover: 3.00 NM value: Cover or less
• Bill Clinton/Gennifer Flowers

4 ❑ Cover: 3.00 NM value: Cover or less
• Tonya Harding/Jeff Gillooly **A:** Mike Apice **W:** Mike Scozelli; Stan Jonathan

5 ❑ Cover: 3.00 NM value: Cover or less
• O.J. Simpson/Nicole Brown **A:** Mike Scozelli; Roberto Andujar **W:** Arthur Meehan

HEX — DC

1 ❑ Sep 1985 Cover: 0.75 NM value: 2.00
Circ: CapCity orders: **13,050**
📖 Once Upon A Time...In The West?!? • continued from Jonah Hex #92 **A:** Mark Texeira **W:** Michael Fleisher ★ Origin of Hex (future Jonah Hex). ★ 1st Appearance of Hex (future Jonah Hex), Stiletta.

2 ❑ Oct 1985 Cover: 0.75 NM value: 1.25
Circ: CapCity orders: **9,350**
📖 Can She Bake a Cherry Pie? **A:** Mark Texeira **W:** Michael Fleisher

3 ❑ Nov 1985 Cover: 0.75 NM value: 1.25
Circ: CapCity orders: **8,250**
📖 The Lotus Eaters! **A:** Mark Texeira **W:** Michael Fleisher

4 ❑ Dec 1985 Cover: 0.75 NM value: 1.25
Circ: CapCity orders: **8,050**
📖 Worms **A:** Ron Wagner **W:** Michael Fleisher

5 ❑ Jan 1986 Cover: 0.75 NM value: 1.25
Circ: CapCity orders: **7,450**
📖 The Seattle Chain Saw Massacre **A:** Mark Texeira **W:** Michael Fleisher

6 ❑ Feb 1986 Cover: 0.75 NM value: 1.25
Circ: CapCity orders: **7,600**

7 ❑ Mar 1986 Cover: 0.75 NM value: 1.25
Circ: CapCity orders: **6,850**

8 ❑ Apr 1986 Cover: 0.75 NM value: 1.25
Circ: CapCity orders: **6,650**
📖 Day of the Cyborg! **A:** Mark Texeira **W:** Michael Fleisher

9 ❑ May 1986 Cover: 0.75 NM value: 1.25
Circ: CapCity orders: **6,450**

10 ❑ Jun 1986 Cover: 0.75 NM value: 1.25
Circ: CapCity orders: **6,250**

11 ❑ Jul 1986 Cover: 0.75 NM value: 1.25
Circ: CapCity orders: **6,250**
📖 Night of the Bat **A:** Mark Texeira **W:** Michael Fleisher ★ Appearance of Batman of future.

12 ❑ Aug 1986 Cover: 0.75 NM value: 1.25
Circ: CapCity orders: **6,200**

13 ❑ Sep 1986 Cover: 0.75 NM value: 1.25
Circ: CapCity orders: **6,150**
📖 The Dogs of War **A:** Carlos Garzon; Mark Texeira **W:** Michael Fleisher ★ 1st Appearance of Dogs of War.

14 ❑ Oct 1986 Cover: 0.75 NM value: 1.25
Circ: CapCity orders: **6,300**

15 ❑ Nov 1986 Cover: 0.75 NM value: 1.25
Circ: CapCity orders: **6,500**
📖 Chain of Doom **A:** Carlos Garzon; Keith Giffen **W:** Michael Fleisher

16 ❑ Dec 1986 Cover: 0.75 NM value: 1.25
Circ: CapCity orders: **6,500**
📖 The Slayer and the Slave! **A:** Keith Giffen **W:** Michael Fleisher

17 ❑ Jan 1987 Cover: 0.75 NM value: 1.25
Circ: CapCity orders: **6,050**

18 ❑ Feb 1987 Cover: 1.00 NM value: 1.25
Circ: CapCity orders: **6,450**
final issue. **A:** Keith Giffen **W:** Michael Fleisher

HEXBREAKER: A BADGER GRAPHIC NOVEL — First

1 ❑ Mar 1988 Cover: 8.95 NM value: Cover or less

HEX OF THE WICKED WITCH — Asylum

0/A ❑ Aug 1999 Cover: 1.95 NM value: Cover or less
0/B ❑ Aug 1999 Cover: 3.95 NM value: Cover or less
• Deluxe edition.

HEY, BOSS! — Visionary

1 ❑ Cover: 1.50 NM value: 2.00

HEY LOOK! (HARVEY KURTZMAN'S...) — Kitchen Sink

Before he became famous as the creator of Mad, Two-Fisted Tales, and Frontline Combat, one of Harvey Kurtzman's comics involvements (along with working in Will Eisner's studio) was producing one-page cartoons called "Hey Look!" These brief gag strips were mostly published in such obscure publications as Joker or Jennie, although a few made it into early Marvel and Timely publications such as Millie the Model and Patsy Walker.

The "Hey Look!" cartoons are collected for the first time in this 1992 Kitchen Sink volume. It's a great showcase for the idiosyncratic, inspired, and groundbreaking talent of one of comics' most influential creators.

1 ❑ Cover: 15.95 NM value: Cover or less

HEY, MISTER — Insomnia

1 ❑ May 1997, b&w Cover: 2.50 NM value: Cover or less
2 ❑ Nov 1997, b&w Cover: 2.50 NM value: Cover or less
3 ❑ Aug 1998, b&w Cover: 2.95 NM value: Cover or less
4 ❑ Dec 1998, b&w Cover: 2.95 NM value: Cover or less

HEY MISTER: AFTERSCHOOL SPECIAL — Top Shelf

1 ❑ b&w Cover: 4.95 NM value: Cover or less
No issue number. • digest. • collects five-issue mini-comics series

HEY NEETERS — Antarctic

Bk 1❑ Jul 1993 Cover: 9.95 NM value: Cover or less
No issue number.

HI-ADVENTURE HEROES — Gold Key

1 ❑ May 1969 Cover: 0.15 NM value: 35.00
• **CGC:** 1 graded, best 9.2
2 ❑ Aug 1969 Cover: 0.15 NM value: 20.00

HICKORY — Quality

1 ❑ Oct 1949 Cover: 0.10 NM value: 65.00
2 ❑ Dec 1949 Cover: 0.10 NM value: 35.00
3 ❑ Feb 1950 Cover: 0.10 NM value: 28.00
4 ❑ Apr 1950 Cover: 0.10 NM value: 28.00
5 ❑ Jun 1950 Cover: 0.10 NM value: 28.00
6 ❑ Aug 1950 Cover: 0.10 NM value: 28.00
• **CGC:** 2 graded, best 8.5

HIDEO LI FILES, THE — Raging Rhino

All issues are adults only.

1 ❑ b&w Cover: 2.95 NM value: Cover or less

HIDEO LI FILES COMIC NOVELLA, THE — Raging Rhino

1 ❑ b&w Cover: 12.95 NM value: Cover or less
cardstock cover. • Oversized.

HIDING PLACE, THE — DC / Piranha

1 ❑ Cover: 12.95 NM value: Cover or less
Circ: CapCity orders: **1,750**

HIEROGLYPH — Dark Horse

Age of Reptiles creator Ricardo Delgado tells an intriguing tale in this four-issue limited series that finds astronaut/explorer Francisco Chavez alone on a planet far from his beloved Earth. Something very much like magic seems an important aspect of the alien cultures he encounters.

On this strange world, Chavez explores his own humanity and finds beauty in a sometimes hostile environment. Delgado's beautiful artwork brings to mind the elegant and intricate drawings of Moebius, and his story is nothing short of spectacular-both emotional and exciting. It's a suitable follow-up to Dark Horse's Two Faces of Tomorrow (by James Hogan and Yukinobu Hoshino), itself an excellent example of science fiction in comics.

1 ❑ Nov 1999 Cover: 2.95 NM value: Cover or less
Circ: Diamd. preorders: **7,995**
2 ❑ Dec 1999 Cover: 2.95 NM value: Cover or less
Circ: Diamd. preorders: **6,186**
3 ❑ Jan 2000 Cover: 2.95 NM value: Cover or less
Circ: Diamd. preorders: **6,035**
4 ❑ Feb 2000 Cover: 2.95 NM value: Cover or less
Circ: Diamd. preorders: **6,095**

HIGHBROW ENTERTAINMENT — Image

Ash 1❑ NM value: 1.00
• Ascan promotional edition.

HIGH CALIBER — Caliber

1 ❑ b&w Cover: 9.95 NM value: Cover or less
• Trade Paperback.

HIGH OCTANE THEATRE — Infiniti

1 ❑ Cover: 2.50 NM value: Cover or less
📖 Codename: Jezebel: Dead Little Lady; Jeremy Sifter: For Hire; It's a Miserable Life **A:** Doug Stephens; Gerimi Burleigh; Hunger **W:** Gerimi Burleigh; Jim Murdoch; John Villalino; Thomas Nealeigh

HIGH SCHOOL AGENT — Sun

1 ❑ Cover: 2.50 NM value: Cover or less

HIGH SHINING BRASS — Apple

1 ❑ b&w Cover: 2.75 NM value: Cover or less
📖 Point **A:** Don Lomax **W:** Don Lomax
2 ❑ b&w Cover: 2.75 NM value: Cover or less
3 ❑ b&w Cover: 2.75 NM value: Cover or less
4 ❑ Cover: 2.95 NM value: Cover or less

HIGH STAKES ADVENTURES — Antarctic

1 ❑ Dec 1998 Cover: 2.95 NM value: Cover or less
Circ: Diamd. preorders: **2,366**
📖 The Big Game; Giant Fighter; S.E.A Force in Glass Hammer; Danger Squad
1/Dlx❑ Dec 1998 Cover: 5.95 NM value: Cover or less
• Deluxe edition. 📖 The Big Game; Giant Fighter; S.E.A Force in Glass Hammer; Danger Squad **A:** Shannon Denton and Kurt Hathaway **W:** Shannon Denton and Kurt Hathaway

HIGHTOP NINJA — Authority

1 ❑ Cover: 2.95 NM value: Cover or less
2 ❑ Cover: 2.95 NM value: Cover or less
3 ❑ Cover: 2.95 NM value: Cover or less
Bk 1❑ Jul 1997 Cover: 5.95 NM value: Cover or less
📖 Getting Aquaintance **A:** Jonathan Hong **W:** Jonathan Hong

HIGH VOLTAGE — Black Out

0 ❑ Cover: 2.95 NM value: Cover or less

HIGHWAY 61 — Vortex

1 ❑ Cover: 11.95 NM value: Cover or less
No issue number.

HILLY ROSE — Astro

Hilly is an investigative reporter for Earth's Rocket Times. She has been given the job by her father, Steeltrap Rose, as a means of keeping her busy and close to home. Steeltrap is of the opinion that Hilly can never make it as a reporter on her own, since he thinks her too young and naive for serious sleuthing. This makes it all the more ironic, when Hilly stumbles onto a story involving corruption and murder-for-hire that winds up pointing back to her own father.

Hilly Rose is a wonderful mix of space fantasy and quick humor, propelled by the wonderful writing of creator B.C. Boyer. The characters in the series seem to be aware of their own cartoon existence and acknowledge it with a wink to the reader. The characters poke fun at everything from comic-book storytelling conventions to the art styles in which they are themselves drawn. Boyer even manages to slip in running gags from such sources as TV's Seinfeld.

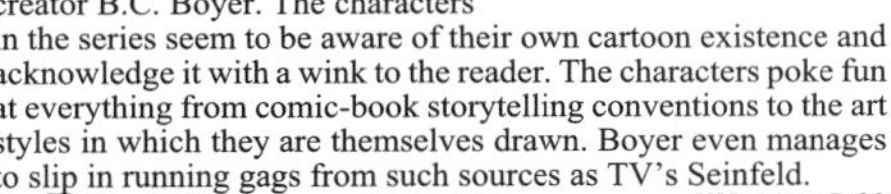

1 ❑ May 1995 Cover: 2.95 NM value: 5.00
Circ: CapCity orders: **2,480**
1/A ❑ Cover: 2.95 NM value: 4.00
2 ❑ Jul 1995 Cover: 2.95 NM value: 4.00
📖 Heartbreak News, Part 2
3 ❑ Oct 1995 Cover: 2.95 NM value: 3.00
4 ❑ Dec 1995 Cover: 2.95 NM value: 3.00
5 ❑ Feb 1996 Cover: 2.95 NM value: 3.00
6 ❑ Apr 1996 Cover: 2.95 NM value: 3.00
7 ❑ Aug 1996 Cover: 2.95 NM value: 3.00
8 ❑ Dec 1996 Cover: 2.95 NM value: 3.00
Circ: Diamd. preorders: **2,792**
9 ❑ Apr 1997 Cover: 2.95 NM value: 3.00
Bk 1❑ Cover: 12.95 NM value: Cover or less

HIM — Birthday Girl Press

Bk 1❑ b&w Cover: 14.00 NM value: Cover or less

HIP FLASK — Comicraft

0.5 ❑ Aug 1998 Cover: 2.95 NM value: Cover or less
• San Dego Comic-Con preview **A:** Ian Churchill **W:** Jeph Loeb

HI-SCHOOL ROMANCE — Home

Hi-School Romance was a teen-romance series that ran from 1949 to 1958. The years following World War II saw a contination of a trend that had begun following World War I—dating as we know it today, with teen-agers being given a great deal of freedom to meet each other without constant adult supervision. This is a true product of that time, full of malt shops, sock hops, and double-dates. In it, starry-eyed schoolgirls do their best to win the man of their dreams. To accomplish this, however, there is always some obstacle to overcome, whether it means fighting off a rival or merely learning how to play the game of love better.

What may be most remarkable about this series is noting how much has changed between men and women in the last few decades—as well as how much has stayed the same.

1 ❑ Oct 1949 Cover: 0.10 NM value: 70.00
• **CGC:** 1 graded, best 7.0
2 ❑ Dec 1949 Cover: 0.10 NM value: 42.00
3 ❑ Feb 1950 Cover: 0.10 NM value: 30.00
4 ❑ ca. 1950 Cover: 0.10 NM value: 30.00
5 ❑ ca. 1950 Cover: 0.10 NM value: 30.00
6 ❑ Dec 1950 Cover: 0.10 NM value: 30.00
7 ❑ Feb 1951 Cover: 0.10 NM value: 30.00
8 ❑ Apr 1951 Cover: 0.10 NM value: 30.00
9 ❑ Jun 1951 Cover: 0.10 NM value: 30.00
10 ❑ Aug 1951 Cover: 0.10 NM value: 30.00
• **CGC:** 1 graded, best 5.0
11 ❑ Oct 1951 Cover: 0.10 NM value: 18.00
12 ❑ Dec 1951 Cover: 0.10 NM value: 18.00
13 ❑ Feb 1952 Cover: 0.10 NM value: 18.00
14 ❑ Apr 1952 Cover: 0.10 NM value: 18.00
15 ❑ Jun 1952 Cover: 0.10 NM value: 18.00
16 ❑ Aug 1952 Cover: 0.10 NM value: 18.00
17 ❑ Oct 1952 Cover: 0.10 NM value: 18.00
18 ❑ Dec 1952 Cover: 0.10 NM value: 18.00
19 ❑ Feb 1953 Cover: 0.10 NM value: 18.00
20 ❑ Apr 1953 Cover: 0.10 NM value: 18.00
21 ❑ Jun 1953 Cover: 0.10 NM value: 15.00
22 ❑ Aug 1953 Cover: 0.10 NM value: 15.00
23 ❑ Oct 1953 Cover: 0.10 NM value: 15.00

CGC-graded: Multiply prices above by **33 for 9.9 M • 16 for 9.8 NM/M • 7 for 9.6 NM+ • 5 for 9.4 NM • 2.5 for 9.2 NM- • 1.5 for 9.0 VF/NM**

24 ❑ Dec 1953 Cover: 0.10 **NM** value: **15.00**
25 ❑ Feb 1954 Cover: 0.10 **NM** value: **15.00**
26 ❑ Apr 1954 Cover: 0.10 **NM** value: **15.00**
27 ❑ May 1954 Cover: 0.10 **NM** value: **15.00**
28 ❑ Jun 1954 Cover: 0.10 **NM** value: **15.00**
📖 I Led Them On; Too Easy to Love; Forbidden Love; Runaway
29 ❑ Jul 1954 Cover: 0.10 **NM** value: **15.00**
30 ❑ Aug 1954 Cover: 0.10 **NM** value: **15.00**
31 ❑ Sep 1954 Cover: 0.10 **NM** value: **15.00**
32 ❑ Oct 1954 Cover: 0.10 **NM** value: **25.00**
33 ❑ Nov 1954 Cover: 0.10 **NM** value: **12.00**
34 ❑ Dec 1954 Cover: 0.10 **NM** value: **12.00**
35 ❑ Jan 1955 Cover: 0.10 **NM** value: **12.00**
36 ❑ Feb 1955 Cover: 0.10 **NM** value: **12.00**
37 ❑ Mar 1955 Cover: 0.10 **NM** value: **12.00**
38 ❑ Apr 1955 Cover: 0.10 **NM** value: **12.00**
39 ❑ May 1955 Cover: 0.10 **NM** value: **12.00**
40 ❑ Jun 1955 Cover: 0.10 **NM** value: **12.00**
41 ❑ Jul 1955 Cover: 0.10 **NM** value: **9.00**
42 ❑ Aug 1955 Cover: 0.10 **NM** value: **9.00**
📖 Very Personally Yours; Framed By Love; My Dream Came True!; I Played A Dangerous Game; Blonde Crazy;
43 ❑ Sep 1955 Cover: 0.10 **NM** value: **9.00**
44 ❑ Oct 1955 Cover: 0.10 **NM** value: **9.00**
45 ❑ Nov 1955 Cover: 0.10 **NM** value: **9.00**
46 ❑ Dec 1955 Cover: 0.10 **NM** value: **9.00**
47 ❑ Jan 1956 Cover: 0.10 **NM** value: **9.00**
48 ❑ Feb 1956 Cover: 0.10 **NM** value: **9.00**
49 ❑ Mar 1956 Cover: 0.10 **NM** value: **9.00**
50 ❑ Apr 1956 Cover: 0.10 **NM** value: **9.00**
51 ❑ May 1956 Cover: 0.10 **NM** value: **9.00**
52 ❑ Jun 1956 Cover: 0.10 **NM** value: **9.00**
53 ❑ Jul 1956 Cover: 0.10 **NM** value: **9.00**
54 ❑ Aug 1956 Cover: 0.10 **NM** value: **9.00**
55 ❑ Sep 1956 Cover: 0.10 **NM** value: **9.00**
56 ❑ Oct 1956 Cover: 0.10 **NM** value: **9.00**
57 ❑ Nov 1956 Cover: 0.10 **NM** value: **9.00**
58 ❑ Dec 1956 Cover: 0.10 **NM** value: **9.00**
59 ❑ Jan 1957 Cover: 0.10 **NM** value: **9.00**
60 ❑ Feb 1957 Cover: 0.10 **NM** value: **9.00**
61 ❑ Mar 1957 Cover: 0.10 **NM** value: **9.00**
62 ❑ Apr 1957 Cover: 0.10 **NM** value: **9.00**
63 ❑ May 1957 Cover: 0.10 **NM** value: **9.00**
64 ❑ Jun 1957 Cover: 0.10 **NM** value: **9.00**
65 ❑ Jul 1957 Cover: 0.10 **NM** value: **9.00**
66 ❑ Aug 1957 Cover: 0.10 **NM** value: **9.00**
📖 Suspicious Of Love; I Flattered Men; A Kiss To Remember; Lovable Yokel!;
67 ❑ Sep 1957 Cover: 0.10 **NM** value: **9.00**
68 ❑ Oct 1957 Cover: 0.10 **NM** value: **9.00**
📖 Odd Girl Out; My Answer; My Sister's Husband; Not Good Enough For Me
69 ❑ Nov 1957 Cover: 0.10 **NM** value: **9.00**
70 ❑ Dec 1957 Cover: 0.10 **NM** value: **9.00**
71 ❑ Jan 1958 Cover: 0.10 **NM** value: **9.00**
72 ❑ Feb 1958 Cover: 0.10 **NM** value: **9.00**
73 ❑ Mar 1958 Cover: 0.10 **NM** value: **9.00**
74 ❑ 1958 Cover: 0.10 **NM** value: **9.00**
75 ❑ 1958 Cover: 0.10 **NM** value: **9.00**

HIS NAME IS...SAVAGE — Adventure House Press

1 ❑ Cover: 0.35 **NM** value: **25.00**
No issue number. • magazine. **A:** Gil Kane

HISTORY OF MARVELS COMICS, THE — Marvel

1 ❑ Jul 2000 Cover: 1.50 **NM** value: **Cover or less**
Circ: Diamd. preorders: **23,061**

HISTORY OF THE DC UNIVERSE — DC

1 ❑ Sep 1986 Cover: 2.95 **NM** value: **3.25**
Circ: CapCity orders: **31,250**
2 ❑ Nov 1986 Cover: 2.95 **NM** value: **3.25**
Circ: CapCity orders: **26,100**

HISTORY OF VIOLENCE — DC / Paradox

1 ❑ b&w Cover: 9.95 **NM** value: **Cover or less**

HITCHHIKER'S GUIDE TO THE GALAXY, THE — DC

1 ❑ Cover: 4.95 **NM** value: **Cover or less**
Circ: CapCity orders: **12,800**
2 ❑ Cover: 4.95 **NM** value: **Cover or less**
Circ: CapCity orders: **9,150**
3 ❑ Cover: 4.95 **NM** value: **Cover or less**
Circ: CapCity orders: **8,150**

HIT COMICS — Quality

Early issues of Hit Comics featured such characters as Hercules, The Red Bee, The Strange Twins, and Neon the Unknown, and dynamic covers featured brawny costumed guys (often, Hercules wearing a cape but no shirt) bopping baddies. With #25 (Dec 42), Kid Eternity was introduced and immediately took over the cover spot and was described on the cover as the "most sensational hero ever to appear in print!"

He was killed, but his death was not supposed to occur. As a result, Mr. Keeper, who was in charge of the list of who was to live and who was to die, was charged with giving the dead lad the remaining 75 years of his life.

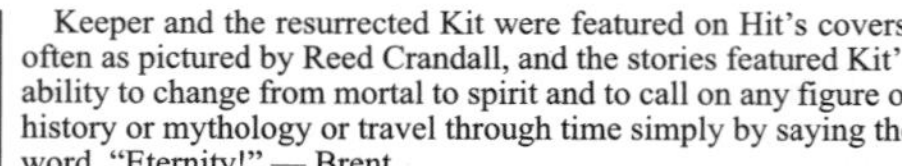

Keeper and the resurrected Kit were featured on Hit's covers, often as pictured by Reed Crandall, and the stories featured Kit's ability to change from mortal to spirit and to call on any figure of history or mythology or travel through time simply by saying the word, "Eternity!" — Brent

1 ❑ Jul 1940 Cover: 0.10 **NM** value: **5000.00**
• **CGC:** 4 graded, best 8.5
2 ❑ Aug 1940 Cover: 0.10 **NM** value: **2500.00**
• **CGC:** 1 graded, best 4.5
3 ❑ Sep 1940 Cover: 0.10 **NM** value: **2000.00**
• **CGC:** 2 graded, best 4.0
4 ❑ Oct 1940 Cover: 0.10 **NM** value: **2000.00**
• **CGC:** 3 graded, best 5.0
5 ❑ Nov 1940 Cover: 0.10 **NM** value: **2000.00**
• **CGC:** 3 graded, best 7.0
6 ❑ Dec 1940 Cover: 0.10 **NM** value: **1500.00**
• **CGC:** 2 graded, best 9.0
7 ❑ Jan 1941 Cover: 0.10 **NM** value: **1500.00**
8 ❑ Feb 1941 Cover: 0.10 **NM** value: **1500.00**
• **CGC:** 2 graded, best 9.0
9 ❑ Mar 1941 Cover: 0.10 **NM** value: **1500.00**
• **CGC:** 3 graded, best 8.5
10 ❑ Apr 1941 Cover: 0.10 **NM** value: **1500.00**
11 ❑ May 1941 Cover: 0.10 **NM** value: **1000.00**
• **CGC:** 2 graded, best 7.5
12 ❑ Jun 1941 Cover: 0.10 **NM** value: **1000.00**
13 ❑ Jul 1941 Cover: 0.10 **NM** value: **1000.00**
• **CGC:** 2 graded, best 7.5
14 ❑ Aug 1941 Cover: 0.10 **NM** value: **1000.00**
15 ❑ Sep 1941 Cover: 0.10 **NM** value: **1000.00**
• **CGC:** 1 graded, best 3.5
16 ❑ Oct 1941 Cover: 0.10 **NM** value: **900.00**
• **CGC:** 2 graded, best 5.0
17 ❑ Nov 1941 Cover: 0.10 **NM** value: **900.00**
18 ❑ Dec 1941 Cover: 0.10 **NM** value: **900.00**
19 ❑ Jan 1942 Cover: 0.10 **NM** value: **900.00**
• **CGC:** 1 graded, best 9.2
20 ❑ Feb 1942 Cover: 0.10 **NM** value: **900.00**
• **CGC:** 1 graded, best 3.5
21 ❑ Apr 1942 Cover: 0.10 **NM** value: **900.00**
22 ❑ Jun 1942 Cover: 0.10 **NM** value: **900.00**
• **CGC:** 1 graded, best 7.0
23 ❑ Aug 1942 Cover: 0.10 **NM** value: **900.00**
• **CGC:** 2 graded, best 7.5
24 ❑ Oct 1942 Cover: 0.10 **NM** value: **900.00**
• **CGC:** 2 graded, best 4.5
25 ❑ Dec 1942 Cover: 0.10 **NM** value: **900.00**
26 ❑ Feb 1943 Cover: 0.10 **NM** value: **700.00**
27 ❑ Apr 1943 Cover: 0.10 **NM** value: **700.00**
28 ❑ Jul 1943 Cover: 0.10 **NM** value: **700.00**
29 ❑ Sep 1943 Cover: 0.10 **NM** value: **700.00**
• **CGC:** 1 graded, best 6.0
30 ❑ Win 1943 Cover: 0.10 **NM** value: **500.00**
• **CGC:** 1 graded, best 9.0
31 ❑ Spr 1944 Cover: 0.10 **NM** value: **500.00**
• **CGC:** 2 graded, best 8.0
32 ❑ Sum 1944 Cover: 0.10 **NM** value: **500.00**
33 ❑ Fal 1944 Cover: 0.10 **NM** value: **500.00**
34 ❑ Win 1944 Cover: 0.10 **NM** value: **500.00**
• **CGC:** 3 graded, best 9.2
35 ❑ Spr 1945 Cover: 0.10 **NM** value: **500.00**
36 ❑ Sum 1945 Cover: 0.10 **NM** value: **350.00**
• **CGC:** 1 graded, best 9.0
37 ❑ Fal 1945 Cover: 0.10 **NM** value: **350.00**
38 ❑ Win 1945 Cover: 0.10 **NM** value: **350.00**
• **CGC:** 1 graded, best 9.2
39 ❑ Spr 1946 Cover: 0.10 **NM** value: **350.00**
40 ❑ May 1946 Cover: 0.10 **NM** value: **300.00**
• **CGC:** 1 graded, best 7.0
41 ❑ Jul 1946 Cover: 0.10 **NM** value: **300.00**
42 ❑ Sep 1946 Cover: 0.10 **NM** value: **300.00**
43 ❑ Nov 1946 Cover: 0.10 **NM** value: **300.00**
44 ❑ Jan 1947 Cover: 0.10 **NM** value: **300.00**
• **CGC:** 1 graded, best 8.0
45 ❑ Mar 1947 Cover: 0.10 **NM** value: **250.00**
46 ❑ May 1947 Cover: 0.10 **NM** value: **250.00**
47 ❑ Jul 1947 Cover: 0.10 **NM** value: **250.00**
48 ❑ Sep 1947 Cover: 0.10 **NM** value: **250.00**
49 ❑ Nov 1947 Cover: 0.10 **NM** value: **250.00**
50 ❑ Jan 1948 Cover: 0.10 **NM** value: **200.00**
51 ❑ Mar 1948 Cover: 0.10 **NM** value: **200.00**
52 ❑ May 1948 Cover: 0.10 **NM** value: **200.00**
53 ❑ Jul 1948 Cover: 0.10 **NM** value: **200.00**
54 ❑ Sep 1948 Cover: 0.10 **NM** value: **200.00**
55 ❑ Nov 1948 Cover: 0.10 **NM** value: **200.00**
56 ❑ Jan 1949 Cover: 0.10 **NM** value: **150.00**
57 ❑ Mar 1949 Cover: 0.10 **NM** value: **150.00**
58 ❑ May 1949 Cover: 0.10 **NM** value: **150.00**
59 ❑ Jul 1949 Cover: 0.10 **NM** value: **150.00**
60 ❑ Sep 1949 Cover: 0.10 **NM** value: **150.00**
61 ❑ Nov 1949 Cover: 0.10 **NM** value: **150.00**
62 ❑ Jan 1950 Cover: 0.10 **NM** value: **150.00**
63 ❑ Mar 1950 Cover: 0.10 **NM** value: **150.00**
64 ❑ May 1950 Cover: 0.10 **NM** value: **150.00**
65 ❑ Jul 1950 Cover: 0.10 **NM** value: **150.00**

Capital City orders are the actual sales of comic books by Capital City Distribution, once one of the largest U.S. sellers of comics to comics shops. Capital City's share of comics shop sales, while not known exactly, increases from around 10-20% in the mid-1980s to 30-35% in the mid-1990s. Capital City's share of comic books sold on newsstands (most Marvels and DCs) will be less.

HITMAN — DC

As the result of an alien assault, Tommy Monaghan has X-ray vision and telepathy, both of which serve him well in his career. Monaghan kills people for money: he's a hitman. He used to make ordinary kills, but since he's acquired his special skills, he contracts for the "weird jobs." Unlike most hitmen, however, Tommy Monaghan comes across as a likable guy with a tedious job and a group of wisecracking friends.

Hitman is one of the few characters from DC's Bloodlines-themed annuals to catch on. Though the title has a dark tone, there is an underlying sense of parody in the stories penned by Garth Ennis, who's also known for his work on Hellblazer and Preacher.

1 ❑ Apr 1996 Cover: 2.25 **NM** value: **5.00**
• **CGC:** 2 graded, best 9.9
📖 A Rage in Arkham, Part 1 **A:** John McCrea **W:** Garth Ennis ★ Appearance of Batman.
2 ❑ Jun 1996 Cover: 2.25 **NM** value: **3.00**
📖 A Rage in Arkham, Part 2 **A:** John McCrea **W:** Garth Ennis ★ Appearance of Joker. ★ Versus Joker.
3 ❑ Jul 1996 Cover: 2.25 **NM** value: **3.00**
4 ❑ Aug 1996 Cover: 2.25 **NM** value: **3.00**
📖 Ten Thousand Bullets, Part 1 **A:** John McCrea **W:** Garth Ennis
5 ❑ Sep 1996 Cover: 2.25 **NM** value: **3.00**
📖 Ten Thousand Bullets, Part 2 **A:** John McCrea **W:** Garth Ennis
6 ❑ Oct 1996 Cover: 2.25 **NM** value: **3.00**
cover says Part 4 of 4. 📖 Ten Thousand Bullets, Part 3 **A:** John McCrea **W:** Garth Ennis
7 ❑ Nov 1996 Cover: 2.25 **NM** value: **2.50**
Circ: Diamd. preorders: **35,319**
📖 Ten Thousand Bullets, Part 4 **A:** John McCrea **W:** Garth Ennis ★ Death of Nightfist. ★ Death of Johnny Navarone.
8 ❑ Dec 1996 Cover: 2.25 **NM** value: **2.50**
Circ: Diamd. preorders: **38,967**
📖 Final Night • Final Night **A:** John McCrea **W:** Garth Ennis ★ Origin of Hitman.
9 ❑ Dec 1996 Cover: 2.25 **NM** value: **2.50**
Circ: Diamd. preorders: **34,447**
📖 Local Hero, Part 1; Local Heroes, Part 1 **A:** John McCrea **W:** Garth Ennis
10 ❑ Jan 1997 Cover: 2.25 **NM** value: **2.50**
Circ: Diamd. preorders: **33,482**
📖 Local Hero, Part 2; Local Heroes, Part 2 **A:** John McCrea **W:** Garth Ennis
11 ❑ Feb 1997 Cover: 2.25 **NM** value: **Cover or less**
Circ: Diamd. preorders: **32,793**
📖 Local Hero, Part 3; Local Heroes, Part 3 **A:** John McCrea **W:** Garth Ennis
12 ❑ Mar 1997 Cover: 2.25 **NM** value: **Cover or less**
Circ: Diamd. preorders: **31,749**
📖 Local Hero, Part 4; Local Heroes, Part 4 **A:** John McCrea **W:** Garth Ennis ★ Appearance of Green Lantern.
13 ❑ Apr 1997 Cover: 2.25 **NM** value: **Cover or less**
Circ: Diamd. preorders: **29,929**
📖 Zombie Night at the Gotham Aquarium, Part 1 **A:** John McCrea **W:** Garth Ennis
14 ❑ May 1997 Cover: 2.25 **NM** value: **Cover or less**
Circ: Diamd. preorders: **29,764**
📖 Zombie Night at the Gotham Aquarium, Part 2; Zombie Night at the Aquarium **A:** John McCrea **W:** Garth Ennis
15 ❑ Jun 1997 Cover: 2.25 **NM** value: **Cover or less**
Circ: Diamd. preorders: **30,010**
📖 Ace of Killers; Ace of Killers, Part 1 **A:** John McCrea **W:** Garth Ennis
16 ❑ Jul 1997 Cover: 2.25 **NM** value: **Cover or less**
Circ: Diamd. preorders: **28,611**
📖 Ace of Killers; Ace of Killers, Part 2 **A:** John McCrea **W:** Garth Ennis ★ Appearance of Catwoman.
17 ❑ Aug 1997 Cover: 2.25 **NM** value: **Cover or less**
Circ: Diamd. preorders: **28,503**
📖 Ace of Killers; Ace of Killers, Part 3 **A:** John McCrea **W:** Garth Ennis
18 ❑ Sep 1997 Cover: 2.25 **NM** value: **Cover or less**
Circ: Diamd. preorders: **27,885**
📖 Ace of Killers; Ace of Killers, Part 4 **A:** John McCrea **W:** Garth Ennis
19 ❑ Oct 1997 Cover: 2.25 **NM** value: **Cover or less**
Circ: Diamd. preorders: **28,182**
📖 Ace of Killers; Ace of Killers, Part 5 **A:** John McCrea **W:** Garth Ennis
20 ❑ Nov 1997 Cover: 2.25 **NM** value: **Cover or less**
Circ: Diamd. preorders: **27,848**
📖 Ace of Killers; Ace of Killers, Part 6 **A:** John McCrea **W:** Garth Ennis
21 ❑ Dec 1997 Cover: 2.25 **NM** value: **Cover or less**
Circ: Diamd. preorders: **27,607**
Face cover. 📖 Kiss Me **A:** Steve Pugh **W:** Garth Ennis
22 ❑ Jan 1998 Cover: 2.25 **NM** value: **Cover or less**
Circ: Diamd. preorders: **26,936**
23 ❑ Feb 1998 Cover: 2.25 **NM** value: **Cover or less**
Circ: Diamd. preorders: **26,345**
📖 Who Dares Wins, Part 1 **A:** John McCrea **W:** Garth Ennis
24 ❑ Mar 1998 Cover: 2.25 **NM** value: **Cover or less**
Circ: Diamd. preorders: **25,625**
📖 Who Dares Wins, Part 2 **A:** John McCrea **W:** Garth Ennis
25 ❑ Apr 1998 Cover: 2.25 **NM** value: **Cover or less**
Circ: Diamd. preorders: **24,916**
26 ❑ May 1998 Cover: 2.25 **NM** value: **Cover or less**

Other grades: Multiply prices above by **1.5 for Mint • 2/3 for Very Fine • 1/3 for Fine • 1/5 for Very Good • 1/8 for Good**

Circ: Diamd. preorders: **25,044**
27 ❑ Jun 1998 Cover: 2.25 **NM** value: **Cover or less**
Circ: Diamd. preorders: **25,628**
28 ❑ Jul 1998 Cover: 2.25 **NM** value: **Cover or less**
Circ: Diamd. preorders: **24,648**
29 ❑ Aug 1998 Cover: 2.25 **NM** value: **Cover or less**
Circ: Diamd. preorders: **24,678**
📖 Tommy's Heroes, Part 1 **A:** John McCrea **W:** Garth Ennis
30 ❑ Sep 1998 Cover: 2.50 **NM** value: **Cover or less**
Circ: Diamd. preorders: **23,699**
📖 Tommy's Heroes, Part 2 **A:** John McCrea **W:** Garth Ennis
31 ❑ Oct 1998 Cover: 2.50 **NM** value: **Cover or less**
Circ: Diamd. preorders: **23,093**
📖 Tommy's Heroes, Part 3 **A:** John McCrea **W:** Garth Ennis
32 ❑ Dec 1998 Cover: 2.50 **NM** value: **Cover or less**
Circ: Diamd. preorders: **22,941**
📖 Tommy's Heroes, Part 4 **A:** John McCrea **W:** Garth Ennis
33 ❑ Jan 1999 Cover: 2.50 **NM** value: **Cover or less**
Circ: Diamd. preorders: **22,406**
📖 Tommy's Heroes, Part 5 **A:** John McCrea **W:** Garth Ennis
34 ❑ Feb 1999 Cover: 2.50 **NM** value: **Cover or less**
Circ: Diamd. preorders: **23,909**
📖 Superfriends? **A:** John McCrea **W:** Garth Ennis ★ Appearance of Superman.
35 ❑ Mar 1999 Cover: 2.50 **NM** value: **Cover or less**
Circ: Diamd. preorders: **22,053**
📖 Katie, Part 1 **A:** John McCrea **W:** Garth Ennis ★ 1st Appearance of Frances Monaghan.
36 ❑ Apr 1999 Cover: 2.50 **NM** value: **Cover or less**
Circ: Diamd. preorders: **21,141**
📖 Katie, Part 2 **A:** John McCrea **W:** Garth Ennis ★ 2nd Appearance of Frances Monaghan. ★ Death of Tommy's mother.
37 ❑ May 1999 Cover: 2.50 **NM** value: **Cover or less**
Circ: Diamd. preorders: **21,651**
📖 Dead Man's Land; Dead Man's Land, Part 1 **A:** John McCrea **W:** Garth Ennis
38 ❑ Jun 1999 Cover: 2.50 **NM** value: **Cover or less**
Circ: Diamd. preorders: **21,921**
📖 Dead Man's Land; Dead Man's Land, Part 2 **A:** John McCrea **W:** Garth Ennis
39 ❑ Jul 1999 Cover: 2.50 **NM** value: **Cover or less**
Circ: Diamd. preorders: **21,338**
📖 For Tomorrow, Part 1 **A:** John McCrea **W:** Garth Ennis
40 ❑ Aug 1999 Cover: 2.50 **NM** value: **Cover or less**
Circ: Diamd. preorders: **21,171**
📖 For Tomorrow, Part 2 **A:** John McCrea **W:** Garth Ennis
41 ❑ Sep 1999 Cover: 2.50 **NM** value: **Cover or less**
Circ: Diamd. preorders: **21,052**
📖 For Tomorrow, Part 3 **A:** John McCrea **W:** Garth Ennis
42 ❑ Oct 1999 Cover: 2.50 **NM** value: **Cover or less**
Circ: Diamd. preorders: **20,827**
📖 For Tomorrow, Part 4 **A:** John McCrea **W:** Garth Ennis
43 ❑ Nov 1999 Cover: 2.50 **NM** value: **Cover or less**
Circ: Diamd. preorders: **20,350**
44 ❑ Dec 1999 Cover: 2.50 **NM** value: **Cover or less**
Circ: Diamd. preorders: **20,567**
📖 Fresh Meat, Part 1 **A:** John McCrea **W:** Garth Ennis
45 ❑ Jan 2000 Cover: 2.50 **NM** value: **Cover or less**
Circ: Diamd. preorders: **19,737**
📖 Fresh Meat, Part 2 **A:** John McCrea **W:** Garth Ennis
46 ❑ Feb 2000 Cover: 2.50 **NM** value: **Cover or less**
Circ: Diamd. preorders: **22,050**
📖 The Old Dog, Part 1 **A:** John McCrea **W:** Garth Ennis
47 ❑ Mar 2000 Cover: 2.50 **NM** value: **Cover or less**
Circ: Diamd. preorders: **19,173**
📖 The Old Dog, Part 2 **A:** John McCrea **W:** Garth Ennis
48 ❑ Apr 2000 Cover: 2.50 **NM** value: **Cover or less**
Circ: Diamd. preorders: **18,194**
49 ❑ May 2000 Cover: 2.50 **NM** value: **Cover or less**
Circ: Diamd. preorders: **18,531**
📖 The Old Dog, Part 3 **A:** John McCrea **W:** Garth Ennis
50 ❑ Jun 2000 Cover: 2.50 **NM** value: **Cover or less**
Circ: Diamd. preorders: **19,586**
51 ❑ Jul 2000 Cover: 2.50 **NM** value: **Cover or less**
Circ: Diamd. preorders: **18,920**
52 ❑ Aug 2000 Cover: 2.50 **NM** value: **Cover or less**
Circ: Diamd. preorders: **19,222**
53 ❑ Sep 2000 Cover: 2.50 **NM** value: **Cover or less**
Circ: Diamd. preorders: **19,477**
📖 Closing Time, Part 1 **A:** John McCrea **W:** Garth Ennis
54 ❑ Oct 2000 Cover: 2.50 **NM** value: **Cover or less**
Circ: Diamd. preorders: **18,302**
📖 Closing Time, Part 2 **A:** John McCrea **W:** Garth Ennis
55 ❑ Nov 2000 Cover: 2.50 **NM** value: **Cover or less**
Circ: Diamd. preorders: **18,584**
📖 Closing Time, Part 3 **A:** John McCrea **W:** Garth Ennis
56 ❑ Dec 2000 Cover: 2.50 **NM** value: **Cover or less**
Circ: Diamd. preorders: **18,556**
📖 Closing Time, Part 4 **A:** John McCrea **W:** Garth Ennis
57 ❑ Jan 2001 Cover: 2.50 **NM** value: **Cover or less**
Circ: Diamd. preorders: **18,595**
📖 Closing Time, Part 5 **A:** John McCrea **W:** Garth Ennis
58 ❑ Feb 2001 Cover: 2.50 **NM** value: **Cover or less**
Circ: Diamd. preorders: **18,420**
📖 Closing Time, Part 6 **A:** John McCrea **W:** Garth Ennis
59 ❑ Mar 2001 Cover: 2.50 **NM** value: **Cover or less**
Circ: Diamd. preorders: **18,215**
📖 Closing Time, Part 7 **A:** John McCrea **W:** Garth Ennis
60 ❑ Jun 2001 Cover: 2.50 **NM** value: **Cover or less**
Circ: Diamd. preorders: **19,144**
📖 Closing Time, Part 8 final issue. **A:** John McCrea **W:** Garth Ennis ★ Death of Hitman.
1000000❑Nov 1998 Cover: 2.50 **NM** value: **Cover or less**
Circ: Diamd. preorders: **30,184**
Anl 1❑ Cover: 3.95 **NM** value: **Cover or less**
• Pulp Heroes; 1997 Annual **A:** John McCrea **W:** Garth Ennis
Bk 1❑ Cover: 9.95 **NM** value: **Cover or less**
• collects issues #1-3, Demon Annual #2, and Batman Chronicles #4; Reprints Hitman stories from Demon Annual #2 (3rd Series), Batman Chronicles #4, Hitman #1-3 **A:** John McCrea **W:** Garth Ennis ★ 1st Appearance of Hitman.
Bk 2❑ Cover: 9.95 **NM** value: **Cover or less**
📖 10, 000 Bullets • collects issues #4-8 **A:** John McCrea **W:** Garth Ennis
Bk 3❑ Cover: 17.95 **NM** value: **Cover or less**
📖 Local Heroes • Local Heroes; collects #9-14, Annual #1 **A:** John McCrea **W:** Garth Ennis ★ Appearance of Green Lantern.

HITMAN/LOBO: THAT STUPID BASTICH — DC
1 ❑ Sep 2000 Cover: 3.95 **NM** value: **Cover or less**

HITOMI 2 — Antarctic
1 ❑ Aug 1993, b&w Cover: 2.50 **NM** value: **Cover or less**
2 ❑ Oct 1993, b&w Cover: 2.75 **NM** value: **Cover or less**
3 ❑ Dec 1993, b&w Cover: 2.75 **NM** value: **Cover or less**
4 ❑ Feb 1994, b&w Cover: 2.75 **NM** value: **Cover or less**
5 ❑ Apr 1994, b&w Cover: 2.75 **NM** value: **Cover or less**
6 ❑ Jul 1994, b&w Cover: 2.75 **NM** value: **Cover or less**
7 ❑ Nov 1994, b&w Cover: 2.75 **NM** value: **Cover or less**
8 ❑ Mar 1995, b&w Cover: 2.75 **NM** value: **Cover or less**
9 ❑ May 1995, b&w Cover: 2.75 **NM** value: **Cover or less**
📖 Shadow Hunter **A:** Dave Wilson **W:** Dave Wilson
10 ❑ May 1997, b&w Cover: 3.95 **NM** value: **Cover or less**

HITOMI AND HER GIRL COMMANDOS — Antarctic
1 ❑ Apr 1992, b&w Cover: 2.50 **NM** value: **Cover or less**
2 ❑ Jun 1992, b&w Cover: 2.50 **NM** value: **Cover or less**
3 ❑ Aug 1992, b&w Cover: 2.50 **NM** value: **Cover or less**
4 ❑ Oct 1992, b&w Cover: 2.50 **NM** value: **Cover or less**

HIT THE BEACH — Antarctic
1 ❑ Jul 1993, b&w Cover: 2.95 **NM** value: **Cover or less**
1/GO❑Jul 1993 Cover: 4.95 **NM** value: **Cover or less**
• Deluxe edition. • gold foil
2 ❑ Jul 1994, b&w Cover: 2.95 **NM** value: **Cover or less**
3 ❑ Jul 1995, b&w Cover: 2.95 **NM** value: **Cover or less**
4 ❑ Jul 1997, b&w Cover: 2.95 **NM** value: **Cover or less**
5 ❑ Jul 1998, b&w Cover: 2.95 **NM** value: **Cover or less**
• regular edition.
5/CS❑Jul 1998, b&w Cover: 4.95 **NM** value: **Cover or less**
• Special edition. • polybagged with postcard
6 ❑ Jul 1999 Cover: 3.95 **NM** value: **Cover or less**

HOBBIT, THE (J.R.R. TOLKIEN'S...) — Eclipse
1 ❑ Cover: 4.95 **NM** value: **Cover or less**
Circ: CapCity orders: **15,500** • **CGC:** 4 graded, best 9.8
2 ❑ Cover: 4.95 **NM** value: **Cover or less**
Circ: CapCity orders: **14,075**
3 ❑ Cover: 4.95 **NM** value: **Cover or less**
Circ: CapCity orders: **15,900**
Bk 1❑ Cover: 12.95 **NM** value: **Cover or less**
Circ: CapCity orders: **2,635**
Bk 1/HC❑ Cover: 39.95 **NM** value: **Cover or less**

HOCKEY MASTERS — Revolutionary
1 ❑ Dec 1993, b&w Cover: 2.95 **NM** value: **Cover or less**

HOE, THE — Thunderball
1 ❑ Cover: 2.50 **NM** value: **Cover or less**

HOGAN'S HEROES — Dell
1 ❑ Jun 1966 Cover: 0.12 **NM** value: **75.00**
• **CGC:** 1 graded, best 8.5
2 ❑ Sep 1966 Cover: 0.12 **NM** value: **50.00**
3 ❑ Nov 1966 Cover: 0.12 **NM** value: **50.00**
4 ❑ Jan 1967 Cover: 0.12 **NM** value: **50.00**
5 ❑ Mar 1967 Cover: 0.12 **NM** value: **45.00**
6 ❑ May 1967 Cover: 0.12 **NM** value: **45.00**
7 ❑ Jul 1967 Cover: 0.12 **NM** value: **45.00**
8 ❑ Sep 1967 Cover: 0.12 **NM** value: **30.00**
9 ❑ Oct 1969 Cover: 0.15 **NM** value: **30.00**

HOKUM & HEX — Marvel
1 ❑ Sep 1993 Cover: 2.50 **NM** value: **Cover or less**
Circ: CapCity orders: **29,100**
Embossed cover. 📖 Strange Angels **A:** Anthony Williams **W:** Frank Lovece ★ Origin of Trip Munroe.
2 ❑ Oct 1993 Cover: 1.75 **NM** value: **Cover or less**
Circ: CapCity orders: **11,500**
📖 A Convocation Of Clowns **A:** Anthony Williams **W:** Frank Lovece ★ Appearance of Felon Bale, Analyzer, Trip Monroe.
3 ❑ Nov 1993 Cover: 1.75 **NM** value: **Cover or less**
Circ: CapCity orders: **9,900**
4 ❑ Dec 1993 Cover: 1.75 **NM** value: **Cover or less**
Circ: CapCity orders: **9,000**
📖 Fire And Rust **A:** Anthony Williams **W:** Frank Lovece ★ Origin of Z-Man. ★ Death of Z-Man.
5 ❑ Jan 1994 Cover: 1.75 **NM** value: **Cover or less**
Circ: CapCity orders: **7,600**
6 ❑ Feb 1994 Cover: 1.75 **NM** value: **Cover or less**
Circ: CapCity orders: **6,100**
📖 Bloodshed, Part 1
7 ❑ Mar 1994 Cover: 1.75 **NM** value: **Cover or less**
Circ: CapCity orders: **9,950**
📖 Bloodshed, Part 2
8 ❑ Apr 1994 Cover: 1.75 **NM** value: **Cover or less**
Circ: CapCity orders: **4,300**
9 ❑ May 1994 Cover: 1.75 **NM** value: **Cover or less**
Circ: CapCity orders: **3,700**
final issue.

HOLIDAY COMICS — Star Publications
1 ❑ Jan 1951 Cover: 0.10 **NM** value: **250.00**
2 ❑ Apr 1951 Cover: 0.10 **NM** value: **200.00**
• **CGC:** 1 graded, best 7.0
3 ❑ Jul 1951 Cover: 0.10 **NM** value: **200.00**
4 ❑ Oct 1951 Cover: 0.10 **NM** value: **175.00**
• **CGC:** 1 graded, best 9.2
5 ❑ Jan 1952 Cover: 0.10 **NM** value: **175.00**
• **CGC:** 1 graded, best 5.0
6 ❑ Apr 1952 Cover: 0.10 **NM** value: **150.00**
7 ❑ Jul 1952 Cover: 0.10 **NM** value: **150.00**
8 ❑ Oct 1952 Cover: 0.10 **NM** value: **150.00**
• **CGC:** 1 graded, best 8.0

HOLIDAY FOR SCREAMS — Malibu
1 ❑ b&w Cover: 4.95 **NM** value: **Cover or less**
No issue number.

HOLIDAY OUT — Renegade
1 ❑ b&w Cover: 2.00 **NM** value: **Cover or less**
2 ❑ b&w Cover: 2.00 **NM** value: **Cover or less**
3 ❑ b&w Cover: 2.00 **NM** value: **Cover or less**

HOLLOW EARTH, THE — Vision
1 ❑ Cover: 2.50 **NM** value: **Cover or less**
2 ❑ Cover: 2.50 **NM** value: **Cover or less**
3 ❑ Jan 1997 Cover: 2.50 **NM** value: **Cover or less**
📖 Follow the Leader **A:** Mark Shaw **W:** Mark Shaw

HOLLYWOOD DETECTIVES — Eternity
Bk 1❑ b&w Cover: 3.95 **NM** value: **Cover or less**

HOLLYWOOD FUNNY FOLKS — DC
Hollywood Funny Folks was a continuation of the simpler-named Funny Folks, which was a "funny animal" comic book with the primary focus of Nutsy Squirrel, created by Rube Grossman. The zany character is chiefly distinguished by his red-and-white-striped long tie — admittedly, nutsy apparel for a squirrel.

The title's evolution was evidently predicated on the cachet that film would increase sales. But before long, there was yet another title change, and the series ended its run simply as Nutsy Squirrel. — Maggie

27 ❑ Aug 1950 Cover: 0.10 **NM** value: **100.00**
• **CGC:** 1 graded, best 6.5
28 ❑ Nov 1950 Cover: 0.10 **NM** value: **60.00**
29 ❑ Dec 1950 Cover: 0.10 **NM** value: **60.00**
30 ❑ Jan 1951 Cover: 0.10 **NM** value: **60.00**
31 ❑ Feb 1951 Cover: 0.10 **NM** value: **60.00**
32 ❑ Mar 1951 Cover: 0.10 **NM** value: **60.00**
33 ❑ Apr 1951 Cover: 0.10 **NM** value: **60.00**
34 ❑ May 1951 Cover: 0.10 **NM** value: **60.00**
35 ❑ Jun 1951 Cover: 0.10 **NM** value: **60.00**
36 ❑ Jul 1951 Cover: 0.10 **NM** value: **60.00**
37 ❑ May 1951 Cover: 0.10 **NM** value: **60.00**
38 ❑ Sep 1951 Cover: 0.10 **NM** value: **60.00**
39 ❑ Oct 1951 Cover: 0.10 **NM** value: **60.00**
40 ❑ Nov 1951 Cover: 0.10 **NM** value: **60.00**
41 ❑ Dec 1951 Cover: 0.10 **NM** value: **45.00**
• **CGC:** 1 graded, best 9.2
42 ❑ Jan 1952 Cover: 0.10 **NM** value: **45.00**
• **CGC:** 1 graded, best 8.0
43 ❑ Feb 1952 Cover: 0.10 **NM** value: **45.00**
44 ❑ Mar 1952 Cover: 0.10 **NM** value: **45.00**
45 ❑ Apr 1952 Cover: 0.10 **NM** value: **45.00**
46 ❑ May 1952 Cover: 0.10 **NM** value: **45.00**
47 ❑ Jun 1952 Cover: 0.10 **NM** value: **45.00**
48 ❑ Aug 1952 Cover: 0.10 **NM** value: **45.00**
49 ❑ Oct 1952 Cover: 0.10 **NM** value: **45.00**
50 ❑ Nov 1952 Cover: 0.10 **NM** value: **45.00**
51 ❑ Jan 1953 Cover: 0.10 **NM** value: **45.00**
52 ❑ Mar 1953 Cover: 0.10 **NM** value: **45.00**
53 ❑ May 1953 Cover: 0.10 **NM** value: **45.00**
54 ❑ Jul 1953 Cover: 0.10 **NM** value: **45.00**
55 ❑ Sep 1953 Cover: 0.10 **NM** value: **45.00**
56 ❑ Nov 1953 Cover: 0.10 **NM** value: **45.00**
57 ❑ Jan 1954 Cover: 0.10 **NM** value: **45.00**
58 ❑ Mar 1954 Cover: 0.10 **NM** value: **45.00**
59 ❑ May 1954 Cover: 0.10 **NM** value: **45.00**
60 ❑ Jul 1954 Cover: 0.10 **NM** value: **45.00**

HOLLYWOOD SUPERSTARS — Marvel / Epic
1 ❑ Nov 1990 Cover: 2.95 **NM** value: **Cover or less**
Circ: CapCity orders: **6,700**
📖 Stuntwork **A:** Don Spiegle; Dan Spiegle **W:** Mark Evanier
2 ❑ Jan 1991 Cover: 2.25 **NM** value: **Cover or less**
Circ: CapCity orders: **4,550**
3 ❑ Feb 1991 Cover: 2.25 **NM** value: **Cover or less**
Circ: CapCity orders: **3,750**
4 ❑ Mar 1991 Cover: 2.25 **NM** value: **Cover or less**
Circ: CapCity orders: **2,900**
5 ❑ Apr 1991 Cover: 2.25 **NM** value: **Cover or less**
Circ: CapCity orders: **2,250**

HOLO BROTHERS, THE — Monster
1 ❑ 1989 b&w Cover: 1.95 **NM** value: **Cover or less**
2 ❑ b&w Cover: 1.95 **NM** value: **Cover or less**
3 ❑ Cover: 2.25 **NM** value: **Cover or less**
4 ❑ Cover: 2.25 **NM** value: **Cover or less**
5 ❑ Cover: 2.25 **NM** value: **Cover or less**
6 ❑ Cover: 2.25 **NM** value: **Cover or less**

CGC-graded: Multiply prices above by **33 for 9.9 M • 16 for 9.8 NM/M • 7 for 9.6 NM+ • 5 for 9.4 NM • 2.5 for 9.2 NM- • 1.5 for 9.0 VF/NM**

7 ❑ Cover: 2.25 **NM** value: **Cover or less**
8 ❑ Cover: 2.25 **NM** value: **Cover or less**
9 ❑ Cover: 2.25 **NM** value: **Cover or less**
10 ❑ Cover: 2.25 **NM** value: **Cover or less**
SE 1❑ Cover: 2.25 **NM** value: **Cover or less**

HOLY AVENGER — Slave Labor
1 ❑ Apr 1996 Cover: 4.95 **NM** value: **Cover or less**

HOLY CROSS — Fantagraphics
0 ❑ b&w Cover: 4.95 **NM** value: **Cover or less**
1 ❑ Cover: 2.95 **NM** value: **Cover or less**
2 ❑ Oct 1994, b&w Cover: 2.95 **NM** value: **Cover or less**

HOMAGE STUDIOS SWIMSUIT SPECIAL — Image
1 ❑ Apr 1993 Cover: 1.95 **NM** value: **2.00**
• **CGC:** 2 graded, best 9.4
• pin-ups **A:** Jason Pearson; J. Scott Campbell; Joe Chiodo; Vic Bridges; Adam Hughes; Cully Hamner; Brett Booth; Trevor Scott; Marc Silvestri; Scott Clark; Jeffrey Scott; Karl Story; Scott Williams; Chris Ivy; Alex Garner

HOME GROWN FUNNIES — Kitchen Sink
1 ❑ Jan 1971 **NM** value: **55.00**
• **CGC:** 3 graded, best 9.8
1-2 ❑ **NM** value: **22.00**
1-3 ❑ **NM** value: **10.00**
1-4 ❑ **NM** value: **6.00**
1-5 ❑ **NM** value: **4.00**
1-6 ❑ **NM** value: **3.00**
1-7 ❑ **NM** value: **3.00**
1-8 ❑ **NM** value: **3.00**
1-9 ❑ **NM** value: **3.00**
1-10❑ **NM** value: **2.50**
1-11❑ **NM** value: **2.50**
1-12❑ **NM** value: **2.50**
1-13❑ **NM** value: **2.50**
1-14❑ **NM** value: **2.50**
1-15❑ Cover: 2.50 **NM** value: **Cover or less**

HOMELANDS ON THE WORLD OF MAGIC: THE GATHERING — Acclaim / Armada
1 ❑ Cover: 5.95 **NM** value: **Cover or less**
Circ: CapCity orders: **8,350**
No issue number. One-shot. • prestige format. • polybagged with Homelands card **A:** Rebecca Guay **W:** D.G. Chicester

HOMICIDE — Dark Horse
1 ❑ Apr 1990, b&w Cover: 1.95 **NM** value: **Cover or less**

HOMICIDE: TEARS OF THE DEAD — Chaos
1 ❑ Cover: 2.95 **NM** value: **Cover or less**

HOMO PATROL — Helpless Anger
All issues are adults only.
1 ❑ b&w Cover: 3.50 **NM** value: **Cover or less**
No issue number.

HONEYMOONERS, THE (LODESTONE) — Lodestone
This one-shot series preceded the longer Honeymooners series, which came out the following year from Triad. Although the publisher's name changed, it was produced by the same creative team.

From the classic lines "Bang, Zoom!" to "Baby, you're the greatest!" Jackie Gleason's Ralph Kramden returned in a faithfully rendered comic book, picking up from the "classic 39" syndicated episodes presented in the 1955 television series, The Honeymooners.

Follow the continuing antics and misadventures of Ralph, Norton, Trixie, Alice, Mrs. Manicotti, and all the other wonderful characters in both new stories, as well as in comic adaptations of "lost episodes." According to the publisher, all stories and artwork in this series were approved personally by Jackie Gleason.

Issues also contain "The $99,000.00 Answer," a fan letter "question and answer page," written by the president of R.A.L.P.H. (The Royal Association for the Longevity and Preservation of Honeymooners).

1 ❑ Oct 1986 Cover: 1.50 **NM** value: **Cover or less**
Photo cover. 📖 The Home Game **A:** Vince Musacchia **W:** Robert Loren Flemming

HONEYMOONERS, THE (TRIAD) — Triad
1 ❑ Sep 1987 Cover: 2.00 **NM** value: **Cover or less**
Photo cover. **W:** Robert Loren Flemming
2 ❑ Sep 1987 Cover: 2.00 **NM** value: **Cover or less**
Circ: CapCity orders: **3,250**
photo back cover. • reprints #1's indicia
3 ❑ Cover: 3.50 **NM** value: **Cover or less**
Circ: CapCity orders: **3,175**
wraparound cover. • Deluxe edition. 📖 She's a Wonderful Wife • squarebound **A:** Win Mortimer **C:** Win Mortimer **W:** Robert Loren Flemming
4 ❑ Jan 1988 Cover: 2.00 **NM** value: **Cover or less**
Circ: CapCity orders: **3,200**
photo back cover. 📖 In the Pink **A:** Vince Musacchia; Win Mortimer **W:** Robert Loren Flemming
5 ❑ Feb 1988 Cover: 2.00 **NM** value: **Cover or less**
Circ: CapCity orders: **3,000**
wraparound cover.
6 ❑ Mar 1988 Cover: 2.00 **NM** value: **Cover or less**
Circ: CapCity orders: **2,600**
photo back cover.
7 ❑ Apr 1988 Cover: 2.00 **NM** value: **Cover or less**
Circ: CapCity orders: **2,450**
wraparound cover. ★ Appearance of Captain Lou Albano.
8 ❑ May 1988 Cover: 2.00 **NM** value: **Cover or less**
wraparound cover.
9 ❑ Jul 1988 Cover: 3.95 **NM** value: **Cover or less**
Circ: CapCity orders: **2,250**
wraparound cover. • squarebound **C:** Jack Davis
10 ❑ Apr 1989 Cover: 2.00 **NM** value: **Cover or less**
Circ: CapCity orders: **2,150**
Photo cover. 📖 Minneapolis Here We Come **A:** Vince Musacchia **W:** Peter Crescenti
11 ❑ Jun 1989 Cover: 2.00 **NM** value: **Cover or less**
Photo cover. 📖 Take Me Out to the Ballgame! **A:** Vince Musacchia; Win Mortimer **W:** Norman Abramoff; Peter Crescenti
12 ❑ Aug 1989 Cover: 2.00 **NM** value: **Cover or less**
Photo cover. 📖 My Fare Lady **A:** Vince Musacchia **W:** Donna McCrohan
13 ❑ Cover: 2.00 **NM** value: **Cover or less**

HONG ON THE RANGE — Image
1 ❑ Dec 1997 Cover: 2.50 **NM** value: **Cover or less**
Circ: Diamd. preorders: **6,132**
📖 I Woke Up Wicked **A:** Jeff Lafferty **W:** Wm. F. Wu
2 ❑ Jan 1998 Cover: 2.50 **NM** value: **Cover or less**
Circ: Diamd. preorders: **4,486**
3 ❑ Feb 1998 Cover: 2.50 **NM** value: **Cover or less**
Circ: Diamd. preorders: **4,118**
📖 The Good, The Bad, and The Control-Natural **A:** Jeff Lafferty **W:** Wm. F. Wu

HONK! — Fantagraphics
1 ❑ Nov 1986, b&w Cover: 2.75 **NM** value: **Cover or less**
2 ❑ Jan 1987, b&w Cover: 2.75 **NM** value: **Cover or less**
3 ❑ Mar 1987, b&w Cover: 2.75 **NM** value: **Cover or less**
4 ❑ May 1987, b&w Cover: 2.75 **NM** value: **Cover or less**
5 ❑ Jul 1987, b&w Cover: 2.75 **NM** value: **Cover or less**

HONKO THE CLOWN — C&T
1 ❑ b&w Cover: 2.00 **NM** value: **Cover or less**

HONOR AMONG THIEVES — Gateway
1 ❑ Cover: 1.50 **NM** value: **Cover or less**

HOOD, THE — South Central
1 ❑ b&w Cover: 2.75 **NM** value: **Cover or less**

HOOD MAGAZINE — Oakland
1 ❑ Cover: 3.00 **NM** value: **Cover or less**
2 ❑ Cover: 3.00 **NM** value: **Cover or less**

HOODOO — 3-D Zone
1 ❑ Nov 1988, b&w Cover: 2.50 **NM** value: **Cover or less**
📖 Old Dave; The Black Cat Bone **A:** Mary Fleener **W:** Mary Fleener

HOOK — Marvel
1 ❑ Feb 1992 Cover: 1.00 **NM** value: **1.25**
Circ: CapCity orders: **9,600**
2 ❑ Feb 1992 Cover: 1.00 **NM** value: **1.25**
Circ: CapCity orders: **6,500**
3 ❑ Mar 1992 Cover: 1.00 **NM** value: **1.25**
Circ: CapCity orders: **6,200**
4 ❑ Mar 1992 Cover: 1.00 **NM** value: **1.25**
Circ: CapCity orders: **5,400**
Bk 1❑ Cover: 5.95 **NM** value: **Cover or less**
No issue number. • bookshelf; Collects series **A:** Denis Rodier; Anna-Maria Cool; John Ridgway; Ray Lago; Craig Hamilton **W:** Charles Vess

HOOK (MAGAZINE) — Marvel
1 ❑ Cover: 2.95 **NM** value: **Cover or less**
No issue number. • magazine.

HOON, THE — Eenieweenie
1 ❑ Jun 1995, b&w Cover: 2.50 **NM** value: **Cover or less**
2 ❑ Cover: 2.50 **NM** value: **Cover or less**
3 ❑ Cover: 2.50 **NM** value: **Cover or less**
4 ❑ Cover: 2.50 **NM** value: **Cover or less**
5 ❑ Cover: 2.50 **NM** value: **Cover or less**
6 ❑ Cover: 2.50 **NM** value: **Cover or less**

HOON, THE (VOL. 2) — Caliber / Tapestry
1 ❑ Cover: 2.95 **NM** value: **Cover or less**
2 ❑ Cover: 2.95 **NM** value: **Cover or less**

HOPALONG CASSIDY & THE FIVE MEN OF EVIL — AC
Bk 1❑ b&w Cover: 12.95 **NM** value: **Cover or less**

HOPSTER'S TRACKS — Bongo
1 ❑ b&w Cover: 2.95 **NM** value: **Cover or less**
Circ: Diamd. preorders: **3,418**
2 ❑ b&w Cover: 2.95 **NM** value: **Cover or less**

HORDE — Swing Shift
1 ❑ b&w Cover: 2.00 **NM** value: **Cover or less**

HORNY BIKER SLUTS — Last Gasp
All issues are adults only.
5 ❑ b&w Cover: 2.95 **NM** value: **Cover or less**

HORNY COMIX & STORIES — Rip Off
All issues are adults only.
1 ❑ Apr 1991, b&w Cover: 2.50 **NM** value: **Cover or less**
2 ❑ Jul 1991, b&w Cover: 2.50 **NM** value: **Cover or less**
3 ❑ Dec 1991, b&w Cover: 2.50 **NM** value: **Cover or less**
4 ❑ May 1992, b&w Cover: 2.50 **NM** value: **Cover or less**

HORNY TOADS (WALLACE WOOD'S...) — Fantagraphics / Eros
All issues are adults only.
1 ❑ b&w Cover: 2.95 **NM** value: **Cover or less**

HOROBI PART 1 — Viz
1 ❑ Mar 1990, b&w Cover: 3.75 **NM** value: **Cover or less**
📖 Omen 1 • Japanese **A:** Yoshihisa Tagami **W:** Yoshihisa Tagami
2 ❑ Apr 1990, b&w Cover: 3.75 **NM** value: **Cover or less**
• Japanese **A:** Yoshihisa Tagami **W:** Yoshihisa Tagami
3 ❑ May 1990, b&w Cover: 3.75 **NM** value: **Cover or less**
• Japanese **A:** Yoshihisa Tagami **W:** Yoshihisa Tagami
4 ❑ Jun 1990, b&w Cover: 3.75 **NM** value: **Cover or less**
• Japanese **A:** Yoshihisa Tagami **W:** Yoshihisa Tagami
5 ❑ Jul 1990, b&w Cover: 3.75 **NM** value: **Cover or less**
• Japanese **A:** Yoshihisa Tagami **W:** Yoshihisa Tagami
6 ❑ Aug 1990, b&w Cover: 3.75 **NM** value: **Cover or less**
• Japanese **A:** Yoshihisa Tagami **W:** Yoshihisa Tagami
7 ❑ Sep 1990, b&w Cover: 3.75 **NM** value: **Cover or less**
• Japanese **A:** Yoshihisa Tagami **W:** Yoshihisa Tagami
8 ❑ Oct 1990, b&w Cover: 3.75 **NM** value: **Cover or less**
• Japanese **A:** Yoshihisa Tagami **W:** Yoshihisa Tagami

HOROBI PART 2 — Viz
1 ❑ Nov 1990, b&w Cover: 4.25 **NM** value: **Cover or less**
📖 Genocide 56 • Japanese **A:** Yoshihisa Tagami **W:** Yoshihisa Tagami
2 ❑ Dec 1990, b&w Cover: 4.25 **NM** value: **Cover or less**
• Japanese **A:** Yoshihisa Tagami **W:** Yoshihisa Tagami
3 ❑ Jan 1991, b&w Cover: 4.25 **NM** value: **Cover or less**
• Japanese **A:** Yoshihisa Tagami **W:** Yoshihisa Tagami
4 ❑ Feb 1991, b&w Cover: 4.25 **NM** value: **Cover or less**
• Japanese **A:** Yoshihisa Tagami **W:** Yoshihisa Tagami
5 ❑ Mar 1991, b&w Cover: 4.25 **NM** value: **Cover or less**
• Japanese **A:** Yoshihisa Tagami **W:** Yoshihisa Tagami
6 ❑ Apr 1991, b&w Cover: 4.25 **NM** value: **Cover or less**
• Japanese **A:** Yoshihisa Tagami **W:** Yoshihisa Tagami
7 ❑ May 1991, b&w Cover: 4.25 **NM** value: **Cover or less**
• Japanese **A:** Yoshihisa Tagami **W:** Yoshihisa Tagami

HORRIBLE TRUTH ABOUT COMICS, THE — Alternative
1 ❑ Jan 1999, b&w Cover: 2.95 **NM** value: **Cover or less**
Circ: Diamd. preorders: **1,715**
No issue number. **A:** James Kochalka **W:** James Kochalka

HORROR HOUSE — AC
1 ❑ Cover: 2.95 **NM** value: **Cover or less**
📖 The Painted Beast! **A:** Wally Wood; Jack Kamen; Bob Powell; Marcus **W:** Wally Wood; Jack Kamen; Bob Powell

HORROR, THE ILLUSTRATED BOOK OF FEARS — Northstar
1 ❑ Cover: 3.95 **NM** value: **4.00**
📖 Timed Exposure; Bug House; Devil's Powder; On my Mind; Crushing Death; The Unforgiven; Perhaps, Dreamed by Many; And of Gideon **A:** Gary McCluskey; Vincent Locke; J.N. Williamson; John Maclay; Mark Bernal; Monty Sheldon; Timothy Walker **W:** Gary McCluskey; J.N. Williamson; John Maclay; Monty Sheldon; Timothy Walker; Bob Weinberg; Mort Castle; Paul Dane Anderson; Richard Christian Matheson
2 ❑ Feb 1990 Cover: 3.95 **NM** value: **4.00**
📖 Hurry Monster; Black Dot; Blood Rape of the Lust Ghouls; Little Holes; Earth Bound; the Wind and the Shadows; The Litter **A:** Dan Day; Ronn Sutton; Dell Barras; Mark Bernal; Myke Maldonado; Timothy Wacker; James O'Barr **W:** Vincent Locke; Timothy Wacker; Cindy Risley; David Schow; Graham Masterton; Jim Kisner; Lynn Hooper; W.C. Rasmussen

HORROR IN THE DARK — Fantagor
All issues are adults only.
1 ❑ b&w Cover: 2.00 **NM** value: **Cover or less**
📖 Tales of the Black Diamond, Blood Birth; Lame lem Love; Forgotten Tomb **A:** Rich Corben **W:** Rich Corben; Rich Margopoulos
2 ❑ b&w Cover: 2.00 **NM** value: **Cover or less**
📖 Tales of the Black Diamond, Bath of Blood; Gogy; Dreaming **A:** Rich Corben; Raul Demingo **W:** Rich Corben; Raul Demingo; Rich Margopoulos
3 ❑ b&w Cover: 2.00 **NM** value: **Cover or less**
4 ❑ b&w Cover: 2.00 **NM** value: **Cover or less**

HORRORIST, THE — DC / Vertigo
1 ❑ Dec 1995 Cover: 5.95 **NM** value: **Cover or less**
📖 Antarctica, Part 1 **A:** David Lloyd **W:** Jamie Delano ★ Appearance of John Constantine.
2 ❑ Jan 1996 Cover: 5.95 **NM** value: **Cover or less**
📖 Antarctica, Part 2 **A:** David Lloyd **W:** Jamie Delano ★ Appearance of John Constantine.

HORROR OF COLLIER COUNTY, THE — Dark Horse
1 ❑ Oct 1999 Cover: 2.95 **NM** value: **Cover or less**
Circ: Diamd. preorders: **6,115**
📖 Them **A:** Rich Tommaso **W:** Rich Tommaso
2 ❑ Cover: 2.95 **NM** value: **Cover or less**
Circ: Diamd. preorders: **4,615**
3 ❑ Cover: 2.95 **NM** value: **Cover or less**
Circ: Diamd. preorders: **4,202**
4 ❑ Cover: 2.95 **NM** value: **Cover or less**
Circ: Diamd. preorders: **3,359**
5 ❑ Cover: 2.95 **NM** value: **Cover or less**
Circ: Diamd. preorders: **2,970**

1 ❑ Apr 1991, b&w Cover: 2.50 **NM** value: **Cover or less**
2 ❑ Jul 1991, b&w Cover: 2.50 **NM** value: **Cover or less**
3 ❑ Dec 1991, b&w Cover: 2.50 **NM** value: **Cover or less**
4 ❑ May 1992, b&w Cover: 2.50 **NM** value: **Cover or less**

HORNY TOADS (WALLACE WOOD'S...) Fantagraphics / Eros

All issues are adults only.

1 ❑ b&w Cover: 2.95 **NM** value: **Cover or less**

HOROBI PART 1 Viz

1 ❑ Mar 1990, b&w Cover: 3.75 **NM** value: **Cover or less**
📖 Omen 1 • Japanese **A:** Yoshihisa Tagami **W:** Yoshihisa Tagami
2 ❑ Apr 1990, b&w Cover: 3.75 **NM** value: **Cover or less**
• Japanese **A:** Yoshihisa Tagami **W:** Yoshihisa Tagami
3 ❑ May 1990, b&w Cover: 3.75 **NM** value: **Cover or less**
• Japanese **A:** Yoshihisa Tagami **W:** Yoshihisa Tagami
4 ❑ Jun 1990, b&w Cover: 3.75 **NM** value: **Cover or less**
• Japanese **A:** Yoshihisa Tagami **W:** Yoshihisa Tagami
5 ❑ Jul 1990, b&w Cover: 3.75 **NM** value: **Cover or less**
• Japanese **A:** Yoshihisa Tagami **W:** Yoshihisa Tagami
6 ❑ Aug 1990, b&w Cover: 3.75 **NM** value: **Cover or less**
• Japanese **A:** Yoshihisa Tagami **W:** Yoshihisa Tagami
7 ❑ Sep 1990, b&w Cover: 3.75 **NM** value: **Cover or less**
• Japanese **A:** Yoshihisa Tagami **W:** Yoshihisa Tagami
8 ❑ Oct 1990, b&w Cover: 3.75 **NM** value: **Cover or less**
• Japanese **A:** Yoshihisa Tagami **W:** Yoshihisa Tagami

HOROBI PART 2 Viz

1 ❑ Nov 1990, b&w Cover: 4.25 **NM** value: **Cover or less**
📖 Genocide 56 • Japanese **A:** Yoshihisa Tagami **W:** Yoshihisa Tagami
2 ❑ Dec 1990, b&w Cover: 4.25 **NM** value: **Cover or less**
• Japanese **A:** Yoshihisa Tagami **W:** Yoshihisa Tagami
3 ❑ Jan 1991, b&w Cover: 4.25 **NM** value: **Cover or less**
• Japanese **A:** Yoshihisa Tagami **W:** Yoshihisa Tagami
4 ❑ Feb 1991, b&w Cover: 4.25 **NM** value: **Cover or less**
• Japanese **A:** Yoshihisa Tagami **W:** Yoshihisa Tagami
5 ❑ Mar 1991, b&w Cover: 4.25 **NM** value: **Cover or less**
• Japanese **A:** Yoshihisa Tagami **W:** Yoshihisa Tagami
6 ❑ Apr 1991, b&w Cover: 4.25 **NM** value: **Cover or less**
• Japanese **A:** Yoshihisa Tagami **W:** Yoshihisa Tagami
7 ❑ May 1991, b&w Cover: 4.25 **NM** value: **Cover or less**
• Japanese **A:** Yoshihisa Tagami **W:** Yoshihisa Tagami

HORRIBLE TRUTH ABOUT COMICS, THE Alternative

1 ❑ Jan 1999, b&w Cover: 2.95 **NM** value: **Cover or less**
Circ: Diamd. preorders: **1,715**
No issue number. **A:** James Kochalka **W:** James Kochalka

HORROR HOUSE AC

1 ❑ Cover: 2.95 **NM** value: **Cover or less**
📖 The Painted Beast! **A:** Wally Wood; Jack Kamen; Bob Powell; Marcus **W:** Wally Wood; Jack Kamen; Bob Powell

HORROR, THE ILLUSTRATED BOOK OF FEARS Northstar

1 ❑ Cover: 3.95 **NM** value: **4.00**
📖 Timed Exposure; Bug House; Devil's Powder; On my Mind; Crushing Death; The Unforgiven; Perhaps, Dreamed by Many; And of Gideon **A:** Gary McCluskey; Vincent Locke; J.N. Williamson; John Maclay; Mark Bernal; Monty Sheldon; Timothy Walker **W:** Gary McCluskey; J.N. Williamson; John Maclay; Monty Sheldon; Timothy Walker; Bob Weinberg; Mort Castle; Paul Dane Anderson; Richard Christian Matheson
2 ❑ Feb 1990 Cover: 3.95 **NM** value: **4.00**
📖 Hurry Monster; Black Dot; Blood Rape of the Lust Ghouls; Little Holes; Earth Bound; the Wind and the Shadows; The Litter **A:** Dan Day; Ronn Sutton; Dell Barras; Mark Bernal; Myke Maldonado; Timothy Wacker; James O'Barr **W:** Vincent Locke; Timothy Wacker; Cindy Risley; David Schow; Graham Masterton; Jim Kisner; Lynn Hooper; W.C. Rasmussen

HORROR IN THE DARK Fantagor

All issues are adults only.

1 ❑ b&w Cover: 2.00 **NM** value: **Cover or less**
📖 Tales of the Black Diamond, Blood Birth; Lame lem Love; Forgotten Tomb **A:** Rich Corben **W:** Rich Corben; Rich Margopoulos
2 ❑ b&w Cover: 2.00 **NM** value: **Cover or less**
📖 Tales of the Black Diamond, Bath of Blood; Gogy; Dreaming **A:** Rich Corben; Raul Demingo **W:** Rich Corben; Raul Demingo; Rich Margopoulos
3 ❑ b&w Cover: 2.00 **NM** value: **Cover or less**
4 ❑ b&w Cover: 2.00 **NM** value: **Cover or less**

HORRORIST, THE DC / Vertigo

1 ❑ Dec 1995 Cover: 5.95 **NM** value: **Cover or less**
📖 Antarctica, Part 1 **A:** David Lloyd **W:** Jamie Delano ★ Appearance of John Constantine.
2 ❑ Jan 1996 Cover: 5.95 **NM** value: **Cover or less**
📖 Antarctica, Part 2 **A:** David Lloyd **W:** Jamie Delano ★ Appearance of John Constantine.

HORROR OF COLLIER COUNTY, THE Dark Horse

1 ❑ Oct 1999 Cover: 2.95 **NM** value: **Cover or less**
Circ: Diamd. preorders: **6,115**
📖 Them **A:** Rich Tommaso **W:** Rich Tommaso
2 ❑ Cover: 2.95 **NM** value: **Cover or less**
Circ: Diamd. preorders: **4,615**
3 ❑ Cover: 2.95 **NM** value: **Cover or less**
Circ: Diamd. preorders: **4,202**
4 ❑ Cover: 2.95 **NM** value: **Cover or less**
Circ: Diamd. preorders: **3,359**
5 ❑ Cover: 2.95 **NM** value: **Cover or less**
Circ: Diamd. preorders: **2,970**

HORRORS OF THE HAUNTER AC

1 ❑ b&w Cover: 2.95 **NM** value: **Cover or less**

HORSE Slave Labor

1 ❑ Sep 1989, b&w Cover: 2.95 **NM** value: **Cover or less**
2 ❑ Cover: 2.95 **NM** value: **Cover or less**
3 ❑ Cover: 2.95 **NM** value: **Cover or less**

HORSEMAN Kevlar

0 ❑ b&w Cover: 2.95 **NM** value: **Cover or less**
no cover price. • Commemorative edition. • published after Crusade issue #1 **A:** Mshindo Kuumba L **W:** Hank Kwon
0/GO❑ May 1996 Cover: 2.95 **NM** value: **Cover or less**
gold foil-embossed cardstock cover. • published after Crusade issue #1 **A:** Mshindo Kuumba L **W:** Hank Kwon
0/SI❑ Cover: 2.95 **NM** value: **Cover or less**
no cover price or indicia. • published after Crusade issue #1
1 ❑ Mar 1996 Cover: 2.95 **NM** value: **Cover or less**
1/A ❑ Nov 1996 Cover: 2.95 **NM** value: **Cover or less**
• Kevlar edition. **A:** Buzz; Mshindo Kuumba I **W:** Hank Kwon; Jonathan Clarke
2 ❑ Jan 1997 Cover: 2.95 **NM** value: **Cover or less**

HOSIE'S HEROINES Slave Labor

All issues are adults only.

1 ❑ Apr 1993 Cover: 2.95 **NM** value: **Cover or less**
📖 The Asteroidisiac; Vic Blister...The Case of the Atomic Tongue **A:** Jeff John **W:** Jeff John

HOSTILE TAKEOVER Malibu

Ash 1❑ Sep 1994 Cover: 0.75 **NM** value: **Cover or less**
No issue number. • ashcan; Ultraverse Preview

HOT DOG Magazine Enterprises

Drawing heavily on funny animal animated shorts for inspiration, Hot Dog's basic premise is familiar. Hot Dog is an irascible type who expends enormous effort on gadgets that fail, and in predictable fashion his plots backfire on him. Blessed with an enormous ego not above underhanded tactics to achieve his aims, there is an obvious resemblance to Donald Duck.

It's not bad reading material, though. The gags work well and can still earn a smile, and the morality of the times always has Hot Dog getting his comeuppance. It's a type of comic book, so prevalent in the 1950s, that is all-too-absent today.

1 ❑ Cover: 0.10 **NM** value: **28.00**
• Indicia reads (A-1 #107)
2 ❑ Cover: 0.10 **NM** value: **18.00**
📖 Harry Hot Dog; Below Par; Complaint Crazy; Shoe Blue; Big Deal; Super Hotdog • Indicia reads (A-1 #113)
3 ❑ Cover: 0.10 **NM** value: **15.00**
• Indicia reads (A-1 #115)
4 ❑ Cover: 0.10 **NM** value: **15.00**
• Indicia reads (A-1 #136)

HOTEL HARBOUR VIEW Viz

1 ❑ b&w Cover: 9.95 **NM** value: **Cover or less**
• Japanese

HOTHEAD PAISAN: HOMICIDAL LESBIAN TERRORIST Giant Ass

13 ❑ Cover: 3.50 **NM** value: **Cover or less**

HOT LINE Eros

1 ❑ Nov 1992 Cover: 2.50 **NM** value: **Cover or less**
📖 Nymphos, Nazis, & Necrophiles **A:** Marti; Tabolina **W:** Marti; Tabolina

HOT MEXICAN LOVE COMICS Hot Mexican Love Comics

1 ❑ Cover: 3.95 **NM** value: **Cover or less**
2 ❑ Cover: 3.95 **NM** value: **Cover or less**

HOT N' COLD HEROES A-Plus

1 ❑ b&w Cover: 2.50 **NM** value: **Cover or less**
📖 The Last Monster Hunter!; Yellow Jacket; That Was No Lady; Mr Muscles: King of the Carnival; The Crash Kid **A:** John Byrne; Mike Zeck; J. Byrne; Jerry Siegel; Roger Beausoleil; Charles Nicholas **W:** Jerry Siegel; Nicola Cutii; Charles Nicholas; Len-Sly; Mike Carson ★ 1st Appearance of Hellsing.
2 ❑ Mar 1991 Cover: 2.50 **NM** value: **Cover or less**
• reprints O: Nemesis, Magicman

HOT NIGHTS IN RANGOON Eros

1 ❑ Cover: 2.95 **NM** value: **Cover or less**
2 ❑ Cover: 2.95 **NM** value: **Cover or less**
3 ❑ Nov 1994 Cover: 2.95 **NM** value: **Cover or less**

HOT PULP! Eclipse

Bk 1❑ b&w Cover: 9.95 **NM** value: **Cover or less**
• pulp stories, art

Looking for further information about a specific comic book or line of comics? Write a letter to ***Comics Buyer's Guide*** at ohso@krause.com — if we don't know, one of our readers always does!

HOT RODS AND RACING CARS Charlton

The reader's interest in this series of wild teenagers, muscle cars, and reckless driving doesn't last long enough to clock a decent time for a quarter mile. Almost every good guy is law-abiding, righteous, and a skillful driver. Almost every bad boy is inexperienced, stubborn, and a reckless driver.

So the formula is simple: bad boy has inflated opinion of his own driving skills, good guy thinks otherwise; then using proper driving techniques, good guy defeats bad boy.

It's hard enough depicting the speed of hurtling cars on the comics page, and it certainly doesn't help that the plots are about as exciting as a school bus drag race. Even the descriptions of the "hot rods" aren't particularly hot.

Auto enthusiasts may be better entertained digging up copies of Car-Toons.

1 ❑ Nov 1951 Cover: 0.10 **NM** value: **135.00**
2 ❑ Jan 1952 Cover: 0.10 **NM** value: **90.00**
3 ❑ Mar 1952 Cover: 0.10 **NM** value: **58.00**
4 ❑ May 1952 Cover: 0.10 **NM** value: **50.00**
5 ❑ Jul 1952 Cover: 0.10 **NM** value: **50.00**
6 ❑ Sep 1952 Cover: 0.10 **NM** value: **50.00**
7 ❑ Nov 1952 Cover: 0.10 **NM** value: **50.00**
8 ❑ Jan 1953 Cover: 0.10 **NM** value: **50.00**
9 ❑ Mar 1953 Cover: 0.10 **NM** value: **50.00**
10 ❑ May 1953 Cover: 0.10 **NM** value: **50.00**
11 ❑ Cover: 0.10 **NM** value: **36.00**
12 ❑ Cover: 0.10 **NM** value: **36.00**
13 ❑ Cover: 0.10 **NM** value: **36.00**
14 ❑ Cover: 0.10 **NM** value: **36.00**
15 ❑ Cover: 0.10 **NM** value: **36.00**
16 ❑ Cover: 0.10 **NM** value: **36.00**
17 ❑ Cover: 0.10 **NM** value: **36.00**
18 ❑ Cover: 0.10 **NM** value: **36.00**
19 ❑ Cover: 0.10 **NM** value: **36.00**
20 ❑ Cover: 0.10 **NM** value: **36.00**
21 ❑ Cover: 0.10 **NM** value: **28.00**
22 ❑ Cover: 0.10 **NM** value: **28.00**
23 ❑ Cover: 0.10 **NM** value: **28.00**
24 ❑ Cover: 0.10 **NM** value: **28.00**
25 ❑ Cover: 0.10 **NM** value: **28.00**
26 ❑ Cover: 0.10 **NM** value: **28.00**
27 ❑ Cover: 0.10 **NM** value: **28.00**
28 ❑ Cover: 0.10 **NM** value: **28.00**
29 ❑ 1957 Cover: 0.10 **NM** value: **28.00**
30 ❑ 1957 Cover: 0.10 **NM** value: **28.00**
31 ❑ Jul 1957 Cover: 0.10 **NM** value: **24.00**
32 ❑ 1957 Cover: 0.10 **NM** value: **24.00**
33 ❑ 1957 Cover: 0.10 **NM** value: **24.00**
34 ❑ Feb 1958 Cover: 0.10 **NM** value: **24.00**
• **CGC:** 1 graded, best 9.0
35 ❑ Jun 1958 Cover: 0.10 **NM** value: **24.00**
36 ❑ 1958 Cover: 0.10 **NM** value: **24.00**
37 ❑ 1958 Cover: 0.10 **NM** value: **24.00**
38 ❑ 1959 Cover: 0.10 **NM** value: **24.00**
39 ❑ 1959 Cover: 0.10 **NM** value: **24.00**
40 ❑ 1959 Cover: 0.10 **NM** value: **24.00**
41 ❑ Jul 1959 Cover: 0.10 **NM** value: **24.00**
42 ❑ 1959 Cover: 0.10 **NM** value: **24.00**
43 ❑ 1959 Cover: 0.10 **NM** value: **24.00**
44 ❑ 1960 Cover: 0.10 **NM** value: **24.00**
45 ❑ 1960 Cover: 0.10 **NM** value: **24.00**
46 ❑ 1960 Cover: 0.10 **NM** value: **24.00**
47 ❑ Aug 1960 Cover: 0.10 **NM** value: **24.00**
48 ❑ Oct 1960 Cover: 0.10 **NM** value: **24.00**
49 ❑ Dec 1960 Cover: 0.10 **NM** value: **24.00**
50 ❑ Feb 1961 Cover: 0.10 **NM** value: **24.00**
Circ: Statement: **125,515**
51 ❑ 1961 Cover: 0.10 **NM** value: **18.00**
Circ: Statement: **125,515**
52 ❑ 1961 Cover: 0.10 **NM** value: **18.00**
Circ: Statement: **125,515**
53 ❑ 1961 Cover: 0.10 **NM** value: **18.00**
Circ: Statement: **125,515**
54 ❑ 1961 Cover: 0.10 **NM** value: **18.00**
Circ: Statement: **125,515**
55 ❑ 1961 Cover: 0.10 **NM** value: **18.00**
Circ: Statement: **125,515**
56 ❑ Mar 1962 Cover: 0.10 **NM** value: **18.00**
57 ❑ 1962 **NM** value: **18.00**
58 ❑ 1962 **NM** value: **18.00**
59 ❑ 1962 **NM** value: **18.00**
60 ❑ 1962 **NM** value: **18.00**
61 ❑ 1962 **NM** value: **13.00**
62 ❑ Mar 1963 Cover: 0.12 **NM** value: **13.00**
63 ❑ May 1963 Cover: 0.12 **NM** value: **13.00**
64 ❑ Jul 1963 Cover: 0.12 **NM** value: **13.00**
65 ❑ Sep 1963 Cover: 0.12 **NM** value: **13.00**
66 ❑ Cover: 0.12 **NM** value: **13.00**
67 ❑ Cover: 0.12 **NM** value: **13.00**
68 ❑ 1964 Cover: 0.12 **NM** value: **13.00**
69 ❑ Jun 1964 Cover: 0.12 **NM** value: **13.00**
70 ❑ Sep 1964 Cover: 0.12 **NM** value: **13.00**
71 ❑ 1964 Cover: 0.12 **NM** value: **13.00**
72 ❑ 1965 Cover: 0.12 **NM** value: **13.00**
Circ: Statement: **143,342**
73 ❑ 1965 Cover: 0.12 **NM** value: **13.00**
Circ: Statement: **143,342**
74 ❑ 1965 Cover: 0.12 **NM** value: **13.00**

CGC-graded: Multiply prices above by **33 for 9.9 M • 16 for 9.8 NM/M • 7 for 9.6 NM+ • 5 for 9.4 NM • 2.5 for 9.2 NM- • 1.5 for 9.0 VF/NM**

📖 Soace Station Dora; The Vanguard; House on Whore Hill; Scarecrow; Orion-Chapter III; Mercy; Kenshi Blade! **A:** Alex Toth; Gray Morrow; Mike Vosburg; Ernie Colon; Bil and Nil Maher; Bob Kline; Dr. William Stillwell **W:** Alex Toth; Gray Morrow; Mike Vosburg; Dr. William Stillwell; Jan Strnad; Bil and Nish Maher; Bob Keenan

5 ❑ 1977 Cover: 1.50 **NM** value: **3.00**
6 ❑ Dec 1977 Cover: 2.00 **NM** value: **3.00**

📖 12 Parts; The Apprentice; The Walls of the City; Hornmania; Manimal; Steel Souls; Winter of '94 **A:** Mike Nasser; Ernie Colon; Rich Larson; Bil Maher; Gail Schlesser **W:** Mike Nasser; Ernie Colon; Bil Maher; Gail Schlesser; Jan Strnad; Steve Grant

7 ❑ Cover: 2.00 **NM** value: **3.00**
8 ❑ Cover: 2.00 **NM** value: **3.00**

HOT STUFF BIG BOOK — Harvey

1 ❑ Nov 1992 Cover: 1.95 **NM** value: **Cover or less**
2 ❑ Cover: 1.95 **NM** value: **Cover or less**

HOT STUFF DIGEST — Harvey

1 ❑ Cover: 2.25 **NM** value: **Cover or less**

📖 Anything You Can Do; Devilish Godfather; Stumbo: Danger from Afar; Richie: Dresses Can Be Dangerous; Strictly From Hunger; Stumbo: What Am I Good For; Richie: The Fast Force; The Little Stranger; Mayda Munny: Missing Miss Misses

2 ❑ Cover: 2.25 **NM** value: **Cover or less**
3 ❑ Cover: 1.75 **NM** value: **Cover or less**
4 ❑ Cover: 1.75 **NM** value: **Cover or less**
5 ❑ Cover: 1.75 **NM** value: **Cover or less**

📖 The Hot Rider; Something Fishy; Tomorrowland; The Big Devil; No Trouble, He Says; Stumbo: The Big Gift Problem; Stumbo: The Spaceman

HOT STUFF GIANT SIZE — Harvey

1 ❑ Oct 1992 Cover: 2.25 **NM** value: **Cover or less**
2 ❑ Jul 1993 Cover: 2.25 **NM** value: **Cover or less**
3 ❑ Oct 1993 Cover: 2.25 **NM** value: **Cover or less**

HOT STUFF, THE LITTLE DEVIL — Harvey

Hot Stuff shares the Enchanted Forest with such popular characters as Casper and Wendy. He's basically a good guy, but it's not really in his nature to be nice all the time. He usually lives up to his name by solving his problems with a blast of fire from his pitchfork.

The cast includes his fiery-haired Auntie and his perpetually cussing Grandpa Blaze, who both want the little devil to act more, well, devilish. Their problem is with the fairy princess Charma, his unlikely little girlfriend. Like the "tuff" ghost Spooky, Hot Stuff's good deeds are often done to impress his best girl.

In addition to 19 years in Devil Kids, Hot Stuff also appeared in Hot Stuff Sizzlers and Creepy Caves. Stumbo the Giant was first introduced in Hot Stuff the Little Devil #2 and remained a regular feature.

1 ❑ Oct 1957 Cover: 0.10 **NM** value: **160.00**
• **CGC:** 2 graded, best 6.0
2 ❑ Dec 1957 Cover: 0.10 **NM** value: **90.00**
3 ❑ Feb 1958 Cover: 0.10 **NM** value: **65.00**
4 ❑ Apr 1958 Cover: 0.10 **NM** value: **65.00**
5 ❑ Jun 1958 Cover: 0.10 **NM** value: **65.00**
6 ❑ Aug 1958 Cover: 0.10 **NM** value: **55.00**
7 ❑ Sep 1958 Cover: 0.10 **NM** value: **55.00**
8 ❑ Dec 1958 Cover: 0.10 **NM** value: **55.00**
9 ❑ Feb 1959 Cover: 0.10 **NM** value: **55.00**
10 ❑ Apr 1959 Cover: 0.10 **NM** value: **55.00**
11 ❑ May 1959 Cover: 0.10 **NM** value: **42.00**
12 ❑ Jun 1959 Cover: 0.10 **NM** value: **42.00**
13 ❑ Jul 1959 Cover: 0.10 **NM** value: **42.00**
14 ❑ Aug 1959 Cover: 0.10 **NM** value: **42.00**
15 ❑ Sep 1959 Cover: 0.10 **NM** value: **42.00**
16 ❑ Oct 1959 Cover: 0.10 **NM** value: **42.00**
17 ❑ Nov 1959 Cover: 0.10 **NM** value: **42.00**
18 ❑ Dec 1959 Cover: 0.10 **NM** value: **42.00**
19 ❑ Jan 1960 Cover: 0.10 **NM** value: **42.00**
20 ❑ Feb 1960 Cover: 0.10 **NM** value: **42.00**
21 ❑ Mar 1960 Cover: 0.10 **NM** value: **30.00**
22 ❑ Apr 1960 Cover: 0.10 **NM** value: **30.00**
23 ❑ May 1960 Cover: 0.10 **NM** value: **30.00**
24 ❑ Jun 1960 Cover: 0.10 **NM** value: **30.00**
25 ❑ Jul 1960 Cover: 0.10 **NM** value: **30.00**
26 ❑ Aug 1960 Cover: 0.10 **NM** value: **30.00**
27 ❑ Sep 1960 Cover: 0.10 **NM** value: **30.00**
28 ❑ Oct 1960 Cover: 0.10 **NM** value: **30.00**
29 ❑ Nov 1960 Cover: 0.10 **NM** value: **30.00**
30 ❑ Dec 1960 Cover: 0.10 **NM** value: **30.00**
31 ❑ Jan 1961 Cover: 0.10 **NM** value: **16.00**
32 ❑ Feb 1961 Cover: 0.10 **NM** value: **16.00**
33 ❑ Mar 1961 Cover: 0.10 **NM** value: **16.00**
34 ❑ Apr 1961 Cover: 0.10 **NM** value: **16.00**
35 ❑ May 1961 Cover: 0.10 **NM** value: **16.00**
36 ❑ Jun 1961 Cover: 0.10 **NM** value: **16.00**
37 ❑ Jul 1961 Cover: 0.10 **NM** value: **16.00**
38 ❑ Aug 1961 Cover: 0.10 **NM** value: **16.00**
39 ❑ Sep 1961 Cover: 0.10 **NM** value: **16.00**
40 ❑ Oct 1961 Cover: 0.10 **NM** value: **16.00**
41 ❑ Nov 1961 Cover: 0.10 **NM** value: **12.00**
42 ❑ Dec 1961 Cover: 0.10 **NM** value: **12.00**
43 ❑ 1962 Cover: 0.12 **NM** value: **12.00**
Circ: Statement: **265,409**
44 ❑ 1962 Cover: 0.12 **NM** value: **12.00**
Circ: Statement: **265,409**
45 ❑ 1962 Cover: 0.12 **NM** value: **12.00**
Circ: Statement: **265,409**
46 ❑ 1962 Cover: 0.12 **NM** value: **12.00**
Circ: Statement: **265,409**
47 ❑ 1962 Cover: 0.12 **NM** value: **12.00**
Circ: Statement: **265,409**
48 ❑ 1962 Cover: 0.12 **NM** value: **12.00**
Circ: Statement: **265,409**
49 ❑ 1962 Cover: 0.12 **NM** value: **12.00**
Circ: Statement: **265,409**
50 ❑ Oct 1962 Cover: 0.12 **NM** value: **12.00**
Circ: Statement: **265,409**
51 ❑ Dec 1962 Cover: 0.12 **NM** value: **10.00**
Circ: Statement: **265,409**
52 ❑ Feb 1963 Cover: 0.12 **NM** value: **10.00**
53 ❑ Apr 1963 Cover: 0.12 **NM** value: **10.00**
54 ❑ Jun 1963 Cover: 0.12 **NM** value: **10.00**
55 ❑ Aug 1963 Cover: 0.12 **NM** value: **10.00**
56 ❑ Oct 1963 Cover: 0.12 **NM** value: **10.00**
57 ❑ Dec 1963 Cover: 0.12 **NM** value: **10.00**
58 ❑ Feb 1964 Cover: 0.12 **NM** value: **10.00**
59 ❑ Apr 1964 Cover: 0.12 **NM** value: **10.00**
60 ❑ Jun 1964 Cover: 0.12 **NM** value: **10.00**
61 ❑ Aug 1964 Cover: 0.12 **NM** value: **10.00**
62 ❑ Oct 1964 Cover: 0.12 **NM** value: **10.00**
63 ❑ Dec 1964 Cover: 0.12 **NM** value: **10.00**
64 ❑ Feb 1965 Cover: 0.12 **NM** value: **10.00**
65 ❑ Apr 1965 Cover: 0.12 **NM** value: **10.00**
66 ❑ Jun 1965 Cover: 0.12 **NM** value: **10.00**
67 ❑ Aug 1965 Cover: 0.12 **NM** value: **10.00**
68 ❑ Oct 1965 Cover: 0.12 **NM** value: **10.00**
69 ❑ Dec 1965 Cover: 0.12 **NM** value: **10.00**
70 ❑ Feb 1966 Cover: 0.12 **NM** value: **10.00**
71 ❑ Apr 1966 Cover: 0.12 **NM** value: **6.00**
72 ❑ Jun 1966 Cover: 0.12 **NM** value: **6.00**
73 ❑ Aug 1966 Cover: 0.12 **NM** value: **6.00**
74 ❑ Oct 1966 Cover: 0.12 **NM** value: **6.00**
75 ❑ Dec 1966 Cover: 0.12 **NM** value: **6.00**
76 ❑ Feb 1967 Cover: 0.12 **NM** value: **6.00**
77 ❑ Apr 1967 Cover: 0.12 **NM** value: **6.00**
78 ❑ Jun 1967 Cover: 0.12 **NM** value: **6.00**
79 ❑ Aug 1967 Cover: 0.12 **NM** value: **6.00**
80 ❑ Oct 1967 Cover: 0.12 **NM** value: **6.00**
81 ❑ Dec 1967 Cover: 0.12 **NM** value: **6.00**
82 ❑ Feb 1968 Cover: 0.12 **NM** value: **6.00**
83 ❑ Apr 1968 Cover: 0.12 **NM** value: **6.00**
84 ❑ Jun 1968 Cover: 0.12 **NM** value: **6.00**
85 ❑ Aug 1968 Cover: 0.12 **NM** value: **6.00**
86 ❑ Oct 1968 Cover: 0.12 **NM** value: **6.00**
87 ❑ Dec 1968 Cover: 0.12 **NM** value: **6.00**
88 ❑ Feb 1969 Cover: 0.12 **NM** value: **6.00**
89 ❑ 1969 Cover: 0.12 **NM** value: **6.00**
90 ❑ May 1969 Cover: 0.12 **NM** value: **6.00**
91 ❑ Jul 1969 Cover: 0.12 **NM** value: **6.00**
92 ❑ 1969 Cover: 0.15 **NM** value: **6.00**
93 ❑ Oct 1969 Cover: 0.15 **NM** value: **6.00**
94 ❑ 1969 Cover: 0.15 **NM** value: **6.00**
95 ❑ Jan 1970 Cover: 0.15 **NM** value: **6.00**
96 ❑ Mar 1970 Cover: 0.15 **NM** value: **6.00**
97 ❑ May 1970 Cover: 0.15 **NM** value: **6.00**
98 ❑ 1970 Cover: 0.15 **NM** value: **6.00**
99 ❑ 1970 Cover: 0.15 **NM** value: **6.00**
100 ❑ 1970 Cover: 0.15 **NM** value: **6.00**
101 ❑ Cover: 0.15 **NM** value: **4.00**
102 ❑ Cover: 0.15 **NM** value: **4.00**
103 ❑ Mar 1971 Cover: 0.15 **NM** value: **4.00**
• **CGC:** 1 graded, best 8.0
104 ❑ May 1971 Cover: 0.15 **NM** value: **4.00**
105 ❑ Jul 1971 Cover: 0.15 **NM** value: **4.00**
106 ❑ Sep 1971 Cover: 0.25 **NM** value: **4.00**
107 ❑ Nov 1971 Cover: 0.25 **NM** value: **4.00**
108 ❑ Jan 1972 Cover: 0.25 **NM** value: **4.00**
Circ: Statement: **130,343**
109 ❑ Mar 1972 Cover: 0.25 **NM** value: **4.00**
Circ: Statement: **130,343**
110 ❑ May 1972 Cover: 0.25 **NM** value: **4.00**
Circ: Statement: **130,343**
111 ❑ Jul 1972 Cover: 0.25 **NM** value: **4.00**
Circ: Statement: **130,343**
112 ❑ Sep 1972 Cover: 0.25 **NM** value: **4.00**
Circ: Statement: **130,343**
113 ❑ Nov 1972 Cover: 0.20 **NM** value: **4.00**
Circ: Statement: **130,343**
114 ❑ Jan 1973 Cover: 0.20 **NM** value: **4.00**
Circ: Statement: **138,353**
115 ❑ Mar 1973 Cover: 0.20 **NM** value: **4.00**
Circ: Statement: **138,353**
116 ❑ May 1973 Cover: 0.20 **NM** value: **4.00**
Circ: Statement: **138,353**
117 ❑ Jul 1973 Cover: 0.20 **NM** value: **4.00**
Circ: Statement: **138,353**
• Has 1972 Statement; avg total paid circ 130,343
118 ❑ Sep 1973 Cover: 0.20 **NM** value: **4.00**
Circ: Statement: **138,353**
119 ❑ Nov 1973 Cover: 0.20 **NM** value: **4.00**
Circ: Statement: **138,353**
120 ❑ Jan 1974 Cover: 0.20 **NM** value: **4.00**
Circ: Statement: **148,014**
121 ❑ Mar 1974 Cover: 0.20 **NM** value: **3.00**
Circ: Statement: **148,014**
122 ❑ May 1974 Cover: 0.25 **NM** value: **3.00**
Circ: Statement: **148,014**
• Has 1973 Statement; avg total paid circ 138,353
123 ❑ Jul 1974 Cover: 0.25 **NM** value: **3.00**
Circ: Statement: **148,014**
124 ❑ Sep 1974 Cover: 0.25 **NM** value: **3.00**
Circ: Statement: **148,014**
125 ❑ Nov 1974 Cover: 0.25 **NM** value: **3.00**
Circ: Statement: **148,014**
126 ❑ Jan 1975 Cover: 0.25 **NM** value: **3.00**
Circ: Statement: **124,021**
127 ❑ Mar 1975 Cover: 0.25 **NM** value: **3.00**
Circ: Statement: **124,021**
128 ❑ May 1975 Cover: 0.25 **NM** value: **3.00**
Circ: Statement: **124,021**
• Has 1974 Statement; avg total paid circ 148,014
129 ❑ Jul 1975 Cover: 0.25 **NM** value: **3.00**
Circ: Statement: **124,021**
130 ❑ Sep 1975 Cover: 0.25 **NM** value: **3.00**
Circ: Statement: **124,021**
131 ❑ Nov 1975 Cover: 0.25 **NM** value: **3.00**
Circ: Statement: **124,021**
132 ❑ Jan 1976 Cover: 0.25 **NM** value: **3.00**
133 ❑ Mar 1976 Cover: 0.25 **NM** value: **3.00**
134 ❑ May 1976 Cover: 0.25 **NM** value: **3.00**
135 ❑ Jul 1976 Cover: 0.30 **NM** value: **3.00**
136 ❑ Sep 1976 Cover: 0.30 **NM** value: **3.00**
137 ❑ Nov 1976 Cover: 0.30 **NM** value: **3.00**
138 ❑ Jan 1977 Cover: 0.30 **NM** value: **3.00**
139 ❑ Mar 1977 Cover: 0.30 **NM** value: **3.00**
140 ❑ May 1977 Cover: 0.30 **NM** value: **3.00**
141 ❑ Jul 1977 Cover: 0.30 **NM** value: **2.00**
142 ❑ Feb 1978 **NM** value: **2.00**
143 ❑ Apr 1978 **NM** value: **2.00**
144 ❑ Jun 1978 Cover: 0.35 **NM** value: **2.00**
145 ❑ Sep 1978 Cover: 0.35 **NM** value: **2.00**
146 ❑ Dec 1978 Cover: 0.35 **NM** value: **2.00**
147 ❑ Feb 1979 Cover: 0.35 **NM** value: **2.00**
148 ❑ Apr 1979 Cover: 0.35 **NM** value: **2.00**
149 ❑ Jun 1979 Cover: 0.35 **NM** value: **2.00**
150 ❑ Aug 1979 **NM** value: **2.00**
151 ❑ Oct 1979 Cover: 0.40 **NM** value: **2.00**
152 ❑ Cover: 0.40 **NM** value: **2.00**
153 ❑ 1980 Cover: 0.40 **NM** value: **2.00**
154 ❑ May 1980 Cover: 0.40 **NM** value: **2.00**
155 ❑ Jul 1980 Cover: 0.40 **NM** value: **2.00**
156 ❑ Sep 1980 Cover: 0.50 **NM** value: **2.00**
157 ❑ Nov 1980 Cover: 0.50 **NM** value: **2.00**
158 ❑ Jan 1981 Cover: 0.50 **NM** value: **2.00**
159 ❑ Mar 1981 Cover: 0.50 **NM** value: **2.00**
160 ❑ May 1981 Cover: 0.50 **NM** value: **2.00**
161 ❑ Jul 1981 Cover: 0.50 **NM** value: **2.00**
162 ❑ Sep 1981 Cover: 0.50 **NM** value: **2.00**
163 ❑ Nov 1981 Cover: 0.50 **NM** value: **2.00**
164 ❑ **NM** value: **2.00**
165 ❑ Oct 1986 Cover: 0.75 **NM** value: **2.00**
166 ❑ Dec 1986 Cover: 0.75 **NM** value: **2.00**
167 ❑ Feb 1987 Cover: 0.75 **NM** value: **2.00**
168 ❑ Apr 1987 Cover: 0.75 **NM** value: **2.00**
169 ❑ Jun 1987 Cover: 0.75 **NM** value: **2.00**
170 ❑ Sep 1987 Cover: 0.75 **NM** value: **2.00**
171 ❑ **NM** value: **2.00**
172 ❑ **NM** value: **2.00**
173 ❑ Sep 1990 Cover: 1.00 **NM** value: **2.00**
174 ❑ Oct 1990 Cover: 1.00 **NM** value: **2.00**
175 ❑ Nov 1990 Cover: 1.00 **NM** value: **2.00**
176 ❑ Dec 1990 Cover: 1.00 **NM** value: **2.00**
177 ❑ Jan 1991 Cover: 1.00 **NM** value: **2.00**

HOT STUFF SIZZLERS — Harvey

1 ❑ Jul 1960 Cover: 0.25 **NM** value: **1.25**

HOT STUFF (VOL. 2) — Harvey

1 ❑ Sep 1991 Cover: 1.00 **NM** value: **1.50**
2 ❑ Dec 1991 Cover: 1.25 **NM** value: **Cover or less**
3 ❑ Mar 1992 Cover: 1.25 **NM** value: **Cover or less**
4 ❑ Jun 1992 Cover: 1.25 **NM** value: **Cover or less**
5 ❑ Sep 1992 Cover: 1.25 **NM** value: **Cover or less**

📖 Story Book Land; Smile-durn You, Smile; Stop Clouding me; The Unseen Invader!

6 ❑ Mar 1993 Cover: 1.25 **NM** value: **Cover or less**
7 ❑ May 1993 Cover: 1.25 **NM** value: **Cover or less**
8 ❑ Aug 1993 Cover: 1.25 **NM** value: **Cover or less**
9 ❑ Nov 1993 Cover: 1.50 **NM** value: **Cover or less**
10 ❑ Jan 1994 Cover: 1.50 **NM** value: **Cover or less**
11 ❑ 1994 Cover: 1.50 **NM** value: **Cover or less**
12 ❑ Jun 1994 Cover: 1.50 **NM** value: **Cover or less**

HOT TAILS — Eros

1 ❑ **NM** value: **3.50**
Circ: Diamd. preorders: **6,125**

HOT WHEELS — DC

1 ❑ Apr 1970 Cover: 0.15 **NM** value: **30.00**
• **CGC:** 3 graded, best 9.4
2 ❑ Jun 1970 Cover: 0.15 **NM** value: **20.00**
3 ❑ Aug 1970 Cover: 0.15 **NM** value: **16.00**
4 ❑ Oct 1970 Cover: 0.15 **NM** value: **16.00**
5 ❑ Dec 1970 Cover: 0.15 **NM** value: **16.00**
• **CGC:** 2 graded, best 9.2
6 ❑ Feb 1971 Cover: 0.15 **NM** value: **16.00**

There are two different pricing tiers in the modern comic-book hobby. **The prices seen above** are the prices we have seen **loose copies** of these issues reliably fetch in a variety of environments. Condition alters the price by the fractions seen on the bar on the bottom of left-hand pages of this book. **Comics graded by CGC** usually sell for more. Use the guide on the bottom of right-hand pages of this book to estimate what copies have brought on eBay.

Other grades: Multiply prices above by **1.5 for Mint • 2/3 for Very Fine • 1/3 for Fine • 1/5 for Very Good • 1/8 for Good**

HOURMAN — DC

OK, you're an android from the 853rd century, and you're programmed with the memories of Rex Tyler, the Golden Age Hourman. After nearly destroying the universe in the DC One Million limited series, you settle down in your past — somewhere around the turn of the 21st century — and give up a good portion of your chronal powers, you decide that you dearly want to be as human as possible. So to whom do you turn for help? Why, former Justice League of America mascot Snapper Carr, that's who! Sure, he's something of a loser, but he needs a purpose in life and it may as well be you.

This was a fun, imaginative super-hero series — certainly one of the best to come out of the late 1990s. Hourman struggled to gain humanity, and it was a thrill to watch him take on such foes as Amazo, The JLAndroids, Epoch the Lord of Time, and his own makers in the 853rd century.

1 ❑ Apr 1999 Cover: 2.50 **NM** value: **Cover or less**
Circ: Diamd. preorders: **37,499**
📖 Through the Hourglass **A:** Rags Morales **W:** Tom Peyer ★ Appearance of Amazo, Justice League of America, Snapper Carr. ★ Versus Amazo.
1/Aut❑ **NM** value: **15.95**
2 ❑ May 1999 Cover: 2.50 **NM** value: **Cover or less**
Circ: Diamd. preorders: **27,623**
3 ❑ Jun 1999 Cover: 2.50 **NM** value: **Cover or less**
Circ: Diamd. preorders: **26,715**
📖 Timepoint **A:** Rags Morales **W:** Tom Peyer
4 ❑ Jul 1999 Cover: 2.50 **NM** value: **Cover or less**
Circ: Diamd. preorders: **24,260**
5 ❑ Aug 1999 Cover: 2.50 **NM** value: **Cover or less**
Circ: Diamd. preorders: **23,070**
📖 The Death of Hourman **A:** Rags Morales **W:** Tom Peyer ★ Appearance of Golden Age Hourman.
6 ❑ Sep 1999 Cover: 2.50 **NM** value: **Cover or less**
Circ: Diamd. preorders: **22,048**
📖 The JLAndroids **A:** Rags Morales **W:** Tom Peyer ★ Versus Amazo.
7 ❑ Oct 1999 Cover: 2.50 **NM** value: **Cover or less**
Circ: Diamd. preorders: **20,399**
📖 The Human League **A:** Rags Morales **W:** Tom Peyer ★ Versus Amazo.
8 ❑ Nov 1999 Cover: 2.50 **NM** value: **Cover or less**
Circ: Diamd. preorders: **21,322**
📖 A Week With No Hourman • Day of Judgment **A:** Rags Morales **W:** Tom Peyer
9 ❑ Dec 1999 Cover: 2.50 **NM** value: **Cover or less**
Circ: Diamd. preorders: **18,827**
📖 Where Does the Time Go? **A:** Rags Morales **W:** Tom Peyer
10 ❑ Jan 2000 Cover: 2.50 **NM** value: **Cover or less**
Circ: Diamd. preorders: **17,639**
📖 Bride of the Gombezi **A:** Rags Morales; Mark Propst **W:** Tom Peyer
11 ❑ Feb 2000 Cover: 2.50 **NM** value: **Cover or less**
Circ: Diamd. preorders: **17,868**
📖 Hourman One Million, Part 1 **A:** Rags Morales **W:** Tom Peyer
12 ❑ Mar 2000 Cover: 2.50 **NM** value: **Cover or less**
Circ: Diamd. preorders: **16,583**
📖 Hourman One Million, Part 2 **A:** Rags Morales **W:** Tom Peyer
13 ❑ Apr 2000 Cover: 2.50 **NM** value: **Cover or less**
Circ: Diamd. preorders: **16,028**
📖 Hourman One Million, Part 3 **A:** Rags Morales **W:** Tom Peyer
14 ❑ May 2000 Cover: 2.50 **NM** value: **Cover or less**
Circ: Diamd. preorders: **16,332**
📖 Secrets and Lies **A:** Rags Morales **W:** Tom Peyer
15 ❑ Jun 2000 Cover: 2.50 **NM** value: **Cover or less**
Circ: Diamd. preorders: **16,241**
📖 Friend of the Devil **A:** Rags Morales **W:** Tom Peyer
16 ❑ Jul 2000 Cover: 2.50 **NM** value: **Cover or less**
Circ: Diamd. preorders: **16,603**
17 ❑ Aug 2000 Cover: 2.50 **NM** value: **Cover or less**
Circ: Diamd. preorders: **15,585**
18 ❑ Sep 2000 Cover: 2.50 **NM** value: **Cover or less**
Circ: Diamd. preorders: **16,105**
19 ❑ Oct 2000 Cover: 2.50 **NM** value: **Cover or less**
Circ: Diamd. preorders: **15,270**
📖 The Thief of Time **A:** Rags Morales **W:** Tom Peyer
20 ❑ Nov 2000 Cover: 2.50 **NM** value: **Cover or less**
Circ: Diamd. preorders: **14,943**
📖 My So-Called Afterlife **A:** Howard Porter; Jason Orfalas **W:** Christopher Priest; Tom Peyer
21 ❑ Dec 2000 Cover: 2.50 **NM** value: **Cover or less**
Circ: Diamd. preorders: **14,717**
📖 Maybe I'm Amazo **A:** Rags Morales **W:** Tom Peyer
22 ❑ Jan 2001 Cover: 2.50 **NM** value: **Cover or less**
Circ: Diamd. preorders: **14,703**
📖 The Chrono-Bums **A:** Tony Harris **W:** Tom Peyer
23 ❑ Feb 2001 Cover: 2.50 **NM** value: **Cover or less**
Circ: Diamd. preorders: **13,987**
📖 The Unbelievable Truth **A:** Rags Morales **W:** Tom Peyer
24 ❑ Mar 2001 Cover: 2.50 **NM** value: **Cover or less**
Circ: Diamd. preorders: **13,565**
📖 Minutes to Go **A:** Rags Morales **W:** Tom Peyer
25 ❑ Apr 2001 Cover: 2.50 **NM** value: **Cover or less**
Circ: Diamd. preorders: **13,679**
📖 ...But You'll Never See the End of the Road if You're Travelling With Me **A:** Rags Morales **W:** Tom Peyer

HOUSE II THE SECOND STORY — Marvel

1 ❑ Oct 1987 Cover: 2.00 **NM** value: **Cover or less**

HOUSE OF FRIGHTENSTEIN — AC

1 ❑ b&w Cover: 2.95 **NM** value: **Cover or less**

HOUSE OF JAVA — NBM

1 ❑ b&w Cover: 8.95 **NM** value: **Cover or less**
• digest.

HOUSE OF MYSTERY — DC

Beginning in 1951, the House of Mystery welcomed its readers into the dark world of the mysterious and macabre. Cain, the caretaker, was the host, as readers reveled in his strange tales of ghosts, witchcraft, demons from beyond the grave, and terror from our own world. No true fear fan dared miss a single issue.

Alas, after 321 issues and more than 30 years, the House had to close its doors. But even in its final issue, the title stayed true to form. In a last story, fictitious DC editors planned to turn the "House of Mystery" into "Condo of Fun." Cain, cantankerous till the end, responded by moving his pet ghouls into the DC publishing offices. Although the strategy failed, it was a fitting send-off to one of the best-loved fright titles of all time.

1 ❑ Dec 1951 Cover: 0.10 **NM** value: **1650.00**
• **CGC:** 11 graded, best 9.4
📖 Wanda Was a Werewolf; I Fell in Love with a Witch; Man--or Monster; The Curse of Seabury Manor
2 ❑ Feb 1952 Cover: 0.10 **NM** value: **690.00**
• **CGC:** 3 graded, best 9.4
📖 I Was a Dead Man; Mark of X; Tree of Doom; Experiment of Dr. Grimm
3 ❑ Apr 1952 Cover: 0.10 **NM** value: **540.00**
• **CGC:** 6 graded, best 9.4
📖 The Dummy of Death
4 ❑ Jun 1952 Cover: 0.10 **NM** value: **425.00**
• **CGC:** 1 graded, best 9.6
📖 The Man With the Evil Eye
5 ❑ Aug 1952 Cover: 0.10 **NM** value: **425.00**
📖 I Was a Witch; Man With the Strangler Hands; Caravan of Miracles; Man Who was Death
6 ❑ Sep 1952 Cover: 0.10 **NM** value: **320.00**
📖 Telltale Hand; The Devil was My Partner
7 ❑ Oct 1952 Cover: 0.10 **NM** value: **320.00**
• **CGC:** 2 graded, best 9.0
📖 The Nine Lives of Roger Denham; Devil Mask of Death; Riddle of the Split-Siamese Twins
8 ❑ Nov 1952 Cover: 0.10 **NM** value: **320.00**
• **CGC:** 3 graded, best 9.2
📖 Tattoos of Doom; The Grim Jester; Nemesis from the Grave
9 ❑ Dec 1952 Cover: 0.10 **NM** value: **320.00**
• **CGC:** 1 graded, best 7.5
📖 Secret of the Little Black Bag; Partners in Fear; Unwanted Guest;Ghost Writer
10 ❑ Jan 1953 Cover: 0.10 **NM** value: **320.00**
📖 Wishes of Doom; The Magician Who Haunted Hollywood; The Bewitched Brush; Weirdest Museum in the World
11 ❑ Feb 1953 Cover: 0.10 **NM** value: **255.00**
• **CGC:** 1 graded, best 8.5
📖 The Grim Game of Ghost; Nine Lives Equals Death; The Demon; The Bewitched Clock
12 ❑ Mar 1953 Cover: 0.10 **NM** value: **255.00**
• **CGC:** 1 graded, best 8.5
📖 Secret of the Matador's Sword; Men Never Die in Cell Thirteen; The Devil's Chessboard; Black Future
13 ❑ Apr 1953 Cover: 0.10 **NM** value: **255.00**
• **CGC:** 1 graded, best 9.0
14 ❑ May 1953 Cover: 0.10 **NM** value: **255.00**
📖 The Deadly Dolls; I Hired a Ghost; Melody of Death; Crimes of the Black Cat
15 ❑ Jun 1953 Cover: 0.10 **NM** value: **255.00**
• **CGC:** 1 graded, best 9.0
📖 The Man Who Could Change People; The Winged Demon; Curse of the Golden Secret; Last Mile Martin
16 ❑ Jul 1953 Cover: 0.10 **NM** value: **195.00**
📖 The Man Who Killed His Shadow; His Name on a Bullet; Lady Luck Wore Black
17 ❑ Aug 1953 Cover: 0.10 **NM** value: **195.00**
📖 Station Ghost; Man With the X-Ray Eyes; Beauty and the Beast; Ordeal of Roger Black
18 ❑ Sep 1953 Cover: 0.10 **NM** value: **195.00**
📖 The Devil-Bird!; Dance of Doom; Bravest Man Alive; The Mechanical Mind
19 ❑ Oct 1953 Cover: 0.10 **NM** value: **195.00**
📖 The Strange Faces of Death; Ghost Writer; Man of Evil; Spirit's Revenge
20 ❑ Nov 1953 Cover: 0.10 **NM** value: **195.00**
📖 Mr. Mortem Was He the Man of Death; The Hex on My House; The Lamp that Changed People; The Beast of Bristol
21 ❑ Dec 1953 Cover: 0.10 **NM** value: **195.00**
• **CGC:** 1 graded, best 8.5
📖 The Magic Spotlight; Madman of Maricombe Island; Sorrow of the Spirits; Man Who Could See Death
22 ❑ Jan 1954 Cover: 0.10 **NM** value: **195.00**
📖 Isle of the Ageless; Phantom's Return; Second Life of General Marcellus
23 ❑ Feb 1954 Cover: 0.10 **NM** value: **195.00**
📖 Stamps of Doom; The Flying Dutchman; Gangster and the Ghost; The Phantom Highwayman Rides Again
24 ❑ Mar 1954 Cover: 0.10 **NM** value: **195.00**
📖 The Bewitched Beauty; Freak Show of Doom; Flaming Treasure; Kill the Black Cat
25 ❑ Apr 1954 Cover: 0.10 **NM** value: **195.00**
📖 The Hands That Could Kill; Devil's Toyshop; The Man with Three Eyes;Whirlpool of Doom
26 ❑ May 1954 Cover: 0.10 **NM** value: **150.00**
• **CGC:** 1 graded, best 9.2
📖 The Human Target; The Man with Magic Ears; Ship From the Past; Dress of Doom
27 ❑ Jun 1954 Cover: 0.10 **NM** value: **150.00**
📖 Fate Held Four Aces; The Mask of Durano; Death's I.O.U.; The Man Who Built a Crazy House
28 ❑ Jul 1954 Cover: 0.10 **NM** value: **150.00**
• **CGC:** 1 graded, best 9.0
📖 The Clock Strikes Death; Wings for Mr. Milo; The Spider Man
29 ❑ Aug 1954 Cover: 0.10 **NM** value: **150.00**
• **CGC:** 2 graded, best 9.4
30 ❑ Sep 1954 Cover: 0.10 **NM** value: **150.00**
• **CGC:** 2 graded, best 9.4
31 ❑ Oct 1954 Cover: 0.10 **NM** value: **150.00**
32 ❑ Nov 1954 Cover: 0.10 **NM** value: **150.00**
33 ❑ Dec 1954 Cover: 0.10 **NM** value: **150.00**
34 ❑ Jan 1955 Cover: 0.10 **NM** value: **150.00**
• **CGC:** 1 graded, best 9.4
35 ❑ Feb 1955 Cover: 0.10 **NM** value: **150.00**
36 ❑ Mar 1955 Cover: 0.10 **NM** value: **125.00**
37 ❑ Apr 1955 Cover: 0.10 **NM** value: **125.00**
38 ❑ May 1955 Cover: 0.10 **NM** value: **125.00**
39 ❑ Jun 1955 Cover: 0.10 **NM** value: **125.00**
• **CGC:** 1 graded, best 9.0
40 ❑ Jul 1955 Cover: 0.10 **NM** value: **125.00**
41 ❑ Aug 1955 Cover: 0.10 **NM** value: **125.00**
• **CGC:** 1 graded, best 7.5
42 ❑ Sep 1955 Cover: 0.10 **NM** value: **125.00**
43 ❑ Oct 1955 Cover: 0.10 **NM** value: **125.00**
44 ❑ Nov 1955 Cover: 0.10 **NM** value: **125.00**
45 ❑ Dec 1955 Cover: 0.10 **NM** value: **125.00**
46 ❑ Jan 1956 Cover: 0.10 **NM** value: **125.00**
47 ❑ Feb 1956 Cover: 0.10 **NM** value: **125.00**
48 ❑ Mar 1956 Cover: 0.10 **NM** value: **125.00**
• **CGC:** 1 graded, best 9.2
49 ❑ Apr 1956 Cover: 0.10 **NM** value: **125.00**
50 ❑ May 1956 Cover: 0.10 **NM** value: **125.00**
51 ❑ Jun 1956 Cover: 0.10 **NM** value: **90.00**
• **CGC:** 1 graded, best 9.0
52 ❑ Jul 1956 Cover: 0.10 **NM** value: **90.00**
53 ❑ Aug 1956 Cover: 0.10 **NM** value: **90.00**
54 ❑ Sep 1956 Cover: 0.10 **NM** value: **90.00**
55 ❑ Oct 1956 Cover: 0.10 **NM** value: **90.00**
56 ❑ Nov 1956 Cover: 0.10 **NM** value: **90.00**
57 ❑ Dec 1956 Cover: 0.10 **NM** value: **90.00**
58 ❑ Jan 1957 Cover: 0.10 **NM** value: **90.00**
59 ❑ Feb 1957 Cover: 0.10 **NM** value: **90.00**
60 ❑ Mar 1957 Cover: 0.10 **NM** value: **90.00**
• **CGC:** 1 graded, best 9.0
61 ❑ Apr 1957 Cover: 0.10 **NM** value: **90.00**
62 ❑ May 1957 Cover: 0.10 **NM** value: **65.00**
• **CGC:** 1 graded, best 7.0
63 ❑ Jun 1957 Cover: 0.10 **NM** value: **85.00**
64 ❑ Jul 1957 Cover: 0.10 **NM** value: **65.00**
65 ❑ Aug 1957 Cover: 0.10 **NM** value: **85.00**
66 ❑ Sep 1957 Cover: 0.10 **NM** value: **65.00**
67 ❑ Oct 1957 Cover: 0.10 **NM** value: **65.00**
68 ❑ Nov 1957 Cover: 0.10 **NM** value: **65.00**
69 ❑ Dec 1957 Cover: 0.10 **NM** value: **65.00**
70 ❑ Jan 1958 Cover: 0.10 **NM** value: **85.00**
71 ❑ Feb 1958 Cover: 0.10 **NM** value: **65.00**
72 ❑ Mar 1958 Cover: 0.10 **NM** value: **65.00**
• **CGC:** 1 graded, best 9.4
73 ❑ Apr 1958 Cover: 0.10 **NM** value: **65.00**
74 ❑ May 1958 Cover: 0.10 **NM** value: **65.00**
75 ❑ Jun 1958 Cover: 0.10 **NM** value: **65.00**
76 ❑ Jul 1958 Cover: 0.10 **NM** value: **85.00**
77 ❑ Aug 1958 Cover: 0.10 **NM** value: **65.00**
78 ❑ Sep 1958 Cover: 0.10 **NM** value: **65.00**
79 ❑ Oct 1958 Cover: 0.10 **NM** value: **65.00**
• **CGC:** 1 graded, best 2.5
80 ❑ Nov 1958 Cover: 0.10 **NM** value: **54.00**
📖 The Ghost Planet
81 ❑ Dec 1958 Cover: 0.10 **NM** value: **54.00**
82 ❑ Jan 1959 Cover: 0.10 **NM** value: **54.00**
83 ❑ Feb 1959 Cover: 0.10 **NM** value: **54.00**
84 ❑ Mar 1959 Cover: 0.10 **NM** value: **85.00**
• **CGC:** 1 graded, best 8.5
85 ❑ Apr 1959 Cover: 0.10 **NM** value: **85.00**
86 ❑ May 1959 Cover: 0.10 **NM** value: **54.00**
87 ❑ Jun 1959 Cover: 0.10 **NM** value: **54.00**
88 ❑ Jul 1959 Cover: 0.10 **NM** value: **54.00**
89 ❑ Aug 1959 Cover: 0.10 **NM** value: **54.00**
90 ❑ Sep 1959 Cover: 0.10 **NM** value: **54.00**
91 ❑ Oct 1959 Cover: 0.10 **NM** value: **54.00**
92 ❑ Nov 1959 Cover: 0.10 **NM** value: **54.00**
93 ❑ Dec 1959 Cover: 0.10 **NM** value: **54.00**
Circ: Statement: **208,000**
94 ❑ Jan 1960 Cover: 0.10 **NM** value: **54.00**
Circ: Statement: **208,000**
95 ❑ Feb 1960 Cover: 0.10 **NM** value: **54.00**
Circ: Statement: **208,000**
96 ❑ Mar 1960 Cover: 0.10 **NM** value: **54.00**
Circ: Statement: **208,000**
97 ❑ Apr 1960 Cover: 0.10 **NM** value: **54.00**
Circ: Statement: **208,000** • **CGC:** 1 graded, best 5.5
98 ❑ May 1960 Cover: 0.10 **NM** value: **54.00**
Circ: Statement: **208,000**
99 ❑ Jun 1960 Cover: 0.10 **NM** value: **54.00**
Circ: Statement: **208,000**
100 ❑ Jul 1960 Cover: 0.10 **NM** value: **65.00**
Circ: Statement: **208,000**
101 ❑ Aug 1960 Cover: 0.10 **NM** value: **45.00**
Circ: Statement: **208,000** • **CGC:** 1 graded, best 8.5

CGC-graded: Multiply prices above by **33 for 9.9 M • 16 for 9.8 NM/M • 7 for 9.6 NM+ • 5 for 9.4 NM • 2.5 for 9.2 NM- • 1.5 for 9.0 VF/NM**

102 ❑ Sep 1960 Cover: 0.10 **NM** value: **45.00**
Circ: Statement: **208,000**
103 ❑ Oct 1960 Cover: 0.10 **NM** value: **45.00**
Circ: Statement: **208,000**
104 ❑ Nov 1960 Cover: 0.10 **NM** value: **45.00**
Circ: Statement: **208,000** • **CGC:** 1 graded, best 8.0
105 ❑ Dec 1960 Cover: 0.10 **NM** value: **45.00**
Circ: Statement: **225,000** • **CGC:** 1 graded, best 8.5
106 ❑ Jan 1961 Cover: 0.10 **NM** value: **45.00**
Circ: Statement: **225,000**
107 ❑ Feb 1961 Cover: 0.10 **NM** value: **45.00**
Circ: Statement: **225,000**
• Has 1960 Statement; avg total paid circ 208,000
108 ❑ Mar 1961 Cover: 0.10 **NM** value: **45.00**
Circ: Statement: **225,000** • **CGC:** 1 graded, best 9.2
109 ❑ Apr 1961 Cover: 0.10 **NM** value: **45.00**
Circ: Statement: **225,000**
110 ❑ May 1961 Cover: 0.10 **NM** value: **45.00**
Circ: Statement: **225,000**
111 ❑ Jun 1961 Cover: 0.10 **NM** value: **45.00**
Circ: Statement: **225,000**
112 ❑ Jul 1961 Cover: 0.10 **NM** value: **45.00**
Circ: Statement: **225,000** • **CGC:** 2 graded, best 9.0
113 ❑ Aug 1961 **NM** value: **45.00**
Circ: Statement: **225,000**
114 ❑ Sep 1961 **NM** value: **45.00**
Circ: Statement: **225,000**
115 ❑ Oct 1961 **NM** value: **45.00**
Circ: Statement: **225,000** • **CGC:** 1 graded, best 8.0
116 ❑ Nov 1961 **NM** value: **45.00**
Circ: Statement: **225,000**
117 ❑ Dec 1961 Cover: 0.12 **NM** value: **35.00**
Circ: Statement: **175,000**
118 ❑ Jan 1962 Cover: 0.12 **NM** value: **35.00**
Circ: Statement: **175,000** • **CGC:** 1 graded, best 8.5
119 ❑ Feb 1962 Cover: 0.12 **NM** value: **35.00**
Circ: Statement: **175,000** • **CGC:** 1 graded, best 8.5
• Has 1961 Statement, filed 10/1/61; avg total paid circ 225,000
120 ❑ Mar 1962 Cover: 0.12 **NM** value: **45.00**
Circ: Statement: **175,000**
121 ❑ Apr 1962 Cover: 0.12 **NM** value: **28.00**
Circ: Statement: **175,000**
122 ❑ May 1962 Cover: 0.12 **NM** value: **28.00**
Circ: Statement: **175,000**
123 ❑ Jun 1962 Cover: 0.12 **NM** value: **28.00**
Circ: Statement: **175,000** • **CGC:** 1 graded, best 9.2
124 ❑ Jul 1962 Cover: 0.12 **NM** value: **28.00**
Circ: Statement: **175,000**
125 ❑ Aug 1962 Cover: 0.12 **NM** value: **28.00**
Circ: Statement: **175,000** • **CGC:** 1 graded, best 9.0
126 ❑ Sep 1962 Cover: 0.12 **NM** value: **28.00**
Circ: Statement: **175,000**
127 ❑ Oct 1962 Cover: 0.12 **NM** value: **28.00**
Circ: Statement: **175,000** • **CGC:** 1 graded, best 5.0
128 ❑ Nov 1962 Cover: 0.12 **NM** value: **28.00**
Circ: Statement: **175,000**
129 ❑ Dec 1962 Cover: 0.12 **NM** value: **28.00**
130 ❑ Jan 1963 Cover: 0.12 **NM** value: **28.00**
131 ❑ Feb 1963 Cover: 0.12 **NM** value: **22.00**
132 ❑ Mar 1963 Cover: 0.12 **NM** value: **22.00**
133 ❑ Apr 1963 Cover: 0.12 **NM** value: **22.00**
• **CGC:** 2 graded, best 9.4
134 ❑ May 1963 Cover: 0.12 **NM** value: **22.00**
135 ❑ Jun 1963 Cover: 0.12 **NM** value: **22.00**
136 ❑ Jul 1963 Cover: 0.12 **NM** value: **22.00**
137 ❑ Sep 1963 Cover: 0.12 **NM** value: **22.00**
138 ❑ Oct 1963 Cover: 0.12 **NM** value: **22.00**
139 ❑ Dec 1963 Cover: 0.12 **NM** value: **22.00**
140 ❑ Jan 1964 Cover: 0.12 **NM** value: **22.00**
141 ❑ Mar 1964 Cover: 0.12 **NM** value: **22.00**
142 ❑ Apr 1964 Cover: 0.12 **NM** value: **22.00**
143 ❑ Jun 1964 Cover: 0.12 **NM** value: **110.00**
• **CGC:** 5 graded, best 9.2
• J'onn J'onzz; Martian Manhunter begins
144 ❑ Jul 1964 Cover: 0.12 **NM** value: **55.00**
• **CGC:** 8 graded, best 9.6
145 ❑ Sep 1964 Cover: 0.12 **NM** value: **45.00**
• **CGC:** 2 graded, best 9.6
146 ❑ Oct 1964 Cover: 0.12 **NM** value: **45.00**
147 ❑ Dec 1964 Cover: 0.12 **NM** value: **45.00**
• **CGC:** 5 graded, best 9.4
148 ❑ Jan 1965 Cover: 0.12 **NM** value: **45.00**
Circ: Statement: **196,677** • **CGC:** 2 graded, best 9.4
149 ❑ Mar 1965 Cover: 0.12 **NM** value: **45.00**
Circ: Statement: **196,677**
• Has 1964 Statement, filed 10/1/64; no circ figures published **A:** Alex Toth
150 ❑ Apr 1965 Cover: 0.12 **NM** value: **45.00**
Circ: Statement: **196,677**
151 ❑ Jun 1965 Cover: 0.12 **NM** value: **45.00**
Circ: Statement: **196,677** • **CGC:** 1 graded, best 9.0
152 ❑ Jul 1965 Cover: 0.12 **NM** value: **45.00**
Circ: Statement: **196,677** • **CGC:** 2 graded, best 9.2
153 ❑ Sep 1965 Cover: 0.12 **NM** value: **45.00**
Circ: Statement: **196,677** • **CGC:** 2 graded, best 9.6
• J'onn J'onzz
154 ❑ Oct 1965 Cover: 0.12 **NM** value: **45.00**
Circ: Statement: **196,677** • **CGC:** 2 graded, best 9.4
155 ❑ Dec 1965 Cover: 0.12 **NM** value: **45.00**
Circ: Statement: **196,677** • **CGC:** 2 graded, best 9.6
156 ❑ Jan 1966 Cover: 0.12 **NM** value: **80.00**
Circ: Statement: **183,934** • **CGC:** 4 graded, best 9.8
157 ❑ Mar 1966 Cover: 0.12 **NM** value: **40.00**
Circ: Statement: **183,934** • **CGC:** 2 graded, best 9.6
158 ❑ Apr 1966 Cover: 0.12 **NM** value: **40.00**
Circ: Statement: **183,934** • **CGC:** 2 graded, best 9.6
159 ❑ Jun 1966 Cover: 0.12 **NM** value: **40.00**
Circ: Statement: **183,934** • **CGC:** 2 graded, best 9.6
160 ❑ Jul 1966 Cover: 0.12 **NM** value: **75.00**
Circ: Statement: **183,934** • **CGC:** 12 graded, best 9.4
• Dial "H" for Hero; Robby Reed becomes Plastic Man; Has 1965 Statement, filed 10/1/65; avg print run 331,000; avg sales 196,000; avg subs 677; avg total paid 196,677; samples 142; max existent 196,819; 41% of run returned
161 ❑ Sep 1966 Cover: 0.12 **NM** value: **35.00**
Circ: Statement: **183,934** • **CGC:** 1 graded, best 7.5
• Dial "H" for Hero
162 ❑ Oct 1966 Cover: 0.12 **NM** value: **35.00**
Circ: Statement: **183,934** • **CGC:** 2 graded, best 9.2
163 ❑ Dec 1966 Cover: 0.12 **NM** value: **35.00**
Circ: Statement: **183,934** • **CGC:** 1 graded, best 9.2
164 ❑ Jan 1967 Cover: 0.12 **NM** value: **35.00**
Circ: Statement: **158,500**
165 ❑ Mar 1967 Cover: 0.12 **NM** value: **35.00**
Circ: Statement: **158,500** • **CGC:** 2 graded, best 9.2
• Has 1966 Statement, filed 10/1/66; avg print run 326,000; avg sales 183,000; avg subs 934; avg total paid 183,934; max existent 183,934; 44% of run returned
166 ❑ Apr 1967 Cover: 0.12 **NM** value: **35.00**
Circ: Statement: **158,500** • **CGC:** 2 graded, best 9.4
167 ❑ Jun 1967 Cover: 0.12 **NM** value: **35.00**
Circ: Statement: **158,500** • **CGC:** 1 graded, best 9.2
168 ❑ Jul 1967 Cover: 0.12 **NM** value: **35.00**
Circ: Statement: **158,500** • **CGC:** 1 graded, best 9.4
169 ❑ Sep 1967 Cover: 0.12 **NM** value: **35.00**
Circ: Statement: **158,500**
170 ❑ Oct 1967 Cover: 0.12 **NM** value: **35.00**
Circ: Statement: **158,500** • **CGC:** 1 graded, best 9.4
171 ❑ Dec 1967 Cover: 0.12 **NM** value: **35.00**
Circ: Statement: **158,500** • **CGC:** 1 graded, best 9.4
📖 The Micro-Monsters!; Manhunter From Mars • Dial "H" for Hero
172 ❑ Feb 1968 Cover: 0.12 **NM** value: **35.00**
Circ: Statement: **156,350** • **CGC:** 1 graded, best 9.6
173 ❑ Apr 1968 Cover: 0.12 **NM** value: **35.00**
Circ: Statement: **156,350** • **CGC:** 2 graded, best 9.4
📖 Revolt of the H-Dial; So You're Faceless!
174 ❑ Jun 1968 Cover: 0.12 **NM** value: **12.00**
Circ: Statement: **156,350** • **CGC:** 3 graded, best 9.4
• Mystery format begins **A:** Neal Adams
175 ❑ Aug 1968 Cover: 0.12 **NM** value: **12.00**
Circ: Statement: **156,350** • **CGC:** 2 graded, best 9.4
176 ❑ Oct 1968 Cover: 0.12 **NM** value: **12.00**
Circ: Statement: **156,350** • **CGC:** 1 graded, best 9.4
177 ❑ Dec 1968 Cover: 0.12 **NM** value: **12.00**
Circ: Statement: **156,350**
178 ❑ Feb 1969 Cover: 0.12 **NM** value: **14.00**
Circ: Statement: **173,206** • **CGC:** 1 graded, best 9.4
179 ❑ Apr 1969 Cover: 0.12 **NM** value: **25.00**
Circ: Statement: **173,206** • **CGC:** 4 graded, best 9.4
📖 Sour Note!; The Man Who Murdered Himself; The Windows Walk; The Dead Tell Tales • Bernie Wrightson's first professional work; Has 1968 Statement, filed 10/1/68; avg print run 295,000; avg sales 156,000; avg subs 350; avg total paid 156,350; office use 386; max existent 156,736; 47% of run returned **A:** Bernie Wrightson; Joe Orlando; Neal Adams
180 ❑ Jun 1969 Cover: 0.12 **NM** value: **9.00**
Circ: Statement: **173,206** • **CGC:** 3 graded, best 9.8
181 ❑ Aug 1969 Cover: 0.15 **NM** value: **9.00**
Circ: Statement: **173,206** • **CGC:** 2 graded, best 9.6
182 ❑ Oct 1969 Cover: 0.15 **NM** value: **9.00**
Circ: Statement: **173,206**
📖 The Devil's Doorway; Grave Results! **A:** Neal Adams; Angelo Torres; Wayne Howard
183 ❑ Dec 1969 Cover: 0.15 **NM** value: **9.00**
Circ: Statement: **173,206**
184 ❑ Feb 1970 Cover: 0.15 **NM** value: **9.00**
Circ: Statement: **180,642** • **CGC:** 1 graded, best 9.4
185 ❑ Apr 1970 Cover: 0.15 **NM** value: **9.00**
Circ: Statement: **180,642**
📖 Voice From The Dead...; The Beautiful Beast; • Has 1969 Statement, filed 10/1/69; avg print run 321,000; avg sales 173,000; avg subs 206; avg total paid 173,206; office use 346; max existent 173,552; 46% of run returned **A:** Al Williamson; Bernie Wrightson; Neal Adams; Wally Wood
186 ❑ Jun 1970 Cover: 0.15 **NM** value: **10.00**
Circ: Statement: **180,642** • **CGC:** 1 graded, best 9.4
187 ❑ Aug 1970 Cover: 0.15 **NM** value: **6.00**
Circ: Statement: **180,642**
188 ❑ Oct 1970 Cover: 0.15 **NM** value: **9.00**
Circ: Statement: **180,642** • **CGC:** 2 graded, best 9.4
189 ❑ Dec 1970 Cover: 0.15 **NM** value: **4.00**
Circ: Statement: **180,642** • **CGC:** 1 graded, best 9.4
190 ❑ Feb 1971 Cover: 0.15 **NM** value: **4.00**
Circ: Statement: **187,408** • **CGC:** 1 graded, best 9.2
191 ❑ Apr 1971 Cover: 0.15 **NM** value: **4.00**
Circ: Statement: **187,408** • **CGC:** 2 graded, best 9.6
📖 No Strings Attached!; Cain's Game Room; The Hanging Tree!; Night Prowler! • Has 1970 Statement, filed 10/1/70; avg print run 333,049; avg sales 180,514; avg subs 128; avg total paid 180,642; office use 122; max existent 180,764; 46% of run returned **A:** Neal Adams
192 ❑ Jun 1971 Cover: 0.15 **NM** value: **4.00**
Circ: Statement: **187,408** • **CGC:** 1 graded, best 9.2
📖 Fright!; A Witch Must Die! **A:** Gray Morrow; Neal Adams
193 ❑ Jul 1971 Cover: 0.15 **NM** value: **4.00**
Circ: Statement: **187,408** • **CGC:** 1 graded, best 9.4
194 ❑ Sep 1971 Cover: 0.25 **NM** value: **4.00**
Circ: Statement: **187,408** • **CGC:** 2 graded, best 9.0
195 ❑ Oct 1971 Cover: 0.25 **NM** value: **10.00**
Circ: Statement: **187,408** • **CGC:** 3 graded, best 9.6
• Swamp Thing prototype? **A:** Bernie Wrightson
196 ❑ Nov 1971 Cover: 0.25 **NM** value: **4.00**
Circ: Statement: **187,408**
197 ❑ Dec 1971 Cover: 0.25 **NM** value: **4.00**
Circ: Statement: **187,408**
198 ❑ Jan 1972 Cover: 0.25 **NM** value: **4.00**
Circ: Statement: **175,134** • **CGC:** 2 graded, best 9.4
199 ❑ Feb 1972 Cover: 0.25 **NM** value: **4.00**
Circ: Statement: **175,134** • **CGC:** 1 graded, best 9.2
200 ❑ Mar 1972 Cover: 0.25 **NM** value: **4.00**
Circ: Statement: **175,134** • **CGC:** 3 graded, best 9.4
• Has 1970 Statement; avg total paid circ 187,408
201 ❑ Apr 1972 Cover: 0.25 **NM** value: **4.00**
Circ: Statement: **175,134** • **CGC:** 2 graded, best 9.6
202 ❑ May 1972 Cover: 0.25 **NM** value: **4.00**
Circ: Statement: **175,134** • **CGC:** 1 graded, best 9.4
203 ❑ Jun 1972 Cover: 0.25 **NM** value: **4.00**
Circ: Statement: **175,134** • **CGC:** 1 graded, best 9.2
204 ❑ Jul 1972 Cover: 0.20 **NM** value: **7.00**
Circ: Statement: **175,134** • **CGC:** 2 graded, best 9.0
205 ❑ Aug 1972 Cover: 0.20 **NM** value: **4.00**
Circ: Statement: **175,134**
206 ❑ Sep 1972 Cover: 0.20 **NM** value: **4.00**
Circ: Statement: **175,134** • **CGC:** 1 graded, best 6.0
207 ❑ Oct 1972 Cover: 0.20 **NM** value: **4.00**
Circ: Statement: **175,134**
208 ❑ Nov 1972 Cover: 0.20 **NM** value: **4.00**
Circ: Statement: **175,134** • **CGC:** 1 graded, best 9.6
209 ❑ Dec 1972 Cover: 0.20 **NM** value: **4.00**
Circ: Statement: **175,134** • **CGC:** 3 graded, best 9.6
210 ❑ Jan 1973 Cover: 0.20 **NM** value: **4.00**
Circ: Statement: **178,025** • **CGC:** 1 graded, best 9.4
211 ❑ Feb 1973 Cover: 0.20 **NM** value: **4.00**
Circ: Statement: **178,025**
212 ❑ Mar 1973 Cover: 0.20 **NM** value: **4.00**
Circ: Statement: **178,025**
• Has 1972 Statement; avg print run 351,000; avg sales 174,697; avg subs 437; avg total paid 175,134; samples 523; office use 408; max existent 175,542; 50% of run returned **A:** Alex Nino; Alex Ni±o
213 ❑ Apr 1973 Cover: 0.20 **NM** value: **4.00**
Circ: Statement: **178,025**
214 ❑ May 1973 Cover: 0.20 **NM** value: **4.00**
Circ: Statement: **178,025**
215 ❑ Jun 1973 Cover: 0.20 **NM** value: **4.00**
Circ: Statement: **178,025**
216 ❑ Jul 1973 Cover: 0.20 **NM** value: **4.00**
Circ: Statement: **178,025**
217 ❑ Sep 1973 Cover: 0.20 **NM** value: **4.00**
Circ: Statement: **178,025**
218 ❑ Oct 1973 Cover: 0.20 **NM** value: **4.00**
Circ: Statement: **178,025**
219 ❑ Nov 1973 Cover: 0.20 **NM** value: **4.00**
Circ: Statement: **178,025**
220 ❑ Dec 1973 Cover: 0.20 **NM** value: **4.00**
Circ: Statement: **178,025**
221 ❑ Jan 1974 Cover: 0.20 **NM** value: **4.00**
Circ: Statement: **174,504** • **CGC:** 6 graded, best 9.4
222 ❑ Feb 1974 Cover: 0.20 **NM** value: **4.00**
Circ: Statement: **174,504** • **CGC:** 1 graded, best 9.2
223 ❑ Mar 1974 Cover: 0.20 **NM** value: **4.00**
Circ: Statement: **174,504**
224 ❑ Apr 1974 Cover: 0.60 **NM** value: **15.00**
Circ: Statement: **174,504** • **CGC:** 1 graded, best 9.0
• Phantom Stranger; Has 1973 Statement; avg total paid circ 178,025 **A:** Bernie Wrightson; Neal Adams; Alex Nino; Alex Ni±o ★ Appearance of Phantom Stranger.
225 ❑ Jun 1974 Cover: 0.60 **NM** value: **9.00**
Circ: Statement: **174,504** • **CGC:** 2 graded, best 9.4
226 ❑ Aug 1974 Cover: 0.60 **NM** value: **9.00**
Circ: Statement: **174,504**
📖 Garden **A:** Bernie Wrightson; Nestor Redondo; Alfredo Alcala; Gerry Talaoc; Bill Ely; Fred Robbin; Jess M. Jodloman **W:** Martin Pasko; Jack Oleck; Mike Pellowski; Robert Kanigher ★ Appearance of Phantom Stranger.
227 ❑ Oct 1974 Cover: 0.60 **NM** value: **9.00**
Circ: Statement: **174,504** • **CGC:** 2 graded, best 9.4
228 ❑ Dec 1974 Cover: 0.60 **NM** value: **9.00**
Circ: Statement: **174,504** • **CGC:** 4 graded, best 9.4
229 ❑ Feb 1975 Cover: 0.60 **NM** value: **9.00**
Circ: Statement: **146,000** • **CGC:** 2 graded, best 9.0
230 ❑ Apr 1975 Cover: 0.25 **NM** value: **3.00**
Circ: Statement: **146,000**
231 ❑ May 1975 Cover: 0.25 **NM** value: **3.00**
Circ: Statement: **146,000** • **CGC:** 1 graded, best 8.0
• Has 1974 Statement; avg print run 365,160; avg sales 173,900; avg subs 604; avg total paid 174,504; samples 100; office use 5,056; max existent 179,560; 51% of run returned
232 ❑ Jun 1975 Cover: 0.25 **NM** value: **3.00**
Circ: Statement: **146,000**
233 ❑ Jul 1975 Cover: 0.25 **NM** value: **3.00**
Circ: Statement: **146,000**
234 ❑ Aug 1975 Cover: 0.25 **NM** value: **3.00**
Circ: Statement: **146,000**
235 ❑ Sep 1975 Cover: 0.25 **NM** value: **3.00**
Circ: Statement: **146,000**
236 ❑ Oct 1975 Cover: 0.25 **NM** value: **3.00**
Circ: Statement: **146,000** • **CGC:** 1 graded, best 8.0
237 ❑ Nov 1975 Cover: 0.25 **NM** value: **3.00**
Circ: Statement: **146,000**
238 ❑ Dec 1975 Cover: 0.25 **NM** value: **3.00**
Circ: Statement: **146,000**
239 ❑ Feb 1976 Cover: 0.25 **NM** value: **3.00**
Circ: Statement: **124,000**
240 ❑ Apr 1976 Cover: 0.30 **NM** value: **3.00**
Circ: Statement: **124,000** • **CGC:** 1 graded, best 9.4
241 ❑ May 1976 Cover: 0.30 **NM** value: **3.00**
Circ: Statement: **124,000** • **CGC:** 1 graded, best 9.2
• Has 1975 Statement; avg print run 351,000; avg sales 145,000; avg subs 1,000; avg total paid 146,000; samples 1,000; office use 2,000; max existent 148,000; 58% of run returned
242 ❑ Jun 1976 Cover: 0.30 **NM** value: **3.00**
Circ: Statement: **124,000**
📖 The Balloon Vendor!; Blood Money
243 ❑ Jul 1976 Cover: 0.30 **NM** value: **3.00**

Other grades: Multiply prices above by **1.5 for Mint • 2/3 for Very Fine • 1/3 for Fine • 1/5 for Very Good • 1/8 for Good**

Circ: Statement: **124,000**
• Bicentennial #10
244 ❑ Aug 1976 Cover: 0.30 **NM** value: **3.00**
Circ: Statement: **124,000**
245 ❑ Sep 1976 Cover: 0.30 **NM** value: **3.00**
Circ: Statement: **124,000** • **CGC:** 1 graded, best 9.0
246 ❑ Oct 1976 Cover: 0.30 **NM** value: **3.00**
Circ: Statement: **124,000** • **CGC:** 1 graded, best 9.2
247 ❑ Nov 1976 Cover: 0.30 **NM** value: **3.00**
Circ: Statement: **124,000**
248 ❑ Dec 1976 Cover: 0.30 **NM** value: **3.00**
Circ: Statement: **124,000**
249 ❑ Jan 1977 Cover: 0.30 **NM** value: **3.00**
Circ: Statement: **109,191** • **CGC:** 1 graded, best 9.2
250 ❑ Feb 1977 Cover: 0.30 **NM** value: **3.00**
Circ: Statement: **109,191**
251 ❑ Mar 1977 Cover: 1.00 **NM** value: **3.00**
Circ: Statement: **109,191** • **CGC:** 1 graded, best 9.6
• giant **A:** Neal Adams; Wally Wood
252 ❑ May 1977 Cover: 1.00 **NM** value: **3.00**
Circ: Statement: **109,191**
• giant; Has 1976 Statement; avg print run 325,000; avg sales 123,000; avg subs 1,000; avg total paid 124,000; samples 1,000; max existent 124,000; 62% of run returned **A:** Neal Adams; Alex Nino; Alex Ni±o
253 ❑ Jul 1977 Cover: 1.00 **NM** value: **3.00**
Circ: Statement: **109,191** • **CGC:** 1 graded, best 9.2
• giant **A:** Neal Adams; Alex Nino; Alex Ni±o
254 ❑ Sep 1977 Cover: 1.00 **NM** value: **3.00**
Circ: Statement: **109,191**
• giant **A:** Steve Ditko; Neal Adams; Wayne Howard
255 ❑ Nov 1977 Cover: 1.00 **NM** value: **3.00**
Circ: Statement: **109,191** • **CGC:** 1 graded, best 8.5
• giant **A:** Bernie Wrightson
256 ❑ Jan 1978 Cover: 1.00 **NM** value: **3.00**
Circ: Statement: **75,650**
• giant **A:** Bernie Wrightson
257 ❑ Mar 1978 Cover: 1.00 **NM** value: **3.00**
Circ: Statement: **75,650**
• giant **A:** Michael Golden
258 ❑ May 1978 Cover: 1.00 **NM** value: **3.00**
Circ: Statement: **75,650**
• giant; Has 1977 Statement; avg print run 285,511; avg sales 108,573; avg subs 618; avg total paid 109,191; samples 400; office use 334; max existent 109,191; 62% of run returned **A:** Steve Ditko
259 ❑ Jul 1978 Cover: 1.00 **NM** value: **3.00**
Circ: Statement: **75,650**
• giant **A:** Don Newton; Michael Golden
260 ❑ Sep 1978 Cover: 1.00 **NM** value: **3.00**
Circ: Statement: **75,650**
261 ❑ Oct 1978 Cover: 0.40 **NM** value: **3.00**
Circ: Statement: **75,650**
262 ❑ Nov 1978 Cover: 0.40 **NM** value: **3.00**
Circ: Statement: **75,650**
263 ❑ Dec 1978 Cover: 0.40 **NM** value: **3.00**
Circ: Statement: **75,650**
264 ❑ Jan 1979 Cover: 0.40 **NM** value: **3.00**
Circ: Statement: **85,569**
265 ❑ Feb 1979 Cover: 0.40 **NM** value: **3.00**
Circ: Statement: **85,569**
266 ❑ Mar 1979 Cover: 0.40 **NM** value: **3.00**
Circ: Statement: **85,569** • **CGC:** 1 graded, best 9.2
267 ❑ Apr 1979 Cover: 0.40 **NM** value: **3.00**
Circ: Statement: **85,569**
📖 The Mouse of History • Has 1978 Statement; avg print run 286,482; avg sales 75,269; avg subs 381; avg total paid 75,650; samples 109; office use 1,142; max existent 76,792; 73% of run returned **C:** Michael W. Kaluta **W:** Don Thompson
268 ❑ May 1979 Cover: 0.40 **NM** value: **3.00**
Circ: Statement: **85,569**
269 ❑ Jun 1979 Cover: 0.40 **NM** value: **3.00**
Circ: Statement: **85,569** • **CGC:** 1 graded, best 9.2
270 ❑ Jul 1979 Cover: 0.40 **NM** value: **3.00**
Circ: Statement: **85,569**
271 ❑ Aug 1979 Cover: 0.40 **NM** value: **3.00**
Circ: Statement: **85,569**
272 ❑ Sep 1979 Cover: 0.40 **NM** value: **3.00**
Circ: Statement: **85,569**
273 ❑ Oct 1979 Cover: 0.40 **NM** value: **3.00**
Circ: Statement: **85,569**
274 ❑ Nov 1979 Cover: 0.40 **NM** value: **3.00**
Circ: Statement: **85,569**
275 ❑ Dec 1979 Cover: 0.40 **NM** value: **3.00**
Circ: Statement: **85,569** • **CGC:** 1 graded, best 9.2
276 ❑ Jan 1980 Cover: 0.40 **NM** value: **3.00**
Circ: Statement: **88,876**
277 ❑ Feb 1980 Cover: 0.40 **NM** value: **3.00**
Circ: Statement: **88,876**
278 ❑ Mar 1980 Cover: 0.40 **NM** value: **3.00**
Circ: Statement: **88,876**
279 ❑ Apr 1980 Cover: 0.40 **NM** value: **3.00**
Circ: Statement: **88,876**
• Has 1979 Statement; avg print run 237,004; avg sales 85,383; avg subs 186; avg total paid 85,569; office use 121; max existent 85,690; 64% of run returned
280 ❑ May 1980 Cover: 0.40 **NM** value: **3.00**
Circ: Statement: **88,876**
281 ❑ Jun 1980 Cover: 0.40 **NM** value: **3.00**
Circ: Statement: **88,876**
282 ❑ Jul 1980 Cover: 0.40 **NM** value: **3.00**
Circ: Statement: **88,876**
283 ❑ Aug 1980 Cover: 0.40 **NM** value: **3.00**
Circ: Statement: **88,876**
284 ❑ Sep 1980 Cover: 0.50 **NM** value: **3.00**
Circ: Statement: **88,876**
285 ❑ Oct 1980 Cover: 0.50 **NM** value: **3.00**
Circ: Statement: **88,876**
286 ❑ Nov 1980 Cover: 0.50 **NM** value: **3.00**
Circ: Statement: **88,876**
287 ❑ Dec 1980 Cover: 0.50 **NM** value: **3.00**
Circ: Statement: **88,876**
288 ❑ Jan 1981 Cover: 0.50 **NM** value: **3.00**
Circ: Statement: **86,962**
289 ❑ Feb 1981 Cover: 0.50 **NM** value: **3.00**
Circ: Statement: **86,962**
290 ❑ Mar 1981 Cover: 0.50 **NM** value: **3.00**
Circ: Statement: **86,962**
• I, Vampire
291 ❑ Apr 1981 Cover: 0.50 **NM** value: **3.00**
Circ: Statement: **86,962**
• I, Vampire; Has 1980 Statement; avg print run 257,865; avg sales 88,218; avg subs 658; avg total paid 88,876; samples 127; office use 2,932; max existent 91,808; 64% of run returned
292 ❑ May 1981 Cover: 0.50 **NM** value: **3.00**
Circ: Statement: **86,962**
293 ❑ Jun 1981 Cover: 0.50 **NM** value: **3.00**
Circ: Statement: **86,962**
• I, Vampire
294 ❑ Jul 1981 Cover: 0.50 **NM** value: **3.00**
Circ: Statement: **86,962**
295 ❑ Aug 1981 Cover: 0.50 **NM** value: **3.00**
Circ: Statement: **86,962**
296 ❑ Sep 1981 Cover: 0.50 **NM** value: **3.00**
Circ: Statement: **86,962**
297 ❑ Oct 1981 Cover: 0.50 **NM** value: **3.00**
Circ: Statement: **86,962** • **CGC:** 1 graded, best 9.4
298 ❑ Nov 1981 Cover: 0.60 **NM** value: **3.00**
Circ: Statement: **86,962**
299 ❑ Dec 1981 Cover: 0.60 **NM** value: **3.00**
Circ: Statement: **86,962**
• I, Vampire
300 ❑ Jan 1982 Cover: 0.60 **NM** value: **3.00**
301 ❑ Feb 1982 Cover: 0.60 **NM** value: **3.00**
302 ❑ Mar 1982 Cover: 0.60 **NM** value: **3.00**
• I, Vampire
303 ❑ Apr 1982 Cover: 0.60 **NM** value: **3.00**
• I, Vampire
304 ❑ May 1982 Cover: 0.60 **NM** value: **3.00**
• I, Vampire; Has 1981 Statement; avg print run 259,942; avg sales 86,227; avg subs 735; avg total paid 86,962; samples 127; office use 3,524; max existent 90,486; 65% of run returned
305 ❑ Jun 1982 Cover: 0.60 **NM** value: **3.00**
• I, Vampire
306 ❑ Jul 1982 Cover: 0.60 **NM** value: **3.00**
• I, Vampire
307 ❑ Aug 1982 Cover: 0.60 **NM** value: **3.00**
• I, Vampire
308 ❑ Sep 1982 Cover: 0.60 **NM** value: **3.00**
• I, Vampire
309 ❑ Oct 1982 Cover: 0.60 **NM** value: **3.00**
• I, Vampire
310 ❑ Nov 1982 Cover: 0.60 **NM** value: **3.00**
📖 Manhattan Interlude • I, Vampire
311 ❑ Dec 1982 Cover: 0.60 **NM** value: **3.00**
• I, Vampire
312 ❑ Jan 1983 Cover: 0.60 **NM** value: **3.00**
• I, Vampire
313 ❑ Feb 1983 Cover: 0.60 **NM** value: **3.00**
314 ❑ Mar 1983 Cover: 0.60 **NM** value: **3.00**
• I, Vampire
315 ❑ Apr 1983 Cover: 0.60 **NM** value: **3.00**
• I, Vampire
316 ❑ May 1983 Cover: 0.60 **NM** value: **3.00**
317 ❑ Jun 1983 Cover: 0.60 **NM** value: **3.00**
318 ❑ Jul 1983 Cover: 0.60 **NM** value: **3.00**
• I, Vampire
319 ❑ Aug 1983 Cover: 0.60 **NM** value: **3.00**
• **CGC:** 1 graded, best 9.0
320 ❑ Sep 1983 Cover: 0.60 **NM** value: **3.00**
321 ❑ Oct 1983 Cover: 0.60 **NM** value: **3.00**
final issue.

HOUSE OF SECRETS — DC

The House of Mystery's Cain has a kinder, gentler brother, Abel, who hosts this exploration of the weird and the supernatural. Witches, goblins, bogey men, and psychotics roam the pages, and the hapless mortals who get caught in their clutches sometimes thwart them and sometimes don't. Some of DC's best artists, including Steve Ditko, Sheldon Mayer, and of course, that master of the macabre himself, Bernie Wrightson, contributed to this series.

The series' title, but little else, returned in the late 1990s as a Vertigo horror series that was more focused on the house itself, rather than the anthology of horror stories.

1 ❑ Nov 1956 Cover: 0.10 **NM** value: **1285.00**
• **CGC:** 2 graded, best 9.2
2 ❑ Jan 1957 Cover: 0.10 **NM** value: **485.00**
3 ❑ Mar 1957 Cover: 0.10 **NM** value: **390.00**
4 ❑ May 1957 Cover: 0.10 **NM** value: **300.00**
5 ❑ Jul 1957 Cover: 0.10 **NM** value: **175.00**
6 ❑ Sep 1957 Cover: 0.10 **NM** value: **175.00**
7 ❑ Nov 1957 Cover: 0.10 **NM** value: **175.00**
• **CGC:** 1 graded, best 7.5
8 ❑ Jan 1958 Cover: 0.10 **NM** value: **225.00**
• **CGC:** 1 graded, best 8.5
9 ❑ Mar 1958 Cover: 0.10 **NM** value: **175.00**
10 ❑ Jun 1958 Cover: 0.10 **NM** value: **175.00**
11 ❑ Aug 1958 Cover: 0.10 **NM** value: **175.00**
12 ❑ Sep 1958 Cover: 0.10 **NM** value: **175.00**
13 ❑ Oct 1958 Cover: 0.10 **NM** value: **100.00**
• **CGC:** 1 graded, best 3.0
14 ❑ Nov 1958 Cover: 0.10 **NM** value: **100.00**
15 ❑ Dec 1958 Cover: 0.10 **NM** value: **100.00**
• **CGC:** 1 graded, best 8.0
16 ❑ Jan 1959 Cover: 0.10 **NM** value: **85.00**
17 ❑ Feb 1959 Cover: 0.10 **NM** value: **85.00**
• **CGC:** 1 graded, best 8.0
18 ❑ Mar 1959 Cover: 0.10 **NM** value: **85.00**
• **CGC:** 1 graded, best 8.0
19 ❑ Apr 1959 Cover: 0.10 **NM** value: **85.00**
20 ❑ May 1959 Cover: 0.10 **NM** value: **85.00**
• **CGC:** 1 graded, best 9.2
21 ❑ Jun 1959 Cover: 0.10 **NM** value: **70.00**
22 ❑ Jul 1959 Cover: 0.10 **NM** value: **70.00**
23 ❑ Aug 1959 Cover: 0.10 **NM** value: **100.00**
24 ❑ Sep 1959 Cover: 0.10 **NM** value: **70.00**
• **CGC:** 1 graded, best 9.0
25 ❑ Oct 1959 Cover: 0.10 **NM** value: **70.00**
• **CGC:** 1 graded, best 9.0
26 ❑ Nov 1959 Cover: 0.10 **NM** value: **70.00**
27 ❑ Dec 1959 Cover: 0.10 **NM** value: **70.00**
Circ: Statement: **194,000**
28 ❑ Jan 1960 Cover: 0.10 **NM** value: **70.00**
Circ: Statement: **194,000**
29 ❑ Feb 1960 Cover: 0.10 **NM** value: **70.00**
Circ: Statement: **194,000**
30 ❑ Mar 1960 Cover: 0.10 **NM** value: **70.00**
Circ: Statement: **194,000** • **CGC:** 1 graded, best 9.0
31 ❑ Apr 1960 Cover: 0.10 **NM** value: **58.00**
Circ: Statement: **194,000**
32 ❑ May 1960 Cover: 0.10 **NM** value: **58.00**
Circ: Statement: **194,000**
33 ❑ Jun 1960 Cover: 0.10 **NM** value: **58.00**
Circ: Statement: **194,000**
34 ❑ Jul 1960 Cover: 0.10 **NM** value: **58.00**
Circ: Statement: **194,000**
35 ❑ Aug 1960 Cover: 0.10 **NM** value: **58.00**
Circ: Statement: **194,000** • **CGC:** 1 graded, best 7.5
36 ❑ Sep 1960 Cover: 0.10 **NM** value: **58.00**
Circ: Statement: **194,000** • **CGC:** 1 graded, best 8.5
37 ❑ Oct 1960 Cover: 0.10 **NM** value: **58.00**
Circ: Statement: **194,000**
38 ❑ Nov 1960 Cover: 0.10 **NM** value: **58.00**
Circ: Statement: **194,000** • **CGC:** 2 graded, best 7.0
39 ❑ Dec 1960 Cover: 0.10 **NM** value: **58.00**
Circ: Statement: **205,000** • **CGC:** 2 graded, best 7.5
40 ❑ Jan 1961 Cover: 0.10 **NM** value: **58.00**
Circ: Statement: **205,000**
41 ❑ Feb 1961 Cover: 0.10 **NM** value: **58.00**
Circ: Statement: **205,000**
• Has 1960 Statement; avg total paid 194,000
42 ❑ Mar 1961 Cover: 0.10 **NM** value: **58.00**
Circ: Statement: **205,000**
43 ❑ Apr 1961 Cover: 0.10 **NM** value: **58.00**
Circ: Statement: **205,000**
44 ❑ May 1961 Cover: 0.10 **NM** value: **58.00**
Circ: Statement: **205,000**
45 ❑ Jun 1961 Cover: 0.10 **NM** value: **58.00**
Circ: Statement: **205,000**
46 ❑ Jul 1961 Cover: 0.10 **NM** value: **58.00**
Circ: Statement: **205,000**
47 ❑ Aug 1961 Cover: 0.10 **NM** value: **58.00**
Circ: Statement: **205,000**
48 ❑ Sep 1961 Cover: 0.10 **NM** value: **58.00**
Circ: Statement: **205,000** • **CGC:** 1 graded, best 8.5
49 ❑ Oct 1961 Cover: 0.10 **NM** value: **58.00**
Circ: Statement: **205,000** • **CGC:** 1 graded, best 9.0
50 ❑ Nov 1961 Cover: 0.10 **NM** value: **58.00**
Circ: Statement: **205,000** • **CGC:** 1 graded, best 7.5
51 ❑ Dec 1961 Cover: 0.12 **NM** value: **48.00**
• **CGC:** 1 graded, best 9.0
52 ❑ Jan 1962 Cover: 0.12 **NM** value: **48.00**
53 ❑ Mar 1962 Cover: 0.12 **NM** value: **48.00**
54 ❑ May 1962 Cover: 0.12 **NM** value: **48.00**
55 ❑ Jul 1962 Cover: 0.12 **NM** value: **48.00**
56 ❑ Sep 1962 Cover: 0.12 **NM** value: **48.00**
57 ❑ Nov 1962 Cover: 0.12 **NM** value: **48.00**
58 ❑ Jan 1963 Cover: 0.12 **NM** value: **48.00**
• **CGC:** 1 graded, best 9.6
59 ❑ Mar 1963 Cover: 0.12 **NM** value: **48.00**
• **CGC:** 2 graded, best 9.4
60 ❑ May 1963 Cover: 0.12 **NM** value: **48.00**
• **CGC:** 1 graded, best 9.6
61 ❑ Jul 1963 Cover: 0.12 **NM** value: **120.00**
• **CGC:** 5 graded, best 9.4
62 ❑ Sep 1963 Cover: 0.12 **NM** value: **75.00**
• **CGC:** 1 graded, best 9.6
63 ❑ Nov 1963 Cover: 0.12 **NM** value: **60.00**
• **CGC:** 2 graded, best 9.4
64 ❑ Jan 1964 Cover: 0.12 **NM** value: **60.00**
• **CGC:** 1 graded, best 9.4
65 ❑ Mar 1964 Cover: 0.12 **NM** value: **60.00**
• **CGC:** 1 graded, best 9.2
• Has 1963 Statement, filed 10/1/63; no numbers printed
66 ❑ May 1964 Cover: 0.12 **NM** value: **75.00**
• **CGC:** 2 graded, best 9.8
Eclipso cover.
67 ❑ Jul 1964 Cover: 0.12 **NM** value: **50.00**
• **CGC:** 2 graded, best 9.4
68 ❑ Sep 1964 Cover: 0.12 **NM** value: **48.00**
• **CGC:** 1 graded, best 9.6
69 ❑ Nov 1964 Cover: 0.12 **NM** value: **48.00**
• **CGC:** 2 graded, best 9.8
70 ❑ Jan 1965 Cover: 0.12 **NM** value: **48.00**

CGC-graded: Multiply prices above by **33 for 9.9 M** • **16 for 9.8 NM/M** • **7 for 9.6 NM+** • **5 for 9.4 NM** • **2.5 for 9.2 NM-** • **1.5 for 9.0 VF/NM**

• **CGC:** 1 graded, best 9.4
71 ❑ Mar 1965 Cover: 0.12 **NM** value: **48.00**
• **CGC:** 1 graded, best 9.6
• Has 1964 Statement, filed 10/1/64; no numbers printed
72 ❑ May 1965 Cover: 0.12 **NM** value: **48.00**
• **CGC:** 1 graded, best 9.6
• Eclipso
73 ❑ Jul 1965 Cover: 0.12 **NM** value: **48.00**
• **CGC:** 1 graded, best 9.4
74 ❑ Sep 1965 Cover: 0.12 **NM** value: **48.00**
• **CGC:** 3 graded, best 9.8
• Eclipso
75 ❑ Nov 1965 Cover: 0.12 **NM** value: **48.00**
• **CGC:** 2 graded, best 9.4
76 ❑ Jan 1966 Cover: 0.12 **NM** value: **48.00**
• **CGC:** 3 graded, best 9.6
• Eclipso
77 ❑ Mar 1966 Cover: 0.12 **NM** value: **48.00**
• **CGC:** 7 graded, best 9.9
• Has 1965 Statement, filed 10/1/65; no numbers printed
78 ❑ May 1966 Cover: 0.12 **NM** value: **48.00**
• **CGC:** 2 graded, best 9.8
79 ❑ Jul 1966 Cover: 0.12 **NM** value: **48.00**
• **CGC:** 3 graded, best 9.4
80 ❑ Sep 1966 Cover: 0.12 **NM** value: **55.00**
• **CGC:** 2 graded, best 8.5
81 ❑ Sep 1969 Cover: 0.15 **NM** value: **12.00**
• **CGC:** 2 graded, best 9.4
• Mystery format begins ★ 1st Appearance of Abel.
82 ❑ Nov 1969 Cover: 0.15 **NM** value: **9.00**
83 ❑ Jan 1970 Cover: 0.15 **NM** value: **9.00**
84 ❑ Mar 1970 Cover: 0.15 **NM** value: **9.00**
85 ❑ May 1970 Cover: 0.15 **NM** value: **9.00**
• **CGC:** 1 graded, best 9.2
86 ❑ Jul 1970 Cover: 0.15 **NM** value: **9.00**
📖 Strain; The Ballard Of Little Joe; The Day After Doomsday... **A:** Gray Morrow **C:** Neal Adams
87 ❑ Sep 1970 Cover: 0.15 **NM** value: **9.00**
• **CGC:** 1 graded, best 9.6
88 ❑ Nov 1970 Cover: 0.15 **NM** value: **9.00**
• **CGC:** 1 graded, best 9.4
89 ❑ Jan 1971 Cover: 0.15 **NM** value: **9.00**
• **CGC:** 1 graded, best 6.5
90 ❑ Mar 1971 Cover: 0.15 **NM** value: **9.00**
• **CGC:** 3 graded, best 8.5
• 1st Buckler DC art **A:** Rich Buckler; Gray Morrow; Neal Adams
91 ❑ May 1971 Cover: 0.15 **NM** value: **9.00**
• **CGC:** 1 graded, best 9.4
92 ❑ Jul 1971 Cover: 0.15 **NM** value: **400.00**
• **CGC:** 121 graded, best 9.6
📖 Swamp Thing; After I Die; It's Better to Give; Trick or Treat **A:** Alan Weiss; Bernie Wrightson; Dick Dillin; Tony DeZuniga; Bill Draut **W:** Dick Dillin; Len Wein; Mark Evanier; Mary Skrenes ★ 1st Appearance of Swamp Thing.
93 ❑ Sep 1971 **NM** value: **5.00**
• **CGC:** 2 graded, best 9.6
94 ❑ Nov 1971 **NM** value: **5.00**
• **CGC:** 3 graded, best 9.2
95 ❑ Jan 1972 **NM** value: **5.00**
Circ: Statement: **168,256** • **CGC:** 4 graded, best 9.4
96 ❑ Mar 1972 **NM** value: **5.00**
Circ: Statement: **168,256** • **CGC:** 2 graded, best 9.4
97 ❑ May 1972 **NM** value: **5.00**
Circ: Statement: **168,256** • **CGC:** 3 graded, best 9.6
98 ❑ Jul 1972 **NM** value: **5.00**
Circ: Statement: **168,256** • **CGC:** 3 graded, best 9.6
99 ❑ Sep 1972 **NM** value: **5.00**
Circ: Statement: **168,256**
100 ❑ Oct 1972 **NM** value: **5.00**
Circ: Statement: **168,256** • **CGC:** 5 graded, best 9.4
101 ❑ Nov 1972 **NM** value: **4.00**
Circ: Statement: **168,256** • **CGC:** 1 graded, best 8.5
102 ❑ Dec 1972 **NM** value: **4.00**
Circ: Statement: **168,256** • **CGC:** 5 graded, best 9.4
103 ❑ Jan 1973 **NM** value: **4.00**
Circ: Statement: **160,154** • **CGC:** 1 graded, best 9.6
104 ❑ Feb 1973 Cover: 0.20 **NM** value: **4.00**
Circ: Statement: **160,154**
105 ❑ Mar 1973 Cover: 0.20 **NM** value: **4.00**
Circ: Statement: **160,154**
106 ❑ Apr 1973 Cover: 0.20 **NM** value: **4.00**
Circ: Statement: **160,154** • **CGC:** 1 graded, best 9.4
107 ❑ May 1973 Cover: 0.20 **NM** value: **4.00**
Circ: Statement: **160,154** • **CGC:** 1 graded, best 9.0
• Has 1972 Statement; avg total paid 168,256
108 ❑ Jun 1973 Cover: 0.20 **NM** value: **4.00**
Circ: Statement: **160,154** • **CGC:** 1 graded, best 9.2
109 ❑ Jul 1973 Cover: 0.20 **NM** value: **4.00**
Circ: Statement: **160,154** • **CGC:** 2 graded, best 9.0
110 ❑ Aug 1973 Cover: 0.20 **NM** value: **4.00**
Circ: Statement: **160,154** • **CGC:** 1 graded, best 9.0
111 ❑ Sep 1973 Cover: 0.20 **NM** value: **3.00**
Circ: Statement: **160,154**
112 ❑ Oct 1973 Cover: 0.20 **NM** value: **3.00**
Circ: Statement: **160,154** • **CGC:** 2 graded, best 9.4
113 ❑ Nov 1973 Cover: 0.20 **NM** value: **3.00**
Circ: Statement: **160,154** • **CGC:** 2 graded, best 9.0
114 ❑ Dec 1973 Cover: 0.20 **NM** value: **3.00**
Circ: Statement: **160,154**
115 ❑ Jan 1974 Cover: 0.20 **NM** value: **3.00**
Circ: Statement: **161,190**
116 ❑ Feb 1974 Cover: 0.20 **NM** value: **3.00**
Circ: Statement: **161,190** • **CGC:** 2 graded, best 9.4
117 ❑ Mar 1974 Cover: 0.20 **NM** value: **3.00**
Circ: Statement: **161,190**
118 ❑ Apr 1974 Cover: 0.20 **NM** value: **3.00**
Circ: Statement: **161,190** • **CGC:** 1 graded, best 9.0
• Has 1973 Statement; avg print run 322,900; avg sales 159,944; avg subs 210; avg total paid 160,154; samples 100; office use 1,294; max existent 161,448; 50% of run returned
119 ❑ May 1974 Cover: 0.20 **NM** value: **3.00**
Circ: Statement: **161,190** • **CGC:** 1 graded, best 9.2
120 ❑ Jun 1974 Cover: 0.20 **NM** value: **3.00**
Circ: Statement: **161,190** • **CGC:** 1 graded, best 9.2
121 ❑ Jul 1974 Cover: 0.20 **NM** value: **3.00**
Circ: Statement: **161,190** • **CGC:** 2 graded, best 9.8
122 ❑ Aug 1974 Cover: 0.20 **NM** value: **3.00**
Circ: Statement: **161,190** • **CGC:** 2 graded, best 9.4
123 ❑ Sep 1974 Cover: 0.20 **NM** value: **3.00**
Circ: Statement: **161,190**
124 ❑ Oct 1974 **NM** value: **3.00**
Circ: Statement: **161,190** • **CGC:** 1 graded, best 9.2
125 ❑ Nov 1974 **NM** value: **3.00**
Circ: Statement: **161,190** • **CGC:** 1 graded, best 9.2
126 ❑ Dec 1974 **NM** value: **3.00**
Circ: Statement: **161,190**
127 ❑ Jan 1975 Cover: 0.25 **NM** value: **3.00**
• **CGC:** 1 graded, best 9.0
128 ❑ Feb 1975 Cover: 0.25 **NM** value: **3.00**
• **CGC:** 1 graded, best 9.6
129 ❑ Mar 1975 Cover: 0.25 **NM** value: **3.00**
130 ❑ Apr 1975 Cover: 0.25 **NM** value: **3.00**
• **CGC:** 1 graded, best 9.2
131 ❑ May 1975 Cover: 0.25 **NM** value: **3.00**
• Has 1974 Statement; avg print run 325,164; avg sales 160,833; avg subs 357; avg total paid 161,190; samples 100; office use 2,624; max existent 163,814; 50% of run returned
132 ❑ Jun 1975 Cover: 0.25 **NM** value: **3.00**
133 ❑ Jul 1975 Cover: 0.25 **NM** value: **3.00**
134 ❑ Aug 1975 Cover: 0.25 **NM** value: **3.00**
135 ❑ Sep 1975 Cover: 0.25 **NM** value: **3.00**
136 ❑ Nov 1975 Cover: 0.25 **NM** value: **3.00**
137 ❑ Jan 1976 Cover: 0.25 **NM** value: **3.00**
Circ: Statement: **116,000**
138 ❑ Mar 1976 Cover: 0.25 **NM** value: **3.00**
Circ: Statement: **116,000**
139 ❑ May 1976 Cover: 0.25 **NM** value: **3.00**
Circ: Statement: **116,000**
140 ❑ Jul 1976 Cover: 0.25 **NM** value: **3.00**
Circ: Statement: **116,000** • **CGC:** 1 graded, best 9.4
141 ❑ Sep 1976 Cover: 0.25 **NM** value: **3.00**
Circ: Statement: **116,000**
142 ❑ Nov 1976 **NM** value: **3.00**
Circ: Statement: **116,000**
143 ❑ Jan 1977 **NM** value: **3.00**
Circ: Statement: **118,766**
144 ❑ Mar 1977 **NM** value: **3.00**
Circ: Statement: **118,766**
145 ❑ May 1977 **NM** value: **3.00**
Circ: Statement: **118,766**
• Has 1976 Statement; avg total paid circ 116,000
146 ❑ Jul 1977 **NM** value: **3.00**
Circ: Statement: **118,766** • **CGC:** 1 graded, best 9.4
147 ❑ Sep 1977 **NM** value: **3.00**
Circ: Statement: **118,766** • **CGC:** 1 graded, best 9.4
148 ❑ Nov 1977 **NM** value: **3.00**
Circ: Statement: **118,766**
149 ❑ Jan 1978 **NM** value: **3.00**
150 ❑ Mar 1978 Cover: 0.35 **NM** value: **3.00**
• **CGC:** 1 graded, best 9.4
151 ❑ May 1978 **NM** value: **3.00**
• **CGC:** 1 graded, best 8.5
152 ❑ Jul 1978 **NM** value: **3.00**
• **CGC:** 1 graded, best 9.2
• Has 1977 Statement; avg total paid circ 118,766
153 ❑ Sep 1978 **NM** value: **3.00**
154 ❑ Nov 1978 Cover: 0.50 **NM** value: **3.00**
• Series continued in The Unexpected

HOUSE OF SECRETS (2ND SERIES) DC / Vertigo

1 ❑ Oct 1996 Cover: 2.50 **NM** value: **4.00**
📖 Foundation, Part 1 **A:** Teddy Kristiansen **W:** Steven Seagle
2 ❑ Nov 1996 Cover: 2.50 **NM** value: **3.00**
Circ: Diamd. preorders: **33,403**
📖 Foundation, Part 2 **A:** Teddy Kristiansen **W:** Steven Seagle
3 ❑ Dec 1996 Cover: 2.50 **NM** value: **3.00**
Circ: Diamd. preorders: **31,870**
📖 Foundation, Part 3 **A:** Teddy Kristiansen **W:** Steven Seagle
4 ❑ Jan 1997 Cover: 2.50 **NM** value: **3.00**
Circ: Diamd. preorders: **30,933**
📖 Foundation, Part 4 **A:** Teddy Kristiansen **W:** Steven Seagle
5 ❑ Feb 1997 Cover: 2.50 **NM** value: **3.00**
Circ: Diamd. preorders: **29,174**
📖 Foundation Epilogue **A:** Teddy Kristiansen **W:** Steven Seagle
6 ❑ Mar 1997 Cover: 2.50 **NM** value: **3.00**
Circ: Diamd. preorders: **27,500**
📖 Other Rooms **A:** Teddy Kristiansen; Duncan Fegredo **W:** Steven Seagle
7 ❑ Apr 1997 Cover: 2.50 **NM** value: **3.00**
Circ: Diamd. preorders: **26,167**
📖 Blueprint: Foundation A **A:** Teddy Kristiansen **W:** Steven Seagle
8 ❑ May 1997 Cover: 2.50 **NM** value: **3.00**
Circ: Diamd. preorders: **25,618**
📖 The Road To You – Getting There, Part 1 **A:** Teddy Kristiansen **W:** Steven Seagle
9 ❑ Jun 1997 Cover: 2.50 **NM** value: **3.00**
Circ: Diamd. preorders: **24,788**
📖 The Road To You – Getting There, Part 2 **A:** Teddy Kristiansen **W:** Steven Seagle
10 ❑ Jul 1997 Cover: 2.50 **NM** value: **3.00**
Circ: Diamd. preorders: **22,328**
📖 The Road To You – Getting There, Part 3 **A:** Teddy Kristiansen **W:** Steven Seagle
11 ❑ Aug 1997 Cover: 2.50 **NM** value: **3.00**
Circ: Diamd. preorders: **21,834**
📖 The Book of Law, Part 1 **A:** Teddy Kristiansen **W:** Steven Seagle
12 ❑ Sep 1997 Cover: 2.50 **NM** value: **3.00**
Circ: Diamd. preorders: **20,590**
📖 The Book of Law, Part 2 **A:** Teddy Kristiansen **W:** Steven Seagle
13 ❑ Oct 1997 Cover: 2.50 **NM** value: **3.00**
Circ: Diamd. preorders: **19,583**
📖 The Book of Law, Part 3 **A:** Teddy Kristiansen **W:** Steven Seagle
14 ❑ Nov 1997 Cover: 2.50 **NM** value: **3.00**
Circ: Diamd. preorders: **19,016**
📖 The Book of Law, Part 4 **A:** Teddy Kristiansen **W:** Steven Seagle
15 ❑ Dec 1997 Cover: 2.50 **NM** value: **3.00**
Circ: Diamd. preorders: **18,609**
📖 The Book of Law, Part 5 **A:** Teddy Kristiansen **W:** Steven Seagle
16 ❑ Feb 1998 Cover: 2.50 **NM** value: **3.00**
Circ: Diamd. preorders: **17,864**
📖 The Book of Law **A:** D'Israeli **W:** Steven Seagle
17 ❑ Mar 1998 Cover: 2.50 **NM** value: **3.00**
Circ: Diamd. preorders: **17,165**
covers form triptych. 📖 The Road To You: Leaving There, Part 1 **A:** Teddy Kristiansen **W:** Steven Seagle
18 ❑ Apr 1998 Cover: 2.50 **NM** value: **3.00**
Circ: Diamd. preorders: **15,696**
covers form triptych. 📖 The Road To You: Leaving There, Part 2 **A:** Teddy Kristiansen **W:** Steven Seagle
19 ❑ May 1998 Cover: 2.50 **NM** value: **3.00**
Circ: Diamd. preorders: **15,526**
covers form triptych. 📖 The Road To You: Leaving There, Part 3 **A:** Teddy Kristiansen **W:** Steven Seagle
20 ❑ Jun 1998 Cover: 2.50 **NM** value: **3.00**
Circ: Diamd. preorders: **15,309**
📖 Other Rooms **A:** Teddy Kristiansen **W:** Steven Seagle
21 ❑ Jul 1998 Cover: 2.50 **NM** value: **Cover or less**
Circ: Diamd. preorders: **11,579**
📖 Basement, Part 1 **A:** Teddy Kristiansen **W:** Steven Seagle
22 ❑ Aug 1998 Cover: 2.50 **NM** value: **Cover or less**
Circ: Diamd. preorders: **14,302**
📖 Basement, Part 2 **A:** Teddy Kristiansen **W:** Steven Seagle
23 ❑ Sep 1998 Cover: 2.50 **NM** value: **Cover or less**
Circ: Diamd. preorders: **13,482**
📖 Basement, Part 3 **A:** Teddy Kristiansen **W:** Steven Seagle
24 ❑ Nov 1998 Cover: 2.50 **NM** value: **Cover or less**
Circ: Diamd. preorders: **13,115**
📖 Attic **A:** Teddy Kristiansen **W:** Steven Seagle
25 ❑ Dec 1998 Cover: 2.50 **NM** value: **Cover or less**
Circ: Diamd. preorders: **12,799**
📖 Blueprint: Elevation B **A:** Teddy Kristiansen **W:** Steven Seagle
Bk 1 ❑ Cover: 14.95 **NM** value: **Cover or less**
📖 Foundation • Foundation; Collects House of Secrets (2nd Series) #1-5 **A:** Teddy Kristiansen **W:** Steven Seagle

HOUSE OF SECRETS: FAÇADE DC / Vertigo

1 ❑ Cover: 5.95 **NM** value: **Cover or less**
Circ: Diamd. preorders: **10,719**
2 ❑ Cover: 5.95 **NM** value: **Cover or less**
Circ: Diamd. preorders: **10,024**

HOUSE ON THE BORDERLAND, THE DC / Vertigo

Bk 1/HC ❑ Cover: 29.95 **NM** value: **Cover or less**

HOUSEWIVES AT PLAY Fantagraphics / Eros

1 ❑ Cover: 2.95 **NM** value: **Cover or less**
Circ: Diamd. preorders: **2,741**
2 ❑ Cover: 2.95 **NM** value: **Cover or less**
Circ: Diamd. preorders: **2,265**
3 ❑ Cover: 2.95 **NM** value: **Cover or less**
Circ: Diamd. preorders: **2,383**

HOWARD THE DUCK (1ST SERIES) Marvel

A hip comic for the cynic in all of us, Howard the Duck depicts a talking duck from another reality who winds up on Earth through a quirk of fate. Needless to say, he doesn't fit in well. The curmudgeonly Mallard spends as much time battling with American morals and culture as he spends in action against strange villains ranging from the Kidney Lady to Le Beaver.

A 1970s cult favorite, Howard the Duck was one of the earliest titles to see a speculative run on its first issue. Stev Gerber's work on the series was some of the quirkiest ever to appear in a mainstream comic book in this period, with an infamous all-text issue standing as the strangest of the run.

But Gerber would clash with marvel over the ownership of the character, and his departure from the series brought a quick end to it. The series returned briefly when Marvel and Gerber sorted out their differences and the long-planned film was released — but the sheer horror of that Hollywood production ran readers screaming from the shelves. — JJM

1 ❑ Jan 1976 Cover: 0.25 **NM** value: **8.00**
• **CGC:** 8 graded, best 9.6
📖 Howard The Barbarian **A:** Frank Brunner **W:** Steve Gerber ★ 1st Appearance of Beverly. ★ Appearance of Spider-Man.
2 ❑ Mar 1976 Cover: 0.25 **NM** value: **2.00**
• **CGC:** 1 graded, best 9.4
📖 Cry Turnip! **A:** Frank Brunner **W:** Steve Gerber
3 ❑ May 1976 Cover: 0.25 **NM** value: **2.00**
📖 Four Feathers of Death! **A:** John Buscema **W:** Steve Gerber
4 ❑ Jul 1976 Cover: 0.25 **NM** value: **2.00**
📖 The Sleep of the Just **A:** Gene Colan **W:** Steve Gerber
5 ❑ Sep 1976 Cover: 0.30 **NM** value: **2.00**
📖 I Want Mo-o-oney! **A:** Gene Colan **W:** Steve Gerber
6 ❑ Nov 1976 Cover: 0.30 **NM** value: **2.00**

Other grades: Multiply prices above by **1.5 for Mint • 2/3 for Very Fine • 1/3 for Fine • 1/5 for Very Good • 1/8 for Good**

• **CGC:** 1 graded, best 9.4
📖 The Secret House of Forbidden Cookies! **A:** Gene Colan **W:** Steve Gerber
7 ❑ Dec 1976 Cover: 0.30 **NM** value: **2.00**
📖 The Way The Cookie Crumbles! **A:** Gene Colan **W:** Steve Gerber
8 ❑ Jan 1977 Cover: 0.30 **NM** value: **2.00**
• **CGC:** 1 graded, best 9.4
📖 Open Season! **A:** Gene Colan **W:** Steve Gerber
9 ❑ Feb 1977 Cover: 0.30 **NM** value: **2.00**
📖 Scandal Plucks Duck **A:** Gene Colan **W:** Steve Gerber
10 ❑ Mar 1977 Cover: 0.30 **NM** value: **2.00**
11 ❑ Apr 1977 Cover: 0.30 **NM** value: **2.00**
📖 Quack-Up **A:** Gene Colan **W:** Steve Gerber
12 ❑ May 1977 Cover: 0.30 **NM** value: **4.00**
• **CGC:** 13 graded, best 9.8
13 ❑ Jun 1977 Cover: 0.30 **NM** value: **3.00**
• **CGC:** 23 graded, best 9.6
📖 Rock, Roll Over, and Writhe; A Duck Possessed **A:** Gene Colan **W:** Steve Gerber ★ Appearance of Kiss (rock group).
14 ❑ Jul 1977 Cover: 0.30 **NM** value: **1.50**
📖 A Duck Possessed! **A:** Gene Colan **W:** Steve Gerber
15 ❑ Aug 1977 Cover: 0.30 **NM** value: **1.50**
📖 The Island of Dr. Bong **A:** Gene Colan **W:** Steve Gerber ★ 1st Appearance of Doctor Bong.
16 ❑ Sep 1977 Cover: 0.30 **NM** value: **1.50**
📖 Zen and the Art of Comic Book Writing • all-text issue **A:** Cast of Thousands **W:** Steve Gerber ★ Origin of Doctor Bong.
17 ❑ Oct 1977 Cover: 0.30 **NM** value: **1.50**
📖 Doctor Bong! **A:** Gene Colan **W:** Steve Gerber ★ Origin of Doctor Bong.
18 ❑ Nov 1977 Cover: 0.35 **NM** value: **1.50**
📖 Metamorphosis **A:** Gene Colan **W:** Steve Gerber
19 ❑ Dec 1977 Cover: 0.35 **NM** value: **1.50**
📖 Howard The Human **A:** Gene Colan **W:** Steve Gerber
20 ❑ Jan 1978 Cover: 0.35 **NM** value: **1.50**
📖 Scrubba-Dub Death! **A:** Gene Colan **W:** Steve Gerber ★ Versus Sudol.
21 ❑ Feb 1978 Cover: 0.35 **NM** value: **1.50**
📖 If You Knew Soofi…! **A:** Carmine Infantino **W:** Steve Gerber ★ Versus Soofi.
22 ❑ Mar 1978 Cover: 0.35 **NM** value: **1.50**
📖 May The Farce Be With You! **A:** Val Mayerik **W:** Steve Gerber
23 ❑ Apr 1978 Cover: 0.35 **NM** value: **1.50**
📖 Star Waaugh **A:** Val Mayerik **W:** Steve Gerber
24 ❑ May 1978 Cover: 0.35 **NM** value: **1.50**
📖 The Night After You Save The Universe? **A:** Gene Colan **W:** Steve Gerber
25 ❑ Jun 1978 Cover: 0.35 **NM** value: **1.50**
📖 Getting Smooth! **A:** Gene Colan **W:** Steve Gerber ★ Appearance of Ringmaster.
26 ❑ Jul 1978 Cover: 0.35 **NM** value: **1.50**
📖 Repercussions…! **A:** Gene Colan **W:** Steve Gerber ★ Appearance of Ringmaster.
27 ❑ Sep 1978 Cover: 0.35 **NM** value: **1.50**
📖 Circus Maximus **A:** Gene Colan **W:** Steve Gerber ★ Appearance of Ringmaster.
28 ❑ Nov 1978 Cover: 0.35 **NM** value: **1.50**
📖 Cooking With Gas **A:** Carmine Infantino **W:** Marv Wolfman
29 ❑ Jan 1979 Cover: 0.35 **NM** value: **1.50**
📖 Help Stamp Out Ducks! **A:** Will Meugniot **W:** Mark Evanier; Steve Gerber
30 ❑ Mar 1979 Cover: 0.35 **NM** value: **1.50**
📖 If This Be Bongsday! **A:** Gene Colan **W:** Bill Mantlo ★ Versus Doctor Bong.
31 ❑ May 1979 Cover: 0.40 **NM** value: **1.50**
📖 The Final Bong! **A:** Al Milgrom; Gene Colan **W:** Bill Mantlo ★ Versus Doctor Bong.
32 ❑ Jan 1986 Cover: 0.65 **NM** value: **1.50**
Circ: CapCity orders: **11,700**
📖 Going Underground **A:** Paul Smith **W:** Steven Grant ★ Origin of Howard the Duck.
33 ❑ Sep 1986 Cover: 1.50 **NM** value: **Cover or less**
Circ: CapCity orders: **11,400**
📖 Material Duck final issue. **A:** Val Mayerik **W:** Christopher Stager
Anl 1❑ Oct 1977 Cover: 0.50 **NM** value: **1.50**
📖 Thief Of Bagmom! **A:** Val Mayerik **W:** Steve Gerber

HOWARD THE DUCK (2ND SERIES) Marvel

1 ❑ Cover: 2.99 **NM** value: **Cover or less**

HOWARD THE DUCK HOLIDAY SPECIAL Marvel

1 ❑ Feb 1997 Cover: 2.50 **NM** value: **Cover or less**
Circ: Direct Market orders: **16,500**
📖 Wreck the Malls with Hydra's Folly! **A:** Pascual Ferry **W:** Larry Hama

HOWARD THE DUCK (MAGAZINE) Marvel

1 ❑ Oct 1979 Cover: 1.00 **NM** value: **3.00**
📖 Thief of Bagmom!; Calling All Carpets!; The Desert Song and Dance • contains nudity **A:** Val Mayerik **W:** Steve Gerber
2 ❑ Dec 1979 Cover: 1.25 **NM** value: **2.00**
📖 Animal Indecency; The Crash of '79 **A:** Gene Colan; Klaus Janson; Dave Simons **W:** Bill Mantlo
3 ❑ Feb 1980 Cover: 1.25 **NM** value: **2.00**
📖 A Christmas for Carol; Duck Soup **A:** Gene Colan; Jerry Bingham; Dave Simons; Joe Rubinstein **W:** Bill Mantlo
4 ❑ Mar 1980 Cover: 1.25 **NM** value: **4.00**
📖 The Maltese Cockroach; The Playduck Interview; The Old Drake's Tale; Duckmate of the Month; Birds in Bondage!; The Prisoner of Ducks; The Dreadcliff Cuckoos; The Playduck Review; The Playduck Advisor **A:** Gene Colan; John Buscema; Klaus Janson; Dave Simons **W:** Bill Mantlo; Mark Gruenwald ★ Appearance of Kiss, Beatles.
5 ❑ May 1980 Cover: 1.25 **NM** value: **2.00**
6 ❑ Jul 1980 Cover: 1.25 **NM** value: **2.00**
7 ❑ Sep 1980 Cover: 1.25 **NM** value: **2.00**
📖 Of Dice & Ducks!; Street People **A:** Gene Colan; Ned Sonntag **W:** Bill Mantlo; Lynn Graeme ★ Appearance of Man-Thing.
8 ❑ Nov 1980 Cover: 1.25 **NM** value: **2.00**
📖 The Grey Panther; How the Duck Got his Pants; Ducktective Comics; Street People • Batman parody **A:** Gene Colan; Marshall Rogers; Ned Sonntag; Steven Grant **W:** Steven Grant; Bill Mantlo; Lynn Graeme
9 ❑ Mar 1981 Cover: 1.25 **NM** value: **2.00**

HOWARD THE DUCK: THE MOVIE Marvel

1 ❑ Dec 1986 Cover: 0.75 **NM** value: **1.00**
Circ: CapCity orders: **9,700**
2 ❑ Jan 1987 Cover: 0.75 **NM** value: **1.00**
Circ: CapCity orders: **8,100**
3 ❑ Feb 1987 Cover: 0.75 **NM** value: **1.00**
Circ: CapCity orders: **7,700**
📖 Duck Day Afternoon **A:** Kyle Baker **W:** Danny Fingeroth

HOWDY DOODY COMICS Dell

One of the most popular characters of early television, freckle-faced and buck-toothed Howdy Doody got the obligatory comics treatment courtesy of Dell, then the reigning champion of kid-friendly fare. Buffalo Bob, the human co-star of the Howdy Doody TV show, is nowhere in sight in the comics-this is strictly a fantasy adaptation of the life and wacky times of the smart-aleck puppet. Howdy and his equally goofy pal Dilly Dally run the gamut of adventures from science-fiction style trips to the moon to surreal excursions to the old West world of cowboys and bandits. All the stories are told in the classic Dell style, blending action and humor with spare dialogue that challenges young kids to read. Howdy Doody's publishing schedule grew increasingly erratic through the 1950s and the title finally ended in 1957.

1 ❑ Jan 1950 Cover: 0.10 **NM** value: **550.00**
2 ❑ May 1950 Cover: 0.10 **NM** value: **225.00**
3 ❑ Jul 1950 Cover: 0.10 **NM** value: **135.00**
4 ❑ Sep 1950 Cover: 0.10 **NM** value: **110.00**
• **CGC:** 1 graded, best 3.0
5 ❑ Nov 1950 Cover: 0.10 **NM** value: **110.00**
• **CGC:** 1 graded, best 8.5
6 ❑ Jan 1951 Cover: 0.10 **NM** value: **125.00**
• Cited in Seduction of the Innocent ("...depicts colored natives as stereotyped characactures...")
7 ❑ Mar 1951 Cover: 0.10 **NM** value: **85.00**
8 ❑ May 1951 Cover: 0.10 **NM** value: **85.00**
9 ❑ Jul 1951 Cover: 0.10 **NM** value: **85.00**
10 ❑ Sep 1951 Cover: 0.10 **NM** value: **85.00**
11 ❑ Nov 1951, four-color Cover: 0.10 **NM** value: **60.00**
• **CGC:** 2 graded, best 9.6
12 ❑ Jan 1952 Cover: 0.10 **NM** value: **60.00**
13 ❑ Mar 1952 Cover: 0.10 **NM** value: **60.00**
14 ❑ May 1952 Cover: 0.10 **NM** value: **60.00**
15 ❑ Jul 1952 Cover: 0.10 **NM** value: **60.00**
16 ❑ Sep 1952 Cover: 0.10 **NM** value: **60.00**
17 ❑ Nov 1952 Cover: 0.10 **NM** value: **60.00**
📖 Howdy Doody in Pet Peeve (text Story); Howdy Doody
18 ❑ Jan 1953 Cover: 0.10 **NM** value: **60.00**
19 ❑ Mar 1953 Cover: 0.10 **NM** value: **60.00**
20 ❑ May 1953 Cover: 0.10 **NM** value: **60.00**
21 ❑ Jul 1953 Cover: 0.10 **NM** value: **45.00**
22 ❑ Sep 1953 Cover: 0.10 **NM** value: **45.00**
23 ❑ Nov 1953 Cover: 0.10 **NM** value: **45.00**
24 ❑ Jan 1954 Cover: 0.10 **NM** value: **45.00**
25 ❑ Mar 1954 Cover: 0.10 **NM** value: **45.00**
26 ❑ May 1954 Cover: 0.10 **NM** value: **45.00**
27 ❑ Jul 1954 Cover: 0.10 **NM** value: **45.00**
28 ❑ Sep 1954 Cover: 0.10 **NM** value: **45.00**
29 ❑ Nov 1954 Cover: 0.10 **NM** value: **45.00**
30 ❑ Jan 1955 Cover: 0.10 **NM** value: **45.00**
31 ❑ Mar 1955 Cover: 0.10 **NM** value: **38.00**
32 ❑ May 1955 Cover: 0.10 **NM** value: **38.00**
33 ❑ Jul 1955 Cover: 0.10 **NM** value: **38.00**
34 ❑ Sep 1955 Cover: 0.10 **NM** value: **38.00**
35 ❑ Nov 1955 Cover: 0.10 **NM** value: **38.00**
36 ❑ Jan 1956 Cover: 0.10 **NM** value: **38.00**
37 ❑ Apr 1956 Cover: 0.10 **NM** value: **38.00**
• **CGC:** 1 graded, best 9.0
38 ❑ Jul 1956 Cover: 0.10 **NM** value: **38.00**

HOWL Eternity

1 ❑ b&w Cover: 2.25 **NM** value: **Cover or less**
2 ❑ b&w Cover: 2.25 **NM** value: **Cover or less**

HOW SLUGGO SURVIVES Kitchen Sink

Bk 1❑ Cover: 7.95 **NM** value: **Cover or less**

HOW THE WEST WAS WON Gold Key

1 ❑ Jul 1963 Cover: 0.12 **NM** value: **18.00**
No issue number.

HOW TO DRAW COMICS COMIC, THE Solson

1 ❑ Cover: 1.95 **NM** value: **Cover or less**

HOW TO DRAW FELIX THE CAT AND HIS FRIENDS Felix

1 ❑ b&w Cover: 2.25 **NM** value: **Cover or less**

HOW TO DRAW TEENAGE MUTANT NINJA TURTLES Solson

1 ❑ Cover: 2.25 **NM** value: **Cover or less**

HOW TO PICK UP GIRLS IF YOU'RE A COMIC BOOK GEEK 3 Finger Prints

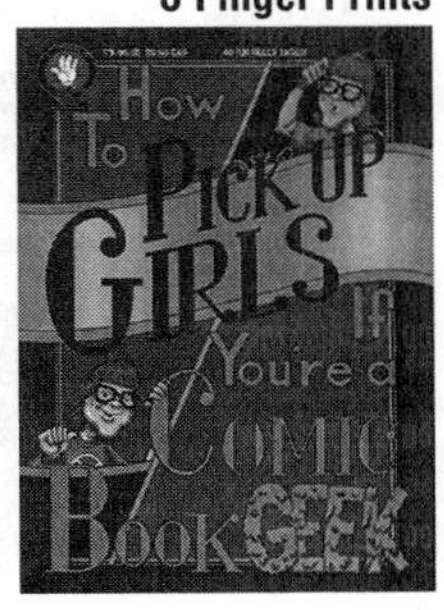

Richard Koslowski finally lets all of comicdom's social outcasts know what it takes to hook up with those exotic creatures known as women. Starring the infamous 3 Geeks (Keith, Allen, and Jim) it points out the common traps that await the unwary comic book geek as they step gingerly into the dating pool. In addition to giving tips on basic hygiene, the issue warns comic book geeks against having unreasonable expectations for their dream girl. (Wonder Woman is not available!). Nor are they to get into debates on on the first date over which super-hero would beat whom.

Sometimes obvious but always funny, this issue is loaded with dating tips, while happily ribbing the stereotypical comic fanboy.

1 ❑ Jul 1997 Cover: 3.95 **NM** value: **Cover or less**
• **CGC:** 1 graded, best 9.8
No issue number. cardstock cover. **A:** Rich Koslowski **W:** Rich Koslowski

HOW TO PUBLISH COMICS Solson

1 ❑ Cover: 2.00 **NM** value: **Cover or less**

H.R. PUFNSTUF Gold Key

1 ❑ Oct 1970 Cover: 0.15 **NM** value: **50.00**
• **CGC:** 19 graded, best 9.6
2 ❑ Jan 1971 Cover: 0.15 **NM** value: **40.00**
• **CGC:** 1 graded, best 9.2
3 ❑ Apr 1971 Cover: 0.15 **NM** value: **40.00**
• **CGC:** 1 graded, best 9.6
4 ❑ Jul 1971 Cover: 0.15 **NM** value: **30.00**
5 ❑ Oct 1971 Cover: 0.15 **NM** value: **30.00**
6 ❑ Jan 1972 Cover: 0.15 **NM** value: **30.00**
7 ❑ Apr 1972 Cover: 0.15 **NM** value: **25.00**
• **CGC:** 1 graded, best 9.4
8 ❑ Jul 1972 Cover: 0.15 **NM** value: **25.00**
• **CGC:** 2 graded, best 9.6

HUCKLEBERRY HOUND & QUICK DRAW MCGRAW GIANT-SIZE FLIP BOOK Harvey

1 ❑ Cover: 2.25 **NM** value: **Cover or less**

HUCKLEBERRY HOUND (GOLD KEY) Gold Key

Close your eyes and let Huckleberry Hound take you back to a time when the world was young and buying comic books was a pleasure, not a business. You could count on the fact that the Hanna-Barbara creation would go on just as many zany adventures as he did on his Saturday morning cartoons.

Broken up into various self-contained shorts, rest assured that the fun loving Huckleberry Hound stars in at least three of his own adventures full of clumsy crime-solving, alien encounters and just about any other wacky plot thread that's sure to draw laughs. Other Hanna-Barbara favorites, like Mr. Jinks, Pixie and Dixie, and even Yogi Bear, are thrown into the mix with their own entertaining shorts. One-page children narratives and reader illustrations round out the fun offerings this playful title provides.

0 ❑ **NM** value: **100.00**
• Four Color Comics #990
1 ❑ May 1959 Cover: 0.10 **NM** value: **65.00**
• Four Color Comics #1050
2 ❑ Oct 1959 Cover: 0.10 **NM** value: **65.00**
• Four Color Comics #1054
3 ❑ Jan 1960 Cover: 0.10 **NM** value: **35.00**
4 ❑ Mar 1960 Cover: 0.10 **NM** value: **35.00**
• **CGC:** 1 graded, best 9.0
5 ❑ May 1960 Cover: 0.10 **NM** value: **35.00**
• **CGC:** 1 graded, best 7.0
6 ❑ Jul 1960 Cover: 0.10 **NM** value: **30.00**
7 ❑ Sep 1960 Cover: 0.10 **NM** value: **30.00**
8 ❑ Nov 1960 Cover: 0.10 **NM** value: **30.00**
9 ❑ Feb 1961 Cover: 0.15 **NM** value: **30.00**
10 ❑ Apr 1961 Cover: 0.15 **NM** value: **30.00**
11 ❑ Jun 1961 Cover: 0.15 **NM** value: **20.00**
12 ❑ Aug 1961 Cover: 0.15 **NM** value: **20.00**
13 ❑ Oct 1961 Cover: 0.15 **NM** value: **20.00**
14 ❑ Cover: 0.15 **NM** value: **20.00**
15 ❑ 1962 Cover: 0.15 **NM** value: **20.00**
16 ❑ 1962 Cover: 0.15 **NM** value: **20.00**
17 ❑ 1962 Cover: 0.12 **NM** value: **20.00**
18 ❑ Oct 1962 Cover: 0.12 **NM** value: **26.00**
• **CGC:** 1 graded, best 8.5
• Giant-size.
19 ❑ Jan 1963 Cover: 0.12 **NM** value: **26.00**
• **CGC:** 2 graded, best 9.6
• Giant-size.
20 ❑ Apr 1963 Cover: 0.12 **NM** value: **20.00**
• Has 1962 Statement, filed 9/27/62; only subscription figures printed; avg subs 7,524

CGC-graded: Multiply prices above by **33 for 9.9 M • 16 for 9.8 NM/M • 7 for 9.6 NM+ • 5 for 9.4 NM • 2.5 for 9.2 NM- • 1.5 for 9.0 VF/NM**

21 ❑ Jul 1963 Cover: 0.12 **NM** value: **15.00**
22 ❑ Oct 1963 Cover: 0.12 **NM** value: **15.00**
23 ❑ Jan 1964 Cover: 0.12 **NM** value: **15.00**
24 ❑ May 1964 Cover: 0.12 **NM** value: **15.00**
25 ❑ Aug 1964 Cover: 0.12 **NM** value: **15.00**
26 ❑ Nov 1964 Cover: 0.12 **NM** value: **15.00**
27 ❑ Jul 1965 Cover: 0.12 **NM** value: **15.00**
28 ❑ 1966 Cover: 0.12 **NM** value: **15.00**
29 ❑ Apr 1967 Cover: 0.12 **NM** value: **15.00**
30 ❑ Jul 1967 Cover: 0.12 **NM** value: **15.00**
31 ❑ Oct 1967 Cover: 0.12 **NM** value: **9.00**
32 ❑ Jan 1968 Cover: 0.12 **NM** value: **9.00**
33 ❑ Apr 1968 Cover: 0.12 **NM** value: **9.00**
34 ❑ Jul 1968 Cover: 0.12 **NM** value: **9.00**
35 ❑ Oct 1968 Cover: 0.15 **NM** value: **9.00**
36 ❑ Jan 1969 Cover: 0.15 **NM** value: **9.00**
37 ❑ Apr 1969 Cover: 0.15 **NM** value: **9.00**
38 ❑ Jul 1969 Cover: 0.15 **NM** value: **9.00**
39 ❑ Oct 1969 Cover: 0.15 **NM** value: **9.00**
• **CGC:** 1 graded, best 9.4
40 ❑ Jan 1970 Cover: 0.15 **NM** value: **6.00**
41 ❑ Apr 1970 Cover: 0.15 **NM** value: **6.00**
42 ❑ Jul 1970 Cover: 0.15 **NM** value: **6.00**
43 ❑ Oct 1970 Cover: 0.15 **NM** value: **6.00**

HUEY, DEWEY, AND LOUIE JUNIOR WOODCHUCKS — Gold Key

Hail Carl Barks, whose creative mind produced some "young adventurer" stories far more interesting than those found in most of juvenile fiction. One may not be able to tell Huey, Dewey, and Louie apart even in Barks' stories, but he's added far more depth to them than they ever had in their animated origins. More than simply foils for their Unca Donald, the kids are responsible members of the Junior Woodchucks, a worldwide organization packed with badges to be earned and leaders with acronymic titles.

Many Woodchucks stories have environmental themes. In one epic, the kids call in scouts from all over (even the Littlest Chickadees) to save a beached whale from the profiteering hands of their own uncle, Scrooge McDuck.

On balance, it's one of the better "comics for kids" series ever produced. — JJM

1 ❑ Cover: 0.12 **NM** value: **35.00**
2 ❑ Aug 1967 Cover: 0.12 **NM** value: **18.00**
3 ❑ Cover: 0.15 **NM** value: **15.00**
4 ❑ Jan 1970 Cover: 0.15 **NM** value: **12.00**
📖 Lost in the Black Forest; Challenge of the Chickadees • Reprinted from Walt Disney's Comics #181 and 227
5 ❑ Apr 1970 Cover: 0.15 **NM** value: **12.00**
📖 Test at Frostbite Pass; Ten Star Generals • Reprinted from Walt Disney's Comics #125 and 132
6 ❑ Jul 1970 Cover: 0.15 **NM** value: **12.00**
📖 Peril of the Black Forest; Life Savers
7 ❑ Oct 1970 Cover: 0.15 **NM** value: **12.00**
📖 Whale of a Good Deed
8 ❑ Jan 1971 Cover: 0.15 **NM** value: **12.00**
📖 Let Sleeping Bones Lie; Bad Day for Troop 'A'
9 ❑ Apr 1971 Cover: 0.15 **NM** value: **12.00**
📖 Looter of the Lake
10 ❑ Jul 1971 Cover: 0.15 **NM** value: **12.00**
📖 Maple Sugar Time (How Sweet It Is!); Bottled Battlers
11 ❑ Oct 1971 Cover: 0.15 **NM** value: **10.00**
📖 Traitor in the Ranks; Eagle Savers
12 ❑ Jan 1972 Cover: 0.15 **NM** value: **10.00**
📖 Hound of the Moaning Hills; Storm Dancers **W:** Carl Barks
13 ❑ Mar 1972 Cover: 0.15 **NM** value: **10.00**
📖 The Day the Mountain Shook; Gold of the '49ers
14 ❑ May 1972 Cover: 0.15 **NM** value: **10.00**
📖 Duckmade Disaster
15 ❑ Jul 1972 Cover: 0.15 **NM** value: **10.00**
📖 Wailing Whalers
16 ❑ Sep 1972 Cover: 0.15 **NM** value: **10.00**
📖 Where There's Smoke
17 ❑ Nov 1972 Cover: 0.15 **NM** value: **10.00**
• **CGC:** 1 graded, best 9.2
📖 Be Leery of Lake Eerie
18 ❑ Jan 1973 Cover: 0.15 **NM** value: **10.00**
19 ❑ Mar 1973 Cover: 0.15 **NM** value: **10.00**
📖 Teahouse of the Waggin' Dragon
20 ❑ May 1973 Cover: 0.20 **NM** value: **10.00**
📖 New Zoo Brews Ado
21 ❑ Jul 1973 Cover: 0.20 **NM** value: **8.00**
📖 Music Hath Charms
22 ❑ Sep 1973 Cover: 0.20 **NM** value: **8.00**
📖 The Phantom Joker; Bubbleweight Champ
23 ❑ Nov 1973 Cover: 0.20 **NM** value: **8.00**
📖 Hark, Hark, the Ark; Medaling Around
24 ❑ Jan 1974 Cover: 0.20 **NM** value: **8.00**
25 ❑ Mar 1974 Cover: 0.20 **NM** value: **8.00**
📖 Captains Outrageous; The Dog-Sitter
26 ❑ May 1974 Cover: 0.20 **NM** value: **8.00**
📖 Under the Polar Ice • Reprinted from Walt Disney's Comics #232
27 ❑ Jul 1974 Cover: 0.25 **NM** value: **8.00**
28 ❑ Sep 1974 Cover: 0.25 **NM** value: **8.00**
29 ❑ Nov 1974 Cover: 0.25 **NM** value: **8.00**
30 ❑ Jan 1975 Cover: 0.25 **NM** value: **8.00**
31 ❑ Mar 1975 Cover: 0.25 **NM** value: **8.00**
32 ❑ May 1975 Cover: 0.25 **NM** value: **8.00**
33 ❑ Jul 1975 Cover: 0.25 **NM** value: **8.00**
34 ❑ Sep 1975 Cover: 0.25 **NM** value: **8.00**
35 ❑ Nov 1975 Cover: 0.25 **NM** value: **8.00**
📖 Whale of a Good Deed • Reprinted from Huey, Dewey and Louie Junior Woodchucks #7
36 ❑ Jan 1976 Cover: 0.25 **NM** value: **8.00**
37 ❑ Mar 1976 Cover: 0.25 **NM** value: **8.00**
38 ❑ May 1976 Cover: 0.25 **NM** value: **8.00**
39 ❑ Jul 1976 Cover: 0.25 **NM** value: **8.00**
40 ❑ Cover: 0.30 **NM** value: **8.00**
41 ❑ Cover: 0.30 **NM** value: **6.00**
📖 Peril of the Black Forest; Life Savers • Reprinted from Huey, Dewey and Louie Junior Woodchucks #6
42 ❑ Mar 1977 Cover: 0.30 **NM** value: **6.00**
43 ❑ Apr 1977 Cover: 0.30 **NM** value: **6.00**
44 ❑ Jun 1977 Cover: 0.30 **NM** value: **6.00**
45 ❑ Aug 1977 Cover: 0.30 **NM** value: **6.00**
46 ❑ Sep 1977 Cover: 0.30 **NM** value: **6.00**
47 ❑ Dec 1977 Cover: 0.35 **NM** value: **6.00**
48 ❑ Feb 1978 Cover: 0.35 **NM** value: **6.00**
49 ❑ Apr 1978 Cover: 0.35 **NM** value: **6.00**
50 ❑ Jun 1978 Cover: 0.35 **NM** value: **6.00**
51 ❑ Aug 1978 Cover: 0.35 **NM** value: **6.00**
52 ❑ Sep 1978 Cover: 0.35 **NM** value: **6.00**
53 ❑ Dec 1978 Cover: 0.35 **NM** value: **6.00**
54 ❑ Feb 1979 Cover: 0.35 **NM** value: **6.00**
55 ❑ Apr 1979 Cover: 0.40 **NM** value: **6.00**
56 ❑ Jun 1979 Cover: 0.40 **NM** value: **6.00**
57 ❑ Jul 1979 Cover: 0.40 **NM** value: **6.00**
58 ❑ Aug 1979 Cover: 0.40 **NM** value: **6.00**
59 ❑ Sep 1979 Cover: 0.40 **NM** value: **6.00**
60 ❑ Dec 1979 Cover: 0.40 **NM** value: **6.00**
61 ❑ Feb 1980 Cover: 0.40 **NM** value: **4.00**
62 ❑ Mar 1980 Cover: 0.40 **NM** value: **4.00**
63 ❑ 1980 Cover: 0.40 **NM** value: **4.00**
64 ❑ 1980 Cover: 0.40 **NM** value: **4.00**
65 ❑ Sep 1980 Cover: 0.40 **NM** value: **4.00**
66 ❑ 1980 Cover: 0.40 **NM** value: **4.00**
67 ❑ Jan 1981 Cover: 0.40 **NM** value: **4.00**
68 ❑ Jun 1981 Cover: 0.50 **NM** value: **4.00**
69 ❑ Aug 1981 Cover: 0.50 **NM** value: **4.00**
70 ❑ 1981 Cover: 0.50 **NM** value: **4.00**
71 ❑ Dec 1981 Cover: 0.50 **NM** value: **4.00**
• **CGC:** 1 graded, best 9.4
72 ❑ 1982 **NM** value: **4.00**
73 ❑ Cover: 0.60 **NM** value: **4.00**
74 ❑ Cover: 0.60 **NM** value: **4.00**
75 ❑ Cover: 0.60 **NM** value: **4.00**
76 ❑ Cover: 0.60 **NM** value: **4.00**
77 ❑ Cover: 0.60 **NM** value: **4.00**
78 ❑ Cover: 0.60 **NM** value: **4.00**
79 ❑ Cover: 0.60 **NM** value: **4.00**
80 ❑ Cover: 0.60 **NM** value: **4.00**
81 ❑ 1984 Cover: 0.60 **NM** value: **4.00**

HUGGA BUNCH — Marvel / Star

1 ❑ Oct 1986 Cover: 0.75 **NM** value: **1.00**
Circ: CapCity orders: **4,150**
2 ❑ Dec 1986 Cover: 0.75 **NM** value: **1.00**
Circ: CapCity orders: **2,150**
3 ❑ Feb 1986 Cover: 0.75 **NM** value: **1.00**
Circ: CapCity orders: **1,900**
4 ❑ Apr 1986 Cover: 0.75 **NM** value: **1.00**
Circ: CapCity orders: **1,600**
📖 Storm Watch
5 ❑ Jun 1986 Cover: 1.00 **NM** value: **Cover or less**
Circ: CapCity orders: **1,100**
6 ❑ Aug 1986 Cover: 1.00 **NM** value: **Cover or less**

HUGO — Fantagraphics

1 ❑ Cover: 1.95 **NM** value: **Cover or less**
2 ❑ Cover: 1.95 **NM** value: **Cover or less**
3 ❑ Jul 1985 Cover: 1.95 **NM** value: **Cover or less**
📖 My Bonnie Lies Under the Ocean **A:** Milton Knight Jr. **W:** Milton Knight Jr.
Bk 1❑ Feb 1995, b&w Cover: 14.95 **NM** value: **Cover or less**
• The Hugo Collection; collects Fantagraphics' Hugo #1-3

HULK — Marvel

After 474 issues, the "powers that be" over at Marvel Comics decided to retire "The Incredible" from the book's title and move Bruce Banner and his monstrous alter ego into a bold new chapter of comics' history. Who better to charge with this task than John Byrne, the king of revamps? But why start over with a title that has been doing so well, you ask? Perception is everything.

Tying up all the loose ends in the character's post-Heroes Return life, Banner has been left without direction, without purpose, and without any active pursuers. This sets the stage for a return to the creature's savage roots. No more intelligent, in control Hulk; instead, expect to see a scrawny, book-smart Banner struggling to gain control of the emotionless and destructive creature resting deep within his subconscious.

After the first year, Marvel quietly put the Incredible adjective back on the title.

1 ❑ Apr 1999 Cover: 2.99 **NM** value: **3.00**
Circ: Diamd. preorders: **77,839** • **CGC:** 5 graded, best 9.8
wraparound cover. 📖 The Gathering Storm **A:** Ron Garney **W:** John Byrne
1/A ❑ Apr 1999 **NM** value: **8.00**
DFE gold foil cover. 📖 The Gathering Storm **A:** Ron Garney **W:** John Byrne
1/Aut❑Apr 1999 **NM** value: **8.00**
📖 The Gathering Storm **A:** Ron Garney **W:** John Byrne
1/GO❑Apr 1999 **NM** value: **5.00**
• **CGC:** 5 graded, best 9.6
DFE gold foil cover. 📖 The Gathering Storm **A:** Ron Garney **W:** John Byrne
2 ❑ May 1999 Cover: 1.99 **NM** value: **2.00**
Circ: Diamd. preorders: **64,618**
3 ❑ Jun 1999 Cover: 1.99 **NM** value: **2.00**
Circ: Diamd. preorders: **56,489**
4 ❑ Jul 1999 Cover: 1.99 **NM** value: **2.00**
Circ: Diamd. preorders: **53,172**
5 ❑ Aug 1999 Cover: 1.99 **NM** value: **2.00**
Circ: Diamd. preorders: **50,950**
6 ❑ Sep 1999 Cover: 1.99 **NM** value: **2.00**
Circ: Diamd. preorders: **48,031**
7 ❑ Oct 1999 Cover: 1.99 **NM** value: **2.00**
Circ: Diamd. preorders: **44,443**
8 ❑ Nov 1999 Cover: 1.99 **NM** value: **2.00**
Circ: Diamd. preorders: **47,724** • **CGC:** 8 graded, best 9.8
• Has 1999 Statement, filed 10/1/99; avg print run 109,800; avg sales 70,156; avg subs 2,342; avg total paid 72,498; samples 600; office use 725; max existent 73,948; 33% of run returned ★ Versus Wolverine.
9 ❑ Dec 1999 Cover: 1.99 **NM** value: **2.00**
Circ: Diamd. preorders: **44,387**
10 ❑ Jan 2000 Cover: 1.99 **NM** value: **2.25**
Circ: Diamd. preorders: **40,631**
11 ❑ Feb 2000 Cover: 1.99 **NM** value: **2.25**
Circ: Diamd. preorders: **43,713**
12 ❑ Mar 2000 Cover: 1.99 **NM** value: **2.25**
13 ❑ Apr 2000 Cover: 1.99 **NM** value: **2.25**
14 ❑ May 2000 Cover: 1.99 **NM** value: **2.25**
15 ❑ Jun 2000 Cover: 2.25 **NM** value: **Cover or less**
16 ❑ Jul 2000 Cover: 2.25 **NM** value: **Cover or less**
17 ❑ Aug 2000 Cover: 2.25 **NM** value: **Cover or less**
18 ❑ Sep 2000 Cover: 2.25 **NM** value: **Cover or less**
📖 The Dogs of War, Part 5 **A:** Ron Garney **W:** Paul Jenkins
19 ❑ Oct 2000 Cover: 2.25 **NM** value: **Cover or less**
📖 The Dogs of War, Part 6 **A:** Ron Garney **W:** Paul Jenkins
20 ❑ Nov 2000 Cover: 2.25 **NM** value: **Cover or less**
📖 The Dogs of War, Part 7 **A:** Ron Garney **W:** Paul Jenkins
21 ❑ Dec 2000 Cover: 2.25 **NM** value: **Cover or less**
📖 Maximum Security; The Truth is Really Out There • Has 2000 Statement, filed 10/1/2000; avg print run 72,300; avg sales 47,961; avg subs 2,158; avg total paid 49,849; samples 600; max existent 50,844; 30% of run returned **A:** Kyle Hotz **W:** Paul Jenkins
22 ❑ Jan 2001 Cover: 2.25 **NM** value: **Cover or less**
📖 Disorganized Crime, Part 1 **A:** Kyle Hotz **W:** Paul Jenkins
23 ❑ Feb 2001 Cover: 2.25 **NM** value: **Cover or less**
📖 Disorganized Crime, Part 2: Chicago Dope **A:** Kyle Hotz **W:** Paul Jenkins
24 ❑ Mar 2001 Cover: 1.99 **NM** value: **Cover or less**
• **CGC:** 1 graded, best 9.6
lower cover price. 📖 Dear Betty ... • part of Marvel's Slashback program **A:** John Romita Jr. **W:** Paul Jenkins ★ Appearance of Abomination, Thunderbolt Ross.
25 ❑ Apr 2001 Cover: 2.99 **NM** value: **Cover or less**
• double-sized. 📖 Always on My Mind **A:** John Romita Jr. **W:** Paul Jenkins ★ Appearance of Abomination.
26 ❑ May 2001 Cover: 2.25 **NM** value: **Cover or less**
📖 Do You Know Where You're Going? **A:** Kyle Hotz **W:** Paul Jenkins; Sean McKeever
27 ❑ Jun 2001 Cover: 2.25 **NM** value: **Cover or less**
28 ❑ Jul 2001 Cover: 2.25 **NM** value: **Cover or less**
29 ❑ Aug 2001 Cover: 2.25 **NM** value: **Cover or less**
30 ❑ Sep 2001 Cover: 2.25 **NM** value: **Cover or less**
31 ❑ Oct 2001 Cover: 2.25 **NM** value: **Cover or less**
32 ❑ Nov 2001 Cover: 2.25 **NM** value: **Cover or less**
33 ❑ Dec 2001 Cover: 3.50 **NM** value: **Cover or less**
34 ❑ Jan 2002 Cover: 2.25 **NM** value: **Cover or less**
35 ❑ Feb 2002 Cover: 2.25 **NM** value: **Cover or less**
• Has 2001 Statement, filed 10/1/2001; avg print run 66,558; avg sales 45,999; avg subs 2,177; avg total paid 48,176; samples 600; max existent 48,776; 27% of run returned
36 ❑ Mar 2002 Cover: 2.25 **NM** value: **Cover or less**
Anl 1999❑Oct 1999 Cover: 3.50 **NM** value: **Cover or less**
Circ: Diamd. preorders: **33,010**
Anl 2000❑ Cover: 3.50 **NM** value: **Cover or less**
📖 Basic Instinct **A:** Mark Texeira **W:** Paul Jenkins ★ Appearance of She-Hulk, Avengers.
Anl 2001❑2001 Cover: 2.99 **NM** value: **Cover or less**

HULK/PITT — Marvel

1 ❑ Dec 1996 Cover: 5.99 **NM** value: **Cover or less**
No issue number.

HULK: PROJECT H.I.D.E. — Marvel

1 ❑ Aug 1998 **NM** value: **1.00**
No issue number. no cover price. • prototype for children's comic

HULK SMASH — Marvel

1 ❑ Mar 2001 Cover: 2.99 **NM** value: **Cover or less**
Circ: Diamd. preorders: **39,792** • **CGC:** 7 graded, best 9.6
2 ❑ Apr 2001 Cover: 2.99 **NM** value: **Cover or less**
Circ: Diamd. preorders: **37,680**

The prices seen above do not represent the highest possible prices seen in online auctions, but rather the prices we have seen these issues reliably fetch in a variety of environments (storefront retail, mail order, auction and convention).

Other grades: Multiply prices above by **1.5 for Mint • 2/3 for Very Fine • 1/3 for Fine • 1/5 for Very Good • 1/8 for Good**

HULK, THE — Marvel

This magazine-sized comic, which began as the Rampaging Hulk, started out in color, switched to partial black-and-white with #24, and gave up on color entirely in the final two issues. The magazine offered several stories in each issue, and also featured columns and articles, including interviews with the stars from the Hulk TV show. It was also noted for backup stories starring fan-favorites Dominic Fortune and Moon Knight.

Most of the stories seen here are less the "Hulk smash!" type found in the long-running Incredible Hulk comic, instead showing the more sensitive, "human" side of the character. Many of the stories deal with significant social issues, including bigotry, cults, and mental retardation.

The magazine also features some of the best writers and artists in the business at the time, including Gene Colan, Alfredo Alcala, John Buscema, and Howard Chaykin.

10 ❑ Aug 1978 Cover: 1.50 **NM** value: **4.00**
• format changes to color magazine. • Title changes to The Hulk

11 ❑ Oct 1978 Cover: 1.50 **NM** value: **5.00**
📖 The Boy Who Cried Hulk; Graven Image of Death **A:** Gene Colan; Ron Wilson; Tony DeZuniga; Fran Matera **W:** Doug Moench

12 ❑ Dec 1978 Cover: 1.50 **NM** value: **3.00**

13 ❑ Feb 1979 Cover: 1.50 **NM** value: **3.00**

14 ❑ Apr 1979 Cover: 1.50 **NM** value: **3.00**
📖 A Cure for Chaos; Countdown to Dark

15 ❑ Jun 1979 Cover: 1.50 **NM** value: **3.00**
📖 The Top Secret!; An Eclipse Waning; An Eclipse Waxing

16 ❑ Aug 1979 Cover: 1.50 **NM** value: **3.00**

17 ❑ Oct 1979 Cover: 1.50 **NM** value: **3.00**

18 ❑ Dec 1979 Cover: 1.50 **NM** value: **3.00**
📖 Cast Away; Shadows in the Heart of the City **A:** Steve Oliff; Bill Sienkiewicz; Ron Wilson; Alfredo Alcala; Klaus Janson **W:** Doug Moench

19 ❑ Feb 1980 Cover: 1.50 **NM** value: **3.00**
📖 Master Mind; It's a Monster; Heaven is a Very Small Place **A:** Steve Oliff; Gene Colan; Herb Trimpe; Alfredo Alcala; John Severin; Marie Severin; Bob Wiacek **W:** Roy Thomas; Doug Moench

20 ❑ Apr 1980 Cover: 1.50 **NM** value: **3.00**

21 ❑ Jun 1980 Cover: 1.50 **NM** value: **3.00**
📖 Into the Myth Realm; Dominic Fortune: All in Color for a Crime **A:** Howard Chaykin; Bob McLeod **W:** Denny O'Neil; Doug Moench

22 ❑ Aug 1980 Cover: 1.50 **NM** value: **3.00**
📖 The Failure of Hydropolis; Ghoul of my Dreams **A:** Ron Wilson; Howard Chaykin **W:** Denny O'Neil; Doug Moench; Jeff Mundo

23 ❑ Oct 1980 Cover: 1.50 **NM** value: **3.00**
📖 A Very Personal Hell; Clothes Call; Moo Over Manhattan **A:** Steve Oliff; John Buscema; Howard Chaykin; Brent Anderson; Alfredo Alcala; John Tartag **W:** Jim Shooter; Roger Stern; Denny O'Neil

24 ❑ Dec 1980 Cover: 1.50 **NM** value: **3.00**
📖 The Man Who Would be President; It's Not Easy Being Green; The Tiny Terror Tumble **A:** Gene Colan; Howard Chaykin **W:** David Kraft; Denny O'Neil; Lora Byrne

25 ❑ Feb 1981 Cover: 1.50 **NM** value: **3.00**
📖 Dreans of Iron…Dreams of Steel!; Carnival of Fools **A:** Gene Colan; Alfredo Alcala; John Tartaglione **W:** Bill Flanagan; Lora Byrne

26 ❑ Apr 1981 Cover: 1.50 **NM** value: **3.00**
📖 Namaste; Where Troops Have Encamped; Oh Boy-Hulk Toys; The River **A:** Gene Colan; Dave Simons **W:** J.M. DeMatteis; Lora Byrne

27 ❑ Jun 1981 Cover: 1.50 **NM** value: **3.00**
📖 Feudin'; Happy Accidents; One for my Baby-And One More for the Hulk final issue. **A:** Gene Colan; John Tartaglione **W:** Steven Grant; J.M. DeMatteis; Lora Byrne

HULK 2099 — Marvel

1 ❑ Dec 1994 Cover: 2.50 **NM** value: **Cover or less**
Circ: CapCity orders: **37,100**
📖 No Exit **A:** Malcolm Davis **W:** Gerard Jones

2 ❑ Jan 1995 Cover: 1.50 **NM** value: **Cover or less**
Circ: CapCity orders: **20,675** • **CGC:** 1 graded, best 5.5

3 ❑ Feb 1995 Cover: 1.50 **NM** value: **Cover or less**
Circ: CapCity orders: **16,500**

4 ❑ Mar 1995 Cover: 1.50 **NM** value: **Cover or less**
Circ: CapCity orders: **13,550**

5 ❑ Apr 1995 Cover: 1.50 **NM** value: **Cover or less**
Circ: CapCity orders: **11,250**

6 ❑ May 1995 Cover: 1.50 **NM** value: **Cover or less**
Circ: CapCity orders: **10,850**

7 ❑ Jun 1995 Cover: 1.95 **NM** value: **Cover or less**
Circ: CapCity orders: **10,275**

8 ❑ Jul 1995 Cover: 1.95 **NM** value: **Cover or less**
Circ: CapCity orders: **9,175**

9 ❑ Aug 1995 Cover: 1.95 **NM** value: **Cover or less**
Circ: CapCity orders: **8,300**

10 ❑ Sep 1995 Cover: 1.95 **NM** value: **Cover or less**
final issue. • continued in 2099 A.D. Apocalypse #1

HULK VERSUS THING — Marvel

1 ❑ Dec 1999 Cover: 3.99 **NM** value: **Cover or less**
📖 The Hulk vs. The Thing; The Avengers Take Over; Battle of the Behemoths; Cry: Monster! • Reprints Fantastic Four #24, 26, 112, Marvel Features #11 **A:** Jim Starlin; John Buscema; Jack Kirby **W:** Len Wein; Stan Lee

📖 indicates **Story Title** or **Storyline** information.
★ indicates **Character Appearance** information.
W = Writer • A = Artist • C = Cover Artist

HUMAN FLY, THE — Marvel

Marvel touted this 1977 series as starring, "The wildest super-hero ever—because he's real!" An Evel-Knievel-type showman, the Human Fly's expolits were fictionalized by Marvel in this series.

The real-life story of the man known as the Human Fly began when, as a young man, he was caught in a tragic auto accident. His body shattered, doctors swore he would never walk again. Years of operations in which bones were replaced with steel made his lot seem hopeless. But he tried with all his might to get his body to do his bidding again, and when the doctors eventually restrained him to keep from injuring himself, he escaped each night, relearning how to walk.

On recovering, he decided to become a symbol for all those who had lost hope, donning the striking red costume of a daredevil and becoming the Human Fly.

1 ❑ Sep 1977 Cover: 0.30 **NM** value: **2.50**
• **CGC:** 9 graded, best 9.6
📖 Death-Walk!; The Making of a Hero! (text) **A:** Lee Elias **W:** Bill Mantlo ★ Origin of Human Fly. ★ 1st Appearance of Human Fly. ★ Appearance of Spider-Man.

2 ❑ Oct 1977 Cover: 0.30 **NM** value: **2.00**
• **CGC:** 2 graded, best 9.6
📖 Race to Destruction! **A:** Carmine Infantino **W:** Bill Mantlo ★ Appearance of Ghost Rider.

3 ❑ Nov 1977 Cover: 0.35 **NM** value: **1.50**
📖 Castle in the Clouds

4 ❑ Dec 1977 Cover: 0.35 **NM** value: **1.50**
📖 Rocky Mounatin Nightmare

5 ❑ Jan 1978 Cover: 0.35 **NM** value: **1.50**
📖 Fire in the Night

6 ❑ Feb 1978 Cover: 0.35 **NM** value: **1.50**
📖 Fear in Funland

7 ❑ Mar 1978 Cover: 0.35 **NM** value: **1.50**
📖 Snow Blind

8 ❑ Apr 1978 Cover: 0.35 **NM** value: **1.50**
📖 The Tiger and the Fly

9 ❑ May 1978 Cover: 0.35 **NM** value: **1.50**
📖 And Daredevil Makes Three ★ Appearance of Daredevil.

10 ❑ Jun 1978 Cover: 0.35 **NM** value: **1.50**
📖 Dark as a Dungeon Down in the Mine

11 ❑ Jul 1978 Cover: 0.35 **NM** value: **1.50**
📖 Silver Charity, Sudden Death

12 ❑ Aug 1978 Cover: 0.35 **NM** value: **1.50**
📖 Arnie's Story

13 ❑ Sep 1978 Cover: 0.35 **NM** value: **1.50**
📖 Slope of Death

14 ❑ Oct 1978 Cover: 0.35 **NM** value: **1.50**
📖 Death Rides the Big Balloons

15 ❑ Nov 1978 Cover: 0.35 **NM** value: **1.50**
📖 War in the Washington Monument

16 ❑ Dec 1978 Cover: 0.35 **NM** value: **1.50**
📖 Niagara Nightmare

17 ❑ Jan 1979 Cover: 0.35 **NM** value: **1.50**
📖 Photo Finish

18 ❑ Feb 1979 Cover: 0.35 **NM** value: **1.50**
📖 A Gathering of Vultures

19 ❑ Mar 1979 Cover: 0.35 **NM** value: **1.50**
📖 Highwire to Heaven final issue.

HUMAN GARGOYLES, THE — Eternity

1 ❑ Jun 1988, b&w Cover: 1.95 **NM** value: **Cover or less**
2 ❑ Aug 1988, b&w Cover: 1.95 **NM** value: **Cover or less**
3 ❑ b&w Cover: 1.95 **NM** value: **Cover or less**
4 ❑ b&w Cover: 1.95 **NM** value: **Cover or less**

HUMAN HEAD COMIX — Iconografix

1 ❑ b&w Cover: 2.50 **NM** value: **Cover or less**

HUMAN POWERHOUSE, THE — Pure Imagination

1 ❑ b&w Cover: 2.00 **NM** value: **Cover or less**
📖 End of A Legend **A:** Theakston **W:** Theakston

HUMAN TARGET — DC / Vertigo

1 ❑ Apr 1999 Cover: 2.95 **NM** value: **Cover or less**
Circ: Diamd. preorders: **17,368**

2 ❑ May 1999 Cover: 2.95 **NM** value: **Cover or less**
Circ: Diamd. preorders: **15,011**

3 ❑ Jun 1999 Cover: 2.95 **NM** value: **Cover or less**
Circ: Diamd. preorders: **15,757**

4 ❑ Jul 1999 Cover: 2.95 **NM** value: **Cover or less**
Circ: Diamd. preorders: **15,787**

Bk 1 ❑ Cover: 12.95 **NM** value: **Cover or less**
• Collects Series **A:** Edvin Biukovic **W:** Peter Milligan

Diamond preorders are the estimated number of comics sold, prior to their release, to comics shops in North America by Diamond Comic Distributors, the largest distributor. These figures underreport the actual number of circulating copies by the amount of reorders Diamond took (usually 5-10% again of the preorders) and sales by publishers to newsstand and bookstore distributors. For many independent publishers, Diamond's preorders may be quite close to the actual number of copies in circulation.

HUMAN TARGET SPECIAL — DC

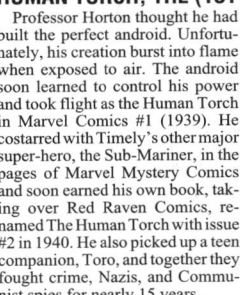

Christopher Chance is in an extremely strange line of work: he impersonates people that are marked for death. He becomes, in effect, a human target, trying to draw the assassin into the open, and stop them before he suffers the ultimate on-the-job-injury. The payoff: he gets 10% of the target's yearly salary, "whether you're Donald Trump, or Donald Trump's gardener."

A minor 1970s character created by Len Wein, the Human Target somehow managed to get his own six-episode midseason replacement series on ABC starring rocker Rick Springfield in the title role. This one-shot reintroduced DC readers to the character and served as a prelude to the TV series. The later, Vertigo version of the character is far darker, as one might expect.

1 ❑ Nov 1991 Cover: 2.00 **NM** value: **Cover or less**
Circ: CapCity orders: **14,650**
One-shot. 📖 The Mack Attack Contract **A:** Dick Giordano; Rick Burchett **W:** Mark Verheiden

HUMAN TORCH, THE (1ST SERIES) — Marvel

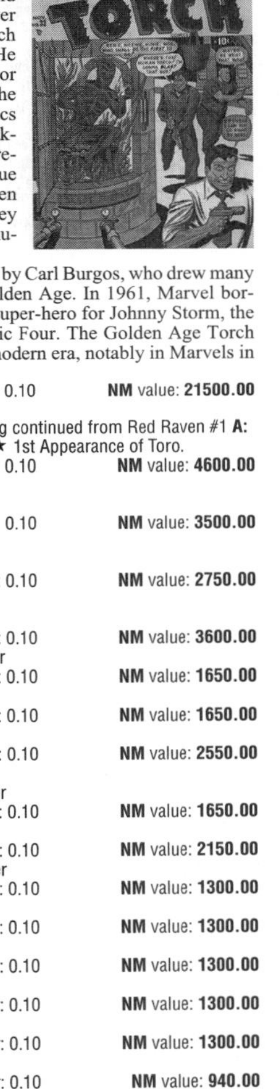

Professor Horton thought he had built the perfect android. Unfortunately, his creation burst into flame when exposed to air. The android soon learned to control his power and took flight as the Human Torch in Marvel Comics #1 (1939). He costarred with Timely's other major super-hero, the Sub-Mariner, in the pages of Marvel Mystery Comics and soon earned his own book, taking over Red Raven Comics, renamed The Human Torch with issue #2 in 1940. He also picked up a teen companion, Toro, and together they fought crime, Nazis, and Communist spies for nearly 15 years.

The Human Torch was created by Carl Burgos, who drew many of his adventures during the Golden Age. In 1961, Marvel borrowed the concept of a flaming super-hero for Johnny Storm, the teenaged member of the Fantastic Four. The Golden Age Torch made a few appearances in the modern era, notably in Marvels in 1995.

1 ❑ Fal 1940 Cover: 0.10 **NM** value: **21500.00**
• **CGC:** 4 graded, best 8.0
#2 on cover. • Series numbering continued from Red Raven #1 **A:** Bill Everett ★ Origin of Toro. ★ 1st Appearance of Toro.

2 ❑ Win 1940 Cover: 0.10 **NM** value: **4600.00**
• **CGC:** 9 graded, best 9.0
#3 on cover.

3 ❑ Spr 1941 Cover: 0.10 **NM** value: **3500.00**
• **CGC:** 12 graded, best 8.5
#4 on cover.

4 ❑ Sum 1941 Cover: 0.10 **NM** value: **2750.00**
• **CGC:** 4 graded, best 8.5
#5 on cover.

5 ❑ Fal 1941 Cover: 0.10 **NM** value: **3600.00**
• Human Torch vs. Sub-Mariner

6 ❑ Win 1941 Cover: 0.10 **NM** value: **1650.00**
• **CGC:** 3 graded, best 8.0

7 ❑ Spr 1942 Cover: 0.10 **NM** value: **1650.00**
• **CGC:** 2 graded, best 9.2

8 ❑ Sum 1942 Cover: 0.10 **NM** value: **2550.00**
• **CGC:** 10 graded, best 9.0
• Human Torch vs. Sub-Mariner

9 ❑ Fal 1942 Cover: 0.10 **NM** value: **1650.00**
• **CGC:** 7 graded, best 9.6

10 ❑ Win 1942 Cover: 0.10 **NM** value: **2150.00**
• Human Torch vs. Sub-Mariner

11 ❑ Spr 1943 Cover: 0.10 **NM** value: **1300.00**
• **CGC:** 4 graded, best 8.0

12 ❑ Sum 1943 Cover: 0.10 **NM** value: **1300.00**
• **CGC:** 4 graded, best 9.0

13 ❑ Fal 1943 Cover: 0.10 **NM** value: **1300.00**
• **CGC:** 2 graded, best 6.5

14 ❑ Win 1943 Cover: 0.10 **NM** value: **1300.00**
• **CGC:** 4 graded, best 8.5

15 ❑ Spr 1944 Cover: 0.10 **NM** value: **1300.00**
• **CGC:** 2 graded, best 4.5

16 ❑ Fal 1944 Cover: 0.10 **NM** value: **940.00**
• **CGC:** 2 graded, best 9.4

17 ❑ Win 1944 Cover: 0.10 **NM** value: **940.00**
• **CGC:** 5 graded, best 9.0

18 ❑ Spr 1945 Cover: 0.10 **NM** value: **940.00**
• **CGC:** 2 graded, best 8.0

19 ❑ Sum 1945 Cover: 0.10 **NM** value: **940.00**
• **CGC:** 8 graded, best 9.0

20 ❑ Fal 1945 Cover: 0.10 **NM** value: **940.00**
• **CGC:** 4 graded, best 8.0

21 ❑ Win 1945 Cover: 0.10 **NM** value: **785.00**
• **CGC:** 3 graded, best 9.2

22 ❑ Spr 1946 Cover: 0.10 **NM** value: **785.00**
• **CGC:** 3 graded, best 8.5

23 ❑ Sum 1946 Cover: 0.10 **NM** value: **785.00**
• **CGC:** 8 graded, best 9.2

24 ❑ Fal 1946 Cover: 0.10 **NM** value: **785.00**
• **CGC:** 1 graded, best 7.5

25 ❑ Win 1946 Cover: 0.10 **NM** value: **785.00**

CGC-graded: Multiply prices above by **33 for 9.9 M • 16 for 9.8 NM/M • 7 for 9.6 NM+ • 5 for 9.4 NM • 2.5 for 9.2 NM- • 1.5 for 9.0 VF/NM**

• **CGC:** 4 graded, best 9.0
26 ❑ Spr 1947 Cover: 0.10 **NM** value: **785.00**
• **CGC:** 6 graded, best 9.0
27 ❑ Sum 1947 Cover: 0.10 **NM** value: **785.00**
• **CGC:** 2 graded, best 9.0
28 ❑ Fal 1947 Cover: 0.10 **NM** value: **785.00**
• **CGC:** 1 graded, best 8.0
29 ❑ Win 1947 Cover: 0.10 **NM** value: **785.00**
• **CGC:** 5 graded, best 7.5
30 ❑ Spr 1948 Cover: 0.10 **NM** value: **785.00**
• **CGC:** 1 graded, best 7.5
31 ❑ Jul 1948 Cover: 0.10 **NM** value: **675.00**
• **CGC:** 3 graded, best 8.0
32 ❑ Sep 1948 Cover: 0.10 **NM** value: **675.00**
33 ❑ Nov 1948 Cover: 0.10 **NM** value: **675.00**
📖 The Ray of Madness! ★ Appearance of Captain America.
34 ❑ Jan 1949 Cover: 0.10 **NM** value: **675.00**
• **CGC:** 1 graded, best 8.0
35 ❑ Mar 1949 Cover: 0.10 **NM** value: **675.00**
• **CGC:** 2 graded, best 7.5
36 ❑ Apr 1954 Cover: 0.10 **NM** value: **625.00**
• **CGC:** 1 graded, best 6.5
37 ❑ Jun 1954 Cover: 0.10 **NM** value: **625.00**
• **CGC:** 3 graded, best 8.5
38 ❑ Aug 1954 Cover: 0.10 **NM** value: **625.00**
• **CGC:** 5 graded, best 9.0
final issue.

HUMAN TORCH, THE (2ND SERIES) — Marvel

1 ❑ Sep 1974 Cover: 0.25 **NM** value: **5.00**
• **CGC:** 4 graded, best 9.4
📖 Johnny Storm, The Human Torch; Horror Hotel • Torch vs. Torch reprinted from Strange Tales #101; Horror Hotel reprinted from The Human Torch (1st series) #33 **A:** Jack Kirby; Dick Ayers **W:** Larry Lieber
2 ❑ Nov 1974 Cover: 0.25 **NM** value: **3.00**
📖 Prisoner Of The Wizard; The Hyena Strikes • Reprints Torch story from Strange Tales #102 and The Human Torch (1st series) #30 **A:** Jack Kirby **W:** Larry Lieber
3 ❑ Jan 1975 Cover: 0.25 **NM** value: **3.00**
📖 Prisoner of the 5th Dimension!; Reptile's Revenge! • Reprints Torch story from Strange Tales #103, Sub-Mariner #23 **A:** Jack Kirby **W:** Larry Lieber; Stan Lee
4 ❑ Mar 1975 Cover: 0.25 **NM** value: **3.00**
📖 The Human Torch Meets Paste-Pot Pete; The World's End • Reprints Torch story from Strange Tales #104, The Human Torch (1st series) #38
5 ❑ May 1975 Cover: 0.25 **NM** value: **3.00**
📖 The Return of the Wizard; In Korea • Reprints Torch story from Strange Tales #105, The Human Torch (1st series) #38
6 ❑ Jul 1975 Cover: 0.25 **NM** value: **3.00**
📖 The Threat of the Torrid Twosome; Flame On • Reprints Torch story from Strange Tales #106, The Human Torch (1st series) #38
7 ❑ Sep 1975 Cover: 0.25 **NM** value: **3.00**
📖 The Master of Flame vs. the Monarch of the Sea; Human Torch – Fugitive At Large • Reprints Torch story from Strange Tales #107, Sub-Mariner #35
8 ❑ Nov 1975 Cover: 0.25 **NM** value: **3.00**
📖 The Painter Of A Thousand Perils!; The Un-Human final issue. • Reprints Torch story from Strange Tales #108, Marvel Super-Heroes #16 **A:** Jack Kirby **W:** R. Berns

HUMAN TORCH COMICS — Marvel

1 ❑ Cover: 3.99 **NM** value: **Cover or less**

HUMMINGBIRD — Slave Labor

1 ❑ Jun 1996 Cover: 4.95 **NM** value: **Cover or less**
📖 Trouble; Jack Shit; Welcome Back (Now, Fuck Off); Death of the Party; Good Cop, Good Doctor, Farewell **A:** Gregory Benton **W:** Gregory Benton

HUMONGOUS MAN — Alternative

1 ❑ Sep 1997, b&w Cover: 2.25 **NM** value: **Cover or less**
📖 Deceiving Appearances **A:** Dan Stepp; Jim Harrison **W:** Dan Stepp; Jim Harrison
2 ❑ Nov 1997, b&w Cover: 2.25 **NM** value: **Cover or less**

HUMOR ON THE CUTTING...EDGE — Edge

1 ❑ b&w Cover: 2.95 **NM** value: **Cover or less**
2 ❑ b&w Cover: 2.95 **NM** value: **Cover or less**
3 ❑ b&w Cover: 2.95 **NM** value: **Cover or less**
4 ❑ b&w Cover: 2.95 **NM** value: **Cover or less**

HUMPHREY COMICS — Harvey

Ham Fisher's Joe Palooka, the happy-go-lucky hillbilly heavyweight fighter, was such a hit with comic-strip and comic-book readers in the 1940s that even his sidekick Humphrey could support his own title. Humphrey is a great big fella with a soft heart and an even softer head. He lives with his dear old mama and shares his pal Palooka's gentlemanly manners. The problem is, he's such a behemoth that every time he sets foot in the ring, he clobbers his opponents with a single swat ("Aw shucks, I didn't mean to hit 'em that hard!") while he's pre-occupied with other matters. Humphrey ambled through a series of lighthearted tales from Harvey Comics from the late 1940s through the early 1950s, featuring a kid-friendly mix of humor and adventure.

In addition to the comedic stories in the series, there were activity pages and a tin toy version of the Humphreymobile, a combination of a small woodshed and a large tricycle that Humphrey peddled around the country.

1 ❑ Oct 1948 Cover: 0.10 **NM** value: **50.00**
📖 Trip to New York; Surprise Knockout; Girl Trouble; True-Thrilling Sport Short; Knobby Gives a Driving Lesson; Sportopics!; Ricky RoonyTellTale Ring **A:** Ham Fisher **W:** Ham Fisher
2 ❑ Dec 1948 Cover: 0.10 **NM** value: **30.00**
3 ❑ Feb 1949 Cover: 0.10 **NM** value: **22.00**
4 ❑ Apr 1949 Cover: 0.10 **NM** value: **20.00**
5 ❑ Jun 1949 Cover: 0.10 **NM** value: **20.00**
6 ❑ Aug 1949 Cover: 0.10 **NM** value: **20.00**
7 ❑ Oct 1949 Cover: 0.10 **NM** value: **20.00**
8 ❑ Dec 1949 Cover: 0.10 **NM** value: **20.00**
9 ❑ Feb 1950 Cover: 0.10 **NM** value: **20.00**
10 ❑ Apr 1950 Cover: 0.10 **NM** value: **20.00**
11 ❑ Jun 1950 Cover: 0.10 **NM** value: **16.00**
12 ❑ Aug 1950 Cover: 0.10 **NM** value: **16.00**
13 ❑ Oct 1950 Cover: 0.10 **NM** value: **16.00**
14 ❑ Dec 1950 Cover: 0.10 **NM** value: **16.00**
15 ❑ Feb 1951 Cover: 0.10 **NM** value: **16.00**
16 ❑ Apr 1951 Cover: 0.10 **NM** value: **16.00**
17 ❑ Jun 1951 Cover: 0.10 **NM** value: **16.00**
18 ❑ Aug 1951 Cover: 0.10 **NM** value: **16.00**
19 ❑ Oct 1951 Cover: 0.10 **NM** value: **16.00**
20 ❑ Dec 1951 Cover: 0.10 **NM** value: **16.00**
21 ❑ Feb 1952 Cover: 0.10 **NM** value: **16.00**
22 ❑ Apr 1952 Cover: 0.10 **NM** value: **16.00**

HUNCHBACK OF NOTRE DAME, THE (DISNEY'S...) — Marvel

1 ❑ Jul 1996 Cover: 4.95 **NM** value: **Cover or less**
cardstock cover. • adapts movie; square binding

HUNTER'S HEART — DC / Paradox

1 ❑ b&w Cover: 5.95 **NM** value: **Cover or less**
Circ: CapCity orders: **3,125**
• digest. **A:** Randy DuBurke **W:** Randy DuBurke
2 ❑ b&w Cover: 5.95 **NM** value: **Cover or less**
Circ: CapCity orders: **2,325**
• digest. **A:** Randy DuBurke **W:** Randy DuBurke
3 ❑ b&w Cover: 5.95 **NM** value: **Cover or less**
• digest. **A:** Randy DuBurke **W:** Randy DuBurke

HUNT FOR BLACK WIDOW, THE — Fleetway-Quality

1 ❑ Cover: 2.95 **NM** value: **Cover or less**
• Judge Dredd

HUNTING, THE — Northstar

1 ❑ Nov 1993 Cover: 3.95 **NM** value: **Cover or less**

HUNTRESS, THE — DC

Think of her as a female Batman without the money, car, or castle. The daughter of a vicious Mafia man, Helena Bertinelli set off on her own and changed her name to Helena Martinez. Now she protects the innocent from crime, and from her father, in a city still squarely under the Mafia's thumb.

This Huntress is actually the third DC character by that name. The first was a seldom-seen Golden Age villainess who made her debut in Sensation Comics #68. The second was Helena Wayne, daughter of Selena Wayne (formerly Catwoman) and Bruce Wayne (Batman) of Earth-2. The newest rendition borrows heavily from the costume and methods of the second Huntress. At the same time, the writers of this series have given her a richer characterization that makes her something much more than a super-hero spinoff.

1 ❑ Apr 1989 Cover: 1.00 **NM** value: **2.00**
Circ: CapCity orders: **27,000**
📖 Darker Still **A:** Michael Netzer **W:** Chuck Dixon ★ Origin of The Huntress III (Helena Bertinelli). ★ 1st Appearance of The Huntress III (Helena Bertinelli).
2 ❑ May 1989 Cover: 1.00 **NM** value: **1.75**
Circ: CapCity orders: **21,000**
📖 Uneasy Lies The Head... **A:** Joe Staton **W:** Joey Cavalieri
3 ❑ Jun 1989 Cover: 1.00 **NM** value: **1.50**
Circ: CapCity orders: **21,400**
4 ❑ Jul 1989 Cover: 1.00 **NM** value: **1.50**
Circ: CapCity orders: **21,250**
5 ❑ Aug 1989 Cover: 1.00 **NM** value: **1.50**
Circ: CapCity orders: **19,000**
6 ❑ Sep 1989 Cover: 1.00 **NM** value: **1.25**
Circ: CapCity orders: **18,050**
7 ❑ Oct 1989 Cover: 1.00 **NM** value: **1.25**
Circ: CapCity orders: **15,450**
8 ❑ Nov 1989 Cover: 1.00 **NM** value: **1.25**
Circ: CapCity orders: **14,150**
9 ❑ Dec 1989 Cover: 1.00 **NM** value: **1.25**
Circ: CapCity orders: **12,550**
10 ❑ Jan 1990 Cover: 1.00 **NM** value: **1.25**
Circ: CapCity orders: **12,350**
11 ❑ Feb 1990 Cover: 1.00 **NM** value: **1.25**
Circ: CapCity orders: **12,350**
12 ❑ Mar 1990 Cover: 1.00 **NM** value: **1.25**
Circ: CapCity orders: **10,950**
13 ❑ Apr 1990 Cover: 1.00 **NM** value: **1.25**
Circ: CapCity orders: **10,100**
14 ❑ May 1990 Cover: 1.00 **NM** value: **1.25**
Circ: CapCity orders: **10,000**
📖 Networking **A:** Joe Staton **W:** Joey Cavalieri
15 ❑ Jun 1990 Cover: 1.25 **NM** value: **Cover or less**
Circ: CapCity orders: **9,450**
16 ❑ Jul 1990 Cover: 1.25 **NM** value: **Cover or less**
Circ: CapCity orders: **9,200**
17 ❑ Aug 1990 Cover: 1.25 **NM** value: **Cover or less**
Circ: CapCity orders: **14,050**
18 ❑ Sep 1990 Cover: 1.25 **NM** value: **Cover or less**
Circ: CapCity orders: **13,950**
19 ❑ Oct 1990 Cover: 1.25 **NM** value: **Cover or less**
Circ: CapCity orders: **14,050**
final issue. ★ Appearance of Batman.

HUNTRESS, THE (MINI-SERIES) — DC

1 ❑ Jun 1994 Cover: 1.50 **NM** value: **Cover or less**
Circ: CapCity orders: **24,050**
📖 Darker Still **A:** Michael Netzer **W:** Chuck Dixon
2 ❑ Jul 1994 Cover: 1.50 **NM** value: **Cover or less**
Circ: CapCity orders: **16,400**
3 ❑ Aug 1994 Cover: 1.50 **NM** value: **Cover or less**
Circ: CapCity orders: **14,500**
4 ❑ Sep 1994 Cover: 1.50 **NM** value: **Cover or less**
Circ: CapCity orders: **13,400**

HUP — Last Gasp

1 ❑ ca. 1986, b&w Cover: 2.50 **NM** value: **Cover or less**
• **CGC:** 1 graded, best 9.0
2 ❑ Cover: 2.50 **NM** value: **Cover or less**
📖 The Mighty Power Fems Versus The Horrible Homunculi; If I Were a King; The Meeting **A:** Robert Crumb **W:** Robert Crumb
3 ❑ Cover: 2.50 **NM** value: **Cover or less**
4 ❑ ca. 1992 Cover: 2.95 **NM** value: **Cover or less**
• **CGC:** 1 graded, best 9.6
📖 Can You Stand Alone And Face The Universe?; Academy Awards; You Can't Have Them All, Magnificent Specimens I Have Seen; A Bitchin' Bod'! **A:** Robert Crumb **W:** Robert Crumb

HURRICANE GIRLS — Antarctic

1 ❑ Jul 1995 Cover: 2.95 **NM** value: **3.50**
Circ: CapCity orders: **2,750**
2 ❑ Sep 1995 Cover: 2.95 **NM** value: **3.50**
3 ❑ Nov 1995 Cover: 2.95 **NM** value: **3.50**
4 ❑ Cover: 2.95 **NM** value: **3.50**
5 ❑ Cover: 2.95 **NM** value: **3.50**
6 ❑ Cover: 2.95 **NM** value: **3.50**
7 ❑ Aug 1996 Cover: 2.95 **NM** value: **3.50**
final issue. **A:** Hiroshi Yakumo **W:** Hiroshi Yakumo

HURRICANE LEROUX — Inferno

1 ❑ Cover: 2.50 **NM** value: **Cover or less**
📖 Bayou Tapestry **A:** Steve Scott **W:** Barry Gregory ★ 1st Appearance of Hurricane LeRoux.

HUSTLER COMIX — L.F.P.

All issues are adults only.
1 ❑ Spr 1997 Cover: 4.99 **NM** value: **Cover or less**
• magazine.
2 ❑ Sum 1997 Cover: 4.99 **NM** value: **Cover or less**
• magazine.
3 ❑ Fal 1997 Cover: 4.99 **NM** value: **Cover or less**
• magazine.
4 ❑ Win 1997 Cover: 4.99 **NM** value: **Cover or less**
• magazine.

HUSTLER COMIX (VOL. 2) — L.F.P.

All issues are adults only.
1 ❑ Spr 1998 Cover: 4.99 **NM** value: **Cover or less**
• magazine. 📖 Venusian Assault; Dead Girl; -Optimo!; Space Chicks and Businessmen; Dino Mansion; Web of the Black Tarantula; Rebel Lovers; Frank Stone; 'Optimo! **A:** O'Clair Albert; Gerald Forton; Mark Beachum; John Heebink; Adam DeKraker; Edde Wagner; Luques; Robert Blue; Ronald Silva **W:** Gerald Forton; Mark Beachum; Bruce David; Luques; Casey Beck; Link Yaco; Russ Miller
2 ❑ May 1998 Cover: 4.99 **NM** value: **Cover or less**
• magazine.
3 ❑ Jul 1998 Cover: 4.99 **NM** value: **Cover or less**
• magazine.
4 ❑ Sep 1998 Cover: 4.99 **NM** value: **Cover or less**
• magazine.
5 ❑ Nov 1998 Cover: 4.99 **NM** value: **Cover or less**
• magazine. final issue.

HUSTLER COMIX XXX — L.F.P.

All issues are adults only.
1 ❑ Jan 1999 Cover: 5.99 **NM** value: **Cover or less**
• magazine.

HUTCH OWEN'S WORKING HARD — New Hat

1 ❑ b&w Cover: 3.95 **NM** value: **Cover or less**

HY-BREED, THE — Division

3 ❑ b&w Cover: 2.25 **NM** value: **Cover or less**
4 ❑ b&w Cover: 2.90 **NM** value: **3.00**
5 ❑ b&w Cover: 2.50 **NM** value: **Cover or less**
6 ❑ b&w Cover: 2.50 **NM** value: **Cover or less**
7 ❑ b&w Cover: 2.50 **NM** value: **Cover or less**

HYBRID: ETHERWORLDS — Dimension 5

1 ❑ Cover: 2.50 **NM** value: **Cover or less**
2 ❑ Cover: 2.50 **NM** value: **Cover or less**
3 ❑ Cover: 2.50 **NM** value: **Cover or less**

HYBRIDS (1ST SERIES) — Continuity

0 ❑ Apr 1993 Cover: 1.00 **NM** value: **Cover or less**
silver and red foil covers. 📖 Deathwatch 2000, Part 2 **A:** Malcolm Davis **W:** Neal Adams; Peter Stone

Other grades: Multiply prices above by **1.5 for Mint • 2/3 for Very Fine • 1/3 for Fine • 1/5 for Very Good • 1/8 for Good**

1 ❑ Apr 1993 Cover: 2.50 **NM** value: **Cover or less**
diecut cardstock cover. 🕮 Deathwatch 2000, Part 4 • trading cards
2 ❑ Jun 1993 Cover: 2.50 **NM** value: **Cover or less**
thermal cover. 🕮 Deathwatch 2000, Part 13 • trading card
3 ❑ Aug 1993 Cover: 2.50 **NM** value: **Cover or less**
🕮 Deathwatch 2000, Part 18 • trading card; Deathwatch 2000 dropped from indicia; Published out of sequence after #5
4 ❑ Cover: 2.50 **NM** value: **Cover or less**
• Published out of sequence after #5, #3
5 ❑ Cover: 2.50 **NM** value: **Cover or less**
🕮 Deathwatch 2000

HYBRIDS (2ND SERIES) — Continuity

1 ❑ Jan 1994 Cover: 2.50 **NM** value: **Cover or less**
Circ: CapCity orders: **12,775**
Embossed cover. 🕮 Rise of Magic **A:** Mike Deodato Jr. **W:** Peter Stone

HYBRIDS: THE ORIGIN — Continuity

1 ❑ Cover: 2.50 **NM** value: **Cover or less**
• really Revengers: Hybrids Special #1
2 ❑ Jul 1993 Cover: 2.50 **NM** value: **Cover or less**
Circ: CapCity orders: **11,425**
"Revengers Special" on cover. 🕮 Who's Really Buried in Grant's Tomb **A:** Malcolm Davis; Larry Stroman **W:** Neal Adams; Elliott S! Maggin; Peter Stone
3 ❑ Sep 1993 Cover: 2.50 **NM** value: **Cover or less**
Circ: CapCity orders: **9,475**
"Revengers Special" on cover.
4 ❑ Dec 1993 Cover: 2.50 **NM** value: **Cover or less**
Circ: CapCity orders: **7,775**
5 ❑ Jan 1994 Cover: 2.50 **NM** value: **Cover or less**
Circ: CapCity orders: **6,525**

HYDE-25 — Harris

0 ❑ Apr 1995 Cover: 2.95 **NM** value: **Cover or less**
Circ: CapCity orders: **12,650**
• Reprints Vampirella (Magazine) #1 in color. 🕮 Storm Before The Calm **A:** Jose Ortiz **W:** Bruce Bezaire ★ 1st Appearance of Vampirella.

HYDROGEN BOMB FUNNIES — Rip Off

1 ❑ Cover: 0.50 **NM** value: **5.00**
🕮 Mr. Sketchum; Wonder Warthog and the Inva **A:** Gilbert Shelton **W:** Gilbert Shelton

HYENA — Tundra

1 ❑ b&w Cover: 3.95 **NM** value: **Cover or less**
2 ❑ b&w Cover: 3.95 **NM** value: **Cover or less**
3 ❑ b&w Cover: 3.95 **NM** value: **Cover or less**
4 ❑ Cover: 3.95 **NM** value: **Cover or less**

HYPER DOLLS — Ironcat

1 ❑ Cover: 2.95 **NM** value: **Cover or less**
Circ: Diamd. preorders: **2,904**
2 ❑ Cover: 2.95 **NM** value: **Cover or less**
Circ: Diamd. preorders: **2,327**

HYPER DOLLS (VOL. 2) — Ironcat

1 ❑ Cover: 2.95 **NM** value: **Cover or less**
Circ: Diamd. preorders: **1,729**
2 ❑ Cover: 2.95 **NM** value: **Cover or less**
Circ: Diamd. preorders: **1,662**
3 ❑ Cover: 2.95 **NM** value: **Cover or less**
Circ: Diamd. preorders: **1,656**
4 ❑ Cover: 2.95 **NM** value: **Cover or less**
Circ: Diamd. preorders: **1,606**
5 ❑ Cover: 2.95 **NM** value: **Cover or less**
6 ❑ Jul 1999 Cover: 2.95 **NM** value: **Cover or less**

HYPERKIND — Marvel / Razorline

Clive Barker's Hyperkind tells of how, in years gone by, a group of super-powered heroes known as the Paxis fought a version of World War I against alien invaders. Seventy-five years later, they would be all but forgotten. But one day, a drunken bum literally drops from the sky — and is attacked by a giant reptilian creature, Thermakk, Lawgiver of Quo. A woman who helps the bum (who's really the last of an alien race) gets an unhappy reward: her bones are replaced with metal, and her body is charged with super-human power. She and three others then became the super-team Hyperkind.

Part of Marvel's Razorline, an attempt to create a comics world based on the owrks of Clive Barker, this and most of the other titles died fast in the glutted environment of the early 1990s.

1 ❑ Sep 1993 Cover: 2.50 **NM** value: **Cover or less**
Circ: CapCity orders: **30,900**
Foil-embossed cover. 🕮 Paxis Reborn **A:** Paris Cullins **W:** Fred Burke ★ Origin of Hyperkind.
2 ❑ Oct 1993 Cover: 1.75 **NM** value: **Cover or less**
Circ: CapCity orders: **11,600**
3 ❑ Nov 1993 Cover: 1.75 **NM** value: **Cover or less**
Circ: CapCity orders: **10,900**
4 ❑ Dec 1993 Cover: 1.75 **NM** value: **Cover or less**
Circ: CapCity orders: **9,800**
5 ❑ Jan 1994 Cover: 1.75 **NM** value: **Cover or less**
Circ: CapCity orders: **8,200**
6 ❑ Feb 1994 Cover: 1.75 **NM** value: **Cover or less**
Circ: CapCity orders: **6,650**
7 ❑ Mar 1994 Cover: 1.75 **NM** value: **Cover or less**
Circ: CapCity orders: **5,350**
8 ❑ Apr 1994 Cover: 1.75 **NM** value: **Cover or less**
Circ: CapCity orders: **4,500**
9 ❑ May 1994 Cover: 1.75 **NM** value: **Cover or less**
Circ: CapCity orders: **4,050**
final issue.

HYPERKIND UNLEASHED! — Marvel

1 ❑ Aug 1994 Cover: 2.95 **NM** value: **Cover or less**
Circ: CapCity orders: **7,250**
🕮 Hyperkind No More **A:** Luke Ross; Fabio Laguna; Manuel Flores **W:** Fred Burke

HYPERSONIC — Dark Horse

1 ❑ Nov 1997 Cover: 2.95 **NM** value: **Cover or less**
Circ: Diamd. preorders: **6,812**
2 ❑ Dec 1997 Cover: 2.95 **NM** value: **Cover or less**
Circ: Diamd. preorders: **5,200**
3 ❑ Jan 1998 Cover: 2.95 **NM** value: **Cover or less**
Circ: Diamd. preorders: **4,409**
4 ❑ Jan 1998 Cover: 2.95 **NM** value: **Cover or less**
Circ: Diamd. preorders: **3,943**

HYPER VIOLENTS — CFD

1 ❑ Jul 1996, b&w Cover: 2.95 **NM** value: **Cover or less**

I AM LEGEND — Eclipse

1 ❑ b&w Cover: 5.95 **NM** value: **Cover or less**
A: Richard Matheson
2 ❑ Cover: 5.95 **NM** value: **Cover or less**
3 ❑ Cover: 5.95 **NM** value: **Cover or less**
4 ❑ Cover: 5.95 **NM** value: **Cover or less**

I BEFORE E — Fantagraphics

1 ❑ b&w Cover: 3.95 **NM** value: **Cover or less**
A: Sam Kieth
1-2 ❑ May 1994 Cover: 3.95 **NM** value: **Cover or less**
2 ❑ b&w Cover: 3.95 **NM** value: **Cover or less**
A: Sam Kieth

IBIS THE INVINCIBLE — Fawcett

Ibis was Fawcett's magic hero, and this sporadically published comic book was packed with his tales. (By the way, while he was on every cover, none of the covers were actually connected with any of the contents of the issues.) As a bonus, though, Basil Wolverton's zany four-page comedy featurette "Mystic Moot and His Magic Snoot" appeared in the last four issues.)

Though there were such other magical characters in comics as the newspaper-strip-featured Mandrake the Magician, Ibis didn't really copy them. A short version of his origin story appeared in Fawcett's Whiz anthology title, but the full version was presented in the initial issue of this series. Ibis' actual name was Amentep, and he was an Egyptian prince 4,000 years earlier. Betrothed to Princess Taia, Ibis was grief-stricken at what appeared to be her violent death. After avenging her, he tried to use his magic wand, the Ibistick, to kill himself. When he found that the Ibistick wouldn't harm him, he used to to put himself into suspended animation and, when he was revived, he revived his beloved, as well. They had numbers of adventures against evil (both fantastic and mundane) in the years that followed. — Maggie

1 ❑ ca. 1942 Cover: 0.10 **NM** value: **1500.00**
• **CGC:** 3 graded, best 9.6
2 ❑ ca. 1943 Cover: 0.10 **NM** value: **750.00**
3 ❑ Win 1945 Cover: 0.10 **NM** value: **600.00**
• **CGC:** 4 graded, best 9.0
4 ❑ Spr 1946 Cover: 0.10 **NM** value: **400.00**
5 ❑ Fal 1946 Cover: 0.10 **NM** value: **400.00**
• **CGC:** 1 graded, best 8.0
6 ❑ Spr 1948 Cover: 0.10 **NM** value: **400.00**
• **CGC:** 2 graded, best 6.0

I•BOTS (ISAAC ASIMOV'S...) (1ST SERIES) — Tekno

In the future, terrorists with high-tech armor wreak havoc in the streets. The police are helpless to stop this wave of crime — until the robot heroes known as the I•Bots burst onto the scene. They're considered vigilantes until they save Gregon Silver, a wealthy industrialist who decides to sponsor them.

Unlike some other series using Tekno's strategy of using names of mainstream creators to sell comics, there was no question of Asimov's further involvement, the author having died several years before. The creators brought in were seasoned veterans, however: Howard Chaykin developed the characters and wrote the plot; Steven Grant scripted; and George Perez penciled. Even so, as with other Tekno series, the presence of a mainstream marquee name alone wasn't enough to ensure the series' longevity.

1 ❑ Dec 1995 Cover: 1.95 **NM** value: **2.00**
🕮 Out of the Blue **A:** George Pérez **W:** Howard Chaykin; Steven Grant ★ 1st Appearance of the I•Bots.
2 ❑ Dec 1995 Cover: 1.95 **NM** value: **2.00**
A: George Pérez **W:** Howard Chaykin; Steven Grant
3 ❑ Jan 1996 Cover: 2.25 **NM** value: **Cover or less**
A: George Pérez **W:** Howard Chaykin; Steven Grant
4 ❑ Feb 1996 Cover: 2.25 **NM** value: **Cover or less**
A: George Pérez **W:** Howard Chaykin; Steven Grant
5 ❑ Mar 1996 Cover: 2.25 **NM** value: **Cover or less**
A: George Pérez **W:** Howard Chaykin; Steven Grant
6 ❑ Apr 1996 Cover: 2.25 **NM** value: **Cover or less**
A: George Pérez **W:** Howard Chaykin; Steven Grant
7 ❑ May 1996 Cover: 2.25 **NM** value: **Cover or less**
A: George Pérez **W:** Howard Chaykin; Steven Grant ★ Appearance of Lady Justice.

I•BOTS (ISAAC ASIMOV'S...) (2ND SERIES) — Big

1 ❑ Jun 1996 Cover: 2.25 **NM** value: **Cover or less**
Circ: CapCity orders: **11,725**
🕮 The Big Crossover, Part 12 **A:** Pat Broderick **W:** Steven Grant ★ Appearance of Lady Justice.
2 ❑ Jul 1996 Cover: 2.25 **NM** value: **Cover or less**
Circ: CapCity orders: **7,500**
C: Gil Kane
3 ❑ Aug 1996 Cover: 2.25 **NM** value: **Cover or less**
Circ: CapCity orders: **5,325**
C: Gil Kane
4 ❑ Sep 1996 Cover: 2.25 **NM** value: **Cover or less**
C: Gil Kane
5 ❑ Oct 1996 Cover: 2.25 **NM** value: **Cover or less**
6 ❑ Nov 1996 Cover: 2.25 **NM** value: **Cover or less**
Circ: Diamd. preorders: **7,038**
E.C. tribute cover.
7 ❑ Dec 1996 Cover: 2.25 **NM** value: **Cover or less**
Circ: Diamd. preorders: **6,973**
🕮 Rebirth, Part 1 • forms triptych
8 ❑ Jan 1997 Cover: 2.25 **NM** value: **Cover or less**
Circ: Diamd. preorders: **5,984**
🕮 Rebirth, Part 2 • forms triptych **A:** Pat Broderick **W:** Brett Brooks; Cliff Biggers
9 ❑ Feb 1997 Cover: 2.25 **NM** value: **Cover or less**
Circ: Diamd. preorders: **5,493**
• forms triptych

ICARUS (AIRCEL) — Aircel

1 ❑ 1987 Cover: 2.00 **NM** value: **Cover or less**
2 ❑ Apr 1987 Cover: 2.00 **NM** value: **Cover or less**
3 ❑ 1987 Cover: 2.00 **NM** value: **Cover or less**
4 ❑ 1987 Cover: 2.00 **NM** value: **Cover or less**
5 ❑ 1987 Cover: 2.00 **NM** value: **Cover or less**

ICARUS (KARDIA) — Kardia

1 ❑ Jun 1992 Cover: 2.25 **NM** value: **Cover or less**
A: Mark McHaley **W:** Dan Yelovich

ICE AGE ON THE WORLD OF MAGIC: THE GATHERING — Acclaim / Armada

1 ❑ Jul 1995 Cover: 2.50 **NM** value: **Cover or less**
Circ: CapCity orders: **52,875**
🕮 The Twilight Kingdom • bound-in Magic card (Chub Toad) **A:** Rafael Kayanan **W:** Jeff Gomez; Jeff G-mez
2 ❑ Aug 1995 Cover: 2.50 **NM** value: **Cover or less**
Circ: CapCity orders: **42,500**
• bound-in Chub Toad card from Ice Age
3 ❑ Sep 1995 Cover: 2.50 **NM** value: **Cover or less**
Circ: CapCity orders: **24,425**
• polybagged with sheet of creature tokens
4 ❑ Oct 1995 Cover: 2.50 **NM** value: **Cover or less**
Circ: CapCity orders: **19,725**
• polybagged with sheet of creature tokens
Bk 1❑ Cover: 4.95 **NM** value: **Cover or less**
• prestige format collection of first two issues; polybagged with sheet of counters
Bk 2❑ Cover: 4.95 **NM** value: **Cover or less**
• prestige format collection of issues #3 and 4; polybagged with sheet of counters

ICE BLADE — Mixx

Bk 1❑ Cover: 11.95 **NM** value: **Cover or less**
Bk 2❑ Cover: 11.95 **NM** value: **Cover or less**

ICEMAN (1ST SERIES) — Marvel

1 ❑ Dec 1984 Cover: 0.75 **NM** value: **2.50**
🕮 The Fuse! **A:** Alan Kupperberg **W:** J.M. DeMatteis ★ Origin of Iceman.
2 ❑ Feb 1985 Cover: 0.75 **NM** value: **2.00**
3 ❑ Apr 1985 Cover: 0.75 **NM** value: **2.00**
4 ❑ Jun 1985 Cover: 0.75 **NM** value: **2.00**
🕮 The Price You Pay! **A:** Alan Kupperberg **W:** J.M. DeMatteis

ICEMAN (2ND SERIES) — Marvel

1 ❑ Dec 2001 Cover: 2.99 **NM** value: **Cover or less**
Circ: Diamd. preorders: **52,095** • **CGC:** 3 graded, best 9.9
2 ❑ Jan 2002 Cover: 2.50 **NM** value: **Cover or less**
Circ: Diamd. preorders: **45,461**
3 ❑ Feb 2002 Cover: 2.50 **NM** value: **Cover or less**
Circ: Diamd. preorders: **44,390**

ICICLE — Hero

1 ❑ Cover: 4.95 **NM** value: **Cover or less**
Circ: CapCity orders: **3,075**
2 ❑ b&w Cover: 3.50 **NM** value: **Cover or less**
3 ❑ b&w Cover: 3.50 **NM** value: **Cover or less**
4 ❑ b&w Cover: 3.50 **NM** value: **Cover or less**
★ Appearance of Chrissie Claus.
5 ❑ b&w Cover: 3.95 **NM** value: **Cover or less**

CGC-graded: Multiply prices above by **33 for 9.9 M • 16 for 9.8 NM/M • 7 for 9.6 NM+ • 5 for 9.4 NM • 2.5 for 9.2 NM- • 1.5 for 9.0 VF/NM**

I COME IN PEACE — Greater Mercury

1 ❑ Cover: 2.50 **NM** value: **Cover or less**
📖 "I" Am The Peace Keeper **A:** Darryl Cobbs **W:** Charles Holland

ICON — DC / Milestone

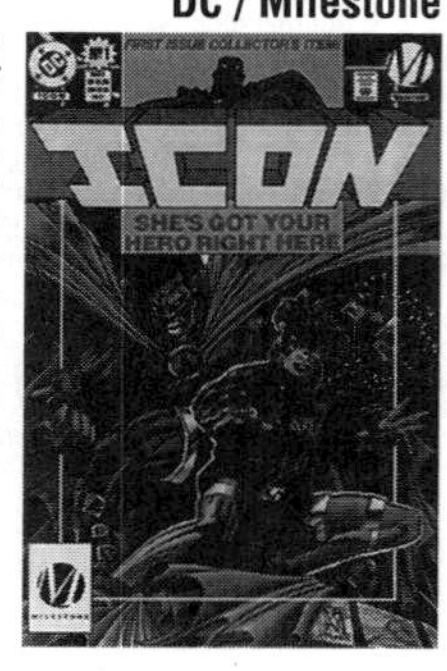

Icon is one of Milestone's more interesting takes on the subject of racial relations. Its title character, Augustus Freeman, is an alien who crashed on our planet more than 150 years ago, taking the form of a black human baby. Extremely long-lived, he is now a conservative lawyer, living in a suburb of the city of Dakota. Until recently, he had concentrated on his own affairs. Then a gang of youngsters broke into his house and tried to burglarize it. The would-be thieves were stunned, however, when Freeman took several shots to the chest, only to rise again, and fly after them.

Later, a young girl named Raquel came to visit Freeman. She had been along with the other teens that night, but when she saw what he could do, she had other thoughts. She returned to challenge Freeman to be an icon — a super-powered symbol of hope to his people. And of course, she, a street-smart liberal, would be his sidekick.

1 ❑ May 1993 Cover: 1.50 **NM** value: **2.00**
Circ: CapCity orders: **43,550**
📖 By Their Own Bootstraps **A:** Mark D. Bright **W:** Dwayne McDuffie ★ Origin of Rocket, Icon. ★ 1st Appearance of S.H.R.E.D., Rocket, Icon.

1/CS❑ May 1993 Cover: 2.95 **NM** value: **Cover or less**
• poster; trading card ★ Origin of Rocket, Icon.

2 ❑ Jun 1993 Cover: 1.50 **NM** value: **Cover or less**
Circ: CapCity orders: **19,150**
★ 1st Appearance of Payback.

3 ❑ Jul 1993 Cover: 1.50 **NM** value: **Cover or less**
Circ: CapCity orders: **16,650**

4 ❑ Aug 1993 Cover: 1.50 **NM** value: **Cover or less**
Circ: CapCity orders: **14,400**
• Rocket's pregnant ★ Appearance of Blood Syndicate.

5 ❑ Sep 1993 Cover: 1.50 **NM** value: **Cover or less**
Circ: CapCity orders: **12,250**
★ Versus Blood Syndicate.

6 ❑ Oct 1993 Cover: 1.50 **NM** value: **Cover or less**
Circ: CapCity orders: **11,200**
★ Versus Blood Syndicate.

7 ❑ Nov 1993 Cover: 1.50 **NM** value: **Cover or less**
Circ: CapCity orders: **9,400**
📖 The Moment of Truth **A:** Erica Helene **W:** Dwayne McDuffie

8 ❑ Dec 1993 Cover: 1.50 **NM** value: **Cover or less**
Circ: CapCity orders: **9,150**
★ Origin of Icon.

9 ❑ Jan 1994 Cover: 1.50 **NM** value: **Cover or less**
Circ: CapCity orders: **12,150**
📖 Shadow War; Shadow War, Part 2

10 ❑ Feb 1994 Cover: 1.50 **NM** value: **Cover or less**
Circ: CapCity orders: **8,050**
★ Versus Holocaust.

11 ❑ Mar 1994 Cover: 1.50 **NM** value: **Cover or less**
Circ: CapCity orders: **7,400**
📖 What I Did on my Vacation **A:** Ron Wilson **W:** Kurt Busiek ★ 1st Appearance of Todd Loomis.

12 ❑ Apr 1994 Cover: 1.50 **NM** value: **Cover or less**
Circ: CapCity orders: **6,750**
★ 1st Appearance of Gideon's Cord.

13 ❑ May 1994 Cover: 1.50 **NM** value: **Cover or less**
Circ: CapCity orders: **6,400**
★ 1st Appearance of Buck Wild.

14 ❑ Jun 1994 Cover: 1.50 **NM** value: **Cover or less**
Circ: CapCity orders: **6,350**

15 ❑ Jul 1994 Cover: 1.75 **NM** value: **Cover or less**
Circ: CapCity orders: **23,150**
📖 Worlds Collide; Worlds Collide, Part 4 ★ Appearance of Superboy.

16 ❑ Aug 1994 Cover: 1.75 **NM** value: **Cover or less**
Circ: CapCity orders: **19,200**
📖 Worlds Collide; Worlds Collide, Part 11 ★ Appearance of Superman.

17 ❑ Sep 1994 Cover: 1.75 **NM** value: **Cover or less**
Circ: CapCity orders: **6,350**
📖 Mothership Connection, Part 1; The Mothership Connection, Part 1

18 ❑ Oct 1994 Cover: 1.75 **NM** value: **Cover or less**
Circ: CapCity orders: **6,600**
📖 Mothership Connection Interlude; The Mothership Connection, Part 2

19 ❑ Nov 1994 Cover: 1.75 **NM** value: **Cover or less**
Circ: CapCity orders: **6,200**
📖 Mothership Connection, Part 2

20 ❑ Dec 1994 Cover: 1.75 **NM** value: **Cover or less**
Circ: CapCity orders: **5,900**
📖 Mothership Connection, Part 3 ★ Appearance of Static, Wise Son, Dharma, Hardware.

21 ❑ Jan 1995 Cover: 1.75 **NM** value: **Cover or less**
Circ: CapCity orders: **5,250**
📖 Mothership Connection Conclusion **A:** M.D. Bright **W:** Dwayne McDuffie

22 ❑ Feb 1995 Cover: 1.75 **NM** value: **Cover or less**
Circ: CapCity orders: **4,725**
★ 1st Appearance of New Rocket. ★ Appearance of Static, Hardware, DMZ.

23 ❑ Mar 1995 Cover: 1.75 **NM** value: **Cover or less**
Circ: CapCity orders: **4,325**

24 ❑ Apr 1995 Cover: 1.75 **NM** value: **Cover or less**
Circ: CapCity orders: **4,100**
• Rocket's baby born

25 ❑ May 1995 Cover: 2.95 **NM** value: **Cover or less**
Circ: CapCity orders: **4,325**
• Giant-size.

26 ❑ Jun 1995 Cover: 1.75 **NM** value: **Cover or less**
Circ: CapCity orders: **4,000**
★ Versus Oblivion.

27 ❑ Jul 1995 Cover: 2.50 **NM** value: **Cover or less**
Circ: CapCity orders: **4,025**
• Icon returns from space

28 ❑ Aug 1995 Cover: 2.50 **NM** value: **Cover or less**
Circ: CapCity orders: **4,075**
📖 Long Hot Summer

29 ❑ Sep 1995 Cover: 2.50 **NM** value: **Cover or less**
Circ: CapCity orders: **4,050**
📖 Long Hot Summer; The Long Hot Summer

30 ❑ Oct 1995 Cover: 2.50 **NM** value: **Cover or less**
Circ: CapCity orders: **3,325**
• Funeral of Buck Wild

31 ❑ Nov 1995 Cover: 0.99 **NM** value: **1.00**

32 ❑ Dec 1995 Cover: 2.50 **NM** value: **Cover or less**

33 ❑ Jan 1996 Cover: 2.50 **NM** value: **Cover or less**
📖 Inertia **A:** M.D. Bright **W:** M.D. Bright

34 ❑ Feb 1996 Cover: 2.50 **NM** value: **Cover or less**
📖 Rocket's Tale **A:** M.D. Bright **W:** Dwayne McDuffie

35 ❑ Mar 1996 Cover: 2.50 **NM** value: **Cover or less**
📖 Arena? **A:** M.D. Bright **W:** Dwayne McDuffie

36 ❑ Apr 1996 Cover: 2.50 **NM** value: **Cover or less**
A: M.D. Bright **W:** Dwayne McDuffie

37 ❑ Sep 1996 Cover: 2.50 **NM** value: **Cover or less**
📖 Rent Man Waiting • Icon in the 1920s **A:** J.J. Birch

38 ❑ Oct 1996 Cover: 2.50 **NM** value: **Cover or less**
📖 Blood Reign, Part 1 **A:** M.D. Bright **W:** Dwayne McDuffie ★ Versus Holocaust.

39 ❑ Nov 1996 Cover: 2.50 **NM** value: **Cover or less**
📖 Blood Reign, Part 2 **A:** M.D. Bright **W:** Dwayne McDuffie ★ Versus Holocaust.

40 ❑ Dec 1996 Cover: 2.50 **NM** value: **Cover or less**
Circ: Diamd. preorders: **6,315**
📖 Blood Reign, Part 3 **A:** M.D. Bright **W:** Dwayne McDuffie ★ Versus Blood Syndicate.

41 ❑ Jan 1997 Cover: 2.50 **NM** value: **Cover or less**
Circ: Diamd. preorders: **6,520**
📖 Blood Reign, Part 4 **A:** M.D. Bright **W:** Dwayne McDuffie

42 ❑ Feb 1997 Cover: 2.50 **NM** value: **Cover or less**
Circ: Diamd. preorders: **6,079**
final issue.

ICON DEVIL — Spider

1 ❑ Cover: 1.60 **NM** value: **Cover or less**
A: Neil Hansen **W:** Neil Hansen

2 ❑ Cover: 1.60 **NM** value: **Cover or less**
A: Neil Hansen **W:** Neil Hansen

ICON DEVIL (VOL. 2) — Spider

2 ❑ b&w Cover: 2.25 **NM** value: **Cover or less**

ICONOGRAFIX SPECIAL — Iconografix

1 ❑ b&w Cover: 2.50 **NM** value: **Cover or less**

ICZER 3 — CPM

1 ❑ Sep 1996, b&w Cover: 2.95 **NM** value: **Cover or less**
Circ: Diamd. preorders: **2,712**
A: Daphne Lage **W:** Daphne Lage; Stacey Rosenstein

2 ❑ Oct 1996, b&w Cover: 2.95 **NM** value: **Cover or less**
A: Daphne Lage **W:** Daphne Lage; Stacey Rosenstein

ID — Fantagraphics / Eros

All issues are adults only.

1 ❑ b&w Cover: 2.50 **NM** value: **Cover or less**
A: Robert Crumb **W:** Robert Crumb

2 ❑ b&w Cover: 2.50 **NM** value: **Cover or less**
A: Robert Crumb **W:** Robert Crumb

3 ❑ b&w Cover: 2.50 **NM** value: **Cover or less**
A: Robert Crumb **W:** Robert Crumb

3-2 ❑ Jun 1995, b&w Cover: 2.95 **NM** value: **Cover or less**

ID4: INDEPENDENCE DAY — Marvel

0 ❑ Jun 1996 Cover: 1.95 **NM** value: **2.50**
• **CGC:** 2 graded, best 9.8
• prequel to movie **A:** Steve Erwin; Rod Whigham; Terry Pallot; Gabriel Gecko **W:** Phil Crain

1 ❑ Jul 1996 Cover: 1.95 **NM** value: **Cover or less**
• adapts movie **A:** Leonard Kirk **W:** Ralph Macchio

2 ❑ Aug 1996 Cover: 1.95 **NM** value: **Cover or less**
• adapts movie **A:** Leonard Kirk **W:** Ralph Macchio

Capital City orders are the actual sales of comic books by Capital City Distribution, once one of the largest U.S. sellers of comics to comics shops. Capital City's share of comics shop sales, while not known exactly, increases from around 10-20% in the mid-1980s to 30-35% in the mid-1990s. Capital City's share of comic books sold on newsstands (most Marvels and DCs) will be less.

IDAHO — Dell

Idaho, an entertaining 1960s Western series from Dell features a hard-riding cowboy hero taking on all the familiar challenges of the old West. Idaho foils bank robbers, guards stagecoach caravans through hostile Indian territory, and frustrates greedy cattle barons with evil intentions against small ranchers — all with a friendly smile and soft-spoken demeanor. Simply drawn and written to appeal to Dell's younger readers, Idaho also featured some gorgeous painted covers and the attractive packaging that made Dell titles stand out from the pack.

1 ❑ Jun 1963 Cover: 0.12 **NM** value: **26.00**
📖 Showdown at Ramrod
2 ❑ Sep 1963 Cover: 0.12 **NM** value: **16.00**
3 ❑ Mar 1964 Cover: 0.12 **NM** value: **16.00**
4 ❑ Jun 1964 Cover: 0.12 **NM** value: **16.00**
5 ❑ Sep 1964 Cover: 0.12 **NM** value: **16.00**
6 ❑ Jan 1965 Cover: 0.12 **NM** value: **16.00**
7 ❑ Apr 1965 Cover: 0.12 **NM** value: **16.00**
8 ❑ Jul 1965 Cover: 0.12 **NM** value: **16.00**

IDEAL — Timely

1 ❑ Jul 1948 Cover: 0.10 **NM** value: **250.00**
2 ❑ Sep 1948 Cover: 0.10 **NM** value: **225.00**
3 ❑ Nov 1948 Cover: 0.10 **NM** value: **200.00**
4 ❑ Jan 1949 Cover: 0.10 **NM** value: **200.00**
5 ❑ Mar 1949 Cover: 0.10 **NM** value: **150.00**

IDEAL COMICS — Timely

1 ❑ Fal 1944 Cover: 0.10 **NM** value: **150.00**
2 ❑ Win 1944 Cover: 0.10 **NM** value: **100.00**
• **CGC:** 1 graded, best 9.2
3 ❑ Sum 1945 Cover: 0.10 **NM** value: **75.00**
• **CGC:** 1 graded, best 9.0
4 ❑ Spr 1946 Cover: 0.10 **NM** value: **75.00**

IDEAL ROMANCE — Key

3 ❑ Apr 1954 Cover: 0.10 **NM** value: **50.00**
4 ❑ Jun 1954 Cover: 0.10 **NM** value: **35.00**
5 ❑ Aug 1954 Cover: 0.10 **NM** value: **35.00**
6 ❑ Oct 1954 Cover: 0.10 **NM** value: **35.00**
7 ❑ Dec 1954 Cover: 0.10 **NM** value: **35.00**
8 ❑ Feb 1955 Cover: 0.10 **NM** value: **35.00**

I DIE AT MIDNIGHT — DC / Vertigo

Distraught by his girlfriend Muriel leaving him just hours away from the Year 2000, Larry pours a glass of wine, fixes a nice meal, writes out a farewell note, and takes half a bottle of sleeping pills. As a result, it's with mixed feelings that he receives a sudden visitor at his door: Muriel, who has changed her mind and wants him back. Now possessed of a reason to live once more, only one thing can save his life, and it's halfway across the city and obstructed by numerous hardships, including the man he stole Muriel away from in the first place. Will he make it by midnight?

Written and drawn in a brilliantly animated, cinematic style by Kyle Baker, this fast-paced tale is a thriller, a comedy, a romance, and a lot of fun. Published in vibrant full-color under DC's Vertigo imprint.

1 ❑ ca. 2000 Cover: 2.95 **NM** value: **Cover or less**
Circ: Diamd. preorders: **13,273** • **CGC:** 1 graded, best 9.6
A: Kyle Baker **W:** Kyle Baker

IDIOTLAND — Fantagraphics

1 ❑ b&w Cover: 2.95 **NM** value: **Cover or less**
2 ❑ b&w Cover: 2.50 **NM** value: **Cover or less**
3 ❑ b&w Cover: 2.50 **NM** value: **Cover or less**
4 ❑ b&w Cover: 2.50 **NM** value: **Cover or less**
5 ❑ b&w Cover: 2.50 **NM** value: **Cover or less**
6 ❑ Aug 1994, b&w Cover: 2.50 **NM** value: **Cover or less**

IDLE WORSHIP — Visceral

1 ❑ Cover: 2.95 **NM** value: **Cover or less**
📖 Breeder; Haze; Mysteriarch; Sticks & Stones; Hel'a **A:** Alan Hagen; Dave Perry; Ken Gallant; Patrick Pautler; Peter Macchione; Rich Leggatt; Terry Visser; Tom Secord; Tom Yeo; Chetan Patel **W:** Alan Hagen; Dave Perry; Ken Gallant; Patrick Pautler; Peter Macchione; Rich Leggatt; Terry Visser; Tom Secord; Tom Yeo; Chetan Patel

IDOL — Marvel / Epic

1 ❑ Cover: 2.95 **NM** value: **Cover or less**
Circ: CapCity orders: **5,400**
A: Ron Randall **W:** Steve Mattsson; Gerard Jones

2 ❑ Cover: 2.95 **NM** value: **Cover or less**
Circ: CapCity orders: **4,150**
A: Ron Randall **W:** Steve Mattsson; Gerard Jones

3 ❑ Cover: 2.95 **NM** value: **Cover or less**
Circ: CapCity orders: **3,800**
📖 The Deep Six **A:** Ron Randall **W:** Steve Mattsson; Gerard Jones

Other grades: Multiply prices above by **1.5 for Mint • 2/3 for Very Fine • 1/3 for Fine • 1/5 for Very Good • 1/8 for Good**

I DREAM OF JEANNIE — Dell

1 ❑ Cover: 0.10 **NM** value: **90.00**
2 ❑ Dec 1966 Cover: 0.10 **NM** value: **65.00**
• **CGC:** 1 graded, best 9.6

I FEEL SICK — Slave Labor

1 ❑ Aug 1999 Cover: 3.95 **NM** value: **Cover or less**
Circ: Diamd. preorders: **14,301**
A: Jhonen Vasquez **W:** Jhonen Vasquez

IF THE DEVIL WOULD TALK — Catholic Guild

1 ❑ ca. 1950 **NM** value: **750.00**
• **CGC:** 2 graded, best 7.5

IF THE DEVIL WOULD TALK (IMPACT) — Impact

1 ❑ ca. 1958 **NM** value: **200.00**
• **CGC:** 4 graded, best 9.6

IGRAT ILLUSTRATIONS, THE — Verotik

All issues are adults only.
1 ❑ Apr 1997 Cover: 3.95 **NM** value: **Cover or less**
Circ: Diamd. preorders: **6,615**
No issue number. embossed cardstock cover. • pin-ups

I HAD A DREAM — King Ink Empire

1 ❑ Jun 1995 Cover: 2.95 **NM** value: **Cover or less**
🕮 The Abyss **A:** Steven Gilbert **W:** Steven Gilbert

ILIAD — Slave Labor / Amaze Ink

1 ❑ Dec 1997, b&w Cover: 2.95 **NM** value: **Cover or less**
🕮 Ikarus: The Plight; Toad **A:** Alex Ogle; Darren Brady **W:** Alex Ogle; Darren Brady
2 ❑ Jan 1998, b&w Cover: 2.95 **NM** value: **Cover or less**
🕮 Ikarus: The Seed; Toad **A:** Alex Ogle; Darren Brady **W:** Alex Ogle; Darren Brady

ILIAD II — Micmac

1 ❑ b&w Cover: 1.70 **NM** value: **2.00**
2 ❑ b&w Cover: 1.70 **NM** value: **2.00**
3 ❑ b&w Cover: 1.70 **NM** value: **2.00**

ILLEGAL ALIEN — Kitchen Sink

1 ❑ Cover: 9.95 **NM** value: **Cover or less**
A: Phil Elliott **W:** James Robinson

ILLEGAL ALIENS — Eclipse

1 ❑ b&w Cover: 2.50 **NM** value: **Cover or less**
No issue number.

ILLUMINATIONS (VOL. 2) — Monolith

1 ❑ Cover: 2.50 **NM** value: **Cover or less**
🕮 Return To The Eve **A:** Holden Morris **W:** Shelly Morris
2 ❑ Cover: 2.50 **NM** value: **Cover or less**
3 ❑ Cover: 2.50 **NM** value: **Cover or less**

ILLUMINATOR — Marvel / Nelson

This joint project between Christian publisher, Nelson, and Marvel Comics stars Andy Prentiss, an average underconfident teenager. His parents send him away to camp for the summer, where his camp mates make fun of him. One night, they trick him into going on a "wampus hunt," and Andy stands in wait for hours in the dark, holding a bag and waiting to trap the mythical "wampus."

Seeing strange lights in the sky, Andy discovers he has great powers, including the ability to fly. But while the powers gave Andy confidence, he doesn't understand what to do with them until an evil spirit begins terrorizing his hometown. An old church caretaker encourages Andy to find his spiritual faith and to battle evil as the Illuminator.

Part of one of Carol Kalish's many projects to widen Marvel's audience, this series saw far more distribution in religious bookstores than through comics shops.

1 ❑ ca. 1993 Cover: 4.99 **NM** value: **Cover or less**
Circ: CapCity orders: **7,400**
🕮 Genesis **A:** Craig Brasfield **W:** Glenn Herdling ★ Origin of Illuminator. ★ 1st Appearance of Illuminator.
2 ❑ ca. 1993 Cover: 4.99 **NM** value: **Cover or less**
Circ: CapCity orders: **4,450**
3 ❑ ca. 1993 Cover: 2.95 **NM** value: **Cover or less**
Circ: CapCity orders: **4,300**

ILLUMINATUS (EYE-N-APPLE) — Eye-N-Apple

1 ❑ Cover: 2.00 **NM** value: **Cover or less**

ILLUMINATUS! (RIP OFF) — Rip Off

1 ❑ Oct 1990, b&w Cover: 2.50 **NM** value: **Cover or less**
2 ❑ Dec 1990, b&w Cover: 2.50 **NM** value: **Cover or less**
3 ❑ Apr 1991, b&w Cover: 2.50 **NM** value: **Cover or less**

ILLUSTRATED CLASSEX — Comic Zone

All issues are adults only.
1 ❑ b&w Cover: 2.75 **NM** value: **Cover or less**

🕮 indicates **Story Title** or **Storyline** information.
★ indicates **Character Appearance** information.

ILLUSTRATED DORE: BOOK OF GENESIS — Tome Press

1 ❑ b&w Cover: 2.50 **NM** value: **Cover or less**
A: Dore

ILLUSTRATED DORE: BOOK OF THE APOCRYPHA — Tome Press

1 ❑ b&w Cover: 2.50 **NM** value: **Cover or less**

ILLUSTRATED EDITIONS — Thwack! Pow!

1 ❑ Feb 1995 Cover: 1.95 **NM** value: **Cover or less**
🕮 The Horned Toad **A:** Garth Haslam **W:** Gerald W. Haslam

ILLUSTRATED LIFE OF SEYMOUR, THE — Sofa Comics

1 ❑ b&w Cover: 2.50 **NM** value: **Cover or less**
2 ❑ b&w Cover: 2.50 **NM** value: **Cover or less**
3 ❑ b&w Cover: 2.50 **NM** value: **Cover or less**
4 ❑ b&w Cover: 2.50 **NM** value: **Cover or less**

ILLUSTRATED STORIES OF THE OPERAS — Bailey

1 ❑ ca. 1943 Cover: 0.25 **NM** value: **400.00**
• **CGC:** 1 graded, best 8.5
• Faust
2 ❑ ca. 1943 Cover: 0.25 **NM** value: **400.00**
3 ❑ ca. 1943 Cover: 0.25 **NM** value: **400.00**
4 ❑ ca. 1943 Cover: 0.25 **NM** value: **400.00**

ILLUSTRATED TALES (JAXON'S...) — FTR

1 ❑ Cover: 1.95 **NM** value: **Cover or less**
🕮 God's Bosom; Bulto...A mountain of Silver **A:** Jaxon **W:** Jaxon

I LOVE LUCY — Eternity

1 ❑ May 1990, b&w Cover: 2.95 **NM** value: **Cover or less**
• strip reprint **A:** Bob Lawrence **W:** Bob Lawrence
2 ❑ Jun 1990, b&w Cover: 2.95 **NM** value: **Cover or less**
• strip reprint **A:** Bob Lawrence **W:** Bob Lawrence
3 ❑ Jul 1990, b&w Cover: 2.95 **NM** value: **Cover or less**
• strip reprint **A:** Bob Lawrence **W:** Bob Lawrence
4 ❑ Aug 1990, b&w Cover: 2.95 **NM** value: **Cover or less**
• strip reprint **A:** Bob Lawrence **W:** Bob Lawrence
5 ❑ Sep 1990, b&w Cover: 2.95 **NM** value: **Cover or less**
• strip reprint **A:** Bob Lawrence **W:** Bob Lawrence
6 ❑ Oct 1990, b&w Cover: 2.95 **NM** value: **Cover or less**
• strip reprint **A:** Bob Lawrence **W:** Bob Lawrence
Bk 1 ❑ b&w Cover: 19.95 **NM** value: **Cover or less**

I LOVE LUCY BOOK TWO — Eternity

1 ❑ Nov 1990, b&w Cover: 2.95 **NM** value: **Cover or less**
• strip reprints **A:** Bob Lawrence **W:** Bob Lawrence
2 ❑ Dec 1990, b&w Cover: 2.95 **NM** value: **Cover or less**
• strip reprints **A:** Bob Lawrence **W:** Bob Lawrence
3 ❑ Jan 1991, b&w Cover: 2.95 **NM** value: **Cover or less**
• strip reprints **A:** Bob Lawrence **W:** Bob Lawrence
4 ❑ Feb 1991, b&w Cover: 2.95 **NM** value: **Cover or less**
• strip reprints **A:** Bob Lawrence **W:** Bob Lawrence
5 ❑ Mar 1991, b&w Cover: 2.95 **NM** value: **Cover or less**
• strip reprints **A:** Bob Lawrence **W:** Bob Lawrence
6 ❑ Apr 1991, b&w Cover: 2.95 **NM** value: **Cover or less**
• strip reprints **A:** Bob Lawrence **W:** Bob Lawrence

I LOVE LUCY COMICS — Dell

I Love Lucy was one of the first indisputable hits of the then-new television medium in the early 1950s. Starring the real-life married couple, Lucille Ball and Desi Arnaz, as Lucy and Ricky Ricardo, with perennial sidekicks William Frawley and Vivian Vance as friends and neighbors, Fred and Ethel Mertz, this comical battle of the sexes reached immortality through reruns.

Whereas the Dell series tells stories developed specifically for the comic-book format, the later Eternity series reprints the daily comic strip which writer Lawrence Nadel and artist Bob Oksner publshed under the name Bob Lawrence.

3 ❑ Aug 1954 Cover: 0.10 **NM** value: **150.00**
• **CGC:** 5 graded, best 8.5
4 ❑ Nov 1954 Cover: 0.10 **NM** value: **150.00**
• **CGC:** 5 graded, best 8.5
5 ❑ Feb 1955 Cover: 0.10 **NM** value: **150.00**
• **CGC:** 6 graded, best 9.4
6 ❑ May 1955 Cover: 0.10 **NM** value: **85.00**
• **CGC:** 6 graded, best 8.5
7 ❑ Aug 1955 Cover: 0.10 **NM** value: **85.00**
• **CGC:** 1 graded, best 8.0
8 ❑ Nov 1955 Cover: 0.10 **NM** value: **8.00**
• **CGC:** 1 graded, best 9.2
9 ❑ Feb 1956 Cover: 0.10 **NM** value: **85.00**
• **CGC:** 1 graded, best 9.2
10 ❑ May 1956 Cover: 0.10 **NM** value: **85.00**
• **CGC:** 1 graded, best 9.4
11 ❑ Jul 1956 Cover: 0.10 **NM** value: **70.00**
• **CGC:** 1 graded, best 9.2
12 ❑ Sep 1956 Cover: 0.10 **NM** value: **70.00**
• **CGC:** 1 graded, best 7.0
13 ❑ Nov 1956 Cover: 0.10 **NM** value: **70.00**
• **CGC:** 1 graded, best 9.2
14 ❑ Jan 1957 Cover: 0.10 **NM** value: **70.00**
• **CGC:** 1 graded, best 9.4
15 ❑ Apr 1957 Cover: 0.10 **NM** value: **70.00**
• **CGC:** 1 graded, best 9.4
16 ❑ Jul 1957 Cover: 0.10 **NM** value: **70.00**
• **CGC:** 1 graded, best 9.2
17 ❑ Oct 1957 Cover: 0.10 **NM** value: **70.00**
• **CGC:** 1 graded, best 9.4
18 ❑ Jan 1958 Cover: 0.10 **NM** value: **70.00**
• **CGC:** 2 graded, best 8.5
19 ❑ Apr 1958 Cover: 0.10 **NM** value: **70.00**
• **CGC:** 2 graded, best 9.2
🕮 The Understudy; It Suits Me; Cyrus Shy in A Close Shave; Don't Step in the Grass; Dyed in the Fool (text) • Has 1957 Statement, filed 9/19/57; no figures published
20 ❑ Jul 1958 Cover: 0.10 **NM** value: **70.00**
• **CGC:** 2 graded, best 9.6
21 ❑ Oct 1958 Cover: 0.10 **NM** value: **50.00**
• **CGC:** 2 graded, best 9.4
22 ❑ Jan 1959 Cover: 0.10 **NM** value: **50.00**
• **CGC:** 1 graded, best 9.2
23 ❑ Apr 1959 Cover: 0.10 **NM** value: **50.00**
• **CGC:** 2 graded, best 8.5
24 ❑ Jul 1959 Cover: 0.10 **NM** value: **50.00**
• **CGC:** 1 graded, best 9.4
25 ❑ Oct 1959 Cover: 0.10 **NM** value: **50.00**
• **CGC:** 1 graded, best 7.5
26 ❑ Jan 1959 Cover: 0.10 **NM** value: **50.00**
• **CGC:** 1 graded, best 8.5
27 ❑ Apr 1960 Cover: 0.10 **NM** value: **50.00**
• **CGC:** 2 graded, best 9.6
28 ❑ Jul 1960 Cover: 0.10 **NM** value: **50.00**
• **CGC:** 1 graded, best 9.0
29 ❑ Oct 1960 Cover: 0.10 **NM** value: **50.00**
• **CGC:** 1 graded, best 9.0
30 ❑ Jan 1961 Cover: 0.10 **NM** value: **50.00**
• **CGC:** 1 graded, best 9.6
31 ❑ Apr 1961 Cover: 0.10 **NM** value: **50.00**
• **CGC:** 1 graded, best 9.2
32 ❑ Jul 1961 Cover: 0.10 **NM** value: **50.00**
• **CGC:** 1 graded, best 8.0
33 ❑ Oct 1961 Cover: 0.10 **NM** value: **50.00**
• **CGC:** 1 graded, best 9.0
34 ❑ Jan 1962 Cover: 0.10 **NM** value: **50.00**
• **CGC:** 1 graded, best 9.2
35 ❑ Apr 1962 Cover: 0.10 **NM** value: **50.00**
• **CGC:** 1 graded, best 8.0

I LOVE LUCY IN 3-D — Eternity

1 ❑ Cover: 3.95 **NM** value: **Cover or less**

I LOVE LUCY IN FULL COLOR — Eternity

1 ❑ Cover: 5.95 **NM** value: **Cover or less**
• comic book reprint; Collects I Love Lucy # 4,5,8,16

I LOVE YOU (AVALON) — Avalon

1 ❑ Cover: 2.95 **NM** value: **Cover or less**
🕮 Devil-May-Care!; My Errant Heart; The Good Fixer (text story); Memory of Love

I LOVE YOU (CHARLTON) — Charlton

Formerly titled In Love, this title is one of Charlton's several long-running contributions to the romance comics genre.

Marriage proposals, reunions with childhood sweethearts, perfetly behaved gentlemen suitors — all are in the stock-in-trade for this series.

Charlton attempted to keep the content of the stories timely, with decidedly mixed results. These attempts included the occasional celebrity appearance, working women — and in the late 1970s, characters with lots and lots of blue eye shadow.

With a 1972 average paid circulation below 120,000, I Love You — as well as most of the other romance (not to mention Charlton) comics inhabited the lower hald of the sales chart.

7 ❑ Sep 1955 Cover: 0.10 **NM** value: **55.00**
• Continued from In Love #6
8 ❑ 1955 Cover: 0.10 **NM** value: **16.00**
9 ❑ Cover: 0.10 **NM** value: **16.00**
10 ❑ 1956 Cover: 0.10 **NM** value: **16.00**
11 ❑ 1956 Cover: 0.10 **NM** value: **14.00**
12 ❑ 1956 Cover: 0.10 **NM** value: **14.00**
13 ❑ Cover: 0.10 **NM** value: **14.00**
14 ❑ 1957 Cover: 0.10 **NM** value: **14.00**
15 ❑ Oct 1957 Cover: 0.10 **NM** value: **14.00**
🕮 Enchanted Hour; Professional Bachelor; Ella's Engagement (text Story); Love is a Voyage; A Wish and a Kiss; A Poor Prospect
16 ❑ Cover: 0.10 **NM** value: **14.00**
17 ❑ 1958 Cover: 0.10 **NM** value: **18.00**
• Giant-size.
18 ❑ 1958 Cover: 0.10 **NM** value: **14.00**
19 ❑ 1958 Cover: 0.10 **NM** value: **14.00**
20 ❑ 1958 Cover: 0.10 **NM** value: **14.00**
21 ❑ Cover: 0.10 **NM** value: **12.00**
22 ❑ Cover: 0.10 **NM** value: **12.00**
23 ❑ 1959 Cover: 0.10 **NM** value: **12.00**
24 ❑ 1959 Cover: 0.10 **NM** value: **12.00**
25 ❑ 1959 Cover: 0.10 **NM** value: **12.00**
26 ❑ 1959 Cover: 0.10 **NM** value: **12.00**
27 ❑ Cover: 0.10 **NM** value: **12.00**
28 ❑ 1960 Cover: 0.10 **NM** value: **12.00**
29 ❑ 1960 Cover: 0.10 **NM** value: **12.00**
30 ❑ 1960 Cover: 0.10 **NM** value: **12.00**
31 ❑ Cover: 0.10 **NM** value: **10.00**

CGC-graded: Multiply prices above by **33 for 9.9 M • 16 for 9.8 NM/M • 7 for 9.6 NM+ • 5 for 9.4 NM • 2.5 for 9.2 NM- • 1.5 for 9.0 VF/NM**

32 ❑ Cover: 0.10 **NM** value: **10.00**
33 ❑ Mar 1961 Cover: 0.10 **NM** value: **10.00**
34 ❑ May 1961 Cover: 0.10 **NM** value: **10.00**
35 ❑ 1961 **NM** value: **10.00**
36 ❑ 1961 **NM** value: **10.00**
37 ❑ 1961 **NM** value: **10.00**
38 ❑ **NM** value: **10.00**
39 ❑ 1962 **NM** value: **10.00**
40 ❑ 1962 **NM** value: **10.00**
41 ❑ 1962 **NM** value: **10.00**
42 ❑ Oct 1962 Cover: 0.12 **NM** value: **10.00**
43 ❑ Dec 1963 Cover: 0.12 **NM** value: **10.00**
44 ❑ Feb 1963 Cover: 0.12 **NM** value: **10.00**
45 ❑ Apr 1963 Cover: 0.12 **NM** value: **10.00**
46 ❑ Jun 1963 Cover: 0.12 **NM** value: **10.00**
47 ❑ Aug 1963 Cover: 0.12 **NM** value: **10.00**
48 ❑ Oct 1963 Cover: 0.12 **NM** value: **10.00**
49 ❑ Feb 1964 Cover: 0.12 **NM** value: **10.00**
50 ❑ Apr 1964 Cover: 0.12 **NM** value: **10.00**
51 ❑ Jun 1964 Cover: 0.12 **NM** value: **8.00**
52 ❑ Aug 1964 Cover: 0.12 **NM** value: **8.00**
53 ❑ Oct 1964 Cover: 0.12 **NM** value: **8.00**
54 ❑ Jan 1965 Cover: 0.12 **NM** value: **8.00**
Circ: Statement: **139,689**
55 ❑ Mar 1965 Cover: 0.12 **NM** value: **8.00**
Circ: Statement: **139,689**
56 ❑ May 1965 Cover: 0.12 **NM** value: **8.00**
Circ: Statement: **139,689**
57 ❑ Jul 1965 Cover: 0.12 **NM** value: **8.00**
Circ: Statement: **139,689**
58 ❑ Sep 1965 Cover: 0.12 **NM** value: **8.00**
Circ: Statement: **139,689**
59 ❑ Nov 1965 Cover: 0.12 **NM** value: **8.00**
Circ: Statement: **139,689**
60 ❑ Jan 1966 Cover: 0.12 **NM** value: **60.00**
• Elvis Presley story
61 ❑ Mar 1966 Cover: 0.12 **NM** value: **4.00**
62 ❑ May 1966 Cover: 0.12 **NM** value: **4.00**
63 ❑ Jul 1966 Cover: 0.12 **NM** value: **4.00**
64 ❑ Sep 1966 Cover: 0.12 **NM** value: **4.00**
65 ❑ Nov 1966 Cover: 0.12 **NM** value: **4.00**
66 ❑ Feb 1967 Cover: 0.12 **NM** value: **4.00**
Circ: Statement: **120,310**
67 ❑ Apr 1967 Cover: 0.12 **NM** value: **4.00**
Circ: Statement: **120,310**
68 ❑ Jun 1967 Cover: 0.12 **NM** value: **4.00**
Circ: Statement: **120,310**
69 ❑ Aug 1967 Cover: 0.12 **NM** value: **4.00**
Circ: Statement: **120,310**
70 ❑ Oct 1967 Cover: 0.12 **NM** value: **3.00**
Circ: Statement: **120,310**
71 ❑ Cover: 0.12 **NM** value: **3.00**
72 ❑ Cover: 0.12 **NM** value: **3.00**
73 ❑ Jun 1968 Cover: 0.12 **NM** value: **3.00**
74 ❑ Aug 1968 Cover: 0.12 **NM** value: **3.00**
75 ❑ Oct 1968 Cover: 0.12 **NM** value: **3.00**
76 ❑ Dec 1968 Cover: 0.12 **NM** value: **3.00**
77 ❑ Jan 1969 Cover: 0.12 **NM** value: **3.00**
78 ❑ Mar 1969 Cover: 0.12 **NM** value: **3.00**
79 ❑ May 1969 Cover: 0.12 **NM** value: **3.00**
80 ❑ Jul 1969 Cover: 0.15 **NM** value: **3.00**
81 ❑ Sep 1969 Cover: 0.15 **NM** value: **3.00**
82 ❑ Nov 1969 Cover: 0.15 **NM** value: **3.00**
83 ❑ Jan 1970 Cover: 0.15 **NM** value: **3.00**
84 ❑ Mar 1970 Cover: 0.15 **NM** value: **3.00**
85 ❑ May 1970 Cover: 0.15 **NM** value: **3.00**
86 ❑ Jul 1970 Cover: 0.15 **NM** value: **3.00**
87 ❑ Sep 1970 Cover: 0.15 **NM** value: **3.00**
88 ❑ Nov 1970 Cover: 0.15 **NM** value: **3.00**
89 ❑ Jan 1971 Cover: 0.15 **NM** value: **3.00**
90 ❑ Mar 1971 Cover: 0.15 **NM** value: **3.00**
91 ❑ May 1971 Cover: 0.15 **NM** value: **2.50**
92 ❑ Jul 1971 Cover: 0.15 **NM** value: **2.50**
93 ❑ Sep 1971 Cover: 0.15 **NM** value: **2.50**
94 ❑ Nov 1971 Cover: 0.20 **NM** value: **2.50**
95 ❑ Jan 1972 Cover: 0.20 **NM** value: **2.50**
Circ: Statement: **118,526**
96 ❑ Mar 1972 Cover: 0.20 **NM** value: **2.50**
Circ: Statement: **118,526**
97 ❑ May 1972 Cover: 0.20 **NM** value: **2.50**
Circ: Statement: **118,526**
98 ❑ Jul 1972 Cover: 0.20 **NM** value: **2.50**
Circ: Statement: **118,526**
99 ❑ Sep 1972 Cover: 0.20 **NM** value: **2.50**
Circ: Statement: **118,526**
100 ❑ Nov 1972 Cover: 0.20 **NM** value: **2.50**
Circ: Statement: **118,526**
101 ❑ Jan 1973 Cover: 0.20 **NM** value: **2.50**
Circ: Statement: **127,041**
102 ❑ Mar 1973 Cover: 0.20 **NM** value: **2.50**
Circ: Statement: **127,041**
103 ❑ May 1973 Cover: 0.20 **NM** value: **2.50**
Circ: Statement: **127,041**
• Has 1972 Statement; avg total paid 118,526
104 ❑ Jul 1973 Cover: 0.20 **NM** value: **2.50**
Circ: Statement: **127,041**
105 ❑ Sep 1973 Cover: 0.20 **NM** value: **2.50**
Circ: Statement: **127,041**
106 ❑ Nov 1973 Cover: 0.20 **NM** value: **2.50**
Circ: Statement: **127,041**
107 ❑ Jun 1974 Cover: 0.25 **NM** value: **2.50**
Circ: Statement: **114,130**
• Has 1973 Statement; avg total paid circ 127,041
108 ❑ Sep 1974 Cover: 0.25 **NM** value: **2.50**
Circ: Statement: **114,130**
109 ❑ Nov 1974 Cover: 0.25 **NM** value: **2.50**
Circ: Statement: **114,130**
110 ❑ Jan 1975 Cover: 0.25 **NM** value: **2.50**
Circ: Statement: **97,660**
111 ❑ Mar 1975 Cover: 0.25 **NM** value: **2.50**
Circ: Statement: **97,660**
112 ❑ May 1975 Cover: 0.25 **NM** value: **2.50**
Circ: Statement: **97,660**
• Has 1974 Statement; avg total paid circ 114,130
113 ❑ 1975 Cover: 0.25 **NM** value: **2.50**
Circ: Statement: **97,660**
114 ❑ Oct 1975 Cover: 0.25 **NM** value: **2.50**
Circ: Statement: **97,660**
115 ❑ Dec 1975 Cover: 0.25 **NM** value: **2.50**
Circ: Statement: **97,660**
116 ❑ Feb 1976 Cover: 0.25 **NM** value: **2.50**
117 ❑ Apr 1976 Cover: 0.25 **NM** value: **2.50**
118 ❑ Jun 1976 Cover: 0.30 **NM** value: **2.50**
119 ❑ Aug 1976 Cover: 0.30 **NM** value: **2.50**
120 ❑ Oct 1976 Cover: 0.30 **NM** value: **2.50**
121 ❑ Dec 1976 Cover: 0.30 **NM** value: **2.50**
• End of original run (1976)
122 ❑ Mar 1979 Cover: 0.40 **NM** value: **1.50**
📖 Lover In Loan; All The Best; All The Beautiful People • Series begins again (1979)
123 ❑ 1979 Cover: 0.40 **NM** value: **1.50**
124 ❑ 1979 Cover: 0.40 **NM** value: **1.50**
125 ❑ 1979 Cover: 0.40 **NM** value: **1.50**
126 ❑ 1979 Cover: 0.40 **NM** value: **1.50**
127 ❑ Cover: 0.40 **NM** value: **1.50**
128 ❑ Feb 1980 Cover: 0.40 **NM** value: **1.50**
129 ❑ Mar 1980 Cover: 0.40 **NM** value: **1.50**
130 ❑ May 1980 Cover: 0.40 **NM** value: **1.50**
• Final issue (1980)

I LOVE YOU SPECIAL — Avalon
1 ❑ b&w Cover: 2.95 **NM** value: **Cover or less**

I, LUSIPHUR — Mulehide
1 ❑ **NM** value: **25.00**
2 ❑ **NM** value: **15.00**
3 ❑ **NM** value: **20.00**
4 ❑ **NM** value: **15.00**
5 ❑ **NM** value: **12.50**
6 ❑ **NM** value: **10.00**
7 ❑ **NM** value: **10.00**
• series continues as Poison Elves

IMAGE — Image
0 ❑ ca. 1993 **NM** value: **4.00**
• **CGC:** 4 graded, best 9.8
📖 Troll; StormWatch; Freak; Blotch; Sweat; Bludd; The Savage Dragon; Stryker; Shadow Hawk • Mail-away coupon-redemption promo from coupons in early Image comics **A:** Jim Valentino; Todd McFarlane; Rob Liefeld; Jim Lee; Marc Silvestri; Erik Larlen **W:** Jim Valentino; Todd McFarlane; Rob Liefeld; Jim Lee; Erik Larsen; Marc Silvestri; Brandon Choi

IMAGE OF THE BEAST, THE — Last Gasp
1 ❑ Cover: 0.75 **NM** value: **3.00**
A: Grizly **W:** Philip Jose Farmer

IMAGE PLUS — Image
1 ❑ May 1993 Cover: 2.25 **NM** value: **Cover or less**
Circ: CapCity orders: **96,850**

IMAGES OF A DISTANT SOIL — Image
1 ❑ Feb 1997, b&w Cover: 2.95 **NM** value: **Cover or less**
• pin-ups by various artists

IMAGES OF OMAHA — Kitchen Sink
All issues are adults only.
1 ❑ b&w Cover: 3.95 **NM** value: **Cover or less**
cardstock cover. • benefit comic; intro by Harlan Ellison; afterword by Neil Gaiman
2 ❑ b&w Cover: 3.95 **NM** value: **Cover or less**
Circ: CapCity orders: **3,200**
cardstock cover. • benefit comic **C:** Dave Sim

IMAGES OF SHADOWHAWK — Image
1 ❑ Sep 1993 Cover: 1.95 **NM** value: **Cover or less**
Circ: CapCity orders: **82,550**
A: Keith Giffen **W:** Keith Giffen; Alan Grant
2 ❑ Oct 1993 Cover: 1.95 **NM** value: **Cover or less**
Circ: CapCity orders: **57,125**
A: Keith Giffen **W:** Keith Giffen; Alan Grant ★ Appearance of Trencher.
3 ❑ Jan 1994 Cover: 1.95 **NM** value: **Cover or less**
Circ: CapCity orders: **47,625**
A: Keith Giffen **W:** Keith Giffen; Alan Grant ★ Appearance of Trencher.

IMAGI-MATION — Imagi-Mation
1 ❑ Cover: 1.75 **NM** value: **Cover or less**
• Gnatman

IMMORTAL COMBAT — Express / Entity
1 ❑ Feb 1995 Cover: 2.95 **NM** value: **Cover or less**
cardstock cover. • Entity Illustrated Novella #5

IMMORTAL DOCTOR FATE, THE — DC
1 ❑ Jan 1985 Cover: 1.25 **NM** value: **1.50**
📖 This Immortal Destiny **A:** Mike Nasser; Keith Giffen; Joe Staton; Walt Simonson **W:** Paul Levitz ★ Origin of Doctor Fate.
2 ❑ Feb 1985 Cover: 1.25 **NM** value: **1.50**
A: Keith Giffen
3 ❑ Mar 1985 Cover: 1.25 **NM** value: **1.50**
A: Keith Giffen

IMMORTAL II — Image
1 ❑ Apr 1997, b&w Cover: 2.50 **NM** value: **Cover or less**
Circ: Diamd. preorders: **17,009**
cover also says May, indicia says Apr. **A:** Mike S. Miller **W:** Mike S. Miller
1/A ❑ Apr 1997, b&w Cover: 2.50 **NM** value: **Cover or less**
cover says Immortal Two, indicia says Immortal II.
2 ❑ Jun 1997, b&w Cover: 2.50 **NM** value: **Cover or less**
Circ: Diamd. preorders: **12,542**
cover says Immortal Two, indicia says Immortal II. **A:** Mike S. Miller **W:** Mike S. Miller
3 ❑ Aug 1997, b&w Cover: 2.50 **NM** value: **Cover or less**
Circ: Diamd. preorders: **11,012**
cover says Immortal Two, indicia says Immortal II. **A:** Mike S. Miller **W:** Mike S. Miller
4 ❑ Sep 1997, b&w Cover: 2.50 **NM** value: **Cover or less**
Circ: Diamd. preorders: **9,777**
cover says Immortal Two, indicia says Immortal II. **A:** Mike S. Miller **W:** Mike S. Miller
5 ❑ Feb 1998, b&w Cover: 2.50 **NM** value: **Cover or less**
Circ: Diamd. preorders: **7,715**
cover says Immortal Two, indicia says Immortal II. **A:** Mike S. Miller **W:** Mike S. Miller

IMMORTALS, THE — Comics By Day
1 ❑ Cover: 1.00 **NM** value: **Cover or less**

IMP — Slave Labor
1 ❑ Jun 1994 Cover: 2.95 **NM** value: **Cover or less**
Circ: CapCity orders: **1,815**

IMPACT — E.C.
There were six E.C. titles in its "New Direction," cover-bannered as "an entirely novel and unique reading experience." The cover of each had a frame with the title on top and an identifying icon down the left side. The "New Direction" was one designed to accommodate the Comics Magazine of America's new Comics Code, though the first issue of each did not carry the Code stamp, and all but one lasted for five issues. The six titles were: Aces High, Extra!, MD, Psychoanalysis, Valor — and Impact.

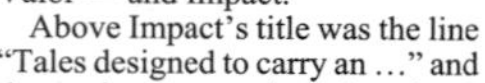

Above Impact's title was the line "Tales designed to carry an ..." and the stories were each designed to have a punch ending. The first issue cover-featured the classic Bernie Krigstein-illustrated "Master Race," and for its time, and considering the restrictions, the series was outstanding. In at least one case (the cover story of #4), Code censorship rendered the story incomprehensible. Nevertheless, the anthology series was powerful, illustrated by Jack Davis, Reed Crandall, Graham Ingels, George Evans, Krigstein, Joe Orlando, and Jack Kamen. — Maggie

1 ❑ Mar 1955 Cover: 0.10 **NM** value: **100.00**
• **CGC:** 2 graded, best 9.2
📖 Tough Cop; Thirty Dollars (Text Story); The Diamond Pendant; The Dress; Master Race; **A:** George Evans; Bernie Krigstein; Reed Crandall; Graham Ingels **W:** George Evans; Bernie Krigstein; Reed Crandall; Graham Ingels
2 ❑ May 1955 Cover: 0.10 **NM** value: **75.00**
• **CGC:** 3 graded, best 9.4
📖 Mother Knows Best; The Suit; The Star (text Story); Paid in Full; The Good Samaritan **A:** Joe Orlando; Reed Crandall; Jack Davis; Graham Ingels **W:** Joe Orlando; Reed Crandall; Jack Davis; Graham Ingels
3 ❑ Jul 1955 Cover: 0.10 **NM** value: **60.00**
• **CGC:** 2 graded, best 9.4
📖 Life Sentence; The Debt; Totally Blind; The Good Fairy; Appointment Cancelled (Text Story) **A:** Reed Crandall; Jack Kamen; Jack Davis; Graham Ingels **W:** Reed Crandall; Jack Kamen; Jack Davis; Graham Ingels
4 ❑ Sep 1955 Cover: 0.10 **NM** value: **60.00**
• **CGC:** 3 graded, best 9.4
📖 The Lonely One; Fall in Winter; The Bitter End; Last Act (Text Story); Country Doctor **A:** George Evans; Reed Crandall; Jack Davis; Graham Ingels **W:** George Evans; Reed Crandall; Jack Davis; Graham Ingels
5 ❑ Nov 1955 Cover: 0.10 **NM** value: **60.00**
• **CGC:** 3 graded, best 9.4
📖 The Art Interest; One Armed Wonder (Text Story); The Travelers; The General; So Much More **A:** George Evans; Joe Orlando; Bernie Krigstein; Graham Ingels **W:** George Evans; Joe Orlando; Bernie Krigstein; Graham Ingels

To find prices for other grades for comic books not graded by CGC, multiply the above prices by:

Mint: 150%	VF-: 55%	VG-: 17%
NM/M:125%	F/VF: 48%	G+: 14%
NM+: 110%	F+: 40%	**Good: 12.5%**
NM-: 90%	**Fine: 33.3%**	G-: 11%
VF/NM: 83%	F-: 30%	FR/G: 10%
VF+: 75%	VG/F: 25%	**Fair: 8%**
Very Fine: 66.6%	VG+: 23%	**Poor: 2%**
	Very Good: 20%	

Other grades: Multiply prices above by **1.5 for Mint • 2/3 for Very Fine • 1/3 for Fine • 1/5 for Very Good • 1/8 for Good**

IMPACT CHRISTMAS SPECIAL — DC / Impact

In the early 1990s, DC licensed the rights to the Archie Comics' super-heroes of the Sixties, (and Radio Comics before that), to launch its Impact imprint. The Shield, The Comet, The Jaguar, The Fly, The Web, and The Black Hood were revived, (albeit with altered origins and identities.

In this one-shot which foreshadowed the return of the team-up title, The Crusaders, the Impact heroes each undertook separate missions to retrieve former members of a group of scientists named The Magi who long ago worked with the crime lord known as Indigo. The scientists testified against Indigo and were given new identities, but now Indigo has escaped and demands that The Magi be surrendered to him to exact revenge. To that end, he kidnapped the president of the United States to use as a hostage.

In the best tradition of super-hero team-up titles, the Impact heroes accomplish their individual assignments and then cooperate to rescue the president.

Although the title of this book is Impact Winter Special, the indicia names it the Impact Christmas Special #1.

1 ❑ Cover: 2.50 **NM** value: **Cover or less**
Circ: CapCity orders: **13,850**
The Gift of Magi; American Crusader; Miracle on Farm Road 139; Immaculate Deception; The Fly; The Black Hood; Transparent Space; **A:** Carmine Infantino; Rick Burchett; Grant Miehm; Mike Parobeck; Tom Artis; Sandra Chiang; Tom Lyle Scott Hanna **W:** William Messner-Loebs; Grant Miehm; Mark Wheatley; Tom Lyle; Len Strazewski; Mark Waid ★ Appearance of Shield, Web, Fly, Comet, Jaguar.

IMPACT COMICS WHO'S WHO — DC / Impact

1 ❑ Cover: 4.95 **NM** value: **Cover or less**
Circ: CapCity orders: **7,600**
2 ❑ Cover: 4.95 **NM** value: **Cover or less**
Circ: CapCity orders: **6,500**
3 ❑ Cover: 4.95 **NM** value: **Cover or less**
Circ: CapCity orders: **4,050**
• trading cards

IMPACT (RCP) — RCP

1 ❑ Apr 1999 Cover: 2.50 **NM** value: **Cover or less**
Circ: Diamd. preorders: **3,892**
Tough Cop; Thirty Dollars (Text Story); The Diamond Pendant; The Dress; Master Race; **A:** George Evans; Bernie Krigstein; Reed Crandall; Graham Ingels **W:** George Evans; Bernie Krigstein; Reed Crandall; Graham Ingels
2 ❑ May 1999 Cover: 2.50 **NM** value: **Cover or less**
Circ: Diamd. preorders: **3,364**
Mother Knows Best; The Suit; The Star (text Story); Paid in Full; The Good Samaritan **A:** Joe Orlando; Reed Crandall; Jack Davis; Graham Ingels **W:** Joe Orlando; Reed Crandall; Jack Davis; Graham Ingels
3 ❑ Jun 1999 Cover: 2.50 **NM** value: **Cover or less**
Circ: Diamd. preorders: **3,412**
Life Sentence; The Debt; Totally Blind; The Good Fairy; Appointment Cancelled (Text Story) **A:** Reed Crandall; Jack Kamen; Jack Davis; Graham Ingels **W:** Reed Crandall; Jack Kamen; Jack Davis; Graham Ingels
4 ❑ Jul 1999 Cover: 2.50 **NM** value: **Cover or less**
Circ: Diamd. preorders: **3,326**
The Lonely One; Fall in Winter; The Bitter End; Last Act (Text Story); Country Doctor **A:** George Evans; Reed Crandall; Jack Davis; Graham Ingels **W:** George Evans; Reed Crandall; Jack Davis; Graham Ingels
5 ❑ Aug 1999 Cover: 2.50 **NM** value: **Cover or less**
Circ: Diamd. preorders: **3,346**
The Art Interest; One Armed Wonder (Text Story); The Travelers; The General; So Much More **A:** George Evans; Joe Orlando; Bernie Krigstein; Graham Ingels **W:** George Evans; Joe Orlando; Bernie Krigstein; Graham Ingels
Anl 1 ❑ Cover: 13.50 **NM** value: **Cover or less**
• Collects Impact (RCP) #1-5 **A:** George Evans; Joe Orlando; Bernie Krigstein; Reed Crandall; Jack Davis; Graham Ingels; Jack Karmen **W:** George Evans; Joe Orlando; Bernie Krigstein; Reed Crandall; Jack Kamen; Jack Davis; Graham Ingels

IMPERIAL GUARD — Marvel

1 ❑ Jan 1997 Cover: 1.99 **NM** value: **Cover or less**
Circ: Direct Market orders: **98,250**
A: Chuck Wojtkiewicz **W:** Brian Augustyn
2 ❑ Feb 1997 Cover: 1.99 **NM** value: **Cover or less**
Circ: Direct Market orders: **48,500**
wraparound cover. Up From The Depths **A:** Chuck Wojtkiewicz **W:** Brian Augustyn
3 ❑ Mar 1997 Cover: 1.99 **NM** value: **Cover or less**
Circ: Direct Market orders: **38,500**
A Mad God Awakens! final issue. **A:** Chuck Wojtkiewicz **W:** Brian Augustyn ★ Appearance of Supreme Intelligence.

IMPOSSIBLE MAN SUMMER VACATION SPECTACULAR — Marvel

1 ❑ Aug 1990 Cover: 2.00 **NM** value: **Cover or less**
Circ: CapCity orders: **16,600**
Impquest **A:** Barry Crain **W:** Michael Gallagher
2 ❑ Aug 1991 Cover: 2.00 **NM** value: **Cover or less**
Circ: CapCity orders: **12,900**

IMPULSE — DC

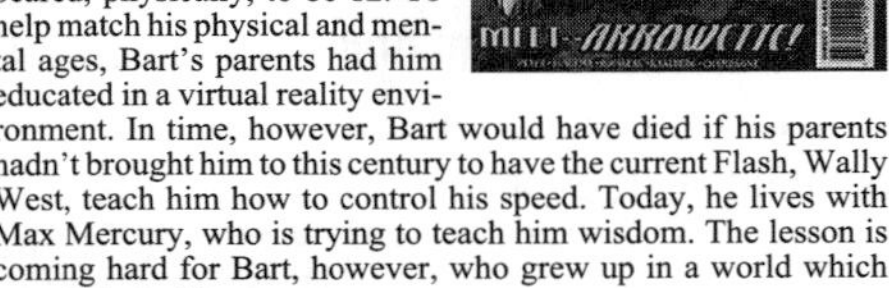

Before Barry Allen — The Flash — died in the Crisis on Infinite Earths, he lived for a time in the future of the 30th century with his wife, Iris. There, she gave birth to twins, Don and Dawn, who became known as the Tornado Twins. In turn, Don eventually had a son named Bart who inherited his grandfather's speed.

Unfortunately, Bart's speed came at a price: his metabolism was accelerated so that by the time he was two years old he appeared, physically, to be 12. To help match his physical and mental ages, Bart's parents had him educated in a virtual reality environment. In time, however, Bart would have died if his parents hadn't brought him to this century to have the current Flash, Wally West, teach him how to control his speed. Today, he lives with Max Mercury, who is trying to teach him wisdom. The lesson is coming hard for Bart, however, who grew up in a world which was all just a big game.

1 ❑ Apr 1995 Cover: 1.50 **NM** value: **4.00**
Circ: CapCity orders: **20,650**
The Single Synapse Theory **A:** Humberto Ramos **W:** Mark Waid ★ Origin of Impulse.
2 ❑ May 1995 Cover: 1.50 **NM** value: **3.50**
Circ: CapCity orders: **14,325**
Crossfire **A:** Humberto Ramos **W:** Mark Waid
3 ❑ Jun 1995 Cover: 1.75 **NM** value: **2.50**
Circ: CapCity orders: **12,600**
How to Win Friends and Influence People **A:** Humberto Ramos **W:** Mark Waid
4 ❑ Jul 1995 Cover: 1.75 **NM** value: **2.50**
Circ: CapCity orders: **12,525**
Bad Influence **A:** Humberto Ramos **W:** Mark Waid ★ 1st Appearance of White Lightning.
5 ❑ Aug 1995 Cover: 1.75 **NM** value: **2.50**
Circ: CapCity orders: **12,150**
Lightning Strikes **A:** Humberto Ramos **W:** Mark Waid
6 ❑ Sep 1995 Cover: 1.75 **NM** value: **2.25**
Circ: CapCity orders: **11,450**
Secret Identity • Child abuse **A:** Humberto Ramos **W:** Mark Waid
7 ❑ Oct 1995 Cover: 1.75 **NM** value: **2.25**
Circ: CapCity orders: **9,800**
W: Mark Waid
8 ❑ Nov 1995 Cover: 1.75 **NM** value: **2.25**
• Underworld Unleashed **W:** Mark Waid ★ Versus Blockbuster.
9 ❑ Dec 1995 Cover: 1.75 **NM** value: **2.25**
Underworld Unleashed **W:** Mark Waid ★ Appearance of Xs.
10 ❑ Jan 1996 Cover: 1.75 **NM** value: **2.00**
Dead Heat, Part 3 • continues in Flash #110 **A:** Humberto Ramos **W:** Mark Waid
11 ❑ Feb 1996 Cover: 1.75 **NM** value: **2.00**
Dead Heat, Part 5 **A:** Humberto Ramos **W:** Mark Waid ★ Death of Johnny Quick.
12 ❑ Mar 1996 Cover: 1.75 **NM** value: **2.00**
Sonic Youth **A:** Humberto Ramos **W:** Mark Waid
13 ❑ May 1996 Cover: 1.75 **NM** value: **2.00**
W: Mark Waid
14 ❑ Jun 1996 Cover: 1.75 **NM** value: **2.00**
W: Mark Waid ★ Versus White Lightning. ★ Versus Trickster.
15 ❑ Jul 1996 Cover: 1.75 **NM** value: **2.00**
W: Mark Waid ★ Versus White Lightning. ★ Versus Trickster.
16 ❑ Aug 1996 Cover: 1.75 **NM** value: **2.00**
• more of Max Mercury's past revealed **W:** Mark Waid
17 ❑ Sep 1996 Cover: 1.75 **NM** value: **2.00**
W: Mark Waid ★ Appearance of Zatanna.
18 ❑ Oct 1996 Cover: 1.75 **NM** value: **2.00**
Virtually Wasted **A:** Anthony Williams **W:** Martin Pasko
19 ❑ Nov 1996 Cover: 1.75 **NM** value: **2.00**
Circ: Diamd. preorders: **34,243**
A Game of Spew **A:** Humberto Ramos **W:** Mark Waid; Tom Peyer
20 ❑ Dec 1996 Cover: 1.75 **NM** value: **Cover or less**
Circ: Diamd. preorders: **34,489**
First Base • Bart plays baseball **A:** Humberto Ramos **W:** Mark Waid
21 ❑ Jan 1997 Cover: 1.75 **NM** value: **Cover or less**
Circ: Diamd. preorders: **33,543**
A Little Knowledge **A:** Craig Rousseau **W:** Mark Waid ★ Appearance of Legion.
22 ❑ Feb 1997 Cover: 1.75 **NM** value: **Cover or less**
Circ: Diamd. preorders: **31,237**
W: Mark Waid ★ Appearance of Jesse Quick.
23 ❑ Mar 1997 Cover: 1.75 **NM** value: **Cover or less**
Circ: Diamd. preorders: **31,610**
Lessons Learned • Impulse's mother returns **A:** Humberto Ramos **W:** Mark Waid
24 ❑ Apr 1997 Cover: 1.75 **NM** value: **Cover or less**
Circ: Diamd. preorders: **30,932**
• Impulse goes to 30th century **W:** Mark Waid
25 ❑ May 1997 Cover: 1.75 **NM** value: **Cover or less**
Circ: Diamd. preorders: **31,015**
You and Me Against the World • Impulse in 30th century **A:** Humberto Ramos **W:** Mark Waid
26 ❑ Jun 1997 Cover: 1.75 **NM** value: **Cover or less**
Circ: Diamd. preorders: **31,397**
• Impulse returns to 20th century **W:** Mark Waid
27 ❑ Jul 1997 Cover: 1.75 **NM** value: **Cover or less**
Circ: Diamd. preorders: **30,446**
W: Mark Waid
28 ❑ Aug 1997 Cover: 1.75 **NM** value: **Cover or less**
Circ: Diamd. preorders: **29,759**
★ 1st Appearance of Arrowette.
29 ❑ Sep 1997 Cover: 1.75 **NM** value: **Cover or less**
Circ: Diamd. preorders: **28,978**
30 ❑ Oct 1997 Cover: 1.75 **NM** value: **Cover or less**
Circ: Diamd. preorders: **30,240**
• Genesis; Impulse gains new powers
31 ❑ Nov 1997 Cover: 1.75 **NM** value: **Cover or less**
Circ: Diamd. preorders: **27,249**
Solving the Puzzle **A:** Craig Rousseau **W:** William Messner-Loebs
32 ❑ Dec 1997 Cover: 1.95 **NM** value: **Cover or less**
Circ: Diamd. preorders: **26,752**
Face cover. Unhealed Wounds **A:** Craig Rousseau **W:** William Messner-Loebs
33 ❑ Jan 1998 Cover: 1.95 **NM** value: **Cover or less**
Circ: Diamd. preorders: **25,681**
★ 1st Appearance of Jasper Pierson. ★ Versus White Lightning.
34 ❑ Feb 1998 Cover: 1.95 **NM** value: **Cover or less**
Circ: Diamd. preorders: **24,534**
• Max and Impulse travel in time
35 ❑ Mar 1998 Cover: 1.95 **NM** value: **Cover or less**
Circ: Diamd. preorders: **23,132**
• Max and Impulse turned into apes
36 ❑ Apr 1998 Cover: 1.95 **NM** value: **Cover or less**
Circ: Diamd. preorders: **21,939**
37 ❑ May 1998 Cover: 1.95 **NM** value: **Cover or less**
Circ: Diamd. preorders: **21,760**
★ 1st Appearance of Glory Shredder.
38 ❑ Jun 1998 Cover: 1.95 **NM** value: **Cover or less**
Circ: Diamd. preorders: **21,653**
• Manchester floods
39 ❑ Jul 1998 Cover: 1.95 **NM** value: **Cover or less**
Circ: Diamd. preorders: **20,432**
★ Appearance of Trickster.
40 ❑ Aug 1998 Cover: 1.95 **NM** value: **Cover or less**
Circ: Diamd. preorders: **20,010**
41 ❑ Sep 1998 Cover: 2.25 **NM** value: **Cover or less**
Circ: Diamd. preorders: **19,066**
★ Appearance of Arrowette.
42 ❑ Oct 1998 Cover: 2.25 **NM** value: **Cover or less**
Circ: Diamd. preorders: **18,268**
• Virtual pets
43 ❑ Dec 1998 Cover: 2.25 **NM** value: **Cover or less**
Circ: Diamd. preorders: **18,099**
44 ❑ Jan 1999 Cover: 2.25 **NM** value: **Cover or less**
Circ: Diamd. preorders: **18,163**
• Halloween
45 ❑ Feb 1999 Cover: 2.25 **NM** value: **Cover or less**
Circ: Diamd. preorders: **17,530**
• Christmas **A:** Craig Rousseau **W:** William Messner-Loebs ★ Appearance of Bart's mother.
46 ❑ Mar 1999 Cover: 2.25 **NM** value: **Cover or less**
Circ: Diamd. preorders: **17,960**
Chain Lightning tie-in; Chain Lightning **A:** Craig Rousseau **W:** William Messner-Loebs ★ Appearance of Flash II (Barry Allen).
47 ❑ Apr 1999 Cover: 2.25 **NM** value: **Cover or less**
Circ: Diamd. preorders: **17,336**
• Superboy cameo **A:** Craig Rousseau **W:** William Messner-Loebs ★ Appearance of Superman.
48 ❑ May 1999 Cover: 2.25 **NM** value: **Cover or less**
Circ: Diamd. preorders: **17,163**
★ Versus Riddler.
49 ❑ Jun 1999 Cover: 2.25 **NM** value: **Cover or less**
Circ: Diamd. preorders: **18,031**
The Old Reform School Dodge **A:** Craig Rousseau **W:** William Messner-Loebs
50 ❑ Jul 1999 Cover: 2.25 **NM** value: **Cover or less**
Circ: Diamd. preorders: **21,297**
First Fool's **A:** Ethan Van Sciver **W:** Todd Dezago ★ Appearance of Batman. ★ Versus Joker.
51 ❑ Aug 1999 Cover: 2.25 **NM** value: **Cover or less**
Circ: Diamd. preorders: **18,218**
It's All Relative **A:** Ethan Van Sciver **W:** Todd Dezago
52 ❑ Sep 1999 Cover: 2.25 **NM** value: **Cover or less**
Circ: Diamd. preorders: **18,813**
Tumbling Down **A:** Ethan Van Sciver; Walt Simonson **W:** Todd Dezago
53 ❑ Oct 1999 Cover: 2.25 **NM** value: **Cover or less**
Circ: Diamd. preorders: **18,392**
Threats **A:** Ethan Van Sciver; Walt Simonson **W:** Todd Dezago ★ Versus Inertia. ★ Versus Kalibak.
54 ❑ Nov 1999 Cover: 2.25 **NM** value: **Cover or less**
Circ: Diamd. preorders: **20,733**
Night of Camping • Day of Judgment **A:** Ethan Van Sciver **W:** Todd Dezago
55 ❑ Dec 1999 Cover: 2.25 **NM** value: **Cover or less**
Circ: Diamd. preorders: **17,915**
It Ain't Easy Being Greenery **A:** Ethan Van Sciver **W:** Shon C. Bury
56 ❑ Jan 2000 Cover: 2.25 **NM** value: **Cover or less**
Circ: Diamd. preorders: **17,989**
The Best of Both **A:** Ethan Van Sciver **W:** Todd Dezago ★ Appearance of Young Justice.
57 ❑ Feb 2000 Cover: 2.25 **NM** value: **Cover or less**
Circ: Diamd. preorders: **17,177**
A Plastic Christmas **A:** Ethan Van Sciver **W:** Todd Dezago ★ Appearance of Plastic Man.
58 ❑ Mar 2000 Cover: 2.25 **NM** value: **Cover or less**
Circ: Diamd. preorders: **16,654**
59 ❑ Apr 2000 Cover: 2.25 **NM** value: **Cover or less**
Circ: Diamd. preorders: **16,023**
60 ❑ May 2000 Cover: 2.25 **NM** value: **Cover or less**
Circ: Diamd. preorders: **16,038**
What Would Flash Do? **A:** Eric Battle **W:** Dwayme McDuffie
61 ❑ Jun 2000 Cover: 2.25 **NM** value: **Cover or less**
Circ: Diamd. preorders: **15,958**
The Sidekick Swap **A:** Eric Battle **W:** Johns
62 ❑ Jul 2000 Cover: 2.25 **NM** value: **Cover or less**
Circ: Diamd. preorders: **15,898**

CGC-graded: Multiply prices above by **33 for 9.9 M • 16 for 9.8 NM/M • 7 for 9.6 NM+ • 5 for 9.4 NM • 2.5 for 9.2 NM- • 1.5 for 9.0 VF/NM**

63 ❑ Aug 2000 Cover: 2.25 **NM** value: **Cover or less**
Circ: Diamd. preorders: **16,041**

64 ❑ Sep 2000 Cover: 2.25 **NM** value: **Cover or less**
Circ: Diamd. preorders: **15,941**

65 ❑ Oct 2000 Cover: 2.50 **NM** value: **Cover or less**
Circ: Diamd. preorders: **14,996**
🕮 Bart Allen's Evil Twin **A:** Ethan Van Sciver **W:** Todd Dezago

66 ❑ Nov 2000 Cover: 2.50 **NM** value: **Cover or less**
Circ: Diamd. preorders: **14,934**
🕮 Mercury Falling **A:** Ethan Van Sciver **W:** Todd Dezago

67 ❑ Dec 2000 Cover: 2.50 **NM** value: **Cover or less**
Circ: Diamd. preorders: **15,103**
🕮 Friends Like These… **A:** Ethan Van Sciver **W:** Todd Dezago

68 ❑ Jan 2001 Cover: 2.50 **NM** value: **Cover or less**
Circ: Diamd. preorders: **15,032**
🕮 I Rann and I Rann and I Rann… **A:** Eric Battle **W:** Todd Dezago

69 ❑ Feb 2001 Cover: 2.50 **NM** value: **Cover or less**
Circ: Diamd. preorders: **15,315**
🕮 Strange Impulses **A:** Eric Battle **W:** Todd Dezago

70 ❑ Mar 2001 Cover: 2.50 **NM** value: **Cover or less**
Circ: Diamd. preorders: **14,749**
🕮 Impulse, the Movie **A:** Carlo Barbieri **W:** Todd Dezago

71 ❑ Apr 2001 Cover: 2.50 **NM** value: **Cover or less**
Circ: Diamd. preorders: **14,520**
🕮 The Return of Lucius Keller, Part 1 **A:** Carlo Barbieri **W:** Todd Dezago

72 ❑ May 2001 Cover: 2.50 **NM** value: **Cover or less**
Circ: Diamd. preorders: **14,366**
🕮 The Return of Lucius Keller, Part 2 **A:** Carlo Barbieri **W:** Todd Dezago

73 ❑ Jun 2001 Cover: 2.50 **NM** value: **Cover or less**
Circ: Diamd. preorders: **14,285**
🕮 Dark Tomorrow **A:** Carlo Barbieri **W:** Todd Dezago

74 ❑ Jul 2001 Cover: 2.50 **NM** value: **Cover or less**
Circ: Diamd. preorders: **14,013**

75 ❑ Aug 2001 Cover: 2.50 **NM** value: **Cover or less**
Circ: Diamd. preorders: **14,255**

76 ❑ Sep 2001 Cover: 2.50 **NM** value: **Cover or less**
Circ: Diamd. preorders: **14,823**

1000000 ❑ Nov 1998 Cover: 2.25 **NM** value: **Cover or less**
Circ: Diamd. preorders: **26,673**
★ Appearance of John Fox.

Anl 1 ❑ ca. 1996 Cover: 2.95 **NM** value: **Cover or less**
• Legends of the Dead Earth **A:** Humberto Ramos; Mike Wieringo; Carlos Pacheco **W:** Mark Waid

Anl 2 ❑ ca. 1997 Cover: 3.95 **NM** value: **Cover or less**
Circ: Diamd. preorders: **23,012**
🕮 Showdown • Pulp Heroes **A:** Craig Rousseau **W:** William Messner-Loebs ★ Appearance of Vigilante.

Bk 1 ❑ Cover: 14.95 **NM** value: **Cover or less**
🕮 Reckless Youth • Reprints Flash #92-94, Impulse #1-6 **A:** Humberto Ramos; Mike Wieringo; Carlos Pacheco **W:** Mark Waid

IMPULSE/ATOM DOUBLE-SHOT — DC

1 ❑ Feb 1998 Cover: 1.95 **NM** value: **Cover or less**
Circ: Diamd. preorders: **24,139**
🕮 Roll Back **A:** Pop Mahn **W:** Dan Jurgens

IMPULSE: BART SAVES THE UNIVERSE — DC

1 ❑ Cover: 5.95 **NM** value: **Cover or less**
Circ: Diamd. preorders: **12,949**
No issue number. • prestige format. • Batman cameo; Flash I (Jay Garrick) cameo; Flash II (Barry Allen) cameo; Flash III (Wally West) cameo **A:** Jason Johnson **W:** Christopher J. Priest ★ Appearance of Extant, Linear Men. ★ Versus Extant.

IMPULSE PLUS — DC

1 ❑ Sep 1997 Cover: 2.95 **NM** value: **Cover or less**
🕮 Speed Freak • continues in Superboy Plus #2 **A:** Anthony Williams **W:** Len Kaminski ★ Appearance of Grossout.

IMP-UNITY — Spoof

1 ❑ b&w Cover: 2.95 **NM** value: **Cover or less**
• parody

INCAL, THE — Marvel / Epic

Bk 1 ❑ Cover: 10.95 **NM** value: **Cover or less**
Circ: CapCity orders: **3,800**

Bk 2 ❑ Cover: 12.95 **NM** value: **Cover or less**
Circ: CapCity orders: **2,500**

Bk 3 ❑ Cover: 10.95 **NM** value: **Cover or less**
Circ: CapCity orders: **2,550**

INCOMPLETE DEATH'S HEAD, THE — Marvel

1 ❑ Jan 1993 Cover: 2.95 **NM** value: **Cover or less**
Circ: CapCity orders: **37,800**
Die-cut cover. • Giant-size. 🕮 Connections; The Crossroads of Time; Here's Death's Head! **A:** Geoff Senior; Simon Coleby **W:** Dan Abnett; John Freeman; Simon Furman ★ 1st Appearance of Death's Head.

2 ❑ Feb 1993 Cover: 1.75 **NM** value: **Cover or less**
Circ: CapCity orders: **22,000**

3 ❑ Mar 1993 Cover: 1.75 **NM** value: **Cover or less**
Circ: CapCity orders: **21,300**
🕮 Contractual Obligations **A:** Bryan Hitch **W:** Simon Furman

4 ❑ Apr 1993 Cover: 1.75 **NM** value: **Cover or less**
Circ: CapCity orders: **24,200**

5 ❑ May 1993 Cover: 1.75 **NM** value: **Cover or less**
Circ: CapCity orders: **20,500**

6 ❑ Jun 1993 Cover: 1.75 **NM** value: **Cover or less**
Circ: CapCity orders: **17,400**
🕮 Do Not Forsake Me Oh My Darling! **A:** John Higgins **W:** Simon Furman

7 ❑ Jul 1993 Cover: 1.75 **NM** value: **Cover or less**
Circ: CapCity orders: **15,100**

8 ❑ Aug 1993 Cover: 1.75 **NM** value: **Cover or less**
Circ: CapCity orders: **12,500**

9 ❑ Sep 1993 Cover: 1.75 **NM** value: **Cover or less**
Circ: CapCity orders: **10,400**

10 ❑ Oct 1993 Cover: 1.75 **NM** value: **Cover or less**
Circ: CapCity orders: **9,000**
A: Geoff Senior **W:** Simon Furman ★ Appearance of Fantastic Four, Hob-Monster, Tuck.

11 ❑ Nov 1993 Cover: 1.75 **NM** value: **Cover or less**
Circ: CapCity orders: **7,550**

12 ❑ Dec 1993 Cover: 2.50 **NM** value: **Cover or less**
Circ: CapCity orders: **6,450**
• double-sized. final issue.

IN-COUNTRY NAM — Survival Arts

1 ❑ Cover: 1.95 **NM** value: **Cover or less**
🕮 Green is the Color of Hell **A:** Ronald F. Ledwell **W:** Ronald F. Ledwell

2 ❑ Cover: 1.95 **NM** value: **Cover or less**
A: Ronald F. Ledwell **W:** Ronald F. Ledwell

INCREDIBLE DRINKIN' BUDDIES — Luxurious

1 ❑ Cover: 2.95 **NM** value: **Cover or less**
🕮 Car Wrecks, Nudity, & Decapitation

INCREDIBLE HULK, THE — Marvel

Bruce Banner was a respected scientist who was working for the military to develop a gamma bomb. Seconds before the gamma bomb was to be tested, he saw a young man driving through the test area. Banner ordered the countdown stopped and raced to save the teen — but a jealous research assistant neglected to stop the countdown, and the bomb was exploded. Although Banner was able to get the boy to safety, he was caught in the gamma radiation released by the bomb. Thereafter, whenever he became angry, he found himself changing into a huge green monster with unbelievable strength. This monster became known as The Incredible Hulk.

In the years since, The Hulk has gone from raging berserker to sharing Banner's intellect and back again.

The Jekyll-and-Hyde-like story has been turned on its ear by Banner's remorse for what his alter-ego does when he's not in control.

-1 ❑ Jul 1997 Cover: 1.99 **NM** value: **2.00**
Circ: Diamd. preorders: **72,542**
🕮 Grave Matters • Flashback **A:** Adam Kubert **W:** Peter David ★ Origin of Hulk.

1 ❑ May 1962 Cover: 0.12 **NM** value: **11000.00**
• **CGC:** 78 graded, best 9.4
🕮 The Coming of the Hulk • Hulk's skin is gray (printing mistake) **A:** Jack Kirby ★ Origin of Hulk. ★ 1st Appearance of General "Thunderbolt" Ross, Hulk, Rick Jones, Betty Ross.

2 ❑ Jul 1962 Cover: 0.12 **NM** value: **2700.00**
• **CGC:** 51 graded, best 9.6
🕮 The Terror of the Toad Men • Hulk's skin is printed in green **A:** Steve Ditko; Jack Kirby ★ Origin of Hulk.

3 ❑ Sep 1962 Cover: 0.12 **NM** value: **1650.00**
• **CGC:** 42 graded, best 9.4
🕮 Banished to Outer Space; The Origin of the Hulk; The Ringmaster **A:** Jack Kirby ★ Origin of Hulk. ★ 1st Appearance of Ringmaster, Cannonball (villain), The Clown, Teena the Fat Lady, Bruto the Strongman.

4 ❑ Nov 1962 Cover: 0.12 **NM** value: **1325.00**
• **CGC:** 52 graded, best 9.4
🕮 The Monster and the Machine; The Gladiator from Outer Space **A:** Jack Kirby ★ Origin of Hulk.

5 ❑ Jan 1963 Cover: 0.12 **NM** value: **1325.00**
• **CGC:** 57 graded, best 9.6
🕮 Beauty and the Beast; The Hordes of General Fang ★ 1st Appearance of Tyrannus.

6 ❑ Mar 1963 Cover: 0.12 **NM** value: **1800.00**
• **CGC:** 58 graded, best 9.6
• Moves to "Tales To Astonish" following this issue **A:** Steve Ditko ★ 1st Appearance of Metal Master, Teen Brigade.

102 ❑ Apr 1968 Cover: 0.12 **NM** value: **150.00**
Circ: Statement: **277,857** • **CGC:** 208 graded, best 9.8
🕮 This World Not His Own • Numbering continued from "Tales To Astonish"; Has 1967 Statement; avg print run 449,213; avg sales 268,182; avg subs 950; avg total paid 269,132; samples 95; max existent 269,227; 40% of run returned ★ Origin of Hulk.

103 ❑ May 1968 Cover: 0.12 **NM** value: **60.00**
Circ: Statement: **277,857** • **CGC:** 18 graded, best 9.6
🕮 And Now, the Space Parasite ★ 1st Appearance of Space Parasite.

104 ❑ Jun 1968 Cover: 0.12 **NM** value: **55.00**
Circ: Statement: **277,857** • **CGC:** 19 graded, best 9.4
🕮 Ring Around the Rhino ★ Versus Rhino.

105 ❑ Jul 1968 Cover: 0.12 **NM** value: **45.00**
Circ: Statement: **277,857** • **CGC:** 29 graded, best 9.6
🕮 This Monster Unleashed ★ 1st Appearance of Missing Link. ★ Versus Gargoyle.

106 ❑ Aug 1968 Cover: 0.12 **NM** value: **45.00**
Circ: Statement: **277,857** • **CGC:** 23 graded, best 9.4
🕮 Above the Earth, A Titan Rages **A:** Herb Trimpe

107 ❑ Sep 1968 Cover: 0.12 **NM** value: **45.00**
Circ: Statement: **277,857** • **CGC:** 30 graded, best 9.8
🕮 Ten Rings Hath the Mandarin **A:** Herb Trimpe ★ Versus Mandarin.

108 ❑ Oct 1968 Cover: 0.12 **NM** value: **45.00**
Circ: Statement: **277,857** • **CGC:** 14 graded, best 9.4
🕮 Monster Triumphant **A:** Herb Trimpe ★ Appearance of Nick Fury.

109 ❑ Nov 1968 Cover: 0.12 **NM** value: **30.00**
Circ: Statement: **277,857** • **CGC:** 19 graded, best 9.6
🕮 The Monster and the Man-Beast! **A:** Herb Trimpe; Frank Giacoia **W:** Stan Lee

110 ❑ Dec 1968 Cover: 0.12 **NM** value: **30.00**
Circ: Statement: **277,857** • **CGC:** 16 graded, best 9.6
🕮 Umbu, the Unliving **A:** Herb Trimpe

111 ❑ Jan 1969 Cover: 0.12 **NM** value: **25.00**
Circ: Statement: **262,472** • **CGC:** 16 graded, best 9.4
🕮 Shanghaied in Space **A:** Herb Trimpe; Dan Adkins

112 ❑ Feb 1969 Cover: 0.12 **NM** value: **25.00**
Circ: Statement: **262,472** • **CGC:** 13 graded, best 9.4
🕮 The Brute Battles On **A:** Herb Trimpe; Dan Adkins

113 ❑ Mar 1969 Cover: 0.12 **NM** value: **25.00**
Circ: Statement: **262,472** • **CGC:** 14 graded, best 9.6
🕮 Where Fall the Shifting Sands? **A:** Herb Trimpe; Dan Adkins ★ Versus Sandman.

114 ❑ Apr 1969 Cover: 0.12 **NM** value: **25.00**
Circ: Statement: **262,472** • **CGC:** 6 graded, best 9.4
🕮 At Last I Will Have My Revenge • Has 1968 Statement, filed 10/1/68; avg print run 430,300; avg sales 276,896; avg subs 961; avg total paid 277,857; samples 400; max existent 278,257; 35% of run returned **A:** Herb Trimpe; Dan Adkins

115 ❑ May 1969 Cover: 0.12 **NM** value: **25.00**
Circ: Statement: **262,472** • **CGC:** 10 graded, best 9.6
🕮 Lo, The Leader Lives

116 ❑ Jun 1969 Cover: 0.12 **NM** value: **25.00**
Circ: Statement: **262,472** • **CGC:** 19 graded, best 9.8
🕮 The Eve of Annihilation

117 ❑ Jul 1969 Cover: 0.12 **NM** value: **25.00**
Circ: Statement: **262,472** • **CGC:** 11 graded, best 9.6
🕮 World's End?

118 ❑ Aug 1969 Cover: 0.15 **NM** value: **18.00**
Circ: Statement: **262,472** • **CGC:** 7 graded, best 9.6
🕮 A Clash of Titans ★ Appearance of Sub-Mariner.

119 ❑ Sep 1969 Cover: 0.15 **NM** value: **18.00**
Circ: Statement: **262,472** • **CGC:** 2 graded, best 9.0
🕮 At the Mercy of Maximus the Mad

120 ❑ Oct 1969 Cover: 0.15 **NM** value: **15.00**
Circ: Statement: **262,472** • **CGC:** 3 graded, best 9.2
🕮 On the Side of the Evil Inhumans

121 ❑ Nov 1969 Cover: 0.15 **NM** value: **15.00**
Circ: Statement: **262,472** • **CGC:** 1 graded, best 9.0
🕮 Within the Swamp, There Stirs a Glob

122 ❑ Dec 1969 Cover: 0.15 **NM** value: **25.00**
Circ: Statement: **262,472** • **CGC:** 14 graded, best 9.4
🕮 The Hulk's Last Fight • Hulk vs. Thing **A:** Herb Trimpe ★ Appearance of Thing.

123 ❑ Jan 1970 Cover: 0.15 **NM** value: **15.00**
Circ: Statement: **222,619** • **CGC:** 3 graded, best 9.8
🕮 No More the Monster

124 ❑ Feb 1970 Cover: 0.15 **NM** value: **15.00**
Circ: Statement: **222,619**
🕮 The Rhino Says No! **A:** Herb Trimpe **W:** Roy Thomas ★ Versus Rhino.

125 ❑ Mar 1970 Cover: 0.15 **NM** value: **15.00**
Circ: Statement: **222,619** • **CGC:** 2 graded, best 9.2
🕮 … And Now, The Absorbing Man! **A:** Herb Trimpe **W:** Roy Thomas ★ Versus Absorbing Man.

126 ❑ Apr 1970 Cover: 0.15 **NM** value: **9.00**
Circ: Statement: **222,619** • **CGC:** 1 graded, best 9.4
🕮 Where Stalks the Night-Crawler • Has 1969 Statement, filed 10/1/69; avg print run 432,345; avg sales 261,489; avg subs 983; avg total paid 262,472; samples 110; max existent 262,582; 37% of run returned

127 ❑ May 1970 Cover: 0.15 **NM** value: **9.00**
Circ: Statement: **222,619** • **CGC:** 7 graded, best 9.4
🕮 Mogol ★ Versus Mogol.

128 ❑ Jun 1970 Cover: 0.15 **NM** value: **9.00**
Circ: Statement: **222,619** • **CGC:** 1 graded, best 9.2
🕮 And In This Corner, The Avengers

129 ❑ Jul 1970 Cover: 0.15 **NM** value: **9.00**
Circ: Statement: **222,619** • **CGC:** 4 graded, best 9.6
🕮 Again, The Glob

130 ❑ Aug 1970 Cover: 0.15 **NM** value: **9.00**
Circ: Statement: **222,619** • **CGC:** 2 graded, best 9.0
🕮 If I Kill You, I Die

131 ❑ Sep 1970 Cover: 0.15 **NM** value: **9.00**
Circ: Statement: **222,619** • **CGC:** 6 graded, best 9.6
🕮 A Titan Stalks the Tenements • Iron Man **A:** Herb Trimpe

132 ❑ Oct 1970 Cover: 0.15 **NM** value: **9.00**
Circ: Statement: **222,619** • **CGC:** 2 graded, best 9.4
🕮 In the Hand of Hydra **A:** Herb Trimpe; John Severin ★ Versus Hydra.

133 ❑ Nov 1970 Cover: 0.15 **NM** value: **9.00**
Circ: Statement: **222,619** • **CGC:** 16 graded, best 9.4
🕮 Day of Thinder, Night of Death

134 ❑ Dec 1970 Cover: 0.15 **NM** value: **9.00**
Circ: Statement: **222,619** • **CGC:** 3 graded, best 9.6
🕮 Among Us Walks the Golem

135 ❑ Jan 1971 Cover: 0.15 **NM** value: **9.00**
Circ: Statement: **232,840** • **CGC:** 3 graded, best 9.6
🕮 Decent into the Time-Storm ★ Versus Kang.

136 ❑ Feb 1971 Cover: 0.15 **NM** value: **9.00**
Circ: Statement: **232,840** • **CGC:** 3 graded, best 9.6
🕮 Klaatu, the Behemoth From Beyond Space ★ 1st Appearance of Xeron.

137 ❑ Mar 1971 Cover: 0.15 **NM** value: **9.00**
Circ: Statement: **232,840** • **CGC:** 8 graded, best 9.4
🕮 The Stars Mine Enemy

138 ❑ Apr 1971 Cover: 0.15 **NM** value: **9.00**
Circ: Statement: **232,840** • **CGC:** 1 graded, best 9.4
🕮 Sincerely, The Sandman • Has 1970 Statement, filed 10/1/70; avg print run 400,196; avg sales 221,808; avg subs 811; avg total paid 222,619; samples 110; max existent 222,729; 44% of run returned

139 ❑ May 1971 Cover: 0.15 **NM** value: **9.00**
Circ: Statement: **232,840** • **CGC:** 1 graded, best 9.4
🕮 Many Foes Has the Hulk

Other grades: Multiply prices above by **1.5 for Mint • 2/3 for Very Fine • 1/3 for Fine • 1/5 for Very Good • 1/8 for Good**

140 ❑ Jun 1971 Cover: 0.15 **NM** value: **9.00**
Circ: Statement: **232,840 • CGC:** 2 graded, best 9.6
🕮 The Brute that Shouted Love at the Heart of the Atom! **A:** Herb Trimpe; Sam Grainger **W:** Roy Thomas; Harlan Ellison ★ 1st Appearance of Jarella.

140-2 ❑ Cover: 0.15 **NM** value: **1.50**

141 ❑ Jul 1971 Cover: 0.15 **NM** value: **20.00**
Circ: Statement: **232,840 • CGC:** 5 graded, best 9.4
🕮 His Name is Samson **A:** Joe Simon; Herb Trimpe ★ Origin of Doc Samson. ★ 1st Appearance of Doc Samson.

142 ❑ Aug 1971 Cover: 0.15 **NM** value: **8.00**
Circ: Statement: **232,840 • CGC:** 1 graded, best 9.0
🕮 They Shoot Hulks, Don't They?

143 ❑ Sep 1971 Cover: 0.15 **NM** value: **8.00**
Circ: Statement: **232,840 • CGC:** 1 graded, best 8.5
🕮 Sanctuary ★ Versus Doctor Doom.

144 ❑ Oct 1971 Cover: 0.15 **NM** value: **8.00**
Circ: Statement: **232,840**
🕮 The Monster and the Madman ★ Versus Doctor Doom.

145 ❑ Nov 1971 Cover: 0.25 **NM** value: **9.00**
Circ: Statement: **232,840 • CGC:** 2 graded, best 9.4
• Giant-size. 🕮 Godspawn **A:** Herb Trimpe; John Severin ★ Origin of Hulk.

146 ❑ Dec 1971 Cover: 0.20 **NM** value: **6.00**
Circ: Statement: **232,840 • CGC:** 2 graded, best 9.6
🕮 And the Measure of a Man is Death **A:** Herb Trimpe; John Severin

147 ❑ Jan 1972 Cover: 0.20 **NM** value: **6.00**
Circ: Statement: **202,223**
🕮 The End of Doc Samson; Heaven is a Very Small Place **A:** Herb Trimpe; John Severin

148 ❑ Feb 1972 Cover: 0.20 **NM** value: **6.00**
Circ: Statement: **202,223 • CGC:** 1 graded, best 9.4
🕮 But Tomorrow the Sun Shall Die • First appearance, Peter Corbeau **A:** Herb Trimpe; John Severin

149 ❑ Mar 1972 Cover: 0.20 **NM** value: **6.00**
Circ: Statement: **202,223**
🕮 The Inheritor **A:** Herb Trimpe; John Severin ★ 1st Appearance of Inheritor.

150 ❑ Apr 1972 Cover: 0.20 **NM** value: **6.00**
Circ: Statement: **202,223 • CGC:** 1 graded, best 9.4
🕮 Cry Hulk, Cry Havok **A:** Herb Trimpe; John Severin ★ 1st Appearance of Viking. ★ Appearance of Lorna Dane, Havoc.

151 ❑ May 1972 Cover: 0.20 **NM** value: **6.00**
Circ: Statement: **202,223 • CGC:** 2 graded, best 9.6
🕮 When Monsters Meet • Has 1971 Statement, filed 9/23/71; avg print run 367,427; avg sales 232,032; avg subs 808; avg total paid 232,840; samples 110; max existent 234,190; 36% of run returned

152 ❑ Jun 1972 Cover: 0.20 **NM** value: **6.00**
Circ: Statement: **202,223 • CGC:** 1 graded, best 9.6
🕮 But Who Will Judge the Hulk?

153 ❑ Jul 1972 Cover: 0.20 **NM** value: **6.00**
Circ: Statement: **202,223 • CGC:** 1 graded, best 9.0
🕮 The World, My Jury ★ Appearance of Fantastic Four, Peter Parker, Matt Murdock.

154 ❑ Aug 1972 Cover: 0.20 **NM** value: **6.00**
Circ: Statement: **202,223 • CGC:** 1 graded, best 9.6
🕮 Hell is a Very Small Hulk ★ Appearance of Ant-Man. ★ Versus Chameleon.

155 ❑ Sep 1972 Cover: 0.20 **NM** value: **6.00**
Circ: Statement: **202,223 • CGC:** 2 graded, best 9.4
🕮 Destination: Nightmare ★ 1st Appearance of Shaper of Worlds. ★ Versus Captain Axis.

156 ❑ Oct 1972 Cover: 0.20 **NM** value: **6.00**
Circ: Statement: **202,223 • CGC:** 1 graded, best 9.4
🕮 Holocaust at the Heart of the Atom

157 ❑ Nov 1972 Cover: 0.20 **NM** value: **6.00**
Circ: Statement: **202,223**
🕮 Name My Vengeance: Rhino

158 ❑ Dec 1972 Cover: 0.20 **NM** value: **6.00**
Circ: Statement: **202,223**
🕮 Frenzy on a Far-Away World ★ Appearance of Warlock. ★ Versus Rhino on Counter-Earth.

159 ❑ Jan 1973 Cover: 0.20 **NM** value: **6.00**
Circ: Statement: **187,318 • CGC:** 1 graded, best 7.0
🕮 Two Years Before the Abomination ★ Versus Abomination.

160 ❑ Feb 1973 Cover: 0.20 **NM** value: **6.00**
Circ: Statement: **187,318**
🕮 Nightmare in Niagara Falls

161 ❑ Mar 1973 Cover: 0.20 **NM** value: **6.00**
Circ: Statement: **187,318 • CGC:** 2 graded, best 9.2
🕮 Beyond the Border Lurks Death • Has 1972 Statement; avg total paid circ 202,223 **A:** Herb Trimpe ★ Appearance of Mimic. ★ Death of Mimic. ★ Versus Beast.

162 ❑ Apr 1973 Cover: 0.20 **NM** value: **7.00**
Circ: Statement: **187,318**
🕮 Spawn of the Flesh-Eater **A:** Herb Trimpe ★ 1st Appearance of Wendigo. ★ Versus Wendigo.

163 ❑ May 1973 Cover: 0.20 **NM** value: **6.00**
Circ: Statement: **187,318**
🕮 Trackdown **A:** Herb Trimpe ★ 1st Appearance of Gremlin.

164 ❑ Jun 1973 Cover: 0.20 **NM** value: **6.00**
Circ: Statement: **187,318**
🕮 The Phantom From 5,000 Fathoms **A:** Herb Trimpe ★ 1st Appearance of Captain Omen.

165 ❑ Jul 1973 Cover: 0.20 **NM** value: **6.00**
Circ: Statement: **187,318**
🕮 The Green-Skinned God **A:** Herb Trimpe ★ Versus Aquon.

166 ❑ Aug 1973 Cover: 0.20 **NM** value: **6.00**
Circ: Statement: **187,318**
🕮 The Destroyer from the Dynamo **A:** Herb Trimpe ★ 1st Appearance of Zzzax.

167 ❑ Sep 1973 Cover: 0.20 **NM** value: **6.00**
Circ: Statement: **187,318 • CGC:** 1 graded, best 9.6
🕮 To Destroy the Monster **A:** Herb Trimpe ★ Versus M.O.D.O.K..

168 ❑ Oct 1973 Cover: 0.20 **NM** value: **6.00**
Circ: Statement: **187,318 • CGC:** 1 graded, best 9.2
🕮 The Hate of the Harpy **A:** Herb Trimpe ★ 1st Appearance of Harpy.

169 ❑ Nov 1973 Cover: 0.20 **NM** value: **6.00**
Circ: Statement: **187,318**
🕮 Calamity in the Clouds **A:** Herb Trimpe **W:** Steve Englehart ★ 1st Appearance of Bi-Beast I. ★ Versus Bi-Beast I.

170 ❑ Dec 1973 Cover: 0.20 **NM** value: **6.00**
Circ: Statement: **187,318 • CGC:** 1 graded, best 9.6
🕮 Death from on High **A:** Herb Trimpe ★ Death of Bi-Beast I.

171 ❑ Jan 1974 Cover: 0.20 **NM** value: **6.00**
Circ: Statement: **202,592**
🕮 Revenge **A:** Herb Trimpe ★ Versus Abomination. ★ Versus Rhino.

172 ❑ Feb 1974 Cover: 0.20 **NM** value: **8.50**
Circ: Statement: **202,592 • CGC:** 1 graded, best 9.2
🕮 And Canst Thou Slay the Juggernaut? **A:** Herb Trimpe ★ Appearance of X-Men.

173 ❑ Mar 1974 Cover: 0.20 **NM** value: **6.00**
Circ: Statement: **202,592**
🕮 Anybody Out There Remember the Cobalt Man? **A:** Herb Trimpe ★ Versus Cobalt Man.

174 ❑ Apr 1974 Cover: 0.20 **NM** value: **6.00**
Circ: Statement: **202,592 • CGC:** 2 graded, best 9.6
🕮 Doomsday Down Under **A:** Herb Trimpe ★ Versus Cobalt Man.

175 ❑ May 1974 Cover: 0.25 **NM** value: **6.00**
Circ: Statement: **202,592 • CGC:** 3 graded, best 9.4
🕮 Man-Brute in the Hidden Land • Has 1973 Statement, filed 9/25/73; avg print run 382,761; avg sales 186,532; avg subs 786; avg total paid 187,318; samples 150; max existent 187,629; 51% of run returned **A:** Herb Trimpe ★ Appearance of Inhumans. ★ Versus Inhumans.

176 ❑ Jun 1974 Cover: 0.25 **NM** value: **7.00**
Circ: Statement: **202,592 • CGC:** 1 graded, best 9.6
🕮 Crisis on Counter-Earth • on Counter-Earth **A:** Herb Trimpe ★ Appearance of Warlock.

177 ❑ Jul 1974 Cover: 0.25 **NM** value: **10.00**
Circ: Statement: **202,592**
🕮 Peril of the Plural Planet **A:** Herb Trimpe ★ Death of Warlock.

178 ❑ Aug 1974 Cover: 0.25 **NM** value: **10.00**
Circ: Statement: **202,592 • CGC:** 1 graded, best 9.6
🕮 Triumph on Terra-Two • Warlock returns **A:** Herb Trimpe ★ Death of Warlock.

179 ❑ Sep 1974 Cover: 0.25 **NM** value: **5.00**
Circ: Statement: **202,592**
🕮 Re-Enter: The Missing Link • Missing Link **A:** Herb Trimpe

180 ❑ Oct 1974 Cover: 0.25 **NM** value: **110.00**
Circ: Statement: **202,592 • CGC:** 101 graded, best 9.8
🕮 And the Wind Howls Wendigo **A:** Herb Trimpe ★ 1st Appearance of Wolverine (cameo). ★ Appearance of Wendigo.

181 ❑ Nov 1974 Cover: 0.25 **NM** value: **600.00**
Circ: Statement: **202,592 • CGC:** 660 graded, best 9.9
🕮 And Now...The Wolverine! • Marvel Value Stamp A/54: Shanna the She-Devil **A:** Herb Trimpe **W:** Len Wein ★ 1st Appearance of Wolverine (full appearance). ★ Appearance of Wendigo.

182 ❑ Dec 1974 Cover: 0.25 **NM** value: **60.00**
Circ: Statement: **202,592 • CGC:** 67 graded, best 9.6
🕮 Between Anvil and Hammer ★ Origin of Hammer, Anvil. ★ 1st Appearance of Hammer, Anvil, Crackajack. ★ Appearance of Wolverine. ★ Versus Hammer. ★ Versus Anvil.

183 ❑ Jan 1975 Cover: 0.25 **NM** value: **4.00**
Circ: Statement: **196,499**
🕮 Fury at 50,000 Volts ★ Versus Zzzax.

184 ❑ Feb 1975 Cover: 0.25 **NM** value: **4.00**
Circ: Statement: **196,499 • CGC:** 1 graded, best 8.5
🕮 Shadow on the Land

185 ❑ Mar 1975 Cover: 0.25 **NM** value: **4.00**
Circ: Statement: **196,499 • CGC:** 2 graded, best 9.2
🕮 Deathknell

186 ❑ Apr 1975 Cover: 0.25 **NM** value: **4.00**
Circ: Statement: **196,499 • CGC:** 1 graded, best 9.2
🕮 The Day of the Devastator ★ 1st Appearance of Devastator I (Kirov Petrovna). ★ Death of Devastator I (Kirov Petrovna).

187 ❑ May 1975 Cover: 0.25 **NM** value: **4.00**
Circ: Statement: **196,499**
🕮 There's a Gremlin in the Works • Has 1974 Statement; avg total paid circ 202,592 ★ Versus Gremlin.

188 ❑ Jun 1975 Cover: 0.25 **NM** value: **4.00**
Circ: Statement: **196,499 • CGC:** 1 graded, best 9.4
🕮 Mind Over Mayhem ★ Versus Gremlin.

189 ❑ Jul 1975 Cover: 0.25 **NM** value: **4.00**
Circ: Statement: **196,499 • CGC:** 1 graded, best 9.0
🕮 None Are So Blind ★ Versus Mole Man.

190 ❑ Aug 1975 Cover: 0.25 **NM** value: **4.00**
Circ: Statement: **196,499 • CGC:** 3 graded, best 9.6
🕮 The Man Who Came Down on a Rainbow ★ 1st Appearance of Glorian. ★ Versus Toad Men.

191 ❑ Sep 1975 Cover: 0.25 **NM** value: **3.75**
Circ: Statement: **196,499 • CGC:** 2 graded, best 9.4
🕮 The Triumph of the Toad ★ Versus Shaper of Worlds.

192 ❑ Oct 1975 Cover: 0.25 **NM** value: **3.75**
Circ: Statement: **196,499 • CGC:** 1 graded, best 9.0
🕮 The Lurker Beneath Loch Fear

193 ❑ Nov 1975 Cover: 0.25 **NM** value: **3.75**
Circ: Statement: **196,499 • CGC:** 1 graded, best 9.2
🕮 The Doctor's Name is Samson ★ Versus Doc Samson.

194 ❑ Dec 1975 Cover: 0.25 **NM** value: **3.75**
Circ: Statement: **196,499**
🕮 The Day of the Locust

195 ❑ Jan 1976 Cover: 0.25 **NM** value: **3.75**
Circ: Statement: **182,460 • CGC:** 1 graded, best 9.4
🕮 Warfare in Wonderland ★ Versus Abomination.

196 ❑ Feb 1976 Cover: 0.25 **NM** value: **3.75**
Circ: Statement: **182,460 • CGC:** 1 graded, best 9.4
🕮 The Abomination Proclamation ★ Versus Abomination.

197 ❑ Mar 1976 Cover: 0.25 **NM** value: **3.75**
Circ: Statement: **182,460**
🕮 And Man-Thing Makes Three ★ Versus Man-Thing. ★ Versus Gardner.

198 ❑ Apr 1976 Cover: 0.25 **NM** value: **3.75**
Circ: Statement: **182,460 • CGC:** 2 graded, best 9.4
🕮 The Shangri-La Syndrome ★ Appearance of Man-Thing.

199 ❑ May 1976 Cover: 0.25 **NM** value: **3.75**
Circ: Statement: **182,460 • CGC:** 3 graded, best 9.0
🕮 ..And S.H.I.E.L.D. Shall Follow! **A:** Sal Buscema; Joe Staton **W:** Len Wein ★ Versus Doc Samson.

200 ❑ Jun 1976 Cover: 0.25 **NM** value: **12.00**
Circ: Statement: **182,460 • CGC:** 35 graded, best 9.8
• 200th anniversary issue. 🕮 An Intruder in the Mind **A:** Sal Buscema; Joe Sinnott ★ Appearance of Surfer and others.

200/A ❑ Jun 1976 Cover: 0.30 **NM** value: **22.00**
• **CGC:** 3 graded, best 9.0
• 200th anniversary issue. 🕮 An Intruder in the Mind **A:** Sal Buscema; Joe Sinnott ★ Appearance of Surfer and others.

201 ❑ Jul 1976 Cover: 0.25 **NM** value: **3.00**
Circ: Statement: **182,460 • CGC:** 1 graded, best 9.0
🕮 The Sword and the Sorceror **A:** Sal Buscema; Joe Sinnott

202 ❑ Aug 1976 Cover: 0.25 **NM** value: **3.00**
Circ: Statement: **182,460**
🕮 Havoc at the Heart of the Atom **A:** Sal Buscema; Joe Sinnott ★ Appearance of Jarella.

203 ❑ Sep 1976 Cover: 0.25 **NM** value: **3.00**
Circ: Statement: **182,460**
🕮 Assault on Psyklop **A:** Sal Buscema; Joe Sinnott ★ Versus Psyklop.

204 ❑ Oct 1976 Cover: 0.30 **NM** value: **3.00**
Circ: Statement: **182,460**
🕮 Vicious Circle **A:** Herb Trimpe; John Severin ★ Origin of Hulk. ★ 1st Appearance of Kronus.

205 ❑ Nov 1976 Cover: 0.30 **NM** value: **3.00**
Circ: Statement: **182,460**
🕮 Do Not Forsake Me! **A:** Sal Buscema; Joe Staton **W:** Len Wein

206 ❑ Dec 1976 Cover: 0.30 **NM** value: **3.00**
Circ: Statement: **182,460**
🕮 A Man-Brute Berserk

207 ❑ Jan 1977 Cover: 0.30 **NM** value: **3.00**
Circ: Statement: **174,287**
🕮 Alone Against the Defenders ★ Appearance of Defenders.

208 ❑ Feb 1977 Cover: 0.30 **NM** value: **3.00**
Circ: Statement: **174,287**
🕮 A Monster in our Midst

209 ❑ Mar 1977 Cover: 0.30 **NM** value: **3.00**
Circ: Statement: **174,287**
🕮 The Absorbing Man is Out for Blood • Has 1976 Statement, filed 9/20/76; avg print run 389,399; avg sales 181,320; avg subs 1,140; avg total paid 182,460; max existent 183,438; 53% of run returned ★ Versus Absorbing Man.

210 ❑ Apr 1977 Cover: 0.30 **NM** value: **3.00**
Circ: Statement: **174,287**
🕮 And Call the Doctor: Druid ★ Appearance of Doctor Druid.

211 ❑ May 1977 Cover: 0.30 **NM** value: **3.00**
Circ: Statement: **174,287**
🕮 The Monster and the Mystic ★ Appearance of Doctor Druid.

212 ❑ Jun 1977 Cover: 0.30 **NM** value: **3.00**
Circ: Statement: **174,287**
🕮 Crushed by the Constrictor ★ 1st Appearance of Constrictor. ★ Versus Constrictor.

213 ❑ Jul 1977 Cover: 0.30 **NM** value: **3.00**
Circ: Statement: **174,287**
🕮 You Just Don't Quarrel with the Quintronic Man ★ Versus Quintronic Man.

214 ❑ Aug 1977 Cover: 0.30 **NM** value: **3.00**
Circ: Statement: **174,287**
🕮 The Jack of Hearts is Wild • Jack of Hearts **A:** Sal Buscema

215 ❑ Sep 1977 Cover: 0.30 **NM** value: **3.00**
Circ: Statement: **174,287**
🕮 Home Is Where The Hurt Is **A:** Ernie Chan; Sal Buscema **W:** Len Wein ★ 1st Appearance of Bi-Beast II.

216 ❑ Oct 1977 Cover: 0.30 **NM** value: **3.00**
Circ: Statement: **174,287**
🕮 Countdown to Catastrophe ★ Versus Bi-Beast II.

217 ❑ Nov 1977 Cover: 0.35 **NM** value: **3.00**
Circ: Statement: **174,287**
🕮 The Circus of Lost Sould ★ Versus Circus of Crime.

218 ❑ Dec 1977 Cover: 0.35 **NM** value: **3.00**
Circ: Statement: **174,287**
🕮 The Rhino Doesn't Stop Here Any More • Doc Samson vs. Rhino

219 ❑ Jan 1978 Cover: 0.35 **NM** value: **3.00**
Circ: Statement: **171,931**
🕮 No Man is an Island

220 ❑ Feb 1978 Cover: 0.35 **NM** value: **3.00**
Circ: Statement: **171,931**
🕮 Fury at 5,000 Fathoms

221 ❑ Mar 1978 Cover: 0.35 **NM** value: **3.00**
Circ: Statement: **171,931**
🕮 Show Me The Way To Go Home • Has 1977 Statement, filed 9/20/77; avg print run 380,845; avg sales 169,195; avg subs 5,092; avg total paid 174,287; samples 200; max existent 175,947; 54% of run returned **A:** Sal Buscema; Alfredo Alcala **W:** Roger Stern ★ Appearance of Stingray.

222 ❑ Apr 1978 Cover: 0.35 **NM** value: **3.00**
Circ: Statement: **171,931**
🕮 Feeding Billy **A:** Jim Starlin; Alfredo Alcala

223 ❑ May 1978 Cover: 0.35 **NM** value: **3.00**
Circ: Statement: **171,931**
🕮 The Curing of Doctor Banner

224 ❑ Jun 1978 Cover: 0.35 **NM** value: **3.00**
Circ: Statement: **171,931 • CGC:** 1 graded, best 9.4
🕮 Follow the Leader

225 ❑ Jul 1978 Cover: 0.35 **NM** value: **3.00**
Circ: Statement: **171,931**
🕮 Is There Hulk After Death?

226 ❑ Aug 1978 Cover: 0.35 **NM** value: **3.00**
Circ: Statement: **171,931**
🕮 Big Monster on Campus

227 ❑ Sep 1978 Cover: 0.35 **NM** value: **3.00**
Circ: Statement: **171,931**
🕮 The Monster's Analyst • Doc Samson

228 ❑ Oct 1978 Cover: 0.35 **NM** value: **3.50**
Circ: Statement: **171,931**

CGC-graded: Multiply prices above by **33 for 9.9 M • 16 for 9.8 NM/M • 7 for 9.6 NM+ • 5 for 9.4 NM • 2.5 for 9.2 NM- • 1.5 for 9.0 VF/NM**

📖 Bad Moon on the Rise! ★ Origin of Moonstone. ★ 1st Appearance of Moonstone.

229 ❑ Nov 1978 Cover: 0.35 **NM** value: **3.00**
Circ: Statement: **171,931**
📖 The Moonstone is a Harsh Mistress ★ Appearance of Moonstone, Doc Samson.

230 ❑ Dec 1978 Cover: 0.35 **NM** value: **3.00**
Circ: Statement: **171,931**
📖 The Harvester from Beyond!

231 ❑ Jan 1979 Cover: 0.35 **NM** value: **3.00**
Circ: Statement: **276,805**
📖 Prelude!

232 ❑ Feb 1979 Cover: 0.35 **NM** value: **3.00**
Circ: Statement: **276,805**
📖 The Battle Below **A:** Sal Buscema ★ Appearance of Captain America.

233 ❑ Mar 1979 Cover: 0.35 **NM** value: **3.00**
Circ: Statement: **276,805 • CGC:** 1 graded, best 9.4
📖 ... At the Bottom of the Bay • Has 1978 Statement, filed 9/25/78; avg print run 379,314; avg sales 159,738; avg subs 12,193; avg total paid 171,931; samples 245; max existent 174,026; 54% of run returned **A:** Sal Buscema ★ Appearance of Marvel Man (Quasar).

234 ❑ Apr 1979 Cover: 0.35 **NM** value: **3.00**
Circ: Statement: **276,805**
📖 Battleground: Berkeley! • (Marvel Man changed name to Quasar); (Marvel Man changed name to Quasar) **A:** Sal Buscema ★ 1st Appearance of Quasar.

235 ❑ May 1979 Cover: 0.40 **NM** value: **3.00**
Circ: Statement: **276,805**
📖 The Monster and the Machine **A:** Sal Buscema ★ Appearance of Machine Man.

236 ❑ Jun 1979 Cover: 0.40 **NM** value: **3.00**
Circ: Statement: **276,805**
📖 Kill Or Be Killed **A:** Sal Buscema; Mike Esposito **W:** Roger Stern ★ Appearance of Machine Man.

237 ❑ Jul 1979 Cover: 0.40 **NM** value: **3.00**
Circ: Statement: **276,805**
📖 When a City Dies! **A:** Sal Buscema

238 ❑ Aug 1979 Cover: 0.40 **NM** value: **3.00**
Circ: Statement: **276,805**
📖 Post Hulk ... Post Holocaust! **A:** Sal Buscema

239 ❑ Sep 1979 Cover: 0.40 **NM** value: **3.00**
Circ: Statement: **276,805**
📖 All That Glitters ... **A:** Sal Buscema

240 ❑ Oct 1979 Cover: 0.40 **NM** value: **3.00**
Circ: Statement: **276,805**
📖 ... And Now El Dorado **A:** Sal Buscema

241 ❑ Nov 1979 Cover: 0.40 **NM** value: **2.50**
Circ: Statement: **276,805**
📖 Partners in Deception **A:** Sal Buscema

242 ❑ Dec 1979 Cover: 0.40 **NM** value: **2.50**
Circ: Statement: **276,805**
📖 Sic Semper Tyrannus! **A:** Sal Buscema ★ Versus Tyranus.

243 ❑ Jan 1980 Cover: 0.40 **NM** value: **2.50**
Circ: Statement: **201,000**
📖 Death – and Destiny! **A:** Sal Buscema ★ Appearance of Power Man and Iron Fist.

244 ❑ Feb 1980 Cover: 0.40 **NM** value: **2.50**
Circ: Statement: **201,000 • CGC:** 1 graded, best 9.4
📖 It Lives! **A:** Sal Buscema ★ Death of It, the Living Colossus.

245 ❑ Mar 1980 Cover: 0.40 **NM** value: **2.50**
Circ: Statement: **201,000**
📖 When the Hulk Comes Raging! • Has 1979 Statement, filed 10/1/79; avg print run 509,287; avg sales 255,636; avg subs 21,169; avg total paid 276,805; samples 596; max existent 278,880; 45% of run returned **A:** Sal Buscema

246 ❑ Apr 1980 Cover: 0.40 **NM** value: **2.50**
Circ: Statement: **201,000**
📖 The Hero and the Hulk! **A:** Sal Buscema ★ Appearance of Captain Marvel.

247 ❑ May 1980 Cover: 0.40 **NM** value: **2.50**
Circ: Statement: **201,000**
📖 Jarella's World **A:** Sal Buscema ★ Appearance of Jarella.

248 ❑ Jun 1980 Cover: 0.40 **NM** value: **2.50**
Circ: Statement: **201,000**
📖 How Green My Garden Grows! **A:** Sal Buscema ★ Versus Gardener.

249 ❑ Jul 1980 Cover: 0.40 **NM** value: **2.50**
Circ: Statement: **201,000 • CGC:** 1 graded, best 9.4
📖 Jack Frost Nipping at Your Soul! **A:** Sal Buscema ★ Appearance of Jack Frost.

250 ❑ Aug 1980 Cover: 0.75 **NM** value: **6.00**
Circ: Statement: **201,000 • CGC:** 7 graded, best 9.6
• Giant-sized. 📖 Monster! **A:** Sal Buscema **W:** Bill Mantlo ★ 1st Appearance of Sabra (cameo). ★ Appearance of Silver Surfer.

251 ❑ Sep 1980 Cover: 0.50 **NM** value: **2.50**
Circ: Statement: **201,000**
📖 Whatever Happened To The 3D Man? **A:** Sal Buscema **W:** Bill Mantlo ★ Appearance of 3-D Man.

252 ❑ Oct 1980 Cover: 0.50 **NM** value: **2.50**
Circ: Statement: **201,000**
📖 The Changelings, Part 1 **A:** Sal Buscema **W:** Bill Mantlo ★ Appearance of Changelings.

253 ❑ Nov 1980 Cover: 0.50 **NM** value: **2.50**
Circ: Statement: **201,000**
📖 The Changelings, Part 2 **A:** Sal Buscema **W:** Bill Mantlo ★ Appearance of Doc Samson, Changelings.

254 ❑ Dec 1980 Cover: 0.50 **NM** value: **2.50**
Circ: Statement: **201,000**
📖 Waiting For The U-Foes! **A:** Sal Buscema **W:** Bill Mantlo ★ Origin of X-Ray, Vector, U-Foes, Ironclad. ★ 1st Appearance of X-Ray, Vector, U-Foes, Ironclad.

255 ❑ Jan 1981 Cover: 0.50 **NM** value: **2.50**
📖 Thunder Under The East River! **A:** Sal Buscema **W:** Bill Mantlo ★ Versus Thor.

256 ❑ Feb 1981 Cover: 0.50 **NM** value: **2.50**
📖 Power In The Promised Land! **A:** Sal Buscema **W:** Bill Mantlo ★ Origin of Sabra. ★ 1st Appearance of Sabra (full).

257 ❑ Mar 1981 Cover: 0.50 **NM** value: **2.50**
📖 Crypt Of Chaos **A:** Sal Buscema **W:** Bill Mantlo ★ Origin of Arabian Knight. ★ 1st Appearance of Arabian Knight.

258 ❑ Apr 1981 Cover: 0.50 **NM** value: **2.50**
📖 ...To Hunt The Hulk! • Has 1980 Statement, filed 10/1/80; avg print run 498,415; avg sales 227,594; avg subs 25,118; avg total paid 252,712; samples 1,082; max existent 258,837; 48% of run returned **A:** Sal Buscema; Frank Miller(cover) **W:** Bill Mantlo ★ Origin of Ursa Major. ★ 1st Appearance of Ursa Major. ★ Versus Soviet Super-Soldiers.

259 ❑ May 1981 Cover: 0.50 **NM** value: **2.50**
📖 The Family That Dies Together **A:** Sal Buscema; Frank Miller(cover) **W:** Bill Mantlo ★ Origin of Presence, Vanguard. ★ Appearance of Soviet Super-Soldiers.

260 ❑ Jun 1981 Cover: 0.50 **NM** value: **2.50**
📖 Sunset Of A Samurai! **A:** Sal Buscema **W:** Bill Mantlo

261 ❑ Jul 1981 Cover: 0.50 **NM** value: **2.50**
📖 Encounter On Easter Island **A:** Sal Buscema; Frank Miller(cover) **W:** Bill Mantlo ★ Versus Absorbing Man.

262 ❑ Aug 1981 Cover: 0.50 **NM** value: **2.50**
📖 People In Glass Houses Shouldn't Hurt hulks! **A:** Sal Buscema **W:** Bill Mantlo

263 ❑ Sep 1981 Cover: 0.50 **NM** value: **2.50**
📖 I Feel The Earth Move Under My Feet, And The Sky Come Tumbling Down **A:** Sal Buscema **W:** Bill Mantlo ★ Versus Landslide, Avalanche.

264 ❑ Oct 1981 Cover: 0.50 **NM** value: **2.50**
📖 He Flies By Night **A:** Sal Buscema; Frank Miller(cover) **W:** Bill Mantlo

265 ❑ Nov 1981 Cover: 0.50 **NM** value: **2.50**
📖 You Can't Always Get What You Want, But If You Try Sometime You Might Just Find You Get What You Need! **A:** Sal Buscema **W:** Bill Mantlo ★ 1st Appearance of Shooting Star, Firebird. ★ Versus Rangers.

266 ❑ Dec 1981 Cover: 0.50 **NM** value: **2.50**
📖 Devolution! **A:** Sal Buscema **W:** Bill Mantlo ★ Versus High Evolutionary.

267 ❑ Jan 1982 Cover: 0.60 **NM** value: **2.50**
📖 The Goliath, The Gargoyle, And The Galaxy Master! **A:** Sal Buscema; Frank Miller(cover) **W:** Bill Mantlo ★ Origin of Glorian. ★ Versus Glorian.

268 ❑ Feb 1982 Cover: 0.60 **NM** value: **2.50**
📖 And They Called The Wind Pariah! **A:** Sal Buscema; Brent Anderson(cover) **W:** Bill Mantlo ★ Origin of Rick Jones.

269 ❑ Mar 1982 Cover: 0.60 **NM** value: **2.50**
📖 Enter: The Hulk Hunters! **A:** Sal Buscema **W:** Bill Mantlo

270 ❑ Apr 1982 Cover: 0.60 **NM** value: **2.50**
A: Sal Buscema

271 ❑ May 1982 Cover: 0.60 **NM** value: **2.50**
• 20th Anniversary Issue. 📖 Rocket Raccoon! **A:** Sal Buscema; Al Milgrom(cover) **W:** Bill Mantlo ★ 1st Appearance of Rocket Raccoon.

272 ❑ Jun 1982 Cover: 0.60 **NM** value: **2.50**
📖 Weidsong Of The Wen-di-go! **A:** Sal Buscema **W:** Bill Mantlo ★ Appearance of Alpha Flight.

273 ❑ Jul 1982 Cover: 0.60 **NM** value: **2.50**
📖 Once A Hulk, Always A Hulk! **A:** Sal Buscema **W:** Bill Mantlo ★ Appearance of Alpha Flight.

274 ❑ Aug 1982 Cover: 0.60 **NM** value: **2.50**
📖 Home The Hard Way! **A:** Sal Buscema **W:** Bill Mantlo

275 ❑ Sep 1982 Cover: 0.60 **NM** value: **2.50**
📖 Megalith! **A:** Sal Buscema; Joe Sinnott **W:** Bill Mantlo ★ Versus Megalith.

276 ❑ Oct 1982 Cover: 0.60 **NM** value: **2.50**
📖 The Return Of The U-Foes! **A:** Sal Buscema; Joe Sinnott **W:** Bill Mantlo ★ Versus U-Foes.

277 ❑ Nov 1982 Cover: 0.60 **NM** value: **2.50**
• **CGC:** 1 graded, best 9.4
📖 What Friends Are For! **A:** Sal Buscema **W:** Bill Mantlo ★ Versus U-Foes.

278 ❑ Dec 1982 Cover: 0.60 **NM** value: **2.50**
📖 Amnesty • Hulk granted amnesty **A:** Sal Buscema; Joe Sinnott **W:** Bill Mantlo

279 ❑ Jan 1983 Cover: 0.60 **NM** value: **2.50**
Circ: Statement: **189,337**
📖 Everybody Loves A Parade, Right? **A:** Sal Buscema; Greg LaRocque **W:** Bill Mantlo; Mark Gruenwald

280 ❑ Feb 1983 Cover: 0.60 **NM** value: **2.50**
Circ: Statement: **189,337**
📖 Alone In A Crowd! **A:** Sal Buscema; Andy Mushynsky **W:** Bill Mantlo

281 ❑ Mar 1983 Cover: 0.60 **NM** value: **2.50**
Circ: Statement: **189,337**
📖 Audition! **A:** Sal Buscema; Joe Sinnott **W:** Bill Mantlo

282 ❑ Apr 1983 Cover: 0.60 **NM** value: **2.50**
Circ: Statement: **189,337**
📖 Again Arsenal! **A:** Sal Buscema; Joe Sinnott **W:** Bill Mantlo ★ Appearance of She-Hulk.

283 ❑ May 1983 Cover: 0.60 **NM** value: **2.50**
Circ: Statement: **189,337**
📖 Follow The Leader! **A:** Sal Buscema ★ Appearance of Avengers.

284 ❑ Jun 1983 Cover: 0.60 **NM** value: **2.50**
Circ: Statement: **189,337**
📖 Time-Lost! **A:** Sal Buscema; Joe Sinnott **W:** Bill Mantlo ★ Appearance of Avengers. ★ Versus Leader.

285 ❑ Jul 1983 Cover: 0.60 **NM** value: **2.50**
Circ: Statement: **189,337 • CGC:** 1 graded, best 9.2
📖 Today Is The First Day Of the Rest Of My Life! **A:** Sal Buscema; Chic Stone **W:** Bill Mantlo

286 ❑ Aug 1983 Cover: 0.60 **NM** value: **2.50**
Circ: Statement: **189,337**
📖 Hero **A:** Sal Buscema; Kim Demulder **W:** Bill Mantlo

287 ❑ Sep 1983 Cover: 0.60 **NM** value: **2.50**
Circ: Statement: **189,337**
📖 Loose Ends! **A:** Sal Buscema; Chic Stone **W:** Bill Mantlo

288 ❑ Oct 1983 Cover: 0.60 **NM** value: **2.50**
Circ: Statement: **189,337**
📖 Yellow Fever?! **A:** Sal Buscema; Jim Mooney **W:** Bill Mantlo ★ Versus M.O.D.O.K..

289 ❑ Nov 1983 Cover: 0.60 **NM** value: **2.50**
Circ: Statement: **189,337**
📖 A.I.M. For The Top! **A:** Sal Buscema; Joe Sinnott **W:** Bill Mantlo ★ Versus A.I.M..

290 ❑ Dec 1983 Cover: 0.60 **NM** value: **2.50**
Circ: Statement: **189,337**
📖 Unholy Alliance **A:** Sal Buscema ★ Versus M.O.D.O.K.. ★ Versus Modame.

291 ❑ Jan 1984 Cover: 0.60 **NM** value: **2.50**
Circ: Statement: **196,567**
📖 Old Soldiers Never Die! • Assistant Editor Month **A:** Sal Buscema ★ Origin of Thunderbolt Ross.

292 ❑ Feb 1984 Cover: 0.60 **NM** value: **2.50**
Circ: Statement: **196,567**
📖 Dragon – Night! **A:** Sal Buscema

293 ❑ Mar 1984 Cover: 0.60 **NM** value: **2.50**
Circ: Statement: **196,567**
📖 Assassin! **A:** Sal Buscema ★ Versus Fantastic Four.

294 ❑ Apr 1984 Cover: 0.60 **NM** value: **2.50**
Circ: Statement: **196,567**
📖 From Out of the Night Comes ... Boomerang! **A:** Sal Buscema

295 ❑ May 1984 Cover: 0.60 **NM** value: **2.50**
Circ: Statement: **196,567**
📖 Turning Point! • Secret Wars aftermath; Has 1983 Statement, filed 10/4/83; avg print run 371,188; avg sales 160,510; avg subs 28,827; avg total paid 189,337; samples 833; max existent 194,826; 48% of run returned **A:** Sal Buscema ★ Versus Boomerang.

296 ❑ Jun 1984 Cover: 0.60 **NM** value: **2.50**
Circ: Statement: **196,567**
📖 To Kill or Cure! **A:** Sal Buscema ★ Versus ROM.

297 ❑ Jul 1984 Cover: 0.60 **NM** value: **2.50**
Circ: Statement: **196,567**
📖 Sleep, My Child ... **A:** Sal Buscema

298 ❑ Aug 1984 Cover: 0.60 **NM** value: **2.50**
Circ: Statement: **196,567**
📖 Sleepwalker! **A:** Sal Buscema ★ Appearance of Nightmare.

299 ❑ Sep 1984 Cover: 0.60 **NM** value: **2.50**
Circ: Statement: **196,567**
📖 Strange Days Have Found Us! **A:** Sal Buscema ★ Appearance of Doctor Strange.

300 ❑ Oct 1984 Cover: 1.00 **NM** value: **4.00**
Circ: Statement: **196,567 • CGC:** 2 graded, best 9.6
• 300th anniversary edition. 📖 Days of Rage! • Hulk banished to Crossroads **A:** Sal Buscema ★ Versus Everybody.

301 ❑ Nov 1984 Cover: 0.60 **NM** value: **2.50**
Circ: Statement: **196,567 • CGC:** 1 graded, best 9.4
📖 You Are Standing At The Crossroads! **A:** Sal Buscema **C:** Bill Sienkiewicz

302 ❑ Dec 1984 Cover: 0.60 **NM** value: **2.50**
Circ: Statement: **196,567**
📖 Lady of Life – City of Death **A:** Sal Buscema **C:** Mike Mignola

303 ❑ Jan 1985 Cover: 0.60 **NM** value: **2.50**
Circ: Statement: **172,033**
📖 Growing Up is Hard to Do! **A:** Sal Buscema

304 ❑ Feb 1985 Cover: 0.60 **NM** value: **2.50**
Circ: Statement: **172,033**
📖 Prisoners! **A:** Sal Buscema **C:** Mike Mignola

305 ❑ Mar 1985 Cover: 0.60 **NM** value: **2.50**
Circ: Statement: **172,033**
📖 Well, Well, Well, Hulk – Fancy Meeting You Here! **A:** Sal Buscema **C:** Mike Mignola ★ Versus U-Foes.

306 ❑ Apr 1985 Cover: 0.65 **NM** value: **2.50**
Circ: Statement: **172,033**
📖 Call Me Ishmael, Call Me ... Hulk! **A:** Sal Buscema **C:** Mike Mignola

307 ❑ May 1985 Cover: 0.65 **NM** value: **2.50**
Circ: Statement: **172,033** CapCity orders: **10,000**
📖 ... The Hunt Across Worlds! **A:** Sal Buscema **C:** Mike Mignola

308 ❑ Jun 1985 Cover: 0.65 **NM** value: **2.50**
Circ: Statement: **172,033** CapCity orders: **10,100**
📖 ... And Here There Be – Demons! • Has 1984 Statement, filed 9/28/84; avg print run 258,727; avg sales 163,228; avg subs 33,339; avg total paid 196,567; samples 190; max existent 197,459; 45% of run returned **A:** Sal Buscema **C:** Mike Mignola

309 ❑ Jul 1985 Cover: 0.65 **NM** value: **2.50**
Circ: Statement: **172,033** CapCity orders: **10,500**
📖 The Triad! **A:** Sal Buscema **C:** Mike Mignola

310 ❑ Aug 1985 Cover: 0.65 **NM** value: **2.50**
Circ: Statement: **172,033** CapCity orders: **10,800**
📖 Banner Redux **A:** Sal Buscema

311 ❑ Sep 1985 Cover: 0.65 **NM** value: **2.50**
Circ: Statement: **172,033** CapCity orders: **10,900**
📖 Life is a Four-Letter Word **A:** Mike Mignola; Sal Buscema **C:** Al Williamson

312 ❑ Oct 1985 Cover: 0.65 **NM** value: **2.50**
Circ: Statement: **172,033** CapCity orders: **19,300**
📖 Monster • Secret Wars II **A:** Mike Mignola **C:** Bill Sienkiewicz

313 ❑ Nov 1985 Cover: 0.65 **NM** value: **2.50**
Circ: Statement: **172,033** CapCity orders: **18,500**
📖 Hook, Line & Sinker! **C:** Mike Mignola ★ Appearance of Alpha Flight.

314 ❑ Dec 1985 Cover: 0.65 **NM** value: **2.50**
Circ: Statement: **172,033** CapCity orders: **27,900**
📖 Call of the Desert; Life Among the Fallen ...; Yesterday's Sorrows; Yesterday's Foes!; **A:** John Byrne ★ Appearance of Doc Samson.

315 ❑ Jan 1986 Cover: 0.65 **NM** value: **3.00**
Circ: Statement: **196,933** CapCity orders: **24,200**
📖 Freedom! • Hulk and Banner separated **A:** John Byrne

316 ❑ Feb 1986 Cover: 0.75 **NM** value: **3.00**
Circ: Statement: **196,933** CapCity orders: **26,200**
📖 Battleground **A:** John Byrne ★ Appearance of Avengers.

317 ❑ Mar 1986 Cover: 0.75 **NM** value: **3.00**
Circ: Statement: **196,933** CapCity orders: **24,200**
📖 You're Probably Wondering Why I Called You Here Today ... **A:** John Byrne

318 ❑ Apr 1986 Cover: 0.75 **NM** value: **3.00**

Other grades: Multiply prices above by **1.5 for Mint • 2/3 for Very Fine • 1/3 for Fine • 1/5 for Very Good • 1/8 for Good**

Circ: Statement: **196,933** CapCity orders: **24,300**
📖 Baptism of Fire • Has 1985 Statement, filed 10/1/85; avg print run 327,017; avg sales 162,458; avg subs 9,575; avg total paid 172,033; samples 373; max existent 173,201; 47% of run returned **A:** John Byrne

319 ❑ May 1986 Cover: 0.75 **NM** value: **3.00**
Circ: Statement: **196,933** CapCity orders: **24,500**
📖 Member of the Wedding • Wedding of Bruce Banner and Betty Ross **A:** John Byrne

320 ❑ Jun 1986 Cover: 0.75 **NM** value: **2.00**
Circ: Statement: **196,933** CapCity orders: **16,500**
📖 Honeymoon's Over!! **A:** Al Milgrom; Dell Barras **W:** Al Milgrom ★ Versus Doc Samson.

321 ❑ Jul 1986 Cover: 0.75 **NM** value: **2.00**
Circ: Statement: **196,933** CapCity orders: **16,300**
📖 ...And The Walls Come Tumbling Down! **A:** Al Milgrom; Dell Barras **W:** Al Milgrom ★ Versus Avengers.

322 ❑ Aug 1986 Cover: 0.75 **NM** value: **2.00**
Circ: Statement: **196,933** CapCity orders: **16,300**
📖 Must The Hulk Die? **A:** Al Milgrom; Dell Barras **W:** Al Milgrom

323 ❑ Sep 1986 Cover: 0.75 **NM** value: **2.00**
Circ: Statement: **196,933** CapCity orders: **15,800**
📖 Certain Intangibles **A:** Al Milgrom; Dell Barras; Dan Bulanadi **W:** Al Milgrom

324 ❑ Oct 1986 Cover: 0.75 **NM** value: **6.00**
Circ: Statement: **196,933** CapCity orders: **16,650** • **CGC:** 6 graded, best 9.4
📖 The More Things Change ... ★ Origin of Hulk. ★ 1st Appearance of Grey Hulk (new).

325 ❑ Nov 1986 Cover: 0.75 **NM** value: **3.00**
Circ: Statement: **196,933** CapCity orders: **16,700**
📖 The New Hulk! ★ 1st Appearance of Rick Jones as green Hulk.

326 ❑ Dec 1986 Cover: 0.75 **NM** value: **3.50**
Circ: Statement: **196,933** CapCity orders: **17,900**
📖 Desert Heat • Green Hulk vs. Grey Hulk

327 ❑ Jan 1987 Cover: 0.75 **NM** value: **2.50**
Circ: Statement: **153,691** CapCity orders: **16,200**
📖 As Others See Us! ★ Versus Zzzax.

328 ❑ Feb 1987 Cover: 0.75 **NM** value: **2.50**
Circ: Statement: **153,691** CapCity orders: **16,300**
📖 Piece of Mind • 1st Peter David writing **W:** Peter David

329 ❑ Mar 1987 Cover: 0.75 **NM** value: **2.00**
Circ: Statement: **153,691** CapCity orders: **15,600**
📖 Outcasts!

330 ❑ Apr 1987 Cover: 0.75 **NM** value: **4.00**
Circ: Statement: **153,691** CapCity orders: **16,000** • **CGC:** 27 graded, best 9.8
📖 Head Games!! (An Old Soldier Dies!) **A:** Todd McFarlane ★ Death of Thunderbolt Ross.

331 ❑ May 1987 Cover: 0.75 **NM** value: **4.00**
Circ: Statement: **153,691** CapCity orders: **14,700** • **CGC:** 3 graded, best 9.4
📖 Inconstant Moon • 2nd Peter David issue; gray Hulk revealed **A:** Todd McFarlane **W:** Peter David

332 ❑ Jun 1987 Cover: 0.75 **NM** value: **4.00**
Circ: Statement: **153,691** CapCity orders: **14,400** • **CGC:** 1 graded, best 9.4
A: Todd McFarlane

333 ❑ Jul 1987 Cover: 0.75 **NM** value: **4.00**
Circ: Statement: **153,691** CapCity orders: **13,800**
A: Todd McFarlane

334 ❑ Aug 1987 Cover: 0.75 **NM** value: **4.00**
Circ: Statement: **153,691** CapCity orders: **14,000** • **CGC:** 3 graded, best 9.6
📖 Grave Circumstances **A:** Todd McFarlane

335 ❑ Sep 1987 Cover: 0.75 **NM** value: **2.00**
Circ: Statement: **153,691** CapCity orders: **15,000** • **CGC:** 1 graded, best 9.4
A: Todd McFarlane

336 ❑ Oct 1987 Cover: 0.75 **NM** value: **3.00**
Circ: Statement: **153,691** CapCity orders: **20,800**
📖 X-tremes! **A:** Todd McFarlane ★ Appearance of X-Factor.

337 ❑ Nov 1987 Cover: 0.75 **NM** value: **3.00**
Circ: Statement: **153,691** CapCity orders: **20,400**
📖 Crossroads **A:** Todd McFarlane ★ Appearance of X-Factor.

338 ❑ Dec 1987 Cover: 0.75 **NM** value: **3.00**
Circ: Statement: **153,691** CapCity orders: **16,200**
📖 Mercy Killing **A:** Todd McFarlane ★ 1st Appearance of Mercy.

339 ❑ Jan 1988 Cover: 0.75 **NM** value: **3.00**
Circ: Statement: **163,850** CapCity orders: **17,400** • **CGC:** 1 graded, best 9.6
📖 Native Son **A:** Todd McFarlane ★ Appearance of Ashcan, Leader.

340 ❑ Feb 1988 Cover: 0.75 **NM** value: **12.00**
Circ: Statement: **163,850** CapCity orders: **32,200** • **CGC:** 217 graded, best 9.8
📖 Vicious Circle **A:** Todd McFarlane ★ Versus Wolverine.

341 ❑ Mar 1988 Cover: 0.75 **NM** value: **2.00**
Circ: Statement: **163,850** CapCity orders: **19,400** • **CGC:** 1 graded, best 9.6
📖 The Savage Bull Doth Bear The Yoke! **A:** Todd McFarlane ★ Versus Man-Bull.

342 ❑ Apr 1988 Cover: 0.75 **NM** value: **2.00**
Circ: Statement: **163,850** CapCity orders: **20,500** • **CGC:** 1 graded, best 9.0
📖 No Human Fears **A:** Todd McFarlane ★ Appearance of Leader.

343 ❑ May 1988 Cover: 0.75 **NM** value: **2.00**
Circ: Statement: **163,850** CapCity orders: **21,100**
📖 Beyond Redemption **A:** Todd McFarlane

344 ❑ Jun 1988 Cover: 0.75 **NM** value: **2.00**
Circ: Statement: **163,850** CapCity orders: **20,950** • **CGC:** 1 graded, best 9.6
📖 Pyrrhic Victory **A:** Todd McFarlane

345 ❑ Jul 1988 Cover: 1.50 **NM** value: **2.00**
Circ: Statement: **163,850** CapCity orders: **22,400** • **CGC:** 1 graded, best 9.2
• Double-size. 📖 Closing Curtain **A:** Todd McFarlane

346 ❑ Aug 1988 Cover: 0.75 **NM** value: **2.00**
Circ: Statement: **163,850** CapCity orders: **22,600**
📖 Whys and Wherefores **A:** Todd McFarlane **W:** Peter David

347 ❑ Sep 1988 Cover: 0.75 **NM** value: **2.00**
Circ: Statement: **163,850** CapCity orders: **22,100**
📖 Crap Shoot • in Vegas **W:** Peter David

348 ❑ Oct 1988 Cover: 0.75 **NM** value: **2.00**
Circ: Statement: **163,850** CapCity orders: **22,300**
📖 Job Security **W:** Peter David ★ Versus Absorbing Man.

349 ❑ Nov 1988 Cover: 0.75 **NM** value: **2.00**
Circ: Statement: **163,850** CapCity orders: **24,700**
📖 Warzone **W:** Peter David ★ Appearance of Spider-Man.

350 ❑ Dec 1988 Cover: 0.75 **NM** value: **3.00**
Circ: Statement: **163,850** CapCity orders: **25,700**
📖 Before the Fall • Hulk vs. Thing **W:** Peter David

351 ❑ Jan 1989 Cover: 0.75 **NM** value: **2.00**
Circ: Statement: **157,892** CapCity orders: **23,500**
📖 Total Recall **W:** Peter David

352 ❑ Feb 1989 Cover: 0.75 **NM** value: **2.00**
Circ: Statement: **157,892** CapCity orders: **23,000**
📖 Fervor **W:** Peter David

353 ❑ Mar 1989 Cover: 0.75 **NM** value: **2.00**
Circ: Statement: **157,892** CapCity orders: **25,000**
📖 Down and Out in ... Las Vegas **W:** Peter David

354 ❑ Apr 1989 Cover: 0.75 **NM** value: **2.00**
Circ: Statement: **157,892** CapCity orders: **25,700**
📖 The Sure Thing **W:** Peter David

355 ❑ May 1989 Cover: 0.75 **NM** value: **2.00**
Circ: Statement: **157,892** CapCity orders: **25,000**
📖 Now You See It ... **W:** Peter David ★ Appearance of Glorian.

356 ❑ Jun 1989 Cover: 0.75 **NM** value: **2.00**
Circ: Statement: **157,892** CapCity orders: **24,200**
📖 Control Problems **W:** Peter David

357 ❑ Jul 1989 Cover: 0.75 **NM** value: **2.00**
Circ: Statement: **157,892** CapCity orders: **23,700**
📖 Possibilities **A:** Jeff Purves **W:** Peter David

358 ❑ Aug 1989 Cover: 0.75 **NM** value: **2.00**
Circ: Statement: **157,892** CapCity orders: **23,800**
📖 Inferno-2 Hulk – – – 0 **A:** Jeff Purves **W:** Peter David

359 ❑ Sep 1989 Cover: 1.00 **NM** value: **2.00**
Circ: Statement: **157,892** CapCity orders: **23,000** • **CGC:** 1 graded, best 8.5
📖 Soul Man **W:** Peter David

360 ❑ Oct 1989 Cover: 1.00 **NM** value: **2.00**
Circ: Statement: **157,892** CapCity orders: **23,100**
📖 Nightmoves **A:** Dan Reed **W:** Bob Harras ★ Versus Nightmare.

361 ❑ Nov 1989 Cover: 1.00 **NM** value: **2.00**
Circ: Statement: **157,892** CapCity orders: **24,400**
📖 Iron Tears • Iron Man **W:** Peter David

362 ❑ Nov 1989 Cover: 1.00 **NM** value: **2.00**
Circ: Statement: **157,892** CapCity orders: **24,300** • **CGC:** 1 graded, best 9.2
📖 Phasing Out **W:** Peter David ★ Appearance of Werewolf by Night.

363 ❑ Dec 1989 Cover: 1.00 **NM** value: **2.00**
Circ: Statement: **157,892** CapCity orders: **25,500**
📖 Acts of Vengeance • Acts of Vengeance **W:** Peter David ★ Versus Grey Gargoyle.

364 ❑ Dec 1989 Cover: 1.00 **NM** value: **2.00**
Circ: Statement: **157,892** CapCity orders: **26,700**
📖 Countdown, Part 1; Abomination **C:** Walt Simonson **W:** Peter David ★ Versus Abomination.

365 ❑ Jan 1990 Cover: 1.00 **NM** value: **2.00**
Circ: Statement: **164,524** CapCity orders: **26,800**
📖 Countdown, Part 2; Fantastic Four **C:** Walt Simonson **W:** Peter David ★ Versus Thing.

366 ❑ Feb 1990 Cover: 1.00 **NM** value: **2.00**
Circ: Statement: **164,524** CapCity orders: **27,000**
📖 Countdown, Part 3; The Leader **C:** Walt Simonson **W:** Peter David ★ Versus Leader.

367 ❑ Mar 1990 Cover: 1.00 **NM** value: **4.00**
Circ: Statement: **164,524** CapCity orders: **28,600** • **CGC:** 2 graded, best 9.8
📖 Countdown, Part 4; Madman • 1st Dale Keown art **A:** Dale Keown **C:** Walt Simonson **W:** Peter David ★ Versus Madman.

368 ❑ Apr 1990 Cover: 1.00 **NM** value: **4.00**
Circ: Statement: **164,524** CapCity orders: **25,800** • **CGC:** 1 graded, best 9.4
📖 Natural Selection **A:** Sam Kieth **W:** Peter David ★ 1st Appearance of Pantheon. ★ Versus Mr. Hyde.

369 ❑ May 1990 Cover: 1.00 **NM** value: **4.00**
Circ: Statement: **164,524** CapCity orders: **27,000**
📖 Silent Screams **W:** Peter David ★ Versus Freedom Force.

370 ❑ Jun 1990 Cover: 1.00 **NM** value: **4.00**
Circ: Statement: **164,524** CapCity orders: **28,700**
📖 Strange Matters **W:** Peter David ★ Appearance of Doctor Strange, Sub-Mariner.

371 ❑ Jul 1990 Cover: 1.00 **NM** value: **4.00**
Circ: Statement: **164,524** CapCity orders: **29,200**
📖 Strange But True **W:** Peter David ★ Appearance of Doctor Strange, Sub-Mariner.

372 ❑ Aug 1990 Cover: 1.00 **NM** value: **5.00**
Circ: Statement: **164,524** CapCity orders: **32,100** • **CGC:** 2 graded, best 9.6
📖 He's Back • Green Hulk returns **W:** Peter David

373 ❑ Sep 1990 Cover: 1.00 **NM** value: **2.50**
Circ: Statement: **164,524** CapCity orders: **30,800**
📖 Mending Fences **W:** Peter David

374 ❑ Oct 1990 Cover: 1.00 **NM** value: **2.50**
Circ: Statement: **164,524** CapCity orders: **30,100**
📖 No Autographs **W:** Peter David ★ Versus Super Skrull.

375 ❑ Nov 1990 Cover: 1.00 **NM** value: **2.50**
Circ: Statement: **164,524** CapCity orders: **30,100**
📖 Night of the Living Skrulls **W:** Peter David ★ Versus Super Skrull.

376 ❑ Dec 1990 Cover: 1.00 **NM** value: **2.50**
Circ: Statement: **164,524** CapCity orders: **30,400**
📖 Personality Conflict • Green Hulk vs. Grey Hulk **W:** Peter David ★ 1st Appearance of Agamemnon (as hologram).

377 ❑ Jan 1991 Cover: 1.00 **NM** value: **4.00**
Circ: Statement: **207,567** CapCity orders: **58,600** • **CGC:** 29 graded, best 9.8
Fluorescent inks on cover. 📖 Honey, I Shrunk The Hulk! **A:** Dale Keown **W:** Peter David ★ 1st Appearance of Hulk (new, smart).

377-2❑ Jan 1991 Cover: 1.00 **NM** value: **2.00**
Fluorescent inks on cover. 📖 Honey, I Shrunk The Hulk! • 2nd printing (gold) **W:** Peter David ★ 1st Appearance of Hulk (new, smart).

377-3❑ Jan 1991 Cover: 1.75 **NM** value: **Cover or less**

378 ❑ Feb 1991 Cover: 1.00 **NM** value: **1.50**
Circ: Statement: **207,567** CapCity orders: **37,600**
📖 Rhino Plastered • Rhino as Santa **W:** Peter David

379 ❑ Mar 1991 Cover: 1.00 **NM** value: **2.00**
Circ: Statement: **207,567** CapCity orders: **42,900** • **CGC:** 1 graded, best 9.6
📖 Hit and Myth **W:** Peter David ★ Appearance of Pantheon.

380 ❑ Apr 1991 Cover: 1.00 **NM** value: **2.00**
Circ: Statement: **207,567** CapCity orders: **37,200**
• Doc Samson solo story; Has 1990 Statement, filed 10/1/90; avg print run 271,132; avg sales 156,541; avg subs 7,983; avg total paid 164,524; samples 150; max existent 165,274; 39% of run returned **W:** Peter David

381 ❑ May 1991 Cover: 1.00 **NM** value: **2.00**
Circ: Statement: **207,567** CapCity orders: **39,000**
📖 Exposition • Hulk joins Pantheon **A:** Dale Keown **W:** Peter David

382 ❑ Jun 1991 Cover: 1.00 **NM** value: **2.00**
Circ: Statement: **207,567** CapCity orders: **42,500**
📖 Moving On **A:** Dale Keown **W:** Peter David

383 ❑ Jul 1991 Cover: 1.00 **NM** value: **2.00**
Circ: Statement: **207,567** CapCity orders: **58,800**
📖 Green Canard **A:** Dale Keown **W:** Peter David ★ Versus Abomination.

384 ❑ Aug 1991 Cover: 1.00 **NM** value: **2.00**
Circ: Statement: **207,567** CapCity orders: **58,500**
📖 Infinity Gauntlet; Small Talk • Infinity Gauntlet; tiny Hulk **A:** Dale Keown **W:** Peter David ★ Versus Abomination.

385 ❑ Sep 1991 Cover: 1.00 **NM** value: **2.00**
Circ: Statement: **207,567** CapCity orders: **59,400**
📖 Infinity Gauntlet • Infinity Gauntlet **A:** Dale Keown **W:** Peter David

386 ❑ Oct 1991 Cover: 1.00 **NM** value: **2.00**
Circ: Statement: **207,567** CapCity orders: **45,900**
📖 Little Hitler **A:** Dale Keown **W:** Peter David ★ Appearance of Sabra.

387 ❑ Nov 1991 Cover: 1.00 **NM** value: **2.00**
Circ: Statement: **207,567** CapCity orders: **45,600**
📖 Hiding Behind Mosques **A:** Dale Keown **W:** Peter David ★ Appearance of Sabra.

388 ❑ Dec 1991 Cover: 1.00 **NM** value: **2.00**
Circ: Statement: **207,567** CapCity orders: **49,500**
📖 Thicker Than Water **A:** Dale Keown **W:** Peter David ★ 1st Appearance of Speedfreek.

389 ❑ Jan 1992 Cover: 1.00 **NM** value: **2.00**
Circ: Statement: **299,775** CapCity orders: **43,800**
📖 Of Man and Man-Thing **W:** Peter David ★ Appearance of Man-Thing.

390 ❑ Feb 1992 Cover: 1.25 **NM** value: **2.00**
Circ: Statement: **299,775** CapCity orders: **49,500** • **CGC:** 1 graded, best 9.6
📖 War & Pieces, Part 1; This Means War **A:** Dale Keown **W:** Peter David

391 ❑ Mar 1992 Cover: 1.25 **NM** value: **2.00**
Circ: Statement: **299,775** CapCity orders: **47,100**
📖 War & Pieces, Part 2; X-Calation **A:** Dale Keown **W:** Peter David ★ Appearance of X-Factor.

392 ❑ Apr 1992 Cover: 1.25 **NM** value: **2.00**
Circ: Statement: **299,775** CapCity orders: **43,500**
📖 War & Pieces, Part 3; War And Pieces: Conclusion Fortunes Of War **A:** Dale Keown **W:** Peter David ★ Appearance of X-Factor.

393 ❑ May 1992 Cover: 2.50 **NM** value: **3.00**
Circ: Statement: **299,775** CapCity orders: **95,400** • **CGC:** 3 graded, best 9.9
• 30th Anniversary of the Hulk, Green Foil Cover. 📖 The Closing Circles; Classic Battles Of The Hulk **A:** Dale Keown **W:** Peter David

393-2❑ May 1992 Cover: 2.50 **NM** value: **Cover or less**

394 ❑ Jun 1992 Cover: 1.25 **NM** value: **1.50**
Circ: Statement: **299,775** CapCity orders: **45,300**
📖 Cold Storage **A:** Andrew Wildman **W:** Peter David ★ 1st Appearance of Trauma.

395 ❑ Jul 1992 Cover: 1.25 **NM** value: **1.50**
Circ: Statement: **299,775** CapCity orders: **55,800**
📖 Return To Vegas **A:** Dale Keown **W:** Peter David ★ Appearance of Punisher.

396 ❑ Aug 1992 Cover: 1.25 **NM** value: **1.50**
Circ: Statement: **299,775** CapCity orders: **62,700**
📖 Frost Bite **A:** Dale Keown **W:** Peter David ★ Appearance of Punisher. ★ Versus Mr. Frost. ★ Versus Doctor Octopus.

397 ❑ Sep 1992 Cover: 1.25 **NM** value: **1.50**
Circ: Statement: **299,775** CapCity orders: **52,500**
📖 Ghost of the Past, Part 1; Ghosts of the Past, Part 1 **A:** Dale Keown **W:** Peter David ★ Versus U-Foes.

398 ❑ Oct 1992 Cover: 1.25 **NM** value: **1.50**
Circ: Statement: **299,775** CapCity orders: **49,900**
📖 Ghost of the Past, Part 2; Ghosts of the Past, Part 2 **A:** Dale Keown **W:** Peter David ★ Versus Leader.

399 ❑ Nov 1992 Cover: 1.25 **NM** value: **1.50**
Circ: Statement: **299,775** CapCity orders: **48,800**
📖 Ghost of the Past, Part 3; Ghosts of the Past, Part 3 **A:** Jan Duursema **W:** Peter David ★ Death of Marlo.

400 ❑ Dec 1992 Cover: 2.50 **NM** value: **3.00**
Circ: Statement: **299,775** CapCity orders: **115,200** • **CGC:** 3 graded, best 9.6
Prism cover. 📖 Ghost of the Past, Part 4; Ghosts of the Past, Part 4 • Marlo revived **A:** Jan Duursema **W:** Peter David ★ Death of Leader.

400-2❑ Dec 1992 Cover: 2.50 **NM** value: **Cover or less**

401 ❑ Jan 1993 Cover: 1.25 **NM** value: **1.50**
Circ: Statement: **277,513** CapCity orders: **45,300**
📖 Filling Slots **A:** Jan Duursema **W:** Peter David ★ 1st Appearance of Agamemnon (physical). ★ Versus U-Foes.

402 ❑ Feb 1993 Cover: 1.25 **NM** value: **1.50**

CGC-graded: Multiply prices above by **33 for 9.9 M • 16 for 9.8 NM/M • 7 for 9.6 NM+ • 5 for 9.4 NM • 2.5 for 9.2 NM- • 1.5 for 9.0 VF/NM**

Circ: Statement: **277,513** CapCity orders: **43,800**
📖 The Forest For The Trees **A:** Jan Duursema **W:** Peter David ★ Appearance of Doc Samson. ★ Versus Juggernaut.
403 ❑ Mar 1993 Cover: 1.25 **NM** value: **1.50**
Circ: Statement: **277,513** CapCity orders: **40,800**
📖 In Memory Not Yet Green **A:** Gary Frank **W:** Peter David ★ Versus Juggernaut.
404 ❑ Apr 1993 Cover: 1.25 **NM** value: **1.50**
Circ: Statement: **277,513** CapCity orders: **42,800**
📖 Disarray, Thataway **W:** Peter David ★ Appearance of Avengers. ★ Versus Juggernaut.
405 ❑ May 1993 Cover: 1.25 **NM** value: **1.50**
Circ: Statement: **277,513** CapCity orders: **41,200**
📖 Downtime **A:** Gary Frank **W:** Peter David
406 ❑ Jun 1993 Cover: 1.25 **NM** value: **1.50**
Circ: Statement: **277,513** CapCity orders: **41,200**
📖 American Pie **A:** Gary Frank **W:** Peter David ★ Appearance of Doc Samson, Captain America.
407 ❑ Jul 1993 Cover: 1.25 **NM** value: **1.50**
Circ: Statement: **277,513** CapCity orders: **42,400**
📖 More Or Ness **A:** Gary Frank **W:** Peter David ★ 1st Appearance of Piecemeal.
408 ❑ Aug 1993 Cover: 1.25 **NM** value: **1.50**
Circ: Statement: **277,513** CapCity orders: **43,500**
📖 A Sinking Feeling **A:** Gary Frank **W:** Peter David ★ Death of Perseus. ★ Versus Madman.
409 ❑ Sep 1993 Cover: 1.25 **NM** value: **1.50**
Circ: Statement: **277,513** CapCity orders: **39,800**
📖 Royal Pain **A:** Gary Frank **W:** Peter David ★ Appearance of Killpower, Motormouth.
410 ❑ Oct 1993 Cover: 1.25 **NM** value: **1.50**
Circ: Statement: **277,513** CapCity orders: **39,100**
📖 Jailhouse Rock **A:** Gary Frank **W:** Peter David ★ Appearance of Doctor Samson, S.H.I.E.L.D., Nick Fury.
411 ❑ Nov 1993 Cover: 1.25 **NM** value: **1.50**
Circ: Statement: **277,513** CapCity orders: **38,800**
📖 Liberation Day **W:** Peter David ★ Appearance of Nick Fury.
412 ❑ Dec 1993 Cover: 1.25 **NM** value: **1.50**
Circ: Statement: **168,192** CapCity orders: **37,800**
📖 Blame That **A:** Paul Pelletier **W:** Peter David ★ Appearance of She-Hulk. ★ Versus Bi-Beast.
413 ❑ Jan 1994 Cover: 1.25 **NM** value: **1.50**
Circ: Statement: **168,192** CapCity orders: **35,800**
📖 Troyjan War, Part 1; The Troyjan War, Part 1 **A:** Gary Frank **W:** Peter David
414 ❑ Feb 1994 Cover: 1.25 **NM** value: **1.50**
Circ: Statement: **168,192** CapCity orders: **36,100**
📖 Troyjan War, Part 2; The Troyjan War, Part 2 **A:** Gary Frank **W:** Peter David ★ Appearance of Silver Surfer.
415 ❑ Mar 1994 Cover: 1.25 **NM** value: **1.50**
Circ: Statement: **168,192** CapCity orders: **36,350**
📖 Troyjan War, Part 3; The Troyjan War, Part 3 **W:** Peter David ★ Appearance of Starjammers.
416 ❑ Apr 1994 Cover: 1.25 **NM** value: **1.50**
Circ: Statement: **168,192** CapCity orders: **35,350**
📖 Troyjan War, Part 4; The Troyjan War, Part 4 **W:** Peter David
417 ❑ May 1994 Cover: 1.50 **NM** value: **Cover or less**
Circ: Statement: **168,192** CapCity orders: **35,550**
📖 Party Animals • Rick's bachelor party **W:** Peter David
418 ❑ Jun 1994 Cover: 1.50 **NM** value: **2.00**
Circ: Statement: **168,192** CapCity orders: **44,850** • **CGC:** 1 graded, best 9.8
📖 We Are Gathered Here • Wedding of Rick Jones and Marlo; Peter David (writer) puts himself in script **A:** Gary Frank **W:** Peter David ★ Appearance of (of Sandman) appearance, (of Sandman) appearance.
418/SC ❑ Jun 1994 Cover: 2.50 **NM** value: **3.00**
Die-cut cover. 📖 We Are Gathered Here • Wedding of Rick Jones and Marlo; Peter David (writer) puts himself in script **A:** Gary Frank **W:** Peter David.
419 ❑ Jul 1994 Cover: 1.50 **NM** value: **Cover or less**
Circ: Statement: **168,192** CapCity orders: **33,800**
📖 The Last Waltz **A:** Roger Cruz **W:** Peter David ★ Versus Talos the Tamed.
420 ❑ Aug 1994 Cover: 1.50 **NM** value: **Cover or less**
Circ: Statement: **168,192** CapCity orders: **35,600**
📖 Lest Darkness Come **W:** Peter David ★ Death of Jim Wilson.
421 ❑ Sep 1994 Cover: 1.50 **NM** value: **Cover or less**
Circ: Statement: **168,192** CapCity orders: **33,700**
📖 Myth Conceptions, Part 1 **W:** Peter David ★ Versus Thor.
422 ❑ Oct 1994 Cover: 1.50 **NM** value: **Cover or less**
Circ: Statement: **168,192** CapCity orders: **31,800**
📖 Myth Conceptions, Part 2 **W:** Peter David
423 ❑ Nov 1994 Cover: 1.50 **NM** value: **Cover or less**
Circ: Statement: **123,003** CapCity orders: **30,800**
📖 Myth Conceptions, Part 3 **W:** Peter David ★ Appearance of Hel.
424 ❑ Dec 1994 Cover: 1.50 **NM** value: **Cover or less**
Circ: Statement: **123,003** CapCity orders: **31,250**
📖 Fall of the Pantheon, Part 1 **W:** Peter David
425 ❑ Jan 1995 Cover: 2.25 **NM** value: **Cover or less**
• **CGC:** 2 graded, best 9.9
• Giant-size. 📖 Fall of the Pantheon, Part 2 **W:** Peter David
425/SC ❑ Jan 1995 Cover: 3.50 **NM** value: **Cover or less**
Circ: Statement: **123,003** CapCity orders: **39,250**
Hologram cover. • Giant-size. 📖 Fall of the Pantheon, Part 2 **W:** Peter David
426 ❑ Feb 1995 Cover: 1.50 **NM** value: **Cover or less**
📖 One Fell Off • Hulk reverts to Banner **A:** Liam Sharp **W:** Peter David
426/Dlx ❑ Feb 1995 Cover: 1.95 **NM** value: **Cover or less**
Circ: Statement: **123,003** CapCity orders: **29,175**
• Deluxe edition. 📖 One Fell Off **A:** Liam Sharp **W:** Peter David
427 ❑ Mar 1995 Cover: 1.95 **NM** value: **Cover or less**
📖 Six Months Later … **W:** Peter David ★ Appearance of Man-Thing.
427/Dlx ❑ Mar 1995 Cover: 1.95 **NM** value: **Cover or less**
Circ: Statement: **123,003** CapCity orders: **28,450**
📖 Six Months Later … **W:** Peter David
428 ❑ Apr 1995 Cover: 1.95 **NM** value: **Cover or less**
📖 Swamped **W:** Peter David ★ Appearance of Man-Thing.
428/Dlx ❑ Apr 1995 Cover: 1.95 **NM** value: **Cover or less**
Circ: Statement: **123,003** CapCity orders: **28,275**
📖 Swamped **W:** Peter David
429 ❑ May 1995 Cover: 1.95 **NM** value: **Cover or less**
📖 A Little Death **W:** Peter David
429/Dlx ❑ May 1995 Cover: 1.95 **NM** value: **Cover or less**
Circ: Statement: **123,003** CapCity orders: **30,025**
📖 A Little Death **W:** Peter David
430 ❑ Jun 1995 Cover: 1.95 **NM** value: **Cover or less**
Circ: Statement: **123,003** CapCity orders: **28,150**
📖 Sliced & Diced **W:** Peter David ★ Versus Speedfreek.
431 ❑ Jul 1995 Cover: 1.95 **NM** value: **Cover or less**
Circ: Statement: **123,003** CapCity orders: **27,400**
📖 Down Under **W:** Peter David ★ Versus Abomination.
432 ❑ Aug 1995 Cover: 1.95 **NM** value: **Cover or less**
Circ: Statement: **123,003** CapCity orders: **27,125**
W: Peter David ★ Versus Abomination.
433 ❑ Sep 1995 Cover: 1.95 **NM** value: **Cover or less**
Circ: Statement: **123,003**
📖 Over the Edge; Punishment Fit The Crime **W:** Peter David ★ Appearance of Punisher, Nick Fury.
434 ❑ Oct 1995 Cover: 1.95 **NM** value: **Cover or less**
Circ: Statement: **114,272**
📖 Funeral Story • Funeral of Nick Fury; OverPower cards inserted **W:** Peter David ★ Appearance of Howling Commandoes.
435 ❑ Nov 1995 Cover: 1.95 **NM** value: **Cover or less**
Circ: Statement: **114,272**
📖 The Unnatural • Casey at the Bat tribute **W:** Peter David ★ Versus Rhino.
436 ❑ Dec 1995 Cover: 1.95 **NM** value: **Cover or less**
Circ: Statement: **114,272**
📖 Ghosts of the Future, Part 1; Uncovered • continued in Cutting Edge #1 **A:** Angel Medina **W:** Peter David ★ Appearance of Maestro.
437 ❑ Jan 1996 Cover: 1.95 **NM** value: **Cover or less**
Circ: Statement: **114,272**
📖 Ghosts of the Future, Part 2; Head Cases • Has 1995 Statement, filed 10/1/95; avg print run 204,799; avg sales 118,737; avg subs 4,266; avg total paid 123,003; samples 750; max existent 124,253; 39% of run returned **W:** Peter David
438 ❑ Feb 1996 Cover: 1.95 **NM** value: **Cover or less**
Circ: Statement: **114,272**
📖 Ghosts of the Future, Part 3; Fragmented Personality **W:** Peter David
439 ❑ Mar 1996 Cover: 1.95 **NM** value: **Cover or less**
Circ: Statement: **114,272**
📖 Ghosts of the Future, Part 4; Scapegoat **A:** Angel Medina **W:** Peter David
440 ❑ Apr 1996 Cover: 1.95 **NM** value: **Cover or less**
Circ: Statement: **114,272**
📖 Ghosts of the Future, Part 5; The Big Bang **A:** Angel Medina **W:** Peter David ★ Versus Thor.
441 ❑ May 1996 Cover: 1.95 **NM** value: **Cover or less**
Circ: Statement: **114,272**
Pulp Fiction tribute cover. 📖 Hulk Fiction **W:** Peter David ★ Appearance of She-Hulk.
442 ❑ Jun 1996 Cover: 1.95 **NM** value: **Cover or less**
Circ: Statement: **114,272**
📖 Private Sessions • no Hulk **W:** Peter David ★ Appearance of She-Hulk, Doc Samson, Molecule Man.
443 ❑ Jul 1996 Cover: 1.95 **NM** value: **Cover or less**
Circ: Statement: **114,272**
📖 Then and Now **W:** Peter David ★ Appearance of Janis.
444 ❑ Aug 1996 Cover: 1.50 **NM** value: **Cover or less**
Circ: Statement: **114,272**
📖 Onslaught: Impact 1; Cable Vision **W:** Peter David ★ Versus Cable.
445 ❑ Sep 1996 Cover: 1.50 **NM** value: **Cover or less**
Circ: Statement: **114,272**
📖 Onslaught: Impact 2; Dancing in the Dark **W:** Peter David ★ Appearance of Avengers.
446 ❑ Oct 1996 Cover: 1.50 **NM** value: **Cover or less**
Circ: Statement: **119,864**
📖 I'll Take Manhattan • post-Onslaught; Hulk turns savage and highly radioactive **W:** Peter David
447 ❑ Nov 1996 Cover: 1.50 **NM** value: **Cover or less**
Circ: Statement: **119,864** Direct Market orders: **170,000**
📖 Survivor's Guilt **W:** Peter David
448 ❑ Dec 1996 Cover: 1.50 **NM** value: **Cover or less**
Circ: Statement: **119,864** Direct Market orders: **87,000**
📖 Line in the Sand **A:** Mike Deodato Jr. **W:** Peter David ★ Appearance of Pantheon.
449 ❑ Jan 1997 Cover: 1.50 **NM** value: **9.00**
Circ: Statement: **119,864** Direct Market orders: **86,750** • **CGC:** 10 graded, best 9.6
• Has 1996 Statement, filed 10/1/96; avg print run 165,977; avg sales 111,653; avg subs 2,619; avg total paid 114,272; samples 600; max existent 114,997; 31% of run returned **A:** Mike Deodato Jr. **W:** Peter David ★ 1st Appearance of The Thunderbolts.
450 ❑ Feb 1997 Cover: 2.95 **NM** value: **5.00**
Circ: Statement: **119,864** Direct Market orders: **84,250**
• Giant-size. 📖 Hurray for Hulk; A Little Leeway • connection to Heroes Reborn universe revealed **A:** Jeff Rebner; Mike Deodato Jr. **W:** Peter David ★ Appearance of Doctor Strange.
451 ❑ Mar 1997 Cover: 1.99 **NM** value: **2.00**
Circ: Statement: **119,864** Direct Market orders: **74,250**
📖 Island Getaway • Hulk takes over Duck Key **A:** Jeff Rebner; Mike Deodato Jr. **W:** Peter David
452 ❑ Apr 1997 Cover: 1.99 **NM** value: **2.00**
Circ: Statement: **119,864** Direct Market orders: **74,000**
📖 Take Charge Guy • Hulk vs. Hurricane Betty **A:** Mike Deodato Jr. **W:** Peter David
453 ❑ May 1997 Cover: 1.99 **NM** value: **2.00**
Circ: Statement: **119,864** Diamd. preorders: **75,794**
📖 Lock and Key • Hulk vs. Hulk **A:** Mike Deodato Jr. **W:** Peter David
454 ❑ Jun 1997 Cover: 1.99 **NM** value: **2.00**
Circ: Statement: **119,864** Diamd. preorders: **83,794**
📖 Best Intentions **A:** Adam Kubert **W:** Peter David
455 ❑ Aug 1997 Cover: 1.99 **NM** value: **2.00**
Circ: Statement: **119,864** Diamd. preorders: **80,731**
• gatefold summary. 📖 Waiting to X-hale • Thunderbolt Ross returns ★ Appearance of Apocalypse. ★ Versus X-Men.
456 ❑ Sep 1997 Cover: 1.99 **NM** value: **2.00**
Circ: Statement: **94,405** Diamd. preorders: **77,527**
• gatefold summary. 📖 War and Remembrance • Apocalypse transforms Hulk into War
457 ❑ Oct 1997 Cover: 1.99 **NM** value: **2.00**
Circ: Statement: **94,405** Diamd. preorders: **76,129**
• gatefold summary. 📖 Of Course You Realize This Means War ★ Versus Juggernaut.
458 ❑ Nov 1997 Cover: 1.99 **NM** value: **2.00**
Circ: Statement: **94,405** Diamd. preorders: **76,411**
• gatefold summary. 📖 Crash and Burn ★ Appearance of Mercy. ★ Versus Mr. Hyde.
459 ❑ Dec 1997 Cover: 1.99 **NM** value: **2.00**
Circ: Statement: **94,405** Diamd. preorders: **76,351**
• gatefold summary. 📖 Last Legs • Has 1997 Statement, filed 10/1/97; avg print run 169,858; avg sales 117,281; avg subs 2,583; avg total paid 119,864; samples 258; max existent 120,247; 29% of run returned ★ Appearance of Mercy. ★ Versus Abomination.
460 ❑ Jan 1998 Cover: 1.99 **NM** value: **2.00**
Circ: Statement: **94,405** Diamd. preorders: **77,021**
• gatefold summary. 📖 Homecoming • The Hulk and Bruce Banner are reunited; return of Maestro
461 ❑ Feb 1998 Cover: 1.99 **NM** value: **2.00**
Circ: Statement: **94,405** Diamd. preorders: **70,408**
• gatefold summary. 📖 Self Destruction ★ Versus Destroyer.
462 ❑ Mar 1998 Cover: 1.99 **NM** value: **2.00**
Circ: Statement: **94,405** Diamd. preorders: **67,760**
• gatefold summary. 📖 Reconciliations
463 ❑ Apr 1998 Cover: 1.99 **NM** value: **2.00**
Circ: Statement: **94,405** Diamd. preorders: **64,603**
• gatefold summary. 📖 College Daze
464 ❑ May 1998 Cover: 1.99 **NM** value: **2.00**
Circ: Statement: **94,405** Diamd. preorders: **64,993**
• gatefold summary. 📖 Battleground Earth **A:** Jack Kirby ★ Appearance of Silver Surfer.
465 ❑ Jun 1998 Cover: 1.99 **NM** value: **2.00**
Circ: Statement: **94,405** Diamd. preorders: **66,534**
• gatefold summary. 📖 Men in Green ★ Appearance of Reed Richards, Tony Stark.
466 ❑ Jul 1998 Cover: 1.99 **NM** value: **2.00**
Circ: Statement: **94,405** Diamd. preorders: **66,327**
• gatefold summary. 📖 Of All Sad Words … ★ Death of Betty Banner.
467 ❑ Aug 1998 Cover: 1.99 **NM** value: **2.00**
Circ: Statement: **94,405** Diamd. preorders: **67,190**
• gatefold summary. 📖 The Lone and Level Sands • final Peter David-written issue
468 ❑ Sep 1998 Cover: 1.99 **NM** value: **2.00**
Circ: Statement: **72,498** Diamd. preorders: **58,890**
• gatefold summary. 📖 A Dark Green Life • 1st Joe Casey issue
469 ❑ Oct 1998 Cover: 1.99 **NM** value: **2.00**
Circ: Statement: **72,498** Diamd. preorders: **55,850**
• gatefold summary. 📖 Adaptive Audience ★ Versus Super-Adaptoid.
470 ❑ Nov 1998 Cover: 1.99 **NM** value: **2.00**
Circ: Statement: **72,498** Diamd. preorders: **53,761**
• gatefold summary. • Has 1998 Statement, filed 10/1/98; avg print run 141,125; avg sales 92,034; avg subs 2,371; avg total paid 94,405; samples 258; max existent 94,788; 33% of run returned ★ Versus Circus of Crime.
471 ❑ Dec 1998 Cover: 1.99 **NM** value: **2.00**
Circ: Statement: **72,498** Diamd. preorders: **51,195**
• gatefold summary. 📖 Odds & Sods ★ Versus Circus of Crime.
472 ❑ Jan 1999 Cover: 1.99 **NM** value: **2.00**
Circ: Statement: **72,498** Diamd. preorders: **46,960**
• gatefold summary. 📖 The Great Astonishment, Part 1; Auld Lang Syne **W:** Joe Casey ★ Appearance of Xantarean.
473 ❑ Feb 1999 Cover: 1.99 **NM** value: **Cover or less**
Circ: Statement: **72,498** Diamd. preorders: **44,501**
• gatefold summary. 📖 The Great Astonishment, Part 2; The Edge of Universal Pain **W:** Joe Casey ★ Appearance of Xanterean, Watchers, Abomination.
474 ❑ Mar 1999 Cover: 2.99 **NM** value: **Cover or less**
Circ: Statement: **72,498** Diamd. preorders: **42,694**
📖 The Great Astonishment, Part 3; It's All True final issue. **W:** Joe Casey ★ Appearance of Xanterean, Watchers, Abomination, Thunderbolt Ross.
Anl 1 ❑ Oct 1968 Cover: 0.25 **NM** value: **50.00**
• **CGC:** 44 graded, best 9.6
📖 A Refuge Divided **C:** Jim Steranko
Anl 2 ❑ Oct 1969 Cover: 0.25 **NM** value: **36.00**
• **CGC:** 3 graded, best 9.6
📖 The Origin of the Hulk; Enter the Chameleon; A Titan Rides the Train; The Horde of Humanoids; On the Rampage Against the Reds; The Power of Doctor Banner • Reprints from Incredible Hulk #3 and Tales to Astonish #62-66
Anl 3 ❑ Jan 1971 Cover: 0.25 **NM** value: **9.00**
• **CGC:** 3 graded, best 9.4
• Cover reads "King-Size Special". 📖 To Live Again; Like A Beast at Bay; Within the Monster Dwells a Man; Another World, Another Foe; The Wisdom of the Watcher • Reprints from Tales to Astonish #70-74
Anl 4 ❑ Jan 1972 Cover: 0.50 **NM** value: **7.00**
• **CGC:** 1 graded, best 6.0
Cover reads "Special". 📖 Not All my Power Can Save Me!; I, Against a World!; Bruce Banner is the Hulk!; The Ever-Lovin' Thung vs. The Inedible Bulk! • Reprints from Tales to Astonish #75-77 and Not Brand Ecch #5 **A:** Jack Kirby; John Romita; Marie Severin; Mickey Demeo; Scott Edward **W:** Stan Lee
Anl 5 ❑ ca. 1976 Cover: 0.50 **NM** value: **7.00**
📖 And Six Shall Crush the Hulk ★ Versus Xemnu. ★ Versus Groot. ★ Versus Diablo. ★ Versus Diablo, Blip. ★ Versus Blip. ★ Versus Taboo. ★ Versus Goom.
Anl 6 ❑ ca. 1977 Cover: 0.60 **NM** value: **3.00**

Other grades: Multiply prices above by **1.5 for Mint • 2/3 for Very Fine • 1/3 for Fine • 1/5 for Very Good • 1/8 for Good**

• **CGC:** 1 graded, best 9.4
📖 Beware the Beehive • Doctor Strange **A:** Herb Trimpe ★ 1st Appearance of Paragon. ★ Appearance of Warlock, Doctor Strange.
Anl 7❑ca. 1978 Cover: 0.60 **NM** value: **3.00**
• **CGC:** 3 graded, best 9.4
📖 The Evil that is Cast **A:** John Byrne; Bob Layton ★ Appearance of Iceman, Angel.
Anl 8❑ca. 1979 Cover: 0.75 **NM** value: **3.00**
📖 Sasquatch! • Alpha Flight
Anl 9❑ca. 1980 Cover: 0.75 **NM** value: **2.50**
📖 A Game Of Monsters And Kings **A:** Al Milgrom; Steve Ditko **W:** Doug Moench
Anl 10❑ca. 1981 Cover: 0.75 **NM** value: **2.50**
📖 Nothing Stops The Hulk! • Captain Universe **A:** Rick Leonardi **W:** Bill Mantlo
Anl 11❑ca. 1982 Cover: 1.00 **NM** value: **2.00**
📖 The Day The Earth Turned Green! • 1st Frank Miller Marvel pencils **A:** Frank Miller
Anl 12❑ca. 1983 Cover: 1.00 **NM** value: **2.00**
📖 Amazing Grace! **A:** Herb Trimpe; Brent Anderson(cover) **W:** Bill Mantlo
Anl 13❑ca. 1984 Cover: 1.00 **NM** value: **2.00**
📖 Friends
Anl 14❑ca. 1985 Cover: 1.25 **NM** value: **2.00**
Circ: CapCity orders: **11,400**
📖 The Weakness of the Flesh
Anl 15❑ca. 1986 Cover: 1.25 **NM** value: **2.25**
📖 Body Double ★ Versus Abomination.
Anl 16❑ca. 1990 Cover: 2.00 **NM** value: **2.50**
Circ: CapCity orders: **35,400**
📖 Lifeform, Part 3; The Quality of Mercy; You Can't Always Get What You Want; The Nightmare Never Ends • Lifeform **A:** Chris Wozniak; Dan Reed; Angel Medina; Herb Trimpe **W:** Bill Mumy; Alan Grant; Gary Barnum; Peter David
Anl 17❑ca. 1991 Cover: 2.00 **NM** value: **Cover or less**
Circ: CapCity orders: **43,100**
📖 Subterranean Wars, Part 2; Vicious Cycle; As Old As The Hills; Mean Joe; Hero Worship; Not to the Swift
Anl 18❑ca. 1992 Cover: 2.25 **NM** value: **2.75**
Circ: CapCity orders: **39,000**
📖 The Return of the Defenders, Part 1; Mano a Mano; Four on the Floor; Things to Come; Nobody Loves the Hulk; The Running Man • Return of Defenders **A:** Travis Charest **W:** Peter David
Anl 19❑ca. 1993 Cover: 2.95 **NM** value: **Cover or less**
Circ: CapCity orders: **39,000**
📖 Dead Man's Hand; Still Dead; A Town Called Hulk • Polybagged with trading card ★ 1st Appearance of Lazarus.
Anl 20❑ca. 1994 Cover: 2.95 **NM** value: **Cover or less**
Circ: CapCity orders: **22,350**
📖 Storytime; Psychobabble; Desert Storm
Anl 1997❑ca. 1997 Cover: 2.99 **NM** value: **Cover or less**
Circ: Diamd. preorders: **53,999**
📖 Sins of the Father; Where the Wild Things Are • Hulk vs. Gladiator; Incredible Hulk '97 **A:** Jeff Rebner; Kevin Lau **W:** Bill Rosemann; Chris Cooper
Anl 1998❑ca. 1998 Cover: 2.99 **NM** value: **Cover or less**
wraparound cover. • gatefold summary. 📖 Lifesblood • Hulk/Sub-Mariner '98 **A:** Doug Wheatley **W:** Chris Cooper
Ash 1❑ Cover: 0.75 **NM** value: **Cover or less**
• ashcan edition.
Bk 1❑ Cover: 19.95 **NM** value: **Cover or less**
📖 Beauty and the Beast
Bk 2❑ Cover: 12.95 **NM** value: **Cover or less**
📖 Ghosts of the Past
Bk 3❑ Cover: 16.95 **NM** value: **Cover or less**
📖 Transformations
GS 1❑ Cover: 0.50 **NM** value: **8.00**
📖 A Refuge Divided • Reprinted from Incredible Hulk Annual #1

INCREDIBLE HULK, THE: A MAN-BRUTE BERSERK! — Marvel

Bk 1❑ Cover: 3.50 **NM** value: **Cover or less**
• (Tor)

INCREDIBLE HULK AND THE THING: THE BIG CHANCE — Marvel

Bk 1❑ Cover: 5.95 **NM** value: **Cover or less**
Circ: CapCity orders: **11,400**

INCREDIBLE HULK AND WOLVERINE — Marvel

1 ❑ Oct 1986 Cover: 2.00 **NM** value: **7.00**
Circ: CapCity orders: **15,900**
• Reprints The Incredible Hulk #181-182, other story
1-2 ❑ **NM** value: **4.00**

INCREDIBLE HULK (FIRESIDE) — Marvel

Bk 1❑ Cover: 7.95 **NM** value: **15.00**
• (Fireside)

Diamond preorders are the estimated number of comics sold, prior to their release, to comics shops in North America by Diamond Comic Distributors, the largest distributor. These figures underreport the actual number of circulating copies by the amount of reorders Diamond took (usually 5-10% again of the preorders) and sales by publishers to newsstand and bookstore distributors. For many independent publishers, Diamond's preorders may be quite close to the actual number of copies in circulation.

INCREDIBLE HULK, THE: FUTURE IMPERFECT — Marvel

Once, Bruce Banner — The Incredible Hulk — was a creature of rage. In Incredible Hulk #377, the brain of Bruce Banner regained dominance over the body of The Hulk, and the monster within was thought to finally be under control. But when Banner was thrust almost 100 years into the future, he discovered a new monster in the form of his future self.

Banner's future self was known as the Maestro, a tyrannical dictator who ruled without conscience or mercy. Banner resolved to stop the Maestro, but doing so wouldn't be easy. The Maestro, after all, was just as strong — and more experienced — than Banner. Moreover, could Banner ultimately avoid becoming the very fiend he battles?

1 ❑ Jan 1993 Cover: 5.95 **NM** value: **6.00**
Circ: CapCity orders: **34,700** • **CGC:** 1 graded, best 9.8
Embossed cover. • prestige format. • indicia lists date as Jan 93 **A:** George Pérez **W:** Peter David ★ 1st Appearance of The Maestro.
2 ❑ Dec 1992 Cover: 5.95 **NM** value: **6.00**
Circ: CapCity orders: **30,250** • **CGC:** 1 graded, best 9.8
Embossed cover. • prestige format. • indicia lists date as Dec 92 **A:** George Pérez **W:** Peter David
Bk 1❑ Cover: 12.95 **NM** value: **Cover or less**
• collects the two-issue mini-series; Reprints Incredible Hulk, The: Future Imperfect #1-2 **A:** George Pérez **W:** Peter David

INCREDIBLE HULK: HERCULES UNLEASHED — Marvel

1 ❑ Oct 1996 Cover: 2.50 **NM** value: **Cover or less**
One-shot. • follows events of Onslaught

INCREDIBLE HULK, THE (LANCER) — Marvel

Bk 1❑ Cover: 0.50 **NM** value: **3.00**
• (Lancer)

INCREDIBLE HULK, THE (MASS-MARKET PAPERBACK) — Marvel

Bk 1❑ Cover: 2.50 **NM** value: **3.00**
• (Marvel); reprints first six issues in mass-market paperback

INCREDIBLE HULK MEGAZINE, THE — Marvel

1 ❑ Dec 1996 Cover: 3.95 **NM** value: **Cover or less**
📖 Quality of Life; Heaven is a Very Small Place; The Abomination; Feeding Billy; People in Glass Houses Shouldn't Hurt Hulks **A:** Adam Kubert; Todd McFarlane **W:** Roy Thomas; Peter David ★ Origin of Hulk, The Abomination. ★ 1st Appearance of The Abomination.

INCREDIBLE HULK, THE (POCKET) — Marvel

Bk 1❑ Cover: 1.95 **NM** value: **Cover or less**
• (Pocket)
Bk 2❑ Cover: 1.95 **NM** value: **Cover or less**
• (Pocket)

INCREDIBLE HULK POSTER MAGAZINE — Marvel

1/A ❑ Cover: 3.95 **NM** value: **Cover or less**
• comics
1/B ❑ Cover: 1.50 **NM** value: **Cover or less**
• TV show

INCREDIBLE HULK, THE (TEMPO) — Marvel

Bk 1❑ Cover: 1.75 **NM** value: **3.00**
• (Tempo, newspaper strips)
Bk 2❑ Cover: 1.95 **NM** value: **3.00**
• (Tempo, newspaper strips)

INCREDIBLE HULK VERSUS QUASIMODO, THE — Marvel

1 ❑ Mar 1983 Cover: 0.60 **NM** value: **1.50**
📖 The Hulk Meets The Hunchback Of Notre Dame! • Based on Saturday morning cartoon **A:** Sal Buscema; Steve Mitchell **W:** Bill Mantlo

INCREDIBLE HULK VS. SUPERMAN — Marvel

1 ❑ Jul 1999 Cover: 5.99 **NM** value: **Cover or less**
• prestige format.

INCREDIBLE HULK VS. VENOM — Marvel

1 ❑ Apr 1994 Cover: 2.50 **NM** value: **Cover or less**
Circ: CapCity orders: **9,824**
No issue number.

INCREDIBLE MR. LIMPET, THE — Dell

1 ❑ Jun 1964 Cover: 0.10 **NM** value: **25.00**
• **CGC:** 3 graded, best 9.6

INCREDIBLE SCIENCE FICTION — E.C.

The Comics Magazine Association of America's implemented the Comics Code, which forbade "all scenes of horror" in newsstand comics and altered possibly offensive titles. So Weird Science-Fantasy changed its name to Incredible Science Fiction, and each issue carried the Code seal. Famously, one story was challenged because fantastic birds in a jungle-planet setting were called satires on angels. And a reprint of "Judgment Day" was initially rejected because, it was claimed, it would offend black readers. E.C. ran both stories, despite pressures to change them. Incredible Science Fiction #33 (Jan 56) was E.C.'s last publication in color comic-book form. — Maggie

30 ❑ Jul 1955 Cover: 0.10 **NM** value: **250.00**
• **CGC:** 3 graded, best 9.6
📖 Clean Start; Marbles; Conditioned Reflex; Barrier
31 ❑ Sep 1955 Cover: 0.10 **NM** value: **250.00**
• **CGC:** 5 graded, best 9.4
📖 You, Rocket; Fulfillment; Time to Leave; Has-Been
32 ❑ Nov 1955 Cover: 0.10 **NM** value: **250.00**
• **CGC:** 5 graded, best 9.4
📖 Fallen Idol; Food for Thought; The Ultimate Weapon; Marked Man
33 ❑ Jan 1956 Cover: 0.10 **NM** value: **250.00**
• **CGC:** 4 graded, best 9.6
📖 Big Moment; Kaleidoscope; One Way Hero; Judgement Day! final issue.

INCUBUS — Palliard Press

All issues are adults only.
1 ❑ b&w Cover: 2.95 **NM** value: **Cover or less**
2 ❑ b&w Cover: 2.95 **NM** value: **Cover or less**

INDEPENDENT PUBLISHER'S GROUP SPOTLIGHT — Hero

0 ❑ Jul 1993 Cover: 3.50 **NM** value: **Cover or less**
📖 Deathrow vs. X-187!: Turf-Wars; Flare: Joyride **W:** Dennis Mallonee; Al Reano; Crag A. Stormon

INDEPENDENT VOICES — Peregrine Entertainment

1 ❑ Sep 1998, b&w Cover: 1.95 **NM** value: **Cover or less**
• SPX '98 anthology
2 ❑ Sep 1999, b&w Cover: 2.95 **NM** value: **Cover or less**
Circ: Diamd. preorders: **4,033** • **CGC:** 2 graded, best 9.6
• CBLDF benefit comic book
36924❑May 2000, b&w Cover: 2.95 **NM** value: **Cover or less**

INDIANA JONES AND THE ARMS OF GOLD — Dark Horse

1 ❑ Feb 1994 Cover: 2.50 **NM** value: **Cover or less**
Circ: CapCity orders: **8,225**
2 ❑ Mar 1994 Cover: 2.50 **NM** value: **Cover or less**
Circ: CapCity orders: **6,975**
3 ❑ Apr 1994 Cover: 2.50 **NM** value: **Cover or less**
Circ: CapCity orders: **6,900**
4 ❑ May 1994 Cover: 2.50 **NM** value: **Cover or less**
Circ: CapCity orders: **6,900**
5 ❑ Cover: 2.50 **NM** value: **Cover or less**
6 ❑ Apr 1994 Cover: 2.50 **NM** value: **Cover or less**

INDIANA JONES AND THE FATE OF ATLANTIS — Dark Horse

Dr. "Indiana" Jones, the noted archaeologist and adventurer returns in this limited series. It began when a strange man appeared, inquiring about the origins of an ancient key. Dr. Jones traced the key to a 3,000 year-old archaeological find, and discovered that the key opened a secret compartment in one of the artifacts from that dig.

No sooner had Jones discovered this than the man, revealed as an S.S. colonel, returned and attempted to seize the artifact. The Nazis felt that it held the key to finding Atlantis, and to a source of limitless power — and only Indiana Jones could stop them from getting it.

Lucasfilm Games created the concept for Indiana Jones and the Fate of Atlantis for use in a computer game by the same name.

1 ❑ Mar 1991 Cover: 2.50 **NM** value: **Cover or less**
Circ: CapCity orders: **23,200**
• trading cards
1-2 ❑ Cover: 2.50 **NM** value: **Cover or less**
2 ❑ May 1991 Cover: 2.50 **NM** value: **Cover or less**
Circ: CapCity orders: **18,650**
• trading cards
3 ❑ Jul 1991 Cover: 2.50 **NM** value: **Cover or less**
Circ: CapCity orders: **17,500**
4 ❑ Sep 1991 Cover: 2.50 **NM** value: **Cover or less**
Circ: CapCity orders: **15,975**
A: Dan Barry; Dave Dorman(cover) **W:** Dan Barry
Bk 1❑ Cover: 13.95 **NM** value: **Cover or less**
• Collects Indiana Jones and the Fate of Atlantis #1-4

INDIANA JONES AND THE GOLDEN FLEECE — Dark Horse

1 ❑ Jun 1994 Cover: 2.50 **NM** value: **Cover or less**
Circ: CapCity orders: **8,300**
A: Ken Hooper **W:** David Rawson; Pat McGreal
2 ❑ Jul 1994 Cover: 2.50 **NM** value: **Cover or less**
Circ: CapCity orders: **7,000**

INDIANA JONES AND THE IRON PHOENIX — Dark Horse

1 ❑ Dec 1994 Cover: 2.50 **NM** value: **Cover or less**
Circ: CapCity orders: **6,350**
A: Leo Durañona; Leo Durañoma **W:** Lee Marrs
2 ❑ Jan 1995 Cover: 2.50 **NM** value: **Cover or less**
Circ: CapCity orders: **5,800**
A: Leo Durañona; Leo Durañoma **W:** Lee Marrs
3 ❑ Feb 1995 Cover: 2.50 **NM** value: **Cover or less**

CGC-graded: Multiply prices above by **33 for 9.9 M** • **16 for 9.8 NM/M** • **7 for 9.6 NM+** • **5 for 9.4 NM** • **2.5 for 9.2 NM-** • **1.5 for 9.0 VF/NM**

Circ: CapCity orders: **5,250**
A: Leo Durañona; Leo Durañoma **W:** Lee Marrs
4 ❑ Mar 1995 Cover: 2.50 **NM** value: **Cover or less**
Circ: CapCity orders: **5,250**
A: Leo Durañona; Leo Durañoma **W:** Lee Marrs

INDIANA JONES AND THE LAST CRUSADE — Marvel

1 ❑ Oct 1989 Cover: 1.00 **NM** value: **Cover or less**
Circ: CapCity orders: **10,000**
• comic book **A:** Brett Blevins **W:** David Michilinie
2 ❑ Oct 1989 Cover: 1.00 **NM** value: **Cover or less**
Circ: CapCity orders: **9,300**
• comic book **A:** Brett Blevins **W:** David Michilinie
3 ❑ Nov 1989 Cover: 1.00 **NM** value: **Cover or less**
Circ: CapCity orders: **8,700**
• comic book **A:** Brett Blevins **W:** David Michilinie
4 ❑ Nov 1989 Cover: 1.00 **NM** value: **Cover or less**
Circ: CapCity orders: **8,700**
• comic book **A:** Brett Blevins **W:** David Michilinie

INDIANA JONES AND THE LAST CRUSADE (MAGAZINE) — Marvel

1 ❑ Aug 1989, b&w Cover: 2.95 **NM** value: **Cover or less**
• magazine.

INDIANA JONES AND THE SARGASSO PIRATES — Dark Horse

1 ❑ Dec 1995 Cover: 2.50 **NM** value: **Cover or less**
A Watery Grave **A:** Karl Kesel; Eduardo Barreto; Paul Guinan **W:** Karl Kesel
2 ❑ Jan 1996 Cover: 2.50 **NM** value: **Cover or less**
A: Karl Kesel; Eduardo Barreto; Paul Guinan **W:** Karl Kesel
3 ❑ Feb 1996 Cover: 2.50 **NM** value: **Cover or less**
A: Karl Kesel; Eduardo Barreto; Paul Guinan **W:** Karl Kesel
4 ❑ Mar 1996 Cover: 2.50 **NM** value: **Cover or less**
final issue. **A:** Karl Kesel; Eduardo Barreto; Paul Guinan **W:** Karl Kesel

INDIANA JONES AND THE SHRINE OF THE SEA DEVIL — Dark Horse

1 ❑ Sep 1994 Cover: 2.50 **NM** value: **Cover or less**
Circ: CapCity orders: **6,325**
One-shot. **A:** Gary Gianni **W:** Gary Gianni

INDIANA JONES AND THE SPEAR OF DESTINY — Dark Horse

1 ❑ Apr 1995 Cover: 2.50 **NM** value: **Cover or less**
Circ: CapCity orders: **6,175**
The Land Below **A:** William Simpson **W:** Elaine Lee
2 ❑ May 1995 Cover: 2.50 **NM** value: **Cover or less**
Circ: CapCity orders: **5,575**
A: William Simpson; Dan Spiegle **W:** Elaine Lee
3 ❑ Jun 1995 Cover: 2.50 **NM** value: **Cover or less**
Circ: CapCity orders: **5,800**
A: William Simpson; Dan Spiegle **W:** Elaine Lee
4 ❑ Jul 1995 Cover: 2.50 **NM** value: **Cover or less**
Circ: CapCity orders: **5,950**
A: William Simpson; Dan Spiegle **W:** Elaine Lee

INDIANA JONES AND THE TEMPLE OF DOOM — Marvel

1 ❑ Sep 1984 Cover: 0.75 **NM** value: **1.50**
A: Jackson Guice **W:** David Michelinie
2 ❑ Oct 1984 Cover: 0.75 **NM** value: **1.50**
A: Jackson Guice **W:** David Michelinie
3 ❑ Nov 1984 Cover: 0.75 **NM** value: **1.50**
A: Jackson Guice **W:** David Michelinie

INDIANA JONES: THUNDER IN THE ORIENT — Dark Horse

1 ❑ Sep 1993 Cover: 2.50 **NM** value: **Cover or less**
Circ: CapCity orders: **10,800**
A: Dan Barry **W:** Dan Barry
2 ❑ Oct 1993 Cover: 2.50 **NM** value: **Cover or less**
Circ: CapCity orders: **8,525**
3 ❑ Nov 1993 Cover: 2.50 **NM** value: **Cover or less**
Circ: CapCity orders: **7,850**
4 ❑ Dec 1993 Cover: 2.50 **NM** value: **Cover or less**
Circ: CapCity orders: **7,625**
A: Dan Barry **W:** Dan Barry
5 ❑ Mar 1994 Cover: 2.50 **NM** value: **Cover or less**
Circ: CapCity orders: **7,125**
6 ❑ Apr 1994 Cover: 2.50 **NM** value: **Cover or less**
Circ: CapCity orders: **6,475**

INDIAN CHIEF — Dell

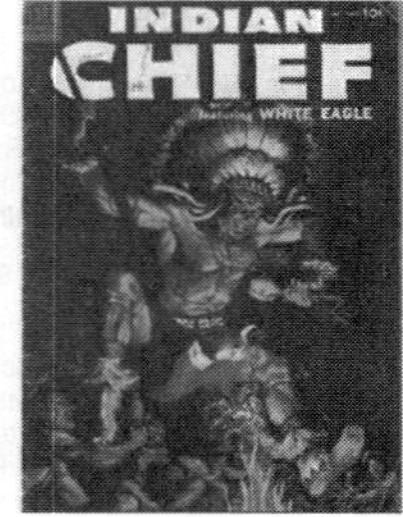

Next to impossible to release today, comic books depicting Native American warriors had their own niche in the 1940s and 1950s. That time saw issues of Indian Chief from Dell, Indians from Fiction House, and — hold onto your hats, political correctness police — Indians on the Warpath from St. John.

But as dated as some of the depictions in this series, which is taken over in mid-run by a whooping White Eagle, might seem, there's no doubt that Indian Chief was home to many powerful painted covers. The back cover to #4 features a Frederick Remington piece depicting frontiersmen fighting off an attack. And the series creators did attempt to convey what knowledge they had about Indian culture; "A Badge of Honor" in #17, for example, explains the meaning of feathers in tribal society. — JJM

3 ❑ Jul 1951 Cover: 0.10 **NM** value: **40.00**
4 ❑ Oct 1951 Cover: 0.10 **NM** value: **30.00**
5 ❑ Jan 1952 Cover: 0.10 **NM** value: **30.00**
6 ❑ Apr 1952 Cover: 0.10 **NM** value: **30.00**
7 ❑ Jul 1952 Cover: 0.10 **NM** value: **30.00**
8 ❑ Oct 1952 Cover: 0.10 **NM** value: **30.00**
9 ❑ Jan 1953 Cover: 0.10 **NM** value: **30.00**
10 ❑ Apr 1953 Cover: 0.10 **NM** value: **30.00**
11 ❑ Jul 1953 Cover: 0.10 **NM** value: **30.00**
12 ❑ Oct 1953 Cover: 0.10 **NM** value: **30.00**
13 ❑ Jan 1954 Cover: 0.10 **NM** value: **25.00**
14 ❑ Apr 1954 Cover: 0.10 **NM** value: **25.00**
15 ❑ Jul 1954 Cover: 0.10 **NM** value: **25.00**
16 ❑ Oct 1954 Cover: 0.10 **NM** value: **25.00**
17 ❑ Jan 1955 Cover: 0.10 **NM** value: **25.00**
18 ❑ Apr 1955 Cover: 0.10 **NM** value: **25.00**
19 ❑ Jul 1955 Cover: 0.10 **NM** value: **25.00**
20 ❑ Oct 1955 Cover: 0.10 **NM** value: **25.00**
21 ❑ Jan 1956 Cover: 0.10 **NM** value: **25.00**
22 ❑ Apr 1956 Cover: 0.10 **NM** value: **25.00**
23 ❑ Jul 1956 Cover: 0.10 **NM** value: **25.00**
24 ❑ Oct 1956 Cover: 0.10 **NM** value: **25.00**
25 ❑ Jan 1957 Cover: 0.10 **NM** value: **25.00**
26 ❑ Apr 1957 Cover: 0.10 **NM** value: **25.00**
27 ❑ Jul 1957 Cover: 0.10 **NM** value: **25.00**
28 ❑ Oct 1957 Cover: 0.10 **NM** value: **25.00**
29 ❑ Jan 1958 Cover: 0.10 **NM** value: **25.00**
30 ❑ Apr 1958 Cover: 0.10 **NM** value: **20.00**
31 ❑ Jul 1958 Cover: 0.10 **NM** value: **20.00**
32 ❑ Oct 1958 Cover: 0.10 **NM** value: **20.00**
33 ❑ Jan 1959 Cover: 0.10 **NM** value: **20.00**

INDIAN FIGHTER — Dell

1 ❑ May 1950 Cover: 0.10 **NM** value: **75.00**
2 ❑ Jul 1950 Cover: 0.10 **NM** value: **50.00**
3 ❑ Sep 1950 Cover: 0.10 **NM** value: **35.00**
4 ❑ Nov 1950 Cover: 0.10 **NM** value: **35.00**
5 ❑ Jan 1951 Cover: 0.10 **NM** value: **35.00**
6 ❑ Mar 1951 Cover: 0.10 **NM** value: **35.00**
7 ❑ May 1951 Cover: 0.10 **NM** value: **35.00**
8 ❑ Jul 1951 Cover: 0.10 **NM** value: **35.00**
9 ❑ Sep 1951 Cover: 0.10 **NM** value: **35.00**
10 ❑ Nov 1951 Cover: 0.10 **NM** value: **35.00**
11 ❑ Jan 1952 Cover: 0.10 **NM** value: **35.00**

INDIANS — Fiction House

1 ❑ Spr 1950 Cover: 0.10 **NM** value: **175.00**
2 ❑ Sum 1950 Cover: 0.10 **NM** value: **125.00**
3 ❑ Fal 1950 Cover: 0.10 **NM** value: **100.00**
4 ❑ Win 1950 Cover: 0.10 **NM** value: **100.00**
5 ❑ Apr 1951 Cover: 0.10 **NM** value: **100.00**
6 ❑ Jun 1951 Cover: 0.10 **NM** value: **75.00**
7 ❑ Aug 1951 Cover: 0.10 **NM** value: **75.00**
8 ❑ Oct 1951 Cover: 0.10 **NM** value: **75.00**
9 ❑ Dec 1951 Cover: 0.10 **NM** value: **75.00**
10 ❑ Feb 1952 Cover: 0.10 **NM** value: **75.00**
11 ❑ Apr 1952 Cover: 0.10 **NM** value: **50.00**
12 ❑ Jun 1952 Cover: 0.10 **NM** value: **50.00**
13 ❑ Aug 1952 Cover: 0.10 **NM** value: **50.00**
14 ❑ Oct 1952 Cover: 0.10 **NM** value: **50.00**
15 ❑ Dec 1952 Cover: 0.10 **NM** value: **50.00**
16 ❑ Feb 1953 Cover: 0.10 **NM** value: **50.00**
17 ❑ Apr 1953 Cover: 0.10 **NM** value: **50.00**

INDIANS ON THE WARPATH — St. John

1 ❑ ca. 1949 Cover: 0.25 **NM** value: **200.00**

INDIAN WARRIORS — Star Publications

7 ❑ Jun 1951 Cover: 0.10 **NM** value: **125.00**
8 ❑ Sep 1951 Cover: 0.10 **NM** value: **100.00**

INDUSTRIAL GOTHIC — DC / Vertigo

1 ❑ Dec 1995 Cover: 2.50 **NM** value: **Cover or less**
Anywhere but Here **A:** Ted McKeever **W:** Ted McKeever
2 ❑ Jan 1996 Cover: 2.50 **NM** value: **Cover or less**
Damn Your Hands **A:** Ted McKeever **W:** Ted McKeever
3 ❑ Feb 1996 Cover: 2.50 **NM** value: **Cover or less**
Traces of Lilac **A:** Ted McKeever **W:** Ted McKeever
4 ❑ Mar 1996 Cover: 2.50 **NM** value: **Cover or less**
The Truncheon's Waltz **A:** Ted McKeever **W:** Ted McKeever
5 ❑ Apr 1996 Cover: 2.50 **NM** value: **Cover or less**
The Aluminum Tower final issue. **A:** Ted McKeever **W:** Ted McKeever

INDUSTRIAL STRENGTH PREVIEW — Silver Skull

1 ❑ b&w Cover: 1.50 **NM** value: **Cover or less**

INEDIBLE ADVENTURES OF CLINT THE CARROT — Hot Leg

1 ❑ Mar 1994, b&w Cover: 2.50 **NM** value: **Cover or less**

INFECTIOUS — Fantaco

1 ❑ Cover: 3.95 **NM** value: **Cover or less**
One-shot. **A:** Kevin Eastman

The prices seen above do not represent the highest possible prices seen in online auctions, but rather the prices we have seen these issues reliably fetch in a variety of environments (storefront retail, mail order, auction and convention).

INFERIOR FIVE, THE — DC

Merryman! Dumb Bunny! The Blimp! White Feather! Awkwardman! This humorous assortment of would-be super-heroes debuted in Showcase #62 and were popular enough in the late 1960s to merit their own book.

With the camp craze in full gear and DC gradually waking up to the new, comparatively older and more "sophisticated" comics audience that Marvel had developed in the 1960s, The Inferior Five was a gesture of wit from the normally staid and traditional publisher. Inferior Five offered lots of broad attempts at humor and some very effective parodies of Stan Lee's histrionic style at Marvel.

1 ❑ Apr 1967 Cover: 0.12 **NM** value: **22.00**
• **CGC:** 1 graded, best 5.0
Poliwko cover. Five Characters In Search Of A Plot **A:** Mike Sekowsky **W:** E. Nelson Bridwell
2 ❑ Jun 1967 Cover: 0.12 **NM** value: **16.00**
• **CGC:** 1 graded, best 4.5
3 ❑ Aug 1967 Cover: 0.12 **NM** value: **14.00**
4 ❑ Oct 1967 Cover: 0.12 **NM** value: **14.00**
5 ❑ Dec 1967 Cover: 0.12 **NM** value: **14.00**
6 ❑ Feb 1968 Cover: 0.12 **NM** value: **14.00**
★ Appearance of DC heroes.
7 ❑ Apr 1968 Cover: 0.12 **NM** value: **14.00**
8 ❑ Jun 1968 Cover: 0.12 **NM** value: **14.00**
9 ❑ Aug 1968 Cover: 0.12 **NM** value: **14.00**
• **CGC:** 1 graded, best 9.4
10 ❑ Oct 1968 Cover: 0.12 **NM** value: **14.00**
• Final issue of original run (1968) ★ Appearance of other heroes.
11 ❑ Sep 1972 Cover: 0.20 **NM** value: **10.00**
• reprints Showcase #62; Series begins again (1972)
12 ❑ Nov 1972 Cover: 0.20 **NM** value: **10.00**
final issue. • reprints Showcase #63

INFERNO (AIRCEL) — Aircel

All issues are adults only.
1 ❑ Oct 1990, b&w Cover: 2.50 **NM** value: **Cover or less**
The White Wolf; Genesis the Magician; Nobody's Perfect
2 ❑ Nov 1990, b&w Cover: 2.50 **NM** value: **Cover or less**
The Hound of Hell; The Axe **A:** Watson Portello **W:** Watson Portello
3 ❑ Dec 1990, b&w Cover: 2.50 **NM** value: **Cover or less**
4 ❑ Jan 1991, b&w Cover: 2.50 **NM** value: **Cover or less**
Metalady; The Avenging Navajo; Power – Parallel
Bk 1 ❑ Cover: 9.95 **NM** value: **Cover or less**

INFERNO (CALIBER) — Caliber

1 ❑ Aug 1995, b&w Cover: 2.95 **NM** value: **Cover or less**

INFERNO (DC) — DC

1 ❑ Oct 1997 Cover: 2.50 **NM** value: **Cover or less**
Circ: Diamd. preorders: **29,554**
Run Come See the Sun • spin-off from Legion of Super-Heroes **A:** Stuart Immonen **W:** Stuart Immonen
2 ❑ Nov 1997 Cover: 2.50 **NM** value: **Cover or less**
Circ: Diamd. preorders: **22,912**
A: Stuart Immonen **W:** Stuart Immonen
3 ❑ Jan 1998 Cover: 2.50 **NM** value: **Cover or less**
Circ: Diamd. preorders: **20,811**
Girls Interrupted **A:** Stuart Immonen **W:** Stuart Immonen
4 ❑ Feb 1998 Cover: 2.50 **NM** value: **Cover or less**
Circ: Diamd. preorders: **17,096**
A: Stuart Immonen **W:** Stuart Immonen

INFINITY CHARADE, THE — Parody Press

1/A ❑ Cover: 2.50 **NM** value: **Cover or less**
1/B ❑ Cover: 2.50 **NM** value: **Cover or less**
1/GO ❑ Cover: 3.95 **NM** value: **4.00**
• Gold limited edition (1500 printed).

INFINITY CRUSADE, THE — Marvel

1 ❑ Jun 1993 Cover: 3.50 **NM** value: **Cover or less**
Circ: CapCity orders: **140,900**
Gold foil cover. ★ 1st Appearance of Goddess.
2 ❑ Jul 1993 Cover: 2.50 **NM** value: **Cover or less**
Circ: CapCity orders: **79,500**
3 ❑ Aug 1993 Cover: 2.50 **NM** value: **Cover or less**
Circ: CapCity orders: **72,400**
4 ❑ Sep 1993 Cover: 2.50 **NM** value: **Cover or less**
Circ: CapCity orders: **58,900**
5 ❑ Oct 1993 Cover: 2.50 **NM** value: **Cover or less**
Circ: CapCity orders: **500**
A: Ron Lim **W:** Jim Starlin ★ Appearance of Hulk, Thanos, Goddess.
6 ❑ Nov 1993 Cover: 2.50 **NM** value: **Cover or less**
Circ: CapCity orders: **47,300**

There are two different pricing tiers in the modern comic-book hobby. **The prices seen above** are the prices we have seen **loose copies** of these issues reliably fetch in a variety of environments. Condition alters the price by the fractions seen on the bar on the bottom of left-hand pages of this book. **Comics graded by CGC** usually sell for more. Use the guide on the bottom of right-hand pages of this book to estimate what copies have brought on eBay.

Other grades: Multiply prices above by **1.5 for Mint • 2/3 for Very Fine • 1/3 for Fine • 1/5 for Very Good • 1/8 for Good**

INFINITY GAUNTLET **Marvel**

It's the end of the universe. Thanos, the mad god who worships death, has gained control of the Infinity Gauntlet: six gems which give him ultimate power over everything. He exerts power that dwarfs that of Galactus. He possesses ultimate knowledge. And with a single thought, he wipes half the living beings in the galaxy from existence.

In a star-spanning, six-part epic by the renowned Jim Starlin, the most powerful beings in the universe unite to try to stop galactic Armageddon. Drawn together by Adam Warlock (who possesses the soul gem — the only infinity gem not in Thanos' control), Earth's heroes must fight an unwinnable battle against an all-powerful foe.

1 ❑ Jul 1991 Cover: 2.50 **NM** value: **3.00**
Circ: CapCity orders: **118,600** • **CGC:** 5 graded, best 9.6
🕮 God **A:** George Pérez **W:** Jim Starlin ★ Appearance of Thanos, Spider-Man, Avengers, Silver Surfer.

2 ❑ Aug 1991 Cover: 2.50 **NM** value: **Cover or less**
Circ: CapCity orders: **93,500**
A: George Pérez **W:** Jim Starlin ★ Appearance of Thanos, Spider-Man, Avengers, Silver Surfer.

3 ❑ Sep 1991 Cover: 2.50 **NM** value: **Cover or less**
Circ: CapCity orders: **97,000**
A: George Pérez **W:** Jim Starlin ★ Appearance of Thanos, Spider-Man, Avengers, Silver Surfer.

4 ❑ Oct 1991 Cover: 2.50 **NM** value: **Cover or less**
Circ: CapCity orders: **91,500** • **CGC:** 1 graded, best 9.8
A: George Pérez **W:** Jim Starlin ★ Appearance of Thanos, Spider-Man, Avengers, Silver Surfer.

5 ❑ Nov 1991 Cover: 2.50 **NM** value: **Cover or less**
Circ: CapCity orders: **88,000**
A: Ron Lim **C:** George Pérez **W:** Jim Starlin

6 ❑ Dec 1991 Cover: 2.50 **NM** value: **Cover or less**
Circ: CapCity orders: **94,300**
A: Ron Lim **C:** George Pérez **W:** Jim Starlin

Bk 1 ❑ Cover: 19.95 **NM** value: **24.95**
Circ: CapCity orders: **3,500**
A: Ron Lim; George Pérez **W:** Jim Starlin ★ Appearance of Thanos.

INFINITY, INC. **DC**

Infinity Inc. was formed by the children and wards of the Justice Society of America. They followed in their parents' footsteps, but they weren't ready to join an old-fashioned type organization like the JSA — though they're quite willing to pitch in to help the older generation if necessary.

Super-offspring who have Infinity affiliations include Nuklon, a seven-foot super-strong party guy with a red Mohawk; Obsidian, the living shadow; Obsidian's sister, Jade, a green equal of her brother; Fury, Wonder Woman's daughter who has inherited her mother's skills; her boyfriend, Silver Scarab, who has inherited Hawkman's — his father's — flight metal and melded it with a device that can fire destructive rays; the new Wildcat, a female boxer and journalist; and Skyman, the gravity-defying leader of the group.

1 ❑ Mar 1984 Cover: 1.25 **NM** value: **2.00**
🕮 Generations **A:** Jerry Ordway; Jerry Conway **W:** Roy Thomas ★ Origin of Infinity Inc.

2 ❑ May 1984 Cover: 1.25 **NM** value: **1.50**
A: Jerry Ordway ★ Origin of ends. ★ Versus Ultra-Humanite.

3 ❑ Jun 1984 Cover: 1.25 **NM** value: **1.50**
A: Jerry Ordway ★ Versus Solomon Grundy.

4 ❑ Jul 1984 Cover: 1.25 **NM** value: **1.50**
A: Jerry Ordway

5 ❑ Aug 1984 Cover: 1.25 **NM** value: **1.50**
A: Jerry Ordway

6 ❑ Sep 1984 Cover: 1.25 **NM** value: **1.50**
A: Jerry Ordway

7 ❑ Oct 1984 Cover: 1.25 **NM** value: **1.50**
A: Jerry Ordway ★ Appearance of E-2 Superman.

8 ❑ Nov 1984 Cover: 1.25 **NM** value: **1.50**
A: Jerry Ordway

9 ❑ Dec 1984 Cover: 1.25 **NM** value: **1.50**
A: Jerry Ordway

10 ❑ Jan 1985 Cover: 1.25 **NM** value: **1.50**
A: Jerry Ordway

11 ❑ Feb 1985 Cover: 1.25 **NM** value: **Cover or less**
• more on Infinity's origin

12 ❑ Mar 1985 Cover: 1.25 **NM** value: **Cover or less**
• Brainwave Junior's new powers ★ 1st Appearance of Yolanda Montez.

13 ❑ Apr 1985 Cover: 1.25 **NM** value: **Cover or less**
★ Versus Thorn.

14 ❑ May 1985 Cover: 1.25 **NM** value: **3.50**
Circ: CapCity orders: **8,950** • **CGC:** 1 graded, best 9.4
A: Todd McFarlane ★ 1st Appearance of Chroma, Marcie Cooper.

15 ❑ Jun 1985 Cover: 1.25 **NM** value: **2.50**
Circ: CapCity orders: **8,950**
A: Todd McFarlane ★ Appearance of Chroma.

16 ❑ Jul 1985 Cover: 1.25 **NM** value: **2.50**
Circ: CapCity orders: **8,650**
A: Todd McFarlane ★ 1st Appearance of Mr. Bones.

17 ❑ Aug 1985 Cover: 1.25 **NM** value: **2.50**
Circ: CapCity orders: **8,550**
A: Todd McFarlane ★ 1st Appearance of Helix.

18 ❑ Sep 1985 Cover: 1.25 **NM** value: **2.50**
Circ: CapCity orders: **8,450**
🕮 Crisis on Infinite Earths • Crisis **A:** Todd McFarlane ★ Versus Helix.

19 ❑ Oct 1985 Cover: 1.25 **NM** value: **2.50**
Circ: CapCity orders: **8,800**
🕮 Crisis on Infinite Earths • Crisis **A:** Todd McFarlane ★ 1st Appearance of Mekanique. ★ Appearance of Steel, JLA.

20 ❑ Nov 1985 Cover: 1.25 **NM** value: **2.50**
Circ: CapCity orders: **11,300**
🕮 Crisis on Infinite Earths • Crisis **A:** Todd McFarlane ★ 1st Appearance of Rick Tyler.

21 ❑ Dec 1985 Cover: 1.50 **NM** value: **2.50**
Circ: CapCity orders: **11,250**
🕮 Crisis on Infinite Earths • Crisis **A:** Todd McFarlane ★ 1st Appearance of Doctor Midnight (new), Hourman II (Rick Tyler).

22 ❑ Jan 1986 Cover: 1.50 **NM** value: **2.50**
Circ: CapCity orders: **13,050**
🕮 Crisis on Infinite Earths • Crisis **A:** Todd McFarlane

23 ❑ Feb 1986 Cover: 1.50 **NM** value: **2.50**
Circ: CapCity orders: **11,450**
🕮 Crisis on Infinite Earths • Crisis **A:** Todd McFarlane ★ Versus Solomon Grundy.

24 ❑ Mar 1986 Cover: 1.50 **NM** value: **2.50**
Circ: CapCity orders: **11,350**
🕮 Crisis on Infinite Earths • Star Spangled Kid, Jonni Thunder vs. Last Criminal; Crisis **A:** Todd McFarlane

25 ❑ Apr 1986 Cover: 1.50 **NM** value: **2.50**
Circ: CapCity orders: **9,700**
• Crisis aftermath; Hourman II joins team; Doctor Midnight joins team; Wildcat II joins team **A:** Todd McFarlane

26 ❑ May 1986 Cover: 1.50 **NM** value: **2.50**
Circ: CapCity orders: **9,550**
A: Todd McFarlane ★ Appearance of Helix.

27 ❑ Jun 1986 Cover: 1.50 **NM** value: **2.50**
Circ: CapCity orders: **9,150**
• Lyta's memories erased **A:** Todd McFarlane

28 ❑ Jul 1986 Cover: 1.50 **NM** value: **2.50**
Circ: CapCity orders: **8,850**
A: Todd McFarlane ★ Versus Mr. Bones.

29 ❑ Jul 1986 Cover: 1.50 **NM** value: **2.50**
Circ: CapCity orders: **8,900**
A: Todd McFarlane ★ Versus Helix.

30 ❑ Sep 1986 Cover: 1.50 **NM** value: **2.50**
Circ: CapCity orders: **9,450**
🕮 What Private Griefs ... • JSA mourned **A:** Todd McFarlane

31 ❑ Oct 1986 Cover: 1.50 **NM** value: **2.50**
Circ: CapCity orders: **9,150**
A: Todd McFarlane ★ 1st Appearance of Skyman. ★ Appearance of Jonni Thunder.

32 ❑ Nov 1986 Cover: 1.50 **NM** value: **2.50**
Circ: CapCity orders: **8,600**
A: Todd McFarlane ★ Versus Psycho Pirate.

33 ❑ Dec 1986 Cover: 1.50 **NM** value: **2.50**
Circ: CapCity orders: **8,600**
A: Todd McFarlane ★ Origin of Obsidian.

34 ❑ Jan 1987 Cover: 1.50 **NM** value: **2.50**
Circ: CapCity orders: **8,850**
A: Todd McFarlane ★ Versus Global Guardians.

35 ❑ Feb 1987 Cover: 1.50 **NM** value: **2.50**
Circ: CapCity orders: **8,750**
A: Todd McFarlane ★ Versus Injustice Unlimited.

36 ❑ Mar 1987 Cover: 1.50 **NM** value: **2.50**
Circ: CapCity orders: **8,600**
A: Todd McFarlane ★ Versus Solomon Grundy.

37 ❑ Apr 1987 Cover: 1.50 **NM** value: **2.50**
Circ: CapCity orders: **8,850**
A: Todd McFarlane ★ Origin of Northwing.

38 ❑ May 1987 Cover: 1.50 **NM** value: **Cover or less**
Circ: CapCity orders: **9,050**

39 ❑ Jun 1987 Cover: 1.50 **NM** value: **Cover or less**
Circ: CapCity orders: **8,700**
🕮 The Saga of Solomon Grundy ★ Origin of Solomon Grundy.

40 ❑ Jul 1987 Cover: 1.50 **NM** value: **Cover or less**
Circ: CapCity orders: **8,800**

41 ❑ Aug 1987 Cover: 1.50 **NM** value: **Cover or less**
Circ: CapCity orders: **9,500**

42 ❑ Sep 1987 Cover: 1.50 **NM** value: **Cover or less**
Circ: CapCity orders: **9,800**
🕮 Farewell To Fury! • Fury leaves team **A:** Vince Argondezzi **W:** Roy Thomas; Dann Thomas

43 ❑ Oct 1987 Cover: 1.50 **NM** value: **Cover or less**
Circ: CapCity orders: **10,000**

44 ❑ Nov 1987 Cover: 1.50 **NM** value: **Cover or less**
Circ: CapCity orders: **10,100**

45 ❑ Dec 1987 Cover: 1.50 **NM** value: **Cover or less**
Circ: CapCity orders: **11,250**
★ Appearance of Titans.

46 ❑ Jan 1988 Cover: 1.75 **NM** value: **Cover or less**
Circ: CapCity orders: **14,750**
• Millennium ★ Versus Floronic Man.

47 ❑ Feb 1988 Cover: 1.75 **NM** value: **Cover or less**
Circ: CapCity orders: **15,550**
• Millennium ★ Versus Harlequin.

48 ❑ Mar 1988 Cover: 1.75 **NM** value: **Cover or less**
Circ: CapCity orders: **11,100**
★ Origin of Nuklon.

49 ❑ Apr 1988 Cover: 1.75 **NM** value: **Cover or less**
Circ: CapCity orders: **11,400**
★ Appearance of Sandman.

50 ❑ May 1988 Cover: 2.50 **NM** value: **Cover or less**
Circ: CapCity orders: **11,700**
• Giant-size.

51 ❑ Jun 1988 Cover: 1.75 **NM** value: **Cover or less**
Circ: CapCity orders: **10,550**
★ Death of Skyman.

52 ❑ Jul 1988 Cover: 1.75 **NM** value: **Cover or less**
Circ: CapCity orders: **10,100**
★ Versus Helix.

53 ❑ Aug 1988 Cover: 1.75 **NM** value: **Cover or less**
Circ: CapCity orders: **10,300**
final issue. ★ Versus Injustice Unlimited.

Anl 1 ❑ Nov 1985 Cover: 2.00 **NM** value: **2.50**
Circ: CapCity orders: **9,250**
• Crisis **A:** Todd McFarlane ★ Origin of Jade and Obsidian.

Anl 2 ❑ Jul 1988 Cover: 2.00 **NM** value: **2.50**
Circ: CapCity orders: **10,200**
• crossover with Young All-Stars Annual #1

SE 1 ❑ ca. 1987 Cover: 1.50 **NM** value: **Cover or less**
Circ: CapCity orders: **10,700**
cover forms diptych with Outsiders Special #1.

INFINITY OF WARRIORS, THE **Ominous**

1 ❑ Oct 1994 Cover: 1.95 **NM** value: **Cover or less**
🕮 The Infinity of Warriors, Revelation of The Molochs **A:** Bart Sears **W:** Bart Sears

INFINITY WAR, THE **Marvel**

1 ❑ Jun 1992 Cover: 2.50 **NM** value: **Cover or less**
Circ: CapCity orders: **139,800**
gatefold cover. **A:** Ron Lim **W:** Jim Starlin

2 ❑ Jul 1992 Cover: 2.50 **NM** value: **Cover or less**
Circ: CapCity orders: **109,200**
gatefold cover. 🕮 Ethereal Revisionism **A:** Ron Lim **W:** Jim Starlin ★ Origin of Magus.

3 ❑ Aug 1992 Cover: 2.50 **NM** value: **Cover or less**
Circ: CapCity orders: **104,700**
gatefold cover. **A:** Ron Lim **W:** Jim Starlin

4 ❑ Sep 1992 Cover: 2.50 **NM** value: **Cover or less**
Circ: CapCity orders: **95,400**
gatefold cover. 🕮 Mortiferous Artifice **A:** Ron Lim **W:** Jim Starlin

5 ❑ Oct 1992 Cover: 2.50 **NM** value: **Cover or less**
Circ: CapCity orders: **92,700**
gatefold cover. 🕮 Psychomachia **A:** Ron Lim **W:** Jim Starlin

6 ❑ Nov 1992 Cover: 2.50 **NM** value: **Cover or less**
Circ: CapCity orders: **89,800**
gatefold cover. 🕮 The Animus Engagement **A:** Ron Lim **W:** Jim Starlin

INFOCHAMELEON: COMPANY CULT **Mediawarp**

1 ❑ Feb 1997, b&w Cover: 4.50 **NM** value: **Cover or less**
One-shot.

INFORMER, THE **Feature**

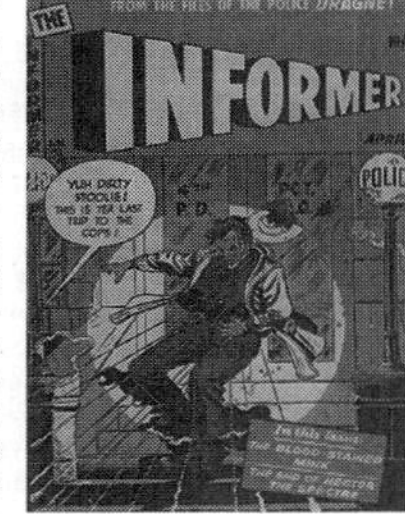

The Informer was a late and relatively minor entry into the then-crowded crime comics genre in the early 1950s. Unlike its more famous and successful competitors like Crime Does Not Pay and Justice Traps the Guilty, The Informer focuses primarily on the straight-laced undercover cops rather than the sensational antics of the criminals. There's a fair share of shoot-em-up violence, but the moral tone is much less dark and cynical than in many other crime books. Some combination of bad sales and the general backlash against adult-themed comics in the mid-50s doomed The Informer before the end of its first year. The artwork, reminiscent of both Milton Caniff (Terry and the Pirates) and Jack Kirby (at that stage of his career the reigning king of the crime comics genre), was provided by Mike Sekowsky, who later went on to become illustrator of DC's Justice League of America.

1 ❑ Apr 1954 Cover: 0.10 **NM** value: **40.00**
• **CGC:** 1 graded, best 7.5
🕮 The Blood Stained Mink; The End of Hector Spectre

2 ❑ Jun 1954 Cover: 0.10 **NM** value: **28.00**

3 ❑ Aug 1954 Cover: 0.10 **NM** value: **24.00**

4 ❑ Oct 1954 Cover: 0.10 **NM** value: **24.00**

5 ❑ Dec 1954 Cover: 0.10 **NM** value: **24.00**

IN HIS STEPS **Marvel**

1 ❑ Cover: 9.99 **NM** value: **Cover or less**
A: Fred Carrillo **W:** Martin Powell

INHUMANOIDS, THE **Marvel / Star**

1 ❑ Jan 1987 Cover: 0.75 **NM** value: **1.00**
Circ: CapCity orders: **7,450**
🕮 The Coming Of The Inhumanoids! **A:** James W. Fry III **W:** Jim Salicrup ★ 1st Appearance of Earth Corps.

2 ❑ Mar 1987 Cover: 0.75 **NM** value: **1.00**
Circ: CapCity orders: **4,850**
A: James W. Fry III **W:** Jim Salicrup

3 ❑ May 1987 Cover: 0.75 **NM** value: **1.00**
Circ: CapCity orders: **320**
A: James W. Fry III **W:** Jim Salicrup

4 ❑ Jul 1987 Cover: 1.00 **NM** value: **Cover or less**
Circ: CapCity orders: **2,600**
A: James W. Fry III **W:** Jim Salicrup

The prices seen above do not represent the highest possible prices seen in online auctions, but rather the prices we have seen these issues reliably fetch in a variety of environments (storefront retail, mail order, auction and convention).

CGC-graded: Multiply prices above by **33 for 9.9 M • 16 for 9.8 NM/M • 7 for 9.6 NM+ • 5 for 9.4 NM • 2.5 for 9.2 NM- • 1.5 for 9.0 VF/NM**

INHUMANS, THE — Marvel

First appearing in Fantastic Four #45, The Inhumans are a race of fantastic beings who make their home in Attilan, a futuristic city located in the Blue Area of the moon.

The Inhumans include Triton, a powerful amphibian; Medusa, who can entangle villains in her scarlet hair; Karnak the Shatterer, who can locate the single weakest point in any object; and Gorgon, whose cloven hoofs can destroy mountains.

They are led by the majestic Black Bolt, who must remain ever silent lest his voice cause a cataclysm.

1 ❑ Oct 1975 Cover: 0.25 **NM** value: **8.00**
• **CGC:** 32 graded, best 9.6
A: George Pérez ★ Versus Blastaar.
2 ❑ Dec 1976 Cover: 0.25 **NM** value: **5.00**
• **CGC:** 1 graded, best 9.2
3 ❑ Feb 1976 Cover: 0.25 **NM** value: **5.00**
4 ❑ Apr 1976 Cover: 0.25 **NM** value: **4.00**
• **CGC:** 1 graded, best 9.4
5 ❑ Jun 1976 Cover: 0.30 **NM** value: **4.00**
6 ❑ Aug 1976 Cover: 0.25 **NM** value: **3.50**
• **CGC:** 1 graded, best 9.0
7 ❑ Oct 1976 Cover: 0.30 **NM** value: **3.50**
8 ❑ Dec 1976 Cover: 0.30 **NM** value: **3.50**
9 ❑ Feb 1977 Cover: 0.30 **NM** value: **3.50**
10 ❑ Apr 1977 Cover: 0.30 **NM** value: **3.00**
11 ❑ Jun 1977 Cover: 0.30 **NM** value: **3.00**
12 ❑ Aug 1977 Cover: 0.30 **NM** value: **3.00**
final issue. ★ Versus Hulk.
Bk 1❑ Cover: 7.95 **NM** value: **Cover or less**
Circ: CapCity orders: **5,200**
SE 1❑ Apr 1990 Cover: 1.50 **NM** value: **2.50**
📖 The Remembrances Of Revolutions Past **A:** Richard Howell **W:** Lou Mougin ★ Origin of Medusa. ★ Appearance of Fantastic Four.

INHUMANS, THE: THE GREAT REFUGE — Marvel

1 ❑ May 1995 Cover: 2.95 **NM** value: **Cover or less**
Circ: CapCity orders: **13,250**

INHUMANS (VOL. 2) — Marvel

1 ❑ Nov 1998 Cover: 2.99 **NM** value: **4.00**
Circ: Diamd. preorders: **56,263** • **CGC:** 4 graded, best 9.6
• gatefold summary. **A:** Jae Lee **W:** Paul Jenkins
1/LE❑ Nov 1998 Cover: 19.95 **NM** value: **Cover or less**
A: Jae Lee **W:** Paul Jenkins
1/SC❑ Nov 1998 Cover: 6.95 **NM** value: **Cover or less**
DFE alternate cover. **A:** Jae Lee **W:** Paul Jenkins
2/A ❑ Dec 1998 Cover: 2.99 **NM** value: **3.50**
Circ: Diamd. preorders: **51,648**
Woman in circle on cover. • gatefold summary. 📖 Genotypical **A:** Jae Lee **W:** Paul Jenkins
2/B ❑ Dec 1998 Cover: 2.99 **NM** value: **3.50**
• gatefold summary. 📖 Genotypical **A:** Jae Lee **W:** Paul Jenkins
3 ❑ Jan 1999 Cover: 2.99 **NM** value: **3.00**
Circ: Diamd. preorders: **46,689**
A: Jae Lee **W:** Paul Jenkins
4 ❑ Feb 1999 Cover: 2.99 **NM** value: **3.00**
Circ: Diamd. preorders: **52,100**
A: Jae Lee **W:** Paul Jenkins
5 ❑ Mar 1999 Cover: 2.99 **NM** value: **3.00**
Circ: Diamd. preorders: **50,819**
• Earth vs. Attilan war **A:** Jae Lee **W:** Paul Jenkins
6 ❑ Apr 1999 Cover: 2.99 **NM** value: **Cover or less**
Circ: Diamd. preorders: **48,500**
A: Jae Lee **W:** Paul Jenkins
7 ❑ May 1999 Cover: 2.99 **NM** value: **Cover or less**
Circ: Diamd. preorders: **48,146**
A: Jae Lee **W:** Paul Jenkins
8 ❑ Jun 1999 Cover: 2.99 **NM** value: **Cover or less**
Circ: Diamd. preorders: **48,850**
📖 Woof **A:** Jae Lee **W:** Paul Jenkins
9 ❑ Jul 1999 Cover: 2.99 **NM** value: **Cover or less**
Circ: Diamd. preorders: **47,438**
A: Jae Lee **W:** Paul Jenkins
10 ❑ Aug 1999 Cover: 2.99 **NM** value: **Cover or less**
Circ: Diamd. preorders: **46,854**
A: Jae Lee **W:** Paul Jenkins
11 ❑ Sep 1999 Cover: 2.99 **NM** value: **Cover or less**
Circ: Diamd. preorders: **46,954**
A: Jae Lee **W:** Paul Jenkins
12 ❑ Oct 1999 Cover: 2.99 **NM** value: **Cover or less**
Circ: Diamd. preorders: **44,414**
A: Jae Lee **W:** Paul Jenkins

INHUMANS (VOL. 3) — Marvel

1 ❑ Jun 2000 Cover: 2.99 **NM** value: **Cover or less**
Circ: Diamd. preorders: **38,408** • **CGC:** 1 graded, best 9.8
📖 Stars Our Destiny **A:** Ladronn **W:** Carlos Pacheco; Rafael Marin
2 ❑ Jul 2000 Cover: 2.99 **NM** value: **Cover or less**
Circ: Diamd. preorders: **34,663**
3 ❑ Aug 2000 Cover: 2.99 **NM** value: **Cover or less**
Circ: Diamd. preorders: **35,579**
4 ❑ Sep 2000 Cover: 2.99 **NM** value: **Cover or less**

INK PUNK — Fantagraphics

Bk 1❑ b&w Cover: 9.95 **NM** value: **Cover or less**
• third collection of Underworld strips

IN LOVE — Mainline

1 ❑ Aug 1954 Cover: 0.10 **NM** value: **150.00**
📖 Bride of the Star
2 ❑ Oct 1954 Cover: 0.10 **NM** value: **85.00**
3 ❑ Dec 1955 Cover: 0.10 **NM** value: **85.00**
4 ❑ Mar 1955 Cover: 0.10 **NM** value: **85.00**
5 ❑ May 1955 Cover: 0.10 **NM** value: **35.00**
6 ❑ Jul 1955 Cover: 0.10 **NM** value: **35.00**

INMATES PRISONERS OF SOCIETY — Delta

1 ❑ Aug 1997 Cover: 2.95 **NM** value: **Cover or less**
A: Chris Meeks **W:** Terrance Griep Jr. Jr.
2 ❑ Mar 1998 Cover: 2.95 **NM** value: **Cover or less**
A: Chris Meeks **W:** Terrance Griep Jr. Jr.
3 ❑ Jul 1998 Cover: 2.95 **NM** value: **Cover or less**
A: Chris Meeks **W:** Terrance Griep Jr. Jr.
4 ❑ Nov 1998 Cover: 2.95 **NM** value: **Cover or less**
A: Chris Meeks **W:** Terrance Griep Jr. Jr.

INNERCIRCLE — Mushroom

0.1 ❑ Feb 1995 Cover: 2.50 **NM** value: **Cover or less**
📖 Assimilation Begins… **A:** Perry S. Yem; Don Figueroa **W:** Robert Lugibihl; Todd Tochioka

INNER-CITY PRODUCTS — Hype

1 ❑ b&w Cover: 2.00 **NM** value: **Cover or less**

INNOCENT BYSTANDER — Ollie Ollie! Oxen Free Press

1 ❑ Cover: 2.50 **NM** value: **2.95**
★ 1st Appearance of Lao Shan, Balac-Soon.
2 ❑ Cover: 2.75 **NM** value: **2.95**
3 ❑ Cover: 2.75 **NM** value: **2.95**
4 ❑ Sum 1997 Cover: 2.75 **NM** value: **2.95**
5 ❑ Win 1998 Cover: 2.95 **NM** value: **Cover or less**
6 ❑ Fal 1998 Cover: 2.95 **NM** value: **Cover or less**

INNOVATION PREVIEW SPECIAL — Innovation

1 ❑ Jun 1989 Cover: 1.00 **NM** value: **Cover or less**
• sampler

INNOVATION SPECTACULAR — Innovation

1 ❑ Dec 1990 Cover: 2.95 **NM** value: **Cover or less**
Circ: CapCity orders: **2,085**
2 ❑ Jan 1991 Cover: 2.95 **NM** value: **Cover or less**

INNOVATION SUMMER FUN SPECIAL — Innovation

1 ❑ Cover: 3.50 **NM** value: **Cover or less**

INOVATORS — Dark Moon

1 ❑ Apr 1995 Cover: 2.50 **NM** value: **Cover or less**
cardstock cover. 📖 Second Chances **A:** Cesar Feliciano **W:** Tom Sniegoski

IN RAGE — CFD

1 ❑ Cover: 2.50 **NM** value: **Cover or less**
📖 Cherokee; Censorshit; F*ck the Moral Minority; Superheroes? The Comic Book; Magic: A Preview; A simple Summer Strip; Cosmic Debris; Candyland; Bleating Hearts; Patriot **A:** Jaxon Renick; Randy Zimmerman; Shannon Wheeler; Hart D. Fischer; Jason Moore; Bob Hollister; Cris Crosby; Cris Edbauer; Deanne Dewitt; Keith Pannell; Michael McNulty; Mike Davis; Scott Harding **W:** Jaxon Renick; Randy Zimmerman; Shannon Wheeler; Hart D. Fischer; Jason Moore; Bob Hollister; Cris Crosby; Cris Edbauer; Deanne Dewitt; Keith Pannell; Michael McNulty; Mike Davis; Scott Harding

INSANE — Dark Horse

1 ❑ Feb 1988 Cover: 1.75 **NM** value: **Cover or less**
📖 Dim Jack; Mundane's Bar; Clodzilla; Mutant **A:** Stephen D. Sullivan; Dave Schwartz; Hilary Barta; Brian Thomas; Mike Richardson **W:** Dave Schwartz; Hilary Barta; Jim Bradrick; Brian Thomas
2 ❑ Cover: 1.75 **NM** value: **Cover or less**

INSANE CLOWN POSSE — Chaos

This may be one of the loudest comics series ever published. Sound effects, screams, splashes of violent color — it's all loud. That's appropriate, since Insane Clown Posse is a band, one which rose to prominence during one of the recording industry's spasmodic reactions against violent lyrics. As loud as the comic book is, the band is probably louder.

Few will find either as loud as the hum coming from Fredric Wertham's grave. In #1, writer Jesse McCann and illustrator Reb serve such an abattoir of a comic book that ConEd could use the Doctor's spinning body to generate electricity for the whole eastern seaboard. Using the magical power of the Dark Carnival, Violent J and Shaggy 2 Dope wreak vengeance through vivisection, among other horrors. We'd say "righteous vengeance," but they enjoy it too much. There's even a stab (well, it's more of a slice) against their corporate enemy, Big D Music.

Fortunately, the series was never discovered by anyone outside its intended heavy-metal listening audience. A random page of this title's unpleasantness appearing on 20/20 could have found us all in front of a Senate Subcommittee again. — JJM

1 ❑ Jun 1999 Cover: 2.95 **NM** value: **Cover or less**
Circ: Diamd. preorders: **14,596**
📖 The Upz & Downz of the Wicked Clownz **A:** Reb **W:** Jesse Leon McCann
1/A ❑ Jun 1999 **NM** value: **8.00**
• Tower Reocrds variant **W:** Jesse Leon McCann
2 ❑ Aug 1999 Cover: 2.95 **NM** value: **Cover or less**
📖 The Amazing Jeckel Brothers **A:** Jerry Beck **W:** Jesse Leon McCann
2/CS❑ Aug 1999 **NM** value: **7.00**
3 ❑ Oct 1999 Cover: 2.95 **NM** value: **Cover or less**
📖 Raze the Desertz of Glass **A:** Jerry Beck **W:** Jesse Leon McCann
3/A ❑ Oct 1999 **NM** value: **10.00**
• Tower Reocrds variant
4 ❑ Jan 2000 Cover: 5.95 **NM** value: **Cover or less**
Says #1 on cover with Pendulum below issue number. 📖 The Pendulum, Part 1 • polybagged with first of 12 Pendulum CDs **A:** Jerry Beck **W:** Jesse Leon McCann
4/CS❑ Jan 2000 **NM** value: **8.00**
5 ❑ 2000 Cover: 2.95 **NM** value: **Cover or less**
5/CS❑ 2000 **NM** value: **8.00**
6 ❑ 2000 Cover: 2.95 **NM** value: **Cover or less**
7 ❑ 2000 Cover: 2.95 **NM** value: **Cover or less**
7/CS❑ 2000 **NM** value: **8.00**
Bk 1❑ Jul 2000 Cover: 8.95 **NM** value: **Cover or less**
No issue number. • Trade Paperback. • collects #1-3 **A:** Jerry Beck **W:** Jesse Leon McCann

IN SEARCH OF THE CASTAWAYS — Gold Key

1 ❑ Mar 1963 **NM** value: **50.00**
• **CGC:** 1 graded, best 8.0

INSIDE CRIME — Fox

2 ❑ Sep 1950 Cover: 0.10 **NM** value: **150.00**
• **CGC:** 3 graded, best 8.5
3 ❑ Jul 1950 Cover: 0.10 **NM** value: **150.00**
• **CGC:** 2 graded, best 9.2

INSIDE OUT KING, THE — Free Fall

1 ❑ Cover: 2.95 **NM** value: **Cover or less**
A: Ron Brown **W:** Ron Brown
1-2 ❑ Cover: 2.95 **NM** value: **Cover or less**

INSOMNIA — Fantagraphics

1 ❑ Cover: 2.95 **NM** value: **Cover or less**
No issue number.

INSTANT PIANO — Dark Horse

1 ❑ Aug 1994, b&w Cover: 3.95 **NM** value: **Cover or less**
Circ: CapCity orders: **3,875**
📖 The Eltingville Comic-Book Science-Fiction Fantasy-Horror and Role-Playing Club **A:** Mark Badger; Evan Dorkin; Kyle Baker; Stephen DeStefano; Robbie Busch **W:** Mark Badger; Evan Dorkin; Kyle Baker; Stephen DeStefano; Robbie Busch
2 ❑ Dec 1994, b&w Cover: 3.95 **NM** value: **Cover or less**
Circ: CapCity orders: **2,125**
A: Mark Badger; Evan Dorkin; Kyle Baker; Stephen DeStefano; Robbie Busch **W:** Mark Badger; Evan Dorkin; Kyle Baker; Stephen DeStefano; Robbie Busch
3 ❑ Feb 1995, b&w Cover: 3.95 **NM** value: **Cover or less**
Circ: CapCity orders: **2,225**
A: Mark Badger; Evan Dorkin; Kyle Baker; Stephen DeStefano; Robbie Busch **W:** Mark Badger; Evan Dorkin; Kyle Baker; Stephen DeStefano; Robbie Busch
4 ❑ Jun 1995, b&w Cover: 3.95 **NM** value: **Cover or less**
A: Mark Badger; Evan Dorkin; Kyle Baker; Stephen DeStefano; Robbie Busch **W:** Mark Badger; Evan Dorkin; Kyle Baker; Stephen DeStefano; Robbie Busch

INTENSE! — Pure Imagination

2 ❑ b&w Cover: 3.00 **NM** value: **Cover or less**
A: Basil Wolverton

INTERACTIVE COMICS — Adventure

1 ❑ Cover: 4.95 **NM** value: **Cover or less**
No issue number. 📖 Saves World
2 ❑ b&w Cover: 4.95 **NM** value: **Cover or less**
No issue number.

INTERFACE — Marvel / Epic

Since time immemorial, two secret cabals of ESPers — The Inner Circle and The Triad — have influenced the actions of governments in order to further their own ends. It explains a lot, actually: all the senseless wars, political struggles, and assorted strife that has plagued mankind throughout history. The cabals subtly bend the wills of world leaders, using the human race as pawns in their eternal battle.

The cabals work in absolute secrecy, and have made a practice of promoting bogus psychics and theories as a way of making the whole idea seem absurd. And those with real psychic abilities are given the choice of either joining them or dying.

James Hudnall's Interface is the story of those who chose a third option: to fight. It's a gripping tale of conspiracy, serial killers, and secret societies.

1 ❑ Dec 1989 Cover: 1.95 **NM** value: **Cover or less**
Circ: CapCity orders: **11,800**
📖 Espers **A:** Paul Johnson **W:** James D. Hudnall
1 ❑ Dec 1989 Cover: 1.95 **NM** value: **Cover or less**
Circ: CapCity orders: **11,800**
📖 Espers **A:** Paul Johnson **W:** James D. Hudnall

Other grades: Multiply prices above by **1.5 for Mint • 2/3 for Very Fine • 1/3 for Fine • 1/5 for Very Good • 1/8 for Good**

2 ❑ Feb 1990 Cover: 1.95 **NM** value: **Cover or less**
Circ: CapCity orders: **8,350**
Assassins **A:** Paul Johnson **W:** James D. Hudnall

2 ❑ Feb 1990 Cover: 1.95 **NM** value: **Cover or less**
Circ: CapCity orders: **8,350**
Assassins **A:** Paul Johnson **W:** James D. Hudnall

3 ❑ Apr 1990 Cover: 1.95 **NM** value: **Cover or less**
Circ: CapCity orders: **6,200**
Awareness **A:** Paul Johnson **W:** James D. Hudnall

3 ❑ Apr 1990 Cover: 1.95 **NM** value: **Cover or less**
Circ: CapCity orders: **6,200**
Awareness **A:** Paul Johnson **W:** James D. Hudnall

4 ❑ Jun 1990 Cover: 1.95 **NM** value: **Cover or less**
Circ: CapCity orders: **5,350**
Information **A:** Paul Johnson **W:** James D. Hudnall

4 ❑ Jun 1990 Cover: 1.95 **NM** value: **Cover or less**
Circ: CapCity orders: **5,350**
Information **A:** Paul Johnson **W:** James D. Hudnall

5 ❑ Aug 1990 Cover: 1.95 **NM** value: **Cover or less**
Circ: CapCity orders: **5,000**
Destruction **A:** Paul Johnson **W:** James D. Hudnall

5 ❑ Aug 1990 Cover: 1.95 **NM** value: **Cover or less**
Circ: CapCity orders: **5,000**
Destruction **A:** Paul Johnson **W:** James D. Hudnall

6 ❑ Oct 1990 Cover: 2.25 **NM** value: **Cover or less**
Circ: CapCity orders: **4,850**
Wet Work **A:** Paul Johnson **W:** James D. Hudnall

6 ❑ Oct 1990 Cover: 2.25 **NM** value: **Cover or less**
Circ: CapCity orders: **4,850**
Wet Work **A:** Paul Johnson **W:** James D. Hudnall

6 ❑ Oct 1990 Cover: 2.25 **NM** value: **Cover or less**
Circ: CapCity orders: **4,850**
Wet Work **A:** Paul Johnson **W:** James D. Hudnall

6 ❑ Oct 1990 Cover: 2.25 **NM** value: **Cover or less**
Circ: CapCity orders: **4,850**
Wet Work **A:** Paul Johnson **W:** James D. Hudnall

7 ❑ Nov 1990 Cover: 2.25 **NM** value: **Cover or less**
Circ: CapCity orders: **4,500**
Fallout **A:** Bill Koeb **W:** James D. Hudnall

7 ❑ Nov 1990 Cover: 2.25 **NM** value: **Cover or less**
Circ: CapCity orders: **4,500**
Fallout **A:** Bill Koeb **W:** James D. Hudnall

7 ❑ Nov 1990 Cover: 2.25 **NM** value: **Cover or less**
Circ: CapCity orders: **4,500**
Fallout **A:** Bill Koeb **W:** James D. Hudnall

7 ❑ Nov 1990 Cover: 2.25 **NM** value: **Cover or less**
Circ: CapCity orders: **4,500**
Fallout **A:** Bill Koeb **W:** James D. Hudnall

8 ❑ Dec 1990 Cover: 2.25 **NM** value: **Cover or less**
Circ: CapCity orders: **4,300**
Closure final issue. **A:** Dan Brereton **W:** James D. Hudnall

8 ❑ Dec 1990 Cover: 2.25 **NM** value: **Cover or less**
Circ: CapCity orders: **4,300**
Closure final issue. **A:** Dan Brereton **W:** James D. Hudnall

8 ❑ Dec 1990 Cover: 2.25 **NM** value: **Cover or less**
Circ: CapCity orders: **4,300**
Closure final issue. **A:** Dan Brereton **W:** James D. Hudnall

8 ❑ Dec 1990 Cover: 2.25 **NM** value: **Cover or less**
Circ: CapCity orders: **4,300**
Closure final issue. **A:** Dan Brereton **W:** James D. Hudnall

Bk 1❑ Cover: 16.95 **NM** value: **Cover or less**
• Collects series **A:** Paul Johnson; Dan Brereton **W:** James D. Hudnall

Bk 1❑ Cover: 16.95 **NM** value: **Cover or less**
• Collects series **A:** Paul Johnson; Dan Brereton **W:** James D. Hudnall

Bk 1❑ Cover: 16.95 **NM** value: **Cover or less**
• Collects series **A:** Paul Johnson; Dan Brereton **W:** James D. Hudnall

INTERNATIONAL COMICS — E.C.

Gardner Fox wrote the stories for this E.C. title which began a morphing sequence which ended as The Crypt of Terror. The Pre-Trend title began as a crime comic book and it had adventures of continuing characters Van Manhattan and Madelon. The first morphing occurred with #6, which was retitled International Crime Patrol, introduced in #5 with the cover copy "Introducing the INTERNATIONAL CRIME-BUSTING PATROL … . featuring Van Manhattan, Igor, Madelon and the Chessmen …. in a thrilling book-length story!" — Maggie

1 ❑ Spr 1947 Cover: 0.10 **NM** value: **500.00**
• **CGC:** 3 graded, best 8.5

2 ❑ Sum 1947 Cover: 0.10 **NM** value: **350.00**
• **CGC:** 2 graded, best 9.4

3 ❑ Jul 1947 Cover: 0.10 **NM** value: **300.00**
• **CGC:** 3 graded, best 8.5

4 ❑ Sep 1947 Cover: 0.10 **NM** value: **300.00**
• **CGC:** 5 graded, best 9.4

5 ❑ Nov 1947 Cover: 0.10 **NM** value: **300.00**
• **CGC:** 3 graded, best 6.0

INTERNATIONAL COWGIRL MAGAZINE — Iconografix

1 ❑ b&w Cover: 2.95 **NM** value: **Cover or less**
2 ❑ b&w Cover: 2.95 **NM** value: **Cover or less**

INTERNATIONAL CRIME PATROL — E.C.

The E.C. title was a one-issue link between the company's International Comics and its Crime Patrol. — Maggie

6 ❑ Spr 1948 Cover: 0.10 **NM** value: **500.00**
• **CGC:** 3 graded, best 6.5

INTERNATIONAL FALLOUT SHELTER ZONE — KHB

1 ❑ b&w Cover: 1.25 **NM** value: **Cover or less**
Blind Allegiance; The Puppeteer: Follow the Leader **A:** Don Michalowski; Bob Farrell **W:** Ken Branch; Michael J. Calleri

2 ❑ b&w Cover: 1.25 **NM** value: **Cover or less**
3 ❑ b&w Cover: 1.25 **NM** value: **Cover or less**
4 ❑ b&w Cover: 1.25 **NM** value: **Cover or less**

INTERPLANETARY LIZARDS OF THE TEXAS PLAINS — Leadbelly

0 ❑ Cover: 2.50 **NM** value: **Cover or less**
1 ❑ b&w Cover: 2.00 **NM** value: **Cover or less**
2 ❑ b&w Cover: 2.00 **NM** value: **Cover or less**
3 ❑ Cover: 2.00 **NM** value: **Cover or less**
The Dark Ages **A:** Alan Jude Summa; Glenn Boyd **W:** Alan Jude Summa; Glenn Boyd

8 ❑ b&w Cover: 2.50 **NM** value: **Cover or less**

INTERVIEW WITH THE VAMPIRE (ANNE RICE'S…) — Innovation

In an adaptation of Anne Rice's classic tale of modern horror, Interview with the Vampire stars the vampire Lestat, eldest of all the undead. For hundreds of years he has lurked about in the shadows of our world, ever since he himself felt the bite of vampiric fangs in his own neck so long ago. Now, the time has come to tell the remarkable story of his life — and unlife. It's a story of power, betrayal, remorse, and the love of the damned. And in telling his story to the hapless interviewer, he sheds light not only on his own existence, but on an entire underworld where love and pain do not stop with death.

1 ❑ ca. 1991 Cover: 2.50 **NM** value: **4.00**
Circ: CapCity orders: **18,355** • **CGC:** 1 graded, best 9.4
The Last Sunrise **A:** Joe Phillips **W:** Anne Rice; Cynthy J. Wood

2 ❑ ca. 1991 Cover: 2.50 **NM** value: **3.00**
Circ: CapCity orders: **12,320**
A: Alexander Jubran **W:** Anne Rice; Faye Perozich

3 ❑ ca. 1991 Cover: 2.50 **NM** value: **Cover or less**
Circ: CapCity orders: **9,605**
A: Alexander Jubran **W:** Anne Rice; Faye Perozich

4 ❑ ca. 1991 Cover: 2.50 **NM** value: **Cover or less**
Circ: CapCity orders: **8,335**
And a Little Child… **A:** Alexander Jubran **W:** Anne Rice; Cynthy J. Wood; Faye Perozich

5 ❑ ca. 1992 Cover: 2.50 **NM** value: **Cover or less**
Circ: CapCity orders: **5,985**
A: Alexander Jubran **W:** Anne Rice; Faye Perozich

6 ❑ ca. 1992 Cover: 2.50 **NM** value: **Cover or less**
Circ: CapCity orders: **6,660**
A: Alexander Jubran **W:** Anne Rice; Faye Perozich

7 ❑ ca. 1992 Cover: 2.50 **NM** value: **Cover or less**
Circ: CapCity orders: **6,750**
In Despair **A:** Alexander Jubran **W:** Anne Rice; Faye Perozich

8 ❑ ca. 1993 Cover: 2.50 **NM** value: **Cover or less**
Circ: CapCity orders: **6,835**
A: Alexander Jubran **W:** Anne Rice; Faye Perozich

9 ❑ ca. 1993 Cover: 2.50 **NM** value: **Cover or less**
Circ: CapCity orders: **6,620**
A: Alexander Jubran **W:** Anne Rice; Faye Perozich

10 ❑ ca. 1993 Cover: 2.50 **NM** value: **Cover or less**
Circ: CapCity orders: **6,850**
Phantoms **A:** Alexander Jubran **W:** Anne Rice; Faye Perozich

11 ❑ ca. 1993 Cover: 2.50 **NM** value: **Cover or less**
Circ: CapCity orders: **6,370**
A: Alexander Jubran **W:** Anne Rice; Faye Perozich

12 ❑ ca. 1993 Cover: 2.50 **NM** value: **Cover or less**
Circ: CapCity orders: **6,150**
A: Alexander Jubran **W:** Anne Rice; Faye Perozich

IN THE DAYS OF THE ACE ROCK 'N' ROLL CLUB — Fantagraphics

1 ❑ b&w Cover: 4.95 **NM** value: **Cover or less**
No issue number.

IN THE DAYS OF THE MOB — DC

1 ❑ Fal 1971 Cover: 0.50 **NM** value: **2.00**
Welcome to Hell; Ma's Boys; Bullets for Big Al; The Breeding Ground; Funeral for a Florist (text); The Kansas City Massacre; Method of Operation

IN THE PRESENCE OF MINE ENEMIES — Spire

1 ❑ Cover: 0.39 **NM** value: **5.00**
A: Al Hartley

IN THIN AIR — Tome Press

1/A ❑ b&w Cover: 2.95 **NM** value: **Cover or less**
• With alternate ending #1 **A:** Ken Holewczynski **W:** Steven Seagle

1/B ❑ b&w Cover: 2.95 **NM** value: **Cover or less**
• With alternate ending #2 **A:** Ken Holewczynski **W:** Steven Seagle

INTIMATE CONFESSIONS (I.W.) — I.W.

9 ❑ ca. 1964 **NM** value: **10.00**
10 ❑ ca. 1964 **NM** value: **10.00**

INTIMATE CONFESSIONS (REALISTIC) — Realistic Comics

1 ❑ Jul 1951 Cover: 0.10 **NM** value: **500.00**
• **CGC:** 2 graded, best 7.0

2 ❑ Sep 1951 Cover: 0.10 **NM** value: **200.00**
3 ❑ Nov 1951 Cover: 0.10 **NM** value: **200.00**
8 ❑ Mar 1953 Cover: 0.10 **NM** value: **150.00**
4 ❑ Jan 1952 Cover: 0.10 **NM** value: **150.00**
5 ❑ Apr 1952 Cover: 0.10 **NM** value: **150.00**
6 ❑ Jun 1952 Cover: 0.10 **NM** value: **150.00**
7 ❑ Aug 1952 Cover: 0.10 **NM** value: **150.00**

INTIMATE LOVE — Standard

Standard stories of romantic complications interspersed between single page fashion and beauty tips, as well as the requisite text story and advice column, comprise the bulk of this title. The romantic complications range from simple, immature misunderstandings to memory-suppressed tragedies. Definitely a product of its times, the moral of these stories taught its generally female audience that true love will solve a multitude of life's problems. Regardless of the severity of the dilemma, a happily-ever-after scenario could always be counted on in eight pages or less.

5 ❑ Jan 1950 Cover: 0.10**NM** value: **50.00**
6 ❑ Mar 1950 Cover: 0.10 **NM** value: **50.00**
7 ❑ Jun 1950 Cover: 0.10 **NM** value: **22.00**
8 ❑ Cover: 0.10 **NM** value: **22.00**
9 ❑ Cover: 0.10 **NM** value: **22.00**
10 ❑ 1951 Cover: 0.10 **NM** value: **22.00**
Jane Russell, Robert Mitchum photo cover.

11 ❑ 1951 Cover: 0.10 **NM** value: **13.00**
12 ❑ 1951 Cover: 0.10 **NM** value: **13.00**
13 ❑ 1951 Cover: 0.10 **NM** value: **13.00**
14 ❑ 1951 Cover: 0.10 **NM** value: **13.00**
15 ❑ Cover: 0.10 **NM** value: **13.00**
16 ❑ Cover: 0.10 **NM** value: **13.00**
17 ❑ 1952 Cover: 0.10 **NM** value: **13.00**
18 ❑ 1952 Cover: 0.10 **NM** value: **13.00**
19 ❑ 1952 Cover: 0.10 **NM** value: **13.00**
20 ❑ Nov 1952 Cover: 0.10 **NM** value: **13.00**
21 ❑ 1953 Cover: 0.10 **NM** value: **9.00**
22 ❑ 1953 Cover: 0.10 **NM** value: **9.00**
23 ❑ 1953 Cover: 0.10 **NM** value: **9.00**
24 ❑ 1953 Cover: 0.10 **NM** value: **9.00**
25 ❑ Cover: 0.10 **NM** value: **9.00**
26 ❑ Cover: 0.10 **NM** value: **9.00**
27 ❑ Cover: 0.10 **NM** value: **9.00**
Borrowed Romance; Love Out West; Conversation Clues; Innocent Sinner; Don't Bet On Love (text story); Stood Up!; Women; Where do. I Belong?; Sweatheart WantedTry These Campus Glamour Tricks

28 ❑ Aug 1954 Cover: 0.10 **NM** value: **9.00**

INTIMATE SECRETS OF ROMANCE — Star Publications

1 ❑ Sep 1953 Cover: 0.10 **NM** value: **100.00**
2 ❑ Apr 1954 Cover: 0.10 **NM** value: **100.00**

INTRAZONE — Brainstorm

1 ❑ Mar 1993, b&w Cover: 2.95 **NM** value: **Cover or less**
Field Report **A:** Scott Harrison **W:** Scott Harrison

1/LE❑ Mar 1993 Cover: 5.95 **NM** value: **Cover or less**
• limited edition. Field Report **A:** Scott Harrison **W:** Scott Harrison

2 ❑ Apr 1993, b&w Cover: 2.95 **NM** value: **Cover or less**
A: Scott Harrison **W:** Scott Harrison

2/LE❑ Apr 1993 Cover: 5.95 **NM** value: **Cover or less**
• limited edition. **A:** Scott Harrison **W:** Scott Harrison

INTRIGUE — Image

1/A ❑ Aug 1999 Cover: 2.50 **NM** value: **Cover or less**
Circ: Diamd. preorders: **13,794**
A: Kaare Andrews **W:** Howard M. Shum

1/B ❑ Aug 1999 Cover: 2.50 **NM** value: **Cover or less**
alternate cover with woman firing directly at reader. • Woman's face in background **A:** Kaare Andrews **W:** Howard M. Shum

2/A ❑ Sep 1999 Cover: 2.50 **NM** value: **Cover or less**
Circ: Diamd. preorders: **9,453**
Woman posting next to target on cover. **A:** Kaare Andrews **W:** Howard M. Shum

2/B ❑ Sep 1999 Cover: 2.50 **NM** value: **Cover or less**
alternate cover. **A:** Kaare Andrews **W:** Howard M. Shum

3 ❑ Oct 1999 Cover: 2.50 **NM** value: **2.95**
Circ: Diamd. preorders: **8,340**
A: Kaare Andrews; Tom Bancroft **W:** Howard M. Shum

INTRIGUE (QUALITY) — Quality

1 ❑ Jan 1955 Cover: 0.10 **NM** value: **250.00**

INTRUDER COMICS MODULE — TSR

1 ❑ Cover: 2.95 **NM** value: **Cover or less**
Circ: CapCity orders: **4,524**
Breakthrough! **A:** Tim Gula; Steven Grant **W:** Tim Gula; Steven Grant

2 ❑ Cover: 2.95 **NM** value: **Cover or less**
Circ: CapCity orders: **3,250**

3 ❑ Cover: 2.95 **NM** value: **Cover or less**
Circ: CapCity orders: **2,450**

4 ❑ Cover: 2.95 **NM** value: **Cover or less**
Circ: CapCity orders: **2,150**

5 ❑ Cover: 2.95 **NM** value: **Cover or less**
Circ: CapCity orders: **1,920**
"Intruder II" on cover. Alexandria; The Intuder Archives **A:** Bruce Zick **W:** Steven Grant

6 ❑ Cover: 2.95 **NM** value: **Cover or less**
Circ: CapCity orders: **1,536**
"Intruder II" on cover. Second Hand Twilight Part 1 **A:** Bruce Zick **W:** Steven Grant

7 ❑ Cover: 2.95 **NM** value: **Cover or less**
Circ: CapCity orders: **1,536**
• Intruder II

CGC-graded: Multiply prices above by **33 for 9.9 M • 16 for 9.8 NM/M • 7 for 9.6 NM+ • 5 for 9.4 NM • 2.5 for 9.2 NM- • 1.5 for 9.0 VF/NM**

8 ❑ Cover: 2.95 **NM** value: **Cover or less**
Circ: CapCity orders: **1,152**
• Intruder II
9 ❑ Cover: 2.95 **NM** value: **Cover or less**
• Intruder II

INU-YASHA — Viz

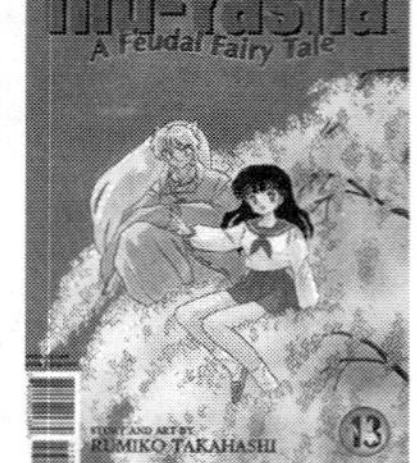

Ranma 1/2 creator Rumiko Takahashi began this feudal fairy tale in 1996 in the pages of the weekly manga magazine Shonen Sunday. Set in medieval Japan, the series features demons, monsters, and a modern-day girl who has been transported back in time by an evil monster that was haunting the shrine her family had taken up residence in.

The girl, Kagome, is hailed as the reincarnation of the ancient people's long-dead priestess Kikyo, who had slain the demon Inu-Yasha with a magic arrow before she, herself died. When Kagome faces other monsters, the truth of her reincarnation seems to be revealed.

Later Kagome learns that Kikyo didn't kill Inu-Yasha, merely trapped him. Kagome frees the demon, who becomes her ally. — Brent

1 ❑ Apr 1997 Cover: 2.95 **NM** value: **Cover or less**
Circ: Diamd. preorders: **9,800**
2 ❑ May 1997 Cover: 2.95 **NM** value: **Cover or less**
Circ: Diamd. preorders: **7,697**
3 ❑ Jun 1997 Cover: 2.95 **NM** value: **Cover or less**
Circ: Diamd. preorders: **7,666**
4 ❑ Jul 1997 Cover: 2.95 **NM** value: **Cover or less**
Circ: Diamd. preorders: **7,861**
5 ❑ Aug 1997 Cover: 2.95 **NM** value: **Cover or less**
Circ: Diamd. preorders: **7,906**
6 ❑ Sep 1997 Cover: 3.25 **NM** value: **Cover or less**
Circ: Diamd. preorders: **8,194**
7 ❑ Oct 1997 Cover: 3.25 **NM** value: **Cover or less**
Circ: Diamd. preorders: **8,035**
8 ❑ Nov 1997 Cover: 3.25 **NM** value: **Cover or less**
Circ: Diamd. preorders: **8,025**
9 ❑ Dec 1997 Cover: 3.25 **NM** value: **Cover or less**
Circ: Diamd. preorders: **7,790**
10 ❑ Jan 1998 Cover: 3.25 **NM** value: **Cover or less**
Circ: Diamd. preorders: **7,536**
11 ❑ Feb 1998 Cover: 3.25 **NM** value: **Cover or less**
Circ: Diamd. preorders: **7,137**
12 ❑ Mar 1998 Cover: 3.25 **NM** value: **Cover or less**
Circ: Diamd. preorders: **7,184**
13 ❑ Apr 1998 Cover: 3.25 **NM** value: **Cover or less**
Circ: Diamd. preorders: **7,235**
14 ❑ May 1998 Cover: 3.25 **NM** value: **Cover or less**
Circ: Diamd. preorders: **6,971**
15 ❑ Jun 1998 Cover: 3.25 **NM** value: **Cover or less**
Circ: Diamd. preorders: **6,916**
Bk 1❑ Mar 1998 Cover: 15.95 **NM** value: **Cover or less**
• Trade Paperback. • collects issues #1 through first half of #6
Bk 2❑ Jul 1998 Cover: 15.95 **NM** value: **Cover or less**
• Trade Paperback. • collects issues #6 (second half) through #11 (first half)
Bk 3❑ Dec 1998 Cover: 15.95 **NM** value: **Cover or less**
• Trade Paperback. • collects issues #11 (second half) through Inu-Yasha Part 2 #1

INU-YASHA PART 2 — Viz

1 ❑ Jul 1998 Cover: 2.95 **NM** value: **Cover or less**
Circ: Diamd. preorders: **6,646**
2 ❑ Aug 1998 Cover: 2.95 **NM** value: **Cover or less**
Circ: Diamd. preorders: **6,311**
3 ❑ Sep 1998 Cover: 3.25 **NM** value: **Cover or less**
Circ: Diamd. preorders: **6,263**
4 ❑ Oct 1998 Cover: 3.25 **NM** value: **Cover or less**
Circ: Diamd. preorders: **6,141**
5 ❑ Nov 1998 Cover: 3.25 **NM** value: **Cover or less**
Circ: Diamd. preorders: **6,030**
6 ❑ Dec 1998 Cover: 3.25 **NM** value: **Cover or less**
Circ: Diamd. preorders: **5,818**
7 ❑ Jan 1999 Cover: 3.25 **NM** value: **Cover or less**
Circ: Diamd. preorders: **5,780**
8 ❑ Feb 1999 Cover: 3.25 **NM** value: **Cover or less**
Circ: Diamd. preorders: **5,626**
9 ❑ Mar 1999 Cover: 3.25 **NM** value: **Cover or less**
Circ: Diamd. preorders: **5,640**

INU-YASHA PART 3 — Viz

1 ❑ Apr 1999 Cover: 3.25 **NM** value: **Cover or less**
Circ: Diamd. preorders: **6,175**
2 ❑ May 1999 Cover: 3.25 **NM** value: **Cover or less**
Circ: Diamd. preorders: **5,780**
3 ❑ Jun 1999 Cover: 3.25 **NM** value: **Cover or less**
Circ: Diamd. preorders: **5,576**
4 ❑ Jul 1999 Cover: 3.25 **NM** value: **Cover or less**
Circ: Diamd. preorders: **5,619**
5 ❑ Aug 1999 Cover: 3.25 **NM** value: **Cover or less**
Circ: Diamd. preorders: **5,533**
6 ❑ Sep 1999 Cover: 3.25 **NM** value: **Cover or less**
Circ: Diamd. preorders: **5,311**
7 ❑ Oct 1999 Cover: 3.25 **NM** value: **Cover or less**
Circ: Diamd. preorders: **5,398**

INVADERS, THE — Marvel

During the 1940s, Marvel had three great heroes: Captain America, The Human Torch, and Namor, The Sub-Mariner. As kid sidekicks were considered necessary for any self-respecting super-hero in those days, we should also count Captain America's sidekick, Bucky, and The Torch's partner, Toro. With World War II raging in the real world, Marvel showed its patriotic spirit by having these super-heroes spend most of their time battling the same Nazi menace.

Three decades later, Marvel hit on the idea of revisiting those days, teaming up its greatest Golden Age heroes as The Invaders. These five, with occasional help from other Golden Age heroes like Miss Liberty and The Whizzer, take on the battle against Axis forces, both at home and abroad.

1 ❑ Aug 1975 Cover: 0.25 **NM** value: **10.00**
• **CGC:** 46 graded, best 9.8
• continued from Giant-Size Invaders #1. The Ring of the Nebulas • Marvel Value Stamp #A/37: The Watcher **A:** Frank Robbins **W:** Roy Thomas
2 ❑ Oct 1975 Cover: 0.25 **NM** value: **7.00**
• **CGC:** 1 graded, best 9.6
Twilight of the Star-Gods ★ 1st Appearance of Mailbag, Brain Drain. ★ Versus Donar.
3 ❑ Nov 1975 Cover: 0.25 **NM** value: **5.00**
• **CGC:** 1 graded, best 9.4
Blitzkrieg at Bermuda • Captain America vs. Namor vs. Torch ★ 1st Appearance of U-Man.
4 ❑ Jan 1976 Cover: 0.25 **NM** value: **5.00**
• **CGC:** 1 graded, best 9.4
U-Man Must Be Stopped ★ Origin of U-Man. ★ Versus U-Man.
5 ❑ Mar 1976 Cover: 0.25 **NM** value: **5.00**
• **CGC:** 1 graded, best 9.6
Red Skull in the Sunset ★ 1st Appearance of Fin. ★ Versus Red Skull.
6 ❑ May 1976 Cover: 0.25 **NM** value: **4.00**
• **CGC:** 2 graded, best 9.2
And Let the Battle Begin ★ Appearance of Liberty Legion.
7 ❑ Jul 1976 Cover: 0.25 **NM** value: **4.00**
• **CGC:** 1 graded, best 9.4
The Blackout Murders of Baron Blood ★ Versus Baron Blood.
8 ❑ Sep 1976 Cover: 0.30 **NM** value: **4.00**
Unio Jack Is Back ★ Appearance of Union Jack.
9 ❑ Oct 1976 Cover: 0.30 **NM** value: **4.00**
In Invader No More ★ Origin of Baron Blood. ★ Versus Baron Blood.
10 ❑ Nov 1976 Cover: 0.30 **NM** value: **3.50**
• **CGC:** 1 graded, best 9.4
The Wrath of the Reaper • reprints Captain America #22 ★ Versus Reaper.
11 ❑ Dec 1976 Cover: 0.30 **NM** value: **3.50**
Night of the Blue Bullet ★ Origin of Spitfire. ★ 1st Appearance of Blue Bullet, Spitfire. ★ Versus Blue Bullet.
12 ❑ Jan 1977 Cover: 0.30 **NM** value: **3.50**
To the Warsaw Ghetto ★ 1st Appearance of Spitfire.
13 ❑ Feb 1977 Cover: 0.30 **NM** value: **3.50**
The Golem Walks Again ★ Appearance of Golem.
14 ❑ Mar 1977 Cover: 0.30 **NM** value: **3.50**
Calling the Crusaders ★ 1st Appearance of Spirit of '76, Dyna-Mite, Crusaders.
15 ❑ Apr 1977 Cover: 0.30 **NM** value: **3.50**
God Save The King! **A:** Frank Robbins; Frank Springer **W:** Roy Thomas ★ Versus Crusaders.
16 ❑ May 1977 Cover: 0.30 **NM** value: **3.50**
The Short, Happy Life of Major Victory ★ Versus Master Man.
17 ❑ Jun 1977 Cover: 0.30 **NM** value: **3.50**
• **CGC:** 1 graded, best 9.4
The Making of Warrior Woman, 1942 ★ 1st Appearance of Warrior Woman. ★ Versus Warrior Woman.
18 ❑ Jul 1977 Cover: 0.30 **NM** value: **3.50**
• **CGC:** 1 graded, best 9.4
★ 1st Appearance of Mighty Destroyer. ★ Appearance of Destroyer.
19 ❑ Aug 1977 Cover: 0.30 **NM** value: **3.50**
• **CGC:** 1 graded, best 9.2
War Comes to the Wilhelmstrasse • Mighty Destroyer becomes Union Jack II; Reprints Motion Picture Funnies Weekly ★ Origin of Union Jack II (Brian Falsworth). ★ 1st Appearance of the Sub-Mariner, Union Jack II (Brian Falsworth). ★ Appearance of Hitler.
20 ❑ Sep 1977 Cover: 0.30 **NM** value: **5.00**
• **CGC:** 1 graded, best 9.0
The Battle of Berlin; The Sub-Mainer • Reprints Sub-Mariner story from Motion Picture Funnies Weekly #1 ★ Origin of Sub-Mariner. ★ 1st Appearance of Sub-Mariner. ★ Appearance of Spitfire, Union Jack.
21 ❑ Oct 1977 Cover: 0.30 **NM** value: **3.00**
• **CGC:** 1 graded, best 9.0
The Battle Of Berlin, Part 2; (Untitled) • Reprints Sub-Mariner story from Marvel Mystery Comics #10 **A:** Frank Robbins; Frank Springer **W:** Roy Thomas
22 ❑ Nov 1977 Cover: 0.35 **NM** value: **3.00**
The Fire That Died ★ Origin of Toro (new origin). ★ Versus Asbestos Lady.
23 ❑ Dec 1977 Cover: 0.35 **NM** value: **3.00**
The Scarab of the Nile ★ 1st Appearance of Scarlet Scarab. ★ Versus Scarlet Scarab.
24 ❑ Jan 1978 Cover: 0.35 **NM** value: **3.00**
The Human Torch and the Sub-Mariner Fighting Side-By-Side • reprints Marvel Mystery Comics #17
25 ❑ Feb 1978 Cover: 0.35 **NM** value: **2.50**
• **CGC:** 1 graded, best 9.4
The Power and the Panzers ★ Versus Scarlet Scarab.
26 ❑ Mar 1978 Cover: 0.35 **NM** value: **2.50**
• **CGC:** 1 graded, best 9.4
Day of Infamy, Day of Shame ★ 1st Appearance of Destroyer II (Roger Aubrey). ★ Versus Agent Axis.
27 ❑ Apr 1978 Cover: 0.35 **NM** value: **2.50**
Agent Axis, Master of Murder
28 ❑ May 1978 Cover: 0.35 **NM** value: **2.50**
Calling the Kid Commandos ★ 1st Appearance of Golden Girl. ★ 1st Appearance of Kid Commandos, Human Top (David Mitchell).
29 ❑ Jun 1978 Cover: 0.35 **NM** value: **2.50**
• **CGC:** 1 graded, best 9.2
Attack Of The Teutonic Knight **A:** Alan Kupperberg **W:** Don Glut ★ Origin of Invaders. ★ 1st Appearance of Teutonic Knight. ★ Versus Teutonic Knight.
30 ❑ Jul 1978 Cover: 0.35 **NM** value: **2.50**
31 ❑ Aug 1978 Cover: 0.35 **NM** value: **2.50**
Heil Frankenstein ★ Versus Frankenstein.
32 ❑ Sep 1978 Cover: 0.35 **NM** value: **2.50**
Thunder in the East ★ Versus Thor.
33 ❑ Oct 1978 Cover: 0.35 **NM** value: **2.50**
• **CGC:** 1 graded, best 9.2
★ Versus Thor.
34 ❑ Nov 1978 Cover: 0.35 **NM** value: **2.50**
• **CGC:** 1 graded, best 6.0
★ Versus Destroyer.
35 ❑ Dec 1978 Cover: 0.35 **NM** value: **2.50**
★ Appearance of Whizzer.
36 ❑ Jan 1979 Cover: 0.35 **NM** value: **2.50**
★ Versus Iron Cross.
37 ❑ Feb 1979 Cover: 0.35 **NM** value: **2.50**
• **CGC:** 1 graded, best 9.4
★ Appearance of Liberty Legion. ★ Versus Iron Cross.
38 ❑ Mar 1979 Cover: 0.35 **NM** value: **2.50**
★ 1st Appearance of Lady Lotus. ★ Appearance of U-Man.
39 ❑ Apr 1979 Cover: 0.35 **NM** value: **2.50**
40 ❑ May 1979 Cover: 0.40 **NM** value: **2.50**
★ Versus Baron Blood.
41 ❑ Sep 1979 Cover: 0.60 **NM** value: **3.50**
• Double-size. final issue. ★ Versus Super Axis (Baron Blood, U-Man, Warrior Woman, Master Man).
Anl 1❑ca. 1977 Cover: 0.50 **NM** value: **5.00**
• **CGC:** 1 graded, best 9.2
Okay, Axis – Here We Come!; The Human Torch; Captain America; Sub-Mariner; Endgame II
GS 1❑ Cover: 0.50 **NM** value: **5.00**
The Coming of the Invaders; A Captain Called America; Enter: The Human Torch; The Sub-Mariner Strikes; Deep-Sea Blitzkrieg

INVADERS FROM HOME — DC / Piranha

1 ❑ Cover: 2.50 **NM** value: **Cover or less**
Circ: CapCity orders: **5,400**
A: John Blair Moore **W:** John Blair Moore
2 ❑ Cover: 2.50 **NM** value: **Cover or less**
Circ: CapCity orders: **4,100**
A: John Blair Moore **W:** John Blair Moore
3 ❑ Cover: 2.50 **NM** value: **Cover or less**
Circ: CapCity orders: **3,500**
A: John Blair Moore **W:** John Blair Moore
4 ❑ Cover: 2.50 **NM** value: **Cover or less**
Circ: CapCity orders: **3,000**
The Faceless Horror **A:** John Blair Moore **W:** John Blair Moore
5 ❑ Cover: 2.50 **NM** value: **Cover or less**
A: John Blair Moore **W:** John Blair Moore
6 ❑ Cover: 2.50 **NM** value: **Cover or less**
Circ: CapCity orders: **2,000**
A: John Blair Moore **W:** John Blair Moore

INVADERS FROM MARS — Eternity

1 ❑ Feb 1990, b&w Cover: 2.50 **NM** value: **Cover or less**
2 ❑ Mar 1990, b&w Cover: 2.50 **NM** value: **Cover or less**
3 ❑ Apr 1990, b&w Cover: 2.50 **NM** value: **Cover or less**
The Son of Man **A:** Sandy Carruthers **W:** Steve Jones

INVADERS FROM MARS (BOOK II) — Eternity

1 ❑ ca. 1990, b&w Cover: 2.50 **NM** value: **Cover or less**
• sequel
2 ❑ ca. 1990, b&w Cover: 2.50 **NM** value: **Cover or less**
• sequel
3 ❑ ca. 1990, b&w Cover: 2.50 **NM** value: **Cover or less**
• sequel

INVADERS (GOLD KEY) — Gold Key

1 ❑ Oct 1967 Cover: 0.12 **NM** value: **75.00**
• **CGC:** 3 graded, best 9.6
2 ❑ Jan 1968 Cover: 0.12 **NM** value: **50.00**
• **CGC:** 2 graded, best 9.4
3 ❑ Jun 1968 Cover: 0.12 **NM** value: **50.00**
• **CGC:** 4 graded, best 9.4
4 ❑ Oct 1968 Cover: 0.12 **NM** value: **50.00**
• **CGC:** 3 graded, best 9.6

INVADERS, THE (LTD. SERIES) — Marvel

1 ❑ May 1993 Cover: 1.75 **NM** value: **Cover or less**
Circ: CapCity orders: **48,700**
The Invaders Return **A:** Dave Hoover **W:** Roy Thomas
2 ❑ Jun 1993 Cover: 1.75 **NM** value: **Cover or less**
Circ: CapCity orders: **27,900**
Havoc In Hollywood **A:** Dave Hoover **W:** Roy Thomas ★ Versus Battle Axis.
3 ❑ Jul 1993 Cover: 1.75 **NM** value: **Cover or less**
Circ: CapCity orders: **22,600**
★ Appearance of Vision.
4 ❑ Aug 1993 Cover: 1.75 **NM** value: **Cover or less**
Circ: CapCity orders: **19,500**

Other grades: Multiply prices above by **1.5 for Mint • 2/3 for Very Fine • 1/3 for Fine • 1/5 for Very Good • 1/8 for Good**

INVASION! DC

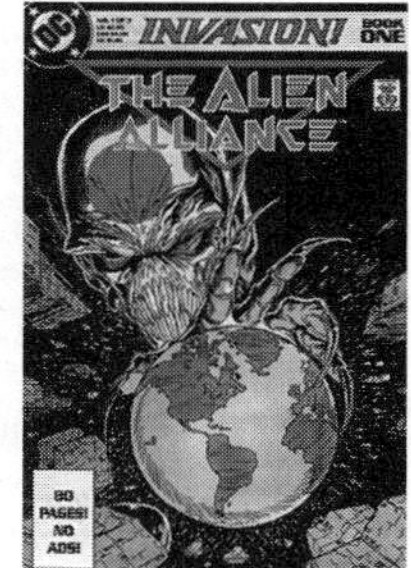

The Dominators, an alien race, were notorious for their ability to plan and scheme. Recently, they had decided that the greatest threat to their security was the planet Earth. For although the galaxy knows many races, none seem to have Earth's capacity for spawning all manner of super-powered individuals. The Dominators could face any hero whose powers they knew, but there seems to be no predicting the super-powers which manifest themselves in Earth's population. For this reason, the Dominators consider Earth dangerous — and have decided that it must be destroyed.

Accordingly, they have formed an alliance of the galaxy's most warlike races, and have proceeded to invade the Earth. Meanwhile, heroes from the Omega Men to Adam Strange have risen in Earth's defense. This series (which contained the first appearance of L.E.G.I.O.N.) tells of Earth's battle for survival against the alien menace.

1 ❑ Jan 1989 Cover: 2.95 **NM** value: **3.00**
Circ: CapCity orders: **39,400**
📖 The Alien Alliance **A:** Todd McFarlane **W:** Keith Giffen; Bill Mantlo ★ Origin of Blasters. ★ 1st Appearance of Garryn Bek, Blasters, Dominators, Vril Dox II.

2 ❑ Feb 1989 Cover: 2.95 **NM** value: **3.00**
Circ: CapCity orders: **37,700**
A: Todd McFarlane ★ 1st Appearance of Strata, L.E.G.I.O.N., Lyrissa Mallor.

3 ❑ Mar 1989 Cover: 2.95 **NM** value: **3.00**
Circ: CapCity orders: **34,750**

INVASION '55 Apple

1 ❑ Oct 1990, b&w Cover: 2.25 **NM** value: **Cover or less**
A: Lito Fernandez **W:** Chuck Dixon

2 ❑ b&w Cover: 2.25 **NM** value: **Cover or less**
A: Lito Fernandez **W:** Chuck Dixon

3 ❑ b&w Cover: 2.25 **NM** value: **Cover or less**
A: Lito Fernandez **W:** Chuck Dixon

INVASION OF THE MIND SAPPERS Fantagraphics

1 ❑ Jan 1996, b&w Cover: 8.95 **NM** value: **Cover or less**
No issue number. cardstock cover.

INVASION OF THE SPACE AMAZONS FROM THE PURPLE PLANET Grizmart Productions

1 ❑ May 1997, b&w Cover: 2.25 **NM** value: **Cover or less**
2 ❑ Fal 1997, b&w Cover: 2.25 **NM** value: **Cover or less**
3 ❑ Win 1997, b&w Cover: 2.25 **NM** value: **Cover or less**

INVERT Caliber

1 ❑ b&w Cover: 2.95 **NM** value: **Cover or less**
No issue number. **A:** Robert De Matteo **W:** Jay Halpern

INVINCIBLE FOUR OF KUNG FU & NINJA Dr. Leung's

1 ❑ Cover: 1.80 **NM** value: **2.00**
Circ: CapCity orders: **2,150**

2 ❑ Cover: 1.80 **NM** value: **2.00**
Circ: CapCity orders: **1,350**

3 ❑ Cover: 1.80 **NM** value: **2.00**
Circ: CapCity orders: **1,200**

4 ❑ Cover: 1.80 **NM** value: **2.00**
Circ: CapCity orders: **750**

5 ❑ Cover: 1.80 **NM** value: **2.00**

INVINCIBLE MAN Junko / Dark Horse

1 ❑ Sum 1998, b&w Cover: 100.00 **NM** value: **Cover or less**
Glossy cover. • 1500 printed **A:** Bob Burden **C:** Bob Burden **W:** Bob Burden

1/LE❑ b&w Cover: 100.00 **NM** value: **Cover or less**
has $100 cover price. • 500 printed **A:** Bob Burden **W:** Bob Burden

INVISIBLE 9 Flypaper

1 ❑ May 1998 Cover: 2.95 **NM** value: **Cover or less**
Bk 1❑ Cover: 12.95 **NM** value: **Cover or less**

INVISIBLE DIRTY OLD MAN, THE Red Giant

1 ❑ **NM** value: **3.50**

INVISIBLE PEOPLE Kitchen Sink

1 ❑ Cover: 2.95 **NM** value: **Cover or less**
Circ: CapCity orders: **4,150**
📖 Sanctum **A:** Will Eisner **W:** Will Eisner

2 ❑ Cover: 3.95 **NM** value: **Cover or less**
📖 The Power **A:** Will Eisner **W:** Will Eisner

3 ❑ Cover: 3.95 **NM** value: **Cover or less**
📖 Mortal Combat **A:** Will Eisner **W:** Will Eisner

The CGC numbers printed in individual listings above represent the **number of copies examined** and given a **Universal** grade by CGC and the **best such copy** graded at press time. For current populations, watch for special ***Comics Buyer's Guide*** issues or check **www.cgccomics.com.**

INVISIBLES, THE DC / Vertigo

Dane McGowan is a smart kid given to running with a bad crowd and hurling Molotov cocktails through the windows of the school library. At school, his teacher counseled him that he needn't be a loser, that if he wanted he could really make something of his life. But Dane already knew what he wanted. He wanted to take on the world.

That is exactly the quality that led King Mob, leader of the Invisibles to recruit him. The Invisibles are the ultimate secret society, employing magic and technology to support subversion in all its forms. They show Dane a world that lies beneath the surface of our own, where shadowy forces conspire to control man's destiny. He learns many secrets — as well as what really happens when you die...

The Invisibles was created by Grant Morrison, a writer known for his genre-expanding work on Animal Man and Doom Patrol (2nd Series).

1 ❑ Sep 1994 Cover: 2.95 **NM** value: **3.50**
Circ: CapCity orders: **19,150**
• Giant-size. 📖 Dead Beatles **A:** Steve Yeowell **W:** Grant Morrison ★ 1st Appearance of King Mob.

2 ❑ Oct 1994 Cover: 1.95 **NM** value: **2.50**
Circ: CapCity orders: **14,500**
📖 Down and Out in Heaven and Hell, Part 1 **A:** Steve Yeowell **W:** Grant Morrison

3 ❑ Nov 1994 Cover: 1.95 **NM** value: **2.50**
Circ: CapCity orders: **13,900**
📖 Down and Out in Heaven and Hell, Part 2 **A:** Steve Yeowell **W:** Grant Morrison

4 ❑ Dec 1994 Cover: 1.95 **NM** value: **2.00**
Circ: CapCity orders: **13,950**
📖 Down and Out in Heaven and Hell, Part 3 **A:** Steve Yeowell **W:** Grant Morrison

5 ❑ Jan 1995 Cover: 1.95 **NM** value: **2.00**
Circ: CapCity orders: **13,050**
There are at least four cover variants, denoted A through D.. 📖 Arcadia, Part 1 **W:** Grant Morrison

6 ❑ Feb 1995 Cover: 1.95 **NM** value: **2.00**
Circ: CapCity orders: **11,850**
📖 Arcadia, Part 2 **W:** Grant Morrison

7 ❑ Mar 1995 Cover: 1.95 **NM** value: **2.00**
Circ: CapCity orders: **11,025**
📖 Arcadia, Part 3 **W:** Grant Morrison

8 ❑ Apr 1995 Cover: 1.95 **NM** value: **2.00**
Circ: CapCity orders: **10,350**
📖 Arcadia, Part 4 **W:** Grant Morrison

9 ❑ Jun 1995 Cover: 2.50 **NM** value: **Cover or less**
Circ: CapCity orders: **9,525**
W: Grant Morrison

10 ❑ Jul 1995 Cover: 2.50 **NM** value: **Cover or less**
Circ: CapCity orders: **9,300**
W: Grant Morrison

11 ❑ Aug 1995 Cover: 2.50 **NM** value: **Cover or less**
Circ: CapCity orders: **9,200**
W: Grant Morrison

12 ❑ Sep 1995 Cover: 2.50 **NM** value: **Cover or less**
Circ: CapCity orders: **8,200**
W: Grant Morrison

13 ❑ Oct 1995 Cover: 2.50 **NM** value: **Cover or less**
Circ: CapCity orders: **7,125**
W: Grant Morrison

14 ❑ Nov 1995 Cover: 2.50 **NM** value: **Cover or less**
W: Grant Morrison

15 ❑ Dec 1995 Cover: 2.50 **NM** value: **Cover or less**
W: Grant Morrison

16 ❑ Jan 1996 Cover: 2.50 **NM** value: **Cover or less**
W: Grant Morrison

17 ❑ Feb 1996 Cover: 2.50 **NM** value: **Cover or less**
📖 Entropy in the U.K., Part 1 **W:** Grant Morrison

18 ❑ Mar 1996 Cover: 2.50 **NM** value: **3.00**
📖 Entropy in the U.K., Part 2 **W:** Grant Morrison

19 ❑ Apr 1996 Cover: 2.50 **NM** value: **3.00**
📖 Entropy in the U.K., Part 3 **W:** Grant Morrison

20 ❑ May 1996 Cover: 2.50 **NM** value: **3.00**
W: Grant Morrison

21 ❑ Jun 1996 Cover: 2.50 **NM** value: **3.00**
W: Grant Morrison

22 ❑ Jul 1996 Cover: 2.50 **NM** value: **3.00**
W: Grant Morrison

23 ❑ Aug 1996 Cover: 2.50 **NM** value: **3.00**
W: Grant Morrison

24 ❑ Sep 1996 Cover: 2.50 **NM** value: **3.00**
W: Grant Morrison

25 ❑ Oct 1996 Cover: 2.50 **NM** value: **4.00**
📖 And a Half Dozen of the Other final issue. **A:** Mark Buckingham **W:** Grant Morrison

Bk 1❑ Cover: 17.95 **NM** value: **Cover or less**
📖 Say You Want a Revolution • Collects The Invisibles #1-8 **A:** Brian Bolland(cover) **W:** Grant Morrison

Bk 2❑ Cover: 19.95 **NM** value: **Cover or less**
• Apocalipstick **A:** John Ridgway; Chris Weston; Steve Parkhouse; Jill Thompson **W:** Grant Morrison

INVISIBLE SCARLET O'NEIL Harvey

1 ❑ Dec 1950 Cover: 0.10 **NM** value: **100.00**
• **CGC:** 2 graded, best 9.0

2 ❑ Feb 1951 Cover: 0.10 **NM** value: **75.00**
• **CGC:** 1 graded, best 8.0

3 ❑ Apr 1951 Cover: 0.10 **NM** value: **75.00**
• **CGC:** 1 graded, best 8.5

INVISIBLES, THE (VOL. 2) DC / Vertigo

1 ❑ Feb 1997 Cover: 2.50 **NM** value: **3.00**
Circ: Diamd. preorders: **24,819**
📖 Black Science, Part 1 **A:** Phil Jimenez **W:** Grant Morrison

2 ❑ Mar 1997 Cover: 2.50 **NM** value: **Cover or less**
Circ: Diamd. preorders: **21,583**
📖 Black Science, Part 2 **A:** Phil Jimenez **W:** Grant Morrison

3 ❑ Apr 1997 Cover: 2.50 **NM** value: **Cover or less**
Circ: Diamd. preorders: **20,754**
📖 Black Science, Part 3 **A:** Phil Jimenez; Brian Bolland(cover) **W:** Grant Morrison

4 ❑ May 1997 Cover: 2.50 **NM** value: **Cover or less**
Circ: Diamd. preorders: **21,376**
W: Grant Morrison

5 ❑ Jun 1997 Cover: 2.50 **NM** value: **Cover or less**
Circ: Diamd. preorders: **22,641**
📖 Time Machine Go **A:** Phil Jimenez; Brian Bolland(cover) **W:** Grant Morrison

6 ❑ Jul 1997 Cover: 2.50 **NM** value: **Cover or less**
Circ: Diamd. preorders: **20,112**
📖 The Girl Most LikelyTo **W:** Grant Morrison

7 ❑ Aug 1997 Cover: 2.50 **NM** value: **Cover or less**
Circ: Diamd. preorders: **20,012**
W: Grant Morrison

8 ❑ Sep 1997 Cover: 2.50 **NM** value: **Cover or less**
Circ: Diamd. preorders: **19,833**
📖 Sensitive Criminals, Part 1 **A:** Phil Jimenez **W:** Grant Morrison

9 ❑ Oct 1997 Cover: 2.50 **NM** value: **Cover or less**
Circ: Diamd. preorders: **19,777**
📖 Sensitive Criminals, Part 2 **A:** Phil Jimenez **W:** Grant Morrison

10 ❑ Nov 1997 Cover: 2.50 **NM** value: **Cover or less**
Circ: Diamd. preorders: **19,877**
📖 Sensitive Criminals, Part 3 **A:** Phil Jimenez; Brian Bolland(cover) **W:** Grant Morrison

11 ❑ Dec 1997 Cover: 2.50 **NM** value: **Cover or less**
Circ: Diamd. preorders: **20,083**
📖 American Death Camp, Part 1 **A:** Phil Jimenez **W:** Grant Morrison

12 ❑ Jan 1998 Cover: 2.50 **NM** value: **Cover or less**
Circ: Diamd. preorders: **19,677**
📖 American Death Camp, Part 2 **A:** Phil Jimenez **W:** Grant Morrison

13 ❑ Feb 1998 Cover: 2.50 **NM** value: **Cover or less**
Circ: Diamd. preorders: **19,523**
📖 American Death Camp, Part 3 **A:** Phil Jimenez **W:** Grant Morrison

14 ❑ Mar 1998 Cover: 2.50 **NM** value: **Cover or less**
Circ: Diamd. preorders: **18,508**
W: Grant Morrison

15 ❑ Apr 1998 Cover: 2.50 **NM** value: **Cover or less**
Circ: Diamd. preorders: **18,454**
W: Grant Morrison

16 ❑ May 1998 Cover: 2.50 **NM** value: **Cover or less**
Circ: Diamd. preorders: **18,695**
W: Grant Morrison

17 ❑ Aug 1998 Cover: 2.50 **NM** value: **Cover or less**
Circ: Diamd. preorders: **18,253**
W: Grant Morrison

18 ❑ Sep 1998 Cover: 2.50 **NM** value: **Cover or less**
Circ: Diamd. preorders: **17,543**
W: Grant Morrison

19 ❑ Oct 1998 Cover: 2.50 **NM** value: **Cover or less**
Circ: Diamd. preorders: **17,356**
W: Grant Morrison

20 ❑ Nov 1998 Cover: 2.50 **NM** value: **Cover or less**
Circ: Diamd. preorders: **17,199**
W: Grant Morrison

21 ❑ Jan 1999 Cover: 2.50 **NM** value: **Cover or less**
Circ: Diamd. preorders: **16,807**
W: Grant Morrison

22 ❑ Feb 1999 Cover: 2.50 **NM** value: **Cover or less**
Circ: Diamd. preorders: **16,579**
📖 The Tower **W:** Grant Morrison

Bk 1❑ Cover: 12.95 **NM** value: **Cover or less**
📖 Bloody Hell in America • Bloody Hell in America **A:** Phil Jimenez **W:** Grant Morrison

Bk 2❑ Cover: 19.95 **NM** value: **Cover or less**
📖 Counting to None • Counting to None **W:** Grant Morrison

INVISIBLES, THE (VOL. 3) DC / Vertigo

12 ❑ Apr 1999 Cover: 2.95 **NM** value: **Cover or less**
Circ: Diamd. preorders: **17,221**
📖 Satanstorm, Part 1 • Issues count from 12 to 1 **A:** Brian Bolland(cover); Phillip Bond **W:** Grant Morrison

11 ❑ May 1999 Cover: 2.95 **NM** value: **Cover or less**
Circ: Diamd. preorders: **16,857**
📖 Satanstorm, Part 2 • **A:** Warren Pleece; Brian Bolland(cover); Phillip Bond **W:** Grant Morrison

10 ❑ Jun 1999 Cover: 2.95 **NM** value: **Cover or less**
Circ: Diamd. preorders: **17,476**
📖 Satanstorm, Part 3 • **A:** Warren Pleece; Brian Bolland(cover); Phillip Bond **W:** Grant Morrison

9 ❑ Jul 1999 Cover: 2.95 **NM** value: **Cover or less**
Circ: Diamd. preorders: **17,434**
📖 Satanstorm, Part 4 • **A:** Warren Pleece; Brian Bolland(cover); Phillip Bond **W:** Grant Morrison

8 ❑ Aug 1999 Cover: 2.95 **NM** value: **Cover or less**
Circ: Diamd. preorders: **17,514**
📖 Karmageddon, Part 1 • **A:** Sean Phillips **W:** Grant Morrison

7 ❑ Oct 1999 Cover: 2.95 **NM** value: **Cover or less**
Circ: Diamd. preorders: **17,530**
📖 Karmageddon, Part 2 • **A:** Sean Phillips **W:** Grant Morrison

6 ❑ Dec 1999 Cover: 2.95 **NM** value: **Cover or less**
Circ: Diamd. preorders: **17,298**
📖 Karmageddon, Part 3 • **A:** Sean Phillips **W:** Grant Morrison

5 ❑ Jan 2000 Cover: 2.95 **NM** value: **Cover or less**
Circ: Diamd. preorders: **16,645**
📖 Karmageddon, Part 4 • **A:** Sean Phillips **W:** Grant Morrison

4 ❑ Mar 2000 Cover: 2.95 **NM** value: **Cover or less**
Circ: Diamd. preorders: **16,037**
📖 The Invisible Kingdom, Part 1 • **W:** Grant Morrison

CGC-graded: Multiply prices above by **33 for 9.9 M • 16 for 9.8 NM/M • 7 for 9.6 NM+ • 5 for 9.4 NM • 2.5 for 9.2 NM- • 1.5 for 9.0 VF/NM**

3 ❑ Apr 2000 Cover: 2.95 **NM value: Cover or less**
Circ: Diamd. preorders: **15,295**
🕮 The Invisible Kingdom, Part 2 • **W:** Grant Morrison
2 ❑ May 2000 Cover: 2.95 **NM value: Cover or less**
Circ: Diamd. preorders: **15,591**
🕮 The Invisible Kingdom, Part 3 • **A:** John Ridgway; Mark Buckingham; Steve Yeowell; Dean Ormston; Arnold Pander; Grant Morrison; Jacob Pander **W:** Grant Morrison
1 ❑ Jun 2000 Cover: 2.95 **NM value: Cover or less**
Circ: Diamd. preorders: **16,636**
final issue. • **W:** Grant Morrison

INVISOWORLD — Eternity
1 ❑ Cover: 1.95 **NM value: Cover or less**

IO — Invictus
1 ❑ Oct 1994 Cover: 2.25 **NM value: Cover or less**
3 ❑ Win 1995, b&w Cover: 2.25 **NM value: Cover or less**
• ashcan

IRONCAT — Ironcat
1 ❑ Jul 1999 Cover: 2.95 **NM value: Cover or less**
Circ: Diamd. preorders: **3,524**
A: Masaomi Kanzaki **W:** Masaomi Kanzaki
2 ❑ Aug 1999 Cover: 2.95 **NM value: Cover or less**
Circ: Diamd. preorders: **2,860**
🕮 The Virgin of Steel **A:** Masaomi Kanzaki **W:** Masaomi Kanzaki

IRON CORPORAL (AVALON) — Avalon
1 ❑ b&w Cover: 2.95 **NM value: Cover or less**
🕮 Here Lies John Williams; Alias Death; The Iron Corporal **A:** Sam Glanzman **W:** Will Franz

IRON CORPORAL, THE (CHARLTON) — Charlton / ACG
23 ❑ Oct 1985 Cover: 0.75 **NM value: 1.50**
• Continues From Army War Heroes
24 ❑ Dec 1985 Cover: 0.75 **NM value: 1.50**
🕮 Alias Death **A:** S.J.G. **W:** Will Franz
25 ❑ Feb 1985 Cover: 0.75 **NM value: 1.50**

IRON DEVIL, THE — Fantagraphics / Eros
All issues are adults only.
1 ❑ b&w Cover: 2.95 **NM value: Cover or less**
A: Frank Thorne **W:** Frank Thorne
2 ❑ b&w Cover: 2.95 **NM value: Cover or less**
A: Frank Thorne **W:** Frank Thorne
3 ❑ Mar 1994, b&w Cover: 2.95 **NM value: Cover or less**
A: Frank Thorne **W:** Frank Thorne

IRON FIST — Marvel

First appearing in Marvel Premiere #15, Iron Fist is really martial artist Daniel Rand. As a child, Daniel had been taken by his parents on an expedition to Tibet, to search for the legendary city of K'un-Lun. His parents were killed in the quest, but Daniel was taken in by the city's inhabitants where he was trained to become a master of the martial arts. Eventually he rose to the ultimate position, received the brand of the dragon on his chest, and learned to focus his chi — his soul force — into an awesomely powerful Iron Fist. Striking with the Iron Fist, however, drained him terribly, leaving him weak for several hours.

In this series, most famous for writer Chris Claremont's introduction of Sabretooth, Iron Fist teams with detectives Colleen Wing and Misty Knight to fight legions of kung-fu-fighting bad guys. He would later join forces with strongman Luke Cage, to form the freelance "Heroes for Hire" service.

1 ❑ Nov 1975 Cover: 0.25 **NM value: 20.00**
• **CGC:** 91 graded, best 9.8
🕮 A Duel of Iron! **A:** John Byrne **W:** Chris Claremont ★ Appearance of Iron Man.
2 ❑ Dec 1975 Cover: 0.25 **NM value: 12.00**
• **CGC:** 21 graded, best 9.8
A: John Byrne **W:** Chris Claremont
3 ❑ Feb 1976 Cover: 0.25 **NM value: 8.00**
• **CGC:** 2 graded, best 9.4
A: John Byrne **W:** Chris Claremont
4 ❑ Apr 1976 Cover: 0.25 **NM value: 8.00**
• **CGC:** 4 graded, best 9.6
A: John Byrne **W:** Chris Claremont
5 ❑ Jun 1976 Cover: 0.25 **NM value: 8.00**
• **CGC:** 3 graded, best 9.6
A: John Byrne **W:** Chris Claremont
6 ❑ Aug 1976 Cover: 0.25 **NM value: 6.00**
🕮 Death Match! **A:** John Byrne **W:** Chris Claremont
7 ❑ Sep 1976 Cover: 0.30 **NM value: 6.00**
A: John Byrne **W:** Chris Claremont
8 ❑ Oct 1976 Cover: 0.30 **NM value: 6.00**
• **CGC:** 3 graded, best 9.4
A: John Byrne **W:** Chris Claremont
9 ❑ Nov 1976 Cover: 0.30 **NM value: 6.00**
• **CGC:** 1 graded, best 9.6
A: John Byrne **W:** Chris Claremont
10 ❑ Dec 1976 Cover: 0.30 **NM value: 6.00**
• **CGC:** 1 graded, best 9.4
A: John Byrne **W:** Chris Claremont
11 ❑ Feb 1977 Cover: 0.30 **NM value: 5.00**
A: John Byrne **W:** Chris Claremont
12 ❑ Apr 1977 Cover: 0.30 **NM value: 5.00**
A: John Byrne **W:** Chris Claremont
13 ❑ Jun 1977 Cover: 0.30 **NM value: 5.00**
• **CGC:** 3 graded, best 9.6
A: John Byrne **W:** Chris Claremont ★ Versus Boomerang.
14 ❑ Aug 1977 Cover: 0.30 **NM value: 80.00**
• **CGC:** 284 graded, best 9.8
🕮 Snowfire **A:** John Byrne **W:** Chris Claremont ★ 1st Appearance of Sabretooth.
15 ❑ Sep 1977 Cover: 0.30 **NM value: 35.00**
• **CGC:** 55 graded, best 9.6
🕮 Enter, the X-Men final issue. **A:** John Byrne **W:** Chris Claremont ★ Appearance of X-Men, Wolverine.
15/A❑ Sep 1977 Cover: 0.35 **NM value: 45.00**
• **CGC:** 2 graded, best 9.2
35¢ cover price. final issue. • Limited distribution **A:** John Byrne ★ Appearance of X-Men.

IRON FIST (2ND SERIES) — Marvel
1 ❑ Sep 1996 Cover: 1.50 **NM value: Cover or less**
🕮 The Descent **A:** Robert Brown **W:** James Felder
2 ❑ Oct 1996 Cover: 1.50 **NM value: Cover or less**
A: Robert Brown **W:** James Felder

IRON FIST (3RD SERIES) — Marvel
1 ❑ Jul 1998 Cover: 2.50 **NM value: Cover or less**
Circ: Diamd. preorders: **33,241**
• gatefold summary.
2 ❑ Aug 1998 Cover: 2.50 **NM value: Cover or less**
Circ: Diamd. preorders: **27,258**
• gatefold summary.
3 ❑ Sep 1998 Cover: 2.50 **NM value: Cover or less**
Circ: Diamd. preorders: **24,794**
• gatefold summary.

IRON FIST: WOLVERINE — Marvel
1 ❑ Nov 2000 Cover: 2.99 **NM value: Cover or less**
Circ: Diamd. preorders: **43,058**
🕮 Dark Horizon **A:** Jamal Igle; Jamal Cole **W:** Jay Faerber
2 ❑ Dec 2000 Cover: 2.99 **NM value: Cover or less**
Circ: Diamd. preorders: **37,768**
🕮 A Gathering of Heroes **A:** Jamal Igle; Jamal Cole **W:** Jay Faerber
3 ❑ Jan 2001 Cover: 2.99 **NM value: Cover or less**
Circ: Diamd. preorders: **35,733**
A: Jamal Igle; Jamal Cole **W:** Jay Faerber
4 ❑ Feb 2001 Cover: 2.99 **NM value: Cover or less**
Circ: Diamd. preorders: **33,657**
🕮 Endgame **A:** Jamal Igle; Jamal Cole **W:** Jay Faerber ★ Appearance of Luke Cage.

IRONHAND OF ALMURIC — Dark Horse
1 ❑ b&w Cover: 2.00 **NM value: Cover or less**
🕮 Crownless In Koth **A:** Mark Winchell **W:** Roy Thomas
2 ❑ b&w Cover: 2.00 **NM value: Cover or less**
3 ❑ b&w Cover: 2.00 **NM value: Cover or less**
4 ❑ b&w Cover: 2.00 **NM value: Cover or less**

IRONJAW — Atlas-Seaboard
1 ❑ Jan 1975 Cover: 0.25 **NM value: 1.50**
• **CGC:** 2 graded, best 9.4
🕮 The Saga of Iron Jaw **A:** Mike Sekowsky **C:** Neal Adams **W:** Michael Fleisher
2 ❑ Mar 1975 Cover: 0.25 **NM value: 1.00**
• **CGC:** 1 graded, best 9.4
🕮 Ironjaw the King! **A:** Pablo Marcos **C:** Neal Adams **W:** Michael Fleisher
3 ❑ May 1975 Cover: 0.25 **NM value: 1.00**
4 ❑ Jul 1975 Cover: 0.25 **NM value: 1.00**
• **CGC:** 1 graded, best 9.4
🕮 And Who Will Forge the Jaw of Iron? **A:** Pablo Marcos **W:** Gary Friedrich ★ Origin of Ironjaw.

IRON LANTERN — Marvel / Amalgam
1 ❑ Jun 1997 Cover: 1.95 **NM value: Cover or less**
Circ: Diamd. preorders: **135,298**
🕮 Showdown at Stark Aircraft! **A:** Paul Smith **W:** Kurt Busiek

IRON MAN & SUB-MARINER — Marvel
Knowing the story behind this unlikely pairing is a true litmus test for determining Marvel Zombiehood.

When Marvel split two double-features into four titles in 1968, it didn't want to launch four "new" series in the same month. So, since Captain America was taking the numbering of Tales of Suspense with #100 and the Hulk was taking the numbering of Tales to Astonish with #102, Marvel chose to wait a month before launching the new new solo titles Iron Man Vol. 1 and Sub-Mariner Vol. 2. To keep readers from thinking the other features were vanishing in the interim, the one-shot Iron Man and Sub-Mariner was released to serve as a bridge between series, continuing their storylines from the previous title. It's a double-feature, too, kind of a Tales of Astonishing Suspense. — JJM

1 ❑ Apr 1968 Cover: 0.12 **NM value: 110.00**
• **CGC:** 162 graded, best 9.9
🕮 Iron Man: The Torrent Without…The Tumult Within!; Sub-Mariner: Call Him Destiny…Or Call Him Death! **A:** Gene Colan; Johnny Craig; Johnny Craig(inks) **W:** Roy Thomas; Archie Goodwin ★ Origin of Destiny.

IRON MAN: BAD BLOOD — Marvel
1 ❑ Sep 2000 Cover: 2.99 **NM value: Cover or less**
Circ: Diamd. preorders: **35,394**
🕮 A Gathering Dark **A:** Bob Layton **W:** Bob Layton; David Michelinie
2 ❑ Oct 2000 Cover: 2.99 **NM value: Cover or less**
Circ: Diamd. preorders: **30,801**
🕮 Smashing Seattle **A:** Bob Layton **W:** Bob Layton; David Michelinie
3 ❑ Nov 2000 Cover: 2.99 **NM value: Cover or less**
Circ: Diamd. preorders: **29,749**
🕮 Enemy Mind **A:** Bob Layton **W:** Bob Layton; David Michelinie
4 ❑ Dec 2000 Cover: 2.99 **NM value: Cover or less**
Circ: Diamd. preorders: **28,483**
🕮 Terminal Space **A:** Bob Layton **W:** Bob Layton; David Michelinie

IRON MAN BATTLEBOOK — Marvel
1 ❑ Cover: 3.99 **NM value: Cover or less**

IRON MAN: CRASH — Marvel / Epic
1 ❑ Cover: 12.95 **NM value: Cover or less**
Circ: CapCity orders: **9,300**
• Computer-generated art **A:** Mike Saenz

IRON MAN: THE IRON AGE — Marvel
1 ❑ Aug 1998 Cover: 5.99 **NM value: Cover or less**
Circ: Diamd. preorders: **36,288**
• prestige format. 🕮 Challenges • retells early Iron Man adventures **A:** Patrick Zircher **W:** Kurt Busiek
2 ❑ Sep 1998 Cover: 5.99 **NM value: Cover or less**
Circ: Diamd. preorders: **31,692**
• prestige format. • retells early Iron Man adventures **A:** Patrick Zircher **W:** Kurt Busiek

IRON MAN: THE LEGEND — Marvel
1 ❑ Sep 1996 Cover: 3.95 **NM value: Cover or less**
One-shot. wraparound cover. • summation of history of character ★ Origin of Iron Man.

IRON MAN 2020 — Marvel
1 ❑ Cover: 5.95 **NM value: Cover or less**
One-shot. **A:** Will Rosado; Bob Wiacek **W:** Walt Simonson; Bob Wiacek

IRON MANUAL — Marvel
1 ❑ ca. 1993 Cover: 1.75 **NM value: 2.00**
Circ: CapCity orders: **25,800**
no cover date. • background info on Iron Man's armor

IRON MAN (VOL. 1) — Marvel
A genius with gadgets, industrialist Tony Stark first put on the armor of Iron Man in Tales of Suspense #39. After sharing that title with Captain America, Shellhead finally received his own series in 1968.

While Stark engages in some selfless super-heroing as Iron Man, many of his adventures involve protecting his business interests from super-villains, who seem far more interested in bothering his factories than, say, Ford's. The most highly regarded runs of Iron Man are by writer David Micheline, who added considerably to the supporting cast and gave Stark a dependency on alcohol. "Demon in a Bottle," in #128, could indeed be considered the story Stark's greatest battle. Sandwiched between Michelinie runs, a storyline by Denny O'Neill takes the alcoholism storyline to a greater extreme, with Stark ending up in the gutter while friend Jim Rhodes subs as Iron Man.

This long-running series was abruptly (and, it would turn out, needlessly) ended to give Marvel a chance to restart the series during "Heroes Reborn." — JJM

1 ❑ May 1968 Cover: 0.12 **NM value: 275.00**
• **CGC:** 356 graded, best 9.9
A: Gene Colan; Johnny Craig ★ Origin of Iron Man.
2 ❑ Jun 1968 Cover: 0.12 **NM value: 80.00**
• **CGC:** 168 graded, best 9.9
A: Johnny Craig ★ 1st Appearance of Demolisher.
3 ❑ Jul 1968 Cover: 0.12 **NM value: 50.00**
• **CGC:** 41 graded, best 9.6
A: Johnny Craig
4 ❑ Aug 1968 Cover: 0.12 **NM value: 48.00**
• **CGC:** 38 graded, best 9.8
A: Johnny Craig
5 ❑ Sep 1968 Cover: 0.12 **NM value: 48.00**
• **CGC:** 25 graded, best 9.4
A: Johnny Craig
6 ❑ Oct 1968 Cover: 0.12 **NM value: 40.00**
• **CGC:** 25 graded, best 9.6
A: Johnny Craig; George Tuska
7 ❑ Nov 1968 Cover: 0.12 **NM value: 40.00**
• **CGC:** 17 graded, best 9.6
🕮 The Maggia Strikes **A:** Johnny Craig; George Tuska **W:** Archie Goodwin
8 ❑ Dec 1968 Cover: 0.12 **NM value: 35.00**
• **CGC:** 21 graded, best 9.6
A: Johnny Craig; George Tuska
9 ❑ Jan 1969 Cover: 0.12 **NM value: 35.00**
• **CGC:** 18 graded, best 9.4
🕮 … There Lives a Green Goliath! **A:** Johnny Craig; George Tuska **W:** Archie Goodwin ★ Versus Hulk (robot).
10 ❑ Feb 1969 Cover: 0.12 **NM value: 35.00**
• **CGC:** 14 graded, best 9.6

Other grades: Multiply prices above by **1.5 for Mint • 2/3 for Very Fine • 1/3 for Fine • 1/5 for Very Good • 1/8 for Good**

A: Johnny Craig; George Tuska
11 ❑ Mar 1969 Cover: 0.12 **NM** value: **28.00**
• **CGC:** 16 graded, best 9.4
★ Versus Mandarin.
12 ❑ Apr 1969 Cover: 0.12 **NM** value: **28.00**
• **CGC:** 9 graded, best 9.6
★ Origin of The Controller. ★ 1st Appearance of The Controller, Janice Cord, Controller.
13 ❑ May 1969 Cover: 0.12 **NM** value: **28.00**
• **CGC:** 8 graded, best 9.6
★ Versus Controller.
14 ❑ Jun 1969 Cover: 0.12 **NM** value: **28.00**
• **CGC:** 5 graded, best 9.2
★ Versus Night Phantom.
15 ❑ Jul 1969 Cover: 0.12 **NM** value: **28.00**
• **CGC:** 7 graded, best 9.6
★ Versus Unicorn.
16 ❑ Aug 1969 Cover: 0.15 **NM** value: **18.00**
• **CGC:** 5 graded, best 9.4
★ Versus Unicorn.
17 ❑ Sep 1969 Cover: 0.15 **NM** value: **18.00**
• **CGC:** 3 graded, best 9.2
★ 1st Appearance of Madame Masque I (Whitney Frost).
18 ❑ Oct 1969 Cover: 0.15 **NM** value: **18.00**
• **CGC:** 4 graded, best 9.0
★ Origin of Madame Masque I.
19 ❑ Nov 1969 Cover: 0.15 **NM** value: **18.00**
• **CGC:** 5 graded, best 9.4
• Tony Stark's heart repaired ★ Origin of Madame Masque I.
20 ❑ Dec 1969 Cover: 0.15 **NM** value: **18.00**
• **CGC:** 4 graded, best 9.4
★ Versus Lucifer.
21 ❑ Jan 1970 Cover: 0.15 **NM** value: **15.00**
• **CGC:** 2 graded, best 9.6
• Tony Stark quits as Iron Man ★ 1st Appearance of Crimson Dynamo III.
22 ❑ Feb 1970 Cover: 0.15 **NM** value: **15.00**
• **CGC:** 1 graded, best 6.5
★ Death of Janice Cord. ★ Versus Crimson Dynamo.
23 ❑ Mar 1970 Cover: 0.15 **NM** value: **15.00**
24 ❑ Apr 1970 Cover: 0.15 **NM** value: **15.00**
★ Versus Minotaur.
25 ❑ May 1970 Cover: 0.15 **NM** value: **15.00**
• **CGC:** 2 graded, best 9.4
★ Appearance of Sub-Mariner. ★ Versus Sub-Mariner.
26 ❑ Jun 1970 Cover: 0.15 **NM** value: **15.00**
• **CGC:** 1 graded, best 9.2
★ Appearance of Val-Larr.
27 ❑ Jul 1970 Cover: 0.15 **NM** value: **15.00**
• **CGC:** 1 graded, best 8.5
★ 1st Appearance of Firebrand (Marvel). ★ Versus Firebrand.
28 ❑ Aug 1970 Cover: 0.15 **NM** value: **15.00**
★ Versus Controller.
29 ❑ Sep 1970 Cover: 0.15 **NM** value: **15.00**
30 ❑ Oct 1970 Cover: 0.15 **NM** value: **15.00**
• **CGC:** 1 graded, best 8.5
31 ❑ Nov 1970 Cover: 0.15 **NM** value: **12.00**
★ 1st Appearance of Kevin O'Brien (later Guardsman). ★ Versus Smashers.
32 ❑ Dec 1970 Cover: 0.15 **NM** value: **12.00**
• **CGC:** 2 graded, best 9.6
★ Versus Mechanoid.
33 ❑ Jan 1971 Cover: 0.15 **NM** value: **12.00**
★ 1st Appearance of Spymaster. ★ Versus Spymaster.
34 ❑ Feb 1971 Cover: 0.15 **NM** value: **12.00**
★ Versus Spymaster.
35 ❑ Mar 1971 Cover: 0.15 **NM** value: **12.00**
★ Appearance of Daredevil.
36 ❑ Apr 1971 Cover: 0.15 **NM** value: **12.00**
• **CGC:** 1 graded, best 7.0
📖 ...Among Men Stalks The Ramrod! **A:** Don Heck **W:** Gerry Conway ★ Versus Ramrod.
37 ❑ May 1971 Cover: 0.15 **NM** value: **12.00**
38 ❑ Jun 1971 Cover: 0.15 **NM** value: **12.00**
• **CGC:** 2 graded, best 9.4
★ Versus Jonah.
39 ❑ Jul 1971 Cover: 0.15 **NM** value: **12.00**
★ Versus White Dragon.
40 ❑ Aug 1971 Cover: 0.15 **NM** value: **12.00**
★ Death of White Dragon I.
41 ❑ Sep 1971 Cover: 0.15 **NM** value: **10.00**
★ Versus Slasher.
42 ❑ Oct 1971 Cover: 0.15 **NM** value: **10.00**
43 ❑ Nov 1971 Cover: 0.25 **NM** value: **10.00**
• **CGC:** 1 graded, best 9.4
• Giant-size. **A:** George Tuska; Jim Mooney ★ 1st Appearance of Guardsman. ★ Versus Mikas.
44 ❑ Jan 1972 Cover: 0.20 **NM** value: **10.00**
• **CGC:** 1 graded, best 9.0
A: George Tuska ★ Versus Night Phantom.
45 ❑ Mar 1972 Cover: 0.20 **NM** value: **10.00**
• **CGC:** 2 graded, best 9.4
A: George Tuska
46 ❑ May 1972 Cover: 0.20 **NM** value: **10.00**
• **CGC:** 1 graded, best 9.4
A: George Tuska ★ 1st Appearance of Marianne Rodgers. ★ Appearance of Guardsman. ★ Death of Guardsman.
47 ❑ Jun 1972 Cover: 0.20 **NM** value: **12.00**
• **CGC:** 4 graded, best 9.6
A: Barry Windsor-Smith; Jim Mooney ★ Origin of Iron Man.
48 ❑ Jul 1972 Cover: 0.20 **NM** value: **8.00**
• **CGC:** 2 graded, best 9.2
★ Versus Firebrand.
49 ❑ Aug 1972 Cover: 0.20 **NM** value: **8.00**
• **CGC:** 2 graded, best 9.4
★ Versus Adaptoid.
50 ❑ Sep 1972 Cover: 0.20 **NM** value: **8.00**
• **CGC:** 2 graded, best 9.2
★ Versus Princess Python.
51 ❑ Oct 1972 Cover: 0.20 **NM** value: **6.00**
• **CGC:** 2 graded, best 8.0
52 ❑ Nov 1972 Cover: 0.20 **NM** value: **6.00**
★ Versus Raga.
53 ❑ Dec 1972 Cover: 0.20 **NM** value: **6.00**
• **CGC:** 1 graded, best 4.5
A: Jim Starlin ★ 1st Appearance of Black Lama. ★ Versus Black Lama.
54 ❑ Jan 1973 Cover: 0.20 **NM** value: **12.00**
• **CGC:** 2 graded, best 9.6
★ 1st Appearance of Moondragon (as "Madame MacEvil"). ★ Appearance of Sub-Mariner. ★ Versus Sub-Mariner.
55 ❑ Feb 1973 Cover: 0.20 **NM** value: **60.00**
• **CGC:** 68 graded, best 9.8
A: Jim Starlin ★ 1st Appearance of Mentor, Drax the Destroyer, Thanos, Kronos, Blood Brothers, Starfox.
56 ❑ Mar 1973 Cover: 0.20 **NM** value: **12.00**
• **CGC:** 2 graded, best 9.4
A: Jim Starlin ★ 1st Appearance of Fangor.
57 ❑ Apr 1973 Cover: 0.20 **NM** value: **6.00**
58 ❑ May 1973 Cover: 0.20 **NM** value: **6.00**
• **CGC:** 2 graded, best 9.6
★ Versus Mandarin.
59 ❑ Jun 1973 Cover: 0.20 **NM** value: **6.00**
60 ❑ Jul 1973 Cover: 0.20 **NM** value: **6.00**
61 ❑ Aug 1973 Cover: 0.20 **NM** value: **6.00**
62 ❑ Sep 1973 Cover: 0.20 **NM** value: **6.00**
63 ❑ Oct 1973 Cover: 0.20 **NM** value: **6.00**
64 ❑ Nov 1973 Cover: 0.20 **NM** value: **6.00**
• survey
65 ❑ Dec 1973 Cover: 0.20 **NM** value: **6.00**
• **CGC:** 1 graded, best 5.5
★ Origin of Doctor Spectrum.
66 ❑ Feb 1974 Cover: 0.20 **NM** value: **6.00**
• Marvel Value Stamp A80 ★ Appearance of Thor.
67 ❑ Apr 1974 Cover: 0.20 **NM** value: **6.00**
• **CGC:** 1 graded, best 9.2
★ Appearance of Sunfire.
68 ❑ Jun 1974 Cover: 0.25 **NM** value: **6.00**
• **CGC:** 1 graded, best 9.6
A: George Tuska ★ Origin of Iron Man. ★ Appearance of Sunfire.
69 ❑ Aug 1974 Cover: 0.25 **NM** value: **6.00**
📖 Confrontation **A:** George Tuska **W:** Mike Friedrich ★ Versus Sunfire. ★ Versus Mandarin. ★ Versus Unicorn. ★ Versus Yellow Claw.
70 ❑ Sep 1974 Cover: 0.25 **NM** value: **6.00**
📖 Who Shall Stop...Ultimo? **A:** George Tuska **W:** Mike Friedrich
71 ❑ Nov 1974 Cover: 0.25 **NM** value: **5.00**
A: George Tuska
72 ❑ Jan 1975 Cover: 0.25 **NM** value: **5.00**
• comic con **A:** George Tuska; Neal Adams
73 ❑ Mar 1975 Cover: 0.25 **NM** value: **5.00**
74 ❑ May 1975 Cover: 0.25 **NM** value: **5.00**
★ Versus M.O.D.O.K..
75 ❑ Jun 1975 Cover: 0.25 **NM** value: **5.00**
76 ❑ Jul 1975 Cover: 0.25 **NM** value: **5.00**
• **CGC:** 1 graded, best 9.4
📖 ...There Lives A Green Goliath **A:** George Tuska **W:** Archie Goodwin
77 ❑ Aug 1975 Cover: 0.25 **NM** value: **5.00**
78 ❑ Sep 1975 Cover: 0.25 **NM** value: **5.00**
• in Vietnam
79 ❑ Oct 1975 Cover: 0.25 **NM** value: **5.00**
80 ❑ Nov 1975 Cover: 0.25 **NM** value: **5.00**
C: Joe Kubert
81 ❑ Dec 1975 Cover: 0.25 **NM** value: **5.00**
• Marvel Value Stamp
82 ❑ Jan 1976 Cover: 0.25 **NM** value: **5.00**
• repeats letter column from #81; Marvel Value Stamp B2
83 ❑ Feb 1976 Cover: 0.25 **NM** value: **5.00**
📖 The Rage of the Red Ghost • Marvel Value Stamp B16 **A:** Herb Trimpe; Marie Severin **W:** Len Wein ★ Versus Red Ghost.
84 ❑ Mar 1976 Cover: 0.25 **NM** value: **5.00**
• **CGC:** 1 graded, best 9.2
📖 Night Of The Walking Bomb • Marvel Value Stamp B56 **A:** Herb Trimpe; John Tartag **W:** Len Wein; Roger Slifer
85 ❑ Apr 1976 Cover: 0.25 **NM** value: **5.00**
86 ❑ May 1976 Cover: 0.25 **NM** value: **5.00**
• Marvel Value Stamp B84 ★ 1st Appearance of Blizzard. ★ Versus Blizzard.
87 ❑ Jun 1976 Cover: 0.25 **NM** value: **5.00**
• Marvel Value Stamp
88 ❑ Jul 1976 Cover: 0.25 **NM** value: **5.00**
📖 Fear Wears Two Faces! • Marvel Value Stamp 66 **A:** George Tuska **W:** Archie Goodwin
89 ❑ Aug 1976 Cover: 0.25 **NM** value: **5.00**
• **CGC:** 1 graded, best 4.0
📖 Brute Fury! **A:** George Tuska; Vince Colletta **W:** Archie Goodwin ★ Appearance of Daredevil.
90 ❑ Sep 1976 Cover: 0.30 **NM** value: **5.00**
91 ❑ Oct 1976 Cover: 0.30 **NM** value: **5.00**
📖 Breakout! **A:** George Tuska **W:** Gerry Conway
92 ❑ Nov 1976 Cover: 0.30 **NM** value: **5.00**
📖 Burn, Hero...Burn **A:** George Tuska **W:** Gerry Conway ★ Versus Melter.
93 ❑ Dec 1976 Cover: 0.30 **NM** value: **5.00**
94 ❑ Jan 1977 Cover: 0.30 **NM** value: **5.00**
📖 Frenzy At Fifty Fathoms **A:** Herb Trimpe **W:** Gerry Conway
95 ❑ Feb 1977 Cover: 0.30 **NM** value: **5.00**
96 ❑ Mar 1977 Cover: 0.30 **NM** value: **5.00**
📖 Only A Friend Can Save Him • Michael O'Brien becomes New Guardsman **A:** George Tuska **W:** Bill Mantlo ★ 1st Appearance of New Guardsman.
97 ❑ Apr 1977 Cover: 0.30 **NM** value: **5.00**
98 ❑ May 1977 Cover: 0.30 **NM** value: **5.00**
99 ❑ Jun 1977 Cover: 0.30 **NM** value: **5.00**
📖 At The Mercy Of The Mandarin! **A:** George Tuska **W:** Bill Mantlo ★ Versus Mandarin.
100 ❑ Jul 1977 Cover: 0.30 **NM** value: **6.00**
• **CGC:** 8 graded, best 9.8
• 100th anniversary issue. • Mandarin **A:** George Tuska **C:** Jim Starlin
101 ❑ Aug 1977 Cover: 0.30 **NM** value: **4.00**
📖 Then Came The Monster! **A:** George Tuska **W:** Bill Mantlo ★ 1st Appearance of Dreadknight.
102 ❑ Sep 1977 Cover: 0.30 **NM** value: **4.00**
• **CGC:** 1 graded, best 9.4
★ Origin of Dreadknight. ★ 1st Appearance of Dreadknight.
103 ❑ Oct 1977 Cover: 0.30 **NM** value: **4.00**
★ Appearance of Jack of Hearts.
104 ❑ Nov 1977 Cover: 0.35 **NM** value: **4.00**
105 ❑ Dec 1977 Cover: 0.35 **NM** value: **4.00**
📖 Every Hand Against Him! **A:** George Tuska **W:** Bill Mantlo ★ Appearance of Jack of Hearts.
106 ❑ Jan 1978 Cover: 0.35 **NM** value: **4.00**
107 ❑ Feb 1978 Cover: 0.35 **NM** value: **4.00**
• **CGC:** 2 graded, best 9.6
📖 And, In the End ... **A:** Keith Pollard **W:** Bill Mantlo ★ Versus Midas.
108 ❑ Mar 1978 Cover: 0.35 **NM** value: **4.00**
• **CGC:** 1 graded, best 9.4
📖 Growing Pains! **A:** Carmine Infantino **W:** Bill Mantlo
109 ❑ Apr 1978 Cover: 0.35 **NM** value: **4.00**
• **CGC:** 1 graded, best 9.6
★ 1st Appearance of Vanguard. ★ Versus Darkstar. ★ Versus Darkstar, Vanguard. ★ Versus Vanguard.
110 ❑ May 1978 Cover: 0.35 **NM** value: **4.00**
📖 Sojourners Through Space! **A:** Keith Pollard; Fred Kida **W:** Bill Mantlo ★ Appearance of Jack of Hearts.
111 ❑ Jun 1978 Cover: 0.35 **NM** value: **4.00**
📖 The Man, the Metal, And The Mayhem • Wundagore
112 ❑ Jul 1978 Cover: 0.35 **NM** value: **4.00**
• **CGC:** 1 graded, best 9.6
📖 Moon Wars! **A:** Keith Pollard; Alfredo Alcala **W:** Bill Mantlo
113 ❑ Aug 1978 Cover: 0.35 **NM** value: **4.00**
• **CGC:** 1 graded, best 9.6
📖 The Horn Of The Unicorn! **A:** Herb Trimpe **W:** Bill Mantlo
114 ❑ Sep 1978 Cover: 0.35 **NM** value: **4.00**
• **CGC:** 2 graded, best 9.6
115 ❑ Oct 1978 Cover: 0.35 **NM** value: **4.00**
📖 Betrayal! **A:** Dan Green **W:** Bill Mantlo
116 ❑ Nov 1978 Cover: 0.35 **NM** value: **4.00**
• **CGC:** 1 graded, best 9.4
📖 Anguish, Once Removed • 1st David Michelinie written issue **A:** Bob Layton; John Romita Jr. **W:** David Michelinie ★ Death of Frog-Man I (Francois LeBlanc). ★ Death of Count Nefaria. ★ Death of Cat-Man I (Townshend Patane). ★ Death of Bird-Man I (Henry Hawk). ★ Death of Ape-Man I (Gordon "Monk" Keefer).
117 ❑ Dec 1978 Cover: 0.35 **NM** value: **4.00**
A: Bob Layton; John Romita Jr. ★ 1st Appearance of Beth Cabe.
118 ❑ Jan 1979 Cover: 0.35 **NM** value: **6.00**
A: John Byrne; Bob Layton ★ 1st Appearance of James Rhodes (Rhodey), Mrs. Arbogast.
119 ❑ Feb 1979 Cover: 0.35 **NM** value: **5.00**
📖 No S.H.I.E.L.D. To Protect Me! • Stark battles with alcohol **A:** Bob Layton; John Romita Jr. **W:** David Michelinie
120 ❑ Mar 1979 Cover: 0.35 **NM** value: **4.00**
• **CGC:** 3 graded, best 9.6
• Stark battles with alcohol ★ 1st Appearance of Justin Hammer. ★ Appearance of Sub-Mariner.
121 ❑ Apr 1979 Cover: 0.35 **NM** value: **4.00**
• Stark battles with alcohol ★ Appearance of Sub-Mariner.
122 ❑ May 1979 Cover: 0.40 **NM** value: **4.00**
• Stark battles with alcohol ★ Origin of Iron Man. ★ Appearance of Sub-Mariner.
123 ❑ Jun 1979 Cover: 0.40 **NM** value: **4.00**
• Stark battles with alcohol
124 ❑ Jul 1979 Cover: 0.40 **NM** value: **4.00**
📖 Pieces Of Hate! • Stark battles with alcohol **A:** John Romita Jr. **W:** David Michelinie
125 ❑ Aug 1979 Cover: 0.40 **NM** value: **4.00**
📖 The Monaco Prelude • Stark battles with alcohol **A:** John Romita Jr. **W:** David Michelinie ★ Appearance of Scott Lang (Ant-Man).
126 ❑ Sep 1979 Cover: 0.40 **NM** value: **4.00**
• Stark battles with alcohol ★ Versus Justin Hammer.
127 ❑ Oct 1979 Cover: 0.40 **NM** value: **4.00**
• Stark battles with alcohol
128 ❑ Nov 1979 Cover: 0.40 **NM** value: **4.00**
• **CGC:** 3 graded, best 8.5
Stark begins recovery from alcohol. 📖 Demon In A Bottle **A:** Bob Layton; John Romita Jr. **W:** David Michelinie
129 ❑ Dec 1979 Cover: 0.40 **NM** value: **3.00**
📖 Dread Night Of the Dreadnought! **A:** Sal Buscema **W:** David Michelinie ★ Versus Dreadnought.
130 ❑ Jan 1980 Cover: 0.40 **NM** value: **3.00**
131 ❑ Feb 1980 Cover: 0.40 **NM** value: **3.00**
★ Appearance of Hulk.
132 ❑ Mar 1980 Cover: 0.40 **NM** value: **3.00**
★ Appearance of Hulk.
133 ❑ Apr 1980 Cover: 0.40 **NM** value: **3.00**
📖 The Hero Within! **A:** Bob Layton; Jerry Bingham **W:** David Michelinie ★ Appearance of Hulk, Ant-Man.
134 ❑ May 1980 Cover: 0.40 **NM** value: **3.00**
📖 The Challenge **A:** Bob Layton; Jerry Bingham **W:** David Michelinie
135 ❑ Jun 1980 Cover: 0.40 **NM** value: **3.00**
📖 Return Of The Hero **A:** Bob Layton; Jerry Bingham **W:** David Michelinie ★ Versus Titanium Man.
136 ❑ Jul 1980 Cover: 0.40 **NM** value: **3.00**
📖 The Beginning Of The Endotherm! **A:** Alan Weiss; Bob Wiacek **W:** David Michelinie
137 ❑ Aug 1980 Cover: 0.40 **NM** value: **3.00**
📖 Fatades! **A:** Bob Layton **W:** David Michelinie
138 ❑ Sep 1980 Cover: 0.50 **NM** value: **3.00**
📖 Fatades And Ruses **A:** Bob Layton; Tom Palmer **W:** David Michelinie ★ 1st Appearance of Dreadnought (silver).

CGC-graded: Multiply prices above by **33 for 9.9 M • 16 for 9.8 NM/M • 7 for 9.6 NM+ • 5 for 9.4 NM • 2.5 for 9.2 NM- • 1.5 for 9.0 VF/NM**

139❑ Oct 1980 Cover: 0.50 **NM** value: **3.00**
📖 Fatades, Ruses, & Masques • Bethany Cabe knows Tony is Iron Man **A:** Bob Layton **W:** David Michelinie
140❑ Nov 1980 Cover: 0.50 **NM** value: **3.00**
📖 The Use Of Deadly Force! **A:** Bob Layton **W:** David Michelinie
141❑ Dec 1980 Cover: 0.50 **NM** value: **3.00**
📖 The Caribbean Connection **A:** Bob Layton; John Romita Jr. **W:** David Michelinie
142❑ Jan 1981 Cover: 0.50 **NM** value: **3.00**
Circ: Statement: **177,520**
📖 Sky Die! **A:** Bob Layton; John Romita Jr. **W:** David Michelinie ★ 1st Appearance of Space Armor.
143❑ Feb 1981 Cover: 0.50 **NM** value: **3.00**
Circ: Statement: **177,520**
📖 Meter On The Sun! **A:** Bob Layton; John Romita Jr. **W:** David Michelinie ★ 1st Appearance of Sunturion.
144❑ Mar 1981 Cover: 0.50 **NM** value: **3.00**
Circ: Statement: **177,520**
📖 Sunfall **A:** Bob Layton; John Romita Jr. **W:** David Michelinie ★ Origin of James Rhodes (Rhodey).
145❑ Apr 1981 Cover: 0.50 **NM** value: **3.00**
Circ: Statement: **177,520**
📖 Raiders' Rampage! **A:** Bob Layton; John Romita Jr. **W:** David Michelinie
146❑ May 1981 Cover: 0.50 **NM** value: **3.00**
Circ: Statement: **177,520**
📖 Blacklash...And The Burning! **A:** Bob Layton; John Romita Jr. **W:** David Michelinie ★ Versus Blacklash.
147❑ Jun 1981 Cover: 0.50 **NM** value: **3.00**
Circ: Statement: **177,520**
📖 Holocaust At High Noon **A:** Bob Layton; John Romita Jr. **W:** David Michelinie
148❑ Jul 1981 Cover: 0.50 **NM** value: **3.00**
Circ: Statement: **177,520**
📖 Siege! **A:** Bob Layton; John Romita Jr. **W:** David Michelinie
149❑ Aug 1981 Cover: 0.50 **NM** value: **3.00**
Circ: Statement: **177,520**
📖 Doomquest **A:** Bob Layton; John Romita Jr. **W:** David Michelinie ★ Versus Dr. Doom. ★ Versus Doctor Doom.
150❑ Sep 1981 Cover: 0.75 **NM** value: **3.50**
Circ: Statement: **177,520** • **CGC:** 2 graded, best 9.6
• double-sized. 📖 Knightmare • In Camelot **A:** Bob Layton; John Romita Jr. **W:** David Michelinie ★ Appearance of Doctor Doom. ★ Versus Dr. Doom. ★ Versus Doctor Doom.
151❑ Oct 1981 Cover: 0.50 **NM** value: **2.50**
Circ: Statement: **177,520**
📖 G.A.R.D.'s Gauntlet **A:** Bob Layton; Luke McDonnell **W:** David Michelinie ★ Appearance of Ant-Man.
152❑ Nov 1981 Cover: 0.50 **NM** value: **2.50**
Circ: Statement: **177,520**
📖 Escape From Heaven's Hand! **A:** Bob Layton; John Romita Jr. **W:** David Michelinie ★ 1st Appearance of Stealth Armor.
153❑ Dec 1981 Cover: 0.50 **NM** value: **2.50**
Circ: Statement: **177,520**
📖 Light Makes Might! **A:** Bob Layton; John Romita Jr. **W:** David Michelinie
154❑ Jan 1982 Cover: 0.60 **NM** value: **2.50**
Circ: Statement: **187,564**
📖 The Other Side Of Madness **A:** Bob Layton; John Romita Jr. **W:** David Michelinie ★ Death of Unicorn I (Milos Masaryk).
155❑ Feb 1982 Cover: 0.60 **NM** value: **2.50**
Circ: Statement: **187,564**
📖 The Back Getters! **A:** Bob Layton; John Romita Jr. **W:** David Michelinie
156❑ Mar 1982 Cover: 0.60 **NM** value: **2.50**
Circ: Statement: **187,564**
📖 The Mauler Mandate! **A:** John Romita Jr.; Pablo Marcos **W:** David Michelinie
157❑ Apr 1982 Cover: 0.60 **NM** value: **2.50**
Circ: Statement: **187,564**
📖 Spores! **A:** Alan Kupperberg **W:** David Michelinie
158❑ May 1982 Cover: 0.60 **NM** value: **2.50**
Circ: Statement: **187,564**
📖 Moms **A:** Carmine Infantino **W:** Denny O'Neil
159❑ Jun 1982 Cover: 0.60 **NM** value: **2.50**
Circ: Statement: **187,564**
📖 When Strikes Diablo • Diablo **A:** Paul Smith **W:** Roger McKenzie
160❑ Jul 1982 Cover: 0.60 **NM** value: **2.50**
Circ: Statement: **187,564**
📖 A Cry Of Beasts • Serpent Squad **A:** Steve Ditko **W:** Denny O'Neil
161❑ Aug 1982 Cover: 0.60 **NM** value: **2.50**
Circ: Statement: **187,564**
📖 If The Moonman Should Fail! • Moon Knight **A:** Luke McDonnell **W:** Denny O'Neil
162❑ Sep 1982 Cover: 0.60 **NM** value: **2.50**
Circ: Statement: **187,564**
📖 The Menace Within! **A:** Mike Vosburg **W:** Denny O'Neil
163❑ Oct 1982 Cover: 0.60 **NM** value: **2.50**
Circ: Statement: **187,564**
📖 Knight's Errand! **A:** Luke McDonnell **W:** Denny O'Neil ★ 1st Appearance of Obadiah Stane (voice only), Chessmen, Indries Moomji, Iron Monger (voice only).
164❑ Nov 1982 Cover: 0.60 **NM** value: **2.50**
Circ: Statement: **187,564**
📖 Deadly Blessing **A:** Luke McDonnell; Brent Anderson(cover) **W:** Denny O'Neil
165❑ Dec 1982 Cover: 0.60 **NM** value: **2.50**
Circ: Statement: **187,564**
📖 Endgame **A:** Luke McDonnell **W:** Denny O'Neil
166❑ Jan 1983 Cover: 0.60 **NM** value: **2.50**
📖 One Of Those Days... **A:** Luke McDonnell **W:** Denny O'Neil ★ 1st Appearance of Obadiah Stane (full appearance), Iron Monger (full appearance).
167❑ Feb 1983 Cover: 0.60 **NM** value: **2.50**
📖 The Empty Shell • Alcohol problem returns **A:** Luke McDonnell **W:** Denny O'Neil
168❑ Mar 1983 Cover: 0.60 **NM** value: **2.50**
📖 The Iron Scream • Machine Man; Stark battles with alcohol **A:** Luke McDonnell **W:** Denny O'Neil
169❑ Apr 1983 Cover: 0.60 **NM** value: **4.00**
• **CGC:** 7 graded, best 9.8
📖 Blackout! • Jim Rhodes takes over Stark's job as Iron Man; Stark battles with alcohol **A:** Luke McDonnell **W:** Denny O'Neil
170❑ May 1983 Cover: 0.60 **NM** value: **4.00**
• **CGC:** 1 graded, best 9.6
📖 And Who Shall Clothe Himself In Iron • Stark battles with alcohol **A:** Luke McDonnell **W:** Denny O'Neil ★ 1st Appearance of Morley Erwin, James Rhodes as Iron Man.
171❑ Jun 1983 Cover: 0.60 **NM** value: **2.50**
📖 Ball And Chain • Stark battles with alcohol **A:** Luke McDonnell **W:** Denny O'Neil ★ 1st Appearance of Clytemnestra Erwin. ★ Versus Thunderball.
172❑ Jul 1983 Cover: 0.60 **NM** value: **2.50**
📖 Firebrand's Revenge! • Stark battles with alcohol **A:** Luke McDonnell **W:** Denny O'Neil ★ Appearance of Captain America.
173❑ Aug 1983 Cover: 0.60 **NM** value: **2.50**
📖 Judas Is A Woman • Stark International becomes Stane International; Stark battles with alcohol **A:** Luke McDonnell **W:** Denny O'Neil
174❑ Sep 1983 Cover: 0.60 **NM** value: **2.50**
📖 Armor Chase • S.H.I.E.L.D. acquires armor; Stark battles with alcohol **A:** Luke McDonnell **W:** Denny O'Neil ★ Versus Chessmen.
175❑ Oct 1983 Cover: 0.60 **NM** value: **2.50**
📖 This Treasure Of Red And Gold • Stark battles with alcohol **A:** Luke McDonnell **W:** Denny O'Neil
176❑ Nov 1983 Cover: 0.60 **NM** value: **2.50**
📖 Turf • Stark battles with alcohol **A:** Luke McDonnell **W:** Denny O'Neil
177❑ Dec 1983 Cover: 0.60 **NM** value: **2.50**
📖 Have Armor, Will Travel • Stark battles with alcohol (alcohol storyline continues through next several issues) **A:** Luke McDonnell **W:** Denny O'Neil ★ Versus Flying Tiger.
178❑ Jan 1984 Cover: 0.60 **NM** value: **2.50**
Circ: Statement: **177,659**
📖 Once An Avenger, Always An Avenger **A:** Luke McDonnell **W:** Denny O'Neil
179❑ Feb 1984 Cover: 0.60 **NM** value: **2.50**
Circ: Statement: **177,659**
📖 Mission Into Darkness **A:** Luke McDonnell **W:** Denny O'Neil ★ Versus Mandarin.
180❑ Mar 1984 Cover: 0.60 **NM** value: **2.50**
Circ: Statement: **177,659**
📖 This Ancient Enemy **A:** Luke McDonnell **W:** Denny O'Neil ★ Versus Mandarin.
181❑ Apr 1984 Cover: 0.60 **NM** value: **2.50**
Circ: Statement: **177,659**
📖 Though My Life Be Forfeit... • Erroneously reprints 1982 Statement of Ownership **A:** Luke McDonnell **W:** Denny O'Neil ★ Versus Mandarin.
182❑ May 1984 Cover: 0.60 **NM** value: **2.50**
Circ: Statement: **177,659**
📖 Deliverance • alcoholism cured again **A:** Luke McDonnell **W:** Denny O'Neil
183❑ Jun 1984 Cover: 0.60 **NM** value: **2.50**
Circ: Statement: **177,659**
📖 All The Kinds Of Fear **A:** Luke McDonnell **W:** Denny O'Neil ★ Versus Taurus.
184❑ Jul 1984 Cover: 0.60 **NM** value: **2.50**
Circ: Statement: **177,659**
📖 On The Road... • Tony Stark founds new company in California **A:** Luke McDonnell **W:** Denny O'Neil
185❑ Aug 1984 Cover: 0.60 **NM** value: **2.50**
Circ: Statement: **177,659**
📖 Terror In Tulaluma! **A:** Luke McDonnell **W:** Denny O'Neil
186❑ Sep 1984 Cover: 0.60 **NM** value: **2.50**
Circ: Statement: **177,659**
📖 Though This Fault Be Mine **A:** Luke McDonnell **W:** Denny O'Neil ★ Origin of Vibro. ★ 1st Appearance of Vibro. ★ Versus Vibro.
187❑ Oct 1984 Cover: 0.60 **NM** value: **2.50**
Circ: Statement: **177,659**
📖 The Vengeance Of Vibro! **A:** Luke McDonnell **W:** Denny O'Neil ★ Versus Vibro.
188❑ Nov 1984 Cover: 0.60 **NM** value: **2.50**
Circ: Statement: **177,659**
📖 And Grimm Shall Be Their Name! **A:** Don Perlin **W:** Denny O'Neil ★ 1st Appearance of Circuits Maximus. ★ Versus Brothers Grimm.
189❑ Dec 1984 Cover: 0.60 **NM** value: **2.50**
Circ: Statement: **177,659**
📖 A Thing That Bores From Within... **A:** Luke McDonnell **W:** Denny O'Neil ★ Versus Termite.
190❑ Jan 1985 Cover: 0.60 **NM** value: **2.50**
Circ: Statement: **201,092**
📖 Losing Touch! **A:** Luke McDonnell **W:** Denny O'Neil ★ Appearance of Scarlet Witch. ★ Versus Termite.
191❑ Feb 1985 Cover: 0.60 **NM** value: **2.50**
Circ: Statement: **201,092**
📖 The Iron Destiny • Tony Stark returns as Iron Man in original armor **A:** Luke McDonnell **W:** Denny O'Neil
192❑ Mar 1985 Cover: 0.60 **NM** value: **2.50**
Circ: Statement: **201,092**
• Iron Man (Stark) vs. Iron Man (Rhodey)
193❑ Apr 1985 Cover: 0.65 **NM** value: **2.50**
Circ: Statement: **201,092**
📖 The Choice And The Challenge • West Coast Avengers learn Tony is Iron Man **A:** Luke McDonnell **W:** Denny O'Neil
194❑ May 1985 Cover: 0.65 **NM** value: **2.50**
Circ: Statement: **201,092** CapCity orders: **16,200**
📖 Otherwhere! **A:** Luke McDonnell **W:** Denny O'Neil ★ 1st Appearance of Scourge. ★ Appearance of West Coast Avengers. ★ Death of Enforcer (Marvel).
195❑ Jun 1985 Cover: 0.65 **NM** value: **2.50**
Circ: Statement: **201,092** CapCity orders: **16,600**
★ Appearance of Shaman.
196❑ Jul 1985 Cover: 0.65 **NM** value: **2.50**
Circ: Statement: **201,092** CapCity orders: **17,000**
197❑ Aug 1985 Cover: 0.65 **NM** value: **2.50**
Circ: Statement: **201,092** CapCity orders: **23,800**
• Secret Wars II
198❑ Sep 1985 Cover: 0.65 **NM** value: **2.50**
Circ: Statement: **201,092** CapCity orders: **18,200**
📖 Revelations! **A:** Sal Buscema **W:** Denny O'Neil ★ Origin of Obadiah Stane, Iron Monger.
199❑ Oct 1985 Cover: 0.65 **NM** value: **2.50**
Circ: Statement: **201,092** CapCity orders: **18,200**
📖 And One Of Them Must Die! • James Rhodes crippled **A:** Herb Trimpe **W:** Denny O'Neil ★ Death of Morley Erwin.
200❑ Nov 1985 Cover: 1.25 **NM** value: **3.00**
Circ: Statement: **201,092** CapCity orders: **25,000**
• double-sized. • Tony Stark returns as Iron Man; New armor (red & white) ★ 1st Appearance of Red and white battlesuit. ★ Appearance of Iron Monger (full. ★ Death of Obadiah Stane. ★ Death of Iron Monger.
201❑ Dec 1985 Cover: 0.60 **NM** value: **2.00**
Circ: Statement: **201,092** CapCity orders: **17,700**
📖 Sky Duel! **A:** Mark D. Bright **W:** Denny O'Neil
202❑ Jan 1986 Cover: 0.60 **NM** value: **2.00**
Circ: Statement: **190,516** CapCity orders: **17,500**
★ Appearance of Ka-Zar. ★ Versus Fixer.
203❑ Feb 1986 Cover: 0.75 **NM** value: **2.00**
Circ: Statement: **190,516** CapCity orders: **19,100**
📖 The Maze **A:** Mark D. Bright **W:** Denny O'Neil
204❑ Mar 1986 Cover: 0.75 **NM** value: **2.00**
Circ: Statement: **190,516** CapCity orders: **19,900**
205❑ Apr 1986 Cover: 0.75 **NM** value: **2.00**
Circ: Statement: **190,516** CapCity orders: **20,200**
★ Versus M.O.D.O.K..
206❑ May 1986 Cover: 0.75 **NM** value: **2.00**
Circ: Statement: **190,516** CapCity orders: **20,500**
📖 Prisons **A:** Mark D. Bright **W:** Denny O'Neil
207❑ Jun 1986 Cover: 0.75 **NM** value: **2.00**
Circ: Statement: **190,516** CapCity orders: **19,800**
📖 Heat **A:** Mark D. Bright **W:** Denny O'Neil
208❑ Jul 1986 Cover: 0.75 **NM** value: **2.00**
Circ: Statement: **190,516** CapCity orders: **19,800**
📖 Firefang! **A:** Mark D. Bright **W:** Denny O'Neil
209❑ Aug 1986 Cover: 0.75 **NM** value: **2.00**
Circ: Statement: **190,516** CapCity orders: **19,700**
📖 A Renaissance Of Magic! **A:** Rick Hoberg **W:** Dennis Mallonee
210❑ Sep 1986 Cover: 0.75 **NM** value: **2.00**
Circ: Statement: **190,516** CapCity orders: **18,700**
📖 Happy's Story **A:** Mark D. Bright **W:** Danny Fingeroth ★ Appearance of Happy Hogan.
211❑ Oct 1986 Cover: 0.75 **NM** value: **2.00**
Circ: Statement: **190,516** CapCity orders: **19,100**
212❑ Nov 1986 Cover: 0.75 **NM** value: **2.00**
Circ: Statement: **190,516** CapCity orders: **19,800**
📖 Precious Legacy **A:** Dwayne Turner **W:** Danny Fingeroth
213❑ Dec 1986 Cover: 0.75 **NM** value: **2.00**
Circ: Statement: **190,516** CapCity orders: **19,200**
★ Appearance of Dominic Fortune.
214❑ Jan 1987 Cover: 0.75 **NM** value: **2.00**
Circ: Statement: **179,567** CapCity orders: **18,100**
📖 Bring Me Spider-Woman! • Construction of Stark Enterprises begins **A:** Tom Morgan **W:** Danny Fingeroth
215❑ Feb 1987 Cover: 0.75 **NM** value: **2.00**
Circ: Statement: **179,567** CapCity orders: **18,800**
📖 The Shattered Sky **A:** Mark D. Bright **W:** David Michelinie
216❑ Mar 1987 Cover: 0.75 **NM** value: **2.00**
Circ: Statement: **179,567** CapCity orders: **19,200**
📖 Requiescat...And Revenge! **A:** Mark D. Bright **W:** David Michelinie ★ Death of Clytemnestra Erwin.
217❑ Apr 1987 Cover: 0.75 **NM** value: **2.00**
Circ: Statement: **179,567** CapCity orders: **18,800**
📖 Metamorphosis Oddity **A:** Mark D. Bright **W:** David Michelinie ★ 1st Appearance of undersea armor.
218❑ May 1987 Cover: 0.75 **NM** value: **2.00**
Circ: Statement: **179,567** CapCity orders: **19,500**
📖 Deep Trouble! **A:** Bob Layton **W:** David Michelinie ★ 1st Appearance of Deep Sea armor.
219❑ Jun 1987 Cover: 0.75 **NM** value: **2.00**
Circ: Statement: **179,567** CapCity orders: **20,100**
📖 Ghost Story **A:** Bob Layton **W:** David Michelinie ★ 1st Appearance of Ghost. ★ Versus Ghost.
220❑ Jul 1987 Cover: 0.75 **NM** value: **2.00**
Circ: Statement: **179,567** CapCity orders: **19,900**
📖 Ghost Of A Chance **A:** Mark D. Bright **W:** David Michelinie ★ Death of Spymaster.
221❑ Aug 1987 Cover: 0.75 **NM** value: **2.00**
Circ: Statement: **179,567** CapCity orders: **20,500**
222❑ Sep 1987 Cover: 0.75 **NM** value: **2.00**
Circ: Statement: **179,567** CapCity orders: **22,600**
📖 The Party **A:** Mark D. Bright **W:** David Michelinie
223❑ Oct 1987 Cover: 0.75 **NM** value: **2.00**
Circ: Statement: **179,567** CapCity orders: **22,100**
📖 Counter Force **A:** Mark D. Bright **W:** David Michelinie ★ 1st Appearance of Rae LaCoste.
224❑ Nov 1987 Cover: 0.75 **NM** value: **2.00**
Circ: Statement: **179,567** CapCity orders: **22,500**
📖 Low Noon **A:** Bob Layton **W:** David Michelinie
225❑ Dec 1987 Cover: 1.25 **NM** value: **3.00**
Circ: Statement: **179,567** CapCity orders: **23,600** • **CGC:** 1 graded, best 9.4
• Giant-size. 📖 Armor Wars, Part 1
226❑ Jan 1988 Cover: 0.75 **NM** value: **2.50**
Circ: Statement: **196,095** CapCity orders: **22,900**
📖 Armor Wars, Part 2
227❑ Feb 1988 Cover: 0.75 **NM** value: **2.50**
Circ: Statement: **196,095** CapCity orders: **25,100**
📖 Armor Wars, Part 3 **A:** Mark D. Bright **W:** David Michelinie
228❑ Mar 1988 Cover: 0.75 **NM** value: **2.50**
Circ: Statement: **196,095** CapCity orders: **27,800**
📖 Armor Wars, Part 4 **A:** Mark D. Bright **W:** David Michelinie
229❑ Apr 1988 Cover: 0.75 **NM** value: **3.00**

Other grades: Multiply prices above by **1.5 for Mint • 2/3 for Very Fine • 1/3 for Fine • 1/5 for Very Good • 1/8 for Good**

Circ: Statement: 196,095 CapCity orders: 28,400
📖 Armor Wars, Part 5 A: Mark D. Bright W: David Michelinie ★ Death of Gremlin a.k.a Titanium Man II.
230 ❑ May 1988 Cover: 0.75 NM value: 2.50
Circ: Statement: 196,095 CapCity orders: 28,600
📖 Armor Wars, Part 6 • apparent death of Iron Man A: Mark D. Bright W: David Michelinie ★ Versus Firepower.
231 ❑ Jun 1988 Cover: 0.75 NM value: 2.50
Circ: Statement: 196,095 CapCity orders: 28,800
📖 Armor Wars, Part 7 • new armor ★ Versus Firepower.
232 ❑ Jul 1988 Cover: 0.75 NM value: 2.50
Circ: Statement: 196,095 CapCity orders: 33,200
📖 Armor Wars, Part 8 • offset A: Barry Windsor-Smith
232/A ❑ Jul 1988 Cover: 0.75 NM value: 2.50
• Flexographic A: Barry Windsor-Smith
233 ❑ Aug 1988 Cover: 0.75 NM value: 2.00
Circ: Statement: 196,095 CapCity orders: 30,300
📖 Slaughterday! A: Jackson Guice W: David Michelinie ★ 1st Appearance of Kathy Dare. ★ Appearance of Ant-Man.
234 ❑ Sep 1988 Cover: 0.75 NM value: 2.00
Circ: Statement: 196,095 CapCity orders: 32,500
📖 Fallout! A: Jackson Guice W: David Michelinie ★ Appearance of Spider-Man.
235 ❑ Oct 1988 Cover: 0.75 NM value: 1.50
Circ: Statement: 196,095 CapCity orders: 33,200
📖 Epitaph In Grey A: Jackson Guice W: David Michelinie
236 ❑ Nov 1988 Cover: 0.75 NM value: 1.50
Circ: Statement: 196,095 CapCity orders: 30,800
📖 Stone Cold! A: Jackson Guice W: David Michelinie
237 ❑ Dec 1988 Cover: 0.75 NM value: 1.50
Circ: Statement: 196,095 CapCity orders: 31,800
📖 Star Hunter! A: Jackson Guice W: David Michelinie
238 ❑ Jan 1989 Cover: 0.75 NM value: 1.50
Circ: Statement: 199,100 CapCity orders: 30,500
📖 Two Live Or Die In L.A.! A: Jackson Guice W: David Michelinie ★ 1st Appearance of Madame Masque II.
239 ❑ Feb 1989 Cover: 0.75 NM value: 1.50
Circ: Statement: 199,100 CapCity orders: 29,200
📖 Unholy Ghost! A: Jackson Guice W: David Michelinie
240 ❑ Mar 1989 Cover: 0.75 NM value: 1.50
Circ: Statement: 199,100 CapCity orders: 29,300
📖 Ghost Righter! A: Jackson Guice W: David Michelinie
241 ❑ Apr 1989 Cover: 0.75 NM value: 1.50
Circ: Statement: 199,100 CapCity orders: 29,900
📖 China See! A: Denys Cowan W: David Michelinie
242 ❑ May 1989 Cover: 0.75 NM value: 1.50
Circ: Statement: 199,100 CapCity orders: 28,400
📖 Master Blaster • Stark shot by Kathy Dare A: Alan Kupperberg W: David Michelinie
243 ❑ Jun 1989 Cover: 0.75 NM value: 2.00
Circ: Statement: 199,100 CapCity orders: 31,300
📖 Heartbeaten • Stark crippled A: Bob Layton W: David Michelinie
244 ❑ Jul 1989 Cover: 1.50 NM value: 3.00
Circ: Statement: 199,100 CapCity orders: 34,700
• Giant-size. • Carl Walker a.k.a. Force becomes Iron Man; New armor to allow Stark to walk again
245 ❑ Aug 1989 Cover: 0.75 NM value: 1.50
Circ: Statement: 199,100 CapCity orders: 31,800
📖 Inside Angry A: Paul Smith W: David Michelinie
246 ❑ Sep 1989 Cover: 1.00 NM value: 1.50
Circ: Statement: 199,100 CapCity orders: 31,400
📖 Heavy Mettle! A: Bob Layton W: David Michelinie
247 ❑ Oct 1989 Cover: 1.00 NM value: 1.50
Circ: Statement: 199,100 CapCity orders: 32,100
📖 Malled! A: Bob Layton W: David Michelinie
248 ❑ Nov 1989 Cover: 1.00 NM value: 1.50
Circ: Statement: 199,100 CapCity orders: 31,300
📖 Footsteps • Stark cured by implanted bio-chip A: Bob Layton W: David Michelinie
249 ❑ Nov 1989 Cover: 1.00 NM value: 1.50
Circ: Statement: 199,100 CapCity orders: 31,100
📖 The Doctor's Passion • Doctor Doom A: Bob Layton W: David Michelinie
250 ❑ Dec 1989 Cover: 1.50 NM value: 1.75
Circ: Statement: 199,100 CapCity orders: 37,300
• double-sized. 📖 Acts of Vengeance, Part 3 • Acts of Vengeance A: Bob Layton W: David Michelinie ★ Versus Doctor Doom.
251 ❑ Dec 1989 Cover: 1.00 NM value: 1.25
Circ: Statement: 199,100 CapCity orders: 33,300
📖 Acts of Vengeance, Part 12 • Acts of Vengeance A: Herb Trimpe W: Dwayne McDuffie ★ Versus Wrecker.
252 ❑ Jan 1990 Cover: 1.00 NM value: 1.25
Circ: Statement: 198,100 CapCity orders: 34,400
📖 Acts of Vengeance, Part 21 • Acts of Vengeance A: Herb Trimpe W: Dwayne McDuffie ★ Versus Chemistro.
253 ❑ Feb 1990 Cover: 1.00 NM value: 1.25
Circ: Statement: 198,100 CapCity orders: 32,200
📖 Laughing All The Way To The Graveyard A: Gene Colan C: John Byrne W: Dwayne McDuffie
254 ❑ Mar 1990 Cover: 1.00 NM value: 1.25
Circ: Statement: 198,100 CapCity orders: 31,200
📖 Graduation Day A: Bob Layton W: Bob Layton
255 ❑ Apr 1990 Cover: 1.00 NM value: 1.25
Circ: Statement: 198,100 CapCity orders: 30,600
📖 Switching Channels A: Herb Trimpe W: Fabian Nicieza; Glenn Herdling
256 ❑ May 1990 Cover: 1.00 NM value: 1.25
Circ: Statement: 198,100 CapCity orders: 36,000
📖 Soliloquy in Silence A: John Romita Jr. W: Bob Layton
257 ❑ Jun 1990 Cover: 1.00 NM value: 1.25
Circ: Statement: 198,100 CapCity orders: 34,500
📖 Retribution A: Rich Yanizeski W: Randall Frenz
258 ❑ Jul 1990 Cover: 1.00 NM value: 1.50
Circ: Statement: 198,100 CapCity orders: 33,300
📖 Armor Wars II, Part 1 A: John Romita Jr. W: John Byrne
259 ❑ Aug 1990 Cover: 1.00 NM value: 1.50
Circ: Statement: 198,100 CapCity orders: 33,900
📖 Armor Wars II, Part 2 A: John Romita Jr. W: John Byrne
260 ❑ Sep 1990 Cover: 1.00 NM value: 1.50
Circ: Statement: 198,100 CapCity orders: 33,600
📖 Armor Wars II, Part 3 A: John Romita Jr. W: John Byrne
261 ❑ Oct 1990 Cover: 1.00 NM value: 1.50
Circ: Statement: 198,100 CapCity orders: 32,700
📖 Armor Wars II, Part 4 A: John Romita Jr. W: John Byrne
262 ❑ Nov 1990 Cover: 1.00 NM value: 1.50
Circ: Statement: 198,100 CapCity orders: 31,500
📖 Armor Wars II, Part 5 A: John Romita Jr. W: John Byrne
263 ❑ Dec 1990 Cover: 1.00 NM value: 1.50
Circ: Statement: 198,100 CapCity orders: 31,500
📖 Armor Wars II, Part 6 A: John Romita Jr. W: John Byrne
264 ❑ Jan 1991 Cover: 1.00 NM value: 1.50
Circ: Statement: 172,450 CapCity orders: 31,500
📖 Armor Wars II, Part 7 A: John Romita Jr. W: John Byrne
265 ❑ Feb 1991 Cover: 1.00 NM value: 1.50
Circ: Statement: 172,450 CapCity orders: 31,800
📖 Armor Wars II, Part 8 A: John Romita Jr. W: John Byrne
266 ❑ Mar 1991 Cover: 1.00 NM value: 1.50
Circ: Statement: 172,450 CapCity orders: 31,200
📖 Armor Wars II
267 ❑ Apr 1991 Cover: 1.00 NM value: 1.50
Circ: Statement: 172,450 CapCity orders: 29,400
📖 The Persistence Of Memory A: Paul Ryan W: John Byrne
268 ❑ May 1991 Cover: 1.00 NM value: 1.50
Circ: Statement: 172,450 CapCity orders: 30,600
📖 First Blood A: Paul Ryan W: John Byrne ★ Origin of Iron Man.
269 ❑ Jun 1991 Cover: 1.00 NM value: 1.50
Circ: Statement: 172,450 CapCity orders: 29,400
📖 The Hallow Man A: Paul Ryan W: John Byrne
270 ❑ Jul 1991 Cover: 1.00 NM value: 1.50
Circ: Statement: 172,450 CapCity orders: 28,800
📖 The Price A: Paul Ryan W: John Byrne
271 ❑ Aug 1991 Cover: 1.00 NM value: 1.50
Circ: Statement: 172,450 CapCity orders: 29,100
📖 The Dragon Seed, Part 1 A: Paul Ryan W: John Byrne
272 ❑ Sep 1991 Cover: 1.00 NM value: 1.50
Circ: Statement: 172,450 CapCity orders: 29,700
📖 The Dragon Seed, Part 2 A: Paul Ryan W: John Byrne
273 ❑ Oct 1991 Cover: 1.00 NM value: 1.50
Circ: Statement: 172,450 CapCity orders: 28,800
📖 The Dragon Seed, Part 3 A: Paul Ryan W: John Byrne
274 ❑ Nov 1991 Cover: 1.00 NM value: 1.50
Circ: Statement: 172,450 CapCity orders: 27,600
📖 The Dragon Seed, Part 4 A: Mark D. Bright W: John Byrne ★ Origin of Fin Fang Foom. ★ Versus Fin Fang Foom.
275 ❑ Dec 1991 Cover: 1.50 NM value: Cover or less
Circ: Statement: 172,450 CapCity orders: 29,100
• Giant-size. 📖 The Dragon Seed, Part 5 A: Paul Ryan W: John Byrne ★ Versus Fin Fang Foom. ★ Versus Mandarin. ★ Versus Dragon Lords.
276 ❑ Jan 1992 Cover: 1.00 NM value: 1.50
Circ: Statement: 156,017 CapCity orders: 27,900
📖 With Friends Like These… A: Paul Ryan W: John Byrne
277 ❑ Feb 1992 Cover: 1.25 NM value: 1.50
Circ: Statement: 156,017 CapCity orders: 26,200
📖 War Games A: Paul Ryan W: John Byrne
278 ❑ Mar 1992 Cover: 1.25 NM value: 1.50
Circ: Statement: 156,017 CapCity orders: 34,200
📖 Operation: Galactic Storm, Part 6 • Galactic Storm A: Paul Ryan W: Len Kaminski ★ 1st Appearance of new Space Armor.
279 ❑ Apr 1992 Cover: 1.25 NM value: 1.50
Circ: Statement: 156,017 CapCity orders: 31,800
📖 Operation: Galactic Storm, Part 13 • Galactic Storm ★ Versus Ronan the Accuser.
280 ❑ May 1992 Cover: 1.25 NM value: 1.50
Circ: Statement: 156,017 CapCity orders: 25,500
📖 Technical Difficulties A: Kev Hopgood W: Len Kaminski ★ Appearance of The Stark.
281 ❑ Jun 1992 Cover: 1.25 NM value: 3.00
Circ: Statement: 156,017 CapCity orders: 26,500
📖 The Masters of Silence A: Kev Hopgood W: Len Kaminski ★ 1st Appearance of War Machine armor.
282 ❑ Jul 1992 Cover: 1.25 NM value: 3.00
Circ: Statement: 156,017 CapCity orders: 27,500
★ 2nd Appearance of War Machine armor.
283 ❑ Aug 1992 Cover: 1.25 NM value: 1.50
Circ: Statement: 156,017 CapCity orders: 26,500
284 ❑ Sep 1992 Cover: 1.25 NM value: 2.00
Circ: Statement: 156,017 CapCity orders: 24,900
📖 Legacy Of Iron A: Kev Hopgood W: Len Kaminski ★ Origin of War Machine. ★ 1st Appearance of War Machine. ★ Death of Tony Stark.
285 ❑ Oct 1992 Cover: 1.25 NM value: Cover or less
Circ: Statement: 156,017 CapCity orders: 28,000
📖 Ashes To Ashes A: Kev Hopgood W: Len Kaminski
286 ❑ Nov 1992 Cover: 1.25 NM value: Cover or less
Circ: Statement: 198,133 CapCity orders: 26,300
📖 Dust To Dust A: Kev Hopgood W: Len Kaminski
287 ❑ Dec 1992 Cover: 1.25 NM value: Cover or less
Circ: Statement: 198,133 CapCity orders: 26,500
📖 Meltdown! A: Kev Hopgood W: Len Kaminski
288 ❑ Jan 1993 Cover: 2.50 NM value: Cover or less
Circ: Statement: 198,133 CapCity orders: 79,900
Embossed cover. • 30th anniversary special. 📖 Ground Zero • Tony Stark revived A: Kev Hopgood W: Len Kaminski
289 ❑ Feb 1993 Cover: 1.25 NM value: Cover or less
Circ: Statement: 198,133 CapCity orders: 34,800
290 ❑ Mar 1993 Cover: 2.95 NM value: 3.50
Circ: Statement: 198,133 CapCity orders: 84,000
Metallic ink cover. 📖 This Years Model • New Armor; Has 1992 Statement, filed 10/1/92; avg print run 246,750; avg sales 151,458; avg subs 4,558; avg total paid 156,017; samples 250; office use 683; max existent 156,949; 36% of run returned A: Kev Hopgood W: Len Kaminski
291 ❑ Apr 1993 Cover: 1.25 NM value: Cover or less
Circ: Statement: 198,133 CapCity orders: 35,800
📖 Judgement Day • James Rhodes leaves to become War Machine A: Kev Hopgood W: Len Kaminski
292 ❑ May 1993 Cover: 1.25 NM value: Cover or less
Circ: Statement: 198,133 CapCity orders: 29,200
📖 Mixed Reactions A: Kev Hopgood W: Len Kaminski
293 ❑ Jun 1993 Cover: 1.25 NM value: Cover or less
Circ: Statement: 198,133 CapCity orders: 28,800
📖 Controlling Interests A: Kev Hopgood W: Len Kaminski
294 ❑ Jul 1993 Cover: 1.25 NM value: Cover or less
Circ: Statement: 198,133 CapCity orders: 33,000
📖 Orbital Resonances A: Kev Hopgood W: Len Kaminski
295 ❑ Aug 1993 Cover: 1.25 NM value: Cover or less
Circ: Statement: 198,133 CapCity orders: 34,200
📖 Infinity Crusade A: Kev Hopgood W: Len Kaminski
296 ❑ Sep 1993 Cover: 1.25 NM value: Cover or less
Circ: Statement: 198,133 CapCity orders: 27,300
📖 Trade War A: Kev Hopgood W: Len Kaminski
297 ❑ Oct 1993 Cover: 1.25 NM value: Cover or less
Circ: Statement: 111,333 CapCity orders: 26,000
📖 Whipsaw! A: Kev Hopgood W: Len Kaminski ★ Appearance of M.O.D.A.M, Omega Red.
298 ❑ Nov 1993 Cover: 1.25 NM value: Cover or less
Circ: Statement: 111,333 CapCity orders: 25,900
299 ❑ Dec 1993 Cover: 1.25 NM value: Cover or less
Circ: Statement: 111,333 CapCity orders: 26,200
W: Len Kaminski ★ Versus Ultimo.
300 ❑ Jan 1994 Cover: 2.50 NM value: Cover or less
Circ: Statement: 111,333 CapCity orders: 49,100
• Giant size. • Stark dons new (modular) armor ★ Appearance of Iron Legion (all substitute Iron Men). ★ Versus Ultimo.
300/SC ❑ Jan 1994 Cover: 3.95 NM value: Cover or less
• Giant size. • Stark dons new (modular) armor
301 ❑ Feb 1994 Cover: 1.25 NM value: Cover or less
Circ: Statement: 111,333 CapCity orders: 25,100
📖 Crash & Burn, Part 1
302 ❑ Mar 1994 Cover: 1.25 NM value: Cover or less
Circ: Statement: 111,333 CapCity orders: 24,150
📖 Crash & Burn, Part 2
303 ❑ Apr 1994 Cover: 1.25 NM value: Cover or less
Circ: Statement: 111,333 CapCity orders: 23,950
📖 Crash & Burn, Part 3
304 ❑ May 1994 Cover: 1.50 NM value: Cover or less
Circ: Statement: 111,333 CapCity orders: 22,350
📖 Crash & Burn, Part 4 ★ 1st Appearance of Hulkbuster Armor.
305 ❑ Jun 1994 Cover: 1.50 NM value: Cover or less
Circ: Statement: 111,333 CapCity orders: 21,900
📖 Crash & Burn, Part 5 A: Kev Hopgood W: Len Kaminski ★ Appearance of Hulk.
306 ❑ Jul 1994 Cover: 1.50 NM value: Cover or less
Circ: Statement: 111,333 CapCity orders: 22,450
📖 Crash & Burn, Part 6 • Stark restructures company A: Kev Hopgood W: Len Kaminski
307 ❑ Aug 1994 Cover: 1.50 NM value: Cover or less
Circ: Statement: 111,333 CapCity orders: 20,850
308 ❑ Sep 1994 Cover: 1.50 NM value: Cover or less
Circ: Statement: 111,333 CapCity orders: 20,400
309 ❑ Oct 1994 Cover: 1.50 NM value: Cover or less
Circ: Statement: 82,469 CapCity orders: 19,550
310 ❑ Nov 1994 Cover: 1.50 NM value: Cover or less
Circ: Statement: 82,469 CapCity orders: 21,850
📖 Friends…And Other Enemies A: Tom Morgan W: Len Kaminski
310/CS ❑ Nov 1994 Cover: 2.95 NM value: Cover or less
Circ: CapCity orders: 21,450
• polybagged with 16-page preview, acetate print, and other items
311 ❑ Dec 1994 Cover: 1.50 NM value: Cover or less
Circ: Statement: 82,469 CapCity orders: 18,825
312 ❑ Jan 1995 Cover: 2.25 NM value: Cover or less
Circ: Statement: 82,469 CapCity orders: 17,250
313 ❑ Feb 1995 Cover: 1.50 NM value: Cover or less
Circ: Statement: 82,469 CapCity orders: 16,375
314 ❑ Mar 1995 Cover: 1.50 NM value: Cover or less
Circ: Statement: 82,469 CapCity orders: 15,975
315 ❑ Apr 1995 Cover: 1.50 NM value: Cover or less
Circ: Statement: 82,469 CapCity orders: 15,250
★ Versus Titanium Man.
316 ❑ May 1995 Cover: 1.50 NM value: Cover or less
Circ: Statement: 82,469 CapCity orders: 14,875
317 ❑ Jun 1995 Cover: 2.50 NM value: Cover or less
Circ: Statement: 82,469 CapCity orders: 14,150
• flip book with War Machine: Brothers in Arms part 3 back-up ★ Death of Titanium Man I.
318 ❑ Jul 1995 Cover: 1.50 NM value: Cover or less
Circ: Statement: 82,469
319 ❑ Aug 1995 Cover: 1.50 NM value: Cover or less
Circ: Statement: 82,469
★ Origin of Iron Man.
320 ❑ Sep 1995 Cover: 1.50 NM value: Cover or less
Circ: Statement: 82,469
321 ❑ Oct 1995 Cover: 1.50 NM value: Cover or less
Circ: Statement: 64,717
• OverPower cards inserted
322 ❑ Nov 1995 Cover: 1.50 NM value: Cover or less
Circ: Statement: 64,717
📖 The Darkest Page to Turn A: Sergio Cariello; Jimmy Cheung W: Terry Kavanagh
323 ❑ Dec 1995 Cover: 1.50 NM value: Cover or less
Circ: Statement: 64,717
📖 Iron Man vs. the Avengers A: Adriana Melo W: Terry Kavanagh ★ Appearance of Avengers, Hawkeye.
324 ❑ Jan 1996 Cover: 1.50 NM value: Cover or less
Circ: Statement: 64,717
325 ❑ Feb 1996 Cover: 2.95 NM value: 3.00
Circ: Statement: 64,717
wraparound cover. • Giant-size. 📖 Avengers: Timeslide • Tony Stark vs. young Tony Stark A: Jim Calafiore; Jimmy Cheung; Hector Collazo W: Terry Kavanagh; Dan Abnett
326 ❑ Mar 1996 Cover: 1.95 NM value: Cover or less
Circ: Statement: 64,717

CGC-graded: Multiply prices above by 33 for 9.9 M • 16 for 9.8 NM/M • 7 for 9.6 NM+ • 5 for 9.4 NM • 2.5 for 9.2 NM- • 1.5 for 9.0 VF/NM

First Sign, Part 3 **A:** Steve Ellis; Jimmy Cheung; Hector Collazo **W:** Terry Kavanagh
327 ❑ Apr 1996 Cover: 1.95 **NM** value: **Cover or less**
Circ: Statement: **64,717**
Frostbite! • reading of Tony Stark's will **A:** Mark McKenna **W:** Jimmy Cheung ★ Versus Frostbite.
328 ❑ May 1996 Cover: 1.50 **NM** value: **Cover or less**
Circ: Statement: **64,717**
329 ❑ Jun 1996 Cover: 1.50 **NM** value: **Cover or less**
Circ: Statement: **64,717**
• Fujikawa International takes over Stark Enterprises
330 ❑ Jul 1996 Cover: 1.50 **NM** value: **Cover or less**
Circ: Statement: **64,717**
331 ❑ Aug 1996 Cover: 1.50 **NM** value: **Cover or less**
Circ: Statement: **64,717**
332 ❑ Sep 1996 Cover: 1.50 **NM** value: **Cover or less**
Circ: Statement: **64,717** • **CGC:** 1 graded, best 9.6
Onslaught: Impact 2 final issue.
Anl 1 ❑ Aug 1970 Cover: 0.25 **NM** value: **20.00**
• **CGC:** 6 graded, best 9.6
War And Remembrance **A:** Jerry Bingham **W:** Ralph Macchio; Peter B. Gillis
Anl 2 ❑ Nov 1971 Cover: 0.25 **NM** value: **9.00**
Anl 3 ❑ ca. 1976 Cover: 0.50 **NM** value: **6.00**
Anl 4 ❑ ca. 1977 Cover: 0.50 **NM** value: **4.00**
• **CGC:** 1 graded, best 9.4
• Cover reads "King-Size Special".
Anl 5 ❑ ca. 1982 Cover: 1.00 **NM** value: **3.00**
Anl 6 ❑ ca. 1983 Cover: 1.00 **NM** value: **3.00**
In Dreams What Death May Come! • New Iron Man appears **A:** Luke McDonnell **W:** Peter B. Gillis ★ Appearance of Eternals. ★ Death of Zuras (spirit leaves body).
Anl 7 ❑ ca. 1984 Cover: 1.00 **NM** value: **3.00**
When Giants Walk The Earth! • West Coast Avengers; Was formerly known as Power Man I **A:** Luke McDonnell **W:** Bob Harras ★ 1st Appearance of Goliath III (Erik Josten).
Anl 8 ❑ ca. 1986 Cover: 1.25 **NM** value: **3.00**
Circ: CapCity orders: **21,800**
When Innocence Dies! **A:** Paul Neary **W:** Bob Harras ★ Appearance of X-Factor.
Anl 9 ❑ ca. 1987 Cover: 1.25 **NM** value: **3.00**
Circ: CapCity orders: **22,400**
Anl 10 ❑ ca. 1989 Cover: 2.00 **NM** value: **2.50**
Circ: CapCity orders: **39,200**
Atlantis Attacks, Part 1 • Atlantis Attacks **A:** Mark Bagley; Paul Smith; Don Perlin **W:** Fabian Nicieza; David Michelinie; David Wohl; Peter Sanderson
Anl 11 ❑ ca. 1990 Cover: 2.00 **NM** value: **Cover or less**
Circ: CapCity orders: **35,300**
The Terminus Factor, Part 2; Terminus Factor ★ Appearance of Machine Man.
Anl 12 ❑ ca. 1991 Cover: 2.00 **NM** value: **Cover or less**
Circ: CapCity orders: **36,500**
Subterranean Wars; Subterranean Odyssey, Part 4 **A:** Tom Morgan; Barry Kitson; Gavin Curtis; John Stanisci **W:** Len Kaminski; Gavin Curtis; Roy Thomas; Dann Thomas; Dwight Jon Zimmerman ★ 1st Appearance of Trapster II.
Anl 13 ❑ ca. 1992 Cover: 2.25 **NM** value: **Cover or less**
Circ: CapCity orders: **28,600**
Assault on Armor City, Part 3; Assault On Armor City **A:** Gene Colan; Chuck Wojtkiewicz; Dave Johnson; Andrew Currie; Cooper Smith **W:** Len Kaminski; John Tomlinson; Mike Kanterovich; Richard Ashford; Tom Brevoort ★ Appearance of Darkhawk, Avengers West Coast.
Anl 14 ❑ ca. 1993 Cover: 2.95 **NM** value: **Cover or less**
Circ: CapCity orders: **31,100**
• trading card
Anl 15 ❑ ca. 1994 Cover: 2.95 **NM** value: **Cover or less**
Circ: CapCity orders: **15,850**
★ Versus Controller.
Ash 1 ❑ Nov 1994 Cover: 1.95 **NM** value: **Cover or less**
"Iron Man & Force Works" on cover. • Collectors' Preview
Bk 1 ❑ Cover: 12.95 **NM** value: **Cover or less**
Circ: CapCity orders: **8,850**
• Armor Wars
Bk 2 ❑ Cover: 12.95 **NM** value: **Cover or less**
• Iron Man vs. Doctor Doom; collects Iron Man #149, 150, 249, and 250
GS 1 ❑ ca. 1975 Cover: 0.50 **NM** value: **5.00**

IRON MAN (VOL. 2) Marvel

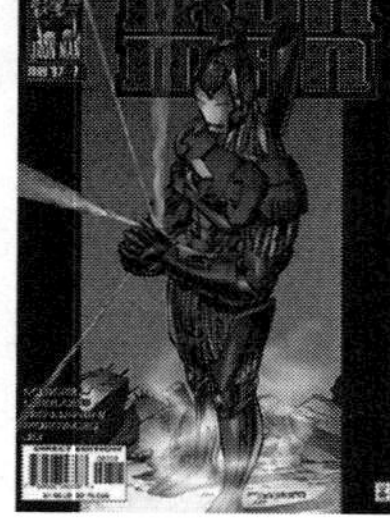

As part of a new strategy called "Heroes Reborn," Marvel Comics hired back the key Image artists (and Marvel expatriates) to revamp some of Marvel's key characters.

In Jim Lee and Whilce Portacio's version, one of his inventor Tony Stark's facilities, housing Bruce Banner's gamma bomb project, is taken over by the forces of Hydra. In an act of desperation, Banner moves the bomb underground, sacrificing himself but sparing the world. The radiation turns him into the Hulk, who downs Stark's helicopter. The accident leaves a piece of shrapnel inches from Stark's heart, and to save himself, he dons a prototype armor and became Iron Man.

Despite the changes to the character's origin, the "Heroes Reborn" Iron Man was somewhat better received than the other versions — if only because what had been going on in the ongoing title, a storyline where Stark had been turned into a child — was so bad.

1 ❑ Nov 1996 Cover: 2.95 **NM** value: **3.50**
Circ: Statement: **184,386** Direct Market orders: **277,500** • **CGC:** 3 graded, best 9.6
• Giant-size. Heart Of The Matter **A:** Whilce Portacio **W:** Jim Lee; Scott Lobdell ★ Origin of Hulk (new), Iron Man (new).
1/A ❑ Nov 1996 Cover: 2.95 **NM** value: **3.50**
• **CGC:** 6 graded, best 9.8
variant cover. • Giant-size. Heart Of The Matter **A:** Whilce Portacio; Ryan Benjamin(cover) **W:** Jim Lee; Scott Lobdell ★ Origin of Iron Man (new).
2 ❑ Dec 1996 Cover: 1.95 **NM** value: **2.00**
Circ: Statement: **184,386** Direct Market orders: **140,000**
Hulk Smash! • Has 1996 Statement, filed 10/1/96 (Alert: Issue went to press BEFORE that date); covers issues from end of Vol. 1; avg print run 117,716; avg sales 62,415; avg subs 2,302; avg total paid 64,717; samples 600; office use 125; max existent 65,442; 44% of run returned **A:** Whilce Portacio **W:** Jim Lee; Scott Lobdell ★ Versus Hulk.
3 ❑ Jan 1997 Cover: 1.95 **NM** value: **2.00**
Circ: Statement: **184,386** Direct Market orders: **138,750**
Misperceptions **A:** Whilce Portacio **W:** Jim Lee; Scott Lobdell ★ 1st Appearance of Whirlwind. ★ Appearance of Fantastic Four.
4 ❑ Feb 1997 Cover: 1.95 **NM** value: **2.00**
Circ: Statement: **184,386**
Bring me the Head of the Hulk! **A:** Ryan Benjamin **W:** Jim Lee; Scott Lobdell ★ Versus Living Laser.
4/A ❑ Feb 1997 Cover: 1.95 **NM** value: **2.00**
variant cover. Bring me the Head of the Hulk! **A:** Ryan Benjamin **W:** Jim Lee; Scott Lobdell
5 ❑ Mar 1997 Cover: 1.95 **NM** value: **Cover or less**
Circ: Statement: **184,386**
Inherit the Whirlwind **A:** Ryan Benjamin **W:** Jim Lee; Scott Lobdell ★ Versus Whirlwind.
6 ❑ Apr 1997 Cover: 1.95 **NM** value: **Cover or less**
Circ: Statement: **184,386**
Industrial Revolution, Part 2 • concludes in Captain America #6 **A:** Whilce Portacio; Ryan Benjamin; Jim Lee **W:** Scott Lobdell ★ Appearance of Onslaught.
7 ❑ May 1997 Cover: 1.95 **NM** value: **Cover or less**
Circ: Statement: **184,386**
Look Back in Anger **A:** Whilce Portacio; Ryan Benjamin **W:** Jim Lee; Scott Lobdell
8 ❑ Jun 1997 Cover: 1.95 **NM** value: **Cover or less**
Circ: Statement: **184,386**
9 ❑ Jul 1997 Cover: 1.95 **NM** value: **Cover or less**
Circ: Statement: **184,386**
10 ❑ Aug 1997 Cover: 1.99 **NM** value: **Cover or less**
Circ: Statement: **184,386**
• gatefold summary.
11 ❑ Sep 1997 Cover: 1.99 **NM** value: **Cover or less**
Circ: Statement: **184,386**
• gatefold summary. ★ Appearance of Doctor Doom.
12 ❑ Oct 1997 Cover: 1.99 **NM** value: **3.50**
Circ: Statement: **151,476**
cover forms quadtych with Fantastic Four #12, Avengers #12, and Captain America #12. • gatefold summary. Heroes Reunited
13 ❑ Nov 1997 Cover: 1.99 **NM** value: **2.50**
Circ: Statement: **151,476**
cover forms quadtych with Fantastic Four #13, Avengers #13, and Captain America #13. • gatefold summary. World War 3

IRON MAN (VOL. 3) Marvel

After the Onslaught affair, everyone in the Marvel universe believed Iron Man had been killed in battle. Having fought his way back from an alternate reality — actually, Marvel having come to its senses following the "Heroes Reborn" debacle — the Armored Avenger is more than eager to get his life back. But, while the world has gotten used to super-powered beings returning from seeming death, the sudden reappearance of Iron Man's alter ego, Tony Stark, is fraught with complications. For one thing, Tony had been legally declared dead, and for some reason just showing up doesn't mean he's not. And then there's the little matter of Stark Industries, which was sold during his absence...

1 ❑ Feb 1998 Cover: 2.99 **NM** value: **3.50**
Circ: Statement: **151,476** Diamd. preorders: **186,327** • **CGC:** 3 graded, best 9.6
wraparound cover. • Giant-size. Looking Forward **A:** Sean Chen **W:** Kurt Busiek ★ 1st Appearance of Stark Solutions.
1/A ❑ Feb 1998 Cover: 2.99 **NM** value: **4.00**
• **CGC:** 1 graded, best 8.5
wraparound cover. • gatefold summary. Looking Forward **A:** Sean Chen **W:** Kurt Busiek ★ 1st Appearance of Stark Solutions.
2 ❑ Mar 1998 Cover: 1.99 **NM** value: **2.00**
Circ: Statement: **151,476** Diamd. preorders: **129,906**
• gatefold summary. Hidden Assets • Has 1997 Statement, filed 10/1/97; covers issues from Vol. 2; avg print run 230,909; avg sales 181,403; avg subs 2,983; avg total paid 184,386; samples 298; office use 125; max existent 184,809; 20% of run returned **A:** Sean Chen **W:** Kurt Busiek
2/SC ❑ Mar 1998 Cover: 1.99 **NM** value: **3.00**
variant cover. Hidden Assets **A:** Sean Chen **W:** Kurt Busiek
3 ❑ Apr 1998 Cover: 1.99 **NM** value: **2.00**
Circ: Statement: **151,476** Diamd. preorders: **99,902**
• gatefold summary. **A:** Sean Chen **W:** Kurt Busiek
4 ❑ May 1998 Cover: 1.99 **NM** value: **2.00**
Circ: Statement: **151,476** Diamd. preorders: **96,977**
• gatefold summary. **A:** Sean Chen **W:** Kurt Busiek ★ Versus Firebrand.
5 ❑ Jun 1998 Cover: 1.99 **NM** value: **2.00**
Circ: Statement: **151,476** Diamd. preorders: **95,684**
• gatefold summary. **A:** Sean Chen **W:** Kurt Busiek ★ Versus Firebrand.
6 ❑ Jul 1998 Cover: 1.99 **NM** value: **2.00**
Circ: Statement: **151,476** Diamd. preorders: **89,751**
• gatefold summary. **A:** Sean Chen **W:** Kurt Busiek ★ Appearance of Black Widow.
7 ❑ Aug 1998 Cover: 1.99 **NM** value: **2.00**
Circ: Statement: **151,476** Diamd. preorders: **91,438**
• gatefold summary. Live Kree or Die!, Part 1 **A:** Sean Chen **W:** Kurt Busiek ★ Appearance of Warbird.
8 ❑ Sep 1998 Cover: 1.99 **NM** value: **2.00**
Circ: Statement: **151,476** Diamd. preorders: **81,609**
• gatefold summary. • Tony beaten **A:** Sean Chen **W:** Kurt Busiek
9 ❑ Oct 1998 Cover: 1.99 **NM** value: **2.00**
Circ: Statement: **92,008** Diamd. preorders: **79,659**
• gatefold summary. Revenge of the Mandarin, Part 1 **A:** Sean Chen **W:** Kurt Busiek ★ Appearance of Winter Guard.
10 ❑ Nov 1998 Cover: 1.99 **NM** value: **2.00**
Circ: Statement: **92,008** Diamd. preorders: **78,570**
• gatefold summary. Revenge of the Mandarin, Part 2 • Has 1998 Statement of Ownership, filed 10/1/98 (Alert: Issue printed before filing date!); avg print run 220,530; avg sales 147,816; avg subs 3,946; avg total paid 151,476; samples 298; office use 125; max existent 152,185; 31% of run returned **A:** Sean Chen **W:** Kurt Busiek
11 ❑ Dec 1998 Cover: 1.99 **NM** value: **2.00**
Circ: Statement: **92,008** Diamd. preorders: **75,350**
• gatefold summary. • new home **A:** Sean Chen **W:** Kurt Busiek ★ Appearance of Warbird. ★ Versus War Machine armor.
12 ❑ Jan 1999 Cover: 1.99 **NM** value: **2.00**
Circ: Statement: **92,008** Diamd. preorders: **71,973**
• gatefold summary. Spoils of War! **A:** Sean Chen; Patrick Zircher **W:** Kurt Busiek ★ Appearance of Warbird. ★ Versus War Machine armor.
13 ❑ Feb 1999 Cover: 2.99 **NM** value: **3.00**
Circ: Statement: **92,008** Diamd. preorders: **69,566**
• double-sized. A Question of Control **A:** Sean Chen; Patrick Zircher **W:** Kurt Busiek ★ Appearance of Controller. ★ Versus Controller.
13/Aut ❑ Feb 1999 Cover: 2.99 **NM** value: **6.00**
A: Sean Chen **W:** Kurt Busiek ★ Appearance of Controller.
14 ❑ Mar 1999 Cover: 1.99 **NM** value: **Cover or less**
Circ: Statement: **92,008** Diamd. preorders: **68,678**
To Challenge the Fantastic • Fantastic Four crossover, part 2 **A:** Sean Chen **W:** Kurt Busiek; Roger Stern ★ Appearance of Fantastic Four, S.H.I.E.L.D., Ronan the Accuser, Watcher. ★ Versus Ronan.
15 ❑ Apr 1999 Cover: 1.99 **NM** value: **Cover or less**
Circ: Statement: **92,008** Diamd. preorders: **63,782**
Exploded View **A:** Salvador Larocca; Sean Chen; Terry Shoemaker **W:** Kurt Busiek; Roger Stern ★ Appearance of Nitro. ★ Versus Nitro.
16 ❑ May 1999 Cover: 1.99 **NM** value: **Cover or less**
Circ: Statement: **92,008** Diamd. preorders: **62,723**
Scale Model **A:** Anthony Williams; Patrick Zircher **W:** Kurt Busiek; Roger Stern
17 ❑ Jun 1999 Cover: 1.99 **NM** value: **Cover or less**
Circ: Statement: **92,008** Diamd. preorders: **63,989**
Your Young Men Shall Slay Dragons! **A:** Sean Chen **W:** Kurt Busiek; Roger Stern ★ Appearance of Fin Fang Foom.
18 ❑ Jul 1999 Cover: 1.99 **NM** value: **Cover or less**
Circ: Statement: **92,008** Diamd. preorders: **60,159**
Machinery of War, Part 1; Sunset Intrigues **A:** Sean Chen **W:** Kurt Busiek; Roger Stern ★ Appearance of Warbird.
19 ❑ Aug 1999 Cover: 1.99 **NM** value: **Cover or less**
Circ: Statement: **92,008** Diamd. preorders: **58,704**
Machinery of War, Part 2; Smart Weapons, Foolish Choices; Smart Weapons, Foolish Choices, Part 2 **A:** Sean Chen **W:** Kurt Busiek; Roger Stern ★ Versus War Machine.
20 ❑ Sep 1999 Cover: 1.99 **NM** value: **Cover or less**
Circ: Statement: **92,008** Diamd. preorders: **57,688**
Machinery of War, Part 3; Cheating Death **A:** Sean Chen; Patrick Zircher **W:** Kurt Busiek; Roger Stern ★ Versus War Machine.
21 ❑ Oct 1999 Cover: 1.99 **NM** value: **Cover or less**
Circ: Statement: **69,257** Diamd. preorders: **56,677**
Eighth Day Prelude; Burning Need • continues in Thor #17 **A:** Mark Bagley **W:** Kurt Busiek; Roger Stern ★ 1st Appearance of Inferno.
22 ❑ Nov 1999 Cover: 1.99 **NM** value: **Cover or less**
Circ: Statement: **69,257** Diamd. preorders: **57,374**
Eighth Day, Part 2; The Thrill of the Chase • continues in Peter Parker, Spider-Man #11; has 1999 Statement, filed 10/1/99 (Alert: Issue printed before filing date); avg print run 129,575; avg sales 88,534; avg subs 3,474; avg total paid 92,008; samples 3,398; office use 125; max existent 95,531; 34% of run returned **A:** Sean Chen **W:** Kurt Busiek; Roger Stern ★ 1st Appearance of Carnivore. ★ Appearance of Thor.
23 ❑ Dec 1999 Cover: 1.99 **NM** value: **Cover or less**
Circ: Statement: **69,257** Diamd. preorders: **54,589**
Ultimate Danger **A:** Sean Chen **W:** Kurt Busiek; Roger Stern ★ Appearance of Ultimo.
24 ❑ Jan 2000 Cover: 1.99 **NM** value: **Cover or less**
Circ: Statement: **69,257** Diamd. preorders: **53,033**
25 ❑ Feb 2000 Cover: 2.99 **NM** value: **Cover or less**
Circ: Statement: **69,257** Diamd. preorders: **55,960**
• double-sized. Ultimate Devastation **A:** Sean Chen **W:** Kurt Busiek; Roger Stern ★ Appearance of Warbird, Ultimo.
26 ❑ Mar 2000 Cover: 1.99 **NM** value: **2.25**
Circ: Statement: **69,257** Diamd. preorders: **52,589**
The Mask in the Iron Man, Part 1; A Boy and His Toys **A:** Sean Chen **W:** Joe Quesada
27 ❑ Apr 2000 Cover: 1.99 **NM** value: **2.25**
Circ: Statement: **69,257** Diamd. preorders: **48,852** • **CGC:** 1 graded, best 9.4
28 ❑ May 2000 Cover: 1.99 **NM** value: **2.25**
Circ: Statement: **69,257** Diamd. preorders: **49,728** • **CGC:** 1 graded, best 9.6
29 ❑ Jun 2000 Cover: 2.25 **NM** value: **Cover or less**
Circ: Statement: **69,257** Diamd. preorders: **49,322**
30 ❑ Jul 2000 Cover: 2.25 **NM** value: **Cover or less**
Circ: Statement: **69,257** Diamd. preorders: **49,226**
31 ❑ Aug 2000 Cover: 2.25 **NM** value: **Cover or less**

Other grades: Multiply prices above by **1.5 for Mint • 2/3 for Very Fine • 1/3 for Fine • 1/5 for Very Good • 1/8 for Good**

Circ: Statement: **69,257** Diamd. preorders: **50,619**
32 ❑ Sep 2000 Cover: 2.25 **NM** value: **Cover or less**
Circ: Statement: **69,257** Diamd. preorders: **50,563**
📖 The Sons of Yinsen, Part 2; Gods & Monsters • concludes in Iron Man Annual 2000 **A:** Alitha Martinez **W:** Joe Quesada; Frank Tieri ★ Appearance of Wong-Chu.
33 ❑ Oct 2000 Cover: 2.25 **NM** value: **Cover or less**
Circ: Statement: **56,557** Diamd. preorders: **48,088**
📖 Power, Part 1; Heroes **A:** Alitha Martinez **W:** Joe Quesada; Frank Tieri
34 ❑ Nov 2000 Cover: 2.25 **NM** value: **Cover or less**
Circ: Statement: **56,557** Diamd. preorders: **48,155**
📖 Power, Part 2; Villain$ **A:** Paul Ryan **W:** Joe Quesada; Frank Tieri
35 ❑ Dec 2000 Cover: 2.25 **NM** value: **Cover or less**
Circ: Statement: **56,557** Diamd. preorders: **48,476**
📖 Maximum Security; Power, Part 3; The Land **A:** Alitha Martinez **W:** Joe Quesada; Frank Tieri
36 ❑ Jan 2001 Cover: 2.25 **NM** value: **Cover or less**
Circ: Statement: **56,557** Diamd. preorders: **45,137**
📖 Danger Deep • Has 2000 Statement, filed 10/1/00; avg print run 102,125; avg sales 66,365 and subs 2,892 (error: figs reversed in issue); avg total paid 69,257; samples 600; office use 125; max existent 69,982; 32% of run returned **A:** Paul Ryan **W:** Chuck Dixon
37 ❑ Feb 2001 Cover: 2.25 **NM** value: **Cover or less**
Circ: Statement: **56,557** Diamd. preorders: **43,768**
📖 Remote Control, Part 1 **A:** Alitha Martinez **W:** Frank Tieri
38 ❑ Mar 2001 Cover: 2.25 **NM** value: **Cover or less**
Circ: Statement: **56,557** Diamd. preorders: **41,843**
📖 Remote Control, Part 2 **A:** Alitha Martinez **W:** Frank Tieri
39 ❑ Apr 2001 Cover: 2.25 **NM** value: **Cover or less**
Circ: Statement: **56,557** Diamd. preorders: **40,635**
📖 Remote Control, Part 3 **A:** Alitha Martinez **W:** Frank Tieri
40 ❑ May 2001 Cover: 2.25 **NM** value: **Cover or less**
Circ: Statement: **56,557** Diamd. preorders: **39,551**
📖 Remote Control, Part 4 **A:** Adam Pollina; Bob Layton; Alitha Martinez; John Romita Sr.; Mike Wieringo; Eric Shanower **W:** Frank Tieri
41 ❑ Jun 2001 Cover: 2.25 **NM** value: **Cover or less**
Circ: Statement: **56,557** Diamd. preorders: **39,507**
42 ❑ Jul 2001 Cover: 2.25 **NM** value: **Cover or less**
Circ: Statement: **56,557** Diamd. preorders: **39,688**
43 ❑ Aug 2001 Cover: 2.25 **NM** value: **Cover or less**
Circ: Statement: **56,557** Diamd. preorders: **39,483**
44 ❑ Sep 2001 Cover: 2.25 **NM** value: **Cover or less**
Circ: Statement: **56,557** Diamd. preorders: **45,715**
45 ❑ Oct 2001 Cover: 2.25 **NM** value: **Cover or less**
Circ: Diamd. preorders: **41,792**
46 ❑ Nov 2001 Cover: 3.50 **NM** value: **Cover or less**
Circ: Diamd. preorders: **39,311**
47 ❑ Dec 2001 Cover: 2.25 **NM** value: **Cover or less**
Circ: Diamd. preorders: **38,342**
48 ❑ Jan 2002 Cover: 2.25 **NM** value: **Cover or less**
Circ: Diamd. preorders: **38,654**
49 ❑ Feb 2002 Cover: 2.25 **NM** value: **Cover or less**
Circ: Diamd. preorders: **38,248**
• Has 2001 Statement, filed 10/1/01; avg print run 80,067; avg sales 54,153; avg subs 2,404; avg total paid 56,557; samples 600; max existent 57,157; 29% of run returned
50 ❑ Mar 2002 Cover: 3.50 **NM** value: **Cover or less**
Circ: Diamd. preorders: **46,259**
Anl 1998❑ca. 1998 Cover: 3.50 **NM** value: **Cover or less**
wraparound cover. 📖 Life & Liberty • Iron Man/Captain America '98 **A:** Patrick Zircher **W:** Mark Waid ★ Versus M.O.D.O.K..
Anl 1999❑Aug 1999 Cover: 3.50 **NM** value: **Cover or less**
Circ: Diamd. preorders: **41,603**
Anl 2000❑ca. 2000 Cover: 3.50 **NM** value: **Cover or less**
Circ: Diamd. preorders: **37,039**
📖 The Sons of Yinsen, Part 3; The Invisible Iron Man **A:** Paul Ryan; Dan Panosian **W:** Joe Quesada; Frank Tieri ★ Death of Wong-Chu.

IRON MAN/X-O MANOWAR: HEAVY METAL — Marvel

1 ❑ Sep 1996 Cover: 2.50 **NM** value: **Cover or less**
• crossover with Acclaim

IRON MARSHAL — Jademan

Jademan Comics, a publisher in Hong Kong, exported this title (in addition to "Buddha's Palm," "Drunken Fist" and "Blood Sword Dynasty") with the aid of Capital City Distribution (whose sales figures can be seen for many comic books in the Standard Catalog. The intention was to serve an American audience eager for martial arts stories.

Much of the comics' appeal can be attributed to the lavish, dynamic artwork, which compensates for the rudimentary plots. Iron Marshal is a supremely gifted martial artist who excels at kung fu and is usually pitted against a plethora of foes. Aside from the physical attraction of the combat, there is often a mystical aspect to the opponents that Iron Marshal faces.

Translated from Chinese, the dialogue often seems stilted and awkward — even by the low standards set by many comic books.

1 ❑ Jul 1990 Cover: 1.75 **NM** value: **Cover or less**
Circ: CapCity orders: **2,800**
A: Lee Chi Ching **W:** Henry Wright
2 ❑ Aug 1990 Cover: 1.75 **NM** value: **Cover or less**
Circ: CapCity orders: **2,000**
A: Lee Chi Ching **W:** Henry Wright
3 ❑ Sep 1990 Cover: 1.75 **NM** value: **Cover or less**
Circ: CapCity orders: **2,000**
A: Lee Chi Ching **W:** Henry Wright
4 ❑ Oct 1990 Cover: 1.75 **NM** value: **Cover or less**
Circ: CapCity orders: **2,000**
A: Lee Chi Ching **W:** Henry Wright
5 ❑ Nov 1990 Cover: 1.75 **NM** value: **Cover or less**
Circ: CapCity orders: **2,000**
A: Lee Chi Ching **W:** Henry Wright
6 ❑ Dec 1990 Cover: 1.75 **NM** value: **Cover or less**
Circ: CapCity orders: **2,000**
A: Lee Chi Ching **W:** Henry Wright
7 ❑ Jan 1991 Cover: 1.75 **NM** value: **Cover or less**
Circ: CapCity orders: **2,000**
A: Lee Chi Ching **W:** Henry Wright
8 ❑ Feb 1991 Cover: 1.75 **NM** value: **Cover or less**
Circ: CapCity orders: **2,000**
A: Lee Chi Ching **W:** Henry Wright
9 ❑ Mar 1991 Cover: 1.75 **NM** value: **Cover or less**
Circ: CapCity orders: **2,000**
A: Lee Chi Ching **W:** Henry Wright
10 ❑ Apr 1991 Cover: 1.75 **NM** value: **Cover or less**
Circ: CapCity orders: **2,000**
A: Lee Chi Ching **W:** Henry Wright
11 ❑ May 1991 Cover: 1.75 **NM** value: **Cover or less**
Circ: CapCity orders: **2,000**
A: Lee Chi Ching **W:** Henry Wright
12 ❑ Jun 1991 Cover: 1.75 **NM** value: **Cover or less**
Circ: CapCity orders: **2,000**
A: Lee Chi Ching **W:** Henry Wright
13 ❑ Jul 1991 Cover: 1.75 **NM** value: **Cover or less**
Circ: CapCity orders: **2,000**
A: Lee Chi Ching **W:** Henry Wright
14 ❑ Aug 1991 Cover: 1.75 **NM** value: **Cover or less**
Circ: CapCity orders: **2,000**
A: Lee Chi Ching **W:** Henry Wright
15 ❑ Sep 1991 Cover: 1.75 **NM** value: **Cover or less**
Circ: CapCity orders: **2,000**
A: Lee Chi Ching **W:** Henry Wright
16 ❑ Oct 1991 Cover: 1.75 **NM** value: **Cover or less**
Circ: CapCity orders: **1,800**
A: Lee Chi Ching **W:** Henry Wright
17 ❑ Nov 1991 Cover: 1.75 **NM** value: **Cover or less**
A: Lee Chi Ching **W:** Henry Wright
18 ❑ Dec 1991 Cover: 1.75 **NM** value: **Cover or less**
A: Lee Chi Ching **W:** Henry Wright
19 ❑ Jan 1992 Cover: 1.75 **NM** value: **Cover or less**
A: Lee Chi Ching **W:** Henry Wright
20 ❑ Feb 1992 Cover: 1.75 **NM** value: **Cover or less**
A: Lee Chi Ching **W:** Henry Wright
21 ❑ Mar 1992 Cover: 1.75 **NM** value: **Cover or less**
A: Lee Chi Ching **W:** Henry Wright
22 ❑ Apr 1992 Cover: 1.75 **NM** value: **Cover or less**
A: Lee Chi Ching **W:** Henry Wright
23 ❑ May 1992 Cover: 1.75 **NM** value: **Cover or less**
A: Lee Chi Ching **W:** Henry Wright
24 ❑ Jun 1992 Cover: 1.75 **NM** value: **Cover or less**
A: Lee Chi Ching **W:** Henry Wright
25 ❑ Jul 1992 Cover: 1.75 **NM** value: **Cover or less**
A: Lee Chi Ching **W:** Henry Wright
26 ❑ Aug 1992 Cover: 1.75 **NM** value: **Cover or less**
📖 A Humiliating Plot **A:** Lee Chi Ching **W:** Henry Wright
27 ❑ Sep 1992 Cover: 1.75 **NM** value: **Cover or less**
A: Lee Chi Ching **W:** Henry Wright
28 ❑ Oct 1992 Cover: 1.75 **NM** value: **Cover or less**
📖 The Exterminator **A:** Lee Chi Ching **W:** Henry Wright
29 ❑ Nov 1992 Cover: 1.75 **NM** value: **Cover or less**
A: Lee Chi Ching **W:** Henry Wright
30 ❑ Dec 1992 Cover: 1.75 **NM** value: **Cover or less**
A: Lee Chi Ching **W:** Henry Wright
31 ❑ Jan 1993 Cover: 1.75 **NM** value: **Cover or less**
A: Lee Chi Ching **W:** Henry Wright
32 ❑ Feb 1993 Cover: 1.75 **NM** value: **Cover or less**
A: Lee Chi Ching **W:** Henry Wright

IRON SAGA'S ANTHOLOGY — Iron Saga

1 ❑ Cover: 1.75 **NM** value: **Cover or less**

IRON WINGS — Action Press

1 ❑ May 1999 Cover: 2.50 **NM** value: **Cover or less**
Circ: Diamd. preorders: **4,093**
A: Jay Juch **W:** Jay Juch

IRON WINGS (VOL. 2) — Image

1 ❑ Apr 2000 Cover: 2.50 **NM** value: **Cover or less**
Circ: Diamd. preorders: **14,894**
📖 The Legends Begin Here... **A:** Jay Juch **W:** Jay Juch

IRONWOLF — DC

1 ❑ ca. 1986 Cover: 2.00 **NM** value: **Cover or less**
Circ: CapCity orders: **10,500**
• Reprints IronWolf adventures from Weird Worlds #8-10 **A:** Howard Chaykin **W:** Howard Chaykin; Denny O'Neil ★ 1st Appearance of IronWolf.

IRONWOLF: FIRES OF THE REVOLUTION — DC

1 ❑ ca. 1992 Cover: 29.95 **NM** value: **Cover or less**

IRONWOOD — Fantagraphics / Eros

All issues are adults only.

1 ❑ b&w Cover: 1.95 **NM** value: **Cover or less**
A: Bill Willingham **W:** Bill Willingham
1 ❑ b&w Cover: 1.95 **NM** value: **Cover or less**
A: Bill Willingham **W:** Bill Willingham
2 ❑ b&w Cover: 2.25 **NM** value: **Cover or less**
A: Bill Willingham **W:** Bill Willingham
3 ❑ b&w Cover: 2.25 **NM** value: **Cover or less**
A: Bill Willingham **W:** Bill Willingham
4 ❑ b&w Cover: 2.25 **NM** value: **Cover or less**
A: Bill Willingham **W:** Bill Willingham
5 ❑ b&w Cover: 2.25 **NM** value: **Cover or less**
A: Bill Willingham **W:** Bill Willingham
6 ❑ 1992b&w Cover: 2.25 **NM** value: **Cover or less**
A: Bill Willingham **W:** Bill Willingham
7 ❑ Mar 1992, b&w Cover: 2.50 **NM** value: **Cover or less**
Circ: CapCity orders: **3,055**
A: Bill Willingham **W:** Bill Willingham
8 ❑ 1992b&w Cover: 2.50 **NM** value: **Cover or less**
Circ: CapCity orders: **3,100**
A: Bill Willingham **W:** Bill Willingham
9 ❑ 1992b&w Cover: 2.50 **NM** value: **Cover or less**
Circ: CapCity orders: **315**
A: Bill Willingham **W:** Bill Willingham
10 ❑ Sep 1994, b&w Cover: 2.75 **NM** value: **Cover or less**
Circ: CapCity orders: **3,035**
A: Bill Willingham **W:** Bill Willingham

I SAW IT — Educomics

Keiji Nakazawa was a six-year-old Japanese boy living in Hiroshima on August 6, 1945. The event of that day influenced the course of his life and forever affected the history of the world. This incredible true story depicts the horror and misery of surviving the blast of an atomic bomb. Most of his family was killed but Keiji lived to witness the aimless procession of living specters with melting flesh and the eventual mass cremations to hinder the stench.

Nakazawa's narrative is a personal recollection of his experiences as he, his mother and brother struggled to survive in post-war Japan. Eventually, Nakazawa became enthralled with comic books. He left his mother and moved to Tokyo to become a cartoonist. He has achieved a measure of notoriety with "Barefoot Gen," a historical fiction graphic novel based on his own life.

Nakazawa's prose and art are somewhat stilted and stiff but the powerful reality of his story overcomes any technical shortcomings.

1 ❑ b&w Cover: 2.00 **NM** value: **Cover or less**
• **CGC:** 7 graded, best 9.4
• Hiroshima **A:** Keji Nakazawa **W:** Keji Nakazawa

ISIS — DC

"Mighty Isis!"

Science teacher Andrea Thomas only had to utter those two words in order to be transformed into an Egyptian goddess during her live-action series every Saturday morning in the mid 1970s. The words work just as well in this eight-issue series adaptation by DC.

While on an archeological expedition in Egypt, Andrea Thomas found a headband which gave her the powers of Isis, including flight, divine strength, powers over the forces of nature and animals, and powers over the mystical regions of the mind. Now whenever disaster strikes, Andrea turns into Isis and saves the day. For some unspecified reason, commands (except for "Mighty Isis!") need to be spoken in rhyming couplets — perhaps nature only understands rap?

A new, different Isis series was announced for 2002.

1 ❑ Oct 1976 Cover: 0.30 **NM** value: **8.00**
• **CGC:** 2 graded, best 9.6
2 ❑ Dec 1976 Cover: 0.30 **NM** value: **5.00**
3 ❑ Feb 1977 Cover: 0.30 **NM** value: **4.00**
📖 The Wrath Of Set! **A:** Mike Vosburg; Vince Colletta **W:** Steve Skeates
4 ❑ Apr 1977 Cover: 0.30 **NM** value: **4.00**
5 ❑ Jun 1977 Cover: 0.30 **NM** value: **4.00**
6 ❑ Aug 1977 Cover: 0.35 **NM** value: **4.00**
7 ❑ Oct 1977 Cover: 0.35 **NM** value: **4.00**
★ Origin of Isis.
8 ❑ Dec 1977 Cover: 0.35 **NM** value: **4.00**
final issue.

ISLAND OF DR. MOREAU, THE — Marvel

1 ❑ Oct 1977 Cover: 0.50 **NM** value: **3.00**
A: Larry Hama **W:** Doug Moench

ISMET — Canis

1 ❑ Cover: 1.25 **NM** value: **Cover or less**
2 ❑ Cover: 1.25 **NM** value: **Cover or less**
3 ❑ Cover: 1.25 **NM** value: **Cover or less**
4 ❑ Cover: 1.25 **NM** value: **Cover or less**
5 ❑ Cover: 1.25 **NM** value: **Cover or less**

I SPY — Gold Key

1 ❑ Aug 1966 Cover: 0.12 **NM** value: **60.00**
• **CGC:** 3 graded, best 9.2
photo cover and pin-up back cover. • based on TV series
2 ❑ Apr 1967 Cover: 0.12 **NM** value: **40.00**
• **CGC:** 2 graded, best 9.6
photo cover and pin-up back cover. • based on TV series
3 ❑ Nov 1967 Cover: 0.12 **NM** value: **40.00**
• **CGC:** 1 graded, best 9.4
photo cover and pin-up back cover. • based on TV series
4 ❑ Feb 1968 Cover: 0.12 **NM** value: **35.00**
• **CGC:** 3 graded, best 9.6
photo cover and pin-up back cover. 📖 Duet for Danger • based on TV series
5 ❑ Jun 1968 Cover: 0.12 **NM** value: **35.00**

CGC-graded: Multiply prices above by **33 for 9.9 M • 16 for 9.8 NM/M • 7 for 9.6 NM+ • 5 for 9.4 NM • 2.5 for 9.2 NM- • 1.5 for 9.0 VF/NM**

• **CGC:** 2 graded, best 9.4
Photo cover. • based on TV series
6 ❑ Sep 1968 Cover: 0.15 **NM** value: **35.00**
Photo cover. 📖 Live Bait • based on TV series

IS THIS TOMORROW? Catechetical Guild
1 ❑ 1947 **NM** value: **150.00**
2 ❑ **NM** value: **150.00**
3 ❑ **NM** value: **150.00**

ITCHY & SCRATCHY COMICS Bongo
1 ❑ ca. 1993 Cover: 2.25 **NM** value: **2.50**
Circ: CapCity orders: **52,275**
📖 Around The World In 80 Pieces **A:** Steve Vance; Mike Milo **W:** Steve Vance
2 ❑ ca. 1993 Cover: 1.95 **NM** value: **2.00**
Circ: CapCity orders: **33,075**
📖 The Itchy & Scratchy Movie II **A:** Steve Vance; Bill Morrison **W:** Dan Castellaneta; Deb Lacusta
3 ❑ ca. 1993 Cover: 2.25 **NM** value: **Cover or less**
Circ: CapCity orders: **27,625**
📖 When Bongos Collide; When Bongos Collide, Part 1 **A:** Steve Vance; Harry McLaughlin; Mike Milo **W:** Steve Vance; Harry McLaughlin; Mike Milo ★ Appearance of Bart Simpson.
HS 1❑ Cover: 1.95 **NM** value: **2.00**
Circ: CapCity orders: **17,000**
• Itchy & Scratchy Holiday Hi-Jinx Special

ITCHY PLANET Fantagraphics
1 ❑ Spr 1988 Cover: 2.25 **NM** value: **Cover or less**
2 ❑ Sum 1988 Cover: 2.25 **NM** value: **Cover or less**
3 ❑ Fal 1988 Cover: 2.25 **NM** value: **Cover or less**

IT REALLY HAPPENED Visual Editions
It Really Happened, a 1940s title from William Wise/Visual Editions, offered wholesome and generally accurate pictorial biographies of famous figures from history. Each issue featured four to six literate, well-illustrated stories about characters from all walks of life — from industrialists like Henry Ford to pirates like Captain Kidd to explorers, adventurers, and scientists. William Wise took its educational mission seriously and strove for factual accuracy and entertainment in equal measure, to inspire children to strive for greatness in their own lives.
1 ❑ ca. 1945 Cover: 0.10 **NM** value: **80.00**
2 ❑ ca. 1945 Cover: 0.10 **NM** value: **55.00**
3 ❑ ca. 1945 Cover: 0.10 **NM** value: **40.00**
4 ❑ ca. 1945 Cover: 0.10 **NM** value: **40.00**
5 ❑ ca. 1945 Cover: 0.10 **NM** value: **40.00**
6 ❑ ca. 1946 Cover: 0.10 **NM** value: **35.00**
7 ❑ ca. 1946 Cover: 0.10 **NM** value: **35.00**
8 ❑ ca. 1947 Cover: 0.10 **NM** value: **70.00**
• Roy Rogers
9 ❑ ca. 1947 Cover: 0.10 **NM** value: **35.00**
📖 William O'Dwyer, Frank Buck, George Eastman, Captain Kidd, Old Ironsides, Carl Norden, Alexandre Dumas
10 ❑ ca. 1947 Cover: 0.10 **NM** value: **50.00**
• Honus Wagner
11 ❑ ca. 1947 Cover: 0.10 **NM** value: **35.00**

IT'S ABOUT TIME Gold Key
1 ❑ Jan 1967 Cover: 0.10 **NM** value: **35.00**
• **CGC:** 2 graded, best 7.5

IT'S A DUCK'S LIFE Atlas
1 ❑ ca. 1950 Cover: 0.10 **NM** value: **100.00**
2 ❑ ca. 1950 Cover: 0.10 **NM** value: **50.00**
3 ❑ ca. 1950 Cover: 0.10 **NM** value: **40.00**
4 ❑ ca. 1950 Cover: 0.10 **NM** value: **40.00**
5 ❑ ca. 1951 Cover: 0.10 **NM** value: **40.00**
6 ❑ ca. 1951 Cover: 0.10 **NM** value: **40.00**
7 ❑ ca. 1951 Cover: 0.10 **NM** value: **35.00**
8 ❑ ca. 1951 Cover: 0.10 **NM** value: **35.00**
9 ❑ ca. 1951 Cover: 0.10 **NM** value: **35.00**
10 ❑ ca. 1951 Cover: 0.10 **NM** value: **35.00**
11 ❑ ca. 1952 Cover: 0.10 **NM** value: **35.00**

IT'S ALL TRUE! Apeshot Studios
Bk 1❑ Sum 1995 Cover: 4.95 **NM** value: **Cover or less**
No issue number. • collects True Artist Tales strips

IT'S FUN TO STAY ALIVE National Automobile Dealers Association
1 ❑ ca. 1947 **NM** value: **125.00**

IT'S GAME TIME DC
1 ❑ Sep 1955 Cover: 0.10 **NM** value: **350.00**
• **CGC:** 1 graded, best 4.0
2 ❑ Nov 1955 Cover: 0.10 **NM** value: **225.00**
3 ❑ Jan 1956 Cover: 0.10 **NM** value: **225.00**
4 ❑ Mar 1957 Cover: 0.10 **NM** value: **200.00**

IT'S LOVE, LOVE, LOVE St. John
1 ❑ Nov 1957 Cover: 0.10 **NM** value: **25.00**
2 ❑ Jan 1958 Cover: 0.10 **NM** value: **25.00**

IT'S ONLY A MATTER OF LIFE AND DEATH Fantagraphics
1 ❑ b&w Cover: 3.95 **NM** value: **Cover or less**

IT'S SCIENCE WITH DR. RADIUM Slave Labor
1 ❑ Sep 1986 Cover: 1.50 **NM** value: **2.00**
📖 Dr. Radium in the King of the KingsLast Chance **A:** Scott Saavedra; Basilio Amaro **W:** Scott Saavedra; Basilio Amaro
2 ❑ Jan 1987 Cover: 1.50 **NM** value: **2.00**
3 ❑ Mar 1987 Cover: 1.50 **NM** value: **2.00**
4 ❑ May 1987 Cover: 1.50 **NM** value: **2.00**
📖 Alien Terror (Oh, My!); A Deal with God **A:** Scott Saavedra **W:** Scott Saavedra
5 ❑ Jul 1987 Cover: 1.50 **NM** value: **2.00**
6 ❑ Oct 1987 Cover: 1.50 **NM** value: **2.00**
7 ❑ Feb 1988 Cover: 1.75 **NM** value: **2.00**
Bk 1❑ Jul 1991, b&w Cover: 17.95 **NM** value: **Cover or less**
• Doctor Radium's Big Book; collects It's Science with Doctor Radium #1-7; Dr. Radium's Big Book; collects It's Science with Dr. Radium #1-7
SE 1❑ Jan 1989, b&w Cover: 2.95 **NM** value: **Cover or less**

IT! THE TERROR FROM BEYOND SPACE Millennium
1 ❑ Cover: 2.50 **NM** value: **Cover or less**
Circ: CapCity orders: **7,875**
Die-cut cover. 📖 Murmur of the Heart **A:** Dean Zachary **W:** Mark Ellis
2 ❑ Cover: 2.50 **NM** value: **Cover or less**
Circ: CapCity orders: **3,650**
3 ❑ Cover: 2.50 **NM** value: **Cover or less**
Circ: CapCity orders: **3,375**
4 ❑ Cover: 2.50 **NM** value: **Cover or less**
Circ: CapCity orders: **2,150**

I WANT TO BE YOUR DOG Fantagraphics / Eros
All issues are adults only.
1 ❑ b&w Cover: 1.95 **NM** value: **Cover or less**
2 ❑ b&w Cover: 1.95 **NM** value: **Cover or less**
3 ❑ b&w Cover: 1.95 **NM** value: **Cover or less**
4 ❑ b&w Cover: 1.95 **NM** value: **Cover or less**
5 ❑ Cover: 2.25 **NM** value: **Cover or less**

J2 Marvel
1 ❑ Oct 1998 Cover: 1.99 **NM** value: **Cover or less**
Circ: Diamd. preorders: **45,949**
• gatefold summary. • son of Juggernaut
1/A ❑ Oct 1998 Cover: 1.99 **NM** value: **Cover or less**
A: Ron Lim **W:** Tom DeFalco
2 ❑ Nov 1998 Cover: 1.99 **NM** value: **Cover or less**
Circ: Diamd. preorders: **43,229**
• gatefold summary. **A:** Ron Lim **W:** Tom DeFalco ★ Versus X-People.
3 ❑ Dec 1998 Cover: 1.99 **NM** value: **Cover or less**
Circ: Diamd. preorders: **38,014**
A: Ron Lim **W:** Tom DeFalco ★ Appearance of Hulk, Dr. Strange, Doctor Strange, Sub-Mariner.
4 ❑ Jan 1999 Cover: 1.99 **NM** value: **Cover or less**
Circ: Diamd. preorders: **36,927**
A: Ron Lim **W:** Tom DeFalco ★ 1st Appearance of Nemesus. ★ Appearance of Doc Magus.
5 ❑ Feb 1999 Cover: 1.99 **NM** value: **Cover or less**
Circ: Diamd. preorders: **35,972**
📖 Here Comes Wild Thing **A:** Ron Lim **W:** Tom DeFalco ★ 1st Appearance of Wild Thing. ★ Appearance of Wolverine, Elektra.
6 ❑ Mar 1999 Cover: 1.99 **NM** value: **Cover or less**
Circ: Diamd. preorders: **32,412**
📖 Majority Rules! • Wild Thing story **A:** Ron Lim **W:** Tom DeFalco ★ Appearance of Magneta.
7 ❑ Apr 1999 Cover: 1.99 **NM** value: **Cover or less**
Circ: Diamd. preorders: **29,178**
📖 The Last Days of the Original Juggernaut; The Day J2 Lost 1,000 Pounds • Wild Thing story **A:** Ron Lim **W:** Tom DeFalco ★ Appearance of Cyclops, Uncanny X-People, Parody.
8 ❑ May 1999 Cover: 1.99 **NM** value: **Cover or less**
Circ: Diamd. preorders: **28,533**
9 ❑ Jun 1999 Cover: 1.99 **NM** value: **Cover or less**
Circ: Diamd. preorders: **27,987**
★ 1st Appearance of Big Julie.
10 ❑ Jul 1999 Cover: 1.99 **NM** value: **Cover or less**
Circ: Diamd. preorders: **27,223**
★ Appearance of Wolverine.
11 ❑ Aug 1999 Cover: 1.99 **NM** value: **Cover or less**
Circ: Diamd. preorders: **26,137**
★ Appearance of Sons of the Tiger, Iron Fist.
12 ❑ Oct 1999 Cover: 1.99 **NM** value: **Cover or less**
Circ: Diamd. preorders: **24,056**

JAB Adhesive
1 ❑ Cover: 2.50 **NM** value: **Cover or less**
2 ❑ Cover: 2.50 **NM** value: **Cover or less**
3 ❑ Spr 1993 Cover: 2.50 **NM** value: **Cover or less**
• bullet hole
4 ❑ Cover: 2.50 **NM** value: **Cover or less**
5 ❑ Cover: 2.50 **NM** value: **Cover or less**
📖 Dead End Cruiser; Untitled; The Urine Squirt Gun; Jesus!; The Wasteland **A:** Shannon Wheeler; Mark Stokes; Al Frank; Mike Washburn; Todd Ramsell **W:** Shannon Wheeler; Al Frank; Todd Ramsell; Aubrey McAuley; Richard Klaw

JAB (CUMMINGS DESIGN) Cummings Design Group
3 ❑ Aut 1994, b&w Cover: 2.95 **NM** value: **Cover or less**

JAB (FUNNY PAPERS) Funny Papers
1 ❑ b&w Cover: 2.50 **NM** value: **Cover or less**
2 ❑ b&w Cover: 2.50 **NM** value: **Cover or less**

JACE PEARSON OF THE TEXAS RANGERS Dell
2 ❑ ca. 1953 Cover: 0.10 **NM** value: **40.00**
• Earlier issue published as Dell Four Color #396
3 ❑ ca. 1953 Cover: 0.10 **NM** value: **25.00**
4 ❑ Nov 1953 Cover: 0.10 **NM** value: **25.00**
• **CGC:** 1 graded, best 9.4

JACK ARMSTRONG Parents' Magazine Institute
The globetrotting adventures of Jack Armstrong and Billy Fairfield were first heard in broadcasts from Chicago radio station in 1933. They briefly appeared in comics form in this series from Parents Magazine Institute.

In an era of super-powered characters running around in Spandex, perhaps these stories about an All-American boy hero, amateur sleuth, and overall upstanding young man seem dated. But it's easy to envision children of the late 1940s being quite entertained by Jack Armstrong's adventure short stories, full-color comics, hobby pages and mystery serials.
1 ❑ Nov 1947 Cover: 0.10 **NM** value: **210.00**
• **CGC:** 1 graded, best 4.0
• Scarce
2 ❑ Dec 1947 Cover: 0.10 **NM** value: **85.00**
3 ❑ Jan 1948 Cover: 0.10 **NM** value: **50.00**
4 ❑ Feb 1948 Cover: 0.10 **NM** value: **50.00**
5 ❑ Mar 1948 Cover: 0.10 **NM** value: **50.00**
6 ❑ May 1948 Cover: 0.10 **NM** value: **45.00**
7 ❑ Jun 1948 Cover: 0.10 **NM** value: **45.00**
8 ❑ Aug 1948 Cover: 0.10 **NM** value: **45.00**
📖 The Flaming Forest; Crime Clues; Crime Lab; Hot Pilot (Text Story); Prisoner of the Jungle; Terror at Top Speed; The Fighting Bird; Mayor for a Day
9 ❑ Dec 1948 Cover: 0.10 **NM** value: **45.00**
10 ❑ Mar 1949 Cover: 0.10 **NM** value: **45.00**
11 ❑ May 1949 Cover: 0.10 **NM** value: **45.00**
12 ❑ Jul 1949 Cover: 0.10 **NM** value: **70.00**
• Limited distribution
13 ❑ Sep 1949 Cover: 0.10 **NM** value: **45.00**

JACKAROO, THE Eternity
1 ❑ Feb 1990, b&w Cover: 2.25 **NM** value: **Cover or less**
📖 Australia Nights • Australian **A:** Gary Chaloner **W:** Gary Chaloner
2 ❑ Mar 1990, b&w Cover: 2.25 **NM** value: **Cover or less**
• Australian
3 ❑ Apr 1990, b&w Cover: 2.25 **NM** value: **Cover or less**
• Australian

JACK FROST Amazing
1 ❑ b&w Cover: 1.95 **NM** value: **Cover or less**
📖 Behold Tomorrow **A:** Kevin Van Hook **W:** Kevin Van Hook; Lee Harmon
2 ❑ b&w Cover: 1.95 **NM** value: **Cover or less**
A: Kevin Van Hook **W:** Kevin Van Hook; Lee Harmon

JACK HUNTER Blackthorne
1 ❑ Mar 1988 Cover: 1.25 **NM** value: **Cover or less**
C: Joe Kubert
Bk 1❑ b&w Cover: 3.50 **NM** value: **Cover or less**
Circ: CapCity orders: **575**
C: Joe Kubert

JACKIE GLEASON St. John
1 ❑ Sep 1955 Cover: 0.10 **NM** value: **500.00**
2 ❑ Oct 1955 Cover: 0.10 **NM** value: **350.00**
3 ❑ Nov 1955 Cover: 0.10 **NM** value: **350.00**
4 ❑ Dec 1955 Cover: 0.10 **NM** value: **350.00**

JACKIE GLEASON AND THE HONEYMOONERS DC
1 ❑ Jul 1956 Cover: 0.10 **NM** value: **700.00**
• **CGC:** 1 graded, best 4.5
2 ❑ Sep 1956 Cover: 0.10 **NM** value: **450.00**
3 ❑ Nov 1956 Cover: 0.10 **NM** value: **400.00**
• **CGC:** 1 graded, best 5.0
4 ❑ Jan 1957 Cover: 0.10 **NM** value: **400.00**
5 ❑ Mar 1957 Cover: 0.10 **NM** value: **350.00**
6 ❑ May 1957 Cover: 0.10 **NM** value: **350.00**
• **CGC:** 1 graded, best 5.0
7 ❑ Jul 1957 Cover: 0.10 **NM** value: **350.00**
8 ❑ Sep 1957 Cover: 0.10 **NM** value: **350.00**
9 ❑ Nov 1957 Cover: 0.10 **NM** value: **350.00**
• **CGC:** 1 graded, best 9.0
10 ❑ Jan 1958 Cover: 0.10 **NM** value: **275.00**
11 ❑ Mar 1958 Cover: 0.10 **NM** value: **275.00**
• **CGC:** 1 graded, best 8.0
12 ❑ May 1958 Cover: 0.10 **NM** value: **300.00**

JACKIE ROBINSON Fawcett
1 ❑ May 1950 Cover: 0.10 **NM** value: **800.00**
• **CGC:** 2 graded, best 8.0
2 ❑ Jul 1950 Cover: 0.10 **NM** value: **450.00**
• **CGC:** 2 graded, best 8.0
3 ❑ Sep 1950 Cover: 0.10 **NM** value: **400.00**
• **CGC:** 1 graded, best 7.0
4 ❑ Nov 1950 Cover: 0.10 **NM** value: **400.00**
5 ❑ ca. 1951 Cover: 0.10 **NM** value: **400.00**
• **CGC:** 1 graded, best 7.5
6 ❑ ca. 1952 Cover: 0.10 **NM** value: **350.00**
• **CGC:** 1 graded, best 8.0

Other grades: Multiply prices above by **1.5 for Mint • 2/3 for Very Fine • 1/3 for Fine • 1/5 for Very Good • 1/8 for Good**

JACK IN THE BOX COMICS — Charlton

11 ❑ Oct 1946 — NM value: **100.00**
• **CGC:** 1 graded, best 7.5
12 ❑ 1947 — NM value: **60.00**
13 ❑ 1947 — NM value: **60.00**
14 ❑ 1947 — NM value: **60.00**
15 ❑ 1947 — NM value: **60.00**
16 ❑ 1947 — NM value: **60.00**

JACK KIRBY TREASURY — Pure Imagination

Bk 2❑ b&w — Cover: 9.95 — NM value: **Cover or less**

JACK OF HEARTS — Marvel

1 ❑ Jan 1984 — Cover: 0.60 — NM value: **1.25**
2 ❑ Feb 1984 — Cover: 0.60 — NM value: **1.25**
📖 Heart To Heart **A:** George Freeman **W:** Bill Mantlo
3 ❑ Mar 1984 — Cover: 0.60 — NM value: **1.25**
A: George Freeman **W:** Bill Mantlo
4 ❑ Apr 1984 — Cover: 0.60 — NM value: **1.25**
📖 Heart Attack **A:** George Freeman **W:** Bill Mantlo

JACKPOT COMICS — Archie

1 ❑ Spr 1941 — Cover: 0.10 — NM value: **1800.00**
• **CGC:** 2 graded, best 7.0
2 ❑ Sum 1941 — Cover: 0.10 — NM value: **1200.00**
3 ❑ Fal 1941 — Cover: 0.10 — NM value: **900.00**
4 ❑ Win 1941 — Cover: 0.10 — NM value: **3000.00**
• **CGC:** 3 graded, best 7.0
5 ❑ Spr 1942 — Cover: 0.10 — NM value: **1250.00**
6 ❑ Sum 1942 — Cover: 0.10 — NM value: **900.00**
7 ❑ Fal 1942 — Cover: 0.10 — NM value: **900.00**
• **CGC:** 1 graded, best 4.5
8 ❑ Win 1942 — Cover: 0.10 — NM value: **900.00**
9 ❑ Spr 1943 — Cover: 0.10 — NM value: **850.00**
• **CGC:** 1 graded, best 9.4

JACK'S LUCK RUNS OUT — Beekeeper Cartoon Amusements

1 ❑ — Cover: 3.50 — NM value: **Cover or less**
No issue number.

JACK THE GIANT KILLER — Dell

1 ❑ Jan 1963 — Cover: 0.12 — NM value: **60.00**
1st printing. • Dell Movie Comic

JACK THE RIPPER — Eternity

1 ❑ b&w — Cover: 2.25 — NM value: **Cover or less**
A: Paul Mendoza **W:** Bruce Balfour
2 ❑ b&w — Cover: 2.25 — NM value: **Cover or less**
A: Chris Jones **W:** Bruce Balfour
3 ❑ b&w — Cover: 2.25 — NM value: **Cover or less**
W: Bruce Balfour
Bk 1❑ — Cover: 9.95 — NM value: **Cover or less**

JACK THE RIPPER (CALIBER) — Caliber / Tome

1 ❑ Jun 1999, b&w — Cover: 2.95 — NM value: **Cover or less**
Circ: Diamd. preorders: **2,347**
One-shot.

JACQUELYN THE RIPPER — Fantagraphics

1 ❑ Oct 1994, b&w — Cover: 2.95 — NM value: **Cover or less**
A: Jim Cheff **W:** Dalia Caravaggi
2 ❑ Oct 1994, b&w — Cover: 2.95 — NM value: **Cover or less**
A: Jim Cheff **W:** Dalia Caravaggi

JACQUE'S VOICE OF DOOM — Doomed Comics

1 ❑ b&w — Cover: 1.50 — NM value: **Cover or less**
• strip reprints

JADEMAN COLLECTION — Jademan

1 ❑ — Cover: 2.50 — NM value: **Cover or less**
Circ: CapCity orders: **2,800**
2 ❑ — Cover: 2.50 — NM value: **Cover or less**
Circ: CapCity orders: **2,200**

JADEMAN KUNG FU SPECIAL — Jademan

1 ❑ — Cover: 1.50 — NM value: **Cover or less**
Circ: CapCity orders: **15,375**
📖 Oriental Heroes; The Blood Sword; Drunken Fist; Force of Buddah's Palm • Perviews of Jademan's Titles **A:** Tony Wong **W:** Tony Wong

JADE WARRIORS — Image

1 ❑ — Cover: 2.50 — NM value: **Cover or less**
Circ: Diamd. preorders: **25,098**
📖 To Die For, Part 1 **A:** Mike Deodato **W:** David Campiti; Mike Buckley
1/A ❑ — Cover: 2.50 — NM value: **Cover or less**
alternate cover. 📖 To Die For, Part 1 • Painted **A:** Mike Deodato **W:** David Campiti; Mike Buckley
2 ❑ Jan 2000 — Cover: 2.50 — NM value: **Cover or less**
Circ: Diamd. preorders: **14,799**
📖 To Die For, Part 2 **A:** Mike Deodato **W:** David Campiti; Mike Buckley

J.A.G. — ThwackPow

1 ❑ — Cover: 1.95 — NM value: **Cover or less**
📖 Tin Man; Savior; Big Wolf **A:** Alberto Melendez; Garth Haslam; Josh Lindeman **W:** Alberto Melendez; Garth Haslam; Josh Lindeman
2 ❑ — Cover: 1.95 — NM value: **Cover or less**
A: Alberto Melendez; Garth Haslam; Josh Lindeman **W:** Alberto Melendez; Garth Haslam; Josh Lindeman
3 ❑ — Cover: 1.95 — NM value: **Cover or less**
A: Alberto Melendez; Garth Haslam; Josh Lindeman **W:** Alberto Melendez; Garth Haslam; Josh Lindeman

JAGUAR, THE — DC / Impact

As soon as Brazilian Maria de Guzman reaches college in Michigan, she begins having strange dreams in which she's a fierce creature stalking through the woods, preying on soldiers and evildoers. The dreams terrify her, but it's not long before she's living them.

Feeling restless one night, she decides to go jogging. Suddenly, she's attacked by wilding youths. In her struggle against them, she changes into the Jaguar — a were-creature whose powers she inherited through her family line. Before long, this shy college student would have to cope not only with fitting in at a big school, but also with cyborg killers, super-villains, and a math teacher who's secretly an agent for The Web.

1 ❑ Aug 1991 — Cover: 1.00 — NM value: **Cover or less**
Circ: CapCity orders: **36,350**
📖 Savage Birthright **A:** David Antoine Williams **W:** William Messner-Loebs ★ Origin of Jaguar. ★ 1st Appearance of The Jaguar (Maria de Guzman), Timon de Guzman, Tracy Dickerson, Maxim Ruiz, Maxx-13, Luiza Timmerman.
2 ❑ Sep 1991 — Cover: 1.00 — NM value: **Cover or less**
Circ: CapCity orders: **20,650**
3 ❑ Oct 1991 — Cover: 1.00 — NM value: **Cover or less**
Circ: CapCity orders: **18,900**
★ Versus Maxx-13.
4 ❑ Nov 1991 — Cover: 1.00 — NM value: **Cover or less**
Circ: CapCity orders: **16,650**
★ 1st Appearance of Victor Drago. ★ Appearance of Black Hood.
5 ❑ Dec 1991 — Cover: 1.00 — NM value: **Cover or less**
Circ: CapCity orders: **15,100**
★ 1st Appearance of Void.
6 ❑ Jan 1992 — Cover: 1.00 — NM value: **Cover or less**
Circ: CapCity orders: **12,350**
7 ❑ Mar 1992 — Cover: 1.00 — NM value: **Cover or less**
Circ: CapCity orders: **10,700**
8 ❑ Apr 1992 — Cover: 1.00 — NM value: **Cover or less**
Circ: CapCity orders: **9,250**
9 ❑ May 1992 — Cover: 1.00 — NM value: **Cover or less**
Circ: CapCity orders: **8,100**
📖 The Coming of The Crusaders, Part 6 • trading card ★ 1st Appearance of Moonlighter.
10 ❑ Jun 1992 — Cover: 1.00 — NM value: **Cover or less**
Circ: CapCity orders: **7,450**
11 ❑ Jul 1992 — Cover: 1.00 — NM value: **1.25**
Circ: CapCity orders: **6,950**
12 ❑ Aug 1992 — Cover: 1.25 — NM value: **Cover or less**
Circ: CapCity orders: **7,150**
13 ❑ Sep 1992 — Cover: 1.25 — NM value: **Cover or less**
Circ: CapCity orders: **6,350**
14 ❑ Oct 1992 — Cover: 1.25 — NM value: **Cover or less**
Circ: CapCity orders: **5,000**
📖 Frightmare in Rio! final issue. **A:** Chuck Wojtkiewicz **W:** William Messner-Loebs
Anl 1❑ ca. 1992 — Cover: 2.50 — NM value: **Cover or less**
Circ: CapCity orders: **7,650**

JAGUAR GOD — Verotik

0 ❑ Feb 1996 — Cover: 2.95 — NM value: **5.00**
Circ: CapCity orders: **12,545**
A: Frank Teran; Frank Frazetta(cover)
1 ❑ Mar 1995 — Cover: 2.95 — NM value: **5.00**
Circ: CapCity orders: **11,300**
A: Frank Teran; Frank Frazetta(cover) **W:** Glenn Danzig
2 ❑ Aug 1995 — Cover: 2.95 — NM value: **4.00**
Circ: CapCity orders: **7,345**
3 ❑ Mar 1996 — Cover: 2.95 — NM value: **3.50**
Circ: CapCity orders: **8,555**
4 ❑ 1996 — Cover: 2.95 — NM value: **3.50**
5 ❑ Sep 1996 — Cover: 2.95 — NM value: **3.50**
6 ❑ Apr 1997 — Cover: 2.95 — NM value: **Cover or less**
Circ: Diamd. preorders: **15,529**
7 ❑ Jun 1997 — Cover: 2.95 — NM value: **Cover or less**
Circ: Diamd. preorders: **14,281**
8 ❑ 1997 — Cover: 2.95 — NM value: **Cover or less**
Circ: Diamd. preorders: **12,834**

JAILBAIT — Fantagraphics / Eros

1 ❑ Dec 1998 — Cover: 2.95 — NM value: **Cover or less**
Circ: Diamd. preorders: **2,071**
A: Dementia **W:** Dementia

JAKE THRASH — Aircel

1 ❑ full color — Cover: 2.00 — NM value: **Cover or less**
Circ: CapCity orders: **2,700**
2 ❑ full color — Cover: 2.00 — NM value: **Cover or less**
Circ: CapCity orders: **1,725**
Bk 1❑ b&w — Cover: 3.95 — NM value: **Cover or less**

JAM, THE — Slave Labor

1 ❑ Nov 1989, b&w — Cover: 1.95 — NM value: **2.50**
A: Bernie Mireault **W:** Bernie Mireault
2 ❑ Jan 1990, b&w — Cover: 1.95 — NM value: **2.00**
A: Bernie Mireault **W:** Bernie Mireault
3 ❑ Mar 1990, b&w — Cover: 1.95 — NM value: **2.00**
A: Bernie Mireault **W:** Bernie Mireault
4 ❑ May 1990 — Cover: 2.25 — NM value: **2.95**
A: Bernie Mireault **W:** Bernie Mireault
5 ❑ Mar 1991 — Cover: 2.25 — NM value: **2.95**
A: Bernie Mireault **W:** Bernie Mireault
6 ❑ — Cover: 2.50 — NM value: **Cover or less**
A: Bernie Mireault **W:** Bernie Mireault
7 ❑ Mar 1994, b&w — Cover: 2.50 — NM value: **Cover or less**
A: Bernie Mireault **W:** Bernie Mireault
8 ❑ Feb 1995, b&w — Cover: 2.50 — NM value: **2.95**
A: Bernie Mireault **W:** Bernie Mireault
9 ❑ Aug 1995, b&w — Cover: 2.95 — NM value: **Cover or less**
A: Bernie Mireault **W:** Bernie Mireault
10 ❑ b&w — Cover: 2.95 — NM value: **Cover or less**
A: Bernie Mireault **W:** Bernie Mireault
11 ❑ b&w — Cover: 2.95 — NM value: **Cover or less**
A: Bernie Mireault **W:** Bernie Mireault
12 ❑ — Cover: 2.95 — NM value: **Cover or less**
A: Bernie Mireault **W:** Bernie Mireault
13 ❑ — Cover: 2.95 — NM value: **Cover or less**
A: Bernie Mireault **W:** Bernie Mireault

JAMAR CHRONICLES, THE — Sweat Shop Press

1 ❑ b&w — Cover: 2.00 — NM value: **Cover or less**

JAMBOREE COMICS — Round

1 ❑ Feb 1946 — Cover: 0.10 — NM value: **175.00**
• **CGC:** 6 graded, best 9.4
2 ❑ Mar 1946 — Cover: 0.10 — NM value: **100.00**
• **CGC:** 4 graded, best 9.6
3 ❑ Apr 1946 — Cover: 0.10 — NM value: **100.00**

JAMES BOND 007: A SILENT ARMAGEDDON — Dark Horse

1 ❑ Mar 1993 — Cover: 2.95 — NM value: **Cover or less**
Circ: CapCity orders: **10,575**
cardstock cover. **A:** John Burns **W:** Simon Jowett
2 ❑ May 1993 — Cover: 2.95 — NM value: **Cover or less**
Circ: CapCity orders: **7,050**
cardstock cover. **A:** John Burns **W:** Simon Jowett

JAMES BOND 007/GOLDENEYE — Topps

1 ❑ Jan 1996 — Cover: 2.95 — NM value: **Cover or less**
A: Jean-Claude St. Aubin **W:** Don McGregor
2 ❑ Feb 1996 — Cover: 2.95 — NM value: **Cover or less**
A: Jean-Claude St. Aubin **W:** Don McGregor
3 ❑ Mar 1996 — Cover: 2.95 — NM value: **Cover or less**
A: Jean-Claude St. Aubin **W:** Don McGregor

JAMES BOND 007: SERPENT'S TOOTH — Dark Horse

James Bond is a member of Her Majesty's Secret Service, double-O branch. As agent 007, he is sent on the most dangerous missions and has a license to kill if necessary.

His latest adventure takes him from the jungles of South America to a vast undersea complex as he tries to stop a madman named Indigo. This mad messiah has stolen nuclear devices and placed them along undersea fault lines. Once triggered, they will create huge tsunamis which threaten to wipe out the 83% of the world's population that lives within 50 miles of the sea. Then, the genetically "perfect" residents of his own underwater Eden will take over and remake the world in Indigo's image.

But unbeknownst to Indigo, there is a snake loose in Eden — a snake with a license to kill.

1 ❑ Jul 1992 — Cover: 4.95 — NM value: **Cover or less**
Circ: CapCity orders: **9,525** • **CGC:** 1 graded, best 9.6
• prestige format. **A:** Paul Gulacy **W:** Doug Moench
2 ❑ Aug 1992 — Cover: 4.95 — NM value: **Cover or less**
Circ: CapCity orders: **6,725**
• prestige format. **A:** Paul Gulacy **W:** Doug Moench
3 ❑ Feb 1993 — Cover: 4.95 — NM value: **Cover or less**
Circ: CapCity orders: **6,600**
• prestige format. **A:** Paul Gulacy **W:** Doug Moench
Bk 1❑ Jan 1995 — Cover: 15.95 — NM value: **Cover or less**
• Trade Paperback. • Collects James Bond 007: Serpent's Tooth #1-3 **A:** Paul Gulacy **W:** Doug Moench

JAMES BOND 007: SHATTERED HELIX — Dark Horse

1 ❑ Jun 1994 — Cover: 2.50 — NM value: **Cover or less**
Circ: CapCity orders: **6,375**
📖 The Greenhouse Effect **A:** David Lloyd; David Jackson **W:** Simon Jowett
2 ❑ Jul 1994 — Cover: 2.50 — NM value: **Cover or less**
Circ: CapCity orders: **5,350**

JAMES BOND 007: THE QUASIMODO GAMBIT — Dark Horse

1 ❑ Jan 1995 — Cover: 3.95 — NM value: **Cover or less**
Circ: CapCity orders: **4,625**
cardstock cover. **A:** Gary Caldwell **W:** Don McGregor
2 ❑ Feb 1995 — Cover: 3.95 — NM value: **Cover or less**
Circ: CapCity orders: **3,625**
cardstock cover.
3 ❑ May 1995 — Cover: 3.95 — NM value: **Cover or less**
Circ: CapCity orders: **3,450**
cardstock cover.

JAMES BOND FOR YOUR EYES ONLY — Marvel

1 ❑ Oct 1981 — Cover: 0.50 — NM value: **1.50**
A: Howard Chaykin **W:** Larry Hama

CGC-graded: Multiply prices above by **33 for 9.9 M • 16 for 9.8 NM/M • 7 for 9.6 NM+ • 5 for 9.4 NM • 2.5 for 9.2 NM- • 1.5 for 9.0 VF/NM**

2 ☐ Nov 1981 Cover: 0.50 **NM** value: **1.50**
A: Howard Chaykin **W:** Larry Hama

JAMES BOND JR. — Marvel

1 ☐ Jan 1992 Cover: 1.00 **NM** value: **Cover or less**
Circ: CapCity orders: **7,300**
📖 The Beginning • TV cartoon **A:** Mario Capaldi **W:** Cal Hamilton; Frank Moss; T. Pederson
2 ☐ Feb 1992 Cover: 1.25 **NM** value: **Cover or less**
Circ: CapCity orders: **5,400**
3 ☐ Mar 1992 Cover: 1.25 **NM** value: **Cover or less**
Circ: CapCity orders: **3,500**
4 ☐ Apr 1992 Cover: 1.25 **NM** value: **Cover or less**
Circ: CapCity orders: **2,900**
5 ☐ May 1992 Cover: 1.25 **NM** value: **Cover or less**
Circ: CapCity orders: **2,200**
6 ☐ Jun 1992 Cover: 1.25 **NM** value: **Cover or less**
7 ☐ Jul 1992 Cover: 1.25 **NM** value: **Cover or less**
8 ☐ Aug 1992 Cover: 1.25 **NM** value: **Cover or less**
9 ☐ Sep 1992 Cover: 1.25 **NM** value: **Cover or less**
10 ☐ Oct 1992 Cover: 1.25 **NM** value: **Cover or less**
11 ☐ Nov 1992 Cover: 1.25 **NM** value: **Cover or less**
12 ☐ Dec 1992 Cover: 1.25 **NM** value: **Cover or less**
final issue.

JAMES BOND: PERMISSION TO DIE — Eclipse

1 ☐ Jul 1991 Cover: 3.95 **NM** value: **5.00**
Circ: CapCity orders: **22,700**
A: Mike Grell **W:** Mike Grell
2 ☐ Aug 1991 Cover: 3.95 **NM** value: **5.00**
Circ: CapCity orders: **13,075**
A: Mike Grell **W:** Mike Grell
3 ☐ Sep 1991 Cover: 4.95 **NM** value: **5.00**
Circ: CapCity orders: **8,800**
A: Mike Grell **W:** Mike Grell

JAM QUACKY — Jq Productions

1 ☐ b&w Cover: 2.00 **NM** value: **Cover or less**

JAM SPECIAL, THE — Matrix

1 ☐ Cover: 2.50 **NM** value: **Cover or less**
Circ: CapCity orders: **3,850**

JAM SUPER COOL COLOR-INJECTED TURBO ADVENTURE FROM HELL — Comico

1 ☐ Cover: 2.50 **NM** value: **Cover or less**

JAM URBAN ADVENTURE, THE — Tundra

1 ☐ full color Cover: 2.95 **NM** value: **Cover or less**
A: Bernie Mireault **W:** Bernie Mireault
2 ☐ full color Cover: 2.95 **NM** value: **Cover or less**
A: Bernie Mireault **W:** Bernie Mireault
3 ☐ full color Cover: 2.95 **NM** value: **Cover or less**
A: Bernie Mireault **W:** Bernie Mireault

JANE ARDEN — St. John

1 ☐ ca. 1948 Cover: 0.10 **NM** value: **100.00**
2 ☐ ca. 1948 Cover: 0.10 **NM** value: **75.00**

JANE BONDAGE — Eros / Eros Comix

1 ☐ Cover: 2.95 **NM** value: **Cover or less**
A: Samuel Savage **W:** Samuel Savage
2 ☐ Sep 1995 Cover: 2.95 **NM** value: **Cover or less**
A: Samuel Savage **W:** Samuel Savage

JANE BOND: THUNDERBALLS — Fantagraphics / Eros Comix

All issues are adults only.
1 ☐ b&w Cover: 2.50 **NM** value: **Cover or less**

JANE DOE — Raging Rhino

All issues are adults only.
1 ☐ b&w Cover: 2.95 **NM** value: **Cover or less**
📖 Androgyne Anger Extreme
2 ☐ b&w Cover: 2.95 **NM** value: **Cover or less**
📖 Slice bySlice
3 ☐ b&w Cover: 2.95 **NM** value: **Cover or less**

JANN OF THE JUNGLE — Atlas

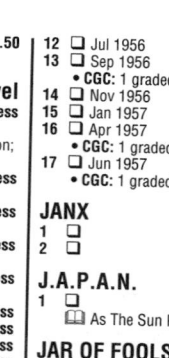

Jann of the Jungle was another of those gorgeous white women who rampaged happily through the under- and overgrowth in a minimum of clothes showing a maximum of leg. She had starred in Jungle Tales before she was given the title, and that meant that her earlier adventures in the series showed not only leg but considerable cleavage. But by the time the title was changed to Jann of the Jungle and given the subtitle "and Other Jungle Tales," there was a big fat CMAA Comics Code stamp on the cover, and suddenly her outfit featured a top without a plunging neckline.

It didn't stop her, however, from continuing to swing from vines, brandishing both knife and spear with equal confidence, and generally hold her own against both wild animals and evil poachers.
— Maggie

8 ☐ Nov 1955 Cover: 0.10 **NM** value: **225.00**
9 ☐ Jan 1956 Cover: 0.10 **NM** value: **130.00**
10 ☐ Mar 1956 Cover: 0.10 **NM** value: **150.00**
11 ☐ May 1956 Cover: 0.10 **NM** value: **130.00**

12 ☐ Jul 1956 Cover: 0.10 **NM** value: **130.00**
13 ☐ Sep 1956 Cover: 0.10 **NM** value: **130.00**
• **CGC:** 1 graded, best 8.5
14 ☐ Nov 1956 Cover: 0.10 **NM** value: **130.00**
15 ☐ Jan 1957 Cover: 0.10 **NM** value: **130.00**
16 ☐ Apr 1957 Cover: 0.10 **NM** value: **150.00**
• **CGC:** 1 graded, best 8.5
17 ☐ Jun 1957 Cover: 0.10 **NM** value: **150.00**
• **CGC:** 1 graded, best 7.5

JANX — Es Graphics

1 ☐ Cover: 1.00 **NM** value: **Cover or less**
2 ☐ Cover: 1.00 **NM** value: **Cover or less**

J.A.P.A.N. — Outerealm

1 ☐ Cover: 1.80 **NM** value: **Cover or less**
📖 As The Sun Rises **A:** Thi Nguyen **W:** Patrick Brockway

JAR OF FOOLS PART ONE — Penny Dreadful

1 ☐ Jun 1994, b&w Cover: 5.95 **NM** value: **Cover or less**
No issue number.

JASON AND THE ARGONAUTS — Tome Press

1 ☐ b&w Cover: 2.50 **NM** value: **Cover or less**
Circ: CapCity orders: **2,640**
A: Patrick Zircher **W:** Patrick Zircher
2 ☐ b&w Cover: 2.50 **NM** value: **Cover or less**
A: Patrick Zircher **W:** Patrick Zircher
3 ☐ b&w Cover: 2.50 **NM** value: **Cover or less**
A: Patrick Zircher **W:** Patrick Zircher
4 ☐ b&w Cover: 2.50 **NM** value: **Cover or less**
A: Patrick Zircher **W:** Patrick Zircher
5 ☐ b&w Cover: 2.50 **NM** value: **Cover or less**
A: Patrick Zircher **W:** Patrick Zircher

JASON GOES TO HELL: THE FINAL FRIDAY — Topps

1 ☐ Jul 1993 Cover: 2.95 **NM** value: **Cover or less**
Circ: CapCity orders: **23,075**
glowing cover. **A:** Cynthia Martin **W:** Andy Mangels
2 ☐ Aug 1993 Cover: 2.95 **NM** value: **Cover or less**
Circ: CapCity orders: **11,950**
A: Bobby Rubio **W:** Andy Mangels
3 ☐ Sep 1993 Cover: 2.95 **NM** value: **Cover or less**
Circ: CapCity orders: **7,000**

JASON MONARCH — Oracle

1 ☐ b&w Cover: 2.00 **NM** value: **Cover or less**
📖 Jason Monarch, Star Menagerie **A:** Jim Craig; Fred Bobb **W:** Fred Bobb; Dave Lillard

JASON VS. LEATHERFACE — Topps

1 ☐ Oct 1995 Cover: 2.95 **NM** value: **Cover or less**
📖 Goin' South **A:** Jeff Butler **W:** David Imhoff; Nancy Collins
2 ☐ Nov 1995 Cover: 2.95 **NM** value: **Cover or less**
3 ☐ Dec 1995 Cover: 2.95 **NM** value: **Cover or less**

JAVA TOWN — Slave Labor

1 ☐ May 1992, b&w Cover: 2.95 **NM** value: **Cover or less**
2 ☐ Nov 1993, b&w Cover: 2.95 **NM** value: **Cover or less**
📖 Java Town; We Want to Own a Coffee Shop B Cuz; The All-New Gertie the Dinosaur; Inspector Ten: Indifference! **A:** Nov-93 **W:** Scott Saavedra
3 ☐ Jul 1994, b&w Cover: 2.95 **NM** value: **Cover or less**
4 ☐ Jul 1995, b&w Cover: 2.95 **NM** value: **Cover or less**
5 ☐ Nov 1995, b&w Cover: 2.95 **NM** value: **Cover or less**
6 ☐ Jun 1996, b&w Cover: 2.95 **NM** value: **Cover or less**

JAVERTS — Firstlight

1 ☐ Cover: 2.95 **NM** value: **Cover or less**
A: Brandt Peters **W:** Mark Lucas; Michael Peters

JAX AND THE HELL HOUND — Blackthorne

1 ☐ Nov 1986 Cover: 1.75 **NM** value: **Cover or less**
📖 Escape **A:** Dennis Francis **W:** Dennis Francis
2 ☐ Feb 1987 Cover: 1.75 **NM** value: **Cover or less**
📖 Death Cance **A:** Dennis Francis **W:** Dennis Francis
3 ☐ 1987 Cover: 1.75 **NM** value: **Cover or less**
A: Dennis Francis **W:** Dennis Francis
4 ☐ 1987 Cover: 1.75 **NM** value: **Cover or less**
A: Dennis Francis **W:** Dennis Francis

JAY ANACLETO SKETCHBOOK — Image

1 ☐ Apr 1999 **NM** value: **2.00**
no cover price. **A:** Jay Anacleto
1/A ☐ Apr 1999 Cover: 5.95 **NM** value: **Cover or less**
Has cover price. **A:** Jay Anacleto

> **Diamond** preorders are the estimated number of comics sold, prior to their release, to comics shops in North America by Diamond Comic Distributors, the largest distributor. These figures underreport the actual number of circulating copies by the amount of reorders Diamond took (usually 5-10% again of the preorders) and sales by publishers to newsstand and bookstore distributors. For many independent publishers, Diamond's preorders may be quite close to the actual number of copies in circulation.

JAY & SILENT BOB — Oni Press

This four-issue mini-series stars the loudmouthed stoner, Jay, and his quiet compatriot, Silent Bob, along with other characters from Kevin Smith's movies.

Smith, who plays Silent Bob in his movies, is a comics fan who made a name for himself with offbeat independent movies such as Clerks, Mallrats, and Chasing Amy, low-budget films telling the tales of various teens living in suburban New Jersey. The films scored points for memorable and bizarre characters, and Jay and Silent Bob appear in them all.

Kevin Smith wrote this humor series starring the duo, who embark in #1 on a quest in search of John Hughes' America. Smith would find himself in demand by other publishers as a writer in this time, and, as a result, the final issue of this limited series took some time to ship.

1 ☐ Jul 1998 Cover: 2.95 **NM** value: **4.00**
Circ: Diamd. preorders: **36,149** • **CGC:** 1 graded, best 9.2
A: Duncan Fegredo; Jimmy Palmiotti(cover); Joe Quesada(cover)
W: Kevin Smith
1/SC ☐ Jul 1998 Cover: 2.95 **NM** value: **5.00**
• **CGC:** 5 graded, best 9.8
Photo cover. **A:** Duncan Fegredo **W:** Kevin Smith
1-2 ☐ Oct 1998 Cover: 2.95 **NM** value: **Cover or less**
Circ: Diamd. preorders: **3,809**
2 ☐ Oct 1998 Cover: 2.95 **NM** value: **3.00**
Circ: Diamd. preorders: **30,402**
A: Duncan Fegredo **W:** Kevin Smith
3 ☐ Dec 1998 Cover: 2.95 **NM** value: **3.00**
Circ: Diamd. preorders: **27,744**
Photo cover. **A:** Duncan Fegredo **W:** Kevin Smith
4 ☐ Oct 1999 Cover: 2.95 **NM** value: **3.00**
Circ: Diamd. preorders: **34,349**
A: Duncan Fegredo **W:** Kevin Smith
Bk 1 ☐ Oct 1999 Cover: 11.95 **NM** value: **Cover or less**
📖 Chasing Dogma • Collects series; introduction by Alanis Morissette **A:** Duncan Fegredo **W:** Kevin Smith

JAZZ — High Impact

1 ☐ 1996 **NM** value: **2.95**
2 ☐ May 1996 **NM** value: **2.95**
A: Jude Millien **W:** Jude Millien

JAZZ AGE CHRONICLES (CALIBER) — Caliber

1 ☐ b&w Cover: 2.50 **NM** value: **Cover or less**
📖 Vote Early and Often Part 1 **A:** Ted Slampyak **W:** Ted Slampyak
2 ☐ May 1990, b&w Cover: 2.50 **NM** value: **Cover or less**
📖 Vote Early and Often Part 2 **A:** Ted Slampyak **W:** Ted Slampyak
3 ☐ b&w Cover: 2.50 **NM** value: **Cover or less**
A: Ted Slampyak **W:** Ted Slampyak
4 ☐ b&w Cover: 2.50 **NM** value: **Cover or less**
A: Ted Slampyak **W:** Ted Slampyak
5 ☐ b&w Cover: 2.50 **NM** value: **Cover or less**
A: Ted Slampyak **W:** Ted Slampyak
Bk 1 ☐ Cover: 9.95 **NM** value: **Cover or less**

JAZZ AGE CHRONICLES (EF) — EF Graphics

1 ☐ Jan 1989 Cover: 1.50 **NM** value: **Cover or less**
📖 The Case of the Beguiling Baroness Part 1 **A:** Ted Slampyak **W:** Ted Slampyak
2 ☐ Mar 1989 Cover: 1.50 **NM** value: **Cover or less**
📖 The Case of the Beguiling Baroness Part 2 **A:** Ted Slampyak **W:** Ted Slampyak
3 ☐ May 1989 Cover: 1.50 **NM** value: **Cover or less**
📖 The Case of the Beguiling Baroness Part 3 **A:** Ted Slampyak **W:** Ted Slampyak

JAZZBO COMICS THAT SWING — Slave Labor

1 ☐ Nov 1994 Cover: 2.95 **NM** value: **Cover or less**
📖 Get Rhythm with Jazzbo! Comics; Yum Cha to Drink Tea and Eat Dim Sum; The Telephone Call; Center of the Universe; Kidney Stone Blues or Wel **A:** Eric Searleman **W:** Eric Searleman
2 ☐ Apr 1995 Cover: 2.95 **NM** value: **Cover or less**
📖 Year of the Egg, Chapter One; Year of the Egg, Chapter Two; Big Shot Gangsters! • Replacement God preview **A:** Eric Searleman **W:** Eric Searleman

JAZZ: SOLITAIRE — High Impact

1 ☐ May 1998 Cover: 2.95 **NM** value: **Cover or less**
Circ: Diamd. preorders: **2,432**
1/A ☐ May 1998 **NM** value: **3.50**
wraparound photo cover.
1/GO ☐ May 1998 **NM** value: **3.50**
no cover price. • gold foil logo
2 ☐ May 1998 Cover: 3.00 **NM** value: **Cover or less**
2/A ☐ Cover: 5.95 **NM** value: **Cover or less**
no cover price.
2/B ☐ Cover: 5.95 **NM** value: **Cover or less**
nude cover (blue background).
3 ☐ Cover: 3.00 **NM** value: **Cover or less**
3/A ☐ Cover: 5.95 **NM** value: **Cover or less**
Nude cover.
3/B ☐ Cover: 5.95 **NM** value: **Cover or less**
wraparound nude cover.

JCP FEATURES — J.C.

1 ☐ Feb 1981 Cover: 2.00 **NM** value: **3.00**
• THUNDER Agents **A:** Dick Giordano; Neal Adams

Other grades: Multiply prices above by **1.5 for Mint • 2/3 for Very Fine • 1/3 for Fine • 1/5 for Very Good • 1/8 for Good**

JEANIE — Timely

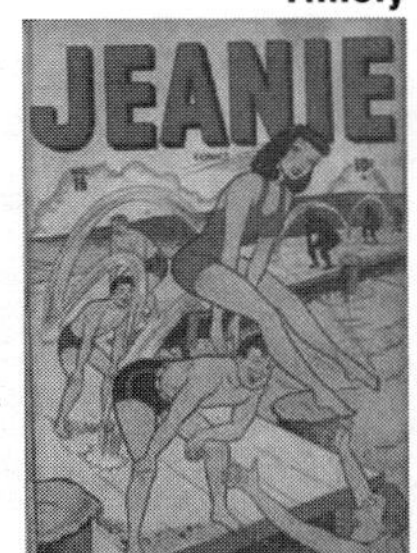

She's "Queen of the Teens," and the perky brunette was quite a change from #12 of the series — which had been titled Daring Comics and cover-featured The Sub-Mariner and The Human Torch and Toro attacking thugs apparently trying to take over a pleasure boat filled with people. The shock to the young comics purchaser wouldn't have been too great, since there'd also been more than a year and a half between Daring #12 and Jeanie #13. The war was over, and the focus (at least in Jeanie) was on teens, dating, and long, shapely legs. At first, the covers went for simple depictions of guys drooling at the sight of her. By #17, the cover come-on described the contents as "another romance-packed mirth-filled magazine," and the emphasis on gags was increased.

And then, suddenly, it morphed, ever so briefly, into Cowgirl Romances. Yikes. — Maggie

13 ❑ 1947 Cover: 0.10 NM value: 125.00
14 ❑ 1947 Cover: 0.10 NM value: 90.00
15 ❑ 1947 Cover: 0.10 NM value: 90.00
16 ❑ 1947 Cover: 0.10 NM value: 90.00
17 ❑ Cover: 0.10 NM value: 90.00
18 ❑ Mar 1948 Cover: 0.10 NM value: 80.00
• CGC: 1 graded, best 9.0
19 ❑ 1948 Cover: 0.10 NM value: 80.00
20 ❑ 1948 Cover: 0.10 NM value: 80.00
21 ❑ 1948 Cover: 0.10 NM value: 80.00
22 ❑ 1948 Cover: 0.10 NM value: 80.00
23 ❑ Cover: 0.10 NM value: 80.00
24 ❑ Cover: 0.10 NM value: 60.00
25 ❑ 1949 Cover: 0.10 NM value: 60.00
26 ❑ 1949 Cover: 0.10 NM value: 60.00
27 ❑ 1949 Cover: 0.10 NM value: 60.00

JEEP COMICS — R.B. Leffingwell

1 ❑ Win 1944 Cover: 0.10 NM value: 400.00
• CGC: 1 graded, best 7.5

JEFF JORDAN, U.S. AGENT — D.S.

1 ❑ NM value: 100.00

JEFFREY DAHMER: AN UNAUTHORIZED BIOGRAPHY OF A SERIAL KILLER — Boneyard Press

1 ❑ Cover: 2.50 NM value: 4.00
A: Al Hanford W: Hart Fisher
1-2 ❑ Cover: 2.75 NM value: Cover or less
A: Al Hanford W: Hart Fisher

JEFFREY DAHMER VS. JESUS CHRIST — Boneyard Press

1 ❑ Feb 1993 Cover: 2.75 NM value: 4.00
Circ: CapCity orders: 4,290
wraparound cover. A: Nelson Danielson W: Hart Fisher
1/Aut❑ Cover: 3.95 NM value: 5.00

JEMM, SON OF SATURN — DC

1 ❑ Sep 1984 Cover: 0.75 NM value: 1.50
🕮 The Arrival A: Gene Colan; Klaus Janson W: Greg Potter ★ 1st Appearance of Jemm, Son of Saturn.
2 ❑ Oct 1984 Cover: 0.75 NM value: 1.00
3 ❑ Nov 1984 Cover: 0.75 NM value: 1.00
★ Origin of Jemm.
4 ❑ Dec 1984 Cover: 0.75 NM value: 1.00
5 ❑ Jan 1985 Cover: 0.75 NM value: 1.00
6 ❑ Feb 1985 Cover: 0.75 NM value: 1.00
7 ❑ Mar 1985 Cover: 0.75 NM value: 1.00
🕮 Firefight A: Gene Colan; Klaus Janson W: Greg Potter
8 ❑ Apr 1985 Cover: 0.75 NM value: 1.00
9 ❑ May 1985 Cover: 0.75 NM value: 1.00
Circ: CapCity orders: 6,850
10 ❑ Jun 1985 Cover: 0.75 NM value: 1.00
Circ: CapCity orders: 6,700
11 ❑ Jul 1985 Cover: 0.75 NM value: 1.00
Circ: CapCity orders: 6,400
12 ❑ Aug 1985 Cover: 0.75 NM value: 1.00
Circ: CapCity orders: 6,100

JENNY FINN — Oni Press

1 ❑ Jun 1999 Cover: 2.95 NM value: Cover or less
Circ: Diamd. preorders: 10,510
A: Troy Nixey W: Mike Mignola; Troy Nixey
2 ❑ Sep 1999 Cover: 2.95 NM value: Cover or less
Circ: Diamd. preorders: 8,375
3 ❑ Nov 1999 Cover: 2.95 NM value: Cover or less
Circ: Diamd. preorders: 7,979
4 ❑ Feb 2000 Cover: 3.95 NM value: Cover or less
Circ: Diamd. preorders: 6,558

JENNY SPARKS: THE SECRET HISTORY OF THE AUTHORITY — WildStorm

1 ❑ Aug 2000 Cover: 2.50 NM value: Cover or less
Circ: Diamd. preorders: 31,707 • CGC: 1 graded, best 9.2
A: John McCrea W: Mark Millar
2 ❑ Sep 2000 Cover: 2.50 NM value: Cover or less
Circ: Diamd. preorders: 28,326
🕮 Rough Trade A: John McCrea W: Mark Millar
3 ❑ Oct 2000 Cover: 2.50 NM value: Cover or less
Circ: Diamd. preorders: 27,362
🕮 A Tale of Two Cities A: John McCrea W: Mark Millar
4 ❑ Nov 2000 Cover: 2.50 NM value: Cover or less
Circ: Diamd. preorders: 29,048
🕮 Many Happy Returns A: John McCrea W: Mark Millar
5 ❑ Dec 2000 Cover: 2.50 NM value: Cover or less
Circ: Diamd. preorders: 29,197
🕮 There's Nothing I Haven't Sung About A: John McCrea W: Mark Millar

JEREMIAH: A FISTFUL OF SAND — Adventure

1 ❑ b&w Cover: 2.50 NM value: Cover or less
2 ❑ b&w Cover: 2.50 NM value: Cover or less

JEREMIAH: BIRDS OF PREY — Adventure

1 ❑ b&w Cover: 2.50 NM value: Cover or less
2 ❑ Apr 1991, b&w Cover: 2.50 NM value: Cover or less

JEREMIAH: THE HEIRS — Adventure

1 ❑ b&w Cover: 2.50 NM value: Cover or less
2 ❑ b&w Cover: 2.50 NM value: Cover or less

JEREMY BROOD — Fantagor

1 ❑ Cover: 11.95 NM value: Cover or less
• graphic album A: Corben

JERRY DRUMMER — Charlton

10 ❑ NM value: 25.00
11 ❑ NM value: 25.00
12 ❑ NM value: 25.00

JERSEY DEVIL — South Jersey Rebellion

1 ❑ 1992 Cover: 2.25 NM value: Cover or less
• no indicia
2 ❑ Cover: 2.95 NM value: Cover or less
3 ❑ Cover: 2.25 NM value: Cover or less
4 ❑ 1997 Cover: 2.25 NM value: Cover or less
5 ❑ 1997 Cover: 2.25 NM value: Cover or less
6 ❑ 1997 Cover: 2.25 NM value: Cover or less
7 ❑ Cover: 2.25 NM value: Cover or less
• no indicia

JESSE JAMES — AC

1 ❑ b&w Cover: 3.95 NM value: Cover or less
A: Jack Kirby

JESSE JAMES (AVON) — Avon

Jesse James (1847-1882) is, like Billy the Kid, one of those real people whose name was propped up to put fresh Western comic-book stories under. In the case of this series, the character begins by being identified as "America's No. 1 Outlaw." Then, looking for a slightly different persona, he's called "Bandit Chieftain of the Wild West." The series doesn't deny his actions outside the law and features such stories as "The San Antonio Stage Robbery," "The California Stagecoach Robberies," "Jesse James' Deadliest Deed," and "Trapped by the Pinkertons!"

Of note in this series is some fine Western art. — Maggie

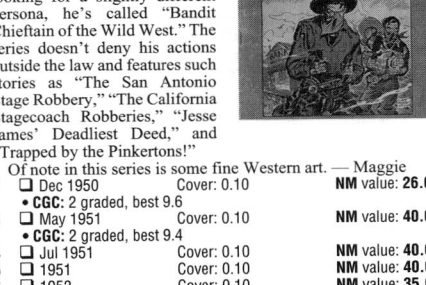

2 ❑ Dec 1950 Cover: 0.10 NM value: 26.00
• CGC: 2 graded, best 9.6
3 ❑ May 1951 Cover: 0.10 NM value: 40.00
• CGC: 2 graded, best 9.4
4 ❑ Jul 1951 Cover: 0.10 NM value: 40.00
5 ❑ 1951 Cover: 0.10 NM value: 40.00
6 ❑ 1952 Cover: 0.10 NM value: 35.00
7 ❑ May 1952 Cover: 0.10 NM value: 35.00
• CGC: 1 graded, best 8.0
8 ❑ Aug 1952 Cover: 0.10 NM value: 35.00
9 ❑ Nov 1952 Cover: 0.10 NM value: 35.00
15 ❑ 1953 Cover: 0.10 NM value: 30.00
16 ❑ Cover: 0.10 NM value: 28.00
17 ❑ Cover: 0.10 NM value: 28.00
18 ❑ 1954 Cover: 0.10 NM value: 28.00
19 ❑ 1954 Cover: 0.10 NM value: 26.00
20 ❑ Oct 1954 Cover: 0.10 NM value: 24.00
21 ❑ Feb 1955 Cover: 0.10 NM value: 24.00
22 ❑ Apr 1955 Cover: 0.10 NM value: 22.00
23 ❑ 1955 Cover: 0.10 NM value: 22.00
24 ❑ 1955 Cover: 0.10 NM value: 22.00
25 ❑ 1955 Cover: 0.10 NM value: 22.00
26 ❑ 1956 Cover: 0.10 NM value: 22.00
27 ❑ Apr 1956 Cover: 0.10 NM value: 22.00
28 ❑ Jun 1956 Cover: 0.10 NM value: 22.00
29 ❑ Aug 1956 Cover: 0.10 NM value: 22.00

JEST — Harry A. Chesler

10 ❑ ca. 1944 Cover: 0.10 NM value: 100.00
11 ❑ ca. 1944 Cover: 0.10 NM value: 100.00

JESTER'S MOON, THE — One Shot Press

1 ❑ Aug 1996, b&w Cover: 0.99 NM value: 1.00
No issue number.

JESUS COMICS (FOOLBERT STURGEON'S...) — Rip Off

1 ❑ Cover: 0.50 NM value: 5.00
2 ❑ Cover: 0.50 NM value: 4.00
3 ❑ Cover: 0.50 NM value: 4.00
🕮 Jesus Joins the Academic Community; Craddock's Crusade, A Will Hatcher Adventure; Jesus Learns a Thing or Two; Jesus Goes to a Faculty Party A: Foolbert Sturgeon; Will Hatcher W: Foolbert Sturgeon; Will Hatcher

JET — Authority

1 ❑ Dec 1996 Cover: 2.95 NM value: Cover or less
A: Jonathan Hong W: Jonathan Hong

JET ACES — Fiction House

1 ❑ ca. 1952 Cover: 0.10 NM value: 90.00
2 ❑ ca. 1952 Cover: 0.10 NM value: 50.00
• CGC: 1 graded, best 9.0
3 ❑ ca. 1952 Cover: 0.10 NM value: 50.00
4 ❑ ca. 1952 Cover: 0.10 NM value: 50.00

JET BLACK — Monolith

1 ❑ Sep 1997 Cover: 2.50 NM value: Cover or less
★ Origin of Jet Black.

JET COMICS — Slave Labor / Amaze Ink

1 ❑ Oct 1997, b&w Cover: 2.95 NM value: Cover or less
🕮 From Out of the Blue A: Steven Martinez W: Josh Olson ★ Origin of Spectrum. ★ 1st Appearance of Spectrum, Alex Chambers.
2 ❑ Feb 1998, b&w Cover: 2.95 NM value: Cover or less
🕮 Whole Lot of Shakin' Goin' On! A: Steven Martinez W: Josh Olson
3 ❑ Mar 1998 Cover: 2.95 NM value: Cover or less
🕮 The Wet and the Wild! final issue. A: Steven Martinez W: Josh Olson

JET DREAM — Gold Key

1 ❑ Jun 1968 Cover: 0.12 NM value: 15.00
• CGC: 1 graded, best 9.2
Painted cover.

JET POWERS — Magazine Enterprises

1 ❑ Cover: 0.10 NM value: 225.00
2 ❑ Cover: 0.10 NM value: 175.00
3 ❑ ca. 1951 Cover: 0.10 NM value: 175.00
4 ❑ ca. 1951 Cover: 0.10 NM value: 175.00

JETSONS, THE (ARCHIE) — Archie

1 ❑ Sep 1995 Cover: 1.50 NM value: Cover or less
Circ: CapCity orders: 3,100
🕮 Journey Back Park; Johnny Space Cadet; Monkey Business; A Hard Dog's Day! ★ Appearance of The Flintstones.
2 ❑ Oct 1995 Cover: 1.50 NM value: Cover or less
Circ: CapCity orders: 1,925
3 ❑ Nov 1995 Cover: 1.50 NM value: Cover or less
4 ❑ Dec 1995 Cover: 1.50 NM value: Cover or less
5 ❑ Jan 1996 Cover: 1.50 NM value: Cover or less
6 ❑ Feb 1996 Cover: 1.50 NM value: Cover or less
7 ❑ Mar 1996 Cover: 1.50 NM value: Cover or less
8 ❑ Apr 1996 Cover: 1.50 NM value: Cover or less
9 ❑ May 1996 Cover: 1.50 NM value: Cover or less
10 ❑ Jun 1996 Cover: 1.50 NM value: Cover or less
11 ❑ Jul 1996 Cover: 1.50 NM value: Cover or less
12 ❑ Aug 1996 Cover: 1.50 NM value: Cover or less

JETSONS BIG BOOK, THE — Harvey

1 ❑ Nov 1992 Cover: 1.95 NM value: Cover or less
🕮 A Visit to Bedrock; Hijacked; Judy's Super Guy; From Tall to Small to Tall; Here, Kitty, Kitty; Astro the Genius; Sloppy but Nice; Rosey's Nervous Breakdown A: Ray Dirgo W: Gwen Krause
2 ❑ Apr 1993 Cover: 1.95 NM value: Cover or less
3 ❑ ca. 1993 Cover: 1.95 NM value: Cover or less

JETSONS, THE (CHARLTON) — Charlton

1 ❑ Nov 1970 Cover: 0.15 NM value: 35.00
2 ❑ Jan 1971 Cover: 0.15 NM value: 22.00
3 ❑ Mar 1971 Cover: 0.15 NM value: 14.00
4 ❑ May 1971 Cover: 0.15 NM value: 14.00
5 ❑ Jul 1971 Cover: 0.15 NM value: 14.00
6 ❑ Sep 1971 Cover: 0.15 NM value: 10.00
7 ❑ Nov 1971 Cover: 0.20 NM value: 10.00
8 ❑ Jan 1972 Cover: 0.20 NM value: 10.00
9 ❑ Mar 1972 Cover: 0.20 NM value: 10.00
10 ❑ May 1972 Cover: 0.20 NM value: 10.00
11 ❑ Jul 1972 Cover: 0.20 NM value: 7.00
12 ❑ Sep 1972 Cover: 0.20 NM value: 7.00
13 ❑ Nov 1972 Cover: 0.20 NM value: 7.00
14 ❑ Jan 1973 Cover: 0.20 NM value: 7.00
15 ❑ Feb 1973 Cover: 0.20 NM value: 7.00
16 ❑ Apr 1973 Cover: 0.20 NM value: 7.00
17 ❑ Jun 1973 Cover: 0.20 NM value: 7.00
18 ❑ Aug 1973 Cover: 0.20 NM value: 7.00
19 ❑ Oct 1973 Cover: 0.20 NM value: 7.00
20 ❑ Dec 1973 Cover: 0.20 NM value: 7.00

JETSONS GIANT SIZE — Harvey

1 ❑ Oct 1992 Cover: 2.25 NM value: 3.00
2 ❑ Mar 1993 Cover: 2.25 NM value: 2.50
3 ❑ ca. 1993 Cover: 2.25 NM value: 2.50

The prices seen above do not represent the highest possible prices seen in online auctions, but rather the prices we have seen these issues reliably fetch in a variety of environments (storefront retail, mail order, auction and convention).

CGC-graded: Multiply prices above by **33 for 9.9 M • 16 for 9.8 NM/M • 7 for 9.6 NM+ • 5 for 9.4 NM • 2.5 for 9.2 NM- • 1.5 for 9.0 VF/NM**

JETSONS, THE (GOLD KEY) — Gold Key

Hanna-Barbera's Jetsons series began as a primetime animated series in the 1960s, when Gold Key licensed the characters for its comic series.

Set in that nebulous future when everyone would be driving flying cars, living in ultra-highrises, having robotic help, and pushing a button to do all their work, the first family of the future found itself dealing with domestic situations not that far removed from their 20th century audience.

Gold Key was the series' first publisher before the license moved to Charlton and, later, to Harvey.
— Brent

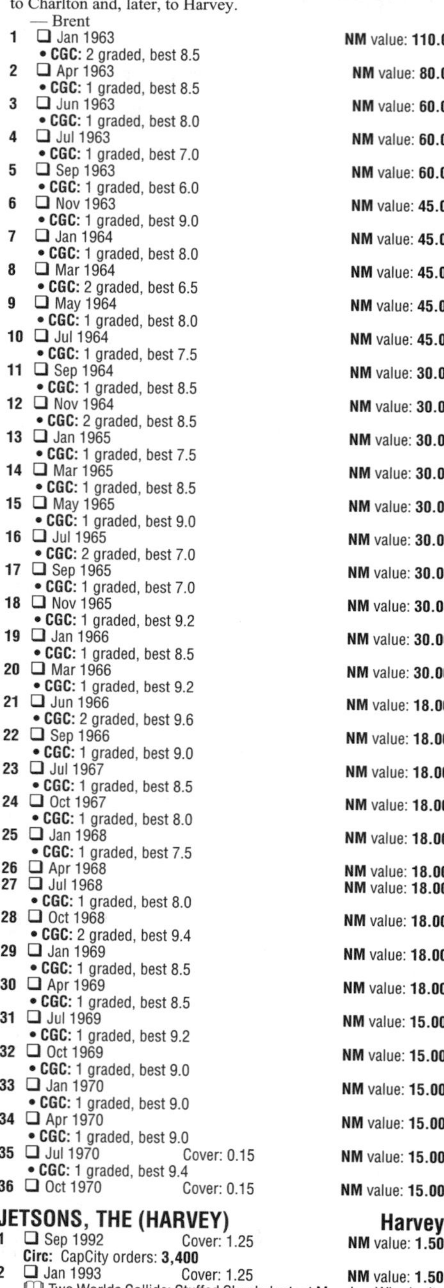

1 ❑ Jan 1963 — **NM** value: **110.00**
• **CGC:** 2 graded, best 8.5
2 ❑ Apr 1963 — **NM** value: **80.00**
• **CGC:** 1 graded, best 8.5
3 ❑ Jun 1963 — **NM** value: **60.00**
• **CGC:** 1 graded, best 8.0
4 ❑ Jul 1963 — **NM** value: **60.00**
• **CGC:** 1 graded, best 7.0
5 ❑ Sep 1963 — **NM** value: **60.00**
• **CGC:** 1 graded, best 6.0
6 ❑ Nov 1963 — **NM** value: **45.00**
• **CGC:** 1 graded, best 9.0
7 ❑ Jan 1964 — **NM** value: **45.00**
• **CGC:** 1 graded, best 8.0
8 ❑ Mar 1964 — **NM** value: **45.00**
• **CGC:** 2 graded, best 6.5
9 ❑ May 1964 — **NM** value: **45.00**
• **CGC:** 1 graded, best 8.0
10 ❑ Jul 1964 — **NM** value: **45.00**
• **CGC:** 1 graded, best 7.5
11 ❑ Sep 1964 — **NM** value: **30.00**
• **CGC:** 1 graded, best 8.5
12 ❑ Nov 1964 — **NM** value: **30.00**
• **CGC:** 2 graded, best 8.5
13 ❑ Jan 1965 — **NM** value: **30.00**
• **CGC:** 1 graded, best 7.5
14 ❑ Mar 1965 — **NM** value: **30.00**
• **CGC:** 1 graded, best 8.5
15 ❑ May 1965 — **NM** value: **30.00**
• **CGC:** 1 graded, best 9.0
16 ❑ Jul 1965 — **NM** value: **30.00**
• **CGC:** 2 graded, best 7.0
17 ❑ Sep 1965 — **NM** value: **30.00**
• **CGC:** 1 graded, best 7.0
18 ❑ Nov 1965 — **NM** value: **30.00**
• **CGC:** 1 graded, best 9.2
19 ❑ Jan 1966 — **NM** value: **30.00**
• **CGC:** 1 graded, best 8.5
20 ❑ Mar 1966 — **NM** value: **30.00**
• **CGC:** 1 graded, best 9.2
21 ❑ Jun 1966 — **NM** value: **18.00**
• **CGC:** 2 graded, best 9.6
22 ❑ Sep 1966 — **NM** value: **18.00**
• **CGC:** 1 graded, best 9.0
23 ❑ Jul 1967 — **NM** value: **18.00**
• **CGC:** 1 graded, best 8.5
24 ❑ Oct 1967 — **NM** value: **18.00**
• **CGC:** 1 graded, best 8.0
25 ❑ Jan 1968 — **NM** value: **18.00**
• **CGC:** 1 graded, best 7.5
26 ❑ Apr 1968 — **NM** value: **18.00**
27 ❑ Jul 1968 — **NM** value: **18.00**
• **CGC:** 1 graded, best 8.0
28 ❑ Oct 1968 — **NM** value: **18.00**
• **CGC:** 2 graded, best 9.4
29 ❑ Jan 1969 — **NM** value: **18.00**
• **CGC:** 1 graded, best 8.5
30 ❑ Apr 1969 — **NM** value: **18.00**
• **CGC:** 1 graded, best 8.5
31 ❑ Jul 1969 — **NM** value: **15.00**
• **CGC:** 1 graded, best 9.2
32 ❑ Oct 1969 — **NM** value: **15.00**
• **CGC:** 1 graded, best 9.0
33 ❑ Jan 1970 — **NM** value: **15.00**
• **CGC:** 1 graded, best 9.0
34 ❑ Apr 1970 — **NM** value: **15.00**
• **CGC:** 1 graded, best 9.0
35 ❑ Jul 1970 — Cover: 0.15 — **NM** value: **15.00**
• **CGC:** 1 graded, best 9.4
36 ❑ Oct 1970 — Cover: 0.15 — **NM** value: **15.00**

JETSONS, THE (HARVEY) — Harvey

1 ❑ Sep 1992 — Cover: 1.25 — **NM** value: **1.50**
Circ: CapCity orders: **3,400**
2 ❑ Jan 1993 — Cover: 1.25 — **NM** value: **1.50**
📖 Two Worlds Collide; Stuffed Skunk; Instant Muscles; Whodunit; A Stich'n Time; Derby Day; Zap Dispose-All; The Go-Go Plant; **A:** Ray Dirgo **W:** Gwen Krause
3 ❑ May 1993 — Cover: 1.25 — **NM** value: **1.50**
4 ❑ Sep 1993 — Cover: 1.25 — **NM** value: **1.50**
5 ❑ Nov 1993 — Cover: 1.50 — **NM** value: **Cover or less**

JETTA OF THE 21ST CENTURY — Standard

5 ❑ Dec 1952 — Cover: 0.10 — **NM** value: **150.00**
6 ❑ Feb 1953 — Cover: 0.10 — **NM** value: **100.00**
7 ❑ Apr 1953 — Cover: 0.10 — **NM** value: **100.00**

JET (WILDSTORM) — DC / Wildstorm

1 ❑ Nov 2000 — Cover: 2.50 — **NM** value: **Cover or less**
Circ: Diamd. preorders: **13,038**
📖 Midnight 2 Midnight, Part 1 **A:** Dustin Nguyen **W:** Andy Lanning; Dan Abnett
2 ❑ Dec 2000 — Cover: 2.50 — **NM** value: **Cover or less**
Circ: Diamd. preorders: **9,473**
📖 Midnight 2 Midnight, Part 2 **A:** Dustin Nguyen **W:** Andy Lanning; Dan Abnett
3 ❑ Jan 2001 — Cover: 2.50 — **NM** value: **Cover or less**
Circ: Diamd. preorders: **9,155**
📖 Midnight 2 Midnight, Part 3 **A:** Dustin Nguyen **W:** Andy Lanning; Dan Abnett
4 ❑ Feb 2001 — Cover: 2.50 — **NM** value: **Cover or less**
Circ: Diamd. preorders: **8,551**
📖 Crimes and Mr. Meaner **A:** Dustin Nguyen **W:** Andy Lanning; Dan Abnett

JEW IN COMMUNIST PRAGUE, A — NBM

1 ❑ — Cover: 11.95 — **NM** value: **Cover or less**
• oversized graphic novel.
2 ❑ — Cover: 11.95 — **NM** value: **Cover or less**
• oversized graphic novel.

JEZEBEL JADE — Comico

1 ❑ Oct 1988 — Cover: 2.00 — **NM** value: **Cover or less**
Circ: CapCity orders: **5,225**
wraparound cover. 📖 The Bones of Galahad **A:** Adam Kubert **C:** Adam Kubert **W:** William Messner-Loebs
2 ❑ Nov 1988 — Cover: 2.00 — **NM** value: **Cover or less**
Circ: CapCity orders: **4,525**
wraparound cover. **A:** Adam Kubert **C:** Adam Kubert **W:** William Messner-Loebs
3 ❑ Dec 1988 — Cover: 2.00 — **NM** value: **Cover or less**
Circ: CapCity orders: **4,625**
wraparound cover. **A:** Adam Kubert **C:** Adam Kubert **W:** William Messner-Loebs

JEZEBELLE — WildStorm

1/A ❑ Mar 2001 — Cover: 2.50 — **NM** value: **Cover or less**
Circ: Diamd. preorders: **13,801**
Woman leaping backward on cover, two hands with energy glow. **A:** Steve Ellis **W:** Ben Raab
1/B ❑ Mar 2001 — Cover: 2.50 — **NM** value: **Cover or less**
Woman standing on cover, one hand in energy ball. **A:** Steve Ellis **W:** Ben Raab
2 ❑ Apr 2001 — Cover: 2.50 — **NM** value: **Cover or less**
Circ: Diamd. preorders: **10,127**
A: Steve Ellis **W:** Ben Raab
3 ❑ May 2001 — Cover: 2.50 — **NM** value: **Cover or less**
Circ: Diamd. preorders: **7,949**
A: Steve Ellis **W:** Ben Raab
4 ❑ Jun 2001 — Cover: 2.50 — **NM** value: **Cover or less**
Circ: Diamd. preorders: **6,505**
A: Steve Ellis **W:** Ben Raab
5 ❑ Jul 2001 — Cover: 2.50 — **NM** value: **Cover or less**
Circ: Diamd. preorders: **5,511**
A: Steve Ellis **W:** Ben Raab
6 ❑ Aug 2001 — Cover: 2.50 — **NM** value: **Cover or less**
Circ: Diamd. preorders: **5,163**
A: Steve Ellis **W:** Ben Raab

JFK ASSASSINATION — Zone

1 ❑ — Cover: 2.95 — **NM** value: **Cover or less**
📖 Frame 313 **A:** Wayne Reid **W:** Jack Herman; Karen Herman

JHEREG — Marvel / Epic

1 ❑ — Cover: 8.95 — **NM** value: **Cover or less**
Circ: CapCity orders: **2,000**
A: John Pierard **W:** Alan Zelenetz; Steven Brust

JIGABOO DEVIL — Millennium

0 ❑ b&w — Cover: 2.95 — **NM** value: **Cover or less**

JIGGS IS BACK — Celtic

1 ❑ — Cover: 12.95 — **NM** value: **Cover or less**
A: George McManus **W:** George McManus; Bill Blackbeard; William Kennedy

JIGSAW — Harvey

Col. Gary Jason is on an orbital mission, photographing stars from space, when his craft is sucked into a strange magnetic vortex. Although he tries to escape, a fossilized tree (yes, a tree) is also caught in the vortex and spears his ship. Jason is pulled out of his ship and flies into the source of the vortex, an alien base on the Moon. The aliens regret their inadvertent capture of Jason, and rebuild his shattered body using special elastic materials to reconnect most of his joints. But the result is uneven, leaving him a virtual jigsaw puzzle.

Jason discovers that these alterations gave him super strength, as well as the ability to stretch his limbs to incredible lengths. These powers let him do everything from rounding up circus animals to saving Earth from aliens. Unfortunately, they can't save this series from its outrageous premise.

1 ❑ Sep 1966 — Cover: 0.12 — **NM** value: **12.00**
• **CGC:** 1 graded, best 9.0
📖 A Nightmare In Space! ★ Origin of Jigsaw (Harvey). ★ 1st Appearance of Jigsaw (Harvey).
2 ❑ — Cover: 0.12 — **NM** value: **7.00**

JIMBO — Bongo / Zongo

All issues are adults only.

1 ❑ b&w — Cover: 2.95 — **NM** value: **Cover or less**
Circ: CapCity orders: **3,825**
A: Gary Panter **W:** Gary Panter
2 ❑ b&w — Cover: 2.95 — **NM** value: **Cover or less**
A: Gary Panter **W:** Gary Panter
3 ❑ — Cover: 2.95 — **NM** value: **Cover or less**
• indicia says #2 **A:** Gary Panter **W:** Gary Panter
4 ❑ b&w — Cover: 2.95 — **NM** value: **Cover or less**
• no indicia **A:** Gary Panter **W:** Gary Panter
5 ❑ — Cover: 2.95 — **NM** value: **Cover or less**
A: Gary Panter **W:** Gary Panter
6 ❑ — Cover: 2.95 — **NM** value: **Cover or less**
A: Gary Panter **W:** Gary Panter
7 ❑ — Cover: 2.95 — **NM** value: **Cover or less**
A: Gary Panter **W:** Gary Panter

JIM DANDY — Lev Gleason

1 ❑ May 1956 — Cover: 0.10 — **NM** value: **40.00**
2 ❑ Jul 1956 — Cover: 0.10 — **NM** value: **25.00**
3 ❑ Sep 1956 — Cover: 0.10 — **NM** value: **25.00**

JIM HARDY — United Feature

1 ❑ ca. 1944 — Cover: 0.25 — **NM** value: **300.00**

JIMMY DURANTE — Magazine Enterprises

1 ❑ Win 1948 — Cover: 0.10 — **NM** value: **350.00**
2 ❑ Win 1948 — Cover: 0.10 — **NM** value: **350.00**
• **CGC:** 1 graded, best 9.6

JIMMY WAKELY — DC

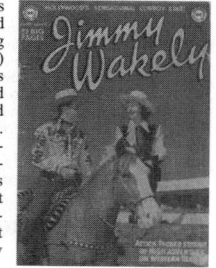

Jimmy Wakely (1914-1982) was another in the classic movie mold of the singing cowboy, appearing (like Roy Rogers and Gene Autry) as "himself" in stories in which his character would become involved in an assortment of adventures and take time out to sing now and then. By 1949, he'd appeared in something like 50 films and had even appeared on the photo cover of DC's Romance Trail #1 — and the first few issues of Jimmy Wakely Comics had photo covers, as well. But that was the last big year of Wakely films.

As with other Western comics of the day, the promise to readers was that there'd be action-packed stories, lots of horses, and a popular performer's new adventures.
— Maggie

1 ❑ Sep 1949 — Cover: 0.10 — **NM** value: **800.00**
• **CGC:** 1 graded, best 9.4
2 ❑ Nov 1949 — Cover: 0.10 — **NM** value: **600.00**
• **CGC:** 1 graded, best 9.4
3 ❑ Jan 1950 — Cover: 0.10 — **NM** value: **550.00**
• **CGC:** 1 graded, best 7.0
4 ❑ Mar 1950 — Cover: 0.10 — **NM** value: **500.00**
5 ❑ May 1950 — Cover: 0.10 — **NM** value: **500.00**
• **CGC:** 1 graded, best 9.6
6 ❑ Jul 1950 — Cover: 0.10 — **NM** value: **500.00**
• **CGC:** 1 graded, best 7.5
7 ❑ Sep 1950 — Cover: 0.10 — **NM** value: **450.00**
8 ❑ Nov 1950 — Cover: 0.10 — **NM** value: **450.00**
9 ❑ Jan 1951 — Cover: 0.10 — **NM** value: **400.00**
10 ❑ Mar 1951 — Cover: 0.10 — **NM** value: **400.00**
11 ❑ May 1951 — Cover: 0.10 — **NM** value: **350.00**
12 ❑ Jul 1951 — Cover: 0.10 — **NM** value: **350.00**
13 ❑ Sep 1951 — Cover: 0.10 — **NM** value: **300.00**
• **CGC:** 1 graded, best 6.0
14 ❑ Nov 1951 — Cover: 0.10 — **NM** value: **300.00**
15 ❑ Jan 1952 — Cover: 0.10 — **NM** value: **300.00**
16 ❑ Mar 1952 — Cover: 0.10 — **NM** value: **250.00**
• **CGC:** 1 graded, best 6.0
17 ❑ May 1952 — Cover: 0.10 — **NM** value: **250.00**
• **CGC:** 1 graded, best 7.0
18 ❑ Jul 1952 — Cover: 0.10 — **NM** value: **250.00**

JIM RAY'S AVIATION SKETCHBOOK — Vital Publications

1 ❑ Feb 1946 — Cover: 0.15 — **NM** value: **275.00**
• **CGC:** 1 graded, best 9.2
2 ❑ May 1946 — Cover: 0.15 — **NM** value: **200.00**

JIM (VOL. 1) — Fantagraphics

1 ❑ — Cover: 2.95 — **NM** value: **10.00**
A: Jim Woodring **W:** Jim Woodring
2 ❑ — Cover: 2.95 — **NM** value: **7.00**
A: Jim Woodring **W:** Jim Woodring
3 ❑ — Cover: 2.95 — **NM** value: **5.00**
A: Jim Woodring **W:** Jim Woodring
4 ❑ — Cover: 2.95 — **NM** value: **5.00**
A: Jim Woodring **W:** Jim Woodring
Bk 1 ❑ — Cover: 17.95 — **NM** value: **Cover or less**
• The Book of Jim **A:** Jim Woodring **W:** Jim Woodring

JIM (VOL. 2) — Fantagraphics

1 ❑ Dec 1993, b&w — Cover: 2.95 — **NM** value: **6.00**
📖 Manhog Beyond The Face **A:** Jim Woodring **W:** Jim Woodring
2 ❑ b&w — Cover: 2.95 — **NM** value: **4.00**
A: Jim Woodring **W:** Jim Woodring
3 ❑ b&w — Cover: 2.95 — **NM** value: **4.00**
A: Jim Woodring **W:** Jim Woodring
4 ❑ b&w — Cover: 2.95 — **NM** value: **3.00**

Other grades: Multiply prices above by **1.5 for Mint • 2/3 for Very Fine • 1/3 for Fine • 1/5 for Very Good • 1/8 for Good**

A: Jim Woodring **W:** Jim Woodring
5 ❑ b&w Cover: 3.50 **NM** value: **Cover or less**
A: Jim Woodring **W:** Jim Woodring
6 ❑ May 1996, b&w Cover: 3.50 **NM** value: **Cover or less**
A: Jim Woodring **W:** Jim Woodring
SE 1❑ Cover: 3.95 **NM** value: **4.00**
• Frank's Real Pa Special Edition. **A:** Jim Woodring **W:** Jim Woodring

JINGLE BELLE — Oni

1 ❑ Nov 1999, b&w Cover: 2.95 **NM** value: **Cover or less**
Circ: Diamd. preorders: **7,168**
2 ❑ Dec 1999, b&w Cover: 2.95 **NM** value: **Cover or less**
Circ: Diamd. preorders: **5,725**
Bk 1❑ Oct 2000, b&w and colorCover: 8.95 **NM** value: **Cover or less**
• Trade Paperback. 📖 Miserable on 34th Street; Santa's Little Hellion; Sanity Clauses; Little Matchstick Girl; Jingle Belle Conquers the Martians • collects #1 and #2, plus story from Oni Double Feature #13, plus new color story **A:** Stephen DeStefano; Barry Caldwell; Lawrence Marvit **W:** Paul Dini

JINGLE BELLE'S ALL-STAR HOLIDAY HULLABALOO — Oni

1 ❑ Nov 2000, b&w Cover: 4.95 **NM** value: **Cover or less**
Circ: Diamd. preorders: **6,148**
📖 A Carol's Christmas, That Olde Christmas Spirit, Visions of Sugar Plums, Blue Belles, Belles' Belles, Coal Comfort **A:** Sergio Aragonés; Stephen DeStefano; Bill Morrison; J. Bone; Jeff Smith; Chynna Clugston-Major; Shane Glines **C:** Frank Cho **W:** Sergio Aragonés; Bill Morrison; Chynna Clugston-Major; Shane Glines; Paul Dini

JINGLE JANGLE COMICS — Eastern Color

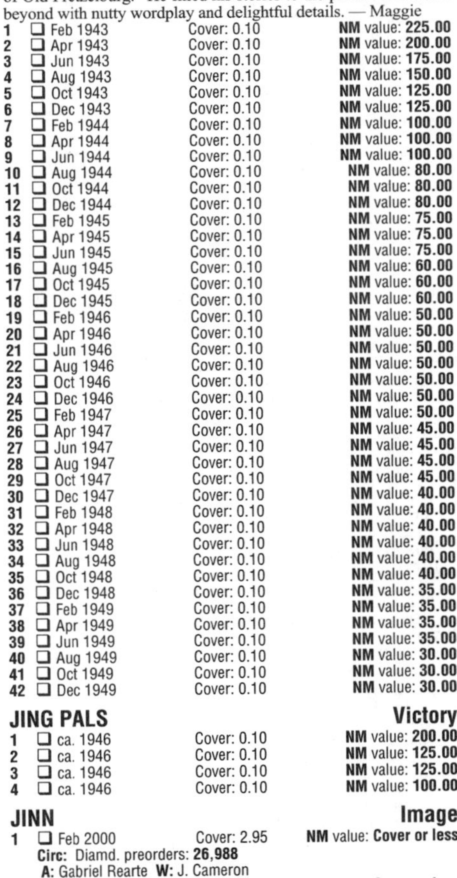

Although there were many characters by an assortment of creators (such as Nostalgia Press' Woody Gelman) featured in their own comedy short stories in Jingle Jangle Comics, the reason the series has drawn much attention from collectors is that it contained the off-the-wall cartooning of George Carlson (1887-1962). Although he was also a "serious" artist (he painted the cover for the first book release of Gone with the Wind), Carlson's comic-book work was goofy fantasy. His two classic features for Jingle Jangle Comics (a name he apparently originated) were "Jingle Jangle Tales" and "The Pie-Face Prince of Old Pretzelburg." He filled his stories to the panel borders and beyond with nutty wordplay and delightful details. — Maggie

1 ❑ Feb 1943 Cover: 0.10 **NM** value: **225.00**
2 ❑ Apr 1943 Cover: 0.10 **NM** value: **200.00**
3 ❑ Jun 1943 Cover: 0.10 **NM** value: **175.00**
4 ❑ Aug 1943 Cover: 0.10 **NM** value: **150.00**
5 ❑ Oct 1943 Cover: 0.10 **NM** value: **125.00**
6 ❑ Dec 1943 Cover: 0.10 **NM** value: **125.00**
7 ❑ Feb 1944 Cover: 0.10 **NM** value: **100.00**
8 ❑ Apr 1944 Cover: 0.10 **NM** value: **100.00**
9 ❑ Jun 1944 Cover: 0.10 **NM** value: **100.00**
10 ❑ Aug 1944 Cover: 0.10 **NM** value: **80.00**
11 ❑ Oct 1944 Cover: 0.10 **NM** value: **80.00**
12 ❑ Dec 1944 Cover: 0.10 **NM** value: **80.00**
13 ❑ Feb 1945 Cover: 0.10 **NM** value: **75.00**
14 ❑ Apr 1945 Cover: 0.10 **NM** value: **75.00**
15 ❑ Jun 1945 Cover: 0.10 **NM** value: **75.00**
16 ❑ Aug 1945 Cover: 0.10 **NM** value: **60.00**
17 ❑ Oct 1945 Cover: 0.10 **NM** value: **60.00**
18 ❑ Dec 1945 Cover: 0.10 **NM** value: **60.00**
19 ❑ Feb 1946 Cover: 0.10 **NM** value: **50.00**
20 ❑ Apr 1946 Cover: 0.10 **NM** value: **50.00**
21 ❑ Jun 1946 Cover: 0.10 **NM** value: **50.00**
22 ❑ Aug 1946 Cover: 0.10 **NM** value: **50.00**
23 ❑ Oct 1946 Cover: 0.10 **NM** value: **50.00**
24 ❑ Dec 1946 Cover: 0.10 **NM** value: **50.00**
25 ❑ Feb 1947 Cover: 0.10 **NM** value: **50.00**
26 ❑ Apr 1947 Cover: 0.10 **NM** value: **45.00**
27 ❑ Jun 1947 Cover: 0.10 **NM** value: **45.00**
28 ❑ Aug 1947 Cover: 0.10 **NM** value: **45.00**
29 ❑ Oct 1947 Cover: 0.10 **NM** value: **45.00**
30 ❑ Dec 1947 Cover: 0.10 **NM** value: **40.00**
31 ❑ Feb 1948 Cover: 0.10 **NM** value: **40.00**
32 ❑ Apr 1948 Cover: 0.10 **NM** value: **40.00**
33 ❑ Jun 1948 Cover: 0.10 **NM** value: **40.00**
34 ❑ Aug 1948 Cover: 0.10 **NM** value: **40.00**
35 ❑ Oct 1948 Cover: 0.10 **NM** value: **40.00**
36 ❑ Dec 1948 Cover: 0.10 **NM** value: **35.00**
37 ❑ Feb 1949 Cover: 0.10 **NM** value: **35.00**
38 ❑ Apr 1949 Cover: 0.10 **NM** value: **35.00**
39 ❑ Jun 1949 Cover: 0.10 **NM** value: **35.00**
40 ❑ Aug 1949 Cover: 0.10 **NM** value: **30.00**
41 ❑ Oct 1949 Cover: 0.10 **NM** value: **30.00**
42 ❑ Dec 1949 Cover: 0.10 **NM** value: **30.00**

JING PALS — Victory

1 ❑ ca. 1946 Cover: 0.10 **NM** value: **200.00**
2 ❑ ca. 1946 Cover: 0.10 **NM** value: **125.00**
3 ❑ ca. 1946 Cover: 0.10 **NM** value: **125.00**
4 ❑ ca. 1946 Cover: 0.10 **NM** value: **100.00**

JINN — Image

1 ❑ Feb 2000 Cover: 2.95 **NM** value: **Cover or less**
Circ: Diamd. preorders: **26,988**
A: Gabriel Rearte **W:** J. Cameron
2 ❑ May 2000 Cover: 2.95 **NM** value: **Cover or less**
Circ: Diamd. preorders: **22,075**
A: Gabriel Rearte **W:** J. Cameron
3 ❑ Oct 2000 Cover: 2.95 **NM** value: **Cover or less**
Circ: Diamd. preorders: **15,604**
A: Gabriel Rearte **W:** J. Cameron

JINX — Caliber

Brian Michael Bendis has become one of those comic-book creators whose name attached to a project means increased interest and higher pre-orders. Jinx was one of his earliest projects, a series devoted to the title character, Jinx Alameda, a female bounty hunter in Cleveland. She's beautiful, she's tough, and she hunts people for money. Bendis not only wrote Jinx; he drew it, using models and lots of photo reference. Readers will find him experimenting with many story-telling devices to tell a compelling thriller in this early stage of his career. The series has traditional "noir" overtones and tells a complete story, with beginning, middle, and end. Crime-novel buffs are in for a treat. — Maggie

1 ❑ b&w Cover: 2.95 **NM** value: **3.50**
• Caliber publishes **A:** Brian Michael Bendis **W:** Brian Michael Bendis
2 ❑ b&w Cover: 2.95 **NM** value: **3.00**
📖 Jinx Meets Goldfish **A:** Brian Michael Bendis **W:** Brian Michael Bendis
3 ❑ b&w Cover: 2.95 **NM** value: **3.00**
📖 Goldfish and Jinx Go on a Date **A:** Brian Michael Bendis **W:** Brian Michael Bendis
4 ❑ b&w Cover: 2.95 **NM** value: **3.00**
📖 The Treasure **A:** Brian Michael Bendis **W:** Brian Michael Bendis
5 ❑ Nov 1996, b&w Cover: 2.95 **NM** value: **3.00**
📖 The Confession **A:** Brian Michael Bendis **W:** Brian Michael Bendis
6 ❑ b&w Cover: 2.95 **NM** value: **3.00**
📖 Jinx and Goldfish Team Up • series moves to Image **A:** Brian Michael Bendis **W:** Brian Michael Bendis
7 ❑ Cover: 2.95 **NM** value: **3.00**
📖 Jinx to the Rescue **A:** Brian Michael Bendis **W:** Brian Michael Bendis
8 ❑ Cover: 4.95 **NM** value: **Cover or less**
• Charity Special **A:** Brian Michael Bendis **W:** Brian Michael Bendis
9 ❑ Cover: 4.95 **NM** value: **Cover or less**
• Homeless Edition. **A:** Brian Michael Bendis **W:** Brian Michael Bendis
10 ❑ b&w Cover: 2.95 **NM** value: **Cover or less**
• Image publishes **A:** Brian Michael Bendis **W:** Brian Michael Bendis
11 ❑ b&w Cover: 2.95 **NM** value: **Cover or less**
A: Brian Michael Bendis **W:** Brian Michael Bendis
12 ❑ Cover: 3.95 **NM** value: **Cover or less**
📖 Stoplights; David Hasselhoff; Everyday of Her Life for a Whole Year; Bad Boys; Sex and Tofrutti; Family Shit; Yaaaahhoohooy **A:** Brian Michael Bendis **W:** Brian Michael Bendis
13 ❑ b&w Cover: 2.95 **NM** value: **3.95**
📖 Follically Challenged; Low Blood Sugar; Sakru; Here's the Deal… **A:** Brian Michael Bendis **W:** Brian Michael Bendis
14 ❑ b&w Cover: 3.95 **NM** value: **Cover or less**
📖 Pitch the Bagel **A:** Brian Michael Bendis **W:** Brian Michael Bendis
15 ❑ Cover: 3.95 **NM** value: **Cover or less**
📖 Borderland; The Kiss Off; Better Living Through Chemistry; Nowheresville; **A:** Brian Michael Bendis **W:** Brian Michael Bendis
16 ❑ Cover: 3.95 **NM** value: **Cover or less**
• Torso **A:** Brian Michael Bendis **W:** Brian Michael Bendis
17 ❑ Cover: 3.95 **NM** value: **Cover or less**
• Torso **A:** Brian Michael Bendis **W:** Brian Michael Bendis
18 ❑ Cover: 2.95 **NM** value: **Cover or less**
• Fire **A:** Brian Michael Bendis **W:** Brian Michael Bendis
19 ❑ Cover: 2.95 **NM** value: **Cover or less**
📖 Defining Moments in Bendis History; A Day in the Life of…a Howard Stern Fan; Another Brian Michael Bendis Celebrity Cameo; Borderland; John Glen • Buried Treasures **A:** Brian Michael Bendis **W:** Brian Michael Bendis; Warren Ellis; Mark Ricketts; Anne Gordon; James D. Hudnall
20 ❑ b&w Cover: 3.95 **NM** value: **Cover or less**
📖 Superman is Dead; Mike; Mall Outing; Brothers and Sisters; Buffalo Chips; Everything You Wanted to Know about Poison Elves Creator Drew Hayes but… (text); Mike (Again); Detroit; Jen; Smokies; Roland; McLife Lessons • True Crime Confessions **A:** Brian Michael Bendis; Michael Avon Oeming **W:** Brian Michael Bendis
21 ❑ Cover: 3.95 **NM** value: **Cover or less**
• Torso **A:** Brian Michael Bendis; Michael Avon Oeming **W:** Brian Michael Bendis
Bk 1❑ b&w Cover: 17.95 **NM** value: **Cover or less**
• collects complete series; Jinx: Essential Collection
Bk 2❑ b&w Cover: 10.95 **NM** value: **Cover or less**
• collects first few issues of Caliber series

JINX POP CULTURE HOO-HAH, THE — Image

1 ❑ b&w Cover: 3.95 **NM** value: **Cover or less**
No issue number. One-shot. 📖 I Married A Sci-Fi-Geek; A Day in the Life of A Film Geek **A:** Brian Michael Bendis **W:** Brian Michael Bendis

JIZZ — Fantagraphics

All issues are adults only.

1 ❑ b&w Cover: 2.00 **NM** value: **Cover or less**
2 ❑ b&w Cover: 2.00 **NM** value: **Cover or less**
3 ❑ b&w Cover: 2.00 **NM** value: **Cover or less**
4 ❑ b&w Cover: 2.00 **NM** value: **Cover or less**
5 ❑ Cover: 2.25 **NM** value: **Cover or less**
6 ❑ Cover: 2.25 **NM** value: **Cover or less**
7 ❑ Cover: 2.25 **NM** value: **Cover or less**
8 ❑ Cover: 2.50 **NM** value: **Cover or less**
9 ❑ Cover: 2.95 **NM** value: **Cover or less**
10 ❑ b&w Cover: 2.50 **NM** value: **Cover or less**

JLA — DC

Grant Morrison breathed new life into the Justice League with this acclaimed series. Since their first appearance as a team in The Brave and the Bold #28, the Justice League of America has been the premier group of super-heroes in DC's stable. The team has been through many changes during the years, including a reorganization into several groups, including Justice League Europe and a Justice League Task Force to handle more covert operations.

Legends on their own — heroes like Superman, Wonder Woman, Green Lantern, and others have often recognized the need to band together against forces too powerful for any one super-hero to defeat. But although their names and costumes have been associated with the League for more than 40 years, the current versions of these characters had never appeared together before, thanks to the continuity-altering effects of such series as Crisis On Infinite Earths and Zero Hour.

1 ❑ Jan 1997 Cover: 1.95 **NM** value: **12.00**
Circ: Diamd. preorders: **104,486** • **CGC:** 87 graded, best 9.9
📖 Them! • Superman, Batman, Flash, Wonder Woman, Green Lantern, Martian Manhunter, Aquaman team **A:** Howard Porter **W:** Grant Morrison
2 ❑ Feb 1997 Cover: 1.95 **NM** value: **10.00**
Circ: Diamd. preorders: **74,517** • **CGC:** 19 graded, best 9.8
A: Howard Porter **W:** Grant Morrison
3 ❑ Mar 1997 Cover: 1.95 **NM** value: **8.00**
Circ: Diamd. preorders: **78,393** • **CGC:** 7 graded, best 9.8
A: Howard Porter **W:** Grant Morrison
4 ❑ Apr 1997 Cover: 1.95 **NM** value: **6.00**
Circ: Diamd. preorders: **81,477** • **CGC:** 7 graded, best 9.6
A: Howard Porter **W:** Grant Morrison
5 ❑ May 1997 Cover: 1.95 **NM** value: **5.00**
Circ: Diamd. preorders: **87,637**
• Membership drive **A:** Howard Porter **W:** Grant Morrison ★ Versus Prof. Ivo. ★ Versus T.O. Morrow.
6 ❑ Jun 1997 Cover: 1.95 **NM** value: **4.00**
Circ: Diamd. preorders: **98,818**
📖 Fire in the Sky **A:** Howard Porter **W:** Grant Morrison ★ 1st Appearance of Zauriel. ★ Appearance of Neron, Ghast, Abnegazar.
7 ❑ Jul 1997 Cover: 1.95 **NM** value: **3.00**
Circ: Diamd. preorders: **103,498**
W: Grant Morrison
8 ❑ Aug 1997 Cover: 1.95 **NM** value: **3.00**
Circ: Diamd. preorders: **104,030**
W: Grant Morrison ★ Versus Key.
9 ❑ Sep 1997 Cover: 1.95 **NM** value: **3.00**
Circ: Diamd. preorders: **104,403**
W: Grant Morrison ★ Versus Key.
10 ❑ Oct 1997 Cover: 1.95 **NM** value: **3.00**
Circ: Diamd. preorders: **104,947**
📖 Rock of Ages, Part 1 **W:** Grant Morrison ★ Versus New Injustice Gang.
11 ❑ Nov 1997 Cover: 1.95 **NM** value: **2.50**
Circ: Diamd. preorders: **104,675**
📖 Rock of Ages, Part 2 **W:** Grant Morrison
12 ❑ Dec 1997 Cover: 1.95 **NM** value: **2.50**
Circ: Diamd. preorders: **107,015**
📖 Rock of Ages, Part 3 **A:** Howard Porter **W:** Grant Morrison
13 ❑ Dec 1997 Cover: 1.95 **NM** value: **2.50**
Circ: Diamd. preorders: **111,217**
Face cover. 📖 Rock of Ages, Part 4 • Aquaman, Green Lantern, and Flash in future **A:** Howard Porter **W:** Grant Morrison
14 ❑ Jan 1998 Cover: 1.95 **NM** value: **2.50**
Circ: Diamd. preorders: **111,425**
📖 Rock of Ages, Part 5 **W:** Grant Morrison
15 ❑ Feb 1998 Cover: 2.95 **NM** value: **Cover or less**
Circ: Diamd. preorders: **109,107**
• Giant-size. 📖 Rock of Ages, Part 6 **W:** Grant Morrison
16 ❑ Mar 1998 Cover: 1.95 **NM** value: **2.00**
Circ: Diamd. preorders: **108,920**
📖 Camelot • Watchtower blueprints **A:** Howard Porter **W:** Grant Morrison ★ Versus Prometheus.
17 ❑ Apr 1998 Cover: 1.95 **NM** value: **2.00**
Circ: Diamd. preorders: **101,430**
W: Grant Morrison ★ Versus Prometheus.
18 ❑ May 1998 Cover: 1.95 **NM** value: **2.00**
Circ: Diamd. preorders: **101,547**
W: Grant Morrison ★ 1st Appearance of Julian September.
19 ❑ Jun 1998 Cover: 1.95 **NM** value: **2.00**
Circ: Diamd. preorders: **104,211**
★ Appearance of Atom.
20 ❑ Jul 1998 Cover: 1.95 **NM** value: **2.00**
Circ: Diamd. preorders: **99,895**
★ Versus Adam Strange.
21 ❑ Aug 1998 Cover: 1.95 **NM** value: **2.00**
Circ: Diamd. preorders: **99,983**
★ Appearance of Aleaa. ★ Versus Adam Strange.
22 ❑ Sep 1998 Cover: 1.99 **NM** value: **2.00**
Circ: Diamd. preorders: **97,296**
★ Appearance of Daniel (Sandman).
23 ❑ Oct 1998 Cover: 1.99 **NM** value: **2.00**
Circ: Diamd. preorders: **95,255**
★ Appearance of Daniel. ★ Versus Star Conqueror.
24 ❑ Dec 1998 Cover: 1.99 **NM** value: **2.00**
Circ: Diamd. preorders: **93,195**
📖 Ultra-Marines Saga, Part 1 ★ 1st Appearance of Ultramarine Corps.

CGC-graded: Multiply prices above by **33 for 9.9 M • 16 for 9.8 NM/M • 7 for 9.6 NM+ • 5 for 9.4 NM • 2.5 for 9.2 NM- • 1.5 for 9.0 VF/NM**

25 ❑ Jan 1999 Cover: 1.99 **NM** value: **2.00**
Circ: Diamd. preorders: **92,178**
Ultra-Marines Saga, Part 2 ★ Versus Ultramarine Corps.
26 ❑ Feb 1999 Cover: 1.99 **NM** value: **2.00**
Circ: Diamd. preorders: **89,254**
Ultra-Marines Saga, Part 3 **W:** Grant Morrison ★ Appearance of Ultra-Marines, Shaggy Man. ★ Versus Shaggy Man.
27 ❑ Mar 1999 Cover: 1.99 **NM** value: **2.00**
Circ: Diamd. preorders: **89,882**
A: Howard Porter **W:** Grant Morrison ★ Appearance of Justice Society of America. ★ Versus Amazo.
28 ❑ Apr 1999 Cover: 1.99 **NM** value: **2.00**
Circ: Diamd. preorders: **85,615**
Crisis Times Five, Part 1 **A:** Howard Porter **W:** Grant Morrison ★ Appearance of Justice Society of America, Triumph.
29 ❑ May 1999 Cover: 1.99 **NM** value: **2.00**
Circ: Diamd. preorders: **85,997**
Crisis Times Five, Part 2 **A:** Howard Porter; Joe Staton **W:** Joe Staton; Grant Morrison ★ Appearance of Justice Society of America, Captain Marvel.
30 ❑ Jun 1999 Cover: 1.99 **NM** value: **2.00**
Circ: Diamd. preorders: **87,952**
Crisis Times Five, Part 3 **A:** Howard Porter **W:** Grant Morrison ★ Appearance of Justice Society of America.
31 ❑ Jul 1999 Cover: 1.99 **NM** value: **2.00**
Circ: Diamd. preorders: **86,456**
Crisis Times Five, Part 4 **A:** Howard Porter **W:** Grant Morrison
32 ❑ Aug 1999 Cover: 1.99 **NM** value: **2.00**
Circ: Diamd. preorders: **86,864**
Inside Job • JLA in No Man's Land **A:** Mark Pajarillo **W:** Devin Grayson; Mark Waid
33 ❑ Sep 1999 Cover: 1.99 **NM** value: **2.00**
Circ: Diamd. preorders: **85,560**
Altered Egos **A:** Mark Pajarillo **W:** Mark Waid
34 ❑ Oct 1999 Cover: 1.99 **NM** value: **2.00**
Circ: Diamd. preorders: **84,007**
The Ant and the Avalanche **A:** Howard Porter **W:** Grant Morrison
35 ❑ Nov 1999 Cover: 1.99 **NM** value: **2.00**
Circ: Diamd. preorders: **83,388**
• Day of Judgment★ Appearance of new Spectre.
36 ❑ Dec 1999 Cover: 1.99 **NM** value: **2.00**
Circ: Diamd. preorders: **83,629**
World War III, Part 1 **A:** Howard Porter **W:** Grant Morrison
37 ❑ Jan 2000 Cover: 1.99 **NM** value: **2.00**
Circ: Diamd. preorders: **80,044**
World War III, Part 2 **A:** Howard Porter **W:** Grant Morrison
38 ❑ Feb 2000 Cover: 1.99 **NM** value: **2.00**
Circ: Diamd. preorders: **84,171**
World War III, Part 3 **A:** Howard Porter **W:** Grant Morrison
39 ❑ Mar 2000 Cover: 1.99 **NM** value: **2.00**
Circ: Diamd. preorders: **78,272**
World War III, Part 4 **A:** Howard Porter **W:** Grant Morrison
40 ❑ Apr 2000 Cover: 1.99 **NM** value: **2.00**
Circ: Diamd. preorders: **75,211**
World War III, Part 5 **A:** Howard Porter **W:** Grant Morrison
41 ❑ May 2000 Cover: 2.99 **NM** value: **Cover or less**
Circ: Diamd. preorders: **77,145**
• Giant-size. World War III, Part 6 **A:** Howard Porter **W:** Grant Morrison
42 ❑ Jun 2000 Cover: 1.99 **NM** value: **Cover or less**
Circ: Diamd. preorders: **73,654**
43 ❑ Jul 2000 Cover: 1.99 **NM** value: **Cover or less**
Circ: Diamd. preorders: **76,922**
Tower of Babel, Part 1 **A:** Howard Porter **W:** Mark Waid
44 ❑ Aug 2000 Cover: 1.99 **NM** value: **Cover or less**
Circ: Diamd. preorders: **76,835**
Tower of Babel, Part 2 **A:** Howard Porter **W:** Mark Waid
45 ❑ Sep 2000 Cover: 2.25 **NM** value: **Cover or less**
Circ: Diamd. preorders: **75,397**
Tower of Babel, Part 3 **A:** Howard Porter **W:** Mark Waid
46 ❑ Oct 2000 Cover: 2.25 **NM** value: **Cover or less**
Circ: Diamd. preorders: **72,048**
Tower of Babel, Part 4 **A:** Steve Scott **W:** Mark Waid
47 ❑ Nov 2000 Cover: 2.25 **NM** value: **Cover or less**
Circ: Diamd. preorders: **76,631**
The Queen of Fables, Part 1 **A:** Bryan Hitch **W:** Mark Waid
48 ❑ Dec 2000 Cover: 2.25 **NM** value: **Cover or less**
Circ: Diamd. preorders: **74,337**
The Queen of Fables, Part 2 **A:** Bryan Hitch **W:** Mark Waid
49 ❑ Jan 2001 Cover: 2.25 **NM** value: **Cover or less**
Circ: Diamd. preorders: **74,274**
The Queen of Fables, Part 3 **A:** Bryan Hitch; Javier Saltares **W:** Mark Waid
50 ❑ Feb 2001 Cover: 3.75 **NM** value: **Cover or less**
Circ: Diamd. preorders: **77,397**
• Giant-size. Dream Team **A:** Phil Jimenez; Bryan Hitch **W:** Mark Waid
51 ❑ Apr 2001 Cover: 2.25 **NM** value: **Cover or less**
Circ: Diamd. preorders: **72,824**
Man and Superman **A:** Mike S. Miller **W:** Mark Waid
52 ❑ May 2001 Cover: 2.25 **NM** value: **Cover or less**
Circ: Diamd. preorders: **72,376**
Element of Surprise **A:** Bryan Hitch **W:** Mark Waid
53 ❑ Jun 2001 Cover: 2.25 **NM** value: **Cover or less**
Circ: Diamd. preorders: **74,293**
54 ❑ Jul 2001 Cover: 2.25 **NM** value: **Cover or less**
Circ: Diamd. preorders: **74,228** • **CGC:** 1 graded, best 9.6
55 ❑ Aug 2001 Cover: 2.25 **NM** value: **Cover or less**
Circ: Diamd. preorders: **75,548**
56 ❑ Sep 2001 Cover: 2.25 **NM** value: **Cover or less**
Circ: Diamd. preorders: **78,649** • **CGC:** 1 graded, best 9.8
1000000❑Nov 1998 Cover: 1.99 **NM** value: **Cover or less**
Circ: Diamd. preorders: **100,278**
Prisoners of the Twentieth Century • One Million **A:** Howard Porter **W:** Grant Morrison
Anl 1❑ca. 1997 Cover: 3.95 **NM** value: **Cover or less**
Circ: Diamd. preorders: **78,580**
Hardboiled Hangover • Pulp Heroes **A:** Ariel Olivetti **W:** Brian Augustyn
Anl 2❑ca. 1998 Cover: 2.95 **NM** value: **3.95**
Circ: Diamd. preorders: **61,851**
• Ghosts
Anl 3❑Sep 1999 Cover: 2.95 **NM** value: **Cover or less**
Circ: Diamd. preorders: **56,730**
Gorilla Warfare • JLApe **A:** Jason Orfalas **W:** Len Kaminski
Bk 1❑ Cover: 5.95 **NM** value: **Cover or less**
New World Order • New World Order; Collects JLA #1-4 **A:** Howard Porter **W:** Grant Morrison
Bk 2❑ Cover: 7.95 **NM** value: **Cover or less**
• American Dreams; Collects JLA #5-9
Bk 3❑ Cover: 9.95 **NM** value: **Cover or less**
Rock of Ages • Rock of Ages; Collects JLA #10-15 **W:** Grant Morrison
Bk 4❑ Cover: 12.95 **NM** value: **Cover or less**
Strength in Numbers • Strength in Numbers; collects #16-23, JLA Secret Files #2, and Prometheus (Villains)
Bk 5❑Dec 1999 Cover: 14.95 **NM** value: **Cover or less**
Justice for All • Collects JLA #24-33 **A:** Howard Porter; Mark Pajarillo **W:** Grant Morrison; Devin Grayson; Mark Millar; Mark Waid
Bk 6❑ Cover: 12.95 **NM** value: **Cover or less**
• World War III; Collects JLA #34-41 **A:** Howard Porter **W:** Grant Morrison
GS 1❑Jul 1998 Cover: 4.95 **NM** value: **Cover or less**
Circ: Diamd. preorders: **54,803**
GS 2❑Nov 1999 Cover: 4.95 **NM** value: **Cover or less**
Circ: Diamd. preorders: **40,820**
The Game; With Friends Like These…!; Average People; Madmen and Mudbaths; Shelter from the Storm; Outside the Box; Tour of Duty **A:** Chris Wozniak; Yanick Paquette; Sal Velluto; Cary Nord; Andy Lanning; Chris Renaud; Antony Wiliams **W:** Fabian Nicieza; Len Wein; Christopher Priest; D. Curtis Johnson; Dan Abnett; Jason Hernandez-Rosenblatt; Tom Peyer
GS 3❑Oct 2000 Cover: 4.95 **NM** value: **Cover or less**
Circ: Diamd. preorders: **36,170**
The Century War II **A:** Dale Eaglesham **W:** D. Curtis Johnson

JLA: ACT OF GOD — DC

1 ❑ Jan 2001 Cover: 4.95 **NM** value: **Cover or less**
Circ: Diamd. preorders: **37,172**
A: Pete Ross **W:** Doug Moench
2 ❑ Feb 2001 Cover: 4.95 **NM** value: **Cover or less**
Circ: Diamd. preorders: **35,509**
A: Pete Ross **W:** Doug Moench
3 ❑ Mar 2001 Cover: 4.95 **NM** value: **Cover or less**
Circ: Diamd. preorders: **34,822**
A: Pete Ross **W:** Doug Moench

JLA: A LEAGUE OF ONE — DC

Bk 1/HC❑ Cover: 24.95 **NM** value: **Cover or less**
A: Christopher Moeller **W:** Christopher Moeller

JLA: BLACK BAPTISM — DC

1 ❑ May 2001 Cover: 2.50 **NM** value: **Cover or less**
Circ: Diamd. preorders: **41,715**
Magicide **A:** Jesus Saiz **W:** Ruben Diaz; Sean Smith
2 ❑ Jun 2001 Cover: 2.50 **NM** value: **Cover or less**
Circ: Diamd. preorders: **40,097**
Trials in Darkness **A:** Jesus Saiz **W:** Ruben Diaz; Sean Smith
3 ❑ Jul 2001 Cover: 2.50 **NM** value: **Cover or less**
Circ: Diamd. preorders: **35,688**
A: Jesus Saiz **W:** Ruben Diaz; Sean Smith
4 ❑ Aug 2001 Cover: 2.50 **NM** value: **Cover or less**
Circ: Diamd. preorders: **33,467**
A: Jesus Saiz **W:** Ruben Diaz; Sean Smith

JLA: CREATED EQUAL — DC

1 ❑ ca. 2000 Cover: 5.95 **NM** value: **Cover or less**
Circ: Diamd. preorders: **34,841**
A: Kevin Maguire **W:** Fabian Nicieza
2 ❑ ca. 2000 Cover: 5.95 **NM** value: **Cover or less**
Circ: Diamd. preorders: **34,036**
The Children of the Spring **A:** Kevin Maguire **W:** Fabian Nicieza

JLA: EARTH 2 — DC

1 ❑ Cover: 14.95 **NM** value: **Cover or less**
A: Frank Quitely **W:** Grant Morrison

JLA: FOREIGN BODIES — DC

1 ❑ ca. 1999 Cover: 5.95 **NM** value: **Cover or less**
Circ: Diamd. preorders: **42,387**
One-shot. • prestige format. **A:** Val Semeiks **W:** Len Kaminski

JLA GALLERY — DC

1 ❑ ca. 1997 Cover: 2.95 **NM** value: **Cover or less**
Circ: Diamd. preorders: **34,530**
No issue number. wraparound cover. • pin-ups

JLA: HEAVEN'S LADDER — DC

1 ❑ Cover: 9.95 **NM** value: **Cover or less**
A: Bryan Hitch **W:** Mark Waid

JLA IN CRISIS SECRET FILES — DC

1 ❑ Nov 1998 Cover: 4.95 **NM** value: **Cover or less**
Circ: Diamd. preorders: **47,503**
• summaries of events from Crisis through One Million **A:** Rags Morales **W:** Tom Peyer

JLA: PARADISE LOST — DC

1 ❑ Jan 1998 Cover: 1.95 **NM** value: **2.00**
Circ: Diamd. preorders: **91,521**
Someone to Watch Over Me **A:** Ariel Olivetti **W:** Mark Millar
2 ❑ Feb 1998 Cover: 1.95 **NM** value: **2.00**
Circ: Diamd. preorders: **83,204**
A: Ariel Olivetti **W:** Mark Millar
3 ❑ Mar 1998 Cover: 1.95 **NM** value: **2.00**
Circ: Diamd. preorders: **74,275**
Revelations **A:** Ariel Olivetti **W:** Mark Millar

JLA: PRIMEVAL — DC

1 ❑ ca. 1999 Cover: 5.95 **NM** value: **Cover or less**
Circ: Diamd. preorders: **34,607**
A: Ariel Olivetti **W:** Andy Lanning; Dan Abnett

JLA SECRET FILES — DC

1 ❑ Sep 1997 Cover: 4.95 **NM** value: **Cover or less**
Circ: Diamd. preorders: **75,505**
Secret Origin; The New Superman Meets the JLA: Day in the Life: Martian Manhunter; Interview: Martian Manhunter; Timeline: JLA; he Roll Call: JLA (Heroes); The Roll Call: JLA: Villains • bios of team members and key villains; timeline **A:** N. Steven Harris; Kelley Jones; John Byrne; Paul Ryan; Howard Porter; Barry Kitson; Darryl Banks; Jim Calafiore; Dave Johnson; Don Hillsman; Dougie Braithwaite; Ray Kryssing **W:** Phil Jimenez; Grant Morrison; Mark Millar ★ Origin of New JLA.
2 ❑ Aug 1998 Cover: 3.95 **NM** value: **Cover or less**
Circ: Diamd. preorders: **57,284**
• bios of team members and key villains★ Origin of new League line-up.
3 ❑ Dec 2000 Cover: 4.95 **NM** value: **Cover or less**
Circ: Diamd. preorders: **35,465**
Blame; Lost Pages; Incarnations of the JLA; The Advance Man; Things to Come **A:** Claude St. Aubin; John McCrea; Doug Mahnke; Steve Scott; Ethan Van Sciver; Dale Eaglesham; Yanick Paquette; Barry Kitson; Greg Land; Pablo Raimondi; Norm Brefogle **W:** D. Curtis Johnson; Mark Waid; Tom Peyer

JLA: SECRET SOCIETY OF SUPER-HEROES — DC

1 ❑ ca. 2000 Cover: 5.95 **NM** value: **Cover or less**
• **CGC:** 1 graded, best 9.8
A: Mike McKone **W:** Howard Chaykin; David Tischman
2 ❑ Cover: 5.95 **NM** value: **Cover or less**
A: Mike McKone **W:** Howard Chaykin; David Tischman

JLA: SEVEN CASKETS — DC

1 ❑ Cover: 5.95 **NM** value: **Cover or less**
A: Dan Brereton **W:** Dan Brereton

JLA SHOWCASE — DC

GS 1❑Feb 2000 Cover: 4.95 **NM** value: **Cover or less**
Circ: Diamd. preorders: **34,365**

JLA: SUPERPOWER — DC

1 ❑ Nov 1999 Cover: 5.95 **NM** value: **Cover or less**
• **CGC:** 1 graded, best 9.6
One-shot. • prestige format. **A:** Scot Eaton **W:** John Arcudi

JLA: THE NAIL — DC

"For want of a nail the shoe was lost. For want of a shoe, the horse was lost. For want of a horse, the knight was lost. For want of a knight, the battle was lost. So it was a kingdom was lost…all for the want of a nail."

In this Elseworlds saga, the kingdom was indeed lost because of a nail. The nail in question punctured the tire of Jonathan and Martha Kent, preventing them from taking that Sunday drive where they otherwise would have found young Kal El as he crashed on Earth as a baby. In our reality, the Kents took the baby in and raised him to become the hero known as Superman. In this other reality, however, young Kal fell into other hands.

So now, 24 years later, the city of Metropolis is under siege, thanks to the Draconian police policies of mayor Lex Luthor. What's more, an anti-metahuman crusade is in full swing, forcing heroes like the JLA to run for cover.

1 ❑ Aug 1998 Cover: 4.95 **NM** value: **5.50**
Circ: Diamd. preorders: **64,794**
• Elseworlds **A:** Alan Davis **W:** Alan Davis
2 ❑ Sep 1998 Cover: 4.95 **NM** value: **5.00**
Circ: Diamd. preorders: **57,848**
• Elseworlds **A:** Alan Davis **W:** Alan Davis
3 ❑ Oct 1998 Cover: 4.95 **NM** value: **5.00**
Circ: Diamd. preorders: **62,015**
• Elseworlds **A:** Alan Davis **W:** Alan Davis
Bk 1❑ Cover: 12.95 **NM** value: **Cover or less**
• collects mini-series; Elseworlds; Collects issues #1-3 **A:** Alan Davis **W:** Alan Davis

JLA/TITANS — DC

1 ❑ Dec 1998 Cover: 2.95 **NM** value: **Cover or less**
Circ: Diamd. preorders: **81,646**
A: Oscar Jimenez **W:** Oscar Jimenez; Devin Grayson
1/LE❑Dec 1998 Cover: 23.95 **NM** value: **Cover or less**
A: Oscar Jimenez **W:** Oscar Jimenez; Devin Grayson
2 ❑ Jan 1999 Cover: 2.95 **NM** value: **Cover or less**
Circ: Diamd. preorders: **71,582**
A: Oscar Jimenez **W:** Oscar Jimenez; Devin Grayson
3 ❑ Feb 1999 Cover: 2.95 **NM** value: **Cover or less**
Circ: Diamd. preorders: **69,696**
A: Oscar Jimenez **W:** Oscar Jimenez; Devin Grayson
Bk 1❑Dec 1999 Cover: 12.95 **NM** value: **Cover or less**
• "The Technis Imperative" trade paperback; Collects series, JLA Secret Files #1 **A:** Oscar Jimenez **W:** Oscar Jimenez; Devin Grayson

Other grades: Multiply prices above by **1.5 for Mint • 2/3 for Very Fine • 1/3 for Fine • 1/5 for Very Good • 1/8 for Good**

JLA: TOMORROW WOMAN — DC

1 ❑ Jun 1998 Cover: 1.95 **NM** value: **Cover or less**
One-shot. 📖 Tomorrow Never Knows • Girlfrenzy; set during events of JLA #5 **A:** Yanick Paquette **W:** Tom Peyer

JLA VERSUS PREDATOR — DC

1 ❑ ca. 2000 Cover: 5.95 **NM** value: **Cover or less**
Circ: Diamd. preorders: **32,928** • **CGC:** 2 graded, best 9.9
A: Graham Nolan **W:** John Ostrander

JLA/WILDC.A.T.S — DC

1 ❑ ca. 1997 Cover: 5.95 **NM** value: **Cover or less**
Circ: Diamd. preorders: **77,034**
No issue number. • prestige format. • crossover with Image; Crime Machine **A:** Val Semeiks; Kevin Conrad **W:** Grant Morrison

JLA/WITCHBLADE — DC

1 ❑ ca. 2000 Cover: 5.95 **NM** value: **Cover or less**
Circ: Diamd. preorders: **46,406**
A: Mark Pajarillo **W:** Len Kaminski

JLA: WORLD WITHOUT GROWN-UPS — DC

1 ❑ Aug 1998 Cover: 4.95 **NM** value: **5.50**
Circ: Diamd. preorders: **55,580**
wraparound cover. • prestige format. **A:** Humberto Ramos; Mike McKone **W:** Todd Dezago
2 ❑ Sep 1998 Cover: 4.95 **NM** value: **5.00**
Circ: Diamd. preorders: **51,430**
A: Humberto Ramos; Mike McKone **W:** Todd Dezago
Bk 1❑ Cover: 9.95 **NM** value: **Cover or less**
A: Humberto Ramos; Mike McKone **W:** Todd Dezago

JLA: YEAR ONE — DC

After a title has achieved a certain measure of longevity, inserting a retroactive continuity to flesh out situations and foreshadow personality conflicts becomes an attractive option. Readers, who were not born when the title started, are anxious to read stories that purport to retell the early days, even though older fans may remember things differently.

JLA: Year One is a 12-issue miniseries featuring characters from the Silver Age with Barry Allen as The Flash, Hal Jordan as Green Lantern, and Black Canary, The Martian Manhunter, and Aquaman rounding out the team. Writer Mark Waid reveals how five disparate strangers mesh to become the Justice League, while behind the scenes, a mysterious group named Locus exhibits an ominous interest in the fledgling alliance.

1 ❑ Jan 1998 Cover: 2.95 **NM** value: **3.50**
Circ: Diamd. preorders: **98,094**
A: Barry Kitson **W:** Brian Augustyn; Mark Waid
2 ❑ Feb 1998 Cover: 1.95 **NM** value: **3.00**
Circ: Diamd. preorders: **88,273**
📖 Group Dynamic **A:** Barry Kitson **W:** Brian Augustyn; Mark Waid
3 ❑ Mar 1998 Cover: 1.95 **NM** value: **3.00**
Circ: Diamd. preorders: **80,239**
A: Barry Kitson **W:** Brian Augustyn; Mark Waid
4 ❑ Apr 1998 Cover: 1.95 **NM** value: **3.00**
Circ: Diamd. preorders: **73,484**
📖 While You Were Out... **A:** Barry Kitson **W:** Brian Augustyn; Mark Waid
5 ❑ May 1998 Cover: 1.95 **NM** value: **3.00**
Circ: Diamd. preorders: **72,012**
📖 A League Divided **A:** Barry Kitson **W:** Brian Augustyn; Mark Waid ★ Appearance of Doom Patrol.
6 ❑ Jun 1998 Cover: 1.95 **NM** value: **Cover or less**
Circ: Diamd. preorders: **72,535**
📖 Sum of Their Parts **A:** Barry Kitson **W:** Brian Augustyn; Mark Waid
7 ❑ Jul 1998 Cover: 1.95 **NM** value: **Cover or less**
Circ: Diamd. preorders: **66,879**
📖 The American Way **A:** Barry Kitson **W:** Brian Augustyn; Mark Waid ★ Appearance of Superman.
8 ❑ Aug 1998 Cover: 1.95 **NM** value: **Cover or less**
Circ: Diamd. preorders: **66,734**
📖 Loose Ends **A:** Barry Kitson **W:** Brian Augustyn; Mark Waid
9 ❑ Sep 1998 Cover: 1.99 **NM** value: **Cover or less**
Circ: Diamd. preorders: **63,342**
📖 Change the World **A:** Barry Kitson **W:** Brian Augustyn; Mark Waid
10 ❑ Oct 1998 Cover: 1.99 **NM** value: **Cover or less**
Circ: Diamd. preorders: **62,321**
📖 Heaven and Earth **A:** Barry Kitson **W:** Brian Augustyn; Mark Waid
11 ❑ Nov 1998 Cover: 1.99 **NM** value: **Cover or less**
Circ: Diamd. preorders: **60,679**
📖 Stalag Earth **A:** Barry Kitson; Joe Staton **W:** Brian Augustyn; Joe Staton; Mark Waid ★ Appearance of Metal Men, Blackhawks, Freedom Fighters, Challengers.
12 ❑ Dec 1998 Cover: 2.95 **NM** value: **Cover or less**
Circ: Diamd. preorders: **60,657**
📖 Justice For All final issue. **A:** Barry Kitson **W:** Brian Augustyn; Mark Waid
Bk 1❑ Cover: 19.95 **NM** value: **Cover or less**
No issue number. • Trade Paperback. • collects series **A:** Barry Kitson **W:** Brian Augustyn; Mark Waid

JLX — DC / Amalgam

1 ❑ Apr 1996 Cover: 1.95 **NM** value: **Cover or less**
📖 A League Of Their Own **A:** Howard Porter **W:** Gerard Jones; Mark Waid

JLX UNLEASHED — DC / Amalgam

1 ❑ Jun 1997 Cover: 1.95 **NM** value: **Cover or less**
Circ: Diamd. preorders: **134,483**
📖 The Unextinguishable Flame! **A:** Oscar Jiminez **W:** Christopher Priest

JOE COLLEGE — Hillman

1 ❑ Fal 1949 Cover: 0.10 **NM** value: **75.00**
2 ❑ Win 1949 Cover: 0.10 **NM** value: **75.00**

JOE DIMAGGIO — Celebrity

1 ❑ Cover: 6.95 **NM** value: **Cover or less**
• trading cards

JOE LOUIS — Fawcett

1 ❑ Sep 1950 Cover: 0.10 **NM** value: **400.00**
• **CGC:** 1 graded, best 7.5
2 ❑ Nov 1950 Cover: 0.10 **NM** value: **300.00**

JOE PALOOKA (1ST SERIES) — Columbia

1 ❑ Jan 1942 Cover: 0.10 **NM** value: **700.00**
• **CGC:** 1 graded, best 8.5
2 ❑ ca. 1943 Cover: 0.10 **NM** value: **400.00**
3 ❑ ca. 1944 Cover: 0.10 **NM** value: **250.00**
4 ❑ ca. 1944 Cover: 0.10 **NM** value: **250.00**

JOE PALOOKA (2ND SERIES) — Harvey

This second Joe Palooka series ran from 1945 until 1961. Its feature character was blonde boxing champ and all-American good guy Joe Palooka. A bruiser in the ring, Joe took on adventure wherever it could be found, from deep sea diving to fighting criminals.

Joe was accompanied by a cast of supporting characters, including Knobby Walsh, his friend and manager; Grey Cloud and the Old Chief, two Indian friends; Smokey, his valet and trusted companion; and a big grizzly bear named Toti. The series also featured Humphrey, a rather large comic character who, when not performing pratfalls, challenged readers with a variety of puzzles and games.

1 ❑ Nov 1945 Cover: 0.10 **NM** value: **350.00**
★ Origin of Joe Palooka.
2 ❑ Jan 1946 Cover: 0.10 **NM** value: **160.00**
3 ❑ Mar 1946 Cover: 0.10 **NM** value: **90.00**
4 ❑ May 1946 Cover: 0.10 **NM** value: **90.00**
5 ❑ Jul 1946 Cover: 0.10 **NM** value: **130.00**
A: Jack Kirby **W:** Joe Simon
6 ❑ Oct 1946 Cover: 0.10 **NM** value: **95.00**
7 ❑ Dec 1946 Cover: 0.10 **NM** value: **95.00**
8 ❑ Mar 1947 Cover: 0.10 **NM** value: **70.00**
📖 Mystery of The Ghost Ship; Sea Fever; A Story of Survival; Invisible Evidence (Text Story); The Flying Fool Chickie Ricks; Ricky Roony **A:** Ham Fisher **W:** Ham Fisher
9 ❑ Apr 1947 Cover: 0.10 **NM** value: **70.00**
10 ❑ May 1947 Cover: 0.10 **NM** value: **70.00**
11 ❑ Jul 1947 Cover: 0.10 **NM** value: **52.00**
• **CGC:** 1 graded, best 9.4
12 ❑ Aug 1947 Cover: 0.10 **NM** value: **52.00**
• **CGC:** 1 graded, best 9.2
13 ❑ Oct 1947 Cover: 0.10 **NM** value: **52.00**
14 ❑ Nov 1947 Cover: 0.10 **NM** value: **52.00**
15 ❑ Dec 1947 Cover: 0.10 **NM** value: **70.00**
★ Origin of Humphrey.
16 ❑ Jan 1948 Cover: 0.10 **NM** value: **52.00**
17 ❑ Feb 1948 Cover: 0.10 **NM** value: **52.00**
📖 Surprise Fight of the Year; Adventures in Hollywood; Joe Palooka and His Bodyguard; Little Max: Baby Service; Little Max: On the Farm; Joe Meets Knobby; Black Cat: Tinhorns are Dumb (text story); Flyin' Fool **A:** Ham Fisher; Bob Powell **W:** Ham Fisher; Bob Powell
18 ❑ Mar 1948 Cover: 0.10 **NM** value: **52.00**
19 ❑ Apr 1948 Cover: 0.10 **NM** value: **52.00**
20 ❑ May 1948 Cover: 0.10 **NM** value: **52.00**
21 ❑ Jun 1948 Cover: 0.10 **NM** value: **40.00**
22 ❑ Jul 1948 Cover: 0.10 **NM** value: **40.00**
• **CGC:** 1 graded, best 9.0
23 ❑ Aug 1948 Cover: 0.10 **NM** value: **40.00**
24 ❑ Sep 1948 Cover: 0.10 **NM** value: **40.00**
25 ❑ Oct 1948 Cover: 0.10 **NM** value: **40.00**
26 ❑ Nov 1948 Cover: 0.10 **NM** value: **40.00**
27 ❑ Dec 1948 Cover: 0.10 **NM** value: **40.00**
28 ❑ Jan 1949 Cover: 0.10 **NM** value: **40.00**
29 ❑ Feb 1949 Cover: 0.10 **NM** value: **40.00**
30 ❑ Mar 1949 Cover: 0.10 **NM** value: **40.00**
31 ❑ Apr 1949 Cover: 0.10 **NM** value: **35.00**
32 ❑ May 1949 Cover: 0.10 **NM** value: **35.00**
33 ❑ Jun 1949 Cover: 0.10 **NM** value: **35.00**
34 ❑ Jul 1949 Cover: 0.10 **NM** value: **35.00**
35 ❑ Aug 1949 Cover: 0.10 **NM** value: **35.00**
36 ❑ Sep 1949 Cover: 0.10 **NM** value: **35.00**
37 ❑ Oct 1949 Cover: 0.10 **NM** value: **35.00**
38 ❑ Nov 1949 Cover: 0.10 **NM** value: **35.00**
39 ❑ Dec 1949 Cover: 0.10 **NM** value: **35.00**
40 ❑ Jan 1950 Cover: 0.10 **NM** value: **35.00**
41 ❑ Feb 1950, four-color Cover: 0.10 **NM** value: **35.00**
42 ❑ Mar 1950, four-color Cover: 0.10 **NM** value: **35.00**
43 ❑ Apr 1950, four-color Cover: 0.10 **NM** value: **35.00**
44 ❑ May 1950, four-color Cover: 0.10 **NM** value: **35.00**
• Wedding of Joe Palooka and Ann Howe
45 ❑ Jun 1950, four-color Cover: 0.10 **NM** value: **28.00**
46 ❑ Jul 1950, four-color Cover: 0.10 **NM** value: **28.00**
47 ❑ Aug 1950, four-color Cover: 0.10 **NM** value: **28.00**
• **CGC:** 1 graded, best 9.0
48 ❑ Sep 1950 Cover: 0.10 **NM** value: **28.00**
• **CGC:** 1 graded, best 9.2
49 ❑ Oct 1950, four-color Cover: 0.10 **NM** value: **28.00**
• **CGC:** 1 graded, best 9.0
50 ❑ Nov 1950, four-color Cover: 0.10 **NM** value: **28.00**
51 ❑ Dec 1950, four-color Cover: 0.10 **NM** value: **28.00**
• series goes on one-year hiatus
52 ❑ Jan 1951, four-color Cover: 0.10 **NM** value: **28.00**
• series resumes after one-year hiatus
53 ❑ Feb 1951, four-color Cover: 0.10 **NM** value: **28.00**
54 ❑ Mar 1951, four-color Cover: 0.10 **NM** value: **28.00**
55 ❑ Apr 1951, four-color Cover: 0.10 **NM** value: **28.00**
56 ❑ May 1951, four-color Cover: 0.10 **NM** value: **28.00**
57 ❑ Jun 1951, four-color Cover: 0.10 **NM** value: **28.00**
58 ❑ Jul 1951, four-color Cover: 0.10 **NM** value: **28.00**
59 ❑ Aug 1951, four-color Cover: 0.10 **NM** value: **28.00**
60 ❑ Sep 1951, four-color Cover: 0.10 **NM** value: **28.00**
61 ❑ Oct 1951, four-color Cover: 0.10 **NM** value: **26.00**
62 ❑ Nov 1951, four-color Cover: 0.10 **NM** value: **42.00**
A: Jack Kirby **W:** Joe Simon
63 ❑ Dec 1951, four-color Cover: 0.10 **NM** value: **26.00**
64 ❑ Jan 1952, four-color Cover: 0.10 **NM** value: **26.00**
65 ❑ Feb 1952, four-color Cover: 0.10 **NM** value: **26.00**
66 ❑ Mar 1952, four-color Cover: 0.10 **NM** value: **26.00**
67 ❑ Apr 1952, four-color Cover: 0.10 **NM** value: **26.00**
68 ❑ May 1952 Cover: 0.10 **NM** value: **26.00**
📖 His Last Grenade!; I Sent My Brother Out to Die!; Night Fighters (Text Story); BattleGrounds; The Most Shocking Secret Behind The War!; Rescue! (Text Story); Voices in Battle (Text Story)
69 ❑ Jun 1952, four-color Cover: 0.10 **NM** value: **26.00**
70 ❑ Jul 1952 Cover: 0.10 **NM** value: **26.00**
71 ❑ Aug 1952 Cover: 0.10 **NM** value: **26.00**
72 ❑ Sep 1952 Cover: 0.10 **NM** value: **26.00**
73 ❑ Oct 1952 Cover: 0.10 **NM** value: **26.00**
74 ❑ Nov 1952 Cover: 0.10 **NM** value: **26.00**
75 ❑ Jan 1953 Cover: 0.10 **NM** value: **26.00**
76 ❑ Mar 1953 Cover: 0.10 **NM** value: **26.00**
77 ❑ May 1953 Cover: 0.10 **NM** value: **26.00**
78 ❑ Jul 1953 Cover: 0.10 **NM** value: **26.00**
79 ❑ Sep 1953 Cover: 0.10 **NM** value: **26.00**
80 ❑ Nov 1953 Cover: 0.10 **NM** value: **26.00**
81 ❑ Jan 1954 Cover: 0.10 **NM** value: **24.00**
82 ❑ Mar 1954 Cover: 0.10 **NM** value: **24.00**
83 ❑ May 1954 Cover: 0.10 **NM** value: **24.00**
84 ❑ Jul 1954 Cover: 0.10 **NM** value: **24.00**
85 ❑ Sep 1954 Cover: 0.10 **NM** value: **24.00**
86 ❑ Nov 1954 Cover: 0.10 **NM** value: **24.00**
87 ❑ Jan 1955 Cover: 0.10 **NM** value: **24.00**
88 ❑ Mar 1955 Cover: 0.10 **NM** value: **24.00**
89 ❑ May 1955 Cover: 0.10 **NM** value: **24.00**
90 ❑ Jul 1955 Cover: 0.10 **NM** value: **24.00**
91 ❑ Sep 1955 Cover: 0.10 **NM** value: **24.00**
92 ❑ Nov 1955 Cover: 0.10 **NM** value: **24.00**
93 ❑ Feb 1956 Cover: 0.10 **NM** value: **24.00**
94 ❑ Apr 1956 Cover: 0.10 **NM** value: **24.00**
95 ❑ Jun 1956 Cover: 0.10 **NM** value: **24.00**
96 ❑ Aug 1956 Cover: 0.10 **NM** value: **24.00**
97 ❑ Oct 1956 Cover: 0.10 **NM** value: **24.00**
98 ❑ Dec 1956 Cover: 0.10 **NM** value: **24.00**
99 ❑ Feb 1957 Cover: 0.10 **NM** value: **24.00**
100 ❑ Apr 1957 Cover: 0.10 **NM** value: **24.00**
• 100th anniversary issue.
101 ❑ Jun 1957 Cover: 0.10 **NM** value: **24.00**
102 ❑ Sep 1957 Cover: 0.10 **NM** value: **24.00**
103 ❑ Nov 1957 Cover: 0.10 **NM** value: **24.00**
104 ❑ Feb 1958 Cover: 0.10 **NM** value: **24.00**
105 ❑ Apr 1958 Cover: 0.10 **NM** value: **24.00**
106 ❑ Jun 1958 Cover: 0.10 **NM** value: **24.00**
107 ❑ Aug 1958 Cover: 0.10 **NM** value: **24.00**
108 ❑ Oct 1958 Cover: 0.10 **NM** value: **24.00**
109 ❑ Dec 1958 Cover: 0.10 **NM** value: **24.00**
110 ❑ Mar 1959 Cover: 0.10 **NM** value: **24.00**
111 ❑ Jun 1959 Cover: 0.10 **NM** value: **24.00**
112 ❑ Sep 1959 Cover: 0.10 **NM** value: **24.00**
113 ❑ Dec 1959 Cover: 0.10 **NM** value: **24.00**
114 ❑ Mar 1960 Cover: 0.10 **NM** value: **24.00**
115 ❑ Jun 1960 Cover: 0.10 **NM** value: **24.00**
116 ❑ Sep 1960 Cover: 0.25 **NM** value: **34.00**
• Giant-size.
117 ❑ Dec 1960 Cover: 0.25 **NM** value: **34.00**
• Giant-size.
118 ❑ Mar 1961 Cover: 0.25 **NM** value: **34.00**
• Giant-size. final issue.

JOE PALOOKA FIGHTS HIS WAY BACK — Harvey

1 ❑ ca. 1945 **NM** value: **100.00**
• **CGC:** 1 graded, best 9.2

JOE PALOOKA HI THERE — American Red Cross

1 ❑ Sep 1949 **NM** value: **75.00**
• **CGC:** 6 graded, best 8.5

JOE PSYCHO & MOO FROG — Goblin Studios

1 ❑ Cover: 2.50 **NM** value: **Cover or less**
2 ❑ ca. 1996 Cover: 2.50 **NM** value: **Cover or less**
Circ: Diamd. preorders: **4,067**
3 ❑ Sep 1997 Cover: 2.50 **NM** value: **Cover or less**
Circ: Diamd. preorders: **3,057**
4 ❑ Cover: 2.50 **NM** value: **Cover or less**
5 ❑ Cover: 2.50 **NM** value: **Cover or less**
Ash 1❑b&w **NM** value: **1.00**
no cover price. • Kinko's Ashcan Edition.

JOE PSYCHO FULL COLOR EXTRAVAGARBONZO — Goblin Studios

1 ❑ ca. 1998 Cover: 2.95 **NM** value: **Cover or less**
Circ: Diamd. preorders: **3,428**
No issue number.

CGC-graded: Multiply prices above by **33 for 9.9 M • 16 for 9.8 NM/M • 7 for 9.6 NM+ • 5 for 9.4 NM • 2.5 for 9.2 NM- • 1.5 for 9.0 VF/NM**

JOE SINN — Caliber
1 ❑ b&w Cover: 2.95 **NM** value: **Cover or less**
Made In Taiwo **A:** Brooks Hagan **W:** Scott Finley
1/LE❑ Cover: 5.95 **NM** value: **Cover or less**
• limited edition.
2 ❑ b&w Cover: 2.95 **NM** value: **Cover or less**
An Open Refrigerator To The Soul • Final issue (others never released) **A:** Brooks Hagan **W:** Scott Finley

JOE YANK — Standard
5 ❑ Mar 1952 Cover: 0.10 **NM** value: **50.00**
6 ❑ May 1952 Cover: 0.10 **NM** value: **55.00**
A: Alex Toth
7 ❑ Aug 1952 Cover: 0.10 **NM** value: **25.00**
8 ❑ Oct 1952 Cover: 0.10 **NM** value: **35.00**
Alex Toth cover.
9 ❑ Dec 1952 Cover: 0.10 **NM** value: **16.00**
10 ❑ Jan 1953 Cover: 0.10 **NM** value: **16.00**
11 ❑ Apr 1953 Cover: 0.10 **NM** value: **16.00**
12 ❑ Jul 1953 Cover: 0.10 **NM** value: **16.00**
13 ❑ Oct 1953 Cover: 0.10 **NM** value: **16.00**
14 ❑ Jan 1954 Cover: 0.10 **NM** value: **16.00**
15 ❑ Apr 1954 Cover: 0.10 **NM** value: **16.00**
16 ❑ Jul 1954 Cover: 0.10 **NM** value: **16.00**
War Of Curves; Trouble Or Nothing, Chain Of Command, Pinhead Perkins, P.F.C., Ever-Lovin' Hero; Ryze And Shyne: The Pick Up Squad final issue.

JOHAN & PEEWIT: THE BLACK ARROW — Fantasy Flight
1 ❑ Cover: 8.95 **NM** value: **Cover or less**

JOHN CARTER OF MARS (EDGAR RICE BURROUGHS'...) — Gold Key
1 ❑ Apr 1964 Cover: 0.12 **NM** value: **28.00**
• **CGC:** 1 graded, best 7.0
2 ❑ Jul 1964 Cover: 0.12 **NM** value: **16.00**
• **CGC:** 1 graded, best 7.0
3 ❑ Oct 1964 Cover: 0.12 **NM** value: **16.00**
• **CGC:** 1 graded, best 7.0

JOHN CARTER, WARLORD OF MARS — Marvel
John Carter was an Earthman who ventured into a cave one day and saw a strange light. When the light touched him, his body seemed split into two, with one body staying behind on Earth, and another being transported to Mars. There he discovered strange races, including green, four-armed giants and ancient humanoid warriors. Carter rose to become a prince on this world, leading a swashbuckling life of space adventure. He also found friendship in the alien known as Tars Tarkas, and true love in the beautiful Dejah Thoris.

John Carter, Warlord of Mars was Edgar Rice Burroughs' first hero, predating his work on Korak and Tarzan. Carter made his comics debut in 1939's The Funnies #30. It appeared sporadically under several different publishers, including a 1972 run in DC's Weird Worlds. Marvel's version began in 1977, and presented Carter's sword and fantasy adventures until issue #28 in 1979.
1 ❑ Jun 1977 Cover: 0.30 **NM** value: **6.00**
• **CGC:** 28 graded, best 9.8
A: Gil Kane; Dave Cockrum ★ Origin of John Carter, Warlord of Mars.
2 ❑ Jul 1977 Cover: 0.30 **NM** value: **4.00**
• **CGC:** 1 graded, best 9.4
A: Gil Kane ★ Versus White Apes.
3 ❑ Aug 1977 Cover: 0.30 **NM** value: **3.00**
• **CGC:** 1 graded, best 9.6
Amazons Of Mars! **A:** Alan Weiss; Gil Kane; Tony DeZuniga **W:** Alan Weiss; Michele Wolfman ★ Versus White Apes.
4 ❑ Sep 1977 Cover: 0.30 **NM** value: **3.00**
• **CGC:** 1 graded, best 9.6
A: Gil Kane
5 ❑ Oct 1977 Cover: 0.30 **NM** value: **3.00**
• **CGC:** 1 graded, best 9.8
A: Gil Kane ★ Versus Stara Kan.
6 ❑ Nov 1977 Cover: 0.35 **NM** value: **2.50**
• **CGC:** 3 graded, best 9.6
7 ❑ Dec 1977 Cover: 0.35 **NM** value: **2.50**
• **CGC:** 1 graded, best 9.4
8 ❑ Jan 1978 Cover: 0.35 **NM** value: **2.50**
• **CGC:** 1 graded, best 9.6
9 ❑ Feb 1978 Cover: 0.35 **NM** value: **2.50**
• **CGC:** 1 graded, best 9.6
10 ❑ Mar 1978 Cover: 0.35 **NM** value: **2.50**
• **CGC:** 1 graded, best 9.4
11 ❑ Apr 1978 Cover: 0.35 **NM** value: **2.50**
★ Origin of Dejah Thoris.
12 ❑ May 1978 Cover: 0.35 **NM** value: **2.50**
13 ❑ Jun 1978 Cover: 0.35 **NM** value: **2.50**
14 ❑ Jul 1978 Cover: 0.35 **NM** value: **2.50**
15 ❑ Aug 1978 Cover: 0.35 **NM** value: **2.50**
16 ❑ Sep 1978 Cover: 0.35 **NM** value: **2.50**
17 ❑ Oct 1978 Cover: 0.35 **NM** value: **2.50**
18 ❑ Nov 1978 Cover: 0.35 **NM** value: **2.50**
• **CGC:** 1 graded, best 9.4
A: Frank Miller
19 ❑ Dec 1978 Cover: 0.35 **NM** value: **2.50**
20 ❑ Jan 1979 Cover: 0.35 **NM** value: **2.50**
21 ❑ Feb 1979 Cover: 0.35 **NM** value: **2.50**
22 ❑ Mar 1979 Cover: 0.35 **NM** value: **2.50**
23 ❑ Apr 1979 Cover: 0.35 **NM** value: **2.50**
24 ❑ May 1979 Cover: 0.40 **NM** value: **2.50**
25 ❑ Jul 1979 Cover: 0.40 **NM** value: **2.50**
A: Frank Miller(cover)
26 ❑ Aug 1979 Cover: 0.40 **NM** value: **2.50**
A: Frank Miller(cover)
27 ❑ Sep 1979 Cover: 0.40 **NM** value: **2.50**
28 ❑ Oct 1979 Cover: 0.40 **NM** value: **2.50**
Anl 1❑ca. 1977 Cover: 0.50 **NM** value: **1.00**
• **CGC:** 1 graded, best 9.2
Anl 2❑ca. 1978 Cover: 0.60 **NM** value: **1.00**
• **CGC:** 1 graded, best 9.8
Anl 3❑ca. 1979 Cover: 0.60 **NM** value: **1.00**
• **CGC:** 1 graded, best 9.6

JOHN F. KENNEDY — Dell
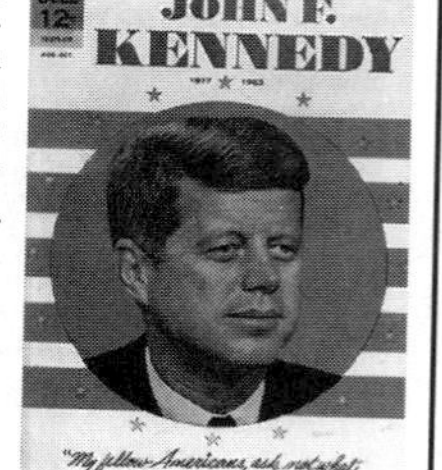

DELL
12¢
JOHN F.
KENNEDY
1917 1963
"My fellow Americans, ask not what your country can do for you; ask what you can do for your country."

The bullets that killed President John F. Kennedy in Dallas on November 22, 1963 left deep scars on American culture, scars that still persist today. The tragic death of the young and vibrant president evoked an almost mythic sense of tragedy, and gave birth to a small industry of memorabilia and commemorative items, among which was the John F. Kennedy life story comic book from Dell. The comic book features a photo of Kennedy against a red, white, and blue background, captioned with his famous call to action, "Ask not what your country can do for you; ask what you can do for your country." Inside is the story of his life and legend, from the heroic rescue of his PT boat crew during World War II to his nervy brinksmanship in diffusing the Cuban Missile Crisis. It's innocent kitsch from a simpler time.
1 ❑ Aug 1964 Cover: 0.12 **NM** value: **42.00**
• **CGC:** 1 graded, best 9.0
• 12-378-410; memorial comic book; Biography **A:** Dick Giordano **W:** Tartaglione
1-2 ❑ ca. 1964 Cover: 0.12 **NM** value: **28.00**
1-3 ❑ ca. 1964 Cover: 0.12 **NM** value: **20.00**

JOHN HIX SCRAPBOOK — Eastern Color
1 ❑ ca. 1937 Cover: 0.10 **NM** value: **250.00**
2 ❑ ca. 1937 Cover: 0.10 **NM** value: **175.00**

JOHN LAW DETECTIVE — Eclipse
1 ❑ Apr 1983 Cover: 1.50 **NM** value: **2.00**
Sand Saref...; Nubbin the Shoeshine Boy and the Strange, Ghastly Affair of the Half Dead Mr. Lox; Ratt Gutt **A:** Will Eisner **W:** Will Eisner

JOHNNY ATOMIC — Eternity
1 ❑ b&w Cover: 2.50 **NM** value: **Cover or less**
2 ❑ b&w Cover: 2.50 **NM** value: **Cover or less**
3 ❑ b&w Cover: 2.50 **NM** value: **Cover or less**

JOHNNY COMET — Avalon
1 ❑ Apr 1999 Cover: 2.95 **NM** value: **Cover or less**
Circ: Diamd. preorders: **1,277**
A: Frank Frazetta **W:** Peter Di Paolo
2 ❑ 1999 Cover: 2.95 **NM** value: **Cover or less**
A: Frank Frazetta **W:** Peter Di Paolo
3 ❑ 1999 Cover: 2.95 **NM** value: **Cover or less**
A: Frank Frazetta **W:** Peter Di Paolo
4 ❑ 1999 Cover: 2.95 **NM** value: **Cover or less**
Slow Joe, The Thinker **A:** Frank Frazetta **W:** Peter Di Paolo
5 ❑ 1999 Cover: 2.95 **NM** value: **Cover or less**
A: Frank Frazetta **W:** Peter Di Paolo
Bk 1❑ Cover: 14.95 **NM** value: **Cover or less**
• strip reprints **A:** Frank Frazetta
Bk 1/HC❑ Cover: 40.00 **NM** value: **Cover or less**
hardcover. • strip reprints **A:** Frank Frazetta

JOHNNY COSMIC — Thorby
1 ❑ Cover: 2.95 **NM** value: **Cover or less**
The Relativity of Reality • Flip-book with Spacegal Comics #2

JOHNNY DANGER — Toby
1 ❑ Aug 1954 Cover: 0.10 **NM** value: **125.00**

JOHNNY DYNAMITE — Dark Horse
1 ❑ Sep 1994, b&w and redCover: 2.95 **NM** value: **Cover or less**
Circ: CapCity orders: **4,725**
Revenge for a Black-Eyed Blonde **A:** Terry Beatty **W:** Max Allan Collins
2 ❑ Oct 1994, b&w and redCover: 2.95 **NM** value: **Cover or less**
Circ: CapCity orders: **3,025**
A: Terry Beatty **W:** Max Allan Collins
3 ❑ Nov 1994, b&w and redCover: 2.95 **NM** value: **Cover or less**
Circ: CapCity orders: **2,675**
A: Terry Beatty **W:** Max Allan Collins
4 ❑ Dec 1994, b&w and redCover: 2.95 **NM** value: **Cover or less**
Circ: CapCity orders: **2,400**
A: Terry Beatty **W:** Max Allan Collins

JOHNNY GAMBIT — Hot
1 ❑ Cover: 1.75 **NM** value: **Cover or less**

JOHNNY HAZARD — Pioneer
1 ❑ Dec 1988, b&w Cover: 2.00 **NM** value: **Cover or less**
C: Howard Chaykin
5 ❑ Aug 1948 Cover: 0.10 **NM** value: **125.00**
6 ❑ Nov 1948 Cover: 0.10 **NM** value: **100.00**
7 ❑ Feb 1949 Cover: 0.10 **NM** value: **100.00**
8 ❑ May 1949 Cover: 0.10 **NM** value: **75.00**

JOHNNY HAZARD QUARTERLY — Dragon Lady
1 ❑ Cover: 5.95 **NM** value: **Cover or less**
C: Alex Toth
2 ❑ Cover: 5.95 **NM** value: **Cover or less**
C: Alex Toth
3 ❑ Cover: 5.95 **NM** value: **Cover or less**
C: Alex Toth
4 ❑ Cover: 5.95 **NM** value: **Cover or less**
C: Alex Toth

JOHNNY LAW, SKY RANGER — Good
1 ❑ May 1955 Cover: 0.10 **NM** value: **50.00**
2 ❑ Jul 1955 Cover: 0.10 **NM** value: **35.00**
3 ❑ Sep 1955 Cover: 0.10 **NM** value: **35.00**
4 ❑ Nov 1955 Cover: 0.10 **NM** value: **35.00**

JOHNNY MACK BROWN COMICS — Dell
2 ❑ Oct 1950 Cover: 0.10 **NM** value: **125.00**
3 ❑ Jan 1951 Cover: 0.10 **NM** value: **100.00**
4 ❑ Apr 1951 Cover: 0.10 **NM** value: **75.00**
5 ❑ Jun 1951 Cover: 0.10 **NM** value: **75.00**
6 ❑ Aug 1951 Cover: 0.10 **NM** value: **60.00**
7 ❑ Oct 1951 Cover: 0.10 **NM** value: **60.00**
8 ❑ Dec 1951 Cover: 0.10 **NM** value: **60.00**
9 ❑ Mar 1952 Cover: 0.10 **NM** value: **75.00**
• **CGC:** 1 graded, best 9.2
10 ❑ Sep 1952 Cover: 0.10 **NM** value: **60.00**

JOHNNY NEMO MAGAZINE, THE — Eclipse
1 ❑ Sep 1995 Cover: 2.75 **NM** value: **Cover or less**
Circ: CapCity orders: **4,300**
The Spice of Death; Sindi Shade **A:** Brett Ewins **W:** Peter Milligan
2 ❑ Cover: 2.75 **NM** value: **Cover or less**
Circ: CapCity orders: **3,075**
A: Brett Ewins **W:** Peter Milligan
3 ❑ Cover: 2.75 **NM** value: **Cover or less**
Circ: CapCity orders: **3,175**
A: Brett Ewins **W:** Peter Milligan
4 ❑ Cover: 2.75 **NM** value: **Cover or less**
• Exists?
5 ❑ Cover: 2.75 **NM** value: **Cover or less**
• Exists?
6 ❑ Cover: 2.75 **NM** value: **Cover or less**
• Exists?

JOHNNY THE HOMICIDAL MANIAC — Slave Labor

For fans of black humor, Johnny the Homicidal Maniac is about as darkly funny as it gets. Jhonen Vasquez' series reads like a Vincent Price movie — the sort where the bad guy is having altogether too much fun.

Nobody knows what it was that sent Johnny over the edge, but he's definitely there now. He lives in house #777, decorated with parts of his victims, a bunny nailed to the wall, and even an evil Pillsbury doughboy cookie jar. When none of them are busy talking to Johnny, he raves on to himself, contemplating suicide routinely before being distracted by a really good commercial on television. It's the combination of murderous intensity and sudden banality that makes for much of this book's humor.
1 ❑ Aug 1995, b&w Cover: 2.95 **NM** value: **26.00**
• **CGC:** 3 graded, best 9.4
Traumatize Thy Neighbor **A:** Jhonen Vasquez **W:** Jhonen Vasquez
★ Appearance of Squee.
1-2 ❑ Dec 1995, b&w Cover: 2.95 **NM** value: **4.50**
1-3 ❑ Aug 1996, b&w Cover: 2.95 **NM** value: **3.00**
Circ: Diamd. preorders: **2,590**
1-4 ❑ May 1997, b&w Cover: 2.95 **NM** value: **3.00**
2 ❑ Nov 1995, b&w Cover: 2.95 **NM** value: **16.00**
• **CGC:** 1 graded, best 9.6
A: Jhonen Vasquez **W:** Jhonen Vasquez
2-2 ❑ Jul 1996, b&w Cover: 2.95 **NM** value: **3.00**
3 ❑ Feb 1996, b&w Cover: 2.95 **NM** value: **12.00**
• **CGC:** 1 graded, best 9.6
A Transient Smile **A:** Jhonen Vasquez **W:** Jhonen Vasquez
3-2 ❑ Jul 1996, b&w Cover: 2.95 **NM** value: **Cover or less**
Circ: Diamd. preorders: **2,661**
4 ❑ May 1996, b&w Cover: 2.95 **NM** value: **9.00**
• **CGC:** 1 graded, best 8.5
A: Jhonen Vasquez **W:** Jhonen Vasquez
4-2 ❑ Apr 1997, b&w Cover: 2.95 **NM** value: **Cover or less**
5 ❑ Aug 1996, b&w Cover: 2.95 **NM** value: **6.00**
• **CGC:** 1 graded, best 7.5
A: Jhonen Vasquez **W:** Jhonen Vasquez
5-2 ❑ Apr 1997, b&w Cover: 2.95 **NM** value: **3.00**
6 ❑ Aug 1996, b&w Cover: 2.95 **NM** value: **4.00**
Circ: Diamd. preorders: **9,522** • **CGC:** 1 graded, best 9.6
A: Jhonen Vasquez **W:** Jhonen Vasquez
7 ❑ Aug 1996, b&w Cover: 2.95 **NM** value: **4.00**
Circ: Diamd. preorders: **9,868** • **CGC:** 1 graded, best 9.0
Wobbly Headed Bob; Meanwhile... Before The Sun Rises **A:** Jhonen Vasquez **W:** Jhonen Vasquez
Bk 1❑ b&w Cover: 19.95 **NM** value: **Cover or less**
• JTHM: Director's Cut; collects stories from Johnny the Homicidal Maniac #1-7 **A:** Jhonen Vasquez **W:** Jhonen Vasquez

Other grades: Multiply prices above by **1.5 for Mint • 2/3 for Very Fine • 1/3 for Fine • 1/5 for Very Good • 1/8 for Good**

Bk 1/HC❑ Cover: 29.95 **NM** value: **Cover or less**
• Hardcover edition. • Collects Johnny the Homicidal Maniac #1-7
A: Jhonen Vasquez **W:** Jhonen Vasquez
SE 1❑ Cover: 20.00 **NM** value: **Cover or less**
Reprints Johnny the Homicidal Maniac #1 with cardstock outer cover.
• Limited to 2000 **A:** Jhonen Vasquez **W:** Jhonen Vasquez

JOHNNY THUNDER — DC

1 ❑ Mar 1973 Cover: 0.20 **NM** value: **12.00**
• **CGC:** 1 graded, best 9.2
2 ❑ May 1973 Cover: 0.20 **NM** value: **8.00**
3 ❑ Aug 1973 Cover: 0.20 **NM** value: **8.00**

JOHN WAYNE ADVENTURE COMICS — Toby

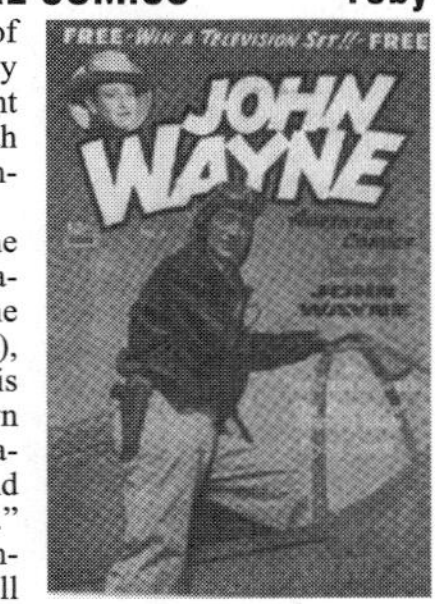

With the big-screen popularity of John Wayne already established by the late 1940s, Toby Press brought the actor's likeness to comics with the 31-issue John Wayne Adventure Comics.

Running from 1949 to 1955, the series featured "The Duke" in a variety of situations, many set in the Old West (his most popular genre), with a smattering of war stories (his second most-popular genre) thrown in for good measure. Back-up features included "Genius Jones" and Harvey Kurtzman's "Potshot Pete." While the stories were stiff and uninteresting, Wayne collectors will go for the photo covers featuring their favorite star. — Brent

1 ❑ Win 1949 Cover: 0.10 **NM** value: **1100.00**
• **CGC:** 1 graded, best 8.0
2 ❑ 1953 Cover: 0.10 **NM** value: **550.00**
3 ❑ Jun 1950 Cover: 0.10 **NM** value: **475.00**
• **CGC:** 3 graded, best 9.2
4 ❑ Jul 1950 Cover: 0.10 **NM** value: **450.00**
5 ❑ Sep 1950 Cover: 0.10 **NM** value: **400.00**
6 ❑ Nov 1950 Cover: 0.10 **NM** value: **400.00**
7 ❑ 1950 Cover: 0.10 **NM** value: **400.00**
8 ❑ 1951 Cover: 0.10 **NM** value: **400.00**
9 ❑ 1951 Cover: 0.10 **NM** value: **400.00**
10 ❑ 1951 Cover: 0.10 **NM** value: **375.00**
11 ❑ 1951 Cover: 0.10 **NM** value: **375.00**
12 ❑ 1951 Cover: 0.10 **NM** value: **375.00**
13 ❑ 1952 Cover: 0.10 **NM** value: **375.00**
14 ❑ 1952 Cover: 0.10 **NM** value: **375.00**
15 ❑ 1952 Cover: 0.10 **NM** value: **350.00**
16 ❑ 1952 Cover: 0.10 **NM** value: **350.00**
17 ❑ 1953 Cover: 0.10 **NM** value: **350.00**
18 ❑ 1953 Cover: 0.10 **NM** value: **350.00**
19 ❑ 1953 Cover: 0.10 **NM** value: **350.00**
20 ❑ 1953 Cover: 0.10 **NM** value: **325.00**
21 ❑ 1953 Cover: 0.10 **NM** value: **325.00**
22 ❑ 1953 Cover: 0.10 **NM** value: **325.00**
23 ❑ Nov 1953 Cover: 0.10 **NM** value: **325.00**
• **CGC:** 1 graded, best 6.5
24 ❑ Dec 1953 Cover: 0.10 **NM** value: **325.00**
25 ❑ 1954 Cover: 0.10 **NM** value: **325.00**
26 ❑ 1954 Cover: 0.10 **NM** value: **300.00**
27 ❑ 1954 Cover: 0.10 **NM** value: **300.00**
28 ❑ 1955 Cover: 0.10 **NM** value: **300.00**
29 ❑ 1955 Cover: 0.10 **NM** value: **300.00**
30 ❑ Mar 1955 Cover: 0.10 **NM** value: **275.00**
31 ❑ May 1955 Cover: 0.10 **NM** value: **275.00**
• **CGC:** 1 graded, best 7.5

JO-JO COMICS — Fox

1 ❑ Spr 1946 Cover: 0.10 **NM** value: **125.00**
• **CGC:** 2 graded, best 9.0
2 ❑ Sum 1946 Cover: 0.10 **NM** value: **75.00**
3 ❑ Fal 1946 Cover: 0.10 **NM** value: **75.00**
4 ❑ Dec 1946 Cover: 0.10 **NM** value: **75.00**
5 ❑ Feb 1947 Cover: 0.10 **NM** value: **75.00**
6 ❑ Apr 1947 Cover: 0.10 **NM** value: **75.00**
7 ❑ Jul 1947 Cover: 0.10 **NM** value: **800.00**
• **CGC:** 2 graded, best 9.2
8 ❑ Sep 1947 Cover: 0.10 **NM** value: **600.00**
• **CGC:** 2 graded, best 9.2
9 ❑ Nov 1947 Cover: 0.10 **NM** value: **450.00**
• **CGC:** 2 graded, best 9.2
10 ❑ Dec 1948 Cover: 0.10 **NM** value: **450.00**
• **CGC:** 1 graded, best 9.0
11 ❑ Jan 1948 Cover: 0.10 **NM** value: **450.00**
12 ❑ Feb 1948 Cover: 0.10 **NM** value: **450.00**
• **CGC:** 2 graded, best 9.0
13 ❑ Mar 1948 Cover: 0.10 **NM** value: **450.00**
14 ❑ Apr 1948 Cover: 0.10 **NM** value: **450.00**
• **CGC:** 1 graded, best 9.4
15 ❑ May 1948 Cover: 0.10 **NM** value: **450.00**
• **CGC:** 1 graded, best 5.0
16 ❑ Jun 1948 Cover: 0.10 **NM** value: **425.00**
17 ❑ Jul 1948 Cover: 0.10 **NM** value: **425.00**
• **CGC:** 1 graded, best 8.0
18 ❑ Aug 1948 Cover: 0.10 **NM** value: **425.00**
19 ❑ Sep 1948 Cover: 0.10 **NM** value: **425.00**
20 ❑ Oct 1948 Cover: 0.10 **NM** value: **400.00**
• **CGC:** 1 graded, best 7.0
21 ❑ Nov 1948 Cover: 0.10 **NM** value: **400.00**
• **CGC:** 1 graded, best 5.0
22 ❑ Dec 1948 Cover: 0.10 **NM** value: **400.00**
23 ❑ Jan 1949 Cover: 0.10 **NM** value: **400.00**
24 ❑ Feb 1949 Cover: 0.10 **NM** value: **400.00**
25 ❑ Mar 1949 Cover: 0.10 **NM** value: **400.00**
• **CGC:** 3 graded, best 9.0
26 ❑ Apr 1949 Cover: 0.10 **NM** value: **375.00**
• **CGC:** 1 graded, best 5.5
27 ❑ May 1949 Cover: 0.10 **NM** value: **375.00**
28 ❑ Jun 1949 Cover: 0.10 **NM** value: **375.00**
29 ❑ Jul 1949 Cover: 0.10 **NM** value: **375.00**

JOKER, THE — DC

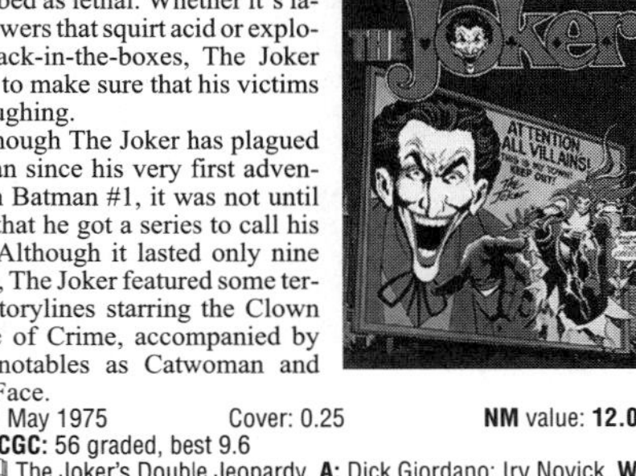

Batman has never had a greater enemy than The Joker: a mad villain whose sense of humor can best be described as lethal. Whether it's lapel flowers that squirt acid or explosive jack-in-the-boxes, The Joker wants to make sure that his victims die laughing.

Although The Joker has plagued Batman since his very first adventure in Batman #1, it was not until 1975 that he got a series to call his own. Although it lasted only nine issues, The Joker featured some terrific storylines starring the Clown Prince of Crime, accompanied by such notables as Catwoman and Two-Face.

1 ❑ May 1975 Cover: 0.25 **NM** value: **12.00**
• **CGC:** 56 graded, best 9.6
📖 The Joker's Double Jeopardy **A:** Dick Giordano; Irv Novick **W:** Denny O'Neil ★ Appearance of Two-Face.
2 ❑ Jul 1975 Cover: 0.25 **NM** value: **8.00**
• **CGC:** 6 graded, best 9.6
3 ❑ Oct 1975 Cover: 0.25 **NM** value: **6.00**
• **CGC:** 6 graded, best 9.6
4 ❑ Dec 1975 Cover: 0.25 **NM** value: **6.00**
• **CGC:** 5 graded, best 9.6
★ Versus Green Arrow.
5 ❑ Feb 1976 Cover: 0.25 **NM** value: **6.00**
• **CGC:** 3 graded, best 9.6
6 ❑ Apr 1976 Cover: 0.25 **NM** value: **5.00**
• **CGC:** 4 graded, best 9.6
7 ❑ Jun 1976 Cover: 0.30 **NM** value: **5.00**
• **CGC:** 3 graded, best 9.4
8 ❑ Aug 1976 Cover: 0.30 **NM** value: **5.00**
• **CGC:** 3 graded, best 9.6
• Bicentennial #7
9 ❑ Sep 1976 Cover: 0.30 **NM** value: **5.00**
• **CGC:** 2 graded, best 9.6
final issue. ★ Appearance of Catwoman.

JOKER COMICS — Timely

1 ❑ Apr 1942 Cover: 0.10 **NM** value: **2000.00**
• **CGC:** 1 graded, best 4.5
2 ❑ Jun 1942 Cover: 0.10 **NM** value: **775.00**
3 ❑ Sep 1942 Cover: 0.10 **NM** value: **400.00**
4 ❑ Nov 1942 Cover: 0.10 **NM** value: **400.00**
5 ❑ Dec 1942 Cover: 0.10 **NM** value: **400.00**
6 ❑ Jan 1943 Cover: 0.10 **NM** value: **350.00**
7 ❑ Feb 1943 Cover: 0.10 **NM** value: **350.00**
8 ❑ Apr 1943 Cover: 0.10 **NM** value: **300.00**
9 ❑ Jun 1943 Cover: 0.10 **NM** value: **300.00**
10 ❑ Jul 1943 Cover: 0.10 **NM** value: **250.00**
11 ❑ Oct 1943 Cover: 0.10 **NM** value: **250.00**
12 ❑ Nov 1943 Cover: 0.10 **NM** value: **250.00**
13 ❑ Dec 1943 Cover: 0.10 **NM** value: **250.00**
14 ❑ Feb 1944 Cover: 0.10 **NM** value: **250.00**
15 ❑ Apr 1944 Cover: 0.10 **NM** value: **225.00**
16 ❑ Jun 1944 Cover: 0.10 **NM** value: **225.00**
17 ❑ Win 1944 Cover: 0.10 **NM** value: **225.00**
18 ❑ Spr 1945 Cover: 0.10 **NM** value: **225.00**
19 ❑ Sum 1945 Cover: 0.10 **NM** value: **225.00**
20 ❑ Fal 1945 Cover: 0.10 **NM** value: **200.00**
21 ❑ Jan 1946 Cover: 0.10 **NM** value: **200.00**
22 ❑ Apr 1946 Cover: 0.10 **NM** value: **200.00**
23 ❑ Jun 1946 Cover: 0.10 **NM** value: **200.00**
24 ❑ Aug 1946 Cover: 0.10 **NM** value: **175.00**
25 ❑ Nov 1946 Cover: 0.10 **NM** value: **175.00**
26 ❑ Jan 1947 Cover: 0.10 **NM** value: **175.00**
27 ❑ May 1947 Cover: 0.10 **NM** value: **175.00**
28 ❑ Sum 1947 Cover: 0.10 **NM** value: **150.00**
29 ❑ Fal 1947 Cover: 0.10 **NM** value: **150.00**
30 ❑ Win 1947 Cover: 0.10 **NM** value: **150.00**
• **CGC:** 1 graded, best 8.0
31 ❑ Spr 1948 Cover: 0.10 **NM** value: **150.00**
32 ❑ Jul 1948 Cover: 0.10 **NM** value: **125.00**
33 ❑ Sep 1948 Cover: 0.10 **NM** value: **125.00**
34 ❑ Nov 1948 Cover: 0.10 **NM** value: **125.00**
35 ❑ Jan 1949 Cover: 0.10 **NM** value: **125.00**
36 ❑ Mar 1949 Cover: 0.10 **NM** value: **100.00**
37 ❑ May 1949 Cover: 0.10 **NM** value: **100.00**
38 ❑ Jul 1949 Cover: 0.10 **NM** value: **100.00**
39 ❑ Sep 1949 Cover: 0.10 **NM** value: **100.00**
40 ❑ Jan 1950 Cover: 0.10 **NM** value: **75.00**
41 ❑ May 1950 Cover: 0.10 **NM** value: **75.00**
42 ❑ Aug 1950 Cover: 0.10 **NM** value: **75.00**

JOKER, THE: DEVIL'S ADVOCATE — DC

Bk 1❑ Cover: 12.95 **NM** value: **Cover or less**
• Joker sentenced to death **A:** Graham Nolan **W:** Chuck Dixon
Bk 1/HC❑ Cover: 24.95 **NM** value: **Cover or less**
hardcover. • Joker sentenced to death **A:** Graham Nolan **W:** Chuck Dixon

JOKER/MASK — Dark Horse

1 ❑ May 2000 Cover: 2.95 **NM** value: **Cover or less**
Circ: Diamd. preorders: **22,603**
A: Ramon F. Bachs **W:** Henry Gilroy and Ronnie del Carmen
2 ❑ Jun 2000 Cover: 2.95 **NM** value: **Cover or less**
Circ: Diamd. preorders: **20,194**
A: Ramon F. Bachs **W:** Henry Gilroy and Ronnie del Carmen
3 ❑ Jul 2000 Cover: 2.95 **NM** value: **Cover or less**
Circ: Diamd. preorders: **19,186**
A: Ramon F. Bachs **W:** Henry Gilroy and Ronnie del Carmen
4 ❑ Aug 2000 Cover: 2.95 **NM** value: **Cover or less**
Circ: Diamd. preorders: **18,435**
A: Ramon F. Bachs **W:** Henry Gilroy and Ronnie del Carmen

JOLLY JACK STARJUMPER SUMMER OF '92 ONE-SHOT, THE — Conquest

1 ❑ b&w Cover: 2.95 **NM** value: **Cover or less**
No issue number.

JOLLY JINGLES — Archie

10 ❑ Sum 1943 Cover: 0.10 **NM** value: **275.00**
11 ❑ Fal 1943 Cover: 0.10 **NM** value: **150.00**
12 ❑ Win 1943 Cover: 0.10 **NM** value: **150.00**
13 ❑ Spr 1944 Cover: 0.10 **NM** value: **125.00**
14 ❑ Sum 1944 Cover: 0.10 **NM** value: **125.00**
15 ❑ Fal 1944 Cover: 0.10 **NM** value: **100.00**
16 ❑ Win 1944 Cover: 0.10 **NM** value: **100.00**

JONAH HEX — DC

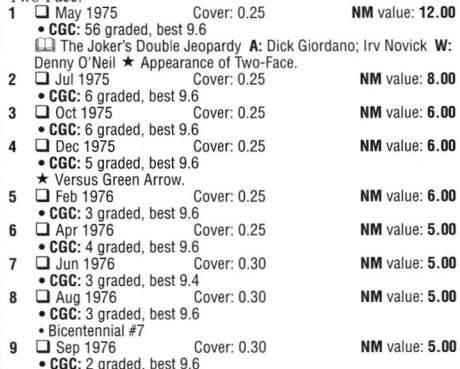

First introduced in All-Star Western (2nd series) #10 in 1972, bounty hunter and mountain man Jonah Hex would travel the west seeking out criminals and bringing them in to face justice. Dressed in Confederate gray, Hex was also distinguished by an ugly bit of scarring on the right side of his face that pulled his face into a perpetual grimace.

When the series switched titles to Weird Western Tales, Hex came along for the ride and, eventually received his own series. Feared both by criminals and most townspeople due to his violent nature, Hex has trouble finding love, since he carries a torch for his ex-wife, Mei Ling.

In addition to the Old West, Hex's adventures took him to the Orient, the South, and the future (in the short-lived, and shorter-named, Hex). In recent years, Jonah has returned to a combination of supernatural and Western tales with a series of mini-series from DC's Vertigo imprint. — Brent

1 ❑ Apr 1977 Cover: 0.30 **NM** value: **28.00**
• **CGC:** 65 graded, best 9.8
2 ❑ Jun 1977 Cover: 0.30 **NM** value: **10.00**
• **CGC:** 3 graded, best 9.0
★ 1st Appearance of El Papagayo. ★ Versus El Papagayo.
3 ❑ Aug 1977 Cover: 0.35 **NM** value: **7.00**
• **CGC:** 1 graded, best 9.4
4 ❑ Sep 1977 Cover: 0.35 **NM** value: **7.00**
• **CGC:** 6 graded, best 9.6
5 ❑ Oct 1977 Cover: 0.35 **NM** value: **7.00**
6 ❑ Nov 1977 Cover: 0.35 **NM** value: **6.00**
7 ❑ Dec 1977 Cover: 0.35 **NM** value: **6.00**
★ Origin of Jonah Hex.
8 ❑ Jan 1978 Cover: 0.35 **NM** value: **5.00**
• **CGC:** 4 graded, best 9.4
★ Origin of Jonah's facial scars.
9 ❑ Feb 1978 Cover: 0.35 **NM** value: **5.00**
• **CGC:** 1 graded, best 9.6
10 ❑ Mar 1978 Cover: 0.35 **NM** value: **5.00**
• **CGC:** 2 graded, best 9.8
11 ❑ Apr 1978 Cover: 0.35 **NM** value: **4.00**
12 ❑ May 1978 Cover: 0.35 **NM** value: **4.00**
• **CGC:** 2 graded, best 9.6
13 ❑ Jun 1978 Cover: 0.35 **NM** value: **4.00**
• **CGC:** 1 graded, best 9.6
14 ❑ Jul 1978 Cover: 0.35 **NM** value: **4.00**
• **CGC:** 1 graded, best 9.2
15 ❑ Aug 1978 Cover: 0.35 **NM** value: **4.00**
16 ❑ Sep 1978 Cover: 0.35 **NM** value: **4.00**
17 ❑ Oct 1978 Cover: 0.35 **NM** value: **4.00**
18 ❑ Nov 1978 Cover: 0.35 **NM** value: **4.00**
• **CGC:** 1 graded, best 9.4
19 ❑ Dec 1978 Cover: 0.35 **NM** value: **4.00**
• **CGC:** 1 graded, best 9.2
20 ❑ Jan 1979 Cover: 0.35 **NM** value: **4.00**
Circ: Statement: **84,200**
21 ❑ Feb 1979 Cover: 0.35 **NM** value: **3.00**
Circ: Statement: **84,200**
22 ❑ Mar 1979 Cover: 0.35 **NM** value: **3.00**
Circ: Statement: **84,200**
23 ❑ Apr 1979 Cover: 0.35 **NM** value: **3.00**
Circ: Statement: **84,200** • **CGC:** 1 graded, best 9.6
24 ❑ May 1979 Cover: 0.35 **NM** value: **3.00**
Circ: Statement: **84,200**
25 ❑ Jun 1979 Cover: 0.35 **NM** value: **3.00**
Circ: Statement: **84,200**
26 ❑ Jul 1979 Cover: 0.35 **NM** value: **3.00**
Circ: Statement: **84,200**
27 ❑ Aug 1979 Cover: 0.35 **NM** value: **3.00**
Circ: Statement: **84,200**
28 ❑ Sep 1979 Cover: 0.35 **NM** value: **3.00**
Circ: Statement: **84,200** • **CGC:** 1 graded, best 9.6
29 ❑ Oct 1979 Cover: 0.35 **NM** value: **3.00**
Circ: Statement: **84,200**
30 ❑ Nov 1979 Cover: 0.35 **NM** value: **3.00**
Circ: Statement: **84,200**
31 ❑ Dec 1979 Cover: 0.35 **NM** value: **3.00**
Circ: Statement: **84,200**

CGC-graded: Multiply prices above by **33 for 9.9 M • 16 for 9.8 NM/M • 7 for 9.6 NM+ • 5 for 9.4 NM • 2.5 for 9.2 NM- • 1.5 for 9.0 VF/NM**

32 ❑ Jan 1980 Cover: 0.40 **NM** value: **3.00**
Circ: Statement: **86,422**
33 ❑ Feb 1980 Cover: 0.40 **NM** value: **3.00**
Circ: Statement: **86,422**
34 ❑ Mar 1980 Cover: 0.40 **NM** value: **3.00**
Circ: Statement: **86,422**
35 ❑ Apr 1980 Cover: 0.40 **NM** value: **3.00**
Circ: Statement: **86,422**
• Has 1979 Statement, filed 10/1/79; avg print run 238,887; avg sales 83,955; avg subs 245; avg total paid 84,200; max existent 84,321; 35% of run returned
36 ❑ May 1980 Cover: 0.40 **NM** value: **3.00**
Circ: Statement: **86,422**
37 ❑ Jun 1980 Cover: 0.40 **NM** value: **3.00**
Circ: Statement: **86,422**
★ Appearance of Stonewall Jackson.
38 ❑ Jul 1980 Cover: 0.40 **NM** value: **3.00**
Circ: Statement: **86,422**
39 ❑ Aug 1980 Cover: 0.40 **NM** value: **3.00**
Circ: Statement: **86,422**
40 ❑ Sep 1980 Cover: 0.50 **NM** value: **3.00**
Circ: Statement: **86,422**
41 ❑ Oct 1980 Cover: 0.50 **NM** value: **3.00**
Circ: Statement: **86,422**
42 ❑ Nov 1980 Cover: 0.50 **NM** value: **3.00**
Circ: Statement: **86,422**
43 ❑ Dec 1980 Cover: 0.50 **NM** value: **3.00**
Circ: Statement: **86,422**
44 ❑ Jan 1981 Cover: 0.50 **NM** value: **3.00**
Circ: Statement: **85,000**
45 ❑ Feb 1981 Cover: 0.50 **NM** value: **3.00**
Circ: Statement: **85,000**
46 ❑ Mar 1981 Cover: 0.50 **NM** value: **3.00**
Circ: Statement: **85,000**
47 ❑ Apr 1981 Cover: 0.50 **NM** value: **3.00**
Circ: Statement: **85,000**
48 ❑ May 1981 Cover: 0.50 **NM** value: **3.00**
Circ: Statement: **85,000**
• Has 1980 Statement, filed 10/1/80; avg print run 250,767; avg sales 85,742; avg subs 680; avg total paid 86,422; samples 127; max existent 88,618; 35% of run returned
49 ❑ Jun 1981 Cover: 0.50 **NM** value: **3.00**
Circ: Statement: **85,000**
50 ❑ Jul 1981 Cover: 0.50 **NM** value: **3.00**
Circ: Statement: **85,000**
51 ❑ Aug 1981 Cover: 0.50 **NM** value: **2.50**
Circ: Statement: **85,000**
52 ❑ Sep 1981 Cover: 0.50 **NM** value: **2.50**
Circ: Statement: **85,000**
53 ❑ Oct 1981 Cover: 0.60 **NM** value: **2.50**
Circ: Statement: **85,000**
54 ❑ Nov 1981 Cover: 0.60 **NM** value: **2.50**
Circ: Statement: **85,000**
55 ❑ Dec 1981 Cover: 0.60 **NM** value: **2.50**
Circ: Statement: **85,000**
56 ❑ Jan 1982 Cover: 0.60 **NM** value: **2.50**
Circ: Statement: **81,032**
57 ❑ Feb 1982 Cover: 0.60 **NM** value: **2.50**
Circ: Statement: **81,032**
• El Diablo back-up
58 ❑ Mar 1982 Cover: 0.60 **NM** value: **2.50**
Circ: Statement: **81,032**
• El Diablo back-up
59 ❑ Apr 1982 Cover: 0.60 **NM** value: **2.50**
Circ: Statement: **81,032**
• El Diablo back-up
60 ❑ May 1982 Cover: 0.60 **NM** value: **2.50**
Circ: Statement: **81,032**
• El Diablo back-up
61 ❑ Jun 1982 Cover: 0.60 **NM** value: **2.50**
Circ: Statement: **81,032**
• in China
62 ❑ Jul 1982 Cover: 0.60 **NM** value: **2.50**
Circ: Statement: **81,032**
• in China
63 ❑ Aug 1982 Cover: 0.60 **NM** value: **2.50**
Circ: Statement: **81,032**
64 ❑ Sep 1982 Cover: 0.60 **NM** value: **2.50**
Circ: Statement: **81,032**
65 ❑ Oct 1982 Cover: 0.60 **NM** value: **2.50**
Circ: Statement: **81,032**
66 ❑ Nov 1982 Cover: 0.60 **NM** value: **2.50**
Circ: Statement: **81,032**
67 ❑ Dec 1982 Cover: 0.60 **NM** value: **2.50**
Circ: Statement: **81,032**
68 ❑ Jan 1983 Cover: 0.60 **NM** value: **2.50**
Circ: Statement: **67,153**
69 ❑ Feb 1983 Cover: 0.60 **NM** value: **2.50**
Circ: Statement: **67,153**
70 ❑ Mar 1983 Cover: 0.60 **NM** value: **2.50**
Circ: Statement: **67,153**
71 ❑ Apr 1983 Cover: 0.60 **NM** value: **2.50**
Circ: Statement: **67,153**
72 ❑ May 1983 Cover: 0.60 **NM** value: **2.50**
Circ: Statement: **67,153**
• Has 1982 Statement, filed 10/1/82; avg print run 252,135; avg sales 80,265; avg subs 767; avg total paid 81,032; samples 677; max existent 83,144; 32% of run returned
73 ❑ Jun 1983 Cover: 0.60 **NM** value: **2.50**
Circ: Statement: **67,153**
74 ❑ Jul 1983 Cover: 0.60 **NM** value: **2.50**
Circ: Statement: **67,153**
75 ❑ Aug 1983 Cover: 0.60 **NM** value: **2.50**
Circ: Statement: **67,153**
76 ❑ Sep 1983 Cover: 0.60 **NM** value: **2.50**
Circ: Statement: **67,153**
Caged! **A:** Dick Ayers; Tony DeZuniga **W:** Michael Fleisher
77 ❑ Oct 1983 Cover: 0.60 **NM** value: **2.50**
Circ: Statement: **67,153**
78 ❑ Nov 1983 Cover: 0.60 **NM** value: **2.50**
Circ: Statement: **67,153**
79 ❑ Dec 1983 Cover: 0.75 **NM** value: **2.50**
Circ: Statement: **67,153**
80 ❑ Jan 1984 Cover: 0.75 **NM** value: **2.50**
Circ: Statement: **55,727**
81 ❑ Feb 1984 Cover: 0.75 **NM** value: **2.50**
Circ: Statement: **55,727**
82 ❑ Mar 1984 Cover: 0.75 **NM** value: **2.50**
Circ: Statement: **55,727**
83 ❑ Apr 1984 Cover: 0.75 **NM** value: **2.50**
Circ: Statement: **55,727**
• Has 1983 Statement, filed 10/1/83; avg print run 220,700; avg sales 6,590; avg subs 563; avg total paid 67,153; samples 664; max existent 9,523; 30% of run returned
84 ❑ May 1984 Cover: 0.75 **NM** value: **2.50**
Circ: Statement: **55,727**
85 ❑ Jun 1984 Cover: 0.75 **NM** value: **2.50**
Circ: Statement: **55,727**
★ Versus Gray Ghost.
86 ❑ Aug 1984 Cover: 0.75 **NM** value: **2.50**
Circ: Statement: **55,727**
87 ❑ Oct 1984 Cover: 0.75 **NM** value: **2.50**
Circ: Statement: **55,727**
88 ❑ Dec 1984 Cover: 0.75 **NM** value: **2.50**
Circ: Statement: **55,727**
89 ❑ Feb 1985 Cover: 0.75 **NM** value: **2.50**
★ Versus Gray Ghost.
90 ❑ Apr 1985 Cover: 0.75 **NM** value: **2.50**
91 ❑ Jun 1985 Cover: 0.75 **NM** value: **2.50**
Circ: CapCity orders: **2,300**
• Has 1984 Statement, filed 10/1/84; avg print run 191,700; avg sales 55,131; avg subs 596; avg total paid 55,727; samples 161; max existent 57,879; 29% of run returned
92 ❑ Aug 1985 Cover: 0.75 **NM** value: **2.50**
Circ: CapCity orders: **4,550**
final issue. • events continue in Hex

JONAH HEX AND OTHER WESTERN TALES — DC

1 ❑ Oct 1979 Cover: 0.95 **NM** value: **6.00**
2 ❑ Dec 1979 Cover: 0.95 **NM** value: **6.00**
3 ❑ Feb 1980 Cover: 0.95 **NM** value: **6.00**

JONAH HEX: RIDERS OF THE WORM AND SUCH — DC / Vertigo

1 ❑ Mar 1995 Cover: 2.95 **NM** value: **3.00**
Circ: CapCity orders: **16,725**
No Rest For The Wicked And The Good Don't Need Any **A:** Tim Truman **W:** Joe Lansdale
2 ❑ Apr 1995 Cover: 2.95 **NM** value: **3.00**
Circ: CapCity orders: **13,075**
Wilde's West **A:** Tim Truman **W:** Joe Lansdale
3 ❑ May 1995 Cover: 2.95 **NM** value: **3.00**
Circ: CapCity orders: **12,400**
Big Worm **A:** Tim Truman **W:** Joe Lansdale
4 ❑ Jun 1995 Cover: 2.95 **NM** value: **3.00**
Circ: CapCity orders: **12,225**
Autumns Of Our Discontent **A:** Tim Truman **W:** Joe Lansdale
5 ❑ Jul 1995 Cover: 2.95 **NM** value: **3.00**
Circ: CapCity orders: **11,975**
A: Tim Truman **W:** Joe Lansdale

JONAH HEX: SHADOWS WEST — DC / Vertigo

1 ❑ Feb 1999 Cover: 2.95 **NM** value: **Cover or less**
Long Tom, Part 1 **A:** Tim Truman **W:** Joe Lansdale
2 ❑ Mar 1999 Cover: 2.95 **NM** value: **Cover or less**
Circ: Diamd. preorders: **17,032**
A: Tim Truman **W:** Joe Lansdale
3 ❑ Apr 1999 Cover: 2.95 **NM** value: **Cover or less**
Circ: Diamd. preorders: **16,101**
A: Tim Truman **W:** Joe Lansdale

JONAH HEX: TWO-GUN MOJO — DC / Vertigo

1 ❑ Aug 1993 Cover: 2.95 **NM** value: **4.00**
Circ: CapCity orders: **20,350**
Slow Go Smith **A:** Tim Truman **W:** Joe Lansdale
1/SI ❑ Aug 1993 **NM** value: **6.00**
• Silver (limited promotional) edition. • platinum **A:** Tim Truman **W:** Joe Lansdale
2 ❑ Sep 1993 Cover: 2.95 **NM** value: **3.00**
Circ: CapCity orders: **13,050**
A: Tim Truman **W:** Joe Lansdale
3 ❑ Oct 1993 Cover: 2.95 **NM** value: **3.00**
Circ: CapCity orders: **12,050**
A: Tim Truman **W:** Joe Lansdale
4 ❑ Nov 1993 Cover: 2.95 **NM** value: **3.00**
Circ: CapCity orders: **14,350**
A: Tim Truman **W:** Joe Lansdale
5 ❑ Dec 1993 Cover: 2.95 **NM** value: **3.00**
Circ: CapCity orders: **14,600**
A: Tim Truman **W:** Joe Lansdale
Bk 1 ❑ Cover: 12.95 **NM** value: **Cover or less**
• Trade Paperback. • Collects Jonah Hex: Two-Gun Mojo #1-5 **A:** Tim Truman **W:** Joe Lansdale

JONAS! (MIKE DEODATO'S...) — Caliber

1 ❑ Cover: 2.95 **NM** value: **Cover or less**
Jonas; Land of Fire **A:** Mike Deodato; Jr. **W:** Mike Deodato; Sr.; Julio E. Braz

JONATHAN FOX — Mariah Graphics

1 ❑ Cover: 2.00 **NM** value: **Cover or less**

JONES TOUCH — Fantagraphics / Eros

All issues are adults only.
1 ❑ Cover: 2.75 **NM** value: **Cover or less**

JONESY — Quality

1 ❑ Aug 1953 Cover: 0.10 **NM** value: **40.00**
• **CGC:** 1 graded, best 7.0
2 ❑ Oct 1953 Cover: 0.10 **NM** value: **25.00**
3 ❑ Dec 1953 Cover: 0.10 **NM** value: **25.00**
4 ❑ Feb 1954 Cover: 0.10 **NM** value: **25.00**
5 ❑ Apr 1954 Cover: 0.10 **NM** value: **20.00**
6 ❑ Jun 1954 Cover: 0.10 **NM** value: **20.00**
7 ❑ Aug 1954 Cover: 0.10 **NM** value: **20.00**
8 ❑ Oct 1954 Cover: 0.10 **NM** value: **20.00**

JON JUAN — Toby

1 ❑ Spr 1950 Cover: 0.10 **NM** value: **500.00**
• **CGC:** 1 graded, best 9.0

JONNI THUNDER — DC

1 ❑ Feb 1985 Cover: 0.75 **NM** value: **1.25**
...Not In The Stars, But In Ourselves...! • origin **A:** Dick Giordano **W:** Roy Thomas; Dann Thomas ★ Origin of Jonni Thunder. ★ 1st Appearance of Jonni Thunder.
2 ❑ Apr 1985 Cover: 0.75 **NM** value: **1.25**
A: Dick Giordano
3 ❑ Jun 1985 Cover: 0.75 **NM** value: **1.25**
Circ: CapCity orders: **7,900**
A: Dick Giordano
4 ❑ Aug 1985 Cover: 0.75 **NM** value: **1.25**
Circ: CapCity orders: **7,650**
A: Dick Giordano

JONNY DEMON — Dark Horse

1 ❑ May 1994 Cover: 2.50 **NM** value: **Cover or less**
Circ: CapCity orders: **5,200**
Living Though It! **A:** Neil Vokes **W:** Kurt Busiek
2 ❑ Jun 1994 Cover: 2.50 **NM** value: **Cover or less**
Circ: CapCity orders: **3,750**
W: Kurt Busiek
3 ❑ Jul 1994 Cover: 2.50 **NM** value: **Cover or less**
W: Kurt Busiek

JONNY DOUBLE — DC / Vertigo

1 ❑ Sep 1998 Cover: 2.95 **NM** value: **Cover or less**
Circ: Diamd. preorders: **13,196**
Two-Finger Discount **A:** Eduardo Risso **W:** Brian Azzarello
2 ❑ Oct 1998 Cover: 2.95 **NM** value: **Cover or less**
Circ: Diamd. preorders: **10,712**
A: Eduardo Risso **W:** Brian Azzarello
3 ❑ Nov 1998 Cover: 2.95 **NM** value: **Cover or less**
Circ: Diamd. preorders: **9,589**
A: Eduardo Risso **W:** Brian Azzarello
4 ❑ Dec 1998 Cover: 2.95 **NM** value: **Cover or less**
Circ: Diamd. preorders: **8,895**
A: Eduardo Risso **W:** Brian Azzarello

JONNY QUEST CLASSICS — Comico

1 ❑ May 1987 Cover: 2.00 **NM** value: **Cover or less**
Circ: CapCity orders: **11,625**
A: Doug Wildey
2 ❑ Jun 1987 Cover: 2.00 **NM** value: **Cover or less**
Circ: CapCity orders: **10,125**
A: Doug Wildey
3 ❑ Jul 1987 Cover: 2.00 **NM** value: **Cover or less**
Circ: CapCity orders: **9,925**
A: Doug Wildey

JONNY QUEST (COMICO) — Comico

Jonny Quest is a blond-haired boy who travels with his father, the eminent Dr. Quest, on a variety of scientific expeditions around the world. They are joined on their journeys by Jonny's friend Hadji, and Dr. Quest's assistant Race Bannon, the quintessential man of action. These four live a life of high adventure, with their scientific expeditions frequently leading them to cross paths with bandits, terrorists, and the odd mad scientist.

A popular animated adventure series of the 1960s, Jonny Quest made his way to Comico in 1986. This series demonstrates Jonny Quest's enduring appeal, and features splendid art by Doug Wildey (Rio at Bay) and Steve Rude (Nexus)

1 ❑ Jun 1986 Cover: 1.50 **NM** value: **3.00**
Circ: CapCity orders: **17,875**
The Sands Of Khasa Tahid
2 ❑ Jul 1986 Cover: 1.50 **NM** value: **2.50**
Circ: CapCity orders: **14,200**
3 ❑ Aug 1986 Cover: 1.50 **NM** value: **2.50**
Circ: CapCity orders: **13,625**
C: Dave Stevens
4 ❑ Sep 1986 Cover: 1.50 **NM** value: **2.50**
Circ: CapCity orders: **14,525**
Marley Frost is Here to Stay **A:** Tom Yeates **W:** William Messner-Loebs
5 ❑ Oct 1986 Cover: 1.50 **NM** value: **2.50**
Circ: CapCity orders: **13,925**
C: Dave Stevens
6 ❑ Nov 1986 Cover: 1.50 **NM** value: **2.00**
Circ: CapCity orders: **12,075**
Philosopher's Stone **A:** Adam Kubert **W:** William Messner-Loebs
7 ❑ Dec 1986 Cover: 1.50 **NM** value: **2.00**
Circ: CapCity orders: **11,150**
8 ❑ Jan 1987 Cover: 1.50 **NM** value: **2.00**
Circ: CapCity orders: **9,875**

Other grades: Multiply prices above by **1.5 for Mint • 2/3 for Very Fine • 1/3 for Fine • 1/5 for Very Good • 1/8 for Good**

9 ❑ Feb 1987 Cover: 1.50 **NM** value: **2.00**
Circ: CapCity orders: **9,550**
📖 Fire in Green Meadows **A:** Murphy Anderson **W:** William Messner-Loebs

10 ❑ Mar 1987 Cover: 1.50 **NM** value: **2.00**
Circ: CapCity orders: **9,525**
📖 Winters of Discontent **A:** Marc Hempel **W:** William Messner-Loebs

11 ❑ Apr 1987 Cover: 1.50 **NM** value: **Cover or less**
Circ: CapCity orders: **9,525**
A: Brent Anderson **C:** Bill Sienkiewicz

12 ❑ May 1987 Cover: 1.50 **NM** value: **Cover or less**
Circ: CapCity orders: **9,625**

13 ❑ Jun 1987 Cover: 1.50 **NM** value: **Cover or less**
Circ: CapCity orders: **9,500**
A: Carmine Infantino

14 ❑ Jul 1987 Cover: 1.50 **NM** value: **Cover or less**
Circ: CapCity orders: **9,250**

15 ❑ Aug 1987 Cover: 1.75 **NM** value: **Cover or less**
Circ: CapCity orders: **8,350**

16 ❑ Sep 1987 Cover: 1.75 **NM** value: **Cover or less**
Circ: CapCity orders: **8,475**

17 ❑ Oct 1987 Cover: 1.75 **NM** value: **Cover or less**
Circ: CapCity orders: **8,300**
📖 Space Ghost **A:** Steve Rude **W:** Mark Evanier

18 ❑ Nov 1987 Cover: 1.75 **NM** value: **Cover or less**
Circ: CapCity orders: **8,000**

19 ❑ Dec 1987 Cover: 1.75 **NM** value: **Cover or less**
Circ: CapCity orders: **7,525**

20 ❑ Jan 1988 Cover: 1.75 **NM** value: **Cover or less**
Circ: CapCity orders: **7,075**

21 ❑ Feb 1988 Cover: 1.75 **NM** value: **Cover or less**
Circ: CapCity orders: **6,400**

22 ❑ Mar 1988 Cover: 1.75 **NM** value: **Cover or less**
Circ: CapCity orders: **6,350**

23 ❑ Apr 1988 Cover: 1.75 **NM** value: **Cover or less**
Circ: CapCity orders: **5,875**

24 ❑ May 1988 Cover: 1.75 **NM** value: **Cover or less**
Circ: CapCity orders: **5,575**

25 ❑ Jun 1988 Cover: 1.75 **NM** value: **Cover or less**
Circ: CapCity orders: **5,450**

26 ❑ Jul 1988 Cover: 1.75 **NM** value: **Cover or less**
Circ: CapCity orders: **5,900**

27 ❑ Aug 1988 Cover: 1.75 **NM** value: **Cover or less**
Circ: CapCity orders: **5,000**

28 ❑ Sep 1988 Cover: 1.75 **NM** value: **Cover or less**
Circ: CapCity orders: **4,925**

29 ❑ Oct 1988 Cover: 1.75 **NM** value: **Cover or less**

30 ❑ Nov 1988 Cover: 1.75 **NM** value: **Cover or less**
Circ: CapCity orders: **4,650**

31 ❑ Dec 1988 Cover: 1.75 **NM** value: **Cover or less**
Circ: CapCity orders: **4,800**

SE 1❑ Sep 1988 Cover: 1.95 **NM** value: **Cover or less**
Circ: CapCity orders: **5,450**
• Special #1

SE 2❑ Oct 1988 Cover: 1.95 **NM** value: **Cover or less**
Circ: CapCity orders: **4,725**
• Special #2

JONNY QUEST (GOLD KEY) — Gold Key

1 ❑ Dec 1964 **NM** value: **375.00**
• **CGC:** 3 graded, best 9.4

JON SABLE, FREELANCE — First

While living in Africa, a brave man named Jon Sable tried to stop a band of poachers from preying on protected species. In retaliation, the poachers killed his family.

Years later, Jon Sable is living in New York, where, under the assumed name of B.B. Flemm, he is a favorite children's book writer. But as Jon Sable, he is a mercenary-a freelance gun for hire. If the pay is right, no job is considered too dangerous. At the same time, he possesses an inner sense of nobility and fair play.

An excellent action-adventure series, Jon Sable, Freelance was created, written, and illustrated by the great Mike Grell.

1 ❑ Jun 1983 Cover: 1.00 **NM** value: **3.00**
• **CGC:** 2 graded, best 9.4
📖 The Iron Monster! **A:** Mike Grell **W:** Mike Grell ★ 1st Appearance of Sable.

2 ❑ Jul 1983 Cover: 1.00 **NM** value: **2.00**
A: Mike Grell **W:** Mike Grell

3 ❑ Aug 1983 Cover: 1.00 **NM** value: **2.00**
A: Mike Grell **W:** Mike Grell ★ Origin of Sable.

4 ❑ Sep 1983 Cover: 1.00 **NM** value: **2.00**
A: Mike Grell **W:** Mike Grell ★ Origin of Sable.

5 ❑ Oct 1983 Cover: 1.00 **NM** value: **2.00**
A: Mike Grell **W:** Mike Grell ★ Origin of Sable.

6 ❑ Nov 1983 Cover: 1.00 **NM** value: **2.00**
A: Mike Grell **W:** Mike Grell ★ Origin of Sable.

7 ❑ Dec 1983 Cover: 1.00 **NM** value: **2.00**
A: Mike Grell **W:** Mike Grell

8 ❑ Jan 1984 Cover: 1.00 **NM** value: **2.00**
A: Mike Grell **W:** Mike Grell

9 ❑ Feb 1984 Cover: 1.00 **NM** value: **2.00**
A: Mike Grell **W:** Mike Grell

10 ❑ Mar 1984 Cover: 1.00 **NM** value: **2.00**
A: Mike Grell **W:** Mike Grell

11 ❑ Apr 1984 Cover: 1.00 **NM** value: **2.00**
A: Mike Grell **W:** Mike Grell

12 ❑ May 1984 Cover: 1.00 **NM** value: **2.00**
A: Mike Grell **W:** Mike Grell

13 ❑ Jun 1984 Cover: 1.00 **NM** value: **2.00**
A: Mike Grell **W:** Mike Grell

14 ❑ Jul 1984 Cover: 1.00 **NM** value: **2.00**
A: Mike Grell **W:** Mike Grell

15 ❑ Aug 1984 Cover: 1.00 **NM** value: **2.00**
A: Mike Grell **W:** Mike Grell

16 ❑ Sep 1984 Cover: 1.00 **NM** value: **2.00**
A: Mike Grell **W:** Mike Grell

17 ❑ Oct 1984 Cover: 1.00 **NM** value: **2.00**
A: Mike Grell **W:** Mike Grell

18 ❑ Oct 1984 Cover: 1.25 **NM** value: **2.00**
A: Mike Grell **W:** Mike Grell

19 ❑ Dec 1984 Cover: 1.25 **NM** value: **2.00**
A: Mike Grell **W:** Mike Grell

20 ❑ Jan 1985 Cover: 1.25 **NM** value: **2.00**
Circ: Statement: **40,015**
A: Mike Grell **W:** Mike Grell

21 ❑ Feb 1985 Cover: 1.25 **NM** value: **1.75**
Circ: Statement: **40,015**
A: Mike Grell **W:** Mike Grell

22 ❑ Mar 1985 Cover: 1.25 **NM** value: **1.75**
Circ: Statement: **40,015**
A: Mike Grell **W:** Mike Grell

23 ❑ Apr 1985 Cover: 1.25 **NM** value: **1.75**
Circ: Statement: **40,015**
A: Mike Grell **W:** Mike Grell

24 ❑ May 1985 Cover: 1.25 **NM** value: **1.75**
Circ: Statement: **40,015** CapCity orders: **8,500**
A: Mike Grell **W:** Mike Grell

25 ❑ Jun 1985 Cover: 1.25 **NM** value: **1.75**
Circ: Statement: **40,015** CapCity orders: **9,700**
• Shatter back-up story **A:** Mike Saenz; Mike Grell **W:** Mike Grell

26 ❑ Jul 1985 Cover: 1.25 **NM** value: **1.75**
Circ: Statement: **40,015** CapCity orders: **9,025**
• Shatter back-up story **A:** Mike Saenz; Mike Grell **W:** Mike Grell

27 ❑ Aug 1985 Cover: 1.25 **NM** value: **1.75**
Circ: Statement: **40,015** CapCity orders: **9,700**
• Shatter back-up story **A:** Mike Saenz; Mike Grell **W:** Mike Grell

28 ❑ Sep 1985 Cover: 1.25 **NM** value: **1.75**
Circ: Statement: **40,015** CapCity orders: **9,875**
• Shatter back-up story **A:** Mike Saenz; Mike Grell **W:** Mike Grell

29 ❑ Oct 1985 Cover: 1.25 **NM** value: **1.75**
Circ: Statement: **40,015** CapCity orders: **10,025**
• Shatter back-up story **A:** Mike Saenz; Mike Grell **W:** Mike Grell

30 ❑ Nov 1985 Cover: 1.25 **NM** value: **1.75**
Circ: Statement: **40,015** CapCity orders: **9,475**
• Shatter back-up story **A:** Mike Saenz; Mike Grell **W:** Mike Grell

31 ❑ Dec 1985 Cover: 1.25 **NM** value: **1.75**
Circ: Statement: **40,015** CapCity orders: **8,950**
A: Mike Grell **W:** Mike Grell

32 ❑ Jan 1986 Cover: 1.25 **NM** value: **1.75**
Circ: CapCity orders: **8,525**
A: Mike Grell **W:** Mike Grell

33 ❑ Feb 1986 Cover: 1.25 **NM** value: **1.75**
Circ: CapCity orders: **8,925**
A: Mike Grell **W:** Mike Grell

34 ❑ Mar 1986 Cover: 1.75 **NM** value: **Cover or less**
Circ: CapCity orders: **8,500**
A: Mike Grell **W:** Mike Grell

35 ❑ Apr 1986 Cover: 1.75 **NM** value: **Cover or less**
Circ: CapCity orders: **8,250**
A: Mike Grell **W:** Mike Grell

36 ❑ May 1986 Cover: 1.75 **NM** value: **Cover or less**
Circ: CapCity orders: **8,425**
A: Mike Grell **W:** Mike Grell

37 ❑ Jun 1986 Cover: 1.75 **NM** value: **Cover or less**
Circ: CapCity orders: **8,250**
A: Mike Grell **W:** Mike Grell

38 ❑ Jul 1986 Cover: 1.75 **NM** value: **Cover or less**
Circ: CapCity orders: **8,225**
A: Mike Grell **W:** Mike Grell

39 ❑ Aug 1986 Cover: 1.75 **NM** value: **Cover or less**
Circ: CapCity orders: **8,175**
A: Mike Grell **W:** Mike Grell

40 ❑ Sep 1986 Cover: 1.75 **NM** value: **Cover or less**
Circ: CapCity orders: **8,125**
A: Mike Grell **W:** Mike Grell

41 ❑ Oct 1986 Cover: 1.75 **NM** value: **Cover or less**
Circ: CapCity orders: **8,150**
A: Mike Grell **W:** Mike Grell

42 ❑ Nov 1986 Cover: 1.75 **NM** value: **Cover or less**
Circ: CapCity orders: **8,000**
A: Mike Grell **W:** Mike Grell

43 ❑ Dec 1986 Cover: 1.75 **NM** value: **Cover or less**
Circ: CapCity orders: **7,875**
A: Mike Grell **W:** Mike Grell

44 ❑ Jan 1987 Cover: 1.75 **NM** value: **Cover or less**
Circ: CapCity orders: **7,150**
A: Mike Grell **C:** Mike Grell **W:** Mike Grell

45 ❑ Mar 1987 Cover: 1.75 **NM** value: **Cover or less**
Circ: CapCity orders: **7,150**
A: Mike Grell **C:** Mike Grell **W:** Mike Grell

46 ❑ Apr 1987 Cover: 1.75 **NM** value: **Cover or less**
Circ: CapCity orders: **6,875**
A: Mike Grell **C:** Mike Grell **W:** Mike Grell

47 ❑ May 1987 Cover: 1.75 **NM** value: **Cover or less**
Circ: CapCity orders: **6,575**
A: Mike Grell **C:** Mike Grell **W:** Mike Grell

48 ❑ Jun 1987 Cover: 1.75 **NM** value: **Cover or less**
Circ: CapCity orders: **6,275**
A: Mike Grell **C:** Mike Grell **W:** Mike Grell

49 ❑ Jul 1987 Cover: 1.75 **NM** value: **Cover or less**
Circ: CapCity orders: **6,250**
A: Mike Grell **C:** Mike Grell **W:** Mike Grell

50 ❑ Aug 1987 Cover: 1.75 **NM** value: **Cover or less**
Circ: CapCity orders: **6,375**
A: Mike Grell **C:** Mike Grell **W:** Mike Grell

51 ❑ Sep 1987 Cover: 1.75 **NM** value: **Cover or less**
Circ: CapCity orders: **6,350**
A: Mike Grell **C:** Mike Grell **W:** Mike Grell

52 ❑ Oct 1987 Cover: 1.75 **NM** value: **Cover or less**
Circ: CapCity orders: **6,250**
A: Mike Grell **C:** Mike Grell **W:** Mike Grell

53 ❑ Nov 1987 Cover: 1.75 **NM** value: **Cover or less**
Circ: CapCity orders: **6,125**
A: Mike Grell **C:** Mike Grell **W:** Mike Grell

54 ❑ Dec 1987 Cover: 1.75 **NM** value: **Cover or less**
Circ: CapCity orders: **5,875**
A: Mike Grell **C:** Mike Grell **W:** Mike Grell

55 ❑ Jan 1988 Cover: 1.75 **NM** value: **Cover or less**
Circ: CapCity orders: **5,425**
A: Mike Grell **C:** Mike Grell **W:** Mike Grell

56 ❑ Feb 1988 Cover: 1.75 **NM** value: **Cover or less**
Circ: CapCity orders: **5,900**
final issue. **A:** Mike Grell **C:** Mike Grell **W:** Mike Grell

JONTAR RETURNS — Miller

1 ❑ b&w Cover: 2.00 **NM** value: **Cover or less**
2 ❑ b&w Cover: 2.00 **NM** value: **Cover or less**
3 ❑ b&w Cover: 2.00 **NM** value: **Cover or less**
4 ❑ b&w Cover: 2.00 **NM** value: **Cover or less**

JOSIE — Archie

Josie, a popular teen-girl back-up feature in Archie comic books, received her own title, She's Josie, in 1963. After a short time, the title changed to simply Josie.

Josie began as typical teen-age comic-book fare. Earning a spot on Archie's cartoon show, Josie would later form a rock band and get a show of her own, "Josie and the Pussycats." That concept would take her title over with issue #45 in 1969.

Dan DeCarlo based the character Josie on his wife Josie. When the character appeared to hit it big again with a feature film in 2001, DeCarlo was at legal loggerheads with Archie Comics over ownership of the character. The film proved to be lackluster, however, and DeCarlo died around the same time that the courts were ruling on his claim.

17 ❑ Dec 1965 Cover: 0.12 **NM** value: **14.00**
• Series continued from She's Josie #16

18 ❑ Feb 1966 Cover: 0.12 **NM** value: **14.00**
19 ❑ Apr 1966 Cover: 0.12 **NM** value: **14.00**
20 ❑ Jun 1966 Cover: 0.12 **NM** value: **14.00**
21 ❑ Aug 1966 Cover: 0.12 **NM** value: **9.00**
22 ❑ Sep 1966 Cover: 0.12 **NM** value: **9.00**
23 ❑ Oct 1966 Cover: 0.12 **NM** value: **9.00**
24 ❑ Dec 1966 Cover: 0.12 **NM** value: **9.00**
25 ❑ Feb 1967 Cover: 0.12 **NM** value: **9.00**
26 ❑ Apr 1967 Cover: 0.12 **NM** value: **9.00**
27 ❑ Jun 1967 Cover: 0.12 **NM** value: **9.00**
28 ❑ Aug 1967 Cover: 0.12 **NM** value: **9.00**
29 ❑ Sep 1967 Cover: 0.12 **NM** value: **9.00**
30 ❑ Oct 1967 Cover: 0.12 **NM** value: **9.00**
31 ❑ Dec 1967 Cover: 0.12 **NM** value: **7.00**
📖 Disco-Dream; Li'l Jinx: Following Orders!

32 ❑ Feb 1968 Cover: 0.12 **NM** value: **7.00**
33 ❑ Apr 1968 Cover: 0.12 **NM** value: **7.00**
34 ❑ Jun 1968 Cover: 0.12 **NM** value: **7.00**
35 ❑ Aug 1968 Cover: 0.12 **NM** value: **7.00**
36 ❑ Sep 1968 Cover: 0.12 **NM** value: **7.00**
37 ❑ Oct 1968 Cover: 0.12 **NM** value: **7.00**
38 ❑ Dec 1968 Cover: 0.12 **NM** value: **7.00**
39 ❑ Feb 1969 Cover: 0.12 **NM** value: **7.00**
40 ❑ Apr 1969 Cover: 0.12 **NM** value: **7.00**
41 ❑ Jun 1969 Cover: 0.12 **NM** value: **7.00**
42 ❑ Aug 1969 Cover: 0.15 **NM** value: **7.00**
43 ❑ Sep 1969 Cover: 0.15 **NM** value: **7.00**
44 ❑ Oct 1969 Cover: 0.15 **NM** value: **7.00**
• series continues as Josie & the Pussycats

JOSIE & THE PUSSYCATS — Archie

45 ❑ Dec 1969 Cover: 0.15 **NM** value: **12.00**
• **CGC:** 1 graded, best 5.0

46 ❑ Feb 1970 Cover: 0.15 **NM** value: **6.00**
Circ: Statement: **196,442**

47 ❑ Apr 1970 Cover: 0.15 **NM** value: **6.00**
Circ: Statement: **196,442**

48 ❑ Jun 1970 Cover: 0.15 **NM** value: **6.00**
Circ: Statement: **196,442**

49 ❑ Aug 1970 Cover: 0.15 **NM** value: **6.00**
Circ: Statement: **196,442**

50 ❑ Sep 1970 Cover: 0.15 **NM** value: **6.00**
Circ: Statement: **196,442**

51 ❑ Oct 1970 Cover: 0.15 **NM** value: **6.00**
Circ: Statement: **196,442**

52 ❑ Dec 1970 Cover: 0.15 **NM** value: **6.00**
Circ: Statement: **196,442**

53 ❑ Feb 1971 Cover: 0.15 **NM** value: **6.00**
54 ❑ Apr 1971 Cover: 0.15 **NM** value: **6.00**
55 ❑ Jun 1971 Cover: 0.25 **NM** value: **6.00**
• Has 1970 Statement filed 10/1/1970; avg print run 364,687; dealer sales 196,406; subs 36; total paid 196,442; max. existing 196,442; 46% of run returned

CGC-graded: Multiply prices above by **33 for 9.9 M • 16 for 9.8 NM/M • 7 for 9.6 NM+ • 5 for 9.4 NM • 2.5 for 9.2 NM- • 1.5 for 9.0 VF/NM**

56 ❑ Aug 1971 Cover: 0.25 **NM** value: **6.00**
57 ❑ Sep 1971 Cover: 0.25 **NM** value: **6.00**
58 ❑ Oct 1971 Cover: 0.25 **NM** value: **6.00**
59 ❑ Dec 1971 Cover: 0.25 **NM** value: **6.00**
60 ❑ Feb 1972 Cover: 0.25 **NM** value: **6.00**
Circ: Statement: **138,871**
61 ❑ Apr 1972 Cover: 0.25 **NM** value: **5.00**
Circ: Statement: **138,871**
62 ❑ Jun 1972 Cover: 0.25 **NM** value: **5.00**
Circ: Statement: **138,871**
63 ❑ Aug 1972 Cover: 0.25 **NM** value: **5.00**
Circ: Statement: **138,871**
64 ❑ Sep 1972 Cover: 0.25 **NM** value: **5.00**
Circ: Statement: **138,871**
65 ❑ Oct 1972 Cover: 0.25 **NM** value: **5.00**
Circ: Statement: **138,871**
66 ❑ Dec 1972 Cover: 0.25 **NM** value: **5.00**
Circ: Statement: **138,871**
67 ❑ Feb 1973 Cover: 0.25 **NM** value: **5.00**
Circ: Statement: **133,576**
68 ❑ Apr 1973 Cover: 0.25 **NM** value: **5.00**
Circ: Statement: **133,576**
• Has 1973 Statement filed 10/1/1973; avg paid circ 138,871
69 ❑ Jun 1973 Cover: 0.25 **NM** value: **5.00**
Circ: Statement: **133,576**
70 ❑ Aug 1973 Cover: 0.25 **NM** value: **5.00**
Circ: Statement: **133,576**
71 ❑ Sep 1973 Cover: 0.25 **NM** value: **4.00**
Circ: Statement: **133,576**
72 ❑ Oct 1973 Cover: 0.25 **NM** value: **4.00**
Circ: Statement: **133,576**
73 ❑ Dec 1973 Cover: 0.25 **NM** value: **4.00**
Circ: Statement: **133,576**
74 ❑ Feb 1974 Cover: 0.25 **NM** value: **4.00**
Circ: Statement: **129,170**
75 ❑ Apr 1974 Cover: 0.25 **NM** value: **4.00**
Circ: Statement: **129,170**
• Has 1973 Statement, filed 10/1/1973; avg print run 289,847; avg dealer sales 132,714; avg subs 862; total avg paid 133,576; max existent 156,271; 54% of run returned
76 ❑ Jun 1974 Cover: 0.25 **NM** value: **4.00**
Circ: Statement: **129,170**
77 ❑ Aug 1974 Cover: 0.25 **NM** value: **4.00**
Circ: Statement: **129,170**
78 ❑ Sep 1974 Cover: 0.25 **NM** value: **4.00**
Circ: Statement: **129,170**
79 ❑ Oct 1974 Cover: 0.25 **NM** value: **4.00**
Circ: Statement: **129,170**
80 ❑ Dec 1974 Cover: 0.25 **NM** value: **4.00**
Circ: Statement: **129,170**
81 ❑ Feb 1975 Cover: 0.25 **NM** value: **4.00**
Circ: Statement: **111,643**
82 ❑ Jun 1975 Cover: 0.25 **NM** value: **4.00**
Circ: Statement: **111,643**
• Has 1974 Statement; avg paid circ 129,170
83 ❑ Aug 1975 Cover: 0.25 **NM** value: **4.00**
Circ: Statement: **111,643**
84 ❑ Sep 1975 Cover: 0.25 **NM** value: **4.00**
Circ: Statement: **111,643**
85 ❑ Oct 1975 Cover: 0.25 **NM** value: **4.00**
Circ: Statement: **111,643**
86 ❑ Dec 1975 Cover: 0.25 **NM** value: **4.00**
Circ: Statement: **111,643**
87 ❑ Feb 1976 Cover: 0.30 **NM** value: **4.00**
Circ: Statement: **98,007**
88 ❑ Apr 1976 Cover: 0.30 **NM** value: **4.00**
Circ: Statement: **98,007**
89 ❑ Jun 1976 Cover: 0.30 **NM** value: **4.00**
Circ: Statement: **98,007**
90 ❑ Aug 1976 Cover: 0.30 **NM** value: **4.00**
Circ: Statement: **98,007**
91 ❑ Sep 1976 Cover: 0.30 **NM** value: **3.00**
Circ: Statement: **98,007**
92 ❑ Oct 1976 Cover: 0.30 **NM** value: **3.00**
Circ: Statement: **98,007**
93 ❑ Dec 1976 Cover: 0.30 **NM** value: **3.00**
Circ: Statement: **98,007**
94 ❑ Feb 1977 Cover: 0.30 **NM** value: **3.00**
95 ❑ Aug 1977 Cover: 0.35 **NM** value: **3.00**
• Has 1976 Statement; avg paid 98,007
96 ❑ **NM** value: **3.00**
97 ❑ **NM** value: **3.00**
98 ❑ **NM** value: **3.00**
99 ❑ 1979 Cover: 0.40 **NM** value: **3.00**
100 ❑ Oct 1979 Cover: 0.40 **NM** value: **3.00**
101 ❑ Cover: 0.50 **NM** value: **3.00**
102 ❑ Cover: 0.50 **NM** value: **3.00**
103 ❑ Cover: 0.50 **NM** value: **3.00**
104 ❑ Cover: 0.50 **NM** value: **3.00**
105 ❑ Cover: 0.60 **NM** value: **3.00**
106 ❑ Oct 1982 Cover: 0.60 **NM** value: **3.00**

JOSIE & THE PUSSYCATS (2ND SERIES) Archie

1 ❑ Cover: 2.00 **NM** value: **Cover or less**
2 ❑ Cover: 2.00 **NM** value: **Cover or less**

JOURNEY Aardvark-Vanaheim

1 ❑ Mar 1983 Cover: 1.60 **NM** value: **4.00**
A: Bill Loebs **W:** Bill Loebs
2 ❑ 1983 Cover: 1.70 **NM** value: **3.00**
A: Bill Loebs **W:** Bill Loebs
3 ❑ 1983 Cover: 1.70 **NM** value: **2.50**
A: Bill Loebs **W:** Bill Loebs
4 ❑ 1983 Cover: 1.70 **NM** value: **2.50**
A: Bill Loebs **W:** Bill Loebs
5 ❑ 1983 Cover: 1.70 **NM** value: **2.50**
A: Bill Loebs **W:** Bill Loebs
6 ❑ Cover: 1.70 **NM** value: **2.50**
A: Bill Loebs **W:** Bill Loebs
7 ❑ Cover: 1.70 **NM** value: **2.50**
A: Bill Loebs **W:** Bill Loebs
8 ❑ Mar 1984 Cover: 1.70 **NM** value: **2.50**
📖 Part 9 Partners; Part 10 Up-Country Shelter **A:** Bill Loebs **W:** Bill Loebs
9 ❑ Apr 1984 Cover: 1.70 **NM** value: **2.50**
A: Bill Loebs **W:** Bill Loebs
10 ❑ May 1984 Cover: 1.70 **NM** value: **2.50**
A: Bill Loebs **W:** Bill Loebs
11 ❑ Jun 1984 Cover: 1.70 **NM** value: **2.00**
A: Bill Loebs **W:** Bill Loebs
12 ❑ Jul 1984 Cover: 1.70 **NM** value: **2.00**
A: Bill Loebs **W:** Bill Loebs
13 ❑ Aug 1984 Cover: 1.70 **NM** value: **2.00**
A: Bill Loebs **W:** Bill Loebs
14 ❑ Sep 1984 Cover: 1.70 **NM** value: **2.00**
A: Bill Loebs **W:** Bill Loebs
15 ❑ Apr 1985 Cover: 2.00 **NM** value: **Cover or less**
16 ❑ May 1985 Cover: 2.00 **NM** value: **Cover or less**
17 ❑ Jun 1985 Cover: 2.00 **NM** value: **Cover or less**
18 ❑ Jul 1985 Cover: 2.00 **NM** value: **Cover or less**
19 ❑ Aug 1985 Cover: 2.00 **NM** value: **Cover or less**
20 ❑ Sep 1985 Cover: 2.00 **NM** value: **Cover or less**
21 ❑ Oct 1985 Cover: 2.00 **NM** value: **Cover or less**
22 ❑ Nov 1985 Cover: 2.00 **NM** value: **Cover or less**
23 ❑ Dec 1985 Cover: 2.00 **NM** value: **Cover or less**
24 ❑ Jan 1986 Cover: 2.00 **NM** value: **Cover or less**
25 ❑ Feb 1986 Cover: 2.00 **NM** value: **Cover or less**
26 ❑ Mar 1986 Cover: 2.00 **NM** value: **Cover or less**
27 ❑ Jul 1986 Cover: 2.00 **NM** value: **Cover or less**

JOURNEY INTO FEAR Superior

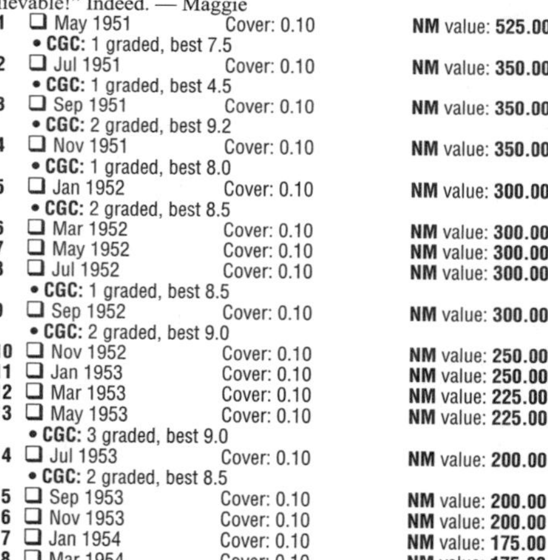

When the Comics Code came in, comics series like Journey into Fear went out. Most of the covers featured busty women being at least terrorized by vampires, skeletal figures, and the like (and, at worst, being actually clutched by said vampires, skeletal figures, and the like). Consider story titles: "Night Screams," "Debt to the Devil," "One of Us Must Die!" "Wandering Corpse," "Invisible Terror," "So Cold a Tomb," "Partners in Blood," "Death Is My Hobby," "Haunt from the Sea," "Bells of the Damned," "Pages of Death," "Out of the Crypt," "Crawling Evil," "Cult of the Dead," "Glove of the Ghoul," "The Green Witch," "Return of the Corpse," and so on and so forth.

All but the first issue carried the overline "Strange and unbelievable!" Indeed. — Maggie

1 ❑ May 1951 Cover: 0.10 **NM** value: **525.00**
• **CGC:** 1 graded, best 7.5
2 ❑ Jul 1951 Cover: 0.10 **NM** value: **350.00**
• **CGC:** 1 graded, best 4.5
3 ❑ Sep 1951 Cover: 0.10 **NM** value: **350.00**
• **CGC:** 2 graded, best 9.2
4 ❑ Nov 1951 Cover: 0.10 **NM** value: **350.00**
• **CGC:** 1 graded, best 8.0
5 ❑ Jan 1952 Cover: 0.10 **NM** value: **300.00**
• **CGC:** 2 graded, best 8.5
6 ❑ Mar 1952 Cover: 0.10 **NM** value: **300.00**
7 ❑ May 1952 Cover: 0.10 **NM** value: **300.00**
8 ❑ Jul 1952 Cover: 0.10 **NM** value: **300.00**
• **CGC:** 1 graded, best 8.5
9 ❑ Sep 1952 Cover: 0.10 **NM** value: **300.00**
• **CGC:** 2 graded, best 9.0
10 ❑ Nov 1952 Cover: 0.10 **NM** value: **250.00**
11 ❑ Jan 1953 Cover: 0.10 **NM** value: **250.00**
12 ❑ Mar 1953 Cover: 0.10 **NM** value: **225.00**
13 ❑ May 1953 Cover: 0.10 **NM** value: **225.00**
• **CGC:** 3 graded, best 9.0
14 ❑ Jul 1953 Cover: 0.10 **NM** value: **200.00**
• **CGC:** 2 graded, best 8.5
15 ❑ Sep 1953 Cover: 0.10 **NM** value: **200.00**
16 ❑ Nov 1953 Cover: 0.10 **NM** value: **200.00**
17 ❑ Jan 1954 Cover: 0.10 **NM** value: **175.00**
18 ❑ Mar 1954 Cover: 0.10 **NM** value: **175.00**
• **CGC:** 1 graded, best 7.5
19 ❑ Cover: 0.10 **NM** value: **175.00**
20 ❑ Cover: 0.10 **NM** value: **150.00**
21 ❑ Cover: 0.10 **NM** value: **150.00**

JOURNEY INTO MYSTERY (1ST SERIES) Marvel

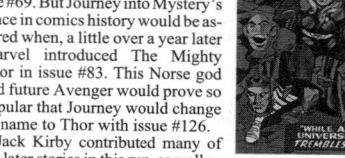

Journey Into Mystery began in 1952, published under the Atlas Comics label. Its contents were a mixed bag of monster and fantasy stories. The monsters and fantasy stories continued when Marvel put its name on the series in 1961's issue #69. But Journey into Mystery's place in comics history would be assured when, a little over a year later Marvel introduced The Mighty Thor in issue #83. This Norse god and future Avenger would prove so popular that Journey would change its name to Thor with issue #126.

Jack Kirby contributed many of the later stories in this run, as well as working with Stan Lee to create Thor. Kirby was the perfect choice to illustrate Thor's fantastic world of gods, monsters, and awe-inspiring sights such as Asgard, home of the Norse gods, and the Rainbow Bridge that spans the space between Asgard and Earth.

An editorial stunt in Thor in the late 1990s led to the series returning to its original name, hence the 378-issue gap. Journey/Thor was Marvel's highest-numbered series when Marvel pointlessly restarted Thor for an insubstantial and temporary sales boost.

-1 ❑ Jul 1997 Cover: 1.99 **NM** value: **2.00**
Circ: Diamd. preorders: **34,789**
• Flashback
1 ❑ Jun 1952 Cover: 0.10 **NM** value: **2650.00**
• **CGC:** 7 graded, best 8.5
2 ❑ Aug 1952 Cover: 0.10 **NM** value: **785.00**
• **CGC:** 3 graded, best 8.5
3 ❑ Oct 1952 Cover: 0.10 **NM** value: **580.00**
• **CGC:** 1 graded, best 6.0
4 ❑ Dec 1952 Cover: 0.10 **NM** value: **580.00**
• **CGC:** 4 graded, best 6.0
5 ❑ Feb 1953 Cover: 0.10 **NM** value: **580.00**
• **CGC:** 1 graded, best 5.0
6 ❑ Mar 1953 Cover: 0.10 **NM** value: **375.00**
• **CGC:** 1 graded, best 6.5
7 ❑ Apr 1953 Cover: 0.10 **NM** value: **375.00**
• **CGC:** 1 graded, best 7.5
8 ❑ May 1953 Cover: 0.10 **NM** value: **375.00**
• **CGC:** 3 graded, best 7.0
9 ❑ Jun 1953 Cover: 0.10 **NM** value: **375.00**
• **CGC:** 2 graded, best 6.5
10 ❑ Jul 1953 Cover: 0.10 **NM** value: **375.00**
• **CGC:** 1 graded, best 5.0
11 ❑ Aug 1953 Cover: 0.10 **NM** value: **375.00**
• **CGC:** 1 graded, best 3.5
12 ❑ Sep 1953 Cover: 0.10 **NM** value: **310.00**
• **CGC:** 2 graded, best 8.5
13 ❑ Dec 1953 Cover: 0.10 **NM** value: **310.00**
14 ❑ Feb 1954 Cover: 0.10 **NM** value: **310.00**
• **CGC:** 3 graded, best 8.5
15 ❑ Apr 1954 Cover: 0.10 **NM** value: **310.00**
• **CGC:** 1 graded, best 7.0
16 ❑ Jun 1954 Cover: 0.10 **NM** value: **310.00**
• **CGC:** 1 graded, best 4.0
17 ❑ Aug 1954 Cover: 0.10 **NM** value: **310.00**
• **CGC:** 1 graded, best 7.0
18 ❑ Oct 1954 Cover: 0.10 **NM** value: **310.00**
• **CGC:** 1 graded, best 4.5
19 ❑ Nov 1954 Cover: 0.10 **NM** value: **310.00**
• **CGC:** 1 graded, best 5.5
20 ❑ Dec 1954 Cover: 0.10 **NM** value: **310.00**
• **CGC:** 1 graded, best 5.0
21 ❑ Jan 1955 Cover: 0.10 **NM** value: **325.00**
• **CGC:** 2 graded, best 8.0
A: Joe Kubert
22 ❑ Feb 1955 Cover: 0.10 **NM** value: **310.00**
• **CGC:** 3 graded, best 8.0
23 ❑ Mar 1955 Cover: 0.10 **NM** value: **195.00**
• **CGC:** 3 graded, best 7.0
24 ❑ May 1955 Cover: 0.10 **NM** value: **195.00**
25 ❑ Jul 1955 Cover: 0.10 **NM** value: **195.00**
26 ❑ Sep 1955 Cover: 0.10 **NM** value: **195.00**
27 ❑ Oct 1955 Cover: 0.10 **NM** value: **195.00**
28 ❑ Nov 1955 Cover: 0.10 **NM** value: **195.00**
• **CGC:** 1 graded, best 8.0
29 ❑ Dec 1955 Cover: 0.10 **NM** value: **195.00**
• **CGC:** 1 graded, best 7.5
30 ❑ Jan 1956 Cover: 0.10 **NM** value: **195.00**
31 ❑ Feb 1956 Cover: 0.10 **NM** value: **195.00**
• **CGC:** 1 graded, best 5.0
32 ❑ Mar 1956 Cover: 0.10 **NM** value: **195.00**
33 ❑ Apr 1956 Cover: 0.10 **NM** value: **215.00**
A: Al Williamson
34 ❑ May 1956 Cover: 0.10 **NM** value: **195.00**
35 ❑ Jun 1956 Cover: 0.10 **NM** value: **195.00**
• **CGC:** 1 graded, best 7.5
36 ❑ Jul 1956 Cover: 0.10 **NM** value: **195.00**
37 ❑ Aug 1956 Cover: 0.10 **NM** value: **195.00**
38 ❑ Sep 1956 Cover: 0.10 **NM** value: **195.00**
• **CGC:** 2 graded, best 7.0
39 ❑ Oct 1956 Cover: 0.10 **NM** value: **195.00**
40 ❑ Nov 1956 Cover: 0.10 **NM** value: **195.00**
41 ❑ Dec 1956 Cover: 0.10 **NM** value: **175.00**
42 ❑ Jan 1957 Cover: 0.10 **NM** value: **155.00**
• **CGC:** 1 graded, best 4.0
43 ❑ Feb 1957 Cover: 0.10 **NM** value: **165.00**
• **CGC:** 3 graded, best 8.0
44 ❑ Mar 1957 Cover: 0.10 **NM** value: **165.00**
45 ❑ Apr 1957 Cover: 0.10 **NM** value: **150.00**
• **CGC:** 2 graded, best 8.5
46 ❑ May 1957 Cover: 0.10 **NM** value: **165.00**
47 ❑ Jun 1957 Cover: 0.10 **NM** value: **145.00**
• **CGC:** 1 graded, best 9.0
48 ❑ Sep 1957 Cover: 0.10 **NM** value: **155.00**
49 ❑ Oct 1957 Cover: 0.10 **NM** value: **165.00**
• **CGC:** 1 graded, best 2.5
50 ❑ Nov 1957 Cover: 0.10 **NM** value: **150.00**
51 ❑ Mar 1959 Cover: 0.10 **NM** value: **145.00**
52 ❑ May 1959 Cover: 0.10 **NM** value: **145.00**
• **CGC:** 1 graded, best 8.5
53 ❑ Jul 1959 Cover: 0.10 **NM** value: **145.00**
54 ❑ Sep 1959 Cover: 0.10 **NM** value: **145.00**
55 ❑ Nov 1959 Cover: 0.10 **NM** value: **145.00**
56 ❑ Jan 1960 Cover: 0.10 **NM** value: **145.00**
57 ❑ Mar 1960 Cover: 0.10 **NM** value: **145.00**
58 ❑ May 1960 Cover: 0.10 **NM** value: **145.00**
59 ❑ Jul 1960 Cover: 0.10 **NM** value: **145.00**
60 ❑ Sep 1960 Cover: 0.10 **NM** value: **145.00**
• **CGC:** 1 graded, best 8.0
61 ❑ Oct 1960 Cover: 0.10 **NM** value: **145.00**
62 ❑ Nov 1960 Cover: 0.10 **NM** value: **210.00**
• **CGC:** 2 graded, best 9.2
★ 1st Appearance of Xemnu: "Hulk" try-out?.
63 ❑ Dec 1960 Cover: 0.10 **NM** value: **130.00**

Other grades: Multiply prices above by **1.5 for Mint • 2/3 for Very Fine • 1/3 for Fine • 1/5 for Very Good • 1/8 for Good**

• **CGC:** 2 graded, best 8.0

64 ❑ Jan 1961 Cover: 0.10 **NM** value: **130.00**
• **CGC:** 1 graded, best 6.5

65 ❑ Feb 1961 Cover: 0.10 **NM** value: **130.00**
• **CGC:** 2 graded, best 8.5

66 ❑ Mar 1961 Cover: 0.10 **NM** value: **130.00**
• **CGC:** 2 graded, best 7.0

67 ❑ Apr 1961 Cover: 0.10 **NM** value: **130.00**
• **CGC:** 1 graded, best 5.0

68 ❑ May 1961 Cover: 0.10 **NM** value: **130.00**
• **CGC:** 1 graded, best 7.0

69 ❑ Jun 1961 Cover: 0.10 **NM** value: **130.00**

70 ❑ Jul 1961 Cover: 0.10 **NM** value: **130.00**

71 ❑ Aug 1961 Cover: 0.10 **NM** value: **130.00**
• **CGC:** 2 graded, best 7.5

72 ❑ Sep 1961 Cover: 0.10 **NM** value: **130.00**

73 ❑ Oct 1961 Cover: 0.10 **NM** value: **130.00**
• **CGC:** 2 graded, best 5.5

74 ❑ Nov 1961 Cover: 0.10 **NM** value: **130.00**

75 ❑ Dec 1961 Cover: 0.10 **NM** value: **130.00**
• **CGC:** 2 graded, best 8.0

76 ❑ Jan 1962 Cover: 0.12 **NM** value: **125.00**
Circ: Statement: **132,113** • **CGC:** 3 graded, best 8.0

77 ❑ Feb 1962 Cover: 0.12 **NM** value: **125.00**
Circ: Statement: **132,113** • **CGC:** 1 graded, best 8.5

78 ❑ Mar 1962 Cover: 0.12 **NM** value: **185.00**
Circ: Statement: **132,113** • **CGC:** 2 graded, best 9.0
• Doctor Strange prototype

79 ❑ Apr 1962 Cover: 0.12 **NM** value: **125.00**
Circ: Statement: **132,113** • **CGC:** 1 graded, best 7.5

80 ❑ May 1962 Cover: 0.12 **NM** value: **125.00**
Circ: Statement: **132,113** • **CGC:** 4 graded, best 8.0

81 ❑ Jun 1962 Cover: 0.12 **NM** value: **125.00**
Circ: Statement: **132,113** • **CGC:** 1 graded, best 8.5

82 ❑ Jul 1962 Cover: 0.12 **NM** value: **125.00**
Circ: Statement: **132,113** • **CGC:** 1 graded, best 7.5

83 ❑ Aug 1962 Cover: 0.12 **NM** value: **4100.00**
Circ: Statement: **132,113** • **CGC:** 79 graded, best 9.6
🕮 The Stone Men from Saturn; The Power of Thor; Thor the Mighty Strikes Back; The Perfect Crime; When the Jungle Sleeps; Discovery (text) **A:** Steve Ditko; Jack Kirby ★ Origin of Thor. ★ 1st Appearance of Thor.

83/GR ❑ ca. 1966 **NM** value: **110.00**
• **CGC:** 10 graded, best 9.6
🕮 The Stone Men from Saturn; The Power of Thor; Thor the Mighty Strikes Back; The Perfect Crime; When the Jungle Sleeps; Discovery (text) • Golden Records reprint (with record)★ Origin of Thor. ★ 1st Appearance of Thor.

84 ❑ Sep 1962 Cover: 0.12 **NM** value: **900.00**
Circ: Statement: **132,113** • **CGC:** 19 graded, best 9.2
🕮 The Mighty Thor vs. the Executioner; The Witching Hour; Somewhere Hides a Thing; The Recipe (text) **A:** Steve Ditko; Don Heck; Jack Kirby ★ 1st Appearance of Executioner. ★ 1st Appearance of Loki, Jane Foster. ★ 2nd Appearance of Thor.

85 ❑ Oct 1962 Cover: 0.12 **NM** value: **550.00**
Circ: Statement: **132,113** • **CGC:** 15 graded, best 9.2
🕮 Trapped By Loki, the God of Mischief; The Vengeance of Loki; Filbert's Frightful Future; Off Limits; The Clock (text) **A:** Steve Ditko; Jack Kirby ★ 1st Appearance of Balder, Loki, Odin, Tyr, Heimdall.

86 ❑ Nov 1962 Cover: 0.12 **NM** value: **325.00**
Circ: Statement: **132,113** • **CGC:** 18 graded, best 9.4
🕮 On the Trail of the Tomorrow Man; Flight to the Future; Humans, Keep Out; The Changeling; Weather Man (text) **A:** Steve Ditko; Don Heck; Jack Kirby ★ 1st Appearance of Tomorrow Man, Odin.

87 ❑ Dec 1962 Cover: 0.12 **NM** value: **240.00**
Circ: Statement: **132,113** • **CGC:** 7 graded, best 9.6
🕮 Prisoner of the Reds; I Know the Secret of the Sea-Monster; The Man on the Endless Stairway; The Comic (text) **A:** Steve Ditko; Jack Kirby

88 ❑ Jan 1963 Cover: 0.12 **NM** value: **240.00**
Circ: Statement: **187,895** • **CGC:** 16 graded, best 9.4
🕮 The Vengeance of Loki; Behind Locked Doors; Long Live the Queen; Masquerade (text) **A:** Steve Ditko; Jack Kirby

89 ❑ Feb 1963 Cover: 0.12 **NM** value: **260.00**
Circ: Statement: **187,895** • **CGC:** 11 graded, best 9.4
🕮 The Thunder God and the Thug; Barker's Body Shop; When the Switch is Pulled; From Outer Space (text) **A:** Steve Ditko; Jack Kirby ★ Origin of Thor.

90 ❑ Mar 1963 Cover: 0.12 **NM** value: **140.00**
Circ: Statement: **187,895** • **CGC:** 5 graded, best 9.2
🕮 Trapped By the Carbon-Copy Man; The Midnight Caller; I Am a Robot; Mystery Mansion (text) **A:** Steve Ditko ★ 1st Appearance of Carbon-Copy.

91 ❑ Apr 1963 Cover: 0.12 **NM** value: **120.00**
Circ: Statement: **187,895** • **CGC:** 7 graded, best 9.2
🕮 Sandu, Master of the Supernatural; The Seedlings; The Manikins; The Party (text) **A:** Steve Ditko; Joe Sinnott ★ 1st Appearance of Sandu.

92 ❑ May 1963 Cover: 0.12 **NM** value: **120.00**
Circ: Statement: **187,895** • **CGC:** 7 graded, best 9.4
🕮 The Day Loki Stole Thor's Magic Hammer; The Man Who Hated Monstro; I Used to Be Human; The Remedy Oil (text) **A:** Steve Ditko; Joe Sinnott ★ 1st Appearance of Frigga. ★ Appearance of Loki.

93 ❑ Jun 1963 Cover: 0.12 **NM** value: **140.00**
Circ: Statement: **187,895** • **CGC:** 7 graded, best 9.4
🕮 The Mysterius Radio-Active Man; The Man Who Wouldn't Die; I Saw a Martian; Over the Moon (text) **A:** Steve Ditko; Jack Kirby ★ 1st Appearance of Radioactive Man (Dr. Chen Lu)-Marvel.

94 ❑ Jul 1963 Cover: 0.12 **NM** value: **120.00**
Circ: Statement: **187,895** • **CGC:** 4 graded, best 9.4
🕮 Thor and Loki Attack the Human Race; Dinner Time on Deimos; The Gentle Old Man; Bird Talk (text) • Loki **A:** Steve Ditko; Joe Sinnott

95 ❑ Aug 1963 Cover: 0.12 **NM** value: **120.00**
Circ: Statement: **187,895** • **CGC:** 5 graded, best 9.4
🕮 The Demon Duplicators; The Tomb of Tut-Amm-Tut; Save Me From the Lizard Men; Time Machine (text) **A:** Steve Ditko; Joe Sinnott

96 ❑ Sep 1963 Cover: 0.12 **NM** value: **120.00**
Circ: Statement: **187,895** • **CGC:** 11 graded, best 9.6
🕮 Mad Merlin; Call Her Medusa; Frederick Fenton's Future; The Traveler, part 1 (text) • Merlin **A:** Steve Ditko; Joe Sinnott

97 ❑ Oct 1963 Cover: 0.12 **NM** value: **140.00**
Circ: Statement: **187,895** • **CGC:** 7 graded, best 9.6
🕮 The Mighty Thor Battles the Lava Man; The Perfect Defense; Tales of Asgard; The Traveler, part 2 (text) • Tales of Asgard backup stories begin **A:** Jack Kirby ★ 1st Appearance of Surtur, Tales of Asgard, Lava Men. ★ Versus Ymir. ★ Versus Molto.

98 ❑ Nov 1963 Cover: 0.12 **NM** value: **100.00**
Circ: Statement: **187,895** • **CGC:** 9 graded, best 9.4
🕮 Challenged By the Human Cobra; The Purple Planet; Odin Battles Ymir, King of the Ice Giants; Snowstorm (text) **A:** Jack Kirby

99 ❑ Dec 1963 Cover: 0.12 **NM** value: **100.00**
Circ: Statement: **187,895** • **CGC:** 8 graded, best 9.6
🕮 The Mysterious Mr. Hyde; Stroom's Strange Solution; Surtur the Fire Demon; The Thread (text) **A:** Jack Kirby ★ 1st Appearance of Mr. Hyde.

100 ❑ Jan 1964 Cover: 0.12 **NM** value: **100.00**
Circ: Statement: **205,075** • **CGC:** 12 graded, best 9.6
🕮 The Master Plan of Mister Hyde; The Unreal; The Storm Giants; Tricky Travel (text) **A:** Jack Kirby

101 ❑ Feb 1964 Cover: 0.12 **NM** value: **70.00**
Circ: Statement: **205,075** • **CGC:** 14 graded, best 9.4
🕮 The Return of Zarrko, the Tomorrow Man; The Enemies; The Invasion of Asgard; The Flying Saucer That Was (text) **A:** Jack Kirby ★ Appearance of Iron Man, Giant Man.

102 ❑ Mar 1964 Cover: 0.12 **NM** value: **75.00**
Circ: Statement: **205,075** • **CGC:** 13 graded, best 9.4
🕮 Slave of Zarrko, the Tomorrow Man; The Menace; Death Comes to Thor; The Green Hat (text) **A:** Jack Kirby ★ 1st Appearance of Hela, Sif, The Norns.

103 ❑ Apr 1964 Cover: 0.12 **NM** value: **75.00**
Circ: Statement: **205,075** • **CGC:** 10 graded, best 9.4
🕮 The Enchantress and the Executioner; To Live Forever; Thor's Mission to Mirmir; Poor Oscar, part 1 (text) **A:** Jack Kirby ★ 1st Appearance of Enchantress. ★ Versus Executioner.

104 ❑ May 1964 Cover: 0.12 **NM** value: **75.00**
Circ: Statement: **205,075** • **CGC:** 9 graded, best 9.4
🕮 Giants Walk the Earth; Revenge; Heimdall, Guardian of the Mystic Rainbow Bridge; Poor Oscar, part 2 (text) • giants **A:** Jack Kirby

105 ❑ Jun 1964 Cover: 0.12 **NM** value: **75.00**
Circ: Statement: **205,075** • **CGC:** 10 graded, best 9.4
🕮 The Cobra and Mr. Hyde; When Heimdall Failed; Marauder, part 1 (text) **A:** Jack Kirby ★ Versus Cobra. ★ Versus Hyde.

106 ❑ Jul 1964 Cover: 0.12 **NM** value: **75.00**
Circ: Statement: **205,075** • **CGC:** 12 graded, best 9.4
🕮 The Thunder God Strikes Back; Balder the Brave; Marauder, part 2 (text) **A:** Jack Kirby ★ Origin of Balder.

107 ❑ Aug 1964 Cover: 0.12 **NM** value: **75.00**
Circ: Statement: **205,075** • **CGC:** 12 graded, best 9.4
🕮 When the Grey Gargoyle Strikes; Baldur Must Die; Traveling Sam, part 1 (text) **A:** Jack Kirby ★ Origin of Grey Gargoyle. ★ 1st Appearance of Grey Gargoyle.

108 ❑ Sep 1964 Cover: 0.12 **NM** value: **75.00**
Circ: Statement: **205,075** • **CGC:** 12 graded, best 9.4
🕮 At the Mercy of Loki, Prince of Evil; Trapped By the Trolls; Traveling Sam, part 2 (text) **A:** Jack Kirby ★ Appearance of Doctor Strange.

109 ❑ Oct 1964 Cover: 0.12 **NM** value: **85.00**
Circ: Statement: **205,075** • **CGC:** 14 graded, best 9.4
🕮 When Magneto Strikes; Banished From Asgard **A:** Jack Kirby ★ Appearance of Magneto.

110 ❑ Nov 1964 Cover: 0.12 **NM** value: **75.00**
Circ: Statement: **205,075** • **CGC:** 13 graded, best 9.4
🕮 Every Hand Against Him; The Defeat of Odin **A:** Jack Kirby ★ Versus Loki. ★ Versus Cobra. ★ Versus Hyde.

111 ❑ Dec 1964 Cover: 0.12 **NM** value: **75.00**
Circ: Statement: **205,075** • **CGC:** 16 graded, best 9.6
🕮 The Power of the Thunder God; The Secret of Sigurd **A:** Jack Kirby ★ Versus Loki. ★ Versus Cobra. ★ Versus Hyde.

112 ❑ Jan 1965 Cover: 0.12 **NM** value: **140.00**
Circ: Statement: **232,644** • **CGC:** 39 graded, best 9.6
🕮 The Mighty Thor Battles the Incredible Hulk; The Coming of Loki **A:** Jack Kirby ★ Versus Hulk.

113 ❑ Feb 1965 Cover: 0.12 **NM** value: **75.00**
Circ: Statement: **232,644** • **CGC:** 19 graded, best 9.6
🕮 A World Gone Mad; The Boyhood of Loki **A:** Jack Kirby ★ Versus Grey Gargoyle.

114 ❑ Mar 1965 Cover: 0.12 **NM** value: **75.00**
Circ: Statement: **232,644** • **CGC:** 21 graded, best 9.6
🕮 The Stronger I Am, the Sooner I Die; The Golden Apples **A:** Jack Kirby ★ Origin of Absorbing Man. ★ 1st Appearance of Absorbing Man.

115 ❑ Apr 1965 Cover: 0.12 **NM** value: **80.00**
Circ: Statement: **232,644** • **CGC:** 21 graded, best 9.6
🕮 The Vengeance of the Thunder God; A Viper In Our Midst **A:** Jack Kirby ★ Origin of Loki.

116 ❑ May 1965 Cover: 0.12 **NM** value: **75.00**
Circ: Statement: **232,644** • **CGC:** 8 graded, best 9.8
🕮 The Trial of the Gods; The Challenge **A:** Jack Kirby ★ Appearance of Daredevil, Loki.

117 ❑ Jun 1965 Cover: 0.12 **NM** value: **65.00**
Circ: Statement: **232,644** • **CGC:** 9 graded, best 9.4
🕮 Into the Blaze of Battle; The Sword in the Scabbard **A:** Jack Kirby ★ Appearance of Loki.

118 ❑ Jul 1965 Cover: 0.12 **NM** value: **65.00**
Circ: Statement: **232,644** • **CGC:** 9 graded, best 9.6
🕮 To Kill a Thunder God; The Crimson Hand **A:** Jack Kirby ★ 1st Appearance of The Destroyer.

119 ❑ Aug 1965 Cover: 0.12 **NM** value: **70.00**
Circ: Statement: **232,644** • **CGC:** 9 graded, best 9.6
🕮 The Day of the Destroyer; Gather, Warriors **A:** Jack Kirby ★ 1st Appearance of Warriors Three, Hogun, Fandrall, Volstagg.

120 ❑ Sep 1965 Cover: 0.12 **NM** value: **65.00**
Circ: Statement: **232,644** • **CGC:** 10 graded, best 9.6
🕮 With My Hammer in Hand; Set Sail **A:** Jack Kirby

121 ❑ Oct 1965 Cover: 0.12 **NM** value: **65.00**
Circ: Statement: **232,644** • **CGC:** 22 graded, best 9.6
🕮 The Power, the Passion, the Pride; Maelstrom **A:** Jack Kirby

122 ❑ Nov 1965 Cover: 0.12 **NM** value: **65.00**
Circ: Statement: **232,644** • **CGC:** 12 graded, best 9.6
🕮 Where Mortals Fear to Tread; The Grim Spectre of Mutiny **A:** Jack Kirby

123 ❑ Dec 1965 Cover: 0.12 **NM** value: **65.00**
Circ: Statement: **232,644** • **CGC:** 11 graded, best 9.6
🕮 While A Universe Trembles!; The Jaws of the Dragon **A:** Jack Kirby **W:** Stan Lee

124 ❑ Jan 1966 Cover: 0.12 **NM** value: **65.00**
Circ: Statement: **296,251** • **CGC:** 40 graded, best 9.6
🕮 The Grandeur and the Glory; Closer Comes the Swarm **A:** Jack Kirby

125 ❑ Feb 1966 Cover: 0.12 **NM** value: **65.00**
Circ: Statement: **296,251** • **CGC:** 17 graded, best 9.6
🕮 When Meet the Immortals; The Queen Commands • Series continues in Thor #126 **A:** Jack Kirby

503 ❑ Nov 1996 Cover: 1.50 **NM** value: **Cover or less**
Circ: Statement: **59,297** Direct Market orders: **66,500**
• Series continued from Thor #502; Has 1996 Statement, filed 10/1/96; avg print run 118,439; avg sales 109,407; avg subs 2,122; avg total paid 111,529; samples 600; office use 125; max existent 112,254; 5% of run returned★ Appearance of Lost Gods. ★ Death of Red Norvell.

504 ❑ Dec 1996 Cover: 1.50 **NM** value: **Cover or less**
Circ: Statement: **59,297** Direct Market orders: **55,500**
🕮 The Lost Gods: If This Be My Quest…! **A:** Deodato Studios **W:** Tom DeFalco ★ Appearance of Ulik.

505 ❑ Jan 1997 Cover: 1.50 **NM** value: **Cover or less**
Circ: Statement: **59,297** Direct Market orders: **48,500**
🕮 The Lost Gods: What Power is This? **A:** Deodato Studios **W:** Tom DeFalco ★ Appearance of Spider-Man. ★ Versus Wrecking Crew.

506 ❑ Feb 1997 Cover: 1.50 **NM** value: **Cover or less**
Circ: Statement: **59,297** Direct Market orders: **41,750**
🕮 The Lost Gods: And Death Be Thy Foe! **A:** Deodato Studios **W:** Tom DeFalco

507 ❑ Mar 1997 Cover: 1.99 **NM** value: **Cover or less**
Circ: Statement: **59,297** Direct Market orders: **37,750**
🕮 The Lost Gods: First Blood **A:** Deodato Studios **W:** Tom DeFalco

508 ❑ Apr 1997 Cover: 1.99 **NM** value: **Cover or less**
Circ: Statement: **59,297** Direct Market orders: **35,750**
🕮 The Lost Gods: Deadly Reunion! **A:** Deodato Studios **W:** Tom DeFalco ★ Versus Red Norvell.

509 ❑ May 1997 Cover: 1.99 **NM** value: **Cover or less**
Circ: Statement: **59,297** Diamd. preorders: **34,157**
🕮 The Lost Gods: Howie's Tale • return of Loki **A:** Deodato Studios **W:** Tom DeFalco

510 ❑ Jun 1997 Cover: 1.99 **NM** value: **Cover or less**
Circ: Statement: **59,297** Diamd. preorders: **33,312**
🕮 The Lost Gods: Lest Despair Doth Claim Thee! **A:** Deodato Studios **W:** Tom DeFalco ★ Versus Red Norvell.

511 ❑ Aug 1997 Cover: 1.99 **NM** value: **Cover or less**
Circ: Statement: **59,297** Diamd. preorders: **31,304**
• gatefold summary. • Loki vs. Seth

512 ❑ Sep 1997 Cover: 1.99 **NM** value: **Cover or less**
Circ: Statement: **59,297** Diamd. preorders: **30,061**
• gatefold summary.

513 ❑ Oct 1997 Cover: 1.99 **NM** value: **Cover or less**
Circ: Diamd. preorders: **30,088**
• gatefold summary. • Asgardian storyline concludes

514 ❑ Nov 1997 Cover: 1.99 **NM** value: **Cover or less**
Circ: Diamd. preorders: **30,156**
• gatefold summary. • Shang-Chi

515 ❑ Dec 1997 Cover: 1.99 **NM** value: **Cover or less**
Circ: Diamd. preorders: **27,708**
• gatefold summary. • Shang-Chi; Has 1997 Statement, filed 10/1/97; avg print run 91,291; avg sales 57,441; avg subs 1,856; avg total paid 59,297; samples 186; office use 125; max existent 59,608; 35% of run returned

516 ❑ Jan 1998 Cover: 1.99 **NM** value: **Cover or less**
Circ: Diamd. preorders: **26,974**
• gatefold summary. • Shang-Chi

517 ❑ Feb 1998 Cover: 1.99 **NM** value: **Cover or less**
Circ: Diamd. preorders: **25,250**
• gatefold summary. • Black Widow

518 ❑ Mar 1998 Cover: 1.99 **NM** value: **Cover or less**
Circ: Diamd. preorders: **21,941**
• gatefold summary. • Black Widow

519 ❑ Apr 1998 Cover: 1.99 **NM** value: **Cover or less**
Circ: Diamd. preorders: **19,666**
• gatefold summary. • Black Widow

520 ❑ May 1998 Cover: 1.99 **NM** value: **Cover or less**
Circ: Diamd. preorders: **18,162**
• gatefold summary. • Hannibal King

521 ❑ Jun 1998 Cover: 1.99 **NM** value: **Cover or less**
Circ: Diamd. preorders: **17,674**
• gatefold summary. final issue. • Hannibal King

Anl 1 ❑ ca. 1965 Cover: 0.25 **NM** value: **125.00**
• **CGC:** 20 graded, best 9.4
• King-Size Annual. 🕮 When Titans Clash; Asgard; Trapped By Loki, God of Mischief; The Mysterious Radio-Active Man; The Mighty Thor Battles the Lava Man • 1st appearance of Hercules; New stories and reprints from JIM #85, 93 and 97; continues as Thor Annual **A:** Jack Kirby ★ 1st Appearance of Hercules. ★ Appearance of Zeus.

JOURNEY INTO MYSTERY (2ND SERIES) Marvel

In this second incarnation of the title, Marvel returned to the monster/science-fiction stories that began the first series of Journey into Mystery.

The second series' high points came in its first few issues, when it featured new stories and adaptations by Robert E. Howard and an H.P. Lovecraft, illustrated by artists including Jim Starlin and Ernie Ploog. Beginning with issue #6, however, it was decided to rely entirely on reprinted material. Not long after, at issue #19, this series was discontinued.

CGC-graded: Multiply prices above by **33 for 9.9 M • 16 for 9.8 NM/M • 7 for 9.6 NM+ • 5 for 9.4 NM • 2.5 for 9.2 NM- • 1.5 for 9.0 VF/NM**

Marvel complicated the card-catalogs of every comics archivist by changing Thor back to Journey into Mystery in 1996. So, effectively, Journey ino Mystery Vol. 1 actually continues again long after Vol. 2 ended!

1 ❑ Oct 1972 Cover: 0.20 **NM** value: **7.00**
• **CGC:** 8 graded, best 9.6
📖 Dig Me No Grave! • Robert Howard adaptation: "Dig Me No Grave" **A:** Gil Kane; Tom Palmer **W:** Roy Thomas
2 ❑ Dec 1972 Cover: 0.20 **NM** value: **4.00**
• **CGC:** 1 graded, best 9.2
3 ❑ Feb 1973 Cover: 0.20 **NM** value: **4.00**
4 ❑ Apr 1973 Cover: 0.20 **NM** value: **3.00**
• **CGC:** 1 graded, best 9.2
• H.P. Lovecraft adaptation: "Haunter of the Dark"
5 ❑ Jun 1973 Cover: 0.20 **NM** value: **3.00**
• Robert Bloch adaptation: "Shadow From the Steeple"
6 ❑ Aug 1973 Cover: 0.20 **NM** value: **2.50**
7 ❑ Oct 1973 Cover: 0.20 **NM** value: **2.50**
8 ❑ Dec 1973 Cover: 0.20 **NM** value: **2.50**
9 ❑ Feb 1974 Cover: 0.20 **NM** value: **2.50**
10 ❑ Apr 1974 Cover: 0.20 **NM** value: **2.50**
11 ❑ Jun 1974 Cover: 0.25 **NM** value: **2.50**
12 ❑ Aug 1974 Cover: 0.25 **NM** value: **2.50**
13 ❑ Oct 1974 Cover: 0.25 **NM** value: **2.50**
14 ❑ Dec 1974 Cover: 0.25 **NM** value: **2.50**
15 ❑ Feb 1975 Cover: 0.25 **NM** value: **2.50**
• **CGC:** 1 graded, best 9.2
16 ❑ Apr 1975 Cover: 0.25 **NM** value: **2.50**
17 ❑ Jun 1975 Cover: 0.25 **NM** value: **2.50**
18 ❑ Aug 1975 Cover: 0.25 **NM** value: **2.50**
19 ❑ Oct 1975 Cover: 0.25 **NM** value: **2.50**
final issue.

JOURNEY INTO UNKNOWN WORLDS — Atlas

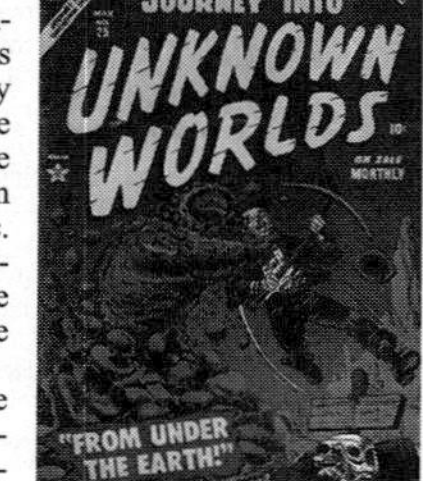

A science-fiction/horror title during the 1950s, Journey Into Unknown Worlds was atypical of Atlas fare of the time in the relative subtlety of its approach. The horror was more of "isn't that strange" flavor than the "eeww! gross!" approach found in such Atlas horror titles as Mystic. And the science fiction was more literary and fantasy-oriented than the bug-eyed monster stories and space operas popular in other titles.

Such top-of-the-line artists as Joe Kubert, Steve Ditko, Al Williamson, Reed Crandall, and the underrated Angelo Torres all graced its pages with fine, detailed work. Journey Into Unknown Worlds therefore did not seem as likely to suffer when the Comics Code came in during the mid-1950s. But, quality notwithstanding, it did not survive the Atlas implosion of 1957.

1 ❑ Sep 1950 Cover: 0.10 **NM** value: **1450.00**
• **CGC:** 6 graded, best 9.0
• #36; Numbering continued from Teen #35
2 ❑ Dec 1950 Cover: 0.10 **NM** value: **675.00**
• **CGC:** 1 graded, best 8.0
• #37; Numbering continued from Teen
3 ❑ Feb 1951 Cover: 0.10 **NM** value: **510.00**
• **CGC:** 2 graded, best 6.5
• #38; Numbering continued from Teen
4 ❑ Apr 1951 Cover: 0.10 **NM** value: **375.00**
5 ❑ Jun 1951 Cover: 0.10 **NM** value: **375.00**
• **CGC:** 2 graded, best 9.0
6 ❑ Aug 1951 Cover: 0.10 **NM** value: **375.00**
• **CGC:** 1 graded, best 5.0
7 ❑ Oct 1951 Cover: 0.10 **NM** value: **550.00**
• **CGC:** 1 graded, best 6.5
A: Basil Wolverton
8 ❑ Dec 1951 Cover: 0.10 **NM** value: **375.00**
• **CGC:** 2 graded, best 8.0
9 ❑ Feb 1952 Cover: 0.10 **NM** value: **375.00**
• **CGC:** 4 graded, best 7.0
10 ❑ Apr 1952 Cover: 0.10 **NM** value: **375.00**
11 ❑ Jun 1952 Cover: 0.10 **NM** value: **240.00**
• **CGC:** 1 graded, best 9.0
12 ❑ Aug 1952 Cover: 0.10 **NM** value: **240.00**
13 ❑ Oct 1952 Cover: 0.10 **NM** value: **240.00**
14 ❑ Dec 1952 Cover: 0.10 **NM** value: **435.00**
A: Basil Wolverton
15 ❑ Feb 1953 Cover: 0.10 **NM** value: **435.00**
• **CGC:** 1 graded, best 7.0
A: Basil Wolverton
16 ❑ Mar 1953 Cover: 0.10 **NM** value: **220.00**
• **CGC:** 1 graded, best 4.5
17 ❑ Apr 1953 Cover: 0.10 **NM** value: **220.00**
18 ❑ May 1953 Cover: 0.10 **NM** value: **220.00**
19 ❑ Jun 1953 Cover: 0.10 **NM** value: **220.00**
20 ❑ Jul 1953 Cover: 0.10 **NM** value: **220.00**
21 ❑ Aug 1953 Cover: 0.10 **NM** value: **150.00**
• **CGC:** 1 graded, best 4.5
22 ❑ Sep 1953 Cover: 0.10 **NM** value: **150.00**
• **CGC:** 2 graded, best 9.0
23 ❑ Dec 1953 Cover: 0.10 **NM** value: **150.00**
• **CGC:** 1 graded, best 4.0
24 ❑ Feb 1954 Cover: 0.10 **NM** value: **150.00**
• **CGC:** 1 graded, best 9.2
25 ❑ Mar 1954 Cover: 0.10 **NM** value: **150.00**
📖 The Castle of Shadows; The Headhunters (text); When Death Comes A-Calling; The World Within; One Extra Head; From Under The Earth **A:** Robert Q. Sale; Doug Wildey; Dan Loprino
26 ❑ Apr 1954 Cover: 0.10 **NM** value: **150.00**
• **CGC:** 2 graded, best 8.5
27 ❑ May 1954 Cover: 0.10 **NM** value: **150.00**
• **CGC:** 1 graded, best 7.0
28 ❑ Jun 1954 Cover: 0.10 **NM** value: **150.00**
• **CGC:** 1 graded, best 5.5
29 ❑ Jul 1954 Cover: 0.10 **NM** value: **150.00**
• **CGC:** 1 graded, best 6.0
30 ❑ Aug 1954 Cover: 0.10 **NM** value: **150.00**
• **CGC:** 1 graded, best 8.5
31 ❑ Oct 1954 Cover: 0.10 **NM** value: **100.00**
32 ❑ Dec 1954 Cover: 0.10 **NM** value: **100.00**
• **CGC:** 2 graded, best 8.0
33 ❑ Feb 1955 Cover: 0.10 **NM** value: **100.00**
• **CGC:** 1 graded, best 7.0
34 ❑ Apr 1955 Cover: 0.10 **NM** value: **100.00**
• **CGC:** 1 graded, best 8.5
35 ❑ Jun 1955 Cover: 0.10 **NM** value: **100.00**
• **CGC:** 1 graded, best 6.0
36 ❑ Aug 1955 Cover: 0.10 **NM** value: **100.00**
• **CGC:** 1 graded, best 8.5
37 ❑ Sep 1955 Cover: 0.10 **NM** value: **100.00**
• **CGC:** 2 graded, best 8.5
38 ❑ Oct 1955 Cover: 0.10 **NM** value: **100.00**
• **CGC:** 1 graded, best 7.0
39 ❑ Nov 1955 Cover: 0.10 **NM** value: **100.00**
• **CGC:** 1 graded, best 7.0
40 ❑ Dec 1955 Cover: 0.10 **NM** value: **100.00**
• **CGC:** 2 graded, best 7.5
41 ❑ Jan 1956 Cover: 0.10 **NM** value: **80.00**
• **CGC:** 1 graded, best 6.5
42 ❑ Feb 1956 Cover: 0.10 **NM** value: **80.00**
• **CGC:** 1 graded, best 5.5
43 ❑ Mar 1956 Cover: 0.10 **NM** value: **80.00**
• **CGC:** 1 graded, best 8.0
44 ❑ Apr 1956 Cover: 0.10 **NM** value: **80.00**
• **CGC:** 1 graded, best 7.5
45 ❑ May 1956 Cover: 0.10 **NM** value: **80.00**
• **CGC:** 1 graded, best 6.5
46 ❑ Jun 1956 Cover: 0.10 **NM** value: **80.00**
• **CGC:** 2 graded, best 9.0
47 ❑ Jul 1956 Cover: 0.10 **NM** value: **80.00**
• **CGC:** 1 graded, best 7.0
48 ❑ Aug 1956 Cover: 0.10 **NM** value: **80.00**
49 ❑ Sep 1956 Cover: 0.10 **NM** value: **80.00**
• **CGC:** 1 graded, best 7.5
50 ❑ Oct 1956 Cover: 0.10 **NM** value: **80.00**
• **CGC:** 1 graded, best 5.0
51 ❑ Nov 1956 Cover: 0.10 **NM** value: **80.00**
• **CGC:** 1 graded, best 7.0
52 ❑ Dec 1956 Cover: 0.10 **NM** value: **80.00**
• **CGC:** 1 graded, best 6.5
53 ❑ Jan 1957 Cover: 0.10 **NM** value: **80.00**
54 ❑ Feb 1957 Cover: 0.10 **NM** value: **80.00**
• **CGC:** 1 graded, best 8.0

JOURNEYMAN — Image

1 ❑ Aug 1999 Cover: 2.95 **NM** value: **Cover or less**
Circ: Diamd. preorders: **6,271**
A: Brandon McKinney **W:** Brandon McKinney
2 ❑ Sep 1999 Cover: 2.95 **NM** value: **Cover or less**
Circ: Diamd. preorders: **5,306**
A: Brandon McKinney **W:** Brandon McKinney
3 ❑ Oct 1999 Cover: 2.95 **NM** value: **Cover or less**
Circ: Diamd. preorders: **3,843**
A: Brandon McKinney **W:** Brandon McKinney

JOURNEYMAN/DARK AGES, THE — Lucid

1 ❑ Sum 1997, b&w Cover: 3.00 **NM** value: **Cover or less**
No issue number. • San Diego edition.

JOURNEY SAGA — Fantagraphics

Bk 1❑ Cover: 6.95 **NM** value: **Cover or less**
• Tall Tales

JOURNEY: WARDRUMS — Fantagraphics

1 ❑ Cover: 2.00 **NM** value: **Cover or less**
2 ❑ Cover: 2.00 **NM** value: **Cover or less**

JR. CARROT PATROL — Dark Horse

1 ❑ b&w Cover: 2.00 **NM** value: **Cover or less**
A: Rick Geary **W:** Rick Geary
2 ❑ b&w Cover: 2.00 **NM** value: **Cover or less**
📖 The Backwards Machine **A:** Rick Geary **W:** Rick Geary

JSA — DC

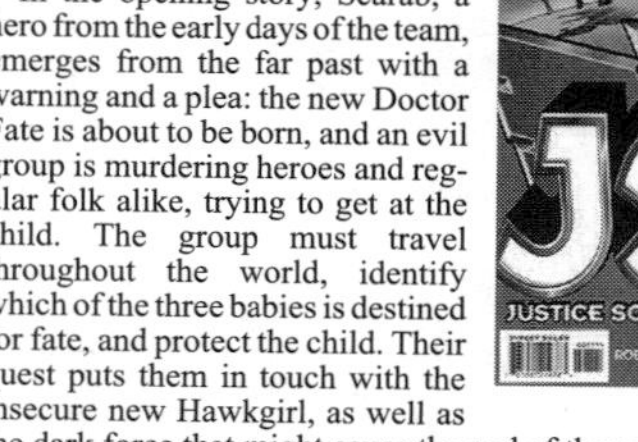

Old and new members of the Justice Society of America are brought together in this story by writers James Robinson and David Goyer, to create the group for a new era.

In the opening story, Scarab, a hero from the early days of the team, emerges from the far past with a warning and a plea: the new Doctor Fate is about to be born, and an evil group is murdering heroes and regular folk alike, trying to get at the child. The group must travel throughout the world, identify which of the three babies is destined for fate, and protect the child. Their quest puts them in touch with the insecure new Hawkgirl, as well as the dark force that might cause the end of them all.

1 ❑ Aug 1999 Cover: 2.50 **NM** value: **Cover or less**
Circ: Diamd. preorders: **69,313** • **CGC:** 8 graded, best 9.8
📖 Justice Be Done **A:** Stephen Sadowski **W:** James Robinson; David Goyer
2 ❑ Sep 1999 Cover: 2.50 **NM** value: **Cover or less**
Circ: Diamd. preorders: **55,885** • **CGC:** 1 graded, best 9.0
📖 The Wheel of Life **A:** Stephen Sadowski **W:** James Robinson; David Goyer ★ Versus Mordru.
3 ❑ Oct 1999 Cover: 2.50 **NM** value: **Cover or less**
Circ: Diamd. preorders: **51,803** • **CGC:** 1 graded, best 9.8
📖 Old Souls **A:** Stephen Sadowski **W:** James Robinson; David Goyer ★ Versus Mordru.
4 ❑ Nov 1999 Cover: 2.50 **NM** value: **Cover or less**
Circ: Diamd. preorders: **49,948**
• identity of new Doctor Fate revealed ★ Versus Mordru.
5 ❑ Dec 1999 Cover: 2.50 **NM** value: **Cover or less**
Circ: Diamd. preorders: **50,250**
📖 Grounded **A:** Aucoin **W:** James Robinson; David Goyer
6 ❑ Jan 2000 Cover: 2.50 **NM** value: **Cover or less**
Circ: Diamd. preorders: **48,616**
📖 Justice, Like Lightning… **A:** Marcos Martin **W:** David Goyer; Geoff Johns
7 ❑ Feb 2000 Cover: 2.50 **NM** value: **Cover or less**
Circ: Diamd. preorders: **50,062**
8 ❑ Mar 2000 Cover: 2.50 **NM** value: **Cover or less**
Circ: Diamd. preorders: **45,590**
9 ❑ Apr 2000 Cover: 2.50 **NM** value: **Cover or less**
Circ: Diamd. preorders: **42,392**
📖 Black Planet **A:** Stephen Sadowski **W:** David Goyer; Geoff Johns
10 ❑ May 2000 Cover: 2.50 **NM** value: **Cover or less**
Circ: Diamd. preorders: **42,813**
📖 Wild Hunt **A:** Stephen Sadowski **W:** David Goyer; Geoff Johns
11 ❑ Jun 2000 Cover: 2.50 **NM** value: **Cover or less**
Circ: Diamd. preorders: **42,370**
12 ❑ Jul 2000 Cover: 2.50 **NM** value: **Cover or less**
Circ: Diamd. preorders: **42,078**
13 ❑ Aug 2000 Cover: 2.50 **NM** value: **Cover or less**
Circ: Diamd. preorders: **42,317**
14 ❑ Sep 2000 Cover: 2.50 **NM** value: **Cover or less**
Circ: Diamd. preorders: **42,297**
📖 Chaos Theory **A:** Stephen Sadowski **W:** David Goyer; Geoff Johns
15 ❑ Oct 2000 Cover: 2.50 **NM** value: **Cover or less**
Circ: Diamd. preorders: **40,085**
📖 Crime and Punishment **A:** Stephen Sadowski **W:** David S. Goyer; Geoff Johns
16 ❑ Nov 2000 Cover: 2.50 **NM** value: **Cover or less**
Circ: Diamd. preorders: **40,250**
📖 Injustice Be Done, Part 1 **A:** Stephen Sadowski **W:** David Goyer; Geoff Johns
17 ❑ Dec 2000 Cover: 2.50 **NM** value: **Cover or less**
Circ: Diamd. preorders: **39,618**
📖 Injustice Be Done, Part 2 **A:** Stephen Sadowski **W:** David Goyer; Geoff Johns
18 ❑ Jan 2001 Cover: 2.50 **NM** value: **Cover or less**
Circ: Diamd. preorders: **39,464**
📖 Injustice Be Done, Part 3 **A:** Stephen Sadowski **W:** David Goyer; Geoff Johns
19 ❑ Feb 2001 Cover: 2.50 **NM** value: **Cover or less**
Circ: Diamd. preorders: **39,005**
📖 Injustice Be Done, Part 4 **A:** Stephen Sadowski **W:** David Goyer; Geoff Johns
20 ❑ Mar 2001 Cover: 2.50 **NM** value: **Cover or less**
Circ: Diamd. preorders: **38,321**
📖 Injustice Be Done, Part 5 **A:** Stephen Sadowski **W:** David Goyer; Geoff Johns
21 ❑ Apr 2001 Cover: 2.50 **NM** value: **Cover or less**
Circ: Diamd. preorders: **38,422**
📖 Guardian Angels **A:** Buzz **W:** David Goyer; Geoff Johns
22 ❑ May 2001 Cover: 2.50 **NM** value: **Cover or less**
Circ: Diamd. preorders: **38,377** • **CGC:** 1 graded, best 9.6
📖 Lost Friends **A:** Michael Bair; Rags Morales; Buzz **W:** David Goyer; Geoff Johns
23 ❑ Jul 2001 Cover: 2.50 **NM** value: **Cover or less**
Circ: Diamd. preorders: **42,558** • **CGC:** 6 graded, best 9.8
24 ❑ Aug 2001 Cover: 2.50 **NM** value: **Cover or less**
Circ: Diamd. preorders: **41,365** • **CGC:** 2 graded, best 9.6
25 ❑ Sep 2001 Cover: 2.50 **NM** value: **Cover or less**
Circ: Diamd. preorders: **44,172**
26 ❑ Oct 2001 Cover: 2.50 **NM** value: **Cover or less**
Circ: Diamd. preorders: **46,203**
Anl 1❑ Oct 2000 Cover: 3.50 **NM** value: **Cover or less**
Circ: Diamd. preorders: **29,617** • **CGC:** 1 graded, best 9.2
📖 Genesis • Planet DC **W:** David Goyer ★ 1st Appearance of Nemesis.
Bk 1❑ Cover: 14.95 **NM** value: **Cover or less**
📖 Justice Be Done • Collects JSA #1-5, JSA Secret Files #1 **A:** Stephen Sadowski **W:** James Robinson; David Goyer

JSA SECRET FILES — DC

1 ❑ Aug 1999 Cover: 4.95 **NM** value: **Cover or less**
Circ: Diamd. preorders: **32,727** • **CGC:** 1 graded, best 9.6
📖 Gathering of Storm; Dead EndsHistory 101 • background information on team's formation and members **A:** Scott Benefiel; Eddy Newell; Chris Weston **W:** James Robinson; Steven Grant; David S. Goyer; Ron Marz
2 ❑ Sep 1999 Cover: 4.95 **NM** value: **Cover or less**
Circ: Diamd. preorders: **27,842**

JSA: THE LIBERTY FILE — DC

1 ❑ Feb 2000 Cover: 6.95 **NM** value: **Cover or less**
Circ: Diamd. preorders: **26,289**
A: Tony Harris; Ray Snyder **W:** Tony Harris; Dan Jolley
2 ❑ Mar 2000 Cover: 6.95 **NM** value: **Cover or less**
Circ: Diamd. preorders: **23,434**
A: Tony Harris; Ray Snyder **W:** Tony Harris; Dan Jolley

JUDE, THE FORGOTTEN SAINT — Catechetical Guild

1 ❑ **NM** value: **10.00**

JUDGE CHILD — Eagle

1 ❑ Cover: 1.50 **NM** value: **2.00**
📖 Judge Dredd: The Judge Child Quest **A:** Brian Bolland; Ron Smith; Mike McMahon **W:** John Wagner

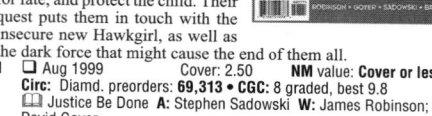

Other grades: Multiply prices above by **1.5 for Mint • 2/3 for Very Fine • 1/3 for Fine • 1/5 for Very Good • 1/8 for Good**

2 ❑ Cover: 1.50 **NM** value: **2.00**
Judge Dredd: The Judge Child Quest
3 ❑ Cover: 1.50 **NM** value: **2.00**
Judge Dredd: The Judge Child Quest
4 ❑ Cover: 1.50 **NM** value: **2.00**
Judge Dredd: The Judge Child Quest
5 ❑ Cover: 1.50 **NM** value: **2.00**
Judge Dredd: The Judge Child Quest
Bk 1❑ Cover: 12.95 **NM** value: **Cover or less**

JUDGE COLT — Gold Key

1 ❑ Oct 1969 Cover: 0.15 **NM** value: **15.00**
2 ❑ Feb 1970 Cover: 0.15 **NM** value: **12.00**
3 ❑ May 1970 Cover: 0.15 **NM** value: **12.00**
4 ❑ Sep 1970 Cover: 0.15 **NM** value: **10.00**
• **CGC:** 1 graded, best 9.6

JUDGE DREDD: AMERICA — Fleetway-Quality

1 ❑ Cover: 2.95 **NM** value: **Cover or less**
Circ: CapCity orders: **3,925**
America
2 ❑ Cover: 2.95 **NM** value: **Cover or less**

JUDGE DREDD: BAD SCIENCE — Fleetway-Quality

Bk 1❑ Cover: 7.95 **NM** value: **Cover or less**
A: Pat Broderick

JUDGE DREDD CLASSICS — Fleetway-Quality

62 ❑ Cover: 1.95 **NM** value: **Cover or less**
63 ❑ Cover: 1.95 **NM** value: **Cover or less**
64 ❑ Cover: 1.95 **NM** value: **Cover or less**
Judge Dredd: Loonies' Moon; Judge Dredd: The Mega-Rackets **A:** Ron Smith; Colin Wilson **W:** T.B. Grover
65 ❑ Cover: 1.95 **NM** value: **Cover or less**
Judge Dredd: The Exo-men, Part 2 **A:** Brian Bolland; Ron Smith **W:** John Howard
66 ❑ Cover: 1.95 **NM** value: **Cover or less**
Judge Dredd: Monkey Business At The Charles Darwin Block **A:** Mike McMahon **W:** John Howard; T.B. Grover
67 ❑ Cover: 1.95 **NM** value: **Cover or less**
The Fink; Date With Destiny **A:** Massimo Belardinelli; Mike McMahon **W:** Mike Cruden; T.B. Grover
68 ❑ Cover: 1.95 **NM** value: **Cover or less**
69 ❑ Cover: 1.95 **NM** value: **Cover or less**
Judge Dredd: Battle of the Black Atlantic; Judge Dredd: Dredd and the Mob Blitzers; Judge Dredd: Sob Story; Judge Dredd: Who Killed Pug Ugly? **A:** Dave Gibbons; Ron Smith **W:** John Howard; T.B. Grover
70 ❑ Cover: 1.95 **NM** value: **Cover or less**
71 ❑ Cover: 1.95 **NM** value: **Cover or less**
Judge Dredd: Bright Eyes…Burning Like Fire!; Judge Dredd: The Weather Man **A:** Ron Smith **W:** John Wagner; T.B. Grover
72 ❑ Cover: 1.95 **NM** value: **Cover or less**
73 ❑ Cover: 1.95 **NM** value: **Cover or less**
Judge Dredd: The Big Sleep; Judge Dredd: The Art of Kenny Who? **A:** Cam Kennedy **W:** T.B. Grover
74 ❑ Cover: 1.95 **NM** value: **Cover or less**
Judge Dredd: High Society; Judge Dredd: The House on Runner's Walk; Judge Dredd: The Executioner; The Killer in the Cab; Judge Dredd: Palais de Boing **A:** Barry Mitchell; Emberton; John Richardson **W:** Alan Moore; John Howard; T.B. Grover
75 ❑ Cover: 1.95 **NM** value: **Cover or less**
Judge Dredd: Death of a Judge; Judge Dredd: Rumble in the Jungle; Resentment **A:** Massimo Belardinelli; Ron Smith; Emberton **W:** Alan Hebden; John Howard; T.B. Grover
76 ❑ Cover: 1.95 **NM** value: **Cover or less**
Judge Dredd: Diary of a Mad Citizen; Judge Dredd: The Mega Rackets **A:** Ron Smith; Emberton **W:** T.B. Grover
77 ❑ Cover: 1.95 **NM** value: **Cover or less**
Judge Dredd: The Falucci Tape final issue. **A:** Cliff Robinson; Cam Kennedy **W:** T.B. Grover

JUDGE DREDD (DC) — DC

1 ❑ Aug 1994 Cover: 1.95 **NM** value: **2.50**
Circ: CapCity orders: **23,600**
A: Michael Avon Oeming **W:** Andy Helfer
2 ❑ Sep 1994 Cover: 1.95 **NM** value: **2.25**
Circ: CapCity orders: **14,250**
3 ❑ Oct 1994 Cover: 1.95 **NM** value: **2.25**
Circ: CapCity orders: **12,200**
4 ❑ Nov 1994 Cover: 1.95 **NM** value: **2.00**
Circ: CapCity orders: **1,100**
48 Hours: A Two-Day Story-Day One: Aftershock **A:** Michael Avon Oeming; Doug Selogy **W:** Andy Helfer
5 ❑ Dec 1994 Cover: 1.95 **NM** value: **2.00**
Circ: CapCity orders: **10,000**
6 ❑ Jan 1995 Cover: 1.95 **NM** value: **2.00**
Circ: CapCity orders: **9,000**
Malice in Wonderland **A:** J.H. Williams III; Cesar Lobo; Doug Selogy **W:** Andy Helfer
7 ❑ Feb 1995 Cover: 1.95 **NM** value: **2.00**
Circ: CapCity orders: **7,825**
8 ❑ Mar 1995 Cover: 1.95 **NM** value: **2.00**
Circ: CapCity orders: **6,950**
9 ❑ Apr 1995 Cover: 1.95 **NM** value: **2.00**
Circ: CapCity orders: **6,150**
• homage to Judge Dredd #1 (first series)
10 ❑ May 1995 Cover: 1.95 **NM** value: **2.00**
Circ: CapCity orders: **4,425**
11 ❑ Jun 1995 Cover: 2.25 **NM** value: **Cover or less**
Circ: CapCity orders: **4,175**
Dredd Again **A:** Randy Green; Christian Alamy; Doug Selogy **W:** Andy Helfer
12 ❑ Jul 1995 Cover: 2.25 **NM** value: **Cover or less**
Circ: CapCity orders: **4,875**
13 ❑ Aug 1995 Cover: 2.25 **NM** value: **Cover or less**
Circ: CapCity orders: **5,600**
Block Wars, Part 1
14 ❑ Sep 1995 Cover: 2.25 **NM** value: **Cover or less**
Circ: CapCity orders: **5,450**
Block Wars, Part 2
15 ❑ Oct 1995 Cover: 2.25 **NM** value: **Cover or less**
Circ: CapCity orders: **4,750**
Block Wars, Part 3 **A:** Tim Gula **W:** D.G. Chichester
16 ❑ Nov 1995 Cover: 2.25 **NM** value: **Cover or less**
17 ❑ Dec 1995 Cover: 2.25 **NM** value: **Cover or less**
18 ❑ Jan 1996 Cover: 2.25 **NM** value: **Cover or less**
final issue.

JUDGE DREDD: EMERALD ISLE — Fleetway-Quality

1 ❑ ca. 1991 Cover: 4.95 **NM** value: **Cover or less**
• **CGC:** 1 graded, best 9.6
No issue number.

JUDGE DREDD: FUTURE CRIME — Fleetway-Quality

Bk 1❑ full color Cover: 7.95 **NM** value: **Cover or less**

JUDGE DREDD: HALL OF JUSTICE — Fleetway-Quality

Bk 1❑ Cover: 7.95 **NM** value: **Cover or less**

JUDGE DREDD: LEGENDS OF THE LAW — DC

In 1994, DC received the rights to begin publishing their own comics featuring Judge Dredd, the legendary futuristic lawman from Britain's 2000 A.D. In order to avoid having to explain the history of almost a thousand Judge Dredd adventures to American readers, DC decided to move Judge Dredd from the 22nd century to the year 2045 — presumably before all the other events of the Judge Dredd continuity had happened.

DC rolled out two new Judge Dredd series in 1994, Judge Dredd (DC), and Judge Dredd: Legends of the Law. Despite the sudden erasure of Dredd history, Legends of the Law was intended to focus on the early exploits of Judge Dredd. As such, the series was modeled after Legends of the Dark Knight. To accomplish this task, DC recruited writers John Wagner (co-creator of Judge Dredd) and Alan Grant (a prolific Dredd storyteller for the series 2000 A.D.), along with a rotating team of artists.

1 ❑ Dec 1994 Cover: 1.95 **NM** value: **2.50**
Circ: CapCity orders: **13,750**
The Organ Donors, Part 1 **A:** Brent Anderson; Dave Dorman(cover) **W:** Alan Grant; John Wagner
2 ❑ Jan 1995 Cover: 1.95 **NM** value: **2.00**
Circ: CapCity orders: **9,200**
The Organ Donors, Part 2 **A:** Brent Anderson **W:** Alan Grant; John Wagner
3 ❑ Feb 1995 Cover: 1.95 **NM** value: **2.00**
Circ: CapCity orders: **7,575**
The Organ Donors, Part 3 **A:** Brent Anderson **W:** Alan Grant; John Wagner
4 ❑ Mar 1995 Cover: 1.95 **NM** value: **2.00**
Circ: CapCity orders: **6,775**
The Organ Donors, Part 4 **A:** Brent Anderson **W:** Alan Grant; John Wagner
5 ❑ Apr 1995 Cover: 1.95 **NM** value: **2.00**
Circ: CapCity orders: **5,775**
Trial by Gunfire, Part 1 **A:** Anthony Williams **W:** D.G. Chichester
6 ❑ May 1995 Cover: 1.95 **NM** value: **2.00**
Circ: CapCity orders: **3,975**
Trial by Gunfire, Part 2 **A:** Anthony Williams **W:** D.G. Chichester
7 ❑ Jun 1995 Cover: 2.25 **NM** value: **Cover or less**
Circ: CapCity orders: **3,825**
Trial by Gunfire, Part 3 **A:** Anthony Williams **W:** D.G. Chichester
8 ❑ Jul 1995 Cover: 2.25 **NM** value: **Cover or less**
Circ: CapCity orders: **4,550**
Fall from Grace, Part 1 **A:** John Byrne
9 ❑ Aug 1995 Cover: 2.25 **NM** value: **Cover or less**
Circ: CapCity orders: **5,150**
Fall from Grace, Part 2 **A:** John Byrne
10 ❑ Sep 1995 Cover: 2.25 **NM** value: **Cover or less**
Circ: CapCity orders: **4,925**
Fall from Grace, Part 3 **A:** John Byrne
11 ❑ Oct 1995 Cover: 2.25 **NM** value: **Cover or less**
Circ: CapCity orders: **4,275**
Dredd of Knight, Part 1 **C:** John Byrne
12 ❑ Nov 1995 Cover: 2.25 **NM** value: **Cover or less**
Dredd of Knight, Part 2
13 ❑ Dec 1995 Cover: 2.25 **NM** value: **Cover or less**
Dredd of Knight, Part 3 final issue.

JUDGE DREDD MEGA-COLLECTION — Fleetway-Quality

Bk 1/HC❑b&w Cover: 14.95 **NM** value: **Cover or less**
hardcover. • strip reprints

JUDGE DREDD: METAL FATIGUE — Fleetway-Quality

Bk 1❑ Cover: 7.95 **NM** value: **Cover or less**

JUDGE DREDD: RAPTAUR — Fleetway-Quality

1 ❑ Cover: 2.95 **NM** value: **Cover or less**
Circ: CapCity orders: **3,925**
Judge Dredd: Raptaur • Judge Dredd
2 ❑ Cover: 2.95 **NM** value: **Cover or less**
Circ: CapCity orders: **2,625**
Judge Dredd: Raptaur • Judge Dredd

JUDGE DREDD'S CRIME FILE (EAGLE) — Eagle

1 ❑ Cover: 1.50 **NM** value: **3.00**
Circ: CapCity orders: **3,475**
2 ❑ Cover: 1.50 **NM** value: **3.00**
Circ: CapCity orders: **2,775**
3 ❑ Cover: 1.50 **NM** value: **3.00**
Circ: CapCity orders: **2,600**
4 ❑ Nov 1985 Cover: 1.50 **NM** value: **3.00**
Circ: CapCity orders: **2,459**
Umpty Baggers **A:** Ron Smith; Ian Gibson **W:** Alan Grant; John Wagner
5 ❑ Cover: 1.50 **NM** value: **3.00**
Palais De Boing; The Psychos!; The Great Muldoon; The Testimonial Of Lips Lazarus **A:** Barry Mitchell **W:** John Wagner
6 ❑ Cover: 1.50 **NM** value: **3.00**

JUDGE DREDD'S CRIME FILE (FLEETWAY) — Fleetway-Quality

1 ❑ Cover: 5.95 **NM** value: **Cover or less**
C: Brian Bolland
2 ❑ Cover: 5.95 **NM** value: **Cover or less**
Judge Dredd: Anatomy Of A Crime; Judge Dredd: Vampire Effect; Robo-Hunter; Judge Dredd: Compulsory Purchase; Judge Dredd: Mega-City Rumble; Judge Dredd: The Big Itch! **A:** Mike McMahon; Ian Gibson; Carlos Ezquerra **C:** Brian Bolland **W:** Alan Grant; John Wagner
3 ❑ Cover: 5.95 **NM** value: **Cover or less**
The Problem With Sonny Bono; The Body Sharks; The Numbers Racket **A:** Ian Gibson; Colin Wilson **C:** Brian Bolland **W:** Alan Grant; John Wagner
4 ❑ Cover: 5.95 **NM** value: **Cover or less**
C: Brian Bolland
Bk 1/CS❑ Cover: 24.95 **NM** value: **Cover or less**
• slipcased set

JUDGE DREDD'S HARDCASE PAPERS — Fleetway-Quality

1 ❑ Cover: 5.95 **NM** value: **Cover or less**
Tarantula; Law of the Jungle; The Dungeon Master **A:** Arthur Ranson; Carlos Ezquerra; Emberton **W:** Alan Grant; John Wagner; Staccato; T.B. Grover
2 ❑ Cover: 5.95 **NM** value: **Cover or less**
3 ❑ Cover: 5.95 **NM** value: **Cover or less**
4 ❑ Cover: 5.95 **NM** value: **Cover or less**
Bk 1❑ Cover: 5.95 **NM** value: **Cover or less**
Bk 2❑ Cover: 5.95 **NM** value: **Cover or less**
Bk 3❑ Cover: 5.95 **NM** value: **Cover or less**

JUDGE DREDD THE EARLY CASES — Eagle

1 ❑ **NM** value: **3.00**
2 ❑ **NM** value: **3.00**
3 ❑ **NM** value: **3.00**
4 ❑ **NM** value: **3.00**
5 ❑ **NM** value: **3.00**
6 ❑ **NM** value: **3.00**

JUDGE DREDD THE MEGAZINE — Fleetway-Quality

1 ❑ Cover: 4.95 **NM** value: **Cover or less**
2 ❑ Cover: 4.95 **NM** value: **Cover or less**
3 ❑ Cover: 4.95 **NM** value: **Cover or less**

JUDGE DREDD: THE OFFICIAL MOVIE ADAPTATION — DC

1 ❑ Cover: 5.95 **NM** value: **Cover or less**
Circ: CapCity orders: **6,775**
No issue number. • prestige format.

JUDGE DREDD (VOL. 1) — Eagle

In the futuristic metropolis Mega-City One, crime has gotten so bad that radical steps have been taken to streamline the process of law enforcement. The police there are known as "judges." It would be more accurate to call them, "judges, juries, and executioners." If you are deemed to have done something in violation of the law, you are simply...dealt with. Despite these Draconian measures, violent crime in Mega-City One is completely out of control. Armed thugs commit brutal and senseless crimes on an almost continual basis, and no citizen is ever safe.

Judge Dredd is out to change all that. With a penchant for violence that inspired RoboCop, and a taste for law and order that makes Joe Friday look like a bleeding-heart liberal, Judge Dredd is the new sheriff in town — and you'd better not forget it.

1 ❑ Nov 1983 Cover: 1.00 **NM** value: **5.00**
• **CGC:** 3 graded, best 9.8
A: Brian Bolland ★ 1st Appearance of Judge Dredd (in U.S.). ★ Appearance of Judge Death.
2 ❑ Dec 1983 Cover: 1.00 **NM** value: **3.50**
A: Brian Bolland
3 ❑ Jan 1984 Cover: 1.00 **NM** value: **3.00**
A: Brian Bolland ★ Appearance of Judge Anderson. ★ Versus Judge Death.
4 ❑ Feb 1984 Cover: 1.00 **NM** value: **3.00**
A: Brian Bolland
5 ❑ Mar 1984 Cover: 1.00 **NM** value: **3.00**
6 ❑ Apr 1984 Cover: 1.00 **NM** value: **2.50**
7 ❑ May 1984 Cover: 1.00 **NM** value: **2.50**

CGC-graded: Multiply prices above by **33 for 9.9 M • 16 for 9.8 NM/M • 7 for 9.6 NM+ • 5 for 9.4 NM • 2.5 for 9.2 NM- • 1.5 for 9.0 VF/NM**

8 ❑ Jun 1984 Cover: 1.00 **NM** value: **2.50**
9 ❑ Jul 1984 Cover: 1.00 **NM** value: **2.50**
10 ❑ Aug 1984 Cover: 1.00 **NM** value: **2.50**
11 ❑ Sep 1984 Cover: 1.00 **NM** value: **2.00**
12 ❑ Oct 1984 Cover: 1.00 **NM** value: **2.00**
13 ❑ Nov 1984 Cover: 1.00 **NM** value: **2.00**
14 ❑ Dec 1984 Cover: 1.00 **NM** value: **2.00**
15 ❑ Jan 1985 Cover: 1.00 **NM** value: **2.00**
📖 Judge Dredd: Block War; Judge Dredd: Umpty Candy; Judge Dredd: The Ape Gang • Umpty Candy
16 ❑ Feb 1985 Cover: 1.00 **NM** value: **2.00**
★ Versus Fink Angel.
17 ❑ Mar 1985 Cover: 1.00 **NM** value: **2.00**
18 ❑ Apr 1985 Cover: 1.00 **NM** value: **2.00**
Circ: CapCity orders: **7,125**
📖 Block Mania
19 ❑ May 1985 Cover: 1.00 **NM** value: **2.00**
Circ: CapCity orders: **7,200**
20 ❑ Jun 1985 Cover: 1.00 **NM** value: **2.00**
Circ: CapCity orders: **7,525**
21 ❑ Jul 1985 Cover: 1.00 **NM** value: **2.00**
Circ: CapCity orders: **7,525**
22 ❑ Aug 1985 Cover: 1.00 **NM** value: **2.00**
Circ: CapCity orders: **7,450**
23 ❑ Sep 1985 Cover: 1.00 **NM** value: **2.00**
Circ: CapCity orders: **7,450**
24 ❑ Oct 1985 Cover: 1.25 **NM** value: **2.00**
Circ: CapCity orders: **7,275**
25 ❑ Nov 1985 Cover: 1.25 **NM** value: **2.00**
Circ: CapCity orders: **6,875**
26 ❑ Dec 1985 Cover: 1.25 **NM** value: **2.00**
Circ: CapCity orders: **6,675**
27 ❑ Jan 1986 Cover: 1.25 **NM** value: **2.00**
Circ: CapCity orders: **6,225**
28 ❑ Feb 1986 Cover: 1.25 **NM** value: **2.00**
Circ: CapCity orders: **6,250**
29 ❑ Mar 1986 Cover: 1.25 **NM** value: **2.00**
Circ: CapCity orders: **5,950**
30 ❑ Apr 1986 Cover: 1.25 **NM** value: **2.00**
Circ: CapCity orders: **5,950**
31 ❑ May 1986 Cover: 1.25 **NM** value: **2.00**
Circ: CapCity orders: **5,725**
★ Versus Judge Child. ★ Versus Mean Machine.
32 ❑ Jun 1986 Cover: 1.25 **NM** value: **2.00**
Circ: CapCity orders: **5,500**
★ Versus Mean Machine.
33 ❑ Jul 1986 Cover: 1.25 **NM** value: **2.00**
Circ: CapCity orders: **5,425**
• League of Fatties
34 ❑ Aug 1986 Cover: 1.25 **NM** value: **2.00**
Circ: CapCity orders: **5,575**
35 ❑ Sep 1986 Cover: 1.25 **NM** value: **2.00**
Circ: CapCity orders: **5,700**
final issue.

JUDGE DREDD (VOL. 2) — Fleetway-Quality

1 ❑ Oct 1986 Cover: 0.75 **NM** value: **3.00**
2 ❑ Nov 1986 **NM** value: **2.50**
📖 Cry of the Werewolf **A:** Steve Dillon **W:** John Wagner
3 ❑ Dec 1986 **NM** value: **2.00**
4 ❑ Jan 1987 **NM** value: **2.00**
5 ❑ Feb 1987 Cover: 0.75 **NM** value: **2.00**
• poster
6 ❑ Mar 1987 Cover: 1.25 **NM** value: **2.00**
• Christmas issue
7 ❑ 1987 Cover: 0.95 **NM** value: **2.00**
8 ❑ Jul 1987 Cover: 1.25 **NM** value: **2.00**
Circ: CapCity orders: **4,675**
wraparound cover.
9 ❑ Aug 1987 Cover: 1.25 **NM** value: **2.00**
Circ: CapCity orders: **4,450**
10 ❑ Sep 1987 Cover: 1.25 **NM** value: **2.00**
Circ: CapCity orders: **4,425**
11 ❑ Oct 1987 Cover: 1.25 **NM** value: **2.00**
Circ: CapCity orders: **4,375**
A: Ron Smith **W:** T.B. Grover
12 ❑ Cover: 1.25 **NM** value: **2.00**
Circ: CapCity orders: **4,550**
dropped publication date from cover and indicia for rest of series.
📖 Starborn Thing, Part 1 **A:** Carlos Ezquerra **W:** T.B. Grover
13 ❑ Cover: 1.25 **NM** value: **2.00**
Circ: CapCity orders: **4,550**
📖 Starborn Thing, Part 2 **A:** Carlos Ezquerra **W:** T.B. Grover
14 ❑ Cover: 1.25 **NM** value: **2.00**
Circ: CapCity orders: **4,300**
📖 Attack Of The 50 Foot Woman; The Switch; Judge Dredd: Varks **A:** Brian Bolland; Gary Leach; Jim Baikie; Kevin O'Neill **W:** Alan Grant; John Howard; John Wagner; T.B. Grover
15 ❑ Cover: 1.25 **NM** value: **2.00**
Circ: CapCity orders: **4,200**
📖 City Of The Damned **A:** Mike McMahon; Kim Raymond **W:** John Howard; T.B. Grover
16 ❑ Cover: 1.25 **NM** value: **2.00**
Circ: CapCity orders: **4,250**
📖 Dredd Angel **A:** Ron Smith; Bart Sears(cover) **W:** T.B. Grover
17 ❑ Cover: 1.25 **NM** value: **2.00**
Circ: CapCity orders: **4,250**
📖 Dredd Angel; Bob's Law; Are You Tired Of Being Mugged? **A:** Ron Smith; Emberton **W:** T.B. Grover
18 ❑ Cover: 1.25 **NM** value: **2.00**
Circ: CapCity orders: **4,350**
W: T.B. Grover
19 ❑ Cover: 1.25 **NM** value: **2.00**
Circ: CapCity orders: **4,450**
📖 Judge Dredd: Condo; Judge Dredd: The Prankster **A:** Carlos Ezquerra **W:** T.B. Grover
20 ❑ Cover: 1.50 **NM** value: **2.00**
Circ: CapCity orders: **4,475**
📖 Channel Illegal **A:** Ron Smith; Cliff Robinson **W:** John Howard; T.B. Grover
21 ❑ Cover: 1.50 **NM** value: **2.00**
Circ: CapCity orders: **4,325**
• double issue #21, 22
22 ❑ Cover: 1.50 **NM** value: **2.00**
Circ: CapCity orders: **4,440**
23 ❑ **NM** value: **2.00**
• double issue #23, 24
24 ❑ Cover: 1.50 **NM** value: **2.00**
Circ: CapCity orders: **4,350**
25 ❑ Cover: 1.50 **NM** value: **2.00**
Circ: CapCity orders: **4,325**
📖 Riders on the Storm!; The Long Sleep; Judge Dredd: He is the Law in Mega City One; A Promised Land; The Mean Machine Goes to Town **A:** Robin Smith; Ian Kennedy; Jeff Anderson; Lalia; McCarthy; Q. Twerk **W:** Peter Milligan; A.N. Other; T.B. Grover
26 ❑ **NM** value: **2.00**
📖 The Urge **A:** Barry Kitson **W:** T.B. Grover
27 ❑ Cover: 1.50 **NM** value: **2.00**
Circ: CapCity orders: **4,300**
28 ❑ Cover: 1.50 **NM** value: **2.00**
Circ: CapCity orders: **4,400**
📖 The Hunters Club **A:** Ron Smith **W:** T.B. Grover
29 ❑ Cover: 1.50 **NM** value: **2.00**
Circ: CapCity orders: **4,225**
📖 Requiem for a Heavy-Weight **A:** Carlos Ezquerra **W:** T.B. Grover
30 ❑ Cover: 1.50 **NM** value: **2.00**
Circ: CapCity orders: **4,250**
31 ❑ Cover: 1.50 **NM** value: **2.00**
Circ: CapCity orders: **4,300**
32 ❑ Cover: 1.50 **NM** value: **2.00**
Circ: CapCity orders: **4,200**
33 ❑ Cover: 1.50 **NM** value: **2.00**
Circ: CapCity orders: **4,150**
📖 Judge Dredd: The Gun, The Badge, The Man; Judge Dredd: Bride Of Death **A:** Cam Kennedy; Ian Gibson **W:** Alan Grant; Charles Gibson; T.B. Grover
34 ❑ Cover: 1.50 **NM** value: **2.00**
Circ: CapCity orders: **4,125**
📖 The Seven Samurai; Bride of Death; Nosferatu **A:** Cam Kennedy; Ian Gibson **W:** Grant; T.B. Grover; Wagner
35 ❑ Cover: 1.50 **NM** value: **2.00**
Circ: CapCity orders: **4,325**
36 ❑ Cover: 1.50 **NM** value: **2.00**
Circ: CapCity orders: **4,350**
📖 Judge Dredd: Tomb Of The Judges!; Judge Dredd In Atlantis **A:** Ian Gibson **W:** Alan Grant; John Wagner
37 ❑ Cover: 1.50 **NM** value: **2.00**
Circ: CapCity orders: **4,375**
📖 Judge Dredd In Atlantis; Rumble In The Jungle, Part 1 **A:** Brendan McCarthy; Emberton **W:** T.B. Grover
38 ❑ Cover: 1.50 **NM** value: **2.00**
Circ: CapCity orders: **4,250**
📖 Rumble In The Jungle, Part 2 **A:** Cam Kennedy; Emberton **W:** T.B. Grover
39 ❑ Cover: 1.75 **NM** value: **2.00**
Circ: CapCity orders: **4,350**
📖 Judge Dredd: The Big Sleep; Judge Dredd: Phantom of the Shoppera **A:** John Higgins; Cam Kennedy **W:** Alan Grant; John Wagner; T.B. Grover
40 ❑ Cover: 1.75 **NM** value: **2.00**
Circ: CapCity orders: **4,200**
41 ❑ Cover: 1.75 **NM** value: **2.00**
Circ: CapCity orders: **4,075**
📖 Judge Dredd: The Lurker; Judge Dredd: The Ugly Mug Ball; Judge Dredd: The Lemming Syndrome; Judge Dredd: Confessions of an Anarchist Flea; In Search of Life… • Reprinted from 2000 A.D. #449; Reprinted from 2000 A.D. #447; Reprinted from 2000 A.D. #445 **A:** Ron Smith; Cliff Robinson **W:** T.B. Grover
42 ❑ Cover: 1.75 **NM** value: **2.00**
Circ: CapCity orders: **4,000**
📖 Judge Dredd: West Side Rumble; Judge Dredd: Thirteenth Assessment; Judge Dredd: Casey's Day Out • Reprints story from 2000 A.D. #434; Reprints story from 2000 A.D. #421; Reprints story from 2000 A.D. #422 **A:** Ron Smith; Cliff Robinson; Ian Gibson **W:** T.B. Grover
43 ❑ Cover: 1.75 **NM** value: **2.00**
Circ: CapCity orders: **3,950**
📖 Judge Dredd: The DNA Man; Judge Dredd: Monsteroso; Tharg's Time Twisters: Que Sera, Sera • Reprints story from 2000 A.D. #113-115; Reprints story from 2000 A.D. #412 **A:** Robin Smith; Brett Ewins; Cam Kennedy **W:** John Howard; T.B. Groover
44 ❑ Cover: 1.75 **NM** value: **2.00**
Circ: CapCity orders: **3,925**
📖 Judge Dredd: Firebug; Judge Dredd: The Genie; Judge Dredd: Prezzel Logic; Judge Dredd: Let's Play Spudbug; Judge Dredd: The Dredd End • Reprint from 2000 A.D. #60; Reprint from 2000 A.D. #514; Reprint from 2000 A.D. #304 **A:** Ron Smith; Cam Kennedy; Emberton; Kim Raymond **W:** Alan Grant; John Wagner; T.B. Grover
45 ❑ Cover: 1.75 **NM** value: **2.00**
Circ: CapCity orders: **3,725**
📖 Judge Dredd: The Secret Diary of Adrian Cockroach; Judge Dredd: Last Voyage of the Flying Dutchman; Judge Dredd: A Tale From Walter's Scrapbook 1; Judge Dredd: A Chief Judge Resigns • Reprint from 2000 A.D. #457; Reprint from 2000 A.D. #458; Reprint from 2000 A.D. #459; Reprint from 2000 A.D. #119 **A:** Bryan Talbot; Ron Smith; Cliff Robinson; Cam Kennedy **W:** John Howard; T.B. Grover
46 ❑ Cover: 1.75 **NM** value: **2.00**
Circ: CapCity orders: **3,475**
47 ❑ Cover: 1.75 **NM** value: **2.00**
Circ: CapCity orders: **3,275**
48 ❑ Cover: 1.75 **NM** value: **2.00**
Circ: CapCity orders: **3,425**
📖 Judge Dredd: An Elm Street Nightmare; Judge Dredd: The Confeshuns Of P.I. Maybe **A:** Mick Austin; Liam Sharp **W:** John Wagner
49 ❑ Cover: 1.75 **NM** value: **2.00**
Circ: CapCity orders: **3,150**
📖 Judge Dredd: Dead Ringer; Judge Dredd: Block War; Judge Dredd: The Peeper; Judge Dredd: Pinboing Replay; Ultimate Warrior • Stories 2000 A.D. #493; From 2000 A.D. #182; From 2000 A.D. #490; From 2000 A.D. #491 **A:** Robin Smith; Barry Kitson; Cliff Robinson **W:** T.B. Grover
50 ❑ Cover: 1.75 **NM** value: **2.00**
Circ: CapCity orders: **3,075**
📖 Judge Dredd: On The Superslab **A:** Steve Dillon; Ron Smith; Cliff Robinson **W:** Alan Grant; John Wagner
51 ❑ Cover: 1.75 **NM** value: **2.00**
Circ: CapCity orders: **2,950**
52 ❑ Cover: 1.95 **NM** value: **2.00**
Circ: CapCity orders: **2,800**
📖 Judge Dredd: On The Air; Judge Dredd: The Witness; Judge Dredd: The Hit **A:** John Higgins; Brendan McCarthy; Dave D'Antiquis; Whittaker **W:** Alan Grant; John Wagner; Larry Watson; T.B. Grover
53 ❑ Cover: 1.95 **NM** value: **2.00**
Circ: CapCity orders: **2,850**
📖 Judge Dredd: The Blood Donor; Judge Dredd: Russell's Inflatable Muscles • Reprinted from 2000 A.D. #519; From 2000 A.D. #25 **A:** John Higgins; Brian Bolland; Brendan McCarthy **W:** Alan Grant; John Howard; John Wagner; T.B. Grover
54 ❑ Cover: 1.95 **NM** value: **2.00**
Circ: CapCity orders: **2,775**
📖 Judge Dredd: Cardboard City; Judge Dredd: Carry on Judging • Reprinted from 2000 A.D. #643-645; Reprinted from 2000 1990 Mega-Special **A:** Cliff Robinson **W:** Alan Grant
55 ❑ Cover: 1.95 **NM** value: **2.00**
Circ: CapCity orders: **2,550**
📖 Judge Dredd: What Would Be Horrible?; Reasons To Be Fearful; Judge Dredd: The Amazing Ant-Man **A:** Carlos Ezquerra **W:** Alan Grant
56 ❑ Cover: 1.95 **NM** value: **2.00**
Circ: CapCity orders: **2,900**
📖 Judge Dredd: Cry of the Werewolf **A:** Steve Dillon **W:** John Wagner
57 ❑ Cover: 1.95 **NM** value: **2.00**
Circ: CapCity orders: **2,700**
58 ❑ Cover: 1.95 **NM** value: **2.00**
Circ: CapCity orders: **2,700**
59 ❑ Cover: 1.95 **NM** value: **Cover or less**
Circ: CapCity orders: **2,675**
📖 Judge Dredd: The Wreckers!; Judge Dredd: The Last Invader; Walter's Works **A:** Steve Dillon **W:** John Wagner
60 ❑ Cover: 1.95 **NM** value: **Cover or less**
Circ: CapCity orders: **3,000**
61 ❑ Cover: 1.95 **NM** value: **Cover or less**
Circ: CapCity orders: **3,000**
• Series continued in Judge Dredd Classics #62
SE 1❑ **NM** value: **2.50**

JUDGE PARKER — Argo

1 ❑ Feb 1956 Cover: 0.10 **NM** value: **35.00**
2 ❑ Apr 1956 Cover: 0.10 **NM** value: **25.00**

J.U.D.G.E.: SECRET RAGE — Image

1 ❑ Mar 2000 Cover: 2.95 **NM** value: **Cover or less**
A: Greg Horn **W:** Greg Horn

JUDGMENT DAY — Awesome

1 ❑ Jun 1997 Cover: 2.50 **NM** value: **Cover or less**
Circ: Diamd. preorders: **32,498**
• Alpha **A:** Rob Liefeld **W:** Alan Moore
1/A ❑ Jun 1997 Cover: 2.50 **NM** value: **Cover or less**
variant cover. • Alpha **A:** Rob Liefeld; Dave Gibbons(cover) **W:** Alan Moore
1-2 ❑ Cover: 2.50 **NM** value: **Cover or less**
2 ❑ Jul 1997 Cover: 2.50 **NM** value: **Cover or less**
Circ: Diamd. preorders: **28,365**
📖 The Trial • Omega **A:** Alan Weiss; Chris Sprouse; Jim Starlin; Terry Dodson; Rob Liefeld; Stephen Platt; Steve Skroce; Al Gordon; Larry Stucker; Rachel Dodson **C:** Rob Liefeld **W:** Alan Moore
2/A ❑ Jul 1997 Cover: 2.50 **NM** value: **Cover or less**
variant cover. 📖 The Trial • Omega **A:** Rob Liefeld; Dave Gibbons(cover) **C:** Dan Panosian **W:** Alan Moore
3 ❑ Cover: 2.50 **NM** value: **Cover or less**
Circ: Diamd. preorders: **28,405**
• Final Judgment **A:** Rob Liefeld **W:** Alan Moore
3/A ❑ Cover: 2.50 **NM** value: **Cover or less**
• Final Judgment **A:** Rob Liefeld; Dave Gibbons(cover) **W:** Alan Moore

JUDGMENT DAY: AFTERMATH — Awesome

1 ❑ Jan 1998 Cover: 3.50 **NM** value: **Cover or less**
Circ: Diamd. preorders: **19,713**
📖 Trial by Tempest **A:** Gil Kane **W:** Alan Moore
1/A ❑ Cover: 3.50 **NM** value: **Cover or less**
Purple cover by Evans. 📖 Trial by Tempest **A:** Gil Kane **W:** Alan Moore

JUDGMENT DAY (LIGHTNING) — Lightning

1/A ❑ Sep 1993 Cover: 3.50 **NM** value: **Cover or less**
Circ: CapCity orders: **10,125**
red foil cover. • Red prism border **A:** Karl Kerschl **W:** Joseph A. Zyskowski
1/B ❑ Sep 1993 Cover: 3.50 **NM** value: **Cover or less**
purple foil cover. **A:** Karl Kerschl **W:** Joseph A. Zyskowski
1/C ❑ Sep 1993 Cover: 3.50 **NM** value: **Cover or less**
• misprint **A:** Karl Kerschl **W:** Joseph A. Zyskowski
1/D ❑ Aug 1993 Cover: 3.50 **NM** value: **Cover or less**
• promotional copy; metallic ink **A:** Karl Kerschl **W:** Joseph A. Zyskowski
1/GO❑Sep 1993 Cover: 3.50 **NM** value: **Cover or less**
Gold foil cover. • Gold prism border **A:** Karl Kerschl **W:** Joseph A. Zyskowski
1/PL❑Aug 1993 Cover: 3.50 **NM** value: **Cover or less**

Other grades: Multiply prices above by **1.5 for Mint • 2/3 for Very Fine • 1/3 for Fine • 1/5 for Very Good • 1/8 for Good**

• promotional copy; platinum **A:** Karl Kerschl **W:** Joseph A. Zyskowski
2 ❑ Oct 1993 Cover: 2.95 **NM** value: **Cover or less**
Circ: CapCity orders: **4,975**
• trading card **A:** Karl Kerschl **W:** Joseph A. Zyskowski
3 ❑ Nov 1993 Cover: 2.95 **NM** value: **Cover or less**
Circ: CapCity orders: **4,850**
A: Karl Kerschl **W:** Joseph A. Zyskowski ★ Origin of X-Treme.
4 ❑ Dec 1993 Cover: 2.95 **NM** value: **Cover or less**
Circ: CapCity orders: **5,125**
A: Karl Kerschl **W:** Joseph A. Zyskowski
5 ❑ Jan 1994 Cover: 2.95 **NM** value: **Cover or less**
Circ: CapCity orders: **5,100**
A: Karl Kerschl **W:** Joseph A. Zyskowski
6 ❑ Feb 1994 Cover: 2.95 **NM** value: **Cover or less**
Circ: CapCity orders: **3,900**
A: Karl Kerschl **W:** Joseph A. Zyskowski ★ Origin of Salubrio.
7 ❑ Mar 1994 Cover: 2.95 **NM** value: **Cover or less**
Circ: CapCity orders: **3,025**
A: Karl Kerschl **W:** Joseph A. Zyskowski ★ Origin of Safeguard.
8 ❑ Apr 1994 Cover: 2.95 **NM** value: **Cover or less**
Circ: CapCity orders: **2,450**
A: Karl Kerschl **W:** Joseph A. Zyskowski

JUDGMENT DAY SOURCEBOOK — Awesome

1 ❑ **NM** value: **1.00**
no cover price. • American Entertainment exclusive preview of series

JUDGMENT PAWNS — Antarctic

1 ❑ Feb 1997, b&w Cover: 2.95 **NM** value: **Cover or less**
Circ: Diamd. preorders: **1,640**
📖 Life is a Game We Play Part 1 **A:** Jean-Sébastien Duberger **W:** Patrick Cabana
2 ❑ Apr 1997, b&w Cover: 2.95 **NM** value: **Cover or less**
📖 Life is a Game We Play Part 2
3 ❑ Jul 1997, b&w Cover: 2.95 **NM** value: **Cover or less**
📖 Life is a Game We Play Part 3 **A:** Jean-Sébastien Duberger **W:** Jean-Sébastien Duberger

JUDO JOE — Jay-Jay Corp.

1 ❑ Aug 1953 Cover: 0.10 **NM** value: **50.00**
2 ❑ Oct 1953 Cover: 0.10 **NM** value: **40.00**
3 ❑ Dec 1953 Cover: 0.10 **NM** value: **40.00**

JUDOMASTER — Charlton

The 1960s comics renaissance known as the Silver Age came late to third-string publisher Charlton, and lasted only until the departure of innovative editor Dick Giordano in 1968. But during that brief flicker of creativity, Charlton produced a few titles that are recognizable as credible super-hero efforts.

Judomaster is at the bottom of that list. It's a simple-minded, martial-arts action series set during World War II. Judomaster is an American trained in the martial arts, set against vicious "Japs and Nazis" in flimsy stories designed to showcase plenty of fighting action.

Written and drawn in obvious haste by the otherwise competent Frank McLaughlin, Judomaster folded after only a short run. In the 1980s, DC acquired the Charlton super-hero properties and Judomaster made an unlikely cameo appearance in the multiple-universe-collapsing epic mini-series Crisis On Infinite Earths.

89 ❑ Jun 1966 Cover: 0.12 **NM** value: **12.00**
• Series continued from Gun Master #89
90 ❑ Aug 1966 Cover: 0.12 **NM** value: **9.00**
91 ❑ Oct 1966 Cover: 0.12 **NM** value: **9.00**
★ Appearance of Sarge Steel.
92 ❑ Dec 1966 Cover: 0.12 **NM** value: **9.00**
93 ❑ Feb 1967 Cover: 0.12 **NM** value: **9.00**
94 ❑ Apr 1967 Cover: 0.12 **NM** value: **9.00**
95 ❑ Jun 1967 Cover: 0.12 **NM** value: **9.00**
• **CGC:** 1 graded, best 8.5
📖 The Plot to Destroy Judomaster; The Art of Stealth; Sarge Steel: Case of the Village Moneyman **A:** Frank McLaughlin; Dick Giordano **W:** Frank McLaughlin; Steve Skeates
96 ❑ Aug 1967 Cover: 0.12 **NM** value: **9.00**
97 ❑ Oct 1967 Cover: 0.12 **NM** value: **9.00**
98 ❑ Dec 1967 Cover: 0.12 **NM** value: **9.00**
final issue.

JUDY CANOVA — Fox

1 ❑ May 1950 Cover: 0.10 **NM** value: **150.00**
2 ❑ Jul 1950 Cover: 0.10 **NM** value: **150.00**
3 ❑ Sep 1950 Cover: 0.10 **NM** value: **125.00**

JUGGERNAUT, THE — Marvel

1 ❑ Apr 1997 Cover: 2.99 **NM** value: **Cover or less**
Circ: Direct Market orders: **70,500**
One-shot. 📖 A Night in Spite **A:** Duncan Rouleau **W:** Joe Kelly

JUGGERNAUT, THE (2ND SERIES) — Marvel

1 ❑ Nov 1999 Cover: 2.99 **NM** value: **Cover or less**
Circ: Diamd. preorders: **41,797**
📖 The Eighth Day, Part 4

Statement of Ownership figures are the average number of copies originally sold, as cited by the publisher to the U.S. Postal Service. These estimate **all** sales, in comics shops and on newsstands.

JUGHEAD (VOL. 1) — Archie

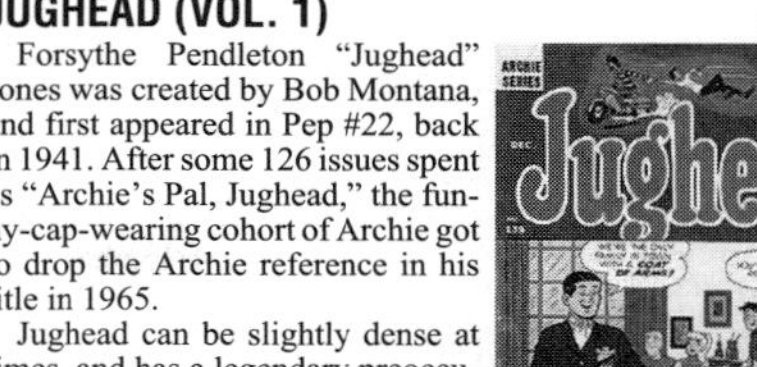

Forsythe Pendleton "Jughead" Jones was created by Bob Montana, and first appeared in Pep #22, back in 1941. After some 126 issues spent as "Archie's Pal, Jughead," the funny-cap-wearing cohort of Archie got to drop the Archie reference in his title in 1965.

Jughead can be slightly dense at times, and has a legendary preoccupation with hamburgers. (Like so much of the Archie iconography, this trait has been used to launch successful marketing campaigns-in this case, for fast food). In some ways, he was the original slacker: falling asleep in class, loafing around, and hanging out at Pop Tate's Chock'Lit Shoppe.

Just to drive comics archivists completely berserk, the series is restarted as Jughead Vol.2 — and then changes its name to Archie's Pal Jughead Comics, exactly the opposite of what happened with the first series!

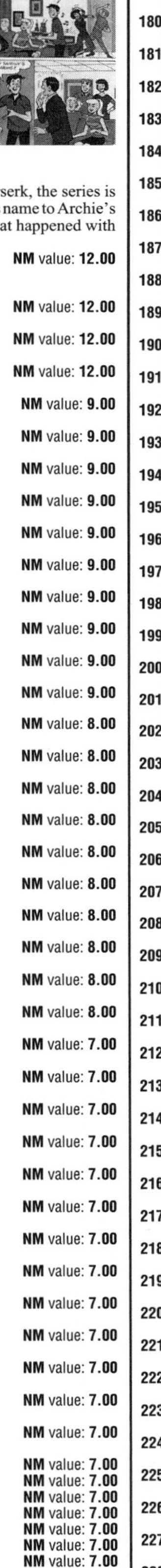

127 ❑ Dec 1965 Cover: 0.12 **NM** value: **12.00**
Circ: Statement: **269,512**
• Formerly Archie's Pal Jughead
128 ❑ Jan 1966 Cover: 0.12 **NM** value: **12.00**
Circ: Statement: **284,928**
129 ❑ Feb 1966 Cover: 0.12 **NM** value: **12.00**
Circ: Statement: **284,928**
130 ❑ Mar 1966 Cover: 0.12 **NM** value: **12.00**
Circ: Statement: **284,928**
131 ❑ Apr 1966 Cover: 0.12 **NM** value: **9.00**
Circ: Statement: **284,928**
132 ❑ May 1966 Cover: 0.12 **NM** value: **9.00**
Circ: Statement: **284,928**
133 ❑ Jun 1966 Cover: 0.12 **NM** value: **9.00**
Circ: Statement: **284,928**
134 ❑ Jul 1966 Cover: 0.12 **NM** value: **9.00**
Circ: Statement: **284,928**
135 ❑ Aug 1966 Cover: 0.12 **NM** value: **9.00**
Circ: Statement: **284,928**
136 ❑ Sep 1966 Cover: 0.12 **NM** value: **9.00**
Circ: Statement: **284,928**
137 ❑ Oct 1966 Cover: 0.12 **NM** value: **9.00**
Circ: Statement: **284,928**
138 ❑ Nov 1966 Cover: 0.12 **NM** value: **9.00**
Circ: Statement: **284,928**
139 ❑ Dec 1966 Cover: 0.12 **NM** value: **9.00**
Circ: Statement: **284,928**
140 ❑ Jan 1967 Cover: 0.12 **NM** value: **9.00**
Circ: Statement: **287,422**
141 ❑ Feb 1967 Cover: 0.12 **NM** value: **8.00**
Circ: Statement: **287,422**
142 ❑ Mar 1967 Cover: 0.12 **NM** value: **8.00**
Circ: Statement: **287,422**
143 ❑ Apr 1967 Cover: 0.12 **NM** value: **8.00**
Circ: Statement: **287,422**
144 ❑ May 1967 Cover: 0.12 **NM** value: **8.00**
Circ: Statement: **287,422**
145 ❑ Jun 1967 Cover: 0.12 **NM** value: **8.00**
Circ: Statement: **287,422**
146 ❑ Jul 1967 Cover: 0.12 **NM** value: **8.00**
Circ: Statement: **287,422**
147 ❑ Aug 1967 Cover: 0.12 **NM** value: **8.00**
Circ: Statement: **287,422**
148 ❑ Sep 1967 Cover: 0.12 **NM** value: **8.00**
Circ: Statement: **287,422**
149 ❑ Oct 1967 Cover: 0.12 **NM** value: **8.00**
Circ: Statement: **287,422**
150 ❑ Nov 1967 Cover: 0.12 **NM** value: **8.00**
Circ: Statement: **287,422**
151 ❑ Dec 1967 Cover: 0.12 **NM** value: **7.00**
Circ: Statement: **287,422**
152 ❑ Jan 1968 Cover: 0.12 **NM** value: **7.00**
Circ: Statement: **345,269**
153 ❑ Feb 1968 Cover: 0.12 **NM** value: **7.00**
Circ: Statement: **345,269**
154 ❑ Mar 1968 Cover: 0.12 **NM** value: **7.00**
Circ: Statement: **345,269**
155 ❑ Apr 1968 Cover: 0.12 **NM** value: **7.00**
Circ: Statement: **345,269**
156 ❑ May 1968 Cover: 0.12 **NM** value: **7.00**
Circ: Statement: **345,269**
157 ❑ Jun 1968 Cover: 0.12 **NM** value: **7.00**
Circ: Statement: **345,269**
158 ❑ Jul 1968 Cover: 0.12 **NM** value: **7.00**
Circ: Statement: **345,269**
159 ❑ Aug 1968 Cover: 0.12 **NM** value: **7.00**
Circ: Statement: **345,269**
160 ❑ Sep 1968 Cover: 0.12 **NM** value: **7.00**
Circ: Statement: **345,269**
161 ❑ Oct 1968 Cover: 0.12 **NM** value: **7.00**
Circ: Statement: **345,269**
162 ❑ Nov 1968 Cover: 0.12 **NM** value: **7.00**
Circ: Statement: **345,269**
163 ❑ Dec 1968 Cover: 0.12 **NM** value: **7.00**
Circ: Statement: **345,269**
164 ❑ Jan 1969 Cover: 0.12 **NM** value: **7.00**
165 ❑ Feb 1969 Cover: 0.12 **NM** value: **7.00**
166 ❑ Mar 1969 Cover: 0.12 **NM** value: **7.00**
167 ❑ Apr 1969 Cover: 0.12 **NM** value: **7.00**
168 ❑ May 1969 Cover: 0.12 **NM** value: **7.00**
169 ❑ Jun 1969 Cover: 0.12 **NM** value: **7.00**
170 ❑ Jul 1969 Cover: 0.15 **NM** value: **7.00**
171 ❑ Aug 1969 Cover: 0.15 **NM** value: **7.00**
172 ❑ Sep 1969 Cover: 0.15 **NM** value: **5.00**
173 ❑ Oct 1969 Cover: 0.15 **NM** value: **5.00**
174 ❑ Nov 1969 Cover: 0.15 **NM** value: **5.00**
175 ❑ Dec 1969 Cover: 0.15 **NM** value: **5.00**
176 ❑ Jan 1970 Cover: 0.15 **NM** value: **5.00**
Circ: Statement: **282,520**
177 ❑ Feb 1970 Cover: 0.15 **NM** value: **5.00**
Circ: Statement: **282,520**
178 ❑ Mar 1970 Cover: 0.15 **NM** value: **5.00**
Circ: Statement: **282,520**
179 ❑ Apr 1970 Cover: 0.15 **NM** value: **5.00**
Circ: Statement: **282,520**
180 ❑ May 1970 Cover: 0.15 **NM** value: **5.00**
Circ: Statement: **282,520**
181 ❑ Jun 1970 Cover: 0.15 **NM** value: **5.00**
Circ: Statement: **282,520**
182 ❑ Jul 1970 Cover: 0.15 **NM** value: **5.00**
Circ: Statement: **282,520**
183 ❑ Aug 1970 Cover: 0.15 **NM** value: **5.00**
Circ: Statement: **282,520**
184 ❑ Sep 1970 Cover: 0.15 **NM** value: **5.00**
Circ: Statement: **282,520**
185 ❑ Oct 1970 Cover: 0.15 **NM** value: **5.00**
Circ: Statement: **282,520**
186 ❑ Nov 1970 Cover: 0.15 **NM** value: **5.00**
Circ: Statement: **282,520**
187 ❑ Dec 1970 Cover: 0.15 **NM** value: **5.00**
Circ: Statement: **282,520**
188 ❑ Jan 1971 Cover: 0.15 **NM** value: **5.00**
Circ: Statement: **286,681**
189 ❑ Feb 1971 Cover: 0.15 **NM** value: **5.00**
Circ: Statement: **286,681**
190 ❑ Mar 1971 Cover: 0.15 **NM** value: **5.00**
Circ: Statement: **286,681**
191 ❑ Apr 1971 Cover: 0.15 **NM** value: **5.00**
Circ: Statement: **286,681**
192 ❑ May 1971 Cover: 0.15 **NM** value: **5.00**
Circ: Statement: **286,681**
193 ❑ Jun 1971 Cover: 0.15 **NM** value: **5.00**
Circ: Statement: **286,681**
194 ❑ Jul 1971 Cover: 0.15 **NM** value: **5.00**
Circ: Statement: **286,681**
195 ❑ Aug 1971 Cover: 0.15 **NM** value: **5.00**
Circ: Statement: **286,681**
196 ❑ Sep 1971 Cover: 0.15 **NM** value: **5.00**
Circ: Statement: **286,681**
197 ❑ Oct 1971 Cover: 0.15 **NM** value: **5.00**
Circ: Statement: **286,681**
198 ❑ Nov 1971 Cover: 0.15 **NM** value: **5.00**
Circ: Statement: **286,681**
199 ❑ Dec 1971 Cover: 0.15 **NM** value: **5.00**
Circ: Statement: **286,681**
200 ❑ Jan 1972 Cover: 0.15 **NM** value: **5.00**
Circ: Statement: **257,415**
201 ❑ Feb 1972 Cover: 0.15 **NM** value: **4.00**
Circ: Statement: **257,415**
202 ❑ Mar 1972 Cover: 0.15 **NM** value: **4.00**
Circ: Statement: **257,415**
203 ❑ Apr 1972 Cover: 0.15 **NM** value: **4.00**
Circ: Statement: **257,415**
204 ❑ May 1972 Cover: 0.20 **NM** value: **4.00**
Circ: Statement: **257,415**
205 ❑ Jun 1972 Cover: 0.20 **NM** value: **4.00**
Circ: Statement: **257,415**
206 ❑ Jul 1972 Cover: 0.20 **NM** value: **4.00**
Circ: Statement: **257,415**
207 ❑ Aug 1972 Cover: 0.20 **NM** value: **4.00**
Circ: Statement: **257,415**
208 ❑ Sep 1972 Cover: 0.20 **NM** value: **4.00**
Circ: Statement: **257,415**
209 ❑ Oct 1972 Cover: 0.20 **NM** value: **4.00**
Circ: Statement: **257,415**
210 ❑ Nov 1972 Cover: 0.20 **NM** value: **4.00**
Circ: Statement: **257,415**
211 ❑ Dec 1972 Cover: 0.20 **NM** value: **4.00**
Circ: Statement: **257,415**
212 ❑ Jan 1973 Cover: 0.20 **NM** value: **4.00**
Circ: Statement: **211,450**
213 ❑ Feb 1973 Cover: 0.20 **NM** value: **4.00**
Circ: Statement: **211,450**
214 ❑ Mar 1973 Cover: 0.20 **NM** value: **4.00**
Circ: Statement: **211,450**
215 ❑ Apr 1973 Cover: 0.20 **NM** value: **4.00**
Circ: Statement: **211,450**
216 ❑ May 1973 Cover: 0.20 **NM** value: **4.00**
Circ: Statement: **211,450**
217 ❑ Jun 1973 Cover: 0.20 **NM** value: **4.00**
Circ: Statement: **211,450**
218 ❑ Jul 1973 Cover: 0.20 **NM** value: **4.00**
Circ: Statement: **211,450**
219 ❑ Aug 1973 Cover: 0.20 **NM** value: **4.00**
Circ: Statement: **211,450**
220 ❑ Sep 1973 Cover: 0.20 **NM** value: **4.00**
Circ: Statement: **211,450**
221 ❑ Oct 1973 Cover: 0.20 **NM** value: **3.00**
Circ: Statement: **211,450**
222 ❑ Nov 1973 Cover: 0.20 **NM** value: **3.00**
Circ: Statement: **211,450**
223 ❑ Dec 1973 Cover: 0.20 **NM** value: **3.00**
Circ: Statement: **211,450**
224 ❑ Jan 1974 Cover: 0.20 **NM** value: **3.00**
Circ: Statement: **204,610**
225 ❑ Feb 1974 Cover: 0.20 **NM** value: **3.00**
Circ: Statement: **204,610**
226 ❑ Mar 1974 Cover: 0.20 **NM** value: **3.00**
Circ: Statement: **204,610**
227 ❑ Apr 1974 Cover: 0.25 **NM** value: **3.00**
Circ: Statement: **204,610**
228 ❑ May 1974 Cover: 0.25 **NM** value: **3.00**
Circ: Statement: **204,610**
229 ❑ Jun 1974 Cover: 0.25 **NM** value: **3.00**
Circ: Statement: **204,610**

CGC-graded: Multiply prices above by **33 for 9.9 M • 16 for 9.8 NM/M • 7 for 9.6 NM+ • 5 for 9.4 NM • 2.5 for 9.2 NM- • 1.5 for 9.0 VF/NM**

230 ❑ Jul 1974 Cover: 0.25 **NM** value: **3.00**
Circ: Statement: **204,610**
231 ❑ Aug 1974 Cover: 0.25 **NM** value: **3.00**
Circ: Statement: **204,610**
232 ❑ Sep 1974 Cover: 0.25 **NM** value: **3.00**
Circ: Statement: **204,610**
233 ❑ Oct 1974 Cover: 0.25 **NM** value: **3.00**
Circ: Statement: **204,610**
234 ❑ Nov 1974 Cover: 0.25 **NM** value: **3.00**
Circ: Statement: **204,610**
235 ❑ Dec 1974 Cover: 0.25 **NM** value: **3.00**
Circ: Statement: **204,610**
236 ❑ Jan 1975 Cover: 0.25 **NM** value: **3.00**
Circ: Statement: **144,619**
237 ❑ Feb 1975 Cover: 0.25 **NM** value: **3.00**
Circ: Statement: **144,619**
238 ❑ Mar 1975 Cover: 0.25 **NM** value: **3.00**
Circ: Statement: **144,619**
239 ❑ Apr 1975 Cover: 0.25 **NM** value: **3.00**
Circ: Statement: **144,619**
240 ❑ May 1975 Cover: 0.25 **NM** value: **3.00**
Circ: Statement: **144,619**
241 ❑ Jun 1975 Cover: 0.25 **NM** value: **2.00**
Circ: Statement: **144,619**
242 ❑ Jul 1975 Cover: 0.25 **NM** value: **2.00**
Circ: Statement: **144,619**
243 ❑ Aug 1975 Cover: 0.25 **NM** value: **2.00**
Circ: Statement: **144,619**
244 ❑ Sep 1975 Cover: 0.25 **NM** value: **2.00**
Circ: Statement: **144,619**
245 ❑ Oct 1975 Cover: 0.25 **NM** value: **2.00**
Circ: Statement: **144,619**
246 ❑ Nov 1975 Cover: 0.25 **NM** value: **2.00**
Circ: Statement: **144,619**
247 ❑ Dec 1975 Cover: 0.25 **NM** value: **2.00**
Circ: Statement: **144,619**
248 ❑ Jan 1976 Cover: 0.25 **NM** value: **2.00**
Circ: Statement: **130,919**
249 ❑ Feb 1976 Cover: 0.30 **NM** value: **2.00**
Circ: Statement: **130,919**
250 ❑ Mar 1976 Cover: 0.30 **NM** value: **2.00**
Circ: Statement: **130,919**
251 ❑ Apr 1976 Cover: 0.30 **NM** value: **2.00**
Circ: Statement: **130,919**
252 ❑ May 1976 Cover: 0.30 **NM** value: **2.00**
Circ: Statement: **130,919**
253 ❑ Jun 1976 Cover: 0.30 **NM** value: **2.00**
Circ: Statement: **130,919**
254 ❑ Jul 1976 Cover: 0.30 **NM** value: **2.00**
Circ: Statement: **130,919**
📖 Fortune Hunters; Li'l Jinx: Fill 'er Up!; Jughead's Gag Bag; Double or Nothing; The Lunch Crunch; Just Kidding ★ Appearance of Reggie, Smithers, Mr. Weatherbee, Betty, Gaston, Li'l Jinx, Archie, Mr. Lodge, Coach Kleats, Jughead, Veronica.
255 ❑ Aug 1976 Cover: 0.30 **NM** value: **2.00**
Circ: Statement: **130,919**
256 ❑ Sep 1976 Cover: 0.30 **NM** value: **2.00**
Circ: Statement: **130,919**
257 ❑ Oct 1976 Cover: 0.30 **NM** value: **2.00**
Circ: Statement: **130,919**
258 ❑ Nov 1976 Cover: 0.30 **NM** value: **2.00**
Circ: Statement: **130,919**
259 ❑ Dec 1976 Cover: 0.30 **NM** value: **2.00**
Circ: Statement: **130,919**
260 ❑ Jan 1977 Cover: 0.30 **NM** value: **2.00**
Circ: Statement: **124,795**
261 ❑ Feb 1977 Cover: 0.30 **NM** value: **2.00**
Circ: Statement: **124,795**
262 ❑ Mar 1977 Cover: 0.30 **NM** value: **2.00**
Circ: Statement: **124,795**
263 ❑ Apr 1977 Cover: 0.30 **NM** value: **2.00**
Circ: Statement: **124,795**
264 ❑ May 1977 Cover: 0.30 **NM** value: **2.00**
Circ: Statement: **124,795**
265 ❑ Jun 1977 Cover: 0.30 **NM** value: **2.00**
Circ: Statement: **124,795**
266 ❑ Jul 1977 Cover: 0.35 **NM** value: **2.00**
Circ: Statement: **124,795**
267 ❑ Aug 1977 Cover: 0.35 **NM** value: **2.00**
Circ: Statement: **124,795**
268 ❑ Sep 1977 Cover: 0.35 **NM** value: **2.00**
Circ: Statement: **124,795**
269 ❑ Oct 1977 Cover: 0.35 **NM** value: **2.00**
Circ: Statement: **124,795**
270 ❑ Nov 1977 Cover: 0.35 **NM** value: **2.00**
Circ: Statement: **124,795**
271 ❑ Dec 1977 Cover: 0.35 **NM** value: **2.00**
Circ: Statement: **124,795**
272 ❑ Jan 1978 Cover: 0.35 **NM** value: **2.00**
273 ❑ Feb 1978 Cover: 0.35 **NM** value: **2.00**
274 ❑ Mar 1978 Cover: 0.35 **NM** value: **2.00**
275 ❑ Apr 1978 Cover: 0.35 **NM** value: **2.00**
276 ❑ May 1978 Cover: 0.35 **NM** value: **2.00**
277 ❑ Jun 1978 Cover: 0.35 **NM** value: **2.00**
278 ❑ Jul 1978 Cover: 0.35 **NM** value: **2.00**
279 ❑ Aug 1978 Cover: 0.35 **NM** value: **2.00**
280 ❑ Sep 1978 Cover: 0.35 **NM** value: **2.00**
281 ❑ Oct 1978 Cover: 0.35 **NM** value: **2.00**
282 ❑ Nov 1978 Cover: 0.35 **NM** value: **2.00**
283 ❑ Dec 1978 Cover: 0.35 **NM** value: **2.00**
284 ❑ Jan 1979 Cover: 0.35 **NM** value: **2.00**
285 ❑ Feb 1979 Cover: 0.35 **NM** value: **2.00**
286 ❑ Mar 1979 Cover: 0.35 **NM** value: **2.00**
287 ❑ Apr 1979 Cover: 0.40 **NM** value: **2.00**
288 ❑ May 1979 Cover: 0.40 **NM** value: **2.00**
289 ❑ Jun 1979 Cover: 0.40 **NM** value: **2.00**
290 ❑ Jul 1979 Cover: 0.40 **NM** value: **2.00**
291 ❑ Aug 1979 Cover: 0.40 **NM** value: **2.00**
292 ❑ Sep 1979 Cover: 0.40 **NM** value: **2.00**
293 ❑ Oct 1979 Cover: 0.40 **NM** value: **2.00**
294 ❑ Nov 1979 Cover: 0.40 **NM** value: **2.00**
295 ❑ Dec 1979 Cover: 0.40 **NM** value: **2.00**
296 ❑ Jan 1980 Cover: 0.40 **NM** value: **2.00**
Circ: Statement: **84,229**
297 ❑ Feb 1980 Cover: 0.40 **NM** value: **2.00**
Circ: Statement: **84,229**
298 ❑ Mar 1980 Cover: 0.40 **NM** value: **2.00**
Circ: Statement: **84,229**
299 ❑ Apr 1980 Cover: 0.40 **NM** value: **2.00**
Circ: Statement: **84,229**
300 ❑ May 1980 Cover: 0.40 **NM** value: **2.00**
Circ: Statement: **84,229**
301 ❑ Jun 1980 Cover: 0.40 **NM** value: **1.50**
Circ: Statement: **84,229**
302 ❑ Jul 1980 Cover: 0.40 **NM** value: **1.50**
Circ: Statement: **84,229**
303 ❑ Aug 1980 Cover: 0.50 **NM** value: **1.50**
Circ: Statement: **84,229**
304 ❑ Sep 1980 Cover: 0.50 **NM** value: **1.50**
Circ: Statement: **84,229**
305 ❑ Oct 1980 Cover: 0.50 **NM** value: **1.50**
Circ: Statement: **84,229**
306 ❑ Nov 1980 Cover: 0.50 **NM** value: **1.50**
Circ: Statement: **84,229**
307 ❑ Dec 1980 Cover: 0.50 **NM** value: **1.50**
Circ: Statement: **84,229**
308 ❑ Jan 1981 Cover: 0.50 **NM** value: **1.50**
309 ❑ Feb 1981 Cover: 0.50 **NM** value: **1.50**
310 ❑ Mar 1981 Cover: 0.50 **NM** value: **1.50**
311 ❑ Apr 1981 Cover: 0.50 **NM** value: **1.50**
312 ❑ May 1981 Cover: 0.50 **NM** value: **1.50**
313 ❑ Jun 1981 Cover: 0.50 **NM** value: **1.50**
314 ❑ Jul 1981 Cover: 0.50 **NM** value: **1.50**
315 ❑ Aug 1981 Cover: 0.50 **NM** value: **1.50**
316 ❑ Sep 1981 Cover: 0.50 **NM** value: **1.50**
317 ❑ Oct 1981 Cover: 0.50 **NM** value: **1.50**
318 ❑ Nov 1981 Cover: 0.50 **NM** value: **1.50**
319 ❑ Dec 1981 Cover: 0.60 **NM** value: **1.50**
320 ❑ Jan 1982 Cover: 0.60 **NM** value: **1.50**
Circ: Statement: **59,186**
321 ❑ Feb 1982 Cover: 0.60 **NM** value: **1.50**
Circ: Statement: **59,186**
322 ❑ Apr 1982 Cover: 0.60 **NM** value: **1.50**
Circ: Statement: **59,186**
323 ❑ Jun 1982 Cover: 0.60 **NM** value: **1.50**
Circ: Statement: **59,186**
324 ❑ Aug 1982 Cover: 0.60 **NM** value: **1.50**
Circ: Statement: **59,186**
325 ❑ Oct 1982 Cover: 0.60 **NM** value: **1.50**
Circ: Statement: **59,186**
326 ❑ Dec 1982 Cover: 0.60 **NM** value: **1.50**
Circ: Statement: **59,186**
327 ❑ Feb 1983 Cover: 0.60 **NM** value: **1.50**
Circ: Statement: **62,454**
328 ❑ 1983 Cover: 0.60 **NM** value: **1.50**
Circ: Statement: **62,454**
329 ❑ 1983 Cover: 0.60 **NM** value: **1.50**
Circ: Statement: **62,454**
330 ❑ Oct 1983 Cover: 0.60 **NM** value: **1.50**
Circ: Statement: **62,454**
331 ❑ Dec 1983 Cover: 0.60 **NM** value: **1.50**
Circ: Statement: **62,454**
332 ❑ Feb 1984 Cover: 0.60 **NM** value: **1.50**
Circ: Statement: **58,377**
333 ❑ Apr 1984 Cover: 0.60 **NM** value: **1.50**
Circ: Statement: **58,377**
334 ❑ Jun 1984 Cover: 0.60 **NM** value: **1.50**
Circ: Statement: **58,377**
335 ❑ Aug 1984 Cover: 0.60 **NM** value: **1.50**
Circ: Statement: **58,377**
336 ❑ Oct 1984 Cover: 0.60 **NM** value: **1.50**
Circ: Statement: **58,377**
337 ❑ Dec 1984 Cover: 0.60 **NM** value: **1.50**
Circ: Statement: **58,377**
338 ❑ Feb 1985 Cover: 0.65 **NM** value: **1.50**
Circ: Statement: **59,126**
339 ❑ Apr 1985 Cover: 0.65 **NM** value: **1.50**
Circ: Statement: **59,126**
340 ❑ Jun 1985 Cover: 0.65 **NM** value: **1.50**
Circ: Statement: **59,126**
341 ❑ Aug 1985 Cover: 0.65 **NM** value: **1.50**
Circ: Statement: **59,126**
342 ❑ Oct 1985 Cover: 0.65 **NM** value: **1.50**
Circ: Statement: **59,126**
343 ❑ Dec 1985 Cover: 0.65 **NM** value: **1.50**
Circ: Statement: **59,126**
344 ❑ Feb 1986 Cover: 0.65 **NM** value: **1.50**
Circ: Statement: **58,859**
345 ❑ Apr 1986 Cover: 0.65 **NM** value: **1.50**
Circ: Statement: **58,859**
346 ❑ Jun 1986 Cover: 0.65 **NM** value: **1.50**
Circ: Statement: **58,859**
347 ❑ Aug 1986 Cover: 0.75 **NM** value: **1.50**
Circ: Statement: **58,859**
348 ❑ Oct 1986 Cover: 0.75 **NM** value: **1.50**
Circ: Statement: **58,859**
349 ❑ Dec 1986 Cover: 0.75 **NM** value: **1.50**
Circ: Statement: **58,859**
350 ❑ Feb 1987 Cover: 0.75 **NM** value: **1.50**
Circ: Statement: **54,227**
351 ❑ Apr 1987 Cover: 0.75 **NM** value: **1.50**
Circ: Statement: **54,227**
352 ❑ Jun 1987 Cover: 0.75 **NM** value: **1.50**
Circ: Statement: **54,227**

JUGHEAD (VOL. 2) — Archie

1 ❑ Aug 1987 Cover: 0.75 **NM** value: **3.00**
Circ: Statement: **54,227**
2 ❑ Oct 1987 Cover: 0.75 **NM** value: **2.00**
Circ: Statement: **54,227**
3 ❑ Dec 1987 Cover: 0.75 **NM** value: **2.00**
Circ: Statement: **54,227**
4 ❑ Feb 1988 Cover: 0.75 **NM** value: **1.50**
Circ: Statement: **60,565**
5 ❑ Apr 1988 Cover: 0.75 **NM** value: **1.50**
Circ: Statement: **60,565**
6 ❑ Jun 1988 Cover: 0.75 **NM** value: **1.50**
Circ: Statement: **60,565**
7 ❑ Aug 1988 Cover: 0.75 **NM** value: **1.50**
Circ: Statement: **60,565**
8 ❑ Oct 1988 Cover: 0.75 **NM** value: **1.50**
Circ: Statement: **60,565**
9 ❑ Dec 1988 Cover: 0.75 **NM** value: **1.50**
Circ: Statement: **60,565**
10 ❑ Feb 1989 Cover: 0.75 **NM** value: **1.50**
Circ: Statement: **56,648**
11 ❑ Apr 1989 Cover: 0.75 **NM** value: **1.50**
Circ: Statement: **56,648**
12 ❑ Jun 1989 Cover: 0.75 **NM** value: **1.50**
Circ: Statement: **56,648**
13 ❑ Aug 1989 Cover: 0.95 **NM** value: **1.50**
Circ: Statement: **56,648**
14 ❑ Oct 1989 Cover: 0.95 **NM** value: **1.50**
Circ: Statement: **56,648**
15 ❑ Dec 1989 Cover: 0.95 **NM** value: **1.50**
Circ: Statement: **56,648**
16 ❑ Feb 1990 Cover: 1.00 **NM** value: **1.50**
Circ: Statement: **48,160**
17 ❑ Apr 1990 Cover: 1.00 **NM** value: **1.50**
Circ: Statement: **48,160**
18 ❑ Jun 1990 Cover: 1.00 **NM** value: **1.50**
Circ: Statement: **48,160**
19 ❑ Aug 1990 Cover: 1.00 **NM** value: **1.50**
Circ: Statement: **48,160**
20 ❑ Oct 1990 Cover: 1.00 **NM** value: **1.50**
Circ: Statement: **48,160**
21 ❑ Dec 1990 Cover: 1.00 **NM** value: **1.50**
Circ: Statement: **48,160**
22 ❑ Feb 1991 Cover: 1.00 **NM** value: **1.50**
Circ: Statement: **36,495**
23 ❑ Apr 1991 Cover: 1.00 **NM** value: **1.50**
Circ: Statement: **36,495**
24 ❑ Jun 1991 Cover: 1.00 **NM** value: **1.50**
Circ: Statement: **36,495**
25 ❑ Aug 1991 Cover: 1.00 **NM** value: **1.50**
Circ: Statement: **36,495**
26 ❑ Oct 1991 Cover: 1.00 **NM** value: **1.50**
Circ: Statement: **36,495**
27 ❑ Nov 1991 Cover: 1.00 **NM** value: **1.50**
Circ: Statement: **36,495**
28 ❑ Dec 1991 Cover: 1.00 **NM** value: **1.50**
Circ: Statement: **36,495**
29 ❑ Jan 1992 Cover: 1.00 **NM** value: **1.50**
Circ: Statement: **29,858**
30 ❑ Feb 1992 Cover: 1.00 **NM** value: **1.50**
Circ: Statement: **29,858**
31 ❑ Mar 1992 Cover: 1.00 **NM** value: **1.50**
Circ: Statement: **29,858**
32 ❑ Apr 1992 Cover: 1.00 **NM** value: **1.50**
Circ: Statement: **29,858**
33 ❑ May 1992 Cover: 1.25 **NM** value: **1.50**
Circ: Statement: **29,858**
34 ❑ Jun 1992 Cover: 1.25 **NM** value: **1.50**
Circ: Statement: **29,858**
35 ❑ Jul 1992 Cover: 1.25 **NM** value: **1.50**
Circ: Statement: **29,858**
📖 A Portrait of the Artist as a Young Jughead; Breaking Up is Hard To Do **A:** Rex Lindsey **W:** Terry Collins
36 ❑ Aug 1992 Cover: 1.25 **NM** value: **1.50**
Circ: Statement: **29,858**
37 ❑ Sep 1992 Cover: 1.25 **NM** value: **1.50**
Circ: Statement: **29,858**
38 ❑ Oct 1992 Cover: 1.25 **NM** value: **1.50**
Circ: Statement: **29,858**
39 ❑ Nov 1992 Cover: 1.25 **NM** value: **1.50**
Circ: Statement: **29,858**
40 ❑ Dec 1992 Cover: 1.25 **NM** value: **1.50**
Circ: Statement: **29,858**
41 ❑ Jan 1993 Cover: 1.25 **NM** value: **1.50**
Circ: Statement: **28,015**
42 ❑ Feb 1993 Cover: 1.25 **NM** value: **1.50**
Circ: Statement: **28,015**
43 ❑ Mar 1993 Cover: 1.25 **NM** value: **1.50**
Circ: Statement: **28,015**
44 ❑ Apr 1993 Cover: 1.25 **NM** value: **1.50**
Circ: Statement: **28,015**
45 ❑ May 1993 Cover: 1.25 **NM** value: **1.50**
Circ: Statement: **28,015**
• Series continued in Archie's Pal Jughead #46

JUGHEAD'S FOLLY — Archie

1 ❑ ca. 1957 Cover: 0.10 **NM** value: **125.00**
• **CGC:** 3 graded, best 5.0

JUGHEAD AS CAPTAIN HERO — Archie

1 ❑ Oct 1966 Cover: 0.12 **NM** value: **25.00**
2 ❑ Dec 1966 Cover: 0.12 **NM** value: **14.00**
3 ❑ Feb 1967 Cover: 0.12 **NM** value: **9.00**
4 ❑ Apr 1967 Cover: 0.12 **NM** value: **6.00**
5 ❑ Jun 1967 Cover: 0.12 **NM** value: **6.00**
6 ❑ Aug 1967 Cover: 0.12 **NM** value: **6.00**
7 ❑ Nov 1967 Cover: 0.12 **NM** value: **6.00**

JUGHEAD JONES DIGEST MAGAZINE, THE — Archie

1 ❑ Jun 1977 Cover: 0.75 **NM** value: **15.00**
A: Neal Adams
2 ❑ Sep 1977 Cover: 0.75 **NM** value: **12.00**
A: Neal Adams

Other grades: Multiply prices above by **1.5 for Mint • 2/3 for Very Fine • 1/3 for Fine • 1/5 for Very Good • 1/8 for Good**

3 ❑ Dec 1977 Cover: 0.75 **NM** value: **6.00**
4 ❑ Mar 1978 **NM** value: **6.00**
5 ❑ Jun 1978 **NM** value: **6.00**
6 ❑ Sep 1978 **NM** value: **6.00**
7 ❑ Dec 1978 **NM** value: **8.00**
8 ❑ Mar 1979 **NM** value: **6.00**
9 ❑ Jun 1979 **NM** value: **6.00**
10 ❑ Sep 1979 **NM** value: **6.00**
11 ❑ Dec 1979 **NM** value: **5.00**
12 ❑ Mar 1980 **NM** value: **5.00**
13 ❑ Jun 1980 **NM** value: **5.00**
14 ❑ Sep 1980 **NM** value: **5.00**
15 ❑ Dec 1980 **NM** value: **5.00**
16 ❑ Mar 1981 **NM** value: **5.00**
17 ❑ Jun 1981 **NM** value: **5.00**
18 ❑ Sep 1981 **NM** value: **5.00**
19 ❑ Dec 1981 **NM** value: **5.00**
20 ❑ Mar 1982 **NM** value: **5.00**
21 ❑ Jun 1982 **NM** value: **4.00**
22 ❑ Sep 1982 **NM** value: **4.00**
23 ❑ Dec 1982 **NM** value: **4.00**
24 ❑ Mar 1983 **NM** value: **4.00**
25 ❑ Jun 1983 **NM** value: **4.00**
26 ❑ Sep 1983 **NM** value: **4.00**
27 ❑ Dec 1983 **NM** value: **4.00**
28 ❑ Mar 1984 **NM** value: **4.00**
29 ❑ Jun 1984 **NM** value: **4.00**
30 ❑ Sep 1984 **NM** value: **4.00**
31 ❑ Dec 1984 **NM** value: **3.00**
32 ❑ Mar 1985 **NM** value: **3.00**
Circ: Statement: **124,174**
33 ❑ Jun 1985 **NM** value: **3.00**
Circ: Statement: **124,174**
34 ❑ Aug 1985 Cover: 1.25 **NM** value: **3.00**
Circ: Statement: **124,174**
35 ❑ Oct 1985 **NM** value: **3.00**
Circ: Statement: **124,174**
36 ❑ Dec 1985 **NM** value: **3.00**
Circ: Statement: **124,174**
37 ❑ Feb 1986 **NM** value: **3.00**
Circ: Statement: **125,458**
38 ❑ Apr 1986 **NM** value: **3.00**
Circ: Statement: **125,458**
39 ❑ Jun 1986 **NM** value: **3.00**
Circ: Statement: **125,458**
40 ❑ Aug 1986 **NM** value: **3.00**
Circ: Statement: **125,458**
41 ❑ Oct 1986 **NM** value: **3.00**
Circ: Statement: **125,458**
42 ❑ Dec 1986 **NM** value: **3.00**
Circ: Statement: **125,458**
43 ❑ Feb 1987 **NM** value: **3.00**
Circ: Statement: **126,997**
44 ❑ Apr 1987 **NM** value: **3.00**
Circ: Statement: **126,997**
45 ❑ Jun 1987 **NM** value: **3.00**
Circ: Statement: **126,997**
46 ❑ Aug 1987 **NM** value: **3.00**
Circ: Statement: **126,997**
47 ❑ Oct 1987 **NM** value: **3.00**
Circ: Statement: **126,997**
48 ❑ Dec 1987 Cover: 1.35 **NM** value: **3.00**
Circ: Statement: **126,997**
49 ❑ Feb 1987 Cover: 1.35 **NM** value: **3.00**
Circ: Statement: **135,478**
50 ❑ Apr 1988 Cover: 1.35 **NM** value: **3.00**
Circ: Statement: **135,478**
• Has 1987 Statement, filed 10/1/87; avg print run 264,245; avg shop sales 126,864; avg subs 133; avg total paid 126,997; office copies 300; max existent 127,297; 52% of run returned
51 ❑ Jun 1988 Cover: 1.35 **NM** value: **2.00**
Circ: Statement: **135,478**
52 ❑ Aug 1988 Cover: 1.35 **NM** value: **2.00**
Circ: Statement: **135,478**
53 ❑ Oct 1988 Cover: 1.35 **NM** value: **2.00**
Circ: Statement: **135,478**
54 ❑ Dec 1988 Cover: 1.35 **NM** value: **2.00**
Circ: Statement: **135,478**
55 ❑ Feb 1989 Cover: 1.35 **NM** value: **2.00**
Circ: Statement: **142,220**
56 ❑ Apr 1989 Cover: 1.35 **NM** value: **2.00**
Circ: Statement: **142,220**
• Has 1988 Statement, filed 10/1/88; avg print run 266,217; avg shop sales 132,758; avg subs 2,720; avg total paid 135,478; samples 614; office 1,367; max existent 137,459; 48% of run returned
57 ❑ Jun 1989 Cover: 1.50 **NM** value: **2.00**
Circ: Statement: **142,220**
58 ❑ Aug 1989 Cover: 1.50 **NM** value: **2.00**
Circ: Statement: **142,220**
59 ❑ Oct 1989 Cover: 1.50 **NM** value: **2.00**
Circ: Statement: **142,220**
60 ❑ Dec 1989 Cover: 1.50 **NM** value: **2.00**
Circ: Statement: **142,220**
61 ❑ Feb 1989 Cover: 1.50 **NM** value: **2.00**
Circ: Statement: **137,596**
62 ❑ Apr 1990 Cover: 1.50 **NM** value: **2.00**
Circ: Statement: **137,596**
63 ❑ Jun 1990 Cover: 1.50 **NM** value: **2.00**
Circ: Statement: **137,596**
64 ❑ Aug 1990 Cover: 1.50 **NM** value: **2.00**
Circ: Statement: **137,596**
65 ❑ Oct 1990 Cover: 1.50 **NM** value: **2.00**
Circ: Statement: **137,596**
66 ❑ Dec 1990 Cover: 1.50 **NM** value: **2.00**
Circ: Statement: **137,596**
67 ❑ Feb 1991 Cover: 1.50 **NM** value: **2.00**
Circ: Statement: **122,695**
68 ❑ Apr 1991 Cover: 1.50 **NM** value: **2.00**
Circ: Statement: **122,695**
• Has 1990 Statement, filed 10/1/1990; avg print run 289,481; avg shop sales 130,569; avg subs 7,027; avg total paid 137,596; samples 542; office copies 2,207; max existent 140,345; 52% of run returned
69 ❑ 1991 Cover: 1.50 **NM** value: **2.00**
Circ: Statement: **122,695**
70 ❑ 1991 Cover: 1.50 **NM** value: **2.00**
Circ: Statement: **122,695**
71 ❑ 1991 Cover: 1.50 **NM** value: **2.00**
Circ: Statement: **122,695**
72 ❑ 1991 Cover: 1.50 **NM** value: **2.00**
Circ: Statement: **122,695**
73 ❑ 1992 Cover: 1.50 **NM** value: **2.00**
74 ❑ 1992 Cover: 1.50 **NM** value: **2.00**
75 ❑ May 1992 Cover: 1.50 **NM** value: **2.00**
• Has 1991 Statement, filed 10/1/91; avg print run 287,755; avg shop sales 121,526; avg subs 1,169; avg total paid 122,695; samples 513; office copies 7,942; max existent 131,150; 54% of run returned
76 ❑ 1992 Cover: 1.50 **NM** value: **2.00**
77 ❑ 1992 Cover: 1.50 **NM** value: **2.00**
78 ❑ Nov 1992 Cover: 1.50 **NM** value: **2.00**
79 ❑ 1993 Cover: 1.50 **NM** value: **2.00**
80 ❑ 1993 Cover: 1.50 **NM** value: **2.00**
81 ❑ 1993 Cover: 1.50 **NM** value: **2.00**
82 ❑ 1993 Cover: 1.50 **NM** value: **2.00**
83 ❑ 1993 Cover: 1.50 **NM** value: **2.00**
84 ❑ 1993 **NM** value: **2.00**
85 ❑ **NM** value: **2.00**
86 ❑ **NM** value: **2.00**
87 ❑ 1994 **NM** value: **2.00**
88 ❑ 1994 **NM** value: **2.00**
89 ❑ 1994 **NM** value: **2.00**
90 ❑ 1994 **NM** value: **2.00**
91 ❑ 1994 **NM** value: **2.00**
92 ❑ Dec 1994 Cover: 1.75 **NM** value: **Cover or less**
93 ❑ Feb 1995 Cover: 1.75 **NM** value: **Cover or less**
Circ: Statement: **92,527**
94 ❑ Apr 1995 Cover: 1.75 **NM** value: **Cover or less**
Circ: Statement: **92,527**
95 ❑ Jun 1995 Cover: 1.75 **NM** value: **Cover or less**
Circ: Statement: **92,527**
96 ❑ Aug 1995 Cover: 1.75 **NM** value: **Cover or less**
Circ: Statement: **92,527**
97 ❑ Oct 1995 Cover: 1.75 **NM** value: **Cover or less**
Circ: Statement: **92,527**
98 ❑ Nov 1995 Cover: 1.75 **NM** value: **Cover or less**
Circ: Statement: **92,527**
99 ❑ Feb 1996 Cover: 1.75 **NM** value: **Cover or less**
100 ❑ May 1996 Cover: 1.75 **NM** value: **Cover or less**
• Has 1995 Statement, filed 10/1/95; avg print run 250,473; avg sales 91,815; avg subs 712; avg total paid 92,527; samples 377; office use 5,721; max existent 98,625; 61% of run returned ★ Appearance of Nathan Jones.

JUGHEAD'S BABY TALES — Archie

1 ❑ Spr 1994 Cover: 2.00 **NM** value: **Cover or less**
2 ❑ Win 1994 Cover: 2.00 **NM** value: **Cover or less**
📖 Monkey Business, Part 1; Monkey Business, Part 2; Picture This!; Sister Act!; Sugar Daddy; Baby Takes a Spin! • Continued from Baby Tales #1 **A**: Stan Goldberg; Dan Parent **W**: Bill Golliher; Dan Parent ★ Appearance of Big Ethel, Archie.

JUGHEAD'S DINER — Archie

1 ❑ Apr 1990 Cover: 1.00 **NM** value: **2.00**
2 ❑ Cover: 1.00 **NM** value: **1.50**
3 ❑ Cover: 1.00 **NM** value: **1.50**
4 ❑ Cover: 1.00 **NM** value: **1.50**
5 ❑ Cover: 1.00 **NM** value: **1.50**
6 ❑ Cover: 1.00 **NM** value: **1.50**
7 ❑ Cover: 1.00 **NM** value: **1.50**

JUGHEAD'S DOUBLE DIGEST — Archie

1 ❑ Oct 1989 Cover: 2.25 **NM** value: **6.00**
2 ❑ Cover: 2.25 **NM** value: **4.00**
3 ❑ **NM** value: **4.00**
4 ❑ **NM** value: **4.00**
5 ❑ **NM** value: **4.00**
6 ❑ **NM** value: **3.00**
7 ❑ **NM** value: **3.00**
8 ❑ **NM** value: **3.00**
9 ❑ **NM** value: **3.00**
10 ❑ Feb 1992 **NM** value: **3.00**
11 ❑ 1992 Cover: 2.50 **NM** value: **3.00**
12 ❑ Jul 1992 Cover: 2.50 **NM** value: **3.00**
13 ❑ Oct 1992 Cover: 2.50 **NM** value: **3.00**
14 ❑ Dec 1992 Cover: 2.50 **NM** value: **3.00**
15 ❑ Feb 1993 Cover: 2.50 **NM** value: **3.00**
16 ❑ 1993 Cover: 2.50 **NM** value: **3.00**
17 ❑ May 1993 Cover: 2.50 **NM** value: **3.00**
18 ❑ **NM** value: **3.00**
19 ❑ **NM** value: **3.00**
20 ❑ **NM** value: **3.00**
21 ❑ **NM** value: **3.00**
22 ❑ 1993 Cover: 2.75 **NM** value: **3.00**
23 ❑ Cover: 2.75 **NM** value: **3.00**
24 ❑ Cover: 2.75 **NM** value: **3.00**
25 ❑ Cover: 2.75 **NM** value: **3.00**
26 ❑ 1994 Cover: 2.75 **NM** value: **3.00**
27 ❑ Dec 1994 Cover: 2.75 **NM** value: **3.00**
28 ❑ Jan 1995 Cover: 2.75 **NM** value: **3.00**
Circ: Statement: **92,918**
29 ❑ Mar 1995 Cover: 2.75 **NM** value: **3.00**
Circ: Statement: **92,918**
30 ❑ May 1995 Cover: 2.75 **NM** value: **3.00**
Circ: Statement: **92,918**
31 ❑ Jul 1995 Cover: 2.75 **NM** value: **Cover or less**
Circ: Statement: **92,918**
32 ❑ Sep 1995 Cover: 2.75 **NM** value: **Cover or less**
Circ: Statement: **92,918**
33 ❑ Nov 1995 Cover: 2.75 **NM** value: **Cover or less**
Circ: Statement: **92,918**
34 ❑ Jan 1996 Cover: 2.75 **NM** value: **Cover or less**
Circ: Statement: **106,257**
35 ❑ Feb 1996 Cover: 2.75 **NM** value: **Cover or less**
Circ: Statement: **106,257**
36 ❑ Apr 1996 Cover: 2.75 **NM** value: **Cover or less**
Circ: Statement: **106,257**
• Has 1995 Statement, filed 10/1/95; avg print run 275,081; avg sales 91,911; avg subs 1,007; avg total paid 92,918; samples 376; max existent 99,833; 34% of run returned
37 ❑ Jun 1996 Cover: 2.75 **NM** value: **Cover or less**
Circ: Statement: **106,257**
38 ❑ Aug 1996 Cover: 2.75 **NM** value: **Cover or less**
Circ: Statement: **106,257**
39 ❑ Sep 1996 Cover: 2.75 **NM** value: **Cover or less**
Circ: Statement: **106,257**
40 ❑ Nov 1996 Cover: 2.75 **NM** value: **Cover or less**
Circ: Statement: **106,257**
• duplicate pages at front
41 ❑ Jan 1997 Cover: 2.75 **NM** value: **Cover or less**
Circ: Statement: **101,017** Diamd. preorders: **3,367**
42 ❑ Feb 1997 Cover: 2.75 **NM** value: **Cover or less**
Circ: Statement: **101,017** Diamd. preorders: **3,070**
43 ❑ Apr 1997 Cover: 2.75 **NM** value: **Cover or less**
Circ: Statement: **101,017** Diamd. preorders: **2,939**
• Has 1996 Statement, filed 9/27/96; avg print run 260,727; avg sales 105,371; avg subs 886; avg total paid 106,257; samples 385; max existent 112,142; 41% of run returned
44 ❑ Jun 1997 Cover: 2.75 **NM** value: **Cover or less**
Circ: Statement: **101,017** Diamd. preorders: **3,290**
45 ❑ Jul 1997 Cover: 2.75 **NM** value: **Cover or less**
Circ: Statement: **101,017**
46 ❑ Sep 1997 Cover: 2.79 **NM** value: **Cover or less**
Circ: Statement: **101,017** Diamd. preorders: **3,752**
47 ❑ Nov 1997 Cover: 2.79 **NM** value: **Cover or less**
Circ: Statement: **101,017**
48 ❑ Dec 1997 Cover: 2.79 **NM** value: **Cover or less**
Circ: Statement: **101,017**
49 ❑ Feb 1998 Cover: 2.95 **NM** value: **Cover or less**
Circ: Statement: **102,989** Diamd. preorders: **3,875**
50 ❑ Apr 1998 Cover: 2.95 **NM** value: **Cover or less**
Circ: Statement: **102,989** Diamd. preorders: **3,653**
• Has 1997 Statement, filed 11/1/97; avg print run 261,180; avg sales 100,137; avg subs 880; avg total paid 101,017; samples 296; max existent 106,477; 39% of run returned
51 ❑ Jun 1998 Cover: 2.95 **NM** value: **Cover or less**
Circ: Statement: **102,989** Diamd. preorders: **3,002**
52 ❑ Jul 1998 Cover: 2.95 **NM** value: **Cover or less**
Circ: Statement: **102,989** Diamd. preorders: **3,578**
53 ❑ Aug 1998 Cover: 2.95 **NM** value: **Cover or less**
Circ: Statement: **102,989** Diamd. preorders: **3,177**
54 ❑ Oct 1998 Cover: 2.95 **NM** value: **Cover or less**
Circ: Statement: **102,989** Diamd. preorders: **2,737**
55 ❑ Nov 1998 Cover: 2.95 **NM** value: **Cover or less**
Circ: Statement: **102,989** Diamd. preorders: **2,873**
A: Dan Decarlo
56 ❑ Jan 1999 Cover: 2.95 **NM** value: **Cover or less**
Circ: Diamd. preorders: **3,170**
57 ❑ Feb 1999 Cover: 2.95 **NM** value: **Cover or less**
Circ: Diamd. preorders: **3,188**
58 ❑ Apr 1999 Cover: 2.99 **NM** value: **Cover or less**
Circ: Diamd. preorders: **2,767**
• Has 1998 Statement, filed 11/1/98; avg print run 247,715; avg sales 102,000' avg subs 989; avg total paid 102,989; samples 280; max existent 110,188; 42% of run returned
59 ❑ Jun 1999 Cover: 2.99 **NM** value: **Cover or less**
Circ: Diamd. preorders: **2,859**
60 ❑ Jul 1999 Cover: 2.99 **NM** value: **Cover or less**
Circ: Diamd. preorders: **2,877**
61 ❑ Aug 1999 Cover: 2.99 **NM** value: **Cover or less**
Circ: Diamd. preorders: **2,864**
62 ❑ Oct 1999 Cover: 2.99 **NM** value: **Cover or less**
Circ: Diamd. preorders: **3,181**
63 ❑ Nov 1999 Cover: 2.99 **NM** value: **Cover or less**
Circ: Diamd. preorders: **3,127**
64 ❑ Jan 2000 Cover: 2.99 **NM** value: **Cover or less**
Circ: Diamd. preorders: **2,451**
65 ❑ Feb 2000 Cover: 2.99 **NM** value: **Cover or less**
Circ: Diamd. preorders: **2,616**
66 ❑ Apr 2000 Cover: 2.99 **NM** value: **Cover or less**
Circ: Diamd. preorders: **2,931**
67 ❑ May 2000 Cover: 2.99 **NM** value: **Cover or less**
Circ: Diamd. preorders: **2,870**
68 ❑ Jul 2000 Cover: 3.19 **NM** value: **Cover or less**
Circ: Diamd. preorders: **2,408**
69 ❑ Aug 2000 Cover: 3.19 **NM** value: **Cover or less**
Circ: Diamd. preorders: **2,720**
70 ❑ Oct 2000 Cover: 3.19 **NM** value: **Cover or less**
Circ: Diamd. preorders: **3,114**
71 ❑ Nov 2000 Cover: 3.19 **NM** value: **Cover or less**
Circ: Diamd. preorders: **2,570**
72 ❑ Jan 2001 Cover: 3.19 **NM** value: **Cover or less**
Circ: Statement: **110,602** Diamd. preorders: **2,569**
73 ❑ Feb 2001 Cover: 3.19 **NM** value: **Cover or less**
Circ: Statement: **110,602** Diamd. preorders: **2,558**
74 ❑ Mar 2001 Cover: 3.19 **NM** value: **Cover or less**
Circ: Statement: **110,602** Diamd. preorders: **2,585**
75 ❑ May 2001 Cover: 3.29 **NM** value: **Cover or less**
Circ: Statement: **110,602** Diamd. preorders: **2,337**
76 ❑ Jun 2001 Cover: 3.29 **NM** value: **Cover or less**
Circ: Statement: **110,602** Diamd. preorders: **2,438**
77 ❑ Aug 2001 Cover: 3.29 **NM** value: **Cover or less**
Circ: Statement: **110,602** Diamd. preorders: **2,790**
78 ❑ Sep 2001 Cover: 3.29 **NM** value: **Cover or less**
Circ: Statement: **110,602** Diamd. preorders: **2,992**
79 ❑ Oct 2001 Cover: 3.29 **NM** value: **Cover or less**

CGC-graded: Multiply prices above by **33 for 9.9 M • 16 for 9.8 NM/M • 7 for 9.6 NM+ • 5 for 9.4 NM • 2.5 for 9.2 NM- • 1.5 for 9.0 VF/NM**

Circ: Statement: **110,602** Diamd. preorders: **3,029**

JUGHEAD'S FANTASY — Archie

1 ❑ Aug 1960 Cover: 0.10 **NM** value: **150.00**
2 ❑ Oct 1960 Cover: 0.10 **NM** value: **100.00**
3 ❑ Dec 1960 Cover: 0.10 **NM** value: **100.00**

JUGHEAD'S PAL HOT DOG — Archie

1 ❑ Jan 1990 Cover: 1.00 **NM** value: **Cover or less**
2 ❑ Jan 1990 Cover: 1.00 **NM** value: **Cover or less**
3 ❑ 1990 Cover: 1.00 **NM** value: **Cover or less**
4 ❑ 1990 Cover: 1.00 **NM** value: **Cover or less**
5 ❑ 1990 Cover: 1.00 **NM** value: **Cover or less**

JUGHEAD'S TIME POLICE — Archie

1 ❑ Jul 1990 Cover: 1.00 **NM** value: **1.25**
2 ❑ Sep 1990 Cover: 1.00 **NM** value: **Cover or less**
3 ❑ Nov 1990 Cover: 1.00 **NM** value: **Cover or less**
4 ❑ Jan 1991 Cover: 1.00 **NM** value: **Cover or less**
5 ❑ Mar 1991 Cover: 1.00 **NM** value: **Cover or less**
★ Appearance of Abe Lincoln.
6 ❑ May 1991 Cover: 1.00 **NM** value: **Cover or less**
★ Origin of Time Beanie.

JUGHEAD WITH ARCHIE DIGEST MAGAZINE — Archie

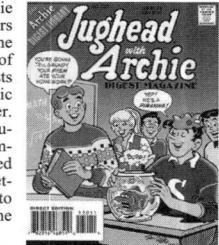

After some thirty years of Archie comic books, Archie's publishers hit upon the idea of repackaging the Archies' adventures in a series of digest magazines. These digests were smaller than a regular comic book in page size, but much thicker. They were often sold alongside supermarket check-out line pamphlets and TV Guides, and proved the perfect present to quiet any fretful children who had been forced to accompany their parents to the store.

Jughead with Archie Digest concentrates a bit more on Archie's best friend Jughead than on the rest of the Riverdale gang. Still, no Archie magazine would be complete without including Betty, Veronica, Archie, Reggie, Moose, and the rest of Jug's friends.

1 ❑ Mar 1974 Cover: 0.60 **NM** value: **12.00**
2 ❑ May 1974 Cover: 0.60 **NM** value: **7.00**
3 ❑ Jul 1974 Cover: 0.60 **NM** value: **7.00**
4 ❑ Sep 1974 Cover: 0.60 **NM** value: **7.00**
5 ❑ Nov 1974 Cover: 0.60 **NM** value: **7.00**
6 ❑ Jan 1975 Cover: 0.60 **NM** value: **7.00**
Circ: Statement: **139,396**
7 ❑ Mar 1975 Cover: 0.60 **NM** value: **7.00**
Circ: Statement: **139,396**
8 ❑ May 1975 Cover: 0.60 **NM** value: **7.00**
Circ: Statement: **139,396**
9 ❑ Jul 1975 Cover: 0.60 **NM** value: **7.00**
Circ: Statement: **139,396**
10 ❑ Sep 1975 Cover: 0.60 **NM** value: **7.00**
Circ: Statement: **139,396**
11 ❑ Nov 1975 Cover: 0.60 **NM** value: **4.00**
Circ: Statement: **139,396**
12 ❑ Jan 1976 Cover: 0.60 **NM** value: **4.00**
Circ: Statement: **154,093**
13 ❑ Mar 1976 Cover: 0.60 **NM** value: **4.00**
Circ: Statement: **154,093**
14 ❑ May 1976 Cover: 0.60 **NM** value: **4.00**
Circ: Statement: **154,093**
• Has 1975 Statement, filed 10/1/1975; avg print run 258,820; avg sales 139,289; avg subs 107; total paid 139,396; office copies 300; max existent 139696; 46% of run returned
15 ❑ Jul 1976 Cover: 0.60 **NM** value: **4.00**
Circ: Statement: **154,093**
16 ❑ Sep 1976 Cover: 0.60 **NM** value: **4.00**
Circ: Statement: **154,093**
17 ❑ Nov 1976 Cover: 0.60 **NM** value: **4.00**
Circ: Statement: **154,093**
18 ❑ Jan 1977 Cover: 0.60 **NM** value: **4.00**
Circ: Statement: **151,872**
19 ❑ Mar 1977 Cover: 0.60 **NM** value: **4.00**
Circ: Statement: **151,872**
20 ❑ May 1977 Cover: 0.60 **NM** value: **4.00**
Circ: Statement: **151,872**
• Has 1976 Statement; total paid 154,093
21 ❑ Jul 1977 Cover: 0.60 **NM** value: **2.50**
Circ: Statement: **151,872**
22 ❑ Sep 1977 Cover: 0.60 **NM** value: **2.50**
Circ: Statement: **151,872**
23 ❑ Nov 1977 **NM** value: **2.50**
Circ: Statement: **151,872**
24 ❑ Jan 1978 **NM** value: **2.50**
25 ❑ Mar 1978 **NM** value: **2.50**
26 ❑ Apr 1978 **NM** value: **2.50**
• Has 1977 Statement; total paid 151,872
27 ❑ Jul 1978 **NM** value: **2.50**
28 ❑ Sep 1978 **NM** value: **2.50**
29 ❑ Nov 1978 **NM** value: **2.50**
30 ❑ Jan 1979 **NM** value: **2.50**
31 ❑ Mar 1979 **NM** value: **2.50**
32 ❑ May 1979 **NM** value: **2.50**
33 ❑ Jul 1979 **NM** value: **2.50**
34 ❑ Sep 1979 **NM** value: **2.50**
35 ❑ Nov 1979 **NM** value: **2.50**
36 ❑ Jan 1980 **NM** value: **2.50**
37 ❑ Mar 1980 **NM** value: **2.50**
38 ❑ May 1980 **NM** value: **2.50**
39 ❑ Jul 1980 **NM** value: **2.50**
40 ❑ Sep 1980 **NM** value: **2.50**
41 ❑ Nov 1980 **NM** value: **2.50**
42 ❑ Jan 1981 **NM** value: **2.50**
43 ❑ Mar 1981 **NM** value: **2.50**
44 ❑ May 1981 **NM** value: **2.50**
45 ❑ Jul 1981 **NM** value: **2.50**
46 ❑ Sep 1981 **NM** value: **2.50**
47 ❑ Nov 1981 **NM** value: **2.50**
48 ❑ Jan 1982 **NM** value: **2.50**
📖 Surprise Flies, Part 1; Surprise Flies, Part 2; A Man and His Dog **A:** Stan Goldberg **W:** Al Hartley
49 ❑ Mar 1982 **NM** value: **2.50**
50 ❑ May 1982 **NM** value: **2.50**
51 ❑ Jul 1982 **NM** value: **2.00**
52 ❑ Sep 1982 **NM** value: **2.00**
53 ❑ Nov 1982 **NM** value: **2.00**
54 ❑ Jan 1983 **NM** value: **2.00**
Circ: Statement: **120,647**
55 ❑ Mar 1983 **NM** value: **2.00**
Circ: Statement: **120,647**
56 ❑ May 1983 **NM** value: **2.00**
Circ: Statement: **120,647**
57 ❑ Jul 1983 **NM** value: **2.00**
Circ: Statement: **120,647**
58 ❑ Sep 1983 Cover: 1.00 **NM** value: **2.00**
Circ: Statement: **120,647**
59 ❑ Nov 1983 Cover: 1.00 **NM** value: **2.00**
Circ: Statement: **120,647**
60 ❑ Jan 1984 Cover: 1.00 **NM** value: **2.00**
Circ: Statement: **132,033**
61 ❑ Mar 1984 Cover: 1.00 **NM** value: **2.00**
Circ: Statement: **132,033**
62 ❑ May 1984 Cover: 1.00 **NM** value: **2.00**
Circ: Statement: **132,033**
• Has 1983 Statement, filed 10/1/1983; avg print run 257,644; avg sales 120,514; avg subs 133; avg total paid 120,647; office use 300; max existent 120,947; 53% of run returned
63 ❑ Jul 1984 Cover: 1.00 **NM** value: **2.00**
Circ: Statement: **132,033**
64 ❑ Sep 1984 Cover: 1.00 **NM** value: **2.00**
Circ: Statement: **132,033**
65 ❑ Nov 1984 Cover: 1.00 **NM** value: **2.00**
Circ: Statement: **132,033**
66 ❑ Jan 1985 **NM** value: **2.00**
Circ: Statement: **136,215**
67 ❑ Mar 1985 **NM** value: **2.00**
Circ: Statement: **136,215**
68 ❑ May 1985 **NM** value: **2.00**
Circ: Statement: **136,215**
69 ❑ Jul 1985 **NM** value: **2.00**
Circ: Statement: **136,215**
70 ❑ Sep 1985 **NM** value: **2.00**
Circ: Statement: **136,215**
71 ❑ Nov 1985 **NM** value: **2.00**
Circ: Statement: **136,215**
72 ❑ Jan 1986 **NM** value: **2.00**
Circ: Statement: **141,796**
73 ❑ Mar 1986 **NM** value: **2.00**
Circ: Statement: **141,796**
74 ❑ May 1986 **NM** value: **2.00**
Circ: Statement: **141,796**
75 ❑ Jul 1986 **NM** value: **2.00**
Circ: Statement: **141,796**
76 ❑ Sep 1986 **NM** value: **2.00**
Circ: Statement: **141,796**
77 ❑ Nov 1986 **NM** value: **2.00**
Circ: Statement: **141,796**
78 ❑ Jan 1987 **NM** value: **2.00**
Circ: Statement: **139,132**
79 ❑ Mar 1987 Cover: 1.35 **NM** value: **2.00**
Circ: Statement: **139,132**
80 ❑ May 1987 Cover: 1.35 **NM** value: **2.00**
Circ: Statement: **139,132**
81 ❑ Jul 1987 Cover: 1.35 **NM** value: **2.00**
Circ: Statement: **139,132**
82 ❑ Sep 1987 Cover: 1.35 **NM** value: **2.00**
Circ: Statement: **139,132**
83 ❑ Nov 1987 Cover: 1.35 **NM** value: **2.00**
Circ: Statement: **139,132**
84 ❑ Jan 1988 Cover: 1.35 **NM** value: **2.00**
Circ: Statement: **145,596**
85 ❑ Mar 1988 Cover: 1.35 **NM** value: **2.00**
Circ: Statement: **145,596**
86 ❑ May 1988 Cover: 1.35 **NM** value: **2.00**
Circ: Statement: **145,596**
87 ❑ Jul 1988 Cover: 1.35 **NM** value: **2.00**
Circ: Statement: **145,596**
88 ❑ Sep 1988 Cover: 1.35 **NM** value: **2.00**
Circ: Statement: **145,596**
89 ❑ Nov 1988 Cover: 1.35 **NM** value: **2.00**
Circ: Statement: **145,596**
90 ❑ Jan 1989 **NM** value: **2.00**
Circ: Statement: **149,295**
91 ❑ Mar 1989 Cover: 1.75 **NM** value: **2.00**
Circ: Statement: **149,295**
92 ❑ May 1989 **NM** value: **2.00**
Circ: Statement: **149,295**
93 ❑ Jul 1989 **NM** value: **2.00**
Circ: Statement: **149,295**
94 ❑ Sep 1989 Cover: 1.50 **NM** value: **2.00**
Circ: Statement: **149,295**
95 ❑ Nov 1989 Cover: 1.50 **NM** value: **2.00**
Circ: Statement: **149,295**
96 ❑ Jan 1990 Cover: 1.50 **NM** value: **2.00**
Circ: Statement: **142,846**
97 ❑ Mar 1990 Cover: 1.50 **NM** value: **2.00**
Circ: Statement: **142,846**
98 ❑ May 1990 Cover: 1.50 **NM** value: **2.00**
Circ: Statement: **142,846**
99 ❑ Jul 1990 Cover: 1.50 **NM** value: **2.00**
Circ: Statement: **142,846**
100 ❑ Sep 1990 Cover: 1.50 **NM** value: **2.00**
Circ: Statement: **142,846**
101 ❑ Nov 1990 Cover: 1.50 **NM** value: **1.75**
Circ: Statement: **142,846**
102 ❑ Jan 1991 Cover: 1.50 **NM** value: **1.75**
103 ❑ Mar 1991 Cover: 1.50 **NM** value: **1.75**
104 ❑ May 1991 Cover: 1.50 **NM** value: **1.75**
105 ❑ Jul 1991 Cover: 1.50 **NM** value: **1.75**
106 ❑ Sep 1991 Cover: 1.50 **NM** value: **1.75**
107 ❑ 1991 Cover: 1.50 **NM** value: **1.75**
108 ❑ Cover: 1.50 **NM** value: **1.75**
109 ❑ 1992 Cover: 1.50 **NM** value: **1.75**
110 ❑ Apr 1992 Cover: 1.50 **NM** value: **1.75**
111 ❑ 1992 Cover: 1.50 **NM** value: **1.75**
112 ❑ 1992 Cover: 1.50 **NM** value: **1.75**
113 ❑ Cover: 1.50 **NM** value: **1.75**
114 ❑ Feb 1993 Cover: 1.50 **NM** value: **1.75**
115 ❑ 1993 Cover: 1.50 **NM** value: **1.75**
116 ❑ Aug 1993 **NM** value: **1.75**
117 ❑ **NM** value: **1.75**
118 ❑ **NM** value: **1.75**
119 ❑ **NM** value: **1.75**
120 ❑ **NM** value: **1.75**
121 ❑ **NM** value: **1.75**
122 ❑ Jan 1995 Cover: 1.75 **NM** value: **Cover or less**
123 ❑ May 1995 Cover: 1.75 **NM** value: **Cover or less**
124 ❑ Aug 1995 Cover: 1.75 **NM** value: **Cover or less**
125 ❑ Oct 1995 Cover: 1.75 **NM** value: **Cover or less**
126 ❑ Jan 1996 Cover: 1.75 **NM** value: **Cover or less**
Circ: Statement: **102,178**
127 ❑ 1996 Cover: 1.75 **NM** value: **Cover or less**
Circ: Statement: **102,178**
128 ❑ Sep 1996 Cover: 1.79 **NM** value: **Cover or less**
Circ: Statement: **102,178**
129 ❑ 1996 Cover: 1.79 **NM** value: **Cover or less**
Circ: Statement: **102,178**
130 ❑ Dec 1997 Cover: 1.79 **NM** value: **Cover or less**
Circ: Statement: **102,178** Diamd. preorders: **2,741**
📖 Glutton For Hire; Double Takes; Fashion Disaster; History Lesson; Snooze Ruse; Sport Report; Food Rude; Paper Chase; Caught In The Act; Retail Whirl; Invader; A Great Team; Present Problems; The Secret Project; A Matter Of Timing; A Spirited Weekend; **A:** Fernando Ruiz **W:** Dan Parent
131 ❑ Feb 1997 Cover: 1.79 **NM** value: **Cover or less**
Circ: Statement: **86,160** Diamd. preorders: **2,860**
132 ❑ Mar 1997 Cover: 1.79 **NM** value: **Cover or less**
Circ: Statement: **86,160** Diamd. preorders: **2,883**
133 ❑ May 1997 Cover: 1.79 **NM** value: **Cover or less**
Circ: Statement: **86,160** Diamd. preorders: **2,523**
• Has 1996 Statement, filed 9/27/96; avg print run 251284; avg sales 101,726; avg subs 453; avg total paid 102178; samples 382; office use 2,186; max existent 104,747; 58% of run returned
134 ❑ Jul 1997 Cover: 1.79 **NM** value: **Cover or less**
Circ: Statement: **86,160**
135 ❑ Aug 1997 Cover: 1.79 **NM** value: **Cover or less**
Circ: Statement: **86,160**
136 ❑ Oct 1997 Cover: 1.79 **NM** value: **Cover or less**
Circ: Statement: **86,160**
137 ❑ Dec 1997 Cover: 1.79 **NM** value: **Cover or less**
Circ: Statement: **86,160**
138 ❑ Jan 1998 Cover: 1.95 **NM** value: **Cover or less**
Circ: Statement: **81,179**
139 ❑ Mar 1998 Cover: 1.95 **NM** value: **Cover or less**
Circ: Statement: **81,179**
140 ❑ May 1998 Cover: 1.95 **NM** value: **Cover or less**
Circ: Statement: **81,179** Diamd. preorders: **3,002**
• Has 1997 Statement, filed 11/1/97; avg print run 250,828; avg sales 85,575; avg subs 585; avg total paid 86,160; samples 452; office use 6,437; max existent 93,049; 63% of run returned
141 ❑ Jun 1998 Cover: 1.95 **NM** value: **Cover or less**
Circ: Statement: **81,179**
142 ❑ Aug 1998 Cover: 1.95 **NM** value: **Cover or less**
Circ: Statement: **81,179**
143 ❑ Oct 1998 Cover: 1.95 **NM** value: **Cover or less**
Circ: Statement: **81,179** Diamd. preorders: **2,820**
A: Dan Decarlo
144 ❑ Nov 1998 Cover: 1.95 **NM** value: **Cover or less**
Circ: Statement: **81,179** Diamd. preorders: **2,688**
145 ❑ Dec 1998 Cover: 1.95 **NM** value: **Cover or less**
Circ: Statement: **81,179** Diamd. preorders: **2,603**
146 ❑ Feb 1999 Cover: 1.95 **NM** value: **Cover or less**
Circ: Diamd. preorders: **2,654**
147 ❑ Apr 1999 Cover: 1.95 **NM** value: **Cover or less**
Circ: Diamd. preorders: **2,592**
148 ❑ May 1999 Cover: 1.99 **NM** value: **Cover or less**
Circ: Diamd. preorders: **2,268**
• Has 1998 Statement, filed 11/1/98; avg print run 227,943; avg sales 80,565; avg subs 614; avg total paid 81,179; samples 392; office use 6,474; max existent 88,045; 58% of run returned
149 ❑ Jun 1999 Cover: 1.99 **NM** value: **Cover or less**
Circ: Diamd. preorders: **2,335**
150 ❑ Aug 1999 Cover: 1.99 **NM** value: **Cover or less**
Circ: Diamd. preorders: **2,448**
151 ❑ Sep 1999 Cover: 1.99 **NM** value: **Cover or less**
Circ: Diamd. preorders: **2,482**
152 ❑ Nov 1999 Cover: 1.99 **NM** value: **Cover or less**
Circ: Diamd. preorders: **2,541**
153 ❑ Dec 1999 Cover: 1.99 **NM** value: **Cover or less**
154 ❑ Feb 2000 Cover: 1.99 **NM** value: **Cover or less**
155 ❑ Mar 2000 Cover: 1.99 **NM** value: **Cover or less**
156 ❑ May 2000 Cover: 1.99 **NM** value: **Cover or less**
Circ: Diamd. preorders: **2,237**
157 ❑ Jul 2000 Cover: 2.19 **NM** value: **Cover or less**

Circ: Diamd. preorders: **2,028**
158 ❑ Aug 2000 Cover: 2.19 **NM** value: **Cover or less**
Circ: Diamd. preorders: **2,397**
159 ❑ Sep 2000 Cover: 2.19 **NM** value: **Cover or less**
Circ: Diamd. preorders: **2,675**
160 ❑ Nov 2000 Cover: 2.19 **NM** value: **Cover or less**
Circ: Diamd. preorders: **2,144**
161 ❑ Dec 2000 Cover: 2.19 **NM** value: **Cover or less**
Circ: Diamd. preorders: **2,124**
162 ❑ Jan 2001 Cover: 2.19 **NM** value: **Cover or less**
Circ: Diamd. preorders: **2,168**
163 ❑ Mar 2001 Cover: 2.19 **NM** value: **Cover or less**
Circ: Diamd. preorders: **2,098**

JUGULAR — Black Out

0 ❑ Cover: 2.95 **NM** value: **Cover or less**
The Immigrants **A:** Brock L. Hor Jr. **W:** Mike Baron

JUKE BOX COMICS — Famous Funnies

1 ❑ Mar 1948 Cover: 0.10 **NM** value: **300.00**
2 ❑ May 1948 Cover: 0.10 **NM** value: **200.00**
3 ❑ Jul 1948 Cover: 0.10 **NM** value: **175.00**
4 ❑ Sep 1948 Cover: 0.10 **NM** value: **175.00**
5 ❑ Nov 1948 Cover: 0.10 **NM** value: **175.00**
6 ❑ Jan 1949 Cover: 0.10 **NM** value: **175.00**

JUMBO COMICS — Fiction House

Jumbo Comics was one of the more important titles of comics' Golden Age and the flagship of the Fiction House publishing enterprise, which was also responsible for Planet Comics, The Spirit, and Jungle Comics. In its first (oversized) issue alone, Jumbo introduced the world to some of the earliest work of comic art king Jack Kirby ("The Count of Monte Cristo," his first professional work), master stylist Will Eisner ("Hawk of the Seas"), and Batman creator Bob Kane ("Peter Pupp")! The star was Mort Meskin's Sheena, Queen of the Jungle, the first significant comics heroine, who went on to star in movie serials and television during the 40s and 50s. Sheena continued to anchor the lineup through 160 issues before Jumbo switched over to science fiction and horror at the end of its run.

Early issues of Jumbo Comics were printed in a 10-1/2-inch-by-14-1/2-inch format-large even by Golden Age standards.

1 ❑ Sep 1938 Cover: 0.10 **NM** value: **18400.00**
• Extremely rare; 1st Jack Kirby comic art **A:** Bob Kane; Mort Meskin; Will Eisner; Jack Kirby ★ 1st Appearance of Sheena.
2 ❑ Oct 1938 Cover: 0.10 **NM** value: **5900.00**
A: Jack Kirby ★ Origin of Sheena.
3 ❑ Nov 1938 Cover: 0.10 **NM** value: **4100.00**
A: Jack Kirby
4 ❑ Dec 1938 Cover: 0.10 **NM** value: **4100.00**
• 1st Lou Fine art in comics **A:** Jack Kirby; Lou Fine ★ Origin of The Hawk.
5 ❑ Jan 1939 Cover: 0.10 **NM** value: **3250.00**
6 ❑ Feb 1939 Cover: 0.10 **NM** value: **2840.00**
7 ❑ Apr 1939 Cover: 0.10 **NM** value: **2840.00**
8 ❑ Jun 1939 Cover: 0.10 **NM** value: **2950.00**
• World's Fair special
9 ❑ Aug 1939 Cover: 0.10 **NM** value: **2475.00**
Sheena cover. • Full color issues begin
10 ❑ Oct 1939 Cover: 0.10 **NM** value: **1430.00**
• **CGC:** 3 graded, best 8.0
11 ❑ Dec 1939 Cover: 0.10 **NM** value: **1125.00**
• **CGC:** 1 graded, best 7.5
12 ❑ Feb 1940 Cover: 0.10 **NM** value: **1125.00**
13 ❑ Mar 1940 Cover: 0.10 **NM** value: **1025.00**
14 ❑ Apr 1940 Cover: 0.10 **NM** value: **1025.00**
• **CGC:** 1 graded, best 8.0
Lightning cover.
15 ❑ May 1940 Cover: 0.10 **NM** value: **725.00**
• Lightning features begin
16 ❑ Jun 1940 Cover: 0.10 **NM** value: **725.00**
17 ❑ Jul 1940 Cover: 0.10 **NM** value: **725.00**
• **CGC:** 2 graded, best 5.5
18 ❑ Aug 1940 Cover: 0.10 **NM** value: **725.00**
19 ❑ Sep 1940 Cover: 0.10 **NM** value: **725.00**
• **CGC:** 1 graded, best 8.0
20 ❑ Oct 1940 Cover: 0.10 **NM** value: **725.00**
21 ❑ Nov 1940 Cover: 0.10 **NM** value: **560.00**
22 ❑ Dec 1940 Cover: 0.10 **NM** value: **560.00**
• **CGC:** 2 graded, best 8.5
23 ❑ Jan 1941 Cover: 0.10 **NM** value: **560.00**
24 ❑ Feb 1941 Cover: 0.10 **NM** value: **560.00**
25 ❑ Mar 1941 Cover: 0.10 **NM** value: **560.00**
26 ❑ Apr 1941 Cover: 0.10 **NM** value: **560.00**
27 ❑ May 1941 Cover: 0.10 **NM** value: **560.00**
28 ❑ Jun 1941 Cover: 0.10 **NM** value: **560.00**
29 ❑ Jul 1941 Cover: 0.10 **NM** value: **560.00**
• **CGC:** 1 graded, best 4.5
30 ❑ Aug 1941 Cover: 0.10 **NM** value: **560.00**
31 ❑ Sep 1941 Cover: 0.10 **NM** value: **460.00**
• **CGC:** 1 graded, best 4.0
32 ❑ Oct 1941 Cover: 0.10 **NM** value: **460.00**
33 ❑ Nov 1941 Cover: 0.10 **NM** value: **460.00**
• **CGC:** 1 graded, best 7.0
34 ❑ Dec 1941 Cover: 0.10 **NM** value: **460.00**
• **CGC:** 1 graded, best 6.5
35 ❑ Jan 1942 Cover: 0.10 **NM** value: **460.00**
36 ❑ Feb 1942 Cover: 0.10 **NM** value: **460.00**
37 ❑ Mar 1942 Cover: 0.10 **NM** value: **460.00**
• **CGC:** 1 graded, best 7.5
38 ❑ Apr 1942 Cover: 0.10 **NM** value: **460.00**
• **CGC:** 2 graded, best 9.0
39 ❑ May 1942 Cover: 0.10 **NM** value: **460.00**
40 ❑ Jun 1942 Cover: 0.10 **NM** value: **460.00**
41 ❑ Jul 1942 Cover: 0.10 **NM** value: **340.00**
42 ❑ Aug 1942 Cover: 0.10 **NM** value: **340.00**
43 ❑ Sep 1942 Cover: 0.10 **NM** value: **340.00**
44 ❑ Oct 1942 Cover: 0.10 **NM** value: **340.00**
45 ❑ Nov 1942 Cover: 0.10 **NM** value: **340.00**
• **CGC:** 1 graded, best 5.5
46 ❑ Dec 1942 Cover: 0.10 **NM** value: **340.00**
47 ❑ Jan 1943 Cover: 0.10 **NM** value: **340.00**
48 ❑ Feb 1943 Cover: 0.10 **NM** value: **340.00**
49 ❑ Mar 1943 Cover: 0.10 **NM** value: **340.00**
50 ❑ Apr 1943 Cover: 0.10 **NM** value: **340.00**
51 ❑ May 1943 Cover: 0.10 **NM** value: **285.00**
• **CGC:** 1 graded, best 8.0
52 ❑ Jun 1943 Cover: 0.10 **NM** value: **285.00**
53 ❑ Jul 1943 Cover: 0.10 **NM** value: **285.00**
54 ❑ Aug 1943 Cover: 0.10 **NM** value: **285.00**
55 ❑ Sep 1943 Cover: 0.10 **NM** value: **285.00**
56 ❑ Oct 1943 Cover: 0.10 **NM** value: **285.00**
57 ❑ Nov 1943 Cover: 0.10 **NM** value: **285.00**
58 ❑ Dec 1943 Cover: 0.10 **NM** value: **285.00**
59 ❑ Jan 1944 Cover: 0.10 **NM** value: **285.00**
60 ❑ Feb 1944 Cover: 0.10 **NM** value: **285.00**
• **CGC:** 1 graded, best 9.0
61 ❑ Mar 1944 Cover: 0.10 **NM** value: **210.00**
62 ❑ Apr 1944 Cover: 0.10 **NM** value: **210.00**
• **CGC:** 1 graded, best 9.2
63 ❑ May 1944 Cover: 0.10 **NM** value: **210.00**
64 ❑ Jun 1944 Cover: 0.10 **NM** value: **210.00**
65 ❑ Jul 1944 Cover: 0.10 **NM** value: **210.00**
66 ❑ Aug 1944 Cover: 0.10 **NM** value: **210.00**
67 ❑ Sep 1944 Cover: 0.10 **NM** value: **210.00**
• **CGC:** 1 graded, best 9.2
68 ❑ Oct 1944 Cover: 0.10 **NM** value: **210.00**
• **CGC:** 1 graded, best 9.2
69 ❑ Nov 1944 Cover: 0.10 **NM** value: **210.00**
70 ❑ Dec 1944 Cover: 0.10 **NM** value: **210.00**
71 ❑ Jan 1945 Cover: 0.10 **NM** value: **175.00**
72 ❑ Feb 1945 Cover: 0.10 **NM** value: **175.00**
73 ❑ Mar 1945 Cover: 0.10 **NM** value: **175.00**
74 ❑ Apr 1945 Cover: 0.10 **NM** value: **175.00**
75 ❑ May 1945 Cover: 0.10 **NM** value: **175.00**
76 ❑ Jun 1945 Cover: 0.10 **NM** value: **175.00**
77 ❑ Jul 1945 Cover: 0.10 **NM** value: **175.00**
78 ❑ Aug 1945 Cover: 0.10 **NM** value: **175.00**
79 ❑ Sep 1945 Cover: 0.10 **NM** value: **175.00**
• **CGC:** 1 graded, best 7.0
80 ❑ Oct 1945 Cover: 0.10 **NM** value: **175.00**
81 ❑ Nov 1945 Cover: 0.10 **NM** value: **150.00**
82 ❑ Dec 1945 Cover: 0.10 **NM** value: **150.00**
83 ❑ Jan 1946 Cover: 0.10 **NM** value: **150.00**
84 ❑ Feb 1946 Cover: 0.10 **NM** value: **150.00**
• **CGC:** 1 graded, best 8.0
85 ❑ Mar 1946 Cover: 0.10 **NM** value: **150.00**
• **CGC:** 3 graded, best 9.4
86 ❑ Apr 1946 Cover: 0.10 **NM** value: **150.00**
• **CGC:** 1 graded, best 9.2
87 ❑ May 1946 Cover: 0.10 **NM** value: **150.00**
• **CGC:** 2 graded, best 9.4
88 ❑ Jun 1946 Cover: 0.10 **NM** value: **150.00**
• **CGC:** 2 graded, best 7.0
89 ❑ Jul 1946 Cover: 0.10 **NM** value: **150.00**
• **CGC:** 2 graded, best 8.0
90 ❑ Aug 1946 Cover: 0.10 **NM** value: **150.00**
91 ❑ Sep 1946 Cover: 0.10 **NM** value: **135.00**
• **CGC:** 2 graded, best 9.0
92 ❑ Oct 1946 Cover: 0.10 **NM** value: **135.00**
• **CGC:** 1 graded, best 8.5
93 ❑ Nov 1946 Cover: 0.10 **NM** value: **135.00**
94 ❑ Dec 1946 Cover: 0.10 **NM** value: **135.00**
Sheena cover. Sheena: Queen of the Jungle; ZX-5; Patsy the Pinup; The Hawk; Sky Girl; Sheena and the Glittering Torture (text story); Hateful Herman; Stuart Taylor: Weird Stories of the Supernatural; The Ghost Gallery **A:** W. Morgan Thomas; Bill Gibson; Curt Davis; Drew Murdoch; Happy Larke; Major Thorpe; Swing Sista; Will Eisner(Willis Rensie) **W:** W. Morgan Thomas; Bill Gibson; Curt Davis; Drew Murdoch; Happy Larke; Major Thorpe; Swing Sista; Will Eisner(Willis Rensie)
95 ❑ Jan 1947 Cover: 0.10 **NM** value: **135.00**
96 ❑ Feb 1947 Cover: 0.10 **NM** value: **135.00**
• **CGC:** 2 graded, best 9.0
97 ❑ Mar 1947 Cover: 0.10 **NM** value: **135.00**
98 ❑ Apr 1947 Cover: 0.10 **NM** value: **135.00**
• **CGC:** 3 graded, best 9.0
99 ❑ May 1947 Cover: 0.10 **NM** value: **135.00**
• **CGC:** 1 graded, best 9.2
100 ❑ Jun 1947 Cover: 0.10 **NM** value: **135.00**
101 ❑ Jul 1947 Cover: 0.10 **NM** value: **135.00**
102 ❑ Aug 1947 Cover: 0.10 **NM** value: **135.00**
103 ❑ Sep 1947 Cover: 0.10 **NM** value: **135.00**
• **CGC:** 1 graded, best 7.5
104 ❑ Oct 1947 Cover: 0.10 **NM** value: **135.00**
• **CGC:** 1 graded, best 7.5
105 ❑ Nov 1947 Cover: 0.10 **NM** value: **135.00**
• **CGC:** 2 graded, best 7.0
106 ❑ Dec 1947 Cover: 0.10 **NM** value: **135.00**
107 ❑ Jan 1948 Cover: 0.10 **NM** value: **135.00**
108 ❑ Feb 1948 Cover: 0.10 **NM** value: **135.00**
109 ❑ Mar 1948 Cover: 0.10 **NM** value: **135.00**
• **CGC:** 1 graded, best 6.5
110 ❑ Apr 1948 Cover: 0.10 **NM** value: **135.00**
111 ❑ May 1948 Cover: 0.10 **NM** value: **100.00**
112 ❑ Jun 1948 Cover: 0.10 **NM** value: **100.00**
113 ❑ Jul 1948 Cover: 0.10 **NM** value: **100.00**
114 ❑ Aug 1948 Cover: 0.10 **NM** value: **100.00**
Sheena cover. Sheena: Queen of the Jungle; The Hawk; The Mud Face (text story); ZX-5; Sky Girl; Stuart Taylor: Weird Stories of the Supernatural; The Ghost Gallery **A:** W. Morgan Thomas; Bill Gibson; Curt Davis; Major Thorpe; Will Eisner(Willis Rensie) **W:** W. Morgan Thomas; Bill Gibson; Curt Davis; Drew Murdoch; Major Thorpe; Will Eisner(Willis Rensie); Tom Alexander
115 ❑ Sep 1948 Cover: 0.10 **NM** value: **100.00**
116 ❑ Oct 1948 Cover: 0.10 **NM** value: **100.00**
117 ❑ Nov 1948 Cover: 0.10 **NM** value: **100.00**
118 ❑ Dec 1948 Cover: 0.10 **NM** value: **100.00**
• **CGC:** 2 graded, best 8.5
119 ❑ Jan 1949 Cover: 0.10 **NM** value: **100.00**
120 ❑ Feb 1949 Cover: 0.10 **NM** value: **100.00**
121 ❑ Mar 1949 Cover: 0.10 **NM** value: **90.00**
• **CGC:** 1 graded, best 8.0
122 ❑ Apr 1949 Cover: 0.10 **NM** value: **90.00**
123 ❑ May 1949 Cover: 0.10 **NM** value: **90.00**
124 ❑ Jun 1949 Cover: 0.10 **NM** value: **90.00**
125 ❑ Jul 1949 Cover: 0.10 **NM** value: **90.00**
126 ❑ Aug 1949 Cover: 0.10 **NM** value: **90.00**
127 ❑ Sep 1949 Cover: 0.10 **NM** value: **90.00**
128 ❑ Oct 1949 Cover: 0.10 **NM** value: **90.00**
129 ❑ Nov 1949 Cover: 0.10 **NM** value: **90.00**
130 ❑ Dec 1949 Cover: 0.10 **NM** value: **90.00**
131 ❑ Jan 1950 Cover: 0.10 **NM** value: **90.00**
• **CGC:** 1 graded, best 8.5
132 ❑ Feb 1950 Cover: 0.10 **NM** value: **90.00**
133 ❑ Mar 1950 Cover: 0.10 **NM** value: **90.00**
134 ❑ Apr 1950 Cover: 0.10 **NM** value: **90.00**
• **CGC:** 1 graded, best 7.5
135 ❑ May 1950 Cover: 0.10 **NM** value: **90.00**
136 ❑ Jun 1950 Cover: 0.10 **NM** value: **90.00**
• **CGC:** 1 graded, best 9.2
137 ❑ Jul 1950 Cover: 0.10 **NM** value: **90.00**
• **CGC:** 3 graded, best 9.4
138 ❑ Aug 1950 Cover: 0.10 **NM** value: **90.00**
• **CGC:** 1 graded, best 8.5
139 ❑ Sep 1950 Cover: 0.10 **NM** value: **90.00**
• **CGC:** 1 graded, best 7.5
140 ❑ Oct 1950 Cover: 0.10 **NM** value: **90.00**
• **CGC:** 3 graded, best 9.0
141 ❑ Nov 1950 Cover: 0.10 **NM** value: **90.00**
• **CGC:** 1 graded, best 9.2
142 ❑ Dec 1950 Cover: 0.10 **NM** value: **90.00**
• **CGC:** 1 graded, best 9.6
143 ❑ Jan 1951 Cover: 0.10 **NM** value: **90.00**
144 ❑ Feb 1951 Cover: 0.10 **NM** value: **90.00**
• **CGC:** 1 graded, best 8.5
145 ❑ Mar 1951 Cover: 0.10 **NM** value: **90.00**
• **CGC:** 1 graded, best 9.0
146 ❑ Apr 1951 Cover: 0.10 **NM** value: **90.00**
• **CGC:** 1 graded, best 7.0
147 ❑ May 1951 Cover: 0.10 **NM** value: **90.00**
148 ❑ Jun 1951 Cover: 0.10 **NM** value: **90.00**
• **CGC:** 1 graded, best 9.0
149 ❑ Jul 1951 Cover: 0.10 **NM** value: **90.00**
150 ❑ Aug 1951 Cover: 0.10 **NM** value: **90.00**
151 ❑ Sep 1951 Cover: 0.10 **NM** value: **90.00**
152 ❑ Oct 1951 Cover: 0.10 **NM** value: **90.00**
• **CGC:** 1 graded, best 9.0
153 ❑ Nov 1951 Cover: 0.10 **NM** value: **90.00**
• **CGC:** 2 graded, best 9.2
154 ❑ Dec 1951 Cover: 0.10 **NM** value: **90.00**
• **CGC:** 3 graded, best 9.0
155 ❑ Jan 1952 Cover: 0.10 **NM** value: **90.00**
156 ❑ Feb 1952 Cover: 0.10 **NM** value: **90.00**
• **CGC:** 2 graded, best 9.4
157 ❑ Mar 1952 Cover: 0.10 **NM** value: **90.00**
158 ❑ Apr 1952 Cover: 0.10 **NM** value: **90.00**
• **CGC:** 1 graded, best 9.0
159 ❑ May 1952 Cover: 0.10 **NM** value: **90.00**
160 ❑ Jun 1952 Cover: 0.10 **NM** value: **90.00**
161 ❑ Jul 1952 Cover: 0.10 **NM** value: **90.00**
162 ❑ Aug 1952 Cover: 0.10 **NM** value: **90.00**
163 ❑ Sep 1952 Cover: 0.10 **NM** value: **90.00**
• **CGC:** 1 graded, best 8.5
164 ❑ Oct 1952 Cover: 0.10 **NM** value: **90.00**
• **CGC:** 1 graded, best 8.5
165 ❑ Dec 1952 Cover: 0.10 **NM** value: **90.00**
• **CGC:** 2 graded, best 8.5
166 ❑ Feb 1953 Cover: 0.10 **NM** value: **90.00**
• **CGC:** 1 graded, best 9.0
167 ❑ Mar 1953 Cover: 0.10 **NM** value: **90.00**
final issue.

JUMPER — Zav

1 ❑ b&w Cover: 3.00 **NM** value: **Cover or less**
Into the Void **A:** Randi Scott **W:** Peter Shawn MacKenzie
2 ❑ b&w Cover: 3.00 **NM** value: **Cover or less**

JUN — Disney

1 ❑ Cover: 1.50 **NM** value: **Cover or less**

JUNGLE TALES — Atlas

1 ❑ Sep 1954 Cover: 0.10 **NM** value: **275.00**
• **CGC:** 1 graded, best 9.0
2 ❑ Nov 1954 Cover: 0.10 **NM** value: **200.00**
3 ❑ Jan 1955 Cover: 0.10 **NM** value: **200.00**
4 ❑ Mar 1955 Cover: 0.10 **NM** value: **200.00**
5 ❑ May 1955 Cover: 0.10 **NM** value: **175.00**
6 ❑ Jul 1955 Cover: 0.10 **NM** value: **175.00**
7 ❑ Sep 1955 Cover: 0.10 **NM** value: **175.00**
• **CGC:** 1 graded, best 7.0

CGC-graded: Multiply prices above by **33 for 9.9 M • 16 for 9.8 NM/M • 7 for 9.6 NM+ • 5 for 9.4 NM • 2.5 for 9.2 NM- • 1.5 for 9.0 VF/NM**

JUNGLE ACTION — Marvel

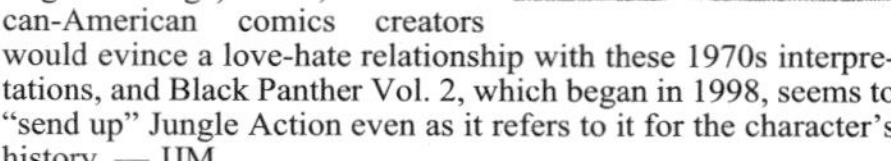

With issue #5, Jungle Action became home to the Black Panther. T'Challa, king of the technologically advanced African nation of Wakanda, had made his first appearance in the Fantastic Four and become an occasional Avenger — and in Jungle Action, used his fighting skills to safeguard his country from villains including Klaw.

Jungle Action also gave cultural-conscious and demographics-mindful Marvel the opportunity to have a second series starring a black character (alongside Hero for Hire, starring Luke Cage). Later, some African-American comics creators would evince a love-hate relationship with these 1970s interpretations, and Black Panther Vol. 2, which began in 1998, seems to "send up" Jungle Action even as it refers to it for the character's history. — JJM

1 ❑ Oct 1972 Cover: 0.20 **NM** value: **6.00**
• **CGC:** 3 graded, best 9.2
Agu the Giant; The Trail of Sudden Death; Striped Fury; Double Danger • Reprints

2 ❑ Dec 1972 Cover: 0.20 **NM** value: **4.00**
Jungle Uprising; The River of No Return; Survival of the Mighty; The Day of Jungle Wrath • Reprints

3 ❑ Feb 1973 Cover: 0.20 **NM** value: **4.00**
Elephant Charge; The Devil's Lagoon; Challenge of the Pit; Rampage • Reprints

4 ❑ Apr 1973 Cover: 0.20 **NM** value: **4.00**
Tharn the Magnificent: Menace From the Past!; Lorna the Jungle Girl: Wildfire!; The Unknown Jungle: The Judgment of the Beasts!; Jann of the Jungle • Reprints

5 ❑ Jul 1973 Cover: 0.20 **NM** value: **4.00**
The Monarch and the Man-Ape • Black Panther; Black Panther begins

6 ❑ Sep 1973 Cover: 0.20 **NM** value: **3.00**
Panther's Rage; Double Danger • Black Panther

7 ❑ Nov 1973 Cover: 0.20 **NM** value: **3.00**
Death Regiments Beneath Wakanda; The Fury of the Tusk • Black Panther

8 ❑ Jan 1974 Cover: 0.20 **NM** value: **3.00**
Malice By Crimson Moonlight!; pin-ups • Black Panther **A:** Rich Buckler; Klaus Janson **W:** Don McGregor ★ Origin of Black Panther.

9 ❑ May 1974 Cover: 0.25 **NM** value: **3.00**
But Now the Spears are Broken • Black Panther

10 ❑ Jul 1974 Cover: 0.25 **NM** value: **2.50**
King Cadaver is Dead and Living in Wakanda; pin-ups • Black Panther

11 ❑ Sep 1974 Cover: 0.25 **NM** value: **2.50**
Once You Slay the Dragon • Black Panther

12 ❑ Nov 1974 Cover: 0.25 **NM** value: **2.50**
Blood Stains on Virgin Snow • Black Panther

13 ❑ Jan 1975 Cover: 0.25 **NM** value: **2.50**
• **CGC:** 1 graded, best 9.4
The God Killer • Black Panther

14 ❑ Mar 1975 Cover: 0.25 **NM** value: **2.50**
Serpents Lurking in Paradise • Black Panther

15 ❑ May 1975 Cover: 0.25 **NM** value: **2.50**
• **CGC:** 1 graded, best 9.2
Thorns in the Flesh, Thorns in the Mind • Black Panther

16 ❑ Jul 1975 Cover: 0.25 **NM** value: **2.50**
• **CGC:** 1 graded, best 9.4
And All Our Past Decades Have Seen Revolutions • Black Panther

17 ❑ Sep 1975 Cover: 0.25 **NM** value: **2.50**
Of Shadows and Rages • Black Panther

18 ❑ Nov 1975 Cover: 0.25 **NM** value: **2.50**
Epilogue • Black Panther

19 ❑ Jan 1976 Cover: 0.25 **NM** value: **2.50**
Blood and Sacrifices • Black Panther ★ 1st Appearance of Baron Macabre.

20 ❑ Mar 1976 Cover: 0.25 **NM** value: **2.50**
• **CGC:** 1 graded, best 9.4
They Told Me a Myth I Wanted to Believe • Black Panther

21 ❑ May 1976 Cover: 0.25 **NM** value: **2.50**
• **CGC:** 1 graded, best 9.2
A Cross Burning Darkly • Black Panther

22 ❑ Jul 1976 Cover: 0.25 **NM** value: **2.50**
Death Riders on the Horizon • Black Panther

23 ❑ Sep 1976 Cover: 0.30 **NM** value: **2.50**
A Life on the Line • Black Panther; reprints Daredevil #69

24 ❑ Nov 1976 Cover: 0.30 **NM** value: **2.50**
Wind Eagle in Flight • Black Panther ★ 1st Appearance of Wind Eagle.

JUNGLE ADVENTURES (SKYWALD) — Skywald

1 ❑ Mar 1971 Cover: 0.25 **NM** value: **10.00**
2 ❑ ca. 1971 Cover: 0.25 **NM** value: **7.00**
3 ❑ ca. 1971 Cover: 0.25 **NM** value: **7.00**
• Zangar

JUNGLE ADVENTURES (SUPER) — Super

10 ❑ ca. 1963 Cover: 0.12 **NM** value: **30.00**
11 ❑ ca. 1963 Cover: 0.12 **NM** value: **30.00**
12 ❑ ca. 1963 Cover: 0.12 **NM** value: **30.00**
13 ❑ ca. 1963 Cover: 0.12 **NM** value: **30.00**
14 ❑ ca. 1963 Cover: 0.12 **NM** value: **30.00**
15 ❑ ca. 1964 Cover: 0.12 **NM** value: **30.00**
16 ❑ ca. 1964 Cover: 0.12 **NM** value: **30.00**
17 ❑ ca. 1964 Cover: 0.12 **NM** value: **30.00**
18 ❑ ca. 1964 Cover: 0.12 **NM** value: **30.00**

JUNGLE BOOK, THE — Disney

1/A ❑ Cover: 2.95 **NM** value: **Cover or less**
• saddle-stitched
1/B ❑ Cover: 5.95 **NM** value: **Cover or less**
• squarebound

JUNGLE BOOK (GOLD KEY) — Gold Key

1 ❑ Mar 1968 **NM** value: **25.00**
• **CGC:** 1 graded, best 9.0

JUNGLE COMICS — Fiction House

In the 1940s, long before the founders of Image were twinkles in their parents' eyes, Fiction House made the important discovery that people would buy comics to look at pictures of half-naked women. Jungle Comics was one of its flagship titles, with a format featuring (white) African adventurers (both male and female) wrestling with lions, discovering lost cities and elephant graveyards, hunting down cruel native kings and craven poachers-all while wearing as little clothing as physically possible.

Among the regular features in Jungle Comics were Ka'a'nga, Lord of the Jungle (the obligatory Tarzan clone), Wambi the Jungle Boy, explorer Terry Thunder, and, of course, Camilla, a variation on their own character Sheena, who appeared in Jumbo Comics. Top artists like Lou Fine and Will Eisner worked on early issues of the run, then left the features in the hands of the workman-like Fiction House staff.

1 ❑ Jan 1940, b&w Cover: 0.10 **NM** value: **3400.00**
• **CGC:** 4 graded, best 9.6
Prey of the Slavers • Kaanga, Terry Thunder, White Hunters of the African Safari, Drums of the Leopard-Men, Camilla, The White Panther, Simba, Taboo ★ Origin of Sheena, Kaanga.

2 ❑ Feb 1940 Cover: 0.10 **NM** value: **1350.00**
• **CGC:** 1 graded, best 9.4
Terror of the Bush • Kaanga, The Red Panther, Wambi, Simba, Tabu

3 ❑ Mar 1940 Cover: 0.10 **NM** value: **1100.00**
• **CGC:** 2 graded, best 9.4
The Crocodiles of Death River • Kaanga, Wambi, Captain Thunder/Congo Lancers

4 ❑ Apr 1940 Cover: 0.10 **NM** value: **985.00**
• **CGC:** 1 graded, best 9.4
Thundering Herds • Kaanga, Wambi, Camilla

5 ❑ May 1940 Cover: 0.10 **NM** value: **915.00**
• **CGC:** 1 graded, best 9.4
Empire of the Ape Men • Kaanga, Terry Thunder, Camilla, Wambi

6 ❑ Jun 1940 Cover: 0.10 **NM** value: **675.00**
• **CGC:** 3 graded, best 9.6
Tigress of the Deep Jungle Swamp; Vengeance on the Veldt; Phantom of the Tree-Tops • Kaanga, Wambi, Roy Lance, Tabu, Terry Thunder, Fantoma

7 ❑ Jul 1940 Cover: 0.10 **NM** value: **600.00**
• **CGC:** 1 graded, best 9.2
Live Sacrifice • Kaanga, Simba, Tabu, Terry Thunder, Wambi, Fantomah, The Red Panther

8 ❑ Aug 1940 Cover: 0.10 **NM** value: **535.00**
• **CGC:** 1 graded, best 9.8
Safari Into Shadowland • Kaanga, Wambi, Fantomah, Roy Lance, Camilla, Tabu, Terry Thunder

9 ❑ Sep 1940 Cover: 0.10 **NM** value: **535.00**
• **CGC:** 1 graded, best 9.6
Captive of the Voodoo Master; Jungle Justice • Kaanga, Wambi, Fantomah, Roy Lance, Camilla, Terry Thunder, Red Panther, Simba

10 ❑ Oct 1940 Cover: 0.10 **NM** value: **535.00**
• **CGC:** 1 graded, best 9.6
Lair of the Renegade Killer; Fight to the Finish • Kaanga, Wambi, Fantomah, Tabu, Roy Lance, Camilla, Terry Thunder, Red Panther

11 ❑ Nov 1940 Cover: 0.10 **NM** value: **465.00**
• **CGC:** 2 graded, best 9.8
• Kaanga, Wambi, Fantomah, Tabu, Roy Lance, Camilla, Terry Thunder

12 ❑ Dec 1940 Cover: 0.10 **NM** value: **465.00**
• **CGC:** 1 graded, best 9.4
The Devil's Death Trap • Kaanga, Camilla, Wambi, Red Panther, Terry Thunder, Fantomah

13 ❑ Jan 1941 Cover: 0.10 **NM** value: **465.00**
• **CGC:** 1 graded, best 9.2
Stalker of the Beasts • Kaanga, Camilla, Wambi, Red Panther, Terry Thunder, Fantomah, Simba

14 ❑ Feb 1941 Cover: 0.10 **NM** value: **465.00**
• **CGC:** 1 graded, best 8.0
Vengeance of the Gorills Hordes • Kaanga, Camilla, Wambi, Red Panther, Terry Thunder, Fantomah, Simba

15 ❑ Mar 1941 Cover: 0.10 **NM** value: **465.00**
• **CGC:** 1 graded, best 9.6
Terror of the Voodoo Cauldron • Kaanga, Camilla, Wambi, Red Panther, Terry Thunder, Fantomah

16 ❑ Apr 1941 Cover: 0.10 **NM** value: **420.00**
• **CGC:** 1 graded, best 9.0
Caveman Killers • Kaanga, Camilla, Wambi, Red Panther, Terry Thunder, Fantomah, Simba

17 ❑ May 1941 Cover: 0.10 **NM** value: **420.00**
• **CGC:** 1 graded, best 9.4
Valley of the Killer-Birds • Kaanga, Wambi, Red Panther, Terry Thunder, Tabu, Simba

18 ❑ Jun 1941 Cover: 0.10 **NM** value: **420.00**
• **CGC:** 1 graded, best 9.2
Trap of the Tawny Killer • Kaanga, Camilla, Wambi, Red Panther, Simba

19 ❑ Jul 1941 Cover: 0.10 **NM** value: **420.00**
• **CGC:** 2 graded, best 9.8
Revolt of the Man-Apes! • Kaanga, Camilla, Wambi, Red Panther, Terry Thunder, Tabu

20 ❑ Aug 1941 Cover: 0.10 **NM** value: **420.00**
• **CGC:** 1 graded, best 9.6
Live-Offering to the Ju-Ju Demon • Kaanga, Camilla, Wambi, Terry Thunder, Tabu, Simba

21 ❑ Sep 1941 Cover: 0.10 **NM** value: **365.00**
• **CGC:** 1 graded, best 9.6
Monster of the Dismal Swamp • Kaanga, Camilla, Wambi, Red Panther, Tabu

22 ❑ Oct 1941 Cover: 0.10 **NM** value: **365.00**
• **CGC:** 1 graded, best 9.6
Lair of the Winged Fiend • Kaanga, Camilla, Wambi, Red Panther, Terry Thunder, Fantomah

23 ❑ Nov 1941 Cover: 0.10 **NM** value: **365.00**
• **CGC:** 1 graded, best 9.4
Man-Eater Jaws • Kaanga, Camilla, Wambi, Red Panther, Terry Thunder, Fantomah, Tabu

24 ❑ Dec 1941 Cover: 0.10 **NM** value: **365.00**
• **CGC:** 1 graded, best 9.4
Battle of the Beasts • Kaanga, Camilla, Wambi, Red Panther, Terry Thunder, Simba

25 ❑ Jan 1942 Cover: 0.10 **NM** value: **365.00**
• **CGC:** 1 graded, best 9.6
Kaghis the Blood God • Kaanga, Camilla, Wambi, Terry Thunder

26 ❑ Feb 1942 Cover: 0.10 **NM** value: **335.00**
• **CGC:** 1 graded, best 8.5
Gorillas of the Witch-Queen • Kaanga, Camilla, Wambi, Terry Thunder, Simba

27 ❑ Mar 1942 Cover: 0.10 **NM** value: **335.00**
• **CGC:** 1 graded, best 9.4
Spoor of the Gold-Raiders • Kaanga, Camilla, Wambi, Terry Thunder, Fantomah

28 ❑ Apr 1942 Cover: 0.10 **NM** value: **335.00**
• **CGC:** 2 graded, best 9.8
Vengeance of the Flame God • Kaanga, Camilla, Wambi, Terry Thunder, Fantomah, Tabu

29 ❑ May 1942 Cover: 0.10 **NM** value: **335.00**
• **CGC:** 1 graded, best 9.4
Juggernaut of Doom • Kaanga, Camilla, Wambi, Simba, Tabu

30 ❑ Jun 1942 Cover: 0.10 **NM** value: **335.00**
• **CGC:** 1 graded, best 9.8
Claws of the Black Terror • Kaanga, Camilla, Wambi, Simba, Tabu, Fantomah

31 ❑ Jul 1942 Cover: 0.10 **NM** value: **285.00**
• **CGC:** 1 graded, best 9.6
Land of the Shrunken Heads • Kaanga, Camilla, Wambi, Simba, Tabu, Fantomah

32 ❑ Aug 1942 Cover: 0.10 **NM** value: **285.00**
• **CGC:** 1 graded, best 9.4
Curse of the King-Beast • Kaanga, Camilla, Wambi, Simba, Tabu, Fantomah

33 ❑ Sep 1942 Cover: 0.10 **NM** value: **285.00**
• **CGC:** 1 graded, best 9.6
Scaly Guardians of Massacre Pool • Kaanga, Camilla, Wambi, Simba, Tabu, Fantomah

34 ❑ Oct 1942 Cover: 0.10 **NM** value: **285.00**
• **CGC:** 1 graded, best 9.6
Bait for the Spotted Fury • Kaanga, Camilla, Wambi, Simba, Tabu

35 ❑ Nov 1942 Cover: 0.10 **NM** value: **285.00**
• **CGC:** 1 graded, best 9.4
Stampede of the Slave Masters • Kaanga, Camilla, Wambi, Simba, Tabu, Fantomah

36 ❑ Dec 1942 Cover: 0.10 **NM** value: **245.00**
• **CGC:** 1 graded, best 9.6
The Flame-Death of Juju Mountain • Kaanga, Camilla, Wambi, Simba, Fantomah

37 ❑ Jan 1943 Cover: 0.10 **NM** value: **245.00**
• **CGC:** 1 graded, best 9.2
Scaly Sentinel of Taboo Swamp • Kaanga, Camilla, Wambi, Simba, Fantomah

38 ❑ Feb 1943 Cover: 0.10 **NM** value: **245.00**
• **CGC:** 1 graded, best 9.4
Duel of the Congo Destroyers • Kaanga, Camilla, Wambi, Simba, Tabu, Terry Thunder

39 ❑ Mar 1943 Cover: 0.10 **NM** value: **245.00**
• **CGC:** 1 graded, best 9.6
Land of the Laughing Bones • Kaanga, Camilla, Wambi, Fantomah

40 ❑ Apr 1943 Cover: 0.10 **NM** value: **245.00**
• **CGC:** 1 graded, best 9.6
Killer Plague • Kaanga, Camilla, Wambi, Simba, Terry Thunder

41 ❑ May 1943 Cover: 0.10 **NM** value: **210.00**
• **CGC:** 1 graded, best 9.8
The King Ape Feeds at Dawn • Kaanga, Camilla, Wambi

42 ❑ Jun 1943 Cover: 0.10 **NM** value: **210.00**
• **CGC:** 1 graded, best 8.5
Master of the Moon Beasts • Kaanga, Camilla, Wambi, Simba

43 ❑ Jul 1943 Cover: 0.10 **NM** value: **210.00**
• **CGC:** 1 graded, best 7.5
The White Sheik • Kaanga, Camilla, Wambi, Simba

44 ❑ Aug 1943 Cover: 0.10 **NM** value: **210.00**
• **CGC:** 1 graded, best 5.0
Monster of the Boiling Pool • Kaanga, Camilla, Wambi, Simba, Congo Lancers

45 ❑ Sep 1943 Cover: 0.10 **NM** value: **210.00**
• **CGC:** 1 graded, best 9.2
Bone-Grinders of B'zambi • Kaanga

46 ❑ Oct 1943 Cover: 0.10 **NM** value: **210.00**
• **CGC:** 1 graded, best 8.5
Blood Raiders of the Tree-Trail • Kaanga, Camilla, Wambi, Simba

47 ❑ Nov 1943 Cover: 0.10 **NM** value: **210.00**
• **CGC:** 1 graded, best 9.6
Monster of the Moon Pool • Kaanga, Camilla, Wambi, Simba, Tabu

48 ❑ Dec 1943 Cover: 0.10 **NM** value: **210.00**
• **CGC:** 1 graded, best 9.4

Other grades: Multiply prices above by **1.5 for Mint • 2/3 for Very Fine • 1/3 for Fine • 1/5 for Very Good • 1/8 for Good**

• Kaanga, Camilla, Wambi, Simba, Tabu
49 ❑ Jan 1944 Cover: 0.10 **NM** value: **210.00**
• **CGC:** 3 graded, best 9.6
📖 Lair of the King Serpent • Kaanga
50 ❑ Feb 1944 Cover: 0.10 **NM** value: **210.00**
• **CGC:** 1 graded, best 9.2
📖 Juggernaut of the Bush • Kaanga, Camilla, Wambi, Simba
51 ❑ Mar 1944 Cover: 0.10 **NM** value: **195.00**
• **CGC:** 1 graded, best 9.4
📖 The Golden Lion of Genghis Khan • Kaanga, Camilla, Simba, Tabu
52 ❑ Apr 1944 Cover: 0.10 **NM** value: **195.00**
• **CGC:** 1 graded, best 9.4
📖 Feast for the River Devils • Kaanga, Wambi, Tabu
53 ❑ May 1944 Cover: 0.10 **NM** value: **195.00**
• **CGC:** 1 graded, best 9.4
📖 Slaves for Horror's Harem • Kaanga, Camilla, Wambi, Terry Thunder
54 ❑ Jun 1944 Cover: 0.10 **NM** value: **195.00**
• **CGC:** 1 graded, best 9.8
📖 Blood Bride of the Crocodile • Kaanga, Camilla, Wambi
55 ❑ Jul 1944 Cover: 0.10 **NM** value: **195.00**
• **CGC:** 1 graded, best 9.2
📖 The Tree Devil • Kaanga
56 ❑ Aug 1944 Cover: 0.10 **NM** value: **195.00**
• **CGC:** 2 graded, best 9.4
• Kaanga, Camilla, Wambi, Simba
57 ❑ Sep 1944 Cover: 0.10 **NM** value: **195.00**
• **CGC:** 1 graded, best 9.6
📖 Fire Gems of T'Ulaki • Kaanga, Camilla, Simba
58 ❑ Oct 1944 Cover: 0.10 **NM** value: **195.00**
• **CGC:** 1 graded, best 9.8
📖 Land of the Cannibal God • Kaanga, Simba, Wambi, Terry Thunder
59 ❑ Nov 1944 Cover: 0.10 **NM** value: **195.00**
• **CGC:** 1 graded, best 9.0
📖 Dwellers of the Mists • Kaanga, Simba
60 ❑ Dec 1944 Cover: 0.10 **NM** value: **195.00**
📖 Bush-Devil's Spoor • Kaanga
61 ❑ Jan 1945 Cover: 0.10 **NM** value: **175.00**
📖 Curse of the Blood Madness • Kaanga, Simba, Wambi, Terry Thunder
62 ❑ Feb 1945 Cover: 0.10 **NM** value: **175.00**
• Kaanga, Wambi, Terry Thunder
63 ❑ Mar 1945 Cover: 0.10 **NM** value: **175.00**
📖 Fire-Birds for the Cliff Dwellers • Kaanga
64 ❑ Apr 1945 Cover: 0.10 **NM** value: **175.00**
📖 Valley of the Ju-Ju Idols • Kaanga, Simba, Wambi, Terry Thunder
65 ❑ May 1945 Cover: 0.10 **NM** value: **175.00**
• **CGC:** 1 graded, best 9.4
📖 Shrine of the Seven Jujus • Kaanga, Camilla, Wambi, Terry Thunder
66 ❑ Jun 1945 Cover: 0.10 **NM** value: **175.00**
📖 Spoor of the Purple Skulls • Kaanga, Camilla, Wambi, Simba
67 ❑ Jul 1945 Cover: 0.10 **NM** value: **175.00**
📖 Devil Beasts of the Golden Temple • Kaanga, Camilla, Tabu
68 ❑ Aug 1945 Cover: 0.10 **NM** value: **175.00**
• **CGC:** 1 graded, best 6.5
📖 Satan's Safari • Kaanga, Camilla, Simba, Terry Thunder
69 ❑ Sep 1945 Cover: 0.10 **NM** value: **175.00**
📖 Brides for the Serpent King • Kaanga, Camilla, Wambi, Simba
70 ❑ Oct 1945 Cover: 0.10 **NM** value: **175.00**
• **CGC:** 1 graded, best 6.5
📖 Brides for the King Beasts • Kaanga
71 ❑ Nov 1945 Cover: 0.10 **NM** value: **160.00**
📖 Congo Prey • Kaanga, Camilla, Wambi, Terry Thunder
72 ❑ Dec 1945 Cover: 0.10 **NM** value: **160.00**
📖 Blood-Brand of the Veldt Cats • Kaanga, Camilla, Tabu
73 ❑ Jan 1946 Cover: 0.10 **NM** value: **160.00**
📖 The Killers of M'Omba Raj • Kaanga, Camilla, Wambi
74 ❑ Feb 1946 Cover: 0.10 **NM** value: **160.00**
📖 Golden Jaws of Ju-Ju River • Kaanga, Camilla, Tabu
75 ❑ Mar 1946 Cover: 0.10 **NM** value: **160.00**
• **CGC:** 1 graded, best 9.0
📖 Congo Kill • Kaanga
76 ❑ Apr 1946 Cover: 0.10 **NM** value: **160.00**
• **CGC:** 1 graded, best 9.0
📖 Blood Thirst of the Golden Tusk • Kaanga
77 ❑ May 1946 Cover: 0.10 **NM** value: **160.00**
• **CGC:** 1 graded, best 7.5
📖 The Golden Gourds Shriek Blood • Kaanga, Camilla, Wambi
78 ❑ Jun 1946 Cover: 0.10 **NM** value: **160.00**
• **CGC:** 4 graded, best 8.0
📖 Ju Ju Kraal of the Flaming Death • Kaanga, Camilla, Wambi, Terry Thunder, Tabu
79 ❑ Jul 1946 Cover: 0.10 **NM** value: **160.00**
• **CGC:** 1 graded, best 9.6
📖 Death Has a Thousand Fangs • Kaanga
80 ❑ Aug 1946 Cover: 0.10 **NM** value: **160.00**
📖 Salome of the Devil-Cats • Kaanga
81 ❑ Sep 1946 Cover: 0.10 **NM** value: **150.00**
• **CGC:** 3 graded, best 9.0
📖 Colossus of the Congo • Kaanga
82 ❑ Oct 1946 Cover: 0.10 **NM** value: **150.00**
📖 Blood Jewels of the Fire-Bird • Kaanga
83 ❑ Nov 1946 Cover: 0.10 **NM** value: **150.00**
• **CGC:** 2 graded, best 8.0
📖 Vampire Veldt • Kaanga
84 ❑ Dec 1946 Cover: 0.10 **NM** value: **150.00**
• **CGC:** 1 graded, best 6.5
📖 Blood Spoor of the Faceless Monster • Kaanga
85 ❑ Jan 1947 Cover: 0.10 **NM** value: **150.00**
📖 Brides for the Man-Apes • Kaanga, Camilla, Simba
86 ❑ Feb 1947 Cover: 0.10 **NM** value: **150.00**
• **CGC:** 1 graded, best 8.0
📖 Firegems of L'Hama Lost • Kaanga
87 ❑ Mar 1947 Cover: 0.10 **NM** value: **150.00**
• **CGC:** 1 graded, best 7.5
📖 Horror Kraal of the Legless One • Kaanga
88 ❑ Apr 1947 Cover: 0.10 **NM** value: **150.00**
• **CGC:** 1 graded, best 8.5
📖 Beyond the Ju-Ju Mists • Kaanga
89 ❑ May 1947 Cover: 0.10 **NM** value: **150.00**
• **CGC:** 3 graded, best 9.2
📖 Blood-Moon Over the Whispering Veldt • Kaanga, Camilla, Tabu, Simba
90 ❑ Jun 1947 Cover: 0.10 **NM** value: **150.00**
• **CGC:** 2 graded, best 9.0
📖 Skulls for the Altar of Doom • Kaanga
91 ❑ Jul 1947 Cover: 0.10 **NM** value: **140.00**
• **CGC:** 2 graded, best 6.5
📖 Monsters from the Mist Lands • Kaanga, Camilla, Tabu
92 ❑ Aug 1947 Cover: 0.10 **NM** value: **140.00**
📖 Vendetta of the Tree Tribes • Kaanga, Camilla, Tabu
93 ❑ Sep 1947 Cover: 0.10 **NM** value: **140.00**
• **CGC:** 1 graded, best 7.0
📖 Witch-Queen of the Hairy Ones • Kaanga, Camilla, Tabu
94 ❑ Oct 1947 Cover: 0.10 **NM** value: **140.00**
• **CGC:** 1 graded, best 7.0
📖 Terror Raid of the Congo Caesar • Kaanga, Camilla, Tabu, Simba
95 ❑ Nov 1947 Cover: 0.10 **NM** value: **140.00**
• **CGC:** 1 graded, best 8.0
📖 Flame-Tongues of the Sky Gods • Kaanga, Camilla, Tabu
96 ❑ Dec 1947 Cover: 0.10 **NM** value: **140.00**
• **CGC:** 3 graded, best 9.0
📖 Phantom Guardians of the Enchanted Lake • Kaanga, Camilla, Simba
97 ❑ Jan 1948 Cover: 0.10 **NM** value: **140.00**
📖 Wizard of the Whirling Doom • Kaanga
98 ❑ Feb 1948 Cover: 0.10 **NM** value: **210.00**
• **CGC:** 1 graded, best 7.0
📖 Ten Tusks of Zulu Ivory • Kaanga; Contains "Hidden pictures within pictures" panel cited in Seduction of the Innocent
99 ❑ Mar 1948 Cover: 0.10 **NM** value: **140.00**
📖 Cannibal Caravans • Kaanga
100 ❑ Apr 1948 Cover: 0.10 **NM** value: **140.00**
📖 Hate Has a Thousand Claws • Kaanga, Camilla, Wambi
101 ❑ May 1948 Cover: 0.10 **NM** value: **130.00**
📖 The Blade of Buddha • Kaanga
102 ❑ Jun 1948 Cover: 0.10 **NM** value: **130.00**
• **CGC:** 1 graded, best 7.5
📖 Queen of the Amazon Lancers • Kaanga
103 ❑ Jul 1948 Cover: 0.10 **NM** value: **130.00**
📖 The Phantoms of Lost Lagoon • Kaanga
104 ❑ Aug 1948 Cover: 0.10 **NM** value: **130.00**
• Kaanga, Camilla, Wambi, Simba, Terry Thunder
105 ❑ Sep 1948 Cover: 0.10 **NM** value: **130.00**
• **CGC:** 3 graded, best 9.2
📖 The Red Witch of Ubangi-Shan • Kaanga, Camilla
106 ❑ Oct 1948 Cover: 0.10 **NM** value: **130.00**
• **CGC:** 1 graded, best 9.2
• Kaanga, Camilla, Wambi
107 ❑ Nov 1948 Cover: 0.10 **NM** value: **130.00**
📖 Banshee Valley • Kaanga, Camilla, Simba **A:** Frank Riddell **W:** Frank Riddell
108 ❑ Dec 1948 Cover: 0.10 **NM** value: **130.00**
• **CGC:** 2 graded, best 9.2
📖 Merchants of Murder • Kaanga, Camilla, Tabu
109 ❑ Jan 1949 Cover: 0.10 **NM** value: **130.00**
• **CGC:** 2 graded, best 9.4
📖 Cavern of the Golden Bones • Kaanga
110 ❑ Feb 1949 Cover: 0.10 **NM** value: **130.00**
• **CGC:** 3 graded, best 9.0
📖 Raid of the Fire-Fangs • Kaanga, Camilla, Wambi, Simba
111 ❑ Mar 1949 Cover: 0.10 **NM** value: **125.00**
• **CGC:** 1 graded, best 9.0
📖 The Trek of the Terror-Paws • Kaanga, Camilla, Wambi
112 ❑ Apr 1949 Cover: 0.10 **NM** value: **125.00**
• **CGC:** 1 graded, best 3.5
📖 Morass of the Mammoths • Kaanga
113 ❑ May 1949 Cover: 0.10 **NM** value: **125.00**
📖 Two-Tusked Terror • Kaanga, Camilla, Tabu, Wambi
114 ❑ Jun 1949 Cover: 0.10 **NM** value: **125.00**
• **CGC:** 2 graded, best 9.4
📖 Mad Jackals Hunt by Night • Kaanga, Camilla, Wambi, Simba
115 ❑ Jul 1949 Cover: 0.10 **NM** value: **125.00**
• **CGC:** 2 graded, best 9.0
📖 Treasure Trove in Vulture Sky • Kaanga, Camilla, Wambi
116 ❑ Aug 1949 Cover: 0.10 **NM** value: **125.00**
• **CGC:** 1 graded, best 8.5
📖 The Banshees of Voodoo Veldt • Kaanga, Camilla, Tabu
117 ❑ Sep 1949 Cover: 0.10 **NM** value: **125.00**
• **CGC:** 1 graded, best 9.4
📖 The Fangs of the Hooded Scorpion • Kaanga, Camilla, Tabu
118 ❑ Oct 1949 Cover: 0.10 **NM** value: **125.00**
• **CGC:** 2 graded, best 9.6
📖 The Muffled Drums of Doom • Kaanga, Camilla, Simba
119 ❑ Nov 1949 Cover: 0.10 **NM** value: **125.00**
• **CGC:** 1 graded, best 9.2
📖 Fury of the Golden Apes • Kaanga, Camilla, Wambi
120 ❑ Dec 1949 Cover: 0.10 **NM** value: **125.00**
• **CGC:** 1 graded, best 8.0
📖 Killer King's Domain • Kaanga
121 ❑ Jan 1950 Cover: 0.10 **NM** value: **125.00**
📖 Wolves of the Desert Night • Kaanga, Camilla, Wambi, Terry Thunder
122 ❑ Feb 1950 Cover: 0.10 **NM** value: **125.00**
📖 The Veldt of Phantom Fangs • Kaanga
123 ❑ Mar 1950 Cover: 0.10 **NM** value: **125.00**
📖 The Ark of the Mist-Maids • Kaanga, Camilla, Wambi
124 ❑ Apr 1950 Cover: 0.10 **NM** value: **125.00**
📖 The Trail of the Pharoh's Eye • Kaanga
125 ❑ May 1950 Cover: 0.10 **NM** value: **125.00**
📖 Skulls for Sale on Dismal River • Kaanga, Camilla, Wambi
126 ❑ Jun 1950 Cover: 0.10 **NM** value: **125.00**
📖 Safari Sinister • Kaanga, Camilla, Wambi, Simba
127 ❑ Jul 1950 Cover: 0.10 **NM** value: **125.00**
• **CGC:** 1 graded, best 8.0
• Kaanga, Camilla, Wambi
128 ❑ Aug 1950 Cover: 0.10 **NM** value: **125.00**
• **CGC:** 1 graded, best 8.0
📖 Dawn-Men of the Congo • Kaanga
129 ❑ Sep 1950 Cover: 0.10 **NM** value: **125.00**
📖 The Captives of Crocodile Swamp • Kaanga
130 ❑ Oct 1950 Cover: 0.10 **NM** value: **125.00**
📖 Phantoms of the Congo • Kaanga
131 ❑ Nov 1950 Cover: 0.10 **NM** value: **115.00**
📖 Treasure Tomb of the Ape-King • Kaanga
132 ❑ Dec 1950 Cover: 0.10 **NM** value: **115.00**
• Kaanga, Camilla, Wambi
133 ❑ Jan 1951 Cover: 0.10 **NM** value: **115.00**
• **CGC:** 1 graded, best 6.0
📖 Scourge of the Soudan • Kaanga, Camilla, Wambi
134 ❑ Feb 1951 Cover: 0.10 **NM** value: **115.00**
📖 The Black Avengers of Kaffir Pass • Kaanga, Camilla, Wambi
135 ❑ Mar 1951 Cover: 0.10 **NM** value: **115.00**
• Kaanga
136 ❑ Apr 1951 Cover: 0.10 **NM** value: **115.00**
📖 The Death Kraals of Kongola • Kaanga
137 ❑ May 1951 Cover: 0.10 **NM** value: **115.00**
📖 The Safari of Golden Ghosts • Kaanga, Camilla, Wambi
138 ❑ Jun 1951 Cover: 0.10 **NM** value: **115.00**
📖 Track of the Black Terror • Kaanga
139 ❑ Jul 1951 Cover: 0.10 **NM** value: **115.00**
📖 Captain Kidd of the Congo • Kaanga
140 ❑ Aug 1951 Cover: 0.10 **NM** value: **115.00**
• **CGC:** 1 graded, best 9.0
📖 The Monsters of Kilmanjabo • Kaanga
141 ❑ Sep 1951 Cover: 0.10 **NM** value: **115.00**
📖 The Death-Hunt of the Man-Cubs • Kaanga
142 ❑ Oct 1951 Cover: 0.10 **NM** value: **115.00**
📖 Sheba of the Terror Claws • Kaanga
143 ❑ Nov 1951 Cover: 0.10 **NM** value: **115.00**
• **CGC:** 2 graded, best 8.5
📖 The Moon of Devil Drums • Kaanga
144 ❑ Dec 1951 Cover: 0.10 **NM** value: **115.00**
📖 The Quest of the Dragon's Claw • Kaanga
145 ❑ Jan 1952 Cover: 0.10 **NM** value: **115.00**
• **CGC:** 1 graded, best 6.5
📖 The Spawn of the Devil's Moon • Kaanga
146 ❑ Feb 1952 Cover: 0.10 **NM** value: **115.00**
• **CGC:** 1 graded, best 6.5
📖 Orphans of the Congo • Kaanga, Camilla, Wambi
147 ❑ Mar 1952 Cover: 0.10 **NM** value: **115.00**
• **CGC:** 1 graded, best 8.0
📖 The Treasure of Tembo Wanculu • Kaanga
148 ❑ Apr 1952 Cover: 0.10 **NM** value: **115.00**
• Kaanga, Camilla, Wambi
149 ❑ May 1952 Cover: 0.10 **NM** value: **115.00**
• **CGC:** 1 graded, best 8.5
• Kaanga
150 ❑ Jun 1952 Cover: 0.10 **NM** value: **115.00**
📖 Rhino Rampage • Kaanga
151 ❑ Jul 1952 Cover: 0.10 **NM** value: **100.00**
• Kaanga, Camilla, Wambi
152 ❑ Aug 1952 Cover: 0.10 **NM** value: **100.00**
📖 The Rogue of Kopje Kull • Kaanga
153 ❑ Sep 1952 Cover: 0.10 **NM** value: **100.00**
• **CGC:** 1 graded, best 8.0
📖 The Wild Men of N'Gara • Kaanga
154 ❑ Oct 1952 Cover: 0.10 **NM** value: **100.00**
📖 The Fire-Wizard • Kaanga, Wambi, Tiger Girl
155 ❑ Nov 1952 Cover: 0.10 **NM** value: **100.00**
📖 Swamp of the Shrieking Dead; The Leopard Juju • Kaanga
156 ❑ Dec 1952 Cover: 0.10 **NM** value: **100.00**
• **CGC:** 1 graded, best 9.0
• Kaanga, Wambi, Tiger Girl
157 ❑ Win 1952 Cover: 0.10 **NM** value: **100.00**
• Kaanga, Wambi, Tiger Girl
158 ❑ Spr 1953 Cover: 0.10 **NM** value: **100.00**
📖 The Rogues of Skullbone Bwana • Kaanga, Sheena
159 ❑ Sum 1953 Cover: 0.10 **NM** value: **100.00**
• **CGC:** 1 graded, best 7.5
📖 The Blow-Gun Kill • Kaanga
160 ❑ Fal 1953 Cover: 0.10 **NM** value: **100.00**
📖 King Fang • Kaanga, Tiger Girl, Jungle Mysteries, Congo Patrol
161 ❑ Win 1953 Cover: 0.10 **NM** value: **100.00**
📖 The Barbarizi Man-Eaters • Kaanga
162 ❑ Spr 1954 Cover: 0.10 **NM** value: **100.00**
• Kaanga, Tiger Girl
163 ❑ Sum 1954 Cover: 0.10 **NM** value: **100.00**
• **CGC:** 1 graded, best 7.5
📖 Jackals at the Kill; final issue. • Kaanga, Tiger Girl

JUNGLE COMICS (A-LIST) — A-List

1 ❑ Spr 1997 Cover: 2.95 **NM** value: **Cover or less**
Circ: Diamd. preorders: **2,620**
• gatefold summary. 📖 Sheena: Queen of the Jungle • Sheena; Reprints Sheena 3-D special #1 in color **A:** W. Morgan Thomas **W:** W. Morgan Thomas
2 ❑ Fal 1997 Cover: 2.95 **NM** value: **Cover or less**
• Wambi
3 ❑ Win 1997 Cover: 2.95 **NM** value: **Cover or less**
📖 Congo King; Death Stalks the Congo; Snarzan the Ape **A:** Jerry Iger; Lionzas; Taylor Tibett **W:** Jerry Iger; Lionzas; Stan Johnson; Taylor Tibett
4 ❑ Mar 1998 Cover: 2.95 **NM** value: **Cover or less**
5 ❑ Oct 1998 Cover: 2.95 **NM** value: **Cover or less**
• Sheena

JUNGLE GIRL — Fawcett

1 ❑ Fal 1942 **NM** value: **1000.00**
• **CGC:** 1 graded, best 9.0

JUNGLE GIRLS — AC

1 ❑ Aug 1988, b&w Cover: 1.95 **NM** value: **2.00**
2 ❑ Cover: 2.25 **NM** value: **Cover or less**

3 ❑ Cover: 2.75 **NM** value: **Cover or less**
4 ❑ Cover: 2.75 **NM** value: **Cover or less**
5 ❑ Cover: 2.75 **NM** value: **Cover or less**
6 ❑ Cover: 2.95 **NM** value: **Cover or less**
A: Matt Baker
7 ❑ Cover: 2.95 **NM** value: **Cover or less**
A: Matt Baker
8 ❑ b&w Cover: 2.95 **NM** value: **Cover or less**
📖 Sheena Queen of the Jungle; Camila Wild Girl of the Congo **A:** W. Morgan Thomas; Victor Ibsen **W:** W. Morgan Thomas; Victor Ibsen
9 ❑ b&w Cover: 2.95 **NM** value: **Cover or less**
10 ❑ b&w Cover: 2.95 **NM** value: **Cover or less**
11 ❑ b&w Cover: 2.95 **NM** value: **Cover or less**
12 ❑ b&w Cover: 2.95 **NM** value: **Cover or less**
13 ❑ b&w Cover: 2.95 **NM** value: **Cover or less**
14 ❑ b&w Cover: 2.95 **NM** value: **Cover or less**
15 ❑ b&w Cover: 2.95 **NM** value: **Cover or less**
16 ❑ b&w Cover: 2.95 **NM** value: **Cover or less**

JUNGLE GIRLS! (ETERNITY) — Eternity

8 ❑ Cover: 2.95 **NM** value: **Cover or less**
Bk 1 ❑ b&w Cover: 9.95 **NM** value: **Cover or less**

JUNGLE JIM (AVALON) — Avalon

1 ❑ Cover: 2.95 **NM** value: **Cover or less**
📖 The Witch Doctor of Borges Island; The One They Fear; The Golden Goddess of Thalthor; Hippo-The River Horse (text); Fatal Mistake (text); How To Become A Werewolf; Men of Magic; Are Zombies Real; The Wizard of Dark Mountain; The Elephant Graveyard • published in 1998 **A:** Wally Wood; indicia says(c) 1995; Newton **W:** Steve Ditko; Nicola Cutii

JUNGLE JIM (CHARLTON) — Charlton

Jungle Jim remains one of the most famous jungle heroes in comics, sharing that distinction with such characters as Tarzan and Congo Bill. Series came from Ace in the late 1940s and Dell in the 1950s before Charlton began chronicling his adventures in 1969.

With his companion Kolu, Jim acts as the jungle's protector. Often this means stopping poachers and those who would shamelessly trample native cultures in search of personal gain.Along with the Jungle Jim stories, issues of this title also include features on African wildlife and a rather interesting series of instructional text pieces teaching readers to speak Swahili.

This issue's numbering theoretically picks up from the Dell series, although the last Dell issue so labeled is #19.

22 ❑ Feb 1969 Cover: 0.12 **NM** value: **24.00**
• Series continued from Jungle Jim (Dell)
23 ❑ Apr 1969 Cover: 0.12 **NM** value: **18.00**
24 ❑ Jun 1969 Cover: 0.12 **NM** value: **18.00**
25 ❑ Aug 1969 Cover: 0.12 **NM** value: **16.00**
📖 The Best of Everything; The Hunters And The Hunted!; The Lamps Of Doom; The Burial Mound! **A:** Pat Boyette **W:** Joe Gill
26 ❑ Oct 1969 Cover: 0.12 **NM** value: **16.00**
27 ❑ Dec 1969 Cover: 0.12 **NM** value: **16.00**
28 ❑ Feb 1970 Cover: 0.15 **NM** value: **16.00**
final issue.

JUNGLE JIM (DELL) — Dell

3 ❑ Oct 1954 Cover: 0.10 **NM** value: **35.00**
• **CGC:** 1 graded, best 6.5
4 ❑ Jan 1955 Cover: 0.10 **NM** value: **35.00**
• **CGC:** 1 graded, best 7.5
5 ❑ 1955 Cover: 0.10 **NM** value: **35.00**
6 ❑ Oct 1955 Cover: 0.10 **NM** value: **35.00**
• **CGC:** 1 graded, best 6.5
7 ❑ Jan 1956 Cover: 0.10 **NM** value: **35.00**
8 ❑ Apr 1956 Cover: 0.10 **NM** value: **35.00**
• **CGC:** 1 graded, best 6.0
9 ❑ Jul 1956 Cover: 0.10 **NM** value: **35.00**
• **CGC:** 1 graded, best 5.0
10 ❑ Oct 1956 Cover: 0.10 **NM** value: **30.00**
• **CGC:** 1 graded, best 7.5
11 ❑ Jan 1957 Cover: 0.10 **NM** value: **30.00**
12 ❑ Apr 1957 Cover: 0.10 **NM** value: **30.00**
13 ❑ Jul 1957 Cover: 0.10 **NM** value: **30.00**
• **CGC:** 1 graded, best 6.0
14 ❑ Oct 1957 Cover: 0.10 **NM** value: **30.00**
15 ❑ Jan 1958 Cover: 0.10 **NM** value: **30.00**
• **CGC:** 1 graded, best 6.0
16 ❑ Apr 1958 Cover: 0.10 **NM** value: **25.00**
• **CGC:** 1 graded, best 7.5
17 ❑ Jul 1958 Cover: 0.10 **NM** value: **25.00**
• **CGC:** 1 graded, best 7.5
18 ❑ Oct 1958 Cover: 0.10 **NM** value: **25.00**
• **CGC:** 1 graded, best 6.5
19 ❑ Jan 1959 Cover: 0.10 **NM** value: **25.00**
• **CGC:** 1 graded, best 7.0

JUNGLE JIM (KING) — King

5 ❑ Dec 1967 Cover: 0.15 **NM** value: **9.00**

JUNGLE JIM (STANDARD) — Standard

11 ❑ Jan 1949 Cover: 0.10 **NM** value: **60.00**
12 ❑ 1949 Cover: 0.10 **NM** value: **55.00**
13 ❑ 1949 Cover: 0.10 **NM** value: **55.00**
14 ❑ Oct 1949 Cover: 0.10 **NM** value: **55.00**
• **CGC:** 1 graded, best 9.4
15 ❑ Cover: 0.10 **NM** value: **55.00**
16 ❑ 1950 Cover: 0.10 **NM** value: **50.00**
17 ❑ 1950 Cover: 0.10 **NM** value: **50.00**
18 ❑ 1950 Cover: 0.10 **NM** value: **50.00**
19 ❑ Cover: 0.10 **NM** value: **45.00**
20 ❑ ca. 1951 Cover: 0.10 **NM** value: **45.00**

JUNGLE JO (FOX) — Fox

1 ❑ Mar 1950 Cover: 0.10 **NM** value: **375.00**
2 ❑ May 1950 Cover: 0.10 **NM** value: **350.00**
• **CGC:** 1 graded, best 5.0
3 ❑ Jul 1950 Cover: 0.10 **NM** value: **350.00**
4 ❑ Sep 1950 Cover: 0.10 **NM** value: **350.00**

JUNGLE JO (SUPERIOR) — Superior

1 ❑ Cover: 0.10 **NM** value: **400.00**
• Canadian version
2 ❑ Cover: 0.10 **NM** value: **375.00**
3 ❑ ca. 1950 Cover: 0.10 **NM** value: **375.00**

JUNGLE LIL — Fox

1 ❑ Apr 1950 Cover: 0.10 **NM** value: **275.00**

JUNGLE LOVE — Aircel

All issues are adults only.

1 ❑ b&w Cover: 2.95 **NM** value: **Cover or less**
2 ❑ b&w Cover: 2.95 **NM** value: **Cover or less**
3 ❑ b&w Cover: 2.95 **NM** value: **Cover or less**

JUNGLE TALES OF TARZAN — Charlton

1 ❑ Jan 1965 Cover: 0.12 **NM** value: **45.00**
• Sam Glanzman credits
2 ❑ Mar 1965 Cover: 0.12 **NM** value: **35.00**
• Sam Glanzman credits
3 ❑ May 1965 Cover: 0.12 **NM** value: **35.00**
• Sam Glanzman credits
4 ❑ Jul 1965 Cover: 0.12 **NM** value: **35.00**
📖 The Lion; Just Jungle (text); A Jungle Joke; Crocodile Tears • Bill Montes and Ernie Bache credits

JUNGLE TWINS, THE — Gold Key

The Jungle Twins live in a world that's like camping out in the backyard: They're far enough from home to have adventures, but close enough to civilization so that help can always be found when it's needed. The two boys were the princes of Glockenberg, but were presumed dead when the plane carrying them and their parents crashed in the jungles of South Africa. Like Tarzan, however, the boys learned to live in the jungles by themselves, making friends with local tribesmen, and taking on the jungle names Tono and Kono.

Their adventures are wonderful flights of boyhood fancy, with battles with slavers, monsters, and giant gorillas. The most interesting struggles, however, are those where elements of the nearby civilization intruded on their jungle life.

This series ran 17 issues from 1972-1975, with a reprint issue #18 appearing in 1982.

1 ❑ Apr 1972 Cover: 0.15 **NM** value: **8.00**
2 ❑ Jul 1972 Cover: 0.15 **NM** value: **5.00**
3 ❑ Oct 1972 Cover: 0.15 **NM** value: **4.00**
📖 The Deadly Arena
4 ❑ Jan 1972 Cover: 0.15 **NM** value: **4.00**
5 ❑ Apr 1972 Cover: 0.15 **NM** value: **4.00**
6 ❑ Jul 1973 Cover: 0.20 **NM** value: **3.00**
7 ❑ Oct 1973 Cover: 0.20 **NM** value: **3.00**
📖 Lair of the Monster Master
8 ❑ Jan 1974 Cover: 0.20 **NM** value: **3.00**
9 ❑ Apr 1974 Cover: 0.20 **NM** value: **3.00**
10 ❑ Jul 1974 Cover: 0.25 **NM** value: **3.00**
11 ❑ Oct 1974 Cover: 0.25 **NM** value: **3.00**
📖 The Island of Dr. Strangekind
12 ❑ Jan 1975 Cover: 0.25 **NM** value: **3.00**
13 ❑ Mar 1975 Cover: 0.25 **NM** value: **3.00**
14 ❑ May 1975 Cover: 0.25 **NM** value: **3.00**
15 ❑ Jul 1975 Cover: 0.25 **NM** value: **3.00**
16 ❑ Sep 1975 Cover: 0.25 **NM** value: **3.00**
17 ❑ Nov 1975 Cover: 0.25 **NM** value: **3.00**
18 ❑ ca. 1982 Cover: 0.60 **NM** value: **2.00**
📖 Royal Warriors; Jon of the Kalahari: The Whisper of Death final issue.

JUNGLE WAR STORIES — Dell

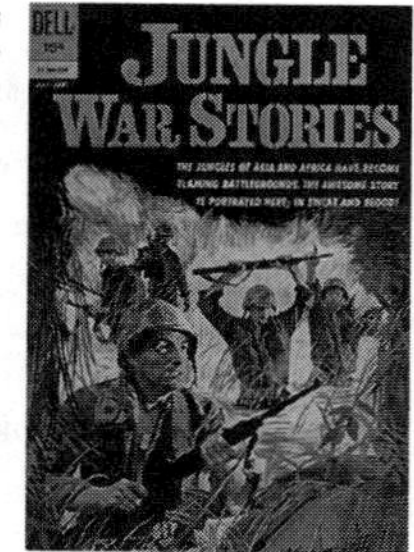

Jungle War Stories comprises the first eleven issues of what later became Guerrilla War. The series began in 1963, just as U.S. involvement in the Vietnam conflict was ramping up. As can be expected, the stories were extremely anti-Communist, with the U.S. soldiers starring as the brave heroes come to save the day. A guide, "Viet Cong: The Face of the Enemy," on one inside front cover, details the torture, village burnings, and other reputed VC activities which justified U.S. involvement.

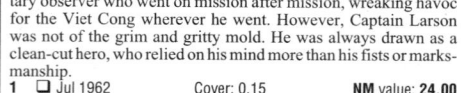

Typical of the U.S. characters was Captain Duke Larson, a military observer who went on mission after mission, wreaking havoc for the Viet Cong wherever he went. However, Captain Larson was not of the grim and gritty mold. He was always drawn as a clean-cut hero, who relied on his mind more than his fists or marksmanship.

1 ❑ Jul 1962 Cover: 0.15 **NM** value: **24.00**
📖 Requiem for a Red...; Doomsday Flight; Vietnam Vengeance; When Ghost Guns Fly...; The Glory Road
2 ❑ Oct 1962 Cover: 0.12 **NM** value: **16.00**
3 ❑ Jan 1963 Cover: 0.12 **NM** value: **16.00**
4 ❑ Apr 1963 Cover: 0.12 **NM** value: **16.00**
📖 Violence in the Air; Mission: Strangle; M-U-D Spells Disaster; Revenge! (text story); The Year of the Cat
5 ❑ Jul 1963 Cover: 0.12 **NM** value: **16.00**
6 ❑ Oct 1963 Cover: 0.12 **NM** value: **14.00**
7 ❑ Jan 1964 Cover: 0.12 **NM** value: **14.00**
8 ❑ Apr 1964 Cover: 0.12 **NM** value: **14.00**
9 ❑ Jul 1964 Cover: 0.12 **NM** value: **14.00**
10 ❑ Oct 1964 Cover: 0.12 **NM** value: **14.00**
11 ❑ Apr 1965 Cover: 0.12 **NM** value: **14.00**
• Series continued in Guerrilla War #12

JUNIE PROM — Dearfield

This title is, each cover assured the reader, "Tops in Teen-Age Fun." And each issue featured the blonde teen surrounded by distractedly admiring guys (little hearts floating romantically around their heads), as she remains cooly provocative and showing a bit of leg. Tops in teen-age fun, indeed.

Dearfield was not a major imprint, briefly producing Dexter Comics (which also featured Junie), Foxy Fagan, Red Rabbit, and this title following World War II and then disappearing, with only Red Rabbit (under another publisher's imprint) continuing after 1949. — Maggie

1 ❑ Win 1947 Cover: 0.10 **NM** value: **75.00**
2 ❑ Spr 1948 Cover: 0.10 **NM** value: **50.00**
3 ❑ Sum 1948 Cover: 0.10 **NM** value: **35.00**
4 ❑ Cover: 0.10 **NM** value: **35.00**
5 ❑ Cover: 0.10 **NM** value: **35.00**
6 ❑ Cover: 0.10 **NM** value: **35.00**
7 ❑ Cover: 0.10 **NM** value: **35.00**

JUNIOR — Fox

9 ❑ Sep 1947 Cover: 0.10 **NM** value: **600.00**
10 ❑ Nov 1947 Cover: 0.10 **NM** value: **575.00**
• **CGC:** 2 graded, best 8.0
11 ❑ Jan 1948 Cover: 0.10 **NM** value: **575.00**
• **CGC:** 2 graded, best 9.2
12 ❑ Mar 1948 Cover: 0.10 **NM** value: **575.00**
• **CGC:** 1 graded, best 4.5
13 ❑ Apr 1948 Cover: 0.10 **NM** value: **550.00**
• **CGC:** 1 graded, best 9.0
14 ❑ May 1948 Cover: 0.10 **NM** value: **550.00**
15 ❑ Jun 1948 Cover: 0.10 **NM** value: **550.00**
• **CGC:** 1 graded, best 8.5
16 ❑ Jul 1948 Cover: 0.10 **NM** value: **550.00**
• **CGC:** 2 graded, best 8.5

JUNIOR HOPP COMICS — Stanmor

1 ❑ Jan 1952 Cover: 0.10 **NM** value: **50.00**
2 ❑ Apr 1952 Cover: 0.10 **NM** value: **35.00**
3 ❑ Jul 1952 Cover: 0.10 **NM** value: **35.00**

JUNIOR JACKALOPE — Nevada City Publishing

1 ❑ b&w Cover: 1.50 **NM** value: **Cover or less**
2 ❑ b&w Cover: 1.50 **NM** value: **Cover or less**

JUNIOR MISS — Timely

24 ❑ Apr 1947 Cover: 0.10 **NM** value: **60.00**
25 ❑ Cover: 0.10 **NM** value: **60.00**
26 ❑ Cover: 0.10 **NM** value: **60.00**
27 ❑ Cover: 0.10 **NM** value: **55.00**
30 ❑ Sum 1948 Cover: 0.10 **NM** value: **50.00**
28 ❑ Cover: 0.10 **NM** value: **55.00**
29 ❑ Cover: 0.10 **NM** value: **55.00**
31 ❑ Nov 1948 Cover: 0.10 **NM** value: **50.00**
32 ❑ Cover: 0.10 **NM** value: **50.00**
33 ❑ Cover: 0.10 **NM** value: **50.00**
34 ❑ Cover: 0.10 **NM** value: **45.00**
35 ❑ Cover: 0.10 **NM** value: **45.00**
36 ❑ Cover: 0.10 **NM** value: **45.00**
37 ❑ Cover: 0.10 **NM** value: **40.00**
38 ❑ Cover: 0.10 **NM** value: **40.00**
39 ❑ Cover: 0.10 **NM** value: **40.00**

JUNIOR WOODCHUCKS (WALT DISNEY'S...) — Disney

1 ❑ Jul 1991 Cover: 1.50 **NM** value: **Cover or less**
Circ: CapCity orders: **6,750**
📖 Bubbleweight Champ **A:** Carl Barks
2 ❑ Aug 1991 Cover: 1.50 **NM** value: **Cover or less**
Circ: CapCity orders: **5,750**
3 ❑ Sep 1991 Cover: 1.50 **NM** value: **Cover or less**
Circ: CapCity orders: **4,900**
4 ❑ Oct 1991 Cover: 1.50 **NM** value: **Cover or less**
Circ: CapCity orders: **4,500**
📖 The Cave Caper!; Sleepy Valley; Doubtful Deeds

Other grades: Multiply prices above by **1.5 for Mint • 2/3 for Very Fine • 1/3 for Fine • 1/5 for Very Good • 1/8 for Good**

JUNK CULTURE — DC / Vertigo
1 ❑ Jul 1997 Cover: 2.50 **NM** value: **Cover or less**
Circ: Diamd. preorders: **16,488**
A: Ted McKeever **W:** Ted McKeever
2 ❑ Aug 1997 Cover: 2.50 **NM** value: **Cover or less**
Circ: Diamd. preorders: **14,070**
A: Ted McKeever **W:** Ted McKeever

JUNKER — Fleetway-Quality
1 ❑ Cover: 2.95 **NM** value: **Cover or less**
A: J. Ridway; T. Perkin **W:** Michael Fleisher
2 ❑ Cover: 2.95 **NM** value: **Cover or less**
A: J. Ridway; T. Perkin **W:** Michael Fleisher
3 ❑ Cover: 2.95 **NM** value: **Cover or less**
A: J. Ridway; T. Perkin **W:** Michael Fleisher
4 ❑ Cover: 2.95 **NM** value: **Cover or less**
A: J. Ridway; T. Perkin **W:** Michael Fleisher

JUNKFOOD NOIR — Oktober Black Press
1 ❑ Jun 1996, b&w Cover: 1.95 **NM** value: **Cover or less**
📖 Murder

JUNKWAFFEL — Print Mint
1 ❑ Cover: 0.50 **NM** value: **5.00**
📖 Tubs; Machines; BMH; Up The Steeple a Comedy in 3 Pages **A:** Vaughn Bodé **W:** Vaughn Bodé
2 ❑ Cover: 0.50 **NM** value: **3.00**
📖 Tubs; Cheech Wizard in His Student Days; The Rudolf; Cobalt 60; War Lizard **A:** Vaughn Bodé **W:** Vaughn Bodé
3 ❑ Cover: 0.50 **NM** value: **3.00**
📖 The Masked Lizard; The Moon of Venus; Gline; The Junkwaffel Papers; **A:** Vaughn Bodé **W:** Vaughn Bodé

JUNKWAFFEL VOL. 2 — Fantagraphics
Bk 1❑ Feb 1995, b&w Cover: 12.95 **NM** value: **Cover or less**
• Oversized.

JUNKYARD ENFORCER — Boxcar Productions
1 ❑ Aug 1998, b&w Cover: 2.95 **NM** value: **Cover or less**

JUPITER — Sandberg
1 ❑ Cover: 2.95 **NM** value: **Cover or less**
2 ❑ Cover: 2.95 **NM** value: **Cover or less**
3 ❑ Cover: 2.95 **NM** value: **Cover or less**

JURASSIC LARK DELUXE EDITION — Parody Press
1 ❑ b&w Cover: 2.95 **NM** value: **Cover or less**

JURASSIC PARK — Topps
Michael Crichton's original novel was first adapted into the blockbuster movie of 1993. Topps then adapted the movie to produce this four-issue mini-series, and the start of a line of related comics.

From blood taken by a primordial mosquito trapped in amber, scientists use dinosaur DNA to recreate dinosaurs. An eccentric billionaire populates an island with them, creating the ultimate wild-animal amusement park, where humans could safely view the dinosaurs. But nature — and the dinosaurs — has other plans!

The first movie created something of a boom in dinosaur popularity with kids, and the comics lasted about as long as the fad did.

0 ❑ Nov 1993 Cover: 2.95 **NM** value: **Cover or less**
📖 Genesis; Betrayal • Polybagged with trade paperback; Flip book with two prequels to the movie **A:** Gil Kane **W:** Walt Simonson
0/DM❑Nov 1993 Cover: 2.95 **NM** value: **3.00**
• trading cards (came packed with trade paperback) **A:** Gil Kane **C:** George Pérez
1 ❑ Jun 1993 Cover: 2.50 **NM** value: **3.00**
A: Gil Kane **C:** Dave Cockrum **W:** Walt Simonson
1/DM❑Jun 1993 Cover: 2.50 **NM** value: **3.00**
Circ: CapCity orders: **56,200** • **CGC:** 1 graded, best 9.6
• trading cards **A:** Gil Kane **C:** Dave Cockrum **W:** Walt Simonson
2 ❑ Jul 1993 Cover: 2.50 **NM** value: **3.00**
A: Gil Kane **W:** Walt Simonson
2/DM❑Jul 1993 Cover: 2.95 **NM** value: **3.00**
Circ: CapCity orders: **34,600**
• trading cards **A:** Gil Kane **W:** Walt Simonson
3 ❑ Jul 1993 Cover: 2.50 **NM** value: **3.00**
A: Gil Kane **W:** Walt Simonson
3/DM❑Jul 1993 Cover: 2.95 **NM** value: **3.00**
Circ: CapCity orders: **33,275**
• trading cards **A:** Gil Kane **W:** Walt Simonson
4 ❑ Aug 1993 Cover: 2.50 **NM** value: **3.00**
A: Gil Kane **W:** Walt Simonson
4/DM❑Aug 1993 Cover: 2.95 **NM** value: **3.00**
Circ: CapCity orders: **33,375**
• hologram card **A:** Gil Kane **W:** Walt Simonson
Bk 1❑ Cover: 9.95 **NM** value: **Cover or less**
A: Gil Kane **W:** Walt Simonson

JURASSIC PARK ADVENTURES — Topps
1 ❑ Jun 1994 Cover: 1.95 **NM** value: **Cover or less**
2 ❑ Cover: 1.95 **NM** value: **Cover or less**
3 ❑ Cover: 1.95 **NM** value: **Cover or less**
4 ❑ Cover: 1.95 **NM** value: **Cover or less**
📖 Animals/Men **A:** Chaz Troug **W:** Steve Englehart
5 ❑ Cover: 1.95 **NM** value: **Cover or less**
6 ❑ Cover: 1.95 **NM** value: **Cover or less**
7 ❑ Cover: 1.95 **NM** value: **Cover or less**
8 ❑ Cover: 1.95 **NM** value: **Cover or less**
9 ❑ Cover: 1.95 **NM** value: **Cover or less**
10 ❑ Cover: 1.95 **NM** value: **Cover or less**

JURASSIC PARK (MAGAZINE) — Dark Horse
1 ❑ **NM** value: **4.00**
2 ❑ **NM** value: **3.00**
3 ❑ **NM** value: **3.00**
4 ❑ **NM** value: **3.00**
5 ❑ **NM** value: **3.00**
6 ❑ **NM** value: **3.00**
7 ❑ **NM** value: **3.00**
8 ❑ **NM** value: **3.00**
9 ❑ **NM** value: **3.00**
10 ❑ **NM** value: **3.00**
11 ❑ **NM** value: **2.50**
12 ❑ **NM** value: **2.50**
13 ❑ **NM** value: **2.50**
14 ❑ **NM** value: **2.50**
15 ❑ **NM** value: **2.50**

JURASSIC PARK: RAPTOR — Topps
1 ❑ Nov 1993 Cover: 2.95 **NM** value: **Cover or less**
Circ: CapCity orders: **38,800**
• Zorro #0
2 ❑ Dec 1993 Cover: 2.95 **NM** value: **Cover or less**
Circ: CapCity orders: **26,500**
📖 Dark Cargo! • cards **A:** Fred Carrillo; Armando Gil; Dell Barras **W:** Steve Englehart

JURASSIC PARK: RAPTORS ATTACK — Topps
1 ❑ Mar 1994 Cover: 2.50 **NM** value: **Cover or less**
Circ: CapCity orders: **18,800**
📖 Rush! **A:** Armando Gil **W:** Steve Englehart
2 ❑ Apr 1994 Cover: 2.50 **NM** value: **Cover or less**
Circ: CapCity orders: **13,450**
3 ❑ May 1994 Cover: 2.50 **NM** value: **Cover or less**
Circ: CapCity orders: **11,670**
📖 Animals/Gods **A:** Chaz Troug **W:** Steve Englehart
4 ❑ Jun 1994 Cover: 2.50 **NM** value: **Cover or less**
Circ: CapCity orders: **10,400**

JURASSIC PARK: RAPTORS HIJACK — Topps
1 ❑ Cover: 2.50 **NM** value: **Cover or less**
Circ: CapCity orders: **8,700**
📖 The Wild! **A:** Neil Vokes **W:** Steve Englehart
2 ❑ Cover: 2.50 **NM** value: **Cover or less**
Circ: CapCity orders: **6,875**
3 ❑ Cover: 2.50 **NM** value: **Cover or less**
Circ: CapCity orders: **6,075**
4 ❑ Cover: 2.50 **NM** value: **Cover or less**
Circ: CapCity orders: **5,900**

JUST A PILGRIM — Black Bull
1 ❑ May 2001 Cover: 2.99 **NM** value: **Cover or less**
Circ: Diamd. preorders: **36,437** • **CGC:** 23 graded, best 9.9
A: Carlos Ezquerra **W:** Garth Ennis
2 ❑ Jun 2001 Cover: 2.99 **NM** value: **Cover or less**
Circ: Diamd. preorders: **32,082** • **CGC:** 7 graded, best 9.8
A: Carlos Ezquerra **W:** Garth Ennis
3 ❑ Jul 2001 Cover: 2.99 **NM** value: **Cover or less**
Circ: Diamd. preorders: **33,123** • **CGC:** 10 graded, best 9.9
A: Carlos Ezquerra **W:** Garth Ennis
4 ❑ Aug 2001 Cover: 2.99 **NM** value: **Cover or less**
Circ: Diamd. preorders: **35,177** • **CGC:** 1 graded, best 9.2
A: Carlos Ezquerra **W:** Garth Ennis
5 ❑ Sep 2001 Cover: 2.99 **NM** value: **Cover or less**
Circ: Diamd. preorders: **36,367** • **CGC:** 1 graded, best 9.0
A: Carlos Ezquerra **W:** Garth Ennis

JUSTICE (ANTARCTIC) — Antarctic
1 ❑ May 1994, b&w Cover: 3.50 **NM** value: **Cover or less**
Circ: CapCity orders: **2,380**

JUSTICE (ATLAS) — Atlas
"It's thrilling because it's true!" "Every case taken from real life!" These were the promises that Justice, one of Atlas' early crime comics, made to its readers.

Formerly an innocuous humor title named Wacky Duck, Justice was born when publisher Martin Goodman caught on to the national interest in crime comics and decided to adopt his usual strategy of saturating the market with similar titles.

The stories themselves were the usual lurid affairs, with stories such as "Dead or Alive!" and "Thicker than Water," full of brazen criminals and plodding policemen. Many were written by a young up-and-comer, Stan Lee, and illustrated by such artists as Russ Heath, George Tuska, and George Wildey.

1 ❑ Fal 1947 Cover: 0.10 **NM** value: **125.00**
#7 on cover. • Numbering continued from Wacky Duck series
2 ❑ Feb 1948 Cover: 0.10 **NM** value: **85.00**
#8 on cover. • Numbering continued from Wacky Duck series
3 ❑ Jun 1948 Cover: 0.10 **NM** value: **70.00**
#9 on cover. • Numbering continued from Wacky Duck series
4 ❑ Aug 1948 Cover: 0.10 **NM** value: **60.00**
5 ❑ Sep 1948 Cover: 0.10 **NM** value: **60.00**
6 ❑ Oct 1948 Cover: 0.10 **NM** value: **50.00**
7 ❑ Dec 1948 Cover: 0.10 **NM** value: **50.00**
• **CGC:** 1 graded, best 8.5
8 ❑ Feb 1949 Cover: 0.10 **NM** value: **50.00**
9 ❑ Apr 1949 Cover: 0.10 **NM** value: **50.00**
10 ❑ May 1949 Cover: 0.10 **NM** value: **60.00**
Photo cover.
11 ❑ Jun 1949 Cover: 0.10 **NM** value: **60.00**
Photo cover.
12 ❑ Jul 1949 Cover: 0.10 **NM** value: **60.00**
Photo cover.
13 ❑ Sep 1949 Cover: 0.10 **NM** value: **60.00**
Photo cover.
14 ❑ Nov 1949 Cover: 0.10 **NM** value: **60.00**
Photo cover.
15 ❑ Feb 1950 Cover: 0.10 **NM** value: **60.00**
Photo cover.
16 ❑ Jun 1950 Cover: 0.10 **NM** value: **50.00**
17 ❑ Sep 1950 Cover: 0.10 **NM** value: **50.00**
18 ❑ Nov 1950 Cover: 0.10 **NM** value: **50.00**
19 ❑ Jan 1951 Cover: 0.10 **NM** value: **50.00**
20 ❑ Mar 1951 Cover: 0.10 **NM** value: **50.00**
21 ❑ May 1951 Cover: 0.10 **NM** value: **45.00**
22 ❑ Jul 1951 Cover: 0.10 **NM** value: **45.00**
23 ❑ Cover: 0.10 **NM** value: **45.00**
24 ❑ Cover: 0.10 **NM** value: **45.00**
25 ❑ Cover: 0.10 **NM** value: **45.00**
26 ❑ 1952 Cover: 0.10 **NM** value: **45.00**
27 ❑ 1952 Cover: 0.10 **NM** value: **45.00**
28 ❑ 1952 Cover: 0.10 **NM** value: **45.00**
29 ❑ 1952 Cover: 0.10 **NM** value: **45.00**
30 ❑ 1952 Cover: 0.10 **NM** value: **45.00**
31 ❑ 1952 Cover: 0.10 **NM** value: **40.00**
32 ❑ 1952 Cover: 0.10 **NM** value: **40.00**
33 ❑ Jan 1953 Cover: 0.10 **NM** value: **40.00**
• **CGC:** 1 graded, best 7.5
34 ❑ 1953 Cover: 0.10 **NM** value: **40.00**
35 ❑ 1953 Cover: 0.10 **NM** value: **40.00**
36 ❑ 1953 Cover: 0.10 **NM** value: **40.00**
37 ❑ 1953 Cover: 0.10 **NM** value: **40.00**
📖 The Crook They Couldn't Catch; Thicker Than Water
38 ❑ 1953 Cover: 0.10 **NM** value: **40.00**
39 ❑ 1953 Cover: 0.10 **NM** value: **40.00**
40 ❑ 1953 Cover: 0.10 **NM** value: **40.00**
41 ❑ Nov 1953 Cover: 0.10 **NM** value: **32.00**
• **CGC:** 1 graded, best 9.0
42 ❑ Cover: 0.10 **NM** value: **32.00**
43 ❑ 1954 Cover: 0.10 **NM** value: **32.00**
44 ❑ 1954 Cover: 0.10 **NM** value: **32.00**
45 ❑ 1954 Cover: 0.10 **NM** value: **32.00**
46 ❑ 1954 Cover: 0.10 **NM** value: **32.00**
47 ❑ 1954 Cover: 0.10 **NM** value: **32.00**
48 ❑ 1954 Cover: 0.10 **NM** value: **32.00**
49 ❑ 1954 Cover: 0.10 **NM** value: **32.00**
50 ❑ 1954 Cover: 0.10 **NM** value: **32.00**
51 ❑ Cover: 0.10 **NM** value: **32.00**
52 ❑ Mar 1955 Cover: 0.10 **NM** value: **32.00**
final issue.

JUSTICE BRIGADE — TCB Comics
1 ❑ b&w Cover: 1.50 **NM** value: **Cover or less**
2 ❑ b&w Cover: 1.50 **NM** value: **Cover or less**
3 ❑ b&w Cover: 1.50 **NM** value: **Cover or less**
4 ❑ b&w Cover: 1.50 **NM** value: **Cover or less**
5 ❑ b&w Cover: 1.50 **NM** value: **Cover or less**
6 ❑ b&w Cover: 1.50 **NM** value: **Cover or less**
7 ❑ b&w Cover: 1.50 **NM** value: **Cover or less**
8 ❑ b&w Cover: 1.50 **NM** value: **Cover or less**

JUSTICE: FOUR BALANCE — Marvel
1 ❑ Sep 1994 Cover: 1.75 **NM** value: **Cover or less**
Circ: CapCity orders: **18,350**
📖 Rock Crushes Scissors **A:** Craig Brasfield **W:** Fabian Nicieza
2 ❑ Oct 1994 Cover: 1.75 **NM** value: **Cover or less**
Circ: CapCity orders: **12,500**
A: Craig Brasfield **W:** Fabian Nicieza
3 ❑ Nov 1994 Cover: 1.75 **NM** value: **Cover or less**
Circ: CapCity orders: **10,800**
📖 Marco-" "-Polo **A:** Craig Brasfield **W:** Fabian Nicieza
4 ❑ Dec 1994 Cover: 1.75 **NM** value: **Cover or less**
Circ: CapCity orders: **9,450**

JUSTICE, INC. — DC
1 ❑ Jun 1975 Cover: 0.25 **NM** value: **3.00**
• **CGC:** 5 graded, best 9.6
📖 This Night, An Avenger Is Born! • adapts Justice Inc. novel **A:** Al McWilliams **W:** Denny O'Neil ★ Origin of The Avenger.
2 ❑ Aug 1975 Cover: 0.25 **NM** value: **2.00**
• adapts The Skywalker **A:** Jack Kirby
3 ❑ Oct 1975 Cover: 0.25 **NM** value: **2.00**
• **CGC:** 1 graded, best 9.2
📖 The Monster Bug! **A:** Jack Kirby **W:** Denny O'Neil ★ 1st Appearance of Fergus MacMurdie.
4 ❑ Dec 1975 Cover: 0.25 **NM** value: **2.00**
A: Jack Kirby **C:** Joe Kubert

JUSTICE, INC. (MINI-SERIES) — DC
1 ❑ Cover: 3.95 **NM** value: **4.00**
• prestige format. 📖 Trust **A:** Kyle Baker; Andy Helfer **W:** Andy Helfer ★ Origin of The Avenger.
2 ❑ Cover: 3.95 **NM** value: **4.00**
• prestige format. 📖 Betrayal **A:** Kyle Baker; Andy Helfer **W:** Andy Helfer

CGC-graded: Multiply prices above by **33 for 9.9 M** • **16 for 9.8 NM/M** • **7 for 9.6 NM+** • **5 for 9.4 NM** • **2.5 for 9.2 NM-** • **1.5 for 9.0 VF/NM**

JUSTICE LEAGUE DC

The Justice League of America had once been the premier super-group in the DC universe. Over the years, however, its key members drifted off, leaving the organization weakened. The death knell of the old Justice League came during the Legends storyline, when Darkseid conspired to move public sentiment against super-heroes. The old Justice League of America was dissolved, only to be reformed in Legends #6 as simply The Justice League.

The new team consisted of Doctor Fate, Batman, Shazam, Guy Gardner, The Martian Manhunter, Black Canary, Mister Miracle, and Blue Beetle. The group was sponsored by Maxwell Lord, a multimillionaire who had fallen under the influence of a sentient super-computer. The computer's plan was to organize the Justice League as a force to bring peace to the world. In issue #7, the computer (via Maxwell Lord) would further this plan by arranging for the team's globalization as Justice League International.

1 ❑ May 1987 Cover: 0.75 **NM** value: **3.50**
Circ: Statement: **164,871** CapCity orders: **35,000 • CGC:** 16 graded, best 9.8
★ 1st Appearance of Maxwell Lord.

2 ❑ Jun 1987 Cover: 0.75 **NM** value: **2.50**
Circ: Statement: **164,871** CapCity orders: **23,900**
★ 1st Appearance of Silver Sorceress, Bluejay, Wandjina.

3 ❑ Jul 1987 Cover: 0.75 **NM** value: **2.50**
Circ: Statement: **164,871** CapCity orders: **25,800 • CGC:** 6 graded, best 9.6
★ Versus Rocket Reds.

3/LE❑ Jul 1987 Cover: 0.75 **NM** value: **15.00**
• **CGC:** 42 graded, best 9.8
alternate cover. • Superman logo on cover (limited edition).

4 ❑ Aug 1987 Cover: 0.75 **NM** value: **2.50**
Circ: Statement: **164,871** CapCity orders: **30,400 • CGC:** 1 graded, best 9.6
• Booster Gold joins team ★ Versus Royal Flush Gang.

5 ❑ Sep 1987 Cover: 0.75 **NM** value: **2.00**
Circ: Statement: **164,871** CapCity orders: **32,500 • CGC:** 2 graded, best 9.8
• Batman vs. Guy Gardner

6 ❑ Oct 1987 Cover: 0.75 **NM** value: **2.00**
Circ: Statement: **164,871** CapCity orders: **34,450 • CGC:** 2 graded, best 9.6
🕮 Massacre In Gray • Series continues in Justice League International #7 **A:** Keith Giffen; Kevin Maguire **W:** Keith Giffen; J.M. DeMatteis

JUSTICE LEAGUE AMERICA DC

The Justice League of America was reformulated in 1987 as part of a great shake-up in DC's titles. As opposed to the old set of veterans who made up the original League, the new League consisted mostly of younger characters, including Mister Miracle, Blue Beetle, and The Martian Manhunter. The series continued to evolve, adding Captain Atom, Rocket Red, and others, while simultaneously retiring other characters.

In an interesting twist, the title took a global bent with issue #7, becoming known as Justice League International. Although the name changed to Justice League America with issue #26, the experiment with globalism saw the birth of Justice League Europe, which then spun off into its own series.

0 ❑ Oct 1994 Cover: 1.50 **NM** value: **2.00**
🕮 Home Again • New team begins: Wonder Woman, Flash III (Wally West), Fire, Metamorpho, Crimson Fox, Hawkman, Obsidian, Nuklon **A:** Chuck Wojtkiewicz **W:** Gerard Jones

26 ❑ May 1989 Cover: 0.75 **NM** value: **1.75**
Circ: CapCity orders: **32,350**
• Continued from "Justice League International" ★ Appearance of Huntress.

27 ❑ Jun 1989 Cover: 0.75 **NM** value: **1.75**
Circ: CapCity orders: **32,600**
Exorcist homage cover.

28 ❑ Jul 1989 Cover: 0.75 **NM** value: **1.75**
Circ: CapCity orders: **34,400**

29 ❑ Aug 1989 Cover: 1.00 **NM** value: **1.75**
Circ: CapCity orders: **34,850**

30 ❑ Sep 1989 Cover: 1.00 **NM** value: **1.75**
Circ: CapCity orders: **35,750**

31 ❑ Oct 1989 Cover: 1.00 **NM** value: **1.75**
Circ: CapCity orders: **35,900**
🕮 Teasdale Imperative, Part 1 ★ Appearance of Justice League Europe.

32 ❑ Nov 1989 Cover: 1.00 **NM** value: **1.75**
Circ: CapCity orders: **39,450**
🕮 Teasdale Imperative, Part 3 ★ Appearance of Justice League Europe.

33 ❑ Dec 1989 Cover: 1.00 **NM** value: **1.75**
Circ: CapCity orders: **36,900**
★ Appearance of Kilowog.

34 ❑ Jan 1990 Cover: 1.00 **NM** value: **1.75**
Circ: CapCity orders: **35,250 • CGC:** 1 graded, best 9.4

35 ❑ Feb 1990 Cover: 1.00 **NM** value: **1.75**
Circ: CapCity orders: **35,050**

36 ❑ Mar 1990 Cover: 1.00 **NM** value: **1.75**
Circ: CapCity orders: **33,600**
★ 1st Appearance of Mr. Nebula, Scarlet Skier. ★ Appearance of G'Nort.

37 ❑ Apr 1990 Cover: 1.00 **NM** value: **1.75**
Circ: CapCity orders: **33,100**

38 ❑ May 1990 Cover: 1.00 **NM** value: **1.75**
Circ: CapCity orders: **32,800**
★ Versus Despero.

39 ❑ Jun 1990 Cover: 1.00 **NM** value: **1.75**
Circ: CapCity orders: **32,200**
★ Versus Despero.

40 ❑ Jul 1990 Cover: 1.00 **NM** value: **1.75**
Circ: CapCity orders: **32,200**
★ Versus Despero.

41 ❑ Aug 1990 Cover: 1.00 **NM** value: **1.75**
Circ: CapCity orders: **30,250**

42 ❑ Sep 1990 Cover: 1.00 **NM** value: **1.75**
Circ: CapCity orders: **30,000**
• membership drive; Return of Mr. Miracle; Orion joins team; Lightray joins team

43 ❑ Oct 1990 Cover: 1.00 **NM** value: **1.75**
Circ: CapCity orders: **29,700**

44 ❑ Nov 1990 Cover: 1.00 **NM** value: **1.75**
Circ: CapCity orders: **28,950**

45 ❑ Jan 1991 Cover: 1.00 **NM** value: **1.75**
Circ: CapCity orders: **29,350**

46 ❑ Jan 1991 Cover: 1.00 **NM** value: **1.75**
Circ: CapCity orders: **28,500**
🕮 Glory Bound, Part 1 • Medley art begins **A:** Linda Medley ★ 1st Appearance of General Glory.

47 ❑ Feb 1991 Cover: 1.00 **NM** value: **1.75**
Circ: CapCity orders: **27,750**
🕮 Glory Bound, Part 2

48 ❑ Mar 1991 Cover: 1.00 **NM** value: **1.75**
Circ: CapCity orders: **27,850**
🕮 Glory Bound, Part 3

49 ❑ Apr 1991 Cover: 1.00 **NM** value: **1.75**
Circ: CapCity orders: **26,450**
🕮 Glory Bound, Part 4

50 ❑ May 1991 Cover: 1.75 **NM** value: **Cover or less**
Circ: CapCity orders: **28,600**
• Double-size. 🕮 Glory Bound, Part 5

51 ❑ Jun 1991 Cover: 1.00 **NM** value: **1.25**
Circ: CapCity orders: **26,500**

52 ❑ Jul 1991 Cover: 1.00 **NM** value: **1.25**
Circ: CapCity orders: **27,950**
• Guy Gardner vs. Blue Beetle

53 ❑ Aug 1991 Cover: 1.00 **NM** value: **1.25**
Circ: CapCity orders: **26,650**
🕮 Breakdowns; Breakdowns, Part 1

54 ❑ Sep 1991 Cover: 1.00 **NM** value: **1.25**
Circ: CapCity orders: **26,650**
🕮 Breakdowns; Breakdowns, Part 3

55 ❑ Oct 1991 Cover: 1.00 **NM** value: **1.25**
Circ: CapCity orders: **28,800**
🕮 Breakdowns; Breakdowns, Part 5 ★ Versus Global Guardians.

56 ❑ Nov 1991 Cover: 1.00 **NM** value: **1.25**
Circ: CapCity orders: **27,400**
🕮 Breakdowns; Breakdowns, Part 7 • back to Happy Harbor

57 ❑ Dec 1991 Cover: 1.00 **NM** value: **1.25**
Circ: CapCity orders: **30,250**
🕮 Breakdowns; Breakdowns, Part 9 ★ Versus Extremists.

58 ❑ Jan 1992 Cover: 1.00 **NM** value: **1.25**
Circ: CapCity orders: **30,050**
🕮 Breakdowns; Breakdowns, Part 11 ★ Appearance of Lobo. ★ Versus Lobo. ★ Versus Despero.

59 ❑ Feb 1992 Cover: 1.00 **NM** value: **1.25**
Circ: CapCity orders: **26,000**
🕮 Breakdowns; Breakdowns, Part 13

60 ❑ Mar 1992 Cover: 1.00 **NM** value: **1.25**
Circ: CapCity orders: **25,550**
🕮 Breakdowns; Breakdowns, Part 15

61 ❑ Apr 1992 Cover: 1.00 **NM** value: **1.25**
Circ: CapCity orders: **28,700**
• new JLA ★ 1st Appearance of Bloodwynd. ★ Versus Weapons Master.

62 ❑ May 1992 Cover: 1.00 **NM** value: **1.25**
Circ: CapCity orders: **24,400**
★ Versus Weapons Master.

63 ❑ Jun 1992 Cover: 1.25 **NM** value: **Cover or less**
Circ: CapCity orders: **24,400**
• Bloodwynd joins team; Guy Gardner leaves team

64 ❑ Jul 1992 Cover: 1.25 **NM** value: **Cover or less**
Circ: CapCity orders: **24,700**
🕮 The Revenge Of Starbreaker **A:** Dan Jurgens **W:** Dan Jurgens ★ Versus Starbreaker.

65 ❑ Aug 1992 Cover: 1.25 **NM** value: **Cover or less**
Circ: CapCity orders: **25,150**
★ Versus Starbreaker.

66 ❑ Sep 1992 Cover: 1.25 **NM** value: **Cover or less**
Circ: CapCity orders: **22,700**
• Guy returns

67 ❑ Oct 1992 Cover: 1.25 **NM** value: **Cover or less**
Circ: CapCity orders: **22,050**
🕮 Transitions, Transmissions, And Transactions **A:** Dan Jurgens **W:** Dan Jurgens

68 ❑ Nov 1992 Cover: 1.25 **NM** value: **Cover or less**
Circ: CapCity orders: **21,250**

69 ❑ Dec 1992 Cover: 1.25 **NM** value: **3.50**
Circ: CapCity orders: **21,550 • CGC:** 6 graded, best 9.6
🕮 Doomsday • Doomsday

69-2❑ Cover: 1.25 **NM** value: **1.75**

70 ❑ Jan 1993 Cover: 1.25 **NM** value: **2.50**
Circ: CapCity orders: **31,000 • CGC:** 3 graded, best 9.6
cover wrapper. 🕮 Funeral For a Friend, Part 1 • Funeral for a Friend **A:** Dan Jurgens **W:** Dan Jurgens

70-2❑ Jan 1993 Cover: 1.25 **NM** value: **1.75**

71 ❑ Feb 1993 Cover: 1.25 **NM** value: **2.00**
Circ: CapCity orders: **22,900**
black cover wrapper. 🕮 A New Look • Wonder Woman joins team; Ray joins team; Agent Liberty joins team; Black Condor joins team **A:** Sal Velluto **W:** Dan Jurgens

71/SC❑ Feb 1993 Cover: 1.25 **NM** value: **2.50**
Split cover. 🕮 A New Look • New team begins **A:** Sal Velluto **W:** Dan Jurgens

72 ❑ Mar 1993 Cover: 1.25 **NM** value: **1.50**
Circ: CapCity orders: **21,800**
★ Versus Doctor Destiny.

73 ❑ Apr 1993 Cover: 1.25 **NM** value: **1.50**
Circ: CapCity orders: **23,200**
🕮 Destiny's Hand, Part 2 **A:** Rick Burchett **W:** Dan Jurgens ★ Versus Doctor Destiny.

74 ❑ May 1993 Cover: 1.25 **NM** value: **1.50**
Circ: CapCity orders: **23,850**
★ Versus Doctor Destiny.

75 ❑ Jun 1993 Cover: 1.25 **NM** value: **1.50**
Circ: CapCity orders: **26,900**
★ Versus Doctor Destiny.

76 ❑ Jul 1993 Cover: 1.25 **NM** value: **1.50**
Circ: CapCity orders: **25,400**

77 ❑ Jul 1993 Cover: 1.25 **NM** value: **1.50**
Circ: CapCity orders: **25,250**

78 ❑ Aug 1993 Cover: 1.25 **NM** value: **1.50**
Circ: CapCity orders: **24,250**
★ Appearance of Jay Garrick.

79 ❑ Aug 1993 Cover: 1.25 **NM** value: **1.50**
Circ: CapCity orders: **27,150**
★ Versus new Extremists.

80 ❑ Sep 1993 Cover: 1.25 **NM** value: **1.50**
Circ: CapCity orders: **23,400**
• Booster gets new armor

81 ❑ Oct 1993 Cover: 1.25 **NM** value: **1.50**
Circ: CapCity orders: **22,150**
• Ray vs. Captain Atom

82 ❑ Nov 1993 Cover: 1.25 **NM** value: **1.50**
Circ: CapCity orders: **20,800**

83 ❑ Dec 1993 Cover: 1.50 **NM** value: **Cover or less**
Circ: CapCity orders: **20,200**

84 ❑ Jan 1994 Cover: 1.50 **NM** value: **Cover or less**
Circ: CapCity orders: **18,650**

85 ❑ Feb 1994 Cover: 1.50 **NM** value: **Cover or less**
Circ: CapCity orders: **17,950**

86 ❑ Mar 1994 Cover: 1.50 **NM** value: **Cover or less**
Circ: CapCity orders: **16,800**
🕮 Cults of the Machine **A:** Marc Campos **W:** Dan Vado

87 ❑ Apr 1994 Cover: 1.50 **NM** value: **Cover or less**
Circ: CapCity orders: **15,600**

88 ❑ May 1994 Cover: 1.50 **NM** value: **Cover or less**
Circ: CapCity orders: **15,300**

89 ❑ Jun 1994 Cover: 1.50 **NM** value: **Cover or less**
Circ: CapCity orders: **15,200**
🕮 Judgment Day

90 ❑ Jul 1994 Cover: 1.50 **NM** value: **Cover or less**
Circ: CapCity orders: **15,350**
🕮 Judgment Day

91 ❑ Aug 1994 Cover: 1.50 **NM** value: **Cover or less**
Circ: CapCity orders: **15,000**
🕮 Heroes Passage • Funeral of Ice **A:** Marc Campos **W:** Dan Vado

92 ❑ Sep 1994 Cover: 1.50 **NM** value: **Cover or less**
Circ: CapCity orders: **19,250**
🕮 The Program • Zero Hour **A:** Luke Ross **W:** Christopher Priest ★ Appearance of Triumph.

93 ❑ Nov 1994 Cover: 1.50 **NM** value: **Cover or less**
Circ: CapCity orders: **15,800**

94 ❑ Dec 1994 Cover: 1.50 **NM** value: **Cover or less**
Circ: CapCity orders: **15,800**

95 ❑ Jan 1995 Cover: 1.50 **NM** value: **Cover or less**
Circ: CapCity orders: **15,750**
🕮 Where the Wild Things Are **A:** Chuck Wojtkiewicz **W:** Gerard Jones

96 ❑ Feb 1995 Cover: 1.50 **NM** value: **Cover or less**
Circ: CapCity orders: **14,825**

97 ❑ Mar 1995 Cover: 1.50 **NM** value: **Cover or less**
Circ: CapCity orders: **13,750**

98 ❑ Apr 1995 Cover: 1.50 **NM** value: **Cover or less**
Circ: CapCity orders: **14,150**

99 ❑ May 1995 Cover: 1.50 **NM** value: **Cover or less**
Circ: CapCity orders: **13,050**

100 ❑ Jun 1995 Cover: 2.95 **NM** value: **Cover or less**
Circ: CapCity orders: **18,900**
• Giant-size anniversary edition.

100/SC❑ Cover: 3.95 **NM** value: **Cover or less**
Holo-grafix cover. • Giant-size anniversary edition.

101 ❑ Jul 1995 Cover: 1.75 **NM** value: **Cover or less**
Circ: CapCity orders: **13,050**
🕮 Way of the Warrior, Part 2

102 ❑ Aug 1995 Cover: 1.75 **NM** value: **Cover or less**
Circ: CapCity orders: **13,025**
🕮 Way of the Warrior, Part 5

103 ❑ Sep 1995 Cover: 1.75 **NM** value: **Cover or less**
Circ: CapCity orders: **12,025**

104 ❑ Oct 1995 Cover: 1.75 **NM** value: **Cover or less**
Circ: CapCity orders: **10,200**

105 ❑ Nov 1995 Cover: 1.75 **NM** value: **Cover or less**
🕮 Underworld Unleashed • Underworld Unleashed

106 ❑ Dec 1995 Cover: 1.75 **NM** value: **Cover or less**
• Underworld Unleashed

107 ❑ Jan 1996 Cover: 1.75 **NM** value: **Cover or less**

108 ❑ Feb 1996 Cover: 1.75 **NM** value: **Cover or less**
🕮 One Hand in Darkness **A:** Chuck Wojtkiewicz **W:** Gerard Jones ★ 1st Appearance of Equinox.

109 ❑ Mar 1996 Cover: 1.75 **NM** value: **Cover or less**
🕮 All that Yazz **A:** Chuck Wojtkiewicz **W:** Gerard Jones ★ Appearance of Equinox.

110 ❑ Apr 1996 Cover: 1.75 **NM** value: **Cover or less**
New Devils for Old **A:** Chuck Wojtkiewicz **W:** Gerard Jones ★ Appearance of El Diablo.

111 ❑ Jun 1996 Cover: 1.75 **NM** value: **Cover or less**
The Purge, Part 1

112 ❑ Jul 1996 Cover: 1.75 **NM** value: **Cover or less**
The Purge, Part 2 **A:** Chuck Wojtkiewicz **W:** Gerard Jones

113 ❑ Aug 1996 Cover: 1.75 **NM** value: **Cover or less**
The Purge, Part 3 final issue.

Anl 4 ❑ ca. 1988 Cover: 2.00 **NM** value: **3.00**
Circ: CapCity orders: **31,750**
• Justice League Antarctica

Anl 5 ❑ ca. 1989 Cover: 2.00 **NM** value: **3.00**
Circ: CapCity orders: **34,950**
• Armageddon 2001

Anl 5-2 ❑ ca. 1990 Cover: 2.00 **NM** value: **2.50**

Anl 6 ❑ ca. 1991 Cover: 2.50 **NM** value: **Cover or less**
Circ: CapCity orders: **28,200**
Eclipso: The Darkness Within, Part 6 • Eclipso **A:** Dave Cockrum **W:** Dan Mishkin

Anl 7 ❑ ca. 1992 Cover: 2.50 **NM** value: **Cover or less**
Only the Lucky Ones Die! • Bloodlines **A:** Greg LaRocque **W:** Bill Loebs ★ 1st Appearance of Terrorsmith.

Anl 8 ❑ ca. 1993 Cover: 2.95 **NM** value: **Cover or less**
Circ: CapCity orders: **12,550**
• Elseworlds

Anl 9 ❑ ca. 1994 Cover: 3.50 **NM** value: **Cover or less**
Circ: CapCity orders: **11,550**
• Year One

Anl 10 ❑ ca. 1996 Cover: 2.95 **NM** value: **Cover or less**
Te Alliance • Legends of the Dead Earth; events continue in Ray #26; 1996 **A:** Sergio Cariello **W:** Christopher Priest

SE 1 ❑ ca. 1990 Cover: 1.50 **NM** value: **Cover or less**
Circ: CapCity orders: **35,050**

SE 2 ❑ ca. 1991 Cover: 2.95 **NM** value: **Cover or less**

SP 1/A ❑ ca. 1992 Cover: 1.50 **NM** value: **2.00**
Circ: CapCity orders: **40,000**
Green Lantern on cover. • Double-size. Team Work • Justice League Spectacular **A:** Dan Jurgens; Ron Randall **W:** Dan Jurgens; Gerard Jones

SP 1/B ❑ ca. 1992 Cover: 1.50 **NM** value: **2.00**
Superman on cover. • Double-size. • Justice League Spectacular **A:** Dan Jurgens; Ron Randall **W:** Dan Jurgens; Gerard Jones

JUSTICE LEAGUE: A MIDSUMMER'S NIGHTMARE — DC

1 ❑ Sep 1996 Cover: 2.95 **NM** value: **Cover or less**
• **CGC:** 1 graded, best 9.6
True Lies • forms triptych with other two issues **A:** Jeff Johnson; Darick Robertson **W:** Fabian Nicieza; Mark Waid

2 ❑ Oct 1996 Cover: 2.95 **NM** value: **Cover or less**
• forms triptych with other two issues **A:** Jeff Johnson; Darick Robertson **W:** Fabian Nicieza; Mark Waid

3 ❑ Nov 1996 Cover: 2.95 **NM** value: **Cover or less**
Circ: Diamd. preorders: **53,244**
• forms triptych with other two issues **A:** Jeff Johnson; Darick Robertson **W:** Fabian Nicieza; Mark Waid

Bk 1 ❑ Cover: 8.95 **NM** value: **Cover or less**
• Collects series **A:** Jeff Johnson; Darick Robertson **W:** Fabian Nicieza; Mark Waid

JUSTICE LEAGUE EUROPE — DC

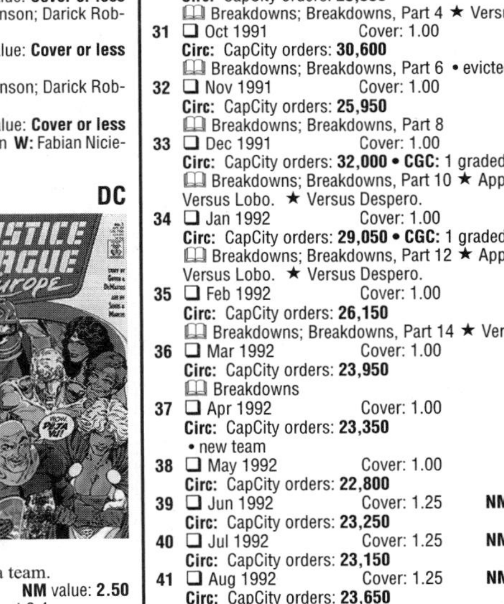

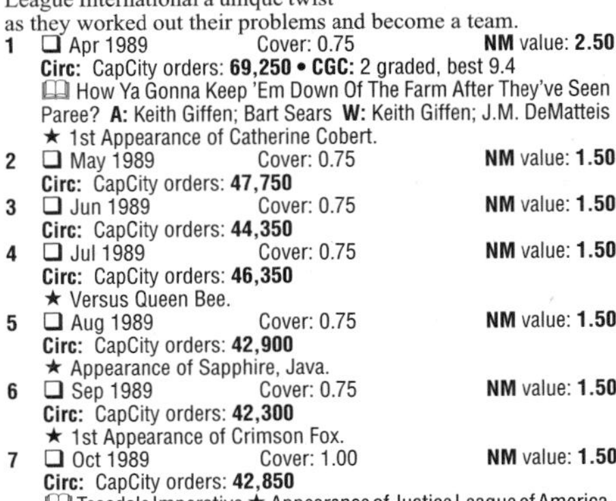

Justice League International eventually spun off a European branch, sending its Russian member, Rocket Red, to Paris with Animal Man, Captain Atom, Wonder Woman, Power Girl, Elongated Man, Metamorpho, and the new Flash. But teamwork was going to come hard: Captain Atom was a nervous new leader, Flash had his eyes on the female members of the team, and Animal Man's costume went up in flames when it was sent over in the teleporter. Paris didn't exactly seem overjoyed to see them either...

The conflicts between the members gave this spinoff from Justice League International a unique twist as they worked out their problems and become a team.

1 ❑ Apr 1989 Cover: 0.75 **NM** value: **2.50**
Circ: CapCity orders: **69,250** • **CGC:** 2 graded, best 9.4
How Ya Gonna Keep 'Em Down Of The Farm After They've Seen Paree? **A:** Keith Giffen; Bart Sears **W:** Keith Giffen; J.M. DeMatteis ★ 1st Appearance of Catherine Cobert.

2 ❑ May 1989 Cover: 0.75 **NM** value: **1.50**
Circ: CapCity orders: **47,750**

3 ❑ Jun 1989 Cover: 0.75 **NM** value: **1.50**
Circ: CapCity orders: **44,350**

4 ❑ Jul 1989 Cover: 0.75 **NM** value: **1.50**
Circ: CapCity orders: **46,350**
★ Versus Queen Bee.

5 ❑ Aug 1989 Cover: 0.75 **NM** value: **1.50**
Circ: CapCity orders: **42,900**
★ Appearance of Sapphire, Java.

6 ❑ Sep 1989 Cover: 0.75 **NM** value: **1.50**
Circ: CapCity orders: **42,300**
★ 1st Appearance of Crimson Fox.

7 ❑ Oct 1989 Cover: 1.00 **NM** value: **1.50**
Circ: CapCity orders: **42,850**
Teasdale Imperative ★ Appearance of Justice League of America.

8 ❑ Nov 1989 Cover: 1.00 **NM** value: **1.50**
Circ: CapCity orders: **39,350**
Teasdale Imperative ★ Appearance of Justice League of America.

9 ❑ Dec 1989 Cover: 1.00 **NM** value: **1.50**
Circ: CapCity orders: **36,850**
★ Appearance of Superman.

10 ❑ Jan 1990 Cover: 1.00 **NM** value: **1.50**
Circ: CapCity orders: **36,100**

11 ❑ Feb 1990 Cover: 1.00 **NM** value: **1.50**
Circ: CapCity orders: **36,050**
• Guy Gardner vs. Metamorpho

12 ❑ Mar 1990 Cover: 1.00 **NM** value: **1.50**
Circ: CapCity orders: **34,700**

13 ❑ Apr 1990 Cover: 1.00 **NM** value: **1.50**
Circ: CapCity orders: **33,650**

14 ❑ May 1990 Cover: 1.00 **NM** value: **1.50**
Circ: CapCity orders: **33,300**

15 ❑ Jun 1990 Cover: 1.00 **NM** value: **1.50**
Circ: CapCity orders: **32,750**
★ 1st Appearance of Extremists.

16 ❑ Jun 1990 Cover: 1.00 **NM** value: **1.50**
Circ: CapCity orders: **31,950**
★ Versus Extremists.

17 ❑ Aug 1990 Cover: 1.00 **NM** value: **1.50**
Circ: CapCity orders: **30,200**
★ Versus Extremists.

18 ❑ Sep 1990 Cover: 1.00 **NM** value: **1.50**
Circ: CapCity orders: **29,300**
★ Versus Extremists.

19 ❑ Oct 1990 Cover: 1.00 **NM** value: **1.50**
Circ: CapCity orders: **28,350**
★ Versus Extremists.

20 ❑ Nov 1990 Cover: 1.00 **NM** value: **1.50**
Circ: CapCity orders: **28,500**

21 ❑ Dec 1990 Cover: 1.00 **NM** value: **1.25**
Circ: CapCity orders: **28,450**

22 ❑ Jan 1991 Cover: 1.00 **NM** value: **1.25**
Circ: CapCity orders: **28,150**

23 ❑ Feb 1991 Cover: 1.00 **NM** value: **1.25**
Circ: CapCity orders: **27,650**

24 ❑ Mar 1991 Cover: 1.00 **NM** value: **1.25**
Circ: CapCity orders: **26,150**

25 ❑ Apr 1991 Cover: 1.00 **NM** value: **1.25**
Circ: CapCity orders: **25,400**

26 ❑ May 1991 Cover: 1.00 **NM** value: **1.25**
Circ: CapCity orders: **25,150**

27 ❑ Jun 1991 Cover: 1.00 **NM** value: **1.25**
Circ: CapCity orders: **25,250**

28 ❑ Jul 1991 Cover: 1.00 **NM** value: **1.25**
Circ: CapCity orders: **25,150**

29 ❑ Aug 1991 Cover: 1.00 **NM** value: **1.25**
Circ: CapCity orders: **25,450**
Breakdowns; Breakdowns, Part 2

30 ❑ Sep 1991 Cover: 1.00 **NM** value: **1.25**
Circ: CapCity orders: **25,550**
Breakdowns; Breakdowns, Part 4 ★ Versus Jack O'Lantern.

31 ❑ Oct 1991 Cover: 1.00 **NM** value: **1.25**
Circ: CapCity orders: **30,600**
Breakdowns; Breakdowns, Part 6 • evicted from JLI Embassy

32 ❑ Nov 1991 Cover: 1.00 **NM** value: **1.25**
Circ: CapCity orders: **25,950**
Breakdowns; Breakdowns, Part 8

33 ❑ Dec 1991 Cover: 1.00 **NM** value: **1.25**
Circ: CapCity orders: **32,000** • **CGC:** 1 graded, best 9.6
Breakdowns; Breakdowns, Part 10 ★ Appearance of Lobo. ★ Versus Lobo. ★ Versus Despero.

34 ❑ Jan 1992 Cover: 1.00 **NM** value: **1.25**
Circ: CapCity orders: **29,050** • **CGC:** 1 graded, best 9.4
Breakdowns; Breakdowns, Part 12 ★ Appearance of Lobo. ★ Versus Lobo. ★ Versus Despero.

35 ❑ Feb 1992 Cover: 1.00 **NM** value: **1.25**
Circ: CapCity orders: **26,150**
Breakdowns; Breakdowns, Part 14 ★ Versus Extremists.

36 ❑ Mar 1992 Cover: 1.00 **NM** value: **1.25**
Circ: CapCity orders: **23,950**
Breakdowns

37 ❑ Apr 1992 Cover: 1.00 **NM** value: **1.25**
Circ: CapCity orders: **23,350**
• new team

38 ❑ May 1992 Cover: 1.00 **NM** value: **1.25**
Circ: CapCity orders: **22,800**

39 ❑ Jun 1992 Cover: 1.25 **NM** value: **Cover or less**
Circ: CapCity orders: **23,250**

40 ❑ Jul 1992 Cover: 1.25 **NM** value: **Cover or less**
Circ: CapCity orders: **23,150**

41 ❑ Aug 1992 Cover: 1.25 **NM** value: **Cover or less**
Circ: CapCity orders: **23,650**

42 ❑ Sep 1992 Cover: 1.25 **NM** value: **Cover or less**
Circ: CapCity orders: **20,450**
• Wonder Woman joins team

43 ❑ Oct 1992 Cover: 1.25 **NM** value: **Cover or less**
Circ: CapCity orders: **20,550**

44 ❑ Oct 1992 Cover: 1.25 **NM** value: **Cover or less**
Circ: CapCity orders: **19,600**

45 ❑ Dec 1992 Cover: 1.25 **NM** value: **Cover or less**
Circ: CapCity orders: **19,000**
Red Winter, Part 1 **A:** Ron Randall **W:** Gerard Jones

46 ❑ Jan 1993 Cover: 1.25 **NM** value: **Cover or less**
Circ: CapCity orders: **18,150**
Red Winter, Part 2

47 ❑ Feb 1993 Cover: 1.25 **NM** value: **Cover or less**
Circ: CapCity orders: **17,450**
Red Winter, Part 3

48 ❑ Mar 1993 Cover: 1.25 **NM** value: **Cover or less**
Circ: CapCity orders: **17,400**
Red Winter, Part 4 ★ Appearance of Justice Society of America.

49 ❑ Apr 1993 Cover: 1.25 **NM** value: **Cover or less**
Circ: CapCity orders: **18,100**
Red Winter, Part 5

50 ❑ May 1993 Cover: 2.50 **NM** value: **Cover or less**
Circ: CapCity orders: **18,000**
Red Winter, Part 6 • Series continues as Justice League International **A:** Ron Randall **W:** Gerard Jones ★ Appearance of Justice Society of America. ★ Versus Sonar.

Anl 1 ❑ Cover: 2.00 **NM** value: **Cover or less**
Circ: CapCity orders: **32,300**
• Global Guardians

Anl 2 ❑ Cover: 2.00 **NM** value: **Cover or less**
Armageddon 2001, Part 13 • Armageddon 2001 ★ Appearance of Demon, Elongated Man, Anthro, Bat Lash, Hex, General Glory, Legion.

Anl 3 ❑ Cover: 2.50 **NM** value: **Cover or less**
Circ: CapCity orders: **24,400**
Eclipso: The Darkness Within, Part 16 • Eclipso; series continues as Justice League International Annual **A:** Tim Hamilton **W:** Will Jacobs; Gerard Jones

JUSTICE LEAGUE INTERNATIONAL — DC

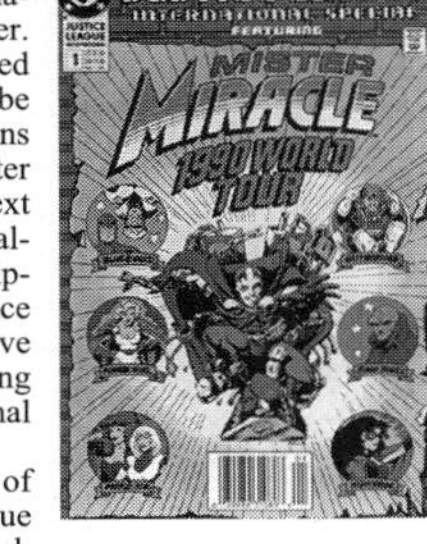

Early in its history, the new Justice League was secretly being manipulated by a sentient computer. That computer had been designed to ensure that world peace would be achieved, regardless of what means were required to ensure this. After forming the Justice League, its next step was to focus on internationalization. The computer thus manipulated Maxwell Lord, the Justice League's rich benefactor, to move the Justice League to Paris, turning it into Justice League International with issue #8.

The new team was composed of Mister Miracle, Booster Gold, Blue Beetle, Guy Gardner, Power Girl, J'onn J'onzz (Martian Manhunter), Fire, Ice, and The Huntress. As Justice League International, they combined super-heroics and silliness in an enjoyable series of adventures. After issue #25, the team split into Justice League America and Justice League Europe. Justice League Europe would later change its name back to Justice League International.

7 ❑ Nov 1987 Cover: 1.25 **NM** value: **2.50**
Circ: Statement: **164,871** CapCity orders: **37,900**
• Title changes to Justice League International; Captain Marvel leaves team; Captain Atom joins team; Rocket Red joins team

8 ❑ Dec 1987 Cover: 0.75 **NM** value: **1.50**
Circ: Statement: **164,871** CapCity orders: **33,850**

9 ❑ Jan 1988 Cover: 0.75 **NM** value: **1.50**
Circ: CapCity orders: **38,400**
• Millennium

10 ❑ Feb 1988 Cover: 0.75 **NM** value: **1.50**
Circ: CapCity orders: **40,700**
• Millennium ★ 1st Appearance of G'Nort.

11 ❑ Mar 1988 Cover: 0.75 **NM** value: **1.25**
Circ: CapCity orders: **36,450**

12 ❑ Apr 1988 Cover: 0.75 **NM** value: **1.25**
Circ: CapCity orders: **36,700**

13 ❑ May 1988 Cover: 0.75 **NM** value: **1.25**
Circ: CapCity orders: **36,200** • **CGC:** 3 graded, best 9.8
★ Appearance of Suicide Squad.

14 ❑ Jun 1988 Cover: 0.75 **NM** value: **1.25**
Circ: CapCity orders: **32,750**

15 ❑ Jul 1988 Cover: 0.75 **NM** value: **1.25**
Circ: CapCity orders: **33,150**
★ 1st Appearance of Manga Khan, L-Ron.

16 ❑ Aug 1988 Cover: 0.75 **NM** value: **1.25**
Circ: CapCity orders: **32,600**

17 ❑ Sep 1988 Cover: 0.75 **NM** value: **1.25**
Circ: CapCity orders: **31,650**

18 ❑ Oct 1988 Cover: 0.75 **NM** value: **1.25**
Circ: CapCity orders: **32,350**
• Bonus Book ★ Appearance of Lobo.

19 ❑ Nov 1988 Cover: 0.75 **NM** value: **1.25**
Circ: CapCity orders: **31,050**
★ Appearance of Lobo.

20 ❑ Dec 1988 Cover: 0.75 **NM** value: **1.25**
Circ: CapCity orders: **31,050**
★ Appearance of Lobo.

21 ❑ Cover: 0.75 **NM** value: **1.25**
Circ: CapCity orders: **31,400**
• no month of publication ★ Appearance of Lobo.

22 ❑ Cover: 0.75 **NM** value: **1.25**
Circ: CapCity orders: **33,150**
• Invasion!; no month of publication; Oberon solo story

23 ❑ Jan 1989 Cover: 0.75 **NM** value: **1.25**
Circ: CapCity orders: **33,050**
• Invasion! ★ 1st Appearance of Injustice League. ★ Versus Injustice League.

24 ❑ Feb 1989 Cover: 1.50 **NM** value: **2.00**
Circ: CapCity orders: **36,750**
• Giant-size. • Bonus Book ★ 1st Appearance of JL Europe.

25 ❑ Apr 1989 Cover: 0.75 **NM** value: **1.25**
Circ: CapCity orders: **31,600**
• becomes Justice League America

51 ❑ Jun 1993 Cover: 1.25 **NM** value: **Cover or less**
Circ: CapCity orders: **17,900**
• was Justice League Europe

52 ❑ Jul 1993 Cover: 1.25 **NM** value: **Cover or less**
Circ: CapCity orders: **16,800**

53 ❑ Aug 1993 Cover: 1.25 **NM** value: **Cover or less**
Circ: CapCity orders: **17,550**

54 ❑ Sep 1993 Cover: 1.25 **NM** value: **Cover or less**
Circ: CapCity orders: **16,000**

55 ❑ Sep 1993 Cover: 1.25 **NM** value: **Cover or less**
Circ: CapCity orders: **15,900**

56 ❑ Oct 1993 Cover: 1.25 **NM** value: **Cover or less**
Circ: CapCity orders: **15,850**

CGC-graded: Multiply prices above by **33 for 9.9 M • 16 for 9.8 NM/M • 7 for 9.6 NM+ • 5 for 9.4 NM • 2.5 for 9.2 NM- • 1.5 for 9.0 VF/NM**

57 ❑ Oct 1993 Cover: 1.25 **NM** value: **Cover or less**
Circ: CapCity orders: **15,850**
58 ❑ Nov 1993 Cover: 1.25 **NM** value: **Cover or less**
Circ: CapCity orders: **15,250**
59 ❑ Dec 1993 Cover: 1.50 **NM** value: **Cover or less**
Circ: CapCity orders: **14,750**
Ordinary People **A:** Will Jacobs **W:** Gerard Jones
60 ❑ Jan 1994 Cover: 1.50 **NM** value: **Cover or less**
Circ: CapCity orders: **14,300**
61 ❑ Feb 1994 Cover: 1.50 **NM** value: **Cover or less**
Circ: CapCity orders: **13,350**
Born of Man and Woman **A:** Will Jacobs **W:** Gerard Jones
62 ❑ Mar 1994 Cover: 1.50 **NM** value: **Cover or less**
Circ: CapCity orders: **12,400**
63 ❑ Apr 1994 Cover: 1.50 **NM** value: **Cover or less**
Circ: CapCity orders: **11,600**
64 ❑ May 1994 Cover: 1.50 **NM** value: **Cover or less**
Circ: CapCity orders: **11,500**
65 ❑ Jun 1994 Cover: 1.50 **NM** value: **Cover or less**
Circ: CapCity orders: **12,000**
Judgment Day; Judgment Day, Part 3 **A:** Chuck Wohtkiewicz **W:** Gerard Jones
66 ❑ Jul 1994 Cover: 1.50 **NM** value: **Cover or less**
Circ: CapCity orders: **12,450**
Judgment Day
67 ❑ Aug 1994 Cover: 1.50 **NM** value: **Cover or less**
Circ: CapCity orders: **12,050**
Aftershocks, Part 3
68 ❑ Sep 1994 Cover: 1.50 **NM** value: **Cover or less**
Circ: CapCity orders: **15,550**
Return of the Hero, Part 3 final issue. • Zero Hour★ Appearance of Triumph.
Anl 1❑ca. 1990 Cover: 1.25 **NM** value: **2.00**
Anl 2❑ca. 1991 Cover: 1.50 **NM** value: **2.00**
• **CGC:** 6 graded, best 9.8
★ Appearance of Joker. ★ Versus Joker.
Anl 3❑ca. 1992 Cover: 1.75 **NM** value: **2.00**
Circ: CapCity orders: **35,100**
Anl 4❑ca. 1993 Cover: 2.50 **NM** value: **Cover or less**
Circ: CapCity orders: **23,100**
Bloodlines • Bloodlines★ 1st Appearance of Lionheart.
Anl 5❑Jun 1994 Cover: 2.95 **NM** value: **Cover or less**
No Rules to Follow • Elseworlds **A:** Kiki Chansamone **W:** Gerard Jones
Bk 1❑ Cover: 12.95 **NM** value: **Cover or less**
Circ: CapCity orders: **5,200**
• A New Beginning
Bk 2❑ Cover: 12.95 **NM** value: **Cover or less**
• The Secret Gospel Of Maxwell Lord
SE 1❑ Cover: 1.50 **NM** value: **Cover or less**
The Show Must Go On…And On…And On…And On… • Mr. Miracle **A:** Joe Phillips; Keith Giffen **W:** Keith Giffen; Len Wein
SE 2❑ Cover: 2.95 **NM** value: **Cover or less**
Circ: CapCity orders: **23,750**
• Huntress

JUSTICE LEAGUE OF AMERICA DC

After their first appearances in The Brave and The Bold #28-30, DC realized that the Justice League of America was a hit. It seemed that if heroes such as Batman, Superman, Flash, Wonder Woman, Green Lantern, and Aquaman were great on their own, they'd be even better together. Thus The Justice League of America was started, gathering these and other heroes together to fight the sort of foes that only their combined might could challenge.

Among the team's most popular adventures were a series of annual crossovers with The Justice Society of America.

1 ❑ Nov 1960 Cover: 0.10 **NM** value: **3450.00**
Circ: Statement: **335,000** • **CGC:** 60 graded, best 9.2
The World of No Return! • Membership consists of Flash, WonderWoman, J'onn J'onzz, Green Lantern, Superman, Batman and Aquaman★ Origin of Despero. ★ 1st Appearance of Despero.
2 ❑ Jan 1961 Cover: 0.10 **NM** value: **810.00**
Circ: Statement: **335,000** • **CGC:** 30 graded, best 9.4
Secret of the Sinister Sorcerers! ★ Appearance of Merlin.
3 ❑ Mar 1961 Cover: 0.10 **NM** value: **610.00**
Circ: Statement: **335,000** • **CGC:** 21 graded, best 8.5
The Slave Ship of Space! ★ Origin of Kanjar Ro. ★ 1st Appearance of Kanjar Ro, Hyathis.
4 ❑ May 1961 Cover: 0.10 **NM** value: **450.00**
Circ: Statement: **335,000** • **CGC:** 15 graded, best 8.5
Doom of the Star Diamond! • Green Arrow joins team; Snapper Carr
5 ❑ Jul 1961 Cover: 0.10 **NM** value: **365.00**
Circ: Statement: **335,000** • **CGC:** 12 graded, best 9.0
When Gravity Went Wild! ★ Origin of Doctor Destiny. ★ 1st Appearance of Doctor Destiny.
6 ❑ Sep 1961 Cover: 0.10 **NM** value: **285.00**
Circ: Statement: **335,000** • **CGC:** 9 graded, best 9.0
The Wheel of Misfortune! ★ 1st Appearance of Professor Amos Fortune.
7 ❑ Nov 1961 Cover: 0.10 **NM** value: **285.00**
Circ: Statement: **335,000** • **CGC:** 19 graded, best 9.0
The Cosmic Fun-House!
8 ❑ Jan 1962 Cover: 0.12 **NM** value: **285.00**
Circ: Statement: **340,000** • **CGC:** 9 graded, best 9.6
For Sale – The Justice League!
9 ❑ Feb 1962 Cover: 0.12 **NM** value: **440.00**
Circ: Statement: **340,000** • **CGC:** 30 graded, best 9.2
The Origin of the Justice League! • Has 1961 Statement, filed 10/1/61; avg total paid 355,000★ Origin of Justice League of America.
10 ❑ Mar 1962 Cover: 0.12 **NM** value: **260.00**
Circ: Statement: **340,000** • **CGC:** 11 graded, best 9.2
The Fantastic Fingers of Felix Faust! ★ 1st Appearance of Lord of Time, Felix Faust.
11 ❑ May 1962 Cover: 0.12 **NM** value: **200.00**
Circ: Statement: **340,000** • **CGC:** 9 graded, best 9.2
One Hour to Doomsday!
12 ❑ Jun 1962 Cover: 0.12 **NM** value: **200.00**
Circ: Statement: **340,000** • **CGC:** 14 graded, best 9.2
The Last Case of the Justice League! ★ Origin of Doctor Light I (Dr. Arthur Light). ★ 1st Appearance of Doctor Light I (Dr. Arthur Light).
13 ❑ Aug 1962 Cover: 0.12 **NM** value: **200.00**
Circ: Statement: **340,000** • **CGC:** 9 graded, best 9.2
Riddle of the Robot Justice League!
14 ❑ Sep 1962 Cover: 0.12 **NM** value: **200.00**
Circ: Statement: **340,000** • **CGC:** 14 graded, best 9.4
The Menace of the "Atom" Bomb! • Atom joins Justice League of America
15 ❑ Nov 1962 Cover: 0.12 **NM** value: **200.00**
Circ: Statement: **340,000** • **CGC:** 17 graded, best 9.6
The Challenge of the Untouchable Aliens!
16 ❑ Dec 1962 Cover: 0.12 **NM** value: **165.00**
Circ: Statement: **340,000** • **CGC:** 5 graded, best 8.5
The Cavern of Deadly Spheres!
17 ❑ Feb 1963 Cover: 0.12 **NM** value: **165.00**
• **CGC:** 16 graded, best 9.4
The Triumpg of the Tornado Tyrant! ★ 1st Appearance of Tornado Champion (Red Tornado).
18 ❑ Mar 1963 Cover: 0.12 **NM** value: **165.00**
• **CGC:** 9 graded, best 9.4
Journey into the Micro-World!
19 ❑ May 1963 Cover: 0.12 **NM** value: **165.00**
• **CGC:** 5 graded, best 9.0
The Super-Exiles of Earth!
20 ❑ Jun 1963 Cover: 0.12 **NM** value: **165.00**
• **CGC:** 8 graded, best 9.2
The Mystery of Spaceman X!
21 ❑ Aug 1963 Cover: 0.12 **NM** value: **340.00**
• **CGC:** 24 graded, best 9.4
Crisis on Earth-One! • Return of Justice Society of America; Justice League of America teams up with Justice Society of America★ 1st Appearance of Earth-2 (named).
22 ❑ Sep 1963 Cover: 0.12 **NM** value: **285.00**
• **CGC:** 23 graded, best 9.4
Crisis on Earth-Two! • Return of Justice Society of America; Justice League of America teams up with Justice Society of America
23 ❑ Nov 1963 Cover: 0.12 **NM** value: **90.00**
• **CGC:** 7 graded, best 9.6
Drones of the Queen Bee! ★ 1st Appearance of Queen Bee.
24 ❑ Dec 1963 Cover: 0.12 **NM** value: **90.00**
• **CGC:** 3 graded, best 9.0
Decoy Missions of the Justice League!
25 ❑ Feb 1964 Cover: 0.12 **NM** value: **90.00**
• **CGC:** 2 graded, best 7.5
Outcasts of Infinity!
26 ❑ Mar 1964 Cover: 0.12 **NM** value: **90.00**
• **CGC:** 2 graded, best 8.0
Four Worlds to Conquer!
27 ❑ May 1964 Cover: 0.12 **NM** value: **90.00**
• **CGC:** 2 graded, best 8.5
The "I" Who Defeated the JusticeLeague!
28 ❑ Jun 1964 Cover: 0.12 **NM** value: **90.00**
• **CGC:** 6 graded, best 9.2
The Case of the Forbidden Super-Powers!
29 ❑ Aug 1964 Cover: 0.12 **NM** value: **115.00**
• **CGC:** 6 graded, best 9.0
Crisis on Earth-Three • Part 1 **A:** Mike Sekowsky; Gardner Fox(cover) **W:** Gardner Fox ★ Origin of Crime Syndicate. ★ 1st Appearance of Earth-3, Crime Syndicate. ★ Appearance of Justice Society of America, Justice Society.
30 ❑ Sep 1964 Cover: 0.12 **NM** value: **115.00**
• **CGC:** 5 graded, best 9.4
The Most Dangerous Earth of All! • Part 2; Justice League of America teams up with Justice Society of America against the Crime Syndicate of America **A:** Mike Sekowsky; Gardner Fox(cover)
31 ❑ Nov 1964 Cover: 0.12 **NM** value: **80.00**
• **CGC:** 5 graded, best 9.4
Riddle of the Runaway Room • Hawkman joins team **A:** Mike Sekowsky; Gardner Fox(cover)
32 ❑ Dec 1964 Cover: 0.12 **NM** value: **52.00**
• **CGC:** 7 graded, best 9.4
Attack of the Star-Bolt Warrior **A:** Mike Sekowsky; Gardner Fox(cover) ★ Origin of Brainstorm. ★ 1st Appearance of Brainstorm. ★ Versus Brain Storm.
33 ❑ Feb 1965 Cover: 0.12 **NM** value: **42.00**
Circ: Statement: **389,285** • **CGC:** 6 graded, best 9.2
Enemy From the Timeless World **A:** Mike Sekowsky; Gardner Fox(cover)
34 ❑ Mar 1965 Cover: 0.12 **NM** value: **58.00**
Circ: Statement: **389,285** • **CGC:** 7 graded, best 9.6
The Deadly Dreams of Doctor Destiny **A:** Mike Sekowsky; Gardner Fox(cover) ★ Appearance of Joker. ★ Versus Doctor Destiny. ★ Versus Dr. Destiny.
35 ❑ May 1965 Cover: 0.12 **NM** value: **42.00**
Circ: Statement: **389,285** • **CGC:** 6 graded, best 9.6
Battle Against the Bodiless Uniforms **A:** Mike Sekowsky; Gardner Fox(cover)
36 ❑ Jun 1965 Cover: 0.12 **NM** value: **42.00**
Circ: Statement: **389,285** • **CGC:** 2 graded, best 9.6
The Case of the Disabled Justice League **A:** Mike Sekowsky; Gardner Fox(cover)
37 ❑ Aug 1965 Cover: 0.12 **NM** value: **85.00**
Circ: Statement: **389,285** • **CGC:** 7 graded, best 9.4
Earth Without a Justice League **A:** Mike Sekowsky; Gardner Fox(cover) ★ 1st Appearance of Earth-A. ★ Appearance of Justice Society of America.
38 ❑ Sep 1965 Cover: 0.12 **NM** value: **85.00**
Circ: Statement: **389,285** • **CGC:** 2 graded, best 9.2
Crisis on Earth-A **A:** Mike Sekowsky; Gardner Fox(cover) ★ Appearance of Justice Society of America.
39 ❑ Nov 1965 Cover: 0.25 **NM** value: **90.00**
Circ: Statement: **389,285** • **CGC:** 7 graded, best 9.6
Starro the Conqueror; Case of the Stolen Super-Powers; When Gravity Went Wild • reprints Brave and the Bold #28, 30, and Justice League of America #5 **A:** Mike Sekowsky; Gardner Fox(cover)
40 ❑ Nov 1965 Cover: 0.12 **NM** value: **42.00**
Circ: Statement: **389,285** • **CGC:** 7 graded, best 9.4
Indestructible Creatures of Nightmare Island • social issue **A:** Mike Sekowsky; Gardner Fox(cover)
41 ❑ Dec 1965 Cover: 0.12 **NM** value: **42.00**
Circ: Statement: **389,285** • **CGC:** 3 graded, best 9.6
The Keymaster of the World! **A:** Mike Sekowsky; Murphy Anderson(cover) **W:** Gardner Fox ★ 1st Appearance of The Key. ★ Versus Key.
42 ❑ Feb 1966 Cover: 0.12 **NM** value: **32.00**
Circ: Statement: **408,219** • **CGC:** 6 graded, best 9.6
Metamorpho Says No! **A:** Mike Sekowsky; Murphy Anderson(cover) **W:** Gardner Fox ★ Appearance of Metamorpho.
43 ❑ Mar 1966 Cover: 0.12 **NM** value: **32.00**
Circ: Statement: **408,219** • **CGC:** 3 graded, best 9.8
The Card Crimes of the Royal Flush Gang! **A:** Mike Sekowsky; Murphy Anderson(cover) **W:** Gardner Fox ★ 1st Appearance of Royal Flush Gang.
44 ❑ May 1966 Cover: 0.12 **NM** value: **32.00**
Circ: Statement: **408,219** • **CGC:** 7 graded, best 9.6
The Plague that Struck the Justice League! **A:** Mike Sekowsky; Murphy Anderson(cover) **W:** Gardner Fox
45 ❑ Jun 1966 Cover: 0.12 **NM** value: **32.00**
Circ: Statement: **408,219** • **CGC:** 5 graded, best 9.6
The Super-Struggle Against Shaggy Man! **A:** Mike Sekowsky; Murphy Anderson(cover) **W:** Gardner Fox ★ 1st Appearance of Shaggy Man. ★ Versus Shaggy Man.
46 ❑ Aug 1966 Cover: 0.12 **NM** value: **105.00**
Circ: Statement: **408,219** • **CGC:** 5 graded, best 9.4
Crisis Between Earth-One and Earth-Two! **A:** Mike Sekowsky; Joe Giella(cover) **W:** Gardner Fox ★ 1st Appearance of Sandman I (in Silver Age). ★ Appearance of Justice Society of America. ★ Versus Solomon Grundy, Blockbuster.
47 ❑ Sep 1966 Cover: 0.12 **NM** value: **48.00**
Circ: Statement: **408,219** • **CGC:** 2 graded, best 9.8
The Bridge Between Earths! **A:** Mike Sekowsky; Joe Giella(cover) **W:** Gardner Fox ★ Appearance of Justice Society of America. ★ Versus Anti-Matter Man.
48 ❑ Oct 1966 Cover: 0.25 **NM** value: **45.00**
Circ: Statement: **408,219** • **CGC:** 11 graded, best 9.8
Challenge of the Weapons Master; Secret of the Sinister Sorcerers; Slave Ship of Space **A:** Mike Sekowsky; Murphy Anderson(cover) **W:** Gardner Fox
49 ❑ Nov 1966 Cover: 0.12 **NM** value: **20.00**
Circ: Statement: **408,219** • **CGC:** 4 graded, best 9.2
Threat of the True-or-False Sorcerer! **A:** Mike Sekowsky; Murphy Anderson(cover) **W:** Gardner Fox
50 ❑ Dec 1966 Cover: 0.12 **NM** value: **20.00**
Circ: Statement: **385,800** • **CGC:** 8 graded, best 9.4
The Lord of Time Attacks the 20th Century! **A:** Mike Sekowsky; Murphy Anderson(cover) **W:** Gardner Fox
51 ❑ Feb 1967 Cover: 0.12 **NM** value: **20.00**
Circ: Statement: **385,800** • **CGC:** 4 graded, best 9.2
Z-As in Zatanna-And Zero Hour! • Has 1966 Statement; avg print run 654,000; avg sales 401,000; avg subs 7,219; avg total paid 408,219; max existent 408,219; 62% of run returned **A:** Mike Sekowsky **W:** Gardner Fox ★ Appearance of Elongated Man.
52 ❑ Mar 1967 Cover: 0.12 **NM** value: **20.00**
Circ: Statement: **385,800** • **CGC:** 4 graded, best 9.6
Missing in Action-5 Justice Leaguers! **A:** Mike Sekowsky **W:** Gardner Fox
53 ❑ May 1967 Cover: 0.12 **NM** value: **20.00**
Circ: Statement: **385,800** • **CGC:** 5 graded, best 9.6
Secret Behind the Stolen Super-Weapons! **A:** Mike Sekowsky **W:** Gardner Fox
54 ❑ Jun 1967 Cover: 0.12 **NM** value: **20.00**
Circ: Statement: **385,800** • **CGC:** 2 graded, best 9.4
History-Making Crimes of the Royal-Flush Gang **A:** Mike Sekowsky **W:** Gardner Fox
55 ❑ Aug 1967 Cover: 0.12 **NM** value: **54.00**
Circ: Statement: **385,800** • **CGC:** 5 graded, best 9.4
The Super-Crisis that Struck Earth-Two • Justice League of America teams up with Justice Society of America **A:** Mike Sekowsky **W:** Gardner Fox
56 ❑ Sep 1967 Cover: 0.12 **NM** value: **38.00**
Circ: Statement: **385,800** • **CGC:** 7 graded, best 9.4
The Negative-Crisis on Earths One-Two • Justice League of America teams up with Justice Society of America **A:** Mike Sekowsky **W:** Gardner Fox
57 ❑ Nov 1967 Cover: 0.12 **NM** value: **18.00**
Circ: Statement: **385,800** • **CGC:** 4 graded, best 9.4
Man, They Name Is-Brother! **A:** Mike Sekowsky **W:** Gardner Fox
58 ❑ Dec 1967 Cover: 0.25 **NM** value: **22.00**
Circ: Statement: **385,800** • **CGC:** 4 graded, best 9.4
• Giant-size. The Wheel of Misfortune!; For Sale-The Justice League!; The World of No Return! • G-41 **A:** Mike Sekowsky **W:** Gardner Fox
59 ❑ Dec 1968 Cover: 0.12 **NM** value: **18.00**
Circ: Statement: **315,500** • **CGC:** 2 graded, best 9.2
The Justice Leaguers' Impossible Adventure! **A:** Mike Sekowsky **W:** Gardner Fox
60 ❑ Feb 1968 Cover: 0.12 **NM** value: **18.00**
Circ: Statement: **315,500** • **CGC:** 6 graded, best 9.4
Winged Warriors of The Immortal Queen! **A:** Mike Sekowsky **W:** Gardner Fox
61 ❑ Mar 1968 Cover: 0.12 **NM** value: **15.00**

Other grades: Multiply prices above by **1.5 for Mint • 2/3 for Very Fine • 1/3 for Fine • 1/5 for Very Good • 1/8 for Good**

Circ: Statement: **315,500** • **CGC:** 5 graded, best 9.4
• Has 1967 Statement; avg print run 630,000; avg sales 381,000; avg subs 4,800; avg total paid 385,800; max existent 385,800; 61% of run returned

62 ❑ May 1968 Cover: 0.12 **NM** value: **15.00**
Circ: Statement: **315,500** • **CGC:** 3 graded, best 9.6

63 ❑ Jun 1968 Cover: 0.12 **NM** value: **15.00**
Circ: Statement: **315,500** • **CGC:** 7 graded, best 9.6

64 ❑ Aug 1968 Cover: 0.12 **NM** value: **15.00**
Circ: Statement: **315,500** • **CGC:** 4 graded, best 9.4
• Return of Red Tornado **A:** Don Perlin ★ Appearance of Justice Society of America.

65 ❑ Sep 1968 Cover: 0.12 **NM** value: **15.00**
Circ: Statement: **315,500** • **CGC:** 5 graded, best 9.6
• Justice League of America teams up with Justice Society of America **A:** Don Perlin ★ Versus T.O.Morrow.

66 ❑ Nov 1968 Cover: 0.12 **NM** value: **15.00**
Circ: Statement: **315,500** • **CGC:** 2 graded, best 9.6
A: Don Perlin

67 ❑ Dec 1968 Cover: 0.25 **NM** value: **15.00**
Circ: Statement: **315,500** • **CGC:** 7 graded, best 9.4

68 ❑ Jan 1969 Cover: 0.12 **NM** value: **15.00**
Circ: Statement: **233,000** • **CGC:** 8 graded, best 9.4
A: Dick Dillin

69 ❑ Feb 1969 Cover: 0.12 **NM** value: **15.00**
Circ: Statement: **233,000** • **CGC:** 6 graded, best 9.8
• Wonder Woman leaves Justice League of America; Has 1969 Statement; avg total paid 233,000 **A:** Dick Dillin

70 ❑ Mar 1969 Cover: 0.12 **NM** value: **15.00**
Circ: Statement: **233,000** • **CGC:** 4 graded, best 9.4
• Has 1968 Statement; avg total paid 315,500 **A:** Dick Dillin ★ Appearance of Creeper.

71 ❑ May 1969 Cover: 0.12 **NM** value: **15.00**
Circ: Statement: **233,000** • **CGC:** 3 graded, best 9.4
• Martian Manhunter leaves Justice League of America **A:** Dick Dillin ★ 1st Appearance of Blue Jay.

72 ❑ Jun 1969 Cover: 0.12 **NM** value: **15.00**
Circ: Statement: **233,000** • **CGC:** 5 graded, best 9.4
A: Dick Dillin

73 ❑ Aug 1969 Cover: 0.15 **NM** value: **15.00**
Circ: Statement: **233,000** • **CGC:** 3 graded, best 9.6
A: Dick Dillin ★ Appearance of Justice Society of America.

74 ❑ Sep 1969 Cover: 0.15 **NM** value: **13.00**
Circ: Statement: **233,000** • **CGC:** 2 graded, best 9.4
Where Death Fears to Tread! • Black Canary goes to Earth-1 **A:** Dick Dillin **W:** Denny O'Neil ★ Appearance of Justice Society. ★ Death of Larry Lance.

75 ❑ Nov 1969 Cover: 0.15 **NM** value: **13.00**
Circ: Statement: **233,000** • **CGC:** 2 graded, best 9.4
A: Dick Dillin ★ 1st Appearance of Black Canary II (Dinah Lance).

76 ❑ Dec 1969 Cover: 0.25 **NM** value: **15.00**
Circ: Statement: **233,000** • **CGC:** 4 graded, best 9.4
• giant; reprints #7 and #12; pin-ups of Justice Society of America and Seven Soldiers **A:** Murphy Anderson; Dick Dillin

77 ❑ Dec 1969 Cover: 0.15 **NM** value: **9.00**
Circ: Statement: **200,715** • **CGC:** 4 graded, best 9.2
A: Dick Dillin

78 ❑ Feb 1970 Cover: 0.15 **NM** value: **9.00**
Circ: Statement: **200,715** • **CGC:** 3 graded, best 9.6
A: Dick Dillin

79 ❑ Mar 1970 Cover: 0.15 **NM** value: **9.00**
Circ: Statement: **200,715** • **CGC:** 1 graded, best 6.5
A: Dick Dillin

80 ❑ May 1970 Cover: 0.15 **NM** value: **9.00**
Circ: Statement: **200,715** • **CGC:** 1 graded, best 4.0
A: Dick Dillin

81 ❑ Jun 1970 Cover: 0.15 **NM** value: **8.00**
Circ: Statement: **200,715** • **CGC:** 3 graded, best 9.4
A: Dick Dillin

82 ❑ Aug 1970 Cover: 0.15 **NM** value: **8.00**
Circ: Statement: **200,715** • **CGC:** 1 graded, best 3.0
A: Dick Dillin

83 ❑ Sep 1970 Cover: 0.15 **NM** value: **8.00**
Circ: Statement: **200,715** • **CGC:** 1 graded, best 7.0
A: Dick Dillin ★ Appearance of Spectre.

84 ❑ Nov 1970 Cover: 0.15 **NM** value: **8.00**
Circ: Statement: **200,715** • **CGC:** 2 graded, best 9.2
A: Dick Dillin

85 ❑ Dec 1970 Cover: 0.25 **NM** value: **12.00**
Circ: Statement: **200,715** • **CGC:** 5 graded, best 9.4
• Giant-size.

86 ❑ Dec 1970 Cover: 0.15 **NM** value: **7.00**
Circ: Statement: **200,715** • **CGC:** 1 graded, best 5.0
A: Dick Dillin

87 ❑ Feb 1971 Cover: 0.15 **NM** value: **7.00**
Circ: Statement: **210,108** • **CGC:** 6 graded, best 9.4
A: Dick Dillin ★ 1st Appearance of Silver Sorceress.

88 ❑ Mar 1971 Cover: 0.15 **NM** value: **7.00**
Circ: Statement: **210,108** • **CGC:** 1 graded, best 4.0
• Has 1970 Statement; avg print run 381,212; avg sales 200,223; avg subs 492; avg total paid 200,223; avg subs 492; avg total paid 200,715; max existent 200,715; 53% of run returned **A:** Dick Dillin

89 ❑ May 1971 Cover: 0.15 **NM** value: **7.00**
Circ: Statement: **210,108** • **CGC:** 3 graded, best 9.4
A: Dick Dillin

90 ❑ Jun 1971 Cover: 0.15 **NM** value: **7.00**
Circ: Statement: **210,108** • **CGC:** 2 graded, best 9.4
A: Dick Dillin

91 ❑ Aug 1971 Cover: 0.25 **NM** value: **7.00**
Circ: Statement: **210,108** • **CGC:** 1 graded, best 3.0
Aftershocks, Part 1 **A:** Dick Dillin

92 ❑ Sep 1971 Cover: 0.25 **NM** value: **7.00**
Circ: Statement: **210,108** • **CGC:** 3 graded, best 9.4
A: Dick Dillin ★ 1st Appearance of Starbreaker.

93 ❑ Nov 1971 Cover: 0.35 **NM** value: **12.00**
Circ: Statement: **210,108** • **CGC:** 3 graded, best 9.4
• Giant-size.

94 ❑ Nov 1971 Cover: 0.25 **NM** value: **40.00**
Circ: Statement: **210,108** • **CGC:** 12 graded, best 9.4
• Reprints Adventure Comics #40 **A:** Neal Adams; Dick Dillin ★ Origin of Sandman I (Wesley Dodds). ★ 1st Appearance of Merlyn. ★ Appearance of Deadman.

95 ❑ Dec 1971 Cover: 0.25 **NM** value: **12.00**
Circ: Statement: **210,108** • **CGC:** 4 graded, best 9.4
• Reprints More Fun Comics #67 and All-American Comics #25 **A:** Dick Dillin ★ Origin of Doctor Midnight, Doctor Fate.

96 ❑ Feb 1972 Cover: 0.25 **NM** value: **12.00**
Circ: Statement: **168,871** • **CGC:** 3 graded, best 9.6
A: Dick Dillin ★ Versus Cosmic Vampire.

97 ❑ Mar 1972 Cover: 0.25 **NM** value: **12.00**
Circ: Statement: **168,871** • **CGC:** 5 graded, best 9.6
• Has 1971 Statement; avg print run 362,500; avg sales 209,835; avg subs' 273; avg total paid 210,108; max existent 210,108; 58% of run returned **A:** Dick Dillin ★ Origin of Justice League of America.

98 ❑ May 1972 Cover: 0.25 **NM** value: **7.00**
Circ: Statement: **168,871** • **CGC:** 6 graded, best 9.4
A: Dick Dillin ★ Appearance of Sargon.

99 ❑ Jun 1972 Cover: 0.25 **NM** value: **12.00**
Circ: Statement: **168,871** • **CGC:** 4 graded, best 9.2
A: Dick Dillin ★ Appearance of Sargon.

100 ❑ Aug 1972 Cover: 0.20 **NM** value: **12.00**
Circ: Statement: **168,871** • **CGC:** 1 graded, best 6.5
• Return of Seven Soldiers of Victory **A:** Dick Dillin

101 ❑ Sep 1972 Cover: 0.20 **NM** value: **10.00**
Circ: Statement: **168,871** • **CGC:** 8 graded, best 9.8
• Justice League of America teams up with Justice Society of America **A:** Dick Dillin

102 ❑ Oct 1972 Cover: 0.20 **NM** value: **10.00**
Circ: Statement: **168,871** • **CGC:** 3 graded, best 9.6
• Justice League of America teams up with Justice Society of America **A:** Dick Dillin ★ Death of Red Tornado.

103 ❑ Dec 1972 Cover: 0.20 **NM** value: **6.00**
Circ: Statement: **168,871** • **CGC:** 2 graded, best 9.4
A: Dick Giordano; Dick Dillin ★ Appearance of Phantom Stranger.

104 ❑ Feb 1973 Cover: 0.20 **NM** value: **6.00**
Circ: Statement: **187,051** • **CGC:** 1 graded, best 9.0
The Shaggy Man Will Get You if You Don't Watch Out! **A:** Dick Giordano; Dick Dillin **W:** Len Wein ★ Versus Hector Hammond. ★ Versus Shaggy Man.

105 ❑ May 1973 Cover: 0.20 **NM** value: **6.00**
Circ: Statement: **187,051**
• Elongated Man joins the Justice League of America; Has 1972 Statement; avg print run 345,000; avg sales 167,296; avg subs 1,575; avg total paid 168,871; max existent 168,871; 49% of run returned **A:** Dick Giordano; Dick Dillin

106 ❑ Aug 1973 Cover: 0.20 **NM** value: **6.00**
Circ: Statement: **187,051** • **CGC:** 2 graded, best 9.2
• Red Tornado (new) joins the Justice League of America **A:** Dick Giordano; Dick Dillin

107 ❑ Oct 1973 Cover: 0.20 **NM** value: **12.00**
Circ: Statement: **187,051** • **CGC:** 2 graded, best 9.0
A: Dick Giordano; Dick Dillin ★ 1st Appearance of Freedom Fighters, Earth-X. ★ Appearance of Justice Society of America.

108 ❑ Dec 1973 Cover: 0.20 **NM** value: **9.00**
Circ: Statement: **187,051** • **CGC:** 7 graded, best 9.6
A: Dick Giordano; Dick Dillin ★ Appearance of Justice Society of America, Freedom Fighters.

109 ❑ Feb 1974 Cover: 0.20 **NM** value: **6.00**
Circ: Statement: **189,392** • **CGC:** 7 graded, best 9.6
• Hawkman resigns from Justice League of America **A:** Dick Giordano; Dick Dillin

110 ❑ Apr 1974 Cover: 0.50 **NM** value: **6.00**
Circ: Statement: **189,392** • **CGC:** 2 graded, best 9.2
The Man Who Murdered Santa Claus; The Plight of a Nation; Z – as in Zatanna – and Zero Hour • Justice Society of America pin-up **A:** Dick Giordano; Dick Dillin **W:** Len Wein

111 ❑ Jun 1974 Cover: 0.60 **NM** value: **6.00**
Circ: Statement: **189,392** • **CGC:** 2 graded, best 9.4
• Has 1973 Statement; avg print run 378,125; avg sales 184,971; avg subs 2,080; avg total paid 187,051; max existent 187,051; 50% of run returned **A:** Dick Giordano; Dick Dillin ★ Versus Libra.

112 ❑ Aug 1974 Cover: 0.60 **NM** value: **6.00**
Circ: Statement: **189,392** • **CGC:** 5 graded, best 9.6
A: Dick Giordano; Dick Dillin ★ Versus Amazo.

113 ❑ Oct 1974 Cover: 0.60 **NM** value: **6.00**
Circ: Statement: **189,392** • **CGC:** 3 graded, best 9.6
A: Dick Giordano; Dick Dillin

114 ❑ Dec 1974 Cover: 0.60 **NM** value: **6.00**
Circ: Statement: **189,392**
The Return of Anakronus!; Crisis on Earth-Three! • Return of Snapper Carr **A:** Dick Giordano; Dick Dillin **W:** Len Wein ★ Versus Anakronus.

115 ❑ Feb 1975 Cover: 0.60 **NM** value: **6.00**
Circ: Statement: **166,000** • **CGC:** 2 graded, best 9.2
A: Dick Giordano; Dick Dillin

116 ❑ Mar 1975 Cover: 0.60 **NM** value: **6.00**
Circ: Statement: **166,000** • **CGC:** 2 graded, best 9.0
• Return of Hawkman **A:** Dick Giordano; Dick Dillin ★ Versus Matter Master.

117 ❑ Apr 1975 Cover: 0.25 **NM** value: **4.00**
Circ: Statement: **166,000**
• Hawkman rejoins JLA **A:** Frank McLaughlin; Dick Dillin

118 ❑ May 1975 Cover: 0.25 **NM** value: **4.00**
Circ: Statement: **166,000**
• Has 1974 Statement; avg total paid 189,392 **A:** Frank McLaughlin; Dick Dillin

119 ❑ Jun 1975 Cover: 0.25 **NM** value: **4.00**
Circ: Statement: **166,000** • **CGC:** 1 graded, best 9.4
A: Frank McLaughlin; Dick Dillin

120 ❑ Jul 1975 Cover: 0.25 **NM** value: **4.00**
Circ: Statement: **166,000** • **CGC:** 1 graded, best 7.0
A: Frank McLaughlin; Dick Dillin ★ Appearance of Adam Strange. ★ Versus Kanjar Ro.

121 ❑ Aug 1975 Cover: 0.25 **NM** value: **4.00**
Circ: Statement: **166,000** • **CGC:** 2 graded, best 9.6
A: Frank McLaughlin; Dick Dillin

122 ❑ Sep 1975 Cover: 0.25 **NM** value: **4.00**
Circ: Statement: **166,000** • **CGC:** 1 graded, best 9.0
A: Frank McLaughlin; Dick Dillin ★ Versus Doctor Light. ★ Versus Dr. Light.

123 ❑ Oct 1975 Cover: 0.25 **NM** value: **4.00**
Circ: Statement: **166,000** • **CGC:** 1 graded, best 9.8
A: Frank McLaughlin; Dick Dillin ★ 1st Appearance of Earth-Prime (named). ★ Appearance of Justice Society of America.

124 ❑ Nov 1975 Cover: 0.25 **NM** value: **4.00**
Circ: Statement: **166,000**
A: Frank McLaughlin; Dick Dillin ★ Appearance of Justice Society of America.

125 ❑ Dec 1975 Cover: 0.25 **NM** value: **4.00**
Circ: Statement: **166,000**
A: Frank McLaughlin; Dick Dillin

126 ❑ Jan 1976 Cover: 0.26 **NM** value: **4.00**
Circ: Statement: **193,000**
• Joker **A:** Frank McLaughlin; Dick Dillin

127 ❑ Feb 1976 Cover: 0.25 **NM** value: **4.00**
Circ: Statement: **193,000**
A: Frank McLaughlin; Dick Dillin

128 ❑ Mar 1976 Cover: 0.25 **NM** value: **4.00**
Circ: Statement: **193,000**
• Wonder Woman rejoins **A:** Frank McLaughlin; Dick Dillin

129 ❑ Apr 1976 Cover: 0.30 **NM** value: **4.00**
Circ: Statement: **193,000** • **CGC:** 1 graded, best 9.6
A: Frank McLaughlin; Dick Dillin ★ Death of Red Tornado (new).

130 ❑ May 1976 Cover: 0.30 **NM** value: **4.00**
Circ: Statement: **193,000** • **CGC:** 1 graded, best 9.6
• Has 1975 Statement; avg print run 357,000; avg sales 162,000; avg subs 4,000; avg total paid 166,000; samples 1,000; max existent 167,000; 47% of run returned **A:** Frank McLaughlin; Dick Dillin

131 ❑ Jun 1976 Cover: 0.30 **NM** value: **3.50**
Circ: Statement: **193,000** • **CGC:** 1 graded, best 9.6
A: Frank McLaughlin; Dick Dillin

132 ❑ Jul 1976 Cover: 0.30 **NM** value: **3.50**
Circ: Statement: **193,000** • **CGC:** 2 graded, best 9.6
• Bicentennial #6 **A:** Frank McLaughlin; Dick Dillin

133 ❑ Aug 1976 Cover: 0.30 **NM** value: **3.50**
Circ: Statement: **193,000** • **CGC:** 1 graded, best 9.4
A: Frank McLaughlin; Dick Dillin

134 ❑ Sep 1976 Cover: 0.30 **NM** value: **3.50**
Circ: Statement: **193,000** • **CGC:** 1 graded, best 9.6
A: Frank McLaughlin; Dick Dillin

135 ❑ Oct 1976 Cover: 0.30 **NM** value: **3.50**
Circ: Statement: **193,000** • **CGC:** 1 graded, best 9.6
Crisis on Earth-S **A:** Frank McLaughlin; Dick Dillin ★ 1st Appearance of Earth-S (named).

136 ❑ Nov 1976 Cover: 0.30 **NM** value: **3.50**
Circ: Statement: **193,000** • **CGC:** 2 graded, best 9.6
Crisis on Earth-S **A:** Frank McLaughlin; Dick Dillin

137 ❑ Dec 1976 Cover: 0.30 **NM** value: **3.50**
Circ: Statement: **193,000**
Crisis on Earth-S • Superman vs. Captain Marvel (Golden Age) **A:** Frank McLaughlin; Dick Dillin ★ Appearance of Marvel Family.

138 ❑ Jan 1977 Cover: 0.30 **NM** value: **3.50**
Circ: Statement: **151,982** • **CGC:** 3 graded, best 9.4
• double-sized. **A:** Frank McLaughlin; Dick Dillin

139 ❑ Feb 1977 Cover: 0.50 **NM** value: **3.50**
Circ: Statement: **151,982**
• double-sized. **A:** Frank McLaughlin; Dick Dillin

140 ❑ Mar 1977 Cover: 0.50 **NM** value: **3.50**
Circ: Statement: **151,982** • **CGC:** 1 graded, best 9.2
• double-sized. **A:** Frank McLaughlin; Dick Dillin ★ Appearance of Manhunters.

141 ❑ Apr 1977 Cover: 0.50 **NM** value: **3.50**
Circ: Statement: **151,982**
• double-sized. **A:** Frank McLaughlin; Dick Dillin ★ Appearance of Manhunters.

142 ❑ May 1977 Cover: 0.50 **NM** value: **3.50**
Circ: Statement: **151,982**
• double-sized. • Has 1976 Statement; avg print run 402,000; avg sales 188,000; avg subs 5,000; avg total paid 193,000; max existent 193,000; 48% of run returned **A:** Frank McLaughlin; Dick Dillin ★ 1st Appearance of The Construct.

143 ❑ Jun 1977 Cover: 0.60 **NM** value: **3.50**
Circ: Statement: **151,982**
• double-sized. **A:** Frank McLaughlin; Dick Dillin ★ 1st Appearance of Privateer.

144 ❑ Jul 1977 Cover: 0.60 **NM** value: **3.50**
Circ: Statement: **151,982** • **CGC:** 1 graded, best 8.5
• double-sized. **A:** Frank McLaughlin; Dick Dillin ★ Origin of Justice League of America.

145 ❑ Aug 1977 Cover: 0.60 **NM** value: **3.50**
Circ: Statement: **151,982**
A: Frank McLaughlin; Dick Dillin

146 ❑ Sep 1977 Cover: 0.60 **NM** value: **3.50**
Circ: Statement: **151,982**
A: Frank McLaughlin; Dick Dillin

147 ❑ Oct 1977 Cover: 0.60 **NM** value: **3.50**
Circ: Statement: **151,982**
A: Frank McLaughlin; Dick Dillin ★ Appearance of Legion. ★ Versus Mordru.

148 ❑ Nov 1977 Cover: 0.60 **NM** value: **3.50**
Circ: Statement: **151,982**
A: Frank McLaughlin; Dick Dillin ★ Appearance of Legion. ★ Versus Mordru.

149 ❑ Dec 1977 Cover: 0.60 **NM** value: **3.50**
Circ: Statement: **151,982**
A: Frank McLaughlin; Dick Dillin ★ 1st Appearance of Star-Tsar.

150 ❑ Jan 1978 Cover: 0.60 **NM** value: **3.50**
Circ: Statement: **126,809** • **CGC:** 1 graded, best 9.4
A: Frank McLaughlin; Dick Dillin ★ Versus Key.

151 ❑ Feb 1978 Cover: 0.60 **NM** value: **3.00**
Circ: Statement: **126,809**
A: Frank McLaughlin; Dick Dillin

152 ❑ Mar 1978 Cover: 0.60 **NM** value: **3.00**
Circ: Statement: **126,809**
A: Frank McLaughlin; Dick Dillin

CGC-graded: Multiply prices above by **33 for 9.9 M** • **16 for 9.8 NM/M** • **7 for 9.6 NM+** • **5 for 9.4 NM** • **2.5 for 9.2 NM-** • **1.5 for 9.0 VF/NM**

153 ❑ Apr 1978 Cover: 0.60 **NM** value: **3.00**
Circ: Statement: **126,809**
A: Frank McLaughlin; Dick Dillin ★ 1st Appearance of Ultraa.

154 ❑ May 1978 Cover: 0.60 **NM** value: **3.00**
Circ: Statement: **126,809**
• Has 1977 Statement; avg total paid 151,982 **A:** Frank McLaughlin; Dick Dillin ★ Versus Doctor Destiny. ★ Versus Dr. Destiny.

155 ❑ Jun 1978 Cover: 0.60 **NM** value: **3.00**
Circ: Statement: **126,809**
A: Frank McLaughlin; Dick Dillin

156 ❑ Jul 1978 Cover: 0.60 **NM** value: **3.00**
Circ: Statement: **126,809**
A: Frank McLaughlin; Dick Dillin ★ Appearance of Phantom Stranger.

157 ❑ Aug 1978 Cover: 0.60 **NM** value: **3.00**
Circ: Statement: **126,809**
A: Frank McLaughlin; Dick Dillin

158 ❑ Sep 1978 Cover: 0.50 **NM** value: **3.00**
Circ: Statement: **126,809**
A: Frank McLaughlin; Dick Dillin

159 ❑ Oct 1978 Cover: 0.60 **NM** value: **3.00**
Circ: Statement: **126,809** • **CGC:** 1 graded, best 6.5
A: Frank McLaughlin; Dick Dillin; Frank McLaughlinJSA **W:** Joe Staton ★ Appearance of Enemy Ace, Justice Society of America, Black Pirate, Viking Prince, Miss Liberty, Jonah Hex.

160 ❑ Nov 1978 Cover: 0.60 **NM** value: **3.00**
Circ: Statement: **126,809** • **CGC:** 1 graded, best 9.0
A: Frank McLaughlin; Dick Dillin; Frank McLaughlinJSA **W:** Joe Staton ★ Appearance of Enemy Ace, Justice Society of America, Black Pirate, Viking Prince, Miss Liberty, Jonah Hex.

161 ❑ Dec 1978 Cover: 0.40 **NM** value: **3.00**
Circ: Statement: **126,809**
• Zatanna joins the Justice League of America **A:** Frank McLaughlin; Dick Dillin

162 ❑ Jan 1979 Cover: 0.40 **NM** value: **3.00**
Circ: Statement: **128,660**
A: Frank McLaughlin; Dick Dillin

163 ❑ Feb 1979 Cover: 0.40 **NM** value: **3.00**
Circ: Statement: **128,660**
A: Frank McLaughlin; Dick Dillin

164 ❑ Mar 1979 Cover: 0.40 **NM** value: **3.00**
Circ: Statement: **128,660**
A: Frank McLaughlin; Dick Dillin

165 ❑ Apr 1979 Cover: 0.40 **NM** value: **3.00**
Circ: Statement: **128,660**
A: Frank McLaughlin; Dick Dillin

166 ❑ May 1979 Cover: 0.40 **NM** value: **3.00**
Circ: Statement: **128,660**
• Has 1978 Statement; avg total paid 126,809 **A:** Frank McLaughlin; Dick Dillin ★ Versus Secret Society of Super-Villains.

167 ❑ Jun 1979 Cover: 0.40 **NM** value: **3.00**
Circ: Statement: **128,660**
A: Frank McLaughlin; Dick Dillin

168 ❑ Jul 1979 Cover: 0.40 **NM** value: **3.00**
Circ: Statement: **128,660**
A: Frank McLaughlin; Dick Dillin ★ Versus Secret Society of Super-Villains.

169 ❑ Aug 1979 Cover: 0.40 **NM** value: **3.00**
Circ: Statement: **128,660**
A: Frank McLaughlin; Dick Dillin

170 ❑ Sep 1979 Cover: 0.40 **NM** value: **3.00**
Circ: Statement: **128,660**
A: Frank McLaughlin; Dick Dillin ★ Appearance of Supergirl.

171 ❑ Oct 1979 Cover: 0.40 **NM** value: **3.00**
Circ: Statement: **128,660**
A: Frank McLaughlin; Dick Dillin ★ Appearance of Justice Society of America. ★ Death of Mr. Terrific.

172 ❑ Nov 1979 Cover: 0.40 **NM** value: **2.50**
Circ: Statement: **128,660** • **CGC:** 1 graded, best 9.8
A: Frank McLaughlin; Dick Dillin ★ Appearance of Justice Society of America.

173 ❑ Dec 1979 Cover: 0.40 **NM** value: **2.50**
Circ: Statement: **128,660**
A: Frank McLaughlin; Dick Dillin ★ Appearance of Black Lightning.

174 ❑ Jan 1980 Cover: 0.40 **NM** value: **2.50**
Circ: Statement: **131,587**
A: Frank McLaughlin; Dick Dillin ★ Appearance of Black Lightning.

175 ❑ Feb 1980 Cover: 0.40 **NM** value: **2.50**
Circ: Statement: **131,587**
A: Frank McLaughlin; Dick Dillin ★ Versus Doctor Destiny. ★ Versus Dr. Destiny.

176 ❑ Mar 1980 Cover: 0.40 **NM** value: **2.50**
Circ: Statement: **131,587**
A: Frank McLaughlin; Dick Dillin ★ Versus Doctor Destiny. ★ Versus Dr. Destiny.

177 ❑ Apr 1980 Cover: 0.40 **NM** value: **2.50**
Circ: Statement: **131,587**
• Has 1979 Statement; avg print run 283,796; avg sales 126,543; avg subs 2,117; avg total paid 128,660; max existent 128,660; 45% of run returned **A:** Frank McLaughlin; Dick Dillin ★ Appearance of J'onn J'onzz. ★ Versus Despero.

178 ❑ May 1980 Cover: 0.40 **NM** value: **2.50**
Circ: Statement: **131,587**
A: Frank McLaughlin; Dick Dillin **C:** Jim Starlin ★ Versus Despero.

179 ❑ Jun 1980 Cover: 0.40 **NM** value: **2.50**
Circ: Statement: **131,587**
• Firestorm joins the Justice League of America **A:** Frank McLaughlin; Dick Dillin **C:** Jim Starlin

180 ❑ Jul 1980 Cover: 0.40 **NM** value: **2.50**
Circ: Statement: **131,587**
A: Frank McLaughlin; Dick Dillin **C:** Jim Starlin

181 ❑ Aug 1980 Cover: 0.40 **NM** value: **2.50**
Circ: Statement: **131,587**
• Green Arrow leaves team **A:** Frank McLaughlin; Dick Dillin ★ Appearance of Snapper Carr.

182 ❑ Sep 1980 Cover: 0.50 **NM** value: **2.50**
Circ: Statement: **131,587**
• Elongated Man back-up **A:** Frank McLaughlin; Dick Dillin **C:** Dave Cockrum ★ Appearance of Felix Faust.

183 ❑ Oct 1980 Cover: 0.50 **NM** value: **2.50**
Circ: Statement: **131,587**
A: Frank McLaughlin; Dick Dillin; Frank McLaughlinJSA **C:** Jim Starlin **W:** Joe Staton ★ Appearance of Orion, Justice Society of America, Metron, Mr. Miracle. ★ Versus Icicle. ★ Versus Shade. ★ Versus Fiddler. ★ Versus Darkseid.

184 ❑ Nov 1980 Cover: 0.50 **NM** value: **2.50**
Circ: Statement: **131,587**
A: Frank McLaughlin; Dick Dillin; Frank McLaughlinJSA **C:** George Pérez **W:** Joe Staton ★ Appearance of Justice Society of America, New Gods. ★ Versus Darkseid. ★ Versus Injustice Society.

185 ❑ Dec 1980 Cover: 0.50 **NM** value: **2.50**
Circ: Statement: **131,587**
A: Frank McLaughlin; Dick Dillin; Frank McLaughlinJSA **C:** Jim Starlin **W:** Joe Staton ★ Appearance of Justice Society of America, New Gods. ★ Versus Darkseid. ★ Versus Injustice Society.

186 ❑ Jan 1981 Cover: 0.50 **NM** value: **2.50**
Circ: Statement: **121,587**
A: Frank McLaughlin; George Pérez ★ Versus Shaggy Man.

187 ❑ Feb 1981 Cover: 0.50 **NM** value: **2.50**
Circ: Statement: **121,587**
A: Frank McLaughlin; Don Heck; Ross Andru **C:** Dick Giordano

188 ❑ Mar 1981 Cover: 0.50 **NM** value: **2.50**
Circ: Statement: **121,587**
A: Frank McLaughlin; Don Heck; Ross Andru **C:** Dick Giordano

189 ❑ Apr 1981 Cover: 0.50 **NM** value: **2.50**
Circ: Statement: **121,587**
A: Frank McLaughlin; Rich Buckler **C:** Brian Bolland ★ Versus Starro.

190 ❑ May 1981 Cover: 0.50 **NM** value: **2.50**
Circ: Statement: **121,587**
• Has 1980 Statement; avg print run 329,301; avg sales 128,042; avg subs 3,545; avg total paid 131,587; max existent 131,587; 40% of run returned **A:** Rich Buckler **C:** Brian Bolland ★ Versus Starro.

191 ❑ Jun 1981 Cover: 0.50 **NM** value: **2.50**
Circ: Statement: **121,587**
A: Rich Buckler **C:** Dick Giordano ★ Versus Amazo. ★ Versus The Key.

192 ❑ Jul 1981 Cover: 0.50 **NM** value: **2.50**
Circ: Statement: **121,587** • **CGC:** 1 graded, best 9.6
A: George Pérez ★ Origin of Red Tornado. ★ Appearance of T.O. Morrow.

193 ❑ Aug 1981 Cover: 0.50 **NM** value: **2.50**
Circ: Statement: **121,587** • **CGC:** 1 graded, best 9.4
A: George Pérez ★ 1st Appearance of Danette Reilly, All-Star Squadron.

194 ❑ Sep 1981 Cover: 0.50 **NM** value: **2.50**
Circ: Statement: **121,587**
A: George Pérez

195 ❑ Oct 1981 Cover: 0.60 **NM** value: **2.50**
Circ: Statement: **121,587**
A: George Pérez ★ Appearance of Justice Society of America. ★ Versus Secret Society of Super-Villains.

196 ❑ Nov 1981 Cover: 0.60 **NM** value: **2.50**
Circ: Statement: **121,587**
A: George Pérez ★ Appearance of Justice Society of America. ★ Versus Secret Society of Super-Villains.

197 ❑ Dec 1981 Cover: 0.60 **NM** value: **2.50**
Circ: Statement: **121,587**
A: George Pérez ★ Appearance of Justice Society of America. ★ Versus Secret Society of Super-Villains.

198 ❑ Jan 1982 Cover: 0.60 **NM** value: **2.50**
Circ: Statement: **131,892**
A: Don Heck; Ross Andru **C:** Dick Giordano ★ Appearance of Scalphunter, Bat Lash, Cinnamon, Jonah Hex. ★ Versus Lord of Time.

199 ❑ Feb 1982 Cover: 0.60 **NM** value: **2.50**
Circ: Statement: **131,892** • **CGC:** 1 graded, best 8.5
A: Don Heck **C:** George Pérez ★ Appearance of Scalphunter, Bat Lash, Cinnamon, Jonah Hex. ★ Versus Lord of Time.

200 ❑ Mar 1982 Cover: 1.50 **NM** value: **4.00**
Circ: Statement: **131,892** • **CGC:** 1 graded, best 9.2
• Anniversary issue. • Green Arrow rejoins **A:** Todd Dezuniga; Carmine Infantino; George Pérez; Dick Giordano; Joe Kubert; Gil Kane ★ Origin of JLA. ★ Appearance of Snapper Carr.

201 ❑ Apr 1982 Cover: 0.60 **NM** value: **2.00**
Circ: Statement: **131,892**
A: Don Heck **C:** George Pérez ★ Versus Ultraa.

202 ❑ May 1982 Cover: 0.60 **NM** value: **2.00**
Circ: Statement: **131,892**
• Has 1981 Statement; avg print run 303,386; avg sales 121,587; avg subs 3,390; avg total paid 121,587; max existent 124,977; 40% of run returned **A:** Don Heck **C:** George Pérez

203 ❑ Jun 1982 Cover: 0.60 **NM** value: **2.00**
Circ: Statement: **131,892**
A: Don Heck **C:** George Pérez ★ Versus Hector Hammond. ★ Versus New Royal Flush Gang.

204 ❑ Jul 1982 Cover: 0.60 **NM** value: **2.00**
Circ: Statement: **131,892**
A: Don Heck **C:** George Pérez ★ Versus Hector Hammond. ★ Versus New Royal Flush Gang.

205 ❑ Aug 1982 Cover: 0.60 **NM** value: **2.00**
Circ: Statement: **131,892**
A: Don Heck **C:** George Pérez ★ Versus Hector Hammond. ★ Versus New Royal Flush Gang.

206 ❑ Sep 1982 Cover: 0.60 **NM** value: **2.00**
Circ: Statement: **131,892**
A: Don Heck; Romeo Tanghal **C:** Dave Cockrum ★ Versus Rath. ★ Versus Ghast. ★ Versus Abnegazar.

207 ❑ Oct 1982 Cover: 0.60 **NM** value: **2.00**
Circ: Statement: **131,892**
• Justice Society of America, Justice League of America, and All-Star Squadron team up **A:** Don Heck; Romeo Tanghal; Romeo TanghalJSA **C:** George Pérez **W:** Joe Staton ★ Appearance of Justice Society of America, All-Star Squadron. ★ Versus Per Degaton. ★ Versus Crime Syndicate.

208 ❑ Nov 1982 Cover: 0.60 **NM** value: **2.00**
Circ: Statement: **131,892**
📖 The Bomb-Blast Heard 'Round the World! • Justice Society of America, Justice League of America, and All-Star Squadron team up **A:** Don Heck; Don HeckJSA **C:** George Pérez **W:** Joe Staton ★ Appearance of Justice Society of America, All-Star Squadron. ★ Versus Per Degaton. ★ Versus Crime Syndicate.

209 ❑ Dec 1982 Cover: 0.60 **NM** value: **1.75**
Circ: Statement: **131,892**
📖 Let Old Acquaintances Be Forgot • Justice Society of America, Justice League of America, and All-Star Squadron team up **A:** Don Heck; Don HeckJSA **C:** George Pérez **W:** Joe Staton ★ Appearance of Justice Society of America, All-Star Squadron. ★ Versus Per Degaton. ★ Versus Crime Syndicate.

210 ❑ Jan 1983 Cover: 0.60 **NM** value: **1.75**
Circ: Statement: **122,397**
• first publication of story slated for 1977 DC tabloid **A:** Rich Buckler

211 ❑ Feb 1983 Cover: 0.60 **NM** value: **1.75**
Circ: Statement: **122,397**
• first publication of story slated for 1977 DC tabloid **A:** Rich Buckler

212 ❑ Mar 1983 Cover: 0.60 **NM** value: **1.75**
Circ: Statement: **122,397**
• concludes story slated for 1977 DC tabloid **A:** Rich Buckler **C:** George Pérez

213 ❑ Apr 1983 Cover: 0.60 **NM** value: **1.75**
Circ: Statement: **122,397**
A: Don Heck; Romeo Tanghal **C:** George Pérez

214 ❑ May 1983 Cover: 0.60 **NM** value: **1.75**
Circ: Statement: **122,397**
• Has 1982 Statement; avg print run 319,248; avg sales 128,275; avg subs 3,617; avg total paid 131,892; max existent 131,892; 41% of run returned **A:** Don Heck; Romeo Tanghal **C:** George Pérez

215 ❑ Jun 1983 Cover: 0.60 **NM** value: **1.75**
Circ: Statement: **122,397**
A: Don Heck; Romeo Tanghal **C:** George Pérez

216 ❑ Jul 1983 Cover: 0.60 **NM** value: **1.75**
Circ: Statement: **122,397**
A: Don Heck

217 ❑ Aug 1983 Cover: 0.60 **NM** value: **1.75**
Circ: Statement: **122,397**
C: George Pérez ★ Death of Garn Daanuth.

218 ❑ Sep 1983 Cover: 0.60 **NM** value: **1.75**
Circ: Statement: **122,397**
★ Appearance of Amazo. ★ Versus Prof. Ivo.

219 ❑ Oct 1983 Cover: 0.60 **NM** value: **1.75**
Circ: Statement: **122,397**
A: Joe Staton **C:** George Pérez **W:** Joe Staton ★ Appearance of Justice Society of America, Thunderbolt.

220 ❑ Nov 1983 Cover: 0.60 **NM** value: **1.75**
Circ: Statement: **122,397**
📖 The Doppelganger Gambit **A:** Joe Staton **C:** George Pérez **W:** Joe Staton ★ Origin of Black Canary. ★ Appearance of Justice Society of America, Sargon.

221 ❑ Dec 1983 Cover: 0.75 **NM** value: **1.50**
Circ: Statement: **122,397**
📖 Beasts **A:** Pablo Marcos; Chuck Patton **W:** Gerry Conway

222 ❑ Jan 1984 Cover: 0.75 **NM** value: **1.50**
Circ: Statement: **110,664**

223 ❑ Feb 1984 Cover: 0.75 **NM** value: **1.50**
Circ: Statement: **110,664**

224 ❑ Mar 1984 Cover: 0.75 **NM** value: **1.50**
Circ: Statement: **110,664**
W: Kurt Busiek ★ Versus Paragon.

225 ❑ Apr 1984 Cover: 0.75 **NM** value: **1.50**
Circ: Statement: **110,664**
• Has 1983 Statement; avg print run 293,990; avg sales 120,285; avg subs 2,112; avg total paid 122,397; 42% of run returned

226 ❑ May 1984 Cover: 0.75 **NM** value: **1.50**
Circ: Statement: **110,664**
C: Ross Andru

227 ❑ Jun 1984 Cover: 0.75 **NM** value: **1.50**
Circ: Statement: **110,664**

228 ❑ Jul 1984 Cover: 0.75 **NM** value: **1.50**
Circ: Statement: **110,664**
• J'onn J'onzz returns

229 ❑ Aug 1984 Cover: 0.75 **NM** value: **1.50**
Circ: Statement: **110,664**

230 ❑ Sep 1984 Cover: 0.75 **NM** value: **1.50**
Circ: Statement: **110,664**

231 ❑ Oct 1984 Cover: 0.75 **NM** value: **1.50**
Circ: Statement: **110,664**
A: Joe Staton **W:** Joe Staton; Kurt Busiek ★ Appearance of Justice Society of America, Supergirl, Phantom Stranger.

232 ❑ Nov 1984 Cover: 0.75 **NM** value: **1.50**
Circ: Statement: **110,664**
A: Joe Staton **W:** Joe Staton; Kurt Busiek ★ Appearance of Justice Society of America, Supergirl. ★ Versus Crime Syndicate.

233 ❑ Dec 1984 Cover: 0.75 **NM** value: **1.50**
Circ: Statement: **110,664**
cover forms four-part poster with issues #234-236. 📖 Rebirth, Part 1 • New team begins ★ Appearance of Vibe.

234 ❑ Jan 1985 Cover: 0.75 **NM** value: **1.50**
Circ: Statement: **96,281**
📖 Rebirth, Part 2 ★ Appearance of Monitor, Vixen.

235 ❑ Feb 1985 Cover: 0.75 **NM** value: **1.50**
Circ: Statement: **96,281**
📖 Rebirth, Part 3 ★ Origin of Steel. ★ 1st Appearance of The Cadre. ★ Versus Overmaster. ★ Versus The Cadre.

236 ❑ Mar 1985 Cover: 0.75 **NM** value: **1.50**
Circ: Statement: **96,281**
📖 Rebirth, Part 4 ★ Appearance of Gypsy. ★ Versus Overmaster. ★ Versus The Cadre.

237 ❑ Apr 1985 Cover: 0.75 **NM** value: **1.50**
Circ: Statement: **96,281**
★ Appearance of Wonder Woman, Superman, The Flash. ★ Versus Mad Maestro.

238 ❑ May 1985 Cover: 0.75 **NM** value: **1.50**
Circ: Statement: **96,281** CapCity orders: **7,700**
📖 Savage Symphony **A:** Chuck Patton **W:** Gerry Conway ★ Death of Anton Allegro.

239 ❑ Jun 1985 Cover: 0.75 **NM** value: **1.50**

Other grades: Multiply prices above by **1.5 for Mint • 2/3 for Very Fine • 1/3 for Fine • 1/5 for Very Good • 1/8 for Good**

Circ: Statement: **96,281** CapCity orders: **7,700**
In the Shadow of the Ox • Wonder Woman leaves Justice League **A:** Rick Hoberg; Chuck Patton **W:** Gerry Conway ★ Death of General Mustapha Maksai.

240 ❑ Jul 1985 Cover: 0.75 **NM value: 1.50**
Circ: Statement: **96,281** CapCity orders: **7,800**
The Future Ain't What it Used to Be **A:** Mike Sekowsky **W:** Kurt Busiek ★ 1st Appearance of Doctor Anomaly.

241 ❑ Aug 1985 Cover: 0.75 **NM value: 1.50**
Circ: Statement: **96,281** CapCity orders: **8,300**
Sea Change **A:** George Tuska **W:** Gerry Conway ★ Versus Amazo.

242 ❑ Sep 1985 Cover: 0.75 **NM value: 1.50**
Circ: Statement: **96,281** CapCity orders: **7,550**
Battle Cry; Assault on Mount Mayhem **A:** George Tuska; Michael Chen **W:** Gerry Conway; Michael Fleisher ★ Versus Amazo.

243 ❑ Oct 1985 Cover: 0.75 **NM value: 1.50**
Circ: Statement: **96,281** CapCity orders: **7,350**
Storm Cloud • Aquaman leaves the Justice League of America **A:** George Tuska **W:** Gerry Conway ★ Versus Amazo.

244 ❑ Nov 1985 Cover: 0.75 **NM value: 1.50**
Circ: Statement: **96,281** CapCity orders: **9,000**
Crisis on Infinite Earths • Crisis; Steel vs. Steel **A:** Joe Staton **W:** Joe Staton; Gerry Conway ★ Appearance of Justice Society of America, Infinity, Inc..

245 ❑ Dec 1985 Cover: 0.75 **NM value: 1.50**
Circ: Statement: **96,281** CapCity orders: **10,450**
Crisis on Infinite Earths • Crisis; Steel in future **A:** Luke McDonnell **W:** Gerry Conway ★ Appearance of Lord of Time.

246 ❑ Jan 1986 Cover: 0.75 **NM value: 1.50**
Circ: Statement: **82,406** CapCity orders: **7,200**
Be It Ever So Humble... • evicted from HQ **A:** Luke McDonnell **W:** Gerry Conway

247 ❑ Feb 1986 Cover: 0.75 **NM value: 1.50**
Circ: Statement: **82,406** CapCity orders: **7,900**
...There' s No Place Like Home • back to Happy Harbor **A:** Luke McDonnell **W:** Gerry Conway

248 ❑ Mar 1986 Cover: 0.75 **NM value: 1.50**
Circ: Statement: **82,406** CapCity orders: **8,000**
Interweavings • J'onn J'onzz solo story **A:** Luke McDonnell **W:** Gerry Conway

249 ❑ Apr 1986 Cover: 0.75 **NM value: 1.50**
Circ: Statement: **82,406** CapCity orders: **7,750**
All Fall Down **A:** Luke McDonnell **W:** Gerry Conway

250 ❑ May 1986 Cover: 1.25 **NM value: 1.50**
Circ: Statement: **82,406** CapCity orders: **8,150**
• Giant-size. The Return of the Justice League of America • Batman rejoins Justice League of America **A:** Luke McDonnell **W:** Gerry Conway ★ Appearance of original JLA.

251 ❑ Jun 1986 Cover: 0.75 **NM value: 1.50**
Circ: Statement: **82,406** CapCity orders: **7,900**
Hunters and Prey **A:** Luke McDonnell **W:** Gerry Conway ★ Versus Despero.

252 ❑ Jul 1986 Cover: 0.75 **NM value: 1.50**
Circ: Statement: **82,406** CapCity orders: **8,150**
Arrival **A:** Luke McDonnell **W:** Gerry Conway ★ Versus Despero.

253 ❑ Aug 1986 Cover: 0.75 **NM value: 1.50**
Circ: Statement: **82,406** CapCity orders: **8,300**
Pyre **A:** Luke McDonnell **W:** Gerry Conway ★ Origin of Despero.

254 ❑ Sep 1986 Cover: 0.75 **NM value: 1.50**
Circ: Statement: **82,406** CapCity orders: **8,450**
Desperate Climax; Secret of the Temple **A:** Luke McDonnell; José Delbo **W:** Joe Orlando; Gerry Conway; Joey Cavalieri ★ Versus Despero.

255 ❑ Oct 1986 Cover: 0.75 **NM value: 1.50**
Circ: Statement: **82,406** CapCity orders: **8,550**
Rising **A:** Luke McDonnell **W:** Gerry Conway; Michael Ellis ★ Origin of Gypsy.

256 ❑ Nov 1986 Cover: 0.75 **NM value: 1.50**
Circ: Statement: **82,406** CapCity orders: **8,600**
Back to Godhead **A:** Luke McDonnell **W:** J.M. DeMatteis

257 ❑ Dec 1986 Cover: 0.75 **NM value: 1.50**
Circ: Statement: **82,406** CapCity orders: **8,900**
Coming Down • Zatanna leaves Justice League **A:** Luke McDonnell **W:** J.M. DeMatteis

258 ❑ Jan 1987 Cover: 0.75 **NM value: 1.50**
Circ: Statement: **164,871** CapCity orders: **14,150**
Legends, Part 5; The End of the Justice League of America, Part 1 • Legends **A:** Luke McDonnell **W:** J.M. DeMatteis ★ Death of Vibe.

259 ❑ Feb 1987 Cover: 0.75 **NM value: 1.50**
Circ: Statement: **164,871** CapCity orders: **15,250**
Legends, Part 9; The End of the Justice League of America, Part 2 • Legends; Gypsy leaves team **A:** Luke McDonnell **W:** J.M. DeMatteis

260 ❑ Mar 1987 Cover: 0.75 **NM value: 1.50**
Circ: Statement: **164,871** CapCity orders: **14,950**
Legends, Part 14; The End of the Justice League of America, Part 3 • Legends **A:** Luke McDonnell **W:** J.M. DeMatteis ★ Death of Steel.

261 ❑ Apr 1987 Cover: 0.75 **NM value: 4.00**
Circ: Statement: **164,871** CapCity orders: **19,150** • **CGC:** 1 graded, best 9.4
Legends, Part 21; The End of the Justice League of America, Part 4 final issue. • group disbands **A:** Luke McDonnell **W:** J.M. DeMatteis

Anl 1 ❑ Oct 1983 Cover: 1.00 **NM value: 4.50**
Circ: CapCity orders: **31,350**
★ Appearance of John Stewart, Sandman, John Stewart, Sandman. ★ Versus Doctor Destiny. ★ Versus Dr. Destiny.

Anl 2 ❑ Oct 1984 Cover: 1.25 **NM value: 3.50**
Circ: CapCity orders: **32,000**
★ Origin of New JLA (Vixen, Vibe, Gypsy, Steel). ★ 1st Appearance of Gypsy, New JLA (Vixen, Vibe, Gypsy, Steel).

Anl 3 ❑ Nov 1985 Cover: 1.25 **NM value: 3.50**
Circ: CapCity orders: **12,250**
Crisis on Infinite Earths • Crisis **A:** Rick Hoberg **W:** Dan Mishkin ★ 1st Appearance of Red Tornado (in current form).

JUSTICE LEAGUE OF AMERICA ARCHIVES — DC

1 ❑ Cover: 39.95 **NM value: Cover or less**
hardcover. • reprints Brave & the Bold #28-30 and Justice League of America #1-6

2 ❑ Cover: 39.95 **NM value: Cover or less**
hardcover. • reprints Justice League of America #7-14

3 ❑ Cover: 39.95 **NM value: Cover or less**
hardcover. • reprints Justice League of America #15-22

4 ❑ Cover: 49.95 **NM value: Cover or less**
hardcover. • reprints Justice League of America #23-30; reprints Justice League of America #31-40

5 ❑ Cover: 49.95 **NM value: Cover or less**
hardcover. Riddle of the Runaway Room; Attack of the Star-Bolt Warrior; Enemy from the Timeless World; The Deadly Dreams of Doctor Destin • reprints Justice League of America #23-31 **A:** Murphy Anderson; Mike Sekowsky **W:** Gardner Fox

6 ❑ Cover: 49.95 **NM value: Cover or less**
hardcover. The Keymaster of the World!; Metamorpho Says No!; The Card Crimes of the Royal Flush Gang!; The Plague that Struck the Justice League!; The Super-Struggle Aga • Reprints Justice League of America #41-50 **A:** Mike Sekowsky; Murphy Anderson(cover) **W:** Mark Evanier; Gardner Fox

7 ❑ Cover: 49.95 **NM value: Cover or less**
hardcover. • Reprints Justice League of America #51-60 **A:** Mike Sekowsky **W:** Gardner Fox; Robert Greenberger

JUSTICE LEAGUE OF AMERICA SUPER SPECTACULAR — DC

1 ❑ ca. 1999 Cover: 5.95 **NM value: Cover or less**

JUSTICE LEAGUE QUARTERLY — DC

Justice League Quarterly kicked off in 1990, featuring giant-sized stories of the world's most contentious gaggle of super-heroes: Justice League International.

The JLI is lovable not so much for their heroics but for the way the different cast members play off each other: Guy Gardner and Wally West (the latest Flash) are fond of needling each other for failing to live up to the reputations of their illustrious predecessors. Blue Beetle and Booster Gold are old friends who sulk and pout as only friends can. And in the midst of it all, J'onn J'onzz, the Martian Manhunter plays the straight man in the style of Mr. Spock from Star Trek. Of course, there are still villains to trounce and people to rescue, but the longer format of this series worked because it gave the characters — not just the plot — space to develop.

1 ❑ Win 1990 Cover: 2.95 **NM value: 3.00**
Circ: CapCity orders: **31,550** • **CGC:** 2 graded, best 9.4
Corporate Maneuvers **A:** Chris Sprouse; Keith Giffen **W:** Keith Giffen; J.M. DeMatteis ★ Origin of The Conglomerate. ★ 1st Appearance of The Conglomerate.

2 ❑ Spr 1991 Cover: 2.95 **NM value: 3.00**
Circ: CapCity orders: **24,800**
★ Versus Mr. Nebula.

3 ❑ Jun 1991 Cover: 2.95 **NM value: 3.00**
Circ: CapCity orders: **22,150**
cover says Sum, indicia says Jun.

4 ❑ Fal 1991 Cover: 2.95 **NM value: 3.00**
Circ: CapCity orders: **21,100**
cover says Aut, indicia says Fal.

5 ❑ Win 1991 Cover: 2.95 **NM value: 3.00**
Circ: CapCity orders: **19,400**
★ Appearance of Global Guardians.

6 ❑ Spr 1992 Cover: 2.95 **NM value: 3.00**
Circ: CapCity orders: **16,250**
★ Appearance of Global Guardians.

7 ❑ Sum 1992 Cover: 3.50 **NM value: Cover or less**
Circ: CapCity orders: **15,350**
★ Appearance of Global Guardians.

8 ❑ Sum 1992 Cover: 3.50 **NM value: Cover or less**
Circ: CapCity orders: **14,250**
cover says Aut, indicia says Sum. • new Conglomerate

9 ❑ Win 1992 Cover: 3.50 **NM value: Cover or less**
Circ: CapCity orders: **12,750**

10 ❑ Spr 1993 Cover: 3.50 **NM value: Cover or less**
Circ: CapCity orders: **11,700**

11 ❑ Sum 1993 Cover: 3.50 **NM value: Cover or less**
Circ: CapCity orders: **12,000**

12 ❑ Sum 1993 Cover: 3.50 **NM value: Cover or less**
Circ: CapCity orders: **11,400**
covers says Aut, indicia says Sum. • Conglomerate

13 ❑ Aut 1993 Cover: 3.50 **NM value: Cover or less**
Circ: CapCity orders: **10,600** • **CGC:** 2 graded, best 9.8
cover says Win, indicia says Aut.

14 ❑ Spr 1994 Cover: 3.50 **NM value: Cover or less**
Circ: CapCity orders: **9,350**
★ Appearance of Nightshade, Thunderbolt, Blue Beetle, Captain Atom.

15 ❑ Jun 1994 Cover: 3.50 **NM value: Cover or less**
Circ: CapCity orders: **8,800**
cover says Sum, indicia says Jun. ★ Appearance of Praxis.

16 ❑ Sep 1994 Cover: 3.50 **NM value: Cover or less**
Circ: CapCity orders: **8,550**
★ Appearance of General Glory.

17 ❑ Win 1994 Cover: 3.50 **NM value: Cover or less**
Circ: CapCity orders: **8,050** • **CGC:** 1 graded, best 9.2
final issue.

Creator Key
W = Writer • A = Artist • C = Cover Artist

JUSTICE LEAGUES: JL? — DC

The six-part Justice Leagues "event" began here and examined the JLA's significance to the DC universe. With the help of Silver Age super-villain Hector Hammond, the enigmatic Advance Man made everyone on Earth forget the Justice League of America so his mysterious client Plura's world-conquering scheme could be set into motion. That is, until Hammond learned the true nature of the plan and encouraged everyone to "remember the Justice League of A..." before being overcome. Still, the Advance Man continued to wreak havoc in his client's name, and even though there was no Justice League of America to oppose him, something drove DC's heaviest hitters to form JLA's of their own to deal with the developing crisis. They were: Justice Leagues: Justice League of Amazons (Part 2), Justice Leagues: Justice League of Atlantis (Part 3), Justice Leagues: Justice League of Arkham (Part 4), and Justice Leagues: Justice League of Aliens (Part 5).

This entertaining, hero-packed storyline concluded in Justice Leagues: JLA (Part 6), and each installment featured a gorgeous cover by artist George Perez.

1 ❑ Mar 2001 Cover: 2.50 **NM value: Cover or less**
Circ: Diamd. preorders: **48,317**
Justice Leagues, Part 1 **A:** Ethan Van Sciver **W:** Tom Peyer

JUSTICE LEAGUES: JLA — DC

1 ❑ Mar 2001 Cover: 2.50 **NM value: Cover or less**
Circ: Diamd. preorders: **46,431** • **CGC:** 1 graded, best 9.8
Justice Leagues, Part 6 **A:** Justiniano **W:** Tom Peyer

JUSTICE LEAGUES: JUSTICE LEAGUE OF ALIENS — DC

1 ❑ Mar 2001 Cover: 2.50 **NM value: Cover or less**
Circ: Diamd. preorders: **43,173**
Justice Leagues, Part 5 **A:** Mike S. Miller **W:** Judd Winick

JUSTICE LEAGUES: JUSTICE LEAGUE OF AMAZONS — DC

1 ❑ Mar 2001 Cover: 2.50 **NM value: Cover or less**
Circ: Diamd. preorders: **42,904**
Justice Leagues, Part 2 **A:** Aluir Amancio **W:** Len Kaminski

JUSTICE LEAGUES:JUSTICE LEAGUE OF ARKHAM — DC

1 ❑ Mar 2001 Cover: 2.50 **NM value: Cover or less**
Circ: Diamd. preorders: **43,923**
Justice Leagues, Part 4 **A:** Coy Turnbull **W:** Paul Grist

JUSTICE LEAGUES: JUSTICE LEAGUE OF ATLANTIS — DC

1 ❑ Mar 2001 Cover: 2.50 **NM value: Cover or less**
Circ: Diamd. preorders: **42,517**
Justice Leagues, Part 3 **A:** Javiar Saltares **W:** Len Kaminski

JUSTICE LEAGUE TASK FORCE — DC

0 ❑ Oct 1994 Cover: 1.50 **NM value: 1.75**
Circ: CapCity orders: **19,050**
The Gathering **A:** Sal Velluto **W:** Mark Waid ★ Appearance of Triumph.

1 ❑ Jun 1993 Cover: 1.25 **NM value: 2.00**
Circ: CapCity orders: **46,600**
The Tyranny Gun! • membership card **A:** Sal Velluto **W:** David Michelinie

2 ❑ Jul 1993 Cover: 1.25 **NM value: 1.50**
Circ: CapCity orders: **23,850**

3 ❑ Aug 1993 Cover: 1.25 **NM value: 1.50**
Circ: CapCity orders: **21,150**

4 ❑ Sep 1993 Cover: 1.25 **NM value: 1.50**
Circ: CapCity orders: **19,550**

5 ❑ Oct 1993 Cover: 1.25 **NM value: 1.50**
Circ: CapCity orders: **84,800**
KnightQuest: The Search

6 ❑ Nov 1993 Cover: 1.25 **NM value: Cover or less**
Circ: CapCity orders: **40,100**
KnightQuest: The Search

7 ❑ Dec 1993 Cover: 1.25 **NM value: 1.50**
Circ: CapCity orders: **17,600**
• transsexual J'onn J'onzz

8 ❑ Jan 1994 Cover: 1.50 **NM value: Cover or less**
Circ: CapCity orders: **17,000**
How Green was my Daalie • transsexual J'onn J'onzz **A:** Sal Velluto **W:** Peter David

9 ❑ Feb 1994 Cover: 1.50 **NM value: Cover or less**
Circ: CapCity orders: **15,950**
Saturday Night's All Right for Fightin'! **A:** Greg Laroque **W:** Jeph Loeb ★ Appearance of New Bloods.

10 ❑ Mar 1994 Cover: 1.50 **NM value: Cover or less**
Circ: CapCity orders: **14,000**
Purification Plague, Part 1 ★ Versus Aryan Brigade.

11 ❑ Apr 1994 Cover: 1.50 **NM value: Cover or less**
Circ: CapCity orders: **12,300**
★ Versus Aryan Brigade.

12 ❑ May 1994 Cover: 1.50 **NM value: Cover or less**
Circ: CapCity orders: **12,050**

13 ❑ Jun 1994 Cover: 1.50 **NM value: Cover or less**
Circ: CapCity orders: **12,150**

CGC-graded: Multiply prices above by **33 for 9.9 M • 16 for 9.8 NM/M • 7 for 9.6 NM+ • 5 for 9.4 NM • 2.5 for 9.2 NM- • 1.5 for 9.0 VF/NM**

Judgment Day; Judgment Day, Part 2 **A:** Sal Velluto **W:** Mark Waid
14 ❑ Jul 1994 Cover: 1.50 **NM** value: **Cover or less**
Circ: CapCity orders: **12,200**
Judgment Day
15 ❑ Aug 1994 Cover: 1.50 **NM** value: **Cover or less**
Circ: CapCity orders: **11,600**
Aftershocks, Part 2
16 ❑ Sep 1994 Cover: 1.50 **NM** value: **Cover or less**
Circ: CapCity orders: **14,750**
• Zero Hour ★ Appearance of Triumph.
17 ❑ Nov 1994 Cover: 1.50 **NM** value: **Cover or less**
Circ: CapCity orders: **12,200**
Savage Legacy, Part 1 **A:** Sal Velluto **W:** Christopher Priest; Mark Waid
18 ❑ Dec 1994 Cover: 1.50 **NM** value: **Cover or less**
Circ: CapCity orders: **12,200**
Savage Legacy, Part 2 **A:** Sal Velluto **W:** Christopher Priest; Mark Waid
19 ❑ Jan 1995 Cover: 1.50 **NM** value: **Cover or less**
Circ: CapCity orders: **12,000**
Savage Legacy, Part 3 **A:** Sal Velluto **W:** Christopher Priest; Mark Waid ★ Versus Vandal Savage.
20 ❑ Feb 1995 Cover: 1.50 **NM** value: **Cover or less**
Circ: CapCity orders: **11,425**
21 ❑ Mar 1995 Cover: 1.50 **NM** value: **Cover or less**
Circ: CapCity orders: **10,375**
22 ❑ Apr 1995 Cover: 1.50 **NM** value: **Cover or less**
Circ: CapCity orders: **9,700**
23 ❑ May 1995 Cover: 1.50 **NM** value: **Cover or less**
Circ: CapCity orders: **9,375**
24 ❑ Jun 1995 Cover: 1.75 **NM** value: **Cover or less**
Circ: CapCity orders: **8,975**
25 ❑ Jul 1995 Cover: 1.75 **NM** value: **Cover or less**
Circ: CapCity orders: **9,000**
26 ❑ Aug 1995 Cover: 1.75 **NM** value: **Cover or less**
Circ: CapCity orders: **8,975**
27 ❑ Sep 1995 Cover: 1.75 **NM** value: **Cover or less**
Circ: CapCity orders: **9,425**
28 ❑ Oct 1995 Cover: 1.75 **NM** value: **Cover or less**
Circ: CapCity orders: **7,075**
29 ❑ Nov 1995 Cover: 1.75 **NM** value: **Cover or less**
30 ❑ Dec 1995 Cover: 1.75 **NM** value: **Cover or less**
• Underworld Unleashed
31 ❑ Jan 1996 Cover: 1.75 **NM** value: **Cover or less**
The Accused **A:** Roger Robinson **W:** Christopher Priest
32 ❑ Feb 1996 Cover: 1.75 **NM** value: **Cover or less**
The Ninth Hour **A:** Roger Robinson **W:** Christopher Priest
33 ❑ Mar 1996 Cover: 1.75 **NM** value: **Cover or less**
The Stand **A:** Ramon Bernado **W:** Christopher Priest
34 ❑ May 1996 Cover: 1.75 **NM** value: **Cover or less**
35 ❑ Jun 1996 Cover: 1.75 **NM** value: **Cover or less**
★ Appearance of Warlord.
36 ❑ Jul 1996 Cover: 1.75 **NM** value: **Cover or less**
37 ❑ Aug 1996 Cover: 1.75 **NM** value: **Cover or less**
final issue.

JUSTICE MACHINE (COMICO) — Comico

The Justice Machine is a sort of super-powered police squad, the ultimate law-enforcers on their home planet of Georwell. Unfortunately, Georwell is a totalitarian state, and its laws are often bent or rewritten to serve the powerful. (Surprise, surprise — Georwell's name is, indeed, derived from from George Orwell, author of 1984.)

This incarnation of the Justice Machine consists of Diviner, a psychic; Titan, a gigantic powerhouse; Blazer, a woman with awesome flame powers; Talisman, a man gifted with unnatural luck; Demon, an egotistical speedster; and their leader, Challenger.

Even though they believe in their cause, the Justice Machine in this series begin to have doubts about their government...

1 ❑ Jan 1987 Cover: 1.50 **NM** value: **2.50**
Circ: CapCity orders: **15,050**
Heroes And Villains **A:** Mike Gustovich **W:** Tony Isabella
2 ❑ Feb 1987 Cover: 1.50 **NM** value: **2.00**
Circ: CapCity orders: **10,125**
A: Mike Gustovich
3 ❑ Mar 1987 Cover: 1.50 **NM** value: **1.75**
Circ: CapCity orders: **9,500**
A: Mike Gustovich
4 ❑ Apr 1987 Cover: 1.50 **NM** value: **1.75**
Circ: CapCity orders: **9,500**
A: Mike Gustovich
5 ❑ May 1987 Cover: 1.50 **NM** value: **1.75**
Circ: CapCity orders: **9,200**
A: Mike Gustovich
6 ❑ Jun 1987 Cover: 1.50 **NM** value: **1.75**
Circ: CapCity orders: **9,425**
A: Mike Gustovich
7 ❑ Jul 1987 Cover: 1.50 **NM** value: **1.75**
Circ: CapCity orders: **9,400**
A: Mike Gustovich
8 ❑ Aug 1987 Cover: 1.50 **NM** value: **1.75**
Circ: CapCity orders: **8,975**
A: Mike Gustovich ★ Death of Demon.
9 ❑ Sep 1987 Cover: 1.50 **NM** value: **1.75**
Circ: CapCity orders: **8,575**
A: Mike Gustovich
10 ❑ Oct 1987 Cover: 1.50 **NM** value: **1.75**
Circ: CapCity orders: **8,375**
A: Mike Gustovich
11 ❑ Nov 1987 Cover: 1.50 **NM** value: **1.75**
Circ: CapCity orders: **8,200**
A: Mike Gustovich
12 ❑ Dec 1987 Cover: 1.50 **NM** value: **1.75**
Circ: CapCity orders: **7,700**
A: Mike Gustovich
13 ❑ Jan 1988 Cover: 1.50 **NM** value: **1.75**
Circ: CapCity orders: **7,100**
A: Mike Gustovich
14 ❑ Feb 1988 Cover: 1.50 **NM** value: **1.75**
Circ: CapCity orders: **6,775**
A: Mike Gustovich
15 ❑ Mar 1988 Cover: 1.75 **NM** value: **Cover or less**
Circ: CapCity orders: **6,350**
16 ❑ Apr 1988 Cover: 1.75 **NM** value: **Cover or less**
Circ: CapCity orders: **6,275**
17 ❑ May 1988 Cover: 1.75 **NM** value: **Cover or less**
Circ: CapCity orders: **5,850**
18 ❑ Jun 1988 Cover: 1.75 **NM** value: **Cover or less**
Circ: CapCity orders: **5,800**
19 ❑ Jul 1988 Cover: 1.75 **NM** value: **Cover or less**
Circ: CapCity orders: **5,375**
20 ❑ Aug 1988 Cover: 1.75 **NM** value: **Cover or less**
Circ: CapCity orders: **5,300**
21 ❑ Sep 1988 Cover: 1.75 **NM** value: **Cover or less**
Circ: CapCity orders: **5,100**
22 ❑ Oct 1988 Cover: 1.75 **NM** value: **Cover or less**
Circ: CapCity orders: **4,825**
23 ❑ Nov 1988 Cover: 1.75 **NM** value: **Cover or less**
Circ: CapCity orders: **4,825**
24 ❑ Dec 1988 Cover: 1.75 **NM** value: **Cover or less**
Circ: CapCity orders: **4,950**
25 ❑ Jan 1989 Cover: 1.75 **NM** value: **Cover or less**
Circ: CapCity orders: **4,700**
26 ❑ Feb 1989 Cover: 1.95 **NM** value: **Cover or less**
Circ: CapCity orders: **4,600**
27 ❑ Mar 1989 Cover: 1.95 **NM** value: **Cover or less**
Circ: CapCity orders: **4,550**
28 ❑ Apr 1989 Cover: 1.95 **NM** value: **Cover or less**
Circ: CapCity orders: **4,600**
29 ❑ May 1989 Cover: 1.95 **NM** value: **Cover or less**
Circ: CapCity orders: **4,550**
final issue.
Anl 1 ❑ Jun 1989 Cover: 2.50 **NM** value: **2.75**
Circ: CapCity orders: **4,750**
★ Appearance of Elementals.

JUSTICE MACHINE FEATURING THE ELEMENTALS — Comico

1 ❑ May 1986 Cover: 2.00 **NM** value: **Cover or less**
Circ: CapCity orders: **15,975**
The Darkforce Affair **A:** Mike Gustovich **W:** Bill Willingham
2 ❑ Jun 1986 Cover: 2.00 **NM** value: **Cover or less**
Circ: CapCity orders: **13,325**
3 ❑ Jul 1986 Cover: 2.00 **NM** value: **Cover or less**
Circ: CapCity orders: **14,050**
4 ❑ Aug 1986 Cover: 2.00 **NM** value: **Cover or less**
Circ: CapCity orders: **14,175**

JUSTICE MACHINE, THE (INNOVATION) — Innovation

1 ❑ Apr 1990 Cover: 1.95 **NM** value: **Cover or less**
Circ: CapCity orders: **4,650**
Burn While You Learn **A:** Rik Levins; Darryl Banks **W:** Mark Ellis
2 ❑ May 1990 Cover: 1.95 **NM** value: **Cover or less**
Circ: CapCity orders: **4,125**
3 ❑ Jul 1990 Cover: 1.95 **NM** value: **Cover or less**
Circ: CapCity orders: **3,625**
4 ❑ Sep 1990 Cover: 1.95 **NM** value: **Cover or less**
Circ: CapCity orders: **3,400**
5 ❑ Nov 1990 Cover: 1.95 **NM** value: **Cover or less**
Circ: CapCity orders: **3,135**
6 ❑ Jan 1991 Cover: 2.25 **NM** value: **Cover or less**
Circ: CapCity orders: **2,835**
7 ❑ Apr 1991 Cover: 2.25 **NM** value: **Cover or less**
Circ: CapCity orders: **2,675**

JUSTICE MACHINE, THE (MILLENNIUM) — Millennium

1 ❑ Cover: 2.50 **NM** value: **Cover or less**
Circ: CapCity orders: **11,075**
The Chimera Conspiracy, Part 1; The Justice Machine: Year One **A:** Darryl Banks **W:** Darryl Banks; Mark Ellis ★ Origin of The Justice Machine.
2 ❑ Cover: 2.50 **NM** value: **Cover or less**
Circ: CapCity orders: **4,075**
The Chimera Conspiracy, Part 2; The Justice Machine: Year Two **A:** Darryl Banks **W:** Darryl Banks; Mark Ellis

JUSTICE MACHINE (NOBLE) — Noble

1 ❑ 1981 **NM** value: **2.50**
A: Mike Gustovich **C:** John Byrne
2 ❑ **NM** value: **2.50**
A: Mike Gustovich **C:** Tony DeZuniga
3 ❑ **NM** value: **2.50**
A: Mike Gustovich
4 ❑ **NM** value: **2.50**
A: Mike Gustovich
5 ❑ Nov 1983 **NM** value: **2.50**
A: Mike Gustovich
Anl 1 ❑ Jan 1984 **NM** value: **5.00**
• THUNDER Agents ★ 1st Appearance of Elementals.

JUSTICE MACHINE SUMMER SPECTACULAR, THE — Innovation

1 ❑ Cover: 2.75 **NM** value: **Cover or less**
Circ: CapCity orders: **4,125**
Machine Musings **A:** Bill Reinhold **W:** William Messner-Loebs

JUSTICE (MARVEL) — Marvel

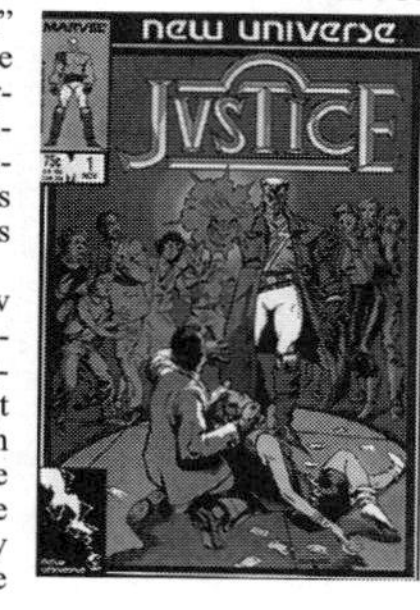

The mysterious "White Event" that birthed Marvel's New Universe acts transforms John Tensen, a narcotics officer working for the Justice Department, into something beyond human. He now has powers beyond imagining, a mission, as well as a new name: Justice.

Now walking the streets of New York, he seeks to fulfill his new mission. His left hand controls an unstoppable force shield, and his right wields an energy "sword" which disintegrates those it strikes. The first to receive its punishment are three thugs who killed an old lady for her Social Security check. The list kind of grows from there...

Mediocre, which for the New Universe puts it in the two or three best.

1 ❑ Nov 1986 Cover: 0.75 **NM** value: **1.25**
Circ: CapCity orders: **32,700**
Brave New World **A:** Geof Isherwood; Jack Fury; Joe Delbeato **W:** Archie Goodwin ★ 1st Appearance of Justice.
2 ❑ Dec 1986 Cover: 0.75 **NM** value: **1.00**
Circ: CapCity orders: **22,300**
3 ❑ Jan 1987 Cover: 0.75 **NM** value: **1.00**
Circ: CapCity orders: **18,200**
4 ❑ Feb 1987 Cover: 0.75 **NM** value: **1.00**
Circ: CapCity orders: **17,300**
5 ❑ Mar 1987 Cover: 0.75 **NM** value: **1.00**
Circ: CapCity orders: **17,900**
6 ❑ Apr 1987 Cover: 0.75 **NM** value: **1.00**
Circ: CapCity orders: **16,500**
Sara **A:** Geof Isherwood **W:** Geof Isherwood
7 ❑ May 1987 Cover: 0.75 **NM** value: **1.00**
Circ: CapCity orders: **15,600**
8 ❑ Jun 1987 Cover: 0.75 **NM** value: **1.00**
Circ: CapCity orders: **13,500**
9 ❑ Jul 1987 Cover: 0.75 **NM** value: **1.00**
Circ: CapCity orders: **12,500**
10 ❑ Aug 1987 Cover: 0.75 **NM** value: **1.00**
Circ: CapCity orders: **12,400**
11 ❑ Sep 1987 Cover: 0.75 **NM** value: **1.00**
Circ: CapCity orders: **12,200**
12 ❑ Oct 1987 Cover: 0.75 **NM** value: **1.00**
Circ: CapCity orders: **11,500**
13 ❑ Nov 1987 Cover: 0.75 **NM** value: **1.00**
Circ: CapCity orders: **11,400**
14 ❑ Dec 1987 Cover: 0.75 **NM** value: **1.00**
Circ: CapCity orders: **10,600**
15 ❑ Jan 1988 Cover: 0.75 **NM** value: **1.00**
Circ: CapCity orders: **11,300**
16 ❑ Feb 1988 Cover: 0.75 **NM** value: **1.00**
Circ: CapCity orders: **12,000**
17 ❑ Mar 1988 Cover: 0.75 **NM** value: **1.00**
Circ: CapCity orders: **11,500**
18 ❑ Apr 1988 Cover: 0.75 **NM** value: **1.25**
Circ: CapCity orders: **13,200**
19 ❑ May 1988 Cover: 1.25 **NM** value: **Cover or less**
Circ: CapCity orders: **11,550**
20 ❑ Jun 1988 Cover: 1.25 **NM** value: **Cover or less**
Circ: CapCity orders: **11,200**
21 ❑ Jul 1988 Cover: 1.25 **NM** value: **Cover or less**
Circ: CapCity orders: **11,600**
22 ❑ Aug 1988 Cover: 1.25 **NM** value: **Cover or less**
Circ: CapCity orders: **11,800**
23 ❑ Sep 1988 Cover: 1.25 **NM** value: **Cover or less**
Circ: CapCity orders: **11,100**
24 ❑ Oct 1988 Cover: 1.25 **NM** value: **Cover or less**
Circ: CapCity orders: **10,800**
25 ❑ Nov 1988 Cover: 1.25 **NM** value: **Cover or less**
Circ: CapCity orders: **10,400**
26 ❑ Dec 1988 Cover: 1.50 **NM** value: **Cover or less**
Circ: CapCity orders: **10,000**
27 ❑ Jan 1989 Cover: 1.50 **NM** value: **Cover or less**
Circ: CapCity orders: **10,600**
28 ❑ Feb 1989 Cover: 1.50 **NM** value: **Cover or less**
Circ: CapCity orders: **8,500**
29 ❑ Mar 1989 Cover: 1.50 **NM** value: **Cover or less**
Circ: CapCity orders: **8,500**
30 ❑ Apr 1989 Cover: 1.50 **NM** value: **Cover or less**
Circ: CapCity orders: **8,300**
Psi Unseen; Psycho Killer **A:** Lee Weeks; Marc McLaurin **W:** Eric Siry; Peter David ★ Appearance of Psi-Force.
31 ❑ May 1989 Cover: 1.50 **NM** value: **Cover or less**
Circ: CapCity orders: **8,400**
32 ❑ Jun 1989 Cover: 1.50 **NM** value: **Cover or less**
Circ: CapCity orders: **8,150**
final issue.

JUSTICE RIDERS — DC

1 ❑ Dec 1996 Cover: 5.95 **NM** value: **Cover or less**
Circ: Diamd. preorders: **26,629**
No issue number. • prestige format. • Elseworlds; Justice League in old West

JUSTICE SOCIETY OF AMERICA — DC

1 ❑ Aug 1992 Cover: 1.25 **NM** value: **1.50**

Circ: CapCity orders: **34,050**
📖 Home Again! **A:** Mike Parobeck **W:** Len Strazewski

2 ❑ Sep 1992 Cover: 1.25 **NM** value: **1.50**
Circ: CapCity orders: **19,100**
📖 Days of Valor **A:** Mike Parobeck **W:** Len Strazewski

3 ❑ Oct 1992 Cover: 1.25 **NM** value: **1.50**
Circ: CapCity orders: **17,050**
📖 Out Of The Past **A:** Mike Parobeck **W:** Len Strazewski ★ Versus Ultra-Humanite.

4 ❑ Nov 1992 Cover: 1.25 **NM** value: **1.50**
Circ: CapCity orders: **15,650**
★ Versus Ultra-Humanite.

5 ❑ Dec 1992 Cover: 1.25 **NM** value: **1.50**
Circ: CapCity orders: **14,400**

6 ❑ Jan 1993 Cover: 1.25 **NM** value: **Cover or less**
Circ: CapCity orders: **13,300**
📖 Give Me Liberty… **A:** Mike Parobeck **W:** Len Strazewski

7 ❑ Feb 1993 Cover: 1.25 **NM** value: **Cover or less**
Circ: CapCity orders: **12,800**
• in Bahdnesia

8 ❑ Mar 1993 Cover: 1.25 **NM** value: **Cover or less**
Circ: CapCity orders: **11,800**

9 ❑ Apr 1993 Cover: 1.25 **NM** value: **Cover or less**
Circ: CapCity orders: **12,950**
• Alan Scott vs. Guy Gardner

10 ❑ May 1993 Cover: 1.25 **NM** value: **Cover or less**
Circ: CapCity orders: **11,950**
final issue.

JUSTICE SOCIETY OF AMERICA (MINI-SERIES) DC

1 ❑ Apr 1991 Cover: 1.00 **NM** value: **2.00**
Circ: CapCity orders: **36,700**
📖 Beware The Savage Skies! • Flash **A:** Rick Burchett **W:** Len Strazewski

2 ❑ May 1991 Cover: 1.00 **NM** value: **1.75**
Circ: CapCity orders: **26,550**
• Black Canary

3 ❑ Jun 1991 Cover: 1.00 **NM** value: **1.75**
Circ: CapCity orders: **23,850**
• Green Lantern

4 ❑ Jul 1991 Cover: 1.00 **NM** value: **1.50**
Circ: CapCity orders: **23,900**
• Hawkman

5 ❑ Aug 1991 Cover: 1.00 **NM** value: **1.50**
Circ: CapCity orders: **22,400**
• Flash, Hawkman

6 ❑ Sep 1991 Cover: 1.00 **NM** value: **1.50**
Circ: CapCity orders: **20,300**
• Green Lantern, Black Canary

7 ❑ Oct 1991 Cover: 1.00 **NM** value: **1.50**
Circ: CapCity orders: **19,600**
• Green Lantern, Black Canary, Hawkman, Flash, Starman

8 ❑ Nov 1991 Cover: 1.00 **NM** value: **1.50**
Circ: CapCity orders: **18,350**
• Green Lantern, Black Canary, Hawkman, Flash, Starman

JUSTICE SOCIETY OF AMERICA 100-PAGE SUPER SPECTACULAR DC

1 ❑ Cover: 6.95 **NM** value: **Cover or less**
📖 Vengeance of the Immortal Villain; The Big Super-Hero Hunt; Finale for a Fiddler; The Sight Stealers; The Mystery of the Vanishing Detectives • 2000 facsimile of 1975 100-Page Super Spectacular; reprints The Flash #137 and #201, All Star Comics #57, The Brave and the Bold #62, and Adventure Comics #418

JUSTICE TRAPS THE GUILTY Headline

One of the pioneering crime comic titles, Justice Traps the Guilty—sometimes simply known as Guilty—is a product of the studios of prolific comics masters Joe Simon and Jack Kirby. By the late 1940s, Kirby's style had matured into one of staggering power and depth, bringing a white-hot intensity to Simon's poignant scripts. In the early issues of Justice Traps the Guilty, action and drama simply explode off the pages.

The creators drew from their own experiences growing up in working-class ethnic neighborhoods in the 1920s and 1930s to create complex and convincing portraits of the criminal underworld, melded with an almost Old Testament brand of justice and retribution.

As Simon and Kirby's involvement diminished and imitators flooded the market with crime comics of lesser quality, Justice Traps the Guilty lost much of its edge, and was squashed after the arrival of the Comics Code.

1 ❑ Oct 1947 Cover: 0.10 **NM** value: **365.00**
📖 I Was a Come-On Girl for Broken Bones, Inc.; The Trial of San Francisco's Strangest Killer; The Firebug; The Head in the Window; The Case Against Scarface • All true crime stories **A:** Jack Kirby **W:** Joe Simon

2 ❑ Jan 1948 Cover: 0.10 **NM** value: **210.00**
• **CGC:** 1 graded, best 5.5
A: Jack Kirby **W:** Joe Simon

3 ❑ Mar 1948 Cover: 0.10 **NM** value: **170.00**
A: Jack Kirby **W:** Joe Simon

4 ❑ May 1948 Cover: 0.10 **NM** value: **160.00**
• **CGC:** 1 graded, best 8.0
A: Jack Kirby **W:** Joe Simon

5 ❑ Jul 1948 Cover: 0.10 **NM** value: **160.00**
• **CGC:** 1 graded, best 6.5
A: Jack Kirby **W:** Joe Simon

6 ❑ Sep 1948 Cover: 0.10 **NM** value: **135.00**
A: Jack Kirby **W:** Joe Simon

7 ❑ Nov 1948 Cover: 0.10 **NM** value: **135.00**
A: Jack Kirby **W:** Joe Simon

8 ❑ Jan 1949 Cover: 0.10 **NM** value: **135.00**
• **CGC:** 1 graded, best 8.0
A: Jack Kirby **W:** Joe Simon

9 ❑ Apr 1949 Cover: 0.10 **NM** value: **135.00**
A: Jack Kirby **W:** Joe Simon

10 ❑ Jun 1949 Cover: 0.10 **NM** value: **135.00**
• **CGC:** 2 graded, best 8.5
A: Jack Kirby **W:** Joe Simon

11 ❑ Aug 1949 Cover: 0.10 **NM** value: **80.00**
A: Jack Kirby **W:** Joe Simon

12 ❑ Oct 1949 Cover: 0.10 **NM** value: **80.00**
A: Jack Kirby **W:** Joe Simon

13 ❑ Dec 1949 Cover: 0.10 **NM** value: **80.00**
• Cited in Seduction of the Innocent **A:** Jack Kirby **W:** Joe Simon

14 ❑ Feb 1950 Cover: 0.10 **NM** value: **54.00**
A: Jack Kirby **W:** Joe Simon

15 ❑ Apr 1950 Cover: 0.10 **NM** value: **54.00**
A: Jack Kirby **W:** Joe Simon

16 ❑ Jun 1950 Cover: 0.10 **NM** value: **54.00**
A: Jack Kirby **W:** Joe Simon

17 ❑ Aug 1950 Cover: 0.10 **NM** value: **54.00**
A: Jack Kirby **W:** Joe Simon

18 ❑ Sep 1950 Cover: 0.10 **NM** value: **54.00**
A: Jack Kirby **W:** Joe Simon

19 ❑ Oct 1950 Cover: 0.10 **NM** value: **54.00**
• **CGC:** 1 graded, best 8.5
A: Jack Kirby **W:** Joe Simon

20 ❑ Nov 1950 Cover: 0.10 **NM** value: **54.00**
A: Jack Kirby **W:** Joe Simon

21 ❑ Dec 1950 Cover: 0.10 **NM** value: **38.00**
A: Jack Kirby **W:** Joe Simon

22 ❑ Jan 1951 Cover: 0.10 **NM** value: **38.00**
23 ❑ Feb 1951 Cover: 0.10 **NM** value: **38.00**
24 ❑ Mar 1951 Cover: 0.10 **NM** value: **38.00**
25 ❑ Apr 1951 Cover: 0.10 **NM** value: **38.00**
26 ❑ May 1951 Cover: 0.10 **NM** value: **38.00**
27 ❑ Jun 1951 Cover: 0.10 **NM** value: **38.00**
📖 Sky Smugglers; Death By Proxy; T-Man Blitz; Mail Fraud!; Houdini of the Underworld

28 ❑ Jul 1951 Cover: 0.10 **NM** value: **38.00**
29 ❑ Aug 1951 Cover: 0.10 **NM** value: **38.00**
30 ❑ Sep 1951 Cover: 0.10 **NM** value: **38.00**
31 ❑ Oct 1951 Cover: 0.10 **NM** value: **24.00**
32 ❑ Nov 1951 Cover: 0.10 **NM** value: **24.00**
33 ❑ Dec 1951 Cover: 0.10 **NM** value: **24.00**
34 ❑ Jan 1952 Cover: 0.10 **NM** value: **24.00**
35 ❑ Feb 1952 Cover: 0.10 **NM** value: **24.00**
36 ❑ Mar 1952 Cover: 0.10 **NM** value: **24.00**
37 ❑ Apr 1952 Cover: 0.10 **NM** value: **24.00**
📖 The Head-hunters!; Photo Finish; Dead Weight!; Breakout!; No Escape

38 ❑ May 1952 Cover: 0.10 **NM** value: **24.00**
39 ❑ Jun 1952 Cover: 0.10 **NM** value: **24.00**
40 ❑ Jul 1952 Cover: 0.10 **NM** value: **24.00**
41 ❑ Aug 1952 Cover: 0.10 **NM** value: **20.00**
42 ❑ Sep 1952 Cover: 0.10 **NM** value: **20.00**
43 ❑ Oct 1952 Cover: 0.10 **NM** value: **20.00**
44 ❑ Nov 1952 Cover: 0.10 **NM** value: **20.00**
45 ❑ Dec 1952 Cover: 0.10 **NM** value: **20.00**
46 ❑ Jan 1953 Cover: 0.10 **NM** value: **20.00**
47 ❑ Feb 1953 Cover: 0.10 **NM** value: **20.00**
48 ❑ Mar 1953 Cover: 0.10 **NM** value: **20.00**
49 ❑ Apr 1953 Cover: 0.10 **NM** value: **20.00**
50 ❑ May 1953 Cover: 0.10 **NM** value: **20.00**
51 ❑ Jun 1953 Cover: 0.10 **NM** value: **18.00**
52 ❑ Jul 1953 Cover: 0.10 **NM** value: **18.00**
📖 The Vandals!; Con Game; Organized for Arson; Fake Alibi; Justice Laughs; Gang Doctor

53 ❑ Aug 1953 Cover: 0.10 **NM** value: **18.00**
📖 The Wreckers; The Victim; Boomerang; Present For Pop

54 ❑ Sep 1953 Cover: 0.10 **NM** value: **18.00**
55 ❑ Oct 1953 Cover: 0.10 **NM** value: **18.00**
56 ❑ Nov 1953 Cover: 0.10 **NM** value: **18.00**
57 ❑ Dec 1953 Cover: 0.10 **NM** value: **18.00**
58 ❑ Jan 1954 Cover: 0.10 **NM** value: **95.00**
• Cited in Seduction of the Innocent

59 ❑ Feb 1954 Cover: 0.10 **NM** value: **18.00**
60 ❑ Mar 1954 Cover: 0.10 **NM** value: **18.00**
61 ❑ Apr 1954 Cover: 0.10 **NM** value: **18.00**
62 ❑ May 1954 Cover: 0.10 **NM** value: **18.00**
63 ❑ Jun 1954 Cover: 0.10 **NM** value: **18.00**
64 ❑ Jul 1954 Cover: 0.10 **NM** value: **18.00**
65 ❑ Aug 1954 Cover: 0.10 **NM** value: **18.00**
66 ❑ Sep 1954 Cover: 0.10 **NM** value: **18.00**
67 ❑ Oct 1954 Cover: 0.10 **NM** value: **18.00**
68 ❑ Nov 1954 Cover: 0.10 **NM** value: **18.00**
69 ❑ Dec 1954 Cover: 0.10 **NM** value: **18.00**
70 ❑ Jan 1955 Cover: 0.10 **NM** value: **18.00**
71 ❑ Feb 1955 Cover: 0.10 **NM** value: **15.00**
72 ❑ Mar 1955 Cover: 0.10 **NM** value: **15.00**
73 ❑ Apr 1955 Cover: 0.10 **NM** value: **15.00**
74 ❑ May 1955 Cover: 0.10 **NM** value: **15.00**
• **CGC:** 1 graded, best 8.0

75 ❑ Jun 1955 Cover: 0.10 **NM** value: **15.00**
76 ❑ Aug 1955 Cover: 0.10 **NM** value: **15.00**
77 ❑ Oct 1955 Cover: 0.10 **NM** value: **15.00**
78 ❑ Dec 1955 Cover: 0.10 **NM** value: **15.00**
79 ❑ Feb 1956 Cover: 0.10 **NM** value: **15.00**
80 ❑ Apr 1956 Cover: 0.10 **NM** value: **15.00**
81 ❑ Jun 1956 Cover: 0.10 **NM** value: **15.00**
82 ❑ Aug 1956 Cover: 0.10 **NM** value: **15.00**
83 ❑ Oct 1956 Cover: 0.10 **NM** value: **15.00**
84 ❑ Dec 1956 Cover: 0.10 **NM** value: **15.00**
85 ❑ Feb 1957 Cover: 0.10 **NM** value: **15.00**
86 ❑ Apr 1957 Cover: 0.10 **NM** value: **15.00**
87 ❑ Jun 1957 Cover: 0.10 **NM** value: **15.00**
88 ❑ Aug 1957 Cover: 0.10 **NM** value: **15.00**
89 ❑ Oct 1957 Cover: 0.10 **NM** value: **15.00**
90 ❑ Dec 1957 Cover: 0.10 **NM** value: **15.00**
91 ❑ Feb 1958 Cover: 0.10 **NM** value: **15.00**
92 ❑ Apr 1958 Cover: 0.10 **NM** value: **15.00**
final issue.

JUST IMAGINE COMICS AND STORIES Just Imagine

1 ❑ **NM** value: **2.00**
2 ❑ **NM** value: **2.00**
3 ❑ **NM** value: **2.00**
4 ❑ **NM** value: **2.00**
5 ❑ **NM** value: **2.00**
6 ❑ **NM** value: **2.00**
7 ❑ **NM** value: **2.00**
8 ❑ **NM** value: **2.00**
9 ❑ Cover: 1.50 **NM** value: **2.00**
📖 The Bunny of Death in SpaceFear; Tit Mouse; Fire Fang; Scavenger Always Win…; Dinosaur Tales **A:** Stan Timmons; Bob Corby; Mark Nelson; Wm. Messner-Loebs **W:** Lenin Delsol; Bob Corby; Mark Nelson; Wm. Messner-Loebs

10 ❑ **NM** value: **2.00**
11 ❑ **NM** value: **2.00**
SE 1❑ **NM** value: **2.00**
• gophers

JUST MARRIED Charlton

Just Married, one of Charlton's numerous love comics, offered up stories of romance, betrayal, jealousy, heartbreak, and heartwarming sentiment in a glossy, standardized, and highly sanitized style. While the social upheavals of the 1960s proved a fertile source of creative ideas for many types of comics, the genre of love and romance comics remained as formulaic and uninspired as ever, dressing up the conventional morality of the 1950s in the new flashy fashions and jet-set backdrops of the 1960s.

Never a trailblazing publisher under the best of circumstances, Charlton set some new standards for mediocrity with some issues of this series.

1 ❑ ca. 1958 Cover: 0.10 **NM** value: **35.00**
2 ❑ ca. 1958 Cover: 0.10 **NM** value: **20.00**
3 ❑ ca. 1958 **NM** value: **12.00**
4 ❑ ca. 1958 Cover: 0.10 **NM** value: **12.00**
5 ❑ ca. 1959 Cover: 0.10 **NM** value: **12.00**
6 ❑ ca. 1959 Cover: 0.10 **NM** value: **9.00**
7 ❑ ca. 1959 Cover: 0.10 **NM** value: **9.00**
8 ❑ ca. 1959 Cover: 0.10 **NM** value: **9.00**
9 ❑ ca. 1959 Cover: 0.10 **NM** value: **9.00**
10 ❑ ca. 1959 Cover: 0.10 **NM** value: **9.00**
11 ❑ ca. 1960 Cover: 0.10 **NM** value: **8.00**
12 ❑ ca. 1960 Cover: 0.10 **NM** value: **8.00**
13 ❑ ca. 1960 Cover: 0.10 **NM** value: **8.00**
14 ❑ Jul 1960 Cover: 0.10 **NM** value: **8.00**
15 ❑ ca. 1960 Cover: 0.10 **NM** value: **8.00**
16 ❑ ca. 1960 Cover: 0.10 **NM** value: **8.00**
17 ❑ ca. 1961 Cover: 0.10 **NM** value: **8.00**
18 ❑ ca. 1961 Cover: 0.10 **NM** value: **8.00**
19 ❑ ca. 1961 Cover: 0.10 **NM** value: **8.00**
20 ❑ ca. 1961 Cover: 0.10 **NM** value: **8.00**
21 ❑ ca. 1961 Cover: 0.10 **NM** value: **6.00**
22 ❑ ca. 1961 Cover: 0.10 **NM** value: **6.00**
23 ❑ ca. 1962 Cover: 0.12 **NM** value: **6.00**
24 ❑ ca. 1962 Cover: 0.12 **NM** value: **6.00**
25 ❑ ca. 1962 Cover: 0.12 **NM** value: **6.00**
26 ❑ ca. 1962 Cover: 0.12 **NM** value: **6.00**
27 ❑ ca. 1962 Cover: 0.12 **NM** value: **6.00**
28 ❑ ca. 1962 Cover: 0.12 **NM** value: **6.00**
29 ❑ ca. 1963 Cover: 0.12 **NM** value: **6.00**
30 ❑ ca. 1963 Cover: 0.12 **NM** value: **6.00**
31 ❑ ca. 1963 Cover: 0.12 **NM** value: **5.00**
32 ❑ ca. 1963 Cover: 0.12 **NM** value: **5.00**
33 ❑ ca. 1963 Cover: 0.12 **NM** value: **5.00**
34 ❑ ca. 1963 Cover: 0.12 **NM** value: **5.00**
35 ❑ ca. 1964 Cover: 0.12 **NM** value: **5.00**
36 ❑ ca. 1964 Cover: 0.12 **NM** value: **5.00**
37 ❑ Jul 1964 Cover: 0.12 **NM** value: **5.00**
38 ❑ ca. 1964 Cover: 0.12 **NM** value: **5.00**
39 ❑ ca. 1964 Cover: 0.12 **NM** value: **5.00**
40 ❑ ca. 1965 Cover: 0.12 **NM** value: **5.00**
41 ❑ ca. 1965 Cover: 0.12 **NM** value: **5.00**
42 ❑ ca. 1965 Cover: 0.12 **NM** value: **5.00**
43 ❑ Sep 1965 Cover: 0.12 **NM** value: **5.00**
44 ❑ ca. 1965 Cover: 0.12 **NM** value: **5.00**
45 ❑ ca. 1966 Cover: 0.12 **NM** value: **5.00**
46 ❑ ca. 1966 Cover: 0.12 **NM** value: **5.00**
47 ❑ ca. 1966 Cover: 0.12 **NM** value: **5.00**
48 ❑ ca. 1966 Cover: 0.12 **NM** value: **5.00**
49 ❑ Oct 1966 Cover: 0.12 **NM** value: **5.00**
50 ❑ ca. 1967 Cover: 0.12 **NM** value: **5.00**
51 ❑ ca. 1967 Cover: 0.12 **NM** value: **5.00**
Circ: Statement: **112,413**

52 ❑ ca. 1967 Cover: 0.12 **NM** value: **5.00**
Circ: Statement: **112,413**

53 ❑ ca. 1967 Cover: 0.12 **NM** value: **5.00**
Circ: Statement: **112,413**

54 ❑ ca. 1967 Cover: 0.12 **NM** value: **5.00**

CGC-graded: Multiply prices above by **33 for 9.9 M • 16 for 9.8 NM/M • 7 for 9.6 NM+ • 5 for 9.4 NM • 2.5 for 9.2 NM- • 1.5 for 9.0 VF/NM**

Circ: Statement: **112,413**
55 ❑ Nov 1967 Cover: 0.12 **NM** value: **5.00**
Circ: Statement: **112,413**
56 ❑ Jan 1968 Cover: 0.12 **NM** value: **5.00**
57 ❑ Mar 1968 Cover: 0.12 **NM** value: **5.00**
58 ❑ May 1968 Cover: 0.12 **NM** value: **5.00**
59 ❑ Jul 1968 Cover: 0.12 **NM** value: **5.00**
60 ❑ Oct 1968 Cover: 0.12 **NM** value: **5.00**
61 ❑ ca. 1968 Cover: 0.12 **NM** value: **4.00**
62 ❑ ca. 1969 Cover: 0.12 **NM** value: **4.00**
63 ❑ ca. 1969 Cover: 0.12 **NM** value: **4.00**
64 ❑ ca. 1969 Cover: 0.12 **NM** value: **4.00**
65 ❑ ca. 1969 Cover: 0.12 **NM** value: **4.00**
66 ❑ Cover: 0.12 **NM** value: **4.00**
📖 My Lonely Days; The Lucky Couple; The Most Beautiful Man in the World **A:** Nicholas Alascia
67 ❑ Oct 1969 Cover: 0.15 **NM** value: **4.00**
68 ❑ Dec 1969 Cover: 0.15 **NM** value: **4.00**
📖 Everyone Must Love Me; First Fight; Time for Tears; One Last Quarrel; Just Jeannette (text); Surrendered Love; What Does a Kiss Mean? **A:** Nicholas Alascia; José Luis Garcia Lopez
69 ❑ Feb 1970 Cover: 0.15 **NM** value: **4.00**
70 ❑ Apr 1970 Cover: 0.15 **NM** value: **4.00**
71 ❑ Jun 1970 Cover: 0.15 **NM** value: **4.00**
72 ❑ Aug 1970 Cover: 0.15 **NM** value: **4.00**
73 ❑ Oct 1970 Cover: 0.15 **NM** value: **4.00**
74 ❑ Dec 1970 Cover: 0.15 **NM** value: **4.00**
75 ❑ Feb 1971 Cover: 0.15 **NM** value: **4.00**
76 ❑ Apr 1971 Cover: 0.15 **NM** value: **4.00**
77 ❑ Jun 1971 Cover: 0.15 **NM** value: **4.00**
78 ❑ Aug 1971 Cover: 0.15 **NM** value: **4.00**
79 ❑ Sep 1971 Cover: 0.20 **NM** value: **4.00**
80 ❑ Nov 1971 Cover: 0.20 **NM** value: **4.00**
81 ❑ Dec 1971 Cover: 0.20 **NM** value: **3.00**
82 ❑ Jan 1972 Cover: 0.20 **NM** value: **3.00**
83 ❑ Mar 1972 Cover: 0.20 **NM** value: **3.00**
Circ: Statement: **127,026**
84 ❑ 1972 Cover: 0.20 **NM** value: **3.00**
Circ: Statement: **127,026**
85 ❑ 1972 Cover: 0.20 **NM** value: **3.00**
Circ: Statement: **127,026**
86 ❑ 1972 Cover: 0.20 **NM** value: **3.00**
Circ: Statement: **127,026**
87 ❑ Aug 1972 Cover: 0.20 **NM** value: **3.00**
Circ: Statement: **127,026**
88 ❑ 1972 Cover: 0.20 **NM** value: **3.00**
Circ: Statement: **127,026**
89 ❑ Nov 1972 Cover: 0.20 **NM** value: **3.00**
Circ: Statement: **127,026**
90 ❑ Dec 1972 Cover: 0.20 **NM** value: **3.00**
Circ: Statement: **127,026**
91 ❑ Jan 1973 Cover: 0.20 **NM** value: **3.00**
Circ: Statement: **119,583**
92 ❑ Feb 1973 Cover: 0.20 **NM** value: **3.00**
Circ: Statement: **119,583**
93 ❑ Mar 1973 Cover: 0.20 **NM** value: **3.00**
Circ: Statement: **119,583**
94 ❑ 1973 Cover: 0.20 **NM** value: **3.00**
Circ: Statement: **119,583**
• Has 1972 Statement; avg total paid circ 127,026
95 ❑ 1973 Cover: 0.20 **NM** value: **3.00**
Circ: Statement: **119,583**
96 ❑ 1973 Cover: 0.20 **NM** value: **3.00**
Circ: Statement: **119,583**
97 ❑ 1973 Cover: 0.20 **NM** value: **3.00**
Circ: Statement: **119,583**
98 ❑ 1973 Cover: 0.20 **NM** value: **3.00**
Circ: Statement: **119,583**
99 ❑ Dec 1973 Cover: 0.20 **NM** value: **3.00**
Circ: Statement: **119,583**
100 ❑ May 1974 Cover: 0.20 **NM** value: **3.00**
Circ: Statement: **112,130**
• Has 1973 Statement; avg total paid circ 119,583
101 ❑ 1974 Cover: 0.20 **NM** value: **3.00**
Circ: Statement: **112,130**
102 ❑ 1974 Cover: 0.25 **NM** value: **3.00**
Circ: Statement: **112,130**
103 ❑ 1974 Cover: 0.25 **NM** value: **3.00**
Circ: Statement: **112,130**
104 ❑ Feb 1975 Cover: 0.25 **NM** value: **3.00**
Circ: Statement: **94,675**
105 ❑ 1975 Cover: 0.25 **NM** value: **3.00**
Circ: Statement: **94,675**
• Has 1974 Statement; avg total paid circ 112,130
106 ❑ 1975 Cover: 0.25 **NM** value: **3.00**
Circ: Statement: **94,675**
107 ❑ Sep 1975 Cover: 0.25 **NM** value: **3.00**
Circ: Statement: **94,675**
108 ❑ Dec 1975 Cover: 0.25 **NM** value: **3.00**
Circ: Statement: **94,675**
109 ❑ Feb 1976 Cover: 0.25 **NM** value: **3.00**
110 ❑ Apr 1976 Cover: 0.25 **NM** value: **3.00**
111 ❑ Jun 1976 Cover: 0.30 **NM** value: **3.00**
112 ❑ Aug 1976 Cover: 0.30 **NM** value: **3.00**
113 ❑ Oct 1976 Cover: 0.30 **NM** value: **3.00**
114 ❑ Dec 1976 Cover: 0.30 **NM** value: **3.00**
final issue.

JUST TWISTED — Necromics

1 ❑ Cover: 2.00 **NM** value: **Cover or less**

JUSTY — Viz

1 ❑ Dec 1988, b&w Cover: 1.75 **NM** value: **Cover or less**
📖 The Tears of Astalis Part 1 • Japanese **A:** Tsuguo Okazaki **W:** Tsuguo Okazaki
2 ❑ Dec 1988, b&w Cover: 1.75 **NM** value: **Cover or less**
📖 The Tears of Astalis Part 2 • Japanese **A:** Tsuguo Okazaki **W:** Tsuguo Okazaki
3 ❑ Jan 1989, b&w Cover: 1.75 **NM** value: **Cover or less**
• Japanese **A:** Tsuguo Okazaki **W:** Tsuguo Okazaki
4 ❑ Jan 1989, b&w Cover: 1.75 **NM** value: **Cover or less**
📖 Hostages Part 1 • Japanese **A:** Tsuguo Okazaki **W:** Tsuguo Okazaki
5 ❑ Feb 1989, b&w Cover: 1.75 **NM** value: **Cover or less**
• Japanese **A:** Tsuguo Okazaki **W:** Tsuguo Okazaki
6 ❑ Feb 1989, b&w Cover: 1.75 **NM** value: **Cover or less**
• Japanese **A:** Tsuguo Okazaki **W:** Tsuguo Okazaki
7 ❑ Mar 1989, b&w Cover: 1.75 **NM** value: **Cover or less**
• Japanese **A:** Tsuguo Okazaki **W:** Tsuguo Okazaki
8 ❑ Mar 1989, b&w Cover: 1.75 **NM** value: **Cover or less**
• Japanese **A:** Tsuguo Okazaki **W:** Tsuguo Okazaki
9 ❑ Apr 1989, b&w Cover: 1.75 **NM** value: **Cover or less**
• Japanese **A:** Tsuguo Okazaki **W:** Tsuguo Okazaki

KA'A'NGA COMICS — Fiction House

Fiction House already ruled the densely forested comics jungle in the late 1940s with such hits as Jumbo Comics, Sheena, and Jungle Comics. Ka'a'nga followed in that same tradition, with another great white jungle lord and his leopard-clad girlfriend making the rain forests and lost cities of the Dark Continent safe against poachers, evil natives, and slave masters. During this time, the brilliant Burne Hogarth, who set a high standard for jungle-king art, was illustrating the Tarzan newspaper strip. Ka'a'nga's Frank Riddell rose to the challenge with elegant, finely crafted, dynamic, and detailed illustrations that brought the standard stories to life. Riddell's art, if not his writing, largely avoided the offensive cliches and crude style of many other Tarzan imitators. And, as required of all Fiction House titles, the women look marvelous.

1 ❑ Spr 1949 Cover: 0.10 **NM** value: **460.00**
• **CGC:** 4 graded, best 9.0
2 ❑ Win 1949 Cover: 0.10 **NM** value: **245.00**
• **CGC:** 1 graded, best 7.5
3 ❑ Spr 1950 Cover: 0.10 **NM** value: **165.00**
• **CGC:** 1 graded, best 7.0
📖 The Return of the Lion-Men; King of the Congo Beasts (Text Story); **A:** Frank Riddell **W:** Frank Riddell
4 ❑ Sum 1950 Cover: 0.10 **NM** value: **135.00**
5 ❑ Fal 1950 Cover: 0.10 **NM** value: **135.00**
6 ❑ Win 1950 Cover: 0.10 **NM** value: **110.00**
7 ❑ Spr 1951 Cover: 0.10 **NM** value: **110.00**
• **CGC:** 1 graded, best 6.5
8 ❑ Sum 1951 Cover: 0.10 **NM** value: **110.00**
9 ❑ Fal 1951 Cover: 0.10 **NM** value: **110.00**
10 ❑ Win 1951 Cover: 0.10 **NM** value: **110.00**
11 ❑ Spr 1952 Cover: 0.10 **NM** value: **85.00**
• **CGC:** 1 graded, best 8.5
12 ❑ Sum 1952 Cover: 0.10 **NM** value: **85.00**
13 ❑ Fal 1952 Cover: 0.10 **NM** value: **85.00**
• **CGC:** 2 graded, best 6.0
14 ❑ Win 1952 Cover: 0.10 **NM** value: **85.00**
15 ❑ Spr 1953 Cover: 0.10 **NM** value: **85.00**
16 ❑ Sum 1953 Cover: 0.10 **NM** value: **85.00**
17 ❑ Fal 1953 Cover: 0.10 **NM** value: **85.00**
18 ❑ Win 1953 Cover: 0.10 **NM** value: **85.00**
19 ❑ Spr 1954 Cover: 0.10 **NM** value: **85.00**
20 ❑ Sum 1954 Cover: 0.10 **NM** value: **85.00**
★ Appearance of final.

KABOOM — Awesome

1 ❑ Sep 1997 Cover: 2.50 **NM** value: **3.00**
Circ: Diamd. preorders: **24,544**
📖 Sixteen Candles **A:** Jeff Matsuda **W:** Jeph Loeb ★ 1st Appearance of Kaboom.
1/A ❑ Sep 1997 Cover: 0.25 **NM** value: **3.00**
📖 Sixteen Candles • Dynamic Forces variant (marked as such); Purple Awesome logo **A:** Jeff Matsuda **W:** Jeph Loeb
1/GO❑ Sep 1997 **NM** value: **4.00**
• Gold edition with silver logo. 📖 Sixteen Candles **A:** Jeff Matsuda **W:** Jeph Loeb ★ 1st Appearance of Kaboom.
2 ❑ Oct 1997 Cover: 2.50 **NM** value: **Cover or less**
Circ: Diamd. preorders: **19,504**
A: Jeff Matsuda **W:** Jeph Loeb
2/Aut❑ Oct 1997 **NM** value: **4.00**
A: Jeff Matsuda **W:** Jeph Loeb
2/GO❑ Oct 1997 **NM** value: **4.00**
• Gold edition. **A:** Jeff Matsuda **W:** Jeph Loeb
3 ❑ Nov 1997 Cover: 2.50 **NM** value: **Cover or less**
Circ: Diamd. preorders: **19,812**
A: Jeff Matsuda **W:** Jeph Loeb
4 ❑ Feb 1998 Cover: 2.50 **NM** value: **Cover or less**
Circ: Diamd. preorders: **16,240**
A: Jeff Matsuda **W:** Jeph Loeb
5 ❑ Mar 1998 Cover: 2.50 **NM** value: **Cover or less**
Circ: Diamd. preorders: **15,968**
A: Jeff Matsuda **W:** Jeph Loeb
Ash 1❑ Feb 1998 **NM** value: **2.50**
• Preview edition. **A:** Jeff Matsuda **W:** Jeph Loeb
Ash 1/GO❑ Feb 1998 **NM** value: **4.00**
• Gold edition. **A:** Jeff Matsuda **W:** Jeph Loeb

KABUKI — Image

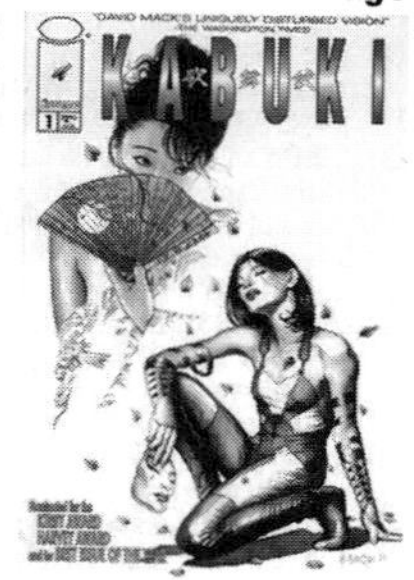

David Mack's impressive series came to Image in 1998, following a legion of one-shots and mini-series at Caliber. Mack uses a multitextured, mixed-media style to illustrate the tale of a girl turned into a weapon of vengeance. It's an intensely psychological series, which explores the story from the private thoughts of the characters, rather than merely filling time between action sequences.

As the series begins, Kabuki is interned in a secret institution designed to house agents who have run amuck or broken down in some way. There, she exchanges countless messages with a fellow inmate called Akemi, all written on tiny squares of paper folded into origami. Over the course of the first four issues, she meets her friend in person, as well as the other members of her circle. Together, they launch a bold plan to break out of the asylum of spies, all the while playing sly games with the doctors who are trying to unlock their secrets.

0.5 ❑ ca. 1999 Cover: 2.95 **NM** value: **4.00**
Circ: Diamd. preorders: **11,226** • **CGC:** 21 graded, best 9.9
• Speckle-foil Wizard variant **A:** David Mack **W:** David Mack
1 ❑ Oct 1997 Cover: 2.95 **NM** value: **4.00**
Circ: Diamd. preorders: **30,623**
📖 Separate Pieces **A:** David Mack **W:** David Mack ★ Origin of Kabuki.
1/A ❑ Oct 1997 Cover: 2.95 **NM** value: **5.00**
Circ: Diamd. preorders: **5,126** • **CGC:** 1 graded, best 9.6
Jim Steranko alternate cover. 📖 Separate Pieces **A:** David Mack; Jim Steranko(cover) **W:** David Mack ★ Origin of Kabuki.
2 ❑ Dec 1997 Cover: 2.95 **NM** value: **3.50**
Circ: Diamd. preorders: **22,144**
📖 Invisible Friends **A:** David Mack **W:** David Mack
3 ❑ Mar 1998 Cover: 2.95 **NM** value: **3.50**
Circ: Diamd. preorders: **19,946**
📖 Retina Escape **A:** David Mack **W:** David Mack
4 ❑ Jun 1998 Cover: 2.95 **NM** value: **3.00**
Circ: Diamd. preorders: **19,855**
📖 Deconstructing Akemi **A:** David Mack **W:** David Mack
5 ❑ Sep 1998 Cover: 2.95 **NM** value: **Cover or less**
Circ: Diamd. preorders: **18,888**
📖 Deeper **A:** David Mack **W:** David Mack
6 ❑ Nov 1998 Cover: 2.95 **NM** value: **Cover or less**
Circ: Diamd. preorders: **18,982**
A: David Mack **W:** David Mack
7 ❑ Feb 1999 Cover: 2.95 **NM** value: **Cover or less**
Circ: Diamd. preorders: **17,967**
A: David Mack **W:** David Mack
8 ❑ Jun 1999 Cover: 2.95 **NM** value: **Cover or less**
Circ: Diamd. preorders: **17,019**
A: David Mack **W:** David Mack
9 ❑ Mar 2000 Cover: 2.95 **NM** value: **Cover or less**
Circ: Diamd. preorders: **16,643**
A: David Mack **W:** David Mack

KABUKI 1996 CALENDAR — Caliber

1 ❑ ca. 1996 Cover: 3.95 **NM** value: **Cover or less**
A: David Mack **W:** David Mack

KABUKI AGENTS — Image

1 ❑ Aug 1999 Cover: 2.95 **NM** value: **Cover or less**
Circ: Diamd. preorders: **14,809**
📖 Synchronicity • Scarab **A:** David Mack **W:** David Mack
1/A ❑ Aug 1999 Cover: 2.95 **NM** value: **Cover or less**
Scarab alternate cover. **A:** David Mack **W:** David Mack
2 ❑ Oct 1999 Cover: 2.95 **NM** value: **Cover or less**
Circ: Diamd. preorders: **13,048**
📖 Chaos by Design • Scarab **A:** David Mack **W:** David Mack; Rick Mays
3 ❑ Nov 1999 Cover: 2.95 **NM** value: **Cover or less**
Circ: Diamd. preorders: **13,091**
📖 Voodoo Doll • Scarab **A:** David Mack **W:** David Mack
4 ❑ Dec 1999 Cover: 2.95 **NM** value: **Cover or less**
Circ: Diamd. preorders: **13,676**
• Scarab **W:** David Mack
5 ❑ Nov 2000 Cover: 2.95 **NM** value: **Cover or less**
Circ: Diamd. preorders: **11,585**
📖 Tale Twp • Scarab **A:** David Mack; Rick Mays **W:** David Mack
6 ❑ Jan 2001 Cover: 2.95 **NM** value: **Cover or less**
Circ: Diamd. preorders: **10,849**
• Scarab **A:** Rick Mays **W:** David Mack
7 ❑ Mar 2001 Cover: 2.95 **NM** value: **Cover or less**
Circ: Diamd. preorders: **10,521**
📖 Lost in Translation • Scarab **A:** Rick Mays **W:** David Mack
8 ❑ Jul 2001 Cover: 2.95 **NM** value: **Cover or less**
Circ: Diamd. preorders: **11,287**
• Scarab

KABUKI: CIRCLE OF BLOOD — Caliber

1 ❑ Jan 1995, b&w Cover: 2.95 **NM** value: **4.00**
Circ: CapCity orders: **7,360**
📖 Ghosts In the Looking Glass **A:** David Mack **W:** David Mack ★ Origin of Kabuki.
1/LE❑ Jan 1995 Cover: 15.00 **NM** value: **Cover or less**
• Limited edition with new, painted cover. 📖 Ghosts In the Looking Glass **A:** David Mack **W:** David Mack ★ Origin of Kabuki.
1-2 ❑ Jul 1995, b&w Cover: 2.95 **NM** value: **3.00**
2 ❑ Mar 1995, b&w Cover: 2.95 **NM** value: **3.00**
Circ: CapCity orders: **7,295**
A: David Mack **W:** David Mack

Other grades: Multiply prices above by **1.5 for Mint • 2/3 for Very Fine • 1/3 for Fine • 1/5 for Very Good • 1/8 for Good**

3 ❑ May 1995, b&w Cover: 2.95 **NM** value: **3.00**
Circ: CapCity orders: **7,675**
• reprints #1's indicia **A:** David Mack **W:** David Mack

4 ❑ Jul 1995, b&w Cover: 2.95 **NM** value: **3.00**
Circ: CapCity orders: **7,715**
A: David Mack **W:** David Mack

5 ❑ Sep 1995, b&w Cover: 2.95 **NM** value: **3.00**
Circ: CapCity orders: **6,150**
A: David Mack **W:** David Mack

6 ❑ Nov 1995, b&w Cover: 2.95 **NM** value: **3.00**
A: David Mack **W:** David Mack

6/LE❑ Nov 1995 Cover: 15.00 **NM** value: **Cover or less**
A: David Mack **W:** David Mack

Bk 1❑ b&w Cover: 17.95 **NM** value: **Cover or less**
• collects mini-series **A:** David Mack **W:** David Mack

Bk 1/HC❑ Cover: 29.95 **NM** value: **Cover or less**
hardcover. **A:** David Mack **W:** David Mack

Bk 1/LE❑ Cover: 49.95 **NM** value: **Cover or less**
A: David Mack **W:** David Mack

Bk 1-2❑b&w Cover: 17.95 **NM** value: **Cover or less**
• collects mini-series; 1st printing published by Caliber **A:** David Mack **W:** David Mack

KABUKI CLASSICS — Image

1 ❑ Feb 1999 Cover: 3.25 **NM** value: **Cover or less**
Circ: Diamd. preorders: **6,760**
📖 Fear the Reaper • Squarebound; Reprints Kabuki: Fear the Reaper **A:** David Mack **W:** David Mack

2 ❑ Mar 1999 Cover: 3.25 **NM** value: **Cover or less**
Circ: Diamd. preorders: **5,914**
📖 Dance of Death • Reprints Kabuki: Dance of Death **A:** David Mack **W:** David Mack

3 ❑ Mar 1999 Cover: 4.95 **NM** value: **Cover or less**
Circ: Diamd. preorders: **5,457**
📖 Circle of Blood, Part 1 • Squarebound **A:** David Mack **W:** David Mack

4 ❑ Apr 1999 Cover: 3.25 **NM** value: **Cover or less**
Circ: Diamd. preorders: **4,767**
📖 Circle of Blood, Part 2 **A:** David Mack **W:** David Mack

5 ❑ Jul 1999 Cover: 3.25 **NM** value: **Cover or less**
Circ: Diamd. preorders: **4,922**
📖 Circle of Blood, Part 3 **A:** David Mack **W:** David Mack

6 ❑ Jul 1999 Cover: 3.25 **NM** value: **Cover or less**
Circ: Diamd. preorders: **4,660**
📖 Circle of Blood, Part 4 **A:** David Mack **W:** David Mack

7 ❑ Aug 1999 Cover: 3.25 **NM** value: **Cover or less**
Circ: Diamd. preorders: **3,762**
📖 Circle of Blood, Part 5 **A:** David Mack **W:** David Mack

8 ❑ Sep 1999 Cover: 3.25 **NM** value: **Cover or less**
Circ: Diamd. preorders: **3,905**
📖 Circle of Blood, Part 6 **A:** David Mack **W:** David Mack

9 ❑ Oct 1999 Cover: 3.25 **NM** value: **Cover or less**
Circ: Diamd. preorders: **3,868**
📖 Masks of the Noh, Part 1 **A:** David Mack **W:** David Mack

10 ❑ Nov 1999 Cover: 3.25 **NM** value: **Cover or less**
Circ: Diamd. preorders: **3,701**
📖 Masks of the Noh, Part 2 **A:** Andrew Robinson; Michael Bair; Buzz; Michael Avon Oeming; David Mack; Rick Mays; Dave Johnson; Caesar; Mahindo Kuumbo **W:** David Mack

11 ❑ Dec 1999 Cover: 3.25 **NM** value: **Cover or less**
Circ: Diamd. preorders: **3,511**
📖 Masks of the Noh, Part 3 **A:** Andrew Robinson; Michael Bair; Buzz; Michael Avon Oeming; David Mack; Rick Mays; Dave Johnson; Caesar; Mahindo Kuumbo **W:** David Mack

12 ❑ Mar 2000 Cover: 3.25 **NM** value: **Cover or less**
Circ: Diamd. preorders: **3,288**
📖 Masks of the Noh, Part 4 **A:** Andrew Robinson; Michael Bair; Buzz; Michael Avon Oeming; David Mack; Rick Mays; Dave Johnson; Caesar; Mahindo Kuumbo **W:** David Mack

KABUKI COLOR SPECIAL — Caliber

1 ❑ Jan 1996 Cover: 2.95 **NM** value: **3.50**
A: Tony Harris; Mike Grell; Buzz; Joe Quesada; Caesar; Bill Tucci **W:** David Mack

KABUKI: DANCE OF DEATH — London Night

1 ❑ Cover: 3.00 **NM** value: **3.50**
Circ: CapCity orders: **8,620**
A: David Mack **W:** David Mack

KABUKI DREAMS — Image

Bk 2❑ Jan 1998, b&w Cover: 4.95 **NM** value: **Cover or less**
Circ: Diamd. preorders: **11,997**
• reprints Kabuki Color Special and Kabuki: Dreams of the Dead **A:** David Mack **W:** David Mack

KABUKI: DREAMS OF THE DEAD — Caliber

1 ❑ Jul 1996 Cover: 2.95 **NM** value: **Cover or less**
No issue number. One-shot.

KABUKI: FEAR THE REAPER — Caliber

1 ❑ Nov 1994 Cover: 3.50 **NM** value: **Cover or less**
Circ: CapCity orders: **8,920** • **CGC:** 2 graded, best 9.6

KABUKI GALLERY — Caliber

1 ❑ Aug 1995 Cover: 2.95 **NM** value: **Cover or less**
Circ: CapCity orders: **7,675**
• pin-ups **A:** Vincent Locke; Andrew Robinson; Ken Meyer Jr.; Paul Pope; Tim Bradstreet; Brian Michael Bendis; Michael Avon Oeming; David Mack; Rick Mays; Greg Land; Andrew Dimitt; Galen Showman; Dave Johnson; Michael Okamoto; Colleen Doran; Kirk Lindo; Arnold Ayala

1/A ❑ Aug 1995 Cover: 15.00 **NM** value: **Cover or less**
• Comic Cavalcade edition. **A:** Vincent Locke; Andrew Robinson; Ken Meyer Jr.; Paul Pope; Tim Bradstreet; Brian Michael Bendis; Michael Avon Oeming; David Mack; Rick Mays; Greg Land; Andrew Dimitt; Galen Showman; Dave Johnson; Michael Okamoto; Colleen Doran; Kirk Lindo; Arnold Ayala

KABUKI-IMAGES — Image

1 ❑ Jul 1998 Cover: 4.95 **NM** value: **Cover or less**
• prestige format. • pin-ups and story; Reprints Kabuki (Image) #1 with new pin-ups **A:** David Mack **W:** David Mack

2 ❑ Jan 1999 Cover: 5.95 **NM** value: **Cover or less**
• prestige format. • collects #2 and 3; Reprints Kabuki (Image) #2-3 **A:** David Mack **W:** David Mack

KABUKI: MASKS OF THE NOH — Image

1 ❑ May 1996 Cover: 2.95 **NM** value: **Cover or less**
A: Andrew Robinson; Michael Bair; Buzz; David Mack; Rick Mays; Caesar **W:** David Mack

2 ❑ 1996 Cover: 2.95 **NM** value: **Cover or less**
A: Andrew Robinson; Michael Bair; Buzz; David Mack; Rick Mays; Caesar **W:** David Mack

3 ❑ 1996 Cover: 2.95 **NM** value: **Cover or less**
A: Andrew Robinson; Michael Bair; Buzz; David Mack; Rick Mays; Caesar **W:** David Mack

4 ❑ Jan 1997 Cover: 2.95 **NM** value: **Cover or less**
Circ: Diamd. preorders: **8,939**
A: Andrew Robinson; Michael Bair; Buzz; David Mack; Rick Mays; Caesar **W:** David Mack

KABUKI REFLECTIONS — Image

1 ❑ Jul 1998 Cover: 4.95 **NM** value: **Cover or less**
no number on cover or in indicia. • prestige format. **A:** David Mack **W:** David Mack

2 ❑ Dec 1998 Cover: 4.95 **NM** value: **Cover or less**
Circ: Diamd. preorders: **10,504**
• prestige format. **A:** David Mack **W:** David Mack

3 ❑ Jan 2000 Cover: 4.95 **NM** value: **Cover or less**
A: David Mack **W:** David Mack

KABUKI: SKIN DEEP — Caliber

1 ❑ Oct 1996 Cover: 2.95 **NM** value: **3.50**
A: David Mack **W:** David Mack

2 ❑ Feb 1997 Cover: 2.95 **NM** value: **3.00**
Circ: Diamd. preorders: **7,480**
A: David Mack **W:** David Mack

2/A ❑ Feb 1997 Cover: 2.95 **NM** value: **3.00**
Circ: Diamd. preorders: **4,746**
Alternate cover by Alex Ross. • white background **A:** David Mack; Alex Ross(cover) **W:** David Mack

2/LE❑ Feb 1997 Cover: 15.00 **NM** value: **Cover or less**
Wraparound cover by David Mack and Alex Ross. **A:** David Mack; Alex Ross(cover) **W:** David Mack

3 ❑ May 1997 Cover: 2.95 **NM** value: **Cover or less**
Circ: Diamd. preorders: **8,591**
A: David Mack **W:** David Mack

KAFKA — Renegade

1 ❑ Apr 1987, b&w Cover: 2.00 **NM** value: **3.00**
2 ❑ May 1987, b&w Cover: 2.00 **NM** value: **2.50**
3 ❑ Jun 1987, b&w Cover: 2.00 **NM** value: **2.50**
4 ❑ Jul 1987, b&w Cover: 2.00 **NM** value: **2.50**
5 ❑ Aug 1987, b&w Cover: 2.00 **NM** value: **2.50**
6 ❑ Sep 1987, b&w Cover: 2.00 **NM** value: **2.50**
Bk 1❑ Cover: 14.95 **NM** value: **Cover or less**

KAFKA: THE EXECUTION — Fantagraphics

1 ❑ b&w Cover: 2.95 **NM** value: **Cover or less**
• Duranona

KAKTUS — Fantagraphics

1 ❑ b&w Cover: 2.50 **NM** value: **Cover or less**

KALAMAZOO COMIX — Discount Hobby

1 ❑ Cover: 1.95 **NM** value: **Cover or less**
2 ❑ Win 1996 Cover: 1.95 **NM** value: **Cover or less**
3 ❑ Win 1996 Cover: 1.95 **NM** value: **Cover or less**
4 ❑ Spr 1997 Cover: 2.95 **NM** value: **Cover or less**
5 ❑ Dec 1997 Cover: 2.95 **NM** value: **Cover or less**
📖 Blind; Mystery At The Center of The Earth; Oh Crap!; Finem Respice; When The U.F.O.'s Come; Doctor Aeon: Always Remember; Roswell: It's All P.C.; Departure; Hero Hold; A Timeliketoon Tribute to Carl Sagan; Cooly Cool Guy; Marilyn Manson in Hell; 3Pals: W **A:** Linc Polderman; Dave Reynolds; Denny Stephens; Douglas Waltz; George Calloway; Jamie Binington; Jason Kahler; Jay Hansen; Marc Palm; Mchael Krupp; Mel Ford; Mikael Van Cleave; Randy Crawford; Rod Pallett; Steve Budzinski; Yul Tolbert; Rich Halpin; Todd Fr **W:** Linc Polderman; Andy Konik; Dave Reynolds; Denny Stephens; Douglas Waltz; George Calloway; Jamie Binington; Jason Kahler; Jay Hansen; Marc Palm; Mchael Krupp; Mel Ford; Mikael Van Cleave; Randy Crawford; Rod Pallett; Steve Budzinski; Yul Tolbert

KALGAN THE GOLDEN — Harrier

1 ❑ Mar 1988 Cover: 1.95 **NM** value: **Cover or less**
A: Ron Turner; John Lawrence **W:** E.C. Tubb; Philip Harbottle

KAMANDI: AT EARTH'S END — DC

1 ❑ Jun 1993 Cover: 1.75 **NM** value: **Cover or less**
Circ: CapCity orders: **20,550**
📖 Dead York City **A:** Frank Gomez **W:** Tom Veitch

2 ❑ Jul 1993 Cover: 1.75 **NM** value: **Cover or less**
Circ: CapCity orders: **17,350**
A: Frank Gomez **W:** Tom Veitch

3 ❑ Aug 1993 Cover: 1.75 **NM** value: **Cover or less**
Circ: CapCity orders: **11,100**
📖 Thunder Road! **A:** Frank Gomez **W:** Tom Veitch

4 ❑ Sep 1993 Cover: 1.75 **NM** value: **Cover or less**
Circ: CapCity orders: **9,700**

5 ❑ Oct 1993 Cover: 1.75 **NM** value: **Cover or less**
Circ: CapCity orders: **8,350**

6 ❑ Nov 1993 Cover: 1.75 **NM** value: **Cover or less**
Circ: CapCity orders: **7,350**

KAMANDI, THE LAST BOY ON EARTH — DC

It has been generations since the shadow of a great devastation blocked out the light of hope for mankind. Finally, one boy emerged from a bunker to see if the world his grandfather told him about still existed. But what the boy — Kamandi — found was more terrible than any story he could have imagined.

In the years since his grandfather first sought the safety of the shelter (Command D), the world had turned upside-down. Humans had lost their civilizations and their intelligence, reverting to an animal-like state. Meanwhile, the other animals: lions, dogs, and even rats, had mastered technology, and had become the new masters of the earth. In fact, these new, civilized animals had taken to keeping humans as pets.

Kamandi is terrific end-of-the-world fiction, told in the incomparable style of the great Jack Kirby himself.

1 ❑ Nov 1972 Cover: 0.20 **NM** value: **18.00**
• **CGC:** 45 graded, best 9.8
📖 The Last Boy on Earth!; Wolf!; The Royal City Kennels! **A:** Jack Kirby **W:** Jack Kirby ★ Origin of Kamandi. ★ 1st Appearance of Kamandi, Dr. Canus, Dr. Canus, Ben Boxer, Ben Boxer.

2 ❑ Jan 1973 Cover: 0.20 **NM** value: **10.00**
• **CGC:** 3 graded, best 9.4
📖 Year of the Rat!; A Short Day's Journey Into Death!; Ordeal! **A:** Jack Kirby **W:** Jack Kirby

3 ❑ Feb 1973 Cover: 0.20 **NM** value: **8.00**
• **CGC:** 1 graded, best 9.4
📖 The Thing that Grew on the Moon!; Encounter with Death! • in Vegas **A:** Jack Kirby **W:** Jack Kirby

4 ❑ Mar 1973 Cover: 0.20 **NM** value: **6.00**
📖 The Devil's Arena!; The Waiting Secret! **A:** Jack Kirby **W:** Jack Kirby ★ 1st Appearance of Prince Tuftan.

5 ❑ Apr 1973 Cover: 0.20 **NM** value: **6.00**
📖 The One-Armed Bandit!; Killing Grounds!; Gamble with Death! **A:** Jack Kirby **W:** Jack Kirby

6 ❑ Jun 1973 Cover: 0.20 **NM** value: **5.00**
📖 Flower; People Hunters!; Death! **A:** Jack Kirby **W:** Jack Kirby

7 ❑ Jul 1973 Cover: 0.20 **NM** value: **5.00**
• **CGC:** 1 graded, best 9.6
📖 The Monster Fetish!; The United States of Lions! **A:** Jack Kirby **W:** Jack Kirby

8 ❑ Aug 1973 Cover: 0.20 **NM** value: **5.00**
📖 Beyond Reason; The Return of Ben Boxer • In Washington, D.C. **A:** Jack Kirby **W:** Jack Kirby

9 ❑ Sep 1973 Cover: 0.20 **NM** value: **5.00**
📖 Tracking Site!; Murdering Misfit! **A:** Jack Kirby **W:** Jack Kirby

10 ❑ Oct 1973 Cover: 0.20 **NM** value: **5.00**
📖 Killer Germ!; Them or Us! **A:** Jack Kirby **W:** Jack Kirby

11 ❑ Nov 1973 Cover: 0.20 **NM** value: **3.50**
📖 The Devil!; Sacker's Department Store!; Unmasked Terror! **A:** Jack Kirby **W:** Jack Kirby

12 ❑ Dec 1973 Cover: 0.20 **NM** value: **3.50**
📖 The Devil and Mr. Sacker!; The Beautiful Dead! **A:** Jack Kirby **W:** Jack Kirby

13 ❑ Jan 1974 Cover: 0.20 **NM** value: **3.50**
📖 Hell at Hialeah!; Death and the Devil! **A:** Jack Kirby **W:** Jack Kirby

14 ❑ Feb 1974 Cover: 0.20 **NM** value: **3.50**
📖 Winner Take All!; The Last Mile! **A:** Jack Kirby **W:** Jack Kirby

15 ❑ Mar 1974 Cover: 0.20 **NM** value: **3.50**
📖 The Watergate Secrets!; Screaming Spirits! **A:** Jack Kirby **W:** Jack Kirby

16 ❑ Apr 1974 Cover: 0.20 **NM** value: **3.50**
📖 The Hospital!; Doomsday Present; The Gift! **A:** Jack Kirby **W:** Jack Kirby

17 ❑ May 1974 Cover: 0.20 **NM** value: **3.50**
📖 The Human Gophers of Ohio!; Vanishville! **A:** Jack Kirby **W:** Jack Kirby

18 ❑ Jun 1974 Cover: 0.20 **NM** value: **3.50**
📖 The Eater!; As the Worm Turns!; In Sudden Flame! **A:** Jack Kirby **W:** Jack Kirby

19 ❑ Jul 1974 Cover: 0.20 **NM** value: **3.50**
📖 The Last Gang in Chicago!; Slaughter on Michigan Avenue! • in Chicago **A:** Jack Kirby **W:** Jack Kirby

20 ❑ Aug 1974 Cover: 0.20 **NM** value: **3.50**
📖 The Electric Chair!; Someone Hidden, Someone Deadly!; Now for the Fantastic, Hope-Destroying Truth! • in Chicago **A:** Jack Kirby **W:** Jack Kirby

21 ❑ Sep 1974 Cover: 0.20 **NM** value: **3.00**
📖 The Fish!; A Legacy of Living Terror!; The One Who Kills! **A:** Jack Kirby **W:** Jack Kirby

22 ❑ Oct 1974 Cover: 0.20 **NM** value: **3.00**
📖 The Red Baron!; The Way of the Dolphins!; Hit-Run Killer! **A:** Jack Kirby **W:** Jack Kirby

23 ❑ Nov 1974 Cover: 0.20 **NM** value: **3.00**
📖 Kamandi and Goliath!; At Any Cost!; Moby Death! **A:** Jack Kirby **W:** Jack Kirby

24 ❑ Dec 1974 Cover: 0.20 **NM** value: **3.00**
📖 The Exorcism!; Evil One!; The Fatal Secret! **A:** Jack Kirby **W:** Jack Kirby

25 ❑ Jan 1975 Cover: 0.25 **NM** value: **3.00**
Circ: Statement: **167,000**
📖 Freak Show!; To Rage Upon the Land!; The Ultimate Fear! **A:** Jack Kirby **W:** Jack Kirby

CGC-graded: Multiply prices above by **33 for 9.9 M • 16 for 9.8 NM/M • 7 for 9.6 NM+ • 5 for 9.4 NM • 2.5 for 9.2 NM- • 1.5 for 9.0 VF/NM**

26 ❑ Feb 1975 Cover: 0.25 **NM** value: **3.00**
Circ: Statement: **167,000**
📖 The Heights of Abraham!; Dominion of the Devils! **A:** Jack Kirby **W:** Jack Kirby

27 ❑ Mar 1975 Cover: 0.25 **NM** value: **3.00**
Circ: Statement: **167,000**
📖 The Mad Marine!; The Ravagers!; Prelude to Fury! **A:** Jack Kirby **W:** Jack Kirby

28 ❑ Apr 1975 Cover: 0.25 **NM** value: **3.00**
Circ: Statement: **167,000**
📖 Enforce the Atlantic Testament!; Murder Alley! **A:** Jack Kirby **W:** Jack Kirby

29 ❑ May 1975 Cover: 0.25 **NM** value: **3.00**
Circ: Statement: **167,000**
📖 Mighty One!; The Legend!; Deceive or Die!; Save the Super-Suit! • Superman's legend **A:** Jack Kirby **W:** Jack Kirby

30 ❑ Jun 1975 Cover: 0.25 **NM** value: **3.00**
Circ: Statement: **167,000**
📖 U.F.O. The Wildest Trip Ever!; The Door! **A:** Jack Kirby **W:** Jack Kirby ★ 1st Appearance of Pyra.

31 ❑ Jul 1975 Cover: 0.25 **NM** value: **3.00**
Circ: Statement: **167,000** • **CGC:** 1 graded, best 7.5
📖 The Gulliver Effect!; It's Alive! **A:** Jack Kirby **W:** Jack Kirby

32 ❑ Aug 1975 Cover: 0.50 **NM** value: **3.00**
Circ: Statement: **167,000** • **CGC:** 3 graded, best 9.2
📖 Me!; No Chance!; Satan in the Sand!; The Last Boy on Earth; Wolf!; The Royal City Kennels!; Jack Kirby – Man with a Pencil (text) • giant; Jack Kirby interview; New story and reprints Kamandi #1 **A:** Jack Kirby **W:** Jack Kirby ★ Origin of Kamandi.

33 ❑ Sep 1975 Cover: 0.25 **NM** value: **3.00**
Circ: Statement: **167,000** • **CGC:** 1 graded, best 9.4
📖 Blood and Fire!; The Birth Bag! **A:** Jack Kirby **W:** Jack Kirby

34 ❑ Oct 1975 Cover: 0.25 **NM** value: **3.00**
Circ: Statement: **167,000**
📖 Pretty Pyra; Thing from Outer Space! **A:** Jack Kirby **C:** Joe Kubert **W:** Jack Kirby

35 ❑ Nov 1975 Cover: 0.25 **NM** value: **3.00**
Circ: Statement: **167,000**
📖 The Soyuz Survivor!; The Thing That Came Out! **A:** Jack Kirby **C:** Joe Kubert **W:** Jack Kirby

36 ❑ Dec 1975 Cover: 0.25 **NM** value: **3.00**
Circ: Statement: **167,000**
📖 The Hotel!; Welcome to Resort!; The Right of Possession!; Come Out and Fight! **A:** Jack Kirby **C:** Joe Kubert **W:** Jack Kirby

37 ❑ Jan 1976 Cover: 0.25 **NM** value: **3.00**
📖 The Crater People; Riders… Red Riders **A:** Jack Kirby **C:** Joe Kubert **W:** Jack Kirby

38 ❑ Feb 1976 Cover: 0.25 **NM** value: **3.00**
📖 Pyra Revealed; The Stalls!; Graveyard **A:** Jack Kirby **C:** Joe Kubert **W:** Jack Kirby

39 ❑ Mar 1976 Cover: 0.25 **NM** value: **3.00**
📖 The Airquarium; To Make Man Free **A:** Jack Kirby **C:** Joe Kubert **W:** Jack Kirby

40 ❑ Apr 1976 Cover: 0.30 **NM** value: **3.00**
📖 Lizard Lords of Los Lorraine!; The Sun Machine!; Let Sleeping Lizards Lie; Blackmail; The Stolen Star **A:** Jack Kirby **C:** Joe Kubert **W:** Jack Kirby

41 ❑ May 1976 Cover: 0.30 **NM** value: **2.00**
📖 The Hollywood Hounds; Night of the Locusts; Kidnapped! • Has 1975 Statement,m filed 10/1/75; avg print run 375,000; avg sales 165,000; avg subs 2,000; avg total paid circ 167,000; samples 1,000; office use 2,000; max existent 170,000; 55% of run returned **C:** Joe Kubert

42 ❑ Jun 1976 Cover: 0.30 **NM** value: **2.00**
📖 Gunfight at Coyote Corral; Attack; The Last Shhot Out!

43 ❑ Jul 1976 Cover: 0.30 **NM** value: **2.00**
📖 A Connecticut Mutant in Great Ceasar's Court; The Heart of the Inferno; Homecoming • Tales of the Great Disaster backup stories begin; Bicentennial #4

44 ❑ Aug 1976 Cover: 0.30 **NM** value: **2.00**
📖 The Merchant of Menace; Sea Battle; The Prince and the Pawn

45 ❑ Sep 1976 Cover: 0.30 **NM** value: **2.00**
📖 This Murder Is X-Rayted!; Betrayal?; The Apocalypse Machine

46 ❑ Oct 1976 Cover: 0.30 **NM** value: **2.00**
📖 The Wrath and the Fury!; The Last Rampage; Finale • Tales of the Great Disaster backup stories end

47 ❑ Nov 1976 Cover: 0.30 **NM** value: **2.00**
📖 Assault on the Clouds!

48 ❑ Jan 1977 Cover: 0.30 **NM** value: **2.00**
Circ: Statement: **110,223**
📖 The Betrayal

49 ❑ Mar 1977 Cover: 0.30 **NM** value: **2.00**
Circ: Statement: **110,223**
📖 Trial By Fear!; Crown Prince of New York!; Knave of the Sidewalks!; King of the Skyscraper!

50 ❑ May 1977 Cover: 0.30 **NM** value: **2.00**
Circ: Statement: **110,223**
📖 The Death Worshippers! • Kamandi reverts to OMAC

51 ❑ Jul 1977 Cover: 0.35 **NM** value: **2.00**
Circ: Statement: **110,223**
📖 The Next to the Last Boy on Earth!

52 ❑ Sep 1977 Cover: 0.35 **NM** value: **2.00**
Circ: Statement: **110,223**
📖 Sing a Song of Survival

53 ❑ Nov 1977 Cover: 0.35 **NM** value: **2.00**
Circ: Statement: **110,223**
📖 The Catnip Connection

54 ❑ Jan 1978 Cover: 0.35 **NM** value: **2.00**
📖 The Eternity Trap!

55 ❑ Mar 1978 Cover: 0.35 **NM** value: **2.00**
📖 The Vortex Beast ★ Versus Vortex Beast.

56 ❑ May 1978 Cover: 0.35 **NM** value: **2.00**
📖 The Sign of Three

57 ❑ Jul 1978 Cover: 0.35 **NM** value: **2.00**
📖 Behold: Evermore! • Has 1977 Statement, filed 10/1/77; avg print run 281,237; avg sales 108,199; avg subs 2,024; avg total paid circ 110,223; samples 200; office use 178; max existent 110,801; 61% of run returned

58 ❑ Sep 1978 Cover: 0.35 **NM** value: **2.00**
📖 Enter: The Legionnaire • Karate Kid ★ Appearance of Karate Kid.

59 ❑ Oct 1978 Cover: 0.50 **NM** value: **3.00**
• **CGC:** 1 graded, best 9.0
📖 The Wondrous Western Wall; The Return of OMAC final issue. • OMAC back-up begins; continues in Warlord #37

KAMA SUTRA (GIRL'S...) — Black Lace

1 ❑ Cover: 2.95 **NM** value: **Cover or less**
A: Taylor **W:** Girl

KAMIKAZE CAT — Pied Piper

1 ❑ Jul 1987 Cover: 1.95 **NM** value: **Cover or less**
📖 The Web of Cat-tastrophe?! **A:** Stephen D. Sullivan **W:** Mark Hamlin; Roger McKenzie

KANE — Dancing Elephant

"Police officers are your friends." That's the advice given to children the world over, but in New Eden, the rule may not apply. Here, the police are just as likely to be the enemy, and a runaway girl has as much to fear from men with badges as she does from men who lurk in alleyways.

After killing his partner and receiving a six-month suspension, Detective Kane returns to the New Eden Police Department. Understandably, the others in the department shun him, and he must adjust to working alone. Kane chronicles the adventures of the anti-hero Detective Kane, as he tries to keep some sense of law and order in New Eden. The series was created by English comic-book artist and writer Paul Grist and deals with the good and bad sides of the law. As the sign says: "Welcome to New Eden...A Better Place to Live."

1 ❑ Cover: 3.50 **NM** value: **5.00**
📖 Living in Eden **A:** Paul Grist **W:** Paul Grist

2 ❑ Cover: 3.50 **NM** value: **4.00**
A: Paul Grist **W:** Paul Grist

3 ❑ Cover: 3.50 **NM** value: **4.00**
A: Paul Grist **W:** Paul Grist

4 ❑ Cover: 3.50 **NM** value: **Cover or less**
A: Paul Grist **W:** Paul Grist

5 ❑ Cover: 3.50 **NM** value: **Cover or less**
A: Paul Grist **W:** Paul Grist

6 ❑ Cover: 3.50 **NM** value: **Cover or less**
A: Paul Grist **W:** Paul Grist

7 ❑ Cover: 3.50 **NM** value: **Cover or less**
A: Paul Grist **W:** Paul Grist

8 ❑ Cover: 3.50 **NM** value: **Cover or less**
A: Paul Grist **W:** Paul Grist

9 ❑ Cover: 3.50 **NM** value: **Cover or less**
A: Paul Grist **W:** Paul Grist

10 ❑ Cover: 3.50 **NM** value: **Cover or less**
A: Paul Grist **W:** Paul Grist

11 ❑ Cover: 3.50 **NM** value: **Cover or less**
A: Paul Grist **W:** Paul Grist

12 ❑ Cover: 3.50 **NM** value: **Cover or less**
A: Paul Grist **W:** Paul Grist

13 ❑ Cover: 3.50 **NM** value: **Cover or less**
A: Paul Grist **W:** Paul Grist

14 ❑ Cover: 3.50 **NM** value: **Cover or less**
A: Paul Grist **W:** Paul Grist

15 ❑ Cover: 3.50 **NM** value: **Cover or less**
A: Paul Grist **W:** Paul Grist

16 ❑ Cover: 3.50 **NM** value: **Cover or less**
A: Paul Grist **W:** Paul Grist

17 ❑ Cover: 3.50 **NM** value: **Cover or less**
A: Paul Grist **W:** Paul Grist

18 ❑ Cover: 3.50 **NM** value: **Cover or less**
A: Paul Grist **W:** Paul Grist

19 ❑ Cover: 3.50 **NM** value: **Cover or less**
A: Paul Grist **W:** Paul Grist

20 ❑ Cover: 3.50 **NM** value: **Cover or less**
A: Paul Grist **W:** Paul Grist

21 ❑ Cover: 3.50 **NM** value: **Cover or less**
A: Paul Grist **W:** Paul Grist

22 ❑ Cover: 3.50 **NM** value: **Cover or less**
A: Paul Grist **W:** Paul Grist

23 ❑ Cover: 2.95 **NM** value: **Cover or less**
A: Paul Grist **W:** Paul Grist

24 ❑ Cover: 2.95 **NM** value: **Cover or less**
A: Paul Grist **W:** Paul Grist

25 ❑ Jan 1999 Cover: 2.95 **NM** value: **Cover or less**
Circ: Diamd. preorders: **1,614**
A: Paul Grist **W:** Paul Grist

26 ❑ Apr 1999 Cover: 2.95 **NM** value: **Cover or less**
Circ: Diamd. preorders: **1,469**
A: Paul Grist **W:** Paul Grist

27 ❑ Cover: 5.00 **NM** value: **Cover or less**
• Giant-size. **A:** Paul Grist **W:** Paul Grist

28 ❑ Cover: 2.95 **NM** value: **Cover or less**
A: Paul Grist **W:** Paul Grist

29 ❑ Cover: 2.95 **NM** value: **Cover or less**
A: Paul Grist **W:** Paul Grist

30 ❑ Nov 2000 Cover: 2.95 **NM** value: **Cover or less**
Circ: Diamd. preorders: **1,439**
A: Paul Grist **W:** Paul Grist

31 ❑ Apr 2001 Cover: 2.95 **NM** value: **Cover or less**
Circ: Diamd. preorders: **1,419**
A: Paul Grist **W:** Paul Grist

32 ❑ Jul 2001 Cover: 2.95 **NM** value: **Cover or less**
Circ: Diamd. preorders: **1,591**
A: Paul Grist **W:** Paul Grist

KANSAS THUNDER — Red Menace

1 ❑ b&w Cover: 2.95 **NM** value: **Cover or less**
📖 Charm; The Romantiks; Organics; Ethereal Tensions; The Gearfisher **A:** Ed Murr; Jared Osborn; John Bugh **W:** Jared Osborn; Keith Karchner

KAOS — Tommy Regalado

1 ❑ Aug 1994, b&w Cover: 2.00 **NM** value: **Cover or less**

KAOS MOON — Caliber

1 ❑ Sep 1996 Cover: 2.95 **NM** value: **Cover or less**
Circ: Diamd. preorders: **7,223**
📖 Full Circle Part 1 **A:** David Boller **W:** David Boller

2 ❑ Nov 1996 Cover: 2.95 **NM** value: **Cover or less**
Circ: Diamd. preorders: **4,181**
📖 Full Circle Part 2 **A:** David Boller **W:** David Boller

3 ❑ Jul 1997 Cover: 2.95 **NM** value: **Cover or less**
Circ: Diamd. preorders: **4,104**

4 ❑ Sep 1997 Cover: 2.95 **NM** value: **Cover or less**
Circ: Diamd. preorders: **3,728**

KAPTAIN KEEN & KOMPANY — Vortex

1 ❑ Dec 1986 Cover: 1.75 **NM** value: **Cover or less**
📖 Super Swine; Codzilla

2 ❑ Cover: 1.75 **NM** value: **Cover or less**
3 ❑ Cover: 1.75 **NM** value: **Cover or less**
4 ❑ Cover: 1.75 **NM** value: **Cover or less**
5 ❑ Cover: 1.75 **NM** value: **Cover or less**
6 ❑ Feb 1988 Cover: 1.75 **NM** value: **Cover or less**

KARATE GIRL — Fantagraphics / Eros

All issues are adults only.

1 ❑ b&w Cover: 2.50 **NM** value: **Cover or less**
2 ❑ b&w Cover: 2.50 **NM** value: **Cover or less**

KARATE GIRL TENGU WARS — Fantagraphics / Eros

1 ❑ Cover: 2.95 **NM** value: **Cover or less**
A: Motoki **W:** Motoki

2 ❑ Cover: 2.95 **NM** value: **Cover or less**
A: Motoki **W:** Motoki

3 ❑ Jun 1995 Cover: 2.95 **NM** value: **Cover or less**
A: Motoki **W:** Motoki

KARATE KID — DC

The 30th century's Val Armorr was born the son of a super-villain (The Black Dragon) and raised by The Sensei, the super-hero that defeated that villain. Trained in the martial arts essentially from birth, Armorr mastered every form of hand-to-hand and armed combat known across the galaxy.

Seeing his mastery as its own super-power, The Legion of Super-Heroes inducted the newly named Karate Kid into its ranks in Adventure Comics #346. As a Legionnaire, Karate Kid met and fell in love with Princess Projectra, the heir to the throne of the planet Orando. To prove himself worthy, Karate Kid went on an extended quest, including a time-traveling trip to the 20th century, where these stories take place. — Brent

1 ❑ Apr 1976 Cover: 0.25 **NM** value: **4.00**
• **CGC:** 4 graded, best 9.4
📖 My World Begins in Yesterday **A:** Joe Staton; Ric Estrada **W:** Paul Levitz

2 ❑ Jun 1976 Cover: 0.30 **NM** value: **2.50**
• **CGC:** 1 graded, best 9.4

3 ❑ Aug 1976 Cover: 0.30 **NM** value: **2.50**
4 ❑ Oct 1976 Cover: 0.30 **NM** value: **2.00**
5 ❑ Dec 1976 Cover: 0.30 **NM** value: **2.00**
6 ❑ Feb 1977 Cover: 0.30 **NM** value: **2.00**
7 ❑ Apr 1977 Cover: 0.30 **NM** value: **2.00**
A: Mike Grell

8 ❑ Jun 1977 Cover: 0.30 **NM** value: **2.00**
📖 Pandemonium…Panic…Pulsar! **A:** Mike Grell; Joe Staton; Ric Estrada **W:** Barry Jameson

9 ❑ Aug 1977 Cover: 0.35 **NM** value: **2.00**
10 ❑ Oct 1977 Cover: 0.35 **NM** value: **2.00**
11 ❑ Dec 1977 Cover: 0.35 **NM** value: **2.00**
12 ❑ Feb 1978 Cover: 0.35 **NM** value: **2.00**
13 ❑ Apr 1978 Cover: 0.35 **NM** value: **2.00**
📖 Tomorrow's Battle…Yesterday **A:** Juan Ortiz **W:** Bob Rozakis

14 ❑ Jun 1978 Cover: 0.35 **NM** value: **2.00**
15 ❑ Aug 1978 Cover: 0.35 **NM** value: **2.00**
final issue.

KARATE KREATURES — Ma

1 ❑ full color Cover: 2.00 **NM** value: **Cover or less**
2 ❑ full color Cover: 2.00 **NM** value: **Cover or less**

KARMATRON Y LOS TRANSFORMABLES — Editorial Antea

1 ❑ Cover: 30.00 **NM** value: **Cover or less**
A: Oscar Gonzçlez Loyo; Oscar Gonzßlez Loyo **W:** Oscar Gonzçlez Loyo; Oscar Gonzßlez Loyo

2 ❑ Cover: 30.00 **NM** value: **Cover or less**
A: Oscar Gonzçlez Loyo; Oscar Gonzßlez Loyo **W:** Oscar Gonzçlez Loyo; Oscar Gonzßlez Loyo

KASCO COMICS — Kasko Grainfeed

1 ❑ **NM** value: **75.00**

Other grades: Multiply prices above by **1.5 for Mint • 2/3 for Very Fine • 1/3 for Fine • 1/5 for Very Good • 1/8 for Good**

2 ❑ ca. 1949 **NM** value: **60.00**

KATHY (ATLAS) Atlas

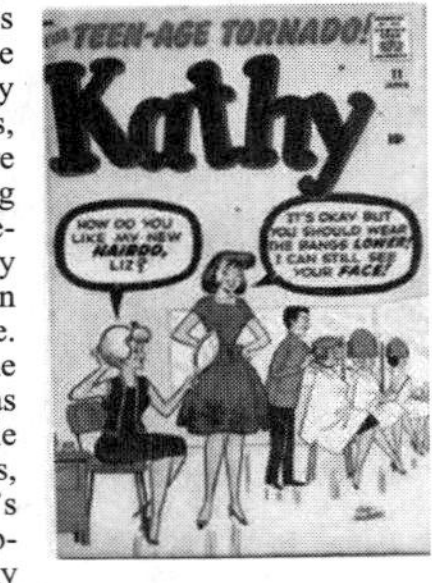

Now, don't confuse Standard's Kathy ("America's Most Lovable Teen-ager") with Atlas' Kathy ("The Teen-Age Tornado"). Yes, they're both blondes. Yes, they are (like such other gorgeous young women titles as Jeanie, Hedy Devine, and Junior Miss) repeatedly the focus of obsessing males thrown into turmoil over her mere presence. But Standard's Kathy lived in the late 1940s and early 1950s, whereas Atlas' Kathy didn't get her own title until the late 1950s. Got it? Oh, yes, and that means that Standard's Kathy wasn't Comics Code-approved (though she demurely showed few cleavage and leg shots, compared to many of her cohorts), whereas Kathy carried a Code seal (and seemed more designed to compete with teens from the Archie line). Class dismissed. — Maggie

1 ❑ Oct 1959 Cover: 0.10 **NM** value: **75.00**
2 ❑ Dec 1959 Cover: 0.10 **NM** value: **75.00**
3 ❑ Feb 1960 Cover: 0.10 **NM** value: **70.00**
4 ❑ Apr 1960 Cover: 0.10 **NM** value: **70.00**
5 ❑ Jun 1960 Cover: 0.10 **NM** value: **70.00**
6 ❑ Aug 1960 Cover: 0.10 **NM** value: **60.00**
7 ❑ Oct 1960 Cover: 0.10 **NM** value: **60.00**
8 ❑ Dec 1960 Cover: 0.10 **NM** value: **60.00**
9 ❑ Feb 1961 Cover: 0.10 **NM** value: **60.00**
10 ❑ Apr 1961 Cover: 0.10 **NM** value: **50.00**
11 ❑ Jun 1961 Cover: 0.10 **NM** value: **50.00**
12 ❑ Aug 1961 Cover: 0.10 **NM** value: **50.00**
13 ❑ Oct 1961 **NM** value: **50.00**
14 ❑ Dec 1961 **NM** value: **50.00**
15 ❑ Feb 1962 **NM** value: **45.00**
16 ❑ Apr 1962 **NM** value: **45.00**
17 ❑ Jun 1962 Cover: 0.12 **NM** value: **45.00**
18 ❑ Aug 1962 Cover: 0.12 **NM** value: **45.00**
19 ❑ Oct 1962 Cover: 0.12 **NM** value: **30.00**
20 ❑ Dec 1962 Cover: 0.12 **NM** value: **40.00**
21 ❑ Feb 1963 Cover: 0.12 **NM** value: **40.00**
22 ❑ Apr 1963 Cover: 0.12 **NM** value: **40.00**
23 ❑ Jun 1963 Cover: 0.12 **NM** value: **40.00**
24 ❑ Aug 1963 Cover: 0.12 **NM** value: **40.00**
25 ❑ Oct 1963 Cover: 0.12 **NM** value: **35.00**
26 ❑ Dec 1963 Cover: 0.12 **NM** value: **35.00**
27 ❑ Feb 1964 Cover: 0.12 **NM** value: **35.00**

KATHY (STANDARD) Standard

1 ❑ Sep 1949 Cover: 0.10 **NM** value: **100.00**
2 ❑ 1950 Cover: 0.10 **NM** value: **90.00**
3 ❑ 1950 Cover: 0.10 **NM** value: **80.00**
4 ❑ 1950 Cover: 0.10 **NM** value: **80.00**
5 ❑ 1950 Cover: 0.10 **NM** value: **75.00**
6 ❑ 1951 Cover: 0.10 **NM** value: **75.00**
7 ❑ 1951 Cover: 0.10 **NM** value: **75.00**
8 ❑ 1951 Cover: 0.10 **NM** value: **60.00**
9 ❑ 1951 Cover: 0.10 **NM** value: **60.00**
10 ❑ 1952 Cover: 0.10 **NM** value: **50.00**
11 ❑ May 1952 Cover: 0.10 **NM** value: **50.00**
12 ❑ 1952 Cover: 0.10 **NM** value: **50.00**
13 ❑ 1952 Cover: 0.10 **NM** value: **50.00**
14 ❑ Mar 1953 Cover: 0.10 **NM** value: **50.00**
15 ❑ 1953 Cover: 0.10 **NM** value: **45.00**
16 ❑ 1953 Cover: 0.10 **NM** value: **45.00**
17 ❑ 1953 Cover: 0.10 **NM** value: **45.00**

KATMANDU Antarctic

All issues are adults only.

1 ❑ Nov 1993, b&w Cover: 2.75 **NM** value: **Cover or less**
A: Terrie Smith **W:** Carole Curtis
2 ❑ Jan 1994, b&w Cover: 2.95 **NM** value: **Cover or less**
A: Terrie Smith **W:** Carole Curtis
3 ❑ Apr 1994, b&w Cover: 2.95 **NM** value: **Cover or less**
A: Terrie Smith **W:** Carole Curtis
4 ❑ Mar 1995, b&w Cover: 2.75 **NM** value: **Cover or less**
Woman of Honor Part 1 **A:** Terrie Smith **W:** Carole Curtis
5 ❑ May 1995, b&w Cover: 2.75 **NM** value: **Cover or less**
Woman of Honor Part 2 **A:** Terrie Smith **W:** Carole Curtis
8 ❑ Jul 1996 Cover: 1.95 **NM** value: **Cover or less**
9 ❑ Jul 1996 Cover: 1.95 **NM** value: **Cover or less**
10 ❑ Jul 1996 Cover: 1.95 **NM** value: **Cover or less**
11 ❑ Jul 1996 Cover: 1.95 **NM** value: **Cover or less**
12 ❑ Jul 1996 Cover: 1.95 **NM** value: **Cover or less**
13 ❑ Sep 1997, b&w Cover: 2.95 **NM** value: **Cover or less**
16 ❑ Apr 1999, b&w Cover: 2.95 **NM** value: **Cover or less**
Circ: Diamd. preorders: **1,391**
Bk 1 ❑ b&w Cover: 8.95 **NM** value: **Cover or less**
• Velites and Hoplites; reprints Antarctic issues

KATO OF THE GREEN HORNET Now

1 ❑ Nov 1991 Cover: 2.50 **NM** value: **Cover or less**
Circ: CapCity orders: **12,900**
Journey Of A Thousand Miles **A:** Brent Anderson **W:** Mike Baron
2 ❑ Dec 1991 Cover: 2.50 **NM** value: **Cover or less**
Circ: CapCity orders: **10,575**
W: Mike Baron
3 ❑ 1992 Cover: 2.50 **NM** value: **Cover or less**
Circ: CapCity orders: **9,875**
W: Mike Baron
4 ❑ 1992 Cover: 2.50 **NM** value: **Cover or less**
Circ: CapCity orders: **8,750**
Demon Sword **A:** Fox **W:** Mike Baron

KATO OF THE GREEN HORNET II Now

1 ❑ Nov 1992 Cover: 2.50 **NM** value: **Cover or less**
Circ: CapCity orders: **6,850**
Bad Boy **A:** Val Mayerik **W:** Mike Baron
2 ❑ Dec 1992 Cover: 2.50 **NM** value: **Cover or less**
Circ: CapCity orders: **4,625**
W: Mike Baron

KATY KEENE (1ST SERIES) Archie

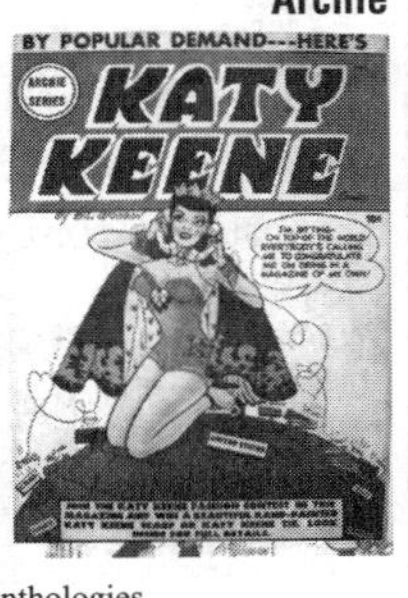

Katy Keene was created by Bill Woggon and was an enormous success, influencing a generation of real-life fashion designers. Nevertheless, throughout much of her Golden Age existence, she was just a feature in teen anthology titles. Introduced in Wilbur #5 (Sum 45), she became established in such other Archie-connected titles as Laugh (starting in #20, Fal 46), Pep (starting in #60, Mar 47), and Suzie (starting in #56, Apr 47). Although such stand-alone titles as Katy Keene (1st series) tended to have short runs, she was of intense interest as a supporting feature in those anthologies.

Though she was a pin-up character, she was a pin-up with a difference: Her clothes (and those of such other characters as her Sis) were based on suggestions from her readers, and those readers were credited — when the outfit was introduced in the story or by the paper doll features that often accompanied her stories. The approach worked to make her audience committed to the feature, feeling involved with its creation, and devoted to Woggon himself as a personality. — Maggie

1 ❑ Cover: 0.10 **NM** value: **600.00**
• **CGC:** 2 graded, best 6.5
2 ❑ Cover: 0.10 **NM** value: **320.00**
3 ❑ Cover: 0.10 **NM** value: **240.00**
4 ❑ Cover: 0.10 **NM** value: **240.00**
• **CGC:** 1 graded, best 7.5
5 ❑ Cover: 0.10 **NM** value: **240.00**
6 ❑ Cover: 0.10 **NM** value: **200.00**
7 ❑ Cover: 0.10 **NM** value: **200.00**
8 ❑ Cover: 0.10 **NM** value: **200.00**
9 ❑ Cover: 0.10 **NM** value: **200.00**
10 ❑ Cover: 0.10 **NM** value: **200.00**
11 ❑ Cover: 0.10 **NM** value: **170.00**
12 ❑ Cover: 0.10 **NM** value: **195.00**
13 ❑ Cover: 0.10 **NM** value: **170.00**
14 ❑ Cover: 0.10 **NM** value: **170.00**
15 ❑ Cover: 0.10 **NM** value: **170.00**
16 ❑ Cover: 0.10 **NM** value: **170.00**
17 ❑ Cover: 0.10 **NM** value: **170.00**
18 ❑ Cover: 0.10 **NM** value: **170.00**
19 ❑ Cover: 0.10 **NM** value: **170.00**
20 ❑ Cover: 0.10 **NM** value: **170.00**
21 ❑ Cover: 0.10 **NM** value: **170.00**
22 ❑ Cover: 0.10 **NM** value: **115.00**
23 ❑ Cover: 0.10 **NM** value: **115.00**
24 ❑ Cover: 0.10 **NM** value: **115.00**
25 ❑ Cover: 0.10 **NM** value: **115.00**
26 ❑ Cover: 0.10 **NM** value: **115.00**
27 ❑ Cover: 0.10 **NM** value: **115.00**
28 ❑ Cover: 0.10 **NM** value: **115.00**
29 ❑ Cover: 0.10 **NM** value: **115.00**
30 ❑ Cover: 0.10 **NM** value: **115.00**
31 ❑ Cover: 0.10 **NM** value: **115.00**
32 ❑ Cover: 0.10 **NM** value: **115.00**
33 ❑ Cover: 0.10 **NM** value: **115.00**
34 ❑ Cover: 0.10 **NM** value: **115.00**
35 ❑ Cover: 0.10 **NM** value: **115.00**
36 ❑ Cover: 0.10 **NM** value: **115.00**
37 ❑ Cover: 0.10 **NM** value: **115.00**
38 ❑ Cover: 0.10 **NM** value: **115.00**
39 ❑ Cover: 0.10 **NM** value: **115.00**
40 ❑ Cover: 0.10 **NM** value: **115.00**
41 ❑ Cover: 0.10 **NM** value: **95.00**
42 ❑ Cover: 0.10 **NM** value: **95.00**
43 ❑ Cover: 0.10 **NM** value: **95.00**
44 ❑ Cover: 0.10 **NM** value: **95.00**
45 ❑ Cover: 0.10 **NM** value: **95.00**
46 ❑ Cover: 0.10 **NM** value: **95.00**
47 ❑ Cover: 0.10 **NM** value: **95.00**
48 ❑ Cover: 0.10 **NM** value: **95.00**
49 ❑ Cover: 0.10 **NM** value: **95.00**
50 ❑ Cover: 0.10 **NM** value: **95.00**
51 ❑ Cover: 0.10 **NM** value: **95.00**
52 ❑ Cover: 0.10 **NM** value: **95.00**
53 ❑ Cover: 0.10 **NM** value: **95.00**
54 ❑ Cover: 0.10 **NM** value: **95.00**
55 ❑ Cover: 0.10 **NM** value: **95.00**
56 ❑ Cover: 0.10 **NM** value: **95.00**
57 ❑ Cover: 0.10 **NM** value: **95.00**
58 ❑ Cover: 0.10 **NM** value: **95.00**
59 ❑ Cover: 0.10 **NM** value: **95.00**
60 ❑ Cover: 0.10 **NM** value: **95.00**
61 ❑ Cover: 0.10 **NM** value: **95.00**
62 ❑ Cover: 0.10 **NM** value: **95.00**

KATY KEENE (2ND SERIES) Archie

8 ❑ 1985 Cover: 0.65 **NM** value: **1.50**
Torn Between Two Loves • Series continued from Katy Keene Special #7 **A:** Don Sherwood **W:** Susan Berkley
9 ❑ 1985 Cover: 0.65 **NM** value: **1.50**
10 ❑ Aug 1985 Cover: 0.65 **NM** value: **1.50**
11 ❑ Oct 1985 Cover: 0.65 **NM** value: **1.50**
12 ❑ Dec 1985 Cover: 0.65 **NM** value: **1.50**
13 ❑ Feb 1986 Cover: 0.65 **NM** value: **1.50**
Circ: Statement: **25,098**
14 ❑ Apr 1986 Cover: 0.65 **NM** value: **1.50**
Circ: Statement: **25,098**
15 ❑ Jun 1986 Cover: 0.75 **NM** value: **1.50**
Circ: Statement: **25,098**
16 ❑ Aug 1986 Cover: 0.75 **NM** value: **1.50**
Circ: Statement: **25,098**
17 ❑ Oct 1986 Cover: 0.75 **NM** value: **1.50**
Circ: Statement: **25,098**
18 ❑ Dec 1986 Cover: 0.75 **NM** value: **1.50**
Circ: Statement: **25,098**
19 ❑ Feb 1987 Cover: 0.75 **NM** value: **1.50**
Circ: Statement: **25,798**
20 ❑ Apr 1987 Cover: 0.75 **NM** value: **1.50**
Circ: Statement: **25,798**
21 ❑ Jun 1987 Cover: 0.75 **NM** value: **1.00**
Circ: Statement: **25,798**
The Surprise; Nostalgia Time; No Choke **A:** John Lucas **W:** John Lucas
22 ❑ Aug 1987 Cover: 0.75 **NM** value: **1.00**
Circ: Statement: **25,798**
23 ❑ Oct 1987 Cover: 0.75 **NM** value: **1.00**
Circ: Statement: **25,798**
24 ❑ Dec 1987 Cover: 0.75 **NM** value: **1.00**
Circ: Statement: **25,798**
25 ❑ Feb 1988 Cover: 0.75 **NM** value: **1.00**
Circ: Statement: **29,429**
26 ❑ May 1988 Cover: 0.75 **NM** value: **1.00**
Circ: Statement: **29,429**
27 ❑ Aug 1988 Cover: 0.75 **NM** value: **1.00**
Circ: Statement: **29,429**
28 ❑ Oct 1988 Cover: 0.75 **NM** value: **1.00**
Circ: Statement: **29,429**
29 ❑ Feb 1989 Cover: 0.75 **NM** value: **1.00**
30 ❑ May 1989 Cover: 0.75 **NM** value: **1.00**
31 ❑ Aug 1989 Cover: 0.95 **NM** value: **1.00**
32 ❑ Oct 1989 Cover: 0.95 **NM** value: **1.00**
33 ❑ Feb 1990 Cover: 1.00 **NM** value: **Cover or less**
Too Many Santas; Burst Her Bubble; Running Late final issue. **A:** John Lucas **W:** John Lucas

KATY KEENE FASHION BOOK MAGAZINE Archie

1 ❑ ca. 1955 Cover: 0.10 **NM** value: **350.00**
2 ❑ ca. 1956 Cover: 0.10 **NM** value: **200.00**
13 ❑ Sum 1956 Cover: 0.10 **NM** value: **175.00**
14 ❑ Fal 1956 Cover: 0.10 **NM** value: **175.00**
15 ❑ Win 1956 Cover: 0.10 **NM** value: **150.00**
16 ❑ Spr 1957 Cover: 0.10 **NM** value: **150.00**
17 ❑ Sum 1957 Cover: 0.10 **NM** value: **140.00**
18 ❑ Fal 1957 Cover: 0.10 **NM** value: **140.00**
19 ❑ Win 1957 Cover: 0.10 **NM** value: **140.00**
20 ❑ Spr 1958 Cover: 0.10 **NM** value: **125.00**
21 ❑ Sum 1958 Cover: 0.10 **NM** value: **125.00**
22 ❑ Fal 1958 Cover: 0.10 **NM** value: **100.00**
23 ❑ Win 1958 Cover: 0.10 **NM** value: **100.00**

KATY KEENE PIN UP PARADE Archie

1 ❑ ca. 1955 Cover: 0.25 **NM** value: **350.00**
• **CGC:** 1 graded, best 9.0
2 ❑ ca. 1956 Cover: 0.25 **NM** value: **325.00**
3 ❑ ca. 1957 Cover: 0.25 **NM** value: **300.00**
4 ❑ ca. 1958 Cover: 0.25 **NM** value: **250.00**
5 ❑ Win 1958 Cover: 0.25 **NM** value: **250.00**
6 ❑ Spr 1959 Cover: 0.25 **NM** value: **250.00**
7 ❑ Sum 1959 Cover: 0.25 **NM** value: **225.00**
8 ❑ Fal 1959 Cover: 0.25 **NM** value: **225.00**
9 ❑ Win 1959 Cover: 0.25 **NM** value: **225.00**
10 ❑ Spr 1960 Cover: 0.25 **NM** value: **200.00**
11 ❑ Sum 1960 Cover: 0.25 **NM** value: **200.00**
12 ❑ Fal 1960 Cover: 0.25 **NM** value: **200.00**
13 ❑ Win 1960 Cover: 0.25 **NM** value: **200.00**
14 ❑ Spr 1961 Cover: 0.25 **NM** value: **175.00**
15 ❑ Sum 1961 Cover: 0.25 **NM** value: **175.00**
• **CGC:** 1 graded, best 6.0

KATY KEENE SPECIAL Archie / Red Circle

1 ❑ Sep 1983 Cover: 1.00 **NM** value: **2.50**
2 ❑ Feb 1984 Cover: 1.00 **NM** value: **2.00**
3 ❑ Apr 1984 Cover: 0.60 **NM** value: **2.00**
4 ❑ Jun 1984 Cover: 0.60 **NM** value: **2.00**
5 ❑ Aug 1984 Cover: 0.60 **NM** value: **2.00**
6 ❑ Oct 1984 Cover: 0.60 **NM** value: **1.50**
7 ❑ Dec 1984 Cover: 0.60 **NM** value: **1.50**
• Series continued in Katy Keene (2nd series) #8

KATZENJAMMER KIDS David McKay

The hugely popular and incredibly long-running strip was among the earliest newspaper comic strips. Created by Rudolph Dirks in 1897, the kids even starred eventually in two strips running simultaneously: The Katzenjammer Kids, then drawn by Harold Knerr, and The Captain and the Kids drawn by Dirks. (Today, Katzenjammer Kids is by Hy Eisman and syndicated by King Features.) Both came to comic books eventually, The Captain and the Kids from United Features Syndicate (including a 50th Anniversary cover, despite the short run of the

CGC-graded: Multiply prices above by **33 for 9.9 M** • **16 for 9.8 NM/M** • **7 for 9.6 NM+** • **5 for 9.4 NM** • **2.5 for 9.2 NM-** • **1.5 for 9.0 VF/NM**

comic book itself; strips ran in Comics on Parade, Sparkler, and Tip Top Comics, too, for a much, much longer run) and The Katzenjammer Kids from David McKay.

McKay also ran the strip as one of the features in its long-running Ace Comics title.) Twins Hans and Fritz plague the lives of the Captain and the Inspector and scheme to contrive complex practical jokes. Skilled writing and art made the strips popular with audiences around the world. — Maggie

1 ❑ Sum 1947 Cover: 0.10 **NM** value: **125.00**
2 ❑ Aut 1947 Cover: 0.10 **NM** value: **100.00**
3 ❑ Win 1947 Cover: 0.10 **NM** value: **75.00**
4 ❑ Spr 1948 Cover: 0.10 **NM** value: **60.00**
5 ❑ Sum 1948 Cover: 0.10 **NM** value: **60.00**
6 ❑ Aut 1948 Cover: 0.10 **NM** value: **50.00**
7 ❑ Win 1948 Cover: 0.10 **NM** value: **50.00**
8 ❑ Spr 1949 Cover: 0.10 **NM** value: **50.00**
9 ❑ Sum 1949 Cover: 0.10 **NM** value: **50.00**
10 ❑ Aut 1949 Cover: 0.10 **NM** value: **45.00**
11 ❑ Win 1949 Cover: 0.10 **NM** value: **45.00**
12 ❑ Spr 1950 Cover: 0.10 **NM** value: **45.00**
13 ❑ Sum 1950 Cover: 0.10 **NM** value: **40.00**
14 ❑ Aut 1950 Cover: 0.10 **NM** value: **40.00**
15 ❑ Win 1950 Cover: 0.10 **NM** value: **40.00**
16 ❑ Spr 1951 Cover: 0.10 **NM** value: **40.00**
17 ❑ Sum 1951 Cover: 0.10 **NM** value: **35.00**
18 ❑ Aut 1951 Cover: 0.10 **NM** value: **35.00**
19 ❑ Win 1951 Cover: 0.10 **NM** value: **35.00**
20 ❑ Spr 1952 Cover: 0.10 **NM** value: **30.00**
21 ❑ Sum 1952 Cover: 0.10 **NM** value: **30.00**
22 ❑ Aut 1952 Cover: 0.10 **NM** value: **30.00**
23 ❑ Win 1952 Cover: 0.10 **NM** value: **25.00**
24 ❑ Spr 1953 Cover: 0.10 **NM** value: **25.00**
25 ❑ Sum 1953 Cover: 0.10 **NM** value: **25.00**
26 ❑ Dec 1953 Cover: 0.10 **NM** value: **25.00**
27 ❑ Feb 1954 Cover: 0.10 **NM** value: **25.00**

KA-ZAR (1ST SERIES) — Marvel

As well as starring in many issues of Astonishing Tales, Ka-Zar got his own — albeit short-lived — series in 1970. Like Astonishing Tales, this was a 25-cent, giant-sized series with several stories per issue. The Ka-Zar stories were reprints from his previous run-ins with such characters as Spider-Man and Daredevil. Ironically, the back-up stories featuring the winged character Angel from The X-Men were the only new material.

By the way, this Ka-Zar is not the same Ka-Zar as the pulp-inspired Ka-Zar who romped through the Congo in Marvel's Golden Age. That Ka-Zar was really David Rand; the Silver Age Ka-Zar is Kevin Plunder, and his jungle ("The Savage Land")is hidden under Antarctica. This series closed down after just three issues, although Marvel would take numerous tries at a Ka-Zar series in the years to come.

1 ❑ Aug 1970 Cover: 0.25 **NM** value: **10.00**
• **CGC:** 7 graded, best 9.4
The Coming of...Ka-Zar; In His Footsteps...The Huntsman of Zeus!!; Daredevil: The Mystery of the Midnight Stalker • giant; reprints X-Men #10 (first series) and Daredevil #24; Hercules back-up **A:** Gene Colan; Jack Kirby; Dick Ayers; Frank Springer **W:** Stan Lee ★ 1st Appearance of Ka-Zar. ★ 1st Appearance of Zabu. ★ Appearance of X-Men.

2 ❑ Dec 1970 Cover: 0.25 **NM** value: **7.00**
• **CGC:** 2 graded, best 9.4
Sightless in a Savage Land; From the Sky...Winged Wrath!; The Secret of Ka-Zar's Origin! • giant; Angel back-up; reprints Daredevil #12 and 13 **A:** George Tuska; Jack Kirby; John Romita **W:** Jerry Siegel; Stan Lee ★ Origin of Ka-Zar. ★ Appearance of Daredevil.

3 ❑ Mar 1971 Cover: 0.25 **NM** value: **7.00**
• **CGC:** 2 graded, best 9.6
The Coming of Ka-Zar; If This Be Justice; In the Den of the Dazzler • giant; reprints Amazing Spider-Man #57 and Daredevil #14; Angel back-up continues in Marvel Tales #30

KA-ZAR (2ND SERIES) — Marvel

1 ❑ Jan 1974 Cover: 0.20 **NM** value: **3.00**
• **CGC:** 4 graded, best 9.8
Return to the Savage Land **A:** Paul Reinman; Mike Royer **W:** Mike Friedrich ★ Origin of Savage Land.

2 ❑ Mar 1974 Cover: 0.20 **NM** value: **2.50**
The Fall Of The Red Wizard! **A:** Don Heck **W:** Mike Friedrich

3 ❑ May 1974 Cover: 0.25 **NM** value: **2.50**
Night of the Man-God! **A:** Don Heck

4 ❑ Jul 1974 Cover: 0.25 **NM** value: **2.50**
Into the Shadows of Chaos **A:** Don Heck

5 ❑ Sep 1974 Cover: 0.25 **NM** value: **2.50**
A Man-God Unleashed; Be This My Destiny **A:** Don Heck

6 ❑ Nov 1974 Cover: 0.25 **NM** value: **2.00**
Waters Of Darkness, River Of Doom! **A:** John Buscema **W:** Gerry Conway

7 ❑ Jan 1975 Cover: 0.25 **NM** value: **2.00**
Revenge Of the River Gods! **A:** John Buscema **W:** Gerry Conway

8 ❑ Mar 1975 Cover: 0.25 **NM** value: **2.00**
Down Into the Volcano! **A:** John Buscema

9 ❑ Jun 1975 Cover: 0.25 **NM** value: **2.00**
The Man Who Hunted Dinosaur! **A:** John Buscema

10 ❑ Aug 1975 Cover: 0.25 **NM** value: **2.00**
Beyond the Veil of Savage Time **A:** John Buscema

11 ❑ Oct 1975 Cover: 0.25 **NM** value: **1.50**
The Devil-God of Sylitha!

12 ❑ Nov 1975 Cover: 0.25 **NM** value: **1.50**

13 ❑ Dec 1975 Cover: 0.25 **NM** value: **1.50**
The Skull of the Lizard-Man!

14 ❑ Feb 1976 Cover: 0.25 **NM** value: **1.50**
• **CGC:** 1 graded, best 9.6
Two Worlds in Frenzy ★ Appearance of Klaw.

15 ❑ Apr 1976 Cover: 0.25 **NM** value: **1.50**
16 ❑ Jun 1976 Cover: 0.30 **NM** value: **1.50**
• **CGC:** 1 graded, best 9.6
17 ❑ Aug 1976 Cover: 0.30 **NM** value: **1.50**
18 ❑ Oct 1976 Cover: 0.30 **NM** value: **1.50**
19 ❑ Dec 1976 Cover: 0.30 **NM** value: **1.50**
• **CGC:** 1 graded, best 9.2
20 ❑ Feb 1977 Cover: 0.30 **NM** value: **1.50**
★ Appearance of Klaw.

KA-ZAR (3RD SERIES) — Marvel

-1 ❑ Jan 1997 Cover: 1.95 **NM** value: **2.00**
Circ: Statement: **74,082**
• Flashback

1 ❑ May 1997 Cover: 1.99 **NM** value: **2.50**
Circ: Statement: **74,082** Diamd. preorders: **50,727** • **CGC:** 9 graded, best 9.8
A: Andy Kubert **W:** Mark Waid

2 ❑ Jun 1997 Cover: 1.99 **NM** value: **2.00**
Circ: Statement: **74,082** Diamd. preorders: **30,010**
Law of the Jungle **A:** Andy Kubert **W:** Mark Waid

2/A ❑ Jun 1997 Cover: 1.99 **NM** value: **2.00**
Circ: Diamd. preorders: **23,669**
alternate cover.

3 ❑ Jul 1997 Cover: 1.99 **NM** value: **2.00**
Circ: Statement: **74,082** Diamd. preorders: **41,587** • **CGC:** 1 graded, best 9.8

4 ❑ Aug 1997 Cover: 1.99 **NM** value: **2.00**
Circ: Statement: **74,082** Diamd. preorders: **43,328** • **CGC:** 1 graded, best 9.6
• gatefold summary.

5 ❑ Sep 1997 Cover: 1.99 **NM** value: **2.00**
Circ: Statement: **74,082** Diamd. preorders: **42,593** • **CGC:** 1 graded, best 9.8
• gatefold summary. ★ Versus Rhino.

6 ❑ Oct 1997 Cover: 1.99 **NM** value: **2.00**
Circ: Statement: **74,082** Diamd. preorders: **41,296**
• gatefold summary.

7 ❑ Nov 1997 Cover: 1.99 **NM** value: **2.00**
Circ: Diamd. preorders: **40,659**
• gatefold summary.

8 ❑ Dec 1997 Cover: 1.99 **NM** value: **2.00**
Circ: Diamd. preorders: **39,362**
• gatefold summary. • Spider-Man CD-ROM inserted

9 ❑ Jan 1998 Cover: 1.99 **NM** value: **2.00**
Circ: Diamd. preorders: **37,439**
• gatefold summary. • Has 1997 Statement, filed 10/1/97 (Alert: Based on only a partial year of series); avg print run 121,760; avg sales 73,972; avg subs 110; avg total paid 74,082; samples 11; office use 125; max existent 74,218; 39% of run returned

10 ❑ Feb 1998 Cover: 1.99 **NM** value: **2.00**
Circ: Diamd. preorders: **35,583**
• gatefold summary.

11 ❑ Mar 1998 Cover: 1.99 **NM** value: **Cover or less**
Circ: Diamd. preorders: **33,852**
• gatefold summary.

12 ❑ Apr 1998 Cover: 1.99 **NM** value: **Cover or less**
Circ: Diamd. preorders: **31,788** • **CGC:** 1 graded, best 9.6
• gatefold summary. ★ Versus High Evolutionary.

13 ❑ May 1998 Cover: 1.99 **NM** value: **Cover or less**
Circ: Diamd. preorders: **31,553**
• gatefold summary. ★ Versus High Evolutionary.

14 ❑ Jun 1998 Cover: 2.99 **NM** value: **Cover or less**
Circ: Diamd. preorders: **31,785**
• Flip-book.

15 ❑ Jul 1998 Cover: 1.99 **NM** value: **Cover or less**
Circ: Diamd. preorders: **27,966**
• gatefold summary. • blinded★ Appearance of Punisher.

16 ❑ Aug 1998 Cover: 1.99 **NM** value: **Cover or less**
Circ: Diamd. preorders: **26,594**
• gatefold summary.

17 ❑ Sep 1998 Cover: 1.99 **NM** value: **Cover or less**
Circ: Diamd. preorders: **23,089**
• gatefold summary.

18 ❑ Oct 1998 Cover: 1.99 **NM** value: **Cover or less**
Circ: Diamd. preorders: **20,703**
• gatefold summary.

19 ❑ Nov 1998 Cover: 1.99 **NM** value: **Cover or less**
Circ: Diamd. preorders: **18,867**
• gatefold summary.

20 ❑ Dec 1998 Cover: 1.99 **NM** value: **Cover or less**
Circ: Diamd. preorders: **17,080**
• gatefold summary. final issue.

Anl 1997❑ca. 1997 Cover: 2.99 **NM** value: **Cover or less**
Circ: Diamd. preorders: **30,704**
wraparound cover. • gatefold summary.

KAZAR OF THE SAVAGE LAND — Marvel

1 ❑ Feb 1997 Cover: 2.50 **NM** value: **Cover or less**
One-shot. wraparound cover. Nature of the Beasts **A:** Frank Teran **W:** Chuck Dixon

KA-ZAR: SIBLING RIVALRY — Marvel

-1 ❑ Jul 1997 Cover: 1.95 **NM** value: **Cover or less**
Circ: Diamd. preorders: **36,297**
• Flashback★ Origin of Ka-Zar.

KA-ZAR THE SAVAGE — Marvel

1 ❑ Apr 1981 Cover: 0.50 **NM** value: **2.50**
Circ: Statement: **226,000**
A New Dawn...A New World **A:** Brent Anderson **W:** Bruce Jones
★ Origin of Ka-Zar.

2 ❑ May 1981 Cover: 0.50 **NM** value: **2.00**
Circ: Statement: **226,000**
To Air Is Human! **A:** Brent Anderson **W:** Bruce Jones

3 ❑ Jun 1981 Cover: 0.50 **NM** value: **1.50**
Circ: Statement: **226,000**
A: Brent Anderson

4 ❑ Jul 1981 Cover: 0.50 **NM** value: **1.50**
Circ: Statement: **226,000**
A: Brent Anderson

5 ❑ Aug 1981 Cover: 0.50 **NM** value: **1.50**
Circ: Statement: **226,000**
A: Brent Anderson

6 ❑ Sep 1981 Cover: 0.50 **NM** value: **1.50**
Circ: Statement: **226,000**
A: Brent Anderson

7 ❑ Oct 1981 Cover: 0.50 **NM** value: **1.50**
Circ: Statement: **226,000**
A: Brent Anderson

8 ❑ Nov 1981 Cover: 0.50 **NM** value: **1.50**
Circ: Statement: **226,000**
A: Brent Anderson

9 ❑ Dec 1981 Cover: 0.50 **NM** value: **1.50**
Circ: Statement: **226,000**
A: Brent Anderson

10 ❑ Jan 1982 Cover: 0.75 **NM** value: **1.50**
Circ: Statement: **129,938**
• direct distribution **A:** Brent Anderson

11 ❑ Feb 1982 Cover: 0.75 **NM** value: **1.50**
Circ: Statement: **129,938**
• Zabu **A:** Brent Anderson; Gil Kane ★ 1st Appearance of Belasco.

12 ❑ Mar 1982 Cover: 0.75 **NM** value: **1.50**
Circ: Statement: **129,938**
• panel missing **A:** Brent Anderson

12-2❑ Cover: 0.75 **NM** value: **1.00**

13 ❑ Apr 1982 Cover: 0.75 **NM** value: **1.50**
Circ: Statement: **129,938**
A: Brent Anderson

14 ❑ May 1982 Cover: 0.75 **NM** value: **1.50**
Circ: Statement: **129,938**
A: Brent Anderson

15 ❑ Jun 1982 Cover: 0.75 **NM** value: **1.50**
Circ: Statement: **129,938**
A: Brent Anderson

16 ❑ Jul 1982 Cover: 0.75 **NM** value: **1.50**
Circ: Statement: **129,938**

17 ❑ Aug 1982 Cover: 0.75 **NM** value: **1.50**
Circ: Statement: **129,938**

18 ❑ Sep 1982 Cover: 0.75 **NM** value: **1.50**
Circ: Statement: **129,938**

19 ❑ Oct 1982 Cover: 0.75 **NM** value: **1.50**
Circ: Statement: **129,938**
A: Brent Anderson

20 ❑ Nov 1982 Cover: 0.75 **NM** value: **1.50**
Circ: Statement: **129,938**

21 ❑ Dec 1982 Cover: 0.75 **NM** value: **1.50**
Circ: Statement: **129,938**

22 ❑ Jan 1983 Cover: 0.75 **NM** value: **1.50**
Circ: Statement: **74,730**

23 ❑ Feb 1983 Cover: 0.75 **NM** value: **1.50**
Circ: Statement: **74,730**

24 ❑ Mar 1983 Cover: 0.75 **NM** value: **1.50**
Circ: Statement: **74,730**

25 ❑ Apr 1983 Cover: 0.75 **NM** value: **1.50**
Circ: Statement: **74,730**
• Has 1982 Statement, filed 10/11/82; avg print run 256,928; avg sales 128,563; avg subs 1,375; avg total paid 129,938; samples 490; office use 4,365; max existent 134,793; 48% of run returned

26 ❑ May 1983 Cover: 0.75 **NM** value: **1.50**
Circ: Statement: **74,730**

27 ❑ Aug 1983 Cover: 0.75 **NM** value: **1.50**
Circ: Statement: **74,730**

28 ❑ Oct 1983 Cover: 0.75 **NM** value: **1.50**
Circ: Statement: **74,730**

29 ❑ Dec 1983 Cover: 1.00 **NM** value: **1.50**
Circ: Statement: **74,730**
• Double-size. • Wedding of Ka-Zar, Shanna

30 ❑ Feb 1984 Cover: 0.75 **NM** value: **1.50**
31 ❑ Apr 1984 Cover: 1.00 **NM** value: **1.50**
32 ❑ Jun 1984 Cover: 1.00 **NM** value: **1.50**
33 ❑ Aug 1984 Cover: 1.00 **NM** value: **1.50**
34 ❑ Oct 1984 Cover: 1.00 **NM** value: **1.50**
final issue.
36862❑ Cover: 0.75 **NM** value: **1.00**

K CHRONICLES, THE — Keith Knight

1 ❑ Cover: 1.50 **NM** value: **Cover or less**
A: Keith Knight **W:** Keith Knight
2 ❑ Cover: 1.50 **NM** value: **Cover or less**
A: Keith Knight **W:** Keith Knight
3 ❑ Cover: 1.50 **NM** value: **Cover or less**
A: Keith Knight **W:** Keith Knight
4 ❑ Cover: 1.50 **NM** value: **Cover or less**
A: Keith Knight **W:** Keith Knight
5 ❑ Cover: 1.50 **NM** value: **Cover or less**
A: Keith Knight **W:** Keith Knight
6 ❑ Cover: 1.50 **NM** value: **Cover or less**
A: Keith Knight **W:** Keith Knight
7 ❑ Cover: 1.50 **NM** value: **Cover or less**
A: Keith Knight **W:** Keith Knight
8 ❑ Cover: 1.50 **NM** value: **Cover or less**
A: Keith Knight **W:** Keith Knight
9 ❑ Cover: 1.50 **NM** value: **Cover or less**
A: Keith Knight **W:** Keith Knight

KEEN DETECTIVE FUNNIES VOL. 1 — Centaur

8 ❑ Jul 1938 Cover: 0.10 **NM** value: **1775.00**
9 ❑ Sep 1938 Cover: 0.10 **NM** value: **900.00**
10 ❑ Oct 1938 Cover: 0.10 **NM** value: **850.00**
11 ❑ Dec 1938 Cover: 0.10 **NM** value: **850.00**

KEEN DETECTIVE FUNNIES VOL. 2 — Centaur

1 ❑ Jan 1939 Cover: 0.10 **NM** value: **825.00**
2 ❑ Feb 1939 Cover: 0.10 **NM** value: **825.00**
3 ❑ Mar 1939 Cover: 0.10 **NM** value: **825.00**
4 ❑ Apr 1939 Cover: 0.10 **NM** value: **825.00**
5 ❑ May 1939 Cover: 0.10 **NM** value: **800.00**
6 ❑ Jun 1939 Cover: 0.10 **NM** value: **800.00**
7 ❑ Jul 1939 Cover: 0.10 **NM** value: **800.00**
8 ❑ Aug 1939 Cover: 0.10 **NM** value: **800.00**
9 ❑ Sep 1939 Cover: 0.10 **NM** value: **800.00**
• **CGC:** 1 graded, best 5.0
10 ❑ Oct 1939 Cover: 0.10 **NM** value: **750.00**
11 ❑ Nov 1939 Cover: 0.10 **NM** value: **750.00**
12 ❑ Dec 1939 Cover: 0.10 **NM** value: **750.00**

KEEN DETECTIVE FUNNIES VOL. 3 — Centaur

18 ❑ Mar 1940 Cover: 0.10 **NM** value: **600.00**
19 ❑ Apr 1940 Cover: 0.10 **NM** value: **600.00**
20 ❑ May 1940 Cover: 0.10 **NM** value: **850.00**
• **CGC:** 1 graded, best 4.0
21 ❑ Jun 1940 Cover: 0.10 **NM** value: **800.00**
22 ❑ Jul 1940 Cover: 0.10 **NM** value: **800.00**
23 ❑ Aug 1940 Cover: 0.10 **NM** value: **750.00**
24 ❑ Sep 1940 Cover: 0.10 **NM** value: **750.00**
• **CGC:** 2 graded, best 9.0

KEEN KOMICS — Centaur

1 ❑ ca. 1939 Cover: 0.10 **NM** value: **900.00**
2 ❑ Sep 1939 Cover: 0.10 **NM** value: **575.00**
3 ❑ Nov 1939 Cover: 0.10 **NM** value: **575.00**

KEEN TEENS — Life's Romances

1 ❑ ca. 1945 Cover: 0.10 **NM** value: **225.00**
2 ❑ ca. 1946 Cover: 0.10 **NM** value: **200.00**
3 ❑ Feb 1947 Cover: 0.10 **NM** value: **100.00**
4 ❑ Apr 1947 Cover: 0.10 **NM** value: **100.00**
5 ❑ Jun 1947 Cover: 0.10 **NM** value: **75.00**
6 ❑ Aug 1947 Cover: 0.10 **NM** value: **75.00**

KEIF LLAMA — Oni Press

1 ❑ Mar 1999 Cover: 2.95 **NM** value: **Cover or less**
Circ: Diamd. preorders: **2,746**
No issue number. 📖 Gas War

KEIF LLAMA XENO-TECH — Fantagraphics

1 ❑ Cover: 2.00 **NM** value: **Cover or less**
2 ❑ Cover: 2.00 **NM** value: **Cover or less**
3 ❑ Cover: 2.00 **NM** value: **Cover or less**
4 ❑ Cover: 2.00 **NM** value: **Cover or less**
5 ❑ Cover: 2.00 **NM** value: **Cover or less**
6 ❑ Cover: 2.00 **NM** value: **Cover or less**

KELLY BELLE POLICE DETECTIVE — Newcomers

1 ❑ Cover: 2.95 **NM** value: **Cover or less**
A: Rob Ewing **W:** James Watson
2 ❑ Cover: 2.95 **NM** value: **Cover or less**
📖 The Case of the Jeweled Scarab, Part 2 **A:** Rob Ewing **W:** James Watson
3 ❑ Cover: 2.95 **NM** value: **Cover or less**
📖 The Case of the Jeweled Scarab, Part 3; Kitty Smith: Hero Worship **A:** Rob Ewing **W:** James Watson

KELVIN MACE — Vortex

1 ❑ Cover: 3.00 **NM** value: **Cover or less**
2 ❑ Cover: 1.75 **NM** value: **Cover or less**

KENDRA: LEGACY OF THE BLOOD — Perrydog

1 ❑ Feb 1987, b&w Cover: 2.00 **NM** value: **Cover or less**
2 ❑ Apr 1987, b&w Cover: 2.00 **NM** value: **Cover or less**

KEN MAYNARD WESTERN — Fawcett

Maynard (1895-1973), the first film singing cowboy, was another of the Western movie stars whose image and name were licensed for comic-book use and whose own professional name in films was (as with Roy Rogers and Gene Autry) the one used as the film character. He was a legitimate trick rider and champion rodeo performer, appearing with Buffalo Bill's Wild West Show and with Ringling Brothers. Though the last of his string of Westerns came basically in 1944, the comics series from Fawcett (which also published such similarly derivative titles as Gabby Hayes, Tom Mix, and Lash LaRue) didn't begin for another six years. That may explain why the series had such a short run at a time when Westerns in general were becoming more and more a part of popular culture. — Maggie

1 ❑ Sep 1950 Cover: 0.10 **NM** value: **375.00**
2 ❑ Nov 1950 Cover: 0.10 **NM** value: **350.00**
3 ❑ Apr 1951 Cover: 0.10 **NM** value: **350.00**
4 ❑ Jun 1951 Cover: 0.10 **NM** value: **300.00**
5 ❑ Aug 1951 Cover: 0.10 **NM** value: **300.00**
6 ❑ Oct 1951 Cover: 0.10 **NM** value: **250.00**
7 ❑ Dec 1951 Cover: 0.10 **NM** value: **250.00**
8 ❑ Feb 1952 Cover: 0.10 **NM** value: **250.00**

KEN SHANNON — Quality

1 ❑ Oct 1951 Cover: 0.10 **NM** value: **300.00**
2 ❑ Dec 1951 Cover: 0.10 **NM** value: **250.00**
3 ❑ Feb 1952 Cover: 0.10 **NM** value: **225.00**
• **CGC:** 1 graded, best 7.0
4 ❑ Apr 1952 Cover: 0.10 **NM** value: **200.00**
5 ❑ Jun 1952 Cover: 0.10 **NM** value: **200.00**
6 ❑ Aug 1952 Cover: 0.10 **NM** value: **175.00**
7 ❑ Oct 1952 Cover: 0.10 **NM** value: **175.00**
8 ❑ Dec 1952 Cover: 0.10 **NM** value: **150.00**
9 ❑ Feb 1953 Cover: 0.10 **NM** value: **150.00**
10 ❑ Apr 1953 Cover: 0.10 **NM** value: **150.00**

KEN STUART — Publication Enterprises

1 ❑ ca. 1949 Cover: 0.10 **NM** value: **50.00**

KENT BLAKE OF THE SECRET SERVICE — Atlas

1 ❑ May 1951 Cover: 0.10 **NM** value: **175.00**
2 ❑ Jul 1951 Cover: 0.10 **NM** value: **150.00**
3 ❑ Sep 1951 Cover: 0.10 **NM** value: **125.00**
4 ❑ Nov 1951 Cover: 0.10 **NM** value: **100.00**
5 ❑ Jan 1952 Cover: 0.10 **NM** value: **100.00**
6 ❑ Mar 1952 Cover: 0.10 **NM** value: **80.00**
7 ❑ May 1952 Cover: 0.10 **NM** value: **80.00**
8 ❑ Jul 1952 Cover: 0.10 **NM** value: **80.00**
9 ❑ Sep 1952 Cover: 0.10 **NM** value: **75.00**
10 ❑ Nov 1952 Cover: 0.10 **NM** value: **75.00**
11 ❑ Jan 1953 Cover: 0.10 **NM** value: **75.00**
12 ❑ Mar 1953 Cover: 0.10 **NM** value: **60.00**
13 ❑ May 1953 Cover: 0.10 **NM** value: **60.00**
14 ❑ Jul 1953 Cover: 0.10 **NM** value: **60.00**

KENTS, THE — DC

Jonathan and Martha Kent, Superman's adoptive parents, welcomed the alien child into their home and into their hearts, thus helping to shape the youth who would become a legend. But who were these people before the alien baby came into their lives, and what events shaped them into such wonderful role models? For the first time, the history of the Kent family is told, and we are shown that the Kents have a habit of producing heroes. Appropriately, the 12-part saga begins with Jonathan's ancestor Silas, the first member of the family to settle in Superman's childhood home of Smallville, Kansas.

Set in the mid-19th century, the series also reveals what may have been the inspiration for Superman's "S" shield.

1 ❑ Aug 1997 Cover: 2.50 **NM** value: **Cover or less**
Circ: Diamd. preorders: **46,470**
📖 Bleeding Kansas, Part 1 • Clark Kent's ancestors in frontier Kansas **A:** Tim Truman **W:** John Ostrander
2 ❑ Sep 1997 Cover: 2.50 **NM** value: **Cover or less**
Circ: Diamd. preorders: **38,320**
📖 Bleeding Kansas, Part 2 **A:** Tim Truman **W:** John Ostrander
3 ❑ Oct 1997 Cover: 2.50 **NM** value: **Cover or less**
Circ: Diamd. preorders: **33,519**
📖 Bleeding Kansas, Part 3 **A:** Tim Truman **W:** John Ostrander
4 ❑ Nov 1997 Cover: 2.50 **NM** value: **Cover or less**
Circ: Diamd. preorders: **29,715**
📖 Bleeding Kansas, Part 4 **A:** Tim Truman **W:** John Ostrander
5 ❑ Dec 1997 Cover: 2.50 **NM** value: **Cover or less**
Circ: Diamd. preorders: **27,331**
📖 Brother vs. Brother, Part 1 **A:** Tim Truman **W:** John Ostrander
6 ❑ Jan 1998 Cover: 2.50 **NM** value: **Cover or less**
Circ: Diamd. preorders: **24,822**
📖 Brother vs. Brother, Part 2 **A:** Tim Truman **W:** John Ostrander
7 ❑ Feb 1998 Cover: 2.50 **NM** value: **Cover or less**
Circ: Diamd. preorders: **23,318**
📖 Brother vs. Brother, Part 3 **A:** Tim Truman **W:** John Ostrander
8 ❑ Mar 1998 Cover: 2.50 **NM** value: **Cover or less**
Circ: Diamd. preorders: **21,915**
📖 Brother vs. Brother, Part 4 **A:** Tim Truman **W:** John Ostrander
9 ❑ Apr 1998 Cover: 2.50 **NM** value: **Cover or less**
Circ: Diamd. preorders: **20,803**
📖 To The Stars by Hard Ways, Part 1 **A:** Tim Truman **W:** John Ostrander
10 ❑ May 1998 Cover: 2.50 **NM** value: **Cover or less**
Circ: Diamd. preorders: **20,367**
📖 To The Stars by Hard Ways, Part 2 **A:** Tim Truman **W:** John Ostrander
11 ❑ Jun 1998 Cover: 2.50 **NM** value: **Cover or less**
Circ: Diamd. preorders: **20,388**
📖 To The Stars by Hard Ways, Part 3 **A:** Tim Truman **W:** John Ostrander
12 ❑ Jul 1998 Cover: 2.50 **NM** value: **Cover or less**
Circ: Diamd. preorders: **19,549**
📖 To The Stars by Hard Ways, Part 4 **A:** Tim Truman **W:** John Ostrander

KERRY DRAKE — Blackthorne

1 ❑ May 1986 Cover: 6.95 **NM** value: **Cover or less**
2 ❑ Jul 1986 Cover: 6.95 **NM** value: **Cover or less**
3 ❑ Dec 1986 Cover: 6.95 **NM** value: **Cover or less**
4 ❑ Feb 1987 Cover: 6.95 **NM** value: **Cover or less**
5 ❑ Jul 1987 Cover: 6.95 **NM** value: **Cover or less**

The prices seen above do not represent the highest possible prices seen in online auctions, but rather the prices we have seen these issues reliably fetch in a variety of environments (storefront retail, mail order, auction and convention).

KERRY DRAKE DETECTIVE CASES — Life's Romances

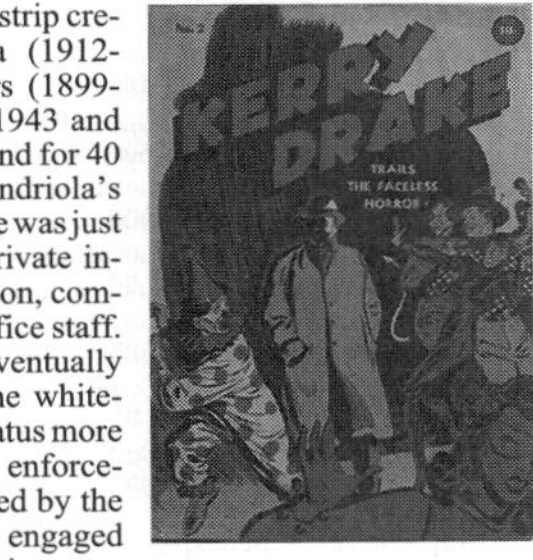

The Kerry Drake comic strip created by Alfred Andriola (1912-1983) and Allen Saunders (1899-1986) was introduced in 1943 and lasted under Andriola's hand for 40 years, ending with Andriola's death. To begin with, Drake was just one of the many, many private investigators in popular fiction, complete with an office and office staff. Unusual developments eventually took over, however, as the white-haired Drake assumed a status more involved with actual law enforcement. He became employed by the District Attorney, became engaged to Sandy, who had been his secretary when the strip began. And then — in a shocking sequence for a newspaper strip — Sandy was murdered, changing the strip's tone and direction. Most of the stories used in the comic book, however, are taken from Drake's P.I. days. — Maggie

2 ❑ ca. 1944 Cover: 0.10 **NM** value: **150.00**
3 ❑ ca. 1944 Cover: 0.10 **NM** value: **125.00**
4 ❑ ca. 1944 Cover: 0.10 **NM** value: **100.00**
5 ❑ ca. 1944 Cover: 0.10 **NM** value: **100.00**
6 ❑ Jan 1948 Cover: 0.10 **NM** value: **85.00**
7 ❑ Mar 1948 Cover: 0.10 **NM** value: **85.00**
8 ❑ May 1948 Cover: 0.10 **NM** value: **85.00**
9 ❑ Jul 1948 Cover: 0.10 **NM** value: **75.00**
10 ❑ Sep 1948 Cover: 0.10 **NM** value: **75.00**
11 ❑ Nov 1948 Cover: 0.10 **NM** value: **75.00**
12 ❑ Jan 1949 Cover: 0.10 **NM** value: **70.00**
13 ❑ Mar 1949 Cover: 0.10 **NM** value: **70.00**
14 ❑ May 1949 Cover: 0.10 **NM** value: **60.00**
15 ❑ Jul 1949 Cover: 0.10 **NM** value: **60.00**
16 ❑ Sep 1949 Cover: 0.10 **NM** value: **60.00**
17 ❑ Nov 1949 Cover: 0.10 **NM** value: **60.00**
18 ❑ Feb 1950 Cover: 0.10 **NM** value: **50.00**
19 ❑ Apr 1950 Cover: 0.10 **NM** value: **50.00**
20 ❑ Jun 1950 Cover: 0.10 **NM** value: **50.00**
21 ❑ Aug 1950 Cover: 0.10 **NM** value: **50.00**
22 ❑ Oct 1950 Cover: 0.10 **NM** value: **50.00**
23 ❑ Dec 1950 Cover: 0.10 **NM** value: **50.00**
24 ❑ Feb 1951 Cover: 0.10 **NM** value: **40.00**
25 ❑ Apr 1951 Cover: 0.10 **NM** value: **40.00**
26 ❑ Jun 1951 Cover: 0.10 **NM** value: **40.00**
27 ❑ Aug 1951 Cover: 0.10 **NM** value: **35.00**
28 ❑ Oct 1951 Cover: 0.10 **NM** value: **35.00**
29 ❑ Dec 1951 Cover: 0.10 **NM** value: **30.00**
30 ❑ Feb 1952 Cover: 0.10 **NM** value: **30.00**
31 ❑ Apr 1952 Cover: 0.10 **NM** value: **30.00**
32 ❑ Jun 1952 Cover: 0.10 **NM** value: **25.00**
33 ❑ Aug 1952 Cover: 0.10 **NM** value: **25.00**

KEWPIES — Will Eisner

1 ❑ Spr 1949 Cover: 0.10 **NM** value: **200.00**

KEY COMICS — Consolidated

1 ❑ Jan 1944 Cover: 0.10 **NM** value: **300.00**
2 ❑ Mar 1944 Cover: 0.10 **NM** value: **200.00**
3 ❑ 1944 Cover: 0.10 **NM** value: **150.00**
4 ❑ 1945 Cover: 0.10 **NM** value: **150.00**
5 ❑ 1946 Cover: 0.10 **NM** value: **175.00**

KEYHOLE — Millennium

1 ❑ Jun 1996 Cover: 2.95 **NM** value: **Cover or less**
2 ❑ Oct 1996 Cover: 2.95 **NM** value: **Cover or less**
3 ❑ 1997 Cover: 2.95 **NM** value: **Cover or less**
4 ❑ May 1997 Cover: 2.95 **NM** value: **Cover or less**
5 ❑ Jun 1998 Cover: 2.95 **NM** value: **Cover or less**

KEY RING COMICS — Dell

1 ❑ ca. 1941 Cover: 0.10 **NM** value: **45.00**
2 ❑ ca. 1941 Cover: 0.10 **NM** value: **45.00**
3 ❑ ca. 1941 Cover: 0.10 **NM** value: **45.00**
4 ❑ ca. 1941 Cover: 0.10 **NM** value: **45.00**
5 ❑ ca. 1941 Cover: 0.10 **NM** value: **45.00**

KICKERS, INC. — Marvel

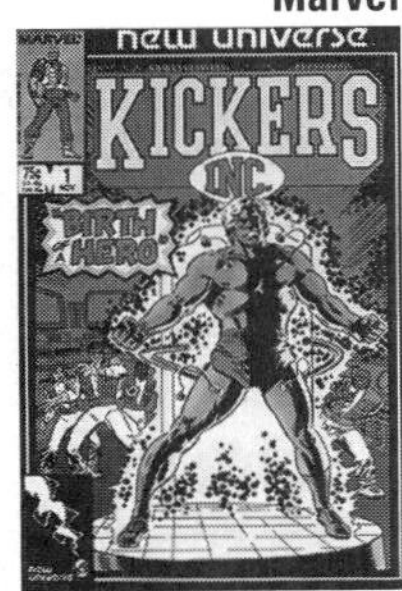

The New York Smashers football team are a colorful lot: dapper wide receiver "Dasher" Corbin, powerhouse Beauford "Brick House" Wohl, the wild "Suicide" Smythe. Leading the team is quarterback Jack Magniconte.

Jack takes the game seriously and is continually looking for an edge to help his playing. His brother, a sports nutritionist, has rigged up a machine called an "intensifier," which he thinks might increase his strength. But this machine might have no effect at all, except that Jack has been exposed to the mysterious "White Event" which transformed Marvel's "New Universe." After that, Jack gains incredible speed and strength — so much so that football is no longer a challenge.

Following his brother's death at the hands of thugs, Jack decides to gather his fellow teammates into Kickers, Inc. — and put some serious "kicking" into crimefighting.

1 ❑ Nov 1986 Cover: 0.75 **NM** value: **1.00**
Circ: CapCity orders: **38,100**

CGC-graded: Multiply prices above by **33 for 9.9 M • 16 for 9.8 NM/M • 7 for 9.6 NM+ • 5 for 9.4 NM • 2.5 for 9.2 NM- • 1.5 for 9.0 VF/NM**

📖 This Legend Born! **A:** Ron Frenz **W:** Tom DeFalco ★ Origin of Kickers, Inc.. ★ 1st Appearance of Kickers, Inc..

2 ☐ Dec 1986 Cover: 0.75 **NM** value: **1.00**
Circ: CapCity orders: **20,000**
3 ☐ Jan 1987 Cover: 0.75 **NM** value: **1.00**
Circ: CapCity orders: **16,400**
4 ☐ Feb 1987 Cover: 0.75 **NM** value: **1.00**
Circ: CapCity orders: **15,500**
5 ☐ Mar 1987 Cover: 0.75 **NM** value: **1.00**
Circ: CapCity orders: **15,400**
6 ☐ Apr 1987 Cover: 0.75 **NM** value: **1.00**
Circ: CapCity orders: **13,000**
7 ☐ May 1987 Cover: 0.75 **NM** value: **1.00**
Circ: CapCity orders: **10,600**
8 ☐ Jun 1987 Cover: 0.75 **NM** value: **1.00**
Circ: CapCity orders: **10,100**
9 ☐ Jul 1987 Cover: 0.75 **NM** value: **1.00**
Circ: CapCity orders: **8,800**
10 ☐ Aug 1987 Cover: 0.75 **NM** value: **1.00**
Circ: CapCity orders: **8,300**
11 ☐ Sep 1987 Cover: 0.75 **NM** value: **1.00**
Circ: CapCity orders: **8,300**
12 ☐ Oct 1987 Cover: 0.75 **NM** value: **1.00**
Circ: CapCity orders: **7,900**

KID ANARCHY — Fantagraphics

1 ☐ b&w Cover: 2.50 **NM** value: **Cover or less**
2 ☐ b&w Cover: 2.75 **NM** value: **Cover or less**
3 ☐ b&w Cover: 2.75 **NM** value: **Cover or less**

KID BLASTOFF — Slave Labor / Amaze Ink

1 ☐ Jun 1996 Cover: 2.75 **NM** value: **Cover or less**
A: Evan Dorkin; Sarah Dyer

KID CANNIBAL — Eternity

1 ☐ Oct 1991 Cover: 2.50 **NM** value: **Cover or less**
• **CGC:** 1 graded, best 8.5
2 ☐ 1991 Cover: 2.50 **NM** value: **Cover or less**
3 ☐ 1992 Cover: 2.50 **NM** value: **Cover or less**
4 ☐ 1992 Cover: 2.50 **NM** value: **Cover or less**

KID CARROTS — St. John

1 ☐ Sep 1953 Cover: 0.10 **NM** value: **40.00**

KID COLT OUTLAW — Marvel

Back when he was young and foolish, Kid Colt killed an outlaw in self-defense. Although innocent, he fled, and has since been hunted as an outlaw. Of course, readers knew that this was no cattle-rustling hombre, but a Robin Hood of the range — a blond knight who came to the aid of ladies, pioneers, and other victims of frontier violence.

A hugely popular series in its heyday, Kid Colt switched to reprints after issue #140, and ran nearly a decade longer, until finally ceasing in 1979.

Colt would later return in Marvel's Blaze of Glory mini-series.

1 ☐ Aug 1948 Cover: 0.10 **NM** value: **650.00**
★ Appearance of Two-Gun Kid.
2 ☐ Oct 1948 Cover: 0.10 **NM** value: **325.00**
3 ☐ Dec 1948 Cover: 0.10 **NM** value: **240.00**
4 ☐ Feb 1949 Cover: 0.10 **NM** value: **240.00**
• **CGC:** 1 graded, best 8.0
5 ☐ May 1949 Cover: 0.10 **NM** value: **240.00**
6 ☐ Jul 1949 Cover: 0.10 **NM** value: **165.00**
7 ☐ Oct 1949 Cover: 0.10 **NM** value: **165.00**
8 ☐ Feb 1950 Cover: 0.10 **NM** value: **165.00**
9 ☐ May 1950 Cover: 0.10 **NM** value: **165.00**
• Has 1949 Statement of Ownership, filed 10/1/49; no sales figures
10 ☐ Jul 1950 Cover: 0.10 **NM** value: **165.00**
11 ☐ Oct 1950 Cover: 0.10 **NM** value: **220.00**
• **CGC:** 2 graded, best 6.5
★ Origin of Kid Colt.
12 ☐ Cover: 0.10 **NM** value: **145.00**
13 ☐ Cover: 0.10 **NM** value: **145.00**
14 ☐ Cover: 0.10 **NM** value: **145.00**
15 ☐ Cover: 0.10 **NM** value: **145.00**
16 ☐ Cover: 0.10 **NM** value: **145.00**
17 ☐ Cover: 0.10 **NM** value: **145.00**
18 ☐ Cover: 0.10 **NM** value: **145.00**
19 ☐ Cover: 0.10 **NM** value: **145.00**
20 ☐ May 1952 Cover: 0.10 **NM** value: **145.00**
21 ☐ Cover: 0.10 **NM** value: **100.00**
22 ☐ Cover: 0.10 **NM** value: **100.00**
23 ☐ Cover: 0.10 **NM** value: **100.00**
24 ☐ Cover: 0.10 **NM** value: **100.00**
25 ☐ Cover: 0.10 **NM** value: **100.00**
26 ☐ Cover: 0.10 **NM** value: **100.00**
27 ☐ Cover: 0.10 **NM** value: **100.00**
28 ☐ Cover: 0.10 **NM** value: **100.00**
29 ☐ Cover: 0.10 **NM** value: **100.00**
30 ☐ Cover: 0.10 **NM** value: **100.00**
31 ☐ Oct 1953 Cover: 0.10 **NM** value: **85.00**
32 ☐ Cover: 0.10 **NM** value: **85.00**
33 ☐ Cover: 0.10 **NM** value: **85.00**
34 ☐ Cover: 0.10 **NM** value: **85.00**
35 ☐ Cover: 0.10 **NM** value: **85.00**
36 ☐ Cover: 0.10 **NM** value: **85.00**
37 ☐ Cover: 0.10 **NM** value: **85.00**
38 ☐ Cover: 0.10 **NM** value: **85.00**
39 ☐ Cover: 0.10 **NM** value: **85.00**
40 ☐ Cover: 0.10 **NM** value: **85.00**
41 ☐ Cover: 0.10 **NM** value: **75.00**
42 ☐ Nov 1954 Cover: 0.10 **NM** value: **75.00**
43 ☐ Dec 1954 Cover: 0.10 **NM** value: **75.00**
44 ☐ Jan 1955 Cover: 0.10 **NM** value: **75.00**
45 ☐ Feb 1955 Cover: 0.10 **NM** value: **75.00**
46 ☐ Mar 1955 Cover: 0.10 **NM** value: **75.00**
47 ☐ Apr 1955 Cover: 0.10 **NM** value: **75.00**
48 ☐ May 1955 Cover: 0.10 **NM** value: **75.00**
49 ☐ Jun 1955 Cover: 0.10 **NM** value: **75.00**
50 ☐ Jul 1955 Cover: 0.10 **NM** value: **75.00**
51 ☐ Aug 1955 Cover: 0.10 **NM** value: **60.00**
52 ☐ Sep 1955 Cover: 0.10 **NM** value: **60.00**
53 ☐ Oct 1955 Cover: 0.10 **NM** value: **60.00**
54 ☐ Nov 1955 Cover: 0.10 **NM** value: **60.00**
55 ☐ Dec 1955 Cover: 0.10 **NM** value: **60.00**
56 ☐ Jan 1956 Cover: 0.10 **NM** value: **60.00**
57 ☐ Feb 1956 Cover: 0.10 **NM** value: **60.00**
58 ☐ Mar 1956 Cover: 0.10 **NM** value: **60.00**
• **CGC:** 1 graded, best 8.5
59 ☐ Apr 1956 Cover: 0.10 **NM** value: **60.00**
• **CGC:** 1 graded, best 9.0
60 ☐ May 1956 Cover: 0.10 **NM** value: **60.00**
61 ☐ Jun 1956 Cover: 0.10 **NM** value: **45.00**
62 ☐ Jul 1956 Cover: 0.10 **NM** value: **45.00**
63 ☐ Aug 1956 Cover: 0.10 **NM** value: **45.00**
64 ☐ Sep 1956 Cover: 0.10 **NM** value: **45.00**
65 ☐ Oct 1956 Cover: 0.10 **NM** value: **45.00**
66 ☐ Nov 1956 Cover: 0.10 **NM** value: **45.00**
67 ☐ Dec 1956 Cover: 0.10 **NM** value: **45.00**
68 ☐ Jan 1957 Cover: 0.10 **NM** value: **45.00**
69 ☐ Feb 1957 Cover: 0.10 **NM** value: **45.00**
70 ☐ Mar 1957 Cover: 0.10 **NM** value: **45.00**
71 ☐ Apr 1957 Cover: 0.10 **NM** value: **38.00**
72 ☐ May 1957 Cover: 0.10 **NM** value: **38.00**
📖 Kid Colt Helps a Lady; Trail of Disaster; Day of Decision; The Coward! **A:** Jack Keller
73 ☐ Jul 1957 Cover: 0.10 **NM** value: **38.00**
74 ☐ Sep 1957 Cover: 0.10 **NM** value: **38.00**
75 ☐ Nov 1957 Cover: 0.10 **NM** value: **38.00**
76 ☐ Jan 1958 Cover: 0.10 **NM** value: **38.00**
77 ☐ Mar 1958 Cover: 0.10 **NM** value: **38.00**
78 ☐ May 1958 Cover: 0.10 **NM** value: **38.00**
79 ☐ Jul 1958 Cover: 0.10 **NM** value: **38.00**
80 ☐ Sep 1958 Cover: 0.10 **NM** value: **38.00**
81 ☐ Nov 1958 Cover: 0.10 **NM** value: **38.00**
82 ☐ Jan 1959 Cover: 0.10 **NM** value: **38.00**
83 ☐ Mar 1959 Cover: 0.10 **NM** value: **38.00**
84 ☐ May 1959 Cover: 0.10 **NM** value: **38.00**
• Has 1958 Statement of Ownership, filed 10/1/1958; no sales figures listed
85 ☐ Jul 1959 Cover: 0.10 **NM** value: **38.00**
86 ☐ Sep 1959 Cover: 0.10 **NM** value: **38.00**
87 ☐ Nov 1959 Cover: 0.10 **NM** value: **38.00**
88 ☐ Jan 1960 Cover: 0.10 **NM** value: **38.00**
Circ: Statement: **144,746**
89 ☐ Mar 1960 Cover: 0.10 **NM** value: **38.00**
Circ: Statement: **144,746**
90 ☐ May 1960 Cover: 0.10 **NM** value: **38.00**
Circ: Statement: **144,746**
91 ☐ Jul 1960 Cover: 0.10 **NM** value: **38.00**
Circ: Statement: **144,746** • **CGC:** 1 graded, best 9.0
92 ☐ Sep 1960 Cover: 0.10 **NM** value: **38.00**
Circ: Statement: **144,746**
93 ☐ Oct 1960 Cover: 0.10 **NM** value: **38.00**
Circ: Statement: **144,746**
94 ☐ Nov 1960 Cover: 0.10 **NM** value: **38.00**
Circ: Statement: **144,746**
95 ☐ Dec 1961 Cover: 0.10 **NM** value: **38.00**
96 ☐ Jan 1961 Cover: 0.10 **NM** value: **38.00**
97 ☐ Mar 1961 Cover: 0.10 **NM** value: **38.00**
98 ☐ May 1961 Cover: 0.10 **NM** value: **38.00**
• Has 1960 Statement, filed 10/1/60; avg paid circ 144,746
99 ☐ Jul 1961 Cover: 0.10 **NM** value: **38.00**
100 ☐ Sep 1961 Cover: 0.10 **NM** value: **38.00**
101 ☐ Nov 1961 Cover: 0.10 **NM** value: **26.00**
102 ☐ Jan 1962 Cover: 0.12 **NM** value: **26.00**
103 ☐ Mar 1962 Cover: 0.12 **NM** value: **26.00**
104 ☐ May 1962 Cover: 0.12 **NM** value: **26.00**
105 ☐ Jul 1962 Cover: 0.12 **NM** value: **26.00**
106 ☐ Sep 1962 Cover: 0.12 **NM** value: **26.00**
107 ☐ Nov 1962 Cover: 0.12 **NM** value: **26.00**
108 ☐ Jan 1963 Cover: 0.12 **NM** value: **26.00**
Circ: Statement: **192,755**
109 ☐ Mar 1963 Cover: 0.12 **NM** value: **26.00**
Circ: Statement: **192,755**
110 ☐ May 1963 Cover: 0.12 **NM** value: **26.00**
Circ: Statement: **192,755**
111 ☐ Jul 1963 Cover: 0.12 **NM** value: **18.00**
Circ: Statement: **192,755**
112 ☐ Sep 1963 Cover: 0.12 **NM** value: **18.00**
Circ: Statement: **192,755**
113 ☐ Nov 1963 Cover: 0.12 **NM** value: **18.00**
Circ: Statement: **192,755**
114 ☐ Jan 1964 Cover: 0.12 **NM** value: **18.00**
Circ: Statement: **184,405**
★ Versus Iron Mask.
115 ☐ Mar 1964 Cover: 0.12 **NM** value: **18.00**
Circ: Statement: **184,405**
116 ☐ May 1964 Cover: 0.12 **NM** value: **18.00**
Circ: Statement: **184,405**
117 ☐ Jul 1964 Cover: 0.12 **NM** value: **18.00**
Circ: Statement: **184,405**
• Has 1963 Statement, filed 10/1/63; avg print run 334,574; avg sals 192,690; avg subs 65; avg total paid 192,755; samples 175; max existing 192,930; 42% of run returned
118 ☐ Sep 1964 Cover: 0.12 **NM** value: **18.00**
Circ: Statement: **184,405**
★ Versus Scorpion. ★ Versus Bull Barton. ★ Versus Doctor Danger.
119 ☐ Nov 1964 Cover: 0.12 **NM** value: **18.00**
Circ: Statement: **184,405**
120 ☐ Jan 1965 Cover: 0.12 **NM** value: **18.00**
Circ: Statement: **193,506**
121 ☐ Mar 1965 Cover: 0.12 **NM** value: **14.00**
Circ: Statement: **193,506**
122 ☐ May 1965 Cover: 0.12 **NM** value: **14.00**
Circ: Statement: **193,506**
• Has 1864 Statement, filed 10/1/64; avg print run 310,000; avg sales 184,300; avg subs 105; avg total paid 184,405; samples 125; max existing 184,530; 41% of run returned
123 ☐ Jul 1965 Cover: 0.12 **NM** value: **14.00**
Circ: Statement: **193,506**
124 ☐ Sep 1965 Cover: 0.12 **NM** value: **14.00**
Circ: Statement: **193,506**
★ Versus Phantom Raider.
125 ☐ Nov 1965 Cover: 0.12 **NM** value: **14.00**
Circ: Statement: **193,506**
★ Appearance of Two-Gun Kid.
126 ☐ Jan 1966 Cover: 0.12 **NM** value: **14.00**
Circ: Statement: **214,555**
127 ☐ Mar 1966 Cover: 0.12 **NM** value: **14.00**
Circ: Statement: **214,555**
★ Versus Iron Mask. ★ Versus Fat Man. ★ Versus Doctor Danger.
128 ☐ May 1966 Cover: 0.12 **NM** value: **14.00**
Circ: Statement: **214,555**
• Has 1965 Statement, filed 10/1/1965; avg print run 330,540; avg sales 193,401; avg subs 105; avg total paid 193,506; samples 60; max existing 193,566; 41% of run returned
129 ☐ Jul 1966 Cover: 0.12 **NM** value: **14.00**
Circ: Statement: **214,555**
130 ☐ Sep 1966 Cover: 0.25 **NM** value: **14.00**
Circ: Statement: **214,555** • **CGC:** 1 graded, best 7.0
• giant ★ Origin of Kid Colt.
131 ☐ Nov 1966 Cover: 0.25 **NM** value: **10.00**
Circ: Statement: **214,555** • **CGC:** 1 graded, best 9.4
• giant
132 ☐ Jan 1967 Cover: 0.25 **NM** value: **10.00**
• **CGC:** 1 graded, best 9.2
• giant
133 ☐ Mar 1967 Cover: 0.12 **NM** value: **10.00**
★ Versus Rammer Ramkin.
134 ☐ May 1967 Cover: 0.12 **NM** value: **10.00**
• Has 1966 Statement, filed 10/1/1966; avg print run 331,344; avg sales 214,355; avg subs 200; avg total print run 214,555; samples 60; max existing 214,615; 35% of run returned
135 ☐ Jul 1967 Cover: 0.12 **NM** value: **10.00**
136 ☐ Sep 1967 Cover: 0.12 **NM** value: **10.00**
137 ☐ Nov 1967 Cover: 0.12 **NM** value: **10.00**
138 ☐ Jan 1968 Cover: 0.12 **NM** value: **10.00**
139 ☐ Mar 1968 Cover: 0.12 **NM** value: **10.00**
• series goes on hiatus
140 ☐ Nov 1969 Cover: 0.15 **NM** value: **5.00**
• Reprints begin
141 ☐ Dec 1969 Cover: 0.15 **NM** value: **5.00**
142 ☐ Jan 1970 Cover: 0.15 **NM** value: **5.00**
143 ☐ Feb 1970 Cover: 0.15 **NM** value: **5.00**
144 ☐ Mar 1970 Cover: 0.15 **NM** value: **5.00**
145 ☐ Apr 1970 Cover: 0.15 **NM** value: **5.00**
146 ☐ May 1970 Cover: 0.15 **NM** value: **5.00**
147 ☐ Jun 1970 Cover: 0.15 **NM** value: **5.00**
148 ☐ Jul 1970 Cover: 0.15 **NM** value: **5.00**
149 ☐ Aug 1970 Cover: 0.15 **NM** value: **5.00**
150 ☐ Oct 1970 Cover: 0.15 **NM** value: **5.00**
151 ☐ Dec 1970 Cover: 0.15 **NM** value: **5.00**
152 ☐ Feb 1971 Cover: 0.15 **NM** value: **5.00**
153 ☐ Apr 1971 Cover: 0.15 **NM** value: **5.00**
154 ☐ Jul 1971 Cover: 0.15 **NM** value: **5.00**
155 ☐ Sep 1971 Cover: 0.15 **NM** value: **5.00**
156 ☐ Nov 1971 Cover: 0.15 **NM** value: **5.00**
• **CGC:** 1 graded, best 9.4
157 ☐ Jan 1972 Cover: 0.15 **NM** value: **5.00**
158 ☐ Mar 1972 Cover: 0.15 **NM** value: **5.00**
159 ☐ May 1972 Cover: 0.15 **NM** value: **5.00**
160 ☐ Jul 1972 Cover: 0.15 **NM** value: **5.00**
161 ☐ Aug 1972 Cover: 0.20 **NM** value: **5.00**
162 ☐ Sep 1972 Cover: 0.20 **NM** value: **5.00**
163 ☐ Oct 1972 Cover: 0.20 **NM** value: **5.00**
164 ☐ Nov 1972 Cover: 0.20 **NM** value: **5.00**
165 ☐ Dec 1972 Cover: 0.20 **NM** value: **5.00**
166 ☐ Jan 1973 Cover: 0.20 **NM** value: **5.00**
167 ☐ Feb 1973 Cover: 0.20 **NM** value: **5.00**
168 ☐ Mar 1973 Cover: 0.20 **NM** value: **5.00**
169 ☐ Apr 1973 Cover: 0.20 **NM** value: **5.00**
170 ☐ May 1973 Cover: 0.20 **NM** value: **5.00**
171 ☐ Jun 1973 Cover: 0.20 **NM** value: **4.00**
172 ☐ Jul 1973 Cover: 0.20 **NM** value: **4.00**
173 ☐ Aug 1973 Cover: 0.20 **NM** value: **4.00**
174 ☐ Sep 1973 Cover: 0.20 **NM** value: **4.00**
175 ☐ Oct 1973 Cover: 0.20 **NM** value: **4.00**
176 ☐ Nov 1973 Cover: 0.20 **NM** value: **4.00**
177 ☐ Dec 1973 Cover: 0.20 **NM** value: **4.00**
178 ☐ Jan 1974 Cover: 0.20 **NM** value: **4.00**
179 ☐ Feb 1974 Cover: 0.20 **NM** value: **4.00**
180 ☐ Mar 1974 Cover: 0.20 **NM** value: **4.00**
181 ☐ Apr 1974 Cover: 0.20 **NM** value: **4.00**
182 ☐ May 1974 Cover: 0.25 **NM** value: **4.00**
183 ☐ Jun 1974 Cover: 0.25 **NM** value: **4.00**
184 ☐ Jul 1974 Cover: 0.25 **NM** value: **4.00**
185 ☐ Aug 1974 Cover: 0.25 **NM** value: **4.00**
186 ☐ Sep 1974 Cover: 0.25 **NM** value: **4.00**
187 ☐ Oct 1974 Cover: 0.25 **NM** value: **4.00**
188 ☐ Nov 1974 Cover: 0.25 **NM** value: **4.00**
189 ☐ Dec 1974 Cover: 0.25 **NM** value: **4.00**
190 ☐ Jan 1975 Cover: 0.25 **NM** value: **4.00**
191 ☐ Feb 1975 Cover: 0.25 **NM** value: **4.00**

Other grades: Multiply prices above by **1.5 for Mint • 2/3 for Very Fine • 1/3 for Fine • 1/5 for Very Good • 1/8 for Good**

192 ❑ Mar 1975 Cover: 0.25 **NM** value: **4.00**
193 ❑ Apr 1975 Cover: 0.25 **NM** value: **4.00**
194 ❑ May 1975 Cover: 0.25 **NM** value: **4.00**
195 ❑ Jun 1975 Cover: 0.25 **NM** value: **4.00**
196 ❑ Jul 1975 Cover: 0.25 **NM** value: **4.00**
197 ❑ Aug 1975 Cover: 0.25 **NM** value: **4.00**
198 ❑ Sep 1975 Cover: 0.25 **NM** value: **4.00**
199 ❑ Oct 1975 Cover: 0.25 **NM** value: **4.00**
200 ❑ Nov 1975 Cover: 0.25 **NM** value: **4.00**
201 ❑ Dec 1975 Cover: 0.25 **NM** value: **3.00**
202 ❑ Jan 1976 Cover: 0.25 **NM** value: **3.00**
203 ❑ Feb 1976 Cover: 0.25 **NM** value: **3.00**
204 ❑ Mar 1976 Cover: 0.25 **NM** value: **3.00**
🕮 Kid Colt Helps a Lady; Trail of Disaster; Day of Decision; The Coward! • Reprints Kid Colt Outlaw #72 **A:** Jack Keller
205 ❑ Apr 1976 Cover: 0.25 **NM** value: **3.00**
206 ❑ May 1976 Cover: 0.25 **NM** value: **3.00**
207 ❑ Jun 1976 Cover: 0.25 **NM** value: **3.00**
208 ❑ Jul 1976 Cover: 0.25 **NM** value: **3.00**
209 ❑ Aug 1976 Cover: 0.25 **NM** value: **3.00**
210 ❑ Sep 1976 Cover: 0.30 **NM** value: **3.00**
211 ❑ Oct 1976 Cover: 0.30 **NM** value: **3.00**
212 ❑ Nov 1976 Cover: 0.30 **NM** value: **3.00**
213 ❑ Dec 1976 Cover: 0.30 **NM** value: **3.00**
214 ❑ Jan 1977 Cover: 0.30 **NM** value: **3.00**
215 ❑ Feb 1977 Cover: 0.30 **NM** value: **3.00**
216 ❑ Mar 1977 Cover: 0.30 **NM** value: **3.00**
217 ❑ Apr 1977 Cover: 0.30 **NM** value: **3.00**
218 ❑ Jun 1977 Cover: 0.30 **NM** value: **3.00**
219 ❑ Aug 1977 Cover: 0.30 **NM** value: **3.00**
220 ❑ Oct 1977 Cover: 0.30 **NM** value: **3.00**
221 ❑ Dec 1977 Cover: 0.35 **NM** value: **3.00**
222 ❑ Feb 1978 Cover: 0.35 **NM** value: **3.00**
223 ❑ Apr 1978 Cover: 0.35 **NM** value: **3.00**
224 ❑ Jun 1978 Cover: 0.35 **NM** value: **3.00**
225 ❑ Aug 1978 Cover: 0.35 **NM** value: **3.00**
226 ❑ Oct 1978 Cover: 0.35 **NM** value: **3.00**
227 ❑ Dec 1978 Cover: 0.35 **NM** value: **3.00**
228 ❑ Feb 1979 Cover: 0.35 **NM** value: **3.00**
229 ❑ Apr 1979 Cover: 0.35 **NM** value: **3.00**
final issue.

KID COWBOY — Ziff-Davis

1 ❑ ca. 1950 Cover: 0.10 **NM** value: **75.00**
2 ❑ ca. 1950 Cover: 0.10 **NM** value: **70.00**
3 ❑ Spr 1951 Cover: 0.10 **NM** value: **60.00**
4 ❑ May 1951 Cover: 0.10 **NM** value: **50.00**
5 ❑ Fal 1951 Cover: 0.10 **NM** value: **45.00**
6 ❑ Win 1951 Cover: 0.10 **NM** value: **45.00**
7 ❑ Spr 1952 Cover: 0.10 **NM** value: **40.00**
8 ❑ Jul 1952 Cover: 0.10 **NM** value: **40.00**
9 ❑ Sep 1952 Cover: 0.10 **NM** value: **40.00**
10 ❑ Fal 1952 Cover: 0.10 **NM** value: **35.00**
11 ❑ ca. 1953 Cover: 0.10 **NM** value: **35.00**
12 ❑ ca. 1953 Cover: 0.10 **NM** value: **30.00**
13 ❑ ca. 1953 Cover: 0.10 **NM** value: **30.00**
14 ❑ Jun 1954 Cover: 0.10 **NM** value: **30.00**

KID DEATH & FLUFFY: HALLOWEEN SPECIAL — Event

1 ❑ Oct 1997 Cover: 2.95 **NM** value: **Cover or less**
Circ: Diamd. preorders: **7,990**
🕮 Slab Happy **A:** John Cebollero **W:** Rick Parker

KID DEATH & FLUFFY SPRING BREAK SPECIAL — Event

1 ❑ Jun 1996 Cover: 2.50 **NM** value: **Cover or less**
🕮 Spring Break Spectacular **A:** Rick Parker; Amanda Conner **W:** Joe Quesada; Jimmy Palmiotti

KIDDIE KAPERS — Kiddie Kapers

1 ❑ Cover: 0.10 **NM** value: **60.00**
2 ❑ Cover: 0.10 **NM** value: **50.00**

KIDDIE KARNIVAL — Ziff-Davis

1 ❑ ca. 1952 Cover: 0.10 **NM** value: **250.00**

KID ETERNITY — DC / Vertigo

1 ❑ May 1993 Cover: 1.95 **NM** value: **2.00**
Circ: CapCity orders: **34,850**
🕮 Even Deadmen Need Friends **A:** Sean Phillips **W:** Ann Nocenti
2 ❑ Jun 1993 Cover: 1.95 **NM** value: **2.00**
Circ: CapCity orders: **20,050**
🕮 Stir It Up **A:** Sean Phillips **W:** Ann Nocenti
3 ❑ Jul 1993 Cover: 1.95 **NM** value: **2.00**
Circ: CapCity orders: **16,600**
🕮 Cupid's Folly **A:** Sean Phillips **W:** Ann Nocenti
4 ❑ Aug 1993 Cover: 1.95 **NM** value: **2.00**
Circ: CapCity orders: **15,250**
5 ❑ Sep 1993 Cover: 1.95 **NM** value: **2.00**
Circ: CapCity orders: **12,250**
6 ❑ Oct 1993 Cover: 1.95 **NM** value: **2.00**
Circ: CapCity orders: **10,750**
7 ❑ Nov 1993 Cover: 1.95 **NM** value: **2.00**
Circ: CapCity orders: **9,450**
🕮 Infinity **A:** Sean Scoffield **W:** Ann Nocenti
8 ❑ Dec 1993 Cover: 1.95 **NM** value: **2.00**
Circ: CapCity orders: **8,800**
9 ❑ Jan 1994 Cover: 1.95 **NM** value: **2.00**
Circ: CapCity orders: **7,900**
10 ❑ Feb 1994 Cover: 1.95 **NM** value: **2.00**
Circ: CapCity orders: **7,400**
11 ❑ Mar 1994 Cover: 1.95 **NM** value: **2.00**
Circ: CapCity orders: **6,650**
12 ❑ May 1994 Cover: 1.95 **NM** value: **2.00**
Circ: CapCity orders: **6,050**
13 ❑ Jun 1994 Cover: 1.95 **NM** value: **2.00**
Circ: CapCity orders: **5,900**
🕮 A Date in Hell, Part 1
14 ❑ Jul 1994 Cover: 1.95 **NM** value: **2.00**
Circ: CapCity orders: **5,400**
🕮 A Date in Hell, Part 2
15 ❑ Aug 1994 Cover: 1.95 **NM** value: **2.00**
Circ: CapCity orders: **5,150**
🕮 A Date in Hell, Part 3
16 ❑ Sep 1994 Cover: 1.95 **NM** value: **2.00**
Circ: CapCity orders: **5,050**
🕮 A Date in Hell, Part 4 final issue.

KID ETERNITY (MINI-SERIES) — DC / Vertigo

1 ❑ May 1991 Cover: 4.95 **NM** value: **Cover or less**
Circ: CapCity orders: **21,500**
🕮 Canto I; Canto II **A:** Duncan Fegredo **W:** Grant Morrison
2 ❑ Jul 1991 Cover: 4.95 **NM** value: **Cover or less**
Circ: CapCity orders: **16,100**
🕮 Canto III; Canto IV **A:** Duncan Fegredo **W:** Grant Morrison
3 ❑ Oct 1991 Cover: 4.95 **NM** value: **Cover or less**
Circ: CapCity orders: **13,600**
🕮 Canto V; Canto VI **A:** Duncan Fegredo **W:** Grant Morrison

KID ETERNITY (QUALITY) — Quality

During World War II, a boy named Kit and his grandfather were out at sea when their ship was torpedoed by a German U-Boat and the survivors were machine-gunned in the water. When Kit and his grandfather arrived at the pearly gates, they were told that it wasn't Kit's time to die yet and Mr. Keeper, who was in charge of the list of who was to live and who was to die, was charged with giving Kit the remaining 75 years of his life.

Keeper or Keep as Kit referred to him, returned Kit's spirit to his mortal body with the power to change from mortal to spirit and to call on any figure of history or mythology or travel through time simply by saying the word, "Eternity!" Kid Eternity's adventures exposed readers to dozens of colorful characters, some familiar and others obscure during the Golden Age.

When DC acquired the Quality characters and the Fawcett characters, a later story established that Freddy Freeman (aka Captain Marvel Jr.) and Kit were actually orphaned brothers who had suffered similar fates (Nazis killing them and their respective grandfathers) and that it was Freddy who was supposed to die during World War II, but the old wizard Shazam gave him the chance to live as part of the Marvel Family. In recent years, Kid Eternity returned in a three-issue mini-series and a short-lived Vertigo series. — Brent

1 ❑ Spr 1946 Cover: 0.10 **NM** value: **700.00**
• **CGC:** 3 graded, best 9.2
2 ❑ Sum 1946 Cover: 0.10 **NM** value: **500.00**
3 ❑ Fal 1946 Cover: 0.10 **NM** value: **500.00**
• **CGC:** 1 graded, best 8.0
4 ❑ Win 1946 Cover: 0.10 **NM** value: **400.00**
5 ❑ Spr 1947 Cover: 0.10 **NM** value: **400.00**
• **CGC:** 1 graded, best 7.5
6 ❑ Sum 1947 Cover: 0.10 **NM** value: **400.00**
7 ❑ Fal 1947 Cover: 0.10 **NM** value: **350.00**
• **CGC:** 1 graded, best 8.5
8 ❑ Win 1947 Cover: 0.10 **NM** value: **350.00**
9 ❑ Spr 1948 Cover: 0.10 **NM** value: **350.00**
10 ❑ Jul 1948 Cover: 0.10 **NM** value: **300.00**
11 ❑ Sep 1948 Cover: 0.10 **NM** value: **300.00**
12 ❑ Nov 1948 Cover: 0.10 **NM** value: **300.00**
13 ❑ Jan 1949 Cover: 0.10 **NM** value: **275.00**
• **CGC:** 1 graded, best 4.0
14 ❑ Mar 1949 Cover: 0.10 **NM** value: **275.00**
15 ❑ May 1949 Cover: 0.10 **NM** value: **275.00**
16 ❑ Jul 1949 Cover: 0.10 **NM** value: **250.00**
17 ❑ Sep 1949 Cover: 0.10 **NM** value: **250.00**
18 ❑ Nov 1949 Cover: 0.10 **NM** value: **250.00**

KID FROM DODGE CITY — Atlas

1 ❑ Jul 1957 Cover: 0.10 **NM** value: **100.00**
2 ❑ Sep 1957 Cover: 0.10 **NM** value: **90.00**

KID FROM TEXAS — Atlas

1 ❑ Jun 1957 Cover: 0.10 **NM** value: **100.00**
• **CGC:** 1 graded, best 9.2
2 ❑ Aug 1957 Cover: 0.10 **NM** value: **90.00**

KID KOMICS — Timely

Though the first issue's main figure is yet another costumed beefy guy punching out Asians in combat, even that cover declares that the issue co-stars kids: Whitewash, Knuckles, Trixie Troubles, Pinto Pete, and Subbie. With the second issue, the line-up at the bottom of the page is identified as The Young Allies, and the lineup now reads: Bucky, Toro, Knuckles, Whitewash, Jeff, and Tubby. From that point on, until it metamorphosed in 1946 to a kids' comic book for one issue before morphing again into a Blondie pastiche called Rusty, it was The Young Allies who took center stage.

Cluttered covers take time to analyze, as in the ninth cover, featuring such details as a bound Tubby suspended over an octopus pit, a hooded villain winching him lower, Bucky aiming an arrow at the octopus, the octopus with an arrow in its head, Toro flamingly separating one of the octopus' tentacles having burned another hooded villain, Jeff in the pit next to the octopus, Knuckles grabbing another hooded villain, and Whitewash preparing to strike with a mallet the winching hooded villain. And, oh, yes, a couple of other hooded types, one brandishing a sword, the other out of commission with one of Bucky's arrows in his back. Classic. — Maggie

1 ❑ Feb 1943 Cover: 0.10 **NM** value: **3500.00**
• **CGC:** 3 graded, best 7.0
2 ❑ Sum 1943 Cover: 0.10 **NM** value: **2500.00**
• **CGC:** 1 graded, best 7.5
3 ❑ Fal 1943 Cover: 0.10 **NM** value: **1775.00**
4 ❑ ca. 1944 Cover: 0.10 **NM** value: **1775.00**
• **CGC:** 1 graded, best 9.2
5 ❑ ca. 1944 Cover: 0.10 **NM** value: **1500.00**
• **CGC:** 2 graded, best 9.2
6 ❑ ca. 1944 Cover: 0.10 **NM** value: **1000.00**
7 ❑ Spr 1945 Cover: 0.10 **NM** value: **1000.00**
• **CGC:** 1 graded, best 8.0
8 ❑ Sum 1945 Cover: 0.10 **NM** value: **750.00**
9 ❑ Fal 1945 Cover: 0.10 **NM** value: **750.00**
• **CGC:** 3 graded, best 9.2
10 ❑ Spr 1946 Cover: 0.10 **NM** value: **750.00**
• **CGC:** 2 graded, best 8.0

KID MONTANA — Charlton

Kid Montana is an intrepid young gunfighter who roams the northern range, protecting honest settlers and foiling the plots of desperados, cattle rustlers, claim jumpers, and other stock Western bad guys. His exploits also bring him into conflict with the region's original inhabitants, the fierce Sioux nation, told in still typical 1950s "cowboys-and-Indians" style. Kid Montana is the product of Charlton Publications, whose meager production values are nevertheless up to the standards of 1950s and 60s Westerns. The early stories, with art by Rocke Mastroserio and (unusually for Charlton) lettered by hand, are crisp, well-told, and illustrated in a clean, if unspectacular, style. Kid Montana changed titles to Gunfighters (Charlton) in the mid-1960s.

9 ❑ Nov 1957 Cover: 0.10 **NM** value: **26.00**
🕮 Kid Montana; Gopher-Face; Dopey Danny Dee; Montana Means Mountain; Wagon Wheels West (Text Story); The Vigilante; Wsurance Agent Agar; Up on the Cliff; Big Hearted; Oh, Doctor • Picks up numbering from Davy Crockett **A:** Mastroserio **W:** Mastroserio
10 ❑ Jan 1958 Cover: 0.10 **NM** value: **16.00**
11 ❑ Mar 1958 Cover: 0.10 **NM** value: **12.00**
12 ❑ May 1958 Cover: 0.10 **NM** value: **12.00**
13 ❑ Jul 1958 Cover: 0.10 **NM** value: **16.00**
14 ❑ ca. 1958 Cover: 0.10 **NM** value: **12.00**
15 ❑ ca. 1958 Cover: 0.10 **NM** value: **12.00**
16 ❑ ca. 1959 Cover: 0.10 **NM** value: **12.00**
17 ❑ Apr 1959 Cover: 0.10 **NM** value: **12.00**
18 ❑ ca. 1959 Cover: 0.10 **NM** value: **12.00**
19 ❑ ca. 1959 Cover: 0.10 **NM** value: **12.00**
20 ❑ ca. 1959 Cover: 0.10 **NM** value: **12.00**
21 ❑ ca. 1959 Cover: 0.10 **NM** value: **8.00**
22 ❑ ca. 1960 Cover: 0.10 **NM** value: **8.00**
23 ❑ ca. 1960 Cover: 0.10 **NM** value: **8.00**
24 ❑ ca. 1960 Cover: 0.10 **NM** value: **8.00**
25 ❑ ca. 1960 Cover: 0.10 **NM** value: **8.00**
26 ❑ ca. 1960 Cover: 0.10 **NM** value: **8.00**
27 ❑ ca. 1960 Cover: 0.10 **NM** value: **8.00**
28 ❑ ca. 1961 Cover: 0.10 **NM** value: **8.00**
29 ❑ ca. 1961 Cover: 0.10 **NM** value: **8.00**
30 ❑ ca. 1961 Cover: 0.10 **NM** value: **8.00**
31 ❑ ca. 1961 Cover: 0.10 **NM** value: **5.00**
32 ❑ ca. 1961 Cover: 0.10 **NM** value: **5.00**
33 ❑ Feb 1962 Cover: 0.10 **NM** value: **5.00**
34 ❑ ca. 1962 Cover: 0.12 **NM** value: **5.00**
35 ❑ ca. 1962 Cover: 0.12 **NM** value: **5.00**
36 ❑ ca. 1962 Cover: 0.12 **NM** value: **5.00**
37 ❑ ca. 1962 Cover: 0.12 **NM** value: **5.00**
38 ❑ ca. 1963 Cover: 0.12 **NM** value: **5.00**
39 ❑ ca. 1963 Cover: 0.12 **NM** value: **5.00**
40 ❑ May 1963 Cover: 0.12 **NM** value: **5.00**
41 ❑ ca. 1963 Cover: 0.12 **NM** value: **3.50**
42 ❑ ca. 1963 Cover: 0.12 **NM** value: **3.50**
43 ❑ ca. 1963 Cover: 0.12 **NM** value: **3.50**
44 ❑ Jan 1964 Cover: 0.12 **NM** value: **3.50**
45 ❑ ca. 1964 Cover: 0.12 **NM** value: **3.50**
46 ❑ Jun 1964 Cover: 0.12 **NM** value: **3.50**
47 ❑ Aug 1964 Cover: 0.12 **NM** value: **3.50**
48 ❑ ca. 1964 Cover: 0.12 **NM** value: **3.50**
49 ❑ ca. 1965 Cover: 0.12 **NM** value: **3.50**
50 ❑ Mar 1965 Cover: 0.12 **NM** value: **3.50**
• Series continued in Gunfighters #51

KID 'N PLAY — Marvel

1 ❑ Feb 1992 Cover: 1.25 **NM** value: **1.50**
Circ: CapCity orders: **4,900**
2 ❑ Mar 1992 Cover: 1.25 **NM** value: **Cover or less**
3 ❑ Apr 1992 Cover: 1.25 **NM** value: **Cover or less**
4 ❑ May 1992 Cover: 1.25 **NM** value: **Cover or less**
5 ❑ Jun 1992 Cover: 1.25 **NM** value: **Cover or less**
6 ❑ Jul 1992 Cover: 1.25 **NM** value: **Cover or less**

7 ❑ Aug 1992 Cover: 1.25 NM value: **Cover or less**
8 ❑ Sep 1992 Cover: 1.25 NM value: **Cover or less**
9 ❑ Oct 1992 Cover: 1.25 NM value: **Cover or less**

KID SUPREME — Image

1 ❑ Mar 1996 Cover: 2.50 NM value: **Cover or less**
Kid Supreme with fist outstretched on cover. 📖 School Daze **A:** Dan Fraga **W:** Dan Fraga
1/A ❑ Mar 1996 Cover: 2.50 NM value: **Cover or less**
Kid Supreme surounded by girls on cover. 📖 School Daze **A:** Dan Fraga **W:** Dan Fraga
2 ❑ Apr 1996 Cover: 2.50 NM value: **Cover or less**
📖 Reptyle! **A:** Dan Fraga **W:** Dan Fraga; Eric Stephenson
3 ❑ Jul 1996 Cover: 2.50 NM value: **Cover or less**
★ Appearance of Glory.
3/A ❑ Jul 1996 Cover: 2.50 NM value: **Cover or less**
alternate cover (green background). ★ Appearance of Glory.

KID TERRIFIC — Image

1 ❑ Nov 1998, b&w Cover: 2.95 NM value: **Cover or less**
Circ: Diamd. preorders: **2,566**
A: Joe Diliberto; Robt. Snyder **W:** Joe Diliberto; Robt. Snyder

KIDZ OF THE KING — King

1 ❑ Cover: 2.95 NM value: **Cover or less**
2 ❑ May 1994 Cover: 2.95 NM value: **Cover or less**
3 ❑ Apr 1995 Cover: 2.95 NM value: **Cover or less**

KID ZOO COMICS — Street & Smith

1 ❑ Jul 1948 Cover: 0.10 NM value: **200.00**
• **CGC:** 1 graded, best 6.5

KI-GORR THE KILLER — AC

1 ❑ Cover: 3.95 NM value: **Cover or less**
📖 Old Thunder; Cave Girl: The Fire Pit Menace!; Fire Beam **A:** Bob Powell; Maurice Whitman **W:** Frank Riddell

KIKU SAN — Aircel

1 ❑ Nov 1988 Cover: 1.95 NM value: **Cover or less**
A: Barry Blair **W:** Barry Blair
2 ❑ Dec 1988 Cover: 1.95 NM value: **Cover or less**
A: Barry Blair **W:** Barry Blair
3 ❑ Jan 1989 Cover: 1.95 NM value: **Cover or less**
A: Barry Blair **W:** Barry Blair
4 ❑ Feb 1989 Cover: 1.95 NM value: **Cover or less**
A: Barry Blair **W:** Barry Blair
5 ❑ Mar 1989 Cover: 1.95 NM value: **Cover or less**
A: Barry Blair **W:** Barry Blair
6 ❑ Apr 1989 Cover: 1.95 NM value: **Cover or less**
A: Barry Blair **W:** Barry Blair

KILGORE — Renegade

1 ❑ Cover: 2.00 NM value: **Cover or less**
2 ❑ Cover: 2.00 NM value: **Cover or less**
3 ❑ Cover: 2.00 NM value: **Cover or less**
4 ❑ May 1988 Cover: 2.00 NM value: **Cover or less**

KILL BARNY — Express / Parody

1 ❑ b&w Cover: 2.50 NM value: **Cover or less**

KILL BARNY 3 — Express / Parody

1 ❑ b&w Cover: 2.75 NM value: **Cover or less**

KILLER AND THE KING, THE — Caliber

Bk 1❑ b&w Cover: 12.95 NM value: **Cover or less**
• collects Deadkiller one-shot and To Kill a King mini-series

KILLER FLY — Slave Labor

1 ❑ Mar 1995 Cover: 2.95 NM value: **Cover or less**
A: Chris Hogg **W:** Chris Butler
2 ❑ Jun 1995 Cover: 2.95 NM value: **Cover or less**
A: Chris Hogg **W:** Chris Butler
3 ❑ Sep 1995 Cover: 2.95 NM value: **Cover or less**
final issue. **A:** Chris Hogg **W:** Chris Butler

KILLER INSTINCT — Acclaim / Armada

1 ❑ Jun 1996 Cover: 2.50 NM value: **Cover or less**
📖 Enemy of My Enemy • based on video game **A:** Bart Sears **W:** Art Holcomb
2 ❑ Jul 1996 Cover: 2.50 NM value: **Cover or less**
• based on video game **W:** Art Holcomb
3 ❑ Jul 1996 Cover: 2.50 NM value: **Cover or less**
📖 The Price of Freedom • based on video game **A:** Steven Butler **W:** Art Holcomb
4 ❑ Sep 1996 Cover: 2.50 NM value: **Cover or less**
📖 Special, Part 1 • based on video game
5 ❑ Oct 1996 Cover: 2.50 NM value: **Cover or less**
📖 Special, Part 2 • based on video game
6 ❑ Nov 1996 Cover: 2.50 NM value: **Cover or less**
📖 Special, Part 3 • based on video game

KILLER INSTINCT NINTENDO POWER EXCLUSIVE EDITION — Acclaim / Armada

1 ❑ NM value: **1.00**
no cover price. • smaller-sized comic book for Nintendo Power.

KILLER INSTINCT TOUR BOOK — Image

1/A ❑ Cover: 5.00 NM value: **Cover or less**
Embossed cover.
1/B ❑ Cover: 5.00 NM value: **Cover or less**
Embossed cover.
1/GO❑ NM value: **3.00**
• Gold edition.

KILLERS — Magazine Enterprises

1 ❑ ca. 1947 Cover: 0.10 NM value: **900.00**
• **CGC:** 1 graded, best 7.5
2 ❑ ca. 1948 Cover: 0.10 NM value: **800.00**
• **CGC:** 2 graded, best 7.5

KILLER...TALES BY TIMOTHY TRUMAN — Eclipse

1 ❑ Mar 1985 Cover: 1.75 NM value: **Cover or less**
📖 Daral: The Savings of Sayera; Braskan Gambit **A:** Tim Truman **W:** Tim Truman

KILL IMAGE — Boneyard

1 ❑ b&w Cover: 2.95 NM value: **4.00**
foil cover. **A:** Joe Duncan **W:** Hart Fisher

KILLING STROKE — Eternity

1 ❑ b&w Cover: 2.50 NM value: **Cover or less**
2 ❑ b&w Cover: 2.50 NM value: **Cover or less**
3 ❑ b&w Cover: 2.50 NM value: **Cover or less**
4 ❑ b&w Cover: 2.50 NM value: **Cover or less**

KILL MARVEL — Boneyard

1/LE❑ Cover: 6.95 NM value: **Cover or less**
• Special "Marvel Can..." edition. **A:** Joe Duncan **W:** Hart Fisher

KILLPOWER: THE EARLY YEARS — Marvel

1 ❑ Sep 1993 Cover: 2.95 NM value: **Cover or less**
Circ: CapCity orders: **22,600**
foil cover. 📖 The Gauntlet **A:** John Ross **W:** Mike W. Barr
2 ❑ Oct 1993 Cover: 1.75 NM value: **Cover or less**
Circ: CapCity orders: **10,800**
A: John Ross **W:** Mike W. Barr
3 ❑ Nov 1993 Cover: 1.75 NM value: **Cover or less**
Circ: CapCity orders: **7,300**
A: John Ross **W:** Mike W. Barr ★ Appearance of Punisher.
4 ❑ Dec 1993 Cover: 1.75 NM value: **Cover or less**
Circ: CapCity orders: **5,350**
A: John Ross **W:** Mike W. Barr

KILLRAVEN — Marvel

H.G. Wells' War of the Worlds really happened: the Martians really did land on Earth. What's more, they enslaved humanity, experimented on them, turned them into gladiators who killed one another for sport. But one man rose up from the human misery to strike back at the alien oppressors. His name? Killraven.

Written and drawn by Joe Linsner (Dawn), this version doesn't exactly pick up where the 1970s Amazing Adventures series or the 1983 Marvel Graphic Novel left off. But Linsner, a self-professed fan of the original series, nevertheless lovingly captures all the flavor of Marvel's futuristic barbarian as Killraven blasts the green baddies, saves a buxom beauty, and makes plans to take his war to Mars itself.

1 ❑ Feb 2001 Cover: 2.99 NM value: **Cover or less**
Circ: Diamd. preorders: **31,052** • **CGC:** 9 graded, best 9.8
📖 Killraven: 2020 **A:** Joseph Michael Linsner **W:** Joseph Michael Linsner

KILL RAZOR SPECIAL — Image

1 ❑ Aug 1995 Cover: 2.50 NM value: **Cover or less**
Circ: CapCity orders: **17,550**
A: Anthony Chun **W:** Brian J. Green

KILL YOUR BOYFRIEND — DC / Vertigo

1 ❑ Jun 1995 Cover: 4.95 NM value: **Cover or less**
Circ: CapCity orders: **8,750**
One-shot. **A:** Philip Bond **W:** Grant Morrison
1-2 ❑ May 1998 Cover: 5.95 NM value: **Cover or less**
Circ: Diamd. preorders: **4,321**
• reprints 1995 one-shot with new afterword and other new material

KILROY IS HERE — Caliber

0 ❑ b&w Cover: 2.95 NM value: **Cover or less**
📖 Sympathy for the Devil; Kilroy **A:** Ken Meyer Jr.; Bill Ruth **C:** Brian Bolland **W:** Joe Pruett
1 ❑ b&w Cover: 2.95 NM value: **Cover or less**
📖 Reflections **A:** Ken Meyer Jr.; Tony Harris; Craig Hamilton; Kenn Bivins; Ray Snyder **W:** Joe Pruett
2 ❑ b&w Cover: 2.95 NM value: **Cover or less**
3 ❑ b&w Cover: 2.95 NM value: **Cover or less**
4 ❑ b&w Cover: 2.95 NM value: **Cover or less**

KILROY: REVELATIONS — Caliber

1 ❑ b&w Cover: 2.95 NM value: **Cover or less**
One-shot.

KILROYS, THE — ACG

The Kilroys ("America's Funniest Family!") combined goofy teen humor with the family situation comedy that was increasingly popular in post-war radio and television. Teen-age daughter Katie provided innocent romantic hi-jinx, young twins Portia and Jackson squeezed laughs out of wise cracks and ugly-jokes, and older brother Wilbur filled the stock role of swaggering high-school jock, all to the grief of the long-suffering parents and teachers. The title was rounded out with the cloddish blonde-joke humor of "Moronica, Miss Nit-Wit of 1952," apparently no relation to America's Funniest Family.

1 ❑ Jun 1947 Cover: 0.10 NM value: **90.00**
2 ❑ Aug 1947 Cover: 0.10 NM value: **55.00**
3 ❑ Oct 1947 Cover: 0.10 NM value: **38.00**
4 ❑ Dec 1947 Cover: 0.10 NM value: **38.00**
5 ❑ Feb 1948 Cover: 0.10 NM value: **38.00**
6 ❑ Mar 1948 Cover: 0.10 NM value: **30.00**
7 ❑ Apr 1948 Cover: 0.10 NM value: **30.00**
8 ❑ May 1948 Cover: 0.10 NM value: **30.00**
9 ❑ Jun 1948 Cover: 0.10 NM value: **30.00**
10 ❑ Jul 1948 Cover: 0.10 NM value: **30.00**
11 ❑ Aug 1948 Cover: 0.10 NM value: **20.00**
12 ❑ Sep 1948 Cover: 0.10 NM value: **20.00**
13 ❑ Oct 1948 Cover: 0.10 NM value: **20.00**
14 ❑ Nov 1948 Cover: 0.10 NM value: **20.00**
15 ❑ Dec 1948 Cover: 0.10 NM value: **20.00**
16 ❑ Feb 1949 Cover: 0.10 NM value: **20.00**
17 ❑ Apr 1949 Cover: 0.10 NM value: **20.00**
18 ❑ Jun 1949 Cover: 0.10 NM value: **20.00**
19 ❑ Aug 1949 Cover: 0.10 NM value: **20.00**
20 ❑ Oct 1949 Cover: 0.10 NM value: **20.00**
21 ❑ Dec 1949 Cover: 0.10 NM value: **16.00**
22 ❑ Feb 1950 Cover: 0.10 NM value: **16.00**
23 ❑ Apr 1950 Cover: 0.10 NM value: **16.00**
24 ❑ Jun 1950 Cover: 0.10 NM value: **16.00**
25 ❑ Aug 1950 Cover: 0.10 NM value: **16.00**
26 ❑ Oct 1950 Cover: 0.10 NM value: **16.00**
27 ❑ Dec 1950 Cover: 0.10 NM value: **16.00**
28 ❑ Mar 1951 Cover: 0.10 NM value: **16.00**
29 ❑ May 1951 Cover: 0.10 NM value: **16.00**
30 ❑ Jul 1951 Cover: 0.10 NM value: **16.00**
31 ❑ Sep 1951 Cover: 0.10 NM value: **14.00**
32 ❑ Nov 1951 Cover: 0.10 NM value: **14.00**
33 ❑ Jan 1952 Cover: 0.10 NM value: **14.00**
34 ❑ Mar 1952 Cover: 0.10 NM value: **14.00**
35 ❑ May 1952 Cover: 0.10 NM value: **14.00**
36 ❑ Jul 1952 Cover: 0.10 NM value: **14.00**
📖 Talk is Cheap; That irresistible Personality! (Text Story); Our Merry Old Jallop!; Scat; Sister; Wily Wilbur; The Grass is Greenest (Text Story); Moronica;
37 ❑ Sep 1952 Cover: 0.10 NM value: **14.00**
38 ❑ Nov 1952 Cover: 0.10 NM value: **14.00**
39 ❑ Jan 1953 Cover: 0.10 NM value: **14.00**
40 ❑ Mar 1953 Cover: 0.10 NM value: **14.00**
41 ❑ May 1953 Cover: 0.10 NM value: **12.00**
42 ❑ Jul 1953 Cover: 0.10 NM value: **12.00**
43 ❑ Sep 1953 Cover: 0.10 NM value: **12.00**
44 ❑ Nov 1953 Cover: 0.10 NM value: **12.00**
45 ❑ Jan 1954 Cover: 0.10 NM value: **12.00**
46 ❑ Mar 1954 Cover: 0.10 NM value: **12.00**
47 ❑ May 1954 Cover: 0.10 NM value: **12.00**
48 ❑ Jul 1954 Cover: 0.10 NM value: **40.00**
• 3-D.
49 ❑ Sep 1954 Cover: 0.10 NM value: **40.00**
• 3-D.
50 ❑ Nov 1954 Cover: 0.10 NM value: **12.00**
51 ❑ Jan 1955 Cover: 0.10 NM value: **12.00**
52 ❑ Mar 1955 Cover: 0.10 NM value: **12.00**
53 ❑ May 1955 Cover: 0.10 NM value: **12.00**
54 ❑ Jul 1955 Cover: 0.10 NM value: **12.00**

KILROY: THE SHORT STORIES — Caliber

1 ❑ b&w Cover: 2.95 NM value: **Cover or less**
One-shot. 📖 Rosewood; Safe Haven; The Accused; Henry; Seasons Change; Kilroy Is Here; Tiennanman Square **A:** Guy Burwell; Andrew Robinson; Ken Meyer Jr.; Tim Bradstreet; Phil Hester; Bill Ruth; Mark Erickson **W:** Joe Pruett

KILROY (VOL. 2) — Caliber

1 ❑ Apr 1998 Cover: 2.95 NM value: **Cover or less**
Circ: Diamd. preorders: **2,390**
1/A ❑ Cover: 2.95 NM value: **Cover or less**

KIMBER, PRINCE OF THE FEYLONS — Antarctic

1 ❑ Apr 1992, b&w Cover: 2.50 NM value: **Cover or less**
2 ❑ Jun 1992, b&w Cover: 2.50 NM value: **Cover or less**

KIMURA — Nightwynd

1 ❑ b&w Cover: 2.50 NM value: **Cover or less**
2 ❑ b&w Cover: 2.50 NM value: **Cover or less**
3 ❑ b&w Cover: 2.50 NM value: **Cover or less**
4 ❑ b&w Cover: 2.50 NM value: **Cover or less**

KIN — Image

1 ❑ Sep 1999 Cover: 2.95 NM value: **Cover or less**
Circ: Diamd. preorders: **7,819**
A: Gary Frank **W:** Gary Frank
2 ❑ Oct 1999 Cover: 2.95 NM value: **Cover or less**
Circ: Diamd. preorders: **7,033**
A: Gary Frank **W:** Gary Frank
3 ❑ Nov 1999 Cover: 2.95 NM value: **Cover or less**
Circ: Diamd. preorders: **6,394**
A: Gary Frank **W:** Gary Frank
4 ❑ Jul 2000 Cover: 2.95 NM value: **Cover or less**
Circ: Diamd. preorders: **17,127**
📖 Friendly Fire **A:** Gary Frank **W:** Gary Frank
5 ❑ Aug 2000 Cover: 2.95 NM value: **Cover or less**
Circ: Diamd. preorders: **16,397**
📖 A Stick in Time **A:** Gary Frank **W:** Gary Frank
6 ❑ Sep 2000 Cover: 3.95 NM value: **Cover or less**
Circ: Diamd. preorders: **16,450**
A: Gary Frank **W:** Gary Frank

KINDRED, THE — Image

1 ❑ Mar 1994 Cover: 2.50 NM value: **Cover or less**
Circ: CapCity orders: **46,625**
A: Brett Booth **W:** Brett Booth; Jim Lee; Brandon Choi; Sean Ruffner
2 ❑ Apr 1994 Cover: 1.95 NM value: **Cover or less**

Other grades: Multiply prices above by **1.5 for Mint • 2/3 for Very Fine • 1/3 for Fine • 1/5 for Very Good • 1/8 for Good**

Circ: CapCity orders: **35,100**
A: Brett Booth **W:** Brett Booth; Jim Lee; Brandon Choi; Sean Ruffner
3 ❑ May 1994 Cover: 1.95 **NM** value: **Cover or less**
Circ: CapCity orders: **40,525**
A: Brett Booth **W:** Brett Booth; Jim Lee; Brandon Choi; Sean Ruffner
3/A ❑ May 1994 Cover: 1.95 **NM** value: **Cover or less**
• **CGC:** 1 graded, best 9.6
alternate cover. **A:** Brett Booth **W:** Brett Booth; Jim Lee; Brandon Choi; Sean Ruffner
4 ❑ Jul 1994 Cover: 2.50 **NM** value: **Cover or less**
Circ: CapCity orders: **43,275**
A: Brett Booth **W:** Brett Booth; Jim Lee; Brandon Choi; Sean Ruffner
Bk 1 ❑ Feb 1995 Cover: 9.95 **NM** value: **Cover or less**

KING ARTHUR AND THE KNIGHTS OF JUSTICE — Marvel

1 ❑ Cover: 1.25 **NM** value: **Cover or less**
Circ: CapCity orders: **7,900**
📖 Opposites Attract **A:** Keith Wilson **W:** Mike Lackey
2 ❑ Cover: 1.25 **NM** value: **Cover or less**
Circ: CapCity orders: **5,400**
3 ❑ Cover: 1.25 **NM** value: **Cover or less**
Circ: CapCity orders: **4,300**

KING COMICS — David McKay

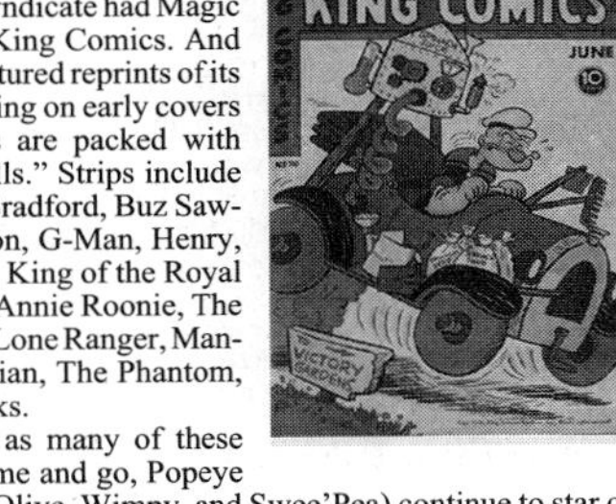

United Features Syndicate had Ace Comics and Sparkler Comics; King Features Syndicate had Magic Comics — and King Comics. And King Comics featured reprints of its comic strips, noting on early covers that its contents are packed with "laughs and thrills." Strips include Blondie, Brick Bradford, Buz Sawyer, Flash Gordon, G-Man, Henry, Hurricane Yank, King of the Royal Mounted, Little Annie Roonie, The Little King, The Lone Ranger, Mandrake the Magician, The Phantom, and Private Bucks.

Nevertheless, as many of these strip reprints come and go, Popeye and his friends (Olive, Wimpy, and Swee'Pea) continue to star on the cover. — Maggie

1 ❑ Apr 1936 Cover: 0.10 **NM** value: **8000.00**
• **CGC:** 1 graded, best 1.0
2 ❑ May 1936 Cover: 0.10 **NM** value: **3000.00**
3 ❑ Jun 1936 Cover: 0.10 **NM** value: **2500.00**
4 ❑ Jul 1936 Cover: 0.10 **NM** value: **2500.00**
5 ❑ Aug 1936 Cover: 0.10 **NM** value: **2000.00**
6 ❑ Sep 1936 Cover: 0.10 **NM** value: **2000.00**
7 ❑ Oct 1936 Cover: 0.10 **NM** value: **1500.00**
8 ❑ Nov 1936 Cover: 0.10 **NM** value: **1500.00**
9 ❑ Dec 1936 Cover: 0.10 **NM** value: **1000.00**
10 ❑ Jan 1937 Cover: 0.10 **NM** value: **1000.00**
11 ❑ Feb 1937 Cover: 0.10 **NM** value: **1000.00**
12 ❑ Mar 1937 Cover: 0.10 **NM** value: **800.00**
13 ❑ Apr 1937 Cover: 0.10 **NM** value: **800.00**
14 ❑ May 1937 Cover: 0.10 **NM** value: **750.00**
15 ❑ Jun 1937 Cover: 0.10 **NM** value: **750.00**
16 ❑ Jul 1937 Cover: 0.10 **NM** value: **700.00**
17 ❑ Aug 1937 Cover: 0.10 **NM** value: **700.00**
18 ❑ Sep 1937 Cover: 0.10 **NM** value: **650.00**
19 ❑ Oct 1937 Cover: 0.10 **NM** value: **650.00**
20 ❑ Nov 1937 Cover: 0.10 **NM** value: **600.00**
21 ❑ Dec 1937 Cover: 0.10 **NM** value: **600.00**
22 ❑ Jan 1938 Cover: 0.10 **NM** value: **550.00**
• **CGC:** 1 graded, best 8.0
23 ❑ Feb 1938 Cover: 0.10 **NM** value: **550.00**
24 ❑ Mar 1938 Cover: 0.10 **NM** value: **550.00**
25 ❑ Apr 1938 Cover: 0.10 **NM** value: **500.00**
26 ❑ May 1938 Cover: 0.10 **NM** value: **500.00**
27 ❑ Jun 1938 Cover: 0.10 **NM** value: **500.00**
28 ❑ Jul 1938 Cover: 0.10 **NM** value: **500.00**
29 ❑ Aug 1938 Cover: 0.10 **NM** value: **500.00**
30 ❑ Sep 1938 Cover: 0.10 **NM** value: **500.00**
31 ❑ Oct 1938 Cover: 0.10 **NM** value: **450.00**
32 ❑ Nov 1938 Cover: 0.10 **NM** value: **450.00**
33 ❑ Dec 1938 Cover: 0.10 **NM** value: **450.00**
34 ❑ Jan 1939 Cover: 0.10 **NM** value: **450.00**
35 ❑ Feb 1939 Cover: 0.10 **NM** value: **450.00**
36 ❑ Mar 1939 Cover: 0.10 **NM** value: **400.00**
37 ❑ Apr 1939 Cover: 0.10 **NM** value: **400.00**
38 ❑ May 1939 Cover: 0.10 **NM** value: **400.00**
39 ❑ Jun 1939 Cover: 0.10 **NM** value: **400.00**
40 ❑ Aug 1939 Cover: 0.10 **NM** value: **350.00**
41 ❑ Sep 1939 Cover: 0.10 **NM** value: **350.00**
42 ❑ Oct 1939 Cover: 0.10 **NM** value: **350.00**
43 ❑ Nov 1939 Cover: 0.10 **NM** value: **350.00**
44 ❑ Dec 1939 Cover: 0.10 **NM** value: **350.00**
45 ❑ Jan 1940 Cover: 0.10 **NM** value: **350.00**
46 ❑ Feb 1940 Cover: 0.10 **NM** value: **300.00**
47 ❑ Mar 1940 Cover: 0.10 **NM** value: **300.00**
48 ❑ Apr 1940 Cover: 0.10 **NM** value: **300.00**
49 ❑ May 1940 Cover: 0.10 **NM** value: **300.00**
50 ❑ Jun 1940 Cover: 0.10 **NM** value: **250.00**
51 ❑ Jul 1940 Cover: 0.10 **NM** value: **250.00**
52 ❑ Aug 1940 Cover: 0.10 **NM** value: **250.00**
53 ❑ Sep 1940 Cover: 0.10 **NM** value: **250.00**
54 ❑ Oct 1940 Cover: 0.10 **NM** value: **250.00**
55 ❑ Nov 1940 Cover: 0.10 **NM** value: **250.00**
56 ❑ Dec 1940 Cover: 0.10 **NM** value: **200.00**
57 ❑ Jan 1941 Cover: 0.10 **NM** value: **200.00**
58 ❑ Feb 1941 Cover: 0.10 **NM** value: **200.00**
59 ❑ Mar 1941 Cover: 0.10 **NM** value: **200.00**
60 ❑ Apr 1941 Cover: 0.10 **NM** value: **175.00**
61 ❑ May 1941 Cover: 0.10 **NM** value: **175.00**
62 ❑ Jun 1941 Cover: 0.10 **NM** value: **175.00**
63 ❑ Jul 1941 Cover: 0.10 **NM** value: **175.00**
64 ❑ Aug 1941 Cover: 0.10 **NM** value: **175.00**
65 ❑ Sep 1941 Cover: 0.10 **NM** value: **175.00**
66 ❑ Oct 1941 Cover: 0.10 **NM** value: **150.00**
67 ❑ Nov 1941 Cover: 0.10 **NM** value: **150.00**
68 ❑ Dec 1941 Cover: 0.10 **NM** value: **150.00**
69 ❑ Jan 1942 Cover: 0.10 **NM** value: **150.00**
70 ❑ Feb 1942 Cover: 0.10 **NM** value: **125.00**
71 ❑ Mar 1942 Cover: 0.10 **NM** value: **125.00**
72 ❑ Apr 1942 Cover: 0.10 **NM** value: **125.00**
73 ❑ May 1942 Cover: 0.10 **NM** value: **125.00**
74 ❑ Jun 1942 Cover: 0.10 **NM** value: **125.00**
75 ❑ Jul 1942 Cover: 0.10 **NM** value: **125.00**
• **CGC:** 1 graded, best 9.0
76 ❑ Aug 1942 Cover: 0.10 **NM** value: **100.00**
77 ❑ Sep 1942 Cover: 0.10 **NM** value: **100.00**
78 ❑ Oct 1942 Cover: 0.10 **NM** value: **100.00**
79 ❑ Nov 1942 Cover: 0.10 **NM** value: **100.00**
80 ❑ Dec 1942 Cover: 0.10 **NM** value: **100.00**
81 ❑ Jan 1943 Cover: 0.10 **NM** value: **100.00**
82 ❑ Feb 1943 Cover: 0.10 **NM** value: **100.00**
83 ❑ Mar 1943 Cover: 0.10 **NM** value: **100.00**
84 ❑ Apr 1943 Cover: 0.10 **NM** value: **100.00**
85 ❑ May 1943 Cover: 0.10 **NM** value: **100.00**
86 ❑ Jun 1943 Cover: 0.10 **NM** value: **100.00**
87 ❑ Jul 1943 Cover: 0.10 **NM** value: **100.00**
88 ❑ Aug 1943 Cover: 0.10 **NM** value: **100.00**
89 ❑ Sep 1943 Cover: 0.10 **NM** value: **100.00**
90 ❑ Oct 1943 Cover: 0.10 **NM** value: **100.00**
91 ❑ Nov 1943 Cover: 0.10 **NM** value: **100.00**
92 ❑ Dec 1943 Cover: 0.10 **NM** value: **100.00**
• **CGC:** 1 graded, best 8.0
93 ❑ Jan 1944 Cover: 0.10 **NM** value: **100.00**
94 ❑ Feb 1944 Cover: 0.10 **NM** value: **100.00**
95 ❑ Mar 1944 Cover: 0.10 **NM** value: **100.00**
96 ❑ Apr 1944 Cover: 0.10 **NM** value: **100.00**
97 ❑ May 1944 Cover: 0.10 **NM** value: **100.00**
98 ❑ Jun 1944 Cover: 0.10 **NM** value: **100.00**
99 ❑ Jul 1944 Cover: 0.10 **NM** value: **100.00**
100 ❑ Aug 1944 Cover: 0.10 **NM** value: **90.00**
101 ❑ Sep 1944 Cover: 0.10 **NM** value: **90.00**
102 ❑ Oct 1944 Cover: 0.10 **NM** value: **90.00**
103 ❑ Nov 1944 Cover: 0.10 **NM** value: **90.00**
104 ❑ Dec 1944 Cover: 0.10 **NM** value: **90.00**
105 ❑ Jan 1945 Cover: 0.10 **NM** value: **90.00**
106 ❑ Feb 1945 Cover: 0.10 **NM** value: **90.00**
107 ❑ Mar 1945 Cover: 0.10 **NM** value: **90.00**
108 ❑ Apr 1945 Cover: 0.10 **NM** value: **90.00**
109 ❑ May 1945 Cover: 0.10 **NM** value: **90.00**
110 ❑ Jun 1945 Cover: 0.10 **NM** value: **85.00**
111 ❑ Jul 1945 Cover: 0.10 **NM** value: **85.00**
112 ❑ Aug 1945 Cover: 0.10 **NM** value: **85.00**
113 ❑ Sep 1945 Cover: 0.10 **NM** value: **85.00**
114 ❑ Oct 1945 Cover: 0.10 **NM** value: **85.00**
• **CGC:** 1 graded, best 9.2
115 ❑ Nov 1945 Cover: 0.10 **NM** value: **85.00**
116 ❑ Dec 1945 Cover: 0.10 **NM** value: **85.00**
117 ❑ Jan 1946 Cover: 0.10 **NM** value: **85.00**
118 ❑ Feb 1946 Cover: 0.10 **NM** value: **85.00**
119 ❑ Mar 1946 Cover: 0.10 **NM** value: **85.00**
120 ❑ Apr 1946 Cover: 0.10 **NM** value: **80.00**
121 ❑ May 1946 Cover: 0.10 **NM** value: **80.00**
122 ❑ Jun 1946 Cover: 0.10 **NM** value: **80.00**
123 ❑ Jul 1946 Cover: 0.10 **NM** value: **80.00**
124 ❑ Aug 1946 Cover: 0.10 **NM** value: **80.00**
125 ❑ Sep 1946 Cover: 0.10 **NM** value: **80.00**
126 ❑ Oct 1946 Cover: 0.10 **NM** value: **80.00**
127 ❑ Nov 1946 Cover: 0.10 **NM** value: **80.00**
128 ❑ Dec 1946 Cover: 0.10 **NM** value: **80.00**
129 ❑ Jan 1947 Cover: 0.10 **NM** value: **80.00**
130 ❑ Feb 1947 Cover: 0.10 **NM** value: **75.00**
131 ❑ Mar 1947 Cover: 0.10 **NM** value: **75.00**
132 ❑ Apr 1947 Cover: 0.10 **NM** value: **75.00**
133 ❑ May 1947 Cover: 0.10 **NM** value: **75.00**
134 ❑ Jun 1947 Cover: 0.10 **NM** value: **75.00**
135 ❑ Jul 1947 Cover: 0.10 **NM** value: **75.00**
136 ❑ Aug 1947 Cover: 0.10 **NM** value: **75.00**
137 ❑ Sep 1947 Cover: 0.10 **NM** value: **75.00**
• **CGC:** 1 graded, best 7.0
138 ❑ Oct 1947 Cover: 0.10 **NM** value: **75.00**
139 ❑ Nov 1947 Cover: 0.10 **NM** value: **75.00**
140 ❑ Dec 1947 Cover: 0.10 **NM** value: **70.00**
141 ❑ Jan 1948 Cover: 0.10 **NM** value: **70.00**
142 ❑ Feb 1948 Cover: 0.10 **NM** value: **70.00**
143 ❑ Mar 1948 Cover: 0.10 **NM** value: **70.00**
144 ❑ Apr 1948 Cover: 0.10 **NM** value: **70.00**
145 ❑ May 1948 Cover: 0.10 **NM** value: **70.00**
146 ❑ Jun 1948 Cover: 0.10 **NM** value: **70.00**
147 ❑ Jul 1948 Cover: 0.10 **NM** value: **70.00**
148 ❑ Sep 1948 Cover: 0.10 **NM** value: **70.00**
149 ❑ Nov 1948 Cover: 0.10 **NM** value: **70.00**
150 ❑ Jan 1949 Cover: 0.10 **NM** value: **60.00**
151 ❑ Mar 1949 Cover: 0.10 **NM** value: **60.00**
152 ❑ May 1949 Cover: 0.10 **NM** value: **60.00**
153 ❑ Jul 1949 Cover: 0.10 **NM** value: **60.00**
154 ❑ Sep 1949 Cover: 0.10 **NM** value: **50.00**
155 ❑ Nov 1949 Cover: 0.10 **NM** value: **50.00**
156 ❑ Spr 1950 Cover: 0.10 **NM** value: **50.00**
157 ❑ Sum 1950 Cover: 0.10 **NM** value: **50.00**
158 ❑ Aut 1950 Cover: 0.10 **NM** value: **50.00**
159 ❑ Win 1950 Cover: 0.10 **NM** value: **50.00**

KING CONAN — Marvel

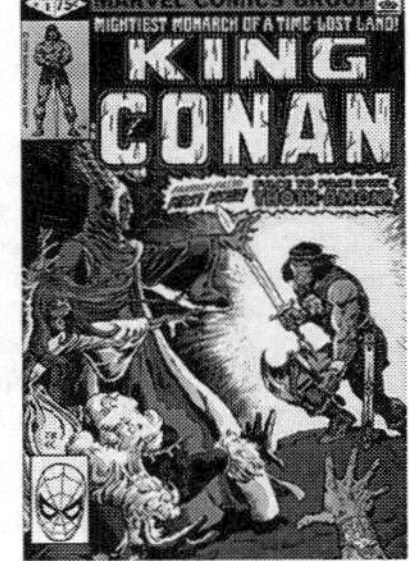

As was destined from the earliest pages of Conan the Barbarian, Conan of Cimmeria became a king. Though the ruler of Aquilonia had long aspired to such a title, he soon found the crown a heavy burden. Taken from a life of adventure, he was, quite simply, bored.

Then his wife was kidnapped by his arch-nemesis Thoth-Amon. That marked the real beginning of the life of Conan the King. After rescuing his queen, he found that danger indeed lurked everywhere. Dread forces were constantly imperiling both his family and his kingdom. Now Conan, who once thought of abandoning the crown, found himself taking on his grandest adventures of all.

A worthwhile series, King Conan (which changed names with issue #20 to become Conan the King) brings a whole new depth to the character of Conan.

1 ❑ Mar 1980 Cover: 0.75 **NM** value: **3.00**
• **CGC:** 5 graded, best 9.9
📖 The Witch of the Mists • wife & son **A:** John Buscema **W:** Roy Thomas ★ Versus Thoth-Amon.
2 ❑ Jun 1980 Cover: 0.75 **NM** value: **2.00**
• **CGC:** 2 graded, best 9.8
A: John Buscema
3 ❑ Sep 1980 Cover: 0.75 **NM** value: **2.00**
• **CGC:** 1 graded, best 9.6
A: John Buscema
4 ❑ Dec 1980 Cover: 0.75 **NM** value: **2.00**
★ Versus Thoth-Amon.
5 ❑ Mar 1981 Cover: 0.75 **NM** value: **2.00**
Circ: Statement: **166,044** • **CGC:** 1 graded, best 9.8
6 ❑ Jun 1981 Cover: 0.75 **NM** value: **2.00**
Circ: Statement: **166,044**
7 ❑ Sep 1981 Cover: 0.75 **NM** value: **2.00**
Circ: Statement: **166,044**
A: Barry Windsor-Smith
8 ❑ Dec 1981 Cover: 0.75 **NM** value: **2.00**
Circ: Statement: **166,044**
A: Barry Windsor-Smith
9 ❑ Mar 1982 Cover: 1.00 **NM** value: **2.00**
Circ: Statement: **142,346**
10 ❑ May 1982 Cover: 1.00 **NM** value: **2.00**
Circ: Statement: **142,346**
• Has 1981 Statement, filed 10/1/81; avg print run 329,066; avg sales 165,835; avg subs 209; avg total paid 166,044; samples 531; office use 1,385; max existent 167,960; 49% of run returned
11 ❑ Jul 1982 Cover: 1.00 **NM** value: **1.50**
Circ: Statement: **142,346**
12 ❑ Sep 1982 Cover: 1.00 **NM** value: **1.50**
Circ: Statement: **142,346**
13 ❑ Nov 1982 Cover: 1.00 **NM** value: **1.50**
Circ: Statement: **142,346**
14 ❑ Jan 1983 Cover: 1.00 **NM** value: **1.50**
Circ: Statement: **141,669**
15 ❑ Mar 1983 Cover: 1.00 **NM** value: **1.50**
Circ: Statement: **141,669**
16 ❑ May 1983 Cover: 1.00 **NM** value: **1.50**
Circ: Statement: **141,669**
17 ❑ Jul 1983 Cover: 1.00 **NM** value: **1.50**
Circ: Statement: **141,669**
• Has 1982 Statement, filed 10/11/82; avg print run 306,190; avg sales 141,480; avg subs 866; avg total paid 142,346; samples 520; office use 695; max existent 143,561; 53% of run returned
18 ❑ Sep 1983 Cover: 1.00 **NM** value: **1.50**
Circ: Statement: **141,669**
19 ❑ Nov 1983 Cover: 1.00 **NM** value: **1.50**
Circ: Statement: **141,669**
• Series continued in Conan the King #20

KINGDOM, THE — DC

1 ❑ Feb 1999 Cover: 2.95 **NM** value: **Cover or less**
Circ: Diamd. preorders: **101,096**
• Elseworlds **A:** Ariel Olivetti; Mike Zeck **W:** Mark Waid
1/Aut ❑ Feb 1999 **NM** value: **8.00**
• Elseworlds **A:** Ariel Olivetti **W:** Mark Waid
2 ❑ Feb 1999 Cover: 2.95 **NM** value: **Cover or less**
Circ: Diamd. preorders: **95,555**
📖 Mighty Rivers • Elseworlds **A:** Mike Zeck **W:** Mark Waid
2/Aut ❑ Feb 1999 **NM** value: **12.00**
• Elseworlds **A:** Mike Zeck **W:** Mark Waid
Bk 1 ❑ Jan 2000 Cover: 14.95 **NM** value: **Cover or less**
• Collects series, other Kingdom specials **A:** Brian Apthorp; Matt Haley; Jerry Ordway; Mark Pajarillo; Frank Quitely; Ariel Olivetti; Barry Kitson; Mike Zeck **W:** Mark Waid

There are two different pricing tiers in the modern comic-book hobby. **The prices seen above** are the prices we have seen **loose copies** of these issues reliably fetch in a variety of environments. Condition alters the price by the fractions seen on the bar on the bottom of left-hand pages of this book. **Comics graded by CGC** usually sell for more. Use the guide on the bottom of right-hand pages of this book to estimate what copies have brought on eBay.

CGC-graded: Multiply prices above by **33 for 9.9 M • 16 for 9.8 NM/M • 7 for 9.6 NM+ • 5 for 9.4 NM • 2.5 for 9.2 NM- • 1.5 for 9.0 VF/NM**

KINGDOM COME — DC

Kingdom Come is an Elseworlds story of what might happen in a different version of the DC universe. In it we see the world of the near future where super-heroes and super-villains have become largely indistinguishable from each other. Both have grown jaded with power, and even the heroes have lost any regard for the mere humans they are meant to protect. In the end, their ceaseless battles eventually result in blasting Kansas into a radioactive ruin.

It's then that an aging pastor is visited by The Spectre and shown what it is that the world has become. It's a place where super-heroes have taken the place of gods, and where the final battle between them threatens to usher in Ragnarok — the end of the world.

A four-issue tour de force by writer Mark Waid (Flash) and painter Alex Ross (Marvels), Kingdom Come was one of the standout series of 1996.

1 ❑ ca. 1996 Cover: 4.95 **NM** value: **6.00**
• **CGC:** 26 graded, best 9.8
📖 Truth And Justice • Elseworlds **A:** Alex Ross **W:** Mark Waid
1-2 ❑ ca. 1996 Cover: 4.95 **NM** value: **Cover or less**
2 ❑ ca. 1996 Cover: 4.95 **NM** value: **5.00**
• **CGC:** 18 graded, best 9.8
📖 Strange Visitor • Elseworlds **A:** Alex Ross **W:** Mark Waid
3 ❑ ca. 1996 Cover: 4.95 **NM** value: **5.00**
• **CGC:** 17 graded, best 9.8
📖 Up In The Sky • return of Captain Marvel; Elseworlds **A:** Alex Ross **W:** Mark Waid
4 ❑ ca. 1996 Cover: 4.95 **NM** value: **5.00**
• **CGC:** 13 graded, best 9.8
📖 Never-Ending Battle • Elseworlds **A:** Alex Ross **W:** Mark Waid ★ Death of Captain Marvel.
Bk 1❑ Cover: 14.95 **NM** value: **Cover or less**
• collects mini-series with additional material; Elseworlds; Collects Kingdom Come #1-4 **A:** Alex Ross **W:** Mark Waid
Bk 1/Aut❑ **NM** value: **29.95**
• Elseworlds; Collects Kingdom Come #1-4 **A:** Alex Ross **W:** Mark Waid
Bk 1/HC❑ Cover: 29.95 **NM** value: **49.95**
hardcover. • Hard-cover edition. • collects mini-series with additional material; Novelization of Kingdom Come mini-series with new artwork; Elseworlds **A:** Alex Ross **W:** Elliott S! Maggin; Mark Waid
Dlx 1❑ Cover: 99.95 **NM** value: **100.00**
• Deluxe slipcase edition with companion book. • collects mini-series with additional material **A:** Alex Ross **W:** Elliott S! Maggin; Mark Waid

KINGDOM, THE: KID FLASH — DC

1 ❑ Feb 1999 Cover: 1.99 **NM** value: **Cover or less**
Circ: Diamd. preorders: **65,540**
• Elseworlds **A:** Mark Pajarillo **W:** Mark Waid

KINGDOM, THE: NIGHTSTAR — DC

1 ❑ Feb 1999 Cover: 1.99 **NM** value: **Cover or less**
Circ: Diamd. preorders: **65,679**
• Elseworlds **A:** Matt Haley **W:** Mark Waid ★ Appearance of Wonder Woman, Superman, Nightwing, Green Lantern, Starfire, Batman.

KINGDOM, THE: OFFSPRING — DC

1 ❑ Feb 1999 Cover: 1.99 **NM** value: **Cover or less**
Circ: Diamd. preorders: **61,641**
• Elseworlds **A:** Frank Quitely **W:** Mark Waid ★ Appearance of Plastic Man.

KINGDOM OF THE DWARFS — Comico

1 ❑ Cover: 4.95 **NM** value: **Cover or less**
Circ: CapCity orders: **4,300**

KINGDOM OF THE WICKED — Caliber

1 ❑ b&w Cover: 2.95 **NM** value: **Cover or less**
A: D'Israeli **W:** Ian Edginton
2 ❑ b&w Cover: 2.95 **NM** value: **Cover or less**
A: D'Israeli **W:** Ian Edginton
3 ❑ b&w Cover: 2.95 **NM** value: **Cover or less**
A: D'Israeli **W:** Ian Edginton
4 ❑ b&w Cover: 2.95 **NM** value: **Cover or less**

KINGDOM, THE: PLANET KRYPTON — DC

1 ❑ Feb 1999 Cover: 1.99 **NM** value: **Cover or less**
Circ: Diamd. preorders: **65,831**
• Elseworlds **A:** Barry Kitson **W:** Mark Waid ★ Appearance of Booster Gold, Gog, Batman.

KINGDOM, THE: SON OF THE BAT — DC

1 ❑ Feb 1999 Cover: 1.99 **NM** value: **Cover or less**
Circ: Diamd. preorders: **68,224**
📖 Convergence • Elseworlds **A:** Brian Apthorp; Mark Farmer(inks) **W:** Mark Waid ★ Appearance of Lex Luthor, Braniac, Superman, Ra's Al Ghul, Gog, Talia Al Ghul, Batman, Ibn al Xu'ffasch.

The prices seen above do not represent the highest possible prices seen in online auctions, but rather the prices we have seen these issues reliably fetch in a variety of environments (storefront retail, mail order, auction and convention).

KING KONG (GOLD KEY) — Gold Key

Perhaps the seminal monstrous creature film, the 1933 movie of Merian Cooper's book, King Kong, remains a timeless example of the public's need to be frightened. Thirty-five years later in 1968, Gold Key published a 64-page adaptation of the classic movie. The publisher was well known for adapting popular TV shows like Star Trek and Man from U.N.C.L.E. for comics.

The artist, Alberto Giolitti, lived in Rome and mailed his pages back to the United States at a time when living in New York was considered a prerequisite for working in comics. He illustrated Gold Key's Star Trek series without actually having seen the show, but presumably he had seen King Kong. His depictions of Skull Island and its fantastic denizens are balanced by his equally impressive representation of 1930s New York in this tragic tale of a monster and his impossible love.

1 ❑ Sep 1968, four-color Cover: 0.25 **NM** value: **12.00**
No issue number. • adapts 1932 film

KING KONG (MONSTER) — Monster

1 ❑ b&w Cover: 2.50 **NM** value: **Cover or less**
A: Donald Simpson; Dave Stevens(cover) **C:** Dave Stevens **W:** Donald Simpson
2 ❑ Cover: 1.95 **NM** value: **2.50**
A: Donald Simpson **W:** Donald Simpson
3 ❑ Cover: 1.95 **NM** value: **2.50**
A: Donald Simpson **W:** Donald Simpson
4 ❑ Cover: 1.95 **NM** value: **2.50**
A: Donald Simpson **W:** Donald Simpson
5 ❑ Nov 1991 Cover: 2.25 **NM** value: **2.50**
A: Donald Simpson **C:** Al Williamson **W:** Donald Simpson
6 ❑ Cover: 2.50 **NM** value: **Cover or less**
A: Donald Simpson **C:** Ken Steacy **W:** Donald Simpson
Bk 1❑ Cover: 9.95 **NM** value: **Cover or less**
• Collects King Kong #1-6 **A:** Donald Simpson **W:** Donald Simpson

KING LEONARDO AND HIS SHORT SUBJECTS — Gold Key

1 ❑ May 1962 Cover: 0.12 **NM** value: **125.00**
• **CGC:** 1 graded, best 6.5
2 ❑ Oct 1962 Cover: 0.12 **NM** value: **100.00**
• **CGC:** 1 graded, best 9.0
3 ❑ Dec 1962 Cover: 0.12 **NM** value: **100.00**
• **CGC:** 1 graded, best 9.2
4 ❑ Mar 1963 Cover: 0.12 **NM** value: **100.00**
• **CGC:** 1 graded, best 8.0

KING LOUIE AND MOWGLI — Gold Key

1 ❑ Sep 1963 Cover: 0.12 **NM** value: **20.00**
• **CGC:** 1 graded, best 8.0

KING OF THE DEAD — Fantaco

0 ❑ Cover: 1.95 **NM** value: **Cover or less**
1 ❑ Cover: 1.95 **NM** value: **Cover or less**
2 ❑ Cover: 1.95 **NM** value: **Cover or less**
3 ❑ Cover: 1.95 **NM** value: **Cover or less**
4 ❑ Cover: 2.95 **NM** value: **Cover or less**

KING OF THE ROYAL MOUNTED — Dell

Whereas Sgt. Preston of the Yukon began on radio (as Challenge of the Yukon) in 1938, ran until 1955 on radio, was transformed into a TV show (1955-1958), and earned a comic-book spin-off in 1951, King of the Royal Mounted preceded it as a popular-fiction look at adventure north of the U.S. border with Canada. King started its existence as a King Features comic strip, beginning in 1935. Though attributed to popular writer Zane Grey, that was apparently simply part of a licensing deal, the character not featured in an inciting Grey novel.</PThe year Preston left radio for TV was the year King of the Royal Mounted left newspaper pages, but his comic-book adventures continued until Preston went off the air. Coincidence? Well, maybe yes. — Maggie

8 ❑ ca. 1952 Cover: 0.10 **NM** value: **40.00**
9 ❑ Sep 1953 Cover: 0.10 **NM** value: **40.00**
10 ❑ Dec 1952 Cover: 0.10 **NM** value: **40.00**
11 ❑ Mar 1953 Cover: 0.10 **NM** value: **40.00**
12 ❑ Jun 1953 Cover: 0.10 **NM** value: **40.00**
13 ❑ Sep 1953 Cover: 0.10 **NM** value: **40.00**
• **CGC:** 1 graded, best 9.0
14 ❑ Dec 1953 Cover: 0.10 **NM** value: **40.00**
• **CGC:** 1 graded, best 9.4
15 ❑ Mar 1954 Cover: 0.10 **NM** value: **40.00**
• **CGC:** 1 graded, best 9.2
16 ❑ Jun 1954 Cover: 0.10 **NM** value: **40.00**
17 ❑ Sep 1954 Cover: 0.10 **NM** value: **40.00**
18 ❑ Dec 1954 Cover: 0.10 **NM** value: **40.00**
19 ❑ Apr 1955 Cover: 0.10 **NM** value: **35.00**
20 ❑ Mar 1956 Cover: 0.10 **NM** value: **35.00**
21 ❑ Jun 1956 Cover: 0.10 **NM** value: **35.00**
22 ❑ Sep 1956 Cover: 0.10 **NM** value: **35.00**
23 ❑ Dec 1956 Cover: 0.10 **NM** value: **35.00**
24 ❑ Mar 1957 Cover: 0.10 **NM** value: **35.00**
25 ❑ Jun 1957 Cover: 0.10 **NM** value: **35.00**
26 ❑ Sep 1957 Cover: 0.10 **NM** value: **35.00**
27 ❑ Dec 1957 Cover: 0.10 **NM** value: **35.00**
28 ❑ Mar 1958 Cover: 0.10 **NM** value: **35.00**

KINGPIN — Marvel

1 ❑ Nov 1997 Cover: 5.99 **NM** value: **Cover or less**
No issue number. One-shot. **A:** John Romita **W:** Stan Lee; Tom DeFalco

KINGS IN DISGUISE — Kitchen Sink

1 ❑ Mar 1988, b&w Cover: 2.00 **NM** value: **Cover or less**
A: Steve Rude(cover) **C:** Steve Rude
2 ❑ May 1988 Cover: 2.00 **NM** value: **Cover or less**
A: Dan Burr **C:** Harvey Kurtzman **W:** James Vance
3 ❑ Jul 1988 Cover: 2.00 **NM** value: **Cover or less**
4 ❑ Sep 1988 Cover: 2.00 **NM** value: **Cover or less**
5 ❑ Mar 1989 Cover: 2.00 **NM** value: **Cover or less**
6 ❑ Sep 1989 Cover: 2.00 **NM** value: **Cover or less**
Bk 1❑ Cover: 14.95 **NM** value: **Cover or less**
• Collects Kings in Disguise #1-6

KINGS OF THE NIGHT — Dark Horse

1 ❑ Cover: 2.25 **NM** value: **Cover or less**
Circ: CapCity orders: **4,700**
📖 Out of the Sunrise **A:** Gary Barker **W:** Roy Thomas
2 ❑ Cover: 2.25 **NM** value: **Cover or less**
Circ: CapCity orders: **4,025**

KING TIGER & MOTORHEAD — Dark Horse

1 ❑ Aug 1996 Cover: 2.95 **NM** value: **Cover or less**
A: Karl Waller **W:** D.G. Chichester
2 ❑ Sep 1996 Cover: 2.95 **NM** value: **Cover or less**
A: Karl Waller **W:** D.G. Chichester

KINKI KLITT KOMICS — Rip Off

All issues are adults only.

1 ❑ Apr 1992, b&w Cover: 2.95 **NM** value: **Cover or less**
2 ❑ Jun 1992, b&w Cover: 2.50 **NM** value: **Cover or less**

KINKY HOOK, THE — Fantagraphics / Eros

All issues are adults only.

1 ❑ b&w Cover: 2.50 **NM** value: **Cover or less**

KIP — Hammer & Anvil

1 ❑ b&w Cover: 2.50 **NM** value: **Cover or less**

KIRBY KING OF THE SERIALS — Blackthorne

1 ❑ Jan 1989, b&w Cover: 2.00 **NM** value: **Cover or less**

KISS — Personality

1 ❑ b&w Cover: 2.95 **NM** value: **3.50**
2 ❑ Cover: 2.95 **NM** value: **3.00**
3 ❑ full color Cover: 2.95 **NM** value: **3.00**

KISS & TELL — Patricia Breen

1 ❑ Dec 1995, b&w Cover: 2.75 **NM** value: **Cover or less**
• magazine. 📖 The Cage

KISS & TELL (VOL. 2) — Sirius

1 ❑ b&w Cover: 2.50 **NM** value: **Cover or less**

KISS CLASSICS — Marvel

1 ❑ Cover: 10.00 **NM** value: **Cover or less**
• Reprints Marvel Super Special #1, #5 **A:** Alan Weiss; Al Milgrom; Sal Buscema **W:** Mark Evanier; Steve Gerber ★ Origin of Kiss (rock group).

KISSES — Spoof

1 ❑ b&w Cover: 2.95 **NM** value: **Cover or less**

KISSING CANVAS — MN Design

1 ❑ full color Cover: 5.50 **NM** value: **Cover or less**
• photos

KISSNATION — Marvel

1 ❑ Cover: 10.00 **NM** value: **Cover or less**
One-shot. • Reprints Marvel Super Specials with new editorial ★ Appearance of X-Men.

KISS OF DEATH — Acme

1 ❑ Cover: 2.00 **NM** value: **Cover or less**

KISS OF THE VAMPIRE — Brainstorm

1 ❑ Cover: 2.95 **NM** value: **Cover or less**
📖 Dark is the Night **A:** Paul Abrams **W:** Paul Abrams; Garry Barnes

KISS PRE-HISTORY — Revolutionary

1 ❑ Apr 1993, b&w Cover: 2.50 **NM** value: **3.00**
A: Scott Pentzer **W:** Spike Steffenhagen
2 ❑ May 1993, b&w Cover: 2.50 **NM** value: **3.00**
3 ❑ Jul 1993, b&w Cover: 2.50 **NM** value: **3.00**

Capital City orders are the actual sales of comic books by Capital City Distribution, once one of the largest U.S. sellers of comics to comics shops. Capital City's share of comics shop sales, while not known exactly, increases from around 10-20% in the mid-1980s to 30-35% in the mid-1990s. Capital City's share of comic books sold on newsstands (most Marvels and DCs) will be less.

Other grades: Multiply prices above by **1.5 for Mint • 2/3 for Very Fine • 1/3 for Fine • 1/5 for Very Good • 1/8 for Good**

KISS: PSYCHO CIRCUS — Image

Published by the Todd McFarlane studio at Image, Kiss: Psycho Circus is more than just an homage to the over-the-top rockers. Like the Marvel Kiss specials that preceded it by some two decades, it attempts to cast the members of a rock glam band as mythical figures. Unlike that earlier effort, however, Kiss: Psycho Circus actually succeeds.

The result is far more surreal than might be imagined. Employing an art style made famous on such comics as Spawn, it tells of a "circus" of sorts where four "creatures of pure spirit, encompassing aspects of both dark and light, heaven and hell" pass judgment upon the living. These are the Demon (aka Gene Simmons in the real band), the Starbearer (Ace Frehley), the Celestial (Paul Stanley), and the King of Beasts (drummer Peter Criss). With not a trace of self-effacement and prose as purple as it comes, Psycho Circus is, nevertheless, effective as pure comic-book fantasy.

1 ❑ Aug 1997 Cover: 1.95 **NM** value: **4.00**
Circ: Diamd. preorders: **80,944 • CGC:** 9 graded, best 9.8
📖 The Witching of Adam Moon, Part 1 **A:** Angel Medina **W:** Brian Holguin

2 ❑ Sep 1997 Cover: 1.95 **NM** value: **3.00**
Circ: Diamd. preorders: **63,475 • CGC:** 4 graded, best 9.8
📖 The Witching of Adam Moon, Part 2 **A:** Angel Medina **W:** Brian Holguin

3 ❑ Oct 1997 Cover: 1.95 **NM** value: **2.50**
Circ: Diamd. preorders: **53,275 • CGC:** 1 graded, best 9.6
A: Angel Medina **W:** Brian Holguin

4 ❑ Nov 1997 Cover: 1.95 **NM** value: **2.50**
Circ: Diamd. preorders: **58,653 • CGC:** 1 graded, best 9.6
📖 Smoke & Mirrors, Part 1 **A:** Angel Medina **W:** Brian Holguin

5 ❑ Dec 1997 Cover: 1.95 **NM** value: **2.50**
Circ: Diamd. preorders: **61,208 • CGC:** 1 graded, best 9.6
📖 Smoke & Mirrors, Part 2 **A:** Angel Medina **W:** Brian Holguin

6 ❑ Jan 1998 Cover: 2.25 **NM** value: **2.50**
Circ: Diamd. preorders: **61,159**
📖 Smoke & Mirrors, Part 3 **A:** Angel Medina **W:** Brian Holguin

7 ❑ Mar 1998 Cover: 2.25 **NM** value: **2.50**
Circ: Diamd. preorders: **56,070**
📖 Bottle Full of Wishes **A:** Angel Medina **W:** Brian Holguin

8 ❑ Apr 1998 Cover: 2.25 **NM** value: **2.50**
Circ: Diamd. preorders: **54,806**
📖 Forever **A:** Angel Medina **W:** Brian Holguin

9 ❑ May 1998 Cover: 2.25 **NM** value: **2.50**
Circ: Diamd. preorders: **55,637**
📖 Four Sides to Every Story **A:** Angel Medina **W:** Brian Holguin

10 ❑ Jun 1998 Cover: 2.25 **NM** value: **2.50**
Circ: Diamd. preorders: **52,851**
covers of #10-12 form quadtych. 📖 Destroyer, Part 1 **A:** Angel Medina **W:** Brian Holguin

11 ❑ Jul 1998 Cover: 2.25 **NM** value: **2.50**
Circ: Diamd. preorders: **51,877**
📖 Destroyer, Part 2 **A:** Angel Medina **W:** Brian Holguin

12 ❑ Aug 1998 Cover: 2.25 **NM** value: **2.50**
Circ: Diamd. preorders: **46,446**
📖 Destroyer, Part 3 **A:** Angel Medina **W:** Brian Holguin

13 ❑ Oct 1998 Cover: 2.25 **NM** value: **Cover or less**
Circ: Diamd. preorders: **46,238**
📖 Destroyer, Part 4 **A:** Angel Medina **W:** Brian Holguin

14 ❑ Nov 1998 Cover: 2.25 **NM** value: **Cover or less**
Circ: Diamd. preorders: **47,757**
📖 Year of the Fox, Part 1 **A:** Angel Medina **W:** Brian Holguin

15 ❑ Dec 1998 Cover: 2.25 **NM** value: **Cover or less**
Circ: Diamd. preorders: **47,730**
📖 Year of the Fox, Part 2 **A:** Angel Medina **W:** Brian Holguin

16 ❑ Feb 1999 Cover: 2.25 **NM** value: **Cover or less**
Circ: Diamd. preorders: **47,145**
📖 World Without Heroes, Part 1 **A:** Angel Medina **W:** Brian Holguin

17 ❑ Mar 1999 Cover: 2.25 **NM** value: **Cover or less**
Circ: Diamd. preorders: **43,729**
📖 World Without Heroes, Part 2 **A:** Angel Medina **W:** Brian Holguin

18 ❑ Apr 1999 Cover: 2.25 **NM** value: **Cover or less**
Circ: Diamd. preorders: **43,055**
📖 Sunburst Finish **A:** Clayton Crain **W:** Brian Holguin

19 ❑ May 1999 Cover: 2.25 **NM** value: **Cover or less**
Circ: Diamd. preorders: **42,799**
📖 Fragments **A:** Clayton Crain **W:** Brian Holguin

20 ❑ Jun 1999 Cover: 2.25 **NM** value: **Cover or less**
Circ: Diamd. preorders: **41,024**
📖 Make Believe, Part 1 **A:** Clayton Crain **W:** Brian Holguin

21 ❑ Jul 1999 Cover: 2.25 **NM** value: **Cover or less**
Circ: Diamd. preorders: **39,162**
📖 Make Believe, Part 2 **A:** Clayton Crain **W:** Brian Holguin

22 ❑ Aug 1999 Cover: 2.25 **NM** value: **Cover or less**
Circ: Diamd. preorders: **37,260**
📖 Mirror Image, Part 1 **A:** Clayton Crain **W:** Brian Holguin

23 ❑ Sep 1999 Cover: 2.25 **NM** value: **Cover or less**
Circ: Diamd. preorders: **35,230**
📖 Mirror Image, Part 2 **A:** Clayton Crain **W:** Brian Holguin

24 ❑ Oct 1999 Cover: 2.25 **NM** value: **Cover or less**
Circ: Diamd. preorders: **33,212**
📖 Cat's Eye **A:** Clayton Crain **W:** Brian Holguin

25 ❑ Nov 1999 Cover: 2.25 **NM** value: **Cover or less**
Circ: Diamd. preorders: **30,569**
📖 The Devil's Tale **A:** Clayton Crain **W:** Brian Holguin

26 ❑ Jan 2000 Cover: 2.25 **NM** value: **Cover or less**
Circ: Diamd. preorders: **30,084**
A: Clayton Crain **W:** Brian Holguin

27 ❑ Feb 2000 Cover: 2.25 **NM** value: **Cover or less**
Circ: Diamd. preorders: **27,640**
📖 The Nightengale's Song **A:** Clayton Crain **W:** Brian Holguin

28 ❑ Apr 2000 Cover: 2.25 **NM** value: **Cover or less**
Circ: Diamd. preorders: **25,386**
📖 Perdition Blues **A:** Clayton Crain **W:** Brian Holguin

29 ❑ Apr 2000 Cover: 2.50 **NM** value: **Cover or less**
Circ: Diamd. preorders: **24,726**
📖 Shadow of the Moon, Part 1 **A:** Clayton Crain **W:** Brian Holguin

30 ❑ May 2000 Cover: 2.50 **NM** value: **Cover or less**
Circ: Diamd. preorders: **24,628**
📖 Shadow of the Moon, Part 2 **A:** Clayton Crain **W:** Brian Holguin

31 ❑ Jun 2000 Cover: 2.50 **NM** value: **Cover or less**
Circ: Diamd. preorders: **24,573**
📖 Shadow of the Moon, Part 3 **A:** Clayton Crain **W:** Brian Holguin

Bk 1 ❑ Sep 1998 Cover: 12.95 **NM** value: **Cover or less**
📖 The Witching of Adam Moon; Smoke & Mirrors • collects issues #1-6 **A:** Angel Medina **W:** Brian Holguin

Bk 2 ❑ Aug 1999 Cover: 9.95 **NM** value: **Cover or less**
📖 Destroyer • Destroyer; Collects Kiss: Psycho Circus #10-13 **A:** Angel Medina **W:** Brian Holguin

SE 1 ❑ **NM** value: **2.00**
• Special Wizard Edition.

KISS: SATAN'S MUSIC? — Celebrity

1 ❑ **NM** value: **4.00**
• trading cards

KISSYFUR — DC

1 ❑ **NM** value: **2.00**
Circ: CapCity orders: **3,550**

KISS: YOU WANTED THE BEST, YOU GOT THE BEST — Wizard

1 ❑ **NM** value: **1.00**

KIT CARSON AND THE BLACKFEET WARRIORS — Realistic Comics

1 ❑ ca. 1953 Cover: 0.10 **NM** value: **50.00**
• **CGC:** 1 graded, best 9.2

KITCHEN SINK CLASSICS — Kitchen Sink

All issues are adults only.

1 ❑ Jan 1994, b&w Cover: 3.95 **NM** value: **4.00**
• reprints Omaha #0

2 ❑ b&w Cover: 2.95 **NM** value: **Cover or less**
• reprints The People's Comics

3 ❑ b&w Cover: 2.95 **NM** value: **Cover or less**
• reprints Death Rattle #8

KITTY — St. John

1 ❑ Oct 1948 Cover: 0.10 **NM** value: **40.00**

KITTY PRYDE & WOLVERINE — Marvel

This story takes place not long after Kitty Pryde joins the X-Men (when she is still called "Ariel"). The tale begins when Kitty learns that her father, a prominent Illinois banker, is being blackmailed by the Yakuza (Japanese mob). They threaten to reveal that he has tampered with his bank's books unless he goes with them to Japan to help them in their money-laundering operations. Kitty overhears the conversation and resolves to follow her father to Japan to rescue him. Quickly discovering that she is way over her head, Kitty calls on fellow X-Man Wolverine, who quickly travels to Japan to aid her.

In this action-packed series, the two struggle together to survive the Yakuza and save Kitty's father. Along the way, they encounter both Yukio, a dangerous ronin with a heart of gold, and Lady Mariko, Wolverine's great love — and the incidental head of a powerful crime family.

1 ❑ Nov 1984 Cover: 0.75 **NM** value: **3.50**
• **CGC:** 2 graded, best 9.6
📖 Lies **A:** Al Milgrom **W:** Chris Claremont

2 ❑ Dec 1984 Cover: 0.75 **NM** value: **2.50**
📖 Terror **A:** Al Milgrom **W:** Chris Claremont

3 ❑ Jan 1985 Cover: 0.75 **NM** value: **2.50**
• **CGC:** 1 graded, best 9.2
📖 Death **A:** Al Milgrom **W:** Chris Claremont

4 ❑ Feb 1985 Cover: 0.75 **NM** value: **2.50**
📖 Rebirth **A:** Al Milgrom **W:** Chris Claremont

5 ❑ Mar 1985 Cover: 0.75 **NM** value: **2.50**
A: Al Milgrom **W:** Chris Claremont

6 ❑ Apr 1985 Cover: 0.75 **NM** value: **2.50**
A: Al Milgrom **W:** Chris Claremont

KITTY PRYDE, AGENT OF SHIELD — Marvel

1 ❑ Dec 1997 Cover: 2.50 **NM** value: **Cover or less**
Circ: Diamd. preorders: **52,165**
• gatefold summary. 📖 The Calling **A:** Jesus Redondo **W:** Larry Hama

2 ❑ Jan 1998 Cover: 2.50 **NM** value: **Cover or less**
Circ: Diamd. preorders: **44,648**
• gatefold summary. **A:** Jesus Redondo **W:** Larry Hama ★ Appearance of Wolverine, Lockheed.

3 ❑ Feb 1998 Cover: 2.50 **NM** value: **Cover or less**
Circ: Diamd. preorders: **39,688**
• gatefold summary. **A:** Jesus Redondo **W:** Larry Hama

KITZ 'N' KATZ KOMIKS — Phantasy

1 ❑ Cover: 1.50 **NM** value: **Cover or less**
2 ❑ b&w Cover: 1.50 **NM** value: **Cover or less**
3 ❑ b&w Cover: 1.50 **NM** value: **Cover or less**
4 ❑ b&w Cover: 1.50 **NM** value: **Cover or less**
5 ❑ Cover: 2.00 **NM** value: **Cover or less**
6 ❑ Cover: 1.50 **NM** value: **Cover or less**

KIWANNI-DAUGHTER OF THE DAWN — C&T

1 ❑ Feb 1988, b&w Cover: 2.25 **NM** value: **Cover or less**
A: Eric Mayer **W:** Eric Mayer

KLOR — Sirius

1 ❑ Cover: 2.95 **NM** value: **Cover or less**
A: Dark One **W:** Dark One

2 ❑ Cover: 2.95 **NM** value: **Cover or less**
A: Dark One **W:** Dark One

3 ❑ Cover: 2.95 **NM** value: **Cover or less**
A: Dark One **W:** Dark One

KNEWTS OF THE ROUND TABLE — Pan

1 ❑ Jul 1998, b&w Cover: 2.50 **NM** value: **Cover or less**
A: Nirut Chamsuwan **W:** Brian Fitzgerald

2 ❑ Sep 1998, b&w Cover: 2.50 **NM** value: **Cover or less**
A: Nirut Chamsuwan **W:** Brian Fitzgerald

3 ❑ Cover: 2.50 **NM** value: **Cover or less**
A: Nirut Chamsuwan **W:** Brian Fitzgerald

4 ❑ Cover: 2.50 **NM** value: **Cover or less**
A: Nirut Chamsuwan **W:** Brian Fitzgerald

5 ❑ Cover: 2.50 **NM** value: **Cover or less**
A: Nirut Chamsuwan **W:** Brian Fitzgerald

KNIGHT — Bear Claw

0 ❑ Oct 1993 Cover: 2.50 **NM** value: **Cover or less**
A: Jake Bear **W:** Jake Bear; Kevin Hill

KNIGHTFOOL: THE FALL OF THE SPLATMAN — Parody Press

1 ❑ Cover: 2.95 **NM** value: **Cover or less**
A: Bill Maus **W:** Bill Maus

KNIGHTHAWK — Acclaim / Windjammer

1 ❑ Sep 1995 Cover: 2.50 **NM** value: **Cover or less**
Circ: CapCity orders: **9,275**
A: Neal Adams **W:** Neal Adams

2 ❑ Sep 1995 Cover: 2.50 **NM** value: **Cover or less**
Circ: CapCity orders: **8,425**

3 ❑ Oct 1995 Cover: 2.50 **NM** value: **Cover or less**
Circ: CapCity orders: **5,850**

4 ❑ Oct 1995 Cover: 2.50 **NM** value: **Cover or less**
Circ: CapCity orders: **5,800**
A: Neal Adams **W:** Neal Adams

5 ❑ Nov 1995 Cover: 2.50 **NM** value: **Cover or less**
Circ: CapCity orders: **4,875**
A: Neal Adams **W:** Neal Adams

6 ❑ Nov 1995 Cover: 2.50 **NM** value: **Cover or less**
Circ: CapCity orders: **4,875**
final issue. **A:** Neal Adams **W:** Neal Adams

KNIGHTMARE (ANTARCTIC) — Antarctic

1 ❑ Jul 1994, b&w Cover: 2.75 **NM** value: **Cover or less**
2 ❑ Sep 1994, b&w Cover: 2.75 **NM** value: **Cover or less**
A: P. Sky Owens **W:** P. Sky Owens

3 ❑ Jan 1995, b&w Cover: 2.75 **NM** value: **Cover or less**
📖 Wedding Knight Part1 **A:** P. Sky Owens **W:** P. Sky Owens

4 ❑ Mar 1995, b&w Cover: 2.75 **NM** value: **Cover or less**
📖 Wedding Knight Part2 **A:** P. Sky Owens **W:** P. Sky Owens

5 ❑ Mar 1995, b&w Cover: 2.75 **NM** value: **Cover or less**
📖 Wedding Knight Part4 **A:** P. Sky Owens **W:** P. Sky Owens

6 ❑ May 1995, b&w Cover: 2.75 **NM** value: **Cover or less**
📖 Wedding Knight Part4 final issue. **A:** P. Sky Owens **W:** Bryan Glass

KNIGHTMARE (IMAGE) — Image

0 ❑ Aug 1995 Cover: 3.50 **NM** value: **Cover or less**
Circ: CapCity orders: **18,050**
chromium cover. 📖 Dulcinea **A:** Marat Mychaels **W:** Rob Liefeld; Robert Loren Flemming ★ Origin of Knightmare. ★ 1st Appearance of Knightmare.

1 ❑ Feb 1995 Cover: 2.50 **NM** value: **Cover or less**
Circ: CapCity orders: **22,675**
W: Rob Liefeld; Robert Loren Flemming

2 ❑ Mar 1995 Cover: 2.50 **NM** value: **Cover or less**
Circ: CapCity orders: **15,925**

3 ❑ Apr 1995 Cover: 2.50 **NM** value: **Cover or less**
Circ: CapCity orders: **14,575**

4 ❑ May 1995 Cover: 2.50 **NM** value: **Cover or less**
Circ: CapCity orders: **14,775**

4/A ❑ May 1995 Cover: 2.50 **NM** value: **Cover or less**
alternate cover.

5 ❑ Jun 1995 Cover: 2.50 **NM** value: **Cover or less**
Circ: CapCity orders: **14,975**
📖 Getting Ugly; Warcry • Flip book with Warcry #1 **A:** John Fang; Mark Pajarillo **W:** Rob Liefeld; Brian Uyeda; Robert Loren Flemming

6 ❑ Cover: 2.50 **NM** value: **Cover or less**
Circ: CapCity orders: **14,450**

7 ❑ Cover: 2.50 **NM** value: **Cover or less**
8 ❑ Cover: 2.50 **NM** value: **Cover or less**
final issue.

The CGC numbers printed in individual listings above represent the **number of copies examined** and given a **Universal** grade by CGC and the **best such copy** graded at press time. For current populations, watch for special ***Comics Buyer's Guide*** issues or check **www.cgccomics.com.**

CGC-graded: Multiply prices above by **33 for 9.9 M • 16 for 9.8 NM/M • 7 for 9.6 NM+ • 5 for 9.4 NM • 2.5 for 9.2 NM- • 1.5 for 9.0 VF/NM**

KNIGHTS OF PENDRAGON, THE (1ST SERIES) Marvel

It began when a series of ghastly murders brings Commander Dai Thomas of Scotland Yard to London. It seems that someone — or something — is settling scores with the Omni Corporation: from a board member of Omni's Swedish whaling subsidiary being killed with a 400 year-old harpoon, to mysterious "food poisoning" killing 87 people in a Tastee Burger (a franchise owned by Omni). Excalibur liaison Alysande Stewart has summoned Dai to add his expertise to this puzzling case.

Unknown to Stewart, the commander has been been having troubling dreams — living out each new nightmare as it happens. Somehow, it's all tied into the Omni Corporation, as well as into the ancient knights of England — in a legacy that is coming alive today.

1 ☐ Jul 1990 Cover: 1.95 **NM** value: **2.50**
Circ: CapCity orders: **28,900**
📖 Brands & Ashes **A:** Gary Erskine **W:** John Tomlinson; Dan Abnett
2 ☐ Aug 1990 Cover: 1.95 **NM** value: **2.00**
Circ: CapCity orders: **22,200**
3 ☐ Oct 1990 Cover: 1.95 **NM** value: **2.00**
Circ: CapCity orders: **18,100**
4 ☐ Oct 1990 Cover: 1.95 **NM** value: **2.00**
Circ: CapCity orders: **16,600**
5 ☐ Nov 1990 Cover: 1.95 **NM** value: **2.00**
Circ: CapCity orders: **15,050**
6 ☐ Dec 1990 Cover: 1.95 **NM** value: **2.00**
Circ: CapCity orders: **13,600**
📖 Once & Future **A:** Gary Erskine **W:** John Tomlinson; Dan Abnett

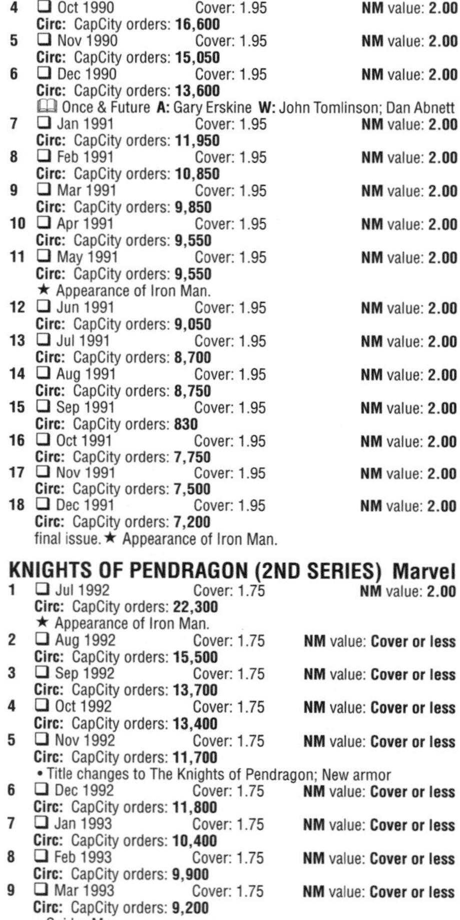

7 ☐ Jan 1991 Cover: 1.95 **NM** value: **2.00**
Circ: CapCity orders: **11,950**
8 ☐ Feb 1991 Cover: 1.95 **NM** value: **2.00**
Circ: CapCity orders: **10,850**
9 ☐ Mar 1991 Cover: 1.95 **NM** value: **2.00**
Circ: CapCity orders: **9,850**
10 ☐ Apr 1991 Cover: 1.95 **NM** value: **2.00**
Circ: CapCity orders: **9,550**
11 ☐ May 1991 Cover: 1.95 **NM** value: **2.00**
Circ: CapCity orders: **9,550**
★ Appearance of Iron Man.
12 ☐ Jun 1991 Cover: 1.95 **NM** value: **2.00**
Circ: CapCity orders: **9,050**
13 ☐ Jul 1991 Cover: 1.95 **NM** value: **2.00**
Circ: CapCity orders: **8,700**
14 ☐ Aug 1991 Cover: 1.95 **NM** value: **2.00**
Circ: CapCity orders: **8,750**
15 ☐ Sep 1991 Cover: 1.95 **NM** value: **2.00**
Circ: CapCity orders: **830**
16 ☐ Oct 1991 Cover: 1.95 **NM** value: **2.00**
Circ: CapCity orders: **7,750**
17 ☐ Nov 1991 Cover: 1.95 **NM** value: **2.00**
Circ: CapCity orders: **7,500**
18 ☐ Dec 1991 Cover: 1.95 **NM** value: **2.00**
Circ: CapCity orders: **7,200**
final issue.★ Appearance of Iron Man.

KNIGHTS OF PENDRAGON (2ND SERIES) Marvel

1 ☐ Jul 1992 Cover: 1.75 **NM** value: **2.00**
Circ: CapCity orders: **22,300**
★ Appearance of Iron Man.
2 ☐ Aug 1992 Cover: 1.75 **NM** value: **Cover or less**
Circ: CapCity orders: **15,500**
3 ☐ Sep 1992 Cover: 1.75 **NM** value: **Cover or less**
Circ: CapCity orders: **13,700**
4 ☐ Oct 1992 Cover: 1.75 **NM** value: **Cover or less**
Circ: CapCity orders: **13,400**
5 ☐ Nov 1992 Cover: 1.75 **NM** value: **Cover or less**
Circ: CapCity orders: **11,700**
• Title changes to The Knights of Pendragon; New armor
6 ☐ Dec 1992 Cover: 1.75 **NM** value: **Cover or less**
Circ: CapCity orders: **11,800**
7 ☐ Jan 1993 Cover: 1.75 **NM** value: **Cover or less**
Circ: CapCity orders: **10,400**
8 ☐ Feb 1993 Cover: 1.75 **NM** value: **Cover or less**
Circ: CapCity orders: **9,900**
9 ☐ Mar 1993 Cover: 1.75 **NM** value: **Cover or less**
Circ: CapCity orders: **9,200**
• Spider-Man
10 ☐ Apr 1993 Cover: 1.75 **NM** value: **Cover or less**
Circ: CapCity orders: **9,100**
📖 Bloodlines, Part 1 **A:** John Royle **W:** John Tomlinson; Dan Abnett
11 ☐ May 1993 Cover: 1.75 **NM** value: **Cover or less**
Circ: CapCity orders: **7,900**
📖 Bloodlines, Part 2 **A:** John Royle **W:** John Tomlinson; Dan Abnett
12 ☐ Jun 1993 Cover: 1.75 **NM** value: **Cover or less**
Circ: CapCity orders: **7,900**
13 ☐ Jul 1993 Cover: 1.75 **NM** value: **Cover or less**
Circ: CapCity orders: **7,200**
14 ☐ Aug 1993 Cover: 1.75 **NM** value: **Cover or less**
Circ: CapCity orders: **6,600**
15 ☐ Sep 1993 Cover: 1.75 **NM** value: **Cover or less**
Circ: CapCity orders: **5,300**
final issue.

Do you have changes or corrections for the **Standard Catalog**? Send your original research to us at
allcomics@krause.com

KNIGHTS OF THE DINNER TABLE Alderac Group

Knights of the Dinner Table began as a series of jokes about gamers (as in Dungeons & Dragons, not Las Vegas) in a gaming magazine. In comic-book form, it probably did more to attract new readers to comic books than any other series in the late 1990s. That may not be saying much, but how many series find the majority of their readership outside of comics shops? It's the case with Knights, which sells about 75% of its copies in game shops.

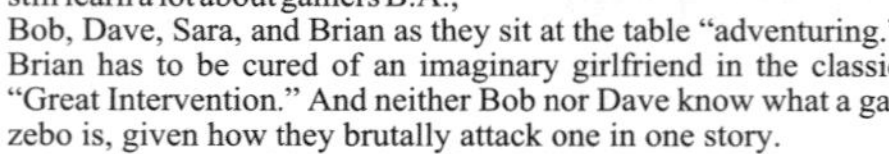

Jolly Blackburn's art is a triumph of minimalism, basically cut-outs that only move when a mouth requires opening. But we still learn a lot about gamers B.A., Bob, Dave, Sara, and Brian as they sit at the table "adventuring." Brian has to be cured of an imaginary girlfriend in the classic "Great Intervention." And neither Bob nor Dave know what a gazebo is, given how they brutally attack one in one story.

Later years would find the title, which started at Alderac and moved to Kenzer early on, attempting to become first a general gaming magazine and then a support magazine for Kenzer's own game line, with mixed success. The real attraction of Knights remains the Knights. — JJM

1 ☐ Jul 1994 Cover: 2.95 **NM** value: **75.00**
• **CGC:** 1 graded, best 7.0
📖 Not Ready for Syndication
2 ☐ Jan 1995 Cover: 2.95 **NM** value: **38.00**
• **CGC:** 1 graded, best 8.5
📖 Gluttons for Punishment
3 ☐ Apr 1995 Cover: 2.95 **NM** value: **22.00**
• **CGC:** 1 graded, best 9.4
📖 License to Loot

KNIGHTS OF THE DINNER TABLE Kenzer

4 ☐ Feb 1997 Cover: 2.95 **NM** value: **22.00**
• **CGC:** 1 graded, best 9.2
📖 Have Dice Will Travel • Gary Con issue
5 ☐ Mar 1997 Cover: 2.95 **NM** value: **22.00**
📖 Master of the Game
6 ☐ Apr 1997 Cover: 2.95 **NM** value: **16.00**
📖 Plays Well With Others
7 ☐ May 1997 Cover: 2.95 **NM** value: **16.00**
📖 The Dice Man Cometh!
8 ☐ Jun 1997 Cover: 2.95 **NM** value: **16.00**
📖 An Orc By Any Other Name
9 ☐ Jul 1997 Cover: 2.95 **NM** value: **16.00**
📖 Two Dice for Sister Sara
10 ☐ Aug 1997 Cover: 2.95 **NM** value: **16.00**
📖 Let the Dice Fall Where They May
11 ☐ Sep 1997 Cover: 2.95 **NM** value: **12.00**
📖 When in Doubt: Hack!!
12 ☐ Oct 1997 Cover: 2.95 **NM** value: **12.00**
📖 The Good The Bad and The Unlucky!
13 ☐ Nov 1997 Cover: 2.95 **NM** value: **12.00**
📖 Men That Hack
14 ☐ Dec 1997 Cover: 2.95 **NM** value: **12.00**
📖 A Fist Full of Dice And A Bad Attitude
15 ☐ Jan 1998 Cover: 2.95 **NM** value: **12.00**
📖 Mama Told Me Not to Play
16 ☐ Feb 1998 Cover: 2.95 **NM** value: **9.00**
📖 The Dice of Wrath
17 ☐ Mar 1998 Cover: 2.95 **NM** value: **9.00**
📖 This Sword for Hire!
18 ☐ Apr 1998 Cover: 2.95 **NM** value: **9.00**
📖 Against All Odds
19 ☐ May 1998 Cover: 2.95 **NM** value: **9.00**
📖 Heroes of the Hack League
20 ☐ Jun 1998 Cover: 2.95 **NM** value: **9.00**
📖 Hack in Space!
21 ☐ Jul 1998 Cover: 2.95 **NM** value: **9.00**
📖 Home is Where You Hang Yer Dicebag • Gary Con issue
22 ☐ Aug 1998 Cover: 2.95 **NM** value: **6.00**
📖 Opportunity Knocks
23 ☐ Sep 1998 Cover: 2.95 **NM** value: **6.00**
Circ: Diamd. preorders: **2,278**
📖 Dice Follies
24 ☐ Oct 1998 Cover: 2.95 **NM** value: **6.00**
Circ: Diamd. preorders: **2,663**
📖 Hackzilla
25 ☐ Nov 1998 Cover: 2.95 **NM** value: **6.00**
Circ: Diamd. preorders: **2,819**
📖 Secrets of the Hackfiles
26 ☐ Dec 1998 Cover: 2.95 **NM** value: **6.00**
Circ: Diamd. preorders: **3,100**
📖 The Mask of El Ravager
27 ☐ Jan 1999 Cover: 2.95 **NM** value: **6.00**
Circ: Diamd. preorders: **3,344**
📖 Hackburger Hill
28 ☐ Feb 1999 Cover: 2.95 **NM** value: **6.00**
Circ: Diamd. preorders: **3,330**
📖 Hoody Freakin' Hoo!!
29 ☐ Mar 1999 Cover: 2.95 **NM** value: **6.00**
Circ: Diamd. preorders: **3,631**
📖 Bad Moon Risin'
30 ☐ Apr 1999 Cover: 2.95 **NM** value: **6.00**
Circ: Diamd. preorders: **4,352**
📖 No Honor
31 ☐ May 1999 Cover: 2.95 **NM** value: **4.00**
Circ: Diamd. preorders: **4,408**
📖 Don't Fear The Reaper

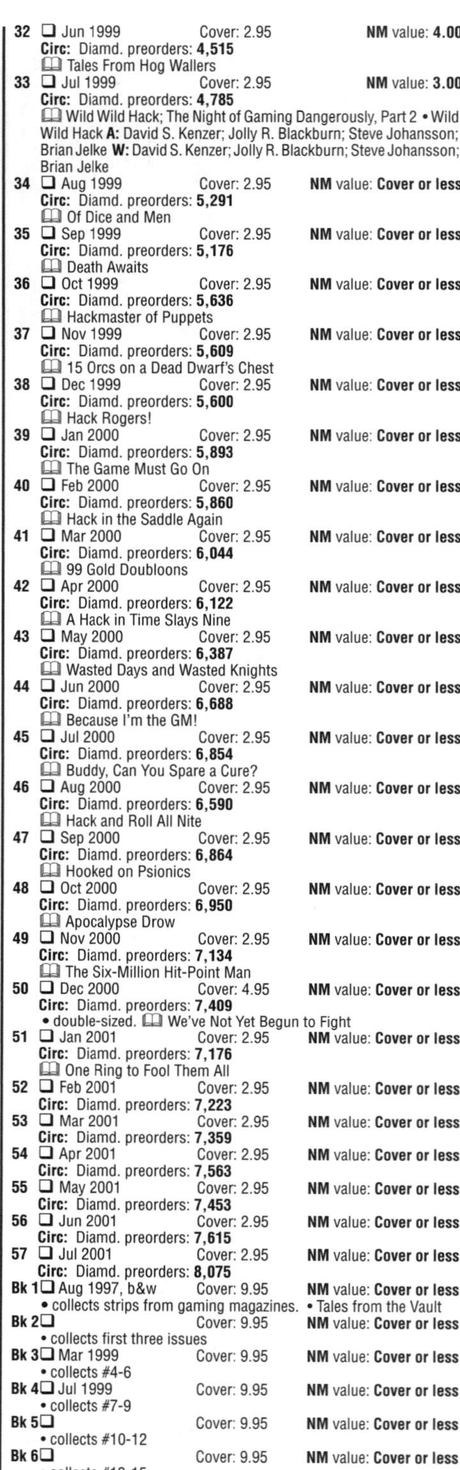

32 ☐ Jun 1999 Cover: 2.95 **NM** value: **4.00**
Circ: Diamd. preorders: **4,515**
📖 Tales From Hog Wallers
33 ☐ Jul 1999 Cover: 2.95 **NM** value: **3.00**
Circ: Diamd. preorders: **4,785**
📖 Wild Wild Hack; The Night of Gaming Dangerously, Part 2 • Wild Wild Hack **A:** David S. Kenzer; Jolly R. Blackburn; Steve Johansson; Brian Jelke **W:** David S. Kenzer; Jolly R. Blackburn; Steve Johansson; Brian Jelke
34 ☐ Aug 1999 Cover: 2.95 **NM** value: **Cover or less**
Circ: Diamd. preorders: **5,291**
📖 Of Dice and Men
35 ☐ Sep 1999 Cover: 2.95 **NM** value: **Cover or less**
Circ: Diamd. preorders: **5,176**
📖 Death Awaits
36 ☐ Oct 1999 Cover: 2.95 **NM** value: **Cover or less**
Circ: Diamd. preorders: **5,636**
📖 Hackmaster of Puppets
37 ☐ Nov 1999 Cover: 2.95 **NM** value: **Cover or less**
Circ: Diamd. preorders: **5,609**
📖 15 Orcs on a Dead Dwarf's Chest
38 ☐ Dec 1999 Cover: 2.95 **NM** value: **Cover or less**
Circ: Diamd. preorders: **5,600**
📖 Hack Rogers!
39 ☐ Jan 2000 Cover: 2.95 **NM** value: **Cover or less**
Circ: Diamd. preorders: **5,893**
📖 The Game Must Go On
40 ☐ Feb 2000 Cover: 2.95 **NM** value: **Cover or less**
Circ: Diamd. preorders: **5,860**
📖 Hack in the Saddle Again
41 ☐ Mar 2000 Cover: 2.95 **NM** value: **Cover or less**
Circ: Diamd. preorders: **6,044**
📖 99 Gold Doubloons
42 ☐ Apr 2000 Cover: 2.95 **NM** value: **Cover or less**
Circ: Diamd. preorders: **6,122**
📖 A Hack in Time Slays Nine
43 ☐ May 2000 Cover: 2.95 **NM** value: **Cover or less**
Circ: Diamd. preorders: **6,387**
📖 Wasted Days and Wasted Knights
44 ☐ Jun 2000 Cover: 2.95 **NM** value: **Cover or less**
Circ: Diamd. preorders: **6,688**
📖 Because I'm the GM!
45 ☐ Jul 2000 Cover: 2.95 **NM** value: **Cover or less**
Circ: Diamd. preorders: **6,854**
📖 Buddy, Can You Spare a Cure?
46 ☐ Aug 2000 Cover: 2.95 **NM** value: **Cover or less**
Circ: Diamd. preorders: **6,590**
📖 Hack and Roll All Nite
47 ☐ Sep 2000 Cover: 2.95 **NM** value: **Cover or less**
Circ: Diamd. preorders: **6,864**
📖 Hooked on Psionics
48 ☐ Oct 2000 Cover: 2.95 **NM** value: **Cover or less**
Circ: Diamd. preorders: **6,950**
📖 Apocalypse Drow
49 ☐ Nov 2000 Cover: 2.95 **NM** value: **Cover or less**
Circ: Diamd. preorders: **7,134**
📖 The Six-Million Hit-Point Man
50 ☐ Dec 2000 Cover: 4.95 **NM** value: **Cover or less**
Circ: Diamd. preorders: **7,409**
• double-sized. 📖 We've Not Yet Begun to Fight
51 ☐ Jan 2001 Cover: 2.95 **NM** value: **Cover or less**
Circ: Diamd. preorders: **7,176**
📖 One Ring to Fool Them All
52 ☐ Feb 2001 Cover: 2.95 **NM** value: **Cover or less**
Circ: Diamd. preorders: **7,223**
53 ☐ Mar 2001 Cover: 2.95 **NM** value: **Cover or less**
Circ: Diamd. preorders: **7,359**
54 ☐ Apr 2001 Cover: 2.95 **NM** value: **Cover or less**
Circ: Diamd. preorders: **7,563**
55 ☐ May 2001 Cover: 2.95 **NM** value: **Cover or less**
Circ: Diamd. preorders: **7,453**
56 ☐ Jun 2001 Cover: 2.95 **NM** value: **Cover or less**
Circ: Diamd. preorders: **7,615**
57 ☐ Jul 2001 Cover: 2.95 **NM** value: **Cover or less**
Circ: Diamd. preorders: **8,075**
Bk 1☐ Aug 1997, b&w Cover: 9.95 **NM** value: **Cover or less**
• collects strips from gaming magazines. • Tales from the Vault
Bk 2☐ Cover: 9.95 **NM** value: **Cover or less**
• collects first three issues
Bk 3☐ Mar 1999 Cover: 9.95 **NM** value: **Cover or less**
• collects #4-6
Bk 4☐ Jul 1999 Cover: 9.95 **NM** value: **Cover or less**
• collects #7-9
Bk 5☐ Cover: 9.95 **NM** value: **Cover or less**
• collects #10-12
Bk 6☐ Cover: 9.95 **NM** value: **Cover or less**
• collects #13-15
Bk 7☐ May 2000 Cover: 9.95 **NM** value: **Cover or less**
• collects #16-18
Bk 8☐ Aug 2000 Cover: 9.95 **NM** value: **Cover or less**
• collects #19-21

KNIGHTS OF THE DINNER TABLE/FAANS CROSSOVER SPECIAL Six Handed Press

1 ☐ Jul 1999, b&w Cover: 2.95 **NM** value: **Cover or less**
Circ: Diamd. preorders: **4,435**

The CGC numbers printed in individual listings above represent the **number of copies examined** and given a **Universal** grade by CGC and the **best such copy** graded at press time. For current populations, watch for special ***Comics Buyer's Guide*** issues or check **www.cgccomics.com.**

Other grades: Multiply prices above by **1.5 for Mint • 2/3 for Very Fine • 1/3 for Fine • 1/5 for Very Good • 1/8 for Good**

KNIGHTS OF THE DINNER TABLE ILLUSTRATED — Kenzer & Company

This series features comic-book retellings of role-playing games featuring the band of adventurers known as the Knights of the Dinner Table.

Join a dwarf, a cleric, a warrior-woman, and an adventurer, as well as many other hirelings, thieves, and other hangers-on, as they travel from dungeons to exotic locales, gathering treasure, killing monsters, and generally harassing the locals.

Each issue contains one or more tales as well as comic-strip dramatizations of the conversations around the gaming table by the players who developed the scenarios.

1 ❑ Jun 2000, b&w Cover: 2.95 **NM** value: **Cover or less**
📖 Lair of the Gazebo; First Impressions; The Cows of War; Sucking Chest Wound; The Farmer Wars **A:** Aaron Williams

2 ❑ Aug 2000, b&w Cover: 2.95 **NM** value: **Cover or less**
📖 Hole Lot of Trouble; Can We Talk?; Wherever You Go – There You Are; Agent of Evil!!; The Streets of Muskeegie **A:** Aaron Williams

3 ❑ Oct 2000, b&w Cover: 2.95 **NM** value: **Cover or less**
📖 Five Green Towels; A Call for Heroes; Coward of the County; Balance of Terror **A:** Aaron Williams **W:** David S. Kenzer; Jolly R. Blackburn; Steve Johansson; Brian Jelke

4 ❑ Dec 2000, b&w Cover: 2.95 **NM** value: **Cover or less**
📖 The Portal; Orcs at the Gates; A Critical Situation; Angel of Mercy; An Orc Too Far; Carvin' Marvin **A:** Brendon Fraim; Brian Fraim **C:** Aaron Williams

KNIGHTS ON BROADWAY — Broadway

1 ❑ Jul 1996 Cover: 2.95 **NM** value: **Cover or less**
A: Geof Isherwood **W:** Joe James

2 ❑ Aug 1996 Cover: 2.95 **NM** value: **Cover or less**
A: Geof Isherwood **W:** Joe James

3 ❑ Oct 1996 Cover: 2.95 **NM** value: **Cover or less**
Circ: Diamd. preorders: **10,090**
A: Geof Isherwood **W:** Joe James

KNIGHT'S ROUND TABLE — Knight Press

1 ❑ Oct 1996, b&w Cover: 2.95 **NM** value: **Cover or less**

KNIGHTSTRIKE — Image

1 ❑ Dec 1995 Cover: 2.50 **NM** value: **Cover or less**
📖 Extreme Destroyer, Part 6 • polybagged with Sentinel card **A:** Robert Napton **W:** Rob Liefeld; Eric Stephenson

KNIGHT WATCHMAN — Image

1 ❑ Jun 1998 Cover: 2.95 **NM** value: **Cover or less**
Circ: Diamd. preorders: **5,832**
cover says May, indicia says Jun. 📖 Graveyard Shift, Part 1 **A:** Ben Torres; John Thompson **W:** Chris Ecker; Gary Carlson

2 ❑ Jul 1998 Cover: 2.95 **NM** value: **Cover or less**
Circ: Diamd. preorders: **3,802**
📖 Graveyard Shift, Part 2 **A:** Ben Torres; John Thompson **W:** Chris Ecker; Gary Carlson

3 ❑ Aug 1998 Cover: 2.95 **NM** value: **Cover or less**
Circ: Diamd. preorders: **3,665**
📖 Graveyard Shift, Part 3 **A:** Ben Torres; John Thompson **W:** Chris Ecker; Gary Carlson

4 ❑ Oct 1998 Cover: 2.95 **NM** value: **3.50**
Circ: Diamd. preorders: **3,616**
📖 Graveyard Shift, Part 4 **A:** Ben Torres **W:** Chris Ecker; Gary Carlson

KNIGHT WATCHMAN: GRAVEYARD SHIFT — Caliber

1 ❑ b&w Cover: 2.95 **NM** value: **Cover or less**
📖 A Hard Day's Night **A:** Ben Torres **W:** Chris Ecker; Gary Carlson

2 ❑ Cover: 2.95 **NM** value: **Cover or less**
📖 Knight Moves **A:** Ben Torres **W:** Chris Ecker; Gary Carlson

3 ❑ Cover: 2.95 **NM** value: **Cover or less**
A: Ben Torres **W:** Chris Ecker; Gary Carlson

4 ❑ Cover: 2.95 **NM** value: **Cover or less**
A: Ben Torres **W:** Chris Ecker; Gary Carlson

KNIGHT WOLF, THE — Five Star

1 ❑ Cover: 2.50 **NM** value: **Cover or less**
📖 Welcome to My Knightmare **A:** Mark A. Lester **W:** Mark A. Lester

2 ❑ Cover: 2.50 **NM** value: **Cover or less**
A: Mark A. Lester **W:** Mark A. Lester

3 ❑ Cover: 2.50 **NM** value: **Cover or less**
A: Mark A. Lester **W:** Mark A. Lester

KNOCKOUT ADVENTURES — Fiction House

1 ❑ ca. 1954 Cover: 0.10 **NM** value: **Cover or less**

> There are two different pricing tiers in the modern comic-book hobby. **The prices seen above** are the prices we have seen **loose copies** of these issues reliably fetch in a variety of environments. Condition alters the price by the fractions seen on the bar on the bottom of left-hand pages of this book. **Comics graded by CGC** usually sell for more. Use the guide on the bottom of right-hand pages of this book to estimate what copies have brought on eBay.

KNUCKLES — Archie

Knuckles is a quick-tempered, gullible Echidna and something of a second banana to Sonic the Hedgehog in assorted Sonic Adventure computer games. He's got red fur, quills, and shoes, a beige muzzle, and a white crescent mark on his upper chest. Oh, yes, and sharp knuckles on his white mitts. In the world of the game, he can use shovel claws, hammer gloves, and special glasses and can teleport. He's the guardian of the Master Emerald on Angel Island.

So, of course, he was a natural to not only appear as one of the gang in Archie's ongoing Sonic the Hedgehog title but also to spin off into his own only four years after Sonic's first comic-book tryout. — Maggie

1 ❑ Apr 1997 Cover: 1.50 **NM** value: **3.00**
📖 The Dark Legion

2 ❑ May 1997 Cover: 1.50 **NM** value: **2.00**
📖 The Dark Legion

3 ❑ Jun 1997 Cover: 1.50 **NM** value: **2.00**
📖 The Dark Legion

4 ❑ Aug 1997 Cover: 1.50 **NM** value: **2.00**
Circ: Diamd. preorders: **5,400**

5 ❑ Sep 1997 Cover: 1.50 **NM** value: **2.00**
Circ: Diamd. preorders: **5,833**

6 ❑ Oct 1997 Cover: 1.50 **NM** value: **2.00**
Circ: Diamd. preorders: **5,887**

7 ❑ Dec 1997 Cover: 1.50 **NM** value: **2.00**
Circ: Diamd. preorders: **6,400**

8 ❑ Jan 1998 Cover: 1.75 **NM** value: **2.00**
Circ: Diamd. preorders: **6,921**

9 ❑ Feb 1998 Cover: 1.75 **NM** value: **2.00**
Circ: Diamd. preorders: **7,325**

10 ❑ Mar 1998 Cover: 1.75 **NM** value: **2.00**
Circ: Diamd. preorders: **6,911**

11 ❑ Apr 1998 Cover: 1.75 **NM** value: **Cover or less**
Circ: Diamd. preorders: **6,571**

12 ❑ May 1998 Cover: 1.75 **NM** value: **Cover or less**
Circ: Diamd. preorders: **6,264**

13 ❑ Jun 1998 Cover: 1.75 **NM** value: **Cover or less**
Circ: Diamd. preorders: **6,445**

14 ❑ Jul 1998 Cover: 1.75 **NM** value: **Cover or less**
Circ: Diamd. preorders: **6,615**

15 ❑ Aug 1998 Cover: 1.75 **NM** value: **Cover or less**
Circ: Diamd. preorders: **6,223**

16 ❑ Sep 1998 Cover: 1.75 **NM** value: **Cover or less**
Circ: Diamd. preorders: **6,450**

17 ❑ Oct 1998 Cover: 1.75 **NM** value: **Cover or less**
Circ: Diamd. preorders: **6,208**

18 ❑ Nov 1998 Cover: 1.75 **NM** value: **Cover or less**
Circ: Diamd. preorders: **5,901**
📖 Debt of Honor! **A:** Andrew Pepoy; Manny Galán **W:** Ken Penders

19 ❑ Dec 1998 Cover: 1.75 **NM** value: **Cover or less**
Circ: Diamd. preorders: **6,045**

20 ❑ Jan 1999 Cover: 1.75 **NM** value: **Cover or less**
Circ: Diamd. preorders: **6,069**

21 ❑ Feb 1999 Cover: 1.75 **NM** value: **Cover or less**
Circ: Diamd. preorders: **5,950**

22 ❑ Mar 1999 Cover: 1.75 **NM** value: **Cover or less**
Circ: Diamd. preorders: **5,862**
cover forms triptych with #23 and #24. 📖 Dark Alliance

23 ❑ Apr 1999 Cover: 1.79 **NM** value: **Cover or less**
Circ: Diamd. preorders: **5,659**
cover forms triptych with #22 and #24. 📖 Dark Alliance

24 ❑ May 1999 Cover: 1.79 **NM** value: **Cover or less**
Circ: Diamd. preorders: **5,388**
cover forms triptych with #22 and #23. 📖 Dark Alliance

25 ❑ Jun 1999 Cover: 1.79 **NM** value: **Cover or less**
Circ: Diamd. preorders: **5,160**
📖 Childhood's End

26 ❑ Jul 1999 Cover: 1.79 **NM** value: **Cover or less**
Circ: Diamd. preorders: **5,406**
📖 The First Date

27 ❑ Aug 1999 Cover: 1.79 **NM** value: **Cover or less**
Circ: Diamd. preorders: **5,208**
📖 The First Date

28 ❑ Sep 1999 Cover: 1.79 **NM** value: **Cover or less**
Circ: Diamd. preorders: **5,105**
📖 The First Date

29 ❑ Oct 1999 Cover: 1.79 **NM** value: **Cover or less**
Circ: Diamd. preorders: **4,957**
• The Echidna

KNUCKLES' CHAOTIX — Archie

1 ❑ Jan 1996 Cover: 2.00 **NM** value: **Cover or less**

KNUCKLES THE MALEVOLENT NUN — Fantagraphics

1 ❑ b&w Cover: 2.25 **NM** value: **Cover or less**
A: Roger Langridge **W:** Cornelius Stone

2 ❑ Cover: 2.00 **NM** value: **2.25**
A: Roger Langridge **W:** Cornelius Stone

> **Statement of Ownership** figures are the average number of copies originally sold, as cited by the publisher to the U.S. Postal Service. These estimate **all** sales, in comics shops and on newsstands.

KOBALT — DC / Milestone

One of the later major additions to the Milestone universe, Kobalt is a grim 'n' gritty bruiser who looks like the bad guy in a pro wrestling match. The fun of this series, however, rests with his sidekick, Ricky Page. Page is the living embodiment of the "before" model in those Charles Atlas ads. He's a kid, constantly victimized by the bullies at school. All the while, he dreams of becoming a super-hero, taking his inspiration from the pages of "Cape and Cowl" magazine.

As luck would have it, Kobalt owes Ricky's dad a favor, and against his wishes, Kobalt takes the kid in and shows him the ropes. The tension between the two provides the series' best moments, although there's plenty of standard beat-up-the-bad-guys action as well.

1 ❑ Jun 1994 Cover: 1.75 **NM** value: **Cover or less**
Circ: CapCity orders: **11,800**
📖 The Gall **A:** Arvell Jones **W:** John Rozum

2 ❑ Jul 1994 Cover: 1.75 **NM** value: **Cover or less**
Circ: CapCity orders: **7,100**
📖 Walking the Plank **A:** Arvell Jones **W:** John Rozum

3 ❑ Aug 1994 Cover: 1.75 **NM** value: **Cover or less**
Circ: CapCity orders: **6,150**

4 ❑ Sep 1994 Cover: 1.75 **NM** value: **Cover or less**
Circ: CapCity orders: **5,800**
★ 1st Appearance of Page.

5 ❑ Oct 1994 Cover: 1.75 **NM** value: **Cover or less**
Circ: CapCity orders: **5,300**

6 ❑ Nov 1994 Cover: 1.75 **NM** value: **Cover or less**
Circ: CapCity orders: **4,600**

7 ❑ Dec 1994 Cover: 1.75 **NM** value: **Cover or less**
Circ: CapCity orders: **4,250**
★ Appearance of Static.

8 ❑ Jan 1995 Cover: 1.75 **NM** value: **Cover or less**
Circ: CapCity orders: **3,650**
★ Appearance of Hardware.

9 ❑ Feb 1995 Cover: 1.75 **NM** value: **Cover or less**
Circ: CapCity orders: **3,150**

10 ❑ Mar 1995 Cover: 1.75 **NM** value: **Cover or less**
Circ: CapCity orders: **2,750**

11 ❑ Apr 1995 Cover: 1.75 **NM** value: **Cover or less**
Circ: CapCity orders: **2,500**

12 ❑ Jun 1995 Cover: 1.75 **NM** value: **Cover or less**
Circ: CapCity orders: **2,325**

13 ❑ Jul 1995 Cover: 2.50 **NM** value: **Cover or less**
Circ: CapCity orders: **2,325**

14 ❑ Jul 1995 Cover: 2.50 **NM** value: **Cover or less**
Circ: CapCity orders: **2,325**
📖 Long Hot Summer

15 ❑ Aug 1995 Cover: 2.50 **NM** value: **Cover or less**
Circ: CapCity orders: **2,325**

16 ❑ Sep 1995 Cover: 2.50 **NM** value: **Cover or less**
Circ: CapCity orders: **2,200**
final issue.

KOBIER AND OSO — Gebhart

1 ❑ Cover: 1.50 **NM** value: **Cover or less**

KOBRA — DC

Twin brothers — one good, one evil — have linked nervous systems. So even as they battle each other as enemies, they must also protect each other or die. One brother, Gemini, is a member of the New York Police Department; the other, Kobra, is the leader of a global crime network. Ironically, the two end up uniting their forces to fight a common enemy in this short-lived, seven-issue series from the mid-Seventies.

Kobra has gone on to be one of the more shadowy super-villains of the DC universe, hatching schemes and attempting a takeover of the League of Assassins.

1 ❑ Mar 1976 Cover: 0.25 **NM** value: **4.00**
• **CGC:** 5 graded, best 9.6
📖 Fangs of the Kobra! **A:** Pablo Marcos; Jack Kirby; D. Bruce Berry **W:** Martin Pasko ★ Origin of Kobra. ★ 1st Appearance of Kobra.

2 ❑ May 1976 Cover: 0.30 **NM** value: **4.00**

3 ❑ Jul 1976 Cover: 0.30 **NM** value: **4.00**
📖 Vengeance In Ultra-Violet **A:** Keith Giffen **W:** Martin Pasko

4 ❑ Sep 1976 Cover: 0.30 **NM** value: **4.00**

5 ❑ Dec 1976 Cover: 0.30 **NM** value: **4.00**

6 ❑ Feb 1977 Cover: 0.30 **NM** value: **4.00**

7 ❑ Apr 1977 Cover: 0.30 **NM** value: **4.00**
final issue.

KOGARATSU: THE LOTUS OF BLOOD — Acme

1 ❑ Cover: 5.95 **NM** value: **Cover or less**

KOKEY KOALA — Toby

1 ❑ May 1952 Cover: 0.10 **NM** value: **24.00**
📖 Kokey Koala and his Magic Button; Home is Where You Find It (text story); Splashy the Platypus: Play Day; Donny Boy; Patrick O'Reilly

CGC-graded: Multiply prices above by **33 for 9.9 M • 16 for 9.8 NM/M • 7 for 9.6 NM+ • 5 for 9.4 NM • 2.5 for 9.2 NM- • 1.5 for 9.0 VF/NM**

KOKO AND KOLA — Magazine Enterprises

1 ❑ ca. 1947 Cover: 0.10 **NM** value: **75.00**
2 ❑ ca. 1947 Cover: 0.10 **NM** value: **40.00**
3 ❑ ca. 1947 Cover: 0.10 **NM** value: **35.00**
4 ❑ ca. 1947 Cover: 0.10 **NM** value: **35.00**
5 ❑ ca. 1947 Cover: 0.10 **NM** value: **35.00**
6 ❑ ca. 1947 Cover: 0.10 **NM** value: **35.00**

K.O. KOMICS — Gerona Publications

KOMIC KARTOONS — Timely

1 ❑ Fal 1945 Cover: 0.10 **NM** value: **125.00**
• **CGC:** 1 graded, best 4.5
2 ❑ Win 1945 Cover: 0.10 **NM** value: **125.00**

KOMIK PAGES — Harry A. Chesler

10 ❑ ca. 1945 Cover: 0.10 **NM** value: **175.00**

KOMODO AND THE DEFIANTS — Victory

1 ❑ Cover: 1.50 **NM** value: **Cover or less**
2 ❑ Cover: 1.50 **NM** value: **Cover or less**

KONA — Dell

Yes, it's a kind of coffee grown in Hawaii. That's not the idea in this series, however. In this case, Kona is a caveman fighting for survival on Monster Isle and elsewhere. Kona's accompanied on many of his adventures by scientist Dr. Dodd and Dodd's daughter and two grandchildren, and Dell's cover text gives much of the flavor of the series: "Kona returns to fight for Monster Isle!" "Attacked … Kona struggles against man-eating plants!" "The Strange End of Captain Krym." "The fantastic plot of the Moleman … to undermine the city!" The covers that are painted are lush and eye-catching; the line-art covers are more traditional.

Art on the series is by Sam Glanzman, best known for such work as "Lonely War of Willie Schultz" for Charlton, The Haunted Tank for DC, Attu for 4Winds, and stories of the U.S.S. Stevens for DC and Marvel. — Maggie

2 ❑ Jul 1962 Cover: 0.12 **NM** value: **15.00**
★ Appearance of Numbering continued from.
3 ❑ Sep 1962 Cover: 0.12 **NM** value: **12.00**
4 ❑ Oct 1962 Cover: 0.12 **NM** value: **12.00**
• Anak stories begin as back-up ★ Origin of Anak. ★ 1st Appearance of Anak.
5 ❑ Jan 1963 Cover: 0.12 **NM** value: **12.00**
6 ❑ Apr 1963 Cover: 0.12 **NM** value: **9.00**
7 ❑ Jul 1963 Cover: 0.12 **NM** value: **9.00**
8 ❑ Oct 1963 Cover: 0.12 **NM** value: **9.00**
9 ❑ Jan 1964 Cover: 0.12 **NM** value: **9.00**
10 ❑ Apr 1964 Cover: 0.12 **NM** value: **9.00**
11 ❑ Jul 1964 Cover: 0.12 **NM** value: **9.00**
12 ❑ Oct 1964 Cover: 0.12 **NM** value: **9.00**
13 ❑ Jan 1965 Cover: 0.12 **NM** value: **9.00**
14 ❑ Apr 1965 Cover: 0.12 **NM** value: **9.00**
15 ❑ Jul 1965 Cover: 0.12 **NM** value: **7.00**
16 ❑ Oct 1965 Cover: 0.12 **NM** value: **7.00**
17 ❑ Jan 1966 Cover: 0.12 **NM** value: **7.00**
18 ❑ Apr 1966 Cover: 0.12 **NM** value: **7.00**
19 ❑ Jul 1966 Cover: 0.12 **NM** value: **7.00**
20 ❑ Oct 1966 Cover: 0.12 **NM** value: **7.00**
21 ❑ Jan 1967 Cover: 0.12 **NM** value: **7.00**
final issue.

KONGA — Charlton

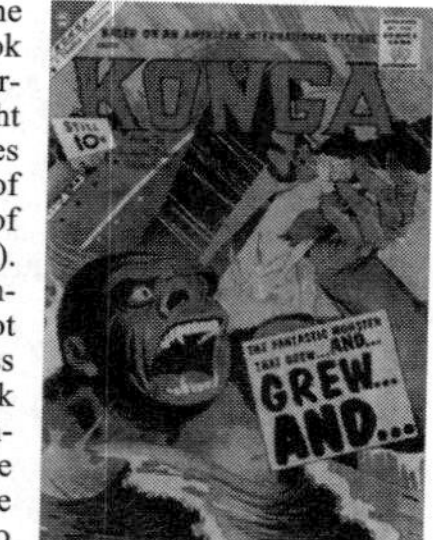

Steve Ditko (1927-) adapted the 1961 Gorgo film to comic-book form; that story features a prehistoric sea monster captured and brought to London with resultant scenes reminiscent of those at the end of King Kong (1933) and of some of the aspects of Godzilla (1956). Though Gorgo was relatively run-of-the-mill (though with a nice plot twist toward the end), the success of the Steve Ditko comic book (where Gorgo's adventures continued long after what happened in the film) led Charlton to go for a Steve Ditko adaptation of Konga (also 1961). In that film, a scientist who's managed to grow plants to a huge size turns a cute chimpanzee into a giant, killer monster. Once again, the series continues long after events that occur in the film. (Note: Not all issues of the comic book contain Ditko art.) — Maggie

1 ❑ ca. 1960 Cover: 0.10 **NM** value: **60.00**
• **CGC:** 2 graded, best 8.5
2 ❑ Aug 1961 Cover: 0.12 **NM** value: **42.00**
• **CGC:** 1 graded, best 7.5
3 ❑ Oct 1961 Cover: 0.12 **NM** value: **30.00**
• **CGC:** 1 graded, best 7.0
4 ❑ Dec 1961 Cover: 0.12 **NM** value: **30.00**
• **CGC:** 1 graded, best 9.0
5 ❑ Mar 1962 Cover: 0.12 **NM** value: **22.00**
• **CGC:** 3 graded, best 9.4
6 ❑ May 1962 Cover: 0.12 **NM** value: **22.00**
7 ❑ Jul 1962 Cover: 0.12 **NM** value: **22.00**
8 ❑ Sep 1962 Cover: 0.12 **NM** value: **22.00**
9 ❑ Nov 1962 Cover: 0.12 **NM** value: **22.00**
10 ❑ Jan 1963 Cover: 0.12 **NM** value: **22.00**
11 ❑ Mar 1963 Cover: 0.12 **NM** value: **15.00**
12 ❑ May 1963 Cover: 0.12 **NM** value: **15.00**
13 ❑ Jul 1963 Cover: 0.12 **NM** value: **15.00**
14 ❑ Sep 1963 Cover: 0.12 **NM** value: **15.00**
15 ❑ Nov 1963 Cover: 0.12 **NM** value: **15.00**
• **CGC:** 1 graded, best 6.0
16 ❑ Jan 1964 Cover: 0.12 **NM** value: **15.00**
17 ❑ Mar 1964 Cover: 0.12 **NM** value: **15.00**
18 ❑ Jun 1964 Cover: 0.12 **NM** value: **15.00**
19 ❑ Sep 1964 Cover: 0.12 **NM** value: **15.00**
20 ❑ Dec 1965 Cover: 0.12 **NM** value: **15.00**
21 ❑ Feb 1965 Cover: 0.12 **NM** value: **13.00**
22 ❑ May 1965 Cover: 0.12 **NM** value: **13.00**
23 ❑ Nov 1965 Cover: 0.12 **NM** value: **13.00**

KONGA'S REVENGE — Charlton

1 ❑ ca. 1963 Cover: 0.12 **NM** value: **9.00**
• Reprints Konga's Revenge #3; Published out of sequence
2 ❑ ca. 1963 Cover: 0.12 **NM** value: **14.00**
3 ❑ ca. 1963 Cover: 0.12 **NM** value: **14.00**

KONG THE UNTAMED — DC

1 ❑ Jul 1975 Cover: 0.25 **NM** value: **4.00**
• **CGC:** 8 graded, best 9.4
A: Alfredo Alcala; Bernie Wrightson(cover) **W:** Jack Oleck ★ Origin of Kong the Untamed.
2 ❑ Sep 1975 Cover: 0.25 **NM** value: **3.00**
W: Jack Oleck
3 ❑ Nov 1975 Cover: 0.25 **NM** value: **3.00**
The Caves of Doom **A:** Alfredo Alcala **W:** Gerry Conway; Jack Oleck
4 ❑ Jan 1976 Cover: 0.25 **NM** value: **3.00**
5 ❑ Mar 1976 Cover: 0.25 **NM** value: **3.00**
final issue.

KONNY AND CZU — Antarctic

1 ❑ Sep 1994, b&w Cover: 2.75 **NM** value: **Cover or less**
Data3 **A:** Matt Howarth; D.M. Kister **W:** Matt Howarth; D.M. Kister
2 ❑ Nov 1994, b&w Cover: 2.75 **NM** value: **Cover or less**
A: Matt Howarth; D.M. Kister **W:** Matt Howarth; D.M. Kister
3 ❑ Jan 1995, b&w Cover: 2.75 **NM** value: **Cover or less**
Totally an Alien Experience! **A:** Matt Howarth; D.M. Kister **W:** Matt Howarth; D.M. Kister
4 ❑ Mar 1995, b&w Cover: 2.75 **NM** value: **Cover or less**
A: Matt Howarth; D.M. Kister **W:** Matt Howarth; D.M. Kister

KOOLAU THE LEPER (JACK LONDON'S...) — Tome Press

1 ❑ b&w Cover: 2.50 **NM** value: **Cover or less**

KOOSH KINS — Archie

1 ❑ Oct 1991 Cover: 1.00 **NM** value: **Cover or less**
Party Time Dudes; Pardon the Eruption; Earth Mirth! **A:** Stan Goldberg **W:** Mike Pellowski
2 ❑ Oct 1991 Cover: 1.00 **NM** value: **Cover or less**
3 ❑ Dec 1991 Cover: 1.00 **NM** value: **Cover or less**
4 ❑ Feb 1992 Cover: 1.00 **NM** value: **Cover or less**

K.O. PUNCH — E.C.

1 ❑ ca. 1952 Cover: 0.10 **NM** value: **750.00**
• **CGC:** 1 graded, best 9.2

KORAK, SON OF TARZAN — Gold Key

Brave Korak, much like his father, can talk to the animals and is leery of civilization. A more youthful version of Tarzan, with greater appeal to younger readers, Korak frequently traveled beyond the jungle and into the outside world. No matter where he went, adventure was sure to follow.

This series began as a Gold Key title. In 1972, it switched over to DC with issue #46. It then continued until issue #60, when it was retitled The Tarzan Family.

Back-ups included adaptations of Burroughs' Carson of Venus stories and a continuation of his one-shot Beyond the Farthest Star.

1 ❑ Jan 1964 Cover: 0.12 **NM** value: **35.00**
• **CGC:** 2 graded, best 9.0
• Gold Key begins publishing **A:** Russ Manning
2 ❑ Mar 1964 Cover: 0.12 **NM** value: **25.00**
• **CGC:** 1 graded, best 7.0
A: Russ Manning
3 ❑ May 1964 Cover: 0.12 **NM** value: **25.00**
• **CGC:** 2 graded, best 9.0
A: Russ Manning
4 ❑ Aug 1964 Cover: 0.12 **NM** value: **25.00**
• **CGC:** 1 graded, best 7.5
A: Russ Manning
5 ❑ Oct 1964 Cover: 0.12 **NM** value: **25.00**
• **CGC:** 1 graded, best 6.0
A: Russ Manning
6 ❑ Dec 1964 Cover: 0.12 **NM** value: **20.00**
• **CGC:** 1 graded, best 7.5
A: Russ Manning
7 ❑ Mar 1965 Cover: 0.12 **NM** value: **20.00**
Circ: Statement: **278,800** • **CGC:** 1 graded, best 7.5
A: Russ Manning
8 ❑ May 1965 Cover: 0.12 **NM** value: **20.00**
Circ: Statement: **278,800** • **CGC:** 1 graded, best 8.0
A: Russ Manning
9 ❑ Jul 1965 Cover: 0.12 **NM** value: **20.00**
Circ: Statement: **278,800** • **CGC:** 1 graded, best 7.0
A: Russ Manning
10 ❑ Sep 1965 Cover: 0.12 **NM** value: **20.00**
Circ: Statement: **278,800** • **CGC:** 1 graded, best 6.0
A: Russ Manning
11 ❑ Nov 1965 Cover: 0.12 **NM** value: **20.00**
Circ: Statement: **278,800** • **CGC:** 1 graded, best 6.5
A: Russ Manning
12 ❑ Mar 1966 Cover: 0.12 **NM** value: **16.00**
Circ: Statement: **270,923** • **CGC:** 1 graded, best 8.0
13 ❑ Jun 1966 Cover: 0.12 **NM** value: **16.00**
Circ: Statement: **270,923** • **CGC:** 1 graded, best 7.5
14 ❑ Sep 1966 Cover: 0.12 **NM** value: **16.00**
Circ: Statement: **270,923** • **CGC:** 1 graded, best 8.0
15 ❑ Dec 1966 Cover: 0.12 **NM** value: **16.00**
Circ: Statement: **270,923** • **CGC:** 1 graded, best 7.0
16 ❑ Mar 1967 Cover: 0.12 **NM** value: **16.00**
Circ: Statement: **270,050** • **CGC:** 2 graded, best 9.0
17 ❑ Jun 1967 Cover: 0.12 **NM** value: **16.00**
Circ: Statement: **270,050** • **CGC:** 1 graded, best 7.0
18 ❑ Aug 1967 Cover: 0.12 **NM** value: **16.00**
Circ: Statement: **270,050** • **CGC:** 1 graded, best 8.0
19 ❑ Oct 1967 Cover: 0.12 **NM** value: **16.00**
Circ: Statement: **270,050** • **CGC:** 1 graded, best 7.0
20 ❑ Dec 1967 Cover: 0.12 **NM** value: **16.00**
Circ: Statement: **270,050** • **CGC:** 1 graded, best 8.5
21 ❑ Feb 1968 Cover: 0.12 **NM** value: **13.00**
• **CGC:** 1 graded, best 8.0
A: Russ Manning
22 ❑ Apr 1968 Cover: 0.12 **NM** value: **13.00**
• **CGC:** 1 graded, best 9.2
23 ❑ Jun 1968 Cover: 0.12 **NM** value: **13.00**
24 ❑ Aug 1968 Cover: 0.12 **NM** value: **13.00**
25 ❑ Oct 1968 Cover: 0.15 **NM** value: **13.00**
26 ❑ Dec 1968 Cover: 0.15 **NM** value: **13.00**
27 ❑ Feb 1969 Cover: 0.15 **NM** value: **13.00**
28 ❑ Apr 1969 Cover: 0.15 **NM** value: **13.00**
29 ❑ Jun 1969 Cover: 0.15 **NM** value: **13.00**
30 ❑ Aug 1969 Cover: 0.15 **NM** value: **13.00**
31 ❑ Oct 1969 Cover: 0.15 **NM** value: **8.00**
32 ❑ Dec 1969 Cover: 0.15 **NM** value: **8.00**
33 ❑ Jan 1970 Cover: 0.15 **NM** value: **8.00**
34 ❑ Mar 1970 Cover: 0.15 **NM** value: **8.00**
35 ❑ May 1970 Cover: 0.15 **NM** value: **8.00**
36 ❑ Jul 1970 Cover: 0.15 **NM** value: **8.00**
37 ❑ Sep 1970 Cover: 0.15 **NM** value: **8.00**
38 ❑ Nov 1970 Cover: 0.15 **NM** value: **8.00**
39 ❑ Jan 1971 Cover: 0.15 **NM** value: **8.00**
40 ❑ Mar 1971 Cover: 0.15 **NM** value: **8.00**
41 ❑ May 1971 Cover: 0.15 **NM** value: **8.00**
42 ❑ Jul 1971 Cover: 0.15 **NM** value: **6.00**
43 ❑ Sep 1971 Cover: 0.15 **NM** value: **6.00**
44 ❑ Nov 1971 Cover: 0.15 **NM** value: **6.00**
45 ❑ Jan 1972 Cover: 0.15 **NM** value: **6.00**
Circ: Statement: **168,381**
46 ❑ May 1972 Cover: 0.25 **NM** value: **4.00**
Circ: Statement: **168,381** • **CGC:** 1 graded, best 5.0
• continues Gold Key numbering; DC begins publishing
47 ❑ Jul 1972 Cover: 0.20 **NM** value: **2.00**
Circ: Statement: **168,381**
48 ❑ Sep 1972 Cover: 0.20 **NM** value: **2.00**
Circ: Statement: **168,381**
49 ❑ Nov 1972 Cover: 0.20 **NM** value: **2.00**
Circ: Statement: **168,381**
50 ❑ Feb 1973 Cover: 0.20 **NM** value: **2.00**
51 ❑ Apr 1973 Cover: 0.20 **NM** value: **2.00**
• Has 1972 Statement; avg total paid circ 168,381
52 ❑ Jul 1973 Cover: 0.20 **NM** value: **2.00**
53 ❑ Sep 1973 Cover: 0.20 **NM** value: **2.00**
• Carson of Venus back-up **C:** Joe Kubert
54 ❑ Nov 1973 Cover: 0.20 **NM** value: **2.00**
• Carson of Venus back-up **C:** Joe Kubert
55 ❑ Jan 1974 Cover: 0.20 **NM** value: **2.00**
Circ: Statement: **183,647**
• Carson of Venus back-up **C:** Joe Kubert
56 ❑ Mar 1974 Cover: 0.20 **NM** value: **2.00**
Circ: Statement: **183,647**
• Carson of Venus back-up **C:** Joe Kubert
57 ❑ Jun 1975 Cover: 0.25 **NM** value: **2.00**
Circ: Statement: **103,000**
The Most Endangered Species • Has 1974 Statement (but only two issues published during year); avg total paid circ 183,647 **A:** Rudy Florese **W:** Robert Kanigher
58 ❑ Aug 1975 Cover: 0.25 **NM** value: **2.00**
Circ: Statement: **103,000**
59 ❑ Oct 1975 Cover: 0.25 **NM** value: **2.00**
Circ: Statement: **103,000**
• Series continued in Tarzan Family #60

KORG: 70,000 B.C. — Charlton

This title derived from the live-action Hanna-Barbera prehistoric-kid television show (1974-75) and stars Korg, a prehistoric man who leads a clan of cave dwellers. In its everyday life, this clan battles incredible dangers just to survive. It must hunt great animals for food, brave iceflows and other natural disasters, and fight huge prehistoric monsters of all kinds. Occasionally, the band encounters other men — including some from strangely advanced civilizations.

Korg's world has a feel of fantasy to it, since the monsters that inhabit

Other grades: Multiply prices above by **1.5 for Mint • 2/3 for Very Fine • 1/3 for Fine • 1/5 for Very Good • 1/8 for Good**

it are so large and powerful — especially in comparison to Korg and his band. That makes their struggle seem all the more heroic, when they win, surviving to face some other danger tomorrow.

1 ❑ May 1975 Cover: 0.25 **NM** value: **8.00**
2 ❑ Aug 1975 Cover: 0.25 **NM** value: **5.00**
3 ❑ Oct 1975 Cover: 0.25 **NM** value: **5.00**
📖 Land Of Milk And Honey **A:** Pat Boyette **W:** Pat Boyette
4 ❑ Dec 1975 Cover: 0.25 **NM** value: **5.00**
5 ❑ Feb 1976 Cover: 0.25 **NM** value: **5.00**
6 ❑ May 1976 Cover: 0.25 **NM** value: **5.00**
7 ❑ Jul 1976 Cover: 0.25 **NM** value: **5.00**
final issue.
8 ❑ Sep 1976 Cover: 0.25 **NM** value: **5.00**
9 ❑ Nov 1976 Cover: 0.25 **NM** value: **5.00**

KORVUS — Arrow
1 ❑ Cover: 2.95 **NM** value: **Cover or less**
2 ❑ Cover: 2.95 **NM** value: **Cover or less**
3 ❑ Spr 1998 Cover: 2.95 **NM** value: **Cover or less**

KORVUS (VOL. 2) — Arrow
1 ❑ Fal 1998 Cover: 2.95 **NM** value: **Cover or less**
2 ❑ Cover: 2.95 **NM** value: **Cover or less**

KOSMIC KAT — Image
1 ❑ Aug 1999 Cover: 2.95 **NM** value: **Cover or less**

KOSMIC KAT ACTIVITY BOOK — Image
1 ❑ Aug 1999 Cover: 2.95 **NM** value: **Cover or less**
Circ: Diamd. preorders: **3,122**
A: Steve Buccellato; Lesean Thomas; Mike O'Hare **W:** Robert Napton; Karl Altstaetter; Brian Buccellato ★ Origin of Kosmic Kat.

KRAZY & IGNATZ: THE KOMPLETE KAT KOMICS — Eclipse
Bk 1❑ ca. 1988, b&w Cover: 9.95 **NM** value: **Cover or less**
• strip reprints
Bk 2❑ b&w Cover: 9.95 **NM** value: **Cover or less**
• strip reprints
Bk 3❑ b&w Cover: 9.95 **NM** value: **Cover or less**
• strip reprints
Bk 4❑ b&w Cover: 9.95 **NM** value: **Cover or less**
• strip reprints
Bk 5❑ b&w Cover: 9.95 **NM** value: **Cover or less**
• strip reprints
Bk 6❑ b&w Cover: 9.95 **NM** value: **Cover or less**
• strip reprints
Bk 7❑ Cover: 14.95 **NM** value: **Cover or less**
• some color
Bk 8❑ b&w Cover: 9.95 **NM** value: **Cover or less**
Bk 9❑ b&w Cover: 9.95 **NM** value: **Cover or less**

KRAZY KAT — Gold Key
1 ❑ Jan 1964 Cover: 0.12 **NM** value: **15.00**
• **CGC:** 1 graded, best 7.0

KRAZY KAT (DELL) — Dell
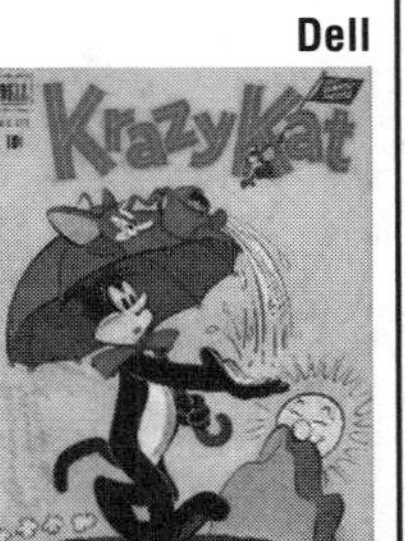

The classic comic strip was written and drawn by George Herriman (1880-1944) and began showing up as a character in The Dingbat Family, finally evolving to its own, solo identity in 1911. Many of Herriman's most devoted admirers were highly educated, and the strips themselves, while seeming to involve little more than the slapstick antics of Ignatz Mouse trying to bean Krazy Kat with a brick, were filled with inventive dialogue and wild, changing environments.

The strip ended with Herriman's death, but Dell for some reason decided to try to make a go of a run-of-the-mill version seven years later with none of Herriman's artistry, either of picture or text. Luckily, actual Kat reprint volumes have been put together in more recent years. — Maggie

1 ❑ ca. 1951 Cover: 0.10 **NM** value: **40.00**
2 ❑ ca. 1952 Cover: 0.10 **NM** value: **25.00**
3 ❑ ca. 1952 Cover: 0.10 **NM** value: **25.00**
4 ❑ ca. 1952 Cover: 0.10 **NM** value: **25.00**
5 ❑ ca. 1952 Cover: 0.10 **NM** value: **25.00**

KRAZY KOMICS — Timely
A spectacularly unappetizing entry in the world of "funny-animal comics" was Krazy Komics, which, for many of the covers of its first several issues featured the exploits of the derby-wearing Toughy Tomcat. He menaced characters like Ziggy Pig and Silly Seal (who would have been of an unidentifiable species had he not been named) with a buzzsaw, a cannon, a hatchet, and so on. Toughy's prey, initially sweating over his desire to eat them, eventually began to turn the tables on him, and the animal world took on a more positive aspect, as characters like Krazy Krow and Super Rabbit joined the mix of characters. — Maggie

1 ❑ Jul 1942 Cover: 0.10 **NM** value: **300.00**
2 ❑ Sep 1942 Cover: 0.10 **NM** value: **200.00**
3 ❑ Nov 1942 Cover: 0.10 **NM** value: **150.00**
4 ❑ 1943 Cover: 0.10 **NM** value: **150.00**
5 ❑ 1943 Cover: 0.10 **NM** value: **150.00**
6 ❑ 1943 Cover: 0.10 **NM** value: **125.00**
7 ❑ 1943 Cover: 0.10 **NM** value: **125.00**
8 ❑ Jun 1943 Cover: 0.10 **NM** value: **125.00**
• **CGC:** 1 graded, best 8.5
9 ❑ Cover: 0.10 **NM** value: **125.00**
10 ❑ 1943 Cover: 0.10 **NM** value: **100.00**
11 ❑ 1943 Cover: 0.10 **NM** value: **100.00**
12 ❑ 1944 Cover: 0.10 **NM** value: **100.00**
13 ❑ 1944 Cover: 0.10 **NM** value: **75.00**
14 ❑ 1944 Cover: 0.10 **NM** value: **75.00**
15 ❑ 1944 Cover: 0.10 **NM** value: **75.00**
16 ❑ 1945 Cover: 0.10 **NM** value: **50.00**
17 ❑ 1945 Cover: 0.10 **NM** value: **50.00**
18 ❑ 1945 Cover: 0.10 **NM** value: **50.00**
19 ❑ 1945 Cover: 0.10 **NM** value: **50.00**
20 ❑ Jan 1946 Cover: 0.10 **NM** value: **30.00**
21 ❑ 1946 Cover: 0.10 **NM** value: **30.00**
22 ❑ 1946 Cover: 0.10 **NM** value: **30.00**
23 ❑ 1946 Cover: 0.10 **NM** value: **25.00**
24 ❑ 1946 Cover: 0.10 **NM** value: **25.00**
25 ❑ 1947 Cover: 0.10 **NM** value: **25.00**
26 ❑ 1947 Cover: 0.10 **NM** value: **25.00**

KRAZY KROW — Marvel
1 ❑ Sum 1945 Cover: 0.10 **NM** value: **150.00**
• **CGC:** 1 graded, best 7.5
2 ❑ Fal 1945 Cover: 0.10 **NM** value: **100.00**
3 ❑ Win 1945 Cover: 0.10 **NM** value: **100.00**

KRAZY LIFE — Fox
1 ❑ ca. 1945 Cover: 0.10 **NM** value: **125.00**
• **CGC:** 1 graded, best 7.0

KREE-SKRULL WAR STARRING THE AVENGERS, THE — Marvel
1 ❑ Sep 1983 Cover: 2.50 **NM** value: **3.00**
📖 The Kree-Skull War, Part 1; The Kree-Skull War, Part 2; The Kree-Skull War, Part 3; The Kree-Skull War, Part 4; The Kree-Skull War, Part 5; The Kree-Skull War, Part 6 **A:** John Buscema; Neal Adams; Walt Simonson **W:** Alan Zelentz; Roy Thomas
2 ❑ Oct 1983 Cover: 2.50 **NM** value: **3.00**
📖 The Kree-Skull War, Part 7; The Kree-Skull War, Part 8; The Kree-Skull War, Part 9 **A:** John Buscema; Neal Adams **W:** Roy Thomas

KREMEN — Grey Productions
1 ❑ Cover: 2.50 **NM** value: **Cover or less**
2 ❑ Cover: 2.50 **NM** value: **Cover or less**
3 ❑ Cover: 2.50 **NM** value: **Cover or less**

KREY — Gauntlet
1 ❑ b&w Cover: 2.50 **NM** value: **Cover or less**
2 ❑ b&w Cover: 2.50 **NM** value: **Cover or less**
3 ❑ b&w Cover: 2.50 **NM** value: **Cover or less**

KROFFT SUPERSHOW — Gold Key
1 ❑ Apr 1978 Cover: 0.35 **NM** value: **6.00**
2 ❑ May 1978 Cover: 0.35 **NM** value: **4.00**
3 ❑ Jun 1978 Cover: 0.35 **NM** value: **4.00**
4 ❑ Sep 1978 Cover: 0.35 **NM** value: **4.00**
📖 Some Party; Bigfoot and Wildboy: Earth Tremors; Wonderbug: Waterbug;
5 ❑ Nov 1978 Cover: 0.35 **NM** value: **4.00**
6 ❑ Jan 1979 Cover: 0.35 **NM** value: **4.00**

KRULL — Marvel
1 ❑ Nov 1983 Cover: 0.60 **NM** value: **1.25**
Photo cover.
2 ❑ Dec 1983 Cover: 0.60 **NM** value: **1.25**
A: Bret Blevins **W:** David Michelinie

KRUSTY COMICS — Bongo
1 ❑ ca. 1995 Cover: 2.25 **NM** value: **2.50**
Circ: CapCity orders: **16,075**
📖 The Rise and Fall of Krustyland, Part 1 **A:** Cary Schramm; Phil Ortiz; Mili Smythe; Shaun Cashman **W:** Jamie Angell
2 ❑ ca. 1995 Cover: 2.25 **NM** value: **2.50**
Circ: CapCity orders: **12,825**
📖 The Rise and Fall of Krustyland, Part 2 **A:** Cary Schramm **W:** Jamie Angell
3 ❑ ca. 1995 Cover: 2.25 **NM** value: **2.50**
Circ: CapCity orders: **12,100**
📖 The Rise and Fall of Krustyland, Part 3 **A:** Cary Schramm; Phil Ortiz; Shaun Cashman **W:** Jamie Angell

KRYPTON CHRONICLES — DC
1 ❑ Sep 1981 Cover: 0.50 **NM** value: **1.50**
• **CGC:** 3 graded, best 9.6
📖 The Search For Superman's Roots! **A:** Curt Swan **W:** E. Nelson Bridwell ★ Appearance of Superman.
2 ❑ Oct 1981 Cover: 0.60 **NM** value: **1.50**
A: Curt Swan ★ Appearance of Black Flame.
3 ❑ Nov 1981 Cover: 0.60 **NM** value: **1.50**
A: Curt Swan ★ Origin of name of Kal-El.

KULL AND THE BARBARIANS — Marvel
1 ❑ May 1975, b&w Cover: 1.00 **NM** value: **5.00**
• magazine. 📖 A King Comes Riding; The Shadow Kingdom; The Valley of the Worm; (text with illustrations) • reprinted from Kull the Conqueror #1 and 2, Supernatural Thrillers #3
2 ❑ Jul 1975, b&w Cover: 1.00 **NM** value: **3.00**
• magazine. 📖 Teeth of the Dragon; The Hills of the Dead; Red Sonja, She-Devil with a Sword; Blackmark vs. the Mind Demons
3 ❑ Sep 1975, b&w Cover: 1.00 **NM** value: **4.00**
• magazine. 📖 The Omen in the Skull; The Day of the Sword; Into the Silent City; Solomon Kane (text) ★ Origin of Red Sonja.

KULL IN 3-D — Blackthorne
1 ❑ Cover: 2.50 **NM** value: **Cover or less**
Circ: CapCity orders: **1,100**
2 ❑ Cover: 2.50 **NM** value: **Cover or less**

KULL THE CONQUEROR (1ST SERIES) — Marvel
Marvel launched Kull in 1971, a year after making a hit with Robert E. Howard's better-known swordsman, Conan the Barbarian. Both characters were barbarians who would slay kings to become kings themselves. Whereas Conan did this toward the end of his life (see King Conan), Kull's adventures really begin when he slew a tyrant so that he might claim the Topaz Throne of fabled Atlantis.

Kull rules in a world that is still young, and which the old gods have not quite departed. Chief among his enemies are the shape-shifting snake men, descendants of the snake gods who once ruled the world. Luckily, Kull has help in fighting them, including his trusted friend (and sometimes rival), Brule the Spear-Slayer, a Pictish savage.

The series changed names with issue #11, becoming "Kull the Destroyer."

Marvel published several Kull series in the 1970s, so careful examination of the indicia is necessary to determine which series is which.

1 ❑ Jun 1971 Cover: 0.15 **NM** value: **8.00**
• **CGC:** 11 graded, best 9.6
📖 A King Comes Riding! **A:** Wally Wood; Ross Andru **W:** Roy Thomas ★ Origin of Kull. ★ 1st Appearance of Brule the Spear-Slayer.
2 ❑ Sep 1971 Cover: 0.15 **NM** value: **4.00**
• **CGC:** 1 graded, best 9.4
📖 The Shadows Kingdom **A:** John Severin; Marie Severin **W:** Roy Thomas
3 ❑ Jul 1972 Cover: 0.20 **NM** value: **3.50**
• **CGC:** 1 graded, best 8.5
📖 The Death-Dance of Thulsa Doom! **A:** John Severin; Marie Severin **W:** Roy Thomas ★ Appearance of Thulsa Doom.
4 ❑ Sep 1972 Cover: 0.20 **NM** value: **2.50**
• **CGC:** 2 graded, best 9.4
📖 The Night of the Red Slayers! **A:** John Severin
5 ❑ Nov 1972 Cover: 0.20 **NM** value: **2.50**
📖 A Kingdom By the Sea! **A:** John Severin; Marie Severin **W:** Gerry Conway
6 ❑ Jan 1973 Cover: 0.20 **NM** value: **2.50**
📖 The Lurker Beneath the Earth! **A:** John Severin; Marie Severin **W:** Gerry Conway
7 ❑ Mar 1973 Cover: 0.20 **NM** value: **2.50**
📖 Delcardes' Cat
8 ❑ May 1973 Cover: 0.20 **NM** value: **2.50**
📖 Wolf's-Head!
9 ❑ Jul 1973 Cover: 0.20 **NM** value: **2.50**
📖 The Scorpion God!
10 ❑ Sep 1973 Cover: 0.20 **NM** value: **2.50**
📖 Swords of the White Queen! • Continued as "Kull the Destroyer"

KULL THE CONQUEROR (2ND SERIES) — Marvel
1 ❑ Dec 1982 Cover: 2.00 **NM** value: **2.50**
📖 The Power And The Kingdom • Brule **A:** John Buscema **W:** Alan Zelentz
2 ❑ Mar 1983 Cover: 2.00 **NM** value: **Cover or less**
📖 The Blood of Kings! • Misareena **A:** John Bolton **W:** Doug Moench

KULL THE CONQUEROR (3RD SERIES) — Marvel
1 ❑ May 1983 Cover: 1.25 **NM** value: **2.00**
• Iraina **A:** John Buscema; Joe Jusko(cover)
2 ❑ Jul 1983 Cover: 1.25 **NM** value: **1.75**
A: John Buscema
3 ❑ Dec 1983 Cover: 1.00 **NM** value: **1.75**
A: John Buscema
4 ❑ Feb 1984 Cover: 1.00 **NM** value: **1.50**
A: John Buscema
5 ❑ Aug 1984 Cover: 0.60 **NM** value: **1.50**
6 ❑ Oct 1984 Cover: 0.60 **NM** value: **1.25**
7 ❑ Dec 1984 Cover: 0.60 **NM** value: **1.25**
8 ❑ Feb 1985 Cover: 0.60 **NM** value: **1.25**
9 ❑ Apr 1985 Cover: 0.65 **NM** value: **1.25**
10 ❑ Jun 1985 Cover: 0.65 **NM** value: **1.25**
Circ: CapCity orders: **5,600**
final issue.

KULL THE DESTROYER — Marvel
11 ❑ Nov 1973 Cover: 0.20 **NM** value: **2.00**
• **CGC:** 1 graded, best 9.6
📖 King Kull Must Die! • Continued from Kull the Conqueror (1st Series) #10
12 ❑ Jan 1974 Cover: 0.20 **NM** value: **2.00**
📖 Moon Of Blood! **A:** Mike Ploog **W:** Steve Englehart
13 ❑ Mar 1974 Cover: 0.20 **NM** value: **2.00**
📖 Torches From Hell! **A:** Mike Ploog **W:** Steve Englehart
14 ❑ May 1974 Cover: 0.25 **NM** value: **2.00**
📖 The Thing from the Black Belfry! **A:** Jim Starlin; Mike Ploog
15 ❑ Aug 1974 Cover: 0.25 **NM** value: **2.00**
📖 Wings of the Night Beast! • series goes on hiatus **A:** Steve Ditko; Mike Ploog
16 ❑ Aug 1976 Cover: 0.25 **NM** value: **2.00**
📖 The Tiger In The Moon **A:** Ed Hannigan **W:** Roy Thomas; Doug Moench

CGC-graded: Multiply prices above by **33 for 9.9 M • 16 for 9.8 NM/M • 7 for 9.6 NM+ • 5 for 9.4 NM • 2.5 for 9.2 NM- • 1.5 for 9.0 VF/NM**

17 ❑ Oct 1976 Cover: 0.30 **NM** value: **2.00**
A: Alfredo Alcala
18 ❑ Dec 1976 Cover: 0.30 **NM** value: **2.00**
A: Alfredo Alcala
19 ❑ Feb 1977 Cover: 0.30 **NM** value: **2.00**
A: Alfredo Alcala
20 ❑ Apr 1977 Cover: 0.30 **NM** value: **2.00**
A: Alfredo Alcala
21 ❑ Jun 1977 Cover: 0.30 **NM** value: **2.00**
22 ❑ Aug 1977 Cover: 0.30 **NM** value: **2.00**
23 ❑ Oct 1977 Cover: 0.30 **NM** value: **2.00**
24 ❑ Dec 1977 Cover: 0.35 **NM** value: **2.00**
25 ❑ Feb 1978 Cover: 0.35 **NM** value: **2.00**
26 ❑ Apr 1978 Cover: 0.35 **NM** value: **2.00**
27 ❑ Jun 1978 Cover: 0.35 **NM** value: **2.00**
28 ❑ Aug 1978 Cover: 0.35 **NM** value: **2.00**
29 ❑ Oct 1978 Cover: 0.35 **NM** value: **2.00**
final issue. ★ Appearance of Thulsa Doom.

KULL: THE VALE OF SHADOW — Marvel

Bk 1❑ Cover: 6.95 **NM** value: **Cover or less**

KUNOICHI — Lightning

1 ❑ Sep 1996 Cover: 3.00 **NM** value: **Cover or less**
• also contains Sinja: Resurrection #1; indicia is for Sinja: Resurrection

KYRA — Elsewhere

From Sheena, Queen of the Jungle, to Nyoka the Jungle Girl, to Shanna the She-Devil, to Rima, the Jungle Girl, the female version of Tarzan has been a recurring figure in comics. Although their origins and backgrounds may have superficial variations, all are lithe, slim, and feminine.

Kyra represents a departure from the standard. Debuting during the black-and-white comics glut mid-1980s when female body builders began to achieve notoriety, creator Robin Ator tapped this new paradigm as inspiration. Kyra is depicted as a large, well-defined, solidly muscled woman. To emphasize the theme, the back cover features photos of female body builders.

1 ❑ b&w Cover: 1.50 **NM** value: **2.00**
2 ❑ Spr 1986, b&w Cover: 1.75 **NM** value: **2.00**
3 ❑ Sum 1986, b&w Cover: 1.75 **NM** value: **2.00**
4 ❑ Dec 1986 Cover: 1.75 **NM** value: **2.00**
📖 Sister Transistor **A:** Robin Ator **W:** Robin Ator
5 ❑ Jun 1987 Cover: 1.75 **NM** value: **2.00**
📖 Leaf in a Furnace! **A:** Robin Ator **W:** Robin Ator
6 ❑ 1987 Cover: 1.75 **NM** value: **2.00**
Bk 1❑ b&w Cover: 6.95 **NM** value: **Cover or less**

K-Z COMICS PRESENTS — K-Z

1 ❑ Jun 1985 Cover: 1.50 **NM** value: **Cover or less**
📖 Colt; Genesis, Part 1 **A:** Dan Berger **W:** Tom Zjaba

LA BLUE GIRL — CPM / Bare Bear

All issues are adults only.

1 ❑ Jul 1996, b&w Cover: 2.95 **NM** value: **Cover or less**
wraparound cover. **A:** Matt Lunsford **W:** Megumi Ichiyanagi; Toshio Maeda
2 ❑ Aug 1996, b&w Cover: 2.95 **NM** value: **Cover or less**
A: Matt Lunsford **W:** Megumi Ichiyanagi; Toshio Maeda
3 ❑ Sep 1996, b&w Cover: 2.95 **NM** value: **Cover or less**
Circ: Diamd. preorders: **6,530**
A: Matt Lunsford **W:** Megumi Ichiyanagi; Toshio Maeda
4 ❑ Oct 1996, b&w Cover: 2.95 **NM** value: **Cover or less**
Circ: Diamd. preorders: **6,007**
A: Matt Lunsford **W:** Megumi Ichiyanagi; Toshio Maeda
5 ❑ Nov 1996, b&w Cover: 2.95 **NM** value: **Cover or less**
Circ: Diamd. preorders: **5,259**
A: Matt Lunsford **W:** Megumi Ichiyanagi; Toshio Maeda
6 ❑ Dec 1996 Cover: 2.95 **NM** value: **Cover or less**
Circ: Diamd. preorders: **4,956**
A: Matt Lunsford **W:** Megumi Ichiyanagi; Toshio Maeda
7 ❑ Jan 1997 Cover: 2.95 **NM** value: **Cover or less**
Circ: Diamd. preorders: **5,026**
A: Matt Lunsford **W:** Megumi Ichiyanagi; Toshio Maeda
8 ❑ Feb 1997 Cover: 2.95 **NM** value: **Cover or less**
Circ: Diamd. preorders: **4,963**
A: Matt Lunsford **W:** Megumi Ichiyanagi; Toshio Maeda
9 ❑ Mar 1997 Cover: 2.95 **NM** value: **Cover or less**
Circ: Diamd. preorders: **4,786**
A: Matt Lunsford **W:** Megumi Ichiyanagi; Toshio Maeda
10 ❑ Apr 1997 Cover: 2.95 **NM** value: **Cover or less**
Circ: Diamd. preorders: **5,028**
A: Matt Lunsford **W:** Megumi Ichiyanagi; Toshio Maeda
11 ❑ May 1997 Cover: 2.95 **NM** value: **Cover or less**
Circ: Diamd. preorders: **4,586**
A: Matt Lunsford **W:** Megumi Ichiyanagi; Toshio Maeda
12 ❑ Jun 1997 Cover: 2.95 **NM** value: **Cover or less**
Circ: Diamd. preorders: **4,791**
A: Matt Lunsford **W:** Megumi Ichiyanagi; Toshio Maeda
Bk 1❑ Cover: 12.95 **NM** value: **Cover or less**
• Graphic novel **A:** Matt Lunsford **W:** Megumi Ichiyanagi; Toshio Maeda

📖 indicates **Story Title** or **Storyline** information.
★ indicates **Character Appearance** information.
W = Writer • A = Artist • C = Cover Artist

LABMAN — Image

Rudy Coby is the self-proclaimed "hippest magician in the world." Certainly, he's one of the more unusual ones. Distinctive in his trademark hairdo and glasses, he takes on the persona of "Labman," a scientific wizard, magician, and crimefighter. His television special, which premiered on the Fox network in 1996, combined stage magic, showbiz razzle-dazzle, and cartoony fun into one entertaining spectacle.

It's only natural that such a comic character would make his way to comic books. In this three-issue series, readers learn how a mild-mannered, licensed scientist discovered a four-legged atomic chicken and stumbled onto the path of super-powered greatness.

1 ❑ Nov 1996 Cover: 3.50 **NM** value: **Cover or less**
Circ: Diamd. preorders: **12,728**
📖 Who Is Labman? **A:** Andy Suriano; Mike Allred; Bill Morrison; Chris Ecker; Marc Gabanna **W:** Rudy Coby ★ 1st Appearance of Labman.
1/A ❑ Nov 1996 Cover: 3.50 **NM** value: **Cover or less**
alternate cover. 📖 Who Is Labman? **A:** Andy Suriano; Mike Allred; Bill Morrison; Chris Ecker; Marc Gabanna **W:** Rudy Coby
1/B ❑ Nov 1996 Cover: 3.50 **NM** value: **Cover or less**
alternate cover. 📖 Who Is Labman? **A:** Andy Suriano; Mike Allred; Bill Morrison; Chris Ecker; Marc Gabanna **W:** Rudy Coby
1/C ❑ Nov 1996 Cover: 3.50 **NM** value: **Cover or less**
alternate cover. 📖 Who Is Labman? **A:** Andy Suriano; Mike Allred; Bill Morrison; Chris Ecker; Marc Gabanna **W:** Rudy Coby
2 ❑ Dec 1996 Cover: 2.95 **NM** value: **Cover or less**
Circ: Diamd. preorders: **8,312**
A: Andy Suriano **W:** Rudy Coby
3 ❑ Jan 1997 Cover: 2.95 **NM** value: **Cover or less**
Circ: Diamd. preorders: **6,897**
A: Andy Suriano **W:** Rudy Coby

LABMAN SOURCEBOOK — Image

1 ❑ Jun 1996 Cover: 2.95 **NM** value: **Cover or less**
• Limited edition giveaway from 1996 San Diego Comic-Con. **A:** Andy Suriano **W:** Rudy Coby

LABOR FORCE — Blackthorne

1 ❑ Sep 1986 Cover: 1.50 **NM** value: **Cover or less**
📖 ...But Somebody's Got to Do It! **A:** David Ammerman **W:** Greg Swan
2 ❑ Cover: 1.50 **NM** value: **Cover or less**
3 ❑ Cover: 1.75 **NM** value: **Cover or less**
4 ❑ Cover: 1.75 **NM** value: **Cover or less**
5 ❑ Mar 1987 Cover: 1.75 **NM** value: **Cover or less**
6 ❑ Cover: 1.75 **NM** value: **Cover or less**
7 ❑ Cover: 1.75 **NM** value: **Cover or less**
8 ❑ Cover: 1.75 **NM** value: **Cover or less**

LABOR IS A PARTNER — Catechetical Guild

1 ❑ ca. 1949 **NM** value: **150.00**

LABOURS OF HERCULES, THE — Malan Classical Enterprises

1 ❑ b&w Cover: 2.95 **NM** value: **Cover or less**
No issue number. **A:** Dore

LABYRINTH OF MADNESS — TSR

1 ❑ **NM** value: **1.00**

LABYRINTH: THE MOVIE — Marvel

1 ❑ Nov 1986 Cover: 0.75 **NM** value: **1.50**
Circ: CapCity orders: **8,600**
A: John Buscema; Romeo Tanghal **W:** Sid Jacobson
2 ❑ Dec 1986 Cover: 0.75 **NM** value: **1.50**
Circ: CapCity orders: **6,600**
A: John Buscema; Romeo Tanghal **W:** Sid Jacobson
3 ❑ Jan 1987 Cover: 0.75 **NM** value: **1.50**
Circ: CapCity orders: **5,300**
A: John Buscema; Romeo Tanghal **W:** Sid Jacobson

L.A. COMICS — Los Angeles

1 ❑ Cover: 0.50 **NM** value: **3.00**
📖 L.A. is...; Mickey Rat; Hey, Boy; Harry the Hop one Wednesday; Them Black Folk; Ozzy Woman and Lotta Hipsworth in The Night Has a Thousand Eyes; Pizza Fella
2 ❑ Cover: 0.50 **NM** value: **3.00**
📖 Famous Lawmen Then,; Sargent Skywatch in Nite Timey Naughties; Dialogue in Black and White; L. A. Breakdown; Future Cop; Th' 1st L.A. Cop; The Metro Squad

LA COSA NOSTROID — Fireman

1 ❑ Mar 1996 Cover: 2.95 **NM** value: **Cover or less**
2 ❑ Jan 1997 Cover: 2.95 **NM** value: **Cover or less**
Circ: Diamd. preorders: **3,293**
3 ❑ May 1997 Cover: 2.95 **NM** value: **Cover or less**
Circ: Diamd. preorders: **3,939**
4 ❑ Jul 1997 Cover: 2.95 **NM** value: **Cover or less**
Circ: Diamd. preorders: **4,149**
5 ❑ Sep 1997 Cover: 2.95 **NM** value: **Cover or less**
Circ: Diamd. preorders: **4,253**
6 ❑ Nov 1997 Cover: 2.95 **NM** value: **Cover or less**
Circ: Diamd. preorders: **6,020**
7 ❑ Jan 1998 Cover: 2.95 **NM** value: **Cover or less**
Circ: Diamd. preorders: **4,629**

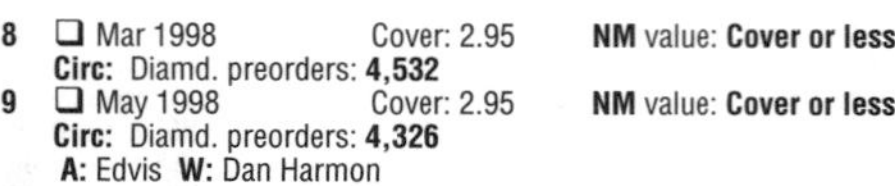

8 ❑ Mar 1998 Cover: 2.95 **NM** value: **Cover or less**
Circ: Diamd. preorders: **4,532**
9 ❑ May 1998 Cover: 2.95 **NM** value: **Cover or less**
Circ: Diamd. preorders: **4,326**
A: Edvis **W:** Dan Harmon

LADY ARCANE — Hero Graphics

1 ❑ Cover: 4.95 **NM** value: **Cover or less**
Circ: CapCity orders: **2,600**
📖 Bats! **A:** Chris Marrinan; Duval Stowers **W:** Dennis Mallonee; Colin Wales ★ Origin of Giant.
2 ❑ b&w Cover: 3.50 **NM** value: **Cover or less**
3 ❑ b&w Cover: 3.50 **NM** value: **Cover or less**
4 ❑ b&w Cover: 2.95 **NM** value: **Cover or less**
final issue. **A:** Joe Martin; Jim Valentino; Duval Stowers **W:** Dennis Mallonee

LADY CRIME — AC

1 ❑ b&w Cover: 2.75 **NM** value: **Cover or less**
📖 Murder For Pennies; The Mystery Of The Underground To Oblivion; The Aristocrat Of Crime; • Bob Powell reprints

LADY DEATH — Chaos!

Lucifer is gone, and Hell's in a state of civil war. Without the authority of The Father of Lies, demons are warring against each other, hoping to set themselves up as rulers of the underworld; and one in particular — Vulbogliagh — seems to have the best shot at the title. At least, that's the case until a certain leather-clad Mistress of the Damned with Partonesque proportions shows up, ready to claim Hell as her own. — While the pale beauty's appearance might be considered somewhat — um — gratuitous, the series is a fairly serious exploration of Hell and its many citizens.

1 ❑ Feb 1998 Cover: 2.95**NM** value: **Cover or less**
Circ: Diamd. preorders: **51,920**
📖 Wicked Ways; Wicked Ways, Part 1 **A:** Steven Hughes **W:** Brian Pulido
1/LE❑ Feb 1998 Cover: 20.00 **NM** value: **Cover or less**
no cover price. • premium limited edition. 📖 Wicked Ways, Part 1 **A:** Steven Hughes **W:** Brian Pulido
2 ❑ Mar 1998 Cover: 2.95 **NM** value: **Cover or less**
Circ: Diamd. preorders: **36,626**
A: Steven Hughes **W:** Brian Pulido
3 ❑ Apr 1998 Cover: 2.95 **NM** value: **Cover or less**
Circ: Diamd. preorders: **35,607**
A: Steven Hughes **W:** Brian Pulido
4 ❑ May 1998 Cover: 2.95 **NM** value: **Cover or less**
Circ: Diamd. preorders: **35,207**
A: Steven Hughes **W:** Brian Pulido
5 ❑ Jun 1998 Cover: 2.95 **NM** value: **Cover or less**
Circ: Diamd. preorders: **34,526**
A: Steven Hughes **W:** Brian Pulido
5/SC❑ Jun 1998 Cover: 6.00 **NM** value: **Cover or less**
variant cover. **A:** Steven Hughes **W:** Brian Pulido
6 ❑ Jul 1998 Cover: 2.95 **NM** value: **Cover or less**
Circ: Diamd. preorders: **33,510**
📖 The Harrowing **A:** Steven Hughes **W:** Brian Pulido
7 ❑ Aug 1998 Cover: 2.95 **NM** value: **Cover or less**
Circ: Diamd. preorders: **31,954**
📖 The Harrowing **A:** Steven Hughes **W:** Brian Pulido
8 ❑ Sep 1998 Cover: 2.95 **NM** value: **Cover or less**
Circ: Diamd. preorders: **30,700**
📖 The Harrowing **A:** Steven Hughes **W:** Brian Pulido
9 ❑ Oct 1998 Cover: 2.95 **NM** value: **Cover or less**
Circ: Diamd. preorders: **29,661**
📖 The Covenant **A:** Steven Hughes **W:** Brian Pulido
10 ❑ Nov 1998 Cover: 2.95 **NM** value: **Cover or less**
Circ: Diamd. preorders: **30,115**
cover says Oct, indicia says Nov. 📖 The Covenant **A:** Steven Hughes **W:** Brian Pulido ★ Appearance of Purgatori.
11 ❑ Dec 1998 Cover: 2.95 **NM** value: **Cover or less**
Circ: Diamd. preorders: **28,508**
📖 The Covenant **A:** Steven Hughes **W:** Brian Pulido
12 ❑ Jan 1999 Cover: 2.95 **NM** value: **Cover or less**
Circ: Diamd. preorders: **27,001**
📖 The Covenant
13 ❑ Feb 1999 Cover: 2.95 **NM** value: **Cover or less**
Circ: Diamd. preorders: **26,430**
📖 Inferno!
14 ❑ Mar 1999 Cover: 2.95 **NM** value: **Cover or less**
Circ: Diamd. preorders: **24,609**
📖 Inferno!
15 ❑ Apr 1999 Cover: 2.95 **NM** value: **Cover or less**
Circ: Diamd. preorders: **23,650**
📖 Inferno!
16 ❑ May 1999 Cover: 2.95 **NM** value: **Cover or less**
Circ: Diamd. preorders: **23,812**
📖 Inferno!

LADY DEATH: DARK MILLENNIUM — Chaos

1 ❑ Feb 2000 Cover: 2.95 **NM** value: **Cover or less**
Circ: Diamd. preorders: **20,835**
2 ❑ Mar 2000 Cover: 2.95 **NM** value: **Cover or less**
Circ: Diamd. preorders: **19,095**
📖 Dark Passage

LADY DEATH: DRAGON WARS — Chaos

1 ❑ Apr 1998 Cover: 2.95 **NM** value: **Cover or less**
Circ: Diamd. preorders: **29,582**

Other grades: Multiply prices above by **1.5 for Mint • 2/3 for Very Fine • 1/3 for Fine • 1/5 for Very Good • 1/8 for Good**

LADY DEATH II: BETWEEN HEAVEN & HELL Chaos!

Having reached new heights of popularity with the Lady Death mini-series, The Mistress of Hell returned in 1995 for another four-issue mini-series. Lady Death II: Between Heaven & Hell, finds her the undisputed ruler of the netherworld. This was a long fall from grace for a girl who was once the very picture of innocence — until her evil father Matthias caused her to be burned at the stake. Arriving in Hell, she eventually came to battle both her father and Lucifer for control. She eventually won, but the battle turned her into what she herself despised.

Now, the only thing that she holds onto is the idea that once she was someone good. Suddenly, however, Lady Death begins remembering her own innocent life in a darker, more evil way. Was she really ever innocent? Or was she always the tainted creature she is now?

1 ❑ Mar 1995 Cover: 2.75 **NM** value: **3.50**
Circ: CapCity orders: **51,525** • **CGC:** 16 graded, best 10.0
chromium cover. **W:** Brian Pulido ★ Origin of Lady Death.
1/A ❑ Mar 1995 **NM** value: **4.00**
• Gold edition. **W:** Brian Pulido
1/B ❑ Mar 1995 Cover: 2.75 **NM** value: **5.00**
• **CGC:** 11 graded, best 9.9
• Black velvet limited edition. **W:** Brian Pulido
1/LE❑ Mar 1995 **NM** value: **5.00**
• **CGC:** 1 graded, best 9.8
W: Brian Pulido
1-2 ❑ Cover: 2.75 **NM** value: **Cover or less**
• Commemorative edition. **W:** Brian Pulido
2 ❑ Apr 1995 Cover: 2.75 **NM** value: **3.00**
Circ: CapCity orders: **40,550** • **CGC:** 2 graded, best 9.6
W: Brian Pulido
3 ❑ May 1995 Cover: 2.75 **NM** value: **3.00**
Circ: CapCity orders: **46,950**
W: Brian Pulido
4 ❑ Jun 1995 Cover: 2.75 **NM** value: **3.00**
Circ: CapCity orders: **48,900** • **CGC:** 2 graded, best 9.6
W: Brian Pulido
4/SC❑Jun 1995 Cover: 2.75 **NM** value: **5.00**
• **CGC:** 2 graded, best 9.6
Lady Demon chase cover. **W:** Brian Pulido
Bk 1❑ Cover: 12.95 **NM** value: **Cover or less**
• collects mini-series **W:** Brian Pulido

LADY DEATH III: THE ODYSSEY Chaos!

-1 ❑ Apr 1996 Cover: 1.50 **NM** value: **Cover or less**
• Sneak Peek Preview; promotional piece for mini-series **A:** Steven Hughes **W:** Brian Pulido
1 ❑ Apr 1996 Cover: 2.95 **NM** value: **3.50**
Gold foil cover. **A:** Steven Hughes **W:** Brian Pulido
1/SC❑Apr 1996 Cover: 3.50 **NM** value: **5.00**
foil embossed cardstock wraparound cover. **A:** Steven Hughes **W:** Brian Pulido
2 ❑ May 1996 Cover: 2.95 **NM** value: **3.00**
A: Steven Hughes **W:** Brian Pulido
3 ❑ Jun 1996 Cover: 2.95 **NM** value: **3.00**
A: Steven Hughes **W:** Brian Pulido
4 ❑ Aug 1996 Cover: 2.95 **NM** value: **3.00**
A: Steven Hughes **W:** Brian Pulido
4/A ❑ Aug 1996 Cover: 2.95 **NM** value: **8.00**
alternate cover by Steven Hughes. **A:** Steven Hughes **W:** Brian Pulido
Bk 1❑ Cover: 9.95 **NM** value: **Cover or less**
A: Steven Hughes **W:** Brian Pulido

LADY DEATH IN LINGERIE Chaos!

1 ❑ Aug 1995 Cover: 2.95 **NM** value: **Cover or less**
Circ: CapCity orders: **67,625** • **CGC:** 9 graded, best 9.8
W: Brian Pulido
1/LE❑ Aug 1995 **NM** value: **8.00**
• **CGC:** 10 graded, best 10.0
no cover price. • foil-stamped leather premium edition. • limited to 10, 000 copies **W:** Brian Pulido

LADY DEATH IV: THE CRUCIBLE Chaos!

0.5 ❑ Nov 1996 **NM** value: **5.00**
• **CGC:** 12 graded, best 10.0
• Wizard promotional edition.
0.5/A❑ **NM** value: **8.00**
Cloth alternate cover. • Wizard promotional edition.
1 ❑ Nov 1996 Cover: 2.95 **NM** value: **3.00**
Circ: Diamd. preorders: **91,718** • **CGC:** 3 graded, best 9.8
1/A ❑ Nov 1996 **NM** value: **1.00**
• **CGC:** 9 graded, best 10.0
• Leather edition.
1/B ❑ Nov 1996 **NM** value: **18.00**
All silver cover. • Limited to 400; Comes with certificate of authenticity
1/SI❑ Nov 1996 Cover: 3.50 **NM** value: **Cover or less**
silver embossed cardstock wraparound cover.
2 ❑ Jan 1997 Cover: 2.95 **NM** value: **Cover or less**
Circ: Diamd. preorders: **59,338**
3 ❑ Mar 1997 Cover: 2.95 **NM** value: **Cover or less**
Circ: Diamd. preorders: **49,818**
4 ❑ Apr 1997 Cover: 2.95 **NM** value: **Cover or less**
Circ: Diamd. preorders: **51,351**
5 ❑ Aug 1997 Cover: 2.95 **NM** value: **Cover or less**
Circ: Diamd. preorders: **48,666**
5/SC❑Aug 1997 **NM** value: **5.00**
no cover price. • Nightmare Premium Edition.
6 ❑ Oct 1997 Cover: 2.95 **NM** value: **Cover or less**
Circ: Diamd. preorders: **41,936**

LADY DEATH: JUDGEMENT WAR Chaos!

1 ❑ Nov 1999 Cover: 2.95 **NM** value: **Cover or less**
Circ: Diamd. preorders: **24,236**
A: Ivan Reis **W:** Len Kaminski; Brian Pulido
2 ❑ Dec 1999 Cover: 2.95 **NM** value: **Cover or less**
Circ: Diamd. preorders: **21,448**
📖 A Device for Damnation **W:** Len Kaminski; Brian Pulido
3 ❑ Jan 2000 Cover: 2.95 **NM** value: **Cover or less**
Circ: Diamd. preorders: **21,542**
📖 A Host for Holocaust **W:** Len Kaminski; Brian Pulido

LADY DEATH: JUDGEMENT WAR PRELUDE Chaos!

1 ❑ Oct 1999 Cover: 2.95 **NM** value: **Cover or less**
Circ: Diamd. preorders: **21,338**
No issue number.

LADY DEATH (MINI-SERIES) Chaos!

0 ❑ Nov 1997 Cover: 2.95 **NM** value: **3.00**
📖 Death Becomes Her **A:** Steven Hughes **W:** Brian Pulido
0.5 ❑ **NM** value: **5.00**
• **CGC:** 1 graded, best 9.2
• Wizard mail-in promotional edition. **A:** Steven Hughes **W:** Brian Pulido
0.5/A❑ **NM** value: **8.00**
• **CGC:** 3 graded, best 9.6
• Wizard mail-in promotional edition. **A:** Steven Hughes **W:** Brian Pulido
0.5/GO❑ **NM** value: **6.00**
• Gold edition. **A:** Steven Hughes **W:** Brian Pulido
1 ❑ Jan 1994 Cover: 2.75 **NM** value: **12.00**
Circ: CapCity orders: **16,275** • **CGC:** 58 graded, best 9.9
A: Steven Hughes **W:** Brian Pulido
1/LE❑ Jan 1994 **NM** value: **15.00**
A: Steven Hughes **W:** Brian Pulido
1-2 ❑ Feb 1994 Cover: 2.75 **NM** value: **Cover or less**
• Commemorative edition. **A:** Steven Hughes **W:** Brian Pulido
2 ❑ Feb 1994 Cover: 2.75 **NM** value: **Cover or less**
Circ: CapCity orders: **10,505** • **CGC:** 4 graded, best 9.6
A: Steven Hughes **W:** Brian Pulido
3 ❑ Mar 1994 Cover: 2.75 **NM** value: **6.00**
Circ: CapCity orders: **9,955** • **CGC:** 5 graded, best 9.8
A: Steven Hughes **W:** Brian Pulido
4 ❑ Apr 1994 Cover: 2.75 **NM** value: **4.00**
A: Steven Hughes **W:** Brian Pulido
Bk 1❑ Cover: 6.95 **NM** value: **Cover or less**
• The Reckoning **A:** Steven Hughes **W:** Brian Pulido
Bk 1/HC❑ Cover: 24.95 **NM** value: **Cover or less**
hardcover. • The Reckoning **A:** Steven Hughes **W:** Brian Pulido
Bk 1-2❑Sep 1996 Cover: 2.95 **NM** value: **Cover or less**
• The Reckoning Encore Presentation; reprints #1 **A:** Steven Hughes **W:** Brian Pulido

LADY DEATH: RETRIBUTION Chaos!

1 ❑ Aug 1998 Cover: 2.95 **NM** value: **Cover or less**
A: Jack Jadsen **W:** Jesse McKann
1/A ❑ Aug 1998 Cover: 2.95 **NM** value: **3.50**
Painted alternate cover. **A:** Jack Jadsen **W:** Jesse McKann
1/LE❑ Aug 1998 **NM** value: **4.00**
• premium edition. **A:** Jack Jadsen **W:** Jesse McKann

LADY DEATH SWIMSUIT SPECIAL Chaos!

1 ❑ May 1994, b&w Cover: 2.50 **NM** value: **Cover or less**
Circ: CapCity orders: **18,645** • **CGC:** 4 graded, best 9.6
1/SC❑May 1994 Cover: 2.50 **NM** value: **8.00**
• **CGC:** 13 graded, best 9.8
• Red Velvet edition.

LADY DEATH: THE RAPTURE Chaos!

1 ❑ Jun 1999 Cover: 2.95 **NM** value: **Cover or less**
Circ: Diamd. preorders: **27,508** • **CGC:** 1 graded, best 9.8
2 ❑ Jul 1999 Cover: 2.95 **NM** value: **Cover or less**
Circ: Diamd. preorders: **23,799**
3 ❑ Aug 1999 Cover: 2.95 **NM** value: **Cover or less**
Circ: Diamd. preorders: **22,823**
📖 Fire In The Sky **A:** Ivan Reis **W:** Len Kaminski; Brian Pulido
4 ❑ Sep 1999 Cover: 2.95 **NM** value: **Cover or less**
Circ: Diamd. preorders: **22,393**

LADY DEATH: TRIBULATION Chaos!

1 ❑ Dec 2000 Cover: 2.95 **NM** value: **Cover or less**
Circ: Diamd. preorders: **19,083** • **CGC:** 11 graded, best 9.8
A: Ivan Reis **W:** Len Kaminski
2 ❑ Jan 2001 Cover: 2.95 **NM** value: **Cover or less**
Circ: Diamd. preorders: **16,350**
A: Ivan Reis **W:** Len Kaminski

LADY DEATH/VAMPIRELLA: DARK HEARTS Chaos!

1 ❑ Mar 1999 Cover: 3.50 **NM** value: **Cover or less**
Circ: Diamd. preorders: **28,785**
No issue number. 📖 Dark Hearts • crossover with Harris
1/A ❑ Mar 1999 **NM** value: **1.00**
• Premium edition (5000 printed).

LADY DEATH VS. PURGATORI Chaos!

1 ❑ Dec 1999 Cover: 2.95 **NM** value: **3.00**
Circ: Diamd. preorders: **23,416**
No issue number. no cover price. 📖 Black, White, and Red All Over! • red foil logo

LADY DEATH V. VAMPIRELLA Chaos

Ash 1❑Feb 2000 Cover: 0.99 **NM** value: **1.00**
Circ: Diamd. preorders: **10,909**
• Lady Death/Vampirella II Preview Book **A:** Mike Deodato Jr.; Luke Ross; ACP; Daerick Gross **W:** Brian Pulido

LADY DEATH: WICKED WAYS Chaos!

1 ❑ Feb 1998 Cover: 2.95 **NM** value: **Cover or less**
1/SC❑Feb 1998 **NM** value: **5.00**
white background cover. • premium edition.

LADY DRACULA Fantaco

1 ❑ Cover: 4.95 **NM** value: **Cover or less**
A: J.J. Goodman **W:** J.J. Goodman
2 ❑ Cover: 4.95 **NM** value: **Cover or less**
📖 Gravy Train **A:** J.J. Goodman **W:** J.J. Goodman

LADY JUSTICE (VOL. 1) (NEIL GAIMAN'S...) Tekno

The idea of Tekno's line was that big-name creators would work out a premise for a specific series and then turn it over to other creators who would actually tell the comic-book stories. So this was called Neil Gaiman's Lady Justice, but the writers were C.J. Henderson and Wendi Lee.

The concept is that Justice is a cosmic force, represented traditionally as a blindfolded woman wielding a sword. She sees, not with human senses and prejudices, but with a faculty all its own, which perceives only justice. Each issue, a different woman is portrayed wearing Lady Justice's blindfold. This is the person whom the spirit of justice has visited for the duration of the story. The rotation of duties allows the writers to expose a wide range of title characters and situations while staying within a broader "super-heroic" context.

1 ❑ Sep 1995 Cover: 1.95 **NM** value: **Cover or less**
Circ: CapCity orders: **14,515**
📖 Hope & Dread **A:** Michael Netzer; Dan Brereton(cover) **W:** C.J. Henderson ★ 1st Appearance of Lady Justice.
2 ❑ Oct 1995 Cover: 1.95 **NM** value: **Cover or less**
Circ: CapCity orders: **13,875**
📖 Stepp'd in Blood **A:** Michael Netzer; Dan Brereton(cover) **W:** C.J. Henderson
3 ❑ Nov 1995 Cover: 1.95 **NM** value: **Cover or less**
Circ: CapCity orders: **13,050**
📖 More Wretched Than He Who Suffers **A:** Georges Jeanty; Jim Webb **W:** C.J. Henderson
4 ❑ Dec 1995 Cover: 1.95 **NM** value: **Cover or less**
Circ: CapCity orders: **11,000**
📖 Wrong Time, Wrong Place, Part 1 • begins new story-arc with new Lady Justice **A:** Greg Boone **W:** Wendi Lee
5 ❑ Dec 1995 Cover: 1.95 **NM** value: **Cover or less**
Circ: CapCity orders: **8,725**
📖 Wrong Time, Wrong Place, Part 2 **A:** Greg Boone **W:** Wendi Lee
6 ❑ Jan 1996 Cover: 2.25 **NM** value: **Cover or less**
Circ: CapCity orders: **6,200**
📖 Wrong Time, Wrong Place, Part 3 **A:** Greg Boone **W:** Wendi Lee
7 ❑ Jan 1996 Cover: 2.25 **NM** value: **Cover or less**
📖 The Chains That Cannot Bind • stand-alone story **A:** Mike Harris; Dan Brereton(cover) **W:** C.J. Henderson
8 ❑ Feb 1996 Cover: 2.25 **NM** value: **Cover or less**
📖 Ravish'd Justice **A:** Steve Lieber **W:** C.J. Henderson
9 ❑ Mar 1996 Cover: 2.25 **NM** value: **Cover or less**
10 ❑ Apr 1996 Cover: 2.25 **NM** value: **Cover or less**
11 ❑ May 1996 Cover: 2.25 **NM** value: **Cover or less**
final issue.

LADY JUSTICE (VOL. 2) (NEIL GAIMAN'S...) Big

1 ❑ Jun 1996 Cover: 2.25 **NM** value: **Cover or less**
📖 The Big Crossover, Part 13; The Big Crossover, Part 14 **A:** Fred Harper **W:** C.J. Henderson
2 ❑ Jul 1996 Cover: 2.25 **NM** value: **Cover or less**
📖 Control Freak Part 1 **A:** Chris Marrinan **W:** Rich Rainey
3 ❑ Aug 1996 Cover: 2.25 **NM** value: **Cover or less**
📖 Control Freak Part 2 **A:** Chris Marrinan **W:** Rich Rainey
4 ❑ Sep 1996 Cover: 2.25 **NM** value: **Cover or less**
📖 Control Freak Part 3 **A:** Chris Marrinan **W:** Rich Rainey
5 ❑ Oct 1996 Cover: 2.25 **NM** value: **Cover or less**
6 ❑ Nov 1996 Cover: 2.25 **NM** value: **Cover or less**
📖 Woman About Town, Part 1; Woman About Time, Part 1 **A:** Dan Brereton; Fred Harper **W:** Dan Brereton
7 ❑ Dec 1996 Cover: 2.25 **NM** value: **Cover or less**
📖 Woman About Town, Part 2; Woman About Time, Part 2 **A:** Dan Brereton; Fred Harper **W:** Dan Brereton
8 ❑ Jan 1997 Cover: 2.25 **NM** value: **Cover or less**
📖 Woman About Town, Part 3; Woman About Time, Part 3 **A:** Dan Brereton; Fred Harper **W:** Dan Brereton
9 ❑ Feb 1997 Cover: 2.25 **NM** value: **Cover or less**
final issue.

LADY LUCK Quality

86 ❑ Dec 1949 Cover: 0.10 **NM** value: **600.00**
• **CGC:** 3 graded, best 8.0
87 ❑ ca. 1950 Cover: 0.10 **NM** value: **400.00**
88 ❑ Apr 1950 Cover: 0.10 **NM** value: **400.00**
• **CGC:** 1 graded, best 6.0
89 ❑ Jun 1950 Cover: 0.10 **NM** value: **350.00**
• **CGC:** 1 graded, best 4.5
90 ❑ Aug 1950 Cover: 0.10 **NM** value: **350.00**
• **CGC:** 2 graded, best 8.0

LADY PENDRAGON GALLERY EDITION Image

1 ❑ Oct 1999 Cover: 2.95 **NM** value: **Cover or less**
Circ: Diamd. preorders: **15,273**
A: David Finch; Jae Lee; Dan Fraga; Marat Mychaels; John Stinsman; Joe Benitez; Joe Jusko; Brandon Peterson; Ed McGuinness; Patrick Lee; Greg Aronowitz; Bruce Brown; Dorian

CGC-graded: Multiply prices above by **33 for 9.9 M** • **16 for 9.8 NM/M** • **7 for 9.6 NM+** • **5 for 9.4 NM** • **2.5 for 9.2 NM-** • **1.5 for 9.0 VF/NM**

1/A ❑ Oct 1999 Cover: 2.95 **NM** value: **Cover or less**
alternate cover. • photo

LADY PENDRAGON: MERLIN — Image

1 ❑ Jan 2000 Cover: 2.95 **NM** value: **Cover or less**
Circ: Diamd. preorders: **18,267**
A: John Stinsman; Peter Vale **W:** Kerri Hawkins; Matt Hawkins

LADY PENDRAGON/MORE THAN MORTAL — Image

1 ❑ May 1999 Cover: 2.50 **NM** value: **Cover or less**
Circ: Diamd. preorders: **29,499**
A: Dan Norton **W:** Matt Hawkins; Matthew Scott; Sharon Scott
1/A ❑ May 1999 Cover: 2.50 **NM** value: **4.00**
alternate cover. • white background
1/B ❑ May 1999 **NM** value: **5.00**
DF alternate cover (holding spear facing forward).
Ash 1❑Feb 1999, b&w **NM** value: **2.00**
No issue number. no cover price. • preview of upcoming crossover

LADY PENDRAGON (VOL. 1) — Maximum

In 540 A.D., King Arthur and his legendary Knights of the Round Table are dead. Three years before, Arthur's wife Guinevere pulled the fabled sword Excalibur from his bastard son Mordred's corpse in the aftermath of the battle where Arthur had been slain. Called to lead Britain back to its past glories, Guinevere embraces the title Pendragon by right of possession of Excalibur. Challenged by the alliance between Constantine, Arthur's cousin and chosen successor to the throne of High King, and Saxon Lord Cheldric's looming invasion from across the sea, the adventure of Lady Pendragon begins.

The legend continues when Jennifer Drake pulls Excalibur from stone and magic returns to present-day Earth. In the aftermath of this prophetic event, all electrical mechanisms have ceased functioning — an omen of things to come.

This intriguing blend of the Arthurian legend and religion contains references that some readers may nonetheless deem heretical.

1 ❑ Mar 1996 Cover: 2.50 **NM** value: **Cover or less**
Rob Liefeld cover. Destiny Embrace **A:** John Stinsman; Rob Liefeld(cover) **W:** Matt Hawkins
1/A ❑ Mar 1996 Cover: 2.50 **NM** value: **Cover or less**
Alternate Cover by Joe Jusko. Destiny Embrace **A:** John Stinsman; Joe Jusko(cover) **W:** Matt Hawkins
1/Aut❑Mar 1996 Cover: 19.95 **NM** value: **Cover or less**
Alternate Cover, Autographed. Destiny Embrace **A:** John Stinsman; Joe Jusko(cover) **W:** Matt Hawkins
1-2 ❑ Mar 1996 Cover: 2.50 **NM** value: **Cover or less**
• Remastered edition. Destiny Embrace **A:** John Stinsman; Rob Liefeld(cover) **W:** Matt Hawkins
Ash 1❑ Cover: 6.95 **NM** value: **Cover or less**
Prelude **A:** John Stinsman **W:** Matt Hawkins
Ash 1/Aut❑ Cover: 19.95 **NM** value: **Cover or less**
Prelude **A:** John Stinsman **W:** Matt Hawkins

LADY PENDRAGON (VOL. 2) — Image

1 ❑ Nov 1998 Cover: 2.50 **NM** value: **3.00**
The Journey Begins **A:** John Stinsman **W:** Matt Hawkins
1/A ❑ Nov 1998 Cover: 5.00 **NM** value: **Cover or less**
alternate cover. • castle
1-2 ❑ Feb 1999 Cover: 2.50 **NM** value: **Cover or less**
• Lady Pendragon Remastered; reprints #1 with corrections
2 ❑ Dec 1998 Cover: 2.50 **NM** value: **3.00**
Photo cover. The Journey Begins **A:** John Stinsman **W:** Matt Hawkins
2/A ❑ Dec 1998 Cover: 2.50 **NM** value: **3.00**
alternate cover.
3 ❑ Jan 1999 Cover: 2.50 **NM** value: **Cover or less**
crucified on cover. **A:** John Stinsman **W:** Matt Hawkins
3/A ❑ Jan 1999 Cover: 2.50 **NM** value: **Cover or less**
manga-style cover.
Ash 1❑Jun 1998 **NM** value: **3.00**
no cover price. • Convention Preview Edition.

LADY PENDRAGON (VOL. 3) — Image

0 ❑ Mar 1999 Cover: 2.50 **NM** value: **Cover or less**
Circ: Diamd. preorders: **27,895**
The Origin • flipbook with origin back-up **A:** Ron Adrian **W:** Matt Hawkins
1 ❑ Mar 1999 Cover: 2.50 **NM** value: **Cover or less**
Circ: Diamd. preorders: **35,068**
A: John Stinsman **W:** Matt Hawkins
2 ❑ Apr 1999 Cover: 2.50 **NM** value: **Cover or less**
Circ: Diamd. preorders: **33,349**
A: John Stinsman **W:** Matt Hawkins
2/A ❑ Apr 1999 Cover: 2.50 **NM** value: **Cover or less**
alternate cover. • Lady Pendragon vanquished
3 ❑ Jul 1999 Cover: 2.50 **NM** value: **Cover or less**
A: Ron Adrian; John Stinsman **W:** Matt Hawkins
4 ❑ Aug 1999 Cover: 2.50 **NM** value: **Cover or less**
A: Ron Adrian; John Stinsman; Joe Jusko(cover) **W:** Matt Hawkins ★ 1st Appearance of Blue.
5 ❑ Sep 1999 Cover: 2.50 **NM** value: **Cover or less**
A: John Stinsman; Peter Vail **W:** Matt Hawkins
6 ❑ Oct 1999 Cover: 2.50 **NM** value: **Cover or less**
A: John Stinsman; Peter Vail **W:** Matt Hawkins
7 ❑ Dec 1999 Cover: 3.95 **NM** value: **Cover or less**
Circ: Diamd. preorders: **20,674**
• Giant-size. Future Prophecy, Part 1 **A:** Dorian Cleavenger **W:** Matt Hawkins
8 ❑ Feb 2000 Cover: 2.50 **NM** value: **Cover or less**
Circ: Diamd. preorders: **18,559**
A: John Stinsman; Joe Jusko(cover) **W:** Matt Hawkins
9 ❑ Apr 2000 Cover: 2.50 **NM** value: **Cover or less**
Circ: Diamd. preorders: **16,991**
10 ❑ Aug 2000 Cover: 2.50 **NM** value: **Cover or less**
Circ: Diamd. preorders: **15,831**
A: John Stinsman; Jennifer Meyer **W:** Kent Hawkins

LADY RAWHIDE — Topps

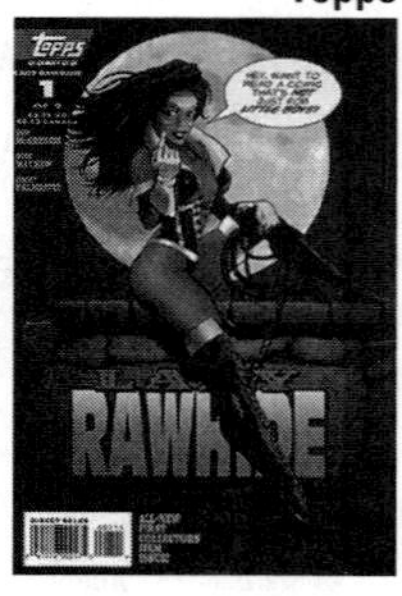

The predominance of "Bad Girl" art in the 1990s introduced this scintillating character to the then-unmined-by-Bad-Girls era of the 1800s. Originating in Zorro #3, Lady Rawhide is Anita Santiago. She adopts this scandalous identity to avenge the blinding of her brother, Ramon. Although her abbreviated, bright, red leather costume could be considered de rigueur for female comics characters in the present, her revealing outfit is daring for the Old West and forms a large part of her offense, since it understandably distracts her male adversaries.

Lady Rawhide stories have more of a storyline than most of the "Bad Girl" ilk, as a testament to its creator, Don McGregor, a writer known for stories with subtext and character motivation. His Black Panther tales in Jungle Action in the early 1970s were prime examples of his talent.

1 ❑ Jul 1995 Cover: 2.95 **NM** value: **Cover or less**
Circ: CapCity orders: **18,975**
It Can't Happen Here, Part 1 **A:** Mike Mayhew **C:** Mike Mayhew **W:** Don McGregor
2 ❑ Sep 1995 Cover: 2.95 **NM** value: **Cover or less**
A: Mike Mayhew **C:** Brian Stelfreeze **W:** Don McGregor
3 ❑ Nov 1995 Cover: 2.95 **NM** value: **Cover or less**
A: Mike Mayhew **C:** Adam Hughes **W:** Don McGregor
4 ❑ Jan 1996 Cover: 2.95 **NM** value: **Cover or less**
A: Mike Mayhew **C:** Michael Golden **W:** Don McGregor
5 ❑ Mar 1996 Cover: 2.95 **NM** value: **Cover or less**
final issue. **A:** Mike Mayhew **C:** Julie Bell **W:** Don McGregor
Bk 1❑ Cover: 10.95 **NM** value: **Cover or less**
• Collects Lady Rawhide #1-5 **A:** Mike Mayhew **W:** Don McGregor
Bk 1-2❑Aug 1999 Cover: 16.95 **NM** value: **Cover or less**
• It Can't Happen Here; Reprints Lady Rawhide #1-5 **A:** Mike Mayhew **W:** Don McGregor

LADY RAWHIDE MINI COMIC — Topps

1 ❑ Jul 1995 **NM** value: **1.00**
no cover price. • Wizard supplement

LADY RAWHIDE: OTHER PEOPLE'S BLOOD — Image

1 ❑ Mar 1999 Cover: 2.95 **NM** value: **Cover or less**
Circ: Diamd. preorders: **7,099**
A: Esteban Maroto **W:** Don McGregor
2 ❑ Apr 1999 Cover: 2.95 **NM** value: **Cover or less**
Circ: Diamd. preorders: **5,630**
A: Esteban Maroto **W:** Don McGregor ★ Versus Scarlet Fever.
3 ❑ May 1999 Cover: 2.95 **NM** value: **Cover or less**
Circ: Diamd. preorders: **4,980**
A: Esteban Maroto **W:** Don McGregor ★ Versus Ansel Plague.
4 ❑ Jun 1999 Cover: 2.95 **NM** value: **Cover or less**
Circ: Diamd. preorders: **4,855**
Intimate Wounds **A:** Esteban Maroto **W:** Don McGregor
5 ❑ Jul 1999 Cover: 2.95 **NM** value: **Cover or less**
Circ: Diamd. preorders: **4,081**
A: Esteban Maroto **W:** Don McGregor

LADY RAWHIDE SPECIAL EDITION — Topps

1 ❑ Jun 1995 Cover: 3.95 **NM** value: **Cover or less**
Circ: CapCity orders: **6,575**
• reprints Zorro #2 and 3

LADY RAWHIDE (VOL. 2) — Topps

0.5 ❑ ca. 1996 **NM** value: **5.00**
• **CGC:** 1 graded, best 9.6
Playing on Violent Emotions **A:** Esteban Maroto; Julie Bell(cover) **W:** Don McGregor ★ 1st Appearance of Star Wolf.
1 ❑ Oct 1996 Cover: 2.95 **NM** value: **Cover or less**
Circ: Diamd. preorders: **26,073**
Other People's Blood, Part 1 **A:** Esteban Maroto; Julie Bell(cover) **C:** Julie Bell **W:** Don McGregor ★ 1st Appearance of Scarlet Fever.
2 ❑ Dec 1996 Cover: 2.95 **NM** value: **Cover or less**
Circ: Diamd. preorders: **18,950**
Other People's Blood, Part 2 **A:** Esteban Maroto **W:** Don McGregor ★ Versus Scarlet Fever.
3 ❑ Feb 1997 Cover: 2.95 **NM** value: **Cover or less**
Circ: Diamd. preorders: **17,321**
4 ❑ Apr 1997, b&w Cover: 2.95 **NM** value: **Cover or less**
Circ: Diamd. preorders: **16,051**
5 ❑ Jun 1997, b&w Cover: 2.95 **NM** value: **Cover or less**
Circ: Diamd. preorders: **15,172**
6 ❑ Aug 1997 Cover: 2.95 **NM** value: **Cover or less**
Circ: Diamd. preorders: **14,622**
• Exists?
7 ❑ Oct 1997 Cover: 2.95 **NM** value: **Cover or less**
Circ: Diamd. preorders: **13,560**
• Exists?

For up-to-the-week CGC ratios, consult the current issue of **Comics Buyer's Guide**.

LADY SPECTRA & SPARKY SPECIAL — J. Kevin Carrier

1 ❑ Jan 1995 Cover: 2.50 **NM** value: **Cover or less**
City Held Hostage **A:** Daniel Nauenberg **W:** J. Kevin Carrier

LADY SUPREME — Image

1 ❑ May 1996 Cover: 2.50 **NM** value: **Cover or less**
aquamarine background cover. Die and Let Die, Part 1 **A:** Deodato Studios; Craig Wagner **C:** Terry Moore **W:** Terry Moore
1/A ❑ May 1996 Cover: 2.50 **NM** value: **Cover or less**
brown background cover. Die and Let Die, Part 1 **A:** Deodato Studios; Craig Wagner **C:** Terry Moore **W:** Terry Moore
2 ❑ Aug 1996 Cover: 2.50 **NM** value: **Cover or less**
• flip-book with New Men Special Preview Edition. Die and Let Die, Part 2 **A:** Deodato Studios; Craig Wagner **W:** Terry Moore

LADY VAMPRÉ — Black Out

0 ❑ Cover: 2.75 **NM** value: **2.95**
Circ: CapCity orders: **5,720**
A: Dave Gutierrez **W:** Bruce Schoengood
1 ❑ Cover: 2.95 **NM** value: **Cover or less**
Circ: CapCity orders: **4,575**
A: Dave Gutierrez **W:** Bruce Schoengood

LADY VAMPRÉ: PLEASURES OF THE FLESH — Black Out

1 ❑ b&w Cover: 2.95 **NM** value: **Cover or less**

LADY VAMPRÉ VS. BLACK LACE — Black Out

1 ❑ Sep 1996 Cover: 2.95 **NM** value: **Cover or less**
Circ: Diamd. preorders: **4,009**
• Flip-book. **A:** Dave Gutierrez; Giampaolo Frizzi **W:** David Pettigrew; Rob Roman

LAFF-A-LYMPICS — Marvel

Probably the best title to come from Marvel's largely unsuccessful stint as a Hanna-Barbera licensee, Laff-a-Lympics captured the spirit of its inspiration, an ABC-TV cartoon from the mid-1970s.

With the 1976 Innsbruck and Austria Olympics fresh in viewer's minds, H-B sent all its characters into sports, with the funny animals playing for the Yogi Yahooeys, the crimefighters playing for the Scooby Doobies, and the villains playing for the Really Rottens.

On TV, the sports segments were used as bumpers surrounding other cartoons, but in the comics, the Laff-a-Lympics events were the whole story. Several issues have clever subplots going on in the background involving some Really Rotten plan, making for generally entertaining issues.

The series also includes well-researched text pieces on individual Hanna-Barbera characters. — JJM

1 ❑ Mar 1978 Cover: 0.35 **NM** value: **8.00**
• **CGC:** 1 graded, best 9.6
• based on Hanna-Barbera animated series
2 ❑ Apr 1978 Cover: 0.35 **NM** value: **6.00**
3 ❑ May 1978 Cover: 0.35 **NM** value: **6.00**
4 ❑ Jun 1978 Cover: 0.35 **NM** value: **6.00**
5 ❑ Jul 1978 Cover: 0.35 **NM** value: **6.00**
6 ❑ Aug 1978 Cover: 0.35 **NM** value: **5.00**
7 ❑ Sep 1978 Cover: 0.35 **NM** value: **5.00**
8 ❑ Oct 1978 Cover: 0.35 **NM** value: **5.00**
9 ❑ Nov 1978 Cover: 0.35 **NM** value: **5.00**
10 ❑ Dec 1978 Cover: 0.35 **NM** value: **5.00**
11 ❑ Jan 1979 Cover: 0.35 **NM** value: **5.00**
12 ❑ Feb 1979 Cover: 0.35 **NM** value: **5.00**
13 ❑ Mar 1979 Cover: 0.35 **NM** value: **5.00**

LAFFIN' GAS — Blackthorne

1 ❑ Jun 1986 Cover: 2.00 **NM** value: **Cover or less**
Adolescent Radioactive Black Belt Hamster: The Untold Story; Radioactive Wrestling Rodents; Colossul Nuclear Bambino Samurai Snails; Adolescent Maniacal Samurai Hares; Pre-Teen Dirty-Gene Kung-Fu Kangaroos **A:** Parsonavich; Andy Ice; Dave Garcia; Lee Marrs **W:** Andy Ice; Cliff MacGillivray; Don Chin; Lee Marrs
2 ❑ 1986 Cover: 2.00 **NM** value: **Cover or less**
The Dark Nightie!; Dork Nyte; The Legend of the Bath-Knight; The Interview; Devil Bat Triumphant; Ye Olde Dark Knight **A:** Andy Ice; Fred Hembeck; William Van Horn; Cliff MacGillivray; Don Chin; Hal Lane **W:** Parsonavich; Andy Ice; Fred Hembeck; Dave Garcia; William Van Horn; Hal Lane
3 ❑ 1986 Cover: 2.00 **NM** value: **Cover or less**
4 ❑ 1986 Cover: 2.00 **NM** value: **Cover or less**
5 ❑ Cover: 2.00 **NM** value: **Cover or less**
6 ❑ Cover: 2.00 **NM** value: **Cover or less**
• 3-D.
7 ❑ Mar 1987 Cover: 2.00 **NM** value: **Cover or less**
8 ❑ 1987 Cover: 2.00 **NM** value: **Cover or less**
9 ❑ 1987 Cover: 2.00 **NM** value: **Cover or less**
10 ❑ 1987 Cover: 2.00 **NM** value: **Cover or less**
11 ❑ Cover: 2.00 **NM** value: **Cover or less**
12 ❑ Cover: 2.00 **NM** value: **Cover or less**

LAFFY-DAFFY COMICS — Rural Home

1 ❑ Feb 1945 Cover: 0.10 **NM** value: **60.00**
2 ❑ Cover: 0.10 **NM** value: **60.00**

Other grades: Multiply prices above by **1.5 for Mint • 2/3 for Very Fine • 1/3 for Fine • 1/5 for Very Good • 1/8 for Good**

LANA — Timely

1 ❑ Aug 1948 Cover: 0.10 **NM** value: **125.00**
2 ❑ Oct 1948 Cover: 0.10 **NM** value: **75.00**
• **CGC:** 1 graded, best 8.5
3 ❑ Dec 1948 Cover: 0.10 **NM** value: **50.00**
4 ❑ Feb 1949 Cover: 0.10 **NM** value: **50.00**
5 ❑ Apr 1949 Cover: 0.10 **NM** value: **50.00**
6 ❑ Jun 1949 Cover: 0.10 **NM** value: **50.00**
7 ❑ Aug 1949 Cover: 0.10 **NM** value: **50.00**

LANCE BARNES: POST NUKE DICK — Marvel / Epic

1 ❑ Apr 1993 Cover: 2.50 **NM** value: **Cover or less**
Circ: CapCity orders: **8,400**
🕮 The Big Bang • Lance accidentally destroys the world **A:** Barry Crain **W:** Stefan Petrucha
2 ❑ May 1993 Cover: 2.50 **NM** value: **Cover or less**
Circ: CapCity orders: **4,600**
🕮 The Big Fit **A:** Barry Crain **W:** Stefan Petrucha
3 ❑ Jun 1993 Cover: 2.50 **NM** value: **Cover or less**
Circ: CapCity orders: **3,800**
🕮 The Big Chip **A:** Barry Crain **W:** Stefan Petrucha
4 ❑ Jul 1993 Cover: 2.50 **NM** value: **Cover or less**
Circ: CapCity orders: **3,300**
A: Barry Crain **W:** Stefan Petrucha

LANCELOT LINK, SECRET CHIMP — Gold Key

1 ❑ May 1971 Cover: 0.15 **NM** value: **18.00**
• **CGC:** 8 graded, best 9.8
🕮 On the Beam; Mummy's the Word; That's the Way the Cookie Crumbles; Leave the Driving to Us
2 ❑ Aug 1971 Cover: 0.15 **NM** value: **12.00**
3 ❑ Nov 1971 Cover: 0.15 **NM** value: **8.00**
4 ❑ Feb 1972 Cover: 0.15 **NM** value: **8.00**
5 ❑ May 1972 Cover: 0.15 **NM** value: **8.00**
6 ❑ Aug 1972 Cover: 0.15 **NM** value: **8.00**
7 ❑ Nov 1972 Cover: 0.15 **NM** value: **8.00**
8 ❑ Feb 1973 Cover: 0.15 **NM** value: **8.00**
• **CGC:** 1 graded, best 9.0

LANCELOT STRONG, THE SHIELD — Archie / Red Circle

1 ❑ Jun 1983 Cover: 1.00 **NM** value: **2.00**
2 ❑ Cover: 1.00 **NM** value: **2.00**

LANCE O'CASEY — Fawcett

1 ❑ Spr 1946 Cover: 0.10 **NM** value: **250.00**
2 ❑ Sum 1946 Cover: 0.10 **NM** value: **150.00**
3 ❑ Fal 1946 Cover: 0.10 **NM** value: **100.00**
4 ❑ Sum 1947 Cover: 0.10 **NM** value: **100.00**

LANDER — Mermaid

Bk 1❑ b&w Cover: 5.00 **NM** value: **Cover or less**
• collects issues #1 and 2 with new material

LAND OF NOD, THE — Dark Horse

1 ❑ Jul 1997, b&w Cover: 2.95 **NM** value: **Cover or less**
Circ: Diamd. preorders: **5,584**
A: Jay Stephens **W:** Jay Stephens
2 ❑ Nov 1997, b&w Cover: 2.95 **NM** value: **Cover or less**
Circ: Diamd. preorders: **3,784**
A: Jay Stephens **W:** Jay Stephens
3 ❑ Feb 1998, b&w Cover: 2.95 **NM** value: **Cover or less**
Circ: Diamd. preorders: **3,256**
A: Jay Stephens **W:** Jay Stephens
4 ❑ Jun 1998, b&w Cover: 2.95 **NM** value: **Cover or less**
Circ: Diamd. preorders: **3,146**
A: Jay Stephens **W:** Jay Stephens
Bk 1❑ Feb 1999, b&w Cover: 13.95 **NM** value: **Cover or less**
• Rockabye Book **A:** Jay Stephens **W:** Jay Stephens

LAND OF OZ, THE — Arrow

1 ❑ Jul 1998 Cover: 2.95 **NM** value: **Cover or less**
Circ: Diamd. preorders: **2,232** • **CGC:** 1 graded, best 9.4
2 ❑ Cover: 2.95 **NM** value: **Cover or less**
• **CGC:** 1 graded, best 9.8
3 ❑ Cover: 2.95 **NM** value: **Cover or less**
• **CGC:** 1 graded, best 9.8
4 ❑ May 1999 Cover: 2.95 **NM** value: **Cover or less**
• **CGC:** 1 graded, best 9.6
5 ❑ Jul 1999 Cover: 2.95 **NM** value: **Cover or less**
• **CGC:** 1 graded, best 9.4
6 ❑ Sep 1999 Cover: 2.95 **NM** value: **Cover or less**
• **CGC:** 1 graded, best 9.9
7 ❑ Nov 1999 Cover: 2.95 **NM** value: **Cover or less**
• **CGC:** 1 graded, best 9.6
8 ❑ Mar 2000 Cover: 2.95 **NM** value: **Cover or less**
• **CGC:** 1 graded, best 9.0
9 ❑ Apr 2000 Cover: 2.95 **NM** value: **Cover or less**

LAND OF THE GIANTS — Gold Key

1 ❑ Nov 1968 Cover: 0.15 **NM** value: **30.00**
• **CGC:** 1 graded, best 9.2
2 ❑ Jan 1969 Cover: 0.15 **NM** value: **15.00**
3 ❑ Mar 1969 Cover: 0.15 **NM** value: **15.00**
• **CGC:** 1 graded, best 9.4
4 ❑ **NM** value: **15.00**
5 ❑ Sep 1969 Cover: 0.15 **NM** value: **15.00**

The prices seen above do not represent the highest possible prices seen in online auctions, but rather the prices we have seen these issues reliably fetch in a variety of environments (storefront retail, mail order, auction and convention).

LAND OF THE LOST COMICS — E.C.

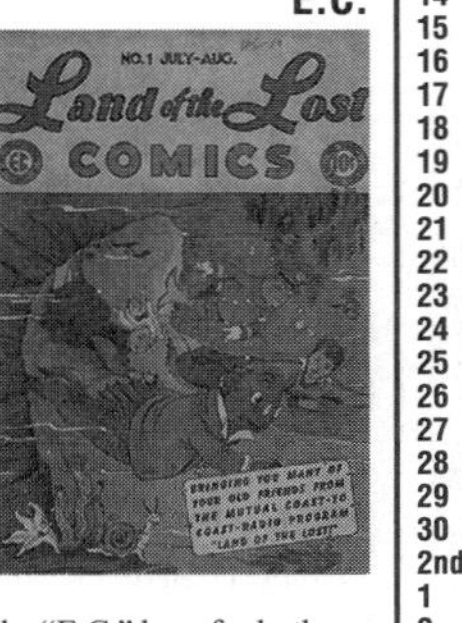

The radio show The Land of the Lost ran on and off from 1943 to 1948, created, written and produced by Isabel Manning Hewson. The land was located at the bottom of the sea, where everything that had been lost wound up. Children Isabel and Billy traveled there with Red Lantern, a talking fish. The show motto was "Never say lost."

E.C. licensed the show, and Hewson wrote the series, mostly drawn by Olive Bailey. Intriguingly, the company imprint changed from "An Educational Comic" to "An Entertaining Comic" with #6. This alternating imprint was typical of the company, which continued to use the "E.C." logo for both. — Maggie

1 ❑ Jul 1946 Cover: 0.10 **NM** value: **250.00**
• **CGC:** 5 graded, best 9.0
2 ❑ Sep 1946 Cover: 0.10 **NM** value: **175.00**
• **CGC:** 1 graded, best 9.0
3 ❑ Win 1946 Cover: 0.10 **NM** value: **125.00**
• **CGC:** 1 graded, best 7.5
4 ❑ Spr 1947 Cover: 0.10 **NM** value: **125.00**
• **CGC:** 2 graded, best 7.0
5 ❑ Sum 1947 Cover: 0.10 **NM** value: **125.00**
• **CGC:** 3 graded, best 9.2
6 ❑ Jul 1947 Cover: 0.10 **NM** value: **125.00**
• **CGC:** 4 graded, best 9.0
7 ❑ Sep 1947 Cover: 0.10 **NM** value: **125.00**
• **CGC:** 3 graded, best 8.5
8 ❑ Nov 1947 Cover: 0.10 **NM** value: **125.00**
• **CGC:** 3 graded, best 8.5
9 ❑ Spr 1948 Cover: 0.10 **NM** value: **125.00**
• **CGC:** 3 graded, best 8.5

LANDRA SPECIAL — Alchemy

1 ❑ b&w Cover: 2.00 **NM** value: **Cover or less**
No issue number.

LANDS OF PRESTER JOHN — Noble

1 ❑ Cover: 15.00 **NM** value: **Cover or less**
A: Mike Gustovich

LANN — Fantagraphics / Eros

All issues are adults only.
1 ❑ b&w Cover: 2.50 **NM** value: **Cover or less**

LA PACIFICA — DC / Paradox

1 ❑ b&w Cover: 4.95 **NM** value: **Cover or less**
Circ: CapCity orders: **4,750**
• digest. **A:** Tayyar Ozkan **W:** Amos Poe; Joel Rose
2 ❑ b&w Cover: 4.95 **NM** value: **Cover or less**
Circ: CapCity orders: **3,675**
• digest. **A:** Tayyar Ozkan **W:** Amos Poe; Joel Rose
3 ❑ b&w Cover: 4.95 **NM** value: **Cover or less**
Circ: CapCity orders: **3,300**
• digest. **A:** Tayyar Ozkan **W:** Amos Poe; Joel Rose

L.A. PHOENIX — David G. Brown Studios

1 ❑ Jul 1994, b&w Cover: 2.00 **NM** value: **Cover or less**
🕮 Rise of the Phoenix **A:** David G. Brown **W:** David G. Brown
2 ❑ Jul 1995, b&w Cover: 2.00 **NM** value: **Cover or less**
🕮 The Conflict **A:** David G. Brown **W:** David G. Brown
3 ❑ Jul 1996, b&w Cover: 2.00 **NM** value: **Cover or less**

L.A. RAPTOR — Morbid

1 ❑ Cover: 2.95 **NM** value: **Cover or less**
A: Mike Michaud **W:** Raymond Cooper

LARGE FEATURE COMICS — Dell

The Large Feature line was one of the early series comprising ongoing changing titles for stand-alone stories, many of which consisted of strip reprints. Some (Lone Ranger, Gang Busters) were based on radio shows; most featured such adventure strips as Dick Tracy, Smilin' Jack, and Terry and the Pirates or such humor features as Private Buck, The Nebbs, Smitty, and Toots and Casper.

Though the contents of the large-size issues were black-and-white, the issues were especially treasured by comics buffs looking for otherwise-unavailable strip reprints. — Maggie

1st Series
1 ❑ ca. 1939 Cover: 0.10 **NM** value: **1200.00**
2 ❑ Cover: 0.10 **NM** value: **1100.00**
3 ❑ Cover: 0.10 **NM** value: **1000.00**
4 ❑ Cover: 0.10 **NM** value: **750.00**
5 ❑ Cover: 0.10 **NM** value: **750.00**
6 ❑ Cover: 0.10 **NM** value: **750.00**
7 ❑ Cover: 0.10 **NM** value: **750.00**
8 ❑ Cover: 0.10 **NM** value: **750.00**
9 ❑ Cover: 0.10 **NM** value: **700.00**
10 ❑ Cover: 0.10 **NM** value: **700.00**
11 ❑ Cover: 0.10 **NM** value: **600.00**
12 ❑ Cover: 0.10 **NM** value: **600.00**
13 ❑ Cover: 0.10 **NM** value: **600.00**
14 ❑ Cover: 0.10 **NM** value: **600.00**
15 ❑ Cover: 0.10 **NM** value: **600.00**
16 ❑ Cover: 0.10 **NM** value: **500.00**
17 ❑ Cover: 0.10 **NM** value: **500.00**
18 ❑ Cover: 0.10 **NM** value: **500.00**
19 ❑ Cover: 0.10 **NM** value: **500.00**
20 ❑ Cover: 0.10 **NM** value: **400.00**
21 ❑ Cover: 0.10 **NM** value: **400.00**
22 ❑ Cover: 0.10 **NM** value: **400.00**
23 ❑ Cover: 0.10 **NM** value: **400.00**
24 ❑ Cover: 0.10 **NM** value: **350.00**
25 ❑ Cover: 0.10 **NM** value: **350.00**
26 ❑ Cover: 0.10 **NM** value: **350.00**
27 ❑ Cover: 0.10 **NM** value: **350.00**
28 ❑ Cover: 0.10 **NM** value: **350.00**
29 ❑ Cover: 0.10 **NM** value: **350.00**
30 ❑ Cover: 0.10 **NM** value: **350.00**
2nd Series
1 ❑ ca. 1942 Cover: 0.10 **NM** value: **450.00**
2 ❑ Cover: 0.10 **NM** value: **450.00**
3 ❑ Cover: 0.10 **NM** value: **450.00**
4 ❑ Cover: 0.10 **NM** value: **400.00**
5 ❑ Cover: 0.10 **NM** value: **400.00**
6 ❑ Cover: 0.10 **NM** value: **400.00**
7 ❑ Cover: 0.10 **NM** value: **400.00**
8 ❑ Cover: 0.10 **NM** value: **780.00**
9 ❑ Cover: 0.10 **NM** value: **500.00**
10 ❑ Cover: 0.10 **NM** value: **500.00**
11 ❑ Cover: 0.10 **NM** value: **400.00**
12 ❑ Cover: 0.10 **NM** value: **400.00**
13 ❑ Cover: 0.10 **NM** value: **400.00**

LARRY DOBY, BASEBALL HERO — Fawcett

1 ❑ ca. 1950 Cover: 0.10 **NM** value: **500.00**
• **CGC:** 1 graded, best 4.5

LARS OF MARS — Ziff-Davis

10 ❑ Apr 1951 Cover: 0.10 **NM** value: **700.00**
• **CGC:** 1 graded, best 7.0
11 ❑ Jul 1951 Cover: 0.10 **NM** value: **500.00**
• **CGC:** 2 graded, best 8.0

LARS OF MARS 3-D — Eclipse

1 ❑ Cover: 2.50 **NM** value: **Cover or less**
Circ: CapCity orders: **2,450**
🕮 When Terrorists Die...; The Earthshaker; The Terror Weapon **A:** Murphy Anderson **W:** Jerry Siegel

LASER ERASER & PRESSBUTTON — Eclipse

Axel Pressbutton is a florist until a Vegan green fungus eats the lower portion of his body and his left hand. When the doctors rebuild him, they give him a pair of robotic legs, a steel midsection, and a razor-sharp cleaver permanently mounted to his new arm. The only consolation is the addition of a big red button on his chest. Pressing it — well, it puts Axel in a very good mood.

His partner is Mysta Mystralis, a "laser eraser" who is as deadly with her laser as she is beautiful. She also knows how to press Axel's button, if you get the drift.

This delightfully depraved duo first appeared in England's Warrior magazine before making its way to America in the Axel Pressbutton deluxe series from Eclipse. This 1985-1987 series brings readers their further adventures in a lower-cost format.

1 ❑ Nov 1985 Cover: 0.75 **NM** value: **1.50**
Circ: CapCity orders: **6,700**
🕮 Laser Eraser and Pressbutton: The Depths of Depravity; Laser Eraser and Pressbutton: The Iniquity From Antiquity; Twilight World, Part 1 **A:** Mike Collins **W:** Pedro Henry; Steve Moore
2 ❑ Dec 1985 Cover: 0.75 **NM** value: **1.50**
Circ: CapCity orders: **5,525**
W: Pedro Henry
3 ❑ Cover: 0.75 **NM** value: **1.50**
Circ: CapCity orders: **5,500**
W: Pedro Henry
4 ❑ Cover: 0.75 **NM** value: **1.50**
Circ: CapCity orders: **5,275**
W: Pedro Henry
5 ❑ Cover: 0.75 **NM** value: **1.50**
Circ: CapCity orders: **4,900**
🕮 Laser Eraser and Pressbutton: The Gates of Hell; Ektryn: Citadel of Lost Souls **A:** Mike Collins; Cam Kennedy **W:** Pedro Henry
6 ❑ Cover: 0.75 **NM** value: **1.50**
Circ: CapCity orders: **4,600**
W: Pedro Henry
3D 1❑ Cover: 2.00 **NM** value: **Cover or less**
Circ: CapCity orders: **4,675**
W: Pedro Henry

Capital City orders are the actual sales of comic books by Capital City Distribution, once one of the largest U.S. sellers of comics to comics shops. Capital City's share of comics shop sales, while not known exactly, increases from around 10-20% in the mid-1980s to 30-35% in the mid-1990s. Capital City's share of comic books sold on newsstands (most Marvels and DCs) will be less.

LASH LARUE WESTERN (FAWCETT) Fawcett

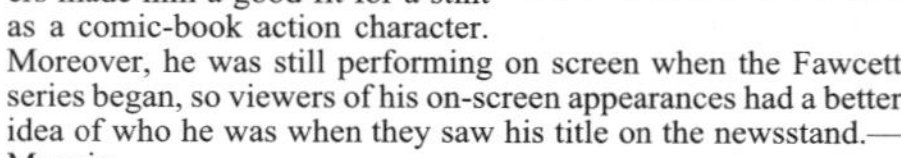

Alfred "Lash" LaRue (1917-1996) was a cowboy movie hero of the late 1940s known for the bull-whip he carried. Like many other Western feature characters, he was most often called by his name, no matter what the plot of the story might happen to be. In many of his appearances, he was accompanied by Al "Fuzzy" St. John and eventually starred in a short-lived TV show in the early 1950s.

He wore a distinctive black outfit and that, plus his whip action and ability to star in dramatic photo covers made him a good fit for a stint as a comic-book action character. Moreover, he was still performing on screen when the Fawcett series began, so viewers of his on-screen appearances had a better idea of who he was when they saw his title on the newsstand.—Maggie

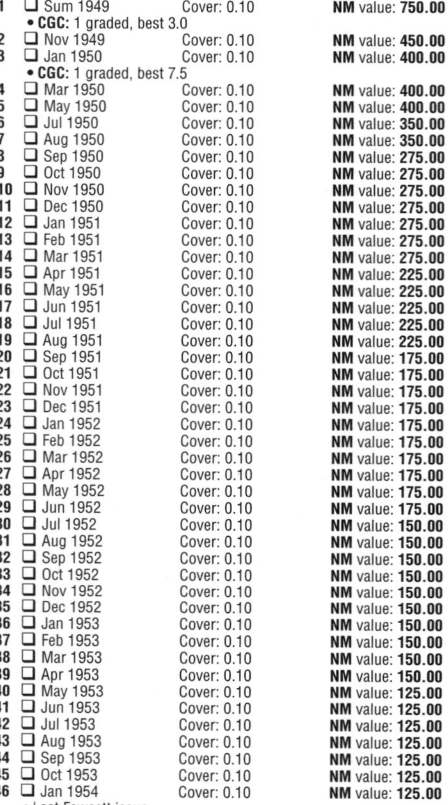

1 ❑ Sum 1949 Cover: 0.10 **NM** value: **750.00**
• **CGC:** 1 graded, best 3.0
2 ❑ Nov 1949 Cover: 0.10 **NM** value: **450.00**
3 ❑ Jan 1950 Cover: 0.10 **NM** value: **400.00**
• **CGC:** 1 graded, best 7.5
4 ❑ Mar 1950 Cover: 0.10 **NM** value: **400.00**
5 ❑ May 1950 Cover: 0.10 **NM** value: **400.00**
6 ❑ Jul 1950 Cover: 0.10 **NM** value: **350.00**
7 ❑ Aug 1950 Cover: 0.10 **NM** value: **350.00**
8 ❑ Sep 1950 Cover: 0.10 **NM** value: **275.00**
9 ❑ Oct 1950 Cover: 0.10 **NM** value: **275.00**
10 ❑ Nov 1950 Cover: 0.10 **NM** value: **275.00**
11 ❑ Dec 1950 Cover: 0.10 **NM** value: **275.00**
12 ❑ Jan 1951 Cover: 0.10 **NM** value: **275.00**
13 ❑ Feb 1951 Cover: 0.10 **NM** value: **275.00**
14 ❑ Mar 1951 Cover: 0.10 **NM** value: **275.00**
15 ❑ Apr 1951 Cover: 0.10 **NM** value: **225.00**
16 ❑ May 1951 Cover: 0.10 **NM** value: **225.00**
17 ❑ Jun 1951 Cover: 0.10 **NM** value: **225.00**
18 ❑ Jul 1951 Cover: 0.10 **NM** value: **225.00**
19 ❑ Aug 1951 Cover: 0.10 **NM** value: **225.00**
20 ❑ Sep 1951 Cover: 0.10 **NM** value: **175.00**
21 ❑ Oct 1951 Cover: 0.10 **NM** value: **175.00**
22 ❑ Nov 1951 Cover: 0.10 **NM** value: **175.00**
23 ❑ Dec 1951 Cover: 0.10 **NM** value: **175.00**
24 ❑ Jan 1952 Cover: 0.10 **NM** value: **175.00**
25 ❑ Feb 1952 Cover: 0.10 **NM** value: **175.00**
26 ❑ Mar 1952 Cover: 0.10 **NM** value: **175.00**
27 ❑ Apr 1952 Cover: 0.10 **NM** value: **175.00**
28 ❑ May 1952 Cover: 0.10 **NM** value: **175.00**
29 ❑ Jun 1952 Cover: 0.10 **NM** value: **175.00**
30 ❑ Jul 1952 Cover: 0.10 **NM** value: **150.00**
31 ❑ Aug 1952 Cover: 0.10 **NM** value: **150.00**
32 ❑ Sep 1952 Cover: 0.10 **NM** value: **150.00**
33 ❑ Oct 1952 Cover: 0.10 **NM** value: **150.00**
34 ❑ Nov 1952 Cover: 0.10 **NM** value: **150.00**
35 ❑ Dec 1952 Cover: 0.10 **NM** value: **150.00**
36 ❑ Jan 1953 Cover: 0.10 **NM** value: **150.00**
37 ❑ Feb 1953 Cover: 0.10 **NM** value: **150.00**
38 ❑ Mar 1953 Cover: 0.10 **NM** value: **150.00**
39 ❑ Apr 1953 Cover: 0.10 **NM** value: **150.00**
40 ❑ May 1953 Cover: 0.10 **NM** value: **125.00**
41 ❑ Jun 1953 Cover: 0.10 **NM** value: **125.00**
42 ❑ Jul 1953 Cover: 0.10 **NM** value: **125.00**
43 ❑ Aug 1953 Cover: 0.10 **NM** value: **125.00**
44 ❑ Sep 1953 Cover: 0.10 **NM** value: **125.00**
45 ❑ Oct 1953 Cover: 0.10 **NM** value: **125.00**
46 ❑ Jan 1954 Cover: 0.10 **NM** value: **125.00**
• Last Fawcett issue

LASH LARUE WESTERN Charlton

47 ❑ Mar 1954 Cover: 0.10 **NM** value: **125.00**
• First Charlton issue
48 ❑ May 1954 Cover: 0.10 **NM** value: **125.00**
49 ❑ Jul 1954 Cover: 0.10 **NM** value: **125.00**
50 ❑ Sep 1954 Cover: 0.10 **NM** value: **100.00**
51 ❑ Nov 1654 Cover: 0.10 **NM** value: **100.00**
52 ❑ ca. 1955 Cover: 0.10 **NM** value: **100.00**
53 ❑ ca. 1955 Cover: 0.10 **NM** value: **100.00**
54 ❑ ca. 1955 Cover: 0.10 **NM** value: **100.00**
55 ❑ ca. 1955 Cover: 0.10 **NM** value: **100.00**
56 ❑ ca. 1955 Cover: 0.10 **NM** value: **100.00**
57 ❑ ca. 1956 Cover: 0.10 **NM** value: **100.00**
58 ❑ ca. 1956 Cover: 0.10 **NM** value: **100.00**
59 ❑ ca. 1956 Cover: 0.10 **NM** value: **100.00**
60 ❑ ca. 1956 Cover: 0.10 **NM** value: **80.00**
61 ❑ ca. 1956 Cover: 0.10 **NM** value: **80.00**
62 ❑ ca. 1957 Cover: 0.10 **NM** value: **80.00**
63 ❑ Mar 1957 Cover: 0.10 **NM** value: **80.00**
64 ❑ ca. 1957 Cover: 0.10 **NM** value: **80.00**
65 ❑ ca. 1957 Cover: 0.10 **NM** value: **80.00**
66 ❑ Nov 1957 Cover: 0.10 **NM** value: **80.00**
67 ❑ ca. 1958 Cover: 0.10 **NM** value: **80.00**
68 ❑ ca. 1958 Cover: 0.10 **NM** value: **80.00**
69 ❑ ca. 1958 Cover: 0.10 **NM** value: **80.00**
70 ❑ ca. 1958 Cover: 0.10 **NM** value: **60.00**
71 ❑ ca. 1958 Cover: 0.10 **NM** value: **60.00**
72 ❑ ca. 1959 Cover: 0.10 **NM** value: **60.00**
73 ❑ ca. 1959 Cover: 0.10 **NM** value: **60.00**
74 ❑ ca. 1959 Cover: 0.10 **NM** value: **60.00**
75 ❑ ca. 1959 Cover: 0.10 **NM** value: **60.00**
76 ❑ ca. 1959 Cover: 0.10 **NM** value: **60.00**
77 ❑ ca. 1960 Cover: 0.10 **NM** value: **60.00**
78 ❑ ca. 1960 Cover: 0.10 **NM** value: **60.00**
79 ❑ ca. 1960 Cover: 0.10 **NM** value: **60.00**
80 ❑ ca. 1960 Cover: 0.10 **NM** value: **50.00**
81 ❑ ca. 1960 Cover: 0.10 **NM** value: **50.00**
82 ❑ Feb 1961 Cover: 0.10 **NM** value: **50.00**
83 ❑ Apr 1961 Cover: 0.10 **NM** value: **50.00**
84 ❑ Jun 1961 Cover: 0.10 **NM** value: **50.00**

LASH LARUE WESTERN Avalon

1 ❑ Cover: 3.50 **NM** value: **Cover or less**
• some color
Anl 1❑b&w Cover: 2.95 **NM** value: **Cover or less**

LASSIE Dell / Gold Key

Smart, resourceful, loyal, brave and furry: that's Lassie, America's favorite pooch and a mainstay on television and in movies and comics from the late 1940s to the early 1970s. The premise of Lassie shows varied slightly through the years, and the original collie eventually gave way to a succession of direct descendents, but the essential boy-and-dog adventure elements remained constant, as Lassie and his nominal owner foiled crimes, searched for treasure, encountered ghosts, and helped each other.

Dell began the comic-book adaptation in 1950. Gold Key, which split off from Dell in the early 1960s, soldiered on with photo-cover issues.

1 ❑ Oct 1950 Cover: 0.10 **NM** value: **85.00**
2 ❑ Jan 1951 Cover: 0.10 **NM** value: **50.00**
3 ❑ Apr 1951 Cover: 0.10 **NM** value: **35.00**
4 ❑ Jul 1951 Cover: 0.10 **NM** value: **35.00**
5 ❑ Oct 1951 Cover: 0.10 **NM** value: **35.00**
6 ❑ Jan 1952 Cover: 0.10 **NM** value: **24.00**
7 ❑ Apr 1952 Cover: 0.10 **NM** value: **24.00**
8 ❑ Jul 1952 Cover: 0.10 **NM** value: **24.00**
9 ❑ Oct 1952 Cover: 0.10 **NM** value: **24.00**
10 ❑ Jan 1953 Cover: 0.10 **NM** value: **24.00**
• **CGC:** 1 graded, best 9.2
11 ❑ Apr 1953 Cover: 0.10 **NM** value: **18.00**
12 ❑ Jul 1953 Cover: 0.10 **NM** value: **18.00**
13 ❑ Oct 1953 Cover: 0.10 **NM** value: **18.00**
14 ❑ Jan 1954 Cover: 0.10 **NM** value: **18.00**
15 ❑ Mar 1954 Cover: 0.10 **NM** value: **18.00**
16 ❑ May 1954 Cover: 0.10 **NM** value: **18.00**
17 ❑ Jul 1954 Cover: 0.10 **NM** value: **18.00**
18 ❑ Sep 1954 Cover: 0.10 **NM** value: **18.00**
19 ❑ Nov 1954 Cover: 0.10 **NM** value: **18.00**
20 ❑ Jan 1955 Cover: 0.10 **NM** value: **18.00**
21 ❑ Mar 1955 Cover: 0.10 **NM** value: **16.00**
• **CGC:** 1 graded, best 9.2
22 ❑ May 1955 Cover: 0.10 **NM** value: **16.00**
23 ❑ Jul 1955 Cover: 0.10 **NM** value: **16.00**
24 ❑ Sep 1955 Cover: 0.10 **NM** value: **15.00**
25 ❑ Nov 1955 Cover: 0.10 **NM** value: **15.00**
26 ❑ Jan 1956 Cover: 0.10 **NM** value: **15.00**
27 ❑ Mar 1956 Cover: 0.10 **NM** value: **15.00**
28 ❑ May 1956 Cover: 0.10 **NM** value: **15.00**
29 ❑ Jul 1956 Cover: 0.10 **NM** value: **15.00**
30 ❑ Sep 1956 Cover: 0.10 **NM** value: **15.00**
31 ❑ Nov 1956 Cover: 0.10 **NM** value: **15.00**
32 ❑ Jan 1957 Cover: 0.10 **NM** value: **15.00**
33 ❑ Mar 1957 Cover: 0.10 **NM** value: **15.00**
34 ❑ May 1957 Cover: 0.10 **NM** value: **15.00**
35 ❑ Jul 1957 Cover: 0.10 **NM** value: **15.00**
36 ❑ Sep 1957 Cover: 0.10 **NM** value: **15.00**
37 ❑ Nov 1957 Cover: 0.10 **NM** value: **15.00**
38 ❑ Jan 1958 Cover: 0.10 **NM** value: **15.00**
39 ❑ Mar 1958 Cover: 0.10 **NM** value: **15.00**
• **CGC:** 1 graded, best 4.5
40 ❑ May 1958 Cover: 0.10 **NM** value: **15.00**
41 ❑ Jul 1958 Cover: 0.10 **NM** value: **15.00**
42 ❑ Sep 1958 Cover: 0.10 **NM** value: **15.00**
43 ❑ Nov 1958 Cover: 0.10 **NM** value: **15.00**
44 ❑ Jan 1959 Cover: 0.10 **NM** value: **15.00**
45 ❑ Apr 1959 Cover: 0.10 **NM** value: **15.00**
46 ❑ Jul 1959 Cover: 0.10 **NM** value: **15.00**
47 ❑ Oct 1959 Cover: 0.10 **NM** value: **15.00**
48 ❑ Jan 1960 Cover: 0.10 **NM** value: **15.00**
• **CGC:** 1 graded, best 9.4
49 ❑ Apr 1960 Cover: 0.10 **NM** value: **15.00**
50 ❑ Jul 1960 Cover: 0.10 **NM** value: **15.00**
51 ❑ Oct 1960 Cover: 0.10 **NM** value: **14.00**
52 ❑ Jan 1961 Cover: 0.10 **NM** value: **14.00**
• **CGC:** 1 graded, best 9.2
53 ❑ 1961 **NM** value: **14.00**
54 ❑ 1961 **NM** value: **14.00**
55 ❑ Dec 1961 Cover: 0.15 **NM** value: **14.00**
56 ❑ Jan 1962 **NM** value: **14.00**
57 ❑ Apr 1962 **NM** value: **14.00**
58 ❑ Jul 1962 **NM** value: **14.00**
59 ❑ Oct 1962 Cover: 0.12 **NM** value: **14.00**
• Gold Key begins as publisher
60 ❑ Jan 1963 Cover: 0.12 **NM** value: **14.00**
61 ❑ Apr 1963 Cover: 0.12 **NM** value: **12.00**
62 ❑ Jul 1963 Cover: 0.12 **NM** value: **12.00**
63 ❑ Oct 1963 Cover: 0.12 **NM** value: **12.00**
• **CGC:** 1 graded, best 6.5
64 ❑ Cover: 0.12 **NM** value: **12.00**
65 ❑ Jan 1966 Cover: 0.12 **NM** value: **12.00**
• **CGC:** 1 graded, best 7.0
66 ❑ Apr 1966 Cover: 0.12 **NM** value: **12.00**
• **CGC:** 1 graded, best 7.5
📖 Old Thunder's Lost Treasure; The Lonely Lookout on Hickory Hill;
67 ❑ Oct 1966 Cover: 0.12 **NM** value: **12.00**
• **CGC:** 1 graded, best 7.5
68 ❑ Sep 1967 Cover: 0.12 **NM** value: **12.00**
• **CGC:** 1 graded, best 2.5
69 ❑ Dec 1967 Cover: 0.12 **NM** value: **12.00**
• **CGC:** 1 graded, best 8.0
70 ❑ Jul 1969 Cover: 0.15 **NM** value: **12.00**
• **CGC:** 1 graded, best 7.0
final issue.

LAST AMERICAN, THE Marvel / Epic

1 ❑ Dec 1990 Cover: 2.25 **NM** value: **Cover or less**
Circ: CapCity orders: **13,500**
📖 Goodnight, Poughkeepsie **A:** Mike McMahon **W:** Alan Grant; John Wagner
2 ❑ Jan 1991 Cover: 2.25 **NM** value: **Cover or less**
A: Mike McMahon **W:** Alan Grant; John Wagner
3 ❑ Feb 1991 Cover: 2.25 **NM** value: **Cover or less**
📖 An American Dream **A:** Mike McMahon **W:** Alan Grant; John Wagner
4 ❑ Mar 1991 Cover: 2.25 **NM** value: **Cover or less**
Circ: CapCity orders: **9,000**
📖 Twilight's Last Gleaming **A:** Mike McMahon **W:** Alan Grant; John Wagner

LAST AVENGERS Marvel

Several years in the future, in a universe parallel to our own, Earth's Mightiest Heroes are about to face their final battle. Most of the old guard are already gone: Thor, Hercules, and The Thing were killed in the Great Cataclysm years before. The Hulk had become utterly evil and attacked his own teammates, killing Tigra and Wonder Man before dying himself. Captain America became president — only to be gunned down in the third year of his office. The rest were gone or retired, and a new group of Avengers took their place. Then someone dropped a bomb on the Avengers' headquarters, slaying the new group.

Afterward, Hank Pym was visited by Ultron-59 and told to warn the surviving heroes. A coalition of villains led by Kang and Ultron-59 were about to wage a final battle against the old Avengers. Pym and the rest were hopelessly outclassed, but it got worse: Kang had already been to the future, read how it would turn out...and was smiling.

The story was based on a script that Peter David originally ran in the pages of Comics Buyer's Guide.

1 ❑ Nov 1995 Cover: 5.95 **NM** value: **Cover or less**
• **CGC:** 1 graded, best 9.6
• Alterniverse story **A:** Ariel Olivetti **W:** Peter David ★ Appearance of Wasp, Cannonball, Ultron, Hank Pym, Hawkeye.
2 ❑ Dec 1995 Cover: 5.95 **NM** value: **Cover or less**
• Alterniverse story **A:** Ariel Olivetti **W:** Peter David ★ Appearance of Wasp, Cannonball, Ultron, Hank Pym, Hawkeye.
Bk 1❑ Cover: 12.95 **NM** value: **Cover or less**

LAST DANGEROUS CHRISTMAS Aeon

1 ❑ b&w Cover: 5.95 **NM** value: **Cover or less**
No issue number. • squarebound; benefit comic for neglected and abused children

LAST DAYS OF HOLLYWOOD, U.S.A. Morgan

1 ❑ **NM** value: **2.95**
A: Mark Thompson **W:** Mark Thompson
2 ❑ **NM** value: **2.95**
A: Mark Thompson **W:** Mark Thompson
3 ❑ **NM** value: **2.95**
A: Mark Thompson **W:** Mark Thompson
4 ❑ **NM** value: **2.95**
A: Mark Thompson **W:** Mark Thompson
5 ❑ Cover: 2.95 **NM** value: **Cover or less**
A: Mark Thompson **W:** Mark Thompson

LAST DAYS OF THE JUSTICE SOCIETY SPECIAL DC

1 ❑ Cover: 2.50 **NM** value: **Cover or less**
Circ: CapCity orders: **13,850**
One-shot. • JSA to Ragnarok after Crisis

LAST DAZE OF THE BAT-GUY Mythic

1 ❑ b&w Cover: 2.95 **NM** value: **Cover or less**

LAST DEFENDER OF CAMELOT, THE Zim

1 ❑ b&w Cover: 4.95 **NM** value: **Cover or less**
No issue number.

LAST DITCH Edge

1 ❑ b&w Cover: 2.50 **NM** value: **Cover or less**

LAST GASP COMICS AND STORIES Last Gasp Eco-Funnies

3 ❑ b&w Cover: 3.95 **NM** value: **Cover or less**

LAST GENERATION, THE Black Tie

1 ❑ 1987 Cover: 1.95 **NM** value: **Cover or less**
📖 From Twin Fires A New Beginning **A:** Mitch Faust **W:** Bill Bryer
2 ❑ Cover: 1.95 **NM** value: **Cover or less**

Other grades: Multiply prices above by **1.5 for Mint • 2/3 for Very Fine • 1/3 for Fine • 1/5 for Very Good • 1/8 for Good**

3 ❑ Cover: 1.95 **NM** value: **Cover or less**
4 ❑ Cover: 1.95 **NM** value: **Cover or less**
5 ❑ 1989 Cover: 1.95 **NM** value: **Cover or less**
Bk 1❑ Cover: 9.95 **NM** value: **Cover or less**
• Reprints The Last Generation #1-3; Published by Caliber

LAST KISS — Eclipse

1 ❑ Feb 2001, b&w Cover: 3.95 **NM** value: **Cover or less**
Circ: Diamd. preorders: **1,188**

LAST OF THE DRAGONS — Marvel / Epic

1 ❑ Cover: 6.95 **NM** value: **Cover or less**
Circ: CapCity orders: **3,150**

LAST OF THE VIKING HEROES, THE — Genesis West

1 ❑ Mar 1987 Cover: 1.50 **NM** value: **Cover or less**
Circ: CapCity orders: **6,850**
📖 Last of the Viking Heroes; The Promise; Challenge!!; Decision! **A:** Michael Thibodeaux **C:** Jack Kirby **W:** Michael Thibodeaux
2 ❑ Jun 1987 Cover: 2.00 **NM** value: **Cover or less**
Circ: CapCity orders: **5,250**
A: Michael Thibodeaux **C:** George Pérez **W:** Michael Thibodeaux
3 ❑ Cover: 1.75 **NM** value: **Cover or less**
Circ: CapCity orders: **5,050**
A: Michael Thibodeaux **C:** John Byrne **W:** Michael Thibodeaux
4 ❑ Cover: 1.75 **NM** value: **Cover or less**
Circ: CapCity orders: **3,950**
A: Michael Thibodeaux **C:** Howard Chaykin **W:** Michael Thibodeaux
5/A ❑ Jun 1988 Cover: 1.95 **NM** value: **Cover or less**
Circ: CapCity orders: **3,100**
A: Jack Kirby; Michael Thibodeaux **C:** Dave Stevens **W:** Michael Thibodeaux
5/B ❑ 1988 Cover: 1.95 **NM** value: **Cover or less**
Circ: CapCity orders: **2,425**
A: Michael Thibodeaux **W:** Michael Thibodeaux
6 ❑ 1988 Cover: 1.95 **NM** value: **Cover or less**
Circ: CapCity orders: **2,975**
A: Michael Thibodeaux **W:** Michael Thibodeaux
7 ❑ Jan 1989 Cover: 1.95 **NM** value: **Cover or less**
Circ: CapCity orders: **3,250**
A: Michael Thibodeaux **W:** Michael Thibodeaux
8 ❑ Jul 1989 Cover: 1.95 **NM** value: **Cover or less**
Circ: CapCity orders: **2,850**
A: Michael Thibodeaux **W:** Michael Thibodeaux
9 ❑ Cover: 1.95 **NM** value: **2.50**
Circ: CapCity orders: **2,525**
A: Michael Thibodeaux **W:** Michael Thibodeaux
10 ❑ Cover: 2.50 **NM** value: **Cover or less**
Circ: CapCity orders: **2,525**
A: Michael Thibodeaux **W:** Michael Thibodeaux
11 ❑ Cover: 2.50 **NM** value: **Cover or less**
A: Michael Thibodeaux **W:** Michael Thibodeaux
12 ❑ Cover: 2.50 **NM** value: **Cover or less**
📖 The Final Confrontation **A:** Michael Thibodeaux **W:** Michael Thibodeaux
Smr 1❑Mar 1988 Cover: 2.50 **NM** value: **Cover or less**
Circ: CapCity orders: **6,075**
• digest. • Summer Special #1 **A:** Michael Thibodeaux; Frank Frazetta(cover) **C:** Frank Frazetta **W:** Jack Kirby; Michael Thibodeaux
Smr 2❑ Cover: 2.50 **NM** value: **Cover or less**
• Signed, numbered edition signed by authors. • Summer Special #2 **A:** Michael Thibodeaux **W:** Michael Thibodeaux ★ Appearance of Teenage Mutant Ninja Turtles.
Smr 3❑Apr 1991 Cover: 2.50 **NM** value: **Cover or less**
Circ: CapCity orders: **7,950**
• Wizard mail-in promotional edition. • Summer Special #3 **A:** Michael Thibodeaux **W:** Michael Thibodeaux ★ Appearance of Teenage Mutant Ninja Turtles.

LAST ONE, THE — DC / Vertigo

1 ❑ Jul 1993 Cover: 2.50 **NM** value: **Cover or less**
Circ: CapCity orders: **22,950**
📖 Beyond The Curtain **A:** Dan Sweetman **W:** J.M. DeMatteis
2 ❑ Aug 1993 Cover: 2.50 **NM** value: **Cover or less**
Circ: CapCity orders: **13,500**
📖 A Memorable Fancy **A:** Dan Sweetman **W:** J.M. DeMatteis
3 ❑ Sep 1993 Cover: 2.50 **NM** value: **Cover or less**
Circ: CapCity orders: **10,750**
A: Dan Sweetman **W:** J.M. DeMatteis
4 ❑ Oct 1993 Cover: 2.50 **NM** value: **Cover or less**
Circ: CapCity orders: **10,450**
📖 Reflections **A:** Dan Sweetman **W:** J.M. DeMatteis
5 ❑ Nov 1993 Cover: 2.50 **NM** value: **Cover or less**
Circ: CapCity orders: **9,800**
📖 Need **A:** Dan Sweetman **W:** J.M. DeMatteis
6 ❑ Dec 1993 Cover: 2.50 **NM** value: **Cover or less**
Circ: CapCity orders: **9,900**
A: Dan Sweetman **W:** J.M. DeMatteis

LAST PLANET, THE — MBS

1 ❑ Cover: 2.50 **NM** value: **Cover or less**
📖 Out Of The Frying Pan; Of Madmen And Gastronomic Ghoulashness; Real Downers **A:** David Pugh **W:** Simon Davies

LAST STARFIGHTER, THE — Marvel

1 ❑ Oct 1984 Cover: 0.75 **NM** value: **2.00**
A: Brett Blevins **W:** Bill Manto
2 ❑ Nov 1984 Cover: 0.75 **NM** value: **2.00**
A: Brett Blevins **W:** Bill Manto
3 ❑ Dec 1984 Cover: 0.75 **NM** value: **2.00**
A: Brett Blevins **W:** Bill Manto

LAST TEMPTATION, THE — Marvel Music

Sandman creator and scribe Neil Gaiman and occasional collaborator Michael Zulli (Sandman, Witchcraft: La Terreur) bring classic shock-rocker Alice Cooper to haunting life as the host of the Theatre of the Real in this limited series based on a Cooper album of the same name.

The cautionary tale concerns a brash boy named Steven and the loss of his innocence, as the harsh realities of life are revealed to him on the theater's stage. The Last Temptation is an interesting, gorgeously illustrated morality play and one of the few offerings from the "Marvel Music" line of comics.

1 ❑ May 1994 Cover: 4.95 **NM** value: **Cover or less**
📖 Bad Place Alone **A:** Michael Zulli **W:** Neil Gaiman ★ Appearance of Alice Cooper.
2 ❑ Aug 1994 Cover: 4.95 **NM** value: **Cover or less**
A: Michael Zulli **W:** Neil Gaiman
3 ❑ Dec 1994 Cover: 4.95 **NM** value: **Cover or less**
📖 Cleanse by Fire **A:** Michael Zulli **W:** Neil Gaiman

LATEST COMICS — Spotlight

1 ❑ ca. 1945 Cover: 0.10 **NM** value: **100.00**
2 ❑ ca. 1945 Cover: 0.10 **NM** value: **75.00**
• **CGC:** 5 graded, best 9.8

LATIGO — Cottonwood

Bk 1❑ Cover: 9.95 **NM** value: **Cover or less**
• 1979-1980
Bk 2❑ Cover: 9.95 **NM** value: **Cover or less**
• 1980-1981 ★ Origin of Latigo.
Bk 3❑ Cover: 9.95 **NM** value: **Cover or less**
Bk 4❑ Cover: 9.95 **NM** value: **Cover or less**

LATIGO KID WESTERN — AC

1 ❑ b&w Cover: 1.95 **NM** value: **Cover or less**
📖 The Bigger They Are…; Red Mask of the Rio Grande; Los Tres Amigos **A:** John Severin; Bill Black **W:** Bill Black

LAUGH COMICS — Archie

One of the major homes of a true cultural icon, Laugh chronicled the adventures of Archie, Jughead, and the rest of the Riverdale gang for almost 40 years. Witness Archie's dating dilemmas: Will he chose the lovely and rich Veronica or the equally fetching Betty? Will either of them give him the time of day, once he does decide? And will Reggie, the perpetual cloud over Archie's parade, ever stop trying to be just a little bit better at everything than his redheaded opponent? Throughout the years, in the pages of Laugh, Archie, his friends, and his adversaries mirrored the fads and fashions that were sweeping the real-world kids who read this classic comic book.

20 ❑ Fal 1946 Cover: 0.10 **NM** value: **185.00**
• Formerly Black Hood
21 ❑ Win 1946 Cover: 0.10 **NM** value: **150.00**
22 ❑ Spr 1947 Cover: 0.10 **NM** value: **150.00**
23 ❑ Sum 1947 Cover: 0.10 **NM** value: **150.00**
24 ❑ Dec 1947 Cover: 0.10 **NM** value: **150.00**
25 ❑ Feb 1948 Cover: 0.10 **NM** value: **150.00**
26 ❑ Apr 1948 Cover: 0.10 **NM** value: **125.00**
27 ❑ Jun 1948 Cover: 0.10 **NM** value: **125.00**
• **CGC:** 1 graded, best 9.4
28 ❑ Aug 1948 Cover: 0.10 **NM** value: **125.00**
29 ❑ Oct 1948 Cover: 0.10 **NM** value: **125.00**
30 ❑ Dec 1948 Cover: 0.10 **NM** value: **125.00**
• **CGC:** 1 graded, best 8.5
31 ❑ Feb 1949 Cover: 0.10 **NM** value: **90.00**
32 ❑ Apr 1949 Cover: 0.10 **NM** value: **90.00**
33 ❑ Jun 1949 Cover: 0.10 **NM** value: **90.00**
34 ❑ Aug 1949 Cover: 0.10 **NM** value: **90.00**
35 ❑ Oct 1949 Cover: 0.10 **NM** value: **90.00**
36 ❑ Dec 1949 Cover: 0.10 **NM** value: **90.00**
37 ❑ Feb 1950 Cover: 0.10 **NM** value: **90.00**
38 ❑ Apr 1950 Cover: 0.10 **NM** value: **90.00**
39 ❑ Jun 1950 Cover: 0.10 **NM** value: **90.00**
40 ❑ Aug 1950 Cover: 0.10 **NM** value: **90.00**
41 ❑ Oct 1950 Cover: 0.10 **NM** value: **60.00**
42 ❑ Dec 1950 Cover: 0.10 **NM** value: **60.00**
43 ❑ Feb 1951 Cover: 0.10 **NM** value: **60.00**
44 ❑ Apr 1951 Cover: 0.10 **NM** value: **60.00**
45 ❑ Jun 1951 Cover: 0.10 **NM** value: **60.00**
46 ❑ Aug 1951 Cover: 0.10 **NM** value: **60.00**
47 ❑ Oct 1951 Cover: 0.10 **NM** value: **60.00**
48 ❑ Dec 1951 Cover: 0.10 **NM** value: **60.00**
• **CGC:** 1 graded, best 9.2
49 ❑ Feb 1952 Cover: 0.10 **NM** value: **60.00**
50 ❑ Apr 1952 Cover: 0.10 **NM** value: **60.00**
51 ❑ Jun 1952 Cover: 0.10 **NM** value: **45.00**
52 ❑ Aug 1952 Cover: 0.10 **NM** value: **45.00**
53 ❑ Oct 1952 Cover: 0.10 **NM** value: **45.00**
54 ❑ Dec 1952 Cover: 0.10 **NM** value: **45.00**
55 ❑ Feb 1953 Cover: 0.10 **NM** value: **45.00**
56 ❑ Apr 1953 Cover: 0.10 **NM** value: **45.00**
57 ❑ Jun 1953 Cover: 0.10 **NM** value: **45.00**
58 ❑ Aug 1953 Cover: 0.10 **NM** value: **45.00**
59 ❑ Oct 1953 Cover: 0.10 **NM** value: **45.00**
60 ❑ Dec 1953 Cover: 0.10 **NM** value: **45.00**
61 ❑ Feb 1954 Cover: 0.10 **NM** value: **28.00**
62 ❑ Apr 1954 Cover: 0.10 **NM** value: **28.00**
63 ❑ Jun 1954 Cover: 0.10 **NM** value: **28.00**
64 ❑ Aug 1954 Cover: 0.10 **NM** value: **28.00**
65 ❑ Oct 1954 Cover: 0.10 **NM** value: **28.00**
66 ❑ Dec 1954 Cover: 0.10 **NM** value: **28.00**
67 ❑ Feb 1955 Cover: 0.10 **NM** value: **28.00**
68 ❑ Apr 1955 Cover: 0.10 **NM** value: **28.00**
69 ❑ Jun 1955 Cover: 0.10 **NM** value: **28.00**
70 ❑ Aug 1955 Cover: 0.10 **NM** value: **28.00**
71 ❑ Oct 1955 Cover: 0.10 **NM** value: **24.00**
72 ❑ Dec 1955 Cover: 0.10 **NM** value: **24.00**
73 ❑ Feb 1956 Cover: 0.10 **NM** value: **24.00**
74 ❑ Apr 1956 Cover: 0.10 **NM** value: **24.00**
75 ❑ Jun 1956 Cover: 0.10 **NM** value: **24.00**
76 ❑ Aug 1956 Cover: 0.10 **NM** value: **24.00**
77 ❑ Oct 1956 Cover: 0.10 **NM** value: **24.00**
78 ❑ Dec 1956 Cover: 0.10 **NM** value: **24.00**
79 ❑ Feb 1957 Cover: 0.10 **NM** value: **24.00**
80 ❑ Apr 1957 Cover: 0.10 **NM** value: **24.00**
81 ❑ Jun 1957 Cover: 0.10 **NM** value: **20.00**
82 ❑ Aug 1957 Cover: 0.10 **NM** value: **20.00**
83 ❑ Oct 1957 Cover: 0.10 **NM** value: **20.00**
84 ❑ Dec 1957 Cover: 0.10 **NM** value: **20.00**
85 ❑ Feb 1958 Cover: 0.10 **NM** value: **20.00**
86 ❑ Apr 1958 Cover: 0.10 **NM** value: **20.00**
87 ❑ Jun 1958 Cover: 0.10 **NM** value: **20.00**
88 ❑ Jul 1958 Cover: 0.10 **NM** value: **20.00**
89 ❑ Aug 1958 Cover: 0.10 **NM** value: **20.00**
90 ❑ Sep 1958 Cover: 0.10 **NM** value: **20.00**
91 ❑ Oct 1958 Cover: 0.10 **NM** value: **18.00**
92 ❑ Nov 1958 Cover: 0.10 **NM** value: **18.00**
93 ❑ Dec 1958 Cover: 0.10 **NM** value: **18.00**
94 ❑ Jan 1959 Cover: 0.10 **NM** value: **18.00**
95 ❑ Feb 1959 Cover: 0.10 **NM** value: **18.00**
96 ❑ Mar 1959 Cover: 0.10 **NM** value: **18.00**
97 ❑ Apr 1959 Cover: 0.10 **NM** value: **18.00**
98 ❑ May 1959 Cover: 0.10 **NM** value: **18.00**
99 ❑ Jun 1959 Cover: 0.10 **NM** value: **18.00**
100 ❑ Jul 1959 Cover: 0.10 **NM** value: **18.00**
101 ❑ Aug 1959 Cover: 0.10 **NM** value: **15.00**
102 ❑ Sep 1959 Cover: 0.10 **NM** value: **15.00**
103 ❑ Oct 1959 Cover: 0.10 **NM** value: **15.00**
104 ❑ Nov 1959 Cover: 0.10 **NM** value: **15.00**
105 ❑ Dec 1959 Cover: 0.10 **NM** value: **15.00**
106 ❑ Jan 1960 Cover: 0.10 **NM** value: **15.00**
107 ❑ Feb 1960 Cover: 0.10 **NM** value: **15.00**
108 ❑ Mar 1960 Cover: 0.10 **NM** value: **15.00**
109 ❑ Apr 1960 Cover: 0.10 **NM** value: **15.00**
110 ❑ May 1960 Cover: 0.10 **NM** value: **15.00**
111 ❑ Jun 1960 Cover: 0.10 **NM** value: **15.00**
112 ❑ Jul 1960 Cover: 0.10 **NM** value: **15.00**
113 ❑ Aug 1960 Cover: 0.10 **NM** value: **15.00**
114 ❑ Sep 1960 Cover: 0.10 **NM** value: **15.00**
115 ❑ Oct 1960 Cover: 0.10 **NM** value: **15.00**
116 ❑ Nov 1960 Cover: 0.10 **NM** value: **15.00**
117 ❑ Dec 1960 Cover: 0.10 **NM** value: **15.00**
118 ❑ Jan 1961 Cover: 0.10 **NM** value: **15.00**
Circ: Statement: **241,416**
119 ❑ Feb 1961 Cover: 0.10 **NM** value: **15.00**
Circ: Statement: **241,416**
120 ❑ Mar 1961 Cover: 0.10 **NM** value: **15.00**
Circ: Statement: **241,416**
121 ❑ Apr 1961 Cover: 0.10 **NM** value: **15.00**
Circ: Statement: **241,416**
122 ❑ May 1961 Cover: 0.10 **NM** value: **15.00**
Circ: Statement: **241,416**
123 ❑ Jun 1961 Cover: 0.10 **NM** value: **15.00**
Circ: Statement: **241,416**
124 ❑ Jul 1961 Cover: 0.10 **NM** value: **15.00**
Circ: Statement: **241,416**
125 ❑ Aug 1961 Cover: 0.10 **NM** value: **15.00**
Circ: Statement: **241,416**
126 ❑ Sep 1961 Cover: 0.10 **NM** value: **15.00**
Circ: Statement: **241,416**
127 ❑ Oct 1961 Cover: 0.10 **NM** value: **15.00**
Circ: Statement: **241,416**
128 ❑ Nov 1961 Cover: 0.10 **NM** value: **15.00**
Circ: Statement: **241,416**
129 ❑ Dec 1961 Cover: 0.10 **NM** value: **15.00**
Circ: Statement: **241,416**
130 ❑ Jan 1962 Cover: 0.12 **NM** value: **15.00**
Circ: Statement: **244,255**
131 ❑ Feb 1962 Cover: 0.12 **NM** value: **12.00**
Circ: Statement: **244,255**
132 ❑ Mar 1962 Cover: 0.12 **NM** value: **12.00**
Circ: Statement: **244,255**
133 ❑ Apr 1962 Cover: 0.12 **NM** value: **12.00**
Circ: Statement: **244,255**
134 ❑ May 1962 Cover: 0.12 **NM** value: **12.00**
Circ: Statement: **244,255**
135 ❑ Jun 1962 Cover: 0.12 **NM** value: **12.00**
Circ: Statement: **244,255**
136 ❑ Jul 1962 Cover: 0.12 **NM** value: **12.00**
Circ: Statement: **244,255**
137 ❑ Aug 1962 Cover: 0.12 **NM** value: **12.00**
Circ: Statement: **244,255**
138 ❑ Sep 1962 Cover: 0.12 **NM** value: **12.00**
Circ: Statement: **244,255**
139 ❑ Oct 1962 Cover: 0.12 **NM** value: **12.00**
Circ: Statement: **244,255**
140 ❑ Nov 1962 Cover: 0.12 **NM** value: **12.00**
Circ: Statement: **244,255**

CGC-graded: Multiply prices above by **33 for 9.9 M • 16 for 9.8 NM/M • 7 for 9.6 NM+ • 5 for 9.4 NM • 2.5 for 9.2 NM- • 1.5 for 9.0 VF/NM**

141 ❑ Dec 1962 Cover: 0.12 **NM** value: **12.00**
Circ: Statement: **244,255**
142 ❑ Jan 1963 Cover: 0.12 **NM** value: **12.00**
Circ: Statement: **264,863**
143 ❑ Feb 1963 Cover: 0.12 **NM** value: **12.00**
Circ: Statement: **264,863**
144 ❑ Mar 1963 Cover: 0.12 **NM** value: **12.00**
Circ: Statement: **264,863**
145 ❑ Apr 1963 Cover: 0.12 **NM** value: **12.00**
Circ: Statement: **264,863**
146 ❑ May 1963 Cover: 0.12 **NM** value: **12.00**
Circ: Statement: **264,863**
147 ❑ Jun 1963 Cover: 0.12 **NM** value: **12.00**
Circ: Statement: **264,863**
148 ❑ Jul 1963 Cover: 0.12 **NM** value: **12.00**
Circ: Statement: **264,863**
149 ❑ Aug 1963 Cover: 0.12 **NM** value: **12.00**
Circ: Statement: **264,863**
150 ❑ Sep 1963 Cover: 0.12 **NM** value: **12.00**
Circ: Statement: **264,863**
151 ❑ Oct 1963 Cover: 0.12 **NM** value: **12.00**
Circ: Statement: **264,863**
152 ❑ Nov 1963 Cover: 0.12 **NM** value: **12.00**
Circ: Statement: **264,863**
153 ❑ Dec 1963 Cover: 0.12 **NM** value: **12.00**
Circ: Statement: **264,863**
154 ❑ Jan 1964 Cover: 0.12 **NM** value: **12.00**
Circ: Statement: **271,122**
155 ❑ Feb 1964 Cover: 0.12 **NM** value: **12.00**
Circ: Statement: **271,122**
156 ❑ Mar 1964 Cover: 0.12 **NM** value: **12.00**
Circ: Statement: **271,122**
157 ❑ Apr 1964 Cover: 0.12 **NM** value: **12.00**
Circ: Statement: **271,122**
158 ❑ May 1964 Cover: 0.12 **NM** value: **12.00**
Circ: Statement: **271,122**
159 ❑ Jun 1964 Cover: 0.12 **NM** value: **12.00**
Circ: Statement: **271,122**
160 ❑ Jul 1964 Cover: 0.12 **NM** value: **12.00**
Circ: Statement: **271,122**
161 ❑ Aug 1964 Cover: 0.12 **NM** value: **12.00**
Circ: Statement: **271,122**
162 ❑ Sep 1964 Cover: 0.12 **NM** value: **12.00**
Circ: Statement: **271,122**
163 ❑ Oct 1964 Cover: 0.12 **NM** value: **12.00**
Circ: Statement: **271,122**
164 ❑ Nov 1964 Cover: 0.12 **NM** value: **12.00**
Circ: Statement: **271,122**
165 ❑ Dec 1964 Cover: 0.12 **NM** value: **12.00**
Circ: Statement: **271,122**
166 ❑ Jan 1965 Cover: 0.12 **NM** value: **12.00**
Circ: Statement: **269,747** • **CGC:** 1 graded, best 8.5
167 ❑ Feb 1965 Cover: 0.12 **NM** value: **12.00**
Circ: Statement: **269,747**
168 ❑ Mar 1965 Cover: 0.12 **NM** value: **12.00**
Circ: Statement: **269,747**
169 ❑ Apr 1965 Cover: 0.12 **NM** value: **12.00**
Circ: Statement: **269,747**
170 ❑ May 1965 Cover: 0.12 **NM** value: **12.00**
Circ: Statement: **269,747**
171 ❑ Jun 1965 Cover: 0.12 **NM** value: **9.00**
Circ: Statement: **269,747**
172 ❑ Jul 1965 Cover: 0.12 **NM** value: **9.00**
Circ: Statement: **269,747**
173 ❑ Aug 1965 Cover: 0.12 **NM** value: **9.00**
Circ: Statement: **269,747**
174 ❑ Sep 1965 Cover: 0.12 **NM** value: **9.00**
Circ: Statement: **269,747**
175 ❑ Oct 1965 Cover: 0.12 **NM** value: **9.00**
Circ: Statement: **269,747**
176 ❑ Nov 1965 Cover: 0.12 **NM** value: **9.00**
Circ: Statement: **269,747**
177 ❑ Dec 1965 Cover: 0.12 **NM** value: **9.00**
Circ: Statement: **269,747**
178 ❑ Jan 1966 Cover: 0.12 **NM** value: **9.00**
Circ: Statement: **282,731**
179 ❑ Feb 1966 Cover: 0.12 **NM** value: **9.00**
Circ: Statement: **282,731**
180 ❑ Mar 1966 Cover: 0.12 **NM** value: **9.00**
Circ: Statement: **282,731**
181 ❑ Apr 1966 Cover: 0.12 **NM** value: **9.00**
Circ: Statement: **282,731**
182 ❑ May 1966 Cover: 0.12 **NM** value: **9.00**
Circ: Statement: **282,731**
183 ❑ Jun 1966 Cover: 0.12 **NM** value: **9.00**
Circ: Statement: **282,731**
184 ❑ Jul 1966 Cover: 0.12 **NM** value: **9.00**
Circ: Statement: **282,731**
185 ❑ Aug 1966 Cover: 0.12 **NM** value: **9.00**
Circ: Statement: **282,731**
186 ❑ Sep 1966 Cover: 0.12 **NM** value: **9.00**
Circ: Statement: **282,731**
187 ❑ Oct 1966 Cover: 0.12 **NM** value: **9.00**
Circ: Statement: **282,731**
188 ❑ Nov 1966 Cover: 0.12 **NM** value: **9.00**
Circ: Statement: **282,731**
189 ❑ Dec 1966 Cover: 0.12 **NM** value: **9.00**
Circ: Statement: **282,731**
190 ❑ Jan 1967 Cover: 0.12 **NM** value: **8.00**
Circ: Statement: **285,544**
191 ❑ Feb 1967 Cover: 0.12 **NM** value: **8.00**
Circ: Statement: **285,544**
192 ❑ Mar 1967 Cover: 0.12 **NM** value: **8.00**
Circ: Statement: **285,544**
193 ❑ Apr 1967 Cover: 0.12 **NM** value: **8.00**
Circ: Statement: **285,544**
194 ❑ May 1967 Cover: 0.12 **NM** value: **8.00**
Circ: Statement: **285,544**
195 ❑ Jun 1967 Cover: 0.12 **NM** value: **8.00**
Circ: Statement: **285,544**
196 ❑ Jul 1967 Cover: 0.12 **NM** value: **8.00**
Circ: Statement: **285,544**
197 ❑ Aug 1967 Cover: 0.12 **NM** value: **8.00**
Circ: Statement: **285,544**
198 ❑ Sep 1967 Cover: 0.12 **NM** value: **8.00**
Circ: Statement: **285,544**
199 ❑ Oct 1967 Cover: 0.12 **NM** value: **8.00**
Circ: Statement: **285,544**
200 ❑ Nov 1967 Cover: 0.12 **NM** value: **8.00**
Circ: Statement: **285,544**
201 ❑ Dec 1967 Cover: 0.12 **NM** value: **6.00**
Circ: Statement: **285,544**
202 ❑ Jan 1968 Cover: 0.12 **NM** value: **6.00**
Circ: Statement: **347,178**
203 ❑ Feb 1968 Cover: 0.12 **NM** value: **6.00**
Circ: Statement: **347,178**
204 ❑ Mar 1968 Cover: 0.12 **NM** value: **6.00**
Circ: Statement: **347,178**
205 ❑ Apr 1968 Cover: 0.12 **NM** value: **6.00**
Circ: Statement: **347,178**
• Has 1967 Statement, filed 10/1/1967; avg print run 459,898; avg sales 283,764; avg subs 1,780; avg total paid 285,544; samples 300; max existent 285,844; 38% of run returned
206 ❑ May 1968 Cover: 0.12 **NM** value: **6.00**
Circ: Statement: **347,178**
207 ❑ Jun 1968 Cover: 0.12 **NM** value: **6.00**
Circ: Statement: **347,178**
208 ❑ Jul 1968 Cover: 0.12 **NM** value: **6.00**
Circ: Statement: **347,178**
209 ❑ Aug 1968 Cover: 0.12 **NM** value: **6.00**
Circ: Statement: **347,178**
210 ❑ Sep 1968 Cover: 0.12 **NM** value: **6.00**
Circ: Statement: **347,178**
211 ❑ Oct 1968 Cover: 0.12 **NM** value: **6.00**
Circ: Statement: **347,178**
212 ❑ Nov 1968 Cover: 0.12 **NM** value: **6.00**
Circ: Statement: **347,178**
213 ❑ Dec 1968 Cover: 0.12 **NM** value: **6.00**
Circ: Statement: **347,178**
214 ❑ Jan 1969 Cover: 0.12 **NM** value: **6.00**
215 ❑ Feb 1969 Cover: 0.12 **NM** value: **6.00**
216 ❑ Mar 1969 Cover: 0.12 **NM** value: **6.00**
217 ❑ Apr 1969 Cover: 0.12 **NM** value: **6.00**
218 ❑ May 1969 Cover: 0.12 **NM** value: **6.00**
• Has 1968 Statement, filed 11/1/1968; avg print run 498,035; avg sales 344,538; avg subs 2,640; avg total paid and max existent 347,178; 30% of run returned
219 ❑ Jun 1969 Cover: 0.12 **NM** value: **6.00**
220 ❑ Jul 1969 Cover: 0.15 **NM** value: **6.00**
221 ❑ Aug 1969 Cover: 0.15 **NM** value: **6.00**
222 ❑ Sep 1969 Cover: 0.15 **NM** value: **6.00**
223 ❑ Oct 1969 Cover: 0.15 **NM** value: **6.00**
224 ❑ Nov 1969 Cover: 0.15 **NM** value: **6.00**
225 ❑ Dec 1969 Cover: 0.15 **NM** value: **6.00**
226 ❑ Jan 1970 Cover: 0.15 **NM** value: **6.00**
Circ: Statement: **290,156**
• Title changes name to Laugh
227 ❑ Feb 1970 Cover: 0.15 **NM** value: **6.00**
Circ: Statement: **290,156**
228 ❑ Mar 1970 Cover: 0.15 **NM** value: **6.00**
Circ: Statement: **290,156**
229 ❑ Apr 1970 Cover: 0.15 **NM** value: **6.00**
Circ: Statement: **290,156**
230 ❑ May 1970 Cover: 0.15 **NM** value: **6.00**
Circ: Statement: **290,156**
231 ❑ Jun 1970 Cover: 0.15 **NM** value: **6.00**
Circ: Statement: **290,156**
232 ❑ Jul 1970 Cover: 0.15 **NM** value: **6.00**
Circ: Statement: **290,156**
233 ❑ Aug 1970 Cover: 0.15 **NM** value: **6.00**
Circ: Statement: **290,156**
234 ❑ Sep 1970 Cover: 0.15 **NM** value: **6.00**
Circ: Statement: **290,156**
235 ❑ Oct 1970 Cover: 0.15 **NM** value: **6.00**
Circ: Statement: **290,156**
236 ❑ Nov 1970 Cover: 0.15 **NM** value: **6.00**
Circ: Statement: **290,156**
237 ❑ Dec 1970 Cover: 0.15 **NM** value: **6.00**
Circ: Statement: **290,156**
238 ❑ Jan 1971 Cover: 0.15 **NM** value: **6.00**
239 ❑ Feb 1971 Cover: 0.15 **NM** value: **6.00**
240 ❑ Mar 1971 Cover: 0.15 **NM** value: **6.00**
241 ❑ Apr 1971 Cover: 0.15 **NM** value: **6.00**
• Has 1970 Statement, filed 10/1/70; avg print run 493,455; avg sales 289,893; avg subs 263; avg total paid and max existent 290,156; 41% of run returned
242 ❑ May 1971 Cover: 0.15 **NM** value: **6.00**
243 ❑ Jun 1971 Cover: 0.15 **NM** value: **6.00**
244 ❑ Jul 1971 Cover: 0.15 **NM** value: **6.00**
245 ❑ Aug 1971 Cover: 0.15 **NM** value: **6.00**
246 ❑ Sep 1971 Cover: 0.15 **NM** value: **6.00**
247 ❑ Oct 1971 Cover: 0.15 **NM** value: **6.00**
248 ❑ Nov 1971 Cover: 0.15 **NM** value: **6.00**
249 ❑ Dec 1971 Cover: 0.15 **NM** value: **6.00**
250 ❑ Jan 1972 Cover: 0.15 **NM** value: **6.00**
Circ: Statement: **258,876**
251 ❑ Feb 1972 Cover: 0.15 **NM** value: **4.00**
Circ: Statement: **258,876**
252 ❑ Mar 1972 Cover: 0.15 **NM** value: **4.00**
Circ: Statement: **258,876**
253 ❑ Apr 1972 Cover: 0.15 **NM** value: **4.00**
Circ: Statement: **258,876**
254 ❑ May 1972 Cover: 0.20 **NM** value: **2.00**
Circ: Statement: **258,876**
255 ❑ Jun 1972 Cover: 0.20 **NM** value: **2.00**
Circ: Statement: **258,876**
256 ❑ Jul 1972 Cover: 0.20 **NM** value: **2.00**
Circ: Statement: **258,876**
257 ❑ Aug 1972 Cover: 0.20 **NM** value: **2.00**
Circ: Statement: **258,876**
258 ❑ Sep 1972 Cover: 0.20 **NM** value: **2.00**
Circ: Statement: **258,876**
259 ❑ Oct 1972 Cover: 0.20 **NM** value: **2.00**
Circ: Statement: **258,876**
260 ❑ Nov 1972 Cover: 0.20 **NM** value: **2.00**
Circ: Statement: **258,876**
261 ❑ Dec 1972 Cover: 0.20 **NM** value: **2.00**
Circ: Statement: **258,876**
262 ❑ Jan 1973 Cover: 0.20 **NM** value: **2.00**
Circ: Statement: **219,111**
263 ❑ Feb 1973 Cover: 0.20 **NM** value: **2.00**
Circ: Statement: **219,111**
264 ❑ Mar 1973 Cover: 0.20 **NM** value: **2.00**
Circ: Statement: **219,111**
265 ❑ Apr 1973 Cover: 0.20 **NM** value: **2.00**
Circ: Statement: **219,111**
• Has 1972 Statement; avg total paid circ 258,876
266 ❑ May 1973 Cover: 0.20 **NM** value: **2.00**
Circ: Statement: **219,111**
267 ❑ Jun 1973 Cover: 0.20 **NM** value: **2.00**
Circ: Statement: **219,111**
268 ❑ Jul 1973 Cover: 0.20 **NM** value: **2.00**
Circ: Statement: **219,111**
269 ❑ Aug 1973 Cover: 0.20 **NM** value: **2.00**
Circ: Statement: **219,111**
270 ❑ Sep 1973 Cover: 0.20 **NM** value: **2.00**
Circ: Statement: **219,111**
271 ❑ Oct 1973 Cover: 0.20 **NM** value: **2.00**
Circ: Statement: **219,111**
272 ❑ Nov 1973 Cover: 0.20 **NM** value: **2.00**
Circ: Statement: **219,111**
273 ❑ Dec 1973 Cover: 0.20 **NM** value: **2.00**
Circ: Statement: **219,111**
274 ❑ Jan 1974 Cover: 0.20 **NM** value: **2.00**
Circ: Statement: **198,709**
275 ❑ Feb 1974 Cover: 0.20 **NM** value: **2.00**
Circ: Statement: **198,709**
276 ❑ Mar 1974 Cover: 0.20 **NM** value: **2.00**
Circ: Statement: **198,709**
277 ❑ Apr 1974 Cover: 0.20 **NM** value: **2.00**
Circ: Statement: **198,709**
• Has 1973 Statement; avg total paid 219,111
278 ❑ May 1974 Cover: 0.20 **NM** value: **2.00**
Circ: Statement: **198,709**
279 ❑ Jun 1974 Cover: 0.20 **NM** value: **2.00**
Circ: Statement: **198,709**
280 ❑ Jul 1974 Cover: 0.20 **NM** value: **2.00**
Circ: Statement: **198,709**
281 ❑ Aug 1974 Cover: 0.20 **NM** value: **2.00**
Circ: Statement: **198,709**
282 ❑ Sep 1974 Cover: 0.20 **NM** value: **2.00**
Circ: Statement: **198,709**
283 ❑ Oct 1974 Cover: 0.20 **NM** value: **2.00**
Circ: Statement: **198,709**
284 ❑ Nov 1974 Cover: 0.20 **NM** value: **2.00**
Circ: Statement: **198,709**
285 ❑ Dec 1974 Cover: 0.20 **NM** value: **2.00**
Circ: Statement: **198,709**
286 ❑ Jan 1975 Cover: 0.20 **NM** value: **2.00**
Circ: Statement: **148,942**
287 ❑ Feb 1975 Cover: 0.20 **NM** value: **2.00**
Circ: Statement: **148,942**
288 ❑ Mar 1975 Cover: 0.20 **NM** value: **2.00**
Circ: Statement: **148,942**
289 ❑ Apr 1975 Cover: 0.20 **NM** value: **2.00**
Circ: Statement: **148,942**
• Has 1974 Statement; avg total paid circ 198,709
290 ❑ May 1975 Cover: 0.25 **NM** value: **4.00**
Circ: Statement: **148,942**
291 ❑ Jun 1975 Cover: 0.25 **NM** value: **4.00**
Circ: Statement: **148,942**
292 ❑ Jul 1975 Cover: 0.25 **NM** value: **4.00**
Circ: Statement: **148,942**
293 ❑ Aug 1975 Cover: 0.25 **NM** value: **4.00**
Circ: Statement: **148,942**
294 ❑ Sep 1975 Cover: 0.25 **NM** value: **4.00**
Circ: Statement: **148,942**
295 ❑ Oct 1975 Cover: 0.25 **NM** value: **4.00**
Circ: Statement: **148,942**
296 ❑ Nov 1975 Cover: 0.25 **NM** value: **4.00**
Circ: Statement: **148,942**
297 ❑ Dec 1975 Cover: 0.25 **NM** value: **4.00**
Circ: Statement: **148,942**
298 ❑ Jan 1976 Cover: 0.25 **NM** value: **4.00**
Circ: Statement: **135,257**
299 ❑ Feb 1976 Cover: 0.30 **NM** value: **4.00**
Circ: Statement: **135,257**
300 ❑ Mar 1976 Cover: 0.30 **NM** value: **4.00**
Circ: Statement: **135,257**
301 ❑ Apr 1976 Cover: 0.30 **NM** value: **2.50**
Circ: Statement: **135,257**
• Has 1975 Statement; avg total paid circ 148,942
302 ❑ May 1976 Cover: 0.30 **NM** value: **2.50**
Circ: Statement: **135,257**
303 ❑ Jun 1976 Cover: 0.30 **NM** value: **2.50**
Circ: Statement: **135,257**
304 ❑ Jul 1976 Cover: 0.30 **NM** value: **2.50**
Circ: Statement: **135,257**
305 ❑ Aug 1976 Cover: 0.30 **NM** value: **2.50**
Circ: Statement: **135,257**
306 ❑ Sep 1976 Cover: 0.30 **NM** value: **2.50**
Circ: Statement: **135,257**
307 ❑ Oct 1976 Cover: 0.30 **NM** value: **2.50**
Circ: Statement: **135,257**

Other grades: Multiply prices above by **1.5 for Mint • 2/3 for Very Fine • 1/3 for Fine • 1/5 for Very Good • 1/8 for Good**

308 ❑ Nov 1976 Cover: 0.30 **NM** value: **2.50**
Circ: Statement: **135,257**
309 ❑ Dec 1976 Cover: 0.30 **NM** value: **2.50**
Circ: Statement: **135,257**
310 ❑ Jan 1977 Cover: 0.30 **NM** value: **2.50**
Circ: Statement: **128,383**
311 ❑ Feb 1977 Cover: 0.30 **NM** value: **2.50**
Circ: Statement: **128,383**
312 ❑ Mar 1977 Cover: 0.30 **NM** value: **2.50**
Circ: Statement: **128,383**
313 ❑ Apr 1977 Cover: 0.30 **NM** value: **2.50**
Circ: Statement: **128,383**
• Has 1976 Statement; avg total paid circ 135,257
314 ❑ May 1977 Cover: 0.30 **NM** value: **2.50**
Circ: Statement: **128,383**
315 ❑ Jun 1977 Cover: 0.30 **NM** value: **2.50**
Circ: Statement: **128,383**
316 ❑ Jul 1977 Cover: 0.35 **NM** value: **2.50**
Circ: Statement: **128,383**
317 ❑ Aug 1977 Cover: 0.35 **NM** value: **2.50**
Circ: Statement: **128,383**
318 ❑ Sep 1977 Cover: 0.35 **NM** value: **2.50**
Circ: Statement: **128,383**
319 ❑ Oct 1977 Cover: 0.35 **NM** value: **2.50**
Circ: Statement: **128,383**
320 ❑ Nov 1977 Cover: 0.35 **NM** value: **2.50**
Circ: Statement: **128,383**
Archie: Breaking Point; Archie: Crash Bash; Archie: Fast Friends; Archie's Gag Bag; Li'l Jinx: Joker's Wild!; Archie: The Wet Look ★ Appearance of Reggie, Betty, Li'l Jinx, Archie, Mr. Lodge, Jughead, Veronica, Moose, Fat Charley.
321 ❑ Dec 1977 Cover: 0.35 **NM** value: **2.50**
Circ: Statement: **128,383**
322 ❑ Jan 1978 Cover: 0.35 **NM** value: **2.50**
323 ❑ Feb 1978 Cover: 0.35 **NM** value: **2.50**
324 ❑ Mar 1978 Cover: 0.35 **NM** value: **2.50**
325 ❑ Apr 1978 Cover: 0.35 **NM** value: **2.50**
• Has 1977 Statement, filed 10/1/77; avg print run 309,556; avg sales 128,179; avg subs 204; avg total paid 128,383; office use 200; max existent 128,683; 59% of run returned
326 ❑ May 1978 Cover: 0.35 **NM** value: **2.50**
327 ❑ Jun 1978 Cover: 0.35 **NM** value: **2.50**
328 ❑ Jul 1978 Cover: 0.35 **NM** value: **2.50**
329 ❑ Aug 1978 Cover: 0.35 **NM** value: **2.50**
330 ❑ Sep 1978 Cover: 0.35 **NM** value: **2.50**
331 ❑ Oct 1978 Cover: 0.35 **NM** value: **2.50**
332 ❑ Nov 1978 Cover: 0.35 **NM** value: **2.50**
333 ❑ Dec 1978 Cover: 0.35 **NM** value: **2.50**
334 ❑ Jan 1979 Cover: 0.35 **NM** value: **2.50**
335 ❑ Feb 1979 Cover: 0.35 **NM** value: **2.50**
336 ❑ Mar 1979 Cover: 0.35 **NM** value: **2.50**
337 ❑ Apr 1979 Cover: 0.40 **NM** value: **2.50**
338 ❑ May 1979 Cover: 0.40 **NM** value: **2.50**
339 ❑ Jun 1979 Cover: 0.40 **NM** value: **2.50**
340 ❑ Jul 1979 Cover: 0.40 **NM** value: **2.50**
341 ❑ Aug 1979 Cover: 0.40 **NM** value: **2.50**
342 ❑ Sep 1979 Cover: 0.40 **NM** value: **2.50**
343 ❑ Oct 1979 Cover: 0.40 **NM** value: **2.50**
344 ❑ Nov 1979 Cover: 0.40 **NM** value: **2.50**
345 ❑ Dec 1979 Cover: 0.40 **NM** value: **2.50**
346 ❑ Jan 1980 Cover: 0.40 **NM** value: **2.50**
347 ❑ Feb 1980 Cover: 0.40 **NM** value: **2.50**
348 ❑ Mar 1980 Cover: 0.40 **NM** value: **2.50**
349 ❑ Apr 1980 Cover: 0.40 **NM** value: **2.50**
350 ❑ May 1980 Cover: 0.40 **NM** value: **2.50**
351 ❑ Jun 1980 Cover: 0.40 **NM** value: **2.00**
352 ❑ Jul 1980 Cover: 0.40 **NM** value: **2.00**
353 ❑ Aug 1980 Cover: 0.50 **NM** value: **2.00**
354 ❑ Sep 1980 Cover: 0.50 **NM** value: **2.00**
355 ❑ Oct 1980 Cover: 0.50 **NM** value: **2.00**
356 ❑ Nov 1980 Cover: 0.50 **NM** value: **2.00**
357 ❑ Dec 1980 Cover: 0.50 **NM** value: **2.00**
358 ❑ Jan 1981 Cover: 0.50 **NM** value: **2.00**
359 ❑ Feb 1981 Cover: 0.50 **NM** value: **2.00**
360 ❑ Mar 1981 Cover: 0.50 **NM** value: **2.00**
361 ❑ Apr 1981 Cover: 0.50 **NM** value: **2.00**
362 ❑ May 1981 Cover: 0.50 **NM** value: **2.00**
363 ❑ Jun 1981 Cover: 0.50 **NM** value: **2.00**
364 ❑ Jul 1981 Cover: 0.50 **NM** value: **2.00**
365 ❑ Aug 1981 Cover: 0.50 **NM** value: **2.00**
366 ❑ Sep 1981 Cover: 0.50 **NM** value: **2.00**
367 ❑ Oct 1981 Cover: 0.50 **NM** value: **2.00**
368 ❑ Nov 1981 Cover: 0.50 **NM** value: **2.00**
369 ❑ Dec 1981 Cover: 0.60 **NM** value: **2.00**
370 ❑ Jan 1982 Cover: 0.60 **NM** value: **2.00**
371 ❑ Feb 1982 Cover: 0.60 **NM** value: **2.00**
372 ❑ May 1982 Cover: 0.60 **NM** value: **2.00**
373 ❑ Jul 1982 Cover: 0.60 **NM** value: **2.00**
374 ❑ Sep 1982 Cover: 0.60 **NM** value: **2.00**
375 ❑ Nov 1982 Cover: 0.60 **NM** value: **2.00**
376 ❑ Jan 1983 Cover: 0.60 **NM** value: **2.00**
Circ: Statement: **60,408**
377 ❑ Apr 1983 Cover: 0.60 **NM** value: **2.00**
Circ: Statement: **60,408**
378 ❑ Jul 1983 Cover: 0.60 **NM** value: **2.00**
Circ: Statement: **60,408**
379 ❑ Oct 1983 Cover: 0.60 **NM** value: **2.00**
Circ: Statement: **60,408**
380 ❑ Dec 1983 Cover: 0.60 **NM** value: **2.00**
Circ: Statement: **60,408**
381 ❑ Feb 1984 Cover: 0.60 **NM** value: **2.00**
Circ: Statement: **62,319**
382 ❑ Apr 1984 Cover: 0.60 **NM** value: **2.00**
Circ: Statement: **62,319**
383 ❑ Jun 1984 Cover: 0.60 **NM** value: **2.00**
Circ: Statement: **62,319**
384 ❑ Aug 1984 Cover: 0.60 **NM** value: **2.00**
Circ: Statement: **62,319**
385 ❑ Oct 1984 Cover: 0.60 **NM** value: **2.00**
Circ: Statement: **62,319**
386 ❑ Dec 1984 Cover: 0.60 **NM** value: **2.00**
Circ: Statement: **62,319**
387 ❑ Feb 1985 Cover: 0.60 **NM** value: **2.00**
Circ: Statement: **60,568**
388 ❑ Apr 1985 Cover: 0.65 **NM** value: **2.00**
Circ: Statement: **60,568**
389 ❑ Jun 1985 Cover: 0.65 **NM** value: **2.00**
Circ: Statement: **60,568**
390 ❑ Aug 1985 Cover: 0.65 **NM** value: **2.00**
Circ: Statement: **60,568**
391 ❑ Oct 1985 Cover: 0.65 **NM** value: **2.00**
Circ: Statement: **60,568**
392 ❑ Dec 1985 Cover: 0.65 **NM** value: **2.00**
Circ: Statement: **60,568**
393 ❑ Feb 1986 Cover: 0.65 **NM** value: **2.00**
Circ: Statement: **59,804**
394 ❑ Apr 1986 Cover: 0.65 **NM** value: **2.00**
Circ: Statement: **59,804**
395 ❑ Jun 1986 Cover: 0.65 **NM** value: **2.00**
Circ: Statement: **59,804**
396 ❑ Aug 1986 Cover: 0.75 **NM** value: **2.00**
Circ: Statement: **59,804**
397 ❑ Oct 1986 Cover: 0.75 **NM** value: **2.00**
Circ: Statement: **59,804**
398 ❑ Dec 1986 Cover: 0.75 **NM** value: **2.00**
Circ: Statement: **59,804**
399 ❑ Feb 1987 Cover: 0.75 **NM** value: **2.00**
Circ: Statement: **53,338**
• Circ figs are provided in Laugh, Vol. 2
400 ❑ Apr 1987 Cover: 0.75 **NM** value: **2.00**
Circ: Statement: **53,338**
• Circ figs are provided in Laugh, Vol. 2

LAUGH COMIX — M.L.J.

46 ❑ Sum 1944 Cover: 0.10 **NM** value: **150.00**
47 ❑ Fal 1944 Cover: 0.10 **NM** value: **100.00**
48 ❑ Win 1944 Cover: 0.10 **NM** value: **100.00**

LAUGH DIGEST MAGAZINE — Archie

The venerable Laugh Comics featuring Archie eventually gave birth to this digest-sized compendium of Archie strips in 1974. This miniature humor comic book began as Laugh Comics Digest and later made minor name changes to become Laugh Comics Digest Magazine, then its present Laugh Digest Magazine. By any name, it's been an affordable way for Archie fans to keep up on the latest antics of the entire Riverdale crew.

Sold frequently in grocery stores (next to the TV Guides), this digest has been an American favorite for more than 30 years. Not only are the comics suitable for young readers, but there was enough material inside to entertain for hours — all for about as much as parents would pay for the week's TV listings.

Early issues of Laugh Digest featured the little-known work of comics great Neal Adams.

1 ❑ Cover: 0.60 **NM** value: **10.00**
A: Neal Adams
2 ❑ Jan 1976 Cover: 0.60 **NM** value: **8.00**
3 ❑ Mar 1976 Cover: 0.60 **NM** value: **8.00**
4 ❑ May 1976 Cover: 0.60 **NM** value: **8.00**
5 ❑ Jul 1976 Cover: 0.60 **NM** value: **8.00**
6 ❑ Sep 1976 Cover: 0.60 **NM** value: **4.00**
7 ❑ Nov 1976 Cover: 0.60 **NM** value: **4.00**
8 ❑ Jan 1977 Cover: 0.60 **NM** value: **4.00**
Circ: Statement: **150,340**
9 ❑ Mar 1977 Cover: 0.60 **NM** value: **4.00**
Circ: Statement: **150,340**
10 ❑ May 1977 Cover: 0.60 **NM** value: **4.00**
Circ: Statement: **150,340**
11 ❑ Jul 1977 Cover: 0.60 **NM** value: **3.00**
Circ: Statement: **150,340**
12 ❑ Sep 1977 Cover: 0.60 **NM** value: **3.00**
Circ: Statement: **150,340**
13 ❑ Nov 1977 Cover: 0.75 **NM** value: **3.00**
Circ: Statement: **150,340**
14 ❑ Jan 1978 Cover: 0.75 **NM** value: **3.00**
Circ: Statement: **142,192**
15 ❑ Mar 1978 Cover: 0.75 **NM** value: **3.00**
Circ: Statement: **142,192**
16 ❑ May 1978 Cover: 0.75 **NM** value: **3.00**
Circ: Statement: **142,192**
• Has 1977 Statement; avg total paid circ 150,340
17 ❑ Jul 1978 Cover: 0.75 **NM** value: **3.00**
Circ: Statement: **142,192**
18 ❑ Sep 1978 Cover: 0.75 **NM** value: **3.00**
Circ: Statement: **142,192**
19 ❑ Nov 1978 Cover: 0.75 **NM** value: **3.00**
Circ: Statement: **142,192**
20 ❑ Jan 1979 Cover: 0.75 **NM** value: **3.00**
21 ❑ Mar 1979 Cover: 0.75 **NM** value: **2.00**
22 ❑ May 1979 Cover: 0.75 **NM** value: **2.00**
• Has 1978 Statement, filed 10/1/78; avg print run 258,046; avg sales 142,150; avg subs 42; avg total paid 142,192; office use 300; max existent 142,492; 45% of run returned
23 ❑ Jul 1979 Cover: 0.75 **NM** value: **2.00**
24 ❑ Sep 1979 Cover: 0.75 **NM** value: **2.00**
25 ❑ Nov 1979 Cover: 0.75 **NM** value: **2.00**
26 ❑ Jan 1980 Cover: 0.75 **NM** value: **2.00**
Circ: Statement: **132,184**
27 ❑ Mar 1980 Cover: 0.75 **NM** value: **2.00**
Circ: Statement: **132,184**
28 ❑ May 1980 Cover: 0.75 **NM** value: **2.00**
Circ: Statement: **132,184**
29 ❑ Jul 1980 Cover: 0.75 **NM** value: **2.00**
Circ: Statement: **132,184**
30 ❑ Sep 1980 Cover: 0.75 **NM** value: **2.00**
Circ: Statement: **132,184**
31 ❑ Nov 1980 Cover: 0.75 **NM** value: **2.00**
Circ: Statement: **132,184**
32 ❑ Jan 1981 Cover: 0.75 **NM** value: **2.00**
33 ❑ Mar 1981 Cover: 0.75 **NM** value: **2.00**
34 ❑ May 1981 **NM** value: **2.00**
• Has 1980 Statement, filed 10/1/80; avg print run 256,733; avg sales 132,167; avg subs 17; avg total paid circ 132,184; office use 300; max existent 132,484; 48% of run returned
35 ❑ Jul 1981 **NM** value: **2.00**
36 ❑ Sep 1981 **NM** value: **2.00**
37 ❑ Nov 1981 Cover: 0.95 **NM** value: **2.00**
38 ❑ Jan 1982 **NM** value: **2.00**
39 ❑ Mar 1982 **NM** value: **2.00**
40 ❑ May 1982 **NM** value: **2.00**
41 ❑ Jul 1982 **NM** value: **1.50**
42 ❑ Sep 1982 **NM** value: **1.50**
43 ❑ Nov 1982 **NM** value: **1.50**
44 ❑ Jan 1983 **NM** value: **1.50**
Circ: Statement: **129,421**
45 ❑ Mar 1983 **NM** value: **1.50**
Circ: Statement: **129,421**
46 ❑ May 1983 **NM** value: **1.50**
Circ: Statement: **129,421**
47 ❑ Jul 1983 **NM** value: **1.50**
Circ: Statement: **129,421**
48 ❑ Sep 1983 **NM** value: **1.50**
Circ: Statement: **129,421**
49 ❑ Nov 1983 **NM** value: **1.50**
Circ: Statement: **129,421**
50 ❑ Jan 1984 **NM** value: **1.50**
Circ: Statement: **144,631**
51 ❑ Mar 1984 **NM** value: **1.50**
Circ: Statement: **144,631**
52 ❑ May 1984 **NM** value: **1.50**
Circ: Statement: **144,631**
• Has 1983 Statement, filed 10/1/83; avg print run 253,471; avg sales 129,314; avg subs 107; avg total paid circ 129,421; office use 300; max existent 129,721; 49% of run returned
53 ❑ Jul 1984 **NM** value: **1.50**
Circ: Statement: **144,631**
54 ❑ Sep 1984 **NM** value: **1.50**
Circ: Statement: **144,631**
55 ❑ Nov 1984 **NM** value: **1.50**
Circ: Statement: **144,631**
56 ❑ Jan 1985 **NM** value: **1.50**
Circ: Statement: **149,728**
57 ❑ Mar 1985 **NM** value: **1.50**
Circ: Statement: **149,728**
58 ❑ May 1985 **NM** value: **1.50**
Circ: Statement: **149,728**
59 ❑ Jul 1985 **NM** value: **1.50**
Circ: Statement: **149,728**
60 ❑ Sep 1985 **NM** value: **1.50**
Circ: Statement: **149,728**
61 ❑ Nov 1985 **NM** value: **1.50**
Circ: Statement: **149,728**
62 ❑ Jan 1986 **NM** value: **1.50**
Circ: Statement: **151,006**
63 ❑ Mar 1986 **NM** value: **1.50**
Circ: Statement: **151,006**
64 ❑ May 1986 **NM** value: **1.50**
Circ: Statement: **151,006**
65 ❑ Jul 1986 **NM** value: **1.50**
Circ: Statement: **151,006**
66 ❑ Sep 1986 **NM** value: **1.50**
Circ: Statement: **151,006**
67 ❑ Nov 1986 **NM** value: **1.50**
Circ: Statement: **151,006**
68 ❑ Jan 1987 **NM** value: **1.50**
Circ: Statement: **154,540**
69 ❑ Mar 1987 Cover: 1.35 **NM** value: **1.50**
Circ: Statement: **154,540**
70 ❑ May 1987 Cover: 1.35 **NM** value: **1.50**
Circ: Statement: **154,540**
71 ❑ Jul 1987 Cover: 1.35 **NM** value: **1.50**
Circ: Statement: **154,540**
72 ❑ Sep 1987 Cover: 1.35 **NM** value: **1.50**
Circ: Statement: **154,540**
73 ❑ Nov 1987 Cover: 1.35 **NM** value: **1.50**
Circ: Statement: **154,540**
74 ❑ Jan 1988 Cover: 1.35 **NM** value: **1.50**
Circ: Statement: **164,187**
75 ❑ Mar 1988 **NM** value: **1.50**
Circ: Statement: **164,187**
76 ❑ May 1988 **NM** value: **1.50**
Circ: Statement: **164,187**
77 ❑ Jul 1988 **NM** value: **1.50**
Circ: Statement: **164,187**
78 ❑ Sep 1988 **NM** value: **1.50**
Circ: Statement: **164,187**
79 ❑ Nov 1988 **NM** value: **1.50**
Circ: Statement: **164,187**
80 ❑ Jan 1989 **NM** value: **1.50**
Circ: Statement: **168,492**
81 ❑ Mar 1989 **NM** value: **1.50**
Circ: Statement: **168,492**
82 ❑ May 1989 **NM** value: **1.50**
Circ: Statement: **168,492**
83 ❑ Jul 1989 Cover: 1.50 **NM** value: **Cover or less**
Circ: Statement: **168,492**

CGC-graded: Multiply prices above by **33 for 9.9 M • 16 for 9.8 NM/M • 7 for 9.6 NM+ • 5 for 9.4 NM • 2.5 for 9.2 NM- • 1.5 for 9.0 VF/NM**

84 ☐ Sep 1989 Cover: 1.50 **NM** value: **Cover or less**
Circ: Statement: **168,492**
85 ☐ Nov 1989 Cover: 1.50 **NM** value: **Cover or less**
Circ: Statement: **168,492**
86 ☐ 1990 Cover: 1.50 **NM** value: **Cover or less**
Circ: Statement: **161,137**
87 ☐ 1990 Cover: 1.50 **NM** value: **Cover or less**
Circ: Statement: **161,137**
88 ☐ 1990 Cover: 1.50 **NM** value: **Cover or less**
Circ: Statement: **161,137**
89 ☐ 1990 Cover: 1.50 **NM** value: **Cover or less**
Circ: Statement: **161,137**
90 ☐ 1990 Cover: 1.50 **NM** value: **Cover or less**
Circ: Statement: **161,137**
91 ☐ Cover: 1.50 **NM** value: **Cover or less**
Circ: Statement: **161,137**
92 ☐ Cover: 1.50 **NM** value: **Cover or less**
93 ☐ 1991 Cover: 1.50 **NM** value: **Cover or less**
94 ☐ 1991 Cover: 1.50 **NM** value: **Cover or less**
95 ☐ 1991 Cover: 1.50 **NM** value: **Cover or less**
96 ☐ Cover: 1.50 **NM** value: **Cover or less**
97 ☐ Cover: 1.50 **NM** value: **Cover or less**
98 ☐ Cover: 1.50 **NM** value: **Cover or less**
99 ☐ Cover: 1.50 **NM** value: **Cover or less**
100 ☐ Cover: 1.50 **NM** value: **Cover or less**
101 ☐ 1992 Cover: 1.50 **NM** value: **Cover or less**
102 ☐ 1992 Cover: 1.50 **NM** value: **Cover or less**
103 ☐ **NM** value: **1.50**
104 ☐ **NM** value: **1.50**
105 ☐ **NM** value: **1.50**
106 ☐ **NM** value: **1.50**
107 ☐ **NM** value: **1.50**
108 ☐ 1993 **NM** value: **1.50**
109 ☐ **NM** value: **1.50**
110 ☐ **NM** value: **1.50**
111 ☐ **NM** value: **1.50**
112 ☐ **NM** value: **1.50**
113 ☐ **NM** value: **1.50**
114 ☐ **NM** value: **1.50**
115 ☐ **NM** value: **1.50**
116 ☐ 1994 Cover: 1.75 **NM** value: **Cover or less**
117 ☐ Nov 1994 Cover: 1.75 **NM** value: **Cover or less**
118 ☐ Jan 1995 Cover: 1.75 **NM** value: **Cover or less**
Circ: Statement: **107,929**
119 ☐ Mar 1995 Cover: 1.75 **NM** value: **Cover or less**
Circ: Statement: **107,929**
120 ☐ May 1995 Cover: 1.75 **NM** value: **Cover or less**
Circ: Statement: **107,929**
121 ☐ Jul 1995 Cover: 1.75 **NM** value: **Cover or less**
Circ: Statement: **107,929**
122 ☐ Sep 1995 Cover: 1.75 **NM** value: **Cover or less**
Circ: Statement: **107,929**
123 ☐ Nov 1995 Cover: 1.75 **NM** value: **Cover or less**
Circ: Statement: **107,929**
124 ☐ Dec 1995 Cover: 1.75 **NM** value: **Cover or less**
Circ: Statement: **107,929**
125 ☐ Feb 1996 Cover: 1.75 **NM** value: **Cover or less**
Circ: Statement: **106,432**
126 ☐ Apr 1996 Cover: 1.75 **NM** value: **Cover or less**
Circ: Statement: **106,432**
• Has 1995 Statement, filed 10/1/95; avg print run 297,953; avg sales 107,044; avg subs 885; avg total paid 107,929; samples 375; office use 7,175; max existent 115,479; 61% of run returned
127 ☐ May 1996 Cover: 1.75 **NM** value: **Cover or less**
Circ: Statement: **106,432**
128 ☐ Jul 1996 Cover: 1.75 **NM** value: **Cover or less**
Circ: Statement: **106,432**
129 ☐ Sep 1996 Cover: 1.79 **NM** value: **Cover or less**
Circ: Statement: **106,432**
130 ☐ Oct 1996 Cover: 1.79 **NM** value: **Cover or less**
Circ: Statement: **106,432**
131 ☐ Dec 1996 Cover: 1.79 **NM** value: **Cover or less**
Circ: Statement: **106,432** Diamd. preorders: **2,771**
📖 Svenson Appreciation Day; Jewels and Justice; Temper, Temper; Peace Pipes; Now You See It; Archie 3000; A Helping Hand; The Great Joke Hunt; Quick Study; Autumn Daze; Tail of Woe; Chef's Special; Torpedo the Sub
132 ☐ Feb 1997 Cover: 1.79 **NM** value: **Cover or less**
Circ: Statement: **101,131** Diamd. preorders: **2,778**
133 ☐ Apr 1997 Cover: 1.79 **NM** value: **Cover or less**
Circ: Statement: **101,131** Diamd. preorders: **2,648**
• Has 1996 Statement; avg print run 272,273; avg sales 105,721; avg subs 710; avg total paid 106,432; samples 385; office use 3,783; max existent 110,599; 59% of run returned
134 ☐ May 1997 Cover: 1.79 **NM** value: **Cover or less**
Circ: Statement: **101,131** Diamd. preorders: **2,493**
135 ☐ Jul 1997 Cover: 1.79 **NM** value: **Cover or less**
Circ: Statement: **101,131**
136 ☐ Sep 1997 Cover: 1.79 **NM** value: **Cover or less**
Circ: Statement: **101,131**
137 ☐ Oct 1997 Cover: 1.79 **NM** value: **Cover or less**
Circ: Statement: **101,131**
138 ☐ Dec 1997 Cover: 1.79 **NM** value: **Cover or less**
Circ: Statement: **101,131**
139 ☐ Jan 1998 Cover: 1.95 **NM** value: **Cover or less**
Circ: Statement: **94,430**
140 ☐ Mar 1998 Cover: 1.95 **NM** value: **Cover or less**
Circ: Statement: **94,430** Diamd. preorders: **3,019**
• Has 1997 Statement, filed 11/1/97; avg print run 275,566; avg sales 100,383; avg subs 748; avg total paid 101,591; samples 460; office use 5,593; max existent 107,184; 61% of run returned
141 ☐ May 1998 Cover: 1.95 **NM** value: **Cover or less**
Circ: Statement: **94,430**
142 ☐ Jul 1998 Cover: 1.95 **NM** value: **Cover or less**
Circ: Statement: **94,430** Diamd. preorders: **2,958**
143 ☐ Aug 1998 Cover: 1.95 **NM** value: **Cover or less**
Circ: Statement: **94,430** Diamd. preorders: **2,906**
144 ☐ Oct 1998 Cover: 1.95 **NM** value: **Cover or less**
Circ: Statement: **94,430** Diamd. preorders: **2,589**
145 ☐ Nov 1998 Cover: 1.95 **NM** value: **Cover or less**
Circ: Statement: **94,430** Diamd. preorders: **2,576**
A: Dan Decarlo
146 ☐ Jan 1999 Cover: 1.95 **NM** value: **Cover or less**
Circ: Diamd. preorders: **2,744**
147 ☐ Mar 1999 Cover: 1.95 **NM** value: **Cover or less**
Circ: Diamd. preorders: **2,618**
148 ☐ Apr 1999 Cover: 1.99 **NM** value: **Cover or less**
Circ: Diamd. preorders: **2,320**
• Has 1998 Statement, filed 11/1/98; avg print run 251,927; avg sales 91,636; avg subs 774; avg total paid 94,430; samples 415 (has minor math error); office use 9,667; max existent 102,492; 59% of run returned
149 ☐ May 1999 Cover: 1.99 **NM** value: **Cover or less**
Circ: Diamd. preorders: **2,309**
150 ☐ Jul 1999 Cover: 1.99 **NM** value: **Cover or less**
Circ: Diamd. preorders: **2,404**
151 ☐ Aug 1999 Cover: 1.99 **NM** value: **Cover or less**
Circ: Diamd. preorders: **2,401**
152 ☐ Oct 1999 Cover: 1.99 **NM** value: **Cover or less**
Circ: Diamd. preorders: **2,486**
153 ☐ Nov 1999 Cover: 1.99 **NM** value: **Cover or less**
Circ: Diamd. preorders: **2,558**
154 ☐ Jan 2000 Cover: 1.99 **NM** value: **Cover or less**
Circ: Diamd. preorders: **2,325**
155 ☐ Mar 2000 Cover: 1.99 **NM** value: **Cover or less**
156 ☐ May 2000 Cover: 1.99 **NM** value: **Cover or less**
Circ: Diamd. preorders: **2,328**
157 ☐ Jul 2000 Cover: 2.19 **NM** value: **Cover or less**
Circ: Diamd. preorders: **2,422**
158 ☐ Aug 2000 Cover: 2.19 **NM** value: **Cover or less**
Circ: Diamd. preorders: **2,483**
159 ☐ Oct 2000 Cover: 2.19 **NM** value: **Cover or less**
Circ: Diamd. preorders: **2,805**
160 ☐ Nov 2000 Cover: 2.19 **NM** value: **Cover or less**
Circ: Diamd. preorders: **2,517**
161 ☐ Dec 2000 Cover: 2.19 **NM** value: **Cover or less**
Circ: Diamd. preorders: **2,271**
162 ☐ Jan 2001 Cover: 2.19 **NM** value: **Cover or less**
Circ: Diamd. preorders: **2,253**
163 ☐ Feb 2001 Cover: 2.19 **NM** value: **Cover or less**
Circ: Diamd. preorders: **2,181**
164 ☐ Apr 2001 Cover: 2.19 **NM** value: **Cover or less**
Circ: Diamd. preorders: **1,980**
165 ☐ May 2001 Cover: 2.19 **NM** value: **Cover or less**
Circ: Diamd. preorders: **2,024**
166 ☐ Jul 2001 Cover: 2.19 **NM** value: **Cover or less**
Circ: Diamd. preorders: **2,208**
167 ☐ Aug 2001 Cover: 2.19 **NM** value: **Cover or less**
Circ: Diamd. preorders: **2,300**
168 ☐ Oct 2001 Cover: 2.19 **NM** value: **Cover or less**
Circ: Diamd. preorders: **2,580**

LAUGH (VOL. 2) — Archie

1 ☐ Jun 1987 Cover: 0.75 **NM** value: **3.00**
Circ: Statement: **53,338**
2 ☐ Aug 1987 Cover: 0.75 **NM** value: **2.00**
Circ: Statement: **53,338**
3 ☐ Oct 1987 Cover: 0.75 **NM** value: **2.00**
Circ: Statement: **53,338**
4 ☐ Dec 1987 Cover: 0.75 **NM** value: **2.00**
Circ: Statement: **53,338**
5 ☐ Feb 1988 Cover: 0.75 **NM** value: **2.00**
Circ: Statement: **57,443**
6 ☐ Apr 1988 Cover: 0.75 **NM** value: **1.00**
Circ: Statement: **57,443**
7 ☐ Jun 1988 Cover: 0.75 **NM** value: **1.00**
Circ: Statement: **57,443**
8 ☐ Jul 1988 Cover: 0.75 **NM** value: **1.00**
Circ: Statement: **57,443**
9 ☐ Aug 1988 Cover: 0.75 **NM** value: **1.00**
Circ: Statement: **57,443**
10 ☐ Oct 1988 Cover: 0.75 **NM** value: **1.00**
Circ: Statement: **57,443**
11 ☐ Dec 1988 Cover: 0.75 **NM** value: **1.00**
Circ: Statement: **57,443**
12 ☐ Feb 1989 Cover: 0.75 **NM** value: **1.00**
Circ: Statement: **55,872**
13 ☐ Apr 1989 Cover: 0.75 **NM** value: **1.00**
Circ: Statement: **55,872**
14 ☐ Jun 1989 Cover: 0.75 **NM** value: **1.00**
Circ: Statement: **55,872**
15 ☐ Jul 1989 Cover: 0.75 **NM** value: **1.00**
Circ: Statement: **55,872**
16 ☐ Aug 1989 Cover: 0.75 **NM** value: **1.00**
Circ: Statement: **55,872**
17 ☐ Oct 1989 Cover: 0.75 **NM** value: **1.00**
Circ: Statement: **55,872**
18 ☐ Dec 1989 Cover: 0.75 **NM** value: **1.00**
Circ: Statement: **55,872**
19 ☐ Feb 1990 Cover: 0.75 **NM** value: **1.00**
Circ: Statement: **47,936**
20 ☐ Apr 1990 Cover: 0.75 **NM** value: **1.00**
Circ: Statement: **47,936**
21 ☐ Jun 1990 Cover: 0.75 **NM** value: **1.00**
Circ: Statement: **47,936**
22 ☐ Jul 1990 Cover: 0.75 **NM** value: **1.00**
Circ: Statement: **47,936**
23 ☐ Aug 1990 Cover: 0.75 **NM** value: **1.00**
Circ: Statement: **47,936**
24 ☐ Oct 1990 Cover: 0.75 **NM** value: **1.00**
Circ: Statement: **47,936**
25 ☐ Dec 1990 Cover: 0.75 **NM** value: **1.00**
Circ: Statement: **47,936**
26 ☐ Feb 1991 Cover: 0.75 **NM** value: **1.00**
27 ☐ Apr 1991 Cover: 0.75 **NM** value: **1.00**
28 ☐ Jun 1991 Cover: 0.75 **NM** value: **1.00**
29 ☐ Aug 1991 Cover: 0.75 **NM** value: **1.00**

LAUNCH! — Elsewhere

1 ☐ Cover: 1.75 **NM** value: **Cover or less**
★ 1st Appearance of Conscience.

LAUNDRYLAND — Fantagraphics

1 ☐ b&w Cover: 2.25 **NM** value: **Cover or less**
2 ☐ b&w Cover: 2.50 **NM** value: **Cover or less**
3 ☐ b&w Cover: 2.50 **NM** value: **Cover or less**
4 ☐ b&w Cover: 2.50 **NM** value: **Cover or less**

LAUREL AND HARDY (DC) — DC

1 ☐ Aug 1972 Cover: 0.20 **NM** value: **40.00**

LAUREL AND HARDY (DELL) — Dell

1 ☐ Aug 1962 Cover: 0.12 **NM** value: **20.00**
• **CGC:** 1 graded, best 9.4
2 ☐ 1963 Cover: 0.12 **NM** value: **15.00**
3 ☐ 1963 Cover: 0.12 **NM** value: **15.00**
4 ☐ Sep 1963 Cover: 0.12 **NM** value: **15.00**
• **CGC:** 2 graded, best 9.0

LAUREL AND HARDY (GOLD KEY) — Gold Key

1 ☐ Jan 1967 Cover: 0.12 **NM** value: **25.00**
• **CGC:** 1 graded, best 6.5
2 ☐ Oct 1967 Cover: 0.12 **NM** value: **20.00**
• **CGC:** 1 graded, best 7.0

LAUREL & HARDY IN 3-D — Blackthorne

1 ☐ Fal 1987 Cover: 2.50 **NM** value: **Cover or less**
• aka Blackthorne 3-D #23
2 ☐ Dec 1987 Cover: 2.50 **NM** value: **Cover or less**
Circ: CapCity orders: **1,750**
• aka Blackthorne 3-D #34

LAVA — Crossbreed

1 ☐ Cover: 2.95 **NM** value: **Cover or less**
A: Ruben Gerard; Gabriela Mottino **W:** Max Espinoza

LAW, THE — Asylum Graphics

1 ☐ b&w Cover: 1.75 **NM** value: **Cover or less**
• no publication date

LAW AGAINST CRIME — Essenkay

1 ☐ Apr 1948 Cover: 0.10 **NM** value: **600.00**
• **CGC:** 3 graded, best 7.0
2 ☐ Jun 1948 Cover: 0.10 **NM** value: **400.00**
3 ☐ Aug 1948 Cover: 0.10 **NM** value: **600.00**
• **CGC:** 2 graded, best 7.0

LAW AND ORDER — Maximum

1 ☐ Sep 1995 Cover: 2.50 **NM** value: **Cover or less**
Circ: CapCity orders: **13,000**
A: Fabio Laguna; Marat Michaels **W:** Marat Michaels; Chris Goffard
★ Origin of Law and Order.
1/A ☐ Sep 1995 Cover: 2.50 **NM** value: **Cover or less**
Alternate cover with women standing atop body. **A:** Fabio Laguna; Marat Michaels **W:** Marat Michaels; Chris Goffard ★ Origin of Law and Order.
2 ☐ Oct 1995 Cover: 2.50 **NM** value: **Cover or less**
Circ: CapCity orders: **7,650**
A: Fabio Laguna; Marat Michaels **W:** Marat Michaels; Chris Goffard
3 ☐ Nov 1995 Cover: 2.50 **NM** value: **Cover or less**
A: Fabio Laguna; Marat Michaels **W:** Marat Michaels; Chris Goffard

LAWBREAKERS ALWAYS LOSE — Atlas

1 ☐ Spr 1948 Cover: 0.10 **NM** value: **250.00**
• **CGC:** 2 graded, best 8.5
2 ☐ Jun 1948 Cover: 0.10 **NM** value: **175.00**
3 ☐ Aug 1948 Cover: 0.10 **NM** value: **100.00**
4 ☐ Oct 1948 Cover: 0.10 **NM** value: **100.00**
5 ☐ Dec 1948 Cover: 0.10 **NM** value: **100.00**
6 ☐ Feb 1949 Cover: 0.10 **NM** value: **75.00**
7 ☐ Apr 1949 Cover: 0.10 **NM** value: **75.00**
8 ☐ Jun 1949 Cover: 0.10 **NM** value: **75.00**
9 ☐ Aug 1949 Cover: 0.10 **NM** value: **75.00**
10 ☐ Oct 1949 Cover: 0.10 **NM** value: **75.00**

LAW BREAKERS SUSPENSE STORIES — Charlton

10 ☐ Jan 1953 Cover: 0.10 **NM** value: **200.00**
11 ☐ Mar 1953 Cover: 0.10 **NM** value: **250.00**
12 ☐ May 1953 Cover: 0.10 **NM** value: **150.00**
13 ☐ Jul 1953 Cover: 0.10 **NM** value: **150.00**
14 ☐ Sep 1953 Cover: 0.10 **NM** value: **150.00**
15 ☐ Nov 1953 Cover: 0.10 **NM** value: **300.00**

LAWDOG — Marvel / Epic

When you travel the highway connecting North Dakota with Hell, you'll want to make darn sure that your van doesn't break down. And, if it does, pray that the man the demons call "Lawdog" finds you before anyone else does.

Lawdog is a highway patrolman of sorts, but his turf isn't limited to the interstates most people know. He's the man who keeps order, when chaos causes reality to drift.

So when you've been driving all night, are getting a bit tired, and decide to stop at the town up the road, make sure the exit isn't marked "Gehenna." If it is, you'd better hope that a certain cop is keeping an eye out for you.

Other grades: Multiply prices above by **1.5 for Mint • 2/3 for Very Fine • 1/3 for Fine • 1/5 for Very Good • 1/8 for Good**

1 ❑ May 1993 Cover: 2.50 **NM** value: **Cover or less**
Circ: CapCity orders: **26,300** • **CGC:** 1 graded, best 9.8
Embossed cover. Lost Highway **A:** Flint Henry **W:** Chuck Dixon
★ 1st Appearance of Lawdog.
2 ❑ Jun 1993 Cover: 1.95 **NM** value: **Cover or less**
Circ: CapCity orders: **10,300** • **CGC:** 1 graded, best 9.8
W: Chuck Dixon
3 ❑ Jul 1993 Cover: 1.95 **NM** value: **Cover or less**
Circ: CapCity orders: **8,500** • **CGC:** 1 graded, best 9.6
W: Chuck Dixon
4 ❑ Aug 1993 Cover: 1.95 **NM** value: **Cover or less**
Circ: CapCity orders: **8,000** • **CGC:** 1 graded, best 9.8
W: Chuck Dixon
5 ❑ Sep 1993 Cover: 1.95 **NM** value: **Cover or less**
Circ: CapCity orders: **5,900** • **CGC:** 1 graded, best 9.6
W: Chuck Dixon
6 ❑ Oct 1993 Cover: 1.95 **NM** value: **Cover or less**
Circ: CapCity orders: **4,700**
A: Flint Henry **W:** Chuck Dixon ★ Appearance of Cleanies, Dr. Freen, 'Lina.
7 ❑ Nov 1993 Cover: 1.95 **NM** value: **Cover or less**
Circ: CapCity orders: **3,900**
W: Chuck Dixon
8 ❑ Dec 1993 Cover: 1.95 **NM** value: **Cover or less**
Circ: CapCity orders: **3,700**
• trading card **W:** Chuck Dixon
9 ❑ Jan 1994 Cover: 1.95 **NM** value: **Cover or less**
Circ: CapCity orders: **3,050**
W: Chuck Dixon
10 ❑ Feb 1994 Cover: 1.95 **NM** value: **Cover or less**
Circ: CapCity orders: **2,650**
final issue. **W:** Chuck Dixon

LAWDOG AND GRIMROD: TERROR AT THE CROSSROADS — Marvel / Epic

1 ❑ Sep 1993 Cover: 3.50 **NM** value: **Cover or less**
Circ: CapCity orders: **4,600**

L.A.W., THE (LIVING ASSAULT WEAPONS) — DC

1 ❑ Sep 1999 Cover: 2.50 **NM** value: **Cover or less**
Avatar Rising **A:** Dick Giordano **W:** Bob Layton
2 ❑ Oct 1999 Cover: 2.50 **NM** value: **Cover or less**
The Way of the Warrior **A:** Dick Giordano **W:** Bob Layton
3 ❑ Nov 1999 Cover: 2.50 **NM** value: **Cover or less**
4 ❑ Dec 1999 Cover: 2.50 **NM** value: **Cover or less**
Martial L.A.W. **A:** Dick Giordano **W:** Bob Layton
5 ❑ Jan 2000 Cover: 2.50 **NM** value: **Cover or less**
To Serve and Protect **A:** Dick Giordano **W:** Bob Layton
6 ❑ Feb 2000 Cover: 2.50 **NM** value: **Cover or less**
A: Dick Giordano **W:** Bob Layton

LAWMAN — Dell

3 ❑ Feb 1960 Cover: 0.10 **NM** value: **50.00**
• **CGC:** 2 graded, best 9.2
4 ❑ May 1960 Cover: 0.10 **NM** value: **50.00**
• **CGC:** 1 graded, best 9.0
5 ❑ Aug 1960 Cover: 0.10 **NM** value: **50.00**
6 ❑ Nov 1960 Cover: 0.10 **NM** value: **50.00**
7 ❑ Apr 1961 Cover: 0.10 **NM** value: **50.00**
8 ❑ Jul 1961 Cover: 0.10 **NM** value: **50.00**
• **CGC:** 2 graded, best 9.6
9 ❑ Oct 1961 Cover: 0.10 **NM** value: **50.00**
• **CGC:** 1 graded, best 9.4
10 ❑ Jan 1962 Cover: 0.10 **NM** value: **50.00**
• **CGC:** 1 graded, best 9.4
11 ❑ Apr 1962 Cover: 0.10 **NM** value: **50.00**

LAW OF DREDD, THE — Fleetway-Quality

1 ❑ Cover: 1.50 **NM** value: **2.50**
Circ: CapCity orders: **5,250**
Judge Dredd: Judge Death • Reprints Judge Dredd stories from 2000 A.D. #149- **A:** Brian Bolland **W:** John Wagner
2 ❑ Cover: 1.50 **NM** value: **2.00**
Circ: CapCity orders: **3,900**
3 ❑ Cover: 1.50 **NM** value: **2.00**
Circ: CapCity orders: **3,650**
★ Versus Judge Death.
4 ❑ Cover: 1.50 **NM** value: **2.00**
Circ: CapCity orders: **3,550**
5 ❑ Cover: 1.50 **NM** value: **2.00**
Circ: CapCity orders: **3,475**
6 ❑ Cover: 1.50 **NM** value: **2.00**
Circ: CapCity orders: **3,450**
7 ❑ Cover: 1.50 **NM** value: **2.00**
Circ: CapCity orders: **3,500**
8 ❑ Cover: 1.50 **NM** value: **2.00**
Circ: CapCity orders: **3,375**
9 ❑ Cover: 1.75 **NM** value: **2.00**
Circ: CapCity orders: **3,500**
10 ❑ Cover: 1.75 **NM** value: **2.00**
Circ: CapCity orders: **3,475**
11 ❑ Cover: 1.75 **NM** value: **2.00**
Circ: CapCity orders: **3,200**
12 ❑ Cover: 1.75 **NM** value: **2.00**
Circ: CapCity orders: **3,150**
13 ❑ Cover: 1.75 **NM** value: **2.00**
Circ: CapCity orders: **3,000**
★ Appearance of Judge Caligula.
14 ❑ Cover: 1.75 **NM** value: **2.00**
Circ: CapCity orders: **2,875**
15 ❑ Cover: 1.75 **NM** value: **2.00**
Circ: CapCity orders: **2,725**
16 ❑ Cover: 1.75 **NM** value: **Cover or less**
Circ: CapCity orders: **2,625**
17 ❑ Cover: 1.75 **NM** value: **Cover or less**
Circ: CapCity orders: **2,475**
18 ❑ Cover: 1.75 **NM** value: **Cover or less**
Circ: CapCity orders: **2,425**
19 ❑ Cover: 1.75 **NM** value: **Cover or less**
Circ: CapCity orders: **2,325**
20 ❑ Cover: 1.75 **NM** value: **Cover or less**
Circ: CapCity orders: **2,225**
21 ❑ Cover: 1.75 **NM** value: **Cover or less**
Circ: CapCity orders: **2,100**
22 ❑ Cover: 1.75 **NM** value: **Cover or less**
Circ: CapCity orders: **1,875**
23 ❑ Cover: 1.75 **NM** value: **Cover or less**
Circ: CapCity orders: **1,900**
24 ❑ Cover: 1.75 **NM** value: **Cover or less**
Circ: CapCity orders: **1,675**
25 ❑ Cover: 1.75 **NM** value: **Cover or less**
26 ❑ Cover: 1.75 **NM** value: **Cover or less**
Circ: CapCity orders: **1,775**
27 ❑ Cover: 1.75 **NM** value: **Cover or less**
Circ: CapCity orders: **1,800**
28 ❑ Cover: 1.75 **NM** value: **Cover or less**
Circ: CapCity orders: **1,725**
29 ❑ Cover: 1.75 **NM** value: **Cover or less**
30 ❑ Cover: 1.75 **NM** value: **1.95**
Circ: CapCity orders: **1,875**
31 ❑ Cover: 1.95 **NM** value: **Cover or less**
32 ❑ Cover: 1.95 **NM** value: **Cover or less**
33 ❑ Cover: 1.95 **NM** value: **Cover or less**
final issue.

LAWRENCE — Dell

1 ❑ ca. 1963 Cover: 0.12 **NM** value: **12.00**

LAZARUS CHURCHYARD — Tundra

1 ❑ Cover: 4.50 **NM** value: **Cover or less**
A: D'Israeli **W:** Warren Ellis
2 ❑ Cover: 4.50 **NM** value: **Cover or less**
A: D'Israeli **W:** Warren Ellis
3 ❑ Cover: 4.95 **NM** value: **Cover or less**
A: D'Israeli **W:** Warren Ellis
Bk 1❑ Cover: 14.95 **NM** value: **Cover or less**
• The Final Cut; Collects series **A:** D'Israeli **W:** Warren Ellis

LAZARUS FIVE — DC

1 ❑ Jul 2000 Cover: 2.50 **NM** value: **Cover or less**
Circ: Diamd. preorders: **15,001**
2 ❑ Aug 2000 Cover: 2.50 **NM** value: **Cover or less**
Circ: Diamd. preorders: **12,479**
3 ❑ Sep 2000 Cover: 2.50 **NM** value: **Cover or less**
Circ: Diamd. preorders: **11,899**
Prodigal Son **A:** Abell **W:** Harris; Jolley; Snyder
4 ❑ Oct 2000 Cover: 2.50 **NM** value: **Cover or less**
Circ: Diamd. preorders: **9,709**
Chosen **A:** Abell **W:** Harris; Jolley; Snyder
5 ❑ Nov 2000 Cover: 2.50 **NM** value: **Cover or less**
Circ: Diamd. preorders: **9,237**

LAZARUS PITS, THE — Boneyard

1 ❑ Cover: 2.75 **NM** value: **4.00**
A: Damon Threet **W:** Mike Ryan

LAZIEST SECRETARY IN THE WORLD, THE — DC / Piranha

Bk 1❑ Cover: 14.95 **NM** value: **Cover or less**
• not comics

LEADING COMICS — DC

Leading Comics — which eventually adjusted its title to Leading Screen Comics — began just as U.S. involvement in World War II was beginning, and it began with DC costumed heroes Star-Spangled Kid, Crimson Avenger, Green Arrow, Vigilante, and Shining Knight. With the war in full swing and including the Kid's sidekick (Stripesy) and Green Arrow's kid pal (Speedy), they became the Seven Soldiers of Victory, battling to right wrongs (though dealing less with Nazis than with criminals and fantasy foes.

In the mid-1940s, though, the direction changed to feature funny animals, with character Nero Fox ("the jive-jumping emperor of ancient Rome") taking over, only to be replaced by Peter Porkchops, constantly outwitting The Big Bad Wolf. — Maggie

1 ❑ Win 1941 Cover: 0.10 **NM** value: **3500.00**
• **CGC:** 5 graded, best 9.2
2 ❑ Spr 1942 Cover: 0.10 **NM** value: **1000.00**
• **CGC:** 2 graded, best 8.0
3 ❑ Sum 1942 Cover: 0.10 **NM** value: **1000.00**
• **CGC:** 3 graded, best 9.2
4 ❑ Fal 1942 Cover: 0.10 **NM** value: **800.00**
• **CGC:** 4 graded, best 9.2
5 ❑ Win 1942 Cover: 0.10 **NM** value: **800.00**
• **CGC:** 1 graded, best 9.6
6 ❑ Spr 1943 Cover: 0.10 **NM** value: **700.00**
• **CGC:** 3 graded, best 9.0
7 ❑ Sum 1943 Cover: 0.10 **NM** value: **700.00**
• **CGC:** 2 graded, best 9.6
8 ❑ Fal 1943 Cover: 0.10 **NM** value: **700.00**
• **CGC:** 3 graded, best 8.0
9 ❑ Win 1943 Cover: 0.10 **NM** value: **700.00**
• **CGC:** 1 graded, best 8.0
10 ❑ Spr 1944 Cover: 0.10 **NM** value: **700.00**
• **CGC:** 5 graded, best 9.2
11 ❑ Sum 1944 Cover: 0.10 **NM** value: **500.00**
• **CGC:** 2 graded, best 9.4
12 ❑ Fal 1944 Cover: 0.10 **NM** value: **500.00**
13 ❑ Win 1944 Cover: 0.10 **NM** value: **500.00**
• **CGC:** 2 graded, best 9.4
14 ❑ Spr 1945 Cover: 0.10 **NM** value: **500.00**
15 ❑ Sum 1945 Cover: 0.10 **NM** value: **200.00**
16 ❑ Fal 1945 Cover: 0.10 **NM** value: **75.00**
17 ❑ Win 1945 Cover: 0.10 **NM** value: **75.00**
18 ❑ Apr 1946 Cover: 0.10 **NM** value: **75.00**
19 ❑ Jun 1946 Cover: 0.10 **NM** value: **75.00**
20 ❑ Aug 1946 Cover: 0.10 **NM** value: **75.00**
21 ❑ Oct 1946 Cover: 0.10 **NM** value: **75.00**
22 ❑ Dec 1946 Cover: 0.10 **NM** value: **75.00**
23 ❑ Feb 1947 Cover: 0.10 **NM** value: **75.00**
24 ❑ Apr 1947 Cover: 0.10 **NM** value: **75.00**
25 ❑ Jun 1947 Cover: 0.10 **NM** value: **75.00**
26 ❑ Aug 1947 Cover: 0.10 **NM** value: **75.00**
27 ❑ Oct 1947 Cover: 0.10 **NM** value: **75.00**
28 ❑ Dec 1947 Cover: 0.10 **NM** value: **75.00**
29 ❑ Feb 1948 Cover: 0.10 **NM** value: **75.00**
30 ❑ Apr 1948 Cover: 0.10 **NM** value: **75.00**
31 ❑ Jun 1948 Cover: 0.10 **NM** value: **75.00**
32 ❑ Aug 1948 Cover: 0.10 **NM** value: **75.00**
33 ❑ Oct 1948 Cover: 0.10 **NM** value: **75.00**
34 ❑ Dec 1948 Cover: 0.10 **NM** value: **75.00**
35 ❑ Feb 1949 Cover: 0.10 **NM** value: **75.00**
• **CGC:** 1 graded, best 3.5
36 ❑ Apr 1949 Cover: 0.10 **NM** value: **75.00**
37 ❑ Jun 1949 Cover: 0.10 **NM** value: **75.00**
38 ❑ Aug 1949 Cover: 0.10 **NM** value: **75.00**
39 ❑ Oct 1949 Cover: 0.10 **NM** value: **75.00**
40 ❑ Dec 1949 Cover: 0.10 **NM** value: **75.00**
41 ❑ Feb 1950 Cover: 0.10 **NM** value: **75.00**

LEADING SCREEN COMICS — DC

42 ❑ Apr 1950 Cover: 0.10 **NM** value: **50.00**
43 ❑ Jun 1950 Cover: 0.10 **NM** value: **40.00**
44 ❑ Aug 1950 Cover: 0.10 **NM** value: **40.00**
45 ❑ Oct 1950 Cover: 0.10 **NM** value: **40.00**
46 ❑ Dec 1950 Cover: 0.10 **NM** value: **40.00**
47 ❑ Feb 1951 Cover: 0.10 **NM** value: **40.00**
48 ❑ Apr 1951 Cover: 0.10 **NM** value: **40.00**
49 ❑ Jun 1951 Cover: 0.10 **NM** value: **40.00**
50 ❑ Aug 1951 Cover: 0.10 **NM** value: **40.00**
51 ❑ Oct 1951 Cover: 0.10 **NM** value: **40.00**
52 ❑ Dec 1951 Cover: 0.10 **NM** value: **40.00**
53 ❑ Feb 1952 Cover: 0.10 **NM** value: **40.00**
• **CGC:** 1 graded, best 8.5
54 ❑ Apr 1952 Cover: 0.10 **NM** value: **40.00**
55 ❑ Jun 1952 Cover: 0.10 **NM** value: **40.00**
56 ❑ Aug 1952 Cover: 0.10 **NM** value: **40.00**
57 ❑ Oct 1952 Cover: 0.10 **NM** value: **40.00**
58 ❑ Dec 1952 Cover: 0.10 **NM** value: **40.00**
59 ❑ Feb 1953 Cover: 0.10 **NM** value: **40.00**
60 ❑ Apr 1953 Cover: 0.10 **NM** value: **40.00**
61 ❑ Jun 1953 Cover: 0.10 **NM** value: **40.00**
62 ❑ Aug 1953 Cover: 0.10 **NM** value: **40.00**
63 ❑ Oct 1953 Cover: 0.10 **NM** value: **40.00**
64 ❑ Dec 1953 Cover: 0.10 **NM** value: **40.00**
65 ❑ Feb 1954 Cover: 0.10 **NM** value: **40.00**
66 ❑ Apr 1954 Cover: 0.10 **NM** value: **40.00**
67 ❑ Jun 1954 Cover: 0.10 **NM** value: **40.00**
68 ❑ Aug 1954 Cover: 0.10 **NM** value: **40.00**
69 ❑ Oct 1954 Cover: 0.10 **NM** value: **40.00**
70 ❑ Dec 1954 Cover: 0.10 **NM** value: **40.00**
71 ❑ Jan 1955 Cover: 0.10 **NM** value: **40.00**
72 ❑ Feb 1955 Cover: 0.10 **NM** value: **40.00**
73 ❑ Mar 1955 Cover: 0.10 **NM** value: **40.00**
74 ❑ Apr 1955 Cover: 0.10 **NM** value: **40.00**
75 ❑ May 1955 Cover: 0.10 **NM** value: **40.00**
76 ❑ Jun 1955 Cover: 0.10 **NM** value: **40.00**
77 ❑ Sep 1955 Cover: 0.10 **NM** value: **40.00**

LEAF — Nab

1 ❑ Cover: 1.95 **NM** value: **Cover or less**
1/Dlx❑ Cover: 4.95 **NM** value: **Cover or less**
• deluxe

LEAGUE OF CHAMPIONS, THE — Hero

1 ❑ Dec 1990 Cover: 2.95 **NM** value: **3.50**
Circ: CapCity orders: **3,455**
The Gods at War; Perceptions **A:** Jim Valentino; Howard Simpson; Chris Marrinan; Dell Barras **W:** Dennis Mallonee; Lou Mougin
2 ❑ Feb 1991 Cover: 2.95 **NM** value: **3.50**
Circ: CapCity orders: **2,460**
★ Origin of Malice (true origin).
3 ❑ Apr 1991 Cover: 2.95 **NM** value: **3.50**
Circ: CapCity orders: **2,215**
4 ❑ b&w Cover: 3.50 **NM** value: **Cover or less**
5 ❑ b&w Cover: 3.50 **NM** value: **Cover or less**
6 ❑ b&w Cover: 3.50 **NM** value: **Cover or less**
7 ❑ b&w Cover: 3.50 **NM** value: **Cover or less**
8 ❑ b&w Cover: 3.50 **NM** value: **Cover or less**
9 ❑ b&w Cover: 3.50 **NM** value: **Cover or less**
Gargoyle! **A:** Cedric Nocon **W:** Dennis Mallonee
10 ❑ b&w Cover: 3.50 **NM** value: **Cover or less**
11 ❑ b&w Cover: 3.95 **NM** value: **Cover or less**
12 ❑ Jul 1993 Cover: 2.95 **NM** value: **Cover or less**

The prices seen above do not represent the highest possible prices seen in online auctions, but rather the prices we have seen these issues reliably fetch in a variety of environments (storefront retail, mail order, auction and convention).

CGC-graded: Multiply prices above by **33 for 9.9 M** • **16 for 9.8 NM/M** • **7 for 9.6 NM+** • **5 for 9.4 NM** • **2.5 for 9.2 NM-** • **1.5 for 9.0 VF/NM**

LEAGUE OF EXTRAORDINARY GENTLEMEN, THE
DC / America's Best Comics

Suppose that there were a villain so evil that Captain Nemo, Alan Quartermain, Dr. Henry Jekyll, John Griffin (the Invisible Man), and Miss Mina Harker (the only survivor of Bram Stoker's Dracula) came together to defeat him. They are the League of Extraordinary Gentlemen. The League is hot on the heels of the Oriental menace, Dr. Fu Manchu, who could destroy the Empire if left unchecked. Numerous references to "cavorite" (an antigravity substance created by H. G. Wells) and Mycroft Holmes (the brother of Sherlock Holmes) only add to the period feel of this masterwork. As a matter of fact, Alan Moore (Watchmen, V for Vendetta) and Kevin O'Neill (Judge Dredd) manage to include some element from just about every piece of English fiction there is.

In addition to the story, there are also period advertisements and a few pages of fiction by Moore entitled "Alan and the Sundered Veil."

1 ❑ Mar 1999 Cover: 2.95 **NM** value: **4.00**
Circ: Diamd. preorders: **36,664** • **CGC:** 12 graded, best 9.8
A: Kevin O'Neill **W:** Alan Moore

1/A ❑ Apr 1999 **NM** value: **6.00**
• **CGC:** 5 graded, best 9.8
• DF Alternate; 5000 copies **A:** Kevin O'Neill **W:** Alan Moore

2 ❑ Apr 1999 Cover: 2.95 **NM** value: **3.50**
Circ: Diamd. preorders: **29,576** • **CGC:** 2 graded, best 9.6
A: Kevin O'Neill **W:** Alan Moore

3 ❑ May 1999 Cover: 2.95 **NM** value: **3.00**
Circ: Diamd. preorders: **30,161** • **CGC:** 2 graded, best 9.6
📖 Mysteries of the East **A:** Kevin O'Neill **W:** Alan Moore

4 ❑ Nov 1999 Cover: 2.95 **NM** value: **Cover or less**
Circ: Diamd. preorders: **43,552** • **CGC:** 3 graded, best 9.6
📖 Gods of Annihilation **A:** Kevin O'Neill **W:** Alan Moore

5 ❑ Jun 2000 Cover: 2.95 **NM** value: **Cover or less**
Circ: Diamd. preorders: **50,863** • **CGC:** 1 graded, best 8.5
A: Kevin O'Neill **W:** Alan Moore

5/A ❑ Jun 2000 Cover: 2.95 **NM** value: **25.00**
• **CGC:** 18 graded, best 9.8
• Contained fake ad for The Marvel; All but est. 200 destroyed by DC
A: Kevin O'Neill **W:** Alan Moore

6 ❑ Sep 2000 Cover: 2.95 **NM** value: **Cover or less**
Circ: Diamd. preorders: **3,455** • **CGC:** 1 graded, best 9.6
📖 Young Helpers League **A:** Kevin O'Neill **W:** Alan Moore

Bk 1❑ Cover: 5.95 **NM** value: **Cover or less**
• Bumper Compendium Edition. • Collects League of Extraordinary Gentlemen #1-2 **A:** Kevin O'Neill **W:** Alan Moore

Bk 2❑ Dec 1999 Cover: 5.95 **NM** value: **Cover or less**
• Bumper Compendium Edition. • Collects League of Extraordinary Gentlemen #3-4 **A:** Kevin O'Neill **W:** Alan Moore

Dlx 1❑ Cover: 24.95 **NM** value: **Cover or less**
• Hardcover edition, collects series. **A:** Kevin O'Neill **W:** Alan Moore

LEAGUE OF JUSTICE
DC

1 ❑ Cover: 5.95 **NM** value: **Cover or less**
• prestige format. 📖 Stave One: Hero Quest • Elseworlds **A:** Ed Hannigan **W:** Ed Hannigan

2 ❑ Cover: 5.95 **NM** value: **Cover or less**
• prestige format. 📖 Stave Two: Hero War • Elseworlds **A:** Ed Hannigan **W:** Ed Hannigan

LEAGUE OF RATS, THE
Caliber / Tome

1 ❑ b&w Cover: 2.95 **NM** value: **Cover or less**

LEAGUE OF SUPER GROOVY CRIMEFIGHTERS
Ancient

This brightly colored title from Ancient Studios flashes back to the swinging years of the 1970s and those bizarre ads for lame novelty items that used to litter comic books: bow-and-arrow sets, martial-arts-training-by-mail, mood rings, X-ray spectacles, bodybuilding courses, croquet mallets, electronics-degrees-by-mail, etc. In this hipster universe, those items and offers worked far better than some of their purchasers could have ever dreamed, inspiring them to band together as the League of Super Groovy Crimefighters and rid New York City of injustice. Funny — if somewhat crudely drawn — this title revisits the slang, the fashions, and the blaxploitation of a bygone era.

1 ❑ Jun 2000 Cover: 2.95 **NM** value: **Cover or less**
• **CGC:** 4 graded, best 9.8
A: Mitch Massey ★ 1st Appearance of Black Belt, Cupid, Thor (Crimefighter), Mr. Phenomenal, X, The Ring, Atlas (crimefighter).

2 ❑ Dec 2000, b&w Cover: 2.95 **NM** value: **Cover or less**
Circ: Diamd. preorders: **1,155**

3 ❑ 2001b&w Cover: 2.95 **NM** value: **Cover or less**

4 ❑ May 2001, b&w Cover: 2.95 **NM** value: **Cover or less**
Circ: Diamd. preorders: **706**
• published after #3, but dated before

5 ❑ 2001 Cover: 2.95 **NM** value: **Cover or less**

LEATHER & LACE
Aircel

All issues are adults only.

Leather & Lace is a sexy comedy-adventure series by Barry Blair. Its storyline has gone through an almost unbelievable number of twists and turns. It all began when an innocent blonde, Pam Wilde, went to the big city in search of her missing sister. Cindy Wilde had been working in a rather kinky nightclub run by Vaughn Stratton III.

Stratton was a villain who specialized in drugging women and turning them into sex slaves. Wilde had cornered Stratton, when he was surprised by Christine Nguyen, a tough female thief. Nguyen had broken into Stratton's club to steal his loot, and her timely arrival allowed Wilde to escape.

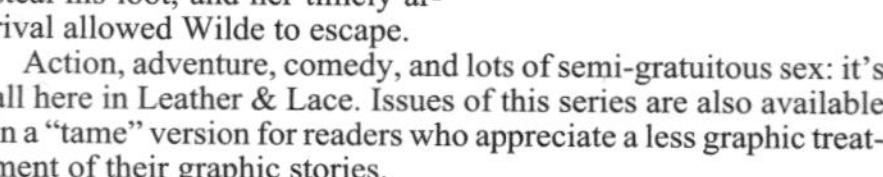

Action, adventure, comedy, and lots of semi-gratuitous sex: it's all here in Leather & Lace. Issues of this series are also available in a "tame" version for readers who appreciate a less graphic treatment of their graphic stories.

1/A ❑ Aug 1989, b&w Cover: 2.50 **NM** value: **Cover or less**
• Adult version **A:** Barry Blair **W:** Barry Blair

1/B ❑ Aug 1989, b&w Cover: 1.95 **NM** value: **Cover or less**
• Tame version **A:** Barry Blair **W:** Barry Blair

2/A ❑ Sep 1989, b&w Cover: 2.50 **NM** value: **Cover or less**
• Adult version **A:** Barry Blair **W:** Barry Blair

2/B ❑ Sep 1989, b&w Cover: 1.95 **NM** value: **Cover or less**
• Tame version **A:** Barry Blair **W:** Barry Blair

3/A ❑ Oct 1989, b&w Cover: 2.50 **NM** value: **Cover or less**
• Adult version **A:** Barry Blair **W:** Barry Blair

3/B ❑ Oct 1989, b&w Cover: 1.95 **NM** value: **Cover or less**
• Tame version **A:** Barry Blair **W:** Barry Blair

4/A ❑ Nov 1989, b&w Cover: 2.50 **NM** value: **Cover or less**
• Adult version **A:** Barry Blair **W:** Barry Blair

4/B ❑ Nov 1989, b&w Cover: 1.95 **NM** value: **Cover or less**
• Tame version **A:** Barry Blair **W:** Barry Blair

5/A ❑ Dec 1989, b&w Cover: 2.50 **NM** value: **Cover or less**
• Adult version **A:** Barry Blair **W:** Barry Blair

5/B ❑ Dec 1989, b&w Cover: 1.95 **NM** value: **Cover or less**
• Tame version **A:** Barry Blair **W:** Barry Blair

6/A ❑ Jan 1990, b&w Cover: 2.50 **NM** value: **Cover or less**
• Adult version **A:** Barry Blair **W:** Barry Blair

6/B ❑ Jan 1990, b&w Cover: 1.95 **NM** value: **Cover or less**
• Tame version **A:** Barry Blair **W:** Barry Blair

7/A ❑ Feb 1990, b&w Cover: 2.50 **NM** value: **Cover or less**
• Adult version **A:** Barry Blair **W:** Barry Blair

7/B ❑ Feb 1990, b&w Cover: 1.95 **NM** value: **Cover or less**
• Tame version **A:** Barry Blair **W:** Barry Blair

8/A ❑ Mar 1990, b&w Cover: 2.50 **NM** value: **Cover or less**
• Adult version **A:** Barry Blair **W:** Barry Blair

8/B ❑ Mar 1990, b&w Cover: 1.95 **NM** value: **Cover or less**
• Tame version **A:** Barry Blair **W:** Barry Blair

9 ❑ Apr 1990, b&w Cover: 2.50 **NM** value: **Cover or less**
A: Barry Blair **W:** Barry Blair

10 ❑ May 1990, b&w Cover: 2.50 **NM** value: **Cover or less**
A: Barry Blair **W:** Barry Blair

11 ❑ Jun 1990, b&w Cover: 2.50 **NM** value: **Cover or less**
A: Barry Blair **W:** Barry Blair

12 ❑ Jul 1990, b&w Cover: 2.50 **NM** value: **Cover or less**
A: Barry Blair **W:** Barry Blair

13 ❑ Aug 1990, b&w Cover: 2.50 **NM** value: **Cover or less**
A: Barry Blair **W:** Barry Blair

14 ❑ Sep 1990, b&w Cover: 2.50 **NM** value: **Cover or less**
A: Barry Blair **W:** Barry Blair

15 ❑ Oct 1990, b&w Cover: 2.50 **NM** value: **Cover or less**
A: Barry Blair **W:** Barry Blair

16 ❑ Nov 1990, b&w Cover: 2.50 **NM** value: **Cover or less**
A: Barry Blair **W:** Barry Blair

17 ❑ Dec 1990, b&w Cover: 2.50 **NM** value: **Cover or less**
A: Barry Blair **W:** Barry Blair

18 ❑ Jan 1991, b&w Cover: 2.50 **NM** value: **Cover or less**
A: Barry Blair **W:** Barry Blair

19 ❑ Feb 1991, b&w Cover: 2.50 **NM** value: **Cover or less**
A: Barry Blair **W:** Barry Blair

20 ❑ Mar 1991, b&w Cover: 2.50 **NM** value: **Cover or less**
A: Barry Blair **W:** Barry Blair

21 ❑ Apr 1991, b&w Cover: 2.50 **NM** value: **Cover or less**
A: Barry Blair **W:** Barry Blair

22 ❑ May 1991, b&w Cover: 2.95 **NM** value: **Cover or less**
A: Barry Blair **W:** Barry Blair

23 ❑ Jun 1991, b&w Cover: 2.95 **NM** value: **Cover or less**
A: Barry Blair **W:** Barry Blair

24 ❑ Jul 1991, b&w Cover: 2.95 **NM** value: **Cover or less**
A: Barry Blair **W:** Barry Blair

25 ❑ Aug 1991, b&w Cover: 2.95 **NM** value: **Cover or less**
final issue. **A:** Barry Blair **W:** Barry Blair

Bk 1❑ b&w Cover: 14.95 **NM** value: **Cover or less**

Bk 2❑ b&w Cover: 9.95 **NM** value: **Cover or less**

Bk 3❑ b&w Cover: 9.95 **NM** value: **Cover or less**

LEATHER & LACE: BLOOD, SEX, & TEARS
Aircel

All issues are adults only.

1 ❑ Oct 1991, b&w Cover: 2.95 **NM** value: **Cover or less**
A: Barry Blair **W:** Barry Blair

2 ❑ Nov 1991, b&w Cover: 2.95 **NM** value: **Cover or less**
A: Barry Blair **W:** Barry Blair

3 ❑ Dec 1991, b&w Cover: 2.95 **NM** value: **Cover or less**
A: Barry Blair **W:** Barry Blair

4 ❑ Jan 1992 Cover: 2.95 **NM** value: **Cover or less**
A: Barry Blair **W:** Barry Blair

LEATHER & LACE SUMMER SPECIAL
Aircel

All issues are adults only.

1 ❑ Jun 1990, b&w Cover: 2.50 **NM** value: **Cover or less**

LEATHERBOY
Eros

1 ❑ Jul 1994 Cover: 2.95 **NM** value: **Cover or less**
A: Craig Maynard **W:** Craig Maynard

2 ❑ Oct 1994 Cover: 2.95 **NM** value: **Cover or less**
📖 The Mayhem- and the Mob! **A:** Craig Maynard **W:** Craig Maynard

3 ❑ Nov 1994 Cover: 2.95 **NM** value: **Cover or less**
📖 The Company She Keeps **A:** Craig Maynard **W:** Craig Maynard

LEATHERFACE
Arpad

1 ❑ Cover: 2.75 **NM** value: **Cover or less**
Circ: CapCity orders: **8,150**

LEATHER UNDERWEAR
Fantagraphics

1 ❑ b&w Cover: 2.50 **NM** value: **Cover or less**

LEAVE IT TO BINKY
DC

Begun in 1948, Leave It to Binky features a lovable, but unlucky teenager whose efforts to impress girls, act chivalrous, or lend a helping hand almost always end in disaster. Binky is joined in his misadventures by his girlfriend, Peggy, and a collection of their teen pals.

For 71 issues through the 1950s and 1960s, Binky would be a poor man's Archie, with typical teen-age situation comedy stories.

The series shortened its name to just Binky with #72 and struggled on with occasional issues until 1977, when the plug was finally pulled.

1 ❑ Feb 1948 Cover: 0.10 **NM** value: **200.00**
• **CGC:** 1 graded, best 7.5

2 ❑ Apr 1948 Cover: 0.10 **NM** value: **150.00**

3 ❑ Jun 1948 Cover: 0.10 **NM** value: **100.00**

4 ❑ Aug 1948 Cover: 0.10 **NM** value: **100.00**

5 ❑ Oct 1948 Cover: 0.10 **NM** value: **100.00**

6 ❑ Dec 1948 Cover: 0.10 **NM** value: **75.00**

7 ❑ Feb 1949 Cover: 0.10 **NM** value: **75.00**
• **CGC:** 1 graded, best 9.8

8 ❑ Apr 1949 Cover: 0.10 **NM** value: **75.00**
• **CGC:** 1 graded, best 8.0

9 ❑ Jun 1949 Cover: 0.10 **NM** value: **75.00**
• **CGC:** 1 graded, best 7.0

10 ❑ Aug 1949 Cover: 0.10 **NM** value: **75.00**

11 ❑ Nov 1949 Cover: 0.10 **NM** value: **50.00**

12 ❑ Jan 1950 Cover: 0.10 **NM** value: **50.00**

13 ❑ Mar 1950 Cover: 0.10 **NM** value: **50.00**
• **CGC:** 1 graded, best 9.4

14 ❑ May 1950 Cover: 0.10 **NM** value: **50.00**

15 ❑ Jul 1950 Cover: 0.10 **NM** value: **50.00**

16 ❑ Sep 1950 Cover: 0.10 **NM** value: **50.00**

17 ❑ Nov 1950 Cover: 0.10 **NM** value: **50.00**

18 ❑ Jan 1951 Cover: 0.10 **NM** value: **50.00**

19 ❑ Mar 1951 Cover: 0.10 **NM** value: **50.00**

20 ❑ May 1951 Cover: 0.10 **NM** value: **50.00**

21 ❑ Jul 1951 Cover: 0.10 **NM** value: **50.00**

22 ❑ Sep 1951 Cover: 0.10 **NM** value: **50.00**

23 ❑ Nov 1951 Cover: 0.10 **NM** value: **50.00**

24 ❑ Jan 1952 Cover: 0.10 **NM** value: **50.00**

25 ❑ Mar 1952 Cover: 0.10 **NM** value: **50.00**

26 ❑ May 1952 Cover: 0.10 **NM** value: **50.00**

27 ❑ Jul 1952 Cover: 0.10 **NM** value: **50.00**

28 ❑ Sep 1952 Cover: 0.10 **NM** value: **50.00**

29 ❑ Nov 1952 Cover: 0.10 **NM** value: **50.00**

30 ❑ Jan 1953 Cover: 0.10 **NM** value: **40.00**

31 ❑ Mar 1953 Cover: 0.10 **NM** value: **40.00**

32 ❑ May 1953 Cover: 0.10 **NM** value: **40.00**

33 ❑ Jul 1953 Cover: 0.10 **NM** value: **40.00**

34 ❑ Sep 1953 Cover: 0.10 **NM** value: **40.00**

35 ❑ Nov 1953 Cover: 0.10 **NM** value: **40.00**

36 ❑ Jan 1954 Cover: 0.10 **NM** value: **40.00**

37 ❑ Mar 1954 Cover: 0.10 **NM** value: **40.00**

38 ❑ May 1954 Cover: 0.10 **NM** value: **40.00**

39 ❑ Jul 1954 Cover: 0.10 **NM** value: **40.00**

40 ❑ Sep 1954 Cover: 0.10 **NM** value: **30.00**

41 ❑ Oct 1954 Cover: 0.10 **NM** value: **30.00**

42 ❑ Nov 1954 Cover: 0.10 **NM** value: **30.00**

43 ❑ Dec 1955 Cover: 0.10 **NM** value: **30.00**

44 ❑ Jan 1955 Cover: 0.10 **NM** value: **30.00**

45 ❑ Feb 1955 Cover: 0.10 **NM** value: **30.00**

46 ❑ Cover: 0.10 **NM** value: **30.00**

47 ❑ Cover: 0.10 **NM** value: **30.00**

48 ❑ Cover: 0.10 **NM** value: **30.00**

49 ❑ Cover: 0.10 **NM** value: **30.00**

50 ❑ Cover: 0.10 **NM** value: **20.00**

51 ❑ Cover: 0.10 **NM** value: **20.00**

52 ❑ Cover: 0.10 **NM** value: **20.00**

53 ❑ Cover: 0.10 **NM** value: **20.00**

54 ❑ May 1957 Cover: 0.10 **NM** value: **20.00**

55 ❑ Jul 1957 Cover: 0.10 **NM** value: **20.00**

56 ❑ Sep 1957 Cover: 0.10 **NM** value: **20.00**

57 ❑ Nov 1957 Cover: 0.10 **NM** value: **20.00**

58 ❑ Jan 1958 Cover: 0.10 **NM** value: **20.00**

59 ❑ Mar 1958 Cover: 0.10 **NM** value: **20.00**

60 ❑ May 1958 Cover: 0.10 **NM** value: **15.00**

61 ❑ Jul 1958 Cover: 0.12 **NM** value: **15.00**

62 ❑ Sep 1958 Cover: 0.12 **NM** value: **15.00**

63 ❑ Nov 1958 Cover: 0.12 **NM** value: **15.00**

64 ❑ Jan 1959 Cover: 0.12 **NM** value: **15.00**

65 ☐ Mar 1959 Cover: 0.12 **NM** value: **15.00**
66 ☐ May 1959 Cover: 0.12 **NM** value: **15.00**
67 ☐ Jul 1959 Cover: 0.15 **NM** value: **15.00**
68 ☐ Sep 1959 Cover: 0.15 **NM** value: **15.00**
69 ☐ Nov 1959 Cover: 0.15 **NM** value: **15.00**
70 ☐ Jan 1960 Cover: 0.15 **NM** value: **15.00**
71 ☐ Mar 1960 Cover: 0.15 **NM** value: **15.00**

LEAVE IT TO CHANCE — Image

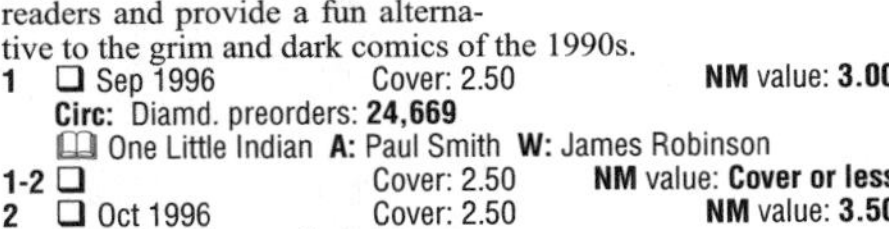

Chance is the daughter of renowned occult investigator Lucas Falconer. While dad is out tangling with demons and vampires, Chance is having adventures of her own in enchanted worlds of fairies as well as in a more sinister world of monster gangsters, accompanied by her pet baby dragon. James Robinson and Paul Smith, creators of the memorable Golden Age mini-series for DC, provide the story and art for this well-crafted series that serves up a refreshingly upbeat take on trendy magical-realism and occult themes. One of Robinson's stated objectives is to appeal to female readers and provide a fun alternative to the grim and dark comics of the 1990s.

1 ☐ Sep 1996 Cover: 2.50 **NM** value: **3.00**
Circ: Diamd. preorders: **24,669**
One Little Indian **A:** Paul Smith **W:** James Robinson
1-2 ☐ Cover: 2.50 **NM** value: **Cover or less**
2 ☐ Oct 1996 Cover: 2.50 **NM** value: **3.50**
Circ: Diamd. preorders: **19,716**
A: Paul Smith **W:** James Robinson
3 ☐ Nov 1996 Cover: 2.50 **NM** value: **3.00**
Circ: Diamd. preorders: **19,804**
Rain **A:** Paul Smith **W:** James Robinson
4 ☐ Feb 1997 Cover: 2.50 **NM** value: **3.00**
Circ: Diamd. preorders: **21,923**
Bad Toad Rising **A:** Paul Smith **W:** James Robinson
5 ☐ May 1997 Cover: 2.50 **NM** value: **3.00**
Circ: Diamd. preorders: **22,794**
A: Paul Smith **W:** James Robinson
6 ☐ Jul 1997 Cover: 2.50 **NM** value: **Cover or less**
Circ: Diamd. preorders: **24,034**
A: Paul Smith **W:** James Robinson
7 ☐ Oct 1997 Cover: 2.50 **NM** value: **Cover or less**
Circ: Diamd. preorders: **23,187**
And Not a Drop to Drink **A:** Paul Smith **W:** James Robinson
8 ☐ Feb 1998 Cover: 2.50 **NM** value: **Cover or less**
Circ: Diamd. preorders: **19,429**
The Phantom of the Mall **A:** Paul Smith **W:** James Robinson
9 ☐ Apr 1998 Cover: 2.50 **NM** value: **Cover or less**
Circ: Diamd. preorders: **18,470**
Midnite Monster Madness **A:** Paul Smith **W:** James Robinson
10 ☐ Jun 1998 Cover: 2.50 **NM** value: **Cover or less**
Circ: Diamd. preorders: **17,315**
Destroy All Monsters **A:** Paul Smith **W:** James Robinson
11 ☐ Sep 1998 Cover: 2.50 **NM** value: **2.95**
Circ: Diamd. preorders: **16,100**
Dead Men Can't Skate **A:** Paul Smith **W:** James Robinson
12 ☐ Jun 1999 Cover: 2.95 **NM** value: **Cover or less**
Circ: Diamd. preorders: **15,907**
The Promise **A:** Paul Smith **W:** James Robinson
Bk 1☐ Cover: 9.95 **NM** value: **Cover or less**
• Shaman's Rain; Collects Leave it to Chance #1-4 **A:** Paul Smith **W:** James Robinson
Bk 2☐ Cover: 12.95 **NM** value: **Cover or less**
• Trick or Threat and Other Stories; collects issues #5-8

LED ZEPPELIN — Personality

1 ☐ b&w Cover: 2.95 **NM** value: **Cover or less**
2 ☐ b&w Cover: 2.95 **NM** value: **Cover or less**
3 ☐ b&w Cover: 2.95 **NM** value: **Cover or less**
4 ☐ b&w Cover: 2.95 **NM** value: **Cover or less**

LED ZEPPELIN EXPERIENCE, THE — Revolutionary

1 ☐ Aug 1992, b&w Cover: 2.50 **NM** value: **Cover or less**
Shapes Off Things To Come **A:** Scott Pentzer **W:** Spike Steffenhagen; Todd Loren
2 ☐ Oct 1992, b&w Cover: 2.50 **NM** value: **Cover or less**
A: Scott Pentzer **W:** Spike Steffenhagen; Todd Loren
3 ☐ Dec 1992, b&w Cover: 2.50 **NM** value: **Cover or less**
A: Scott Pentzer **W:** Spike Steffenhagen; Todd Loren
4 ☐ Jan 1993, b&w Cover: 2.50 **NM** value: **Cover or less**
A: Scott Pentzer **W:** Spike Steffenhagen; Todd Loren
5 ☐ Feb 1993, b&w Cover: 2.50 **NM** value: **Cover or less**
A: Scott Pentzer **W:** Spike Steffenhagen; Todd Loren

LEFT-FIELD FUNNIES — Apex Novelties

1 ☐ Cover: 0.50 **NM** value: **4.00**
Artie Schnopp the Happy Cop; Merton: **A:** Gary Hallgren; Bobby London; Shary Flenniken; Will Murray **W:** Gary Hallgren; Bobby London; Shary Flenniken; Will Murray

LEGACY — Majestic

0 ☐ Aug 1993 **NM** value: **2.25**
0/GO☐Aug 1993 **NM** value: **2.25**
• gold
1 ☐ Oct 1993 Cover: 2.25 **NM** value: **Cover or less**
Circ: CapCity orders: **15,355**
Pledge For Allegiance **A:** Tom Morgan **W:** Fred Schiller
2 ☐ Jan 1994 Cover: 2.25 **NM** value: **Cover or less**
Circ: CapCity orders: **8,125**

LEGACY (FRED PERRY'S...) — Antarctic

1 ☐ Aug 1999 Cover: 2.99 **NM** value: **Cover or less**
Circ: Diamd. preorders: **4,660**

LEGACY OF KAIN: SOUL REAVER — Top Cow

1 ☐ Oct 1999 **NM** value: **2.00**
A: David Boller **W:** Matt Hawkins

LEGEND LORE (ARROW) — Arrow

1 ☐ b&w Cover: 2.00 **NM** value: **Cover or less**
Before the Storm **A:** Guy Davis **W:** Ralph Griffith; Stuart Kerr
2 ☐ b&w Cover: 2.00 **NM** value: **Cover or less**
A: Guy Davis **W:** Ralph Griffith; Stuart Kerr

LEGENDLORE (CALIBER) — Caliber

1 ☐ Cover: 2.95 **NM** value: **Cover or less**
A: Philip Xavier **W:** Joe Martin
2 ☐ Cover: 2.95 **NM** value: **Cover or less**
A: Philip Xavier **W:** Joe Martin
3 ☐ Cover: 2.95 **NM** value: **Cover or less**
A: Philip Xavier **W:** Joe Martin
4 ☐ Cover: 2.95 **NM** value: **Cover or less**
A: Philip Xavier **W:** Joe Martin
Bk 1☐ Cover: 8.95 **NM** value: **Cover or less**
• Realm reprints

LEGEND OF JEDIT OJANEN ON THE WORLD OF MAGIC: THE GATHERING — Acclaim / Armada

1 ☐ Mar 1996 Cover: 2.50 **NM** value: **Cover or less**
• polybagged with card **A:** David Boller **W:** Kenn Bell
2 ☐ Apr 1996 Cover: 2.50 **NM** value: **Cover or less**
Jedits Tales final issue. **A:** David Boller **W:** Kenn Bell

LEGEND OF JESSE JAMES — Gold Key

1 ☐ Feb 1966 Cover: 0.12 **NM** value: **25.00**
• **CGC:** 2 graded, best 9.2

LEGEND OF KAMUI, THE — Eclipse / Viz

1 ☐ May 1987, b&w Cover: 1.50 **NM** value: **3.00**
Circ: CapCity orders: **9,825**
Ichijiro (One White), Part 1 • Japanese **A:** Akame Productions; Sanpei Shirato **W:** Akame Productions; Sanpei Shirato
1-2 ☐ Cover: 1.50 **NM** value: **Cover or less**
2 ☐ Jun 1987 Cover: 1.50 **NM** value: **2.00**
Circ: CapCity orders: **6,625**
Ichijiro (One White), Part 2 **A:** Akame Productions; Sanpei Shirato **W:** Akame Productions; Sanpei Shirato
2-2 ☐ Cover: 1.50 **NM** value: **Cover or less**
3 ☐ Jun 1987 Cover: 1.50 **NM** value: **2.00**
Circ: CapCity orders: **6,350**
Red Medusas, Part 1 **A:** Akame Productions; Sanpei Shirato **W:** Akame Productions; Sanpei Shirato
3-2 ☐ Cover: 1.50 **NM** value: **Cover or less**
Red Medusas, Part 1 **A:** Akame Productions; Sanpei Shirato **W:** Akame Productions; Sanpei Shirato
4 ☐ Jul 1987 Cover: 1.50 **NM** value: **Cover or less**
Red Medusas, Part 2 **A:** Akame Productions; Sanpei Shirato **W:** Akame Productions; Sanpei Shirato
5 ☐ Jul 1987 Cover: 1.50 **NM** value: **Cover or less**
A: Akame Productions; Sanpei Shirato **W:** Akame Productions; Sanpei Shirato
6 ☐ Aug 1987 Cover: 1.50 **NM** value: **Cover or less**
Circ: CapCity orders: **7,025**
A: Akame Productions; Sanpei Shirato **W:** Akame Productions; Sanpei Shirato
7 ☐ Aug 1987 Cover: 1.50 **NM** value: **Cover or less**
Circ: CapCity orders: **7,025**
A: Akame Productions; Sanpei Shirato **W:** Akame Productions; Sanpei Shirato
8 ☐ Sep 1987 Cover: 1.50 **NM** value: **Cover or less**
A: Akame Productions; Sanpei Shirato **W:** Akame Productions; Sanpei Shirato
9 ☐ Sep 1987 Cover: 1.50 **NM** value: **Cover or less**
A: Akame Productions; Sanpei Shirato **W:** Akame Productions; Sanpei Shirato
10 ☐ Oct 1987 Cover: 1.50 **NM** value: **Cover or less**
A: Akame Productions; Sanpei Shirato **W:** Akame Productions; Sanpei Shirato
11 ☐ Oct 1987 Cover: 1.50 **NM** value: **Cover or less**
A: Akame Productions; Sanpei Shirato **W:** Akame Productions; Sanpei Shirato
12 ☐ Nov 1987 Cover: 1.50 **NM** value: **Cover or less**
A: Akame Productions; Sanpei Shirato **W:** Akame Productions; Sanpei Shirato
13 ☐ Nov 1987 Cover: 1.50 **NM** value: **Cover or less**
A: Akame Productions; Sanpei Shirato **W:** Akame Productions; Sanpei Shirato
14 ☐ Dec 1987 Cover: 1.50 **NM** value: **Cover or less**
A: Akame Productions; Sanpei Shirato **W:** Akame Productions; Sanpei Shirato
15 ☐ Dec 1987 Cover: 1.50 **NM** value: **Cover or less**
A: Akame Productions; Sanpei Shirato **W:** Akame Productions; Sanpei Shirato
16 ☐ Jan 1988 Cover: 1.50 **NM** value: **Cover or less**
After Sunset, Part 1 **A:** Akame Productions; Sanpei Shirato **W:** Akame Productions; Sanpei Shirato
17 ☐ Jan 1988 Cover: 1.50 **NM** value: **Cover or less**
After Sunset, Part 2 **A:** Akame Productions; Sanpei Shirato **W:** Akame Productions; Sanpei Shirato
18 ☐ Feb 1988 Cover: 1.95 **NM** value: **Cover or less**
A: Akame Productions; Sanpei Shirato **W:** Akame Productions; Sanpei Shirato
19 ☐ Feb 1988 Cover: 1.50 **NM** value: **Cover or less**
A: Akame Productions; Sanpei Shirato **W:** Akame Productions; Sanpei Shirato
20 ☐ Mar 1988 Cover: 1.50 **NM** value: **Cover or less**
A: Akame Productions; Sanpei Shirato **W:** Akame Productions; Sanpei Shirato
21 ☐ Mar 1988 Cover: 1.50 **NM** value: **Cover or less**
A: Akame Productions; Sanpei Shirato **W:** Akame Productions; Sanpei Shirato
22 ☐ Apr 1988 Cover: 1.50 **NM** value: **Cover or less**
A: Akame Productions; Sanpei Shirato **W:** Akame Productions; Sanpei Shirato
23 ☐ Apr 1988 Cover: 1.50 **NM** value: **Cover or less**
A: Akame Productions; Sanpei Shirato **W:** Akame Productions; Sanpei Shirato
24 ☐ May 1988 Cover: 1.50 **NM** value: **Cover or less**
A: Akame Productions; Sanpei Shirato **W:** Akame Productions; Sanpei Shirato
25 ☐ May 1988 Cover: 1.50 **NM** value: **Cover or less**
A: Akame Productions; Sanpei Shirato **W:** Akame Productions; Sanpei Shirato
26 ☐ Jun 1988 Cover: 1.50 **NM** value: **Cover or less**
A: Akame Productions; Sanpei Shirato **W:** Akame Productions; Sanpei Shirato
27 ☐ Jun 1988 Cover: 1.50 **NM** value: **Cover or less**
A: Akame Productions; Sanpei Shirato **W:** Akame Productions; Sanpei Shirato
28 ☐ Jul 1988 Cover: 1.50 **NM** value: **Cover or less**
A: Akame Productions; Sanpei Shirato **W:** Akame Productions; Sanpei Shirato
29 ☐ Jul 1988 Cover: 1.50 **NM** value: **Cover or less**
A: Akame Productions; Sanpei Shirato **W:** Akame Productions; Sanpei Shirato
30 ☐ Aug 1988 Cover: 1.50 **NM** value: **Cover or less**
A: Akame Productions; Sanpei Shirato **W:** Akame Productions; Sanpei Shirato
31 ☐ Aug 1988 Cover: 1.50 **NM** value: **Cover or less**
A: Akame Productions; Sanpei Shirato **W:** Akame Productions; Sanpei Shirato
32 ☐ Sep 1988 Cover: 1.50 **NM** value: **Cover or less**
A: Akame Productions; Sanpei Shirato **W:** Akame Productions; Sanpei Shirato
33 ☐ Sep 1988 Cover: 1.50 **NM** value: **Cover or less**
A: Akame Productions; Sanpei Shirato **W:** Akame Productions; Sanpei Shirato
34 ☐ Oct 1988 Cover: 1.50 **NM** value: **Cover or less**
A: Akame Productions; Sanpei Shirato **W:** Akame Productions; Sanpei Shirato
35 ☐ Oct 1988 Cover: 1.50 **NM** value: **Cover or less**
A: Akame Productions; Sanpei Shirato **W:** Akame Productions; Sanpei Shirato
36 ☐ Nov 1988 Cover: 1.50 **NM** value: **Cover or less**
A: Akame Productions; Sanpei Shirato **W:** Akame Productions; Sanpei Shirato
37 ☐ Nov 1988 Cover: 1.50 **NM** value: **Cover or less**
final issue. **A:** Akame Productions; Sanpei Shirato **W:** Akame Productions; Sanpei Shirato
Bk 1☐ Cover: 16.95 **NM** value: **Cover or less**
• Island of Sugaru
Bk 2☐ Cover: 16.95 **NM** value: **Cover or less**
• Island of Sugaru
Bk 3☐ Aug 1998 Cover: 16.95 **NM** value: **Cover or less**
• Perfect Collection

LEGEND OF LEMNEAR — CPM

Legend of Lemnear was originally published in Japan and was brought to America by CPM Manga. The series was created by artist Satoshi Urushihara (known also for his work on Midnight Panther and Chirality), working with writer Kinji Yoshimoto.

The gods have grown tired of mankind's constant battles. To foil man, they create evil — first a force within man, but later as a personified force in itself. The plan is to force mankind to unite against the common foe — rising over petty squabbles to something greater. Instead, a good proportion of mankind decides to serve this new "animate evil." Embarrassed by this turn of events, the gods then appoint knights of valor (such as the heroine Lemnear) to fight evil.

A good adventure series, Legend of Lemnear is marred by pointless nudity and groping.

1 ☐ Jan 1998 Cover: 2.95 **NM** value: **3.00**
Circ: Diamd. preorders: **6,371**
wraparound cover. Legend of the Descent **A:** Satoshi Urushihara **W:** Kinji Yoshimoto
2 ☐ Feb 1998 Cover: 2.95 **NM** value: **3.00**
Circ: Diamd. preorders: **4,662**
Unexpected Compassion **A:** Satoshi Urushihara **W:** Kinji Yoshimoto
3 ☐ Mar 1998 Cover: 2.95 **NM** value: **3.00**
Circ: Diamd. preorders: **4,548**
Vestiges of War **A:** Satoshi Urushihara **W:** Kinji Yoshimoto
4 ☐ Apr 1998 Cover: 2.95 **NM** value: **3.00**
Circ: Diamd. preorders: **4,844**
Impure Bronze, Part 1 **A:** Satoshi Urushihara **W:** Kinji Yoshimoto
5 ☐ May 1998 Cover: 2.95 **NM** value: **3.00**
Circ: Diamd. preorders: **4,371**
Impure Bronze, Part 2 **A:** Satoshi Urushihara **W:** Kinji Yoshimoto
6 ☐ Jun 1998 Cover: 2.95 **NM** value: **3.00**
Circ: Diamd. preorders: **4,312**
wraparound cover. Pulsating Anguish **A:** Satoshi Urushihara **W:** Kinji Yoshimoto
7 ☐ Jul 1998 Cover: 2.95 **NM** value: **3.00**
Circ: Diamd. preorders: **4,079**
wraparound cover. The Face of Absurdity **A:** Satoshi Urushihara **W:** Kinji Yoshimoto
8 ☐ Aug 1998 Cover: 2.95 **NM** value: **Cover or less**
Circ: Diamd. preorders: **3,994**

CGC-graded: Multiply prices above by **33 for 9.9 M • 16 for 9.8 NM/M • 7 for 9.6 NM+ • 5 for 9.4 NM • 2.5 for 9.2 NM- • 1.5 for 9.0 VF/NM**

🕮 The Dilemma of Destiny **A:** Satoshi Urushihara **W:** Kinji Yoshimoto
9 ❑ Sep 1998 Cover: 2.95 **NM** value: **Cover or less**
Circ: Diamd. preorders: **3,843**
10 ❑ Oct 1998 Cover: 2.95 **NM** value: **Cover or less**
11 ❑ Nov 1998 Cover: 2.95 **NM** value: **Cover or less**
12 ❑ Dec 1998 Cover: 2.95 **NM** value: **Cover or less**
13 ❑ Jan 1999 Cover: 2.95 **NM** value: **Cover or less**
Circ: Diamd. preorders: **3,406**
wraparound cover.
14 ❑ Feb 1999 Cover: 2.95 **NM** value: **Cover or less**
Circ: Diamd. preorders: **3,453**

LEGEND OF LILITH — Image
0 ❑ Cover: 4.95 **NM** value: **Cover or less**
• no date

LEGEND OF MOTHER SARAH — Dark Horse / Manga
1 ❑ Apr 1995, b&w Cover: 2.95 **NM** value: **3.50**
Circ: CapCity orders: **6,200**
A: Takumi Nagayasu **W:** Katsuhiro Otomo
2 ❑ May 1995, b&w Cover: 2.95 **NM** value: **3.00**
Circ: CapCity orders: **5,150**
A: Takumi Nagayasu **W:** Katsuhiro Otomo
3 ❑ Jun 1995, b&w Cover: 2.95 **NM** value: **3.00**
Circ: CapCity orders: **5,225**
A: Takumi Nagayasu **W:** Katsuhiro Otomo
4 ❑ Jul 1995, b&w Cover: 2.95 **NM** value: **Cover or less**
Circ: CapCity orders: **5,225**
A: Takumi Nagayasu **W:** Katsuhiro Otomo
5 ❑ Aug 1995, b&w Cover: 2.95 **NM** value: **Cover or less**
Circ: CapCity orders: **4,900**
A: Takumi Nagayasu **W:** Katsuhiro Otomo
6 ❑ Sep 1995, b&w Cover: 2.95 **NM** value: **Cover or less**
Circ: CapCity orders: **4,325**
A: Takumi Nagayasu **W:** Katsuhiro Otomo
7 ❑ Oct 1995, b&w Cover: 2.95 **NM** value: **Cover or less**
A: Takumi Nagayasu **W:** Katsuhiro Otomo
8 ❑ Nov 1995, b&w Cover: 2.95 **NM** value: **Cover or less**
final issue. **A:** Takumi Nagayasu **W:** Katsuhiro Otomo
Bk 1 ❑ Mar 1996 Cover: 18.95 **NM** value: **Cover or less**
• Tunnel Town trade paperback **A:** Takumi Nagayasu **W:** Katsuhiro Otomo

LEGEND OF MOTHER SARAH, THE: CITY OF THE ANGELS — Dark Horse / Manga
In the aftermath of a nuclear war, scientists attempt to bury the nuclear devastation under ice by tilting the Earth on its axis. As humans return to the radically-changed planet from their orbital space stations, bands of technofascists and environmentalists battle over the remains of civilization. Caught between environmental disaster and war are streams of refugees, including a young mother called Mother Sarah, who emerges as a hero of this tattered world.

Sarah: City of the Angels is an ambitious manga epic by Katshuiro Otomo and Takumi Nagayasu, brought out in a nine-issue mini-series of 48-page books from Dark Horse. The intense, principled storytelling and dramatic, detailed black-and-white art help Sarah stand out from the pack of Japanese imports and realize its high artistic goals.
1 ❑ Oct 1997 Cover: 3.95 **NM** value: **Cover or less**
Circ: Diamd. preorders: **10,194**
A: Takumi Nagayasu **W:** Katsuhiro Otomo
2 ❑ Dec 1997 Cover: 3.95 **NM** value: **Cover or less**
Circ: Diamd. preorders: **5,742**
A: Takumi Nagayasu **W:** Katsuhiro Otomo
3 ❑ Jan 1998 Cover: 3.95 **NM** value: **Cover or less**
Circ: Diamd. preorders: **6,055**
A: Takumi Nagayasu **W:** Katsuhiro Otomo
4 ❑ Feb 1998 Cover: 3.95 **NM** value: **Cover or less**
Circ: Diamd. preorders: **5,577**
A: Takumi Nagayasu **W:** Katsuhiro Otomo
5 ❑ Mar 1998 Cover: 3.95 **NM** value: **Cover or less**
Circ: Diamd. preorders: **5,313**
A: Takumi Nagayasu **W:** Katsuhiro Otomo
6 ❑ Apr 1998 Cover: 3.95 **NM** value: **Cover or less**
Circ: Diamd. preorders: **5,209**
A: Takumi Nagayasu **W:** Katsuhiro Otomo
7 ❑ May 1998 Cover: 3.95 **NM** value: **Cover or less**
Circ: Diamd. preorders: **4,763**
A: Takumi Nagayasu **W:** Katsuhiro Otomo
8 ❑ Jun 1998 Cover: 3.95 **NM** value: **Cover or less**
Circ: Diamd. preorders: **4,708**
A: Takumi Nagayasu **W:** Katsuhiro Otomo
9 ❑ Jul 1998 Cover: 3.95 **NM** value: **Cover or less**
Circ: Diamd. preorders: **4,513**
A: Takumi Nagayasu **W:** Katsuhiro Otomo

LEGEND OF MOTHER SARAH, THE: CITY OF THE CHILDREN — Dark Horse / Manga
1 ❑ Jan 1996 Cover: 3.95 **NM** value: **Cover or less**
A: Takumi Nagayasu **W:** Katsuhiro Otomo
2 ❑ Feb 1996 Cover: 3.95 **NM** value: **Cover or less**
A: Takumi Nagayasu **W:** Katsuhiro Otomo
3 ❑ Mar 1996 Cover: 3.95 **NM** value: **Cover or less**
A: Takumi Nagayasu **W:** Katsuhiro Otomo
4 ❑ Apr 1996 Cover: 3.95 **NM** value: **Cover or less**
A: Takumi Nagayasu **W:** Katsuhiro Otomo
5 ❑ May 1996 Cover: 3.95 **NM** value: **Cover or less**
A: Takumi Nagayasu **W:** Katsuhiro Otomo
6 ❑ Jun 1996 Cover: 3.95 **NM** value: **Cover or less**
A: Takumi Nagayasu **W:** Katsuhiro Otomo
7 ❑ Jul 1996 Cover: 3.95 **NM** value: **Cover or less**
A: Takumi Nagayasu **W:** Katsuhiro Otomo

LEGEND OF SLEEPY HOLLOW, THE — Tundra
1 ❑ Cover: 6.95 **NM** value: **Cover or less**
No issue number. **A:** Bo Hampton

LEGEND OF SUPREME — Image
1 ❑ Dec 1994 Cover: 2.50 **NM** value: **Cover or less**
A: Jeff Johnson **W:** Keith Giffen; Robert Loren Flemming ★ Origin of Supreme.
2 ❑ Jan 1995 Cover: 2.50 **NM** value: **Cover or less**
A: Jeff Johnson **W:** Keith Giffen; Robert Loren Flemming ★ Origin of Supreme.
3 ❑ Feb 1995 Cover: 2.50 **NM** value: **Cover or less**
A: Jeff Johnson **W:** Keith Giffen; Robert Loren Flemming ★ Origin of Supreme.

LEGEND OF THE DC UNIVERSE: SUPERMAN — DC
1 ❑ Cover: 1.95 **NM** value: **Cover or less**
🕮 U.L.T.R.A. Humanite, Part 1, Madness and Science **A:** Val Semeiks **W:** James Robinson
2 ❑ Cover: 1.95 **NM** value: **Cover or less**
3 ❑ Cover: 1.95 **NM** value: **Cover or less**

LEGEND OF THE ELFLORD — Davdez
1 ❑ Jul 1998 Cover: 2.95 **NM** value: **Cover or less**
2 ❑ Sep 1998 Cover: 2.95 **NM** value: **Cover or less**
3 ❑ Cover: 2.95 **NM** value: **Cover or less**

LEGEND OF THE HAWKMAN — DC
1 ❑ Sep 2000 Cover: 4.95 **NM** value: **Cover or less**
Circ: Diamd. preorders: **21,170**
A: Michael Lark **W:** Ben Raab
2 ❑ Oct 2000 Cover: 4.95 **NM** value: **Cover or less**
Circ: Diamd. preorders: **18,019**
A: Michael Lark **W:** Ben Raab
3 ❑ Nov 2000 Cover: 4.95 **NM** value: **Cover or less**
Circ: Diamd. preorders: **17,540**
🕮 Flight of Faith **A:** Michael Lark **W:** Ben Raab

LEGEND OF THE SHIELD, THE — DC / Impact
1 ❑ Jul 1991 Cover: 1.00 **NM** value: **Cover or less**
Circ: CapCity orders: **41,600**
🕮 The Glory Makers **A:** Grant Miehm **W:** Grant Miehm; Mark Waid ★ Origin of Shield.
2 ❑ Aug 1991 Cover: 1.00 **NM** value: **Cover or less**
Circ: CapCity orders: **25,350**
3 ❑ Sep 1991 Cover: 1.00 **NM** value: **Cover or less**
Circ: CapCity orders: **19,300**
★ 1st Appearance of The Weapon, Bert Watson, The Black Hood (Wayne Sidmonson), Millie Mazda.
4 ❑ Oct 1991 Cover: 1.00 **NM** value: **Cover or less**
Circ: CapCity orders: **18,650**
🕮 The Dark Mirror!! **A:** Grant Miehm **W:** Grant Miehm; Mark Waid ★ Versus Weapon.
5 ❑ Nov 1991 Cover: 1.00 **NM** value: **Cover or less**
Circ: CapCity orders: **16,550**
★ 1st Appearance of Dusty Madigan.
6 ❑ Dec 1991 Cover: 1.00 **NM** value: **Cover or less**
Circ: CapCity orders: **15,750**
★ 1st Appearance of Theo Carver. ★ Appearance of Fly.
7 ❑ Jan 1992 Cover: 1.00 **NM** value: **Cover or less**
Circ: CapCity orders: **13,100**
★ Appearance of Fly.
8 ❑ Feb 1992 Cover: 1.00 **NM** value: **Cover or less**
Circ: CapCity orders: **11,300**
★ 1st Appearance of The Shield I (Roger Higgins). ★ Versus Weapon.
9 ❑ Mar 1992 Cover: 1.00 **NM** value: **Cover or less**
Circ: CapCity orders: **9,700**
10 ❑ Apr 1992 Cover: 1.00 **NM** value: **Cover or less**
Circ: CapCity orders: **8,450**
11 ❑ May 1992 Cover: 1.00 **NM** value: **Cover or less**
Circ: CapCity orders: **8,500**
• trading card
12 ❑ Jun 1992 Cover: 1.25 **NM** value: **Cover or less**
Circ: CapCity orders: **7,650**
13 ❑ Jul 1992 Cover: 1.25 **NM** value: **Cover or less**
Circ: CapCity orders: **7,250**
🕮 The Glory Machine **A:** Grant Miehm **W:** Grant Miehm
14 ❑ Aug 1992 Cover: 1.25 **NM** value: **Cover or less**
Circ: CapCity orders: **7,050**
15 ❑ Sep 1992 Cover: 1.25 **NM** value: **Cover or less**
Circ: CapCity orders: **6,150**
16 ❑ Oct 1992 Cover: 1.25 **NM** value: **Cover or less**
Circ: CapCity orders: **5,750**
final issue.
Anl 1 ❑ Cover: 2.50 **NM** value: **Cover or less**
Circ: CapCity orders: **8,400**
🕮 Earth Quest, Part 2

LEGEND OF WONDER WOMAN, THE — DC
1 ❑ May 1986 Cover: 1.00 **NM** value: **1.50**
🕮 Legends Live Forever **A:** Kurt Busiek; Trina Robbins **W:** Kurt Busiek
2 ❑ Jun 1986 Cover: 1.00 **NM** value: **1.50**
A: Kurt Busiek; Trina Robbins **W:** Kurt Busiek
3 ❑ Jul 1986 Cover: 1.00 **NM** value: **1.50**
A: Kurt Busiek; Trina Robbins **W:** Kurt Busiek
4 ❑ Aug 1986 Cover: 1.00 **NM** value: **1.50**
A: Kurt Busiek; Trina Robbins **W:** Kurt Busiek

LEGEND OF YOUNG DICK TURPIN — Gold Key
1 ❑ May 1966 Cover: 0.12 **NM** value: **25.00**
• **CGC:** 1 graded, best 6.5

LEGEND OF ZELDA, THE — Valiant
1 ❑ ca. 19990 Cover: 1.95 **NM** value: **Cover or less**
Circ: CapCity orders: **4,300**
2 ❑ ca. 19990 Cover: 1.95 **NM** value: **Cover or less**
Circ: CapCity orders: **2,200**
3 ❑ ca. 19990 Cover: 1.95 **NM** value: **Cover or less**
Circ: CapCity orders: **1,900**
4 ❑ ca. 19990 Cover: 1.95 **NM** value: **Cover or less**
Circ: CapCity orders: **1,500**
5 ❑ ca. 19990 Cover: 1.95 **NM** value: **Cover or less**

LEGEND OF ZELDA, THE (2ND SERIES) — Valiant
1 ❑ ca. 19990 Cover: 1.50 **NM** value: **Cover or less**
2 ❑ ca. 19990 Cover: 1.50 **NM** value: **Cover or less**
3 ❑ ca. 19990 Cover: 1.50 **NM** value: **Cover or less**
4 ❑ ca. 19990 Cover: 1.50 **NM** value: **Cover or less**
5 ❑ ca. 19990 Cover: 1.50 **NM** value: **Cover or less**

LEGENDS — DC
On the cold world of Apokolips, the evil Darkseid had just quashed another rebellion. Still, he felt uneasy. In turning toward Earth, he saw always the same heroes that rose to defeat him time and time again. It was time, he thought, to put an end to them. This time, he would attack not the heroes, but the very ideals — the legends — themselves.

Darkseid sent Doctor Bedlam and Glorious Godfrey to Earth. There, they quickly engineered it so that Billy Batson (aka Shazam) would accidentally murder a super-villain, and accordingly become so ashamed that he would abandon his super-hero identity. At the same time, "Dr. G. Gordon Godfrey" appeared on television to whip the public into an anti-super-hero frenzy.

This series crossed over through countless DC titles in 1986 and served as the birthplace for the new Suicide Squad and the revamped Justice League (which dropped the "of America" from its name).
1 ❑ Nov 1986 Cover: 0.75 **NM** value: **2.00**
Circ: CapCity orders: **57,250**
🕮 Once Upon A Time…! **A:** John Byrne **W:** Len Wein; John Ostrander ★ 1st Appearance of Amanda Waller.
2 ❑ Dec 1986 Cover: 0.75 **NM** value: **1.50**
Circ: CapCity orders: **51,650**
A: John Byrne
3 ❑ Jan 1987 Cover: 0.75 **NM** value: **2.00**
Circ: CapCity orders: **45,150**
A: John Byrne ★ 1st Appearance of Suicide Squad (modern).
4 ❑ Feb 1987 Cover: 0.75 **NM** value: **1.50**
Circ: CapCity orders: **39,450**
A: John Byrne
5 ❑ Mar 1987 Cover: 0.75 **NM** value: **1.50**
Circ: CapCity orders: **38,200**
A: John Byrne
6 ❑ Apr 1987 Cover: 0.75 **NM** value: **3.00**
Circ: CapCity orders: **34,600** • **CGC:** 1 graded, best 9.0
A: John Byrne ★ 1st Appearance of Justice League.

LEGENDS AND FOLKLORE — Zone
1 ❑ b&w Cover: 2.95 **NM** value: **Cover or less**
2 ❑ b&w Cover: 2.95 **NM** value: **Cover or less**

LEGENDS OF DANIEL BOONE — DC
1 ❑ Nov 1955 Cover: 0.10 **NM** value: **400.00**
2 ❑ Dec 1955 Cover: 0.10 **NM** value: **200.00**
3 ❑ Jan 1956 Cover: 0.10 **NM** value: **200.00**
4 ❑ Mar 1956 Cover: 0.10 **NM** value: **150.00**
5 ❑ Apr 1956 Cover: 0.10 **NM** value: **150.00**
6 ❑ Jun 1956 Cover: 0.10 **NM** value: **150.00**
• **CGC:** 1 graded, best 7.0
7 ❑ Aug 1956 Cover: 0.10 **NM** value: **150.00**
8 ❑ Oct 1956 Cover: 0.10 **NM** value: **150.00**

LEGENDS OF ELFINWILD, THE — Wehner
1 ❑ b&w Cover: 1.75 **NM** value: **Cover or less**
A: Pasquale D. Gabriele **W:** Sandra I.H. Wehner

LEGENDS OF KID DEATH & FLUFFY — Event
1 ❑ Feb 1997 Cover: 2.95 **NM** value: **Cover or less**
Circ: Diamd. preorders: **12,730**
🕮 No Good Deed Goes Unpunished; I "Bone" New York; Never Send a Man to do a Boy's Job **W:** Rick Parker; Amanda Conner; John Cebollero

LEGENDS OF LUXURA — Brainstorm
1 ❑ Feb 1996, b&w Cover: 2.95 **NM** value: **Cover or less**
• collects Luxura stories
1/LE ❑ Feb 1996 **NM** value: **5.00**
no cover price. • Special edition. • limited to 1000 copies

LEGENDS OF NASCAR, THE — Vortex
1 ❑ Cover: 3.00 **NM** value: **3.50**
Circ: CapCity orders: **6,085**
• Bill Elliott **A:** Herb Trimpe **W:** Herb Trimpe; Steve Waid
1-2 ❑ Cover: 3.00 **NM** value: **Cover or less**
1-3 ❑ Cover: 3.00 **NM** value: **Cover or less**

Other grades: Multiply prices above by **1.5 for Mint • 2/3 for Very Fine • 1/3 for Fine • 1/5 for Very Good • 1/8 for Good**

2 ❑ Cover: 2.00 NM value: **Cover or less**
Circ: CapCity orders: **7,445**
• Richard Petty; no indicia

2/SC❑ Cover: 5.00 NM value: **Cover or less**
• hologram

3 ❑ Cover: 2.00 NM value: **Cover or less**
Circ: CapCity orders: **9,970**
• Ken Shrader

4 ❑ Cover: 2.00 NM value: **Cover or less**
Circ: CapCity orders: **7,295**
• Bobby Allison **A:** Don Spiegle

5 ❑ Cover: 2.00 NM value: **Cover or less**
Circ: CapCity orders: **5,280**
• Sterling Marlin

6 ❑ Cover: 2.00 NM value: **Cover or less**
Circ: CapCity orders: **5,920**

7 ❑ Cover: 2.00 NM value: **Cover or less**
Circ: CapCity orders: **4,125**

8 ❑ Cover: 2.00 NM value: **Cover or less**
Circ: CapCity orders: **4,115**
• Benny Parsons **A:** Don Heck

9 ❑ Cover: 2.00 NM value: **Cover or less**
Circ: CapCity orders: **4,415**
• Rusty Wallace

10 ❑ Cover: 2.00 NM value: **Cover or less**
Circ: CapCity orders: **3,510**
• Talladega Story

11 ❑ Cover: 2.00 NM value: **Cover or less**
Circ: CapCity orders: **3,550**
• Morgan Shepherd

12 ❑ Cover: 2.00 NM value: **Cover or less**
Circ: CapCity orders: **3,115**

13 ❑ Cover: 2.00 NM value: **Cover or less**

14 ❑ Cover: 2.00 NM value: **Cover or less**

15 ❑ Cover: 2.00 NM value: **Cover or less**

16 ❑ Cover: 2.00 NM value: **Cover or less**

LEGENDS OF THE DARK CLAW — DC / Amalgam

1 ❑ Apr 1996 Cover: 1.95 NM value: **2.00**
📖 Through A Glass Darkly **A:** Jim Balent **W:** Larry Hama ★ Origin of The Hyena, The Dark Claw.

LEGENDS OF THE DCU: CRISIS ON INFINITE EARTHS — DC

1 ❑ Feb 1999 Cover: 4.95 NM value: **Cover or less**
Circ: Diamd. preorders: **45,157 • CGC:** 1 graded, best 9.8
📖 The Untold Story • Takes place between Crisis of Infinite Earths #4 and #5; Supergirl I (Kara Zor-El) **A:** Paul Ryan **W:** Marv Wolfman ★ Appearance of Flash II (Barry Allen.

1/Aut❑Feb 1999 Cover: 4.95 NM value: **18.95**
• Takes place between Crisis of Infinite Earths #4 and #5; Supergirl I (Kara Zor-El) **A:** Paul Ryan **W:** Marv Wolfman ★ Appearance of Flash II (Barry Allen).

LEGENDS OF THE DC UNIVERSE — DC

Featuring rotating creative teams (a la Legends of the Dark Knight) and superstar leads, Legends of the DC Universe brings to light untold tales of the post-Crisis on Infinite Earths and post-Zero Hour DC Comics continuity. Superman's first battle with the U.L.T.R.A.-Humanite is chronicled in the series' first three issues, while later issues feature the first meeting of Hal (Green Lantern) Jordan and Oliver (Green Arrow) Queen. There is also a Kirby-era Jimmy Olsen adventure, additional facts about the origin of the New Teen Titans, and tales set early in the careers of Barry Allen — the Silver Age Flash — and the Modern Age Wonder Woman.

Boasting such stellar creators as James Robinson, Denny O'Neil, Marv Wolfman, Steven Grant, Mike Zeck, Gil Kane, and Steve Rude, Legends of the DC Universe is a modern comics classic...and a must-see!

1 ❑ Feb 1998 Cover: 1.95 NM value: **3.00**
Circ: Diamd. preorders: **47,600 • CGC:** 1 graded, best 8.0
• Superman

2 ❑ Mar 1998 Cover: 1.95 NM value: **2.50**
Circ: Diamd. preorders: **37,858 • CGC:** 1 graded, best 9.2
• Superman

3 ❑ Apr 1998 Cover: 1.95 NM value: **2.50**
Circ: Diamd. preorders: **34,400 • CGC:** 1 graded, best 9.6
• Superman

4 ❑ May 1998 Cover: 1.95 NM value: **2.50**
Circ: Diamd. preorders: **35,522**
• Wonder Woman

5 ❑ Jun 1998 Cover: 1.95 NM value: **2.50**
Circ: Diamd. preorders: **34,572**
• Wonder Woman

6 ❑ Jul 1998 Cover: 1.95 NM value: **2.25**
Circ: Diamd. preorders: **30,987**
• Robin, Superman

7 ❑ Aug 1998 Cover: 1.95 NM value: **2.25**
Circ: Diamd. preorders: **33,961**
• Green Lantern/Green Arrow

8 ❑ Sep 1998 Cover: 1.99 NM value: **2.25**
Circ: Diamd. preorders: **31,092**
• Green Lantern/Green Arrow

9 ❑ Oct 1998 Cover: 1.99 NM value: **2.25**
Circ: Diamd. preorders: **30,161**
• Green Lantern/Green Arrow

10 ❑ Nov 1998 Cover: 1.99 NM value: **2.25**
Circ: Diamd. preorders: **33,700**
• Batgirl

11 ❑ Dec 1998 Cover: 1.99 NM value: **2.25**
Circ: Diamd. preorders: **31,302**
• Batgirl

12 ❑ Jan 1999 Cover: 1.99 NM value: **2.25**
Circ: Diamd. preorders: **32,706**
📖 Critical Mass, Part 1 • JLA

13 ❑ Feb 1999 Cover: 1.99 NM value: **2.25**
Circ: Diamd. preorders: **31,274**
📖 Critical Mass, Part 2 • JLA **A:** Ken Lashley **W:** Christopher Priest

14 ❑ Mar 1999 Cover: 3.95 NM value: **Cover or less**
Circ: Diamd. preorders: **29,698**
A: Steve Rude **W:** Jack Kirby; Mark Evanier ★ Appearance of Jimmy Olsen, Simyan, Superman, Darkseid, Guardian, Mokkari.

15 ❑ Apr 1999 Cover: 1.99 NM value: **2.25**
Circ: Diamd. preorders: **27,330**
📖 Dark Matters, Part 1 **A:** Richard Case **W:** Michael Jan Friedman ★ Appearance of Flash II (Barry Allen).

16 ❑ May 1999 Cover: 1.99 NM value: **2.25**
Circ: Diamd. preorders: **26,638**
📖 Dark Matters, Part 2 **A:** Richard Case **W:** Michael Jan Friedman ★ Appearance of Flash II (Barry Allen).

17 ❑ Jun 1999 Cover: 1.99 NM value: **2.25**
Circ: Diamd. preorders: **25,422**
📖 Dark Matters, Part 3 **A:** Richard Case **W:** Michael Jan Friedman ★ Appearance of Flash II (Barry Allen).

18 ❑ Jul 1999 Cover: 1.99 NM value: **2.25**
Circ: Diamd. preorders: **24,889**
📖 Conflicting Emotions • Kid Flash, Raven **A:** Jackson Guice **W:** Marv Wolfman

19 ❑ Aug 1999 Cover: 1.99 NM value: **2.25**
Circ: Diamd. preorders: **21,983**
📖 Manchester Monkey Business • Impulse; prelude to JLApe Annuals **A:** Pop Mahn **W:** Jason Hernandez Rosenblatt

20 ❑ Sep 1999 Cover: 1.99 NM value: **2.25**
Circ: Diamd. preorders: **24,373**
📖 The Trail of the Traitor Part 1 • Green Lantern: Abin Sur **A:** Mike Zeck **W:** Steven Grant

21 ❑ Oct 1999 Cover: 1.99 NM value: **Cover or less**
Circ: Diamd. preorders: **22,777**
📖 The Trail of the Traitor Part 2 • Green Lantern: Abin Sur **A:** Mike Zeck **W:** Steven Grant

22 ❑ Nov 1999 Cover: 1.99 NM value: **Cover or less**
Circ: Diamd. preorders: **22,838**
📖 Transilvane, Part 1; Supremum Vale **A:** J.O. Ladronn **W:** Jean-Marc Lofficier; Randy Lofficier

23 ❑ Dec 1999 Cover: 1.99 NM value: **Cover or less**
Circ: Diamd. preorders: **22,191**
📖 Dies Irae **A:** J.O. Ladronn **W:** Jean-Marc Lofficier; Randy Lofficier

24 ❑ Jan 2000 Cover: 1.99 NM value: **Cover or less**
Circ: Diamd. preorders: **19,188**
📖 The Jump, Part 1 **A:** Steve Pugh **W:** Jamie Delano

25 ❑ Feb 2000 Cover: 1.99 NM value: **Cover or less**
Circ: Diamd. preorders: **20,056**

26 ❑ Mar 2000 Cover: 1.99 NM value: **Cover or less**
Circ: Diamd. preorders: **19,132**

27 ❑ Apr 2000 Cover: 1.99 NM value: **Cover or less**
Circ: Diamd. preorders: **18,649**
📖 Reign of the Joker! **A:** Trevor Von Eeden **W:** Steve Englehart

28 ❑ May 2000 Cover: 1.99 NM value: **Cover or less**
Circ: Diamd. preorders: **21,536**
📖 Traitor's Revenge, Part 1 **A:** Gil Kane; Klaus Janson **W:** Steven Grant

29 ❑ Jun 2000 Cover: 1.99 NM value: **Cover or less**
Circ: Diamd. preorders: **21,129**
📖 Traitor's Revenge, Part 2 **A:** Gil Kane; Klaus Janson **W:** Steven Grant

30 ❑ Jul 2000 Cover: 1.99 NM value: **Cover or less**
Circ: Diamd. preorders: **18,563**

31 ❑ Aug 2000 Cover: 2.50 NM value: **Cover or less**
Circ: Diamd. preorders: **19,057**

32 ❑ Sep 2000 Cover: 2.50 NM value: **Cover or less**
Circ: Diamd. preorders: **18,774**
📖 The 18th Letter **A:** Karl Waller; Pablo Raimond **W:** Christopher Priest

33 ❑ Oct 2000 Cover: 2.50 NM value: **Cover or less**
Circ: Diamd. preorders: **21,128**
📖 Destroyer of Worlds, Part 1 **A:** Michael Zulli **W:** J.M. DeMatteis

34 ❑ Nov 2000 Cover: 2.50 NM value: **Cover or less**
Circ: Diamd. preorders: **21,103**
📖 Destroyer of Worlds, Part 2 **A:** Michael Zulli **W:** J.M. DeMatteis

35 ❑ Dec 2000 Cover: 2.50 NM value: **Cover or less**
Circ: Diamd. preorders: **21,304**
📖 Destroyer of Worlds, Part 3 **A:** Michael Zulli **W:** J.M. DeMatteis

36 ❑ Jan 2001 Cover: 2.50 NM value: **Cover or less**
Circ: Diamd. preorders: **21,855**
📖 Destroyer of Worlds, Part 4 **A:** Michael Zulli **W:** J.M. DeMatteis

37 ❑ Feb 2001 Cover: 2.50 NM value: **Cover or less**
Circ: Diamd. preorders: **19,771**
📖 The Tragedy of the Traitor, Part 1 **A:** Scott Kolins **W:** Steven Grant

38 ❑ Mar 2001 Cover: 2.50 NM value: **Cover or less**
Circ: Diamd. preorders: **19,304**
📖 The Tragedy of the Traitor, Part 2 **A:** Scott Kolins **W:** Steven Grant

39 ❑ Apr 2001 Cover: 2.50 NM value: **Cover or less**
Circ: Diamd. preorders: **19,397**
📖 Sole Survivor of Earth **A:** Randy Green **W:** Danny Fingeroth

40 ❑ May 2001 Cover: 2.50 NM value: **Cover or less**
Circ: Diamd. preorders: **17,683**
📖 Lessons in Time, Part 1 **A:** Drew Johnson **W:** Rich Faber; Todd Dezago

GS 1❑Sep 1998 Cover: 4.95 NM value: **Cover or less**
Circ: Diamd. preorders: **28,231**
• Spectre, Hawkman, Teen Titans, Adam Strange, Chronos, Doom Patrol, Rip Hunter, Linear Men

GS 2❑Jan 2000 Cover: 4.95 NM value: **Cover or less**
Circ: Diamd. preorders: **18,821**
📖 The Great Unknown; Twisted; Passenger 15B; A Little Goes a Long Way; Heart of Tin; Carnival in Armagetto; Bedtime Story **A:** Arthur Adams; Scott Kolins; Stuart Immonen; George Freeman; Justiniano; Phil Winslade; Eduardo Barreto; Klaus Janson **W:** Michael Jan Friedman; Karl Kesel; Paul Levitz; Walt Simonson; Ben Raab; Dan Curtis Johnson; Geoff Johns; Tom Peyer

LEGENDS OF THE DC UNIVERSE 3-D GALLERY — DC

1 ❑ Dec 1998 Cover: 2.95 NM value: **Cover or less**
Circ: Diamd. preorders: **19,480**
• pin-ups **A:** Adam Warren; Tony Harris; Leonard Kirk; Eric Battle; Mark Buckingham; Howard Porter; Yanick Paquette; Jim Balent; Greg Luzniak; Steve Epting; Peter Krause; Angel Unzueta; Art Thibert; Todd Nauck

LEGENDS OF THE LEGION — DC

1 ❑ Feb 1998 Cover: 2.25 NM value: **Cover or less**
Circ: Diamd. preorders: **24,876**
★ Origin of Ultra Boy.

2 ❑ Mar 1998 Cover: 2.25 NM value: **Cover or less**
Circ: Diamd. preorders: **21,430**
📖 Resistance **A:** Jeffrey Moyer **W:** Barry Kitson; Tom Peyer ★ Origin of Spark.

3 ❑ Apr 1998 Cover: 2.25 NM value: **Cover or less**
Circ: Diamd. preorders: **19,819**
★ Origin of Umbra.

4 ❑ May 1998 Cover: 2.25 NM value: **Cover or less**
Circ: Diamd. preorders: **19,299**
★ Origin of Star Boy.

LEGENDS OF THE LIVING DEAD — Fantaco

1 ❑ Cover: 3.95 NM value: **Cover or less**

LEGENDS OF THE STARGRAZERS — Innovation

1 ❑ Aug 1989 Cover: 1.95 NM value: **Cover or less**
Circ: CapCity orders: **3,950**
📖 Here There Be Dragons **A:** Matt Thompson **W:** David Campiti; Cynthy J. Wood

2 ❑ Cover: 1.95 NM value: **Cover or less**
Circ: CapCity orders: **3,050**

3 ❑ Cover: 1.95 NM value: **Cover or less**
Circ: CapCity orders: **320**

4 ❑ Cover: 1.95 NM value: **Cover or less**
Circ: CapCity orders: **3,075**

5 ❑ Cover: 1.95 NM value: **Cover or less**
Circ: CapCity orders: **2,975**

6 ❑ Cover: 1.95 NM value: **Cover or less**
Circ: CapCity orders: **2,800**

Bk 1❑ Cover: 9.95 NM value: **Cover or less**

Bk 2❑ Cover: 9.95 NM value: **Cover or less**

LEGENDS OF THE WORLD'S FINEST — DC

1 ❑ ca. 1994 Cover: 4.95 NM value: **Cover or less**
Circ: CapCity orders: **30,500**
📖 Perchance To Dream **A:** Dan Brereton **W:** Walt Simonson

2 ❑ ca. 1994 Cover: 4.95 NM value: **Cover or less**
Circ: CapCity orders: **20,150**
A: Dan Brereton **W:** Walt Simonson

3 ❑ ca. 1994 Cover: 4.95 NM value: **Cover or less**
Circ: CapCity orders: **17,850**
• Superman, Batman

Bk 1❑ Cover: 14.95 NM value: **Cover or less**
• Collects Legends of the World's Finest #1-3

L.E.G.I.O.N. — DC

A group that traces its origins to the Invasion! mini-series, L.E.G.I.O.N. is the "Licensed Extra-Governmental Interstellar Operatives Network." They are a futuristic fighting force which serves as a peacekeeping force for hire. Unfortunately, they seem to have a talent for getting involved on worlds where the conflicts are not always clear, and where the natives don't always appreciate their intervention.

Led by the hard-nosed Commander Vril Dox II, L.E.G.I.O.N. is remarkable in that its membership includes Lobo, who otherwise would seem to be the ultimate loner. Lobo joined L.E.G.I.O.N. after Dox actually beat him in battle and forced him to make a promise — knowing that Lobo's one virtue is that he always keeps his word.

1 ❑ Feb 1989 Cover: 1.50 NM value: **2.50**
Circ: CapCity orders: **28,250**
📖 Homecoming • L.E.G.I.O.N. '89 starts **A:** Barry Kitson **W:** Keith Giffen; Alan Grant ★ Origin of L.E.G.I.O.N.. ★ 1st Appearance of Stealth.

2 ❑ Mar 1989 Cover: 1.50 NM value: **2.00**
Circ: CapCity orders: **19,500**

3 ❑ Apr 1989 Cover: 1.50 NM value: **2.00**
Circ: CapCity orders: **18,200**

4 ❑ May 1989 Cover: 1.50 NM value: **2.00**
Circ: CapCity orders: **18,450**
★ Appearance of Lobo.

5 ❑ Jun 1989 Cover: 1.50 NM value: **2.00**
Circ: CapCity orders: **18,750**
• Lobo joins team

6 ❑ Jul 1989 Cover: 1.50 NM value: **1.75**
Circ: CapCity orders: **18,350**

7 ❑ Aug 1989 Cover: 1.50 NM value: **1.75**
Circ: CapCity orders: **19,150**

8 ❑ Sep 1989 Cover: 1.50 NM value: **1.75**
Circ: CapCity orders: **19,100**

9 ❑ Nov 1989 Cover: 1.50 NM value: **1.75**

CGC-graded: Multiply prices above by **33 for 9.9 M • 16 for 9.8 NM/M • 7 for 9.6 NM+ • 5 for 9.4 NM • 2.5 for 9.2 NM- • 1.5 for 9.0 VF/NM**

Circ: CapCity orders: **18,750**
★ Appearance of Phantom Girl.
10 ❑ Dec 1989 Cover: 1.50 **NM** value: **1.75**
Circ: CapCity orders: **17,100**
11 ❑ Jan 1990 Cover: 1.50 **NM** value: **Cover or less**
Circ: CapCity orders: **16,450**
• L.E.G.I.O.N. '90 starts
12 ❑ Feb 1990 Cover: 1.50 **NM** value: **Cover or less**
Circ: CapCity orders: **16,550**
★ Appearance of Emerald Eye.
13 ❑ Mar 1990 Cover: 1.50 **NM** value: **Cover or less**
Circ: CapCity orders: **16,200**
14 ❑ Apr 1990 Cover: 1.50 **NM** value: **Cover or less**
Circ: CapCity orders: **15,200**
15 ❑ May 1990 Cover: 1.50 **NM** value: **Cover or less**
Circ: CapCity orders: **15,300**
16 ❑ Jun 1990 Cover: 1.50 **NM** value: **Cover or less**
Circ: CapCity orders: **15,600**
★ Appearance of Lar Gand.
17 ❑ Jul 1990 Cover: 1.50 **NM** value: **Cover or less**
Circ: CapCity orders: **15,600**
18 ❑ Aug 1990 Cover: 1.50 **NM** value: **Cover or less**
Circ: CapCity orders: **15,200**
19 ❑ Sep 1990 Cover: 1.50 **NM** value: **Cover or less**
Circ: CapCity orders: **15,350**
20 ❑ Oct 1990 Cover: 1.50 **NM** value: **Cover or less**
Circ: CapCity orders: **15,050**
21 ❑ Nov 1990 Cover: 1.50 **NM** value: **Cover or less**
Circ: CapCity orders: **15,100**
22 ❑ Dec 1990 Cover: 1.50 **NM** value: **Cover or less**
Circ: CapCity orders: **15,200**
★ Appearance of Lady Quark.
23 ❑ Jan 1991 Cover: 2.50 **NM** value: **Cover or less**
Circ: CapCity orders: **15,300**
• L.E.G.I.O.N. '91 starts
24 ❑ Feb 1991 Cover: 1.50 **NM** value: **Cover or less**
Circ: CapCity orders: **15,050**
25 ❑ Mar 1991 Cover: 1.50 **NM** value: **Cover or less**
Circ: CapCity orders: **14,550**
26 ❑ Apr 1991 Cover: 1.50 **NM** value: **Cover or less**
Circ: CapCity orders: **15,450**
27 ❑ May 1991 Cover: 1.50 **NM** value: **Cover or less**
Circ: CapCity orders: **14,700**
28 ❑ Jun 1991 Cover: 1.50 **NM** value: **Cover or less**
Circ: CapCity orders: **15,250**
📖 Hard Labor **A:** George Pratt **W:** Keith Giffen; Alan Grant
29 ❑ Jul 1991 Cover: 1.50 **NM** value: **Cover or less**
Circ: CapCity orders: **17,900**
30 ❑ Aug 1991 Cover: 1.50 **NM** value: **Cover or less**
Circ: CapCity orders: **18,550**
★ 1st Appearance of Ig'nea.
31 ❑ Sep 1991 Cover: 1.50 **NM** value: **Cover or less**
Circ: CapCity orders: **23,100**
Painted cover. 📖 War of the Gods, Part 5 • Lobo vs. Captain Marvel; Lobo vs. Capt. Marvel
32 ❑ Oct 1991 Cover: 1.50 **NM** value: **Cover or less**
Circ: CapCity orders: **19,450**
★ 1st Appearance of Ice Man.
33 ❑ Nov 1991 Cover: 1.50 **NM** value: **Cover or less**
Circ: CapCity orders: **18,850**
34 ❑ Dec 1991 Cover: 1.50 **NM** value: **Cover or less**
Circ: CapCity orders: **19,550**
35 ❑ Jan 1992 Cover: 1.50 **NM** value: **Cover or less**
Circ: CapCity orders: **20,800**
• L.E.G.I.O.N. '92 starts
36 ❑ Feb 1992 Cover: 1.25 **NM** value: **1.50**
Circ: CapCity orders: **17,450**
37 ❑ Mar 1992 Cover: 1.25 **NM** value: **1.50**
Circ: CapCity orders: **16,350**
38 ❑ Apr 1992 Cover: 1.25 **NM** value: **1.50**
Circ: CapCity orders: **15,750**
39 ❑ May 1992 Cover: 1.50 **NM** value: **Cover or less**
Circ: CapCity orders: **14,600**
40 ❑ Jun 1992 Cover: 1.50 **NM** value: **Cover or less**
Circ: CapCity orders: **14,750**
📖 Costs **A:** Barry Kitson **W:** Barry Kitson
41 ❑ Jul 1992 Cover: 1.50 **NM** value: **Cover or less**
Circ: CapCity orders: **14,700**
42 ❑ Jul 1992 Cover: 1.50 **NM** value: **Cover or less**
Circ: CapCity orders: **15,000**
📖 Revolution **A:** Robin Smith; Barry Kitson **W:** Barry Kitson
43 ❑ Aug 1992 Cover: 1.50 **NM** value: **Cover or less**
Circ: CapCity orders: **14,650**
44 ❑ Aug 1992 Cover: 1.50 **NM** value: **Cover or less**
Circ: CapCity orders: **14,600**
45 ❑ Sep 1992 Cover: 1.50 **NM** value: **Cover or less**
Circ: CapCity orders: **13,550**
46 ❑ Nov 1992 Cover: 1.50 **NM** value: **Cover or less**
Circ: CapCity orders: **14,200**
47 ❑ Dec 1992 Cover: 1.50 **NM** value: **Cover or less**
Circ: CapCity orders: **14,400**
• Lobo vs. Green Lantern (Hal Jordan)
48 ❑ Jan 1993 Cover: 1.75 **NM** value: **Cover or less**
Circ: CapCity orders: **13,100**
• L.E.G.I.O.N. '93 starts
49 ❑ Feb 1993 Cover: 1.75 **NM** value: **Cover or less**
Circ: CapCity orders: **13,150**
50 ❑ Mar 1993 Cover: 3.50 **NM** value: **Cover or less**
Circ: CapCity orders: **14,250**
• Double-size. • L.E.G.I.O.N. '67 back-up
51 ❑ Apr 1993 Cover: 1.75 **NM** value: **Cover or less**
Circ: CapCity orders: **14,550**
52 ❑ May 1993 Cover: 1.75 **NM** value: **Cover or less**
Circ: CapCity orders: **14,450**
53 ❑ Jun 1993 Cover: 1.75 **NM** value: **Cover or less**
Circ: CapCity orders: **13,750**
54 ❑ Jun 1993 Cover: 1.75 **NM** value: **Cover or less**
Circ: CapCity orders: **13,750**
55 ❑ Jul 1993 Cover: 1.75 **NM** value: **Cover or less**
Circ: CapCity orders: **13,150**
56 ❑ Jul 1993 Cover: 1.75 **NM** value: **Cover or less**
Circ: CapCity orders: **13,050**
57 ❑ Aug 1993 Cover: 1.75 **NM** value: **Cover or less**
Circ: CapCity orders: **18,950**
📖 Trinity
58 ❑ Sep 1993 Cover: 1.75 **NM** value: **Cover or less**
Circ: CapCity orders: **15,550**
📖 Trinity
59 ❑ Oct 1993 Cover: 1.75 **NM** value: **Cover or less**
Circ: CapCity orders: **11,850**
60 ❑ Nov 1993 Cover: 1.75 **NM** value: **Cover or less**
Circ: CapCity orders: **12,250**
61 ❑ Dec 1993 Cover: 1.75 **NM** value: **Cover or less**
Circ: CapCity orders: **12,550**
📖 Death of the Party! **A:** Arnie Jorgensen **W:** Tom Peyer
62 ❑ Jan 1994 Cover: 1.75 **NM** value: **Cover or less**
Circ: CapCity orders: **13,850**
• L.E.G.I.O.N. '94 starts
63 ❑ Feb 1994 Cover: 1.75 **NM** value: **Cover or less**
Circ: CapCity orders: **14,200**
📖 We Fight and Fight and Fight **A:** Arnie Jorgensen **W:** Tennessee Peyer
64 ❑ Mar 1994 Cover: 1.75 **NM** value: **Cover or less**
Circ: CapCity orders: **10,250**
65 ❑ Apr 1994 Cover: 1.75 **NM** value: **Cover or less**
Circ: CapCity orders: **9,350**
66 ❑ May 1994 Cover: 1.75 **NM** value: **Cover or less**
Circ: CapCity orders: **9,850**
67 ❑ Jun 1994 Cover: 1.75 **NM** value: **Cover or less**
Circ: CapCity orders: **9,650**
68 ❑ Jul 1994 Cover: 1.75 **NM** value: **Cover or less**
Circ: CapCity orders: **9,850**
69 ❑ Aug 1994 Cover: 1.75 **NM** value: **Cover or less**
Circ: CapCity orders: **10,600**
★ Appearance of Ultra Boy.
70 ❑ Sep 1994 Cover: 2.50 **NM** value: **Cover or less**
Circ: CapCity orders: **12,450**
• Giant-size. final issue. • Zero Hour; story continues in R.E.B.E.L.S. '94 #0; L.E.G.I.O.N. goes renegade (becomes R.E.B.E.L.S.)
Anl 1❑ca. 1990 Cover: 2.95 **NM** value: **Cover or less**
Circ: CapCity orders: **17,950**
• Vril Dox vs. Brainiac ★ Appearance of Superman.
Anl 2❑ca. 1991 Cover: 2.95 **NM** value: **Cover or less**
📖 Armageddon 2001, Part 9 • Armageddon 2001
Anl 3❑ca. 1992 Cover: 2.95 **NM** value: **Cover or less**
Circ: CapCity orders: **18,900**
📖 Eclipso: The Darkness Within, Part 15 • Eclipso
Anl 4❑ca. 1993 Cover: 3.50 **NM** value: **Cover or less**
Circ: CapCity orders: **17,700**
📖 Bloodlines • Bloodlines: Deathstorm ★ 1st Appearance of Pax.
Anl 5❑ca. 1994 Cover: 3.50 **NM** value: **Cover or less**
Circ: CapCity orders: **10,000**
• Elseworlds; L.E.G.I.O.N. 007

LEGION ANTHOLOGY — Limelight

1 ❑ b&w Cover: 2.95 **NM** value: **Cover or less**
📖 Binary Angel; Atria the Grim; Magical Princess Saccharine • manga **A:** Kokoro Grafix; Roy Sato; Terry Karvonen **W:** Kokoro Grafix; Florencio Lim Jr.; Kevin Karvonen
2 ❑ Cover: 2.95 **NM** value: **Cover or less**

LEGION LOST — DC

Name an often-used formula in the comic book industry to infuse a waning title with new life: Take the title's main character(s) and drop him/them into a completely new environment with no apparent way back. Such is the case in DC's Legion Lost. Best described as a cross between the Legionnaires and Star Trek: Voyager, the series takes members of the 30th century's popular super-hero team and drops them in the outer reaches of known space, far from home. Both physically and emotionally lost, the group must learn to put their differences aside (no small task for this diverse bunch) and work together if they plan on ever seeing Earth again.

Apparition, Brainiac 5.1, Chameleon, Kid Quantum, Live Wire, Monstress, Saturn Girl, Ultra Boy, Umbra, and a tag along from the local parts of the galaxy, float aimlessly through space grappling with the fact that they may never find home. Add to that an alien race known as the Progeny, whose sole purpose is to exterminate any life form they deem unpure, and you've got a super-hero version of a classic SF television series.

1 ❑ May 2000 Cover: 2.50 **NM** value: **Cover or less**
Circ: Diamd. preorders: **21,829** • CGC: 3 graded, best 9.8
📖 Legion Lost **W:** Andy Lanning; Dan Abnett
2 ❑ Jun 2000 Cover: 2.50 **NM** value: **Cover or less**
Circ: Diamd. preorders: **19,965**
📖 Enigma Variations **A:** Olivier Coipel **W:** Andy Lanning; Dan Abnett
3 ❑ Jul 2000 Cover: 2.50 **NM** value: **Cover or less**
Circ: Diamd. preorders: **21,923**
📖 Lone Star State **W:** Andy Lanning; Dan Abnett
4 ❑ Aug 2000 Cover: 2.50 **NM** value: **Cover or less**
Circ: Diamd. preorders: **22,744**
📖 Phantoms and Menaces **W:** Andy Lanning; Dan Abnett
5 ❑ Sep 2000 Cover: 2.50 **NM** value: **Cover or less**
Circ: Diamd. preorders: **22,883**
📖 Omniphagos **W:** Andy Lanning; Dan Abnett
6 ❑ Oct 2000 Cover: 2.50 **NM** value: **Cover or less**
Circ: Diamd. preorders: **21,348**
📖 Burnout **A:** Pascal Alixe **W:** Andy Lanning; Dan Abnett
7 ❑ Nov 2000 Cover: 2.50 **NM** value: **Cover or less**
Circ: Diamd. preorders: **21,423**
📖 Singularity **W:** Andy Lanning; Dan Abnett
8 ❑ Dec 2000 Cover: 2.50 **NM** value: **Cover or less**
Circ: Diamd. preorders: **20,949**
📖 Lost & Found **A:** Olivier Coipel **W:** Andy Lanning; Dan Abnett
9 ❑ Jan 2001 Cover: 2.50 **NM** value: **Cover or less**
Circ: Diamd. preorders: **20,665**
📖 Lost & Alone **A:** Pascal Alike **W:** Andy Lanning; Dan Abnett
10 ❑ Feb 2001 Cover: 2.50 **NM** value: **Cover or less**
Circ: Diamd. preorders: **20,403**
📖 Rosette **A:** Olivier Coipel **W:** Andy Lanning; Dan Abnett
11 ❑ Mar 2001 Cover: 2.50 **NM** value: **Cover or less**
Circ: Diamd. preorders: **19,827**
📖 One Billion Years of Solitude **A:** Olivier Coipel **W:** Andy Lanning; Dan Abnett
12 ❑ Apr 2001 Cover: 2.50 **NM** value: **Cover or less**
Circ: Diamd. preorders: **20,178**
📖 First & Last **A:** Olivier Coipel **W:** Andy Lanning; Dan Abnett

LEGION MANGA ANTHOLOGY — Limelight

1 ❑ Cover: 2.95 **NM** value: **Cover or less**
2 ❑ Cover: 2.95 **NM** value: **Cover or less**
3 ❑ Cover: 2.95 **NM** value: **Cover or less**
4 ❑ Cover: 2.95 **NM** value: **Cover or less**
📖 Atria the Grim; Vampire Cat; Binary Angel **A:** Florencia Lim Jr.; Kokoro Grafix **W:** Florencia Lim Jr.; Kokoro Grafix

LEGIONNAIRES — DC

The Legionnaires are a group of super-heroes who live in a future of a thousand years from now. By 2995, man destroyed Earth from abuse and neglect, forcing the remaining inhabitants to live in domed cities in space. The Legionnaires protect those cities using their extraordinary powers.

Their ranks include scores of heroes: from Cosmic Boy, who fights with magnetic powers, to Brainiac 5, latter-day descendent of the super-genius Braniac. New characters were constantly being added and dropped. Although this could be confusing at times, it gave the title almost infinite possibilities for character development and plot lines.

0 ❑ Oct 1994 Cover: 1.50 **NM** value: **2.25**
Circ: CapCity orders: **18,400**
📖 Close Encounters • revised Legion origin; continues in Legion of Super-Heroes #62 and Legionnaires #19 **A:** Jeffrey Moy **W:** Mark Waid; Tom McCraw
1 ❑ Apr 1993 Cover: 1.25 **NM** value: **3.00**
Circ: CapCity orders: **46,150**
📖 Baptism By Fire! • with trading card **A:** Chris Sprouse **W:** Mary Bierbaum; Tom Bierbaum
2 ❑ May 1993 Cover: 1.25 **NM** value: **2.00**
Circ: CapCity orders: **23,550**
covers of issues #2-6 form one image. 📖 In Death's Grip **A:** Chris Sprouse **W:** Mary Bierbaum; Tom Bierbaum ★ Versus Fatal Five.
3 ❑ Jun 1993 Cover: 1.25 **NM** value: **2.00**
Circ: CapCity orders: **20,750**
📖 The Beast Below **A:** Chris Sprouse **W:** Mary Bierbaum; Tom Bierbaum ★ Versus Fatal Five.
4 ❑ Jul 1993 Cover: 1.25 **NM** value: **2.00**
Circ: CapCity orders: **19,100**
📖 If Looks Could Kill ★ Versus Fatal Five.
5 ❑ Aug 1993 Cover: 1.25 **NM** value: **2.00**
Circ: CapCity orders: **18,750**
📖 New Life, New Death! ★ Versus Fatal Five.
6 ❑ Sep 1993 Cover: 1.25 **NM** value: **1.50**
Circ: CapCity orders: **16,500**
📖 An Eye For an Eye ★ Versus Fatal Five.
7 ❑ Oct 1993 Cover: 1.25 **NM** value: **1.50**
Circ: CapCity orders: **15,950**
📖 Devils in the Deep **C:** Adam Hughes
8 ❑ Nov 1993 Cover: 1.25 **NM** value: **1.50**
Circ: CapCity orders: **14,800**
📖 In Heart and Conscience Free • Brainiac 5 leaves team
9 ❑ Dec 1993 Cover: 1.50 **NM** value: **Cover or less**
Circ: CapCity orders: **14,300**
📖 Skin Deep
10 ❑ Jan 1994 Cover: 1.50 **NM** value: **Cover or less**
Circ: CapCity orders: **13,900**
📖 Little White Lies
11 ❑ Feb 1994 Cover: 1.50 **NM** value: **Cover or less**
Circ: CapCity orders: **13,200**
📖 The Astonishing Return of Kid Quantum • Kid Quantum joins team
12 ❑ Mar 1994 Cover: 1.50 **NM** value: **Cover or less**
Circ: CapCity orders: **12,600**
📖 Street Justice
13 ❑ Apr 1994 Cover: 1.50 **NM** value: **Cover or less**
Circ: CapCity orders: **11,900**
📖 Chain Gang • Matter-Eater Lad becomes a girl
14 ❑ May 1994 Cover: 1.50 **NM** value: **Cover or less**
Circ: CapCity orders: **11,950**
📖 Grim Reality
15 ❑ Jun 1994 Cover: 1.50 **NM** value: **Cover or less**
Circ: CapCity orders: **11,700**
📖 Worst Nightmares
16 ❑ Jul 1994 Cover: 1.50 **NM** value: **Cover or less**
Circ: CapCity orders: **12,850**
📖 Saved By Zero • Return of Dream Girl
17 ❑ Aug 1994 Cover: 1.50 **NM** value: **Cover or less**

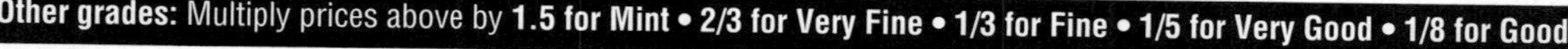
Other grades: Multiply prices above by **1.5 for Mint • 2/3 for Very Fine • 1/3 for Fine • 1/5 for Very Good • 1/8 for Good**

Circ: CapCity orders: **13,500**
End of an Era, Part 1: History Lesson • End of an Era Conclusion
18 ❑ Sep 1994 Cover: 1.50 **NM** value: **Cover or less**
Circ: CapCity orders: **14,300**
End of an Era, Part 4: Changing Times • Zero Hour
19 ❑ Nov 1994 Cover: 1.50 **NM** value: **Cover or less**
Circ: CapCity orders: **12,500**
The Quick and the Dead
20 ❑ Dec 1994 Cover: 1.50 **NM** value: **Cover or less**
Circ: CapCity orders: **12,450**
The Descent of Mano! **A:** Jeffrey Moy ★ Versus Mano.
21 ❑ Jan 1995 Cover: 1.50 **NM** value: **Cover or less**
Circ: CapCity orders: **12,250**
Enter the Workforce! **A:** Jeffrey Moy **W:** Tom Peyer ★ 1st Appearance of Work Force.
22 ❑ Feb 1995 Cover: 1.50 **NM** value: **Cover or less**
Circ: CapCity orders: **11,650**
Hard Time! **A:** Jeffrey Moy
23 ❑ Mar 1995 Cover: 1.50 **NM** value: **Cover or less**
Circ: CapCity orders: **10,975**
A: Jeffrey Moy
24 ❑ Apr 1995 Cover: 1.50 **NM** value: **Cover or less**
Circ: CapCity orders: **10,225**
Me, Myself and I! **A:** Jeffrey Moy
25 ❑ May 1995 Cover: 1.50 **NM** value: **Cover or less**
Circ: CapCity orders: **10,050**
26 ❑ Jun 1995 Cover: 1.75 **NM** value: **Cover or less**
Circ: CapCity orders: **9,775**
Authority **A:** Jeffrey Moy
27 ❑ Jul 1995 Cover: 2.25 **NM** value: **Cover or less**
Circ: CapCity orders: **9,850**
Eyes of Hate!
28 ❑ Aug 1995 Cover: 2.25 **NM** value: **Cover or less**
Circ: CapCity orders: **9,875**
Nightfall ★ 1st Appearance of Legion Espionage Squad.
29 ❑ Sep 1995 Cover: 2.25 **NM** value: **Cover or less**
Circ: CapCity orders: **9,375**
A: Jeffrey Moy ★ 1st Appearance of Dirk Morgna.
30 ❑ Oct 1995 Cover: 2.25 **NM** value: **Cover or less**
Circ: CapCity orders: **8,125**
Struck By Lightning! • Lightning Lad turning point **A:** Jeffrey Moy
31 ❑ Nov 1995 Cover: 2.25 **NM** value: **Cover or less**
One Thousand Years of Solitude • Future Tense, Part 3; Superboy made honorary member; Valor released into 30th century **A:** Jeffrey Moy
32 ❑ Dec 1995 Cover: 2.25 **NM** value: **Cover or less**
Here and Now • Underworld Unleashed **A:** Jeffrey Moy ★ Appearance of Chronos.
33 ❑ Jan 1996 Cover: 2.25 **NM** value: **Cover or less**
The Inhuman Touch • Kinetix finds Emerald Eye; [L1996-2] **A:** Jeffrey Moy **W:** Tom Peyerm Tom McCraw
34 ❑ Feb 1996 Cover: 2.25 **NM** value: **Cover or less**
Fallen Star • [L1996-4] **A:** Jeffrey Moy **W:** Tom McCraw; Tom Peyer
35 ❑ Mar 1996 Cover: 2.25 **NM** value: **Cover or less**
While You Were Out… • XS returns to 30th century; [L1996-6] **A:** Jeffrey Moy **W:** Roger Stern; Tom McCraw
36 ❑ May 1996 Cover: 2.25 **NM** value: **Cover or less**
To the Rescue! • [L1996-8] **A:** Jeffrey Moy
37 ❑ Jun 1996 Cover: 2.25 **NM** value: **Cover or less**
Decisions • [L1996-10] ★ Origin of M'onel.
38 ❑ Jul 1996 Cover: 2.25 **NM** value: **Cover or less**
Trouble on Titan • [L1996-12]
39 ❑ Aug 1996 Cover: 2.25 **NM** value: **Cover or less**
Wishful Thinking • Triad's three personalities become distinct; [L1996-14]
40 ❑ Sep 1996 Cover: 2.25 **NM** value: **Cover or less**
Emerald/Violet • [L1996-16]
41 ❑ Oct 1996 Cover: 2.25 **NM** value: **Cover or less**
Aftermath • [L1996-18] **A:** Jeffrey Moy **W:** Roger Stern; Tom McCraw
42 ❑ Nov 1996 Cover: 2.25 **NM** value: **Cover or less**
Circ: Diamd. preorders: **25,391**
When Strikes the Sorceress! • [L1996-20] **A:** Jeffrey Moy **W:** Roger Stern; Tom McGraw
43 ❑ Dec 1996 Cover: 2.25 **NM** value: **Cover or less**
Circ: Diamd. preorders: **27,298**
New Blood • Legion try-outs; Magno joins team; Umbra joins team; Sensor joins team; [L1996-22] **A:** Jeffrey Moy **W:** Roger Stern; Tom McGraw
44 ❑ Jan 1997 Cover: 2.25 **NM** value: **Cover or less**
Circ: Diamd. preorders: **26,168**
Taking a Licking • [L1997-1] **A:** Jeffrey Moy **W:** Tom McCraw; Tom Peyer
45 ❑ Feb 1997 Cover: 2.25 **NM** value: **Cover or less**
Circ: Diamd. preorders: **25,835**
Things Change • [L1997-3] ★ Versus Mantis Morlo.
46 ❑ Mar 1997 Cover: 2.25 **NM** value: **Cover or less**
Circ: Diamd. preorders: **25,692**
Questions • [L1997-5] **A:** Jeffrey Moy; Philip Moy **W:** Roger Stern; Tom McGraw
47 ❑ Apr 1997 Cover: 2.25 **NM** value: **Cover or less**
Circ: Diamd. preorders: **25,488**
Lost in Time • [L1997-7]
48 ❑ May 1997 Cover: 2.25 **NM** value: **Cover or less**
Circ: Diamd. preorders: **25,546**
Dawn of the Dark Lord • [L1997-9] ★ Versus Mordru.
49 ❑ Jun 1997 Cover: 2.25 **NM** value: **Cover or less**
Circ: Diamd. preorders: **26,308**
Let the Call Go Forth • [L1997-11] ★ Appearance of Workforce, Heroes of Xanthu. ★ Death of Atom'x. ★ Versus Mordru.
50 ❑ Jul 1997 Cover: 3.95 **NM** value: **Cover or less**
Circ: Diamd. preorders: **28,319**
• Giant-size. The Bride of Mordru • Poster; Mysa becomes young; [L1997-13] ★ Versus Mordru.
51 ❑ Aug 1997 Cover: 2.25 **NM** value: **Cover or less**
Circ: Diamd. preorders: **25,684**
Picking Up the Pieces • [L1997-15]
52 ❑ Sep 1997 Cover: 2.25 **NM** value: **Cover or less**
Circ: Diamd. preorders: **25,205**
Big Trouble • Vi's new powers manifest; [L1997-17]
53 ❑ Oct 1997 Cover: 2.25 **NM** value: **Cover or less**
Circ: Diamd. preorders: **25,402**
Fitting In • Monstress joins team; Magno leaves team; [L1997-19]
54 ❑ Nov 1997 Cover: 2.25 **NM** value: **Cover or less**
Circ: Diamd. preorders: **25,204**
(Untitled) • Golden Age story; [L1997-21] **A:** Jeffrey Moy **W:** Tom Peyer
55 ❑ Dec 1997 Cover: 2.25 **NM** value: **Cover or less**
Circ: Diamd. preorders: **25,131**
Face cover. Control • [L1997-23] **A:** Jeffrey Moy **W:** Roger Stern; Tom McGraw ★ Versus Composite Man.
56 ❑ Jan 1998 Cover: 2.25 **NM** value: **Cover or less**
Circ: Diamd. preorders: **25,055**
The Better Part of Valor • M'onel returns to Daxam; [L1998-1]
57 ❑ Feb 1998 Cover: 2.25 **NM** value: **Cover or less**
Circ: Diamd. preorders: **24,387**
Troubled Minds • [L1998-3]
58 ❑ Mar 1998 Cover: 2.25 **NM** value: **Cover or less**
Circ: Diamd. preorders: **23,765**
If a Man Be Made of Iron… • [L1998-5]
59 ❑ Apr 1998 Cover: 2.25 **NM** value: **Cover or less**
Circ: Diamd. preorders: **23,139**
Friends, Lovers and the Calm Before the Storm • [L1998-7]
60 ❑ May 1998 Cover: 2.25 **NM** value: **Cover or less**
Circ: Diamd. preorders: **23,125**
Scandalous • Chameleon leaves team; Sensor leaves team; Karate Kid joins team; Kid Quantum joins team; [L1998-9]
61 ❑ Jun 1998 Cover: 2.25 **NM** value: **Cover or less**
Circ: Diamd. preorders: **24,169**
If I Could Turn Back Time… • Multiple time shifts; [L1998-11] ★ Appearance of Superman (from Time and Time Again).
62 ❑ Jul 1998 Cover: 2.25 **NM** value: **Cover or less**
Circ: Diamd. preorders: **22,836**
Balance of Power • Dark Circle Rising, Part 1: Crossfire!; [L1998-13]
63 ❑ Aug 1998 Cover: 2.25 **NM** value: **Cover or less**
Circ: Diamd. preorders: **23,070**
Winds of War? • Dark Circle Rising, Part 3: Resignation!; [L1998-15]
64 ❑ Sep 1998 Cover: 2.50 **NM** value: **Cover or less**
Circ: Diamd. preorders: **22,432**
Time Out! • Dark Circle Rising, Part 5: Enlightenment!; [L1998-17]
65 ❑ Oct 1998 Cover: 2.50 **NM** value: **Cover or less**
Circ: Diamd. preorders: **21,615**
Days of Reckoning! • Dark Circle falls; [L1998-19]
66 ❑ Dec 1998 Cover: 2.50 **NM** value: **Cover or less**
Circ: Diamd. preorders: **20,921**
Missing Persons • [L1998-21] ★ 1st Appearance of Charma.
67 ❑ Jan 1999 Cover: 2.50 **NM** value: **Cover or less**
Circ: Diamd. preorders: **20,685**
Here Be Heroes! • [L1999-1] ★ Appearance of Kono.
68 ❑ Feb 1999 Cover: 2.50 **NM** value: **Cover or less**
Circ: Diamd. preorders: **20,096**
When Robots Attack • Monstress changes color; [L1999-3] **A:** Jeffrey Moy **W:** Roger Stern; Tom McCraw
69 ❑ Mar 1999 Cover: 2.50 **NM** value: **Cover or less**
Circ: Diamd. preorders: **19,795**
Secrets and Lies! • [L1999-5] **A:** Jeffrey Moy **W:** Roger Stern; Tom McCraw ★ Appearance of Plasma.
70 ❑ Apr 1999 Cover: 2.50 **NM** value: **Cover or less**
Circ: Diamd. preorders: **18,932**
Enter: Domain! • Cosmic Boy vs. Domain; [L1999-7] **A:** Jeffrey Moy **W:** Roger Stern; Tom McCraw
71 ❑ May 1999 Cover: 2.50 **NM** value: **Cover or less**
Circ: Diamd. preorders: **18,890**
The Elements of Disaster • [L1999-9] ★ Versus Elements of Disaster.
72 ❑ Jun 1999 Cover: 2.50 **NM** value: **Cover or less**
Circ: Diamd. preorders: **19,044**
Enemies of Science! • [L1999-11] **A:** Jeffrey Moy **W:** Roger Stern; Tom McCraw
73 ❑ Jul 1999 Cover: 2.50 **NM** value: **Cover or less**
Circ: Diamd. preorders: **18,505**
The Final Gathering • Star Boy solo; [L1999-13] **A:** Jeffrey Moy **W:** Roger Stern; Tom McCraw
74 ❑ Aug 1999 Cover: 2.50 **NM** value: **Cover or less**
Circ: Diamd. preorders: **18,104**
Aftershocks • [L1999-15] **A:** Jeffrey Moy **W:** Roger Stern; Tom Peyer
75 ❑ Sep 1999 Cover: 2.50 **NM** value: **Cover or less**
Circ: Diamd. preorders: **18,274**
Tyrants Three • [L1999-17] **A:** Jeffrey Moy **W:** Tom Peyer
76 ❑ Oct 1999 Cover: 2.50 **NM** value: **Cover or less**
Circ: Diamd. preorders: **17,919**
The Fire This Time • [L1999-19] **A:** Jeffrey Moy **W:** Roger Stern; Tom McCraw ★ Origin of Wildfire.
77 ❑ Nov 1999 Cover: 2.50 **NM** value: **Cover or less**
Circ: Diamd. preorders: **17,418**
Endless Summer! • [L1999-21] **A:** Jeffrey Moy **W:** Roger Stern; Tom McCraw
78 ❑ Dec 2000 Cover: 2.50 **NM** value: **Cover or less**
Circ: Diamd. preorders: **17,952**
Emissary • [L1999-23] **A:** Jeffrey Moy **W:** Andy Lanning; Dan Abnett
79 ❑ Jan 2000 Cover: 2.50 **NM** value: **Cover or less**
Circ: Diamd. preorders: **17,482**
Legionnaires of the Damned, Part 2 • [L2000-1] **A:** Olivier Coipel **W:** Andy Lanning; Dan Abnett
80 ❑ Feb 2000 Cover: 2.50 **NM** value: **Cover or less**
Circ: Diamd. preorders: **17,198**
Legionnaires of the Damned, Part 4 • [L2000-3] **A:** Olivier Coipel **W:** Andy Lanning; Dan Abnett
1000000 ❑ Nov 1998 Cover: 2.50 **NM** value: **Cover or less**
Circ: Diamd. preorders: **29,268**
Come Together • set 1, 000 years after events of One Million **A:** Sean Phillips **W:** Tom Peyer
Anl 1 ❑ ca. 1994 Cover: 2.95 **NM** value: **Cover or less**
Circ: CapCity orders: **10,700**
Castles in the Air • Elseworlds; Futuristic Camelot
Anl 2 ❑ ca. 1995 Cover: 3.95 **NM** value: **Cover or less**
Circ: CapCity orders: **9,100**
Four Horsemen • Andromeda leaves team ★ Death of Apparition.
Anl 3 ❑ ca. 1996 Cover: 3.50 **NM** value: **Cover or less**
Circ: Diamd. preorders: **24,267**
The Long Road Home • Legends of the Dead Earth; XS' travels in time; 1996 Annual **A:** Chuck Wojtkiewicz; Dan Jurgens; Tony Castrillo **W:** Roger Stern ★ Appearance of Barry Allen.

LEGIONNAIRES THREE — DC

1 ❑ Feb 1986 Cover: 0.75 **NM** value: **1.25**
Circ: CapCity orders: **15,100**
Future Shock! **A:** Ernie Colon **W:** Keith Giffen; Mindy Newell ★ Versus Time Trapper.
2 ❑ Mar 1986 Cover: 0.75 **NM** value: **1.00**
Circ: CapCity orders: **13,150**
From Hell to Eternity
3 ❑ Apr 1986 Cover: 0.75 **NM** value: **1.00**
Circ: CapCity orders: **12,450**
And Then There Were Two!
4 ❑ May 1986 Cover: 0.75 **NM** value: **1.00**
Circ: CapCity orders: **11,700**
Countdown

LEGION OF MONSTERS, THE — Marvel

1 ❑ Cover: 1.00 **NM** value: **6.00**
• magazine, b&w.

LEGION OF NIGHT, THE — Marvel

1 ❑ Nov 1991 Cover: 4.95 **NM** value: **Cover or less**
Circ: CapCity orders: **19,600**
Messenger From The Dead Part 1 **A:** Whilce Portacio **W:** Steve Gerber
2 ❑ Dec 1991 Cover: 4.95 **NM** value: **Cover or less**
Circ: CapCity orders: **15,700**
Messenger From The Dead Part 2 **A:** Whilce Portacio **W:** Steve Gerber

LEGION OF STUPID HEROES — Alternate Concepts

Not to be confused with the one-shot Legion of the Stupid-Heroes, this title nevertheless takes on the same mission of lampooning popular costumed characters. Published by Johnny Lauck (The Comic Book Index) and Alternate Concepts, it's a series of gag strips starring such characters as Tubs-Mariner, Flaming Armpit, Captain Almost, and Puff-a dragon.

The gags are mostly short, one-page affairs, reminiscent of Britain's Beano. A letterhack whose note appeared in issue #3's letter column probably summed it up the best when he wrote "It looks pretty good, and the jokes, while juvenile and silly and gross, nonetheless work."

1 ❑ Jul 1997 Cover: 2.50 **NM** value: **Cover or less**
One Day at the Olympics **A:** Chas Gillen **W:** Johnny Lauck
2 ❑ Sep 1997 Cover: 2.50 **NM** value: **Cover or less**
Vomit!; Once Upon a Morning Shave **A:** Chas Gillen; Brian Briggs; Charles Burgoon; Danny Watson; Dustin Krcatovich; Linc Polderman; Randall Davis; Richard Tomasic **W:** Dustin Krcatovich; Linc Polderman; Rick Schmitz; John Barrett; Johnny Lauck
3 ❑ Cover: 2.50 **NM** value: **Cover or less**
Blambo and Tubs-Mariner: Play it Again Sam!; The Great Pumpkin **A:** Chas Gillen; Charles Burgoon; Danny Watson; Donnie Page; Earl Geier; Richard Tomasic; Rick Schmitz **W:** Richard Tomasic; John Barrett; Johnny Lauck
4 ❑ Mar 1998 Cover: 2.50 **NM** value: **Cover or less**
Innocent as a Baby…Rat! **A:** Chas Gillen; Charles Burgoon; Danny Watson; Donnie Page; Earl Geier; Rick Schmitz **W:** Rick Schmitz; John Barrett; Johnny Lauck

LEGION OF STUPID KNIGHTS — Alternate Concepts

SE 1 ❑ Feb 1998, b&w Cover: 2.50 **NM** value: **Cover or less**
A: Danny Watson; Earl Geier; Richard Tomasic; Rick Schmitz **W:** Johnny Lauck

LEGION OF SUBSTITUTE HEROES SPECIAL — DC

1 ❑ Cover: 1.25 **NM** value: **2.00**
Circ: CapCity orders: **15,250**
You Can't Keep a Good Villain Down **A:** Keith Giffen **W:** Paul Levitz

To find the median price offered on eBay at press time for pre-1990 **CGC-graded comics**, multiply by:

9.9 (M): **33**	8.5 (VF+): **1.25**
9.8(NM/M): **16**	8.0 (VF): **0.85**
9.6 (NM+): **7**	7.5 (VF-): **0.6**
9.4 (NM): **5**	7.0 (F/VF): **0.5**
9.2 (NM-): **2.5**	6.5 (F+): **0.4**
9.0 (VF/NM): **1.5**	6.0 (F-): **0.33**

These are median prices of all CGC comics auctioned on eBay; prices for individual issues will vary.

CGC-graded: Multiply prices above by **33 for 9.9 M • 16 for 9.8 NM/M • 7 for 9.6 NM+ • 5 for 9.4 NM • 2.5 for 9.2 NM- • 1.5 for 9.0 VF/NM**

LEGION OF SUPER-HEROES (1ST SERIES) DC

The Legion of Super-Heroes' story began when 30th century teens Garth Ranzz (Lightning Lad), Rokk Krinn (Cosmic Boy), and Imra Ardeen (Saturn Girl) saved the life of R.J. Brande, possibly the universe's richest man. Brande repaid the teens by helping them set up the Legion of Super-Heroes. It was to be a club of sorts, open to super-powered youngsters under the age of 18. Thanks to the wonders of time travel, this soon included Superboy, followed by 30th century teens such as Matter Eater Lad.

This short-lived early 1970s Legion of Super-Heroes series reprinted the Legion's early adventures from Action Comics and Adventure Comics. Although the Legion had appeared as a regular feature with Superboy since 1949, in Superboy and the Legion of Super-Heroes, this was the first title which bore their name alone. A few years later, the Superboy series would change names to become The Legion of Super-Heroes (2nd Series).

1 ❑ Feb 1973 Cover: 0.20 **NM** value: **11.50**
• **CGC:** 3 graded, best 9.6
📖 The Lad Who Wrecked the Legion!; The Secret of the Legion Rookie?!; Our Strange Universe; Professor Eureka (1/2 page, untitled); The Riddle of the Space Rainbow; Legion of Super-Heroes Membership List, Part 1 (text); The Legion Constitution (text) • Tales of the Legion of Super-Heroes; Tommy Tomorrow reprint

2 ❑ Mar 1973 Cover: 0.20 **NM** value: **7.00**
• **CGC:** 1 graded, best 9.2
📖 The War Between Krypton and Earth!; The Civil War of the Legion!; The Toys That Stopped Space Crime; Legion of Super-Heroes Membership List, Part 2 (text) • Tales of the Legion of Super-Heroes; Tommy Tomorrow reprint

3 ❑ May 1973 Cover: 0.20 **NM** value: **6.00**
• **CGC:** 1 graded, best 9.6
📖 Computo The Conqueror!; The Trial of Tommy Tomorrow; The Timeless Legion (text) • Tales of the Legion of Super-Heroes; Tommy Tomorrow reprint ★ Versus Computo.

4 ❑ Aug 1973 Cover: 0.20 **NM** value: **6.00**
📖 Colossal Boy's One-Man War!; The Strategy of Braniac 5!; The Forbidden Robots; The Legion Outpost (text) • Tales of the Legion of Super-Heroes; Tommy Tomorrow reprint ★ Versus Computo.

LEGION OF SUPER-HEROES, THE (2ND SERIES) DC

First appearing in Adventure Comics #247, the Legion of Super-Heroes is a group of teenaged heroes from the 30th century. Over time, their membership has included Mon-El, Phantom Girl, Dawnstar, Timber Wolf, Brainiac, Ultra Boy, Saturn Girl, Star Boy, Chemical King, the Invisible Kid, and numerous others.

This series, which picked up the numbering of Superboy (1st series), starred the youthful Kryptonian throughout most of its run. When Superboy left the series in issue #259 in 1980, it became known simply as "The Legion of Super-Heroes." Superboy returned to the series in issue #280, though he was never again mentioned in the title.

259 ❑ Jan 1980 Cover: 0.40 **NM** value: **3.50**
Circ: Statement: **130,478**
• Superboy leaves team; Continued from "Superboy and the Legion of Super-Heroes"

260 ❑ Feb 1980 Cover: 0.40 **NM** value: **2.75**
Circ: Statement: **130,478**
📖 Come to the Circus and Die! ★ Versus Circus of Crime.

261 ❑ Mar 1980 Cover: 0.40 **NM** value: **2.50**
Circ: Statement: **130,478**
📖 Space Circus of Death! ★ Versus Circus of Crime.

262 ❑ Apr 1980 Cover: 0.40 **NM** value: **2.50**
Circ: Statement: **130,478**
📖 The Planet That Captured the Legion • Has 1979 Statement; avg print run 322,106; avg sales 160,395; avg subs 1,870; avg total paid 162,265; max existent 162,265; 50% of run returned

263 ❑ May 1980 Cover: 0.40 **NM** value: **2.50**
Circ: Statement: **130,478**
📖 Day of Judgment

264 ❑ Jun 1980 Cover: 0.40 **NM** value: **2.50**
Circ: Statement: **130,478**
📖 Dagons Cavern of Doom!

265 ❑ Jul 1980 Cover: 0.40 **NM** value: **2.50**
Circ: Statement: **130,478**
📖 The Brigadoon Syndrome!; The Computers That Saved Metropolis! • bonus Superman story starring the TRS-80 Computer Whiz Kids (Radio Shack sponsored story) ★ Origin of Tyroc.

266 ❑ Aug 1980 Cover: 0.40 **NM** value: **2.50**
Circ: Statement: **130,478**
📖 Kantuu • Return of Bouncing Boy; Return of Duo Damsel

267 ❑ Sep 1980 Cover: 0.50 **NM** value: **2.50**
Circ: Statement: **130,478**
📖 To Bottle a Genie!; The Grounded Legionnaires • Secret of the Legion Flight Rings ★ Origin of Legion Flight Rings.

268 ❑ Oct 1980 Cover: 0.50 **NM** value: **2.50**
Circ: Statement: **130,478**
📖 Life After Life After Life **A:** Steve Ditko

269 ❑ Nov 1980 Cover: 0.50 **NM** value: **2.50**
Circ: Statement: **130,478**
📖 Who Shall Name the Dark Man? ★ Versus Fatal Five.

270 ❑ Dec 1980 Cover: 0.50 **NM** value: **2.50**
Circ: Statement: **130,478**
📖 Who Is the Dark Man? • Dark Man's identity revealed

271 ❑ Jan 1981 Cover: 0.50 **NM** value: **1.75**
Circ: Statement: **117,038**
📖 What Is the Dark Man? ★ Origin of Dark Man.

272 ❑ Feb 1981 Cover: 0.50 **NM** value: **1.75**
Circ: Statement: **117,038**
📖 The Secret Origin of Blok!; Who Are the Heroes? • Blok joins Legion of Super-Heroes; Dial 'H' For Hero preview story ★ Origin of Blok. ★ 1st Appearance of Dial 'H' for Hero (new).

273 ❑ Mar 1981 Cover: 0.50 **NM** value: **1.75**
Circ: Statement: **117,038**
📖 A Murderer Among Us?

274 ❑ Apr 1981 Cover: 0.50 **NM** value: **1.75**
Circ: Statement: **117,038**
📖 The Exaggerated Death of Ultra Boy • Ultra Boy becomes pirate **A:** Steve Ditko

275 ❑ May 1981 Cover: 0.50 **NM** value: **1.75**
Circ: Statement: **117,038**
• Has 1980 Statement; avg print run 320,922; avg sales 127,143; avg subs 3,335; avg total paid 130,478; max existent 130,478; 58% of run returned

276 ❑ Jun 1981 Cover: 0.50 **NM** value: **1.75**
Circ: Statement: **117,038**

277 ❑ Jul 1981 Cover: 0.50 **NM** value: **1.75**
Circ: Statement: **117,038**

278 ❑ Aug 1981 Cover: 0.50 **NM** value: **1.75**
Circ: Statement: **117,038**
📖 Tragedy at the Top of the World! ★ Appearance of Reflecto. ★ Versus Grimbor.

279 ❑ Sep 1981 Cover: 0.50 **NM** value: **1.75**
Circ: Statement: **117,038**
• Reflecto's identity revealed

280 ❑ Oct 1981 Cover: 0.60 **NM** value: **1.75**
Circ: Statement: **117,038**
📖 O! Call Back Yesterday! • Superboy rejoins

281 ❑ Nov 1981 Cover: 0.60 **NM** value: **1.75**
Circ: Statement: **117,038**
📖 Madness Is the Molecule Master **A:** Steve Ditko ★ Versus Molecule Master.

282 ❑ Dec 1981 Cover: 0.60 **NM** value: **1.75**
Circ: Statement: **117,038**
📖 If Answers There Be... • Ultra Boy returns **A:** Paul Levitz **W:** Roy Thomas ★ Origin of Reflecto.

283 ❑ Jan 1982 Cover: 0.60 **NM** value: **1.75**
Circ: Statement: **127,037**
📖 The Startling Secret of Wildfire! • Wildfire story ★ Origin of Wildfire.

284 ❑ Feb 1982 Cover: 0.60 **NM** value: **1.75**
Circ: Statement: **127,037** • **CGC:** 1 graded, best 9.6
📖 The Soul- Thief From the Stars

285 ❑ Mar 1982 Cover: 0.60 **NM** value: **2.50**
Circ: Statement: **127,037**
📖 Night Never Falls at Nullport • Keith Giffen plots begin **A:** Keith Giffen; Pat Broderick

286 ❑ Apr 1982 Cover: 0.60 **NM** value: **2.00**
Circ: Statement: **127,037**
📖 Old Friends, New Relatives and Other Corpses! **A:** Pat Broderick ★ Versus Doctor Regulus. ★ Versus Dr. Regulus.

287 ❑ May 1982 Cover: 0.60 **NM** value: **2.00**
Circ: Statement: **127,037**
• Has 1981 Statement; avg print run 282,442; avg sales 114,016; avg subs 3,022; avg total paid 117,038; max existent 117,038; 57% of run returned **A:** Keith Giffen ★ Versus Kharlak.

288 ❑ Jun 1982 Cover: 0.60 **NM** value: **2.00**
Circ: Statement: **127,037**
📖 The Legionnaires Made for Burning **A:** Keith Giffen

289 ❑ Jul 1982 Cover: 0.60 **NM** value: **2.00**
Circ: Statement: **127,037**
📖 A Cold and Lonely Corner of Hell! **A:** Keith Giffen

290 ❑ Aug 1982 Cover: 0.60 **NM** value: **2.00**
Circ: Statement: **127,037**
📖 And the Servant Shall Be a Sign... • Great Darkness Saga, Part 1 **A:** Keith Giffen

291 ❑ Sep 1982 Cover: 0.60 **NM** value: **2.00**
Circ: Statement: **127,037**
📖 ...A Sign of Darkness Dawning • Great Darkness Saga, Part 2 **A:** Keith Giffen

292 ❑ Oct 1982 Cover: 0.60 **NM** value: **2.00**
Circ: Statement: **127,037**
📖 Darkness Transcendent • Great Darkness Saga, Part 3 **A:** Keith Giffen

293 ❑ Nov 1982 Cover: 0.60 **NM** value: **2.00**
Circ: Statement: **127,037**
📖 Within the Darkness...; Fate Is the Killer • Great Darkness Saga, Part 4; Masters of the Universe preview story **A:** Keith Giffen

294 ❑ Dec 1982 Cover: 1.00 **NM** value: **2.00**
Circ: Statement: **127,037**
📖 Darkseid • Great Darkness Saga, Part 5; giant-size issue **A:** Keith Giffen

295 ❑ Jan 1983 Cover: 0.60 **NM** value: **1.50**
Circ: Statement: **166,733**
📖 The Origin of the Universe File ★ Origin of Universo (possible origin), Green Lantern Corps.

296 ❑ Feb 1983 Cover: 0.60 **NM** value: **1.50**
Circ: Statement: **166,733**
📖 What Do You Do on the Day After Domsday?

297 ❑ Mar 1983 Cover: 0.60 **NM** value: **1.50**
Circ: Statement: **166,733**
📖 (Untitled) • Cosmic Boy solo story ★ Origin of Legion of Super-Heroes.

298 ❑ Apr 1983 Cover: 0.60 **NM** value: **1.50**
Circ: Statement: **166,733**
📖 The Edge of Nowhere; Duel in Dark Magic! • Amethyst, Princess of Gemworld preview story ★ 1st Appearance of Gemworld, Dark Opal, Amethyst.

299 ❑ May 1983 Cover: 0.60 **NM** value: **1.50**
Circ: Statement: **166,733**
📖 Not a Ghost of a Chance • Invisible Kid II meets Invisible Kid I; Has 1982 Statement; avg print run 288,045; avg sales 123,556; avg subs 3,481; avg total paid 127,037; max existent 127,037; 55% of run returned

300 ❑ Jun 1983 Cover: 1.50 **NM** value: **2.00**
Circ: Statement: **166,733** • **CGC:** 1 graded, best 9.6
• Double-size. 📖 The Future Is Forever! • Tales of the Adult Legion; alternate futures

301 ❑ Jul 1983 Cover: 0.60 **NM** value: **1.50**
Circ: Statement: **166,733**
📖 Different Paths, Different Dooms

302 ❑ Aug 1983 Cover: 0.60 **NM** value: **1.50**
Circ: Statement: **166,733**
📖 Family Matters • Lightning Lad vs. Lightning Lord

303 ❑ Sep 1983 Cover: 0.60 **NM** value: **1.50**
Circ: Statement: **166,733**
📖 Those Emerald Eyes Are Shining... ★ Versus Emerald Empress.

304 ❑ Oct 1983 Cover: 0.60 **NM** value: **1.50**
Circ: Statement: **166,733**
📖 Siege Perilous • Legion Academy

305 ❑ Nov 1983 Cover: 0.60 **NM** value: **1.50**
Circ: Statement: **166,733**
📖 Violet's Story • Shrinking Violet revealed as Durlan; real Shrinking Violet returns

306 ❑ Dec 1983 Cover: 0.75 **NM** value: **1.50**
Circ: Statement: **166,733**
📖 Born Under a Lucky Star ★ Origin of Star Boy.

307 ❑ Jan 1984 Cover: 0.75 **NM** value: **1.50**
Circ: Statement: **140,018**
📖 The Prophet Shall Speak ★ Versus Prophet.

308 ❑ Feb 1984 Cover: 0.75 **NM** value: **1.50**
Circ: Statement: **140,018**
📖 And the Sky Itself Shall Burn! ★ Versus Prophet.

309 ❑ Mar 1984 Cover: 0.75 **NM** value: **1.50**
Circ: Statement: **140,018**
📖 As the Sky Burns ★ Versus Prophet.

310 ❑ Apr 1984 Cover: 0.75 **NM** value: **1.50**
Circ: Statement: **140,018**
📖 Omen • Has 1983 Statement; avg print run 329,965; avg sales 164,280; avg subs 2,453; avg total paid 166,733; max existent 166,733; 48% of run returned ★ Versus Omen.

311 ❑ May 1984 Cover: 0.75 **NM** value: **1.50**
Circ: Statement: **140,018**
📖 Destruction By Design

312 ❑ Jun 1984 Cover: 0.75 **NM** value: **1.50**
Circ: Statement: **140,018**
📖 Good Cop, Bad Cop?

313 ❑ Jul 1984 Cover: 0.75 **NM** value: **1.50**
Circ: Statement: **140,018**
📖 Death Threat • series continues as Tales of the Legion of Super-Heroes

Anl 1 ❑ ca. 1982 Cover: 1.00 **NM** value: **2.50**
📖 Monster in a Little Girl's Mind! **A:** Keith Giffen ★ 1st Appearance of Invisible Kid II (Jacques Foccart).

Anl 2 ❑ ca. 1983 Cover: 1.00 **NM** value: **2.00**
📖 Whatever Gods There Be... • Wedding of Karate Kid and Princess Projectra; Karate Kid and Princess Projectra leave Legion of Super-Heroes **A:** Dave Gibbons; Keith Giffen **W:** Paul Levitz

Anl 3 ❑ ca. 1984 Cover: 1.25 **NM** value: **2.00**
📖 The Curse **A:** Curt Swan ★ Origin of Validus.

Bk 1 ❑ Nov 1989 Cover: 17.95 **NM** value: **Cover or less**
• The Great Darkness Saga

LEGION OF SUPER-HEROES (3RD SERIES) DC

This third series of DC's super-team of the future ran concurrently with Legion of Super-Heroes (2nd series), which had changed its name to Tales of the Legion. The third series began as a direct-market only title printed on better quality paper and able to tell slightly more mature (but not adult) stories of the super-team of the future. Tales of the Legion began reprinting these stories a year after they originally ran.

The watchword of this title seemed to be "change" — hard, rapid change. It took only until the fourth issue for DC to kill longtime Legion of Super-Heroes member Karate Kid. Nemesis Kid joined him in that fate in the next issue. Later issues would see a great change in the membership roster as Magnetic Kid, Mentalla, Quislet, Tellus, and Sensor Girl replaced original members Cosmic Boy, Lightning Lad, and Saturn Girl.

All that, of course, was nothing compared to the great upheaval that took place in the Crisis on Infinite Earths and the subsequent revamps to the legend of Superman, including the elimination of Legion inspiration Superboy.

1 ❑ Aug 1984 Cover: 1.25 **NM** value: **3.00**
• **CGC:** 3 graded, best 9.8
Silver ink cover. 📖 Here a Villain, There a Villain... **A:** Keith Giffen **W:** Keith Giffen; Paul Levitz ★ Versus Legion of Super-Villains.

2 ❑ Sep 1984 Cover: 1.25 **NM** value: **2.50**
📖 ...Where a Villain? **A:** Keith Giffen ★ 1st Appearance of Kono. ★ Versus Legion of Super-Villains.

3 ❑ Oct 1984 Cover: 1.25 **NM** value: **2.50**
📖 Everywhere a Villain? **A:** Keith Giffen ★ Versus Legion of Super-Villains.

Other grades: Multiply prices above by **1.5 for Mint • 2/3 for Very Fine • 1/3 for Fine • 1/5 for Very Good • 1/8 for Good**

4 ❑ Nov 1984 Cover: 1.25 **NM** value: **2.50**
📖 Lest Villainy Triumph **A:** Keith Giffen ★ Death of Karate Kid. ★ Versus Legion of Super-Villains.

5 ❑ Dec 1984 Cover: 1.25 **NM** value: **2.50**
📖 An Eye for an Eye, a Villain for a Hero **A:** Keith Giffen ★ Death of Nemesis Kid.

6 ❑ Jan 1985 Cover: 1.25 **NM** value: **2.25**
📖 Silver Linings • Spotlight on Lightning Lass ★ 1st Appearance of Laurel Gand.

7 ❑ Feb 1985 Cover: 1.25 **NM** value: **2.25**
📖 A Choice of Dooms

8 ❑ Mar 1985 Cover: 1.25 **NM** value: **2.25**
📖 To Destroy a World!

9 ❑ Apr 1985 Cover: 1.25 **NM** value: **2.25**
📖 Reunion

10 ❑ May 1985 Cover: 1.25 **NM** value: **2.25**
Circ: CapCity orders: **13,900**
📖 Election Day

11 ❑ Jun 1985 Cover: 1.25 **NM** value: **2.00**
Circ: CapCity orders: **14,150**
📖 Taking Care of Business: Old Business; New Business • Bouncing Boy back-up

12 ❑ Jul 1985 Cover: 1.25 **NM** value: **2.00**
Circ: CapCity orders: **12,800**
📖 The More Things Change; The More Things Stay the Same

13 ❑ Aug 1985 Cover: 1.25 **NM** value: **2.00**
Circ: CapCity orders: **12,450**

14 ❑ Sep 1985 Cover: 1.25 **NM** value: **2.00**
Circ: CapCity orders: **12,350**
• New members ★ 1st Appearance of Quislet.

15 ❑ Oct 1985 Cover: 1.25 **NM** value: **2.00**
Circ: CapCity orders: **14,800**
📖 Hostage on a Hostile Star

16 ❑ Nov 1985 Cover: 1.25 **NM** value: **2.00**
Circ: CapCity orders: **11,900**
📖 Baptism • Crisis

17 ❑ Dec 1985 Cover: 1.25 **NM** value: **2.00**
Circ: CapCity orders: **12,300**
📖 A New Beginning; Legionnaires' Fact File

18 ❑ Jan 1986 Cover: 1.50 **NM** value: **2.00**
Circ: CapCity orders: **11,650**
• Crisis

19 ❑ Feb 1986 Cover: 1.50 **NM** value: **2.00**
Circ: CapCity orders: **11,850**
📖 No Good Deed Goes Unpunished; Freedom of Choice

20 ❑ Mar 1986 Cover: 1.50 **NM** value: **2.00**
Circ: CapCity orders: **11,850**
📖 To Control a World; Night of Madness ★ Versus Tyr.

21 ❑ Apr 1986 Cover: 1.50 **NM** value: **2.00**
Circ: CapCity orders: **11,800**
📖 Obsession; Training Session ★ Versus Emerald Empress.

22 ❑ May 1986 Cover: 1.50 **NM** value: **2.00**
Circ: CapCity orders: **11,300**
📖 Dead End

23 ❑ Jun 1986 Cover: 1.50 **NM** value: **2.00**
Circ: CapCity orders: **11,000**

24 ❑ Jul 1986 Cover: 1.50 **NM** value: **2.00**
Circ: CapCity orders: **10,950**

25 ❑ Aug 1986 Cover: 1.50 **NM** value: **2.00**
Circ: CapCity orders: **11,250**

26 ❑ Sep 1986 Cover: 1.50 **NM** value: **2.00**
Circ: CapCity orders: **11,150**

27 ❑ Oct 1986 Cover: 1.50 **NM** value: **2.00**
Circ: CapCity orders: **11,250**
📖 Going Home ★ Versus Mordru.

28 ❑ Nov 1986 Cover: 1.50 **NM** value: **2.00**
Circ: CapCity orders: **11,450**
📖 The Lost Hero

29 ❑ Dec 1986 Cover: 1.50 **NM** value: **2.00**
Circ: CapCity orders: **11,800**
📖 No Star Shall Shine! ★ Versus Starfinger.

30 ❑ Jan 1987 Cover: 1.50 **NM** value: **2.00**
Circ: CapCity orders: **11,750**

31 ❑ Feb 1987 Cover: 1.50 **NM** value: **1.75**
Circ: CapCity orders: **11,850**
📖 Knights in Shining Armor • Karate Kid, Princess Projectra, Ferro Lad story

32 ❑ Mar 1987 Cover: 1.50 **NM** value: **1.75**
Circ: CapCity orders: **11,600**
📖 Forgotten Heroes • Universo Project, Chapter 1

33 ❑ Apr 1987 Cover: 1.50 **NM** value: **1.75**
Circ: CapCity orders: **11,450**
📖 Forgotten Planet • Universo Project, Chapter 2

34 ❑ May 1987 Cover: 1.50 **NM** value: **1.75**
Circ: CapCity orders: **11,100**
📖 Forgotten Foe • Universo Project, Chapter 3 **A:** Greg La Rocque **W:** Paul Levitz

35 ❑ Jun 1987 Cover: 1.50 **NM** value: **1.75**
Circ: CapCity orders: **11,300**
• Universo Project, Chapter 4

36 ❑ Jul 1987 Cover: 1.50 **NM** value: **1.75**
Circ: CapCity orders: **11,450**
📖 Peace, Quiet and Impending Doom • Legion elections

37 ❑ Aug 1987 Cover: 1.50 **NM** value: **8.00**
Circ: CapCity orders: **14,700** • **CGC:** 3 graded, best 9.8
📖 A Twist in Time • Fate of Superboy revealed; Return of Star Boy and Sun Girl

38 ❑ Sep 1987 Cover: 1.50 **NM** value: **8.00**
Circ: CapCity orders: **15,800** • **CGC:** 1 graded, best 9.6
📖 The Greatest Hero of Them All • Death of Superboy ★ Death of Superboy.

39 ❑ Oct 1987 Cover: 1.50 **NM** value: **1.75**
Circ: CapCity orders: **13,900**
📖 The One That Got Away **A:** Curt Swan ★ Origin of Colossal Boy.

40 ❑ Nov 1987 Cover: 1.75 **NM** value: **Cover or less**
Circ: CapCity orders: **15,050**
📖 What Starfinger Touches… ★ Versus Starfinger.

41 ❑ Dec 1987 Cover: 1.75 **NM** value: **Cover or less**
Circ: CapCity orders: **15,050**
📖 Shall Ne'er Burn So Bright ★ Versus Starfinger.

42 ❑ Jan 1988 Cover: 1.75 **NM** value: **Cover or less**
Circ: CapCity orders: **19,650**
📖 To Sleep a Thousand Years… • Millennium ★ Versus Laurel Kent.

43 ❑ Feb 1988 Cover: 1.75 **NM** value: **Cover or less**
Circ: CapCity orders: **19,700**
📖 …and Wake to Find a Dream • Millennium ★ Versus Laurel Kent.

44 ❑ Mar 1988 Cover: 1.75 **NM** value: **Cover or less**
Circ: CapCity orders: **14,900**
📖 Quislet's Story **A:** Stuart Immonen; Ron Boyd **W:** Mary Bierbaum; Tom Bierbaum ★ Origin of Quislet.

45 ❑ Apr 1988 Cover: 2.95 **NM** value: **3.00**
Circ: CapCity orders: **18,700**
• Double-size. 📖 Unlucky Streak • 30th Anniversary Issue

46 ❑ May 1988 Cover: 1.75 **NM** value: **Cover or less**
Circ: CapCity orders: **16,050**
📖 On the Fourth Hand

47 ❑ Jun 1988 Cover: 1.75 **NM** value: **Cover or less**
Circ: CapCity orders: **14,500**
📖 Conspiracy Theory ★ Versus Starfinger.

48 ❑ Jul 1988 Cover: 1.75 **NM** value: **Cover or less**
Circ: CapCity orders: **14,750**
📖 A Time to Die ★ Versus Starfinger.

49 ❑ Aug 1988 Cover: 1.75 **NM** value: **Cover or less**
Circ: CapCity orders: **14,250**
📖 A Time to Live ★ Versus Starfinger.

50 ❑ Sep 1988 Cover: 2.50 **NM** value: **Cover or less**
Circ: CapCity orders: **14,850**
• Giant-size. 📖 Life and Death at the End of Time • Mon-El wounded ★ Death of Duo Damsel (half). ★ Death of Time Trapper (possible death). ★ Death of Infinite Man.

51 ❑ Oct 1988 Cover: 1.75 **NM** value: **Cover or less**
Circ: CapCity orders: **14,050**
📖 The Trial of Braniac Five

52 ❑ Nov 1988 Cover: 1.75 **NM** value: **Cover or less**
Circ: CapCity orders: **13,100**
📖 Rites of Passage

53 ❑ Dec 1988 Cover: 1.75 **NM** value: **Cover or less**
Circ: CapCity orders: **13,200**
📖 Hunters and Hunted

54 ❑ Win 1988 Cover: 1.75 **NM** value: **Cover or less**
Circ: CapCity orders: **13,050**
cover says Winter. 📖 Strength in Numbers • no month of publication; "Winter"

55 ❑ Hol 1989 Cover: 1.75 **NM** value: **Cover or less**
Circ: CapCity orders: **12,500**
cover says Holiday. 📖 Different Paths • no month of publication; "Holiday"

56 ❑ Jan 1989 Cover: 1.75 **NM** value: **Cover or less**
Circ: CapCity orders: **12,800**
📖 By Hope Ensnared

57 ❑ Feb 1989 Cover: 1.75 **NM** value: **Cover or less**
Circ: CapCity orders: **13,400**
📖 Under a Watchful Eye

58 ❑ Mar 1989 Cover: 1.75 **NM** value: **Cover or less**
Circ: CapCity orders: **13,300**
📖 If Thine Eye Offend Thee ★ Death of Emerald Empress.

59 ❑ Apr 1989 Cover: 1.75 **NM** value: **Cover or less**
Circ: CapCity orders: **13,350**
📖 Ghosts in the Clubhouse

60 ❑ May 1989 Cover: 1.75 **NM** value: **Cover or less**
Circ: CapCity orders: **14,600**
📖 When Magic Shall Return **A:** Keith Giffen **W:** Paul Levitz

61 ❑ Jun 1989 Cover: 1.75 **NM** value: **Cover or less**
Circ: CapCity orders: **14,550**
📖 The Magic Wars, Part 2 **A:** Keith Giffen **W:** Paul Levitz

62 ❑ Jul 1989 Cover: 1.75 **NM** value: **Cover or less**
Circ: CapCity orders: **14,900**
📖 The Magic Wars, Part 3 **A:** Keith Giffen **W:** Paul Levitz ★ Death of Magnetic Kid.

63 ❑ Aug 1989 Cover: 1.75 **NM** value: **Cover or less**
Circ: CapCity orders: **15,550**
📖 The Magic Wars, Part 4 final issue. **A:** Keith Giffen **W:** Paul Levitz

Anl 1 ❑ ca. 1985 Cover: 2.00 **NM** value: **Cover or less**
Circ: CapCity orders: **13,100**
📖 Who Shot Laurel Kent? **A:** Keith Giffen

Anl 2 ❑ ca. 1986 Cover: 2.00 **NM** value: **Cover or less**
Circ: CapCity orders: **12,450**
📖 Child of Darkness, Child of Light ★ Versus Validus.

Anl 3 ❑ ca. 1987 Cover: 2.25 **NM** value: **Cover or less**
Circ: CapCity orders: **13,650**
📖 There's No Substitute for the Real Thing ★ Origin of new Legion of Substitute Heroes.

Anl 4 ❑ ca. 1988 Cover: 2.50 **NM** value: **Cover or less**
Circ: CapCity orders: **13,100**
📖 Secrets Within the Star; Private Lives • 1988 annual ★ Origin of Starfinger.

LEGION OF SUPER-HEROES (4TH SERIES) DC

Written by Keith Giffen and begun in 1989, this series was set five years after the end of the previous series, with a universe beset by an alien invasion and a disbanded Legion whose scattered members have dropped their code names for the most part, reverting to their original names. Eventually, a second group of younger Legionnaires, clones of the originals, came on the scene, leading to further confusion and a spin-off series. This fourth series ended with a second, nastier alien invasion that destroyed the easy methods of interstellar transportation and sent one group of Legionnaires far, far from home. Their adventures are covered in Legion Lost. — Brent

0 ❑ Oct 1994 Cover: 1.95 **NM** value: **2.00**
Circ: CapCity orders: **18,400**
📖 Time and Chance • continues in Legion of Super-Heroes #62 and Legionnaires #19 **A:** Keith Giffen; Al Gordon **W:** Keith Giffen; Al Gordon; Mary Bierbaum; Tom Bierbaum ★ Origin of Legion of Super-Heroes (revised).

1 ❑ Nov 1989 Cover: 1.75 **NM** value: **2.50**
Circ: CapCity orders: **33,750**
📖 Five Years Later… • Begins five years after previous series **A:** Keith Giffen **W:** Keith Giffen; Al Gordon; Mary Bierbaum; Tom Bierbaum

2 ❑ Dec 1989 Cover: 1.75 **NM** value: **2.00**
Circ: CapCity orders: **22,450**
📖 Untitled

3 ❑ Jan 1990 Cover: 1.75 **NM** value: **2.00**
Circ: CapCity orders: **20,150**
📖 Untitled ★ Versus Roxxas.

4 ❑ Feb 1990 Cover: 1.75 **NM** value: **2.00**
Circ: CapCity orders: **20,650**
📖 Untitled **A:** Keith Giffen **W:** Keith Giffen; Al Gordon; Mary Bierbaum; Tom Bierbaum ★ Appearance of Mon-El.

5 ❑ Mar 1990 Cover: 1.75 **NM** value: **2.00**
Circ: CapCity orders: **19,900**
📖 Untitled

6 ❑ Apr 1990 Cover: 1.75 **NM** value: **2.00**
Circ: CapCity orders: **19,150**
📖 Untitled

7 ❑ May 1990 Cover: 1.75 **NM** value: **2.00**
Circ: CapCity orders: **19,400**
📖 Untitled

8 ❑ Jun 1990 Cover: 1.75 **NM** value: **2.00**
Circ: CapCity orders: **19,500**
📖 Untitled • origin

9 ❑ Jul 1990 Cover: 1.75 **NM** value: **2.00**
Circ: CapCity orders: **19,300**
📖 Laurel's Story

10 ❑ Aug 1990 Cover: 1.75 **NM** value: **2.00**
Circ: CapCity orders: **18,800**
📖 Roxxas Strikes! ★ Versus Roxxas.

11 ❑ Sep 1990 Cover: 1.75 **NM** value: **2.00**
Circ: CapCity orders: **18,600**
📖 Tenzil Kem Takes a Bite Out of Crime! ★ Appearance of Matter-Eater Lad.

12 ❑ Oct 1990 Cover: 1.75 **NM** value: **2.00**
Circ: CapCity orders: **18,050**
📖 Rebirth! • Legion reformed

13 ❑ Nov 1990 Cover: 1.75 **NM** value: **2.00**
Circ: CapCity orders: **18,200**
📖 State of the Universe • poster

14 ❑ Jan 1991 Cover: 1.75 **NM** value: **2.00**
Circ: CapCity orders: **17,900**
📖 Untitled

15 ❑ Feb 1991 Cover: 1.75 **NM** value: **2.00**
Circ: CapCity orders: **18,100**
📖 Untitled

16 ❑ Mar 1991 Cover: 1.75 **NM** value: **2.00**
Circ: CapCity orders: **17,750**
📖 Untitled

17 ❑ Apr 1991 Cover: 1.75 **NM** value: **2.00**
Circ: CapCity orders: **16,850**
📖 The Last Battle

18 ❑ May 1991 Cover: 1.75 **NM** value: **2.00**
Circ: CapCity orders: **16,700**
📖 Untitled ★ Versus Dark Circle.

19 ❑ Jun 1991 Cover: 1.75 **NM** value: **2.00**
Circ: CapCity orders: **17,750**
📖 Untitled

20 ❑ Jul 1991 Cover: 1.75 **NM** value: **2.00**
Circ: CapCity orders: **16,750**
📖 Venado Bay

21 ❑ Aug 1991 Cover: 1.75 **NM** value: **Cover or less**
Circ: CapCity orders: **21,000**
📖 The Quiet Darkness, Part 1

22 ❑ Sep 1991 Cover: 1.75 **NM** value: **Cover or less**
Circ: CapCity orders: **20,400**
📖 The Quiet Darkness, Part 2

23 ❑ Oct 1991 Cover: 1.75 **NM** value: **Cover or less**
Circ: CapCity orders: **21,100**
📖 The Quiet Darkness, Part 3 ★ Versus Lobo.

24 ❑ Dec 1991 Cover: 1.75 **NM** value: **Cover or less**
Circ: CapCity orders: **19,450**
📖 The Quiet Darkness, Part 4

25 ❑ Jan 1992 Cover: 1.75 **NM** value: **Cover or less**
Circ: CapCity orders: **17,900**
📖 Untitled

26 ❑ Feb 1992 Cover: 1.75 **NM** value: **Cover or less**
Circ: CapCity orders: **17,050**
📖 The Terra Mosaic: Battered By B.I.O.N. • contains map of Legion headquarters

27 ❑ Mar 1992 Cover: 1.75 **NM** value: **Cover or less**
Circ: CapCity orders: **15,850**
📖 Showdown! ★ Versus B.I.O.N..

28 ❑ Apr 1992 Cover: 1.75 **NM** value: **Cover or less**
Circ: CapCity orders: **15,300**
📖 The Sizzling Story of Sun Boy! ★ Appearance of Sun Boy.

29 ❑ May 1992 Cover: 1.75 **NM** value: **Cover or less**
Circ: CapCity orders: **15,250**
📖 Untitled

30 ❑ Jun 1992 Cover: 1.75 **NM** value: **Cover or less**
Circ: CapCity orders: **15,250**
📖 Ambush! • The Terra Mosaic

31 ❑ Jul 1992 Cover: 1.75 **NM** value: **Cover or less**
Circ: CapCity orders: **14,900**
romance cover. 📖 The Elements of Heartbreak! • The Terra Mosaic

32 ❑ Aug 1992 Cover: 1.75 **NM** value: **Cover or less**
Circ: CapCity orders: **15,350**
📖 The First to Fall • The Terra Mosaic

33 ❑ Sep 1992 Cover: 1.75 **NM** value: **Cover or less**

CGC-graded: Multiply prices above by **33 for 9.9 M • 16 for 9.8 NM/M • 7 for 9.6 NM+ • 5 for 9.4 NM • 2.5 for 9.2 NM- • 1.5 for 9.0 VF/NM**

Circ: CapCity orders: **13,900**
Whatever Happened to Kid Quantum? • The Terra Mosaic; Fate of Kid Quantum
34 ❑ Oct 1992 Cover: 1.75 **NM** value: **Cover or less**
Circ: CapCity orders: **14,200**
Untitled • The Terra Mosaic; Timber Wolf mini-series preview
35 ❑ Nov 1992 Cover: 1.75 **NM** value: **Cover or less**
Circ: CapCity orders: **13,750**
Sun Boy Meets Sun Boy?!! • The Terra Mosaic; Sun Boy meets Sun Boy
36 ❑ Nov 1992 Cover: 1.75 **NM** value: **Cover or less**
Circ: CapCity orders: **13,700**
Bounty vs. Sade! • The Terra Mosaic conclusion
37 ❑ Dec 1992 Cover: 1.75 **NM** value: **Cover or less**
Circ: CapCity orders: **13,250**
Star Boy Returns in a League of His Own! • Star Boy and Dream Girl return
38 ❑ Dec 1992 Cover: 1.75 **NM** value: **2.50**
Circ: CapCity orders: **13,700**
The End • Earth destroyed
39 ❑ Jan 1993 Cover: 1.75 **NM** value: **Cover or less**
Circ: CapCity orders: **13,150**
Beginnings
40 ❑ Feb 1993 Cover: 1.75 **NM** value: **Cover or less**
Circ: CapCity orders: **13,750**
Guess Who's Back? Wrong!
41 ❑ Mar 1993 Cover: 1.75 **NM** value: **Cover or less**
Circ: CapCity orders: **14,100**
Introducing the Legionnaires ★ 1st Appearance of Legionnaires.
42 ❑ Apr 1993 Cover: 1.75 **NM** value: **Cover or less**
Circ: CapCity orders: **14,900**
The Enemy Within!
43 ❑ May 1993 Cover: 1.75 **NM** value: **Cover or less**
Circ: CapCity orders: **14,800**
The Witch Is Back! • White Witch returns
44 ❑ Jun 1993 Cover: 1.75 **NM** value: **Cover or less**
Circ: CapCity orders: **14,950**
Projectra Returns!
45 ❑ Jul 1993 Cover: 1.75 **NM** value: **Cover or less**
Circ: CapCity orders: **14,400**
New Members? New Problems!
46 ❑ Aug 1993 Cover: 1.75 **NM** value: **Cover or less**
Circ: CapCity orders: **15,000**
Untitled
47 ❑ Sep 1993 Cover: 1.75 **NM** value: **Cover or less**
Circ: CapCity orders: **13,900**
Last Rites for the Legion of Super-Heroes ★ Versus dead heroes.
48 ❑ Oct 1993 Cover: 1.75 **NM** value: **Cover or less**
Circ: CapCity orders: **13,300**
Mordru Triumphant! ★ Versus Mordru.
49 ❑ Nov 1993 Cover: 1.75 **NM** value: **Cover or less**
Circ: CapCity orders: **13,300**
50 ❑ Nov 1993 Cover: 3.50 **NM** value: **Cover or less**
Circ: CapCity orders: **15,200**
• Wedding of Matter-Eater Lad and Saturn Queen
51 ❑ Dec 1993 Cover: 1.75 **NM** value: **Cover or less**
Circ: CapCity orders: **12,850**
A Li'l Legion Adventure
52 ❑ Dec 1993 Cover: 1.75 **NM** value: **Cover or less**
Circ: CapCity orders: **12,850**
Broken Dreams, Fuzzy Memories ★ Origin of Timber Wolf.
53 ❑ Jan 1994 Cover: 1.75 **NM** value: **Cover or less**
Circ: CapCity orders: **12,400**
A Moment in Time ★ Versus Glorith.
54 ❑ Feb 1994 Cover: 2.95 **NM** value: **Cover or less**
Circ: CapCity orders: **13,350**
Die-cut cover. Time's Change
55 ❑ Mar 1994 Cover: 1.75 **NM** value: **Cover or less**
Circ: CapCity orders: **11,250**
56 ❑ Apr 1994 Cover: 1.75 **NM** value: **Cover or less**
Circ: CapCity orders: **10,750**
Dragon's Fury!
57 ❑ May 1994 Cover: 1.75 **NM** value: **Cover or less**
Circ: CapCity orders: **11,250**
Friends and Foes
58 ❑ Jun 1994 Cover: 1.75 **NM** value: **Cover or less**
Circ: CapCity orders: **11,200**
Deadly Encounter
59 ❑ Jul 1994 Cover: 1.95 **NM** value: **Cover or less**
Circ: CapCity orders: **12,100**
A Time of Loss
60 ❑ Aug 1994 Cover: 1.95 **NM** value: **Cover or less**
Circ: CapCity orders: **12,800**
End of an Era, Part 3: Infinite Possibilities • Crossover with Legionnaires and Valor
61 ❑ Sep 1994 Cover: 1.95 **NM** value: **Cover or less**
Circ: CapCity orders: **14,050**
End of an Era, The Real Conclusion:Borrowed Time! • Zero Hour; end of original Legion of Super-Heroes
62 ❑ Nov 1994 Cover: 1.95 **NM** value: **Cover or less**
Circ: CapCity orders: **12,150**
Forced Friends, Deadly Cosequences!
63 ❑ Dec 1994 Cover: 1.95 **NM** value: **Cover or less**
Circ: CapCity orders: **12,150**
Things at hand! • Tenzil Kem hired as chef ★ 1st Appearance of Athramites, new Legion headquarters.
64 ❑ Jan 1995 Cover: 1.95 **NM** value: **Cover or less**
Circ: CapCity orders: **12,200**
Sibling Rivalry • Return of Ultra Boy **A:** Yancey Labat; Lee Moder **W:** Mark Waid; Tom McCraw
65 ❑ Feb 1995 Cover: 1.95 **NM** value: **Cover or less**
Circ: CapCity orders: **11,700**
Breakout!
66 ❑ Mar 1995 Cover: 1.95 **NM** value: **Cover or less**
Circ: CapCity orders: **11,125**
Membership Drive • Andromeda, Shrinking Violet and Kinetix join team ★ Appearance of Laurel Gand.
67 ❑ Apr 1995 Cover: 1.95 **NM** value: **Cover or less**
Circ: CapCity orders: **10,425**
Insect Fear
68 ❑ May 1995 Cover: 1.95 **NM** value: **Cover or less**
Circ: CapCity orders: **10,200**
69 ❑ Jun 1995 Cover: 2.25 **NM** value: **Cover or less**
Circ: CapCity orders: **9,900**
Absolute Power
70 ❑ Jul 1995 Cover: 2.25 **NM** value: **Cover or less**
Circ: CapCity orders: **10,025**
71 ❑ Aug 1995 Cover: 2.25 **NM** value: **Cover or less**
Circ: CapCity orders: **10,150**
Heaven and Hell • Trom destroyed
72 ❑ Sep 1995 Cover: 2.25 **NM** value: **Cover or less**
Circ: CapCity orders: **9,525**
73 ❑ Oct 1995 Cover: 2.25 **NM** value: **Cover or less**
Circ: CapCity orders: **8,300**
End of the Road ★ Appearance of Mekt Ranz.
74 ❑ Nov 1995 Cover: 2.25 **NM** value: **Cover or less**
Prisoner of the Super-Heroes • Future Tense, Part 2; Concludes in Legionnaires #31 ★ Appearance of Superboy, Scavenger.
75 ❑ Dec 1995 Cover: 2.25 **NM** value: **Cover or less**
2-Timer • Underworld Unleashed ★ Appearance of Chronos.
76 ❑ Jan 1996 Cover: 2.25 **NM** value: **Cover or less**
Bouncing Back • Star Boy and Gates joins team; [L1996-1]
77 ❑ Feb 1996 Cover: 2.25 **NM** value: **Cover or less**
Lock Up • [L1996-3] **A:** Lee Moder **W:** Tom McCraw; Tom Peyer ★ Origin of Brainiac Five.
78 ❑ Mar 1996 Cover: 2.25 **NM** value: **Cover or less**
The Gathering Doom • [L1996-5] **A:** Lee Moder **W:** Tom McCraw; Tom Peyer ★ Origin of Fatal Five. ★ 1st Appearance of Fatal Five.
79 ❑ Apr 1996 Cover: 2.25 **NM** value: **Cover or less**
The Fatal Five! • [L1996-7] **A:** Lee Moder **W:** Tom McCraw; Tom Peyer ★ Versus Fatal Five.
80 ❑ May 1996 Cover: 2.25 **NM** value: **Cover or less**
Trust • [L1996-9]
81 ❑ Jun 1996 Cover: 2.25 **NM** value: **Cover or less**
Sundown • Dirk Morgna becomes Sun Boy; Brainiac 5 quits; [L1996-11]
82 ❑ Jul 1996 Cover: 2.25 **NM** value: **Cover or less**
Lifestyles of the Dead • Apparition returns; [L1996-13]
83 ❑ Aug 1996 Cover: 2.25 **NM** value: **Cover or less**
Big Tears • Violet possessed by Emerald Eye; [L1996-15] ★ Death of Leviathan.
84 ❑ Sep 1996 Cover: 2.25 **NM** value: **Cover or less**
Emerald Legion • [L1996-17]
85 ❑ Oct 1996 Cover: 2.25 **NM** value: **Cover or less**
Metropolis Now! • Seven Legionnaires, Inferno, and Shvaughn Erin in 20th century; [L1996-19] **A:** Lee Moder **W:** Tom McCraw; Tom Peyer ★ Appearance of Superman.
86 ❑ Nov 1996 Cover: 2.25 **NM** value: **Cover or less**
Circ: Diamd. preorders: **33,130**
Heart of Iron • Final Night; [L1996-21] **A:** Lee Moder **W:** Tom McCraw; Tom Peyer ★ Appearance of Ferro.
87 ❑ Dec 1996 Cover: 2.25 **NM** value: **Cover or less**
Circ: Diamd. preorders: **27,788**
She's Not There • [L1996-23] **A:** Mike Collins; Lee Moder **W:** Tom McCraw; Tom Peyer ★ Appearance of Deadman, Phase.
88 ❑ Jan 1997 Cover: 2.25 **NM** value: **Cover or less**
Circ: Diamd. preorders: **28,683**
Fast Times • [L1997-2] **A:** Lee Moder **W:** Tom McCraw; Tom Peyer ★ Appearance of Impulse.
89 ❑ Feb 1997 Cover: 2.25 **NM** value: **Cover or less**
Circ: Diamd. preorders: **27,494**
She's Electric! • [L1997-4] ★ Appearance of Doctor Psycho.
90 ❑ Mar 1997 Cover: 2.25 **NM** value: **Cover or less**
Circ: Diamd. preorders: **27,286**
Face to Face • [L1997-6] **A:** Lee Moder **W:** Tom McCraw; Tom Peyer ★ Versus Doctor Psycho.
91 ❑ Apr 1997 Cover: 2.25 **NM** value: **Cover or less**
Circ: Diamd. preorders: **26,961**
No Exit • Legion visits several DC eras; [L1997-8]
92 ❑ May 1997 Cover: 2.25 **NM** value: **Cover or less**
Circ: Diamd. preorders: **26,695**
Swan's Way • 20th century group lands in 1958 Happy Harbor; [L1997-10]
93 ❑ Jun 1997 Cover: 2.25 **NM** value: **Cover or less**
Circ: Diamd. preorders: **27,232**
Knight Shift • [L1997-12] ★ Death of Douglas Nolan.
94 ❑ Jul 1997 Cover: 2.25 **NM** value: **Cover or less**
Circ: Diamd. preorders: **26,472**
22 Pages About the Legion of Super-Heroes • [L1997-14]
95 ❑ Aug 1997 Cover: 2.25 **NM** value: **Cover or less**
Circ: Diamd. preorders: **26,122**
The Emerald Doom! • [L1997-16] ★ Appearance of Metal Men.
96 ❑ Sep 1997 Cover: 2.25 **NM** value: **Cover or less**
Circ: Diamd. preorders: **25,519**
Til Death • Wedding of Ultra Boy and Apparition; Cosmic Boy revives; [L1997-18]
97 ❑ Oct 1997 Cover: 2.25 **NM** value: **Cover or less**
Circ: Diamd. preorders: **27,748**
Dwarfing the Infinite • Genesis; Spark gains gravity powers; [L1997-20] ★ Versus Mantis.
98 ❑ Nov 1997 Cover: 2.25 **NM** value: **Cover or less**
Circ: Diamd. preorders: **25,779**
Computo the Conqueror, Part 1 • Phase meets Apparition; [L1997-22] **A:** Lee Moder **W:** Tom McCraw; Tom Peyer
99 ❑ Dec 1997 Cover: 2.25 **NM** value: **Cover or less**
Circ: Diamd. preorders: **26,121**
Face cover. When the Reign Comes • [L1997-24] **A:** Lee Moder; Derec Aucoin **W:** Tom McCraw; Tom Peyer
100 ❑ Jan 1998 Cover: 5.95 **NM** value: **Cover or less**
Circ: Diamd. preorders: **29,805**
gatefold cover. OK Computo; Legion Day; All Together Now!; The Braniac Adventures: It's a Wonderful Legion; The Fires of Creation; • Legionnaires return from 20th century; Pin-ups; [L1998-2]
101 ❑ Feb 1998 Cover: 2.25 **NM** value: **Cover or less**
Circ: Diamd. preorders: **25,018**
Jump • Spark gets her lightning powers back; [L1998-4]
102 ❑ Mar 1998 Cover: 2.25 **NM** value: **Cover or less**
Circ: Diamd. preorders: **24,491**
Heroes • [L1998-6] ★ Appearance of Heroes of Xanthu.
103 ❑ Apr 1998 Cover: 2.25 **NM** value: **Cover or less**
Circ: Diamd. preorders: **23,901**
A Storm in Heaven • Karate Kid quits McCauley Industries; [L1998-8]
104 ❑ May 1998 Cover: 2.25 **NM** value: **Cover or less**
Circ: Diamd. preorders: **24,092**
Heroes' Return • time shifts to 2968; [L1998-10] ★ Appearance of Kono.
105 ❑ Jun 1998 Cover: 2.25 **NM** value: **Cover or less**
Circ: Diamd. preorders: **24,711**
Time Won't Let Me • [L1998-12] ★ Versus Time Trapper.
106 ❑ Jul 1998 Cover: 2.25 **NM** value: **Cover or less**
Circ: Diamd. preorders: **23,243**
High Crimes • Dark Circle Rising, Part 2: Assassination!; [L1998-14]
107 ❑ Aug 1998 Cover: 2.25 **NM** value: **Cover or less**
Circ: Diamd. preorders: **23,436**
Brainspotting • Dark Circle Rising, Part 4: Duplicity!; [L1998-16]
108 ❑ Sep 1998 Cover: 2.50 **NM** value: **Cover or less**
Circ: Diamd. preorders: **22,723**
The End • Dark Circle Rising, Part 6: Revelation!; [L1998-18]
109 ❑ Oct 1998 Cover: 2.50 **NM** value: **Cover or less**
Circ: Diamd. preorders: **21,853**
Wish Fulfillment • [L1998-20] ★ Versus Emerald Eye.
110 ❑ Dec 1998 Cover: 2.50 **NM** value: **Cover or less**
Circ: Diamd. preorders: **21,401**
The Power of Thunder! • Thunder joins team; [L1998-22]
111 ❑ Jan 1999 Cover: 2.50 **NM** value: **Cover or less**
Circ: Diamd. preorders: **20,889**
Possession • Karate Kid vs. M'onel; [L1999-2]
112 ❑ Feb 1999 Cover: 2.50 **NM** value: **Cover or less**
Circ: Diamd. preorders: **20,387**
Bound Together • [L1999-4] **A:** Scott Kolins **W:** Tom McCraw; Tom Peyer
113 ❑ Mar 1999 Cover: 2.50 **NM** value: **Cover or less**
Circ: Diamd. preorders: **20,247**
The Anywhere Machine! • [L1999-6] **A:** Scott Kolins **W:** Tom McCraw; Tom Peyer
114 ❑ Apr 1999 Cover: 2.50 **NM** value: **Cover or less**
Circ: Diamd. preorders: **19,609**
Imperfect Strangers • [L1999-8] **A:** Scott Kolins **W:** Tom McCraw; Tom Peyer ★ 1st Appearance of Bizarro Legion.
115 ❑ May 1999 Cover: 2.50 **NM** value: **Cover or less**
Circ: Diamd. preorders: **19,365**
Imperfect Strangers: Bizzaros Forever! • [L1999-10] **A:** Scott Kolins **W:** Tom McCraw; Tom Peyer
116 ❑ Jun 1999 Cover: 2.50 **NM** value: **Cover or less**
Circ: Diamd. preorders: **19,532**
Cold Irons Bound • Thunder vs. Pernisius; [L1999-12] **A:** Keron Grant **W:** Tom McCraw; Tom Peyer
117 ❑ Jul 1999 Cover: 2.50 **NM** value: **Cover or less**
Circ: Diamd. preorders: **18,838**
The Machine in the Ghost • [L1999-14] **A:** Scott Kolins **W:** Tom McCraw; Tom Peyer
118 ❑ Aug 1999 Cover: 2.50 **NM** value: **Cover or less**
Circ: Diamd. preorders: **18,590**
Shadow of the Sun • [L1999-16] **A:** Scott Kolins **W:** Tom McCraw; Tom Peyer ★ Versus Pernisius.
119 ❑ Sep 1999 Cover: 2.50 **NM** value: **Cover or less**
Circ: Diamd. preorders: **18,603**
Eat the Poor • M'Onel and Apparition tell a L.E.G.I.O.N. story; [L1999-18] **A:** Scott Kolins **W:** Tom McCraw; Tom Peyer
120 ❑ Oct 1999 Cover: 2.50 **NM** value: **Cover or less**
Circ: Diamd. preorders: **18,302**
The Fatal Four…Plus One! • [L1999-20] **A:** Scott Kolins **W:** Tom McCraw; Tom Peyer ★ Versus Fatal Five.
121 ❑ Nov 1999 Cover: 2.50 **NM** value: **Cover or less**
Circ: Diamd. preorders: **17,795**
End of the Line • [L1999-22] **A:** Olivier Coipel **W:** Andy Lanning; Dan Abnett
122 ❑ Dec 1999 Cover: 2.50 **NM** value: **Cover or less**
Circ: Diamd. preorders: **19,012**
Legion of the Damned, Part 1 • [L1999-24] **A:** Olivier Coipel **W:** Andy Lanning; Dan Abnett
123 ❑ Jan 2000 Cover: 2.50 **NM** value: **Cover or less**
Circ: Diamd. preorders: **17,948**
Legion of the Damned, Part 3: Damned If We Don't! • [L2000-2] **A:** Olivier Coipel **W:** Andy Lanning; Dan Abnett
1000000 ❑ Nov 1998 Cover: 2.50 **NM** value: **Cover or less**
Circ: Diamd. preorders: **29,339**
1,000 Years Later • set 1, 000 years after events of One Million+E12681 **A:** Keith Giffen **W:** Tom Peyer
Anl 1 ❑ ca. 1990 Cover: 3.50 **NM** value: **Cover or less**
Circ: CapCity orders: **18,050**
Charane ★ Origin of Glorith, Ultra Boy, Legion.
Anl 2 ❑ ca. 1991 Cover: 3.50 **NM** value: **Cover or less**
Circ: CapCity orders: **16,400**
The Legend of Valor ★ Origin of Valor.
Anl 3 ❑ ca. 1992 Cover: 3.50 **NM** value: **Cover or less**
Circ: CapCity orders: **15,400**
Full Moon Fever; (Untitled) • Timber Wolf goes to 20th century
Anl 4 ❑ ca. 1993 Cover: 3.50 **NM** value: **Cover or less**
Circ: CapCity orders: **21,700**
Bloodlines, Part 12 • Bloodlines: Earthplague; 1993 annual **A:** Joe Phillips; Stuart Immonen; Darryl Banks; Nick Napolitano; Christopher Taylor **W:** Mary Bierbaum; Tom Bierbaum ★ Origin of Jamm. ★ 1st Appearance of Jamm.
Anl 5 ❑ ca. 1994 Cover: 3.50 **NM** value: **Cover or less**
Circ: CapCity orders: **13,450**
The Long Road Home • Elseworlds; Legion in Oz
Anl 6 ❑ ca. 1995 Cover: 3.95 **NM** value: **Cover or less**
Circ: CapCity orders: **9,225**
Deep Background; XS Running Scared; Kinetix: From Dawn to Darkness; Leviathan in Greater Good • Year One; 0: XS; Legion Headquarters Map; Legion Equipment ★ Origin of Leviathan, Kinetix.
Anl 7 ❑ ca. 1996 Cover: 3.50 **NM** value: **Cover or less**
One Shot • Legends of the Dead Earth; 1996 annual **A:** Mike Collins **W:** Tom Peyer ★ Appearance of Wildfire.

Other grades: Multiply prices above by **1.5 for Mint • 2/3 for Very Fine • 1/3 for Fine • 1/5 for Very Good • 1/8 for Good**

Bk 1❑ Cover: 17.95 **NM** value: **Cover or less**
Circ: CapCity orders: **2,900**
• Trade Paperback. • The Beginning of Tomorrow; collects origin stories **A:** Scott Benefiel; Brian Apthorp; Stuart Immonen; Lee Moder; Jeffrey Moy; Yancy Labat **W:** Mark Waid; Tom McCraw; Tom Peyer

LEGION OF SUPER-HEROES ARCHIVES — DC

1 ❑ Cover: 39.95 **NM** value: **Cover or less**
• Reprints Legion stories from Action Comics #267, 276, 287, 289, Superboy #86, 89, 98, and Superman #147; No contents
2 ❑ Cover: 39.95 **NM** value: **Cover or less**
• Reprints Legion stories from Adventure Comics #306-317, Superman's Pal Jimmy Olsen #72
3 ❑ Cover: 39.95 **NM** value: **Cover or less**
• Reprints Legion stories from Adventure Comics #318-328, Superman's Pal Jimmy Olsen #76, Superboy (1st Series) #117
4 ❑ Cover: 39.95 **NM** value: **Cover or less**
• Reprints Legion stories from Adventure Comics #329-339, Superboy (1st Series) #124, 125
5 ❑ Cover: 39.95 **NM** value: **Cover or less**
• Reprints Legion stories from Adventure Comics #340-349
6 ❑ Cover: 49.95 **NM** value: **Cover or less**
• Reprints Legion stories from Adventure Comics #350-358
7 ❑ Cover: 49.95 **NM** value: **Cover or less**
• Reprints Legion stories from Adventure Comics #359-367, Superman's Pal Jimmy Olsen #106
8 ❑ Cover: 49.95 **NM** value: **Cover or less**
• Reprints Legion stories from Adventure Comics #368-376, Superboy (1st Series) #147
9 ❑ Cover: 49.95 **NM** value: **Cover or less**
• Reprints Legion stories from adventure Comics #377-380, Action Comics #377-392 **A:** Jim Shooter; Win Mortimer; Neal Adams **W:** Jim Shooter; Cary Bates; E. Nelson Bridwell
10 ❑ Cover: 49.95 **NM** value: **Cover or less**
• Reprints Legion stories from Adventure Comics #403, Superboy (1st Series) #172-202 **A:** George Tuska; Dave Cockrum; Ross Andru **W:** Cary Bates; E. Nelson Bridwell
11 ❑ Cover: 49.95 **NM** value: **Cover or less**

LEGION OF SUPER-HEROES INDEX — Eclipse / Independent

1 ❑ Cover: 2.00 **NM** value: **Cover or less**
Circ: CapCity orders: **4,275**
2 ❑ Jan 1987 Cover: 2.00 **NM** value: **Cover or less**
Circ: CapCity orders: **4,025**
3 ❑ Feb 1987 Cover: 2.00 **NM** value: **Cover or less**
Circ: CapCity orders: **3,525**
4 ❑ Mar 1987 Cover: 2.00 **NM** value: **Cover or less**
Circ: CapCity orders: **3,375**
5 ❑ May 1987 Cover: 2.00 **NM** value: **Cover or less**
Circ: CapCity orders: **3,300**

LEGION OF SUPER-HEROES SECRET FILES — DC

1 ❑ Jan 1998 Cover: 4.95 **NM** value: **Cover or less**
Circ: Diamd. preorders: **23,673**
📖 Legionnaires Three; What Did the Legion Do for Money When They Were Stranded in the 20th Century?; Timeline: LSH; Guided Tour: Legion Outpost; The Roll Call; Interview: Shvaughn Erin • bios on members and villains **A:** Cully Hamner; Chris Sprouse; Mike Collins; Leonard Kirk; Humberto Ramos; Paul Pelletier; Phil Jimenez; Barry Kitson; Dan Jurgens; Lee Moder; Jeffrey Moy; Jason Armstrong; Colleen Doran; Todd Nauck; Philip Moy; Ron Boyd; W.C. Carani **W:** Tom McCraw; Tom Peyer ★ Origin of Legion.
2 ❑ Jun 1999 Cover: 4.95 **NM** value: **Cover or less**
Circ: Diamd. preorders: **16,406**
📖 Unknown Point of Origin, Part 2; The Legion Constitution; Interview with United Planets President R.J. Brande; A Partial Listing of the United Planets and Affiliated Planets • bios on members and villains; Legion constitution **A:** Cully Hamner; Matt Haley; Chuck Wojtkiewicz; Phil Jimenez; Sean Phillips; Olivier Coipel; Jeffrey Moy; Greg Luzniak; Derec Aucoin; Kilian Plunkett; Dusty Abell; Keith Champagne **W:** Andy Lanning; Dan Abnett; Matt Brady; Tom McCraw; Tom Peyer

LEGION OF THE STUPID-HEROES — Blackthorne

1 ❑ b&w Cover: 1.75 **NM** value: **Cover or less**
• parody

LEGION: SCIENCE POLICE — DC

1 ❑ Aug 1998 Cover: 2.25 **NM** value: **Cover or less**
Circ: Diamd. preorders: **18,525**
📖 Ringers, Part 1 **A:** Paul Ryan **W:** David Michelinie
2 ❑ Sep 1998 Cover: 2.25 **NM** value: **Cover or less**
Circ: Diamd. preorders: **15,886**
📖 Ringers, Part 2 **A:** Paul Ryan **W:** David Michelinie
3 ❑ Oct 1998 Cover: 2.25 **NM** value: **Cover or less**
Circ: Diamd. preorders: **14,465**
📖 Ringers, Part 3 **A:** Paul Ryan **W:** David Michelinie
4 ❑ Nov 1998 Cover: 2.25 **NM** value: **Cover or less**
Circ: Diamd. preorders: **13,350**
📖 Ringers, Part 4 **A:** Paul Ryan **W:** David Michelinie

LEGIONS OF LUDICROUS HEROES — C&T

1 ❑ b&w Cover: 2.00 **NM** value: **Cover or less**

LEGION X-1 (VOL. 2) — Greater Mercury

1 ❑ Aug 1989 Cover: 2.00 **NM** value: **Cover or less**
📖 Return of the Eradicators, Part 1 **A:** Brandon McKinney **W:** Kristoffer A. Silver

LEJENTIA — Opus

1 ❑ Cover: 1.95 **NM** value: **Cover or less**
A: Steven S. Crompton **W:** Holly Bennett
2 ❑ Cover: 2.25 **NM** value: **Cover or less**

LEMONADE KID — AC

1 ❑ Cover: 2.50 **NM** value: **Cover or less**
• Powell reprints

LENORE — Slave Labor

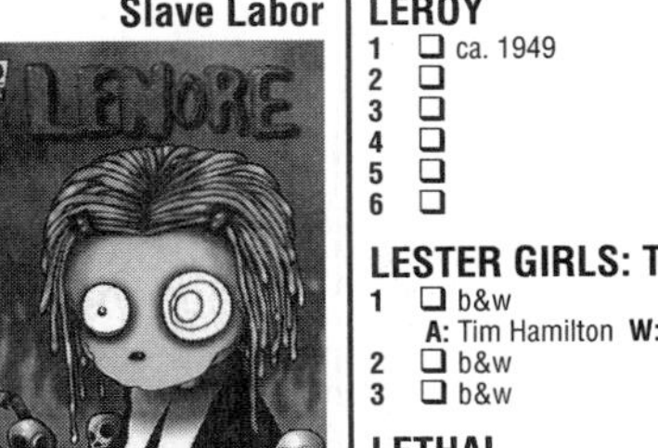

Subtitled "The Adventures of a Cute Little Dead Girl," Lenore draws much of its style from such sources as Edgar Allan Poe, Edward Gorey, Charles Addams, and Tim Burton — so a dark sense of humor is required to appreciate the antics of the waif from Nevermore.

Embalmed but cute as a button, the title character encounters such interesting folks as Soilent Green, a paraplegic cannibal; Timmy, an ebullient blind mouse; and Ragamuffin, a vampire who has been cursed to spend eternity as a ragdoll. This is drop-dead hilarious stuff from the mind of Roman Dirge (Something at the Window Is Scratching).

1 ❑ Feb 1998 Cover: 2.95 **NM** value: **3.25**
Circ: Diamd. preorders: **7,026** • **CGC:** 1 graded, best 9.4
📖 B **A:** Roman Dirge **W:** Roman Dirge
2 ❑ Jun 1998 Cover: 2.95 **NM** value: **3.00**
Circ: Diamd. preorders: **6,287**
📖 The Raven; Little Bunny Foo Foo; The Crooked Man; One Day Above the Highway; A Walk in the City; The 'Lil Ballerina; Tormented; Snack Time at the Movies; The Possum King; Babysitting 2, The Return of Little Edward **A:** Roman Dirge **W:** Roman Dirge
3 ❑ Sep 1998 Cover: 2.95 **NM** value: **Cover or less**
Circ: Diamd. preorders: **6,263**
📖 Ragamuffin; Georgie Porgie; The Boy with His Heart in a Box; Chinese Food; Little Miss Muffet; Roman Dirge...Things Involving Me; Kityty #46; Dance of the Butterfly; Mr. Puffy; Roman Dirge and Jhonen Vaszuez...The Comic I Pulled from My Ass **A:** Roman Dirge; Jhonen Vaszuez **W:** Roman Dirge; Jhonen Vaszuez
4 ❑ Jan 1999 Cover: 2.95 **NM** value: **Cover or less**
Circ: Diamd. preorders: **6,795**
📖 The Return of Mr. Gosh; The Last Robot; The Sing Along; Taxidermy; Leap Froggy; The Sinus Problem; A New Toy!!; Magic Muffin; Things Involving Me; Hemic **A:** Roman Dirge; Xu Mal **W:** Roman Dirge; Xu Mal
5 ❑ Mar 1999 Cover: 2.95 **NM** value: **Cover or less**
Circ: Diamd. preorders: **6,674**
A: Roman Dirge **W:** Roman Dirge
6 ❑ Jul 1999 Cover: 2.95 **NM** value: **Cover or less**
Circ: Diamd. preorders: **7,202**
A: Roman Dirge **W:** Roman Dirge
7 ❑ Dec 1999 Cover: 2.95 **NM** value: **Cover or less**
Circ: Diamd. preorders: **8,217**
📖 The Dream Catcher; Skin-Less; Dope Ass Tattoo Flash; Buggie Zap!; Kitty #53; Things Involving Me' Medical Miracles!; Therapy **A:** Roman Dirge **W:** Roman Dirge
Bk 1❑ Cover: 11.95 **NM** value: **Cover or less**
• Collects Lenore #1-4 **A:** Roman Dirge **W:** Roman Dirge

LENSMAN — Eternity

1 ❑ Feb 1990, b&w Cover: 2.25 **NM** value: **Cover or less**
1/SC❑ Feb 1990, b&w Cover: 3.95 **NM** value: **Cover or less**
cardstock cover. • Special edition. 📖 The Secret of the Lens: Arrival • Includes Episode Guide; History; Story Timeline; Cycroader info; Galactic Patrol & Eddore Organizational charts; Vital Statistics on characters, vehicles and weapons
2 ❑ Cover: 2.25 **NM** value: **Cover or less**
3 ❑ Cover: 2.25 **NM** value: **Cover or less**
4 ❑ Cover: 2.25 **NM** value: **Cover or less**
5 ❑ Cover: 2.25 **NM** value: **Cover or less**
6 ❑ Cover: 2.25 **NM** value: **Cover or less**
Bk 1❑ Cover: 5.95 **NM** value: **Cover or less**
• Birth of a Lensman
Bk 2❑ Cover: 5.95 **NM** value: **Cover or less**
• The Secret Of The Lens

LENSMAN: WAR OF THE GALAXIES — Eternity

1 ❑ Nov 1990, b&w Cover: 2.25 **NM** value: **Cover or less**
📖 Birth of a Lensman **A:** Tim Eldred **W:** Paul O'Conner
2 ❑ 1991b&w Cover: 2.25 **NM** value: **Cover or less**
A: Tim Eldred **W:** Paul O'Conner
3 ❑ 1991b&w Cover: 2.25 **NM** value: **Cover or less**
A: Tim Eldred **W:** Paul O'Conner
4 ❑ 1991b&w Cover: 2.25 **NM** value: **Cover or less**
A: Tim Eldred **W:** Paul O'Conner
5 ❑ 1991b&w Cover: 2.25 **NM** value: **Cover or less**
A: Tim Eldred **W:** Paul O'Conner
6 ❑ Jun 1991, b&w Cover: 2.25 **NM** value: **Cover or less**
A: Tim Eldred **W:** Paul O'Conner
7 ❑ Jul 1991, b&w Cover: 2.25 **NM** value: **Cover or less**
📖 Tregonsee **A:** Tim Eldred **W:** Tim Eldred

LEONARD NIMOY — Celebrity

1 ❑ b&w Cover: 5.95 **NM** value: **Cover or less**

LEONARDO TEENAGE MUTANT NINJA TURTLE — Mirage

1 ❑ Dec 1986 Cover: 1.50 **NM** value: **2.00**
• **CGC:** 4 graded, best 9.4
• continues in Teenage Mutant Ninja Turtles #10

LEOPOLD AND BRINK — Faultline Press

1 ❑ Jun 1997, b&w Cover: 2.50 **NM** value: **Cover or less**
• **CGC:** 1 graded, best 9.8
A: C. Alan Fink **W:** C. Alan Fink
2 ❑ Nov 1997, b&w Cover: 2.50 **NM** value: **Cover or less**
3 ❑ Jan 1998, b&w Cover: 2.95 **NM** value: **Cover or less**

LEROY — Standard

1 ❑ ca. 1949 Cover: 0.10 **NM** value: **50.00**
2 ❑ Cover: 0.10 **NM** value: **35.00**
3 ❑ Cover: 0.10 **NM** value: **25.00**
4 ❑ Cover: 0.10 **NM** value: **25.00**
5 ❑ Cover: 0.10 **NM** value: **25.00**
6 ❑ Cover: 0.10 **NM** value: **25.00**

LESTER GIRLS: THE LIZARD'S TRAIL — Eternity

1 ❑ b&w Cover: 2.50 **NM** value: **Cover or less**
A: Tim Hamilton **W:** Will Jacobs; Gerard Jones
2 ❑ b&w Cover: 2.50 **NM** value: **Cover or less**
3 ❑ b&w Cover: 2.50 **NM** value: **Cover or less**

LETHAL — Image

1 ❑ Feb 1996 Cover: 2.50 **NM** value: **Cover or less**
📖 One Step Forward, Two Steps Back

LETHAL FOES OF SPIDER-MAN — Marvel

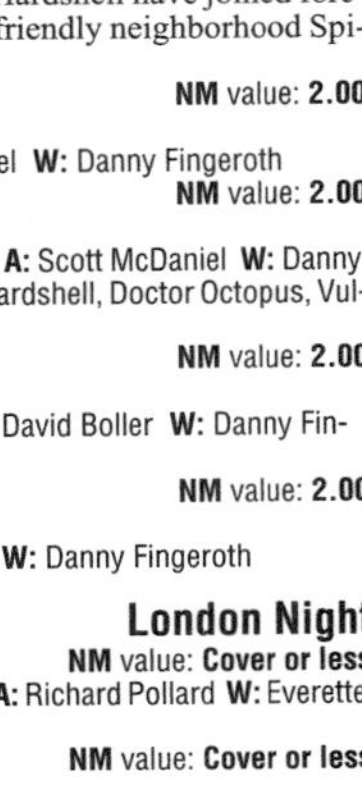

The bad guys are back-in force — in this follow-up to the Deadly Foes of Spider-Man limited series. It begins with the imprisoned Otto Octavius forced to sit helplessly by as government agents destroy the mechanical arms that had once made him Doctor Octopus. Octavius still shares a bond with the arms, however, and he feels their destruction even though he is physically some 2,000 miles away from them when it happens.

Then, someone — or something — contacts Octavius over the same psychic link that had once connected him to his arms. It turns out that the criminal once known as the Answer has regained an incorporeal awareness after his apparent disintegration in Spectacular Spider-Man #96. Now he seeks Octavius' help in recovering his physical form. Meanwhile, The Vulture, The Rhino, Boomerang, and Hardshell have joined forces...all in order to gain revenge on the friendly neighborhood Spider-Man!

1 ❑ Sep 1993 Cover: 1.75 **NM** value: **2.00**
Circ: CapCity orders: **57,200**
📖 Deadly Reunion **A:** Scott McDaniel **W:** Danny Fingeroth
2 ❑ Oct 1993 Cover: 1.75 **NM** value: **2.00**
Circ: CapCity orders: **37,200**
📖 Hate Is A Many Splendored Thing **A:** Scott McDaniel **W:** Danny Fingeroth ★ Appearance of Answer, Hardshell, Doctor Octopus, Vulture.
3 ❑ Nov 1993 Cover: 1.75 **NM** value: **2.00**
Circ: CapCity orders: **34,500**
📖 Power Struggle **A:** Keith Pollard; David Boller **W:** Danny Fingeroth
4 ❑ Dec 1993 Cover: 1.75 **NM** value: **2.00**
Circ: CapCity orders: **29,300**
📖 Re-Disunited **A:** Scott McDaniel **W:** Danny Fingeroth

LETHAL STRIKE — London Night

0 ❑ Cover: 5.95 **NM** value: **Cover or less**
• Commemorative edition. 📖 Ice... **A:** Richard Pollard **W:** Everette Hartsoe; Kevin Hill
0.5 ❑ Cover: 3.00 **NM** value: **Cover or less**
Circ: CapCity orders: **11,625**
📖 London Night **A:** Jude Millien; Everette Hartsoe **W:** Jude Millien; Everette Hartsoe
1 ❑ Jun 1995 Cover: 3.00 **NM** value: **Cover or less**
A: Jude Millien; Everette Hartsoe **W:** Jude Millien; Everette Hartsoe
2 ❑ Cover: 3.00 **NM** value: **Cover or less**
A: Jude Millien; Everette Hartsoe **W:** Jude Millien; Everette Hartsoe
3 ❑ Cover: 3.00 **NM** value: **Cover or less**
A: Jude Millien; Everette Hartsoe **W:** Jude Millien; Everette Hartsoe
Anl 1❑ Cover: 3.00 **NM** value: **Cover or less**

LETHAL STRIKE/DOUBLE IMPACT: LETHAL IMPACT — London Night

1 ❑ May 1996 Cover: 3.00 **NM** value: **Cover or less**
• crossover with High Impact

LETHARGIC COMICS — Alpha

Lethargic Comics picks up after the three-issue Tales of Lethargy series, bringing the madcap world of Greg Hyland, Steve Remen, and the rest of the Lethargic gang to readers everywhere. Here are the continuing adventures of the inimitable (because he's so sketchily drawn) Lethargic Lad, the gung-ho Guy-With-a-Gun (a Punisher spoof), Spawn-envying Walrus Boy, and the hopelessly nice No-Mutants (a low-key parody of the New Mutants).

Of course, no Lethargic title would be truly complete without featuring Much Much More, including that most unlikely of all super-heroes, the Zit. The Zit is normally a mild-mannered man in the crowd but, when danger calls, he chomps down a chocolate bar, his face breaks out instantly, and a quick costume change is all that's required to turn him into his super-hero identity. And no, you do not want to know his super-power.

1 ❑ b&w Cover: 2.50 **NM** value: **3.50**

CGC-graded: Multiply prices above by **33 for 9.9 M • 16 for 9.8 NM/M • 7 for 9.6 NM+ • 5 for 9.4 NM • 2.5 for 9.2 NM- • 1.5 for 9.0 VF/NM**

Spawn/Cerebus parody cover. Lethargic Lad Is Dead!; Guy With A Gun; The Grad; No-Mutants **A:** Greg Hyland **W:** Greg Hyland; John Migliore

2 ❑ Feb 1994, b&w Cover: 2.50 **NM** value: **3.00**
Ladfall, Part 1; Guy-With-A-Gun: Interlude #1, Guy-With-A-Gun: Interlude #2; The Zit; The Grad; No-Mutants **A:** Greg Hyland **W:** Greg Hyland; Mary Bierbaum; Tom Bierbaum; John Migliore

3 ❑ Mar 1994, b&w Cover: 2.50 **NM** value: **3.00**

3.14❑ Apr 1994, b&w Cover: 2.50 **NM** value: **3.00**
Suicide, Part 1; The Zit; The Grad • Issue #pi **A:** Greg Hyland; Steve Reman; Brian Lemay **W:** Greg Hyland; Steve Reman; Brian Lemay; Mary Bierbaum; Tom Bierbaum; John Migliore

4 ❑ May 1994, b&w Cover: 2.50 **NM** value: **3.00**
Marvels #4 parody cover. Guy-With-A-Gun; Robo-Guy; The Zit; The Grad **A:** Greg Hyland; Brian Lemay **W:** Greg Hyland; Brian Lemay

5 ❑ Jul 1994, b&w Cover: 2.50 **NM** value: **3.00**
Dot-It-Yerself cover. Lethargic Lad Returns; Roboguy; The Zit; The Grad; No-Mutants **A:** Greg Hyland; Bob Cram Jr. **W:** Greg Hyland; Mary Bierbaum; Tom Bierbaum; John Migliore

6 ❑ b&w Cover: 2.50 **NM** value: **Cover or less**
Sin City parody cover. Lethargic Lad; Guy-With-A-Gun; The Zit; The Grad: The Shindig; No-Mutants; Roboguy **A:** Paul Pelletier; Greg Hyland; Brian Lemay **W:** Greg Hyland; Brian Lemay; Mary Bierbaum; Tom Bierbaum

7 ❑ b&w Cover: 2.50 **NM** value: **Cover or less**
Spawn/Batman parody cover.

8 ❑ b&w Cover: 2.50 **NM** value: **Cover or less**

9 ❑ Apr 1995, b&w Cover: 2.50 **NM** value: **Cover or less**
Bone cover. Midieval Lethargic Lad; Dangling Plotline Theater with: Robo-Guy!; The Zit:The Grad: Deader Than Alive!; The No-Mutants; Self-Indulgent Auto-Biographical Boy in "But I Digress..." • Bone

10 ❑ b&w Cover: 2.50 **NM** value: **Cover or less**
Sin City parody cover.

11 ❑ Aug 1995, b&w Cover: 2.95 **NM** value: **Cover or less**
These Guys Battle This Guy; Guy-With-A-Gun; The Zit; The Grad in: Coalhead Chainsawhands!; Him • Milk & Cheese **A:** Evan Dorkin(cover)

12 ❑ b&w Cover: 2.50 **NM** value: **Cover or less**
Shi cover. ★ Appearance of Shi.

13 ❑ Cover: 2.50 **NM** value: **Cover or less**
A: Dave Dorman(cover)

14 ❑ Cover: 2.50 **NM** value: **Cover or less**
A: Dave Sim(cover)

LETHARGIC COMICS, WEAKLY — Lethargic

1 ❑ Jun 1991, b&w Cover: 1.95 **NM** value: **5.00**
Action Comics #601 parody cover. Lethargic Lad; Guy-With-A-Gun; The Zit; Walrus-Boy!The Grad: The Story Must Be Told!; Him; The No-Mutants ★ 1st Appearance of Guy with a Gun, No Mutants, Lethargic Lad, Walrus Boy, Him, The Grad, The Zit.

2 ❑ b&w Cover: 1.95 **NM** value: **4.00**
Detective Comics #27 parody cover.

3 ❑ b&w Cover: 1.95 **NM** value: **3.50**
Spider-Man #1 parody cover.

4 ❑ b&w Cover: 1.75 **NM** value: **3.00**
X-Men #1 parody cover.

5 ❑ b&w Cover: 1.95 **NM** value: **3.00**
Dark Knight #1 parody cover.

6 ❑ b&w Cover: 1.95 **NM** value: **2.50**
Dark Knight #4 parody cover.

7 ❑ Cover: 2.50 **NM** value: **Cover or less**
Crisis on Infinite Earths #12 parody cover.

8 ❑ Cover: 2.50 **NM** value: **Cover or less**
Avengers #4 parody cover.

9 ❑ Cover: 2.50 **NM** value: **Cover or less**
Spider-Man #16 parody cover. • Issue reads sideways

10 ❑ Cover: 2.25 **NM** value: **2.50**
Adventures of Captain America parody cover. • Captain America parody

11 ❑ Cover: 2.50 **NM** value: **Cover or less**
Youngblood #1 parody cover.

12 ❑ b&w Cover: 2.50 **NM** value: **Cover or less**
Superman #75 parody cover. • Alpha begins publishing

LETHARGIC LAD (1ST SERIES) — Crusade

1 ❑ Cover: 2.95 **NM** value: **Cover or less**

2 ❑ Cover: 2.95 **NM** value: **Cover or less**

3 ❑ Sep 1996, b&w Cover: 2.95 **NM** value: **Cover or less**
wraparound cover. • Kingdom Come parody **C:** Alex Ross

LETHARGIC LAD (2ND SERIES) — Crusade

1 ❑ Oct 1997 Cover: 2.95 **NM** value: **Cover or less**
Lethargic Lad; Lethagic Lad Team-Up, Episode 4: A New Hope! • Team-up with Him ★ Origin of Guy with a Gun.

2 ❑ Dec 1997 Cover: 2.95 **NM** value: **Cover or less**

3 ❑ Mar 1998 Cover: 2.95 **NM** value: **Cover or less**
Lethargic Lad; Lethargigotchi "The Lovable Keychain!"; Sailor Steve; Creator-Owned Team-Up; Lethargic Team-Up, Episode 6: A New Hope 3 • Thieves & Kings

4 ❑ Apr 1998 Cover: 2.95 **NM** value: **Cover or less**
Lethargic Lad; Him • Starro'David, The Captain Company (Starro and Avengers parodies); Batman origin parody

5 ❑ Jun 1998 Cover: 2.95 **NM** value: **Cover or less**
★ Appearance of Lethargic Lad-Red.

6 ❑ Sep 1998 Cover: 2.95 **NM** value: **Cover or less**
★ Appearance of new Lethargic Lass.

7 ❑ Nov 1998 Cover: 2.95 **NM** value: **Cover or less**

8 ❑ Jan 1999 Cover: 2.95 **NM** value: **Cover or less**
Circ: Diamd. preorders: **1,085**
★ Appearance of past Lethargic Lads.

9 ❑ Mar 1999 Cover: 2.95 **NM** value: **Cover or less**

LET'S PRETEND — D.S.

1 ❑ ca. 1950 Cover: 0.10 **NM** value: **100.00**

2 ❑ ca. 1950 Cover: 0.10 **NM** value: **75.00**

3 ❑ ca. 1950 Cover: 0.10 **NM** value: **75.00**

LET'S TAKE A TRIP — Pines

1 ❑ ca. 1958 Cover: 0.10 **NM** value: **25.00**

LEVEL X — Caliber

1 ❑ b&w Cover: 3.95 **NM** value: **Cover or less**

2 ❑ b&w Cover: 3.95 **NM** value: **Cover or less**

LEWD MOANA — Eros

1 ❑ Cover: 2.95 **NM** value: **Cover or less**
A: Tayyar Ozkan **W:** Tayyar Ozkan

LEX LUTHOR: THE UNAUTHORIZED BIOGRAPHY — DC

1 ❑ Jul 1989 Cover: 3.95 **NM** value: **4.00**
Circ: CapCity orders: **27,700**
Painted cover. **A:** Adam Kubert; Eduardo Barreto **W:** James D. Hudnall ★ Origin of Luthor.

LIAISONS DELICIEUSES — Fantagraphics / Eros

All issues are adults only.

1 ❑ b&w Cover: 1.95 **NM** value: **Cover or less**

2 ❑ b&w Cover: 1.95 **NM** value: **Cover or less**

3 ❑ Cover: 2.25 **NM** value: **Cover or less**

4 ❑ Cover: 2.25 **NM** value: **Cover or less**

5 ❑ Cover: 2.25 **NM** value: **Cover or less**

LIBBY ELLIS (ETERNITY) — Eternity

1 ❑ Jun 1988 Cover: 1.95 **NM** value: **Cover or less**
Rocket Coaster; Sharp Stalks the Dark, Part 1 **A:** Norm Dwyer; John McColloch **W:** Dennis Pimple

2 ❑ Jul 1988 Cover: 1.95 **NM** value: **Cover or less**
W: Dennis Pimple

3 ❑ Aug 1988 Cover: 1.95 **NM** value: **Cover or less**
W: Dennis Pimple

4 ❑ Sep 1988 Cover: 1.95 **NM** value: **Cover or less**
W: Dennis Pimple

LIBBY ELLIS (MALIBU) — Malibu

1 ❑ Cover: 1.95 **NM** value: **Cover or less**

2 ❑ Cover: 1.95 **NM** value: **Cover or less**

3 ❑ Cover: 1.95 **NM** value: **Cover or less**

4 ❑ Cover: 1.95 **NM** value: **Cover or less**

LIBERATOR — Malibu

1 ❑ Dec 1987, b&w Cover: 1.95 **NM** value: **Cover or less**
Looking at a Memory **A:** Butch Burcham(inks); Jim Chadwick **W:** Paul O'Conner ★ 1st Appearance of Liberator.

2 ❑ Feb 1988 Cover: 1.95 **NM** value: **Cover or less**
A: Butch Burcham(inks); Jim Chadwick **W:** Paul O'Conner

3 ❑ Mar 1988 Cover: 1.95 **NM** value: **Cover or less**
A: Butch Burcham(inks); Jim Chadwick **W:** Paul O'Conner

4 ❑ Jun 1988 Cover: 1.95 **NM** value: **Cover or less**
A: Butch Burcham(inks); Jim Chadwick **W:** Paul O'Conner

5 ❑ Oct 1988 Cover: 1.95 **NM** value: **Cover or less**
A: Butch Burcham(inks); Jim Chadwick **W:** Paul O'Conner

6 ❑ Dec 1988 Cover: 1.95 **NM** value: **Cover or less**
A: Butch Burcham(inks); Jim Chadwick **W:** Paul O'Conner

LIBERTINE, THE — Fantagraphics / Eros

All issues are adults only.

1 ❑ b&w Cover: 2.25 **NM** value: **Cover or less**

2 ❑ Cover: 2.50 **NM** value: **Cover or less**

LIBERTY COMICS — Green Publications

5 ❑ 1945 Cover: 0.10 **NM** value: **100.00**

6 ❑ 1945 Cover: 0.10 **NM** value: **100.00**

7 ❑ 1945 Cover: 0.10 **NM** value: **100.00**

8 ❑ 1945 Cover: 0.10 **NM** value: **100.00**

9 ❑ 1945 Cover: 0.10 **NM** value: **100.00**

10 ❑ ca. 1945 Cover: 0.10 **NM** value: **75.00**
• **CGC:** 5 graded, best 9.0

11 ❑ Jan 1946 Cover: 0.10 **NM** value: **75.00**
• **CGC:** 7 graded, best 9.4

12 ❑ Mar 1946 Cover: 0.10 **NM** value: **75.00**
• **CGC:** 3 graded, best 8.5

13 ❑ Apr 1946 Cover: 0.10 **NM** value: **75.00**

14 ❑ May 1946 Cover: 0.10 **NM** value: **75.00**

15 ❑ Jun 1946 Cover: 0.10 **NM** value: **75.00**
• **CGC:** 1 graded, best 8.5

LIBERTY GUARDS — Chicago Mail Order

1 ❑ ca. 1942 **NM** value: **250.00**

LIBERTY MEADOWS — Insight Studios

Fans of Frank Cho's newspaper strip had their requests for a collected version answered when Cho's Insight Studios began reprinting the strip in comic-book form in 1999. In addition to strips that appeared in the newspapers, Cho also included unedited strips that had been rejected or changed by his syndicate.

The strip is set at an animal preserve where Frank (no relation or resemblance to Cho) has been hired as the veterinarian. He pines for the voluptous Brandy who cares for the animals, who include Leslie, a hypochondriac bullfrog; Ralph, a midget circus bear; Dean, a male chauvinist pig (a real swine); and Truman, a baby duckling. The strips deal with the pains of unrequited love, various bits of pop culture, and the strange behavior of the bizarre anthropomorphic animals. Cho occasionally draws himself in the strip as a talking monkey. In late 2001, Cho ended the newspaper strip and moved new adventures to the comic book, which moved to Image in 2002. — Brent

1 ❑ Jun 1999 Cover: 2.95 **NM** value: **8.00**
Circ: Diamd. preorders: **6,879** • **CGC:** 5 graded, best 9.8
• Reprints first eight weeks of Liberty Meadows **A:** Frank Cho **W:** Frank Cho

1=2 ❑ Cover: 2.95 **NM** value: **4.00**

2 ❑ Aug 1999 Cover: 2.95 **NM** value: **5.00**
Circ: Diamd. preorders: **6,762** • **CGC:** 2 graded, best 9.6
• Reprints weeks 9-16 of Liberty Meadows strip **A:** Frank Cho **W:** Frank Cho

3 ❑ Oct 1999 Cover: 2.95 **NM** value: **4.00**
Circ: Diamd. preorders: **7,760**
• Reprints weeks 17-24 of Liberty Meadows strip **A:** Frank Cho **W:** Frank Cho

4 ❑ Nov 1999 Cover: 2.95 **NM** value: **4.00**
Circ: Diamd. preorders: **8,068**
• Reprints weeks 25-32 of Liberty Meadows strip **A:** Frank Cho **W:** Frank Cho

5 ❑ Dec 1999 Cover: 2.95 **NM** value: **4.00**
Circ: Diamd. preorders: **8,913**
• 42 strips plus 3 Sunday strip reprints **A:** Frank Cho **W:** Frank Cho

6 ❑ Jan 2000 Cover: 2.95 **NM** value: **3.50**
Circ: Diamd. preorders: **9,293**
A: Frank Cho **W:** Frank Cho

7 ❑ Feb 2000 Cover: 2.95 **NM** value: **3.50**
Circ: Diamd. preorders: **9,377**
A: Frank Cho **W:** Frank Cho

8 ❑ Mar 2000 Cover: 2.95 **NM** value: **3.50**
Circ: Diamd. preorders: **9,954**
A: Frank Cho **W:** Frank Cho

9 ❑ Apr 2000 Cover: 2.95 **NM** value: **3.50**
Circ: Diamd. preorders: **10,822**
A: Frank Cho **W:** Frank Cho

10 ❑ May 2000 Cover: 2.95 **NM** value: **3.50**
Circ: Diamd. preorders: **11,384**
A: Frank Cho **W:** Frank Cho

11 ❑ Jun 2000 Cover: 2.95 **NM** value: **Cover or less**
Circ: Diamd. preorders: **11,803**
A: Frank Cho **W:** Frank Cho

12 ❑ Jul 2000 Cover: 2.95 **NM** value: **Cover or less**
Circ: Diamd. preorders: **12,205**
A: Frank Cho **W:** Frank Cho

13 ❑ Aug 2000 Cover: 2.95 **NM** value: **Cover or less**
Circ: Diamd. preorders: **11,886**
A: Frank Cho **W:** Frank Cho

14 ❑ Sep 2000 Cover: 2.95 **NM** value: **Cover or less**
Circ: Diamd. preorders: **12,374**
A: Frank Cho **W:** Frank Cho

15 ❑ Nov 2000 Cover: 2.95 **NM** value: **Cover or less**
Circ: Diamd. preorders: **12,167**
• reader requests **A:** Frank Cho **W:** Frank Cho

16 ❑ Dec 2000 Cover: 2.95 **NM** value: **Cover or less**
Circ: Diamd. preorders: **12,615**
• Wiener Dog Race **A:** Frank Cho **W:** Frank Cho

17 ❑ Jan 2001 Cover: 2.95 **NM** value: **Cover or less**
Circ: Diamd. preorders: **12,529**
A: Frank Cho **W:** Frank Cho

18 ❑ Feb 2001 Cover: 2.95 **NM** value: **Cover or less**
Circ: Diamd. preorders: **12,872**
A: Frank Cho **W:** Frank Cho

19 ❑ Mar 2001 Cover: 2.95 **NM** value: **Cover or less**
Circ: Diamd. preorders: **12,719**
A: Frank Cho **W:** Frank Cho

20 ❑ May 2001 Cover: 2.95 **NM** value: **Cover or less**
Circ: Diamd. preorders: **13,745**
A: Frank Cho **W:** Frank Cho

21 ❑ Jul 2001 Cover: 2.95 **NM** value: **Cover or less**
Circ: Diamd. preorders: **14,086**
A: Frank Cho **W:** Frank Cho

LIBERTY PROJECT, THE — Eclipse

Rosalita Vasquez was a tempest with super-human strength. First she ripped open a slot machine that wouldn't pay out, then she assaulted the cops who came to arrest her, eventually tossing their own squad car at them. Naturally, Rosalita wound up in jail. Similar turns of fate befell bankrobber Nicholas "Slick" Wallace (who could form areas of frictionless space — the ultimate oil slick), Lee "Crackshot" Alexander (who never missed a target he aimed for), and Beatrice "Burnout" Keough (who could burn through any material).

Noting that super-heroes tend not to reform once they're released, the government tried something new: the Liberty Project. These four felons were offered parole if they would use their powers to fight crime as part of a special task force. It was a terrible gamble betting on four such misfits, but if it worked, the results might be nothing less than spectacular!

The series was an early super-team title for writer Kurt Busiek.

1 ❑ Jun 1987 Cover: 1.75 **NM** value: **2.00**
Circ: CapCity orders: **5,175**
I Fought The Law **A:** James W. Fry III **W:** Kurt Busiek ★ Origin of The Liberty Project. ★ 1st Appearance of Cimmaron, Burnout, Crackshot, The Liberty Project, Slick.

Other grades: Multiply prices above by **1.5 for Mint • 2/3 for Very Fine • 1/3 for Fine • 1/5 for Very Good • 1/8 for Good**

2 ❑ Jul 1987 Cover: 1.75 **NM** value: **Cover or less**
Circ: CapCity orders: **3,825**
A: James W. Fry III **W:** Kurt Busiek

3 ❑ Aug 1987 Cover: 1.75 **NM** value: **Cover or less**
Circ: CapCity orders: **3,775**
A: James W. Fry III **W:** Kurt Busiek

4 ❑ Sep 1987 Cover: 1.75 **NM** value: **Cover or less**
Circ: CapCity orders: **3,800**
A: James W. Fry III **W:** Kurt Busiek

5 ❑ Oct 1987 Cover: 1.75 **NM** value: **Cover or less**
Circ: CapCity orders: **3,875**
A: James W. Fry III **W:** Kurt Busiek

6 ❑ Nov 1987 Cover: 1.75 **NM** value: **Cover or less**
Circ: CapCity orders: **4,100**
A: James W. Fry III **W:** Kurt Busiek ★ Appearance of Valkyrie.

7 ❑ Dec 1987 Cover: 1.75 **NM** value: **Cover or less**
Circ: CapCity orders: **3,875**
A: James W. Fry III **W:** Kurt Busiek

8 ❑ May 1988 Cover: 1.75 **NM** value: **Cover or less**
Circ: CapCity orders: **3,775**
A: James W. Fry III **W:** Kurt Busiek

LIBERTY SCOUTS — Centaur

2 ❑ Jun 1941 Cover: 0.10 **NM** value: **750.00**
• **CGC:** 1 graded, best 6.5

3 ❑ Aug 1941 Cover: 0.10 **NM** value: **500.00**

LIBRA — Eternity

1 ❑ Apr 1987 Cover: 1.95 **NM** value: **Cover or less**
A: Delfin Barral **W:** Delfin Barral

LIBRARIAN, THE — Fantagraphics

1 ❑ b&w Cover: 2.75 **NM** value: **Cover or less**
A: Penny Moran Van Horn **W:** Penny Moran Van Horn

LICENSE TO KILL — Eclipse

1 ❑ Cover: 7.95 **NM** value: **Cover or less**
Circ: CapCity orders: **3,650**
A: Mike Grell; Tom Yeates; Stan Woch; Chuck Austen **W:** Richard Ashford

LIDSVILLE — Gold Key

1 ❑ Oct 1972 Cover: 0.15 **NM** value: **40.00**
• **CGC:** 1 graded, best 6.0

2 ❑ Jan 1973 Cover: 0.15 **NM** value: **25.00**
• **CGC:** 1 graded, best 7.0

3 ❑ Apr 1973 Cover: 0.15 **NM** value: **25.00**
• **CGC:** 1 graded, best 6.5

4 ❑ Jul 1973 Cover: 0.20 **NM** value: **25.00**
• **CGC:** 1 graded, best 6.0

5 ❑ Oct 1973 Cover: 0.20 **NM** value: **25.00**
• **CGC:** 1 graded, best 5.5

LIEUTENANT BLUEBERRY: GENERAL GOLDEN MANE — Marvel / Epic

1 ❑ Cover: 14.95 **NM** value: **Cover or less**

LIFE AND TIMES OF DEATH'S HEAD — Marvel

Bk 1❑ Cover: 12.95 **NM** value: **Cover or less**
• Trade Paperback.

L.I.F.E. BRIGADE, THE — Blue Comet

1 ❑ Cover: 2.00 **NM** value: **Cover or less**
📖 L.I.F.E. Brigade: Beginning or End; Blazing Tales **A:** Glenn Wong; Craig A. Stormon **W:** Glenn Wong; Craig A. Stormon

1-2 ❑ Cover: 1.80 **NM** value: **2.00**

2 ❑ Cover: 1.80 **NM** value: **2.00**

3 ❑ Cover: 1.80 **NM** value: **2.00**
• Title changes to New L.I.F.E. Brigade

LIFE FORCE, A — Kitchen Sink Press

1 ❑ b&w Cover: 12.95 **NM** value: **Cover or less**
A: Will Eisner **W:** Will Eisner

1-2 ❑ b&w Cover: 12.95 **NM** value: **Cover or less**

LIFE OF CAPTAIN MARVEL, THE — Marvel

1 ❑ Aug 1985 Cover: 2.00 **NM** value: **3.00**
Circ: CapCity orders: **11,100**
📖 Beware The…Blood Brothers! • Baxter reprint **A:** Jim Starlin **W:** Jim Starlin; Mike Friedrich

2 ❑ Sep 1985 Cover: 2.00 **NM** value: **2.50**
Circ: CapCity orders: **9,300**
📖 Betrayal! • Baxter reprint **A:** Jim Starlin **W:** Jim Starlin; Mike Friedrich

3 ❑ Oct 1985 Cover: 2.00 **NM** value: **2.50**
Circ: CapCity orders: **7,700**
• Baxter reprint **A:** Jim Starlin

4 ❑ Nov 1985 Cover: 2.00 **NM** value: **2.50**
Circ: CapCity orders: **7,450**
• Baxter reprint **A:** Jim Starlin

5 ❑ Dec 1985 Cover: 2.00 **NM** value: **2.50**
Circ: CapCity orders: **6,950**
• Baxter reprint **A:** Jim Starlin

Bk 1❑ Dec 1990 Cover: 14.95 **NM** value: **Cover or less**
Circ: CapCity orders: **2,600**
• Collects series **A:** Jim Starlin

LIFE OF CHRIST, THE — Marvel / Nelson

1 ❑ Feb 1993 Cover: 2.99 **NM** value: **3.00**
Circ: CapCity orders: **7,000**
📖 The Christmas Story **A:** Mary Wilshire **W:** Louise Simonson

LIFE OF CHRIST, THE: THE EASTER STORY — Marvel / Nelson

1 ❑ Cover: 2.95 **NM** value: **3.00**
Circ: CapCity orders: **5,400**
📖 The Easter Story **A:** Mary Wilshire **W:** Louise Simonson

LIFE OF GROO — Marvel / Epic

Bk 1❑ Mar 1993 Cover: 8.95 **NM** value: **Cover or less**
Circ: CapCity orders: **11,775**
No issue number. **A:** Sergio Aragonés ★ Origin of Groo.

Bk 1-2❑ Cover: 12.95 **NM** value: **Cover or less**
Circ: CapCity orders: **3,725**
No issue number. • reprints Marvel/Epic graphic novel **A:** Sergio Aragonés ★ Origin of Groo.

LIFE OF POPE JOHN PAUL II, THE — Marvel

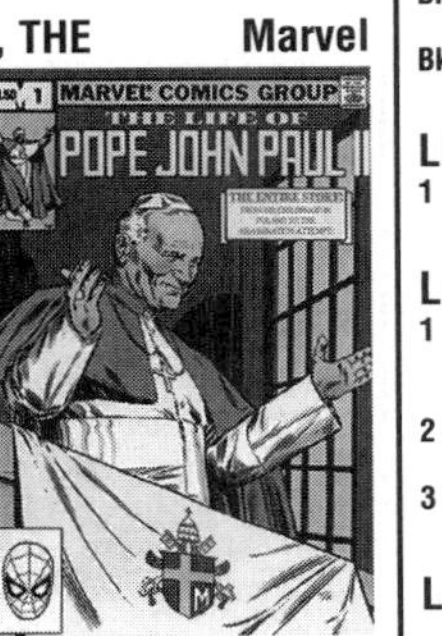

Marvel commissioned this title 1981, putting the life story of the then-new Pope into comics form, from his birth in Poland to the attempt on his life while Pope. Father Mieczyslaw Malinski, a lifelong friend of the first non-Italian pope, collaborated with Marvel artists and writers on this project.

The comic book gives readers insight concerning this popular Pope's younger days in Poland, when he narrowly escaped being placed in a concentration camp for his pro-Resistance views by studying for the priesthood. He wrote poetry and could have aspired to a career as an actor, had he not responded to the spirituality that led him to give his life and talents to the church and the world.

1 ❑ Jan 1983 Cover: 1.50 **NM** value: **2.50**
A: Joe Sinnott; John Tartaglione **W:** Steven Grant

LIFE ON ANOTHER PLANET — DC

1 ❑ Cover: 12.95 **NM** value: **Cover or less**
• Reprints Signal From Space **A:** Will Eisner **W:** Will Eisner

LIFE STORY — Fawcett

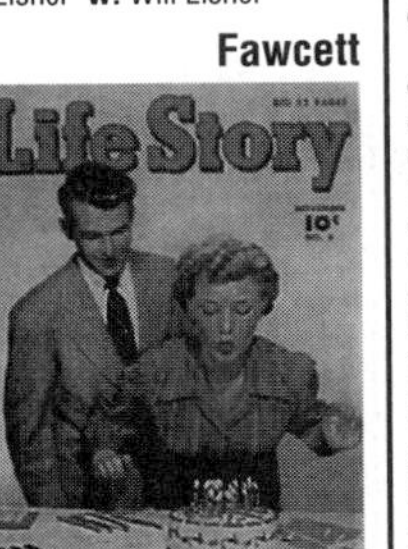

Though it sounds as though it could be some sort of adventure publication, Life Story is just another romance comic book from the late 1940's and early 1950's.

Photo covers from this series often featured a guy and a gal just staring at each other, possibly simply typical model shots from photo services of the day.

Story titles include "The Troubled Heart," "None but the Lonely," "I Destroyed My Love," "The Way of My Heart," "On the Altar of Romance," "Too Young to Know," "Goodbye, My Love," and "No Life of My Own." — Maggie

#	Date	Cover	NM value
1	❑ Apr 1949	Cover: 0.10	**NM** value: **100.00**
2	❑ May 1949	Cover: 0.10	**NM** value: **50.00**
3	❑ Jun 1949	Cover: 0.10	**NM** value: **30.00**
4	❑ Jul 1949	Cover: 0.10	**NM** value: **30.00**
5	❑ Aug 1949	Cover: 0.10	**NM** value: **30.00**
6	❑ Sep 1949	Cover: 0.10	**NM** value: **30.00**
7	❑ Oct 1949	Cover: 0.10	**NM** value: **30.00**
8	❑ Nov 1949	Cover: 0.10	**NM** value: **30.00**
9	❑ Dec 1949	Cover: 0.10	**NM** value: **30.00**
10	❑ Jan 1950	Cover: 0.10	**NM** value: **25.00**
11	❑ Feb 1950	Cover: 0.10	**NM** value: **25.00**
12	❑ Mar 1950	Cover: 0.10	**NM** value: **25.00**
13	❑ Apr 1950	Cover: 0.10	**NM** value: **25.00**
14	❑ May 1950	Cover: 0.10	**NM** value: **25.00**
15	❑ Jun 1950	Cover: 0.10	**NM** value: **25.00**
16	❑ Jul 1950	Cover: 0.10	**NM** value: **25.00**
17	❑ Aug 1950	Cover: 0.10	**NM** value: **25.00**
18	❑ Sep 1950	Cover: 0.10	**NM** value: **25.00**
19	❑ Oct 1950	Cover: 0.10	**NM** value: **25.00**
20	❑ Nov 1950	Cover: 0.10	**NM** value: **25.00**
21	❑ Dec 1950	Cover: 0.10	**NM** value: **25.00**
22	❑ Jan 1951	Cover: 0.10	**NM** value: **25.00**
23	❑ Feb 1951	Cover: 0.10	**NM** value: **25.00**
24	❑ Mar 1951	Cover: 0.10	**NM** value: **25.00**
25	❑ Apr 1951	Cover: 0.10	**NM** value: **25.00**
26	❑ May 1951	Cover: 0.10	**NM** value: **25.00**
27	❑ Jun 1951	Cover: 0.10	**NM** value: **25.00**
28	❑ Jul 1951	Cover: 0.10	**NM** value: **25.00**
29	❑ Aug 1951	Cover: 0.10	**NM** value: **25.00**
30	❑ Sep 1951	Cover: 0.10	**NM** value: **20.00**
31	❑ Oct 1951	Cover: 0.10	**NM** value: **20.00**
32	❑ Nov 1951	Cover: 0.10	**NM** value: **20.00**
33	❑ Dec 1951	Cover: 0.10	**NM** value: **20.00**
34	❑ Jan 1952	Cover: 0.10	**NM** value: **20.00**
35	❑ Feb 1952	Cover: 0.10	**NM** value: **20.00**
36	❑ Mar 1952	Cover: 0.10	**NM** value: **20.00**
37	❑ Apr 1952	Cover: 0.10	**NM** value: **20.00**
38	❑ May 1952	Cover: 0.10	**NM** value: **20.00**
39	❑ Jun 1952	Cover: 0.10	**NM** value: **20.00**
40	❑ 1952	Cover: 0.10	**NM** value: **20.00**
41	❑ 1952	Cover: 0.10	**NM** value: **20.00**
42	❑ 1952	Cover: 0.10	**NM** value: **20.00**
43	❑ 1952	Cover: 0.10	**NM** value: **20.00**
44	❑ 1952	Cover: 0.10	**NM** value: **20.00**
45	❑ 1953	Cover: 0.10	**NM** value: **20.00**
46	❑ 1953	Cover: 0.10	**NM** value: **20.00**
47	❑ Apr 1953	Cover: 0.10	**NM** value: **20.00**

The CGC numbers printed in individual listings above represent the **number of copies examined** and given a **Universal** grade by CGC and the **best such copy** graded at press time. For current populations, watch for special ***Comics Buyer's Guide*** issues or check **www.cgccomics.com**.

LIFE STORY OF THE FLASH, THE — DC

Bk 1❑ Cover: 12.95 **NM** value: **Cover or less**
No issue number. softcover. • 1st mention of Flash's twin brother

Bk 1/HC❑ Cover: 24.95 **NM** value: **Cover or less**
No issue number. hardcover. • 1st mention of Flash's twin brother

LIFE UNDER SANCTIONS — Fantagraphics

1 ❑ Feb 1994, b&w Cover: 2.95 **NM** value: **Cover or less**
No issue number. **A:** Aleksandar Zograf **W:** Aleksandar Zograf

LIFE, THE UNIVERSE AND EVERYTHING — DC

1 ❑ Cover: 6.95 **NM** value: **Cover or less**
• prestige format. • adapts Douglas Adams book **A:** Neil Vokes; Paris Cullins **W:** Douglas Adams; John Carnell

2 ❑ Cover: 6.95 **NM** value: **Cover or less**
• prestige format. • adapts Douglas Adams book

3 ❑ Cover: 6.95 **NM** value: **Cover or less**
• prestige format. • adapts Douglas Adams book

LIFE WITH ARCHIE — Archie

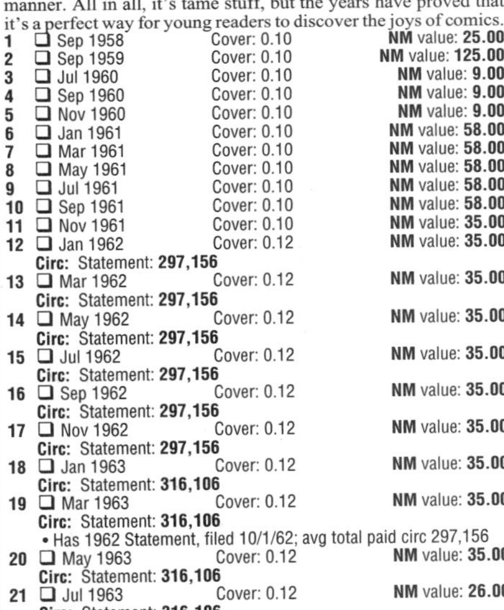

Running from 1958 to 1991, Life With Archie was one of many comics to feature Archie Andrews and the rest of his pals from Riverdale High. Throughout the years, Archie has proved one of the most enduring comics, using good-natured humor and light adventure to draw in its audience of primarily young readers.

There was nothing particularly different to set Life With Archie apart from such other Archie series as Laugh Digest, Archie, or Pep. It focused equally on the entire Riverdale crew, following them on adventures ranging from getting lost on road trips, or even (yes) turning into werewolves. Of course, by issue's end, all problems are resolved, typically in a humorous manner. All in all, it's tame stuff, but the years have proved that it's a perfect way for young readers to discover the joys of comics.

#	Date	Cover	NM value
1	❑ Sep 1958	Cover: 0.10	**NM** value: **25.00**
2	❑ Sep 1959	Cover: 0.10	**NM** value: **125.00**
3	❑ Jul 1960	Cover: 0.10	**NM** value: **9.00**
4	❑ Sep 1960	Cover: 0.10	**NM** value: **9.00**
5	❑ Nov 1960	Cover: 0.10	**NM** value: **9.00**
6	❑ Jan 1961	Cover: 0.10	**NM** value: **58.00**
7	❑ Mar 1961	Cover: 0.10	**NM** value: **58.00**
8	❑ May 1961	Cover: 0.10	**NM** value: **58.00**
9	❑ Jul 1961	Cover: 0.10	**NM** value: **58.00**
10	❑ Sep 1961	Cover: 0.10	**NM** value: **58.00**
11	❑ Nov 1961	Cover: 0.10	**NM** value: **35.00**

12 ❑ Jan 1962 Cover: 0.12 **NM** value: **35.00**
Circ: Statement: **297,156**

13 ❑ Mar 1962 Cover: 0.12 **NM** value: **35.00**
Circ: Statement: **297,156**

14 ❑ May 1962 Cover: 0.12 **NM** value: **35.00**
Circ: Statement: **297,156**

15 ❑ Jul 1962 Cover: 0.12 **NM** value: **35.00**
Circ: Statement: **297,156**

16 ❑ Sep 1962 Cover: 0.12 **NM** value: **35.00**
Circ: Statement: **297,156**

17 ❑ Nov 1962 Cover: 0.12 **NM** value: **35.00**
Circ: Statement: **297,156**

18 ❑ Jan 1963 Cover: 0.12 **NM** value: **35.00**
Circ: Statement: **316,106**

19 ❑ Mar 1963 Cover: 0.12 **NM** value: **35.00**
Circ: Statement: **316,106**
• Has 1962 Statement, filed 10/1/62; avg total paid circ 297,156

20 ❑ May 1963 Cover: 0.12 **NM** value: **35.00**
Circ: Statement: **316,106**

21 ❑ Jul 1963 Cover: 0.12 **NM** value: **26.00**
Circ: Statement: **316,106**

22 ❑ Aug 1963 Cover: 0.12 **NM** value: **26.00**
Circ: Statement: **316,106**

23 ❑ 1963 Cover: 0.12 **NM** value: **26.00**
Circ: Statement: **316,106**

24 ❑ 1963 Cover: 0.12 **NM** value: **26.00**
Circ: Statement: **316,106**

25 ❑ 1964 Cover: 0.12 **NM** value: **26.00**
Circ: Statement: **311,744**

26 ❑ Mar 1964 Cover: 0.12 **NM** value: **26.00**
Circ: Statement: **311,744**

27 ❑ May 1964 Cover: 0.12 **NM** value: **26.00**
Circ: Statement: **311,744**
• Has 1963 Statement, filed 10/1/63; avg print run 490,187; avg sales 316,106; no subs; avg total paid 316,106; samples 300; max existent 316,406; 36% of run returned

28 ❑ Jul 1964 Cover: 0.12 **NM** value: **26.00**
Circ: Statement: **311,744**

29 ❑ 1964 Cover: 0.12 **NM** value: **26.00**
Circ: Statement: **311,744**

30 ❑ Oct 1964 Cover: 0.12 **NM** value: **26.00**
Circ: Statement: **311,744**

31 ❑ Nov 1964 Cover: 0.12 **NM** value: **26.00**
Circ: Statement: **311,744**

32 ❑ Dec 1964 Cover: 0.12 **NM** value: **18.00**
Circ: Statement: **311,744**

CGC-graded: Multiply prices above by **33 for 9.9 M • 16 for 9.8 NM/M • 7 for 9.6 NM+ • 5 for 9.4 NM • 2.5 for 9.2 NM- • 1.5 for 9.0 VF/NM**

33 ☐ Jan 1965 Cover: 0.12 **NM** value: **18.00**
Circ: Statement: **293,651**
34 ☐ Feb 1965 Cover: 0.12 **NM** value: **18.00**
Circ: Statement: **293,651**
35 ☐ Mar 1965 Cover: 0.12 **NM** value: **18.00**
Circ: Statement: **293,651**
36 ☐ Apr 1965 Cover: 0.12 **NM** value: **18.00**
Circ: Statement: **293,651**
37 ☐ May 1965 Cover: 0.12 **NM** value: **18.00**
Circ: Statement: **293,651**
• Has 1964 Statement, files 10/1/64; avg print run 501,824; avg sales 311,744; no subs; avg total paid 311,744; samples 200; max existent 311,944; 38% of run returned
38 ☐ Jun 1965 Cover: 0.12 **NM** value: **18.00**
Circ: Statement: **293,651**
39 ☐ Jul 1965 Cover: 0.12 **NM** value: **18.00**
Circ: Statement: **293,651**
40 ☐ Aug 1965 Cover: 0.12 **NM** value: **18.00**
Circ: Statement: **293,651**
41 ☐ Sep 1965 Cover: 0.12 **NM** value: **13.00**
Circ: Statement: **293,651**
42 ☐ Oct 1965 Cover: 0.12 **NM** value: **13.00**
Circ: Statement: **293,651**
43 ☐ Nov 1965 Cover: 0.12 **NM** value: **13.00**
Circ: Statement: **293,651**
44 ☐ Dec 1965 Cover: 0.12 **NM** value: **13.00**
Circ: Statement: **293,651**
45 ☐ Jan 1966 Cover: 0.12 **NM** value: **13.00**
Circ: Statement: **300,954**
46 ☐ Feb 1966 Cover: 0.12 **NM** value: **13.00**
Circ: Statement: **300,954**
47 ☐ Mar 1966 Cover: 0.12 **NM** value: **13.00**
Circ: Statement: **300,954**
48 ☐ Apr 1966 Cover: 0.12 **NM** value: **13.00**
Circ: Statement: **300,954**
49 ☐ May 1966 Cover: 0.12 **NM** value: **13.00**
Circ: Statement: **300,954**
• Has 1965 Statement, filed 10/1/65; avg print run 494,027; avg sales 293,651; avg subs no subs; avg total paid 293,651; max existent 293,651; 41% of run returned
50 ☐ Jun 1966 Cover: 0.12 **NM** value: **13.00**
Circ: Statement: **300,954**
51 ☐ Jul 1966 Cover: 0.12 **NM** value: **9.00**
Circ: Statement: **300,954**
52 ☐ Aug 1966 Cover: 0.12 **NM** value: **9.00**
Circ: Statement: **300,954**
53 ☐ Sep 1966 Cover: 0.12 **NM** value: **9.00**
Circ: Statement: **300,954**
54 ☐ Oct 1966 Cover: 0.12 **NM** value: **9.00**
Circ: Statement: **300,954**
55 ☐ Nov 1966 Cover: 0.12 **NM** value: **9.00**
Circ: Statement: **300,954**
56 ☐ Dec 1966 Cover: 0.12 **NM** value: **9.00**
Circ: Statement: **300,954**
57 ☐ Jan 1967 Cover: 0.12 **NM** value: **9.00**
Circ: Statement: **275,099**
58 ☐ Feb 1967 Cover: 0.12 **NM** value: **9.00**
Circ: Statement: **275,099**
59 ☐ Mar 1967 Cover: 0.12 **NM** value: **9.00**
Circ: Statement: **275,099**
60 ☐ Apr 1967 Cover: 0.12 **NM** value: **9.00**
Circ: Statement: **275,099**
61 ☐ May 1967 Cover: 0.12 **NM** value: **6.00**
Circ: Statement: **275,099**
62 ☐ Jun 1967 Cover: 0.12 **NM** value: **6.00**
Circ: Statement: **275,099**
63 ☐ Jul 1967 Cover: 0.12 **NM** value: **6.00**
Circ: Statement: **275,099**
64 ☐ Aug 1967 Cover: 0.12 **NM** value: **6.00**
Circ: Statement: **275,099**
65 ☐ Sep 1967 Cover: 0.12 **NM** value: **6.00**
Circ: Statement: **275,099**
66 ☐ Oct 1967 Cover: 0.12 **NM** value: **6.00**
Circ: Statement: **275,099**
67 ☐ Nov 1967 Cover: 0.12 **NM** value: **6.00**
Circ: Statement: **275,099**
68 ☐ Dec 1967 Cover: 0.12 **NM** value: **6.00**
Circ: Statement: **275,099**
69 ☐ Jan 1968 Cover: 0.12 **NM** value: **6.00**
70 ☐ Feb 1968 Cover: 0.12 **NM** value: **6.00**
71 ☐ Mar 1968 Cover: 0.12 **NM** value: **4.50**
72 ☐ Apr 1968 Cover: 0.12 **NM** value: **4.50**
73 ☐ May 1968 Cover: 0.12 **NM** value: **4.50**
74 ☐ Jun 1968 Cover: 0.12 **NM** value: **4.50**
75 ☐ Jul 1968 Cover: 0.12 **NM** value: **4.50**
76 ☐ Aug 1968 Cover: 0.12 **NM** value: **4.50**
77 ☐ Sep 1968 Cover: 0.12 **NM** value: **4.50**
78 ☐ Oct 1968 Cover: 0.12 **NM** value: **4.50**
79 ☐ Nov 1968 Cover: 0.12 **NM** value: **4.50**
80 ☐ Dec 1968 Cover: 0.12 **NM** value: **4.50**
81 ☐ Jan 1969 Cover: 0.12 **NM** value: **3.50**
Circ: Statement: **326,488**
82 ☐ Feb 1969 Cover: 0.12 **NM** value: **3.50**
Circ: Statement: **326,488**
83 ☐ Mar 1969 Cover: 0.12 **NM** value: **3.50**
Circ: Statement: **326,488**
84 ☐ Apr 1969 Cover: 0.12 **NM** value: **3.50**
Circ: Statement: **326,488**
85 ☐ May 1969 Cover: 0.12 **NM** value: **3.50**
Circ: Statement: **326,488**
86 ☐ Jun 1969 Cover: 0.12 **NM** value: **3.50**
Circ: Statement: **326,488**
87 ☐ Jul 1969 **NM** value: **3.50**
Circ: Statement: **326,488**
88 ☐ Aug 1969 Cover: 0.15 **NM** value: **3.50**
Circ: Statement: **326,488**
89 ☐ Sep 1969 Cover: 0.15 **NM** value: **3.50**
Circ: Statement: **326,488**
90 ☐ Oct 1969 Cover: 0.15 **NM** value: **3.50**
Circ: Statement: **326,488**
91 ☐ Nov 1969 Cover: 0.15 **NM** value: **3.00**
Circ: Statement: **326,488**
92 ☐ Dec 1969 Cover: 0.15 **NM** value: **3.00**
Circ: Statement: **326,488**
93 ☐ Jan 1970 Cover: 0.15 **NM** value: **3.00**
Circ: Statement: **286,935**
94 ☐ Feb 1970 Cover: 0.15 **NM** value: **3.00**
Circ: Statement: **286,935**
95 ☐ Mar 1970 Cover: 0.15 **NM** value: **3.00**
Circ: Statement: **286,935**
96 ☐ Apr 1970 Cover: 0.15 **NM** value: **3.00**
Circ: Statement: **286,935**
• Has 1969 Statement, filed 10/1/69; avg print run 530,994; avg sales 326,198; avg subs 290; avg total paid 326,488; max existent 326,488; 62% of run returned
97 ☐ May 1970 Cover: 0.15 **NM** value: **3.00**
Circ: Statement: **286,935**
98 ☐ Jun 1970 Cover: 0.15 **NM** value: **3.00**
Circ: Statement: **286,935**
99 ☐ Jul 1970 Cover: 0.15 **NM** value: **3.00**
Circ: Statement: **286,935**
100 ☐ Aug 1970 Cover: 0.15 **NM** value: **3.00**
Circ: Statement: **286,935**
101 ☐ Sep 1970 Cover: 0.15 **NM** value: **2.50**
Circ: Statement: **286,935**
102 ☐ Oct 1970 Cover: 0.15 **NM** value: **2.50**
Circ: Statement: **286,935**
103 ☐ Nov 1970 Cover: 0.15 **NM** value: **2.50**
Circ: Statement: **286,935**
104 ☐ Dec 1970 Cover: 0.15 **NM** value: **2.50**
Circ: Statement: **286,935**
105 ☐ Jan 1971 Cover: 0.15 **NM** value: **2.50**
Circ: Statement: **301,045**
106 ☐ Feb 1971 Cover: 0.15 **NM** value: **2.50**
Circ: Statement: **301,045**
107 ☐ Mar 1971 Cover: 0.15 **NM** value: **2.50**
Circ: Statement: **301,045**
108 ☐ Apr 1971 Cover: 0.15 **NM** value: **2.50**
Circ: Statement: **301,045**
109 ☐ May 1971 Cover: 0.15 **NM** value: **2.50**
Circ: Statement: **301,045**
• Has 1970 Statement, filed 10/1/70; avg print run 482,357; avg sales 286,694; avg subs 241; avg total paid 286,935; max existent 286,935; 60% of run returned
110 ☐ Jun 1971 Cover: 0.15 **NM** value: **2.50**
Circ: Statement: **301,045**
111 ☐ Jul 1971 Cover: 0.15 **NM** value: **2.50**
Circ: Statement: **301,045**
112 ☐ Aug 1971 Cover: 0.15 **NM** value: **2.50**
Circ: Statement: **301,045**
113 ☐ Sep 1971 Cover: 0.15 **NM** value: **2.50**
Circ: Statement: **301,045**
114 ☐ Oct 1971 Cover: 0.15 **NM** value: **2.50**
Circ: Statement: **301,045**
115 ☐ Nov 1971 Cover: 0.15 **NM** value: **2.50**
Circ: Statement: **301,045**
116 ☐ Dec 1971 Cover: 0.15 **NM** value: **2.50**
Circ: Statement: **301,045**
117 ☐ Jan 1972 Cover: 0.15 **NM** value: **2.50**
Circ: Statement: **263,434**
118 ☐ Feb 1972 Cover: 0.15 **NM** value: **2.50**
Circ: Statement: **263,434**
119 ☐ Mar 1972 Cover: 0.15 **NM** value: **2.50**
Circ: Statement: **263,434**
120 ☐ Apr 1972 Cover: 0.15 **NM** value: **2.50**
Circ: Statement: **263,434**
• Has 1971 Statement, filed 10/1/71; avg print run 514,173; avg sales 300,695; avg subs 350; avg total paid 301,045; max existent 301,045; 59% of run returned
121 ☐ May 1972 Cover: 0.20 **NM** value: **2.00**
Circ: Statement: **263,434**
122 ☐ Jun 1972 Cover: 0.20 **NM** value: **2.00**
Circ: Statement: **263,434**
123 ☐ Jul 1972 Cover: 0.20 **NM** value: **2.00**
Circ: Statement: **263,434**
124 ☐ Aug 1972 Cover: 0.20 **NM** value: **2.00**
Circ: Statement: **263,434**
125 ☐ Sep 1972 Cover: 0.20 **NM** value: **2.00**
Circ: Statement: **263,434**
126 ☐ Oct 1972 Cover: 0.20 **NM** value: **2.00**
Circ: Statement: **263,434**
127 ☐ Nov 1972 Cover: 0.20 **NM** value: **2.00**
Circ: Statement: **263,434**
128 ☐ Dec 1972 Cover: 0.20 **NM** value: **2.00**
Circ: Statement: **263,434**
129 ☐ Jan 1973 Cover: 0.20 **NM** value: **2.00**
Circ: Statement: **228,041**
130 ☐ Feb 1973 Cover: 0.20 **NM** value: **2.00**
Circ: Statement: **228,041**
131 ☐ Mar 1973 Cover: 0.20 **NM** value: **2.00**
Circ: Statement: **228,041**
132 ☐ Apr 1973 Cover: 0.20 **NM** value: **2.00**
Circ: Statement: **228,041**
• Has 1972 Statement, filed 10/1/72; avg print run 485,371; avg sales 300,695; avg subs 100; avg total paid 263,434; max existent 263,434; 54% of run returned
133 ☐ May 1973 Cover: 0.20 **NM** value: **2.00**
Circ: Statement: **228,041**
134 ☐ Jun 1973 Cover: 0.20 **NM** value: **2.00**
Circ: Statement: **228,041**
135 ☐ Jul 1973 Cover: 0.20 **NM** value: **2.00**
Circ: Statement: **228,041**
136 ☐ Aug 1973 Cover: 0.20 **NM** value: **2.00**
Circ: Statement: **228,041**
137 ☐ Sep 1973 Cover: 0.20 **NM** value: **2.00**
Circ: Statement: **228,041**
138 ☐ Oct 1973 Cover: 0.20 **NM** value: **2.00**
Circ: Statement: **228,041**
139 ☐ Nov 1973 Cover: 0.20 **NM** value: **2.00**
Circ: Statement: **228,041**
140 ☐ Dec 1973 Cover: 0.20 **NM** value: **2.00**
Circ: Statement: **228,041**
141 ☐ Jan 1974 Cover: 0.20 **NM** value: **2.00**
Circ: Statement: **206,361**
142 ☐ Feb 1974 Cover: 0.20 **NM** value: **2.00**
Circ: Statement: **206,361**
143 ☐ Mar 1974 Cover: 0.20 **NM** value: **2.00**
Circ: Statement: **206,361**
144 ☐ Apr 1974 Cover: 0.25 **NM** value: **2.00**
Circ: Statement: **206,361**
• Has 1973 Statement, filed 10/1/73; avg print run 456,003; avg sales 226,901; avg subs 1,140; avg total paid 228,041; max existent 228,041; 50% of run returned
145 ☐ May 1974 Cover: 0.25 **NM** value: **2.00**
Circ: Statement: **206,361**
146 ☐ Jun 1974 Cover: 0.25 **NM** value: **2.00**
Circ: Statement: **206,361**
147 ☐ Jul 1974 Cover: 0.25 **NM** value: **2.00**
Circ: Statement: **206,361**
148 ☐ Aug 1974 Cover: 0.25 **NM** value: **2.00**
Circ: Statement: **206,361**
149 ☐ Sep 1974 Cover: 0.25 **NM** value: **2.00**
Circ: Statement: **206,361**
150 ☐ Oct 1974 Cover: 0.25 **NM** value: **2.00**
Circ: Statement: **206,361**
151 ☐ Nov 1974 Cover: 0.25 **NM** value: **1.75**
Circ: Statement: **206,361**
152 ☐ Dec 1974 Cover: 0.25 **NM** value: **1.75**
Circ: Statement: **206,361**
153 ☐ Jan 1975 Cover: 0.25 **NM** value: **1.75**
Circ: Statement: **153,467**
154 ☐ Feb 1975 Cover: 0.25 **NM** value: **1.75**
Circ: Statement: **153,467**
155 ☐ Mar 1975 Cover: 0.25 **NM** value: **1.75**
Circ: Statement: **153,467**
156 ☐ Apr 1975 Cover: 0.25 **NM** value: **1.75**
Circ: Statement: **153,467**
• Has 1974 Statement; avg total paid 206,361
157 ☐ May 1975 Cover: 0.25 **NM** value: **1.75**
Circ: Statement: **153,467**
158 ☐ Jun 1975 Cover: 0.25 **NM** value: **1.75**
Circ: Statement: **153,467**
159 ☐ Jul 1975 Cover: 0.25 **NM** value: **1.75**
Circ: Statement: **153,467**
160 ☐ Aug 1975 Cover: 0.25 **NM** value: **1.75**
Circ: Statement: **153,467**
161 ☐ Sep 1975 Cover: 0.25 **NM** value: **1.75**
Circ: Statement: **153,467**
162 ☐ Oct 1975 Cover: 0.25 **NM** value: **1.75**
Circ: Statement: **153,467**
163 ☐ Nov 1975 Cover: 0.25 **NM** value: **1.75**
Circ: Statement: **153,467**
164 ☐ Dec 1975 Cover: 0.25 **NM** value: **1.75**
Circ: Statement: **153,467**
165 ☐ Jan 1976 Cover: 0.25 **NM** value: **1.75**
Circ: Statement: **142,353**
166 ☐ Feb 1976 Cover: 0.25 **NM** value: **1.75**
Circ: Statement: **142,353**
167 ☐ Mar 1976 Cover: 0.30 **NM** value: **1.75**
Circ: Statement: **142,353**
168 ☐ Apr 1976 Cover: 0.30 **NM** value: **1.75**
Circ: Statement: **142,353**
• Has 1975 Statement; avg total paid 153,467
169 ☐ May 1976 Cover: 0.30 **NM** value: **1.75**
Circ: Statement: **142,353**
170 ☐ Jun 1976 Cover: 0.30 **NM** value: **1.75**
Circ: Statement: **142,353**
171 ☐ Jul 1976 Cover: 0.30 **NM** value: **1.50**
Circ: Statement: **142,353**
172 ☐ Aug 1976 Cover: 0.30 **NM** value: **1.50**
Circ: Statement: **142,353**
173 ☐ Sep 1976 Cover: 0.30 **NM** value: **1.50**
Circ: Statement: **142,353**
174 ☐ Oct 1976 Cover: 0.30 **NM** value: **1.50**
Circ: Statement: **142,353**
175 ☐ Nov 1976 Cover: 0.30 **NM** value: **1.50**
Circ: Statement: **142,353**
176 ☐ Dec 1976 Cover: 0.30 **NM** value: **1.50**
Circ: Statement: **142,353**
177 ☐ Jan 1977 Cover: 0.30 **NM** value: **1.50**
Circ: Statement: **130,746**
178 ☐ Feb 1977 Cover: 0.30 **NM** value: **1.50**
Circ: Statement: **130,746**
179 ☐ Mar 1977 Cover: 0.30 **NM** value: **1.50**
Circ: Statement: **130,746**
180 ☐ Apr 1977 Cover: 0.30 **NM** value: **1.50**
Circ: Statement: **130,746**
• Has 1976 Statement, filed 10/1/76; avg print run 326,685; avg sales 142,087; avg subs 266; avg total paid 142,353; samples 300; max existent 142,653; 44% of run returned
181 ☐ May 1977 Cover: 0.30 **NM** value: **1.50**
Circ: Statement: **130,746**
182 ☐ Jun 1977 Cover: 0.35 **NM** value: **1.50**
Circ: Statement: **130,746**
183 ☐ Jul 1977 Cover: 0.35 **NM** value: **1.50**
Circ: Statement: **130,746**
184 ☐ Aug 1977 Cover: 0.35 **NM** value: **1.50**
Circ: Statement: **130,746**
185 ☐ Sep 1977 Cover: 0.35 **NM** value: **1.50**
Circ: Statement: **130,746**
186 ☐ Oct 1977 Cover: 0.35 **NM** value: **1.50**
Circ: Statement: **130,746**
187 ☐ Nov 1977 Cover: 0.35 **NM** value: **1.50**
Circ: Statement: **130,746**

Other grades: Multiply prices above by **1.5 for Mint • 2/3 for Very Fine • 1/3 for Fine • 1/5 for Very Good • 1/8 for Good**

188 ❑ Dec 1977 Cover: 0.35 **NM** value: **1.50**
Circ: Statement: **130,746**
189 ❑ Jan 1978 Cover: 0.35 **NM** value: **1.50**
Circ: Statement: **109,732**
190 ❑ Feb 1978 Cover: 0.35 **NM** value: **1.50**
Circ: Statement: **109,732**
191 ❑ Mar 1978 Cover: 0.35 **NM** value: **1.50**
Circ: Statement: **109,732**
192 ❑ Apr 1978 Cover: 0.35 **NM** value: **1.50**
Circ: Statement: **109,732**
• Has 1977 Statement; avg total paid 130,746
193 ❑ May 1978 Cover: 0.35 **NM** value: **1.50**
Circ: Statement: **109,732**
194 ❑ Jun 1978 Cover: 0.35 **NM** value: **1.50**
Circ: Statement: **109,732**
195 ❑ Jul 1978 Cover: 0.35 **NM** value: **1.50**
Circ: Statement: **109,732**
196 ❑ Aug 1978 Cover: 0.35 **NM** value: **1.50**
Circ: Statement: **109,732**
197 ❑ Sep 1978 Cover: 0.35 **NM** value: **1.50**
Circ: Statement: **109,732**
198 ❑ Oct 1978 Cover: 0.35 **NM** value: **1.50**
Circ: Statement: **109,732**
📖 Lost Valley; Prowling Peril
199 ❑ Nov 1978 Cover: 0.35 **NM** value: **1.50**
Circ: Statement: **109,732**
200 ❑ Dec 1978 Cover: 0.35 **NM** value: **1.50**
Circ: Statement: **109,732**
201 ❑ Jan 1979 Cover: 0.35 **NM** value: **1.25**
202 ❑ Feb 1979 Cover: 0.35 **NM** value: **1.25**
203 ❑ Mar 1979 Cover: 0.35 **NM** value: **1.25**
204 ❑ Apr 1979 Cover: 0.40 **NM** value: **1.25**
• Has 1978 Statement; avg print run 298,596, avg sales 109,703; avg subs 29; avg total paid 109,732; max existent 110,032; 37% of run returned
205 ❑ Jun 1979 Cover: 0.40 **NM** value: **1.25**
206 ❑ Jul 1979 Cover: 0.40 **NM** value: **1.25**
207 ❑ Aug 1979 Cover: 0.40 **NM** value: **1.25**
208 ❑ Sep 1979 Cover: 0.40 **NM** value: **1.25**
209 ❑ Nov 1979 Cover: 0.40 **NM** value: **1.25**
210 ❑ Dec 1979 Cover: 0.40 **NM** value: **1.25**
211 ❑ Feb 1980 Cover: 0.40 **NM** value: **1.25**
Circ: Statement: **90,039**
212 ❑ Mar 1980 Cover: 0.40 **NM** value: **1.25**
Circ: Statement: **90,039**
213 ❑ Apr 1980 Cover: 0.40 **NM** value: **1.25**
Circ: Statement: **90,039**
214 ❑ Jun 1980 Cover: 0.40 **NM** value: **1.25**
Circ: Statement: **90,039**
215 ❑ Jul 1980 Cover: 0.40 **NM** value: **1.25**
Circ: Statement: **90,039**
216 ❑ Aug 1980 Cover: 0.50 **NM** value: **1.25**
Circ: Statement: **90,039**
217 ❑ Sep 1980 Cover: 0.50 **NM** value: **1.25**
Circ: Statement: **90,039**
218 ❑ Nov 1980 Cover: 0.50 **NM** value: **1.25**
Circ: Statement: **90,039**
219 ❑ Dec 1980 Cover: 0.50 **NM** value: **1.25**
Circ: Statement: **90,039**
220 ❑ Feb 1981 Cover: 0.50 **NM** value: **1.25**
Circ: Statement: **84,886**
221 ❑ Mar 1981 Cover: 0.50 **NM** value: **1.25**
Circ: Statement: **84,886**
222 ❑ Apr 1981 Cover: 0.50 **NM** value: **1.25**
Circ: Statement: **84,886**
• Has 1980 Statement, filed 10/1/80; avg print run 252,085; avg sales 89,952; avg subs 87; avg total paid 90,039; max existent 90,339; 36% of run returned
223 ❑ Jun 1981 Cover: 0.50 **NM** value: **1.25**
Circ: Statement: **84,886**
224 ❑ Jul 1981 Cover: 0.50 **NM** value: **1.25**
Circ: Statement: **84,886**
225 ❑ Aug 1981 Cover: 0.50 **NM** value: **1.25**
Circ: Statement: **84,886**
226 ❑ Sep 1981 Cover: 0.50 **NM** value: **1.25**
Circ: Statement: **84,886**
227 ❑ Nov 1981 Cover: 0.50 **NM** value: **1.25**
Circ: Statement: **84,886**
228 ❑ Dec 1981 Cover: 0.60 **NM** value: **1.25**
Circ: Statement: **84,886**
229 ❑ Feb 1982 Cover: 0.60 **NM** value: **1.25**
Circ: Statement: **66,150**
230 ❑ Mar 1982 Cover: 0.60 **NM** value: **1.25**
Circ: Statement: **66,150**
231 ❑ May 1982 Cover: 0.60 **NM** value: **1.25**
Circ: Statement: **66,150**
232 ❑ Jul 1982 Cover: 0.60 **NM** value: **1.25**
Circ: Statement: **66,150**
233 ❑ Sep 1982 Cover: 0.60 **NM** value: **1.25**
Circ: Statement: **66,150**
234 ❑ Nov 1982 Cover: 0.60 **NM** value: **1.25**
Circ: Statement: **66,150**
235 ❑ Jan 1983 Cover: 0.60 **NM** value: **1.25**
Circ: Statement: **66,111**
236 ❑ Apr 1983 Cover: 0.60 **NM** value: **1.25**
Circ: Statement: **66,111**
237 ❑ 1983 Cover: 0.60 **NM** value: **1.25**
Circ: Statement: **66,111**
238 ❑ 1983 Cover: 0.60 **NM** value: **1.25**
Circ: Statement: **66,111**
239 ❑ Nov 1983 Cover: 0.60 **NM** value: **1.25**
Circ: Statement: **66,111**
240 ❑ Jan 1984 Cover: 0.60 **NM** value: **1.25**
Circ: Statement: **58,704**
241 ❑ Mar 1984 Cover: 0.60 **NM** value: **1.25**
Circ: Statement: **58,704**
242 ❑ May 1984 Cover: 0.60 **NM** value: **1.25**
Circ: Statement: **58,704**
243 ❑ Jul 1984 Cover: 0.60 **NM** value: **1.25**
Circ: Statement: **58,704**
244 ❑ Sep 1984 Cover: 0.60 **NM** value: **1.25**
Circ: Statement: **58,704**
245 ❑ Nov 1984 Cover: 0.60 **NM** value: **1.25**
Circ: Statement: **58,704**
246 ❑ Jan 1985 Cover: 0.60 **NM** value: **1.25**
Circ: Statement: **54,735**
247 ❑ Mar 1985 Cover: 0.65 **NM** value: **1.25**
Circ: Statement: **54,735**
248 ❑ May 1985 Cover: 0.65 **NM** value: **1.25**
Circ: Statement: **54,735**
249 ❑ Jul 1985 Cover: 0.65 **NM** value: **1.25**
Circ: Statement: **54,735**
250 ❑ Sep 1985 Cover: 0.65 **NM** value: **1.25**
Circ: Statement: **54,735**
251 ❑ Nov 1985 Cover: 0.65 **NM** value: **1.00**
Circ: Statement: **54,735**
252 ❑ Jan 1986 Cover: 0.65 **NM** value: **1.00**
Circ: Statement: **57,256**
253 ❑ Mar 1986 Cover: 0.65 **NM** value: **1.00**
Circ: Statement: **57,256**
254 ❑ May 1986 Cover: 0.65 **NM** value: **1.00**
Circ: Statement: **57,256**
255 ❑ Jul 1986 Cover: 0.75 **NM** value: **1.00**
Circ: Statement: **57,256**
256 ❑ Sep 1986 Cover: 0.75 **NM** value: **1.00**
Circ: Statement: **57,256**
257 ❑ Nov 1986 Cover: 0.75 **NM** value: **1.00**
Circ: Statement: **57,256**
258 ❑ Jan 1987 Cover: 0.75 **NM** value: **1.00**
Circ: Statement: **50,943**
259 ❑ Mar 1987 Cover: 0.75 **NM** value: **1.00**
Circ: Statement: **50,943**
260 ❑ May 1987 Cover: 0.75 **NM** value: **1.00**
Circ: Statement: **50,943**
261 ❑ Jul 1987 Cover: 0.75 **NM** value: **1.00**
Circ: Statement: **50,943**
262 ❑ Sep 1987 Cover: 0.75 **NM** value: **1.00**
Circ: Statement: **50,943**
263 ❑ Nov 1987 Cover: 0.75 **NM** value: **1.00**
Circ: Statement: **50,943**
264 ❑ Jan 1988 Cover: 0.75 **NM** value: **1.00**
Circ: Statement: **52,290**
265 ❑ Mar 1988 Cover: 0.75 **NM** value: **1.00**
Circ: Statement: **52,290**
266 ❑ May 1988 Cover: 0.75 **NM** value: **1.00**
Circ: Statement: **52,290**
267 ❑ Jul 1988 Cover: 0.75 **NM** value: **1.00**
Circ: Statement: **52,290**
268 ❑ Sep 1988 Cover: 0.75 **NM** value: **1.00**
Circ: Statement: **52,290**
269 ❑ Nov 1988 Cover: 0.75 **NM** value: **1.00**
Circ: Statement: **52,290**
270 ❑ Jan 1989 Cover: 0.75 **NM** value: **1.00**
Circ: Statement: **54,506**
271 ❑ Mar 1989 Cover: 0.75 **NM** value: **1.00**
Circ: Statement: **54,506**
272 ❑ May 1989 Cover: 0.75 **NM** value: **1.00**
Circ: Statement: **54,506**
273 ❑ Jul 1989 Cover: 0.95 **NM** value: **1.00**
Circ: Statement: **54,506**
274 ❑ Sep 1989 Cover: 0.95 **NM** value: **1.00**
Circ: Statement: **54,506**
275 ❑ Nov 1989 Cover: 0.95 **NM** value: **1.00**
Circ: Statement: **54,506**
276 ❑ Jan 1990 Cover: 1.00 **NM** value: **Cover or less**
Circ: Statement: **46,480**
277 ❑ Mar 1990 Cover: 1.00 **NM** value: **Cover or less**
Circ: Statement: **46,480**
278 ❑ May 1990 Cover: 1.00 **NM** value: **Cover or less**
Circ: Statement: **46,480**
279 ❑ Jul 1990 Cover: 1.00 **NM** value: **Cover or less**
Circ: Statement: **46,480**
280 ❑ Sep 1990 Cover: 1.00 **NM** value: **Cover or less**
Circ: Statement: **46,480**
281 ❑ Nov 1990 Cover: 1.00 **NM** value: **Cover or less**
Circ: Statement: **46,480**
282 ❑ Jan 1991 Cover: 1.00 **NM** value: **Cover or less**
283 ❑ Mar 1991 Cover: 1.00 **NM** value: **Cover or less**
284 ❑ May 1991 Cover: 1.00 **NM** value: **Cover or less**
285 ❑ Jul 1991 Cover: 1.00 **NM** value: **Cover or less**
• Final issue

LIFE WITH MILLIE — Atlas

8 ❑ Dec 1960 Cover: 0.10 **NM** value: **50.00**
9 ❑ Feb 1961 Cover: 0.10 **NM** value: **40.00**
10 ❑ Apr 1961 Cover: 0.10 **NM** value: **35.00**
11 ❑ Jun 1961 Cover: 0.10 **NM** value: **35.00**
12 ❑ Aug 1961 Cover: 0.10 **NM** value: **35.00**
13 ❑ Oct 1961 Cover: 0.10 **NM** value: **30.00**
14 ❑ Dec 1961 Cover: 0.10 **NM** value: **30.00**
15 ❑ Feb 1962 Cover: 0.12 **NM** value: **30.00**
Circ: Statement: **143,476**
16 ❑ Apr 1962 Cover: 0.12 **NM** value: **25.00**
Circ: Statement: **143,476**
17 ❑ Jun 1962 Cover: 0.12 **NM** value: **25.00**
Circ: Statement: **143,476**
18 ❑ Aug 1962 Cover: 0.12 **NM** value: **25.00**
Circ: Statement: **143,476**
19 ❑ Oct 1962 Cover: 0.12 **NM** value: **25.00**
Circ: Statement: **143,476**
20 ❑ Dec 1962 Cover: 0.12 **NM** value: **25.00**
Circ: Statement: **143,476**

LIFE WITH SNARKY PARKER — Fox

1 ❑ Aug 1950 Cover: 0.10 **NM** value: **150.00**

LIGHT AND DARKNESS WAR, THE — Marvel / Epic

1 ❑ Oct 1988 Cover: 1.95 **NM** value: **Cover or less**
Circ: CapCity orders: **16,000**
A: Cam Kennedy **W:** Tom Veitch
2 ❑ Nov 1988 Cover: 1.95 **NM** value: **Cover or less**
Circ: CapCity orders: **11,200**
A: Cam Kennedy **W:** Tom Veitch
3 ❑ Jan 1989 Cover: 1.95 **NM** value: **Cover or less**
Circ: CapCity orders: **10,700**
A: Cam Kennedy **W:** Tom Veitch
4 ❑ Feb 1989 Cover: 1.95 **NM** value: **Cover or less**
Circ: CapCity orders: **11,500**
A: Cam Kennedy **W:** Tom Veitch
5 ❑ Apr 1989 Cover: 1.95 **NM** value: **Cover or less**
Circ: CapCity orders: **11,700**
A: Cam Kennedy **W:** Tom Veitch
6 ❑ Sep 1989 Cover: 1.95 **NM** value: **Cover or less**
A: Cam Kennedy **W:** Tom Veitch

LIGHT FANTASTIC, THE (TERRY PRATCHETT'S...) — Innovation

0 ❑ Cover: 2.50 **NM** value: **Cover or less**
A: Steven Ross **W:** Scott Rockwell
1 ❑ Jun 1992 Cover: 2.50 **NM** value: **Cover or less**
Circ: CapCity orders: **3,530**
A: Steven Ross **W:** Scott Rockwell
2 ❑ Cover: 2.50 **NM** value: **Cover or less**
A: Steven Ross **W:** Scott Rockwell
3 ❑ Cover: 2.50 **NM** value: **Cover or less**
A: Steven Ross **W:** Scott Rockwell
4 ❑ Cover: 2.50 **NM** value: **Cover or less**
A: Steven Ross **W:** Scott Rockwell

LIGHTNING COMICS — Feature

4 ❑ Oct 1940 Cover: 0.10 **NM** value: **800.00**
5 ❑ Feb 1941 Cover: 0.10 **NM** value: **600.00**
6 ❑ Apr 1941 Cover: 0.10 **NM** value: **600.00**
7 ❑ Jun 1941 Cover: 0.10 **NM** value: **500.00**
8 ❑ Aug 1941 Cover: 0.10 **NM** value: **500.00**
9 ❑ Oct 1941 Cover: 0.10 **NM** value: **500.00**
10 ❑ Dec 1941 Cover: 0.10 **NM** value: **400.00**
11 ❑ Feb 1942 Cover: 0.10 **NM** value: **400.00**
12 ❑ Apr 1942 Cover: 0.10 **NM** value: **400.00**
13 ❑ Jun 1942 Cover: 0.10 **NM** value: **400.00**

LIGHTNING COMICS PRESENTS — Lightning

1 ❑ May 1994 Cover: 3.50 **NM** value: **Cover or less**
📖 Triple Crossed **A:** Terral Lawrence **W:** Steven Zyskowski

LIGHTNING NUDE COLLECTION — Lightning

All issues are adults only.
Bk 1 ❑ Jan 1997, b&w Cover: 9.95 **NM** value: **Cover or less**
reproduces nude covers.

LI'L ABNER — Harvey

Al Capp's Li'l Abner featured a group of mountain folk in the fictional hamlet of Dogpatch, U.S.A. The principal family was the Yokums, Mammy, Pappy, and their son Abner. The Dogpatchers simplistic existence was often upset by the influence of outside parties including General Bullmoose, a turnip termite invasion, the cute and cuddly (and edible) Shmoos, and the annual Sadie Hawkins Day, in which the eligible bachelors of Dogpatch were pursued by the single women whose ultimate goal was matrimony. The series spawned two films and a Broadway play.

Harvey's comic-book series took the original strips, cut them up, and relaid them out to tell a semi-cohesive story. A much better way to get a sampling of Capp's genius is to pick up the strip collections by Kitchen Sink Press. — Brent

61 ❑ Dec 1947 Cover: 0.10 **NM** value: **200.00**
• **CGC:** 1 graded, best 8.0
62 ❑ Feb 1948 Cover: 0.10 **NM** value: **175.00**
63 ❑ Apr 1948 Cover: 0.10 **NM** value: **125.00**
• **CGC:** 1 graded, best 9.6
64 ❑ Jun 1948 Cover: 0.10 **NM** value: **100.00**
• **CGC:** 3 graded, best 9.4
65 ❑ Aug 1948 Cover: 0.10 **NM** value: **100.00**
• **CGC:** 1 graded, best 9.6
66 ❑ Oct 1948 Cover: 0.10 **NM** value: **100.00**
67 ❑ Dec 1948 Cover: 0.10 **NM** value: **100.00**
• **CGC:** 2 graded, best 4.5
68 ❑ Jan 1949 Cover: 0.10 **NM** value: **75.00**
• **CGC:** 1 graded, best 7.5
69 ❑ Feb 1949 Cover: 0.10 **NM** value: **75.00**
• **CGC:** 1 graded, best 5.0
70 ❑ 1949 Cover: 0.10 **NM** value: **75.00**
71 ❑ 1949 Cover: 0.10 **NM** value: **75.00**
72 ❑ 1949 Cover: 0.10 **NM** value: **50.00**
73 ❑ 1949 Cover: 0.10 **NM** value: **50.00**
74 ❑ 1950 Cover: 0.10 **NM** value: **40.00**
75 ❑ 1950 Cover: 0.10 **NM** value: **40.00**
76 ❑ 1950 Cover: 0.10 **NM** value: **40.00**
77 ❑ 1950 Cover: 0.10 **NM** value: **40.00**
78 ❑ 1950 Cover: 0.10 **NM** value: **35.00**
79 ❑ Nov 1950 Cover: 0.10 **NM** value: **35.00**
80 ❑ Jan 1951 Cover: 0.10 **NM** value: **35.00**
81 ❑ Mar 1951 Cover: 0.10 **NM** value: **35.00**
82 ❑ May 1951 Cover: 0.10 **NM** value: **35.00**
83 ❑ Jul 1951 Cover: 0.10 **NM** value: **30.00**

CGC-graded: Multiply prices above by **33 for 9.9 M • 16 for 9.8 NM/M • 7 for 9.6 NM+ • 5 for 9.4 NM • 2.5 for 9.2 NM- • 1.5 for 9.0 VF/NM**

84 ❑ Sep 1951 Cover: 0.10 **NM** value: **30.00**
85 ❑ Nov 1951 Cover: 0.10 **NM** value: **30.00**
86 ❑ Jan 1952 Cover: 0.10 **NM** value: **30.00**
87 ❑ Mar 1952 Cover: 0.10 **NM** value: **30.00**
88 ❑ May 1952 Cover: 0.10 **NM** value: **25.00**
89 ❑ Jul 1952 Cover: 0.10 **NM** value: **25.00**
90 ❑ Sep 1952 Cover: 0.10 **NM** value: **25.00**
91 ❑ Nov 1952 Cover: 0.10 **NM** value: **25.00**
92 ❑ Jan 1953 Cover: 0.10 **NM** value: **25.00**
93 ❑ Cover: 0.10 **NM** value: **25.00**
94 ❑ Cover: 0.10 **NM** value: **25.00**
95 ❑ Cover: 0.10 **NM** value: **25.00**
96 ❑ Nov 1954 Cover: 0.10 **NM** value: **20.00**
97 ❑ Jan 1955 Cover: 0.10 **NM** value: **20.00**

LI'L GENIUS — Charlton

What comic book could one create with exasperated parents, a mischievous son, and a female nemesis? Perhaps a comic book named Dennis the Menace? Well, not in this case. Li'l Genius is an easily forgettable, poor imitation of Dennis. Some of the best children's comic books include satire, crisp dialog, and an adult's perspective of humor and themes. Sadly, these qualities are missing and the entire series suffers. A sharp reader will quickly determine the writing is aimed at younger readers, since the jokes are simple wordplay and sight gags. This book is written only for the 10-year-old and under group.

5 ❑ ca. 1955 Cover: 0.10 **NM** value: **10.00**
6 ❑ ca. 1955 Cover: 0.10 **NM** value: **10.00**
7 ❑ Sep 1955 Cover: 0.10 **NM** value: **10.00**
8 ❑ ca. 1956 Cover: 0.10 **NM** value: **10.00**
9 ❑ ca. 1956 Cover: 0.10 **NM** value: **10.00**
10 ❑ ca. 1956 Cover: 0.10 **NM** value: **10.00**
11 ❑ ca. 1956 Cover: 0.10 **NM** value: **10.00**
12 ❑ ca. 1957 Cover: 0.10 **NM** value: **10.00**
13 ❑ ca. 1957 Cover: 0.10 **NM** value: **10.00**
14 ❑ ca. 1957 Cover: 0.10 **NM** value: **10.00**
15 ❑ ca. 1957 Cover: 0.10 **NM** value: **10.00**
16 ❑ Jan 1958 Cover: 0.15 **NM** value: **10.00**
17 ❑ Apr 1958 Cover: 0.15 **NM** value: **10.00**
• **CGC:** 2 graded, best 8.5
18 ❑ Cover: 0.10 **NM** value: **10.00**
19 ❑ Cover: 0.10 **NM** value: **10.00**
20 ❑ Cover: 0.10 **NM** value: **10.00**
21 ❑ Cover: 0.10 **NM** value: **10.00**
22 ❑ Cover: 0.10 **NM** value: **10.00**
23 ❑ Cover: 0.10 **NM** value: **10.00**
24 ❑ Cover: 0.10 **NM** value: **10.00**
25 ❑ Cover: 0.10 **NM** value: **10.00**
26 ❑ Cover: 0.10 **NM** value: **10.00**
27 ❑ Jun 1960 Cover: 0.10 **NM** value: **10.00**
28 ❑ Aug 1960 Cover: 0.10 **NM** value: **10.00**
29 ❑ Oct 1960 Cover: 0.10 **NM** value: **10.00**
30 ❑ Dec 1960 Cover: 0.10 **NM** value: **10.00**
31 ❑ Feb 1961 Cover: 0.10 **NM** value: **8.00**
32 ❑ Apr 1961 Cover: 0.10 **NM** value: **8.00**
33 ❑ Jun 1961 Cover: 0.10 **NM** value: **8.00**
34 ❑ Aug 1961 Cover: 0.10 **NM** value: **8.00**
• **CGC:** 1 graded, best 8.5
35 ❑ Oct 1961 Cover: 0.10 **NM** value: **8.00**
36 ❑ **NM** value: **8.00**
37 ❑ 1962 Cover: 0.12 **NM** value: **8.00**
38 ❑ 1962 Cover: 0.12 **NM** value: **8.00**
39 ❑ 1962 Cover: 0.12 **NM** value: **8.00**
40 ❑ 1962 Cover: 0.12 **NM** value: **8.00**
41 ❑ Nov 1962 Cover: 0.12 **NM** value: **8.00**
42 ❑ Jan 1963 Cover: 0.12 **NM** value: **8.00**
43 ❑ Mar 1963 Cover: 0.12 **NM** value: **8.00**
44 ❑ May 1963 Cover: 0.12 **NM** value: **8.00**
45 ❑ Jul 1963 Cover: 0.12 **NM** value: **8.00**
46 ❑ Sep 1963 Cover: 0.12 **NM** value: **8.00**
47 ❑ Nov 1963 Cover: 0.12 **NM** value: **8.00**
48 ❑ Jan 1964 Cover: 0.12 **NM** value: **8.00**
49 ❑ Mar 1964 Cover: 0.12 **NM** value: **8.00**
50 ❑ Aug 1964 Cover: 0.12 **NM** value: **8.00**
51 ❑ Nov 1964 Cover: 0.12 **NM** value: **8.00**
52 ❑ Jan 1965 Cover: 0.12 **NM** value: **8.00**
53 ❑ Cover: 0.12 **NM** value: **8.00**
54 ❑ Oct 1985 Cover: 0.75 **NM** value: **8.00**
• Final issue of original run
55 ❑ Jan 1986 Cover: 0.75 **NM** value: **1.00**
📖 New Baby; On Wings of Song; Li'l Lumberjack…Animal Charmer; Visitin'; Li'l Genius and Li'l Tomboy **A:** Frank Johnson **W:** Frank Johnson ★ Appearance of Li'l Tomboy, Li'l Lumberjack.

LILI — Image

0 ❑ ca. 1999 Cover: 4.95 **NM** value: **Cover or less**
Circ: Diamd. preorders: **5,117**
A: Jason Waltrip; John Waltrip **W:** Brian Michael Bendis; Michael Yanover

LI'L JINX — Archie

11 ❑ Nov 1956 Cover: 0.10 **NM** value: **75.00**
12 ❑ Jan 1957 Cover: 0.10 **NM** value: **50.00**
13 ❑ Mar 1957 Cover: 0.10 **NM** value: **50.00**
14 ❑ Cover: 0.10 **NM** value: **50.00**
15 ❑ Cover: 0.10 **NM** value: **50.00**
16 ❑ Cover: 0.10 **NM** value: **50.00**

LI'L KIDS — Marvel

1 ❑ Jul 1970 Cover: 0.15 **NM** value: **50.00**
• **CGC:** 3 graded, best 9.0
2 ❑ Oct 1970 Cover: 0.15 **NM** value: **25.00**
3 ❑ Nov 1971 Cover: 0.15 **NM** value: **25.00**
4 ❑ Feb 1972 Cover: 0.20 **NM** value: **25.00**
5 ❑ Apr 1972 Cover: 0.20 **NM** value: **25.00**
6 ❑ Jun 1972 Cover: 0.20 **NM** value: **25.00**
7 ❑ Aug 1972 Cover: 0.20 **NM** value: **25.00**
• **CGC:** 1 graded, best 9.2
8 ❑ Oct 1972 Cover: 0.20 **NM** value: **25.00**
9 ❑ 1973 Cover: 0.20 **NM** value: **25.00**
10 ❑ Feb 1973 **NM** value: **30.00**
• **CGC:** 1 graded, best 9.2
11 ❑ Apr 1973 Cover: 0.20 **NM** value: **30.00**
12 ❑ Jun 1973 Cover: 0.20 **NM** value: **30.00**

LILLITH: DEMON PRINCESS — Antarctic

0 ❑ Mar 1998 Cover: 2.95 **NM** value: **Cover or less**
Circ: Diamd. preorders: **8,911**
📖 Faith and Sin **A:** Ben Dunn **W:** Ben Dunn
0/SC ❑ Mar 1998 Cover: 5.00 **NM** value: **Cover or less**
Special limited cover (Lilith flying w/green swish). 📖 Faith and Sin **A:** Ben Dunn **W:** Ben Dunn
1 ❑ Aug 1996 Cover: 2.95 **NM** value: **5.00**
A: Jeff Henderson **W:** Barry Lyga
2 ❑ Oct 1996 Cover: 2.95 **NM** value: **5.00**
Circ: Diamd. preorders: **8,786**
A: Jeff Henderson; Shawn Atkinson; Mark Heike; David Jacob Beckett; Sam De La Rosa **W:** Barry Lyga
3 ❑ Feb 1997 Cover: 2.95 **NM** value: **5.00**
Circ: Diamd. preorders: **5,612**
A: Shawn Atkinson **W:** Barry Lyga

LI'L MENACE — Fago

1 ❑ ca. 1958 Cover: 0.10 **NM** value: **40.00**
2 ❑ ca. 1959 Cover: 0.10 **NM** value: **30.00**
3 ❑ ca. 1959 Cover: 0.10 **NM** value: **25.00**

LI'L PAN — Fox

6 ❑ Dec 1946 Cover: 0.10 **NM** value: **60.00**
7 ❑ Feb 1947 Cover: 0.10 **NM** value: **40.00**
8 ❑ Apr 1947 Cover: 0.10 **NM** value: **40.00**

LI'L RASCAL TWINS — Charlton

6 ❑ May 1957 Cover: 0.10 **NM** value: **2.00**
7 ❑ Aug 1957 Cover: 0.10 **NM** value: **12.00**
8 ❑ Nov 1957 Cover: 0.10 **NM** value: **12.00**
9 ❑ Feb 1957 Cover: 0.10 **NM** value: **12.00**
10 ❑ May 1957 Cover: 0.10 **NM** value: **12.00**
11 ❑ Aug 1958 Cover: 0.10 **NM** value: **8.00**
12 ❑ Nov 1958 Cover: 0.10 **NM** value: **8.00**
13 ❑ ca. 1959 Cover: 0.10 **NM** value: **8.00**
14 ❑ ca. 1959 Cover: 0.10 **NM** value: **8.00**
15 ❑ ca. 1959 Cover: 0.10 **NM** value: **8.00**
16 ❑ ca. 1959 Cover: 0.10 **NM** value: **8.00**
17 ❑ ca. 1959 Cover: 0.10 **NM** value: **8.00**
18 ❑ ca. 1960 Cover: 0.10 **NM** value: **8.00**

LIMITED COLLECTORS' EDITION — DC

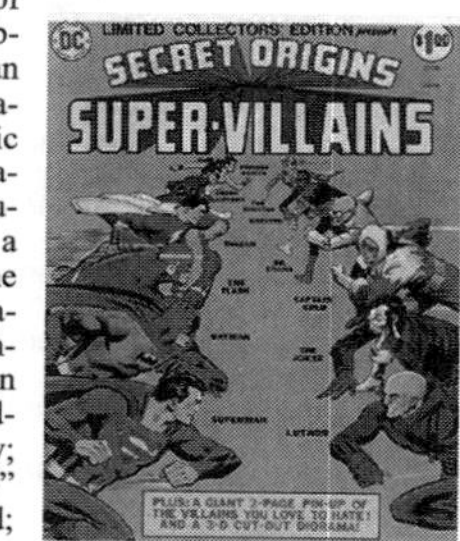

DC's popular series of 10x13.5-inch treasury- or tabloid-sized reprint comics ran from 1972 until 1978 and featured a wide variety of classic Golden Age and Silver Age material. Of course, DC stalwart Superman was represented in a number of issues, but some of the more interesting editions featured such gems as the 1946 Sunday comic strips starring Batman and Two-Face; Golden Age adventures of the Marvel Family; 1943-44 "Dick Tracy vs. Flattop" comic strips by Chester Gould; the Batman/Ra's al Ghul saga by Denny O'Neil, Neal Adams, and Irv Novick; the first battle between the Legion of Super-Heroes and Mordru; and Joe Kubert's complete adaptation of the origin of Tarzan. One issue of Limited Collectors' Edition even presented all-new adaptations of Bible stories by Kubert, Sheldon Mayer, and Nestor Redondo.

20 ❑ Cover: 1.00 **NM** value: **3.00**
• really C-20; Rudolph the Red-Nosed Reindeer
21 ❑ Sum 1973 Cover: 1.00 **NM** value: **16.00**
• really C-21; Shazam!; reprints Golden Age Marvel Family stories
22 ❑ Fal 1973 Cover: 1.00 **NM** value: **14.00**
• really C-22; Tarzan **A:** Jack Kirby; Joe Kubert
23 ❑ Cover: 1.00 **NM** value: **16.00**
• really C-23; House of Mystery
24 ❑ Cover: 1.00 **NM** value: **25.00**
• really C-24; Rudolph the Red-Nosed Reindeer
25 ❑ Cover: 1.00 **NM** value: **28.00**
• really C-25; Batman **A:** Neal Adams
27 ❑ Cover: 1.00 **NM** value: **16.00**
• really C-27; Shazam!; reprints Golden Age Marvel Family stories
29 ❑ Cover: 1.00 **NM** value: **Cover or less**
• really C-29; Tarzan **A:** Jack Kirby
30 ❑ Cover: 1.00 **NM** value: **12.00**
• really C-30; Superman
31 ❑ Nov 1974 Cover: 1.00 **NM** value: **15.00**
• really C-31; Superman
32 ❑ Jan 1975 Cover: 1.00 **NM** value: **Cover or less**
• really C-32; Ghosts
33 ❑ Feb 1975 Cover: 1.00 **NM** value: **15.00**
• really C-33; Rudolph the Red-Nosed Reindeer
34 ❑ Mar 1975 Cover: 1.00 **NM** value: **12.00**
• really C-34; Christmas With the Super-Heroes
35 ❑ May 1975 Cover: 1.00 **NM** value: **Cover or less**
• really C-35; Shazam!
36 ❑ Jul 1975 Cover: 1.00 **NM** value: **15.00**
📖 The Creation; The Garden of Eden; Digging into the Past; Cain and Abel; The Generations of Adam; Noah and the Flood; School Days in Bible Times; The Ziggurat; The Tower of Babel; Soldiers in the Time of Abraham; The Story of Abraham; Sodom and Gomorrah • really C-36; The Bible **A:** Nestor Redondo; Jack Kirby; Joe Kubert **W:** Sheldon Mayer
37 ❑ Sep 1975 Cover: 1.00 **NM** value: **2.00**
• really C-37; Batman
38 ❑ Nov 1975 Cover: 1.00 **NM** value: **Cover or less**
• really C-38; Superman
39 ❑ Nov 1975 Cover: 1.00 **NM** value: **Cover or less**
📖 The Man Behind the Red Hood!; How Luthor Met Superboy; The Coldest Man on Earth!; Capt. Marvel; The Origin of Terra-Man • really C-39; Secret Origins of Super Villains **A:** Bob Kane; Carmine Infantino; Neal Adams; Dick Dillin; C.C. Beck; Frank Giacoia; Al Plastino **W:** Bob Kane; Cary Bates; John Broome
40 ❑ Nov 1975 Cover: 1.00 **NM** value: **12.00**
• really C-40; Dick Tracy
41 ❑ Jan 1976 Cover: 1.00 **NM** value: **Cover or less**
• really C-41; Super Friends
42 ❑ Mar 1976 Cover: 1.00 **NM** value: **Cover or less**
• really C-42; Rudolph the Red-Nosed Reindeer
43 ❑ Mar 1976 Cover: 1.00 **NM** value: **Cover or less**
• really C-43; Christmas With the Super-Heroes
44 ❑ Jul 1976 Cover: 1.00 **NM** value: **12.00**
• really C-44; Batman
45 ❑ Jul 1976 Cover: 1.00 **NM** value: **Cover or less**
• really C-45; More Secret Origins of Super-Villains
46 ❑ Sep 1976 Cover: 1.00 **NM** value: **Cover or less**
• really C-46; Justice League of America
47 ❑ Sep 1976 Cover: 1.00 **NM** value: **Cover or less**
• really C-47; Superman Salutes the Bicentennial; reprints Tomahawk stories
48 ❑ Nov 1976 Cover: 1.00 **NM** value: **12.00**
• really C-48; Superman vs. Flash
49 ❑ Nov 1976 Cover: 1.00 **NM** value: **Cover or less**
• really C-49; Legion
50 ❑ Cover: 2.00 **NM** value: **Cover or less**
• really C-50; Rudolph the Red-Nosed Reindeer; poster
51 ❑ Aug 1977 Cover: 2.00 **NM** value: **12.00**
• really C-51; Batman vs. Ra's Al Ghul
52 ❑ Cover: 2.00 **NM** value: **Cover or less**
• really C-52; Best of DC **A:** Neal Adams
57 ❑ Cover: 2.00 **NM** value: **12.00**
• really C-57; Welcome Back, Kotter
59 ❑ Cover: 2.00 **NM** value: **14.00**
• Series continued in All-New Collectors' Edition. • really C-59; Batman's Strangest Cases

LINCOLN-16 — Skarwood Productions

1 ❑ Aug 1997 Cover: 2.95 **NM** value: **Cover or less**

LINDA — Ajax

1 ❑ Apr 1954 Cover: 0.10 **NM** value: **100.00**
2 ❑ Jun 1954 Cover: 0.10 **NM** value: **75.00**
3 ❑ Aug 1954 Cover: 0.10 **NM** value: **50.00**
4 ❑ Oct 1954 Cover: 0.10 **NM** value: **50.00**

LINDA CARTER, STUDENT NURSE — Atlas

1 ❑ Sep 1961 Cover: 0.10 **NM** value: **40.00**
• **CGC:** 1 graded, best 6.5
2 ❑ Nov 1961 Cover: 0.10 **NM** value: **25.00**
• **CGC:** 1 graded, best 7.5
3 ❑ Jan 1962 Cover: 0.10 **NM** value: **25.00**
4 ❑ Mar 1962 Cover: 0.12 **NM** value: **25.00**
5 ❑ May 1962 Cover: 0.12 **NM** value: **25.00**
6 ❑ Jul 1962 Cover: 0.12 **NM** value: **20.00**
7 ❑ Sep 1962 Cover: 0.12 **NM** value: **20.00**
8 ❑ Nov 1962 Cover: 0.12 **NM** value: **20.00**
9 ❑ Jan 1963 Cover: 0.12 **NM** value: **20.00**

LIONHEART — Awesome

1/A ❑ Aug 1999 Cover: 2.99 **NM** value: **5.00**
Circ: Diamd. preorders: **30,041**
• Dynamic Forces variant **A:** Ian Churchill **W:** Jeph Loeb; Ian Churchill
1/B ❑ Aug 1999 Cover: 2.99 **NM** value: **Cover or less**
Women, treasure chest on cover. **A:** Ian Churchill **W:** Jeph Loeb; Ian Churchill
Ash 1 ❑ Jul 1999 **NM** value: **3.00**
• Wizard World '99 preview edition. **A:** Ian Churchill **W:** Jeph Loeb; Ian Churchill

LION KING, THE (DISNEY'S...) — Marvel

1 ❑ Jul 1994 Cover: 2.50 **NM** value: **Cover or less**
Circ: CapCity orders: **10,500** • **CGC:** 1 graded, best 7.5
A: Sparky Moore **W:** Bobbi J.G. Weiss

LIPPY THE LION AND HARDY HAR HAR — Gold Key

1 ❑ Mar 1963 **NM** value: **100.00**
• **CGC:** 1 graded, best 6.5

LIPSTICK — Rip Off

All issues are adults only.

1 ❑ May 1992, b&w Cover: 2.50 **NM** value: **Cover or less**

LISA COMICS — Bongo

1 ❑ Cover: 2.25 **NM** value: **Cover or less**
Circ: CapCity orders: **15,000**
One-shot. 📖 Lisa in Wordland; Lisa's Adventures in Wordland **A:** Bill Morrison; Chris Clements; Matt Groening(cover); Mili Smythe; Stephanie Gladden **W:** Mary Trainor

Other grades: Multiply prices above by **1.5 for Mint • 2/3 for Very Fine • 1/3 for Fine • 1/5 for Very Good • 1/8 for Good**

LITA FORD: THE QUEEN OF HEAVY METAL

Rock-It Comics

1 ❑ Cover: 3.95 **NM** value: **5.00**
Circ: CapCity orders: **4,900**

LITTLE AL OF THE FBI

Ziff-Davis

10 ❑ ca. 1950 Cover: 0.10 **NM** value: **100.00**
• **CGC:** 1 graded, best 7.0
11 ❑ Apr 1951 Cover: 0.10 **NM** value: **75.00**

LITTLE AL OF THE SECRET SERVICE

Ziff-Davis

1 ❑ Jul 1951 Cover: 0.10 **NM** value: **100.00**
2 ❑ Sep 1951 Cover: 0.10 **NM** value: **75.00**
• **CGC:** 1 graded, best 8.0
3 ❑ Win 1951 Cover: 0.10 **NM** value: **75.00**

LITTLE AMBROSE

Archie

1 ❑ Sep 1958 Cover: 0.10 **NM** value: **100.00**

LITTLE ANGEL

Pines

5 ❑ ca. 1954 Cover: 0.10 **NM** value: **24.00**
• Previous issues exist?
6 ❑ ca. 1955 Cover: 0.10 **NM** value: **2.00**
7 ❑ ca. 1956 Cover: 0.10 **NM** value: **2.00**
8 ❑ ca. 1956 Cover: 0.10 **NM** value: **2.00**
9 ❑ ca. 1956 Cover: 0.10 **NM** value: **2.00**
10 ❑ ca. 1957 Cover: 0.10 **NM** value: **16.00**
11 ❑ ca. 1957 Cover: 0.10 **NM** value: **16.00**
12 ❑ ca. 1957 Cover: 0.10 **NM** value: **16.00**
13 ❑ ca. 1958 Cover: 0.10 **NM** value: **16.00**
14 ❑ ca. 1958 Cover: 0.10 **NM** value: **16.00**
15 ❑ ca. 1958 Cover: 0.10 **NM** value: **16.00**
16 ❑ ca. 1959 Cover: 0.10 **NM** value: **16.00**

LITTLE ANNIE ROONEY

David McKay

1 ❑ ca. 1948 Cover: 0.10 **NM** value: **100.00**
2 ❑ ca. 1948 Cover: 0.10 **NM** value: **50.00**
3 ❑ ca. 1948 Cover: 0.10 **NM** value: **50.00**

LITTLE ARCHIE

Archie

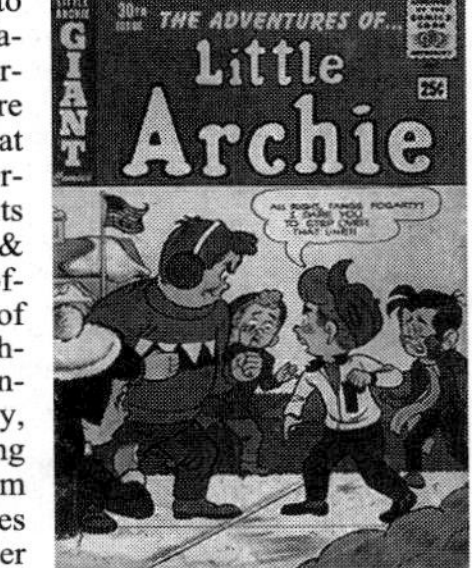

Although the series purports to tell the stories of America's favorite teenager as a boy, Little Archie is in many ways more mature and absorbing than the series that spawned it. Thanks to the masterful drawing and scripting of its creator Bob Bolling (Archie & Friends, Betty), Little Archie offers a highly entertaining mix of humor and adventure. Throughout the series young Archie Andrews, his faithful dog Spotty, and the rest of the Riverdale gang encounter dangers ranging from irate teachers and school bullies to natural disasters and sinister criminals. The title enjoyed a long run as a monthly comic and giant-sized quarterly before ending in 1983. Many of the original stories were reprinted in several of the Archie Digest titles.

1 ❑ ca. 1956 Cover: 0.10 **NM** value: **425.00**
• **CGC:** 2 graded, best 7.0
2 ❑ Cover: 0.10 **NM** value: **160.00**
3 ❑ Cover: 0.25 **NM** value: **110.00**
4 ❑ Cover: 0.25 **NM** value: **75.00**
5 ❑ Cover: 0.25 **NM** value: **75.00**
6 ❑ 1958 Cover: 0.25 **NM** value: **52.00**
7 ❑ 1958 Cover: 0.25 **NM** value: **52.00**
8 ❑ 1958 Cover: 0.25 **NM** value: **52.00**
9 ❑ Cover: 0.25 **NM** value: **52.00**
10 ❑ Spr 1959 Cover: 0.25 **NM** value: **52.00**
• **CGC:** 1 graded, best 9.0
11 ❑ Sum 1959 Cover: 0.25 **NM** value: **34.00**
12 ❑ Fal 1959 Cover: 0.25 **NM** value: **34.00**
13 ❑ Win 1959 Cover: 0.25 **NM** value: **34.00**
14 ❑ Spr 1960 Cover: 0.25 **NM** value: **34.00**
Circ: Statement: **210,089**
15 ❑ Sum 1960 Cover: 0.25 **NM** value: **34.00**
Circ: Statement: **210,089**
16 ❑ Fal 1960 Cover: 0.25 **NM** value: **34.00**
Circ: Statement: **210,089**
17 ❑ Win 1960 Cover: 0.25 **NM** value: **34.00**
Circ: Statement: **210,089**
18 ❑ Spr 1961 Cover: 0.25 **NM** value: **34.00**
19 ❑ Sum 1961 Cover: 0.25 **NM** value: **34.00**
20 ❑ Fal 1961 Cover: 0.25 **NM** value: **34.00**
21 ❑ Win 1961 Cover: 0.25 **NM** value: **22.00**
22 ❑ Spr 1962 Cover: 0.25 **NM** value: **22.00**
23 ❑ Sum 1962 Cover: 0.25 **NM** value: **22.00**
24 ❑ Fal 1962 Cover: 0.25 **NM** value: **22.00**
25 ❑ Win 1962 Cover: 0.25 **NM** value: **22.00**
26 ❑ Spr 1963 Cover: 0.25 **NM** value: **22.00**
Circ: Statement: **195,414**
27 ❑ Sum 1963 Cover: 0.25 **NM** value: **22.00**
Circ: Statement: **195,414**
28 ❑ Fal 1963 Cover: 0.25 **NM** value: **22.00**
Circ: Statement: **195,414**
29 ❑ Win 1963 Cover: 0.25 **NM** value: **22.00**
Circ: Statement: **195,414**
30 ❑ Spr 1964 Cover: 0.25 **NM** value: **22.00**
📖 Bully For You; Spoty Takes the Cake; Li'l Jinx: Off the Hook; The Glacier Glow Gun; The Great Chief (text story); Stampede; A Happy Holiday; The Adventure in Money; Like Cats and Dogs (text story); With a Mission;
31 ❑ Sum 1964 Cover: 0.25 **NM** value: **22.00**
32 ❑ Fal 1964 Cover: 0.25 **NM** value: **22.00**
33 ❑ Win 1964 Cover: 0.25 **NM** value: **22.00**
34 ❑ Spr 1965 Cover: 0.25 **NM** value: **22.00**
35 ❑ Sum 1965 Cover: 0.25 **NM** value: **22.00**
36 ❑ Fal 1965 Cover: 0.25 **NM** value: **22.00**
37 ❑ Win 1965 Cover: 0.25 **NM** value: **22.00**
38 ❑ Spr 1966 Cover: 0.25 **NM** value: **22.00**
Circ: Statement: **206,321**
39 ❑ Sum 1966 Cover: 0.25 **NM** value: **22.00**
Circ: Statement: **206,321**
40 ❑ Fal 1966 Cover: 0.25 **NM** value: **22.00**
Circ: Statement: **206,321**
41 ❑ Win 1966 Cover: 0.25 **NM** value: **15.00**
Circ: Statement: **206,321**
42 ❑ Spr 1967 Cover: 0.25 **NM** value: **15.00**
Circ: Statement: **191,623**
43 ❑ Sum 1967 Cover: 0.25 **NM** value: **15.00**
Circ: Statement: **191,623**
44 ❑ Fal 1967 Cover: 0.25 **NM** value: **15.00**
Circ: Statement: **191,623**
45 ❑ Win 1967 Cover: 0.25 **NM** value: **15.00**
Circ: Statement: **191,623**
46 ❑ Spr 1968 Cover: 0.25 **NM** value: **15.00**
Circ: Statement: **230,347**
47 ❑ Sum 1968 Cover: 0.25 **NM** value: **15.00**
Circ: Statement: **230,347**
48 ❑ Jul 1968 Cover: 0.25 **NM** value: **15.00**
Circ: Statement: **230,347**
49 ❑ Sep 1968 Cover: 0.25 **NM** value: **15.00**
Circ: Statement: **230,347**
50 ❑ Nov 1968 Cover: 0.25 **NM** value: **15.00**
Circ: Statement: **230,347**
51 ❑ Jan 1969 Cover: 0.25 **NM** value: **15.00**
52 ❑ Mar 1969 Cover: 0.25 **NM** value: **15.00**
53 ❑ May 1969 Cover: 0.25 **NM** value: **15.00**
• Has 1968 Statement, filed 11/1/68; avg print run 370,424; avg sales 228,072; avg subs 2,275; avg total paid and max existent 230,347; 38% of run returned
54 ❑ Jul 1969 Cover: 0.25 **NM** value: **15.00**
55 ❑ Sep 1969 Cover: 0.25 **NM** value: **15.00**
56 ❑ Nov 1969 Cover: 0.25 **NM** value: **15.00**
57 ❑ Jan 1970 Cover: 0.25 **NM** value: **15.00**
Circ: Statement: **223,561**
58 ❑ Mar 1970 Cover: 0.25 **NM** value: **15.00**
Circ: Statement: **223,561**
59 ❑ May 1970 Cover: 0.25 **NM** value: **15.00**
Circ: Statement: **223,561**
60 ❑ Jul 1970 Cover: 0.25 **NM** value: **15.00**
Circ: Statement: **223,561**
61 ❑ Sep 1970 Cover: 0.25 **NM** value: **11.00**
Circ: Statement: **223,561**
62 ❑ Nov 1970 Cover: 0.25 **NM** value: **11.00**
Circ: Statement: **223,561**
63 ❑ Jan 1971 Cover: 0.25 **NM** value: **11.00**
Circ: Statement: **211,357**
64 ❑ Mar 1971 Cover: 0.25 **NM** value: **11.00**
Circ: Statement: **211,357**
65 ❑ May 1971 Cover: 0.25 **NM** value: **11.00**
Circ: Statement: **211,357**
• Has 1970 Statement, filed 10/1/1970; avg print run 384,485; avg sales 220,941; avg subs 2,620; avg total paid and max existent 223,561; 42% of run returned
66 ❑ Jul 1971 Cover: 0.25 **NM** value: **11.00**
Circ: Statement: **211,357**
67 ❑ Sep 1971 Cover: 0.25 **NM** value: **11.00**
Circ: Statement: **211,357**
68 ❑ Nov 1971 Cover: 0.25 **NM** value: **11.00**
Circ: Statement: **211,357**
69 ❑ Jan 1972 Cover: 0.25 **NM** value: **11.00**
Circ: Statement: **191,219**
70 ❑ Mar 1972 Cover: 0.25 **NM** value: **11.00**
Circ: Statement: **191,219**
71 ❑ May 1972 Cover: 0.25 **NM** value: **11.00**
Circ: Statement: **191,219**
• Has 1971 Statement, filed 10/1/1971; avg print run 388,254; avg sales 208,739; avg subs 2,618; avg total paid and max existent 211,357; 43% of run returned
72 ❑ Jul 1972 Cover: 0.25 **NM** value: **11.00**
Circ: Statement: **191,219**
73 ❑ Sep 1972 Cover: 0.25 **NM** value: **11.00**
Circ: Statement: **191,219**
74 ❑ Oct 1972 Cover: 0.25 **NM** value: **11.00**
Circ: Statement: **191,219**
75 ❑ Dec 1972 Cover: 0.25 **NM** value: **11.00**
Circ: Statement: **191,219**
76 ❑ Feb 1973 Cover: 0.25 **NM** value: **11.00**
Circ: Statement: **184,395**
77 ❑ Apr 1973 Cover: 0.25 **NM** value: **11.00**
Circ: Statement: **184,395**
78 ❑ May 1973 Cover: 0.25 **NM** value: **11.00**
Circ: Statement: **184,395**
• Has 1972 Statement; avg total paid circ 191,219
79 ❑ Jul 1973 Cover: 0.25 **NM** value: **11.00**
Circ: Statement: **184,395**
80 ❑ Aug 1973 Cover: 0.25 **NM** value: **11.00**
Circ: Statement: **184,395**
81 ❑ Sep 1973 Cover: 0.25 **NM** value: **8.00**
Circ: Statement: **184,395**
82 ❑ Oct 1973 Cover: 0.25 **NM** value: **8.00**
Circ: Statement: **184,395**
83 ❑ Dec 1973 Cover: 0.25 **NM** value: **8.00**
Circ: Statement: **184,395**
84 ❑ Feb 1974 Cover: 0.25 **NM** value: **8.00**
Circ: Statement: **178,824**
85 ❑ Apr 1974 Cover: 0.25 **NM** value: **8.00**
Circ: Statement: **178,824**
• Has 1973 Statement, filed 10/1/73; avg print run 376,385; avg sales 183,195; avg subs 1,200; avg total paid and max existent 184,395; 51% of run returned
86 ❑ May 1974 Cover: 0.25 **NM** value: **8.00**
Circ: Statement: **178,824**
87 ❑ Jul 1974 Cover: 0.25 **NM** value: **8.00**
Circ: Statement: **178,824**
88 ❑ Aug 1974 Cover: 0.25 **NM** value: **8.00**
Circ: Statement: **178,824**
89 ❑ Sep 1974 Cover: 0.25 **NM** value: **8.00**
Circ: Statement: **178,824**
90 ❑ Oct 1974 Cover: 0.25 **NM** value: **8.00**
Circ: Statement: **178,824**
91 ❑ Dec 1974 Cover: 0.25 **NM** value: **8.00**
Circ: Statement: **178,824**
92 ❑ Feb 1975 Cover: 0.25 **NM** value: **8.00**
Circ: Statement: **151,253**
93 ❑ Mar 1975 Cover: 0.25 **NM** value: **8.00**
Circ: Statement: **151,253**
94 ❑ Apr 1975 Cover: 0.25 **NM** value: **8.00**
Circ: Statement: **151,253**
• Has 1974 Statement, filed 10/1/74; avg print run 357,871; avg sales 177,531; avg subs 1,293; avg total paid and max existent 178,824; 50% of run returned
95 ❑ May 1975 Cover: 0.25 **NM** value: **8.00**
Circ: Statement: **151,253**
96 ❑ Jul 1975 Cover: 0.25 **NM** value: **8.00**
Circ: Statement: **151,253**
97 ❑ Aug 1975 Cover: 0.25 **NM** value: **8.00**
Circ: Statement: **151,253**
98 ❑ Sep 1975 Cover: 0.25 **NM** value: **8.00**
Circ: Statement: **151,253**
99 ❑ Oct 1975 Cover: 0.25 **NM** value: **8.00**
Circ: Statement: **151,253**
100 ❑ Nov 1975 Cover: 0.25 **NM** value: **8.00**
Circ: Statement: **151,253**
101 ❑ Dec 1975 Cover: 0.25 **NM** value: **4.50**
Circ: Statement: **151,253**
102 ❑ Jan 1976 Cover: 0.25 **NM** value: **4.50**
Circ: Statement: **134,597**
103 ❑ Feb 1976 Cover: 0.30 **NM** value: **4.50**
Circ: Statement: **134,597**
104 ❑ Mar 1976 Cover: 0.30 **NM** value: **4.50**
Circ: Statement: **134,597**
105 ❑ Apr 1976 Cover: 0.30 **NM** value: **4.50**
Circ: Statement: **134,597**
106 ❑ May 1976 Cover: 0.30 **NM** value: **4.50**
Circ: Statement: **134,597**
107 ❑ Jun 1976 Cover: 0.30 **NM** value: **4.50**
Circ: Statement: **134,597**
108 ❑ Jul 1976 Cover: 0.30 **NM** value: **4.50**
Circ: Statement: **134,597**
109 ❑ Aug 1976 Cover: 0.30 **NM** value: **4.50**
Circ: Statement: **134,597**
110 ❑ Sep 1976 Cover: 0.30 **NM** value: **4.50**
Circ: Statement: **134,597**
111 ❑ Oct 1976 Cover: 0.30 **NM** value: **4.50**
Circ: Statement: **134,597**
112 ❑ Nov 1976 Cover: 0.30 **NM** value: **4.50**
Circ: Statement: **134,597**
113 ❑ Dec 1976 Cover: 0.30 **NM** value: **4.50**
Circ: Statement: **134,597**
114 ❑ Jan 1977 Cover: 0.30 **NM** value: **4.50**
Circ: Statement: **124,932**
115 ❑ Feb 1977 Cover: 0.30 **NM** value: **4.50**
Circ: Statement: **124,932**
116 ❑ Mar 1977 Cover: 0.30 **NM** value: **4.50**
Circ: Statement: **124,932**
117 ❑ Apr 1977 Cover: 0.30 **NM** value: **4.50**
Circ: Statement: **124,932**
• Has 1976 Statement, filed 10/1/76; avg print run 313,638; avg sales 134,260; avg subs 337; avg total paid 134,597; office use 300; max existent 134,897; 58% of run returned
118 ❑ May 1977 Cover: 0.30 **NM** value: **4.50**
Circ: Statement: **124,932**
119 ❑ Jun 1977 Cover: 0.30 **NM** value: **4.50**
Circ: Statement: **124,932**
120 ❑ Jul 1977 Cover: 0.35 **NM** value: **4.50**
Circ: Statement: **124,932**
121 ❑ Aug 1977 Cover: 0.35 **NM** value: **3.00**
Circ: Statement: **124,932**
122 ❑ Sep 1977 Cover: 0.35 **NM** value: **3.00**
Circ: Statement: **124,932**
123 ❑ Oct 1977 Cover: 0.35 **NM** value: **3.00**
Circ: Statement: **124,932**
124 ❑ Nov 1977 Cover: 0.35 **NM** value: **3.00**
Circ: Statement: **124,932**
125 ❑ Dec 1977 Cover: 0.35 **NM** value: **3.00**
Circ: Statement: **124,932**
126 ❑ Jan 1978 Cover: 0.35 **NM** value: **3.00**
Circ: Statement: **106,314**
127 ❑ Feb 1978 Cover: 0.35 **NM** value: **3.00**
Circ: Statement: **106,314**
128 ❑ Mar 1978 Cover: 0.35 **NM** value: **3.00**
Circ: Statement: **106,314**
129 ❑ Apr 1978 Cover: 0.35 **NM** value: **3.00**
Circ: Statement: **106,314**
• Has 1977 Statement; avg total paid circ 124,932
130 ❑ May 1978 Cover: 0.35 **NM** value: **3.00**
Circ: Statement: **106,314**
131 ❑ Jun 1978 Cover: 0.35 **NM** value: **3.00**
Circ: Statement: **106,314**
132 ❑ Jul 1978 Cover: 0.35 **NM** value: **3.00**
Circ: Statement: **106,314**
133 ❑ Aug 1978 Cover: 0.35 **NM** value: **3.00**
Circ: Statement: **106,314**
134 ❑ Sep 1978 Cover: 0.35 **NM** value: **3.00**
Circ: Statement: **106,314**
135 ❑ Oct 1978 Cover: 0.35 **NM** value: **3.00**
Circ: Statement: **106,314**
136 ❑ Nov 1978 Cover: 0.35 **NM** value: **3.00**
Circ: Statement: **106,314**

CGC-graded: Multiply prices above by **33 for 9.9 M • 16 for 9.8 NM/M • 7 for 9.6 NM+ • 5 for 9.4 NM • 2.5 for 9.2 NM- • 1.5 for 9.0 VF/NM**

137 ❑ Dec 1978 Cover: 0.35 **NM** value: **3.00**
Circ: Statement: **106,314**
138 ❑ Jan 1979 Cover: 0.35 **NM** value: **3.00**
139 ❑ Feb 1979 Cover: 0.35 **NM** value: **3.00**
140 ❑ Mar 1979 Cover: 0.35 **NM** value: **3.00**
141 ❑ Apr 1979 Cover: 0.40 **NM** value: **2.25**
• Has 1978 Statement, filed 10/1/78; avg print run 291,579; avg sales 106,242; avg subs 72; avg total paid 106,314; office use 300; max existent 106,614; 63% of run returned
142 ❑ May 1979 Cover: 0.40 **NM** value: **2.25**
143 ❑ Jun 1979 Cover: 0.40 **NM** value: **2.25**
144 ❑ Jul 1979 Cover: 0.40 **NM** value: **2.25**
145 ❑ Aug 1979 Cover: 0.40 **NM** value: **2.25**
146 ❑ Sep 1979 Cover: 0.40 **NM** value: **2.25**
147 ❑ Oct 1979 Cover: 0.40 **NM** value: **2.25**
148 ❑ Nov 1979 Cover: 0.40 **NM** value: **2.25**
149 ❑ Dec 1979 Cover: 0.40 **NM** value: **2.25**
150 ❑ Jan 1980 Cover: 0.40 **NM** value: **2.25**
151 ❑ Feb 1980 Cover: 0.40 **NM** value: **2.25**
152 ❑ Mar 1980 Cover: 0.40 **NM** value: **2.25**
153 ❑ Apr 1980 Cover: 0.40 **NM** value: **2.25**
154 ❑ May 1980 Cover: 0.40 **NM** value: **2.25**
155 ❑ Jun 1980 Cover: 0.40 **NM** value: **2.25**
156 ❑ Jul 1980 Cover: 0.40 **NM** value: **2.25**
157 ❑ Aug 1980 Cover: 0.50 **NM** value: **2.25**
158 ❑ Sep 1980 Cover: 0.50 **NM** value: **2.25**
159 ❑ Oct 1980 Cover: 0.50 **NM** value: **2.25**
160 ❑ Nov 1980 Cover: 0.50 **NM** value: **2.25**
161 ❑ Dec 1980 Cover: 0.50 **NM** value: **2.25**
162 ❑ Jan 1981 Cover: 0.50 **NM** value: **2.25**
163 ❑ Feb 1981 Cover: 0.50 **NM** value: **2.25**
164 ❑ Mar 1981 Cover: 0.50 **NM** value: **2.25**
165 ❑ Apr 1981 Cover: 0.50 **NM** value: **2.25**
166 ❑ May 1981 Cover: 0.50 **NM** value: **2.25**
167 ❑ Jun 1981 Cover: 0.50 **NM** value: **2.25**
168 ❑ Jul 1981 Cover: 0.50 **NM** value: **2.25**
169 ❑ Aug 1981 Cover: 0.50 **NM** value: **2.25**
170 ❑ Sep 1981 Cover: 0.50 **NM** value: **2.25**
171 ❑ Oct 1981 Cover: 0.50 **NM** value: **2.25**
172 ❑ Nov 1981 Cover: 0.50 **NM** value: **2.25**
173 ❑ 1982 Cover: 0.60 **NM** value: **2.25**
174 ❑ 1982 Cover: 0.60 **NM** value: **2.25**
175 ❑ 1982 Cover: 0.60 **NM** value: **2.25**
176 ❑ 1982 Cover: 0.60 **NM** value: **2.25**
177 ❑ 1982 Cover: 0.60 **NM** value: **2.25**
178 ❑ 1982 Cover: 0.60 **NM** value: **2.25**
179 ❑ 1982 Cover: 0.60 **NM** value: **2.25**
180 ❑ ca. 1983 Cover: 0.60 **NM** value: **3.00**

LITTLE ARCHIE DIGEST MAGAZINE — Archie

1 ❑ 1991 Cover: 1.50 **NM** value: **3.00**
2 ❑ 1991 Cover: 1.50 **NM** value: **2.00**
3 ❑ 1991 Cover: 1.50 **NM** value: **2.00**
4 ❑ 1991 Cover: 1.50 **NM** value: **2.00**
5 ❑ 1992 Cover: 1.50 **NM** value: **2.00**
6 ❑ 1992 Cover: 1.50 **NM** value: **2.00**
7 ❑ 1992 Cover: 1.50 **NM** value: **2.00**
8 ❑ 1992 Cover: 1.50 **NM** value: **2.00**
9 ❑ 1992 Cover: 1.50 **NM** value: **2.00**
10 ❑ **NM** value: **2.00**
11 ❑ Cover: 1.75 **NM** value: **Cover or less**
12 ❑ Cover: 1.75 **NM** value: **Cover or less**
13 ❑ Cover: 1.75 **NM** value: **Cover or less**
14 ❑ Aug 1995 Cover: 1.75 **NM** value: **Cover or less**
15 ❑ Oct 1995 Cover: 1.75 **NM** value: **Cover or less**
16 ❑ Jun 1996 Cover: 1.75 **NM** value: **Cover or less**
17 ❑ Sep 1996 Cover: 1.79 **NM** value: **Cover or less**
18 ❑ Mar 1997 Cover: 1.79 **NM** value: **Cover or less**
19 ❑ Jun 1997 Cover: 1.79 **NM** value: **Cover or less**
Circ: Diamd. preorders: **2,213**
20 ❑ Sep 1997 Cover: 1.79 **NM** value: **Cover or less**
21 ❑ Mar 1998 Cover: 1.95 **NM** value: **Cover or less**
22 ❑ Cover: 1.95 **NM** value: **Cover or less**
23 ❑ Cover: 1.95 **NM** value: **Cover or less**
24 ❑ Cover: 1.95 **NM** value: **Cover or less**
25 ❑ Cover: 1.95 **NM** value: **Cover or less**

LITTLE ARCHIE MYSTERY — Archie

1 ❑ Aug 1963 Cover: 0.12 **NM** value: **100.00**
2 ❑ Oct 1963 Cover: 0.12 **NM** value: **50.00**

LITTLE ASPIRIN — Marvel

1 ❑ Jul 1949 Cover: 0.10 **NM** value: **100.00**
2 ❑ Sep 1949 Cover: 0.10 **NM** value: **65.00**
3 ❑ Nov 1949 Cover: 0.10 **NM** value: **35.00**

LITTLE AUDREY (ST. JOHN) — St. John

1 ❑ Apr 1948 Cover: 0.10 **NM** value: **300.00**
2 ❑ Jul 1948 Cover: 0.10 **NM** value: **150.00**
3 ❑ Oct 1948 Cover: 0.10 **NM** value: **100.00**
4 ❑ Jan 1949 Cover: 0.10 **NM** value: **100.00**
5 ❑ Apr 1949 Cover: 0.10 **NM** value: **100.00**
6 ❑ Jul 1949 Cover: 0.10 **NM** value: **75.00**
7 ❑ 1949 Cover: 0.10 **NM** value: **75.00**
8 ❑ 1949 Cover: 0.10 **NM** value: **75.00**
9 ❑ 1950 Cover: 0.10 **NM** value: **75.00**
10 ❑ 1950 Cover: 0.10 **NM** value: **75.00**
11 ❑ Jul 1950 Cover: 0.10 **NM** value: **50.00**
12 ❑ Sep 1950 Cover: 0.10 **NM** value: **50.00**
13 ❑ Nov 1950 Cover: 0.10 **NM** value: **50.00**
14 ❑ Jan 1951 Cover: 0.10 **NM** value: **50.00**
15 ❑ Mar 1951 Cover: 0.10 **NM** value: **50.00**
16 ❑ May 1951 Cover: 0.10 **NM** value: **50.00**
17 ❑ ca. 1951 Cover: 0.10 **NM** value: **50.00**
18 ❑ ca. 1951 Cover: 0.10 **NM** value: **50.00**
19 ❑ ca. 1951 Cover: 0.10 **NM** value: **50.00**
20 ❑ ca. 1951 Cover: 0.10 **NM** value: **40.00**
21 ❑ ca. 1951 Cover: 0.10 **NM** value: **40.00**
22 ❑ ca. 1952 Cover: 0.10 **NM** value: **40.00**
23 ❑ ca. 1952 Cover: 0.10 **NM** value: **40.00**
24 ❑ ca. 1952 Cover: 0.10 **NM** value: **40.00**

LITTLE AUDREY (HARVEY) — Harvey

29 ❑ Apr 1953 Cover: 0.10 **NM** value: **60.00**
38 ❑ Oct 1954 Cover: 0.10 **NM** value: **45.00**
39 ❑ Dec 1954 Cover: 0.10 **NM** value: **45.00**
40 ❑ Feb 1955 Cover: 0.10 **NM** value: **45.00**
41 ❑ Apr 1955 Cover: 0.10 **NM** value: **45.00**
42 ❑ Jun 1955 Cover: 0.10 **NM** value: **45.00**
43 ❑ Aug 1955 Cover: 0.10 **NM** value: **45.00**
44 ❑ Oct 1945 Cover: 0.10 **NM** value: **45.00**
45 ❑ Dec 1955 Cover: 0.10 **NM** value: **45.00**
46 ❑ Feb 1956 Cover: 0.10 **NM** value: **40.00**
47 ❑ Apr 1956 Cover: 0.10 **NM** value: **40.00**
48 ❑ Jun 1956 Cover: 0.10 **NM** value: **40.00**
49 ❑ Aug 1956 Cover: 0.10 **NM** value: **40.00**
50 ❑ Oct 1956 Cover: 0.10 **NM** value: **40.00**
51 ❑ Dec 1956 Cover: 0.10 **NM** value: **40.00**
52 ❑ Feb 1957 Cover: 0.10 **NM** value: **40.00**
53 ❑ Apr 1957 Cover: 0.10 **NM** value: **40.00**
25 ❑ Aug 1952 Cover: 0.10 **NM** value: **100.00**
26 ❑ Oct 1952 Cover: 0.10 **NM** value: **60.00**
27 ❑ Dec 1952 Cover: 0.10 **NM** value: **60.00**
28 ❑ Feb 1953 Cover: 0.10 **NM** value: **60.00**
30 ❑ Jun 1953 Cover: 0.10 **NM** value: **60.00**
31 ❑ Aug 1953 Cover: 0.10 **NM** value: **50.00**
32 ❑ Oct 1953 Cover: 0.10 **NM** value: **50.00**
33 ❑ Dec 1953 Cover: 0.10 **NM** value: **50.00**
34 ❑ Feb 1954 Cover: 0.10 **NM** value: **50.00**
35 ❑ Apr 1954 Cover: 0.10 **NM** value: **50.00**
36 ❑ Jun 1954 Cover: 0.10 **NM** value: **45.00**
37 ❑ Aug 1954 Cover: 0.10 **NM** value: **45.00**

LITTLE AUDREY (VOL. 2) — Harvey

1 ❑ Aug 1992 Cover: 1.25 **NM** value: **1.50**
📖 It Walks Like a Man; You Make Me Laugh; A moose Named Marvin
2 ❑ 1992 Cover: 1.25 **NM** value: **Cover or less**
3 ❑ 1992 Cover: 1.25 **NM** value: **Cover or less**
4 ❑ 1992 Cover: 1.25 **NM** value: **Cover or less**
5 ❑ 1993 Cover: 1.25 **NM** value: **Cover or less**
6 ❑ 1993 Cover: 1.50 **NM** value: **Cover or less**
7 ❑ 1993 Cover: 1.50 **NM** value: **Cover or less**
8 ❑ 1993 Cover: 1.50 **NM** value: **Cover or less**
9 ❑ 1993 Cover: 1.25 **NM** value: **Cover or less**

LITTLE AUDREY AND MELVIN — Harvey

Little Audrey and Melvin are two mischievous kids in the time-honored tradition of Little Lulu. In fact, Little Audrey was created when Paramount's Famous Studios found its Little Lulu cartoons to be doing so well that it could drop her and keep all the money, if it introduced the new character. Cartoon plots featured her in fantasy adventures from which she learned lessons.

In comic books, Audrey is the brains of the operation, frequently foiling her freckle-faced pal Melvin with harmless kid-mischief pranks. The stories cover themes popular with young readers, like dealing with parents who just don't get it, ways to get out of doing chores, the tedium of shopping for clothes, and misunderstandings that crop up when kids play "grown up." Audrey and Melvin stories run about four pages, with frequent gags leading to a punchline or finish. This series is not to be confused with Little Audrey or the longer Playful Little Audrey.

1 ❑ May 1962 Cover: 0.12 **NM** value: **45.00**
2 ❑ Jul 1962 Cover: 0.12 **NM** value: **25.00**
3 ❑ Sep 1962 Cover: 0.12 **NM** value: **18.00**
4 ❑ Nov 1962 Cover: 0.12 **NM** value: **18.00**
5 ❑ Jan 1963 Cover: 0.12 **NM** value: **18.00**
6 ❑ 1963 Cover: 0.12 **NM** value: **14.00**
7 ❑ 1963 Cover: 0.12 **NM** value: **14.00**
8 ❑ 1963 Cover: 0.12 **NM** value: **14.00**
9 ❑ 1963 Cover: 0.12 **NM** value: **14.00**
10 ❑ 1964 Cover: 0.12 **NM** value: **14.00**
11 ❑ 1964 Cover: 0.12 **NM** value: **12.00**
12 ❑ 1964 Cover: 0.12 **NM** value: **12.00**
13 ❑ 1964 Cover: 0.12 **NM** value: **12.00**
14 ❑ Sep 1964 Cover: 0.12 **NM** value: **12.00**
15 ❑ Nov 1964 Cover: 0.12 **NM** value: **12.00**
16 ❑ Jan 1965 Cover: 0.12 **NM** value: **12.00**
17 ❑ Mar 1965 Cover: 0.12 **NM** value: **12.00**
18 ❑ May 1965 Cover: 0.12 **NM** value: **12.00**
19 ❑ Jul 1965 Cover: 0.12 **NM** value: **12.00**
20 ❑ Sep 1965 Cover: 0.12 **NM** value: **12.00**
📖 A Dollar the Hard Way; Instant Make-Up; The Mystery Machine; Sly Like a Fox (text story); Temper Test;
21 ❑ Nov 1965 Cover: 0.12 **NM** value: **9.00**
22 ❑ Jan 1966 Cover: 0.12 **NM** value: **9.00**
23 ❑ Mar 1966 Cover: 0.12 **NM** value: **9.00**
24 ❑ May 1966 Cover: 0.12 **NM** value: **9.00**
25 ❑ Jul 1966 Cover: 0.12 **NM** value: **9.00**
26 ❑ Sep 1966 Cover: 0.12 **NM** value: **9.00**
27 ❑ Oct 1966 Cover: 0.12 **NM** value: **9.00**
28 ❑ Jan 1967 Cover: 0.12 **NM** value: **9.00**
29 ❑ Mar 1967 Cover: 0.12 **NM** value: **9.00**
30 ❑ May 1967 Cover: 0.12 **NM** value: **9.00**
31 ❑ Jul 1967 Cover: 0.12 **NM** value: **6.00**
32 ❑ Sep 1967 Cover: 0.12 **NM** value: **6.00**
33 ❑ Nov 1967 Cover: 0.12 **NM** value: **6.00**
34 ❑ Jan 1968 Cover: 0.12 **NM** value: **6.00**
35 ❑ Sep 1968 Cover: 0.12 **NM** value: **6.00**
36 ❑ Nov 1968 Cover: 0.12 **NM** value: **6.00**
37 ❑ Jan 1969 Cover: 0.12 **NM** value: **6.00**
38 ❑ Mar 1969 Cover: 0.12 **NM** value: **6.00**
39 ❑ Apr 1969 Cover: 0.12 **NM** value: **6.00**
40 ❑ Jun 1969 Cover: 0.12 **NM** value: **6.00**
41 ❑ Aug 1969 **NM** value: **4.00**
42 ❑ Oct 1969 Cover: 0.15 **NM** value: **4.00**
43 ❑ Dec 1969 Cover: 0.15 **NM** value: **4.00**
44 ❑ Feb 1970 Cover: 0.15 **NM** value: **4.00**
45 ❑ Apr 1970 Cover: 0.15 **NM** value: **4.00**
46 ❑ Aug 1970 Cover: 0.15 **NM** value: **4.00**
47 ❑ Oct 1970 Cover: 0.15 **NM** value: **4.00**
48 ❑ Nov 1970 Cover: 0.15 **NM** value: **4.00**
49 ❑ 1971 Cover: 0.15 **NM** value: **4.00**
50 ❑ Aug 1971 Cover: 0.15 **NM** value: **4.00**
51 ❑ Sep 1971 Cover: 0.25 **NM** value: **4.00**
52 ❑ Nov 1971 Cover: 0.25 **NM** value: **4.00**
53 ❑ 1972 Cover: 0.25 **NM** value: **4.00**
54 ❑ Sep 1972 Cover: 0.25 **NM** value: **4.00**
55 ❑ Nov 1972 Cover: 0.20 **NM** value: **4.00**
56 ❑ Feb 1973 Cover: 0.20 **NM** value: **4.00**
57 ❑ Apr 1973 Cover: 0.20 **NM** value: **4.00**
58 ❑ Jun 1973 Cover: 0.20 **NM** value: **4.00**
59 ❑ Aug 1973 Cover: 0.20 **NM** value: **4.00**
60 ❑ Oct 1973 Cover: 0.20 **NM** value: **4.00**
61 ❑ Dec 1973 Cover: 0.20 **NM** value: **4.00**

LITTLE AUDREY TV FUNTIME — Harvey

1 ❑ Sep 1962 Cover: 0.25 **NM** value: **75.00**
2 ❑ Dec 1962 Cover: 0.25 **NM** value: **50.00**
3 ❑ Mar 1963 Cover: 0.25 **NM** value: **50.00**
4 ❑ Jun 1963 Cover: 0.25 **NM** value: **40.00**
5 ❑ Sep 1963 Cover: 0.25 **NM** value: **40.00**
6 ❑ Dec 1963 Cover: 0.25 **NM** value: **25.00**
7 ❑ Mar 1964 Cover: 0.25 **NM** value: **25.00**
8 ❑ Jun 1964 Cover: 0.25 **NM** value: **25.00**
9 ❑ Sep 1964 Cover: 0.25 **NM** value: **25.00**
10 ❑ Dec 1964 Cover: 0.25 **NM** value: **25.00**
11 ❑ Mar 1965 Cover: 0.25 **NM** value: **25.00**
12 ❑ Jun 1965 Cover: 0.25 **NM** value: **25.00**
13 ❑ Sep 1965 Cover: 0.25 **NM** value: **25.00**
14 ❑ Dec 1965 Cover: 0.25 **NM** value: **25.00**
15 ❑ Mar 1966 Cover: 0.25 **NM** value: **20.00**
16 ❑ 1966 Cover: 0.25 **NM** value: **20.00**
17 ❑ Nov 1966 Cover: 0.25 **NM** value: **20.00**
18 ❑ Mar 1967 Cover: 0.25 **NM** value: **20.00**
19 ❑ 1967 Cover: 0.25 **NM** value: **20.00**
20 ❑ Oct 1967 Cover: 0.25 **NM** value: **20.00**
21 ❑ Dec 1967 Cover: 0.25 **NM** value: **20.00**
22 ❑ 1968 Cover: 0.25 **NM** value: **20.00**
23 ❑ 1968 Cover: 0.25 **NM** value: **20.00**
24 ❑ Sep 1968 Cover: 0.25 **NM** value: **20.00**
• **CGC:** 1 graded, best 9.6
25 ❑ Cover: 0.25 **NM** value: **20.00**
26 ❑ Cover: 0.25 **NM** value: **15.00**
27 ❑ Cover: 0.25 **NM** value: **15.00**
28 ❑ Aug 1969 Cover: 0.25 **NM** value: **15.00**
29 ❑ Cover: 0.25 **NM** value: **15.00**
30 ❑ Dec 1970 Cover: 0.25 **NM** value: **15.00**
31 ❑ Cover: 0.25 **NM** value: **15.00**
32 ❑ Cover: 0.25 **NM** value: **15.00**
33 ❑ Cover: 0.25 **NM** value: **15.00**

LITTLE BEAVER — Dell

3 ❑ Oct 1951 Cover: 0.10 **NM** value: **25.00**
4 ❑ Jan 1952 Cover: 0.10 **NM** value: **25.00**
5 ❑ Apr 1952 Cover: 0.10 **NM** value: **25.00**
6 ❑ Jul 1952 Cover: 0.10 **NM** value: **25.00**
7 ❑ Oct 1952 Cover: 0.10 **NM** value: **25.00**
8 ❑ Jan 1953 Cover: 0.10 **NM** value: **25.00**

LITTLE BIT — St. John

1 ❑ Mar 1949 Cover: 0.10 **NM** value: **25.00**
2 ❑ Jun 1949 Cover: 0.10 **NM** value: **25.00**

LITTLE DOT (VOL. 1) — Harvey

This cute little girl is charming, but she's a girl possessed. She simply can't get enough of dots. She wears dotted clothes, has dotted toys, and keeps a huge collection of dots packed into every drawer and closet in the house. Of course, when your name is Dot (and your Dad's name is "Polka"), it's probably destiny.

A sweet, funny girl, Little Dot is joined in her adventures by a collection of friends, particularly her large and powerful best friend, Little Lotta. Richie Rich, "the poor little rich boy." also appears in this series, having made his first comic-book appearance in issue #1.

1 ❑ Sep 1953 Cover: 0.10 **NM** value: **675.00**
★ 1st Appearance of Richie Rich, Little Dot.
2 ❑ Nov 1953 Cover: 0.10 **NM** value: **340.00**
3 ❑ Jan 1954 Cover: 0.10 **NM** value: **215.00**
4 ❑ Mar 1954 Cover: 0.10 **NM** value: **160.00**
5 ❑ May 1954 Cover: 0.10 **NM** value: **320.00**
• **CGC:** 1 graded, best 5.5
★ Origin of Little Dot's dots on dress.
6 ❑ Jul 1954 Cover: 0.10 **NM** value: **185.00**
First Richie Rich cover.
7 ❑ Sep 1954 Cover: 0.10 **NM** value: **85.00**

Other grades: Multiply prices above by **1.5 for Mint • 2/3 for Very Fine • 1/3 for Fine • 1/5 for Very Good • 1/8 for Good**

8 ☐ Nov 1954 Cover: 0.10 **NM** value: **85.00**
9 ☐ Jan 1955 Cover: 0.10 **NM** value: **85.00**
10 ☐ Mar 1955 Cover: 0.10 **NM** value: **85.00**
11 ☐ May 1955 Cover: 0.10 **NM** value: **64.00**
12 ☐ Jul 1955 Cover: 0.10 **NM** value: **64.00**
13 ☐ Sep 1955 Cover: 0.10 **NM** value: **64.00**
14 ☐ Nov 1955 Cover: 0.10 **NM** value: **64.00**
15 ☐ Jan 1956 Cover: 0.10 **NM** value: **64.00**
16 ☐ Mar 1956 Cover: 0.10 **NM** value: **64.00**
17 ☐ May 1956 Cover: 0.10 **NM** value: **64.00**
18 ☐ Jul 1956 Cover: 0.10 **NM** value: **64.00**
19 ☐ Sep 1956 Cover: 0.10 **NM** value: **64.00**
20 ☐ Nov 1956 Cover: 0.10 **NM** value: **64.00**
21 ☐ Jan 1957 Cover: 0.10 **NM** value: **36.00**
22 ☐ Mar 1957 Cover: 0.10 **NM** value: **36.00**
23 ☐ May 1957 Cover: 0.10 **NM** value: **36.00**
24 ☐ Jul 1957 Cover: 0.10 **NM** value: **36.00**
25 ☐ Sep 1957 Cover: 0.10 **NM** value: **36.00**
26 ☐ Nov 1957 Cover: 0.10 **NM** value: **36.00**
27 ☐ Dec 1957 Cover: 0.10 **NM** value: **36.00**
28 ☐ Jan 1958 Cover: 0.10 **NM** value: **36.00**
29 ☐ Feb 1958 Cover: 0.10 **NM** value: **36.00**
30 ☐ Mar 1958 Cover: 0.10 **NM** value: **36.00**
31 ☐ Apr 1958 Cover: 0.10 **NM** value: **32.00**
32 ☐ May 1958 Cover: 0.10 **NM** value: **32.00**
33 ☐ Jun 1958 Cover: 0.10 **NM** value: **32.00**
34 ☐ Jul 1958 Cover: 0.10 **NM** value: **32.00**
35 ☐ Aug 1958 Cover: 0.10 **NM** value: **32.00**
36 ☐ Sep 1958 Cover: 0.10 **NM** value: **32.00**
37 ☐ Oct 1958 Cover: 0.10 **NM** value: **32.00**
38 ☐ Nov 1958 Cover: 0.10 **NM** value: **32.00**
39 ☐ Dec 1958 Cover: 0.10 **NM** value: **32.00**
40 ☐ Jan 1959 Cover: 0.10 **NM** value: **32.00**
41 ☐ Feb 1959 Cover: 0.10 **NM** value: **18.00**
42 ☐ Mar 1959 Cover: 0.10 **NM** value: **18.00**
43 ☐ Apr 1959 Cover: 0.10 **NM** value: **18.00**
44 ☐ May 1959 Cover: 0.10 **NM** value: **18.00**
45 ☐ Jun 1959 Cover: 0.10 **NM** value: **18.00**
46 ☐ Jul 1959 Cover: 0.10 **NM** value: **18.00**
47 ☐ Aug 1959 Cover: 0.10 **NM** value: **18.00**
48 ☐ Sep 1959 Cover: 0.10 **NM** value: **18.00**
49 ☐ Oct 1959 Cover: 0.10 **NM** value: **18.00**
50 ☐ Nov 1959 Cover: 0.10 **NM** value: **18.00**
51 ☐ Dec 1959 Cover: 0.10 **NM** value: **13.00**
52 ☐ Jan 1960 Cover: 0.10 **NM** value: **13.00**
53 ☐ Feb 1960 Cover: 0.10 **NM** value: **13.00**
54 ☐ Mar 1960 Cover: 0.10 **NM** value: **13.00**
55 ☐ Apr 1960 Cover: 0.10 **NM** value: **13.00**
56 ☐ May 1960 Cover: 0.10 **NM** value: **13.00**
57 ☐ Jun 1960 Cover: 0.10 **NM** value: **13.00**
58 ☐ Jul 1960 Cover: 0.10 **NM** value: **13.00**
59 ☐ Aug 1960 Cover: 0.10 **NM** value: **13.00**
60 ☐ Sep 1960 Cover: 0.10 **NM** value: **13.00**
61 ☐ Oct 1960 Cover: 0.10 **NM** value: **11.00**
62 ☐ Nov 1960 Cover: 0.10 **NM** value: **11.00**
63 ☐ Dec 1960 Cover: 0.10 **NM** value: **11.00**
64 ☐ Jan 1961 Cover: 0.10 **NM** value: **11.00**
65 ☐ Feb 1961 Cover: 0.10 **NM** value: **11.00**
66 ☐ Mar 1961 Cover: 0.10 **NM** value: **11.00**
67 ☐ Apr 1961 Cover: 0.10 **NM** value: **11.00**
68 ☐ May 1961 Cover: 0.10 **NM** value: **11.00**
69 ☐ Jun 1961 Cover: 0.10 **NM** value: **11.00**
70 ☐ Jul 1961 Cover: 0.10 **NM** value: **11.00**
71 ☐ Aug 1961 Cover: 0.10 **NM** value: **9.00**
72 ☐ Sep 1961 Cover: 0.10 **NM** value: **9.00**
73 ☐ Oct 1961 Cover: 0.10 **NM** value: **9.00**
74 ☐ Nov 1961 Cover: 0.10 **NM** value: **9.00**
75 ☐ Dec 1961 Cover: 0.10 **NM** value: **9.00**
76 ☐ Jan 1962 **NM** value: **9.00**
77 ☐ Feb 1962 **NM** value: **9.00**
78 ☐ Mar 1962 **NM** value: **9.00**
79 ☐ Apr 1962 **NM** value: **9.00**
80 ☐ May 1962 Cover: 0.12 **NM** value: **9.00**
81 ☐ Jun 1962 Cover: 0.12 **NM** value: **8.00**
82 ☐ Aug 1962 Cover: 0.12 **NM** value: **8.00**
83 ☐ Oct 1962 Cover: 0.12 **NM** value: **8.00**
84 ☐ Dec 1962 Cover: 0.12 **NM** value: **8.00**
85 ☐ Feb 1963 Cover: 0.12 **NM** value: **8.00**
86 ☐ Apr 1963 Cover: 0.12 **NM** value: **8.00**
87 ☐ Jun 1963 Cover: 0.12 **NM** value: **8.00**
88 ☐ Aug 1963 Cover: 0.12 **NM** value: **8.00**
89 ☐ Oct 1963 Cover: 0.12 **NM** value: **8.00**
90 ☐ Dec 1963 Cover: 0.12 **NM** value: **8.00**
91 ☐ Feb 1964 Cover: 0.12 **NM** value: **8.00**
Circ: Statement: **171,642**
92 ☐ Apr 1964 Cover: 0.12 **NM** value: **8.00**
Circ: Statement: **171,642**
93 ☐ Jun 1964 Cover: 0.12 **NM** value: **8.00**
Circ: Statement: **171,642**
94 ☐ Aug 1964 Cover: 0.12 **NM** value: **8.00**
Circ: Statement: **171,642**
95 ☐ Oct 1964 Cover: 0.12 **NM** value: **8.00**
Circ: Statement: **171,642**
96 ☐ Dec 1964 Cover: 0.12 **NM** value: **8.00**
Circ: Statement: **171,642**
97 ☐ Feb 1965 Cover: 0.12 **NM** value: **8.00**
98 ☐ Apr 1965 Cover: 0.12 **NM** value: **8.00**
99 ☐ Jun 1965 Cover: 0.12 **NM** value: **8.00**
• Has 1964 Statement, filed 1/1/1964 (late); avg print run 314,100; avg sales 171,595; avg subs 47; avg total paid circ 171,642; samples 345; max copies existent 171,987; 45% of run returned
100 ☐ Aug 1965 Cover: 0.12 **NM** value: **8.00**
101 ☐ Oct 1965 Cover: 0.12 **NM** value: **4.50**
102 ☐ Dec 1965 Cover: 0.12 **NM** value: **4.50**
103 ☐ Feb 1966 Cover: 0.12 **NM** value: **4.50**
104 ☐ Apr 1966 Cover: 0.12 **NM** value: **4.50**
105 ☐ Jun 1966 Cover: 0.12 **NM** value: **4.50**
106 ☐ Aug 1966 Cover: 0.12 **NM** value: **4.50**
107 ☐ Oct 1966 Cover: 0.12 **NM** value: **4.50**
108 ☐ Dec 1966 Cover: 0.12 **NM** value: **4.50**
109 ☐ Feb 1967 Cover: 0.12 **NM** value: **4.50**
Circ: Statement: **179,592**
110 ☐ Apr 1967 Cover: 0.12 **NM** value: **4.50**
Circ: Statement: **179,592**
111 ☐ Jun 1967 Cover: 0.12 **NM** value: **4.50**
Circ: Statement: **179,592**
112 ☐ Aug 1967 Cover: 0.12 **NM** value: **4.50**
Circ: Statement: **179,592**
113 ☐ Oct 1967 Cover: 0.12 **NM** value: **4.50**
Circ: Statement: **179,592**
114 ☐ Dec 1967 Cover: 0.12 **NM** value: **4.50**
Circ: Statement: **179,592**
115 ☐ Feb 1968 Cover: 0.12 **NM** value: **4.50**
116 ☐ Apr 1968 Cover: 0.12 **NM** value: **4.50**
117 ☐ Jun 1968 Cover: 0.12 **NM** value: **4.50**
118 ☐ Aug 1968 Cover: 0.12 **NM** value: **4.50**
119 ☐ Oct 1968 Cover: 0.12 **NM** value: **4.50**
120 ☐ Dec 1968 Cover: 0.12 **NM** value: **4.50**
121 ☐ Feb 1969 Cover: 0.12 **NM** value: **4.50**
122 ☐ 1969 Cover: 0.12 **NM** value: **4.50**
Circ: Statement: **213,070**
123 ☐ 1969 Cover: 0.12 **NM** value: **4.50**
Circ: Statement: **213,070**
124 ☐ Jul 1969 Cover: 0.12 **NM** value: **4.50**
Circ: Statement: **213,070**
125 ☐ 1969 Cover: 0.12 **NM** value: **4.50**
Circ: Statement: **213,070**
126 ☐ Oct 1969 Cover: 0.15 **NM** value: **4.50**
Circ: Statement: **213,070**
127 ☐ Dec 1969 Cover: 0.15 **NM** value: **4.50**
Circ: Statement: **213,070**
128 ☐ Jan 1970 Cover: 0.15 **NM** value: **4.50**
129 ☐ Mar 1970 Cover: 0.15 **NM** value: **4.50**
130 ☐ May 1970 Cover: 0.15 **NM** value: **4.50**
• Has 1969 Statement, filed 10/1/1969; avg print run 351,228; avg sales 213,016; avg subs 54; avg total paid circ 213,070; 345 samples; max existent 213,415; 39% of run returned
131 ☐ Jul 1970 Cover: 0.15 **NM** value: **4.50**
132 ☐ Sep 1970 Cover: 0.15 **NM** value: **4.50**
133 ☐ Oct 1970 Cover: 0.15 **NM** value: **4.50**
134 ☐ Nov 1970 Cover: 0.15 **NM** value: **4.50**
135 ☐ Jan 1971 Cover: 0.15 **NM** value: **4.50**
136 ☐ Mar 1971 Cover: 0.15 **NM** value: **4.50**
137 ☐ May 1971 Cover: 0.15 **NM** value: **4.50**
138 ☐ Jul 1971 Cover: 0.15 **NM** value: **4.50**
139 ☐ 1971 Cover: 0.15 **NM** value: **4.50**
140 ☐ 1971 Cover: 0.15 **NM** value: **4.50**
141 ☐ Nov 1971 Cover: 0.15 **NM** value: **4.50**
142 ☐ Mar 1972 Cover: 0.25 **NM** value: **6.00**
Circ: Statement: **174,721**
• Giant-size.
143 ☐ May 1972 Cover: 0.25 **NM** value: **6.00**
Circ: Statement: **174,721**
• Giant-size.
144 ☐ Jul 1972 Cover: 0.25 **NM** value: **6.00**
Circ: Statement: **174,721**
• Giant-size.
145 ☐ Sep 1972 Cover: 0.25 **NM** value: **6.00**
Circ: Statement: **174,721**
• Giant-size.
146 ☐ Nov 1972 Cover: 0.25 **NM** value: **2.50**
Circ: Statement: **174,721**
147 ☐ Jan 1973 Cover: 0.20 **NM** value: **2.50**
Circ: Statement: **160,982**
148 ☐ Mar 1973 Cover: 0.20 **NM** value: **2.50**
Circ: Statement: **160,982**
149 ☐ May 1973 Cover: 0.20 **NM** value: **2.50**
Circ: Statement: **160,982**
150 ☐ Jul 1973 Cover: 0.20 **NM** value: **2.50**
Circ: Statement: **160,982**
• Has 1972 Statement; avg total paid circ 174,721
151 ☐ Sep 1973 Cover: 0.20 **NM** value: **2.50**
Circ: Statement: **160,982**
152 ☐ **NM** value: **2.50**
Circ: Statement: **132,986**
153 ☐ Jun 1974 **NM** value: **2.50**
Circ: Statement: **132,986**
• Has 1973 Statement (Alert: Reports partial year only); avg total paid circ 160,982
154 ☐ Aug 1974 Cover: 0.25 **NM** value: **2.50**
Circ: Statement: **132,986**
155 ☐ Oct 1974 Cover: 0.25 **NM** value: **2.50**
Circ: Statement: **132,986**
156 ☐ Dec 1974 Cover: 0.25 **NM** value: **2.50**
Circ: Statement: **132,986**
157 ☐ Feb 1975 Cover: 0.25 **NM** value: **2.50**
158 ☐ Apr 1975 Cover: 0.25 **NM** value: **2.50**
159 ☐ Jun 1975 Cover: 0.25 **NM** value: **2.50**
• Has 1974 Statement; avg total paid circ 132,986
160 ☐ Aug 1975 Cover: 0.25 **NM** value: **2.50**
161 ☐ Oct 1975 Cover: 0.25 **NM** value: **2.50**
162 ☐ Dec 1975 Cover: 0.25 **NM** value: **2.50**
163 ☐ Feb 1976 Cover: 0.25 **NM** value: **2.50**
164 ☐ Apr 1976 Cover: 0.25 **NM** value: **2.50**
final issue.

LITTLE DOT (VOL. 2) — Harvey

1 ☐ Sep 1992 Cover: 1.25 **NM** value: **1.50**
📖 Little Dot: The Dot Demon; Little Dot: Poor Old Uncle Charlie; Little Lotta: Voodoo Booboo; Richie Rich: Robot Law and Order
2 ☐ Cover: 1.25 **NM** value: **1.50**
3 ☐ Jun 1993 Cover: 1.25 **NM** value: **1.50**
4 ☐ 1993 Cover: 1.25 **NM** value: **1.50**
5 ☐ Jan 1994 Cover: 1.50 **NM** value: **Cover or less**
📖 Dot's Dot; Little Dot Meets Uncle Bull Dozer; Little Lotta in Mr. Thundermaker; Richie Rich Meets Windblow
6 ☐ Apr 1994 Cover: 1.50 **NM** value: **Cover or less**
📖 Little Dot in the Hiding Place; Little Lotta; Little Dot in Uncle Dabby; Little Lotta in Vacation Daze; Richie Rich and the Boiling Butler
7 ☐ Jun 1994 Cover: 1.50 **NM** value: **Cover or less**

LITTLE DOT IN 3-D — Blackthorne

1 ☐ Cover: 2.50 **NM** value: **Cover or less**
📖 Sittin' Pretty; Dash It All; The Duchess; Meets Uncle Tytfist

LITTLE DOT'S UNCLES AND AUNTS — Harvey

1 ☐ ca. 1961 Cover: 0.25 **NM** value: **100.00**
• **CGC:** 1 graded, best 9.4
2 ☐ Aug 1962 Cover: 0.25 **NM** value: **50.00**
• **CGC:** 1 graded, best 9.4
3 ☐ Cover: 0.25 **NM** value: **50.00**
4 ☐ Cover: 0.25 **NM** value: **40.00**
5 ☐ Cover: 0.25 **NM** value: **40.00**
6 ☐ Cover: 0.25 **NM** value: **30.00**
7 ☐ Cover: 0.25 **NM** value: **30.00**
8 ☐ Cover: 0.25 **NM** value: **30.00**
9 ☐ Cover: 0.25 **NM** value: **30.00**
10 ☐ Cover: 0.25 **NM** value: **30.00**
11 ☐ Nov 1964 Cover: 0.25 **NM** value: **25.00**
12 ☐ 1965 Cover: 0.25 **NM** value: **25.00**
13 ☐ 1965 Cover: 0.25 **NM** value: **25.00**
14 ☐ Aug 1965 Cover: 0.25 **NM** value: **25.00**
15 ☐ Cover: 0.25 **NM** value: **25.00**
16 ☐ Cover: 0.25 **NM** value: **25.00**
17 ☐ 1966 Cover: 0.25 **NM** value: **25.00**
18 ☐ Sep 1966 Cover: 0.25 **NM** value: **25.00**
19 ☐ Nov 1966 Cover: 0.25 **NM** value: **25.00**
20 ☐ Aug 1967 Cover: 0.25 **NM** value: **25.00**
21 ☐ Nov 1967 Cover: 0.25 **NM** value: **25.00**
22 ☐ Feb 1968 Cover: 0.25 **NM** value: **25.00**
• **CGC:** 1 graded, best 8.5
23 ☐ Jul 1968 Cover: 0.25 **NM** value: **25.00**
24 ☐ Oct 1968 Cover: 0.25 **NM** value: **25.00**
25 ☐ Dec 1968 Cover: 0.25 **NM** value: **25.00**
26 ☐ 1969 Cover: 0.25 **NM** value: **25.00**
27 ☐ Jun 1969 Cover: 0.25 **NM** value: **25.00**
28 ☐ Aug 1969 Cover: 0.25 **NM** value: **25.00**
• **CGC:** 1 graded, best 9.0
29 ☐ Oct 1969 Cover: 0.25 **NM** value: **25.00**
• **CGC:** 1 graded, best 8.5
30 ☐ Nov 1969 Cover: 0.25 **NM** value: **25.00**
• **CGC:** 1 graded, best 9.4
31 ☐ Mar 1970 Cover: 0.25 **NM** value: **25.00**
32 ☐ Jun 1970 Cover: 0.25 **NM** value: **25.00**
33 ☐ Aug 1970 Cover: 0.25 **NM** value: **25.00**
34 ☐ 1970 Cover: 0.25 **NM** value: **25.00**
35 ☐ Nov 1970 Cover: 0.25 **NM** value: **25.00**
36 ☐ Mar 1971 Cover: 0.25 **NM** value: **15.00**
37 ☐ 1971 Cover: 0.25 **NM** value: **15.00**
38 ☐ Aug 1971 Cover: 0.25 **NM** value: **15.00**
39 ☐ Oct 1971 Cover: 0.25 **NM** value: **15.00**
40 ☐ Cover: 0.25 **NM** value: **15.00**
41 ☐ 1972 Cover: 0.25 **NM** value: **15.00**
42 ☐ Jun 1972 Cover: 0.25 **NM** value: **15.00**
43 ☐ 1972 Cover: 0.25 **NM** value: **15.00**
44 ☐ Dec 1972 Cover: 0.25 **NM** value: **15.00**
45 ☐ Feb 1973 Cover: 0.25 **NM** value: **15.00**
46 ☐ Apr 1973 Cover: 0.25 **NM** value: **15.00**
47 ☐ Jun 1973 Cover: 0.25 **NM** value: **15.00**
48 ☐ Aug 1973 Cover: 0.25 **NM** value: **15.00**
49 ☐ Oct 1973 Cover: 0.25 **NM** value: **15.00**
50 ☐ Dec 1973 Cover: 0.25 **NM** value: **15.00**
51 ☐ Feb 1974 Cover: 0.25 **NM** value: **15.00**
52 ☐ Apr 1974 Cover: 0.25 **NM** value: **15.00**

LITTLE DRACULA — Harvey

1 ☐ Jan 1992 Cover: 1.25 **NM** value: **1.50**
Circ: CapCity orders: **2,350**
2 ☐ Mar 1992 Cover: 1.25 **NM** value: **1.50**
3 ☐ May 1992 Cover: 1.25 **NM** value: **1.50**

LITTLE EVA 3-D — St. John

1 ☐ Oct 1953 Cover: 0.25 **NM** value: **150.00**
2 ☐ Nov 1953 Cover: 0.25 **NM** value: **150.00**

LITTLE FIR TREE — W.T. Grant

1 ☐ ca. 1943 **NM** value: **50.00**

LITTLE GHOST — St. John

1 ☐ 1959 Cover: 0.10 **NM** value: **50.00**
2 ☐ 1959 Cover: 0.10 **NM** value: **25.00**
3 ☐ 1959 Cover: 0.10 **NM** value: **25.00**

LITTLE GIANT COMICS — Centaur

1 ☐ ca. 1938 Cover: 0.10 **NM** value: **500.00**
2 ☐ Aug 1938 Cover: 0.10 **NM** value: **400.00**
3 ☐ Oct 1938 Cover: 0.10 **NM** value: **400.00**
4 ☐ Feb 1939 Cover: 0.10 **NM** value: **400.00**

LITTLE GIANT DETECTIVE FUNNIES — Centaur

1 ☐ Oct 1938 Cover: 0.10 **NM** value: **500.00**
2 ☐ Nov 1938 Cover: 0.10 **NM** value: **400.00**
3 ☐ Dec 1938 Cover: 0.10 **NM** value: **400.00**
4 ☐ Jan 1939 Cover: 0.10 **NM** value: **400.00**

The prices seen above do not represent the highest possible prices seen in online auctions, but rather the prices we have seen these issues reliably fetch in a variety of environments (storefront retail, mail order, auction and convention).

CGC-graded: Multiply prices above by **33 for 9.9 M • 16 for 9.8 NM/M • 7 for 9.6 NM+ • 5 for 9.4 NM • 2.5 for 9.2 NM- • 1.5 for 9.0 VF/NM**

LITTLE GIANT MOVIE FUNNIES — Centaur

#	Issue	Cover	NM value
1	❑ Aug 1938	Cover: 0.10	NM value: 500.00
2	❑ Oct 1938	Cover: 0.10	NM value: 400.00

LITTLE GLOOMY — Slave Labor

#	Issue	Cover	NM value
1	❑ Oct 1999	Cover: 2.95	NM value: Cover or less
	Circ: Diamd. preorders: 5,920		

LITTLE GRETA GARBAGE — Rip Off

All issues are adults only.

#	Issue	Cover	NM value
1	❑ Jul 1990, b&w	Cover: 2.50	NM value: Cover or less
2	❑ Jun 1991, b&w	Cover: 2.50	NM value: Cover or less

LITTLE GREY MAN — Image

#	Issue	Cover	NM value
1	❑	Cover: 6.95	NM value: Cover or less
	• graphic novel		

LITTLE GROUCHO — Reston

#	Issue	Cover	NM value
1	❑ Mar 1955	Cover: 0.10	NM value: 50.00
2	❑ Jun 1955	Cover: 0.10	NM value: 30.00

LITTLE IKE — St. John

#	Issue	Cover	NM value
1	❑ Apr 1953	Cover: 0.10	NM value: 50.00
2	❑ Jun 1953	Cover: 0.10	NM value: 30.00
3	❑ Aug 1953	Cover: 0.10	NM value: 25.00
4	❑ Oct 1953	Cover: 0.10	NM value: 25.00

LITTLE IODINE — Dell

Jimmy Hatlo (1898-1963) so tapped into the national experience with the title "They'll do it every time" that he was able to cull "you ain't heard nothing yet" experiences from his audience for decades. The King Features newspaper feature began in 1936. The concept was somewhat along the lines of "My mother says I should keep my phone calls short but" (next panel) "When she gets on the phone she doesn't get off for an hour." And it has been so popular that it's still running, now done by Al Scaduto.

The suburban Tremblechin family's red-haired little girl eventually became so popular she earned her own strip, which ran from 1943 to 1986, and Little Iodine starred in her own comic book for some time. Much of the comic-book version was original material, consisting of short stories with beginning, middle, and end. — Maggie

#	Issue	Cover	NM value
1	❑ Mar 1950	Cover: 0.10	NM value: 100.00
2	❑ Jun 1950	Cover: 0.10	NM value: 35.00
3	❑ 1950	Cover: 0.10	NM value: 35.00
4	❑ 1951	Cover: 0.10	NM value: 35.00
5	❑ Apr 1951	Cover: 0.10	NM value: 35.00
6	❑ Jun 1951	Cover: 0.10	NM value: 30.00
7	❑ Aug 1951	Cover: 0.10	NM value: 30.00
8	❑ Oct 1951	Cover: 0.10	NM value: 30.00
9	❑ Dec 1951	Cover: 0.10	NM value: 30.00
10	❑ Feb 1952	Cover: 0.10	NM value: 30.00
11	❑ Apr 1952	Cover: 0.10	NM value: 25.00
12	❑ Jun 1952	Cover: 0.10	NM value: 25.00
13	❑ Aug 1952	Cover: 0.10	NM value: 25.00
14	❑ Oct 1952	Cover: 0.10	NM value: 25.00
15	❑ Dec 1952	Cover: 0.10	NM value: 25.00
16	❑ Feb 1953	Cover: 0.10	NM value: 25.00
17	❑ Apr 1953	Cover: 0.10	NM value: 25.00
18	❑ Jun 1953	Cover: 0.10	NM value: 25.00
19	❑ Aug 1953	Cover: 0.10	NM value: 25.00
20	❑ Oct 1953	Cover: 0.10	NM value: 20.00
21	❑ Dec 1953	Cover: 0.10	NM value: 20.00
22	❑ Feb 1954	Cover: 0.10	NM value: 20.00
23	❑ Apr 1954	Cover: 0.10	NM value: 20.00
24	❑ Jun 1954	Cover: 0.10	NM value: 20.00
25	❑ Aug 1954	Cover: 0.10	NM value: 20.00
26	❑ Oct 1954	Cover: 0.10	NM value: 20.00
27	❑ Jan 1955	Cover: 0.10	NM value: 20.00
28	❑ Apr 1955	Cover: 0.10	NM value: 20.00
29	❑ Jul 1955	Cover: 0.10	NM value: 20.00
30	❑ Oct 1955	Cover: 0.10	NM value: 15.00
31	❑ Jan 1956	Cover: 0.10	NM value: 15.00
32	❑ Apr 1956	Cover: 0.10	NM value: 15.00
33	❑ Jul 1956	Cover: 0.10	NM value: 15.00
34	❑ Oct 1956	Cover: 0.10	NM value: 15.00
35	❑ Jan 1957	Cover: 0.10	NM value: 15.00
36	❑ Apr 1957	Cover: 0.10	NM value: 15.00
37	❑ Jul 1957	Cover: 0.10	NM value: 15.00
38	❑ Oct 1957	Cover: 0.10	NM value: 15.00
39	❑ Jan 1958	Cover: 0.10	NM value: 15.00
40	❑ Apr 1958	Cover: 0.10	NM value: 10.00
41	❑ Jul 1958	Cover: 0.10	NM value: 10.00
42	❑ Oct 1958	Cover: 0.10	NM value: 10.00
43	❑ Jan 1959	Cover: 0.10	NM value: 10.00
44	❑ Apr 1959	Cover: 0.10	NM value: 10.00
45	❑ Jul 1959	Cover: 0.10	NM value: 10.00
46	❑ Oct 1959	Cover: 0.10	NM value: 10.00
47	❑ Jan 1960	Cover: 0.10	NM value: 10.00
48	❑ Apr 1960	Cover: 0.10	NM value: 10.00
49	❑ Jul 1960	Cover: 0.10	NM value: 10.00
50	❑ Oct 1960	Cover: 0.10	NM value: 10.00
51	❑ Jan 1961	Cover: 0.10	NM value: 10.00
52	❑ Apr 1961	Cover: 0.10	NM value: 10.00
53	❑ Jul 1961	Cover: 0.10	NM value: 10.00
54	❑ Oct 1961	Cover: 0.10	NM value: 10.00
55	❑ Jan 1962	Cover: 0.10	NM value: 10.00
56	❑ Apr 1962	Cover: 0.10	NM value: 10.00

LITTLE ITALY — Fantagraphics

#	Issue	Cover	NM value
1	❑ b&w	Cover: 3.95	NM value: Cover or less

LITTLE JACK FROST — Avon

#	Issue	Cover	NM value
1	❑ ca. 1952	Cover: 0.10	NM value: 50.00

LITTLE JIM-BOB BIG FOOT — Jump Back Productions

#	Issue	Cover	NM value
1	❑ b&w	Cover: 2.95	NM value: Cover or less
	final issue. A: Doug Baron W: Doug Baron		
2	❑ Jan 1998, b&w	Cover: 2.95	NM value: Cover or less

LITTLE JOE — St. John

#	Issue	Cover	NM value
1	❑ ca. 1953	Cover: 0.10	NM value: 25.00

LITTLE LANA — Marvel

#	Issue	Cover	NM value
8	❑ Nov 1949	Cover: 0.10	NM value: 50.00
9	❑ Feb 1950	Cover: 0.10	NM value: 50.00

LITTLE LENNY — Marvel

#	Issue	Cover	NM value
1	❑ Jun 1949	Cover: 0.10	NM value: 75.00
2	❑ Aug 1949	Cover: 0.10	NM value: 40.00
3	❑ Oct 1949	Cover: 0.10	NM value: 40.00

LITTLE LIZZIE (1ST SERIES) — Marvel

#	Issue	Cover	NM value
1	❑ Jun 1949	Cover: 0.10	NM value: 75.00
2	❑ Aug 1949	Cover: 0.10	NM value: 50.00
3	❑ Oct 1949	Cover: 0.10	NM value: 50.00
4	❑ Jan 1950	Cover: 0.10	NM value: 50.00
5	❑ Apr 1950	Cover: 0.10	NM value: 50.00

LITTLE LIZZIE (2ND SERIES) — Marvel

#	Issue	Cover	NM value
1	❑ Sep 1953	Cover: 0.10	NM value: 50.00
2	❑ Nov 1953	Cover: 0.10	NM value: 40.00
3	❑ Jan 1954	Cover: 0.10	NM value: 40.00

LITTLE LOTTA (VOL. 1) — Harvey

Modern-day P.C. police might think about running away. Very, very fast.

Several Harvey characters are built around an excess of one sort or another (Richie Rich's money, Little Dot's exuberance for circular objects, or Hot Stuff's desire for fire). With Lotta, it's food. It isn't that this series starring an enormous child has many fat jokes — rather, some stories make a point of establishing that Lotta exercises frequently and uses her considerable strength in admirable exploits.

But let's be honest: She's not just "big for her age." Many of the series' writers see to it that she earns her heft, with stories and cover gags depicting her voracious appetite for sweets. One of the spinoff series is Little Lotta's Foodland. Could today's comics fans see "Tony Stark's Hip Flask?"

Still, it's a piece of Comics Americana that may not be coming around again. Harvey tried to bring her back in the early 1990s without much luck. — JJM

#	Issue	Cover	NM value
1	❑ Nov 1955	Cover: 0.10	NM value: 225.00
	• CGC: 1 graded, best 7.5		
2	❑ Jan 1956	Cover: 0.10	NM value: 90.00
3	❑ Mar 1956	Cover: 0.10	NM value: 75.00
	• CGC: 1 graded, best 9.4		
4	❑ May 1956	Cover: 0.10	NM value: 55.00
	• CGC: 1 graded, best 8.0		
5	❑ Jul 1956	Cover: 0.10	NM value: 55.00
6	❑ Sep 1956	Cover: 0.10	NM value: 40.00
7	❑ Nov 1956	Cover: 0.10	NM value: 40.00
8	❑ Jan 1957	Cover: 0.10	NM value: 40.00
9	❑ Mar 1957	Cover: 0.10	NM value: 40.00
10	❑ May 1957	Cover: 0.10	NM value: 40.00
11	❑ Jul 1957	Cover: 0.10	NM value: 28.00
12	❑ Sep 1957	Cover: 0.10	NM value: 28.00
13	❑ Nov 1957	Cover: 0.10	NM value: 28.00
14	❑ Jan 1958	Cover: 0.10	NM value: 28.00
15	❑ Mar 1958	Cover: 0.10	NM value: 28.00
16	❑ May 1958	Cover: 0.10	NM value: 28.00
17	❑ Jul 1958	Cover: 0.10	NM value: 28.00
18	❑ Sep 1958	Cover: 0.10	NM value: 28.00
19	❑ Nov 1958	Cover: 0.10	NM value: 28.00
20	❑ Feb 1959	Cover: 0.10	NM value: 28.00
21	❑ Apr 1959	Cover: 0.10	NM value: 22.00
22	❑ Jun 1959	Cover: 0.10	NM value: 22.00
23	❑ Aug 1959	Cover: 0.10	NM value: 22.00
24	❑ Oct 1959	Cover: 0.10	NM value: 22.00
25	❑ Dec 1959	Cover: 0.10	NM value: 22.00
26	❑ 1960	Cover: 0.10	NM value: 22.00
27	❑ 1960	Cover: 0.10	NM value: 22.00
28	❑ 1960	Cover: 0.10	NM value: 22.00
29	❑ 1960	Cover: 0.10	NM value: 22.00
30	❑ 1960	Cover: 0.10	NM value: 22.00
31	❑ 1960	Cover: 0.10	NM value: 18.00
32	❑ 1961	Cover: 0.10	NM value: 18.00
33	❑ 1961	Cover: 0.10	NM value: 18.00
34	❑ 1961	Cover: 0.10	NM value: 18.00
35	❑ 1961	Cover: 0.10	NM value: 18.00
36	❑ 1961	Cover: 0.10	NM value: 18.00
37	❑ Sep 1961	Cover: 0.10	NM value: 18.00
38	❑ Nov 1961	Cover: 0.10	NM value: 18.00
39	❑ Jan 1962	Cover: 0.12	NM value: 18.00
40	❑ Mar 1962	Cover: 0.12	NM value: 18.00
41	❑ May 1962	Cover: 0.12	NM value: 15.00
42	❑ Jul 1962	Cover: 0.12	NM value: 15.00
43	❑ Sep 1962	Cover: 0.12	NM value: 15.00
44	❑ Nov 1962	Cover: 0.12	NM value: 15.00
45	❑ Jan 1963	Cover: 0.12	NM value: 15.00
46	❑ Mar 1963	Cover: 0.12	NM value: 15.00
47	❑ May 1963	Cover: 0.12	NM value: 15.00
48	❑ Jul 1963	Cover: 0.12	NM value: 15.00
49	❑ Sep 1963	Cover: 0.12	NM value: 15.00
50	❑ Nov 1963	Cover: 0.12	NM value: 15.00
51	❑ Jan 1964	Cover: 0.12	NM value: 12.00
52	❑ Mar 1964	Cover: 0.12	NM value: 12.00
53	❑ May 1964	Cover: 0.12	NM value: 12.00
54	❑ Jul 1964	Cover: 0.12	NM value: 12.00
55	❑ Sep 1964	Cover: 0.12	NM value: 12.00
56	❑ Nov 1964	Cover: 0.12	NM value: 12.00
57	❑ Jan 1965	Cover: 0.12	NM value: 12.00
58	❑ Mar 1965	Cover: 0.12	NM value: 12.00
59	❑ May 1965	Cover: 0.12	NM value: 12.00
60	❑ Jul 1965	Cover: 0.12	NM value: 12.00
61	❑ Sep 1965	Cover: 0.12	NM value: 12.00
62	❑ Nov 1965	Cover: 0.12	NM value: 12.00
63	❑ Jan 1966	Cover: 0.12	NM value: 12.00
64	❑ Mar 1966	Cover: 0.12	NM value: 12.00
65	❑ May 1966	Cover: 0.12	NM value: 12.00
66	❑ Jul 1966	Cover: 0.12	NM value: 12.00
67	❑ Sep 1966	Cover: 0.12	NM value: 12.00
68	❑ Nov 1966	Cover: 0.12	NM value: 12.00
69	❑ Jan 1967	Cover: 0.12	NM value: 12.00
	Circ: Statement: 171,055		
70	❑ Mar 1967	Cover: 0.12	NM value: 12.00
	Circ: Statement: 171,055		
71	❑ May 1967	Cover: 0.12	NM value: 8.00
	Circ: Statement: 171,055		
72	❑ Jul 1967	Cover: 0.12	NM value: 8.00
	Circ: Statement: 171,055		
73	❑ Sep 1967	Cover: 0.12	NM value: 8.00
	Circ: Statement: 171,055		
74	❑ Nov 1967	Cover: 0.12	NM value: 8.00
	Circ: Statement: 171,055		
75	❑ Jan 1968	Cover: 0.12	NM value: 8.00
76	❑ Mar 1968	Cover: 0.12	NM value: 8.00
77	❑ May 1968	Cover: 0.12	NM value: 8.00
78	❑ Jul 1968	Cover: 0.12	NM value: 8.00
79	❑ Sep 1968	Cover: 0.12	NM value: 8.00
80	❑ Nov 1968	Cover: 0.12	NM value: 8.00
81	❑ Jan 1969	Cover: 0.12	NM value: 8.00
	Circ: Statement: 211,039		
82	❑ Mar 1969	Cover: 0.12	NM value: 8.00
	Circ: Statement: 211,039		
83	❑ May 1969	Cover: 0.12	NM value: 8.00
	Circ: Statement: 211,039		
84	❑ Jul 1969	Cover: 0.12	NM value: 8.00
	Circ: Statement: 211,039		
85	❑ 1969		NM value: 8.00
	Circ: Statement: 211,039		
86	❑ Oct 1969	Cover: 0.15	NM value: 8.00
	Circ: Statement: 211,039		
87	❑ Dec 1969	Cover: 0.15	NM value: 8.00
	Circ: Statement: 211,039		
88	❑ Jan 1970	Cover: 0.15	NM value: 8.00
89	❑ Apr 1970	Cover: 0.15	NM value: 8.00
	• Has 1969 Statement, filed 10/1/69; avg print run 341,883; avg sales 210,985; avg subs 54; avg total paid circ 211,039; samples 345; max existent 211,384; 38% of run returned		
90	❑ Jul 1970	Cover: 0.15	NM value: 8.00
91	❑ 1970	Cover: 0.15	NM value: 5.00
92	❑ Oct 1970	Cover: 0.15	NM value: 5.00
93	❑ Nov 1970	Cover: 0.15	NM value: 5.00
94	❑ Jan 1971	Cover: 0.15	NM value: 5.00
95	❑ Mar 1971	Cover: 0.15	NM value: 5.00
96	❑ May 1971	Cover: 0.15	NM value: 5.00
97	❑ Jul 1971	Cover: 0.15	NM value: 5.00
98	❑ Sep 1971	Cover: 0.15	NM value: 5.00
99	❑ Nov 1971	Cover: 0.15	NM value: 6.00
100	❑ 1972		NM value: 6.00
	Circ: Statement: 166,478		
101	❑ May 1972	Cover: 0.25	NM value: 6.00
	Circ: Statement: 166,478		
102	❑ Jul 1972	Cover: 0.25	NM value: 6.00
	Circ: Statement: 166,478		
103	❑ Sep 1972	Cover: 0.25	NM value: 3.00
	Circ: Statement: 166,478		
104	❑ Nov 1972	Cover: 0.20	NM value: 3.00
	Circ: Statement: 166,478		
105	❑ Jan 1973	Cover: 0.20	NM value: 3.00
	Circ: Statement: 166,478		
106	❑ Mar 1973	Cover: 0.20	NM value: 3.00
107	❑ May 1973		NM value: 3.00
108	❑ Jul 1973		NM value: 3.00
	• Has 1972 Statement; avg total paid circ 166,478		
109	❑ 1974		NM value: 3.00
	Circ: Statement: 178,576		
110	❑ 1974		NM value: 3.00
	Circ: Statement: 178,576		
111	❑ 1974		NM value: 3.00
	Circ: Statement: 178,576		
112	❑ 1974		NM value: 3.00
	Circ: Statement: 178,576		
113	❑ Jan 1975	Cover: 0.25	NM value: 3.00
114	❑ Mar 1975	Cover: 0.25	NM value: 3.00
115	❑ May 1975	Cover: 0.25	NM value: 3.00
	• Has 1974 Statement; avg total paid circ 178,576		
116	❑ Jul 1975	Cover: 0.25	NM value: 3.00
117	❑ Sep 1975	Cover: 0.25	NM value: 3.00
118	❑ Nov 1975	Cover: 0.25	NM value: 3.00
119	❑ Jan 1976	Cover: 0.25	NM value: 3.00
120	❑ Mar 1976	Cover: 0.25	NM value: 3.00

Other grades: Multiply prices above by **1.5 for Mint • 2/3 for Very Fine • 1/3 for Fine • 1/5 for Very Good • 1/8 for Good**

LITTLE LOTTA (VOL. 2) Harvey

1 ❑ Oct 1992 Cover: 1.25 **NM** value: **1.50**
📖 Dynamic Dot; Special Police; Bigger And Better!; Aunt Elastic
2 ❑ Jan 1993 Cover: 1.25 **NM** value: **1.50**
📖 I Promise You a Rose Garden; The Spectator; The Town Guard; Gerald's Ordeal **A:** Dom Sileo; Sig Couchey
3 ❑ Apr 1993 Cover: 1.25 **NM** value: **1.50**
4 ❑ Jul 1993 Cover: 1.25 **NM** value: **1.50**

LITTLE LOTTA FOODLAND Harvey

1 ❑ Sep 1963 Cover: 0.25 **NM** value: **100.00**
2 ❑ Dec 1963 Cover: 0.25 **NM** value: **75.00**
• **CGC:** 1 graded, best 9.4
3 ❑ Mar 1964 Cover: 0.25 **NM** value: **75.00**
• **CGC:** 1 graded, best 9.6
4 ❑ 1964 Cover: 0.25 **NM** value: **50.00**
5 ❑ 1964 Cover: 0.25 **NM** value: **50.00**
6 ❑ 1964 Cover: 0.25 **NM** value: **50.00**
7 ❑ 1965 Cover: 0.25 **NM** value: **50.00**
8 ❑ 1965 Cover: 0.25 **NM** value: **50.00**
9 ❑ 1965 Cover: 0.25 **NM** value: **50.00**
10 ❑ Jan 1966 Cover: 0.25 **NM** value: **45.00**
11 ❑ Apr 1966 Cover: 0.25 **NM** value: **45.00**
12 ❑ 1966 Cover: 0.25 **NM** value: **45.00**
13 ❑ 1967 Cover: 0.25 **NM** value: **45.00**
14 ❑ 1967 Cover: 0.25 **NM** value: **45.00**
15 ❑ Oct 1968 Cover: 0.25 **NM** value: **45.00**
16 ❑ 1969 Cover: 0.25 **NM** value: **40.00**
17 ❑ 1969 Cover: 0.25 **NM** value: **40.00**
18 ❑ Dec 1969 Cover: 0.25 **NM** value: **40.00**
19 ❑ Sep 1970 Cover: 0.25 **NM** value: **40.00**
20 ❑ 1970 Cover: 0.25 **NM** value: **25.00**
21 ❑ Feb 1971 Cover: 0.25 **NM** value: **25.00**
22 ❑ May 1971 Cover: 0.25 **NM** value: **25.00**
23 ❑ Aug 1971 Cover: 0.25 **NM** value: **25.00**
• **CGC:** 2 graded, best 9.6
24 ❑ Oct 1971 Cover: 0.25 **NM** value: **25.00**
• **CGC:** 1 graded, best 9.6
25 ❑ Dec 1971 Cover: 0.25 **NM** value: **25.00**
• **CGC:** 1 graded, best 9.6
26 ❑ Feb 1972 Cover: 0.25 **NM** value: **20.00**
27 ❑ May 1972 Cover: 0.20 **NM** value: **20.00**
28 ❑ Aug 1972 Cover: 0.20 **NM** value: **20.00**
29 ❑ Oct 1972 Cover: 0.20 **NM** value: **20.00**

LITTLE LULU AND HER SPECIAL FRIENDS (MARGE'S...) Dell / Gold Key/Whitman

3 ❑ Mar 1955 Cover: 0.25 **NM** value: **125.00**
• **CGC:** 1 graded, best 6.0
• Dell giant

LITTLE LULU AND TUBBY AT SUMMER CAMP (MARGE'S ...) Dell

1 ❑ Cover: 0.25 **NM** value: **35.00**
2 ❑ Oct 1958 Cover: 0.25 **NM** value: **35.00**
• **CGC:** 3 graded, best 9.4

LITTLE LULU AND TUBBY HALLOWEEN FUN (MARGE'S ...) Dell

1 ❑ **NM** value: **35.00**

LITTLE LULU AND TUBBY IN ALASKA (MARGE'S ...) Dell

1 ❑ Jul 1959 Cover: 0.25 **NM** value: **35.00**
• **CGC:** 3 graded, best 9.0

LITTLE LULU (MARGE'S...) Dell / Gold Key/Whitman

Little Lulu, by "Marge" (Marjorie Henderson Buell) began as a gag panel in the Saturday Evening Post magazine in 1935, replacing Henry. Marge successfully licensed the strip for versions in animated cartoons, advertising, newspaper strips, and comic books. She carefully monitored what was done with the character, including what happened in the comic-book stories scripted and roughed by John Stanley, who worked anonymously. In 1972, Gold Key picked up the rights and began a new series of humorous adventures.

In Stanley's hands, Lulu is a sensible problem solver, contending with such challenges as the boys' gang whose policies include "Mumday," in which they will not speak to girls and with little Alvin, who constantly blackmails her into telling him a story.

Those stories eventually focused on Witch Hazel (who eventually got her own strip). Lulu's other activities often involved her friend Tubby, who eventually got his own comic book. Stanley's stories are classic and collectible for their inventive plotting and outstanding scripting. An HBO series of Lulu's stories managed to use Stanley's plots (without credit) without conveying the brilliance of the material.

1 ❑ Jan 1948 Cover: 0.10 **NM** value: **550.00**
• Lulu's Diary feature begins; Dell publishes
2 ❑ Mar 1948 Cover: 0.10 **NM** value: **285.00**
★ 1st Appearance of Miss Feeney, Gloria (Little Lulu's friend).
3 ❑ May 1948 Cover: 0.10 **NM** value: **225.00**
• **CGC:** 1 graded, best 8.5
4 ❑ Jul 1948 Cover: 0.10 **NM** value: **200.00**
5 ❑ Sep 1948 Cover: 0.10 **NM** value: **200.00**
6 ❑ Nov 1948 Cover: 0.10 **NM** value: **165.00**
7 ❑ Jan 1949 Cover: 0.10 **NM** value: **165.00**
★ 1st Appearance of Annie.
8 ❑ Feb 1949 Cover: 0.10 **NM** value: **165.00**
9 ❑ Mar 1949 Cover: 0.10 **NM** value: **165.00**
10 ❑ Apr 1949 Cover: 0.10 **NM** value: **165.00**
11 ❑ May 1949 Cover: 0.10 **NM** value: **125.00**
12 ❑ Jun 1949 Cover: 0.10 **NM** value: **125.00**
13 ❑ Jul 1949 Cover: 0.10 **NM** value: **125.00**
14 ❑ Aug 1949 Cover: 0.10 **NM** value: **125.00**
15 ❑ Sep 1949 Cover: 0.10 **NM** value: **125.00**
16 ❑ Oct 1949 Cover: 0.10 **NM** value: **125.00**
17 ❑ Nov 1949 Cover: 0.10 **NM** value: **125.00**
18 ❑ Dec 1949 Cover: 0.10 **NM** value: **125.00**
19 ❑ Jan 1950 Cover: 0.10 **NM** value: **125.00**
★ 1st Appearance of Wilbur.
20 ❑ Feb 1950 Cover: 0.10 **NM** value: **125.00**
★ 1st Appearance of Mr. McNabbem.
21 ❑ Mar 1950 Cover: 0.10 **NM** value: **150.00**
22 ❑ Apr 1950 Cover: 0.10 **NM** value: **150.00**
23 ❑ May 1950 Cover: 0.10 **NM** value: **150.00**
24 ❑ Jun 1950 Cover: 0.10 **NM** value: **150.00**
25 ❑ Jul 1950 Cover: 0.10 **NM** value: **150.00**
26 ❑ Aug 1950 Cover: 0.10 **NM** value: **150.00**
27 ❑ Sep 1950 Cover: 0.10 **NM** value: **150.00**
28 ❑ Oct 1950 Cover: 0.10 **NM** value: **150.00**
29 ❑ Nov 1950 Cover: 0.10 **NM** value: **150.00**
30 ❑ Dec 1950 Cover: 0.10 **NM** value: **150.00**
31 ❑ Jan 1951 Cover: 0.10 **NM** value: **90.00**
32 ❑ Feb 1951 Cover: 0.10 **NM** value: **90.00**
33 ❑ Mar 1951 Cover: 0.10 **NM** value: **90.00**
34 ❑ Apr 1951 Cover: 0.10 **NM** value: **90.00**
35 ❑ May 1951 Cover: 0.10 **NM** value: **90.00**
36 ❑ Jun 1951 Cover: 0.10 **NM** value: **90.00**
37 ❑ Jul 1951 Cover: 0.10 **NM** value: **90.00**
38 ❑ Aug 1951 Cover: 0.10 **NM** value: **90.00**
39 ❑ Sep 1951 Cover: 0.10 **NM** value: **125.00**
★ 1st Appearance of Witch Hazel.
40 ❑ Oct 1951 Cover: 0.10 **NM** value: **90.00**
41 ❑ Nov 1951 Cover: 0.10 **NM** value: **70.00**
42 ❑ Dec 1951 Cover: 0.10 **NM** value: **70.00**
43 ❑ Jan 1952 Cover: 0.10 **NM** value: **70.00**
44 ❑ Feb 1952 Cover: 0.10 **NM** value: **70.00**
45 ❑ Mar 1952 Cover: 0.10 **NM** value: **70.00**
★ 2nd Appearance of Witch Hazel.
46 ❑ Apr 1952 Cover: 0.10 **NM** value: **70.00**
47 ❑ May 1952 Cover: 0.10 **NM** value: **70.00**
48 ❑ Jun 1952 Cover: 0.10 **NM** value: **70.00**
49 ❑ Jul 1952 Cover: 0.10 **NM** value: **70.00**
50 ❑ Aug 1952 Cover: 0.10 **NM** value: **70.00**
51 ❑ Sep 1952 Cover: 0.10 **NM** value: **60.00**
52 ❑ Oct 1952 Cover: 0.10 **NM** value: **60.00**
53 ❑ Nov 1952 Cover: 0.10 **NM** value: **60.00**
• **CGC:** 1 graded, best 7.5
54 ❑ Dec 1952 Cover: 0.10 **NM** value: **60.00**
• **CGC:** 1 graded, best 9.4
55 ❑ Jan 1953 Cover: 0.10 **NM** value: **60.00**
• **CGC:** 1 graded, best 8.5
56 ❑ Feb 1953 Cover: 0.10 **NM** value: **60.00**
• **CGC:** 1 graded, best 9.4
57 ❑ Mar 1953 Cover: 0.10 **NM** value: **60.00**
58 ❑ Apr 1953 Cover: 0.10 **NM** value: **60.00**
59 ❑ May 1953 Cover: 0.10 **NM** value: **60.00**
60 ❑ Jun 1953 Cover: 0.10 **NM** value: **60.00**
61 ❑ Jul 1953 Cover: 0.10 **NM** value: **55.00**
62 ❑ Aug 1953 Cover: 0.10 **NM** value: **55.00**
63 ❑ Sep 1953 Cover: 0.10 **NM** value: **55.00**
★ 1st Appearance of Chubby.
64 ❑ Oct 1953 Cover: 0.10 **NM** value: **55.00**
65 ❑ Nov 1953 Cover: 0.10 **NM** value: **55.00**
66 ❑ Dec 1953 Cover: 0.10 **NM** value: **55.00**
67 ❑ Jan 1954 Cover: 0.10 **NM** value: **55.00**
68 ❑ Feb 1954 Cover: 0.10 **NM** value: **55.00**
69 ❑ Mar 1954 Cover: 0.10 **NM** value: **55.00**
70 ❑ Apr 1954 Cover: 0.10 **NM** value: **55.00**
71 ❑ May 1954 Cover: 0.10 **NM** value: **45.00**
72 ❑ Jun 1954 Cover: 0.10 **NM** value: **45.00**
• **CGC:** 1 graded, best 9.2
73 ❑ Jul 1954 Cover: 0.10 **NM** value: **45.00**
74 ❑ Aug 1954 Cover: 0.10 **NM** value: **45.00**
75 ❑ Sep 1954 Cover: 0.10 **NM** value: **45.00**
76 ❑ Oct 1954 Cover: 0.10 **NM** value: **45.00**
77 ❑ Nov 1954 Cover: 0.10 **NM** value: **45.00**
78 ❑ Dec 1954 Cover: 0.10 **NM** value: **45.00**
79 ❑ Jan 1955 Cover: 0.10 **NM** value: **45.00**
80 ❑ Feb 1955 Cover: 0.10 **NM** value: **45.00**
81 ❑ Mar 1955 Cover: 0.10 **NM** value: **40.00**
82 ❑ Apr 1955 Cover: 0.10 **NM** value: **40.00**
83 ❑ May 1955 Cover: 0.10 **NM** value: **40.00**
84 ❑ Jun 1955 Cover: 0.10 **NM** value: **40.00**
85 ❑ Jul 1955 Cover: 0.10 **NM** value: **40.00**
86 ❑ Aug 1955 Cover: 0.10 **NM** value: **40.00**
87 ❑ Sep 1955 Cover: 0.10 **NM** value: **40.00**
88 ❑ Oct 1955 Cover: 0.10 **NM** value: **40.00**
89 ❑ Nov 1955 Cover: 0.10 **NM** value: **40.00**
90 ❑ Dec 1955 Cover: 0.10 **NM** value: **40.00**
91 ❑ Jan 1956 Cover: 0.10 **NM** value: **35.00**
92 ❑ Feb 1956 Cover: 0.10 **NM** value: **35.00**
93 ❑ Mar 1956 Cover: 0.10 **NM** value: **35.00**
94 ❑ Apr 1956 Cover: 0.10 **NM** value: **35.00**
95 ❑ May 1956 Cover: 0.10 **NM** value: **35.00**
96 ❑ Jun 1956 Cover: 0.10 **NM** value: **35.00**
97 ❑ Jul 1956 Cover: 0.10 **NM** value: **35.00**
98 ❑ Aug 1956 Cover: 0.10 **NM** value: **35.00**
99 ❑ Sep 1956 Cover: 0.10 **NM** value: **35.00**
100 ❑ Oct 1956 Cover: 0.10 **NM** value: **50.00**
101 ❑ Nov 1956 Cover: 0.10 **NM** value: **30.00**
102 ❑ Dec 1956 Cover: 0.10 **NM** value: **30.00**
103 ❑ Jan 1957 Cover: 0.10 **NM** value: **30.00**
104 ❑ Feb 1957 Cover: 0.10 **NM** value: **30.00**
105 ❑ Mar 1957 Cover: 0.10 **NM** value: **30.00**
106 ❑ Apr 1957 Cover: 0.10 **NM** value: **30.00**
107 ❑ May 1957 Cover: 0.10 **NM** value: **30.00**
108 ❑ Jun 1957 Cover: 0.10 **NM** value: **30.00**
109 ❑ Jul 1957 Cover: 0.10 **NM** value: **30.00**
110 ❑ Aug 1957 Cover: 0.10 **NM** value: **30.00**
111 ❑ Sep 1957 Cover: 0.10 **NM** value: **30.00**
112 ❑ Oct 1957 Cover: 0.10 **NM** value: **30.00**
113 ❑ Nov 1957 Cover: 0.10 **NM** value: **30.00**
114 ❑ Dec 1957 Cover: 0.10 **NM** value: **30.00**
115 ❑ Jan 1958 Cover: 0.10 **NM** value: **30.00**
116 ❑ Feb 1958 Cover: 0.10 **NM** value: **30.00**
117 ❑ Mar 1958 Cover: 0.10 **NM** value: **30.00**
118 ❑ Apr 1958 Cover: 0.10 **NM** value: **30.00**
119 ❑ May 1958 Cover: 0.10 **NM** value: **30.00**
120 ❑ Jun 1958 Cover: 0.10 **NM** value: **30.00**
121 ❑ Jul 1958 Cover: 0.10 **NM** value: **28.00**
122 ❑ Aug 1958 Cover: 0.10 **NM** value: **28.00**
123 ❑ Sep 1958 Cover: 0.10 **NM** value: **28.00**
124 ❑ Oct 1958 Cover: 0.10 **NM** value: **28.00**
125 ❑ Nov 1958 Cover: 0.10 **NM** value: **28.00**
126 ❑ Dec 1958 Cover: 0.10 **NM** value: **28.00**
127 ❑ Jan 1959 Cover: 0.10 **NM** value: **28.00**
128 ❑ Feb 1959 Cover: 0.10 **NM** value: **28.00**
129 ❑ Mar 1959 Cover: 0.10 **NM** value: **28.00**
130 ❑ Apr 1959 Cover: 0.10 **NM** value: **28.00**
131 ❑ May 1959 Cover: 0.10 **NM** value: **28.00**
132 ❑ Jun 1959 Cover: 0.10 **NM** value: **28.00**
133 ❑ Jul 1959 Cover: 0.10 **NM** value: **28.00**
134 ❑ Aug 1959 Cover: 0.10 **NM** value: **28.00**
135 ❑ Sep 1959 Cover: 0.10 **NM** value: **28.00**
136 ❑ Oct 1959 Cover: 0.10 **NM** value: **28.00**
137 ❑ Nov 1959 Cover: 0.10 **NM** value: **28.00**
138 ❑ Dec 1959 Cover: 0.10 **NM** value: **28.00**
139 ❑ Jan 1960 Cover: 0.10 **NM** value: **28.00**
140 ❑ Feb 1960 Cover: 0.10 **NM** value: **28.00**
141 ❑ Mar 1960 Cover: 0.10 **NM** value: **25.00**
142 ❑ Apr 1960 Cover: 0.10 **NM** value: **25.00**
143 ❑ May 1960 Cover: 0.10 **NM** value: **25.00**
144 ❑ Jun 1960 Cover: 0.10 **NM** value: **25.00**
145 ❑ Jul 1960 Cover: 0.10 **NM** value: **25.00**
146 ❑ Aug 1960 Cover: 0.10 **NM** value: **25.00**
147 ❑ Sep 1960 Cover: 0.10 **NM** value: **25.00**
148 ❑ Oct 1960 Cover: 0.10 **NM** value: **25.00**
149 ❑ Nov 1960 **NM** value: **25.00**
150 ❑ Dec 1960 **NM** value: **25.00**
151 ❑ Jan 1961 **NM** value: **25.00**
152 ❑ Feb 1961 **NM** value: **25.00**
153 ❑ Mar 1961 **NM** value: **25.00**
154 ❑ Apr 1961 Cover: 0.15 **NM** value: **25.00**
155 ❑ 1961 **NM** value: **25.00**
156 ❑ 1961 **NM** value: **25.00**
157 ❑ 1961 **NM** value: **25.00**
158 ❑ 1961 **NM** value: **25.00**
159 ❑ 1961 **NM** value: **25.00**
160 ❑ 1961 **NM** value: **25.00**
161 ❑ 1962 **NM** value: **20.00**
162 ❑ 1962 **NM** value: **20.00**
163 ❑ May 1962 Cover: 0.15 **NM** value: **20.00**
164 ❑ Jul 1962 Cover: 0.15 **NM** value: **20.00**
165 ❑ Oct 1962 Cover: 0.25 **NM** value: **70.00**
• **CGC:** 1 graded, best 9.4
• Giant-size.
166 ❑ Jan 1963 Cover: 0.25 **NM** value: **70.00**
• **CGC:** 1 graded, best 8.5
• Giant-size.
167 ❑ 1963 **NM** value: **20.00**
Circ: Statement: **247,530**
168 ❑ 1963 **NM** value: **20.00**
Circ: Statement: **247,530**
169 ❑ 1963 **NM** value: **20.00**
Circ: Statement: **247,530**
170 ❑ **NM** value: **20.00**
Circ: Statement: **247,530**
171 ❑ Mar 1964 **NM** value: **20.00**
Circ: Statement: **239,376**
172 ❑ Jun 1964 Cover: 0.12 **NM** value: **20.00**
Circ: Statement: **239,376** • **CGC:** 1 graded, best 9.4
173 ❑ Sep 1964 Cover: 0.12 **NM** value: **20.00**
Circ: Statement: **239,376**
174 ❑ Dec 1964 Cover: 0.12 **NM** value: **20.00**
Circ: Statement: **239,376**
175 ❑ Mar 1965 Cover: 0.12 **NM** value: **20.00**
Circ: Statement: **246,650**
176 ❑ Jun 1965 Cover: 0.12 **NM** value: **20.00**
Circ: Statement: **246,650**
177 ❑ Sep 1965 Cover: 0.12 **NM** value: **20.00**
Circ: Statement: **246,650**
178 ❑ Dec 1965 Cover: 0.12 **NM** value: **20.00**
Circ: Statement: **246,650**
179 ❑ Mar 1966 Cover: 0.12 **NM** value: **20.00**
Circ: Statement: **245,000**
180 ❑ Jun 1966 Cover: 0.12 **NM** value: **20.00**
Circ: Statement: **245,000**
181 ❑ Sep 1966 Cover: 0.12 **NM** value: **15.00**
Circ: Statement: **245,000**
182 ❑ Dec 1966 Cover: 0.12 **NM** value: **15.00**
Circ: Statement: **245,000**
183 ❑ Mar 1967 Cover: 0.12 **NM** value: **15.00**
Circ: Statement: **224,800**

CGC-graded: Multiply prices above by **33 for 9.9 M • 16 for 9.8 NM/M • 7 for 9.6 NM+ • 5 for 9.4 NM • 2.5 for 9.2 NM- • 1.5 for 9.0 VF/NM**

184 ❑ Jun 1967 Cover: 0.12 **NM** value: **15.00**
Circ: Statement: **224,800**
• Has 1966 Statement, filed 9/28/66; avg print run 408,364; avg sales 243,875; avg subs 1,125; avg total paid 245,000; 568 samples; max existent 245,568; 36% of run returned
185 ❑ Sep 1967 Cover: 0.12 **NM** value: **15.00**
Circ: Statement: **224,800**
186 ❑ Dec 1967 Cover: 0.12 **NM** value: **15.00**
Circ: Statement: **224,800**
187 ❑ Mar 1968 Cover: 0.12 **NM** value: **15.00**
188 ❑ Jun 1968 Cover: 0.12 **NM** value: **15.00**
189 ❑ Sep 1968 Cover: 0.15 **NM** value: **15.00**
190 ❑ Dec 1968 Cover: 0.15 **NM** value: **15.00**
191 ❑ Mar 1969 Cover: 0.15 **NM** value: **15.00**
192 ❑ Jun 1969 Cover: 0.15 **NM** value: **15.00**
193 ❑ Sep 1969 Cover: 0.15 **NM** value: **15.00**
194 ❑ Dec 1969 Cover: 0.15 **NM** value: **15.00**
195 ❑ Mar 1970 Cover: 0.15 **NM** value: **15.00**
196 ❑ Jun 1970 Cover: 0.15 **NM** value: **15.00**
197 ❑ Sep 1970 Cover: 0.15 **NM** value: **15.00**
198 ❑ Dec 1970 Cover: 0.15 **NM** value: **15.00**
199 ❑ Mar 1971 Cover: 0.15 **NM** value: **15.00**
Circ: Statement: **208,875**
📖 Little Lulu Tames Tubby; The Doll Doctor; Breakfast In Bed; Witch Hazel; Turtle In A Tree
200 ❑ Jun 1971 Cover: 0.15 **NM** value: **15.00**
Circ: Statement: **208,875**
201 ❑ Sep 1971 Cover: 0.15 **NM** value: **9.00**
Circ: Statement: **208,875**
202 ❑ Dec 1971 Cover: 0.15 **NM** value: **9.00**
Circ: Statement: **208,875**
203 ❑ Mar 1972 Cover: 0.15 **NM** value: **9.00**
204 ❑ May 1972 Cover: 0.15 **NM** value: **9.00**
205 ❑ Jul 1972 Cover: 0.15 **NM** value: **9.00**
• Has 1971 Statement; avg print run 323,914; avg total paid circ 208,875; 64% or less of run returned
206 ❑ Aug 1972 Cover: 0.15 **NM** value: **9.00**
• **CGC:** 2 graded, best 9.4
207 ❑ Sep 1972 Cover: 0.15 **NM** value: **9.00**
📖 The Case of the Doll-Napper, Miss Junior Witch, The Case of the Big Squeeze
208 ❑ Nov 1972, four-color Cover: 0.15 **NM** value: **9.00**
📖 Gobble Trouble; Wedding Belles; Mr. McNabbem We Love You!
209 ❑ Dec 1972 Cover: 0.15 **NM** value: **9.00**
210 ❑ Jan 1973 Cover: 0.15 **NM** value: **9.00**
📖 A Doll Named Tubby, Who Crows There?, Puny Express
211 ❑ Mar 1973 Cover: 0.15 **NM** value: **9.00**
212 ❑ May 1973 Cover: 0.20 **NM** value: **9.00**
213 ❑ Jul 1973 Cover: 0.20 **NM** value: **9.00**
214 ❑ Sep 1973 Cover: 0.20 **NM** value: **9.00**
215 ❑ Nov 1973 Cover: 0.20 **NM** value: **9.00**
216 ❑ Jan 1974 Cover: 0.20 **NM** value: **9.00**
217 ❑ Mar 1974 Cover: 0.20 **NM** value: **9.00**
218 ❑ May 1974 Cover: 0.20 **NM** value: **9.00**
219 ❑ Jul 1974 Cover: 0.25 **NM** value: **9.00**
220 ❑ Aug 1974 Cover: 0.25 **NM** value: **9.00**
221 ❑ Sep 1974 Cover: 0.25 **NM** value: **6.00**
222 ❑ Nov 1974 Cover: 0.25 **NM** value: **6.00**
223 ❑ Jan 1975 Cover: 0.25 **NM** value: **6.00**
224 ❑ Mar 1975 Cover: 0.25 **NM** value: **6.00**
225 ❑ May 1975 Cover: 0.25 **NM** value: **6.00**
226 ❑ Jul 1975 Cover: 0.25 **NM** value: **6.00**
227 ❑ Aug 1975 Cover: 0.25 **NM** value: **6.00**
228 ❑ Sep 1975 Cover: 0.25 **NM** value: **6.00**
229 ❑ Nov 1975 Cover: 0.25 **NM** value: **6.00**
230 ❑ Jan 1976 Cover: 0.25 **NM** value: **6.00**
231 ❑ 1976 Cover: 0.25 **NM** value: **6.00**
232 ❑ 1976 Cover: 0.25 **NM** value: **6.00**
233 ❑ 1976 **NM** value: **6.00**
234 ❑ 1976 **NM** value: **6.00**
235 ❑ 1976 Cover: 0.30 **NM** value: **6.00**
236 ❑ 1976 Cover: 0.30 **NM** value: **6.00**
237 ❑ 1977 Cover: 0.30 **NM** value: **6.00**
238 ❑ 1977 Cover: 0.30 **NM** value: **6.00**
239 ❑ 1977 Cover: 0.30 **NM** value: **6.00**
240 ❑ 1977 Cover: 0.30 **NM** value: **6.00**
241 ❑ 1977 Cover: 0.30 **NM** value: **4.00**
242 ❑ 1977 Cover: 0.30 **NM** value: **4.00**
243 ❑ 1977 **NM** value: **4.00**
244 ❑ 1978 **NM** value: **4.00**
245 ❑ 1978 Cover: 0.35 **NM** value: **4.00**
246 ❑ 1978 Cover: 0.35 **NM** value: **4.00**
247 ❑ 1978 Cover: 0.35 **NM** value: **4.00**
248 ❑ Sep 1978 Cover: 0.35 **NM** value: **4.00**
249 ❑ **NM** value: **4.00**
250 ❑ **NM** value: **4.00**
251 ❑ **NM** value: **3.00**
252 ❑ 1979 **NM** value: **3.00**
253 ❑ 1979 **NM** value: **3.00**
254 ❑ Aug 1979 Cover: 0.40 **NM** value: **3.00**
255 ❑ 1979 Cover: 0.40 **NM** value: **3.00**
256 ❑ Nov 1979 Cover: 0.40 **NM** value: **3.00**
257 ❑ Jan 1980 Cover: 0.40 **NM** value: **3.00**
258 ❑ Mar 1980 Cover: 0.40 **NM** value: **3.00**
259 ❑ May 1980 Cover: 0.40 **NM** value: **3.00**
260 ❑ **NM** value: **2.00**
261 ❑ **NM** value: **2.00**
262 ❑ 1981 **NM** value: **2.00**
263 ❑ 1981 **NM** value: **2.00**
264 ❑ Feb 1982 Cover: 0.60 **NM** value: **2.00**
265 ❑ **NM** value: **2.00**
266 ❑ **NM** value: **2.00**
267 ❑ **NM** value: **2.00**
268 ❑ **NM** value: **2.00**
final issue.

LITTLE MAX COMICS — Harvey

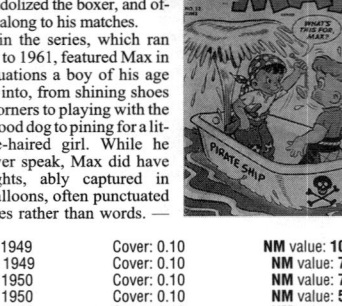

Joe Palooka's mute friend, Max, is the star of this long-running series. The little red-headed boy wore a large straw hat, idolized the boxer, and often tagged along to his matches.

Stories in the series, which ran from 1949 to 1961, featured Max in typical situations a boy of his age would get into, from shining shoes on street corners to playing with the neighborhood dog to pining for a little blonde-haired girl. While he would never speak, Max did have big thoughts, ably captured in thought balloons, often punctuated with images rather than words. — Brent

1 ❑ Oct 1949 Cover: 0.10 **NM** value: **100.00**
2 ❑ Dec 1949 Cover: 0.10 **NM** value: **75.00**
3 ❑ Feb 1950 Cover: 0.10 **NM** value: **75.00**
4 ❑ Apr 1950 Cover: 0.10 **NM** value: **50.00**
5 ❑ Jun 1950 Cover: 0.10 **NM** value: **40.00**
6 ❑ Aug 1950 Cover: 0.10 **NM** value: **35.00**
7 ❑ Oct 1950 Cover: 0.10 **NM** value: **35.00**
8 ❑ Dec 1950 Cover: 0.10 **NM** value: **35.00**
9 ❑ Feb 1951 Cover: 0.10 **NM** value: **35.00**
10 ❑ Apr 1951 Cover: 0.10 **NM** value: **30.00**
11 ❑ Jun 1951 Cover: 0.10 **NM** value: **30.00**
12 ❑ Aug 1951 Cover: 0.10 **NM** value: **30.00**
13 ❑ Oct 1951 Cover: 0.10 **NM** value: **30.00**
14 ❑ Dec 1951 Cover: 0.10 **NM** value: **30.00**
15 ❑ Feb 1952 Cover: 0.10 **NM** value: **30.00**
16 ❑ Apr 1952 Cover: 0.10 **NM** value: **30.00**
17 ❑ Jun 1952 Cover: 0.10 **NM** value: **30.00**
18 ❑ Aug 1952 Cover: 0.10 **NM** value: **30.00**
19 ❑ Oct 1952 Cover: 0.10 **NM** value: **30.00**
20 ❑ Dec 1952 Cover: 0.10 **NM** value: **25.00**
21 ❑ Feb 1953 Cover: 0.10 **NM** value: **25.00**
22 ❑ Apr 1953 Cover: 0.10 **NM** value: **25.00**
23 ❑ Jun 1953 Cover: 0.10 **NM** value: **25.00**
24 ❑ Aug 1953 Cover: 0.10 **NM** value: **25.00**
25 ❑ Oct 1953 Cover: 0.10 **NM** value: **25.00**
26 ❑ Dec 1953 Cover: 0.10 **NM** value: **25.00**
27 ❑ Feb 1954 Cover: 0.10 **NM** value: **25.00**
28 ❑ Apr 1954 Cover: 0.10 **NM** value: **25.00**
29 ❑ Jun 1954 Cover: 0.10 **NM** value: **25.00**
30 ❑ Aug 1954 Cover: 0.10 **NM** value: **25.00**
31 ❑ Oct 1954 Cover: 0.10 **NM** value: **25.00**
32 ❑ Dec 1954 Cover: 0.10 **NM** value: **25.00**
33 ❑ Feb 1955 Cover: 0.10 **NM** value: **25.00**
34 ❑ Apr 1955 Cover: 0.10 **NM** value: **25.00**
35 ❑ Jun 1955 Cover: 0.10 **NM** value: **25.00**
36 ❑ Aug 1955 Cover: 0.10 **NM** value: **25.00**
37 ❑ Oct 1955 Cover: 0.10 **NM** value: **25.00**
38 ❑ Dec 1955 Cover: 0.10 **NM** value: **25.00**
39 ❑ Feb 1956 Cover: 0.10 **NM** value: **25.00**
40 ❑ Apr 1956 Cover: 0.10 **NM** value: **20.00**
41 ❑ Jun 1956 Cover: 0.10 **NM** value: **20.00**
42 ❑ Aug 1956 Cover: 0.10 **NM** value: **20.00**
43 ❑ Oct 1956 Cover: 0.10 **NM** value: **20.00**
44 ❑ Dec 1956 Cover: 0.10 **NM** value: **20.00**
45 ❑ Feb 1957 Cover: 0.10 **NM** value: **20.00**
46 ❑ Apr 1957 Cover: 0.10 **NM** value: **20.00**
47 ❑ Jun 1957 Cover: 0.10 **NM** value: **20.00**
48 ❑ Aug 1957 Cover: 0.10 **NM** value: **20.00**
49 ❑ Oct 1957 Cover: 0.10 **NM** value: **20.00**
50 ❑ Dec 1957 Cover: 0.10 **NM** value: **20.00**
51 ❑ Feb 1958 Cover: 0.10 **NM** value: **20.00**
52 ❑ Apr 1958 Cover: 0.10 **NM** value: **20.00**
53 ❑ Jun 1958 Cover: 0.10 **NM** value: **20.00**
54 ❑ Aug 1958 Cover: 0.10 **NM** value: **20.00**
55 ❑ Oct 1958 Cover: 0.10 **NM** value: **20.00**
56 ❑ Jan 1959 Cover: 0.10 **NM** value: **20.00**
57 ❑ Mar 1959 Cover: 0.10 **NM** value: **20.00**
58 ❑ May 1959 Cover: 0.10 **NM** value: **20.00**
59 ❑ Jul 1959 Cover: 0.10 **NM** value: **20.00**
60 ❑ Sep 1959 Cover: 0.10 **NM** value: **15.00**
61 ❑ Nov 1959 Cover: 0.10 **NM** value: **15.00**
62 ❑ Jan 1960 Cover: 0.10 **NM** value: **15.00**
63 ❑ Mar 1960 Cover: 0.10 **NM** value: **15.00**
64 ❑ May 1960 Cover: 0.10 **NM** value: **15.00**
65 ❑ Jul 1960 Cover: 0.10 **NM** value: **15.00**
66 ❑ Sep 1960 Cover: 0.10 **NM** value: **15.00**
67 ❑ Nov 1960 Cover: 0.10 **NM** value: **15.00**
68 ❑ Jan 1961 Cover: 0.10 **NM** value: **15.00**
69 ❑ Mar 1961 Cover: 0.10 **NM** value: **15.00**
70 ❑ May 1961 Cover: 0.10 **NM** value: **15.00**
71 ❑ Jul 1961 Cover: 0.10 **NM** value: **15.00**
72 ❑ Sep 1961 Cover: 0.10 **NM** value: **15.00**
73 ❑ Nov 1961 Cover: 0.10 **NM** value: **15.00**

LITTLE MERMAID, THE (DISNEY'S...) — Marvel

1 ❑ Sep 1994 Cover: 1.50 **NM** value: **2.50**
Circ: CapCity orders: **14,550**
📖 Sink Or Swim **A:** Mary Wilshire **W:** Trina Robbins
2 ❑ Oct 1994 Cover: 1.50 **NM** value: **2.00**
Circ: CapCity orders: **9,900**
3 ❑ Nov 1994 Cover: 1.50 **NM** value: **2.00**
Circ: CapCity orders: **9,150**
4 ❑ Dec 1994 Cover: 1.50 **NM** value: **2.00**
Circ: CapCity orders: **7,000**
5 ❑ Jan 1995 Cover: 1.50 **NM** value: **2.00**
Circ: CapCity orders: **6,350**
6 ❑ Feb 1995 Cover: 1.50 **NM** value: **2.00**
Circ: CapCity orders: **5,375**
7 ❑ Mar 1995 Cover: 1.50 **NM** value: **2.00**
Circ: CapCity orders: **4,525**
8 ❑ Apr 1995 Cover: 1.50 **NM** value: **2.00**
Circ: CapCity orders: **3,950**
9 ❑ May 1995 Cover: 1.50 **NM** value: **2.00**
Circ: CapCity orders: **3,850**
10 ❑ Jun 1995 Cover: 1.50 **NM** value: **2.00**
Circ: CapCity orders: **3,700**
11 ❑ Jul 1995 Cover: 1.50 **NM** value: **2.00**
Circ: CapCity orders: **3,425**
12 ❑ Aug 1995 Cover: 1.50 **NM** value: **2.00**
Circ: CapCity orders: **3,450**
final issue.

LITTLE MERMAID LIMITED SERIES, THE (DISNEY'S...) — Disney

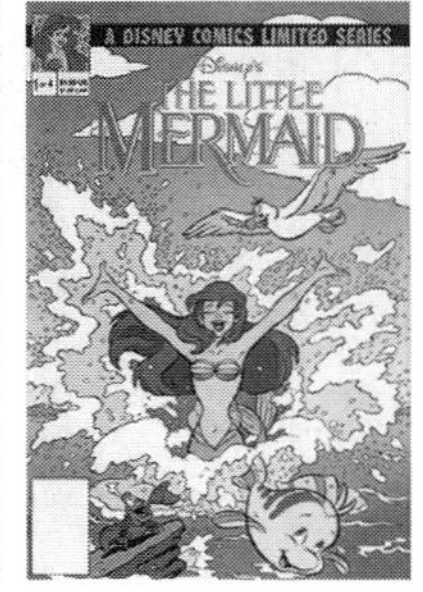

OK, so you just couldn't get enough of the winsome Ariel in the now classic Disney film The Little Mermaid? Here's a limited series from Disney Comics that reveals some of young Ariel's adventures prior to her cinematic encounter with the handsome Prince Eric. All of your favorite characters from the film are here: the hapless Flounder, the powerful King Triton, the evil Ursula, and the delightful Sebastian. And there are some new friends and foes to boot! Thrill as Ariel faces the frightening Serpentine in this excellent four-parter from writer Peter David and artist Chuck Austen.

1 ❑ Feb 1992 Cover: 1.50 **NM** value: **2.00**
Circ: CapCity orders: **17,750**
2 ❑ Mar 1992 Cover: 1.50 **NM** value: **2.00**
Circ: CapCity orders: **9,850**
3 ❑ May 1992 Cover: 1.50 **NM** value: **2.00**
Circ: CapCity orders: **8,100**
4 ❑ Jun 1992 Cover: 1.50 **NM** value: **2.00**
Circ: CapCity orders: **8,200**

LITTLE MERMAID (ONE-SHOT) — W.D.

1 ❑ Cover: 3.50 **NM** value: **Cover or less**
No issue number. 📖 Under the Sea

LITTLE MERMAID, THE: UNDERWATER ENGAGEMENTS (DISNEY'S...) — Acclaim

1 ❑ Cover: 4.50 **NM** value: **Cover or less**
• flip-book digest set before movie.

LITTLE MERMAID, THE (WALT DISNEY'S...) — Disney

1 ❑ Cover: 2.50 **NM** value: **Cover or less**
Circ: CapCity orders: **3,900**
• stapled **A:** Gutenberghus Publishing Service **W:** Tom Anderson
1/DM ❑ Cover: 5.95 **NM** value: **Cover or less**
• squarebound

LITTLE MISS MUFFET — Best

11 ❑ ca. 1948 Cover: 0.10 **NM** value: **50.00**
• **CGC:** 1 graded, best 9.0
12 ❑ ca. 1949 Cover: 0.10 **NM** value: **30.00**
13 ❑ ca. 1949 Cover: 0.10 **NM** value: **30.00**

LITTLE MISS STRANGE — Millennium

1 ❑ Cover: 2.95 **NM** value: **Cover or less**

LITTLE MISS SUNBEAM — Magazine Enterprises

1 ❑ Jun 1950 Cover: 0.10 **NM** value: **100.00**
2 ❑ Aug 1950 Cover: 0.10 **NM** value: **50.00**
3 ❑ Oct 1950 Cover: 0.10 **NM** value: **50.00**
4 ❑ Dec 1950 Cover: 0.10 **NM** value: **50.00**
• **CGC:** 1 graded, best 6.5

LITTLE MISTER MAN — Slave Labor

1 ❑ Nov 1995, b&w Cover: 2.95 **NM** value: **Cover or less**
A: James Kochalka **W:** James Kochalka
2 ❑ Dec 1995, b&w Cover: 2.95 **NM** value: **Cover or less**
A: James Kochalka **W:** James Kochalka
3 ❑ Feb 1996, b&w Cover: 2.95 **NM** value: **Cover or less**
final issue. **A:** James Kochalka **W:** James Kochalka

LITTLE MONSTERS — Now

1 ❑ Jan 1990 Cover: 1.75 **NM** value: **Cover or less**
Circ: CapCity orders: **2,850**
A: Kurt Anderson **W:** Katherine Llewellyn
2 ❑ Feb 1990 Cover: 1.75 **NM** value: **Cover or less**
📖 Run Amuck **A:** Kurt Anderson **W:** Katherine Llewellyn
3 ❑ Mar 1990 Cover: 1.75 **NM** value: **Cover or less**
Circ: CapCity orders: **1,900**
📖 Pie Party **A:** Kurt Anderson **W:** Katherine Llewellyn
4 ❑ Apr 1990 Cover: 1.75 **NM** value: **Cover or less**
📖 Mindwarp **A:** Kurt Anderson **W:** Katherine Llewellyn
5 ❑ May 1990 Cover: 1.75 **NM** value: **Cover or less**
Circ: CapCity orders: **1,050**
📖 Rampant Royalty **A:** Kurt Anderson **W:** Katherine Llewellyn
6 ❑ Jun 1990 Cover: 1.75 **NM** value: **Cover or less**
Circ: CapCity orders: **950**
📖 Sweet Revenge **A:** Kurt Anderson **W:** Katherine Llewellyn

Statement of Ownership figures are the average number of copies originally sold, as cited by the publisher to the U.S. Postal Service. These estimate **all** sales, in comics shops and on newsstands.

Other grades: Multiply prices above by **1.5 for Mint • 2/3 for Very Fine • 1/3 for Fine • 1/5 for Very Good • 1/8 for Good**

LITTLE MONSTERS, THE (GOLD KEY) Gold Key

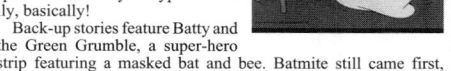

'Orrible Orvie and Awful Annie star in this humor series, yet another depicting the family life of weird but amiable monsters. (See also The Addams Family, The Munsters, Mr. and Mrs. J. Evil Scientist, among others.)

Orvie and Annie are the children of a pair of Frankenstein-style monsters, and their lives are filled with gruesome humor. The kids sleep beds of nails, Dad breathes fire when he's angry, and Mom knits spider webs. Just your typical family, basically!

Back-up stories feature Batty and the Green Grumble, a super-hero strip featuring a masked bat and bee. Batmite still came first, though... — JJM

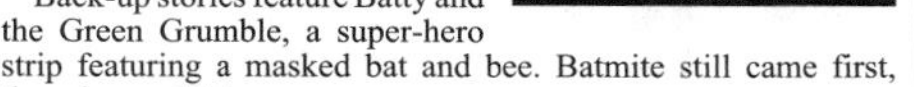

1 ❑ Nov 1964 Cover: 0.12 **NM** value: **2.00**
2 ❑ Feb 1965 Cover: 0.12 **NM** value: **12.00**
3 ❑ Nov 1965 Cover: 0.12 **NM** value: **8.00**
4 ❑ 1966 Cover: 0.12 **NM** value: **8.00**
5 ❑ Jul 1966 Cover: 0.12 **NM** value: **8.00**
6 ❑ Oct 1966 Cover: 0.12 **NM** value: **6.00**
7 ❑ Dec 1966 Cover: 0.12 **NM** value: **6.00**
8 ❑ Feb 1967 Cover: 0.12 **NM** value: **6.00**
9 ❑ Apr 1967 Cover: 0.12 **NM** value: **6.00**
10 ❑ Jun 1967 Cover: 0.12 **NM** value: **5.00**
11 ❑ Cover: 0.12 **NM** value: **5.00**
12 ❑ Dec 1970 Cover: 0.12 **NM** value: **5.00**
13 ❑ ca. 1971 **NM** value: **5.00**
14 ❑ Sep 1971 Cover: 0.15 **NM** value: **5.00**
15 ❑ Dec 1971 Cover: 0.15 **NM** value: **5.00**
16 ❑ Mar 1972 Cover: 0.15 **NM** value: **5.00**
17 ❑ Jun 1972 Cover: 0.15 **NM** value: **5.00**
18 ❑ Sep 1972 Cover: 0.15 **NM** value: **5.00**
19 ❑ Dec 1972 Cover: 0.15 **NM** value: **5.00**
20 ❑ Mar 1973 **NM** value: **5.00**
21 ❑ Jun 1973 Cover: 0.20 **NM** value: **4.00**
• **CGC:** 1 graded, best 9.2
22 ❑ Sep 1973 Cover: 0.20 **NM** value: **4.00**
• **CGC:** 1 graded, best 9.0
23 ❑ Dec 1973 Cover: 0.20 **NM** value: **4.00**
24 ❑ Mar 1974 Cover: 0.20 **NM** value: **4.00**
25 ❑ Jun 1974 Cover: 0.20 **NM** value: **4.00**
26 ❑ Sep 1974 Cover: 0.25 **NM** value: **4.00**
27 ❑ Dec 1974 Cover: 0.25 **NM** value: **4.00**
28 ❑ Mar 1975 Cover: 0.25 **NM** value: **4.00**
29 ❑ Jun 1975 Cover: 0.25 **NM** value: **4.00**
30 ❑ Sep 1975 Cover: 0.25 **NM** value: **4.00**
31 ❑ Dec 1975 Cover: 0.25 **NM** value: **4.00**
32 ❑ Feb 1976 Cover: 0.25 **NM** value: **4.00**
33 ❑ Apr 1976 Cover: 0.25 **NM** value: **4.00**
34 ❑ Jun 1976 Cover: 0.25 **NM** value: **4.00**
35 ❑ Aug 1976 Cover: 0.25 **NM** value: **4.00**
36 ❑ Oct 1976 Cover: 0.30 **NM** value: **4.00**
37 ❑ Dec 1976 Cover: 0.30 **NM** value: **4.00**
38 ❑ Feb 1977 Cover: 0.30 **NM** value: **4.00**
39 ❑ Apr 1977 Cover: 0.30 **NM** value: **4.00**
40 ❑ Jun 1977 Cover: 0.30 **NM** value: **4.00**
41 ❑ Aug 1977 Cover: 0.30 **NM** value: **4.00**
42 ❑ Oct 1977 Cover: 0.30 **NM** value: **4.00**
43 ❑ Dec 1977 Cover: 0.35 **NM** value: **4.00**
44 ❑ Feb 1978 Cover: 0.35 **NM** value: **4.00**

LITTLE NEMO IN SLUMBERLAND 3-D Blackthorne

1 ❑ Cover: 2.50 **NM** value: **Cover or less**

LITTLE ORPHAN ANNIE David McKay

Harold Gray (1894-1968) introduced Little Orphan Annie in 1924 as something of a humorous character in a humorous strip, nevertheless featuring the adventures of a spunky little orphan girl. Shortly after the strip began, she was adopted by industrialist (well, look at his name) "Daddy" Warbucks. The following year, she teamed up with her dog, Sandy, and the pair plunged into a series of up again, down again adventures, often reunited with and then separated from Warbucks.

Eventually, of course, the series spawned its own musical, Annie, but, long before that, the girl starred in her own title for three issues of strip reprints. — Maggie

1 ❑ Mar 1948 Cover: 0.10 **NM** value: **150.00**
2 ❑ Jun 1948 Cover: 0.10 **NM** value: **100.00**
3 ❑ Sep 1948 Cover: 0.10 **NM** value: **100.00**

LITTLE RED HOT: CHANE OF FOOLS Image

1 ❑ Feb 1999 Cover: 2.95 **NM** value: **Cover or less**
Circ: Diamd. preorders: **5,736**
📖 Chane of Fools **A:** Dawn Brown **W:** Dawn Brown
2 ❑ Mar 1999 Cover: 2.95 **NM** value: **Cover or less**
📖 Rain **A:** Dawn Brown **W:** Dawn Brown
3 ❑ Apr 1999 Cover: 2.95 **NM** value: **Cover or less**
📖 Prelude to a Kiss **A:** Dawn Brown **W:** Dawn Brown
Bk 1❑ Cover: 12.95 **NM** value: **Cover or less**
• The Foolish Connection; Collects mini-series

LITTLE RONZO IN SLUMBERLAND Slave Labor

1 ❑ Jul 1987 Cover: 1.75 **NM** value: **Cover or less**
A: Jim Bricker **W:** Jim Bricker

LITTLE ROQUEFORT St. John

1 ❑ ca. 1952 Cover: 0.10 **NM** value: **60.00**
2 ❑ ca. 1952 Cover: 0.10 **NM** value: **30.00**
3 ❑ ca. 1952 Cover: 0.10 **NM** value: **25.00**
4 ❑ ca. 1952 Cover: 0.10 **NM** value: **25.00**
5 ❑ ca. 1953 Cover: 0.10 **NM** value: **25.00**
6 ❑ ca. 1953 Cover: 0.10 **NM** value: **25.00**
7 ❑ Cover: 0.10 **NM** value: **25.00**
8 ❑ Cover: 0.10 **NM** value: **25.00**
9 ❑ Cover: 0.10 **NM** value: **25.00**
10 ❑ **NM** value: **25.00**

LITTLE SAD SACK Harvey

1 ❑ Oct 1964 Cover: 0.12 **NM** value: **40.00**
• **CGC:** 1 graded, best 9.4
2 ❑ Dec 1964 Cover: 0.12 **NM** value: **20.00**
3 ❑ Feb 1964 Cover: 0.12 **NM** value: **20.00**
4 ❑ Apr 1965 Cover: 0.12 **NM** value: **20.00**
5 ❑ Jun 1965 Cover: 0.12 **NM** value: **20.00**
6 ❑ Aug 1965 Cover: 0.12 **NM** value: **20.00**
7 ❑ Oct 1965 Cover: 0.12 **NM** value: **20.00**
8 ❑ Dec 1965 Cover: 0.12 **NM** value: **20.00**
9 ❑ Feb 1966 Cover: 0.12 **NM** value: **20.00**
10 ❑ Apr 1966 Cover: 0.12 **NM** value: **15.00**
11 ❑ Jun 1966 Cover: 0.12 **NM** value: **15.00**
12 ❑ Sep 1966 Cover: 0.12 **NM** value: **15.00**
13 ❑ Nov 1966 Cover: 0.12 **NM** value: **15.00**
14 ❑ Jan 1966 Cover: 0.12 **NM** value: **15.00**
15 ❑ Mar 1966 Cover: 0.12 **NM** value: **15.00**
16 ❑ May 1966 Cover: 0.12 **NM** value: **15.00**
17 ❑ Jul 1966 Cover: 0.12 **NM** value: **15.00**
18 ❑ Sep 1966 Cover: 0.12 **NM** value: **15.00**
19 ❑ Nov 1966 Cover: 0.12 **NM** value: **15.00**

LITTLE SCOUTS Dell

2 ❑ Oct 1951 Cover: 0.10 **NM** value: **15.00**
3 ❑ Jan 1952 Cover: 0.10 **NM** value: **15.00**
4 ❑ Apr 1952 Cover: 0.10 **NM** value: **15.00**
5 ❑ Jul 1952 Cover: 0.10 **NM** value: **15.00**
6 ❑ Oct 1952 Cover: 0.10 **NM** value: **15.00**

LITTLE SHOP OF HORRORS DC

1 ❑ Mar 1987 Cover: 2.00 **NM** value: **Cover or less**
A: Gene Colan; Dave Hunt **W:** Michael Fleisher

LITTLE STOOGES Gold Key

1 ❑ Sep 1972 Cover: 0.15 **NM** value: **25.00**
• **CGC:** 2 graded, best 9.2
2 ❑ Dec 1972 Cover: 0.15 **NM** value: **15.00**
• **CGC:** 1 graded, best 8.5
3 ❑ Mar 1973 Cover: 0.15 **NM** value: **15.00**
• **CGC:** 22 graded, best 9.8
4 ❑ Jun 1973 Cover: 0.20 **NM** value: **15.00**
• **CGC:** 1 graded, best 7.5
5 ❑ Sep 1973 Cover: 0.20 **NM** value: **15.00**
• **CGC:** 1 graded, best 8.5
6 ❑ Dec 1973 Cover: 0.20 **NM** value: **15.00**
• **CGC:** 1 graded, best 7.5
7 ❑ Mar 1974 Cover: 0.20 **NM** value: **15.00**
• **CGC:** 1 graded, best 6.0

LITTLE WHITE MOUSE Caliber

1 ❑ Nov 1997, b&w Cover: 2.95 **NM** value: **Cover or less**
📖 A Day in the Life of a Mouse in the Field **A:** Paul Sizer **W:** Paul Sizer
2 ❑ Jan 1998, b&w Cover: 2.95 **NM** value: **Cover or less**
A: Paul Sizer **W:** Paul Sizer
3 ❑ 1998 Cover: 2.95 **NM** value: **Cover or less**
A: Paul Sizer **W:** Paul Sizer
4 ❑ Jan 2001 Cover: 2.95 **NM** value: **Cover or less**
Circ: Diamd. preorders: **679**
A: Paul Sizer **W:** Paul Sizer

LIVING BIBLE Living Bible

1 ❑ Fal 1945 Cover: 0.10 **NM** value: **300.00**
2 ❑ Win 1945 Cover: 0.10 **NM** value: **200.00**
3 ❑ Spr 1946 Cover: 0.10 **NM** value: **200.00**

LIVINGSTONE MOUNTAIN Adventure

1 ❑ Jul 1991, b&w Cover: 2.50 **NM** value: **Cover or less**
A: Steve Moncuse **W:** Steve Moncuse
2 ❑ Aug 1991, b&w Cover: 2.50 **NM** value: **Cover or less**
A: Steve Moncuse **W:** Steve Moncuse
3 ❑ Sep 1991, b&w Cover: 2.50 **NM** value: **Cover or less**
A: Steve Moncuse **W:** Steve Moncuse
4 ❑ Oct 1991, b&w Cover: 2.50 **NM** value: **Cover or less**
A: Steve Moncuse **W:** Steve Moncuse

LIZ AND BETH (VOL. 1) Fantagraphics / Eros

All issues are adults only.

1 ❑ b&w Cover: 2.25 **NM** value: **3.00**
A: G. Levis **W:** G. Levis
2 ❑ b&w Cover: 2.25 **NM** value: **3.00**
A: G. Levis **W:** G. Levis
3 ❑ b&w Cover: 2.25 **NM** value: **3.00**
A: G. Levis **W:** G. Levis
4 ❑ Cover: 2.50 **NM** value: **3.00**
A: G. Levis **W:** G. Levis

LIZ AND BETH (VOL. 2) Fantagraphics / Eros

All issues are adults only.

1 ❑ b&w Cover: 2.50 **NM** value: **Cover or less**
A: G. Levis **W:** G. Levis
2 ❑ b&w Cover: 2.50 **NM** value: **Cover or less**
A: G. Levis **W:** G. Levis
3 ❑ b&w Cover: 2.50 **NM** value: **Cover or less**
A: G. Levis **W:** G. Levis
4 ❑ Cover: 2.50 **NM** value: **Cover or less**
A: G. Levis **W:** G. Levis

LIZ AND BETH (VOL. 3) Fantagraphics / Eros

All issues are adults only.

1 ❑ b&w Cover: 2.50 **NM** value: **Cover or less**
2 ❑ b&w Cover: 2.50 **NM** value: **Cover or less**
3 ❑ b&w Cover: 2.50 **NM** value: **Cover or less**
4 ❑ b&w Cover: 2.50 **NM** value: **Cover or less**
5 ❑ b&w Cover: 2.50 **NM** value: **Cover or less**
6 ❑ b&w Cover: 2.50 **NM** value: **Cover or less**
7 ❑ b&w Cover: 2.50 **NM** value: **Cover or less**

LIZARD LADY Aircel

All issues are adults only.

1 ❑ b&w Cover: 2.95 **NM** value: **Cover or less**
2 ❑ b&w Cover: 2.95 **NM** value: **Cover or less**
3 ❑ b&w Cover: 2.95 **NM** value: **Cover or less**
4 ❑ b&w Cover: 2.95 **NM** value: **Cover or less**

LIZARDS SUMMER FUN SPECIAL Caliber

1 ❑ b&w Cover: 3.50 **NM** value: **Cover or less**

LLOYD LLEWELLYN Fantagraphics

1 ❑ Apr 1986 Cover: 2.25 **NM** value: **Cover or less**
Circ: CapCity orders: **1,425**
2 ❑ Jun 1986 Cover: 2.25 **NM** value: **Cover or less**
3 ❑ Aug 1986 Cover: 2.25 **NM** value: **Cover or less**
4 ❑ Oct 1986 Cover: 2.25 **NM** value: **Cover or less**
5 ❑ Jan 1987 Cover: 2.25 **NM** value: **Cover or less**
6 ❑ Jun 1987 Cover: 2.25 **NM** value: **Cover or less**
SE 1❑ Cover: 2.50 **NM** value: **Cover or less**
SE 1-2❑ Cover: 2.95 **NM** value: **Cover or less**

LOBO DC

After what seemed like countless mini-series and specials, Lobo finally got his own ongoing series in December 1993. The opening of this series finds the Czarnian plying his usual trade as a bounty hunter, although no longer for Ramona's Unisex Hair Salon and Bail Bonds. Now he's hunting down everyone from alimony-dodgers to mobsters for Bunsen's Bounty, a scummy establishment run by a mook who would double-cross Lobo just for the satisfaction of taking him down.

Of course, messing with the Main Man is dangerous business. For that matter, befriending Lobo, letting him eat in your restaurant, or practically anything else involving The Main Man is bound to be hazardous to your health. Lobo, to put it mildly, is Bad News incarnate. And there's nobody like Lobo for dishing up the entertainment value while destroying everything in sight.

0 ❑ Oct 1994 Cover: 1.95 **NM** value: **2.50**
Circ: CapCity orders: **29,750**
📖 Reservoir Mooks • 10/94 **A:** Val Semeiks **W:** Alan Grant ★ Origin of Lobo.
1 ❑ Dec 1993 Cover: 2.95 **NM** value: **4.00**
Circ: CapCity orders: **49,800**
foil cover. 📖 The Quigley Affair, Part 1 **A:** Val Semeiks **W:** Alan Grant
2 ❑ Feb 1994 Cover: 1.75 **NM** value: **3.00**
Circ: CapCity orders: **30,000**
📖 The Quigley Affair, Part 2 **A:** Val Semeiks **W:** Alan Grant
3 ❑ Mar 1994 Cover: 1.75 **NM** value: **3.00**
Circ: CapCity orders: **25,050**
W: Alan Grant
4 ❑ Apr 1994 Cover: 1.75 **NM** value: **3.00**
Circ: CapCity orders: **22,200**
W: Alan Grant
5 ❑ May 1994 Cover: 1.75 **NM** value: **2.50**
Circ: CapCity orders: **22,650**
W: Alan Grant
6 ❑ Jun 1994 Cover: 1.75 **NM** value: **2.50**
Circ: CapCity orders: **26,050**
W: Alan Grant
7 ❑ Jul 1994 Cover: 1.75 **NM** value: **2.50**
Circ: CapCity orders: **23,200**
W: Alan Grant
8 ❑ Aug 1994 Cover: 1.75 **NM** value: **2.50**
Circ: CapCity orders: **22,550**
W: Alan Grant
9 ❑ Sep 1994 Cover: 1.95 **NM** value: **2.50**
Circ: CapCity orders: **21,700**
W: Alan Grant
10 ❑ Nov 1994 Cover: 1.95 **NM** value: **2.50**
Circ: CapCity orders: **19,950**
W: Alan Grant
11 ❑ Dec 1994 Cover: 1.95 **NM** value: **2.00**
Circ: CapCity orders: **19,550**
📖 Preacher Wars, Part 2 **A:** Val Semeiks **W:** Alan Grant
12 ❑ Jan 1995 Cover: 1.95 **NM** value: **2.00**
Circ: CapCity orders: **19,100**
W: Alan Grant
13 ❑ Feb 1995 Cover: 1.95 **NM** value: **2.00**
Circ: CapCity orders: **17,650**
W: Alan Grant
14 ❑ Mar 1995 Cover: 1.95 **NM** value: **2.00**

CGC-graded: Multiply prices above by **33 for 9.9 M • 16 for 9.8 NM/M • 7 for 9.6 NM+ • 5 for 9.4 NM • 2.5 for 9.2 NM- • 1.5 for 9.0 VF/NM**

Circ: CapCity orders: **16,325**
Lobo, P.I., Part 1 **W:** Alan Grant
15 ❑ Apr 1995 Cover: 1.95 **NM** value: **2.00**
Circ: CapCity orders: **15,525**
W: Alan Grant
16 ❑ Jun 1995 Cover: 2.25 **NM** value: **Cover or less**
Circ: CapCity orders: **15,125**
W: Alan Grant
17 ❑ Jul 1995 Cover: 2.25 **NM** value: **Cover or less**
Circ: CapCity orders: **15,000**
W: Alan Grant
18 ❑ Aug 1995 Cover: 2.25 **NM** value: **Cover or less**
Circ: CapCity orders: **15,050**
W: Alan Grant
19 ❑ Sep 1995 Cover: 2.25 **NM** value: **Cover or less**
Circ: CapCity orders: **14,325**
W: Alan Grant
20 ❑ Oct 1995 Cover: 2.25 **NM** value: **Cover or less**
Circ: CapCity orders: **12,150**
W: Alan Grant
21 ❑ Nov 1995 Cover: 2.25 **NM** value: **Cover or less**
W: Alan Grant ★ Appearance of Space Cabby.
22 ❑ Dec 1995 Cover: 2.25 **NM** value: **Cover or less**
• Underworld Unleashed **W:** Alan Grant
23 ❑ Jan 1996 Cover: 2.25 **NM** value: **Cover or less**
Stargaze Rally, Part 1 **W:** Alan Grant
24 ❑ Feb 1996 Cover: 2.25 **NM** value: **Cover or less**
Stargaze Rally, Part 2 **A:** Warren Ellis **W:** Alan Grant
25 ❑ Mar 1996 Cover: 2.25 **NM** value: **Cover or less**
Lobo's Big Birfday Bash **A:** Warren Ellis **W:** Alan Grant
26 ❑ Apr 1996 Cover: 2.25 **NM** value: **Cover or less**
The Duel **A:** Alex Horley **W:** Alan Grant
27 ❑ May 1996 Cover: 2.25 **NM** value: **Cover or less**
W: Alan Grant
28 ❑ Jun 1996 Cover: 2.25 **NM** value: **Cover or less**
The Heiress, Part 1 **W:** Alan Grant
29 ❑ Jul 1996 Cover: 2.25 **NM** value: **Cover or less**
The Heiress, Part 2 **W:** Alan Grant
30 ❑ Aug 1996 Cover: 2.25 **NM** value: **Cover or less**
The Heiress, Part 3 **W:** Alan Grant
31 ❑ Sep 1996 Cover: 2.25 **NM** value: **Cover or less**
The Heiress, Part 4 **W:** Alan Grant
32 ❑ Oct 1996 Cover: 2.25 **NM** value: **Cover or less**
STance on a Wet Afternoon • Lobo's body is destroyed **A:** Carl Critchlow **W:** Alan Grant
33 ❑ Nov 1996 Cover: 2.25 **NM** value: **Cover or less**
Circ: Diamd. preorders: **24,212**
Wetterworld **A:** Carl Critchlow **W:** Alan Grant
34 ❑ Dec 1996 Cover: 2.25 **NM** value: **Cover or less**
Circ: Diamd. preorders: **23,916**
Bo on a Dolphin **A:** Frank Gomez **W:** Alan Grant
35 ❑ Jan 1997 Cover: 2.25 **NM** value: **Cover or less**
Circ: Diamd. preorders: **22,495**
Death Trek 100 **A:** Carl Critchlow; Mark Propst **W:** Alan Grant
36 ❑ Feb 1997 Cover: 2.25 **NM** value: **Cover or less**
Circ: Diamd. preorders: **22,339**
W: Alan Grant ★ Appearance of Hemingway, Poe, Mark Twain, Chaucer, Shakespeare.
37 ❑ Mar 1997 Cover: 2.25 **NM** value: **Cover or less**
Circ: Diamd. preorders: **21,836**
Lobo's Guide to Girls **A:** Barry Kitson; David Roach; Shaun McManus **W:** Alan Grant
38 ❑ Apr 1997 Cover: 2.25 **NM** value: **Cover or less**
Circ: Diamd. preorders: **21,090**
Last 'Bo on Earth **W:** Alan Grant
39 ❑ May 1997 Cover: 2.25 **NM** value: **Cover or less**
Circ: Diamd. preorders: **20,503**
• Lobo as a pirate **W:** Alan Grant
40 ❑ Jun 1997 Cover: 2.25 **NM** value: **Cover or less**
Circ: Diamd. preorders: **20,824**
• Lobo inside a whale **W:** Alan Grant
41 ❑ Jul 1997 Cover: 2.25 **NM** value: **Cover or less**
Circ: Diamd. preorders: **19,364**
W: Alan Grant
42 ❑ Aug 1997 Cover: 2.25 **NM** value: **Cover or less**
Circ: Diamd. preorders: **19,275**
W: Alan Grant
43 ❑ Sep 1997 Cover: 2.25 **NM** value: **Cover or less**
Circ: Diamd. preorders: **18,375**
W: Alan Grant
44 ❑ Oct 1997 Cover: 2.25 **NM** value: **Cover or less**
Circ: Diamd. preorders: **20,446**
• Genesis **W:** Alan Grant
45 ❑ Nov 1997 Cover: 2.25 **NM** value: **Cover or less**
Circ: Diamd. preorders: **17,859**
The Big Brawl, Part 1 **A:** Carl Critchlow **W:** Alan Grant ★ Versus Jackie Chin.
46 ❑ Dec 1997 Cover: 2.25 **NM** value: **Cover or less**
Circ: Diamd. preorders: **18,091**
Face cover. The Big Brawl, Part 2 **A:** Alex Ronald **W:** Alan Grant
47 ❑ Jan 1998 Cover: 2.25 **NM** value: **Cover or less**
Circ: Diamd. preorders: **17,341**
W: Alan Grant
48 ❑ Feb 1998 Cover: 2.25 **NM** value: **Cover or less**
Circ: Diamd. preorders: **16,970**
W: Alan Grant
49 ❑ Mar 1998 Cover: 2.25 **NM** value: **Cover or less**
Circ: Diamd. preorders: **16,468**
Don Alfonszo's Dinner **A:** Carl Critchlow **W:** Alan Grant
50 ❑ Apr 1998 Cover: 2.25 **NM** value: **Cover or less**
Circ: Diamd. preorders: **19,047**
W: Alan Grant ★ Appearance of Keith Giffen. ★ Death of Everyone.
51 ❑ May 1998 Cover: 2.25 **NM** value: **Cover or less**
Circ: Diamd. preorders: **16,005**
W: Alan Grant
52 ❑ Jun 1998 Cover: 2.25 **NM** value: **Cover or less**
Circ: Diamd. preorders: **16,069**
W: Alan Grant
53 ❑ Jul 1998 Cover: 2.25 **NM** value: **Cover or less**
Circ: Diamd. preorders: **15,805**
W: Alan Grant
54 ❑ Aug 1998 Cover: 2.25 **NM** value: **Cover or less**
Circ: Diamd. preorders: **15,460**
W: Alan Grant
55 ❑ Sep 1998 Cover: 2.50 **NM** value: **Cover or less**
Circ: Diamd. preorders: **14,572**
W: Alan Grant
56 ❑ Oct 1998 Cover: 2.50 **NM** value: **Cover or less**
Circ: Diamd. preorders: **14,086**
W: Alan Grant
57 ❑ Dec 1998 Cover: 2.50 **NM** value: **Cover or less**
Circ: Diamd. preorders: **13,479**
• at police convention **W:** Alan Grant
58 ❑ Jan 1999 Cover: 2.50 **NM** value: **Cover or less**
Circ: Diamd. preorders: **13,422**
W: Alan Grant ★ Appearance of Orion, Superman.
59 ❑ Feb 1999 Cover: 2.50 **NM** value: **Cover or less**
Circ: Diamd. preorders: **13,036**
• in miniature world **A:** Greg Luzniak **W:** Alan Grant ★ Appearance of Bad Wee Bastards.
60 ❑ Mar 1999 Cover: 2.50 **NM** value: **Cover or less**
Circ: Diamd. preorders: **12,862**
The All-New, Nonviolent Adventures of Superbo, Part 1 • Lobo reforms **A:** Greg Luzniak **W:** Alan Grant ★ 1st Appearance of Superbo.
61 ❑ Apr 1999 Cover: 2.50 **NM** value: **Cover or less**
Circ: Diamd. preorders: **12,144**
The All-New, Nonviolent Adventures of Superbo, Part 2 **A:** Greg Luzniak **W:** Alan Grant ★ 2nd Appearance of Superbo. ★ Appearance of Savage Six.
62 ❑ May 1999 Cover: 2.50 **NM** value: **Cover or less**
Circ: Diamd. preorders: **11,973**
The All-New, Nonviolent Adventures of Superbo, Part 3 **A:** Greg Luzniak **W:** Alan Grant
63 ❑ Jun 1999 Cover: 2.50 **NM** value: **Cover or less**
Circ: Diamd. preorders: **12,547**
Soul Brothers, Part 1 **A:** Ariel Olivetti **W:** Alan Grant ★ Appearance of Demon.
64 ❑ Jul 1999 Cover: 2.50 **NM** value: **Cover or less**
Circ: Diamd. preorders: **12,413**
Soul Brothers, Part 2 final issue. **A:** Ariel Olivetti **W:** Alan Grant ★ Appearance of Demon.
1000000 ❑ Nov 1998 Cover: 2.50 **NM** value: **Cover or less**
Circ: Diamd. preorders: **21,314**
Lobo's Last Job **A:** Greg Luzniak **W:** Alan Grant ★ 1st Appearance of Layla.
Anl 1 ❑ ca. 1993 Cover: 3.50 **NM** value: **Cover or less**
Circ: CapCity orders: **46,850**
Bloodlines, Part 1; Hounds of Blood
Anl 2 ❑ ca. 1994 Cover: 3.50 **NM** value: **Cover or less**
Circ: CapCity orders: **18,350**
• Elseworlds
Anl 3 ❑ ca. 1995 Cover: 3.95 **NM** value: **Cover or less**
• Year One

LOBO: A CONTRACT ON GAWD — DC

1 ❑ Apr 1994 Cover: 1.75 **NM** value: **2.00**
Circ: CapCity orders: **23,450**
Trouble in Paradise **A:** Kieron Dwyer **W:** Alan Grant
2 ❑ May 1994 Cover: 1.75 **NM** value: **2.00**
Circ: CapCity orders: **20,750**
A: Kieron Dwyer **W:** Alan Grant
3 ❑ Jun 1994 Cover: 1.75 **NM** value: **2.00**
Circ: CapCity orders: **19,650**
A: Kieron Dwyer **W:** Alan Grant
4 ❑ Jul 1994 Cover: 1.75 **NM** value: **2.00**
Circ: CapCity orders: **19,150**
A: Kieron Dwyer **W:** Alan Grant

LOBO: BLAZING CHAIN OF LOVE — DC

1 ❑ Sep 1992 Cover: 1.50 **NM** value: **2.00**
Circ: CapCity orders: **70,500**
A: Denys Cowan **W:** Alan Grant

LOBO: BOUNTY HUNTING FOR FUN AND PROFIT — DC

1 ❑ Cover: 4.95 **NM** value: **Cover or less**
No issue number. • prestige format. **A:** Kieron Dwyer; Frank Gomez; Martin Emond; Robert McCallum; Simon Bisley(cover); Kevin O'Neill **W:** Alan Grant

LOBO: CHAINED — DC

1 ❑ May 1997 Cover: 2.50 **NM** value: **Cover or less**
Circ: Diamd. preorders: **20,688**
One-shot. • Lobo goes to jail

LOBO CONVENTION SPECIAL — DC

1 ❑ Cover: 1.75 **NM** value: **2.00**
Circ: CapCity orders: **30,700**
Lobo-Con • Set at 1993 San Diego Comic Convention **A:** Kevin O'Neill **W:** Keith Giffen; Alan Grant

LOBOCOP — DC

1 ❑ Feb 1994 Cover: 1.95 **NM** value: **2.00**
Circ: CapCity orders: **26,550**
A: Martin Emond **W:** Alan Grant

LOBO/DEADMAN: THE BRAVE AND THE BALD — DC

1 ❑ Feb 1995 Cover: 3.50 **NM** value: **Cover or less**
No issue number. One-shot. Deadmen Don't Wear Plaid **A:** Martin Elmond **W:** Alan Grant

LOBO: DEATH AND TAXES — DC

1 ❑ Oct 1996 Cover: 2.25 **NM** value: **Cover or less**
A: Alex Horley **W:** Alan Grant; Kieth Giffen
2 ❑ Nov 1996 Cover: 2.25 **NM** value: **Cover or less**
Circ: Diamd. preorders: **24,271**
A: Alex Horley **W:** Alan Grant; Kieth Giffen
3 ❑ Dec 1996 Cover: 2.25 **NM** value: **Cover or less**
Circ: Diamd. preorders: **23,314**
A: Alex Horley **W:** Alan Grant; Kieth Giffen
4 ❑ Jan 1997 Cover: 2.25 **NM** value: **Cover or less**
Circ: Diamd. preorders: **21,817**
final issue. **A:** Alex Horley **W:** Alan Grant; Kieth Giffen

LOBO/DEMON: HELLOWEEN — DC

1 ❑ Dec 1996 Cover: 2.25 **NM** value: **Cover or less**
Circ: Diamd. preorders: **26,171**
One-shot. **A:** Vince Giarrano **W:** Alan Grant

LOBO: FRAGTASTIC VOYAGE — DC

1 ❑ ca. 1998 Cover: 5.95 **NM** value: **Cover or less**
Circ: Diamd. preorders: **14,907**
No issue number. One-shot. • prestige format.

LOBO GALLERY, THE: PORTRAITS OF A BASTICH — DC

1 ❑ Sep 1995 Cover: 3.50 **NM** value: **Cover or less**
• pin-ups **A:** Kieron Dwyer; Vince Giarrano; Kyle Baker; Keith Giffen; Liam Sharp; John Byrne; Denys Cowan; Howard Porter; Val Semeiks; Simon Bisley; Darryl Banks; Frank Gomez; Mike Zeck; Mike Wieringo; Christian Alamy; Dusty Abell; John Dell

LOBO GOES TO HOLLYWOOD — DC

1 ❑ Aug 1996 Cover: 2.25 **NM** value: **Cover or less**
One-shot.

LOBO: INFANTICIDE — DC

1 ❑ Oct 1992 Cover: 1.50 **NM** value: **2.00**
Circ: CapCity orders: **77,200**
The Theory Of Relativity **A:** Keith Giffen **W:** Keith Giffen; Alan Grant
2 ❑ Nov 1992 Cover: 1.50 **NM** value: **2.00**
Circ: CapCity orders: **56,000**
Your In The Army Now! **A:** Keith Giffen **W:** Keith Giffen; Alan Grant
3 ❑ Dec 1992 Cover: 1.50 **NM** value: **2.00**
Circ: CapCity orders: **48,550**
What Did You Do in the War, Daddy? **A:** Keith Giffen **W:** Keith Giffen; Alan Grant
4 ❑ Jan 1993 Cover: 1.50 **NM** value: **2.00**
Circ: CapCity orders: **44,750**
To The Devil A Daughter! **A:** Keith Giffen **W:** Keith Giffen; Alan Grant

LOBO: IN THE CHAIR — DC

1 ❑ Aug 1994 Cover: 1.95 **NM** value: **Cover or less**
Circ: CapCity orders: **24,000**
One-shot. **W:** Alan Grant

LOBO: I QUIT — DC

1 ❑ Dec 1995 Cover: 2.25 **NM** value: **2.75**
One-shot. • Lobo stops smoking **A:** Carlos Ezquerra **W:** Alan Grant

LOBO/JUDGE DREDD: PSYCHO-BIKERS VS. THE MUTANTS FROM HELL — DC

1 ❑ Cover: 4.95 **NM** value: **Cover or less**
No issue number. • prestige format. **A:** Val Semeiks **W:** Alan Grant; John Wagner

LOBO/MASK — DC

1 ❑ Feb 1997 Cover: 5.95 **NM** value: **Cover or less**
Circ: Diamd. preorders: **23,107**
• prestige format crossover with Dark Horse
2 ❑ Mar 1997 Cover: 5.95 **NM** value: **Cover or less**
Circ: Diamd. preorders: **19,452**
final issue. • prestige format crossover with Dark Horse

LOBO (MINI-SERIES) — DC

Lobo's first solo series begins when Commander Dox recruits him to capture the person Lobo hates most in the world: his second grade teacher, Ms. Tribb. Knowing Lobo's legendary temper, he planned to stoke his rage into an inferno, then use the resultant mayhem to eliminate "some tricky little problems" of his own.

This strange plan was soon complicated even further by the trouble that follows Lobo wherever he goes. Before this four-issue mini-series is over, Lobo will have torn a swath through a legion of paramilitary grannies, fragged a gang of space-bikers, amputated the legs of his second grade teacher, and become an unwilling contestant in a "spell-or-die" spelling bee.

1 ❑ Nov 1990 Cover: 0.99 **NM** value: **3.00**
Circ: CapCity orders: **51,600** • **CGC:** 7 graded, best 9.9
The Last Czarnian, Part 1 **A:** Keith Giffen; Simon Bisley(cover) **W:** Alan Grant
1-2 ❑ Nov 1990 Cover: 0.99 **NM** value: **2.00**
2 ❑ Dec 1990 Cover: 1.50 **NM** value: **2.00**
Circ: CapCity orders: **35,250**
The Last Czarnian, Part 2 **A:** Keith Giffen; Simon Bisley(cover) **W:** Alan Grant
3 ❑ Jan 1991 Cover: 1.50 **NM** value: **2.00**
Circ: CapCity orders: **42,250**
The Last Czarnian, Part 3 **A:** Keith Giffen; Simon Bisley(cover) **W:** Alan Grant
4 ❑ Feb 1991 Cover: 1.50 **NM** value: **2.00**

Circ: CapCity orders: **53,650**
The Last Czarnian, Part 4 **A:** Keith Giffen; Simon Bisley(cover) **W:** Alan Grant

LOBO PARAMILITARY CHRISTMAS SPECIAL — DC
1 ❑ Jan 1991 Cover: 2.39 **NM** value: **3.00**
Circ: CapCity orders: **62,250** • **CGC:** 1 graded, best 9.4
The Lobo Xmas Sanction **A:** Keith Giffen; Simon Bisley **W:** Keith Giffen; Alan Grant ★ Death of Santa Claus.

LOBO: PORTRAIT OF A VICTIM — DC
1 ❑ Cover: 1.75 **NM** value: **2.00**
Circ: CapCity orders: **52,150**
A: Val Semeiks **W:** Alan Grant

LOBO'S BACK — DC
1 ❑ May 1992 Cover: 1.50 **NM** value: **2.00**
Circ: CapCity orders: **78,050**
Variant covers exist. **A:** Keith Giffen; Simon Bisley(cover) **W:** Alan Grant ★ 1st Appearance of Ramona.
2 ❑ Jun 1992 Cover: 1.50 **NM** value: **2.00**
Circ: CapCity orders: **67,700**
Heaven Is A Four Letter Word **A:** Keith Giffen; Simon Bisley(cover) **W:** Alan Grant
3 ❑ Oct 1992 Cover: 1.50 **NM** value: **2.00**
Circ: CapCity orders: **60,950**
A: Keith Giffen; Simon Bisley(cover) **W:** Alan Grant
4 ❑ Nov 1992 Cover: 1.50 **NM** value: **2.00**
Circ: CapCity orders: **60,000**
A: Keith Giffen; Simon Bisley(cover) **W:** Alan Grant
Bk 1❑ Cover: 9.95 **NM** value: **Cover or less**
• Collects Lobo's Back #1-4 **A:** Keith Giffen; Simon Bisley(cover) **W:** Alan Grant

LOBO'S BIG BABE SPRING BREAK SPECIAL — DC
1 ❑ Spr 1995 Cover: 1.95 **NM** value: **Cover or less**
No issue number. **A:** Jim Balent **W:** Alan Grant

LOBO SLIPCASE PACKAGE — DC
Bk 1/CS❑ Cover: 29.87 **NM** value: **Cover or less**
No issue number. • three trade paperbacks in case

LOBO THE DUCK — DC / Amalgam
1 ❑ Jun 1997 Cover: 1.95 **NM** value: **Cover or less**
Circ: Diamd. preorders: **108,625**
A: Val Semeiks **W:** Alan Grant

LOBO: UN-AMERICAN GLADIATORS — DC
1 ❑ Jun 1993 Cover: 1.75 **NM** value: **2.00**
Circ: CapCity orders: **44,400**
Fragituri Te Salutamus! **A:** Cam Kennedy **W:** Alan Grant; John Wagner
2 ❑ Jul 1993 Cover: 1.75 **NM** value: **2.00**
Circ: CapCity orders: **35,300**
Veni, Vidi, Fragi! **A:** Cam Kennedy **W:** Alan Grant; John Wagner
3 ❑ Aug 1993 Cover: 1.75 **NM** value: **2.00**
Circ: CapCity orders: **31,650**
A: Cam Kennedy **W:** Alan Grant; John Wagner
4 ❑ Sep 1993 Cover: 1.75 **NM** value: **2.00**
Circ: CapCity orders: **26,550**
A: Cam Kennedy **W:** Alan Grant; John Wagner

LOCO VS. PULVERINE — Eclipse
1 ❑ Jul 1992, b&w Cover: 2.50 **NM** value: **Cover or less**
Circ: CapCity orders: **3,475**
No issue number. wraparound cover. • parody

LOGAN: PATH OF THE WARLORD — Marvel
1 ❑ Feb 1996 Cover: 5.95 **NM** value: **6.00**
A: John Paul Leon **W:** Howard Mackie

LOGAN: SHADOW SOCIETY — Marvel
1 ❑ Dec 1996 Cover: 5.95 **NM** value: **6.00**
Circ: Direct Market orders: **58,750**
No issue number. **A:** Octavio Cariello; Tomm Coker; Keith Aiken **W:** Mark Jason

LOGAN'S RUN (ADVENTURE) — Adventure
1 ❑ Cover: 2.25 **NM** value: **2.50**
• Introduction by William F. Nolan **A:** Barry Blair; Paul Gulacy(cover) **W:** Barry Blair; Chris Ulm; Tom Mason
2 ❑ Jul 1990 Cover: 2.25 **NM** value: **2.50**
A: Barry Blair **W:** Barry Blair; Chris Ulm; Tom Mason
3 ❑ Cover: 2.25 **NM** value: **2.50**
A: Barry Blair **W:** Barry Blair; Chris Ulm; Tom Mason
4 ❑ Oct 1990 Cover: 2.25 **NM** value: **2.50**
A: Barry Blair **W:** Barry Blair; Chris Ulm; Tom Mason
5 ❑ Mar 1991 Cover: 2.25 **NM** value: **2.50**
A: Barry Blair **W:** Barry Blair; Chris Ulm; Tom Mason
6 ❑ Apr 1991 Cover: 2.25 **NM** value: **2.50**
A: Barry Blair **W:** Barry Blair; Chris Ulm; Tom Mason

Diamond preorders are the estimated number of comics sold, prior to their release, to comics shops in North America by Diamond Comic Distributors, the largest distributor. These figures underreport the actual number of circulating copies by the amount of reorders Diamond took (usually 5-10% again of the preorders) and sales by publishers to newsstand and bookstore distributors. For many independent publishers, Diamond's preorders may be quite close to the actual number of copies in circulation.

LOGAN'S RUN (MARVEL) — Marvel
Logan's Run is notable for both its dynamic adaptation of the stunning science-fiction movie and for a little-noticed backup story in #6, the first solo story for the now-infamous galactic powerhouse Thanos.

In the world of Logan's Run, mankind has decided that, in order to support the growing population, it is necessary to limit the time people are allowed to live. A crystal life-clock is now placed in the palms of all newborns. It glows yellow for the first 10 years of life, then blue for a decade, then red. At the age of 31, citizens are required to die.

Of course, some people do not submit so easily — they run. That's where the Sandmen come in: They track down the "runners" and terminate them. But some runners have spoken of a place called "Sanctuary," where they can live and grow old. Logan-6 is assigned to become a runner and find Sanctuary — and then destroy it.

1 ❑ Jan 1977 Cover: 0.30 **NM** value: **4.00**
• **CGC:** 14 graded, best 9.8
A: George Pérez **W:** Gerry Conway
2 ❑ Feb 1977 Cover: 0.30 **NM** value: **3.00**
• **CGC:** 1 graded, best 8.0
Cathedral Kill **A:** George Pérez **W:** David Anthony Kraft
3 ❑ Mar 1977 Cover: 0.30 **NM** value: **3.00**
• **CGC:** 1 graded, best 9.2
Sanctuary!? **A:** George Pérez **W:** David Anthony Kraft
4 ❑ Apr 1977 Cover: 0.30 **NM** value: **2.50**
• **CGC:** 1 graded, best 8.0
Enter the eternal Ice-World of Box **A:** George Pérez **W:** David Anthony Kraft
5 ❑ May 1977 Cover: 0.30 **NM** value: **2.50**
• **CGC:** 1 graded, best 9.4
End*Run **A:** George Pérez **W:** David Anthony Kraft
6 ❑ Jun 1977 Cover: 0.30 **NM** value: **5.00**
• **CGC:** 2 graded, best 9.6
Aftermath! • New stories begin; Back-up story is first solo story featuring Thanos **A:** Tom Sutton; Terry Austin **W:** John Wagner ★ Appearance of Thanos.
7 ❑ Jul 1977 Cover: 0.30 **NM** value: **2.50**
Cathedral Prime! **A:** George Pérez **W:** David Anthony Kraft

LOGAN'S WORLD — Adventure
1 ❑ May 1991 Cover: 2.50 **NM** value: **Cover or less**
2 ❑ Cover: 2.50 **NM** value: **Cover or less**
3 ❑ Cover: 2.50 **NM** value: **Cover or less**
4 ❑ Cover: 2.50 **NM** value: **Cover or less**
5 ❑ Cover: 2.50 **NM** value: **Cover or less**
6 ❑ Cover: 2.50 **NM** value: **Cover or less**

LOIS AND CLARK, THE NEW ADVENTURES OF SUPERMAN — DC
1 ❑ Cover: 9.95 **NM** value: **Cover or less**
• Trade Paperback. The Story of the Century; Tears for Titano; Metropolis-900 Mi; The Name Game; Lois Lane; Headhunter; Homeless for the Holidays; The Limits of Power; Survival • collects issues of Action Comics, Adv. of Superman, Man of Steel, Superman Annual, and Superman; Introduction by John Byrne **A:** Karl Kesel; Brett Breeding; Jerry Ordway; John Byrne; Dan Jurgens; Ron Frenz; Bob McLeod; Kurt Schaffenberger **W:** Jerry Ordway; John Byrne; Ron Frenz; Roger Stern

LOIS LANE — DC
1 ❑ Aug 1986 Cover: 1.50 **NM** value: **2.00**
Circ: CapCity orders: **9,750** • **CGC:** 5 graded, best 9.2
When It Rains, God Is Crying **A:** Gray Morrow **W:** Mindy Newell
2 ❑ Sep 1986 Cover: 1.50 **NM** value: **2.00**
Circ: CapCity orders: **8,000** • **CGC:** 6 graded, best 9.4
Quicksand! **A:** Gray Morrow **W:** Mindy Newell

LONELY HEART — Ajax
9 ❑ 1955 Cover: 0.10 **NM** value: **75.00**
10 ❑ 1955 Cover: 0.10 **NM** value: **50.00**
11 ❑ 1955 Cover: 0.10 **NM** value: **35.00**
12 ❑ 1955 Cover: 0.10 **NM** value: **35.00**
13 ❑ 1955 Cover: 0.10 **NM** value: **35.00**
14 ❑ 1956 Cover: 0.10 **NM** value: **35.00**

LONELY NIGHTS COMICS — Last Gasp
1 ❑ Cover: 2.00 **NM** value: **Cover or less**
Laundry Day Delight!; Fuck Story; Abused; Take a Walk on the Sleazy Side; It Makes Me Feel so Real; Random Thoughts; Of Human Bondage and Discipline; The Artist Reputation Gets Ruined; Orgy at the Women's Retreat! **A:** Bob Davis; Dori Seda; Joe O. **W:** Bob Davis; Dori Seda; Joe O.

LONELY WAR OF WILLY SCHULTZ, THE — Avalon
1 ❑ b&w Cover: 2.95 **NM** value: **Cover or less**
A: Sam Glanzman **W:** Will Franz
2 ❑ Cover: 2.95 **NM** value: **Cover or less**
A: Sam Glanzman **W:** Will Franz
3 ❑ Cover: 2.95 **NM** value: **Cover or less**
A: Sam Glanzman **W:** Will Franz
4 ❑ Cover: 2.95 **NM** value: **Cover or less**
Escape **A:** Sam Glanzman **W:** Will Franz

LONER — Fleetway-Quality
1 ❑ Cover: 1.95 **NM** value: **Cover or less**
2 ❑ Cover: 1.95 **NM** value: **Cover or less**
3 ❑ Cover: 1.95 **NM** value: **Cover or less**

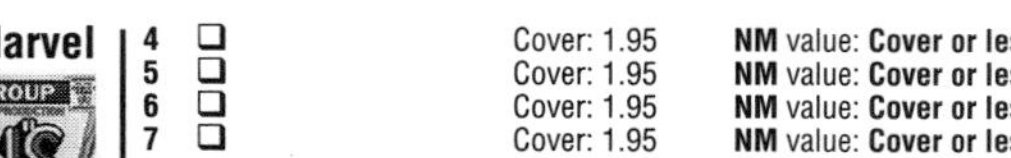

4 ❑ Cover: 1.95 **NM** value: **Cover or less**
5 ❑ Cover: 1.95 **NM** value: **Cover or less**
6 ❑ Cover: 1.95 **NM** value: **Cover or less**
7 ❑ Cover: 1.95 **NM** value: **Cover or less**

LONE RANGER AND TONTO, THE — Topps
1 ❑ Aug 1994 Cover: 2.50 **NM** value: **Cover or less**
Circ: CapCity orders: **15,425**
It Crawls, Part 1 **A:** Tim Truman **W:** Joe Lansdale
1/SC❑Aug 1994 Cover: 2.50 **NM** value: **4.00**
• foil edition. It Crawls, Part 1 **A:** Tim Truman **W:** Joe Lansdale
2 ❑ Sep 1994 Cover: 2.50 **NM** value: **Cover or less**
Circ: CapCity orders: **11,575**
It Crawls, Part 2 **A:** Tim Truman **W:** Joe Lansdale
2/SC❑Sep 1994 **NM** value: **3.50**
• limited edition. It Crawls, Part 2 **A:** Tim Truman **W:** Joe Lansdale
3 ❑ Oct 1994 Cover: 2.50 **NM** value: **Cover or less**
Circ: CapCity orders: **11,200**
It Crawls, Part 3 **A:** Tim Truman **W:** Joe Lansdale
3/SC❑Oct 1994 **NM** value: **3.00**
• limited edition. It Crawls, Part 3 **A:** Tim Truman **W:** Joe Lansdale
4 ❑ Nov 1994 Cover: 2.50 **NM** value: **Cover or less**
Circ: CapCity orders: **10,300**
It Crawls, Part 4 **A:** Tim Truman **W:** Joe Lansdale
4/SC❑Nov 1994 **NM** value: **3.00**
• limited edition. It Crawls, Part 4 **A:** Tim Truman **W:** Joe Lansdale
Bk 1❑ Cover: 9.95 **NM** value: **Cover or less**
It Crawls • Reprints The Lone Ranger and Tonto #1-4 **A:** Tim Truman **W:** Joe Lansdale

LONE RANGER COMICS (LONE RANGER) — Lone Ranger Inc.
1 ❑ ca. 1939 **NM** value: **4000.00**
• **CGC:** 1 graded, best 5.0

LONE RANGER, THE (DELL) — Dell
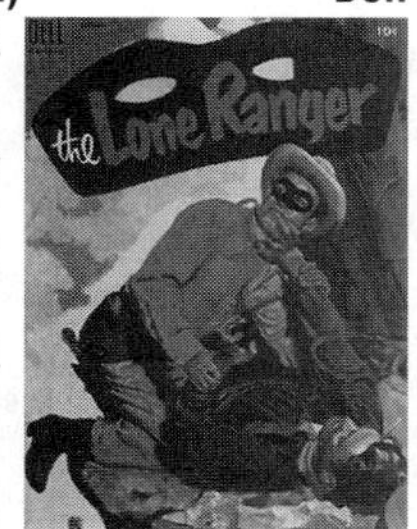

With a successful radio series that ran from 1933 to 1956, a series of movies, and a television series, The Lone Ranger is probably one of the best-known Western characters of all time. This Dell series, which began in 1948 and ran until 1962, captured much of the spirit of the other media's adventures.

The story of the Lone Ranger began with the ambush of a group of Texas Rangers by the notorious Butch Cavendish gang. Left for dead, the sole survivor of the ambush was found by Tonto, an Indian the Ranger, John Reid, had befriended years earlier. Nursed back to health, Reid vowed to devote his life, and the fortune he and his late brother (the leader of that group of Rangers) had amassed in a silver mine, to fighting evil throughout the West. The Lone Ranger was a clean-cut hero who didn't drink, smoke, or curse. He shot silver bullets (perhaps there were werewolves in the Old West?) and even named his horse Silver.

Beautiful painted covers graced early issues of the series, while later issues had photo covers featuring Clayton Moore, who had played the Lone Ranger in the movies. — Brent

1 ❑ Jan 1948 Cover: 0.10 **NM** value: **6.00**
• **CGC:** 10 graded, best 9.6
2 ❑ Mar 1948 Cover: 0.10 **NM** value: **34.00**
• **CGC:** 1 graded, best 7.0
3 ❑ May 1948 Cover: 0.10 **NM** value: **25.00**
• **CGC:** 1 graded, best 9.4
4 ❑ Jul 1948 Cover: 0.10 **NM** value: **22.00**
• **CGC:** 2 graded, best 9.2
5 ❑ Sep 1948 Cover: 0.10 **NM** value: **22.00**
• **CGC:** 1 graded, best 8.5
6 ❑ Nov 1948 Cover: 0.10 **NM** value: **185.00**
7 ❑ Jan 1949 Cover: 0.10 **NM** value: **185.00**
8 ❑ Feb 1949 Cover: 0.10 **NM** value: **235.00**
★ Origin of the Lone Ranger.
9 ❑ Mar 1949 Cover: 0.10 **NM** value: **185.00**
10 ❑ Apr 1949 Cover: 0.10 **NM** value: **185.00**
11 ❑ May 1949 Cover: 0.10 **NM** value: **130.00**
12 ❑ Jun 1949 Cover: 0.10 **NM** value: **130.00**
13 ❑ Jul 1949 Cover: 0.10 **NM** value: **130.00**
14 ❑ Aug 1949 Cover: 0.10 **NM** value: **130.00**
15 ❑ Sep 1949 Cover: 0.10 **NM** value: **130.00**
16 ❑ Oct 1949 Cover: 0.10 **NM** value: **130.00**
• **CGC:** 1 graded, best 8.5
17 ❑ Nov 1949 Cover: 0.10 **NM** value: **130.00**
18 ❑ Dec 1949 Cover: 0.10 **NM** value: **130.00**
19 ❑ Jan 1950 Cover: 0.10 **NM** value: **130.00**
• **CGC:** 1 graded, best 9.0
20 ❑ Feb 1950 Cover: 0.10 **NM** value: **130.00**
• **CGC:** 1 graded, best 8.5
21 ❑ Mar 1950 Cover: 0.10 **NM** value: **95.00**
22 ❑ Apr 1950 Cover: 0.10 **NM** value: **95.00**
23 ❑ May 1950 Cover: 0.10 **NM** value: **95.00**
24 ❑ Jun 1950 Cover: 0.10 **NM** value: **95.00**
25 ❑ Jul 1950 Cover: 0.10 **NM** value: **95.00**
26 ❑ Aug 1950 Cover: 0.10 **NM** value: **95.00**
• **CGC:** 1 graded, best 9.2
27 ❑ Sep 1950 Cover: 0.10 **NM** value: **95.00**
• **CGC:** 1 graded, best 9.2
28 ❑ Oct 1950 Cover: 0.10 **NM** value: **95.00**
• **CGC:** 1 graded, best 7.5
29 ❑ Nov 1950 Cover: 0.10 **NM** value: **95.00**
• **CGC:** 1 graded, best 7.5
30 ❑ Dec 1950 Cover: 0.10 **NM** value: **95.00**
31 ❑ Jan 1951 Cover: 0.10 **NM** value: **75.00**

CGC-graded: Multiply prices above by **33 for 9.9 M • 16 for 9.8 NM/M • 7 for 9.6 NM+ • 5 for 9.4 NM • 2.5 for 9.2 NM- • 1.5 for 9.0 VF/NM**

32 ❑ Feb 1951 Cover: 0.10 **NM** value: **75.00**
33 ❑ Mar 1951 Cover: 0.10 **NM** value: **75.00**
34 ❑ Apr 1951 Cover: 0.10 **NM** value: **75.00**
35 ❑ May 1951 Cover: 0.10 **NM** value: **75.00**
36 ❑ Jun 1951 Cover: 0.10 **NM** value: **75.00**
37 ❑ Jul 1951 Cover: 0.10 **NM** value: **75.00**
38 ❑ Aug 1951 Cover: 0.10 **NM** value: **75.00**
39 ❑ Sep 1951 Cover: 0.10 **NM** value: **75.00**
40 ❑ Oct 1951 Cover: 0.10 **NM** value: **75.00**
41 ❑ Nov 1951 Cover: 0.10 **NM** value: **58.00**
42 ❑ Dec 1951 Cover: 0.10 **NM** value: **58.00**
43 ❑ Jan 1952 Cover: 0.10 **NM** value: **58.00**
44 ❑ Feb 1952 Cover: 0.10 **NM** value: **58.00**
45 ❑ Mar 1952 Cover: 0.10 **NM** value: **58.00**
46 ❑ Apr 1952 Cover: 0.10 **NM** value: **58.00**
47 ❑ May 1952 Cover: 0.10 **NM** value: **58.00**
48 ❑ Jun 1952 Cover: 0.10 **NM** value: **58.00**
49 ❑ Jul 1952 Cover: 0.10 **NM** value: **58.00**
50 ❑ Aug 1952 Cover: 0.10 **NM** value: **58.00**
51 ❑ Sep 1952 Cover: 0.10 **NM** value: **50.00**
52 ❑ Oct 1952 Cover: 0.10 **NM** value: **50.00**
53 ❑ Nov 1952 Cover: 0.10 **NM** value: **50.00**
54 ❑ Dec 1952 Cover: 0.10 **NM** value: **50.00**
55 ❑ Jan 1953 Cover: 0.10 **NM** value: **50.00**
56 ❑ Feb 1953 Cover: 0.10 **NM** value: **50.00**
• **CGC:** 1 graded, best 9.2
57 ❑ Mar 1953 Cover: 0.10 **NM** value: **50.00**
58 ❑ Apr 1953 Cover: 0.10 **NM** value: **50.00**
59 ❑ May 1953 Cover: 0.10 **NM** value: **50.00**
60 ❑ Jun 1953 Cover: 0.10 **NM** value: **50.00**
61 ❑ Jul 1953 Cover: 0.10 **NM** value: **48.00**
62 ❑ Aug 1953 Cover: 0.10 **NM** value: **48.00**
63 ❑ Sep 1953 Cover: 0.10 **NM** value: **48.00**
64 ❑ Oct 1953 Cover: 0.10 **NM** value: **48.00**
65 ❑ Nov 1953 Cover: 0.10 **NM** value: **48.00**
66 ❑ Dec 1953 Cover: 0.10 **NM** value: **48.00**
• **CGC:** 1 graded, best 9.2
67 ❑ Jan 1954 Cover: 0.10 **NM** value: **48.00**
• **CGC:** 1 graded, best 9.2
68 ❑ Feb 1954 Cover: 0.10 **NM** value: **48.00**
• **CGC:** 1 graded, best 9.4
69 ❑ Mar 1954 Cover: 0.10 **NM** value: **48.00**
• **CGC:** 1 graded, best 8.5
70 ❑ Apr 1954 Cover: 0.10 **NM** value: **48.00**
71 ❑ May 1954 Cover: 0.10 **NM** value: **38.00**
• **CGC:** 1 graded, best 9.2
72 ❑ Jun 1954 Cover: 0.10 **NM** value: **38.00**
73 ❑ Jul 1954 Cover: 0.10 **NM** value: **38.00**
• **CGC:** 1 graded, best 9.4
74 ❑ Aug 1954 Cover: 0.10 **NM** value: **38.00**
75 ❑ Sep 1954 Cover: 0.10 **NM** value: **38.00**
• **CGC:** 2 graded, best 8.0
76 ❑ Oct 1954 Cover: 0.10 **NM** value: **38.00**
📖 The Fight over Death Gorge; The Tommy Knockers (Text Story); Young Hawk
77 ❑ Nov 1954 Cover: 0.10 **NM** value: **38.00**
78 ❑ Dec 1954 Cover: 0.10 **NM** value: **38.00**
79 ❑ Jan 1955 Cover: 0.10 **NM** value: **38.00**
80 ❑ Feb 1955 Cover: 0.10 **NM** value: **38.00**
📖 Trouble Shooting; Pursuit; Friend of the Family (Text Story); Young Hawk
81 ❑ Mar 1955 Cover: 0.10 **NM** value: **34.00**
• **CGC:** 1 graded, best 9.2
82 ❑ Apr 1955 Cover: 0.10 **NM** value: **34.00**
83 ❑ May 1955 Cover: 0.10 **NM** value: **34.00**
84 ❑ Jun 1955 Cover: 0.10 **NM** value: **34.00**
85 ❑ Jul 1955 Cover: 0.10 **NM** value: **34.00**
86 ❑ Aug 1955 Cover: 0.10 **NM** value: **34.00**
87 ❑ Sep 1955 Cover: 0.10 **NM** value: **34.00**
88 ❑ Oct 1955 Cover: 0.10 **NM** value: **34.00**
89 ❑ Nov 1955 Cover: 0.10 **NM** value: **34.00**
90 ❑ Dec 1955 Cover: 0.10 **NM** value: **34.00**
91 ❑ Jan 1956 Cover: 0.10 **NM** value: **34.00**
• **CGC:** 1 graded, best 8.5
92 ❑ Feb 1956 Cover: 0.10 **NM** value: **34.00**
93 ❑ Mar 1956 Cover: 0.10 **NM** value: **34.00**
94 ❑ Apr 1956 Cover: 0.10 **NM** value: **34.00**
• **CGC:** 1 graded, best 9.2
95 ❑ May 1956 Cover: 0.10 **NM** value: **34.00**
96 ❑ Jun 1956 Cover: 0.10 **NM** value: **34.00**
97 ❑ Jul 1956 Cover: 0.10 **NM** value: **34.00**
• **CGC:** 2 graded, best 9.6
98 ❑ Aug 1956 Cover: 0.10 **NM** value: **34.00**
99 ❑ Sep 1956 Cover: 0.10 **NM** value: **34.00**
100 ❑ Oct 1956 Cover: 0.10 **NM** value: **34.00**
• **CGC:** 1 graded, best 8.5
101 ❑ Nov 1956 Cover: 0.10 **NM** value: **30.00**
102 ❑ Dec 1956 Cover: 0.10 **NM** value: **30.00**
• **CGC:** 1 graded, best 9.4
103 ❑ Jan 1957 Cover: 0.10 **NM** value: **30.00**
• **CGC:** 1 graded, best 9.6
104 ❑ Feb 1957 Cover: 0.10 **NM** value: **30.00**
105 ❑ Mar 1957, four-color Cover: 0.10 **NM** value: **30.00**
106 ❑ Apr 1957 Cover: 0.10 **NM** value: **30.00**
• **CGC:** 1 graded, best 9.4
107 ❑ May 1957 Cover: 0.10 **NM** value: **30.00**
• **CGC:** 1 graded, best 7.5
108 ❑ Jun 1957 Cover: 0.10 **NM** value: **30.00**
109 ❑ Jul 1957 Cover: 0.10 **NM** value: **30.00**
110 ❑ Aug 1957 Cover: 0.10 **NM** value: **30.00**
111 ❑ Sep 1957 Cover: 0.10 **NM** value: **30.00**
112 ❑ Oct 1957 Cover: 0.10 **NM** value: **55.00**
Photo cover.
113 ❑ Nov 1957 Cover: 0.10 **NM** value: **45.00**
Photo cover.
114 ❑ Dec 1957 Cover: 0.10 **NM** value: **45.00**
Photo cover.
115 ❑ Jan 1958 Cover: 0.10 **NM** value: **45.00**
Photo cover.
116 ❑ Feb 1958 Cover: 0.10 **NM** value: **45.00**
Photo cover.
117 ❑ Mar 1958 Cover: 0.10 **NM** value: **45.00**
Photo cover.
118 ❑ Apr 1958 Cover: 0.10 **NM** value: **45.00**
Photo cover. ★ Origin of Lone Ranger.
119 ❑ May 1958 Cover: 0.10 **NM** value: **45.00**
• **CGC:** 1 graded, best 9.4
Photo cover.
120 ❑ Jun 1958 Cover: 0.10 **NM** value: **45.00**
• **CGC:** 1 graded, best 4.5
Photo cover.
121 ❑ Jul 1958 Cover: 0.10 **NM** value: **45.00**
Photo cover.
122 ❑ Aug 1958 Cover: 0.10 **NM** value: **45.00**
Photo cover.
123 ❑ Sep 1958 Cover: 0.10 **NM** value: **45.00**
Photo cover.
124 ❑ Oct 1958 Cover: 0.10 **NM** value: **45.00**
Photo cover.
125 ❑ Dec 1958 Cover: 0.10 **NM** value: **45.00**
Photo cover.
126 ❑ Feb 1959 Cover: 0.10 **NM** value: **45.00**
Photo cover.
127 ❑ Apr 1959 Cover: 0.10 **NM** value: **45.00**
• **CGC:** 1 graded, best 9.4
Photo cover.
128 ❑ Jun 1959 Cover: 0.10 **NM** value: **45.00**
Photo cover.
129 ❑ Aug 1959 Cover: 0.10 **NM** value: **45.00**
Photo cover.
130 ❑ Oct 1959 Cover: 0.10 **NM** value: **45.00**
• **CGC:** 2 graded, best 9.4
Photo cover.
131 ❑ Dec 1959 Cover: 0.10 **NM** value: **45.00**
Circ: Statement: **408,711**
Photo cover.
132 ❑ Feb 1960 Cover: 0.10 **NM** value: **45.00**
Circ: Statement: **408,711** • **CGC:** 1 graded, best 9.4
Photo cover.
133 ❑ Apr 1960 Cover: 0.10 **NM** value: **45.00**
Circ: Statement: **408,711**
Photo cover.
134 ❑ Jun 1960 Cover: 0.10 **NM** value: **45.00**
Circ: Statement: **408,711** • **CGC:** 1 graded, best 9.0
Photo cover.
135 ❑ Aug 1960 **NM** value: **45.00**
Circ: Statement: **408,711** • **CGC:** 2 graded, best 9.6
Photo cover.
136 ❑ Oct 1960 **NM** value: **45.00**
Circ: Statement: **408,711**
Photo cover.
137 ❑ Dec 1960 **NM** value: **45.00**
• **CGC:** 1 graded, best 9.2
Photo cover.
138 ❑ Feb 1961 Cover: 0.15 **NM** value: **45.00**
• **CGC:** 1 graded, best 9.2
Photo cover. • Has 1960 Statement, filed 10/1/1960; no print run listed; avg paid circ 408,711
139 ❑ Apr 1961 Cover: 0.15 **NM** value: **45.00**
Photo cover.
140 ❑ Jun 1961 Cover: 0.15 **NM** value: **45.00**
• **CGC:** 1 graded, best 9.0
Photo cover.
141 ❑ Aug 1961 Cover: 0.15 **NM** value: **45.00**
Photo cover.
142 ❑ Oct 1961 Cover: 0.15 **NM** value: **45.00**
• **CGC:** 1 graded, best 7.5
Photo cover.
143 ❑ Dec 1961 Cover: 0.15 **NM** value: **45.00**
• **CGC:** 1 graded, best 7.5
Photo cover.
144 ❑ Feb 1961 Cover: 0.15 **NM** value: **45.00**
• **CGC:** 1 graded, best 8.0
Photo cover.
145 ❑ May 1962 Cover: 0.15 **NM** value: **45.00**
• **CGC:** 1 graded, best 7.5
Photo cover. final issue.

LONE RANGER GOLDEN WEST (GOLD KEY) — Gold Key

1 ❑ ca. 1966 Cover: 0.25 **NM** value: **75.00**
• **CGC:** 2 graded, best 9.0

LONE RANGER, THE (GOLD KEY) — Gold Key

1 ❑ Sep 1964 Cover: 0.12 **NM** value: **32.00**
• **CGC:** 1 graded, best 7.0
2 ❑ Dec 1964 Cover: 0.12 **NM** value: **15.00**
• **CGC:** 1 graded, best 8.0
3 ❑ Mar 1965 Cover: 0.12 **NM** value: **12.00**
• **CGC:** 1 graded, best 8.0
4 ❑ Aug 1965 Cover: 0.12 **NM** value: **10.00**
• **CGC:** 1 graded, best 9.0
5 ❑ Jan 1966 Cover: 0.12 **NM** value: **10.00**
• **CGC:** 1 graded, best 5.0
6 ❑ Apr 1966 Cover: 0.12 **NM** value: **10.00**
7 ❑ Jul 1966 Cover: 0.12 **NM** value: **10.00**
📖 The Lone Ranger: Silver Gets Through; Small Bear: Till the Rope is Cut; Geronimo: The Restless One; The Lone Ranger: The Siege; The Lone Ranger: The Blocked Train; True Gold (text story)
8 ❑ Oct 1966 Cover: 0.12 **NM** value: **10.00**
9 ❑ Jan 1967 Cover: 0.12 **NM** value: **10.00**
10 ❑ Apr 1967 Cover: 0.12 **NM** value: **10.00**
11 ❑ Jul 1967 Cover: 0.12 **NM** value: **9.00**
12 ❑ Oct 1968 Cover: 0.15 **NM** value: **9.00**
13 ❑ Mar 1969 Cover: 0.15 **NM** value: **9.00**
14 ❑ Jun 1969 Cover: 0.15 **NM** value: **9.00**
15 ❑ Sep 1969 Cover: 0.15 **NM** value: **9.00**
16 ❑ Dec 1969 Cover: 0.15 **NM** value: **9.00**
17 ❑ ca. 1972 Cover: 0.15 **NM** value: **9.00**
📖 The Wide Missouri; Valley of Danger
18 ❑ Sep 1974 Cover: 0.25 **NM** value: **9.00**
• **CGC:** 1 graded, best 8.5
19 ❑ Dec 1974 Cover: 0.25 **NM** value: **9.00**
20 ❑ Mar 1975 Cover: 0.25 **NM** value: **9.00**
📖 Terror Trail; The Gunfight
21 ❑ Jun 1975 Cover: 0.25 **NM** value: **5.00**
22 ❑ Sep 1975 Cover: 0.25 **NM** value: **5.00**
23 ❑ Dec 1975 Cover: 0.25 **NM** value: **5.00**
24 ❑ Mar 1976 Cover: 0.25 **NM** value: **5.00**
25 ❑ Jun 1976 Cover: 0.25 **NM** value: **5.00**
26 ❑ Sep 1976 Cover: 0.30 **NM** value: **5.00**
27 ❑ Dec 1976 Cover: 0.30 **NM** value: **5.00**
28 ❑ Mar 1977 Cover: 0.30 **NM** value: **5.00**
final issue.

LONE RANGER IN MILK FOR BIG MIKE — Dell

1 ❑ ca. 1955 **NM** value: **100.00**
• **CGC:** 31 graded, best 9.8

LONE RANGER MOVIE STORY — Dell

1 ❑ ca. 1956 Cover: 0.25 **NM** value: **500.00**
• **CGC:** 3 graded, best 9.0

LONE RANGER, THE (PURE IMAGINATION) — Pure Imagination

1 ❑ b&w Cover: 3.00 **NM** value: **Cover or less**
• reprints newspaper strip

LONE RANGER'S COMPANION TONTO, THE — Dell

Although there are several versions of his origin story, the first states that as a boy, Tonto was wounded by renegade Indians and left for dead. Luckily, a young John Reid stumbled across him and nursed him back to health. From that point on, they became fast friends. Reid later became a Texas Ranger, and when his troop was ambushed by outlaws and Reid was left for dead, his old friend Tonto appeared to return the favor done him years earlier.

With the outlaws thinking Reid was dead, Reid decided to don a mask and ride out as the The Lone Ranger. Tonto, his faithful friend, rode with him and the two became legends of books, radio, and the silver screen.

In this 1951 series, Tonto at last got a comic book of his own, where he tried to help keep the peace between farmers, ranchers, and Indians in the Old West.

2 ❑ Aug 1951 Cover: 0.10 **NM** value: **5.00**
• Series continued from Four Color Comics #312
3 ❑ Nov 1951 Cover: 0.10 **NM** value: **32.00**
4 ❑ 1952 Cover: 0.10 **NM** value: **32.00**
5 ❑ 1952 Cover: 0.10 **NM** value: **32.00**
6 ❑ 1952 Cover: 0.10 **NM** value: **25.00**
7 ❑ 1952 Cover: 0.10 **NM** value: **25.00**
8 ❑ Nov 1952 Cover: 0.10 **NM** value: **25.00**
9 ❑ 1953 Cover: 0.10 **NM** value: **25.00**
10 ❑ Mar 1953 Cover: 0.10 **NM** value: **25.00**
11 ❑ 1953 Cover: 0.10 **NM** value: **22.00**
12 ❑ Aug 1953 Cover: 0.10 **NM** value: **22.00**
13 ❑ Nov 1953 Cover: 0.10 **NM** value: **22.00**
14 ❑ Feb 1954 Cover: 0.10 **NM** value: **22.00**
15 ❑ May 1954 Cover: 0.10 **NM** value: **22.00**
16 ❑ Aug 1954 Cover: 0.10 **NM** value: **22.00**
17 ❑ Nov 1954 Cover: 0.10 **NM** value: **22.00**
18 ❑ Feb 1955 Cover: 0.10 **NM** value: **22.00**
19 ❑ May 1955 Cover: 0.10 **NM** value: **22.00**
20 ❑ Aug 1955 Cover: 0.10 **NM** value: **22.00**
21 ❑ Nov 1955 Cover: 0.10 **NM** value: **18.00**
• **CGC:** 1 graded, best 9.2
22 ❑ Feb 1956 Cover: 0.10 **NM** value: **18.00**
23 ❑ May 1956 Cover: 0.10 **NM** value: **18.00**
24 ❑ Aug 1956 Cover: 0.10 **NM** value: **18.00**
25 ❑ Nov 1956 Cover: 0.10 **NM** value: **18.00**
26 ❑ Feb 1957 Cover: 0.10 **NM** value: **18.00**
27 ❑ May 1957 Cover: 0.10 **NM** value: **18.00**
• The Barbed Wire Warpath; The Risk Takers; The Waterhole (text story); The Painted Pony; Trail Boss
28 ❑ Aug 1957 Cover: 0.10 **NM** value: **18.00**
29 ❑ Nov 1957 Cover: 0.10 **NM** value: **18.00**
30 ❑ Feb 1958 Cover: 0.10 **NM** value: **18.00**
31 ❑ May 1958 Cover: 0.10 **NM** value: **18.00**
32 ❑ Aug 1958 Cover: 0.10 **NM** value: **18.00**
33 ❑ Nov 1958 Cover: 0.10 **NM** value: **18.00**
final issue.

LONE RANGER'S FAMOUS HORSE HI-YO SILVER — Dell

3 ❑ Jul 1952 Cover: 0.10 **NM** value: **35.00**
4 ❑ Oct 1952 Cover: 0.10 **NM** value: **35.00**
5 ❑ Jan 1953 Cover: 0.10 **NM** value: **35.00**
6 ❑ Apr 1953 Cover: 0.10 **NM** value: **35.00**
7 ❑ Jul 1953 Cover: 0.10 **NM** value: **35.00**
8 ❑ Oct 1953 Cover: 0.10 **NM** value: **35.00**
9 ❑ Jan 1954 Cover: 0.10 **NM** value: **35.00**
10 ❑ Apr 1954 Cover: 0.10 **NM** value: **25.00**
11 ❑ Jul 1954 Cover: 0.10 **NM** value: **25.00**
12 ❑ Oct 1954 Cover: 0.10 **NM** value: **25.00**
13 ❑ Jan 1955 Cover: 0.10 **NM** value: **25.00**
14 ❑ Apr 1955 Cover: 0.10 **NM** value: **25.00**

Other grades: Multiply prices above by **1.5 for Mint • 2/3 for Very Fine • 1/3 for Fine • 1/5 for Very Good • 1/8 for Good**

15 ❑ Jul 1955 Cover: 0.10 **NM** value: **25.00**
16 ❑ Oct 1955 Cover: 0.10 **NM** value: **25.00**
17 ❑ Jan 1956 Cover: 0.10 **NM** value: **25.00**
18 ❑ Apr 1956 Cover: 0.10 **NM** value: **25.00**
19 ❑ Jul 1956 Cover: 0.10 **NM** value: **25.00**
20 ❑ Oct 1956 Cover: 0.10 **NM** value: **25.00**
21 ❑ Jan 1957 Cover: 0.10 **NM** value: **20.00**
22 ❑ Apr 1957 Cover: 0.10 **NM** value: **20.00**
23 ❑ Jul 1957 Cover: 0.10 **NM** value: **20.00**
24 ❑ Oct 1957 Cover: 0.10 **NM** value: **20.00**
25 ❑ Jan 1958 Cover: 0.10 **NM** value: **20.00**
26 ❑ Apr 1958 Cover: 0.10 **NM** value: **20.00**
27 ❑ Jul 1958 Cover: 0.10 **NM** value: **20.00**
28 ❑ Oct 1958 Cover: 0.10 **NM** value: **20.00**
29 ❑ Jan 1959 Cover: 0.10 **NM** value: **20.00**
30 ❑ Apr 1959 Cover: 0.10 **NM** value: **20.00**
31 ❑ Jul 1959 Cover: 0.10 **NM** value: **20.00**
32 ❑ Oct 1959 Cover: 0.10 **NM** value: **20.00**
33 ❑ Jan 1960 Cover: 0.10 **NM** value: **20.00**
34 ❑ Apr 1960 Cover: 0.10 **NM** value: **20.00**
35 ❑ Jul 1960 Cover: 0.10 **NM** value: **20.00**
36 ❑ Oct 1960 Cover: 0.10 **NM** value: **20.00**

LONE RANGER'S GOLDEN WEST (DELL) — Dell

3 ❑ Aug 1955 Cover: 0.25 **NM** value: **75.00**
• **CGC:** 1 graded, best 8.5

LONE RANGER'S WESTERN TREASURY — Dell

1 ❑ Sep 1953 Cover: 0.25 **NM** value: **300.00**
• **CGC:** 3 graded, best 9.6
2 ❑ Aug 1954 Cover: 0.25 **NM** value: **200.00**
• **CGC:** 3 graded, best 9.4

LONE RIDER — Superior

1 ❑ Apr 1951 Cover: 0.10 **NM** value: **125.00**
2 ❑ Jun 1951 Cover: 0.10 **NM** value: **75.00**
3 ❑ Aug 1951 Cover: 0.10 **NM** value: **60.00**
4 ❑ Oct 1951 Cover: 0.10 **NM** value: **60.00**
5 ❑ Dec 1951 Cover: 0.10 **NM** value: **60.00**
6 ❑ Feb 1952 Cover: 0.10 **NM** value: **60.00**
7 ❑ Apr 1952 Cover: 0.10 **NM** value: **50.00**
8 ❑ Jun 1952 Cover: 0.10 **NM** value: **50.00**
9 ❑ Aug 1952 Cover: 0.10 **NM** value: **50.00**
10 ❑ Oct 1952 Cover: 0.10 **NM** value: **50.00**
11 ❑ Dec 1952 Cover: 0.10 **NM** value: **50.00**
12 ❑ Feb 1953 Cover: 0.10 **NM** value: **50.00**
13 ❑ Apr 1953 Cover: 0.10 **NM** value: **50.00**
14 ❑ Jun 1953 Cover: 0.10 **NM** value: **50.00**
15 ❑ Aug 1953 Cover: 0.10 **NM** value: **50.00**
16 ❑ Oct 1953 Cover: 0.10 **NM** value: **40.00**
17 ❑ Dec 1953 Cover: 0.10 **NM** value: **40.00**
18 ❑ Feb 1954 Cover: 0.10 **NM** value: **40.00**
19 ❑ Apr 1954 Cover: 0.10 **NM** value: **40.00**
20 ❑ Jun 1954 Cover: 0.10 **NM** value: **35.00**
21 ❑ Aug 1954 Cover: 0.10 **NM** value: **35.00**
22 ❑ Oct 1954 Cover: 0.10 **NM** value: **35.00**
23 ❑ Dec 1954 Cover: 0.10 **NM** value: **35.00**
24 ❑ Feb 1955 Cover: 0.10 **NM** value: **35.00**
25 ❑ Apr 1955 Cover: 0.10 **NM** value: **35.00**
26 ❑ Jun 1955 Cover: 0.10 **NM** value: **35.00**

LONE WOLF AND CUB — First

Itto Ogami was once the official executioner for a Japanese shogun. This was a position of extreme power and was coveted by all, especially the Yagyu clan. This scheming family framed Ogami for treason, toppling him from his position, and throwing him into a state of dishonor. When ordered to commit ritual suicide (seppuku), Ogami fought back, killing all present. The Yagyu clan retaliated by killing Ogami's wife.

Ogami now wanders throughout Japan with his infant son, Daigoro, always plotting to return and exact his revenge.

Lone Wolf and Cub was originally printed in Japan, and was brought to the U.S. and translated by First Comics. The English edition featured cover artwork by Frank Miller, Bill Sienkiewicz, and Mike Ploog.

1 ❑ May 1987 Cover: 1.95 **NM** value: **6.00**
Circ: CapCity orders: **14,900** • **CGC:** 5 graded, best 9.9
📖 The Assassin's Road **A:** Goseki Kojima; Frank Miller(cover) **C:** Frank Miller **W:** Kazuo Koike
1-2 ❑ Cover: 1.95 **NM** value: **2.50**
1-3 ❑ Cover: 1.95 **NM** value: **2.50**
2 ❑ Jun 1987 Cover: 1.95 **NM** value: **4.00**
Circ: CapCity orders: **11,800**
A: Goseki Kojima; Frank Miller(cover) **C:** Frank Miller **W:** Kazuo Koike
2-2 ❑ Jun 1987 Cover: 1.95 **NM** value: **2.50**
3 ❑ Jul 1987 Cover: 1.95 **NM** value: **4.00**
Circ: CapCity orders: **16,500** • **CGC:** 1 graded, best 9.6
📖 The Gateless Barrier **A:** Goseki Kojima; Frank Miller(cover) **C:** Frank Miller **W:** Kazuo Koike
3-2 ❑ Cover: 1.95 **NM** value: **2.50**
4 ❑ Aug 1987 Cover: 1.95 **NM** value: **3.00**
A: Goseki Kojima; Frank Miller(cover) **C:** Frank Miller **W:** Kazuo Koike
5 ❑ Sep 1987 Cover: 1.95 **NM** value: **3.00**
A: Goseki Kojima; Frank Miller(cover) **C:** Frank Miller **W:** Kazuo Koike
6 ❑ Oct 1987 Cover: 1.95 **NM** value: **3.00**
A: Goseki Kojima; Frank Miller(cover) **C:** Frank Miller **W:** Kazuo Koike ★ Origin of Lone Wolf.
7 ❑ Nov 1987 Cover: 1.95 **NM** value: **3.00**
A: Goseki Kojima; Frank Miller(cover) **C:** Frank Miller **W:** Kazuo Koike ★ Origin of Lone Wolf.
8 ❑ Dec 1987 Cover: 1.95 **NM** value: **3.00**
A: Goseki Kojima; Frank Miller(cover) **C:** Frank Miller **W:** Kazuo Koike
9 ❑ Jan 1988 Cover: 1.95 **NM** value: **3.00**
A: Goseki Kojima; Frank Miller(cover) **C:** Frank Miller **W:** Kazuo Koike
10 ❑ Feb 1988 Cover: 1.95 **NM** value: **3.00**
A: Goseki Kojima; Frank Miller(cover) **C:** Frank Miller **W:** Kazuo Koike
11 ❑ Mar 1988 Cover: 2.50 **NM** value: **Cover or less**
A: Goseki Kojima; Frank Miller(cover) **C:** Frank Miller **W:** Kazuo Koike
12 ❑ Apr 1988 Cover: 2.50 **NM** value: **Cover or less**
A: Goseki Kojima; Frank Miller(cover) **C:** Frank Miller **W:** Kazuo Koike
13 ❑ May 1988 Cover: 2.50 **NM** value: **Cover or less**
A: Goseki Kojima; Bill Sienkiewicz(cover) **C:** Bill Sienkiewicz **W:** Kazuo Koike
14 ❑ Jun 1988 Cover: 2.50 **NM** value: **Cover or less**
A: Goseki Kojima; Bill Sienkiewicz(cover) **C:** Bill Sienkiewicz **W:** Kazuo Koike
15 ❑ Jul 1988 Cover: 2.50 **NM** value: **Cover or less**
A: Goseki Kojima; Bill Sienkiewicz(cover) **C:** Bill Sienkiewicz **W:** Kazuo Koike
16 ❑ Aug 1988 Cover: 2.50 **NM** value: **Cover or less**
A: Goseki Kojima; Bill Sienkiewicz(cover) **C:** Bill Sienkiewicz **W:** Kazuo Koike
17 ❑ Sep 1988 Cover: 2.50 **NM** value: **Cover or less**
A: Goseki Kojima; Bill Sienkiewicz(cover) **C:** Bill Sienkiewicz **W:** Kazuo Koike
18 ❑ Oct 1988 Cover: 2.50 **NM** value: **Cover or less**
A: Goseki Kojima; Bill Sienkiewicz(cover) **C:** Bill Sienkiewicz **W:** Kazuo Koike
19 ❑ Nov 1988 Cover: 2.50 **NM** value: **Cover or less**
A: Goseki Kojima; Bill Sienkiewicz(cover) **C:** Bill Sienkiewicz **W:** Kazuo Koike
20 ❑ Dec 1988 Cover: 2.50 **NM** value: **Cover or less**
A: Goseki Kojima; Bill Sienkiewicz(cover) **C:** Bill Sienkiewicz **W:** Kazuo Koike
21 ❑ Jan 1989 Cover: 2.50 **NM** value: **Cover or less**
A: Goseki Kojima; Bill Sienkiewicz(cover) **C:** Bill Sienkiewicz **W:** Kazuo Koike
22 ❑ Feb 1989 Cover: 2.50 **NM** value: **Cover or less**
A: Goseki Kojima; Bill Sienkiewicz(cover) **C:** Bill Sienkiewicz **W:** Kazuo Koike
23 ❑ Mar 1989 Cover: 2.50 **NM** value: **Cover or less**
A: Goseki Kojima; Bill Sienkiewicz(cover) **C:** Bill Sienkiewicz **W:** Kazuo Koike
24 ❑ Apr 1989 Cover: 2.50 **NM** value: **Cover or less**
A: Goseki Kojima; Bill Sienkiewicz(cover) **C:** Bill Sienkiewicz **W:** Kazuo Koike
25 ❑ May 1989 Cover: 2.95 **NM** value: **Cover or less**
A: Goseki Kojima; Matt Wagner(cover) **C:** Matt Wagner **W:** Kazuo Koike
26 ❑ Jun 1989 Cover: 2.95 **NM** value: **Cover or less**
A: Goseki Kojima; Matt Wagner(cover) **C:** Matt Wagner **W:** Kazuo Koike
27 ❑ Jul 1989 Cover: 2.95 **NM** value: **3.00**
A: Goseki Kojima; Matt Wagner(cover) **C:** Matt Wagner **W:** Kazuo Koike
28 ❑ Aug 1989 Cover: 2.95 **NM** value: **3.00**
A: Goseki Kojima; Matt Wagner(cover) **C:** Matt Wagner **W:** Kazuo Koike
29 ❑ Sep 1989 Cover: 2.95 **NM** value: **3.00**
A: Goseki Kojima; Matt Wagner(cover) **C:** Matt Wagner **W:** Kazuo Koike
30 ❑ Oct 1989 Cover: 2.95 **NM** value: **3.00**
A: Goseki Kojima; Matt Wagner(cover) **C:** Matt Wagner **W:** Kazuo Koike
31 ❑ Jan 1990 Cover: 3.25 **NM** value: **Cover or less**
A: Goseki Kojima **C:** Matt Wagner **W:** Kazuo Koike
32 ❑ Apr 1990 Cover: 3.25 **NM** value: **Cover or less**
A: Goseki Kojima **C:** Matt Wagner **W:** Kazuo Koike
33 ❑ May 1990 Cover: 3.25 **NM** value: **Cover or less**
A: Goseki Kojima **C:** Matt Wagner **W:** Kazuo Koike
34 ❑ Jun 1990 Cover: 3.25 **NM** value: **Cover or less**
A: Goseki Kojima **C:** Matt Wagner **W:** Kazuo Koike
35 ❑ Jun 1990 Cover: 3.25 **NM** value: **Cover or less**
A: Goseki Kojima **C:** Matt Wagner **W:** Kazuo Koike
36 ❑ Jul 1990 Cover: 3.25 **NM** value: **Cover or less**
A: Goseki Kojima **C:** Matt Wagner **W:** Kazuo Koike
37 ❑ Aug 1990 Cover: 3.25 **NM** value: **Cover or less**
A: Goseki Kojima; Mike Ploog(cover) **C:** Mike Ploog **W:** Kazuo Koike
38 ❑ Sep 1990 Cover: 3.25 **NM** value: **Cover or less**
A: Goseki Kojima; Mike Ploog(cover) **C:** Mike Ploog **W:** Kazuo Koike
39 ❑ Oct 1990 Cover: 3.25 **NM** value: **6.00**
• Giant-size. **A:** Goseki Kojima; Mike Ploog(cover) **C:** Mike Ploog **W:** Kazuo Koike
40 ❑ Nov 1990 Cover: 3.25 **NM** value: **Cover or less**
A: Goseki Kojima; Mike Ploog(cover) **C:** Mike Ploog **W:** Kazuo Koike
41 ❑ Dec 1990 Cover: 3.25 **NM** value: **4.00**
A: Goseki Kojima; Mike Ploog(cover) **C:** Mike Ploog **W:** Kazuo Koike
42 ❑ Jan 1991 Cover: 3.25 **NM** value: **4.00**
A: Goseki Kojima; Mike Ploog(cover) **C:** Mike Ploog **W:** Kazuo Koike
43 ❑ Feb 1991 Cover: 3.25 **NM** value: **4.00**
A: Goseki Kojima; Mike Ploog(cover) **C:** Mike Ploog **W:** Kazuo Koike
44 ❑ Mar 1991 Cover: 3.25 **NM** value: **4.00**
A: Goseki Kojima; Mike Ploog(cover) **C:** Mike Ploog **W:** Kazuo Koike
45 ❑ Apr 1991 Cover: 3.25 **NM** value: **4.00**
A: Goseki Kojima; Mike Ploog(cover) **C:** Mike Ploog **W:** Kazuo Koike
46 ❑ May 1991 Cover: 3.95 **NM** value: **4.00**
A: Goseki Kojima; Mike Ploog(cover) **W:** Kazuo Koike
47 ❑ Jun 1991 Cover: 3.95 **NM** value: **4.00**
A: Goseki Kojima; Mike Ploog(cover) **W:** Kazuo Koike
48 ❑ Jul 1991 Cover: 3.95 **NM** value: **4.00**
A: Goseki Kojima **W:** Kazuo Koike
49 ❑ Aug 1991 Cover: 3.95 **NM** value: **4.00**
A: Goseki Kojima **W:** Kazuo Koike
Bk 1❑ Cover: 19.95 **NM** value: **Cover or less**
• Reprints Lone Wolf & Cub #1-7 **A:** Goseki Kojima **W:** Kazuo Koike

LONG BOW — Fiction House

1 ❑ ca. 1951 Cover: 0.10 **NM** value: **100.00**
2 ❑ ca. 1951 Cover: 0.10 **NM** value: **65.00**
3 ❑ ca. 1951 Cover: 0.10 **NM** value: **50.00**
4 ❑ ca. 1951 Cover: 0.10 **NM** value: **50.00**
5 ❑ ca. 1952 Cover: 0.10 **NM** value: **50.00**
6 ❑ ca. 1952 Cover: 0.10 **NM** value: **50.00**
7 ❑ Sum 1952 Cover: 0.10 **NM** value: **50.00**
8 ❑ Fal 1952 Cover: 0.10 **NM** value: **50.00**
9 ❑ Win 1952 Cover: 0.10 **NM** value: **50.00**

LONG, HOT SUMMER, THE — DC / Milestone

1 ❑ Jul 1995 Cover: 2.95 **NM** value: **Cover or less**
Circ: CapCity orders: **4,525**
enhanced cover.
2 ❑ Aug 1995 Cover: 2.50 **NM** value: **Cover or less**
Circ: CapCity orders: **3,475**
3 ❑ Sep 1995 Cover: 2.50 **NM** value: **Cover or less**
Circ: CapCity orders: **3,150**

LONGSHOT — Marvel

This six-part limited series introduced readers to both Longshot, its tousled namesake, and the entire universe of Mojo-world. Both have become regular features in the X-Men/mutant titles.

Readers first meet Longshot when he crosses from dimension to elude a group of heavily armed pursuers. In crossing, however, he loses his memory and can no longer tell who he is or why he was being chased. He needn't have worried, since his pursuers, the denizens of a twisted world, named "Mojo-world" after its (literally) spineless ruler, catch up to him on Earth. Now, using only his throwing

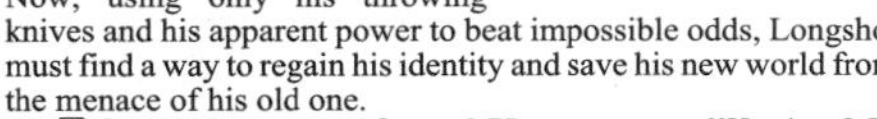

knives and his apparent power to beat impossible odds, Longshot must find a way to regain his identity and save his new world from the menace of his old one.

1 ❑ Sep 1985 Cover: 0.75 **NM** value: **3.50**
Circ: CapCity orders: **23,000** • **CGC:** 6 graded, best 9.8
A: Arthur Adams **W:** Ann Nocenti ★ 1st Appearance of Longshot.
2 ❑ Oct 1985 Cover: 0.75 **NM** value: **3.00**
Circ: CapCity orders: **15,800** • **CGC:** 1 graded, best 9.6
A: Arthur Adams **W:** Ann Nocenti ★ 1st Appearance of Ricochet Rita.
3 ❑ Nov 1985 Cover: 0.75 **NM** value: **2.50**
Circ: CapCity orders: **15,700** • **CGC:** 1 graded, best 9.8
📖 Just Let Me Die **A:** Arthur Adams **W:** Ann Nocenti ★ 1st Appearance of Mojo, Spiral.
4 ❑ Dec 1985 Cover: 0.75 **NM** value: **2.50**
Circ: CapCity orders: **15,000** • **CGC:** 1 graded, best 9.4
📖 Can't Give It All Away **A:** Arthur Adams **W:** Ann Nocenti ★ Appearance of Spider-Man.
5 ❑ Jan 1986 Cover: 0.75 **NM** value: **2.00**
Circ: CapCity orders: **15,300** • **CGC:** 1 graded, best 9.8
📖 Deadly Lies **A:** Arthur Adams **W:** Ann Nocenti
6 ❑ Feb 1986 Cover: 1.25 **NM** value: **2.50**
Circ: CapCity orders: **16,100** • **CGC:** 1 graded, best 9.8
• Double-size. 📖 A Snake Coils… **A:** Arthur Adams **W:** Ann Nocenti
Bk 1❑ Cover: 16.95 **NM** value: **Cover or less**
• Double-size. **A:** Arthur Adams **W:** Ann Nocenti

LONGSHOT (2ND SERIES) — Marvel

1 ❑ Feb 1998 Cover: 3.99 **NM** value: **Cover or less**
One-shot. wraparound cover. 📖 Fools **A:** Michael Zulli **W:** J.M. DeMatteis

LONGSHOT COMICS — Slave Labor

1 ❑ Jun 1995 Cover: 2.95 **NM** value: **Cover or less**
📖 The Long and Unlearned Life of Roland Gethers **A:** Shane Simmons **W:** Shane Simmons
1-2 ❑ Feb 1996 Cover: 2.95 **NM** value: **Cover or less**
2 ❑ Jul 1997, b&w Cover: 2.95 **NM** value: **Cover or less**
📖 The Failed Promise of Bradley Gethers **A:** Shane Simmons **W:** Shane Simmons

LOOKERS — Avatar

1 ❑ Cover: 3.00 **NM** value: **Cover or less**
A: Rob Durham **W:** Mark Seifert; William A. Christensen
2 ❑ Cover: 3.00 **NM** value: **Cover or less**
A: Rob Durham **W:** Mark Seifert; William A. Christensen

LOOKERS: SLAVES OF ANUBIS — Avatar

1 ❑ Cover: 3.50 **NM** value: **Cover or less**
A: Pat Quinn **W:** Barry Gregory

Diamond preorders are the estimated number of comics sold, prior to their release, to comics shops in North America by Diamond Comic Distributors, the largest distributor. These figures underreport the actual number of circulating copies by the amount of reorders Diamond took (usually 5-10% again of the preorders) and sales by publishers to newsstand and bookstore distributors. For many independent publishers, Diamond's preorders may be quite close to the actual number of copies in circulation.

CGC-graded: Multiply prices above by **33 for 9.9 M • 16 for 9.8 NM/M • 7 for 9.6 NM+ • 5 for 9.4 NM • 2.5 for 9.2 NM- • 1.5 for 9.0 VF/NM**

LOONEY TUNES AND MERRIE MELODIES COMICS
Dell

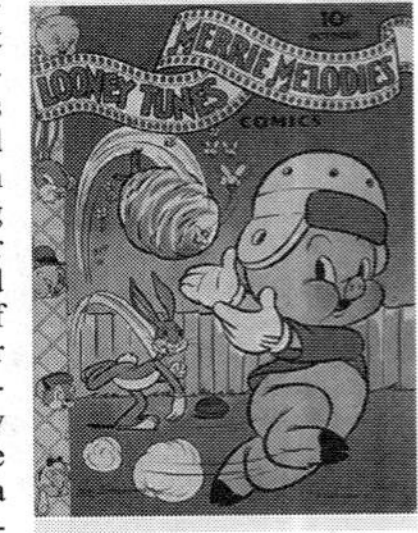

The comic book (carrying Producer Leon Schlesinger's credit line, much as Walt Disney's associated comics carried his name as their creator) of Looney Tunes and Merrie Melodies was primarily an anthology of short stories featuring characters introduced in Warner Brothers cartoons. These included Porky Pig and Bugs Bunny, of course. Even Sniffles was a Warner Brothers character, though the comic-book creators memorably teamed the little mouse with a little girl named Mary Jane. (The idea was that she could magically become as small as the mouse and at first accomplished this by tossing magic sand over herself accompanied by the chant, "Magic sand, magic sand, make me small at my command!" When mothers complained about having to wash sand out of their children's hair, the spell was changed to "Magic words of poof, poof, piffles, make me just as small as Sniffles." It didn't work, either, but it didn't make a mess.)

Not all the characters originated in movies; "Pat, Patsy, and Pete," for example, were only to be found in comic books.

— Maggie

1 ❑ 1941 Cover: 0.10 **NM** value: **10000.00**
• **CGC:** 3 graded, best 8.5
• Extremely rare; Less than 200 thought to exist
2 ❑ Dec 1941 Cover: 0.10 **NM** value: **1800.00**
3 ❑ Jan 1942 Cover: 0.10 **NM** value: **1200.00**
4 ❑ Feb 1942 Cover: 0.10 **NM** value: **900.00**
5 ❑ Mar 1942 Cover: 0.10 **NM** value: **900.00**
6 ❑ Apr 1942 Cover: 0.10 **NM** value: **585.00**
7 ❑ May 1942 Cover: 0.10 **NM** value: **585.00**
8 ❑ Jun 1942 Cover: 0.10 **NM** value: **585.00**
9 ❑ Jul 1942 Cover: 0.10 **NM** value: **585.00**
10 ❑ Aug 1942 Cover: 0.10 **NM** value: **585.00**
11 ❑ Sep 1942 Cover: 0.10 **NM** value: **425.00**
• **CGC:** 1 graded, best 9.0
12 ❑ Oct 1942 Cover: 0.10 **NM** value: **425.00**
• **CGC:** 1 graded, best 9.0
13 ❑ Nov 1942 Cover: 0.10 **NM** value: **425.00**
14 ❑ Dec 1942 Cover: 0.10 **NM** value: **425.00**
• **CGC:** 1 graded, best 9.0
15 ❑ Jan 1943 Cover: 0.10 **NM** value: **425.00**
16 ❑ Feb 1943 Cover: 0.10 **NM** value: **350.00**
17 ❑ Mar 1943 Cover: 0.10 **NM** value: **350.00**
18 ❑ Apr 1943 Cover: 0.10 **NM** value: **350.00**
19 ❑ May 1943 Cover: 0.10 **NM** value: **350.00**
20 ❑ Jun 1943 Cover: 0.10 **NM** value: **350.00**
21 ❑ Jul 1943 Cover: 0.10 **NM** value: **265.00**
• **CGC:** 1 graded, best 8.0
22 ❑ Aug 1943 Cover: 0.10 **NM** value: **265.00**
23 ❑ Sep 1943 Cover: 0.10 **NM** value: **265.00**
24 ❑ Oct 1943 Cover: 0.10 **NM** value: **265.00**
25 ❑ Nov 1943 Cover: 0.10 **NM** value: **265.00**
26 ❑ Dec 1943 Cover: 0.10 **NM** value: **265.00**
27 ❑ Jan 1944 Cover: 0.10 **NM** value: **265.00**
28 ❑ Feb 1944 Cover: 0.10 **NM** value: **265.00**
29 ❑ Mar 1944 Cover: 0.10 **NM** value: **265.00**
30 ❑ Apr 1944 Cover: 0.10 **NM** value: **200.00**
31 ❑ May 1944 Cover: 0.10 **NM** value: **200.00**
32 ❑ Jun 1944 Cover: 0.10 **NM** value: **200.00**
33 ❑ Jul 1944 Cover: 0.10 **NM** value: **200.00**
34 ❑ Aug 1944 Cover: 0.10 **NM** value: **200.00**
35 ❑ Sep 1944 Cover: 0.10 **NM** value: **200.00**
36 ❑ Oct 1944 Cover: 0.10 **NM** value: **200.00**
37 ❑ Nov 1944 Cover: 0.10 **NM** value: **200.00**
38 ❑ Dec 1944 Cover: 0.10 **NM** value: **200.00**
39 ❑ Jan 1945 Cover: 0.10 **NM** value: **200.00**
40 ❑ Feb 1945 Cover: 0.10 **NM** value: **200.00**
41 ❑ Mar 1945 Cover: 0.10 **NM** value: **140.00**
42 ❑ Apr 1945 Cover: 0.10 **NM** value: **140.00**
43 ❑ May 1945 Cover: 0.10 **NM** value: **140.00**
44 ❑ Jun 1945 Cover: 0.10 **NM** value: **140.00**
45 ❑ Jul 1945 Cover: 0.10 **NM** value: **140.00**
46 ❑ Aug 1945 Cover: 0.10 **NM** value: **140.00**
47 ❑ Sep 1945 Cover: 0.10 **NM** value: **140.00**
48 ❑ Oct 1945 Cover: 0.10 **NM** value: **140.00**
49 ❑ Nov 1945 Cover: 0.10 **NM** value: **140.00**
50 ❑ Dec 1945 Cover: 0.10 **NM** value: **140.00**
51 ❑ Jan 1946 Cover: 0.10 **NM** value: **110.00**
52 ❑ Feb 1946 Cover: 0.10 **NM** value: **110.00**
53 ❑ Mar 1946 Cover: 0.10 **NM** value: **110.00**
54 ❑ Apr 1946 Cover: 0.10 **NM** value: **110.00**
55 ❑ May 1946 Cover: 0.10 **NM** value: **110.00**
56 ❑ Jun 1946 Cover: 0.10 **NM** value: **110.00**
• **CGC:** 1 graded, best 2.5
57 ❑ Jul 1946 Cover: 0.10 **NM** value: **110.00**
58 ❑ Aug 1946 Cover: 0.10 **NM** value: **110.00**
59 ❑ Sep 1946 Cover: 0.10 **NM** value: **110.00**
60 ❑ Oct 1946 Cover: 0.10 **NM** value: **110.00**
61 ❑ Nov 1946 Cover: 0.10 **NM** value: **85.00**
62 ❑ Dec 1946 Cover: 0.10 **NM** value: **85.00**
63 ❑ Jan 1947 Cover: 0.10 **NM** value: **85.00**
64 ❑ Feb 1947 Cover: 0.10 **NM** value: **85.00**
65 ❑ Mar 1947 Cover: 0.10 **NM** value: **85.00**
66 ❑ Apr 1947 Cover: 0.10 **NM** value: **85.00**
67 ❑ May 1947 Cover: 0.10 **NM** value: **85.00**
68 ❑ Jun 1947 Cover: 0.10 **NM** value: **85.00**
69 ❑ Jul 1947 Cover: 0.10 **NM** value: **85.00**
70 ❑ Aug 1947 Cover: 0.10 **NM** value: **85.00**
71 ❑ Sep 1947 Cover: 0.10 **NM** value: **60.00**
72 ❑ Oct 1947 Cover: 0.10 **NM** value: **60.00**
73 ❑ Nov 1947 Cover: 0.10 **NM** value: **60.00**
74 ❑ Dec 1947 Cover: 0.10 **NM** value: **60.00**
75 ❑ Jan 1948 Cover: 0.10 **NM** value: **60.00**
76 ❑ Feb 1948 Cover: 0.10 **NM** value: **60.00**
77 ❑ Mar 1948 Cover: 0.10 **NM** value: **60.00**
78 ❑ Apr 1948 Cover: 0.10 **NM** value: **60.00**
79 ❑ May 1948 Cover: 0.10 **NM** value: **60.00**
80 ❑ Jun 1948 Cover: 0.10 **NM** value: **60.00**
81 ❑ Jul 1948 Cover: 0.10 **NM** value: **45.00**
82 ❑ Aug 1948 Cover: 0.10 **NM** value: **45.00**
83 ❑ Sep 1948 Cover: 0.10 **NM** value: **45.00**
84 ❑ Oct 1948 Cover: 0.10 **NM** value: **45.00**
85 ❑ Nov 1948 Cover: 0.10 **NM** value: **45.00**
86 ❑ Dec 1948 Cover: 0.10 **NM** value: **45.00**
87 ❑ Jan 1949 Cover: 0.10 **NM** value: **45.00**
88 ❑ Feb 1949 Cover: 0.10 **NM** value: **45.00**
89 ❑ Mar 1949 Cover: 0.10 **NM** value: **45.00**
90 ❑ Apr 1949 Cover: 0.10 **NM** value: **45.00**
91 ❑ May 1949 Cover: 0.10 **NM** value: **32.00**
92 ❑ Jun 1949 Cover: 0.10 **NM** value: **32.00**
93 ❑ Jul 1949 Cover: 0.10 **NM** value: **32.00**
94 ❑ Aug 1949 Cover: 0.10 **NM** value: **32.00**
📖 Untitled stories; Dumb Bunny (text) • Bugs Bunny, Sniffle and Mary Jane, Porky Pig, Henery Hawk, Elmer Fudd
95 ❑ Sep 1949 Cover: 0.10 **NM** value: **32.00**
96 ❑ Oct 1949 Cover: 0.10 **NM** value: **32.00**
97 ❑ Nov 1949 Cover: 0.10 **NM** value: **32.00**
98 ❑ Dec 1949 Cover: 0.10 **NM** value: **32.00**
99 ❑ Jan 1950 Cover: 0.10 **NM** value: **32.00**
100 ❑ Feb 1950 Cover: 0.10 **NM** value: **38.00**
101 ❑ Mar 1950 Cover: 0.10 **NM** value: **22.00**
102 ❑ Apr 1950 Cover: 0.10 **NM** value: **22.00**
103 ❑ May 1950 Cover: 0.10 **NM** value: **22.00**
104 ❑ Jun 1950 Cover: 0.10 **NM** value: **22.00**
105 ❑ Jul 1950 Cover: 0.10 **NM** value: **22.00**
106 ❑ Aug 1950 Cover: 0.10 **NM** value: **22.00**
107 ❑ Sep 1950 Cover: 0.10 **NM** value: **22.00**
108 ❑ Oct 1950 Cover: 0.10 **NM** value: **22.00**
109 ❑ Nov 1950 Cover: 0.10 **NM** value: **22.00**
110 ❑ Dec 1950 Cover: 0.10 **NM** value: **22.00**
111 ❑ Jan 1951 Cover: 0.10 **NM** value: **20.00**
112 ❑ Feb 1951 Cover: 0.10 **NM** value: **20.00**
113 ❑ Mar 1951 Cover: 0.10 **NM** value: **20.00**
114 ❑ Apr 1951 Cover: 0.10 **NM** value: **20.00**
115 ❑ May 1951 Cover: 0.10 **NM** value: **20.00**
116 ❑ Jun 1951 Cover: 0.10 **NM** value: **20.00**
117 ❑ Jul 1951 Cover: 0.10 **NM** value: **20.00**
118 ❑ Aug 1951 Cover: 0.10 **NM** value: **20.00**
119 ❑ Sep 1951 Cover: 0.10 **NM** value: **20.00**
120 ❑ Oct 1951 Cover: 0.10 **NM** value: **20.00**
121 ❑ Nov 1951 Cover: 0.10 **NM** value: **18.00**
• **CGC:** 1 graded, best 9.4
122 ❑ Dec 1951 Cover: 0.10 **NM** value: **18.00**
123 ❑ Jan 1952 Cover: 0.10 **NM** value: **18.00**
📖 Untitled stories; Double Feature Trouble (text) • Bugs Bunny, Porky Pig, Elmer Fudd and Daffy, Mary Jane and Sniffles, Henery Hawk
124 ❑ Feb 1952 Cover: 0.10 **NM** value: **18.00**
125 ❑ Mar 1952 Cover: 0.10 **NM** value: **18.00**
126 ❑ Apr 1952 Cover: 0.10 **NM** value: **18.00**
127 ❑ May 1952 Cover: 0.10 **NM** value: **18.00**
128 ❑ Jun 1952 Cover: 0.10 **NM** value: **18.00**
129 ❑ Jul 1952 Cover: 0.10 **NM** value: **18.00**
130 ❑ Aug 1952 Cover: 0.10 **NM** value: **18.00**
131 ❑ Sep 1952 Cover: 0.10 **NM** value: **15.00**
132 ❑ Oct 1952 Cover: 0.10 **NM** value: **15.00**
133 ❑ Nov 1952 Cover: 0.10 **NM** value: **15.00**
134 ❑ Dec 1952 Cover: 0.10 **NM** value: **15.00**
135 ❑ Jan 1953 Cover: 0.10 **NM** value: **15.00**
136 ❑ Feb 1953 Cover: 0.10 **NM** value: **15.00**
137 ❑ Mar 1953 Cover: 0.10 **NM** value: **15.00**
138 ❑ Apr 1953 Cover: 0.10 **NM** value: **15.00**
139 ❑ May 1953 Cover: 0.10 **NM** value: **15.00**
140 ❑ Jun 1953 Cover: 0.10 **NM** value: **15.00**
141 ❑ Jul 1953 Cover: 0.10 **NM** value: **12.00**
142 ❑ Aug 1953 Cover: 0.10 **NM** value: **12.00**
143 ❑ Sep 1953 Cover: 0.10 **NM** value: **12.00**
144 ❑ Oct 1953 Cover: 0.10 **NM** value: **12.00**
145 ❑ Nov 1953 Cover: 0.10 **NM** value: **12.00**
146 ❑ Dec 1953 Cover: 0.10 **NM** value: **12.00**
147 ❑ Jan 1954 Cover: 0.10 **NM** value: **12.00**
148 ❑ Feb 1954 Cover: 0.10 **NM** value: **12.00**
149 ❑ Mar 1954 Cover: 0.10 **NM** value: **12.00**
150 ❑ Apr 1954 Cover: 0.10 **NM** value: **12.00**
151 ❑ May 1954 Cover: 0.10 **NM** value: **10.00**
152 ❑ Jun 1954 Cover: 0.10 **NM** value: **10.00**
153 ❑ Jul 1954 Cover: 0.10 **NM** value: **10.00**
154 ❑ Aug 1954 Cover: 0.10 **NM** value: **10.00**
155 ❑ Sep 1954 Cover: 0.10 **NM** value: **10.00**
156 ❑ Oct 1954 Cover: 0.10 **NM** value: **10.00**
157 ❑ Nov 1954 Cover: 0.10 **NM** value: **10.00**
158 ❑ Dec 1954 Cover: 0.10 **NM** value: **10.00**
159 ❑ Jan 1955 Cover: 0.10 **NM** value: **10.00**
160 ❑ Feb 1955 Cover: 0.10 **NM** value: **10.00**
161 ❑ Mar 1955 Cover: 0.10 **NM** value: **10.00**
162 ❑ Apr 1955 Cover: 0.10 **NM** value: **10.00**
163 ❑ May 1955 Cover: 0.10 **NM** value: **10.00**
164 ❑ Jun 1955 Cover: 0.10 **NM** value: **10.00**
165 ❑ Jul 1955 Cover: 0.10 **NM** value: **10.00**
166 ❑ Aug 1955 Cover: 0.10 **NM** value: **10.00**
167 ❑ Sep 1955 Cover: 0.10 **NM** value: **10.00**
168 ❑ Oct 1955 Cover: 0.10 **NM** value: **10.00**
169 ❑ Nov 1955 Cover: 0.10 **NM** value: **10.00**
170 ❑ Dec 1955 Cover: 0.10 **NM** value: **10.00**
171 ❑ Jan 1956 Cover: 0.10 **NM** value: **8.00**
172 ❑ Feb 1956 Cover: 0.10 **NM** value: **8.00**
173 ❑ Mar 1956 Cover: 0.10 **NM** value: **8.00**
174 ❑ Apr 1956 Cover: 0.10 **NM** value: **8.00**
175 ❑ May 1956 Cover: 0.10 **NM** value: **8.00**
176 ❑ Jun 1956 Cover: 0.10 **NM** value: **8.00**
177 ❑ Jul 1956 Cover: 0.10 **NM** value: **8.00**
178 ❑ Aug 1956 Cover: 0.10 **NM** value: **8.00**
179 ❑ Sep 1956 Cover: 0.10 **NM** value: **8.00**
180 ❑ Oct 1956 Cover: 0.10 **NM** value: **8.00**
181 ❑ Nov 1956 Cover: 0.10 **NM** value: **8.00**
182 ❑ Dec 1956 Cover: 0.10 **NM** value: **8.00**
183 ❑ Jan 1957 Cover: 0.10 **NM** value: **8.00**
184 ❑ Feb 1957 Cover: 0.10 **NM** value: **8.00**
185 ❑ Mar 1957 Cover: 0.10 **NM** value: **8.00**
186 ❑ Apr 1957 Cover: 0.10 **NM** value: **8.00**
187 ❑ May 1957 Cover: 0.10 **NM** value: **8.00**
188 ❑ Jun 1957 Cover: 0.10 **NM** value: **8.00**
189 ❑ Jul 1957 Cover: 0.10 **NM** value: **8.00**
• **CGC:** 1 graded, best 9.0
190 ❑ Aug 1957 Cover: 0.10 **NM** value: **8.00**
191 ❑ Sep 1957 Cover: 0.10 **NM** value: **8.00**
192 ❑ Oct 1957 Cover: 0.10 **NM** value: **8.00**
193 ❑ Nov 1957 Cover: 0.10 **NM** value: **8.00**
194 ❑ Dec 1957 Cover: 0.10 **NM** value: **8.00**
195 ❑ Jan 1958 Cover: 0.10 **NM** value: **8.00**
196 ❑ Feb 1958 Cover: 0.10 **NM** value: **8.00**
197 ❑ Mar 1958 Cover: 0.10 **NM** value: **8.00**
198 ❑ Apr 1958 Cover: 0.10 **NM** value: **8.00**
199 ❑ May 1958 Cover: 0.10 **NM** value: **8.00**
200 ❑ Jun 1958 Cover: 0.10 **NM** value: **8.00**
201 ❑ Jul 1958 Cover: 0.10 **NM** value: **6.00**
202 ❑ Aug 1958 Cover: 0.10 **NM** value: **6.00**
203 ❑ Sep 1958 Cover: 0.10 **NM** value: **6.00**
204 ❑ Oct 1958 Cover: 0.10 **NM** value: **6.00**
205 ❑ Nov 1958 Cover: 0.10 **NM** value: **6.00**
206 ❑ Dec 1958 Cover: 0.10 **NM** value: **6.00**
207 ❑ Jan 1959 Cover: 0.10 **NM** value: **6.00**
208 ❑ Feb 1959 Cover: 0.10 **NM** value: **6.00**
209 ❑ Mar 1959 Cover: 0.10 **NM** value: **6.00**
210 ❑ Apr 1959 Cover: 0.10 **NM** value: **6.00**
211 ❑ May 1959 Cover: 0.10 **NM** value: **6.00**
212 ❑ Jun 1959 Cover: 0.10 **NM** value: **6.00**
213 ❑ Jul 1959 Cover: 0.10 **NM** value: **6.00**
214 ❑ Aug 1959 Cover: 0.10 **NM** value: **6.00**
215 ❑ Sep 1959 Cover: 0.10 **NM** value: **6.00**
216 ❑ Oct 1959 Cover: 0.10 **NM** value: **6.00**
217 ❑ Nov 1959 Cover: 0.10 **NM** value: **6.00**
218 ❑ Dec 1959 Cover: 0.10 **NM** value: **6.00**
219 ❑ Jan 1960 Cover: 0.10 **NM** value: **6.00**
Circ: Statement: **459,344**
220 ❑ Feb 1960 Cover: 0.10 **NM** value: **6.00**
Circ: Statement: **459,344**
221 ❑ Mar 1960 Cover: 0.10 **NM** value: **6.00**
Circ: Statement: **459,344**
222 ❑ Apr 1960 Cover: 0.10 **NM** value: **4.00**
Circ: Statement: **459,344**
223 ❑ May 1960 Cover: 0.10 **NM** value: **4.00**
Circ: Statement: **459,344**
224 ❑ Jun 1960 Cover: 0.10 **NM** value: **4.00**
Circ: Statement: **459,344**
225 ❑ Jul 1960 Cover: 0.10 **NM** value: **4.00**
Circ: Statement: **459,344**
226 ❑ Aug 1960 Cover: 0.10 **NM** value: **4.00**
Circ: Statement: **459,344**
227 ❑ Sep 1960 Cover: 0.10 **NM** value: **4.00**
Circ: Statement: **459,344**
228 ❑ Oct 1960 Cover: 0.10 **NM** value: **4.00**
Circ: Statement: **459,344**
229 ❑ Nov 1960 Cover: 0.10 **NM** value: **4.00**
Circ: Statement: **459,344**
230 ❑ Dec 1960 Cover: 0.10 **NM** value: **4.00**
Circ: Statement: **459,344**
231 ❑ Jan 1961 Cover: 0.10 **NM** value: **4.00**
232 ❑ Feb 1961 Cover: 0.15 **NM** value: **4.00**
233 ❑ Mar 1961 Cover: 0.15 **NM** value: **4.00**
234 ❑ Apr 1961 Cover: 0.15 **NM** value: **4.00**
235 ❑ May 1961 Cover: 0.15 **NM** value: **4.00**
236 ❑ Jun 1961 Cover: 0.15 **NM** value: **4.00**
237 ❑ Jul 1961 Cover: 0.15 **NM** value: **4.00**
238 ❑ Aug 1961 Cover: 0.15 **NM** value: **4.00**
239 ❑ Sep 1961 Cover: 0.15 **NM** value: **4.00**
240 ❑ Oct 1961 Cover: 0.15 **NM** value: **4.00**
241 ❑ Nov 1961 Cover: 0.15 **NM** value: **4.00**
242 ❑ Dec 1961 Cover: 0.15 **NM** value: **4.00**
243 ❑ 1962 Cover: 0.15 **NM** value: **4.00**
244 ❑ May 1962 Cover: 0.15 **NM** value: **4.00**
245 ❑ Jul 1962 Cover: 0.15 **NM** value: **4.00**
246 ❑ Sep 1962 Cover: 0.12 **NM** value: **4.00**
final issue.

LOONEY TUNES (DC)
DC

This series features the popular Warner Brothers cartoon characters who were first given their own series back in 1941 and who ran as comic-book characters for years under the Dell and Gold Key imprints. DC's 1994 rendition brings back all the favorites, including Marvin the Martian, Bugs Bunny, Daffy Duck, the Roadrunner, Wyle E. Coyote, Speedy Gonzalez, and many more. Geared to cater to the children's market, the series also contains activity pages like word scrambles and connect-the-dots puzzles. It all comes recommended for children, but it's fun for children of all ages.

Other grades: Multiply prices above by **1.5 for Mint • 2/3 for Very Fine • 1/3 for Fine • 1/5 for Very Good • 1/8 for Good**

1 Apr 1994 Cover: 1.50 **NM** value: **2.25**
Circ: CapCity orders: **23,900**
Earthstruck; The Shot Felt 'Round the World; Down Under Mousers **A:** George Wildman; Dilapsa Studio **W:** Brett Koth; Jack Enyart ★ Appearance of Marvin Martian.

2 May 1994 Cover: 1.50 **NM** value: **2.00**
Circ: CapCity orders: **13,550**
• Road Runner, Coyote

3 Jun 1994 Cover: 1.50 **NM** value: **2.00**
Circ: CapCity orders: **11,700**
Take Me Out to the Ballgame; Half-Baked Romance • Baseball issue **A:** Chuck Fiala; Stephanie Gladden **W:** Dave King; Jack Enyart

4 Jul 1994 Cover: 1.50 **NM** value: **2.00**
Circ: CapCity orders: **11,300**
Makeover Mayhem; Peking Duck; Swat to Trot **A:** John Costanza; Alvaro Flores; Horacio Saavedra **W:** Brett Koth; Jack Enyart ★ Appearance of Witch Hazel.

5 Aug 1994 Cover: 1.50 **NM** value: **1.75**
Circ: CapCity orders: **10,050**
Spaced-Out Coyote; Brawl Or Nothing • Coyote, Martians **A:** George Wildman; Dilapsa Studios **W:** Jack Enyart

6 Sep 1994 Cover: 1.50 **NM** value: **Cover or less**
Circ: CapCity orders: **8,600**
• Tazmanian Devil

7 Oct 1994 Cover: 1.50 **NM** value: **Cover or less**
Circ: CapCity orders: **7,200**

8 Nov 1994 Cover: 1.50 **NM** value: **Cover or less**
Circ: CapCity orders: **6,350**

9 Dec 1994 Cover: 1.50 **NM** value: **Cover or less**
Circ: CapCity orders: **6,000**
If It's Tuesday, this Must be Love; The Duck with no Name; The Last Laugh! **A:** George Wildman **W:** Jack Enyart

10 Jan 1995 Cover: 1.50 **NM** value: **Cover or less**
Circ: CapCity orders: **5,500**
• Christmas issue

11 Feb 1995 Cover: 1.50 **NM** value: **Cover or less**
Circ: CapCity orders: **4,600**

12 Mar 1995 Cover: 1.50 **NM** value: **Cover or less**
Circ: CapCity orders: **4,100**

13 Apr 1995 Cover: 1.50 **NM** value: **Cover or less**
Circ: CapCity orders: **3,650**
• Coyote

14 May 1995 Cover: 1.50 **NM** value: **Cover or less**
Circ: CapCity orders: **3,550**

15 Jun 1995 Cover: 1.50 **NM** value: **Cover or less**
Circ: CapCity orders: **3,375**

16 Jul 1995 Cover: 1.50 **NM** value: **Cover or less**
Circ: CapCity orders: **3,250**
• Daffy, Speedy Gonzales

17 Aug 1995 Cover: 1.50 **NM** value: **Cover or less**
Circ: CapCity orders: **3,250**

18 Sep 1995 Cover: 1.50 **NM** value: **Cover or less**
Circ: CapCity orders: **3,075**
• Duck Dodgers

19 Oct 1995 Cover: 1.50 **NM** value: **Cover or less**
Circ: CapCity orders: **2,575**

20 Nov 1995 Cover: 1.50 **NM** value: **Cover or less**
• Yosemite Sam

21 Feb 1996 Cover: 1.50 **NM** value: **Cover or less**
• Tazmanian Devil

22 Apr 1996 Cover: 1.50 **NM** value: **Cover or less**
Fudd Hunt; Punch 'n Tweety **A:** Eduardo Savid; Horacio Saavedra **W:** David Cody Weiss; Bobbi J.G. Weiss

23 Jun 1996 Cover: 1.75 **NM** value: **Cover or less**

24 Aug 1996 Cover: 1.75 **NM** value: **Cover or less**
Get Tweety

25 Oct 1996 Cover: 1.75 **NM** value: **Cover or less**
• Indiana Itz Mine

26 Nov 1996 Cover: 1.75 **NM** value: **Cover or less**
Circ: Diamd. preorders: **6,287**
indicia says Nov, cover says Dec. Psylvester; Modem Operandi; Survival of the Unfit • Sylvester, Tweety **A:** Horacio Saavedra; Nelson Luty; Pablo Zamboni **W:** Allison Heartinger; Dan Slott; Dana Kurtin; Sean Carolan

27 Jan 1997 Cover: 1.75 **NM** value: **Cover or less**
Circ: Diamd. preorders: **6,093**
indicia says Jan, cover says Feb. One a Toon...Always a Toon **A:** Cosme Quartieri **W:** Allison Heartinger; C.M. Baldwin

28 Feb 1997 Cover: 1.75 **NM** value: **Cover or less**
Circ: Diamd. preorders: **5,721**
cover says Apr 96, indicia says Feb 97. I Love Goosey; I'll Take Manhattan • Valentine's issue **A:** Horacio Ottolini; Nelson Luty **W:** Allison Heartinger; Michael Eury

29 May 1997 Cover: 1.75 **NM** value: **Cover or less**
Circ: Diamd. preorders: **5,725**
• Coyote

30 Jul 1997 Cover: 1.75 **NM** value: **Cover or less**
Circ: Diamd. preorders: **5,476**
Twilight Zone cover.

31 Aug 1997 Cover: 1.75 **NM** value: **Cover or less**
Circ: Diamd. preorders: **5,562**

32 Sep 1997 Cover: 1.75 **NM** value: **Cover or less**
Circ: Diamd. preorders: **5,461**
• Hercules parody

33 Oct 1997 Cover: 1.75 **NM** value: **Cover or less**
Circ: Diamd. preorders: **5,425**
• Back to School issue

34 Nov 1997 Cover: 1.75 **NM** value: **Cover or less**
Circ: Diamd. preorders: **5,304**
Sidekicked; Inherit the Windbag; The Envelope Please • Daffy versus Dinky Downunder **A:** Horacio Saavedra; Pablo Zamboni **W:** Bill Matheny; Michael Eury; Terry Collins

35 Dec 1997 Cover: 1.95 **NM** value: **Cover or less**
Circ: Diamd. preorders: **5,396**
Agent Duck; Agent Daffy; The Hungry Hypnotist; Extreme Coyote! • Agent Daffy **A:** Horacio Ottolini; Nelson Luty; Pablo Zamboni **W:** Dave King; Terry Collins

36 Jan 1998 Cover: 1.95 **NM** value: **Cover or less**
Circ: Diamd. preorders: **5,063**
• Sylvester, Tweety

37 Feb 1998 Cover: 1.95 **NM** value: **Cover or less**
Circ: Diamd. preorders: **4,842**
★ Versus Crusher.

38 Mar 1998 Cover: 1.95 **NM** value: **Cover or less**
Circ: Diamd. preorders: **4,961**
The Trouble with Mars!; Puppy Love **A:** Cosme Quartieri; Pablo Zamboni **W:** Dana Kurtin; Terry Collins ★ Appearance of Marvin Martian.

39 Apr 1998 Cover: 1.95 **NM** value: **Cover or less**
Circ: Diamd. preorders: **4,329**
• Foghorn Leghorn

40 May 1998 Cover: 1.95 **NM** value: **Cover or less**
Circ: Diamd. preorders: **4,468**
• Sylvester

41 Jun 1998 Cover: 1.95 **NM** value: **Cover or less**
Circ: Diamd. preorders: **4,505**
• Sylvester, Porky

42 Jul 1998 Cover: 1.95 **NM** value: **Cover or less**
Circ: Diamd. preorders: **4,396**
• Speedy Gonzales, Sylvester

43 Aug 1998 Cover: 1.95 **NM** value: **Cover or less**
Circ: Diamd. preorders: **4,574**
• Bugs and Daffy do Magic

44 Sep 1998 Cover: 1.99 **NM** value: **Cover or less**
Circ: Diamd. preorders: **4,441**
• Tweety and Sylvester

45 Oct 1998 Cover: 1.99 **NM** value: **Cover or less**
Circ: Diamd. preorders: **4,149**
• Marvin Martian

46 Nov 1998 Cover: 1.99 **NM** value: **Cover or less**
Circ: Diamd. preorders: **4,017**
• Bugs and Taz

47 Dec 1998 Cover: 1.99 **NM** value: **Cover or less**
Circ: Diamd. preorders: **4,067**
• Christmas issue

48 Jan 1999 Cover: 1.99 **NM** value: **Cover or less**
Circ: Diamd. preorders: **4,007**
★ Appearance of Rocky and Mugsy.

49 Feb 1999 Cover: 1.99 **NM** value: **Cover or less**
Circ: Diamd. preorders: **3,929**
Swoon; Cityscrape • Pepe is stalked

50 Mar 1999 Cover: 1.99 **NM** value: **Cover or less**
Circ: Diamd. preorders: **4,554**

51 Apr 1999 Cover: 1.99 **NM** value: **Cover or less**
Circ: Diamd. preorders: **3,526**

52 May 1999 Cover: 1.99 **NM** value: **Cover or less**
Circ: Diamd. preorders: **3,522**
Shake Well Before Ewes; Love's Capture; Desert Fleethearts; Roll Playing; The Old Brawl Game **A:** David Alvarez **W:** Barry Leibermann; Dan Slott

53 Jun 1999 Cover: 1.99 **NM** value: **Cover or less**
Circ: Diamd. preorders: **3,635**
The Postman Always Brings Mice; One for the Books; Checkstand and Deliver **A:** David Alvarez **W:** Terry Laban; Jennifer Moore; Bill Mattheny; Sean Carolan

54 Jul 1999 Cover: 1.99 **NM** value: **Cover or less**
Circ: Diamd. preorders: **3,862**
Rumble on the Red Planet; Be My Pest; You've Got Mayhem **A:** David Alvarez **W:** Terry Laban; Barry Leibmann; Bill Mattheny

55 Aug 1999 Cover: 1.99 **NM** value: **Cover or less**
Circ: Diamd. preorders: **3,439**
Twuce or Consequences; Trampolined Underfoot; Sylvester Jr., Jr.; Losing Your Lunch; Rival Story **A:** David Alvarez **W:** Jennifer Moore; Barry Leibmann; Chuck Kim; Sean Carolan

56 Sep 1999 Cover: 1.99 **NM** value: **Cover or less**
Circ: Diamd. preorders: **3,601**
Block Herds; Touchdown Tweety; Produckt Placement; Mars Needs Dogs; Glide Control **A:** David Alvarez **W:** Jennifer Moore; Chuck Kim; Sean Carolan

57 Oct 1999 Cover: 1.99 **NM** value: **Cover or less**
Circ: Diamd. preorders: **3,657**
Claws & Effect; Taking the Plunge; X Marks the Bugs; **A:** David Alvarez **W:** Terry Laban; Brett Koth; Dan Slott

58 Nov 1999 Cover: 1.99 **NM** value: **Cover or less**
Circ: Diamd. preorders: **3,413**
Femme Fatale; The Missing Link; Stiff Upper Beak; For My Sweet-Tea; Old Dawg, New Tricks **A:** David Alvarez; Walter Carzon; Leo Batic **W:** Terry Laban; Barry Liebmann; Brett Koth; Michael Eury

59 Dec 1999 Cover: 1.99 **NM** value: **Cover or less**
Circ: Diamd. preorders: **3,521**

60 Jan 2000 Cover: 1.99 **NM** value: **Cover or less**
Circ: Diamd. preorders: **3,385**
Tweety Temps!; Spring Fling!; Barnyard Banzai; Con-Fuse-Ion Take Two; The Temple of Thetzalatlhui **A:** David Alvarez; Stephanie Gladden **W:** Jennifer Moore; Bill Matheny; Brett Koth; Chuck Kim; Sean Carolan

61 Feb 2000 Cover: 1.99 **NM** value: **Cover or less**
Circ: Diamd. preorders: **3,328**
Roll out the Bunny; Takin' Care of Business; The Predator Group; All's Weight that ends Weight **A:** David Alvarez; Jennifer Moore **W:** Frank Strom; Terry Laban; Chuck Kim; Sean Carolan

62 Mar 2000 Cover: 1.99 **NM** value: **Cover or less**
Circ: Diamd. preorders: **3,150**

63 Apr 2000 Cover: 1.99 **NM** value: **Cover or less**
Circ: Diamd. preorders: **3,023**

64 May 2000 Cover: 1.99 **NM** value: **Cover or less**
Circ: Diamd. preorders: **3,173**
Moldy Locks; The Wabbit Season Pwoject; The Unpredictable Psychic; Little Orphan Marvin **A:** David Alvarez **W:** Earl Kress; Paul S. Newman; Sam Henderson

65 Jun 2000 Cover: 1.99 **NM** value: **Cover or less**
Circ: Diamd. preorders: **3,349**

66 Jul 2000 Cover: 1.99 **NM** value: **Cover or less**
Circ: Diamd. preorders: **3,128**

67 Aug 2000 Cover: 1.99 **NM** value: **Cover or less**
Circ: Diamd. preorders: **3,416**

68 Sep 2000 Cover: 1.99 **NM** value: **Cover or less**
Circ: Diamd. preorders: **3,293**

69 Oct 2000 Cover: 1.99 **NM** value: **Cover or less**
Circ: Diamd. preorders: **3,055**
Image is Everything; True Hollyweird Mysteries!; Lights, Camera, Traction! **A:** David Alvarez; Brian Garvey; John Costanza **W:** Chuck Kim; Karl Kress; Terry Collins

70 Nov 2000 Cover: 1.99 **NM** value: **Cover or less**
Circ: Diamd. preorders: **3,173**
Reach Out and Bugs Someone; So You Want a Million Bucks, Eh?; Goldyrobber and the Three Bears; Danger Line **A:** Howard Simpson; Brian Garvey; John Costanza; Neal Sternecky **W:** Frank Strom; Barry Liebmann; Brett Koth; Dan Slott

71 Dec 2000 Cover: 1.99 **NM** value: **Cover or less**
Circ: Diamd. preorders: **3,259**
Hare-A 51; The Shiny; Tazzy -Doo, Where Are You? **A:** David Alvarez; Wlater Carzon **W:** Craig Boldman; Chuck Kim; Jesse Leon McCann

72 Jan 2001 Cover: 1.99 **NM** value: **Cover or less**
Circ: Diamd. preorders: **3,171**
What Dis Country Needs; Bad News Cat; Who You Callin' Chicken? **A:** Howard Simpson; John Costanza; Leo Batic **W:** Frank Strom; Terry Laban; Mark McKain

73 Feb 2001 Cover: 1.99 **NM** value: **Cover or less**
Circ: Diamd. preorders: **3,193**
Looney Yule **A:** David Alvarez **W:** Earl Kress; Paul S. Newman; Sam Henderson

74 Mar 2001 Cover: 1.99 **NM** value: **Cover or less**
Circ: Diamd. preorders: **3,069**
The K-9 Files; Heading for Trouble; Cannon Fodder; A Doctor in the Mouse **A:** David Alvarez; Garvey; Neal Sternecky; Omar Aranda **W:** Frank Strom; Jesse Leon McCann; Koth

75 Apr 2001 Cover: 1.99 **NM** value: **Cover or less**
Circ: Diamd. preorders: **4,019**
A Hare Gone Conclusion **A:** David Alvarez **W:** Dan Slott

76 May 2001 Cover: 1.99 **NM** value: **Cover or less**
Circ: Diamd. preorders: **3,084**
Sea Monkey Business; Foes Afloat; Rabbit Seasoning! **A:** David Alvarez; John Costanza; Leo Batic **W:** Terry Laban; Jennifer Moore; James Denning; Sean Carolan

77 Jun 2001 Cover: 1.99 **NM** value: **Cover or less**
Circ: Diamd. preorders: **3,193**
Fowled Out; My Fair Doggy; Sleeping Daffy **A:** Leo Batic; Neal Sternecky; Waltern Carzon **W:** Mike DeCarlo; Neal Sternecky; Debbie Sternecky; James Denning

78 Jul 2001 Cover: 1.99 **NM** value: **Cover or less**
Circ: Diamd. preorders: **3,167**

79 Aug 2001 Cover: 1.99 **NM** value: **Cover or less**
Circ: Diamd. preorders: **3,335**

80 Sep 2001 Cover: 1.99 **NM** value: **Cover or less**
Circ: Diamd. preorders: **3,455**

LOONEY TUNES (GOLD KEY) Gold Key

The Warner Brothers' stable of cartoon characters has been a mainstay of comic books almost as long as the animated versions, which started out as short features at movie theaters and then migrated to television. This title from Gold Key contained stories highlighting all of the most popular characters like Sylvester and Tweety, Foghorn Leghorn, Roadrunner, and Wile E. Coyote, and, of course, Daffy Duck and Bugs Bunny.

Even though issues contained different self-contained stories, some had running gags that appeared throughout. In one issue, Daffy did cameos in all the other characters' stories, with his subplot wrapping up in his own story, later in ths issue.

#	Date	Cover	NM value
1	Apr 1975	Cover: 0.25	**NM** value: **12.00**
2	Jun 1975	Cover: 0.25	**NM** value: **7.00**
3	Aug 1975	Cover: 0.25	**NM** value: **5.00**
4	Oct 1975	Cover: 0.25	**NM** value: **5.00**
5	Dec 1975	Cover: 0.25	**NM** value: **5.00**
6	Feb 1976	Cover: 0.25	**NM** value: **3.50**
7	Apr 1976	Cover: 0.25	**NM** value: **3.50**
8	Jun 1976	Cover: 0.25	**NM** value: **3.50**
9	Aug 1976	Cover: 0.25	**NM** value: **3.50**

Sagebrush Songster; Pet Peeve; The Wall Scrawler; Dear Diary; Maurice is Missing

#	Date	Cover	NM value
10	Oct 1976	Cover: 0.30	**NM** value: **3.50**
11	Dec 1976	Cover: 0.30	**NM** value: **2.50**
12	Feb 1977	Cover: 0.30	**NM** value: **2.50**
13	Apr 1977	Cover: 0.30	**NM** value: **2.50**
14	Jun 1977	Cover: 0.30	**NM** value: **2.50**
15	Aug 1977	Cover: 0.35	**NM** value: **2.50**
16	Oct 1977	Cover: 0.35	**NM** value: **2.50**
17	Dec 1977	Cover: 0.35	**NM** value: **2.50**
18	Feb 1978	Cover: 0.35	**NM** value: **2.50**
19	Apr 1978	Cover: 0.35	**NM** value: **2.50**
20	Jun 1978	Cover: 0.35	**NM** value: **2.50**
21	Aug 1978	Cover: 0.35	**NM** value: **2.00**
22	Oct 1978	Cover: 0.35	**NM** value: **2.00**
23	Dec 1978	Cover: 0.35	**NM** value: **2.00**
24	Feb 1979	Cover: 0.35	**NM** value: **2.00**
25	Apr 1979	Cover: 0.40	**NM** value: **2.00**
26	Jun 1979	Cover: 0.40	**NM** value: **2.00**
27	Aug 1979	Cover: 0.40	**NM** value: **2.00**
28	Oct 1979	Cover: 0.40	**NM** value: **2.00**
29	Dec 1979	Cover: 0.40	**NM** value: **2.00**
30	Feb 1980	Cover: 0.40	**NM** value: **2.00**
31	Apr 1980	Cover: 0.40	**NM** value: **2.00**
32	Jun 1980	Cover: 0.40	**NM** value: **2.00**
33	Aug 1980	Cover: 0.40	**NM** value: **2.00**
34	Oct 1980	Cover: 0.40	**NM** value: **2.00**

CGC-graded: Multiply prices above by **33 for 9.9 M • 16 for 9.8 NM/M • 7 for 9.6 NM+ • 5 for 9.4 NM • 2.5 for 9.2 NM- • 1.5 for 9.0 VF/NM**

35 ❑ Dec 1980 Cover: 0.40 **NM** value: **2.00**
36 ❑ Feb 1981 Cover: 0.50 **NM** value: **2.00**
37 ❑ Apr 1981 Cover: 0.50 **NM** value: **2.00**
38 ❑ Jun 1981 Cover: 0.50 **NM** value: **2.00**
39 ❑ Aug 1981 Cover: 0.50 **NM** value: **2.00**
40 ❑ Oct 1981 Cover: 0.50 **NM** value: **2.00**
41 ❑ Dec 1981 Cover: 0.50 **NM** value: **1.50**
42 ❑ Feb 1982 Cover: 0.60 **NM** value: **1.50**
43 ❑ Apr 1982 Cover: 0.60 **NM** value: **1.50**
44 ❑ Jun 1982 Cover: 0.60 **NM** value: **1.50**
45 ❑ Aug 1982 Cover: 0.60 **NM** value: **1.50**
46 ❑ Oct 1982 Cover: 0.60 **NM** value: **1.50**
47 ❑ Dec 1982 Cover: 0.60 **NM** value: **1.50**

LOONEY TUNES MAGAZINE — DC

1 ❑ Cover: 1.95 **NM** value: **2.50**
Circ: CapCity orders: **5,550**
• Bugs Bunny
2 ❑ Cover: 1.95 **NM** value: **2.00**
Circ: CapCity orders: **4,050**
• Batman parody
3 ❑ Cover: 1.95 **NM** value: **2.00**
Circ: CapCity orders: **2,450**
4 ❑ Cover: 1.95 **NM** value: **2.00**
Circ: CapCity orders: **2,000**
5 ❑ Cover: 1.95 **NM** value: **2.00**
Circ: CapCity orders: **2,150**
6 ❑ Cover: 1.95 **NM** value: **Cover or less**
Circ: CapCity orders: **1,850**
7 ❑ Cover: 1.95 **NM** value: **Cover or less**
Circ: CapCity orders: **1,550**
8 ❑ Cover: 1.95 **NM** value: **Cover or less**
9 ❑ Cover: 1.95 **NM** value: **Cover or less**
10 ❑ Cover: 1.95 **NM** value: **Cover or less**
11 ❑ Cover: 1.95 **NM** value: **Cover or less**
• Title changes to Bugs Bunny & The Looney Tunes magazine.
12 ❑ Cover: 1.95 **NM** value: **Cover or less**
13 ❑ Cover: 1.95 **NM** value: **Cover or less**
14 ❑ Cover: 1.95 **NM** value: **Cover or less**
15 ❑ Cover: 1.95 **NM** value: **Cover or less**
16 ❑ Cover: 1.95 **NM** value: **Cover or less**
• trading cards
17 ❑ Spr 1994 Cover: 1.95 **NM** value: **Cover or less**
19 ❑ Fal 1994 Cover: 1.50 **NM** value: **Cover or less**
20 ❑ Win 1995 Cover: 1.95 **NM** value: **Cover or less**

LOOSE CANNON — DC

By day, he's Eddie Walker, a crutch-bound homicide detective for the Metropolis Police Force. What really sets Walker apart, however, is the alien blood which courses through his system (as seen in the Bloodlines crossover storyline, specifically, Action Comics Annual #5). By night, this turns Walker into a gigantic blue behemoth with immense strength. Unfortunately, it also places him squarely in the middle of the battle against the alien trust, which deems him a traitor.

In this, his first mini-series, Loose Cannon must survive a collection of alien killers, while at the same time eluding the super-powered bounty hunters sent by the police, who believe he is responsible for "murdering" his alter-ego, Eddie Walker.

1 ❑ Jun 1995 Cover: 1.75 **NM** value: **Cover or less**
Circ: CapCity orders: **8,500**
📖 Mad **A:** Scott Baumann **W:** Jeph Loeb
2 ❑ Jul 1995 Cover: 1.75 **NM** value: **Cover or less**
Circ: CapCity orders: **5,100**
3 ❑ Aug 1995 Cover: 1.75 **NM** value: **Cover or less**
★ Versus Eradicator.
4 ❑ Sep 1995 Cover: 1.75 **NM** value: **Cover or less**
Circ: CapCity orders: **4,525**

LOOSE TEETH — Fantagraphics

1 ❑ b&w Cover: 2.75 **NM** value: **Cover or less**
2 ❑ b&w Cover: 2.75 **NM** value: **Cover or less**
3 ❑ b&w Cover: 2.75 **NM** value: **Cover or less**

LORD FARRIS: SLAVEMASTER — Eros

1 ❑ Feb 1996 Cover: 2.95 **NM** value: **Cover or less**
A: Peter Noga Jr. **W:** Roland Cordell
2 ❑ May 1996 Cover: 2.95 **NM** value: **Cover or less**
A: Peter Noga Jr. **W:** Roland Cordell

LORD OF THE DEAD — Conquest

1 ❑ b&w Cover: 2.95 **NM** value: **Cover or less**

LORD PUMPKIN — Malibu / Ultraverse

0 ❑ Oct 1994 Cover: 2.50 **NM** value: **Cover or less**
Circ: CapCity orders: **12,150**
📖 The Return of th Great Pumpkin **A:** Aaron Lopresti **W:** Dan Danko

LORD PUMPKIN/NECROMANTRA — Malibu / Ultraverse

1 ❑ Cover: 2.95 **NM** value: **Cover or less**
Circ: CapCity orders: **8,100**
📖 The Last Pumpkin **A:** Kyle Jotz **W:** Dan Danko
2 ❑ Cover: 2.95 **NM** value: **Cover or less**
Circ: CapCity orders: **6,550**
A: Kyle Jotz **W:** Dan Danko

LORDS — Legend (Not Dark Horse Imprint)

1 ❑ Cover: 2.15 **NM** value: **2.25**
Circ: CapCity orders: **6,350**

LORDS OF MISRULE (ATOMEKA) — Atomeka

1 ❑ Cover: 6.95 **NM** value: **Cover or less**

LORDS OF MISRULE, THE (DARK HORSE) — Dark Horse

1 ❑ Jan 1997, b&w Cover: 2.95 **NM** value: **Cover or less**
Circ: Diamd. preorders: **8,680**
📖 The Callow Heart **A:** Peter Snejbjerg **W:** Steve White; John Tomlinson; Dan Abnett
2 ❑ Feb 1997, b&w Cover: 2.95 **NM** value: **Cover or less**
Circ: Diamd. preorders: **6,261**
📖 Far From Home **A:** Peter Snejbjerg **W:** Steve White; John Tomlinson; Dan Abnett
3 ❑ Mar 1997, b&w Cover: 2.95 **NM** value: **Cover or less**
Circ: Diamd. preorders: **5,258**
📖 Hag Ride **A:** Peter Snejbjerg **W:** Steve White; John Tomlinson; Dan Abnett
4 ❑ Apr 1997, b&w Cover: 2.95 **NM** value: **Cover or less**
Circ: Diamd. preorders: **4,335**
A: Peter Snejbjerg **W:** Steve White; John Tomlinson; Dan Abnett
5 ❑ May 1997, b&w Cover: 2.95 **NM** value: **Cover or less**
Circ: Diamd. preorders: **3,618**
A: Peter Snejbjerg **W:** Steve White; John Tomlinson; Dan Abnett
6 ❑ Jun 1997, b&w Cover: 2.95 **NM** value: **Cover or less**
Circ: Diamd. preorders: **3,567**
A: Peter Snejbjerg **W:** Steve White; John Tomlinson; Dan Abnett

LORDS OF THE ULTRA-REALM — DC

1 ❑ Jun 1986 Cover: 1.50 **NM** value: **Cover or less**
Circ: CapCity orders: **11,250**
2 ❑ Jul 1986 Cover: 1.50 **NM** value: **Cover or less**
Circ: CapCity orders: **9,650**
3 ❑ Aug 1986 Cover: 1.50 **NM** value: **Cover or less**
Circ: CapCity orders: **9,350**
4 ❑ Sep 1986 Cover: 1.50 **NM** value: **Cover or less**
Circ: CapCity orders: **10,900**
5 ❑ Oct 1986 Cover: 1.50 **NM** value: **Cover or less**
Circ: CapCity orders: **12,850**
6 ❑ Nov 1986 Cover: 1.50 **NM** value: **Cover or less**
Circ: CapCity orders: **11,000**
SE 1 ❑ Cover: 2.25 **NM** value: **Cover or less**
Circ: CapCity orders: **10,700**

LORELEI — Starwarp

1 ❑ b&w Cover: 2.50 **NM** value: **Cover or less**

LORELEI OF THE RED MIST — Conquest

1 ❑ b&w Cover: 2.95 **NM** value: **Cover or less**
2 ❑ b&w Cover: 2.95 **NM** value: **Cover or less**

LORI LOVECRAFT: MY FAVORITE REDHEAD — Caliber

1 ❑ Feb 1997 Cover: 3.95 **NM** value: **Cover or less**
Circ: Diamd. preorders: **3,767**
A: Mike Vosburg **W:** Mike Vosburg

LORI LOVECRAFT: THE BIG COMEBACK — Caliber

1 ❑ Cover: 2.95 **NM** value: **Cover or less**
A: Mike Vosburg **W:** Mike Vosburg; Pete Ventrella

LORI LOVECRAFT: THE DARK LADY — Caliber

1 ❑ Cover: 2.95 **NM** value: **Cover or less**
A: Mike Vosburg **W:** Mike Vosburg; Pete Ventrella

LORNA THE JUNGLE GIRL — Atlas

Her father is a big-game hunter, now a disabled widower, and Lorna's there to help him, thanks to her expertise in hunting. Oh, yes, and she fights jungle crime and begins her cover credits as "Lorna, the Jungle Queen," soon demoted to "Lorna, the Jungle Girl." The cover of her first issue says it all: "One valiant girl, alone and unafraid, against the savage terrors of the jungle!" It's the usual stuff: headhunters, elephants, gorillas, lions, and similar jungly threats. To equip herself to best jungle mobility, she wears a knife on a belt over a sort of one-piece or two-piece swimsuit outfit that may be made out of tiger and leopard skins. She also wears one of those necklaces made of predator teeth. Oh, yes, and there's a romantic tension between big-game-hunter Greg Knight and Lorna. — Maggie

1 ❑ Jul 1953 Cover: 0.10 **NM** value: **300.00**
• **CGC:** 1 graded, best 7.5
2 ❑ Aug 1953 Cover: 0.10 **NM** value: **250.00**
3 ❑ Sep 1953 Cover: 0.10 **NM** value: **250.00**
4 ❑ Dec 1953 Cover: 0.10 **NM** value: **200.00**
5 ❑ Feb 1954 Cover: 0.10 **NM** value: **200.00**
6 ❑ Mar 1954 Cover: 0.10 **NM** value: **150.00**
7 ❑ May 1954 Cover: 0.10 **NM** value: **150.00**
8 ❑ Jul 1954 Cover: 0.10 **NM** value: **100.00**
9 ❑ Sep 1954 Cover: 0.10 **NM** value: **100.00**
10 ❑ Nov 1954 Cover: 0.10 **NM** value: **100.00**
11 ❑ Jan 1955 Cover: 0.10 **NM** value: **75.00**
12 ❑ Mar 1955 Cover: 0.10 **NM** value: **75.00**
13 ❑ May 1955 Cover: 0.10 **NM** value: **75.00**
14 ❑ Jul 1955 Cover: 0.10 **NM** value: **75.00**
15 ❑ Sep 1955 Cover: 0.10 **NM** value: **60.00**
16 ❑ Nov 1955 Cover: 0.10 **NM** value: **60.00**
17 ❑ Jan 1956 Cover: 0.10 **NM** value: **60.00**
18 ❑ Mar 1956 Cover: 0.10 **NM** value: **60.00**
19 ❑ May 1956 Cover: 0.10 **NM** value: **60.00**
20 ❑ Jul 1956 Cover: 0.10 **NM** value: **50.00**
21 ❑ Sep 1956 Cover: 0.10 **NM** value: **50.00**
22 ❑ Nov 1956 Cover: 0.10 **NM** value: **50.00**
23 ❑ Jan 1957 Cover: 0.10 **NM** value: **50.00**
24 ❑ Mar 1957 Cover: 0.10 **NM** value: **50.00**
25 ❑ May 1957 Cover: 0.10 **NM** value: **50.00**
26 ❑ Jul 1957 Cover: 0.10 **NM** value: **50.00**

LORTNOC — Radio

1 ❑ Aug 1998, b&w Cover: 2.95 **NM** value: **Cover or less**

LOSERS SPECIAL — DC

The Losers were some of DC's best-loved war comics characters. First appearing in G.I. Combat #138, their number included Gunner and Sarge, ill-fated P.T. boat commander Capt. Storm, and Native American Johnny Cloud. All of them had seen those they fought with die, while somehow, they survived. But survival never felt like victory when the costs were so high — thus they called themselves "the Losers."

The gang was united for one final special (the first title to bear their name). Unfortunately, this was to be their swan song. After relating the origins of the various team members, the special told the tale of their final battle. The Losers finally met their end, in a special edition that tied in with the Crisis On Infinite Earths, DC's ultimate universe-destroying event.

1 ❑ Sep 1985 Cover: 1.25 **NM** value: **2.50**
Circ: CapCity orders: **8,150**
📖 Crisis on Infinite Earths • Crisis **A:** Sam Glanzman; Judith Hunt; Mike Esposito **W:** Robert Kanigher ★ Origin of Pooch (Gunner's Dog), Johnny Cloud, Captain Storm. ★ Death of The Losers.

LOST ANGEL — Caliber

1 ❑ b&w Cover: 2.95 **NM** value: **Cover or less**

LOST, THE (CALIBER) — Caliber

1 ❑ Oct 1996, b&w Cover: 2.95 **NM** value: **Cover or less**
Circ: Diamd. preorders: **4,277**
2 ❑ Dec 1996, b&w Cover: 2.95 **NM** value: **Cover or less**
Circ: Diamd. preorders: **3,000**

LOST, THE (CHAOS) — Chaos

1 ❑ Dec 1997, b&w Cover: 2.95 **NM** value: **Cover or less**
Circ: Diamd. preorders: **8,669**
2 ❑ Jan 1998, b&w Cover: 2.95 **NM** value: **Cover or less**
Circ: Diamd. preorders: **6,990**
3 ❑ Feb 1998, b&w Cover: 2.95 **NM** value: **Cover or less**
Circ: Diamd. preorders: **7,209**
cover says Feb 97. • a misprint

LOST CONTINENT — Eclipse

1 ❑ b&w Cover: 3.50 **NM** value: **Cover or less**
• Japanese **A:** Akihiro Yamada **W:** Akihiro Yamada
2 ❑ b&w Cover: 3.50 **NM** value: **Cover or less**
• Japanese **A:** Akihiro Yamada **W:** Akihiro Yamada
3 ❑ b&w Cover: 3.50 **NM** value: **Cover or less**
• Japanese **A:** Akihiro Yamada **W:** Akihiro Yamada
4 ❑ b&w Cover: 3.50 **NM** value: **Cover or less**
• Japanese **A:** Akihiro Yamada **W:** Akihiro Yamada
5 ❑ b&w Cover: 3.50 **NM** value: **Cover or less**
• Japanese **A:** Akihiro Yamada **W:** Akihiro Yamada
6 ❑ b&w Cover: 3.50 **NM** value: **Cover or less**
• Japanese **A:** Akihiro Yamada **W:** Akihiro Yamada

LOST GIRL — NBM / ComicsLit

1 ❑ b&w Cover: 9.95 **NM** value: **Cover or less**
No issue number. • smaller than normal comic book

LOST GIRLS — Kitchen Sink

All issues are adults only.

1 ❑ Nov 1995 Cover: 5.95 **NM** value: **Cover or less**
cardstock cover. • Oversized. **W:** Alan Moore
2 ❑ Feb 1996 Cover: 5.95 **NM** value: **Cover or less**
cardstock cover. • Oversized. **W:** Alan Moore

LOST HEROES — Davdez

0 ❑ Mar 1998 Cover: 2.95 **NM** value: **Cover or less**
1 ❑ Apr 1998 Cover: 2.95 **NM** value: **Cover or less**
Circ: Diamd. preorders: **5,709**
2 ❑ May 1998 Cover: 2.95 **NM** value: **Cover or less**
Circ: Diamd. preorders: **4,983**
3 ❑ Jun 1998 Cover: 2.95 **NM** value: **Cover or less**
Circ: Diamd. preorders: **4,594**
4 ❑ Aug 1998 Cover: 2.95 **NM** value: **Cover or less**
Circ: Diamd. preorders: **4,279**

LOST IN SPACE (DARK HORSE) — Dark Horse

1 ❑ Apr 1998 Cover: 2.95 **NM** value: **Cover or less**
Circ: Diamd. preorders: **24,143**
A: Gordon Purcell **W:** Brian McDonald
2 ❑ May 1998 Cover: 2.95 **NM** value: **Cover or less**
Circ: Diamd. preorders: **17,898**
A: Gordon Purcell **W:** Brian McDonald

3 ❑ Jul 1998 Cover: 2.95 **NM** value: **Cover or less**
Circ: Diamd. preorders: **12,320**
A: Gordon Purcell **W:** Brian McDonald
Bk 1❑ Aug 1998 Cover: 7.95 **NM** value: **Cover or less**
• collects movie adaptation **A:** Gordon Purcell **W:** Brian McDonald

LOST IN SPACE (INNOVATION) — Innovation

Once a popular television show, Lost In Space is the star-crossed tale of the Robinson family. The Robinsons were to have been the first family in space, accompanied by Major West and a robot named simply Robot. Unfortunately, the duplicitous Dr. Smith brought catastrophe on the crew, sending them spinning out of control into the far reaches of space. Ironically, Dr. Smith was trapped aboard the Jupiter 2 with the rest of the crew.

Everyone had plenty of time to chew Smith out as they tried to find their way back home. In the meanwhile, they had countless adventures on a variety of strange worlds. Unfortunately, Smith seems not to have learned from his mistakes, and his greedy, cowardly nature never failed to lead the crew into trouble.

This Innovation series was set a few years after the events of the TV series with the Robinsons and Smith still trying to find a way home.

1 ❑ Aug 1991 Cover: 2.50 **NM** value: **3.00**
Circ: CapCity orders: **6,315**
📖 Seduction of the Innocent **A:** Eddy Newell; Mark Jones **W:** Matt Thompson; George Broderick Jr.; David Campiti
2 ❑ Nov 1991 Cover: 2.50 **NM** value: **2.75**
Circ: CapCity orders: **5,180**
A: Bill Mumy
3 ❑ Dec 1991 Cover: 2.50 **NM** value: **2.75**
Circ: CapCity orders: **4,710**
A: Bill Mumy **W:** Bill Mumy
4 ❑ Feb 1992 Cover: 2.50 **NM** value: **Cover or less**
Circ: CapCity orders: **5,170**
A: Bill Mumy **W:** Bill Mumy
5 ❑ Mar 1992 Cover: 2.50 **NM** value: **Cover or less**
Circ: CapCity orders: **5,240**
📖 The Perils Of Penelope **A:** Bill Mumy **W:** George Broderick Jr.
6 ❑ May 1992 Cover: 2.50 **NM** value: **Cover or less**
Circ: CapCity orders: **5,105**
📖 In Unity There is Strength **A:** John Garcia **W:** Terry Collins
7 ❑ Jun 1992 Cover: 2.50 **NM** value: **Cover or less**
Circ: CapCity orders: **4,695**
📖 Don's Dilemma **A:** Dan Day; David Day **W:** George Broderick Jr.; Mark Goddard
8 ❑ Aug 1992 Cover: 2.50 **NM** value: **Cover or less**
Circ: CapCity orders: **4,550**
A: Bill Mumy
9 ❑ Oct 1992 Cover: 2.50 **NM** value: **Cover or less**
A: Bill Mumy
10 ❑ Nov 1992 Cover: 2.50 **NM** value: **Cover or less**
Circ: CapCity orders: **6,840**
A: Bill Mumy
11 ❑ Dec 1992 Cover: 2.50 **NM** value: **Cover or less**
Circ: CapCity orders: **5,885**
• Judy's story **A:** Bill Mumy
12 ❑ 1993 Cover: 2.50 **NM** value: **Cover or less**
Circ: CapCity orders: **6,400**
A: Bill Mumy
13 ❑ Aug 1993 Cover: 2.50 **NM** value: **4.95**
enhanced cardstock cover. 📖 Voyage to the Bottom of the Soul, Part 1; Journey to the Bottom of the Soul, Part 1 **A:** Bill Mumy
13/GO❑Aug 1993 Cover: 4.95 **NM** value: **5.00**
enhanced cardstock cover. • Gold edition. 📖 Voyage to the Bottom of the Soul, Part 1; Journey to the Bottom of the Soul, Part 1 **A:** Bill Mumy
14 ❑ Sep 1993 Cover: 2.50 **NM** value: **Cover or less**
📖 Voyage to the Bottom of the Soul, Part 2; Journey to the Bottom of the Soul, Part 2 **A:** Bill Mumy **W:** Michal Dutkiewicz
15 ❑ Aug 1993 Cover: 2.50 **NM** value: **Cover or less**
📖 Voyage to the Bottom of the Soul, Part 3; Journey to the Bottom of the Soul, Part 3 **A:** Bill Mumy
16 ❑ Sep 1993 Cover: 2.50 **NM** value: **Cover or less**
📖 Voyage to the Bottom of the Soul, Part 4; Journey to the Bottom of the Soul, Part 4 **A:** Bill Mumy
17 ❑ Oct 1993 Cover: 2.50 **NM** value: **Cover or less**
📖 Voyage to the Bottom of the Soul, Part 5; Journey to the Bottom of the Soul, Part 5 **A:** Bill Mumy
18 ❑ Nov 1993 Cover: 2.50 **NM** value: **Cover or less**
📖 Voyage to the Bottom of the Soul, Part 6; Journey to the Bottom of the Soul, Part 6 final issue. **A:** Bill Mumy
Anl 1❑ca. 1991 Cover: 2.95 **NM** value: **Cover or less**
A: Bill Mumy **W:** Miguel Ferrer
Anl 2❑ca. 1992 Cover: 2.95 **NM** value: **Cover or less**
Circ: CapCity orders: **5,685**
A: Bill Mumy **W:** Bill Mumy; Peter David
Bk 1❑ Mar 1993 Cover: 5.95 **NM** value: **Cover or less**
• reprints #3 and #4
SE 1❑ Cover: 2.50 **NM** value: **Cover or less**
• amended reprint of #1
SE 2❑ Cover: 2.50 **NM** value: **Cover or less**

LOST IN SPACE: PROJECT ROBINSON — Innovation

1 ❑ Nov 1993 Cover: 2.50 **NM** value: **Cover or less**
Circ: CapCity orders: **5,690**
📖 It's A Little Secret, Just The Robinson's Affair **A:** Mike Deodato; Luke Ross **W:** Christine Hantzopulos-Hunt

LOST LAUGHTER — Bad Habit

1 ❑ b&w Cover: 2.50 **NM** value: **Cover or less**
2 ❑ b&w Cover: 2.50 **NM** value: **Cover or less**
3 ❑ b&w Cover: 2.50 **NM** value: **Cover or less**
4 ❑ Apr 1994, b&w Cover: 2.50 **NM** value: **Cover or less**

LOST ONES, THE: FOR YOUR EYES ONLY — Image

1 ❑ Mar 2000 Cover: 2.95 **NM** value: **Cover or less**
Circ: Diamd. preorders: **4,815**
No issue number. • special preview; no price

LOST PLANET — Eclipse

Filled with dragons, pointy-eared forest dwellers, and lots of magic, this intricate fantasy mini-series reads like a well-plotted game of Advanced Dungeons & Dragons.

A wizard, an Air Force pilot, and a young woman on a mysterious quest join forces on a "lost planet" accessible only through magic corridors. As Ambrose Bierce, a self-taught wizard who disappeared from Earth in 1914, tells them, when the evil Zorrin family conquered the planet Iriel, they killed its scientists so it could be dominated by the Zorrins' magic. Before they can return to Earth, the heroes have to destroy the lotus potion which subjugates the world's populace to the Zorrins' will.

1 ❑ May 1987 Cover: 1.75 **NM** value: **2.00**
Circ: CapCity orders: **6,000**
A: Bo Hampton **W:** Bo Hampton
2 ❑ Jul 1987 Cover: 1.75 **NM** value: **2.00**
Circ: CapCity orders: **4,450**
A: Bo Hampton **W:** Bo Hampton
3 ❑ Sep 1987 Cover: 2.00 **NM** value: **Cover or less**
Circ: CapCity orders: **4,350**
A: Bo Hampton **W:** Bo Hampton
4 ❑ Dec 1987 Cover: 2.00 **NM** value: **Cover or less**
Circ: CapCity orders: **4,300**
📖 Through Past Darkly **A:** Bo Hampton **W:** Bo Hampton
5 ❑ Feb 1988 Cover: 2.00 **NM** value: **Cover or less**
Circ: CapCity orders: **3,525**
A: Bo Hampton **W:** Bo Hampton
6 ❑ Mar 1989 Cover: 2.00 **NM** value: **Cover or less**
Circ: CapCity orders: **2,950**
📖 My Soul to Take... **A:** Bo Hampton **W:** Bo Hampton

LOST UNIVERSE (GENE RODDENBERRY'S...) — Tekno

Dr. Grange returns to his home planet, Malay, anxious see his family and the idyllic paradise he remembers. Some time ago, he'd been in in an accident that had left him in coma. He's not sure how long he was out, but it couldn't have been more than five years, could it?

But things on Malay don't quite reconcile with his recollections. Cities are gone; his brother's farm has been overgrown with vegetation and is inhabited by a colony of hostile Payeru, the large flying, furry creatures that he remembers as being civilized. It's almost as though centuries have passed...

Comics series by celebrities was Tekno-Comix' stock-in-trade, but some readers suspected how much the celebrities were creatively involved — beyond their participation in Tekno's expensive public promotions, that is. Given Roddenberry's death years before, this title tended to provide fuel to critics of the Tekno strategy.

0 ❑ Cover: 2.25 **NM** value: **Cover or less**
Circ: CapCity orders: **11,850**
📖 O Brave New World **A:** Jim Callahan **W:** Lawrence Watt-Evans Evans
1 ❑ Apr 1995 Cover: 1.95 **NM** value: **Cover or less**
Circ: CapCity orders: **37,125**
📖 O Brave New World **A:** Jim Callahan **W:** Lawrence Watt-Evans Evans
2 ❑ May 1995 Cover: 1.95 **NM** value: **Cover or less**
Circ: CapCity orders: **27,275**
📖 A Riddle Wrapped in an Enigma **A:** Mike Harris **W:** Lawrence Watt-Evans Evans
3 ❑ Jun 1995 Cover: 1.95 **NM** value: **Cover or less**
Circ: CapCity orders: **22,475**
• trading card **W:** Lawrence Watt-Evans Evans
3/A ❑ Jun 1995 Cover: 1.95 **NM** value: **Cover or less**
variant cover. **W:** Lawrence Watt-Evans Evans
4 ❑ Jul 1995 Cover: 1.95 **NM** value: **Cover or less**
Circ: CapCity orders: **12,585**
• bound-in trading card **W:** Lawrence Watt-Evans Evans
5 ❑ Aug 1995 Cover: 1.95 **NM** value: **Cover or less**
Circ: CapCity orders: **13,600**
W: Lawrence Watt-Evans Evans ★ 1st Appearance of Xander.
6 ❑ Sep 1995 Cover: 1.95 **NM** value: **Cover or less**
Circ: CapCity orders: **11,925**
W: Lawrence Watt-Evans Evans
7 ❑ Oct 1995 Cover: 1.95 **NM** value: **Cover or less**
Circ: CapCity orders: **10,875**
final issue.

LOST WORLD, THE — Millennium

1 ❑ Jan 1996 Cover: 2.95 **NM** value: **Cover or less**
cover says Mar, indicia says Jan.
2 ❑ Mar 1996 Cover: 2.95 **NM** value: **Cover or less**

LOST WORLD, THE: JURASSIC PARK — Topps

1 ❑ May 1997 Cover: 2.95 **NM** value: **Cover or less**
Circ: Diamd. preorders: **16,453**
A: Jeff Butler **W:** Don McGregor
2 ❑ Jun 1997 Cover: 2.95 **NM** value: **Cover or less**
Circ: Diamd. preorders: **12,761**
A: Jeff Butler **W:** Don McGregor
3 ❑ Jul 1997 Cover: 2.95 **NM** value: **Cover or less**
Circ: Diamd. preorders: **10,042**
A: Jeff Butler **W:** Don McGregor

LOST WORLDS — Standard

5 ❑ Oct 1952 Cover: 0.10 **NM** value: **300.00**
• **CGC:** 2 graded, best 8.0
6 ❑ Dec 1952 Cover: 0.10 **NM** value: **200.00**
• **CGC:** 2 graded, best 9.2

LOUD CANNOLI — Crazyfish / MJ-12

1 ❑ Cover: 2.95 **NM** value: **Cover or less**
No issue number.

LOUDER THAN WORDS (SERGIO ARAGONÉS'...) — Dark Horse

1 ❑ Jul 1997 Cover: 2.95 **NM** value: **Cover or less**
A: Sergio Aragonés **W:** Sergio Aragonés
2 ❑ Aug 1997 Cover: 2.95 **NM** value: **Cover or less**
A: Sergio Aragonés **W:** Sergio Aragonés
3 ❑ Sep 1997 Cover: 2.95 **NM** value: **Cover or less**
A: Sergio Aragonés **W:** Sergio Aragonés
4 ❑ Oct 1997 Cover: 2.95 **NM** value: **Cover or less**
A: Sergio Aragonés **W:** Sergio Aragonés
5 ❑ Nov 1997 Cover: 2.95 **NM** value: **Cover or less**
A: Sergio Aragonés **W:** Sergio Aragonés
6 ❑ Dec 1997 Cover: 2.95 **NM** value: **Cover or less**
A: Sergio Aragonés **W:** Sergio Aragonés

LOU FINE TREASURY — Pure Imagination

Bk 1❑ b&w Cover: 19.95 **NM** value: **Cover or less**

LOUIS VS. ALI — Revolutionary

1 ❑ Dec 1993, b&w Cover: 2.95 **NM** value: **Cover or less**

LOVE ADVENTURES — Marvel

1 ❑ Oct 1949 Cover: 0.10 **NM** value: **100.00**
2 ❑ Jan 1950 Cover: 0.10 **NM** value: **100.00**
3 ❑ Feb 1951 Cover: 0.10 **NM** value: **50.00**
4 ❑ Apr 1951 Cover: 0.10 **NM** value: **50.00**
5 ❑ Jun 1951 Cover: 0.10 **NM** value: **50.00**
6 ❑ Aug 1951 Cover: 0.10 **NM** value: **50.00**
7 ❑ Oct 1951 Cover: 0.10 **NM** value: **50.00**
8 ❑ Dec 1951 Cover: 0.10 **NM** value: **50.00**
9 ❑ Feb 1952 Cover: 0.10 **NM** value: **50.00**
10 ❑ Apr 1952 Cover: 0.10 **NM** value: **1.00**
11 ❑ Jun 1952 Cover: 0.10 **NM** value: **50.00**
12 ❑ Aug 1952 Cover: 0.10 **NM** value: **50.00**

LOVE AND MARRIAGE — Superior

Hard as it is to believe considering the formulaic rut that the romance comics genre slipped into following the arrival of the Comics Code, this series used to be among the most sharp and sophisticated comics on the stands. While few titles achieved the excellence of Simon and Kirby's Young Love and Young Romance, some, like Love and Marriage, maintained high standards of art and writing and obviously catered to adult readers. Love and Marriage, despite its innocuous title, features edgy stories of divorce and deception, seduction and infidelity, and violent emotional turbulence. The unsigned art is more reminiscent of Golden Age angularity and Charles Biro-style "comics noir" atmosphere than of the well-scrubbed suburban fantasy look that came to dominate romance comics after the Code. IW reprinted issues from the early 50s Superior Comics series in the mid-1960s, which, significantly, appeared without the ubiquitous Comics Code insignia.

1 ❑ Mar 1952 Cover: 0.10 **NM** value: **6.00**
2 ❑ May 1952 Cover: 0.10 **NM** value: **35.00**
3 ❑ Jul 1952 Cover: 0.10 **NM** value: **24.00**
4 ❑ Sep 1952 Cover: 0.10 **NM** value: **24.00**
5 ❑ Nov 1952 Cover: 0.10 **NM** value: **24.00**
6 ❑ Jan 1953 Cover: 0.10 **NM** value: **2.00**
7 ❑ Mar 1953 Cover: 0.10 **NM** value: **2.00**
• **CGC:** 1 graded, best 8.5
8 ❑ May 1953 Cover: 0.10 **NM** value: **2.00**
9 ❑ Jul 1953 Cover: 0.10 **NM** value: **2.00**
10 ❑ Sep 1953 Cover: 0.10 **NM** value: **2.00**
11 ❑ Nov 1953 Cover: 0.10 **NM** value: **16.00**
12 ❑ Jan 1954 Cover: 0.10 **NM** value: **16.00**
13 ❑ Mar 1954 Cover: 0.10 **NM** value: **16.00**
14 ❑ May 1954 Cover: 0.10 **NM** value: **16.00**
15 ❑ Jul 1954 Cover: 0.10 **NM** value: **16.00**
16 ❑ Sep 1954 Cover: 0.10 **NM** value: **16.00**
final issue.

CGC-graded: Multiply prices above by **33 for 9.9 M • 16 for 9.8 NM/M • 7 for 9.6 NM+ • 5 for 9.4 NM • 2.5 for 9.2 NM- • 1.5 for 9.0 VF/NM**

LOVE & ROCKETS — Fantagraphics

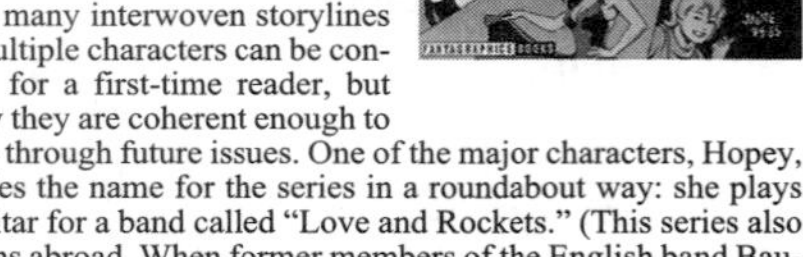

The brothers who created this series, Jaime and Gilbert Hernandez, have a strong understanding of and empathy for women, since it features some of the best-developed and compelling female characters in comics. Racially diverse, the women deal with such contemporary topics as homosexuality, infidelity, drug use, and sexual harassment without ever overwhelming a storyline or the characters' integrity.

The many interwoven storylines and multiple characters can be confusing for a first-time reader, but luckily they are coherent enough to follow through future issues. One of the major characters, Hopey, provides the name for the series in a roundabout way: she plays the guitar for a band called "Love and Rockets." (This series also had fans abroad. When former members of the English band Bauhaus formed a new band in the mid-1980s, they named themselves after this series and became, in effect, Hopey's band.

1 ❑ Fal 1982 Cover: 2.95 **NM** value: **28.00**
A: Gilbert Hernandez; Jaime Hernandez **W:** Gilbert Hernandez; Jaime Hernandez
1-2 ❑ Cover: 3.95 **NM** value: **4.00**
1-3 ❑ Cover: 3.95 **NM** value: **Cover or less**
1-4 ❑ Cover: 4.95 **NM** value: **Cover or less**
2 ❑ Spr 1983 Cover: 2.95 **NM** value: **14.00**
• Spring 1983 **A:** Gilbert Hernandez; Jaime Hernandez **W:** Gilbert Hernandez; Jaime Hernandez
2-2 ❑ Cover: 3.95 **NM** value: **Cover or less**
3 ❑ Cover: 2.95 **NM** value: **10.00**
A: Gilbert Hernandez; Jaime Hernandez **W:** Gilbert Hernandez; Jaime Hernandez
3-2 ❑ Apr 1991 Cover: 3.95 **NM** value: **Cover or less**
4 ❑ Cover: 2.95 **NM** value: **8.00**
A: Gilbert Hernandez; Jaime Hernandez **W:** Gilbert Hernandez; Jaime Hernandez
4-2 ❑ Apr 1991 Cover: 3.95 **NM** value: **Cover or less**
4-3 ❑ Cover: 3.95 **NM** value: **Cover or less**
5 ❑ Cover: 1.95 **NM** value: **7.00**
A: Gilbert Hernandez; Jaime Hernandez **W:** Gilbert Hernandez; Jaime Hernandez
5-2 ❑ May 1991 Cover: 2.50 **NM** value: **Cover or less**
6 ❑ Cover: 1.95 **NM** value: **5.00**
A: Gilbert Hernandez; Jaime Hernandez **W:** Gilbert Hernandez; Jaime Hernandez
6-2 ❑ May 1991 Cover: 2.50 **NM** value: **Cover or less**
7 ❑ Jul 1984 Cover: 1.95 **NM** value: **5.00**
A: Gilbert Hernandez; Jaime Hernandez **W:** Gilbert Hernandez; Jaime Hernandez
7-2 ❑ May 1991 Cover: 2.50 **NM** value: **Cover or less**
8 ❑ Cover: 1.95 **NM** value: **5.00**
A: Gilbert Hernandez; Jaime Hernandez **W:** Gilbert Hernandez; Jaime Hernandez
8-2 ❑ Aug 1991 Cover: 2.50 **NM** value: **Cover or less**
9 ❑ Cover: 1.95 **NM** value: **5.00**
A: Gilbert Hernandez; Jaime Hernandez **W:** Gilbert Hernandez; Jaime Hernandez
9-2 ❑ Oct 1991 Cover: 2.50 **NM** value: **Cover or less**
10 ❑ Cover: 2.50 **NM** value: **5.00**
A: Gilbert Hernandez; Jaime Hernandez **W:** Gilbert Hernandez; Jaime Hernandez
10-2 ❑ Dec 1991 Cover: 2.95 **NM** value: **Cover or less**
11 ❑ Cover: 1.95 **NM** value: **4.00**
A: Gilbert Hernandez; Jaime Hernandez **W:** Gilbert Hernandez; Jaime Hernandez
11-2 ❑ Feb 1992 Cover: 2.50 **NM** value: **Cover or less**
12 ❑ Jul 1985 Cover: 1.95 **NM** value: **4.00**
A: Gilbert Hernandez; Jaime Hernandez **W:** Gilbert Hernandez; Jaime Hernandez
12-2 ❑ Aug 1992 Cover: 2.50 **NM** value: **Cover or less**
13 ❑ Cover: 2.25 **NM** value: **4.00**
A: Gilbert Hernandez; Jaime Hernandez **W:** Gilbert Hernandez; Jaime Hernandez
13-2 ❑ Oct 1992 Cover: 2.50 **NM** value: **Cover or less**
14 ❑ Nov 1985 Cover: 2.25 **NM** value: **4.00**
A: Gilbert Hernandez; Jaime Hernandez **W:** Gilbert Hernandez; Jaime Hernandez
14-2 ❑ Feb 1993 Cover: 2.50 **NM** value: **Cover or less**
15 ❑ Jan 1986 Cover: 2.25 **NM** value: **4.00**
A: Gilbert Hernandez; Jaime Hernandez **W:** Gilbert Hernandez; Jaime Hernandez
15-2 ❑ Aug 1993 Cover: 2.50 **NM** value: **Cover or less**
16 ❑ Mar 1986 Cover: 2.25 **NM** value: **3.00**
A: Gilbert Hernandez; Jaime Hernandez **W:** Gilbert Hernandez; Jaime Hernandez
16-2 ❑ Oct 1993 Cover: 2.95 **NM** value: **Cover or less**
17 ❑ Jun 1986 Cover: 2.25 **NM** value: **3.00**
A: Gilbert Hernandez; Jaime Hernandez **W:** Gilbert Hernandez; Jaime Hernandez
18 ❑ Sep 1986 Cover: 2.25 **NM** value: **3.00**
A: Gilbert Hernandez; Jaime Hernandez **W:** Gilbert Hernandez; Jaime Hernandez
19 ❑ Jan 1987 Cover: 2.25 **NM** value: **3.00**
A: Gilbert Hernandez; Jaime Hernandez **W:** Gilbert Hernandez; Jaime Hernandez
20 ❑ Apr 1987 Cover: 2.25 **NM** value: **3.00**
A: Gilbert Hernandez; Jaime Hernandez **W:** Gilbert Hernandez; Jaime Hernandez
21 ❑ Jul 1987 Cover: 2.25 **NM** value: **Cover or less**
A: Gilbert Hernandez; Jaime Hernandez **W:** Gilbert Hernandez; Jaime Hernandez
22 ❑ Aug 1987 Cover: 2.25 **NM** value: **Cover or less**
A: Gilbert Hernandez; Jaime Hernandez **W:** Gilbert Hernandez; Jaime Hernandez
23 ❑ Oct 1987 Cover: 2.25 **NM** value: **Cover or less**
A: Gilbert Hernandez; Jaime Hernandez **W:** Gilbert Hernandez; Jaime Hernandez
24 ❑ Dec 1987 Cover: 2.25 **NM** value: **Cover or less**
A: Gilbert Hernandez; Jaime Hernandez **W:** Gilbert Hernandez; Jaime Hernandez
25 ❑ Mar 1988 Cover: 2.25 **NM** value: **Cover or less**
A: Gilbert Hernandez; Jaime Hernandez **W:** Gilbert Hernandez; Jaime Hernandez
26 ❑ Jun 1988 Cover: 2.25 **NM** value: **Cover or less**
A: Gilbert Hernandez; Jaime Hernandez **W:** Gilbert Hernandez; Jaime Hernandez
27 ❑ Aug 1988 Cover: 2.25 **NM** value: **Cover or less**
A: Gilbert Hernandez; Jaime Hernandez **W:** Gilbert Hernandez; Jaime Hernandez
28 ❑ Nov 1988 Cover: 2.95 **NM** value: **Cover or less**
A: Gilbert Hernandez; Jaime Hernandez **W:** Gilbert Hernandez; Jaime Hernandez
28-2 ❑ Apr 1995 Cover: 2.95 **NM** value: **Cover or less**
29 ❑ Mar 1989 Cover: 2.25 **NM** value: **2.75**
A: Gilbert Hernandez; Jaime Hernandez **W:** Gilbert Hernandez; Jaime Hernandez
29-2 ❑ Mar 1992 Cover: 2.25 **NM** value: **Cover or less**
30 ❑ Jul 1989 Cover: 2.25 **NM** value: **2.95**
A: Gilbert Hernandez; Jaime Hernandez **W:** Gilbert Hernandez; Jaime Hernandez
30-2 ❑ Mar 1992 Cover: 2.95 **NM** value: **Cover or less**
31 ❑ Dec 1989 Cover: 2.50 **NM** value: **Cover or less**
A: Gilbert Hernandez; Jaime Hernandez **W:** Gilbert Hernandez; Jaime Hernandez
31-2 ❑ Apr 1992 Cover: 2.50 **NM** value: **Cover or less**
32 ❑ May 1990 Cover: 2.50 **NM** value: **Cover or less**
A: Gilbert Hernandez; Jaime Hernandez **W:** Gilbert Hernandez; Jaime Hernandez
33 ❑ Aug 1990 Cover: 2.50 **NM** value: **Cover or less**
A: Gilbert Hernandez; Jaime Hernandez **W:** Gilbert Hernandez; Jaime Hernandez
34 ❑ Nov 1990 Cover: 2.50 **NM** value: **Cover or less**
A: Gilbert Hernandez; Jaime Hernandez **W:** Gilbert Hernandez; Jaime Hernandez
35 ❑ Mar 1991 Cover: 2.75 **NM** value: **Cover or less**
A: Gilbert Hernandez; Jaime Hernandez **W:** Gilbert Hernandez; Jaime Hernandez
36 ❑ Nov 1991 Cover: 2.75 **NM** value: **Cover or less**
A: Gilbert Hernandez; Jaime Hernandez **W:** Gilbert Hernandez; Jaime Hernandez
37 ❑ Feb 1992 Cover: 2.75 **NM** value: **Cover or less**
A: Gilbert Hernandez; Jaime Hernandez **W:** Gilbert Hernandez; Jaime Hernandez
38 ❑ Apr 1992 Cover: 2.75 **NM** value: **Cover or less**
A: Gilbert Hernandez; Jaime Hernandez **W:** Gilbert Hernandez; Jaime Hernandez
39 ❑ Aug 1992 Cover: 2.75 **NM** value: **Cover or less**
Circ: CapCity orders: **4,200**
A: Gilbert Hernandez; Jaime Hernandez **W:** Gilbert Hernandez; Jaime Hernandez
40 ❑ Jan 1993 Cover: 3.50 **NM** value: **Cover or less**
Circ: CapCity orders: **4,625**
A: Gilbert Hernandez; Jaime Hernandez **W:** Gilbert Hernandez; Jaime Hernandez
41 ❑ Apr 1993 Cover: 2.95 **NM** value: **Cover or less**
Circ: CapCity orders: **4,400**
A: Gilbert Hernandez; Jaime Hernandez **W:** Gilbert Hernandez; Jaime Hernandez
42 ❑ Aug 1993 Cover: 2.95 **NM** value: **Cover or less**
Circ: CapCity orders: **4,120**
A: Gilbert Hernandez; Jaime Hernandez **W:** Gilbert Hernandez; Jaime Hernandez
43 ❑ Nov 1993 Cover: 2.95 **NM** value: **Cover or less**
Circ: CapCity orders: **3,730**
A: Gilbert Hernandez; Jaime Hernandez **W:** Gilbert Hernandez; Jaime Hernandez
44 ❑ Mar 1994 Cover: 2.95 **NM** value: **Cover or less**
Circ: CapCity orders: **3,741**
A: Gilbert Hernandez; Jaime Hernandez **W:** Gilbert Hernandez; Jaime Hernandez
45 ❑ Jul 1994 Cover: 2.95 **NM** value: **Cover or less**
Circ: CapCity orders: **3,490**
A: Gilbert Hernandez; Jaime Hernandez **W:** Gilbert Hernandez; Jaime Hernandez
46 ❑ Nov 1994 Cover: 2.95 **NM** value: **Cover or less**
Circ: CapCity orders: **3,437**
A: Gilbert Hernandez; Jaime Hernandez **W:** Gilbert Hernandez; Jaime Hernandez
47 ❑ Apr 1995 Cover: 2.95 **NM** value: **Cover or less**
Circ: CapCity orders: **3,381**
A: Gilbert Hernandez; Jaime Hernandez **W:** Gilbert Hernandez; Jaime Hernandez
48 ❑ Jul 1995 Cover: 2.95 **NM** value: **Cover or less**
Circ: CapCity orders: **3,280**
A: Gilbert Hernandez; Jaime Hernandez **W:** Gilbert Hernandez; Jaime Hernandez
49 ❑ Nov 1995 Cover: 2.95 **NM** value: **Cover or less**
A: Gilbert Hernandez; Jaime Hernandez **W:** Gilbert Hernandez; Jaime Hernandez
50 ❑ Apr 1996, b&w Cover: 4.95 **NM** value: **Cover or less**
final issue. **A:** Gilbert Hernandez; Jaime Hernandez **W:** Gilbert Hernandez; Jaime Hernandez
Bk 1 ❑ Cover: 9.95 **NM** value: **Cover or less**
Bk 2 ❑ Cover: 9.95 **NM** value: **Cover or less**
Bk 3 ❑ Cover: 9.95 **NM** value: **Cover or less**
Bk 4 ❑ Cover: 9.95 **NM** value: **Cover or less**
Bk 5 ❑ Cover: 9.95 **NM** value: **Cover or less**
Bk 6 ❑ Cover: 12.95 **NM** value: **Cover or less**
Bk 7 ❑ Cover: 12.95 **NM** value: **Cover or less**
Bk 8 ❑ Cover: 12.95 **NM** value: **Cover or less**
Bk 13 ❑ Jul 1996 Cover: 18.95 **NM** value: **Cover or less**
• Chester Square; reprints several issues of Love & Rockets

LOVE & ROCKETS BONANZA — Fantagraphics

1 ❑ Mar 1989, b&w Cover: 2.95 **NM** value: **Cover or less**
1-2 ❑ Feb 1992, b&w Cover: 2.95 **NM** value: **Cover or less**

LOVE AT FIRST SIGHT — Ace

1 ❑ Oct 1949 Cover: 0.10 **NM** value: **75.00**
2 ❑ 1950 Cover: 0.10 **NM** value: **50.00**
3 ❑ 1950 Cover: 0.10 **NM** value: **30.00**
4 ❑ 1950 Cover: 0.10 **NM** value: **30.00**
5 ❑ 1950 Cover: 0.10 **NM** value: **30.00**
6 ❑ 1950 Cover: 0.10 **NM** value: **30.00**
7 ❑ Cover: 0.10 **NM** value: **30.00**
8 ❑ 1951 Cover: 0.10 **NM** value: **30.00**
9 ❑ 1951 Cover: 0.10 **NM** value: **30.00**
10 ❑ 1951 Cover: 0.10 **NM** value: **25.00**
11 ❑ Sep 1951 Cover: 0.10 **NM** value: **25.00**
12 ❑ 1951 Cover: 0.10 **NM** value: **25.00**
13 ❑ Cover: 0.10 **NM** value: **25.00**
14 ❑ 1952 Cover: 0.10 **NM** value: **25.00**
15 ❑ 1952 Cover: 0.10 **NM** value: **25.00**
16 ❑ 1952 Cover: 0.10 **NM** value: **25.00**
17 ❑ 1952 Cover: 0.10 **NM** value: **25.00**
18 ❑ 1952 Cover: 0.10 **NM** value: **25.00**
19 ❑ Cover: 0.10 **NM** value: **25.00**
20 ❑ 1953 Cover: 0.10 **NM** value: **25.00**
21 ❑ 1953 Cover: 0.10 **NM** value: **20.00**
22 ❑ 1953 Cover: 0.10 **NM** value: **20.00**
23 ❑ 1953 Cover: 0.10 **NM** value: **20.00**
24 ❑ 1953 Cover: 0.10 **NM** value: **20.00**
25 ❑ Cover: 0.10 **NM** value: **20.00**
26 ❑ Cover: 0.10 **NM** value: **20.00**
27 ❑ Apr 1954 Cover: 0.10 **NM** value: **20.00**
28 ❑ 1954 Cover: 0.10 **NM** value: **20.00**
29 ❑ 1954 Cover: 0.10 **NM** value: **20.00**
30 ❑ 1954 Cover: 0.10 **NM** value: **20.00**
31 ❑ Cover: 0.10 **NM** value: **20.00**
32 ❑ Cover: 0.10 **NM** value: **20.00**
33 ❑ Cover: 0.10 **NM** value: **20.00**
34 ❑ Apr 1955 Cover: 0.10 **NM** value: **20.00**
35 ❑ 1955 Cover: 0.10 **NM** value: **20.00**
36 ❑ 1955 Cover: 0.10 **NM** value: **15.00**
37 ❑ 1955 Cover: 0.10 **NM** value: **15.00**
38 ❑ 1955 Cover: 0.10 **NM** value: **15.00**
39 ❑ 1955 Cover: 0.10 **NM** value: **15.00**
40 ❑ 1956 Cover: 0.10 **NM** value: **15.00**
41 ❑ 1956 Cover: 0.10 **NM** value: **15.00**
42 ❑ 1956 Cover: 0.10 **NM** value: **15.00**
43 ❑ 1956 Cover: 0.10 **NM** value: **15.00**

LOVE BITES — Fantagraphics / Eros

All issues are adults only.
1 ❑ b&w Cover: 2.25 **NM** value: **Cover or less**
2 ❑ Cover: 2.25 **NM** value: **Cover or less**

LOVE BITES (RADIO COMIX) — Radio Comix

1 ❑ Oct 2000 Cover: 2.95 **NM** value: **Cover or less**
📖 The Wedding **A:** Daniel Fu **W:** Daniel Fu

LOVE BOMB — Abaculus

1 ❑ Cover: 2.95 **NM** value: **Cover or less**
A: Paul B. Rainey **W:** Paul B. Rainey
2 ❑ Cover: 2.95 **NM** value: **Cover or less**
📖 Son of Thatcher; Kurious Middle: Almost Heaven; Damon Hill; Swill the Alien **A:** Paul B. Rainey **W:** Paul B. Rainey

LOVE CLASSICS — Marvel

1 ❑ ca. 1949 Cover: 0.10 **NM** value: **75.00**
2 ❑ ca. 1950 Cover: 0.10 **NM** value: **75.00**

LOVE CONFESSIONS — Quality

"I stole my way into a career! But I couldn't steal romance!" "As I dreamed of Bill's passionate kisses on my lips, my cold selfishness melted away!" (See Princess of the Five and Ten.) "I plunged headlong toward ecstasy — only to encounter disaster! (Read Torment.) "I had to choose between two ways of life — work and worry or champagne and mink — " (Read The man I Choose.)

This was the sort of cover copy typical of newsstand magazines of the day, and Quality happily adopted it for its covers. One intriguing evolution of Love Confession's covers was from line art to photo covers, some featuring such stars of the day as Van Johnson, Jane Russell, and Robert Mitchum.

— Maggie

1 ❑ Oct 1949 Cover: 0.10 **NM** value: **200.00**
2 ❑ Dec 1949 Cover: 0.10 **NM** value: **100.00**
3 ❑ Feb 1950 Cover: 0.10 **NM** value: **50.00**
4 ❑ Apr 1950 Cover: 0.10 **NM** value: **50.00**
5 ❑ Jun 1950 Cover: 0.10 **NM** value: **50.00**
6 ❑ Aug 1950 Cover: 0.10 **NM** value: **35.00**
7 ❑ Oct 1950 Cover: 0.10 **NM** value: **35.00**
8 ❑ Dec 1950 Cover: 0.10 **NM** value: **35.00**
9 ❑ Feb 1951 Cover: 0.10 **NM** value: **35.00**
10 ❑ Apr 1951 Cover: 0.10 **NM** value: **50.00**
11 ❑ ca. 1951 Cover: 0.10 **NM** value: **40.00**
12 ❑ ca. 1951 Cover: 0.10 **NM** value: **40.00**
13 ❑ ca. 1951 Cover: 0.10 **NM** value: **40.00**
14 ❑ Nov 1951 Cover: 0.10 **NM** value: **40.00**
15 ❑ Cover: 0.10 **NM** value: **40.00**

16 ❑ ca. 1952 Cover: 0.10 **NM** value: **40.00**
17 ❑ ca. 1952 Cover: 0.10 **NM** value: **40.00**
18 ❑ ca. 1952 Cover: 0.10 **NM** value: **40.00**
19 ❑ ca. 1952 Cover: 0.10 **NM** value: **40.00**
20 ❑ ca. 1952 Cover: 0.10 **NM** value: **40.00**
21 ❑ Jul 1952 Cover: 0.10 **NM** value: **30.00**
22 ❑ 1952 Cover: 0.10 **NM** value: **30.00**
23 ❑ 1952 Cover: 0.10 **NM** value: **30.00**
24 ❑ 1953 Cover: 0.10 **NM** value: **30.00**
25 ❑ 1953 Cover: 0.10 **NM** value: **30.00**
26 ❑ 1953 Cover: 0.10 **NM** value: **30.00**
27 ❑ 1953 Cover: 0.10 **NM** value: **30.00**
28 ❑ 1953 Cover: 0.10 **NM** value: **30.00**
29 ❑ 1953 Cover: 0.10 **NM** value: **30.00**
30 ❑ 1953 Cover: 0.10 **NM** value: **30.00**
31 ❑ 1953 Cover: 0.10 **NM** value: **25.00**
32 ❑ 1953 Cover: 0.10 **NM** value: **25.00**
33 ❑ 1954 Cover: 0.10 **NM** value: **25.00**
34 ❑ 1954 Cover: 0.10 **NM** value: **25.00**
35 ❑ 1954 Cover: 0.10 **NM** value: **25.00**
36 ❑ 1954 Cover: 0.10 **NM** value: **25.00**
37 ❑ 1954 Cover: 0.10 **NM** value: **25.00**
38 ❑ 1954 Cover: 0.10 **NM** value: **25.00**
39 ❑ 1954 Cover: 0.10 **NM** value: **25.00**
40 ❑ 1954 Cover: 0.10 **NM** value: **20.00**
41 ❑ 1955 Cover: 0.10 **NM** value: **20.00**
42 ❑ 1955 Cover: 0.10 **NM** value: **20.00**
43 ❑ 1955 Cover: 0.10 **NM** value: **20.00**
44 ❑ 1955 Cover: 0.10 **NM** value: **20.00**
45 ❑ 1955 Cover: 0.10 **NM** value: **20.00**
46 ❑ 1955 Cover: 0.10 **NM** value: **20.00**
47 ❑ 1955 Cover: 0.10 **NM** value: **20.00**
48 ❑ 1955 Cover: 0.10 **NM** value: **20.00**
49 ❑ 1956 Cover: 0.10 **NM** value: **20.00**
50 ❑ 1956 Cover: 0.10 **NM** value: **20.00**
51 ❑ 1956 Cover: 0.10 **NM** value: **20.00**
52 ❑ 1956 Cover: 0.10 **NM** value: **20.00**
53 ❑ 1956 Cover: 0.10 **NM** value: **20.00**
54 ❑ 1956 Cover: 0.10 **NM** value: **20.00**

LOVECRAFT — Adventure

1 ❑ Cover: 2.95 **NM** value: **Cover or less**
Circ: CapCity orders: **4,970**
📖 The Lurking Fear **A:** Octavio Cariello **W:** Octavio Cariello; H.P. Lovecraft; Steve Jones
1/LE❑ Cover: 5.95 **NM** value: **Cover or less**
Circ: CapCity orders: **2,560**
• limited edition.
2 ❑ Cover: 2.95 **NM** value: **Cover or less**
Circ: CapCity orders: **3,360**
W: H.P. Lovecraft
3 ❑ Cover: 2.95 **NM** value: **Cover or less**
Circ: CapCity orders: **3,310**
📖 The Tomb **A:** Katy Llewellyn **W:** Octavio Cariello; H.P. Lovecraft; Steve Jones
4 ❑ Cover: 2.95 **NM** value: **Cover or less**
Circ: CapCity orders: **3,550**
📖 The Alchemist **W:** H.P. Lovecraft

LOVE DIARY (CHARLTON) — Charlton

This long-running romance comic book kept up with the times in its almost two-decade-long run. By the mid-1970s, Love Diary had moved beyond the typical girl-meets-boy, boy-proposes-to girl formula to stories such as a conniving jealous girl disrupting an already dysfunctional relationship; a woman leaving her boring boyfriend for a more exciting man; and a woman dating another man despite her engagement to the one she loves.

Like many romance comics, the framing device used throughout was a sort of "Dear Diary" entry in which the female storyteller would recount the romantic scenario.

1 ❑ Jul 1958 Cover: 0.10 **NM** value: **45.00**
2 ❑ Cover: 0.10 **NM** value: **24.00**
3 ❑ Cover: 0.10 **NM** value: **16.00**
4 ❑ Cover: 0.10 **NM** value: **16.00**
5 ❑ Cover: 0.10 **NM** value: **14.00**
• **CGC:** 1 graded, best 9.0
6 ❑ Cover: 0.10 **NM** value: **20.00**
A: Joe Torres
7 ❑ Cover: 0.10 **NM** value: **14.00**
8 ❑ Cover: 0.10 **NM** value: **14.00**
9 ❑ Mar 1960 Cover: 0.10 **NM** value: **14.00**
10 ❑ Jun 1960 Cover: 0.10 **NM** value: **14.00**
11 ❑ Aug 1960 Cover: 0.10 **NM** value: **12.00**
12 ❑ Oct 1960 Cover: 0.10 **NM** value: **12.00**
13 ❑ Dec 1960 Cover: 0.10 **NM** value: **12.00**
14 ❑ Feb 1961 Cover: 0.10 **NM** value: **12.00**
15 ❑ Apr 1961 Cover: 0.10 **NM** value: **12.00**
16 ❑ Jun 1961 Cover: 0.10 **NM** value: **10.00**
17 ❑ Aug 1961 Cover: 0.10 **NM** value: **10.00**
18 ❑ Oct 1961 Cover: 0.10 **NM** value: **10.00**
19 ❑ Dec 1961 Cover: 0.10 **NM** value: **10.00**
• **CGC:** 1 graded, best 8.0
20 ❑ Mar 1962 Cover: 0.10 **NM** value: **10.00**
• **CGC:** 1 graded, best 9.2
21 ❑ 1962 Cover: 0.12 **NM** value: **7.00**
22 ❑ 1962 Cover: 0.12 **NM** value: **7.00**
23 ❑ 1962 Cover: 0.12 **NM** value: **7.00**
24 ❑ 1962 Cover: 0.12 **NM** value: **7.00**
25 ❑ Jan 1963 Cover: 0.12 **NM** value: **7.00**
26 ❑ 1963 Cover: 0.12 **NM** value: **7.00**
27 ❑ 1963 Cover: 0.12 **NM** value: **7.00**
28 ❑ 1963 Cover: 0.12 **NM** value: **7.00**
29 ❑ 1963 Cover: 0.12 **NM** value: **7.00**
30 ❑ Cover: 0.12 **NM** value: **7.00**
31 ❑ 1964 Cover: 0.12 **NM** value: **5.00**
32 ❑ 1964 Cover: 0.12 **NM** value: **5.00**
33 ❑ 1964 Cover: 0.12 **NM** value: **5.00**
34 ❑ 1964 Cover: 0.12 **NM** value: **5.00**
35 ❑ Cover: 0.12 **NM** value: **5.00**
36 ❑ 1965 Cover: 0.12 **NM** value: **5.00**
Circ: Statement: **141,333**
37 ❑ 1965 Cover: 0.12 **NM** value: **5.00**
Circ: Statement: **141,333**
38 ❑ 1965 Cover: 0.12 **NM** value: **5.00**
Circ: Statement: **141,333**
39 ❑ 1965 Cover: 0.12 **NM** value: **5.00**
Circ: Statement: **141,333**
40 ❑ Oct 1965 Cover: 0.12 **NM** value: **5.00**
Circ: Statement: **141,333**
41 ❑ Dec 1965 Cover: 0.12 **NM** value: **4.00**
Circ: Statement: **141,333**
42 ❑ Feb 1966 Cover: 0.12 **NM** value: **4.00**
43 ❑ Apr 1966 Cover: 0.12 **NM** value: **4.00**
44 ❑ Jun 1966 Cover: 0.12 **NM** value: **4.00**
45 ❑ Sep 1966 Cover: 0.12 **NM** value: **4.00**
46 ❑ Nov 1966 Cover: 0.12 **NM** value: **4.00**
47 ❑ Jan 1967 Cover: 0.12 **NM** value: **4.00**
Circ: Statement: **115,412**
48 ❑ Mar 1967 Cover: 0.12 **NM** value: **4.00**
Circ: Statement: **115,412**
49 ❑ 1967 Cover: 0.12 **NM** value: **4.00**
Circ: Statement: **115,412**
50 ❑ 1967 Cover: 0.12 **NM** value: **4.00**
Circ: Statement: **115,412**
51 ❑ 1967 Cover: 0.12 **NM** value: **4.00**
Circ: Statement: **115,412**
52 ❑ 1968 Cover: 0.12 **NM** value: **4.00**
53 ❑ 1968 Cover: 0.12 **NM** value: **4.00**
54 ❑ Jun 1968 Cover: 0.12 **NM** value: **4.00**
55 ❑ Aug 1968 Cover: 0.12 **NM** value: **4.00**
56 ❑ Oct 1968 Cover: 0.12 **NM** value: **4.00**
57 ❑ Dec 1968 Cover: 0.12 **NM** value: **4.00**
58 ❑ Feb 1969 Cover: 0.12 **NM** value: **4.00**
59 ❑ Apr 1969 Cover: 0.12 **NM** value: **4.00**
📖 My Love Shall Live Again; Nothing in Common; Your Kind of Woman **A:** Nicholas Alascia
60 ❑ Jun 1969 Cover: 0.12 **NM** value: **4.00**
61 ❑ Aug 1969 Cover: 0.15 **NM** value: **2.50**
62 ❑ Oct 1969 Cover: 0.15 **NM** value: **2.50**
63 ❑ Dec 1969 Cover: 0.15 **NM** value: **2.50**
64 ❑ Feb 1970 Cover: 0.15 **NM** value: **2.50**
65 ❑ Apr 1970 Cover: 0.15 **NM** value: **2.50**
66 ❑ Jun 1970 Cover: 0.15 **NM** value: **2.50**
67 ❑ Aug 1970 Cover: 0.15 **NM** value: **2.50**
68 ❑ Oct 1970 Cover: 0.15 **NM** value: **2.50**
69 ❑ Dec 1970 Cover: 0.15 **NM** value: **2.50**
70 ❑ Jan 1971 Cover: 0.15 **NM** value: **2.50**
71 ❑ Mar 1971 Cover: 0.15 **NM** value: **2.50**
72 ❑ May 1971 Cover: 0.15 **NM** value: **2.50**
73 ❑ Jul 1971 Cover: 0.15 **NM** value: **2.50**
74 ❑ Sep 1971 Cover: 0.20 **NM** value: **2.50**
75 ❑ Nov 1971 Cover: 0.20 **NM** value: **2.50**
76 ❑ Jan 1972 Cover: 0.20 **NM** value: **2.50**
Circ: Statement: **160,033**
77 ❑ Mar 1972 Cover: 0.20 **NM** value: **2.50**
Circ: Statement: **160,033**
78 ❑ May 1972 Cover: 0.20 **NM** value: **2.50**
Circ: Statement: **160,033**
79 ❑ Jul 1972 Cover: 0.20 **NM** value: **2.50**
Circ: Statement: **160,033**
80 ❑ 1972 Cover: 0.20 **NM** value: **2.50**
Circ: Statement: **160,033**
81 ❑ Dec 1972 Cover: 0.20 **NM** value: **2.50**
Circ: Statement: **160,033**
82 ❑ 1973 Cover: 0.20 **NM** value: **2.50**
Circ: Statement: **132,043**
83 ❑ Mar 1973 Cover: 0.20 **NM** value: **2.50**
Circ: Statement: **132,043**
84 ❑ May 1973 Cover: 0.20 **NM** value: **2.50**
Circ: Statement: **132,043**
• Has 1972 Statement; avg total paid 160,033
85 ❑ Jul 1973 Cover: 0.20 **NM** value: **2.50**
Circ: Statement: **132,043**
86 ❑ Sep 1973 Cover: 0.20 **NM** value: **2.50**
Circ: Statement: **132,043**
87 ❑ Nov 1973 Cover: 0.20 **NM** value: **2.50**
Circ: Statement: **132,043**
88 ❑ Jun 1974 **NM** value: **2.50**
Circ: Statement: **114,080**
• Has 1973 Statement; avg total paid circ 132,043
89 ❑ 1974 **NM** value: **2.50**
Circ: Statement: **114,080**
90 ❑ 1974 **NM** value: **2.50**
Circ: Statement: **114,080**
91 ❑ **NM** value: **2.50**
Circ: Statement: **114,080**
92 ❑ Mar 1975 Cover: 0.25 **NM** value: **2.50**
Circ: Statement: **96,170**
93 ❑ May 1975 Cover: 0.25 **NM** value: **2.50**
Circ: Statement: **96,170**
• Has 1974 Statement; avg total paid circ 114,080
94 ❑ 1975 Cover: 0.25 **NM** value: **2.50**
Circ: Statement: **96,170**
95 ❑ 1975 Cover: 0.25 **NM** value: **2.50**
Circ: Statement: **96,170**
96 ❑ 1975 Cover: 0.25 **NM** value: **2.50**
Circ: Statement: **96,170**
97 ❑ Feb 1976 Cover: 0.25 **NM** value: **2.50**
98 ❑ 1976 **NM** value: **2.50**
99 ❑ 1976 Cover: 0.30 **NM** value: **2.50**
📖 In Just One Day; I'll Always Love Him…; Big Mystery; A Stranger's Kiss
100 ❑ 1976 **NM** value: **2.50**
101 ❑ Oct 1976 Cover: 0.30 **NM** value: **2.50**
102 ❑ Dec 1976 Cover: 0.30 **NM** value: **2.50**
final issue.

LOVE DIARY (OUR PUBLISHING) — Our

The romance comic book was one of the best-selling genres of comics in the post-World War II era. Love Diary was targeted at teen-age girls and young women, with "True Confessions"-type stories. The quality was generally competent — and standard for the time. Each issue also had the helpful advice of Ray Mann, "Love Diary's Human Relations Counselor." Ray Mann provided a text article, an advice column for the readers who (allegedly) had written in, and occasionally stepped into a comics story himself. It was a pretty good romance series and a good representation of post-war American society.

1 ❑ Jul 1949 Cover: 0.10 **NM** value: **9.00**
2 ❑ Oct 1949 Cover: 0.10 **NM** value: **6.00**
3 ❑ Dec 1949 Cover: 0.10 **NM** value: **5.00**
4 ❑ Jan 1950 Cover: 0.10 **NM** value: **3.00**
📖 I Lied To My Heart; Miss "X": The Girl Without A Past; Prescription For Happiness; Movie Crazy; I Hated Men;
5 ❑ Mar 1950 Cover: 0.10 **NM** value: **3.00**
6 ❑ 1950 Cover: 0.10 **NM** value: **25.00**
7 ❑ 1950 Cover: 0.10 **NM** value: **25.00**
8 ❑ 1950 Cover: 0.10 **NM** value: **25.00**
9 ❑ 1950 Cover: 0.10 **NM** value: **25.00**
10 ❑ 1950 Cover: 0.10 **NM** value: **25.00**
11 ❑ 1950 Cover: 0.10 **NM** value: **22.00**
12 ❑ 1950 Cover: 0.10 **NM** value: **22.00**
13 ❑ Cover: 0.10 **NM** value: **22.00**
14 ❑ 1951 Cover: 0.10 **NM** value: **22.00**
15 ❑ 1951 Cover: 0.10 **NM** value: **22.00**
16 ❑ 1951 Cover: 0.10 **NM** value: **22.00**
17 ❑ 1951 Cover: 0.10 **NM** value: **22.00**
18 ❑ Jul 1951 Cover: 0.10 **NM** value: **22.00**
19 ❑ Aug 1951 Cover: 0.10 **NM** value: **22.00**
20 ❑ Sep 1951 Cover: 0.10 **NM** value: **22.00**
21 ❑ 1951 Cover: 0.10 **NM** value: **16.00**
22 ❑ 1951 Cover: 0.10 **NM** value: **16.00**
23 ❑ Cover: 0.10 **NM** value: **16.00**
24 ❑ 1952 Cover: 0.10 **NM** value: **16.00**
25 ❑ 1952 Cover: 0.10 **NM** value: **16.00**
26 ❑ 1952 Cover: 0.10 **NM** value: **16.00**
27 ❑ 1952 Cover: 0.10 **NM** value: **16.00**
28 ❑ 1952 Cover: 0.10 **NM** value: **16.00**
29 ❑ 1952 Cover: 0.10 **NM** value: **16.00**
30 ❑ 1952 Cover: 0.10 **NM** value: **16.00**
31 ❑ Cover: 0.10 **NM** value: **13.00**
32 ❑ 1953 Cover: 0.10 **NM** value: **13.00**
33 ❑ 1953 Cover: 0.10 **NM** value: **13.00**
34 ❑ 1953 Cover: 0.10 **NM** value: **13.00**
35 ❑ 1953 Cover: 0.10 **NM** value: **13.00**
36 ❑ 1953 Cover: 0.10 **NM** value: **13.00**
37 ❑ 1953 Cover: 0.10 **NM** value: **13.00**
38 ❑ Cover: 0.10 **NM** value: **13.00**
39 ❑ Cover: 0.10 **NM** value: **13.00**
40 ❑ 1954 Cover: 0.10 **NM** value: **13.00**
📖 Behind Closed Doors!; Girl With a Past!; Prescription for Happiness; Dance for Me, Darling!
41 ❑ 1954 Cover: 0.10 **NM** value: **1.00**
42 ❑ Apr 1954 Cover: 0.10 **NM** value: **1.00**
43 ❑ May 1954 Cover: 0.10 **NM** value: **1.00**
44 ❑ Jun 1954 Cover: 0.10 **NM** value: **1.00**
45 ❑ Jul 1954 Cover: 0.10 **NM** value: **1.00**
46 ❑ 1954 Cover: 0.10 **NM** value: **1.00**
47 ❑ 1954 Cover: 0.10 **NM** value: **1.00**
48 ❑ 1954 Cover: 0.10 **NM** value: **1.00**
final issue.

LOVE DIARY (QUALITY) — Quality

1 ❑ Sep 1949 Cover: 0.10 **NM** value: **200.00**

LOVE DRAMAS — Marvel

1 ❑ **NM** value: **100.00**
2 ❑ **NM** value: **75.00**

LOVE ETERNAL: A TORTURED SOUL — Vlad Ent.

1 ❑ b&w Cover: 2.00 **NM** value: **Cover or less**

LOVE EXPERIENCES — Ace

1 ❑ Oct 1949 Cover: 0.10 **NM** value: **6.00**
2 ❑ Cover: 0.10 **NM** value: **3.00**
3 ❑ 1950 Cover: 0.10 **NM** value: **22.00**
4 ❑ 1950 Cover: 0.10 **NM** value: **22.00**
5 ❑ 1950 Cover: 0.10 **NM** value: **22.00**
6 ❑ 1950 Cover: 0.10 **NM** value: **16.00**
7 ❑ 1950 Cover: 0.10 **NM** value: **16.00**
8 ❑ Cover: 0.10 **NM** value: **16.00**
9 ❑ 1951 Cover: 0.10 **NM** value: **16.00**
10 ❑ 1951 Cover: 0.10 **NM** value: **16.00**
11 ❑ 1951 Cover: 0.10 **NM** value: **13.00**
12 ❑ 1951 Cover: 0.10 **NM** value: **13.00**
13 ❑ 1951 Cover: 0.10 **NM** value: **13.00**

CGC-graded: Multiply prices above by **33 for 9.9 M • 16 for 9.8 NM/M • 7 for 9.6 NM+ • 5 for 9.4 NM • 2.5 for 9.2 NM- • 1.5 for 9.0 VF/NM**

14 ❑ Cover: 0.10 **NM** value: **13.00**
15 ❑ 1952 Cover: 0.10 **NM** value: **13.00**
16 ❑ Cover: 0.10 **NM** value: **13.00**
Photo cover. 📖 Love was my Career; My Name was Glamour; Blamed by Everyone; I'll Follow My Man
17 ❑ Feb 1953 Cover: 0.10 **NM** value: **13.00**
18 ❑ 1953 Cover: 0.10 **NM** value: **13.00**
19 ❑ 1953 Cover: 0.10 **NM** value: **13.00**
20 ❑ 1953 Cover: 0.10 **NM** value: **13.00**
21 ❑ 1953 Cover: 0.10 **NM** value: **11.00**
22 ❑ 1953 Cover: 0.10 **NM** value: **11.00**
23 ❑ Cover: 0.10 **NM** value: **11.00**
24 ❑ 1954 Cover: 0.10 **NM** value: **11.00**
25 ❑ 1954 Cover: 0.10 **NM** value: **11.00**
26 ❑ 1954 Cover: 0.10 **NM** value: **11.00**
27 ❑ 1954 Cover: 0.10 **NM** value: **11.00**
28 ❑ 1954 Cover: 0.10 **NM** value: **11.00**
29 ❑ 1954 Cover: 0.10 **NM** value: **11.00**
30 ❑ Feb 1955 Cover: 0.10 **NM** value: **11.00**
31 ❑ Apr 1955 Cover: 0.10 **NM** value: **1.00**
32 ❑ Jun 1955 Cover: 0.10 **NM** value: **1.00**
33 ❑ Aug 1955 Cover: 0.10 **NM** value: **1.00**
34 ❑ Oct 1955 Cover: 0.10 **NM** value: **1.00**
35 ❑ Dec 1955 Cover: 0.10 **NM** value: **1.00**
36 ❑ Feb 1956 Cover: 0.10 **NM** value: **1.00**
37 ❑ Apr 1956 Cover: 0.10 **NM** value: **1.00**
38 ❑ Jun 1956 Cover: 0.10 **NM** value: **1.00**
final issue.

LOVE FANTASY — Renegade

1 ❑ b&w Cover: 2.00 **NM** value: **Cover or less**
📖 Check-Out Girl; The Perfect Guy; Royal Con Interlude **A:** Gabriel Morrissette; Jacques Boivin **W:** Arn Saba; Mike Baron; Mark Shainblum

LOVE IN TIGHTS — Slave Labor

1 ❑ Nov 1998, b&w Cover: 2.95 **NM** value: **Cover or less**
📖 While You Were Sleeping; Crash Course; Dork Tower; Fatal Hestitation; Cosmic Carrot • First heart throbbin' issue **A:** Brian Clopper; John Kovalic; Francis Manapul; Takeshi Miyazawa; Cayetano Garza Jr **W:** John Kovalic; Takeshi Miyazawa; Cayetano Garza Jr; J. Torres

LOVE JOURNAL — Our

10 ❑ Oct 1951 Cover: 0.10 **NM** value: **50.00**
• **CGC:** 1 graded, best 4.0
11 ❑ Dec 1951 Cover: 0.10 **NM** value: **25.00**
12 ❑ Feb 1952 Cover: 0.10 **NM** value: **25.00**
13 ❑ Apr 1952 Cover: 0.10 **NM** value: **25.00**
14 ❑ Jun 1952 Cover: 0.10 **NM** value: **25.00**
15 ❑ Aug 1952 Cover: 0.10 **NM** value: **25.00**
16 ❑ Oct 1952 Cover: 0.10 **NM** value: **25.00**
17 ❑ Dec 1952 Cover: 0.10 **NM** value: **25.00**
18 ❑ Feb 1953 Cover: 0.10 **NM** value: **25.00**
19 ❑ Apr 1953 Cover: 0.10 **NM** value: **25.00**
20 ❑ Jun 1953 Cover: 0.10 **NM** value: **25.00**
21 ❑ Aug 1953 Cover: 0.10 **NM** value: **20.00**
22 ❑ Oct 1953 Cover: 0.10 **NM** value: **20.00**
23 ❑ Dec 1953 Cover: 0.10 **NM** value: **20.00**
24 ❑ Feb 1954 Cover: 0.10 **NM** value: **20.00**
25 ❑ Apr 1954 Cover: 0.10 **NM** value: **20.00**

LOVELAND — Marvel

1 ❑ Nov 1949 Cover: 0.10 **NM** value: **50.00**
2 ❑ Feb 1950 Cover: 0.10 **NM** value: **50.00**

LOVE LESSONS — Harvey

1 ❑ Oct 1949 Cover: 0.10 **NM** value: **75.00**
• **CGC:** 1 graded, best 9.2
2 ❑ Dec 1949 Cover: 0.10 **NM** value: **40.00**
3 ❑ Feb 1950 Cover: 0.10 **NM** value: **30.00**
• **CGC:** 1 graded, best 9.4
4 ❑ Apr 1950 Cover: 0.10 **NM** value: **30.00**
5 ❑ Jun 1950 Cover: 0.10 **NM** value: **30.00**

LOVE LETTERS — Quality

The late 1940s are generally thought of as a low point in comics history because of the demise of the Golden Age super-heroes and funny-animal comics, but in fact comics never before and rarely since enjoyed a larger, more diverse, and more adult readership than in those years. As a result, several genres, including romance, crime, and horror comics, emerged to cater to older readers, with more sophisticated stories and themes and a harder edge to their material. Love Letters, from Quality Comics, came out quickly on the heels of the first romance comics from Simon and Kirby, Young Love and Young Romance. Love Letters took its cue from those pioneering titles, offering bittersweet tales of temptation, betrayal, class conflict, and emotional violence that belied the image of sappy sentimentalism that later overtook the genre. Artists like Bill Ward and Reed Crandall helped lift the standard even higher.

1 ❑ Nov 1949 Cover: 0.10 **NM** value: **110.00**
2 ❑ Jan 1950 Cover: 0.10 **NM** value: **85.00**
3 ❑ Mar 1950 Cover: 0.10 **NM** value: **60.00**
4 ❑ May 1950 Cover: 0.10 **NM** value: **80.00**
5 ❑ Jul 1950 Cover: 0.10 **NM** value: **20.00**
6 ❑ Sep 1950 Cover: 0.10 **NM** value: **20.00**
7 ❑ Mar 1951 Cover: 0.10 **NM** value: **20.00**
8 ❑ Apr 1951 Cover: 0.10 **NM** value: **20.00**
9 ❑ May 1951 Cover: 0.10 **NM** value: **20.00**
10 ❑ Jun 1951 Cover: 0.10 **NM** value: **20.00**
Photo cover. • Cover depicts Robert Mitchum and Faith Dommergue
11 ❑ Jul 1951 Cover: 0.10 **NM** value: **20.00**
12 ❑ Aug 1951 Cover: 0.10 **NM** value: **16.00**
13 ❑ Sep 1951 Cover: 0.10 **NM** value: **16.00**
14 ❑ Oct 1951 Cover: 0.10 **NM** value: **16.00**
15 ❑ Nov 1951 Cover: 0.10 **NM** value: **16.00**
16 ❑ Dec 1951 Cover: 0.10 **NM** value: **16.00**
17 ❑ Feb 1952 Cover: 0.10 **NM** value: **16.00**
18 ❑ 1952 Cover: 0.10 **NM** value: **16.00**
19 ❑ 1952 Cover: 0.10 **NM** value: **16.00**
20 ❑ 1952 Cover: 0.10 **NM** value: **16.00**
21 ❑ 1952 Cover: 0.10 **NM** value: **12.00**
22 ❑ 1952 Cover: 0.10 **NM** value: **12.00**
23 ❑ 1952 Cover: 0.10 **NM** value: **12.00**
24 ❑ 1952 Cover: 0.10 **NM** value: **12.00**
25 ❑ 1952 Cover: 0.10 **NM** value: **12.00**
26 ❑ 1952 Cover: 0.10 **NM** value: **12.00**
📖 Starved for Kisses; I'll Fight For You; Broken Dreams; I'll Be Waiting
27 ❑ 1952 Cover: 0.10 **NM** value: **12.00**
28 ❑ Cover: 0.10 **NM** value: **12.00**
29 ❑ 1953 Cover: 0.10 **NM** value: **12.00**
30 ❑ Apr 1953 Cover: 0.10 **NM** value: **12.00**
31 ❑ Jun 1953 Cover: 0.10 **NM** value: **12.00**
32 ❑ Feb 1954 Cover: 0.10 **NM** value: **10.00**
33 ❑ Apr 1954 Cover: 0.10 **NM** value: **10.00**
34 ❑ Jun 1954 Cover: 0.10 **NM** value: **10.00**
35 ❑ ca. 1954 Cover: 0.10 **NM** value: **10.00**
36 ❑ ca. 1954 Cover: 0.10 **NM** value: **10.00**
37 ❑ ca. 1954 Cover: 0.10 **NM** value: **10.00**
38 ❑ ca. 1954 Cover: 0.10 **NM** value: **10.00**
39 ❑ ca. 1955 Cover: 0.10 **NM** value: **10.00**
40 ❑ ca. 1955 Cover: 0.10 **NM** value: **10.00**
41 ❑ ca. 1955 Cover: 0.10 **NM** value: **10.00**
42 ❑ ca. 1955 Cover: 0.10 **NM** value: **10.00**
43 ❑ ca. 1955 Cover: 0.10 **NM** value: **10.00**
44 ❑ ca. 1955 Cover: 0.10 **NM** value: **10.00**
45 ❑ ca. 1955 Cover: 0.10 **NM** value: **10.00**
46 ❑ ca. 1956 Cover: 0.10 **NM** value: **10.00**
47 ❑ ca. 1956 Cover: 0.10 **NM** value: **10.00**
48 ❑ ca. 1956 Cover: 0.10 **NM** value: **10.00**
49 ❑ Jul 1956 Cover: 0.10 **NM** value: **35.00**
50 ❑ Cover: 0.10 **NM** value: **35.00**
A: Matt Baker
51 ❑ Cover: 0.10 **NM** value: **24.00**
final issue. **C:** Matt Baker

LOVE LETTERS IN THE HAND — Fantagraphics / Eros

All issues are adults only.

1 ❑ b&w Cover: 2.25 **NM** value: **Cover or less**
2 ❑ b&w Cover: 2.25 **NM** value: **Cover or less**
3 ❑ b&w Cover: 2.50 **NM** value: **Cover or less**

LOVELORN — ACG

Subtitled "Stirring stories of real romance," the series featured tales of such torment as the heroine's trying to decide which truly pays off, love or money (in "My Heart Went Astray"). Early issues cover-featured major traumas for the characters shown; some later ones were more decoratively devoted to clinches simple (on the Coney Island Ferry) and complex (both kissing while on trapezes).

In the mid-1950s, ACG faced up to the challenge presented by 3-D comics by announcing a "TrueVision" story in the issue. Boasting "Full color!" and "No glasses!" the approach consisted of having characters depicted in front of their panel borders. — Maggie

1 ❑ Aug 1949 Cover: 0.10 **NM** value: **100.00**
2 ❑ Oct 1949 Cover: 0.10 **NM** value: **50.00**
3 ❑ Dec 1949 Cover: 0.10 **NM** value: **50.00**
4 ❑ Feb 1950 Cover: 0.10 **NM** value: **40.00**
5 ❑ Apr 1950 Cover: 0.10 **NM** value: **40.00**
6 ❑ Jun 1950 Cover: 0.10 **NM** value: **40.00**
7 ❑ Aug 1950 Cover: 0.10 **NM** value: **40.00**
8 ❑ Oct 1950 Cover: 0.10 **NM** value: **40.00**
9 ❑ Dec 1950 Cover: 0.10 **NM** value: **40.00**
10 ❑ Feb 1951 Cover: 0.10 **NM** value: **35.00**
11 ❑ Mar 1951 Cover: 0.10 **NM** value: **35.00**
12 ❑ Apr 1951 Cover: 0.10 **NM** value: **35.00**
13 ❑ May 1951 Cover: 0.10 **NM** value: **35.00**
14 ❑ Jun 1951 Cover: 0.10 **NM** value: **35.00**
15 ❑ Jul 1951 Cover: 0.10 **NM** value: **35.00**
16 ❑ Aug 1951 Cover: 0.10 **NM** value: **35.00**
17 ❑ Sep 1951 Cover: 0.10 **NM** value: **35.00**
18 ❑ Oct 1951 Cover: 0.10 **NM** value: **35.00**
19 ❑ Nov 1951 Cover: 0.10 **NM** value: **35.00**
20 ❑ Dec 1951 Cover: 0.10 **NM** value: **30.00**
21 ❑ Jan 1952 Cover: 0.10 **NM** value: **30.00**
22 ❑ Feb 1952 Cover: 0.10 **NM** value: **30.00**
23 ❑ Mar 1952 Cover: 0.10 **NM** value: **30.00**
24 ❑ Apr 1952 Cover: 0.10 **NM** value: **30.00**
25 ❑ May 1952 Cover: 0.10 **NM** value: **30.00**
26 ❑ Jun 1952 Cover: 0.10 **NM** value: **30.00**
27 ❑ Jul 1952 Cover: 0.10 **NM** value: **30.00**
28 ❑ Aug 1952 Cover: 0.10 **NM** value: **30.00**
29 ❑ Sep 1952 Cover: 0.10 **NM** value: **30.00**
30 ❑ Oct 1952 Cover: 0.10 **NM** value: **25.00**
31 ❑ Nov 1952 Cover: 0.10 **NM** value: **25.00**
32 ❑ Dec 1952 Cover: 0.10 **NM** value: **25.00**
33 ❑ Jan 1953 Cover: 0.10 **NM** value: **25.00**
34 ❑ Feb 1953 Cover: 0.10 **NM** value: **25.00**
35 ❑ Mar 1953 Cover: 0.10 **NM** value: **25.00**
36 ❑ Apr 1953 Cover: 0.10 **NM** value: **25.00**
37 ❑ May 1953 Cover: 0.10 **NM** value: **25.00**
38 ❑ Jun 1953 Cover: 0.10 **NM** value: **25.00**
39 ❑ Jul 1953 Cover: 0.10 **NM** value: **25.00**
40 ❑ Aug 1953 Cover: 0.10 **NM** value: **20.00**
41 ❑ Sep 1953 Cover: 0.10 **NM** value: **20.00**
42 ❑ Oct 1953 Cover: 0.10 **NM** value: **20.00**
43 ❑ Nov 1953 Cover: 0.10 **NM** value: **20.00**
44 ❑ Dec 1953 Cover: 0.10 **NM** value: **20.00**
45 ❑ Jan 1954 Cover: 0.10 **NM** value: **20.00**
46 ❑ Feb 1954 Cover: 0.10 **NM** value: **20.00**
47 ❑ Mar 1954 Cover: 0.10 **NM** value: **20.00**
48 ❑ Apr 1954 Cover: 0.10 **NM** value: **20.00**
49 ❑ May 1954 Cover: 0.10 **NM** value: **20.00**
50 ❑ Jun 1954 Cover: 0.10 **NM** value: **20.00**
51 ❑ Jul 1954 Cover: 0.10 **NM** value: **20.00**

LOVELY AS A LIE — Illustration

1 ❑ Nov 1994 Cover: 3.25 **NM** value: **Cover or less**
📖 Mortal Sins **A:** Jim Taylor; Rich Longmore **W:** Ian Stigliani; Paul Wishinsky

LOVELY LADIES — Caliber

1 ❑ b&w Cover: 3.50 **NM** value: **Cover or less**
• pin-ups

LOVELY PRUDENCE — Modern

3 ❑ b&w Cover: 2.95 **NM** value: **Cover or less**

LOVE MEMORIES — Fawcett

1 ❑ ca. 1949 Cover: 0.10 **NM** value: **75.00**
2 ❑ Win 1949 Cover: 0.10 **NM** value: **40.00**
3 ❑ May 1950 Cover: 0.10 **NM** value: **40.00**
4 ❑ ca. 1950 Cover: 0.10 **NM** value: **40.00**

LOVE MYSTERY — Fawcett

1 ❑ Jun 1950 Cover: 0.10 **NM** value: **100.00**
2 ❑ Aug 1950 Cover: 0.10 **NM** value: **75.00**
3 ❑ Oct 1950 Cover: 0.10 **NM** value: **75.00**

LOVE ROMANCES — Timely

6 ❑ May 1949 Cover: 0.10 **NM** value: **100.00**
7 ❑ Jul 1949 Cover: 0.10 **NM** value: **75.00**
8 ❑ 1949 Cover: 0.10 **NM** value: **75.00**
9 ❑ Cover: 0.10 **NM** value: **75.00**
10 ❑ Feb 1950 Cover: 0.10 **NM** value: **75.00**
📖 I Married For Money! • Wanda Hendrix Photo Cover
11 ❑ 1950 Cover: 0.10 **NM** value: **65.00**
12 ❑ 1950 Cover: 0.10 **NM** value: **65.00**
13 ❑ 1950 Cover: 0.10 **NM** value: **65.00**
14 ❑ Cover: 0.10 **NM** value: **65.00**
15 ❑ Cover: 0.10 **NM** value: **65.00**
16 ❑ 1951 Cover: 0.10 **NM** value: **65.00**
17 ❑ 1951 Cover: 0.10 **NM** value: **65.00**
18 ❑ 1951 Cover: 0.10 **NM** value: **65.00**
19 ❑ 1951 Cover: 0.10 **NM** value: **65.00**
20 ❑ Jan 1952 Cover: 0.20 **NM** value: **65.00**
21 ❑ 1952 Cover: 0.10 **NM** value: **65.00**
22 ❑ 1952 Cover: 0.10 **NM** value: **65.00**
23 ❑ 1952 Cover: 0.10 **NM** value: **65.00**
24 ❑ 1952 Cover: 0.10 **NM** value: **65.00**
25 ❑ 1952 Cover: 0.10 **NM** value: **65.00**
26 ❑ 1952 Cover: 0.10 **NM** value: **65.00**
27 ❑ Cover: 0.10 **NM** value: **65.00**
28 ❑ 1953 Cover: 0.10 **NM** value: **65.00**
29 ❑ 1953 Cover: 0.10 **NM** value: **65.00**
30 ❑ 1953 Cover: 0.10 **NM** value: **65.00**
31 ❑ 1953 Cover: 0.10 **NM** value: **65.00**
32 ❑ 1953 Cover: 0.10 **NM** value: **65.00**
33 ❑ 1953 Cover: 0.10 **NM** value: **65.00**
34 ❑ Cover: 0.10 **NM** value: **65.00**
35 ❑ Cover: 0.10 **NM** value: **65.00**
36 ❑ Cover: 0.10 **NM** value: **65.00**
37 ❑ 1954 Cover: 0.10 **NM** value: **65.00**
38 ❑ 1954 Cover: 0.10 **NM** value: **65.00**
39 ❑ 1954 Cover: 0.10 **NM** value: **65.00**
40 ❑ 1954 Cover: 0.10 **NM** value: **65.00**
41 ❑ 1954 Cover: 0.10 **NM** value: **65.00**
42 ❑ 1954 Cover: 0.10 **NM** value: **65.00**
43 ❑ 1954 Cover: 0.10 **NM** value: **65.00**
44 ❑ 1954 Cover: 0.10 **NM** value: **65.00**
45 ❑ Cover: 0.10 **NM** value: **65.00**
46 ❑ Jan 1955 Cover: 0.10 **NM** value: **65.00**
47 ❑ Feb 1955 Cover: 0.10 **NM** value: **65.00**
48 ❑ Mar 1955 Cover: 0.10 **NM** value: **65.00**
49 ❑ Apr 1955 Cover: 0.10 **NM** value: **65.00**
50 ❑ May 1955 Cover: 0.10 **NM** value: **65.00**
51 ❑ Jun 1955 Cover: 0.10 **NM** value: **60.00**
52 ❑ Jul 1955 Cover: 0.10 **NM** value: **60.00**
53 ❑ Aug 1955 Cover: 0.10 **NM** value: **60.00**
54 ❑ Sep 1955 Cover: 0.10 **NM** value: **60.00**
55 ❑ Oct 1955 Cover: 0.10 **NM** value: **60.00**
56 ❑ Nov 1955 Cover: 0.10 **NM** value: **60.00**
57 ❑ Dec 1955 Cover: 0.10 **NM** value: **60.00**
58 ❑ Jan 1956 Cover: 0.10 **NM** value: **60.00**
59 ❑ Feb 1956 Cover: 0.10 **NM** value: **60.00**
60 ❑ Mar 1956 Cover: 0.10 **NM** value: **60.00**
61 ❑ Apr 1956 Cover: 0.10 **NM** value: **60.00**
62 ❑ May 1956 Cover: 0.10 **NM** value: **60.00**
63 ❑ Jun 1956 Cover: 0.10 **NM** value: **60.00**
64 ❑ Jul 1956 Cover: 0.10 **NM** value: **60.00**
65 ❑ Sep 1956 Cover: 0.10 **NM** value: **60.00**
66 ❑ Nov 1956 Cover: 0.10 **NM** value: **60.00**
67 ❑ Jan 1957 Cover: 0.10 **NM** value: **60.00**
68 ❑ Mar 1957 Cover: 0.10 **NM** value: **60.00**

69 ❑ May 1957 Cover: 0.10 **NM** value: **60.00**
70 ❑ Jul 1957 Cover: 0.10 **NM** value: **55.00**
71 ❑ Sep 1957 Cover: 0.10 **NM** value: **55.00**
72 ❑ Nov 1957 Cover: 0.10 **NM** value: **55.00**
73 ❑ Jan 1958 Cover: 0.10 **NM** value: **55.00**
74 ❑ Mar 1958 Cover: 0.10 **NM** value: **55.00**
75 ❑ May 1958 Cover: 0.10 **NM** value: **55.00**
76 ❑ Jul 1958 Cover: 0.10 **NM** value: **55.00**
77 ❑ Sep 1958 Cover: 0.10 **NM** value: **55.00**
78 ❑ Nov 1958 Cover: 0.10 **NM** value: **55.00**
79 ❑ Jan 1959 Cover: 0.10 **NM** value: **55.00**
80 ❑ Mar 1959 Cover: 0.10 **NM** value: **55.00**
81 ❑ May 1959 Cover: 0.10 **NM** value: **55.00**
82 ❑ Jul 1959 Cover: 0.10 **NM** value: **55.00**
83 ❑ Sep 1959 Cover: 0.10 **NM** value: **55.00**
84 ❑ Nov 1959 Cover: 0.10 **NM** value: **55.00**
85 ❑ Jan 1960 Cover: 0.10 **NM** value: **55.00**
86 ❑ Mar 1960 Cover: 0.10 **NM** value: **55.00**
87 ❑ May 1960 Cover: 0.10 **NM** value: **55.00**
88 ❑ Jul 1960 Cover: 0.10 **NM** value: **55.00**
89 ❑ Sep 1960 Cover: 0.10 **NM** value: **55.00**
90 ❑ Nov 1960 Cover: 0.10 **NM** value: **50.00**
91 ❑ Jan 1961 Cover: 0.10 **NM** value: **50.00**
92 ❑ Mar 1961 Cover: 0.10 **NM** value: **50.00**
93 ❑ May 1961 Cover: 0.10 **NM** value: **50.00**
94 ❑ Jul 1961 Cover: 0.10 **NM** value: **50.00**
95 ❑ Sep 1961 Cover: 0.10 **NM** value: **50.00**
96 ❑ Nov 1961 Cover: 0.10 **NM** value: **50.00**
• **CGC:** 1 graded, best 7.5
97 ❑ Jan 1962 Cover: 0.12 **NM** value: **50.00**
📖 My Life is Yours; Little Girl; And So We Meet; The Kiss
98 ❑ Mar 1962 Cover: 0.12 **NM** value: **50.00**
📖 I'm Lost Without You; Second Best; My Kind of Man; Lover's Quarrel
99 ❑ May 1962 Cover: 0.12 **NM** value: **50.00**
📖 Teenager and the Truck Driver; In My Sister's Shadow; Fungirl; Don't Break My Heart
100 ❑ Jul 1962 Cover: 0.12 **NM** value: **50.00**
📖 My Life, My Love; The Dream of Doris Drake; I Dare Not Love You; Two Loves Had Helen
101 ❑ Sep 1962 Cover: 0.12 **NM** value: **50.00**
102 ❑ Nov 1962 Cover: 0.12 **NM** value: **50.00**
103 ❑ Jan 1963 Cover: 0.12 **NM** value: **50.00**
• **CGC:** 1 graded, best 7.0
104 ❑ Mar 1963 Cover: 0.12 **NM** value: **50.00**
105 ❑ May 1963 Cover: 0.12 **NM** value: **50.00**
• **CGC:** 1 graded, best 7.0
106 ❑ Jul 1963 Cover: 0.12 **NM** value: **50.00**

LOVERS **Marvel**

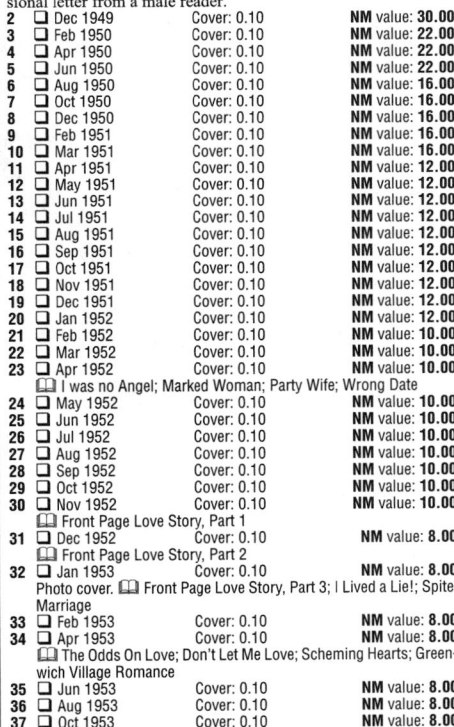

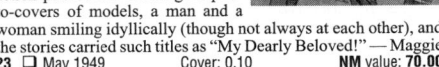

Remember The Blonde Phantom? She was one of those Golden Age costumed characters it's so much fun to trot out when describing over-the-top Golden Age crime-fighters: When she prepared to confront the forces of evil, she'd pause to put on a floor-length gown (slit at the knee to display shapely legs) and domino mask before venturing out. She seemed to be doing well enough in #22 , but in the spring of 1949, wham! Her series' title was changed to Lovers (subtitled "True-to-life stories"), and the covers went from action-packed line drawings to photo-covers of models, a man and a woman smiling idyllically (though not always at each other), and the stories carried such titles as "My Dearly Beloved!" — Maggie

23 ❑ May 1949 Cover: 0.10 **NM** value: **70.00**
• Continued from Blonde Phantom #22
24 ❑ Sep 1949 Cover: 0.10 **NM** value: **40.00**
25 ❑ Dec 1949 Cover: 0.10 **NM** value: **40.00**
26 ❑ Feb 1950 Cover: 0.10 **NM** value: **30.00**
27 ❑ Apr 1950 Cover: 0.10 **NM** value: **30.00**
28 ❑ Jun 1950 Cover: 0.10 **NM** value: **30.00**
29 ❑ Aug 1950 Cover: 0.10 **NM** value: **30.00**
30 ❑ Oct 1950 Cover: 0.10 **NM** value: **30.00**
31 ❑ Dec 1950 Cover: 0.10 **NM** value: **30.00**
32 ❑ Feb 1951 Cover: 0.10 **NM** value: **30.00**
33 ❑ Apr 1951 Cover: 0.10 **NM** value: **30.00**
34 ❑ Jun 1951 Cover: 0.10 **NM** value: **30.00**
35 ❑ Aug 1951 Cover: 0.10 **NM** value: **30.00**
36 ❑ Oct 1951 Cover: 0.10 **NM** value: **30.00**
37 ❑ Dec 1951 Cover: 0.10 **NM** value: **30.00**
38 ❑ Feb 1952 Cover: 0.10 **NM** value: **30.00**
39 ❑ Apr 1952 Cover: 0.10 **NM** value: **30.00**
40 ❑ Jun 1952 Cover: 0.10 **NM** value: **30.00**
41 ❑ Aug 1952 Cover: 0.10 **NM** value: **24.00**
42 ❑ Oct 1952 Cover: 0.10 **NM** value: **24.00**
43 ❑ Dec 1952 Cover: 0.10 **NM** value: **24.00**
44 ❑ Feb 1953 Cover: 0.10 **NM** value: **24.00**
45 ❑ Apr 1953 Cover: 0.10 **NM** value: **24.00**
46 ❑ Jun 1953 Cover: 0.10 **NM** value: **24.00**
47 ❑ Jul 1953 Cover: 0.10 **NM** value: **24.00**
48 ❑ Aug 1953 Cover: 0.10 **NM** value: **24.00**
49 ❑ Sep 1953 Cover: 0.10 **NM** value: **24.00**
50 ❑ Oct 1953 Cover: 0.10 **NM** value: **24.00**
51 ❑ Nov 1953 Cover: 0.10 **NM** value: **24.00**
52 ❑ Dec 1953 Cover: 0.10 **NM** value: **24.00**
53 ❑ Jan 1954 Cover: 0.10 **NM** value: **24.00**
54 ❑ Feb 1954 Cover: 0.10 **NM** value: **24.00**
55 ❑ Mar 1954 Cover: 0.10 **NM** value: **24.00**
56 ❑ Apr 1954 Cover: 0.10 **NM** value: **24.00**
57 ❑ May 1954 Cover: 0.10 **NM** value: **24.00**
58 ❑ Jun 1954 Cover: 0.10 **NM** value: **24.00**
59 ❑ Jul 1954 Cover: 0.10 **NM** value: **24.00**
60 ❑ Aug 1954 Cover: 0.10 **NM** value: **24.00**
61 ❑ Sep 1954 Cover: 0.10 **NM** value: **20.00**
62 ❑ Oct 1954 Cover: 0.10 **NM** value: **20.00**
63 ❑ Nov 1954 Cover: 0.10 **NM** value: **20.00**
64 ❑ Dec 1954 Cover: 0.10 **NM** value: **20.00**
65 ❑ Jan 1955 Cover: 0.10 **NM** value: **20.00**
66 ❑ Feb 1955 Cover: 0.10 **NM** value: **20.00**
67 ❑ Mar 1955 Cover: 0.10 **NM** value: **20.00**
📖 I Do...; Big Man on Campus! **A:** Jay Scott Piza
68 ❑ 1955 Cover: 0.10 **NM** value: **20.00**
69 ❑ 1955 Cover: 0.10 **NM** value: **20.00**
70 ❑ 1955 Cover: 0.10 **NM** value: **20.00**
71 ❑ 1955 Cover: 0.10 **NM** value: **18.00**
72 ❑ 1955 Cover: 0.10 **NM** value: **18.00**
73 ❑ 1955 Cover: 0.10 **NM** value: **18.00**
74 ❑ 1955 Cover: 0.10 **NM** value: **18.00**
75 ❑ Cover: 0.10 **NM** value: **18.00**
76 ❑ Cover: 0.10 **NM** value: **18.00**
77 ❑ Cover: 0.10 **NM** value: **18.00**
78 ❑ 1956 Cover: 0.10 **NM** value: **18.00**
79 ❑ 1956 Cover: 0.10 **NM** value: **18.00**
80 ❑ 1956 Cover: 0.10 **NM** value: **18.00**
81 ❑ 1956 Cover: 0.10 **NM** value: **18.00**
82 ❑ 1956 Cover: 0.10 **NM** value: **18.00**
83 ❑ Cover: 0.10 **NM** value: **18.00**
84 ❑ 1957 Cover: 0.10 **NM** value: **18.00**
85 ❑ 1957 Cover: 0.10 **NM** value: **18.00**
86 ❑ 1957 Cover: 0.10 **NM** value: **18.00**
• Final issue?

LOVERS' LANE **Lev Gleason**

Lovers' Lane was a rarity: a romance comic book with enough action and adventure to attract and keep a male audience. Lev Gleason, the publisher, borrowed heavily from the formula behind his successful Crime Must Pay the Penalty in order to make this series work.

Begun in 1949 and running until the coming of the Comics Code Authority in 1954, Lovers' Lane was full of desperate women, deceit, treachery, crime, and violence. This was a heady mix for the relatively tame world of romance comics, and it gave Lovers' Lane a definite edge. It also was innovative in its occasional use of longer, multi-issue storylines wherein the romance was part of a larger adventure or crime saga. Of course, it also carried the obligatory advice column ("Eloise Taylor Answers Your Love Problems"), which even indicated receipt of an occasional letter from a male reader.

2 ❑ Dec 1949 Cover: 0.10 **NM** value: **30.00**
3 ❑ Feb 1950 Cover: 0.10 **NM** value: **22.00**
4 ❑ Apr 1950 Cover: 0.10 **NM** value: **22.00**
5 ❑ Jun 1950 Cover: 0.10 **NM** value: **22.00**
6 ❑ Aug 1950 Cover: 0.10 **NM** value: **16.00**
7 ❑ Oct 1950 Cover: 0.10 **NM** value: **16.00**
8 ❑ Dec 1950 Cover: 0.10 **NM** value: **16.00**
9 ❑ Feb 1951 Cover: 0.10 **NM** value: **16.00**
10 ❑ Mar 1951 Cover: 0.10 **NM** value: **16.00**
11 ❑ Apr 1951 Cover: 0.10 **NM** value: **12.00**
12 ❑ May 1951 Cover: 0.10 **NM** value: **12.00**
13 ❑ Jun 1951 Cover: 0.10 **NM** value: **12.00**
14 ❑ Jul 1951 Cover: 0.10 **NM** value: **12.00**
15 ❑ Aug 1951 Cover: 0.10 **NM** value: **12.00**
16 ❑ Sep 1951 Cover: 0.10 **NM** value: **12.00**
17 ❑ Oct 1951 Cover: 0.10 **NM** value: **12.00**
18 ❑ Nov 1951 Cover: 0.10 **NM** value: **12.00**
19 ❑ Dec 1951 Cover: 0.10 **NM** value: **12.00**
20 ❑ Jan 1952 Cover: 0.10 **NM** value: **12.00**
21 ❑ Feb 1952 Cover: 0.10 **NM** value: **10.00**
22 ❑ Mar 1952 Cover: 0.10 **NM** value: **10.00**
23 ❑ Apr 1952 Cover: 0.10 **NM** value: **10.00**
📖 I was no Angel; Marked Woman; Party Wife; Wrong Date
24 ❑ May 1952 Cover: 0.10 **NM** value: **10.00**
25 ❑ Jun 1952 Cover: 0.10 **NM** value: **10.00**
26 ❑ Jul 1952 Cover: 0.10 **NM** value: **10.00**
27 ❑ Aug 1952 Cover: 0.10 **NM** value: **10.00**
28 ❑ Sep 1952 Cover: 0.10 **NM** value: **10.00**
29 ❑ Oct 1952 Cover: 0.10 **NM** value: **10.00**
30 ❑ Nov 1952 Cover: 0.10 **NM** value: **10.00**
📖 Front Page Love Story, Part 1
31 ❑ Dec 1952 Cover: 0.10 **NM** value: **8.00**
📖 Front Page Love Story, Part 2
32 ❑ Jan 1953 Cover: 0.10 **NM** value: **8.00**
Photo cover. 📖 Front Page Love Story, Part 3; I Lived a Lie!; Spite Marriage
33 ❑ Feb 1953 Cover: 0.10 **NM** value: **8.00**
34 ❑ Apr 1953 Cover: 0.10 **NM** value: **8.00**
📖 The Odds On Love; Don't Let Me Love; Scheming Hearts; Greenwich Village Romance
35 ❑ Jun 1953 Cover: 0.10 **NM** value: **8.00**
36 ❑ Aug 1953 Cover: 0.10 **NM** value: **8.00**
37 ❑ Oct 1953 Cover: 0.10 **NM** value: **8.00**
38 ❑ Dec 1953 Cover: 0.10 **NM** value: **8.00**
39 ❑ Feb 1954 Cover: 0.10 **NM** value: **8.00**
40 ❑ Apr 1954 Cover: 0.10 **NM** value: **8.00**
41 ❑ Jun 1954 Cover: 0.10 **NM** value: **8.00**
final issue.

LOVE SCANDALS **Quality**

1 ❑ Feb 1950 Cover: 0.10 **NM** value: **175.00**
2 ❑ Apr 1950 Cover: 0.10 **NM** value: **100.00**
3 ❑ Jun 1950 Cover: 0.10 **NM** value: **100.00**
4 ❑ Aug 1950 Cover: 0.10 **NM** value: **100.00**
5 ❑ Oct 1950 Cover: 0.10 **NM** value: **100.00**

LOVE SECRETS (MARVEL) **Marvel**

1 ❑ ca. 1949 Cover: 0.10 **NM** value: **75.00**
2 ❑ ca. 1950 Cover: 0.10 **NM** value: **50.00**

LOVE SECRETS (QUALITY) **Quality**

32 ❑ Aug 1953 Cover: 0.10 **NM** value: **12.00**
33 ❑ Oct 1953 Cover: 0.10 **NM** value: **12.00**
34 ❑ Nov 1953 Cover: 0.10 **NM** value: **12.00**
35 ❑ Dec 1953 Cover: 0.10 **NM** value: **12.00**
36 ❑ Feb 1954 Cover: 0.10 **NM** value: **12.00**
37 ❑ Apr 1954 Cover: 0.10 **NM** value: **12.00**
38 ❑ Jun 1954 Cover: 0.10 **NM** value: **12.00**
📖 How I Got My Man; I Wanted His Arms Around Me; What Is Love; My Heavy Date
39 ❑ Aug 1954 Cover: 0.10 **NM** value: **12.00**
40 ❑ Oct 1954 Cover: 0.10 **NM** value: **12.00**
41 ❑ Dec 1954 Cover: 0.10 **NM** value: **12.00**
42 ❑ Feb 1955 Cover: 0.10 **NM** value: **12.00**
43 ❑ Apr 1955 Cover: 0.10 **NM** value: **12.00**
44 ❑ Jun 1955 Cover: 0.10 **NM** value: **12.00**
45 ❑ Aug 1955 Cover: 0.10 **NM** value: **12.00**
46 ❑ Oct 1955 Cover: 0.10 **NM** value: **12.00**
47 ❑ Nov 1956 Cover: 0.10 **NM** value: **12.00**
48 ❑ 1956 Cover: 0.10 **NM** value: **12.00**

LOVE SONG **Viz**

Bk 1 ❑ Dec 1997, b&w Cover: 15.95 **NM** value: **Cover or less**

LOVE STORIES OF MARY WORTH **Harvey**

1 ❑ Sep 1949 Cover: 0.10 **NM** value: **40.00**
2 ❑ Nov 1949 Cover: 0.10 **NM** value: **25.00**
3 ❑ Jan 1950 Cover: 0.10 **NM** value: **25.00**
• **CGC:** 1 graded, best 8.5
4 ❑ Mar 1950 Cover: 0.10 **NM** value: **25.00**
5 ❑ May 1950 Cover: 0.10 **NM** value: **25.00**
• **CGC:** 1 graded, best 8.0

LOVE SUCKS **Ace**

Created by Kevin Hayes and Jay Juch, and published by Ace Comics, Love Sucks centers its self-contained, black-and-white stories around Nelson, Adrian, and Wendy, three single friends and their relationship woes in New York City.

Each character represents a facet of American dating. Nelson is sensitive and dependent, just coming out of a serious relationship and feeling he will never embrace that love again. Adrian is the self-proclaimed ladies' man, cocky and brash-he has no trouble meeting the women-it's the part after that scares him to death. The beautiful Wendy can't get a break: every guy who looks like a dream ends up a nightmare.

Funny anecdotes and witty narratives, like how Nelson earned the name "Submarine Boy" in a drunken bar scene, or how Adrian was beaten up by his lover's girlfriend, adds to the realism.

1 ❑ Cover: 2.95 **NM** value: **Cover or less**

LOVE TALES **Marvel**

36 ❑ May 1949 Cover: 0.10 **NM** value: **75.00**
37 ❑ 1949 Cover: 0.10 **NM** value: **50.00**
38 ❑ 1949 Cover: 0.10 **NM** value: **40.00**
39 ❑ Dec 1949 Cover: 0.10 **NM** value: **40.00**
40 ❑ 1950 Cover: 0.10 **NM** value: **40.00**
41 ❑ May 1950 Cover: 0.10 **NM** value: **40.00**
42 ❑ 1950 Cover: 0.10 **NM** value: **40.00**
43 ❑ 1950 Cover: 0.10 **NM** value: **40.00**
44 ❑ 1950 Cover: 0.10 **NM** value: **40.00**
45 ❑ Mar 1951 Cover: 0.10 **NM** value: **40.00**
46 ❑ 1951 Cover: 0.10 **NM** value: **40.00**
47 ❑ 1951 Cover: 0.10 **NM** value: **40.00**
48 ❑ 1951 Cover: 0.10 **NM** value: **40.00**
49 ❑ 1951 Cover: 0.10 **NM** value: **40.00**
50 ❑ Cover: 0.10 **NM** value: **40.00**
51 ❑ Cover: 0.10 **NM** value: **35.00**
52 ❑ Cover: 0.10 **NM** value: **35.00**
53 ❑ 1952 Cover: 0.10 **NM** value: **35.00**
54 ❑ 1952 Cover: 0.10 **NM** value: **35.00**
55 ❑ 1952 Cover: 0.10 **NM** value: **35.00**
56 ❑ Jun 1952 Cover: 0.10 **NM** value: **35.00**
57 ❑ Jul 1952 Cover: 0.10 **NM** value: **35.00**
58 ❑ Aug 1952 Cover: 0.10 **NM** value: **35.00**
59 ❑ ca. 1954 Cover: 0.10 **NM** value: **35.00**
60 ❑ ca. 1955 Cover: 0.10 **NM** value: **35.00**
61 ❑ 1955 Cover: 0.10 **NM** value: **30.00**
62 ❑ 1955 Cover: 0.10 **NM** value: **30.00**
63 ❑ 1955 Cover: 0.10 **NM** value: **30.00**
64 ❑ 1955 Cover: 0.10 **NM** value: **30.00**
65 ❑ Cover: 0.10 **NM** value: **30.00**
66 ❑ 1956 Cover: 0.10 **NM** value: **30.00**
67 ❑ 1956 Cover: 0.10 **NM** value: **30.00**
68 ❑ 1956 Cover: 0.10 **NM** value: **30.00**
69 ❑ 1956 Cover: 0.10 **NM** value: **30.00**
70 ❑ 1956 Cover: 0.10 **NM** value: **30.00**
71 ❑ 1957 Cover: 0.10 **NM** value: **25.00**
72 ❑ 1957 Cover: 0.10 **NM** value: **25.00**
73 ❑ 1957 Cover: 0.10 **NM** value: **25.00**
74 ❑ 1957 Cover: 0.10 **NM** value: **25.00**
75 ❑ 1957 Cover: 0.10 **NM** value: **25.00**

LOVE TRAILS **Marvel**

1 ❑ Dec 1949 Cover: 0.10 **NM** value: **75.00**
2 ❑ Cover: 0.10 **NM** value: **75.00**

CGC-graded: Multiply prices above by **33 for 9.9 M • 16 for 9.8 NM/M • 7 for 9.6 NM+ • 5 for 9.4 NM • 2.5 for 9.2 NM- • 1.5 for 9.0 VF/NM**

LOWLIFE — Caliber

1 ❑ b&w Cover: 2.50 **NM** value: **Cover or less**
2 ❑ b&w Cover: 2.50 **NM** value: **Cover or less**
3 ❑ b&w Cover: 2.50 **NM** value: **Cover or less**
4 ❑ Feb 1994, b&w Cover: 2.50 **NM** value: **Cover or less**

L.T. CAPER — Spotlight

1 ❑ Cover: 1.75 **NM** value: **Cover or less**
The Phoenix Caper **A:** Rich Maurizio **W:** Rich Maurizio

LUBA — Fantagraphics

1 ❑ Feb 1998 Cover: 2.95 **NM** value: **Cover or less**
Circ: Diamd. preorders: **6,222**
Luba in America; The Sisters, the Cousins, and the Kids; The Old Man Sets Up; F*ckin' Steve!; El Show Super Duper Sensacional de Doralis; That Family Thing Again **A:** Gilbert Hernandez **W:** Gilbert Hernandez
2 ❑ Jul 1998 Cover: 2.95 **NM** value: **Cover or less**
Circ: Diamd. preorders: **5,034**
A: Gilbert Hernandez **W:** Gilbert Hernandez
3 ❑ Dec 1998 Cover: 2.95 **NM** value: **Cover or less**
Circ: Diamd. preorders: **4,393**
A: Gilbert Hernandez **W:** Gilbert Hernandez

LUCIFER'S HAMMER — Innovation

1 ❑ Nov 1993 Cover: 2.50 **NM** value: **Cover or less**
Circ: CapCity orders: **5,410**
The Anvil **A:** Roger Vilela **W:** Terry Collins
2 ❑ Cover: 2.50 **NM** value: **Cover or less**
Circ: CapCity orders: **3,465**
Hammer Fever **A:** Roger Vilela **W:** Terry Collins
3 ❑ Cover: 2.50 **NM** value: **Cover or less**
Circ: CapCity orders: **3,070**
W: Terry Collins
4 ❑ Cover: 2.50 **NM** value: **Cover or less**
Circ: CapCity orders: **2,670**
W: Terry Collins
5 ❑ Cover: 2.50 **NM** value: **Cover or less**
Circ: CapCity orders: **2,290**
W: Terry Collins
6 ❑ Cover: 2.50 **NM** value: **Cover or less**
W: Terry Collins

LUCIFER (TRIDENT) — Trident

1 ❑ b&w Cover: 1.95 **NM** value: **Cover or less**
2 ❑ b&w Cover: 1.95 **NM** value: **Cover or less**
3 ❑ b&w Cover: 1.95 **NM** value: **Cover or less**

LUCIFER (VERTIGO) — DC / Vertigo

One of the most intriguing characters introduced by Neil Gaiman in his landmark Sandman series was Lucifer — the most beautiful of all the angels, the Morningstar and the Prince of Hell. He gave up his wings and his God-given powers and walked away from the Underworld. Now, he owns an exclusive nightclub in Los Angeles.

In this ongoing series from writer Mike Carey (Petrefax), Lucifer is ready to get back into the game of being bad and divine. And so begins the pursuit of both his wings and his powers; however, not everyone wants Lucifer to return to his former state of being. And therein lies the conflict at the heart of this series. Carey leads the Morningstar to such exotic locales as the House of Windowless rooms, where he encounters Izanami, the Queen of Death who's looking to take out the anti-hero.

While it's hard to equal Sandman, Carey proves that he's more than capable of playing in Gaiman's sandbox. This series is a worthy successor to Gaiman's seminal work.

1 ❑ Jun 2000 Cover: 2.50 **NM** value: **3.00**
Circ: Diamd. preorders: **23,401** • **CGC:** 3 graded, best 9.8
A Six-Card Spread **A:** Chris Weston **W:** Mike Carey
2 ❑ Jul 2000 Cover: 2.50 **NM** value: **Cover or less**
Circ: Diamd. preorders: **19,666**
W: Mike Carey
3 ❑ Aug 2000 Cover: 2.50 **NM** value: **Cover or less**
Circ: Diamd. preorders: **20,029**
W: Mike Carey
4 ❑ Sep 2000 Cover: 2.50 **NM** value: **Cover or less**
Circ: Diamd. preorders: **19,540**
W: Mike Carey
5 ❑ Oct 2000 Cover: 2.50 **NM** value: **Cover or less**
Circ: Diamd. preorders: **18,211**
The House of Windowless Rooms, Part 1 **A:** Peter Gross **W:** Mike Carey
6 ❑ Nov 2000 Cover: 2.50 **NM** value: **Cover or less**
Circ: Diamd. preorders: **17,901**
The House of Windowless Rooms, Part 2 **A:** Peter Gross **W:** Mike Carey
7 ❑ Dec 2000 Cover: 2.50 **NM** value: **Cover or less**
Circ: Diamd. preorders: **17,851**
The House of Windowless Rooms, Part 3 **A:** Peter Gross **W:** Mike Carey
8 ❑ Jan 2001 Cover: 2.50 **NM** value: **Cover or less**
Circ: Diamd. preorders: **17,226**
The House of Windowless Rooms, Part 4 **A:** Peter Gross; Ryan Kelly **W:** Mike Carey
9 ❑ Feb 2001 Cover: 2.50 **NM** value: **Cover or less**
Circ: Diamd. preorders: **16,796**
Children and Monsters **A:** Dean Ormston **W:** Mike Carey
10 ❑ Mar 2001 Cover: 2.50 **NM** value: **Cover or less**
Circ: Diamd. preorders: **16,291**
Children and Monsters, Part 1 **A:** Peter Gross; Ryan Kelly **W:** Mike Carey
11 ❑ Apr 2001 Cover: 2.50 **NM** value: **Cover or less**
Circ: Diamd. preorders: **16,090**
Children and Monsters, Part 2 **A:** Peter Gross; Ryan Kelly **W:** Mike Carey
12 ❑ May 2001 Cover: 2.50 **NM** value: **Cover or less**
Circ: Diamd. preorders: **15,601**
Children and Monsters, Part 3 **A:** Peter Gross; Ryan Kelly **W:** Mike Carey
13 ❑ Jun 2001 Cover: 2.50 **NM** value: **Cover or less**
Circ: Diamd. preorders: **15,674**
Children and Monsters, Part 4 **A:** Peter Gross; Ryan Kelly **W:** Mike Carey
14 ❑ Jul 2001 Cover: 2.50 **NM** value: **Cover or less**
Circ: Diamd. preorders: **15,439**
15 ❑ Aug 2001 Cover: 2.50 **NM** value: **Cover or less**
Circ: Diamd. preorders: **15,608**
16 ❑ Sep 2001 Cover: 2.50 **NM** value: **Cover or less**
Circ: Diamd. preorders: **16,541**

LUCK OF THE DRAW — Radio Comix

All issues are adults only.

1 ❑ Jun 2000, b&w Cover: 3.95 **NM** value: **Cover or less**

LUCKY 7 — Runaway Graphics

1 ❑ Apr 1993 Cover: 1.95 **NM** value: **Cover or less**
Martyrs & Mayhem **A:** Ben Alvarez; Roland Paris **W:** Ben Alvarez; Frank Matijevich; Vernon Firestone

LUCKY COMICS — Holyoke

1 ❑ Jan 1944 Cover: 0.10 **NM** value: **150.00**
2 ❑ Sum 1945 Cover: 0.10 **NM** value: **75.00**
3 ❑ Win 1945 Cover: 0.10 **NM** value: **75.00**
4 ❑ May 1946 Cover: 0.10 **NM** value: **75.00**
5 ❑ Aug 1946 Cover: 0.10 **NM** value: **75.00**
• **CGC:** 2 graded, best 8.5

LUCKY DUCK — Standard

5 ❑ ca. 1953 Cover: 0.10 **NM** value: **75.00**
6 ❑ ca. 1953 Cover: 0.10 **NM** value: **50.00**
7 ❑ ca. 1953 Cover: 0.10 **NM** value: **50.00**
8 ❑ ca. 1953 Cover: 0.10 **NM** value: **50.00**

LUCKY FIGHTS IT THROUGH — E.C.

1 ❑ ca. 1949 **NM** value: **750.00**
• **CGC:** 1 graded, best 8.0

LUCKY LUKE: JESSE JAMES — Fantasy Flight

1 ❑ Cover: 8.95 **NM** value: **Cover or less**

LUCKY LUKE: THE STAGE COACH — Fantasy Flight

1 ❑ Cover: 8.95 **NM** value: **Cover or less**

LUCKY "7" — Howard

1 ❑ ca. 1945 Cover: 0.10 **NM** value: **300.00**
• **CGC:** 1 graded, best 7.0

LUCKY STAR — Nationwide

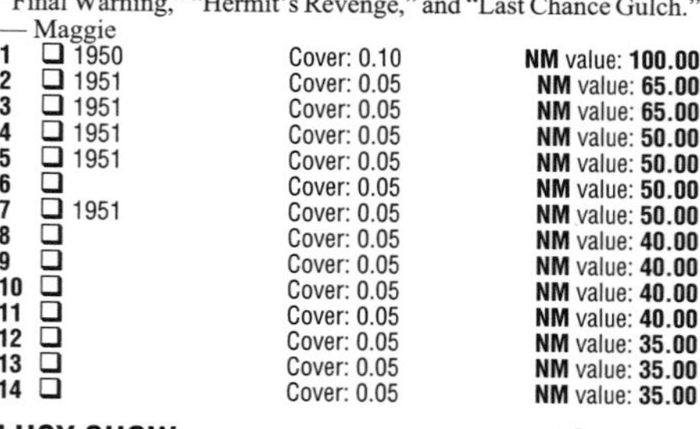

The Lucky Star Western comic book was published by Chicago's Nation-Wide company in the early 1950s. Although it contained the usual 52 pages, all but the first issue were priced at only 5 cents. That's a price that's seldom seen in the comic-book world, though the first actually carried the price in its title: Nickel Comics. (Two years later, Fawcett tried its own series under the same name; it lasted for eight issues before folding, and a short-lived line of 5-cent titles actually had their own display rack in the 1950s.)

Covers display Lucky astride his horse and waving a lasso (often terrorizing Indians while doing so), and issues feature such story titles as "The Lost Treasure," "Final Warning," "Hermit's Revenge," and "Last Chance Gulch." — Maggie

1 ❑ 1950 Cover: 0.10 **NM** value: **100.00**
2 ❑ 1951 Cover: 0.05 **NM** value: **65.00**
3 ❑ 1951 Cover: 0.05 **NM** value: **65.00**
4 ❑ 1951 Cover: 0.05 **NM** value: **50.00**
5 ❑ 1951 Cover: 0.05 **NM** value: **50.00**
6 ❑ Cover: 0.05 **NM** value: **50.00**
7 ❑ 1951 Cover: 0.05 **NM** value: **50.00**
8 ❑ Cover: 0.05 **NM** value: **40.00**
9 ❑ Cover: 0.05 **NM** value: **40.00**
10 ❑ Cover: 0.05 **NM** value: **40.00**
11 ❑ Cover: 0.05 **NM** value: **40.00**
12 ❑ Cover: 0.05 **NM** value: **35.00**
13 ❑ Cover: 0.05 **NM** value: **35.00**
14 ❑ Cover: 0.05 **NM** value: **35.00**

LUCY SHOW — Gold Key

1 ❑ Jun 1963 Cover: 0.12 **NM** value: **100.00**
• **CGC:** 1 graded, best 3.5
2 ❑ Sep 1963 Cover: 0.12 **NM** value: **75.00**
3 ❑ Dec 1963 Cover: 0.12 **NM** value: **50.00**
• **CGC:** 1 graded, best 4.0
4 ❑ Mar 1964 Cover: 0.12 **NM** value: **50.00**
5 ❑ Jun 1964 Cover: 0.12 **NM** value: **50.00**

LUDWIG VON DRAKE (WALT DISNEY'S...) — Dell

1 ❑ Nov 1961 Cover: 0.10 **NM** value: **2.00**
• **CGC:** 3 graded, best 8.0
2 ❑ Jan 1962 Cover: 0.10 **NM** value: **12.00**
• **CGC:** 1 graded, best 7.0
3 ❑ Mar 1962 Cover: 0.10 **NM** value: **12.00**
• **CGC:** 1 graded, best 6.5
4 ❑ Jun 1962 Cover: 0.10 **NM** value: **12.00**
• **CGC:** 1 graded, best 7.0

LUFTWAFFE: 1946 TECHNICAL MANUAL — Antarctic

1 ❑ Feb 1998 Cover: 3.95 **NM** value: **4.00**
Circ: Diamd. preorders: **3,547**
• Projekt Saucer **A:** Ben Dunn; Ted Nomura **W:** Ted Nomura
2 ❑ Apr 1999 Cover: 3.99 **NM** value: **4.00**
Circ: Diamd. preorders: **3,323**
• Hitler's Kamikazes **A:** Ben Dunn; Ted Nomura **W:** Ted Nomura

LUFTWAFFE: 1946 (VOL. 1) — Antarctic

This four-issue mini-series is set in the same alternate universe occupied by the Tigers of Terra. Here, the Axis powers were the victors in World War II, and the Nazis have created a dazzling variety of aircraft which helped pave the way for their victory. Creator Ted Nomura was a longtime fan of World War II stories but, as a Japanese-American, he had a hard time relating to the parade of war stories in which the Japanese were the "bad guys." He thus turned to science-fiction to create a reality full of neat planes (expertly drawn by Nomura and Ben Dunn), but piloted by members of "the other side."

1 ❑ Jul 1996, b&w Cover: 2.95 **NM** value: **5.00**
Fires of Faith **A:** Ben Dunn; Ted Nomura **W:** Ted Nomura
2 ❑ Sep 1996, b&w Cover: 2.95 **NM** value: **4.00**
Circ: Diamd. preorders: **4,466**
Clash of the Neptunes **A:** Ben Dunn; Ted Nomura **W:** Ted Nomura
3 ❑ Nov 1996, b&w Cover: 2.95 **NM** value: **4.00**
Circ: Diamd. preorders: **5,015**
Conquest of Space **A:** Ben Dunn; Ted Nomura **W:** Ted Nomura
4 ❑ Jan 1997, b&w Cover: 2.95 **NM** value: **4.00**
Circ: Diamd. preorders: **4,709**
Victory or Death final issue. **A:** Ben Dunn; Ted Nomura **W:** Ted Nomura
Anl 1 ❑ Apr 1998, b&w Cover: 2.95 **NM** value: **4.00**
Bk 1 ❑ Jun 1997 Cover: 10.95 **NM** value: **Cover or less**
Victory or Death **A:** Ben Dunn; Ted Nomura **W:** Ted Nomura

LUFTWAFFE: 1946 (VOL. 2) — Antarctic

1 ❑ Mar 1997 Cover: 2.95 **NM** value: **4.00**
Luftsturm, Part 1 **A:** Ben Dunn; Ted Nomura **W:** Ted Nomura
2 ❑ Apr 1997 Cover: 2.95 **NM** value: **3.50**
Circ: Diamd. preorders: **5,168**
Luftsturm, Part 2 • contains indicia for issue #1 **A:** Ben Dunn; Ted Nomura **W:** Ted Nomura
3 ❑ May 1997 Cover: 2.95 **NM** value: **3.50**
Circ: Diamd. preorders: **5,283**
Luftsturm, Part 3 **A:** Ben Dunn; Ted Nomura **W:** Ted Nomura
4 ❑ Jul 1997 Cover: 2.95 **NM** value: **3.50**
Circ: Diamd. preorders: **4,743**
Luftsturm, Part 4 **A:** Ben Dunn; Ted Nomura **W:** Ted Nomura
5 ❑ Aug 1997 Cover: 2.95 **NM** value: **3.00**
Circ: Diamd. preorders: **4,768**
Luftsturm, Part 5 **A:** Ben Dunn; Ted Nomura **W:** Ted Nomura
6 ❑ Oct 1997 Cover: 2.95 **NM** value: **3.00**
Circ: Diamd. preorders: **4,693**
Projekt Saucer, Part 1 **A:** Ben Dunn; Ted Nomura **W:** Ted Nomura
7 ❑ Nov 1997 Cover: 2.95 **NM** value: **3.00**
Circ: Diamd. preorders: **4,867**
Projekt Saucer, Part 2 **A:** Ben Dunn; Ted Nomura **W:** Ted Nomura
8 ❑ Feb 1998 Cover: 2.95 **NM** value: **3.00**
Circ: Diamd. preorders: **4,721**
• 50th "Families of Altered Wars" issue **A:** Ben Dunn; Ted Nomura **W:** Ted Nomura
9 ❑ Apr 1998 Cover: 2.95 **NM** value: **3.00**
Circ: Diamd. preorders: **4,787**
Projekt Saucer, Part 3 **A:** Ben Dunn; Ted Nomura **W:** Ted Nomura
10 ❑ May 1998 Cover: 2.95 **NM** value: **3.00**
Circ: Diamd. preorders: **4,722**
Projekt Saucer, Part 4 **A:** Ben Dunn; Ted Nomura **W:** Ted Nomura
11 ❑ Jun 1998 Cover: 2.95 **NM** value: **3.00**
Circ: Diamd. preorders: **4,683**
Projekt Saucer, Part 5 **A:** Ben Dunn; Ted Nomura **W:** Ted Nomura
12 ❑ Jul 1998 Cover: 2.95 **NM** value: **3.00**
Circ: Diamd. preorders: **4,418**
Projekt Saucer, Part 6 **A:** Ben Dunn; Ted Nomura **W:** Ted Nomura
13 ❑ Aug 1998 Cover: 2.95 **NM** value: **3.00**
Circ: Diamd. preorders: **4,273**
Jagdgeschwader, Part 1 **A:** Ben Dunn; Ted Nomura **W:** Ted Nomura
14 ❑ Oct 1998 Cover: 2.95 **NM** value: **3.00**
Circ: Diamd. preorders: **4,076**
Jagdgeschwader, Part 2 **A:** Ben Dunn; Ted Nomura **W:** Ted Nomura
15 ❑ Feb 1999 Cover: 2.99 **NM** value: **3.00**
Circ: Diamd. preorders: **3,851**
Jagdgeschwader, Part 3 **A:** Ben Dunn; Ted Nomura **W:** Ted Nomura
16 ❑ Mar 1999 Cover: 2.99 **NM** value: **3.00**
Circ: Diamd. preorders: **3,735**
Jagdgeschwader, Part 4 **A:** Ben Dunn; Ted Nomura **W:** Ted Nomura

Other grades: Multiply prices above by **1.5 for Mint • 2/3 for Very Fine • 1/3 for Fine • 1/5 for Very Good • 1/8 for Good**

Anl 1❑ca. 1998 Cover: 2.95 **NM** value: **3.00**
Circ: Diamd. preorders: **3,656**
🕮 Airkid; Kid War; Wars Series; Comrade Birdboy; Sturmvogel; Hitler's Angels of Death; Eagles of the Iron Cross; Angels of the Luftwaffe; Panzerducks; Battle of the Lousewake; The Last Samurai • 1998 Annual **A:** Ben Dunn; Joseph Wight; Ted Nomura; C.E. Davis; Patricia Lynn McGullam **W:** Ted Nomura

Bk 2❑ Jan 1998 Cover: 10.95 **NM** value: **Cover or less**
🕮 Luftsturm • Collects Luftsturm #1-5 **A:** Ben Dunn; Joseph Wight; Ted Nomura; C.E. Davis; Patricia Lynn McGullam **W:** Ted Nomura

Bk 3❑ Dec 1998 Cover: 10.95 **NM** value: **Cover or less**
• Project Saucer; Collects Project Saucer #1-6 **A:** Ben Dunn; Joseph Wight; Ted Nomura; C.E. Davis; Patricia Lynn McGullam **W:** Ted Nomura

SE 1❑ Apr 1998 Cover: 2.95 **NM** value: **4.00**
🕮 Luftwaffe 1946, Eagles of the Sky • Color Special **A:** Ben Dunn; Ted Nomura **W:** Ted Nomura

SE 2❑ Feb 1997, b&w Cover: 2.95 **NM** value: **4.00**
One-shot. 🕮 Triebflƒgel; Triebflngel • Triebflƒgel Special; German rocketry; Triebflngel Special **A:** Ben Dunn; Ted Nomura **W:** Ted Nomura

LUGER — Eclipse

1 ❑ Oct 1986 Cover: 1.75 **NM** value: **2.00**
Circ: CapCity orders: **7,450**
A: Bo Hampton; Tom Yeates **W:** Bruce Jones

2 ❑ Dec 1986 Cover: 1.75 **NM** value: **2.00**
Circ: CapCity orders: **5,400**
A: Bo Hampton; Tom Yeates **W:** Bruce Jones

3 ❑ Feb 1987 Cover: 1.75 **NM** value: **2.00**
Circ: CapCity orders: **3,950**
A: Bo Hampton; Tom Yeates **W:** Bruce Jones

LUGH, LORD OF LIGHT — Flagship

1 ❑ Cover: 1.75 **NM** value: **Cover or less**
2 ❑ Jun 1987 Cover: 1.75 **NM** value: **Cover or less**
3 ❑ Cover: 1.75 **NM** value: **Cover or less**
4 ❑ Cover: 1.75 **NM** value: **Cover or less**

LUGO — Lost Boys

0.5 ❑ **NM** value: **1.00**
• Promotional edition. **A:** Giovanni Barberi Cavazos **W:** Carlos Garcia Campillo; Salvador Vazquez Mtz.

LUM URUSEI*YATSURA — Viz

Aliens land on Earth. To remain free, a random contestant will face off with the alien champion in their national sport: tag. Unfortunately, they chose Ataru Moroboshi, the unluckiest, most lecherous, lout in Japan. He agrees, when he sees the beautiful Lum, but finds out too late that she can fly. Astonishingly, he wins!

When Lum misinterprets his victory cry, she moves in as his fiancee and enforces his monogamy with her powerful electric zap. What's a guy to do?

This is the zaniest of Rumiko Takahashi's works. The whole series is full of puns that the translators do their best to make work in English. She has also written Ranma 1/2, Mermaid Forest, and Maison Ikkoku.

1 ❑ b&w Cover: 2.95 **NM** value: **4.00**
🕮 A Good Catch; Poor Little Devil • Japanese **A:** Rumiko Takahashi **W:** Rumiko Takahashi

2 ❑ b&w Cover: 2.95 **NM** value: **3.50**
• Japanese **A:** Rumiko Takahashi **W:** Rumiko Takahashi

3 ❑ b&w Cover: 2.95 **NM** value: **3.50**
• Japanese **A:** Rumiko Takahashi **W:** Rumiko Takahashi

4 ❑ b&w Cover: 2.95 **NM** value: **3.25**
• Japanese **A:** Rumiko Takahashi **W:** Rumiko Takahashi

5 ❑ Cover: 3.25 **NM** value: **Cover or less**
A: Rumiko Takahashi **W:** Rumiko Takahashi

6 ❑ Cover: 2.95 **NM** value: **3.25**
A: Rumiko Takahashi **W:** Rumiko Takahashi

7 ❑ Cover: 3.25 **NM** value: **Cover or less**
A: Rumiko Takahashi **W:** Rumiko Takahashi

8 ❑ Cover: 3.25 **NM** value: **Cover or less**

Bk 1❑ Cover: 19.95 **NM** value: **Cover or less**
• Perfect Collection

Bk 1-2❑b&w Cover: 14.95 **NM** value: **Cover or less**
• Trade Paperback.

Bk 1-3❑b&w Cover: 14.95 **NM** value: **Cover or less**
• Trade Paperback.

LUNAR DONUT — Lunar Donut

0 ❑ b&w Cover: 2.50 **NM** value: **Cover or less**
cardstock cover. • says (Honey-Glazed)

1 ❑ b&w Cover: 2.50 **NM** value: **Cover or less**
cover says (With Sprinkles). • Flip-book.

2 ❑ b&w Cover: 2.50 **NM** value: **Cover or less**
cover says (Cherry-Filled). • Flip-book.

3 ❑ b&w Cover: 2.50 **NM** value: **Cover or less**
cover says (Jelly-Filled). • Flip-book.

LUNATIC BINGE — Eternity

1 ❑ Cover: 1.95 **NM** value: **3.95**

2 ❑ Cover: 3.95 **NM** value: **Cover or less**
🕮 I Married Twins; Look at this Year's Horror Video; Sonny Boy; When Only A Right Shoe is Left; Saturday; The Alien Came; Acid Rain; Soul Sacrifice **A:** Evan Dorkin; Gary Fields; Brian Carrol; Cliff Mott; Madman; Stuart Meyer **W:** Evan Dorkin; Gary Fields; Brian Carrol; Cliff Mott; Madman; Stuart Meyer

LUNATIC FRINGE, THE — Innovation

1 ❑ Jul 1989 Cover: 1.75 **NM** value: **Cover or less**
Circ: CapCity orders: **5,225**
A: John Statema **W:** Scott Rockwell; David Lawrence ★ Origin of Lunatic Fringe.

2 ❑ Aug 1989 Cover: 1.75 **NM** value: **Cover or less**
Circ: CapCity orders: **2,625**
A: John Statema **W:** Scott Rockwell; David Lawrence

LUNATIK — Marvel

1 ❑ Dec 1995 Cover: 1.95 **NM** value: **Cover or less**
A: Duncan Rouleau **W:** Lovern Kindzierski ★ Origin of Lunatik II (alien). ★ 1st Appearance of Lunatik II (alien). ★ Death of Lunatik I.

2 ❑ Jan 1996 Cover: 1.95 **NM** value: **Cover or less**
A: Duncan Rouleau **W:** Lovern Kindzierski ★ Versus Avengers.

3 ❑ Feb 1996 Cover: 1.95 **NM** value: **Cover or less**
🕮 Fool's Errand final issue. **A:** Duncan Rouleau **W:** Lovern Kindzierski

LURID TALES — Fantagraphics / Eros

All issues are adults only.

1 ❑ b&w Cover: 2.95 **NM** value: **Cover or less**
Circ: Diamd. preorders: **4,979**

LUST — Fantagraphics / Eros

1 ❑ Apr 1997 Cover: 2.95 **NM** value: **Cover or less**
Circ: Diamd. preorders: **4,313**
A: Tenjiku Ronin **W:** Tenjiku Ronin

2 ❑ May 1997 Cover: 2.95 **NM** value: **Cover or less**
Circ: Diamd. preorders: **4,369**
A: Tenjiku Ronin **W:** Tenjiku Ronin

3 ❑ Jun 1997 Cover: 2.95 **NM** value: **Cover or less**
Circ: Diamd. preorders: **4,138**
A: Tenjiku Ronin **W:** Tenjiku Ronin

4 ❑ Jul 1997 Cover: 2.95 **NM** value: **Cover or less**
Circ: Diamd. preorders: **4,263**
A: Tenjiku Ronin **W:** Tenjiku Ronin

5 ❑ Aug 1997 Cover: 2.95 **NM** value: **Cover or less**
Circ: Diamd. preorders: **4,404**
A: Tenjiku Ronin **W:** Tenjiku Ronin

6 ❑ Sep 1997 Cover: 2.95 **NM** value: **Cover or less**
A: Tenjiku Ronin **W:** Tenjiku Ronin

LUST FOR LIFE — Slave Labor

1 ❑ Feb 1997, b&w Cover: 2.95 **NM** value: **Cover or less**
Circ: Diamd. preorders: **1,718**
🕮 Who Am I?; Episode 415; Hayes Mansion (text) **A:** Jeff Levine **W:** Jeff Levine

2 ❑ May 1997, b&w Cover: 2.95 **NM** value: **Cover or less**
A: Jeff Levine **W:** Jeff Levine

3 ❑ Aug 1997, b&w Cover: 2.95 **NM** value: **Cover or less**
🕮 Lush Life; One; The Final Days of Luxury (text); Two **A:** Jeff Levine **W:** Jeff Levine; Billy Strayhorn

4 ❑ Jan 1998 Cover: 2.95 **NM** value: **Cover or less**
🕮 I Work in a Video Store; Scary Stories; The Cat Got My Tongue; October; True Medical Tales **A:** Jeff Levine **W:** Jeff Levine; Jason Levine

LUST OF THE NAZI WEASEL WOMEN — Fantagraphics

1 ❑ b&w Cover: 2.25 **NM** value: **Cover or less**
2 ❑ b&w Cover: 2.25 **NM** value: **Cover or less**
3 ❑ b&w Cover: 2.25 **NM** value: **Cover or less**
4 ❑ b&w Cover: 2.25 **NM** value: **Cover or less**

LUX & ALBY SIGN ON AND SAVE THE UNIVERSE — Dark Horse

1 ❑ b&w Cover: 2.50 **NM** value: **Cover or less**
A: Simon Fraser **W:** Martin Millar

2 ❑ May 1993, b&w Cover: 2.50 **NM** value: **Cover or less**
A: Simon Fraser **W:** Martin Millar

3 ❑ Jun 1993, b&w Cover: 2.50 **NM** value: **Cover or less**
A: Simon Fraser **W:** Martin Millar

4 ❑ Cover: 2.50 **NM** value: **Cover or less**
A: Simon Fraser **W:** Martin Millar

5 ❑ Cover: 2.50 **NM** value: **Cover or less**
A: Simon Fraser **W:** Martin Millar

6 ❑ Cover: 2.50 **NM** value: **Cover or less**
A: Simon Fraser **W:** Martin Millar

7 ❑ Cover: 2.50 **NM** value: **Cover or less**
A: Simon Fraser **W:** Martin Millar

8 ❑ Oct 1993 Cover: 2.50 **NM** value: **Cover or less**
A: Simon Fraser **W:** Martin Millar

9 ❑ Dec 1993 Cover: 2.50 **NM** value: **Cover or less**
A: Simon Fraser **W:** Martin Millar

LUXURA & VAMPFIRE — Brainstorm

1 ❑ Cover: 2.95 **NM** value: **Cover or less**

LUXURA COLLECTION (KIRK LINDO'S...) — Brainstorm

All issues are adults only.

1 ❑ Cover: 4.95 **NM** value: **Cover or less**
No issue number. cardstock cover. • stories and pin-ups

LUXURA LEATHER SPECIAL — Brainstorm

1 ❑ Mar 1996 Cover: 2.95 **NM** value: **Cover or less**
No issue number.

LYCANTHROPE LEO — Viz

1 ❑ b&w Cover: 2.95 **NM** value: **Cover or less**
Circ: CapCity orders: **4,825**
A: Kenji Okamura **W:** Kengo Kaji

2 ❑ b&w Cover: 2.95 **NM** value: **Cover or less**
Circ: CapCity orders: **3,025**
A: Kenji Okamura **W:** Kengo Kaji

3 ❑ b&w Cover: 2.95 **NM** value: **Cover or less**
Circ: CapCity orders: **2,925**
A: Kenji Okamura **W:** Kengo Kaji

4 ❑ b&w Cover: 2.95 **NM** value: **Cover or less**
Circ: CapCity orders: **2,700**
A: Kenji Okamura **W:** Kengo Kaji

5 ❑ b&w Cover: 2.95 **NM** value: **Cover or less**
A: Kenji Okamura **W:** Kengo Kaji

6 ❑ b&w Cover: 2.95 **NM** value: **Cover or less**
A: Kenji Okamura **W:** Kengo Kaji

7 ❑ b&w Cover: 2.95 **NM** value: **Cover or less**
A: Kenji Okamura **W:** Kengo Kaji

Bk 1❑ b&w Cover: 17.95 **NM** value: **Cover or less**

LYCEUM — Hunter Productions

1 ❑ Oct 1996, b&w Cover: 2.95 **NM** value: **Cover or less**
2 ❑ Aug 1997, b&w Cover: 2.95 **NM** value: **Cover or less**

LYCRA-WOMAN AND SPANDEX-GIRL — Comic Zone

1 ❑ Dec 1992, b&w Cover: 2.95 **NM** value: **Cover or less**
🕮 Slave 2 Fashion **A:** Michael Avon Oeming **W:** Bryan J.L. Glass

LYCRA WOMAN AND SPANDEX GIRL CHRISTMAS '77 SPECIAL — Comic Zone

1 ❑ b&w Cover: 2.95 **NM** value: **Cover or less**

LYCRA WOMAN AND SPANDEX GIRL HALLOWEEN SPECIAL — Lost Cause

1 ❑ b&w Cover: 2.95 **NM** value: **Cover or less**

LYCRA WOMAN AND SPANDEX GIRL JURASSIC DINOSAUR SPECIAL — Comic Zone

1 ❑ b&w Cover: 2.95 **NM** value: **Cover or less**

LYCRA WOMAN AND SPANDEX GIRL SUMMER VACATION SPECIAL — Comic Zone

1 ❑ b&w Cover: 2.95 **NM** value: **Cover or less**

LYCRA WOMAN AND SPANDEX GIRL TIME TRAVEL SPECIAL — Comic Zone

1 ❑ b&w Cover: 2.95 **NM** value: **Cover or less**

LYCRA WOMAN AND SPANDEX GIRL VALENTINE SPECIAL — Comic Zone

1 ❑ b&w Cover: 2.95 **NM** value: **Cover or less**

LYNCH — Image

1 ❑ May 1997 Cover: 2.50 **NM** value: **Cover or less**
Circ: Diamd. preorders: **25,333**
One-shot. 🕮 The Sword of Viracocha • no indicia **A:** Trevor Scott **W:** Shon Bury

LYNCH MOB — Chaos

1 ❑ ca. 1994 Cover: 2.50 **NM** value: **Cover or less**
Circ: CapCity orders: **9,420**
🕮 Mayhem Comes **A:** Roman Morales III **W:** Brian Pulido

2 ❑ ca. 1994 Cover: 2.50 **NM** value: **Cover or less**
Circ: CapCity orders: **6,475**
A: Roman Morales III **W:** Brian Pulido

3 ❑ ca. 1994 Cover: 2.50 **NM** value: **Cover or less**
Circ: CapCity orders: **6,875**
A: Roman Morales III **W:** Brian Pulido

4 ❑ ca. 1994 Cover: 2.50 **NM** value: **Cover or less**
Circ: CapCity orders: **5,925**
A: Roman Morales III **W:** Brian Pulido

LYNX: AN ELFLORD TALE — Peregrine Entertainment

1 ❑ Mar 1999, b&w Cover: 2.95 **NM** value: **Cover or less**

M — Eclipse

1 ❑ Cover: 4.95 **NM** value: **Cover or less**
Circ: CapCity orders: **4,925**
A: Jon J. Muth

2 ❑ Cover: 4.95 **NM** value: **Cover or less**
Circ: CapCity orders: **4,975**
A: Jon J. Muth

3 ❑ Cover: 4.95 **NM** value: **Cover or less**
Circ: CapCity orders: **4,975**
A: Jon J. Muth

4 ❑ Cover: 5.95 **NM** value: **Cover or less**
Circ: CapCity orders: **3,550**

MACABRE — Lighthouse

1 ❑ 1989b&w Cover: 2.00 **NM** value: **Cover or less**
2 ❑ 1989b&w Cover: 2.00 **NM** value: **Cover or less**
3 ❑ 1989b&w Cover: 2.00 **NM** value: **Cover or less**
4 ❑ 1989 Cover: 2.00 **NM** value: **Cover or less**
5 ❑ 1989 Cover: 2.00 **NM** value: **Cover or less**
6 ❑ Aug 1989 Cover: 2.00 **NM** value: **Cover or less**
🕮 Shadows; St. Peter Judgement **A:** Angelo DeCicco **W:** Angelo DeCicco; John Rigitano

MACABRE (VOL. 2) — Lighthouse

1 ❑ 1989 Cover: 2.00 **NM** value: **Cover or less**
2 ❑ 1989 Cover: 2.00 **NM** value: **Cover or less**

M.A.C.H. 1 — Fleetway-Quality

1 ❑ b&w Cover: 1.95 **NM** value: **2.00**
★ 1st Appearance of John Probe.
2 ❑ b&w Cover: 1.95 **NM** value: **2.00**
3 ❑ b&w Cover: 1.95 **NM** value: **2.00**
4 ❑ b&w Cover: 1.95 **NM** value: **2.00**

CGC-graded: Multiply prices above by **33 for 9.9 M • 16 for 9.8 NM/M • 7 for 9.6 NM+ • 5 for 9.4 NM • 2.5 for 9.2 NM- • 1.5 for 9.0 VF/NM**

5 ❑ b&w Cover: 1.95 **NM** value: **2.00**
6 ❑ b&w Cover: 1.95 **NM** value: **2.00**
7 ❑ b&w Cover: 1.95 **NM** value: **2.00**
8 ❑ b&w Cover: 1.95 **NM** value: **2.00**
9 ❑ b&w Cover: 1.95 **NM** value: **2.00**

MACHINE, THE — Dark Horse

1 ❑ Nov 1994 Cover: 2.50 **NM** value: **Cover or less**
Circ: CapCity orders: **7,625**
📖 Judgment Hour **A:** Ted Naifeh **W:** John Arcudi
2 ❑ Dec 1994 Cover: 2.50 **NM** value: **Cover or less**
Circ: CapCity orders: **4,850**
📖 Top of the ?Heap **A:** Ted Naifeh; Kelly Krantz **W:** John Arcudi
3 ❑ Jan 1995 Cover: 2.50 **NM** value: **Cover or less**
Circ: CapCity orders: **3,925**
📖 Heaven In Hell **A:** Ted Naifeh **W:** John Arcudi
4 ❑ Feb 1995 Cover: 2.50 **NM** value: **Cover or less**
Circ: CapCity orders: **3,600**
A: Ted Naifeh **W:** John Arcudi

MACHINE MAN — Marvel

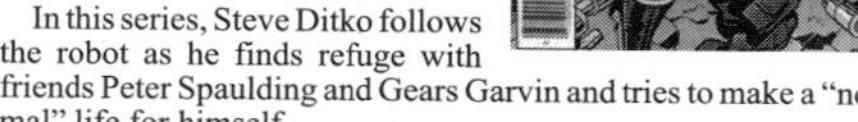
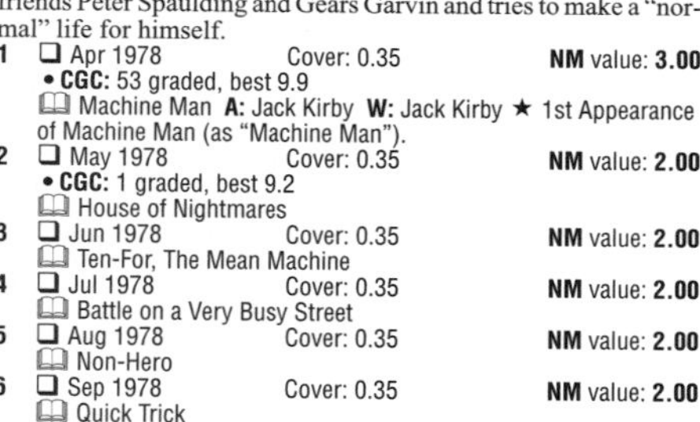

Springing from the pages of Marvel's bizarre "adaptation" of 2001, Jack Kirby's Machine Man was originally known by his experiment number: X-51. The brainchild of Dr. Abel Stack, Machine Man was the first and only success of an experiment to create robotic life. In all ways that matter, X-51 had become a living, sentient creature

Dr. Stack raised X-51 as if he were his own son. When he was given the order to terminate the experiment, Stack sacrificed his own life to save the life of X-51.

In this series, Steve Ditko follows the robot as he finds refuge with friends Peter Spaulding and Gears Garvin and tries to make a "normal" life for himself.

1 ❑ Apr 1978 Cover: 0.35 **NM** value: **3.00**
• **CGC:** 53 graded, best 9.9
📖 Machine Man **A:** Jack Kirby **W:** Jack Kirby ★ 1st Appearance of Machine Man (as "Machine Man").
2 ❑ May 1978 Cover: 0.35 **NM** value: **2.00**
• **CGC:** 1 graded, best 9.2
📖 House of Nightmares
3 ❑ Jun 1978 Cover: 0.35 **NM** value: **2.00**
📖 Ten-For, The Mean Machine
4 ❑ Jul 1978 Cover: 0.35 **NM** value: **2.00**
📖 Battle on a Very Busy Street
5 ❑ Aug 1978 Cover: 0.35 **NM** value: **2.00**
📖 Non-Hero
6 ❑ Sep 1978 Cover: 0.35 **NM** value: **2.00**
📖 Quick Trick
7 ❑ Oct 1978 Cover: 0.35 **NM** value: **2.00**
8 ❑ Nov 1978 Cover: 0.35 **NM** value: **2.00**
📖 Super Escape
9 ❑ Dec 1978 Cover: 0.35 **NM** value: **2.00**
10 ❑ Aug 1979 Cover: 0.40 **NM** value: **2.00**
11 ❑ Oct 1979 Cover: 0.40 **NM** value: **2.00**
12 ❑ Dec 1979 Cover: 0.40 **NM** value: **2.00**
13 ❑ Feb 1980 Cover: 0.40 **NM** value: **2.00**
14 ❑ Apr 1980 Cover: 0.40 **NM** value: **2.00**
15 ❑ Jun 1980 Cover: 0.40 **NM** value: **2.00**
★ Origin of Ion. ★ 1st Appearance of Ion.
16 ❑ Aug 1980 Cover: 0.40 **NM** value: **2.00**
★ 1st Appearance of Baron Brimstone.
17 ❑ Oct 1980 Cover: 0.50 **NM** value: **2.00**
18 ❑ Dec 1980 Cover: 0.50 **NM** value: **2.00**
• **CGC:** 1 graded, best 9.2
★ Appearance of Alpha Flight.
19 ❑ Feb 1981 Cover: 0.50 **NM** value: **12.50**
• **CGC:** 1 graded, best 9.4
• Macendale becomes Hobgoblin II in Amazing Spider-Man #289 **A:** Frank Miller(cover) ★ 1st Appearance of Jack O'Lantern I (Jason Macendale).

MACHINE MAN/BASTION '98 — Marvel

1 ❑ ca. 1998 Cover: 2.99 **NM** value: **Cover or less**
No issue number. wraparound cover. • gatefold summary. 📖 Engines of Destruction, Part 2 • Marvel Annual ★ Appearance of Cable.

MACHINE MAN (LTD. SERIES) — Marvel

1 ❑ Oct 1984 Cover: 0.75 **NM** value: **1.50**
📖 He Lives Again! **A:** Barry Windsor-Smith; Herb Trimpe **W:** Tom DeFalco
2 ❑ Nov 1984 Cover: 0.75 **NM** value: **1.50**
📖 If This Be Sanctuary?! **A:** Barry Windsor-Smith; Herb Trimpe **W:** Tom DeFalco ★ 1st Appearance of Iron Man 2020.
3 ❑ Dec 1984 Cover: 0.75 **NM** value: **1.50**
📖 Ancient Wrecker! **A:** Barry Windsor-Smith; Herb Trimpe **W:** Tom DeFalco
4 ❑ Jan 1985 Cover: 0.75 **NM** value: **1.50**
📖 Victory **A:** Barry Windsor-Smith; Herb Trimpe **W:** Barry Windsor-Smith; Tom DeFalco
Bk 1 ❑ Feb 1989 Cover: 6.95 **NM** value: **Cover or less**
Circ: CapCity orders: **2,100**
A: Barry Windsor-Smith; Herb Trimpe

MACHINE MAN 2020 — Marvel

1 ❑ Aug 1994 Cover: 2.00 **NM** value: **Cover or less**
Circ: CapCity orders: **12,500**
2 ❑ Sep 1994 Cover: 2.00 **NM** value: **Cover or less**
Circ: CapCity orders: **9,750**

MACK BOLAN: THE EXECUTIONER (DON PENDLETON'S...) — Innovation

The continuing character Mack Bolan first appeared in 1969, created by adventure writer Don Pendleton (1927-1995). He later licensed the Executioner characters, and there are more than 400 novels featuring Pendleton's characters, who spun off into companion series such as Able Team and Phoenix Force. One of those licenses went to Innovation during the comic-book boom of the early 1990s.

The short-lived series, with three variant first issues, adapted Pendleton's first Bolan Book, War Against the Mafia, and began adapting Death Squad before its cancellation with #4.

— Maggie

1 ❑ Jul 1993 Cover: 2.95 **NM** value: **Cover or less**
Circ: CapCity orders: **5,885**
enhanced cardstock cover. • adapts War Against the Mafia
1/A ❑ Jul 1993 Cover: 3.95 **NM** value: **Cover or less**
Indestructible Tyvek cover. 📖 War Against The Mafia **A:** Sandu Florea **W:** Don Pendleton; Linda Pendleton
1/B ❑ Jul 1993 Cover: 3.50 **NM** value: **Cover or less**
black outer cover with red X. • Double-cover edition. 📖 War Against The Mafia **A:** Sandu Florea **W:** Don Pendleton; Linda Pendleton
2 ❑ Aug 1993 Cover: 2.50 **NM** value: **Cover or less**
Circ: CapCity orders: **4,285**
• Adapts War Against the Mafia **A:** Sandu Florea **W:** Don Pendleton; Linda Pendleton
3 ❑ Nov 1993 Cover: 2.50 **NM** value: **Cover or less**
Circ: CapCity orders: **4,380**
• Adapts War Against the Mafia **A:** Sandu Florea **W:** Don Pendleton; Linda Pendleton
4 ❑ Cover: 2.50 **NM** value: **Cover or less**
Circ: CapCity orders: **3,935**
A: Sandu Florea **W:** Don Pendleton; Linda Pendleton

MACKENZIE QUEEN — Matrix

1 ❑ Cover: 1.50 **NM** value: **Cover or less**
2 ❑ b&w Cover: 1.50 **NM** value: **Cover or less**
3 ❑ Cover: 1.50 **NM** value: **Cover or less**
4 ❑ Cover: 1.50 **NM** value: **Cover or less**
5 ❑ Cover: 1.50 **NM** value: **Cover or less**
Bk 1 ❑ b&w Cover: 14.95 **NM** value: **Cover or less**

MACK THE KNIFE: MONOCHROME MEMORIES — Caliber

1 ❑ b&w Cover: 2.50 **NM** value: **Cover or less**

MACROSS II — Viz

1 ❑ ca. 1992 Cover: 2.75 **NM** value: **Cover or less**
Circ: CapCity orders: **8,600**
📖 Contact **W:** Tsuguo Okazaki; James D. Hudnall; Matt Thorn
2 ❑ ca. 1992 Cover: 2.75 **NM** value: **Cover or less**
Circ: CapCity orders: **6,400**
3 ❑ ca. 1992 Cover: 2.75 **NM** value: **Cover or less**
Circ: CapCity orders: **6,095**
4 ❑ ca. 1992 Cover: 2.75 **NM** value: **Cover or less**
Circ: CapCity orders: **5,750**
5 ❑ ca. 1992 Cover: 2.75 **NM** value: **Cover or less**
Circ: CapCity orders: **5,600**
6 ❑ ca. 1992 Cover: 2.75 **NM** value: **Cover or less**
Circ: CapCity orders: **5,275**
7 ❑ ca. 1993 Cover: 2.75 **NM** value: **Cover or less**
Circ: CapCity orders: **5,425**
8 ❑ ca. 1993 Cover: 2.75 **NM** value: **Cover or less**
Circ: CapCity orders: **5,025**
9 ❑ ca. 1993 Cover: 2.75 **NM** value: **Cover or less**
Circ: CapCity orders: **4,750**
10 ❑ ca. 1993 Cover: 2.75 **NM** value: **Cover or less**
Circ: CapCity orders: **4,675**
Bk 1 ❑ Cover: 16.95 **NM** value: **Cover or less**

MACROSS II: THE MICRON CONSPIRACY — Viz

1 ❑ b&w Cover: 2.75 **NM** value: **3.00**
Circ: CapCity orders: **4,225**
📖 The Terrorists **A:** Schulhoff Tam **W:** James D. Hudnall
2 ❑ b&w Cover: 2.75 **NM** value: **Cover or less**
Circ: CapCity orders: **3,375**
3 ❑ b&w Cover: 2.75 **NM** value: **Cover or less**
Circ: CapCity orders: **2,975**
4 ❑ b&w Cover: 2.75 **NM** value: **Cover or less**
Circ: CapCity orders: **2,575**
5 ❑ b&w Cover: 2.75 **NM** value: **Cover or less**
Circ: CapCity orders: **2,500**

There are two different pricing tiers in the modern comic-book hobby. **The prices seen above** are the prices we have seen **loose copies** of these issues reliably fetch in a variety of environments. Condition alters the price by the fractions seen on the bar on the bottom of left-hand pages of this book. **Comics graded by CGC** usually sell for more. Use the guide on the bottom of right-hand pages of this book to estimate what copies have brought on eBay.

MAD — E.C.

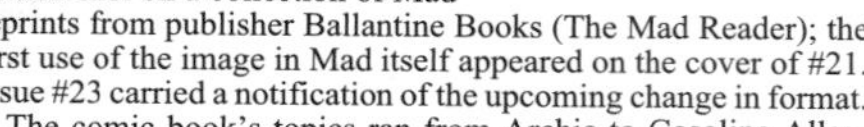

This series, carrying the spine-long text "Humor in a jugular vein" and the top-of cover lead-in "Tales calculated to drive you," was one of two of Editor Harvey Kurtzman's major projects at E.C. (The other was Frontline Combat.)

Mad began as a color comic book, shifted to black-and-white magazine format with #24. Several of the early covers were by Kurtzman, and the satiric title carried parodies even on many of its covers.

The face of "Alfred E. Neuman" as connected with Mad actually appeared first on a collection of Mad reprints from publisher Ballantine Books (The Mad Reader); the first use of the image in Mad itself appeared on the cover of #21. Issue #23 carried a notification of the upcoming change in format.

The comic book's topics ran from Archie to Gasoline Alley, from Sherlock Holmes to Flash Gordon, from G.I. Joe to Pogo, and from Mickey Mouse to The Shadow. No issue of Mad carried the seal of the Comics Magazine Association of America.

When the shift came to the magazine format, more text was introduced and initial contributions from such mainstream comedy sources as Bob and Ray, Ernie Kovacs, and Tom Lehrer appeared. Kurtzman departed, Al Feldstein took over as editor, and the title continues to this day, with "What — Me Worry?" kid Neuman as a mascot and satire directed more toward media and society than other comic art staples. Entire books have been devoted to the series.

— Maggie

1 ❑ Oct 1952 Cover: 0.10 **NM** value: **5450.00**
• **CGC:** 32 graded, best 9.8
2 ❑ Dec 1952 Cover: 0.10 **NM** value: **1300.00**
• **CGC:** 26 graded, best 9.8
3 ❑ Jan 1953 Cover: 0.10 **NM** value: **725.00**
• **CGC:** 15 graded, best 9.6
4 ❑ Apr 1953 Cover: 0.10 **NM** value: **725.00**
• **CGC:** 17 graded, best 9.8
5 ❑ Jun 1953 Cover: 0.10 **NM** value: **1300.00**
• **CGC:** 9 graded, best 9.6
• Low distribution
6 ❑ Aug 1953 Cover: 0.10 **NM** value: **540.00**
• **CGC:** 6 graded, best 9.4
7 ❑ Oct 1953 Cover: 0.10 **NM** value: **540.00**
• **CGC:** 9 graded, best 9.6
8 ❑ Dec 1953 Cover: 0.10 **NM** value: **540.00**
• **CGC:** 11 graded, best 9.4
9 ❑ Mar 1954 Cover: 0.10 **NM** value: **540.00**
• **CGC:** 13 graded, best 9.2
10 ❑ Apr 1954 Cover: 0.10 **NM** value: **540.00**
• **CGC:** 8 graded, best 9.4
11 ❑ May 1954 Cover: 0.10 **NM** value: **540.00**
• **CGC:** 8 graded, best 9.4
12 ❑ Jun 1954 Cover: 0.10 **NM** value: **440.00**
• **CGC:** 10 graded, best 9.8
13 ❑ Jul 1954 Cover: 0.10 **NM** value: **440.00**
• **CGC:** 9 graded, best 9.4
14 ❑ Aug 1954 Cover: 0.10 **NM** value: **440.00**
• **CGC:** 8 graded, best 9.4
15 ❑ Sep 1954 Cover: 0.10 **NM** value: **440.00**
• **CGC:** 10 graded, best 9.4
16 ❑ Oct 1954 Cover: 0.10 **NM** value: **440.00**
• **CGC:** 17 graded, best 9.6
17 ❑ Nov 1954 Cover: 0.10 **NM** value: **440.00**
• **CGC:** 9 graded, best 9.8
18 ❑ Dec 1954 Cover: 0.10 **NM** value: **440.00**
• **CGC:** 12 graded, best 9.2
19 ❑ Jan 1955 Cover: 0.10 **NM** value: **440.00**
• **CGC:** 17 graded, best 9.6
20 ❑ Feb 1955 Cover: 0.10 **NM** value: **325.00**
• **CGC:** 12 graded, best 9.4
21 ❑ Mar 1955 Cover: 0.10 **NM** value: **325.00**
• **CGC:** 12 graded, best 9.6
22 ❑ Apr 1955 Cover: 0.10 **NM** value: **325.00**
• **CGC:** 16 graded, best 9.8
📖 The Child!; The Boy!; The Young Artist!; The Commercial Artist!; The old Pro'! • "Art Issue" **A:** Bill Elder **W:** Harvey Kurtzman
23 ❑ May 1955 Cover: 0.10 **NM** value: **325.00**
• **CGC:** 14 graded, best 9.2
📖 Scenes We'd Like to See!; Gopo Gossum!; Ripup's Believe it or Don't; The Barefoot Nocountessa! • "Think" **A:** Wally Wood; Jack Davis **W:** Harvey Kurtzman
24 ❑ Jul 1955 Cover: 0.25 **NM** value: **810.00**
• Mad switches to magazine format.
25 ❑ Sep 1955 Cover: 0.25 **NM** value: **325.00**
26 ❑ Nov 1955 Cover: 0.25 **NM** value: **275.00**
27 ❑ Apr 1956 Cover: 0.25 **NM** value: **275.00**
• Has 1955 Statement, filed 10/1/55; no numbers printed
28 ❑ Jun 1956 Cover: 0.25 **NM** value: **250.00**
29 ❑ Sep 1956 Cover: 0.25 **NM** value: **250.00**
30 ❑ Dec 1956 Cover: 0.25 **NM** value: **375.00**
Alfred E. Neuman cover.
31 ❑ Feb 1957 Cover: 0.25 **NM** value: **215.00**
32 ❑ Apr 1957 Cover: 0.25 **NM** value: **180.00**
33 ❑ Jun 1957 Cover: 0.25 **NM** value: **175.00**
34 ❑ Aug 1957 Cover: 0.25 **NM** value: **145.00**
35 ❑ Oct 1957 Cover: 0.25 **NM** value: **145.00**
36 ❑ Dec 1957 Cover: 0.25 **NM** value: **110.00**
37 ❑ Jan 1958 Cover: 0.25 **NM** value: **110.00**
38 ❑ Mar 1958 Cover: 0.25 **NM** value: **110.00**
39 ❑ May 1958 Cover: 0.25 **NM** value: **110.00**
40 ❑ Jul 1958 Cover: 0.25 **NM** value: **110.00**
41 ❑ Sep 1958 Cover: 0.25 **NM** value: **80.00**
42 ❑ Nov 1958 Cover: 0.25 **NM** value: **80.00**

Other grades: Multiply prices above by **1.5 for Mint • 2/3 for Very Fine • 1/3 for Fine • 1/5 for Very Good • 1/8 for Good**

43 ❑ Dec 1958 Cover: 0.25 **NM** value: **80.00**
44 ❑ Jan 1959 Cover: 0.25 **NM** value: **80.00**
45 ❑ Mar 1959 Cover: 0.25 **NM** value: **80.00**
46 ❑ Apr 1959 Cover: 0.25 **NM** value: **80.00**
47 ❑ Jun 1959 Cover: 0.25 **NM** value: **80.00**
48 ❑ Jul 1959 Cover: 0.25 **NM** value: **80.00**
49 ❑ Sep 1959 Cover: 0.25 **NM** value: **80.00**
50 ❑ Oct 1959 Cover: 0.25 **NM** value: **80.00**
51 ❑ Dec 1959 Cover: 0.25 **NM** value: **60.00**
52 ❑ Jan 1960 Cover: 0.25 **NM** value: **60.00**
Circ: Statement: **1,048,550**
53 ❑ Mar 1960 Cover: 0.25 **NM** value: **60.00**
Circ: Statement: **1,048,550**
• Has 1959 Statement; no numbers printed
54 ❑ Apr 1960 Cover: 0.25 **NM** value: **60.00**
Circ: Statement: **1,048,550**
55 ❑ Jun 1960 Cover: 0.25 **NM** value: **60.00**
Circ: Statement: **1,048,550**
56 ❑ Jul 1960 Cover: 0.25 **NM** value: **60.00**
Circ: Statement: **1,048,550**
57 ❑ Sep 1960 Cover: 0.25 **NM** value: **60.00**
Circ: Statement: **1,048,550**
58 ❑ Oct 1960 Cover: 0.25 **NM** value: **60.00**
Circ: Statement: **1,048,550**
59 ❑ Dec 1960 Cover: 0.25 **NM** value: **60.00**
Circ: Statement: **1,048,550**
60 ❑ Jan 1961 Cover: 0.25 **NM** value: **60.00**
Circ: Statement: **1,209,918**
61 ❑ Mar 1961 Cover: 0.25 **NM** value: **48.00**
Circ: Statement: **1,209,918**
• Has 1960 Statement; avg sales 1,000,000; avg subs 48,550; avg total paid 1,048,550; max existent 1,048,550
62 ❑ Apr 1961 Cover: 0.25 **NM** value: **48.00**
Circ: Statement: **1,209,918**
63 ❑ Jun 1961 Cover: 0.25 **NM** value: **48.00**
Circ: Statement: **1,209,918**
64 ❑ Jul 1961 Cover: 0.25 **NM** value: **48.00**
Circ: Statement: **1,209,918**
65 ❑ Sep 1961 Cover: 0.25 **NM** value: **48.00**
Circ: Statement: **1,209,918**
66 ❑ Oct 1961 Cover: 0.25 **NM** value: **48.00**
Circ: Statement: **1,209,918**
67 ❑ Dec 1961 Cover: 0.25 **NM** value: **48.00**
Circ: Statement: **1,209,918**
68 ❑ Jan 1962 Cover: 0.25 **NM** value: **48.00**
Circ: Statement: **1,293,705**
69 ❑ Mar 1962 Cover: 0.25 **NM** value: **48.00**
Circ: Statement: **1,293,705**
• Has 1961 Statement; avg total paid 1,209,918
70 ❑ Apr 1962 Cover: 0.25 **NM** value: **48.00**
Circ: Statement: **1,293,705**
71 ❑ Jun 1962 Cover: 0.25 **NM** value: **36.00**
Circ: Statement: **1,293,705**
72 ❑ Jul 1962 Cover: 0.25 **NM** value: **36.00**
Circ: Statement: **1,293,705**
73 ❑ Sep 1962 Cover: 0.25 **NM** value: **36.00**
Circ: Statement: **1,293,705**
74 ❑ Oct 1962 Cover: 0.25 **NM** value: **36.00**
Circ: Statement: **1,293,705**
75 ❑ Dec 1962 Cover: 0.25 **NM** value: **36.00**
Circ: Statement: **1,293,705**
76 ❑ Jan 1963 Cover: 0.25 **NM** value: **36.00**
Circ: Statement: **1,429,080**
77 ❑ Mar 1963 Cover: 0.25 **NM** value: **36.00**
Circ: Statement: **1,429,080**
• Has 1962 Statement; avg total paid 1,293,705
78 ❑ Apr 1963 Cover: 0.25 **NM** value: **36.00**
Circ: Statement: **1,429,080**
79 ❑ Jun 1963 Cover: 0.25 **NM** value: **36.00**
Circ: Statement: **1,429,080**
80 ❑ Jul 1963 Cover: 0.25 **NM** value: **36.00**
Circ: Statement: **1,429,080**
81 ❑ Sep 1963 Cover: 0.25 **NM** value: **32.00**
Circ: Statement: **1,429,080**
82 ❑ Oct 1963 Cover: 0.25 **NM** value: **32.00**
Circ: Statement: **1,429,080**
83 ❑ Dec 1963 Cover: 0.25 **NM** value: **32.00**
Circ: Statement: **1,429,080**
84 ❑ Jan 1964 Cover: 0.25 **NM** value: **32.00**
Circ: Statement: **1,424,628**
85 ❑ Mar 1964 Cover: 0.25 **NM** value: **32.00**
Circ: Statement: **1,424,628**
• Has 1963 Statement; avg print run 1,891,062; avg subs 55,070; avg total paid 1,429,080; max existent 1,429,080; 24% of run returned
86 ❑ Apr 1964 Cover: 0.25 **NM** value: **32.00**
Circ: Statement: **1,424,628**
• 1st fold-in
87 ❑ Jun 1964 Cover: 0.25 **NM** value: **32.00**
Circ: Statement: **1,424,628**
88 ❑ Jul 1964 Cover: 0.25 **NM** value: **32.00**
Circ: Statement: **1,424,628**
89 ❑ Sep 1964 Cover: 0.25 **NM** value: **32.00**
Circ: Statement: **1,424,628**
90 ❑ Oct 1964 Cover: 0.25 **NM** value: **32.00**
Circ: Statement: **1,424,628**
91 ❑ Dec 1964 Cover: 0.25 **NM** value: **32.00**
Circ: Statement: **1,424,628**
92 ❑ Jan 1965 Cover: 0.25 **NM** value: **32.00**
Circ: Statement: **1,532,926**
93 ❑ Mar 1965 Cover: 0.25 **NM** value: **32.00**
Circ: Statement: **1,532,926**
• Has 1964 Statement; avg print run 1,936,000; avg sales 1,369,373; avg subs 55,255; avg total paid 1,424,628; max existent 1,424,628; 26% of run returned
94 ❑ Apr 1965 Cover: 0.25 **NM** value: **32.00**
Circ: Statement: **1,532,926**
95 ❑ Jun 1965 Cover: 0.30 **NM** value: **32.00**
Circ: Statement: **1,532,926**
96 ❑ Jul 1965 Cover: 0.30 **NM** value: **32.00**
Circ: Statement: **1,532,926**
97 ❑ Sep 1965 Cover: 0.30 **NM** value: **32.00**
Circ: Statement: **1,532,926**
98 ❑ Oct 1965 Cover: 0.30 **NM** value: **32.00**
Circ: Statement: **1,532,926**
99 ❑ Dec 1965 Cover: 0.30 **NM** value: **32.00**
Circ: Statement: **1,532,926**
100 ❑ Jan 1966 Cover: 0.30 **NM** value: **32.00**
Circ: Statement: **1,635,612**
101 ❑ Mar 1966 Cover: 0.30 **NM** value: **18.00**
Circ: Statement: **1,635,612**
• Has 1965 Statement; avg print run 1,957,148; avg sales 1,473,223; avg subs 59,703; avg total paid 1,532,926; max existent 1,532,926; 22% of run returned
102 ❑ Apr 1966 Cover: 0.30 **NM** value: **18.00**
Circ: Statement: **1,635,612**
103 ❑ Jun 1966 Cover: 0.30 **NM** value: **18.00**
Circ: Statement: **1,635,612**
104 ❑ Jul 1966 Cover: 0.30 **NM** value: **18.00**
Circ: Statement: **1,635,612**
105 ❑ Sep 1966 Cover: 0.30 **NM** value: **18.00**
Circ: Statement: **1,635,612**
• Batman TV-show parody
106 ❑ Oct 1966 Cover: 0.30 **NM** value: **18.00**
Circ: Statement: **1,635,612**
107 ❑ Dec 1966 Cover: 0.30 **NM** value: **18.00**
Circ: Statement: **1,635,612**
108 ❑ Jan 1967 Cover: 0.30 **NM** value: **18.00**
Circ: Statement: **1,789,555**
109 ❑ Mar 1967 Cover: 0.30 **NM** value: **18.00**
Circ: Statement: **1,789,555**
• Has 1966 Statement; avg print run 2,121,960; avg sales 1,564,111; avg subs 71,501; avg total paid 1,635,612; max existent 1,635,612; 23% of run returned
110 ❑ Apr 1967 Cover: 0.30 **NM** value: **18.00**
Circ: Statement: **1,789,555**
111 ❑ Jun 1967 Cover: 0.30 **NM** value: **18.00**
Circ: Statement: **1,789,555**
112 ❑ Jul 1967 Cover: 0.30 **NM** value: **18.00**
Circ: Statement: **1,789,555**
113 ❑ Sep 1967 Cover: 0.30 **NM** value: **18.00**
Circ: Statement: **1,789,555**
114 ❑ Oct 1967 Cover: 0.30 **NM** value: **18.00**
Circ: Statement: **1,789,555**
115 ❑ Dec 1967 Cover: 0.30 **NM** value: **18.00**
Circ: Statement: **1,789,555**
116 ❑ Jan 1968 Cover: 0.30 **NM** value: **18.00**
Circ: Statement: **1,831,648**
117 ❑ Mar 1968 Cover: 0.30 **NM** value: **18.00**
Circ: Statement: **1,831,648**
• Has 1967 Statement; avg print run 2,370,336; avg sales 1,703,254; avg subs 77,301
avg total paid 1,789,555; max existent 1,780,555; 25% of run returned
118 ❑ Apr 1968 Cover: 0.30 **NM** value: **18.00**
Circ: Statement: **1,831,648**
119 ❑ Jun 1968 Cover: 0.35 **NM** value: **18.00**
Circ: Statement: **1,831,648**
120 ❑ Jul 1968 Cover: 0.35 **NM** value: **18.00**
Circ: Statement: **1,831,648**
121 ❑ Sep 1968 Cover: 0.35 **NM** value: **22.00**
Circ: Statement: **1,831,648**
• Beatles parody
122 ❑ Oct 1968 Cover: 0.35 **NM** value: **18.00**
Circ: Statement: **1,831,648**
123 ❑ Dec 1968 Cover: 0.35 **NM** value: **15.00**
Circ: Statement: **1,831,648**
124 ❑ Jan 1969 Cover: 0.35 **NM** value: **15.00**
Circ: Statement: **1,884,502**
125 ❑ Mar 1969 Cover: 0.35 **NM** value: **15.00**
Circ: Statement: **1,884,502**
• Has 1968 Statement; avg print run 2,434,137; avg sales 1,746,261; avg subs 85,387; avg total paid 1,831,648; samples 25; max existent 1,831,673; 25% of run returned
126 ❑ Apr 1969 Cover: 0.35 **NM** value: **15.00**
Circ: Statement: **1,884,502**
127 ❑ Jun 1969 Cover: 0.35 **NM** value: **15.00**
Circ: Statement: **1,884,502**
128 ❑ Jul 1969 Cover: 0.35 **NM** value: **15.00**
Circ: Statement: **1,884,502**
129 ❑ Sep 1969 Cover: 0.35 **NM** value: **15.00**
Circ: Statement: **1,884,502**
130 ❑ Oct 1969 Cover: 0.35 **NM** value: **15.00**
Circ: Statement: **1,884,502**
131 ❑ Dec 1969 Cover: 0.35 **NM** value: **15.00**
Circ: Statement: **1,884,502**
132 ❑ Jan 1970 Cover: 0.35 **NM** value: **15.00**
Circ: Statement: **1,864,443**
133 ❑ Mar 1970 Cover: 0.35 **NM** value: **15.00**
Circ: Statement: **1,864,443**
• Has 1969 Statement; avg print run 2,466,650; avg sales 1,782,713; avg subs 101,789; avg total paid 1,884,502; samples 56; max existent 1,884,558; 24% of run returned
134 ❑ Apr 1970 Cover: 0.35 **NM** value: **15.00**
Circ: Statement: **1,864,443**
135 ❑ Jun 1970 Cover: 0.35 **NM** value: **15.00**
Circ: Statement: **1,864,443**
136 ❑ Jul 1970 Cover: 0.35 **NM** value: **15.00**
Circ: Statement: **1,864,443**
137 ❑ Sep 1970 Cover: 0.35 **NM** value: **15.00**
Circ: Statement: **1,864,443**
138 ❑ Oct 1970 Cover: 0.35 **NM** value: **15.00**
Circ: Statement: **1,864,443**
139 ❑ Dec 1970 Cover: 0.35 **NM** value: **15.00**
Circ: Statement: **1,864,443**
140 ❑ Jan 1971 Cover: 0.35 **NM** value: **15.00**
Circ: Statement: **1,845,325**
141 ❑ Mar 1971 Cover: 0.35 **NM** value: **12.00**
Circ: Statement: **1,845,325**
142 ❑ Apr 1971 Cover: 0.35 **NM** value: **12.00**
Circ: Statement: **1,845,325**
143 ❑ Jun 1971 Cover: 0.40 **NM** value: **12.00**
Circ: Statement: **1,845,325**
144 ❑ Jul 1971 Cover: 0.40 **NM** value: **12.00**
Circ: Statement: **1,845,325**
145 ❑ Sep 1971 Cover: 0.40 **NM** value: **12.00**
Circ: Statement: **1,845,325**
146 ❑ Oct 1971 Cover: 0.40 **NM** value: **12.00**
Circ: Statement: **1,845,325**
147 ❑ Dec 1971 Cover: 0.40 **NM** value: **12.00**
Circ: Statement: **1,845,325**
148 ❑ Jan 1972 Cover: 0.40 **NM** value: **12.00**
Circ: Statement: **1,905,973**
149 ❑ Mar 1972 Cover: 0.40 **NM** value: **12.00**
Circ: Statement: **1,905,973**
150 ❑ Apr 1972 Cover: 0.40 **NM** value: **12.00**
Circ: Statement: **1,905,973**
151 ❑ Jun 1972 Cover: 0.40 **NM** value: **9.00**
Circ: Statement: **1,905,973**
152 ❑ Jul 1972 Cover: 0.40 **NM** value: **9.00**
Circ: Statement: **1,905,973**
153 ❑ Sep 1972 Cover: 0.40 **NM** value: **9.00**
Circ: Statement: **1,905,973**
154 ❑ Oct 1972 Cover: 0.40 **NM** value: **9.00**
Circ: Statement: **1,905,973**
155 ❑ Dec 1972 Cover: 0.40 **NM** value: **9.00**
Circ: Statement: **1,905,973**
156 ❑ Jan 1973 Cover: 0.40 **NM** value: **9.00**
Circ: Statement: **2,059,236**
157 ❑ Mar 1973 Cover: 0.40 **NM** value: **9.00**
Circ: Statement: **2,059,236**
158 ❑ Apr 1973 Cover: 0.40 **NM** value: **9.00**
Circ: Statement: **2,059,236**
159 ❑ Jun 1973 Cover: 0.40 **NM** value: **9.00**
Circ: Statement: **2,059,236**
160 ❑ Jul 1973 Cover: 0.40 **NM** value: **9.00**
Circ: Statement: **2,059,236**
161 ❑ Sep 1973 Cover: 0.40 **NM** value: **8.00**
Circ: Statement: **2,059,236**
162 ❑ Oct 1973 Cover: 0.40 **NM** value: **8.00**
Circ: Statement: **2,059,236**
163 ❑ Dec 1973 Cover: 0.40 **NM** value: **8.00**
Circ: Statement: **2,059,236**
164 ❑ Jan 1974 Cover: 0.40 **NM** value: **8.00**
Circ: Statement: **2,132,655**
165 ❑ Mar 1974 Cover: 0.40 **NM** value: **8.00**
Circ: Statement: **2,132,655**
166 ❑ Apr 1974 Cover: 0.40 **NM** value: **8.00**
Circ: Statement: **2,132,655**
167 ❑ Jun 1974 Cover: 0.40 **NM** value: **8.00**
Circ: Statement: **2,132,655**
168 ❑ Jul 1974 Cover: 0.40 **NM** value: **8.00**
Circ: Statement: **2,132,655**
169 ❑ Sep 1974 Cover: 0.40 **NM** value: **8.00**
Circ: Statement: **2,132,655**
170 ❑ Oct 1974 Cover: 0.40 **NM** value: **8.00**
Circ: Statement: **2,132,655**
171 ❑ Dec 1974 Cover: 0.50 **NM** value: **6.50**
Circ: Statement: **2,132,655**
172 ❑ Jan 1975 Cover: 0.50 **NM** value: **6.50**
Circ: Statement: **1,928,139**
173 ❑ Mar 1975 Cover: 0.50 **NM** value: **6.50**
Circ: Statement: **1,928,139**
174 ❑ Apr 1975 Cover: 0.50 **NM** value: **6.50**
Circ: Statement: **1,928,139**
175 ❑ Jun 1975 Cover: 0.50 **NM** value: **6.50**
Circ: Statement: **1,928,139**
176 ❑ Jul 1975 Cover: 0.50 **NM** value: **6.50**
Circ: Statement: **1,928,139**
177 ❑ Sep 1975 Cover: 0.50 **NM** value: **6.50**
Circ: Statement: **1,928,139**
178 ❑ Oct 1975 Cover: 0.50 **NM** value: **6.50**
Circ: Statement: **1,928,139**
179 ❑ Dec 1975 Cover: 0.50 **NM** value: **6.50**
Circ: Statement: **1,928,139**
180 ❑ Jan 1976 Cover: 0.50 **NM** value: **6.50**
Circ: Statement: **1,787,928**
181 ❑ Mar 1976 Cover: 0.50 **NM** value: **6.50**
Circ: Statement: **1,787,928**
182 ❑ Apr 1976 Cover: 0.50 **NM** value: **6.50**
Circ: Statement: **1,787,928**
183 ❑ Jun 1976 Cover: 0.50 **NM** value: **6.50**
Circ: Statement: **1,787,928**
184 ❑ Jul 1976 Cover: 0.50 **NM** value: **6.50**
Circ: Statement: **1,787,928**
185 ❑ Sep 1976 Cover: 0.50 **NM** value: **6.50**
Circ: Statement: **1,787,928**
186 ❑ Oct 1976 Cover: 0.50 **NM** value: **6.50**
Circ: Statement: **1,787,928**
• Star Trek parody
187 ❑ Dec 1976 Cover: 0.50 **NM** value: **6.50**
Circ: Statement: **1,787,928**
188 ❑ Jan 1977 Cover: 0.50 **NM** value: **6.50**
Circ: Statement: **1,721,515**
189 ❑ Mar 1977 Cover: 0.50 **NM** value: **6.50**
Circ: Statement: **1,721,515**
190 ❑ Apr 1977 Cover: 0.50 **NM** value: **5.00**
Circ: Statement: **1,721,515**
191 ❑ Jun 1977 Cover: 0.50 **NM** value: **5.00**
Circ: Statement: **1,721,515**
192 ❑ Jul 1977 Cover: 0.60 **NM** value: **5.00**
Circ: Statement: **1,721,515**
193 ❑ Sep 1977 Cover: 0.60 **NM** value: **5.00**
Circ: Statement: **1,721,515**
194 ❑ Oct 1977 Cover: 0.60 **NM** value: **5.00**
Circ: Statement: **1,721,515**

CGC-graded: Multiply prices above by **33 for 9.9 M • 16 for 9.8 NM/M • 7 for 9.6 NM+ • 5 for 9.4 NM • 2.5 for 9.2 NM- • 1.5 for 9.0 VF/NM**

195 ❑ Dec 1977 Cover: 0.60 **NM** value: **5.00**
Circ: Statement: **1,721,515**

196 ❑ Jan 1978 Cover: 0.60 **NM** value: **5.00**
Circ: Statement: **1,626,452**

197 ❑ Mar 1978 Cover: 0.60 **NM** value: **5.00**
Circ: Statement: **1,626,452**

198 ❑ Apr 1978 Cover: 0.60 **NM** value: **5.00**
Circ: Statement: **1,626,452**

199 ❑ Jun 1978 Cover: 0.60 **NM** value: **5.00**
Circ: Statement: **1,626,452**

200 ❑ Jul 1978 Cover: 0.60 **NM** value: **5.00**
Circ: Statement: **1,626,452**

201 ❑ Sep 1978 Cover: 0.60 **NM** value: **4.00**
Circ: Statement: **1,626,452**

202 ❑ Oct 1978 Cover: 0.60 **NM** value: **4.00**
Circ: Statement: **1,626,452**

203 ❑ Dec 1978 Cover: 0.60 **NM** value: **4.00**
Circ: Statement: **1,626,452**

204 ❑ Jan 1979 Cover: 0.60 **NM** value: **4.00**
Circ: Statement: **1,561,327**

205 ❑ Mar 1979 Cover: 0.60 **NM** value: **4.00**
Circ: Statement: **1,561,327**

206 ❑ Apr 1979 Cover: 0.60 **NM** value: **4.00**
Circ: Statement: **1,561,327**

207 ❑ Jun 1979 Cover: 0.60 **NM** value: **4.00**
Circ: Statement: **1,561,327**

208 ❑ Jul 1979 Cover: 0.60 **NM** value: **4.00**
Circ: Statement: **1,561,327**

209 ❑ Sep 1979 Cover: 0.75 **NM** value: **4.00**
Circ: Statement: **1,561,327**

210 ❑ Oct 1979 Cover: 0.75 **NM** value: **4.00**
Circ: Statement: **1,561,327**

211 ❑ Dec 1979 Cover: 0.75 **NM** value: **4.00**
Circ: Statement: **1,561,327**

212 ❑ Jan 1980 Cover: 0.75 **NM** value: **4.00**
Circ: Statement: **1,342,640**

213 ❑ Mar 1980 Cover: 0.75 **NM** value: **4.00**
Circ: Statement: **1,342,640**

214 ❑ Apr 1980 Cover: 0.75 **NM** value: **4.00**
Circ: Statement: **1,342,640**

215 ❑ Jun 1980 Cover: 0.75 **NM** value: **4.00**
Circ: Statement: **1,342,640**

216 ❑ Jul 1980 Cover: 0.75 **NM** value: **4.00**
Circ: Statement: **1,342,640**

217 ❑ Sep 1980 Cover: 0.75 **NM** value: **4.00**
Circ: Statement: **1,342,640**

218 ❑ Oct 1980 Cover: 0.75 **NM** value: **4.00**
Circ: Statement: **1,342,640**

219 ❑ Dec 1980 Cover: 0.75 **NM** value: **4.00**
Circ: Statement: **1,342,640**

220 ❑ Jan 1981 Cover: 0.75 **NM** value: **4.00**
Circ: Statement: **1,094,085**

221 ❑ Mar 1981 Cover: 0.75 **NM** value: **3.00**
Circ: Statement: **1,094,085**

222 ❑ Apr 1981 Cover: 0.90 **NM** value: **3.00**
Circ: Statement: **1,094,085**

223 ❑ Jun 1981 Cover: 0.90 **NM** value: **3.00**
Circ: Statement: **1,094,085**

224 ❑ Jul 1981 Cover: 0.90 **NM** value: **3.00**
Circ: Statement: **1,094,085**

225 ❑ Sep 1981 Cover: 0.90 **NM** value: **3.00**
Circ: Statement: **1,094,085**

226 ❑ Oct 1981 Cover: 0.90 **NM** value: **3.00**
Circ: Statement: **1,094,085**

227 ❑ Dec 1981 Cover: 0.90 **NM** value: **3.00**
Circ: Statement: **1,094,085**

228 ❑ Jan 1982 Cover: 0.90 **NM** value: **3.00**
Circ: Statement: **1,001,724**

229 ❑ Mar 1982 Cover: 0.90 **NM** value: **3.00**
Circ: Statement: **1,001,724**

230 ❑ Apr 1982 Cover: 0.90 **NM** value: **3.00**
Circ: Statement: **1,001,724**

231 ❑ Jun 1982 Cover: 0.90 **NM** value: **3.00**
Circ: Statement: **1,001,724**

232 ❑ Jul 1982 Cover: 1.00 **NM** value: **3.00**
Circ: Statement: **1,001,724**

233 ❑ Sep 1982 Cover: 1.00 **NM** value: **3.00**
Circ: Statement: **1,001,724**

234 ❑ Oct 1982 Cover: 1.00 **NM** value: **3.00**
Circ: Statement: **1,001,724**

235 ❑ Dec 1982 Cover: 1.00 **NM** value: **3.00**
Circ: Statement: **1,001,724**

236 ❑ Jan 1983 Cover: 1.00 **NM** value: **3.00**
Circ: Statement: **879,075**

237 ❑ Mar 1983 Cover: 1.00 **NM** value: **3.00**
Circ: Statement: **879,075**

238 ❑ Apr 1983 Cover: 1.00 **NM** value: **3.00**
Circ: Statement: **879,075**

239 ❑ Jun 1983 Cover: 1.00 **NM** value: **3.00**
Circ: Statement: **879,075**

240 ❑ Jul 1983 Cover: 1.00 **NM** value: **3.00**
Circ: Statement: **879,075**

241 ❑ Sep 1983 Cover: 1.00 **NM** value: **2.50**
Circ: Statement: **879,075**

242 ❑ Oct 1983 Cover: 1.00 **NM** value: **2.50**
Circ: Statement: **879,075**

243 ❑ Dec 1983 Cover: 1.00 **NM** value: **2.50**
Circ: Statement: **879,075**

244 ❑ Jan 1984 Cover: 1.00 **NM** value: **2.50**
Circ: Statement: **783,192**

245 ❑ Mar 1984 Cover: 1.00 **NM** value: **2.50**
Circ: Statement: **783,192**

246 ❑ Apr 1984 Cover: 1.25 **NM** value: **2.50**
Circ: Statement: **783,192**

247 ❑ Jun 1984 Cover: 1.25 **NM** value: **2.50**
Circ: Statement: **783,192**

248 ❑ Jul 1984 Cover: 1.25 **NM** value: **2.50**
Circ: Statement: **783,192**

249 ❑ Sep 1984 Cover: 1.25 **NM** value: **2.50**
Circ: Statement: **783,192**

250 ❑ Oct 1984 Cover: 1.25 **NM** value: **2.50**
Circ: Statement: **783,192**

251 ❑ Dec 1984 Cover: 1.25 **NM** value: **2.50**
Circ: Statement: **783,192**

252 ❑ Jan 1985 Cover: 1.25 **NM** value: **2.50**
Circ: Statement: **744,817**

253 ❑ Mar 1985 Cover: 1.25 **NM** value: **2.50**
Circ: Statement: **744,817**

254 ❑ Apr 1985 Cover: 1.25 **NM** value: **2.50**
Circ: Statement: **744,817**

255 ❑ Jun 1985 Cover: 1.25 **NM** value: **2.50**
Circ: Statement: **744,817**

256 ❑ Jul 1985 Cover: 1.25 **NM** value: **2.50**
Circ: Statement: **744,817**

257 ❑ Sep 1985 Cover: 1.25 **NM** value: **2.50**
Circ: Statement: **744,817**

258 ❑ Oct 1985 Cover: 1.25 **NM** value: **2.50**
Circ: Statement: **744,817**

259 ❑ Dec 1985 Cover: 1.25 **NM** value: **2.50**
Circ: Statement: **744,817**

260 ❑ Jan 1986 Cover: 1.25 **NM** value: **2.50**
Circ: Statement: **740,442**

261 ❑ Mar 1986 Cover: 1.35 **NM** value: **2.25**
Circ: Statement: **740,442**

262 ❑ Apr 1986 Cover: 1.35 **NM** value: **2.25**
Circ: Statement: **740,442**

263 ❑ Jun 1986 Cover: 1.35 **NM** value: **2.25**
Circ: Statement: **740,442**

264 ❑ Jul 1986 Cover: 1.35 **NM** value: **2.25**
Circ: Statement: **740,442**

265 ❑ Sep 1986 Cover: 1.35 **NM** value: **2.25**
Circ: Statement: **740,442**

266 ❑ Oct 1986 Cover: 1.35 **NM** value: **2.25**
Circ: Statement: **740,442**

267 ❑ Dec 1986 Cover: 1.35 **NM** value: **2.25**
Circ: Statement: **740,442**

268 ❑ Jan 1987 Cover: 1.35 **NM** value: **2.25**
Circ: Statement: **742,743**

269 ❑ Mar 1987 Cover: 1.35 **NM** value: **2.25**
Circ: Statement: **742,743**

270 ❑ Apr 1987 Cover: 1.35 **NM** value: **2.25**
Circ: Statement: **742,743**

271 ❑ Jun 1987 Cover: 1.35 **NM** value: **2.25**
Circ: Statement: **742,743**

272 ❑ Jul 1987 Cover: 1.35 **NM** value: **2.25**
Circ: Statement: **742,743**

273 ❑ Sep 1987 Cover: 1.35 **NM** value: **2.25**
Circ: Statement: **742,743**

274 ❑ Oct 1987 Cover: 1.35 **NM** value: **2.25**
Circ: Statement: **742,743**

275 ❑ Dec 1987 Cover: 1.35 **NM** value: **2.25**
Circ: Statement: **742,743**

276 ❑ Jan 1988 Cover: 1.35 **NM** value: **2.25**
Circ: Statement: **763,335**

277 ❑ Mar 1988 Cover: 1.50 **NM** value: **2.25**
Circ: Statement: **763,335**

278 ❑ Apr 1988 Cover: 1.50 **NM** value: **2.25**
Circ: Statement: **763,335**

279 ❑ Jun 1988 Cover: 1.50 **NM** value: **2.25**
Circ: Statement: **763,335**

280 ❑ Jul 1988 Cover: 1.50 **NM** value: **2.25**
Circ: Statement: **763,335**

281 ❑ Sep 1988 Cover: 1.50 **NM** value: **2.25**
Circ: Statement: **763,335**

282 ❑ Oct 1988 Cover: 1.50 **NM** value: **2.25**
Circ: Statement: **763,335**

283 ❑ Dec 1988 Cover: 1.50 **NM** value: **2.25**
Circ: Statement: **763,335**

284 ❑ Jan 1989 Cover: 1.50 **NM** value: **2.25**
Circ: Statement: **784,206**

285 ❑ Mar 1989 Cover: 1.50 **NM** value: **2.25**
Circ: Statement: **784,206**

286 ❑ Apr 1989 Cover: 1.50 **NM** value: **2.25**
Circ: Statement: **784,206**

287 ❑ Jun 1989 Cover: 1.50 **NM** value: **2.25**
Circ: Statement: **784,206**

288 ❑ Jul 1989 Cover: 1.50 **NM** value: **2.25**
Circ: Statement: **784,206**

289 ❑ Sep 1989 Cover: 1.50 **NM** value: **2.25**
Circ: Statement: **784,206**
• Batman parody

290 ❑ Oct 1989 Cover: 1.50 **NM** value: **2.25**
Circ: Statement: **784,206**

291 ❑ Dec 1989 Cover: 1.50 **NM** value: **2.25**
Circ: Statement: **784,206**
• Teenage Mutant Ninja Turtles parody

292 ❑ Jan 1990 Cover: 1.50 **NM** value: **2.25**
Circ: Statement: **681,726**

293 ❑ Mar 1990 Cover: 1.75 **NM** value: **2.25**
Circ: Statement: **681,726**

294 ❑ Apr 1990 Cover: 1.75 **NM** value: **2.25**
Circ: Statement: **681,726**

295 ❑ Jun 1990 Cover: 1.75 **NM** value: **2.25**
Circ: Statement: **681,726**

296 ❑ Jul 1990 Cover: 1.75 **NM** value: **2.25**
Circ: Statement: **681,726**

297 ❑ Sep 1990 Cover: 1.75 **NM** value: **2.25**
Circ: Statement: **681,726**

298 ❑ Oct 1990 Cover: 1.75 **NM** value: **2.25**
Circ: Statement: **681,726**

299 ❑ Dec 1990 Cover: 1.75 **NM** value: **2.25**
Circ: Statement: **681,726**

300 ❑ Jan 1991 Cover: 1.75 **NM** value: **2.25**
Circ: Statement: **584,684**

301 ❑ Mar 1991 Cover: 1.75 **NM** value: **2.00**
Circ: Statement: **584,684**

302 ❑ Apr 1991 Cover: 1.75 **NM** value: **2.00**
Circ: Statement: **584,684**

303 ❑ Jun 1991 Cover: 1.75 **NM** value: **2.00**
Circ: Statement: **584,684**

304 ❑ Jul 1991 Cover: 1.75 **NM** value: **2.00**
Circ: Statement: **584,684**

305 ❑ Sep 1991 Cover: 1.75 **NM** value: **2.00**
Circ: Statement: **584,684**

306 ❑ Oct 1991 Cover: 1.75 **NM** value: **2.00**
Circ: Statement: **584,684**

307 ❑ Dec 1991 Cover: 1.75 **NM** value: **2.00**
Circ: Statement: **584,684**

308 ❑ Jan 1992 Cover: 1.75 **NM** value: **2.00**
Circ: Statement: **503,576**

309 ❑ Mar 1992 Cover: 1.75 **NM** value: **2.00**
Circ: Statement: **503,576**

310 ❑ Apr 1992 Cover: 1.75 **NM** value: **2.00**
Circ: Statement: **503,576**

311 ❑ Jun 1992 Cover: 1.75 **NM** value: **2.00**
Circ: Statement: **503,576**

312 ❑ Jul 1992 Cover: 1.75 **NM** value: **2.00**
Circ: Statement: **503,576**

313 ❑ Sep 1992 Cover: 1.75 **NM** value: **2.00**
Circ: Statement: **503,576**

314 ❑ Oct 1992 Cover: 1.75 **NM** value: **2.00**
Circ: Statement: **503,576**

315 ❑ Dec 1992 Cover: 1.75 **NM** value: **2.00**
Circ: Statement: **503,576**

316 ❑ Jan 1993 Cover: 1.75 **NM** value: **2.00**
Circ: Statement: **478,385**

317 ❑ Mar 1993 Cover: 1.75 **NM** value: **2.00**
Circ: Statement: **478,385**

318 ❑ Apr 1993 Cover: 1.75 **NM** value: **2.00**
Circ: Statement: **478,385**

319 ❑ Jun 1993 Cover: 1.75 **NM** value: **2.00**
Circ: Statement: **478,385**

320 ❑ Jul 1993 Cover: 1.75 **NM** value: **2.00**
Circ: Statement: **478,385**

321 ❑ Sep 1993 Cover: 1.75 **NM** value: **2.00**
Circ: Statement: **478,385**
• Star Trek: Deep Space Nine parody

322 ❑ Oct 1993 Cover: 1.75 **NM** value: **2.00**
Circ: Statement: **478,385**

323 ❑ Dec 1993 Cover: 1.95 **NM** value: **2.00**
Circ: Statement: **478,385**

324 ❑ Jan 1994 Cover: 1.95 **NM** value: **2.00**
Circ: Statement: **409,344**

325 ❑ Feb 1994 Cover: 1.95 **NM** value: **2.00**
Circ: Statement: **409,344**

326 ❑ Mar 1994 Cover: 1.95 **NM** value: **2.00**
Circ: Statement: **409,344**

327 ❑ May 1994 Cover: 1.95 **NM** value: **2.00**
Circ: Statement: **409,344**

328 ❑ Jun 1994 Cover: 1.95 **NM** value: **2.00**
Circ: Statement: **409,344**

329 ❑ Jul 1994 Cover: 1.95 **NM** value: **2.00**
Circ: Statement: **409,344**

330 ❑ Sep 1994 Cover: 1.95 **NM** value: **2.00**
Circ: Statement: **409,344**

331 ❑ Oct 1994 Cover: 1.95 **NM** value: **Cover or less**
Circ: Statement: **409,344**

332 ❑ Dec 1994 Cover: 1.95 **NM** value: **Cover or less**
Circ: Statement: **409,344**

333 ❑ Jan 1995 Cover: 1.95 **NM** value: **Cover or less**
Circ: Statement: **359,936**

334 ❑ Mar 1995 Cover: 1.95 **NM** value: **Cover or less**
Circ: Statement: **359,936**

335 ❑ May 1995 Cover: 1.95 **NM** value: **Cover or less**
Circ: Statement: **359,936** CapCity orders: **2,075**

336 ❑ Jun 1995 Cover: 1.99 **NM** value: **Cover or less**
Circ: Statement: **359,936**

337 ❑ Jul 1995 Cover: 1.99 **NM** value: **Cover or less**
Circ: Statement: **359,936**

338 ❑ Aug 1995 Cover: 1.99 **NM** value: **Cover or less**
Circ: Statement: **359,936**

339 ❑ Sep 1995 Cover: 1.99 **NM** value: **Cover or less**
Circ: Statement: **359,936**

340 ❑ Oct 1995 Cover: 1.99 **NM** value: **Cover or less**
Circ: Statement: **359,936**

341 ❑ Dec 1995 Cover: 1.99 **NM** value: **Cover or less**
Circ: Statement: **309,911**

342 ❑ Jan 1996 Cover: 1.99 **NM** value: **2.00**
Circ: Statement: **309,911**

343 ❑ Mar 1996 Cover: 2.50 **NM** value: **Cover or less**
Circ: Statement: **309,911**

344 ❑ Apr 1996 Cover: 2.50 **NM** value: **Cover or less**
Circ: Statement: **309,911**

345 ❑ May 1996 Cover: 2.50 **NM** value: **Cover or less**
Circ: Statement: **309,911**

346 ❑ Jun 1996 Cover: 2.50 **NM** value: **Cover or less**
Circ: Statement: **309,911**

347 ❑ Jul 1996 Cover: 2.50 **NM** value: **Cover or less**
Circ: Statement: **309,911**

348 ❑ Aug 1996 Cover: 2.50 **NM** value: **Cover or less**
Circ: Statement: **309,911**

349 ❑ Sep 1996 Cover: 2.50 **NM** value: **Cover or less**
Circ: Statement: **309,911**

350 ❑ Oct 1996 Cover: 2.50 **NM** value: **Cover or less**
Circ: Statement: **309,911**

351 ❑ Nov 1996 Cover: 2.50 **NM** value: **Cover or less**
Circ: Statement: **309,660**

352 ❑ Dec 1996 Cover: 2.50 **NM** value: **Cover or less**
Circ: Statement: **309,660**

353 ❑ Jan 1997 Cover: 2.50 **NM** value: **Cover or less**
Circ: Statement: **309,660**

354 ❑ Feb 1997 Cover: 2.50 **NM** value: **Cover or less**
Circ: Statement: **309,660**

355 ❑ Mar 1997 Cover: 2.50 **NM** value: **Cover or less**
Circ: Statement: **309,660**

356 ❑ Apr 1997 Cover: 2.50 **NM** value: **Cover or less**
Circ: Statement: **309,660**

Other grades: Multiply prices above by **1.5 for Mint • 2/3 for Very Fine • 1/3 for Fine • 1/5 for Very Good • 1/8 for Good**

357 ❑ May 1997 Cover: 2.50 **NM** value: **Cover or less**
Circ: Statement: **309,660**
358 ❑ Jun 1997 Cover: 2.50 **NM** value: **Cover or less**
Circ: Statement: **309,660**
359 ❑ Jul 1997 Cover: 2.50 **NM** value: **Cover or less**
Circ: Statement: **309,660**
360 ❑ Aug 1997 Cover: 2.50 **NM** value: **Cover or less**
Circ: Statement: **309,660**
361 ❑ Sep 1997 Cover: 2.50 **NM** value: **Cover or less**
Circ: Statement: **309,660**
362 ❑ Oct 1997 Cover: 2.50 **NM** value: **Cover or less**
Circ: Statement: **309,660**
363 ❑ Nov 1997 Cover: 2.50 **NM** value: **Cover or less**
364 ❑ Dec 1997 Cover: 2.50 **NM** value: **Cover or less**
365 ❑ Jan 1998 Cover: 2.50 **NM** value: **Cover or less**
366 ❑ Feb 1998 Cover: 2.50 **NM** value: **Cover or less**
367 ❑ Mar 1998 Cover: 2.50 **NM** value: **Cover or less**
368 ❑ Apr 1998 Cover: 2.50 **NM** value: **Cover or less**
369 ❑ May 1998 Cover: 2.50 **NM** value: **Cover or less**
370 ❑ Jun 1998 Cover: 2.50 **NM** value: **Cover or less**
371 ❑ Jul 1998 Cover: 2.50 **NM** value: **Cover or less**
372 ❑ Aug 1998 Cover: 2.50 **NM** value: **Cover or less**
373 ❑ Sep 1998 Cover: 2.50 **NM** value: **Cover or less**
374 ❑ Oct 1998 Cover: 2.50 **NM** value: **Cover or less**
375 ❑ Nov 1998 Cover: 2.50 **NM** value: **Cover or less**
376 ❑ Dec 1998 Cover: 2.50 **NM** value: **Cover or less**
377 ❑ Jan 1999 Cover: 2.95 **NM** value: **Cover or less**
📖 Mad's 20 Dumbest People, Events, and Things
378 ❑ Feb 1999 Cover: 2.50 **NM** value: **Cover or less**
379 ❑ Mar 1999 Cover: 2.50 **NM** value: **Cover or less**
380 ❑ Apr 1999 Cover: 2.50 **NM** value: **Cover or less**
381 ❑ May 1999 Cover: 2.75 **NM** value: **Cover or less**
382 ❑ Jun 1999 Cover: 2.75 **NM** value: **Cover or less**
383 ❑ Jul 1999 Cover: 2.75 **NM** value: **Cover or less**
384 ❑ Aug 1999 Cover: 2.75 **NM** value: **Cover or less**
385 ❑ Sep 1999 Cover: 2.75 **NM** value: **Cover or less**
386 ❑ Oct 1999 Cover: 2.75 **NM** value: **Cover or less**
387 ❑ Nov 1999 Cover: 2.75 **NM** value: **Cover or less**
388 ❑ Dec 1999 Cover: 2.75 **NM** value: **Cover or less**
389 ❑ Jan 2000 Cover: 2.95 **NM** value: **Cover or less**
390 ❑ Feb 2000 Cover: 2.99 **NM** value: **Cover or less**
391 ❑ Mar 2000 Cover: 2.99 **NM** value: **Cover or less**
392 ❑ Apr 2000 Cover: 2.99 **NM** value: **Cover or less**
393 ❑ May 2000 Cover: 2.99 **NM** value: **Cover or less**
394 ❑ Jun 2000 Cover: 2.99 **NM** value: **Cover or less**
395 ❑ Jul 2000 Cover: 2.99 **NM** value: **Cover or less**
396 ❑ Aug 2000 Cover: 2.99 **NM** value: **Cover or less**
397 ❑ Sep 2000 Cover: 2.99 **NM** value: **Cover or less**
398 ❑ Oct 2000 Cover: 2.99 **NM** value: **Cover or less**
399 ❑ Nov 2000 Cover: 2.99 **NM** value: **Cover or less**
400 ❑ Dec 2000 Cover: 2.99 **NM** value: **Cover or less**
401 ❑ Jan 2001 Cover: 2.99 **NM** value: **Cover or less**
402 ❑ Feb 2001 Cover: 2.99 **NM** value: **Cover or less**
403 ❑ Mar 2001 Cover: 2.99 **NM** value: **Cover or less**
404 ❑ Apr 2001 Cover: 2.99 **NM** value: **Cover or less**
405 ❑ May 2001 Cover: 2.99 **NM** value: **Cover or less**
406 ❑ Jun 2001 Cover: 2.99 **NM** value: **Cover or less**
407 ❑ Jul 2001 Cover: 2.99 **NM** value: **Cover or less**
408 ❑ Aug 2001 Cover: 2.99 **NM** value: **Cover or less**

MAD 2992, THE — Graphic Image

Ash 2 ❑ **NM** value: **1.00**
📖 From The Future **A:** Bill Byrne **W:** Bill Byrne

MAD ABOUT MILLIE — Marvel

Millie the Model began her long run in 1945, and her "home" series ended in 1973. Marvel published several Millie titles over the years: Life with Millie, A Date with Millie, and this one, Mad about Millie, which ran from 1969 until 1970. Millie is a fashion model who gets into all sorts of Archie Andrews-esque situations, including competitions with her Reggie Mantle-esque rival, Chili. Like Archie comics, the Millie titles are designed to appeal to younger teens, particularly girls, and their emphasis is on lighthearted fun. Because this title's short run fell in the heart of the bell-bottom era, the fashions are indicative of the early 1970s: lots of beads, flared pants legs, and wild prints. And, hey, many of the stories were written by Stan "The Man" Lee himself!

1 ❑ Apr 1969 Cover: 0.15 **NM** value: **35.00**
• **CGC:** 1 graded, best 9.2
2 ❑ ca. 1969 Cover: 0.15 **NM** value: **28.00**
3 ❑ ca. 1969 Cover: 0.15 **NM** value: **25.00**
4 ❑ ca. 1969 Cover: 0.15 **NM** value: **15.00**
5 ❑ Nov 1969 Cover: 0.15 **NM** value: **15.00**
📖 Chili Strikes Again!; New Summer Pants Fashions for Millie (pinup); Her Hair-Raising Tale!; Millie's Summer Party Outfits (pinup); Dolly Dimly: A Shrinker's a Clinker!; Millie's Mini Poster; The Miss Gets a Kiss **A:** Stan Goldberg **W:** Stan Lee ★ Appearance of Clicker, Dolly Dimly, Chili, Daisy.
6 ❑ Dec 1969 Cover: 0.15 **NM** value: **12.00**
7 ❑ Jan 1970 Cover: 0.15 **NM** value: **12.00**
8 ❑ Feb 1970 Cover: 0.15 **NM** value: **12.00**
9 ❑ Mar 1970 Cover: 0.15 **NM** value: **12.00**
10 ❑ Apr 1970 Cover: 0.15 **NM** value: **10.00**
11 ❑ May 1970 Cover: 0.15 **NM** value: **10.00**
12 ❑ Jun 1970 Cover: 0.15 **NM** value: **10.00**
13 ❑ Jul 1970 Cover: 0.15 **NM** value: **10.00**
14 ❑ Aug 1970 Cover: 0.15 **NM** value: **10.00**
15 ❑ Sep 1970 Cover: 0.15 **NM** value: **10.00**
16 ❑ Oct 1970 Cover: 0.15 **NM** value: **10.00**
17 ❑ Nov 1970 Cover: 0.15 **NM** value: **10.00**
• Never published?
Anl 1 ❑ **NM** value: **15.00**

MAD ABOUT TV — E.C.

1 ❑ Cover: 14.95 **NM** value: **Cover or less**

MADAME XANADU — DC

1 ❑ Jul 1981 Cover: 2.00 **NM** value: **3.00**
• **CGC:** 1 graded, best 9.2
📖 Dance for Two Demons; Falling Down to Heaven... **A:** Brian Bolland; Marshall Rogers **W:** J.M. DeMatteis; Steve Englehart ★ Origin of Madame Xanadu.

MADBALLS — Marvel / Star

1 ❑ Sep 1986 Cover: 0.75 **NM** value: **1.00**
Circ: CapCity orders: **5,600**
📖 The Evil Dr. Frankenbeans **A:** Howie Post **W:** Michael Gallagher ★ Origin of Madballs. ★ 1st Appearance of Madballs, Colonel Corn.
2 ❑ Oct 1986 Cover: 0.75 **NM** value: **1.00**
Circ: CapCity orders: **3,700**
3 ❑ Nov 1986 Cover: 0.75 **NM** value: **1.00**
Circ: CapCity orders: **3,300**
4 ❑ Jun 1987 Cover: 1.00 **NM** value: **Cover or less**
Circ: CapCity orders: **2,650**
5 ❑ Aug 1987 Cover: 1.00 **NM** value: **Cover or less**
Circ: CapCity orders: **1,750**
6 ❑ Oct 1987 Cover: 1.00 **NM** value: **Cover or less**
7 ❑ Dec 1987 Cover: 1.00 **NM** value: **Cover or less**
8 ❑ Feb 1988 Cover: 1.00 **NM** value: **Cover or less**
Circ: CapCity orders: **1,500**
9 ❑ Apr 1988 Cover: 1.00 **NM** value: **Cover or less**
Circ: CapCity orders: **1,400**
10 ❑ Jun 1988 Cover: 1.00 **NM** value: **Cover or less**
Circ: CapCity orders: **1,100**

MAD BATHROOM COMPANION, THE — E.C.

1 ❑ Cover: 9.95 **NM** value: **Cover or less**

MAD-DOG — Marvel

Comics imitate TV imitating comics in this novel title. In 1992, television's Bob Newhart starred in a new series, "Bob," playing a comic artist from the Golden Age. Asked to update his comic book for the 1990s, he's teamed up with egotistical "graphic novelist" Harlan Stone. This team has more than its share of tension, with Bob's "Goody Two-Shoes" style conflicting with the "gritty realism" of Harlan's vision for the hero.

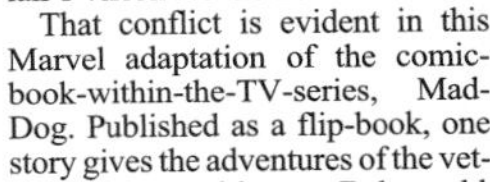

That conflict is evident in this Marvel adaptation of the comic-book-within-the-TV-series, Mad-Dog. Published as a flip-book, one story gives the adventures of the veterinarian-turned-hero as Bob would have told them, full of silly villains and wholesome dialog. The flip side has a more contemporary feel, complete with the obligatory "ghastly experiment at the hands of shadowy powers" origin, and lots of street thugs to beat up.

The TV show became Newhart's one failure on CBS, laden with far too much baggage and far too little Bob. The comic book, while a strange artifact, shows just how many comics Marvel was willing to put out in this period.

1 ❑ May 1993 Cover: 1.25 **NM** value: **Cover or less**
📖 Mad-Dog vs. The Truly Amazing Space Creatures From The Omega Galaxy **A:** Ty Templeton **W:** Ty Templeton; Bob McKay
2 ❑ Jun 1993 Cover: 1.25 **NM** value: **Cover or less**
📖 All-Out Action Ish **A:** Ty Templeton **W:** Ty Templeton; Bob McKay ★ Origin of Mad-Dog.
3 ❑ Jul 1993 Cover: 1.25 **NM** value: **Cover or less**
4 ❑ Aug 1993 Cover: 1.25 **NM** value: **Cover or less**
5 ❑ Sep 1993 Cover: 1.25 **NM** value: **Cover or less**
6 ❑ Oct 1993 Cover: 1.25 **NM** value: **Cover or less**
📖 Dogs of War final issue. **A:** Gordon Purcell; Ty Templeton **W:** Evan Dorkin; Ty Templeton

MAD DOG MAGAZINE — Blackthorne

1 ❑ Cover: 1.75 **NM** value: **Cover or less**
2 ❑ Cover: 1.75 **NM** value: **Cover or less**
3 ❑ Mar 1987 Cover: 1.75 **NM** value: **Cover or less**

MAD DOGS — Eclipse

1 ❑ Cover: 2.50 **NM** value: **Cover or less**
Circ: CapCity orders: **2,725**
A: Victor Toppi **W:** Chuck Dixon
2 ❑ Cover: 2.50 **NM** value: **Cover or less**
3 ❑ Cover: 2.50 **NM** value: **Cover or less**

MAD GROSS BOOK, THE — E.C.

1 ❑ Cover: 9.95 **NM** value: **Cover or less**
A: Sergio Aragonés; Harvey Kurtzman; Peter Kuper; Dave Berg; Al Jaffee; Don Martin; John Caldwell; John Pound; Kevin Pope; Tom Bunk **W:** Sergio Aragonés; Peter Kuper; Al Jaffee; Don Martin; Tom Bunk; Will Elder; David Shayne; Desmond Devlin; Duck Edwing

MAD HATTER — O.W.

1 ❑ Jan 1946 Cover: 0.10 **NM** value: **750.00**
• **CGC:** 1 graded, best 9.0
2 ❑ Sep 1946 Cover: 0.10 **NM** value: **300.00**
• **CGC:** 1 graded, best 9.2

MAD HOUSE — Red Circle

The publishing history of Mad House is one of the more convoluted in Archie's history. While the Mad House part of the name stayed with the title, it began as Archie's Madhouse in 1959. In 1969, it became Madhouse Ma-ad for a short time(adding Jokes to the title at one point and, later, Freak-Out to the title after Jokes was dropped). In the early 1970s, it changed title again to Madhouse Glads before changing once again to just simply Mad House in 1974, a title it retained until its cancellation in 1982.

The simple humor series deviated from the typical Archie model of teen-age romantic comedy with silly super-hero stories, mirthful monster tales, and screwy science-fiction scenes. While the Archie gang did make cover appearances in the early going, by this part of the overall series, they were nowhere to be found. — Brent

95 ❑ Sep 1974 Cover: 0.25 **NM** value: **4.00**
Circ: Statement: **121,728**
96 ❑ Nov 1974 Cover: 0.25 **NM** value: **4.00**
Circ: Statement: **121,728**
📖 Mever Bother a Dead Man; Demon Kiss; The Respect for the Dead (text story); The Devil's Matchmaker; The Gentlest Dog on the Block! **A:** Bruce Jones; Sal Amendola; Jesse Santos **W:** Bruce Jones; John Jacobson; Marvin Channing
97 ❑ Jan 1975 Cover: 0.25 **NM** value: **3.00**
Circ: Statement: **104,823**
98 ❑ Aug 1975 Cover: 0.25 **NM** value: **3.00**
Circ: Statement: **104,823**
• Has 1974 Statement, filed 10/1/74; avg print run 273,017; avg sales 121,368; avg subs 360; avg total paid 121,728; 55% of run returned
99 ❑ Sep 1975 Cover: 0.25 **NM** value: **3.00**
Circ: Statement: **104,823**
100 ❑ Nov 1975 Cover: 0.25 **NM** value: **3.00**
Circ: Statement: **104,823**
101 ❑ Feb 1976 Cover: 0.25 **NM** value: **2.50**
Circ: Statement: **99,411**
102 ❑ May 1976 Cover: 0.30 **NM** value: **2.50**
Circ: Statement: **99,411**
103 ❑ 1976 **NM** value: **2.50**
Circ: Statement: **99,411**
104 ❑ Sep 1976 Cover: 0.30 **NM** value: **2.50**
Circ: Statement: **99,411**
105 ❑ Nov 1976 Cover: 0.30 **NM** value: **2.50**
Circ: Statement: **99,411**
106 ❑ Feb 1977 Cover: 0.30 **NM** value: **2.50**
Circ: Statement: **89,755**
107 ❑ May 1977 Cover: 0.30 **NM** value: **2.50**
Circ: Statement: **89,755**
• Has 1976 Statement; avg total paid circ 99,411
108 ❑ 1977 **NM** value: **2.50**
Circ: Statement: **89,755**
109 ❑ Sep 1977 Cover: 0.35 **NM** value: **2.50**
Circ: Statement: **89,755**
110 ❑ Nov 1977 Cover: 0.35 **NM** value: **2.50**
Circ: Statement: **89,755**
111 ❑ Feb 1978 Cover: 0.35 **NM** value: **2.50**
112 ❑ May 1978 Cover: 0.35 **NM** value: **2.50**
• Has 1977 Statement, filed 10/1/1997; avg print run 228,939; avg sales 89,595; avg subs 160; avg total paid 89,755; office use 300; max existent 90,055; 61% of run returned
113 ❑ Aug 1978 Cover: 0.35 **NM** value: **2.50**
114 ❑ Nov 1978 Cover: 0.35 **NM** value: **2.50**
115 ❑ Feb 1979 Cover: 0.35 **NM** value: **2.50**
116 ❑ May 1979 Cover: 0.40 **NM** value: **2.50**
117 ❑ Aug 1979 Cover: 0.40 **NM** value: **2.50**
118 ❑ Nov 1979 Cover: 0.40 **NM** value: **2.50**
119 ❑ Feb 1980 Cover: 0.40 **NM** value: **2.50**
120 ❑ May 1980 Cover: 0.40 **NM** value: **2.50**
121 ❑ Aug 1980 Cover: 0.50 **NM** value: **2.50**
122 ❑ Nov 1980 Cover: 0.50 **NM** value: **2.50**
123 ❑ Feb 1981 Cover: 0.50 **NM** value: **2.50**
124 ❑ May 1981 Cover: 0.50 **NM** value: **2.50**
125 ❑ Aug 1981 Cover: 0.50 **NM** value: **2.50**
126 ❑ Oct 1981 Cover: 0.50 **NM** value: **2.50**
127 ❑ Mar 1982 Cover: 0.60 **NM** value: **2.50**
128 ❑ Jun 1982 Cover: 0.60 **NM** value: **2.50**
129 ❑ Aug 1982 Cover: 0.60 **NM** value: **2.50**
130 ❑ Oct 1982 Cover: 0.60 **NM** value: **2.50**

MADHOUSE (AJAX) — Ajax

1 ❑ Mar 1954 Cover: 0.10 **NM** value: **200.00**
2 ❑ May 1954 Cover: 0.10 **NM** value: **125.00**
• **CGC:** 1 graded, best 7.0
3 ❑ Jul 1954 Cover: 0.10 **NM** value: **125.00**
4 ❑ Sep 1954 Cover: 0.10 **NM** value: **125.00**

MADHOUSE GLADS — Archie

73 ❑ May 1970 Cover: 0.15 **NM** value: **3.00**
Circ: Statement: **186,736**
1st printing. • Previous issues published as Madhouse Ma-ad Freakout
74 ❑ Jul 1970 Cover: 0.15 **NM** value: **3.00**
Circ: Statement: **186,736**
75 ❑ Sep 1970 Cover: 0.15 **NM** value: **3.00**
Circ: Statement: **186,736**
76 ❑ Nov 1970 Cover: 0.15 **NM** value: **3.00**
Circ: Statement: **186,736**
77 ❑ Feb 1971 Cover: 0.15 **NM** value: **3.00**
78 ❑ May 1971 Cover: 0.25 **NM** value: **5.00**
• Has 1970 Statement, filed 10/1/1970; avg print run 359,997; avg sales 186,736; no subscriptions reported; avg total paid 186,736

CGC-graded: Multiply prices above by **33 for 9.9 M • 16 for 9.8 NM/M • 7 for 9.6 NM+ • 5 for 9.4 NM • 2.5 for 9.2 NM- • 1.5 for 9.0 VF/NM**

79 ❑ Aug 1971 Cover: 0.25 **NM** value: **5.00**
80 ❑ Sep 1971 Cover: 0.25 **NM** value: **5.00**
81 ❑ Nov 1971 Cover: 0.25 **NM** value: **5.00**
82 ❑ Feb 1972 Cover: 0.25 **NM** value: **5.00**
Circ: Statement: **143,371**
83 ❑ May 1972 Cover: 0.25 **NM** value: **5.00**
Circ: Statement: **143,371**
84 ❑ Aug 1972 Cover: 0.25 **NM** value: **5.00**
Circ: Statement: **143,371**
85 ❑ Oct 1972 Cover: 0.25 **NM** value: **5.00**
Circ: Statement: **143,371**
86 ❑ Dec 1972 Cover: 0.25 **NM** value: **5.00**
Circ: Statement: **143,371**
87 ❑ Feb 1973 Cover: 0.25 **NM** value: **5.00**
Circ: Statement: **127,045**
88 ❑ May 1973 Cover: 0.25 **NM** value: **5.00**
Circ: Statement: **127,045**
• Has 1972 Statement, filed 10/1/1972; avg print run 314,922; avg sales 143,371; no subscriptions reported; avg total paid 143,371
89 ❑ Aug 1973 Cover: 0.25 **NM** value: **5.00**
Circ: Statement: **127,045**
90 ❑ Oct 1973 Cover: 0.25 **NM** value: **5.00**
Circ: Statement: **127,045**
91 ❑ Dec 1973 Cover: 0.25 **NM** value: **5.00**
Circ: Statement: **127,045**
92 ❑ Feb 1974 Cover: 0.25 **NM** value: **5.00**
Circ: Statement: **121,728**
93 ❑ May 1974 Cover: 0.25 **NM** value: **3.00**
Circ: Statement: **121,728**
• Has 1973 Statement; avg total paid circ 127,045
94 ❑ Aug 1974 Cover: 0.25 **NM** value: **3.00**
Circ: Statement: **121,728**
• Later issues published as Madhouse

MADHOUSE MA-AD JOKES — Archie

66 ❑ Feb 1969 Cover: 0.12 **NM** value: **3.50**
Circ: Statement: **209,897**
• Previous issues published as Archie's Madhouse
67 ❑ Apr 1969 Cover: 0.12 **NM** value: **3.50**
Circ: Statement: **209,897**
68 ❑ Jun 1969 Cover: 0.12 **NM** value: **3.50**
Circ: Statement: **209,897**
69 ❑ Aug 1969 Cover: 0.15 **NM** value: **3.50**
Circ: Statement: **209,897**
70 ❑ Oct 1969 Cover: 0.15 **NM** value: **3.50**
Circ: Statement: **209,897**
final issue. • Series continues as Madhouse Ma-ad Freakout

MADHOUSE MA-AD FREAKOUT — Archie

71 ❑ ca. 1969 Cover: 0.15 **NM** value: **3.00**
Circ: Statement: **209,897**
• Earlier issues published as Madhouse Ma-ad Jokes
72 ❑ Jan 1970 Cover: 0.15 **NM** value: **3.00**
Circ: Statement: **186,736**
• Later issues published as Madhouse Glads

MADMAN — Tundra

Mike Allred's Madman is one of the strongest and strangest comics of the 1990s. Madman is a disturbed young man who goes around in a baggy costume and a mask with the mouth sewn shut. He has an unusual sensitivity that allows him to sense guilty secrets within people, but his inability to focus and concentrate gets him into all kinds of trouble. Allred's handling of the material maximizes the disturbing qualities of the story, as he abruptly intrudes on an amusing sequence with an intensely violent image or inserts a subversive element that makes the reader doubt the entire sense of reality Allred has created in Madman's world. This psychotic, detached ambiguity is Madman's singular achievement and one which gives it a literary gravity that is impossible to ignore.

1 ❑ Mar 1992, b&w Cover: 3.95 **NM** value: **10.00**
• **CGC:** 1 graded, best 9.2
• prestige format. 🕮 Trapped By Gravity • flip-action corners **A:** Mike Allred **W:** Mike Allred
1-2 ❑ Cover: 3.95 **NM** value: **5.00**
1-3 ❑ Cover: 3.95 **NM** value: **4.00**
2 ❑ Apr 1992 Cover: 3.95 **NM** value: **8.00**
• **CGC:** 1 graded, best 9.2
A: Mike Allred **W:** Mike Allred
3 ❑ May 1992 Cover: 3.95 **NM** value: **8.00**
A: Mike Allred **W:** Mike Allred
Bk 1❑ **NM** value: **12.95**
• The Oddity Odyssey **A:** Mike Allred **W:** Mike Allred
Bk 1-2❑ Cover: 12.95 **NM** value: **Cover or less**

MADMAN ADVENTURES — Tundra

1 ❑ ca. 1993 Cover: 2.95 **NM** value: **5.00**
Circ: CapCity orders: **4,975**
A: Mike Allred **W:** Mike Allred
2 ❑ ca. 1993 Cover: 2.95 **NM** value: **4.00**
Circ: CapCity orders: **3,944**
A: Mike Allred **W:** Mike Allred
3 ❑ ca. 1993 Cover: 2.95 **NM** value: **4.00**
Circ: CapCity orders: **4,175**
🕮 Inevitability of the Impossible **A:** Mike Allred **W:** Mike Allred
Bk 1❑ Cover: 14.95 **NM** value: **Cover or less**
• Collects series **A:** Mike Allred **W:** Mike Allred

MADMAN BOOGALOO — Dark Horse

Bk 1❑ Jun 1999 Cover: 8.95 **NM** value: **Cover or less**
• Starring Nexus & The Jam

MADMAN COMICS — Dark Horse

Madman's first name is Frank. Last name: Einstein. At least, that's the name they gave him when he was brought back from the dead. Before that, he was an average John Doe: terrible car crash, dug up from the grave, reanimated — all the usual stuff.

Now he's a happy guy living in Snap City. He dresses up in the lightning bolt costume due to both a recovered memory of childhood hero Mr. Excitement and because it helps hide the scars. He leads a normal life, hanging out with his girlfriend Joe (who thinks he's really "gingy!") and assisting Dr. Flem and his bandaged assistant Gail in the laboratory. Oh, yeah, he occasionally takes on street beatniks with his toy disc gun (modified to actually hurt when they get hit) and battles the odd space alien or two. It's OK, though, because, when one knocks him unconscious and drags him into the heart of its ship, there's a pretty fair chance that it just wants to ask him to be its friend.

1 ❑ Apr 1994 Cover: 2.95 **NM** value: **4.00**
Circ: CapCity orders: **19,075**
🕮 The Living End **A:** Mike Allred; Frank Miller(back cover) **W:** Mike Allred ★ Origin of Madman.
2 ❑ Jun 1994 Cover: 2.95 **NM** value: **3.50**
Circ: CapCity orders: **13,725**
A: Mike Allred **W:** Mike Allred
3 ❑ Aug 1994 Cover: 2.95 **NM** value: **3.50**
Circ: CapCity orders: **12,500**
A: Mike Allred **W:** Mike Allred
4 ❑ Oct 1994 Cover: 2.95 **NM** value: **3.00**
Circ: CapCity orders: **11,725**
A: Mike Allred **W:** Mike Allred
5 ❑ Jan 1995 Cover: 2.95 **NM** value: **3.00**
Circ: CapCity orders: **9,650**
A: Mike Allred **W:** Mike Allred
6 ❑ Mar 1995 Cover: 2.95 **NM** value: **3.00**
Circ: CapCity orders: **10,200**
A: Mike Allred **W:** Mike Allred
7 ❑ May 1995 Cover: 2.95 **NM** value: **3.00**
Circ: CapCity orders: **9,425**
A: Mike Allred **W:** Mike Allred
8 ❑ Jul 1995 Cover: 2.95 **NM** value: **3.00**
Circ: CapCity orders: **9,500**
A: Mike Allred **W:** Mike Allred
9 ❑ Oct 1995 Cover: 2.95 **NM** value: **3.00**
A: Mike Allred **W:** Mike Allred
10 ❑ Jan 1996 Cover: 2.95 **NM** value: **Cover or less**
A: Mike Allred **W:** Mike Allred
11 ❑ Oct 1996 Cover: 2.95 **NM** value: **Cover or less**
Circ: Diamd. preorders: **22,327**
🕮 The Truth About Everything…And All the Rest! **A:** Mike Allred **W:** Mike Allred
12 ❑ Apr 1999 Cover: 2.95 **NM** value: **Cover or less**
Circ: Diamd. preorders: **15,668**
🕮 The Exit of Dr. Boiffard, Part 1 • Doctor Robot back-up; Dr. Robot back-up **A:** Mike Allred **W:** Mike Allred
13 ❑ May 1999 Cover: 2.95 **NM** value: **Cover or less**
Circ: Diamd. preorders: **14,981**
🕮 The Exit of Dr. Boiffard, Part 2 • Doctor Robot back-up; Dr. Robot back-up **A:** Mike Allred **W:** Mike Allred
14 ❑ Jun 1999 Cover: 2.95 **NM** value: **Cover or less**
Circ: Diamd. preorders: **14,664**
🕮 The Exit of Dr. Boiffard, Part 3 • Doctor Robot back-up; Dr. Robot back-up **A:** Mike Allred **W:** Mike Allred
15 ❑ Jul 1999 Cover: 2.95 **NM** value: **Cover or less**
Circ: Diamd. preorders: **13,866**
🕮 The Exit of Dr. Boiffard, Part 4 • Doctor Robot back-up; Dr. Robot back-up **A:** Mike Allred **W:** Mike Allred
16 ❑ Dec 1999 Cover: 2.95 **NM** value: **Cover or less**
Circ: Diamd. preorders: **12,898**
🕮 Frank Einstein's Holi-Daze Adventure **A:** Mike Allred **W:** Mike Allred
17 ❑ Aug 2000 Cover: 2.95 **NM** value: **Cover or less**
🕮 G-Men From Hell, Part 1 **A:** Mike Allred **W:** Mike Allred
18 ❑ Sep 2000 Cover: 2.95 **NM** value: **Cover or less**
🕮 G-Men From Hell, Part 2 **A:** Mike Allred **W:** Mike Allred
19 ❑ Oct 2000 Cover: 2.99 **NM** value: **Cover or less**
🕮 G-Men From Hell, Part 3 **A:** Mike Allred **W:** Mike Allred
20 ❑ Dec 2000 Cover: 2.99 **NM** value: **Cover or less**
🕮 G-Men From Hell, Part 4 **A:** Mike Allred **W:** Mike Allred
Bk 1❑ Nov 1996 Cover: 17.95 **NM** value: **Cover or less**
• The Complete Madman Comics; collects issues #6-10 **A:** Mike Allred **W:** Mike Allred
YB 1995❑ Jan 1996 Cover: 17.95 **NM** value: **Cover or less**
• Yearbook '95. • collects Madman Comics #1-5 **A:** Mike Allred **W:** Mike Allred

MADMAN/THE JAM — Dark Horse

1 ❑ Jul 1998 Cover: 2.95 **NM** value: **Cover or less**
Circ: Diamd. preorders: **15,015**
🕮 House of Escher I **A:** Bernie Mireault; Mike Allred **W:** Bernie Mireault; Mike Allred
2 ❑ Aug 1998 Cover: 2.95 **NM** value: **Cover or less**
Circ: Diamd. preorders: **13,521**
🕮 House of Escher II **A:** Bernie Mireault; Mike Allred **W:** Bernie Mireault; Mike Allred

MADMAN: TWO TRILOGIES — Graphitti

Bk 1/LE❑ Cover: 79.95 **NM** value: **Cover or less**
hardcover. • collects Tundra-published stories

MAD MONSTER PARTY — Dell

1 ❑ Sep 1967 Cover: 0.12 **NM** value: **50.00**
• **CGC:** 1 graded, best 9.6

MAD MONSTER PARTY ADAPTATION — Black Bear

1 ❑ **NM** value: **2.95**
2 ❑ **NM** value: **2.95**
3 ❑ **NM** value: **2.95**
4 ❑ **NM** value: **2.95**

MADONNA — Personality

1 ❑ b&w Cover: 2.95 **NM** value: **Cover or less**
1/Aut❑ b&w Cover: 3.95 **NM** value: **Cover or less**
2 ❑ b&w Cover: 2.95 **NM** value: **Cover or less**
2/Aut❑ b&w Cover: 3.95 **NM** value: **Cover or less**

MADONNA SEX GODDESS — Friendly

1 ❑ ca. 1990 Cover: 2.95 **NM** value: **Cover or less**
2 ❑ ca. 1991 Cover: 2.95 **NM** value: **Cover or less**
3 ❑ ca. 1991 Cover: 2.95 **NM** value: **Cover or less**

MADONNA SPECIAL — Revolutionary

1 ❑ Aug 1993, b&w Cover: 2.50 **NM** value: **Cover or less**

MADONNA VS. MARILYN — Celebrity

1 ❑ Cover: 2.95 **NM** value: **Cover or less**

MAD RACCOONS — Mu

1 ❑ Jul 1991 Cover: 2.50 **NM** value: **Cover or less**
2 ❑ Sep 1992 Cover: 2.50 **NM** value: **Cover or less**
3 ❑ Aug 1993 Cover: 2.50 **NM** value: **Cover or less**
4 ❑ Aug 1994 Cover: 2.95 **NM** value: **Cover or less**
5 ❑ Aug 1995 Cover: 2.95 **NM** value: **Cover or less**
cardstock cover.
6 ❑ Jul 1996 Cover: 2.95 **NM** value: **Cover or less**
cardstock cover.
Bk 1❑ Jul 1995 Cover: 14.95 **NM** value: **Cover or less**
• collects issues #1-4 plus additional material

MADRAVEN HALLOWEEN SPECIAL — Hamilton

1 ❑ Oct 1995 Cover: 2.95 **NM** value: **Cover or less**
No issue number. One-shot. 🕮 Song of the Silkie **A:** Gray Morrow; Jan Duursema **W:** Nicola Cutii; Gary Gabner ★ Appearance of Wolff & Byrd, Hoo-Hah back-up.

MAD SUPER SPECIAL — E.C.

Begun as a series of lengthier reprints of "the worst" of Mad, the Mad Super Specials evolved into a more regular reprint series in the late 1960s and early 1970s, adding such bonuses as flexi-disc records, pages of stickers, pull-out posters, and other ephemera.

At one point, comic-book sized reprints of color material from the first 23 issues of the series (when it was in a comic-book-sized format) were included as an extra bonus, allowing readers who came along late in the game to experience those early issues. — Brent

1 ❑ Fal 1970 Cover: 0.60 **NM** value: **90.00**
2 ❑ Spr 1971 Cover: 0.60 **NM** value: **54.00**
3 ❑ 1971 Cover: 0.60 **NM** value: **44.00**
4 ❑ 1971 Cover: 0.60 **NM** value: **44.00**
5 ❑ 1971 Cover: 0.60 **NM** value: **44.00**
6 ❑ 1971 Cover: 0.60 **NM** value: **38.00**
7 ❑ 1972 Cover: 0.60 **NM** value: **38.00**
8 ❑ 1972 Cover: 0.60 **NM** value: **38.00**
9 ❑ 1972 Cover: 0.60 **NM** value: **38.00**
10 ❑ 1973 Cover: 0.60 **NM** value: **38.00**
11 ❑ 1973 Cover: 0.75 **NM** value: **26.00**
12 ❑ Cover: 0.75 **NM** value: **26.00**
13 ❑ Cover: 0.75 **NM** value: **26.00**
14 ❑ 1974 Cover: 0.75 **NM** value: **26.00**
15 ❑ 1974 Cover: 0.75 **NM** value: **26.00**
16 ❑ Cover: 1.00 **NM** value: **20.00**
17 ❑ 1975 Cover: 1.00 **NM** value: **20.00**
18 ❑ Cover: 1.00 **NM** value: **20.00**
19 ❑ 1976 Cover: 1.00 **NM** value: **20.00**
20 ❑ 1976 Cover: 1.00 **NM** value: **20.00**
21 ❑ 1976 Cover: 1.00 **NM** value: **16.00**
22 ❑ 1977 Cover: 1.00 **NM** value: **16.00**
23 ❑ 1977 Cover: 1.00 **NM** value: **16.00**
24 ❑ 1977 Cover: 1.00 **NM** value: **16.00**
25 ❑ Cover: 1.25 **NM** value: **16.00**
26 ❑ 1978 Cover: 1.25 **NM** value: **12.00**
27 ❑ 1978 Cover: 1.25 **NM** value: **12.00**
28 ❑ Fal 1979 Cover: 1.25 **NM** value: **12.00**
29 ❑ Win 1979 Cover: 1.25 **NM** value: **12.00**
30 ❑ Spr 1980 Cover: 1.25 **NM** value: **12.00**
31 ❑ Sum 1980 Cover: 1.50 **NM** value: **10.00**
32 ❑ Fal 1980 Cover: 1.50 **NM** value: **10.00**
33 ❑ Win 1980 Cover: 1.50 **NM** value: **10.00**
34 ❑ Spr 1981 Cover: 1.50 **NM** value: **10.00**
35 ❑ Sum 1981 Cover: 1.50 **NM** value: **10.00**
36 ❑ Fal 1981 Cover: 1.50 **NM** value: **10.00**
37 ❑ Win 1981 Cover: 1.75 **NM** value: **10.00**
38 ❑ Spr 1982 Cover: 1.75 **NM** value: **10.00**
39 ❑ Sum 1982 Cover: 1.75 **NM** value: **10.00**
40 ❑ Fal 1982 Cover: 2.00 **NM** value: **10.00**

Other grades: Multiply prices above by **1.5 for Mint • 2/3 for Very Fine • 1/3 for Fine • 1/5 for Very Good • 1/8 for Good**

41 ❑ Win 1982 Cover: 2.00 NM value: 6.00
42 ❑ Win 1983 Cover: 2.00 NM value: 6.00
43 ❑ Spr 1983 Cover: 2.00 NM value: 6.00
44 ❑ Sum 1983 Cover: 2.00 NM value: 6.00
45 ❑ Fal 1983 Cover: 2.00 NM value: 6.00
46 ❑ Spr 1984 Cover: 2.00 NM value: 6.00
47 ❑ Sum 1984 NM value: 6.00
48 ❑ Fal 1984 Cover: 2.50 NM value: 6.00
49 ❑ Win 1984 Cover: 2.50 NM value: 6.00
50 ❑ Spr 1985 Cover: 2.50 NM value: 6.00
51 ❑ Sum 1985 Cover: 2.50 NM value: 4.50
52 ❑ Fal 1985 Cover: 2.50 NM value: 4.50
53 ❑ Win 1985 Cover: 2.50 NM value: 4.50
54 ❑ Spr 1986 Cover: 2.50 NM value: 4.50
55 ❑ Sum 1986 Cover: 2.50 NM value: 4.50
56 ❑ Fal 1986 Cover: 2.75 NM value: 4.50
57 ❑ Win 1986 Cover: 2.75 NM value: 4.50
58 ❑ Spr 1987 Cover: 2.75 NM value: 4.50
59 ❑ Sum 1987 Cover: 2.75 NM value: 4.50
60 ❑ Fal 1987 Cover: 2.75 NM value: 4.50
61 ❑ Win 1987 Cover: 2.75 NM value: 4.00
62 ❑ Spr 1988 Cover: 2.75 NM value: 4.00
63 ❑ Sum 1988 Cover: 2.75 NM value: 4.00
64 ❑ Fal 1988 Cover: 2.95 NM value: 4.00
65 ❑ Win 1988 Cover: 2.95 NM value: 4.00
66 ❑ Spr 1989 Cover: 2.95 NM value: 4.00
67 ❑ Sum 1989 Cover: 2.95 NM value: 4.00
68 ❑ Fal 1989 Cover: 2.95 NM value: 4.00
69 ❑ Win 1989 Cover: 2.95 NM value: 4.00
70 ❑ Spr 1990 Cover: 2.95 NM value: 4.00
71 ❑ Sum 1990 Cover: 3.50 NM value: Cover or less
72 ❑ Fal 1990 Cover: 3.50 NM value: Cover or less
73 ❑ Win 1990 Cover: 3.50 NM value: Cover or less
74 ❑ Spr 1991 Cover: 3.50 NM value: Cover or less
75 ❑ Sum 1991 Cover: 3.50 NM value: Cover or less
76 ❑ Fal 1991 Cover: 3.50 NM value: Cover or less
77 ❑ Win 1991 Cover: 3.50 NM value: Cover or less
78 ❑ Jan 1992 Cover: 3.50 NM value: Cover or less
79 ❑ Feb 1992 Cover: 3.50 NM value: Cover or less
80 ❑ Mar 1992 Cover: 3.50 NM value: Cover or less
81 ❑ May 1992 Cover: 3.50 NM value: Cover or less
82 ❑ Jul 1992 Cover: 4.50 NM value: Cover or less
83 ❑ Sep 1992 Cover: 3.50 NM value: Cover or less
84 ❑ Nov 1992 Cover: 3.50 NM value: Cover or less
85 ❑ Jan 1993 Cover: 3.50 NM value: Cover or less
86 ❑ Mar 1993 Cover: 3.50 NM value: Cover or less
87 ❑ May 1993 Cover: 3.50 NM value: Cover or less
88 ❑ Jul 1993 Cover: 3.50 NM value: Cover or less
89 ❑ Sep 1993 Cover: 3.50 NM value: Cover or less
90 ❑ Nov 1993 Cover: 3.50 NM value: Cover or less
91 ❑ Jan 1994 Cover: 3.50 NM value: Cover or less
92 ❑ Mar 1994 Cover: 3.50 NM value: Cover or less
93 ❑ May 1994 Cover: 3.95 NM value: Cover or less
94 ❑ Jul 1994 Cover: 3.95 NM value: Cover or less
95 ❑ Sep 1994 Cover: 3.95 NM value: Cover or less
96 ❑ Cover: 3.95 NM value: Cover or less
97 ❑ Cover: 3.95 NM value: Cover or less
98 ❑ Cover: 3.95 NM value: Cover or less
99 ❑ Cover: 3.95 NM value: Cover or less
100 ❑ Cover: 3.99 NM value: Cover or less
101 ❑ Cover: 3.99 NM value: Cover or less
102 ❑ Spr 1995 Cover: 3.99 NM value: Cover or less
103 ❑ Apr 1995 Cover: 3.99 NM value: Cover or less
104 ❑ Jun 1995 Cover: 3.99 NM value: Cover or less
105 ❑ Jul 1995 Cover: 3.99 NM value: Cover or less
106 ❑ 1995 Cover: 3.99 NM value: Cover or less
107 ❑ Oct 1995 Cover: 3.99 NM value: Cover or less
108 ❑ 1995 Cover: 3.99 NM value: Cover or less
109 ❑ 1996 Cover: 3.99 NM value: Cover or less
110 ❑ 1996 Cover: 3.99 NM value: Cover or less
111 ❑ 1996 Cover: 3.99 NM value: Cover or less
112 ❑ 1996 Cover: 3.99 NM value: Cover or less
113 ❑ 1996 Cover: 3.99 NM value: Cover or less
114 ❑ Jul 1996 Cover: 3.99 NM value: Cover or less
115 ❑ 1996 Cover: 3.99 NM value: Cover or less
116 ❑ Oct 1996 Cover: 3.99 NM value: Cover or less
117 ❑ Dec 1996 Cover: 3.99 NM value: Cover or less
118 ❑ Feb 1997 Cover: 3.99 NM value: Cover or less
119 ❑ Apr 1997 Cover: 3.99 NM value: Cover or less
120 ❑ 1997 Cover: 3.99 NM value: Cover or less
121 ❑ 1997 Cover: 3.99 NM value: Cover or less
122 ❑ 1997 Cover: 3.99 NM value: Cover or less
123 ❑ 1997 Cover: 3.99 NM value: Cover or less
124 ❑ 1997 Cover: 3.99 NM value: Cover or less
125 ❑ 1997 Cover: 3.99 NM value: Cover or less
126 ❑ Jan 1998 Cover: 3.99 NM value: Cover or less
127 ❑ Mar 1998 Cover: 3.99 NM value: Cover or less
128 ❑ Jun 1998 Cover: 3.99 NM value: Cover or less
129 ❑ Jul 1998 Cover: 3.99 NM value: Cover or less
130 ❑ Aug 1998 Cover: 3.99 NM value: Cover or less
131 ❑ Oct 1998 Cover: 3.99 NM value: Cover or less
132 ❑ Nov 1998 Cover: 3.99 NM value: Cover or less
133 ❑ Jan 1998 Cover: 3.99 NM value: Cover or less
134 ❑ Mar 1999 Cover: 3.99 NM value: Cover or less
135 ❑ Jun 1999 Cover: 3.99 NM value: Cover or less
📖 Ecch-Rated Mad #6

MAD TV — E.C.

1 ❑ 2000 Cover: 2.99 NM value: 3.50

MAD XL — E.C.

1 ❑ Jan 2000 Cover: 4.99 NM value: Cover or less
A: Sergio Aragonés; Don Martin W: Frank Jacobs
2 ❑ Mar 2000 Cover: 4.99 NM value: Cover or less
3 ❑ Jun 2000 Cover: 4.99 NM value: Cover or less
4 ❑ Jul 2000 Cover: 4.99 NM value: Cover or less
5 ❑ Aug 2000 Cover: 4.99 NM value: Cover or less
6 ❑ Nov 2000 Cover: 4.99 NM value: Cover or less
7 ❑ Jan 2001 Cover: 4.99 NM value: Cover or less
8 ❑ Mar 2001 Cover: 4.99 NM value: Cover or less
9 ❑ Jun 2001 Cover: 4.99 NM value: Cover or less
10 ❑ Jul 2001 Cover: 4.99 NM value: Cover or less
11 ❑ Aug 2001 Cover: 4.99 NM value: Cover or less

MAEL'S RAGE — Ominous

2 ❑ Aug 1994 Cover: 2.50 NM value: Cover or less
A: Bart Sears W: Bart Sears
2/SC❑ Aug 1994 Cover: 2.50 NM value: Cover or less
cardstock outer cover. A: Bart Sears W: Bart Sears

MAELSTROM — Aircel

1 ❑ Jun 1987 Cover: 1.70 NM value: Cover or less
2 ❑ Jul 1987 Cover: 1.70 NM value: Cover or less
3 ❑ Aug 1987 Cover: 1.70 NM value: Cover or less
4 ❑ Sep 1987 Cover: 1.70 NM value: Cover or less
5 ❑ Oct 1987 Cover: 1.50 NM value: Cover or less
6 ❑ Nov 1987 Cover: 1.50 NM value: Cover or less
7 ❑ Dec 1987 Cover: 1.50 NM value: Cover or less
8 ❑ Jan 1988 Cover: 1.50 NM value: Cover or less
9 ❑ Feb 1988 Cover: 1.50 NM value: Cover or less
10 ❑ Mar 1988 Cover: 1.50 NM value: Cover or less

MAGDALENA, THE — Image

1 ❑ Apr 2000 Cover: 2.50 NM value: Cover or less
Circ: Diamd. preorders: 76,364 • CGC: 4 graded, best 9.8
📖 Blood Divine, Part 1 A: Joe Benitez W: Joe Benitez; Marcia Chen
2 ❑ Jun 2000 Cover: 2.50 NM value: Cover or less
Circ: Diamd. preorders: 42,036
A: Joe Benitez W: Joe Benitez; Marcia Chen
3 ❑ Jan 2001 Cover: 2.50 NM value: Cover or less
Circ: Diamd. preorders: 40,823
A: Joe Benitez W: Joe Benitez; Marcia Chen

MAGE — Comico

Matt Wagner's Mage is a complex mix of mythology and action-adventure. Its hero is a man named Kevin, who finds himself reluctantly cast as a hero, then discovers he is unable to part with the power once he has it. On the surface, Mage is about Kevin's struggle against shapeshifters called the Grackleflinks. But the true story is played out on many levels, as Kevin discovers his true role as a latter-day King Arthur and realizes that his enemies are agents of a primal evil.

Wagner's Grendel plays a pivotal role in this series (and, indeed, is killed in #13). Fans of the Grendel series would be well advised to check out Mage, as well.

1 ❑ May 1984 Cover: 1.50 NM value: 9.00
• CGC: 3 graded, best 8.5
📖 Outrageous Slings and Arrows A: Matt Wagner W: Matt Wagner ★ 1st Appearance of Kevin Matchstick.
2 ❑ Jul 1984 Cover: 1.50 NM value: 7.00
• CGC: 3 graded, best 9.6
📖 Too, Too Solid Flesh A: Matt Wagner W: Matt Wagner
3 ❑ Sep 1984 Cover: 1.50 NM value: 5.00
• CGC: 1 graded, best 9.0
📖 The Mouse Trap A: Matt Wagner W: Matt Wagner
4 ❑ Nov 1984 Cover: 1.50 NM value: 5.00
• CGC: 1 graded, best 7.5
📖 O What A Rash And Bloody Deed A: Matt Wagner W: Matt Wagner
5 ❑ Jan 1985 Cover: 1.50 NM value: 5.00
📖 Come What Come May A: Matt Wagner W: Matt Wagner
6 ❑ Mar 1985 Cover: 1.50 NM value: 20.00
• CGC: 9 graded, best 9.6
• Grendel A: Matt Wagner W: Matt Wagner ★ 1st Appearance of Grendel I (Hunter Rose) (in color).
7 ❑ May 1985 Cover: 1.50 NM value: 10.00
Circ: CapCity orders: 3,825 • CGC: 1 graded, best 9.2
A: Matt Wagner W: Matt Wagner ★ Appearance of Grendel I (Hunter Rose).
8 ❑ Jul 1985 Cover: 1.50 NM value: 5.00
Circ: CapCity orders: 3,800
A: Matt Wagner W: Matt Wagner ★ Appearance of Grendel I (Hunter Rose).
9 ❑ Sep 1985 Cover: 1.50 NM value: 4.00
Circ: CapCity orders: 4,625 • CGC: 1 graded, best 9.2
A: Matt Wagner W: Matt Wagner ★ Appearance of Grendel I (Hunter Rose).
10 ❑ Dec 1985 Cover: 1.50 NM value: 4.00
Circ: CapCity orders: 6,500
A: Matt Wagner W: Matt Wagner ★ Appearance of Grendel I (Hunter Rose).
11 ❑ Feb 1986 Cover: 1.50 NM value: 4.00
Circ: CapCity orders: 5,375 • CGC: 1 graded, best 8.5
A: Matt Wagner W: Matt Wagner ★ Appearance of Grendel I (Hunter Rose).
12 ❑ Apr 1986 Cover: 1.50 NM value: 4.00
Circ: CapCity orders: 5,425 • CGC: 1 graded, best 9.2
A: Matt Wagner W: Matt Wagner ★ Appearance of Grendel I (Hunter Rose).
13 ❑ Jun 1986 Cover: 1.50 NM value: 5.00
Circ: CapCity orders: 5,875 • CGC: 1 graded, best 9.0
📖 Mark Me A: Matt Wagner W: Matt Wagner ★ Death of Grendel I (Hunter Rose). ★ Death of Edsel.
14 ❑ Aug 1986 Cover: 1.50 NM value: 4.00
Circ: CapCity orders: 5,600
📖 ...Or Not to Be A: Matt Wagner W: Matt Wagner ★ Appearance of Grendel.
15 ❑ Dec 1986 Cover: 2.95 NM value: 7.00
Circ: CapCity orders: 8,550 • CGC: 2 graded, best 9.4
• Giant-size. 📖 Pass With Your Best Violence final issue. A: Matt Wagner W: Matt Wagner
Bk 1❑ Oct 1998 Cover: 5.95 NM value: Cover or less
The Hero Discovered Book 1. 📖 Outrageous Slings and Arrows; Too, Too Solid Flesh • Collects issues #1-2 A: Matt Wagner W: Matt Wagner
Bk 2❑ Cover: 5.95 NM value: Cover or less
The Hero Discovered Book 2. 📖 The Mouse Trap; O What A Rash and Bloody Deed • Collects issues #3-4 A: Matt Wagner W: Matt Wagner
Bk 3❑ Jan 1999 Cover: 5.95 NM value: Cover or less
The Hero Discovered Book 3. 📖 Rosencrantz and Guilderstern; Alas, Poor Ghost • Collects issues #5-6 A: Matt Wagner W: Matt Wagner
Bk 4❑ Feb 1999 Cover: 5.95 NM value: Cover or less
The Hero Discovered Book 4. 📖 Lady, Shall I Lie in Your Lap?; Against A Sea of Troubles • Collects issues #7-8 A: Matt Wagner W: Matt Wagner
Bk 5❑ Apr 1999 Cover: 6.95 NM value: Cover or less
The Hero Discovered Book 5. 📖 And by Opposing, End Them; To Sleep, Perchance to Dream • Collects issues #9-10 A: Matt Wagner W: Matt Wagner
Bk 6❑ Jun 1999 Cover: 6.95 NM value: Cover or less
The Hero Discovered Book 6. 📖 Most Foul, Strange and Unusual; Defend Me Friends, I am but Hurt • Collects issues #11-12 A: Matt Wagner W: Matt Wagner
Bk 7❑ Jul 1999 Cover: 6.95 NM value: Cover or less
The Hero Discovered Book 7. 📖 Mark Me; ...Or Not to Be • Collects issues #13-14 A: Matt Wagner W: Matt Wagner
Bk 8❑ Sep 1999 Cover: 6.95 NM value: Cover or less
The Hero Discovered Book 8. 📖 Pass With Your Best Violence; • Collects issues #15-16 A: Matt Wagner W: Matt Wagner

MAGEBOOK — Comico

1 ❑ Cover: 8.95 NM value: Cover or less
2 ❑ Cover: 7.95 NM value: Cover or less
Circ: CapCity orders: 765

MAGE (IMAGE) — Image

Mage, the Hero Defined, is the continuation of Mage, the Hero Discovered, a cult favorite in the 1980s. In this series from Image Comics, creator Matt Wagner (Grendel) explores his personal perspective on the heroic archetype in comics, while weaving aspects of mythology and fantasy into the mix. His characters are down-to-Earth regular people who just happen to possess supernatural abilities. In particular, Kevin Matchstick is a latter-day King Arthur. When he grasps his Excalibur, a glowing baseball bat, he gains the agility and dexterity of a supreme athlete.

Matchstick is accompanied on his travels by compatriots Joe Phat, the reincarnation of the Iroquois chief, Hiawatha, and a Hercules metaphor, Kirby Hero, whose name is a respectful reference to the legendary artist Jack Kirby.

0 ❑ Jul 1997 NM value: 3.00
• American Entertainment Exclusive
0/AUT❑ Jul 1997 NM value: 7.00
1 ❑ Jul 1997 Cover: 2.50 NM value: 4.00
Circ: Diamd. preorders: 39,744 • CGC: 1 graded, best 9.2
📖 The Handle Towards My Hand A: Matt Wagner W: Matt Wagner
1/3D❑ Feb 1998 Cover: 4.95 NM value: Cover or less
Circ: Diamd. preorders: 4,943
• 3-D edition. 📖 The Handle Towards My Hand • with glasses A: Matt Wagner W: Matt Wagner
2 ❑ Aug 1997 Cover: 2.50 NM value: 3.50
Circ: Diamd. preorders: 31,660
📖 When We Three Shall Meet A: Matt Wagner W: Matt Wagner
3 ❑ Sep 1997 Cover: 2.50 NM value: 3.50
Circ: Diamd. preorders: 32,163
📖 Two Truths are Told A: Matt Wagner W: Matt Wagner
4 ❑ Nov 1997 Cover: 2.50 NM value: 3.00
Circ: Diamd. preorders: 33,223
📖 Bubble, Bubble, Toil and Trouble A: Matt Wagner W: Matt Wagner
5 ❑ Jan 1998 Cover: 2.50 NM value: 3.00
Circ: Diamd. preorders: 32,605
📖 Come What Come May A: Matt Wagner W: Matt Wagner
6 ❑ Mar 1998 Cover: 2.50 NM value: Cover or less
Circ: Diamd. preorders: 31,940
📖 Lay on, MacDuff A: Matt Wagner W: Matt Wagner
7 ❑ Apr 1998 Cover: 2.50 NM value: Cover or less
Circ: Diamd. preorders: 30,367
📖 Infirm of Purpose A: Matt Wagner W: Matt Wagner
8 ❑ Jun 1998 Cover: 2.50 NM value: Cover or less
Circ: Diamd. preorders: 28,828
📖 So Weary With Disasters A: Matt Wagner W: Matt Wagner
9 ❑ Sep 1998 Cover: 2.50 NM value: Cover or less
Circ: Diamd. preorders: 29,208
📖 The Weird Sisters A: Matt Wagner W: Matt Wagner
10 ❑ Dec 1998 Cover: 2.50 NM value: Cover or less
Circ: Diamd. preorders: 28,150
📖 Foul is Fair A: Matt Wagner W: Matt Wagner
11 ❑ Feb 1999 Cover: 2.50 NM value: Cover or less
Circ: Diamd. preorders: 27,302
📖 Dwindle, Peak and Pine A: Matt Wagner W: Matt Wagner
12 ❑ Apr 1999 Cover: 2.50 NM value: Cover or less
Circ: Diamd. preorders: 27,055
📖 A Charmed Life A: Matt Wagner W: Matt Wagner

CGC-graded: Multiply prices above by 33 for 9.9 M • 16 for 9.8 NM/M • 7 for 9.6 NM+ • 5 for 9.4 NM • 2.5 for 9.2 NM- • 1.5 for 9.0 VF/NM

13/A❑ Jun 1999 Cover: 2.50 **NM** value: **Cover or less**
Circ: Diamd. preorders: **25,596**
covers form triptych.
13/B❑ Jun 1999 Cover: 2.50 **NM** value: **Cover or less**
Mage cover.
13/C❑ Jun 1999 Cover: 2.50 **NM** value: **Cover or less**
Joe Phat cover.
14 ❑ Aug 1999 Cover: 2.50 **NM** value: **Cover or less**
Circ: Diamd. preorders: **23,416**
📖 When the Battle's Lost and Won **A:** Matt Wagner **W:** Matt Wagner
15 ❑ Oct 1999 Cover: 2.50 **NM** value: **Cover or less**
Circ: Diamd. preorders: **23,189** • **CGC:** 2 graded, best 9.8
📖 All that may Become a Man **A:** Matt Wagner **W:** Matt Wagner
Bk 1❑ Cover: 9.95 **NM** value: **Cover or less**
• collects issues #1-4 **A:** Matt Wagner **W:** Matt Wagner
Bk 2❑ Dec 1998 Cover: 9.95 **NM** value: **Cover or less**
• collects issues #5-8 **A:** Matt Wagner **W:** Matt Wagner

MAGGIE AND HOPEY COLOR SPECIAL
Fantagraphics

1 ❑ May 1997 Cover: 3.50 **NM** value: **Cover or less**
Circ: Diamd. preorders: **7,181**

MAGGIE THE CAT
Image

1 ❑ Jan 1996 Cover: 2.50 **NM** value: **Cover or less**
📖 Master Piece, Part 1 **A:** Mike Grell **W:** Mike Grell
2 ❑ Mar 1996 Cover: 2.50 **NM** value: **Cover or less**
📖 Master Piece, Part 2 **A:** Mike Grell **W:** Mike Grell

MAGGOTS
Hamilton

1 ❑ Nov 1991, b&w Cover: 3.95 **NM** value: **Cover or less**
2 ❑ 1992b&w Cover: 3.95 **NM** value: **Cover or less**
3 ❑ 1992b&w Cover: 3.95 **NM** value: **Cover or less**

MAGICAL MATES
Antarctic

1 ❑ Feb 1996 Cover: 2.95 **NM** value: **Cover or less**
A: Mio Odagi **W:** Mio Odagi
2 ❑ Apr 1996 Cover: 2.95 **NM** value: **Cover or less**
A: Mio Odagi **W:** Mio Odagi
3 ❑ Jun 1996 Cover: 2.95 **NM** value: **Cover or less**
A: Mio Odagi **W:** Mio Odagi
4 ❑ Aug 1996 Cover: 2.95 **NM** value: **Cover or less**
A: Mio Odagi **W:** Mio Odagi
5 ❑ Oct 1996 Cover: 2.95 **NM** value: **Cover or less**
A: Mio Odagi **W:** Mio Odagi
6 ❑ Dec 1996 Cover: 2.95 **NM** value: **Cover or less**
A: Mio Odagi **W:** Mio Odagi
7 ❑ 1997 Cover: 2.95 **NM** value: **Cover or less**
A: Mio Odagi **W:** Mio Odagi
8 ❑ 1997 Cover: 2.95 **NM** value: **Cover or less**
A: Mio Odagi **W:** Mio Odagi
9 ❑ 1997 Cover: 2.95 **NM** value: **Cover or less**
A: Mio Odagi **W:** Mio Odagi

MAGICAL NYMPHINI, THE
Rip Off

All issues are adults only.

1 ❑ Feb 1991, b&w Cover: 2.50 **NM** value: **Cover or less**
1-2 ❑ Cover: 2.50 **NM** value: **Cover or less**
2 ❑ Apr 1991, b&w Cover: 2.50 **NM** value: **Cover or less**
2-2 ❑ Cover: 2.50 **NM** value: **Cover or less**
3 ❑ Aug 1991, b&w Cover: 2.50 **NM** value: **Cover or less**
3-2 ❑ Cover: 2.50 **NM** value: **Cover or less**
4 ❑ Dec 1991, b&w Cover: 2.95 **NM** value: **Cover or less**
4-2 ❑ Cover: 2.95 **NM** value: **Cover or less**
5 ❑ Aug 1992, b&w Cover: 2.95 **NM** value: **Cover or less**
5-2 ❑ Cover: 2.95 **NM** value: **Cover or less**

MAGICAL TWILIGHT
Graphic Visions

1 ❑ Cover: 2.95 **NM** value: **Cover or less**
Circ: CapCity orders: **2,310**
A: Yuki **W:** Yuki

MAGIC BOY AND GIRLFRIEND
Top Shelf

1 ❑ Jul 1998, b&w Cover: 8.95 **NM** value: **Cover or less**
No issue number.

MAGIC BOY & THE ROBOT ELF
Slave Labor

1 ❑ May 1996 Cover: 9.95 **NM** value: **Cover or less**
A: James Jochalka **W:** James Jochalka

MAGIC CARPET
Shanda Fantasy Arts

1 ❑ Apr 1999, b&w Cover: 4.50 **NM** value: **Cover or less**

MAGIC COMICS
David McKay

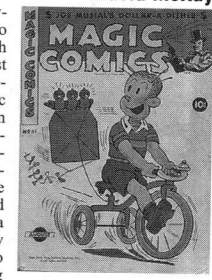

In the early days of comics, several titles were created in order to keep printing plants provided with material in their off-hours. For fast content, it was most simple to repackage existing content: comic strips that had already appeared in newspapers. So Magic Comics began as a repackager of King Features Syndicate strips. The first-issue cover feature was the pantomime boy star Henry. Created by Carl Anderson (1865-1948) as a panel cartoon for the Saturday Evening Post, Henry jumped to newspapers in 1934. Following Henry's covers (even co-starring with Henry on a few) was Mandrake (written by Lee Falk, drawn by Phil Davis), and finally Chic Young's Blondie and Dagwood (and their kids and dogs). There were more King Features strips inside. — Maggie

1 ❑ Aug 1939 Cover: 0.10 **NM** value: **2000.00**
2 ❑ Sep 1939 Cover: 0.10 **NM** value: **1000.00**
3 ❑ Oct 1939 Cover: 0.10 **NM** value: **750.00**
4 ❑ Nov 1939 Cover: 0.10 **NM** value: **500.00**
5 ❑ Dec 1939 Cover: 0.10 **NM** value: **400.00**
• **CGC:** 1 graded, best 9.0
6 ❑ Jan 1940 Cover: 0.10 **NM** value: **350.00**
7 ❑ Feb 1940 Cover: 0.10 **NM** value: **350.00**
8 ❑ Mar 1940 Cover: 0.10 **NM** value: **350.00**
9 ❑ Apr 1940 Cover: 0.10 **NM** value: **350.00**
10 ❑ May 1940 Cover: 0.10 **NM** value: **350.00**
11 ❑ Jun 1940 Cover: 0.10 **NM** value: **275.00**
12 ❑ Jul 1940 Cover: 0.10 **NM** value: **275.00**
13 ❑ Aug 1940 Cover: 0.10 **NM** value: **275.00**
14 ❑ Sep 1940 Cover: 0.10 **NM** value: **250.00**
15 ❑ Oct 1940 Cover: 0.10 **NM** value: **250.00**
16 ❑ Nov 1940 Cover: 0.10 **NM** value: **250.00**
17 ❑ Dec 1940 Cover: 0.10 **NM** value: **175.00**
18 ❑ Jan 1941 Cover: 0.10 **NM** value: **175.00**
19 ❑ Feb 1941 Cover: 0.10 **NM** value: **175.00**
20 ❑ Mar 1941 Cover: 0.10 **NM** value: **175.00**
21 ❑ Apr 1941 Cover: 0.10 **NM** value: **150.00**
22 ❑ May 1941 Cover: 0.10 **NM** value: **150.00**
23 ❑ Jun 1941 Cover: 0.10 **NM** value: **150.00**
24 ❑ Jul 1941 Cover: 0.10 **NM** value: **150.00**
25 ❑ Aug 1941 Cover: 0.10 **NM** value: **150.00**
• **CGC:** 1 graded, best 9.0
26 ❑ Sep 1941 Cover: 0.10 **NM** value: **150.00**
27 ❑ Oct 1941 Cover: 0.10 **NM** value: **150.00**
28 ❑ Nov 1941 Cover: 0.10 **NM** value: **150.00**
29 ❑ Dec 1941 Cover: 0.10 **NM** value: **150.00**
30 ❑ Jan 1942 Cover: 0.10 **NM** value: **150.00**
31 ❑ Feb 1942 Cover: 0.10 **NM** value: **125.00**
32 ❑ Mar 1942 Cover: 0.10 **NM** value: **125.00**
33 ❑ Apr 1942 Cover: 0.10 **NM** value: **125.00**
34 ❑ May 1942 Cover: 0.10 **NM** value: **125.00**
35 ❑ Jun 1942 Cover: 0.10 **NM** value: **125.00**
36 ❑ Jul 1942 Cover: 0.10 **NM** value: **125.00**
37 ❑ Aug 1942 Cover: 0.10 **NM** value: **125.00**
38 ❑ Sep 1942 Cover: 0.10 **NM** value: **125.00**
39 ❑ Oct 1942 Cover: 0.10 **NM** value: **125.00**
40 ❑ Nov 1942 Cover: 0.10 **NM** value: **125.00**
41 ❑ Dec 1942 Cover: 0.10 **NM** value: **100.00**
42 ❑ Jan 1943 Cover: 0.10 **NM** value: **100.00**
43 ❑ Feb 1943 Cover: 0.10 **NM** value: **100.00**
44 ❑ Mar 1943 Cover: 0.10 **NM** value: **100.00**
45 ❑ Apr 1943 Cover: 0.10 **NM** value: **100.00**
46 ❑ May 1943 Cover: 0.10 **NM** value: **100.00**
47 ❑ Jun 1943 Cover: 0.10 **NM** value: **100.00**
48 ❑ Jul 1943 Cover: 0.10 **NM** value: **100.00**
49 ❑ Aug 1943 Cover: 0.10 **NM** value: **100.00**
50 ❑ Sep 1943 Cover: 0.10 **NM** value: **100.00**
51 ❑ Oct 1943 Cover: 0.10 **NM** value: **100.00**
52 ❑ Nov 1943 Cover: 0.10 **NM** value: **100.00**
53 ❑ Dec 1943 Cover: 0.10 **NM** value: **100.00**
54 ❑ Jan 1944 Cover: 0.10 **NM** value: **100.00**
55 ❑ Feb 1944 Cover: 0.10 **NM** value: **100.00**
56 ❑ Mar 1944 Cover: 0.10 **NM** value: **100.00**
57 ❑ Apr 1944 Cover: 0.10 **NM** value: **100.00**
58 ❑ May 1944 Cover: 0.10 **NM** value: **100.00**
59 ❑ Jun 1944 Cover: 0.10 **NM** value: **100.00**
60 ❑ Jul 1944 Cover: 0.10 **NM** value: **75.00**
61 ❑ Aug 1944 Cover: 0.10 **NM** value: **75.00**
• **CGC:** 1 graded, best 3.5
62 ❑ Sep 1944 Cover: 0.10 **NM** value: **75.00**
63 ❑ Oct 1944 Cover: 0.10 **NM** value: **75.00**
64 ❑ Nov 1944 Cover: 0.10 **NM** value: **75.00**
65 ❑ Dec 1944 Cover: 0.10 **NM** value: **75.00**
66 ❑ Jan 1945 Cover: 0.10 **NM** value: **75.00**
67 ❑ Feb 1945 Cover: 0.10 **NM** value: **75.00**
68 ❑ Mar 1945 Cover: 0.10 **NM** value: **75.00**
69 ❑ Apr 1945 Cover: 0.10 **NM** value: **75.00**
70 ❑ May 1945 Cover: 0.10 **NM** value: **75.00**
71 ❑ Jun 1945 Cover: 0.10 **NM** value: **75.00**
72 ❑ Jul 1945 Cover: 0.10 **NM** value: **75.00**
73 ❑ Aug 1945 Cover: 0.10 **NM** value: **75.00**
74 ❑ Sep 1945 Cover: 0.10 **NM** value: **75.00**
75 ❑ Oct 1945 Cover: 0.10 **NM** value: **75.00**
76 ❑ Nov 1945 Cover: 0.10 **NM** value: **75.00**
77 ❑ Dec 1945 Cover: 0.10 **NM** value: **75.00**
78 ❑ Jan 1946 Cover: 0.10 **NM** value: **75.00**
79 ❑ Feb 1946 Cover: 0.10 **NM** value: **75.00**
80 ❑ Mar 1946 Cover: 0.10 **NM** value: **60.00**
81 ❑ Apr 1946 Cover: 0.10 **NM** value: **60.00**
82 ❑ May 1946 Cover: 0.10 **NM** value: **60.00**
83 ❑ Jun 1946 Cover: 0.10 **NM** value: **60.00**
84 ❑ Jul 1946 Cover: 0.10 **NM** value: **60.00**
85 ❑ Aug 1946 Cover: 0.10 **NM** value: **60.00**
86 ❑ Sep 1946 Cover: 0.10 **NM** value: **60.00**
87 ❑ Oct 1946 Cover: 0.10 **NM** value: **60.00**
88 ❑ Nov 1946 Cover: 0.10 **NM** value: **60.00**
89 ❑ Dec 1946 Cover: 0.10 **NM** value: **60.00**
90 ❑ Jan 1947 Cover: 0.10 **NM** value: **50.00**
91 ❑ Feb 1947 Cover: 0.10 **NM** value: **50.00**
92 ❑ Mar 1947 Cover: 0.10 **NM** value: **50.00**
93 ❑ Apr 1947 Cover: 0.10 **NM** value: **50.00**
94 ❑ May 1947 Cover: 0.10 **NM** value: **50.00**
95 ❑ Jun 1947 Cover: 0.10 **NM** value: **50.00**
96 ❑ Jul 1947 Cover: 0.10 **NM** value: **50.00**
97 ❑ Aug 1947 Cover: 0.10 **NM** value: **50.00**
98 ❑ Sep 1947 Cover: 0.10 **NM** value: **50.00**
99 ❑ Oct 1947 Cover: 0.10 **NM** value: **50.00**
100 ❑ Nov 1947 Cover: 0.10 **NM** value: **50.00**
101 ❑ Dec 1947 Cover: 0.10 **NM** value: **30.00**
102 ❑ Jan 1948 Cover: 0.10 **NM** value: **30.00**
103 ❑ Feb 1948 Cover: 0.10 **NM** value: **30.00**
104 ❑ Mar 1948 Cover: 0.10 **NM** value: **30.00**
105 ❑ Apr 1948 Cover: 0.10 **NM** value: **30.00**
106 ❑ May 1948 Cover: 0.10 **NM** value: **30.00**
107 ❑ Jun 1948 Cover: 0.10 **NM** value: **30.00**
108 ❑ Jul 1948 Cover: 0.10 **NM** value: **30.00**
109 ❑ Aug 1948 Cover: 0.10 **NM** value: **30.00**
110 ❑ Sep 1948 Cover: 0.10 **NM** value: **30.00**
111 ❑ Oct 1948 Cover: 0.10 **NM** value: **30.00**
112 ❑ Nov 1948 Cover: 0.10 **NM** value: **30.00**
113 ❑ Dec 1948 Cover: 0.10 **NM** value: **30.00**
114 ❑ Jan 1949 Cover: 0.10 **NM** value: **30.00**
115 ❑ Feb 1949 Cover: 0.10 **NM** value: **30.00**
116 ❑ Mar 1949 Cover: 0.10 **NM** value: **30.00**
117 ❑ Apr 1949 Cover: 0.10 **NM** value: **30.00**
118 ❑ May 1949 Cover: 0.10 **NM** value: **30.00**
119 ❑ Jun 1949 Cover: 0.10 **NM** value: **30.00**
120 ❑ Jul 1949 Cover: 0.10 **NM** value: **30.00**
121 ❑ Aug 1949 Cover: 0.10 **NM** value: **30.00**
122 ❑ Sep 1949 Cover: 0.10 **NM** value: **30.00**
123 ❑ Nov 1949 Cover: 0.10 **NM** value: **30.00**

MAGIC FLUTE, THE
Eclipse

1 ❑ Cover: 4.95 **NM** value: **Cover or less**
Circ: CapCity orders: **3,925**
2 ❑ Cover: 4.95 **NM** value: **Cover or less**
Circ: CapCity orders: **3,300**
3 ❑ Cover: 4.95 **NM** value: **Cover or less**
Circ: CapCity orders: **3,250**

MAGICIANS' VILLAGE
Mad Monkey

1 ❑ ca. 1995 Cover: 2.45 **NM** value: **Cover or less**

MAGIC KNIGHT RAYEARTH
Mixx

Bk 1❑ Cover: 11.95 **NM** value: **Cover or less**
Bk 2❑ Cover: 11.95 **NM** value: **Cover or less**

MAGICMAN
A-Plus

1 ❑ b&w Cover: 2.50 **NM** value: **2.95**
📖 Magicman!; The Case of the Young Old Men **A:** Pete Costanza
W: Zev Zimmer

MAGIC PRIEST
Antarctic

1 ❑ Jun 1998, b&w Cover: 2.95 **NM** value: **Cover or less**
Circ: Diamd. preorders: **2,886**
📖 A Murder of Crowe's **A:** Neil Googe **W:** Barry Lyga

MAGIC: THE GATHERING-ANTIQUITIES WAR
Acclaim / Armada

1 ❑ Nov 1995 Cover: 2.50 **NM** value: **Cover or less**
A: Paul Smith **W:** Jerry Prosser ★ Origin of Urza and Mishra.
2 ❑ Dec 1995 Cover: 2.50 **NM** value: **Cover or less**
Circ: CapCity orders: **11,350**
A: Paul Smith **W:** Jerry Prosser
3 ❑ Jan 1996 Cover: 2.50 **NM** value: **Cover or less**
Circ: CapCity orders: **8,200**
A: Paul Smith **W:** Jerry Prosser
4 ❑ Feb 1996 Cover: 2.50 **NM** value: **Cover or less**
A: Paul Smith **W:** Jerry Prosser

MAGIC: THE GATHERING-ELDER DRAGONS
Acclaim / Armada

1 ❑ Apr 1996 Cover: 2.50 **NM** value: **Cover or less**
📖 The Tikery Man **A:** Doug Tropea Wheatly **W:** Art Holcomb
2 ❑ May 1996 Cover: 2.50 **NM** value: **Cover or less**

MAGIC: THE GATHERING: GERARD'S QUEST
Dark Horse

Magic: The Gathering was a trading-card game that single-handedly launched a new genre in gaming. It was such a mighty success that many comics stores found a large part of their revenue suddenly shifted to eager gamers snatching up packs of Magic cards. It was not surprising that Magic: The Gathering eventually worked its way to comic books, with a number of Magic series enjoying mixed success at Acclaim under its Armada imprint.

In 1998, Dark Horse picked up the Magic comics, launching this new series written by Mike Grell (Green Arrow). This hard-to-follow title follows a group of adventurers out to reclaim some vague "legacy" from the Lords of the Wastes. Gerard, the key figure in this struggle, is a reluctant messiah. Although he's been schooled since birth to fulfill his destiny, he would just as soon let history pass him by. Only the love of endangered friends makes him press on.

1 ❑ Mar 1998 Cover: 2.95 **NM** value: **Cover or less**
Circ: Diamd. preorders: **11,541**
A: Pop Mhan **W:** Mike Grell
2 ❑ Apr 1998 Cover: 2.95 **NM** value: **Cover or less**
Circ: Diamd. preorders: **9,667**
📖 Legacy **A:** Pop Mhan **W:** Mike Grell
3 ❑ May 1998 Cover: 2.95 **NM** value: **Cover or less**
Circ: Diamd. preorders: **8,888**
📖 Crucible **A:** Pop Mhan **W:** Mike Grell
4 ❑ Sep 1998 Cover: 2.95 **NM** value: **Cover or less**
📖 Destiny **A:** Pop Mhan **W:** Mike Grell
Bk 1❑ Apr 1999 Cover: 12.95 **NM** value: **Cover or less**
• Trade Paperback. • collects mini-series

Do you have changes or corrections for the **Standard Catalog**? Send your original research to us at
allcomics@krause.com

Other grades: Multiply prices above by **1.5 for Mint • 2/3 for Very Fine • 1/3 for Fine • 1/5 for Very Good • 1/8 for Good**

MAGIC: THE GATHERING-NIGHTMARE
Acclaim / Armada

1 ❑ ca. 1995 Cover: 2.50 **NM** value: **Cover or less**
Circ: CapCity orders: **16,850**
📖 Vanishing Lands **A:** Anthony Castrillo **W:** Hilary Bader

MAGIC: THE GATHERING-SHANDALAR
Acclaim / Armada

1 ❑ Mar 1996 Cover: 2.50 **NM** value: **Cover or less**
2 ❑ Apr 1996 Cover: 2.50 **NM** value: **Cover or less**
📖 The Threshold final issue. **A:** Bo Hampton **W:** David Quinn

MAGIC: THE GATHERING-THE SHADOW MAGE
Acclaim / Armada

1 ❑ Jul 1995 Cover: 2.50 **NM** value: **Cover or less**
Circ: CapCity orders: **52,225**
• bound-in Fireball card
2 ❑ Aug 1995 Cover: 2.50 **NM** value: **Cover or less**
Circ: CapCity orders: **40,950**
• bound-in Blue Elemental card
3 ❑ Sep 1995 Cover: 2.50 **NM** value: **Cover or less**
Circ: CapCity orders: **23,950**
• bagged with Magic: The Gathering tokens and counters
4 ❑ Oct 1995 Cover: 2.50 **NM** value: **Cover or less**
Circ: CapCity orders: **19,425**
• polybagged with sheet of creature tokens
Bk 1 ❑ Dec 1995 Cover: 4.95 **NM** value: **Cover or less**
• prestige format collection of first two issues; polybagged with sheet of creature tokens
Bk 2 ❑ Dec 1995 Cover: 4.95 **NM** value: **Cover or less**
• prestige format collection of final two issues; polybagged with sheet of creature tokens

MAGIC: THE GATHERING-WAYFARER
Acclaim / Armada

1 ❑ Nov 1995 Cover: 2.50 **NM** value: **Cover or less**
Circ: CapCity orders: **16,725**
📖 A Need for Monsters **A:** Val Mayerik **W:** Jeff Gomez; Jeff G-mez
2 ❑ Dec 1995 Cover: 2.50 **NM** value: **Cover or less**
Circ: CapCity orders: **11,450**
A: Val Mayerik **W:** Jeff Gomez; Jeff G-mez
3 ❑ Jan 1996 Cover: 2.50 **NM** value: **Cover or less**
Circ: CapCity orders: **8,200**
A: Val Mayerik **W:** Jeff Gomez; Jeff G-mez
4 ❑ Feb 1996 Cover: 2.50 **NM** value: **Cover or less**
📖 Lovers & Comrades **A:** Val Mayerik **W:** Jeff Gomez; Jeff G-mez
5 ❑ Mar 1996 Cover: 2.50 **NM** value: **Cover or less**
A: Val Mayerik **W:** Jeff Gomez; Jeff G-mez

MAGIC WHISTLE
Alternative

1 ❑ b&w Cover: 2.95 **NM** value: **Cover or less**
2 ❑ b&w Cover: 2.95 **NM** value: **Cover or less**

MAGIK
Marvel

In Uncanny X-Men #160, future New Mutants member Illyana Rasputin (kid sister of Peter Rasputin, a.k.a. Colossus) was abducted by Belasco and pulled into a demonic realm known as Limbo. When the X-Men came to rescue her, they managed to (literally) pull her out of that dark domain, but Kitty Pryde momentarily lost her grip on Illyana. Illyana fell back into Limbo for what was only a second or so in our reality, but which was seven years in Limbo.

This mini-series takes place during those years in Limbo. There, Illyana is torn between Belasco, who seduces her into the black arts, and an older version of Storm, who has become a powerful sorceress in Limbo, and who tries to save Illyana's soul from corruption by Belasco.

1 ❑ Dec 1983 Cover: 0.60 **NM** value: **2.25**
📖 Inferno **A:** Tom Palmer **W:** Chris Claremont
2 ❑ Jan 1984 Cover: 0.60 **NM** value: **2.00**
📖 Inferno **A:** Tom Palmer **W:** Chris Claremont
3 ❑ Feb 1984 Cover: 0.60 **NM** value: **2.00**
📖 Inferno **A:** Tom Palmer **W:** Chris Claremont
4 ❑ Mar 1984 Cover: 0.60 **NM** value: **2.00**
📖 Inferno **A:** Tom Palmer **W:** Chris Claremont

MAGIK (2ND SERIES)
Marvel

1 ❑ Dec 2000 Cover: 2.99 **NM** value: **Cover or less**
📖 The Crossing Guard **A:** Liam McCormack-Sharp **W:** Andy Lanning; Dan Abnett
2 ❑ Jan 2001 Cover: 2.99 **NM** value: **Cover or less**
📖 A Gathering of Foes **A:** Liam McCormack-Sharp **W:** Andy Lanning; Dan Abnett
3 ❑ Feb 2001 Cover: 2.99 **NM** value: **Cover or less**
📖 The Fall of Hades **A:** Liam McCormack-Sharp **W:** Andy Lanning; Dan Abnett
4 ❑ Mar 2001 Cover: 2.99 **NM** value: **Cover or less**
📖 Bound for Destruction **A:** Liam McCormack-Sharp **W:** Andy Lanning; Dan Abnett

MAGILLA GORILLA (GOLD KEY)
Gold Key

1 ❑ ca. 1964 Cover: 0.12 **NM** value: **35.00**
📖 The Explorer; The Gunslinger; The Midnight Raid Of Zit And Zat; Pop Went The Circle; Once Upon A Time Machine
2 ❑ ca. 1964 Cover: 0.12 **NM** value: **18.00**
3 ❑ Dec 1964 Cover: 0.12 **NM** value: **15.00**
4 ❑ ca. 1965 Cover: 0.12 **NM** value: **15.00**
5 ❑ ca. 1965 Cover: 0.12 **NM** value: **15.00**
📖 Magilla Gorilla: The Explorer; Ricochet Rabbit and Droop-a-Long Coyote: The Gunslinger; Magilla Gorilla: The Midnight Raid of Zit and Zat; Punkin Puss and Mushmouse: Pop Went the Cicle; Magilla Gorilla: Once Upon a Time Machine
6 ❑ Aug 1965 Cover: 0.12 **NM** value: **13.00**
7 ❑ Nov 1965 Cover: 0.12 **NM** value: **13.00**
8 ❑ Jul 1966 Cover: 0.12 **NM** value: **13.00**
9 ❑ Cover: 0.12 **NM** value: **13.00**
10 ❑ Dec 1968 Cover: 0.15 **NM** value: **13.00**
final issue.

MAGNA-MAN: THE LAST SUPERHERO
Comics Interview

1 ❑ b&w Cover: 1.95 **NM** value: **Cover or less**
2 ❑ Sum 1988, b&w Cover: 1.95 **NM** value: **Cover or less**
3 ❑ Sum 1988, b&w Cover: 1.95 **NM** value: **Cover or less**

MAGNESIUM ARC
Iconografix

1 ❑ Cover: 3.50 **NM** value: **Cover or less**
A: Matt Howarth **W:** Matt Howarth

MAGNETIC MEN FEATURING MAGNETO
Marvel / Amalgam

1 ❑ Jun 1997 Cover: 1.95 **NM** value: **Cover or less**
Circ: Diamd. preorders: **134,349**
📖 Born Again **A:** Barry Kitson **W:** Tom Peyer

MAGNETO
Marvel

0 ❑ Sep 1993 **NM** value: **3.00**
• **CGC:** 5 graded, best 9.6
no cover price. • retailer giveaway. 📖 A Fire In The Sky; I Magneto; Magneto Seminar • Promotional give-away; Reprints "A Fire in the Sky" from X-Men Classic #19; Reprints "I Magneto" From X-Men Classic #12 **A:** John Bolton; Jan Duursema **W:** Fabian Nicieza; Chris Claremont ★ Origin of Magneto.

MAGNETO AND THE MAGNETIC MEN
Marvel / Amalgam

1 ❑ Apr 1996 Cover: 1.95 **NM** value: **Cover or less**
📖 Opposites Attract **A:** Jeff Matsuda **W:** Gerard Jones

MAGNETO ASCENDANT
Marvel / Amalgam

1 ❑ Apr 1999 Cover: 3.99 **NM** value: **Cover or less**
📖 The Triumph of Magneto; If Iceman Should Fail; The Gentleman's Name is Magneto; Please Allow Me to Introduce Myself… • Reprints Magneto Stories from X-Men (1st Series) **A:** Rick Leonardi; Jack Kirby; Dave Cockrum; Jay Gavin **W:** Stan Lee; Bill Mantlo; Chris Claremont

MAGNETO: DARK SEDUCTION
Marvel

1 ❑ Jun 2000 Cover: 2.99 **NM** value: **Cover or less**
Circ: Diamd. preorders: **54,903**
📖 The Masada Maneuver **A:** Roger Cruz **W:** Fabian Nicieza

MAGNETO (LTD. SERIES)
Marvel

When Magneto's orbiting citadel, Avalon, crashes near the Andes Mountains, his loyal devotees gather debris and erect a shrine. Meanwhile, in the desolate Arctic, another citadel called New Avalon thrives, supervised by Magneto's greatest disciple, Exodus. He plans to launch his fortress in an attempt to mirror the accomplishments of his absent mentor, regardless of the worldwide destruction this event may cause.

Having no memory of his past deeds as Magneto, an unassuming man called Joseph decides to pretend to be the man he once was in order to dissuade Exodus from his precarious course. Can this absolve the guilt that Joseph feels for deeds he no longer remembers, or will it have even greater consequences for the new-found serenity of the man who was once The X-Men's greatest foe?

1 ❑ Nov 1996 Cover: 1.99 **NM** value: **Cover or less**
Circ: Direct Market orders: **139,000**
📖 Return Of The Messiah **A:** Kelley Jones **W:** Jorge Gonzalez; Peter Milligan
2 ❑ Dec 1996 Cover: 1.99 **NM** value: **Cover or less**
Circ: Direct Market orders: **117,000**
A: Kelley Jones **W:** Jorge Gonzalez; Peter Milligan
3 ❑ Jan 1997 Cover: 1.99 **NM** value: **Cover or less**
Circ: Direct Market orders: **107,500**
📖 Killzone **A:** Kelley Jones **W:** Jorge Gonzalez; Peter Milligan
4 ❑ Feb 1997 Cover: 1.99 **NM** value: **Cover or less**
Circ: Direct Market orders: **93,750**
📖 Spectres final issue. **A:** Kelley Jones **W:** Jorge Gonzalez; Peter Milligan

MAGNETO REX
Marvel

1 ❑ Apr 1999 Cover: 2.50 **NM** value: **Cover or less**
Circ: Diamd. preorders: **82,514**
2 ❑ Jun 1999 Cover: 2.50 **NM** value: **Cover or less**
Circ: Diamd. preorders: **72,247**
3 ❑ Jul 1999 Cover: 2.50 **NM** value: **Cover or less**
Circ: Diamd. preorders: **70,160**

MAGNETS: ROBOT DISMANTLER
Parody Press

1 ❑ b&w Cover: 2.95 **NM** value: **Cover or less**
Foil-embossed cover. **A:** Dan Nelson **W:** Bob Schmidt; Stacy Freeman

MAGNUS ROBOT FIGHTER (ACCLAIM)
Acclaim

1 ❑ May 1997 Cover: 2.50 **NM** value: **Cover or less**
Circ: Diamd. preorders: **21,608**
📖 Kick the Can **A:** Mike McKone **W:** Tom Peyer
1/SC ❑ May 1997 Cover: 2.50 **NM** value: **Cover or less**
alternate painted cover.
2 ❑ Jun 1997 Cover: 2.50 **NM** value: **Cover or less**
Circ: Diamd. preorders: **16,001**
📖 It Is Not Dying **A:** Mike McKone **W:** Tom Peyer
3 ❑ Jul 1997 Cover: 2.50 **NM** value: **Cover or less**
Circ: Diamd. preorders: **15,136**
A: Mike McKone **W:** Tom Peyer
4 ❑ Aug 1997 Cover: 2.50 **NM** value: **Cover or less**
Circ: Diamd. preorders: **14,683**
📖 Hell to the Chief! **A:** Mike McKone **W:** Tom Peyer
5 ❑ Sep 1997 Cover: 2.50 **NM** value: **Cover or less**
Circ: Diamd. preorders: **13,583**
6 ❑ Oct 1997 Cover: 2.50 **NM** value: **Cover or less**
Circ: Diamd. preorders: **12,680**
7 ❑ Nov 1997 Cover: 2.50 **NM** value: **Cover or less**
Circ: Diamd. preorders: **11,724**
Gold Key homage cover.
8 ❑ Dec 1997 Cover: 2.50 **NM** value: **Cover or less**
Circ: Diamd. preorders: **10,827**
9 ❑ Jan 1998 Cover: 2.50 **NM** value: **Cover or less**
Circ: Diamd. preorders: **10,005**
10 ❑ Feb 1998 Cover: 2.50 **NM** value: **Cover or less**
Circ: Diamd. preorders: **9,549**
11 ❑ Mar 1998 Cover: 2.50 **NM** value: **Cover or less**
Circ: Diamd. preorders: **8,836**
12 ❑ Apr 1998 Cover: 2.50 **NM** value: **Cover or less**
Circ: Diamd. preorders: **8,211**
13 ❑ Jan 1998 Cover: 2.50 **NM** value: **Cover or less**
Circ: Diamd. preorders: **7,736**
no cover date. • indicia says Jan
14 ❑ Feb 1998 Cover: 2.50 **NM** value: **Cover or less**
Circ: Diamd. preorders: **7,147**
no cover date. • indicia says Feb
15 ❑ Mar 1998 Cover: 2.50 **NM** value: **Cover or less**
Circ: Diamd. preorders: **6,971**
16 ❑ Apr 1998 Cover: 2.50 **NM** value: **Cover or less**
Circ: Diamd. preorders: **6,834**
17 ❑ May 1998 Cover: 2.50 **NM** value: **Cover or less**
Ash 1 ❑ Jan 1997, b&w **NM** value: **1.00**
no cover price. • preview of upcoming series

MAGNUS, ROBOT FIGHTER (GOLD KEY)
Gold Key

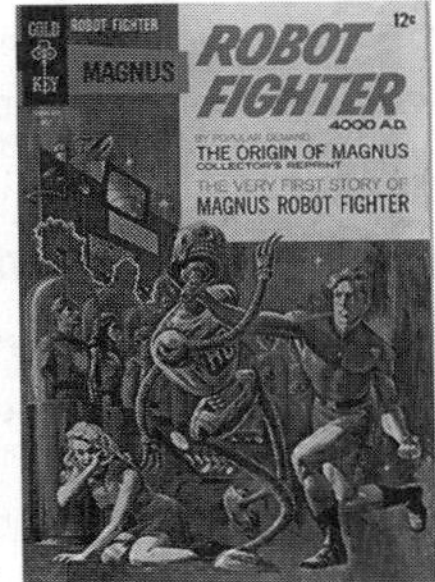

When robots gain free will and stage a revolt in the 41st century, it's up to one man, Magnus, who knows how to disable them to stop their rampage. Magnus learned his skills from the first robot to achieve free will, 1A, and has to be careful about revealing that knowledge lest the old robot is found out.

Magnus moves to North Am, a large continent-spanning city, where he is befriended by Leeja Clane and her father, who's one of the city's most influential senators. Later adventures take Magnus to the lower levels of the high-rise city and into outer space where he faces additional robotic threats.

Fondly remembered for its imaginative art by Russ Manning, the series would find new interest when Valiant Comics updated Magnus for the 1990s and collectors began seeking out the original series. — Brent

1 ❑ Feb 1963 Cover: 0.12 **NM** value: **100.00**
• **CGC:** 7 graded, best 9.2
★ Origin of Magnus. ★ 1st Appearance of Leeja Clane, Magnus.
2 ❑ May 1963 Cover: 0.12 **NM** value: **60.00**
• **CGC:** 3 graded, best 9.0
3 ❑ Aug 1963 Cover: 0.12 **NM** value: **60.00**
• **CGC:** 1 graded, best 8.5
4 ❑ Nov 1963 Cover: 0.12 **NM** value: **35.00**
• **CGC:** 1 graded, best 5.0
5 ❑ Feb 1964 Cover: 0.12 **NM** value: **35.00**
Circ: Statement: **247,279** • **CGC:** 1 graded, best 7.5
6 ❑ May 1964 Cover: 0.12 **NM** value: **35.00**
Circ: Statement: **247,279**
7 ❑ Aug 1964 Cover: 0.12 **NM** value: **35.00**
Circ: Statement: **247,279**
8 ❑ Nov 1964 Cover: 0.12 **NM** value: **35.00**
Circ: Statement: **247,279**
9 ❑ Feb 1965 Cover: 0.12 **NM** value: **35.00**
Circ: Statement: **236,713**
10 ❑ May 1965 Cover: 0.12 **NM** value: **35.00**
Circ: Statement: **236,713** • **CGC:** 1 graded, best 7.5
• Has 1964 Statement, filed 9/28/64; avg print run 378,176; avg sales 246,700; avg subs 579; avg total paid 247,279; samples 451; max existent 247,279
11 ❑ Aug 1965 Cover: 0.12 **NM** value: **25.00**
Circ: Statement: **236,713**
12 ❑ Nov 1965 Cover: 0.12 **NM** value: **25.00**
Circ: Statement: **236,713**
13 ❑ Feb 1966 Cover: 0.12 **NM** value: **25.00**
Circ: Statement: **236,304** • **CGC:** 1 graded, best 8.0
★ 1st Appearance of Doctor Noel.
14 ❑ May 1966 Cover: 0.12 **NM** value: **25.00**
Circ: Statement: **236,304**
• Has 1965 Statement, filed 9/28/1965; avg print run 392,076; avg sales 235,500; avg subs 1,213; avg total paid 236,713; samples 763; max existent 237,476; 39% of run returned
15 ❑ Aug 1966 Cover: 0.12 **NM** value: **25.00**
Circ: Statement: **236,304** • **CGC:** 1 graded, best 9.2

CGC-graded: Multiply prices above by **33 for 9.9 M • 16 for 9.8 NM/M • 7 for 9.6 NM+ • 5 for 9.4 NM • 2.5 for 9.2 NM- • 1.5 for 9.0 VF/NM**

16 ❑ Nov 1966 Cover: 0.12 **NM** value: **25.00**
Circ: Statement: **236,304**
17 ❑ Feb 1967 Cover: 0.12 **NM** value: **25.00**
Circ: Statement: **215,100**
18 ❑ May 1967 Cover: 0.12 **NM** value: **25.00**
Circ: Statement: **215,100** • **CGC:** 1 graded, best 9.2
19 ❑ Aug 1967 Cover: 0.12 **NM** value: **25.00**
Circ: Statement: **215,100** • **CGC:** 1 graded, best 9.4
20 ❑ Nov 1967 Cover: 0.12 **NM** value: **25.00**
Circ: Statement: **215,100**
21 ❑ Feb 1968 Cover: 0.12 **NM** value: **15.00**
22 ❑ May 1968 Cover: 0.12 **NM** value: **15.00**
• **CGC:** 1 graded, best 9.4
• reprints origin and first story; Reprints Magnus, Robot Fighter (Gold Key) #1 ★ Origin of Magnus. ★ 1st Appearance of Leeja Clane, Magnus.
23 ❑ Aug 1968 Cover: 0.12 **NM** value: **15.00**
A: Dan Spiegle
24 ❑ Nov 1968 Cover: 0.15 **NM** value: **15.00**
• Destruction of Malev-6
25 ❑ Feb 1969 Cover: 0.15 **NM** value: **15.00**
26 ❑ May 1969 Cover: 0.15 **NM** value: **15.00**
27 ❑ Aug 1969 Cover: 0.15 **NM** value: **15.00**
28 ❑ Nov 1969 Cover: 0.15 **NM** value: **15.00**
• goes on hiatus
29 ❑ Nov 1971 Cover: 0.15 **NM** value: **6.00**
30 ❑ Jan 1972 Cover: 0.15 **NM** value: **6.00**
31 ❑ Apr 1972 Cover: 0.15 **NM** value: **6.00**
32 ❑ Jul 1972 Cover: 0.15 **NM** value: **6.00**
33 ❑ Oct 1972 Cover: 0.15 **NM** value: **6.00**
34 ❑ Jan 1973 Cover: 0.15 **NM** value: **6.00**
The Evil Ark of Doctor Noel
35 ❑ May 1974 Cover: 0.20 **NM** value: **6.00**
36 ❑ Aug 1974 Cover: 0.25 **NM** value: **6.00**
37 ❑ Nov 1974 Cover: 0.25 **NM** value: **6.00**
38 ❑ Feb 1975 Cover: 0.25 **NM** value: **6.00**
39 ❑ May 1975 Cover: 0.25 **NM** value: **6.00**
40 ❑ Aug 1975 Cover: 0.25 **NM** value: **6.00**
41 ❑ Nov 1975 Cover: 0.25 **NM** value: **6.00**
42 ❑ Jan 1976 Cover: 0.25 **NM** value: **6.00**
43 ❑ May 1976 Cover: 0.25 **NM** value: **6.00**
44 ❑ Aug 1976 Cover: 0.25 **NM** value: **6.00**
45 ❑ Oct 1976 Cover: 0.30 **NM** value: **6.00**
• **CGC:** 1 graded, best 9.2
46 ❑ Jan 1977 Cover: 0.30 **NM** value: **6.00**

MAGNUS ROBOT FIGHTER/NEXUS
Valiant / Dark Horse

1 ❑ Dec 1993 Cover: 2.95 **NM** value: **3.00**
Circ: CapCity orders: **41,400**
covers says Mar, indicia says Dec. The Gift Horse, Part 1
2 ❑ Apr 1994 Cover: 2.95 **NM** value: **3.00**
Circ: CapCity orders: **26,650**
The Gift Horse, Part 2 **A:** Steve Rude **W:** Mike Baron

MAGNUS ROBOT FIGHTER (VALIANT)
Valiant

In the "perfect society" of North Am in 4000 A.D., humans have become dependent on robots for most work. Most robots are just that — robots — but a few developed minds of their own and seek to liberate all robots from enslavement by annihilating humanity.

Coddled by robots for most of their lives, humans are easy victims, so it falls upon the shoulders of one chosen savior to fight the renegade robots. Magnus has been trained his entire life for this battle. The renegade robots, called "freewills," are quick to take advantage of Magnus' human mind and constantly throw psychological curves his way, when they're not busy trying to rip him to shreds. This Valiant version of the Gold Key series is a fast-paced adventure, set in a future in which man's technology has turned against him.

0 ❑ ca. 1992 Cover: 1.75 **NM** value: **4.00**
no cover price. • Promotional "0" edition (from redeeming coupons in issues 1-8). • sendaway ★ Origin of Magnus.
0/A ❑ ca. 1992 Cover: 1.75 **NM** value: **3.00**
no cover price. • Promotional "0" edition without trading card. • sendaway; without trading card ★ Origin of Magnus.
1 ❑ May 1991 Cover: 1.75 **NM** value: **3.50**
Circ: CapCity orders: **20,500** • **CGC:** 9 graded, best 9.8
Steel Nation, Part 1 • trading cards **A:** Art Nichols **W:** Jim Shooter ★ Origin of Magnus.
2 ❑ Jul 1991 Cover: 1.75 **NM** value: **2.50**
Circ: CapCity orders: **13,400** • **CGC:** 1 graded, best 9.6
Steel Nation, Part 2 **A:** Art Nichols **W:** Jim Shooter
3 ❑ Aug 1991 Cover: 1.75 **NM** value: **2.50**
Circ: CapCity orders: **13,500**
Steel Nation, Part 3 **A:** Art Nichols **W:** Jim Shooter ★ 1st Appearance of Tekla.
4 ❑ Sep 1991 Cover: 1.75 **NM** value: **2.50**
Circ: CapCity orders: **14,900**
Steel Nation, Part 4 **A:** Art Nichols **W:** Jim Shooter
5 ❑ Oct 1991 Cover: 1.75 **NM** value: **2.00**
Circ: CapCity orders: **16,300**
• Flip-book. Invasion, Part 1 • Flip-book with Rai #1 **A:** Paul Creddick **W:** Jim Shooter ★ 1st Appearance of Rai.
6 ❑ Nov 1991 Cover: 1.75 **NM** value: **2.00**
Circ: CapCity orders: **17,000**
• Flip-book. **W:** Jim Shooter ★ Appearance of Rai, Solar.
7 ❑ Dec 1991 Cover: 1.75 **NM** value: **2.00**
Circ: CapCity orders: **16,800**
• Flip-book. **W:** Jim Shooter ★ Appearance of Rai. ★ Versus Rai.
8 ❑ Jan 1992 Cover: 1.95 **NM** value: **2.00**
Circ: CapCity orders: **17,700**
• Flip-book. **W:** Jim Shooter ★ Appearance of Rai.
9 ❑ Feb 1992 Cover: 1.95 **NM** value: **2.00**
Circ: CapCity orders: **15,900**
W: Jim Shooter
10 ❑ Mar 1992 Cover: 1.95 **NM** value: **2.00**
Circ: CapCity orders: **13,800**
W: Jim Shooter
11 ❑ Apr 1992 Cover: 1.95 **NM** value: **2.00**
Circ: CapCity orders: **12,900**
W: Jim Shooter
12 ❑ May 1992 Cover: 3.25 **NM** value: **5.00**
Circ: CapCity orders: **11,800** • **CGC:** 5 graded, best 9.6
• Giant-size. Stone and Steel! **A:** Gonzalo Mayo **W:** Jim Shooter; Faye Perozich ★ 1st Appearance of Turok (Valiant). ★ Appearance of Turok.
13 ❑ Jun 1992 Cover: 2.25 **NM** value: **Cover or less**
Circ: CapCity orders: **11,200**
W: Jim Shooter
14 ❑ Jul 1992 Cover: 2.25 **NM** value: **Cover or less**
Circ: CapCity orders: **12,100**
W: Jim Shooter
15 ❑ Aug 1992 Cover: 2.25 **NM** value: **Cover or less**
Circ: CapCity orders: **27,600**
Unity, Part 4 • Unity **A:** Frank Miller(cover) **W:** Jim Shooter; Roger Stern
16 ❑ Sep 1992 Cover: 2.25 **NM** value: **Cover or less**
Circ: CapCity orders: **31,500**
Unity, Part 12 • Unity **A:** Howard Simpson **C:** Walt Simonson **W:** Jim Shooter; Roger Stern
17 ❑ Nov 1992 Cover: 2.25 **NM** value: **Cover or less**
Circ: CapCity orders: **18,000**
W: Roger Stern
18 ❑ Nov 1992 Cover: 2.25 **NM** value: **Cover or less**
Circ: CapCity orders: **17,500**
W: Jim Shooter; Steve Ditko; David Michelinie
19 ❑ Dec 1992 Cover: 2.25 **NM** value: **Cover or less**
Circ: CapCity orders: **18,400**
W: Jim Shooter
20 ❑ Jan 1993 Cover: 2.25 **NM** value: **Cover or less**
Circ: CapCity orders: **18,300**
Hit Or Kiss **A:** Ernie Colon **W:** Jim Shooter; Fred Pierce
21 ❑ Feb 1993 Cover: 2.25 **NM** value: **Cover or less**
Circ: CapCity orders: **29,100**
Holocaust 4002, Part 1 • New logo
21/GO ❑ Feb 1993 Cover: 2.25 **NM** value: **3.00**
• Gold edition. Holocaust 4002, Part 1 • New logo
22 ❑ Mar 1993 Cover: 2.25 **NM** value: **Cover or less**
Circ: CapCity orders: **31,400**
Holocaust 4002, Part 2
23 ❑ Apr 1993 Cover: 2.25 **NM** value: **Cover or less**
Circ: CapCity orders: **38,000**
Holocaust 4002, Part 3 **A:** James Brock **W:** John Ostrander
24 ❑ May 1993 Cover: 2.25 **NM** value: **Cover or less**
Circ: CapCity orders: **90,100**
Holocaust 4002, Part 4; The Fall of North Am • Story leads into Rai and the Future Force #9 **A:** James Brock; Peter Grau **W:** John Ostrander
25 ❑ Jun 1993 Cover: 2.95 **NM** value: **Cover or less**
Circ: CapCity orders: **196,900**
Silver embossed cover. Flesh And Steel **A:** James Brock **W:** John Ostrander
25/LE ❑ Jun 1993 Cover: 2.95 **NM** value: **3.00**
Silver embossed cover. Flesh And Steel **A:** James Brock **W:** John Ostrander
26 ❑ Jul 1993 Cover: 2.25 **NM** value: **Cover or less**
Circ: CapCity orders: **78,900**
Exemplar **A:** Jim Calafiore **W:** John Ostrander
27 ❑ Aug 1993 Cover: 2.25 **NM** value: **Cover or less**
Circ: CapCity orders: **70,200**
The Enemy Of My Enemy **A:** Jim Calafiore **W:** John Ostrander
28 ❑ Sep 1993 Cover: 2.25 **NM** value: **Cover or less**
Circ: CapCity orders: **61,600**
Will Of Iron **A:** Jim Calafiore **W:** John Ostrander
29 ❑ Oct 1993 Cover: 2.25 **NM** value: **Cover or less**
Circ: CapCity orders: **49,200**
Indomitable **A:** Jim Calafiore **W:** John Ostrander ★ Appearance of Eternal Warrior.
30 ❑ Nov 1993 Cover: 2.25 **NM** value: **Cover or less**
Circ: CapCity orders: **42,375**
The Battle For South Am, Part 2 **A:** Jim Calafiore **W:** John Ostrander ★ Appearance of X-O.
31 ❑ Dec 1993 Cover: 2.25 **NM** value: **Cover or less**
Circ: CapCity orders: **37,900**
The Battle For South Am, Part 4 **A:** Jim Calafiore **W:** John Ostrander
32 ❑ Jan 1994 Cover: 2.25 **NM** value: **Cover or less**
Circ: CapCity orders: **34,175**
Mal-Adjusted **A:** Jim Calafiore **W:** Antony J.L. Bedard
33 ❑ Feb 1994 Cover: 2.25 **NM** value: **Cover or less**
Circ: CapCity orders: **30,675**
If This Is Tuesday, This Must Be...North Am? **A:** Jim Calafiore **W:** John Ostrander ★ Appearance of Timewalker.
34 ❑ Mar 1994 Cover: 2.25 **NM** value: **Cover or less**
Circ: CapCity orders: **25,925**
Christmas Eve: Minutes To Midnight **A:** Jim Calafiore **W:** Dave DeVries
35 ❑ Apr 1994 Cover: 2.25 **NM** value: **Cover or less**
Circ: CapCity orders: **22,625**
36 ❑ May 1994 Cover: 2.25 **NM** value: **Cover or less**
Circ: CapCity orders: **26,625**
• trading card
37 ❑ Jun 1994 Cover: 2.25 **NM** value: **Cover or less**
Circ: CapCity orders: **19,575**
★ Appearance of Starwatchers, Rai.
38 ❑ Aug 1994 Cover: 2.25 **NM** value: **Cover or less**
Circ: CapCity orders: **17,700**
39 ❑ Sep 1994 Cover: 2.25 **NM** value: **Cover or less**
Circ: CapCity orders: **18,825**
★ Appearance of Torque.
40 ❑ Oct 1994 Cover: 2.25 **NM** value: **Cover or less**
Circ: CapCity orders: **16,475**
41 ❑ Nov 1994 Cover: 2.25 **NM** value: **Cover or less**
Circ: CapCity orders: **21,625**
The Chaos Effect: Epsilon, Part 4 • Chaos Effect
42 ❑ Dec 1994 Cover: 2.25 **NM** value: **Cover or less**
Circ: CapCity orders: **13,600**
43 ❑ Jan 1995 Cover: 2.25 **NM** value: **Cover or less**
Circ: CapCity orders: **12,350**
The Geomancer Quest, Part 1
44 ❑ Feb 1995 Cover: 2.25 **NM** value: **Cover or less**
Circ: CapCity orders: **11,350**
The Geomancer Quest, Part 2
45 ❑ Mar 1995 Cover: 2.25 **NM** value: **Cover or less**
Circ: CapCity orders: **9,800**
The Geomancer Quest, Part 3
46 ❑ Apr 1995 Cover: 2.25 **NM** value: **Cover or less**
Circ: CapCity orders: **9,000**
The Geomancer Quest, Part 4
47 ❑ May 1995 Cover: 2.25 **NM** value: **Cover or less**
Circ: CapCity orders: **8,175**
War & Remembrance; Cold Blooded, Part 1
48 ❑ Jun 1995 Cover: 2.25 **NM** value: **Cover or less**
Circ: CapCity orders: **7,325**
Cold Blooded, Part 2
49 ❑ Jul 1995 Cover: 2.50 **NM** value: **Cover or less**
Circ: CapCity orders: **7,950**
50 ❑ Jul 1995 Cover: 2.25 **NM** value: **Cover or less**
Circ: CapCity orders: **7,500**
• Birthquake
51 ❑ Aug 1995 Cover: 2.25 **NM** value: **Cover or less**
Circ: CapCity orders: **6,825**
• Birthquake
52 ❑ Aug 1995 Cover: 2.25 **NM** value: **Cover or less**
Circ: CapCity orders: **6,825**
• Birthquake
53 ❑ Sep 1995 Cover: 2.25 **NM** value: **Cover or less**
Circ: CapCity orders: **6,600**
54 ❑ Sep 1995 Cover: 2.25 **NM** value: **Cover or less**
Circ: CapCity orders: **6,600**
55 ❑ Oct 1995 Cover: 2.50 **NM** value: **Cover or less**
Circ: CapCity orders: **6,550**
56 ❑ Oct 1995 Cover: 2.50 **NM** value: **Cover or less**
Circ: CapCity orders: **6,550**
57 ❑ Nov 1995 Cover: 2.50 **NM** value: **Cover or less**
Circ: CapCity orders: **6,325**
58 ❑ Nov 1995 Cover: 2.50 **NM** value: **Cover or less**
Circ: CapCity orders: **6,350**
59 ❑ Dec 1995 Cover: 2.50 **NM** value: **Cover or less**
Circ: CapCity orders: **5,500**
60 ❑ Dec 1995 Cover: 2.50 **NM** value: **Cover or less**
Circ: CapCity orders: **5,525**
61 ❑ Jan 1996 Cover: 2.50 **NM** value: **Cover or less**
Circ: CapCity orders: **4,675**
62 ❑ Jan 1996 Cover: 2.50 **NM** value: **Cover or less**
Circ: CapCity orders: **4,675**
• Torque becomes a Psi-Lord
63 ❑ Feb 1996 Cover: 2.50 **NM** value: **Cover or less**
64 ❑ Feb 1996 Cover: 2.50 **NM** value: **Cover or less**
final issue. ★ Death of Magnus, Robot Fighter (Valiant).
YB 1 ❑ Cover: 3.95 **NM** value: **Cover or less**
Circ: CapCity orders: **15,450**
cardstock cover. • 1994 Yearbook.

MAGUS
Caliber

1 ❑ Cover: 2.95 **NM** value: **Cover or less**
A: Craig Brasfield **W:** Gary Reed
1/A ❑ Cover: 2.95 **NM** value: **Cover or less**
Variant cover of Girl praying in foreground, Magus behind. **A:** Craig Brasfield **W:** Gary Reed
2 ❑ Cover: 2.95 **NM** value: **Cover or less**

MAINE ZOMBIE LOBSTERMEN
Maine Stream Comics

1 ❑ b&w Cover: 2.50 **NM** value: **Cover or less**
2 ❑ b&w Cover: 2.50 **NM** value: **Cover or less**
3 ❑ b&w Cover: 3.50 **NM** value: **Cover or less**

MAI, THE PSYCHIC GIRL
Eclipse / Viz

Mai is a 14-year-old Japanese girl pursued by the sinister Wisdom Alliance, which wants to control and exploit the psionic power she wields. After the death of her father, Mai is rescued and aided by Tokyo University student Intetsu, who, with the help of his college friends, decides to oppose the forces that want to enslave her.

Translated from the original Japanese, Mai, the Psychic Girl, has the unusual quality and pacing of such other manga titles as Ranma 1/2 and Akira. There is a sense of anticipation due to the abundant use of facial close-ups with no dialogue and a complete absence of thought balloons. Scenes can change from deadly serious to humorous to absurd in the space of a page.

1 ❑ May 1987, b&w Cover: 1.50 **NM** value: **3.50**
Mai, The Psychic Girl, Part 1 • Japanese **A:** Ryoichi Ikegami **W:** Kazuya Kudo
1-2 ❑ 1987 Cover: 1.50 **NM** value: **2.00**
2 ❑ Jun 1987 Cover: 1.50 **NM** value: **2.50**
Circ: CapCity orders: **6,400**
Mai, The Psychic Girl, Part 2 **A:** Ryoichi Ikegami **W:** Kazuya Kudo

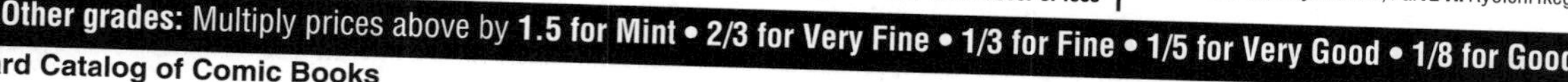

2-2 ❑ 1987 Cover: 1.50 NM value: 2.00
3 ❑ Jun 1987 Cover: 1.50 NM value: 2.50
Circ: CapCity orders: 6,175
Mai, the Psychic Girl, Part 3; Mai, the Psychic Girl, Part 4 A: Ryoichi Ikegami W: Kazuya Kudo
4 ❑ Jul 1987 Cover: 1.50 NM value: 2.00
Mai, The Psychic Girl, Part 5; Mai, The Psychic Girl, Part 6 A: Ryoichi Ikegami W: Kazuya Kudo
5 ❑ Jul 1987 Cover: 1.50 NM value: 2.00
Mai, The Psychic Girl, Part 7; Mai, The Psychic Girl, Part 8 A: Ryoichi Ikegami W: Kazuya Kudo
6 ❑ Aug 1987 Cover: 1.50 NM value: 1.75
Circ: CapCity orders: 6,700
Mai, The Psychic Girl, Part 9; Mai, The Psychic Girl, Part 10 A: Ryoichi Ikegami W: Kazuya Kudo
7 ❑ Aug 1987 Cover: 1.50 NM value: 1.75
Circ: CapCity orders: 6,700
Mai, The Psychic Girl, Part 11; Mai, The Psychic Girl, Part 12 A: Ryoichi Ikegami W: Kazuya Kudo
8 ❑ Sep 1987 Cover: 1.50 NM value: 1.75
Mai, The Psychic Girl, Part 13; Mai, The Psychic Girl, Part 14 A: Ryoichi Ikegami W: Kazuya Kudo
9 ❑ Sep 1987 Cover: 1.50 NM value: 1.75
Mai, the Psychic Girl, Part 15; Mai, the Psychic Girl, Part 16 A: Ryoichi Ikegami W: Kazuya Kudo
10 ❑ Oct 1987 Cover: 1.50 NM value: 1.75
A: Ryoichi Ikegami W: Kazuya Kudo
11 ❑ Oct 1987 Cover: 1.50 NM value: 1.75
A: Ryoichi Ikegami W: Kazuya Kudo
12 ❑ Nov 1987 Cover: 1.50 NM value: 1.75
A: Ryoichi Ikegami W: Kazuya Kudo
13 ❑ Nov 1987 Cover: 1.50 NM value: 1.75
A: Ryoichi Ikegami W: Kazuya Kudo
14 ❑ Dec 1987 Cover: 1.50 NM value: 1.75
A: Ryoichi Ikegami W: Kazuya Kudo
15 ❑ Dec 1987 Cover: 1.50 NM value: 1.75
A: Ryoichi Ikegami W: Kazuya Kudo
16 ❑ Jan 1988 Cover: 1.50 NM value: 1.75
A: Ryoichi Ikegami W: Kazuya Kudo
17 ❑ Jan 1988 Cover: 1.50 NM value: 1.75
A: Ryoichi Ikegami W: Kazuya Kudo
18 ❑ Feb 1988 Cover: 1.50 NM value: 1.75
A: Ryoichi Ikegami W: Kazuya Kudo
19 ❑ Feb 1988 Cover: 1.50 NM value: 1.75
A: Ryoichi Ikegami W: Kazuya Kudo
20 ❑ Mar 1988 Cover: 1.50 NM value: 1.75
A: Ryoichi Ikegami W: Kazuya Kudo
21 ❑ Mar 1988 Cover: 1.50 NM value: 1.75
A: Ryoichi Ikegami W: Kazuya Kudo
22 ❑ Apr 1988 Cover: 1.50 NM value: 1.75
A: Ryoichi Ikegami W: Kazuya Kudo
23 ❑ Apr 1988 Cover: 1.50 NM value: 1.75
Part 43, Ryu's Arrival; Part 44, Ryu's Plan A: Ryoichi Ikegami W: Kazuya Kudo
24 ❑ May 1988 Cover: 1.50 NM value: 1.75
A: Ryoichi Ikegami W: Kazuya Kudo
25 ❑ May 1988 Cover: 1.50 NM value: 1.75
A: Ryoichi Ikegami W: Kazuya Kudo
26 ❑ Jun 1988 Cover: 1.50 NM value: 1.75
A: Ryoichi Ikegami W: Kazuya Kudo
27 ❑ Jun 1988 Cover: 1.50 NM value: 1.75
A: Ryoichi Ikegami W: Kazuya Kudo
28 ❑ Jul 1988 Cover: 1.50 NM value: 1.75
final issue. A: Ryoichi Ikegami W: Kazuya Kudo
Bk 1❑ Cover: 16.95 NM value: 19.95
A: Ryoichi Ikegami W: Kazuya Kudo
Bk 2❑ Cover: 16.95 NM value: 19.95
A: Ryoichi Ikegami W: Kazuya Kudo
Bk 3❑ Cover: 16.95 NM value: 19.95
A: Ryoichi Ikegami W: Kazuya Kudo
Bk 4❑ Cover: 16.95 NM value: Cover or less
A: Ryoichi Ikegami W: Kazuya Kudo

MAI, THE PSYCHIC GIRL PERFECT COLLECTION Viz

Bk 1❑ Cover: 19.95 NM value: Cover or less
A: Ryoichi Ikegami W: Kazuya Kudo
Bk 2❑ Cover: 19.95 NM value: Cover or less
A: Ryoichi Ikegami W: Kazuya Kudo
Bk 3❑ Cover: 19.95 NM value: Cover or less
A: Ryoichi Ikegami W: Kazuya Kudo

MAISON IKKOKU PART 1 Viz

Rumiko Takashi's long-running romance manga mixes slapstick comedy with truly touching moments. The male love-interest is Yusaku Godai, who lives at the boarding house Maison Ikkoku, which has such other tenants as a club hostess. He falls for Kyoko Otonashi, the widowed manager of the establishment, but he's too embarrassed to convey his feelings to her.

This sequence starts a series that actually has a beginning, middle, and end; the art communicates the characters' emotions without getting bogged down in gratuitous detail, and the manga was adapted as a Japanese TV series and film.

1 ❑ Jun 1992 Cover: 2.95 NM value: 4.00
Circ: CapCity orders: 4,200
A: Rumiko Takahashi W: Rumiko Takahashi
2 ❑ Jul 1992 Cover: 2.95 NM value: 3.50
Circ: CapCity orders: 3,050
A: Rumiko Takahashi W: Rumiko Takahashi
3 ❑ Aug 1992 Cover: 2.95 NM value: 3.50
Circ: CapCity orders: 2,975
A: Rumiko Takahashi W: Rumiko Takahashi
4 ❑ Sep 1992 Cover: 2.95 NM value: 3.50
A: Rumiko Takahashi W: Rumiko Takahashi
5 ❑ Oct 1992 Cover: 2.95 NM value: 3.50
Circ: CapCity orders: 2,825
A: Rumiko Takahashi W: Rumiko Takahashi
6 ❑ Nov 1992 Cover: 2.95 NM value: 3.50
Circ: CapCity orders: 2,725
A: Rumiko Takahashi W: Rumiko Takahashi
7 ❑ Dec 1992 Cover: 2.95 NM value: 3.50
Circ: CapCity orders: 2,750
A: Rumiko Takahashi W: Rumiko Takahashi
Bk 1❑ Cover: 16.95 NM value: Cover or less
• collects first series A: Rumiko Takahashi W: Rumiko Takahashi

MAISON IKKOKU PART 2 Viz

1 ❑ Jan 1993 Cover: 2.95 NM value: 3.50
Circ: CapCity orders: 2,925
A: Rumiko Takahashi W: Rumiko Takahashi
2 ❑ Feb 1993 Cover: 2.95 NM value: 3.00
Circ: CapCity orders: 2,725
A: Rumiko Takahashi W: Rumiko Takahashi
3 ❑ Mar 1993 Cover: 2.95 NM value: 3.00
Circ: CapCity orders: 2,725
A: Rumiko Takahashi W: Rumiko Takahashi
4 ❑ Apr 1993 Cover: 2.95 NM value: 3.00
Circ: CapCity orders: 2,875
A: Rumiko Takahashi W: Rumiko Takahashi
5 ❑ May 1993 Cover: 2.95 NM value: 3.00
Circ: CapCity orders: 3,100
A: Rumiko Takahashi W: Rumiko Takahashi
6 ❑ Jun 1993 Cover: 2.95 NM value: 3.00
Circ: CapCity orders: 3,200
A: Rumiko Takahashi W: Rumiko Takahashi
Bk 2❑ Cover: 16.95 NM value: Cover or less
• Family Affairs A: Rumiko Takahashi W: Rumiko Takahashi

MAISON IKKOKU PART 3 Viz

1 ❑ Jul 1993 Cover: 2.95 NM value: Cover or less
A: Rumiko Takahashi W: Rumiko Takahashi
2 ❑ Aug 1993 Cover: 2.95 NM value: Cover or less
Circ: CapCity orders: 3,300
A: Rumiko Takahashi W: Rumiko Takahashi
3 ❑ Sep 1993 Cover: 2.95 NM value: Cover or less
Circ: CapCity orders: 3,125
A: Rumiko Takahashi W: Rumiko Takahashi
4 ❑ Oct 1993 Cover: 2.95 NM value: Cover or less
Circ: CapCity orders: 3,075
A: Rumiko Takahashi W: Rumiko Takahashi
5 ❑ Nov 1993 Cover: 2.95 NM value: Cover or less
Circ: CapCity orders: 2,950
A: Rumiko Takahashi W: Rumiko Takahashi
6 ❑ Dec 1993 Cover: 2.95 NM value: Cover or less
Circ: CapCity orders: 2,975
A: Rumiko Takahashi W: Rumiko Takahashi
Bk 3❑ Cover: 15.95 NM value: Cover or less
• Home Sweet Home A: Rumiko Takahashi W: Rumiko Takahashi

MAISON IKKOKU PART 4 Viz

1 ❑ Jan 1994 Cover: 2.95 NM value: Cover or less
Circ: CapCity orders: 3,025
Embraced by Illness A: Rumiko Takahashi W: Rumiko Takahashi
2 ❑ Feb 1994 Cover: 2.75 NM value: Cover or less
Circ: CapCity orders: 2,800
A: Rumiko Takahashi W: Rumiko Takahashi
3 ❑ Apr 1994 Cover: 2.75 NM value: Cover or less
Circ: CapCity orders: 2,875
A: Rumiko Takahashi W: Rumiko Takahashi
4 ❑ May 1994 Cover: 2.95 NM value: Cover or less
Circ: CapCity orders: 2,800
A: Rumiko Takahashi W: Rumiko Takahashi
5 ❑ Jun 1994 Cover: 2.95 NM value: Cover or less
Circ: CapCity orders: 2,750
A: Rumiko Takahashi W: Rumiko Takahashi
6 ❑ Jul 1994 Cover: 2.95 NM value: Cover or less
Circ: CapCity orders: 2,825
A: Rumiko Takahashi W: Rumiko Takahashi
7 ❑ Aug 1994 Cover: 2.95 NM value: Cover or less
Circ: CapCity orders: 2,900
A: Rumiko Takahashi W: Rumiko Takahashi
8 ❑ Sep 1994 Cover: 2.95 NM value: Cover or less
Circ: CapCity orders: 2,725
A: Rumiko Takahashi W: Rumiko Takahashi
9 ❑ Oct 1994 Cover: 2.95 NM value: Cover or less
Circ: CapCity orders: 2,525
A: Rumiko Takahashi W: Rumiko Takahashi
10 ❑ Nov 1994 Cover: 2.95 NM value: Cover or less
A: Rumiko Takahashi W: Rumiko Takahashi
Bk 4❑ Cover: 15.95 NM value: Cover or less
• Good Housekeeping A: Rumiko Takahashi W: Rumiko Takahashi
Bk 5❑ Cover: 15.95 NM value: Cover or less
• Empty Nest A: Rumiko Takahashi W: Rumiko Takahashi

MAISON IKKOKU PART 5 Viz

1 ❑ Nov 1995 Cover: 2.95 NM value: Cover or less
A: Rumiko Takahashi W: Rumiko Takahashi
2 ❑ Dec 1995 Cover: 2.95 NM value: Cover or less
A: Rumiko Takahashi W: Rumiko Takahashi
3 ❑ Jan 1996 Cover: 3.50 NM value: Cover or less
A: Rumiko Takahashi W: Rumiko Takahashi
4 ❑ Feb 1996 Cover: 3.50 NM value: Cover or less
A: Rumiko Takahashi W: Rumiko Takahashi
5 ❑ Mar 1996 Cover: 3.50 NM value: Cover or less
A: Rumiko Takahashi W: Rumiko Takahashi
6 ❑ Apr 1996 Cover: 2.95 NM value: Cover or less
A: Rumiko Takahashi W: Rumiko Takahashi
7 ❑ May 1996 Cover: 3.50 NM value: Cover or less
A: Rumiko Takahashi W: Rumiko Takahashi
8 ❑ Jun 1996 Cover: 3.50 NM value: Cover or less
A: Rumiko Takahashi W: Rumiko Takahashi
9 ❑ Jul 1996 Cover: 2.75 NM value: Cover or less
A: Rumiko Takahashi W: Rumiko Takahashi
Bk 6❑ Cover: 15.95 NM value: Cover or less
• Bedside Manners A: Rumiko Takahashi W: Rumiko Takahashi
Bk 7❑ Cover: 15.95 NM value: Cover or less
• Intensive Care A: Rumiko Takahashi W: Rumiko Takahashi

MAISON IKKOKU PART 6 Viz

1 ❑ Aug 1996 Cover: 3.50 NM value: Cover or less
A: Rumiko Takahashi W: Rumiko Takahashi
2 ❑ Sep 1996 Cover: 2.95 NM value: Cover or less
Circ: Diamd. preorders: 6,478
A: Rumiko Takahashi W: Rumiko Takahashi
3 ❑ Oct 1996 Cover: 3.50 NM value: Cover or less
Circ: Diamd. preorders: 6,336
A: Rumiko Takahashi W: Rumiko Takahashi
4 ❑ Nov 1996 Cover: 3.50 NM value: Cover or less
Circ: Diamd. preorders: 6,154
A: Rumiko Takahashi W: Rumiko Takahashi
5 ❑ Dec 1996 Cover: 2.95 NM value: Cover or less
Circ: Diamd. preorders: 6,021
A: Rumiko Takahashi W: Rumiko Takahashi
6 ❑ Jan 1997 Cover: 3.50 NM value: Cover or less
Circ: Diamd. preorders: 5,974
A: Rumiko Takahashi W: Rumiko Takahashi
7 ❑ Feb 1997 Cover: 2.95 NM value: Cover or less
Circ: Diamd. preorders: 5,600
A: Rumiko Takahashi W: Rumiko Takahashi
8 ❑ Mar 1997 Cover: 2.95 NM value: Cover or less
Circ: Diamd. preorders: 5,611
A: Rumiko Takahashi W: Rumiko Takahashi
9 ❑ Apr 1997 Cover: 2.95 NM value: Cover or less
Circ: Diamd. preorders: 5,666
A: Rumiko Takahashi W: Rumiko Takahashi
10 ❑ May 1997 Cover: 2.95 NM value: Cover or less
Circ: Diamd. preorders: 5,336
A: Rumiko Takahashi W: Rumiko Takahashi
11 ❑ Jun 1997 Cover: 2.95 NM value: 3.50
Circ: Diamd. preorders: 5,406
A: Rumiko Takahashi W: Rumiko Takahashi
Bk 8❑ Nov 1997 Cover: 15.95 NM value: Cover or less
• Domestic Dispute A: Rumiko Takahashi W: Rumiko Takahashi
Bk 9❑ Jan 1998 Cover: 16.95 NM value: Cover or less
• Learning Curves A: Rumiko Takahashi W: Rumiko Takahashi

MAISON IKKOKU PART 7 Viz

1 ❑ Jul 1997 Cover: 3.50 NM value: Cover or less
Circ: Diamd. preorders: 5,859
A: Rumiko Takahashi W: Rumiko Takahashi
2 ❑ Aug 1997 Cover: 3.50 NM value: Cover or less
Circ: Diamd. preorders: 5,618
A: Rumiko Takahashi W: Rumiko Takahashi
3 ❑ Sep 1997 Cover: 3.25 NM value: Cover or less
Circ: Diamd. preorders: 5,690
A: Rumiko Takahashi W: Rumiko Takahashi
4 ❑ Oct 1997 Cover: 3.25 NM value: Cover or less
Circ: Diamd. preorders: 5,531
A: Rumiko Takahashi W: Rumiko Takahashi
5 ❑ Nov 1997 Cover: 3.25 NM value: Cover or less
Circ: Diamd. preorders: 5,672
A: Rumiko Takahashi W: Rumiko Takahashi
6 ❑ Dec 1997 Cover: 3.25 NM value: Cover or less
Circ: Diamd. preorders: 5,458
A: Rumiko Takahashi W: Rumiko Takahashi
7 ❑ Jan 1998 Cover: 3.25 NM value: Cover or less
Circ: Diamd. preorders: 5,211
A: Rumiko Takahashi W: Rumiko Takahashi
8 ❑ Feb 1998 Cover: 3.25 NM value: Cover or less
Circ: Diamd. preorders: 5,149
A: Rumiko Takahashi W: Rumiko Takahashi
9 ❑ Mar 1998 Cover: 3.25 NM value: Cover or less
Circ: Diamd. preorders: 5,180
A: Rumiko Takahashi W: Rumiko Takahashi
10 ❑ Apr 1998 Cover: 3.25 NM value: Cover or less
Circ: Diamd. preorders: 5,084
A: Rumiko Takahashi W: Rumiko Takahashi
11 ❑ May 1998 Cover: 3.25 NM value: Cover or less
Circ: Diamd. preorders: 5,014
A: Rumiko Takahashi W: Rumiko Takahashi
12 ❑ Jun 1998 Cover: 3.25 NM value: Cover or less
Circ: Diamd. preorders: 4,975
A: Rumiko Takahashi W: Rumiko Takahashi
13 ❑ Jul 1998 Cover: 3.25 NM value: Cover or less
Circ: Diamd. preorders: 4,803
A: Rumiko Takahashi W: Rumiko Takahashi
Bk 10❑Apr 1998 Cover: 17.95 NM value: Cover or less
• Dogged Pursuit A: Rumiko Takahashi W: Rumiko Takahashi
Bk 11❑Feb 1999 Cover: 16.95 NM value: Cover or less
• Student Affairs A: Rumiko Takahashi W: Rumiko Takahashi

MAISON IKKOKU PART 8 Viz

1 ❑ Aug 1998 Cover: 3.25 NM value: Cover or less
Circ: Diamd. preorders: 4,843
A: Rumiko Takahashi W: Rumiko Takahashi
2 ❑ Sep 1998 Cover: 3.50 NM value: Cover or less
Circ: Diamd. preorders: 4,660
A: Rumiko Takahashi W: Rumiko Takahashi
3 ❑ Oct 1998 Cover: 2.95 NM value: Cover or less
Circ: Diamd. preorders: 4,647
A: Rumiko Takahashi W: Rumiko Takahashi
4 ❑ Nov 1998 Cover: 3.50 NM value: Cover or less
Circ: Diamd. preorders: 4,638
A: Rumiko Takahashi W: Rumiko Takahashi

CGC-graded: Multiply prices above by **33 for 9.9 M • 16 for 9.8 NM/M • 7 for 9.6 NM+ • 5 for 9.4 NM • 2.5 for 9.2 NM- • 1.5 for 9.0 VF/NM**

5 ❑ Dec 1998 Cover: 3.50 **NM** value: **Cover or less**
Circ: Diamd. preorders: **4,429**
A: Rumiko Takahashi **W:** Rumiko Takahashi
6 ❑ Jan 1999 Cover: 3.50 **NM** value: **Cover or less**
Circ: Diamd. preorders: **4,458**
A: Rumiko Takahashi **W:** Rumiko Takahashi
7 ❑ Feb 1999 Cover: 3.50 **NM** value: **Cover or less**
Circ: Diamd. preorders: **4,327**
A: Rumiko Takahashi **W:** Rumiko Takahashi
8 ❑ Mar 1999 Cover: 3.25 **NM** value: **Cover or less**
Circ: Diamd. preorders: **4,354**
A: Rumiko Takahashi **W:** Rumiko Takahashi

MAISON IKKOKU PART 9 — Viz

1 ❑ Apr 1999 Cover: 3.25 **NM** value: **Cover or less**
Circ: Diamd. preorders: **4,881**
A: Rumiko Takahashi **W:** Rumiko Takahashi
2 ❑ May 1999 Cover: 3.25 **NM** value: **Cover or less**
Circ: Diamd. preorders: **4,600**
A: Rumiko Takahashi **W:** Rumiko Takahashi
3 ❑ Jun 1999 Cover: 3.25 **NM** value: **Cover or less**
Circ: Diamd. preorders: **4,515**
A: Rumiko Takahashi **W:** Rumiko Takahashi
4 ❑ Jul 1999 Cover: 3.25 **NM** value: **Cover or less**
Circ: Diamd. preorders: **4,462**
A: Rumiko Takahashi **W:** Rumiko Takahashi
5 ❑ Aug 1999 Cover: 3.25 **NM** value: **Cover or less**
Circ: Diamd. preorders: **4,372**
A: Rumiko Takahashi **W:** Rumiko Takahashi
6 ❑ Sep 1999 Cover: 3.25 **NM** value: **Cover or less**
Circ: Diamd. preorders: **4,266**
A: Rumiko Takahashi **W:** Rumiko Takahashi
7 ❑ Oct 1999 Cover: 3.25 **NM** value: **Cover or less**
Circ: Diamd. preorders: **4,397**
A: Rumiko Takahashi **W:** Rumiko Takahashi

MAJCANS, THE — P.S.

1 ❑ Cover: 1.00 **NM** value: **Cover or less**

MAJOR BUMMER — DC

John Arcudi and Doug Mahnke had the perfect, 1990s idea for a super-hero with the creation of "Major Bummer." The title character is Lou Martin, the archetypal slacker teen who spent most of his life playing videogames and loafing in front of the TV. Then came the fateful day he opened a strange package that had been left on his doorstep by an unknown party. There was a blinding flash of light, Lou was knocked unconscious...and when he woke up, he had been transformed from a gangly teen into a super-heroic hunk.

The next day, Lou was unaware of the changes in him — even after he zoned out while fixing a VCR and accidentally turned it into a futuristic ray gun. The revelation came when he foiled a holdup at the local convenience store while going on a munchie run to feed his suddenly ravenous appetite. Like so many events in this series, the comedy comes from Lou's utter apathy in the face of extraordinary events.

1 ❑ Aug 1997 Cover: 2.50 **NM** value: **3.50**
Circ: Diamd. preorders: **23,799**
📖 What the Hell…?? **A:** Doug Mahnke **W:** John Arcudi ★ Origin of Major Bummer. ★ 1st Appearance of The Gecko, Major Bummer.
2 ❑ Sep 1997 Cover: 2.50 **NM** value: **3.00**
Circ: Diamd. preorders: **15,504**
A: Doug Mahnke **W:** John Arcudi
3 ❑ Oct 1997 Cover: 2.50 **NM** value: **3.00**
Circ: Diamd. preorders: **14,868**
📖 Alone Against the Other Guys! **A:** Doug Mahnke **W:** John Arcudi
4 ❑ Nov 1997 Cover: 2.50 **NM** value: **Cover or less**
Circ: Diamd. preorders: **14,907**
A: Doug Mahnke **W:** John Arcudi
5 ❑ Dec 1997 Cover: 2.50 **NM** value: **Cover or less**
Circ: Diamd. preorders: **14,844**
Face cover. 📖 No Matter or How I Started Worrying and Saved the World **A:** Doug Mahnke **W:** John Arcudi
6 ❑ Jan 1998 Cover: 2.50 **NM** value: **Cover or less**
Circ: Diamd. preorders: **13,916**
A: Doug Mahnke **W:** John Arcudi
7 ❑ Feb 1998 Cover: 2.50 **NM** value: **Cover or less**
Circ: Diamd. preorders: **13,259**
A: Doug Mahnke **W:** John Arcudi
8 ❑ Mar 1998 Cover: 2.50 **NM** value: **Cover or less**
Circ: Diamd. preorders: **12,478**
A: Doug Mahnke **W:** John Arcudi
9 ❑ Apr 1998 Cover: 2.50 **NM** value: **Cover or less**
Circ: Diamd. preorders: **11,710**
A: Doug Mahnke **W:** John Arcudi
10 ❑ May 1998 Cover: 2.50 **NM** value: **Cover or less**
Circ: Diamd. preorders: **11,972**
A: Doug Mahnke **W:** John Arcudi
11 ❑ Jun 1998 Cover: 2.50 **NM** value: **Cover or less**
Circ: Diamd. preorders: **12,699**
A: Doug Mahnke **W:** John Arcudi
12 ❑ Jul 1998 Cover: 2.50 **NM** value: **Cover or less**
Circ: Diamd. preorders: **12,236**
13 ❑ Aug 1998 Cover: 2.50 **NM** value: **Cover or less**
Circ: Diamd. preorders: **12,396**
14 ❑ Sep 1998 Cover: 2.50 **NM** value: **Cover or less**
Circ: Diamd. preorders: **12,006**
15 ❑ Oct 1998 Cover: 2.50 **NM** value: **Cover or less**
Circ: Diamd. preorders: **11,628**

MAJOR DAMAGE — Invictus

1 ❑ Oct 1994 Cover: 2.25 **NM** value: **Cover or less**
📖 Above and Beyond **A:** C.E. Sutherland III **W:** C.E. Sutherland III
2 ❑ Cover: 2.25 **NM** value: **Cover or less**

MAJOR POWER AND SPUNKY — Eros

1 ❑ Oct 1994 Cover: 3.50 **NM** value: **Cover or less**
• one shot

MAJOR VICTORY COMICS — Harry A. Chesler

1 ❑ ca. 1944 Cover: 0.10 **NM** value: **500.00**
2 ❑ Spr 1945 Cover: 0.10 **NM** value: **300.00**
• **CGC:** 1 graded, best 7.0
3 ❑ Sum 1945 Cover: 0.10 **NM** value: **250.00**
• **CGC:** 2 graded, best 9.2

MAKEBELIEVE — Liar

1 ❑ Cover: 2.95 **NM** value: **Cover or less**
A: Paul Barbabosa **W:** Dean Poisso

MALCOLM-10 — Onli Studios

1 ❑ b&w Cover: 2.00 **NM** value: **Cover or less**
A: Rhymism; Turtel Onli **W:** Turtel Onli; Punkin X

MALCOLM X — Millennium

1 ❑ Cover: 3.95 **NM** value: **Cover or less**

MALIBU ASHCAN: ULTRAFORCE — Malibu / Ultraverse

1 ❑ Jun 1994 Cover: 0.75 **NM** value: **Cover or less**
No issue number.

MALIBU SIGNATURE SERIES — Malibu

1993❑ **NM** value: **0.25**
• autograph book giveaway.
1994❑ **NM** value: **0.25**
• autograph book giveaway.

MALICE IN WONDERLAND — Fantagraphics / Eros

All issues are adults only.
1 ❑ Aug 1993, b&w Cover: 2.75 **NM** value: **Cover or less**
A: Wally Wood

MALLIMALOU — Chance

1 ❑ Cover: 1.50 **NM** value: **Cover or less**

MALLRATS — Kitchen Sink

Bk 1❑ Oct 1995 Cover: 14.95 **NM** value: **Cover or less**
• movie background

MALU IN THE LAND OF ADVENTURE — I.W.

1 ❑ ca. 1964 Cover: 0.12 **NM** value: **50.00**

MAMMOTH COMICS — K.K.

1 ❑ ca. 1939 **NM** value: **1500.00**

MAN AGAINST TIME — Image

1 ❑ May 1996 Cover: 2.25 **NM** value: **Cover or less**
📖 Every Hero **A:** Gino Dicicco **W:** Brett Lewis
1/A ❑ May 1996 Cover: 2.25 **NM** value: **Cover or less**
2 ❑ Jun 1996 Cover: 2.25 **NM** value: **Cover or less**
📖 Tomorrow's Persuasion **A:** Gino Dicicco **W:** Brett Lewis
3 ❑ Jul 1996 Cover: 2.25 **NM** value: **Cover or less**
A: Gino Dicicco **W:** Brett Lewis
4 ❑ Aug 1996 Cover: 2.25 **NM** value: **Cover or less**
A: Gino Dicicco **W:** Brett Lewis
5 ❑ Sep 1996 Cover: 2.25 **NM** value: **Cover or less**
A: Gino Dicicco **W:** Brett Lewis
6 ❑ Oct 1996 Cover: 2.25 **NM** value: **Cover or less**
A: Gino Dicicco **W:** Brett Lewis

MAN-BAT (1ST SERIES) — DC

In the early 70s, a new generation of creators restored Batman from the 1960s campy TV star to his original stature as Dark Knight of Gotham. For the 400th issue of Detective Comics, writer Frank Robbins and artists Neal Adams and Dick Giordano created a macabre menace known as the Man-Bat — a scientist transformed into a giant bat creature through an experiment gone awry. Not really a villain, Man-Bat was a tragic figure torn between savage animal instincts and remaining traces of humanity. His early conflicts with Batman are some of the highlights of Batman's 60-year history. Man-Bat also starred in this short-lived title in the 1970s and in backup stories in Batman Family. He has appeared sporadically in the DC universe to the present day.

1 ❑ Dec 1975 Cover: 0.25 **NM** value: **8.00**
• **CGC:** 14 graded, best 9.8
📖 Beware the Eyes of Baron Tyme **A:** Steve Ditko **W:** Gerry Conway
2 ❑ Feb 1976 Cover: 0.25 **NM** value: **5.00**
📖 Fugitive From Blind Justice **A:** Steve Ditko **W:** Gerry Conway

MAN-BAT (2ND SERIES) — DC

1 ❑ Dec 1984 Cover: 2.50 **NM** value: **Cover or less**
One-shot. 📖 Challenge of the Man-Bat; Man or Bat?; Marriage: Impossible **A:** Dick Giordano; Neal Adams **W:** Frank Robbins

MAN-BAT (MINI-SERIES) — DC

1 ❑ Feb 1996 Cover: 2.25 **NM** value: **2.50**
📖 Gotham Skies **A:** Flint Henry **W:** Chuck Dixon
2 ❑ Mar 1996 Cover: 2.25 **NM** value: **2.50**
📖 Dark of the Moon **A:** Flint Henry **W:** Chuck Dixon ★ Appearance of Killer Croc.
3 ❑ Apr 1996 Cover: 2.25 **NM** value: **2.50**
📖 The Deadly Sky final issue. **A:** Flint Henry **W:** Chuck Dixon

MAN CALLED A-X, THE — Malibu / Bravura

Never has a place been more appropriately named than the city of Bedlam. Here the police, the mayor, and virtually the entire populace are held tightly by the grip of corruption and unseen forces. Then the man called A-X appeared...and made things even worse.

The first to die were businessmen Andrew and Edward Taliss. A month later, an attempt was made on the life of Bedlam's "favorite son" Garrison Gage. This was followed later by more murders and the destruction of the city's power transmitters, leaving the entire city plunged into blackness. One after another, prominent figures fell before this seemingly unstoppable assassin. But who was the man called A-X? Not even he knew. His only identity came from a voice in his head which commanded him to kill the city's criminals. What's more, it seemed that his body could recover from virtually any injury — even, it seems, death itself.

0 ❑ Cover: 2.95 **NM** value: **Cover or less**
Circ: CapCity orders: **6,800**
📖 Bedlam! **A:** Shawn McManus **W:** Marv Wolfman
1 ❑ Nov 1994 Cover: 2.95 **NM** value: **Cover or less**
Circ: CapCity orders: **15,925**
A: Shawn McManus **W:** Marv Wolfman
1/A ❑ Nov 1994 Cover: 2.95 **NM** value: **Cover or less**
2 ❑ Dec 1994 Cover: 2.95 **NM** value: **Cover or less**
Circ: CapCity orders: **9,075**
A: Shawn McManus **W:** Marv Wolfman
3 ❑ Jan 1995 Cover: 2.95 **NM** value: **Cover or less**
Circ: CapCity orders: **7,300**
📖 Silicon Skies **A:** Shawn McManus **W:** Marv Wolfman
4 ❑ Feb 1995 Cover: 2.95 **NM** value: **Cover or less**
Circ: CapCity orders: **5,150**
A: Shawn McManus **W:** Marv Wolfman
5 ❑ Mar 1995 Cover: 2.95 **NM** value: **Cover or less**
Circ: CapCity orders: **4,650**
A: Shawn McManus **W:** Marv Wolfman

MAN CALLED A-X, THE (DC) — DC

1 ❑ Oct 1997 Cover: 2.50 **NM** value: **Cover or less**
📖 A-Ten • follows events in Malibu/Bravura series **A:** Shawn McManus **W:** Marv Wolfman
2 ❑ Nov 1997 Cover: 2.50 **NM** value: **Cover or less**
Circ: Diamd. preorders: **11,129**
📖 Massacre at Mercy General! **A:** Shawn McManus **W:** Marv Wolfman
3 ❑ Dec 1997 Cover: 2.50 **NM** value: **Cover or less**
Circ: Diamd. preorders: **9,527**
📖 Battle over Bedlam **A:** Shawn McManus **W:** Marv Wolfman
4 ❑ Jan 1998 Cover: 2.50 **NM** value: **Cover or less**
Circ: Diamd. preorders: **7,357**
A: Shawn McManus **W:** Marv Wolfman
5 ❑ Feb 1998 Cover: 2.50 **NM** value: **Cover or less**
Circ: Diamd. preorders: **6,169**
A: Shawn McManus **W:** Marv Wolfman
6 ❑ Mar 1998 Cover: 2.50 **NM** value: **Cover or less**
Circ: Diamd. preorders: **5,217**
📖 The Blight Before Christmas! **A:** Shawn McManus **W:** Marv Wolfman
7 ❑ Apr 1998 Cover: 2.50 **NM** value: **Cover or less**
Circ: Diamd. preorders: **4,419**
📖 New Year's Eve! **A:** Sergio Cariello **W:** Marv Wolfman
8 ❑ May 1998 Cover: 2.50 **NM** value: **Cover or less**
Circ: Diamd. preorders: **4,383**
final issue. **A:** Shawn McManus **W:** Marv Wolfman

MAN CALLED LOCO, A — Avalon

1 ❑ Cover: 2.50 **NM** value: **Cover or less**
A: P.A.M. **W:** Sergius O'Shaugnessy

MAN COMICS — Marvel

One of the early Atlas war comics, Man Comics specialized in tales of combat, courage, and daring in the face of danger. In its early issues, Man Comics was originally a crime and adventure series, but switched to war tales with #9.

Although the stories were not exceptional, Man Comics was lucky to feature early work by several of the medium's legendary artists. Included were #1 and #2's pages by George Tuska, various issues by Gene Colan (Tomb of Dracula), and Bernie Krigstein's unsettling style seen in #22, which became better known at E.C. on such titles as Shock SuspenStories.

1 ❑ Dec 1949 Cover: 0.10 **NM** value: **100.00**
2 ❑ Mar 1950 Cover: 0.10 **NM** value: **65.00**

Other grades: Multiply prices above by **1.5 for Mint • 2/3 for Very Fine • 1/3 for Fine • 1/5 for Very Good • 1/8 for Good**

3 ❑ Jun 1950 Cover: 0.10 **NM** value: **45.00**
4 ❑ Oct 1950 Cover: 0.10 **NM** value: **45.00**
5 ❑ Dec 1950 Cover: 0.10 **NM** value: **45.00**
6 ❑ Feb 1951 Cover: 0.10 **NM** value: **38.00**
7 ❑ Apr 1951 Cover: 0.10 **NM** value: **38.00**
8 ❑ Jun 1951 Cover: 0.10 **NM** value: **38.00**
9 ❑ Aug 1951 Cover: 0.10 **NM** value: **38.00**
10 ❑ Oct 1951 Cover: 0.10 **NM** value: **38.00**
11 ❑ Dec 1951 Cover: 0.10 **NM** value: **32.00**
12 ❑ Feb 1952 Cover: 0.10 **NM** value: **32.00**
13 ❑ Apr 1952 Cover: 0.10 **NM** value: **32.00**
14 ❑ May 1952 Cover: 0.10 **NM** value: **32.00**
15 ❑ Jun 1952 Cover: 0.10 **NM** value: **32.00**
16 ❑ Jul 1952 Cover: 0.10 **NM** value: **32.00**
17 ❑ Aug 1952 Cover: 0.10 **NM** value: **32.00**
18 ❑ Sep 1952 Cover: 0.10 **NM** value: **32.00**
19 ❑ Oct 1952 Cover: 0.10 **NM** value: **32.00**
20 ❑ Nov 1952 Cover: 0.10 **NM** value: **32.00**
• **CGC:** 1 graded, best 8.5
21 ❑ Dec 1952 Cover: 0.10 **NM** value: **28.00**
22 ❑ Jan 1953 Cover: 0.10 **NM** value: **28.00**
23 ❑ Feb 1953 Cover: 0.10 **NM** value: **28.00**
📖 Close-Up; Bonaparte at Bat!; The Marines from Mars(text story); Hit and Run; Fire at Will **A:** Gene Colan; Gil Evans
24 ❑ Mar 1953 Cover: 0.10 **NM** value: **28.00**
25 ❑ Apr 1953 Cover: 0.10 **NM** value: **28.00**
26 ❑ May 1953 Cover: 0.10 **NM** value: **28.00**
27 ❑ Jul 1953 Cover: 0.10 **NM** value: **28.00**
28 ❑ Sep 1953 Cover: 0.10 **NM** value: **28.00**

MANDRAKE — Pioneer

1 ❑ b&w Cover: 4.95 **NM** value: **Cover or less**

MANDRAKE THE MAGICIAN — Marvel

1 ❑ Apr 1995 Cover: 2.95 **NM** value: **Cover or less**
Circ: CapCity orders: **5,450**
cardstock cover. 📖 The Quest For The 13th Scroll **A:** Rob Ortaleza **W:** Mike W. Barr
2 ❑ May 1995 Cover: 2.95 **NM** value: **Cover or less**
Circ: CapCity orders: **3,900**
cardstock cover.

MANDRAKE THE MAGICIAN (KING) — King

Mandrake the Magician began as a Sunday newspaper strip in 1934, the creation of Lee Falk, who also brought The Phantom to life. Mandrake is a stage magician, complete with top hat and cape, who can control people's minds with hypnotic gestures. Together with his gigantic African servant Lothar (often seen wearing a fez and leopard-skin cummerbund), they tackle all kinds of criminals, spies, pirates, and other menaces. If this sounds cliched, it's not Mandrake's fault; he was the first crime-fighting magician in the comics, and all the imitations that followed were based on his huge popularity.

Comic books often reprinted complete Mandrake adventures after they had been serialized in Sunday newspaper strips. In the 1960s, however, King Comics published this series of new Mandrake adventures, credited to original writer Falk.

1 ❑ Sep 1966 Cover: 0.12 **NM** value: **30.00**
📖 Menace of the Jungle!; The Phantom: SOS Phantom; The Flying Phantom
2 ❑ Nov 1966 Cover: 0.12 **NM** value: **18.00**
3 ❑ Jan 1967 Cover: 0.12 **NM** value: **13.00**
4 ❑ Mar 1967 Cover: 0.12 **NM** value: **12.00**
5 ❑ May 1967 Cover: 0.12 **NM** value: **12.00**
• **CGC:** 5 graded, best 9.4
📖 Cape Cod Caper; The Fear Mongers; Brick Bradford • Flying saucer story
6 ❑ Jul 1967 Cover: 0.12 **NM** value: **9.00**
7 ❑ Aug 1967 Cover: 0.12 **NM** value: **9.00**
8 ❑ Sep 1967 Cover: 0.12 **NM** value: **16.00**
• **CGC:** 6 graded, best 9.2
A: Jeff Jones
9 ❑ Oct 1967 Cover: 0.12 **NM** value: **9.00**
10 ❑ Nov 1967 Cover: 0.12 **NM** value: **24.00**
A: Alex Raymond

MAN-EATING COW — NEC

1 ❑ Jul 1992 Cover: 2.75 **NM** value: **4.00**
2 ❑ Nov 1992 Cover: 2.75 **NM** value: **3.00**
3 ❑ Jan 1993 Cover: 2.75 **NM** value: **3.00**
4 ❑ Apr 1993 Cover: 2.75 **NM** value: **3.00**
• Scarcer
5 ❑ Jun 1993 Cover: 2.75 **NM** value: **3.00**
6 ❑ Aug 1993 Cover: 2.75 **NM** value: **Cover or less**
7 ❑ Nov 1993 Cover: 2.75 **NM** value: **Cover or less**
📖 A Spooky House on a Hill Near a Graveyard **A:** Alan Hopkins **W:** Clay Griffith
8 ❑ Jan 1994 Cover: 2.75 **NM** value: **Cover or less**
📖 Hunting Heather **A:** Alan Hopkins **W:** Clay Griffith
9 ❑ 1994 Cover: 2.75 **NM** value: **3.00**
★ Appearance of The Tick.
10 ❑ 1994 Cover: 2.75 **NM** value: **3.00**
★ Appearance of The Tick.
Bk 1❑ Cover: 9.00 **NM** value: **Cover or less**
• Collects Man-Eating Cow #1-4
Bk 2❑ Cover: 5.00 **NM** value: **Cover or less**
• Collects Man-Eating Cow #5-8

MAN-FROG — Mad Dog

1 ❑ b&w Cover: 2.00 **NM** value: **Cover or less**
2 ❑ b&w Cover: 2.00 **NM** value: **Cover or less**

MAN FROM ATLANTIS — Marvel

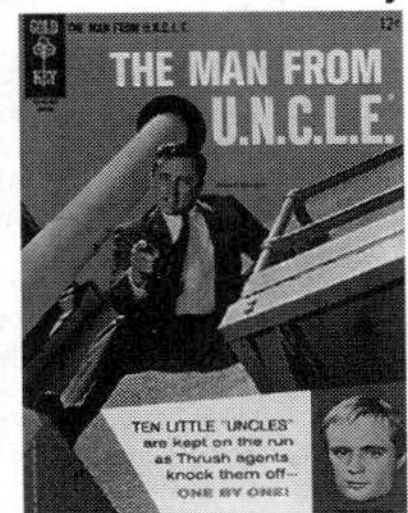

Fans of so-so sci-fi will recall that, long before Dallas, Patrick Duffy flopped around on the beach with flippers for NBC during the single season of The Man from Atlantis. Well, not flippers, actually, but he did have webbed fingers and the abilities to breathe underwater and communicate with sea animals.

Sensing these talents would come in handy, Foundation for Oceanic Research took in the Atlantean refugee, naming him Mark Harris and sending him out to battle mad scientists and aliens.

Marvel cranked out seven imaginative issues of its adaptation, but by 1978 both it and the TV series were sunk. — JJM

1 ❑ Feb 1978 Cover: 1.00 **NM** value: **3.00**
• **CGC:** 1 graded, best 9.2
• Giant-size. 📖 Birthright • TV series; giant **A:** Tom Sutton; Sonny Trinidad **W:** Bill Mantlo
2 ❑ Mar 1978 Cover: 0.35 **NM** value: **2.00**
📖 Into the Bermuda Triangle **A:** Frank Robbins **W:** Bill Mantlo
3 ❑ Apr 1978 Cover: 0.35 **NM** value: **2.00**
4 ❑ May 1978 Cover: 0.35 **NM** value: **2.00**
📖 The Killer Spores! **A:** Frank Robbins **W:** Bill Mantlo
5 ❑ Jun 1978 Cover: 0.35 **NM** value: **2.00**
6 ❑ Jul 1978 Cover: 0.35 **NM** value: **2.00**
7 ❑ Aug 1978 Cover: 0.35 **NM** value: **2.00**
📖 Man Dogs And Dinosaurs final issue. **A:** Frank Robbins **W:** Bill Mantlo

MAN FROM U.N.C.L.E., THE — Gold Key

The success of James Bond dramas, starting with 1962's Dr. No, unleashed a flood of stories of super-spies out to save the world from the clutches of villainous conspiracies. Preeminent among the Bond wannabes was the 1964-68 TV series The Man from U.N.C.L.E., starring Robert Vaughn as Napoleon Solo and David McCallum as Illya Kuryakin: two operatives of the United Network Command for Law and Enforcement, the secret agency that protects the world from the diabolical organization THRUSH.

Like the Bond series, Man from U.N.C.L.E. provided lots of exotic locales, mysterious women, car chases, explosions, and intrigue. The comic book from Gold Key faithfully reproduced the key ingredients of the series.

1 ❑ Feb 1965 Cover: 0.12 **NM** value: **60.00**
• **CGC:** 2 graded, best 9.6
• based on TV series
2 ❑ Oct 1965 Cover: 0.12 **NM** value: **35.00**
• **CGC:** 1 graded, best 9.6
3 ❑ Nov 1965 Cover: 0.12 **NM** value: **24.00**
4 ❑ Jan 1966 Cover: 0.12 **NM** value: **24.00**
5 ❑ Mar 1966 Cover: 0.12 **NM** value: **24.00**
• **CGC:** 1 graded, best 9.0
📖 The Ten Little Uncles Affair
6 ❑ May 1966 Cover: 0.12 **NM** value: **18.00**
7 ❑ Jul 1966 Cover: 0.12 **NM** value: **18.00**
8 ❑ Sep 1966 Cover: 0.12 **NM** value: **18.00**
📖 The Floating People Affair; Jet Dream: The Spider and the Spy • 10146-609
9 ❑ Nov 1966 Cover: 0.12 **NM** value: **18.00**
10 ❑ Jan 1967 Cover: 0.12 **NM** value: **18.00**
Circ: Statement: **411,235**
11 ❑ Mar 1967 Cover: 0.12 **NM** value: **16.00**
Circ: Statement: **411,235**
12 ❑ May 1967 Cover: 0.12 **NM** value: **16.00**
Circ: Statement: **411,235**
13 ❑ Jul 1967 Cover: 0.12 **NM** value: **16.00**
Circ: Statement: **411,235**
14 ❑ Sep 1967 Cover: 0.12 **NM** value: **16.00**
Circ: Statement: **411,235**
15 ❑ Nov 1967 Cover: 0.12 **NM** value: **16.00**
Circ: Statement: **411,235**
16 ❑ Jan 1968 Cover: 0.12 **NM** value: **16.00**
17 ❑ Mar 1968 Cover: 0.12 **NM** value: **16.00**
18 ❑ May 1968 Cover: 0.12 **NM** value: **16.00**
19 ❑ Jul 1968 Cover: 0.12 **NM** value: **16.00**
20 ❑ Oct 1968 Cover: 0.15 **NM** value: **16.00**
21 ❑ Jan 1969 Cover: 0.15 **NM** value: **10.00**
22 ❑ Apr 1969 Cover: 0.15 **NM** value: **10.00**
final issue.

MAN FROM U.N.C.L.E., THE (2ND SERIES) — Entertainment

1 ❑ Jan 1987, b&w Cover: 1.50 **NM** value: **2.00**
2 ❑ Feb 1987 Cover: 1.50 **NM** value: **2.00**
3 ❑ Apr 1987 Cover: 1.50 **NM** value: **2.00**
4 ❑ Aug 1987 Cover: 1.50 **NM** value: **2.00**

5 ❑ Dec 1987 Cover: 1.50 **NM** value: **2.00**
6 ❑ Feb 1988 Cover: 1.75 **NM** value: **2.00**
7 ❑ May 1988 Cover: 1.75 **NM** value: **2.00**
8 ❑ Jul 1988 Cover: 1.75 **NM** value: **2.00**
9 ❑ Aug 1988 Cover: 1.75 **NM** value: **2.00**
10 ❑ Sep 1988 Cover: 1.75 **NM** value: **2.00**
11 ❑ Sep 1988 Cover: 1.75 **NM** value: **2.00**

MAN FROM U.N.C.L.E., THE: THE BIRDS OF PREY AFFAIR — Millennium

1 ❑ Mar 1993 Cover: 2.95 **NM** value: **Cover or less**
📖 The Birds of Prey Affair, Part 1 **A:** Nick Choles **W:** Mark Ellis
2 ❑ Sep 1993 Cover: 2.95 **NM** value: **Cover or less**
📖 The Birds of Prey Affair, Part 2 **A:** Nick Choles **W:** Mark Ellis

MANGA HORROR — Avalon

1 ❑ b&w Cover: 2.95 **NM** value: **Cover or less**
📖 The Port in the Rain; A Girl in the Castle!; Murder!; Bloody Mermaid!; She Must Be Destroyed!; To Live in Peace!; Strange Valley • reprints Ghostly Tales **A:** Sanho Kim **W:** Sanho Kim; Joe Gill

MANGAPHILE — Radio Comix

1 ❑ Aug 1999, b&w Cover: 2.95 **NM** value: **Cover or less**
Circ: Diamd. preorders: **2,671**
2 ❑ Oct 1999, b&w Cover: 2.95 **NM** value: **Cover or less**
3 ❑ Dec 1999, b&w Cover: 2.95 **NM** value: **Cover or less**
4 ❑ Feb 2000, b&w Cover: 2.95 **NM** value: **Cover or less**
5 ❑ Apr 2000, b&w Cover: 2.95 **NM** value: **Cover or less**
6 ❑ Jun 2000, b&w Cover: 2.95 **NM** value: **Cover or less**
7 ❑ Aug 2000, b&w Cover: 2.95 **NM** value: **Cover or less**

MANGA SHI — Crusade

1 ❑ Aug 1996 Cover: 2.95 **NM** value: **Cover or less**
📖 Shiseiji **A:** Nelson Asencio **W:** Brian David-Marshall

MANGA SHI 2000 — Crusade

1 ❑ Feb 1997 Cover: 2.95 **NM** value: **Cover or less**
Circ: Diamd. preorders: **33,210**
• flip book with Shi: Heaven and Earth preview back-up; In the Killer Skies **A:** Jason Orfalas **W:** Bill Tucci; Dan Mishkin
2 ❑ Apr 1997 Cover: 2.95 **NM** value: **Cover or less**
Circ: Diamd. preorders: **26,016**
A: Jason Orfalas **W:** Bill Tucci; Dan Mishkin
3 ❑ Jun 1997 Cover: 2.95 **NM** value: **Cover or less**
Circ: Diamd. preorders: **26,203**
A: Jason Orfalas **W:** Bill Tucci; Dan Mishkin

MANGA SURPRISE ! — Morning & Afternoon, Kodansha Ltd.

1 ❑ Jul 1996, b&w **NM** value: **2.00**
No issue number.

MANGA VIZION — Viz

This series more resembles a magazine than a comic book. Beginning in 1995, this black-and-white series staked its claim as North America's only manga monthly. Along with entertaining existing fans, the series was dedicated to coax new readers into the world of Japanese comics. Although it was relatively expensive at cover price of $4.95, each issue had almost 100 pages.

Most manga in Japan is published in large anthologies. Viz Communications, Manga Vizion's publisher, saw to it that this tradition would be carried on in the United States. Manga Vizion printed one-shot stories alongside serial manga. Among the artists featured in Manga Vizion are Rumiko Takahashi (Maison Ikkoku, Ranma 1/2, and the Mermaid Saga) Ryoichi Ikegami (Mai, The Psychic Girl), and Kei Kusunoki (Shonen).

1 ❑ Mar 1995 Cover: 4.95 **NM** value: **Cover or less**
📖 The Tragedy of P; Samurai Crusader: The Kumomaru Chronicles; Ogre Slayer **A:** Ryoichi Ikegami; Rumiko Takahashi; Kei Kusunoki **W:** Rumiko Takahashi; Hiroi Oji; Kei Kusunoki
2 ❑ Apr 1995 Cover: 4.95 **NM** value: **Cover or less**
Circ: CapCity orders: **2,150**
3 ❑ May 1995 Cover: 4.95 **NM** value: **Cover or less**
Circ: CapCity orders: **2,150**
4 ❑ Jun 1995 Cover: 4.95 **NM** value: **Cover or less**
Circ: CapCity orders: **2,275**
5 ❑ Jul 1995 Cover: 4.95 **NM** value: **Cover or less**
Circ: CapCity orders: **2,450**
6 ❑ Aug 1995 Cover: 4.95 **NM** value: **Cover or less**
Circ: CapCity orders: **2,250**
📖 Rumic Theater: Exrta-Large Size Happiness; Samurai Crusader: The Kumomaru Chronicles; A, A' **A:** Rumiko Takahashi; Moto Hagio; Hiroi Oji **W:** Rumiko Takahashi; Moto Hagio; Hiroi Oji
7 ❑ Sep 1995 Cover: 4.95 **NM** value: **Cover or less**
Circ: CapCity orders: **2,100**
8 ❑ Oct 1995 Cover: 4.95 **NM** value: **Cover or less**
9 ❑ Nov 1995 Cover: 4.95 **NM** value: **Cover or less**
10 ❑ Dec 1995 Cover: 4.95 **NM** value: **Cover or less**

MANGA VIZION (VOL. 2) — Viz

1 ❑ Jan 1996 Cover: 4.95 **NM** value: **Cover or less**
2 ❑ Feb 1996 Cover: 4.95 **NM** value: **Cover or less**
3 ❑ Mar 1996 Cover: 4.95 **NM** value: **Cover or less**
4 ❑ Apr 1996 Cover: 4.95 **NM** value: **Cover or less**
5 ❑ May 1996 Cover: 4.95 **NM** value: **Cover or less**
6 ❑ Jun 1996 Cover: 4.95 **NM** value: **Cover or less**
7 ❑ Jul 1996 Cover: 4.95 **NM** value: **Cover or less**
8 ❑ Aug 1996 Cover: 4.95 **NM** value: **Cover or less**

CGC-graded: Multiply prices above by **33 for 9.9 M • 16 for 9.8 NM/M • 7 for 9.6 NM+ • 5 for 9.4 NM • 2.5 for 9.2 NM- • 1.5 for 9.0 VF/NM**

9 ❑ Sep 1996 Cover: 4.95 **NM** value: **Cover or less**
10 ❑ Oct 1996 Cover: 4.95 **NM** value: **Cover or less**
Circ: Diamd. preorders: **4,242**
11 ❑ Nov 1996 Cover: 4.95 **NM** value: **Cover or less**
Circ: Diamd. preorders: **3,917**
12 ❑ Dec 1996 Cover: 4.95 **NM** value: **Cover or less**
Circ: Diamd. preorders: **3,781**

MANGA VIZION (VOL. 3) — Viz

1 ❑ Jan 1997 Cover: 4.95 **NM** value: **Cover or less**
Circ: Diamd. preorders: **3,786**
2 ❑ Feb 1997 Cover: 4.95 **NM** value: **Cover or less**
Circ: Diamd. preorders: **3,707**
3 ❑ Mar 1997 Cover: 4.95 **NM** value: **Cover or less**
Circ: Diamd. preorders: **3,494**
4 ❑ Apr 1997 Cover: 4.95 **NM** value: **Cover or less**
Circ: Diamd. preorders: **3,648**
5 ❑ 1997 Cover: 4.95 **NM** value: **Cover or less**
6 ❑ 1997 Cover: 4.95 **NM** value: **Cover or less**
7 ❑ 1997 Cover: 4.95 **NM** value: **Cover or less**
8 ❑ 1997 Cover: 4.95 **NM** value: **Cover or less**

MANGA VIZION (VOL. 4) — Viz

1 ❑ Cover: 4.95 **NM** value: **Cover or less**
2 ❑ Cover: 4.95 **NM** value: **Cover or less**
3 ❑ Cover: 4.95 **NM** value: **Cover or less**
4 ❑ Cover: 4.95 **NM** value: **Cover or less**
5 ❑ Cover: 4.95 **NM** value: **Cover or less**
6 ❑ Cover: 4.95 **NM** value: **Cover or less**
7 ❑ Cover: 4.95 **NM** value: **Cover or less**
8 ❑ Cover: 4.95 **NM** value: **Cover or less**

MANGA ZEN — Zen Comics

1 ❑ b&w Cover: 2.50 **NM** value: **Cover or less**

MANGAZINE — Antarctic

Antarctic Press, one of the first and best purveyors of "American manga," established Mangazine to spread the word about all forms of anime, sentai, and manga-style comic books. Less a comic book than a magazine, it includes film news, reviews, and synopses of popular anime films, along with interviews with both American and Japanese manga creators.

This is a valiant effort to provide an insight into the esoteric world of anime, manga and Japanese animation. There is something for everyone with extra stories and art in a huge package of anime and manga-inspired adventures for U.S. readers.

1 ❑ ca. 1985, b&w Cover: 1.25 **NM** value: **4.00**
newsprint cover. • first Antarctic publication; company name misspelled throughout
1-2 ❑ Cover: 1.50 **NM** value: **2.00**
2 ❑ ca. 1985 Cover: 1.50 **NM** value: **3.50**
3 ❑ ca. 1986 Cover: 1.50 **NM** value: **1.75**
📖 Hedrax, Part 2; Cybersmash, Part 2; The Magician **A:** Ben Dunn; Steve Stamatiadis; George Brycki **W:** Ben Dunn; Ian Gould; James Mission
4 ❑ ca. 1986 Cover: 1.50 **NM** value: **3.50**
5 ❑ ca. 1986 Cover: 1.50 **NM** value: **3.50**

MANGAZINE (VOL. 2) — Antarctic

1 ❑ Jan 1989 Cover: 3.00 **NM** value: **3.50**
2 ❑ Cover: 3.00 **NM** value: **Cover or less**
3 ❑ Cover: 1.75 **NM** value: **2.00**
4 ❑ Cover: 1.95 **NM** value: **2.00**
5 ❑ Cover: 1.95 **NM** value: **2.00**
6 ❑ Cover: 1.95 **NM** value: **3.00**
7 ❑ Cover: 1.95 **NM** value: **3.00**
8 ❑ Cover: 1.95 **NM** value: **3.00**
9 ❑ Cover: 1.95 **NM** value: **3.00**
10 ❑ Cover: 2.25 **NM** value: **3.00**
11 ❑ Cover: 2.25 **NM** value: **3.00**
12 ❑ Cover: 2.25 **NM** value: **3.00**
13 ❑ Cover: 2.25 **NM** value: **3.00**
14 ❑ Cover: 2.95 **NM** value: **3.00**
15 ❑ Cover: 2.95 **NM** value: **3.00**
📖 A View From The Castle; Machine Dog/Part 2; The Caravan Plague/Part 1; Oh Gord! **A:** Christina Hanson; Eric Burza; Myke Maldonado; Pat MacDonald **W:** Christina Hanson; Eric Burza; Pat MacDonald; William Rasmussen
16 ❑ Cover: 2.95 **NM** value: **3.00**
17 ❑ Nov 1992 Cover: 2.95 **NM** value: **3.00**
18 ❑ Dec 1992 Cover: 2.95 **NM** value: **3.00**
• Urusei Yatsura special issue
19 ❑ Jan 1993 Cover: 2.95 **NM** value: **3.00**
20 ❑ Feb 1993 Cover: 2.95 **NM** value: **3.00**
21 ❑ Mar 1993 Cover: 2.95 **NM** value: **3.00**
22 ❑ Apr 1993 Cover: 2.95 **NM** value: **3.00**
23 ❑ May 1993 Cover: 2.95 **NM** value: **3.00**
24 ❑ Jun 1993 Cover: 2.95 **NM** value: **3.00**
25 ❑ Jul 1993 Cover: 3.95 **NM** value: **Cover or less**
26 ❑ Aug 1993 Cover: 2.95 **NM** value: **3.00**
27 ❑ Sep 1993 Cover: 2.95 **NM** value: **3.00**
28 ❑ Oct 1993 Cover: 2.95 **NM** value: **3.00**
29 ❑ Nov 1993 Cover: 2.95 **NM** value: **3.00**
30 ❑ Dec 1993 Cover: 2.95 **NM** value: **3.00**
31 ❑ Jan 1994 Cover: 2.95 **NM** value: **Cover or less**
32 ❑ Feb 1994 Cover: 2.95 **NM** value: **Cover or less**
• Super Cat Nuku-Nuku
33 ❑ May 1994 Cover: 2.95 **NM** value: **Cover or less**
34 ❑ Jul 1994 Cover: 2.95 **NM** value: **Cover or less**
35 ❑ Sep 1994 Cover: 2.95 **NM** value: **Cover or less**
36 ❑ Nov 1994 Cover: 2.95 **NM** value: **Cover or less**
37 ❑ Jan 1995 Cover: 3.95 **NM** value: **Cover or less**
38 ❑ Mar 1995 Cover: 2.95 **NM** value: **Cover or less**
39 ❑ May 1995 Cover: 2.95 **NM** value: **Cover or less**
40 ❑ Sep 1995 Cover: 2.95 **NM** value: **Cover or less**
41 ❑ Sep 1995 Cover: 2.95 **NM** value: **Cover or less**
• Samurai Troopers
42 ❑ Sep 1995 Cover: 2.95 **NM** value: **Cover or less**
43 ❑ Sep 1995 Cover: 2.95 **NM** value: **Cover or less**
• Samurai Troopers Episode Guide, Part 2
44 ❑ May 1996 Cover: 2.95 **NM** value: **Cover or less**

MANGAZINE (VOL. 3) — Antarctic

Bk 1 ❑ Jul 1999 Cover: 8.99 **NM** value: **Cover or less**
📖 Gold Digger; Warrior Nun Areala; Ninja High School; Shadow Gear; Powderburn Data Book **A:** Ben Dunn; Fred Perry; Locke; Ted Nomura **W:** Ben Dunn; Fred Perry; Locke; Ted Nomura; Brian Farrens

MANGLE TANGLE TALES — Innovation

1 ❑ Cover: 2.95 **NM** value: **Cover or less**
Circ: CapCity orders: **1,814**
📖 Harry Hart Farkule & The Crane of Thorns; Cliffed Palate; Weird Atomic Broccoli; My Son3; Harry Hart Farkule Goes to the Pall Mall; Walrussticities • Intro by Harlan Ellison **A:** George Broderick; J.T. Casey; R.T. Schneider **W:** Scott Rockwell

MANHUNT — Print Mint

1 ❑ Cover: 0.50 **NM** value: **4.00**
📖 I Loved a Vampire… and Lived; Yell Queen,; Hot Breakfast; Henry Henpeck: Henpeck Breaks Out; My Fat Came; Little League; Dr. Reuben Ruin my Sex Life; The Left-Overs: Boys will be Boys; Slum Goddess; The Blow Job; Can This Marriage be Destroyed? **W:** Ted Richards; Gary Hallgren; Aline Kominsky-Crumb; Bobby London; Lee Marrs; Lora Fountain; Michele Brand; Sharon Rudahl; Shary Flenniken; Shelby; Willy Murphy; Gail Madonia; Gary King; Nancy Griffith; Terry Richards
2 ❑ Cover: 0.75 **NM** value: **3.00**
📖 I Was a Fag Hag; M **A:** Ted Richards; Trina; Gary Hallgren; Justine Green; Lee Marrs; Leslie Cabago; Sharon Rudahl; Sheridan Anderson; T. Stanley; Willy Murphy **W:** Ted Richards; Gary Hallgren; Justine Green; Lee Marrs; Leslie Cabago; Sharon Rudahl; Sheridan Anderson; Willy Murphy; Lola Bennet

MANHUNTER (1ST SERIES) — DC

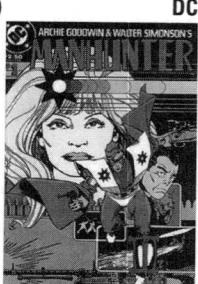

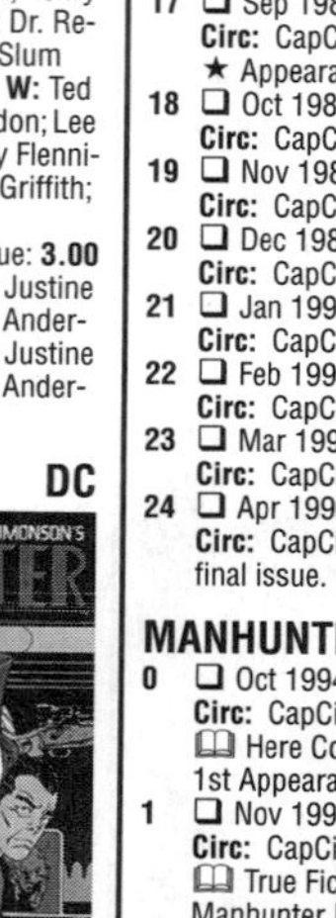

Manhunter was an obscure hero of the Golden Age. Disillusioned after the war, he is almost glad when a stampeding elephant tramples him to death while on safari.

But he doesn't stay dead. A group of 10 brilliant scientists called The Council store his body in suspended animation and eventually succeed in bringing him back from the dead. The Council, which claims to be out to save mankind from itself, has brought Manhunter back to head their "enforcement division." But when Manhunter discovers that this "enforcement" involves killing people to further the Council's evil ends, he turns against them.

This special gathers the Manhunter stories as they appeared in Detective Comics #447-443. An artistic triumph, these stories garnered six critical awards in their brief seven-issue run.

1 ❑ ca. 1984 Cover: 2.50 **NM** value: **Cover or less**
One-shot. • Double-size. • reprints serial from Detective Comics; Archie Goodwin **A:** Walt Simonson **W:** Archie Goodwin ★ Origin of Manhunter.

MANHUNTER (2ND SERIES) — DC

The second incarnation of Manhunter is Mark Shaw, introduced in First Issue Special #5. He begins his path to power as a member of the "Manhunter Cult." Eventually, he discovers that his fellow members are actually a group of alien androids, created as guardians of the galaxy by the Oans, a technologically advanced race. The Manhunters' evolution took a wrong turn, however, and they were corrupted. Eventually, they were "discarded" and the Oans replaced them with their second effort: the Green Lantern Corps.

By the time Shaw discovers the Manhunters' true nature, he no longer cares: He is too intoxicated with power. He is eventually reeled in by The Justice League International's Red Tornado and spends time in prison. Now reformed, he uses his Manhunter identity to be a bounty hunter of costumed criminals.

1 ❑ Jul 1988 Cover: 1.00 **NM** value: **1.50**
Circ: CapCity orders: **24,700**
📖 Visible Objects **A:** Sam Keith; Doug Rice **W:** Kim Yale; John Ostrander ★ Appearance of appearance Manhunter II (Mark Shaw).
2 ❑ Aug 1988 Cover: 1.00 **NM** value: **1.25**
Circ: CapCity orders: **17,250**
A: Sam Kieth
3 ❑ Sep 1988 Cover: 1.00 **NM** value: **1.25**
Circ: CapCity orders: **15,800**
A: Sam Kieth
4 ❑ Oct 1988 Cover: 1.00 **NM** value: **1.25**
Circ: CapCity orders: **16,100**
5 ❑ Nov 1988 Cover: 1.00 **NM** value: **1.25**
Circ: CapCity orders: **14,550**
6 ❑ Dec 1988 Cover: 1.00 **NM** value: **1.25**
Circ: CapCity orders: **14,100**
7 ❑ Dec 1988 Cover: 1.00 **NM** value: **1.25**
Circ: CapCity orders: **14,300**
★ Versus Count Vertigo.
8 ❑ Jan 1989 Cover: 1.00 **NM** value: **1.25**
Circ: CapCity orders: **14,700**
• Invasion! ★ Appearance of Flash.
9 ❑ Jan 1989 Cover: 1.00 **NM** value: **1.25**
Circ: CapCity orders: **13,650**
• Invasion! ★ Appearance of Flash.
10 ❑ Feb 1989 Cover: 1.00 **NM** value: **1.25**
Circ: CapCity orders: **11,750**
★ Appearance of Checkmate.
11 ❑ Mar 1989 Cover: 1.00 **NM** value: **1.25**
Circ: CapCity orders: **11,150**
12 ❑ Apr 1989 Cover: 1.00 **NM** value: **1.25**
Circ: CapCity orders: **10,900**
13 ❑ May 1989 Cover: 1.00 **NM** value: **1.25**
Circ: CapCity orders: **10,800**
14 ❑ Jun 1989 Cover: 1.00 **NM** value: **1.25**
Circ: CapCity orders: **11,450**
📖 Janus Directive
15 ❑ Jul 1989 Cover: 1.00 **NM** value: **1.25**
Circ: CapCity orders: **12,500**
16 ❑ Aug 1989 Cover: 1.00 **NM** value: **1.25**
Circ: CapCity orders: **9,950**
17 ❑ Sep 1989 Cover: 1.00 **NM** value: **1.25**
Circ: CapCity orders: **13,650**
★ Appearance of Batman.
18 ❑ Oct 1989 Cover: 1.00 **NM** value: **1.25**
Circ: CapCity orders: **10,150**
19 ❑ Nov 1989 Cover: 1.00 **NM** value: **1.25**
Circ: CapCity orders: **9,500**
20 ❑ Dec 1989 Cover: 1.00 **NM** value: **1.25**
Circ: CapCity orders: **9,700**
21 ❑ Jan 1990 Cover: 1.00 **NM** value: **1.25**
Circ: CapCity orders: **9,550**
22 ❑ Feb 1990 Cover: 1.00 **NM** value: **1.25**
Circ: CapCity orders: **9,300**
23 ❑ Mar 1990 Cover: 1.00 **NM** value: **1.25**
Circ: CapCity orders: **9,200**
24 ❑ Apr 1990 Cover: 1.00 **NM** value: **1.25**
Circ: CapCity orders: **8,700**
final issue.

MANHUNTER (3RD SERIES) — DC

0 ❑ Oct 1994 Cover: 1.95 **NM** value: **2.25**
Circ: CapCity orders: **20,100**
📖 Here Comes The Night **A:** Vince Giarrano **W:** Steven Grant ★ 1st Appearance of Manhunter III (Chase Lawler).
1 ❑ Nov 1994 Cover: 1.95 **NM** value: **2.25**
Circ: CapCity orders: **16,150**
📖 True Fiction **A:** Vince Giarrano **W:** Steven Grant ★ Origin of Manhunter III (Chase Lawler).
2 ❑ Dec 1994 Cover: 1.95 **NM** value: **2.00**
Circ: CapCity orders: **12,350**
★ Origin of Manhunter III (Chase Lawler).
3 ❑ Jan 1995 Cover: 1.95 **NM** value: **2.00**
Circ: CapCity orders: **11,250**
4 ❑ Feb 1995 Cover: 1.95 **NM** value: **2.00**
Circ: CapCity orders: **8,925**
5 ❑ Mar 1995 Cover: 1.95 **NM** value: **2.00**
Circ: CapCity orders: **7,150**
6 ❑ Apr 1995 Cover: 1.95 **NM** value: **2.00**
Circ: CapCity orders: **5,775**
7 ❑ Jun 1995 Cover: 2.25 **NM** value: **Cover or less**
Circ: CapCity orders: **4,700**
8 ❑ Jul 1995 Cover: 2.25 **NM** value: **Cover or less**
Circ: CapCity orders: **4,250**
9 ❑ Aug 1995 Cover: 2.25 **NM** value: **Cover or less**
Circ: CapCity orders: **4,050**
10 ❑ Sep 1995 Cover: 2.25 **NM** value: **Cover or less**
Circ: CapCity orders: **3,600**
11 ❑ Oct 1995 Cover: 2.25 **NM** value: **Cover or less**
Circ: CapCity orders: **2,875**
12 ❑ Nov 1995 Cover: 2.25 **NM** value: **Cover or less**
📖 Underworld Unleashed final issue. • Underworld Unleashed

MANHUNTER: THE SPECIAL EDITION — DC

1 ❑ ca. 1999 Cover: 9.95 **NM** value: **Cover or less**
No issue number. One-shot. • collects serial from Detective Comics plus new story **A:** Walt Simonson **W:** Archie Goodwin

MANHUNT (MAGAZINE ENTERPRISES) — Magazine Enterprises

1 ❑ Oct 1947 Cover: 0.10 **NM** value: **400.00**
• **CGC:** 1 graded, best 4.5
2 ❑ Nov 1947 Cover: 0.10 **NM** value: **300.00**
3 ❑ Dec 1947 Cover: 0.10 **NM** value: **250.00**
4 ❑ Jan 1948 Cover: 0.10 **NM** value: **250.00**
5 ❑ Feb 1948 Cover: 0.10 **NM** value: **250.00**
6 ❑ Mar 1948 Cover: 0.10 **NM** value: **250.00**
• **CGC:** 1 graded, best 6.0
7 ❑ Apr 1948 Cover: 0.10 **NM** value: **200.00**
• **CGC:** 1 graded, best 5.0
8 ❑ May 1948 Cover: 0.10 **NM** value: **200.00**
9 ❑ Jun 1948 Cover: 0.10 **NM** value: **200.00**
10 ❑ Jul 1948 Cover: 0.10 **NM** value: **200.00**
11 ❑ Aug 1948 Cover: 0.10 **NM** value: **200.00**

Creator Key
W = Writer • A = Artist • C = Cover Artist

Other grades: Multiply prices above by **1.5 for Mint • 2/3 for Very Fine • 1/3 for Fine • 1/5 for Very Good • 1/8 for Good**

MANIK — **Millennium**

1 ❑ Sep 1995 Cover: 2.95 **NM** value: **Cover or less**
foil cover. **A:** Ben Fogletto Jr. **W:** Mitchell Reichgut
2 ❑ 1995 Cover: 2.95 **NM** value: **Cover or less**
A: Ben Fogletto Jr. **W:** Mitchell Reichgut
3 ❑ 1996 Cover: 2.95 **NM** value: **Cover or less**
A: Ben Fogletto Jr. **W:** Mitchell Reichgut

MANIMAL — **Renegade**

1 ❑ Jan 1986, b&w Cover: 1.70 **NM** value: **Cover or less**

MAN IN BLACK — **Recollections**

1 ❑ b&w Cover: 2.00 **NM** value: **Cover or less**
2 ❑ Jul 1991, b&w Cover: 2.00 **NM** value: **Cover or less**

MAN IN BLACK (HARVEY) — **Harvey**

1 ❑ Sep 1957 Cover: 0.10 **NM** value: **100.00**
• **CGC:** 1 graded, best 8.5
2 ❑ Nov 1957 Cover: 0.10 **NM** value: **75.00**
3 ❑ Jan 1958 Cover: 0.10 **NM** value: **75.00**
4 ❑ Mar 1958 Cover: 0.10 **NM** value: **75.00**

MANKIND — **Chaos**

1 ❑ Sep 1999 Cover: 2.95 **NM** value: **Cover or less**
Circ: Diamd. preorders: **22,540**

MANN AND SUPERMAN — **DC**

1 ❑ ca. 2000 Cover: 5.95 **NM** value: **Cover or less**
Circ: Diamd. preorders: **17,718**
A: Michael T. Gilbert **W:** Michael T. Gilbert

MAN OF RUST — **Blackthorne**

1/A ❑ Nov 1986 Cover: 1.50 **NM** value: **Cover or less**
A: Rick Burchett **W:** Cliff MacGillivray
1/B ❑ Nov 1986 Cover: 1.50 **NM** value: **Cover or less**
A: Rick Burchett **W:** Cliff MacGillivray

MAN OF STEEL, THE (MINI-SERIES) — **DC**

This 1986 series began a major overhaul of the Superman legend, continued later in Superman (2nd series). Artist and writer John Byrne retold the origin of Superman, only this time, the Man of Steel was different. As a baby, Kal-El was sent off into space, escaping the destruction of the planet Krypton. Only this time, he was the only escapee. Kara Zor-El (Supergirl) and the assorted people in the bottle city of Kandor didn't make it. The stories featuring them were said to have happened in another reality — giving us, in effect, retroactive continuity.

And there's more: Superman never fully discovered his powers until he was nearly 18, thus the adventures of Superboy never took place on our Earth. And, even now that he's Superman, his powers are nowhere near the level they were in the stories of yore. This new "Superman of the 80s" came as a shock to many fans, but it ultimately laid the groundwork for a new level of characterization.

1 ❑ Oct 1986 Cover: 0.75 **NM** value: **3.00**
Circ: CapCity orders: **51,500** • **CGC:** 1 graded, best 9.0
• newsstand **A:** John Byrne **W:** John Byrne
1/SC❑ Oct 1986 Cover: 0.75 **NM** value: **3.00**
Circ: CapCity orders: **125,400** • **CGC:** 3 graded, best 9.4
• direct **A:** John Byrne; Dick Giordano **W:** John Byrne
1/SI❑ Oct 1986 Cover: 1.95 **NM** value: **3.00**
• silver edition. **A:** John Byrne **W:** John Byrne
2 ❑ Oct 1986 Cover: 0.75 **NM** value: **2.50**
A: John Byrne **W:** John Byrne
2/SI❑ Nov 1986 Cover: 1.95 **NM** value: **2.50**
Circ: CapCity orders: **95,300**
• silver edition. **A:** John Byrne **W:** John Byrne
3 ❑ Nov 1986 Cover: 0.75 **NM** value: **2.50**
A: John Byrne **W:** John Byrne
3/SI❑ Nov 1986 Cover: 1.95 **NM** value: **2.50**
Circ: CapCity orders: **85,000**
• silver edition. **A:** John Byrne **W:** John Byrne
4 ❑ Nov 1986 Cover: 0.75 **NM** value: **2.50**
A: John Byrne **W:** John Byrne
4/SI❑ Nov 1986 Cover: 1.95 **NM** value: **2.50**
Circ: CapCity orders: **85,000**
• silver edition. **A:** John Byrne **W:** John Byrne
5 ❑ Dec 1986 Cover: 0.75 **NM** value: **2.50**
A: John Byrne **W:** John Byrne
5/SI❑ Dec 1986 Cover: 1.95 **NM** value: **2.50**
Circ: CapCity orders: **81,450**
• silver edition. **A:** John Byrne **W:** John Byrne
6 ❑ Dec 1986 Cover: 0.75 **NM** value: **2.50**
A: John Byrne **W:** John Byrne
6/SI❑ Jan 1986 Cover: 1.95 **NM** value: **2.50**
Circ: CapCity orders: **80,950**
• silver edition. **A:** John Byrne **W:** John Byrne

MAN OF THE ATOM — **Acclaim / Valiant**

1 ❑ Jan 1997 Cover: 3.95 **NM** value: **Cover or less**
Circ: Diamd. preorders: **19,111**
no cover price. • preview of upcoming one-shot

MAN OF WAR (CENTAUR) — **Centaur**

1 ❑ Nov 1941 Cover: 0.10 **NM** value: **1000.00**
• **CGC:** 2 graded, best 9.0
2 ❑ Jan 1942 Cover: 0.10 **NM** value: **750.00**

MAN OF WAR (ECLIPSE) — **Eclipse**

1 ❑ Aug 1987 Cover: 1.75 **NM** value: **Cover or less**
Circ: CapCity orders: **5,000**
📖 All This And The Big Bang Two **A:** Rick Burchett **W:** Bruce Jones ★ Origin of Man of War.
2 ❑ Dec 1987 Cover: 1.75 **NM** value: **Cover or less**
Circ: CapCity orders: **3,775**
3 ❑ Feb 1988 Cover: 1.75 **NM** value: **Cover or less**
Circ: CapCity orders: **3,250**

MAN OF WAR (MALIBU) — **Malibu**

1 ❑ ca. 1993 Cover: 2.50 **NM** value: **Cover or less**
Circ: CapCity orders: **10,200**
📖 A Man At War **A:** Bryan Lee **W:** Dan Danko; Tom Mason
2 ❑ ca. 1993 Cover: 2.50 **NM** value: **Cover or less**
Circ: CapCity orders: **6,725**
3 ❑ ca. 1993 Cover: 2.50 **NM** value: **Cover or less**
Circ: CapCity orders: **5,500**
4 ❑ ca. 1993 Cover: 2.50 **NM** value: **Cover or less**
Circ: CapCity orders: **4,275**
5 ❑ ca. 1993 Cover: 2.25 **NM** value: **2.50**
Circ: CapCity orders: **4,000**
📖 Only the Good Die Young **A:** Glenn Brown **W:** Dan Danko; Tom Mason
6 ❑ ca. 1993 Cover: 2.25 **NM** value: **Cover or less**
Circ: CapCity orders: **6,075**
7 ❑ ca. 1994 Cover: 2.25 **NM** value: **Cover or less**
Circ: CapCity orders: **5,175**
8 ❑ ca. 1994 Cover: 2.25 **NM** value: **Cover or less**
Circ: CapCity orders: **4,200**

MAN O' MARS — **Fiction House**

1 ❑ ca. 1954 Cover: 0.10 **NM** value: **300.00**
• **CGC:** 1 graded, best 9.0

MANOSAURS — **Express / Entity**

1 ❑ Cover: 2.95 **NM** value: **Cover or less**
📖 The Armageddon Agenda Part 1 **A:** Ben Go; Kevin MacKenzie **W:** Steve Stern
2 ❑ Cover: 2.95 **NM** value: **Cover or less**
📖 The Armageddon Agenda Part 2 **A:** Ben Go; Kevin MacKenzie

MANTECH ROBOT WARRIORS — **Archie**

1 ❑ Sep 1984 Cover: 0.75 **NM** value: **1.00**
📖 Siege Of The Renegade Robots **A:** Dick Ayers **W:** Rich Margopoulos ★ Origin of The Mantechs. ★ 1st Appearance of The Mantechs.
2 ❑ Dec 1984 Cover: 0.75 **NM** value: **1.00**
3 ❑ Feb 1985 Cover: 0.75 **NM** value: **1.00**
4 ❑ May 1985 Cover: 0.75 **NM** value: **1.00**
📖 Invaders from Earth final issue. **A:** Dick Ayers **W:** Rich Margopoulos

MAN-THING (VOL. 1) — **Marvel**

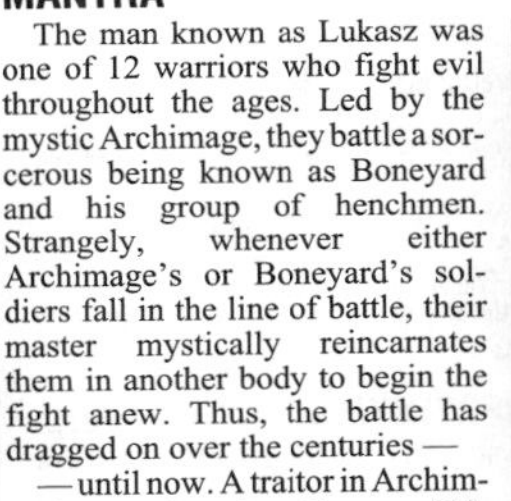

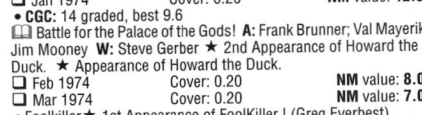

Chemist Ted Sallis has a terrible accident in his lab. The ghastly event turns his entire body into a mucky substance. He's man-like only in that he stands upright on two legs and has two arms. Where eyes once were, two red, unblinking orbs stare out from between three long strands of orange proboscises. His mind is shattered, and, lacking vocal cords, he couldn't speak, even if he remembered how. Nonetheless, this Man-Thing understands intent and shows compassion to other living beings, even though some of them seek to destroy him. Oh, but beware: Whatever knows fear burns at The Man-Thing's touch.

1 ❑ Jan 1974 Cover: 0.20 **NM** value: **12.00**
• **CGC:** 14 graded, best 9.6
📖 Battle for the Palace of the Gods! **A:** Frank Brunner; Val Mayerik; Jim Mooney **W:** Steve Gerber ★ 2nd Appearance of Howard the Duck. ★ Appearance of Howard the Duck.
2 ❑ Feb 1974 Cover: 0.20 **NM** value: **8.00**
3 ❑ Mar 1974 Cover: 0.20 **NM** value: **7.00**
• Foolkiller★ 1st Appearance of FoolKiller I (Greg Everbest).
4 ❑ Apr 1974 Cover: 0.20 **NM** value: **5.00**
• Foolkiller★ Origin of FoolKiller I (Greg Everbest). ★ Death of FoolKiller I (Greg Everbest).
5 ❑ May 1974 Cover: 0.25 **NM** value: **4.00**
6 ❑ Jun 1974 Cover: 0.25 **NM** value: **3.00**
A: Mike Ploog
7 ❑ Jul 1974 Cover: 0.25 **NM** value: **3.00**
A: Mike Ploog
8 ❑ Aug 1974 Cover: 0.25 **NM** value: **3.00**
A: Mike Ploog
9 ❑ Sep 1974 Cover: 0.25 **NM** value: **3.00**
A: Mike Ploog
10 ❑ Oct 1974 Cover: 0.25 **NM** value: **3.00**
A: Mike Ploog
11 ❑ Nov 1974 Cover: 0.25 **NM** value: **2.50**
A: Mike Ploog
12 ❑ Dec 1974 Cover: 0.25 **NM** value: **2.50**
13 ❑ Jan 1975 Cover: 0.25 **NM** value: **2.50**
14 ❑ Feb 1975 Cover: 0.25 **NM** value: **2.50**
15 ❑ Mar 1975 Cover: 0.25 **NM** value: **2.50**
16 ❑ Apr 1975 Cover: 0.25 **NM** value: **2.50**
17 ❑ May 1975 Cover: 0.25 **NM** value: **2.50**
18 ❑ Jun 1975 Cover: 0.25 **NM** value: **2.50**
19 ❑ Jul 1975 Cover: 0.25 **NM** value: **2.50**
★ 1st Appearance of Scavenger.
20 ❑ Aug 1975 Cover: 0.25 **NM** value: **2.50**
A: Jim Mooney
21 ❑ Sep 1975 Cover: 0.25 **NM** value: **2.50**
★ Origin of Scavenger.
22 ❑ Oct 1975 Cover: 0.25 **NM** value: **3.00**
A: Jim Mooney ★ Appearance of Howard the Duck.

MAN-THING (VOL. 2) — **Marvel**

1 ❑ Nov 1979 Cover: 0.40 **NM** value: **2.50**
• **CGC:** 5 graded, best 9.8
📖 Regeneration-And Rebirth **A:** Jim Mooney **W:** Michael Fleisher
2 ❑ Jan 1980 Cover: 0.40 **NM** value: **2.00**
📖 Nowhere To Go But Down! **A:** Val Mayerik **W:** Steve Gerber
3 ❑ Mar 1980 Cover: 0.40 **NM** value: **2.00**
4 ❑ May 1980 Cover: 0.40 **NM** value: **2.00**
5 ❑ Jul 1980 Cover: 0.40 **NM** value: **2.00**
6 ❑ Sep 1990 Cover: 0.50 **NM** value: **2.00**
7 ❑ Nov 1990 Cover: 0.50 **NM** value: **2.00**
8 ❑ Jan 1981 Cover: 0.50 **NM** value: **2.00**
9 ❑ Mar 1981 Cover: 0.50 **NM** value: **2.00**
10 ❑ May 1981 Cover: 0.50 **NM** value: **2.00**
11 ❑ Jul 1981 Cover: 0.50 **NM** value: **2.00**

MAN-THING (VOL. 3) — **Marvel**

1 ❑ Dec 1997 Cover: 2.99 **NM** value: **Cover or less**
Circ: Diamd. preorders: **37,624**
wraparound cover. • gatefold summary. 📖 Shame **A:** Liam Sharp **W:** J.M. DeMatteis
2 ❑ Jan 1998 Cover: 2.99 **NM** value: **Cover or less**
Circ: Diamd. preorders: **33,915**
• gatefold summary. 📖 The Journey **A:** Liam Sharp **W:** J.M. DeMatteis
3 ❑ Feb 1998 Cover: 2.99 **NM** value: **Cover or less**
Circ: Diamd. preorders: **22,960**
• gatefold summary.
4 ❑ Mar 1998 Cover: 2.99 **NM** value: **Cover or less**
Circ: Diamd. preorders: **19,412**
• gatefold summary. 📖 Silent Night **A:** Liam Sharp **W:** J.M. DeMatteis
5 ❑ Apr 1998 Cover: 2.99 **NM** value: **Cover or less**
Circ: Diamd. preorders: **16,695**
• gatefold summary.
6 ❑ May 1998 Cover: 2.99 **NM** value: **Cover or less**
Circ: Diamd. preorders: **15,117**
• gatefold summary.
7 ❑ Jun 1998 Cover: 2.99 **NM** value: **Cover or less**
Circ: Diamd. preorders: **13,793**
• gatefold summary. ★ Appearance of Sub-Mariner.
8 ❑ Jul 1998 Cover: 2.99 **NM** value: **Cover or less**
Circ: Diamd. preorders: **12,467**
• gatefold summary. ★ Appearance of Sub-Mariner.

MANTRA — **Malibu / Ultraverse**

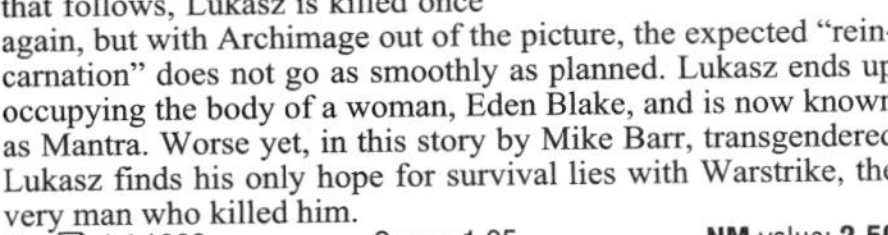

The man known as Lukasz was one of 12 warriors who fight evil throughout the ages. Led by the mystic Archimage, they battle a sorcerous being known as Boneyard and his group of henchmen. Strangely, whenever either Archimage's or Boneyard's soldiers fall in the line of battle, their master mystically reincarnates them in another body to begin the fight anew. Thus, the battle has dragged on over the centuries —

— until now. A traitor in Archimage's camp has given Boneyard his greatest secret, which has led to Archimage's defeat. In the battle that follows, Lukasz is killed once again, but with Archimage out of the picture, the expected "reincarnation" does not go as smoothly as planned. Lukasz ends up occupying the body of a woman, Eden Blake, and is now known as Mantra. Worse yet, in this story by Mike Barr, transgendered Lukasz finds his only hope for survival lies with Warstrike, the very man who killed him.

1 ❑ Jul 1993 Cover: 1.95 **NM** value: **2.50**
Circ: CapCity orders: **32,600**
• Ultraverse **W:** Mike W. Barr ★ Origin of Mantra I (Eden Blake). ★ 1st Appearance of Boneyard, Warstrike, Mantra I (Eden Blake).
1/Hol❑ Jul 1993 **NM** value: **5.00**
Hologram cover. **W:** Mike W. Barr ★ Origin of Mantra I (Eden Blake). ★ 1st Appearance of Boneyard, Warstrike, Mantra I (Eden Blake).
1/LE❑ Jul 1993 Cover: 1.95 **NM** value: **3.00**
• Ultra Limited edition. **W:** Mike W. Barr
2 ❑ Aug 1993 Cover: 1.95 **NM** value: **2.25**
Circ: CapCity orders: **18,900**
W: Mike W. Barr
3 ❑ Sep 1993 Cover: 1.95 **NM** value: **2.25**
Circ: CapCity orders: **20,825**
📖 Sister Act **A:** Henry Martinez **W:** Mike W. Barr ★ 1st Appearance of Kismet Deadly.
4 ❑ Oct 1993 Cover: 2.50 **NM** value: **Cover or less**
Circ: CapCity orders: **29,900**
📖 Rune, Part J • Rune **A:** Barry Windsor-Smith **W:** Mike W. Barr
5 ❑ Nov 1993 Cover: 1.95 **NM** value: **2.00**
Circ: CapCity orders: **22,800**
W: Mike W. Barr
6 ❑ Dec 1993 Cover: 1.95 **NM** value: **2.00**
Circ: CapCity orders: **22,050**
📖 Break-Thru • Break-Thru **W:** Mike W. Barr
7 ❑ Jan 1994 Cover: 1.95 **NM** value: **2.00**
Circ: CapCity orders: **19,325**
W: Mike W. Barr
8 ❑ Feb 1994 Cover: 1.95 **NM** value: **2.00**
Circ: CapCity orders: **16,825**
W: Mike W. Barr

CGC-graded: Multiply prices above by **33 for 9.9 M • 16 for 9.8 NM/M • 7 for 9.6 NM+ • 5 for 9.4 NM • 2.5 for 9.2 NM- • 1.5 for 9.0 VF/NM**

9 ❑ Mar 1994 Cover: 1.95 **NM** value: **2.00**
Circ: CapCity orders: **15,425**
W: Mike W. Barr

10 ❑ Apr 1994 Cover: 3.50 **NM** value: **Cover or less**
Circ: CapCity orders: **17,525**
• Flip-book with Ultraverse Premiere #2 **W:** Mike W. Barr

11 ❑ May 1994 Cover: 1.95 **NM** value: **Cover or less**
Circ: CapCity orders: **14,825**
W: Mike W. Barr

12 ❑ Jun 1994 Cover: 1.95 **NM** value: **Cover or less**
Circ: CapCity orders: **14,125**
📖 The Archimage Quest, Part 3 **A:** Terry Dodson; Bryan Hitch(cover) **W:** Mike W. Barr

13 ❑ Aug 1994 Cover: 1.95 **NM** value: **Cover or less**
Circ: CapCity orders: **12,200**
issue has two different covers. 📖 The Archimage Quest, Part 5 **A:** Bryan Hitch; Jason Armstrong **W:** Mike W. Barr ★ Death of Boneyard's Wives.

13/A❑ Cover: 1.95 **NM** value: **Cover or less**
variant cover. 📖 The Archimage Quest, Part 5 **A:** Bryan Hitch; Jason Armstrong **W:** Mike W. Barr ★ Death of Boneyard's Wives.

14 ❑ Sep 1994 Cover: 1.95 **NM** value: **Cover or less**
Circ: CapCity orders: **11,050**
📖 The Archimage Quest, Part 6 **A:** Mark Heike **W:** Mike W. Barr ★ 1st Appearance of Mantra II (Lauren). ★ Death of Archimage.

15 ❑ Oct 1994 Cover: 1.95 **NM** value: **Cover or less**
Circ: CapCity orders: **10,375**
📖 The Archimage Quest **A:** Mark Heike; Keith Conroy(cover) **W:** Mike W. Barr ★ Appearance of Prime. ★ Death of Notch.

16 ❑ Nov 1994 Cover: 1.95 **NM** value: **Cover or less**
Circ: CapCity orders: **9,525**
📖 Wedding Knight **A:** Jason Armstrong **W:** Mike W. Barr

17 ❑ Dec 1994 Cover: 2.50 **NM** value: **Cover or less**
Circ: CapCity orders: **8,775**
📖 Body Building **A:** Jason Armstrong **W:** Mike W. Barr ★ 1st Appearance of NecroMantra. ★ Versus Necro Mantra.

18 ❑ Feb 1995 Cover: 2.50 **NM** value: **Cover or less**
Circ: CapCity orders: **7,425**
📖 Should Auld Acquaintance…! **A:** Scott Lee; Jason Armstrong(cover) **W:** Mike W. Barr

19 ❑ Mar 1995 Cover: 2.50 **NM** value: **Cover or less**
Circ: CapCity orders: **7,300**
📖 Mother and Child Reunion **A:** Robb Phipps **W:** Mike W. Barr

20 ❑ Apr 1995 Cover: 2.50 **NM** value: **Cover or less**
Circ: CapCity orders: **7,000**
📖 Not Without Her My Daughter **A:** Aaron Lopresti; Brock Hor Jr. **W:** Mike W. Barr ★ 1st Appearance of Overlord. ★ Death of Overlord.

21 ❑ May 1995 Cover: 2.50 **NM** value: **Cover or less**
Circ: CapCity orders: **6,475**
📖 Little Miss Mantras **A:** Bryan Hitch(cover); Jim Amash **W:** Mike W. Barr

22 ❑ Jun 1995 Cover: 2.50 **NM** value: **Cover or less**
Circ: CapCity orders: **7,600**
W: Mike W. Barr

23 ❑ Jul 1995 Cover: 2.50 **NM** value: **Cover or less**
W: Mike W. Barr

24 ❑ Aug 1995 Cover: 2.50 **NM** value: **Cover or less**
final issue. **W:** Mike W. Barr

GS 1❑ca. 1994 Cover: 3.50 **NM** value: **Cover or less**
Circ: CapCity orders: **13,075**
• Giant-Size Mantra #1. 📖 The Archimage Quest, Part 4 **A:** Mark Heike; David Williams **W:** Mike W. Barr ★ 1st Appearance of Topaz, Opal Queen, Sapphire Queen.

MANTRA: SPEAR OF DESTINY — Malibu / Ultraverse

1 ❑ ca. 1995 Cover: 2.50 **NM** value: **Cover or less**
Circ: CapCity orders: **7,025**
📖 The Woman From Aladdin, Part 1 **A:** Paul Abrams; Joel Adams(cover) **W:** Mike W. Barr ★ 1st Appearance of The Herronvolk.

2 ❑ ca. 1995 Cover: 2.50 **NM** value: **Cover or less**
Circ: CapCity orders: **5,875**
📖 The Woman From Aladdin, Part 2 **A:** Paul Abrams; Bryan Hitch(cover) **W:** Mike W. Barr

MANTRA (VOL. 2) — Malibu / Ultraverse

0 ❑ Sep 1995 Cover: 1.50 **NM** value: **Cover or less**
• # Infinity **A:** Dave Roberts ★ Origin of New Mantra.

0/A ❑ Sep 1995 Cover: 1.50 **NM** value: **Cover or less**
alternate cover. ★ Origin of New Mantra.

1 ❑ Oct 1995 Cover: 1.50 **NM** value: **2.00**
📖 My So Called Magic Life **A:** Dave Roberts ★ Origin of Coven. ★ 1st Appearance of Coven.

2 ❑ Nov 1995 Cover: 1.50 **NM** value: **Cover or less**

3 ❑ Dec 1995 Cover: 1.50 **NM** value: **Cover or less**
★ Versus Necro Mantra.

4 ❑ Jan 1996 Cover: 1.50 **NM** value: **Cover or less**

5 ❑ Feb 1996 Cover: 1.50 **NM** value: **Cover or less**
★ Versus N-ME.

6 ❑ Mar 1996 Cover: 1.50 **NM** value: **Cover or less**
final issue. • Mantra gets new costume ★ Appearance of Rush.

7 ❑ Apr 1996 Cover: 1.50 **NM** value: **Cover or less**

MANTUS FILES — Eternity

1 ❑ b&w Cover: 2.50 **NM** value: **Cover or less**
2 ❑ b&w Cover: 2.50 **NM** value: **Cover or less**
3 ❑ b&w Cover: 2.50 **NM** value: **Cover or less**
4 ❑ b&w Cover: 2.50 **NM** value: **Cover or less**

MAN WHO WOULD BE KING, THE — Tome

1 ❑ Cover: 2.95 **NM** value: **Cover or less**
No issue number.

MANY DEATHS OF THE BATMAN — DC

Bk 1❑ Cover: 3.95 **NM** value: **Cover or less**
Circ: CapCity orders: **6,200**
A: Pat Broderick; Jim Aparo

MANY GHOSTS OF DR. GRAVES, THE — Charlton

The Many Ghosts of Doctor Graves was a long-lived and relatively successful horror and mystery title from Charlton. Featuring the tried-and-true format of the horror "host" — in this case, the dapper Doctor Graves — introducing short tales of (Code-approved) terror and suspense, The Many Ghosts of Doctor Graves presented eight-page chillers of monsters, vampires, werewolves, and other supernatural creatures.

Charlton was not a prestige market for comics creators and often presented opportunities for young talent to gain professional experience. Among those whose early work appears in the pages of Graves are Jim Aparo, Don Newton, Joe Staton, and John Byrne — plus the talented Steve Ditko, an alrleady-accomplished master of comic art.

1 ❑ May 1967 Cover: 0.12 **NM** value: **14.00**
2 ❑ Jul 1967 Cover: 0.12 **NM** value: **10.00**
3 ❑ Sep 1967 Cover: 0.12 **NM** value: **10.00**
4 ❑ Nov 1967 Cover: 0.12 **NM** value: **8.00**
5 ❑ Jan 1968 Cover: 0.12 **NM** value: **8.00**
6 ❑ May 1968 Cover: 0.12 **NM** value: **7.00**
7 ❑ Jul 1968 Cover: 0.12 **NM** value: **7.00**
8 ❑ Aug 1968 Cover: 0.12 **NM** value: **7.00**
9 ❑ Oct 1968 Cover: 0.12 **NM** value: **7.00**
10 ❑ Nov 1968 Cover: 0.12 **NM** value: **7.00**
11 ❑ Jan 1969 Cover: 0.12 **NM** value: **5.00**
12 ❑ Feb 1969 Cover: 0.12 **NM** value: **5.00**
13 ❑ Apr 1969 Cover: 0.12 **NM** value: **5.00**
14 ❑ Jun 1969 Cover: 0.12 **NM** value: **5.00**
15 ❑ Aug 1969 Cover: 0.12 **NM** value: **5.00**
• **CGC:** 1 graded, best 9.4
16 ❑ Oct 1969 Cover: 0.15 **NM** value: **5.00**
• **CGC:** 1 graded, best 9.4
17 ❑ Dec 1969 Cover: 0.15 **NM** value: **5.00**
18 ❑ Feb 1970 Cover: 0.15 **NM** value: **5.00**
19 ❑ Apr 1970 Cover: 0.15 **NM** value: **5.00**
20 ❑ Jun 1970 Cover: 0.15 **NM** value: **5.00**
21 ❑ Aug 1970 Cover: 0.15 **NM** value: **4.00**
22 ❑ Oct 1970 Cover: 0.15 **NM** value: **4.00**
23 ❑ Dec 1970 Cover: 0.15 **NM** value: **4.00**
24 ❑ Feb 1971 Cover: 0.15 **NM** value: **4.00**
25 ❑ Apr 1971 Cover: 0.15 **NM** value: **4.00**
26 ❑ Jun 1971 Cover: 0.15 **NM** value: **4.00**
• **CGC:** 1 graded, best 8.5
27 ❑ Aug 1971 Cover: 0.15 **NM** value: **4.00**
28 ❑ Oct 1971 Cover: 0.20 **NM** value: **4.00**
29 ❑ Dec 1971 Cover: 0.20 **NM** value: **4.00**
30 ❑ Feb 1972 Cover: 0.20 **NM** value: **4.00**
31 ❑ Apr 1972 Cover: 0.20 **NM** value: **4.00**
32 ❑ Jun 1972 Cover: 0.20 **NM** value: **4.00**
33 ❑ Aug 1972 Cover: 0.20 **NM** value: **4.00**
34 ❑ Oct 1972 Cover: 0.20 **NM** value: **4.00**
35 ❑ Dec 1972 Cover: 0.20 **NM** value: **4.00**
36 ❑ Jan 1973 Cover: 0.20 **NM** value: **4.00**
• **CGC:** 1 graded, best 9.4
37 ❑ Mar 1973 Cover: 0.20 **NM** value: **4.00**
38 ❑ May 1973 Cover: 0.20 **NM** value: **4.00**
39 ❑ Jun 1973 Cover: 0.20 **NM** value: **4.00**
40 ❑ Jul 1973 Cover: 0.20 **NM** value: **4.00**
41 ❑ Sep 1973 Cover: 0.20 **NM** value: **2.50**
42 ❑ Oct 1973 Cover: 0.20 **NM** value: **2.50**
43 ❑ Dec 1973 Cover: 0.20 **NM** value: **2.50**
44 ❑ Jan 1974 Cover: 0.20 **NM** value: **2.50**
45 ❑ May 1974 Cover: 0.25 **NM** value: **2.50**
46 ❑ Jul 1974 Cover: 0.25 **NM** value: **2.50**
47 ❑ Sep 1974 Cover: 0.25 **NM** value: **2.50**
48 ❑ Nov 1974 Cover: 0.25 **NM** value: **2.50**
49 ❑ Jan 1975 Cover: 0.25 **NM** value: **2.50**
📖 Bed Time Story!; The Hades Germ; Death in the Storm! **A:** Tom Sutton; M. Postell; Newton **W:** Joe Gill; Nicola Cutti; Joe Malloy
50 ❑ Mar 1975 Cover: 0.25 **NM** value: **2.50**
51 ❑ May 1975 Cover: 0.25 **NM** value: **2.50**
52 ❑ Jul 1975 Cover: 0.25 **NM** value: **2.50**
53 ❑ Oct 1975 Cover: 0.25 **NM** value: **2.50**
54 ❑ Dec 1975 Cover: 0.25 **NM** value: **2.50**
55 ❑ Feb 1976 Cover: 0.25 **NM** value: **2.50**
56 ❑ Apr 1976 Cover: 0.25 **NM** value: **2.50**
57 ❑ Jun 1976 Cover: 0.30 **NM** value: **2.50**
58 ❑ Aug 1976 Cover: 0.30 **NM** value: **2.50**
59 ❑ Oct 1976 Cover: 0.30 **NM** value: **2.50**
60 ❑ Dec 1976 Cover: 0.30 **NM** value: **2.50**
61 ❑ Sep 1977 Cover: 0.35 **NM** value: **2.50**
62 ❑ Oct 1977 Cover: 0.35 **NM** value: **2.50**
63 ❑ Feb 1978 Cover: 0.35 **NM** value: **2.50**
64 ❑ Mar 1978 Cover: 0.35 **NM** value: **2.50**
65 ❑ Apr 1978 Cover: 0.35 **NM** value: **2.50**
66 ❑ Jun 1981 Cover: 0.50 **NM** value: **2.50**
67 ❑ 1981 Cover: 0.50 **NM** value: **2.50**
68 ❑ Sep 1981 Cover: 0.50 **NM** value: **2.50**
69 ❑ Nov 1981 Cover: 0.50 **NM** value: **2.50**
70 ❑ Jan 1982 Cover: 0.60 **NM** value: **2.50**
71 ❑ Mar 1982 Cover: 0.60 **NM** value: **2.50**
72 ❑ May 1982 Cover: 0.60 **NM** value: **2.50**

📖 indicates **Story Title** or **Storyline** information.
★ indicates **Character Appearance** information.
W = Writer • A = Artist • C = Cover Artist

MANY LOVES OF DOBIE GILLIS — DC

"My name is Dobie Gillis, and I like girls. What am I saying? I love girls! … I just want one, one beautiful, gorgeous, soft, round, creamy girl for my very own. That's all I want! One lousy girl!" So said the teen (played by Dwayne Hickman) on the sitcom (1959-63) based on the novel of the same name by Max Shulman (1919-1988, author of such other books as Rally Round the Flag Boys! and the film The Tender Trap and the Broadway play How Now, Dow Jones). Gillis' buddy on the TV show, Maynard G. Krebs, was played by Bob Denver.

The comic-book series ran roughly as long as the TV series and featured art by Bob Oksner. DC completists who picked up the short-lived Windy & Willy in the late 1960s were amused to discover that that series consisted of revamps of Dobie and Maynard, complete with new bellbottom trousers. — Maggie

1 ❑ Jun 1960 Cover: 0.10 **NM** value: **90.00**
2 ❑ Aug 1960 Cover: 0.10 **NM** value: **65.00**
3 ❑ Oct 1960 Cover: 0.10 **NM** value: **50.00**
4 ❑ Dec 1960 Cover: 0.10 **NM** value: **45.00**
5 ❑ Feb 1961 Cover: 0.10 **NM** value: **45.00**
6 ❑ Apr 1961 Cover: 0.10 **NM** value: **35.00**
7 ❑ Jun 1961 Cover: 0.10 **NM** value: **35.00**
8 ❑ Aug 1961 Cover: 0.10 **NM** value: **35.00**
9 ❑ Oct 1961 Cover: 0.10 **NM** value: **35.00**
10 ❑ Dec 1961 Cover: 0.12 **NM** value: **35.00**
11 ❑ Feb 1962 Cover: 0.12 **NM** value: **26.00**
12 ❑ Apr 1962 Cover: 0.12 **NM** value: **26.00**
13 ❑ Jun 1962 Cover: 0.12 **NM** value: **26.00**
14 ❑ Aug 1962 Cover: 0.12 **NM** value: **26.00**
15 ❑ Oct 1962 Cover: 0.12 **NM** value: **26.00**
16 ❑ Dec 1962 Cover: 0.12 **NM** value: **26.00**
17 ❑ Feb 1963 Cover: 0.12 **NM** value: **26.00**
18 ❑ Apr 1963 Cover: 0.12 **NM** value: **26.00**
19 ❑ Jun 1963 Cover: 0.12 **NM** value: **26.00**
20 ❑ Aug 1963 Cover: 0.12 **NM** value: **26.00**
21 ❑ Oct 1963 Cover: 0.12 **NM** value: **24.00**
22 ❑ Dec 1963 Cover: 0.12 **NM** value: **24.00**
23 ❑ Feb 1964 Cover: 0.12 **NM** value: **24.00**
24 ❑ Apr 1964 Cover: 0.12 **NM** value: **24.00**
25 ❑ Sep 1964 Cover: 0.12 **NM** value: **24.00**
26 ❑ Oct 1964 Cover: 0.12 **NM** value: **24.00**

MANY REINCARNATIONS OF LAZARUS, THE (VOL. 2) — Fisher Media Publications

1 ❑ Dec 1998 Cover: 3.00 **NM** value: **Cover or less**
📖 The Risen and the Re-Risen: A Tale of a Restless Soul **A:** Zak Hennessey **W:** Zak Hennessey

Ash 1❑b&w **NM** value: **1.00**
No issue number. no cover price.

MARA — Aircel

1 ❑ May 1991 Cover: 2.50 **NM** value: **Cover or less**
2 ❑ Cover: 2.50 **NM** value: **Cover or less**
3 ❑ Cover: 2.50 **NM** value: **Cover or less**
4 ❑ Jan 1992 Cover: 2.95 **NM** value: **Cover or less**

MARA CELTIC SHAMANESS — Eros

1 ❑ Cover: 2.95 **NM** value: **Cover or less**
📖 Twilight **A:** Dennis Cramer **W:** Dennis Cramer

2 ❑ Cover: 2.95 **NM** value: **Cover or less**
A: Dennis Cramer **W:** Dennis Cramer

3 ❑ Cover: 2.95 **NM** value: **Cover or less**
A: Dennis Cramer **W:** Dennis Cramer

4 ❑ Cover: 2.95 **NM** value: **Cover or less**
A: Dennis Cramer **W:** Dennis Cramer

5 ❑ Cover: 2.95 **NM** value: **Cover or less**
A: Dennis Cramer **W:** Dennis Cramer

6 ❑ Cover: 2.95 **NM** value: **Cover or less**
A: Dennis Cramer **W:** Dennis Cramer

MARA CELTIC SHAMANESS BOOK 2 — Eros

1 ❑ Cover: 2.95 **NM** value: **Cover or less**
A: Dennis Cramer **W:** Dennis Cramer

2 ❑ Cover: 2.95 **NM** value: **Cover or less**
A: Dennis Cramer **W:** Dennis Cramer

3 ❑ Cover: 2.95 **NM** value: **Cover or less**
A: Dennis Cramer **W:** Dennis Cramer

4 ❑ Cover: 2.95 **NM** value: **Cover or less**
A: Dennis Cramer **W:** Dennis Cramer

5 ❑ May 1997 Cover: 2.95 **NM** value: **Cover or less**
A: Dennis Cramer **W:** Dennis Cramer

MARADA THE SHE-WOLF — Marvel

Bk 1❑ Cover: 5.95 **NM** value: **Cover or less**

MARA OF THE CELTS BOOK 1 — Rip Off

All issues are adults only.

SE 1❑ Sep 1993, b&w Cover: 2.95 **NM** value: **Cover or less**
Circ: CapCity orders: **2,330**
A: Dennis Cramer **W:** Dennis Cramer

MARA OF THE CELTS BOOK 2 — Eros

1 ❑ Cover: 2.95 **NM** value: **Cover or less**

MARAUDER — Silverline

1 ❑ Jan 1998 Cover: 2.95 **NM** value: **Cover or less**
📖 Seldom an Ill Wind **A:** Jaxon Renick **W:** Sidney Williams

Other grades: Multiply prices above by **1.5 for Mint • 2/3 for Very Fine • 1/3 for Fine • 1/5 for Very Good • 1/8 for Good**

2 ❑ 1998 Cover: 2.95 **NM** value: **Cover or less**
3 ❑ 1998 Cover: 2.95 **NM** value: **Cover or less**
4 ❑ 1998 Cover: 2.95 **NM** value: **Cover or less**

MARCH HARE, THE — Lodestone

1 ❑ b&w Cover: 1.50 **NM** value: **Cover or less**
Circ: CapCity orders: **5,775**
📖 Home Sweet Hitman **A:** Keith Giffen **W:** Robert Loren Fleming

MARCH OF COMICS (BOYS' AND GIRLS'...) K.K.

March of Comics was one of the longest-running comic titles, surviving from the mid-1940s all the way into the 80s. Its formula for success was to serve up nothing but favorites issue after issue like newspaper comic strip hits Tarzan, Henry, Krazy Kat and Popeye. Also, blue-chip animation stars like Bugs Bunny, Mickey Mouse, Porky Pig, Woody Woodpecker, Scooby Doo and the Pink Panther; and movie and TV tie-ins like The Three Stooges, Our Gang, Lassie, Gene Autry, and the Lone Ranger. In fact, the titles were those to which Western Printing had access over the years, whether it used Dell or Gold Key or other imprints.

Over the years, the publisher experimented on the giveaway, trying shorter page counts (16 instead of 32), uncoated cover stock (rough, not slick), oblong format, photo covers, full advertiser sponsorships, and more. A number of issues appear not to have been published; if they come to our attention we'll add them to the database.

1 ❑ ca. 1946 **NM** value: **300.00**
No issue number. • Goldilocks
2 ❑ ca. 1947 **NM** value: **235.00**
No issue number. • Santa Claus
3 ❑ ca. 1947 **NM** value: **285.00**
No issue number. 📖 Our Gang and the Old House Mystery • Our Gang **A:** Walt Kelly **W:** Walt Kelly
4 ❑ ca. 1947 **NM** value: **4850.00**
• **CGC:** 1 graded, best 3.5
No issue number. 📖 Maharajah Donald; The Peaceful Hills • Donald Duck **A:** Carl Barks
5 ❑ ca. 1947 • Andy Panda **NM** value: **170.00**
6 ❑ ca. 1947 • Fairy Tales **NM** value: **155.00**
7 ❑ ca. 1947 • Oswald the Rabbit **NM** value: **125.00**
8 ❑ ca. 1947 • Mickey Mouse **NM** value: **390.00**
9 ❑ ca. 1947 • Gloomy Bunny **NM** value: **75.00**
10 ❑ ca. 1947 • Santa Claus **NM** value: **75.00**
11 ❑ ca. 1947 • Santa Claus **NM** value: **60.00**
12 ❑ ca. 1947 • Santa's Toys **NM** value: **55.00**
13 ❑ ca. 1947 • Santa's Surprise **NM** value: **55.00**
14 ❑ ca. 1947 • Santa's Kitchen **NM** value: **55.00**
15 ❑ ca. 1947 • Hip-It-Ty Hop **NM** value: **45.00**
16 ❑ ca. 1947 • Woody Woodpecker **NM** value: **85.00**
17 ❑ ca. 1947 • Roy Rogers **NM** value: **160.00**
18 ❑ ca. 1947 • Fairy Tales **NM** value: **90.0**
19 ❑ ca. 1948 • Uncle Wiggily **NM** value: **80.00**
20 ❑ ca. 1948 **NM** value: **3100.00**
📖 Darkest Africa • Donald Duck **A:** Carl Barks
21 ❑ ca. 1948 • Tom and Jerry **NM** value: **80.00**
22 ❑ ca. 1948 • Andy Panda **NM** value: **85.00**
23 ❑ ca. 1948 • Raggedy Ann & Andy **NM** value: **100.00**
24 ❑ ca. 1948 • Felix the Cat **NM** value: **200.00**
25 ❑ ca. 1948 • Gene Autry **NM** value: **185.00**
26 ❑ ca. 1948 **NM** value: **200.00**
📖 Our Gang and the Skeleton River Mystery • Our Gang **A:** Walt Kelly **W:** Walt Kelly
27 ❑ ca. 1948 **NM** value: **240.00**
• **CGC:** 2 graded, best 8.5
• Mickey Mouse
28 ❑ ca. 1948 • Gene Autry **NM** value: **175.00**
29 ❑ ca. 1948 • Easter **NM** value: **40.00**
30 ❑ ca. 1948 • Santa Claus **NM** value: **40.00**
31 ❑ ca. 1948 • Santa Claus **NM** value: **40.00**
33 ❑ ca. 1948 • A Christmas Carol **NM** value: **40.00**
34 ❑ ca. 1949 • Woody Woodpecker **NM** value: **70.00**
35 ❑ ca. 1949 • Roy Rogers **NM** value: **160.00**
36 ❑ ca. 1949 • Felix the Cat **NM** value: **140.00**
37 ❑ ca. 1949 • Popeye **NM** value: **110.00**
38 ❑ ca. 1949 • Oswald the Rabbit **NM** value: **45.00**
39 ❑ ca. 1949 • Gene Autry **NM** value: **160.00**
40 ❑ ca. 1949 • Andy and Woody **NM** value: **60.00**
41 ❑ ca. 1949 **NM** value: **2700.00**
• **CGC:** 1 graded, best 4.0
📖 Race to the South Seas • Donald Duck in Darkest Africa **A:** Carl Barks
42 ❑ ca. 1949 • Porky Pig **NM** value: **60.00**
43 ❑ ca. 1949 • Henry **NM** value: **45.00**
44 ❑ ca. 1949 • Bug Bunny **NM** value: **70.00**
45 ❑ ca. 1949 • Mickey Mouse **NM** value: **200.00**
46 ❑ ca. 1949 • Tom and Jerry **NM** value: **65.00**
47 ❑ ca. 1949 • Roy Rogers **NM** value: **140.00**
48 ❑ ca. 1949 • Santa Claus **NM** value: **35.00**
49 ❑ ca. 1950 • Santa Claus **NM** value: **35.00**
50 ❑ ca. 1950 • Santa Claus **NM** value: **35.00**
51 ❑ ca. 1950 • Felix the Cat **NM** value: **115.00**
52 ❑ ca. 1950 • Popeye **NM** value: **90.00**
53 ❑ ca. 1950 • Oswald the Rabbit **NM** value: **40.00**
54 ❑ ca. 1950 **NM** value: **160.00**
📖 The Masked Marauders • Gene Autry
55 ❑ ca. 1950 • Andy and Woody **NM** value: **55.00**
56 ❑ ca. 1950 • Donald Duck **NM** value: **250.00**
57 ❑ ca. 1950 • Porky Pig **NM** value: **55.00**
58 ❑ ca. 1950 • Henry **NM** value: **40.00**
59 ❑ ca. 1950 • Bugs Bunny **NM** value: **70.00**
60 ❑ ca. 1950 • Mickey Mouse **NM** value: **185.00**
61 ❑ ca. 1950 • Tom and Jerry **NM** value: **55.00**
62 ❑ ca. 1950 • Roy Rogers **NM** value: **140.00**
63 ❑ ca. 1950 • Santa Claus **NM** value: **30.00**
64 ❑ ca. 1950 • Santa Claus **NM** value: **30.00**
65 ❑ ca. 1950 • Jingle Bells **NM** value: **30.00**
66 ❑ ca. 1950 • Popeye **NM** value: **80.00**
67 ❑ ca. 1950 • Oswald the Rabbit **NM** value: **30.00**
68 ❑ ca. 1951 • Roy Rogers **NM** value: **110.00**
69 ❑ ca. 1951 **NM** value: **180.00**
• **CGC:** 1 graded, best 9.6
• Donald Duck
70 ❑ ca. 1951 • Tom and Jerry **NM** value: **45.00**
71 ❑ ca. 1951 • Porky Pig **NM** value: **50.00**
72 ❑ ca. 1951 • Krazy Kat **NM** value: **60.00**
73 ❑ ca. 1951 • Roy Rogers **NM** value: **100.00**
74 ❑ ca. 1951 • Mickey Mouse **NM** value: **165.00**
75 ❑ ca. 1951 **NM** value: **45.00**
• **CGC:** 1 graded, best 8.5
• Bugs Bunny
76 ❑ ca. 1951 • Andy and Woody **NM** value: **50.00**
77 ❑ ca. 1951 • Roy Rogers **NM** value: **100.00**
78 ❑ ca. 1951 **NM** value: **85.00**
• **CGC:** 1 graded, best 9.0
• Gene Autry
79 ❑ • Andy Panda **NM** value: **30.00**
80 ❑ • Popeye **NM** value: **65.00**
81 ❑ ca. 1952 • Oswald the Rabbit **NM** value: **25.00**
82 ❑ ca. 1952 • Tarzan **NM** value: **90.00**
83 ❑ ca. 1952 • Bugs Bunny **NM** value: **40.00**
84 ❑ ca. 1952 • Henry **NM** value: **35.00**
85 ❑ ca. 1952 • Woody Woodpecker **NM** value: **30.00**
86 ❑ ca. 1952 • Roy Rogers **NM** value: **115.00**
87 ❑ ca. 1952 • Krazy Kat **NM** value: **55.00**
88 ❑ ca. 1952 • Tom and Jerry **NM** value: **45.00**
89 ❑ ca. 1952 • Porky Pig **NM** value: **30.00**
90 ❑ ca. 1952 • Gene Autry **NM** value: **115.00**
91 ❑ • Roy Rogers & Santa **NM** value: **105.00**
92 ❑ • Christmas with Santa **NM** value: **25.00**
93 ❑ ca. 1953 • Woody Woodpecker **NM** value: **20.00**
94 ❑ ca. 1953 • Indian Chief **NM** value: **55.00**
95 ❑ ca. 1953 • Oswald the Rabbit **NM** value: **25.00**
96 ❑ ca. 1953 • Popeye **NM** value: **50.00**
97 ❑ ca. 1953 • Bugs Bunny **NM** value: **35.00**
98 ❑ ca. 1953 • Tarzan **NM** value: **85.00**
99 ❑ ca. 1953 • Porky Pig **NM** value: **25.00**
100 ❑ ca. 1953 • Roy Rogers **NM** value: **80.00**
101 ❑ ca. 1953 • Henry **NM** value: **20.00**
102 ❑ ca. 1953 • Tom Corbett, Space Cadet **NM** value: **105.00**
103 ❑ ca. 1953 • Tom and Jerry **NM** value: **25.00**
104 ❑ ca. 1953 • Gene Autry **NM** value: **75.00**
105 ❑ • Roy Rogers **NM** value: **60.00**
106 ❑ • Santa's Helpers **NM** value: **25.00**
108 ❑ • Fun with Santa Claus **NM** value: **25.00**
109 ❑ • Woody Woodpecker **NM** value: **20.00**
110 ❑ • Indian Chief **NM** value: **40.00**
111 ❑ ca. 1954 • Oswald the Rabbit **NM** value: **25.00**
112 ❑ ca. 1954 • Henry **NM** value: **20.00**
113 ❑ ca. 1954 • Porky Pig **NM** value: **20.00**
114 ❑ ca. 1954 • Tarzan **NM** value: **80.00**
115 ❑ ca. 1954 • Bugs Bunny **NM** value: **25.00**
116 ❑ ca. 1954 • Roy Rogers **NM** value: **60.00**
117 ❑ ca. 1954 • Popeye **NM** value: **50.00**
118 ❑ ca. 1954 • Flash Gordon **NM** value: **75.00**
119 ❑ ca. 1954 • Tom and Jerry **NM** value: **20.00**
120 ❑ ca. 1954 • Gene Autry **NM** value: **65.00**
121 ❑ ca. 1954 • Roy Rogers **NM** value: **65.00**
122 ❑ • Santa's Surprise **NM** value: **23.00**
123 ❑ • Santa's Christmas Book **NM** value: **23.00**
124 ❑ • Woody Woodpecker **NM** value: **18.00**
125 ❑ • Tarzan **NM** value: **80.00**
126 ❑ • Oswald the Rabbit **NM** value: **20.00**
127 ❑ • Indian Chief **NM** value: **35.00**
128 ❑ • Tom and Jerry **NM** value: **20.00**
129 ❑ • Henry **NM** value: **20.00**
130 ❑ • Porky Pig **NM** value: **20.00**
131 ❑ 1955 • Roy Rogers **NM** value: **65.00**
132 ❑ 1955 • Bugs Bunny **NM** value: **20.00**
133 ❑ 1955 • Flash Gordon **NM** value: **70.00**
134 ❑ 1955 • Popeye **NM** value: **40.00**
135 ❑ 1955 • Gene Autry **NM** value: **60.00**
136 ❑ 1955 • Roy Rogers **NM** value: **60.00**
137 ❑ • Gifts From Santa **NM** value: **20.00**
138 ❑ • Fun at Christmas **NM** value: **20.00**
139 ❑ • Woody Woodpecker **NM** value: **18.00**
140 ❑ • Indian Chief **NM** value: **30.00**
141 ❑ • Oswald the Rabbit **NM** value: **18.00**
142 ❑ ca. 1956 • Flash Gordon **NM** value: **70.00**
143 ❑ ca. 1956 • Porky Pig **NM** value: **18.00**
144 ❑ ca. 1956 • Tarzan **NM** value: **80.00**
145 ❑ ca. 1956 • Tom and Jerry **NM** value: **18.00**
146 ❑ ca. 1956 • Roy Rogers **NM** value: **55.00**
147 ❑ ca. 1956 • Henry **NM** value: **18.00**
148 ❑ ca. 1956 • Popeye **NM** value: **40.00**
149 ❑ ca. 1956 • Bugs Bunny **NM** value: **18.00**
150 ❑ ca. 1956 • Gene Autry **NM** value: **60.00**
151 ❑ • Roy Rogers **NM** value: **60.00**
152 ❑ • The Night Before Christmas **NM** value: **20.00**
153 ❑ • Merry Christmas **NM** value: **20.00**
154 ❑ • Tom and Jerry **NM** value: **18.00**
155 ❑ • Tarzan **NM** value: **75.00**
156 ❑ • Oswald the Rabbit **NM** value: **18.00**
157 ❑ • Popeye **NM** value: **35.00**
158 ❑ • Woody Woodpecker **NM** value: **18.00**
159 ❑ • Indian Chief **NM** value: **30.00**
160 ❑ • Bugs Bunny **NM** value: **18.00**
161 ❑ ca. 1957 • Roy Rogers **NM** value: **50.00**
162 ❑ ca. 1957 • Henry **NM** value: **18.00**
163 ❑ ca. 1957 • Rin Tin Tin **NM** value: **50.00**
164 ❑ • Porky Pig **NM** value: **18.00**
165 ❑ • The Lone Ranger **NM** value: **60.00**
166 ❑ • Santa and His Reindeer **NM** value: **20.00**
167 ❑ • Roy Rogers & Santa **NM** value: **55.00**
168 ❑ • Santa Claus' Workshop **NM** value: **20.00**
169 ❑ ca. 1958 • Popeye **NM** value: **30.00**
170 ❑ ca. 1958 • Indian Chief **NM** value: **30.00**
171 ❑ ca. 1958 • Oswald the Rabbit **NM** value: **18.00**
172 ❑ ca. 1958 • Tarzan **NM** value: **70.00**
173 ❑ ca. 1958 • Tom and Jerry **NM** value: **18.00**
174 ❑ ca. 1958 • The Lone Ranger **NM** value: **55.00**
175 ❑ ca. 1958 • Porky Pig **NM** value: **18.00**
176 ❑ ca. 1958 • Roy Rogers **NM** value: **50.00**
177 ❑ • Woody Woodpecker **NM** value: **18.00**
178 ❑ • Henry **NM** value: **18.00**
179 ❑ • Bugs Bunny **NM** value: **18.00**
180 ❑ • Rin Tin Tin **NM** value: **45.00**
181 ❑ • Happy Holiday **NM** value: **15.00**
182 ❑ • Happi Tim **NM** value: **15.00**
183 ❑ • Welcome Santa **NM** value: **18.00**
184 ❑ ca. 1959 • Woody Woodpecker **NM** value: **15.00**
185 ❑ ca. 1959 • Tarzan **NM** value: **65.00**
186 ❑ ca. 1959 • Oswald the Rabbit **NM** value: **15.00**
187 ❑ ca. 1959 • Indian Chief **NM** value: **30.00**
188 ❑ ca. 1959 • Bugs Bunny **NM** value: **15.00**
189 ❑ ca. 1959 • Henry **NM** value: **15.00**
190 ❑ ca. 1959 • Tom and Jerry **NM** value: **15.00**
191 ❑ ca. 1959 • Roy Rogers **NM** value: **45.00**
192 ❑ ca. 1959 • Porky Pig **NM** value: **15.00**
193 ❑ • The Lone Ranger **NM** value: **55.00**
194 ❑ • Popeye **NM** value: **30.00**
195 ❑ • Rin Tin Tin **NM** value: **40.00**
197 ❑ • Santa is Coming **NM** value: **18.00**
198 ❑ • Santa's Helpers **NM** value: **18.00**
199 ❑ • Huckleberry Hound **NM** value: **40.00**
200 ❑ ca. 1960 • Fury **NM** value: **25.00**
201 ❑ ca. 1960 • Bugs Bunny **NM** value: **15.00**
202 ❑ ca. 1960 **NM** value: **50.00**
• **CGC:** 1 graded, best 8.5
• Space Explorer
203 ❑ ca. 1960 • Woody Woodpecker **NM** value: **15.00**
204 ❑ ca. 1960 • Tarzan **NM** value: **60.00**
205 ❑ ca. 1960 **NM** value: **35.00**
• **CGC:** 1 graded, best 9.0
• Mighty Mouse
206 ❑ • Roy Rogers **NM** value: **45.00**
207 ❑ • Tom and Jerry **NM** value: **15.00**
208 ❑ **NM** value: **55.00**
• **CGC:** 2 graded, best 9.4
• The Lone Ranger
209 ❑ • Porky Pig **NM** value: **15.00**
210 ❑ • Lassie **NM** value: **35.00**
212 ❑ • Christmas Eve **NM** value: **15.00**
213 ❑ • Here Comes Santa **NM** value: **15.00**
214 ❑ • Huckleberry Hound **NM** value: **30.00**
215 ❑ • Hi Yo Silver **NM** value: **40.00**
216 ❑ • Rocky and his Friends **NM** value: **50.00**
217 ❑ • Lassie **NM** value: **30.00**
218 ❑ • Porky Pig **NM** value: **10.00**
219 ❑ • Journey to the Sun **NM** value: **25.00**
220 ❑ • Bugs Bunny **NM** value: **10.00**
221 ❑ ca. 1961 • Roy and Dale **NM** value: **35.00**
222 ❑ ca. 1961 • Woody Woodpecker **NM** value: **10.00**
223 ❑ ca. 1961 • Tarzan **NM** value: **55.00**
224 ❑ ca. 1961 • Tom and Jerry **NM** value: **10.00**
225 ❑ ca. 1961 • The Lone Ranger **NM** value: **45.00**
226 ❑ ca. 1961 • Christmas Treasury **NM** value: **15.00**
228 ❑ • Letters to Santa **NM** value: **15.00**
229 ❑ • The Flintstones **NM** value: **50.00**
230 ❑ • Lassie **NM** value: **30.00**
231 ❑ ca. 1962 • Bugs Bunny **NM** value: **10.00**
232 ❑ ca. 1962 • Three Stooges **NM** value: **55.00**
233 ❑ ca. 1962 • Bullwinkle **NM** value: **50.00**
234 ❑ ca. 1962 • Smokey the Bear **NM** value: **25.00**
235 ❑ ca. 1962 • Huckleberry Hound **NM** value: **25.00**
236 ❑ ca. 1962 • Roy and Dale **NM** value: **30.00**
237 ❑ • Mighty Mouse **NM** value: **30.00**
238 ❑ • The Lone Ranger **NM** value: **40.00**
239 ❑ • Woody Woodpecker **NM** value: **10.00**
240 ❑ • Tarzan **NM** value: **50.00**
241 ❑ • Santa Claus Around the World **NM** value: **15.00**
242 ❑ • Santa's Toyland **NM** value: **15.00**
243 ❑ ca. 1963 **NM** value: **40.00**
• **CGC:** 1 graded, best 9.4
• The Flintstones
244 ❑ ca. 1963 **NM** value: **35.00**
• **CGC:** 1 graded, best 9.4
• Mr. Ed
245 ❑ • Bugs Bunny **NM** value: **10.00**
246 ❑ • Popeye **NM** value: **25.00**
247 ❑ • Mighty Mouse **NM** value: **25.00**
248 ❑ • Three Stooges **NM** value: **50.00**
249 ❑ • Woody Woodpecker **NM** value: **10.00**
250 ❑ • Roy and Dale **NM** value: **30.00**
251 ❑ • Little Lulu and Witch Hazel **NM** value: **85.00**
252 ❑ • Tarzan **NM** value: **45.00**
253 ❑ • Yogi Bear **NM** value: **40.00**
254 ❑ • Lassie **NM** value: **30.00**
255 ❑ • Santa's Christmas List **NM** value: **15.00**
256 ❑ • Christmas Party **NM** value: **15.00**
257 ❑ ca. 1964 • Mighty Mouse **NM** value: **25.00**

CGC-graded: Multiply prices above by **33 for 9.9 M • 16 for 9.8 NM/M • 7 for 9.6 NM+ • 5 for 9.4 NM • 2.5 for 9.2 NM- • 1.5 for 9.0 VF/NM**

No.	Date	Title	Value
258 ❑	ca. 1964	• The Sword in the Stone	NM value: 40.00
259 ❑	ca. 1964	• Bugs Bunny	NM value: 10.00
260 ❑	ca. 1964	• Mr. Ed	NM value: 20.00
261 ❑	ca. 1964	• Woody Woodpecker	NM value: 10.00
262 ❑	ca. 1964	• Tarzan	NM value: 40.00
263 ❑		• Donald Duck	NM value: 45.00
264 ❑		• Popeye	NM value: 20.00
265 ❑		• Yogi Bear	NM value: 30.00
266 ❑		• Lassie	NM value: 25.00
267 ❑		• Little Lulu	NM value: 70.00
268 ❑		• Three Stooges	NM value: 45.00
269 ❑		• A Jolly Christmas	NM value: 15.00
270 ❑		• Santa's Little Helpers	NM value: 15.00
271 ❑		• The Flintstones	NM value: 40.00
272 ❑		• Tarzan	NM value: 40.00
273 ❑	ca. 1965	• Bugs Bunny	NM value: 10.00
274 ❑	ca. 1965	• Popeye	NM value: 20.00
275 ❑	ca. 1965	• Little Lulu	NM value: 60.00
276 ❑	ca. 1965	• The Jetsons	NM value: 75.00
277 ❑	ca. 1965	• Daffy Duck	NM value: 10.00
278 ❑	ca. 1965	• Lassie	NM value: 20.00
279 ❑	ca. 1965	• Yogi Bear	NM value: 25.00
280 ❑	ca. 1965	• Three Stooges	NM value: 45.00
281 ❑	ca. 1965	• Tom and Jerry	NM value: 10.00
282 ❑	ca. 1965	• Mr. Ed	NM value: 20.00
283 ❑		• Santa's Visit	NM value: 15.00
284 ❑		• Christmas Parade	NM value: 15.00
285 ❑	Jan 1966	• **CGC:** 1 graded, best 5.5 • Astro Boy	NM value: 140.00
286 ❑		• Tarzan	NM value: 35.00
287 ❑		• Bugs Bunny	NM value: 10.00
288 ❑		• Daffy Duck	NM value: 10.00
289 ❑		• The Flintstones	NM value: 35.00
290 ❑		• Mr. Ed	NM value: 15.00
291 ❑		• Yogi Bear	NM value: 20.00
292 ❑		• Three Stooges	NM value: 40.00
293 ❑		• Little Lulu	NM value: 35.00
294 ❑		• Popeye	NM value: 20.00
295 ❑		• Tom and Jerry	NM value: 10.00
296 ❑		• Lassie	NM value: 15.00
297 ❑		• Christmas Bells	NM value: 15.00
298 ❑		• Santa's Sleigh	NM value: 15.00
299 ❑		• The Flintstones	NM value: 30.00
300 ❑		• Tarzan	NM value: 30.00
301 ❑		• Bugs Bunny	NM value: 10.00
302 ❑		• Laurel and Hardy	NM value: 25.00
303 ❑		• Daffy Duck	NM value: 10.00
304 ❑		• Three Stooges	NM value: 40.00
305 ❑		• Tom and Jerry	NM value: 10.00
306 ❑		• Daniel Boone	NM value: 30.00
307 ❑		• Little Lulu	NM value: 30.00
308 ❑		• Lassie	NM value: 15.00
309 ❑		• Yogi Bear	NM value: 20.00
310 ❑		• The Lone Ranger	NM value: 40.00
311 ❑		• Santa's Show	NM value: 15.00
312 ❑		• Christmas Album	NM value: 15.00
313 ❑		• Daffy Duck	NM value: 10.00
314 ❑		• Laurel and Hardy	NM value: 25.00
315 ❑		• Bugs Bunny	NM value: 10.00
316 ❑		• Three Stooges	NM value: 35.00
317 ❑		• The Flintstones	NM value: 30.00
318 ❑		• Tarzan	NM value: 30.00
319 ❑		• Yogi Bear	NM value: 20.00
320 ❑		• Space Family Robinson	NM value: 65.00
321 ❑		• Tom and Jerry	NM value: 10.00
322 ❑		• The Lone Ranger	NM value: 35.00
323 ❑		• Little Lulu	NM value: 20.00
324 ❑		• Lassie	NM value: 15.00
325 ❑		• Fun with Santa	NM value: 15.00
326 ❑		• Christmas Story	NM value: 15.00
327 ❑		• The Flintstones	NM value: 30.00
328 ❑		• Space Family Robinson	NM value: 60.00
329 ❑		• Bugs Bunny	NM value: 10.00
330 ❑		• The Jetsons	NM value: 50.00
331 ❑		• Daffy Duck	NM value: 8.00
332 ❑		• Tarzan	NM value: 25.00
333 ❑		• Tom and Jerry	NM value: 8.00
334 ❑		• Lassie	NM value: 15.00
335 ❑		• Little Lulu	NM value: 20.00
336 ❑		• Three Stooges	NM value: 30.00
337 ❑		• Yogi Bear	NM value: 20.00
338 ❑		• The Lone Ranger	NM value: 35.00
340 ❑		• Here Comes Santa	NM value: 15.00
341 ❑		• The Flintstones	NM value: 25.00
342 ❑		• Tarzan	NM value: 25.00
343 ❑		• Bugs Bunny	NM value: 8.00
344 ❑		• Yogi Bear	NM value: 15.00
345 ❑		• Tom and Jerry	NM value: 8.00
346 ❑		• Lassie	NM value: 15.00
347 ❑		• Daffy Duck	NM value: 8.00
348 ❑		• The Jetsons	NM value: 40.00
349 ❑		• Little Lulu	NM value: 20.00
350 ❑		• The Lone Ranger	NM value: 30.00
351 ❑		• Road Runner	NM value: 10.00
352 ❑		• Space Family Robinson	NM value: 50.00
353 ❑		• Road Runner	NM value: 8.00
354 ❑		• Tarzan	NM value: 20.00
355 ❑		• Little Lulu	NM value: 20.00
356 ❑		• Scooby Doo	NM value: 35.00
357 ❑		• Daffy Duck	NM value: 8.00
358 ❑		• Lassie	NM value: 15.00
359 ❑	ca. 1971	• Baby Snoots	NM value: 10.00
360 ❑		• H.R. Pufnstuff	NM value: 40.00
361 ❑		• Tom and Jerry	NM value: 8.00
362 ❑		• Smokey the Bear	NM value: 15.00
363 ❑		• Bugs Bunny and Yosemite Sam	NM value: 8.00
364 ❑		• The Banana Splits	NM value: 25.00
365 ❑		• Tom and Jerry	NM value: 6.00
366 ❑		• Tarzan	NM value: 20.00
367 ❑		• Bugs Bunny & Porky Pig	NM value: 8.00
368 ❑		• Scooby Doo	NM value: 25.00
369 ❑		• Little Lulu	NM value: 15.00
370 ❑		• Lassie	NM value: 15.00
371 ❑	ca. 1972	• Baby Snoots	NM value: 6.00
372 ❑		• Smokey the Bear	NM value: 15.00
373 ❑		• Three Stooges	NM value: 25.00
374 ❑		• Wacky Witch	NM value: 6.00
375 ❑		• The Road Runner & Daffy Duck	NM value: 6.00
376 ❑		• Pink Panther	NM value: 10.00
377 ❑		• Baby Snoots	NM value: 6.00
378 ❑		• Turok	NM value: 50.00
379 ❑		• Heckle & Jeckle	NM value: 6.00
380 ❑		• Bugs Bunny & Yosemite Sam	NM value: 6.00
381 ❑		• Lassie	NM value: 10.00
382 ❑		• Scooby Doo	NM value: 15.00
383 ❑		• Smokey the Bear	NM value: 10.00
384 ❑		• Pink Panther	NM value: 6.00
385 ❑		• Little Lulu	NM value: 15.00
386 ❑		• Wacky Witch	NM value: 6.00
387 ❑	ca. 1973	• Road Runner & Daffy Duck	NM value: 6.00
388 ❑	ca. 1973	• Tom and Jerry	NM value: 6.00
389 ❑		• Little Lulu	NM value: 15.00
390 ❑		• Pink Panther	NM value: 6.00
391 ❑		• Scooby Doo	NM value: 15.00
392 ❑		• Bugs Bunny & Yosemite Sam	NM value: 5.00
393 ❑		• Heckle & Jeckle	NM value: 5.00
394 ❑		• Lassie	NM value: 10.00
395 ❑		• Woodsy Owl	NM value: 8.00
396 ❑	ca. 1974	• Baby Snoots	NM value: 5.00
397 ❑		• Road Runner & Daffy Duck	NM value: 5.00
398 ❑		• Wacky Witch	NM value: 5.00
399 ❑		• Turok	NM value: 40.00
400 ❑		• Tom and Jerry	NM value: 5.00
401 ❑		• Baby Snoots	NM value: 4.00
402 ❑		• Daffy Duck	NM value: 4.00
403 ❑		• Bugs Bunny	NM value: 4.00
404 ❑		• Space Family Robinson	NM value: 35.00
405 ❑		• Cracky	NM value: 5.00
406 ❑		• Little Lulu	NM value: 10.00
407 ❑		• Smokey the Bear	NM value: 8.00
408 ❑		• Turok	NM value: 30.00
409 ❑		• Pink Panther	NM value: 4.00
410 ❑		• Wacky Witch	NM value: 4.00
411 ❑		• Lassie	NM value: 10.00
412 ❑		• Terrytoons	NM value: 4.00
413 ❑		• Daffy Duck	NM value: 3.50
414 ❑		• Space Family Robinson	NM value: 30.00
415 ❑		• Bugs Bunny	NM value: 3.50
416 ❑		• Road Runner	NM value: 3.50
417 ❑		• Little Lulu	NM value: 10.00
418 ❑		• Pink Panther	NM value: 3.50
419 ❑	ca. 1973	• Baby Snoots	NM value: 3.50
420 ❑	ca. 1976	• Woody Woodpecker	NM value: 3.50
421 ❑	ca. 1976	• Tweety & Sylvester	NM value: 3.50
422 ❑		• Wacky Witch	NM value: 3.50
423 ❑		• Little Monsters	NM value: 3.50
424 ❑		• Cracky	NM value: 3.50
425 ❑		• Daffy Duck	NM value: 3.50
426 ❑		• Underdog	NM value: 15.00
427 ❑	ca. 1977	• Little Lulu	NM value: 6.00
428 ❑	ca. 1977	• Bugs Bunny	NM value: 3.50
429 ❑	ca. 1977	• Pink Panther	NM value: 3.50
430 ❑	ca. 1977	• Road Runner	NM value: 3.50
431 ❑	ca. 1977	• Baby Snoots	NM value: 3.50
432 ❑	ca. 1977	• Lassie	NM value: 4.00
433 ❑	ca. 1977	• Tweety & Sylvester	NM value: 3.50
434 ❑	ca. 1977	• Wacky Witch	NM value: 3.50
435 ❑	ca. 1977	• Terrytoons	NM value: 3.50
436 ❑		• Cracky	NM value: 3.50
437 ❑	ca. 1978	• Daffy Duck	NM value: 3.50
438 ❑	ca. 1978	• Underdog	NM value: 12.00
439 ❑	ca. 1978	• Little Lulu	NM value: 5.00
440 ❑	ca. 1978	• Bugs Bunny	NM value: 3.50
441 ❑	ca. 1978	• Pink Panther	NM value: 3.50
442 ❑	ca. 1978	• Road Runner	NM value: 3.50
443 ❑	ca. 1978	• Baby Snoots	NM value: 3.50
444 ❑	ca. 1978	• Tom and Jerry	NM value: 3.50
445 ❑	ca. 1978	• Tweety & Sylvester	NM value: 3.50
446 ❑		• Wacky Witch	NM value: 3.50
447 ❑		• Mighty Mouse	NM value: 5.00
448 ❑		• Cracky	NM value: 3.50
449 ❑		• Pink Panther	NM value: 3.50
450 ❑		• Baby Snoots	NM value: 3.50
451 ❑		• Tom and Jerry	NM value: 3.50
452 ❑		• Bugs Bunny	NM value: 3.50
453 ❑		• Popeye	NM value: 3.50
454 ❑		• Woody Woodpecker	NM value: 3.50
455 ❑		• Road Runner	NM value: 3.50
456 ❑	ca. 1979	• Little Lulu	NM value: 4.00
457 ❑		• Tweety & Sylvester	NM value: 3.00
458 ❑		• Wacky Witch	NM value: 3.00
459 ❑		• Mighty Mouse	NM value: 4.00
460 ❑		• Daffy Duck	NM value: 3.00
461 ❑		• Pink Panther	NM value: 3.50
462 ❑		• Baby Snoots	NM value: 3.50
463 ❑		• Tom and Jerry	NM value: 3.50
464 ❑		• Bugs Bunny	NM value: 3.50
465 ❑		• Popeye	NM value: 3.50
466 ❑		• Woody Woodpecker	NM value: 3.50
467 ❑		• Underdog	NM value: 8.00
468 ❑		• Little Lulu	NM value: 3.50
469 ❑		• Tweety & Sylvester	NM value: 3.50
470 ❑		• Wacky Witch	NM value: 3.50
471 ❑		• Mighty Mouse	NM value: 3.50
472 ❑		• Heckle & Jeckle	NM value: 3.50
473 ❑		• Pink Panther	NM value: 3.50
474 ❑		• Baby Snoots	NM value: 3.50
475 ❑		• Little Lulu	NM value: 3.50
476 ❑		• Bugs Bunny	NM value: 3.50
477 ❑		• Popeye	NM value: 3.50
478 ❑		• Woody Woodpecker	NM value: 3.50
479 ❑		• Underdog	NM value: 6.00
480 ❑		• Tom and Jerry	NM value: 3.50
481 ❑		• Tweety & Sylvester	NM value: 3.50
482 ❑		• Wacky Witch	NM value: 3.50
483 ❑		• Mighty Mouse	NM value: 3.50
484 ❑		• Heckle & Jeckle	NM value: 3.50
485 ❑		• Baby Snoots	NM value: 3.50
486 ❑		• Pink Panther	NM value: 3.50
487 ❑	ca. 1982	• Bugs Bunny	NM value: 3.50
488 ❑		final issue. • Little Lulu	NM **value: 3.50**

MARCH OF CRIME — Fox

No.	Date	Cover	Value
1	❑ Jul 1950	Cover: 0.10	NM value: 300.00
2	❑ Sep 1950	Cover: 0.10	NM value: 275.00
3	❑ Sep 1951	Cover: 0.10	NM value: 125.00

MARCO POLO — Charlton

No.	Date	Cover	Value
1	❑ ca. 1962	Cover: 0.12	NM value: 100.00

MARC SPECTOR: MOON KNIGHT — Marvel

Marc Spector is a cold-hearted mercenary, willing to fight for whatever army pays the most money. All that changes, when he rebels at his commander's wholesale slaughter of a Egyptian village's townsfolk. His commander, a madman named Bushman, knocks Spector unconscious and orders that Marc be dropped in the middle of the desert. Left to die in the blazing heat, Marc crawls across the sand for miles, eventually happening upon an ancient temple of the moon god Khonshu. There, under a statue of Khonshu, "Marc Spector" dies. What emerges later from the temple is a new man — a Marc Spector who will take on the garb and weapons of Khonshu and use them to fight evil. Marc Spector has become Moon Knight.

In this, the third Moon Knight series, Marc Spector's war rages on.

1 ❑ Jun 1989 — Cover: 1.50 — NM value: **2.50**
Circ: CapCity orders: **31,800** • **CGC:** 1 graded, best 9.8
📖 New Moon **A:** Sal Velluto **W:** Chuck Dixon

2 ❑ Jul 1989 — Cover: 1.50 — NM value: **2.00**
Circ: CapCity orders: **24,700**
A: Sal Velluto **W:** Chuck Dixon

3 ❑ Mar 1989 — Cover: 1.50 — NM value: **2.00**
Circ: CapCity orders: **24,100**
📖 Butcher's Moon **A:** Sal Velluto **W:** Chuck Dixon

4 ❑ Sep 1989 — Cover: 1.50 — NM value: **2.00**
Circ: CapCity orders: **25,200**

5 ❑ Oct 1989 — Cover: 1.50 — NM value: **2.00**
Circ: CapCity orders: **25,100**

6 ❑ Nov 1989 — Cover: 1.50 — NM value: **2.00**
Circ: CapCity orders: **24,900**
• Brother Voodoo

7 ❑ Nov 1989 — Cover: 1.50 — NM value: **2.00**
Circ: CapCity orders: **25,100**
• Brother Voodoo

8 ❑ Dec 1989 — Cover: 1.50 — NM value: **3.00**
Circ: CapCity orders: **27,900**
📖 Acts of Vengeance • Acts of Vengeance★ Appearance of Punisher.

9 ❑ Dec 1989 — Cover: 1.50 — NM value: **3.00**
Circ: CapCity orders: **28,800**
📖 Acts of Vengeance • Acts of Vengeance★ Appearance of Punisher.

10 ❑ Jan 1990 — Cover: 1.50 — NM value: **2.00**
Circ: Statement: **96,426** CapCity orders: **23,400**
📖 Acts of Vengeance • Acts of Vengeance★ 1st Appearance of Ringer II.

11 ❑ Feb 1990 — Cover: 1.50 — NM value: **2.00**
Circ: Statement: **96,426** CapCity orders: **21,300**

12 ❑ Mar 1990 — Cover: 1.50 — NM value: **2.00**
Circ: Statement: **96,426** CapCity orders: **20,600**

13 ❑ Apr 1990 — Cover: 1.50 — NM value: **2.00**
Circ: Statement: **96,426** CapCity orders: **20,400**

14 ❑ May 1990 — Cover: 1.50 — NM value: **2.00**
Circ: Statement: **96,426** CapCity orders: **19,000**

15 ❑ Jun 1990 — Cover: 1.50 — NM value: **2.00**
Circ: Statement: **96,426** CapCity orders: **18,600**
📖 Trial

16 ❑ Jul 1990 — Cover: 1.50 — NM value: **2.00**
Circ: Statement: **96,426** CapCity orders: **17,800**
📖 Trial

17 ❑ Aug 1990 — Cover: 1.50 — NM value: **2.00**
Circ: Statement: **96,426** CapCity orders: **16,600**
📖 Trial

18 ❑ Sep 1990 — Cover: 1.50 — NM value: **2.00**
Circ: Statement: **96,426** CapCity orders: **17,000**
📖 Trial

19 ❑ Oct 1990 — Cover: 1.50 — NM value: **3.00**
Circ: Statement: **96,426** CapCity orders: **36,400**
★ Appearance of Punisher, Spider-Man.

Other grades: Multiply prices above by **1.5 for Mint • 2/3 for Very Fine • 1/3 for Fine • 1/5 for Very Good • 1/8 for Good**

20 ❑ Nov 1990 Cover: 1.50 **NM** value: **3.00**
Circ: Statement: **96,426** CapCity orders: **33,000**
★ Appearance of Punisher, Spider-Man.
21 ❑ Dec 1990 Cover: 1.50 **NM** value: **3.00**
Circ: Statement: **96,426** CapCity orders: **37,800**
★ Appearance of Punisher, Spider-Man.
22 ❑ Jan 1991 Cover: 1.50 **NM** value: **3.00**
Circ: CapCity orders: **19,000**
23 ❑ Feb 1991 Cover: 1.50 **NM** value: **3.00**
Circ: CapCity orders: **18,600**
24 ❑ Mar 1991 Cover: 1.50 **NM** value: **3.00**
Circ: CapCity orders: **19,400**
25 ❑ Apr 1991 Cover: 2.50 **NM** value: **Cover or less**
Circ: CapCity orders: **37,200**
• Giant-size. ★ Appearance of Ghost Rider.
26 ❑ May 1991 Cover: 1.50 **NM** value: **2.00**
Circ: CapCity orders: **18,300**
27 ❑ Jun 1991 Cover: 1.50 **NM** value: **2.00**
Circ: CapCity orders: **17,300**
28 ❑ Jul 1991 Cover: 1.50 **NM** value: **2.00**
Circ: CapCity orders: **17,700**
29 ❑ Aug 1991 Cover: 1.50 **NM** value: **2.00**
Circ: CapCity orders: **17,600**
30 ❑ Sep 1991 Cover: 1.50 **NM** value: **2.00**
Circ: CapCity orders: **17,200**
31 ❑ Oct 1991 Cover: 1.50 **NM** value: **2.00**
Circ: CapCity orders: **19,500**
32 ❑ Nov 1991 Cover: 1.50 **NM** value: **3.00**
Circ: CapCity orders: **20,100**
★ Appearance of Hobgoblin.
33 ❑ Dec 1991 Cover: 1.50 **NM** value: **3.00**
Circ: CapCity orders: **24,400**
★ Appearance of Hobgoblin.
34 ❑ Jan 1992 Cover: 1.50 **NM** value: **2.00**
Circ: CapCity orders: **25,800**
35 ❑ Feb 1992 Cover: 1.75 **NM** value: **2.00**
Circ: CapCity orders: **24,300**
📖 Blood Brothers, Part 1 **A:** Ron Garney **W:** Terry Kavanagh ★ Appearance of Punisher.
36 ❑ Mar 1992 Cover: 1.75 **NM** value: **2.00**
Circ: CapCity orders: **23,400**
📖 Blood Brothers, Part 2 **A:** Ron Garney **W:** Terry Kavanagh ★ Appearance of Punisher.
37 ❑ Apr 1992 Cover: 1.75 **NM** value: **2.00**
Circ: CapCity orders: **21,300**
📖 Blood Brothers, Part 3 **A:** Ron Garney **W:** Terry Kavanagh ★ Appearance of Punisher.
38 ❑ May 1992 Cover: 1.75 **NM** value: **2.00**
Circ: CapCity orders: **22,800**
📖 Blood Brothers, Part 4 **A:** Ron Garney **W:** Terry Kavanagh ★ Appearance of Punisher.
39 ❑ Jun 1992 Cover: 1.75 **NM** value: **2.00**
Circ: CapCity orders: **23,400**
📖 Impending Doom! **A:** Gary Kwapisz **W:** Ron Garney; Terry Kavanagh ★ Versus Doctor Doom.
40 ❑ Jul 1992 Cover: 1.75 **NM** value: **2.00**
Circ: CapCity orders: **20,200**
41 ❑ Aug 1992 Cover: 1.75 **NM** value: **2.00**
Circ: CapCity orders: **30,300**
42 ❑ Sep 1992 Cover: 1.75 **NM** value: **2.00**
Circ: CapCity orders: **30,000**
43 ❑ Oct 1992 Cover: 1.75 **NM** value: **2.00**
Circ: CapCity orders: **29,100**
📖 Infinity War **A:** Gary Kwapisz **W:** Terry Kavanagh
44 ❑ Nov 1992 Cover: 1.75 **NM** value: **2.00**
Circ: CapCity orders: **25,100**
📖 Infinity War
45 ❑ Dec 1992 Cover: 1.75 **NM** value: **2.00**
Circ: CapCity orders: **17,300**
46 ❑ Jan 1993 Cover: 1.75 **NM** value: **2.00**
Circ: CapCity orders: **15,800**
📖 Death Watch **A:** James W. Fry III **W:** Terry Kavanagh
47 ❑ Feb 1993 Cover: 1.75 **NM** value: **2.00**
Circ: CapCity orders: **15,400**
48 ❑ Mar 1993 Cover: 1.75 **NM** value: **2.00**
Circ: CapCity orders: **14,500**
49 ❑ Apr 1993 Cover: 1.75 **NM** value: **2.00**
Circ: CapCity orders: **14,000**
50 ❑ May 1993 Cover: 2.95 **NM** value: **Cover or less**
Circ: CapCity orders: **39,100**
Die-cut cover.
51 ❑ Jun 1993 Cover: 1.75 **NM** value: **Cover or less**
Circ: CapCity orders: **15,800**
52 ❑ Jul 1993 Cover: 1.75 **NM** value: **Cover or less**
Circ: CapCity orders: **14,800**
53 ❑ Aug 1993 Cover: 1.75 **NM** value: **Cover or less**
Circ: CapCity orders: **13,500**
54 ❑ Sep 1993 Cover: 1.75 **NM** value: **Cover or less**
Circ: CapCity orders: **11,200**
55 ❑ Oct 1993 Cover: 1.75 **NM** value: **3.00**
Circ: CapCity orders: **10,500** • **CGC:** 3 graded, best 9.6
• 1st professional Stephen Platt art **A:** Stephen Platt **W:** Terry Kavanagh ★ 1st Appearance of Sunstreak.
56 ❑ Nov 1993 Cover: 1.75 **NM** value: **3.00**
Circ: CapCity orders: **9,150**
A: Stephen Platt
57 ❑ Dec 1993 Cover: 1.75 **NM** value: **3.00**
Circ: CapCity orders: **9,350** • **CGC:** 1 graded, best 9.6
A: Stephen Platt
58 ❑ Jan 1994 Cover: 1.75 **NM** value: **2.00**
Circ: CapCity orders: **12,400** • **CGC:** 1 graded, best 9.6
59 ❑ Feb 1994 Cover: 1.75 **NM** value: **2.00**
Circ: CapCity orders: **13,500**
60 ❑ Mar 1994 Cover: 1.75 **NM** value: **2.00**
Circ: CapCity orders: **22,950**
final issue.

SE 1❑ ca. 1992 Cover: 2.50 **NM** value: **Cover or less**
📖 Explosion At The Center Of A Madman's Crown • Team-up with Shang-Chi, Master of Kung Fu **A:** Art Nichols **W:** Doug Moench

MARILYN MONROE: SUICIDE OR MURDER? — Revolutionary

1 ❑ Sep 1993, b&w Cover: 2.50 **NM** value: **Cover or less**
A: Hugh Fleming; Pete Mullins **W:** Herbert Shapiro

MARILYN: THE STORY OF A WOMAN — Seven Stories

Bk 1❑ b&w Cover: 14.95 **NM** value: **Cover or less**
• Marilyn Monroe biography

MARINES IN ACTION — Atlas

1 ❑ Jun 1955 Cover: 0.10 **NM** value: **60.00**
2 ❑ ca. 1955 Cover: 0.10 **NM** value: **40.00**
3 ❑ ca. 1955 Cover: 0.10 **NM** value: **40.00**
4 ❑ Cover: 0.10 **NM** value: **40.00**
5 ❑ Feb 1956 Cover: 0.10 **NM** value: **40.00**
6 ❑ ca. 1956 Cover: 0.10 **NM** value: **40.00**
7 ❑ ca. 1956 Cover: 0.10 **NM** value: **40.00**
8 ❑ Sep 1956 Cover: 0.10 **NM** value: **40.00**
9 ❑ ca. 1957 Cover: 0.10 **NM** value: **40.00**
10 ❑ ca. 1957 Cover: 0.10 **NM** value: **40.00**
11 ❑ ca. 1957 Cover: 0.10 **NM** value: **35.00**
12 ❑ ca. 1957 Cover: 0.10 **NM** value: **35.00**
13 ❑ Jul 1957 Cover: 0.10 **NM** value: **35.00**
14 ❑ ca. 1957 Cover: 0.10 **NM** value: **35.00**

MARINES IN BATTLE — Marvel

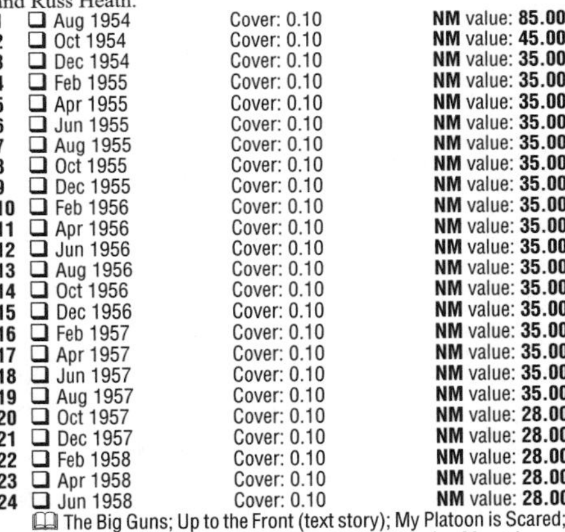

The marines have long been an outstanding, versatile fighting force, taking on the enemy (as the song says) "on air, on land, and sea." This makes them versatile heroes for war comics, as well, allowing writers to set their adventures virtually any time in the past 200 years and in any campaign or mission.

Marines in Battle does just that, with daring adventures set from the Civil War to the then-raging war in Korea. As befits the times, Marines in Battle took particular aim at communist forces, whether in China, Korea, or elsewhere. And, while the stories were rarely "true to life," they were universally well-illustrated by a cadre of artists including Reed Crandall, Al Williamson, and Russ Heath.

1 ❑ Aug 1954 Cover: 0.10 **NM** value: **85.00**
2 ❑ Oct 1954 Cover: 0.10 **NM** value: **45.00**
3 ❑ Dec 1954 Cover: 0.10 **NM** value: **35.00**
4 ❑ Feb 1955 Cover: 0.10 **NM** value: **35.00**
5 ❑ Apr 1955 Cover: 0.10 **NM** value: **35.00**
6 ❑ Jun 1955 Cover: 0.10 **NM** value: **35.00**
7 ❑ Aug 1955 Cover: 0.10 **NM** value: **35.00**
8 ❑ Oct 1955 Cover: 0.10 **NM** value: **35.00**
9 ❑ Dec 1955 Cover: 0.10 **NM** value: **35.00**
10 ❑ Feb 1956 Cover: 0.10 **NM** value: **35.00**
11 ❑ Apr 1956 Cover: 0.10 **NM** value: **35.00**
12 ❑ Jun 1956 Cover: 0.10 **NM** value: **35.00**
13 ❑ Aug 1956 Cover: 0.10 **NM** value: **35.00**
14 ❑ Oct 1956 Cover: 0.10 **NM** value: **35.00**
15 ❑ Dec 1956 Cover: 0.10 **NM** value: **35.00**
16 ❑ Feb 1957 Cover: 0.10 **NM** value: **35.00**
17 ❑ Apr 1957 Cover: 0.10 **NM** value: **35.00**
18 ❑ Jun 1957 Cover: 0.10 **NM** value: **35.00**
19 ❑ Aug 1957 Cover: 0.10 **NM** value: **35.00**
20 ❑ Oct 1957 Cover: 0.10 **NM** value: **28.00**
21 ❑ Dec 1957 Cover: 0.10 **NM** value: **28.00**
22 ❑ Feb 1958 Cover: 0.10 **NM** value: **28.00**
23 ❑ Apr 1958 Cover: 0.10 **NM** value: **28.00**
24 ❑ Jun 1958 Cover: 0.10 **NM** value: **28.00**
📖 The Big Guns; Up to the Front (text story); My Platoon is Scared; Blockade; Jeb Stuart's Raiders!; Thunderbolt! **A:** Joe Maneely
25 ❑ Aug 1958 Cover: 0.10 **NM** value: **28.00**
final issue. **A:** Angelo Torres

MARINE WAR HEROES — Charlton

War comics, like their polar opposite, romance comics, exist to satisfy a narrow spectrum of fantasies for an audience presumed to despise any variation from tried and true formulas. Some war comics have risen to greater creative heights than love comics, since the male creators may have had more sympathy for and insight into their material, but at their most formulaic — in comics like Marine War Heroes — there is little real difference, once you substitute buzz cuts for beehives, green khaki for white lace, and bullets for wedding rings. Marine War Heroes runs grimly through the register of stock plots — the reluctant soldier, bravery under fire, seeking revenge for a fallen friend, one man against an entire division — all rendered in the artless, low-budget Charlton house style. It was mustered out of the Charlton lineup in 1967, when the threat of real war dampened the public appetite for war fantasies.

1 ❑ Jan 1964 Cover: 0.12 **NM** value: **14.00**
2 ❑ Apr 1964 Cover: 0.12 **NM** value: **10.00**
3 ❑ Jun 1964 Cover: 0.12 **NM** value: **10.00**
4 ❑ Aug 1964 Cover: 0.12 **NM** value: **8.00**
5 ❑ Nov 1964 Cover: 0.12 **NM** value: **8.00**
6 ❑ Jan 1965 Cover: 0.12 **NM** value: **6.00**
7 ❑ Apr 1965 Cover: 0.12 **NM** value: **6.00**
8 ❑ Jun 1965 Cover: 0.12 **NM** value: **6.00**
📖 The Silent Foe; The Town Taker; If One Survived; Final Score; Two For Trouble; Not Very Brave
9 ❑ Aug 1965 Cover: 0.12 **NM** value: **6.00**
10 ❑ Oct 1965 Cover: 0.12 **NM** value: **6.00**
11 ❑ Dec 1965 Cover: 0.12 **NM** value: **4.00**
12 ❑ Jan 1966 Cover: 0.12 **NM** value: **4.00**
13 ❑ Apr 1966 Cover: 0.12 **NM** value: **4.00**
14 ❑ Jun 1966 Cover: 0.12 **NM** value: **4.00**
15 ❑ Aug 1966 Cover: 0.12 **NM** value: **4.00**
16 ❑ Nov 1966 Cover: 0.12 **NM** value: **4.00**
17 ❑ Jan 1967 Cover: 0.12 **NM** value: **4.00**
18 ❑ Mar 1967 Cover: 0.12 **NM** value: **4.00**

MARIONETTE — Raven

1 ❑ b&w Cover: 0.75 **NM** value: **1.00**

MARIONETTE, THE — Alpha Productions

1 ❑ b&w Cover: 2.50 **NM** value: **Cover or less**
2 ❑ b&w Cover: 2.50 **NM** value: **Cover or less**

MARK TRAIL — Standard

1 ❑ ca. 1955 Cover: 0.10 **NM** value: **35.00**

MARK, THE (1ST SERIES) — Dark Horse

1 ❑ Sep 1987 Cover: 1.75 **NM** value: **2.00**
Circ: CapCity orders: **5,075**
2 ❑ Dec 1987 Cover: 1.95 **NM** value: **2.00**
Circ: CapCity orders: **4,075**
3 ❑ Aug 1988 Cover: 1.75 **NM** value: **2.00**
Circ: CapCity orders: **3,650**
4 ❑ Sep 1988 Cover: 1.75 **NM** value: **2.00**
Circ: CapCity orders: **2,900**
5 ❑ Nov 1988 Cover: 1.75 **NM** value: **2.00**
A: Gary Barker **W:** Jerry Prosser
6 ❑ Jan 1989 Cover: 1.75 **NM** value: **2.00**
📖 History Lesson **A:** Robert Caracol **W:** Jerry Prosser

MARK, THE (2ND SERIES) — Dark Horse

1 ❑ Dec 1993 Cover: 2.50 **NM** value: **Cover or less**
Circ: CapCity orders: **5,775**
📖 American Tune **A:** Brad Rader **W:** Mike W. Barr
2 ❑ Jan 1994 Cover: 2.50 **NM** value: **Cover or less**
Circ: CapCity orders: **3,750**
📖 American Success Story **A:** Brad Rader **W:** Mike W. Barr
3 ❑ Feb 1994 Cover: 2.50 **NM** value: **Cover or less**
Circ: CapCity orders: **2,975**
📖 America…Love It Or Leave **A:** Brad Rader **W:** Mike W. Barr
4 ❑ Mar 1994 Cover: 2.50 **NM** value: **Cover or less**
Circ: CapCity orders: **2,500**

MARKAM — Gauntlet

1 ❑ Cover: 2.50 **NM** value: **Cover or less**
📖 The Demons of Fate **A:** Steve Stamatiadis **W:** Steve Stamatiadis

MARK HAZZARD: MERC — Marvel

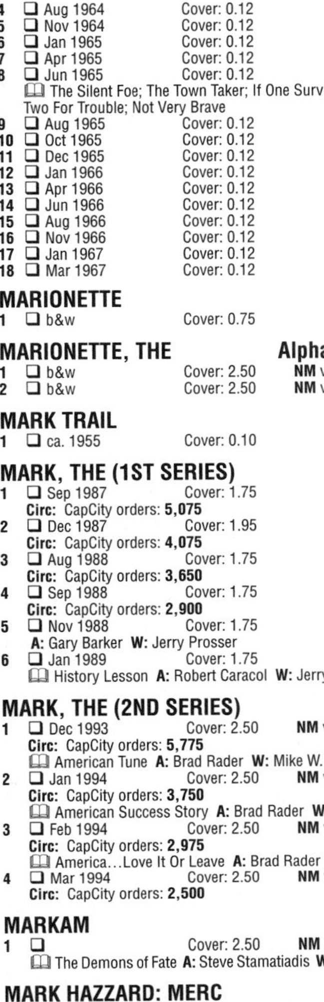

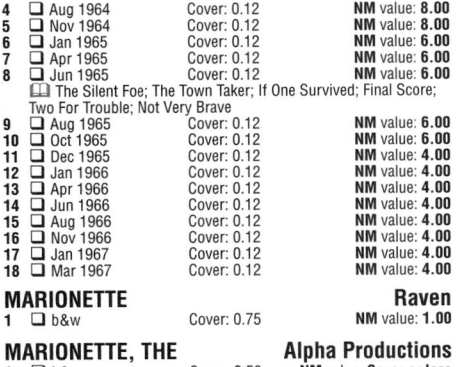

Mark's parents were stunned when he dropped out of West Point to fight as an infantryman in Vietnam. He took the most dangerous duties he could find, serving a total of three tours. After that, he realized he was addicted to life on the edge, and became a soldier of fortune.

His chosen profession cost him the love of his parents, his marriage, and endangered his relationship with his son. The worst casualty is his conscience, for Mark wants to see himself as one of the good guys. However, it's all too often that he realizes that the people he works for are no better than the people he fights. When that happens, Mark rewrites the rules of the game.

Written by The Incredible Hulk's Peter David, Mark Hazard: Merc was easily one of the best of Marvel's New Universe line of comics.

1 ❑ Nov 1986 Cover: 0.75 **NM** value: **1.25**
Circ: CapCity orders: **36,300**
📖 Bad For Business **A:** Gray Morrow **W:** Peter David ★ 1st Appearance of Mark Hazzard.
2 ❑ Dec 1986 Cover: 0.75 **NM** value: **1.00**
Circ: CapCity orders: **21,900**
3 ❑ Jan 1987 Cover: 0.75 **NM** value: **1.00**
Circ: CapCity orders: **18,400**
4 ❑ Feb 1987 Cover: 0.75 **NM** value: **1.00**
Circ: CapCity orders: **17,800**
5 ❑ Mar 1987 Cover: 0.75 **NM** value: **1.00**
Circ: CapCity orders: **16,800**
6 ❑ Apr 1987 Cover: 0.75 **NM** value: **1.00**
Circ: CapCity orders: **14,400**
7 ❑ May 1987 Cover: 0.75 **NM** value: **1.00**
Circ: CapCity orders: **12,000**
8 ❑ Jun 1987 Cover: 0.75 **NM** value: **1.00**
Circ: CapCity orders: **11,200**
9 ❑ Jul 1987 Cover: 0.75 **NM** value: **1.00**
Circ: CapCity orders: **10,700**
10 ❑ Aug 1987 Cover: 0.75 **NM** value: **1.00**
Circ: CapCity orders: **10,100**
📖 Iran Slam **A:** Gray Morrow **W:** Doug Murray
11 ❑ Sep 1987 Cover: 0.75 **NM** value: **1.00**
Circ: CapCity orders: **9,800**

CGC-graded: Multiply prices above by **33 for 9.9 M** • **16 for 9.8 NM/M** • **7 for 9.6 NM+** • **5 for 9.4 NM** • **2.5 for 9.2 NM-** • **1.5 for 9.0 VF/NM**

12 ❑ Oct 1987 Cover: 0.75 NM value: 1.00
Circ: CapCity orders: 9,100
Anl 1❑Nov 1987 Cover: 1.25 NM value: Cover or less
Circ: CapCity orders: 9,500
★ Death of Hazzard.

MARKSMAN, THE — Hero

1 ❑ Jan 1988 Cover: 1.95 NM value: Cover or less
Circ: CapCity orders: 2,875
📖 The Origin Of The Marksman A: Pete McDonnell W: Steve Perrin
★ Origin of The Marksman.
2 ❑ Feb 1988 Cover: 1.95 NM value: Cover or less
Circ: CapCity orders: 2,050
3 ❑ Apr 1988 Cover: 1.95 NM value: Cover or less
Circ: CapCity orders: 1,775
4 ❑ Jun 1988 Cover: 1.95 NM value: Cover or less
Circ: CapCity orders: 1,625
5 ❑ Aug 1988 Cover: 1.95 NM value: Cover or less
Circ: CapCity orders: 1,300
Anl 1❑Dec 1988 Cover: 2.75 NM value: Cover or less
Circ: CapCity orders: 1,200

MARMADUKE MOUSE — Quality

Although sometimes regarded as a rip-off of Tom & Jerry, Marmaduke Mouse had a quirky charm that was its own. Granted, the stories did follow a simple formula: Hapless Marmaduke blunders from adventure to adventure trying to bail his friend (and employer), loony King Louie the lion, out of trouble. But, like many of the best funny-animal comics and cartoons, Marmaduke Mouse holds a fun-house mirror up to American society in the 1950s. Some stories revolve around a growing obsession with television (and some of the characters featured are thinly disguised representations of many celebrities of the day, including Milton Berle), the rise of suburban sprawl, and even the threat of communism. When Quality Comics folded and DC bought most of its properties, Marmaduke Mouse was canceled and never revived as a comic book.

1 ❑ Spr 1946 Cover: 0.10 NM value: 70.00
2 ❑ Sum 1946 Cover: 0.10 NM value: 40.00
3 ❑ Fal 1946 Cover: 0.10 NM value: 28.00
4 ❑ Win 1946 Cover: 0.10 NM value: 28.00
5 ❑ Spr 1947 Cover: 0.10 NM value: 28.00
6 ❑ Sum 1947 Cover: 0.10 NM value: 20.00
7 ❑ Fal 1947 Cover: 0.10 NM value: 20.00
8 ❑ Win 1947 Cover: 0.10 NM value: 20.00
9 ❑ Spr 1948 Cover: 0.10 NM value: 20.00
10 ❑ Fal 1948 Cover: 0.10 NM value: 20.00
11 ❑ Win 1948 Cover: 0.10 NM value: 16.00
12 ❑ Spr 1949 Cover: 0.10 NM value: 16.00
13 ❑ Sum 1949 Cover: 0.10 NM value: 16.00
14 ❑ Fal 1949 Cover: 0.10 NM value: 16.00
15 ❑ Win 1949 Cover: 0.10 NM value: 16.00
16 ❑ Jan 1950 Cover: 0.10 NM value: 16.00
17 ❑ Mar 1950 Cover: 0.10 NM value: 16.00
18 ❑ May 1950 Cover: 0.10 NM value: 16.00
19 ❑ Jul 1950 Cover: 0.10 NM value: 16.00
20 ❑ Sep 1950 Cover: 0.10 NM value: 16.00
21 ❑ Nov 1950 Cover: 0.10 NM value: 12.00
22 ❑ Jan 1951 Cover: 0.10 NM value: 12.00
23 ❑ Mar 1951 Cover: 0.10 NM value: 12.00
24 ❑ May 1951 Cover: 0.10 NM value: 12.00
25 ❑ Jul 1951 Cover: 0.10 NM value: 12.00
26 ❑ Sep 1951 Cover: 0.10 NM value: 12.00
27 ❑ Nov 1951 Cover: 0.10 NM value: 12.00
28 ❑ Jan 1952 Cover: 0.10 NM value: 12.00
29 ❑ Mar 1952 Cover: 0.10 NM value: 12.00
📖 Mamaduke's Time (text story); The Boasting Miner
30 ❑ May 1952 Cover: 0.10 NM value: 12.00
31 ❑ Jul 1952 Cover: 0.10 NM value: 12.00
32 ❑ Aug 1952 Cover: 0.10 NM value: 12.00
33 ❑ Oct 1952 Cover: 0.10 NM value: 12.00
34 ❑ Dec 1952 Cover: 0.10 NM value: 12.00
35 ❑ Jan 1953 Cover: 0.10 NM value: 12.00
36 ❑ ca. 1953 Cover: 0.10 NM value: 12.00
37 ❑ ca. 1953 Cover: 0.10 NM value: 12.00
38 ❑ ca. 1953 Cover: 0.10 NM value: 12.00
39 ❑ Jul 1953 Cover: 0.10 NM value: 12.00
40 ❑ Aug 1953 Cover: 0.10 NM value: 12.00
41 ❑ Sep 1953 Cover: 0.10 NM value: 9.00
42 ❑ Nov 1953 Cover: 0.10 NM value: 9.00
43 ❑ Cover: 0.10 NM value: 9.00
44 ❑ ca. 1954 Cover: 0.10 NM value: 9.00
45 ❑ ca. 1954 Cover: 0.10 NM value: 9.00
46 ❑ ca. 1954 Cover: 0.10 NM value: 9.00
47 ❑ Jul 1954 Cover: 0.10 NM value: 9.00
48 ❑ Sep 1954 Cover: 0.10 NM value: 9.00
49 ❑ Nov 1954 Cover: 0.10 NM value: 9.00
50 ❑ Cover: 0.10 NM value: 9.00
51 ❑ ca. 1955 Cover: 0.10 NM value: 9.00
52 ❑ ca. 1955 Cover: 0.10 NM value: 9.00
53 ❑ ca. 1955 Cover: 0.10 NM value: 9.00
54 ❑ Oct 1955 Cover: 0.10 NM value: 9.00
55 ❑ Nov 1955 Cover: 0.10 NM value: 9.00
56 ❑ Dec 1955 Cover: 0.10 NM value: 9.00
57 ❑ Jan 1956 Cover: 0.10 NM value: 9.00
58 ❑ Feb 1956 Cover: 0.10 NM value: 9.00
59 ❑ Mar 1956 Cover: 0.10 NM value: 9.00
60 ❑ ca. 1956 Cover: 0.10 NM value: 9.00
61 ❑ ca. 1956 Cover: 0.10 NM value: 9.00
62 ❑ ca. 1956 Cover: 0.10 NM value: 9.00
63 ❑ ca. 1956 Cover: 0.10 NM value: 9.00
64 ❑ Oct 1956 Cover: 0.10 NM value: 9.00
65 ❑ Dec 1956 Cover: 0.10 NM value: 9.00

MAROONED! — Fantagraphics / Eros

All issues are adults only.
1 ❑ b&w Cover: 1.95 NM value: Cover or less
A: Richard Green W: Richard Green

MARQUIS, THE: DANSE MACABRE — Oni

1 ❑ b&w Cover: 2.95 NM value: Cover or less
A: Guy Davis W: Guy Davis
2 ❑ Jul 2000, b&w Cover: 2.95 NM value: Cover or less
A: Guy Davis W: Guy Davis
3 ❑ Oct 2000, b&w Cover: 2.95 NM value: Cover or less
A: Guy Davis W: Guy Davis

MARRIAGE OF HERCULES AND XENA, THE — Topps

1 ❑ Jul 1998 Cover: 2.95 NM value: Cover or less
A: Aaron Lopresti; June Brigman; Alex Ross(cover) W: Mary Bierbaum; Tom Bierbaum

MARRIED...WITH CHILDREN 3-D SPECIAL — Now

1 ❑ Jun 1993 Cover: 2.95 NM value: Cover or less
📖 The Nanny Scam, Inc. A: Tom Richmond W: Katy Llewellyn

MARRIED...WITH CHILDREN: BUCK'S TALE — Now

1 ❑ ca. 1994 Cover: 1.95 NM value: 2.00
Circ: CapCity orders: 2,850
📖 Buck's Tale A: Eddie Pittman W: Geoff White ★ Origin of Buck (the Bundy Family dog).

MARRIED...WITH CHILDREN: BUD BUNDY, FANBOY IN PARADISE — Now

1 ❑ Cover: 2.95 NM value: Cover or less
📖 Fanboy In Paradise A: Tom Richmond W: Geoff White; Todd Ruttle

MARRIED...WITH CHILDREN: FLASHBACK SPECIAL — Now

1 ❑ Jan 1993 Cover: 1.95 NM value: 2.00
• Al & Peg's First Date
2 ❑ Feb 1993 Cover: 1.95 NM value: 2.00
• Al & Peg's Wedding
3 ❑ Mar 1993 Cover: 1.95 NM value: 2.00
📖 Father Knows Worst A: Tom Richmond W: Ty Addams

MARRIED...WITH CHILDREN: KELLY BUNDY — Now

1 ❑ Aug 1992 Cover: 1.95 NM value: 2.25
Circ: CapCity orders: 6,900
Photo cover.
2 ❑ Sep 1992 Cover: 1.95 NM value: 2.25
Circ: CapCity orders: 4,600
Photo cover. 📖 One Flew Over The Bundy's Nest A: Tom Richmond W: James Bradshaw
3 ❑ Oct 1992 Cover: 1.95 NM value: 2.25
Circ: CapCity orders: 4,275
Photo cover. 📖 Happy Birthday and Get Out! A: Mark Braun W: Barry Petersen

MARRIED...WITH CHILDREN: KELLY GOES TO KOLLEGE — Now

1 ❑ Cover: 2.95 NM value: Cover or less
Circ: CapCity orders: 2,700
📖 A Mind Is A Terrible Thing A: Tom Richmond W: Joe Colombero; Joe Locicero
2 ❑ Cover: 2.95 NM value: Cover or less
3 ❑ Cover: 2.95 NM value: Cover or less

MARRIED...WITH CHILDREN: OFF BROADWAY — Now

1 ❑ Sep 1993 Cover: 1.95 NM value: 2.00
📖 Off Broadway A: Eddie Pittman W: Geoff White

MARRIED...WITH CHILDREN: QUANTUM QUARTET — Now

1 ❑ Oct 1993 Cover: 1.95 NM value: 2.00
Circ: CapCity orders: 3,075
• parody
2 ❑ Nov 1993 Cover: 1.95 NM value: 2.00
Circ: CapCity orders: 2,700
• parody
3 ❑ Fal 1994 Cover: 2.95 NM value: Cover or less
• The Big Wrap-Up; combines issues #3 and 4 into flipbook; no indicia; parody

MARRIED...WITH CHILDREN: 2099 — Now

1 ❑ Jun 1993 Cover: 1.95 NM value: 2.00
Circ: CapCity orders: 3,525
📖 Recognizing Authority • Terminator spoof A: Tom Richmond; Barb Kaalberg W: James Caputo
2 ❑ Jul 1993 Cover: 1.95 NM value: 2.00
Circ: CapCity orders: 3,050
3 ❑ Aug 1993 Cover: 1.95 NM value: 2.00
Circ: CapCity orders: 3,175

MARRIED...WITH CHILDREN (VOL. 1) — Now

Think of the Bundy family as sort of the anti-Brady Bunch. Whereas the Bradys were always the high achievers, with warm, supportive relationships between them, the Bundy family is a real mess. They have a failed shoe salesman for a father, a lazy shrew for a mother, a son who will probably never get a date, and a daughter who's a helium-headed tramp.

It all sounds rather pathetic, but when you're Married...With Children, it becomes outrageously funny. An incredibly popular television show, the Bundy's antics and misadventures are even funnier in comic-book form. If nothing else, the Bundy's will make you feel a lot better about your own family.

1 ❑ Jun 1990 Cover: 1.75 NM value: 2.50
Circ: CapCity orders: 10,575
📖 The All American Family or Just Act Natural A: Dave Schwartz W: Katherine Llewelyn
1-2 ❑ Cover: 1.75 NM value: 2.00
2 ❑ Jul 1990 Cover: 1.75 NM value: 2.00
Circ: CapCity orders: 6,475
Photo cover. 📖 Viva Las Bundys A: Dave Schwartz W: Katherine Llewellyn
3 ❑ Aug 1990 Cover: 1.75 NM value: 2.00
Circ: CapCity orders: 5,675
4 ❑ Sep 1990 Cover: 1.75 NM value: 2.00
Circ: CapCity orders: 5,925
📖 Big Man Bundy A: Mark Braun W: Katherine Llewellyn
5 ❑ Oct 1990 Cover: 1.75 NM value: 2.00
Circ: CapCity orders: 4,925
Photo cover. 📖 Shoe Zombies A: Dave Schwartz W: Katherine Llewellyn
6 ❑ Nov 1990 Cover: 1.75 NM value: 2.00
Circ: CapCity orders: 4,350
Photo cover. 📖 TV or not TV A: Tom Richmond; Joseph Allen W: Katherine Llewellyn
7 ❑ Feb 1991 Cover: 1.75 NM value: 2.00
Circ: CapCity orders: 3,875
final issue.

MARRIED...WITH CHILDREN (VOL. 2) — Now

1 ❑ Sep 1991 Cover: 1.95 NM value: 2.50
Circ: CapCity orders: 7,775
Photo cover. 📖 The Love Line A: Marc Hansen W: Marc Hansen; Katherine Llewellyn
2 ❑ Oct 1991 Cover: 1.95 NM value: 2.25
Circ: CapCity orders: 6,250
📖 Sweet Revenge • Peggy invents bon-bon filling detector A: Tom Richmond W: Diane Piron
3 ❑ Nov 1991 Cover: 1.95 NM value: 2.25
Circ: CapCity orders: 5,950
📖 Psychodad • Al turns into Psychodad A: Tom Richmond W: Marc Hansen
4 ❑ Dec 1991 Cover: 1.95 NM value: 2.00
Circ: CapCity orders: 7,900
Photo cover.
5 ❑ Jan 1992 Cover: 1.95 NM value: 2.00
Circ: CapCity orders: 8,650
6 ❑ Mar 1992 Cover: 1.95 NM value: 2.00
Circ: CapCity orders: 9,525
Photo cover. 📖 Hog Heaven! A: Tom Richmond W: Ty Addams
7 ❑ Apr 1992 Cover: 1.95 NM value: 2.00
Circ: CapCity orders: 8,975
📖 Attack Of The Job Huntress! final issue. A: Tom Richmond W: Ty Addams
Anl 1994❑ca. 194 Cover: 2.50 NM value: Cover or less
• Annual
SE 1❑Jul 1992 Cover: 1.95 NM value: 2.00
Photo cover. • Special; with poster

MARS — First

1 ❑ Jan 1984 Cover: 1.25 NM value: 1.50
📖 Rebirth A: Marc Hempel W: Mark Wheatley
2 ❑ Feb 1984 Cover: 1.25 NM value: Cover or less
📖 Mars Attacks! A: Marc Hempel W: Mark Wheatley
3 ❑ Mar 1984 Cover: 1.25 NM value: Cover or less
A: Marc Hempel W: Mark Wheatley
4 ❑ Apr 1984 Cover: 1.25 NM value: Cover or less
A: Marc Hempel W: Mark Wheatley
5 ❑ May 1984 Cover: 1.25 NM value: Cover or less
A: Marc Hempel W: Mark Wheatley
6 ❑ Jun 1984 Cover: 1.25 NM value: Cover or less
A: Marc Hempel W: Mark Wheatley
7 ❑ Jul 1984 Cover: 1.25 NM value: Cover or less
A: Marc Hempel W: Mark Wheatley
8 ❑ Aug 1984 Cover: 1.25 NM value: Cover or less
A: Marc Hempel W: Mark Wheatley
9 ❑ Sep 1984 Cover: 1.25 NM value: Cover or less
A: Marc Hempel W: Mark Wheatley
10 ❑ Oct 1984 Cover: 1.25 NM value: Cover or less
A: Marc Hempel W: Mark Wheatley
11 ❑ Nov 1984 Cover: 1.25 NM value: Cover or less
A: Marc Hempel W: Mark Wheatley
12 ❑ Dec 1984 Cover: 1.25 NM value: Cover or less
A: Marc Hempel W: Mark Wheatley

MARS ATTACKS BASEBALL SPECIAL — Topps

1 ❑ Jun 1996 Cover: 2.95 NM value: Cover or less
One-shot. Simon Bisley cover.

Other grades: Multiply prices above by **1.5 for Mint • 2/3 for Very Fine • 1/3 for Fine • 1/5 for Very Good • 1/8 for Good**

MARS ATTACKS HIGH SCHOOL — Topps

1 ❑ May 1997 Cover: 2.95 **NM** value: **Cover or less**
Circ: Diamd. preorders: **14,095**
A: Hugh Haynes **W:** Dwight Jon Zimmerman

2 ❑ Sep 1997 Cover: 2.95 **NM** value: **Cover or less**
Circ: Diamd. preorders: **11,466**
A: Hugh Haynes **W:** Dwight Jon Zimmerman

MARS ATTACKS IMAGE — Image

1 ❑ Dec 1996 Cover: 2.50 **NM** value: **Cover or less**
Circ: Diamd. preorders: **46,918**
• crossover with Topps **A:** Bill Sienkiewicz; Andy Smith **W:** Keith Giffen

2 ❑ Jan 1997 Cover: 2.50 **NM** value: **Cover or less**
Circ: Diamd. preorders: **37,047**
A: Bill Sienkiewicz; Andy Smith **W:** Keith Giffen; Gary Carlson ★ Appearance of Shadowhawk, Witchblade, SuperPatriot, Spawn.

3 ❑ Mar 1997 Cover: 2.50 **NM** value: **Cover or less**
Circ: Diamd. preorders: **31,816**
A: Bill Sienkiewicz; Andy Smith **W:** Keith Giffen ★ Appearance of Shadowhawk, Witchblade, SuperPatriot, Spawn.

4 ❑ Apr 1997 Cover: 2.50 **NM** value: **Cover or less**
Circ: Diamd. preorders: **27,240**
A: Bill Sienkiewicz; Andy Smith **W:** Keith Giffen ★ Death of U.S. Male.

MARS ATTACKS! (MINI-COMICS) — Pocket

1 ❑ Cover: 1.00 **NM** value: **Cover or less**
• mini-comics

2 ❑ Cover: 1.00 **NM** value: **Cover or less**
• mini-comics

3 ❑ Cover: 1.00 **NM** value: **Cover or less**
• mini-comics

4 ❑ Cover: 1.00 **NM** value: **Cover or less**
• mini-comics

MARS ATTACKS THE SAVAGE DRAGON — Topps

1 ❑ Dec 1996 Cover: 2.95 **NM** value: **Cover or less**
Circ: Diamd. preorders: **25,893**
• crossover with Image; trading cards **A:** Jean-Claude St. Aubin **W:** Dwight Jon Zimmerman

2 ❑ Jan 1997 Cover: 2.95 **NM** value: **Cover or less**
Circ: Diamd. preorders: **20,963**
• crossover with Image **A:** Jean-Claude St. Aubin **W:** Dwight Jon Zimmerman

3 ❑ Feb 1997 Cover: 2.95 **NM** value: **Cover or less**
Circ: Diamd. preorders: **19,462**
Killer Monday! • crossover with Image **A:** Jean-Claude St. Aubin **W:** Dwight Jon Zimmerman

4 ❑ Mar 1997 Cover: 2.95 **NM** value: **Cover or less**
Circ: Diamd. preorders: **16,740**
Hard Rain! • crossover with Image **A:** Jean-Claude St. Aubin **W:** Dwight Jon Zimmerman

MARS ATTACKS (VOL. 1) — Topps

The Martians once visited our planet seeking peace, but met their deaths. Now they've come back to Earth to return the favor.

In 1962, the Topps bubblegum card company released an outrageous set of cards entitled "Mars Attacks." The series depicted an alien invasion of Earth, complete with genetically mutated ants, nuclear explosions, and lots of bug-eyed Martians. The set didn't sell very well at the time, while drawing lots of scandalizing media attention for Topps. Not surprisingly, Topps canceled the series, although it has since become a cult classic. More than 30 years later, many of the same artists who either worked on or grew up reading the Mars Attacks cards joined forces to bring readers this updated comic-book adaptation of the card series.

1 ❑ May 1994 Cover: 2.95 **NM** value: **3.50**
Circ: CapCity orders: **9,575**
• Flip-book format **A:** Charles Adlard; Keith Giffen **W:** Keith Giffen; Len Brown

1/ACE❑ May 1994 **NM** value: **15.00**
acetate overlay cover. • Wizard Ace Edition #11. • sendaway from Wizard #65

1/LE❑ May 1994 **NM** value: **4.00**
• Limited edition promotional edition (5,000 printed). • Flip-book format

2 ❑ Jun 1994 Cover: 2.95 **NM** value: **3.00**
Circ: CapCity orders: **6,950**

3 ❑ Aug 1994 Cover: 2.95 **NM** value: **3.00**
Circ: CapCity orders: **6,625**

4 ❑ Sep 1994 Cover: 2.95 **NM** value: **3.00**
Circ: CapCity orders: **6,400**

5 ❑ Oct 194 Cover: 2.95 **NM** value: **3.00**
Circ: CapCity orders: **6,100**

Bk 1❑ Cover: 12.95 **NM** value: **Cover or less**

MARS ATTACKS (VOL. 2) — Topps

1 ❑ Aug 1995 Cover: 2.95 **NM** value: **3.50**
Circ: CapCity orders: **7,825**
Counterstrike, Part 1 **A:** Charles Adlard **W:** Keith Giffen; Dwight Jon Zimmerman

2 ❑ Sep 1995 Cover: 2.95 **NM** value: **3.00**
Circ: CapCity orders: **5,775**
Counterstrike, Part 2

3 ❑ Oct 1995 Cover: 2.95 **NM** value: **3.00**
Counterstrike, Part 3

4 ❑ Jan 1996 Cover: 2.95 **NM** value: **3.00**
Counterstrike, Part 4

5 ❑ Jan 1996 Cover: 2.95 **NM** value: **3.00**
Counterstrike, Part 5

6 ❑ Mar 1996 Cover: 2.95 **NM** value: **3.00**
Claws of the Tiger, Part 1

7 ❑ May 1996 Cover: 2.95 **NM** value: **3.00**
Claws of the Tiger, Part 2 **C:** Dan Brereton

MARSHAL LAW — Marvel / Epic

1 ❑ Oct 1987 Cover: 1.95 **NM** value: **3.50**
Circ: CapCity orders: **14,350**
A: Kevin O'Neill **W:** Pat Mills

2 ❑ Feb 1988 Cover: 1.95 **NM** value: **2.50**
Circ: CapCity orders: **13,200**
A: Kevin O'Neill **W:** Pat Mills

3 ❑ Apr 1988 Cover: 1.95 **NM** value: **2.50**
Circ: CapCity orders: **15,100**
Super Hero Messiah **A:** Kevin O'Neill **W:** Pat Mills

4 ❑ Aug 1988 Cover: 1.95 **NM** value: **2.50**
Circ: CapCity orders: **13,500**
A: Kevin O'Neill **W:** Pat Mills

5 ❑ Dec 1988 Cover: 1.95 **NM** value: **2.50**
Circ: CapCity orders: **12,500**
A: Kevin O'Neill **W:** Pat Mills

6 ❑ Apr 1989 Cover: 1.95 **NM** value: **2.50**
Circ: CapCity orders: **11,300**
Nemesis **A:** Kevin O'Neill **W:** Pat Mills

Bk 1❑ Cover: 14.95 **NM** value: **Cover or less**
Circ: CapCity orders: **2,300**
• Fear and Loathing

MARSHAL LAW: KINGDOM OF THE BLIND — Apocalypse

1 ❑ Cover: 3.95 **NM** value: **Cover or less**
Circ: CapCity orders: **1,725**
No issue number. • newsstand

1/DM❑ Cover: 5.95 **NM** value: **Cover or less**
Circ: CapCity orders: **8,025**
No issue number. • squarebound

MARSHAL LAW: SECRET TRIBUNAL — Dark Horse

1 ❑ Sep 1993 Cover: 2.95 **NM** value: **Cover or less**
cardstock cover.

2 ❑ Apr 1994 Cover: 2.95 **NM** value: **Cover or less**
cardstock cover.

MARSHAL LAW: SUPER BABYLON — Dark Horse

1 ❑ May 1992 Cover: 4.95 **NM** value: **Cover or less**
Circ: CapCity orders: **7,700**
No issue number. • prestige format.

MARSHAL LAW: THE HATEFUL DEAD — Apocalypse

1 ❑ Cover: 5.95 **NM** value: **Cover or less**
Circ: CapCity orders: **6,325**
No issue number. • prestige format.

MARS ON EARTH — DC / Piranha

Bk 1❑ b&w Cover: 12.95 **NM** value: **Cover or less**
• not comics **A:** Pat Broderick

M.A.R.S. PATROL TOTAL WAR — Gold Key

3 ❑ Sep 1966 Cover: 0.12 **NM** value: **10.00**
• Series continued from Total War #2 **A:** Wally Wood

4 ❑ Oct 1967 Cover: 0.12 **NM** value: **8.00**
• **CGC:** 1 graded, best 6.5

5 ❑ May 1968 Cover: 0.12 **NM** value: **8.00**
Mystery Beachhead

6 ❑ Aug 1968 Cover: 0.12 **NM** value: **7.00**

7 ❑ Nov 1968 Cover: 0.12 **NM** value: **7.00**

8 ❑ Feb 1969 Cover: 0.12 **NM** value: **7.00**

9 ❑ May 1969 Cover: 0.12 **NM** value: **7.00**

10 ❑ Aug 1969 Cover: 0.12 **NM** value: **7.00**
final issue.

MARTHA SPLATTERHEAD'S WEIRDEST STORIES EVER TOLD — Monster

All issues are adults only.

1 ❑ b&w Cover: 3.50 **NM** value: **Cover or less**

MARTHA WASHINGTON GOES TO WAR — Dark Horse / Legend

Frank Miller and Dave Gibbons' Give Me Liberty was the powerful tale of a young black girl named Martha Washington, who somehow rose out of a life of despair to become a hero in the corporate wars of the next century. In all these situations, she triumphed merely by surviving.

Now, in this five-issue mini-series, Martha Washington goes back to war. Once again, she's fighting for the Pax forces, this time in the second American Civil War. Like too many wars, this one is fought for trivialities. Here, the forces of Fat Boy Hamburgers have marshaled the beef-raising state of Texas into a bloody general war.

Grievously wounded in the battle for Texas, Martha finds herself placed in the tender care of the Surgeon General, whom she herself killed in the last series. Other friends, long thought dead, also reappear, followed by a fear that the ghosts of the war dead had returned.

1 ❑ May 1994 Cover: 2.95 **NM** value: **3.00**
Circ: CapCity orders: **20,400**
cardstock cover. The Killing Fields **A:** Dave Gibbons **W:** Frank Miller

2 ❑ Jun 1994 Cover: 2.95 **NM** value: **3.00**
Circ: CapCity orders: **18,625**
cardstock cover. Harmony **A:** Dave Gibbons **W:** Frank Miller

3 ❑ Jul 1994 Cover: 2.95 **NM** value: **3.00**
Circ: CapCity orders: **17,775**
cardstock cover. The Valley Of Death **A:** Dave Gibbons **W:** Frank Miller

4 ❑ Aug 1994 Cover: 2.95 **NM** value: **3.00**
Circ: CapCity orders: **17,075**
cardstock cover. **A:** Dave Gibbons **W:** Frank Miller

5 ❑ Nov 1994 Cover: 2.95 **NM** value: **3.00**
Circ: CapCity orders: **16,150**
cardstock cover. **A:** Dave Gibbons **W:** Frank Miller

Bk 1❑ Nov 1995 Cover: 17.95 **NM** value: **Cover or less**
• Trade Paperback. • Collects Martha Washington Goes to War #1-5 **A:** Dave Gibbons **W:** Frank Miller

MARTHA WASHINGTON SAVES THE WORLD — Dark Horse

1 ❑ Dec 1997 Cover: 2.95 **NM** value: **3.00**
Circ: Diamd. preorders: **22,444**
cardstock cover. Comin' in on a Wing and a Prayer **A:** Dave Gibbons **W:** Frank Miller

2 ❑ Jan 1998 Cover: 2.95 **NM** value: **3.00**
Circ: Diamd. preorders: **20,342**
cardstock cover. Tomorrow, When The World is Free **A:** Dave Gibbons **W:** Frank Miller

3 ❑ Feb 1998 Cover: 2.95 **NM** value: **3.00**
Circ: Diamd. preorders: **18,857**
cardstock cover. When The Lights Go On Again All Over the World **A:** Dave Gibbons **W:** Frank Miller

Bk 1❑ Apr 1999 Cover: 12.95 **NM** value: **Cover or less**
No issue number. • Trade Paperback. • collects mini-series

MARTHA WASHINGTON: STRANDED IN SPACE — Dark Horse / Legend

1 ❑ Nov 1995 Cover: 2.95 **NM** value: **3.00**
No issue number. cardstock cover. Crossover • reprints story from Dark Horse Presents **A:** Dave Gibbons **W:** Frank Miller ★ Appearance of The Big Guy.

MARTIAN MANHUNTER — DC

After almost 40 years, the Martian Manhunter, J'onn J'onzz, finally received his own series in 1998. The Martian Manhunter was the last Martian who was accidentally brought to Earth by a scientist who activated an abandoned Martian teleport device. The Manhunter stayed on Earth, eventually becoming one of the mainstays of the Justice League. The Manhunter went through several special issues before the official first issue — an annual, a #0 issue, and then a "#1,000,000" issue which was a tie-in to the DC One Million crossover event. In his series, the Manhunter fought such foes as the Headmaster and Ma'alefa'ak, in hardboiled and intense stories written by John Ostrander.

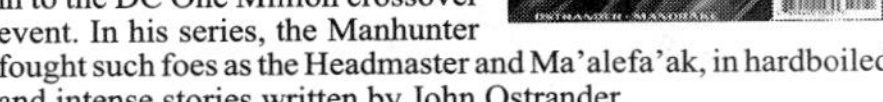

0 ❑ Oct 1998 Cover: 1.99 **NM** value: **3.00**
Circ: Diamd. preorders: **43,272**
Pilgrimage **A:** Tom Mandrake **W:** John Ostrander

1 ❑ Dec 1998 Cover: 1.99 **NM** value: **2.50**
Circ: Diamd. preorders: **40,533**
Duty **A:** Tom Mandrake **W:** John Ostrander

2 ❑ Jan 1999 Cover: 1.99 **NM** value: **2.00**
Circ: Diamd. preorders: **34,610**
A: Tom Mandrake **W:** John Ostrander

3 ❑ Feb 1999 Cover: 1.99 **NM** value: **2.00**
Circ: Diamd. preorders: **32,412**
A: Tom Mandrake **W:** John Ostrander ★ Appearance of Bette Noir.

4 ❑ Mar 1999 Cover: 1.99 **NM** value: **2.00**
Circ: Diamd. preorders: **29,702**
A: Tom Mandrake **W:** John Ostrander ★ Death of Karen Smith.

5 ❑ Apr 1999 Cover: 1.99 **NM** value: **2.00**
Circ: Diamd. preorders: **27,161**
A: Jan Duursema **W:** John Arcudi

6 ❑ May 1999 Cover: 1.99 **NM** value: **2.00**
Circ: Diamd. preorders: **27,212**
W: John Arcudi ★ Versus JLA.

7 ❑ Jun 1999 Cover: 1.99 **NM** value: **2.00**
Circ: Diamd. preorders: **26,975**
My Brother's Keeper **A:** Tom Mandrake **W:** John Ostrander

8 ❑ Jul 1999 Cover: 1.99 **NM** value: **2.00**
Circ: Diamd. preorders: **26,983**
Abandon All Hope **A:** Tom Mandrake **W:** John Ostrander

9 ❑ Aug 1999 Cover: 1.99 **NM** value: **2.00**
Circ: Diamd. preorders: **26,277**
The Burning Grave **A:** Tom Mandrake **W:** John Ostrander ★ Appearance of JLA.

10 ❑ Sep 1999 Cover: 1.99 **NM** value: **2.00**
Circ: Diamd. preorders: **25,186**
Good Faith **A:** Phil Winslade **W:** John Ostrander ★ Appearance of Fire.

11 ❑ Oct 1999 Cover: 1.99 **NM** value: **2.00**
Circ: Diamd. preorders: **24,428**
Pilgrims **A:** Bryan Hitch **W:** John Ostrander

12 ❑ Nov 1999 Cover: 1.99 **NM** value: **2.00**
Circ: Diamd. preorders: **26,303**
Past Saving • Day of Judgment **A:** Tom Mandrake **W:** John Ostrander ★ Appearance of Steel, Crimson Fox, Ice, Vibe.

CGC-graded: Multiply prices above by **33 for 9.9 M • 16 for 9.8 NM/M • 7 for 9.6 NM+ • 5 for 9.4 NM • 2.5 for 9.2 NM- • 1.5 for 9.0 VF/NM**

13 ❑ Dec 1999 Cover: 1.99 **NM** value: **2.00**
Circ: Diamd. preorders: **23,372**
📖 Rings of Saturn, Part 1 **A:** Tom Mandrake **W:** John Ostrander
14 ❑ Jan 2000 Cover: 1.99 **NM** value: **Cover or less**
Circ: Diamd. preorders: **22,123**
📖 Rings of Saturn, Part 2 **A:** Tom Mandrake **W:** John Ostrander
15 ❑ Feb 2000 Cover: 1.99 **NM** value: **Cover or less**
Circ: Diamd. preorders: **21,186**
📖 Rings of Saturn, Part 3 **A:** Tom Mandrake **W:** John Ostrander
16 ❑ Mar 2000 Cover: 1.99 **NM** value: **Cover or less**
Circ: Diamd. preorders: **20,223**
A: Tom Mandrake **W:** John Ostrander
17 ❑ Apr 2000 Cover: 1.99 **NM** value: **Cover or less**
Circ: Diamd. preorders: **18,951**
A: Tom Mandrake **W:** John Ostrander
18 ❑ May 2000 Cover: 1.99 **NM** value: **Cover or less**
Circ: Diamd. preorders: **19,357**
📖 One for All **A:** Tom Mandrake **W:** John Ostrander ★ Appearance of JSA.
19 ❑ Jun 2000 Cover: 1.99 **NM** value: **Cover or less**
Circ: Diamd. preorders: **19,135**
📖 All for One **A:** Tom Mandrake **W:** John Ostrander
20 ❑ Jul 2000 Cover: 1.99 **NM** value: **Cover or less**
Circ: Diamd. preorders: **19,636**
📖 Revelations, Part 1 **A:** Tom Mandrake **W:** John Ostrander
21 ❑ Aug 2000 Cover: 1.99 **NM** value: **Cover or less**
Circ: Diamd. preorders: **19,848**
📖 Revelations, Part 2 **A:** Tom Mandrake **W:** John Ostrander
22 ❑ Sep 2000 Cover: 1.99 **NM** value: **Cover or less**
Circ: Diamd. preorders: **20,709**
📖 Revelations, Part 3 **A:** Tom Mandrake **W:** John Ostrander
23 ❑ Oct 2000 Cover: 2.50 **NM** value: **Cover or less**
Circ: Diamd. preorders: **19,674**
📖 Revelations, Part 4 **A:** Tom Mandrake **W:** John Ostrander
24 ❑ Nov 2000 Cover: 2.50 **NM** value: **Cover or less**
Circ: Diamd. preorders: **19,202**
📖 Double Stuff **A:** Doug Mahnke **W:** John Ostrander
25 ❑ Dec 2000 Cover: 2.50 **NM** value: **Cover or less**
Circ: Diamd. preorders: **18,942**
📖 Renegades of Mars, Part 1 **A:** Tom Mandrake **W:** John Ostrander
26 ❑ Jan 2001 Cover: 2.50 **NM** value: **Cover or less**
Circ: Diamd. preorders: **18,919**
📖 Renegades of Mars, Part 2 **A:** Tom Mandrake **W:** John Ostrander
27 ❑ Feb 2001 Cover: 2.50 **NM** value: **Cover or less**
Circ: Diamd. preorders: **18,249**
📖 Renegades of Mars, Part 3 **A:** Tom Mandrake **W:** John Ostrander
28 ❑ Mar 2001 Cover: 2.50 **NM** value: **Cover or less**
Circ: Diamd. preorders: **17,456**
📖 Torn Asunder **A:** Tom Mandrake **W:** John Ostrander
29 ❑ Apr 2001 Cover: 2.50 **NM** value: **Cover or less**
Circ: Diamd. preorders: **17,141**
📖 Altered Egos, Part 1 **A:** Tom Mandrake **W:** John Ostrander
30 ❑ May 2001 Cover: 2.50 **NM** value: **Cover or less**
Circ: Diamd. preorders: **16,719**
📖 Altered Egos, Part 2 **A:** Tom Mandrake **W:** John Ostrander
31 ❑ Jun 2001 Cover: 2.50 **NM** value: **Cover or less**
Circ: Diamd. preorders: **16,898**
📖 Altered Egos, Part 3 **A:** Tom Mandrake **W:** John Ostrander
32 ❑ Jul 2001 Cover: 2.50 **NM** value: **Cover or less**
Circ: Diamd. preorders: **16,479**
33 ❑ Aug 2001 Cover: 2.50 **NM** value: **Cover or less**
Circ: Diamd. preorders: **16,711**
34 ❑ Sep 2001 Cover: 2.50 **NM** value: **Cover or less**
Circ: Diamd. preorders: **17,138**
1000000❑Nov 1998 Cover: 1.99 **NM** value: **2.00**
Circ: Diamd. preorders: **39,653**
📖 The Abyss of Time **A:** Tom Mandrake **W:** John Ostrander
Anl 1❑ca. 1998 Cover: 2.95 **NM** value: **Cover or less**
Circ: Diamd. preorders: **29,167**
• Ghosts
Anl 2❑Oct 1999 Cover: 2.95 **NM** value: **Cover or less**
Circ: Diamd. preorders: **24,473**
📖 Fear and Loathing on the Planet of the Apes • JLApe **A:** Gus Vasquez **W:** Len Kaminski

MARTIAN MANHUNTER: AMERICAN SECRETS DC

1 ❑ ca. 1992 Cover: 4.95 **NM** value: **Cover or less**
Circ: CapCity orders: **13,750**
• prestige format. **A:** Eduardo Barreto **W:** Gerald Jones
2 ❑ ca. 1992 Cover: 4.95 **NM** value: **Cover or less**
Circ: CapCity orders: **10,600**
• prestige format. **A:** Eduardo Barreto **W:** Gerald Jones
3 ❑ ca. 1992 Cover: 4.95 **NM** value: **Cover or less**
Circ: CapCity orders: **9,600**
• prestige format. **A:** Eduardo Barreto **W:** Gerald Jones

MARTIAN MANHUNTER (MINI-SERIES) DC

J'onn J'onzz — the Martian Manhunter — first appeared in Detective Comics #225. As we had heard it, J'onn J'onzz was accidentally brought to Earth by Doctor Mark Erdel's Miracle Machine. Once here, he had assumed the guise of a human police officer, "John Jones." As the need arises, however, he can change into his natural green form and use newfound Earth super-powers to fight crime. In this manner, he became one of Earth's better-known super-heroes, frequently appearing with the Justice League of America.

That, at least, is the way we had heard it until now.

J.M. DeMatteis and Mark Badger remade the Manhunter in this four-part series. Here, we find out the true story of Doctor Erdel and J'onn J'onzz, discover the nature of life on Mars, and uncover the real reason why J'onn is afraid of fire.

1 ❑ May 1988 Cover: 1.25 **NM** value: **1.50**
Circ: CapCity orders: **28,800**
📖 Fever Dream **A:** Mark Badger **W:** J.M. DeMatteis ★ Origin of Martian Manhunter.
2 ❑ Jun 1988 Cover: 1.25 **NM** value: **1.50**
Circ: CapCity orders: **21,550**
A: Mark Badger **W:** J.M. DeMatteis
3 ❑ Jul 1988 Cover: 1.25 **NM** value: **1.50**
Circ: CapCity orders: **18,850**
A: Mark Badger **W:** J.M. DeMatteis
4 ❑ Aug 1988 Cover: 1.25 **NM** value: **1.50**
Circ: CapCity orders: **17,200**
📖 Welcome Home **A:** Mark Badger **W:** J.M. DeMatteis

MARTIAN MANHUNTER SPECIAL DC

1 ❑ ca. 1996 Cover: 3.50 **NM** value: **Cover or less**

MARTIN KANE Fox

1 ❑ Jun 1949 Cover: 0.10 **NM** value: **200.00**
2 ❑ Aug 1949 Cover: 0.10 **NM** value: **150.00**

MARTIN MYSTERY Dark Horse

1 ❑ Mar 1999 Cover: 4.95 **NM** value: **Cover or less**
Circ: Diamd. preorders: **6,481**
A: Giancarlo Alessandrini **W:** Alfredo Castelli
2 ❑ Apr 1999 Cover: 4.95 **NM** value: **Cover or less**
Circ: Diamd. preorders: **5,292**
A: Giancarlo Alessandrini **W:** Alfredo Castelli
3 ❑ May 1999 Cover: 4.95 **NM** value: **Cover or less**
Circ: Diamd. preorders: **4,200**
A: Giancarlo Alessandrini **W:** Alfredo Castelli
4 ❑ Jun 1999 Cover: 4.95 **NM** value: **Cover or less**
Circ: Diamd. preorders: **3,822**
A: Giancarlo Alessandrini **W:** Alfredo Castelli
5 ❑ Jul 1999 Cover: 4.95 **NM** value: **Cover or less**
Circ: Diamd. preorders: **3,671**
A: Giancarlo Alessandrini **W:** Alfredo Castelli
6 ❑ Aug 1999 Cover: 4.95 **NM** value: **Cover or less**
Circ: Diamd. preorders: **3,499**
A: Giancarlo Alessandrini **W:** Alfredo Castelli

MARTIN THE SATANIC RACCOON Gabe Martinez

1 ❑ Cover: 1.00 **NM** value: **Cover or less**
📖 Kiss Babies; How to Get Money out of Animal Rights Activists **A:** Gabe Martinez **W:** Gabe Martinez
2 ❑ Cover: 2.00 **NM** value: **Cover or less**
📖 The Sh't Present; Cannibal Corpse **A:** Gabe Martinez **W:** Gabe Martinez

MARVEL ACTION HOUR, FEATURING IRON MAN Marvel

Encouraged by the success of its X-Men Adventures animated series on Saturday morning television, Marvel relaunched its animated Marvel Action Hour in 1994 with segments featuring Iron Man and the Fantastic Four. Dutifully, Marvel followed with series adapting the TV shows.

The Iron Man segment was actually a team-up between Tony Stark (the original Iron Man) and Force Works, a super-hero group comprising War Machine, the Scarlet Witch, Hawkeye, U.S. Agent, a revamped Spider-Woman, and Century. The comics adaptation finds these heroes battling a cast of classic villains such as the Mandarin, Whirlwind, and Fin Fang Foom. The emphasis is on fast-paced action, dispensing with the angst and complicated subplots characteristic of the regular Iron Man series.

The TV series failed, and both comics adaptations went away.

1 ❑ Nov 1994 Cover: 1.50 **NM** value: **Cover or less**
Circ: CapCity orders: **17,750**
📖 The Sea Shall Give Up Its Dead **A:** Anthony Williams **W:** Eric Fein
1/CS❑Nov 1994 Cover: 2.95 **NM** value: **Cover or less**
📖 The Sea Shall Give Up Its Dead • Collector's set: includes animation cel **A:** Anthony Williams **W:** Eric Fein
2 ❑ Dec 1994 Cover: 1.50 **NM** value: **Cover or less**
Circ: CapCity orders: **10,750**
3 ❑ Jan 1995 Cover: 1.50 **NM** value: **Cover or less**
Circ: CapCity orders: **8,825**
📖 Ultimo **A:** Dario Carrasco **W:** Eric Fein
4 ❑ Feb 1995 Cover: 1.50 **NM** value: **Cover or less**
Circ: CapCity orders: **6,725**
5 ❑ Mar 1995 Cover: 1.50 **NM** value: **Cover or less**
Circ: CapCity orders: **4,800**
📖 Origins, Part 1
6 ❑ Apr 1995 Cover: 1.50 **NM** value: **Cover or less**
Circ: CapCity orders: **3,675**
📖 Origins, Part 2 ★ Origin of The Mandarin.
7 ❑ May 1995 Cover: 1.50 **NM** value: **Cover or less**
Circ: CapCity orders: **2,900**
📖 Origins, Part 3
8 ❑ Jun 1995 Cover: 1.50 **NM** value: **Cover or less**
Circ: CapCity orders: **2,675**

MARVEL ACTION HOUR, FEATURING THE FANTASTIC FOUR Marvel

1 ❑ Nov 1994 Cover: 1.50 **NM** value: **Cover or less**
Circ: CapCity orders: **18,550**
📖 How It All Began **A:** Enrique Alcatena **W:** Joey Cavalieri
1/CS❑Nov 1994 Cover: 2.95 **NM** value: **Cover or less**
📖 How It All Began • Collector's set: includes animation cel **A:** Enrique Alcatena **W:** Joey Cavalieri
2 ❑ Dec 1994 Cover: 1.50 **NM** value: **Cover or less**
Circ: CapCity orders: **1,800**
A: Enrique Alcatena **W:** Joey Cavalieri
3 ❑ Jan 1995 Cover: 1.50 **NM** value: **Cover or less**
Circ: CapCity orders: **9,550**
A: Enrique Alcatena **W:** Joey Cavalieri
4 ❑ Feb 1995 Cover: 1.50 **NM** value: **Cover or less**
Circ: CapCity orders: **7,125**
A: Enrique Alcatena **W:** Joey Cavalieri
5 ❑ Mar 1995 Cover: 1.50 **NM** value: **Cover or less**
Circ: CapCity orders: **5,050**
A: Enrique Alcatena **W:** Joey Cavalieri
6 ❑ Apr 1995 Cover: 1.50 **NM** value: **Cover or less**
Circ: CapCity orders: **3,875**
A: Enrique Alcatena **W:** Joey Cavalieri
7 ❑ May 1995 Cover: 1.50 **NM** value: **Cover or less**
Circ: CapCity orders: **3,050**
A: Enrique Alcatena **W:** Joey Cavalieri
8 ❑ Jun 1995 Cover: 1.50 **NM** value: **Cover or less**
Circ: CapCity orders: **2,750**
A: Enrique Alcatena **W:** Joey Cavalieri

MARVEL ACTION UNIVERSE Marvel

1 ❑ Jan 1989 Cover: 1.00 **NM** value: **Cover or less**
Circ: CapCity orders: **10,300**
📖 The Triumph of the Green Goblin • Reprints Spider-Man and His Amazing Friends #1 **A:** Dan Spiegle **W:** Dennis Marks

MARVEL ADVENTURE Marvel

1 ❑ Dec 1975 Cover: 0.25 **NM** value: **3.00**
• **CGC:** 1 graded, best 9.4
📖 The Tri-Man Lives! • Reprints Daredevil #22 **A:** Gene Colan **W:** Stan Lee
2 ❑ Feb 1976 Cover: 0.25 **NM** value: **2.00**
• Reprints Daredevil #23
3 ❑ Apr 1976 Cover: 0.25 **NM** value: **2.00**
• Reprints Daredevil #24
4 ❑ Jun 1976 Cover: 0.25 **NM** value: **2.00**
• Reprints Daredevil #25
5 ❑ Aug 1976 Cover: 0.25 **NM** value: **2.00**
• Reprints Daredevil #26
6 ❑ Oct 1976 Cover: 0.30 **NM** value: **2.00**
• Reprints Daredevil #27

MARVEL ADVENTURES Marvel

1 ❑ Apr 1997 Cover: 1.50 **NM** value: **Cover or less**
Circ: Statement: **203,756** Direct Market orders: **25,000**
📖 A Titan in Torment! **A:** Andy Kuhn **W:** Ralph Macchio ★ Appearance of Hulk. ★ Versus Leader. ★ Versus Abomination.
2 ❑ May 1997 Cover: 1.50 **NM** value: **Cover or less**
Circ: Statement: **203,756** Diamd. preorders: **20,031**
📖 The Name of the Game **A:** Ben Herrera **W:** Ralph Macchio ★ Appearance of Spider-Man. ★ Versus Scorpion.
3 ❑ Jun 1997 Cover: 1.50 **NM** value: **Cover or less**
Circ: Statement: **203,756** Diamd. preorders: **19,127**
📖 Hexed **A:** Ben Herrera **W:** Ralph Macchio ★ Appearance of X-Men. ★ Versus Magneto.
4 ❑ Jul 1997 Cover: 1.50 **NM** value: **Cover or less**
Circ: Statement: **203,756** Diamd. preorders: **14,326**
★ Appearance of Hulk. ★ Versus Brotherhood of Evil Mutants.
5 ❑ Aug 1997 Cover: 1.50 **NM** value: **Cover or less**
Circ: Statement: **203,756** Diamd. preorders: **13,061**
★ Appearance of X-Men, Spider-Man. ★ Versus Abomination. ★ Versus Magneto.
6 ❑ Sep 1997 Cover: 1.50 **NM** value: **Cover or less**
Circ: Statement: **203,756** Diamd. preorders: **11,237**
★ Appearance of Torch, Spider-Man. ★ Versus Lava Men.
7 ❑ Oct 1997 Cover: 1.50 **NM** value: **Cover or less**
Circ: Statement: **203,756** Diamd. preorders: **9,788**
★ Appearance of Hulk. ★ Versus Tyrannus.
8 ❑ Nov 1997 Cover: 1.50 **NM** value: **Cover or less**
Circ: Diamd. preorders: **10,765**
★ Appearance of X-Men.
9 ❑ Dec 1997 Cover: 1.50 **NM** value: **Cover or less**
Circ: Diamd. preorders: **9,116**
★ Appearance of Fantastic Four.
10 ❑ Jan 1998 Cover: 1.50 **NM** value: **Cover or less**
Circ: Diamd. preorders: **8,286**
• Has 1997 Statement, filed 10/1/97; avg print run 213,133; avg sales 104,472; avg subs 99,284 (Alert: Reported subscription numbers are VERY high; regard with caution); avg total paid 203,756; samples 600; office use 125; max existent 204,481; 4% of run returned ★ Appearance of Silver Surfer. ★ Versus Gladiator.
11 ❑ Feb 1998 Cover: 1.50 **NM** value: **Cover or less**
Circ: Diamd. preorders: **7,779**
★ Appearance of Spider-Man. ★ Versus Sandman.
12 ❑ Mar 1998 Cover: 1.50 **NM** value: **Cover or less**
Circ: Diamd. preorders: **6,969**
13 ❑ Apr 1998 Cover: 1.50 **NM** value: **Cover or less**
Circ: Diamd. preorders: **7,078**
14 ❑ May 1998 Cover: 1.50 **NM** value: **Cover or less**
Circ: Diamd. preorders: **6,525**
★ Appearance of Hulk, Doctor Strange, Juggernaut.
15 ❑ Jun 1998 Cover: 1.50 **NM** value: **Cover or less**
Circ: Diamd. preorders: **7,532**
★ Appearance of Wolverine.
16 ❑ Jul 1998 Cover: 1.50 **NM** value: **Cover or less**
Circ: Diamd. preorders: **6,193**
★ Appearance of Silver Surfer. ★ Versus Skrulls.
17 ❑ Aug 1998 Cover: 1.50 **NM** value: **Cover or less**
Circ: Diamd. preorders: **6,945**
★ Appearance of Iron Man, Spider-Man. ★ Versus Grey Gargoyle.
18 ❑ Sep 1998 Cover: 1.50 **NM** value: **Cover or less**
Circ: Diamd. preorders: **6,327**
final issue.

Other grades: Multiply prices above by **1.5 for Mint • 2/3 for Very Fine • 1/3 for Fine • 1/5 for Very Good • 1/8 for Good**

MARVEL AGE Marvel

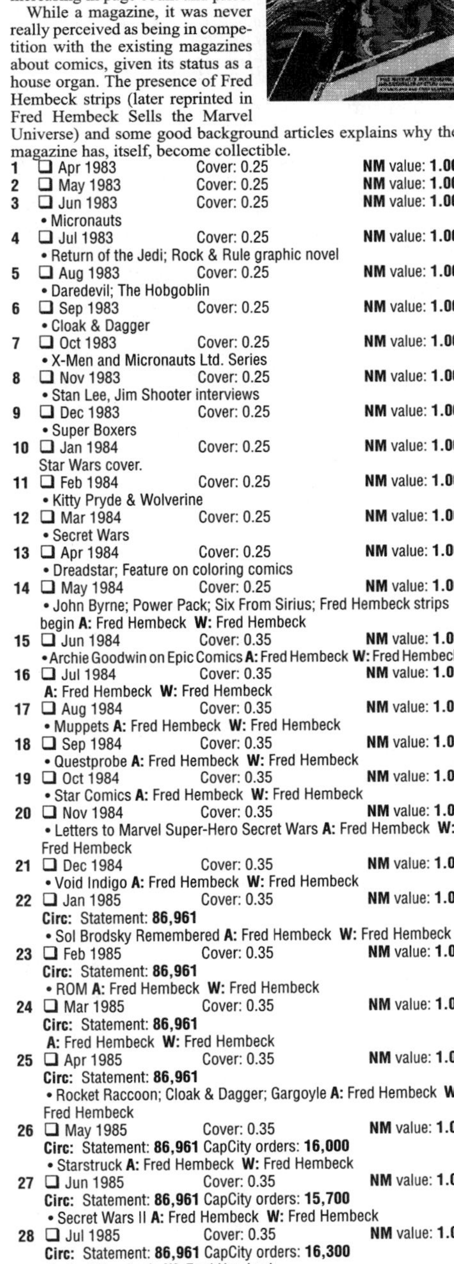

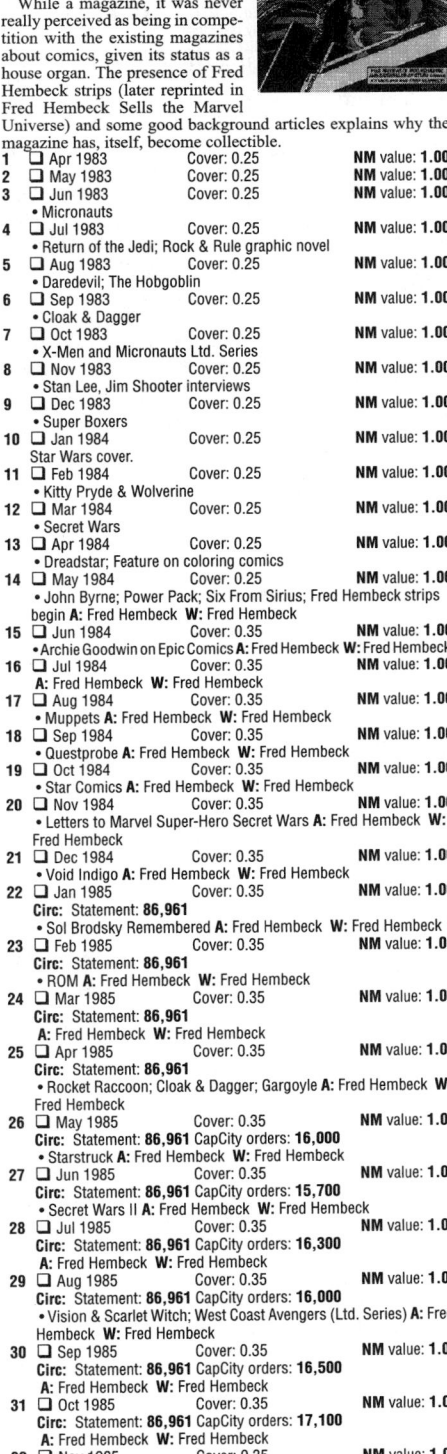

Not a comic book but included here because of its massive distribution by the largest comics publisher, Marvel Age served as Marvel's carnival barker in the 1980s and early 1990s, announcing new projects and information from behind-the-scenes. The first 16-page comic-book sized issue was priced to move at 25 cents, with later issues increasing in page count and price.

While a magazine, it was never really perceived as being in competition with the existing magazines about comics, given its status as a house organ. The presence of Fred Hembeck strips (later reprinted in Fred Hembeck Sells the Marvel Universe) and some good background articles explains why the magazine has, itself, become collectible.

1 ❑ Apr 1983 Cover: 0.25 **NM** value: **1.00**
2 ❑ May 1983 Cover: 0.25 **NM** value: **1.00**
3 ❑ Jun 1983 Cover: 0.25 **NM** value: **1.00**
• Micronauts
4 ❑ Jul 1983 Cover: 0.25 **NM** value: **1.00**
• Return of the Jedi; Rock & Rule graphic novel
5 ❑ Aug 1983 Cover: 0.25 **NM** value: **1.00**
• Daredevil; The Hobgoblin
6 ❑ Sep 1983 Cover: 0.25 **NM** value: **1.00**
• Cloak & Dagger
7 ❑ Oct 1983 Cover: 0.25 **NM** value: **1.00**
• X-Men and Micronauts Ltd. Series
8 ❑ Nov 1983 Cover: 0.25 **NM** value: **1.00**
• Stan Lee, Jim Shooter interviews
9 ❑ Dec 1983 Cover: 0.25 **NM** value: **1.00**
• Super Boxers
10 ❑ Jan 1984 Cover: 0.25 **NM** value: **1.00**
Star Wars cover.
11 ❑ Feb 1984 Cover: 0.25 **NM** value: **1.00**
• Kitty Pryde & Wolverine
12 ❑ Mar 1984 Cover: 0.25 **NM** value: **1.00**
• Secret Wars
13 ❑ Apr 1984 Cover: 0.25 **NM** value: **1.00**
• Dreadstar; Feature on coloring comics
14 ❑ May 1984 Cover: 0.25 **NM** value: **1.00**
• John Byrne; Power Pack; Six From Sirius; Fred Hembeck strips begin **A:** Fred Hembeck **W:** Fred Hembeck
15 ❑ Jun 1984 Cover: 0.35 **NM** value: **1.00**
• Archie Goodwin on Epic Comics **A:** Fred Hembeck **W:** Fred Hembeck
16 ❑ Jul 1984 Cover: 0.35 **NM** value: **1.00**
A: Fred Hembeck **W:** Fred Hembeck
17 ❑ Aug 1984 Cover: 0.35 **NM** value: **1.00**
• Muppets **A:** Fred Hembeck **W:** Fred Hembeck
18 ❑ Sep 1984 Cover: 0.35 **NM** value: **1.00**
• Questprobe **A:** Fred Hembeck **W:** Fred Hembeck
19 ❑ Oct 1984 Cover: 0.35 **NM** value: **1.00**
• Star Comics **A:** Fred Hembeck **W:** Fred Hembeck
20 ❑ Nov 1984 Cover: 0.35 **NM** value: **1.00**
• Letters to Marvel Super-Hero Secret Wars **A:** Fred Hembeck **W:** Fred Hembeck
21 ❑ Dec 1984 Cover: 0.35 **NM** value: **1.00**
• Void Indigo **A:** Fred Hembeck **W:** Fred Hembeck
22 ❑ Jan 1985 Cover: 0.35 **NM** value: **1.00**
Circ: Statement: **86,961**
• Sol Brodsky Remembered **A:** Fred Hembeck **W:** Fred Hembeck
23 ❑ Feb 1985 Cover: 0.35 **NM** value: **1.00**
Circ: Statement: **86,961**
• ROM **A:** Fred Hembeck **W:** Fred Hembeck
24 ❑ Mar 1985 Cover: 0.35 **NM** value: **1.00**
Circ: Statement: **86,961**
A: Fred Hembeck **W:** Fred Hembeck
25 ❑ Apr 1985 Cover: 0.35 **NM** value: **1.00**
Circ: Statement: **86,961**
• Rocket Raccoon; Cloak & Dagger; Gargoyle **A:** Fred Hembeck **W:** Fred Hembeck
26 ❑ May 1985 Cover: 0.35 **NM** value: **1.00**
Circ: Statement: **86,961** CapCity orders: **16,000**
• Starstruck **A:** Fred Hembeck **W:** Fred Hembeck
27 ❑ Jun 1985 Cover: 0.35 **NM** value: **1.00**
Circ: Statement: **86,961** CapCity orders: **15,700**
• Secret Wars II **A:** Fred Hembeck **W:** Fred Hembeck
28 ❑ Jul 1985 Cover: 0.35 **NM** value: **1.00**
Circ: Statement: **86,961** CapCity orders: **16,300**
A: Fred Hembeck **W:** Fred Hembeck
29 ❑ Aug 1985 Cover: 0.35 **NM** value: **1.00**
Circ: Statement: **86,961** CapCity orders: **16,000**
• Vision & Scarlet Witch; West Coast Avengers (Ltd. Series) **A:** Fred Hembeck **W:** Fred Hembeck
30 ❑ Sep 1985 Cover: 0.35 **NM** value: **1.00**
Circ: Statement: **86,961** CapCity orders: **16,500**
A: Fred Hembeck **W:** Fred Hembeck
31 ❑ Oct 1985 Cover: 0.35 **NM** value: **1.00**
Circ: Statement: **86,961** CapCity orders: **17,100**
A: Fred Hembeck **W:** Fred Hembeck
32 ❑ Nov 1985 Cover: 0.35 **NM** value: **1.00**
Circ: Statement: **86,961** CapCity orders: **18,300**
A: Arthur Adams; Fred Hembeck **W:** Fred Hembeck
33 ❑ Dec 1985 Cover: 0.35 **NM** value: **1.00**
Circ: Statement: **86,961** CapCity orders: **18,400**
• X-Factor **A:** Fred Hembeck **W:** Fred Hembeck
34 ❑ Jan 1986 Cover: 0.35 **NM** value: **1.00**
Circ: Statement: **91,483** CapCity orders: **18,300**
• G.I. Joes **A:** Fred Hembeck **W:** Fred Hembeck
35 ❑ Feb 1986 Cover: 0.35 **NM** value: **1.00**
Circ: Statement: **91,483** CapCity orders: **19,900**
• A Day in the Life of Marvel Comics **A:** Fred Hembeck **W:** Fred Hembeck
36 ❑ Mar 1986 Cover: 0.35 **NM** value: **1.00**
Circ: Statement: **91,483** CapCity orders: **20,900**
A: Fred Hembeck **W:** Fred Hembeck
37 ❑ Apr 1986 Cover: 0.35 **NM** value: **1.00**
Circ: Statement: **91,483** CapCity orders: **21,500**
A: Fred Hembeck **W:** Fred Hembeck
38 ❑ May 1986 Cover: 0.35 **NM** value: **1.00**
Circ: Statement: **91,483** CapCity orders: **20,750**
• He-Man **A:** Fred Hembeck **W:** Fred Hembeck
39 ❑ Jun 1986 Cover: 0.35 **NM** value: **1.00**
Circ: Statement: **91,483** CapCity orders: **21,600**
• Has 1985 Statement, filed 10/1/1985; avg print run 88,681; avg sales 85,291; avg subs 1,670; avg total paid 86,961; samples 100; office use 1,620; max existent 88,681; no newsstand sales **A:** Fred Hembeck **W:** Fred Hembeck
40 ❑ Jul 1986 Cover: 0.35 **NM** value: **1.00**
Circ: Statement: **91,483** CapCity orders: **21,100**
A: Fred Hembeck **W:** Fred Hembeck
41 ❑ Aug 1986 Cover: 0.50 **NM** value: **1.00**
Circ: Statement: **91,483** CapCity orders: **19,200**
A: Fred Hembeck **W:** Fred Hembeck
42 ❑ Sep 1986 Cover: 0.50 **NM** value: **1.00**
Circ: Statement: **91,483** CapCity orders: **18,600**
A: Fred Hembeck **W:** Fred Hembeck
43 ❑ Oct 1986 Cover: 0.50 **NM** value: **1.00**
Circ: Statement: **91,483** CapCity orders: **19,100**
A: Fred Hembeck **W:** Fred Hembeck
44 ❑ Nov 1986 Cover: 0.50 **NM** value: **1.00**
Circ: Statement: **91,483** CapCity orders: **20,000**
A: Fred Hembeck **W:** Fred Hembeck
45 ❑ Dec 1986 Cover: 0.50 **NM** value: **1.00**
Circ: Statement: **91,483** CapCity orders: **19,200**
A: Fred Hembeck **W:** Fred Hembeck
46 ❑ Jan 1987 Cover: 0.50 **NM** value: **1.00**
Circ: Statement: **82,042** CapCity orders: **18,800**
A: Fred Hembeck **W:** Fred Hembeck
47 ❑ Feb 1987 Cover: 0.50 **NM** value: **1.00**
Circ: Statement: **82,042** CapCity orders: **19,400**
A: Fred Hembeck **W:** Fred Hembeck
48 ❑ Mar 1987 Cover: 0.50 **NM** value: **1.00**
Circ: Statement: **82,042** CapCity orders: **16,700**
A: Fred Hembeck **W:** Fred Hembeck
49 ❑ Apr 1987 Cover: 0.50 **NM** value: **1.00**
Circ: Statement: **82,042** CapCity orders: **16,600**
• Has 1986 Statement, filed 10/6/86; avg print run 94,408; avg sales 88,258; avg subs 2,625; avg total paid 91,483; samples 1,487; office use 1,438; max existent 94,408; no newsstand sales **A:** Fred Hembeck **W:** Fred Hembeck
50 ❑ May 1987 Cover: 0.50 **NM** value: **1.00**
Circ: Statement: **82,042** CapCity orders: **15,500**
A: Fred Hembeck **W:** Fred Hembeck
51 ❑ Jun 1987 Cover: 0.50 **NM** value: **1.00**
Circ: Statement: **82,042** CapCity orders: **14,900**
A: Fred Hembeck **W:** Fred Hembeck
52 ❑ Jul 1987 Cover: 0.50 **NM** value: **1.00**
Circ: Statement: **82,042** CapCity orders: **14,200**
A: Fred Hembeck **W:** Fred Hembeck
53 ❑ Aug 1987 Cover: 0.50 **NM** value: **1.00**
Circ: Statement: **82,042** CapCity orders: **14,700**
A: Fred Hembeck **W:** Fred Hembeck
54 ❑ Sep 1987 Cover: 0.50 **NM** value: **1.00**
Circ: Statement: **82,042** CapCity orders: **17,200**
• Spider-Man wedding **A:** Fred Hembeck **W:** Fred Hembeck
55 ❑ Oct 1987 Cover: 0.50 **NM** value: **1.00**
Circ: Statement: **82,042** CapCity orders: **16,100**
A: Fred Hembeck **W:** Fred Hembeck
56 ❑ Nov 1987 Cover: 0.50 **NM** value: **1.00**
Circ: Statement: **82,042** CapCity orders: **16,200**
A: Fred Hembeck **W:** Fred Hembeck
57 ❑ Dec 1987 Cover: 0.50 **NM** value: **1.00**
Circ: Statement: **82,042** CapCity orders: **15,100**
A: Fred Hembeck **W:** Fred Hembeck
58 ❑ Jan 1988 Cover: 0.50 **NM** value: **1.00**
Circ: Statement: **68,000** CapCity orders: **17,100**
A: Fred Hembeck **W:** Fred Hembeck
59 ❑ Feb 1988 Cover: 0.50 **NM** value: **1.00**
Circ: Statement: **68,000** CapCity orders: **16,700**
A: Fred Hembeck **W:** Fred Hembeck
60 ❑ Mar 1988 Cover: 0.50 **NM** value: **1.00**
Circ: Statement: **68,000** CapCity orders: **19,500**
A: Fred Hembeck **W:** Fred Hembeck
61 ❑ Apr 1988 Cover: 0.50 **NM** value: **1.00**
Circ: Statement: **68,000** CapCity orders: **19,000**
A: Fred Hembeck **W:** Fred Hembeck
62 ❑ May 1988 Cover: 0.50 **NM** value: **1.00**
Circ: Statement: **68,000** CapCity orders: **17,800**
A: Fred Hembeck **W:** Fred Hembeck
63 ❑ Jun 1988 Cover: 0.50 **NM** value: **1.00**
Circ: Statement: **68,000** CapCity orders: **17,400**
A: Fred Hembeck **W:** Fred Hembeck
64 ❑ Jul 1988 Cover: 0.50 **NM** value: **1.00**
Circ: Statement: **68,000** CapCity orders: **16,800**
A: Fred Hembeck **W:** Fred Hembeck
65 ❑ Aug 1988 Cover: 0.50 **NM** value: **1.00**
Circ: Statement: **68,000** CapCity orders: **17,000**
A: Fred Hembeck **W:** Fred Hembeck
66 ❑ Sep 1988 Cover: 0.50 **NM** value: **1.00**
Circ: Statement: **68,000** CapCity orders: **18,000**
A: Fred Hembeck **W:** Fred Hembeck
67 ❑ Oct 1988 Cover: 0.50 **NM** value: **1.00**
Circ: Statement: **68,000** CapCity orders: **18,500**
A: Fred Hembeck **W:** Fred Hembeck
68 ❑ Nov 1988 Cover: 0.50 **NM** value: **1.00**
Circ: Statement: **68,000** CapCity orders: **18,100**
A: Fred Hembeck **W:** Fred Hembeck
69 ❑ Dec 1988 Cover: 0.50 **NM** value: **1.00**
Circ: Statement: **68,000** CapCity orders: **17,100**
A: Fred Hembeck **W:** Fred Hembeck
70 ❑ Jan 1989 Cover: 0.50 **NM** value: **1.00**
Circ: Statement: **65,900** CapCity orders: **17,700**
A: Fred Hembeck **W:** Fred Hembeck
71 ❑ Feb 1989 Cover: 0.50 **NM** value: **1.00**
Circ: Statement: **65,900** CapCity orders: **17,000**
A: Fred Hembeck **W:** Fred Hembeck
72 ❑ Mar 1989 Cover: 0.50 **NM** value: **1.00**
Circ: Statement: **65,900** CapCity orders: **17,800**
A: Fred Hembeck **W:** Fred Hembeck
73 ❑ Apr 1989 Cover: 0.50 **NM** value: **1.00**
Circ: Statement: **65,900** CapCity orders: **17,500**
A: Fred Hembeck **W:** Fred Hembeck
74 ❑ May 1989 Cover: 0.50 **NM** value: **1.00**
Circ: Statement: **65,900** CapCity orders: **16,900**
A: Fred Hembeck **W:** Fred Hembeck
75 ❑ Jun 1989 Cover: 0.50 **NM** value: **1.00**
Circ: Statement: **65,900** CapCity orders: **16,950**
A: Fred Hembeck **W:** Fred Hembeck
76 ❑ Jul 1989 Cover: 0.50 **NM** value: **1.00**
Circ: Statement: **65,900** CapCity orders: **17,700**
• Atlantis Attacks **A:** Fred Hembeck **W:** Fred Hembeck
77 ❑ Aug 1989 Cover: 0.50 **NM** value: **1.00**
Circ: Statement: **65,900** CapCity orders: **17,800**
A: Fred Hembeck **W:** Fred Hembeck
78 ❑ Sep 1989 Cover: 0.50 **NM** value: **1.00**
Circ: Statement: **65,900** CapCity orders: **17,500**
A: Fred Hembeck **W:** Fred Hembeck
79 ❑ Oct 1989 Cover: 0.75 **NM** value: **1.00**
Circ: Statement: **65,900** CapCity orders: **17,100**
A: Fred Hembeck **W:** Fred Hembeck
80 ❑ Nov 1989 Cover: 0.75 **NM** value: **1.00**
Circ: Statement: **65,900** CapCity orders: **16,700**
A: Fred Hembeck **W:** Fred Hembeck
81 ❑ Nov 1989 Cover: 0.75 **NM** value: **1.00**
Circ: Statement: **65,900** CapCity orders: **16,400**
A: Fred Hembeck **W:** Fred Hembeck
82 ❑ Dec 1989 Cover: 0.75 **NM** value: **1.00**
Circ: Statement: **65,900** CapCity orders: **15,400**
• Squadron Supreme **A:** Fred Hembeck **W:** Fred Hembeck
83 ❑ Dec 1989 Cover: 0.75 **NM** value: **1.00**
Circ: Statement: **65,900** CapCity orders: **15,300**
A: Fred Hembeck **W:** Fred Hembeck
84 ❑ Jan 1990 Cover: 0.75 **NM** value: **1.00**
Circ: Statement: **96,678** CapCity orders: **16,600**
A: Fred Hembeck **W:** Fred Hembeck
85 ❑ Feb 1990 Cover: 0.75 **NM** value: **1.00**
Circ: Statement: **96,678** CapCity orders: **16,400**
A: Fred Hembeck **W:** Fred Hembeck
86 ❑ Mar 1990 Cover: 1.00 **NM** value: **Cover or less**
Circ: Statement: **96,678** CapCity orders: **15,900**
A: Fred Hembeck **W:** Fred Hembeck
87 ❑ Apr 1990 Cover: 1.00 **NM** value: **Cover or less**
Circ: Statement: **96,678** CapCity orders: **14,200**
A: Fred Hembeck **W:** Fred Hembeck
88 ❑ May 1990 Cover: 1.00 **NM** value: **Cover or less**
Circ: Statement: **96,678** CapCity orders: **13,800**
• Guardians of the Galaxy; Has 1989 Statement, filed 11/1/89; avg print run 66,625; avg sales 64,600; avg subs 1,300; avg total paid 65,900; samples 125; office use 600; max existent 66,500; no newsstand sales **A:** Fred Hembeck **W:** Fred Hembeck
89 ❑ Jun 1990 Cover: 1.00 **NM** value: **Cover or less**
Circ: Statement: **96,678** CapCity orders: **13,800**
A: Fred Hembeck **W:** Fred Hembeck
90 ❑ Jul 1990 Cover: 1.00 **NM** value: **Cover or less**
Circ: Statement: **96,678** CapCity orders: **17,000**
A: Fred Hembeck **W:** Fred Hembeck
91 ❑ Aug 1990 Cover: 1.00 **NM** value: **Cover or less**
Circ: Statement: **96,678** CapCity orders: **13,600**
A: Fred Hembeck **W:** Fred Hembeck
92 ❑ Sep 1990 Cover: 1.00 **NM** value: **Cover or less**
Circ: Statement: **96,678** CapCity orders: **13,500**
A: Fred Hembeck **W:** Fred Hembeck
93 ❑ Oct 1990 Cover: 1.00 **NM** value: **Cover or less**
Circ: Statement: **96,678** CapCity orders: **13,200**
A: Fred Hembeck **W:** Fred Hembeck
94 ❑ Nov 1990 Cover: 1.00 **NM** value: **Cover or less**
Circ: Statement: **96,678** CapCity orders: **12,700**
A: Fred Hembeck **W:** Fred Hembeck
95 ❑ Dec 1990 Cover: 1.00 **NM** value: **Cover or less**
Circ: Statement: **96,678** CapCity orders: **13,400**
• Captain America issue **A:** Fred Hembeck **W:** Fred Hembeck
96 ❑ Jan 1991 Cover: 1.00 **NM** value: **Cover or less**
Circ: CapCity orders: **12,900**
A: Fred Hembeck **W:** Fred Hembeck
97 ❑ Feb 1991 Cover: 1.00 **NM** value: **Cover or less**
Circ: CapCity orders: **12,700**
A: Fred Hembeck **W:** Fred Hembeck
98 ❑ Mar 1991 Cover: 1.00 **NM** value: **Cover or less**
Circ: CapCity orders: **11,800**
A: Fred Hembeck **W:** Fred Hembeck
99 ❑ Apr 1991 Cover: 1.00 **NM** value: **Cover or less**
Circ: CapCity orders: **11,100**
A: Fred Hembeck **W:** Fred Hembeck

CGC-graded: Multiply prices above by **33 for 9.9 M • 16 for 9.8 NM/M • 7 for 9.6 NM+ • 5 for 9.4 NM • 2.5 for 9.2 NM- • 1.5 for 9.0 VF/NM**

100 ❑ May 1991 Cover: 1.00 **NM** value: **Cover or less**
Circ: CapCity orders: **15,100**
A: Fred Hembeck **W:** Fred Hembeck

101 ❑ Jun 1991 Cover: 1.00 **NM** value: **Cover or less**
Circ: CapCity orders: **11,200**
A: Fred Hembeck **W:** Fred Hembeck

102 ❑ Jul 1991 Cover: 1.00 **NM** value: **Cover or less**
Circ: CapCity orders: **10,500**
A: Fred Hembeck **W:** Fred Hembeck

103 ❑ Aug 1991 Cover: 1.00 **NM** value: **Cover or less**
Circ: CapCity orders: **10,500**
A: Fred Hembeck **W:** Fred Hembeck

104 ❑ Sep 1991 Cover: 1.00 **NM** value: **Cover or less**
Circ: CapCity orders: **13,100**
A: Fred Hembeck **W:** Fred Hembeck

105 ❑ Oct 1991 Cover: 1.00 **NM** value: **Cover or less**
Circ: CapCity orders: **10,900**
A: Fred Hembeck **W:** Fred Hembeck

106 ❑ Nov 1991 Cover: 1.00 **NM** value: **Cover or less**
Circ: CapCity orders: **10,200**
A: Fred Hembeck **W:** Fred Hembeck

107 ❑ Dec 1991 Cover: 1.00 **NM** value: **Cover or less**
Circ: CapCity orders: **11,000**
A: Fred Hembeck **W:** Fred Hembeck

108 ❑ Jan 1992 Cover: 1.00 **NM** value: **Cover or less**
Circ: Statement: **81,567** CapCity orders: **10,700**
A: Fred Hembeck **W:** Fred Hembeck

109 ❑ Feb 1992 Cover: 1.00 **NM** value: **Cover or less**
Circ: Statement: **81,567** CapCity orders: **9,800**
A: Fred Hembeck **W:** Fred Hembeck

110 ❑ Mar 1992 Cover: 1.00 **NM** value: **Cover or less**
Circ: Statement: **81,567** CapCity orders: **9,100**
A: Fred Hembeck **W:** Fred Hembeck

111 ❑ Apr 1992 Cover: 1.00 **NM** value: **Cover or less**
Circ: Statement: **81,567** CapCity orders: **8,200**
A: Fred Hembeck **W:** Fred Hembeck

112 ❑ May 1992 Cover: 1.00 **NM** value: **Cover or less**
Circ: Statement: **81,567** CapCity orders: **8,100**
A: Fred Hembeck **W:** Fred Hembeck

113 ❑ Jun 1992 Cover: 1.00 **NM** value: **Cover or less**
Circ: Statement: **81,567** CapCity orders: **8,200**
A: Fred Hembeck **W:** Fred Hembeck

114 ❑ Jul 1992 Cover: 1.00 **NM** value: **Cover or less**
Circ: Statement: **81,567** CapCity orders: **8,400**
• Spider-Man's 30th anniversary. **A:** Fred Hembeck **W:** Fred Hembeck

115 ❑ Aug 1992 Cover: 1.00 **NM** value: **Cover or less**
Circ: Statement: **81,567** CapCity orders: **8,700**
A: Fred Hembeck **W:** Fred Hembeck

116 ❑ Sep 1992 Cover: 1.00 **NM** value: **Cover or less**
Circ: Statement: **81,567** CapCity orders: **9,600**
• X-Men **A:** Fred Hembeck **W:** Fred Hembeck

117 ❑ Oct 1992 Cover: 1.00 **NM** value: **Cover or less**
Circ: Statement: **81,567** CapCity orders: **10,300**
• 2099 **A:** Fred Hembeck **W:** Fred Hembeck

118 ❑ Nov 1992 Cover: 1.50 **NM** value: **Cover or less**
Circ: Statement: **81,567** CapCity orders: **45,800**
• with card **A:** Fred Hembeck **W:** Fred Hembeck

119 ❑ Dec 1992 Cover: 1.00 **NM** value: **Cover or less**
Circ: Statement: **81,567** CapCity orders: **9,300**
A: Fred Hembeck **W:** Fred Hembeck

120 ❑ Jan 1993 Cover: 1.00 **NM** value: **Cover or less**
Circ: CapCity orders: **10,000**
A: Fred Hembeck **W:** Fred Hembeck

121 ❑ Feb 1993 Cover: 1.00 **NM** value: **Cover or less**
Circ: CapCity orders: **9,600**
• Ren & Stimpy **A:** Fred Hembeck **W:** Fred Hembeck

122 ❑ Mar 1993 Cover: 1.00 **NM** value: **Cover or less**
Circ: CapCity orders: **9,600**
A: Fred Hembeck **W:** Fred Hembeck

123 ❑ Apr 1993 Cover: 1.00 **NM** value: **Cover or less**
Circ: CapCity orders: **11,000**
A: Fred Hembeck **W:** Fred Hembeck

124 ❑ May 1993 Cover: 1.00 **NM** value: **Cover or less**
Circ: CapCity orders: **9,900**
A: Fred Hembeck **W:** Fred Hembeck

125 ❑ Jun 1993 Cover: 1.00 **NM** value: **Cover or less**
Circ: CapCity orders: **10,500**
A: Fred Hembeck **W:** Fred Hembeck

126 ❑ Jul 1993 Cover: 1.00 **NM** value: **Cover or less**
Circ: CapCity orders: **9,500**
A: Fred Hembeck **W:** Fred Hembeck

127 ❑ Aug 1993 Cover: 1.00 **NM** value: **Cover or less**
A: Fred Hembeck **W:** Fred Hembeck

128 ❑ Sep 1993 Cover: 1.00 **NM** value: **Cover or less**
Circ: CapCity orders: **8,900**
A: Fred Hembeck **W:** Fred Hembeck

129 ❑ Oct 1993 Cover: 1.00 **NM** value: **1.25**
Circ: CapCity orders: **8,850**
X-Men/Avengers cover. • Flip-book. • 1/2 X-Men/Avengers crossover poster; Biker Mice from Mars preview; Hellraiser/Marshal Law preview; Heavy Hitters Preview **A:** Fred Hembeck; Adam Hughes(cover); George Pérez(cover) **W:** Fred Hembeck

130 ❑ Nov 1993 Cover: 1.25 **NM** value: **Cover or less**
Circ: CapCity orders: **8,650**
• Marvels; poster **A:** Fred Hembeck **W:** Fred Hembeck

131 ❑ Dec 1993 Cover: 1.00 **NM** value: **1.25**
Circ: CapCity orders: **7,850**
• Excalibur **A:** Adam Kubert; Fred Hembeck; Andy Kubert **W:** Fred Hembeck

132 ❑ Jan 1994 Cover: 1.00 **NM** value: **1.25**
Circ: CapCity orders: **7,850**
• Force Works, ClanDestine **A:** Fred Hembeck **W:** Fred Hembeck

133 ❑ Feb 1994 Cover: 1.00 **NM** value: **1.25**
Circ: CapCity orders: **9,100**
• X-Wedding, War Machine; Has 1992 Statement, filed 10/1/93; avg print run 159,567; avg sales 81,142; avg subs 425; avg total paid 81,567; samples 125; office use 500; max existent 82,067; 49% of run returned **A:** Fred Hembeck **W:** Fred Hembeck

134 ❑ Mar 1994 Cover: 1.00 **NM** value: **1.50**
Circ: CapCity orders: **11,950**
• Beavis & Butt-Head **A:** Fred Hembeck **W:** Fred Hembeck

135 ❑ Apr 1994 Cover: 1.25 **NM** value: **Cover or less**
Circ: CapCity orders: **6,450**
• Ghost Rider 2099; Conan the Adventurer **A:** Fred Hembeck **W:** Fred Hembeck

136 ❑ May 1994 Cover: 1.25 **NM** value: **Cover or less**
Circ: CapCity orders: **6,400**
A: Fred Hembeck **W:** Fred Hembeck

137 ❑ Jun 1994 Cover: 1.50 **NM** value: **Cover or less**
Circ: CapCity orders: **7,500**
A: Fred Hembeck **W:** Fred Hembeck

138 ❑ Jul 1994 Cover: 1.25 **NM** value: **1.50**
Circ: CapCity orders: **6,050**
• Giant-size. • remembering Jack Kirby; Spider-Man Animated Series, Blaze **A:** Fred Hembeck **W:** Fred Hembeck

139 ❑ Aug 1994 Cover: 1.25 **NM** value: **Cover or less**
Circ: CapCity orders: **6,000**
• Batman and the Punisher **A:** Fred Hembeck **W:** Fred Hembeck

140 ❑ Sep 1994 Cover: 1.25 **NM** value: **Cover or less**
Circ: CapCity orders: **5,500**
final issue. • Marvel Action Hour **A:** Fred Hembeck **W:** Fred Hembeck

Anl 1 ❑ Sep 1985 Cover: 0.50 **NM** value: **1.00**
Circ: CapCity orders: **18,400**

Anl 2 ❑ Sep 1986 Cover: 0.50 **NM** value: **1.00**
Circ: CapCity orders: **16,600**

Anl 3 ❑ Sep 1987 Cover: 0.75 **NM** value: **1.00**
Circ: CapCity orders: **18,300**
A: Fred Hembeck; John Buscema; Tony DeZuniga; Marshall Rogers

Anl 4 ❑ Sep 1988 Cover: 0.75 **NM** value: **1.00**
Circ: CapCity orders: **23,400**
• Wolverine

MARVEL AGE PREVIEW — Marvel

1 ❑ Apr 1990 Cover: 1.50 **NM** value: **Cover or less**
Circ: CapCity orders: **18,000**

2 ❑ Cover: 2.25 **NM** value: **Cover or less**

MARVEL AND DC PRESENT — Marvel / DC

In 1982, crossovers between publishers were rare and special events, and none were as much anticipated as the get-together between Marvel's Uncanny X-Men and DC's New Teen Titans — the two hottest titles then on the stands. The two super-groups are united, when DC's baddest bad guy, Darkseid of Apokolips, revives the all-powerful Dark Phoenix, who has just met her demise after an action-packed (and top-selling) series in The X-Men. The New Gods' Metron and Titan villain Deathstroke the Terminator make guest appearances.

Len Wein, who had a hand in creating both groups, writes the epic, and artists Walter Simonson and Terry Austin do a good job synthesizing the styles of John Byrne and George Perez to give the crossover an appearance consistent with the art in both series.

1 ❑ Nov 1982 Cover: 2.00 **NM** value: **12.00**
• **CGC:** 40 graded, best 9.8
Apokolips…Now. • X-Men & Titans; Early Marvel/DC crossover **A:** Tony DeZuniga; Walt Simonson **W:** Chris Claremont

MARVEL BOY — Marvel

1 ❑ Aug 2000 Cover: 2.99 **NM** value: **Cover or less**
Circ: Diamd. preorders: **47,843** • **CGC:** 5 graded, best 9.8
Hello Cruel World **A:** J.G. Jones **W:** Grant Morrison

2 ❑ Sep 2000 Cover: 2.99 **NM** value: **Cover or less**
Circ: Diamd. preorders: **37,392**
A: J.G. Jones **W:** Grant Morrison

3 ❑ Oct 2000 Cover: 2.99 **NM** value: **Cover or less**
Circ: Diamd. preorders: **35,649**
A: J.G. Jones **W:** Grant Morrison

4 ❑ Nov 2000 Cover: 2.99 **NM** value: **Cover or less**
Circ: Diamd. preorders: **34,452**
A: J.G. Jones **W:** Grant Morrison

5 ❑ Dec 2000 Cover: 2.99 **NM** value: **Cover or less**
Circ: Diamd. preorders: **33,062**
Zero Zero: Year of Love **A:** J.G. Jones **W:** Grant Morrison

6 ❑ Mar 2001 Cover: 2.99 **NM** value: **Cover or less**
Circ: Diamd. preorders: **32,566**
Mindless: The End **A:** J.G. Jones **W:** Grant Morrison

MARVEL BOY (1ST SERIES) — Marvel

1 ❑ Dec 1950 Cover: 0.10 **NM** value: **800.00**
Marvel Boy and the Lost World; Panic; Eyes of Death; The Case of the Cat (text)

2 ❑ Feb 1951 Cover: 0.10 **NM** value: **600.00**
The Zero Hour; Blast of Doom; Planetary Error; Circus Terror; The Clay Pipe (text)

MARVEL CHILLERS — Marvel

1 ❑ Nov 1975 Cover: 0.25 **NM** value: **4.00**
• **CGC:** 10 graded, best 9.4
Magic Is Alive! **A:** Yong Montaño **W:** Bill Mantlo ★ 1st Appearance of The Other (Chthon). ★ 1st Appearance of Modred the Mystic.

2 ❑ Jan 1976 Cover: 0.25 **NM** value: **3.00**
• Modred ★ Appearance of Tigra.

3 ❑ Mar 1976 Cover: 0.25 **NM** value: **5.00**
• **CGC:** 4 graded, best 9.4
• Tigra ★ Origin of Tigra. ★ 1st Appearance of The Darkhold.

4 ❑ May 1976 Cover: 0.25 **NM** value: **2.50**
★ Appearance of Tigra, Kraven.

5 ❑ Jun 1976 Cover: 0.25 **NM** value: **2.50**
★ Appearance of Tigra.

6 ❑ Aug 1976 Cover: 0.25 **NM** value: **2.50**
A: John Byrne ★ Appearance of Tigra.

7 ❑ Oct 1976 Cover: 0.30 **NM** value: **2.50**
★ Appearance of Tigra.

MARVEL CHILLERS: SHADES OF GREEN MONSTERS — Marvel

1 ❑ Mar 1997 Cover: 2.99 **NM** value: **Cover or less**
No issue number. • mostly text story

MARVEL CHILLERS: THE THING IN THE GLASS CASE — Marvel

1 ❑ Mar 1997 Cover: 2.99 **NM** value: **Cover or less**
No issue number. • mostly text story **A:** Pat Chau **W:** Larry Hama

MARVEL CLASSICS COMICS — Marvel

No doubt inspired by Classics Illustrated, Marvel Comics decided to produce its own line of literary adaptations between 1976 and 1978. The series kicked off with an adaptation of Dr. Jekyll and Mr. Hyde, and moved on to present tales ranging from The Odyssey to The Pit and The Pendulum. In all, the series ran 36 issues, bringing adventure and horror stories from conventional fiction into the four-color world of comics.

As a bonus for collectors, back covers often featured artwork from upcoming issues, allowing them to anticipate those releases.

1 ❑ Jan 1976 Cover: 0.50 **NM** value: **6.00**
• **CGC:** 4 graded, best 9.6
Dr. Jekyll and Mr. Hyde • Doctor Jekyll and Mr. Hyde; Dr. Jekyll and Mr. Hyde

2 ❑ Feb 1976 Cover: 0.50 **NM** value: **4.00**
• **CGC:** 1 graded, best 9.2
The Time Machine • The Time Machine

3 ❑ Mar 1976 Cover: 0.50 **NM** value: **4.00**
• **CGC:** 1 graded, best 9.0
The Hunchback of Notre Dame • The Hunchback of Notre Dame

4 ❑ Apr 1976 Cover: 0.50 **NM** value: **4.00**
20,000 Leagues Under the Sea • 20, 000 Leagues Under the Sea

5 ❑ May 1976 Cover: 0.50 **NM** value: **4.00**
Black Beauty • Black Beauty

6 ❑ Jun 1976 Cover: 0.50 **NM** value: **3.50**
Gulliver's Travels • Gulliver's Travels

7 ❑ Jul 1976 Cover: 0.50 **NM** value: **3.50**
Tom Sawyer • Tom Sawyer

8 ❑ Aug 1976 Cover: 0.50 **NM** value: **3.50**
Moby Dick • Moby Dick

9 ❑ Sep 1976 Cover: 0.50 **NM** value: **3.50**
Dracula • Dracula

10 ❑ Oct 1976 Cover: 0.50 **NM** value: **3.50**
Red Badge of Courage • Red Badge of Courage

11 ❑ Nov 1976 Cover: 0.50 **NM** value: **3.50**
Mysterious Island of Dr. Moreau • Mysterious Island

12 ❑ Dec 1976 Cover: 0.50 **NM** value: **3.50**
The Three Musketeers • Three Musketeers

13 ❑ Jan 1977 Cover: 0.50 **NM** value: **3.50**
Last of the Mohicans • Last of the Mohicans

14 ❑ Feb 1977 Cover: 0.50 **NM** value: **3.50**
War of the Worlds • War of the Worlds

15 ❑ Mar 1977 Cover: 0.50 **NM** value: **3.50**
Treasure Island • Treasure Island

16 ❑ Apr 1977 Cover: 0.50 **NM** value: **3.50**
Ivanhoe • Ivanhoe

17 ❑ May 1977 Cover: 0.50 **NM** value: **3.50**
The Count of Monte Cristo • Count of Monte Cristo

18 ❑ Jun 1977 Cover: 0.50 **NM** value: **3.50**
The Odyssey • Odyssey

19 ❑ Jul 1977 Cover: 0.50 **NM** value: **3.50**
Robinson Crusoe • Robinson Crusoe **A:** The Tribe **W:** Daniel Defoe; Doug Moench

20 ❑ Aug 1977 Cover: 0.50 **NM** value: **3.50**
Frankenstein • Frankenstein

21 ❑ Sep 1977 Cover: 0.50 **NM** value: **3.50**
Master of the World • Master of the World

22 ❑ Oct 1977 Cover: 0.50 **NM** value: **3.50**
Food of the Gods • Food of the Gods

23 ❑ Nov 1977 Cover: 0.50 **NM** value: **3.50**
The Moonstone • The Moonstone

24 ❑ Dec 1977 Cover: 0.50 **NM** value: **3.50**
She • She

25 ❑ Jan 1978 Cover: 0.50 **NM** value: **3.50**
The Invisible Man • Invisible Man

26 ❑ Feb 1978 Cover: 0.50 **NM** value: **3.50**
The Iliad • Iliad

27 ❑ Mar 1978 Cover: 0.60 **NM** value: **3.50**
Kidnapped • Kidnapped

28 ❑ Apr 1978 Cover: 0.60 **NM** value: **7.00**
The Pit and the Pendulum • Pit & Pendulum; Mike Golden's first professional art **A:** Michael Golden

29 ❑ May 1978 Cover: 0.60 **NM** value: **3.50**
The Prisoner of Zenda • Prisoner of Zenda **A:** Rico Rival **W:** Doug Moench

30 ❑ Jun 1978 Cover: 0.60 **NM** value: **3.50**
The Arabian Nights • The Arabian Nights

31 ❑ Jul 1978 Cover: 0.60 **NM** value: **3.50**
The First Men In the Moon • First Man in the Moon

Other grades: Multiply prices above by **1.5 for Mint • 2/3 for Very Fine • 1/3 for Fine • 1/5 for Very Good • 1/8 for Good**

32 ❑ Aug 1978 Cover: 0.60 **NM** value: **3.50**
📖 White Fang • White Fang
33 ❑ Sep 1978 Cover: 0.60 **NM** value: **3.50**
📖 The Prince and the Pauper • The Prince and the Pauper
34 ❑ Oct 1978 Cover: 0.60 **NM** value: **3.50**
📖 Robin Hood • Robin Hood
35 ❑ Nov 1978 Cover: 0.60 **NM** value: **3.50**
📖 Alice In Wonderland • Alice in Wonderland
36 ❑ Dec 1978 Cover: 0.60 **NM** value: **3.50**
📖 A Christmas Carol • A Christmas Carol

MARVEL COLLECTIBLE CLASSICS: AMAZING SPIDER-MAN — Marvel

300❑ Cover: 13.50 **NM** value: **Cover or less**
Chromium wraparound cover. • Reprints Amazing Spider-Man #300 **A:** Todd McFarlane ★ 1st Appearance of Venom.
300/Aut❑ **NM** value: **29.99**
Chromium wraparound cover. • Reprints Amazing Spider-Man #300 **A:** Todd McFarlane ★ 1st Appearance of Venom.

MARVEL COLLECTIBLE CLASSICS: AVENGERS (VOL. 3) — Marvel

1 ❑ Nov 1998 Cover: 13.50 **NM** value: **Cover or less**
Circ: Diamd. preorders: **3,260** • **CGC:** 16 graded, best 10.0
Chromium wraparound cover.

MARVEL COLLECTIBLE CLASSICS: X-MEN — Marvel

1 ❑ Aug 1998 Cover: 13.50 **NM** value: **Cover or less**
• **CGC:** 6 graded, best 9.8
Chromium wraparound cover. • Reprints X-Men #1
GS 1❑Nov 1998 Cover: 13.50 **NM** value: **Cover or less**
Circ: Diamd. preorders: **4,567**
Chromium wraparound cover. • Reprints Giant Size X-Men #1.

MARVEL COLLECTIBLE CLASSICS: X-MEN (VOL. 2) — Marvel

1 ❑ Oct 1998 Cover: 13.50 **NM** value: **Cover or less**
Circ: Diamd. preorders: **3,963**
Chromium wraparound cover. **A:** Jim Lee
1/Aut❑Oct 1998 **NM** value: **29.99**
Chromium wraparound cover. **A:** Jim Lee

MARVEL COLLECTOR'S EDITION — Marvel

This special edition was offered as a 1992 promotion with the makers of Charleston Chew candy bars. For 50 cents and a wrapper from a Charleston Chew, you were sent this limited edition flip-book featuring Spider-Man and Silver Surfer stories on one side, and Wolverine and Ghost Rider stories on the other.

The Spider-Man tale kicks off with the webslinger looking for some good photo opportunities so he can sell the pictures to the Bugle and buy Mary Jane a brooch. What he finds is a showdown with electric villain The Eel. This was followed by a Silver Surfer story in which he aids a woman warrior in the fight to take back her world from machines run amok.

The flip-side finds the X-Men's Wolverine and Jubilee doing some hazardous cleaning up in the Danger Room, followed by Ghost Rider saving a boy and making a friend.

1 ❑ 1992 Cover: 1.50 **NM** value: **2.50**
• **CGC:** 1 graded, best 8.0
📖 Gimme A Break • Spider-Man, Wolverine, Ghost Rider; Charleston Chew promotion, $.50 and a candy bar wrapper; Flip-book format **A:** Sam Kieth **W:** Richard Howell; Larry Hama

MARVEL COLLECTORS' ITEM CLASSICS — Marvel

For a mere 25 cents, readers of Marvel Collector's Item Classics got four separate stories from earlier in Marvel's Silver Age. These giant-sized editions, published between 1965 and 1969, featured early exploits of the Fantastic Four, Iron Man, Doctor Strange, Thor, and many more of Marvel's greatest heroes. Perhaps the most remarkable thing about this series is that a company so young had already begun reprinting its "classics."

The series still offers affordable reprints of those early issues, many of which are outside the price range of today's collectors.

1 ❑ Feb 1966 Cover: 0.25 **NM** value: **45.00**
• **CGC:** 10 graded, best 9.4
2 ❑ Apr 1966 Cover: 0.25 **NM** value: **28.00**
• **CGC:** 3 graded, best 9.2
3 ❑ Jun 1966 Cover: 0.25 **NM** value: **25.00**
• **CGC:** 4 graded, best 9.4
• reprints Fantastic Four (Vol. 1) #4, Tales of Suspense #40, Incredible Hulk #3, Tales of Suspense #49, Strange Tales #110
4 ❑ Aug 1966 Cover: 0.25 **NM** value: **25.00**
• **CGC:** 3 graded, best 9.4
5 ❑ Oct 1966 Cover: 0.25 **NM** value: **14.00**
6 ❑ Dec 1966 Cover: 0.25 **NM** value: **14.00**
7 ❑ Feb 1967 Cover: 0.25 **NM** value: **14.00**
• **CGC:** 1 graded, best 9.2
8 ❑ Apr 1967 Cover: 0.25 **NM** value: **14.00**
• **CGC:** 1 graded, best 9.0
9 ❑ Jun 1967 Cover: 0.25 **NM** value: **14.00**
10 ❑ Aug 1967 Cover: 0.25 **NM** value: **14.00**
11 ❑ Oct 1967 Cover: 0.25 **NM** value: **12.00**
12 ❑ Dec 1967 Cover: 0.25 **NM** value: **12.00**
13 ❑ Feb 1968 Cover: 0.25 **NM** value: **12.00**
14 ❑ Apr 1968 Cover: 0.25 **NM** value: **12.00**
15 ❑ Jun 1968 Cover: 0.25 **NM** value: **12.00**
• **CGC:** 2 graded, best 9.4
16 ❑ Aug 1968 Cover: 0.25 **NM** value: **12.00**
• **CGC:** 1 graded, best 9.2
17 ❑ Oct 1968 Cover: 0.25 **NM** value: **12.00**
• **CGC:** 4 graded, best 9.4
18 ❑ Dec 1968 Cover: 0.25 **NM** value: **12.00**
• **CGC:** 1 graded, best 9.4
19 ❑ Feb 1969 Cover: 0.25 **NM** value: **12.00**
📖 The Search For Sub-Mariner!; The Primitive; The Death Of Tony Stark **A:** Don Heck; Jack Kirby **W:** Stan Lee
20 ❑ Apr 1969 Cover: 0.25 **NM** value: **12.00**
21 ❑ Jun 1969 Cover: 0.25 **NM** value: **10.00**
22 ❑ Aug 1969 Cover: 0.25 **NM** value: **10.00**
• Series continued in Marvel's Greatest Comics #23

MARVEL COMICS — Marvel

1 ❑ Nov 1939 Cover: 0.10 **NM** value: **118000.00**
• **CGC:** 4 graded, best 9.0
• This is the first Marvel Comic; One-shot as "Marvel Comics" ★ Origin of Human Torch. ★ 1st Appearance of Ka-Zar, Human Torch, The Angel I, Sub-Mariner.
1-2/HC❑ Cover: 17.95 **NM** value: **Cover or less**
hardcover.

MARVEL COMICS PRESENTS — Marvel

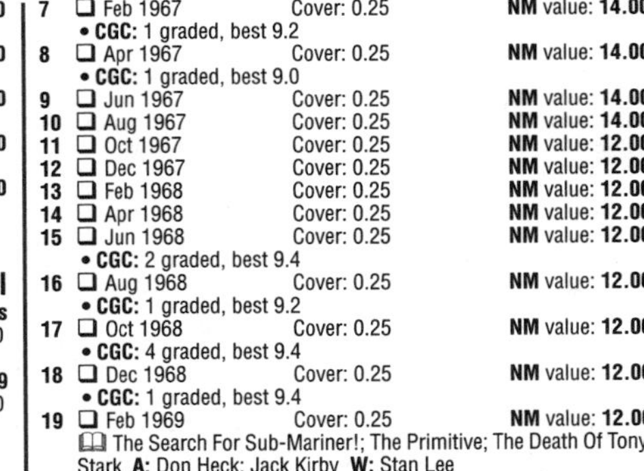

Marvel Comics Presents was a bit like the old adventure reels in Saturday afternoon cinema. It takes four different storylines and presented them as serials, with a new issue every two weeks. This let Marvel experiment with a number of new story ideas while staying reasonably sure that if one didn't appeal to the readers, the other three would.

In most issues, at least one of the stories featured the X-Men's Wolverine. The other stories covered diverse characters from Ghost Rider to Nth Man. However, many people will remember the series for the 12-part story entitled "Weapon X." This series by Barry Windsor-Smith served as a sort of origin for Wolverine, telling the story of the grisly experiment which laced his bones with adamantium, and of the brutal methods by which the experimenters tried to turn him into a human killing machine.

1 ❑ Sep 1988 Cover: 1.25 **NM** value: **3.50**
Circ: CapCity orders: **70,100** • **CGC:** 26 graded, best 9.8
📖 Wolverine: Save The Tiger, Part 1; Man-Thing: Elements Of Terror, Part 1; Master Of Kung-Fu: Crossing Lines, Part 1; Silver Surfer: Fear Itself • Wolverine features begin **A:** Al Milgrom; Tom Sutton; John Buscema; Tom Grindberg **W:** Al Milgrom; Chris Claremont; Doug Moench; Steve Gerber
2 ❑ Sep 1988 Cover: 1.25 **NM** value: **2.50**
Circ: CapCity orders: **54,500** • **CGC:** 3 graded, best 9.4
📖 Wolverine: Save The Tiger, Part 2; Man-Thing: Elements Of Terror, Part 2; Master Of Kung-Fu: Crossing Lines, Part 2 • Wolverine **A:** Tom Sutton; John Buscema; Tom Grindberg **W:** Chris Claremont; Doug Moench; Steve Gerber
3 ❑ Sep 1988 Cover: 1.25 **NM** value: **2.50**
Circ: CapCity orders: **54,500**
📖 Wolverine: Save The Tiger, Part 3; Man-Thing: Elements Of Terror, Part 3; Master Of Kung-Fu: Crossing Lines, Part 3 • Wolverine **A:** Tom Sutton; John Buscema; Tom Grindberg **W:** Chris Claremont; Doug Moench; Steve Gerber
4 ❑ Oct 1988 Cover: 1.25 **NM** value: **2.50**
Circ: CapCity orders: **48,600**
📖 Wolverine: Save The Tiger, Part 4; Man-Thing: Elements Of Terror, Part 4; Master Of Kung-Fu: Crossing Lines, Part 4 • Wolverine **A:** Tom Sutton; John Buscema; Tom Grindberg **W:** Chris Claremont; Doug Moench; Steve Gerber
5 ❑ Oct 1988 Cover: 1.25 **NM** value: **2.50**
Circ: CapCity orders: **47,200**
📖 Wolverine: Save The Tiger, Part 5; Man-Thing: Elements Of Terror, Part 5; Master Of Kung-Fu: Crossing Lines, Part 5 • Wolverine **A:** Tom Sutton; John Buscema; Tom Grindberg **W:** Chris Claremont; Doug Moench; Steve Gerber
6 ❑ Nov 1988 Cover: 1.25 **NM** value: **2.00**
Circ: CapCity orders: **43,800**
📖 Wolverine: Save The Tiger, Part 6; Man-Thing: Elements Of Terror, Part 6; Master Of Kung-Fu: Crossing Lines, Part 6; The Incredible Hulk: Risky Business • Wolverine **A:** Tom Sutton; John Buscema; Jeff Purves; Tom Grindberg **W:** Bobbie Chase; Chris Claremont; Doug Moench; Steve Gerber ★ Appearance of Sub-Mariner.
7 ❑ Nov 1988 Cover: 1.25 **NM** value: **2.00**
Circ: CapCity orders: **43,800**
📖 Wolverine: Save The Tiger, Part 7; Man-Thing: Elements Of Terror, Part 7; Master Of Kung-Fu: Crossing Lines, Part 7; Sub-Mariner: From Sea To Deadly Sea • Wolverine **A:** Tom Sutton; John Buscema; Tom Grindberg; Hollis Bright **W:** Steve Ditko; Chris Claremont; Doug Moench; Steve Gerber
8 ❑ Dec 1988 Cover: 1.25 **NM** value: **2.00**
Circ: CapCity orders: **42,000**
📖 Wolverine: Save The Tiger, Part 8; Man-Thing: Elements Of Terror, Part 8; Master Of Kung-Fu: Crossing Lines, Part 8; Iron Man: One Day At A Time • Wolverine **A:** Tom Sutton; John Buscema; Javier Saltares; Tom Grindberg **W:** Chris Claremont; Doug Moench; Sholly Fisch; Steve Gerber
9 ❑ Dec 1988 Cover: 1.25 **NM** value: **2.00**
Circ: CapCity orders: **41,700**
📖 Wolverine: Save The Tiger, Part 9; Man-Thing: Elements Of Terror, Part 9; Cloak: In The Dark; El Aguila: A Piece Of Cake • Wolverine **A:** Tom Sutton; John Buscema; Tony Salmons; Larry Alexander; Brad Joyce **W:** Scott Lobdell; Marc McLaurin; Chris Claremont; Steve Gerber
10 ❑ Jan 1989 Cover: 1.25 **NM** value: **2.00**
Circ: Statement: **163,525** CapCity orders: **38,900**
📖 Wolverine: Save The Tiger, Part 10; Man-Thing: Elements Of Terror, Part 10; Colossus: God's Country, Part 1 • Wolverine; Colossus features begin **A:** Tom Sutton; John Buscema **W:** Chris Claremont; Steve Gerber
11 ❑ Jan 1989 Cover: 1.25 **NM** value: **1.50**
Circ: Statement: **163,525** CapCity orders: **32,700**
📖 Man-Thing: Elements Of Terror, Part 11; Colossus: God's Country, Part 2; Ant-Man: Drain Storm; Slag Of Wolfpack: Over And Over • Colossus **A:** Tom Sutton; Ron Wilson; Rick Leonardi; Bob Layton; Don Hudson **W:** Len Wein; Ann Nocenti; John Figueroa; Steve Gerber
12 ❑ Feb 1989 Cover: 1.25 **NM** value: **1.50**
Circ: Statement: **163,525** CapCity orders: **30,100**
• Colossus, Man-Thing **A:** Tom Sutton; Rick Leonardi; Don Heck; Frank Springer **W:** Scott Lobdell; C.J. Henderson; Ann Nocenti; Steve Gerber
13 ❑ Feb 1989 Cover: 1.25 **NM** value: **1.50**
Circ: Statement: **163,525** CapCity orders: **30,000**
📖 Colossus: God's Country, Part 4; Black Panther: Panther's Quest, Part 1; Mr. Fantastic And The Invisible Woman: Reed's On The Roof And We Cant Get Him Down; Shanna The She-Devil: A Tooth For A Tooth • Colossus **A:** Gene Colan; Rick Leonardi; Mike Harris; Bruce Jones **W:** Bruce Jones; C.J. Henderson; Ann Nocenti; Don McGregor
14 ❑ Mar 1989 Cover: 1.25 **NM** value: **1.50**
Circ: Statement: **163,525** CapCity orders: **28,100**
📖 Colossus: God's Country, Part 5; Black Panther: Panther's Quest, Part 2; Speedball: The Feathered Felon; Nomad: Angel In The Snow • Colossus **A:** Gene Colan; Rick Leonardi; Larry Alexander; Mary Jo Duffy **W:** Steve Ditko; Fabian Nicieza; Ann Nocenti; Don McGregor
15 ❑ Mar 1989 Cover: 1.25 **NM** value: **1.50**
Circ: Statement: **163,525** CapCity orders: **29,000**
📖 Colossus: God's Country, Part 6; Black Panther: Panther's Quest, Part 3; Marvel Girl: The Maiden Phoenix; Red Wolf: Desert Tears • Colossus **A:** Gene Colan; Rick Leonardi; Dwayne Turner; Javier Saltares **W:** Fabian Nicieza; Ann Nocenti; Bobbie Chase; Don McGregor
16 ❑ Mar 1989 Cover: 1.25 **NM** value: **1.50**
Circ: Statement: **163,525** CapCity orders: **27,500**
📖 Colossus: God's Country, Part 7; Black Panther: Panther's Quest, Part 4 • Colossus **A:** Gene Colan; Rick Leonardi **W:** Ann Nocenti; Don McGregor
17 ❑ Apr 1989 Cover: 1.25 **NM** value: **1.50**
Circ: Statement: **163,525** CapCity orders: **27,100**
📖 Colossus: God's Country, Part 8; Black Panther: Panther's Quest, Part 5, Cyclops: The Retribution Affair, Part 1 • Cyclops features begin **A:** Tom Sutton; Gene Colan; Rick Leonardi; Ron Lim **W:** Scott Lobdell; Ann Nocenti; Bob Harras; Don McGregor
18 ❑ Apr 1989 Cover: 1.25 **NM** value: **1.50**
Circ: Statement: **163,525** CapCity orders: **23,800**
📖 Black Panther: Panther's Quest, Part 6; Cyclops: The Retribution Affair, Part 2; She-Hulk: X-Mas Tease; Willie Lumpkin: A Christmas Card • She-Hulk, Cyclops **A:** Richard Howell; Gene Colan; Ron Lim; John Byrne **W:** John Byrne; Bob Harras; Don McGregor; Glenn Herdling
19 ❑ May 1989 Cover: 1.25 **NM** value: **1.50**
Circ: Statement: **163,525** CapCity orders: **23,700**
📖 Black Panther: Panther's Quest, Part 7; Cyclops: The Retribution Affair, Part 3; Dr. Strange: Nightmare In Suburbia, Part 1; Damage Control: Overture • Cyclops **A:** Mark Badger; Gene Colan; Ron Lim; Ernie Colon **W:** Dwayne McDuffie; Fabian Nicieza; Bob Harras; Don McGregor ★ 1st Appearance of Damage Control.
20 ❑ May 1989 Cover: 1.25 **NM** value: **1.50**
Circ: Statement: **163,525** CapCity orders: **22,500**
📖 Black Panther: Panther's Quest, Part 8; Cyclops: The Retribution Affair, Part 4; Dr. Strange: Nightmare In Suburbia, Part 2; Clea: At The Bottom Of My Garden • Cyclops **A:** Mark Badger; Gene Colan; Ron Lim **W:** Fabian Nicieza; Bob Harras; Don McGregor; Peter B. Gillis
21 ❑ Jun 1989 Cover: 1.25 **NM** value: **1.50**
Circ: Statement: **163,525** CapCity orders: **22,500**
📖 Black Panther: Panther's Quest, Part 9; Cyclops: The Retribution Affair, Part 5; Paladin: Let's Take It From Where I Swing In And Rescue You; The Thing: The First Cut • Cyclops **A:** Gene Colan; Ron Wilson; Ron Lim; Kevin VanHook **W:** Scott Lobdell; Marc McLaurin; Bob Harras; Don McGregor
22 ❑ Jun 1989 Cover: 1.25 **NM** value: **1.50**
Circ: Statement: **163,525** CapCity orders: **22,800**
📖 Black Panther: Panther's Quest, Part 10; Cyclops: The Retribution Affair, Part 6; Starfox: New Worlds To Conquer; Wolfsbane & Mirage: Suffer A Wolf To Live • Cyclops **A:** Gene Colan; Ron Lim; Dave Cockrum; Rodney Ramos **W:** Bob Harras; Don McGregor; Peter B. Gillis; Sue Flaxman
23 ❑ Jul 1989 Cover: 1.25 **NM** value: **1.50**
Circ: Statement: **163,525** CapCity orders: **22,300**
📖 Black Panther: Panther's Quest, Part 11; Cyclops: The Retribution Affair, Part 7; The Falcon: The Forest For The Trees; Wheels Of Wolfpack: Lady Jane • Cyclops **A:** Gene Colan; Ron Wilson; Ron Lim; Dave Cockrum **W:** Fabian Nicieza; Bob Harras; Don McGregor; John Figueroa
24 ❑ Jul 1989 Cover: 1.25 **NM** value: **1.50**
Circ: Statement: **163,525** CapCity orders: **22,400**
📖 Black Panther: Panther's Quest, Part 12; Cyclops: The Retribution Affair, Part 8; Shamrock: Haven't Got Time For The Pain; Havok: Pharaoh's Legacy, Part 1 • Cyclops, Havok **A:** Rich Buckler; Gene Colan; Ron Lim; Dennis Jensen; Joe Rubinstein **W:** Scott Lobdell; Howard Mackie; Bob Harras; Don McGregor
25 ❑ Aug 1989 Cover: 1.25 **NM** value: **1.50**
Circ: Statement: **163,525** CapCity orders: **22,200**

Black Panther: Panther's Quest, Part 13; Havok: Pharaoh's Legacy, Part 2; Nth Man: ...From Little Acorns Grow; Ursa Major: Sophia • Havok **A:** Rich Buckler; Ron Wagner; Gene Colan; Don Hudson; Joe Rubinstein **W:** Larry Hama; Scott Lobdell; Howard Mackie; Don McGregor ★ Origin of Nth Man. ★ 1st Appearance of Nth Man.

26 ❑ Aug 1989 Cover: 1.25 **NM** value: **1.50**
Circ: Statement: **163,525** CapCity orders: **21,500**
Black Panther: Panther's Quest, Part 14; Havok: Pharaoh's Legacy, Part 3; The Incredible Hulk: Splashdown; Coldblood: Rise And Shine, Part 1 • Havok **A:** Rich Buckler; Gene Colan; Paul Gulacy; Joe Rubinstein **W:** Howard Mackie; Don McGregor; Doug Moench ★ 1st Appearance of Coldblood.

27 ❑ Sep 1989 Cover: 1.25 **NM** value: **1.50**
Circ: Statement: **163,525** CapCity orders: **21,500**
Black Panther: Panther's Quest, Part 15; Havok: Pharaoh's Legacy, Part 4; Coldblood: Rise And Shine, Part 2; American Eagle: Just Another Shade Of Hate • Havok **A:** Rich Buckler; Gene Colan; Ron Wilson; Paul Gulacy; Joe Rubinstein **W:** Scott Lobdell; Howard Mackie; Don McGregor; Doug Moench

28 ❑ Sep 1989 Cover: 1.25 **NM** value: **1.50**
Circ: Statement: **163,525** CapCity orders: **21,300**
Black Panther: Panther's Quest, Part 16; Havok: Pharaoh's Legacy, Part 5; Coldblood: Rise And Shine, Part 3; Triton: Giving Peace A Chance • Havok **A:** Rich Buckler; Gene Colan; Paul Gulacy; Javier Saltares; Joe Rubinstein **W:** Howard Mackie; Robert Campanella; Don McGregor; Doug Moench

29 ❑ Sep 1989 Cover: 1.25 **NM** value: **1.50**
Circ: Statement: **163,525** CapCity orders: **22,800**
Black Panther: Panther's Quest, Part 17; Havok: Pharaoh's Legacy, Part 6; Coldblood: Rise And Shine, Part 4; Quasar: It Came From Within... • Havok **A:** Rich Buckler; Gene Colan; Paul Ryan; Paul Gulacy; Joe Rubinstein **W:** Howard Mackie; Don McGregor; Doug Moench; Mark Gruenwald

30 ❑ Oct 1989 Cover: 1.25 **NM** value: **1.50**
Circ: Statement: **163,525** CapCity orders: **22,500**
Black Panther: Panther's Quest, Part 18; Havok: Pharaoh's Legacy, Part 7; Coldblood: Rise And Shine, Part 5; Leir: Lord Of Lightning • Havok **A:** Rich Buckler; Gene Colan; Tom Morgan; Paul Gulacy; Joe Rubinstein **W:** Howard Mackie; Don McGregor; Doug Moench; Sue Flaxman ★ Appearance of Wolverine.

31 ❑ Oct 1989 Cover: 1.25 **NM** value: **1.50**
Circ: Statement: **163,525** CapCity orders: **23,300**
Black Panther: Panther's Quest, Part 19; Havok: Pharaoh's Legacy, Part 8; Coldblood: Rise And Shine, Part 6; Excalibur: Having A Wild Weekend, Part 1 • Havok, Excalibur **A:** Rich Buckler; Gene Colan; Paul Gulacy; Erik Larsen; Terry Austin; Joe Rubinstein **W:** Howard Mackie; Don McGregor; Doug Moench; Michael Higgins ★ Origin of Coldblood.

32 ❑ Nov 1989 Cover: 1.25 **NM** value: **1.50**
Circ: Statement: **163,525** CapCity orders: **23,900**
Black Panther: Panther's Quest, Part 20; Coldblood: Rise And Shine, Part 7; Excalibur: Having A Wild Weekend, Part 2; Sunfire: The Dreaded Deadline Doom • Excalibur **A:** Gene Colan; Don Heck; Paul Gulacy; Erik Larsen **C:** Todd McFarlane **W:** Scott Lobdell; Don McGregor; Doug Moench; Michael Higgins

33 ❑ Nov 1989 Cover: 1.25 **NM** value: **1.50**
Circ: Statement: **163,525**
Black Panther: Panther's Quest, Part 21; Coldblood: Rise And Shine, Part 8; Excalibur: Having A Wild Weekend, Part 3 • Excalibur **A:** Gene Colan; Paul Gulacy; Jim Lee; Erik Larsen **W:** Don McGregor; Doug Moench; Michael Higgins

34 ❑ Dec 1989 Cover: 1.25 **NM** value: **1.50**
Circ: Statement: **163,525** CapCity orders: **23,900**
Black Panther: Panther's Quest, Part 22; Coldblood: Rise And Shine, Part 9; Excalibur: Having A Wild Weekend, Part 4; Captain America: Past And Present Sins • Excalibur **A:** Gene Colan; Paul Gulacy; Erik Larsen; Jack Sparling **W:** Don McGregor; Doug Moench; Michael Higgins; Sholly Fisch

35 ❑ Dec 1989 Cover: 1.25 **NM** value: **1.50**
Circ: Statement: **163,525** CapCity orders: **23,100**
Black Panther: Panther's Quest, Part 23; Coldblood: Rise And Shine, Part 10; Excalibur: Having A Wild Weekend, Part 5; Her: Gods R' Us • Excalibur **A:** Gene Colan; Paul Gulacy; Erik Larsen **W:** Fabian Nicieza; Don McGregor; Doug Moench; Michael Higgins ★ 1st Appearance of Starduster.

36 ❑ Jan 1989 Cover: 1.25 **NM** value: **1.50**
Circ: Statement: **132,201** CapCity orders: **22,800**
Black Panther: Panther's Quest, Part 24; Excalibur: Having A Wild Weekend, Part 6 • Excalibur **A:** Gene Colan; Erik Larsen **W:** Don McGregor; Michael Higgins

37 ❑ Jan 1989 Cover: 1.25 **NM** value: **1.50**
Circ: Statement: **132,201** CapCity orders: **22,600**
Black Panther: Panther's Quest, Part 25; Excalibur: Having A Wild Weekend, Part 7; Devil Slayer: To Slay The Devil • Excalibur **A:** Gene Colan; Rodney Ramos; Erik Larsen **W:** Don McGregor; Dwight Jon Zimmerman; Michael Higgins

38 ❑ Feb 1989 Cover: 1.25 **NM** value: **2.00**
Circ: Statement: **132,201** CapCity orders: **29,300**
Excalibur: Having A Wild Weekend, Part 8; Hulk: Art For Art's Sake; Wolverine: Black Shadow White Shadow, Part 1; Wonder Man: Stardust Miseries, Part 1 • Excalibur **A:** John Buscema; Erik Larsen; Javier Saltares; Marshall Rogers **W:** Bill Mumy; Marv Wolfman; Michael Higgins

39 ❑ Feb 1989 Cover: 1.25 **NM** value: **1.50**
Circ: Statement: **132,201** CapCity orders: **28,000**
Wolverine: Black Shadow White Shadow, Part 2; Wonder Man: Stardust Miseries, Part 2; Hercules: All In The Family, Part 1; Spider-Man: With Liberty And Justice For All • Wolverine **A:** Aaron Lopresti; John Buscema; Bob Layton; Erik Larsen; Javier Saltares **W:** Bob Layton; Bill Mumy; Marv Wolfman; Michael Higgins

40 ❑ Mar 1989 Cover: 1.25 **NM** value: **1.50**
Circ: Statement: **132,201** CapCity orders: **27,700**
Wolverine: Black Shadow White Shadow, Part 3; Wonder Man: Stardust Miseries, Part 3; Hercules: All In The Family, Part 2; Overmind: Anything • Wolverine **A:** John Buscema; Bob Layton; Don Heck; Javier Saltares **W:** Bob Layton; Scott Lobdell; Marv Wolfman; Michael Higgins

41 ❑ Mar 1990 Cover: 1.25 **NM** value: **1.50**
Circ: Statement: **132,201** CapCity orders: **27,600**
Wolverine: Black Shadow White Shadow, Part 4; Wonder Man: Stardust Miseries, Part 4; Hercules: All In The Family, Part 3; Freedom Force: Forced Fed! • Wolverine **A:** John Buscema; Bob Layton; Dave Cockrum; Javier Saltares **W:** Bob Layton; Scott Lobdell; Marv Wolfman; Michael Higgins

42 ❑ Mar 1990 Cover: 1.25 **NM** value: **1.50**
Circ: Statement: **132,201** CapCity orders: **27,800**
Wolverine: Black Shadow White Shadow, Part 5; Wonder Man: Stardust Miseries, Part 5 • Wolverine **A:** John Buscema; Javier Saltares **W:** Marv Wolfman; Michael Higgins

43 ❑ Apr 1990 Cover: 1.25 **NM** value: **1.50**
Circ: Statement: **132,201** CapCity orders: **26,300**
Wolverine: Black Shadow White Shadow, Part 6; Wonder Man: Stardust Miseries, Part 6; Iron Man: Donovan's Brains; Siryn: Hello Little Girl...Is Your Father Home? • Wolverine **A:** Mark Bagley; John Buscema; Javier Saltares; Larry Stroman **W:** Scott Lobdell; Ed Simmons; Marv Wolfman; Michael Higgins

44 ❑ Apr 1990 Cover: 1.25 **NM** value: **1.50**
Circ: Statement: **132,201** CapCity orders: **26,300**
Wolverine: Black Shadow White Shadow, Part 7; Wonder Man: Stardust Miseries, Part 7; Dr. Strange: Trashed; Puma: ...And Not A Drop To Drink • Wolverine **A:** John Buscema; Javier Saltares; Dave Simons; Gavin Curtis **W:** Roy Thomas; Dan Mishkin; Marv Wolfman; Michael Higgins

45 ❑ May 1990 Cover: 1.25 **NM** value: **1.50**
Circ: Statement: **132,201** CapCity orders: **24,200**
Wolverine: Black Shadow White Shadow, Part 8; Wonder Man: Stardust Miseries, Part 8 • Wolverine **A:** John Buscema; Javier Saltares **W:** Marv Wolfman; Michael Higgins

46 ❑ May 1990 Cover: 1.25 **NM** value: **1.50**
Circ: Statement: **132,201** CapCity orders: **24,000**
Wolverine: Black Shadow White Shadow, Part 9; Devil Slayer: Lost Souls, Part 1; Aquarian: A Gift Of Death; Sub-Mariner: The Eye That Sees • Wolverine **A:** John Buscema; Hugh Haynes; Rodney Ramos; Dell Barras **W:** Fabian Nicieza; Hollis Bright; Dwight Jon Zimmerman; Marv Wolfman

47 ❑ Apr 1990 Cover: 1.25 **NM** value: **1.50**
Circ: Statement: **132,201** CapCity orders: **24,500**
Wolverine: Black Shadow White Shadow, Part 10; Devil Slayer: Lost Souls, Part 2 • Wolverine; cover dates, which only appeared in the indicia or in Marvel's catalog copy, actually do go backwards for a while at this point **A:** John Buscema; Rodney Ramos **W:** Dwight Jon Zimmerman; Marv Wolfman

48 ❑ Apr 1990 Cover: 1.25 **NM** value: **2.00**
Circ: Statement: **132,201** CapCity orders: **23,500**
Wolverine/Spider-Man: Life's End, Part 1; Devil Slayer: Lost Souls, Part 3 • Spider-Man, Wolverine **A:** Rodney Ramos **W:** Dwight Jon Zimmerman

49 ❑ May 1990 Cover: 1.25 **NM** value: **2.00**
Circ: Statement: **132,201** CapCity orders: **25,200**
Wolverine/Spider-Man: Life's End, Part 2; Devil Slayer: Lost Souls, Part 4 • Spider-Man, Wolverine; Has 1989 Statement, filed 11/1/89; avg print run 281,765; avg sales 163,295; avg subs 230; avg total paid 163,525; samples 125; office use 600; max existent 164,250; 42% of run returned **A:** Rodney Ramos **W:** Dwight Jon Zimmerman ★ 1st Appearance of Whiplash II.

50 ❑ May 1990 Cover: 1.25 **NM** value: **2.00**
Circ: Statement: **132,201** CapCity orders: **23,000**
Wolverine/Spider-Man: Life's End, Part 3 • Spider-Man, Wolverine ★ Origin of Captain Ultra.

51 ❑ Jun 1990 Cover: 1.25 **NM** value: **2.00**
Circ: Statement: **132,201** CapCity orders: **23,400**
• Wolverine **A:** Rob Liefeld

52 ❑ Jun 1990 Cover: 1.25 **NM** value: **2.00**
Circ: Statement: **132,201**
• Wolverine **A:** Rob Liefeld

53 ❑ Jul 1990 Cover: 1.25 **NM** value: **2.00**
Circ: Statement: **132,201** CapCity orders: **24,200**
Stingray: Family Matters, Part 1 • Wolverine **A:** Rob Liefeld; Jim Fern **W:** Len Wein

54 ❑ Jul 1990 Cover: 1.25 **NM** value: **2.50**
Circ: Statement: **132,201** CapCity orders: **25,600**
Stingray: Family Matters, Part 2; Wolverine: On The Road, Part 1; Werewolf: Children Of The Beast, Part 1 • Wolverine & Hulk **A:** James W. Fry III; Dave Ross; Jim Fern **W:** Len Kaminski; Len Wein; Michael Higgins

55 ❑ Jul 1990 Cover: 1.25 **NM** value: **2.50**
Circ: Statement: **132,201** CapCity orders: **25,200**
Stingray: Family Matters, Part 3; Wolverine: On The Road, Part 2; Werewolf: Children Of The Beast, Part 2 • Wolverine & Hulk **A:** James W. Fry III; Dave Ross; Jim Fern **W:** Len Kaminski; Len Wein; Michael Higgins

56 ❑ Aug 1990 Cover: 1.25 **NM** value: **2.50**
Circ: Statement: **132,201** CapCity orders: **25,600**
Stingray: Family Matters, Part 4; Wolverine: On The Road, Part 3; Werewolf: Children Of The Beast, Part 3; Speedball: Any Number Can Play • Wolverine & Hulk **A:** James W. Fry III; Dave Ross; Jim Fern; Mary Jo Duffy **W:** Len Kaminski; Steve Ditko; Len Wein; Michael Higgins

57 ❑ Aug 1990 Cover: 1.25 **NM** value: **2.50**
Circ: Statement: **132,201** CapCity orders: **25,700**
Wolverine: On The Road, Part 4; Werewolf: Children Of The Beast, Part 4; Sub-Mariner: Neptunes Eye, Part 1; Black Cat: The Crown Jewel Caper • Wolverine & Hulk **A:** Mike Collins; James W. Fry III; Mike Harris; Dave Ross **W:** Len Kaminski; Dwight Jon Zimmerman; Michael Higgins; Robert Denatale

58 ❑ Sep 1990 Cover: 1.25 **NM** value: **2.50**
Circ: Statement: **132,201** CapCity orders: **25,600**
Wolverine: On The Road, Part 5; Werewolf: Children Of The Beast, Part 5; Sub-Mariner: Neptunes Eye, Part 2; Iron Man: Neutralizing Effects • Wolverine & Hulk **A:** Mike Collins; James W. Fry III; Dave Ross; Hollis Bright **W:** Len Kaminski; Steve Ditko; Michael Higgins; Robert Denatale

59 ❑ Sep 1990 Cover: 1.25 **NM** value: **2.50**
Circ: Statement: **132,201** CapCity orders: **26,100**
Wolverine: On The Road, Part 6; Sub-Mariner: Neptunes Eye, Part 3; Werewolf: Children Of The Beast, Part 6; Punisher: The Real Thing • Wolverine & Hulk **A:** Mike Collins; Dan Reed; James W. Fry III; Dave Ross **W:** Len Kaminski; Marcus McLauren; Michael Higgins; Robert Denatale

60 ❑ Oct 1990 Cover: 1.25 **NM** value: **2.50**
Circ: Statement: **132,201** CapCity orders: **24,600**
Wolverine: On The Road, Part 7; Poison: Vandals Of The Heart, Part 1; Scarlet Witch: Yesterdays, Part 1; Captain America: The American Way • Wolverine & Hulk **A:** Richard Howell; Cynthia Martin; Dave Ross; Tom Lyle **W:** Richard Howell; John Figueroa; Michael Higgins; Steve Gerber

61 ❑ Oct 1990 Cover: 1.25 **NM** value: **2.50**
Circ: Statement: **132,201** CapCity orders: **24,400**
Wolverine: On The Road, Part 8; Poison: Vandals Of The Heart, Part 2; Scarlet Witch: Yesterdays, Part 2; Dr. Strange: The Librarian • Wolverine & Hulk **A:** Richard Howell; Cynthia Martin; Dave Ross; Chris Tsuda **W:** Richard Howell; Michael Higgins; Peter B. Gillis; Steve Gerber

62 ❑ Nov 1990 Cover: 1.25 **NM** value: **2.50**
Circ: CapCity orders: **24,000**
Poison: Vandals Of The Heart, Part 3; Scarlet Witch: Yesterdays, Part 3; Wolverine: The Quest Of Abdul Alhazred, Part 1; Deathlok: Test Run • Wolverine **A:** Richard Howell; Jackson Guice; Paul Ryan; Cynthia Martin **W:** Greg Wright; Richard Howell; Dwayne McDuffie; Dwight Jon Zimmerman; Steve Gerber

63 ❑ Nov 1990 Cover: 1.25 **NM** value: **2.00**
Circ: CapCity orders: **23,100**
Poison: Vandals Of The Heart, Part 4; Scarlet Witch: Yesterdays, Part 4; Wolverine: The Quest Of Abdul Alhazred, Part 2; Thor: Norse Blood • Wolverine **A:** Richard Howell; Paul Ryan; Don Heck; Cynthia Martin **W:** Len Kaminski; Richard Howell; Dwight Jon Zimmerman; Steve Gerber

64 ❑ Dec 1990 Cover: 1.25 **NM** value: **2.00**
Circ: CapCity orders: **36,800**
Wolverine and Ghost Rider: Acts of Vengeance, Part 1; Poison: Vandals Of The Heart, Part 5; Fantastic Four: Deadly Dimensions, Part 1 • Wolverine, Ghost Rider **A:** Mark Texeira; Paul Ryan; Tom Morgan; Cynthia Martin **W:** Howard Mackie; Dwight Jon Zimmerman; Robert Denatale; Steve Gerber

65 ❑ Dec 1990 Cover: 1.25 **NM** value: **2.00**
Circ: CapCity orders: **34,200**
Wolverine and Ghost Rider: Acts of Vengeance, Part 2; Poison: Vandals Of The Heart, Part 6; Fantastic Four: Deadly Dimensions, Part 2 • Wolverine, Ghost Rider **A:** Tom Morgan; Cynthia Martin; Robert Texeira **W:** Howard Mackie; Robert Denatale; Steve Gerber

66 ❑ Dec 1990 Cover: 1.25 **NM** value: **2.00**
Circ: CapCity orders: **33,200**
Wolverine and Ghost Rider: Acts of Vengeance, Part 3; Poison: Vandals Of The Heart, Part 7; Fantastic Four: Deadly Dimensions, Part 3; Volstagg: The Thief Of Asgard • Wolverine, Ghost Rider **A:** Tom Morgan; Cynthia Martin; Sam Grainger; Robert Texeira **W:** Howard Mackie; Robert Denatale; Sholly Fisch; Steve Gerber

67 ❑ Jan 1991 Cover: 1.25 **NM** value: **2.00**
Circ: CapCity orders: **35,100**
Wolverine and Ghost Rider: Acts of Vengeance, Part 4; Poison: Vandals Of The Heart, Part 8; Fantastic Four: Deadly Dimensions, Part 4, Spider-Man: Slow Burn • Wolverine, Ghost Rider **A:** Tom Morgan; Cynthia Martin; Dean Ormston; Robert Texeira **W:** Howard Mackie; Len Wein; Robert Denatale; Steve Gerber

68 ❑ Jan 1991 Cover: 1.25 **NM** value: **2.00**
Circ: CapCity orders: **34,800**
Wolverine and Ghost Rider: Acts of Vengeance, Part 5; Fantastic Four: Deadly Dimensions, Part 5; Lockjaw: Sparky The Wonder Dog; Shanna: The Bush Of Ghosts, Part 1 • Wolverine, Ghost Rider **A:** Mark Texeira; Tom Morgan; Paul Gulacy; José Delbo **W:** Scott Lobdell; Howard Mackie; Gerard Jones; Robert Denatale

69 ❑ Feb 1991 Cover: 1.25 **NM** value: **2.00**
Circ: CapCity orders: **34,200**
Wolverine and Ghost Rider: Acts of Vengeance, Part 6; Shanna: The Bush Of Ghosts, Part 2; Daredevil: Redemption Song, Part 1 • Wolverine, Ghost Rider **A:** Mark Texeira; Paul Gulacy; Sandy Plunkett **W:** Sandy Plunkett; Gerard Jones; Robert Mackie

70 ❑ Feb 1991 Cover: 1.25 **NM** value: **2.00**
Circ: CapCity orders: **34,300**
Wolverine and Ghost Rider: Acts of Vengeance, Part 7; Shanna: The Bush Of Ghosts, Part 3; Daredevil: Redemption Song, Part 2 • Wolverine, Ghost Rider **A:** Mark Texeira; Paul Gulacy; Sandy Plunkett **W:** Sandy Plunkett; Gerard Jones; Robert Mackie

71 ❑ Mar 1991 Cover: 1.25 **NM** value: **2.00**
Circ: CapCity orders: **55,800**
Wolverine and Ghost Rider: Acts of Vengeance, Part 8; Shanna: The Bush Of Ghosts, Part 4, Warlock: Warlock And The Fleshtones; Daredevil: Redemption Song, Part 3 • Wolverine, Ghost Rider; Has 1990 Statement, filed 10/1/90; avg print run 230,744; avg sales 131,788; avg subs 413; avg total paid 132,201; samples 10; office use 600; max existent 132,901; 42% of run returned **A:** Mark Texeira; Paul Gulacy; Scott McDaniel; Sandy Plunkett **W:** Sandy Plunkett; Scott Lobdell; Gerard Jones; Robert Mackie

72 ❑ Mar 1991 Cover: 1.25 **NM** value: **4.00**
Circ: CapCity orders: **34,900** • **CGC:** 7 graded, best 9.8
Weapon X; Shanna: The Bush Of Ghosts, Part 5; Daredevil: Redemption Song, Part 4; Red Wolf: Flesh Of My Flesh • Weapon X **A:** Barry Windsor-Smith; Paul Gulacy; Sandy Plunkett; Javier Saltares **W:** Barry Windsor-Smith; Sandy Plunkett; Fabian Nicieza; Gerard Jones

73 ❑ Mar 1991 Cover: 1.25 **NM** value: **2.50**
Circ: CapCity orders: **48,000** • **CGC:** 3 graded, best 9.6
Weapon X, Part 1; Shanna: The Bush Of Ghosts, Part 6; Sub-Mariner: The Sea Enemy; Black Knight: Sands Of Time • Weapon X **A:** Barry Windsor-Smith; Paul Gulacy; Jim Mooney; Russel Lyman **W:** Barry Windsor-Smith; Gerard Jones; Jason Balgobis; John Morelli

Other grades: Multiply prices above by **1.5 for Mint • 2/3 for Very Fine • 1/3 for Fine • 1/5 for Very Good • 1/8 for Good**

74 ❑ Apr 1991 Cover: 1.25 **NM** value: **2.50**
Circ: CapCity orders: **47,100 • CGC:** 3 graded, best 9.6
Weapon X, Part 2; Shanna: The Bush Of Ghosts, Part 7; Constrictor: The Freebie; Iceman/Torch: Absolute Zero • Weapon X **A:** Barry Windsor-Smith; Paul Gulacy; Joe Staton; Scott McDaniel **W:** Barry Windsor-Smith; Scott Lobdell; Dan Mishkin; Gerard Jones

75 ❑ Apr 1991 Cover: 1.25 **NM** value: **2.50**
Circ: CapCity orders: **4,900 • CGC:** 2 graded, best 9.6
Weapon X, Part 3; Shanna: The Bush Of Ghosts, Part 8 • Weapon X **A:** Barry Windsor-Smith; Paul Gulacy **W:** Barry Windsor-Smith; Gerard Jones

76 ❑ May 1991 Cover: 1.25 **NM** value: **2.50**
Circ: CapCity orders: **48,600 • CGC:** 2 graded, best 9.6
Weapon X, Part 4; Shanna: The Bush Of Ghosts, Part 9 • Weapon X **A:** Barry Windsor-Smith; Paul Gulacy **W:** Barry Windsor-Smith; Gerard Jones

77 ❑ May 1991 Cover: 1.25 **NM** value: **2.50**
Circ: CapCity orders: **57,300 • CGC:** 2 graded, best 9.8
Weapon X, Part 5; Shanna: The Bush Of Ghosts, Part 10; Sgt. Fury/Dracula: Rumanian Rumble, Part 1; Sub-Mariner: The Tides That Bind • Weapon X **A:** Barry Windsor-Smith; Paul Gulacy; Grant Miehm; Tom Lyle **W:** Barry Windsor-Smith; Robert Campanella; Doug Murray; Gerard Jones

78 ❑ Jun 1991 Cover: 1.25 **NM** value: **2.50**
Circ: CapCity orders: **57,000 • CGC:** 3 graded, best 9.6
Weapon X, Part 6; Sgt. Fury/Dracula: Rumanian Rumble, Part 2; Iron Man: Games; Hulk/Selene: Not Interested • Weapon X **A:** Brian Stelfreeze; Barry Windsor-Smith; Ken Steacy; Tom Lyle **W:** Barry Windsor-Smith; Doug Murray; Dwight Jon Zimmerman

79 ❑ Jun 1991 Cover: 1.25 **NM** value: **2.50**
Circ: CapCity orders: **56,700 • CGC:** 2 graded, best 9.4
Weapon X, Part 7; Sgt. Fury/Dracula: Rumanian Rumble, Part 3; Sunspot: The Tender And The Vulgar; Dr. Strange: A Nightmare On Bleecker Street • Weapon X **A:** John Byrne; Barry Windsor-Smith; Tom Lyle; Steve Geiger **W:** Barry Windsor-Smith; Robert Campanella; Daryl Edelman; Doug Murray

80 ❑ Jul 1991 Cover: 1.25 **NM** value: **2.50**
Circ: CapCity orders: **63,600 • CGC:** 2 graded, best 9.6
Weapon X, Part 8; Captain America: Wargod, Part 1; Daughters Of The Dragon: Child's Play; Mr. Fantastic: Fantastic Foray • Weapon X **A:** Steve Ditko; Barry Windsor-Smith; Chris Tsuda; Dennis Jensen **W:** Steve Ditko; Barry Windsor-Smith; Mary Jo Duffy; Danny Fingeroth

81 ❑ Jul 1991 Cover: 1.25 **NM** value: **2.50**
Circ: CapCity orders: **63,000 • CGC:** 2 graded, best 9.6
Weapon X, Part 9; Ant-Man: The Bomb; Daredevil: The Call; Captain America: Wargod, Part 2 • Weapon X; Daredevil **A:** Steve Ditko; James W. Fry III; Barry Windsor-Smith; Marshall Rogers **W:** Steve Ditko; Barry Windsor-Smith; Dana Moreshead; Robert Denatale

82 ❑ Aug 1991 Cover: 1.25 **NM** value: **2.50**
Circ: CapCity orders: **64,800 • CGC:** 2 graded, best 9.6
Weapon X, Part 10; Firestar: Life During War Time, Part 1; Power Man: Hero In Hiding; Iron Man: Making Real Progress • Weapon X **A:** Dwayne Turner; Barry Windsor-Smith; Sal Velluto; Steve Leialoha **W:** Barry Windsor-Smith; Bill Mumy; Marc McLaurin; Marie Javins

83 ❑ Aug 1991 Cover: 1.25 **NM** value: **2.50**
Circ: CapCity orders: **64,500 • CGC:** 2 graded, best 9.6
Weapon X, Part 11; Firestar: Life During War Time, Part 2; Human Torch: The Matchstick And The Moth; Hawkeye: The Distance • Weapon X **A:** Dwayne Turner; Barry Windsor-Smith; Erik Larsen; John Stanisci **W:** Steve Ditko; Barry Windsor-Smith; Fabian Nicieza; Marc McLaurin; Marie Javins

84 ❑ Sep 1991 Cover: 1.25 **NM** value: **2.50**
Circ: CapCity orders: **68,400 • CGC:** 2 graded, best 9.8
Weapon X, Part 12; Firestar: Life During War Time, Part 3 • Weapon X **A:** Dwayne Turner; Barry Windsor-Smith **W:** Barry Windsor-Smith; Marc McLaurin; Marie Javins

85 ❑ Sep 1991 Cover: 1.25 **NM** value: **2.50**
Circ: CapCity orders: **50,900**
Firestar: Life During War Time, Part 4; Wolverine: Blood Hungry, Part 1; Beast: Just Friends, Part 1; Speedball: The Dude In The Really Rad Armor! • Wolverine; 1st Kieth art on Wolverine **A:** Ron Wilson; Sam Kieth; Jae Lee; Dwayne Turner; Rob Liefeld **W:** Scott Lobdell; Marc McLaurin; Marie Javins; Peter David ★ 1st Appearance of Cyber.

86 ❑ Oct 1991 Cover: 1.25 **NM** value: **2.50**
Circ: CapCity orders: **46,500**
Firestar: Life During War Time, Part 5; Wolverine: Blood Hungry, Part 2; Beast: Just Friends, Part 2; Paladin: Take Me Out To The Bomb Game • Wolverine **A:** Ron Wilson; Sam Kieth; Jae Lee; Dwayne Turner; Rob Liefeld; J. Adam J. Walters **W:** Scott Lobdell; Marc McLaurin; Eric Fein; Marie Javins; Peter David

87 ❑ Oct 1991 Cover: 1.25 **NM** value: **2.00**
Circ: CapCity orders: **45,000**
Wolverine: Blood Hungry, Part 3; Beast: Just Friends, Part 3; Shroud: To Touch The Darkness • Wolverine **A:** Ron Wilson; Jae Lee; Rob Liefeld **W:** Scott Lobdell; Eric Fein; Peter David

88 ❑ Nov 1991 Cover: 1.25 **NM** value: **2.00**
Circ: CapCity orders: **42,900**
Wolverine: Blood Hungry, Part 4; Beast: Just Friends, Part 4; Solo: Hero Of The People; Volcana: Shopping • Wolverine **A:** Sam Kieth; Jae Lee; James Brock; Mark Runyan **W:** James Brock; Scott Lobdell; Eric Fein; Peter David

89 ❑ Nov 1991 Cover: 1.25 **NM** value: **2.00**
Circ: CapCity orders: **42,600 • CGC:** 1 graded, best 8.5
Wolverine: Blood Hungry, Part 5; Beast: Just Friends, Part 5; Spitfire: Young Blood; Mojo: What's Wrong With This Picture • Wolverine **A:** Sam Kieth; Jae Lee; Joe Madureira; Rita Fagiani **W:** Scott Lobdell; Dan Slott; Peter David

90 ❑ Dec 1991 Cover: 1.25 **NM** value: **2.00**
Circ: CapCity orders: **68,100**
Flip-book covers begin. Ghost Rider and Cable: Servants of the Dead, Part 1; Wolverine: Blood Hungry, Part 6; Beast: Just Friends, Part 6; Nightmare: Fangu Lives! • Wolverine **A:** Guang Yap; Sam Kieth; Jae Lee; Steve Buccellato **W:** Scott Lobdell; Steve Buccellato; Howard Mackie; Peter David ★ Appearance of Ghost Rider, Cable.

91 ❑ Dec 1991 Cover: 1.25 **NM** value: **1.50**
Circ: CapCity orders: **62,400**
Ghost Rider and Cable: Servants of the Dead, Part 2; Wolverine: Blood Hungry, Part 7; Beast: Just Friends, Part 7; Impossible Man: Truth Or Daredevil • Wolverine **A:** Guang Yap; Sam Kieth; Jae Lee; Dave Manak **W:** Scott Lobdell; Dave Manak; Howard Mackie; Peter David ★ Appearance of Ghost Rider, Cable.

92 ❑ Dec 1991 Cover: 1.25 **NM** value: **1.50**
Circ: CapCity orders: **60,300**
Ghost Rider and Cable: Servants of the Dead, Part 3; Wolverine: Blood Hungry, Part 8; Beast: Just Friends, Part 8; Northstar: Separate Allies • Wolverine **A:** Guang Yap; Sam Kieth; Jae Lee; Joe Madureira **W:** Scott Lobdell; Howard Mackie; Antonia Matias; Karl Bollers; Peter David ★ Appearance of Ghost Rider, Cable.

93 ❑ Jan 1992 Cover: 1.25 **NM** value: **1.50**
Circ: CapCity orders: **54,600**
Ghost Rider and Cable: Servants of the Dead, Part 4; Nova: And Ye Shall Remember This Day, Part 1; Wolverine: Wild Frontier, Part 1; Daredevil/Black Widow: Split Second • Wolverine **A:** Guang Yap; Dwayne Turner; Todd Fox; Gavin Curtis **W:** Tim Truman; Howard Mackie; Dan Slott; Susan Kennedy ★ Appearance of Ghost Rider, Cable.

94 ❑ Jan 1992 Cover: 1.25 **NM** value: **1.50**
Circ: CapCity orders: **53,400**
Ghost Rider and Cable: Servants of the Dead, Part 5; Thing: Grimm's Tale; Nova: And Ye Shall Remember This Day, Part 2; Wolverine: Wild Frontier, Part 2 • Wolverine **A:** Guang Yap; Ron Wilson; Todd Fox; Gavin Curtis **W:** Tim Truman; Howard Mackie; John Figueroa; Susan Kennedy ★ Appearance of Ghost Rider, Cable.

95 ❑ Feb 1992 Cover: 1.50 **NM** value: **Cover or less**
Circ: CapCity orders: **52,200**
Ghost Rider and Cable: Servants of the Dead, Part 6; Nova: And Ye Shall Remember This Day, Part 3; Wolverine: Wild Frontier, Part 3; Hulk: Heroes • Wolverine **A:** Vince Evans; Guang Yap; Todd Fox; Gavin Curtis **W:** Tim Truman; Howard Mackie; Danny Fingeroth; Susan Kennedy ★ Appearance of Ghost Rider, Cable.

96 ❑ Feb 1992 Cover: 1.50 **NM** value: **Cover or less**
Circ: CapCity orders: **51,900**
Ghost Rider and Cable: Servants of the Dead, Part 7; Nova: And Ye Shall Remember This Day, Part 4; Wolverine: Wild Frontier, Part 4; Speedball: Class Clown • Wolverine **A:** Guang Yap; Todd Fox; Dennis Jensen; Gavin Curtis **W:** Tim Truman; Scott Lobdell; Gavin Curtis; Howard Mackie; Susan Kennedy ★ Appearance of Ghost Rider, Cable.

97 ❑ Mar 1992 Cover: 1.50 **NM** value: **Cover or less**
Circ: CapCity orders: **45,900**
Ghost Rider and Cable: Servants of the Dead, Part 8; Wolverine: Wild Frontier, Part 5; Silver Surfer: Collision Course; Bar With No Name: Where Everyone Knows Your Alias • Wolverine **W:** Tim Truman; Howard Mackie; John Figueroa; Sholly Fisch ★ Appearance of Ghost Rider, Cable.

98 ❑ Mar 1992 Cover: 1.50 **NM** value: **Cover or less**
Circ: CapCity orders: **43,500**
Wolverine: Wild Frontier, Part 6; Ghost Rider: D'Spryte Times, D'Spryte Measures, Part 1 • Wolverine **A:** Todd Fox; Jimmy Palmiotti **W:** Tim Truman; Dan Slott

99 ❑ Apr 1992 Cover: 1.50 **NM** value: **Cover or less**
Circ: CapCity orders: **67,800**
Wolverine: Hauntings; Puck: Razor's Edge; Ghost Rider: D'Spryte Times, D'Spryte Measures, Part 2; Spider-Man: Has Anybody Seen My Gal? • Wolverine **A:** Malcolm Davis; Howard Mackie; Jimmy Palmiotti; Paula Foye **W:** Rob Liefeld; Paula Foye; Dan Slott; Raz Mesinai; Susan Kennedy

100 ❑ Apr 1992 Cover: 1.50 **NM** value: **Cover or less**
Circ: CapCity orders: **42,500**
• Anniversary issue. Dr. Doom: Dreams Of Doom; Ghost Rider: Whose Nightmare Is It Anyway; Wolverine: Mutant Dreams; Nightmare: Awakenings • Wolverine **A:** Sam Kieth **W:** Howard Mackie ★ Appearance of Ghost Rider. ★ Versus Doctor Doom.

101 ❑ May 1992 Cover: 1.50 **NM** value: **Cover or less**
Circ: CapCity orders: **38,000**
Wolverine/Nightcrawler: Male Bonding, Part 1; Young Gods: Against A Rogue God, Part 1; Ghost Rider/Dr. Strange: Doorway To Darkness, Part 1; Punisher: Vices • Wolverine, Nightcrawler **A:** Tom Sutton; Scott Kolins; Gene Colan; Rick Leonardi **W:** Scott Lobdell; Howard Mackie; Gerry Conway; Ron Marz

102 ❑ May 1992 Cover: 1.50 **NM** value: **Cover or less**
Circ: CapCity orders: **37,200**
Wolverine/Nightcrawler: Male Bonding, Part 2; Young Gods: Against A Rogue God, Part 2; Ghost Rider/Dr. Strange: Doorway To Darkness, Part 2; Phantom Rider: Stunt Show • Wolverine, Nightcrawler **A:** Tom Sutton; Gene Colan; Rick Leonardi; Dave Hoover **W:** Scott Lobdell; Howard Mackie; Gary Barnum; Gerry Conway

103 ❑ May 1992 Cover: 1.50 **NM** value: **Cover or less**
Circ: CapCity orders: **36,900**
Wolverine/Nightcrawler: Male Bonding, Part 3; Young Gods: Against A Rogue God, Part 3; Ghost Rider/Dr. Strange: Doorway To Darkness, Part 3; Rintrah: Stage Fright • Wolverine, Nightcrawler **A:** Tom Sutton; Gene Colan; Rick Leonardi; Larry Alexander **W:** Scott Lobdell; Howard Mackie; Gerry Conway; James Felder

104 ❑ Jun 1992 Cover: 1.50 **NM** value: **Cover or less**
Circ: CapCity orders: **34,200**
Wolverine/Nightcrawler: Male Bonding, Part 4; Young Gods: Against A Rogue God, Part 4; Ghost Rider/Dr. Strange: Doorway To Darkness, Part 4; U.S. Agent: Fight The Right Thing • Wolverine, Nightcrawler **A:** Tom Sutton; Gene Colan; Rick Leonardi; Paula Foye **W:** Scott Lobdell; Howard Mackie; Gerry Conway

105 ❑ Jun 1992 Cover: 1.50 **NM** value: **Cover or less**
Circ: CapCity orders: **34,200**
Wolverine/Nightcrawler: Male Bonding, Part 5; Young Gods: Against A Rogue God, Part 5; Ghost Rider/Dr. Strange: Doorway To Darkness, Part 5; The Thing: Crystal Quest • Wolverine, Nightcrawler **A:** Tom Sutton; Gene Colan; Rick Leonardi; Joel Zulueta **W:** Scott Lobdell; Howard Mackie; Gerry Conway; Skip Dietz

106 ❑ Jul 1992 Cover: 1.50 **NM** value: **Cover or less**
Circ: CapCity orders: **33,100**
Wolverine/Nightcrawler: Male Bonding, Part 6; Young Gods: Against A Rogue God, Part 6; Ghost Rider/Dr. Strange: Doorway To Darkness, Part 6; Gabriel: One Nation Under Hades • Wolverine, Nightcrawler **A:** Tom Sutton; Gene Colan; Rick Leonardi; Bret Blevins **W:** Scott Lobdell; Howard Mackie; Robert Campanella; Gerry Conway

107 ❑ Jul 1992 Cover: 1.50 **NM** value: **Cover or less**
Circ: CapCity orders: **32,800**
Wolverine/Nightcrawler: Male Bonding, Part 7; Young Gods: Against A Rogue God, Part 7, Red Wolf: Fuel For The Fire; Ghost Rider/Werewolf By Night: Return Of The Braineaters, Part 1 • Wolverine, Nightcrawler **A:** Tom Sutton; Gene Colan; James Blackburn; John Stanisci **W:** Scott Lobdell; Fabian Nicieza; Chris Cooper; Gerry Conway

108 ❑ Aug 1992 Cover: 1.50 **NM** value: **Cover or less**
Circ: CapCity orders: **39,300**
Wolverine/Nightcrawler: Male Bonding, Part 8; Young Gods: Against A Rogue God, Part 8; Ghost Rider/Werewolf By Night: Return Of The Braineaters, Part 2; Thanos: I Thanos, Part 1 • Wolverine, Ghost Rider **A:** Tom Sutton; Gene Colan; John Stanisci **W:** Scott Lobdell; Chris Cooper; Gerry Conway

109 ❑ Aug 1992 Cover: 1.50 **NM** value: **Cover or less**
Circ: CapCity orders: **38,700**
Young Gods: Against A Rogue God, Part 9; Typhoid's Kiss, Part 1; Ghost Rider/Werewolf By Night: Return Of The Braineaters, Part 3; Thanos: I, Thanos, Part 2 • Wolverine, Ghost Rider **A:** Scott Kolins; Shawn McManus; Steve Lightle; John Stanisci **W:** Jim Starlin; Ann Nocenti; Chris Cooper; Eric Fein; Gerry Conway ★ Appearance of Typhoid Mary.

110 ❑ Sep 1992 Cover: 1.50 **NM** value: **Cover or less**
Circ: CapCity orders: **36,300**
Typhoid's Kiss, Part 2; Ghost Rider/Werewolf By Night: Return Of The Braineaters, Part 4; Nightcrawler: Night Of The Ripper; Thanos: I Thanos, Part 3 • Wolverine, Ghost Rider **A:** Shawn McManus; Steve Lightle; John Stanisci; Mark Runyan **W:** Jim Starlin; Ann Nocenti; Barry Dutter; Chris Cooper ★ Appearance of Typhoid Mary.

111 ❑ Sep 1992 Cover: 1.50 **NM** value: **Cover or less**
Circ: CapCity orders: **36,000**
Typhoid's Kiss, Part 3; Ghost Rider/Werewolf By Night: Return Of The Braineaters, Part 5; Thanos: I Thanos, Part 4; Iron Fist: Menace Of The Mad Abbot • Infinity War; Wolverine, Ghost Rider **A:** Alexander Morrissey; Shawn McManus; Steve Lightle; John Stanisci **W:** Jim Starlin; Ann Nocenti; Chris Cooper; Joey Cavalieri ★ Appearance of Typhoid Mary.

112 ❑ Oct 1992 Cover: 1.50 **NM** value: **Cover or less**
Circ: CapCity orders: **25,500**
Typhoid's Kiss, Part 4; Ghost Rider/Werewolf By Night: Return Of The Braineaters, Part 6; Demogoblin: Demogoblin's Lament; Pip The Troll: Picnic • Wolverine, Ghost Rider **A:** Gene Colan; Steve Lightle; John Stanisci; Rita Fagiani **W:** Jim Starlin; Ann Nocenti; Chris Cooper; Danny Fingeroth ★ Appearance of Typhoid Mary.

113 ❑ Oct 1992 Cover: 1.50 **NM** value: **Cover or less**
Circ: CapCity orders: **25,500**
Typhoid's Kiss, Part 5; Giant-Man: The Third Life Of Bill Foster, Part 1; Ghost Rider/Iron Fist: The Night Has A Thousand Eyes, Part 1; Werewolf: Mercy Mission • Wolverine, Ghost Rider **A:** Vince Mielcarek; Ron Wilson; Shawn McManus; Steve Lightle **W:** Len Kaminski; Dwayne McDuffie; Ann Nocenti; Joey Cavalieri ★ Appearance of Typhoid Mary.

114 ❑ Oct 1992 Cover: 1.50 **NM** value: **Cover or less**
Circ: CapCity orders: **23,900**
Typhoid's Kiss, Part 6; Giant-Man: The Third Life Of Bill Foster, Part 2; Ghost Rider/Iron Fist: The Night Has A Thousand Eyes, Part 2; Arabian Knight: Bazar Tales • Wolverine, Ghost Rider **A:** Ron Wilson; Shawn McManus; Steve Lightle; James Blackburn **W:** Dwayne McDuffie; Ann Nocenti; Gary Barnum; Joey Cavalieri ★ Appearance of Typhoid Mary.

115 ❑ Nov 1992 Cover: 1.50 **NM** value: **Cover or less**
Circ: CapCity orders: **23,900**
Typhoid's Kiss, Part 7; Giant-Man: The Third Life Of Bill Foster, Part 3; Ghost Rider/Iron Fist: The Night Has A Thousand Eyes, Part 3; Cloak & Dagger: On The Dark Side Of The Street • Wolverine, Ghost Rider **A:** Ron Wilson; Shawn McManus; Steve Lightle; John Stanisci **W:** Dwayne McDuffie; Ann Nocenti; Eric Fein; Joey Cavalieri ★ Appearance of Typhoid Mary.

116 ❑ Nov 1992 Cover: 1.50 **NM** value: **Cover or less**
Circ: CapCity orders: **23,900**
Typhoid's Kiss, Part 8; Giant-Man: The Third Life Of Bill Foster, Part 4; Ghost Rider/Iron Fist: The Night Has A Thousand Eyes, Part 4; Two-Gun-Kid: Just Deserts • Wolverine, Ghost Rider **A:** Ron Wilson; Gil Kane; Shawn McManus; Steve Lightle **W:** Dwayne McDuffie; Ann Nocenti; Dan Slott; Joey Cavalieri ★ Appearance of Typhoid Mary.

117 ❑ Dec 1992 Cover: 1.50 **NM** value: **Cover or less**
Circ: CapCity orders: **33,900**
Giant-Man: The Third Life Of Bill Foster, Part 5; Ghost Rider/Iron Fist: The Night Has A Thousand Eyes, Part 5; Wolverine/Venom: Claws And Webs, Part 1 • Wolverine, Ghost Rider; Ravage 2099 preview **A:** Ron Wilson; Sam Kieth; Shawn McManus **W:** Dwayne McDuffie; Howard Mackie; Joey Cavalieri ★ 1st Appearance of Ravage 2099. ★ Appearance of Venom.

118 ❑ Dec 1992 Cover: 1.50 **NM** value: **Cover or less**
Circ: CapCity orders: **32,600**
Giant-Man: The Third Life Of Bill Foster, Part 6; Ghost Rider/Iron Fist: The Night Has A Thousand Eyes, Part 6; Wolverine/Venom: Claws And Webs, Part 2 • Wolverine; Doom 2099 preview **A:** Ron Wilson; Sam Kieth; Shawn McManus **W:** Dwayne McDuffie; Howard Mackie; Joey Cavalieri ★ 1st Appearance of Doom 2099. ★ Appearance of Venom.

119 ❑ Jan 1993 Cover: 1.50 **NM** value: **Cover or less**
Circ: Statement: **433,492**
Ghost Rider/Cloak & Dagger: And Let There Be Light, Part 1; Wolverine/Venom: Claws And Webs, Part 3; The Constrictor: Doin' The Toe Jam, Part 1 • Wolverine **A:** Alexander Morrissey; Sam Kieth; Mark Powers **W:** Howard Mackie; Paula Foye ★ Appearance of Venom.

120 ❑ Jan 1993 Cover: 1.50 **NM** value: **Cover or less**
Circ: Statement: **433,492** CapCity orders: **27,500**

CGC-graded: Multiply prices above by **33 for 9.9 M • 16 for 9.8 NM/M • 7 for 9.6 NM+ • 5 for 9.4 NM • 2.5 for 9.2 NM- • 1.5 for 9.0 VF/NM**

Ghost Rider/Cloak & Dagger: And Let There Be Light, Part 2; Spider-Man: Along Came A Child; Wolverine/Venom: Claws And Webs, Part 4; The Constrictor: Doin' The Toe Jam, Part 2 • Wolverine **A:** Alexander Morrissey; Sam Kieth; Ed Murr; Mark Powers **W:** Howard Mackie; Paula Foye; Keith Planit ★ Appearance of Venom.

121 ❑ Feb 1993 Cover: 1.50 **NM** value: **Cover or less**
Circ: Statement: **433,492** CapCity orders: **27,400** • **CGC:** 1 graded, best 9.0
Ghost Rider/Cloak & Dagger: And Let There Be Light, Part 3; Wolverine/Venom: Claws And Webs, Part 5; Mirage: Of Faith And Fable, Andromeda: Civil Disabilities • Wolverine **A:** Alexander Morrissey; Sam Kieth; Mark Moretti; Joe Madureira **W:** Howard Mackie; Paula Foye; Jaye Gardner; Karl Bollers

122 ❑ Feb 1993 Cover: 1.50 **NM** value: **Cover or less**
Circ: Statement: **433,492** CapCity orders: **29,900**
Ghost Rider/Cloak & Dagger: And Let There Be Light, Part 4; Wolverine/Venom: Claws And Webs, Part 6; Speedball: Taped Confessions; Knights Of Pendragon: Seeds Of Winter • Wolverine **A:** Alexander Morrissey; Sam Kieth; Hoang Nguyen; Paris Karounos **W:** Fabian Nicieza; Howard Mackie; Paula Foye; Skip Dietz

123 ❑ Mar 1993 Cover: 1.50 **NM** value: **Cover or less**
Circ: Statement: **433,492** CapCity orders: **29,600**
Ghost Rider/Typhoid Mary: The Walking Wounded, Part 1; Master Man: The Doomed Man; She-Hulk: Adrenazon's Revenge, Part 1; Wolverine/Lynx: Passion Play, Part 1 • Wolverine **A:** Scott Kolins; Dave Hoover; Steve Lightle; Dennis Jensen **W:** Scott Kolins; Scott Lobdell; Ann Nocenti; Kelly Corvese

124 ❑ Mar 1993 Cover: 1.50 **NM** value: **Cover or less**
Circ: Statement: **433,492** CapCity orders: **23,800**
Ghost Rider/Typhoid Mary: The Walking Wounded, Part 2; Wolverine/Lynx: Passion Play, Part 2; She-Hulk: Adrenazon's Revenge, Part 2; Solo: Death Flight • Wolverine **A:** Mark Bagley; Dave Hoover; Steve Lightle; Dennis Jensen **W:** Scott Lobdell; Ann Nocenti; Eric Fein; Kelly Corvese

125 ❑ Apr 1993 Cover: 1.50 **NM** value: **Cover or less**
Circ: Statement: **433,492** CapCity orders: **23,200**
Ghost Rider/Typhoid Mary: The Walking Wounded, Part 3; Wolverine/Lynx: Passion Play, Part 3; She-Hulk: Adrenazon's Revenge, Part 3; Iron Fist: The Book Of Changes, Part 1 • Wolverine **A:** Dave Hoover; Steve Lightle; Dennis Jensen **W:** Scott Lobdell; Ann Nocenti; Joey Cavalieri; Kelly Corvese

126 ❑ Apr 1993 Cover: 1.50 **NM** value: **Cover or less**
Circ: Statement: **433,492** CapCity orders: **23,100**
Ghost Rider/Typhoid Mary: The Walking Wounded, Part 4; Wolverine/Lynx: Passion Play, Part 4; She-Hulk: Adrenazon's Revenge, Part 4; Iron Fist: The Book Of Changes, Part 2 • Wolverine **A:** Dave Hoover; Steve Lightle; Dennis Jensen **W:** Scott Lobdell; Ann Nocenti; Joey Cavalieri; Kelly Corvese

127 ❑ May 1993 Cover: 1.50 **NM** value: **Cover or less**
Circ: Statement: **433,492** CapCity orders: **22,100**
Ghost Rider/Typhoid Mary: The Walking Wounded, Part 5; Wolverine/Lynx: Passion Play, Part 5; Iron Fist: The Book Of Changes, Part 3; Speedball: The Big Time • Wolverine **A:** Dave Hoover; Don Perlin; Steve Lightle; Dennis Jensen **W:** Scott Lobdell; Ann Nocenti; Danny Fingeroth; Joey Cavalieri

128 ❑ May 1993 Cover: 1.50 **NM** value: **Cover or less**
Circ: Statement: **433,492** CapCity orders: **22,100**
Ghost Rider/Typhoid Mary: The Walking Wounded, Part 6; Wolverine/Lynx: Passion Play, Part 6; Iron Fist: The Book Of Changes, Part 4; American Eagle: The Hunter And The Hunted • Wolverine **A:** Ron Wilson; Dave Hoover; Steve Lightle; Dennis Jensen **W:** Scott Lobdell; Ann Nocenti; Joey Cavalieri; John Figueroa

129 ❑ May 1993 Cover: 1.50 **NM** value: **Cover or less**
Circ: Statement: **433,492** CapCity orders: **22,100**
Ghost Rider/Typhoid Mary: The Walking Wounded, Part 7; Wolverine/Lynx: Passion Play, Part 7; Iron Fist: The Book Of Changes, Part 5; Crossbones: A Time To Die • Wolverine **A:** Ron Wilson; Dave Hoover; Steve Lightle; Dennis Jensen **W:** Scott Lobdell; Ann Nocenti; Joey Cavalieri; John Figueroa

130 ❑ Jun 1993 Cover: 1.50 **NM** value: **Cover or less**
Circ: Statement: **433,492** CapCity orders: **20,700**
Ghost Rider/Typhoid Mary: The Walking Wounded, Part 8; Wolverine/Lynx: Passion Play, Part 8; Iron Fist: The Book Of Changes, Part 6; American Eagle: Screams • Wolverine **A:** Ron Wilson; Dave Hoover; Steve Lightle; Dennis Jensen **W:** Scott Lobdell; Ann Nocenti; Joey Cavalieri; John Figueroa

131 ❑ Jun 1993 Cover: 1.50 **NM** value: **Cover or less**
Circ: Statement: **433,492** CapCity orders: **20,600**
Wolverine: These Foolish Things; Ant-Man: Late For Supper; Iron Fist: The Book Of Changes, Part 7; Ghost Rider/Cage: Heart And Soul, Part 1 • Wolverine **A:** Dave Hoover; Freddy Mendez; Sandy Plunkett; Dennis Jensen **W:** Sandy Plunkett; James Felder; Joey Cavalieri; Karl Bollers

132 ❑ Jul 1993 Cover: 1.50 **NM** value: **Cover or less**
Circ: Statement: **433,492** CapCity orders: **20,300**
Iron Fist: The Book Of Changes, Part 8; Ghost Rider/Cage: Heart And Soul, Part 2; Ghost Rider/Cage: Heart And Soul, Part 2 • Wolverine **A:** Dave Hoover; Freddy Mendez **W:** Joey Cavalieri; Karl Bollers

133 ❑ Jul 1993 Cover: 1.50 **NM** value: **Cover or less**
Circ: Statement: **433,492** CapCity orders: **20,100**
Ghost Rider/Cage: Heart And Soul, Part 3 • Wolverine **A:** Freddy Mendez **W:** Karl Bollers

134 ❑ Aug 1993 Cover: 1.50 **NM** value: **Cover or less**
Circ: Statement: **433,492** CapCity orders: **19,300**
Ghost Rider/Cage: Heart And Soul, Part 4 • Wolverine **A:** Freddy Mendez **W:** Karl Bollers

135 ❑ Aug 1993 Cover: 1.50 **NM** value: **Cover or less**
Circ: Statement: **433,492** CapCity orders: **19,300**
Ghost Rider/Cage: Heart And Soul, Part 5 • Wolverine **A:** Freddy Mendez **W:** Karl Bollers

136 ❑ Sep 1993 Cover: 1.50 **NM** value: **Cover or less**
Circ: Statement: **433,492** CapCity orders: **17,600**
Ghost Rider/Cage: Heart And Soul, Part 6 • Wolverine **A:** Freddy Mendez **W:** Karl Bollers

137 ❑ Sep 1993 Cover: 1.50 **NM** value: **Cover or less**
Circ: Statement: **433,492** CapCity orders: **17,600**
• Wolverine

138 ❑ Sep 1993 Cover: 1.50 **NM** value: **Cover or less**
Circ: Statement: **433,492** CapCity orders: **16,600**
Wolverine: Rumble in the Jungle, Part 1; Spellbound, Part 1; Excalibur; Ghost Rider/Masters of Silence, Part 2 **A:** Chris Marrinan; Ron Wilson; James W. Fry III; Terry Shoemaker **W:** Len Kaminski; Erik Larsen; Bobbie Chase; John Figueroa ★ Appearance of Masters of Silence, Ghost Rider, Wolverine, Wusin, Spellbound, Nightcrawler.

139 ❑ Oct 1993 Cover: 1.50 **NM** value: **Cover or less**
Circ: Statement: **433,492** CapCity orders: **16,600**
Wolverine: Rumble in the Jungle, Part 2; Spellbound, Part 2; The Foreigner; Ghost Rider/Masters of Silence, Part 3 **A:** Chris Marrinan; James W. Fry III; Terry Shoemaker; Derek Yaniger **W:** Len Kaminski; Erik Larsen; Bobbie Chase; Simon Furman ★ Appearance of Masters of Silence, Ghost Rider, Wolverine, Wusin, Foreigner, Spellbound, Zzzax.

140 ❑ Oct 1993 Cover: 1.50 **NM** value: **Cover or less**
Circ: Statement: **433,492** CapCity orders: **16,500**
Wolverine: Rumble in the Jungle, Part 3; Spellbound, Part 3; Captain Universe; Ghost Rider/Masters of Silence, Part 4 **A:** Chris Marrinan; James W. Fry III; Bill Wylie; Terry Shoemaker **W:** Len Kaminski; Erik Larsen; Bobbie Chase; Dan Slott ★ Origin of Captain Universe. ★ Appearance of Masters of Silence, Ghost Rider, Wolverine, Wusin, Captain Universe, Spellbound, Zzzax.

141 ❑ Nov 1993 Cover: 1.50 **NM** value: **Cover or less**
Circ: Statement: **433,492** CapCity orders: **15,600**

142 ❑ Nov 1993 Cover: 1.50 **NM** value: **Cover or less**
Circ: Statement: **433,492** CapCity orders: **15,400**

143 ❑ Dec 1993 Cover: 1.75 **NM** value: **Cover or less**
Circ: Statement: **433,492** CapCity orders: **17,100**
Siege of Darkness, Part 3; Werewolf: Goblin Night, Part 1; Scarlet Witch: Digital Terror, Part 1; Devil-Slayer: Out of Time, in the Time Out Hotel • Ghost Rider

144 ❑ Dec 1993 Cover: 1.75 **NM** value: **Cover or less**
Circ: Statement: **433,492** CapCity orders: **22,300**
Siege of Darkness, Part 6 • Ghost Rider

145 ❑ Jan 1994 Cover: 1.75 **NM** value: **Cover or less**
Circ: CapCity orders: **18,000**
• Ghost Rider

146 ❑ Jan 1994 Cover: 1.75 **NM** value: **Cover or less**
Circ: CapCity orders: **18,200**

147 ❑ Feb 1994 Cover: 1.50 **NM** value: **1.75**
Circ: CapCity orders: **12,400**
Vengeance, Part 1 • Has 1993 Statement, filed 10/1/93; avg print run 207,833; avg sales 133,067; avg subs 425; avg total paid 133,492; samples 125; office use 500; max existent 134,117; 36% of run returned **W:** Steve Lieber

148 ❑ Feb 1994 Cover: 1.50 **NM** value: **1.75**
Circ: CapCity orders: **12,300**
Vengeance, Part 2

149 ❑ Mar 1994 Cover: 1.50 **NM** value: **1.75**
Circ: CapCity orders: **18,100**

150 ❑ Mar 1994 Cover: 1.50 **NM** value: **1.75**
Circ: CapCity orders: **15,600**

151 ❑ Apr 1994 Cover: 1.50 **NM** value: **1.75**
Circ: CapCity orders: **13,050**

152 ❑ Apr 1994 Cover: 1.50 **NM** value: **1.75**
Circ: CapCity orders: **13,050**

153 ❑ May 1994 Cover: 1.75 **NM** value: **Cover or less**
Circ: CapCity orders: **12,000**

154 ❑ May 1994 Cover: 1.75 **NM** value: **Cover or less**
Circ: CapCity orders: **11,850**

155 ❑ May 1994 Cover: 1.75 **NM** value: **Cover or less**
Circ: CapCity orders: **11,100**

156 ❑ Jun 1994 Cover: 1.75 **NM** value: **Cover or less**
Circ: CapCity orders: **11,100**

157 ❑ Jun 1994 Cover: 1.75 **NM** value: **Cover or less**

158 ❑ Jul 1994 Cover: 1.75 **NM** value: **Cover or less**
Circ: CapCity orders: **12,100**

159 ❑ Jul 1994 Cover: 1.75 **NM** value: **Cover or less**
Circ: CapCity orders: **11,650**

160 ❑ Aug 1994 Cover: 1.75 **NM** value: **Cover or less**
Circ: CapCity orders: **10,300**

161 ❑ Aug 1994 Cover: 1.75 **NM** value: **Cover or less**
Circ: CapCity orders: **10,250**

162 ❑ Sep 1994 Cover: 1.75 **NM** value: **Cover or less**
Circ: CapCity orders: **9,200**

163 ❑ Sep 1994 Cover: 1.75 **NM** value: **Cover or less**
Circ: CapCity orders: **9,200**

164 ❑ Oct 1994 Cover: 1.75 **NM** value: **Cover or less**
Circ: CapCity orders: **8,150**

165 ❑ Oct 1994 Cover: 1.75 **NM** value: **Cover or less**
Circ: CapCity orders: **8,150**

166 ❑ Oct 1994 Cover: 1.75 **NM** value: **Cover or less**
Circ: CapCity orders: **8,150**

167 ❑ Nov 1994 Cover: 1.75 **NM** value: **Cover or less**
Circ: CapCity orders: **7,650**

168 ❑ Nov 1994 Cover: 1.75 **NM** value: **Cover or less**
Circ: CapCity orders: **7,650**

169 ❑ Dec 1994 Cover: 1.75 **NM** value: **Cover or less**
Circ: CapCity orders: **7,350**

170 ❑ Dec 1994 Cover: 1.75 **NM** value: **Cover or less**
Circ: CapCity orders: **7,300**

171 ❑ Jan 1995 Cover: 1.75 **NM** value: **Cover or less**
Circ: CapCity orders: **6,175**

172 ❑ Jan 1995 Cover: 1.75 **NM** value: **Cover or less**
Circ: CapCity orders: **6,150**

173 ❑ Feb 1995 Cover: 1.75 **NM** value: **Cover or less**
Circ: CapCity orders: **5,225**

174 ❑ Feb 1995 Cover: 1.75 **NM** value: **Cover or less**
Circ: CapCity orders: **5,200**

175 ❑ Mar 1995 Cover: 1.75 **NM** value: **Cover or less**
Circ: CapCity orders: **5,575**
final issue.

Bk 1/HC ❑ Cover: 19.95 **NM** value: **Cover or less**
hardcover. • Weapon X; collects Marvel Comics Presents #72-84 **A:** Barry Windsor-Smith

Bk 2 ❑ Cover: 6.95 **NM** value: **Cover or less**
• Wolverine: Typhoid's Kiss; collects story from Marvel Comics Presents #109-116

MARVEL COMICS PRESENTS SPIDER-MAN — Marvel

1 ❑ **NM** value: **1.50**
Spider-Man vs. the Chameleon!; Spider-Man Tackles the Torch! • Reprints Amazing Spider-Man #1 **A:** Steve Ditko; Jack Kirby **W:** Stan Lee

MARVEL COMICS PRESENTS THE X-MEN — Marvel

1 ❑ **NM** value: **1.50**
The Rage of Blastaar! **A:** Barry Windsor Smith **W:** Arnold Drake

MARVEL DOUBLE FEATURE — Marvel

1 ❑ Dec 1973 Cover: 0.20 **NM** value: **5.00**
• **CGC:** 4 graded, best 9.0
2 ❑ Feb 1974 Cover: 0.20 **NM** value: **4.00**
3 ❑ Apr 1974 Cover: 0.20 **NM** value: **4.00**
• **CGC:** 1 graded, best 9.2
4 ❑ Jun 1974 Cover: 0.25 **NM** value: **3.00**
5 ❑ Aug 1974 Cover: 0.25 **NM** value: **3.00**
6 ❑ Oct 1974 Cover: 0.25 **NM** value: **3.00**
7 ❑ Dec 1974 Cover: 0.25 **NM** value: **2.50**
8 ❑ Feb 1975 Cover: 0.25 **NM** value: **2.50**
9 ❑ Apr 1975 Cover: 0.25 **NM** value: **2.50**
10 ❑ Jun 1975 Cover: 0.25 **NM** value: **2.50**
11 ❑ Aug 1975 Cover: 0.25 **NM** value: **2.50**
12 ❑ Oct 1975 Cover: 0.25 **NM** value: **2.50**
13 ❑ Dec 1975 Cover: 0.25 **NM** value: **2.50**
14 ❑ Feb 1976 Cover: 0.25 **NM** value: **2.50**
15 ❑ Apr 1976 Cover: 0.25 **NM** value: **2.50**
16 ❑ Jun 1976 Cover: 0.25 **NM** value: **2.50**
17 ❑ Aug 1976 Cover: 0.25 **NM** value: **2.50**
• Reprints Iron Man vs. Sub-Mariner #1
18 ❑ Oct 1976 Cover: 0.30 **NM** value: **2.50**
• Reprints story from Iron Man #1
19 ❑ Dec 1976 Cover: 0.30 **NM** value: **2.50**
20 ❑ Feb 1977 Cover: 0.30 **NM** value: **2.50**
21 ❑ Apr 1977 Cover: 0.30 **NM** value: **2.50**

MARVEL FAMILY, THE — Fawcett

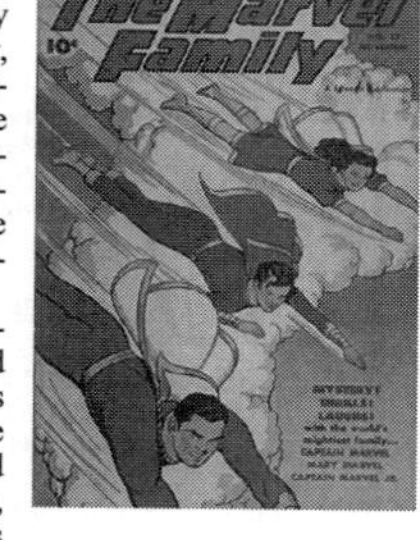

Begun in 1945, The Marvel Family united Captain Marvel, Mary Marvel, and Captain Marvel Junior, giving the key Fawcett super-heroes a chance to interact, and take on bad guys that could not be defeated by the heroes working individually. Uncle Marvel and the three Lieutenant Marvels also appeared in this series.

The fun-loving aspect of Fawcett's super-heroes stands in marked contrast to the angst-ridden antics of contemporary teams such as the X-Men. The characters here treated fighting evil as a great adventure, and often indulged in comic capers as well as super-heroic exploits.

1 ❑ Dec 1945 Cover: 0.10 **NM** value: **1325.00**
• **CGC:** 4 graded, best 7.5
★ Origin of Uncle Marvel, Captain Marvel Jr., Captain Marvel, Mary Marvel.
2 ❑ Jun 1946 Cover: 0.10 **NM** value: **585.00**
• **CGC:** 8 graded, best 9.6
3 ❑ Jul 1946 Cover: 0.10 **NM** value: **460.00**
4 ❑ Sep 1946 Cover: 0.10 **NM** value: **340.00**
5 ❑ Oct 1946 Cover: 0.10 **NM** value: **340.00**
• **CGC:** 1 graded, best 9.2
6 ❑ Nov 1946 Cover: 0.10 **NM** value: **285.00**
7 ❑ Dec 1946 Cover: 0.10 **NM** value: **285.00**
• **CGC:** 1 graded, best 9.2
8 ❑ Feb 1947 Cover: 0.10 **NM** value: **285.00**
9 ❑ Mar 1947 Cover: 0.10 **NM** value: **285.00**
10 ❑ Apr 1947 Cover: 0.10 **NM** value: **285.00**
11 ❑ May 1947 Cover: 0.10 **NM** value: **215.00**
12 ❑ Jun 1947 Cover: 0.10 **NM** value: **215.00**
13 ❑ Jul 1947 Cover: 0.10 **NM** value: **215.00**
14 ❑ Aug 1947 Cover: 0.10 **NM** value: **215.00**
15 ❑ Sep 1947 Cover: 0.10 **NM** value: **215.00**
16 ❑ Oct 1947 Cover: 0.10 **NM** value: **215.00**
17 ❑ Nov 1947 Cover: 0.10 **NM** value: **215.00**
18 ❑ Dec 1947 Cover: 0.10 **NM** value: **215.00**
19 ❑ Jan 1948 Cover: 0.10 **NM** value: **215.00**
20 ❑ Feb 1948 Cover: 0.10 **NM** value: **215.00**
21 ❑ Mar 1948 Cover: 0.10 **NM** value: **175.00**
22 ❑ Apr 1948 Cover: 0.10 **NM** value: **175.00**
23 ❑ May 1948 Cover: 0.10 **NM** value: **175.00**
24 ❑ Jun 1948 Cover: 0.10 **NM** value: **175.00**
25 ❑ Jul 1948 Cover: 0.10 **NM** value: **175.00**
26 ❑ Aug 1948 Cover: 0.10 **NM** value: **175.00**
27 ❑ Sep 1948 Cover: 0.10 **NM** value: **175.00**
28 ❑ Oct 1948 Cover: 0.10 **NM** value: **175.00**
29 ❑ Nov 1948 Cover: 0.10 **NM** value: **175.00**
30 ❑ Dec 1948 Cover: 0.10 **NM** value: **175.00**
31 ❑ Jan 1949 Cover: 0.10 **NM** value: **140.00**
32 ❑ Feb 1949 Cover: 0.10 **NM** value: **140.00**
33 ❑ Mar 1949 Cover: 0.10 **NM** value: **140.00**
34 ❑ Apr 1949 Cover: 0.10 **NM** value: **140.00**
35 ❑ May 1949 Cover: 0.10 **NM** value: **140.00**
36 ❑ Jun 1949 Cover: 0.10 **NM** value: **140.00**
37 ❑ Jul 1949 Cover: 0.10 **NM** value: **140.00**
• **CGC:** 1 graded, best 7.0
38 ❑ Aug 1949 Cover: 0.10 **NM** value: **140.00**
• **CGC:** 1 graded, best 8.0
39 ❑ Sep 1949 Cover: 0.10 **NM** value: **140.00**
• **CGC:** 1 graded, best 8.0
40 ❑ Oct 1949 Cover: 0.10 **NM** value: **140.00**

Other grades: Multiply prices above by **1.5 for Mint • 2/3 for Very Fine • 1/3 for Fine • 1/5 for Very Good • 1/8 for Good**

41 ❑ Nov 1949 Cover: 0.10 **NM** value: **110.00**
42 ❑ Dec 1949 Cover: 0.10 **NM** value: **110.00**
43 ❑ Jan 1950 Cover: 0.10 **NM** value: **110.00**
44 ❑ Feb 1950 Cover: 0.10 **NM** value: **110.00**
45 ❑ Mar 1950 Cover: 0.10 **NM** value: **110.00**
46 ❑ Apr 1950 Cover: 0.10 **NM** value: **110.00**
47 ❑ May 1950 Cover: 0.10 **NM** value: **110.00**
Flying saucer cover. 📖 The Marvel Family and the Interplanetary Theft!; Capt. Marvel Jr. and the Worm that Grew!; Mary Marvel Meets the Chameleon Girl!; Captain Marvel and the Mysterious Migration
48 ❑ Jun 1950 Cover: 0.10 **NM** value: **110.00**
49 ❑ Jul 1950 Cover: 0.10 **NM** value: **110.00**
• **CGC:** 1 graded, best 3.5
50 ❑ Aug 1950 Cover: 0.10 **NM** value: **110.00**
• **CGC:** 1 graded, best 2.5
51 ❑ Sep 1950 Cover: 0.10 **NM** value: **110.00**
• **CGC:** 1 graded, best 9.2
52 ❑ Oct 1950 Cover: 0.10 **NM** value: **110.00**
📖 The Flying Broom Stick;
53 ❑ Nov 1950 Cover: 0.10 **NM** value: **110.00**
54 ❑ Dec 1950 Cover: 0.10 **NM** value: **110.00**
• **CGC:** 1 graded, best 9.0
55 ❑ Jan 1951 Cover: 0.10 **NM** value: **110.00**
56 ❑ Feb 1951 Cover: 0.10 **NM** value: **110.00**
57 ❑ Mar 1951 Cover: 0.10 **NM** value: **110.00**
58 ❑ Apr 1951 Cover: 0.10 **NM** value: **110.00**
59 ❑ May 1951 Cover: 0.10 **NM** value: **110.00**
60 ❑ Jun 1951 Cover: 0.10 **NM** value: **110.00**
61 ❑ Jul 1951 Cover: 0.10 **NM** value: **110.00**
62 ❑ Aug 1951 Cover: 0.10 **NM** value: **110.00**
63 ❑ Sep 1951 Cover: 0.10 **NM** value: **110.00**
64 ❑ Oct 1951 Cover: 0.10 **NM** value: **110.00**
65 ❑ Nov 1951 Cover: 0.10 **NM** value: **110.00**
• **CGC:** 1 graded, best 6.0
66 ❑ Dec 1951 Cover: 0.10 **NM** value: **110.00**
67 ❑ Jan 1952 Cover: 0.10 **NM** value: **110.00**
68 ❑ Feb 1952 Cover: 0.10 **NM** value: **110.00**
69 ❑ Mar 1952 Cover: 0.10 **NM** value: **110.00**
70 ❑ Apr 1952 Cover: 0.10 **NM** value: **110.00**
71 ❑ May 1952 Cover: 0.10 **NM** value: **90.00**
72 ❑ Jun 1952 Cover: 0.10 **NM** value: **90.00**
73 ❑ Jul 1952 Cover: 0.10 **NM** value: **90.00**
74 ❑ Aug 1952 Cover: 0.10 **NM** value: **90.00**
75 ❑ Sep 1952 Cover: 0.10 **NM** value: **90.00**
76 ❑ Oct 1952 Cover: 0.10 **NM** value: **90.00**
77 ❑ Nov 1952 Cover: 0.10 **NM** value: **90.00**
78 ❑ Dec 1952 Cover: 0.10 **NM** value: **90.00**
79 ❑ Jan 1953 Cover: 0.10 **NM** value: **90.00**
📖 The Marvel Family Battles The Dynasty of Horror
80 ❑ Feb 1953 Cover: 0.10 **NM** value: **90.00**
81 ❑ Mar 1953 Cover: 0.10 **NM** value: **90.00**
final issue.
82 ❑ Apr 1953 Cover: 0.10 **NM** value: **75.00**
83 ❑ May 1953 Cover: 0.10 **NM** value: **75.00**
84 ❑ Jun 1953 Cover: 0.10 **NM** value: **75.00**
85 ❑ Jul 1953 Cover: 0.10 **NM** value: **75.00**
86 ❑ Aug 1953 Cover: 0.10 **NM** value: **75.00**
87 ❑ Sep 1953 Cover: 0.10 **NM** value: **75.00**
88 ❑ Oct 1953 Cover: 0.10 **NM** value: **75.00**
89 ❑ Jan 1954 Cover: 0.10 **NM** value: **75.00**

MARVEL FANFARE Marvel

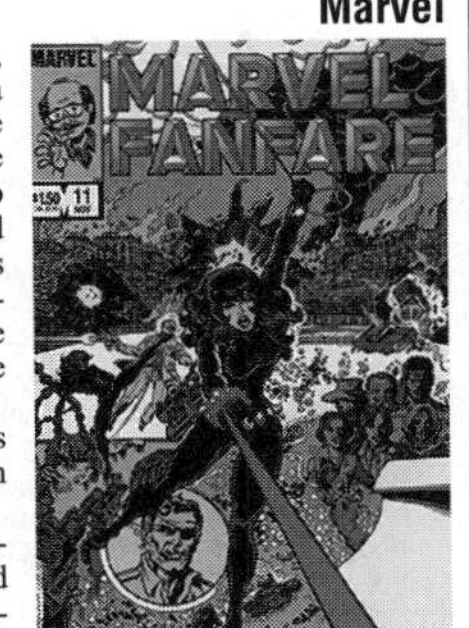

A deluxe, bimonthly series, Marvel Fanfare was announced a way for Marvel to spotlight some of its artistic rising stars while giving the writers a chance to stretch the bounds of established characters. Indeed, early issues were just that, with Chris Claremont returning the X-Men to the Savage Land to face Sauron in the series opener.

Other guest stars in the series included Iron Man, Moon Knight, and the Black Widow.

While some stories were compelling — and certainly benefited from the better paper — eventually some fans regarded the series as a dumping ground for unused file stories. And if you didn't have a particular interest in a character or characters, an extended story could put you off for good. Such is the life of the anthology!

1 ❑ Mar 1982 Cover: 1.25 **NM** value: **4.50**
• **CGC:** 10 graded, best 9.6
• Spider-Man; Daredevil; Angel **A:** Michael Golden; Tony DeZuniga; Frank Miller(cover) ★ 1st Appearance of Vertigo II.
2 ❑ May 1982 Cover: 1.25 **NM** value: **3.25**
• Spider-Man; Angel; Ka-Zar; Fantastic Four **A:** Michael Golden
3 ❑ Jul 1982 Cover: 1.25 **NM** value: **3.25**
• **CGC:** 2 graded, best 9.6
• X-Men **A:** Dave Cockrum
4 ❑ Sep 1982 Cover: 1.25 **NM** value: **2.50**
• **CGC:** 6 graded, best 9.8
📖 Cause and Effect • X-Men; Deathlok **A:** Michael Golden; Paul Smith; Tony DeZuniga; Steven Jones **W:** Jaimie Campos
5 ❑ Nov 1982 Cover: 1.25 **NM** value: **2.50**
📖 To Steal The Sorcerer's Soul! • Doctor Strange **A:** P. Craig Russell; Marshall Rogers **W:** Chris Claremont
6 ❑ Jan 1983 Cover: 1.25 **NM** value: **2.00**
Circ: Statement: **115,232**
📖 Switch Witch • Spider-Man; Doctor Strange; Scarlet Witch **A:** Sandy Plunkett **W:** Mike W. Barr
7 ❑ Mar 1983 Cover: 1.25 **NM** value: **2.00**
Circ: Statement: **115,232**
📖 With Friends Like These… • Hulk; Daredevil **A:** Dick Dillin; Joe Barney **W:** Steven Grant
8 ❑ May 1983 Cover: 1.50 **NM** value: **2.00**
Circ: Statement: **115,232**
📖 The Light That Never Was! • Doctor Strange; Mowgli **A:** Carmine Infantino **W:** Peter B. Gillis
9 ❑ Jul 1983 Cover: 1.50 **NM** value: **2.00**
Circ: Statement: **115,232**
📖 Rock 'n' Soul! • Man-Thing; Mowgli **A:** Joe Brozowski **W:** J.M. DeMatteis
10 ❑ Aug 1983 Cover: 1.50 **NM** value: **2.00**
Circ: Statement: **115,232**
📖 Widow • Black Widow; Mowgli **A:** George Pérez **C:** George Pérez **W:** Ralph Macchio
11 ❑ Nov 1983 Cover: 1.50 **NM** value: **2.00**
Circ: Statement: **115,232**
📖 Back In The USSR • Black Widow **A:** George Pérez **W:** Ralph Macchio
12 ❑ Jan 1984 Cover: 1.50 **NM** value: **2.00**
• Black Widow **A:** George Pérez
13 ❑ Mar 1984 Cover: 1.50 **NM** value: **2.00**
• Black Widow **A:** George Pérez **C:** Arthur Adams
14 ❑ May 1984 Cover: 1.50 **NM** value: **2.00**
• Vision; Quicksilver; Has 1983 Statement, filed 10/3/1983; avg print run 118,262; avg sales 114,536; avg subs 696; avg total paid 115,232; samples 483; office use 2,547; max existent 118,262; no newsstand sales
15 ❑ Jul 1984 Cover: 1.50 **NM** value: **2.00**
• Thing **A:** Barry Windsor-Smith
16 ❑ Sep 1984 Cover: 1.50 **NM** value: **2.00**
• Skywolf **A:** Dave Cockrum **W:** Marv Wolfman
17 ❑ Nov 1984 Cover: 1.50 **NM** value: **2.00**
• Skywolf **A:** Dave Cockrum **W:** Marv Wolfman
18 ❑ Jan 1985 Cover: 1.50 **NM** value: **2.00**
• Captain America **A:** Frank Miller
19 ❑ Mar 1985 Cover: 1.50 **NM** value: **2.00**
• Cloak & Dagger **A:** Jim Starlin
20 ❑ May 1985 Cover: 1.50 **NM** value: **2.00**
Circ: CapCity orders: **14,500**
📖 The Clash • Thing; Hulk; Doctor Strange **A:** Jim Starlin; Jim Novak **W:** Jim Starlin
21 ❑ Jul 1985 Cover: 1.50 **NM** value: **2.00**
Circ: CapCity orders: **13,750**
• Thing; Hulk **A:** Jim Starlin
22 ❑ Sep 1985 Cover: 1.50 **NM** value: **2.00**
Circ: CapCity orders: **12,850**
📖 Night Of The Octopus • Thing; Hulk; Iron Man **A:** Jim Starlin; Ken Steacy **W:** Roger McKenzie
23 ❑ Nov 1985 Cover: 1.50 **NM** value: **2.00**
Circ: CapCity orders: **12,500**
📖 From The Ashes • Thing; Hulk; Iron Man **A:** Jim Starlin; Ken Steacy **W:** Roger McKenzie
24 ❑ Jan 1986 Cover: 1.50 **NM** value: **2.00**
Circ: Statement: **61,691** CapCity orders: **11,500** • **CGC:** 1 graded, best 9.4
• Weirdworld
25 ❑ Mar 1986 Cover: 1.50 **NM** value: **2.00**
Circ: Statement: **61,691** CapCity orders: **10,950**
📖 Raven's Dark Sorcery • Dave Sim pin-up section; Weirdworld; Dave Sims pin-up section **A:** Pat Broderick **W:** Doug Moench
26 ❑ May 1986 Cover: 1.50 **NM** value: **2.00**
Circ: Statement: **61,691** CapCity orders: **9,950**
📖 The Goblin Spree • Weirdworld **A:** Pat Broderick **W:** Doug Moench
27 ❑ Jul 1986 Cover: 1.50 **NM** value: **2.00**
Circ: Statement: **61,691** CapCity orders: **11,650**
📖 Cars • Weirdworld; Spider-Man; Daredevil **A:** Tony Salmons **W:** Bill Mantlo
28 ❑ Sep 1986 Cover: 1.50 **NM** value: **2.00**
Circ: Statement: **61,691** CapCity orders: **13,650**
📖 Murder By Numbers 1,2,3… • Alpha Flight **A:** Ken Steacy **W:** Bill Mantlo
29 ❑ Nov 1986 Cover: 1.50 **NM** value: **2.00**
Circ: Statement: **61,691** CapCity orders: **15,400**
• Hulk ★ Death of Hammer. ★ Death of Anvil.
30 ❑ Jan 1987 Cover: 1.50 **NM** value: **2.00**
Circ: Statement: **66,300** CapCity orders: **11,000**
Painted cover. 📖 Real To Reel • Moon Knight **A:** Brent Anderson **W:** Ann Nocenti
31 ❑ Mar 1987 Cover: 1.50 **NM** value: **2.00**
Circ: Statement: **66,300** CapCity orders: **10,900**
📖 A Plague Of Frogs • Captain America **A:** Kerry Gammill **W:** J.M. DeMatteis
32 ❑ May 1987 Cover: 1.50 **NM** value: **2.00**
Circ: Statement: **66,300** CapCity orders: **10,600**
• Captain America
33 ❑ Jul 1987 Cover: 1.50 **NM** value: **2.00**
Circ: Statement: **66,300** CapCity orders: **23,150**
📖 Shadows on the Soul! • Wolverine; X-Men **A:** June Brigman; Terry Austin(inks) **W:** Chris Claremont
34 ❑ Sep 1987 Cover: 1.50 **NM** value: **2.00**
Circ: Statement: **66,300** CapCity orders: **11,300**
• Warriors Three
35 ❑ Nov 1987 Cover: 1.50 **NM** value: **2.00**
Circ: Statement: **66,300** CapCity orders: **11,500**
📖 Hogun's Goat • Warriors Three **A:** Alan Zelentz **W:** Alan Zelentz
36 ❑ Jan 1988 Cover: 1.50 **NM** value: **2.00**
Circ: Statement: **50,840** CapCity orders: **11,600**
• Warriors Three
37 ❑ Mar 1988 Cover: 1.50 **NM** value: **2.00**
Circ: Statement: **50,840** CapCity orders: **12,100**
• Warriors Three
38 ❑ Apr 1988 Cover: 1.50 **NM** value: **2.00**
Circ: Statement: **50,840** CapCity orders: **13,800**
• Moon Knight
39 ❑ Aug 1988 Cover: 1.95 **NM** value: **2.00**
Circ: Statement: **50,840** CapCity orders: **11,800**
• Hawkeye; Moon Knight; Has 1987 Statement; avg print run 71,595; avg sales 65,116; avg subs 1,184; avg total paid 66,300; samples 132; office use 730; max existent 67,162; 6% of run returned
40 ❑ Oct 1988 Cover: 1.95 **NM** value: **2.00**
Circ: Statement: **50,840** CapCity orders: **18,350**
📖 Chiaroscuro • Angel; Storm **A:** David Mazzucchelli **W:** Ann Nocenti
41 ❑ Dec 1988 Cover: 1.95 **NM** value: **2.00**
Circ: Statement: **50,840** CapCity orders: **12,000**
• Doctor Strange **A:** Dick Giordano
42 ❑ Feb 1989 Cover: 1.95 **NM** value: **2.00**
Circ: Statement: **50,300** CapCity orders: **13,300**
📖 Windfall! • Spider-Man **A:** Carl Potts; Terry Shoemaker **W:** Carl Potts
43 ❑ Apr 1989 Cover: 1.95 **NM** value: **2.00**
Circ: Statement: **50,300** CapCity orders: **11,350**
• Sub-Mariner; Human Torch
44 ❑ Jun 1989 Cover: 1.95 **NM** value: **2.00**
Circ: Statement: **50,300** CapCity orders: **12,400**
📖 Doom Bug • Iron Man; Iron Man vs. Doctor Doom **A:** Ken Steacy **W:** Ken Steacy
45 ❑ Aug 1989 Cover: 1.95 **NM** value: **2.00**
Circ: Statement: **50,300** CapCity orders: **14,500**
• all pin-ups **C:** John Byrne
46 ❑ Oct 1989 Cover: 1.95 **NM** value: **2.00**
Circ: Statement: **50,300** CapCity orders: **12,000**
• Fantastic Four
47 ❑ Nov 1989 Cover: 1.95 **NM** value: **2.00**
Circ: Statement: **50,300** CapCity orders: **17,650**
• Spider-Man; Hulk
48 ❑ Dec 1989 Cover: 1.95 **NM** value: **2.00**
Circ: Statement: **50,300** CapCity orders: **16,550**
• She-Hulk
49 ❑ Feb 1990 Cover: 1.95 **NM** value: **2.00**
Circ: Statement: **51,338** CapCity orders: **13,100**
• Doctor Strange; Dr. Strange
50 ❑ Apr 1990 Cover: 2.25 **NM** value: **Cover or less**
Circ: Statement: **51,338** CapCity orders: **13,900**
• X-Factor
51 ❑ Jun 1990 Cover: 2.95 **NM** value: **Cover or less**
Circ: Statement: **51,338** CapCity orders: **14,300**
• Silver Surfer; Has 1989 Statement; avg print run 51,025; avg sales 49,335; avg subs 965; avg total paid 50,300; samples 125; office use 600; max existent 51,025; no newsstand sales
52 ❑ Aug 1990 Cover: 2.25 **NM** value: **Cover or less**
Circ: Statement: **51,338** CapCity orders: **10,050**
• Black Knight; Fantastic Four
53 ❑ Oct 1990 Cover: 2.25 **NM** value: **Cover or less**
Circ: Statement: **51,338** CapCity orders: **9,800**
• Black Knight; Doctor Strange
54 ❑ Dec 1990 Cover: 2.25 **NM** value: **Cover or less**
Circ: Statement: **51,338** CapCity orders: **8,700**
• Black Knight; Wolverine
55 ❑ Feb 1991 Cover: 2.25 **NM** value: **Cover or less**
Circ: CapCity orders: **8,100**
• Power Pack; Wolverine
56 ❑ Apr 1991 Cover: 2.25 **NM** value: **Cover or less**
Circ: CapCity orders: **7,550**
• Shanna the She-Devil
57 ❑ Jun 1991 Cover: 2.25 **NM** value: **Cover or less**
Circ: CapCity orders: **7,500**
• Captain Marvel; Shanna the She-Devil
58 ❑ Aug 1991 Cover: 2.25 **NM** value: **Cover or less**
Circ: CapCity orders: **7,500**
• Shanna the She-Devil; Vision II (android); Scarlet Witch
59 ❑ Oct 1991 Cover: 2.25 **NM** value: **Cover or less**
Circ: CapCity orders: **6,900**
• Shanna the She-Devil
60 ❑ Jan 1992 Cover: 2.25 **NM** value: **Cover or less**
Circ: CapCity orders: **8,400**
final issue. • Black Panther; Rogue; Daredevil **A:** Denys Cowan

MARVEL FANFARE (2ND SERIES) Marvel

1 ❑ Sep 1996 Cover: 0.99 **NM** value: **1.00**
📖 Fateful Choices **A:** Scott Kolins; Robert Brown; Bruce Jones **W:** Jaimie Campos ★ Appearance of Captain America, Deathlok, Falcon.
2 ❑ Oct 1996 Cover: 0.99 **NM** value: **1.00**
📖 Instinct, Part 1 **A:** Pop Mhan **W:** Joe Kelly ★ Appearance of Wendigo, Hulk, Wolverine.
3 ❑ Nov 1996 Cover: 0.99 **NM** value: **1.00**
Circ: Direct Market orders: **32,750**
📖 Instinct, Part 2 **A:** Pop Mhan; Mike Witherby **W:** Joe Kelly ★ Appearance of Ghost Rider, Spider-Man.
4 ❑ Dec 1996 Cover: 0.99 **NM** value: **1.00**
Circ: Direct Market orders: **40,500**
★ Appearance of Longshot.
5 ❑ Jan 1997 Cover: 0.99 **NM** value: **1.00**
Circ: Direct Market orders: **36,500**
📖 Life Lessons **A:** Stephen Jones **W:** Jaimie Campos ★ Appearance of Dazzler, Longshot. ★ Versus Spiral.
6 ❑ Feb 1997 Cover: 0.99 **NM** value: **1.00**
Circ: Direct Market orders: **26,500**
📖 Direct Chances **A:** Stephen Jones; Gabe Alberola **W:** Jaimie Campos ★ Appearance of Sabretooth, Power Man, Iron Fist. ★ Versus Sabretooth.

Diamond preorders are the estimated number of comics sold, prior to their release, to comics shops in North America by Diamond Comic Distributors, the largest distributor. These figures underreport the actual number of circulating copies by the amount of reorders Diamond took (usually 5-10% again of the preorders) and sales by publishers to newsstand and bookstore distributors. For many independent publishers, Diamond's preorders may be quite close to the actual number of copies in circulation.

CGC-graded: Multiply prices above by **33 for 9.9 M • 16 for 9.8 NM/M • 7 for 9.6 NM+ • 5 for 9.4 NM • 2.5 for 9.2 NM- • 1.5 for 9.0 VF/NM**

MARVEL FEATURE (1ST SERIES) — Marvel

In its 12-issue run, this title served as the catalyst for a remarkable number of events. The first issue of Marvel Feature is the first appearance of The Defenders, a group consisting at this point of The Incredible Hulk, The Sub-Mariner, and Doctor Strange. Later issues reintroduce the long-neglected Ant-Man, present an early appearance of Thanos, and give readers the famous Thing vs. The Hulk battle.

The second series of Marvel Feature showcased Red Sonja in what many consider to be her finest stories and, beginning with a color reprint of Savage Sword of Conan #1, it soon turned to original storylines, culminating in #7's famous battle with Conan the Barbarian.

1 ❑ Dec 1971 Cover: 0.25 **NM** value: **75.00**
• **CGC:** 53 graded, best 9.6
📖 The Day of the Defenders! **A:** Ross Andru **C:** Neal Adams **W:** Roy Thomas ★ Origin of Defenders. ★ 1st Appearance of Omegatron, Defenders. ★ Death of Yandroth (physical body).

2 ❑ Mar 1972 Cover: 0.25 **NM** value: **36.00**
• **CGC:** 9 graded, best 9.4
• Sub-Mariner reprint **A:** Bill Everett ★ 2nd Appearance of Defenders.

3 ❑ Jun 1972 Cover: 0.20 **NM** value: **35.00**
• **CGC:** 10 graded, best 9.6
• Defenders **A:** Bill Everett ★ Appearance of Defenders.

4 ❑ Jul 1972 Cover: 0.20 **NM** value: **12.00**
• **CGC:** 2 graded, best 9.4
★ Appearance of Peter Parker, Ant-Man.

5 ❑ Sep 1972 Cover: 0.20 **NM** value: **6.00**
• **CGC:** 2 graded, best 9.4
★ Appearance of Ant-Man.

6 ❑ Nov 1972 Cover: 0.20 **NM** value: **6.00**
★ Appearance of Ant-Man.

7 ❑ Jan 1973 Cover: 0.20 **NM** value: **6.00**
A: Gil Kane ★ Appearance of Ant-Man.

8 ❑ Mar 1973 Cover: 0.20 **NM** value: **6.00**
★ Origin of Wasp, Ant-Man.

9 ❑ May 1973 Cover: 0.20 **NM** value: **6.00**
📖 The Killer Is My Wife **A:** P. Craig Russell **W:** Mike Friedrich ★ Appearance of Iron Man, Ant-Man.

10 ❑ Jul 1973 Cover: 0.20 **NM** value: **6.00**
• **CGC:** 1 graded, best 9.6
📖 Ant-Man No More! **A:** P. Craig Russell **W:** Mike Friedrich ★ Appearance of Ant-Man.

11 ❑ Sep 1973 Cover: 0.20 **NM** value: **11.00**
• **CGC:** 9 graded, best 9.6
• Thing vs. Hulk

12 ❑ Nov 1973 Cover: 0.20 **NM** value: **9.00**
★ Appearance of Thing, Iron Man, Thanos.

MARVEL FEATURE (2ND SERIES) — Marvel

1 ❑ Nov 1975 Cover: 0.25 **NM** value: **4.50**
• **CGC:** 4 graded, best 9.6
📖 The Temple Of Abomination • Red Sonja stories begin; Reprints Savage Sword of Conan #1 **A:** Dick Giordano; Neal Adams **W:** Roy Thomas; Robert E. Howard

2 ❑ Jan 1976 Cover: 0.25 **NM** value: **2.75**
📖 Blood Of The Hunter **A:** Frank Thorne **W:** Bruce Jones

3 ❑ Mar 1976 Cover: 0.25 **NM** value: **2.75**
📖 Balek-Lives! **A:** Frank Thorne **W:** Bruce Jones

4 ❑ May 1976 Cover: 0.25 **NM** value: **2.75**
• **CGC:** 1 graded, best 8.0
📖 Eyes Of The Gorgon **A:** Frank Thorne **W:** Bruce Jones

5 ❑ Jul 1976 Cover: 0.25 **NM** value: **2.75**
📖 The Bear Gold Walks! **A:** Frank Thorne **W:** Bruce Jones

6 ❑ Sep 1976 Cover: 0.30 **NM** value: **2.75**
📖 Beware The Sacred Sons Of Set! ★ Appearance of Conan.

7 ❑ Nov 1976 Cover: 0.30 **NM** value: **2.75**
• **CGC:** 1 graded, best 9.4
📖 The Battle Of The Barbarians • Red Sonja vs. Conan

MARVEL FRONTIER COMICS UNLIMITED — Marvel

1 ❑ Jan 1994 Cover: 2.95 **NM** value: **Cover or less**
Circ: CapCity orders: **6,600**
📖 Immortalis: That Sleep of Death,Savage Illusions; Children of Voyager; A Bloodseed Story; The Locked Room; Troubling Deaf Heaven **A:** Charles Adlard; Paul Johnson; D'isreali **W:** Nick Abadzis; David Hine; Nicholas Vince; Simon Jowett

MARVEL FUMETTI BOOK, THE — Marvel

1 ❑ Apr 1984, b&w Cover: 1.00 **NM** value: **2.00**
• photos with balloon captions

MARVEL GRAPHIC NOVEL — Marvel

The Marvel Graphic Novels feature book-length (OK, short book-length) stories with good writing and are propelled by the visual impact of comics. Freed from poor-quality printing and length restrictions of comic books, the creative teams on a graphic novel can be at their best.

And some of these are impressive. Early issues of The Marvel Graphic Novel series feature The Death of Captain Marvel, the introduction of The New Mutants, and the Holocaust-like cautionary tale "God Loves, Man Kills," starring The Uncanny X-Men. Later issues continue the tradition, demonstrating that comic art need not be limited to the bubble-gum crowd.

1 ❑ ca. 1982 Cover: 5.95 **NM** value: **12.50**
A: Jim Starlin **W:** Jim Starlin ★ Death of Captain Marvel.

1-2 ❑ Cover: 5.95 **NM** value: **6.00**

1-3 ❑ Cover: 5.95 **NM** value: **6.00**

2 ❑ Cover: 4.95 **NM** value: **7.00**
• Elric **A:** P. Craig Russell **W:** Roy Thomas

3 ❑ Cover: 4.95 **NM** value: **7.50**
• Dreadstar **A:** Jim Starlin **W:** Jim Starlin

4 ❑ Cover: 4.95 **NM** value: **10.00**
A: Bob McLeod **W:** Chris Claremont ★ Origin of Mirage II (Danielle "Dani" Moonstar), Sunspot, New Mutants. ★ 1st Appearance of Mirage II (Danielle "Dani" Moonstar), Sunspot, New Mutants.

4-2 ❑ Cover: 4.95 **NM** value: **6.00**

4-3 ❑ Cover: 4.95 **NM** value: **5.00**

5 ❑ Cover: 5.95 **NM** value: **10.00**
• X-Men: God Loves, Man Kills **A:** Brent Anderson **W:** Chris Claremont

5-2 ❑ Cover: 5.95 **NM** value: **7.00**

5-3 ❑ Cover: 5.95 **NM** value: **6.00**

5-4 ❑ Cover: 5.95 **NM** value: **6.00**

5-5 ❑ Cover: 5.95 **NM** value: **6.00**

6 ❑ Cover: 5.95 **NM** value: **6.00**
• Star Slammers **A:** Walt Simonson **W:** Walt Simonson

7 ❑ Cover: 5.95 **NM** value: **6.00**
• Killraven **A:** P. Craig Russell **W:** Don McGregor

8 ❑ Cover: 5.95 **NM** value: **6.00**
• Super Boxers **A:** John Byrne; Armando Gil **W:** Ron Wilson

9 ❑ Cover: 5.95 **NM** value: **6.00**
• The Futurians **A:** Dave Cockrum **W:** Dave Cockrum

10 ❑ Cover: 5.95 **NM** value: **6.00**
• Heartburst **A:** Rick Veitch **W:** Rick Veitch

11 ❑ Cover: 5.95 **NM** value: **6.00**
• Void Indigo **A:** Val Mayerik **W:** Steve Gerber

12 ❑ Cover: 5.95 **NM** value: **6.00**
• Dazzler: The Movie **A:** Frank Springer; Vince Colletta **W:** Jim Shooter

13 ❑ Cover: 5.95 **NM** value: **6.00**
• Starstruck **A:** Michael W. Kaluta **W:** Elaine Lee

14 ❑ Cover: 5.95 **NM** value: **6.00**
• Swords of the Swashbucklers **A:** Jackson Guice **W:** Bill Mantlo

15 ❑ Cover: 5.95 **NM** value: **6.00**
Circ: CapCity orders: **5,050**
• Raven Banner **A:** Charles Vess **W:** Alan Zelentz

16 ❑ Cover: 5.95 **NM** value: **6.00**
Circ: CapCity orders: **5,200**
• Aladdin Effect **A:** Greg LaRocque; Vince Colletta **W:** Jim Shooter; David Michelinie

17 ❑ Cover: 5.95 **NM** value: **6.00**
Circ: CapCity orders: **5,500**
• Living Monolith **A:** Geof Isherwood; Marc Silvestri **W:** David Michelinie

18 ❑ Cover: 6.95 **NM** value: **7.00**
Circ: CapCity orders: **5,950**
• She-Hulk **A:** Kim Demulder; Petra Scotese **W:** John Byrne

19 ❑ Cover: 6.95 **NM** value: **7.00**
Circ: CapCity orders: **3,750**
📖 The Witch Queen of Acheron • Conan the Barbarian **A:** Gary Kwapisz; Art Nichols **W:** Don Kraar

20 ❑ Cover: 6.95 **NM** value: **7.00**
Circ: CapCity orders: **9,000**
• Greenberg the Vampire **A:** Mark Badger **W:** J.M. DeMatteis

21 ❑ Cover: 6.95 **NM** value: **7.00**
Circ: CapCity orders: **5,200**
• Marada the She-Wolf **A:** John Bolton **W:** Chris Claremont

22 ❑ Cover: 6.95 **NM** value: **9.00**
Circ: CapCity orders: **11,250**
• Amazing Spider-Man **A:** Bernie Wrightson **W:** Susan K. Putney

23 ❑ Cover: 6.95 **NM** value: **7.00**
Circ: CapCity orders: **5,500**
📖 Shamballa • Dr. Strange **A:** Dan Green **W:** J.M. DeMatteis

24 ❑ Cover: 6.95 **NM** value: **7.50**
Circ: CapCity orders: **4,650**
• Daredevil

25 ❑ Cover: 6.95 **NM** value: **7.00**
Circ: CapCity orders: **6,800**
• Dracula

26 ❑ Cover: 6.95 **NM** value: **7.00**
• Alien Legion

27 ❑ Cover: 6.95 **NM** value: **Cover or less**
• Avengers ★ Death of The Purple Man.

28 ❑ Cover: 6.95 **NM** value: **Cover or less**
• Conan the Reaver

29 ❑ Cover: 6.95 **NM** value: **8.00**
• Thing vs. Hulk

30 ❑ Cover: 6.95 **NM** value: **Cover or less**
• Sailor's Story

31 ❑ Cover: 6.95 **NM** value: **Cover or less**
• Wolfpack ★ Origin of Wolfpack. ★ 1st Appearance of Wolfpack.

32 ❑ Cover: 6.95 **NM** value: **10.00**
★ Death of Groo.

33 ❑ Cover: 6.95 **NM** value: **Cover or less**
• Thor

34 ❑ Cover: 6.95 **NM** value: **Cover or less**
• Cloak & Dagger

35 ❑ Cover: 6.95 **NM** value: **Cover or less**
hardcover. • Shadow 1941

36 ❑ Cover: 12.95 **NM** value: **Cover or less**
• Willow

37 ❑ Cover: 6.95 **NM** value: **7.00**
• Hercules

38 ❑ Cover: 14.95 **NM** value: **16.00**
• Silver Surfer

MARVEL GRAPHIC NOVEL: ARENA — Marvel

1 ❑ Cover: 5.95 **NM** value: **Cover or less**
A: Bruce Jones **W:** Bruce Jones

MARVEL GRAPHIC NOVEL: CLOAK AND DAGGER AND POWER PACK: SHELTER FROM THE STORM — Marvel

1 ❑ Cover: 7.95 **NM** value: **Cover or less**
A: Sal Velluto **W:** Bill Mantlo

MARVEL GRAPHIC NOVEL: EMPEROR DOOM-STARRING THE MIGHTY AVENGERS — Marvel

1 ❑ Cover: 5.95 **NM** value: **Cover or less**
A: Bob Hall **W:** David Michelinie

MARVEL GRAPHIC NOVEL: KA-ZAR: GUNS OF THE SAVAGE LAND — Marvel

1 ❑ Cover: 8.95 **NM** value: **Cover or less**
A: Timothy Truman **W:** Chuck Dixon

MARVEL GRAPHIC NOVEL: RICK MASON, THE AGENT — Marvel

1 ❑ Cover: 9.95 **NM** value: **Cover or less**
A: John Ridgway **W:** James D. Hudnall

MARVEL GRAPHIC NOVEL: ROGER RABBIT IN THE RESURRECTION OF DOOM — Marvel

1 ❑ Cover: 8.95 **NM** value: **Cover or less**
📖 The Resurrection of Doom; Tummy Trouble **A:** Dan Spiegle; Mike Kazaleh **W:** Bob Foster

MARVEL GRAPHIC NOVEL: WHO FRAMED ROGER RABBIT? — Marvel

1 ❑ Cover: 6.95 **NM** value: **Cover or less**
A: Dan Spiegle; Daan Jippes **W:** Daan Jippes; Don Ferguson

MARVEL GUIDE TO COLLECTING COMICS, THE — Marvel

1 ❑ Sep 1982 **NM** value: **2.00**
no cover price.

MARVEL HALLOWEEN: SUPERNATURALS TOUR BOOK — Marvel

1 ❑ Nov 1998 Cover: 2.99 **NM** value: **Cover or less**
Circ: Diamd. preorders: **10,755**

MARVEL: HEROES & LEGENDS — Marvel

1 ❑ Oct 1996 Cover: 2.95 **NM** value: **Cover or less**
wraparound cover. 📖 For Better And For Worse! • backstory on Reed and Sue's wedding **A:** Steve Ditko; Gene Colan; John Buscema; Sal Buscema; John Romita Jr.; Ron Frenz; Marie Severin **W:** Fabian Nicieza; Stan Lee

2 ❑ Nov 1997 Cover: 2.99 **NM** value: **Cover or less**
No issue number. • untold Avengers story; Hawkeye, Quicksilver, Scarlet Witch joins team

MARVEL HOLIDAY SPECIAL — Marvel

1 ❑ Cover: 2.25 **NM** value: **3.00**
No issue number. no cover date or date in indicia. 📖 A Miracle A Few Blocks Down From 34th Street; A Christmas Coda; Midnight Drear; Twas A Midwinter's Night; Precious Gifts; Ghosts Of Christmas Past; It Came And Went On A Midnight Clear; A Spider-Man Carol **A:** Arthur Adams; Ron Garney; Sal Buscema; Ron Lim; Dave Cockrum; Klaus Janson; Dennis Jensen **W:** Len Kaminski; Walt Simonson; Scott Lobdell; Steven Grant; Tom DeFalco; Danny Fingeroth

1992 ❑ Jan 1993 Cover: 2.95 **NM** value: **3.00**
No issue number. • for 1992 holiday season

1993 ❑ Jan 1994 Cover: 2.95 **NM** value: **3.00**
Circ: CapCity orders: **16,900**
No issue number. • for 1993 holiday season **A:** Arthur Adams

1994 ❑ Jan 1995 Cover: 2.95 **NM** value: **3.00**
No issue number. 📖 Catastrophe on 34th Street; A Midnight Clear; Losin' the Blues; The Eternal Game; Star of the Show; The Night Before X-Mas • for 1994 holiday season **A:** Tom Mandrake; Gray Morrow; Sal Buscema; Rick Leonardi; James W. Fry III; Mike Manley **W:** Greg Wright; Kurt Busiek; J.M. DeMatteis; John Ostrander; Karl Bollers; Mindy Newell

1996 ❑ Jan 1997 Cover: 2.95 **NM** value: **Cover or less**
Circ: Direct Market orders: **27,250**

MARVEL ILLUSTRATED: SWIMSUIT ISSUE — Marvel

1 ❑ Mar 1991 Cover: 3.95 **NM** value: **Cover or less**
Circ: CapCity orders: **5,850**

MARVEL KIDS — Marvel

1 ❑ Cover: 3.49 **NM** value: **Cover or less**
📖 Franklin's Adventures • Fantastic Four

2 ❑ Cover: 3.49 **NM** value: **Cover or less**
📖 Project Hide • Incredible Hulk

3 ❑ Cover: 3.49 **NM** value: **Cover or less**
📖 Spider-Man Mysteries • Spider-Man

4 ❑ Cover: 3.49 **NM** value: **Cover or less**
📖 Mutant Search R.U.1? • X-Men

MARVEL KNIGHTS — Marvel

1 ❑ Jul 2000 Cover: 2.99 **NM** value: **Cover or less**
Circ: Diamd. preorders: **60,445**
📖 The Burrowers **A:** Eduardo Barreto **W:** Chuck Dixon

1/A ❑ Jul 2000 **NM** value: **6.50**
• **CGC:** 4 graded, best 9.8
Daredevil close-up cover. 📖 The Burrowers **A:** Eduardo Barreto **W:** Chuck Dixon

2 ❑ Aug 2000 Cover: 2.99 **NM** value: **Cover or less**
Circ: Diamd. preorders: **55,418** • **CGC:** 1 graded, best 9.4

Other grades: Multiply prices above by **1.5 for Mint • 2/3 for Very Fine • 1/3 for Fine • 1/5 for Very Good • 1/8 for Good**

📖 Thunder Below **A:** Eduardo Barreto **W:** Chuck Dixon ★ Appearance of Ulik.
3 ❑ Sep 2000 Cover: 2.99 **NM** value: **Cover or less**
Circ: Diamd. preorders: **44,145**
📖 The Destroyers **A:** Eduardo Barreto **W:** Chuck Dixon ★ Appearance of Ulik.
4 ❑ Oct 2000 Cover: 2.99 **NM** value: **Cover or less**
Circ: Diamd. preorders: **43,634**
📖 Zaran **A:** Eduardo Barreto **W:** Chuck Dixon
5 ❑ Nov 2000 Cover: 2.99 **NM** value: **Cover or less**
Circ: Diamd. preorders: **41,890**
📖 Family and Friends **A:** Eduardo Barreto **W:** Chuck Dixon
6 ❑ Dec 2000 Cover: 2.99 **NM** value: **Cover or less**
Circ: Diamd. preorders: **40,201**
📖 Maximum Security; The Reckoning **A:** Eduardo Barreto **W:** Chuck Dixon
7 ❑ Jan 2001 Cover: 2.99 **NM** value: **Cover or less**
Circ: Diamd. preorders: **37,687**
📖 Strange Matters **A:** Eduardo Barreto **W:** Chuck Dixon
8 ❑ Feb 2001 Cover: 2.99 **NM** value: **Cover or less**
Circ: Diamd. preorders: **36,029**
📖 Dark Matters **A:** Eduardo Barreto **W:** Chuck Dixon
9 ❑ Mar 2001 Cover: 2.99 **NM** value: **Cover or less**
Circ: Diamd. preorders: **34,605**
📖 Final Matters **A:** Eduardo Barreto **W:** Chuck Dixon
10 ❑ Apr 2001 Cover: 2.99 **NM** value: **Cover or less**
Circ: Diamd. preorders: **33,827**
📖 The Good with the Bad **A:** Eduardo Barreto **W:** Chuck Dixon
11 ❑ 2001 Cover: 2.99 **NM** value: **Cover or less**
Circ: Diamd. preorders: **32,716**
12 ❑ 2001 Cover: 2.99 **NM** value: **Cover or less**
Circ: Diamd. preorders: **32,247**
13 ❑ 2001 Cover: 2.99 **NM** value: **Cover or less**
Circ: Diamd. preorders: **31,030**
14 ❑ 2001 Cover: 2.99 **NM** value: **Cover or less**
Circ: Diamd. preorders: **30,738**
15 ❑ 2001 Cover: 2.99 **NM** value: **Cover or less**
Circ: Diamd. preorders: **31,216**

MARVEL KNIGHTS MAGAZINE — Marvel
2 ❑ Cover: 3.99 **NM** value: **Cover or less**
3 ❑ Cover: 3.99 **NM** value: **Cover or less**
4 ❑ Cover: 3.99 **NM** value: **Cover or less**
5 ❑ Cover: 3.99 **NM** value: **Cover or less**
6 ❑ Cover: 3.99 **NM** value: **Cover or less**

MARVEL KNIGHTS/MARVEL BOY GENESIS EDITION — Marvel
1 ❑ Jun 2000 **NM** value: **1.00**
• Polybagged with Punisher (5th Series) #3 **A:** Eduardo Barreto **W:** Mike Raicht

MARVEL KNIGHTS: MILLENNIAL VISIONS — Marvel
1 ❑ Feb 2002 Cover: 3.99 **NM** value: **Cover or less**
Circ: Diamd. preorders: **18,171**

MARVEL KNIGHTS SKETCHBOOK — Marvel
1 ❑ **NM** value: **1.00**
• Bundled with Wizard #84 **A:** Mark Texeira; Bernie Wrightson; Jae Lee; Joe Quesada

MARVEL KNIGHTS TOUR BOOK — Marvel
1 ❑ Oct 1998 Cover: 2.99 **NM** value: **Cover or less**
Circ: Diamd. preorders: **16,709**
No issue number. • previews and interviews

MARVEL KNIGHTS WAVE 2 SKETCHBOOK — Marvel
1 ❑ **NM** value: **0.50**
• Special free edition from Marvel in Wizard #90. • Sketchbook **A:** Tony Harris; J.G. Jones; Joe Jusko; Joe Quesada; Patrick Lee **W:** Tony Harris; David Mack; J.G. Jones; Joe Jusko; Joe Quesada; Patrick Lee; Jimmy Palmiotti; Devin Grayson

MARVEL MAGAZINE — Marvel
1 ❑ Cover: 1.25 **NM** value: **Cover or less**
2 ❑ Cover: 1.25 **NM** value: **Cover or less**
3 ❑ Cover: 1.25 **NM** value: **Cover or less**
4 ❑ Cover: 1.25 **NM** value: **Cover or less**
5 ❑ Cover: 1.25 **NM** value: **Cover or less**
6 ❑ Cover: 1.25 **NM** value: **Cover or less**

MARVEL MASTERPIECES 2 COLLECTION, THE — Marvel
1 ❑ Jul 1994 Cover: 2.95 **NM** value: **Cover or less**
• Pin-ups
2 ❑ Aug 1994 Cover: 2.95 **NM** value: **Cover or less**
3 ❑ Sep 1994 Cover: 2.95 **NM** value: **Cover or less**

MARVEL MASTERPIECES COLLECTION — Marvel
1 ❑ May 1993 Cover: 2.95 **NM** value: **Cover or less**
Circ: CapCity orders: **41,200**
A: Joe Jusko
2 ❑ Jun 1993 Cover: 2.95 **NM** value: **Cover or less**
Circ: CapCity orders: **28,900**
A: Joe Jusko
3 ❑ Jul 1993 Cover: 2.95 **NM** value: **Cover or less**
Circ: CapCity orders: **25,800**
A: Joe Jusko
4 ❑ Aug 1993 Cover: 2.95 **NM** value: **Cover or less**
Circ: CapCity orders: **29,600**
A: Joe Jusko

MARVEL MASTERWORKS — Marvel
1 ❑ Apr 1988 Cover: 29.95 **NM** value: **Cover or less**
• Spider-Man; Collects Amazing Fantasy #15 and Amazing Spider-Man #1-10 **A:** Steve Ditko **W:** Stan Lee ★ Origin of Spider-Man. ★ 1st Appearance of Spider-Man, Aunt May.
2 ❑ Apr 1988 Cover: 29.95 **NM** value: **Cover or less**
• Fantastic Four; Collects Fantastic Four #1-10
3 ❑ Apr 1988 Cover: 29.95 **NM** value: **Cover or less**
• X-Men; Collects X-Men (1st Series) #1-10
4 ❑ Jan 1989 Cover: 29.95 **NM** value: **Cover or less**
• Avengers
5 ❑ Feb 1989 Cover: 29.95 **NM** value: **Cover or less**
• Spider-Man; Collects Amazing Spider-Man #11-20
6 ❑ Feb 1989 Cover: 29.95 **NM** value: **100.00**
• Fantastic Four; Collects Fantastic Four #11-20
7 ❑ Mar 1989 Cover: 29.95 **NM** value: **Cover or less**
• X-Men; Collects X-Men (1st Series) #11-21
8 ❑ Nov 1989 Cover: 24.95 **NM** value: **Cover or less**
• Hulk; Collects The Incredible Hulk #1-6
9 ❑ Dec 1989 Cover: 29.95 **NM** value: **Cover or less**
• Avengers
10 ❑ Dec 1989 Cover: 29.95 **NM** value: **Cover or less**
• Spider-Man; Collects Amazing Spider-Man #21-30, Anl #1
11 ❑ Jan 1990 Cover: 29.95 **NM** value: **Cover or less**
• Collects X-Men #94-100, Giant-Size X-Men #1. • X-Men
12 ❑ Oct 1990 Cover: 29.95 **NM** value: **Cover or less**
• X-Men; Collects X-Men #101-110
13 ❑ Nov 1990 Cover: 34.95 **NM** value: **150.00**
• Fantastic Four; Collects Fantastic Four #21-30, Anl #1
14 ❑ Dec 1990 Cover: 34.95 **NM** value: **Cover or less**
• Captain America; Reprints Captain America stories from Tales of Suspense #59-81
15 ❑ Aug 1991 Cover: 34.95 **NM** value: **100.00**
• Surfer; Collects Silver Surfer #1-5
16 ❑ Sep 1991 Cover: 34.95 **NM** value: **115.00**
• Spider-Man; Collects Amazing Spider-Man #31-40, Anl 2
17 ❑ Oct 1991 Cover: 34.95 **NM** value: **Cover or less**
• Daredevil; Collects Daredevil #1-11
18 ❑ Nov 1991 Cover: 34.95 **NM** value: **Cover or less**
• Thor; Collects Journey into Mystery #83-100
19 ❑ Dec 1991 Cover: 44.95 **NM** value: **120.00**
• Silver Surfer; Collects Silver Surfer #6-18
20 ❑ ca. 1992 Cover: 34.95 **NM** value: **105.00**
• Iron Man; Collects Tales of Suspense #39-50
21 ❑ ca. 1992 Cover: 34.95 **NM** value: **225.00**
• Fantastic Four; Collects Fantastic Four #31-40, Anl #2
22 ❑ ca. 1992 Cover: 34.95 **NM** value: **100.00**
• Spider-Man; Collects Amazing Spider-Man #41-50, Anl #3
23 ❑ ca. 1992 Cover: 39.95 **NM** value: **Cover or less**
• Doctor Strange
24 ❑ ca. 1992 Cover: 24.95 **NM** value: **Cover or less**
• Collects X-Men (1st Series) #111-120 **A:** John Byrne **W:** Chris Claremont
25 ❑ ca. 1993 Cover: 34.95 **NM** value: **105.00**
• Collects Fantastic Four #41-50, Anl 3
26 ❑ ca. 1993 Cover: 34.95 **NM** value: **Cover or less**
• Collects Journey into Mystery #101-110
27 ❑ ca. 1993 Cover: 34.95 **NM** value: **200.00**
• Collects Avengers #21-30

MARVEL MAZES TO DRIVE YOU MAD! — Marvel
Bk 1 ❑ Cover: 2.95 **NM** value: **Cover or less**
• (Fireside)

MARVEL MILESTONE EDITION: AMAZING FANTASY — Marvel
15 ❑ Mar 1992 Cover: 2.95 **NM** value: **Cover or less**
📖 Spider-Man!; The Bell Ringer; Man in the Mummy Case! • Reprints of Amazing Fantasy # 15: Spider-man's Origin **A:** Steve Ditko **W:** Stan Lee

MARVEL MILESTONE EDITION: AMAZING SPIDER-MAN — Marvel
The Marvel Milestone Editions are reprints of some of the most famous comics Marvel has ever published. The Amazing Spider-Man editions include reprints of Amazing Spider-Man #1 (his first regular comic and the first appearance of J. Jonah Jameson), Amazing Spider-Man #3 (where the nefarious Doctor Octopus came into being), and Amazing Spider-Man #129 (the first appearance of the Punisher and the Jackal).

Each $2.95 milestone edition reprints the original comic in full, along with the letters pages and ads. They're a wonderful step back in time, and a great way for readers to experience the wonder of the early Marvel universe.
1 ❑ Jan 1993 Cover: 2.95 **NM** value: **Cover or less**
📖 The Chameleon Strikes! • Reprints Amazing Spider-Man #1 **A:** Steve Ditko **W:** Stan Lee ★ Origin of Spider-Man. ★ 1st Appearance of John Jameson, J. Jonah Jameson, Chameleon. ★ Appearance of Fantastic Four.
3 ❑ Mar 1995 Cover: 2.95 **NM** value: **Cover or less**
📖 Spider-Man Versus Doctor Octopus • Reprints Amazing Spider-Man #3 **A:** Steve Ditko **W:** Stan Lee ★ Origin of Doctor Octopus. ★ 1st Appearance of Doctor Octopus.
129 ❑ Cover: 2.95 **NM** value: **Cover or less**
• Reprints Amazing Spider-Man #129 ★ Origin of Punisher. ★ 1st Appearance of the Punisher, Jackal.
149 ❑ Nov 1994 Cover: 2.95 **NM** value: **Cover or less**
• indicia says Marvel Milestone Edition: Amazing Spider-Man #1.
📖 Even If I Live, I Die! • Reprints Amazing Spider-Man #149 **A:** Ross Andru **W:** Gerry Conway ★ 1st Appearance of Ben Reilly (Spider-Man clone).

MARVEL MILESTONE EDITION: AVENGERS — Marvel
1 ❑ Sep 1993 Cover: 2.95 **NM** value: **Cover or less**
• Reprints The Avengers #1; Thor, Iron Man, Ant-man, Wasp, Hulk **A:** Jack Kirby **W:** Stan Lee ★ Origin of Avengers.
4 ❑ Mar 1995 Cover: 2.95 **NM** value: **Cover or less**
• Reprints The Avengers #4; Captain America Joins **A:** Jack Kirby **W:** Stan Lee
16 ❑ Cover: 2.95 **NM** value: **Cover or less**
📖 The Old Order Changeth • Reprints The Avengers #16; New team begins: Captain America, Hawkeye, Quicksilver, and Scarlet Witch **A:** Jack Kirby **W:** Jack Kirby; Stan Lee

MARVEL MILESTONE EDITION: CAPTAIN AMERICA — Marvel
1 ❑ Mar 1995 Cover: 3.95 **NM** value: **Cover or less**
• Reprints Captain America #1 **A:** Joe Simon; Jack Kirby **W:** Joe Simon; Jack Kirby

MARVEL MILESTONE EDITION: FANTASTIC FOUR — Marvel
1 ❑ Nov 1991 Cover: 2.95 **NM** value: **Cover or less**
Circ: CapCity orders: **24,300**
5 ❑ Nov 1992 Cover: 2.95 **NM** value: **Cover or less**

MARVEL MILESTONE EDITION: GIANT-SIZE X-MEN — Marvel
1 ❑ 1991 Cover: 3.95 **NM** value: **Cover or less**
Circ: CapCity orders: **33,000** • **CGC:** 1 graded, best 4.0

MARVEL MILESTONE EDITION: INCREDIBLE HULK — Marvel
1 ❑ Mar 1991 Cover: 2.95 **NM** value: **Cover or less**
Circ: CapCity orders: **19,100**
📖 The Coming of The Hulk; The Hulk Strikes; The Search for the Hulk; Enter the Gargoyle…; The Hulk Triumph • Reprints Incredible Hulk #1 **A:** Jack Kirby; Stan Lee **W:** Jack Kirby; Stan Lee

MARVEL MILESTONE EDITION: IRON FIST — Marvel
14 ❑ Cover: 2.95 **NM** value: **Cover or less**
📖 Snowfire **A:** John Byrne **W:** Chris Claremont ★ 1st Appearance of Sabretooth.

MARVEL MILESTONE EDITION: IRON MAN — Marvel
55 ❑ Nov 1992 Cover: 2.95 **NM** value: **Cover or less**
📖 Beware the Blood Brothers! • Reprints Iron Man #55 **A:** Jim Starlin **W:** Jim Starlin; Mike Friedrich ★ 1st Appearance of Thanos, Drax, Starfox.

MARVEL MILESTONE EDITION: TALES OF SUSPENSE — Marvel
39 ❑ Nov 1994 Cover: 2.95 **NM** value: **Cover or less**
📖 Iron Man is Born; Gundar • Reprints Tales of Suspense #39 **A:** Steve Ditko; Don Heck **W:** Larry Lieber; Stan Lee ★ Origin of Iron Man. ★ 1st Appearance of Iron Man.

MARVEL MILESTONE EDITION: X-MEN — Marvel
1 ❑ 1991 Cover: 2.95 **NM** value: **Cover or less**
Circ: CapCity orders: **44,400** • **CGC:** 3 graded, best 9.8
📖 X-Men • reprint (first series) **A:** Jack Kirby **W:** Stan Lee ★ Origin of X-Men. ★ 1st Appearance of X-Men, Magneto.
9 ❑ Oct 1993 Cover: 2.95 **NM** value: **Cover or less**
• Reprints X-Men (1st Series) #9 **A:** Jack Kirby **W:** Stan Lee ★ 1st Appearance of Lucifer. ★ Appearance of Avengers.
28 ❑ Nov 1994 Cover: 2.95 **NM** value: **Cover or less**
• indicia says Marvel Milestone Edition: X-Men #1. • Reprints X-Men (1st Series) #28 ★ 1st Appearance of Banshee.

MARVEL MOVIE PREMIERE — Marvel
1 ❑ b&w Cover: 1.00 **NM** value: **3.00**
• magazine. 📖 The Land that Time Forgot

MARVEL MYSTERY COMICS — Marvel

Marvel Comics #1, dated October (with some cover-stamped November) 1939, was the first newsstand comic book from fledgling Marvel Comics. Its inaugural issue introduced newsstand buyers to such characters as the original Human Torch, The Sub-Mariner, and jungle hero Ka-Zar.

With #2, the title changed names to Marvel Mystery Comics. During this time of escalating global tensions, it found a ready audience for such patriotic heroes as The Patriot and Miss America. The Human Torch (with kid sidekick Toro) would soon stop fighting each other and begin battling side by side against Axis forces. Captain America would also make appearances in later issues.

Although these heroes could conquer the Nazis, they eventually fell to the post-war super-hero malaise. With #93, the series dropped its super-hero stories and became Marvel Tales (1st Series).

CGC-graded: Multiply prices above by **33 for 9.9 M • 16 for 9.8 NM/M • 7 for 9.6 NM+ • 5 for 9.4 NM • 2.5 for 9.2 NM- • 1.5 for 9.0 VF/NM**

2 ❑ Dec 1939 Cover: 0.10 **NM** value: **20000.00**
• **CGC:** 1 graded, best 8.0
• Series continued from Marvel Comics #1
3 ❑ Jan 1940 Cover: 0.10 **NM** value: **9500.00**
• **CGC:** 1 graded, best 5.0
4 ❑ Feb 1940 Cover: 0.10 **NM** value: **7400.00**
5 ❑ Mar 1940 Cover: 0.10 **NM** value: **15400.00**
• **CGC:** 3 graded, best 4.5
Human Torch cover. • scarce
6 ❑ Apr 1940 Cover: 0.10 **NM** value: **4800.00**
• **CGC:** 2 graded, best 6.0
7 ❑ May 1940 Cover: 0.10 **NM** value: **4800.00**
• **CGC:** 2 graded, best 8.0
8 ❑ Jun 1940 Cover: 0.10 **NM** value: **6300.00**
• **CGC:** 2 graded, best 8.5
• Human Torch vs. Sub-Mariner
9 ❑ Jul 1940 Cover: 0.10 **NM** value: **15300.00**
• **CGC:** 5 graded, best 6.5
• Human Torch vs. Sub-Mariner; scarce
10 ❑ Aug 1940 Cover: 0.10 **NM** value: **4800.00**
• **CGC:** 4 graded, best 7.0
11 ❑ Sep 1940 Cover: 0.10 **NM** value: **3000.00**
• **CGC:** 2 graded, best 9.0
12 ❑ Oct 1940 Cover: 0.10 **NM** value: **2900.00**
• **CGC:** 6 graded, best 8.5
13 ❑ Nov 1940 Cover: 0.10 **NM** value: **3800.00**
• **CGC:** 5 graded, best 9.2
★ 1st Appearance of The Vision I.
14 ❑ Dec 1940 Cover: 0.10 **NM** value: **2000.00**
• **CGC:** 8 graded, best 6.5
15 ❑ Jan 1941 Cover: 0.10 **NM** value: **2000.00**
• **CGC:** 3 graded, best 8.5
16 ❑ Feb 1941 Cover: 0.10 **NM** value: **2000.00**
• **CGC:** 1 graded, best 9.2
17 ❑ Mar 1941 Cover: 0.10 **NM** value: **2100.00**
• Sub-Mariner/Human Torch team-up
18 ❑ Apr 1941 Cover: 0.10 **NM** value: **1650.00**
• **CGC:** 5 graded, best 9.0
19 ❑ May 1941 Cover: 0.10 **NM** value: **1800.00**
• **CGC:** 3 graded, best 9.2
★ Origin of Toro.
20 ❑ Jun 1941 Cover: 0.10 **NM** value: **1800.00**
• **CGC:** 5 graded, best 8.5
21 ❑ Jul 1941 Cover: 0.10 **NM** value: **1550.00**
• **CGC:** 1 graded, best 7.5
★ 1st Appearance of The Patriot.
22 ❑ Aug 1941 Cover: 0.10 **NM** value: **1400.00**
• **CGC:** 3 graded, best 9.0
23 ❑ Sep 1941 Cover: 0.10 **NM** value: **1400.00**
• **CGC:** 3 graded, best 9.0
24 ❑ Oct 1941 Cover: 0.10 **NM** value: **1400.00**
• **CGC:** 3 graded, best 8.0
25 ❑ Nov 1941 Cover: 0.10 **NM** value: **1400.00**
• **CGC:** 1 graded, best 8.5
26 ❑ Dec 1941 Cover: 0.10 **NM** value: **1300.00**
• **CGC:** 1 graded, best 8.0
27 ❑ Jan 1942 Cover: 0.10 **NM** value: **1300.00**
• **CGC:** 4 graded, best 9.4
28 ❑ Feb 1942 Cover: 0.10 **NM** value: **1300.00**
• **CGC:** 2 graded, best 8.0
29 ❑ Mar 1942 Cover: 0.10 **NM** value: **1300.00**
• **CGC:** 1 graded, best 5.5
30 ❑ Apr 1942 Cover: 0.10 **NM** value: **1300.00**
• **CGC:** 4 graded, best 8.0
31 ❑ May 1942 Cover: 0.10 **NM** value: **1200.00**
32 ❑ Jun 1942 Cover: 0.10 **NM** value: **1200.00**
• **CGC:** 2 graded, best 7.0
★ 1st Appearance of The Boboes.
33 ❑ Jul 1942 Cover: 0.10 **NM** value: **1200.00**
• **CGC:** 1 graded, best 9.2
34 ❑ Aug 1942 Cover: 0.10 **NM** value: **1200.00**
• **CGC:** 3 graded, best 8.5
35 ❑ Sep 1942 Cover: 0.10 **NM** value: **1200.00**
• **CGC:** 2 graded, best 9.2
36 ❑ Oct 1942 Cover: 0.10 **NM** value: **1200.00**
• **CGC:** 2 graded, best 8.0
37 ❑ Nov 1942 Cover: 0.10 **NM** value: **1200.00**
• **CGC:** 6 graded, best 8.5
38 ❑ Dec 1942 Cover: 0.10 **NM** value: **1200.00**
• **CGC:** 1 graded, best 3.5
39 ❑ Jan 1943 Cover: 0.10 **NM** value: **1200.00**
40 ❑ Feb 1943 Cover: 0.10 **NM** value: **1200.00**
• **CGC:** 2 graded, best 8.5
41 ❑ Mar 1943 Cover: 0.10 **NM** value: **1200.00**
• **CGC:** 1 graded, best 4.5
42 ❑ Apr 1943 Cover: 0.10 **NM** value: **1020.00**
• **CGC:** 2 graded, best 9.0
43 ❑ May 1943 Cover: 0.10 **NM** value: **1020.00**
• **CGC:** 2 graded, best 9.0
44 ❑ Jun 1943 Cover: 0.10 **NM** value: **1020.00**
• **CGC:** 1 graded, best 9.4
45 ❑ Jul 1943 Cover: 0.10 **NM** value: **1020.00**
• **CGC:** 1 graded, best 4.5
46 ❑ Aug 1943 Cover: 0.10 **NM** value: **1020.00**
• **CGC:** 2 graded, best 7.5
47 ❑ Sep 1943 Cover: 0.10 **NM** value: **1020.00**
• **CGC:** 4 graded, best 9.2
48 ❑ Oct 1943 Cover: 0.10 **NM** value: **1020.00**
• **CGC:** 4 graded, best 5.5
49 ❑ Nov 1943 Cover: 0.10 **NM** value: **1250.00**
• **CGC:** 4 graded, best 9.0
★ Origin of Miss America.
50 ❑ Dec 1943 Cover: 0.10 **NM** value: **1020.00**
• **CGC:** 2 graded, best 6.5
51 ❑ Jan 1944 Cover: 0.10 **NM** value: **900.00**
• **CGC:** 2 graded, best 7.5
52 ❑ Feb 1944 Cover: 0.10 **NM** value: **900.00**
• **CGC:** 2 graded, best 9.2
53 ❑ Mar 1944 Cover: 0.10 **NM** value: **900.00**
• **CGC:** 1 graded, best 8.5
54 ❑ Apr 1944 Cover: 0.10 **NM** value: **900.00**
55 ❑ May 1944 Cover: 0.10 **NM** value: **900.00**
56 ❑ Jun 1944 Cover: 0.10 **NM** value: **900.00**
• **CGC:** 2 graded, best 5.0
57 ❑ Jul 1944 Cover: 0.10 **NM** value: **900.00**
• **CGC:** 3 graded, best 7.5
58 ❑ Sep 1944 Cover: 0.10 **NM** value: **900.00**
• **CGC:** 5 graded, best 7.5
59 ❑ Oct 1944 Cover: 0.10 **NM** value: **900.00**
60 ❑ Dec 1944 Cover: 0.10 **NM** value: **900.00**
61 ❑ Jan 1945 Cover: 0.10 **NM** value: **900.00**
• **CGC:** 1 graded, best 2.0
62 ❑ Mar 1945 Cover: 0.10 **NM** value: **900.00**
• **CGC:** 1 graded, best 5.0
63 ❑ Apr 1945 Cover: 0.10 **NM** value: **900.00**
64 ❑ Jun 1945 Cover: 0.10 **NM** value: **900.00**
• **CGC:** 2 graded, best 9.0
65 ❑ Jul 1945 Cover: 0.10 **NM** value: **900.00**
• **CGC:** 5 graded, best 9.4
66 ❑ Sep 1945 Cover: 0.10 **NM** value: **900.00**
• **CGC:** 4 graded, best 6.5
67 ❑ Nov 1945 Cover: 0.10 **NM** value: **900.00**
• **CGC:** 2 graded, best 8.0
68 ❑ Jan 1946 Cover: 0.10 **NM** value: **790.00**
• **CGC:** 5 graded, best 8.5
69 ❑ Feb 1946 Cover: 0.10 **NM** value: **790.00**
• **CGC:** 2 graded, best 4.5
70 ❑ Mar 1946 Cover: 0.10 **NM** value: **790.00**
• **CGC:** 2 graded, best 9.4
71 ❑ Apr 1946 Cover: 0.10 **NM** value: **790.00**
• **CGC:** 5 graded, best 9.4
72 ❑ May 1946 Cover: 0.10 **NM** value: **790.00**
• **CGC:** 3 graded, best 9.6
73 ❑ Jun 1946 Cover: 0.10 **NM** value: **790.00**
• **CGC:** 2 graded, best 8.0
74 ❑ Jul 1946 Cover: 0.10 **NM** value: **790.00**
• **CGC:** 5 graded, best 9.2
75 ❑ Aug 1946 Cover: 0.10 **NM** value: **790.00**
• **CGC:** 5 graded, best 9.0
76 ❑ Sep 1946 Cover: 0.10 **NM** value: **790.00**
• **CGC:** 4 graded, best 8.0
77 ❑ Oct 1946 Cover: 0.10 **NM** value: **790.00**
• **CGC:** 1 graded, best 8.0
78 ❑ Nov 1946 Cover: 0.10 **NM** value: **790.00**
• **CGC:** 5 graded, best 9.2
79 ❑ Dec 1946 Cover: 0.10 **NM** value: **740.00**
• **CGC:** 4 graded, best 9.0
80 ❑ Jan 1947 Cover: 0.10 **NM** value: **1100.00**
• **CGC:** 4 graded, best 9.0
★ Appearance of Captain America.
81 ❑ Mar 1947 Cover: 0.10 **NM** value: **860.00**
• **CGC:** 3 graded, best 7.0
★ Appearance of Captain America.
82 ❑ May 1947 Cover: 0.10 **NM** value: **1600.00**
• **CGC:** 8 graded, best 9.4
• Sub-Mariner/Namora team-up ★ Origin of Namora.
83 ❑ Aug 1947 Cover: 0.10 **NM** value: **715.00**
• **CGC:** 2 graded, best 6.0
84 ❑ Oct 1947 Cover: 0.10 **NM** value: **1050.00**
• **CGC:** 4 graded, best 8.0
• Blonde Phantom features start
85 ❑ Dec 1947 Cover: 0.10 **NM** value: **715.00**
• **CGC:** 1 graded, best 7.5
86 ❑ Mar 1948 Cover: 0.10 **NM** value: **815.00**
★ Appearance of Captain America.
87 ❑ Aug 1948 Cover: 0.10 **NM** value: **710.00**
• **CGC:** 5 graded, best 8.5
★ Appearance of Captain America.
88 ❑ Oct 1948 Cover: 0.10 **NM** value: **865.00**
• **CGC:** 7 graded, best 9.2
★ Appearance of Captain America.
89 ❑ Dec 1948 Cover: 0.10 **NM** value: **865.00**
★ Appearance of Captain America.
90 ❑ Feb 1949 Cover: 0.10 **NM** value: **865.00**
• **CGC:** 1 graded, best 8.0
• Blonde Phantom's identity revealed
91 ❑ Apr 1949 Cover: 0.10 **NM** value: **865.00**
• **CGC:** 1 graded, best 4.5
92 ❑ Jun 1949 Cover: 0.10 **NM** value: **1650.00**
• **CGC:** 7 graded, best 9.2
• Series continued as Marvel Tales #93 ★ Origin of The Human Torch.

MARVEL MYSTERY COMICS (2ND SERIES) Marvel

1 ❑ Dec 1999 Cover: 3.95 **NM** value: **Cover or less**
Circ: Diamd. preorders: **15,590** • **CGC:** 1 graded, best 9.8
📖 Human Torch: The Parrot Strikes Back!; The Vision; Submariner; Hurricane; The Angel; Silver Scorpion; Captain America and the White Death **A:** Bill Everett; Jack Kirby; Carl Burgos **W:** Joe Simon

Do you have changes or corrections for the **Standard Catalog**? Send your original research to us at **allcomics@krause.com**

MARVEL NO-PRIZE BOOK, THE Marvel

Marvel's intrepid Stan Lee is nothing if not a grand promoter. And nowhere is his particular genius more evident than in the "No-Prize." In the 1960s and 1970s, this "award" was sent to fans who pointed out blunders in Marvel books. So, when you read a comic where Captain America administered the coup de grace to an opponent, challenging, "Only one of us is going to leave this room alive ... and it won't be me!" — or when heroes referred to each other by their (supposedly unknown) real names, you could rest assured that a no-prize was in the mail to the fan who first pointed out the mistake.

In reality, the no-prizes were urgently inscribed — but empty — envelopes. That didn't stop millions of fans from wanting to be the first on the block to earn one of these coveted awards by catching Marvel's mistakes, the biggest and best of which are collected in this compilation of Marvel's greatest goofs.

1 ❑ Jan 1983 Cover: 1.00 **NM** value: **2.00**
• **CGC:** 2 graded, best 9.4
📖 Lest We Should Goof…! • mistakes **A:** Jack Kirby **W:** Stan Lee

MARVELOUS DRAGON CLAN Lunar

1 ❑ Jul 1994, b&w Cover: 2.50 **NM** value: **Cover or less**
2 ❑ Sep 1994, b&w Cover: 2.50 **NM** value: **Cover or less**

MARVELOUS WIZARD OF OZ (MGM'S...) Marvel / DC

1 ❑ Cover: 1.50 **NM** value: **15.00**
• treasury-sized movie adaptation.

MARVEL: PORTRAITS OF A UNIVERSE Marvel

1 ❑ Mar 1995 Cover: 2.95 **NM** value: **Cover or less**
Circ: CapCity orders: **12,525**
A: Dave Gibbons; Simon Bisley; Colin MacNeil; Kevin Walker; Bret Blevins; Ken Steacy; Mark A. Nelson; Ricardo Villagran; John Estes; John Van Fleet; Bob Larkin; Dennis Calero; Nick Percival; Terese Nielsen; Alan Craddock; Lou Harrison
2 ❑ Apr 1995 Cover: 2.95 **NM** value: **Cover or less**
Circ: CapCity orders: **9,075**
3 ❑ May 1995 Cover: 2.95 **NM** value: **Cover or less**
Circ: CapCity orders: **6,950**
4 ❑ Jun 1995 Cover: 2.95 **NM** value: **Cover or less**
Circ: CapCity orders: **6,025**
A: Vince Evans; Steve Sampson; John Higgins; Joe Phillips; Christopher Moeller; Ariel Olivetti; Simon Bisley; Bret Blevins; Dan Lawlis; Tony Luke; Brian Ashmore; Doug Gregory; Glenn Kim; Lou Harrison

MARVEL POSTER BOOK Marvel

1 ❑ Jan 1991 Cover: 2.50 **NM** value: **Cover or less**
Circ: CapCity orders: **26,800**
A: Todd McFarlane

MARVEL PREMIERE Marvel

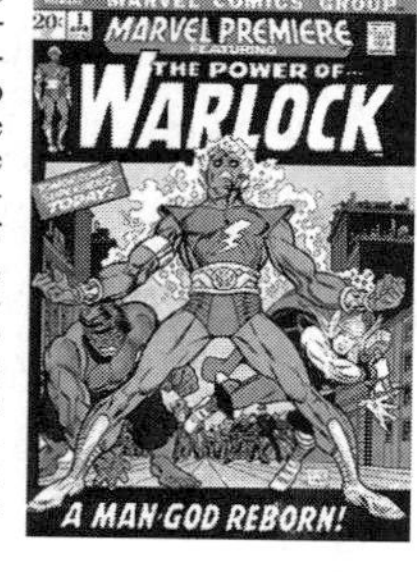

In its nearly decade-long run, Marvel Premiere served as a proving ground for a host of new characters. Iron Fist, Woodgod, Caleb Hammer, The Liberty Legion, The 3-D Man, and many others made first appearances in Marvel Premiere. Other characters, like Doctor Strange, The Falcon, Morbius, Ghost Rider, and Jack of Hearts were featured here in their first solo stories. Marvel even tried out its own Elfquest-like series with Weirdworld in #38. And yes, Marvel Premiere was also the venue in which Alice Cooper made his first comic book appearance.

1 ❑ Apr 1972 Cover: 0.20 **NM** value: **22.00**
• **CGC:** 36 graded, best 9.6
📖 And Men Shall Call Him…Warlock! **A:** Gil Kane **W:** Roy Thomas
★ Origin of Counter-Earth, Warlock.
2 ❑ May 1972 Cover: 0.20 **NM** value: **13.00**
• **CGC:** 7 graded, best 9.8
• Yellow Claw **A:** Jack Kirby ★ Appearance of Warlock.
3 ❑ Jul 1972 Cover: 0.20 **NM** value: **20.00**
• **CGC:** 2 graded, best 9.4
A: Barry Windsor-Smith ★ Appearance of Doctor Strange.
4 ❑ Sep 1972 Cover: 0.20 **NM** value: **9.00**
• **CGC:** 5 graded, best 9.8
A: Frank Brunner; Barry Windsor-Smith ★ Appearance of Doctor Strange.
5 ❑ Nov 1972 Cover: 0.20 **NM** value: **7.00**
A: Mike Ploog; P. Craig Russell ★ Appearance of Doctor Strange.
6 ❑ Jan 1973 Cover: 0.20 **NM** value: **7.00**
A: Frank Brunner; Mike Ploog ★ Appearance of Doctor Strange.
7 ❑ Mar 1973 Cover: 0.20 **NM** value: **7.00**
A: Mike Ploog; P. Craig Russell ★ Appearance of Doctor Strange.
8 ❑ May 1973 Cover: 0.20 **NM** value: **7.00**
• **CGC:** 1 graded, best 9.4
A: Jim Starlin ★ Appearance of Doctor Strange.
9 ❑ Jul 1973 Cover: 0.20 **NM** value: **7.00**
A: Frank Brunner ★ Appearance of Doctor Strange.
10 ❑ Sep 1973 Cover: 0.20 **NM** value: **8.00**
A: Frank Brunner; Neal Adams ★ Appearance of Doctor Strange.
★ Death of The Ancient One.

Other grades: Multiply prices above by **1.5 for Mint • 2/3 for Very Fine • 1/3 for Fine • 1/5 for Very Good • 1/8 for Good**

11 ❑ Oct 1973 Cover: 0.20 **NM** value: **5.00**
A: Frank Brunner; Neal Adams ★ Appearance of Doctor Strange.
12 ❑ Nov 1973 Cover: 0.20 **NM** value: **5.00**
A: Frank Brunner; Neal Adams ★ Appearance of Doctor Strange.
13 ❑ Jan 1974 Cover: 0.20 **NM** value: **5.00**
A: Frank Brunner; Neal Adams ★ 1st Appearance of Sise-Neg (as Cagliostro). ★ Appearance of Doctor Strange.
14 ❑ Mar 1974 Cover: 0.20 **NM** value: **5.00**
A: Frank Brunner; Neal Adams ★ Appearance of Sise-Neg, Doctor Strange.
15 ❑ May 1974 Cover: 0.25 **NM** value: **35.00**
• **CGC:** 49 graded, best 9.8
A: Gil Kane ★ Origin of Iron Fist. ★ 1st Appearance of Iron Fist.
16 ❑ Jul 1974 Cover: 0.25 **NM** value: **18.00**
• **CGC:** 3 graded, best 9.6
★ 2nd Appearance of Iron Fist.
17 ❑ Sep 1974 Cover: 0.25 **NM** value: **9.00**
• **CGC:** 1 graded, best 8.5
★ Appearance of Iron Fist.
18 ❑ Oct 1974 Cover: 0.25 **NM** value: **9.00**
• **CGC:** 3 graded, best 9.4
★ Appearance of Iron Fist.
19 ❑ Nov 1974 Cover: 0.25 **NM** value: **9.00**
★ 1st Appearance of Colleen Wing. ★ Appearance of Iron Fist.
20 ❑ Jan 1975 Cover: 0.25 **NM** value: **9.00**
• **CGC:** 1 graded, best 9.4
★ Appearance of Iron Fist.
21 ❑ Mar 1975 Cover: 0.25 **NM** value: **9.00**
• **CGC:** 1 graded, best 9.2
★ Appearance of Iron Fist.
22 ❑ Jun 1975 Cover: 0.25 **NM** value: **9.00**
★ Appearance of Iron Fist.
23 ❑ Aug 1975 Cover: 0.25 **NM** value: **9.00**
• **CGC:** 1 graded, best 9.6
A: Pat Broderick ★ Appearance of Iron Fist.
24 ❑ Sep 1975 Cover: 0.25 **NM** value: **9.00**
• **CGC:** 2 graded, best 9.6
A: Pat Broderick ★ Appearance of Iron Fist.
25 ❑ Oct 1975 Cover: 0.25 **NM** value: **14.00**
• **CGC:** 2 graded, best 9.0
A: John Byrne ★ Appearance of Iron Fist.
26 ❑ Nov 1975 Cover: 0.25 **NM** value: **4.00**
A: Jack Kirby ★ Appearance of Hercules.
27 ❑ Dec 1975 Cover: 0.25 **NM** value: **4.00**
★ Appearance of Satana.
28 ❑ Feb 1976 Cover: 0.25 **NM** value: **5.00**
• **CGC:** 5 graded, best 9.4
★ Appearance of Werewolf, Man-Thing, Ghost Rider, Legion of Monsters, Morbius.
29 ❑ Apr 1976 Cover: 0.25 **NM** value: **3.00**
• **CGC:** 1 graded, best 9.0
A: Jack Kirby ★ Origin of Whizzer, Red Raven, Thin Man, Blue Diamond, Miss America. ★ 1st Appearance of Patriot, Jack Frost I, Thin Man, Blue Diamond. ★ Appearance of Liberty Legion.
30 ❑ Jun 1976 Cover: 0.25 **NM** value: **2.50**
• **CGC:** 1 graded, best 9.2
A: Jack Kirby ★ Appearance of Liberty Legion.
31 ❑ Aug 1976 Cover: 0.25 **NM** value: **2.00**
A: Jack Kirby ★ Origin of Woodgod. ★ 1st Appearance of Woodgod.
32 ❑ Oct 1976 Cover: 0.30 **NM** value: **2.00**
• Monark Starstalker **A:** Howard Chaykin
33 ❑ Dec 1976 Cover: 0.30 **NM** value: **2.00**
• Monark **A:** Howard Chaykin ★ Appearance of Solomon Kane.
34 ❑ Feb 1977 Cover: 0.30 **NM** value: **2.00**
A: Howard Chaykin ★ Appearance of Solomon Kane.
35 ❑ Apr 1977 Cover: 0.30 **NM** value: **2.00**
📖 The 3-D Man! **A:** Jim Craig **W:** Roy Thomas ★ Origin of 3-D Man. ★ 1st Appearance of 3-D Man.
36 ❑ Jun 1977 Cover: 0.30 **NM** value: **2.00**
📖 The Devil's Music **A:** Jim Craig **W:** Roy Thomas ★ Appearance of 3-D Man.
37 ❑ Aug 1977 Cover: 0.30 **NM** value: **2.00**
• **CGC:** 1 graded, best 9.0
📖 Code-Name: The Cold Warrior! **A:** Jim Craig **W:** Roy Thomas ★ Appearance of 3-D Man.
38 ❑ Oct 1977 Cover: 0.30 **NM** value: **2.00**
★ 1st Appearance of Weirdworld.
39 ❑ Dec 1977 Cover: 0.35 **NM** value: **2.00**
★ Appearance of Torpedo.
40 ❑ Feb 1978 Cover: 0.35 **NM** value: **2.00**
★ 1st Appearance of Bucky II (Fred Davis). ★ Appearance of Torpedo.
41 ❑ Apr 1978 Cover: 0.35 **NM** value: **2.00**
📖 The Dying Sun! **A:** Tom Sutton **W:** Doug Moench ★ Appearance of Seeker 3000.
42 ❑ Jun 1978 Cover: 0.35 **NM** value: **2.00**
📖 Nightmare's Evolution • Tigra **A:** Ernie Chan; Mike Vosburg **W:** Ed Hannigan; John Wagner ★ Appearance of Tigra.
43 ❑ Aug 1978 Cover: 0.35 **NM** value: **2.00**
📖 In Manhattan, They Play For Keeps **A:** Tom Sutton **W:** Don McGregor ★ 1st Appearance of Paladin.
44 ❑ Oct 1978 Cover: 0.35 **NM** value: **2.00**
• Jack of Hearts **A:** Keith Giffen ★ Appearance of Jack of Hearts.
45 ❑ Dec 1978 Cover: 0.35 **NM** value: **2.00**
• Man-Wolf ★ Appearance of Man-Wolf.
46 ❑ Feb 1979 Cover: 0.35 **NM** value: **2.00**
Circ: Statement: **131,264**
• War God **A:** George Pérez ★ Appearance of Man-Wolf.
47 ❑ Apr 1979 Cover: 0.35 **NM** value: **2.00**
Circ: Statement: **131,264**
A: John Byrne ★ 1st Appearance of Ant-Man.
48 ❑ Jun 1979 Cover: 0.40 **NM** value: **2.00**
Circ: Statement: **131,264**
📖 The Price Of A Heart! **A:** John Byrne; Bob Layton **W:** David Michelinie ★ Appearance of Ant-Man.
49 ❑ Aug 1979 Cover: 0.40 **NM** value: **2.00**
Circ: Statement: **131,264**
A: Frank Miller(cover) ★ Appearance of The Falcon.
50 ❑ Oct 1979 Cover: 0.40 **NM** value: **8.00**
Circ: Statement: **131,264** • **CGC:** 3 graded, best 9.6
📖 From The Inside ★ 1st Appearance of Alice Cooper.
51 ❑ Dec 1979 Cover: 0.40 **NM** value: **2.00**
Circ: Statement: **131,264** • **CGC:** 1 graded, best 9.4
★ Appearance of Black Panther.
52 ❑ Feb 1980 Cover: 0.40 **NM** value: **2.00**
Circ: Statement: **124,852**
★ Appearance of Black Panther.
53 ❑ Apr 1980 Cover: 0.40 **NM** value: **2.00**
Circ: Statement: **124,852**
A: Frank Miller(cover) ★ Appearance of Black Panther.
54 ❑ Jun 1980 Cover: 0.40 **NM** value: **2.00**
Circ: Statement: **124,852**
A: Gene Day ★ 1st Appearance of Caleb Hammer.
55 ❑ Aug 1980 Cover: 0.40 **NM** value: **2.00**
Circ: Statement: **124,852**
★ Appearance of Wonder Man.
56 ❑ Oct 1980 Cover: 0.50 **NM** value: **2.00**
Circ: Statement: **124,852**
A: Howard Chaykin; Tony DeZuniga ★ Appearance of Dominic Fortune.
57 ❑ Dec 1980 Cover: 0.50 **NM** value: **3.00**
Circ: Statement: **124,852** • **CGC:** 4 graded, best 9.8
• Has 1979 Statement, filed 10/1/79 (Alert: Appeared VERY late in year); avg print run 269,621; avg sales 130,725; avg subs 539; avg total paid 131,264; samples 550; office use 2,220; max existent 134,034; 50% of run returned **A:** Walt Simonson ★ 1st Appearance of Doctor Who (in U.S.).
58 ❑ Feb 1981 Cover: 0.50 **NM** value: **2.50**
A: Frank Miller; Tony DeZuniga; Frank Miller(cover) ★ Appearance of Doctor Who.
59 ❑ Apr 1981 Cover: 0.50 **NM** value: **2.50**
• Has 1980 Statement, flied 10/1/80; avg print run 254,611; avg sales 124,044; avg subs 808; avg total paid 124,852; samples 577; office use 1,237; max existent 126,666; 50% of run returned ★ Appearance of Doctor Who.
60 ❑ Jun 1981 Cover: 0.50 **NM** value: **2.50**
• **CGC:** 1 graded, best 9.6
A: Walt Simonson ★ Appearance of Doctor Who.
61 ❑ Aug 1981 Cover: 0.50 **NM** value: **2.00**
A: Tom Sutton ★ Appearance of Star-Lord.

MARVEL PRESENTS **Marvel**

1 ❑ Oct 1975 Cover: 0.25 **NM** value: **4.00**
• **CGC:** 3 graded, best 9.4
📖 Dweller From The Depths! **A:** Mike Vosburg **W:** John Warner ★ Origin of Bloodstone. ★ 1st Appearance of Bloodstone.
2 ❑ Dec 1975 Cover: 0.25 **NM** value: **3.00**
• **CGC:** 1 graded, best 9.6
📖 The Hellfire Helix Hex! **A:** Sonny Trinidad **W:** John Warner ★ Origin of Bloodstone.
3 ❑ Feb 1976 Cover: 0.25 **NM** value: **4.00**
• **CGC:** 2 graded, best 9.4
★ Appearance of Guardians of the Galaxy.
4 ❑ May 1976 Cover: 0.25 **NM** value: **4.00**
• **CGC:** 1 graded, best 9.4
★ Origin of Nikki. ★ 1st Appearance of Nikki. ★ Appearance of Guardians of the Galaxy.
5 ❑ Jun 1976 Cover: 0.25 **NM** value: **4.00**
• **CGC:** 2 graded, best 9.0
★ Appearance of Guardians of the Galaxy.
6 ❑ Aug 1976 Cover: 0.25 **NM** value: **3.50**
• **CGC:** 3 graded, best 9.4
★ Appearance of Guardians of the Galaxy. ★ Versus Planetary Man.
7 ❑ Nov 1976 Cover: 0.30 **NM** value: **3.50**
★ Appearance of Guardians of the Galaxy.
8 ❑ Dec 1976 Cover: 0.30 **NM** value: **3.50**
• reprints Silver Surfer #2 ★ Appearance of Guardians of the Galaxy.
9 ❑ Feb 1977 Cover: 0.30 **NM** value: **3.50**
★ Origin of Starhawk II (Aleta). ★ Appearance of Guardians of the Galaxy.
10 ❑ Apr 1977 Cover: 0.30 **NM** value: **3.50**
• **CGC:** 1 graded, best 8.5
★ Origin of Starhawk II (Aleta). ★ Appearance of Guardians of the Galaxy.
11 ❑ Jun 1977 Cover: 0.30 **NM** value: **3.50**
• **CGC:** 1 graded, best 9.2
★ Appearance of Guardians of the Galaxy.
12 ❑ Aug 1977 Cover: 0.30 **NM** value: **3.50**
★ Appearance of Guardians of the Galaxy.

MARVEL PREVIEW **Marvel**

Marvel set out to stretch the bounds of what a comic book could be, when it introduced Marvel Preview, a comics magazine consisting of adult-oriented stories featuring a number of familiar and new characters. In its black-and-white, magazine format, it could reach out to a new group of readers and approach issues that might be too adult for the traditional comic-book medium. As a result, the writers got a chance to create terrific stories.

One of these early stories tells of an ex-marine named Frank Castle, who barely survives when his family is murdered by mobsters. In that origin story (which appeared in Marvel Preview #2), readers see for the first time the origin of the man now known as The Punisher. Marvel Preview also contains the origins or early appearances of such greats as Dominic Fortune, Star-Lord, Kull the Conqueror, and Moon Knight. With #25, Marvel Preview switches names to become Bizarre Adventures.

1 ❑ Sum 1975 Cover: 1.00 **NM** value: **2.50**
• Man Gods From Beyond the Stars
2 ❑ 1975 Cover: 1.00 **NM** value: **25.00**
★ Origin of the Punisher. ★ 1st Appearance of Dominic Fortune.
3 ❑ Sep 1975 Cover: 1.00 **NM** value: **5.00**
• Blade the Vampire Slayer
4 ❑ Jan 1976 Cover: 1.00 **NM** value: **4.00**
★ Origin of Star-Lord. ★ 1st Appearance of Star-Lord.
5 ❑ Cover: 1.00 **NM** value: **3.00**
• Sherlock Holmes
6 ❑ Cover: 1.00 **NM** value: **3.00**
• Sherlock Holmes
7 ❑ Sep 1976 Cover: 1.00 **NM** value: **3.00**
• Satanna ★ 1st Appearance of Rocket Raccoon.
8 ❑ Fal 1976 Cover: 1.00 **NM** value: **5.00**
• Morbius, Blade ★ Appearance of Legion of Monsters.
9 ❑ Apr 1977 Cover: 1.00 **NM** value: **3.00**
• Man-God ★ Origin of Star Hawk.
10 ❑ Jul 1977 Cover: 1.00 **NM** value: **3.00**
• Thor **A:** Jim Starlin
11 ❑ Oct 1977 Cover: 1.00 **NM** value: **3.00**
• Star-Lord
12 ❑ Jan 1978 Cover: 1.00 **NM** value: **3.00**
• Haunt of Horror
13 ❑ Apr 1978 Cover: 1.00 **NM** value: **3.00**
• UFO
14 ❑ Aug 1978 Cover: 1.00 **NM** value: **3.00**
• Star-Lord
15 ❑ Oct 1978 Cover: 1.00 **NM** value: **3.00**
• Star-Lord
16 ❑ Mar 1979 Cover: 1.00 **NM** value: **3.00**
• Detectives
17 ❑ May 1979 Cover: 1.00 **NM** value: **3.00**
• Blackmark
18 ❑ Aug 1979 Cover: 1.25 **NM** value: **3.00**
• Star-Lord
19 ❑ Nov 1979 Cover: 1.25 **NM** value: **3.00**
★ Appearance of Kull.
20 ❑ Mar 1980 Cover: 1.25 **NM** value: **3.00**
• Bizarre Adventures
21 ❑ May 1980 Cover: 1.25 **NM** value: **3.00**
★ Appearance of Moon Knight.
22 ❑ Aug 1980 Cover: 1.25 **NM** value: **3.00**
• Merlin; King Arthur
23 ❑ Nov 1980 Cover: 1.25 **NM** value: **3.00**
• Bizarre Adventures **A:** Frank Miller
24 ❑ Feb 1981 Cover: 1.25 **NM** value: **3.00**
• Paradox; Title continues as "Bizarre Adventures" with #25

MARVEL PREVIEW '93 **Marvel**

1 ❑ ca. 1993 Cover: 3.95 **NM** value: **Cover or less**

MARVEL RIOT **Marvel**

1 ❑ Dec 1995 Cover: 1.95 **NM** value: **Cover or less**
One-shot. wraparound cover. • parodies Age of Apocalypse **A:** Rurik Tyler; Hilary Barta; Steve Bunche **W:** Scott Lobdell

MARVELS **Marvel**

Countless comics readers have grown up in the Marvel universe, where the exploits of Spider-Man, The Fantastic Four, and The X-Men interweave naturally with each other, and with people and events from the real world. Such strong continuity was rare in comic books when Marvel started out, but the creation of coherent "comics universes" has since become almost mandatory for any line of comics.

After 30 years in the Marvel universe, readers take for granted that Norse gods walk the streets of New York alongside winged mutants and human fireballs. This series, however, makes it all seem fresh again, recapturing the wonder of the early days of Marvel. Written by Kurt Busiek, it's told through the eyes of an ace photographer, who recounts the story of when The Marvels first appeared. The fully painted artwork by Alex Ross only adds to the magical feel.

0 ❑ Aug 1994 Cover: 2.95 **NM** value: **3.50**
Circ: CapCity orders: **53,500** • **CGC:** 6 graded, best 9.6
Plastic dust cover. • collects promo art and Human Torch story from Marvel Age; Fully painted **A:** Alex Ross **W:** Kurt Busiek
1 ❑ Jan 1994 Cover: 4.95 **NM** value: **5.00**
Circ: CapCity orders: **37,300** • **CGC:** 40 graded, best 9.9
wraparound acetate outer cover. 📖 A Time Of Marvel • Torch, Sub-Mariner, Captain America; Torch, Sub-Mariner, Capt. America; Fully painted **A:** Alex Ross **W:** Kurt Busiek
1-2 ❑ Apr 1996 Cover: 2.95 **NM** value: **Cover or less**
2 ❑ Feb 1994 Cover: 5.95 **NM** value: **Cover or less**
Circ: CapCity orders: **29,350** • **CGC:** 21 graded, best 9.8
wraparound acetate outer cover. 📖 Monsters • Fully painted **A:** Alex Ross **W:** Kurt Busiek
2-2 ❑ May 1996 Cover: 2.95 **NM** value: **Cover or less**
3 ❑ Mar 1994 Cover: 5.95 **NM** value: **Cover or less**
Circ: CapCity orders: **32,400** • **CGC:** 17 graded, best 9.9
wraparound acetate outer cover. 📖 Judgement Day • Coming of Galactus; Fully painted **A:** Alex Ross **W:** Kurt Busiek
3-2 ❑ May 1996 Cover: 2.95 **NM** value: **5.95**
4 ❑ Apr 1994 Cover: 5.95 **NM** value: **Cover or less**
Circ: CapCity orders: **43,975** • **CGC:** 26 graded, best 9.8
wraparound acetate outer cover. 📖 The Day She Died • Fully painted **A:** Alex Ross **W:** Kurt Busiek ★ Death of Gwen Stacy.
4-2 ❑ Jun 1996 Cover: 2.95 **NM** value: **Cover or less**

CGC-graded: Multiply prices above by **33 for 9.9 M** • **16 for 9.8 NM/M** • **7 for 9.6 NM+** • **5 for 9.4 NM** • **2.5 for 9.2 NM-** • **1.5 for 9.0 VF/NM**

MARVEL SAGA — Marvel

One of the unique things about Marvel is that it has created a Marvel universe within the real one, and has taken great pains over the years to be true to it. Marvel Saga traced the evolution of the Marvel universe, beginning with the spaceshot that created the Fantastic Four, up through the coming of Galactus and the origin of The Silver Surfer.

Marvel Saga presented the origins of every major Marvel character, along with the key elements in each one's lives. What's more, it followed the many crossed paths of these characters, showing us how things interrelated at each moment.

1 ❑ Dec 1985 Cover: 1.00 **NM** value: **2.00**
Circ: CapCity orders: **27,000**
The Saga Begins...! **A:** Brett Breeding; Ron Wilson; Sal Buscema; John Byrne; Don Heck; Jack Kirby; Dick Ayers; Joe Sinnott; Hilary Barta; Art Simek **W:** John Byrne; Larry Lieber; Stan Lee; H.E. Huntley ★ Origin of X-Men, Fantastic Four, Alpha Flight.

2 ❑ Jan 1986 Cover: 1.00 **NM** value: **1.50**
Circ: CapCity orders: **18,400**
Transformation And Rebirth **A:** Paul Reinman; Steve Ditko; Jack Kirby; Greg LaRocque; Dick Ayers; Bob Wiacek; Sol Brodsky **W:** Roger Stern; Stan Lee ★ Origin of Hulk, Spider-Man.

3 ❑ Feb 1986 Cover: 1.00 **NM** value: **1.50**
Circ: CapCity orders: **20,900**
★ Origin of Sub-Mariner, Doom.

4 ❑ Mar 1986 Cover: 1.00 **NM** value: **1.50**
Circ: CapCity orders: **21,000**
Of Gods And Mutants **A:** Alex Toth; John Buscema; John Byrne; Herb Trimpe; Jack Kirby; Frank Miller; Brent Anderson; Dave Cockrum; Dick Ayers; Bob Hall; Frank Giacoia; Terry Austin; Werner Roth; Bob Wiacek; Joe Rubinstein; John Verpoorten; Vince Colletta **W:** Alan Zelentz; Larry Lieber; Roy Thomas; Stan Lee; Chris Claremont ★ Origin of Thor.

5 ❑ Apr 1986 Cover: 1.00 **NM** value: **1.50**
Circ: CapCity orders: **19,400**
★ Origin of Iceman, Angel.

6 ❑ May 1986 Cover: 1.00 **NM** value: **1.50**
Circ: CapCity orders: **18,100**
Love, Hate...And Sacrifice! **A:** John Buscema; Don Heck; George Tuska; Jack Kirby; Gil Kane; Dick Ayers; Walt Simonson; George Roussos; John Tartaglione; John Verpoorten; Mike Esposito; Vince Colletta **W:** Alan Zelentz; Walt Simonson; Larry Lieber; Gary Friedrich; Stan Lee; Gerry Conway; Steve Englehart ★ Origin of Iron Man, Asgard, Odin.

7 ❑ Jun 1986 Cover: 1.00 **NM** value: **1.50**
Circ: CapCity orders: **18,400**
The Ties That bind! **A:** Steve Ditko; Bob Layton; Barry Windsor-Smith; John Romita Jr.; Don Heck; Jack Kirby; Dick Ayers; Jim Mooney **W:** Larry Lieber; Roy Thomas; Stan Lee; David Michelinie

8 ❑ Jul 1986 Cover: 1.00 **NM** value: **1.50**
Circ: CapCity orders: **18,000**
Fateful Encounters! **A:** Steve Ditko; Don Heck; Jack Kirby; Dick Ayers; Sol Brodsky **W:** Larry Lieber; Roy Thomas; Stan Lee; Robert Bernstein

9 ❑ Aug 1986 Cover: 1.00 **NM** value: **1.50**
Circ: CapCity orders: **17,200**
★ Origin of Vulture.

10 ❑ Sep 1986 Cover: 1.00 **NM** value: **1.50**
Circ: CapCity orders: **16,800**
The Stand United! **A:** Paul Reinman; Steve Ditko; John Buscema; Bill Everett; Jack Kirby; Dick Ayers; John Tartaglione; John Verpoorten **W:** Stan Lee; Arnold Drake; Chris Claremont; Denny O'Neil ★ Origin of Marvel Girl, Beast, Avengers.

11 ❑ Oct 1986 Cover: 1.00 **NM** value: **1.50**
Circ: CapCity orders: **16,400**
★ Origin of Molecule Man.

12 ❑ Nov 1986 Cover: 1.00 **NM** value: **1.50**
Circ: CapCity orders: **16,300**
• Captain America revived

13 ❑ Dec 1986 Cover: 1.00 **NM** value: **1.50**
Circ: CapCity orders: **15,000**
Evil Dared **A:** Paul Reinman; Steve Ditko; Gene Colan; John Buscema; Bill Everett; Don Heck; Steve Rude; Jack Kirby; Frank Miller; Tom Palmer; Chic Stone; Klaus Janson; George Roussos; Joe Rubinstein **W:** Frank Miller; Roy Thomas; Stan Lee; Gerry Conway; N. Korak; Roger McKenzie ★ Origin of Daredevil.

14 ❑ Jan 1987 Cover: 1.00 **NM** value: **1.50**
Circ: CapCity orders: **13,900**
Confrontations! **A:** Paul Reinman; Al Milgrom; Steve Ditko; John Byrne; Dan Green; John Romita Jr.; Jack Kirby; Chic Stone; Joe Sinnott; George Roussos; Mike Esposito; Vince Colletta **W:** Stan Lee; Steven Grant; David Michelinie; Mark Gruenwald ★ Origin of Scarlet Witch, Quicksilver.

15 ❑ Feb 1987 Cover: 1.00 **NM** value: **1.50**
Circ: CapCity orders: **13,500**
★ Origin of Wonder Man, Hawkeye.

16 ❑ Mar 1987 Cover: 1.00 **NM** value: **1.50**
Circ: CapCity orders: **13,200**
Dread Reckonings! **A:** Steve Ditko; Gene Colan; Paul Smith; Don Heck; Jack Kirby; Gil Kane; Dick Ayers; Chic Stone; Dan Adkins; Frank Chiaramonte; George Roussos; Vince Colletta **W:** Ralph Macchio; Len Wein; Roger Stern; Stan Lee; Mark Gruenwald; Steve Englehart ★ Origin of Frightful Four, Dormammu.

17 ❑ Apr 1987 Cover: 1.00 **NM** value: **1.50**
Circ: CapCity orders: **12,900**
Man's Inhumanity **A:** Steve Ditko; Val Mayerik; Don Heck; Jack Kirby; Gil Kane; Dick Ayers; Chic Stone; Joe Sinnott; Frank Giacoia; George Roussos **W:** Bruce Jones; Roy Thomas; Stan Lee ★ Origin of Ka-Zar, Leader.

18 ❑ May 1987 Cover: 1.00 **NM** value: **1.50**
Circ: CapCity orders: **11,400**
The Triumph And The Tragedy! **A:** Steve Ditko; Don Heck; Jack Kirby; Dick Ayers; Jim Steranko; Chic Stone; Joe Sinnott; Frank Giacoia; Bob Powell; Mike Esposito; Vince Colletta **W:** Steve Ditko; Stan Lee; Larry Ivie ★ Origin of S.H.I.E.L.D..

19 ❑ Jun 1987 Cover: 1.00 **NM** value: **1.50**
Circ: CapCity orders: **11,300**
• new Avengers team

20 ❑ Jul 1987 Cover: 1.00 **NM** value: **1.50**
Circ: CapCity orders: **10,700**

21 ❑ Aug 1987 Cover: 1.00 **NM** value: **1.50**
Circ: CapCity orders: **10,900**
• X-Men

22 ❑ Sep 1987 Cover: 1.00 **NM** value: **1.50**
Circ: CapCity orders: **13,100**
★ Origin of Mary Jane.

23 ❑ Oct 1987 Cover: 1.00 **NM** value: **1.50**
Circ: CapCity orders: **11,000**
• Inhumans

24 ❑ Nov 1987 Cover: 1.00 **NM** value: **1.50**
Circ: CapCity orders: **10,900**
A: John Buscema; Jack Kirby; Joe Sinnott; George Klein; Vince Colletta **W:** Jack Kirby; Stan Lee ★ Origin of Galactus.

25 ❑ Dec 1987 Cover: 1.00 **NM** value: **1.50**
Circ: CapCity orders: **11,500**
Reborn! final issue. **A:** John Buscema; Jack Kirby; Joe Sinnott; George Klein; Vince Colletta **W:** Jack Kirby; Stan Lee ★ Origin of Silver Surfer.

MARVELS COMICS: CAPTAIN AMERICA — Marvel

1 ❑ Jul 2000 Cover: 2.25 **NM** value: **Cover or less**
Circ: Diamd. preorders: **30,648**
Time Rip, Part 5 **A:** Mark Bagley; Ron Frenz; Joe Sinnott; Al Vey **W:** Peter David

MARVELS COMICS: DAREDEVIL — Marvel

1 ❑ Jun 2000 Cover: 2.25 **NM** value: **Cover or less**
Circ: Diamd. preorders: **32,255**
Angel **A:** Eddy Newell **W:** Tony Isabella

MARVELS COMICS: FANTASTIC FOUR — Marvel

1 ❑ May 2000 Cover: 2.25 **NM** value: **Cover or less**
Circ: Diamd. preorders: **32,582**
The Life Fantastic! **A:** Paul Smith **W:** Karl Kesel

MARVELS COMICS: SPIDER-MAN — Marvel

1 ❑ Jul 2000 Cover: 2.25 **NM** value: **Cover or less**
Circ: Diamd. preorders: **32,733**
The Menace of Spider-Man **A:** Kyle Hotz **W:** Paul Grist

MARVELS COMICS: THOR — Marvel

1 ❑ Jul 2000 Cover: 2.25 **NM** value: **Cover or less**
Circ: Diamd. preorders: **30,955**
Friendly Fire **A:** Derec Aucoin **W:** Ty Templeton

MARVELS COMICS: X-MEN — Marvel

1 ❑ Jun 2000 Cover: 2.25 **NM** value: **Cover or less**
Circ: Diamd. preorders: **44,445**
How I Learned to Love the Bomb **A:** Sean Phillips; Duncan Fegredo **W:** Mark Millar

MARVEL SELECTS: FANTASTIC FOUR — Marvel

1 ❑ Jan 2000 Cover: 2.75 **NM** value: **Cover or less**
Circ: Diamd. preorders: **9,465**
And Now...The Thing! **A:** John Buscema **W:** Stan Lee

MARVEL SELECTS: SPIDER-MAN — Marvel

1 ❑ Jan 2000 Cover: 2.75 **NM** value: **Cover or less**
Circ: Diamd. preorders: **9,947**
The Spider or the Man? • Reprints Amazing Spider-Man #100 **A:** Gil Kane **W:** Stan Lee

2 ❑ Feb 2000 Cover: 2.75 **NM** value: **Cover or less**
Circ: Diamd. preorders: **8,735**

3 ❑ Mar 2000 Cover: 2.75 **NM** value: **Cover or less**
Circ: Diamd. preorders: **6,346**

MARVEL'S GREATEST COMICS — Marvel

Marvel's Greatest Comics is a continuation of Marvel Collectors' Item Classics, with the name changing as of issue #23. The series ran from 1969 until 1981 when it concluded with issue #96. In that time, it reprinted some of the most colorful and important issues of Fantastic Four. These included the first appearance of The Silver Surfer, Galactus, and The Inhumans. Illustrated by Jack Kirby and written by Stan Lee, there was a feeling of wonder about these early issues that has not been matched since.

Like the title it continued, these issues are an affordable way for fans to read those early stories without breaking the bank.

23 ❑ Oct 1969 Cover: 0.25 **NM** value: **6.00**
• Giant-size. • Title continued from "Marvel Collector's Item Classics"

24 ❑ Dec 1969 Cover: 0.25 **NM** value: **6.00**
• Giant-size.

25 ❑ Feb 1970 Cover: 0.25 **NM** value: **6.00**
• Giant-size.

26 ❑ Apr 1970 Cover: 0.25 **NM** value: **6.00**
• Giant-size.

27 ❑ Jun 1970 Cover: 0.25 **NM** value: **6.00**
• Giant-size.

28 ❑ Aug 1970 Cover: 0.25 **NM** value: **6.00**
• **CGC:** 1 graded, best 8.5
• Giant-size.

29 ❑ Dec 1970 Cover: 0.25 **NM** value: **6.00**
• **CGC:** 3 graded, best 8.5
• Giant-size. • Reprinted from Fantastic Four #12 and 31

30 ❑ Mar 1971 Cover: 0.25 **NM** value: **6.00**
• Giant-size. • Reprinted from Fantastic Four #37 and 38

31 ❑ Jun 1971 Cover: 0.25 **NM** value: **6.00**
• Giant-size. • Reprinted from Fantastic Four #39 and 40

32 ❑ Sep 1971 Cover: 0.25 **NM** value: **6.00**
• **CGC:** 1 graded, best 9.2
• Giant-size. • Reprinted from Fantastic Four #41 and 42

33 ❑ Dec 1971 Cover: 0.25 **NM** value: **6.00**
• Giant-size. • Reprinted from Fantastic Four #44 and 45

34 ❑ Mar 1972 Cover: 0.25 **NM** value: **6.00**
• **CGC:** 1 graded, best 9.0
• Giant-size. • Reprinted from Fantastic Four #46 and 47

35 ❑ Jun 1972 Cover: 0.20 **NM** value: **5.00**
• **CGC:** 1 graded, best 9.4
• Reprinted from Fantastic Four #48 ★ Appearance of Silver Surfer.

36 ❑ Jul 1972 Cover: 0.20 **NM** value: **5.00**
• Reprinted from Fantastic Four #49

37 ❑ Sep 1972 Cover: 0.20 **NM** value: **5.00**
• Reprinted from Fantastic Four #50

38 ❑ Oct 1972 Cover: 0.20 **NM** value: **3.50**
• Reprinted from Fantastic Four #51

39 ❑ Nov 1972 Cover: 0.20 **NM** value: **3.50**
• Reprinted from Fantastic Four #52

40 ❑ Jan 1973 Cover: 0.20 **NM** value: **3.50**
• Reprinted from Fantastic Four #53

41 ❑ Mar 1973 Cover: 0.20 **NM** value: **3.50**
• Reprinted from Fantastic Four #54

42 ❑ May 1973 Cover: 0.20 **NM** value: **3.50**
• Reprinted from Fantastic Four #55

43 ❑ Jul 1973 Cover: 0.20 **NM** value: **3.50**
• Reprinted from Fantastic Four #56

44 ❑ Sep 1973 Cover: 0.20 **NM** value: **3.50**
• Reprinted from Fantastic Four #61

45 ❑ Oct 1973 Cover: 0.20 **NM** value: **3.50**
• Reprinted from Fantastic Four #62

46 ❑ Nov 1973 Cover: 0.20 **NM** value: **3.50**
• Reprinted from Fantastic Four #63

47 ❑ Jan 1974 Cover: 0.20 **NM** value: **3.50**
• Reprinted from Fantastic Four #64

48 ❑ Mar 1974 Cover: 0.20 **NM** value: **3.50**
• Reprinted from Fantastic Four #65

49 ❑ May 1974 Cover: 0.25 **NM** value: **3.50**
• Reprinted from Fantastic Four #66

50 ❑ Jul 1974 Cover: 0.25 **NM** value: **4.00**
• Reprinted from Fantastic Four #67 ★ Appearance of Warlock (Him).

51 ❑ Sep 1974 Cover: 0.25 **NM** value: **3.00**
• Reprinted from Fantastic Four #68

52 ❑ Oct 1974 Cover: 0.25 **NM** value: **2.50**
• Reprinted from Fantastic Four #69

53 ❑ Nov 1974 Cover: 0.25 **NM** value: **2.50**
• Reprinted from Fantastic Four #70

54 ❑ Jan 1975 Cover: 0.25 **NM** value: **2.50**
• Reprinted from Fantastic Four #71

55 ❑ Mar 1975 Cover: 0.25 **NM** value: **2.50**
• Reprinted from Fantastic Four #73

56 ❑ May 1975 Cover: 0.25 **NM** value: **2.50**
• Reprinted from Fantastic Four #74

57 ❑ Jul 1975 Cover: 0.25 **NM** value: **2.50**
• Reprinted from Fantastic Four #75

58 ❑ Sep 1975 Cover: 0.25 **NM** value: **2.50**
• Reprinted from Fantastic Four #76

59 ❑ Oct 1975 Cover: 0.25 **NM** value: **2.50**
• Reprinted from Fantastic Four #77

60 ❑ Nov 1975 Cover: 0.25 **NM** value: **2.50**
• Reprinted from Fantastic Four #78

61 ❑ Jan 1976 Cover: 0.25 **NM** value: **2.50**
• Reprinted from Fantastic Four #79

62 ❑ Mar 1976 Cover: 0.25 **NM** value: **2.50**
• Reprinted from Fantastic Four #80

63 ❑ May 1976 Cover: 0.25 **NM** value: **2.50**
• Reprinted from Fantastic Four #81

64 ❑ Jul 1976 Cover: 0.25 **NM** value: **2.50**
• Reprinted from Fantastic Four #82

65 ❑ Sep 1976 Cover: 0.30 **NM** value: **2.50**
• Reprinted from Fantastic Four #83

66 ❑ Oct 1976 Cover: 0.30 **NM** value: **2.50**
• Reprinted from Fantastic Four #84

67 ❑ Nov 1976 Cover: 0.30 **NM** value: **2.50**
• Reprinted from Fantastic Four #85

68 ❑ Jan 1977 Cover: 0.30 **NM** value: **2.50**
• Reprinted from Fantastic Four #86

69 ❑ Mar 1977 Cover: 0.30 **NM** value: **2.50**
• Reprinted from Fantastic Four #87

70 ❑ May 1977 Cover: 0.30 **NM** value: **2.50**
• Reprinted from Fantastic Four #88

71 ❑ Jul 1977 Cover: 0.30 **NM** value: **2.00**
• Reprinted from Fantastic Four #89

72 ❑ Sep 1977 Cover: 0.30 **NM** value: **2.00**
• Reprinted from Fantastic Four #90

73 ❑ Oct 1977 Cover: 0.30 **NM** value: **2.00**
• Reprinted from Fantastic Four #91

74 ❑ Nov 1977 Cover: 0.35 **NM** value: **2.00**
• Reprinted from Fantastic Four #92

75 ❑ Jan 1978 Cover: 0.35 **NM** value: **2.00**
• Reprinted from Fantastic Four #93

76 ❑ Mar 1978 Cover: 0.35 **NM** value: **2.00**
• Reprinted from Fantastic Four #95

77 ❑ May 1978 Cover: 0.35 **NM** value: **2.00**
• Reprinted from Fantastic Four #96

78 ❑ Jul 1978 Cover: 0.35 **NM** value: **2.00**
• Reprinted from Fantastic Four #97
79 ❑ Sep 1978 Cover: 0.35 **NM** value: **2.00**
• Reprinted from Fantastic Four #98
80 ❑ Nov 1978 Cover: 0.35 **NM** value: **2.00**
• Reprinted from Fantastic Four #99
81 ❑ Jan 1979 Cover: 0.35 **NM** value: **2.00**
• Reprinted from Fantastic Four #100
82 ❑ Mar 1979 Cover: 0.35 **NM** value: **2.00**
• Reprinted from Fantastic Four #102
83 ❑ Dec 1979 Cover: 0.35 **NM** value: **2.00**
• Reprinted from Fantastic Four #103
84 ❑ Jan 1980 Cover: 0.35 **NM** value: **2.00**
• Reprinted from Fantastic Four #104
85 ❑ Feb 1980 Cover: 0.35 **NM** value: **2.00**
• Reprinted from Fantastic Four #105
86 ❑ Mar 1980 Cover: 0.35 **NM** value: **2.00**
• Reprinted from Fantastic Four #116
87 ❑ Apr 1980 Cover: 0.35 **NM** value: **2.00**
• Reprinted from Fantastic Four #107
88 ❑ May 1980 Cover: 0.40 **NM** value: **2.00**
• Reprinted from Fantastic Four #108
89 ❑ Jun 1980 Cover: 0.40 **NM** value: **2.00**
• Reprinted from Fantastic Four #109
90 ❑ Jul 1980 Cover: 0.40 **NM** value: **2.00**
• Reprinted from Fantastic Four #110
91 ❑ Aug 1980 Cover: 0.40 **NM** value: **2.00**
• Reprinted from Fantastic Four #111
92 ❑ Sep 1980 Cover: 0.50 **NM** value: **2.00**
• Reprinted from Fantastic Four #112
93 ❑ Oct 1980 Cover: 0.40 **NM** value: **2.00**
94 ❑ Nov 1980 Cover: 0.40 **NM** value: **2.00**
95 ❑ Dec 1980 Cover: 0.40 **NM** value: **2.00**
96 ❑ Jan 1981 Cover: 0.40 **NM** value: **2.00**

MARVEL'S GREATEST SUPERHERO BATTLES Marvel

Bk 1❑ Cover: 6.95 **NM** value: **10.00**
• (Fireside)

MARVEL: SHADOWS & LIGHT Marvel

1 ❑ Feb 1997, b&w Cover: 2.95 **NM** value: **Cover or less**
wraparound cover. 📖 Wolverine: The Spoon Job; Dracula: Into the Tomb; Captain Marvel: Prisoners of the Red Ghost; Dr. Strange: Strange Reflections • Wolverine, Dracula, Doctor Strange, Captain Marvel **A:** Michael Golden; J.O. Ladronn; John Paul Leon; Wilfred **W:** Michael Golden; John Paul Leon; Alex Leon; James Felder; John Rozum

MARVELS OF SCIENCE Charlton

1 ❑ Mar 1946 Cover: 0.10 **NM** value: **150.00**
2 ❑ Apr 1946 Cover: 0.10 **NM** value: **100.00**
3 ❑ May 1946 Cover: 0.10 **NM** value: **100.00**
4 ❑ Jun 1946 Cover: 0.10 **NM** value: **100.00**

MARVEL SPECIAL EDITION FEATURING CLOSE ENCOUNTERS OF THE THIRD KIND Marvel

3 ❑ ca. 1978 Cover: 1.50 **NM** value: **7.00**
• treasury-sized. • adapts Close Encounters of the Third Kind

MARVEL SPECIAL EDITION FEATURING SPECTACULAR SPIDER-MAN Marvel

1 ❑ ca. 1975 Cover: 1.50 **NM** value: **10.00**
• treasury-sized.

MARVEL SPECIAL EDITION FEATURING STAR WARS Marvel

1 ❑ ca. 1977 Cover: 1.00 **NM** value: **12.00**
• treasury-sized adaption of Star Wars.
2 ❑ ca. 1977 Cover: 1.00 **NM** value: **10.00**
• treasury-sized adaption of Star Wars.
3 ❑ ca. 1978 Cover: 2.50 **NM** value: **12.00**
• treasury-sized. • collects previous two issues

MARVEL SPECTACULAR Marvel

1 ❑ Aug 1973 Cover: 0.20 **NM** value: **5.00**
• **CGC:** 1 graded, best 7.0
• reprints Thor #128 **A:** Jack Kirby **W:** Stan Lee
2 ❑ Sep 1973 Cover: 0.20 **NM** value: **3.00**
• reprints Thor #129 **A:** Jack Kirby **W:** Stan Lee
3 ❑ Oct 1973 Cover: 0.20 **NM** value: **3.00**
📖 Thunder in the Netherworld! • reprints Thor #130 **A:** Jack Kirby **W:** Stan Lee ★ 1st Appearance of Tana Nile (in real form).
4 ❑ Nov 1973 Cover: 0.20 **NM** value: **3.00**
• reprints Thor #133 **A:** Jack Kirby **W:** Stan Lee
5 ❑ Jan 1974 Cover: 0.20 **NM** value: **3.00**
• reprints Thor #134 **A:** Jack Kirby **W:** Stan Lee
6 ❑ Mar 1974 Cover: 0.20 **NM** value: **3.00**
• reprints Tales of Asgard from Journey Into Mystery #121 and Thor #135 **A:** Jack Kirby **W:** Stan Lee
7 ❑ May 1974 Cover: 0.25 **NM** value: **3.00**
• reprints Thor #136 **A:** Jack Kirby **W:** Stan Lee
8 ❑ Jul 1974 Cover: 0.25 **NM** value: **3.00**
• reprints Thor #137 **A:** Jack Kirby **W:** Stan Lee
9 ❑ Sep 1974 Cover: 0.25 **NM** value: **3.00**
• reprints Thor #138 **A:** Jack Kirby **W:** Stan Lee
10 ❑ Oct 1974 Cover: 0.25 **NM** value: **3.00**
• reprints Thor #139 **A:** Jack Kirby **W:** Stan Lee
11 ❑ Nov 1974 Cover: 0.25 **NM** value: **2.00**
• reprints Thor #140 **A:** Jack Kirby **W:** Stan Lee
12 ❑ Dec 1974 Cover: 0.25 **NM** value: **2.00**
• reprints Thor #141 **A:** Jack Kirby **W:** Stan Lee
13 ❑ Jan 1975 Cover: 0.25 **NM** value: **2.00**
• reprints Thor #142 **A:** Jack Kirby **W:** Stan Lee
14 ❑ Mar 1975 Cover: 0.25 **NM** value: **2.00**
• reprints Thor #143 **A:** Jack Kirby **W:** Stan Lee
15 ❑ Jun 1975 Cover: 0.25 **NM** value: **2.00**
• reprints Thor #144 **A:** Jack Kirby **W:** Stan Lee
16 ❑ Jul 1975 Cover: 0.25 **NM** value: **2.00**
• reprints Thor #145 **A:** Jack Kirby **W:** Stan Lee
17 ❑ Sep 1975 Cover: 0.25 **NM** value: **2.00**
• reprints Thor #146 **A:** Jack Kirby **W:** Stan Lee
18 ❑ Oct 1975 Cover: 0.25 **NM** value: **2.00**
• reprints Thor #147 **A:** Jack Kirby **W:** Stan Lee
19 ❑ Nov 1975 Cover: 0.25 **NM** value: **2.00**
• reprints Thor #148 **A:** Jack Kirby **W:** Stan Lee

MARVEL SPOTLIGHT (VOL. 1) Marvel

Marvel Spotlight is primarily a means for Marvel to experiment with new characters. By giving each new character an issue or two, Marvel was able to showcase a number of real winners who might otherwise have been considered too risky.

First among these winners was the #5 first appearance and origin of today's Ghost Rider, a complete revamp of the Western character created in the Golden Age. The fiery-headed avenger was an instant success, and Marvel soon featured him in his own series and found him of star quality.

Later issues of Marvel Spotlight gave readers the first appearances or solo stories of The Son of Satan, Moon Knight, Red Wolf, and Spider-Woman.

1 ❑ Nov 1971 Cover: 0.15 **NM** value: **15.00**
• **CGC:** 18 graded, best 9.8
A: Syd Shores; Neal Adams; Wally Wood **W:** Gardner Fox ★ Origin of Red Wolf. ★ Appearance of Red Wolf.
2 ❑ Feb 1972 Cover: 0.25 **NM** value: **35.00**
• **CGC:** 49 graded, best 9.6
A: Frank Miller(cover) ★ Origin of Werewolf. ★ 1st Appearance of Werewolf.
3 ❑ May 1972 Cover: 0.20 **NM** value: **15.00**
• **CGC:** 9 graded, best 9.8
★ Appearance of Werewolf.
4 ❑ Jun 1972 Cover: 0.20 **NM** value: **15.00**
• **CGC:** 10 graded, best 9.6
★ Appearance of Werewolf.
5 ❑ Aug 1972 Cover: 0.20 **NM** value: **50.00**
• **CGC:** 52 graded, best 9.6
A: Steve Ditko; Mike Ploog; Frank Miller(cover) ★ Origin of Ghost Rider I (Johnny Blaze). ★ 1st Appearance of Zarathos (Ghost Rider's Spirit of Vengeance), Ghost Rider I (Johnny Blaze), Johnny Blaze.
6 ❑ Oct 1972 Cover: 0.20 **NM** value: **20.00**
• **CGC:** 5 graded, best 9.6
★ Appearance of Ghost Rider.
7 ❑ Dec 1972 Cover: 0.20 **NM** value: **16.00**
• **CGC:** 4 graded, best 9.2
A: Frank Miller(cover) ★ Appearance of Ghost Rider.
8 ❑ Feb 1973 Cover: 0.20 **NM** value: **16.00**
• **CGC:** 2 graded, best 9.6
A: Frank Miller ★ Appearance of Ghost Rider.
9 ❑ Apr 1973 Cover: 0.20 **NM** value: **12.00**
• **CGC:** 2 graded, best 9.2
★ Appearance of Ghost Rider.
10 ❑ Jun 1973 Cover: 0.20 **NM** value: **12.00**
• **CGC:** 3 graded, best 9.4
★ Appearance of Ghost Rider.
11 ❑ Aug 1973 Cover: 0.20 **NM** value: **12.00**
• **CGC:** 4 graded, best 9.6
★ Appearance of Ghost Rider.
12 ❑ Oct 1973 Cover: 0.20 **NM** value: **12.00**
• **CGC:** 7 graded, best 9.2
A: Steve Ditko ★ Origin of Son of Satan. ★ 1st Appearance of Son of Satan (full appearance), Son of Satan.
13 ❑ Jan 1974 Cover: 0.20 **NM** value: **6.00**
★ Origin of Satana. ★ Appearance of Son of Satan.
14 ❑ Mar 1974 Cover: 0.20 **NM** value: **5.00**
★ Appearance of Son of Satan.
15 ❑ May 1974 Cover: 0.25 **NM** value: **5.00**
★ Appearance of Son of Satan.
16 ❑ Jul 1974 Cover: 0.25 **NM** value: **4.00**
★ Appearance of Son of Satan.
17 ❑ Sep 1974 Cover: 0.25 **NM** value: **4.00**
★ Appearance of Son of Satan.
18 ❑ Oct 1974 Cover: 0.25 **NM** value: **4.00**
★ Appearance of Son of Satan.
19 ❑ Dec 1974 Cover: 0.25 **NM** value: **4.00**
★ Appearance of Son of Satan.
20 ❑ Feb 1975 Cover: 0.25 **NM** value: **4.00**
★ Appearance of Son of Satan.
21 ❑ Apr 1975 Cover: 0.25 **NM** value: **4.00**
★ Appearance of Son of Satan.
22 ❑ Jun 1975 Cover: 0.25 **NM** value: **5.00**
★ Appearance of Ghost Rider, Son of Satan.
23 ❑ Aug 1975 Cover: 0.25 **NM** value: **4.00**
• **CGC:** 1 graded, best 7.0
★ Appearance of Son of Satan.
24 ❑ Oct 1975 Cover: 0.25 **NM** value: **4.00**
• Last Son of Satan in Marvel Spotlight ★ Appearance of Son of Satan.
25 ❑ Dec 1975 Cover: 0.25 **NM** value: **3.00**
★ Appearance of Sinbad.
26 ❑ Feb 1976 Cover: 0.25 **NM** value: **3.00**
★ Appearance of Scarecrow (Marvel).
27 ❑ Apr 1976 Cover: 0.25 **NM** value: **3.00**
★ Appearance of Sub-Mariner.
28 ❑ Jun 1976 Cover: 0.25 **NM** value: **8.00**
• **CGC:** 12 graded, best 9.4
• 1st solo story for Moon Knight ★ Appearance of Moon Knight.
29 ❑ Aug 1976 Cover: 0.25 **NM** value: **6.00**
• **CGC:** 8 graded, best 9.6
A: Jack Kirby ★ Appearance of Moon Knight.
30 ❑ Oct 1976 Cover: 0.30 **NM** value: **3.00**
A: John Buscema ★ Appearance of Warriors Three.
31 ❑ Dec 1976 Cover: 0.30 **NM** value: **3.00**
A: Howard Chaykin; John Severinn ★ Appearance of Nick Fury.
32 ❑ Feb 1977 Cover: 0.30 **NM** value: **8.00**
• **CGC:** 11 graded, best 9.6
📖 Dark Destiny! **A:** Sal Buscema; Jim Mooney **W:** Archie Goodwin ★ Origin of Spider-Woman I (Jessica Drew). ★ 1st Appearance of Spider-Woman I (Jessica Drew).
33 ❑ Apr 1977 Cover: 0.30 **NM** value: **3.00**
• **CGC:** 2 graded, best 9.4
★ 1st Appearance of Devil-Slayer. ★ Appearance of Deathlok.

MARVEL SPOTLIGHT (VOL. 2) Marvel

1 ❑ Jul 1979 Cover: 0.40 **NM** value: **3.00**
• **CGC:** 1 graded, best 9.6
📖 The Saturn Storm! **A:** Pat Broderick **W:** Doug Moench ★ Appearance of Captain Marvel.
2 ❑ Sep 1979 Cover: 0.40 **NM** value: **2.00**
A: Tony DeZuniga **C:** Frank Miller ★ Appearance of Captain Marvel.
3 ❑ Nov 1979 Cover: 0.40 **NM** value: **2.00**
📖 Blue-Red-Blue **A:** Pat Broderick **W:** Doug Moench ★ Appearance of Captain Marvel.
4 ❑ Jan 1980 Cover: 0.40 **NM** value: **2.00**
📖 Shadow Doom! **A:** Steve Ditko **C:** Frank Miller **W:** Archie Goodwin ★ Appearance of Dragon Lord.
5 ❑ Mar 1980 Cover: 0.40 **NM** value: **2.00**
📖 A Hero Is Also A Man! **A:** Steve Ditko **C:** Frank Miller **W:** Marv Wolfman ★ Appearance of Dragon Lord, Captain Marvel.
6 ❑ May 1980 Cover: 0.40 **NM** value: **2.00**
📖 The Saga Of Star-Lord **A:** Tom Sutton **W:** Doug Moench ★ Origin of Star-Lord.
7 ❑ Jul 1980 Cover: 0.40 **NM** value: **2.00**
📖 Tears For The World Called Heaven **A:** Tom Sutton **W:** Doug Moench ★ Appearance of Star-Lord.
8 ❑ Sep 1980 Cover: 0.50 **NM** value: **2.00**
• **CGC:** 1 graded, best 9.2
A: Frank Miller; Tony DeZuniga ★ Appearance of Captain Marvel.
9 ❑ Nov 1980 Cover: 0.50 **NM** value: **2.00**
A: Steve Ditko ★ Appearance of Captain Universe.
10 ❑ Jan 1981 Cover: 0.50 **NM** value: **2.00**
A: Steve Ditko ★ Appearance of Captain Universe.
11 ❑ Mar 1981 Cover: 0.50 **NM** value: **2.00**
A: Steve Ditko ★ Appearance of Captain Universe.

MARVEL SPRING SPECIAL Marvel

1 ❑ Nov 1988 **NM** value: **2.50**
• Elvira

MARVEL SUPER ACTION Marvel

1 ❑ May 1977 Cover: 0.30 **NM** value: **4.00**
• **CGC:** 4 graded, best 9.6
• reprints Captain America #100 **A:** Jack Kirby
2 ❑ Jul 1977 Cover: 0.30 **NM** value: **2.50**
• Reprints Captain America #101 **A:** Jack Kirby
3 ❑ Sep 1977 Cover: 0.30 **NM** value: **2.50**
• **CGC:** 1 graded, best 7.5
• Reprints Captain America #102 **A:** Jack Kirby
4 ❑ Nov 1977 Cover: 0.35 **NM** value: **2.50**
• Reprints Marvel Boy #1 **A:** Jack Kirby ★ Origin of Marvel Boy.
5 ❑ Jan 1978 Cover: 0.35 **NM** value: **2.00**
• Reprints Captain America #103 **A:** Jack Kirby
6 ❑ Mar 1978 Cover: 0.35 **NM** value: **2.00**
• Reprints Captain America #104 **A:** Jack Kirby
7 ❑ Apr 1978 Cover: 0.35 **NM** value: **2.00**
• Reprints Captain America #105 **A:** Jack Kirby
8 ❑ Jun 1978 Cover: 0.35 **NM** value: **2.00**
• Reprints Captain America #106 **A:** Jack Kirby
9 ❑ Aug 1978 Cover: 0.35 **NM** value: **2.00**
• Reprints Captain America #107 **A:** Jack Kirby
10 ❑ Oct 1978 Cover: 0.35 **NM** value: **2.00**
• Reprints Captain America #108 **A:** Jack Kirby
11 ❑ Dec 1978 Cover: 0.35 **NM** value: **2.00**
• Reprints Captain America #109 **A:** Jack Kirby
12 ❑ Feb 1979 Cover: 0.35 **NM** value: **2.00**
• Reprints Captain America #110 **A:** Jim Steranko ★ Appearance of Hulk.
13 ❑ Apr 1979 Cover: 0.35 **NM** value: **2.00**
• Reprints Captain America #111 **A:** Jim Steranko
14 ❑ Dec 1979 Cover: 0.40 **NM** value: **1.50**
• reprints Avengers #55
15 ❑ Jan 1980 Cover: 0.40 **NM** value: **1.50**
Circ: Statement: **94,267**
• reprints Avengers #56
16 ❑ Feb 1980 Cover: 0.40 **NM** value: **1.50**
Circ: Statement: **94,267**
• reprints Avengers Annual #2
17 ❑ Mar 1980 Cover: 0.40 **NM** value: **1.50**
Circ: Statement: **94,267**
• reprints Avengers Annual #2
18 ❑ Apr 1980 Cover: 0.40 **NM** value: **1.50**
Circ: Statement: **94,267**
• reprints Avengers #57
19 ❑ May 1980 Cover: 0.40 **NM** value: **1.50**
Circ: Statement: **94,267**
• reprints Avengers #58
20 ❑ Jun 1980 Cover: 0.40 **NM** value: **1.50**
Circ: Statement: **94,267**
• reprints Avengers #59
21 ❑ Jul 1980 Cover: 0.40 **NM** value: **1.50**
Circ: Statement: **94,267**
• reprints Avengers #60
22 ❑ Aug 1980 Cover: 0.40 **NM** value: **1.50**
Circ: Statement: **94,267**
• reprints Avengers #61

CGC-graded: Multiply prices above by **33 for 9.9 M • 16 for 9.8 NM/M • 7 for 9.6 NM+ • 5 for 9.4 NM • 2.5 for 9.2 NM- • 1.5 for 9.0 VF/NM**

23 ❑ Sep 1980 Cover: 0.50 **NM** value: **1.50**
Circ: Statement: **94,267**
• reprints Avengers #62

24 ❑ Oct 1980 Cover: 0.50 **NM** value: **1.50**
Circ: Statement: **94,267**
• reprints Avengers #63

25 ❑ Nov 1980 Cover: 0.50 **NM** value: **1.50**
Circ: Statement: **94,267**
• reprints Avengers #64

26 ❑ Dec 1980 Cover: 0.50 **NM** value: **1.50**
Circ: Statement: **94,267**
• reprints Avengers #65

27 ❑ Jan 1981 Cover: 0.50 **NM** value: **1.50**
• reprints Avengers #66

28 ❑ Feb 1981 Cover: 0.50 **NM** value: **1.50**
• reprints Avengers #67

29 ❑ Mar 1981 Cover: 0.50 **NM** value: **1.50**
• reprints Avengers #68

30 ❑ Apr 1981 Cover: 0.50 **NM** value: **1.50**
• reprints Avengers #69; has 1980 Statement, filed 10/1/80; avg print run 254,725; avg sales 94,154; avg subs 113; avg total paid circ 94,267; samples 582; office use 1,660; max existent 96,509; 62% of run returned

31 ❑ May 1981 Cover: 0.50 **NM** value: **1.50**
• reprints Avengers #70

32 ❑ Jun 1981 Cover: 0.50 **NM** value: **1.50**
• reprints Avengers #71

33 ❑ Jul 1981 Cover: 0.50 **NM** value: **1.50**
• reprints Avengers #72

34 ❑ Aug 1981 Cover: 0.50 **NM** value: **1.50**
• reprints Avengers #73

35 ❑ Sep 1981 Cover: 0.50 **NM** value: **1.50**
• reprints Avengers #74

36 ❑ Oct 1981 Cover: 0.50 **NM** value: **1.50**
• reprints Avengers #75

37 ❑ Nov 1981 Cover: 0.50 **NM** value: **1.50**
• reprints Avengers #76

MARVEL SUPER ACTION (MAGAZINE) Marvel

1 ❑ Jan 1976, b&w Cover: 1.00 **NM** value: **28.00**
One-shot. • Weird World and Punisher stories ★ Origin of Dominic Fortune. ★ 1st Appearance of Mockingbird (as "Huntress"). ★ 2nd Appearance of Dominic Fortune.

MARVEL SUPER HERO CONTEST OF CHAMPIONS Marvel

Marvel's first limited series actually announced as such, 1982's Marvel Super Hero Contest of Champions began when every living super-hero was abruptly snatched from Earth and taken to a stadium in space. They had been called there to settle a bet between a powerful being known as the Grandmaster and a cloaked adversary called "the Unknown." The super-heroes were to divide into teams and search for the four pieces of the Golden Globe of Life, hidden in various places around the planet. If the Grandmaster's team won, the Unknown would be forced to resurrect the Grandmaster's dead brother. If the Grandmaster lost, the Unknown would claim the Grandmaster's life.

This three-issue title was one of Marvel's first limited series. It served as an excuse to introduce several minor super-heroes such as Le Peregrine and Talisman. As a bonus, it included an index to Marvel characters major and minor a la the Marvel Universe handbooks.

1 ❑ Jun 1982 Cover: 0.25 **NM** value: **4.00**
• **CGC:** 4 graded, best 9.6
🕮 A Gathering of Heroes! • Alpha Flight **A:** John Romita Jr. **W:** Steven Grant; Bill Mantlo; Mark Gruenwald ★ 1st Appearance of Shamrock, Le Peregrine, Blitzkrieg, Talisman I, Collective Man.

2 ❑ Jul 1982 Cover: 0.25 **NM** value: **3.50**
• **CGC:** 1 graded, best 9.2
🕮 Frenzy In The Frozen North! • X-Men **A:** John Romita Jr. **W:** Steven Grant; Bill Mantlo; Mark Gruenwald

3 ❑ Aug 1982 Cover: 0.25 **NM** value: **3.50**
• **CGC:** 1 graded, best 9.4
🕮 Siege In The City Of The Dead! • X-Men **A:** John Romita Jr. **W:** Steven Grant; Bill Mantlo; Mark Gruenwald

MARVEL SUPER-HEROES MEGAZINE Marvel

1 ❑ Oct 1994 Cover: 2.95 **NM** value: **Cover or less**
🕮 Fantastic Four: Back To The Basics!; Iron Man: Betrayal; Hulk: Call Of The Desert; Daredevil: Marked For Murder **A:** John Byrne; John Romita Jr.; Frank Miller **W:** John Byrne; Bill Mantlo; Roger McKenzie

2 ❑ Nov 1994 Cover: 2.95 **NM** value: **Cover or less**
🕮 Fantastic Four: Mission For A Dead Man!; Daredevil: In The Hands Of Bullseye; Iron Man: Anguish, Once Removed; Hulk: Freedom **A:** John Byrne; John Romita Jr.; Frank Miller **W:** John Byrne; David Michelinie; Roger McKenzie

3 ❑ Dec 1994 Cover: 2.95 **NM** value: **Cover or less**
A: Frank Miller

4 ❑ Jan 1995 Cover: 2.95 **NM** value: **Cover or less**
A: Frank Miller

5 ❑ Feb 1995 Cover: 2.95 **NM** value: **Cover or less**

6 ❑ Mar 1995 Cover: 2.95 **NM** value: **Cover or less**
final issue.

🕮 indicates **Story Title** or **Storyline** information.
★ indicates **Character Appearance** information.
W = Writer • A = Artist • C = Cover Artist

MARVEL SUPER HEROES SECRET WARS Marvel

In May, 1984, Marvel editor in chief Jim Shooter decided to shake up the Marvel universe a bit. To do this, the company created the Secret Wars, a 12-issue limited series that involved almost every major Marvel character. In this series, Earth's heroes were kidnapped by an almost omnipotent being known as The Beyonder, and pitted against their deadliest enemies. The members of the winning side were promised their fondest desire — but the losers would be granted no mercy.

The Secret Wars changed the lives of all involved, particularly The Amazing Spider-Man. As part of his involvement, he was given a black alien costume which gave him special powers. Eventually, however, it was revealed that this "costume" was actually a living being — a symbiote. When Spider-Man rejected bonding with it, it found another host and became known as the super-villain Venom.

Like DC's Super Powers line, this series also spawned a companion toy line.

1 ❑ May 1984 Cover: 0.75 **NM** value: **3.00**
• **CGC:** 24 graded, best 9.8
• X-Men, Avengers, Fantastic Four in all **A:** Mike Zeck ★ 1st Appearance of Beyonder (voice only).

2 ❑ Jun 1984 Cover: 0.75 **NM** value: **2.00**
• **CGC:** 2 graded, best 9.6
A: Mike Zeck

3 ❑ Jul 1984 Cover: 0.75 **NM** value: **2.00**
• **CGC:** 1 graded, best 9.6
A: Mike Zeck ★ Origin of Volcana. ★ 1st Appearance of Volcana.

4 ❑ Aug 1984 Cover: 0.75 **NM** value: **2.00**
• **CGC:** 2 graded, best 9.8
A: Mike Zeck

5 ❑ Sep 1984 Cover: 0.75 **NM** value: **2.00**
• **CGC:** 1 graded, best 9.4
A: Mike Zeck

6 ❑ Oct 1984 Cover: 0.75 **NM** value: **2.00**
A: Mike Zeck ★ Death of Wasp.

7 ❑ Nov 1984 Cover: 0.75 **NM** value: **3.00**
• **CGC:** 1 graded, best 9.6
A: Mike Zeck ★ 1st Appearance of Spider-Woman II (Julia Carpenter).

8 ❑ Dec 1984 Cover: 0.75 **NM** value: **9.00**
• **CGC:** 231 graded, best 9.8
A: Mike Zeck ★ Origin of Spider-Man's black costume. ★ 1st Appearance of Alien costume (later Venom).

9 ❑ Jan 1985 Cover: 0.75 **NM** value: **2.00**
• **CGC:** 1 graded, best 9.8
A: Mike Zeck

10 ❑ Feb 1985 Cover: 0.75 **NM** value: **2.00**
• **CGC:** 1 graded, best 9.2
A: Mike Zeck

11 ❑ Mar 1985 Cover: 0.75 **NM** value: **2.00**
• **CGC:** 1 graded, best 9.8
A: Mike Zeck

12 ❑ Apr 1985 Cover: 1.00 **NM** value: **2.00**
• **CGC:** 2 graded, best 9.8
• Giant-size. • Conclusion **A:** Mike Zeck

Bk 1❑ Cover: 19.95 **NM** value: **Cover or less**

MARVEL SUPER-HEROES (VOL. 1) Marvel

Formerly entitled Fantasy Masterpieces, this series began as Marvel Super-Heroes with issue #12. It featured multiple storylines in each issue — a combination of new stories and characters alongside reprints of classic material from the 1950s. The new stories included the first appearances of both Captain Marvel and the Guardians of the Galaxy.

Beginning with issue #32, the format changed again — this time to a regular-sized comic book featuring reprints of Tales to Astonish starring the Sub-Mariner and the Incredible Hulk.

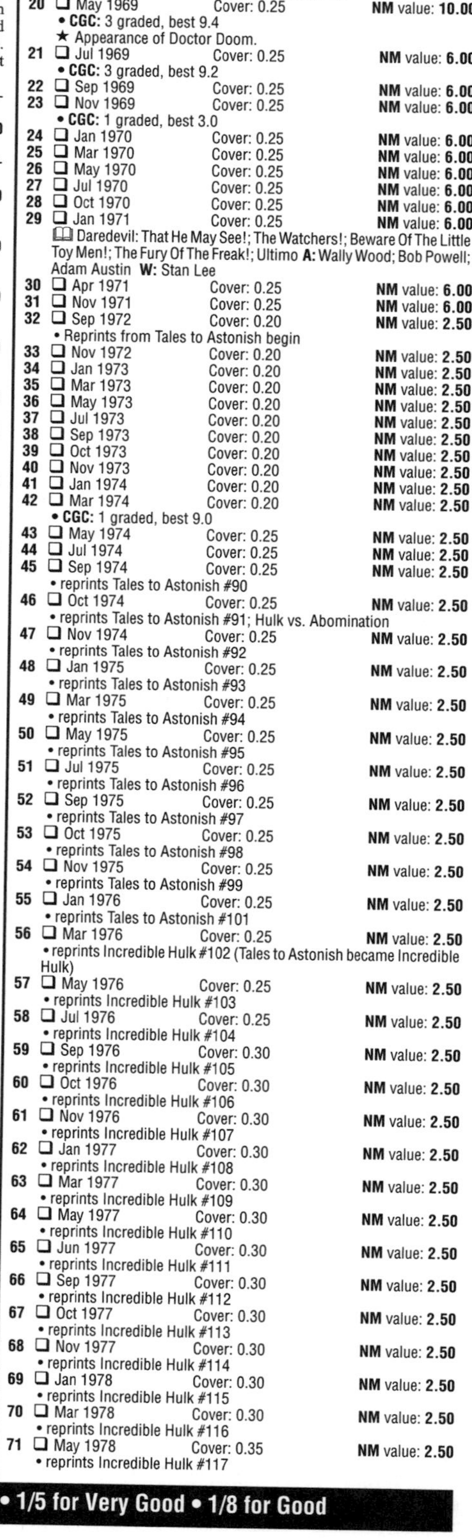

12 ❑ Dec 1967 Cover: 0.25 **NM** value: **50.00**
• **CGC:** 35 graded, best 9.6
• Title continued from "Fantasy Masterpieces" ★ Origin of Captain Marvel. ★ 1st Appearance of Captain Marvel.

13 ❑ Mar 1968 Cover: 0.25 **NM** value: **30.00**
• **CGC:** 2 graded, best 9.4
★ 1st Appearance of Carol Danvers. ★ 2nd Appearance of Captain Marvel.

14 ❑ May 1968 Cover: 0.25 **NM** value: **45.00**
• **CGC:** 12 graded, best 9.6
• Reprints 1st Kirby art at Marvel **A:** Jack Kirby ★ Appearance of Spider-Man.

15 ❑ Jul 1968 Cover: 0.25 **NM** value: **12.00**
• **CGC:** 1 graded, best 8.0
🕮 Let The Silence Shatter!; Black Knight; The Dawn Of The Sub-Mariner; The Black Marvel; Captain America • Medusa **A:** Gene Colan **W:** Archie Goodwin

16 ❑ Sep 1968 Cover: 0.25 **NM** value: **12.00**
• **CGC:** 3 graded, best 9.2
🕮 The Phantom Eagle; The Human Torch; Captain America: The Cargo Of Death; Black Knight; The Patriot; Sub-Mariner **A:** Herb Trimpe **W:** Gary Friedrich ★ Origin of Phantom Eagle. ★ 1st Appearance of Phantom Eagle.

17 ❑ Nov 1968 Cover: 0.25 **NM** value: **12.00**
• **CGC:** 1 graded, best 9.2
🕮 The Black Knight Reborn!; The Original Human Torch; Sub-Mariner: Wings On His Feet; The All Winners Squad; Captain America: The Green Plague; The Whizzer • Reprints All-Winners Squad #21 **A:** Howard Purcell **W:** Roy Thomas ★ Origin of Black Knight III (Dane Whitman). ★ Death of Black Knight I (Sir Percy of Scandia).

18 ❑ Jan 1969 Cover: 0.25 **NM** value: **25.00**
• **CGC:** 9 graded, best 9.6
★ Origin of Vance Astro, Guardians of the Galaxy. ★ 1st Appearance of Vance Astro, Yondu, Guardians of the Galaxy, Charlie-27, Zarek.

19 ❑ Mar 1969 Cover: 0.25 **NM** value: **10.00**
• **CGC:** 1 graded, best 9.2
🕮 My Father, My Enemy!; The Human Torch; Verdict By Magic; Black Knight; Sub-Mariner • Ka-Zar **A:** George Tuska **W:** Steve Parkhouse; Arnold Drake ★ Appearance of Ka-Zar.

20 ❑ May 1969 Cover: 0.25 **NM** value: **10.00**
• **CGC:** 3 graded, best 9.4
★ Appearance of Doctor Doom.

21 ❑ Jul 1969 Cover: 0.25 **NM** value: **6.00**
• **CGC:** 3 graded, best 9.2

22 ❑ Sep 1969 Cover: 0.25 **NM** value: **6.00**

23 ❑ Nov 1969 Cover: 0.25 **NM** value: **6.00**
• **CGC:** 1 graded, best 3.0

24 ❑ Jan 1970 Cover: 0.25 **NM** value: **6.00**

25 ❑ Mar 1970 Cover: 0.25 **NM** value: **6.00**

26 ❑ May 1970 Cover: 0.25 **NM** value: **6.00**

27 ❑ Jul 1970 Cover: 0.25 **NM** value: **6.00**

28 ❑ Oct 1970 Cover: 0.25 **NM** value: **6.00**

29 ❑ Jan 1971 Cover: 0.25 **NM** value: **6.00**
🕮 Daredevil: That He May See!; The Watchers!; Beware Of The Little Toy Men!; The Fury Of The Freak!; Ultimo **A:** Wally Wood; Bob Powell; Adam Austin **W:** Stan Lee

30 ❑ Apr 1971 Cover: 0.25 **NM** value: **6.00**

31 ❑ Nov 1971 Cover: 0.25 **NM** value: **6.00**

32 ❑ Sep 1972 Cover: 0.20 **NM** value: **2.50**
• Reprints from Tales to Astonish begin

33 ❑ Nov 1972 Cover: 0.20 **NM** value: **2.50**

34 ❑ Jan 1973 Cover: 0.20 **NM** value: **2.50**

35 ❑ Mar 1973 Cover: 0.20 **NM** value: **2.50**

36 ❑ May 1973 Cover: 0.20 **NM** value: **2.50**

37 ❑ Jul 1973 Cover: 0.20 **NM** value: **2.50**

38 ❑ Sep 1973 Cover: 0.20 **NM** value: **2.50**

39 ❑ Oct 1973 Cover: 0.20 **NM** value: **2.50**

40 ❑ Nov 1973 Cover: 0.20 **NM** value: **2.50**

41 ❑ Jan 1974 Cover: 0.20 **NM** value: **2.50**

42 ❑ Mar 1974 Cover: 0.20 **NM** value: **2.50**
• **CGC:** 1 graded, best 9.0

43 ❑ May 1974 Cover: 0.25 **NM** value: **2.50**

44 ❑ Jul 1974 Cover: 0.25 **NM** value: **2.50**

45 ❑ Sep 1974 Cover: 0.25 **NM** value: **2.50**
• reprints Tales to Astonish #90

46 ❑ Oct 1974 Cover: 0.25 **NM** value: **2.50**
• reprints Tales to Astonish #91; Hulk vs. Abomination

47 ❑ Nov 1974 Cover: 0.25 **NM** value: **2.50**
• reprints Tales to Astonish #92

48 ❑ Jan 1975 Cover: 0.25 **NM** value: **2.50**
• reprints Tales to Astonish #93

49 ❑ Mar 1975 Cover: 0.25 **NM** value: **2.50**
• reprints Tales to Astonish #94

50 ❑ May 1975 Cover: 0.25 **NM** value: **2.50**
• reprints Tales to Astonish #95

51 ❑ Jul 1975 Cover: 0.25 **NM** value: **2.50**
• reprints Tales to Astonish #96

52 ❑ Sep 1975 Cover: 0.25 **NM** value: **2.50**
• reprints Tales to Astonish #97

53 ❑ Oct 1975 Cover: 0.25 **NM** value: **2.50**
• reprints Tales to Astonish #98

54 ❑ Nov 1975 Cover: 0.25 **NM** value: **2.50**
• reprints Tales to Astonish #99

55 ❑ Jan 1976 Cover: 0.25 **NM** value: **2.50**
• reprints Tales to Astonish #101

56 ❑ Mar 1976 Cover: 0.25 **NM** value: **2.50**
• reprints Incredible Hulk #102 (Tales to Astonish became Incredible Hulk)

57 ❑ May 1976 Cover: 0.25 **NM** value: **2.50**
• reprints Incredible Hulk #103

58 ❑ Jul 1976 Cover: 0.25 **NM** value: **2.50**
• reprints Incredible Hulk #104

59 ❑ Sep 1976 Cover: 0.30 **NM** value: **2.50**
• reprints Incredible Hulk #105

60 ❑ Oct 1976 Cover: 0.30 **NM** value: **2.50**
• reprints Incredible Hulk #106

61 ❑ Nov 1976 Cover: 0.30 **NM** value: **2.50**
• reprints Incredible Hulk #107

62 ❑ Jan 1977 Cover: 0.30 **NM** value: **2.50**
• reprints Incredible Hulk #108

63 ❑ Mar 1977 Cover: 0.30 **NM** value: **2.50**
• reprints Incredible Hulk #109

64 ❑ May 1977 Cover: 0.30 **NM** value: **2.50**
• reprints Incredible Hulk #110

65 ❑ Jun 1977 Cover: 0.30 **NM** value: **2.50**
• reprints Incredible Hulk #111

66 ❑ Sep 1977 Cover: 0.30 **NM** value: **2.50**
• reprints Incredible Hulk #112

67 ❑ Oct 1977 Cover: 0.30 **NM** value: **2.50**
• reprints Incredible Hulk #113

68 ❑ Nov 1977 Cover: 0.30 **NM** value: **2.50**
• reprints Incredible Hulk #114

69 ❑ Jan 1978 Cover: 0.30 **NM** value: **2.50**
• reprints Incredible Hulk #115

70 ❑ Mar 1978 Cover: 0.30 **NM** value: **2.50**
• reprints Incredible Hulk #116

71 ❑ May 1978 Cover: 0.35 **NM** value: **2.50**
• reprints Incredible Hulk #117

Other grades: Multiply prices above by **1.5 for Mint • 2/3 for Very Fine • 1/3 for Fine • 1/5 for Very Good • 1/8 for Good**

72 ❑ Jul 1978 Cover: 0.35 **NM** value: **2.50**
73 ❑ Aug 1978 Cover: 0.35 **NM** value: **2.50**
• reprints Incredible Hulk #120
74 ❑ Sep 1978 Cover: 0.35 **NM** value: **2.50**
75 ❑ Oct 1978 Cover: 0.35 **NM** value: **2.50**
76 ❑ Nov 1978 Cover: 0.35 **NM** value: **2.50**
• reprints Incredible Hulk #124
77 ❑ Dec 1978 Cover: 0.35 **NM** value: **2.50**
• reprints Incredible Hulk #125
78 ❑ Jan 1979 Cover: 0.35 **NM** value: **2.50**
• reprints Incredible Hulk #126
79 ❑ Mar 1979 Cover: 0.35 **NM** value: **2.50**
• reprints Incredible Hulk #127
80 ❑ May 1979 Cover: 0.40 **NM** value: **2.50**
• reprints Incredible Hulk #128
81 ❑ Jul 1979 Cover: 0.35 **NM** value: **2.00**
• reprints Incredible Hulk #129
82 ❑ Aug 1979 Cover: 0.35 **NM** value: **2.00**
• reprints Incredible Hulk #130
83 ❑ Sep 1979 Cover: 0.35 **NM** value: **2.00**
• reprints Incredible Hulk #131
84 ❑ Oct 1979 Cover: 0.35 **NM** value: **2.00**
• reprints Incredible Hulk #132
85 ❑ Nov 1979 Cover: 0.35 **NM** value: **2.00**
• reprints Incredible Hulk #133
86 ❑ Jan 1980 Cover: 0.35 **NM** value: **2.00**
• reprints Incredible Hulk #134
87 ❑ Mar 1980 Cover: 0.35 **NM** value: **2.00**
88 ❑ May 1980 Cover: 0.35 **NM** value: **2.00**
89 ❑ Jul 1980 Cover: 0.40 **NM** value: **2.00**
• reprints Incredible Hulk #139
90 ❑ Aug 1980 Cover: 0.35 **NM** value: **2.00**
📖 The Summons OF Psyklop • reprints Avengers #88 **A:** Sal Buscema **W:** Roy Thomas; Harlan Ellison
91 ❑ Sep 1980 Cover: 0.50 **NM** value: **2.00**
📖 Brute That Shouted Love at the Heart of the Atom • reprints Incredible Hulk #140 **W:** Harlan Ellison
92 ❑ Oct 1980 Cover: 0.40 **NM** value: **2.00**
93 ❑ Nov 1980 Cover: 0.40 **NM** value: **2.00**
94 ❑ Jan 1981 Cover: 0.40 **NM** value: **2.00**
95 ❑ Mar 1981 Cover: 0.50 **NM** value: **2.00**
96 ❑ Apr 1981 Cover: 0.50 **NM** value: **2.00**
97 ❑ May 1981 Cover: 0.50 **NM** value: **2.00**
98 ❑ Jun 1981 Cover: 0.50 **NM** value: **2.00**
99 ❑ Jul 1981 Cover: 0.50 **NM** value: **2.00**
• reprints Incredible Hulk #150
100 ❑ Aug 1981 Cover: 0.75 **NM** value: **2.00**
• reprints Incredible Hulk #151-152
101 ❑ Sep 1981 Cover: 0.50 **NM** value: **2.00**
• reprints Incredible Hulk #153
102 ❑ Oct 1981 Cover: 0.40 **NM** value: **2.00**
• reprints Incredible Hulk #154
103 ❑ Nov 1981 Cover: 0.40 **NM** value: **2.00**
• reprints Incredible Hulk #155
104 ❑ Dec 1981 Cover: 0.40 **NM** value: **2.00**
• reprints Incredible Hulk #156
105 ❑ Jan 1982 Cover: 0.40 **NM** value: **2.00**
• reprints Incredible Hulk #157
SE 1 ❑ Oct 1966 Cover: 0.25 **NM** value: **45.00**
📖 The Avengers Battle the Space Phantom; The Origin of Daredevil; The Human Torch and the Sub-Mariner Meet!!! • One-shot from 1966; Reprints stories from Avengers #2, Daredevil #1, Marvel Mystery Comics #8; Human Torch meets Sub-Mariner **A:** Bill Everett; Jack Kirby **W:** Stan Lee ★ Origin of Daredevil. ★ 1st Appearance of Daredevil.

MARVEL SUPER-HEROES (VOL. 2) — Marvel

1 ❑ May 1990 Cover: 2.95 **NM** value: **3.50**
Circ: CapCity orders: **28,700**
📖 Moon Knight: Old Business; Hercules: I Shot an Arrow Into the Sky!; Hellcat: The Sacrifice; Brother Voodoo: Do That Voodoo You Do So Well; Speedball: Pulitzer Patty; Magik: Who Wants to Live Forever?; The Black Panther: Conflagration • Spring 1990 **A:** Steve Ditko; Fred Hembeck; Ron Lim; Keith Pollard; Mike Gustovich; Rodney Ramos; Kim Demulder; Dennis Jensen **W:** Scott Lobdell; Fabian Nicieza; D.G. Chichester; Margaret Clark; Richard Bensam; Robert Ingersoll; Sue Flaxman ★ Origin of Raptor.
2 ❑ Jul 1990 Cover: 2.95 **NM** value: **3.25**
Circ: CapCity orders: **21,800**
3 ❑ Oct 1990 Cover: 2.95 **NM** value: **3.25**
Circ: CapCity orders: **16,900**
4 ❑ Dec 1990 Cover: 2.95 **NM** value: **3.25**
Circ: CapCity orders: **14,450**
5 ❑ Apr 1991 Cover: 2.95 **NM** value: **3.25**
Circ: CapCity orders: **10,700**
6 ❑ Jul 1991 Cover: 2.25 **NM** value: **3.25**
Circ: CapCity orders: **16,500**
C: Arthur Adams
7 ❑ Oct 1991 Cover: 2.25 **NM** value: **3.25**
Circ: CapCity orders: **17,000**
8 ❑ Dec 1991 Cover: 2.25 **NM** value: **3.25**
Circ: CapCity orders: **15,450**
9 ❑ Apr 1992 Cover: 2.50 **NM** value: **3.25**
W: Kurt Busiek ★ Appearance of Cupid.
10 ❑ Jul 1992 Cover: 2.50 **NM** value: **3.25**
Circ: CapCity orders: **12,800**
• Oversized format. ★ Appearance of Sabretooth.
11 ❑ Oct 1992 Cover: 2.50 **NM** value: **3.00**
Circ: CapCity orders: **11,200**
• Ghost Rider
12 ❑ Jan 1993 Cover: 2.50 **NM** value: **Cover or less**
Circ: CapCity orders: **8,400**
W: Kurt Busiek
13 ❑ Apr 1993 Cover: 2.75 **NM** value: **Cover or less**
Circ: CapCity orders: **11,400**
• Iron Man **W:** Kurt Busiek
14 ❑ Jul 1993 Cover: 2.75 **NM** value: **Cover or less**
Circ: CapCity orders: **10,100**
15 ❑ Oct 1993 Cover: 2.75 **NM** value: **Cover or less**
Circ: CapCity orders: **8,700**
📖 Volstagg's Mostly Greatest Adventure; The Theft of Thor's Hammer; Heart of Power final issue. **A:** Keith Pollard; Don Heck; Joe Barney **W:** Len Kaminski; Walt Simonson; David Anthony Kraft; Bill Mantlo ★ Appearance of Iron Man, Thor.

MARVEL SUPER SPECIAL — Marvel

Marvel Super Special began as a large-format book featuring the first appearance of the rock group Kiss in a comic book. In a fantastic publicity stunt, the group even arranged to mix drops of their own blood into the ink used in the print run, thus playing up their "Satan-rock" image. Other special issues included a feature on The Beatles and a proof-quality limited run of the Weirdworld storyline, with each copy signed by the artists.

Most issues, however, were rather straightforward movie adaptations. The features ranged from Battlestar Galactica to Annie, although science-fiction and fantasy films of one sort or another dominated the series.

1 ❑ Sep 1977 Cover: 1.50 **NM** value: **35.00**
• Group mixed drops of their blood into the printer's ink in publicity stunt **W:** Steve Gerber ★ Origin of Kiss (rock group).
2 ❑ Mar 1978 Cover: 1.50 **NM** value: **5.00**
• Conan
3 ❑ Jun 1978 Cover: 1.50 **NM** value: **5.00**
• Close Encounters of the Third Kind
4 ❑ Aug 1978 Cover: 1.50 **NM** value: **15.00**
• The Beatles
5 ❑ Dec 1978 Cover: 1.50 **NM** value: **20.00**
• Title changes to Marvel Super Special; Jaws 2; Kiss
6 ❑ Dec 1978 Cover: 1.50 **NM** value: **4.00**
• Kiss; Jaws 2
7 ❑ Dec 1978 Cover: 1.50 **NM** value: **3.00**
• Nonexistent?
8 ❑ Cover: 1.50 **NM** value: **5.00**
• Battlestar Galactica; tabloid
9 ❑ Feb 1979 Cover: 1.50 **NM** value: **5.00**
• Conan
10 ❑ Jun 1979 Cover: 1.50 **NM** value: **5.00**
• Star-Lord
11 ❑ Sep 1979 Cover: 1.50 **NM** value: **4.00**
• Warriors of Shadow Realm; Weirdworld
12 ❑ Nov 1979 Cover: 1.50 **NM** value: **4.00**
• Warriors of Shadow Realm; Weirdworld
13 ❑ Jan 1980 Cover: 1.50 **NM** value: **4.00**
• Warriors of Shadow Realm; Weirdworld
14 ❑ Feb 1980 Cover: 1.50 **NM** value: **3.00**
📖 Meteor • Meteor **A:** Gene Colan; Tom Palmer **W:** Ralph Macchio
15 ❑ Mar 1980 Cover: 1.50 **NM** value: **5.00**
• Star Trek: The Motion Picture
16 ❑ Aug 1980 Cover: 2.00 **NM** value: **6.00**
• Empire Strikes Back
17 ❑ Nov 1980 Cover: 2.00 **NM** value: **3.00**
• Xanadu
18 ❑ Sep 1981 Cover: 2.50 **NM** value: **3.00**
• Raiders of the Lost Ark
19 ❑ Oct 1981 Cover: 2.50 **NM** value: **3.00**
• For Your Eyes Only
20 ❑ Oct 1981 Cover: 2.50 **NM** value: **3.00**
• Dragonslayer
21 ❑ Aug 1982 Cover: 2.50 **NM** value: **3.00**
• Conan movie
22 ❑ Sep 1982 Cover: 2.50 **NM** value: **3.00**
• Comic size. • Blade Runner
23 ❑ Sep 1982 Cover: 2.50 **NM** value: **3.00**
• Annie
24 ❑ Mar 1983 Cover: 2.50 **NM** value: **3.00**
• Dark Crystal
25 ❑ Aug 1983 Cover: 2.50 **NM** value: **3.00**
• Comic size. 📖 Rock & Rule **W:** Bob Budiansky; Bill Mantlo; Clive Smith
26 ❑ Sep 1983 Cover: 2.50 **NM** value: **3.00**
• Octopussy
27 ❑ Sep 1983 Cover: 2.50 **NM** value: **3.00**
• Return of the Jedi
28 ❑ Oct 1983 Cover: 2.50 **NM** value: **3.00**
• Krull
29 ❑ Jul 1984 Cover: 2.00 **NM** value: **3.00**
• Tarzan of the Apes
30 ❑ Aug 1984 Cover: 2.50 **NM** value: **3.00**
• Indiana Jones and the Temple of Doom
31 ❑ Sep 1984 Cover: 2.50 **NM** value: **3.00**
• The Last Starfighter
32 ❑ Oct 1984 Cover: 2.50 **NM** value: **3.00**
• The Muppets Take Manhattan
33 ❑ Nov 1984 Cover: 2.50 **NM** value: **3.00**
• Buckaroo Banzai
34 ❑ Nov 1984 Cover: 2.50 **NM** value: **3.00**
• Sheena
35 ❑ Dec 1984 Cover: 2.50 **NM** value: **3.00**
• Conan the Destroyer
36 ❑ Apr 1985 Cover: 2.50 **NM** value: **3.00**
• Dune
37 ❑ Apr 1985 Cover: 2.00 **NM** value: **3.00**
• 2010
38 ❑ Nov 1985 Cover: 2.00 **NM** value: **3.00**
Circ: CapCity orders: **3,100**
📖 Into the Realm of Darkness • Red Sonja **A:** Mary Wilshier **W:** Louise Simonson
39 ❑ Mar 1985 Cover: 2.50 **NM** value: **3.00**
Circ: CapCity orders: **2,300**
• Santa Claus: the Movie
40 ❑ Oct 1986 Cover: 2.50 **NM** value: **3.00**
Circ: CapCity orders: **2,400**
• Labyrinth
41 ❑ Nov 1986 Cover: 2.50 **NM** value: **3.00**
Circ: CapCity orders: **4,600**
• Howard the Duck movie adaptation **A:** Kyle Baker **W:** Danny Fingeroth

MARVEL SWIMSUIT SPECIAL — Marvel

1 ❑ ca. 1992 Cover: 3.95 **NM** value: **4.00**
• 1992; in Wakanda
2 ❑ ca. 1993 Cover: 4.50 **NM** value: **Cover or less**
Circ: CapCity orders: **49,700**
• 1993; on Monster Island
3 ❑ ca. 1994 Cover: 4.50 **NM** value: **Cover or less**
Circ: CapCity orders: **27,875**
4 ❑ ca. 1995 Cover: 4.95 **NM** value: **5.00**
A: Greg Hildebrandt(cover); Tim Hildebrandt(cover)

MARVEL TAILS — Marvel

1 ❑ Nov 1983 Cover: 0.60 **NM** value: **1.50**
📖 If He Should Punch Me! **A:** Mark Armstrong **W:** Tom DeFalco ★ 1st Appearance of Peter Porker.

MARVEL TALES (1ST SERIES) — Marvel

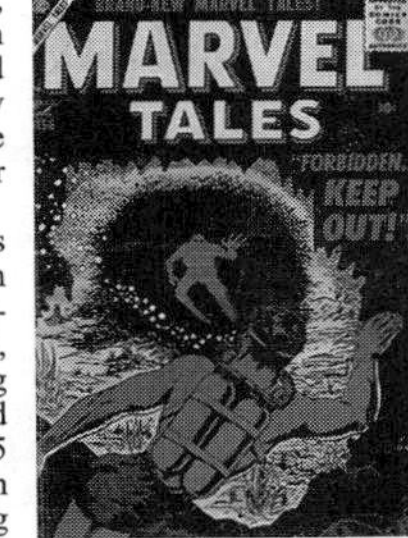

Marvel Comics' premiere title, Marvel Mystery Comics had fallen on tough times in the post-World War II years. As strange as it may seem today, super-heroes like The Human Torch and The Sub-Mariner simply weren't selling.

In 1949, the title changed its name to Marvel Tales and began presenting a collection of science-fiction and monster stories. Sadly, Marvel Tales lacked the storytelling flair that made E.C. titles like Weird Science so memorable. 1955 brought with it the Comics Code, an industry response to the growing pressure to tone down the content of comic books. Although never especially daring to begin with, the Code forced Marvel Tales to become further watered-down. With anti-comics sentiment running strong, and the Code doing its part to make comics less interesting, sales of all comics dropped dramatically. In 1957, Marvel Tales was canceled along with the rest of the Atlas line of comics.

93 ❑ Aug 1949 Cover: 0.10 **NM** value: **940.00**
• **CGC:** 3 graded, best 6.5
• Series continued from Marvel Mystery Comics #92
94 ❑ Nov 1949 Cover: 0.10 **NM** value: **685.00**
95 ❑ Mar 1950 Cover: 0.10 **NM** value: **490.00**
96 ❑ Jun 1950 Cover: 0.10 **NM** value: **490.00**
• **CGC:** 4 graded, best 9.2
97 ❑ Sep 1950 Cover: 0.10 **NM** value: **550.00**
• **CGC:** 4 graded, best 9.2
98 ❑ Dec 1950 Cover: 0.10 **NM** value: **490.00**
• **CGC:** 2 graded, best 8.5
99 ❑ Feb 1951 Cover: 0.10 **NM** value: **490.00**
• **CGC:** 2 graded, best 9.2
100 ❑ Apr 1951 Cover: 0.10 **NM** value: **490.00**
• **CGC:** 3 graded, best 8.0
101 ❑ Jun 1951 Cover: 0.10 **NM** value: **490.00**
• **CGC:** 2 graded, best 9.2
102 ❑ Aug 1951 Cover: 0.10 **NM** value: **600.00**
• **CGC:** 2 graded, best 9.0
A: Basil Wolverton
103 ❑ Oct 1951 Cover: 0.10 **NM** value: **450.00**
• **CGC:** 2 graded, best 7.5
104 ❑ Dec 1951 Cover: 0.10 **NM** value: **525.00**
• **CGC:** 3 graded, best 9.2
A: Basil Wolverton
105 ❑ Feb 1952 Cover: 0.10 **NM** value: **390.00**
• **CGC:** 1 graded, best 8.0
106 ❑ Apr 1952 Cover: 0.10 **NM** value: **345.00**
• **CGC:** 2 graded, best 9.4
107 ❑ Jun 1952 Cover: 0.10 **NM** value: **345.00**
108 ❑ Aug 1952 Cover: 0.10 **NM** value: **345.00**
109 ❑ Oct 1952 Cover: 0.10 **NM** value: **245.00**
• **CGC:** 1 graded, best 8.5
110 ❑ Dec 1952 Cover: 0.10 **NM** value: **245.00**
• **CGC:** 2 graded, best 9.2
111 ❑ Feb 1953 Cover: 0.10 **NM** value: **245.00**
112 ❑ Mar 1953 Cover: 0.10 **NM** value: **245.00**
• **CGC:** 2 graded, best 9.2
113 ❑ Apr 1953 Cover: 0.10 **NM** value: **245.00**
• **CGC:** 2 graded, best 8.5
114 ❑ May 1953 Cover: 0.10 **NM** value: **245.00**
115 ❑ Jun 1953 Cover: 0.10 **NM** value: **245.00**
• **CGC:** 1 graded, best 6.5
116 ❑ Jul 1953 Cover: 0.10 **NM** value: **245.00**
• **CGC:** 1 graded, best 7.0
117 ❑ Aug 1953 Cover: 0.10 **NM** value: **245.00**
• **CGC:** 3 graded, best 7.5
118 ❑ Sep 1953 Cover: 0.10 **NM** value: **245.00**
• **CGC:** 1 graded, best 7.5
119 ❑ Dec 1953 Cover: 0.10 **NM** value: **245.00**
120 ❑ Feb 1954 Cover: 0.10 **NM** value: **245.00**
121 ❑ Mar 1954 Cover: 0.10 **NM** value: **195.00**
• **CGC:** 1 graded, best 5.0
122 ❑ Apr 1954 Cover: 0.10 **NM** value: **195.00**
A: Joe Kubert
123 ❑ May 1954 Cover: 0.10 **NM** value: **195.00**
• **CGC:** 2 graded, best 7.5

CGC-graded: Multiply prices above by **33 for 9.9 M • 16 for 9.8 NM/M • 7 for 9.6 NM+ • 5 for 9.4 NM • 2.5 for 9.2 NM- • 1.5 for 9.0 VF/NM**

124 ❑ Jun 1954 Cover: 0.10 **NM** value: **195.00**
• **CGC:** 1 graded, best 6.0
125 ❑ Jul 1954 Cover: 0.10 **NM** value: **195.00**
• **CGC:** 1 graded, best 6.0
126 ❑ Aug 1954 Cover: 0.10 **NM** value: **195.00**
• **CGC:** 3 graded, best 8.5
127 ❑ Oct 1954 Cover: 0.10 **NM** value: **195.00**
• **CGC:** 1 graded, best 8.5
128 ❑ Nov 1954 Cover: 0.10 **NM** value: **195.00**
129 ❑ Dec 1954 Cover: 0.10 **NM** value: **195.00**
• **CGC:** 1 graded, best 8.5
130 ❑ Jan 1955 Cover: 0.10 **NM** value: **195.00**
131 ❑ Feb 1955 Cover: 0.10 **NM** value: **175.00**
• **CGC:** 1 graded, best 9.0
132 ❑ Mar 1955 Cover: 0.10 **NM** value: **135.00**
133 ❑ Apr 1955 Cover: 0.10 **NM** value: **135.00**
• **CGC:** 1 graded, best 7.5
134 ❑ May 1955 Cover: 0.10 **NM** value: **155.00**
A: Joe Kubert
135 ❑ Jun 1955 Cover: 0.10 **NM** value: **135.00**
• **CGC:** 1 graded, best 6.0
136 ❑ Jul 1955 Cover: 0.10 **NM** value: **135.00**
• **CGC:** 1 graded, best 9.0
137 ❑ Aug 1955 Cover: 0.10 **NM** value: **135.00**
• **CGC:** 1 graded, best 9.0
138 ❑ Sep 1955 Cover: 0.10 **NM** value: **135.00**
• **CGC:** 1 graded, best 6.5
139 ❑ Oct 1955 Cover: 0.10 **NM** value: **135.00**
• **CGC:** 2 graded, best 8.5
140 ❑ Nov 1955 Cover: 0.10 **NM** value: **135.00**
• **CGC:** 2 graded, best 9.0
141 ❑ Dec 1955 Cover: 0.10 **NM** value: **135.00**
• **CGC:** 1 graded, best 5.0
142 ❑ Jan 1956 Cover: 0.10 **NM** value: **135.00**
143 ❑ Feb 1956 Cover: 0.10 **NM** value: **135.00**
144 ❑ Mar 1956 Cover: 0.10 **NM** value: **135.00**
• **CGC:** 1 graded, best 3.0
A: Al Williamson
145 ❑ Apr 1956 Cover: 0.10 **NM** value: **135.00**
146 ❑ May 1956 Cover: 0.10 **NM** value: **115.00**
147 ❑ Jun 1956 Cover: 0.10 **NM** value: **115.00**
A: Steve Ditko
148 ❑ Jul 1956 Cover: 0.10 **NM** value: **115.00**
• **CGC:** 1 graded, best 7.5
149 ❑ Aug 1956 Cover: 0.10 **NM** value: **115.00**
150 ❑ Sep 1956 Cover: 0.10 **NM** value: **115.00**
• **CGC:** 1 graded, best 7.5
151 ❑ Oct 1956 Cover: 0.10 **NM** value: **115.00**
• **CGC:** 1 graded, best 8.5
152 ❑ Nov 1956 Cover: 0.10 **NM** value: **115.00**
• **CGC:** 1 graded, best 7.5
A: Wally Wood
153 ❑ Dec 1956 Cover: 0.10 **NM** value: **115.00**
• **CGC:** 1 graded, best 3.0
154 ❑ Jan 1957 Cover: 0.10 **NM** value: **115.00**
• **CGC:** 1 graded, best 8.0
155 ❑ Feb 1957 Cover: 0.10 **NM** value: **115.00**
• **CGC:** 1 graded, best 7.5
156 ❑ Mar 1957 Cover: 0.10 **NM** value: **115.00**
• **CGC:** 1 graded, best 8.0
157 ❑ 1957 Cover: 0.10 **NM** value: **115.00**
158 ❑ 1957 Cover: 0.10 **NM** value: **115.00**
159 ❑ Aug 1957 Cover: 0.10 **NM** value: **115.00**
final issue.

MARVEL TALES (2ND SERIES) — Marvel

Marvel Tales gave newer readers a way to catch up on the early adventures of Marvel's favorite heroes. Although it began with reprints of various characters' first issues, Marvel Tales soon focused its reprint efforts on The Amazing Spider-Man.

For more than 30 years, the series served as a retrospective on the web-slinger's career, from his premiere in Amazing Fantasy #15 to his relatively recent struggles.

Most of the reprints came from Amazing Spider-Man, but a few issues of Marvel Team-Up also made the cut.

1 ❑ ca. 1964 Cover: 0.25 **NM** value: **160.00**
• **CGC:** 20 graded, best 9.4
• Giant-size. 📖 Spider-Man!; The Coming of the Hulk!; Return of the Ant-Man; The Birth of Giant-Man!; Sgt. Furt, and his Howling Commandos; Iron Man is Born! • Amazing Fantasy #15; Listed as Marvel Tales Annual #1 in indicia **A:** Steve Ditko; Jack Kirby **W:** Stan Lee ★ Origin of Iron Man, Ant-Man, Spider-Man, The Hulk, Giant-Man. ★ 1st Appearance of Spider-Man.
2 ❑ ca. 1965 Cover: 0.25 **NM** value: **75.00**
• **CGC:** 13 graded, best 9.4
• Giant-size. • Reprints Uncanny X-Men #1, Incredible Hulk #3, Avengers #1★ Origin of X-Men.
3 ❑ Jul 1966 Cover: 0.25 **NM** value: **36.00**
• **CGC:** 2 graded, best 9.4
• Giant-size. • reprints Amazing Spider-Man #6
4 ❑ Sep 1966 Cover: 0.25 **NM** value: **20.00**
• **CGC:** 3 graded, best 9.6
• Giant-size. • Amazing Spider-Man #7 **A:** Steve Ditko
5 ❑ Nov 1966 Cover: 0.25 **NM** value: **20.00**
• **CGC:** 2 graded, best 9.6
• Giant-size. • Amazing Spider-Man #8 **A:** Steve Ditko
6 ❑ Jan 1967 Cover: 0.25 **NM** value: **15.00**
• **CGC:** 4 graded, best 9.6
• Giant-size. • Amazing Spider-Man #9 **A:** Steve Ditko
7 ❑ Mar 1967 Cover: 0.25 **NM** value: **15.00**
• **CGC:** 2 graded, best 9.2
• Giant-size. • Amazing Spider-Man #10 **A:** Steve Ditko
8 ❑ May 1967 Cover: 0.25 **NM** value: **15.00**
• **CGC:** 2 graded, best 8.5
• Giant-size. • Amazing Spider-Man #13 **A:** Steve Ditko
9 ❑ Jul 1967 Cover: 0.25 **NM** value: **16.00**
• **CGC:** 3 graded, best 9.2
• Giant-size. • Amazing Spider-Man #14 **A:** Steve Ditko
10 ❑ Sep 1967 Cover: 0.25 **NM** value: **14.00**
• Giant-size. • Amazing Spider-Man #15 **A:** Steve Ditko
11 ❑ Nov 1967 Cover: 0.25 **NM** value: **9.00**
• **CGC:** 2 graded, best 8.0
• Giant-size. • Amazing Spider-Man #16 **A:** Steve Ditko
12 ❑ Jan 1968 Cover: 0.25 **NM** value: **9.00**
• Giant-size. 📖 The Return of the Green Goblin!; The Magician and the Maiden!; The Human Torch vs. The Wizard and Paste-Pot Pete!; Challenged by the Human Cobra!" • Reprints stories from Amazing Spider-Man #17, Strange Tales #110, Tales to Astonish #58, Tales to Astonish #98 **A:** Steve Ditko; Don Heck; Dick Ayers; Larry Lieber **W:** Larry Lieber; Stan Lee ★ 1st Appearance of the Trapster ("Paste-Pot Pete").
13 ❑ Mar 1968 Cover: 0.25 **NM** value: **9.00**
• **CGC:** 1 graded, best 9.8
• Giant-size. • Amazing Spider-Man #18; Reprints Marvel Boy #1 **A:** Steve Ditko ★ Origin of Marvel Boy.
14 ❑ May 1968 Cover: 0.25 **NM** value: **9.00**
• **CGC:** 2 graded, best 9.4
• Giant-size. • Marvel Boy; Amazing Spider-Man #19 **A:** Steve Ditko
15 ❑ Jul 1968 Cover: 0.25 **NM** value: **9.00**
• **CGC:** 1 graded, best 8.5
• Giant-size. • Marvel Boy; Amazing Spider-Man #20 **A:** Steve Ditko
16 ❑ Sep 1968 Cover: 0.25 **NM** value: **9.00**
• **CGC:** 3 graded, best 9.6
• Giant-size. • Marvel Boy; Amazing Spider-Man #21 **A:** Steve Ditko
17 ❑ Nov 1968 Cover: 0.25 **NM** value: **9.00**
• **CGC:** 2 graded, best 9.4
• Giant-size. • Amazing Spider-Man #22 **A:** Steve Ditko
18 ❑ Jan 1969 Cover: 0.25 **NM** value: **9.00**
• **CGC:** 1 graded, best 8.0
• Giant-size. • Amazing Spider-Man #23 **A:** Steve Ditko
19 ❑ Mar 1969 Cover: 0.25 **NM** value: **9.00**
• Giant-size. • Amazing Spider-Man #24 **A:** Steve Ditko
20 ❑ May 1969 Cover: 0.25 **NM** value: **9.00**
• **CGC:** 1 graded, best 9.4
• Giant-size. • Amazing Spider-Man #25 **A:** Steve Ditko
21 ❑ Jul 1969 Cover: 0.25 **NM** value: **8.00**
• Giant-size. • Amazing Spider-Man #26 **A:** Steve Ditko
22 ❑ Sep 1969 Cover: 0.25 **NM** value: **8.00**
• Giant-size. • Amazing Spider-Man #27 **A:** Steve Ditko
23 ❑ Nov 1969 Cover: 0.25 **NM** value: **8.00**
• Giant-size. 📖 The Claws of the Cat; Every Hand Against Him!; Prisoner of the Plantman!
24 ❑ Jan 1970 Cover: 0.25 **NM** value: **8.00**
• **CGC:** 1 graded, best 9.4
• Giant-size. • Amazing Spider-Man #31 **A:** Steve Ditko
25 ❑ Mar 1970 Cover: 0.25 **NM** value: **8.00**
• **CGC:** 1 graded, best 8.5
• Giant-size. • Amazing Spider-Man #32 **A:** Steve Ditko
26 ❑ May 1970 Cover: 0.25 **NM** value: **8.00**
• **CGC:** 2 graded, best 9.4
• Giant-size. • Amazing Spider-Man #33 **A:** Steve Ditko
27 ❑ Jul 1970 Cover: 0.25 **NM** value: **8.00**
• **CGC:** 1 graded, best 7.0
• Giant-size. • Amazing Spider-Man #34 **A:** Steve Ditko
28 ❑ Oct 1970 Cover: 0.25 **NM** value: **8.00**
• **CGC:** 2 graded, best 8.5
• Giant-size. • Amazing Spider-Man #35 and #36 **A:** Steve Ditko
29 ❑ Jan 1971 Cover: 0.25 **NM** value: **8.00**
• **CGC:** 2 graded, best 9.6
• Giant-size. • Amazing Spider-Man #39 and #40 **A:** John Romita ★ Origin of Green Goblin.
30 ❑ Apr 1971 Cover: 0.25 **NM** value: **8.00**
• Giant-size. • Amazing Spider-Man #58 and #41; conclusion of Angel back-up from Ka-Zar #3 **A:** John Romita
31 ❑ Jul 1971 Cover: 0.25 **NM** value: **8.00**
• Giant-size. • Amazing Spider-Man #37 and #42 **A:** Steve Ditko; John Romita
32 ❑ Nov 1971 Cover: 0.25 **NM** value: **8.00**
• **CGC:** 1 graded, best 8.5
• Last giant-size issue. **A:** John Romita
33 ❑ Feb 1972 Cover: 0.25 **NM** value: **3.00**
• Amazing Spider-Man #45 and #47 **A:** John Romita
34 ❑ Apr 1972 Cover: 0.20 **NM** value: **3.00**
• Amazing Spider-Man #48 **A:** John Romita
35 ❑ Jun 1972 Cover: 0.20 **NM** value: **3.00**
• Amazing Spider-Man #49 **A:** John Romita
36 ❑ Aug 1972 Cover: 0.20 **NM** value: **3.00**
• Amazing Spider-Man #51 **A:** John Romita
37 ❑ Sep 1972 Cover: 0.20 **NM** value: **3.00**
• Amazing Spider-Man #52 **A:** John Romita
38 ❑ Oct 1972 Cover: 0.20 **NM** value: **3.00**
• Amazing Spider-Man #53 **A:** John Romita
39 ❑ Nov 1972 Cover: 0.20 **NM** value: **3.00**
• Amazing Spider-Man #54 **A:** John Romita
40 ❑ Dec 1972 Cover: 0.20 **NM** value: **3.00**
• Amazing Spider-Man #55 **A:** John Romita
41 ❑ Feb 1973 Cover: 0.20 **NM** value: **3.00**
• Amazing Spider-Man #56 **A:** John Romita
42 ❑ Apr 1973 Cover: 0.20 **NM** value: **3.00**
• Amazing Spider-Man #59 **A:** John Romita
43 ❑ Jun 1973 Cover: 0.20 **NM** value: **3.00**
• Amazing Spider-Man #60 **A:** John Romita
44 ❑ Aug 1973 Cover: 0.20 **NM** value: **3.00**
45 ❑ Sep 1973 Cover: 0.20 **NM** value: **3.00**
46 ❑ Oct 1973 Cover: 0.20 **NM** value: **3.00**
47 ❑ Nov 1973 Cover: 0.20 **NM** value: **3.00**
48 ❑ Dec 1973 Cover: 0.20 **NM** value: **3.00**
• **CGC:** 2 graded, best 9.4
49 ❑ Feb 1974 Cover: 0.20 **NM** value: **3.00**
50 ❑ Apr 1974 Cover: 0.20 **NM** value: **3.00**
• **CGC:** 1 graded, best 9.4
51 ❑ Jun 1974 Cover: 0.25 **NM** value: **2.50**
52 ❑ Aug 1974 Cover: 0.25 **NM** value: **2.50**
53 ❑ Sep 1974 Cover: 0.25 **NM** value: **2.50**
• **CGC:** 1 graded, best 9.6
54 ❑ Oct 1974 Cover: 0.25 **NM** value: **2.50**
55 ❑ Nov 1974 Cover: 0.25 **NM** value: **2.50**
56 ❑ Dec 1974 Cover: 0.25 **NM** value: **2.50**
57 ❑ Feb 1975 Cover: 0.25 **NM** value: **2.50**
58 ❑ Apr 1975 Cover: 0.25 **NM** value: **2.50**
59 ❑ Jun 1975 Cover: 0.25 **NM** value: **2.50**
60 ❑ Aug 1975 Cover: 0.25 **NM** value: **2.50**
61 ❑ Sep 1975 Cover: 0.25 **NM** value: **2.50**
62 ❑ Oct 1975 Cover: 0.25 **NM** value: **2.50**
63 ❑ Nov 1975 Cover: 0.25 **NM** value: **2.50**
64 ❑ Jan 1976 Cover: 0.25 **NM** value: **2.50**
• **CGC:** 12 graded, best 9.8
65 ❑ Mar 1976 Cover: 0.25 **NM** value: **2.50**
66 ❑ Apr 1976 Cover: 0.25 **NM** value: **2.50**
67 ❑ May 1976 Cover: 0.25 **NM** value: **2.50**
68 ❑ Jun 1976 Cover: 0.25 **NM** value: **2.50**
69 ❑ Jul 1976 Cover: 0.25 **NM** value: **2.50**
70 ❑ Aug 1976 Cover: 0.25 **NM** value: **2.50**
71 ❑ Sep 1976 Cover: 0.30 **NM** value: **2.00**
72 ❑ Oct 1976 Cover: 0.30 **NM** value: **2.00**
73 ❑ Nov 1976 Cover: 0.30 **NM** value: **2.00**
74 ❑ Dec 1976 Cover: 0.30 **NM** value: **2.00**
75 ❑ Jan 1977 Cover: 0.30 **NM** value: **2.00**
76 ❑ Feb 1977 Cover: 0.30 **NM** value: **2.00**
77 ❑ Mar 1977 Cover: 0.30 **NM** value: **2.00**
78 ❑ Apr 1977 Cover: 0.30 **NM** value: **2.00**
79 ❑ May 1977 Cover: 0.30 **NM** value: **2.00**
80 ❑ Jun 1977 Cover: 0.30 **NM** value: **2.00**
81 ❑ Jul 1977 Cover: 0.30 **NM** value: **2.00**
82 ❑ Aug 1977 Cover: 0.30 **NM** value: **2.00**
83 ❑ Sep 1977 Cover: 0.30 **NM** value: **2.00**
84 ❑ Oct 1977 Cover: 0.30 **NM** value: **2.00**
85 ❑ Nov 1977 Cover: 0.30 **NM** value: **2.00**
86 ❑ Dec 1977 Cover: 0.35 **NM** value: **2.00**
87 ❑ Jan 1978 Cover: 0.35 **NM** value: **2.00**
88 ❑ Feb 1978 Cover: 0.35 **NM** value: **2.00**
89 ❑ Mar 1978 Cover: 0.35 **NM** value: **2.00**
90 ❑ Apr 1978 Cover: 0.35 **NM** value: **2.00**
91 ❑ May 1978 Cover: 0.35 **NM** value: **2.00**
92 ❑ Jun 1978 Cover: 0.35 **NM** value: **2.00**
93 ❑ Jul 1978 Cover: 0.35 **NM** value: **2.00**
94 ❑ Aug 1978 Cover: 0.35 **NM** value: **2.00**
95 ❑ Sep 1978 Cover: 0.35 **NM** value: **2.00**
96 ❑ Oct 1978 Cover: 0.35 **NM** value: **2.00**
97 ❑ Nov 1978 Cover: 0.35 **NM** value: **2.00**
98 ❑ Dec 1978 Cover: 0.35 **NM** value: **2.25**
★ Death of Gwen Stacy.
99 ❑ Jan 1979 Cover: 0.35 **NM** value: **2.25**
★ Death of Green Goblin.
100 ❑ Feb 1979 Cover: 0.60 **NM** value: **2.00**
• **CGC:** 2 graded, best 9.6
A: Mike Nasser; Steve Ditko; Gil Kane; Tony DeZuniga
101 ❑ Mar 1979 Cover: 0.35 **NM** value: **2.00**
102 ❑ Apr 1979 Cover: 0.35 **NM** value: **2.00**
103 ❑ May 1979 Cover: 0.35 **NM** value: **2.00**
104 ❑ Jun 1979 Cover: 0.35 **NM** value: **2.00**
105 ❑ Jul 1979 Cover: 0.35 **NM** value: **2.00**
106 ❑ Aug 1979 Cover: 0.40 **NM** value: **3.50**
• Reprints Amazing Spider-Man #129★ 1st Appearance of Punisher, Jackal.
107 ❑ Sep 1979 Cover: 0.40 **NM** value: **2.00**
108 ❑ Oct 1979 Cover: 0.40 **NM** value: **2.00**
109 ❑ Nov 1979 Cover: 0.40 **NM** value: **2.00**
110 ❑ Dec 1979 Cover: 0.40 **NM** value: **2.00**
111 ❑ Jan 1980 Cover: 0.40 **NM** value: **2.00**
• Punisher
112 ❑ Feb 1980 Cover: 0.40 **NM** value: **2.00**
• Punisher
113 ❑ Mar 1980 Cover: 0.40 **NM** value: **2.00**
114 ❑ Apr 1980 Cover: 0.40 **NM** value: **2.00**
115 ❑ May 1980 Cover: 0.40 **NM** value: **2.00**
116 ❑ Jun 1980 Cover: 0.40 **NM** value: **2.00**
117 ❑ Jul 1980 Cover: 0.40 **NM** value: **2.00**
118 ❑ Aug 1980 Cover: 0.40 **NM** value: **2.00**
119 ❑ Sep 1980 Cover: 0.50 **NM** value: **2.00**
120 ❑ Oct 1980 Cover: 0.40 **NM** value: **2.00**
121 ❑ Nov 1980 Cover: 0.50 **NM** value: **2.00**
122 ❑ Dec 1980 Cover: 0.50 **NM** value: **2.00**
123 ❑ Jan 1981 Cover: 0.50 **NM** value: **2.00**
124 ❑ Feb 1981 Cover: 0.50 **NM** value: **2.00**
125 ❑ Mar 1981 Cover: 0.50 **NM** value: **2.00**
126 ❑ Apr 1981 Cover: 0.50 **NM** value: **2.00**
127 ❑ May 1981 Cover: 0.50 **NM** value: **2.00**
128 ❑ Jun 1981 Cover: 0.50 **NM** value: **2.00**
129 ❑ Jul 1981 Cover: 0.50 **NM** value: **2.00**
130 ❑ Aug 1981 Cover: 0.50 **NM** value: **2.00**
131 ❑ Sep 1981 Cover: 0.50 **NM** value: **2.00**
132 ❑ Oct 1981 Cover: 0.50 **NM** value: **2.00**
133 ❑ Nov 1981 Cover: 0.50 **NM** value: **2.00**
134 ❑ Dec 1981 Cover: 0.50 **NM** value: **2.00**
135 ❑ Jan 1982 Cover: 0.60 **NM** value: **2.00**
136 ❑ Feb 1982 Cover: 0.50 **NM** value: **2.00**
137 ❑ Mar 1982 Cover: 0.60 **NM** value: **4.00**
• Reprints Amazing Fantasy #15★ Origin of Spider-Man. ★ 1st Appearance of Spider-Man.
138 ❑ Apr 1982 Cover: 0.60 **NM** value: **4.00**
• Reprints Amazing Spider-Man #1
139 ❑ May 1982 Cover: 0.60 **NM** value: **2.50**
• Reprints Amazing Spider-Man #2

Other grades: Multiply prices above by **1.5 for Mint • 2/3 for Very Fine • 1/3 for Fine • 1/5 for Very Good • 1/8 for Good**

140 ❑ Jun 1982 Cover: 0.60 **NM** value: **2.50**
• Reprints Amazing Spider-Man #3
141 ❑ Jul 1982 Cover: 0.60 **NM** value: **2.50**
• Reprints Amazing Spider-Man #4
142 ❑ Aug 1982 Cover: 0.60 **NM** value: **2.50**
• Reprints Amazing Spider-Man #5
143 ❑ Sep 1982 Cover: 0.60 **NM** value: **2.50**
• Reprints Amazing Spider-Man #6
144 ❑ Oct 1982 Cover: 0.60 **NM** value: **2.50**
• Reprints Amazing Spider-Man #7
145 ❑ Nov 1982 Cover: 0.60 **NM** value: **2.00**
146 ❑ Dec 1982 Cover: 0.60 **NM** value: **2.00**
• **CGC:** 1 graded, best 5.0
147 ❑ Jan 1983 Cover: 0.60 **NM** value: **2.00**
Circ: Statement: **113,066**
148 ❑ Feb 1983 Cover: 0.60 **NM** value: **2.00**
Circ: Statement: **113,066**
149 ❑ Mar 1983 Cover: 0.60 **NM** value: **2.00**
Circ: Statement: **113,066**
150 ❑ Apr 1983 Cover: 0.60 **NM** value: **2.00**
Circ: Statement: **113,066**
• Giant-size.
151 ❑ May 1983 Cover: 0.60 **NM** value: **2.00**
Circ: Statement: **113,066**
152 ❑ Jun 1983 Cover: 0.60 **NM** value: **2.00**
Circ: Statement: **113,066**
153 ❑ Jul 1983 Cover: 0.60 **NM** value: **2.00**
Circ: Statement: **113,066**
154 ❑ Aug 1983 Cover: 0.60 **NM** value: **2.00**
Circ: Statement: **113,066**
155 ❑ Sep 1983 Cover: 0.60 **NM** value: **2.00**
Circ: Statement: **113,066**
156 ❑ Oct 1983 Cover: 0.60 **NM** value: **2.00**
Circ: Statement: **113,066**
157 ❑ Nov 1983 Cover: 0.60 **NM** value: **2.00**
Circ: Statement: **113,066**
158 ❑ Dec 1983 Cover: 0.60 **NM** value: **2.00**
Circ: Statement: **113,066**
159 ❑ Jan 1984 Cover: 0.60 **NM** value: **2.00**
Circ: Statement: **110,681**
160 ❑ Feb 1984 Cover: 0.60 **NM** value: **2.00**
Circ: Statement: **110,681**
161 ❑ Mar 1984 Cover: 0.60 **NM** value: **2.00**
Circ: Statement: **110,681**
162 ❑ Apr 1984 Cover: 0.60 **NM** value: **2.00**
Circ: Statement: **110,681**
163 ❑ May 1984 Cover: 0.60 **NM** value: **2.00**
Circ: Statement: **110,681**
• Has 1983 Statement, filed 1/5/1983 (date is likely in error); avg print run 268,350; avg sales 111,295; avg subs 1,771; avg total paid 113,066; samples 690; office use 1,563; max existent 115,319; 57% of run returned
164 ❑ Jun 1984 Cover: 0.60 **NM** value: **2.00**
Circ: Statement: **110,681**
165 ❑ Jul 1984 Cover: 0.60 **NM** value: **2.00**
Circ: Statement: **110,681**
166 ❑ Aug 1984 Cover: 0.60 **NM** value: **2.00**
Circ: Statement: **110,681**
167 ❑ Sep 1984 Cover: 0.60 **NM** value: **2.00**
Circ: Statement: **110,681**
168 ❑ Oct 1984 Cover: 0.60 **NM** value: **2.00**
Circ: Statement: **110,681**
169 ❑ Nov 1984 Cover: 0.60 **NM** value: **2.00**
Circ: Statement: **110,681**
170 ❑ Dec 1984 Cover: 0.60 **NM** value: **2.00**
Circ: Statement: **110,681**
171 ❑ Jan 1985 Cover: 0.60 **NM** value: **2.00**
Circ: Statement: **120,059**
172 ❑ Feb 1985 Cover: 0.60 **NM** value: **2.00**
Circ: Statement: **120,059**
173 ❑ Mar 1985 Cover: 0.60 **NM** value: **2.00**
Circ: Statement: **120,059**
174 ❑ Apr 1985 Cover: 0.65 **NM** value: **2.00**
Circ: Statement: **120,059**
175 ❑ May 1985 Cover: 0.65 **NM** value: **2.00**
Circ: Statement: **120,059** CapCity orders: **4,900**
176 ❑ Jun 1985 Cover: 0.65 **NM** value: **2.00**
Circ: Statement: **120,059** CapCity orders: **5,100**
177 ❑ Jul 1985 Cover: 0.65 **NM** value: **2.00**
Circ: Statement: **120,059** CapCity orders: **5,100**
178 ❑ Aug 1985 Cover: 0.65 **NM** value: **2.00**
Circ: Statement: **120,059** CapCity orders: **5,500**
179 ❑ Sep 1985 Cover: 0.65 **NM** value: **2.00**
Circ: Statement: **120,059** CapCity orders: **5,300**
180 ❑ Oct 1985 Cover: 0.65 **NM** value: **2.00**
Circ: Statement: **120,059** CapCity orders: **4,900**
181 ❑ Nov 1985 Cover: 0.65 **NM** value: **2.00**
Circ: Statement: **120,059** CapCity orders: **5,100**
182 ❑ Dec 1985 Cover: 0.65 **NM** value: **2.00**
Circ: Statement: **120,059** CapCity orders: **5,000**
183 ❑ Jan 1986 Cover: 0.65 **NM** value: **2.00**
Circ: Statement: **101,832** CapCity orders: **6,300**
184 ❑ Feb 1986 Cover: 0.75 **NM** value: **2.00**
Circ: Statement: **101,832** CapCity orders: **5,000**
185 ❑ Mar 1986 Cover: 0.75 **NM** value: **2.00**
Circ: Statement: **101,832** CapCity orders: **4,800**
186 ❑ Apr 1986 Cover: 0.75 **NM** value: **2.00**
Circ: Statement: **101,832** CapCity orders: **4,900**
187 ❑ May 1986 Cover: 0.75 **NM** value: **2.00**
Circ: Statement: **101,832** CapCity orders: **4,800**
188 ❑ Jun 1986 Cover: 0.75 **NM** value: **2.00**
Circ: Statement: **101,832** CapCity orders: **4,700**
189 ❑ Jul 1986 Cover: 0.75 **NM** value: **2.00**
Circ: Statement: **101,832** CapCity orders: **4,700**
190 ❑ Aug 1986 Cover: 0.75 **NM** value: **2.00**
Circ: Statement: **101,832** CapCity orders: **4,900**
191 ❑ Sep 1986 Cover: 0.75 **NM** value: **2.00**
Circ: Statement: **101,832** CapCity orders: **5,750**
192 ❑ Oct 1986 Cover: 0.75 **NM** value: **2.00**
Circ: Statement: **101,832** CapCity orders: **6,500**
• Giant-size. • Reprints Amazing Spider-Man #121-122
193 ❑ Nov 1986 Cover: 0.75 **NM** value: **2.00**
Circ: Statement: **101,832** CapCity orders: **6,700**
194 ❑ Dec 1986 Cover: 0.75 **NM** value: **2.00**
Circ: Statement: **101,832** CapCity orders: **6,500**
195 ❑ Jan 1987 Cover: 0.75 **NM** value: **2.00**
Circ: Statement: **105,700** CapCity orders: **6,000**
196 ❑ Feb 1987 Cover: 0.75 **NM** value: **2.00**
Circ: Statement: **105,700** CapCity orders: **6,900**
197 ❑ Mar 1987 Cover: 0.75 **NM** value: **2.00**
Circ: Statement: **105,700** CapCity orders: **6,500**
198 ❑ Apr 1987 Cover: 0.75 **NM** value: **2.00**
Circ: Statement: **105,700** CapCity orders: **6,500**
199 ❑ May 1987 Cover: 0.75 **NM** value: **2.00**
Circ: Statement: **105,700** CapCity orders: **6,500**
200 ❑ Jun 1987 Cover: 1.25 **NM** value: **2.00**
Circ: Statement: **105,700** CapCity orders: **7,400**
• Giant-size. • Reprints Amazing Spider-Man Annual #14 **A:** Frank Miller(cover) **C:** Todd McFarlane
201 ❑ Jul 1987 Cover: 0.75 **NM** value: **1.50**
Circ: Statement: **105,700** CapCity orders: **6,200**
C: Todd McFarlane
202 ❑ Aug 1987 Cover: 0.75 **NM** value: **1.50**
Circ: Statement: **105,700** CapCity orders: **6,000**
C: Todd McFarlane
203 ❑ Sep 1987 Cover: 0.75 **NM** value: **1.50**
Circ: Statement: **105,700** CapCity orders: **6,500**
C: Todd McFarlane
204 ❑ Oct 1987 Cover: 0.75 **NM** value: **1.50**
Circ: Statement: **105,700** CapCity orders: **6,400**
C: Todd McFarlane
205 ❑ Nov 1987 Cover: 0.75 **NM** value: **1.50**
Circ: Statement: **105,700** CapCity orders: **6,700**
C: Todd McFarlane
206 ❑ Dec 1987 Cover: 0.75 **NM** value: **1.50**
Circ: Statement: **105,700** CapCity orders: **6,400**
C: Todd McFarlane
207 ❑ Jan 1988 Cover: 0.75 **NM** value: **1.50**
Circ: CapCity orders: **6,300**
C: Todd McFarlane
208 ❑ Feb 1988 Cover: 0.75 **NM** value: **1.50**
Circ: CapCity orders: **6,600**
C: Todd McFarlane
209 ❑ Mar 1988 Cover: 0.75 **NM** value: **1.50**
Circ: CapCity orders: **10,400**
C: Todd McFarlane ★ 1st Appearance of Punisher, Jackal.
210 ❑ Apr 1988 Cover: 0.75 **NM** value: **1.50**
Circ: CapCity orders: **9,300**
C: Todd McFarlane ★ Appearance of Punisher.
211 ❑ May 1988 Cover: 0.75 **NM** value: **1.50**
Circ: CapCity orders: **8,900**
C: Todd McFarlane ★ Appearance of Punisher.
212 ❑ Jun 1988 Cover: 0.75 **NM** value: **1.50**
Circ: CapCity orders: **9,000**
C: Todd McFarlane ★ Appearance of Punisher.
213 ❑ Jul 1988 Cover: 0.75 **NM** value: **1.50**
Circ: CapCity orders: **9,200**
C: Todd McFarlane ★ Appearance of Punisher.
214 ❑ Aug 1988 Cover: 0.75 **NM** value: **1.50**
Circ: CapCity orders: **9,100**
C: Todd McFarlane ★ Appearance of Punisher.
215 ❑ Sep 1988 Cover: 0.75 **NM** value: **1.50**
Circ: CapCity orders: **9,100**
C: Todd McFarlane ★ Appearance of Punisher.
216 ❑ Oct 1988 Cover: 0.75 **NM** value: **1.50**
Circ: CapCity orders: **8,600**
C: Todd McFarlane ★ Appearance of Punisher.
217 ❑ Nov 1988 Cover: 0.75 **NM** value: **1.50**
Circ: CapCity orders: **8,600**
C: Todd McFarlane ★ Appearance of Punisher.
218 ❑ Dec 1988 Cover: 0.75 **NM** value: **1.50**
Circ: CapCity orders: **8,700**
C: Todd McFarlane ★ Appearance of Punisher.
219 ❑ Jan 1989 Cover: 0.75 **NM** value: **1.50**
Circ: Statement: **93,892** CapCity orders: **8,200**
C: Todd McFarlane ★ Appearance of Punisher.
220 ❑ Feb 1989 Cover: 0.75 **NM** value: **1.50**
Circ: Statement: **93,892** CapCity orders: **8,100**
C: Todd McFarlane ★ Appearance of Punisher.
221 ❑ Mar 1989 Cover: 0.75 **NM** value: **1.50**
Circ: Statement: **93,892** CapCity orders: **8,050**
C: Todd McFarlane ★ Appearance of Punisher.
222 ❑ Apr 1989 Cover: 0.75 **NM** value: **1.50**
Circ: Statement: **93,892** CapCity orders: **8,500**
C: Todd McFarlane ★ Appearance of Punisher.
223 ❑ May 1989 Cover: 0.75 **NM** value: **1.50**
Circ: Statement: **93,892** CapCity orders: **8,100**
A: Todd McFarlane(cover) **C:** Todd McFarlane
224 ❑ Jun 1989 Cover: 0.75 **NM** value: **1.50**
Circ: Statement: **93,892** CapCity orders: **7,600** • **CGC:** 3 graded, best 9.4
A: Todd McFarlane(cover) **C:** Todd McFarlane
225 ❑ Jul 1989 Cover: 0.75 **NM** value: **1.50**
Circ: Statement: **93,892** CapCity orders: **8,300**
A: Todd McFarlane(cover) **C:** Todd McFarlane
226 ❑ Aug 1989 Cover: 0.75 **NM** value: **1.50**
Circ: Statement: **93,892** CapCity orders: **7,900**
A: Todd McFarlane(cover) **C:** Todd McFarlane
227 ❑ Sep 1989 Cover: 1.00 **NM** value: **1.50**
Circ: Statement: **93,892** CapCity orders: **7,700**
A: Todd McFarlane(cover) **C:** Todd McFarlane
228 ❑ Oct 1989 Cover: 1.00 **NM** value: **1.50**
Circ: Statement: **93,892** CapCity orders: **7,800**
A: Todd McFarlane(cover) **C:** Todd McFarlane
229 ❑ Nov 1989 Cover: 1.00 **NM** value: **1.50**
Circ: Statement: **93,892** CapCity orders: **7,900**
A: Todd McFarlane(cover) **C:** Todd McFarlane
230 ❑ Nov 1989 Cover: 1.00 **NM** value: **1.50**
Circ: Statement: **93,892** CapCity orders: **8,200**
A: Todd McFarlane(cover) **C:** Todd McFarlane
231 ❑ Dec 1989 Cover: 1.00 **NM** value: **1.50**
Circ: Statement: **93,892** CapCity orders: **8,100**
A: Todd McFarlane(cover) **C:** Todd McFarlane
232 ❑ Dec 1989 Cover: 1.00 **NM** value: **1.50**
Circ: Statement: **93,892** CapCity orders: **7,600**
A: Todd McFarlane(cover) **C:** Todd McFarlane
233 ❑ Jan 1990 Cover: 1.00 **NM** value: **1.50**
Circ: Statement: **88,749** CapCity orders: **9,300**
A: Todd McFarlane(cover) **C:** Todd McFarlane
234 ❑ Feb 1990 Cover: 1.00 **NM** value: **1.50**
Circ: Statement: **88,749** CapCity orders: **8,800**
A: Todd McFarlane(cover) **C:** Todd McFarlane
235 ❑ Mar 1990 Cover: 1.00 **NM** value: **1.50**
Circ: Statement: **88,749** CapCity orders: **9,400**
A: Todd McFarlane(cover) **C:** Todd McFarlane
236 ❑ Apr 1990 Cover: 1.00 **NM** value: **1.50**
Circ: Statement: **88,749** CapCity orders: **9,100**
A: Todd McFarlane(cover) **C:** Todd McFarlane
237 ❑ May 1990 Cover: 1.00 **NM** value: **1.50**
Circ: Statement: **88,749** CapCity orders: **9,200**
A: Todd McFarlane(cover) **C:** Todd McFarlane
238 ❑ Jun 1990 Cover: 1.00 **NM** value: **1.50**
Circ: Statement: **88,749** CapCity orders: **9,400**
A: Todd McFarlane(cover) **C:** Todd McFarlane
239 ❑ Jul 1990 Cover: 1.00 **NM** value: **1.50**
Circ: Statement: **88,749** CapCity orders: **11,000**
A: Todd McFarlane(cover) **C:** Todd McFarlane
240 ❑ Aug 1990 Cover: 1.00 **NM** value: **1.50**
Circ: Statement: **88,749** CapCity orders: **10,100**
241 ❑ Sep 1990 Cover: 1.00 **NM** value: **1.50**
Circ: Statement: **88,749** CapCity orders: **8,400**
242 ❑ Oct 1990 Cover: 1.00 **NM** value: **1.50**
Circ: Statement: **88,749** CapCity orders: **8,100**
243 ❑ Nov 1990 Cover: 1.00 **NM** value: **1.50**
Circ: Statement: **88,749** CapCity orders: **8,600**
244 ❑ Dec 1990 Cover: 1.00 **NM** value: **1.50**
Circ: Statement: **88,749** CapCity orders: **7,400**
245 ❑ Jan 1991 Cover: 1.00 **NM** value: **1.50**
Circ: CapCity orders: **7,000**
246 ❑ Feb 1991 Cover: 1.00 **NM** value: **1.50**
Circ: CapCity orders: **7,200**
247 ❑ Mar 1991 Cover: 1.00 **NM** value: **1.50**
Circ: CapCity orders: **6,900**
248 ❑ Apr 1991 Cover: 1.00 **NM** value: **1.50**
Circ: CapCity orders: **6,600**
249 ❑ May 1991 Cover: 1.00 **NM** value: **1.50**
Circ: CapCity orders: **6,900**
250 ❑ Jun 1991 Cover: 1.50 **NM** value: **Cover or less**
Circ: CapCity orders: **7,400**
• Giant-size. • Reprints Marvel Team-Up #100 **A:** Frank Miller(cover) ★ Origin of Storm.
251 ❑ Jul 1991 Cover: 1.00 **NM** value: **1.50**
Circ: CapCity orders: **7,400**
252 ❑ Aug 1991 Cover: 1.00 **NM** value: **1.50**
Circ: CapCity orders: **7,200**
📖 A Monster Called Morbius • Reprints Amazing Spider-Man #101 **A:** Gil Kane **W:** Gil Kane; Roy Thomas; Stan Lee ★ 1st Appearance of Morbius.
253 ❑ Sep 1991 Cover: 1.50 **NM** value: **Cover or less**
Circ: CapCity orders: **7,200**
• Giant-size. 📖 Vampire at Large; The Way It Began; The Curse and the Cure • Reprints Amazing Spider-Man #102 **A:** Gil Kane **C:** Moebius **W:** Gil Kane; Roy Thomas; Stan Lee ★ Origin of Morbius.
254 ❑ Oct 1991 Cover: 1.00 **NM** value: **1.50**
Circ: CapCity orders: **10,200**
255 ❑ Nov 1991 Cover: 1.00 **NM** value: **1.50**
Circ: CapCity orders: **9,600**
📖 Panic On Pier One! **A:** Sal Buscema; Pablo Marcos **W:** Chris Claremont
256 ❑ Dec 1991 Cover: 1.00 **NM** value: **1.50**
Circ: CapCity orders: **10,000**
257 ❑ Jan 1992 Cover: 1.00 **NM** value: **1.50**
Circ: Statement: **85,642** CapCity orders: **9,700**
258 ❑ Feb 1992 Cover: 1.25 **NM** value: **1.50**
Circ: Statement: **85,642** CapCity orders: **8,800**
259 ❑ Mar 1992 Cover: 1.25 **NM** value: **1.50**
Circ: Statement: **85,642** CapCity orders: **7,900**
260 ❑ Apr 1992 Cover: 1.25 **NM** value: **1.50**
Circ: Statement: **85,642** CapCity orders: **7,300**
261 ❑ May 1992 Cover: 1.25 **NM** value: **1.50**
Circ: Statement: **85,642** CapCity orders: **7,400**
262 ❑ Jun 1992 Cover: 1.25 **NM** value: **1.50**
Circ: Statement: **85,642** CapCity orders: **7,000**
• X-Men
263 ❑ Jul 1992 Cover: 1.25 **NM** value: **1.50**
Circ: Statement: **85,642** CapCity orders: **6,800**
264 ❑ Aug 1992 Cover: 1.25 **NM** value: **1.50**
Circ: Statement: **85,642** CapCity orders: **8,900**
• reprints Amazing Spider-Man Annual #5
265 ❑ Sep 1992 Cover: 1.25 **NM** value: **1.50**
Circ: Statement: **85,642** CapCity orders: **7,100**
• reprints Amazing Spider-Man Annual #6
266 ❑ Oct 1992 Cover: 1.25 **NM** value: **1.50**
Circ: Statement: **85,642**
267 ❑ Nov 1992 Cover: 1.25 **NM** value: **1.50**
Circ: Statement: **85,642** CapCity orders: **6,100**
268 ❑ Dec 1992 Cover: 1.25 **NM** value: **1.50**
Circ: Statement: **85,642** CapCity orders: **6,200**
269 ❑ Jan 1993 Cover: 1.25 **NM** value: **1.50**
Circ: CapCity orders: **5,900**
270 ❑ Feb 1993 Cover: 1.25 **NM** value: **1.50**
Circ: CapCity orders: **5,900**
271 ❑ Mar 1993 Cover: 1.25 **NM** value: **1.50**
Circ: CapCity orders: **6,700**

CGC-graded: Multiply prices above by **33 for 9.9 M • 16 for 9.8 NM/M • 7 for 9.6 NM+ • 5 for 9.4 NM • 2.5 for 9.2 NM- • 1.5 for 9.0 VF/NM**

• Has 1992 Statement, filed 10/1/1992; avg print run 163,850; avg sales 83,442; avg subs 2,200; avg total paid 85,642; samples 250; office use 500; max existent 86,392; 47% of run returned

272 ❑ Apr 1993 Cover: 1.25 **NM** value: **1.50**
Circ: CapCity orders: **7,300**

273 ❑ May 1993 Cover: 1.25 **NM** value: **1.50**
Circ: CapCity orders: **6,500**

274 ❑ Jun 1993 Cover: 1.25 **NM** value: **1.50**
Circ: CapCity orders: **6,300**

275 ❑ Jul 1993 Cover: 1.25 **NM** value: **1.50**
Circ: CapCity orders: **7,000**

276 ❑ Aug 1993 Cover: 1.25 **NM** value: **1.50**
Circ: CapCity orders: **6,800**

277 ❑ Sep 1993 Cover: 1.25 **NM** value: **1.50**
Circ: CapCity orders: **6,500**
★ 1st Appearance of Silver Sable.

278 ❑ Oct 1993 Cover: 1.25 **NM** value: **1.50**
Circ: CapCity orders: **6,000**
• Reprints Amazing Spider-Man #268 **A:** Ron Frenz; Ron Lim(cover) **W:** Tom DeFalco ★ Appearance of Kingpin, Beyonder.

279 ❑ Nov 1993 Cover: 1.25 **NM** value: **1.50**
Circ: CapCity orders: **5,600**

280 ❑ Dec 1993 Cover: 1.25 **NM** value: **1.50**
Circ: CapCity orders: **5,350**

281 ❑ Jan 1994 Cover: 1.25 **NM** value: **1.50**
Circ: CapCity orders: **5,350**

282 ❑ Feb 1994 Cover: 1.25 **NM** value: **1.50**
Circ: CapCity orders: **4,950**

283 ❑ Mar 1994 Cover: 1.25 **NM** value: **1.50**
Circ: CapCity orders: **4,650**
• double-sized. The Choice And The Challenge • Reprints Amazing Spider-Man #275; Hobgoblin story **A:** Ron Frenz **W:** Tom DeFalco ★ Origin of Spider-Man.

284 ❑ Apr 1994 Cover: 1.25 **NM** value: **1.50**
Circ: CapCity orders: **4,300**
Unmasked! • Reprints Amazing Spider-Man #276 **A:** Ron Frenz **W:** Tom DeFalco ★ Appearance of Hobgoblin. ★ Death of Fly.

285 ❑ May 1994 Cover: 1.25 **NM** value: **1.50**
Circ: CapCity orders: **3,900**
The Rules Of The Game • Reprints Amazing Spider-Man #277 **A:** Ron Frenz **W:** Tom DeFalco

286 ❑ Jun 1994 Cover: 1.50 **NM** value: **Cover or less**
Circ: CapCity orders: **2,000**
• Reprints Amazing Spider-Man #278 ★ Death of Wraith.

286-2 ❑ Jun 1994 Cover: 2.95 **NM** value: **Cover or less**
Circ: CapCity orders: **11,750**
• Collector's set; Includes animation cel, 16 page preview

287 ❑ Jul 1994 Cover: 1.25 **NM** value: **1.50**
Circ: CapCity orders: **4,450**
Jack O'Lantern cover/story. Savage Is The Sable • Reprints Amazing Spider-Man #279 **A:** Rick Leonardi **W:** Tom DeFalco

288 ❑ Aug 1994 Cover: 1.25 **NM** value: **1.50**
Circ: CapCity orders: **3,900**
• Reprints Amazing Spider-Man #280

289 ❑ Sep 1994 Cover: 1.25 **NM** value: **1.50**
Circ: CapCity orders: **3,950**
• Reprints Amazing Spider-Man #281 ★ Appearance of Jack O'Lantern.

290 ❑ Oct 1994 Cover: 1.50 **NM** value: **Cover or less**
Circ: CapCity orders: **4,000**
The Fury Of X-Factor • Reprints Amazing Spider-Man #282 **A:** Rick Leonardi **W:** Tom DeFalco

291 ❑ Nov 1994 Cover: 1.50 **NM** value: **Cover or less**
Circ: CapCity orders: **3,400**
final issue. • Amazing Spider-Man #283

MARVEL TEAM-UP — Marvel

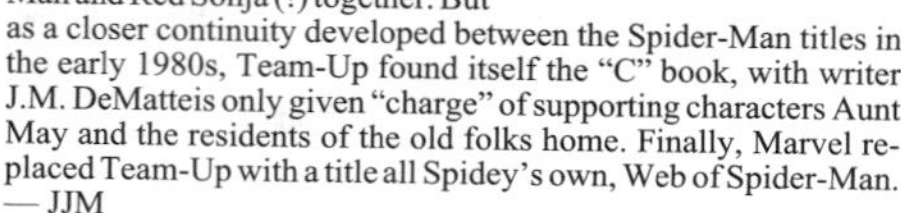

A cynic might call this series, "Trademark Renewal Theater." Here, all Marvel's characters who couldn't support a regular series of their own were given exposure through team-ups with Spider-Man. (There are a few non-Spidey stories in this series' 150-issue run, but they're the exception.) Frog-Man, Valkyrie, Hercules — even the Not Ready For Prime-Time Players found their logos proudly displayed beneath Spidey's marquee.

Some of the pairings took some creative engineering, such as Chris Claremont's story bringing Spider-Man and Red Sonja (!) together. But as a closer continuity developed between the Spider-Man titles in the early 1980s, Team-Up found itself the "C" book, with writer J.M. DeMatteis only given "charge" of supporting characters Aunt May and the residents of the old folks home. Finally, Marvel replaced Team-Up with a title all Spidey's own, Web of Spider-Man. — JJM

1 ❑ Mar 1972 Cover: 0.20 **NM** value: **50.00**
• **CGC:** 58 graded, best 9.8
Have Yourself a Sandman Little Christmas • Spider-Man; Human Torch **A:** Ross Andru **C:** Gil Kane **W:** Roy Thomas ★ 1st Appearance of Misty Knight. ★ Versus Sandman.

2 ❑ May 1972 Cover: 0.20 **NM** value: **24.00**
• **CGC:** 12 graded, best 9.6
And Spidey Makes Four • Spider-Man; Human Torch **A:** Ross Andru **C:** Gil Kane

3 ❑ Jul 1972 Cover: 0.20 **NM** value: **28.00**
• **CGC:** 16 graded, best 9.6
The Power to Purge • Spider-Man; Human Torch **A:** Ross Andru **C:** Gil Kane ★ Appearance of Morbius.

4 ❑ Sep 1972 Cover: 0.20 **NM** value: **28.00**
• **CGC:** 15 graded, best 9.6
And Then, the X-Men • Spider-Man; X-Men **A:** Gil Kane ★ Appearance of Morbius.

5 ❑ Nov 1972 Cover: 0.20 **NM** value: **9.00**
• **CGC:** 2 graded, best 9.4
A Passion of the Mind • Spider-Man; Vision **A:** Gil Kane ★ 1st Appearance of Ballox ("The Monstroid").

6 ❑ Jan 1973 Cover: 0.20 **NM** value: **9.00**
As Those Who Will Not See • Spider-Man; Thing **A:** Gil Kane ★ Origin of Puppet Master.

7 ❑ Mar 1973 Cover: 0.20 **NM** value: **9.00**
A Hitch in Time • Spider-Man; Thor **A:** Ross Andru **C:** Gil Kane ★ 1st Appearance of Kryllk the Cruel.

8 ❑ Apr 1973 Cover: 0.20 **NM** value: **9.00**
The Man-Killer Moves at Midnight • Spider-Man; The Cat **A:** Jim Mooney ★ 1st Appearance of The Man-Killer.

9 ❑ May 1973 Cover: 0.20 **NM** value: **9.00**
• **CGC:** 1 graded, best 8.0
The Tomorrow War • Spider-Man; Iron Man; Spider-Man, Iron Man **A:** Ross Andru **C:** John Romita

10 ❑ Jun 1973 Cover: 0.20 **NM** value: **9.00**
• **CGC:** 2 graded, best 9.2
Time Bomb • Spider-Man; Human Torch **A:** Jim Mooney **C:** John Romita

11 ❑ Jul 1973 Cover: 0.20 **NM** value: **7.00**
The Doomsday Gambit • Spider-Man; Inhumans **A:** Jim Mooney **C:** John Romita

12 ❑ Aug 1973 Cover: 0.20 **NM** value: **7.00**
• **CGC:** 2 graded, best 9.2
Wolf at Bay • Spider-Man; Werewolf **A:** Ross Andru **C:** Gil Kane ★ 1st Appearance of Moondark.

13 ❑ Sep 1973 Cover: 0.20 **NM** value: **7.00**
• **CGC:** 1 graded, best 9.4
The Granite Sky • Spider-Man; Captain America **A:** Gil Kane

14 ❑ Oct 1973 Cover: 0.20 **NM** value: **7.00**
• **CGC:** 2 graded, best 9.4
Mayhem is the Man-Fish! • Spider-Man; Sub-Mariner **A:** Gil Kane ★ 1st Appearance of The Aquanoids.

15 ❑ Nov 1973 Cover: 0.20 **NM** value: **7.00**
• **CGC:** 5 graded, best 9.6
If an Eye Offend Thee! • Spider-Man; Ghost Rider **A:** Ross Andru **C:** Gil Kane ★ Origin of Orb. ★ 1st Appearance of Orb.

16 ❑ Dec 1973 Cover: 0.20 **NM** value: **7.00**
• **CGC:** 1 graded, best 9.2
Beware the Basilisk, My Son • Spider-Man; Captain Marvel **A:** Gil Kane ★ Origin of The Basilisk I (Basil Elks). ★ 1st Appearance of The Basilisk I (Basil Elks).

17 ❑ Jan 1974 Cover: 0.20 **NM** value: **7.00**
• **CGC:** 1 graded, best 9.2
Chaos at the Earth's Core • Spider-Man; Mr. Fantastic **A:** Gil Kane ★ Versus Basilisk. ★ Versus Mole Man.

18 ❑ Feb 1974 Cover: 0.20 **NM** value: **7.00**
• **CGC:** 4 graded, best 9.4
Where Bursts The Bomb! • Human Torch; Hulk **A:** Gil Kane **W:** Len Wein

19 ❑ Mar 1974 Cover: 0.20 **NM** value: **7.00**
The Coming of Stegron, the Dinosaur Man! • Spider-Man; Ka-Zar **A:** Gil Kane ★ 1st Appearance of Stegron, the Dinosaur Man.

20 ❑ Apr 1974 Cover: 0.20 **NM** value: **7.00**
• **CGC:** 1 graded, best 9.2
Dinosaurs on Broadway • Spider-Man; Black Panther **A:** Sal Buscema **C:** Gil Kane

21 ❑ May 1974 Cover: 0.25 **NM** value: **6.00**
• **CGC:** 1 graded, best 9.4
The Spider and the Sorcerer • Spider-Man; Doctor Strange **A:** Sal Buscema **C:** Gil Kane

22 ❑ Jun 1974 Cover: 0.25 **NM** value: **6.00**
The Messiah Machine • Spider-Man; Hawkeye **A:** Sal Buscema **C:** John Romita **W:** Len Wein

23 ❑ Jul 1974 Cover: 0.25 **NM** value: **6.00**
The Night of the Frozen Inferno • Human Torch; Iceman; X-Men **A:** Gil Kane ★ Appearance of X-Men.

24 ❑ Aug 1974 Cover: 0.25 **NM** value: **6.00**
Moondog Is Another Name For Murder! • Spider-Man; Brother Voodoo **A:** Jim Mooney; Sal Trapani **C:** Gil Kane **W:** Len Wein

25 ❑ Sep 1974 Cover: 0.25 **NM** value: **6.00**
Three Into Two Won't Go! • Spider-Man; Daredevil **A:** Jim Mooney; Frank Giacoia **C:** Gil Kane **W:** Len Wein

26 ❑ Oct 1974 Cover: 0.25 **NM** value: **6.00**
• **CGC:** 1 graded, best 9.0
The Fire This Time...! • Human Torch; Thor **A:** Jim Mooney **C:** Gil Kane **W:** Len Wein

27 ❑ Nov 1974 Cover: 0.25 **NM** value: **6.00**
• **CGC:** 1 graded, best 8.0
A Friend in Need • Spider-Man; Hulk **A:** Jim Mooney **C:** Jim Starlin

28 ❑ Dec 1974 Cover: 0.25 **NM** value: **6.00**
The City Stealers • Spider-Man; Hercules **A:** Jim Mooney **C:** Gil Kane **W:** Gerry Conway

29 ❑ Jan 1975 Cover: 0.25 **NM** value: **6.00**
Beware the Coming of Infinitus • Human Torch; Iron Man **A:** Jim Mooney **C:** John Romita

30 ❑ Feb 1975 Cover: 0.25 **NM** value: **6.00**
• **CGC:** 1 graded, best 9.2
All That Glitters Is Not Gold • Spider-Man; The Falcon **A:** Jim Mooney **C:** Gil Kane

31 ❑ Mar 1975 Cover: 0.25 **NM** value: **6.00**
• **CGC:** 1 graded, best 9.0
For a Few Fists More • Spider-Man; Iron Fist **A:** Jim Mooney **C:** Gil Kane

32 ❑ Apr 1975 Cover: 0.25 **NM** value: **4.00**
All the Fires in Hell; The Possessed; A Vision Born in Hell; The Flame and the Fire • Human Torch; Son of Satan **A:** Sal Buscema **C:** Gil Kane

33 ❑ May 1975 Cover: 0.25 **NM** value: **4.00**
Anybody Here Know a Guy Named Meteor Man? • Spider-Man; Nighthawk **A:** Sal Buscema; Vince Colleta **C:** Gil Kane ★ Versus Meteor Man.

34 ❑ Jun 1975 Cover: 0.25 **NM** value: **4.00**
Beware of the Death Crusade; A Gift for Violence; The Innocents of Hell; The Savior Syndrome • Spider-Man; Valkyrie **A:** Sal Buscema; Vince Colleta **C:** Gil Kane ★ Versus Meteor Man.

35 ❑ Jul 1975 Cover: 0.25 **NM** value: **4.00**
Blood Church; Dark Immortal; Church of Blood; The Flames of Battle • Human Torch; Doctor Strange; Doctor Strange team-up **A:** Sal Buscema; Vince Colleta **C:** Gil Kane

36 ❑ Aug 1975 Cover: 0.25 **NM** value: **4.00**
• **CGC:** 1 graded, best 9.4
Once Upon a Time, in a Castle; The Cold Wind of Doom; To Make a Monster • Spider-Man; Frankenstein **A:** Sal Buscema

37 ❑ Sep 1975 Cover: 0.25 **NM** value: **4.00**
Snow Death; Madhouse!; Wolfpack; Survival; Epilogue • Spider-Man; Man-Wolf **A:** Sal Buscema

38 ❑ Oct 1975 Cover: 0.25 **NM** value: **4.00**
Night Of The Griffin • Spider-Man; Beast **A:** Sal Buscema **W:** Bill Mantlo

39 ❑ Nov 1975 Cover: 0.25 **NM** value: **4.00**
Any Number Can Slay • Spider-Man; Human Torch **A:** Sal Buscema

40 ❑ Dec 1975 Cover: 0.25 **NM** value: **4.00**
• **CGC:** 1 graded, best 9.6
Murder's Better the Second Time Around • Spider-Man; Sons of Tiger; Human Torch; Sons of the Tiger **A:** Sal Buscema

41 ❑ Jan 1976 Cover: 0.25 **NM** value: **4.00**
A Witch in Time • Spider-Man; Scarlet Witch **A:** Sal Buscema **C:** Gil Kane

42 ❑ Feb 1976 Cover: 0.25 **NM** value: **4.00**
Visions of Hate • Spider-Man; Scarlet Witch; Vision **A:** Sal Buscema

43 ❑ Mar 1976 Cover: 0.25 **NM** value: **4.00**
A Past Gone Mad • Spider-Man; Doctor Doom **A:** Sal Buscema **C:** Gil Kane ★ Appearance of Doctor Doom.

44 ❑ Apr 1976 Cover: 0.25 **NM** value: **4.00**
Death in the Year Before Yesterday • Spider-Man; Moondragon **A:** Sal Buscema **C:** Gil Kane

45 ❑ May 1976 Cover: 0.25 **NM** value: **4.00**
Future-Shock! • Spider-Man; Killraven **A:** Sal Buscema **C:** Gil Kane

46 ❑ Jun 1976 Cover: 0.25 **NM** value: **4.00**
Am I Now or Have I Ever Been? • Spider-Man; Deathlok **A:** Sal Buscema **C:** Rich Buckler

47 ❑ Jul 1976 Cover: 0.25 **NM** value: **3.00**
• **CGC:** 1 graded, best 9.6
I Have to Fight the Basilisk • Spider-Man; Thing **C:** Gil Kane ★ Versus Basilisk.

48 ❑ Aug 1976 Cover: 0.25 **NM** value: **3.00**
• **CGC:** 1 graded, best 9.8
A Fine Night For Dying • Spider-Man; Iron Man **A:** Sal Buscema **C:** John Romita ★ 1st Appearance of Wraith.

49 ❑ Sep 1976 Cover: 0.30 **NM** value: **3.00**
Madness Is All in the Mind • Spider-Man; Iron Man; Doctor Strange **A:** Sal Buscema **C:** John Romita ★ Origin of Wraith.

50 ❑ Oct 1976 Cover: 0.25 **NM** value: **3.00**
The Mystery Of the Wraith! • Spider-Man; Doctor Strange; Iron Man **A:** Sal Buscema **C:** Gil Kane **W:** Sal Buscema; Bill Mantlo

51 ❑ Nov 1976 Cover: 0.30 **NM** value: **3.00**
The Trial of the Wraith • Spider-Man; Iron Man **A:** Sal Buscema **C:** Gil Kane

52 ❑ Dec 1976 Cover: 0.30 **NM** value: **3.00**
Danger: Demon on a Rampage! • Spider-Man; Captain America **A:** Sal Buscema **W:** Gerry Conway ★ Appearance of Batroc.

53 ❑ Jan 1977 Cover: 0.30 **NM** value: **6.00**
• **CGC:** 31 graded, best 9.8
Nightmare in New Mexico • Spider-Man; Hulk; Woodgod; X-Men; 1st John Byrne art on X-Men **A:** John Byrne **C:** Dave Cockrum ★ Appearance of X-Men, Woodgod.

54 ❑ Feb 1977 Cover: 0.30 **NM** value: **3.50**
Spider in the Middle • Spider-Man; Hulk **A:** John Byrne **C:** Gil Kane ★ Appearance of Woodgod.

55 ❑ Mar 1977 Cover: 0.30 **NM** value: **3.50**
Spider, Spider on the Moon • Spider-Man; Warlock **A:** John Byrne **C:** Dave Cockrum ★ 1st Appearance of the Gardener. ★ Versus Gardener.

56 ❑ Apr 1977 Cover: 0.30 **NM** value: **2.00**
Double Danger at the Daily Bugle • Spider-Man; Daredevil **A:** Sal Buscema **C:** John Romita Jr. ★ Versus Blizzard. ★ Versus Electro.

57 ❑ May 1977 Cover: 0.30 **NM** value: **2.00**
When Slays the Silver Samurai • Spider-Man; Black Widow **A:** Sal Buscema **C:** Dave Cockrum

58 ❑ Jun 1977 Cover: 0.30 **NM** value: **2.00**
Panic On Pier One! • Spider-Man; Ghost Rider **A:** Sal Buscema; Dave Cockrum **C:** Al Milgrom

59 ❑ Jul 1977 Cover: 0.30 **NM** value: **2.00**
Some Say Spidey Will Die By Fire...Some Say By Ice! • Spider-Man; Yellowjacket; The Wasp **A:** John Byrne **C:** Dave Cockrum **W:** Chris Claremont

60 ❑ Aug 1977 Cover: 0.30 **NM** value: **2.00**
A Matter Of Love...And Death! • Spider-Man; The Wasp **A:** John Byrne **C:** Al Milgrom **W:** Chris Claremont ★ Appearance of Yellow-jacket.

61 ❑ Sep 1977 Cover: 0.30 **NM** value: **2.00**
• **CGC:** 1 graded, best 9.4
Not All The Powers Can Save Thee! • Spider-Man; Human Torch **A:** John Byrne **C:** Ross Andru **W:** Chris Claremont ★ Versus Super-Skrull.

62 ❑ Oct 1977 Cover: 0.30 **NM** value: **2.00**
All This And The QE2 • Spider-Man; Ms. Marvel **A:** John Byrne **C:** Gil Kane **W:** Chris Claremont ★ Versus Super-Skrull.

63 ❑ Nov 1977 Cover: 0.35 **NM** value: **2.00**
• **CGC:** 2 graded, best 9.4
Night Of The Dragon • Spider-Man; Iron Fist **A:** John Byrne **C:** Dave Cockrum **W:** Chris Claremont

64 ❑ Dec 1977 Cover: 0.35 **NM** value: **2.00**
If Death Be My Destiny... • Spider-Man; Daughters of Dragon; Daughters of the Dragon **A:** John Byrne **C:** Dave Cockrum **W:** Chris Claremont

65 ❑ Jan 1978 Cover: 0.35 **NM** value: **2.00**
• **CGC:** 1 graded, best 9.4
Introducing, Captain Britain • Spider-Man; Captain Britain **A:** John Byrne **C:** George Pérez **W:** Chris Claremont ★ 1st Appearance of Arcade, Captain Britain (U.S.).

66 ❑ Feb 1978 Cover: 0.35 **NM** value: **2.00**

Other grades: Multiply prices above by **1.5 for Mint • 2/3 for Very Fine • 1/3 for Fine • 1/5 for Very Good • 1/8 for Good**

Murder World • Spider-Man; Captain Britain **A:** John Byrne **W:** Chris Claremont ★ Versus Arcade.

67 ❑ Mar 1978 Cover: 0.35 **NM** value: **2.00**
Tigra Tigra, Burning Bright! • Spider-Man; Tigra **A:** John Byrne **W:** Chris Claremont ★ Appearance of Tigra. ★ Versus Kraven.

68 ❑ Apr 1978 Cover: 0.35 **NM** value: **2.00**
The Measure Of A Man! • Spider-Man; Man-Thing **A:** John Byrne **W:** Chris Claremont ★ 1st Appearance of D'Spayre. ★ Appearance of Man-Thing.

69 ❑ May 1978 Cover: 0.35 **NM** value: **2.00**
Night Of The Living God! • Spider-Man; Havok **A:** John Byrne **C:** Dave Cockrum **W:** Chris Claremont ★ Appearance of Havok.

70 ❑ Jun 1978 Cover: 0.35 **NM** value: **2.00**
Whom Gods Destroy! • Spider-Man; Thor **A:** John Byrne **W:** Chris Claremont ★ Versus Living Monolith.

71 ❑ Jul 1978 Cover: 0.35 **NM** value: **2.00**
Deathgarden • Spider-Man; The Falcon

72 ❑ Aug 1978 Cover: 0.35 **NM** value: **2.00**
Crack of the Whip! • Spider-Man; Iron Man **A:** Jim Mooney **C:** John Byrne

73 ❑ Sep 1978 Cover: 0.35 **NM** value: **2.00**
A Fluttering of Wings Most Foul • Spider-Man; Daredevil **C:** Keith Pollard

74 ❑ Oct 1978 Cover: 0.35 **NM** value: **3.00**
Live From New York, It's Saturday Night! • Spider-Man; The Not-Ready-For-Prime-Time-Players (SNL) **C:** Dave Cockrum ★ Appearance of Not Ready For Prime Time Players (Saturday Night Live).

75 ❑ Nov 1978 Cover: 0.35 **NM** value: **2.00**
The Smoke OF That Great Burning! • Spider-Man; Power Man **A:** John Byrne **W:** Ralph Macchio; Chris Claremont

76 ❑ Dec 1978 Cover: 0.35 **NM** value: **2.00**
If Not For Love... • Spider-Man; Doctor Strange **A:** Howard Chaykin; J. Ortiz; Jeff Aclin **C:** John Byrne **W:** Chris Claremont

77 ❑ Jan 1979 Cover: 0.35 **NM** value: **2.00**
Circ: Statement: **218,021**
• Spider-Man; Ms. Marvel **A:** Howard Chaykin **C:** John Romita Jr.

78 ❑ Feb 1979 Cover: 0.35 **NM** value: **2.00**
Circ: Statement: **218,021**
Claws! • Spider-Man; Wonder Man **A:** Don Perlin **C:** Al Milgrom **W:** Bill Kunkel

79 ❑ Mar 1979 Cover: 0.35 **NM** value: **2.00**
Circ: Statement: **218,021**
Sword Of The She-Devil • Spider-Man; Red Sonja **A:** John Byrne **W:** Chris Claremont

80 ❑ Apr 1979 Cover: 0.35 **NM** value: **2.00**
Circ: Statement: **218,021**
A Sorcerer Possessed! • Spider-Man; Doctor Strange; Clea **A:** Mike Vosburg **C:** Rich Buckler **W:** Chris Claremont

81 ❑ May 1979 Cover: 0.40 **NM** value: **2.00**
Circ: Statement: **218,021**
Last Rites • Spider-Man; Satana **C:** Al Milgrom ★ Death of Satana.

82 ❑ Jun 1979 Cover: 0.40 **NM** value: **2.00**
Circ: Statement: **218,021**
No Way to Treat a Lady • Spider-Man; Black Widow **A:** Sal Buscema **C:** Rich Buckler

83 ❑ Jul 1979 Cover: 0.40 **NM** value: **2.00**
Circ: Statement: **218,021**
Slaughter on 10th Avenue • Spider-Man; Nick Fury **A:** Sal Buscema **C:** Rich Buckler

84 ❑ Aug 1979 Cover: 0.40 **NM** value: **2.00**
Circ: Statement: **218,021**
Catch A Falling Hero • Spider-Man; Shang-Chi **A:** Sal Buscema; Steve Leialoha **W:** Chris Claremont

85 ❑ Sep 1979 Cover: 0.40 **NM** value: **2.00**
Circ: Statement: **218,021**
The Woman Who Never Was • Spider-Man; Shang-Chi; Nick Fury; Black Widow **A:** Sal Buscema; Steve Leialoha **C:** Al Milgrom **W:** Chris Claremont

86 ❑ Oct 1979 Cover: 0.40 **NM** value: **2.00**
Circ: Statement: **218,021**
Story Of The Year! • Spider-Man; Guardians of Galaxy **A:** Bob McLeod **W:** Chris Claremont

87 ❑ Nov 1979 Cover: 0.40 **NM** value: **2.00**
Circ: Statement: **218,021**
The Razor's Edge • Spider-Man; Black Panther **A:** Gene Colan **C:** Al Milgrom ★ 1st Appearance of Hellrazor.

88 ❑ Dec 1979 Cover: 0.40 **NM** value: **2.00**
Circ: Statement: **218,021**
A Child Is Waiting • Spider-Man; Invisible Girl **A:** Sal Buscema **C:** Rich Buckler

89 ❑ Jan 1980 Cover: 0.40 **NM** value: **2.00**
Shoot Out Over Center Ring • Spider-Man; Nightcrawler **A:** Mike Nasser; Rich Buckler **W:** Chris Claremont ★ 1st Appearance of Cut-throat.

90 ❑ Feb 1980 Cover: 0.40 **NM** value: **2.00**
Death on the Air • Spider-Man; Beast **C:** Al Milgrom

91 ❑ Mar 1980 Cover: 0.40 **NM** value: **2.00**
Carnival of Souls • Spider-Man; Ghost Rider; Has 1979 Statement, filed 10/1/79; avg print run 426,418; avg sales 210,351; avg subs 7,670; avg total paid 218,021; samples 590; office use 1,066; max existent 219,677; 49% of run returned **A:** Pat Broderick **C:** Rich Buckler

92 ❑ Apr 1980 Cover: 0.40 **NM** value: **2.00**
Fear! • Spider-Man; Hawkeye **A:** Carmine Infantino **C:** Al Milgrom **W:** Steven Grant ★ 1st Appearance of Mister Fear IV (Alan Fagan).

93 ❑ May 1980 Cover: 0.40 **NM** value: **2.00**
Rags To Riches! • Spider-Man; Werewolf; Werewolf by Night **A:** Tom Sutton; Carmine Infantino **C:** Don Perlin **W:** Steven Grant

94 ❑ Jun 1980 Cover: 0.40 **NM** value: **2.00**
Darkness, Darkness... • Spider-Man; Shroud **A:** Mike Zeck **C:** Al Milgrom **W:** Steven Grant

95 ❑ Jul 1980 Cover: 0.40 **NM** value: **2.00**
...And No Birds Sing! • Spider-Man **A:** Bruce Patterson; Frank Miller(cover); Jimmy Janes **C:** Frank Miller **W:** Steven Grant ★ 1st Appearance of Mockingbird, Huntress as Mockingbird.

96 ❑ Aug 1980 Cover: 0.40 **NM** value: **2.00**
Panic in the Streets • Spider-Man; Howard the Duck

97 ❑ Sep 1980 Cover: 0.50 **NM** value: **2.00**
Doctor Of Madness • Hulk; Spider-Woman **A:** Carmine Infantino **W:** Steven Grant

98 ❑ Oct 1980 Cover: 0.50 **NM** value: **2.00**
(Untitled) • Spider-Man; Black Widow **A:** Will Meugniot **C:** Al Milgrom **W:** Marv Wolfman; Roger McKenzie

99 ❑ Nov 1980 Cover: 0.50 **NM** value: **2.00**
And Machine Man Makes 3 • Spider-Man; Machine Man **A:** Jerry Bingham; Frank Miller(cover) **C:** Frank Miller **W:** Tom DeFalco

100 ❑ Dec 1980 Cover: 0.75 **NM** value: **5.00**
• **CGC:** 2 graded, best 9.6
• double-sized. And Introducing-Karma! She Possesses People!; Cry–Vengeance • Spider-Man; Fantastic Four; Black Panther **A:** John Byrne; Frank Miller **W:** Frank Miller; Chris Claremont ★ Origin of Karma, Storm. ★ 1st Appearance of Karma.

101 ❑ Jan 1981 Cover: 0.50 **NM** value: **2.00**
Circ: Statement: **185,818**
To Judge A Nighthawk!; Don't Let the Sun Come Up on Me • Spider-Man; Nighthawk **A:** Jerry Bingham **W:** J.M. DeMatteis

102 ❑ Feb 1981 Cover: 0.50 **NM** value: **2.00**
Circ: Statement: **185,818**
Samson And Delilah! • Spider-Man; Doc Samson **A:** Frank Springer; Mike Esposito **C:** Frank Miller **W:** Mike W. Barr

103 ❑ Mar 1981 Cover: 0.50 **NM** value: **2.00**
Circ: Statement: **185,818**
The Assassin Academy • Spider-Man; Ant-Man **A:** Jerry Bingham **W:** David Michelinie

104 ❑ Apr 1981 Cover: 0.50 **NM** value: **2.00**
Circ: Statement: **185,818**
Madok Must Triumph • Hulk; Ka-Zar **A:** Jerry Bingham **C:** Al Milgrom **W:** Roger McKenzie

105 ❑ May 1981 Cover: 0.50 **NM** value: **2.00**
Circ: Statement: **185,818**
A Small Circle of Hate; Wolves oin Designer's Clothing • Power Man; Iron Fist; Hulk **A:** Carmine Infantino **C:** Al Milgrom

106 ❑ Jun 1981 Cover: 0.50 **NM** value: **2.00**
Circ: Statement: **185,818**
A Savage Sting Has the Scorpion • Spider-Man; Captain America **A:** Herb Trimpe; Frank Miller(cover) **C:** Frank Miller ★ Versus Scorpion.

107 ❑ Jul 1981 Cover: 0.50 **NM** value: **2.00**
Circ: Statement: **185,818**
This Rumor of Revolution • Spider-Man; She-Hulk **A:** Herb Trimpe

108 ❑ Aug 1981 Cover: 0.50 **NM** value: **2.00**
Circ: Statement: **185,818**
Something Wicked This Way Rules • Spider-Man; Paladin **A:** Herb Trimpe

109 ❑ Sep 1981 Cover: 0.50 **NM** value: **2.00**
Circ: Statement: **185,818**
Critical Mass • Spider-Man; Dazzler **A:** Herb Trimpe **C:** John Romita Jr.

110 ❑ Oct 1981 Cover: 0.50 **NM** value: **2.00**
Circ: Statement: **185,818**
Magma Force • Spider-Man; Iron Man **A:** Herb Trimpe **C:** Bob Layton

111 ❑ Nov 1981 Cover: 0.50 **NM** value: **2.00**
Circ: Statement: **185,818**
Of Spiders and Serpents • Spider-Man; Devil-Slayer **A:** Herb Trimpe

112 ❑ Dec 1981 Cover: 0.50 **NM** value: **2.00**
Circ: Statement: **185,818**
A King Comes Riding • Spider-Man; King Kull **A:** Herb Trimpe

113 ❑ Jan 1982 Cover: 0.60 **NM** value: **2.00**
Circ: Statement: **179,032**
• Spider-Man; Quasar

114 ❑ Feb 1982 Cover: 0.60 **NM** value: **2.00**
Circ: Statement: **179,032**
• Spider-Man; The Falcon

115 ❑ Mar 1982 Cover: 0.60 **NM** value: **2.00**
Circ: Statement: **179,032**
• Spider-Man; Thor

116 ❑ Apr 1982 Cover: 0.60 **NM** value: **2.00**
Circ: Statement: **179,032**
• Spider-Man; Valkyrie; Has 1981 Statement, filed 10/1/81; avg print run 418,687; avg sales 177,178; avg subs 8,640; avg total paid 185,818; samples 595; office use 4,795; max existent 191,208; 54% of run returned

117 ❑ May 1982 Cover: 0.60 **NM** value: **4.00**
Circ: Statement: **179,032** • **CGC:** 9 graded, best 9.8
• Spider-Man; Wolverine ★ 1st Appearance of Professor Power.

118 ❑ Jun 1982 Cover: 0.60 **NM** value: **2.00**
Circ: Statement: **179,032**
Meeting Of The Minds • Spider-Man; Professor X **A:** Herb Trimpe **W:** J.M. DeMatteis ★ Origin of Professor Power.

119 ❑ Jul 1982 Cover: 0.60 **NM** value: **2.00**
Circ: Statement: **179,032**
• Spider-Man; Gargoyle **A:** Kerry Gammill

120 ❑ Aug 1982 Cover: 0.60 **NM** value: **2.00**
Circ: Statement: **179,032**
• Spider-Man; Dominic Fortune **A:** Kerry Gammill

121 ❑ Sep 1982 Cover: 0.60 **NM** value: **2.00**
Circ: Statement: **179,032**
• Spider-Man; Human Torch **A:** Kerry Gammill ★ 1st Appearance of Frog-Man II.

122 ❑ Oct 1982 Cover: 0.60 **NM** value: **2.00**
Circ: Statement: **179,032**
• Man-Thing **A:** Dick Dillin

123 ❑ Nov 1982 Cover: 0.60 **NM** value: **2.00**
Circ: Statement: **179,032**
• Man-Thing; Daredevil **A:** Dick Dillin

124 ❑ Dec 1982 Cover: 0.60 **NM** value: **2.00**
Circ: Statement: **179,032**
The Ties That Bind! • Spider-Man; The Beast **A:** Kerry Gammill **W:** J.M. DeMatteis ★ Origin of Professor Power.

125 ❑ Jan 1983 Cover: 0.60 **NM** value: **2.00**
Circ: Statement: **177,253**
Tigra! • Spider-Man; Tigra **A:** Kerry Gammill **W:** J.M. DeMatteis

126 ❑ Feb 1983 Cover: 0.60 **NM** value: **2.00**
Circ: Statement: **177,253**
• Spider-Man; Hulk; Power Man; Son of Satan **A:** Bob Hall

127 ❑ Mar 1983 Cover: 0.60 **NM** value: **2.00**
Circ: Statement: **177,253**
Small Miracles • Spider-Man; The Watcher **A:** Kerry Gammill **W:** J.M. DeMatteis

128 ❑ Apr 1983 Cover: 0.60 **NM** value: **2.00**
Circ: Statement: **177,253**
Photo cover. • Spider-Man; Captain America

129 ❑ May 1983 Cover: 0.60 **NM** value: **2.00**
Circ: Statement: **177,253**
...And Much To Ponder Before The Dawn • Spider-Man; Vision; The Vision **A:** Kerry Gammill **W:** J.M. DeMatteis

130 ❑ Jun 1983 Cover: 0.60 **NM** value: **2.00**
Circ: Statement: **177,253**
Till Death Do Us Part! • Spider-Man; Scarlet Witch; The Scarlet Witch; Has 1982 Statement, filed 10/11/82; avg print run 387,534; avg sales 171,087; avg subs 7,945; avg total paid 179,032; samples 713; office use 2,748; max existent 182,493; 53% of run returned **A:** Sal Buscema **W:** J.M. DeMatteis

131 ❑ Jul 1983 Cover: 0.60 **NM** value: **2.00**
Circ: Statement: **177,253**
The Best Things In Life Are Free...But Everything Else Costs Money! • Spider-Man; Frogman **A:** Kerry Gammill **W:** J.M. DeMatteis

132 ❑ Aug 1983 Cover: 0.60 **NM** value: **2.00**
Circ: Statement: **177,253**
• Spider-Man; Mr. Fantastic

133 ❑ Sep 1983 Cover: 0.60 **NM** value: **2.00**
Circ: Statement: **177,253**
The World According To...Faustus! • Spider-Man; Fantastic Four **A:** Sal Buscema; Mike Esposito **W:** J.M. DeMatteis

134 ❑ Oct 1983 Cover: 0.60 **NM** value: **2.00**
Circ: Statement: **177,253**
The Boy's Night Out! • Spider-Man; Jack of Hearts **A:** Ron Frenz; Mike Esposito **W:** Bill Mantlo

135 ❑ Nov 1983 Cover: 0.60 **NM** value: **2.00**
Circ: Statement: **177,253**
• Spider-Man; Kitty Pryde

136 ❑ Dec 1983 Cover: 0.60 **NM** value: **2.00**
Circ: Statement: **177,253**
Webs • Spider-Man; Wonder Man **A:** Ron Frenz; Mike Esposito **W:** David Michelinie

137 ❑ Jan 1984 Cover: 0.60 **NM** value: **2.00**
• Spider-Man; Aunt May; Franklin Richards; Assistant Editor's Month ★ Origin of Doctor Faustus.

138 ❑ Feb 1984 Cover: 0.60 **NM** value: **2.00**
Starting Over! • Spider-Man; Sandman (Marvel); Nick Fury **A:** Greg LaRocque; Mike Esposito **W:** Tom DeFalco

139 ❑ Mar 1984 Cover: 0.60 **NM** value: **2.00**
• Spider-Man; Sandman (Marvel); Nick Fury

140 ❑ Apr 1984 Cover: 0.60 **NM** value: **2.00**
• Spider-Man; Black Widow; Has 1983 Statement, filed 10/3/83; avg print run 365,308; avg sales 168,308; avg subs 8,909; avg total paid 177,253; samples 752; office use 3,039; max existent 181,044; % of run returned

141 ❑ May 1984 Cover: 0.60 **NM** value: **2.00**
• Spider-Man new costume; Daredevil

142 ❑ Jun 1984 Cover: 0.60 **NM** value: **2.00**
• Spider-Man; Captain Marvel (female, new)

143 ❑ Jul 1984 Cover: 0.60 **NM** value: **2.00**
• Spider-Man; Starfox

144 ❑ Aug 1984 Cover: 0.60 **NM** value: **2.00**
• Spider-Man; Moon Knight

145 ❑ Sep 1984 Cover: 0.60 **NM** value: **2.00**
• Spider-Man; Iron Man

146 ❑ Oct 1984 Cover: 0.60 **NM** value: **2.00**
• Spider-Man; Nomad

147 ❑ Nov 1984 Cover: 0.60 **NM** value: **2.00**
• Spider-Man; Human Torch

148 ❑ Dec 1984 Cover: 0.60 **NM** value: **2.00**
A Child Shall Lead Them! • Spider-Man; Thor **A:** Greg LaRocque **W:** Cary Burkett

149 ❑ Jan 1985 Cover: 0.60 **NM** value: **2.00**
• Spider-Man; Cannonball

150 ❑ Feb 1985 Cover: 1.00 **NM** value: **3.00**
• Giant-size. final issue. • Spider-Man; X-Men

Anl 1 ❑ ca. 1976 Cover: 0.50 **NM** value: **15.00**
• **CGC:** 22 graded, best 9.4
The Lords of Light and Darkness; The Nest; Day of the Demons; Into--- Hellpit!; A Gathering of Gods • Spider-Man; X-Men **A:** Sal Buscema **C:** Dave Cockrum

Anl 2 ❑ ca. 1979 Cover: 0.75 **NM** value: **4.00**
Murder in Cathedral Canyon; A Friend in Need; Brother, Can You Spare a Hulk?; Rochy Mountain High; A Man's Life – Or a World? • Spider-Man; Hulk **A:** Sal Buscema **C:** Al Milgrom

Anl 3 ❑ ca. 1980 Cover: 0.75 **NM** value: **3.00**
Mayhem in Middle America; Monster in the Meadow; Payoff; Hearoes for Hire; The Men and the Machine; Confrontation • Hulk; Power Man; Iron Fist; Machine Man **A:** Herb Trimpe; Frank Miller(cover) **C:** Frank Miller **W:** Roger Stern

Anl 4 ❑ ca. 1981 Cover: 0.75 **NM** value: **2.50**
• **CGC:** 1 graded, best 9.4
Power Play • Spider-Man; Iron Fist; Power Man; Daredevil; Moon Knight **A:** Herb Trimpe; Frank Miller **C:** Frank Miller **W:** Frank Miller

Anl 5 ❑ Nov 1981 Cover: 1.00 **NM** value: **2.50**
• Spider-Man; Thing; Scarlet Witch; Vision; Quasar

Anl 6 ❑ Oct 1983 Cover: 1.00 **NM** value: **2.50**
The Hunters And The Hunted! • New Mutants; Cloak & Dagger **A:** Ron Frenz; Kevin Dzuban **W:** Bill Mantlo

Anl 7 ❑ Oct 1984 Cover: 1.00 **NM** value: **2.00**
• Alpha Flight

MARVEL TEAM-UP (2ND SERIES) Marvel

1 ❑ Sep 1997 Cover: 1.99 **NM** value: **2.00**
Circ: Diamd. preorders: **54,643**

CGC-graded: Multiply prices above by **33 for 9.9 M** • **16 for 9.8 NM/M** • **7 for 9.6 NM+** • **5 for 9.4 NM** • **2.5 for 9.2 NM-** • **1.5 for 9.0 VF/NM**

• gatefold summary. 📖 D.E.A.D. to Rights! • Spider-Man; Generation X; Story takes place before Generation X #32 **A:** Patrick Olliffe **W:** Tom Peyer

2 ❑ Oct 1997 Cover: 1.99 **NM** value: **2.00**
Circ: Diamd. preorders: **43,513**
• gatefold summary. • Spider-Man; Hercules

3 ❑ Nov 1997 Cover: 1.99 **NM** value: **2.00**
Circ: Diamd. preorders: **34,175**
• gatefold summary. • Spider-Man; Sandman; Sandman (Marvel) ★ Appearance of Silver Sable.

4 ❑ Dec 1997 Cover: 1.99 **NM** value: **2.00**
Circ: Diamd. preorders: **32,638**
• gatefold summary. • Spider-Man; Man-Thing

5 ❑ Jan 1998 Cover: 1.99 **NM** value: **2.00**
Circ: Diamd. preorders: **30,269**
• Spider-Man ★ Appearance of Authority. ★ Versus Authority.

6 ❑ Feb 1998 Cover: 1.99 **NM** value: **2.00**
Circ: Diamd. preorders: **27,750**
• Spider-Man; Sub-Mariner ★ Appearance of Wrecking Crew. ★ Versus Wrecking Crew.

7 ❑ Mar 1998 Cover: 1.99 **NM** value: **2.00**
Circ: Diamd. preorders: **24,782**
• Spider-Man; Blade

8 ❑ Apr 1998 Cover: 1.99 **NM** value: **2.00**
Circ: Diamd. preorders: **21,263**
• Sub-Mariner; Doctor Strange

9 ❑ May 1998 Cover: 1.99 **NM** value: **2.00**
Circ: Diamd. preorders: **21,733**
• Sub-Mariner; Captain America

10 ❑ Jun 1998 Cover: 1.99 **NM** value: **2.00**
Circ: Diamd. preorders: **19,862**
• Sub-Mariner; Thing

11 ❑ Jul 1998 Cover: 1.99 **NM** value: **2.00**
Circ: Diamd. preorders: **19,052**
final issue. • Sub-Mariner; Iron Man ★ Appearance of Wrecking Crew. ★ Versus Wrecking Crew.

MARVEL: THE LOST GENERATION — Marvel

In the years between World War II and the introduction of such heroes as The Fantastic Four and The Avengers, an entire generation of Earth's super-human population was brutally slaughtered by a Skrull invasion force. Propelled continuously backwards through time, scientist Cassandra Locke must bear witness to this terrible tragedy. As she sees the events unfold in reverse, Cassandra seems helpless to save these forgotten heroes. But armed with the knowledge of her own future era, as well as the information gleaned on her strange journey, she may actually hold the key to averting these terrible events at their very outset. But can she change history, when she's already lived through it? Even if Cassandra decides it's possible, powerful beings like the sorcerous Dr. Strange and the cosmic Watcher might not give her the chance.

This 12-issue series ran in reverse, beginning with #12 and finishing with #1.

12 ❑ Mar 2000 Cover: 2.95 **NM** value: **Cover or less**
Circ: Diamd. preorders: **34,935**
• #1 in sequence **A:** John Byrne **W:** John Byrne; Roger Stern

11 ❑ Apr 2000 Cover: 2.95 **NM** value: **Cover or less**
Circ: Diamd. preorders: **27,217**
• #2 in sequence **A:** John Byrne **W:** John Byrne; Roger Stern

10 ❑ May 2000 Cover: 2.95 **NM** value: **Cover or less**
Circ: Diamd. preorders: **26,421**
📖 Mad to Live • #3 in sequence **A:** John Byrne; Roger Stern **W:** John Byrne; Roger Stern

9 ❑ Jun 2000 Cover: 2.95 **NM** value: **Cover or less**
Circ: Diamd. preorders: **25,384**
• #4 in sequence **A:** John Byrne **W:** John Byrne; Roger Stern

8 ❑ Jul 2000 Cover: 2.95 **NM** value: **Cover or less**
Circ: Diamd. preorders: **25,157**
• #5 in sequence **A:** John Byrne **W:** John Byrne; Roger Stern

7 ❑ Aug 2000 Cover: 2.99 **NM** value: **Cover or less**
Circ: Diamd. preorders: **24,918**
📖 Highly Placed Sources • #6 in sequence **A:** John Byrne **W:** John Byrne; Roger Stern ★ Appearance of Fantastic Four, Sub-Mariner.

6 ❑ Sep 2000 Cover: 2.99 **NM** value: **Cover or less**
Circ: Diamd. preorders: **24,226**
📖 Crisis of Conscience • #7 in sequence **A:** John Byrne **W:** John Byrne; Roger Stern

5 ❑ Oct 2000 Cover: 2.99 **NM** value: **Cover or less**
Circ: Diamd. preorders: **22,295**
📖 Wild in the Streets • #8 in sequence **A:** John Byrne **W:** John Byrne; Roger Stern ★ Appearance of Venus, Thor, Odin.

4 ❑ Nov 2000 Cover: 2.99 **NM** value: **Cover or less**
Circ: Diamd. preorders: **22,051**
📖 Lightning in the Day • #9 in sequence **A:** John Byrne **W:** John Byrne; Roger Stern

3 ❑ Dec 2000 Cover: 2.99 **NM** value: **Cover or less**
Circ: Diamd. preorders: **21,645**
📖 Mad to Live • #10 in sequence **A:** John Byrne **W:** John Byrne; Roger Stern ★ Appearance of Yellow Claw, Sub-Mariner.

2 ❑ Jan 2001 Cover: 2.99 **NM** value: **Cover or less**
Circ: Diamd. preorders: **21,402**
📖 After ... • #11 in sequence **A:** John Byrne **W:** John Byrne; Roger Stern

1 ❑ Feb 2001 Cover: 2.99 **NM** value: **Cover or less**
Circ: Diamd. preorders: **21,201**
📖 It's Starting Again • #12 in sequence **A:** John Byrne **W:** John Byrne; Roger Stern

MARVEL TREASURY EDITION — Marvel

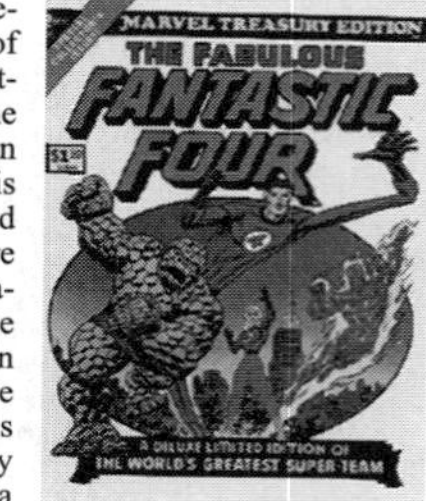

The Marvel Treasury Edition series stands out (literally) as some of the largest comic books ever printed. Published in the mid-1970s, the series kicked off with a Spider-Man special that reprinted some of his earliest adventures in an enlarged format. This was followed by more than two dozen other specials featuring everyone from Conan the Barbarian to Howard the Duck (in a Defenders issue). Although the oversized format of these specials was a headache for retailers, they were favorites with collectors. As a final send-off to the series, Marvel and DC joined forces to publish a Spider-Man/Superman team-up.

1 ❑ ca. 1974 Cover: 1.50 **NM** value: **10.00**
• The Spectacular Spider-Man **A:** Steve Ditko

2 ❑ Dec 1974 Cover: 1.50 **NM** value: **7.50**
📖 Captives of the Deadly Duo!; The Impossible Man; A Visit With the Fantastic Four; The Coming of Galactus • The Fabulous Fantastic Four; Reprints early Fantastic Four issues **A:** Jack Kirby **W:** Stan Lee ★ 1st Appearance of Galactus, The Silver Surfer. ★ Appearance of Sub-Mariner.

3 ❑ ca. 1974 Cover: 1.50 **NM** value: **7.50**
📖 When Meet the Immortals!; Whom the Gods Would Destroy!; The Hammer and the Holocaust!; The Power of Pluto; The Verdict of Zeus; Thunder in the Netherworld • The Mighty Thor; reprints Thor #125-130 **A:** Jack Kirby **W:** Stan Lee ★ Versus Hercules.

4 ❑ ca. 1975 Cover: 1.50 **NM** value: **7.50**
📖 An Informal History of the Thomas/Smith Conan; Rogues in the House; The Road to Aquilonia; Red Nails • Conan **A:** Barry Windsor-Smith **W:** Roy Thomas

5 ❑ ca. 1975 Cover: 1.50 **NM** value: **7.50**
📖 The Origin of The Hulk; Let There be Battle!; Many Foes Has the Hulk!; His Name is...Samson!; Cry: Monster! • reprints Hulk #3, 139, 141, Tales to Astonish #79, 100, and Marvel Feature #11 **A:** Jim Starlin; Herb Trimpe; John Severin; Joe Sinnott; Marie Severin; Dan Adkins **W:** Len Wein; Roy Thomas; Stan Lee

6 ❑ ca. 1975 Cover: 1.50 **NM** value: **7.50**
📖 The End...at Last!; The Origin of the Ancient One!; The End of the Ancient One; To Dream...Perchance to Die!; Face-to-Face With the Magic of Baron Mordo!; The Cult and the Curse; Finally, Suma-Gorath! • Doctor Strange **A:** Steve Ditko; Gene Colan; Frank Brunner; Bill Everett; Marie Severin; Dan Adkins **W:** Roy Thomas; Stan Lee; Denny O'Neil; Steve Englehart ★ Origin of The Ancient One.

7 ❑ ca. 1975 Cover: 1.50 **NM** value: **7.50**
• Avengers

8 ❑ Hol 1975 Cover: 1.50 **NM** value: **7.50**
📖 Twas the Night Before Christmas; Spidey Gone Mad!; Jungle Bombs!; Heaven is a Very Small Place!; Eternity! Eternity! • Giant Super-Hero Holiday Grab Bag; The Incredible Hulk #147, Luke Cage, Hero for Hire #7 **A:** Steve Ditko; Billy Graham; Gene Colan; Herb Trimpe; George Tuska; Frank Springer **W:** Gary Friedrich; Roy Thomas; Stan Lee; Steve Englehart

9 ❑ ca. 1976 Cover: 1.50 **NM** value: **7.50**
📖 In the Rage of Battle; In Combat with Captain America!; The Mighty Thor Battles the Incredible Hulk!; The Surfer and the Spider! • Giant Superhero Team-up; Reprints Prince Namor, the Sub-Mariner #8, Journey into Mystery #112, Silver Surfer (Vol. 1) #14, Daredevil #43; Namor vs. Human-Torch; Daredevil vs. Captain America; Thor vs. Hulk; Silver Surfer vs. Spider-Man **A:** John Buscema; Jack Kirby **W:** John Buscema; Roy Thomas; Stan Lee

10 ❑ ca. 1976 Cover: 1.50 **NM** value: **7.50**
📖 To Wake the Mangog!; Now Ends the Universe; The Hammer and the Holocaust; Behind him Ragnarok • The Mighty Thor; Reprints Thor #154-157 **A:** Jack Kirby **W:** Stan Lee

11 ❑ ca. 1976 Cover: 1.50 **NM** value: **7.50**
• Fantastic Four **A:** Frank Frazetta

12 ❑ ca. 1976 Cover: 1.50 **NM** value: **7.50**
• Reprints Howard the Duck #1, Giant-Size Man-Thing #4, 5, with new Defenders story. 📖 The Duck and the Defenders; The Way it All Began!; Frog Death!; Hellcow!; Howard the Barbarian • Howard the Duck **A:** Frank Brunner; Val Mayerik; Sal Buscema; Tom Palmer; Klaus Janson; Sal Trapani; Steve Leialoha **W:** Steve Gerber

13 ❑ ca. 1976 Cover: 1.50 **NM** value: **7.50**
• Giant Super-Hero Holiday Grab-Bag

14 ❑ ca. 1977 Cover: 1.50 **NM** value: **7.50**
• Amazing Spider-Man; reprints Amazing Spider-Man #100-102 and Not Brand Echh #6

15 ❑ ca. 1977 Cover: 1.50 **NM** value: **7.50**
• Conan; Red Sonja **A:** Barry Windsor-Smith

16 ❑ ca. 1977 Cover: 1.50 **NM** value: **7.50**
• Defenders

17 ❑ ca. 1978 Cover: 1.50 **NM** value: **7.50**
📖 Within the Swamp, there Stirs...a Glob!; Among us Walks the Golem; Cry Hulk, Cry Havok; Frenzy on a Far-Away World • The Incredible Hulk; Reprints The Incredible Hulk #121, 134, 150 **A:** Sal Buscema; Herb Trimpe; John Severin; Sal Trapani **W:** Roy Thomas; Archie Goodwin; Steve Gerber

18 ❑ ca. 1978 Cover: 2.00 **NM** value: **7.50**
• Spider-Man; X-Men

19 ❑ ca. 1978 Cover: 2.00 **NM** value: **7.50**
• Conan

20 ❑ ca. 1979 Cover: 2.00 **NM** value: **7.50**
• Hulk; reprints Incredible Hulk #136, 137, 143, 144; pin-up gallery

21 ❑ ca. 1979 Cover: 2.00 **NM** value: **7.50**
• Fantastic Four **A:** Frank Frazetta

22 ❑ ca. 1979 Cover: 2.00 **NM** value: **7.50**
• Spider-Man

23 ❑ ca. 1979 Cover: 2.00 **NM** value: **7.50**
• Conan

24 ❑ ca. 1979 Cover: 2.00 **NM** value: **7.50**
• Incredible Hulk; reprints Incredible Hulk #167-170; Wolverine and Hercules new back-up story

25 ❑ ca. 1980 Cover: 2.00 **NM** value: **7.50**
• Spider-Man and Hulk at Winter Olympics

26 ❑ ca. 1980 Cover: 2.00 **NM** value: **8.00**
• Hulk; Wolverine; Hercules

27 ❑ ca. 1980 Cover: 2.00 **NM** value: **7.50**
• Marvel Team-Up; reprints MTU #9-11 and 27; new Angel story

28 ❑ Jul 1981 Cover: 2.50 **NM** value: **15.00**
• Spider-Man and Superman ★ Appearance of Wonder Woman, Hulk. ★ Versus Parasite. ★ Versus Doctor Doom.

MARVEL TREASURY OF OZ — Marvel

1 ❑ ca. 1975 Cover: 1.50 **NM** value: **10.00**
• adapts Baum's Land of Oz

MARVEL TREASURY SPECIAL FEATURING CAPTAIN AMERICA'S BICENTENNIAL BATTLES — Marvel

1 ❑ ca. 1976 Cover: 1.50 **NM** value: **14.00**
• Captain America's Bicentennial Battles **A:** Jack Kirby **W:** Jack Kirby

MARVEL TREASURY SPECIAL, GIANT SUPERHERO HOLIDAY GRAB-BAG — Marvel

1 ❑ ca. 1974 Cover: 1.50 **NM** value: **7.50**
📖 Have Yourself a Sandman, Little Christmas; In Mortal Combat with The Sub-Mariner!; ...And To All a Good Night!; The Hulk vs. The Thing!; The Avengers Take Over! • Giant Super-Hero Holiday Grab Bag; reprints MTU #1, Fantastic Four #25-26, DD #7, and Amazing Adventures; reprints Marvel Team-Up #1, Fantastic Four #25-26, Daredevil #7, and Amazing Adventures **A:** Gene Colan; Jack Kirby; Wally Wood; Ross Andru **W:** Roy Thomas; Stan Lee

MARVEL TRIPLE ACTION — Marvel

1 ❑ Feb 1972 Cover: 0.25 **NM** value: **5.00**
• **CGC:** 3 graded, best 9.4
• reprints Avengers

2 ❑ Apr 1972 Cover: 0.20 **NM** value: **3.00**
3 ❑ Jun 1972 Cover: 0.20 **NM** value: **3.00**
4 ❑ Aug 1972 Cover: 0.20 **NM** value: **3.00**
• **CGC:** 1 graded, best 9.2
5 ❑ Sep 1972 Cover: 0.20 **NM** value: **3.00**
6 ❑ Oct 1972 Cover: 0.20 **NM** value: **2.00**
📖 This Hostage Earth! **A:** Don Heck **W:** Stan Lee
7 ❑ Nov 1972 Cover: 0.20 **NM** value: **2.00**
8 ❑ Jan 1973 Cover: 0.20 **NM** value: **2.00**
9 ❑ Feb 1973 Cover: 0.20 **NM** value: **2.00**
10 ❑ Apr 1973 Cover: 0.20 **NM** value: **2.00**
11 ❑ Jun 1973 Cover: 0.20 **NM** value: **2.00**
12 ❑ Aug 1973 Cover: 0.20 **NM** value: **2.00**
13 ❑ Sep 1973 Cover: 0.20 **NM** value: **2.00**
14 ❑ Oct 1973 Cover: 0.20 **NM** value: **2.00**
📖 Vengeance is Ours! **A:** Don Heck **W:** Stan Lee
15 ❑ Nov 1973 Cover: 0.20 **NM** value: **2.00**
16 ❑ Jan 1974 Cover: 0.20 **NM** value: **2.00**
17 ❑ Mar 1974 Cover: 0.20 **NM** value: **2.00**
18 ❑ May 1974 Cover: 0.25 **NM** value: **2.00**
19 ❑ Jul 1974 Cover: 0.25 **NM** value: **2.00**
20 ❑ Sep 1974 Cover: 0.25 **NM** value: **2.00**
21 ❑ Oct 1974 Cover: 0.25 **NM** value: **2.00**
22 ❑ Nov 1974 Cover: 0.25 **NM** value: **2.00**
📖 Four Against the Floodtide! • reprints Avengers #28 **A:** Don Heck **W:** Stan Lee
23 ❑ Jan 1975 Cover: 0.25 **NM** value: **2.00**
24 ❑ Mar 1975 Cover: 0.25 **NM** value: **2.00**
25 ❑ Sep 1975 Cover: 0.25 **NM** value: **2.00**
26 ❑ Nov 1975 Cover: 0.25 **NM** value: **2.00**
27 ❑ Jan 1976 Cover: 0.25 **NM** value: **2.00**
28 ❑ Mar 1976 Cover: 0.25 **NM** value: **2.00**
29 ❑ May 1976 Cover: 0.25 **NM** value: **2.00**
30 ❑ Jul 1976 Cover: 0.25 **NM** value: **2.00**
31 ❑ Sep 1976 Cover: 0.30 **NM** value: **2.00**
32 ❑ Nov 1976 Cover: 0.30 **NM** value: **2.00**
33 ❑ Jan 1977 Cover: 0.30 **NM** value: **2.00**
34 ❑ Mar 1977 Cover: 0.30 **NM** value: **2.00**
35 ❑ May 1977 Cover: 0.30 **NM** value: **2.00**
36 ❑ Jul 1977 Cover: 0.30 **NM** value: **2.00**
37 ❑ Sep 1977 Cover: 0.30 **NM** value: **2.00**
38 ❑ Nov 1977 Cover: 0.30 **NM** value: **2.00**
39 ❑ Jan 1978 Cover: 0.30 **NM** value: **2.00**
40 ❑ Mar 1978 Cover: 0.30 **NM** value: **2.00**
41 ❑ Apr 1978 Cover: 0.30 **NM** value: **2.00**
42 ❑ Jun 1978 Cover: 0.30 **NM** value: **2.00**
43 ❑ Aug 1978 Cover: 0.30 **NM** value: **2.00**
44 ❑ Oct 1978 Cover: 0.30 **NM** value: **2.00**
45 ❑ Dec 1978 Cover: 0.30 **NM** value: **2.00**
★ Appearance of X-Men.
46 ❑ Feb 1979 Cover: 0.30 **NM** value: **2.00**
47 ❑ Apr 1979 Cover: 0.30 **NM** value: **2.00**
GS 1 ❑ ca. 1975 Cover: 0.50 **NM** value: **4.00**
GS 2 ❑ ca. 1975 Cover: 0.50 **NM** value: **4.00**

MARVEL TWO-IN-ONE — Marvel

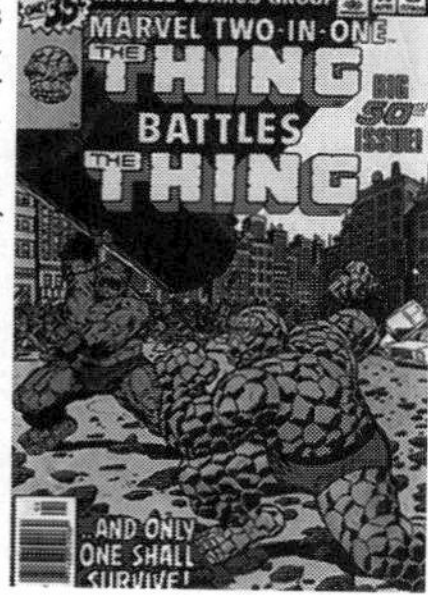

Another "team-up" series, this one featured the Fantastic Four's Thing in a series of adventures involving a wide collection of other characters. Marvel Two-In-One introduced us to a number of new heroes, including Maelstrom and the Impossible Woman. It also told of the demise of at least two characters: Issue #54 brought us the death of Luther Manning, the original Deathlok; and tragedy struck again in issue #93 with the death of Jocasta, a female "living robot" and member of the Avengers. Jocasta was eventually rebuilt, however, and made an appearance in the futuristic Machine Man limited series.

Other grades: Multiply prices above by **1.5 for Mint • 2/3 for Very Fine • 1/3 for Fine • 1/5 for Very Good • 1/8 for Good**

Following #100's tale of an alternate future in which New York had been devastated — featuring a depiction of a destroyed World Trade Center, spookily enough — the series was restarted as The Thing.

1 ❑ Jan 1974 Cover: 0.20 **NM** value: **22.00**
• **CGC:** 27 graded, best 9.6
• Man-Thing

2 ❑ Mar 1974 Cover: 0.20 **NM** value: **9.00**
• **CGC:** 5 graded, best 9.4
• Sub-Mariner; Namor

3 ❑ May 1974 Cover: 0.25 **NM** value: **7.00**
• **CGC:** 4 graded, best 9.6
• Daredevil ★ Appearance of Black Widow.

4 ❑ Jul 1974 Cover: 0.25 **NM** value: **7.00**
• **CGC:** 4 graded, best 9.6
• Captain America

5 ❑ Sep 1974 Cover: 0.25 **NM** value: **8.00**
• **CGC:** 1 graded, best 5.5
• Guardians of the Galaxy

6 ❑ Nov 1974 Cover: 0.25 **NM** value: **8.00**
• **CGC:** 2 graded, best 9.6
• Doctor Strange

7 ❑ Jan 1975 Cover: 0.25 **NM** value: **5.00**
• **CGC:** 1 graded, best 7.5
• Valkyrie ★ Appearance of Doctor Strange.

8 ❑ Mar 1975 Cover: 0.25 **NM** value: **5.00**
• Ghost Rider

9 ❑ May 1975 Cover: 0.25 **NM** value: **5.00**
• **CGC:** 1 graded, best 7.5
• Thor

10 ❑ Jul 1975 Cover: 0.25 **NM** value: **5.00**
• Black Widow

11 ❑ Sep 1975 Cover: 0.25 **NM** value: **3.00**
• Golem

12 ❑ Nov 1975 Cover: 0.25 **NM** value: **3.00**
• Iron Man

13 ❑ Jan 1976 Cover: 0.25 **NM** value: **3.00**
📖 I Created Braggadoom! • Power Man **A:** Ron Wilson **W:** Len Wein; Roger Slifer

14 ❑ Mar 1976 Cover: 0.25 **NM** value: **3.00**
• Son of Satan

15 ❑ May 1976 Cover: 0.25 **NM** value: **3.00**
• Morbius

16 ❑ Jun 1976 Cover: 0.25 **NM** value: **3.00**
• Ka-Zar

17 ❑ Jul 1976 Cover: 0.25 **NM** value: **3.00**
• Spider-Man ★ Appearance of Basilisk I (Basil Elks).

18 ❑ Aug 1976 Cover: 0.25 **NM** value: **3.00**
• Scarecrow; Spider-Man

18/A ❑ Aug 1976 Cover: 0.30 **NM** value: **8.00**
30Û Cover price. • Scarecrow; Spider-Man

19 ❑ Sep 1976 Cover: 0.30 **NM** value: **3.00**
• Tigra

20 ❑ Oct 1976 Cover: 0.30 **NM** value: **3.00**
• Liberty Legion; continued from Marvel Two-In-One Annual #1

21 ❑ Nov 1976 Cover: 0.30 **NM** value: **3.00**
• Doc Savage ★ Appearance of Human Torch.

22 ❑ Dec 1976 Cover: 0.30 **NM** value: **3.00**
• **CGC:** 1 graded, best 9.4
• Human Torch; Thor

23 ❑ Jan 1977 Cover: 0.30 **NM** value: **3.00**
• Human Torch; Thor

24 ❑ Feb 1977 Cover: 0.30 **NM** value: **3.00**
• **CGC:** 1 graded, best 9.4
• Black Goliath **A:** Sal Buscema

25 ❑ Mar 1977 Cover: 0.30 **NM** value: **3.00**
• Iron Fist

26 ❑ Apr 1977 Cover: 0.30 **NM** value: **2.00**
• Nick Fury

27 ❑ May 1977 Cover: 0.30 **NM** value: **2.00**
• Deathlok

28 ❑ Jun 1977 Cover: 0.30 **NM** value: **2.00**
• Sub-Mariner

29 ❑ Jul 1977 Cover: 0.30 **NM** value: **2.00**
📖 Two Against Hydra • Shang-Chi **A:** Ron Wilson **W:** Marv Wolfman

30 ❑ Aug 1977 Cover: 0.30 **NM** value: **2.00**
A: John Buscema ★ 2nd Appearance of Spider-Woman I (Jessica Drew).

31 ❑ Sep 1977 Cover: 0.30 **NM** value: **2.00**
• Spider-Woman I (Jessica Drew)

32 ❑ Oct 1977 Cover: 0.30 **NM** value: **2.00**
• Invisible Girl

33 ❑ Nov 1977 Cover: 0.35 **NM** value: **2.00**
• Mordred

34 ❑ Dec 1977 Cover: 0.35 **NM** value: **2.00**
• Nighthawk

35 ❑ Jan 1978 Cover: 0.35 **NM** value: **2.00**
• Skull the Slayer

36 ❑ Feb 1978 Cover: 0.35 **NM** value: **2.00**
• Mr. Fantastic

37 ❑ Mar 1978 Cover: 0.35 **NM** value: **2.00**
• Matt Murdock

38 ❑ Apr 1978 Cover: 0.35 **NM** value: **2.00**
• Daredevil

39 ❑ May 1978 Cover: 0.35 **NM** value: **2.00**
• Vision; Daredevil

40 ❑ Jun 1978 Cover: 0.35 **NM** value: **2.00**
• Black Panther

41 ❑ Jul 1978 Cover: 0.35 **NM** value: **2.00**
• Brother Voodoo

42 ❑ Aug 1978 Cover: 0.35 **NM** value: **2.00**
• Captain America

43 ❑ Sep 1978 Cover: 0.35 **NM** value: **2.00**
• Man-Thing **A:** John Byrne

44 ❑ Oct 1978 Cover: 0.35 **NM** value: **2.00**
• Hercules **A:** Gene Day

45 ❑ Nov 1978 Cover: 0.35 **NM** value: **2.00**
📖 The Andromeda Rub-Out! • Captain Marvel **A:** Alan Kupperberg; Gene Day; Mike Esposito **W:** Peter Gillis

46 ❑ Dec 1978 Cover: 0.35 **NM** value: **2.00**
• Hulk

47 ❑ Jan 1979 Cover: 0.35 **NM** value: **2.00**
• Yancy Street Gang **A:** Gene Day ★ 1st Appearance of Machinesmith.

48 ❑ Feb 1979 Cover: 0.35 **NM** value: **2.00**
• Jack of Hearts

49 ❑ Mar 1979 Cover: 0.35 **NM** value: **2.00**
• Doctor Strange **A:** Gene Day

50 ❑ Apr 1979 Cover: 0.35 **NM** value: **2.00**
• **CGC:** 1 graded, best 9.4
📖 Remembrance Of Things Past! • Thing vs. Thing **A:** John Byrne; John Severin; Joe Sinnott **W:** John Byrne

51 ❑ May 1979 Cover: 0.40 **NM** value: **3.00**
• **CGC:** 1 graded, best 9.4
• Beast; Wonder Man; Ms. Marvel; Nick Fury **A:** Frank Miller; Bob McLeod

52 ❑ Jun 1979 Cover: 0.40 **NM** value: **2.00**
• Moon Knight

53 ❑ Jul 1979 Cover: 0.40 **NM** value: **2.00**
• Quasar **A:** John Byrne; John Severin

54 ❑ Aug 1979 Cover: 0.40 **NM** value: **4.00**
• Deathlok **A:** John Byrne; John Severin ★ 1st Appearance of Screaming Mimi, Poundcakes. ★ Death of Deathlok I (Luther Manning).

55 ❑ Sep 1979 Cover: 0.40 **NM** value: **2.00**
• Giant Man II (Bill Foster) **A:** John Byrne; John Severin

56 ❑ Oct 1979 Cover: 0.40 **NM** value: **1.50**
• Thundra **A:** George Pérez; Gene Day ★ 1st Appearance of Letha.

57 ❑ Nov 1979 Cover: 0.40 **NM** value: **1.50**
• Wundarr **A:** George Pérez; Gene Day

58 ❑ Dec 1979 Cover: 0.40 **NM** value: **1.50**
• Aquarian; Quasar **A:** George Pérez; Gene Day

59 ❑ Jan 1980 Cover: 0.40 **NM** value: **1.50**
📖 Trial And Error! • Human Torch **A:** Chic Stone **W:** Ralph Macchio; Marv Wolfman

60 ❑ Feb 1980 Cover: 0.40 **NM** value: **1.50**
• Impossible Man **A:** George Pérez; Gene Day ★ 1st Appearance of Impossible Woman.

61 ❑ Mar 1980 Cover: 0.40 **NM** value: **1.50**
• Starhawk **A:** Gene Day ★ 1st Appearance of Her.

62 ❑ Apr 1980 Cover: 0.40 **NM** value: **1.50**
📖 The Taking Of Counter-Earth • Moondragon **A:** Jerry Bingham; Gene Day **W:** Mark Gruenwald

63 ❑ May 1980 Cover: 0.40 **NM** value: **1.50**
• Warlock **A:** Gene Day

64 ❑ Jun 1980 Cover: 0.40 **NM** value: **1.50**
• Stingray **A:** George Pérez; Gene Day ★ 1st Appearance of Black Mamba, Anaconda, Death-Adder.

65 ❑ Jul 1980 Cover: 0.40 **NM** value: **1.50**
• Triton **A:** George Pérez; Gene Day

66 ❑ Aug 1980 Cover: 0.40 **NM** value: **1.50**
📖 A Congress Of Crowns! • Scarlet Witch **A:** Jerry Bingham; Gene Day **W:** Ralph Macchio; Mark Gruenwald ★ Appearance of Arcade.

67 ❑ Sep 1980 Cover: 0.50 **NM** value: **1.50**
• Hyperion; Thundra

68 ❑ Oct 1980 Cover: 0.50 **NM** value: **1.50**
• Angel ★ Appearance of Arcade.

69 ❑ Nov 1980 Cover: 0.50 **NM** value: **1.50**
• Guardians of the Galaxy

70 ❑ Dec 1980 Cover: 0.50 **NM** value: **1.50**
• Inhumans

71 ❑ Jan 1981 Cover: 0.50 **NM** value: **1.50**
• Mr. Fantastic ★ 1st Appearance of Maelstrom, Gronk, Phobius, Helio.

72 ❑ Feb 1981 Cover: 0.50 **NM** value: **1.50**
• Stingray

73 ❑ Mar 1981 Cover: 0.50 **NM** value: **1.50**
• Quasar

74 ❑ Apr 1981 Cover: 0.50 **NM** value: **1.50**
• Puppet Master

75 ❑ May 1981 Cover: 0.50 **NM** value: **1.50**
📖 By Blastaar Betrayed • Avengers **A:** Alan Kupperberg; Chic Stone **W:** Tom DeFalco ★ Origin of Blastaar.

76 ❑ Jun 1981 Cover: 0.50 **NM** value: **1.50**
• Iceman ★ Origin of Ringmaster.

77 ❑ Jul 1981 Cover: 0.50 **NM** value: **1.50**
• Man-Thing

78 ❑ Aug 1981 Cover: 0.50 **NM** value: **1.50**
• Wonder Man

79 ❑ Sep 1981 Cover: 0.50 **NM** value: **1.50**
• Blue Diamond ★ 1st Appearance of Star-Dancer.

80 ❑ Oct 1981 Cover: 0.50 **NM** value: **1.50**
• Ghost Rider

81 ❑ Nov 1981 Cover: 0.50 **NM** value: **1.50**
• Sub-Mariner

82 ❑ Dec 1981 Cover: 0.50 **NM** value: **1.50**
• Captain America

83 ❑ Jan 1982 Cover: 0.60 **NM** value: **1.50**
• Sasquatch

84 ❑ Feb 1982 Cover: 0.60 **NM** value: **1.50**
• Alpha Flight

85 ❑ Mar 1982 Cover: 0.60 **NM** value: **1.50**
• Giant-Man; Spider-Woman

86 ❑ Apr 1982 Cover: 0.60 **NM** value: **1.50**
📖 Time Runs Like Sand! • Sandman (Marvel) **A:** Ron Wilson **W:** Tom DeFalco

87 ❑ May 1982 Cover: 0.60 **NM** value: **1.50**
📖 Menace Of The Microworld! • Ant-Man **A:** Ron Wilson **W:** Tom DeFalco

88 ❑ Jun 1982 Cover: 0.60 **NM** value: **1.50**
• She-Hulk

89 ❑ Jul 1982 Cover: 0.60 **NM** value: **1.50**
• Torch; Human Torch

90 ❑ Aug 1982 Cover: 0.60 **NM** value: **1.50**
• Spider-Man

91 ❑ Sep 1982 Cover: 0.60 **NM** value: **1.50**
• Sphinx

92 ❑ Oct 1982 Cover: 0.60 **NM** value: **1.50**
📖 This Evil Returning! • Jocasta; Machine Man **A:** Ron Wilson **W:** Tom DeFalco ★ Versus Ultron.

93 ❑ Nov 1982 Cover: 0.60 **NM** value: **1.50**
★ Appearance of Machine Man. ★ Death of Jocasta.

94 ❑ Dec 1982 Cover: 0.60 **NM** value: **1.50**
• Power Man; Iron Fist

95 ❑ Jan 1983 Cover: 0.60 **NM** value: **1.50**
• Living Mummy

96 ❑ Feb 1983 Cover: 0.60 **NM** value: **1.50**
• Marvel Heroes; Sandman (Marvel)

97 ❑ Mar 1983 Cover: 0.60 **NM** value: **1.50**
• Iron Man

98 ❑ Apr 1983 Cover: 0.60 **NM** value: **1.50**
• Franklin Richards

99 ❑ May 1983 Cover: 0.60 **NM** value: **1.50**
• ROM

100 ❑ Jun 1983 Cover: 1.00 **NM** value: **2.50**
• Double-size. final issue. • Ben Grimm **W:** John Byrne

Anl 1 ❑ ca. 1976 Cover: 0.50 **NM** value: **4.00**
• **CGC:** 2 graded, best 9.4
📖 Their Name Is Legion! • Liberty Legion **A:** Sal Buscema **W:** Roy Thomas

Anl 2 ❑ Dec 1977 Cover: 0.60 **NM** value: **15.00**
• **CGC:** 14 graded, best 9.6
• Thanos transformed to stone **A:** Jim Starlin ★ 1st Appearance of Lord Chaos, Champion of the Universe, Master Order. ★ Death of Warlock. ★ Death of Thanos.

Anl 3 ❑ Aug 1978 Cover: 0.60 **NM** value: **2.00**
• **CGC:** 1 graded, best 9.4
• Nova

Anl 4 ❑ Oct 1979 Cover: 0.60 **NM** value: **2.00**
• Black Bolt

Anl 5 ❑ Sep 1980 Cover: 0.75 **NM** value: **2.50**
• Hulk **A:** Alan Kupperberg; Pablo Marcos **W:** Alan Kupperberg

Anl 6 ❑ Oct 1981 Cover: 0.75 **NM** value: **2.00**
★ 1st Appearance of American Eagle.

Anl 7 ❑ Oct 1982 Cover: 1.00 **NM** value: **2.00**
• Champion ★ 1st Appearance of Champion of the Universe.

MARVEL UNIVERSE — Marvel

1 ❑ Jun 1998 Cover: 1.99 **NM** value: **2.99**
Circ: Diamd. preorders: **41,036**
• gatefold summary. 📖 The Spoils of War! • Invaders **A:** Steve Epting **W:** Roger Stern

2 ❑ Jul 1998 Cover: 1.99 **NM** value: **Cover or less**
Circ: Diamd. preorders: **39,063**
• gatefold summary. • Invaders **C:** John Byrne

2/A ❑ Jul 1998 Cover: 1.99 **NM** value: **Cover or less**
alternate cover. • gatefold summary. • Invaders **C:** John Byrne

3 ❑ Aug 1998 Cover: 1.99 **NM** value: **Cover or less**
Circ: Diamd. preorders: **30,817**
• gatefold summary. 📖 The Eve of Destruction • Invaders **A:** Steve Epting **W:** Roger Stern

4 ❑ Sep 1998 Cover: 1.99 **NM** value: **Cover or less**
Circ: Diamd. preorders: **26,093**
• gatefold summary. • Monster Hunters

5 ❑ Oct 1998 Cover: 1.99 **NM** value: **Cover or less**
Circ: Diamd. preorders: **22,227**
• gatefold summary. • Monster Hunters

6 ❑ Nov 1998 Cover: 1.99 **NM** value: **Cover or less**
Circ: Diamd. preorders: **20,410**
• gatefold summary. • Monster Hunters

7 ❑ Dec 1998 Cover: 1.99 **NM** value: **Cover or less**
Circ: Diamd. preorders: **17,469**
• gatefold summary. final issue. • Monster Hunters ★ Origin of Mole Man.

MARVEL UNIVERSE: MILLENNIAL VISIONS — Marvel

1 ❑ Feb 2002 Cover: 3.99 **NM** value: **Cover or less**
Circ: Diamd. preorders: **18,780**

MARVEL VALENTINE SPECIAL — Marvel

1 ❑ Apr 1997 Cover: 1.99 **NM** value: **2.00**
Circ: Direct Market orders: **20,000**
One-shot. 📖 My Fair Spidey; Love Hurts; Venus: Atom-Age Amore; The Greatest Gift; Cyclops and Phoenix: The Way • romance anthology **A:** Kyle Holtz; Mary Mitchell; Mark Buckingham; Dan Decarlo; Dan Lawlis **W:** Tom DeFalco; John OstranderFrank Strom; Tom Peyer ★ Appearance of Cyclops, Venus, Daredevil, Spider-Man, Phoenix, Absorbing Man.

MARVEL VERSUS DC/DC VERSUS MARVEL — DC / Marvel

In early 1996, the two largest publishers of comic books decided to team up to produce an epic storyline in which characters from one publisher would fight characters from the other. Fans have long wondered who would win if, for example, Superman battled the Hulk, or if Namor fought against Aquaman. The outcome of these battles were decided solely by fan votes.

In the midst of the series, the Marvel and DC universes actually merged, creating an "Amalgam" universe. Here, the world was populated by super-hero hybrids such as Spider-Boy, Speed Demon, Doctor Strangefate, Super Soldier, and Bruce Wayne: Agent of S.H.I.E.L.D.

1 ❑ Mar 1996 Cover: 3.95 **NM** value: **4.00**
• **CGC:** 6 graded, best 10.0

CGC-graded: Multiply prices above by **33 for 9.9 M • 16 for 9.8 NM/M • 7 for 9.6 NM+ • 5 for 9.4 NM • 2.5 for 9.2 NM- • 1.5 for 9.0 VF/NM**

cardstock cover. • crossover with Marvel; continues in Marvel versus DC #2 **A:** Dan Jurgens; Claudio Castellini **W:** Ron Marz ★ 1st Appearance of Access (out of costume).

2 ❑ Mar 1996 Cover: 3.95 **NM** value: **4.00**
• **CGC:** 4 graded, best 10.0
cardstock cover. • crossover with DC **A:** Dan Jurgens; Claudio Castellini **W:** Peter David

3 ❑ Apr 1996 Cover: 3.95 **NM** value: **4.00**
• **CGC:** 3 graded, best 9.8
cardstock cover. • crossover with DC; voting results; Marvel and DC universes joined; Stories continued in Amalgam titles **A:** Dan Jurgens; Claudio Castellini **W:** Ron Marz ★ 1st Appearance of Access.

4 ❑ Apr 1996 Cover: 3.95 **NM** value: **4.00**
• **CGC:** 1 graded, best 9.4
cardstock cover. final issue. • continued from Marvel versus DC #3 **A:** Dan Jurgens; Claudio Castellini **W:** Peter David

Ash 1❑ **NM** value: **1.00**
No issue number. • Consumer Preview; free preview of crossover series; with trading card and ballot

Bk 1❑ Cover: 12.95 **NM** value: **Cover or less**
• Collects series **A:** Dan Jurgens; Claudio Castellini **W:** Peter David; Ron Marz

MARVEL X-MEN COLLECTION, THE — Marvel

1 ❑ Jan 1994 Cover: 2.95 **NM** value: **Cover or less**
• Pin-Ups **A:** Jim Lee
2 ❑ Feb 1994 Cover: 2.95 **NM** value: **Cover or less**
A: Jim Lee
3 ❑ Mar 1994 Cover: 2.95 **NM** value: **Cover or less**
A: Jim Lee

MARVEL YEAR IN REVIEW — Marvel

1 ❑ ca. 1989 Cover: 3.95 **NM** value: **Cover or less**
Circ: CapCity orders: **18,150**
C: Todd McFarlane
2 ❑ ca. 1990 Cover: 3.95 **NM** value: **Cover or less**
Circ: CapCity orders: **12,250**
3 ❑ ca. 1991 Cover: 3.95 **NM** value: **Cover or less**
4 ❑ ca. 1992 Cover: 3.95 **NM** value: **Cover or less**
Circ: CapCity orders: **17,300**
5 ❑ ca. 1993 Cover: 3.95 **NM** value: **Cover or less**
Circ: CapCity orders: **12,100**
6 ❑ ca. 1994 Cover: 2.95 **NM** value: **Cover or less**

MARVIN MOUSE — Atlas

1 ❑ Sep 1957 Cover: 0.10 **NM** value: **75.00**

MARY MARVEL — Fawcett

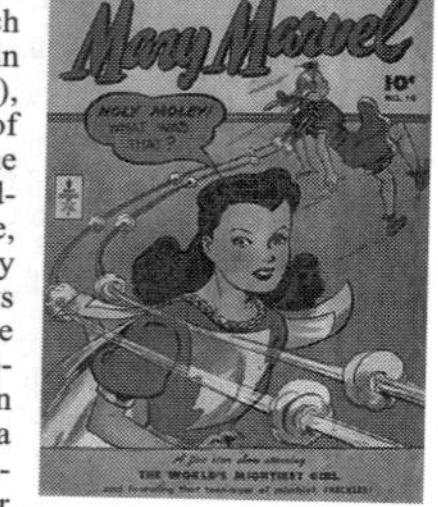

The third member of Fawcett's burgeoning Marvel Family (which included Captain Marvel, Captain Marvel, Jr. and assorted others), Mary was the long-lost sister of Cap's alter-ego, Billy Batson. She was granted the powers of the goddesses Selena, Hippolyta, Ariadne, Sephyrus, Aurora, and Minerva by the old wizard Shazam and fights evil in the guise of super-heroine Mary Marvel. After some memorable guest appearances in Captain Marvel and Whiz Comics, plus a permanent spot in the team-up feature Marvel Family, Mary got her own book in 1945 where she entertained with lighthearted adventures in the endearing Fawcett style. She was revived along with her super-siblings by DC in the 70s and again in The Power of Shazam.

1 ❑ Dec 1945 Cover: 0.10 **NM** value: **1600.00**
• **CGC:** 9 graded, best 9.6
2 ❑ Jun 1946 Cover: 0.10 **NM** value: **700.00**
3 ❑ Jul 1946 Cover: 0.10 **NM** value: **485.00**
4 ❑ Aug 1946 Cover: 0.10 **NM** value: **425.00**
• **CGC:** 1 graded, best 4.5
5 ❑ Sep 1946 Cover: 0.10 **NM** value: **300.00**
6 ❑ Oct 1946 Cover: 0.10 **NM** value: **265.00**
7 ❑ Nov 1946 Cover: 0.10 **NM** value: **265.00**
• **CGC:** 1 graded, best 8.5
8 ❑ Dec 1946 Cover: 0.10 **NM** value: **265.00**
9 ❑ Feb 1947 Cover: 0.10 **NM** value: **265.00**
10 ❑ Mar 1947 Cover: 0.10 **NM** value: **265.00**
📖 The Man Who Talks to Animals!; Horse Sense; Freckles' Jackpot; The Ghost of Finnegan's Heights (Text Story); Reversed Impulses; Dizzy Daisy; Freddy Freshman Rides Again; Meets Dr. Whirro! The Birdmobile; **A:** Jack Binder
11 ❑ Apr 1947 Cover: 0.10 **NM** value: **175.00**
12 ❑ May 1947 Cover: 0.10 **NM** value: **175.00**
13 ❑ Jun 1947 Cover: 0.10 **NM** value: **175.00**
14 ❑ Jul 1947 Cover: 0.10 **NM** value: **175.00**
15 ❑ Aug 1947 Cover: 0.10 **NM** value: **175.00**
16 ❑ Sep 1947 Cover: 0.10 **NM** value: **175.00**
17 ❑ Oct 1947 Cover: 0.10 **NM** value: **175.00**
18 ❑ Nov 1947 Cover: 0.10 **NM** value: **175.00**
• **CGC:** 1 graded, best 8.0
19 ❑ Dec 1947 Cover: 0.10 **NM** value: **175.00**
• **CGC:** 1 graded, best 7.0
20 ❑ Jan 1948 Cover: 0.10 **NM** value: **175.00**
21 ❑ Feb 1948 Cover: 0.10 **NM** value: **150.00**
22 ❑ Mar 1948 Cover: 0.10 **NM** value: **150.00**
23 ❑ Apr 1948 Cover: 0.10 **NM** value: **150.00**
24 ❑ May 1948 Cover: 0.10 **NM** value: **150.00**
25 ❑ Jun 1948 Cover: 0.10 **NM** value: **150.00**
26 ❑ Jul 1948 Cover: 0.10 **NM** value: **150.00**
27 ❑ Aug 1948 Cover: 0.10 **NM** value: **150.00**
28 ❑ Sep 1948 Cover: 0.10 **NM** value: **150.00**

MARY POPPINS — Gold Key

1 ❑ Jan 1965 **NM** value: **35.00**
• **CGC:** 2 graded, best 9.2

MARY WORTH — Argo

1 ❑ Mar 1956 Cover: 0.10 **NM** value: **35.00**

MASK, THE — Dark Horse

1 ❑ Feb 1995 Cover: 2.50 **NM** value: **3.00**
Circ: CapCity orders: **15,700**
📖 Strikes Back, Part 1; The Mask Strikes Back, Part 1 **A:** Doug Mahnke **W:** John Arcudi
2 ❑ Mar 1995 Cover: 2.50 **NM** value: **Cover or less**
Circ: CapCity orders: **11,175**
📖 Strikes Back, Part 2; The Mask Strikes Back, Part 2 **A:** Doug Mahnke **W:** John Arcudi
3 ❑ Apr 1995 Cover: 2.50 **NM** value: **Cover or less**
Circ: CapCity orders: **10,425**
📖 Strikes Back, Part 3; The Mask Strikes Back, Part 3 **A:** Doug Mahnke **W:** John Arcudi
4 ❑ May 1995 Cover: 2.50 **NM** value: **Cover or less**
Circ: CapCity orders: **10,250**
📖 Strikes Back, Part 4; The Mask Strikes Back, Part 4 **A:** Doug Mahnke **W:** John Arcudi
5 ❑ Jun 1995 Cover: 2.50 **NM** value: **Cover or less**
Circ: CapCity orders: **9,950**
📖 Strikes Back, Part 5; The Mask Strikes Back, Part 5 **A:** Doug Mahnke **W:** John Arcudi
6 ❑ Jul 1995 Cover: 2.50 **NM** value: **Cover or less**
📖 The Hunt for Green October, Part 1
7 ❑ Aug 1995 Cover: 2.50 **NM** value: **Cover or less**
📖 The Hunt for Green October, Part 2
8 ❑ Sep 1995 Cover: 2.50 **NM** value: **Cover or less**
📖 The Hunt for Green October, Part 3
9 ❑ Oct 1995 Cover: 2.50 **NM** value: **Cover or less**
📖 The Hunt for Green October, Part 4
10 ❑ Dec 1995 Cover: 2.50 **NM** value: **Cover or less**
📖 World Tour, Part 1 **A:** Gary Erskine **W:** Robert Loren Flemming ★ Appearance of Hero Zero, King Tiger.
11 ❑ Jan 1996 Cover: 2.50 **NM** value: **Cover or less**
📖 World Tour, Part 2 **A:** Gary Erskine **W:** Robert Loren Flemming ★ Appearance of Barb Wire, The Machine.
12 ❑ Feb 1996 Cover: 2.50 **NM** value: **Cover or less**
📖 World Tour, Part 3 **A:** Gary Erskine **W:** Robert Loren Flemming ★ Appearance of X, Ghost, King Tiger.
13 ❑ Mar 1996 Cover: 2.50 **NM** value: **Cover or less**
📖 World Tour, Part 4 **A:** Gary Erskine **W:** Robert Loren Flemming ★ Appearance of Warmaker, King Tiger, Vortex.
14 ❑ Apr 1996 Cover: 2.50 **NM** value: **Cover or less**
📖 Southern Discomfort, Part 1 **A:** Goran Delic **W:** Rich Hedden
15 ❑ May 1996 Cover: 2.50 **NM** value: **Cover or less**
📖 Southern Discomfort, Part 2 **A:** Goran Delic **W:** Rich Hedden ★ Appearance of Lt. Kellaway.
16 ❑ Jun 1996 Cover: 2.50 **NM** value: **Cover or less**
📖 Southern Discomfort, Part 3 **A:** Goran Delic **W:** Rich Hedden
17 ❑ Jul 1996 Cover: 2.50 **NM** value: **Cover or less**
📖 Southern Discomfort, Part 4 **A:** Goran Delic **W:** Rich Hedden
Bk 1❑ Cover: 14.95 **NM** value: **Cover or less**

MASK (1ST SERIES) — DC

1 ❑ Dec 1985 Cover: 1.00 **NM** value: **Cover or less**
Circ: CapCity orders: **11,750**
A: Curt Swan; Kurt Schaffenberger
2 ❑ Jan 1986 Cover: 1.00 **NM** value: **Cover or less**
Circ: CapCity orders: **9,200**
A: Curt Swan; Kurt Schaffenberger
3 ❑ Feb 1986 Cover: 1.00 **NM** value: **Cover or less**
Circ: CapCity orders: **7,950**
A: Curt Swan; Kurt Schaffenberger
4 ❑ Mar 1986 Cover: 1.00 **NM** value: **Cover or less**
Circ: CapCity orders: **6,850**
A: Curt Swan; Kurt Schaffenberger

MASK (2ND SERIES) — DC

1 ❑ Feb 1987 Cover: 1.00 **NM** value: **Cover or less**
Circ: CapCity orders: **12,950**
📖 The Ice Age Cometh **A:** Curt Swan; Kurt Schaffenberger **C:** Murphy Anderson **W:** Michael Fleisher
2 ❑ Mar 1987 Cover: 1.00 **NM** value: **Cover or less**
Circ: CapCity orders: **10,150**
📖 Masquerade **A:** Curt Swan; Kurt Schaffenberger **C:** Murphy Anderson **W:** Michael Fleisher
3 ❑ Apr 1987 Cover: 1.00 **NM** value: **Cover or less**
Circ: CapCity orders: **8,800**
📖 The Switchblade Conspiracy **A:** Curt Swan; Kurt Schaffenberger **C:** Murphy Anderson **W:** Michael Fleisher
4 ❑ May 1987 Cover: 1.00 **NM** value: **Cover or less**
Circ: CapCity orders: **6,650**
📖 Matt Trakker- Outlaw **A:** Curt Swan; Kurt Schaffenberger **C:** Murphy Anderson **W:** Michael Fleisher
5 ❑ Jun 1987 Cover: 1.00 **NM** value: **Cover or less**
Circ: CapCity orders: **5,400**
A: Curt Swan; Kurt Schaffenberger **C:** Murphy Anderson
6 ❑ Jul 1987 Cover: 1.00 **NM** value: **Cover or less**
Circ: CapCity orders: **4,750**
A: Curt Swan; Kurt Schaffenberger **C:** Murphy Anderson
7 ❑ Aug 1987 Cover: 1.00 **NM** value: **Cover or less**
Circ: CapCity orders: **4,400**
A: Curt Swan; Kurt Schaffenberger **C:** Murphy Anderson
8 ❑ Sep 1987 Cover: 1.00 **NM** value: **Cover or less**
Circ: CapCity orders: **4,300**
A: Curt Swan; Kurt Schaffenberger **C:** Murphy Anderson
9 ❑ Oct 1987 Cover: 1.00 **NM** value: **Cover or less**
Circ: CapCity orders: **4,110**

MASK COMICS — Rural Home

1 ❑ Feb 1945 Cover: 0.10 **NM** value: **2000.00**
• **CGC:** 3 graded, best 7.0
2 ❑ Fal 1945 Cover: 0.10 **NM** value: **1200.00**
• **CGC:** 4 graded, best 7.0

MASK CONSPIRACY, THE — Ink & Feathers

1 ❑ Cover: 6.95 **NM** value: **Cover or less**
A: Jim Ridings; Myke Feinman **W:** Jim Ridings; Myke Feinman

MASKED MAN, THE — Eclipse

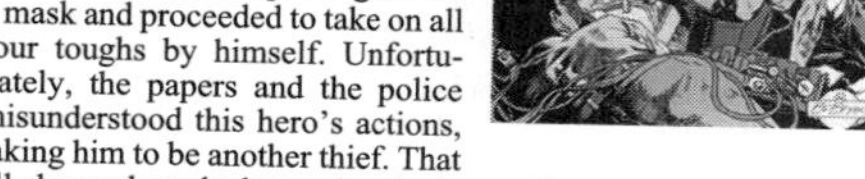

It all started the night reporter John Athens was mugged. Although Athens had been roughed up, he followed his reporter's instincts and decided to go after the story. He followed the group of ruffians for several blocks, then watched as they broke into a costume shop. The thieves were busy looting the shop when a man passed by on the street, saw what was going on, then jumped through the broken window into the shop. He grabbed a mask and proceeded to take on all four toughs by himself. Unfortunately, the papers and the police misunderstood this hero's actions, taking him to be another thief. That all changed weeks later when he jumped into a tense hostage situation and saved the day using nothing but his fists.

The Masked Man is an inspiring figure, a normal guy who decides he's not willing to sit by when crime strikes his neighborhood. He has no weapons, no super-powers, and this isn't even "his job." He is simply a hero.

1 ❑ Dec 1984, full color Cover: 1.75 **NM** value: **2.00**
📖 The Idol **W:** B.C. Boyer ★ Origin of Masked Man.
2 ❑ Feb 1985, full color Cover: 1.75 **NM** value: **2.00**
Circ: CapCity orders: **3,825**
3 ❑ Apr 1985, full color Cover: 1.75 **NM** value: **2.00**
Circ: CapCity orders: **3,850**
4 ❑ Jun 1985, full color Cover: 1.75 **NM** value: **2.00**
Circ: CapCity orders: **3,600**
5 ❑ Aug 1985, full color Cover: 1.75 **NM** value: **2.00**
Circ: CapCity orders: **3,575**
6 ❑ Oct 1985, full color Cover: 1.75 **NM** value: **2.00**
Circ: CapCity orders: **2,825**
7 ❑ Dec 1985, full color Cover: 2.00 **NM** value: **Cover or less**
Circ: CapCity orders: **2,800**
8 ❑ Feb 1986, full color Cover: 2.00 **NM** value: **Cover or less**
Circ: CapCity orders: **2,750**
9 ❑ Apr 1986, full color Cover: 2.00 **NM** value: **Cover or less**
Circ: CapCity orders: **2,500**
10 ❑ b&w Cover: 2.00 **NM** value: **Cover or less**
11 ❑ b&w Cover: 2.00 **NM** value: **Cover or less**
12 ❑ Apr 1988, b&w Cover: 2.00 **NM** value: **Cover or less**

MASKED MARVEL — Centaur

1 ❑ Sep 1940 Cover: 0.10 **NM** value: **1200.00**
• **CGC:** 4 graded, best 9.2
2 ❑ Oct 1940 Cover: 0.10 **NM** value: **1000.00**
• **CGC:** 1 graded, best 3.5
3 ❑ Dec 1940 Cover: 0.10 **NM** value: **1000.00**

MASKED RANGER — Premier

1 ❑ Apr 1954 Cover: 0.10 **NM** value: **300.00**
2 ❑ Jun 1954 Cover: 0.10 **NM** value: **100.00**
3 ❑ Aug 1954 Cover: 0.10 **NM** value: **100.00**
4 ❑ Oct 1954 Cover: 0.10 **NM** value: **100.00**
5 ❑ Dec 1954 Cover: 0.10 **NM** value: **100.00**
6 ❑ Feb 1955 Cover: 0.10 **NM** value: **100.00**
7 ❑ Apr 1955 Cover: 0.10 **NM** value: **100.00**
8 ❑ Jun 1955 Cover: 0.10 **NM** value: **100.00**
9 ❑ Aug 1955 Cover: 0.10 **NM** value: **100.00**

MASKED RIDER — Marvel

1 ❑ Apr 1996 Cover: 2.95 **NM** value: **Cover or less**
• based on Saban television series, one-shot **A:** Rurik Tyler; Tod Smith **W:** Frank Lovece ★ Appearance of Mighty Morphin Power Rangers, Ninja Rangers.

MASKED WARRIOR X — Antarctic

1 ❑ Apr 1996, b&w Cover: 2.95 **NM** value: **3.50**
📖 Warrior X, Part 1 **A:** Masayuki Fujihara **W:** Masayuki Fujihara
2 ❑ Jun 1996, b&w Cover: 2.95 **NM** value: **Cover or less**
3 ❑ Aug 1996, b&w Cover: 3.50 **NM** value: **Cover or less**
4 ❑ Oct 1996, b&w Cover: 2.95 **NM** value: **Cover or less**

MASK/MARSHAL LAW, THE — Dark Horse

1 ❑ Feb 1998 Cover: 2.95 **NM** value: **Cover or less**
Circ: Diamd. preorders: **7,866**
A: Kevin O'Neill **W:** Pat Mills
2 ❑ Mar 1998 Cover: 2.95 **NM** value: **Cover or less**
Circ: Diamd. preorders: **7,067**
• Law dons the Mask **A:** Kevin O'Neill **W:** Pat Mills

Capital City orders are the actual sales of comic books by Capital City Distribution, once one of the largest U.S. sellers of comics to comics shops. Capital City's share of comics shop sales, while not known exactly, increases from around 10-20% in the mid-1980s to 30-35% in the mid-1990s. Capital City's share of comic books sold on newsstands (most Marvels and DCs) will be less.

Other grades: Multiply prices above by **1.5 for Mint • 2/3 for Very Fine • 1/3 for Fine • 1/5 for Very Good • 1/8 for Good**

MASK, THE (MINI-SERIES) — Dark Horse

Long before Jim Carrey inherited the ancient face-gear, the original comics series existed, and was a very different beast, running as The Masque in Dark Horse Presents #10-15 and #18-21. A make-over resulted in a more familiar version, where ultraviolence with high body counts and rivers of blood is tempered with slapstick humor and bad jokes. The first mini-series [reprinted here from Mayhem #1-4] has Stanley Ipkiss, a "loser" of a bank teller from Edge City, discovering an old mask. When he puts the mask on he's transformed into a maniacal, bloodthirsty, wisecracking vigilante. To prevent some gangsters from robbing his bank, Stanley destroys half the city, and consequently makes an enemy for life in the mute, unstoppable thug known only as Walter. The strengths of the series lie in the ludicrous props The Mask seems to pull from thin air and the imaginative way he dispatches his enemies in the fashion of an acid-crazed merging of Tom & Jerry and Charles Manson.

0 ❑ ca. 1991 Cover: 4.95 **NM** value: **Cover or less**
Circ: CapCity orders: **6,800**
• Reprints Mask stories from Mayhem **A:** Doug Mahnke **W:** John Arcudi

1 ❑ Aug 1991 Cover: 2.50 **NM** value: **4.00**
Circ: CapCity orders: **7,625** • **CGC:** 1 graded, best 9.4
📖 Mask Justice **A:** Doug Mahnke **W:** John Arcudi

2 ❑ Sep 1991 Cover: 2.50 **NM** value: **3.50**
Circ: CapCity orders: **4,650** • **CGC:** 1 graded, best 9.2
A: Doug Mahnke **W:** John Arcudi

3 ❑ Oct 1991 Cover: 2.50 **NM** value: **3.00**
Circ: CapCity orders: **4,350**
A: Doug Mahnke **W:** John Arcudi

4 ❑ Nov 1991 Cover: 2.50 **NM** value: **3.00**
Circ: CapCity orders: **5,700**
A: Doug Mahnke **W:** John Arcudi

Bk 1❑ Cover: 14.95 **NM** value: **Cover or less**
A: Doug Mahnke **W:** John Arcudi

MASK OF DR. FU MANCHU — Avon

1 ❑ ca. 1951 Cover: 0.10 **NM** value: **500.00**
• **CGC:** 5 graded, best 8.5

MASK, THE: OFFICIAL MOVIE ADAPTATION — Dark Horse

1 ❑ Jul 1994 Cover: 2.50 **NM** value: **Cover or less**
Circ: CapCity orders: **9,350**
A: Kilian Plunkett **W:** Mark Verheiden; Mike Fallon

2 ❑ Aug 1994 Cover: 2.50 **NM** value: **Cover or less**
Circ: CapCity orders: **8,750**
A: Kilian Plunkett **W:** Mark Verheiden; Mike Fallon

MASK OF ZORRO, THE — Image

1 ❑ Aug 1998 Cover: 2.95 **NM** value: **Cover or less**
Circ: Diamd. preorders: **12,159**
A: Ron Wagner **W:** Don McGregor

2 ❑ Sep 1998 Cover: 2.95 **NM** value: **Cover or less**
Circ: Diamd. preorders: **9,134**
A: Ron Wagner **W:** Don McGregor

2/SC❑ Sep 1998 Cover: 2.95 **NM** value: **Cover or less**
alternate cover. • photo

3 ❑ Oct 1998 Cover: 2.95 **NM** value: **Cover or less**
Circ: Diamd. preorders: **8,553**
Photo cover. • indicia says Oct **A:** Ron Wagner **W:** Don McGregor

3/SC❑ Oct 1998 Cover: 2.95 **NM** value: **Cover or less**
alternate cover. • Zorro photo

4 ❑ Dec 1998 Cover: 2.95 **NM** value: **Cover or less**
Circ: Diamd. preorders: **7,477**
cover says Jan, indicia says Dec. **A:** Ron Wagner **W:** Don McGregor

4/SC❑ Dec 1998 Cover: 2.95 **NM** value: **Cover or less**
Photo cover.

MASK RETURNS, THE — Dark Horse

1 ❑ Dec 1992 Cover: 2.50 **NM** value: **4.00**
Circ: CapCity orders: **14,850**
• with Mask mask **A:** Doug Mahnke **W:** John Arcudi

2 ❑ Jan 1993 Cover: 2.50 **NM** value: **3.00**
Circ: CapCity orders: **10,625**
A: Doug Mahnke **W:** John Arcudi

3 ❑ Feb 1993 Cover: 2.50 **NM** value: **3.00**
Circ: CapCity orders: **9,700**
A: Doug Mahnke **W:** John Arcudi

4 ❑ Mar 1993 Cover: 2.50 **NM** value: **3.00**
Circ: CapCity orders: **10,375**
• Walter dons Mask **A:** Doug Mahnke **W:** John Arcudi

Bk 1❑ Cover: 14.95 **NM** value: **Cover or less**
A: Doug Mahnke **W:** John Arcudi

MASK SUMMER VACATION, THE — Dark Horse

Bk 1/HC❑ Jul 1995 Cover: 10.95 **NM** value: **Cover or less**
No issue number. hardcover. **A:** Rick Geary **W:** Rick Geary

MASK, THE: TOYS IN THE ATTIC — Dark Horse

1 ❑ Aug 1998 Cover: 2.95 **NM** value: **Cover or less**
Circ: Diamd. preorders: **4,856**
A: Sibin **W:** Bob Fingerman

2 ❑ Sep 1998 Cover: 2.95 **NM** value: **Cover or less**
Circ: Diamd. preorders: **4,306**
A: Sibin **W:** Bob Fingerman ★ Appearance of Kellaway.

3 ❑ Oct 1998 Cover: 2.95 **NM** value: **Cover or less**
Circ: Diamd. preorders: **3,492**
A: Sibin **W:** Bob Fingerman

4 ❑ Nov 1998 Cover: 2.95 **NM** value: **Cover or less**
Circ: Diamd. preorders: **3,126**
A: Sibin **W:** Bob Fingerman

MASK, THE: VIRTUAL SURREALITY — Dark Horse

1 ❑ Jul 1997 Cover: 2.95 **NM** value: **Cover or less**
Circ: Diamd. preorders: **7,239**
No issue number. One-shot. 📖 The Age of Barbarians; Maskman Vs. Lavender Lass; Gug Soth-Yog Sugoth; Macy's: 3099; Tuber Frenzy **A:** Aaron Lopresti; Sergio Aragonés; Mike Mignola; Ivan Reis; Dave Cooper; David Taylor; Edde Wagner **W:** Michael Eury

MASQUE OF THE RED DEATH, THE — Dell

1 ❑ Oct 1964 Cover: 0.12 **NM** value: **20.00**
Phoo cover.

MASQUERADE — Mad Monkey

1 ❑ Cover: 3.95 **NM** value: **Cover or less**
2 ❑ Cover: 3.95 **NM** value: **Cover or less**
Ash 1❑ Cover: 2.45 **NM** value: **Cover or less**

MASQUES (J.N. WILLIAMSON'S...) — Innovation

1 ❑ Jul 1992 Cover: 4.95 **NM** value: **Cover or less**
Circ: CapCity orders: **6,075**
📖 Rail Rider; Nightcrawlers; The Crushing Death **A:** James Kisner; Mark Evans; Mike Okamoto **W:** Wayne Allen Sallee; Bob Weinberg; Robert R. McCammon

2 ❑ Cover: 4.95 **NM** value: **Cover or less**
Circ: CapCity orders: **3,355**

MASTER, THE — New Comics

1 ❑ b&w Cover: 2.25 **NM** value: **Cover or less**
2 ❑ b&w Cover: 2.25 **NM** value: **Cover or less**

MASTER COMICS — Fawcett

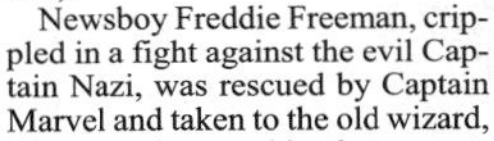

Master Comics was one of the cornerstones of the Fawcett lineup during the 1940s. Originally featuring a mix of adventure, Western, and generic super-hero stories — and, for a while, the home of Bulletman, a popular second-string Fawcett hero — Master Comics began featuring the adventures of Captain Marvel, Jr. with issues #21-22 (crossing over into Whiz Comics #25).

Newsboy Freddie Freeman, crippled in a fight against the evil Captain Nazi, was rescued by Captain Marvel and taken to the old wizard, Shazam, who gave him the power to become the world's mightiest boy by uttering the words "Captain Marvel." Junior's adventures were generally grittier than those of the other Marvels, partly due to the superb realistic artwork of Mac Raboy.

This series also introduced Nyoka the Jungle Girl, Tom Mix, and Hopalong Cassidy.

1 ❑ Mar 1940 Cover: 0.15 **NM** value: **7800.00**
• Oversized format. ★ Origin of Masterman. ★ 1st Appearance of Masterman.

2 ❑ May 1940 Cover: 0.15 **NM** value: **2100.00**
• Oversized format.

3 ❑ Jun 1940 Cover: 0.15 **NM** value: **1400.00**
• Oversized format.

4 ❑ Jul 1940 Cover: 0.10 **NM** value: **1175.00**
• Oversized format.

5 ❑ Aug 1940 Cover: 0.10 **NM** value: **1175.00**
• Oversized format.

6 ❑ Sep 1940 Cover: 0.10 **NM** value: **1100.00**
• Oversized format.

7 ❑ Oct 1940 Cover: 0.10 **NM** value: **1900.00**
• Bulletman features begin

8 ❑ Nov 1940 Cover: 0.10 **NM** value: **1150.00**
• **CGC:** 2 graded, best 3.0

9 ❑ Dec 1940 Cover: 0.10 **NM** value: **925.00**
• **CGC:** 1 graded, best 1.0

10 ❑ Jan 1941 Cover: 0.10 **NM** value: **925.00**

11 ❑ Feb 1941 Cover: 0.10 **NM** value: **2000.00**
• **CGC:** 1 graded, best 1.5
★ Origin of Minute-Man. ★ 1st Appearance of Minute-Man.

12 ❑ Mar 1941 Cover: 0.10 **NM** value: **975.00**
• **CGC:** 1 graded, best 9.2
★ Appearance of Bulletman.

13 ❑ Apr 1941 Cover: 0.10 **NM** value: **1550.00**
• **CGC:** 1 graded, best 9.6
★ Origin of Bulletgirl. ★ 1st Appearance of Bulletgirl.

14 ❑ May 1941 Cover: 0.10 **NM** value: **825.00**
• **CGC:** 2 graded, best 9.4

15 ❑ Jun 1941 Cover: 0.10 **NM** value: **825.00**
• **CGC:** 1 graded, best 9.6

16 ❑ Jul 1941 Cover: 0.10 **NM** value: **775.00**
• **CGC:** 2 graded, best 9.8

17 ❑ Aug 1941 Cover: 0.10 **NM** value: **775.00**
• **CGC:** 2 graded, best 9.0

18 ❑ Sep 1941 Cover: 0.10 **NM** value: **775.00**
• **CGC:** 1 graded, best 9.6

19 ❑ Oct 1941 Cover: 0.10 **NM** value: **775.00**
• **CGC:** 1 graded, best 9.2

20 ❑ Nov 1941 Cover: 0.10 **NM** value: **775.00**
• **CGC:** 2 graded, best 9.4

21 ❑ Dec 1941 Cover: 0.10 **NM** value: **3950.00**
• **CGC:** 3 graded, best 9.6
• Captain Marvel & Bulletman vs. Captain Nazi ★ Origin of Captain Nazi. ★ 1st Appearance of Captain Nazi.

22 ❑ Jan 1942 Cover: 0.10 **NM** value: **3450.00**
• **CGC:** 5 graded, best 9.6
• Captain Marvel Jr. features begin

23 ❑ Feb 1942 Cover: 0.10 **NM** value: **2100.00**
• **CGC:** 3 graded, best 9.4

24 ❑ Mar 1942 Cover: 0.10 **NM** value: **725.00**

25 ❑ Apr 1942 Cover: 0.10 **NM** value: **725.00**
• **CGC:** 2 graded, best 9.2

26 ❑ May 1942 Cover: 0.10 **NM** value: **725.00**
• **CGC:** 2 graded, best 9.6

27 ❑ Jun 1942 Cover: 0.10 **NM** value: **725.00**
• **CGC:** 1 graded, best 9.4

28 ❑ Jul 1942 Cover: 0.10 **NM** value: **725.00**

29 ❑ Aug 1942 Cover: 0.10 **NM** value: **725.00**
• **CGC:** 4 graded, best 9.4

30 ❑ Sep 1942 Cover: 0.10 **NM** value: **725.00**
• **CGC:** 1 graded, best 7.0

31 ❑ Oct 1942 Cover: 0.10 **NM** value: **520.00**
• **CGC:** 1 graded, best 9.4

32 ❑ Nov 1942 Cover: 0.10 **NM** value: **520.00**
• **CGC:** 1 graded, best 9.4

33 ❑ Dec 1942 Cover: 0.10 **NM** value: **520.00**
• **CGC:** 1 graded, best 9.6

34 ❑ Jan 1943 Cover: 0.10 **NM** value: **520.00**
• **CGC:** 1 graded, best 9.6

35 ❑ Feb 1943 Cover: 0.10 **NM** value: **520.00**
• **CGC:** 2 graded, best 9.6

36 ❑ Mar 1943 Cover: 0.10 **NM** value: **520.00**
• **CGC:** 1 graded, best 8.5

37 ❑ Apr 1943 Cover: 0.10 **NM** value: **520.00**
• **CGC:** 1 graded, best 9.2

38 ❑ May 1943 Cover: 0.10 **NM** value: **520.00**
• **CGC:** 2 graded, best 9.0

39 ❑ Jun 1943 Cover: 0.10 **NM** value: **520.00**
• **CGC:** 1 graded, best 9.0

40 ❑ Jul 1943 Cover: 0.10 **NM** value: **520.00**

41 ❑ Aug 1943 Cover: 0.10 **NM** value: **415.00**
• **CGC:** 2 graded, best 9.2

42 ❑ Sep 1943 Cover: 0.10 **NM** value: **320.00**
• **CGC:** 1 graded, best 9.8

43 ❑ Oct 1943 Cover: 0.10 **NM** value: **320.00**

44 ❑ Nov 1943 Cover: 0.10 **NM** value: **320.00**
• **CGC:** 1 graded, best 9.2

45 ❑ Dec 1943 Cover: 0.10 **NM** value: **320.00**
• **CGC:** 2 graded, best 9.0

46 ❑ Jan 1944 Cover: 0.10 **NM** value: **320.00**
• **CGC:** 1 graded, best 9.6

47 ❑ Feb 1944 Cover: 0.10 **NM** value: **320.00**
• **CGC:** 1 graded, best 7.5

48 ❑ Mar 1944 Cover: 0.10 **NM** value: **350.00**
• **CGC:** 2 graded, best 9.6
★ 1st Appearance of Bulletboy.

49 ❑ Apr 1944 Cover: 0.10 **NM** value: **320.00**
• **CGC:** 1 graded, best 8.5

50 ❑ May 1944 Cover: 0.10 **NM** value: **360.00**
★ 1st Appearance of Nyoka the Jungle Girl, Radar.

51 ❑ Jun 1944 Cover: 0.10 **NM** value: **210.00**
• **CGC:** 2 graded, best 9.0

52 ❑ Jul 1944 Cover: 0.10 **NM** value: **210.00**

53 ❑ Aug 1944 Cover: 0.10 **NM** value: **210.00**
• **CGC:** 2 graded, best 8.0

54 ❑ Sep 1944 Cover: 0.10 **NM** value: **210.00**

55 ❑ Oct 1944 Cover: 0.10 **NM** value: **210.00**
• **CGC:** 4 graded, best 9.4

56 ❑ Nov 1944 Cover: 0.10 **NM** value: **175.00**

57 ❑ Jan 1945 Cover: 0.10 **NM** value: **175.00**

58 ❑ Feb 1945 Cover: 0.10 **NM** value: **175.00**

59 ❑ Mar 1945 Cover: 0.10 **NM** value: **175.00**

60 ❑ Apr 1945 Cover: 0.10 **NM** value: **175.00**
• **CGC:** 1 graded, best 9.2

61 ❑ May 1945 Cover: 0.10 **NM** value: **175.00**
• **CGC:** 1 graded, best 9.6

62 ❑ Jul 1945 Cover: 0.10 **NM** value: **175.00**

63 ❑ Sep 1945 Cover: 0.10 **NM** value: **175.00**

64 ❑ Nov 1945 Cover: 0.10 **NM** value: **175.00**

65 ❑ Jan 1946 Cover: 0.10 **NM** value: **175.00**

66 ❑ Mar 1946 Cover: 0.10 **NM** value: **120.00**

67 ❑ Apr 1946 Cover: 0.10 **NM** value: **120.00**
• **CGC:** 1 graded, best 9.2

68 ❑ May 1946 Cover: 0.10 **NM** value: **120.00**
• **CGC:** 1 graded, best 9.4

69 ❑ Jun 1946 Cover: 0.10 **NM** value: **120.00**
• **CGC:** 1 graded, best 9.8

70 ❑ Jul 1946 Cover: 0.10 **NM** value: **120.00**
• **CGC:** 2 graded, best 9.4

71 ❑ Aug 1946 Cover: 0.10 **NM** value: **120.00**

72 ❑ Sep 1946 Cover: 0.10 **NM** value: **120.00**

73 ❑ Oct 1946 Cover: 0.10 **NM** value: **120.00**

74 ❑ Nov 1946 Cover: 0.10 **NM** value: **120.00**

75 ❑ Dec 1946 Cover: 0.10 **NM** value: **120.00**
• **CGC:** 1 graded, best 9.4

76 ❑ Feb 1947 Cover: 0.10 **NM** value: **120.00**

77 ❑ Mar 1947 Cover: 0.10 **NM** value: **120.00**
• **CGC:** 4 graded, best 9.2

78 ❑ Apr 1947 Cover: 0.10 **NM** value: **120.00**
• **CGC:** 1 graded, best 9.6

79 ❑ May 1947 Cover: 0.10 **NM** value: **120.00**
• **CGC:** 3 graded, best 9.0

80 ❑ Jun 1947 Cover: 0.10 **NM** value: **120.00**
• **CGC:** 1 graded, best 9.6

81 ❑ Jul 1947 Cover: 0.10 **NM** value: **100.00**
• **CGC:** 1 graded, best 9.4

82 ❑ Aug 1947 Cover: 0.10 **NM** value: **100.00**
• **CGC:** 1 graded, best 9.6

83 ❑ Sep 1947 Cover: 0.10 **NM** value: **100.00**
• **CGC:** 1 graded, best 9.6

84 ❑ Oct 1947 Cover: 0.10 **NM** value: **100.00**
• **CGC:** 1 graded, best 9.2

CGC-graded: Multiply prices above by **33 for 9.9 M • 16 for 9.8 NM/M • 7 for 9.6 NM+ • 5 for 9.4 NM • 2.5 for 9.2 NM- • 1.5 for 9.0 VF/NM**

85 ❑ Nov 1947 Cover: 0.10 **NM** value: **100.00**
86 ❑ Dec 1947 Cover: 0.10 **NM** value: **100.00**
87 ❑ Jan 1948 Cover: 0.10 **NM** value: **100.00**
• **CGC:** 1 graded, best 9.0
88 ❑ Feb 1948 Cover: 0.10 **NM** value: **100.00**
• **CGC:** 1 graded, best 9.6
89 ❑ Mar 1948 Cover: 0.10 **NM** value: **100.00**
90 ❑ Apr 1948 Cover: 0.10 **NM** value: **100.00**
• **CGC:** 1 graded, best 8.5
91 ❑ May 1948 Cover: 0.10 **NM** value: **90.00**
• **CGC:** 3 graded, best 8.5
92 ❑ Jun 1948 Cover: 0.10 **NM** value: **90.00**
• **CGC:** 1 graded, best 9.0
93 ❑ Jul 1948 Cover: 0.10 **NM** value: **90.00**
• **CGC:** 1 graded, best 9.6
94 ❑ Aug 1948 Cover: 0.10 **NM** value: **90.00**
95 ❑ Sep 1948 Cover: 0.10 **NM** value: **90.00**
• **CGC:** 2 graded, best 9.2
96 ❑ Oct 1948 Cover: 0.10 **NM** value: **90.00**
• **CGC:** 1 graded, best 9.2
97 ❑ Nov 1948 Cover: 0.10 **NM** value: **90.00**
• **CGC:** 1 graded, best 9.6
98 ❑ Dec 1948 Cover: 0.10 **NM** value: **90.00**
• **CGC:** 1 graded, best 9.6
99 ❑ Jan 1949 Cover: 0.10 **NM** value: **90.00**
• **CGC:** 1 graded, best 7.0
100 ❑ Feb 1949 Cover: 0.10 **NM** value: **90.00**
101 ❑ Mar 1949 Cover: 0.10 **NM** value: **85.00**
• **CGC:** 1 graded, best 9.6
102 ❑ Apr 1949 Cover: 0.10 **NM** value: **85.00**
103 ❑ May 1949 Cover: 0.10 **NM** value: **85.00**
• **CGC:** 1 graded, best 7.0
104 ❑ Jun 1949 Cover: 0.10 **NM** value: **85.00**
105 ❑ Jul 1949 Cover: 0.10 **NM** value: **85.00**
• **CGC:** 2 graded, best 8.0
106 ❑ Aug 1949 Cover: 0.10 **NM** value: **85.00**
107 ❑ Sep 1949 Cover: 0.10 **NM** value: **85.00**
108 ❑ Oct 1949 Cover: 0.10 **NM** value: **85.00**
• **CGC:** 1 graded, best 9.2
109 ❑ Nov 1949 Cover: 0.10 **NM** value: **85.00**
• **CGC:** 1 graded, best 9.2
110 ❑ Dec 1949 Cover: 0.10 **NM** value: **85.00**
• **CGC:** 1 graded, best 6.0
111 ❑ Jan 1950 Cover: 0.10 **NM** value: **85.00**
112 ❑ Feb 1950 Cover: 0.10 **NM** value: **85.00**
113 ❑ Mar 1950 Cover: 0.10 **NM** value: **85.00**
114 ❑ Apr 1950 Cover: 0.10 **NM** value: **85.00**
115 ❑ May 1950 Cover: 0.10 **NM** value: **85.00**
• **CGC:** 1 graded, best 7.0
116 ❑ Jun 1950 Cover: 0.10 **NM** value: **85.00**
117 ❑ Aug 1950 Cover: 0.10 **NM** value: **85.00**
• **CGC:** 1 graded, best 7.5
118 ❑ Oct 1950 Cover: 0.10 **NM** value: **85.00**
119 ❑ Dec 1950 Cover: 0.10 **NM** value: **85.00**
120 ❑ Feb 1951 Cover: 0.10 **NM** value: **85.00**
• **CGC:** 1 graded, best 8.5
121 ❑ Apr 1951 Cover: 0.10 **NM** value: **85.00**
122 ❑ Jun 1951 Cover: 0.10 **NM** value: **85.00**
123 ❑ Aug 1951 Cover: 0.10 **NM** value: **85.00**
• **CGC:** 1 graded, best 7.0
124 ❑ Oct 1951 Cover: 0.10 **NM** value: **85.00**
125 ❑ Dec 1951 Cover: 0.10 **NM** value: **85.00**
126 ❑ Feb 1952 Cover: 0.10 **NM** value: **85.00**
127 ❑ Apr 1952 Cover: 0.10 **NM** value: **85.00**
128 ❑ Jun 1952 Cover: 0.10 **NM** value: **85.00**
• **CGC:** 1 graded, best 7.5
129 ❑ Aug 1952 Cover: 0.10 **NM** value: **85.00**
• **CGC:** 1 graded, best 4.0
130 ❑ Oct 1952 Cover: 0.10 **NM** value: **85.00**
• **CGC:** 1 graded, best 4.0
131 ❑ Dec 1952 Cover: 0.10 **NM** value: **85.00**
Captain Marvel Jr.: The Deadly Fraud; Nyoka the Jungle Girl: The Mask of Death!; Ozzie: The Meeting on the High Seas!; Tom Mix: Shadows on the Grave!
132 ❑ Feb 1953 Cover: 0.10 **NM** value: **85.00**
• **CGC:** 2 graded, best 8.0
133 ❑ Apr 1953 Cover: 0.10 **NM** value: **90.00**
• **CGC:** 1 graded, best 8.0
final issue.

MASTER OF KUNG FU — Marvel

Continuing the numbering began by Special Marvel Edition, Master of Kung Fu followed the adventures of Shang Chi, son of Fu Manchu from the Sax Rohmer books. Rejecting his father's evil, the thoughtful martial artist became the charge of Sir Denis Nayland Smith and worked frequently with Smith's partners-in-espiopnage, Black Jack Tarr, Clive Reston, and Leiko Wu.

As written for most of its run by Doug Moench and drawn by Paul Gulacy and later Gene Day, Master of Kung Fu was often regarded as Marvel's most thoughtful, introspective, and, during Day's run, visually inventive title. But sales were never up to those of Spandex-wearing characters, and the series was cancelled at #125. — JJM

17 ❑ Apr 1974 Cover: 0.20 **NM** value: **10.00**
• **CGC:** 5 graded, best 9.6
• Series continued from "Special Marvel Edition". Lair of the Lost! **A:** Jim Starlin ★ 1st Appearance of Black Jack Tarr.
18 ❑ Jun 1974 Cover: 0.25 **NM** value: **5.50**
• **CGC:** 1 graded, best 9.2
Attack! **A:** Paul Gulacy
19 ❑ Aug 1974 Cover: 0.25 **NM** value: **5.50**
• **CGC:** 2 graded, best 9.4
Retreat • Man-Thing **A:** Paul Gulacy ★ Appearance of Man-Thing.
20 ❑ Sep 1974 Cover: 0.25 **NM** value: **5.50**
• **CGC:** 1 graded, best 9.4
Weapon of the Soul **A:** Paul Gulacy
21 ❑ Oct 1974 Cover: 0.25 **NM** value: **3.00**
• **CGC:** 1 graded, best 9.6
Season of Vengeance
22 ❑ Nov 1974 Cover: 0.25 **NM** value: **3.00**
A Fortune of Death! **A:** Paul Gulacy
23 ❑ Dec 1974 Cover: 0.25 **NM** value: **3.00**
River of Death!
24 ❑ Jan 1975 Cover: 0.25 **NM** value: **3.00**
• **CGC:** 1 graded, best 9.6
Massacre Along the Amazon! **A:** Jim Starlin; Walt Simonson
25 ❑ Feb 1975 Cover: 0.25 **NM** value: **3.00**
• **CGC:** 1 graded, best 9.4
Rites of Courage, Fists of Death! **A:** Paul Gulacy
26 ❑ Mar 1975 Cover: 0.25 **NM** value: **3.00**
Daughter of Darkness!
27 ❑ Apr 1975 Cover: 0.25 **NM** value: **3.00**
Confrontation
28 ❑ May 1975 Cover: 0.25 **NM** value: **3.00**
• **CGC:** 1 graded, best 8.5
A Small Spirit Slowly Shaped
29 ❑ Jun 1975 Cover: 0.25 **NM** value: **3.00**
• **CGC:** 1 graded, best 9.6
The Crystal Connection **A:** Paul Gulacy ★ 1st Appearance of Razor-Fist I. ★ Death of Razor-Fist I.
30 ❑ Jul 1975 Cover: 0.25 **NM** value: **3.00**
A Gulf of Lions **A:** Paul Gulacy
31 ❑ Aug 1975 Cover: 0.25 **NM** value: **2.50**
Snowbuster **A:** Paul Gulacy
32 ❑ Sep 1975 Cover: 0.25 **NM** value: **2.50**
Assault on an Angry Sea!
33 ❑ Oct 1975 Cover: 0.25 **NM** value: **2.50**
Wicked Messenger of Madness **A:** Paul Gulacy **W:** Doug Moench ★ 1st Appearance of Leiko Wu.
34 ❑ Nov 1975 Cover: 0.25 **NM** value: **2.50**
Cyclone at the Center of a Madman's Crown! **A:** Paul Gulacy
35 ❑ Dec 1975 Cover: 0.25 **NM** value: **2.50**
Death-Hand and the Son of Mordillo **A:** Paul Gulacy
36 ❑ Jan 1976 Cover: 0.25 **NM** value: **2.50**
• **CGC:** 1 graded, best 9.4
Cages of Myth, Menagerie of Mirrors!
37 ❑ Feb 1976 Cover: 0.25 **NM** value: **2.50**
Web of Dark Death!
38 ❑ Mar 1976 Cover: 0.25 **NM** value: **2.50**
Cat **A:** Paul Gulacy
39 ❑ Apr 1976 Cover: 0.25 **NM** value: **2.50**
Fight Without Pity **A:** Paul Gulacy
40 ❑ May 1976 Cover: 0.25 **NM** value: **2.50**
The Murder Agency **A:** Paul Gulacy
41 ❑ Jun 1976 Cover: 0.25 **NM** value: **2.50**
Slain in Secrecy, and by Illusion!
42 ❑ Jul 1976 Cover: 0.25 **NM** value: **2.50**
The Clock of Shattered Time **A:** Paul Gulacy ★ 1st Appearance of Shockwave.
43 ❑ Aug 1976 Cover: 0.25 **NM** value: **2.50**
A Flash of Purple Sparks **A:** Paul Gulacy
44 ❑ Sep 1976 Cover: 0.30 **NM** value: **2.50**
• **CGC:** 1 graded, best 9.2
Prelude: Golden Daggers (A Death Run) **A:** Paul Gulacy
45 ❑ Oct 1976 Cover: 0.30 **NM** value: **2.50**
Part 1 (Shang-Chi): The Death Seed! **A:** Paul Gulacy
46 ❑ Nov 1976 Cover: 0.30 **NM** value: **2.50**
Part 2 (Clive Reston): The Spider Spell! **A:** Paul Gulacy
47 ❑ Dec 1976 Cover: 0.30 **NM** value: **2.50**
Part 3 (Leiko Wu): Phantom Sand **A:** Paul Gulacy
48 ❑ Jan 1977 Cover: 0.30 **NM** value: **2.50**
Part 4 (Black Jack Tarr): City in the Top of the World **A:** Paul Gulacy
49 ❑ Feb 1977 Cover: 0.30 **NM** value: **2.50**
Part 5 (Sir Denis Nayland Smith): The Affair of the Agent Who Died! **A:** Paul Gulacy **W:** Doug Moench
50 ❑ Mar 1977 Cover: 0.30 **NM** value: **2.50**
Part 6 (Fu Manchu): The Dreamslayer! **A:** Paul Gulacy
51 ❑ Apr 1977 Cover: 0.30 **NM** value: **2.50**
Epilogue: Brass and Blackness (A Death Move!!) **A:** Paul Gulacy
52 ❑ May 1977 Cover: 0.30 **NM** value: **2.00**
A Night at the 1000 Nights
53 ❑ Jun 1977 Cover: 0.30 **NM** value: **2.00**
• **CGC:** 1 graded, best 9.2
Weapon of the Soul • reprints Master of Kung Fu #20
54 ❑ Jul 1977 Cover: 0.30 **NM** value: **2.00**
The Story of War-Yore
55 ❑ Aug 1977 Cover: 0.30 **NM** value: **2.00**
• **CGC:** 1 graded, best 9.2
The Ages of Death!
56 ❑ Sep 1977 Cover: 0.30 **NM** value: **2.00**
Of Heroes Past and Battles Present!
57 ❑ Oct 1977 Cover: 0.30 **NM** value: **2.00**
The Saga of War-Yore III: Call It Thunder!
58 ❑ Nov 1977 Cover: 0.35 **NM** value: **2.00**
59 ❑ Dec 1977 Cover: 0.35 **NM** value: **2.00**
The Phoenix Gambit, Part 1: The Temples of Time
60 ❑ Jan 1978 Cover: 0.35 **NM** value: **2.00**
The Phoenix Gambit, Part 2: End-Game • Dr. Doom ★ Versus Dr. Doom. ★ Versus Doctor Doom.
61 ❑ Feb 1978 Cover: 0.35 **NM** value: **2.00**
• **CGC:** 1 graded, best 9.4
Glass Orchids
62 ❑ Mar 1978 Cover: 0.35 **NM** value: **2.00**
Red Seas
63 ❑ Apr 1978 Cover: 0.35 **NM** value: **2.00**
• **CGC:** 1 graded, best 9.4
Hiding Cats
64 ❑ May 1978 Cover: 0.35 **NM** value: **2.00**
65 ❑ Jun 1978 Cover: 0.35 **NM** value: **2.00**
66 ❑ Jul 1978 Cover: 0.35 **NM** value: **2.00**
67 ❑ Aug 1978 Cover: 0.35 **NM** value: **2.00**
Dark Encounters
68 ❑ Sep 1978 Cover: 0.35 **NM** value: **2.00**
Final Combats ★ Versus The Cat.
69 ❑ Oct 1978 Cover: 0.35 **NM** value: **2.00**
Stairway to Rage!
70 ❑ Nov 1978 Cover: 0.35 **NM** value: **2.00**
Home to Die
71 ❑ Dec 1978 Cover: 0.35 **NM** value: **2.00**
Nightimes
72 ❑ Jan 1979 Cover: 0.35 **NM** value: **2.00**
Circ: Statement: **128,103**
Traitors to the Crown
73 ❑ Feb 1979 Cover: 0.35 **NM** value: **2.00**
Circ: Statement: **128,103**
Prisoners of the Crown
74 ❑ Mar 1979 Cover: 0.35 **NM** value: **2.00**
Circ: Statement: **128,103**
Brynocki Triumphant
75 ❑ Apr 1979 Cover: 0.35 **NM** value: **2.00**
Circ: Statement: **128,103**
Shattered Crowns
76 ❑ May 1979 Cover: 0.40 **NM** value: **2.00**
Circ: Statement: **128,103**
Smoke, Beads and Blood!
77 ❑ Jun 1979 Cover: 0.40 **NM** value: **2.00**
Circ: Statement: **128,103**
Weapons ★ Origin of Zaran. ★ 1st Appearance of Zaran.
78 ❑ Jul 1979 Cover: 0.40 **NM** value: **2.00**
Circ: Statement: **128,103**
Tread the Night Softly
79 ❑ Aug 1979 Cover: 0.40 **NM** value: **2.00**
Circ: Statement: **128,103**
To Sleep… This Side of Death
80 ❑ Sep 1979 Cover: 0.40 **NM** value: **2.00**
Circ: Statement: **128,103**
The Pride of Leopards
81 ❑ Oct 1979 Cover: 0.40 **NM** value: **2.00**
Circ: Statement: **128,103**
Breathless
82 ❑ Nov 1979 Cover: 0.40 **NM** value: **2.00**
Circ: Statement: **128,103**
Like a God, Weeping Fire
83 ❑ Dec 1979 Cover: 0.40 **NM** value: **2.00**
Circ: Statement: **128,103**
Warriors of the Golden Dawn, Part 1: The Phoenix and the Snake ★ Versus Fu Manchu.
84 ❑ Jan 1980 Cover: 0.40 **NM** value: **2.00**
Circ: Statement: **129,874**
Warriors of the Golden Dawn, Part 2: The Bull and the Dragon
85 ❑ Feb 1980 Cover: 0.40 **NM** value: **2.00**
Circ: Statement: **129,874**
Warriors of the Golden Dawn, Part 3: The Ram and the Dove
86 ❑ Mar 1980 Cover: 0.40 **NM** value: **2.00**
Circ: Statement: **129,874**
Warriors of the Golden Dawn, Part 4: The Phoenix and the Dragon • Has 1979 Statement, filed 10/1/79; avg print run 301,744; avg sales 125,699; avg subs 2,404; avg total paid 128,103; samples 560; office use 1,286; max existent 129,949; 56.9% of run returned
87 ❑ Apr 1980 Cover: 0.40 **NM** value: **2.00**
Circ: Statement: **129,874**
Warriors of the Golden Dawn, Part 5: The Chrysalis and the Peacock
88 ❑ May 1980 Cover: 0.40 **NM** value: **2.00**
Circ: Statement: **129,874**
Warriors of the Golden Dawn, Part 6: The Leopard and the Dove
89 ❑ Jun 1980 Cover: 0.40 **NM** value: **2.00**
Circ: Statement: **129,874**
Warriors of the Golden Dawn, Part 7: The Dragons ★ Versus Fu Manchu.
90 ❑ Jul 1980 Cover: 0.40 **NM** value: **2.00**
Circ: Statement: **129,874**
Triumphs of the Flesh
91 ❑ Aug 1980 Cover: 0.40 **NM** value: **2.00**
Circ: Statement: **129,874**
Triumphs of the Spirit **A:** Gene Day
92 ❑ Sep 1980 Cover: 0.50 **NM** value: **2.00**
Circ: Statement: **129,874**
Shadows of a Silent Past **A:** Gene Day
93 ❑ Oct 1980 Cover: 0.50 **NM** value: **2.00**
Circ: Statement: **129,874**
Midnight Wind **A:** Gene Day
94 ❑ Nov 1980 Cover: 0.50 **NM** value: **2.00**
Circ: Statement: **129,874**
Agent Syn's Nightmare **A:** Gene Day
95 ❑ Dec 1980 Cover: 0.50 **NM** value: **2.00**
Circ: Statement: **129,874** • **CGC:** 1 graded, best 9.4
The Samisdat Secret! **A:** Gene Day
96 ❑ Jan 1981 Cover: 0.50 **NM** value: **2.00**
Circ: Statement: **120,600**
Carter's Super Midnight **A:** Gene Day
97 ❑ Feb 1981 Cover: 0.50 **NM** value: **2.00**
Circ: Statement: **120,600**
Lost Art **A:** Gene Day
98 ❑ Mar 1981 Cover: 0.50 **NM** value: **2.00**
Circ: Statement: **120,600**
The Journey as Goal **A:** Gene Day
99 ❑ Apr 1981 Cover: 0.50 **NM** value: **2.00**
Circ: Statement: **120,600**
Bitter Harvest • Has 1980 Statement, filed 10/1/80; avg print run 275,823; avg sales127,506; avg subs 2,368; avg total paid 129,874; samples 575; office use 2,124; max existent 132,573; 52% of run returned **A:** Gene Day
100 ❑ May 1981 Cover: 0.75 **NM** value: **2.50**
Circ: Statement: **120,600** • **CGC:** 1 graded, best 9.8
• Giant-size. Red of Fang and Claw, All Love Lost; Then – The Immortal Caravan; Later – The Ancient Mystery; Now – The Whitechapel Madness **A:** Gene Day

Other grades: Multiply prices above by **1.5 for Mint • 2/3 for Very Fine • 1/3 for Fine • 1/5 for Very Good • 1/8 for Good**

101 ❑ Jun 1981 Cover: 0.50 **NM** value: **1.50**
Circ: Statement: **120,600**
📖 Not Smoke, Nor Beads, Nor Blood! **A:** Gene Day
102 ❑ Jul 1981 Cover: 0.50 **NM** value: **1.50**
Circ: Statement: **120,600**
📖 A Vision of Winter in Spring! **A:** Gene Day ★ 1st Appearance of Day pencils.
103 ❑ Aug 1981 Cover: 0.50 **NM** value: **1.50**
Circ: Statement: **120,600**
📖 A City Asea **A:** Gene Day
104 ❑ Sep 1981 Cover: 0.50 **NM** value: **1.50**
Circ: Statement: **120,600**
📖 Fight Without Reason!
105 ❑ Oct 1981 Cover: 0.50 **NM** value: **1.50**
Circ: Statement: **120,600**
📖 The Razor-Fist Connection ★ 1st Appearance of Razor-Fist II, Razor-Fist III. ★ Death of Razor-Fist III.
106 ❑ Nov 1981 Cover: 0.50 **NM** value: **1.50**
Circ: Statement: **120,600**
📖 The Assassin Master **A:** Gene Day ★ Origin of Razor-Fist II, Razor-Fist III. ★ Appearance of Velcro.
107 ❑ Dec 1981 Cover: 0.50 **NM** value: **1.50**
Circ: Statement: **120,600**
📖 A Painless Result of Having Lived **A:** Gene Day ★ Appearance of Sata.
108 ❑ Jan 1982 Cover: 0.60 **NM** value: **1.50**
📖 Chameleons **A:** Gene Day
109 ❑ Feb 1982 Cover: 0.60 **NM** value: **1.50**
📖 The Dark Angel's Kiss **A:** Gene Day
110 ❑ Mar 1982 Cover: 0.60 **NM** value: **1.50**
• **CGC:** 1 graded, best 9.6
📖 Perilous Reign • Has 1981 Statement, filed 10/1/81; avg print run 255,967; avg sales 118,654; avg subs 1,946; avg total paid 120,600; samples 523; office use 6,052; max existent 127,175; 50% of run returned **A:** Gene Day
111 ❑ Apr 1982 Cover: 0.60 **NM** value: **1.50**
📖 Deadly Rain **A:** Gene Day
112 ❑ May 1982 Cover: 0.60 **NM** value: **1.50**
📖 Commit and Destroy **A:** Gene Day
113 ❑ Jun 1982 Cover: 0.60 **NM** value: **1.50**
📖 Learn & Burn **A:** Gene Day
114 ❑ Jul 1982 Cover: 0.60 **NM** value: **1.50**
📖 A Fantasy of the Autumn Moon
115 ❑ Aug 1982 Cover: 0.60 **NM** value: **1.50**
📖 Deals **A:** Gene Day
116 ❑ Sep 1982 Cover: 0.60 **NM** value: **1.50**
📖 Blood of His Blood **A:** Gene Day
117 ❑ Oct 1982 Cover: 0.60 **NM** value: **1.50**
📖 Devil Deeds Done in Darkness **A:** Gene Day
118 ❑ Nov 1982 Cover: 1.00 **NM** value: **1.50**
• double-sized. 📖 Flesh of My Flesh **A:** Gene Day ★ Death of Fu Manchu.
119 ❑ Dec 1982 Cover: 0.60 **NM** value: **1.50**
📖 Brynocki's Marauders **A:** Gene Day
120 ❑ Jan 1983 Cover: 0.60 **NM** value: **1.50**
📖 Dweller By The Dark Stream **A:** Gene Day
121 ❑ Feb 1983 Cover: 0.60 **NM** value: **1.50**
📖 Passing Strangers!
122 ❑ Mar 1983 Cover: 0.60 **NM** value: **1.50**
📖 The Madhouse Effect
123 ❑ Apr 1983 Cover: 0.60 **NM** value: **1.50**
📖 The Sins of the Son!
124 ❑ May 1983 Cover: 0.60 **NM** value: **1.50**
📖 Retribution!
125 ❑ Jun 1983 Cover: 1.00 **NM** value: **2.00**
• Double-size. 📖 Atonement final issue. **A:** William Johnson **W:** Alan Zelentz
Anl 1 ❑ ca. 1976 Cover: 0.50 **NM** value: **5.00**
📖 The Fortress of Sahra Sharn! • 1976 Annual **A:** Keith Pollard **W:** Doug Moench
GS 1 ❑ Sep 1974 Cover: 0.50 **NM** value: **8.00**
GS 2 ❑ Dec 1974 Cover: 0.50 **NM** value: **4.00**
GS 3 ❑ Mar 1975 Cover: 0.50 **NM** value: **4.00**
GS 4 ❑ Jun 1975 Cover: 0.50 **NM** value: **4.00**

MASTER OF KUNG FU: BLEEDING BLACK — Marvel

1 ❑ Feb 1991 Cover: 2.95 **NM** value: **3.00**
📖 Bleeding Black+D6037 **A:** Dan Day; David Day **W:** Doug Moench

MASTER OF MYSTICS: THE DEMONCRAFT — Chakra

1 ❑ Cover: 1.50 **NM** value: **Cover or less**
A: Jadurani Harinam **W:** Jadurani Harinam
2 ❑ Cover: 1.50 **NM** value: **Cover or less**
A: Jadurani Harinam **W:** Jadurani Harinam

MASTER OF THE VOID — Iron Hammer

1 ❑ Dec 1993 Cover: 2.95 **NM** value: **Cover or less**
📖 Surtur **A:** Stephen Stanley **W:** Stephen Stanley

MASTERS OF THE UNIVERSE — Marvel / Star

Animated TV stars Masters of the Universe returned to the comics with this 1986 series. Prince Adam is the heir to the throne of the fantastic land of Eternia. He is accompanied on his adventures by a group of loyal friends, including the diminutive magician Orko and the talking cat Battlecat.

Unfortunately, Prince Adam also has his enemies, including Hordak and the dread Skeletor. These evildoers would like nothing better than to take over the bright land of Eternia. Luckily, Prince Adam and his friends are more than a match for them—especially when Adam uses his Power Sword to transform himself into the mighty warrior He-Man.

1 ❑ May 1986 Cover: 0.75 **NM** value: **1.00**
Circ: CapCity orders: **19,250** • **CGC:** 5 graded, best 9.8
📖 The Coming of Hordak!
2 ❑ Jul 1986 Cover: 0.75 **NM** value: **1.00**
Circ: CapCity orders: **14,250** • **CGC:** 1 graded, best 9.6
3 ❑ Sep 1986 Cover: 0.75 **NM** value: **1.00**
Circ: CapCity orders: **9,250**
📖 The Garden Of Evil **A:** Ron Wilson **W:** Mike Carlin
4 ❑ Nov 1986 Cover: 0.75 **NM** value: **1.00**
Circ: CapCity orders: **6,700**
5 ❑ Jan 1987 Cover: 0.75 **NM** value: **1.00**
Circ: CapCity orders: **5,450**
6 ❑ Mar 1987 Cover: 0.75 **NM** value: **1.00**
Circ: CapCity orders: **4,700**
7 ❑ May 1987 Cover: 1.00 **NM** value: **Cover or less**
Circ: CapCity orders: **3,550**
8 ❑ Jul 1987 Cover: 1.00 **NM** value: **Cover or less**
Circ: CapCity orders: **3,000**
9 ❑ Sep 1987 Cover: 1.00 **NM** value: **Cover or less**
Circ: CapCity orders: **2,650**
10 ❑ Nov 1987 Cover: 1.00 **NM** value: **Cover or less**
Circ: CapCity orders: **2,550**
11 ❑ Jan 1988 Cover: 1.00 **NM** value: **Cover or less**
Circ: CapCity orders: **2,300**
12 ❑ Mar 1988 Cover: 1.00 **NM** value: **Cover or less**
Circ: CapCity orders: **2,400**
final issue.
13 ❑ May 1988 Cover: 1.00 **NM** value: **Cover or less**
Circ: CapCity orders: **1,950**

MASTERS OF THE UNIVERSE (MINI-SERIES) — DC

1 ❑ Dec 1982 Cover: 1.50 **NM** value: **Cover or less**
• **CGC:** 7 graded, best 9.4
📖 To Tempt The Gods **A:** George Tuska; Alfredo Alcala **W:** Paul Kupperberg
2 ❑ Jan 1983 Cover: 1.00 **NM** value: **Cover or less**
3 ❑ Feb 1983 Cover: 1.00 **NM** value: **Cover or less**

MASTER'S SERIES — Avalon

1 ❑ Cover: 2.50 **NM** value: **Cover or less**
📖 One-Man Mission!; The Prisoner in Chateau in Beaujais; Lone Defender!; The Underwater Avenger; D-Day for the Fighting Airborne; Iwo Jima • Wally Wood War **A:** Wally Wood **W:** Wally Wood

MASTERWORKS SERIES OF GREAT COMIC BOOK ARTISTS, THE — DC / Seagate

1 ❑ Spr 1983 Cover: 1.50 **NM** value: **2.50**
• **CGC:** 1 graded, best 9.0
📖 Shining Knights • Reprints Shining Knight stories from Adventure Comics (1950-1951) **A:** Frank Frazetta
2 ❑ Jul 1983 Cover: 1.50 **NM** value: **2.50**
📖 Spores From Space **A:** Frank Frazetta
3 ❑ Oct 1983 Cover: 1.50 **NM** value: **2.50**
📖 Molded In Evil **A:** Bernie Wrightson

MATT CHAMPION — Metro

1 ❑ Cover: 2.00 **NM** value: **Cover or less**

MATTERBABY — Antarctic

1 ❑ Feb 1997, b&w Cover: 2.95 **NM** value: **Cover or less**
Anl 1 ❑ Cover: 2.95 **NM** value: **Cover or less**
📖 Core of Evil; Drop of Doom; Mall on the Moon; Die, Lobster Die!; Concrete Conquest; **A:** John Marshall **W:** John Marshall

MATT SLADE, GUNFLIGHTER — Atlas

1 ❑ May 1956 Cover: 0.10 **NM** value: **150.00**
2 ❑ Jul 1956 Cover: 0.10 **NM** value: **75.00**
3 ❑ Sep 1956 Cover: 0.10 **NM** value: **50.00**
4 ❑ Nov 1956 Cover: 0.10 **NM** value: **50.00**

MAUS: A SURVIVOR'S TALE — Pantheon

Art Spiegelman's Maus stands at the height of the comics art form. It's the sort of work that makes people who don't read comics swear that a work this moving can't really be "just a comic book." Perhaps it's not so surprising then that the two-volume work was the first comic book to win the Pulitzer Prize in Literature.

Maus is the tale of Art's father and how he survived the Holocaust during World War II. It's also a story of Art as a grown man, struggling to come to terms with his aging father. Spiegelman uses the device of portraying his characters as cartoon animals: the Nazis as cats, the Jews as mice. This provides an apt parallel to a saga in which millions of innocents were systematically dehumanized and sent to be slaughtered at places like Buchenwald and Auschwitz. Ironically, it probably also gives the reader a stronger emotional bond to the characters involved than if they were portrayed as humans.

1 ❑ ca. 1986 Cover: 8.95 **NM** value: **Cover or less**
📖 My Father Bleeds History **A:** Art Spiegelman **W:** Art Spiegelman
1/HC ❑ Cover: 20.00 **NM** value: **Cover or less**
hardcover. 📖 My Father Bleeds History **A:** Art Spiegelman **W:** Art Spiegelman
1-2 ❑ Cover: 14.95 **NM** value: **Cover or less**
2 ❑ ca. 1991 Cover: 14.00 **NM** value: **Cover or less**
📖 And Here My Troubles Began **A:** Art Spiegelman **W:** Art Spiegelman
2/HC ❑ Cover: 20.00 **NM** value: **Cover or less**
hardcover. 📖 And Here My Troubles Began **A:** Art Spiegelman **W:** Art Spiegelman
2-2 ❑ Cover: 14.95 **NM** value: **Cover or less**

MAVERICK — Marvel

1 ❑ Sep 1997 Cover: 2.99 **NM** value: **3.00**
Circ: Diamd. preorders: **55,961**
wraparound cover. • gatefold summary. 📖 Overture **W:** Jorge Gonzalez
2 ❑ Oct 1997 Cover: 1.99 **NM** value: **Cover or less**
Circ: Diamd. preorders: **51,930**
wraparound cover. • gatefold summary.
2/SC ❑ Oct 1997 Cover: 1.95 **NM** value: **Cover or less**
variant cover.
3 ❑ Nov 1997 Cover: 1.99 **NM** value: **Cover or less**
Circ: Diamd. preorders: **41,101**
wraparound cover. • gatefold summary. ★ Appearance of Alpha Flight.
4 ❑ Dec 1997 Cover: 1.99 **NM** value: **Cover or less**
Circ: Diamd. preorders: **41,450**
wraparound cover. • gatefold summary. ★ Appearance of Alpha Flight.
5 ❑ Jan 1998 Cover: 1.99 **NM** value: **Cover or less**
Circ: Diamd. preorders: **37,359**
• gatefold summary.
6 ❑ Feb 1998 Cover: 1.99 **NM** value: **Cover or less**
Circ: Diamd. preorders: **34,762**
• gatefold summary.
7 ❑ Mar 1998 Cover: 1.99 **NM** value: **Cover or less**
Circ: Diamd. preorders: **31,711**
• gatefold summary.
8 ❑ Apr 1998 Cover: 1.99 **NM** value: **Cover or less**
Circ: Diamd. preorders: **28,886**
• gatefold summary.
9 ❑ May 1998 Cover: 1.99 **NM** value: **Cover or less**
Circ: Diamd. preorders: **27,313**
• gatefold summary.
10 ❑ Jun 1998 Cover: 1.99 **NM** value: **Cover or less**
Circ: Diamd. preorders: **26,571**
• gatefold summary.
11 ❑ Jul 1998 Cover: 1.99 **NM** value: **Cover or less**
Circ: Diamd. preorders: **24,448**
• gatefold summary.
12 ❑ Aug 1998 Cover: 1.99 **NM** value: **2.99**
Circ: Diamd. preorders: **23,594**
• Giant-size. final issue.

MAVERICK (DELL) — Dell

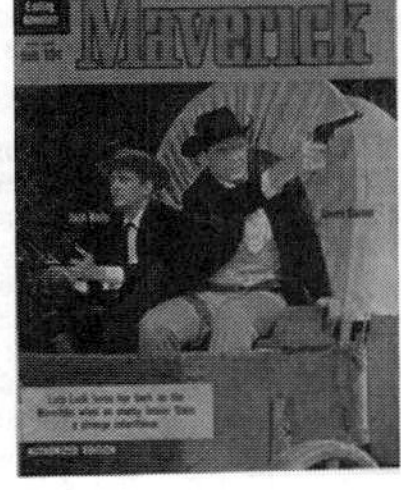

The comic-book title picked up from the character's appearances in Dell's special-numbered Four-Color series. The Warner Brothers Western TV series ran from 1957 to 1962 and opened with James Garner playing Bret Maverick, though he left the series before it concluded. Bret and Bart were poker-playing brothers who roamed the West. Though perceived as gamblers, they contended poker was a game of skill and they were averse to anything that was truly a game of chance. (As Bret said in the 1981 Bret Maverick show, "Luck don't have a thing to do with how you play the game; Maverick didn't come here to lose.") Stories often involved them and other Mavericks in con games.

One of the attractions of the comic books is their photo covers.

— Maggie

7 ❑ Oct 1959 Cover: 0.10 **NM** value: **95.00**
• **CGC:** 1 graded, best 9.0
8 ❑ Jan 1960 Cover: 0.10 **NM** value: **95.00**
• **CGC:** 1 graded, best 9.4
9 ❑ Mar 1960 Cover: 0.10 **NM** value: **95.00**
10 ❑ May 1960 Cover: 0.10 **NM** value: **95.00**
• **CGC:** 1 graded, best 8.0
11 ❑ Jul 1960 Cover: 0.10 **NM** value: **75.00**
• **CGC:** 1 graded, best 8.5
12 ❑ Sep 1960 Cover: 0.10 **NM** value: **75.00**
• **CGC:** 1 graded, best 9.0
13 ❑ Nov 1960 Cover: 0.10 **NM** value: **75.00**
• **CGC:** 1 graded, best 9.4
14 ❑ Jan 1961 Cover: 0.10 **NM** value: **75.00**
• **CGC:** 1 graded, best 9.4
15 ❑ Jun 1961 Cover: 0.15 **NM** value: **75.00**
16 ❑ Sep 1961 Cover: 0.15 **NM** value: **50.00**
17 ❑ Dec 1961 Cover: 0.15 **NM** value: **50.00**
18 ❑ Mar 1962 Cover: 0.15 **NM** value: **50.00**
19 ❑ Jun 1962 Cover: 0.15 **NM** value: **50.00**

MAVERICK MARSHAL — Charlton

1 ❑ 1957 Cover: 0.10 **NM** value: **30.00**
2 ❑ 1958 Cover: 0.10 **NM** value: **20.00**
3 ❑ Mar 1958 Cover: 0.10 **NM** value: **20.00**
4 ❑ 1958 Cover: 0.10 **NM** value: **20.00**
5 ❑ 1959 Cover: 0.10 **NM** value: **20.00**
6 ❑ 1959 Cover: 0.10 **NM** value: **20.00**
7 ❑ 1959 Cover: 0.10 **NM** value: **20.00**

MAVERICK (MINI-SERIES) — Marvel

1 ❑ Jan 1997 Cover: 2.95 **NM** value: **Cover or less**
Circ: Direct Market orders: **76,000**
One-shot. • Giant-size. 📖 The Sword Sung on a Barren Heath **A:** Wilfred Santiago **W:** Larry Hama

CGC-graded: Multiply prices above by **33 for 9.9 M** • **16 for 9.8 NM/M** • **7 for 9.6 NM+** • **5 for 9.4 NM** • **2.5 for 9.2 NM-** • **1.5 for 9.0 VF/NM**

MAVERICKS (DAGGER) — Dagger

1 ❑ Jan 1994 Cover: 2.50 **NM** value: **Cover or less**
Circ: CapCity orders: **5,710**
2 ❑ Feb 1994 Cover: 2.50 **NM** value: **Cover or less**
Circ: CapCity orders: **2,660**
3 ❑ Mar 1994 Cover: 2.50 **NM** value: **Cover or less**
4 ❑ Apr 1994 Cover: 2.50 **NM** value: **Cover or less**
5 ❑ May 1994 Cover: 2.50 **NM** value: **Cover or less**
A: Charley Parker **W:** Paul Danner

MAVERICKS: THE NEW WAVE — Dagger

1 ❑ Cover: 2.50 **NM** value: **Cover or less**
Circ: CapCity orders: **2,935**
2 ❑ Cover: 2.50 **NM** value: **Cover or less**
3 ❑ Cover: 2.50 **NM** value: **Cover or less**

MAX BREWSTER: THE UNIVERSAL SOLDIER — Fleetway-Quality

1 ❑ Cover: 2.95 **NM** value: **Cover or less**
2 ❑ Cover: 2.95 **NM** value: **Cover or less**
3 ❑ Cover: 2.95 **NM** value: **Cover or less**
📖 Never Say Die **A:** Ewins & Sandler **W:** Alan McKenzie

MAX BURGER PI — Graphic Image

1 ❑ b&w Cover: 2.00 **NM** value: **Cover or less**
A: Bill Byrne **W:** Bill Byrne ★ 1st Appearance of Max Burger.
2 ❑ b&w Cover: 2.50 **NM** value: **Cover or less**
A: Bill Byrne **W:** Bill Byrne

MAX DAMAGE: PANIC! — Head Press

1 ❑ Jul 1995, b&w Cover: 2.75 **NM** value: **Cover or less**
A: Michael Anthony Lagocki **W:** Robert Luedke; Michael Anthony Lagoki

MAXIMAGE — Image

1 ❑ Dec 1995 Cover: 2.50 **NM** value: **Cover or less**
📖 Second Coming **A:** Fabio Laguna; Rob Liefeld(cover) **W:** Rob Liefeld; Eric Stephenson ★ Origin of Maximage. ★ 1st Appearance of The Ancient, Maximage.
2 ❑ Jan 1996 Cover: 2.50 **NM** value: **Cover or less**
📖 Extreme Destroyer, Part 2 • polybagged with card
3 ❑ Feb 1996 Cover: 2.50 **NM** value: **Cover or less**
4 ❑ Mar 1996 Cover: 2.50 **NM** value: **Cover or less**
📖 Rage of Angels, Part 5 • continued from Glory #10
5 ❑ Apr 1996 Cover: 2.50 **NM** value: **Cover or less**
6 ❑ May 1996 Cover: 2.50 **NM** value: **Cover or less**
7 ❑ Jun 1996 Cover: 2.50 **NM** value: **Cover or less**
8 ❑ Jul 1996 Cover: 2.50 **NM** value: **Cover or less**
9 ❑ Aug 1996 Cover: 2.50 **NM** value: **Cover or less**
10 ❑ Sep 1996 Cover: 2.50 **NM** value: **Cover or less**
Circ: Diamd. preorders: **18,138**

MAXIMORTAL, THE — Tundra

1 ❑ Aug 1992 Cover: 3.95 **NM** value: **4.00**
Circ: CapCity orders: **9,625**
📖 Cheek, Chin, Knuckle, or Knee **A:** Rick Veitch **W:** Rick Veitch
2 ❑ Oct 1992 Cover: 3.95 **NM** value: **4.00**
Circ: CapCity orders: **5,475**
A: Rick Veitch **W:** Rick Veitch
3 ❑ Dec 1992 Cover: 3.95 **NM** value: **4.00**
Circ: CapCity orders: **5,000**
A: Rick Veitch **W:** Rick Veitch ★ Appearance of Holmes.
4 ❑ Mar 1993 Cover: 3.95 **NM** value: **4.00**
Circ: CapCity orders: **3,922**
A: Rick Veitch **W:** Rick Veitch
5 ❑ May 1993 Cover: 2.95 **NM** value: **3.00**
Circ: CapCity orders: **4,150**
A: Rick Veitch **W:** Rick Veitch
6 ❑ Jul 1993 Cover: 2.95 **NM** value: **3.00**
Circ: CapCity orders: **3,850**
A: Rick Veitch **W:** Rick Veitch
7 ❑ Dec 1993 Cover: 2.95 **NM** value: **Cover or less**
Circ: CapCity orders: **3,500**

MAXIMUM SECURITY — Marvel

1 ❑ Dec 2000 Cover: 2.99 **NM** value: **Cover or less**
Circ: Diamd. preorders: **45,872**
📖 Illegal Aliens **A:** Jerry Ordway **W:** Kurt Busiek
2 ❑ Dec 2000 Cover: 2.99 **NM** value: **Cover or less**
Circ: Diamd. preorders: **43,115**
📖 A World of Hurt **A:** Jerry Ordway **W:** Kurt Busiek
3 ❑ Jan 2001 Cover: 2.99 **NM** value: **Cover or less**
Circ: Diamd. preorders: **40,317**
📖 Whatever the Cost! **A:** Jerry Ordway **W:** Kurt Busiek

MAXIMUM SECURITY DANGEROUS PLANET — Marvel

1 ❑ Oct 2000 Cover: 2.99 **NM** value: **Cover or less**
Circ: Diamd. preorders: **36,701**
📖 A Very Dangerous Planet • lead-in to Maximum Security **A:** Jerry Ordway **W:** Kurt Busiek

MAXIMUM SECURITY: THOR VS. EGO — Marvel

1 ❑ Nov 2000 Cover: 2.99 **NM** value: **Cover or less**
Circ: Diamd. preorders: **17,775**
📖 Behold ... The Living Planet!; And Now ... Galactus!; Shall a God Prevail? • reprints Thor #133, #160, and #161; Reprints Thor #133, 160, 161 **A:** Jack Kirby; Vince Colletta **W:** Stan Lee ★ Appearance of Recorder, Ego.

MAXION — CPM Manga

1 ❑ Dec 1999, b&w Cover: 2.95 **NM** value: **Cover or less**
Circ: Diamd. preorders: **3,328**
📖 A Beautiful Girl Suddenly Appears **A:** Takeshi Takebayashi **W:** Takeshi Takebayashi
2 ❑ Jan 2000, b&w Cover: 2.95 **NM** value: **Cover or less**
Circ: Diamd. preorders: **2,477**
📖 Private Beach of Love **A:** Takeshi Takebayashi **W:** Takeshi Takebayashi
3 ❑ Feb 2000, b&w Cover: 2.95 **NM** value: **Cover or less**
Circ: Diamd. preorders: **2,189**
📖 The Infinite Power of Love **A:** Takeshi Takebayashi **W:** Takeshi Takebayashi
4 ❑ Mar 2000, b&w Cover: 2.95 **NM** value: **Cover or less**
Circ: Diamd. preorders: **2,258**
📖 Latent Power **A:** Takeshi Takebayashi **W:** Takeshi Takebayashi
5 ❑ Apr 2000, b&w Cover: 2.95 **NM** value: **Cover or less**
Circ: Diamd. preorders: **2,120**
📖 I Want Them Both **A:** Takeshi Takebayashi **W:** Takeshi Takebayashi
6 ❑ May 2000, b&w Cover: 2.95 **NM** value: **Cover or less**
Circ: Diamd. preorders: **2,095**
📖 Hold Me **A:** Takeshi Takebayashi **W:** Takeshi Takebayashi
7 ❑ Jun 2000 Cover: 2.95 **NM** value: **Cover or less**
Circ: Diamd. preorders: **2,144**
8 ❑ Jul 2000 Cover: 2.95 **NM** value: **Cover or less**
Circ: Diamd. preorders: **2,071**
9 ❑ Aug 2000 Cover: 2.95 **NM** value: **Cover or less**
10 ❑ Sep 2000 Cover: 2.95 **NM** value: **Cover or less**
11 ❑ Oct 2000 Cover: 2.95 **NM** value: **Cover or less**
Circ: Diamd. preorders: **1,831**
12 ❑ Nov 2000 Cover: 2.95 **NM** value: **Cover or less**
Circ: Diamd. preorders: **1,768**
13 ❑ Dec 2000 Cover: 2.95 **NM** value: **Cover or less**
Circ: Diamd. preorders: **1,731**
14 ❑ Jan 2001 Cover: 2.95 **NM** value: **Cover or less**
Circ: Diamd. preorders: **1,692**
15 ❑ Feb 2001 Cover: 2.95 **NM** value: **Cover or less**
Circ: Diamd. preorders: **1,668**
16 ❑ Mar 2001 Cover: 2.95 **NM** value: **Cover or less**
Circ: Diamd. preorders: **1,656**
17 ❑ Apr 2001 Cover: 2.95 **NM** value: **Cover or less**
Circ: Diamd. preorders: **1,662**
18 ❑ May 2001 Cover: 2.95 **NM** value: **Cover or less**
Circ: Diamd. preorders: **1,564**
19 ❑ Jun 2001 Cover: 2.95 **NM** value: **Cover or less**
Circ: Diamd. preorders: **1,577**
20 ❑ Jul 2001 Cover: 2.95 **NM** value: **Cover or less**
Circ: Diamd. preorders: **1,652**
Bk 1 ❑ Oct 2000, b&w Cover: 15.95 **NM** value: **Cover or less**
📖 I Want Them Both • collects #1-6 **A:** Takeshi Takebayashi **W:** Takeshi Takebayashi

MAX OF THE REGULATORS — Atlantic

1 ❑ Cover: 1.50 **NM** value: **Cover or less**
2 ❑ Cover: 1.75 **NM** value: **Cover or less**
3 ❑ Cover: 1.75 **NM** value: **Cover or less**
4 ❑ Cover: 1.75 **NM** value: **Cover or less**

MAX REP IN THE AGE OF THE ASTROTITANS — Dumbbell Press

1 ❑ Jun 1997, b&w Cover: 2.75 **NM** value: **Cover or less**
2 ❑ Mar 1998, b&w Cover: 2.75 **NM** value: **Cover or less**

MAX THE MAGNIFICENT — Slave Labor

1 ❑ Jul 1987 Cover: 1.50 **NM** value: **Cover or less**
A: Jim Valentino **W:** Jim Valentino

MAXWELL MOUSE FOLLIES — Renegade

1 ❑ Feb 1986, b&w Cover: 1.70 **NM** value: **2.00**
2 ❑ Apr 1986, b&w Cover: 1.70 **NM** value: **2.00**
3 ❑ Jun 1986, b&w Cover: 1.70 **NM** value: **2.00**
4 ❑ Sep 1986, b&w Cover: 2.00 **NM** value: **Cover or less**
5 ❑ Dec 1986 Cover: 2.00 **NM** value: **Cover or less**
6 ❑ Mar 1987 Cover: 2.00 **NM** value: **Cover or less**

MAXWELL THE MAGIC CAT — Acme

1 ❑ Cover: 4.95 **NM** value: **Cover or less**
W: Alan Moore
2 ❑ Cover: 4.95 **NM** value: **Cover or less**
W: Alan Moore
3 ❑ Cover: 4.95 **NM** value: **Cover or less**
W: Alan Moore
4 ❑ Cover: 5.95 **NM** value: **Cover or less**
W: Alan Moore

MAXX — Image

Huge. Powerful. Purple. It's that last part about being purple (along with his general confusion about life) that separates The Maxx from the other musclebound mooks you're likely to encounter. Of undetermined origin, The Maxx seems convinced that he's some sort of super-hero, but other than getting beaten up by bad guys, he is not exactly sure of what he's supposed to do. Frankly, he would much rather just go home and watch Cheers.

Created, written, and drawn by Sam Kieth, The Maxx comes off like Image's answer to Groo the Wanderer. Upon further examination, however, it turns out that Kieth has created one of the more complex psychodramas to be seen in comic books. The real story revolves around a girl, Julie, who suffered abuse as a child and has grown into an incredibly shy adult. The Outback is her dreamland, where she appears as a jungle princess. The Maxx is actually just a homeless bum whom Julie took in.

The comics series eventually spawned an MTV animated series of the same name.

0.5 ❑ Jun 1993 Cover: 1.95 **NM** value: **4.00**
• **CGC:** 8 graded, best 9.6
• Wizard promotional edition. **A:** Sam Kieth **W:** Sam Kieth
0.5/GO ❑ Jun 1993 Cover: 1.95 **NM** value: **12.00**
• Gold edition. **A:** Sam Kieth **W:** Sam Kieth
1 ❑ Mar 1993 Cover: 1.95 **NM** value: **3.00**
Circ: CapCity orders: **295,400** • **CGC:** 19 graded, best 9.8
A: Sam Kieth; Jim Sinclair **W:** William Messner-Loebs; Sam Kieth
1/3D ❑ Jan 1998 Cover: 4.95 **NM** value: **5.00**
Circ: Diamd. preorders: **9,958**
• 3-D edition. • bound-in glasses **A:** Sam Kieth; Jim Sinclair **W:** William Messner-Loebs; Sam Kieth
1/SC ❑ Mar 1993 Cover: 1.95 **NM** value: **8.00**
• **CGC:** 4 graded, best 9.6
glow in the dark cover. • Glow-in-the-dark promotional edition. **A:** Sam Kieth; Jim Sinclair **W:** William Messner-Loebs; Sam Kieth
2 ❑ Apr 1993 Cover: 1.95 **NM** value: **2.50**
Circ: CapCity orders: **169,425** • **CGC:** 1 graded, best 9.0
A: Sam Kieth **W:** Sam Kieth
3 ❑ May 1993 Cover: 1.95 **NM** value: **2.50**
Circ: CapCity orders: **130,700**
A: Sam Kieth **W:** Sam Kieth
4 ❑ Aug 1993 Cover: 1.95 **NM** value: **2.50**
Circ: CapCity orders: **115,975**
A: Sam Kieth **W:** Sam Kieth
5 ❑ Sep 1993 Cover: 1.95 **NM** value: **2.50**
Circ: CapCity orders: **89,350**
A: Sam Kieth **W:** Sam Kieth
6 ❑ Nov 1993 Cover: 1.95 **NM** value: **2.50**
Circ: CapCity orders: **78,125**
cover says Oct, indicia says Nov. **A:** Sam Kieth **W:** Sam Kieth
7 ❑ Mar 1994 Cover: 1.95 **NM** value: **2.50**
Circ: CapCity orders: **51,150**
A: Sam Kieth **W:** Sam Kieth ★ Appearance of Pitt.
8 ❑ May 1994 Cover: 1.95 **NM** value: **2.50**
Circ: CapCity orders: **44,250**
A: Sam Kieth **W:** Sam Kieth ★ Appearance of Pitt.
9 ❑ Jun 1994 Cover: 1.95 **NM** value: **2.50**
Circ: CapCity orders: **39,700**
A: Sam Kieth **W:** Sam Kieth
10 ❑ Aug 1994 Cover: 1.95 **NM** value: **2.50**
Circ: CapCity orders: **40,800**
A: Sam Kieth **W:** Sam Kieth
11 ❑ Oct 1994 Cover: 1.95 **NM** value: **2.00**
Circ: CapCity orders: **36,050**
A: Sam Kieth **W:** Sam Kieth
12 ❑ Dec 1994 Cover: 1.95 **NM** value: **2.00**
Circ: CapCity orders: **33,650**
A: Sam Kieth **W:** Sam Kieth
13 ❑ Jan 1995 Cover: 1.95 **NM** value: **2.00**
Circ: CapCity orders: **25,625**
A: Sam Kieth **W:** Sam Kieth
14 ❑ Feb 1995 Cover: 1.95 **NM** value: **2.00**
Circ: CapCity orders: **23,225**
A: Sam Kieth **W:** Sam Kieth
15 ❑ Apr 1995 Cover: 1.95 **NM** value: **2.00**
Circ: CapCity orders: **21,200**
cover says February, indicia says Apr. **A:** Sam Kieth **W:** Sam Kieth
16 ❑ Jun 1995 Cover: 1.95 **NM** value: **2.00**
Circ: CapCity orders: **18,475**
cover says Feb, indicia says Jun. **A:** Sam Kieth **W:** Sam Kieth
17 ❑ Jul 1995 Cover: 1.95 **NM** value: **2.00**
Circ: CapCity orders: **20,750**
A: Sam Kieth **W:** Sam Kieth
18 ❑ Aug 1995 Cover: 1.95 **NM** value: **Cover or less**
Circ: CapCity orders: **20,425**
A: Sam Kieth **W:** Sam Kieth
19 ❑ Sep 1995 Cover: 1.95 **NM** value: **Cover or less**
Circ: CapCity orders: **20,425**
A: Sam Kieth **W:** Sam Kieth
20 ❑ Nov 1995 Cover: 1.95 **NM** value: **Cover or less**
Circ: CapCity orders: **18,200**
A: Sam Kieth **W:** Sam Kieth
21 ❑ Jan 1996 Cover: 1.95 **NM** value: **Cover or less**
Circ: CapCity orders: **13,475**
A: Sam Kieth **W:** Sam Kieth
22 ❑ Feb 1996 Cover: 1.95 **NM** value: **Cover or less**
A: Sam Kieth **W:** Sam Kieth
23 ❑ Mar 1996 Cover: 1.95 **NM** value: **Cover or less**
A: Sam Kieth **W:** Sam Kieth
24 ❑ May 1996 Cover: 1.95 **NM** value: **Cover or less**
A: Sam Kieth **W:** Sam Kieth
25 ❑ Jun 1996 Cover: 1.95 **NM** value: **Cover or less**
cover says Jul, indicia says Jun. **A:** Sam Kieth **W:** Sam Kieth
26 ❑ Aug 1996 Cover: 1.95 **NM** value: **Cover or less**
A: Sam Kieth **W:** Sam Kieth ★ Origin of Mr. Gone.
27 ❑ Sep 1996 Cover: 1.95 **NM** value: **Cover or less**
Circ: Diamd. preorders: **39,137**
A: Sam Kieth **W:** Sam Kieth
28 ❑ Jan 1997 Cover: 1.95 **NM** value: **Cover or less**
Circ: Diamd. preorders: **36,972**
📖 Pool of Tears **A:** Sam Kieth **W:** Sam Kieth
29 ❑ Apr 1997 Cover: 1.95 **NM** value: **Cover or less**
Circ: Diamd. preorders: **32,971**
A: Sam Kieth **W:** Sam Kieth
30 ❑ Jun 1997 Cover: 1.95 **NM** value: **Cover or less**
Circ: Diamd. preorders: **30,961**
A: Sam Kieth **W:** Sam Kieth
31 ❑ Jul 1997 Cover: 1.95 **NM** value: **Cover or less**
Circ: Diamd. preorders: **28,872**
A: Sam Kieth **W:** Sam Kieth
32 ❑ Sep 1997 Cover: 1.95 **NM** value: **Cover or less**

Other grades: Multiply prices above by **1.5 for Mint • 2/3 for Very Fine • 1/3 for Fine • 1/5 for Very Good • 1/8 for Good**

Circ: Diamd. preorders: **28,410**
🕮 Glorie's Story **A:** Sam Kieth **W:** Sam Kieth

33 ❑ Oct 1997 Cover: 1.95 **NM** value: **Cover or less**
Circ: Diamd. preorders: **27,736**
🕮 The Love for Three Oranges **A:** Sam Kieth; Jim Sinclair **W:** Sam Kieth

34 ❑ Dec 1997 Cover: 1.95 **NM** value: **Cover or less**
Circ: Diamd. preorders: **26,657**
A: Sam Kieth **W:** Sam Kieth

35 ❑ Feb 1998 Cover: 1.95 **NM** value: **Cover or less**
Circ: Diamd. preorders: **25,908**
🕮 Endings and Beginnings final issue. **A:** Sam Kieth; Jim Sinclair **W:** Sam Kieth

36 ❑ Mar 1998 Cover: 1.95 **NM** value: **Cover or less**
Circ: Diamd. preorders: **22,785**
A: Sam Kieth **W:** Sam Kieth

37 ❑ Apr 1998 Cover: 1.95 **NM** value: **Cover or less**
Circ: Diamd. preorders: **22,914**
A: Sam Kieth **W:** Sam Kieth

Bk 1❑ Apr 1995 Cover: 12.95 **NM** value: **Cover or less**
• collects issues #1-6 **A:** Sam Kieth **W:** Sam Kieth

Bk 2❑ Jun 1997 Cover: 12.95 **NM** value: **Cover or less**
• collects issues #7-12 **A:** Sam Kieth **W:** Sam Kieth

M.A.X. YEARBOOK — Marvel

Bk 1❑ 1993 Cover: 19.95 **NM** value: **Cover or less**
• **CGC:** 4 graded, best 9.6

MAYHEM — Dark Horse

1 ❑ May 1989, b&w Cover: 2.50 **NM** value: **5.00**
• **CGC:** 1 graded, best 9.0
🕮 The Mask: Who's Laughing Now?; The Mark: Beyond Good and Evil, Part 1; Mecha: Deliverance **A:** Doug Mahnke; Robert Caracol; Harrison Fong; Wayne Tanaka **W:** Tim Eldred; Jerry Prosser; John Arcudi

2 ❑ Jun 1989, b&w Cover: 2.50 **NM** value: **4.00**
🕮 The Mask: What Revenge Means to Me; The Mark: Beyond Good and Evil; Mecha: Freefall **A:** Doug Mahnke; Robert Caracol; Harrison Fong; Wayne Tanaka **W:** Tim Eldred; Jerry Prosser; John Arcudi

3 ❑ Jul 1989, b&w Cover: 2.50 **NM** value: **4.00**
🕮 The Mask: Have Gun, Will Use; The Mark: Beyond Good and Evil, Part 3 Mecha: Triangle **A:** Doug Mahnke; Robert Caracol; Harrison Fong; Wayne Tanaka **W:** Tim Eldred; Jerry Prosser; John Arcudi

4 ❑ Aug 1989, b&w Cover: 2.50 **NM** value: **4.00**
🕮 The Mask: Final Kick; The Mark: Beyond Good and Evil, Part 4; Mecha: White Water **A:** Doug Mahnke; Robert Caracol; Harrison Fong; Wayne Tanaka **W:** Tim Eldred; Jerry Prosser; John Arcudi

MAYHEM (KELVA) — Kelva

1 ❑ Cover: 1.25 **NM** value: **Cover or less**
🕮 Care Your Dreams Away; Planet Mars; Bloodbath **A:** Baron Mrkva; Bob Waterman **W:** Baron Mrkva; Bob Waterman

MAZE, THE — Metaphrog

1 ❑ Aug 1997, b&w Cover: 3.65 **NM** value: **3.75**
🕮 Metaphrog • no indicia

MAZE AGENCY, THE — Comico

The Maze Agency is a group of detectives headed by the lovely and capable Jennifer Mays. She is joined in her efforts by Gabriel Webb, her somewhat overanalytical guy Friday. Each issue posed an interesting puzzle for the reader, with just enough clues being dropped so that a clever reader could puzzle out the solution before it was revealed in the end.

Much like TV's "Moonlighting," The Maze Agency was as much about the developing romance of the lead characters in the detective agency as it was about solving crimes. The romantic aspect was made particularly interesting due to their remarkably believable characterizations — credit going to writer Mike W. Barr.

1 ❑ Dec 1988 Cover: 1.95 **NM** value: **3.00**
Circ: CapCity orders: **9,650**
★ 1st Appearance of The Maze Agency.

2 ❑ Jan 1989 Cover: 1.95 **NM** value: **2.50**
Circ: CapCity orders: **6,575**
🕮 Murder-The Lost Episodes **A:** Adam Hughes **W:** Mike W. Barr

3 ❑ Feb 1989 Cover: 1.95 **NM** value: **2.50**
Circ: CapCity orders: **5,950**

4 ❑ Mar 1989 Cover: 1.95 **NM** value: **2.00**
Circ: CapCity orders: **5,700**

5 ❑ Apr 1989 Cover: 1.95 **NM** value: **2.00**
Circ: CapCity orders: **5,200**

6 ❑ May 1989 Cover: 1.95 **NM** value: **2.00**
Circ: CapCity orders: **5,000**

7 ❑ Jun 1989 Cover: 2.50 **NM** value: **Cover or less**
Circ: CapCity orders: **4,650**

8 ❑ Dec 1989 Cover: 1.95 **NM** value: **2.00**
Circ: CapCity orders: **4,325**

9 ❑ Feb 1990 Cover: 1.95 **NM** value: **2.00**
Circ: CapCity orders: **4,100**
🕮 The English Channeler Mystery • Ellery Queen **A:** Adam Hughes **W:** Mike W. Barr

10 ❑ Apr 1990 Cover: 1.95 **NM** value: **2.00**
Circ: CapCity orders: **3,950**

11 ❑ Apr 1990 Cover: 1.95 **NM** value: **2.00**
Circ: CapCity orders: **3,950**
🕮 ...Twas The Crime Before Christmas **A:** Robb Phipps **W:** Mike W. Barr

12 ❑ May 1990 Cover: 2.50 **NM** value: **Cover or less**
Circ: CapCity orders: **4,025**

13 ❑ Jun 1990 Cover: 1.95 **NM** value: **2.00**
Circ: CapCity orders: **4,075**

14 ❑ Jul 1990 Cover: 1.95 **NM** value: **2.00**
Circ: CapCity orders: **4,000**

15 ❑ Aug 1990 Cover: 1.95 **NM** value: **2.00**
Circ: CapCity orders: **3,900**

16 ❑ Oct 1990 Cover: 2.50 **NM** value: **Cover or less**
Circ: CapCity orders: **3,750**

17 ❑ Dec 1990 Cover: 2.50 **NM** value: **Cover or less**
Circ: CapCity orders: **3,620**

18 ❑ Feb 1991 Cover: 2.50 **NM** value: **Cover or less**
Circ: CapCity orders: **3,690**

19 ❑ Mar 1991 Cover: 2.50 **NM** value: **Cover or less**
Circ: CapCity orders: **3,515**

20 ❑ May 1991 Cover: 2.50 **NM** value: **Cover or less**
Circ: CapCity orders: **3,315**

21 ❑ Jun 1991 Cover: 2.50 **NM** value: **Cover or less**
Circ: CapCity orders: **3,050**

22 ❑ Jul 1991 Cover: 2.50 **NM** value: **Cover or less**
Circ: CapCity orders: **2,800**

23 ❑ Aug 1991 Cover: 2.50 **NM** value: **Cover or less**
Circ: CapCity orders: **2,865**

Anl 1❑ Aug 1990 Cover: 2.75 **NM** value: **3.00**
Circ: CapCity orders: **3,870**
• Spirit parody **C:** Mike Ploog

Bk 1❑ b&w Cover: 10.95 **NM** value: **Cover or less**
• Trade Paperback. • Collects The Maze Agency #1-4

SE 1❑ May 1990 Cover: 2.75 **NM** value: **3.00**
Circ: CapCity orders: **3,875**

Xmas 1❑ **NM** value: **3.00**
Circ: CapCity orders: **2,580**
• Special edition.

MAZIE AND HER BOYFRIENDS — Harvey

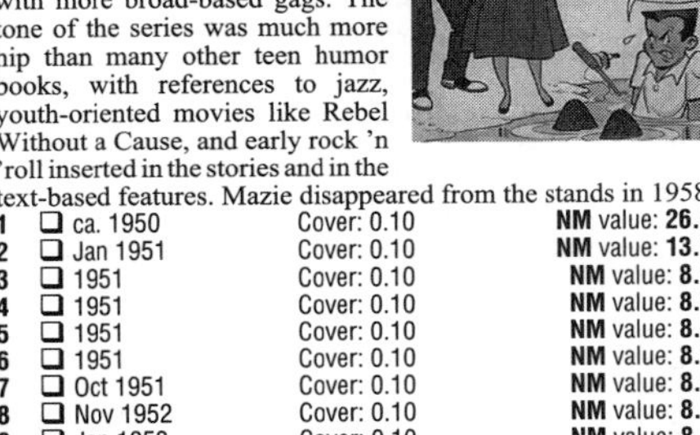

Mazie and her pals at Greenview High School kept teens and their younger siblings entertained throughout the 1950s in a series of innocuous humor stories in the Archie vein. Mazie, the blond flirt, was the titular star of the series, but her suitors Stevie and Flat-Top, rival Jeanie, geekish pal Mortie, and little brother Brod often stole the show with more broad-based gags. The tone of the series was much more hip than many other teen humor books, with references to jazz, youth-oriented movies like Rebel Without a Cause, and early rock 'n 'roll inserted in the stories and in the text-based features. Mazie disappeared from the stands in 1958.

#	Date	Cover	NM value
1 ❑	ca. 1950	Cover: 0.10	**NM** value: **26.00**
2 ❑	Jan 1951	Cover: 0.10	**NM** value: **13.00**
3 ❑	1951	Cover: 0.10	**NM** value: **8.50**
4 ❑	1951	Cover: 0.10	**NM** value: **8.50**
5 ❑	1951	Cover: 0.10	**NM** value: **8.50**
6 ❑	1951	Cover: 0.10	**NM** value: **8.50**
7 ❑	Oct 1951	Cover: 0.10	**NM** value: **8.50**
8 ❑	Nov 1952	Cover: 0.10	**NM** value: **8.50**
9 ❑	Jan 1953	Cover: 0.10	**NM** value: **8.50**
10 ❑	1953	Cover: 0.10	**NM** value: **8.50**
11 ❑	1953	Cover: 0.10	**NM** value: **6.00**
12 ❑	Dec 1953	Cover: 0.10	**NM** value: **6.00**
13 ❑	Mar 1954	Cover: 0.10	**NM** value: **6.00**
14 ❑	1954	Cover: 0.10	**NM** value: **6.00**
15 ❑	1954	Cover: 0.10	**NM** value: **6.00**
16 ❑	1955	Cover: 0.10	**NM** value: **6.00**
17 ❑	1955	Cover: 0.10	**NM** value: **6.00**
18 ❑	1955	Cover: 0.10	**NM** value: **6.00**
19 ❑	1956	Cover: 0.10	**NM** value: **6.00**
20 ❑	1956	Cover: 0.10	**NM** value: **6.00**
21 ❑	1956	Cover: 0.10	**NM** value: **6.00**
22 ❑	1957	Cover: 0.10	**NM** value: **6.00**
23 ❑	1957	Cover: 0.10	**NM** value: **6.00**
24 ❑	Nov 1957	Cover: 0.10	**NM** value: **6.00**

🕮 Oh, Brother; Clothes Shmoes; Sale Silly; Fooler Dueler; Club Women;

#	Date	Cover	NM value
25 ❑	1958	Cover: 0.10	**NM** value: **6.00**
26 ❑	1958	Cover: 0.10	**NM** value: **6.00**
27 ❑	1958	Cover: 0.10	**NM** value: **6.00**
28 ❑	ca. 1958	Cover: 0.10	**NM** value: **6.00**

'MAZING MAN — DC

This could easily have become a cutesy, fluffy, or satirical title. Instead, 'Mazing Man has a charm and innocence that rises above all that, becoming a cult favorite even to this day.

The hero is Siegfried Horatio Hunch III, also known as the diminutive super-hero 'Mazing Man. He's really just an ordinary (albeit short) guy who gets involved when others stand aside. Even if that makes him a bit crazy, it's probably the true definition of a hero.

But of course, a hero is nothing without his supporting cast. It includes Guido, the car-crazy macho man; Eddie and Brenda, the quintessentially happy couple, and comic writer Denton Fixx — who, for no apparent reason, has puppy dog ears. Sure it's silly — but it's also touching and charmingly human.

1 ❑ Jan 1986 Cover: 0.75 **NM** value: **1.00**
Circ: CapCity orders: **9,150**

2 ❑ Feb 1986 Cover: 0.75 **NM** value: **1.00**
Circ: CapCity orders: **7,900**

3 ❑ Mar 1986 Cover: 0.75 **NM** value: **1.00**
Circ: CapCity orders: **7,250**
🕮 I Hates Frog Legs; How To Create A Comic Book: The Plotting Session; Co-Operations **A:** Stephen DeStefano **W:** Bob Rozakis

4 ❑ Apr 1986 Cover: 0.75 **NM** value: **1.00**
Circ: CapCity orders: **6,450**

5 ❑ May 1986 Cover: 0.75 **NM** value: **1.00**
Circ: CapCity orders: **5,950**

6 ❑ Jun 1986 Cover: 0.75 **NM** value: **1.00**
Circ: CapCity orders: **5,450**

7 ❑ Jul 1986 Cover: 0.75 **NM** value: **1.00**
Circ: CapCity orders: **5,300**

8 ❑ Aug 1986 Cover: 0.75 **NM** value: **1.00**
Circ: CapCity orders: **5,200**

9 ❑ Sep 1986 Cover: 0.75 **NM** value: **1.00**
Circ: CapCity orders: **5,200**

10 ❑ Oct 1986 Cover: 0.75 **NM** value: **1.00**
Circ: CapCity orders: **5,400**

11 ❑ Nov 1986 Cover: 0.75 **NM** value: **1.00**
Circ: CapCity orders: **5,250**

12 ❑ Dec 1986 Cover: 0.75 **NM** value: **1.00**
Circ: CapCity orders: **6,000**

SE 1❑ Jul 1987 Cover: 2.00 **NM** value: **Cover or less**
• Special #1

SE 2❑ Apr 1988 Cover: 2.00 **NM** value: **Cover or less**
• Special #2

SE 3❑ Sep 1990 Cover: 2.00 **NM** value: **Cover or less**
• Special #3 **A:** Kyle Baker; Ty Templeton; Stephen DeStefano **W:** Bob Rozakis

MCHALE'S NAVY — Dell

1 ❑ May 1963 Cover: 0.12 **NM** value: **50.00**
• **CGC:** 1 graded, best 9.4

2 ❑ Aug 1963 Cover: 0.12 **NM** value: **40.00**
• **CGC:** 1 graded, best 9.4

3 ❑ Nov 1963 Cover: 0.12 **NM** value: **40.00**
• **CGC:** 1 graded, best 9.0

MCKEEVER AND THE COLONEL — Dell

1 ❑ Cover: 0.12 **NM** value: **28.00**
Photo cover.

2 ❑ Cover: 0.12 **NM** value: **20.00**
Photo cover.

3 ❑ Aug 1963 Cover: 0.12 **NM** value: **20.00**
Photo cover. 🕮 The Rugged Life!

M.D. (E.C.) — E.C.

There were six E.C. titles in its "New Direction," cover-bannered as "an entirely novel and unique reading experience." The cover of each had a frame with the title on top and an identifying icon down the left side. The "New Direction" was one designed to accommodate the Comics Magazine of America's new Comics Code, though the first issue of each did not carry the Code stamp, and all but one lasted for five issues. The six titles were: Aces High, Extra!, Impact, Psychoanalysis, Valor — and MD.

The stories were heavy with text and technical terms, but each had a point, and many were affecting, dealing with topics like amputation and diagnosis. Each cover was by Johnny Craig, and interiors were by Graham Ingels, George Evans, Joe Orlando, Reed Crandall, and Jack Davis. — Maggie

1 ❑ Apr 1955 Cover: 0.10 **NM** value: **75.00**
• **CGC:** 4 graded, best 9.4
🕮 The Fight for Life; Janie Some Day; To Fill the Bill; The Pain Killers (text story); The Antidote **A:** George Evans; Joe Orlando; Reed Crandall; Johnny Craig(cover) **W:** George Evans; Joe Orlando; Reed Crandall

2 ❑ Jun 1955 Cover: 0.10 **NM** value: **60.00**
• **CGC:** 2 graded, best 9.2

3 ❑ Aug 1955 Cover: 0.10 **NM** value: **60.00**
• **CGC:** 3 graded, best 9.2
🕮 When You Know How; The Right Cure; Shock Treatment; The Lesson **A:** George Evans; Joe Orlando; Reed Crandall; Graham Ingels **W:** George Evans; Joe Orlando; Reed Crandall; Graham Ingels

4 ❑ Oct 1955 Cover: 0.10 **NM** value: **60.00**
• **CGC:** 2 graded, best 9.6

5 ❑ Dec 1955 Cover: 0.10 **NM** value: **60.00**
• **CGC:** 2 graded, best 9.2

There are two different pricing tiers in the modern comic-book hobby. **The prices seen above** are the prices we have seen **loose copies** of these issues reliably fetch in a variety of environments. Condition alters the price by the fractions seen on the bar on the bottom of left-hand pages of this book. **Comics graded by CGC** usually sell for more. Use the guide on the bottom of right-hand pages of this book to estimate what copies have brought on eBay.

CGC-graded: Multiply prices above by **33 for 9.9 M • 16 for 9.8 NM/M • 7 for 9.6 NM+ • 5 for 9.4 NM • 2.5 for 9.2 NM- • 1.5 for 9.0 VF/NM**

M.D. GEIST — CPM

For more than 100 years, the Nexrum Alliance on the planet Jerra has been fighting Earth's loyalists for independence. But Earth's regular army would rather annihilate Jerra completely than give it to the Nexrum Alliance. In its desperation, the regular army unleashes a genetically engineered soldier with supernatural fighting abilities, Most Dangerous (M.D.) Geist. Too late, they find M.D. Geist is a force they can never control, and so lock him away.

Geist has broken loose, and the regular army has all but completely lost ground to the more organized and determined Nexrum Alliance. He quickly becomes the leader of a mercenary group, which includes the calculatingly sly Vaiya. Now only lots of battles in Robotech-style armor will determine whom Geist is fighting for, if he's fighting for anyone at all.

1 ❑ Jun 1995 Cover: 2.95 **NM** value: **Cover or less**
Circ: CapCity orders: **3,230**
A: Tim Eldred; Koichi Ohata **W:** Tim Eldred; Koichi Ohata
2 ❑ Jul 1995 Cover: 2.95 **NM** value: **Cover or less**
Circ: CapCity orders: **2,435**
A: Tim Eldred; Koichi Ohata **W:** Tim Eldred; Koichi Ohata
3 ❑ Aug 1995 Cover: 2.95 **NM** value: **Cover or less**
Circ: CapCity orders: **2,125**
A: Tim Eldred; Koichi Ohata **W:** Tim Eldred; Koichi Ohata
Bk 1❑ Jun 1996 Cover: 9.95 **NM** value: **Cover or less**
• Data Album #1; Collects M.D. Geist #1-3 and concept sketches **A:** Tim Eldred; Koichi Ohata **W:** Tim Eldred; Koichi Ohata

M.D. GEIST: GROUND ZERO — CPM

1 ❑ Mar 1996 Cover: 2.95 **NM** value: **Cover or less**
• prequel to M.D. Geist, Armored Trooper Votoms preview back-up
A: Tim Eldred **W:** Tim Eldred; Koichi Ohata; John Ott
2 ❑ Apr 1996 Cover: 2.95 **NM** value: **Cover or less**
• prequel to M.D. Geist, Armored Trooper Votoms preview back-up
A: Tim Eldred **W:** Tim Eldred; Koichi Ohata; John Ott
3 ❑ May 1996 Cover: 2.95 **NM** value: **Cover or less**
• prequel to M.D. Geist, Armored Trooper Votoms preview back-up
A: Tim Eldred **W:** Tim Eldred; Koichi Ohata; John Ott

M.D. (GEMSTONE) — Gemstone

1 ❑ Sep 1999 Cover: 2.50 **NM** value: **Cover or less**
Circ: Diamd. preorders: **3,369**
📖 The Fight for Life; Janie Some Day; To Fill the Bill; The Pain Killers (text story); The Antidote **A:** George Evans; Joe Orlando; Reed Crandall; Johnny Craig(cover) **W:** George Evans; Joe Orlando; Reed Crandall
2 ❑ Oct 1999 Cover: 2.50 **NM** value: **Cover or less**
Circ: Diamd. preorders: **2,885**
3 ❑ Nov 1999 Cover: 2.50 **NM** value: **Cover or less**
Circ: Diamd. preorders: **2,885**
📖 When You Know How; The Right Cure; Shock Treatment; The Lesson **A:** George Evans; Joe Orlando; Reed Crandall; Graham Ingels **W:** George Evans; Joe Orlando; Reed Crandall; Graham Ingels
4 ❑ Dec 1999 Cover: 2.50 **NM** value: **Cover or less**
Circ: Diamd. preorders: **2,825**
5 ❑ Jan 2000 Cover: 2.50 **NM** value: **Cover or less**
Circ: Diamd. preorders: **2,652**

MEA CULPA — Four Walls Eight Windows

1 ❑ Oct 1990 Cover: 12.95 **NM** value: **Cover or less**
A: Peter Kalberkamp **W:** Peter Kalberkamp

ME-A DAY WITH ELVIS — Invincible

1 ❑ **NM** value: **0.50**
A: Chris Higginson **W:** Chris Higginson

MEADOWLARK — Parody Press

1 ❑ b&w Cover: 2.95 **NM** value: **Cover or less**
Shadowhawksilver foil cover parody.

ME AND HER — Fantagraphics / Eros

All issues are adults only.
1 ❑ b&w Cover: 1.95 **NM** value: **2.00**
📖 It's Moving Day **A:** Mike Melillo **W:** Mike Melillo
1-2 ❑ Cover: 1.95 **NM** value: **2.00**
2 ❑ b&w Cover: 1.95 **NM** value: **2.00**
A: Mike Melillo **W:** Mike Melillo
3 ❑ Cover: 1.95 **NM** value: **2.00**
A: Mike Melillo **W:** Mike Melillo
SE 1❑ b&w Cover: 2.50 **NM** value: **Cover or less**
• Special edition. **A:** Mike Melillo **W:** Mike Melillo

MEAN, GREEN BONDO MACHINE — Mu Press

1 ❑ Jul 1992 Cover: 2.50 **NM** value: **Cover or less**

MEAN MACHINE — Fleetway-Quality

1 ❑ Cover: 4.95 **NM** value: **Cover or less**
Circ: CapCity orders: **2,750**
📖 Mean Machine: Travels with muh Shrink; Judge Dredd: The Gipper's Big Night • Judge Dredd; no date of publication; Reprints Mean Machine stories from 2000 A.D. #730-736 **A:** Richard Dolan **W:** John Wagner

MEANWHILE... — Crow

1 ❑ b&w Cover: 2.95 **NM** value: **Cover or less**
📖 Cohen and Melish; Pandora; Space Story; Suzie Sunshine; Keepsake; Midnight Confessions; Gandaft; My Life With Glasses; Calling You Out; Hairy Mary's handbag **A:** Eddie Campbell; Craig Conlan; Donald Rhooum; James Peaty; Jane Schofield; Mercy Van Vlack; Ralph Horsley; Stephen Lowther; John Anderson **W:** Craig Conlan; Donald Rhooum; Howard Stangroom; James Peaty; Jane Schofield; Mercy Van Vlack; Ralph Horsley; Paul Rafferty; Sam Hunt
2 ❑ b&w Cover: 2.95 **NM** value: **Cover or less**

MEASLES — Fantagraphics

1 ❑ 1998 Cover: 2.95 **NM** value: **Cover or less**
Circ: Diamd. preorders: **3,847**
📖 The New Adventures of Venus; Little Frogs; Olaf Oedwards, Kid Firechief; The Boomerang; Space on the Loose!; Professor Eggrod and "Nibblett" **A:** Rick Altergott; Jim Woodring; Gilbert Hernandez; Lewis Trondheim; Mario Hernandez; Steven Weissman **W:** Rick Altergott; Jim Woodring; Gilbert Hernandez; Lewis Trondheim; Mario Hernandez; Steven Weissman
2 ❑ 1999 Cover: 2.95 **NM** value: **Cover or less**
Circ: Diamd. preorders: **2,739**
3 ❑ Sum 1999 Cover: 2.95 **NM** value: **Cover or less**
Circ: Diamd. preorders: **2,591**
4 ❑ Sum 1999 Cover: 2.95 **NM** value: **Cover or less**
Circ: Diamd. preorders: **2,417**
5 ❑ Win 2000 Cover: 2.95 **NM** value: **Cover or less**
6 ❑ Spr 2000 Cover: 2.95 **NM** value: **Cover or less**
Circ: Diamd. preorders: **2,185**
7 ❑ 2000 Cover: 2.95 **NM** value: **Cover or less**
Circ: Diamd. preorders: **2,119**

MEAT CAKE (FANTAGRAPHICS) — Fantagraphics

1 ❑ b&w Cover: 2.50 **NM** value: **Cover or less**
2 ❑ b&w Cover: 2.50 **NM** value: **Cover or less**
3 ❑ b&w Cover: 2.50 **NM** value: **Cover or less**
4 ❑ b&w Cover: 2.50 **NM** value: **Cover or less**
5 ❑ Nov 1995, b&w Cover: 2.95 **NM** value: **Cover or less**
6 ❑ Jan 1996, b&w Cover: 2.95 **NM** value: **Cover or less**
7 ❑ 1997b&w Cover: 2.95 **NM** value: **Cover or less**
8 ❑ Jun 1998, b&w Cover: 2.95 **NM** value: **Cover or less**
9 ❑ Apr 1999 Cover: 2.95 **NM** value: **Cover or less**
Circ: Diamd. preorders: **2,482**
W: Alan Moore
10 ❑ Cover: 2.95 **NM** value: **Cover or less**
11 ❑ Cover: 3.95 **NM** value: **Cover or less**

MEAT CAKE (ICONOGRAFIX) — Iconografix

1 ❑ b&w Cover: 2.50 **NM** value: **Cover or less**

MEATFACE THE AMAZING FLESH — Monster

1 ❑ b&w Cover: 2.50 **NM** value: **Cover or less**

MECHA — Dark Horse

1 ❑ Jun 1987, full color Cover: 1.50 **NM** value: **1.75**
Circ: CapCity orders: **5,700**
📖 First Contact **A:** Harrison Fong **W:** Randy Stradley
2 ❑ Aug 1987, full color Cover: 1.50 **NM** value: **1.75**
Circ: CapCity orders: **4,000**
3 ❑ Oct 1987, b&w Cover: 1.50 **NM** value: **1.75**
Circ: CapCity orders: **3,775**
4 ❑ Dec 1987, b&w Cover: 1.50 **NM** value: **1.75**
Circ: CapCity orders: **3,050**
5 ❑ Feb 1988, b&w Cover: 1.50 **NM** value: **1.75**
Circ: CapCity orders: **2,325**
6 ❑ Apr 1988 Cover: 1.50 **NM** value: **1.75**

MECHAMEN — Antarctic

Bk 1❑ b&w Cover: 6.95 **NM** value: **Cover or less**
No issue number.

MECHANIC, THE — Image

1 ❑ Oct 1998 Cover: 5.95 **NM** value: **Cover or less**
Circ: Diamd. preorders: **13,334**
No issue number. One-shot. • prestige format.

MECHANICAL MAN BLUES — Radio

1 ❑ Dec 1998, b&w Cover: 2.95 **NM** value: **Cover or less**
Circ: Diamd. preorders: **3,191**
A: Tsukasa Kotobuki **W:** Tsukasa Kotobuki

MECHANICS — Fantagraphics

1 ❑ Cover: 2.00 **NM** value: **Cover or less**
Circ: CapCity orders: **5,950**
A: Jaime Hernandez
2 ❑ Cover: 2.00 **NM** value: **Cover or less**
Circ: CapCity orders: **5,150**
A: Jaime Hernandez
3 ❑ Cover: 2.00 **NM** value: **Cover or less**
Circ: CapCity orders: **4,425**
A: Jaime Hernandez

MECHANIMALS — Novelle

1 ❑ b&w Cover: 3.50 **NM** value: **Cover or less**
2 ❑ b&w Cover: 2.50 **NM** value: **Cover or less**

MECHANIMOIDS SPECIAL X ANNIVERSARY — Mu

1 ❑ b&w Cover: 3.50 **NM** value: **Cover or less**
cardstock cover.

MECHANISMO — Fleetway-Quality

Bk 1❑ Cover: 7.95 **NM** value: **Cover or less**
No issue number. • Judge Dredd

MECHANOIDS — Caliber

1 ❑ b&w Cover: 3.50 **NM** value: **Cover or less**
A: Mark Winfrey **W:** Gary Reed
2 ❑ Cover: 3.50 **NM** value: **Cover or less**
3 ❑ Cover: 3.50 **NM** value: **Cover or less**

MECH DESTROYER — Image

1 ❑ Mar 2001 Cover: 2.95 **NM** value: **Cover or less**
Circ: Diamd. preorders: **14,233** • **CGC:** 1 graded, best 9.6
A: Jae Kim **W:** Robert Chong

MECHOVERSE — Airbrush

1 ❑ Cover: 1.50 **NM** value: **Cover or less**
• Airbrushed
2 ❑ Cover: 1.50 **NM** value: **Cover or less**
• Airbrushed
3 ❑ Cover: 1.50 **NM** value: **Cover or less**
• Airbrushed

MECHTHINGS — Renegade

1 ❑ Jul 1987, b&w Cover: 2.00 **NM** value: **Cover or less**
2 ❑ Sep 1987, b&w Cover: 2.00 **NM** value: **Cover or less**
3 ❑ Nov 1987, b&w Cover: 2.00 **NM** value: **Cover or less**
4 ❑ Feb 1988, b&w Cover: 2.00 **NM** value: **Cover or less**

MEDAL OF HONOR — Dark Horse

The Congressional Medal of Honor is America's highest military honor, given to those brave few who rise far beyond the call of duty, risking their lives in the service of their country. In 1994, Dark Horse Comics produced this mini-series to tell the real stories of winners of the honor.

Among those was Lt. Charles Q. Williams, who served in the early days of the war in Viet Nam. Back in 1965, Americans were merely advisors in the conflict, but when Williams' base was attacked, they became more than observers. Wounded in the initial skirmish, he led his men through an all-night fire fight, putting back the V.C. advance. In the morning, an air strike leveled the compound, but the helicopters due to evacuate them were ambushed by V.C. forces. After several hours of fierce fighting, rescue was finally at hand. Although he had been hit multiple times, Williams insisted that others be evacuated before him.

1 ❑ Oct 1994 Cover: 2.50 **NM** value: **Cover or less**
Circ: CapCity orders: **3,300**
📖 Richard Bong: Honor Bound; Julius Langbein: The Little Drummer Boy **A:** Wayne Vansant; John Garcia **W:** Doug Murray
2 ❑ Nov 1994 Cover: 2.50 **NM** value: **Cover or less**
Circ: CapCity orders: **2,450**
📖 Firefly Fight; Gridiron to Glory **A:** Steve Lieber; Mark Wheatley **W:** Doug Murray
3 ❑ Dec 1994 Cover: 2.50 **NM** value: **Cover or less**
📖 The Andrews Raid; The Black Watch **A:** Bernie Mireault; Ted Naifeh **W:** Doug Murray
4 ❑ Jan 1995 Cover: 2.50 **NM** value: **Cover or less**
5 ❑ Cover: 2.50 **NM** value: **Cover or less**
SE 1❑ Apr 1994 Cover: 2.50 **NM** value: **Cover or less**
Circ: CapCity orders: **4,175**
• Special edition. 📖 Lt. Charles Q. Williams: Night in Hell; Sgt. Desmond Doss: The Bible Tells Me So **A:** Steve Lieber; Joe Kubert **W:** Doug Murray

MEDIA*STARR — Innovation

1 ❑ Jul 1989 Cover: 1.95 **NM** value: **Cover or less**
Circ: CapCity orders: **2,452**
2 ❑ Aug 1989 Cover: 1.95 **NM** value: **Cover or less**
Circ: CapCity orders: **1,850**
3 ❑ Sep 1989 Cover: 1.95 **NM** value: **Cover or less**
Circ: CapCity orders: **1,675**
Bk 1❑ Cover: 8.95 **NM** value: **Cover or less**

MEDIEVAL SPAWN — Image

1 ❑ Cover: 2.95 **NM** value: **Cover or less**
• three-part story; polybagged with Fan
2 ❑ Cover: 2.95 **NM** value: **Cover or less**
• three-part story; polybagged with Fan
3 ❑ Cover: 2.95 **NM** value: **Cover or less**
• three-part story; polybagged with Fan

MEDIEVAL SPAWN/WITCHBLADE — Image

1 ❑ May 1996 Cover: 2.95 **NM** value: **3.50**
• **CGC:** 4 graded, best 9.8
A: Brandon Peterson **W:** Garth Ennis
1/AE❑ **NM** value: **4.50**
Gold cover. • American Entertainment exclusive
1/GO❑May 1996 **NM** value: **4.50**
• **CGC:** 2 graded, best 9.4
• Gold edition.
1/PL❑ **NM** value: **18.00**
• Platinum edition.
2 ❑ Jun 1996 Cover: 2.95 **NM** value: **3.50**
W: Garth Ennis
3 ❑ Jun 1996 Cover: 2.95 **NM** value: **3.00**
cover says Jul, indicia says Jun. final issue. **W:** Garth Ennis
Bk 1❑ Jun 1997 Cover: 9.95 **NM** value: **Cover or less**
• Collects issues #1-3 **W:** Garth Ennis

MEDORA — Lobster

1 ❑ Dec 1999 Cover: 2.95 **NM** value: **Cover or less**
A: M. Gerald Delaney **W:** Alvero Fracassi

MEDUSA COMICS — Triangle

1 ❑ Cover: 1.50 **NM** value: **Cover or less**

MEEF COMIX — Print Mint

1 ❑ Cover: 0.50 **NM** value: **4.00**
📖 Records; What's This Lame We play in the Mirror; The Late Show; High Steppin' John; The Man Who Knows Everything **A:** F.Shrier **W:** F.Shrier

Other grades: Multiply prices above by **1.5 for Mint • 2/3 for Very Fine • 1/3 for Fine • 1/5 for Very Good • 1/8 for Good**

2 ❑ Cover: 0.50 **NM** value: **4.00**
The Electronic Concert; Beer; The Highjacking; Dog; A Zen Fable; Quick Sketches; Bedspring; Honky Motherfunny **A:** F.Shrier **W:** F.Shrier

MEET CORLISS ARCHER — Fox

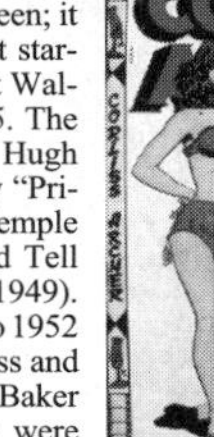

The radio sitcom was another comedy radio show focusing on the goings-on of an irrepressible teen; it aired from 1943 to 1956, first starring Priscilla Lyon, then Janet Waldo as Corliss, 14 going on 15. The characters were created by F. Hugh Herbert in the magazine story "Private Affair," and Shirley Temple starred as Corliss in Kiss and Tell (1945) and A Kiss for Corliss (1949). The TV series ran from 1951 to 1952 with Lugene Sanders as Corliss and from 1954 to 1955 with Ann Baker as Corliss. Other characters were Corliss' parents, Harry and Janet; her boyfriend, Dexter Franklin; brat Raymond Ames; Mildred, Corliss' best friend; and Betty Cameron, Corliss' rival.

In other words, the property was far more successful in media other than comic books, where she was played on covers as a "headlights" character, though the cover also carried the notation "America's favorite teen-age radio and screen star!!!" — Maggie

1 ❑ Mar 1948 Cover: 0.10 **NM** value: **450.00**
• **CGC:** 2 graded, best 8.0
2 ❑ May 1948 Cover: 0.10 **NM** value: **350.00**
3 ❑ Jul 1948 Cover: 0.10 **NM** value: **250.00**

MEET MERTON — Toby

1 ❑ ca. 1953 Cover: 0.10 **NM** value: **50.00**
2 ❑ ca. 1954 Cover: 0.10 **NM** value: **30.00**
3 ❑ ca. 1954 Cover: 0.10 **NM** value: **25.00**

MEET MISS BLISS — Atlas

1 ❑ May 1955 Cover: 0.10 **NM** value: **75.00**
• **CGC:** 1 graded, best 5.0
2 ❑ Jul 1955 Cover: 0.10 **NM** value: **50.00**
3 ❑ Sep 1955 Cover: 0.10 **NM** value: **50.00**
4 ❑ Nov 1955 Cover: 0.10 **NM** value: **50.00**

MEET MISS PEPPER — St. John

5 ❑ ca. 1954 Cover: 0.10 **NM** value: **80.00**
6 ❑ ca. 1954 Cover: 0.10 **NM** value: **65.00**

MEGA DRAGON & TIGER — Image

1 ❑ Mar 1999 Cover: 2.95 **NM** value: **Cover or less**
Circ: Diamd. preorders: **8,203**
A: Tony Wong **W:** Tony Wong; James D. Hudnall
2 ❑ Apr 1999 Cover: 2.95 **NM** value: **Cover or less**
Circ: Diamd. preorders: **6,502**
A: Tony Wong **W:** Tony Wong; James D. Hudnall
3 ❑ May 1999 Cover: 2.95 **NM** value: **Cover or less**
Circ: Diamd. preorders: **6,414**
A: Tony Wong **W:** Tony Wong; James D. Hudnall
4 ❑ Jun 1999 Cover: 2.95 **NM** value: **Cover or less**
Circ: Diamd. preorders: **7,003**
A: Tony Wong **W:** Tony Wong; James D. Hudnall
5 ❑ Jul 1999 Cover: 2.95 **NM** value: **Cover or less**
Circ: Diamd. preorders: **6,911**
A: Tony Wong **W:** Tony Wong; James D. Hudnall

MEGAHURTZ — Image

1 ❑ Aug 1997 Cover: 2.95 **NM** value: **Cover or less**
Circ: Diamd. preorders: **6,404**
Gods Born of Dreams and Demons **A:** Joe St. Pierre; David Chlystek **W:** Joe St. Pierre; David Chlystek
1/A ❑ Aug 1997 Cover: 2.95 **NM** value: **Cover or less**
no cover price. Gods Born of Dreams and Demons **A:** Joe St. Pierre; David Chlystek **W:** Joe St. Pierre; David Chlystek
1/B ❑ Aug 1997 Cover: 2.95 **NM** value: **Cover or less**
no cover price. Gods Born of Dreams and Demons **A:** Joe St. Pierre; David Chlystek **W:** Joe St. Pierre; David Chlystek
2 ❑ Sep 1997 Cover: 2.95 **NM** value: **Cover or less**
Circ: Diamd. preorders: **4,712**
Alise in Wonderland **A:** Joe St. Pierre; David Chlystek **W:** Joe St. Pierre; David Chlystek
3 ❑ Oct 1997 Cover: 2.95 **NM** value: **Cover or less**
Circ: Diamd. preorders: **4,451**
Seeing Red **A:** Joe St. Pierre; David Chlystek **W:** Joe St. Pierre; David Chlystek

MEGALITH — Continuity

1 ❑ 1990 Cover: 2.00 **NM** value: **Cover or less**
Circ: CapCity orders: **30,025**
2 ❑ 1990 Cover: 2.00 **NM** value: **Cover or less**
Circ: CapCity orders: **22,900**
3 ❑ 1990 Cover: 2.00 **NM** value: **Cover or less**
Circ: CapCity orders: **29,150**
4 ❑ Nov 1990 Cover: 2.00 **NM** value: **Cover or less**
Circ: CapCity orders: **13,250**
5 ❑ Jan 1991 Cover: 2.00 **NM** value: **Cover or less**
Circ: CapCity orders: **10,300**
• Rise of Magic storyline **A:** Ernesto Infante **W:** Peter Stone
6 ❑ Jun 1991 Cover: 2.00 **NM** value: **Cover or less**
Circ: CapCity orders: **8,700**
7 ❑ Jul 1991 Cover: 2.00 **NM** value: **Cover or less**
Circ: CapCity orders: **8,675**
8 ❑ Dec 1991 Cover: 2.00 **NM** value: **Cover or less**
Circ: CapCity orders: **7,100**
9 ❑ Mar 1992 Cover: 2.00 **NM** value: **Cover or less**
Circ: CapCity orders: **3,450**

MEGALITH (2ND SERIES) — Continuity

0 ❑ Apr 1993 Cover: 1.00 **NM** value: **Cover or less**
silver foil cover. Deathwatch 2000, Part 1 • silver foil issue number; prelude to Deathwatch 2000 **A:** Ernesto Infante **W:** Neal Adams; Peter Stone
0/A ❑ Apr 1993 Cover: 1.00 **NM** value: **Cover or less**
red foil cover. Deathwatch 2000, Part 1 **A:** Ernesto Infante **W:** Neal Adams; Peter Stone
1 ❑ Apr 1993 Cover: 2.50 **NM** value: **Cover or less**
Circ: CapCity orders: **6,800**
Deathwatch 2000, Part 5 • trading cards **A:** Ernesto Infante **W:** Neal Adams; Peter Stone
2 ❑ Jun 1993 Cover: 2.50 **NM** value: **Cover or less**
Circ: CapCity orders: **3,450**
Deathwatch 2000, Part10 • trading cards **A:** Vincente Alcazar **W:** Neal Adams; Peter Stone
3 ❑ Aug 1993 Cover: 2.50 **NM** value: **Cover or less**
Circ: CapCity orders: **2,925**
Deathwatch 2000, Part16 **A:** Ernesto Infante **W:** Neal Adams; Peter Stone
4 ❑ Oct 1993 Cover: 2.50 **NM** value: **Cover or less**
Circ: CapCity orders: **2,950**
5 ❑ Dec 1993 Cover: 2.50 **NM** value: **Cover or less**
Circ: CapCity orders: **2,950**
6 ❑ Dec 1993 Cover: 2.50 **NM** value: **Cover or less**
Circ: CapCity orders: **2,350**
7 ❑ Jan 1994 Cover: 2.50 **NM** value: **Cover or less**
Circ: CapCity orders: **2,325**

MEGATON — Megaton

1 ❑ Nov 1983 Cover: 2.00 **NM** value: **4.00**
• **CGC:** 1 graded, best 9.0
Ultragirl: Sins of the Father; The City at Sunrise; Megaton: The Pulsar Project; Berzerker; Vanguard; Sentinel: Sidekicks; The Skull: Night of the Skull; Ethrian; Wizards of War: The Summoning **A:** Ralph Cabrera; Dan Reed; Jackson Guice; Mike Gustovich; Gene Day; Erik Larsen; Ken Landgraf; Chris Ecker; Frank Fosco; James Cassara; Sam De La Rosa **W:** Gary Carlson; John Cosgriff ★ 1st Appearance of Megaton. ★ Appearance of Vanguard.
2 ❑ Oct 1985 Cover: 2.00 **NM** value: **3.00**
A: Erik Larsen
3 ❑ Feb 1986 Cover: 2.00 **NM** value: **5.00**
• **CGC:** 1 graded, best 9.2
A: Erik Larsen **W:** Erik Larsen ★ 1st Appearance of Savage Dragon.
4 ❑ Apr 1986 Cover: 2.00 **NM** value: **3.00**
5 ❑ Jun 1986 Cover: 1.50 **NM** value: **3.00**
6 ❑ Dec 1986 Cover: 1.50 **NM** value: **3.00**
7 ❑ Apr 1987 Cover: 1.50 **NM** value: **3.00**
8 ❑ Aug 1987 Cover: 1.50 **NM** value: **4.00**
HS 1❑ Cover: 2.95 **NM** value: **3.00**
says 1994 on cover, 1993 in indicia. Vanguard: First Noel **A:** Steve Adams **W:** Gary Carlson

MEGATON MAN — Kitchen Sink

In his badly-kept secret identity of Trent Phloog, he's just another hulking, goggled reporter. But as Megaton Man, he's a hulking, goggled super-hero! (You see the difference, right?)

Of course, it's not all fighting super-villains (like the dread "Bad Guy") for our hero. No, he has a sensitive, romantic side as well. For instance, he has an impossible crush on ace reporter Pamela Jointly. Strangely, despite his sensitive cries of "Woo! Pammy Baby!" she is somehow convinced that Trent is a macho jerk. In contrast, the nubile "See-Thru Girl" is dying to do some "patrolling" with him. The only problem: she's married to super-hero Phil Flaccid.

Created by Donald Simpson, Megaton Man is a hilarious send-up of the super-hero genre, poking fun at everyone from Superman to the Fantastic Four.

1 ❑ Nov 1984 Cover: 2.00 **NM** value: **3.00**
They Call the Doctor...Software! **A:** Donald Simpson **W:** Donald Simpson ★ Origin of Megaton Man.
1-2 ❑ Cover: 2.00 **NM** value: **Cover or less**
2 ❑ Feb 1985 Cover: 2.00 **NM** value: **2.50**
Circ: CapCity orders: **2,945**
A: Donald Simpson **W:** Donald Simpson
3 ❑ Apr 1985 Cover: 2.00 **NM** value: **2.50**
Circ: CapCity orders: **5,075**
I Am Called Bad Guy, Mortal! **A:** Donald Simpson **W:** Donald Simpson
4 ❑ Jun 1985 Cover: 2.00 **NM** value: **2.50**
Circ: CapCity orders: **5,100**
News Of The World **A:** Donald Simpson **W:** Donald Simpson
5 ❑ Aug 1985 Cover: 2.00 **NM** value: **2.50**
Circ: CapCity orders: **4,300**
Stella's Story **A:** Donald Simpson **W:** Donald Simpson
6 ❑ Oct 1985 Cover: 2.00 **NM** value: **2.50**
Circ: CapCity orders: **4,950**
The Death of Megaton Man; Border Worlds, Part 1 • Border Worlds storyline begins **A:** Donald Simpson **W:** Donald Simpson
7 ❑ Dec 1985 Cover: 2.00 **NM** value: **2.50**
Circ: CapCity orders: **4,300**
No Bag Guy Shall Escape My Patrol!; Border Worlds, Part 2 **A:** Donald Simpson **W:** Donald Simpson
8 ❑ Feb 1986 Cover: 2.00 **NM** value: **2.50**
Circ: CapCity orders: **4,450**
Megaton Man's All-Collegiate Issue!; Border Worlds, Part 3 • Border Worlds back-up **A:** Donald Simpson **W:** Donald Simpson
9 ❑ Apr 1986 Cover: 2.00 **NM** value: **2.50**
Circ: CapCity orders: **4,500**
Border Worlds, Part 4 **A:** Donald Simpson **W:** Donald Simpson
10 ❑ Jun 1986 Cover: 2.00 **NM** value: **2.50**
Circ: CapCity orders: **4,750**
Over-Kill!; Border Worlds, Part 5 final issue. **A:** Donald Simpson **W:** Donald Simpson

MEGATON MAN: BOMBSHELL — Image

1 ❑ Jul 1999 Cover: 2.95 **NM** value: **Cover or less**
Circ: Diamd. preorders: **2,734**
Megaton Man versus Unleash; Megaton Man versus Bombshell **A:** Donald Simpson **W:** Donald Simpson

MEGATON MAN: HARDCOPY — Image

1 ❑ Feb 1999, b&w Cover: 2.95 **NM** value: **Cover or less**
Circ: Diamd. preorders: **3,595**
• collects Internet strips **A:** Donald Simpson **W:** Donald Simpson
2 ❑ Apr 1999, b&w Cover: 2.95 **NM** value: **Cover or less**
Circ: Diamd. preorders: **2,882**
Mammaw Voodoo! • collects Internet strips **A:** Donald Simpson **W:** Donald Simpson

MEGATON MAN MEETS THE UNCATEGORIZABLE X+THEMS — Kitchen Sink

1 ❑ Apr 1989, b&w Cover: 2.00 **NM** value: **Cover or less**
• X-Men parody **A:** Donald Simpson **W:** Donald Simpson

MEGAZZAR DUDE — Slave Labor

1 ❑ Nov 1991, b&w Cover: 2.95 **NM** value: **Cover or less**

MEL ALLEN SPORTS COMICS — Standard

1 ❑ ca. 1949 Cover: 0.10 **NM** value: **80.00**
Dick Hardy at Somerset; Mel Allen, the Voice of the Yankees; Chester Makes the Team (text story); Junior Baseball; Football Cavalcade; Danny Glover **A:** Dave Sheridan; F.Schrier **W:** Dave Sheridan; F.Schrier
2 ❑ ca. 1950 Cover: 0.10 **NM** value: **55.00**
#6 on cover.

MELISSA MOORE: BODYGUARD — Draculina

1 ❑ b&w Cover: 2.95 **NM** value: **Cover or less**

MELODY — Kitchen Sink

All issues are adults only.

1 ❑ b&w Cover: 2.00 **NM** value: **2.50**
A: Gabriel Morrissette; Jacques Boivin **W:** Sylvie Rancourt
2 ❑ b&w Cover: 2.00 **NM** value: **2.25**
Lunatic Lola **A:** Gabriel Morrissette; Jacques Boivin **W:** Sylvie Rancourt
3 ❑ b&w Cover: 2.00 **NM** value: **Cover or less**
A: Gabriel Morrissette; Jacques Boivin **W:** Sylvie Rancourt
4 ❑ b&w Cover: 2.00 **NM** value: **Cover or less**
Debauchery **A:** Gabriel Morrissette; Jacques Boivin **W:** Sylvie Rancourt
5 ❑ b&w Cover: 2.00 **NM** value: **Cover or less**
A Father's Ire **A:** Gabriel Morrissette; Jacques Boivin **W:** Sylvie Rancourt
6 ❑ b&w Cover: 2.00 **NM** value: **Cover or less**
Isosceles **A:** Gabriel Morrissette; Jacques Boivin **W:** Sylvie Rancourt
7 ❑ b&w Cover: 2.25 **NM** value: **Cover or less**
A: Gabriel Morrissette; Jacques Boivin **W:** Sylvie Rancourt
8 ❑ b&w Cover: 2.50 **NM** value: **Cover or less**
Big City Welcome **A:** Gabriel Morrissette; Jacques Boivin **W:** Sylvie Rancourt
Bk 1❑ Cover: 14.95 **NM** value: **Cover or less**
The Orgies of Abitibi • Collects Melody #1-4 **A:** Gabriel Morrissette; Jacques Boivin **W:** Sylvie Rancourt

MELONPOOL CHRONICLES, THE — Para-Troop

1 ❑ Cover: 2.95 **NM** value: **Cover or less**
Crash Course! **A:** Steve Troop **W:** Steve Troop

MELTING POT — Kitchen Sink

1 ❑ Dec 1993 Cover: 2.95 **NM** value: **Cover or less**
Circ: CapCity orders: **15,375**
A: Kevin Eastman; Simon Bisley; Eric Talbot **W:** Kevin Eastman
2 ❑ 1994 Cover: 2.95 **NM** value: **Cover or less**
Circ: CapCity orders: **9,770**
3 ❑ 1994 Cover: 2.95 **NM** value: **Cover or less**
Circ: CapCity orders: **8,710**
4 ❑ Sep 1994 Cover: 3.50 **NM** value: **Cover or less**
Circ: CapCity orders: **7,475**
Bk 1❑ Jul 1995 Cover: 19.95 **NM** value: **Cover or less**
Bk 1/LE❑ Cover: 50.00 **NM** value: **Cover or less**
hardcover.

MELTY FEELING — Antarctic / Venus

All issues are adults only.

1 ❑ Oct 1996, b&w Cover: 3.50 **NM** value: **Cover or less**
Circ: Diamd. preorders: **3,416**
2 ❑ Dec 1996, b&w Cover: 3.50 **NM** value: **Cover or less**
Circ: Diamd. preorders: **2,903**
The Daily Grind **A:** Komashi Mamiya **W:** Komashi Mamiya
3 ❑ Jan 1997, b&w Cover: 3.50 **NM** value: **Cover or less**
Circ: Diamd. preorders: **3,161**
A Thief on Delight **A:** Komashi Mamiya **W:** Komashi Mamiya
4 ❑ Feb 1997, b&w Cover: 3.50 **NM** value: **Cover or less**
Circ: Diamd. preorders: **3,298**
Summer Nana **A:** Komashi Mamiya **W:** Komashi Mamiya

MELVIN MONSTER (DELL) — Dell

1 ❑ Apr 1965 Cover: 0.12 **NM** value: **100.00**
• **CGC:** 2 graded, best 9.6
2 ❑ Jul 1965 Cover: 0.12 **NM** value: **75.00**
• **CGC:** 3 graded, best 9.4
3 ❑ Dec 1965 Cover: 0.12 **NM** value: **75.00**
• **CGC:** 2 graded, best 9.0

CGC-graded: Multiply prices above by **33 for 9.9 M • 16 for 9.8 NM/M • 7 for 9.6 NM+ • 5 for 9.4 NM • 2.5 for 9.2 NM- • 1.5 for 9.0 VF/NM**

4 ❑ Jul 1966 Cover: 0.12 **NM** value: **75.00**
5 ❑ Oct 1966 Cover: 0.12 **NM** value: **75.00**
6 ❑ 1967 Cover: 0.12 **NM** value: **75.00**
7 ❑ 1967 Cover: 0.12 **NM** value: **75.00**
8 ❑ 1967 Cover: 0.12 **NM** value: **75.00**
9 ❑ Aug 1967 Cover: 0.12 **NM** value: **75.00**
• **CGC:** 1 graded, best 9.4
10 ❑ Oct 1969 Cover: 0.12 **NM** value: **75.00**

MELVIN THE MONSTER (ATLAS) — Atlas

1 ❑ Jul 1956 Cover: 0.10 **NM** value: **75.00**
2 ❑ Sep 1956 Cover: 0.10 **NM** value: **50.00**
3 ❑ Nov 1956 Cover: 0.10 **NM** value: **50.00**
4 ❑ Jan 1957 Cover: 0.10 **NM** value: **50.00**
5 ❑ Mar 1957 Cover: 0.10 **NM** value: **50.00**

MELVIS — Chameleon

1 ❑ Jul 1994 **NM** value: **2.00**
• 2, 500 copies
2 ❑ 1994 **NM** value: **2.00**
3 ❑ 1994 **NM** value: **2.00**
4 ❑ 1994 **NM** value: **2.00**

MEMENTO MORI — Memento Mori

1 ❑ 1995 **NM** value: **2.00**
2 ❑ Mar 1995, b&w **NM** value: **2.00**
no cover price.

MEMORIES — Marvel / Epic

1 ❑ b&w Cover: 2.50 **NM** value: **Cover or less**
Circ: CapCity orders: **5,400**
• Japanese **A:** Katsuhiro Otomo **W:** Katsuhiro Otomo

MEMORYMAN — David Markoff

1/Ash❑ **NM** value: **0.50**
• Ashcan edition given as promo at 1995 San Diego Comicon. **A:** David Markoff **W:** David Markoff ★ 1st Appearance of Memoryman.

MEMORY MAN (EMERGENCY STOP) — Esp

1 ❑ b&w Cover: 2.95 **NM** value: **Cover or less**
Some of the Spare Men **A:** Paul Rainey **W:** Paul Rainey
2 ❑ Cover: 1.50 **NM** value: **2.25**
• Promotional edition (black & white). The Independent State of The Jurassic Rock Cafe **A:** Paul Rainey **W:** Paul Rainey ★ 1st Appearance of Memory Man (Emergency Stop).
3 ❑ **NM** value: **2.25**
W: Paul Rainey
4 ❑ b&w Cover: 2.95 **NM** value: **Cover or less**
W: Paul Rainey
5 ❑ Cover: 2.95 **NM** value: **Cover or less**
The Firestarter **A:** Marc Laming; John Welding **W:** Paul Rainey
Ash 1❑ Cover: 1.50 **NM** value: **3.00**
• Promotional edition (black & white). The Independent State of The Jurassic Rock Cafe **A:** Paul Rainey **W:** Paul Rainey ★ 1st Appearance of Memory Man (Emergency Stop).

MENACE — Atlas

1 ❑ Mar 1953 Cover: 0.10 **NM** value: **500.00**
• **CGC:** 3 graded, best 9.2
2 ❑ Apr 1953 Cover: 0.10 **NM** value: **400.00**
• **CGC:** 2 graded, best 7.5
3 ❑ May 1953 Cover: 0.10 **NM** value: **350.00**
• **CGC:** 2 graded, best 7.5
4 ❑ Jun 1953 Cover: 0.10 **NM** value: **350.00**
• **CGC:** 1 graded, best 9.2
5 ❑ Jul 1953 Cover: 0.10 **NM** value: **275.00**
• **CGC:** 2 graded, best 6.0
6 ❑ Aug 1953 Cover: 0.10 **NM** value: **275.00**
7 ❑ Sep 1953 Cover: 0.10 **NM** value: **225.00**
8 ❑ Oct 1953 Cover: 0.10 **NM** value: **225.00**
9 ❑ Jan 1954 Cover: 0.10 **NM** value: **225.00**
10 ❑ Mar 1954 Cover: 0.10 **NM** value: **225.00**
11 ❑ May 1954 Cover: 0.10 **NM** value: **225.00**

MENAGERIE — Chrome Tiger

1 ❑ Nov 1987 Cover: 1.95 **NM** value: **Cover or less**
Scarycat and Mousekanaut; Iron Crosses **A:** Mike Raabe; Chris Johnson **W:** Clifton Jackson; Paula Shoudy

MENDY AND THE GOLEM — Mendy

1 ❑ Cover: 2.00 **NM** value: **2.50**
2 ❑ Cover: 2.00 **NM** value: **Cover or less**
3 ❑ Cover: 2.00 **NM** value: **Cover or less**
4 ❑ Cover: 2.00 **NM** value: **Cover or less**
5 ❑ Cover: 2.00 **NM** value: **Cover or less**
6 ❑ Cover: 2.00 **NM** value: **Cover or less**
7 ❑ Cover: 2.00 **NM** value: **Cover or less**
8 ❑ Cover: 2.00 **NM** value: **Cover or less**
9 ❑ Cover: 2.00 **NM** value: **Cover or less**
10 ❑ Cover: 2.00 **NM** value: **Cover or less**
11 ❑ Cover: 2.00 **NM** value: **Cover or less**
12 ❑ Cover: 2.00 **NM** value: **Cover or less**
13 ❑ Cover: 2.00 **NM** value: **Cover or less**
14 ❑ Cover: 2.00 **NM** value: **Cover or less**
15 ❑ Cover: 2.00 **NM** value: **Cover or less**
16 ❑ Cover: 2.00 **NM** value: **Cover or less**
17 ❑ Cover: 2.00 **NM** value: **Cover or less**
18 ❑ Cover: 2.00 **NM** value: **Cover or less**
19 ❑ Cover: 2.00 **NM** value: **Cover or less**

MEN FROM EARTH — Future-Fun

1 ❑ Cover: 2.00 **NM** value: **Cover or less**

MEN IN ACTION (1ST SERIES) — Marvel

1 ❑ Apr 1952 Cover: 0.10 **NM** value: **50.00**
2 ❑ May 1952 Cover: 0.10 **NM** value: **36.00**
• **CGC:** 1 graded, best 9.0
3 ❑ Jun 1952 Cover: 0.10 **NM** value: **28.00**
4 ❑ Jul 1952 Cover: 0.10 **NM** value: **28.00**
At Dawn They Die; Fight Another Day (text story); Platoon Sergeant; The Gun!; Squad Charge **A:** Robert Q. Sale; Joe Maneely **W:** Hank Chapman
5 ❑ Aug 1952 Cover: 0.10 **NM** value: **28.00**
6 ❑ Sep 1952 Cover: 0.10 **NM** value: **28.00**
7 ❑ Oct 1952 Cover: 0.10 **NM** value: **32.00**
A: Bernie Krigstein
8 ❑ Nov 1952 Cover: 0.10 **NM** value: **28.00**
9 ❑ Dec 1952 Cover: 0.10 **NM** value: **28.00**
• Series continued in Battle Brady #10

MEN IN ACTION (2ND SERIES) — Ajax

1 ❑ Apr 1957 Cover: 0.10 **NM** value: **35.00**
2 ❑ ca. 1957 Cover: 0.10 **NM** value: **25.00**
3 ❑ ca. 1957 Cover: 0.10 **NM** value: **15.00**
4 ❑ ca. 1957 Cover: 0.10 **NM** value: **15.00**
5 ❑ ca. 1958 Cover: 0.10 **NM** value: **15.00**
6 ❑ ca. 1958 Cover: 0.10 **NM** value: **15.00**

MEN IN BLACK, THE — Aircel

They are the chosen few. They observe. They protect. They control. They are...the Men in Black.

Jay was just an undercover DEA agent, until the day that Kay, one of the deadly Men in Black, recruited him. Now his past is expunged, he wears Ray-Bans and black suits, and carries a neurolyser that can erase an innocent bystander's memory in a flash.

The MIB exist to suppress socially explosive incidents, including, but not limited to, the appearance of UFOs. Kay will face a variety of threats such as desert drug cultists who practice human sacrifice, and aliens sent to Earth on gigantic scavenger hunts.

If Jay can adjust to the secrecy of the organization, and survive the dangers of having a partner who doesn't mind using him as bait, he may learn to love being part of the most bizarre law enforcement agency on the planet.

The Lowell Cunningham series was eventually the basis for a pair of feature films starring Tommy Lee Jones as Kay and Will Smith as Jay.

1 ❑ Jan 1990, b&w Cover: 2.25 **NM** value: **10.00**
• **CGC:** 1 graded, best 9.0
Initiation **A:** Sandy Carruthers **W:** Lowell Cunningham
2 ❑ Feb 1990, b&w Cover: 2.25 **NM** value: **8.00**
Encounter **A:** Sandy Carruthers **W:** Lowell Cunningham
3 ❑ Mar 1990, b&w Cover: 2.25 **NM** value: **7.00**
Invocation **A:** Sandy Carruthers **W:** Lowell Cunningham
Bk 1❑ Cover: 7.95 **NM** value: **Cover or less**

MEN IN BLACK, THE (BOOK II) — Aircel

1 ❑ May 1991, b&w Cover: 2.50 **NM** value: **10.00**
Wolf in the Fold **A:** Sandy Carruthers **W:** Lowell Cunningham
2 ❑ Jun 1991, b&w Cover: 2.50 **NM** value: **6.00**
A: Sandy Carruthers **W:** Lowell Cunningham
3 ❑ Jul 1991, b&w Cover: 2.50 **NM** value: **5.00**
A: Sandy Carruthers **W:** Lowell Cunningham

MEN IN BLACK: FAR CRY — Marvel

1 ❑ Aug 1997 Cover: 3.99 **NM** value: **Cover or less**
Circ: Diamd. preorders: **11,293**
One-shot. • Jay and Kay are reunited

MEN IN BLACK: RETRIBUTION — Marvel

1 ❑ Dec 1997 Cover: 3.99 **NM** value: **Cover or less**
A: Rod Whigham **W:** Lowell Cunningham

MEN IN BLACK: THE MOVIE — Marvel

1 ❑ Oct 1997 Cover: 3.99 **NM** value: **Cover or less**
Circ: Diamd. preorders: **9,902**
One-shot. • adapts movie

MEN OF WAR — DC

This war series focused more on good writing than on weapons specifications, offering its readers a number of unique storylines in each issue: The Gravedigger series followed the fearless Ulysses Hazard into the front lines of Nazi-occupied Europe. There, together with Allied troops, he embarked on missions no one expects him to return from alive — although he always does so, victoriously.

New Enemy Ace stories by Howard Chaykin took the unusual twist of tracking the actions of a German pilot, Baron Hans von Hammer.

The third feature, Dateline: Frontline, focused on a war correspondent as he struggled to report the action as the world collapsed around him.

1 ❑ Aug 1977 Cover: 0.35 **NM** value: **4.00**
• **CGC:** 1 graded, best 9.4
Code Name: Gravedigger; Enemy Ace: Death is a Wild Beast! • Enemy Ace back-up **A:** Ed Davis **W:** Bob Kanigher; David Michelinie ★ Origin of Gravedigger. ★ 1st Appearance of Gravedigger.
2 ❑ Sep 1977 Cover: 0.35 **NM** value: **3.00**
• Enemy Ace back-up **C:** Joe Kubert
3 ❑ Nov 1977 Cover: 0.35 **NM** value: **3.00**
• Enemy Ace back-up **C:** Joe Kubert
4 ❑ Jan 1978 Cover: 0.35 **NM** value: **3.00**
• Dateline: Frontline back-up **C:** Joe Kubert
5 ❑ Mar 1978 Cover: 0.35 **NM** value: **3.00**
6 ❑ May 1978 Cover: 0.35 **NM** value: **2.50**
7 ❑ Jul 1978 Cover: 0.35 **NM** value: **2.50**
8 ❑ Sep 1978 Cover: 0.35 **NM** value: **2.50**
9 ❑ Oct 1978 Cover: 0.50 **NM** value: **2.50**
10 ❑ Nov 1978 Cover: 0.50 **NM** value: **2.50**
• Enemy Ace and Dateline: Frontline back-ups **C:** Joe Kubert
11 ❑ Dec 1978 Cover: 0.40 **NM** value: **2.50**
12 ❑ Jan 1979 Cover: 0.40 **NM** value: **2.50**
13 ❑ Feb 1979 Cover: 0.40 **NM** value: **2.50**
Project Gravedigger-Plus One **A:** Dick Ayers; Romeo Tanghal **W:** Jack Harris
14 ❑ Mar 1979 Cover: 0.40 **NM** value: **2.50**
• Enemy Ace back-up **C:** Joe Kubert
15 ❑ Apr 1979 Cover: 0.40 **NM** value: **2.50**
C: Joe Kubert
16 ❑ May 1979 Cover: 0.40 **NM** value: **2.50**
17 ❑ Jun 1979 Cover: 0.40 **NM** value: **2.50**
18 ❑ Jul 1979 Cover: 0.40 **NM** value: **2.50**
19 ❑ Aug 1979 Cover: 0.40 **NM** value: **2.50**
20 ❑ Sep 1979 Cover: 0.40 **NM** value: **2.50**
C: Joe Kubert
21 ❑ Oct 1979 Cover: 0.40 **NM** value: **2.50**
22 ❑ Nov 1979 Cover: 0.40 **NM** value: **2.50**
23 ❑ Dec 1979 Cover: 0.40 **NM** value: **2.50**
24 ❑ Jan 1980 Cover: 0.40 **NM** value: **2.50**
25 ❑ Feb 1980 Cover: 0.40 **NM** value: **2.50**
26 ❑ Mar 1980 Cover: 0.40 **NM** value: **2.50**
final issue.

MEN'S ADVENTURE COMIX — Penthouse International

1 ❑ May 1995 Cover: 4.95 **NM** value: **6.00**
Circ: CapCity orders: **5,650**
• Comic-sized. Action Figures, Part 1; Generation Sex, Part 1; Slim & Nun, Part 1; LA-X, Part 1; Salem, Part 1; Hericane, Part 1; Miss Adventure, Part 1 **A:** Jason Pearson; Mark Texeira; Dan Barry; Kevin Maguire; Cary Polkovitz; Terry Austin; Boris Vallejo(cover); Joe Rubinstein; Karl Story; Doug Gregory; Les Edwards **W:** George Caragonne; Tom Thornton ★ Origin of Miss Adventure. ★ 1st Appearance of Hericane, Miss Adventure.
2 ❑ Jul 1995 Cover: 4.95 **NM** value: **5.00**
Circ: CapCity orders: **5,995**
3 ❑ Sep 1995 Cover: 4.95 **NM** value: **5.00**
Circ: CapCity orders: **4,250**
4 ❑ Nov 1995 Cover: 4.95 **NM** value: **5.00**
5 ❑ Dec 1995 Cover: 4.95 **NM** value: **5.00**
6 ❑ Feb 1996 Cover: 4.95 **NM** value: **5.00**
7 ❑ Apr 1996 Cover: 4.95 **NM** value: **5.00**

MEN'S ADVENTURES — Atlas

4 ❑ Jul 1950 Cover: 0.10 **NM** value: **125.00**
• **CGC:** 1 graded, best 5.5
5 ❑ Nov 1950 Cover: 0.10 **NM** value: **80.00**
• **CGC:** 1 graded, best 8.0
6 ❑ Feb 1951 Cover: 0.10 **NM** value: **70.00**
• **CGC:** 1 graded, best 8.5
7 ❑ Apr 1951 Cover: 0.10 **NM** value: **70.00**
• **CGC:** 1 graded, best 9.0
8 ❑ Jun 1951 Cover: 0.10 **NM** value: **70.00**
• **CGC:** 2 graded, best 9.0
9 ❑ Aug 1951 Cover: 0.10 **NM** value: **40.00**
• **CGC:** 1 graded, best 4.5
10 ❑ Oct 1951 Cover: 0.10 **NM** value: **40.00**
11 ❑ Dec 1951 Cover: 0.10 **NM** value: **40.00**
12 ❑ Feb 1952 Cover: 0.10 **NM** value: **40.00**
13 ❑ Apr 1952 Cover: 0.10 **NM** value: **40.00**
14 ❑ Jun 1952 Cover: 0.10 **NM** value: **40.00**
15 ❑ Aug 1952 Cover: 0.10 **NM** value: **40.00**
16 ❑ Oct 1952 Cover: 0.10 **NM** value: **40.00**
17 ❑ Dec 1952 Cover: 0.10 **NM** value: **40.00**
18 ❑ Feb 1953 Cover: 0.10 **NM** value: **40.00**
19 ❑ Mar 1953 Cover: 0.10 **NM** value: **40.00**
20 ❑ Apr 1953 Cover: 0.10 **NM** value: **40.00**
21 ❑ May 1953 Cover: 0.10 **NM** value: **35.00**
22 ❑ Jun 1953 Cover: 0.10 **NM** value: **35.00**
23 ❑ Sep 1953 Cover: 0.10 **NM** value: **35.00**
24 ❑ Nov 1953 Cover: 0.10 **NM** value: **35.00**
• **CGC:** 1 graded, best 2.5
25 ❑ Jan 1954 Cover: 0.10 **NM** value: **35.00**
• **CGC:** 1 graded, best 7.0
26 ❑ Mar 1954 Cover: 0.10 **NM** value: **35.00**
27 ❑ May 1954 Cover: 0.10 **NM** value: **35.00**
• **CGC:** 1 graded, best 5.5
28 ❑ Jul 1954 Cover: 0.10 **NM** value: **35.00**
• **CGC:** 1 graded, best 4.0

MENTHU — Black Inc!

1 ❑ Jan 1998 Cover: 2.95 **NM** value: **Cover or less**
Tributary **A:** Robert Roach **W:** Robert Roach
2 ❑ 1998 Cover: 2.95 **NM** value: **Cover or less**
A: Robert Roach **W:** Robert Roach
3 ❑ 1998 Cover: 2.95 **NM** value: **Cover or less**
A: Robert Roach **W:** Robert Roach
4 ❑ 1998 Cover: 2.95 **NM** value: **Cover or less**
A: Robert Roach **W:** Robert Roach

MENZ INSANA — DC / Vertigo

1 ❑ Cover: 7.95 **NM** value: **Cover or less**
No issue number. One-shot. • prestige format. Mortals and Portals; Let's Get Normal; Big Night Out; Trains, Boats, and Insane Planes; On the Level; The Snow Job; Home Truths, Part 1 and 2 **A:** John Bolton **W:** Christopher Fowler

Other grades: Multiply prices above by **1.5 for Mint • 2/3 for Very Fine • 1/3 for Fine • 1/5 for Very Good • 1/8 for Good**

MEPHISTO VS... — Marvel

1 ❑ Apr 1987 Cover: 1.50 **NM** value: **2.50**
Circ: CapCity orders: **36,800**
Give The Devil His Due • Fantastic Four **A:** John Buscema **W:** Al Milgrom

2 ❑ May 1987 Cover: 1.50 **NM** value: **2.00**
Circ: CapCity orders: **32,900**
Sympathy For The Devil • X-Factor **A:** John Buscema **W:** Al Milgrom

3 ❑ Jun 1987 Cover: 1.50 **NM** value: **2.00**
Circ: CapCity orders: **31,900**
The Devil You Say! • X-Men **A:** John Buscema

4 ❑ Jul 1987 Cover: 1.50 **NM** value: **2.00**
Circ: CapCity orders: **30,400**
His Satanic Majesty's Requiest • Avengers **A:** John Buscema

MERCEDES — Angus

1 ❑ 1995 Cover: 2.95 **NM** value: **Cover or less**
A: Grant Fuhst **W:** Mike Friedland

2 ❑ Jan 1996 Cover: 2.95 **NM** value: **Cover or less**
A: Grant Fuhst **W:** Mike Friedland

3 ❑ Feb 1996 Cover: 2.95 **NM** value: **Cover or less**
A: Grant Fuhst **W:** Mike Friedland

4 ❑ Mar 1996 Cover: 2.95 **NM** value: **Cover or less**
A: Grant Fuhst **W:** Mike Friedland

5 ❑ Apr 1996 Cover: 2.95 **NM** value: **Cover or less**
Six Bullets, Part 1 **A:** Grant Fuhst **W:** Mike Friedland

6 ❑ Cover: 2.95 **NM** value: **Cover or less**
Six Bullets, Part 2 **A:** Grant Fuhst **W:** Mike Friedland

7 ❑ Cover: 2.95 **NM** value: **Cover or less**
Six Bullets, Part 3 **A:** Grant Fuhst **W:** Mike Friedland

8 ❑ Cover: 2.95 **NM** value: **Cover or less**
Six Bullets, Part 4 **A:** Grant Fuhst **W:** Mike Friedland

9 ❑ Cover: 2.95 **NM** value: **Cover or less**
Six Bullets, Part 5 **A:** Grant Fuhst **W:** Mike Friedland

10 ❑ Cover: 2.95 **NM** value: **Cover or less**
Six Bullets, Part 6 **A:** Grant Fuhst **W:** Mike Friedland

11 ❑ Cover: 2.95 **NM** value: **Cover or less**
The Wicked, Part 1 **A:** Grant Fuhst **W:** Mike Friedland

12 ❑ Cover: 2.95 **NM** value: **Cover or less**
The Wicked, Part 2 **A:** Grant Fuhst **W:** Mike Friedland

MERCHANTS OF DEATH — Eclipse

1 ❑ Jul 1988, b&w Cover: 3.50 **NM** value: **Cover or less**
Circ: CapCity orders: **2,650**
• magazine. The Hero **A:** Jose Luis Salinas **W:** Carlos Trillo

2 ❑ b&w Cover: 3.50 **NM** value: **Cover or less**
Circ: CapCity orders: **2,125**
• magazine.

3 ❑ b&w Cover: 3.50 **NM** value: **Cover or less**
Circ: CapCity orders: **1,650**
• magazine.

4 ❑ b&w Cover: 3.50 **NM** value: **Cover or less**
Circ: CapCity orders: **1,300**
• magazine.

MERCHANTS OF VENUS, THE — DC

1 ❑ Cover: 5.95 **NM** value: **6.00**
A: Victoria Petersen **W:** Frederik Pohl; Neal McPheeters

MERCY — DC / Vertigo

1 ❑ Cover: 5.95 **NM** value: **6.00**
No issue number. **A:** Paul Johnson **W:** J.M. DeMatteis

MERIDIAN — CrossGen

In the interwoven worlds of the CrossGen universe, Demetria is a world that suffered from an ancient cataclysm that led to toxic zones jeopardizing the city-states of the planet. The title island, Meridian, is the first of the cities that survivors created to float in the sky.

The focal character is the Sigil-bearing 16-year-old Sephie, the only daughter of the late Minister of Meridian. Her adventures range from dealing with political intrigue to the physical adventures of visiting other floating islands while coping with inter-city conflicts. Elaborate layouts provide views of the various city islands and the land below. —Maggie

1 ❑ Jul 2000 Cover: 2.95 **NM** value: **Cover or less**
Circ: Diamd. preorders: **27,989** • **CGC:** 23 graded, best 9.9
A: Joshua Middleton **W:** Barbara Kesel

2 ❑ Aug 2000 Cover: 2.95 **NM** value: **Cover or less**
Circ: Diamd. preorders: **22,169** • **CGC:** 1 graded, best 9.0
A: Joshua Middleton **W:** Barbara Kesel

3 ❑ Sep 2000 Cover: 2.95 **NM** value: **Cover or less**
Circ: Diamd. preorders: **21,060**
A: Joshua Middleton **W:** Barbara Kesel

4 ❑ Oct 2000 Cover: 2.95 **NM** value: **Cover or less**
Circ: Diamd. preorders: **20,768**
A: Joshua Middleton **W:** Barbara Kesel

5 ❑ Nov 2000 Cover: 2.95 **NM** value: **Cover or less**
Circ: Diamd. preorders: **20,424**

6 ❑ Dec 2000 Cover: 2.95 **NM** value: **Cover or less**
Circ: Diamd. preorders: **20,496**

7 ❑ Jan 2001 Cover: 2.95 **NM** value: **Cover or less**
Circ: Diamd. preorders: **19,446**

8 ❑ Feb 2001 Cover: 2.95 **NM** value: **Cover or less**
Circ: Diamd. preorders: **18,988**

9 ❑ Mar 2001 Cover: 2.95 **NM** value: **Cover or less**
Circ: Diamd. preorders: **18,153**

10 ❑ Apr 2001 Cover: 2.95 **NM** value: **Cover or less**
Circ: Diamd. preorders: **17,412**

11 ❑ May 2001 Cover: 2.95 **NM** value: **Cover or less**
Circ: Diamd. preorders: **17,176**

12 ❑ Jun 2001 Cover: 2.95 **NM** value: **Cover or less**
Circ: Diamd. preorders: **16,882**

13 ❑ Jul 2001 Cover: 2.95 **NM** value: **Cover or less**
Circ: Diamd. preorders: **16,645**

14 ❑ Aug 2001 Cover: 2.95 **NM** value: **Cover or less**
Circ: Diamd. preorders: **17,061**

15 ❑ Sep 2001 Cover: 2.95 **NM** value: **Cover or less**

16 ❑ Oct 2001 Cover: 2.95 **NM** value: **Cover or less**

17 ❑ Nov 2001 Cover: 2.95 **NM** value: **Cover or less**

18 ❑ Dec 2001 Cover: 2.95 **NM** value: **Cover or less**

19 ❑ Jan 2002 Cover: 2.95 **NM** value: **Cover or less**

20 ❑ Feb 2002 Cover: 2.95 **NM** value: **Cover or less**

21 ❑ Mar 2002 Cover: 2.95 **NM** value: **Cover or less**

MERLIN — Adventure

1 ❑ Dec 1990, b&w Cover: 2.50 **NM** value: **Cover or less**

2 ❑ Jan 1991, b&w Cover: 2.50 **NM** value: **Cover or less**

3 ❑ Feb 1991, b&w Cover: 2.50 **NM** value: **Cover or less**
Where Madness Lies

4 ❑ Mar 1991, b&w Cover: 2.50 **NM** value: **Cover or less**
Belle du Lac

5 ❑ Apr 1991, b&w Cover: 2.50 **NM** value: **Cover or less**
Dark Desires

6 ❑ May 1991, b&w Cover: 2.50 **NM** value: **Cover or less**
Circle Of Fire final issue. **A:** Bob Davis **W:** R.A. Jones

MERLIN: IDYLLS OF THE KING — Adventure

1 ❑ b&w Cover: 2.50 **NM** value: **Cover or less**

2 ❑ b&w Cover: 2.50 **NM** value: **Cover or less**

MERLINREALM 3-D — Blackthorne

1 ❑ Oct 1985 Cover: 2.00 **NM** value: **2.25**
When Illusions of Life Becom Deathdreams Realized **A:** Nicholas Koenig **W:** Mark Wayne Harris

MERMAID — Alternative

1 ❑ May 1998, b&w Cover: 2.95 **NM** value: **Cover or less**
No issue number.

MERMAID FOREST — Viz

1 ❑ b&w Cover: 2.75 **NM** value: **Cover or less**
Circ: CapCity orders: **3,850**
A: Rumiko Takahashi **W:** Rumiko Takahashi

2 ❑ b&w Cover: 2.75 **NM** value: **Cover or less**
Circ: CapCity orders: **2,925**
A: Rumiko Takahashi **W:** Rumiko Takahashi

3 ❑ b&w Cover: 2.75 **NM** value: **Cover or less**
Circ: CapCity orders: **2,600**
A: Rumiko Takahashi **W:** Rumiko Takahashi

4 ❑ b&w Cover: 2.75 **NM** value: **Cover or less**
Circ: CapCity orders: **2,600**
A: Rumiko Takahashi **W:** Rumiko Takahashi

Bk 1 ❑ b&w Cover: 16.95 **NM** value: **Cover or less**
• Collects Mermaid Forest #1-4 **A:** Rumiko Takahashi **W:** Rumiko Takahashi

MERMAID'S DREAM — Viz

1 ❑ Oct 1985, b&w Cover: 2.75 **NM** value: **Cover or less**
Circ: CapCity orders: **3,300**
When Illusions of Life Become Death Dream Realized **A:** Rumiko Takahashi **W:** Rumiko Takahashi

2 ❑ b&w Cover: 2.75 **NM** value: **Cover or less**
Circ: CapCity orders: **2,825**
The Ash Princess **A:** Rumiko Takahashi **W:** Rumiko Takahashi

3 ❑ b&w Cover: 2.75 **NM** value: **Cover or less**
Circ: CapCity orders: **2,675**
A: Rumiko Takahashi **W:** Rumiko Takahashi

MERMAID'S GAZE — Viz

1 ❑ b&w Cover: 2.75 **NM** value: **Cover or less**
Circ: CapCity orders: **3,050**
A: Rumiko Takahashi **W:** Rumiko Takahashi

2 ❑ b&w Cover: 2.75 **NM** value: **Cover or less**
Circ: CapCity orders: **2,650**
A: Rumiko Takahashi **W:** Rumiko Takahashi

3 ❑ b&w Cover: 2.75 **NM** value: **Cover or less**
Circ: CapCity orders: **2,600**
A: Rumiko Takahashi **W:** Rumiko Takahashi

4 ❑ b&w Cover: 2.75 **NM** value: **Cover or less**
Circ: CapCity orders: **2,625**
A: Rumiko Takahashi **W:** Rumiko Takahashi

Bk 1 ❑ b&w Cover: 15.95 **NM** value: **Cover or less**

MERMAID'S MASK — Viz

1 ❑ b&w Cover: 2.75 **NM** value: **Cover or less**
Circ: CapCity orders: **3,050**
A: Rumiko Takahashi **W:** Rumiko Takahashi

2 ❑ b&w Cover: 2.75 **NM** value: **Cover or less**
Circ: CapCity orders: **2,600**
A: Rumiko Takahashi **W:** Rumiko Takahashi

3 ❑ b&w Cover: 2.75 **NM** value: **Cover or less**
Circ: CapCity orders: **2,400**
A: Rumiko Takahashi **W:** Rumiko Takahashi

4 ❑ Cover: 2.75 **NM** value: **Cover or less**
A: Rumiko Takahashi **W:** Rumiko Takahashi

MERMAID'S PROMISE — Viz

1 ❑ b&w Cover: 2.75 **NM** value: **Cover or less**
Circ: CapCity orders: **3,850**
A: Rumiko Takahashi **W:** Rumiko Takahashi

2 ❑ b&w Cover: 2.75 **NM** value: **Cover or less**
Circ: CapCity orders: **3,175**
A: Rumiko Takahashi **W:** Rumiko Takahashi

3 ❑ b&w Cover: 2.75 **NM** value: **Cover or less**
Circ: CapCity orders: **3,150**
A: Rumiko Takahashi **W:** Rumiko Takahashi

4 ❑ b&w Cover: 2.75 **NM** value: **Cover or less**
Circ: CapCity orders: **2,975**
A: Rumiko Takahashi **W:** Rumiko Takahashi

MERMAID'S SCAR — Viz

1 ❑ b&w Cover: 2.75 **NM** value: **Cover or less**
Circ: CapCity orders: **3,575**
A: Rumiko Takahashi **W:** Rumiko Takahashi

2 ❑ b&w Cover: 2.75 **NM** value: **Cover or less**
Circ: CapCity orders: **3,150**
A: Rumiko Takahashi **W:** Rumiko Takahashi

3 ❑ b&w Cover: 2.75 **NM** value: **Cover or less**
Circ: CapCity orders: **3,175**
A: Rumiko Takahashi **W:** Rumiko Takahashi

4 ❑ b&w Cover: 2.75 **NM** value: **Cover or less**
A: Rumiko Takahashi **W:** Rumiko Takahashi

Bk 1 ❑ b&w Cover: 17.95 **NM** value: **Cover or less**

MERRY COMICS — Charlton

1 ❑ ca. 1946 Cover: 0.10 **NM** value: **150.00**

MERRY MOUSE — Avon

1 ❑ Jun 1953 Cover: 0.10 **NM** value: **50.00**

2 ❑ Aug 1953 Cover: 0.10 **NM** value: **35.00**

3 ❑ Oct 1953 Cover: 0.10 **NM** value: **35.00**

4 ❑ Dec 1953 Cover: 0.10 **NM** value: **35.00**

MERTON OF THE MOVEMENT — Last Gasp

1 ❑ Cover: 0.50 **NM** value: **3.50**
Doctor Dope; 1st Demonstration; Dopin' Dan; Pollyanna Pals; Trots Bonnie; Why Bobby Seale is not Black **A:** Ted Richards; Gary Hallgren; Bobby London; Shary Flenniken **W:** Ted Richards; Gary Hallgren; Bobby London; Shary Flenniken

MESSENGER, THE — Image

1 ❑ Jul 2000 Cover: 5.95 **NM** value: **Cover or less**
Circ: Diamd. preorders: **7,373**
A: Jerry Ordway **W:** Jerry Ordway

MESSENGER 29 — September

1 ❑ b&w Cover: 1.95 **NM** value: **2.00**

MESSIAH — Pinnacle

1 ❑ b&w Cover: 1.50 **NM** value: **Cover or less**

MESSOZOIC — Kitchen Sink

1 ❑ Cover: 2.95 **NM** value: **Cover or less**
No issue number.

META-4 — First

1 ❑ Feb 1991 Cover: 3.95 **NM** value: **Cover or less**
Circ: CapCity orders: **5,850**
The Unbearable Being Of Lightness **A:** Ian Gibson **W:** Stefan Petrucha ★ Origin of Meta-4. ★ 1st Appearance of Meta-4.

2 ❑ Mar 1991 Cover: 2.25 **NM** value: **Cover or less**
Circ: CapCity orders: **4,125**
Disparate Liaisons **A:** Ian Gibson **W:** Stefan Petrucha

3 ❑ Apr 1991 Cover: 2.25 **NM** value: **Cover or less**
Circ: CapCity orders: **4,075**
A: Ian Gibson **W:** Stefan Petrucha

METABARONS, THE — Humanoids

1 ❑ Jan 2000 Cover: 2.95 **NM** value: **Cover or less**
A: Juan Gimenez **W:** Alexander Jodorowsky

2 ❑ 2000 Cover: 2.95 **NM** value: **Cover or less**
A: Juan Gimenez **W:** Alexander Jodorowsky

3 ❑ 2000 Cover: 2.95 **NM** value: **Cover or less**
A: Juan Gimenez **W:** Alexander Jodorowsky

4 ❑ 2000 Cover: 2.95 **NM** value: **Cover or less**
A: Juan Gimenez **W:** Alexander Jodorowsky

5 ❑ Jun 2000 Cover: 2.95 **NM** value: **Cover or less**
A: Juan Gimenez **W:** Alexander Jodorowsky

6 ❑ Jul 2000 Cover: 2.95 **NM** value: **Cover or less**

7 ❑ Aug 2000 Cover: 2.95 **NM** value: **Cover or less**
Circ: Diamd. preorders: **3,851**

8 ❑ Oct 2000 Cover: 2.95 **NM** value: **Cover or less**
Circ: Diamd. preorders: **4,236**

9 ❑ Nov 2000 Cover: 2.95 **NM** value: **Cover or less**
Circ: Diamd. preorders: **4,328**

10 ❑ Dec 2000 Cover: 2.95 **NM** value: **Cover or less**
Circ: Diamd. preorders: **4,437**

11 ❑ Jan 2001 Cover: 2.95 **NM** value: **Cover or less**
Circ: Diamd. preorders: **4,586**

12 ❑ Mar 2001 Cover: 2.95 **NM** value: **Cover or less**
Circ: Diamd. preorders: **4,577**

13 ❑ Apr 2001 Cover: 2.95 **NM** value: **Cover or less**
Circ: Diamd. preorders: **4,970**

14 ❑ Apr 2001 Cover: 2.95 **NM** value: **Cover or less**
Circ: Diamd. preorders: **5,462**

METACOPS — Fantagraphics / Monster

1 ❑ Feb 1991, b&w Cover: 1.95 **NM** value: **Cover or less**

2 ❑ Mar 1991, b&w Cover: 1.95 **NM** value: **Cover or less**

3 ❑ Jul 1991, b&w Cover: 1.95 **NM** value: **Cover or less**

METAL BIKINI — Eternity

1 ❑ Oct 1990, b&w Cover: 2.25 **NM** value: **Cover or less**
A: Jason Waltrip **W:** Jason Waltrip

2 ❑ 1990b&w Cover: 2.25 **NM** value: **Cover or less**
A: Jason Waltrip **W:** Jason Waltrip

3 ❑ 1991b&w Cover: 2.25 **NM** value: **Cover or less**
A: Jason Waltrip **W:** Jason Waltrip

CGC-graded: Multiply prices above by **33 for 9.9 M • 16 for 9.8 NM/M • 7 for 9.6 NM+ • 5 for 9.4 NM • 2.5 for 9.2 NM- • 1.5 for 9.0 VF/NM**

4 ❑ 1991b&w Cover: 2.25 NM value: Cover or less
A: Jason Waltrip W: Jason Waltrip
5 ❑ 1991b&w Cover: 2.25 NM value: Cover or less
A: Jason Waltrip W: Jason Waltrip
6 ❑ 1991b&w Cover: 2.25 NM value: Cover or less
A: Jason Waltrip W: Jason Waltrip

METAL GUARDIAN FAUST — Viz

1 ❑ Mar 1997 Cover: 2.95 NM value: Cover or less
Circ: Diamd. preorders: 5,145
A: Tetsuro Ueyama W: Tetsuro Ueyama
2 ❑ Apr 1997 Cover: 2.95 NM value: Cover or less
Circ: Diamd. preorders: 4,201
A: Tetsuro Ueyama W: Tetsuro Ueyama
3 ❑ May 1997 Cover: 2.95 NM value: Cover or less
Circ: Diamd. preorders: 3,641
A: Tetsuro Ueyama W: Tetsuro Ueyama
4 ❑ Jun 1997 Cover: 2.95 NM value: Cover or less
📖 Dream of an Angel A: Tetsuro Ueyama W: Tetsuro Ueyama
5 ❑ Jul 1997 Cover: 2.95 NM value: Cover or less
A: Tetsuro Ueyama W: Tetsuro Ueyama
6 ❑ Aug 1997 Cover: 2.95 NM value: Cover or less
A: Tetsuro Ueyama W: Tetsuro Ueyama
7 ❑ Sep 1997 Cover: 2.95 NM value: Cover or less
A: Tetsuro Ueyama W: Tetsuro Ueyama
8 ❑ Oct 1997 Cover: 2.95 NM value: Cover or less
A: Tetsuro Ueyama W: Tetsuro Ueyama
Bk 1❑ Mar 1998 Cover: 16.95 NM value: Cover or less
A: Tetsuro Ueyama W: Tetsuro Ueyama

METALLICA (CELEBRITY) — Celebrity

1/A ❑ Cover: 2.95 NM value: Cover or less
1/B ❑ Cover: 6.95 NM value: Cover or less
• trading cards

METALLICA (FORBIDDEN FRUIT) — Forbidden Fruit

All issues are adults only.
1 ❑ b&w Cover: 2.95 NM value: Cover or less
📖 My Ferrous Lady
2 ❑ b&w Cover: 2.95 NM value: Cover or less

METALLICA (ROCK-IT) — Rock-It Comics

1 ❑ Cover: 4.95 NM value: 5.00

METALLICA'S GREATEST HITS — Revolutionary

1 ❑ Sep 1993, b&w Cover: 2.50 NM value: Cover or less

METAL MEN — DC

The Metal Men were a group of robots created by Dr. Will Magnus. They took their names and their powers from the metals from which they were created. Lead was able to block bullets and radiation; Gold was able to stretch himself to incredible thinness; Iron was super-strong and nearly indestructible; Mercury could turn himself into a collection of liquid globules at room temperature; Tina (Platinum) also had amazing stretching and springing abilities — as well as a schoolgirl crush on Doc Magnus; and Tin, the coward of the bunch, seemed mostly good for laughs.

This strange but lovable bunch debuted in Showcase #37 before beginning this, their first solo series. They appeared regularly throughout the Sixties and Seventies, but seemed to vanish afterward. That changed in 1993, when DC revisited this old favorite in a brand new mini-series.

1 ❑ May 1963 Cover: 0.12 NM value: 285.00
• CGC: 22 graded, best 9.4
2 ❑ Jul 1963 Cover: 0.12 NM value: 125.00
• CGC: 2 graded, best 9.6
3 ❑ Sep 1963 Cover: 0.12 NM value: 80.00
• CGC: 2 graded, best 8.5
4 ❑ Nov 1963 Cover: 0.12 NM value: 80.00
• CGC: 2 graded, best 9.6
5 ❑ Jan 1964 Cover: 0.12 NM value: 80.00
Circ: Statement: 295,513
6 ❑ Mar 1964 Cover: 0.12 NM value: 52.00
Circ: Statement: 295,513 • CGC: 1 graded, best 9.2
7 ❑ May 1964 Cover: 0.12 NM value: 52.00
Circ: Statement: 295,513 • CGC: 1 graded, best 7.5
8 ❑ Jul 1964 Cover: 0.12 NM value: 52.00
Circ: Statement: 295,513
9 ❑ Sep 1964 Cover: 0.12 NM value: 52.00
Circ: Statement: 295,513 • CGC: 1 graded, best 7.5
10 ❑ Nov 1964 Cover: 0.12 NM value: 52.00
Circ: Statement: 295,513
11 ❑ Jan 1965 Cover: 0.12 NM value: 35.00
Circ: Statement: 334,245
12 ❑ Mar 1965 Cover: 0.12 NM value: 35.00
Circ: Statement: 334,245 • CGC: 2 graded, best 9.0
• Has 1964 Statement, filed 10/1/64; avg print run 410,000; avg sales 290,000; avg subs 4,126; avg total paid 295,513; samples 387; max existent 295,513; 28% of run returned
13 ❑ May 1965 Cover: 0.12 NM value: 35.00
Circ: Statement: 334,245 • CGC: 1 graded, best 5.0
★ 1st Appearance of Tin's girlfriend. ★ Versus Skyscraper Robot.
14 ❑ Jul 1965 Cover: 0.12 NM value: 35.00
Circ: Statement: 334,245
15 ❑ Sep 1965 Cover: 0.12 NM value: 35.00
Circ: Statement: 334,245 • CGC: 1 graded, best 9.4
16 ❑ Nov 1965 Cover: 0.12 NM value: 35.00
Circ: Statement: 334,245 • CGC: 1 graded, best 9.0
17 ❑ Jan 1966 Cover: 0.12 NM value: 35.00
Circ: Statement: 396,506
18 ❑ Mar 1966 Cover: 0.12 NM value: 35.00
Circ: Statement: 396,506 • CGC: 1 graded, best 9.4
19 ❑ May 1966 Cover: 0.12 NM value: 35.00
Circ: Statement: 396,506 • CGC: 1 graded, best 9.4
• Has 1965 Statement, filed 10/1/65; avg print run 505,000; avg sales 328,000; avg subs 6,245; avg total paid 334,245; samples 142; max existent 334,387; 34% of run returned
20 ❑ Jul 1966 Cover: 0.12 NM value: 35.00
Circ: Statement: 396,506 • CGC: 1 graded, best 8.5
21 ❑ Sep 1966 Cover: 0.12 NM value: 30.00
Circ: Statement: 396,506 • CGC: 1 graded, best 9.4
22 ❑ Nov 1966 Cover: 0.12 NM value: 30.00
Circ: Statement: 396,506
23 ❑ Jan 1967 Cover: 0.12 NM value: 30.00
Circ: Statement: 239,700 • CGC: 1 graded, best 9.2
24 ❑ Mar 1967 Cover: 0.12 NM value: 30.00
Circ: Statement: 239,700 • CGC: 1 graded, best 9.4
• Has 1966 Statement, filed 10/1/66; avg print run 642,000; avg sales 391,000; avg subs 5,506; avg total paid 396,506; samples 265; max existent 396,771; 38% of run returned
25 ❑ May 1967 Cover: 0.12 NM value: 30.00
Circ: Statement: 239,700
26 ❑ Jul 1967 Cover: 0.12 NM value: 30.00
Circ: Statement: 239,700 • CGC: 1 graded, best 9.4
27 ❑ Sep 1967 Cover: 0.12 NM value: 55.00
Circ: Statement: 239,700
★ Origin of Metal Men.
28 ❑ Nov 1967 Cover: 0.12 NM value: 24.00
Circ: Statement: 239,700 • CGC: 1 graded, best 8.5
29 ❑ Jan 1968 Cover: 0.12 NM value: 24.00
Circ: Statement: 206,555
30 ❑ Mar 1968 Cover: 0.12 NM value: 24.00
Circ: Statement: 206,555 • CGC: 1 graded, best 9.2
• Has 1967 Statement, filed 10/1/67; avg print run 439,000; avg sales 236,000; avg subs 3,700; avg total paid 239,700; samples 340; max existent 240,040; 45% of run returned
31 ❑ May 1968 Cover: 0.12 NM value: 16.00
Circ: Statement: 206,555
32 ❑ Jul 1968 Cover: 0.12 NM value: 16.00
Circ: Statement: 206,555 • CGC: 1 graded, best 9.4
33 ❑ Sep 1968 Cover: 0.12 NM value: 16.00
Circ: Statement: 206,555 • CGC: 1 graded, best 8.5
34 ❑ Nov 1968 Cover: 0.12 NM value: 16.00
Circ: Statement: 206,555
📖 Death Comes Calling
35 ❑ Jan 1969 Cover: 0.12 NM value: 16.00
36 ❑ Mar 1969 Cover: 0.12 NM value: 16.00
37 ❑ May 1969 Cover: 0.12 NM value: 16.00
• Has 1968 Statement, filed 10/1/68; avg print run 387,000; avg sales 205,000; avg subs 1,555; avg total paid 206,555; samples 386; max existent 206,941; 47% of run returned
38 ❑ Jul 1969 Cover: 0.12 NM value: 16.00
39 ❑ Sep 1969 Cover: 0.12 NM value: 16.00
40 ❑ Nov 1969 Cover: 0.15 NM value: 16.00
41 ❑ Dec 1969 Cover: 0.15 NM value: 16.00
• series put on hiatus
42 ❑ Mar 1973 Cover: 0.20 NM value: 9.00
• Series begins again (1973)
43 ❑ May 1973 Cover: 0.20 NM value: 9.00
44 ❑ Jul 1973 Cover: 0.20 NM value: 9.00
• back to hiatus ★ Versus Missile Men.
45 ❑ May 1976 Cover: 0.30 NM value: 4.00
• Series begins again (1976) A: Walt Simonson
46 ❑ Jul 1976 Cover: 0.30 NM value: 4.00
A: Walt Simonson
47 ❑ Sep 1976 Cover: 0.30 NM value: 4.00
A: Walt Simonson ★ Versus Plutonium Man.
48 ❑ Nov 1976 Cover: 0.30 NM value: 4.00
A: Walt Simonson ★ Versus Eclipso.
49 ❑ Jan 1977 Cover: 0.30 NM value: 4.00
A: Walt Simonson ★ Versus Eclipso.
50 ❑ Mar 1977 Cover: 0.30 NM value: 4.00
• CGC: 1 graded, best 9.2
A: Walt Simonson
51 ❑ May 1977 Cover: 0.30 NM value: 4.00
A: Walt Simonson ★ Versus Vox.
52 ❑ Jul 1977 Cover: 0.35 NM value: 4.00
• CGC: 1 graded, best 9.0
C: Walt Simonson
53 ❑ Sep 1977 Cover: 0.35 NM value: 4.00
54 ❑ Nov 1977 Cover: 0.35 NM value: 4.00
★ Appearance of Green Lantern.
55 ❑ Jan 1978 Cover: 0.35 NM value: 4.00
★ Versus Missile Men.
56 ❑ Mar 1978 Cover: 0.35 NM value: 4.00
final issue. ★ Versus Inheritor.

METAL MEN (MINI-SERIES) — DC

1 ❑ Oct 1993 Cover: 2.50 NM value: Cover or less
Circ: CapCity orders: 31,650 • CGC: 1 graded, best 8.5
foil cover. 📖 Thanks For The Memories A: Dan Jurgens W: Mike Carlin
2 ❑ Nov 1993 Cover: 1.25 NM value: 1.50
Circ: CapCity orders: 16,350
A: Dan Jurgens W: Mike Carlin
3 ❑ Dec 1993 Cover: 1.25 NM value: 1.50
Circ: CapCity orders: 13,800
📖 Metalurgency A: Dan Jurgens W: Mike Carlin
4 ❑ Jan 1994 Cover: 1.25 NM value: 1.50
Circ: CapCity orders: 14,750
📖 ThePeriodic Tables Turn! A: Dan Jurgens W: Mike Carlin

METAL MEN OF MARS & OTHER IMPROBABLE TALES — Slave Labor

1 ❑ Jan 1989, b&w Cover: 1.95 NM value: 2.00
📖 Metal Men of Mars; The Pharaoh of Fear; Fururama A: Ken Holewczynski W: Ken Holewczynski ★ Appearance of Tasma, Captain Daring.

METAL MILITIA — Express / Entity

1 ❑ Aug 1995 Cover: 2.50 NM value: Cover or less
Circ: CapCity orders: 2,890
A: Hoang Nguyen W: Hoang Nguyen; Lam Duy
2 ❑ 1995 Cover: 2.50 NM value: Cover or less
Circ: CapCity orders: 1,855
A: Hoang Nguyen W: Hoang Nguyen; Lam Duy
3 ❑ 1995 Cover: 2.50 NM value: Cover or less
📖 Lost A: Hoang Nguyen W: Hoang Nguyen; Lam Duy

METAMORPHO — DC

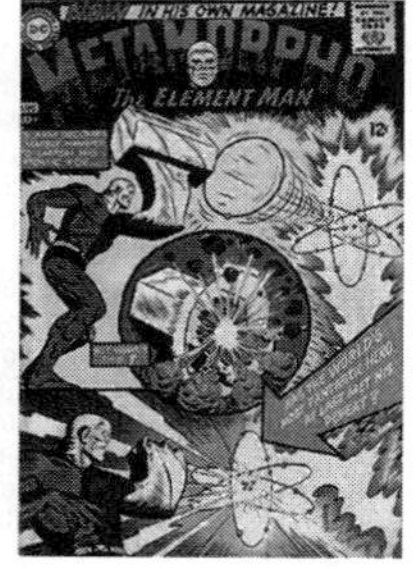

Originally created in The Brave and the Bold #57 (Jan 1965), archaelogist Rex Mason was tricked into attempting to recover the Orb of Ra, a mystic relic rumored to have great powers.

Millionaire Simon Stagg, whose daughter Sapphire was Mason's fiancee, set Mason on the quest and double-crossed the unsuspecting adventurer when Stagg's henchman, the resurrected Neanderthal Java, trapped Mason in a chamber with the Orb. The object's radiations changed Mason, giving him the ability to transform his body into any combination of the chemical elements and shaping those forms into any shape he pleases. In the years since, Mason has attempted to find a cure for his condition so he can become human once again and marry the girl of his dreams. — Brent

1 ❑ Aug 1965 Cover: 0.12 NM value: 40.00
• CGC: 8 graded, best 9.6
2 ❑ Oct 1965 Cover: 0.12 NM value: 20.00
• CGC: 2 graded, best 9.8
3 ❑ Dec 1965 Cover: 0.12 NM value: 18.00
• CGC: 2 graded, best 9.6
4 ❑ Feb 1966 Cover: 0.12 NM value: 15.00
• Metamorpho in Mexico
5 ❑ Apr 1966 Cover: 0.12 NM value: 15.00
• CGC: 1 graded, best 9.2
• Metamorpho vs. Metamorpho
6 ❑ Jun 1966 Cover: 0.12 NM value: 12.00
7 ❑ Aug 1966 Cover: 0.12 NM value: 12.00
8 ❑ Oct 1966 Cover: 0.12 NM value: 12.00
★ Versus Doc Dread.
9 ❑ Dec 1966 Cover: 0.12 NM value: 12.00
• CGC: 1 graded, best 8.0
10 ❑ Feb 1967 Cover: 0.12 NM value: 14.00
★ 1st Appearance of Element Girl.
11 ❑ Apr 1967 Cover: 0.12 NM value: 10.00
• CGC: 2 graded, best 7.5
12 ❑ Jun 1967 Cover: 0.12 NM value: 10.00
13 ❑ Aug 1967 Cover: 0.12 NM value: 10.00
14 ❑ Oct 1967 Cover: 0.12 NM value: 10.00
15 ❑ Dec 1967 Cover: 0.12 NM value: 10.00
16 ❑ Feb 1968 Cover: 0.12 NM value: 10.00
17 ❑ Apr 1968 Cover: 0.12 NM value: 10.00
final issue.

METAMORPHO (MINI-SERIES) — DC

1 ❑ Aug 1993 Cover: 1.50 NM value: Cover or less
Circ: CapCity orders: 26,200
📖 Like Father Like Son A: Graham Nolan W: Graham Nolan; Mark Waid
2 ❑ Sep 1993 Cover: 1.50 NM value: Cover or less
Circ: CapCity orders: 13,600
📖 Chemical Bonds A: Graham Nolan W: Graham Nolan; Mark Waid
3 ❑ Oct 1993 Cover: 1.50 NM value: Cover or less
Circ: CapCity orders: 11,600
📖 Chemical Imbalance A: Graham Nolan W: Graham Nolan; Mark Waid
4 ❑ Nov 1993 Cover: 1.50 NM value: Cover or less
Circ: CapCity orders: 9,900
A: Graham Nolan W: Graham Nolan; Mark Waid

METAPHYSIQUE — Eclipse

1 ❑ Cover: 2.50 NM value: Cover or less
📖 The Path A: Norm Breyfogle W: Norm Breyfogle

METAPHYSIQUE (MALIBU) — Malibu

1 ❑ ca. 1995 Cover: 2.95 NM value: Cover or less
Circ: CapCity orders: 8,150
📖 The Oneironauts Session One: Inner Worlds A: Norm Breyfogle W: Norm Breyfogle
2 ❑ ca. 1995 Cover: 2.95 NM value: Cover or less
Circ: CapCity orders: 5,250
A: Norm Breyfogle W: Norm Breyfogle
3 ❑ ca. 1995 Cover: 2.95 NM value: Cover or less
Circ: CapCity orders: 5,050
A: Norm Breyfogle W: Norm Breyfogle
4 ❑ ca. 1995 Cover: 2.95 NM value: Cover or less
A: Norm Breyfogle W: Norm Breyfogle
5 ❑ ca. 1995 Cover: 2.95 NM value: Cover or less
A: Norm Breyfogle W: Norm Breyfogle
6 ❑ ca. 1995 Cover: 2.95 NM value: Cover or less
📖 Apocalyptic Armageddon A: Norm Breyfogle W: Norm Breyfogle
★ Appearance of Superius.
Ash 1❑ Cover: 0.99 NM value: 1.00

Other grades: Multiply prices above by **1.5 for Mint • 2/3 for Very Fine • 1/3 for Fine • 1/5 for Very Good • 1/8 for Good**

METEOR COMICS — Baird

1 ❑ Nov 1945 Cover: 0.10 **NM** value: **300.00**
• **CGC:** 1 graded, best 8.0

METEOR MAN — Marvel

1 ❑ Aug 1993 Cover: 1.25 **NM** value: **Cover or less**
Circ: CapCity orders: **13,400**
2 ❑ Sep 1993 Cover: 1.25 **NM** value: **Cover or less**
Circ: CapCity orders: **6,800**
3 ❑ Oct 1993 Cover: 1.25 **NM** value: **Cover or less**
Circ: CapCity orders: **5,300**
A: Robert Walker **W:** Bert Hubbard; Dwight Coye ★ Appearance of Spider-Man.
4 ❑ Nov 1993 Cover: 1.25 **NM** value: **Cover or less**
Circ: CapCity orders: **4,750**
📖 To the Third Power! **A:** Robert Walker **W:** Bert Hubbard; Dwight Coye ★ Appearance of Night Thrasher.
5 ❑ Dec 1993 Cover: 1.25 **NM** value: **Cover or less**
Circ: CapCity orders: **3,650**
📖 All Out War!
6 ❑ Jan 1994 Cover: 1.25 **NM** value: **Cover or less**
Circ: CapCity orders: **3,250**

METEOR MAN: THE MOVIE — Marvel

1 ❑ Cover: 2.25 **NM** value: **Cover or less**
Circ: CapCity orders: **15,600**
A: Robert Walker **W:** Dwight Coye

METROPOL A.D. (VOL. 2, TED MCKEEVER'S...) — Marvel / Epic

1 ❑ Oct 1992 Cover: 3.50 **NM** value: **Cover or less**
Circ: CapCity orders: **4,400**
📖 Like A Babe In Arms **A:** Ted McKeever **W:** Ted McKeever
2 ❑ Nov 1992 Cover: 3.50 **NM** value: **Cover or less**
Circ: CapCity orders: **3,700**
📖 The Smell Of Rust And Gunpowder **A:** Ted McKeever **W:** Ted McKeever
3 ❑ Dec 1992 Cover: 3.50 **NM** value: **Cover or less**
Circ: CapCity orders: **3,600**
A: Ted McKeever **W:** Ted McKeever

METROPOLIS S.C.U. — DC

1 ❑ Nov 1994 Cover: 1.50 **NM** value: **Cover or less**
Circ: CapCity orders: **18,350**
📖 Sawyer's Blue **A:** Peter Krause **W:** Cindy Goff
2 ❑ Dec 1994 Cover: 1.50 **NM** value: **Cover or less**
Circ: CapCity orders: **12,950**
📖 Cop Out! **A:** Peter Krause **W:** Cindy Goff
3 ❑ Jan 1995 Cover: 1.50 **NM** value: **Cover or less**
Circ: CapCity orders: **11,800**
A: Peter Krause **W:** Cindy Goff
4 ❑ Feb 1995 Cover: 1.50 **NM** value: **Cover or less**
Circ: CapCity orders: **8,850**
A: Peter Krause **W:** Cindy Goff

METROPOL (TED MCKEEVER'S...) — Marvel / Epic

1 ❑ ca. 1991 Cover: 2.95 **NM** value: **Cover or less**
Circ: CapCity orders: **9,400**
📖 Secrets and Revelations **A:** Ted McKeever **W:** Ted McKeever
2 ❑ ca. 1991 Cover: 2.95 **NM** value: **Cover or less**
Circ: CapCity orders: **6,200**
📖 My Bones, My Pulse **A:** Ted McKeever **W:** Ted McKeever
3 ❑ ca. 1991 Cover: 2.95 **NM** value: **Cover or less**
Circ: CapCity orders: **6,000**
📖 You Can Only Experience Death Once **A:** Ted McKeever **W:** Ted McKeever
4 ❑ ca. 1991 Cover: 2.95 **NM** value: **Cover or less**
Circ: CapCity orders: **5,500**
📖 The Breath Of Reptiles **A:** Ted McKeever **W:** Ted McKeever
5 ❑ ca. 1991 Cover: 2.95 **NM** value: **Cover or less**
Circ: CapCity orders: **5,200**
A: Ted McKeever **W:** Ted McKeever
6 ❑ ca. 1991 Cover: 2.95 **NM** value: **Cover or less**
Circ: CapCity orders: **4,900**
A: Ted McKeever **W:** Ted McKeever
7 ❑ ca. 1991 Cover: 2.95 **NM** value: **Cover or less**
Circ: CapCity orders: **4,800**
A: Ted McKeever **W:** Ted McKeever
8 ❑ ca. 1991 Cover: 2.95 **NM** value: **Cover or less**
Circ: CapCity orders: **4,300**
A: Ted McKeever **W:** Ted McKeever
9 ❑ ca. 1991 Cover: 2.95 **NM** value: **Cover or less**
Circ: CapCity orders: **4,000**
A: Ted McKeever **W:** Ted McKeever
10 ❑ ca. 1991 Cover: 2.95 **NM** value: **Cover or less**
Circ: CapCity orders: **3,900**
A: Ted McKeever **W:** Ted McKeever
11 ❑ ca. 1992 Cover: 2.95 **NM** value: **Cover or less**
Circ: CapCity orders: **3,600**
A: Ted McKeever **W:** Ted McKeever
12 ❑ ca. 1992 Cover: 2.95 **NM** value: **Cover or less**
Circ: CapCity orders: **3,500**
A: Ted McKeever **W:** Ted McKeever

MEZ — C.A.P.

1 ❑ May 1997, b&w Cover: 3.00 **NM** value: **Cover or less**
Canadian cover price only.
2 ❑ Mar 1998, b&w Cover: 3.00 **NM** value: **Cover or less**
Canadian cover price only.

MEZZ: GALACTIC TOUR 2494 — Dark Horse

1 ❑ Cover: 2.50 **NM** value: **Cover or less**
Circ: CapCity orders: **2,825**
A: Mike Vosburg **W:** Mike Baron

M FALLING — Vagabond Press

1 ❑ Cover: 3.50 **NM** value: **Cover or less**
No issue number.

MFI: THE GHOSTS OF CHRISTMAS — Image

1 ❑ Dec 1999 Cover: 3.95 **NM** value: **Cover or less**
A: Francis Manapul **W:** J. Torres

MIAMI MICE — Rip Off

1 ❑ Apr 1986 Cover: 2.00 **NM** value: **Cover or less**
📖 The Mice Meet the Big Cheez; Scureface **A:** Mark Bodé **W:** Mark Bodé; S. Hajicek-Dobberstein
1-2 ❑ May 1986 Cover: 2.00 **NM** value: **Cover or less**
1-3 ❑ May 1986 Cover: 2.00 **NM** value: **Cover or less**
2 ❑ Jul 1986, b&w Cover: 2.00 **NM** value: **Cover or less**
📖 The Deadly Cheese Dust Caper **A:** Mark Bodé **W:** Mark Bodé
3 ❑ Oct 1986, b&w Cover: 2.00 **NM** value: **Cover or less**
📖 Pie in Der' Sky **A:** Mark Bodé **W:** Mark Bodé; Larry Todd
3/A ❑ Oct 1986, b&w Cover: 5.00 **NM** value: **Cover or less**
📖 Pie in Der' Sky • flexi-disc; w/ soundsheet **A:** Mark Bodé **W:** Mark Bodé; Larry Todd
4 ❑ Jan 1987, b&w Cover: 2.00 **NM** value: **Cover or less**

MICHAELANGELO CHRISTMAS SPECIAL — Mirage

1 ❑ Dec 1990, b&w Cover: 1.75 **NM** value: **2.00**

MICHAELANGELO TEENAGE MUTANT NINJA TURTLE — Mirage

1 ❑ Cover: 1.50 **NM** value: **2.50**
📖 The Christmas Aliens **A:** Kevin Eastman; Peter Laird **W:** Kevin Eastman; Peter Laird

MICHAEL JORDAN TRIBUTE — Revolutionary

1 ❑ Cover: 2.95 **NM** value: **Cover or less**
A: Ken Landgraf **W:** Mitsi Herrera

MICKEY AND DONALD (WALT DISNEY'S...) — Gladstone

1 ❑ Mar 1988 Cover: 0.95 **NM** value: **2.00**
Circ: CapCity orders: **8,350**
A: Carl Barks
2 ❑ 1988 Cover: 0.95 **NM** value: **2.00**
Circ: CapCity orders: **5,425**
A: Carl Barks
3 ❑ Jul 1988 Cover: 0.95 **NM** value: **2.00**
Circ: CapCity orders: **5,450**
A: Carl Barks
4 ❑ Aug 1988 Cover: 0.95 **NM** value: **2.00**
Circ: CapCity orders: **5,500**
A: Carl Barks
5 ❑ Sep 1988 Cover: 0.95 **NM** value: **2.00**
Circ: CapCity orders: **5,300**
A: Carl Barks **C:** Walt Kelly
6 ❑ Oct 1988 Cover: 0.95 **NM** value: **2.00**
Circ: CapCity orders: **5,300**
A: Carl Barks
7 ❑ Nov 1988 Cover: 0.95 **NM** value: **2.00**
Circ: CapCity orders: **5,050**
A: Carl Barks
8 ❑ Dec 1988 Cover: 0.95 **NM** value: **2.00**
Circ: CapCity orders: **5,150**
A: Carl Barks
9 ❑ 1989 Cover: 0.95 **NM** value: **2.00**
Circ: CapCity orders: **5,550**
A: Carl Barks
10 ❑ 1989 Cover: 0.95 **NM** value: **2.00**
Circ: CapCity orders: **5,400**
A: Carl Barks
11 ❑ 1989 Cover: 0.95 **NM** value: **2.00**
Circ: CapCity orders: **5,500**
A: Carl Barks
12 ❑ Aug 1989 Cover: 0.95 **NM** value: **2.00**
Circ: CapCity orders: **5,600**
A: Carl Barks
13 ❑ Sep 1989 Cover: 0.95 **NM** value: **2.00**
Circ: CapCity orders: **5,550**
A: Carl Barks
14 ❑ Oct 1989 Cover: 0.95 **NM** value: **2.00**
Circ: CapCity orders: **6,550**
A: Carl Barks
15 ❑ Nov 1989 Cover: 0.95 **NM** value: **2.00**
Circ: CapCity orders: **5,650**
A: Carl Barks
16 ❑ Jan 1990 Cover: 0.95 **NM** value: **2.00**
Circ: CapCity orders: **5,600**
📖 Beanstalk **A:** Carl Barks
17 ❑ Mar 1990 Cover: 1.95 **NM** value: **Cover or less**
Circ: CapCity orders: **5,500**
📖 Mickey Mouse and Goofy; Donald Duck; Mickey Mouse and the Riddle of the Red Hat **A:** Carl Barks; Floyd Gottfredson; Don Rosa
18 ❑ May 1990 Cover: 1.95 **NM** value: **Cover or less**
Circ: CapCity orders: **5,400**
• series continues as Donald and Mickey **A:** Carl Barks; Floyd Gottfredson **C:** Walt Kelly

MICKEY & MINNIE — W.D.

1 ❑ Cover: 3.50 **NM** value: **Cover or less**
No issue number. 📖 Mystery in Mouseton

Do you have changes or corrections for the **Standard Catalog**? Send your original research to us at
allcomics@krause.com

MICKEY FINN — Eastern

Mickey Finn is an Irish cop on the beat whose humorous adventures focus at least as much on the comic interplay of the stereotyped characters as on the ostensible crime and action storyline. Drawn by Lank Leonard in a goofy, funny-pages style that's one part Dick Tracy and two parts Barney Google, Mickey Finn's crime-busting antics take him to all manner of settings, from the inner city to the rural countryside.

Fast-moving, fun, and innocently unsophisticated, Mickey Finn is nonetheless marred by the gratuitous use of racial and ethnic stereotypes of Irish, Blacks, Jews, and Asians that is conspicuous and notably offensive even for the 1940s. Early issues feature backup stories of "Bo," a saucer-eyed orphan and his dog.

1 ❑ ca. 1942 Cover: 0.10 **NM** value: **80.00**
• **CGC:** 1 graded, best 6.5
A: Lank Leonard **W:** Lank Leonard
2 ❑ ca. 1943 Cover: 0.10 **NM** value: **40.00**
A: Lank Leonard **W:** Lank Leonard
3 ❑ ca. 1943 Cover: 0.10 **NM** value: **28.00**
A: Lank Leonard **W:** Lank Leonard
4 ❑ ca. 1943 Cover: 0.10 **NM** value: **20.00**
A: Lank Leonard **W:** Lank Leonard
5 ❑ ca. 1943 Cover: 0.10 **NM** value: **20.00**
A: Lank Leonard **W:** Lank Leonard
6 ❑ Cover: 0.10 **NM** value: **18.00**
A: Lank Leonard **W:** Lank Leonard
7 ❑ Cover: 0.10 **NM** value: **18.00**
A: Lank Leonard **W:** Lank Leonard
8 ❑ Cover: 0.10 **NM** value: **18.00**
A: Lank Leonard **W:** Lank Leonard
9 ❑ Cover: 0.10 **NM** value: **18.00**
A: Lank Leonard **W:** Lank Leonard
10 ❑ Cover: 0.10 **NM** value: **18.00**
A: Lank Leonard **W:** Lank Leonard
11 ❑ Cover: 0.10 **NM** value: **18.00**
A: Lank Leonard **W:** Lank Leonard
12 ❑ ca. 1949 Cover: 0.10 **NM** value: **18.00**
A: Lank Leonard **W:** Lank Leonard
13 ❑ Cover: 0.10 **NM** value: **18.00**
A: Lank Leonard **W:** Lank Leonard
14 ❑ Cover: 0.10 **NM** value: **18.00**
A: Lank Leonard **W:** Lank Leonard
15 ❑ Cover: 0.10 **NM** value: **18.00**
A: Lank Leonard **W:** Lank Leonard

MICKEY MANTLE — Magnum

1 ❑ Dec 1991 Cover: 1.75 **NM** value: **2.00**
Circ: CapCity orders: **9,725**
Photo cover. 📖 The Mickey Mantle Story **A:** Joe Sinnott **W:** Tom Peyer
2 ❑ **NM** value: **2.00**
Circ: CapCity orders: **6,050**

MICKEY MOUSE ADVENTURES — Disney

1 ❑ Jun 1990 Cover: 1.50 **NM** value: **2.00**
Circ: CapCity orders: **9,550**
2 ❑ Jul 1990 Cover: 1.50 **NM** value: **Cover or less**
Circ: CapCity orders: **6,600**
3 ❑ Aug 1990 Cover: 1.50 **NM** value: **Cover or less**
Circ: CapCity orders: **7,200**
★ Versus Phantom Blot.
4 ❑ Sep 1990 Cover: 1.50 **NM** value: **Cover or less**
Circ: CapCity orders: **7,400**
5 ❑ Oct 1990 Cover: 1.50 **NM** value: **Cover or less**
Circ: CapCity orders: **7,300**
6 ❑ Nov 1990 Cover: 1.50 **NM** value: **Cover or less**
Circ: CapCity orders: **6,550**
7 ❑ Dec 1990 Cover: 1.50 **NM** value: **Cover or less**
Circ: CapCity orders: **6,100**
8 ❑ Jan 1991 Cover: 1.50 **NM** value: **Cover or less**
Circ: CapCity orders: **6,250**
C: John Byrne
9 ❑ Feb 1991 Cover: 1.50 **NM** value: **Cover or less**
Circ: CapCity orders: **6,750**
• Fantasia
10 ❑ Mar 1991 Cover: 1.50 **NM** value: **Cover or less**
Circ: CapCity orders: **5,800**
11 ❑ Apr 1991 Cover: 1.50 **NM** value: **Cover or less**
Circ: CapCity orders: **5,050**
12 ❑ May 1991 Cover: 1.50 **NM** value: **Cover or less**
Circ: CapCity orders: **4,950**
13 ❑ Jun 1991 Cover: 1.50 **NM** value: **Cover or less**
Circ: CapCity orders: **4,950**
14 ❑ Jul 1991 Cover: 1.50 **NM** value: **Cover or less**
Circ: CapCity orders: **4,800**
15 ❑ Aug 1991 Cover: 1.50 **NM** value: **Cover or less**
Circ: CapCity orders: **4,850**
16 ❑ Sep 1991 Cover: 1.50 **NM** value: **Cover or less**
Circ: CapCity orders: **4,700**
A: Kurt Busiek
17 ❑ Oct 1991 Cover: 1.50 **NM** value: **Cover or less**
Circ: CapCity orders: **4,650**
• Dinosaur
18 ❑ Nov 1991 Cover: 1.50 **NM** value: **Cover or less**
Circ: CapCity orders: **4,500**
• Dinosaur

CGC-graded: Multiply prices above by **33 for 9.9 M • 16 for 9.8 NM/M • 7 for 9.6 NM+ • 5 for 9.4 NM • 2.5 for 9.2 NM- • 1.5 for 9.0 VF/NM**

MICKEY MOUSE BIRTHDAY PARTY — Dell

1 ❑ Sep 1953 — **NM** value: **500.00**
• **CGC:** 2 graded, best 8.0

MICKEY MOUSE CLUB PARADE — Dell

1 ❑ Dec 1955 — **NM** value: **350.00**
• **CGC:** 4 graded, best 7.5

MICKEY MOUSE DIGEST — Gladstone

1 ❑ ca. 1986 — Cover: 1.25 — **NM** value: **5.00**
Circ: CapCity orders: **2,175**
2 ❑ ca. 1986 — Cover: 1.25 — **NM** value: **4.00**
Circ: CapCity orders: **2,000**
3 ❑ ca. 1986 — Cover: 1.50 — **NM** value: **3.00**
Circ: CapCity orders: **1,575**
4 ❑ ca. 1986 — Cover: 1.50 — **NM** value: **3.00**
Circ: CapCity orders: **1,375**
5 ❑ ca. 1987 — Cover: 1.50 — **NM** value: **3.00**
Circ: CapCity orders: **1,400**

MICKEY MOUSE IN FANTASYLAND — Dell

1 ❑ May 1957 — Cover: 0.25 — **NM** value: **200.00**
• **CGC:** 1 graded, best 9.4

MICKEY MOUSE IN FRONTIERLAND — Dell

1 ❑ May 1956 — Cover: 0.25 — **NM** value: **200.00**
• **CGC:** 2 graded, best 9.4

MICKEY MOUSE (ONE-SHOT) — Disney

1 ❑ — **NM** value: **4.00**
No issue number. • in Russian

MICKEY MOUSE SUMMER FUN — Dell

1 ❑ May 1958 — Cover: 0.25 — **NM** value: **200.00**
• **CGC:** 2 graded, best 9.0

MICKEY MOUSE SURPRISE PARTY — Gold Key

1 ❑ Jan 1969 — Cover: 0.25 — **NM** value: **25.00**
• **CGC:** 1 graded, best 7.5

MICKEY MOUSE (WALT DISNEY'S...) — Dell / Gold Key / Gladstone

Walt Disney's Mickey Mouse is the world's most recognized comics character, star of stage, screen, television, ice shows, merchandise, parade floats, and, oh, yeah — comic books.

Dell began publishing Mickey Mouse as a comic book in 1941, picking up from the Mickey Mouse magazine that carried his adventures previously and appearances in Four Color Comics. The stories picked up from the character as presented in Disney's shorts, and some adventures were adapted from Floyd Gottfredson's daily newspaper strip. Virtually all comics creators working in the Disney fields were forced to work anonymously. The tales are, nevertheless, funny, fast-paced, and familiar to anyone with the most passing interest in pop culture. In the comics, by the way, Mickey's nephews permit the comics to accommodate stories initially scripted for other comic-book characters.

28 ❑ — Cover: 0.10 — **NM** value: **24.00**
29 ❑ Feb 1953 — Cover: 0.10 — **NM** value: **24.00**
• **CGC:** 1 graded, best 9.4
30 ❑ ca. 1953 — Cover: 0.10 — **NM** value: **24.00**
31 ❑ ca. 1953 — Cover: 0.10 — **NM** value: **20.00**
32 ❑ ca. 1953 — Cover: 0.10 — **NM** value: **20.00**
📖 Mickey Mouse: Westward Whoa!
33 ❑ ca. 1953 — Cover: 0.10 — **NM** value: **20.00**
34 ❑ Feb 1954 — Cover: 0.10 — **NM** value: **20.00**
35 ❑ Apr 1954 — Cover: 0.10 — **NM** value: **20.00**
36 ❑ Jun 1954 — Cover: 0.10 — **NM** value: **20.00**
37 ❑ Aug 1954 — Cover: 0.10 — **NM** value: **20.00**
38 ❑ Oct 1954 — Cover: 0.10 — **NM** value: **20.00**
39 ❑ Dec 1954 — Cover: 0.10 — **NM** value: **20.00**
40 ❑ Feb 1955 — Cover: 0.10 — **NM** value: **20.00**
• **CGC:** 1 graded, best 9.4
41 ❑ Apr 1955 — Cover: 0.10 — **NM** value: **18.00**
📖 Diamond in the Rough; Hot Water
42 ❑ Jun 1955 — Cover: 0.10 — **NM** value: **18.00**
43 ❑ Aug 1955 — Cover: 0.10 — **NM** value: **18.00**
44 ❑ Oct 1955 — Cover: 0.10 — **NM** value: **18.00**
45 ❑ Dec 1955 — Cover: 0.10 — **NM** value: **18.00**
46 ❑ Feb 1956 — Cover: 0.10 — **NM** value: **18.00**
47 ❑ Apr 1956 — Cover: 0.10 — **NM** value: **18.00**
48 ❑ Jun 1956 — Cover: 0.10 — **NM** value: **18.00**
49 ❑ Aug 1956 — Cover: 0.10 — **NM** value: **18.00**
50 ❑ Oct 1956 — Cover: 0.10 — **NM** value: **18.00**
• **CGC:** 1 graded, best 8.0
51 ❑ Dec 1956 — Cover: 0.10 — **NM** value: **15.00**
52 ❑ Feb 1957 — Cover: 0.10 — **NM** value: **15.00**
53 ❑ Apr 1957 — Cover: 0.10 — **NM** value: **15.00**
54 ❑ Jun 1957 — Cover: 0.10 — **NM** value: **15.00**
55 ❑ Aug 1957 — Cover: 0.10 — **NM** value: **15.00**
56 ❑ Oct 1957 — Cover: 0.10 — **NM** value: **15.00**
57 ❑ Dec 1957 — Cover: 0.10 — **NM** value: **15.00**
58 ❑ Feb 1958 — Cover: 0.10 — **NM** value: **15.00**
59 ❑ Apr 1958 — Cover: 0.10 — **NM** value: **15.00**
60 ❑ Jun 1958 — Cover: 0.10 — **NM** value: **15.00**
61 ❑ Aug 1958 — Cover: 0.10 — **NM** value: **14.00**
62 ❑ Oct 1958 — Cover: 0.10 — **NM** value: **14.00**
63 ❑ Dec 1958 — Cover: 0.10 — **NM** value: **14.00**
64 ❑ Feb 1959 — Cover: 0.10 — **NM** value: **14.00**
65 ❑ Apr 1959 — Cover: 0.10 — **NM** value: **14.00**
66 ❑ Jun 1959 — Cover: 0.10 — **NM** value: **14.00**
67 ❑ Aug 1959 — Cover: 0.10 — **NM** value: **14.00**
68 ❑ Oct 1959 — Cover: 0.10 — **NM** value: **14.00**
69 ❑ Dec 1959 — Cover: 0.10 — **NM** value: **14.00**
70 ❑ Feb 1960 — Cover: 0.10 — **NM** value: **14.00**
Circ: Statement: **568,803**
71 ❑ Apr 1960 — Cover: 0.10 — **NM** value: **13.00**
Circ: Statement: **568,803**
72 ❑ Jun 1960 — Cover: 0.10 — **NM** value: **13.00**
Circ: Statement: **568,803**
📖 Baffled By Boatnappers; Cabin Cutups; The Big Fish Flop; Pet Competition
73 ❑ Aug 1960 — Cover: 0.10 — **NM** value: **13.00**
Circ: Statement: **568,803**
74 ❑ Oct 1960 — Cover: 0.10 — **NM** value: **13.00**
Circ: Statement: **568,803**
75 ❑ Dec 1960 — Cover: 0.10 — **NM** value: **13.00**
Circ: Statement: **568,803**
76 ❑ Mar 1961 — Cover: 0.15 — **NM** value: **13.00**
77 ❑ ca. 1961 — Cover: 0.15 — **NM** value: **13.00**
78 ❑ Jun 1961 — Cover: 0.15 — **NM** value: **13.00**
79 ❑ ca. 1961 — Cover: 0.15 — **NM** value: **13.00**
80 ❑ Nov 1961 — Cover: 0.15 — **NM** value: **13.00**
81 ❑ Jan 1962 — Cover: 0.15 — **NM** value: **11.00**
82 ❑ Mar 1962 — Cover: 0.15 — **NM** value: **11.00**
83 ❑ Jun 1962 — Cover: 0.15 — **NM** value: **11.00**
84 ❑ Sep 1962 — Cover: 0.12 — **NM** value: **11.00**
85 ❑ Nov 1962 — Cover: 0.12 — **NM** value: **11.00**
86 ❑ Feb 1963 — Cover: 0.12 — **NM** value: **11.00**
87 ❑ May 1963 — Cover: 0.12 — **NM** value: **11.00**
88 ❑ Jul 1963 — Cover: 0.12 — **NM** value: **11.00**
89 ❑ Sep 1963 — Cover: 0.12 — **NM** value: **11.00**
90 ❑ Nov 1963 — Cover: 0.12 — **NM** value: **11.00**
91 ❑ Dec 1963 — Cover: 0.12 — **NM** value: **11.00**
92 ❑ Feb 1964 — Cover: 0.12 — **NM** value: **11.00**
93 ❑ ca. 1964 — Cover: 0.12 — **NM** value: **11.00**
94 ❑ ca. 1964 — Cover: 0.12 — **NM** value: **11.00**
95 ❑ Jul 1964 — Cover: 0.12 — **NM** value: **11.00**
96 ❑ ca. 1964 — Cover: 0.12 — **NM** value: **11.00**
97 ❑ Oct 1964 — Cover: 0.12 — **NM** value: **11.00**
98 ❑ Nov 1964 — Cover: 0.12 — **NM** value: **11.00**
Circ: Statement: **231,814**
99 ❑ Feb 1965 — Cover: 0.12 — **NM** value: **11.00**
Circ: Statement: **231,814**
100 ❑ Apr 1965 — Cover: 0.12 — **NM** value: **11.00**
Circ: Statement: **231,814**
101 ❑ Jun 1965 — Cover: 0.12 — **NM** value: **10.00**
Circ: Statement: **231,814**
102 ❑ Aug 1965 — Cover: 0.12 — **NM** value: **10.00**
Circ: Statement: **231,814**
103 ❑ Oct 1965 — Cover: 0.12 — **NM** value: **10.00**
Circ: Statement: **231,814**
104 ❑ Dec 1965 — Cover: 0.12 — **NM** value: **10.00**
Circ: Statement: **225,716**
105 ❑ Feb 1966 — Cover: 0.12 — **NM** value: **10.00**
Circ: Statement: **225,716**
• Has 1965 Statement, filed 9/28/65; avg print run 398,250; avg sales 280,943; avg subs 2,871; avg total paid 231,814; samples 850; max existent 232,664; 37% of run returned
106 ❑ Apr 1966 — Cover: 0.12 — **NM** value: **10.00**
Circ: Statement: **225,716**
107 ❑ Jun 1966 — Cover: 0.12 — **NM** value: **10.00**
Circ: Statement: **225,716**
108 ❑ Aug 1966 — Cover: 0.12 — **NM** value: **10.00**
Circ: Statement: **225,716**
109 ❑ Oct 1966 — Cover: 0.12 — **NM** value: **10.00**
Circ: Statement: **225,716**
110 ❑ Dec 1966 — Cover: 0.12 — **NM** value: **10.00**
Circ: Statement: **205,083**
111 ❑ Feb 1967 — Cover: 0.12 — **NM** value: **10.00**
Circ: Statement: **205,083**
112 ❑ Apr 1967 — Cover: 0.12 — **NM** value: **10.00**
Circ: Statement: **205,083**
113 ❑ Jun 1967 — Cover: 0.12 — **NM** value: **10.00**
Circ: Statement: **205,083**
114 ❑ Aug 1967 — Cover: 0.12 — **NM** value: **10.00**
Circ: Statement: **205,083**
115 ❑ Nov 1967 — Cover: 0.12 — **NM** value: **10.00**
Circ: Statement: **205,083**
116 ❑ Feb 1968 — Cover: 0.12 — **NM** value: **10.00**
117 ❑ May 1968 — Cover: 0.12 — **NM** value: **10.00**
• Has 1967 Statement; avg print run 395,790; avg sales 203,900; avg subs 1,183; avg total paid 205,083; samples 557; max existent 205,640; 48% of run returned
118 ❑ Aug 1968 — Cover: 0.12 — **NM** value: **10.00**
119 ❑ Nov 1968 — Cover: 0.15 — **NM** value: **10.00**
120 ❑ Feb 1969 — Cover: 0.15 — **NM** value: **10.00**
121 ❑ May 1969 — Cover: 0.15 — **NM** value: **9.00**
122 ❑ Aug 1969 — Cover: 0.15 — **NM** value: **9.00**
123 ❑ Nov 1969 — Cover: 0.15 — **NM** value: **9.00**
124 ❑ Feb 1970 — Cover: 0.15 — **NM** value: **9.00**
125 ❑ May 1970 — Cover: 0.15 — **NM** value: **9.00**
126 ❑ Aug 1970 — Cover: 0.15 — **NM** value: **9.00**
127 ❑ Nov 1970 — Cover: 0.15 — **NM** value: **9.00**
Circ: Statement: **210,361**
128 ❑ Feb 1971 — Cover: 0.15 — **NM** value: **9.00**
Circ: Statement: **210,361**
129 ❑ Apr 1971 — Cover: 0.15 — **NM** value: **9.00**
Circ: Statement: **210,361**
130 ❑ Jun 1971 — Cover: 0.15 — **NM** value: **9.00**
Circ: Statement: **210,361**
131 ❑ Aug 1971 — Cover: 0.15 — **NM** value: **9.00**
Circ: Statement: **210,361**
132 ❑ Oct 1971 — Cover: 0.15 — **NM** value: **9.00**
Circ: Statement: **210,361**
133 ❑ Dec 1971 — Cover: 0.15 — **NM** value: **9.00**
134 ❑ Feb 1972 — Cover: 0.15 — **NM** value: **9.00**
• Has 1971 Statement; avg print run 327,008; avg total paid circ 210,361
135 ❑ Apr 1972 — Cover: 0.15 — **NM** value: **9.00**
136 ❑ Jun 1972 — Cover: 0.15 — **NM** value: **9.00**
137 ❑ Aug 1972 — Cover: 0.15 — **NM** value: **9.00**
138 ❑ Oct 1972 — Cover: 0.15 — **NM** value: **9.00**
139 ❑ Dec 1972 — Cover: 0.15 — **NM** value: **9.00**
140 ❑ Feb 1973 — Cover: 0.15 — **NM** value: **9.00**
• **CGC:** 12 graded, best 9.6
141 ❑ Apr 1973 — Cover: 0.15 — **NM** value: **7.00**
142 ❑ Jun 1973 — Cover: 0.20 — **NM** value: **7.00**
143 ❑ Aug 1973 — Cover: 0.20 — **NM** value: **7.00**
144 ❑ Sep 1973 — Cover: 0.20 — **NM** value: **7.00**
145 ❑ Oct 1973 — Cover: 0.20 — **NM** value: **7.00**
146 ❑ Dec 1973 — Cover: 0.20 — **NM** value: **7.00**
147 ❑ Feb 1974 — Cover: 0.20 — **NM** value: **7.00**
148 ❑ Apr 1974 — Cover: 0.20 — **NM** value: **7.00**
149 ❑ Jun 1974 — Cover: 0.20 — **NM** value: **7.00**
150 ❑ Aug 1974 — Cover: 0.25 — **NM** value: **7.00**
151 ❑ Sep 1974 — Cover: 0.25 — **NM** value: **7.00**
152 ❑ Oct 1974 — Cover: 0.25 — **NM** value: **7.00**
153 ❑ Dec 1974 — Cover: 0.25 — **NM** value: **7.00**
154 ❑ Feb 1975 — Cover: 0.25 — **NM** value: **7.00**
155 ❑ Apr 1975 — Cover: 0.25 — **NM** value: **7.00**
156 ❑ Jun 1975 — Cover: 0.25 — **NM** value: **7.00**
157 ❑ Aug 1975 — Cover: 0.25 — **NM** value: **7.00**
158 ❑ Sep 1975 — Cover: 0.25 — **NM** value: **7.00**
159 ❑ Oct 1975 — Cover: 0.25 — **NM** value: **7.00**
160 ❑ Nov 1975 — Cover: 0.25 — **NM** value: **7.00**
161 ❑ Jan 1976 — Cover: 0.25 — **NM** value: **6.00**
162 ❑ Apr 1976 — Cover: 0.25 — **NM** value: **6.00**
163 ❑ Jun 1976 — Cover: 0.25 — **NM** value: **6.00**
164 ❑ Aug 1976 — Cover: 0.25 — **NM** value: **6.00**
165 ❑ Sep 1976 — Cover: 0.25 — **NM** value: **6.00**
166 ❑ Oct 1976 — Cover: 0.30 — **NM** value: **6.00**
167 ❑ Nov 1976 — Cover: 0.30 — **NM** value: **6.00**
168 ❑ Dec 1976 — Cover: 0.30 — **NM** value: **6.00**
169 ❑ Feb 1977 — Cover: 0.30 — **NM** value: **6.00**
170 ❑ Apr 1977 — Cover: 0.30 — **NM** value: **6.00**
171 ❑ May 1977 — Cover: 0.30 — **NM** value: **6.00**
172 ❑ Jun 1977 — Cover: 0.30 — **NM** value: **6.00**
173 ❑ Jul 1977 — Cover: 0.30 — **NM** value: **6.00**
174 ❑ Aug 1977 — Cover: 0.30 — **NM** value: **6.00**
175 ❑ Sep 1977 — Cover: 0.30 — **NM** value: **6.00**
176 ❑ Oct 1977 — Cover: 0.30 — **NM** value: **6.00**
177 ❑ Nov 1977 — Cover: 0.30 — **NM** value: **6.00**
178 ❑ Dec 1977 — Cover: 0.35 — **NM** value: **6.00**
179 ❑ Jan 1978 — Cover: 0.35 — **NM** value: **6.00**
180 ❑ Feb 1978 — Cover: 0.35 — **NM** value: **6.00**
181 ❑ Mar 1978 — Cover: 0.35 — **NM** value: **5.00**
182 ❑ Apr 1978 — Cover: 0.35 — **NM** value: **5.00**
183 ❑ May 1978 — Cover: 0.35 — **NM** value: **5.00**
184 ❑ Jun 1978 — Cover: 0.35 — **NM** value: **5.00**
185 ❑ Jul 1978 — Cover: 0.35 — **NM** value: **5.00**
186 ❑ Aug 1978 — Cover: 0.35 — **NM** value: **5.00**
187 ❑ Sep 1978 — Cover: 0.35 — **NM** value: **5.00**
188 ❑ Oct 1978 — Cover: 0.35 — **NM** value: **5.00**
189 ❑ Nov 1978 — Cover: 0.35 — **NM** value: **5.00**
190 ❑ Dec 1978 — Cover: 0.35 — **NM** value: **5.00**
191 ❑ Jan 1979 — Cover: 0.35 — **NM** value: **5.00**
192 ❑ Feb 1979 — Cover: 0.35 — **NM** value: **5.00**
193 ❑ Mar 1979 — Cover: 0.35 — **NM** value: **5.00**
194 ❑ Apr 1979 — Cover: 0.40 — **NM** value: **5.00**
195 ❑ May 1979 — Cover: 0.40 — **NM** value: **5.00**
196 ❑ Jun 1979 — Cover: 0.40 — **NM** value: **5.00**
197 ❑ Jul 1979 — Cover: 0.40 — **NM** value: **5.00**
198 ❑ Aug 1979 — Cover: 0.40 — **NM** value: **5.00**
199 ❑ Sep 1979 — Cover: 0.40 — **NM** value: **5.00**
200 ❑ Oct 1979 — Cover: 0.40 — **NM** value: **5.00**
201 ❑ Nov 1979 — Cover: 0.40 — **NM** value: **4.00**
202 ❑ Dec 1979 — Cover: 0.40 — **NM** value: **4.00**
203 ❑ Jan 1980 — Cover: 0.40 — **NM** value: **4.00**
204 ❑ Feb 1980 — Cover: 0.40 — **NM** value: **4.00**
205 ❑ Apr 1980 — Cover: 0.40 — **NM** value: **4.00**
206 ❑ Jun 1980 — Cover: 0.40 — **NM** value: **4.00**
207 ❑ Jul 1980 — Cover: 0.40 — **NM** value: **4.00**
208 ❑ Aug 1980 — Cover: 0.40 — **NM** value: **4.00**
• **CGC:** 3 graded, best 9.6
209 ❑ — **NM** value: **4.00**
210 ❑ — **NM** value: **4.00**
211 ❑ Jun 1981 — Cover: 0.50 — **NM** value: **3.00**
212 ❑ Aug 1981 — Cover: 0.50 — **NM** value: **3.00**
213 ❑ Sep 1981 — Cover: 0.50 — **NM** value: **3.00**
214 ❑ Dec 1981 — Cover: 0.50 — **NM** value: **3.00**
215 ❑ Feb 1982 — Cover: 0.60 — **NM** value: **3.00**
216 ❑ — **NM** value: **3.00**
217 ❑ — **NM** value: **3.00**
218 ❑ — Cover: 0.75 — **NM** value: **3.00**
• Last Gold Key issue
219 ❑ Oct 1986 — Cover: 0.75 — **NM** value: **3.00**
Circ: CapCity orders: **3,450** • **CGC:** 1 graded, best 9.4
A: Floyd Gottfredson • First Gladstone issue
220 ❑ Nov 1986 — Cover: 0.75 — **NM** value: **3.00**
Circ: CapCity orders: **3,375**
A: Floyd Gottfredson
221 ❑ Dec 1986 — Cover: 0.75 — **NM** value: **2.50**
Circ: CapCity orders: **3,575**
A: Floyd Gottfredson
222 ❑ Jan 1987 — Cover: 0.75 — **NM** value: **2.50**
Circ: Statement: **73,806** CapCity orders: **4,500**
A: Floyd Gottfredson
223 ❑ Feb 1987 — Cover: 0.75 — **NM** value: **2.50**

Circ: Statement: **73,806** CapCity orders: **5,450**
A: Floyd Gottfredson

224 ❑ Mar 1987 Cover: 0.75 **NM** value: **2.50**
Circ: Statement: **73,806** CapCity orders: **6,175**
A: Floyd Gottfredson

225 ❑ Apr 1987 Cover: 0.75 **NM** value: **2.50**
Circ: Statement: **73,806** CapCity orders: **5,125**
A: Floyd Gottfredson

226 ❑ May 1987 Cover: 0.75 **NM** value: **2.50**
Circ: Statement: **73,806** CapCity orders: **4,225**
A: Floyd Gottfredson

227 ❑ Jun 1987 Cover: 0.95 **NM** value: **2.50**
Circ: Statement: **73,806** CapCity orders: **4,250**
A: Floyd Gottfredson

228 ❑ Jul 1987 Cover: 0.95 **NM** value: **2.50**
Circ: Statement: **73,806** CapCity orders: **4,175**
A: Floyd Gottfredson

229 ❑ Aug 1987 Cover: 0.95 **NM** value: **2.50**
Circ: Statement: **73,806** CapCity orders: **4,375**
A: Floyd Gottfredson

230 ❑ Sep 1987 Cover: 0.95 **NM** value: **2.50**
Circ: Statement: **73,806** CapCity orders: **4,525**
A: Floyd Gottfredson

231 ❑ Oct 1987 Cover: 0.95 **NM** value: **2.50**
Circ: Statement: **73,806** CapCity orders: **4,600**
A: Floyd Gottfredson

232 ❑ Nov 1987 Cover: 0.95 **NM** value: **2.50**
Circ: Statement: **73,806** CapCity orders: **4,525**
A: Floyd Gottfredson

233 ❑ Dec 1987 Cover: 0.95 **NM** value: **2.50**
Circ: Statement: **73,806** CapCity orders: **4,350**
A: Floyd Gottfredson

234 ❑ Jan 1988 Cover: 0.95 **NM** value: **2.50**
Circ: Statement: **63,119** CapCity orders: **4,525**
A: Floyd Gottfredson

235 ❑ Mar 1988 Cover: 0.95 **NM** value: **2.50**
Circ: Statement: **63,119** CapCity orders: **4,725**
A: Floyd Gottfredson

236 ❑ Apr 1988 Cover: 0.95 **NM** value: **2.50**
Circ: Statement: **63,119** CapCity orders: **4,700**
A: Floyd Gottfredson

237 ❑ Jun 1988 Cover: 0.95 **NM** value: **2.50**
Circ: Statement: **63,119** CapCity orders: **4,500**
A: Floyd Gottfredson

238 ❑ Jul 1988 Cover: 0.95 **NM** value: **2.50**
Circ: Statement: **63,119** CapCity orders: **4,550**
A: Floyd Gottfredson

239 ❑ Aug 1988 Cover: 0.95 **NM** value: **2.50**
Circ: Statement: **63,119** CapCity orders: **4,550**
A: Floyd Gottfredson

240 ❑ Sep 1988 Cover: 0.95 **NM** value: **2.50**
Circ: Statement: **63,119** CapCity orders: **4,500**
A: Floyd Gottfredson

241 ❑ Oct 1988 Cover: 0.95 **NM** value: **2.00**
Circ: Statement: **63,119** CapCity orders: **4,700**
A: Floyd Gottfredson

242 ❑ Nov 1988 Cover: 0.95 **NM** value: **2.00**
Circ: Statement: **63,119** CapCity orders: **4,550**
A: Floyd Gottfredson

243 ❑ Dec 1988 Cover: 0.95 **NM** value: **2.00**
Circ: Statement: **63,119** CapCity orders: **4,550**
A: Floyd Gottfredson

244 ❑ Jan 1989 Cover: 2.95 **NM** value: **Cover or less**
Circ: Statement: **63,183** CapCity orders: **5,100**
• 60th anniversary, 100 pages. 📖 The Miracle Master; Society Dog Show • Daily Strips compilation **A:** Floyd Gottfredson

245 ❑ Mar 1989 Cover: 0.95 **NM** value: **2.00**
Circ: Statement: **63,183** CapCity orders: **4,850**
📖 Mickey Mouse and Pluto Battle the Giant Ants **A:** Floyd Gottfredson; Bill Wright

246 ❑ Apr 1989 Cover: 0.95 **NM** value: **2.00**
Circ: Statement: **63,183** CapCity orders: **4,950**
A: Floyd Gottfredson

247 ❑ Jun 1989 Cover: 0.95 **NM** value: **2.00**
Circ: Statement: **63,183** CapCity orders: **4,800**
A: Floyd Gottfredson

248 ❑ Jul 1989 Cover: 0.95 **NM** value: **2.00**
Circ: Statement: **63,183** CapCity orders: **5,000**
A: Floyd Gottfredson

249 ❑ Aug 1989 Cover: 0.95 **NM** value: **2.00**
Circ: Statement: **63,183** CapCity orders: **5,000**
A: Floyd Gottfredson

250 ❑ Sep 1989 Cover: 0.95 **NM** value: **2.00**
Circ: Statement: **63,183** CapCity orders: **5,050**
A: Floyd Gottfredson

251 ❑ Oct 1989 Cover: 0.95 **NM** value: **2.00**
Circ: Statement: **63,183** CapCity orders: **5,150**
A: Floyd Gottfredson

252 ❑ Nov 1989 Cover: 0.95 **NM** value: **2.00**
Circ: Statement: **63,183** CapCity orders: **5,150**
A: Floyd Gottfredson

253 ❑ Dec 1989 Cover: 0.95 **NM** value: **2.00**
Circ: Statement: **63,183** CapCity orders: **5,100**
A: Floyd Gottfredson

254 ❑ Jan 1990 Cover: 0.95 **NM** value: **2.00**
Circ: CapCity orders: **5,200**
A: Floyd Gottfredson

255 ❑ Feb 1990 Cover: 1.95 **NM** value: **2.00**
Circ: CapCity orders: **4,850**

256 ❑ Apr 1990 Cover: 1.95 **NM** value: **2.00**
Circ: CapCity orders: **5,000**
final issue.

MICKEY RAT — Los Angeles Comic Book Co.

All issues are adults only.

1 ❑ May 1972, b&w Cover: 0.50 **NM** value: **5.00**
A: Robert Armstrong **W:** Robert Armstrong

2 ❑ Oct 1972, b&w Cover: 0.50 **NM** value: **4.00**
📖 Feelin' Kinda Disney; The Coming of the Rat-Man; Incense Reaction; The Rot Expedition **A:** Robert Armstrong **W:** Robert Armstrong

3 ❑ Jul 1980, b&w Cover: 1.25 **NM** value: **3.00**
A: Robert Armstrong **W:** Robert Armstrong

4 ❑ b&w Cover: 1.50 **NM** value: **3.00**
📖 ...Nothing Like a Nice Day in the Park; The Life of the Party; Dizzy Ratstein: Beyond the Pedestrian; Hot Time in the Old Town; The Couch Potatoes; On the Youth Scene; The Helping Hand; Jamming in the Groove; The Survivor **A:** Robert Armstrong **W:** Robert Armstrong

MICRA: MIND CONTROLLED REMOTE AUTOMATON — Comics Interview

1 ❑ Nov 1986 Cover: 1.75 **NM** value: **Cover or less**
📖 The Beginning **A:** Ted Boonthanakit **W:** Lamar Waldron

2 ❑ 1987 Cover: 1.75 **NM** value: **Cover or less**
3 ❑ Feb 1987 Cover: 1.75 **NM** value: **Cover or less**
4 ❑ 1987 Cover: 1.75 **NM** value: **Cover or less**
5 ❑ 1987 Cover: 1.75 **NM** value: **Cover or less**
6 ❑ 1987 Cover: 1.75 **NM** value: **Cover or less**
7 ❑ 1987 Cover: 1.75 **NM** value: **Cover or less**
Bk 1 ❑ Cover: 4.95 **NM** value: **Cover or less**
• collects #1-3

MICROBOTS, THE — Gold Key

1 ❑ Dec 1971 Cover: 0.15 **NM** value: **10.00**
📖 This is the Way the World Ends

MICRONAUTS (VOL. 1) — Marvel

The toys were never that popular, but Marvel's comic books still give Generation X-ers the warm fuzzies. In adapting Mego's toys to a comics title, Marvel delivered a surprisingly strong series which brought a whole new dimension, the "Microverse," to the Marvel Universe.

The Micronauts chronicles the struggle of a band of freedom fighters as they battle the empire's "dog-soldiers" and the dread Baron Karza. Taking place in a microcosmic world somehow located within our own, the rebels battle against impossible odds, in a war that occasionally spills over into our own dimension — thanks to the manufacturer's far-sighted willingness to allow their characters to exist in the Marvel universe proper.

Partway through its run, Micronauts became one of the first Marvel series to leave newsstands entirely, selling to comics shops only.

1 ❑ Jan 1979 Cover: 0.35 **NM** value: **3.00**
• **CGC:** 19 graded, best 9.8
A: Michael Golden ★ Origin of Micronauts. ★ 1st Appearance of The Micronauts, Baron Karza, Space Glider, Biotron, Marionette.

2 ❑ Feb 1979 Cover: 0.35 **NM** value: **2.50**
• **CGC:** 3 graded, best 9.4
A: Michael Golden

3 ❑ Mar 1979 Cover: 0.35 **NM** value: **2.25**
• **CGC:** 4 graded, best 9.8
A: Michael Golden

4 ❑ Apr 1979 Cover: 0.35 **NM** value: **2.25**
• **CGC:** 1 graded, best 9.0
A: Michael Golden

5 ❑ May 1979 Cover: 0.40 **NM** value: **2.25**
A: Michael Golden

6 ❑ Jun 1979 Cover: 0.40 **NM** value: **2.00**
• **CGC:** 1 graded, best 9.6
A: Michael Golden

7 ❑ Jul 1979 Cover: 0.40 **NM** value: **2.00**
• **CGC:** 1 graded, best 9.4
A: Michael Golden ★ Appearance of Man-Thing.

8 ❑ Aug 1979 Cover: 0.40 **NM** value: **2.25**
A: Michael Golden ★ 1st Appearance of Captain Universe. ★ Appearance of Captain Universe.

9 ❑ Sep 1979 Cover: 0.40 **NM** value: **2.00**
A: Michael Golden

10 ❑ Oct 1979 Cover: 0.40 **NM** value: **2.00**
A: Michael Golden

11 ❑ Nov 1979 Cover: 0.40 **NM** value: **1.50**
A: Michael Golden

12 ❑ Dec 1979 Cover: 0.40 **NM** value: **1.50**
A: Michael Golden

13 ❑ Jan 1980 Cover: 0.40 **NM** value: **1.50**
14 ❑ Feb 1980 Cover: 0.40 **NM** value: **1.50**
15 ❑ Mar 1980 Cover: 0.40 **NM** value: **1.50**
★ Appearance of Fantastic Four. ★ Death of Microtron.

16 ❑ Apr 1980 Cover: 0.40 **NM** value: **1.50**
★ Appearance of Fantastic Four.

17 ❑ May 1980 Cover: 0.40 **NM** value: **1.50**
★ Appearance of Fantastic Four. ★ Death of Jasmine.

18 ❑ Jun 1980 Cover: 0.40 **NM** value: **1.50**
19 ❑ Jul 1980 Cover: 0.40 **NM** value: **1.50**
20 ❑ Aug 1980 Cover: 0.40 **NM** value: **1.50**
★ Appearance of Ant-Man.

21 ❑ Sep 1980 Cover: 0.50 **NM** value: **1.25**
22 ❑ Oct 1980 Cover: 0.50 **NM** value: **1.25**
23 ❑ Nov 1980 Cover: 0.50 **NM** value: **1.25**
★ Versus Molecule Man.

24 ❑ Dec 1980 Cover: 0.50 **NM** value: **1.25**
25 ❑ Jan 1981 Cover: 0.50 **NM** value: **1.25**
Circ: Statement: **132,000**
★ Origin of Baron Karza. ★ Versus Mentallo.

26 ❑ Feb 1981 Cover: 0.50 **NM** value: **1.25**
Circ: Statement: **132,000**
A: Pat Broderick

27 ❑ Mar 1981 Cover: 0.50 **NM** value: **1.25**
Circ: Statement: **132,000**
A: Pat Broderick ★ Death of Biotron.

28 ❑ Apr 1981 Cover: 0.50 **NM** value: **1.25**
Circ: Statement: **132,000**
A: Pat Broderick ★ Appearance of Nick Fury.

29 ❑ May 1981 Cover: 0.50 **NM** value: **1.25**
Circ: Statement: **132,000**
A: Pat Broderick ★ Appearance of Nick Fury.

30 ❑ Jun 1981 Cover: 0.50 **NM** value: **1.25**
Circ: Statement: **132,000**
A: Pat Broderick

31 ❑ Jul 1981 Cover: 0.50 **NM** value: **1.25**
Circ: Statement: **132,000**
A: Pat Broderick; Frank Miller(cover) ★ Appearance of Doctor Strange.

32 ❑ Aug 1981 Cover: 0.50 **NM** value: **1.25**
Circ: Statement: **132,000**
A: Pat Broderick ★ Appearance of Doctor Strange.

33 ❑ Sep 1981 Cover: 0.50 **NM** value: **1.25**
Circ: Statement: **132,000**
A: Pat Broderick ★ Appearance of Doctor Strange.

34 ❑ Oct 1981 Cover: 0.50 **NM** value: **1.25**
Circ: Statement: **132,000**
A: Pat Broderick ★ Appearance of Doctor Strange.

35 ❑ Nov 1981 Cover: 0.75 **NM** value: **1.25**
Circ: Statement: **132,000**
• double-sized. ★ Origin of Microverse. ★ Appearance of Doctor Strange.

36 ❑ Dec 1981 Cover: 0.50 **NM** value: **1.25**
Circ: Statement: **132,000**

37 ❑ Jan 1982 Cover: 0.60 **NM** value: **1.50**
★ Appearance of X-Men, Nightcrawler.

38 ❑ Feb 1982 Cover: 0.75 **NM** value: **1.50**
• Direct sales (only) begin

39 ❑ Mar 1982 Cover: 0.75 **NM** value: **1.25**
40 ❑ Apr 1982 Cover: 0.75 **NM** value: **1.25**
★ Appearance of Fantastic Four.

41 ❑ May 1982 Cover: 0.75 **NM** value: **1.25**
★ Versus Dr. Doom. ★ Versus Doctor Doom.

42 ❑ Jun 1982 Cover: 0.75 **NM** value: **1.25**
43 ❑ Jul 1982 Cover: 0.75 **NM** value: **1.25**
44 ❑ Aug 1982 Cover: 0.75 **NM** value: **1.25**
45 ❑ Sep 1982 Cover: 0.75 **NM** value: **1.25**
46 ❑ Oct 1982 Cover: 0.75 **NM** value: **1.25**
47 ❑ Nov 1982 Cover: 0.75 **NM** value: **1.25**
48 ❑ Dec 1982 Cover: 0.75 **NM** value: **1.25**
• 1st Guice **A:** Jackson Guice

49 ❑ Jan 1983 Cover: 0.75 **NM** value: **1.25**
Circ: Statement: **80,685**

50 ❑ Feb 1983 Cover: 0.75 **NM** value: **1.25**
Circ: Statement: **80,685**

51 ❑ Mar 1983 Cover: 0.75 **NM** value: **1.25**
Circ: Statement: **80,685**

52 ❑ May 1983 Cover: 0.75 **NM** value: **1.25**
Circ: Statement: **80,685**

53 ❑ Jul 1983 Cover: 0.75 **NM** value: **1.25**
Circ: Statement: **80,685**

54 ❑ Sep 1983 Cover: 0.75 **NM** value: **1.25**
Circ: Statement: **80,685**

55 ❑ Nov 1983 Cover: 0.75 **NM** value: **1.25**
Circ: Statement: **80,685**

56 ❑ Jan 1984 Cover: 0.75 **NM** value: **1.25**
57 ❑ Mar 1984 Cover: 1.00 **NM** value: **1.25**
• double-sized.

58 ❑ May 1984 Cover: 0.75 **NM** value: **1.25**
• Has 1983 Statement, filed 10/3/83; avg print run 82,258; avg sales 69,807; avg subs 10,878; avg total paid circ 80,685; samples 491; office use 1,082; max existent 82,258; no newsstand sales this year

59 ❑ Aug 1984 Cover: 0.75 **NM** value: **1.25**
📖 Homeworld final issue. **A:** Kelley Jones **W:** Peter B. Gillis

Anl 1 ❑ Dec 1979 Cover: 0.75 **NM** value: **2.00**
• **CGC:** 1 graded, best 9.2
A: Steve Ditko

Anl 2 ❑ Oct 1980 Cover: 0.75 **NM** value: **1.50**
• **CGC:** 1 graded, best 9.8
A: Steve Ditko ★ Versus Toymaster.

SE 1 ❑ Dec 1983 Cover: 2.00 **NM** value: **Cover or less**
SE 2 ❑ Jan 1984 Cover: 2.00 **NM** value: **Cover or less**
SE 3 ❑ Feb 1984 Cover: 2.00 **NM** value: **Cover or less**
SE 4 ❑ Mar 1984 Cover: 2.00 **NM** value: **Cover or less**
SE 5 ❑ Apr 1984 Cover: 2.00 **NM** value: **Cover or less**

MICRONAUTS (VOL. 2) — Marvel

By the end of their first series, the Micronauts had finally defeated their dread enemy Baron Karza. Nevertheless, the battle had cost them dearly: they had lost friends and lovers, and had seen multitudes killed in the struggle against Karza's rule. Victory was not sweet.

At the start of this second series, the Micronauts are on a journey to find peace within themselves. Acroyear was once the warrior king of Spartak, but has turned from war to become a priest. Similarly, Huntarr, who was bio-engineered in Karza's body banks to be the ultimate instrument of war, must discover how to live during peacetime.

Released a long time after the toys came out — but too soon for nostalgia to kick in — this second series failed to find many of the old fans.

1 ❑ Oct 1984 Cover: 0.60 **NM** value: **1.50**
• **CGC:** 1 graded, best 9.2
📖 Shadow Of The Makers • Makers **A:** Kelley Jones **W:** Peter B. Gillis

CGC-graded: Multiply prices above by **33 for 9.9 M • 16 for 9.8 NM/M • 7 for 9.6 NM+ • 5 for 9.4 NM • 2.5 for 9.2 NM- • 1.5 for 9.0 VF/NM**

2 ❑ Nov 1984 Cover: 0.60 **NM** value: **1.00**
Life-Cycles **A:** Kelley Jones **W:** Peter B. Gillis
3 ❑ Dec 1984 Cover: 0.60 **NM** value: **1.00**
4 ❑ Jan 1985 Cover: 0.60 **NM** value: **1.00**
5 ❑ Feb 1985 Cover: 0.60 **NM** value: **1.00**
6 ❑ Mar 1985 Cover: 0.60 **NM** value: **1.00**
7 ❑ Apr 1985 Cover: 0.65 **NM** value: **1.00**
8 ❑ May 1985 Cover: 0.65 **NM** value: **1.00**
Circ: CapCity orders: **11,100**
9 ❑ Jun 1985 Cover: 0.65 **NM** value: **1.00**
Circ: CapCity orders: **10,400**
10 ❑ Jul 1985 Cover: 0.65 **NM** value: **1.00**
Circ: CapCity orders: **10,000**
11 ❑ Aug 1985 Cover: 0.65 **NM** value: **1.00**
Circ: CapCity orders: **9,900**
12 ❑ Sep 1985 Cover: 0.65 **NM** value: **1.00**
Circ: CapCity orders: **9,700**
13 ❑ Oct 1985 Cover: 0.65 **NM** value: **1.00**
Circ: CapCity orders: **9,300**
14 ❑ Nov 1985 Cover: 0.65 **NM** value: **1.00**
Circ: CapCity orders: **8,800**
15 ❑ Dec 1985 Cover: 0.65 **NM** value: **1.00**
Circ: CapCity orders: **8,600**
16 ❑ Jan 1986 Cover: 0.65 **NM** value: **1.00**
Circ: CapCity orders: **16,100**
• Secret Wars II
17 ❑ Feb 1986 Cover: 0.75 **NM** value: **1.00**
Circ: CapCity orders: **8,700**
18 ❑ Mar 1986 Cover: 0.75 **NM** value: **1.00**
Circ: CapCity orders: **8,800**
And One Clear Call for Me! **A:** Kelley Jones **W:** Peter B. Gillis
19 ❑ Apr 1986 Cover: 0.75 **NM** value: **1.00**
Circ: CapCity orders: **8,600**
20 ❑ May 1986 Cover: 0.75 **NM** value: **1.00**
Circ: CapCity orders: **9,700**

MIDDLE CLASS FANTASIES — Cartoonists Co-Op

1 ❑ Cover: 0.50 **NM** value: **3.00**
The Frogman; A Night at Motel 6 **A:** Jerry Lane **W:** Jerry Lane
2 ❑ Cover: 1.00 **NM** value: **3.00**
The Return of the Frogman; chicken Noodle Goes West **A:** Jerry Lane **W:** Jerry Lane

MIDGET COMICS — St. John

1 ❑ ca. 1950 Cover: 0.10 **NM** value: **100.00**
2 ❑ ca. 1950 Cover: 0.10 **NM** value: **50.00**

MIDNIGHT — Ajax

1 ❑ Apr 1957 Cover: 0.10 **NM** value: **50.00**
• **CGC:** 2 graded, best 9.2
2 ❑ 1958 Cover: 0.10 **NM** value: **35.00**
3 ❑ Cover: 0.10 **NM** value: **25.00**
4 ❑ Cover: 0.10 **NM** value: **25.00**
5 ❑ Feb 1958 Cover: 0.10 **NM** value: **25.00**
The Mightiest Force in the World!; He Sailed into Silence!; Double Terror (text); Doing the Turkey Trot!; The Last Laugh!
6 ❑ Cover: 0.10 **NM** value: **25.00**

MIDNIGHT DAYS (NEIL GAIMAN'S...) — DC / Vertigo

1 ❑ Jan 2000 Cover: 17.95 **NM** value: **Cover or less**
Jack in the Green; Brothers, Shaggy God Stories, Hold Me • Reprints Neil Gaiman stories from Swamp Thing, Hellblazer, Sandman Midnight Theatre **A:** Richard Piers Rayner; Mike Hoffman; Dave McKean; Mike Mignola; Stephen R. Bissette **W:** Matt Wagner; Neil Gaiman

MIDNIGHT EYE GOKU — Viz

1 ❑ Cover: 4.95 **NM** value: **Cover or less**
Circ: CapCity orders: **3,800**
2 ❑ Cover: 4.95 **NM** value: **Cover or less**
Circ: CapCity orders: **2,675**
3 ❑ Cover: 4.95 **NM** value: **Cover or less**
4 ❑ Cover: 4.95 **NM** value: **Cover or less**
Circ: CapCity orders: **2,700**
5 ❑ Cover: 4.95 **NM** value: **Cover or less**
Circ: CapCity orders: **2,575**
6 ❑ Cover: 4.95 **NM** value: **Cover or less**
Circ: CapCity orders: **2,475**

MIDNIGHT MEN — Marvel / Epic

1 ❑ Jun 1993 Cover: 2.50 **NM** value: **Cover or less**
Circ: CapCity orders: **29,400**
Embossed cover. **A:** Howard Chaykin **W:** Howard Chaykin
2 ❑ Jul 1993 Cover: 1.95 **NM** value: **Cover or less**
Circ: CapCity orders: **12,500**
A: Howard Chaykin **W:** Howard Chaykin
3 ❑ Aug 1993 Cover: 1.95 **NM** value: **Cover or less**
Circ: CapCity orders: **9,500**
A: Howard Chaykin **W:** Howard Chaykin
4 ❑ Sep 1993 Cover: 1.95 **NM** value: **Cover or less**
Circ: CapCity orders: **7,500**
A: Howard Chaykin **W:** Howard Chaykin

MIDNIGHT MYSTERY — ACG

1 ❑ Cover: 0.10 **NM** value: **55.00**
2 ❑ Cover: 0.10 **NM** value: **35.00**
Spacemen Against The Supernatural
3 ❑ Cover: 0.10 **NM** value: **28.00**
4 ❑ Cover: 0.10 **NM** value: **28.00**
5 ❑ Cover: 0.10 **NM** value: **28.00**
6 ❑ Cover: 0.10 **NM** value: **28.00**
Clem Never Does Anything Big!; The White Apeman; The Gladiator
7 ❑ Cover: 0.10 **NM** value: **28.00**

MIDNIGHT NATION — Image

J. Michael Straczynski strikes again. After wowing audiences with his comic-book debut Rising Stars, the writer made famous as the creator of the TV series Babylon 5 launches his own imprint (Joe's Comics) under the Top Cow banner with the flagship title Midnight Nation. Complementing text with imagery that is both attractive and otherworldly, penciller Gary Frank is as much a visual storyteller as Straczynski is a verbal one.

Detective David Grey is trying to solve a murder that no one wants or even cares about helping to solve. In his search for the killer, the detective comes across The Men — other-worldly beings that kill at will. But David's encounter with them leaves him shouldering a fate worse than death — the loss of his soul. Transported to the "World In-Between" — an eerie ghost world populated by forgotten souls — David and his beautiful guide Laurel fight to reclaim the man's soul. If he does not accomplish his mission within 11 months, he will turn into one of The Men and live a life trapped in an eternal hell.

1/A ❑ Oct 2000 Cover: 2.50 **NM** value: **3.00**
Circ: Diamd. preorders: **65,513** • **CGC:** 6 graded, best 9.9
Cover A. **A:** Gary Frank **W:** J. Michael Straczynski
1/B ❑ Oct 2000 Cover: 2.50 **NM** value: **3.00**
• **CGC:** 2 graded, best 9.8
Cover B. • Dynamic Forces Exclusive **A:** Gary Frank **W:** J. Michael Straczynski
1/C ❑ Oct 2000 **NM** value: **10.00**
A: Gary Frank **W:** J. Michael Straczynski
1/D ❑ Oct 2000 Cover: 3.00 **NM** value: **5.00**
Circ: Diamd. preorders: **2,047**
• Convention exclusive edition. **A:** Gary Frank **W:** J. Michael Straczynski
2 ❑ Nov 2000 Cover: 2.50 **NM** value: **Cover or less**
Circ: Diamd. preorders: **42,805**
A: Gary Frank **W:** J. Michael Straczynski
3 ❑ Dec 2000 Cover: 2.50 **NM** value: **Cover or less**
Circ: Diamd. preorders: **44,613** • **CGC:** 1 graded, best 9.8
A: Gary Frank **W:** J. Michael Straczynski
4 ❑ Jan 2001 Cover: 2.50 **NM** value: **Cover or less**
Circ: Diamd. preorders: **43,318**
A: Gary Frank **W:** J. Michael Straczynski
5 ❑ Mar 2001 Cover: 2.50 **NM** value: **Cover or less**
Circ: Diamd. preorders: **40,777**
A: Gary Frank **W:** J. Michael Straczynski
6 ❑ Apr 2001 Cover: 2.50 **NM** value: **Cover or less**
Circ: Diamd. preorders: **40,386**
A: Gary Frank **W:** J. Michael Straczynski

MIDNIGHT PANTHER — CPM

1 ❑ Apr 1997 Cover: 2.95 **NM** value: **Cover or less**
Circ: Diamd. preorders: **5,125**
2 ❑ May 1997 Cover: 2.95 **NM** value: **Cover or less**
Circ: Diamd. preorders: **3,512**
3 ❑ Jun 1997 Cover: 2.95 **NM** value: **Cover or less**
Circ: Diamd. preorders: **3,873**
4 ❑ Jul 1997 Cover: 2.95 **NM** value: **Cover or less**
5 ❑ Aug 1997 Cover: 2.95 **NM** value: **Cover or less**
6 ❑ Sep 1997 Cover: 2.95 **NM** value: **Cover or less**
Circ: Diamd. preorders: **3,828**
7 ❑ Oct 1997 Cover: 2.95 **NM** value: **Cover or less**
Circ: Diamd. preorders: **3,978**
8 ❑ Nov 1997 Cover: 2.95 **NM** value: **Cover or less**
Circ: Diamd. preorders: **3,931**
9 ❑ Dec 1997 Cover: 2.95 **NM** value: **Cover or less**
10 ❑ Jan 1998 Cover: 2.95 **NM** value: **Cover or less**
Circ: Diamd. preorders: **3,847**
11 ❑ Feb 1998 Cover: 2.95 **NM** value: **Cover or less**
Circ: Diamd. preorders: **3,552**
12 ❑ Mar 1998 Cover: 2.95 **NM** value: **Cover or less**
Circ: Diamd. preorders: **3,719**
Bk 1❑ May 1998 Cover: 15.95 **NM** value: **Cover or less**
• I'll Love You to Death; collects Midnight Panther #1-6

MIDNIGHT PANTHER: FEUDAL FANTASY — CPM

1 ❑ Sep 1998 Cover: 2.95 **NM** value: **Cover or less**
Circ: Diamd. preorders: **3,641**
wraparound cover.
2 ❑ Oct 1998 Cover: 2.95 **NM** value: **Cover or less**
Circ: Diamd. preorders: **3,519**

MIDNIGHT PANTHER: SCHOOL DAZE — CPM

1 ❑ Apr 1998 Cover: 2.95 **NM** value: **Cover or less**
Circ: Diamd. preorders: **4,333**
wraparound cover.
2 ❑ May 1998 Cover: 2.95 **NM** value: **Cover or less**
Circ: Diamd. preorders: **3,633**
3 ❑ Jun 1998 Cover: 2.95 **NM** value: **Cover or less**
Circ: Diamd. preorders: **3,767**
wraparound cover.
4 ❑ Jul 1998 Cover: 2.95 **NM** value: **Cover or less**
Circ: Diamd. preorders: **3,489**
5 ❑ Aug 1998 Cover: 2.95 **NM** value: **Cover or less**
Circ: Diamd. preorders: **3,306**

MIDNIGHT SCREAMS — Mystery Graphix

1 ❑ Cover: 2.50 **NM** value: **Cover or less**
2 ❑ Cover: 2.50 **NM** value: **Cover or less**

MIDNIGHT SONS UNLIMITED — Marvel

1 ❑ Apr 1993 Cover: 3.95 **NM** value: **4.00**
Circ: CapCity orders: **50,600**
Eyes Of The Beholder; From The Light, Darkness; On The Wings Of Angles; Blood Is Thicker **A:** Jerry Bingham; Cynthia Martin; Klaus Janson; Joe Quesada **W:** Howard Mackie; Len Wein; Chris Cooper; D.G. Chichester
2 ❑ Jul 1993 Cover: 3.95 **NM** value: **4.00**
Circ: CapCity orders: **30,700**
3 ❑ Oct 1993 Cover: 3.95 **NM** value: **4.00**
Circ: CapCity orders: **20,900**
A: Javier Saltares; Dougie Braithwaite; John Romita Jr.(cover) **W:** Mort Todd ★ Appearance of Spider-Man.
4 ❑ Jan 1994 Cover: 3.95 **NM** value: **Cover or less**
Circ: CapCity orders: **19,000**
5 ❑ Apr 1994 Cover: 3.95 **NM** value: **Cover or less**
Circ: CapCity orders: **13,250**
6 ❑ Jul 1994 Cover: 3.95 **NM** value: **Cover or less**
Circ: CapCity orders: **11,850**
7 ❑ Oct 1994 Cover: 3.95 **NM** value: **Cover or less**
Circ: CapCity orders: **8,800**
8 ❑ Jan 1995 Cover: 3.95 **NM** value: **Cover or less**
Circ: CapCity orders: **6,800**
9 ❑ May 1995 Cover: 3.95 **NM** value: **Cover or less**
Circ: CapCity orders: **5,525**
★ Appearance of Destroyer, Union Jack, Blazing Skull.
Ash 1❑ Cover: 0.75 **NM** value: **Cover or less**
• Previews the Midnight Sons titles **A:** James DeSimone **W:** Jim Krueger

MIDNIGHT TALES — Charlton

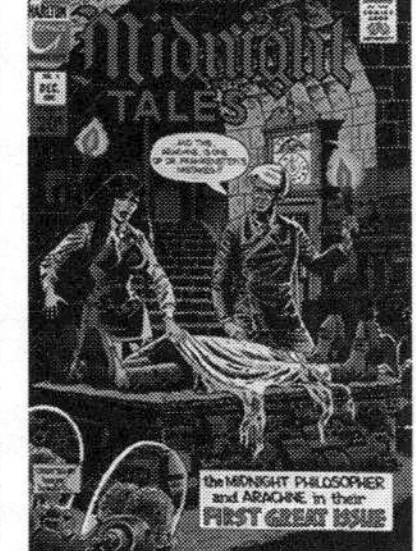

In the early 1970s, some Charlton comics were sold in polybagged three-packs at airports, so that Mom and Pop could give junior his comics fix to keep him quiet on the plane ride to visit the grandparents in Florida. This was shrewd marketing, because it assumed that, to parents, a comic book was a comic book ("Spider-Man, E-Man, what's the difference?"), even if every kid knew that Charltons were the airplane food of the comics cafeteria. Midnight Tales is a typical 1970s Charlton horror-mystery anthology title "hosted" by voluptuous young Arachne and her mentor, the Midnight Philosopher. Artist Wayne Howard was clearly imitating the style of comic-art great Wally Wood ,right down to his gothic signature, but at least he aimed high in his tribute. Consequently, Midnight Tales has the look of a seedy, off-register knock-off of an E.C. horror title — putting it at the top of Charlton's quality spectrum.

1 ❑ Dec 1972 Cover: 0.20 **NM** value: **6.00**
The Midnight Philosopher; Weave me A Web!; The Doll; Last of It's Kind; **A:** Joe Staton **W:** Nicola Cutii
2 ❑ Feb 1973 Cover: 0.20 **NM** value: **4.00**
3 ❑ May 1973 Cover: 0.20 **NM** value: **4.00**
Game Preserve; Malfunction; Lost in Transit; **A:** Joe Staton **W:** Nicola Cutii
4 ❑ Jul 1973 Cover: 0.20 **NM** value: **4.00**
5 ❑ Sep 1973 Cover: 0.20 **NM** value: **4.00**
6 ❑ Nov 1973 Cover: 0.20 **NM** value: **3.00**
7 ❑ Jun 1974 Cover: 0.25 **NM** value: **3.00**
8 ❑ Jul 1974 Cover: 0.25 **NM** value: **3.00**
9 ❑ Oct 1974 Cover: 0.25 **NM** value: **3.00**
10 ❑ Dec 1974 Cover: 0.25 **NM** value: **3.00**
11 ❑ Feb 1975 Cover: 0.25 **NM** value: **3.00**
The Library; Jason; The Oracle **A:** Don Newton; Joe Staton **W:** Nicola Cutii
12 ❑ Apr 1975 Cover: 0.25 **NM** value: **2.00**
13 ❑ Jun 1975 Cover: 0.25 **NM** value: **3.00**
14 ❑ Sep 1975 Cover: 0.25 **NM** value: **3.00**
The Midnight Philosopher: The Time Machine; Love Thy Neighbor; Know Thyself; Criminal Offense **A:** Don Newton; Joe Staton; Marie-Lynn Hammond **W:** Marie-Lynn Hammond; Nicola Cutii
15 ❑ Nov 1975 Cover: 0.25 **NM** value: **3.00**
16 ❑ Jan 1976 Cover: 0.25 **NM** value: **3.00**
17 ❑ Mar 1976 Cover: 0.25 **NM** value: **2.00**
18 ❑ May 1976 Cover: 0.30 **NM** value: **3.00**

MIDNITE — Blackthorne

1 ❑ Nov 1986 Cover: 1.75 **NM** value: **Cover or less**
2 ❑ Jan 1987 Cover: 1.75 **NM** value: **Cover or less**
3 ❑ Mar 1987 Cover: 1.75 **NM** value: **Cover or less**

MIDNITE SKULKER, THE — Target

1 ❑ Jun 1986 Cover: 1.50 **NM** value: **1.75**
2 ❑ Aug 1986, b&w Cover: 1.50 **NM** value: **1.75**
Return of the Duck Knight
3 ❑ Oct 1986 Cover: 1.50 **NM** value: **1.75**
The Black Event **A:** E. Larry Dobias; Stephen Jahner **W:** E. Larry Dobias; Scott Myers
4 ❑ Dec 1986 Cover: 1.75 **NM** value: **Cover or less**
5 ❑ Feb 1987 Cover: 1.75 **NM** value: **Cover or less**
6 ❑ Apr 1987 Cover: 1.75 **NM** value: **Cover or less**
7 ❑ Aug 1987 Cover: 1.75 **NM** value: **Cover or less**

MIDNITE'S QUICKIES — One Shot

1 ❑ b&w Cover: 3.50 **NM** value: **Cover or less**
2 ❑ b&w Cover: 2.95 **NM** value: **Cover or less**
SE 1❑ Oct 1997, b&w **NM** value: **3.00**
no cover price. • no indicia; published in Oct 97
SE 1/A❑ Jan 1998, b&w **NM** value: **3.00**
no cover price. • center color poster

Other grades: Multiply prices above by **1.5 for Mint • 2/3 for Very Fine • 1/3 for Fine • 1/5 for Very Good • 1/8 for Good**

SE 1/B ❑ Oct 1997, b&w **NM** value: **3.00**
foil variant cover.

MIDVALE — Mu Press

1 ❑ b&w Cover: 2.50 **NM** value: **Cover or less**
2 ❑ Oct 1990, b&w Cover: 2.00 **NM** value: **Cover or less**

MIGHTILY MURDERED POWER RINGERS — Express / Parody Press

1 ❑ b&w Cover: 2.50 **NM** value: **Cover or less**

MIGHTY ACE, THE — Omega 7

1 ❑ Cover: 2.00 **NM** value: **Cover or less**
A: Alonzo Washington; Palmer Talley **W:** Alonzo Washington; Palmer Talley
2 ❑ Cover: 2.50 **NM** value: **Cover or less**
• indicia indicates 1992 copyright, probably not year of publication **A:** Alonzo Washington; Palmer Talley **W:** Alonzo Washington; Palmer Talley

MIGHTY ATOM — Magazine Enterprises

1 ❑ Nov 1957 Cover: 0.10 **NM** value: **20.00**
2 ❑ Jan 1958 Cover: 0.10 **NM** value: **20.00**
3 ❑ Mar 1958 Cover: 0.10 **NM** value: **20.00**
4 ❑ May 1958 Cover: 0.10 **NM** value: **20.00**
5 ❑ Jul 1958 Cover: 0.10 **NM** value: **20.00**
6 ❑ Sep 1958 Cover: 0.10 **NM** value: **20.00**

MIGHTY BOMB — Antarctic

1 ❑ Jul 1997, b&w Cover: 2.95 **NM** value: **Cover or less**
Fishkill **A:** Steve Wilhite **W:** John Marshall

MIGHTY BOMBSHELLS, THE — Antarctic

1 ❑ Sep 1993, b&w Cover: 2.95 **NM** value: **Cover or less**
2 ❑ Oct 1993, b&w Cover: 2.75 **NM** value: **Cover or less**
A: Yujin Ishikawa **W:** Yujin Ishikawa

MIGHTY CARTOON HEROES — Karl Art

0 ❑ Cover: 2.95 **NM** value: **Cover or less**
Chameleon Kat; The Aquahounds; Space Bananas in Orland's Dilemma **A:** Chris Allan; Gary St. Lawrence; Tim Perkins; Brendan Spillane **W:** Joe Dator; Barry Kraus

MIGHTY COMICS — Archie

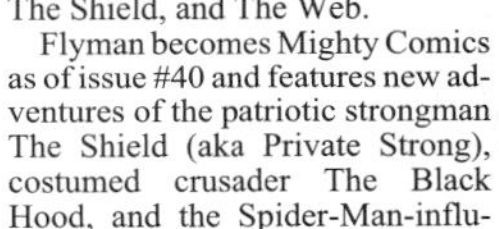

In the early 1940s, MLJ publications produced a number of super-hero comics before stumbling onto a more lucrative formula: the teen humor of Archie and his pals. The reemergence and popularity of super-heroes in the 1960s led MLJ, by then known as Archie Publications, to dust off some of their own Golden Age characters, including The Fly, The Shield, and The Web.

Flyman becomes Mighty Comics as of issue #40 and features new adventures of the patriotic strongman The Shield (aka Private Strong), costumed crusader The Black Hood, and the Spider-Man-influenced Web. Later issues feature The Hangman, a grim vigilante, and Steel Sterling, a Flash Gordon-style science-fiction adventure strip.

Mighty Comics made an earnest attempt to emulate the art and packaging of 1960s Marvel titles but was retired when the series didn't gain similar reader interest.

40 ❑ Nov 1966 Cover: 0.12 **NM** value: **12.00**
• Series continued from Fly Man #39
41 ❑ Dec 1966 Cover: 0.12 **NM** value: **12.00**
42 ❑ Jan 1967 Cover: 0.12 **NM** value: **12.00**
• **CGC:** 1 graded, best 9.6
43 ❑ Feb 1967 Cover: 0.12 **NM** value: **12.00**
The Shield; The Blackhood And His Secret Ordeal; The Web Vs. The Viperous Villains • Black Hood appearace ★ 1st Appearance of The Storm King, The Stunner. ★ Appearance of The Web, The Shield.
44 ❑ Mar 1967 Cover: 0.12 **NM** value: **12.00**
• **CGC:** 1 graded, best 9.2
45 ❑ Apr 1967 Cover: 0.12 **NM** value: **12.00**
46 ❑ May 1967 Cover: 0.12 **NM** value: **12.00**
47 ❑ Jun 1967 Cover: 0.12 **NM** value: **12.00**
• **CGC:** 1 graded, best 9.6
48 ❑ Jul 1967 Cover: 0.12 **NM** value: **12.00**
• **CGC:** 1 graded, best 9.4
49 ❑ 1967 Cover: 0.12 **NM** value: **12.00**
50 ❑ Oct 1967 Cover: 0.12 **NM** value: **12.00**
• **CGC:** 1 graded, best 9.6
final issue.

To find the median price offered on eBay at press time for pre-1990 **CGC-graded comics**, multiply by:

9.9 (M): **32**	8.5 (VF+): **1.25**
9.8(NM/M): **16**	8.0 (VF): **0.85**
9.6 (NM+): **7**	7.5 (VF-): **0.6**
9.4 (NM): **5**	7.0 (F/VF): **0.5**
9.2 (NM-): **2.5**	6.5 (F+): **0.4**
9.0 (VF/NM): **1.5**	6.0 (F-): **0.33**

These are median prices of all CGC comics auctioned on eBay; prices for individual issues will vary.

MIGHTY CRUSADERS, THE (1ST SERIES) — Archie

The Mighty Crusaders is Radio Comics' super-hero team-up title, similar to Marvel's Avengers and DC's Justice League of America. The Mighty Crusaders were Radio's leading super-heroes: The Comet, Black Hood, The Shield, Fly Man, and Fly Girl. They join to battle Inferno the Destroyer and other devious (and ridiculous) would-be world conquerors. In addition to the main story, many issues of this series retell the origins of the team's members in back-up features.

Almost two decades after the end of this 1965-1966 series, Archie revived it, along with the individual members. Several years after that, DC also had a go at it with its 1993 title The Crusaders. It should be noted that DC's Crusaders mentions "previous history" which does not match events from either of the other two series.

1 ❑ Nov 1965 Cover: 0.12 **NM** value: **24.00**
• **CGC:** 1 graded, best 9.2
The Mighty Crusaders vs. The Brain Emperor; The Fly-Man's Ultra-Pals; The Origin of The Shield ★ Origin of The Shield.
2 ❑ 1966 Cover: 0.12 **NM** value: **15.00**
Inferno, The Destroyer ★ Origin of The Comet.
3 ❑ Mar 1966 Cover: 0.12 **NM** value: **12.00**
• **CGC:** 2 graded, best 9.4
★ Origin of Fly Man.
4 ❑ Apr 1966 Cover: 0.12 **NM** value: **9.00**
• **CGC:** 1 graded, best 9.0
• "Too Many Superheroes"
5 ❑ Jun 1966 Cover: 0.12 **NM** value: **9.00**
★ 1st Appearance of The Terrific Three.
6 ❑ Aug 1966 Cover: 0.12 **NM** value: **9.00**
7 ❑ Oct 1966 Cover: 0.12 **NM** value: **9.00**
★ Origin of Fly Girl.

MIGHTY CRUSADERS (2ND SERIES) — Archie / Red Circle

1 ❑ 1983 Cover: 1.00 **NM** value: **1.50**
2 ❑ 1983 Cover: 1.00 **NM** value: **Cover or less**
3 ❑ 1983 Cover: 1.00 **NM** value: **Cover or less**
4 ❑ Nov 1983 Cover: 1.00 **NM** value: **Cover or less**
5 ❑ Jan 1984 Cover: 1.00 **NM** value: **Cover or less**
6 ❑ Mar 1984 Cover: 0.75 **NM** value: **1.00**
7 ❑ May 1984 Cover: 0.75 **NM** value: **1.00**
8 ❑ Jul 1984 Cover: 0.75 **NM** value: **1.00**
9 ❑ Sep 1984 Cover: 0.75 **NM** value: **1.00**
10 ❑ Dec 1984 Cover: 0.75 **NM** value: **1.00**
11 ❑ Mar 1985 Cover: 0.75 **NM** value: **1.00**
12 ❑ Jun 1985 Cover: 0.75 **NM** value: **1.00**
13 ❑ Sep 1985 Cover: 0.75 **NM** value: **1.00**

MIGHTYGUY — C&T

1 ❑ May 1987 Cover: 1.50 **NM** value: **Cover or less**
The Origin of Mightyguy **A:** Tim Corrigan **W:** Tim Corrigan ★ Origin of Mightyguy. ★ 1st Appearance of Mightyguy.
2 ❑ 1987 Cover: 1.50 **NM** value: **Cover or less**
A: Tim Corrigan **W:** Tim Corrigan
3 ❑ 1987 Cover: 1.50 **NM** value: **Cover or less**
A: Tim Corrigan **W:** Tim Corrigan
4 ❑ 1987 Cover: 1.50 **NM** value: **Cover or less**
A: Tim Corrigan **W:** Tim Corrigan
5 ❑ 1987 Cover: 1.50 **NM** value: **Cover or less**
A: Tim Corrigan **W:** Tim Corrigan

MIGHTY HEROES, THE — Marvel / Paramount

1 ❑ Jan 1998 Cover: 2.99 **NM** value: **Cover or less**
Circ: Diamd. preorders: **8,292**
• based on Terrytoons feature **A:** Rurik Tyler **W:** Scott Lobdell ★ Origin of The Mighty Heroes.

MIGHTY I, THE — Image

1 ❑ May 1995 Cover: 1.25 **NM** value: **Cover or less**
Circ: CapCity orders: **8,825**
• Image Comics Fan Club...
2 ❑ Jul 1995 Cover: 1.25 **NM** value: **Cover or less**
Circ: CapCity orders: **6,825**
• Image Comics Fan Club...

MIGHTY MAGNOR, THE — Malibu

This title was created by Sergio Aragones and Mark Evanier, the team who brought us Groo the Wanderer. It features C.J. Delaney and Gil Gillman, two fledgling comic artists. C.J. and Gil have submitted dozens of comic book proposals to their editor, Charles "Attila" Hunsecker, only to receive the same reply: "The readers want super-heroes! And nothing but super-heroes!" In desperation, the two starving creators tried creating a super-hero, but any idea they could come up with had been done at least 97 times before. They were just on the verge of giving up when they spied a huge, costumed man in the alley, reciting TV commercial slogans...

They took him home, gave him a costume, and called him Magnor. Magnor then read through C.J.'s comic book collection and began speaking in comic book cliches. Combined with his apparent strength and super-powers, Magnor became the hero they'd been waiting for.

1 ❑ Apr 1993 Cover: 1.95 **NM** value: **2.25**
A: Sergio Aragonés **W:** Mark Evanier ★ 1st Appearance of The Mighty Magnor.
1/SC ❑ Apr 1993 Cover: 3.95 **NM** value: **Cover or less**
Circ: CapCity orders: **15,225**
Pop-up cover. **A:** Sergio Aragonés **W:** Mark Evanier ★ 1st Appearance of The Mighty Magnor.
2 ❑ May 1993 Cover: 1.95 **NM** value: **Cover or less**
Circ: CapCity orders: **8,100**
A: Sergio Aragonés **W:** Mark Evanier
3 ❑ Jun 1993 Cover: 1.95 **NM** value: **Cover or less**
Circ: CapCity orders: **8,175**
A: Sergio Aragonés **W:** Mark Evanier
4 ❑ Jul 1993 Cover: 1.95 **NM** value: **Cover or less**
Circ: CapCity orders: **7,625**
A: Sergio Aragonés **W:** Mark Evanier
5 ❑ Dec 1993 Cover: 1.95 **NM** value: **Cover or less**
Circ: CapCity orders: **7,350**
A: Sergio Aragonés **W:** Mark Evanier
6 ❑ Apr 1994 Cover: 1.95 **NM** value: **Cover or less**
Circ: CapCity orders: **6,675**
final issue. **A:** Sergio Aragonés **W:** Mark Evanier

MIGHTY MARVEL COMICS STRENGTH AND FITNESS BOOK — Marvel

Bk 1 ❑ Cover: 3.95 **NM** value: **5.00**
• (Fireside)

MIGHTY MARVEL SUPERHEROES FUN BOOK — Marvel

Bk 1 ❑ Cover: 2.95 **NM** value: **3.50**
• (Fireside)
Bk 2 ❑ Cover: 2.95 **NM** value: **3.50**
• (Fireside)
Bk 3 ❑ Cover: 2.95 **NM** value: **3.50**
• Mighty Marvel Fun Book (Fireside)
Bk 4 ❑ Cover: 2.95 **NM** value: **3.50**
• Mighty Marvel Fun Book (Fireside)
Bk 5 ❑ Cover: 2.95 **NM** value: **3.50**
• Mighty Marvel Fun Book (Fireside)

MIGHTY MARVEL TEAM-UP THRILLERS — Marvel

Bk 1 ❑ Mar 1984 Cover: 5.95 **NM** value: **Cover or less**

MIGHTY MARVEL WESTERN, THE — Marvel

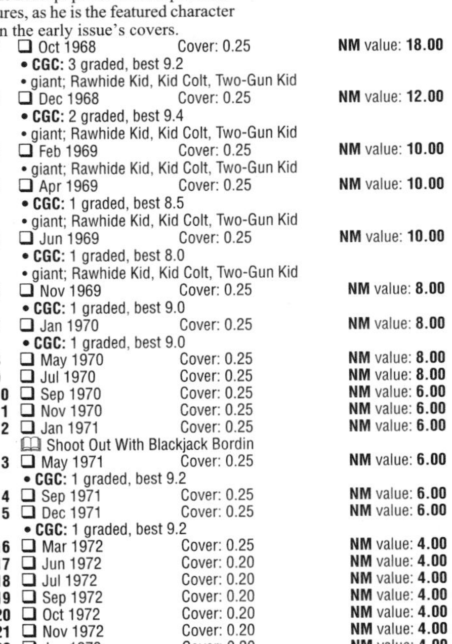

The Mighty Marvel Western was a giant-sized title that reprinted the best of Marvel's various western series. Each issue contained several stories, featuring the early exploits of gunslingers like The Rawhide Kid, Kid Colt, and The Two-Gun Kid. Although the characters follow a familiar formula ("dashing young gunfighter who is hunted by the law for a crime he didn't commit, or committed in self-defense"), the stories are fast-paced and solidly written.

Apparently, Rawhide Kid was the most popular of the reprint features, as he is the featured character on the early issue's covers.

1 ❑ Oct 1968 Cover: 0.25 **NM** value: **18.00**
• **CGC:** 3 graded, best 9.2
• giant; Rawhide Kid, Kid Colt, Two-Gun Kid
2 ❑ Dec 1968 Cover: 0.25 **NM** value: **12.00**
• **CGC:** 2 graded, best 9.4
• giant; Rawhide Kid, Kid Colt, Two-Gun Kid
3 ❑ Feb 1969 Cover: 0.25 **NM** value: **10.00**
• giant; Rawhide Kid, Kid Colt, Two-Gun Kid
4 ❑ Apr 1969 Cover: 0.25 **NM** value: **10.00**
• **CGC:** 1 graded, best 8.5
• giant; Rawhide Kid, Kid Colt, Two-Gun Kid
5 ❑ Jun 1969 Cover: 0.25 **NM** value: **10.00**
• **CGC:** 1 graded, best 8.0
• giant; Rawhide Kid, Kid Colt, Two-Gun Kid
6 ❑ Nov 1969 Cover: 0.25 **NM** value: **8.00**
• **CGC:** 1 graded, best 9.0
7 ❑ Jan 1970 Cover: 0.25 **NM** value: **8.00**
• **CGC:** 1 graded, best 9.0
8 ❑ May 1970 Cover: 0.25 **NM** value: **8.00**
9 ❑ Jul 1970 Cover: 0.25 **NM** value: **8.00**
10 ❑ Sep 1970 Cover: 0.25 **NM** value: **6.00**
11 ❑ Nov 1970 Cover: 0.25 **NM** value: **6.00**
12 ❑ Jan 1971 Cover: 0.25 **NM** value: **6.00**
Shoot Out With Blackjack Bordin
13 ❑ May 1971 Cover: 0.25 **NM** value: **6.00**
• **CGC:** 1 graded, best 9.2
14 ❑ Sep 1971 Cover: 0.25 **NM** value: **6.00**
15 ❑ Dec 1971 Cover: 0.25 **NM** value: **6.00**
• **CGC:** 1 graded, best 9.2
16 ❑ Mar 1972 Cover: 0.25 **NM** value: **4.00**
17 ❑ Jun 1972 Cover: 0.20 **NM** value: **4.00**
18 ❑ Jul 1972 Cover: 0.20 **NM** value: **4.00**
19 ❑ Sep 1972 Cover: 0.20 **NM** value: **4.00**
20 ❑ Oct 1972 Cover: 0.20 **NM** value: **4.00**
21 ❑ Nov 1972 Cover: 0.20 **NM** value: **4.00**
22 ❑ Jan 1973 Cover: 0.20 **NM** value: **4.00**
23 ❑ Mar 1973 Cover: 0.20 **NM** value: **4.00**
24 ❑ May 1973 Cover: 0.20 **NM** value: **4.00**
25 ❑ Jul 1973 Cover: 0.20 **NM** value: **4.00**

CGC-graded: Multiply prices above by **33 for 9.9 M • 16 for 9.8 NM/M • 7 for 9.6 NM+ • 5 for 9.4 NM • 2.5 for 9.2 NM- • 1.5 for 9.0 VF/NM**

26 ❑ Sep 1973 Cover: 0.20 **NM** value: **4.00**
27 ❑ Oct 1973 Cover: 0.20 **NM** value: **4.00**
28 ❑ Dec 1973 Cover: 0.20 **NM** value: **4.00**
29 ❑ Jan 1974 Cover: 0.20 **NM** value: **4.00**
30 ❑ Mar 1974 Cover: 0.20 **NM** value: **4.00**
31 ❑ May 1974 Cover: 0.20 **NM** value: **3.00**
32 ❑ Jul 1974 Cover: 0.20 **NM** value: **3.00**
33 ❑ Aug 1974 Cover: 0.20 **NM** value: **3.00**
34 ❑ Sep 1974 Cover: 0.25 **NM** value: **3.00**
35 ❑ Oct 1974 Cover: 0.25 **NM** value: **3.00**
36 ❑ Dec 1974 Cover: 0.25 **NM** value: **3.00**
37 ❑ Jan 1975 Cover: 0.25 **NM** value: **3.00**
38 ❑ Mar 1975 Cover: 0.25 **NM** value: **3.00**
39 ❑ May 1975 Cover: 0.25 **NM** value: **3.00**
40 ❑ Jul 1975 Cover: 0.25 **NM** value: **3.00**
41 ❑ Sep 1975 Cover: 0.25 **NM** value: **3.00**
42 ❑ Oct 1975 Cover: 0.25 **NM** value: **3.00**
43 ❑ Dec 1975 Cover: 0.25 **NM** value: **3.00**
44 ❑ Mar 1976 Cover: 0.25 **NM** value: **3.00**
45 ❑ Jun 1976 Cover: 0.25 **NM** value: **3.00**
• **CGC:** 2 graded, best 9.0
46 ❑ Sep 1976 Cover: 0.25 **NM** value: **3.00**
final issue.

MIGHTY MITES, THE (VOL. 1) — Eternity

The first release from "The Great Big Comicbook Company of New York" (Eternity, Scott Rosenberg's first comic-book company), the issue shows li'l kid versions of The X-Men (though, obviously, not really The X-Men or there'd have been a lawsuit). There is nothing wrong with the idea, since Marvel would later appropriate it for its own X-Babies specials, and the art is appealing enough, albeit lacking in background. No, the problem is in the writing. This X-Men parody goes for the obvious joke every time, most based on such attributes as the soul-searching found in the source material as it was then.

1 ❑ Oct 1986 Cover: 1.80 **NM** value: **2.00**
• X-Men parody **A:** Nicholas Conti **W:** John Nubbin; Sparky
2/A ❑ Jan 1987 Cover: 1.80 **NM** value: **2.00**
• Batman parody
2/B ❑ Jan 1987 Cover: 1.80 **NM** value: **2.00**
• Batman parody
3 ❑ Mar 1987, b&w and colorCover: 1.95 **NM** value: **2.00**

MIGHTY MITES, THE (VOL. 2) — Eternity

1 ❑ May 1987 Cover: 1.95 **NM** value: **Cover or less**
📖 A Mite on the Town **A:** Conti **W:** John Nubbin; Sparky ★ Appearance of Godzilla.
2 ❑ Jul 1987 Cover: 1.95 **NM** value: **Cover or less**

MIGHTY MORPHIN POWER RANGERS: NINJA RANGERS/VR TROOPERS (SABAN'S...) — Marvel

1 ❑ Dec 1995 Cover: 1.75 **NM** value: **2.50**
📖 Cheaters Never Prosper and Winners Never Cheat!; Father Figure • flip book with VR Troopers back-up **A:** John Ross; Tod Smith **W:** Fabian Nicieza; Frank Lovece
2 ❑ Jan 1996 Cover: 1.75 **NM** value: **2.00**
Power Rangers cover says Dec 95.
3 ❑ Feb 1996 Cover: 1.75 **NM** value: **2.00**
• flip book with VR Troopers back-up
4 ❑ Mar 1996 Cover: 1.75 **NM** value: **2.00**
📖 Loyalty; Ghost Of A Chance • flip book with VR Troopers back-up **A:** Steve Ditko; Bart Schmidt **W:** Frank Strom; Fabian Nicieza
5 ❑ Apr 1996 Cover: 1.75 **NM** value: **2.00**
📖 Weather Witch; The Boy Trooper • flip book with VR Troopers back-up **A:** Steve Ditko; Tod Smith **W:** Frank Strom; Fabian Nicieza
6 ❑ May 1996 Cover: 1.75 **NM** value: **2.00**
7 ❑ Jun 1996 Cover: 1.75 **NM** value: **2.00**
8 ❑ Jul 1996 Cover: 1.75 **NM** value: **2.00**
final issue.

MIGHTY MORPHIN POWER RANGERS (SABAN'S...) — Marvel

In the early 1990s, the Japanese company Saban Entertainment introduced The Mighty Morphin Power Rangers to American audiences. Children went crazy over the new super-hero team. The Rangers were so popular that they unseated The Teenage Mutant Ninja Turtles as the reigning leaders of children's heroes. Of course, a comic-book series soon followed.

In 1995, Marvel's rendition of Mighty Morphin Power Rangers was released. The series reintroduces the heroes from Angel City: Billy, the Blue Ranger; Trini, the Yellow Ranger; Kimberly, the Pink Ranger; Zack, the Black Ranger; and Jason, the Red Ranger. They continually fight their hopelessly hokey arch-enemies Rita Repulsa and Lord Zed, along with their army of putty warriors — yes, putty warriors. It's campy in the extreme, but the concept proved a winner, combining elements of King Arthur, big dinosaurs, kung fu, and Transformers-like machines.

1 ❑ Nov 1995 Cover: 1.75 **NM** value: **2.50**
📖 The Menace of Dracula
2 ❑ Dec 1995 Cover: 1.75 **NM** value: **2.00**
A: Ron Lim **W:** Fabian Nicieza
3 ❑ Dec 1995 Cover: 1.75 **NM** value: **2.00**
cover says Jan, indicia says Dec. 📖 It's Not the End of the World! **A:** Al Bigley **W:** Jack Harris
4 ❑ Feb 1996 Cover: 1.75 **NM** value: **2.00**
5 ❑ Mar 1996 Cover: 1.75 **NM** value: **2.00**
📖 Vortex **A:** Ron Lim **W:** Fabian Nicieza
6 ❑ Apr 1996 Cover: 1.75 **NM** value: **2.00**
📖 Elementary **A:** Ron Lim **W:** Fabian Nicieza
7 ❑ May 1996 Cover: 1.75 **NM** value: **2.00**
A: Ron Lim **W:** Fabian Nicieza
8 ❑ Jun 1996 Cover: 1.75 **NM** value: **2.00**
A: Ron Lim **W:** Fabian Nicieza
9 ❑ Jul 1996 Cover: 1.75 **NM** value: **2.00**
final issue. **A:** Ron Lim **W:** Fabian Nicieza

MIGHTY MORPHIN POWER RANGERS SAGA (SABAN'S...) — Hamilton

1 ❑ Dec 1994 Cover: 1.95 **NM** value: **2.50**
Circ: CapCity orders: **7,425**
A: Sparky Moore; John Heebink; Aaron McClellan **W:** Don Markstein ★ Origin of the Power Rangers.
2 ❑ 1995 Cover: 1.95 **NM** value: **2.50**
Circ: CapCity orders: **5,050**
W: Don Markstein
3 ❑ 1995 Cover: 1.95 **NM** value: **2.50**
Circ: CapCity orders: **4,275** • **CGC:** 1 graded, best 9.8
W: Don Markstein

MIGHTY MORPHIN POWER RANGERS: THE MOVIE — Marvel

1 ❑ Sep 1995 Cover: 2.95 **NM** value: **Cover or less**
No issue number. **A:** Ron Lim **W:** Nel Yomtov
1/SC❑Sep 1995 Cover: 3.95 **NM** value: **Cover or less**
No issue number. cardstock cover. **A:** Ron Lim **W:** Nel Yomtov

MIGHTY MOUSE ADVENTURE MAGAZINE — Spotlight

1 ❑ b&w Cover: 2.00 **NM** value: **Cover or less**

MIGHTY MOUSE ADVENTURES — St. John

1 ❑ Nov 1951 Cover: 0.10 **NM** value: **250.00**
• **CGC:** 1 graded, best 4.0

MIGHTY MOUSE AND FRIENDS HOLIDAY SPECIAL — Spotlight

1 ❑ Cover: 1.75 **NM** value: **2.00**
Circ: CapCity orders: **3,350**

MIGHTY MOUSE COMICS — Timely

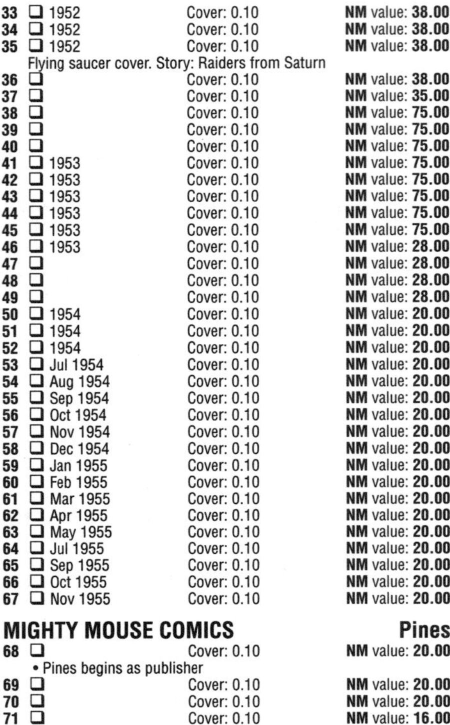

Aside from giving a new direction to the comic-book industry, the initial popularity of Superman generated characters that were meant to parallel his image. One of these was a mouse. "The Mouse of Tomorrow" was a 1942 animated cartoon from the Terrytoons studio with a character called Super Mouse. He can fly, is invulnerable, and is incredibly strong — and changes his name to Mighty Mouse in all the ensuing cartoon shorts, eventually adding the element of a pseudo-operatic style of singing to the mix.

The comic-book stories were funny and lighthearted, consisting of formulaic tales of "good" mice and "bad" cats. Defending Mouseland from the schemes of a band of villains, such as the Sphinx and Oil Can Harry, is a routine task.

In addition to Mighty Mouse, this series from the 1940s and 1950s also featured the misadventures of Heckle and Jeckle, two cunning and crafty crows also from cartoons from the Terrytoons studio.

1 ❑ Fal 1946 Cover: 0.10 **NM** value: **675.00**
• Marvel (Timely) publishes
2 ❑ Win 1946 Cover: 0.10 **NM** value: **350.00**
3 ❑ Spr 1947 Cover: 0.10 **NM** value: **265.00**
4 ❑ Sum 1947 Cover: 0.10 **NM** value: **265.00**

MIGHTY MOUSE COMICS — St. John

5 ❑ Aug 1947 Cover: 0.10 **NM** value: **215.00**
• St. John begins as publisher
6 ❑ 1947 Cover: 0.10 **NM** value: **135.00**
7 ❑ 1947 Cover: 0.10 **NM** value: **135.00**
8 ❑ Feb 1948 Cover: 0.10 **NM** value: **135.00**
9 ❑ 1948 Cover: 0.10 **NM** value: **110.00**
10 ❑ 1948 Cover: 0.10 **NM** value: **110.00**
11 ❑ 1948 Cover: 0.10 **NM** value: **75.00**
12 ❑ 1949 Cover: 0.10 **NM** value: **75.00**
13 ❑ 1949 Cover: 0.10 **NM** value: **75.00**
14 ❑ 1949 Cover: 0.10 **NM** value: **75.00**
15 ❑ 1949 Cover: 0.10 **NM** value: **75.00**
16 ❑ 1950 Cover: 0.10 **NM** value: **75.00**
17 ❑ 1950 Cover: 0.10 **NM** value: **75.00**
18 ❑ 1950 Cover: 0.10 **NM** value: **75.00**
19 ❑ 1950 Cover: 0.10 **NM** value: **75.00**
📖 Mighty Mouse **A:** Art Bartsch
20 ❑ Nov 1950 Cover: 0.10 **NM** value: **75.00**
21 ❑ Dec 1950 Cover: 0.10 **NM** value: **50.00**
22 ❑ Jan 1951 Cover: 0.10 **NM** value: **50.00**
23 ❑ Feb 1951 Cover: 0.10 **NM** value: **50.00**
24 ❑ Mar 1951 Cover: 0.10 **NM** value: **50.00**
25 ❑ 1951 Cover: 0.10 **NM** value: **50.00**
26 ❑ 1951 Cover: 0.10 **NM** value: **50.00**
27 ❑ 1951 Cover: 0.10 **NM** value: **50.00**
28 ❑ 1952 Cover: 0.10 **NM** value: **50.00**
29 ❑ 1952 Cover: 0.10 **NM** value: **50.00**
30 ❑ 1952 Cover: 0.10 **NM** value: **50.00**
31 ❑ 1952 Cover: 0.10 **NM** value: **38.00**
32 ❑ 1952 Cover: 0.10 **NM** value: **38.00**
33 ❑ 1952 Cover: 0.10 **NM** value: **38.00**
34 ❑ 1952 Cover: 0.10 **NM** value: **38.00**
35 ❑ 1952 Cover: 0.10 **NM** value: **38.00**
Flying saucer cover. Story: Raiders from Saturn
36 ❑ Cover: 0.10 **NM** value: **38.00**
37 ❑ Cover: 0.10 **NM** value: **35.00**
38 ❑ Cover: 0.10 **NM** value: **75.00**
39 ❑ Cover: 0.10 **NM** value: **75.00**
40 ❑ Cover: 0.10 **NM** value: **75.00**
41 ❑ 1953 Cover: 0.10 **NM** value: **75.00**
42 ❑ 1953 Cover: 0.10 **NM** value: **75.00**
43 ❑ 1953 Cover: 0.10 **NM** value: **75.00**
44 ❑ 1953 Cover: 0.10 **NM** value: **75.00**
45 ❑ 1953 Cover: 0.10 **NM** value: **75.00**
46 ❑ 1953 Cover: 0.10 **NM** value: **28.00**
47 ❑ Cover: 0.10 **NM** value: **28.00**
48 ❑ Cover: 0.10 **NM** value: **28.00**
49 ❑ Cover: 0.10 **NM** value: **28.00**
50 ❑ 1954 Cover: 0.10 **NM** value: **20.00**
51 ❑ 1954 Cover: 0.10 **NM** value: **20.00**
52 ❑ 1954 Cover: 0.10 **NM** value: **20.00**
53 ❑ Jul 1954 Cover: 0.10 **NM** value: **20.00**
54 ❑ Aug 1954 Cover: 0.10 **NM** value: **20.00**
55 ❑ Sep 1954 Cover: 0.10 **NM** value: **20.00**
56 ❑ Oct 1954 Cover: 0.10 **NM** value: **20.00**
57 ❑ Nov 1954 Cover: 0.10 **NM** value: **20.00**
58 ❑ Dec 1954 Cover: 0.10 **NM** value: **20.00**
59 ❑ Jan 1955 Cover: 0.10 **NM** value: **20.00**
60 ❑ Feb 1955 Cover: 0.10 **NM** value: **20.00**
61 ❑ Mar 1955 Cover: 0.10 **NM** value: **20.00**
62 ❑ Apr 1955 Cover: 0.10 **NM** value: **20.00**
63 ❑ May 1955 Cover: 0.10 **NM** value: **20.00**
64 ❑ Jul 1955 Cover: 0.10 **NM** value: **20.00**
65 ❑ Sep 1955 Cover: 0.10 **NM** value: **20.00**
66 ❑ Oct 1955 Cover: 0.10 **NM** value: **20.00**
67 ❑ Nov 1955 Cover: 0.10 **NM** value: **20.00**

MIGHTY MOUSE COMICS — Pines

68 ❑ Cover: 0.10 **NM** value: **20.00**
• Pines begins as publisher
69 ❑ Cover: 0.10 **NM** value: **20.00**
70 ❑ Cover: 0.10 **NM** value: **20.00**
71 ❑ Cover: 0.10 **NM** value: **16.00**
72 ❑ Cover: 0.10 **NM** value: **16.00**
73 ❑ Cover: 0.10 **NM** value: **16.00**
74 ❑ Cover: 0.10 **NM** value: **16.00**
75 ❑ Cover: 0.10 **NM** value: **16.00**
76 ❑ Cover: 0.10 **NM** value: **16.00**
77 ❑ Mar 1958 Cover: 0.10 **NM** value: **16.00**
78 ❑ 1958 Cover: 0.10 **NM** value: **16.00**
79 ❑ 1958 Cover: 0.10 **NM** value: **16.00**
80 ❑ Cover: 0.10 **NM** value: **16.00**
81 ❑ Cover: 0.10 **NM** value: **16.00**
82 ❑ Cover: 0.10 **NM** value: **16.00**
83 ❑ Jun 1959 Cover: 0.10 **NM** value: **16.00**
final issue.

MIGHTY MOUSE (MARVEL) — Marvel

1 ❑ Oct 1990 Cover: 1.00 **NM** value: **2.00**
Circ: CapCity orders: **14,400**
Dark Knight parody cover. 📖 The Dark Might Returns **A:** Ernie Colon **W:** Michael Gallagher
2 ❑ Nov 1990 Cover: 1.00 **NM** value: **1.50**
Circ: CapCity orders: **8,200**
3 ❑ Dec 1990 Cover: 1.00 **NM** value: **1.50**
Circ: CapCity orders: **7,900**
📖 Cooler Heads Prevail • Sub-Mariner parody **A:** Mike Kazaleh **W:** Michael Gallagher ★ 1st Appearance of Bat-Bat.
4 ❑ Jan 1991 Cover: 1.00 **NM** value: **1.50**
Circ: CapCity orders: **5,500**
• Crisis parody **C:** George Pérez
5 ❑ Feb 1991 Cover: 1.00 **NM** value: **1.50**
Circ: CapCity orders: **6,800**
• Crisis parody
6 ❑ Mar 1991 Cover: 1.00 **NM** value: **1.50**
• McFarlane parody
7 ❑ Apr 1991 Cover: 1.00 **NM** value: **1.50**
• computer art
8 ❑ May 1991 Cover: 1.00 **NM** value: **1.50**
Circ: CapCity orders: **5,500**
9 ❑ Jun 1991 Cover: 1.00 **NM** value: **1.50**
Circ: CapCity orders: **5,600**
10 ❑ Jul 1991 Cover: 1.00 **NM** value: **1.50**
Circ: CapCity orders: **4,900**
• Letterman parody

MIGHTY MOUSE (SPOTLIGHT) — Spotlight

1 ❑ ca. 1987 Cover: 1.50 **NM** value: **2.00**
Circ: CapCity orders: **3,875**
2 ❑ ca. 1987 Cover: 1.50 **NM** value: **2.00**
Circ: CapCity orders: **2,850**

MIGHTY MOUSE (TIMELY) — Timely

1 ❑ Fal 1946 Cover: 0.10 **NM** value: **750.00**
• **CGC:** 1 graded, best 8.5
2 ❑ Win 1946 Cover: 0.10 **NM** value: **350.00**
• **CGC:** 1 graded, best 6.0
3 ❑ Spr 1947 Cover: 0.10 **NM** value: **200.00**
4 ❑ Sum 1947 Cover: 0.10 **NM** value: **200.00**

MIGHTY MUTANIMALS — Archie

1 ❑ Apr 1992 Cover: 1.25 **NM** value: **Cover or less**
Circ: CapCity orders: **8,050**
📖 The Mighty Mutanimals **A:** Garrett Ho **W:** Dean Carrain
2 ❑ Jun 1992 Cover: 1.25 **NM** value: **Cover or less**
Circ: CapCity orders: **6,025**
W: Dean Carrain
3 ❑ Aug 1992 Cover: 1.25 **NM** value: **Cover or less**

Other grades: Multiply prices above by **1.5 for Mint • 2/3 for Very Fine • 1/3 for Fine • 1/5 for Very Good • 1/8 for Good**

Circ: CapCity orders: **5,525**
W: Dean Carrain
4 ❑ Sep 1992 Cover: 1.25 **NM** value: **Cover or less**
Circ: CapCity orders: **1,825**
W: Dean Carrain
5 ❑ Oct 1992 Cover: 1.25 **NM** value: **Cover or less**
W: Dean Carrain
6 ❑ Dec 1992 Cover: 1.25 **NM** value: **Cover or less**
📖 United We Stand…Divided We Fall **A:** Mike Kazaleh **W:** Dean Carrain
7 ❑ Feb 1993 Cover: 1.25 **NM** value: **Cover or less**
W: Dean Carrain
8 ❑ Apr 1993 Cover: 1.25 **NM** value: **Cover or less**
W: Dean Carrain

MIGHTY MUTANIMALS (MINI-SERIES) — Archie

1 ❑ May 1991 Cover: 1.25 **NM** value: **1.50**
📖 The Wild Angels • TMNT spin-off **A:** Garrett Ho; Ken Mitchroney **W:** Dean Clarrain
2 ❑ 1991 Cover: 1.25 **NM** value: **Cover or less**
• TMNT spin-off **A:** Garrett Ho; Ken Mitchroney **W:** Dean Clarrain
3 ❑ 1991 Cover: 1.25 **NM** value: **Cover or less**
• TMNT spin-off **A:** Garrett Ho; Ken Mitchroney **W:** Dean Clarrain

MIGHTY SAMSON — Gold Key

Nuclear war has laid waste to the world. Those who were not killed immediately fell victim to the radioactive fallout. And the few survivors lived in a world that had literally been bombed into a new Stone Age. Here, technology was lost and strange, mutated plants and animals posed a constant threat to the humans that remained.

Into this world rose a hero called Samson. Like his world, he is a mix of the old and the new. He wears an eyepatch and the skin of a beast, and possesses strength worthy of his biblical namesake. Along with Mindor, a scientist, and Mindor's daughter Sharmaine, they set out to reclaim this strange new primitive world.

1 ❑ Jul 1964 Cover: 0.12 **NM** value: **30.00**
• **CGC:** 1 graded, best 8.5
back cover pin-up. ★ Origin of Samson. ★ 1st Appearance of Samson.
2 ❑ Jun 1965 Cover: 0.12 **NM** value: **18.00**
back cover pin-up. ★ 1st Appearance of Terra of Jerz.
3 ❑ Sep 1965 Cover: 0.12 **NM** value: **18.00**
back cover pin-up.
4 ❑ Dec 1965 Cover: 0.12 **NM** value: **12.00**
back cover pin-up.
5 ❑ Mar 1966 Cover: 0.12 **NM** value: **12.00**
Circ: Statement: **254,725**
back cover pin-up.
6 ❑ Jun 1966 Cover: 0.12 **NM** value: **10.00**
Circ: Statement: **254,725**
back cover pin-up. 📖 The Death Geysers
7 ❑ Sep 1966 Cover: 0.12 **NM** value: **10.00**
Circ: Statement: **254,725**
back cover pin-up.
8 ❑ Dec 1966 Cover: 0.12 **NM** value: **10.00**
Circ: Statement: **254,725**
9 ❑ Mar 1967 Cover: 0.12 **NM** value: **10.00**
Circ: Statement: **238,075**
• In Washington, D.C.
10 ❑ Jun 1967 Cover: 0.12 **NM** value: **10.00**
Circ: Statement: **238,075**
11 ❑ Aug 1967 Cover: 0.12 **NM** value: **8.00**
Circ: Statement: **238,075**
12 ❑ Nov 1967 Cover: 0.12 **NM** value: **8.00**
Circ: Statement: **238,075**
13 ❑ Feb 1968 Cover: 0.12 **NM** value: **8.00**
14 ❑ May 1968 Cover: 0.12 **NM** value: **8.00**
15 ❑ Aug 1968 Cover: 0.12 **NM** value: **8.00**
16 ❑ Nov 1968 Cover: 0.15 **NM** value: **8.00**
17 ❑ Feb 1969 Cover: 0.15 **NM** value: **8.00**
18 ❑ May 1969 Cover: 0.15 **NM** value: **8.00**
19 ❑ Aug 1969 Cover: 0.15 **NM** value: **8.00**
• N'Yark floods
20 ❑ Nov 1969 Cover: 0.15 **NM** value: **8.00**
21 ❑ Aug 1972 Cover: 0.15 **NM** value: **5.00**
22 ❑ Dec 1973 Cover: 0.20 **NM** value: **5.00**
23 ❑ Mar 1974 Cover: 0.20 **NM** value: **5.00**
24 ❑ Jun 1974 Cover: 0.20 **NM** value: **5.00**
25 ❑ Sep 1974 Cover: 0.25 **NM** value: **5.00**
26 ❑ Dec 1974 Cover: 0.25 **NM** value: **5.00**
27 ❑ Mar 1975 Cover: 0.25 **NM** value: **5.00**
28 ❑ Jun 1975 Cover: 0.25 **NM** value: **5.00**
29 ❑ Sep 1975 Cover: 0.25 **NM** value: **5.00**
30 ❑ Dec 1975 Cover: 0.25 **NM** value: **5.00**
• In Macy's
31 ❑ Mar 1976 Cover: 0.25 **NM** value: **5.00**
★ Versus giant moths.
32 ❑ Apr 1982 Cover: 0.60 **NM** value: **3.00**
📖 Peril From The Past; The Desperate Mission final issue. • 1982 revival

MIGHTY THOR: ALONE AGAINST THE CELESTIALS — Marvel

Bk 1❑ Cover: 5.95 **NM** value: **Cover or less**

MIGHTY THOR: BALLAD OF BETA RAY BILL — Marvel

Bk 1❑ Feb 1990 Cover: 8.95 **NM** value: **Cover or less**
A: Walt Simonson

MIGHTY THOR: I, WHOM THE GODS WOULD DESTROY — Marvel

Bk 1❑ Cover: 5.95 **NM** value: **Cover or less**

MIGHTY THOR!, THE (LANCER) — Marvel

Bk 1❑ Cover: 0.50 **NM** value: **4.00**
• (Lancer)

MIGHTY TINY — Antarctic

1 ❑ b&w Cover: 1.75 **NM** value: **2.00**
2 ❑ b&w Cover: 1.75 **NM** value: **2.00**
3 ❑ b&w Cover: 1.75 **NM** value: **2.00**
4 ❑ b&w Cover: 1.75 **NM** value: **2.00**
5 ❑ Cover: 2.50 **NM** value: **Cover or less**

MIGHTY TINY: TALES OF THE OLD EMPIRE — Antarctic

Bk 1❑ Jul 1996, b&w Cover: 14.95 **NM** value: **Cover or less**
• Trade Paperback. • collects series

MIGHTY TINY: THE MOUSE MARINES — Antarctic

1 ❑ b&w Cover: 2.50 **NM** value: **Cover or less**
📖 The Wisdom Of The Poet **A:** Pat Duke **W:** Pat Duke
Bk 1❑ Cover: 7.95 **NM** value: **Cover or less**
• collection **A:** Pat Broderick

MIKE BARNETT, MAN AGAINST CRIME — Fawcett

1 ❑ Dec 1951 Cover: 0.10 **NM** value: **150.00**
2 ❑ Feb 1952 Cover: 0.10 **NM** value: **100.00**
3 ❑ Apr 1952 Cover: 0.10 **NM** value: **75.00**
4 ❑ Jun 1952 Cover: 0.10 **NM** value: **75.00**
5 ❑ Aug 1952 Cover: 0.10 **NM** value: **75.00**
6 ❑ Oct 1952 Cover: 0.10 **NM** value: **75.00**

MIKE DANGER (VOL. 1) (MICKEY SPILLANE'S...) — Tekno

Better known for his tough-guy private eye, Mike Hammer, novelist Mickey Spillane did write for comic books at an early stage in his career. One unpublished comic-book tale of Spillane's was Mike Danger, a precursor to Mike Hammer.

In the 1990s, Max Allan Collins and Spillane brought Mike Danger to Tekno Comics. Rather than hard-boiled detective stories, this series takes a science-fiction angle. While on an investigation in 1952, Mike Danger uncovers a former Nazi scientist working with cryogenics to revive Nazis in hibernation. In the ensuing shootout, Danger takes refuge in a cryogenic chamber and becomes trapped, when the device activates. He wakes 100 years later to a greatly changed world. Mike Danger, a pulp-fiction, no-nonsense, private eye, is a man out of his time in a world where his brand of forthright justice is as much of an anomaly as red meat or love and marriage.

1 ❑ Sep 1995 Cover: 1.95 **NM** value: **Cover or less**
Circ: Statement: **125,989** CapCity orders: **11,950**
📖 Danger Ahead **A:** Eduardo Barreto **W:** Max Allan Collins
2 ❑ Oct 1995 Cover: 1.95 **NM** value: **Cover or less**
Circ: Statement: **125,989** CapCity orders: **10,525**
📖 Danger in the Future **A:** Eduardo Barreto **W:** Max Allan Collins
3 ❑ Nov 1995 Cover: 1.95 **NM** value: **Cover or less**
Circ: Statement: **125,989** CapCity orders: **9,500**
A: Eduardo Barreto **W:** Max Allan Collins
4 ❑ Dec 1995 Cover: 1.95 **NM** value: **Cover or less**
Circ: CapCity orders: **7,850**
A: Eduardo Barreto **W:** Max Allan Collins
5 ❑ Dec 1995 Cover: 1.95 **NM** value: **Cover or less**
Circ: CapCity orders: **6,775**
A: Eduardo Barreto **W:** Max Allan Collins
6 ❑ Jan 1996 Cover: 2.25 **NM** value: **Cover or less**
📖 Man Out of Time **A:** Eduardo Barreto **W:** Max Allan Collins
7 ❑ Jan 1996 Cover: 2.25 **NM** value: **Cover or less**
📖 Death in Duplicate, Part 1 • Has 1995 Statement of Onwership, filed 10/11/1995 (Alert: Printed VERY early and on little data); avg print run 232,898; avg sales 125,929; avg subs 60; avg total paid 125,989; samples 1,850; office use 3,124; max existent 130,963; 44% or run returned **A:** Peter Grau **W:** Max Allan Collins
8 ❑ Feb 1996 Cover: 2.25 **NM** value: **Cover or less**
A: Peter Grau **W:** Max Allan Collins
9 ❑ Mar 1996 Cover: 2.25 **NM** value: **Cover or less**
A: Peter Grau **W:** Max Allan Collins
10 ❑ Apr 1996 Cover: 2.25 **NM** value: **Cover or less**
A: Peter Grau **W:** Max Allan Collins
11 ❑ May 1996 Cover: 2.25 **NM** value: **Cover or less**
A: Peter Grau **W:** Max Allan Collins

MIKE DANGER (VOL. 2) (MICKEY SPILLANE'S...) — Big

1 ❑ Jun 1996 Cover: 2.25 **NM** value: **Cover or less**
📖 The Big Crossover Chapter 11; Virtual Man; The Big Crossover, Part 11 **A:** Rich Buckler; Peter Grau **W:** Max Allan Collins; Ron Fortier
2 ❑ Jul 1996 Cover: 2.25 **NM** value: **Cover or less**
• Mike's head is separated from his body
3 ❑ Aug 1996 Cover: 2.25 **NM** value: **Cover or less**
4 ❑ Sep 1996 Cover: 2.25 **NM** value: **Cover or less**
📖 A Woman Called Mann **A:** Peter Grau **W:** Max Allan Collins ★ Versus Mann.
5 ❑ Oct 1996 Cover: 2.25 **NM** value: **Cover or less**
6 ❑ Nov 1996 Cover: 2.25 **NM** value: **Cover or less**
Circ: Diamd. preorders: **10,141**
7 ❑ Dec 1996 Cover: 2.25 **NM** value: **Cover or less**
Circ: Diamd. preorders: **9,781**
📖 Red Menace, Part 1
8 ❑ Jan 1996 Cover: 2.25 **NM** value: **Cover or less**
Circ: Diamd. preorders: **9,231**
📖 Red Menace, Part 2
9 ❑ Feb 1996 Cover: 2.25 **NM** value: **Cover or less**
Circ: Diamd. preorders: **8,605**
📖 Red Menace, Part 3
10 ❑ Apr 1996 Cover: 2.25 **NM** value: **Cover or less**
Circ: Diamd. preorders: **7,342**
📖 Red Menace, Part 4

MIKE MAUSER FILES — Avalon

1 ❑ Cover: 2.95 **NM** value: **Cover or less**
📖 The Cayugan Curse; Dog Days; Sleazze!; The Things in the Subway **A:** Joe Staton **W:** Nicola Cuti

MIKE MIST MINUTE MIST-ERIES — Eclipse

1 ❑ Apr 1981, b&w Cover: 1.50 **NM** value: **Cover or less**

MIKE REGAN — Hardboiled

1 ❑ b&w Cover: 2.95 **NM** value: **Cover or less**

MIKE SHAYNE PRIVATE EYE — Dell

1 ❑ Nov 1962 Cover: 0.15 **NM** value: **15.00**
📖 The Gangster Era (text); The Private Practice of Michael Shayne; Danny the Dip (text); A Plot to Murder; Landmarks of Crime: Paradise Square (text); Crime Notes: Rigor Mortis (text)
2 ❑ Feb 1968 Cover: 0.12 **NM** value: **9.00**
3 ❑ May 1962 Cover: 0.12 **NM** value: **9.00**
📖 The Gangster Era: John Torrio (text); Heads…You Lose; The Deadly Hour (text); The Rumble; Casebook: The Lime Pit… (text)

MILIKARDO KNIGHTS — Mad Badger

1 ❑ Mar 1997, b&w Cover: 3.00 **NM** value: **Cover or less**
2 ❑ Jan 1998, b&w Cover: 3.00 **NM** value: **Cover or less**

MILITARY COMICS — Comic Magazines

This 1941 series trumpets itself as "stories of military action on land and at sea." It contains an assortment of war strips along those lines, ranging from the naval adventure "PT Boat" to the air/sea flight team of the Atlantic Patrol. A comic piece with the unlikely name of "Death Patrol" paints the Japanese as a collection of goggle-eyed, buck-toothed stooges that are easily routed by a kid-led flight squad. Another long-running feature, The Sniper, is practically a prototype of the later Green Arrow, albeit armed with a rifle instead of a bow and arrow.

The best-known feature of Military Comics is the elite flight squadron known as The Blackhawks. The strip eschews the normal super-heroics and fantasy plots for grim war adventures — a difference that helps account for its huge and long-running popularity. After running through every issue of Military (later Modern Comics), they star in several incarnations of their own series.

1 ❑ Aug 1941 Cover: 0.10 **NM** value: **7800.00**
• **CGC:** 1 graded, best 9.4
📖 The Origin of Blackhawk • Stories of the Army and Navy; Blackhawk **A:** Chuck Cuidera ★ Origin of Blackhawk. ★ 1st Appearance of Blackhawk.
2 ❑ Sep 1941 Cover: 0.10 **NM** value: **2100.00**
• **CGC:** 1 graded, best 9.0
📖 The Coward Dies Twice • Blackhawk
3 ❑ Oct 1941 Cover: 0.10 **NM** value: **1750.00**
• **CGC:** 1 graded, best 9.2
📖 The Doomed Battalion • Blackhawk ★ Origin of Chop Chop. ★ 1st Appearance of Chop Chop.
4 ❑ Nov 1941 Cover: 0.10 **NM** value: **1375.00**
• **CGC:** 1 graded, best 9.2
📖 Desert Death • Blackhawk
5 ❑ Dec 1941 Cover: 0.10 **NM** value: **1200.00**
• **CGC:** 1 graded, best 9.0
📖 Scavengers of Doom • Blackhawk
6 ❑ Jan 1942 Cover: 0.10 **NM** value: **985.00**
• **CGC:** 1 graded, best 9.6
📖 The Vial of Death • Blackhawk
7 ❑ Feb 1942 Cover: 0.10 **NM** value: **985.00**
• **CGC:** 1 graded, best 5.0
📖 The Return of Genghis Khan • Blackhawk
8 ❑ Mar 1942 Cover: 0.10 **NM** value: **875.00**
• **CGC:** 1 graded, best 9.4
📖 The Sunken Island of Death; The Song of the Blackhawks • Blackhawk
9 ❑ Apr 1942 Cover: 0.10 **NM** value: **875.00**
• **CGC:** 1 graded, best 9.2
📖 The Man in the Iron Mask • Blackhawk
10 ❑ Jun 1942 Cover: 0.10 **NM** value: **875.00**
• **CGC:** 1 graded, best 9.6
📖 Trapped in the Devil's Oven • Blackhawk
11 ❑ Aug 1942 Cover: 0.10 **NM** value: **775.00**
• **CGC:** 1 graded, best 9.6
📖 Fury in the Philippines • Blackhawk
12 ❑ Oct 1942 Cover: 0.10 **NM** value: **775.00**
• **CGC:** 2 graded, best 9.6
📖 The Curse of Xanukhara • Blackhawk **A:** Reed Crandall

CGC-graded: Multiply prices above by **33 for 9.9 M** • **16 for 9.8 NM/M** • **7 for 9.6 NM+** • **5 for 9.4 NM** • **2.5 for 9.2 NM-** • **1.5 for 9.0 VF/NM**

13 ❑ Nov 1942 Cover: 0.10 **NM** value: **700.00**
• **CGC:** 1 graded, best 9.4
Blackhawk vs. the Butcher • Blackhawk **A:** Reed Crandall
14 ❑ Dec 1942 Cover: 0.10 **NM** value: **700.00**
• **CGC:** 1 graded, best 9.4
Tondeleyo • Blackhawk **A:** Reed Crandall
15 ❑ Jan 1943 Cover: 0.10 **NM** value: **700.00**
• **CGC:** 1 graded, best 5.0
Men Who Never Came Back • Blackhawk **A:** Reed Crandall
16 ❑ Feb 1943 Cover: 0.10 **NM** value: **600.00**
• **CGC:** 1 graded, best 9.2
Blackhawk vs. the Fox • Blackhawk **A:** Reed Crandall
17 ❑ Mar 1943 Cover: 0.10 **NM** value: **600.00**
• **CGC:** 1 graded, best 9.4
The Golden Bell of Soong-Toy! • Blackhawk **A:** Reed Crandall
18 ❑ Apr 1943 Cover: 0.10 **NM** value: **600.00**
• **CGC:** 1 graded, best 9.4
A: Reed Crandall
19 ❑ May 1943 Cover: 0.10 **NM** value: **600.00**
• **CGC:** 2 graded, best 9.6
A: Reed Crandall
20 ❑ Jul 1943 Cover: 0.10 **NM** value: **600.00**
• **CGC:** 1 graded, best 9.2
A: Reed Crandall
21 ❑ Aug 1943 Cover: 0.10 **NM** value: **525.00**
A: Reed Crandall
22 ❑ Sep 1943 Cover: 0.10 **NM** value: **525.00**
• **CGC:** 1 graded, best 9.0
A: Reed Crandall
23 ❑ Oct 1943 Cover: 0.10 **NM** value: **440.00**
• **CGC:** 1 graded, best 4.5
24 ❑ Nov 1943 Cover: 0.10 **NM** value: **440.00**
• **CGC:** 3 graded, best 8.0
Blackhawk: The Man with the Heavy Glasses; Death Patrol; The Sniper; Pt. Boat; Curse of the Chimus (text story); The Atlantic Patrol **A:** Al Stahl; Vernon Henkel **W:** Al Stahl; Vernon Henkel
25 ❑ Jan 1944 Cover: 0.10 **NM** value: **440.00**
• **CGC:** 1 graded, best 8.0
26 ❑ Feb 1944 Cover: 0.10 **NM** value: **440.00**
• **CGC:** 3 graded, best 9.0
27 ❑ Mar 1944 Cover: 0.10 **NM** value: **440.00**
• **CGC:** 2 graded, best 9.0
28 ❑ Apr 1944 Cover: 0.10 **NM** value: **440.00**
• **CGC:** 3 graded, best 9.0
29 ❑ May 1944 Cover: 0.10 **NM** value: **440.00**
• **CGC:** 2 graded, best 9.0
30 ❑ Jul 1944 Cover: 0.10 **NM** value: **440.00**
• **CGC:** 1 graded, best 8.0
31 ❑ Aug 1944 Cover: 0.10 **NM** value: **440.00**
• **CGC:** 2 graded, best 9.2
32 ❑ Sep 1944 Cover: 0.10 **NM** value: **440.00**
• **CGC:** 1 graded, best 7.0
33 ❑ Oct 1944 Cover: 0.10 **NM** value: **440.00**
34 ❑ Nov 1944 Cover: 0.10 **NM** value: **440.00**
• **CGC:** 1 graded, best 7.5
35 ❑ Jan 1945 Cover: 0.10 **NM** value: **440.00**
• **CGC:** 3 graded, best 8.5
36 ❑ Feb 1945 Cover: 0.10 **NM** value: **440.00**
• **CGC:** 2 graded, best 8.0
37 ❑ Mar 1945 Cover: 0.10 **NM** value: **440.00**
• **CGC:** 1 graded, best 8.5
38 ❑ Apr 1945 Cover: 0.10 **NM** value: **440.00**
• **CGC:** 1 graded, best 8.5
39 ❑ May 1945 Cover: 0.10 **NM** value: **440.00**
40 ❑ Jul 1945 Cover: 0.10 **NM** value: **440.00**
• **CGC:** 2 graded, best 8.5
41 ❑ Aug 1945 Cover: 0.10 **NM** value: **440.00**
• **CGC:** 2 graded, best 6.5
42 ❑ Sep 1945 Cover: 0.10 **NM** value: **440.00**
43 ❑ Oct 1945 Cover: 0.10 **NM** value: **440.00**
• **CGC:** 1 graded, best 8.0
• Series continued in Modern Comics #44

MILK — Radio

All issues are adults only.

1 ❑ Sep 1997, b&w Cover: 2.95 **NM** value: **Cover or less**
Circ: Diamd. preorders: **4,415**
2 ❑ Nov 1997, b&w Cover: 2.95 **NM** value: **Cover or less**
3 ❑ Jan 1998, b&w Cover: 2.95 **NM** value: **Cover or less**
Circ: Diamd. preorders: **3,638**
4 ❑ Mar 1998, b&w Cover: 2.95 **NM** value: **Cover or less**
Circ: Diamd. preorders: **3,661**
5 ❑ May 1998, b&w Cover: 2.95 **NM** value: **Cover or less**
Circ: Diamd. preorders: **3,438**
6 ❑ Jul 1998, b&w Cover: 2.95 **NM** value: **Cover or less**
Circ: Diamd. preorders: **3,275**
7 ❑ Sep 1998, b&w Cover: 2.95 **NM** value: **Cover or less**
Circ: Diamd. preorders: **2,976**
8 ❑ Nov 1998, b&w Cover: 2.95 **NM** value: **Cover or less**
Circ: Diamd. preorders: **3,246**
9 ❑ Jan 1999, b&w Cover: 2.95 **NM** value: **Cover or less**
Circ: Diamd. preorders: **2,940**
10 ❑ Mar 1999, b&w Cover: 2.95 **NM** value: **Cover or less**
Circ: Diamd. preorders: **2,765**
11 ❑ May 1999, b&w Cover: 2.95 **NM** value: **Cover or less**
Circ: Diamd. preorders: **2,885**
12 ❑ Jul 1999, b&w Cover: 2.95 **NM** value: **Cover or less**
Circ: Diamd. preorders: **2,799**
13 ❑ Sep 1999, b&w Cover: 2.95 **NM** value: **Cover or less**
Circ: Diamd. preorders: **2,725**
14 ❑ Nov 1999, b&w Cover: 2.95 **NM** value: **Cover or less**
Circ: Diamd. preorders: **2,595**
15 ❑ Jan 2000, b&w Cover: 2.95 **NM** value: **Cover or less**
Circ: Diamd. preorders: **2,533**
16 ❑ Mar 2000, b&w Cover: 2.95 **NM** value: **Cover or less**
Circ: Diamd. preorders: **2,552**
17 ❑ May 2000, b&w Cover: 2.95 **NM** value: **Cover or less**
Circ: Diamd. preorders: **2,397**
18 ❑ Jul 2000, b&w Cover: 2.95 **NM** value: **Cover or less**
Circ: Diamd. preorders: **2,503**
19 ❑ Sep 2000, b&w Cover: 2.95 **NM** value: **Cover or less**
Circ: Diamd. preorders: **2,445**

MILK & CHEESE — Slave Labor

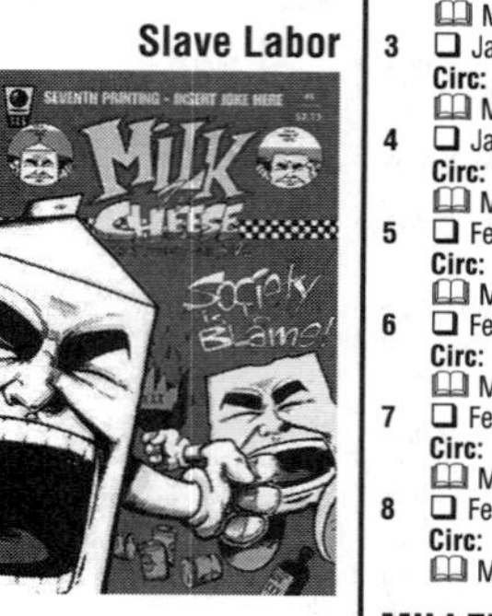

Creator Evan Dorkin sums it up nicely in his intro to issue #7 of this infamous series: "There's this milk and there's this cheese, see, and they don't like much of anything and they do stuff." What they do is primarily get loaded on anything intoxicating they can lay their mitts on while creating incredible mayhem. These "dairy products gone bad" are foul-mouthed alcoholics with a hate-on for just about everyone. Oh yes, and they're incredibly funny.

Published sporadically since 1991, Evan Dorkin delights in confounding collectors with odd issue numberings (the first six issues were called Milk & Cheese #1, Milk & Cheese's 2nd #1, 3rd #1, 4th #1, Other #1 and #666 respectively). He also eviscerates comic store owners, Weight Watchers, Renaissance fairs, and other sitting-duck targets. Ironically, the sheer spite of the comic accounts for much of its appeal — and even Hollywood has sought the rights to feature these unlovable characters.

1 ❑ Mar 1991, b&w Cover: 2.50 **NM** value: **80.00**
• **CGC:** 2 graded, best 9.0
Vas is Milk and Cheese?; Hercules of Hate!; Jury Duty; Wo-Hoppin'!; Dress Up, Get Down, Get Trendy; Bowl-O-Rama; Home Sweet Home Shopping Network; Mall-Bound; War on Drugs; Merv Griffin **A:** Evan Dorkin **W:** Evan Dorkin
1-2 ❑ Sep 1991, b&w Cover: 2.50 **NM** value: **6.00**
1-3 ❑ Sep 1992, b&w Cover: 2.50 **NM** value: **5.00**
1-4 ❑ Aug 1993, b&w Cover: 2.50 **NM** value: **3.00**
1-5 ❑ Oct 1994, b&w Cover: 2.50 **NM** value: **3.00**
1-6 ❑ Sep 1995, b&w Cover: 2.75 **NM** value: **3.00**
1-7 ❑ Feb 1997, b&w Cover: 2.75 **NM** value: **Cover or less**
Circ: Diamd. preorders: **1,946**
2 ❑ Mar 1992, b&w Cover: 2.50 **NM** value: **40.00**
• **CGC:** 1 graded, best 9.6
has Doctor Radium ad on back cover. • Other Number One **A:** Evan Dorkin **W:** Evan Dorkin
2-2 ❑ Jun 1993 Cover: 2.50 **NM** value: **5.00**
2-3 ❑ Oct 1994 Cover: 2.50 **NM** value: **4.00**
2-4 ❑ Jan 1996 Cover: 2.75 **NM** value: **Cover or less**
2-5 ❑ Cover: 2.75 **NM** value: **Cover or less**
3 ❑ Aug 1992, b&w Cover: 2.50 **NM** value: **32.00**
has Rats ad on back cover. • Third #1 **A:** Evan Dorkin **W:** Evan Dorkin
3-2 ❑ May 1993 Cover: 2.50 **NM** value: **4.00**
3-3 ❑ Oct 1994 Cover: 2.50 **NM** value: **3.00**
3-4 ❑ Feb 1996 Cover: 2.75 **NM** value: **Cover or less**
3-5 ❑ Cover: 2.75 **NM** value: **Cover or less**
4 ❑ Apr 1993, b&w Cover: 2.50 **NM** value: **20.00**
has Fine Dairy Products ad on back cover. • Fourth #1 **A:** Evan Dorkin **W:** Evan Dorkin
4-2 ❑ Mar 1995 Cover: 2.50 **NM** value: **3.00**
4-3 ❑ Aug 1996 Cover: 2.75 **NM** value: **Cover or less**
5 ❑ Apr 1994, b&w Cover: 2.50 **NM** value: **20.00**
• **CGC:** 1 graded, best 9.6
has APE ad on back cover. • First Second Issue **A:** Evan Dorkin **W:** Evan Dorkin
5-2 ❑ Nov 1994 Cover: 2.50 **NM** value: **3.00**
5-3 ❑ Feb 1996 Cover: 2.75 **NM** value: **3.00**
5-4 ❑ Cover: 2.75 **NM** value: **Cover or less**
6 ❑ Apr 1995, b&w Cover: 2.50 **NM** value: **8.00**
Circ: CapCity orders: **4,135** • **CGC:** 1 graded, best 9.2
• Six Six Six **A:** Evan Dorkin **W:** Evan Dorkin
6-2 ❑ Sep 1996 Cover: 2.75 **NM** value: **Cover or less**
Circ: Diamd. preorders: **3,206**
7 ❑ Jun 1997, b&w Cover: 2.95 **NM** value: **3.00**
Circ: Diamd. preorders: **13,603**
There's No Busine$$...; Alcoholics Unanimous; The Devil Made them Do It; Small Pre$$ Sales Blitz; Renaissance Madmen; Chubby Chasers!; Mummy's the Word!; Cult Heroes; Sex; Get Tat Fly! • Latest Thing! **A:** Evan Dorkin **W:** Evan Dorkin

MILLENNIUM — DC

Millennium was DC's mega-crossover event of 1988, running for eight weekly issues with dozens of related title crossovers. It was a story which really began billions of years ago, and which would shape the future of Earth for ages to come. Long before intelligent life on Earth, the Oans created a race of androids called the Manhunters to help them enforce order in the universe. After half a billion years, the Manhunters turned on them and the Oans were forced to strip them of power. The Oans tried again, and the result was the Green Lantern Corps.

In the wake of the Crisis on Infinite Earths, the Oans decided the time had come to create the next generation of immortals. They came to Earth intending to choose 10 people for this gift. They needed the aid of Earth's super-heroes to protect the chosen ones from the Manhunters, which had gained new powers and had been living secretly among humans for generations.

1 ❑ Jan 1988 Cover: 0.75 **NM** value: **2.00**
Circ: CapCity orders: **59,850**
Millennium: Week One Over **A:** Ian Gibson; Joe Staton **W:** Steve Englehart
2 ❑ Jan 1988 Cover: 0.75 **NM** value: **1.50**
Circ: CapCity orders: **51,350**
Millennium
3 ❑ Jan 1988 Cover: 0.75 **NM** value: **1.50**
Circ: CapCity orders: **49,150**
Millennium
4 ❑ Jan 1988 Cover: 0.75 **NM** value: **1.50**
Circ: CapCity orders: **48,300**
Millennium
5 ❑ Feb 1988 Cover: 0.75 **NM** value: **1.50**
Circ: CapCity orders: **47,150**
Millennium
6 ❑ Feb 1988 Cover: 0.75 **NM** value: **1.50**
Circ: CapCity orders: **46,900**
Millennium
7 ❑ Feb 1988 Cover: 0.75 **NM** value: **1.50**
Circ: CapCity orders: **46,750**
Millennium
8 ❑ Feb 1988 Cover: 0.75 **NM** value: **1.50**
Circ: CapCity orders: **46,900**
Millennium

MILLENNIUM 2.5 A.D. — Avalon

1 ❑ Cover: 2.95 **NM** value: **Cover or less**
The Saga of Buck Rogers

MILLENNIUM EDITION: ACTION COMICS — DC

As Superman has celebrated his milestone anniversaries in the past, DC has reprinted his first appearance in Action Comics #1 from June 1938. Often, these thin reprints only have that original story and ignore the other material in the issue, which included stories featuring Zatara the magician, adventurer Tex Thomson, rancher Chuck Dawson, and explorer Marco Polo.

In 2000, in anticipation of the new millenium, DC began reprinting significant first issues or first appearances in its Millenium Edition line. Fans were asked to vote for several of their favorites, most of which came from later in DC's history.

The Action #1 reprint included all those early features, giving readers a chance to experience what readers of the late 1930s might have held in their hands at the time. — Brent

1 ❑ Feb 2000 Cover: 3.95 **NM** value: **Cover or less**
Superman; "Chuck" Dawson; Zatara; South Sea Strategy; Sticky-Mitt Stimson; The Adventures of Marco Polo; Pep Morgan; Scoop Scanlon, Five Star Reporter; Tex Thompson; Stardust **A:** Joe Shuster; Bernard Baily; Bill Alger; Fred Guardineer; Hugh Fleming; Sven Elven; Will Ely **W:** Bernard Baily; Bill Alger; Fred Guardineer; Hugh Fleming; Jerry Siegel; Sven Elven; Will Ely ★ Origin of Superman. ★ 1st Appearance of Superman.

MILLENNIUM EDITION: ADVENTURE COMICS — DC

61 ❑ Dec 2000 Cover: 3.95 **NM** value: **Cover or less**
Circ: Diamd. preorders: **10,223**
Starman; Mark Lansing of Mikishawm; Facts; Federal Men; Steve Conrad, Adventurer; Peter and His Pup; The Quiz Page; Hourman; Paul Kirk, Manhunter; Cotton Carver, Defender of Barlunda; Case of the Black Cat; The Sandman **A:** Henry Boltinoff; Jack Burnley; Howard Purcell; Bernard Baily; Chad Grothkopf; Creig Flessel; Ed Moore; Jack Lehti; Ray McGirk; T.C. O'Neil **W:** Henry Boltinoff; Howard Purcell; Ed Moore; Jack Lehti; Jerry Siegel; Ray McGirk; Gardner Fox; Ken Fitch; T.C. O'Neil ★ 1st Appearance of Starman I (Ted Knight).
247 ❑ Nov 2000 Cover: 2.50 **NM** value: **Cover or less**
Circ: Diamd. preorders: **10,377**
• The Legion of Super-Heroes; The 13 Superstition Arrows; Aquaman's Super Sea-Squad **W:** Ramona Fradon; Al Plastino; George Papp

MILLENNIUM EDITION: ALL STAR COMICS — DC

3 ❑ Jun 2000 Cover: 3.95 **NM** value: **Cover or less**
Circ: Diamd. preorders: **11,050**
A: Howard Sherman; Sheldon Mayer; Ben Flinton; Bernard Baily; Craig Flessel; Everett E. Hibbard; Martin Nodell; Sheldon Moldoff **W:** Gardner Fox ★ 1st Appearance of the Justice Society of America.
3/SC ❑ Jun 2000 **NM** value: **10.00**
Circ: Diamd. preorders: **4,690** • **CGC:** 2 graded, best 9.8
chromium cover. **A:** Howard Sherman; Sheldon Mayer; Ben Flinton; Bernard Baily; Craig Flessel; Everett E. Hibbard; Martin Nodell; Sheldon Moldoff **W:** Gardner Fox ★ 1st Appearance of the Justice Society of America.
8 ❑ Feb 2001 Cover: 3.95 **NM** value: **Cover or less**
Circ: Diamd. preorders: **10,338**
Two New Members Win Their Spurs; Introducing Wonder Woman; Sky Cutups **A:** Jack Burnley; Ben Flinton; Bernard Baily; Cliff Young; Everett E. Hibbard; Harry G. Peter; Sheldon Moldoff **W:** Gardner Fox; William Moulton Marston ★ Origin of Wonder Woman. ★ 1st Appearance of Wonder Woman.

MILLENNIUM EDITION: ALL-STAR WESTERN — DC

10 ❑ Apr 2000 Cover: 2.50 **NM** value: **Cover or less**
Jonah Hex: Welcome to Paradise; El Diablo: The Devil's Secret; Bat Lash • Reprints All-Star Western #10 **A:** Gray Morrow; Tony DeZuniga; Nick Cardy; Tony DeZuñiga **W:** Sergio Aragonés; John Albano; Denny O'Neil; Robert Kanigher ★ 1st Appearance of Jonah Hex.

MILLENNIUM EDITION: BATMAN DC

1 ❑ Feb 2001 Cover: 3.95 **NM** value: **Cover or less**
Circ: Diamd. preorders: **13,499**
📖 The Legend of Batman-Who He Is and How He Came to Be!; The Joker; Major Bigsbe an' Botts; Professor Hugo Strange and the Monsters; Strictly Publicity; Meet the artist!; The Cat; Two Aces; Ginger Snap; Fantastic Facts; The Joker Returns **A:** Bob Kane; George Papp; Paul Gustavson; Ted Raye **W:** George Papp; Paul Gustavson; Ted Raye; Gardner Fox; George Shute; Guy Monroe

MILLENNIUM EDITION: BATMAN: THE DARK KNIGHT RETURNS DC

1 ❑ Oct 2000 Cover: 5.95 **NM** value: **Cover or less**
Circ: Diamd. preorders: **8,483**
📖 The Dark Knight Returns • Reprints Batman: The Dark Knight #1 **A:** Klaus Janson **W:** Frank Miller

MILLENNIUM EDITION: CRISIS ON INFINITE EARTHS DC

1 ❑ ca. 2000 Cover: 2.50 **NM** value: **Cover or less**
• Reprints Crisis on Infinite Earths #1

MILLENNIUM EDITION: DETECTIVE COMICS DC

1 ❑ Jan 2001 Cover: 3.95 **NM** value: **Cover or less**
Circ: Diamd. preorders: **11,651**
📖 Speed Saunders; Cosmo, the Phantom of Disguise; Bret Lawton; The Claws of the Red Dragon; Gumshoe Gus; Bart Regan, Spy; Eagle-Eyed Jake; Silly Sleuths; Buck Marshall, Range Detective; Slam Bradley • Reprints Detective Comics #1 **A:** Joe Shuster; Bill Patrick; E.C. Stoner; Fred Schwab; Homer Fleming; Russell Cole; Sven Elven; Tom Hickey **W:** Bill Patrick; E.C. Stoner; Fred Schwab; Homer Fleming; Jerry Siegel; Russell Cole; Sven Elven; Major Malcolm Wheeler-Nicholson

27 ❑ Feb 2000 Cover: 3.95 **NM** value: **Cover or less**
📖 The Bat-Man: The Case of the Chemical Syndicate; Speed Saunders Ace Investigator **A:** Bob Kane; Joe Shuster; Bill Alger; Fred Guardineer; Hugh Fleming; James Chambers; Paul Gustavson; Sven Elven **W:** Bill Alger; Bill Finger; Fred Guardineer; Hugh Fleming; James Chambers; Jerry Siegel; Paul Gustavson; Sven Elven; Tom Hickey; Paul Dean; Sax Rohmer ★ 1st Appearance of Commissioner Gordon, Batman.

38 ❑ ca. 2000 Cover: 3.95 **NM** value: **Cover or less**
📖 Robin-The Boy Wonder; Spy; Red Logan; The Crimson Avenger; Speed Saunders: The Kidnapped Singer; Steve Malone; Cliff Crosby; Slam Bradley **A:** Bob Kane; Dennis Neville; Don Lynch; Fred Guardineer; Jack Lehti; Maurice Kashuba **W:** Bill Finger; Don Lynch; Fred Guardineer; Jack Lehti; Jerry Siegel ★ 1st Appearance of Robin I (Dick Grayson).

225 ❑ Dec 2000 Cover: 2.50 **NM** value: **Cover or less**
Circ: Diamd. preorders: **10,834**
📖 If I were Batman; Roy Raymond, TV Detective: The Money that Came to Life; Casey the Cop; Varsity Vic; Four Tricks of the Detective's Trade; The Strange Experiment of Dr. Erdell; Homer **A:** Henry Boltinoff; Joe Certa; Ruben Moreira; Sheldon Moldoff **W:** Henry Boltinoff; Edmond Hamilton; Jack Miller; Joe Samachson ★ Origin of Martian Manhunter. ★ 1st Appearance of Martian Manhunter.

359 ❑ Oct 2000 Cover: 3.95 **NM** value: **Cover or less**
Circ: Diamd. preorders: **12,163**
📖 The Million Dollar Debut of Batgirl; Riddle of the Sleepytime Tax! **A:** Murphy Anderson; Carmine Infantino **W:** Gardner Fox; John Broome

MILLENNIUM EDITION: FLASH COMICS DC

1 ❑ Sep 2000 Cover: 3.95 **NM** value: **Cover or less**
Circ: Diamd. preorders: **13,093**
📖 The Flash; "Cliff" Cornwall Special Agent; The Hawkman; Johnny Thunderbolt; Warfarein Space; The Demon Dummy; The Whip • Reprints Flash Comics #1 **A:** Denis Neville; Ed Wheelan; George Storm; Harry Lampert; Sheldon Moldoff; Stan Asch **W:** Ed Wheelan; Sheldon Moldoff; Gardner Fox; John B. Wentworth ★ Origin of The Flash I (Jay Garrick). ★ 1st Appearance of The Flash I (Jay Garrick).

MILLENNIUM EDITION: GREEN LANTERN DC

76 ❑ ca. 2000 Cover: 2.50 **NM** value: **Cover or less**

MILLENNIUM EDITION: HELLBLAZER DC

1 ❑ Jul 2000 Cover: 2.95 **NM** value: **Cover or less**
Circ: Diamd. preorders: **5,964**
📖 Hunger • Reprints Hellblazer #1 **A:** John Ridgway **W:** Jamie Delano

MILLENNIUM EDITION: HOUSE OF MYSTERY DC

1 ❑ Sep 2000 Cover: 2.50 **NM** value: **Cover or less**
Circ: Diamd. preorders: **9,644**
📖 I Fell in Love With a Witch!; Man or Monster?; The Ghost of Paris!; The Curse of Seabury Manor; Casey the Cop; Wanda Was a Werewolf; Superstitious Lover! • Reprints House of Mystery #1 **A:** Henry Boltinoff; Curt Swan; Bob Brown; John Prentice; Morris Waldinger **W:** Henry Boltinoff

MILLENNIUM EDITION: HOUSE OF SECRETS DC

92 ❑ May 2000 Cover: 2.50 **NM** value: **Cover or less**
Circ: Diamd. preorders: **8,671**
📖 Swamp Thing; After I Die; It's Better to Give; Trick or Treat **A:** Alan Weiss; Bernie Wrightson; Dick Dillin; Tony DeZuniga; Bill Draut **W:** Dick Dillin; Len Wein; Mark Evanier; Mary Skrenes ★ 1st Appearance of Swamp Thing.

MILLENNIUM EDITION: JLA DC

1 ❑ ca. 2000 Cover: 2.50 **NM** value: **Cover or less**
Circ: Diamd. preorders: **11,286**

MILLENNIUM EDITION: JUSTICE LEAGUE DC

1 ❑ Jul 2000 Cover: 2.50 **NM** value: **Cover or less**
Circ: Diamd. preorders: **7,042**
📖 Born Again • Reprints Justice League #1 **A:** Keith Giffen; Kevin Maguire **W:** Keith Giffen; J.M. DeMatteis

MILLENNIUM EDITION: MILITARY COMICS DC

1 ❑ Oct 2000 Cover: 3.95 **NM** value: **Cover or less**
Circ: Diamd. preorders: **8,831**
📖 Blackhawk; Loops and Banks; Blue Tracer; Archie Atkins; Shot and Shell; Yankee Eagle; Death Patrol; Sabotage; Miss America; Gone with the Draft; Q-Boat **A:** Klaus Nordling; Jack Cole; Fred Guardineer; Bud Ernest; Dick Scopes; Frank Frollo; Carl Kiefer; Charles Cuidera; Elmer Wexler; Phillip "Tex" Blaisdell; William A. Smith **W:** Klaus Nordling; Jack Cole; Bud Ernest; Dick Scopes; Frank Frollo; John Steward; S.R. Powell

MILLENNIUM EDITION: MORE FUN COMICS DC

73 ❑ Jan 2001 Cover: 3.95 **NM** value: **Cover or less**
Circ: Diamd. preorders: **10,528**
📖 Doctor Fate; The Green Arrow; Radio Squad; Johnny Quick; Who Did It?; Clip Carson; The Spectre; Aquaman **A:** Howard Sherman; Bernard Baily; Chad Grothkopf; Ed Moore; George Papp; Paul Norris **W:** Jerry Siegel; Gardner Fox; Mort Weisinger; Wilton Weston

101 ❑ Nov 2000 Cover: 2.95 **NM** value: **Cover or less**
Circ: Diamd. preorders: **10,153**
📖 Formula for Doom!; Orphans of the Sea!; Superboy!; A Personal Reason (text story); An Investment in Happiness!; The Unsafe Safe **A:** Mort Meskin; Maurice Del Bourgo; Bernard Baily; Louis Cazeneuve **W:** Don Cameron; Joe Samachson; Joseph Greene

MILLENNIUM EDITION: NEW GODS DC

1 ❑ Jun 2000 Cover: 2.50 **NM** value: **Cover or less**
Circ: Diamd. preorders: **8,277**
📖 Orion Fights for Earth! **A:** Jack Kirby **W:** Jack Kirby

MILLENNIUM EDITION: OUR ARMY AT WAR DC

81 ❑ Jun 2000 Cover: 2.50 **NM** value: **Cover or less**
Circ: Diamd. preorders: **10,013**
📖 The Rock of Easy Co.!; Fighting Footsteps; The Liberators; Umbrella Pilot; No Pocket for Easy; The Unsafe Safe **A:** Joe Kubert; Ross Andru; Russ Heath; Jack Abel **W:** Bob Haney; Robert Kanigher ★ 1st Appearance of Sgt. Rock.

MILLENNIUM EDITION: PLOP! DC

1 ❑ Jul 2000 Cover: 2.50 **NM** value: **Cover or less**
Circ: Diamd. preorders: **7,072**
📖 Plops; The Escape; A Plop is Born; Kongzilla; The Message; The Gourmet • Reprints Plop! #1 **A:** George Evans; Sergio Aragonés; Alfredo Alcala; Berni Wrightson **W:** Sergio Aragonés; Frank Robbins; Paul Levitz; Sheldon Mayer; Steve Skeates

MILLENNIUM EDITION: POLICE COMICS DC

1 ❑ Sep 2000 Cover: 3.95 **NM** value: **Cover or less**
Circ: Diamd. preorders: **10,983**
📖 Firebrand; 711; Super Snooper; Eagle Evans, Flier of Fortune; Chic Carter; Plastic Man; Steele Kerrigan; The Mouthpiece; Vengeance; Phantom Lady; Dewey Drip; The Human Bomb • Reprints Police Comics #1 **A:** Gill Fox; Will Eisner; Reed Crandall; Jack Cole; Fred Guardineer; Clark Williams; George E. Brenner; John Devlin; Paul Carroll; Al Bryant; Arthur Peddy **W:** Gill Fox; Will Eisner; Jack Cole; Fred Guardineer; Clark Williams; George E. Brenner; John Devlin; Paul Carroll; Robert M. Hyatt ★ 1st Appearance of Plastic Man, Firebrand.

MILLENNIUM EDITION: PREACHER DC

1 ❑ Oct 2000 Cover: 2.95 **NM** value: **Cover or less**
Circ: Diamd. preorders: **7,536**
📖 The Time of the Preacher **A:** Steve Dillon **W:** Garth Ennis

MILLENNIUM EDITION: SENSATION COMICS DC

1 ❑ Oct 2000 Cover: 3.95 **NM** value: **Cover or less**
Circ: Diamd. preorders: **9,905**
📖 Wonder Woman; Black Pirate; Mr. Terrific; The Gay Ghost; Gunner Godbee; Little Boy Blue and the Blue Boys; Wildcat • Reprints Sensation Comics #1 **A:** Hal Sharp; Howard Purcell; Harry G. Peter; Irwin Hasen; Jon L. Blummer; Sheldon Moldoff **W:** Bill Finger; Charles Reizenstein; Gardner Fox; George S. Hurst Jr.; William Moulton Marston

MILLENNIUM EDITION: SHOWCASE DC

4 ❑ ca. 2000 Cover: 2.50 **NM** value: **Cover or less**
• Reprints Showcase #4 ★ 1st Appearance of Flash II (Barry Allen).

9 ❑ Jan 2001 Cover: 2.50 **NM** value: **Cover or less**
Circ: Diamd. preorders: **9,830**
📖 The Girl in Superman's Past; Odd Newspaper Items!; The New Lois Lane; Jerry the Jitterbug; Newspaper Talk; Sleuths in Skirts; Mrs. Superman; Ollie • Reprints Showcase #9 **A:** Henry Boltinoff; Al Plastino; Ruben Moreiro **W:** Henry Boltinoff; Jerry Coleman; Otto Binder

22 ❑ Dec 2000 Cover: 2.50 **NM** value: **Cover or less**
Circ: Diamd. preorders: **10,618**
📖 SOS Green Lantern • Reprints Showcase #22 **A:** Gil Kane; Joe Giella **W:** John Broome ★ 1st Appearance of Green Lantern II (Hal Jordan).

MILLENNIUM EDITION: SUPERBOY DC

1 ❑ Feb 2001 Cover: 2.95 **NM** value: **Cover or less**
Circ: Diamd. preorders: **10,709**
📖 The Man Who Could See Tomorrow!; Rocket Plane; Shorty; The Boy Vandals; Daffy & Doodle; The Language of the Sea; Sagebrush Sam; Superboy Meets Mighty Boy!; Homer **A:** Henry Boltinoff; Win Mortimer; Ed Dobrotka; John Sikela; Lit-Win **W:** Henry Boltinoff; Lit-Win; Cliff Rhodes; Edmond Hamilton

MILLENNIUM EDITION: SUPERMAN DC

75 ❑ ca. 2000 Cover: 2.95 **NM** value: **Cover or less**
Circ: Diamd. preorders: **8,191**

MILLENNIUM EDITION: SUPERMAN (1ST SERIES) DC

1 ❑ Dec 2000 Cover: 3.95 **NM** value: **Cover or less**
Circ: Diamd. preorders: **14,115**
📖 Superman-Champion of the Oppressed!; Scientific Explanation of Superman's Amazing Strength!; Cave-In at the Blakely Mine!; Superman-Football Hero!; Superman • Reprints Superman (1st Series) #1 **A:** Joe Shuster **W:** Jerry Siegel

76 ❑ ca. 2000 Cover: 2.95 **NM** value: **Cover or less**
Circ: Diamd. preorders: **14,073**
📖 The Mightiest Team in the World; The Misfit Manhunter; The Gatling Gun (text story); Jerry the Jitterbug; Mrs. Superman **A:** Henry Boltinoff; Curt Swan; Wayne Boring **W:** Henry Boltinoff; Ben Galloway; Edmond Hamilton

233 ❑ Jan 2001 Cover: 2.50 **NM** value: **Cover or less**
Circ: Diamd. preorders: **9,453**
📖 Superman Breaks Loose; Super-Turtle; Jor-El's Golden Folly; A New Year Brings a New Beginning for Superman **A:** Henry Boltinoff; Murphy Anderson; Curt Swan **W:** Henry Boltinoff; Denny O'Neil; E. Nelson Bridwell

MILLENNIUM EDITION: SUPERMAN'S PAL JIMMY OLSEN DC

1 ❑ Apr 2000 Cover: 2.95 **NM** value: **Cover or less**
Circ: Diamd. preorders: **13,115**
📖 The Boy of 100 Faces!; Case of the Lumberjack Jinx!; Peg; Cruelist Critter in the Sea (text story); The Man of Steel's Substitute!; Varsity Vic • Reprints Superman's Pal Jimmy Olsen #1 **A:** Curt Swan **W:** Otto Binder

MILLENNIUM EDITION: TALES CALCULATED TO DRIVE YOU MAD DC

1 ❑ ca. 2000 **NM** value: **2.95**

MILLENNIUM EDITION: THE BRAVE AND THE BOLD DC

28 ❑ Feb 2000 Cover: 2.50 **NM** value: **Cover or less**
📖 Starro the Conqueror! **A:** Mike Sekowsky **W:** Gardner Fox ★ 1st Appearance of The Justice League of America, Snapper Carr.

85 ❑ Nov 2000 Cover: 2.50 **NM** value: **Cover or less**
Circ: Diamd. preorders: **9,292**
📖 The Senator's Been Shot! **A:** Neal Adams **W:** Bob Haney

MILLENNIUM EDITION: THE FLASH DC

123 ❑ May 2000 Cover: 2.50 **NM** value: **Cover or less**
Circ: Diamd. preorders: **13,566**
📖 Flash of Two Worlds! • Reprints The Flash (1st Series) #1 **A:** Carmine Infantino **W:** Gardner Fox

MILLENNIUM EDITION: THE MAN OF STEEL DC

1 ❑ ca. 2000 Cover: 2.50 **NM** value: **Cover or less**

MILLENNIUM EDITION: THE NEW TEEN TITANS DC

1 ❑ Dec 2000 Cover: 2.50 **NM** value: **Cover or less**
Circ: Diamd. preorders: **6,415**
📖 You Can Go Home Again **A:** George Pérez **W:** Marv Wolfman

MILLENNIUM EDITION: THE SAGA OF THE SWAMP THING DC

21 ❑ Feb 2000 Cover: 2.50 **NM** value: **Cover or less**
Circ: Diamd. preorders: **6,530**
📖 Sleep of the Just • Reprints Sandman #1 **A:** Sam Kieth **W:** Neil Gaiman ★ 1st Appearance of Sanman II (Morpheus).

MILLENNIUM EDITION: THE SANDMAN DC

1 ❑ Feb 2000 Cover: 2.95 **NM** value: **Cover or less**
📖 Sleep of the Just • Reprints Sandman #1 **A:** Sam Kieth **W:** Neil Gaiman ★ 1st Appearance of Sanman II (Morpheus).

MILLENNIUM EDITION: THE SHADOW DC

1 ❑ Feb 2001 Cover: 2.50 **NM** value: **Cover or less**
Circ: Diamd. preorders: **7,339**
📖 The Doom Puzzle; The Shadow Knows (text story) **A:** Michael W. Kaluta **W:** Denny O'Neil

MILLENNIUM EDITION: THE SPIRIT DC

1 ❑ Jul 2000 Cover: 2.95 **NM** value: **Cover or less**
Circ: Diamd. preorders: **11,047**
📖 Wanted for Murder; Tony Zacco, Public Enemy No. 1; Dressed to Kill; A Clock Stops; The Eyes Have It; Manhunt • Reprints The Spirit #1 **A:** Will Eisner; Lou Fine **W:** Will Eisner

MILLENNIUM EDITION: WATCHMEN DC

1 ❑ ca. 2000 Cover: 2.50 **NM** value: **Cover or less**
Circ: Diamd. preorders: **7,565**
• Reprints Watchmen #1 **A:** Dave Gibbons **W:** Alan Moore

MILLENNIUM EDITION: WHIZ COMICS DC

1 ❑ Mar 2000 Cover: 3.95 **NM** value: **Cover or less**
Circ: Diamd. preorders: **12,056**

MILLENNIUM EDITION: WILDC.A.T.S DC

1 ❑ ca. 2000 Cover: 2.50 **NM** value: **Cover or less**
Circ: Diamd. preorders: **5,495**

MILLENNIUM EDITION: WONDER WOMAN (2ND SERIES) DC

1 ❑ May 2000 Cover: 2.50 **NM** value: **Cover or less**
Circ: Diamd. preorders: **8,775**
📖 The Princess and the Power! • Reprints Wonder Woman (2nd Series) #1 **A:** George Pérez **W:** George Pérez; Greg Potter

CGC-graded: Multiply prices above by **33 for 9.9 M • 16 for 9.8 NM/M • 7 for 9.6 NM+ • 5 for 9.4 NM • 2.5 for 9.2 NM- • 1.5 for 9.0 VF/NM**

MILLENNIUM EDITION: YOUNG ROMANCE COMICS — DC

1 ❑ Apr 2000 Cover: 2.95 **NM** value: **Cover or less**
Circ: Diamd. preorders: **8,372**
📖 I Was a Pick-Up!; The Farmer's Wife; Misguided Heart; The Plight of the Suspicious Bride Groom; Young Hearts Sing a Summer Song • Reprints Young Romance (DC) #1; 1st romance comic **A:** Joe Simon; Jack Kirby; Bill Draut **W:** Joe Simon

MILLENNIUM FEVER — DC / Vertigo

1 ❑ Oct 1995 Cover: 2.50 **NM** value: **Cover or less**
Circ: CapCity orders: **6,825**
A: Duncan Fegredo **W:** Nick Abadzis
2 ❑ Nov 1995 Cover: 2.50 **NM** value: **Cover or less**
📖 Fear of Rain **A:** Duncan Fegredo **W:** Nick Abadzis
3 ❑ Dec 1995 Cover: 2.50 **NM** value: **Cover or less**
A: Duncan Fegredo **W:** Nick Abadzis
4 ❑ Jan 1996 Cover: 2.50 **NM** value: **Cover or less**
📖 A Way of Seeing Things final issue. **A:** Duncan Fegredo **W:** Nick Abadzis
Ash 1❑ **NM** value: **0.75**
A: Duncan Fegredo **W:** Nick Abadzis

MILLENNIUM INDEX — Eclipse

1 ❑ Mar 1988 Cover: 2.00 **NM** value: **Cover or less**
Circ: CapCity orders: **4,000**
2 ❑ Mar 1988 Cover: 2.00 **NM** value: **Cover or less**
Circ: CapCity orders: **3,925**

MILLIE THE LOVABLE MONSTER — Dell

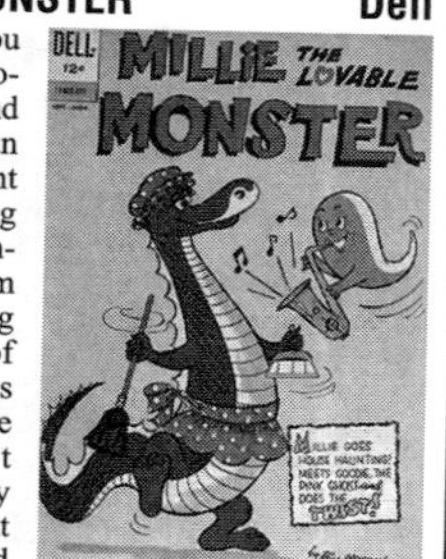

Here's a wild idea: Suppose you have a big purple and green dinosaur with great big eyelashes and lots of charm that loves to have fun and play with kids. Think it might catch on? Dell Comics was hoping so, with Millie the Loveable Monster, a wholesome comic book from the early 1960s aimed at very young kids. Millie comes to the town of Midway and immediately captures the hearts of everyone except one old sourpuss industrialist who can't believe that people would really love a giant purple monster. But Millie's pleasant nature and big old eyelashes carry the day, and soon the millionaire builds Millie her own haunted house to live in with other supernatural friends. Despite the obvious potential, Millie the Loveable Monster must have been too far ahead of her time, since the comics appeared only sporadically until the early 1970s.

1 ❑ ca. 1962 Cover: 0.12 **NM** value: **25.00**
📖 Millie the Lovable Monster comes to Midway; Millie Goes House Haunting; Millie Does the Twist; Millie Goes to Hollywood • (#12-523-211) **A:** Bill Woggon **W:** Bill Woggon
2 ❑ ca. 1963 Cover: 0.12 **NM** value: **20.00**
A: Bill Woggon **W:** Bill Woggon
3 ❑ ca. 1964 Cover: 0.12 **NM** value: **20.00**
A: Bill Woggon **W:** Bill Woggon
4 ❑ Jul 1972 Cover: 0.15 **NM** value: **14.00**
A: Bill Woggon **W:** Bill Woggon
5 ❑ Oct 1972 Cover: 0.15 **NM** value: **14.00**
A: Bill Woggon **W:** Bill Woggon
6 ❑ Jan 1973 Cover: 0.15 **NM** value: **14.00**
A: Bill Woggon **W:** Bill Woggon

MILLIE THE MODEL COMICS — Marvel

Millie Collins is the good-hearted star of this glamour series. She works as a model at the Hanover Agency with her good friend Toni and the catty Chili. The action in the series revolves around the world of fashion, where the women vie for choice jobs, try out the latest clothes and hairstyles, and struggle with more romantic entanglements than most soap operas.

This series is a rarity among Marvel titles, running without interruption from the end of World War II through 1972. This incredible longevity is, no doubt, due to the remarkable support it enjoyed from its readers, many of whom submitted hairstyles and fashion ideas for Millie. Marvel honored these readers by using many different looks for Millie in each issue, making special note of the names of the readers who had suggested them in a device initiated in this sort of comic book by Bill Woggon with his Katy Keene.

1 ❑ ca. 1945 Cover: 0.10 **NM** value: **475.00**
• **CGC:** 2 graded, best 7.5
★ Origin of Millie the Model.
2 ❑ Oct 1946 Cover: 0.10 **NM** value: **285.00**
3 ❑ Dec 1946 Cover: 0.10 **NM** value: **180.00**
4 ❑ ca. 1947 Cover: 0.10 **NM** value: **180.00**
5 ❑ ca. 1947 Cover: 0.10 **NM** value: **180.00**
6 ❑ ca. 1947 Cover: 0.10 **NM** value: **180.00**
7 ❑ Sep 1947 Cover: 0.10 **NM** value: **180.00**
8 ❑ Oct 1947 Cover: 0.10 **NM** value: **180.00**
9 ❑ Dec 1947 Cover: 0.10 **NM** value: **175.00**
A: Basil Wolverton
10 ❑ Feb 1948 Cover: 0.10 **NM** value: **140.00**
• **CGC:** 1 graded, best 7.5
11 ❑ Apr 1948 Cover: 0.10 **NM** value: **100.00**
12 ❑ Jun 1948 Cover: 0.10 **NM** value: **85.00**
13 ❑ Aug 1948 Cover: 0.10 **NM** value: **110.00**
A: Harvey Kurtzman
14 ❑ Oct 1948 Cover: 0.10 **NM** value: **110.00**
A: Harvey Kurtzman
15 ❑ Dec 1948 Cover: 0.10 **NM** value: **85.00**
16 ❑ ca. 1949 Cover: 0.10 **NM** value: **110.00**
A: Harvey Kurtzman
17 ❑ ca. 1949 Cover: 0.10 **NM** value: **85.00**
18 ❑ ca. 1949 Cover: 0.10 **NM** value: **85.00**
19 ❑ ca. 1949 Cover: 0.10 **NM** value: **85.00**
20 ❑ ca. 1950 Cover: 0.10 **NM** value: **85.00**
21 ❑ ca. 1950 Cover: 0.10 **NM** value: **60.00**
22 ❑ ca. 1950 Cover: 0.10 **NM** value: **60.00**
23 ❑ ca. 1950 Cover: 0.10 **NM** value: **60.00**
24 ❑ Sep 1950 Cover: 0.10 **NM** value: **60.00**
25 ❑ Nov 1950 Cover: 0.10 **NM** value: **60.00**
26 ❑ Jan 1951 Cover: 0.10 **NM** value: **60.00**
27 ❑ Mar 1951 Cover: 0.10 **NM** value: **60.00**
28 ❑ May 1951 Cover: 0.10 **NM** value: **60.00**
29 ❑ Jul 1951 Cover: 0.10 **NM** value: **60.00**
30 ❑ Sep 1951 Cover: 0.10 **NM** value: **60.00**
31 ❑ Nov 1951 Cover: 0.10 **NM** value: **38.00**
32 ❑ Jan 1952 Cover: 0.10 **NM** value: **38.00**
33 ❑ Mar 1952 Cover: 0.10 **NM** value: **38.00**
34 ❑ May 1952 Cover: 0.10 **NM** value: **38.00**
35 ❑ Jul 1952 Cover: 0.10 **NM** value: **38.00**
36 ❑ Sep 1952 Cover: 0.10 **NM** value: **38.00**
37 ❑ Nov 1952 Cover: 0.10 **NM** value: **38.00**
38 ❑ Jan 1953 Cover: 0.10 **NM** value: **38.00**
39 ❑ Feb 1953 Cover: 0.10 **NM** value: **38.00**
40 ❑ Mar 1953 Cover: 0.10 **NM** value: **35.00**
41 ❑ Apr 1953 Cover: 0.10 **NM** value: **35.00**
42 ❑ May 1953 Cover: 0.10 **NM** value: **35.00**
43 ❑ Jun 1953 Cover: 0.10 **NM** value: **35.00**
44 ❑ Jul 1953 Cover: 0.10 **NM** value: **35.00**
45 ❑ Aug 1953 Cover: 0.10 **NM** value: **35.00**
46 ❑ Sep 1953 Cover: 0.10 **NM** value: **35.00**
47 ❑ Oct 1953 Cover: 0.10 **NM** value: **35.00**
48 ❑ Nov 1953 Cover: 0.10 **NM** value: **35.00**
49 ❑ Dec 1953 Cover: 0.10 **NM** value: **35.00**
50 ❑ Jan 1954 Cover: 0.10 **NM** value: **35.00**
51 ❑ 1954 Cover: 0.10 **NM** value: **35.00**
52 ❑ 1954 Cover: 0.10 **NM** value: **35.00**
53 ❑ 1954 Cover: 0.10 **NM** value: **35.00**
54 ❑ 1954 Cover: 0.10 **NM** value: **35.00**
55 ❑ 1954 Cover: 0.10 **NM** value: **35.00**
56 ❑ Oct 1954 Cover: 0.10 **NM** value: **35.00**
57 ❑ Cover: 0.10 **NM** value: **35.00**
58 ❑ 1955 Cover: 0.10 **NM** value: **35.00**
59 ❑ 1955 Cover: 0.10 **NM** value: **35.00**
60 ❑ 1955 Cover: 0.10 **NM** value: **35.00**
61 ❑ 1955 Cover: 0.10 **NM** value: **28.00**
62 ❑ Sep 1955 Cover: 0.10 **NM** value: **28.00**
63 ❑ Oct 1955 Cover: 0.10 **NM** value: **28.00**
64 ❑ 1955 Cover: 0.10 **NM** value: **28.00**
65 ❑ Cover: 0.10 **NM** value: **28.00**
66 ❑ 1956 Cover: 0.10 **NM** value: **28.00**
67 ❑ Mar 1956 Cover: 0.10 **NM** value: **28.00**
68 ❑ 1956 Cover: 0.10 **NM** value: **28.00**
69 ❑ 1956 Cover: 0.10 **NM** value: **28.00**
70 ❑ 1956 Cover: 0.10 **NM** value: **28.00**
71 ❑ 1956 Cover: 0.10 **NM** value: **25.00**
72 ❑ Nov 1956 Cover: 0.10 **NM** value: **25.00**
73 ❑ Dec 1956 Cover: 0.10 **NM** value: **25.00**
74 ❑ Jan 1957 Cover: 0.10 **NM** value: **25.00**
75 ❑ Feb 1957 Cover: 0.10 **NM** value: **25.00**
76 ❑ Mar 1957 Cover: 0.10 **NM** value: **25.00**
77 ❑ Apr 1957 Cover: 0.10 **NM** value: **25.00**
78 ❑ May 1957 Cover: 0.10 **NM** value: **25.00**
79 ❑ 1957 Cover: 0.10 **NM** value: **25.00**
80 ❑ 1957 Cover: 0.10 **NM** value: **25.00**
81 ❑ Nov 1957 Cover: 0.10 **NM** value: **25.00**
82 ❑ Jan 1958 Cover: 0.10 **NM** value: **25.00**
83 ❑ Mar 1958 Cover: 0.10 **NM** value: **25.00**
84 ❑ May 1958 Cover: 0.10 **NM** value: **25.00**
85 ❑ Jul 1958 Cover: 0.10 **NM** value: **25.00**
86 ❑ Sep 1958 Cover: 0.10 **NM** value: **25.00**
87 ❑ Nov 1958 Cover: 0.10 **NM** value: **25.00**
88 ❑ Jan 1959 Cover: 0.10 **NM** value: **25.00**
89 ❑ Mar 1959 Cover: 0.10 **NM** value: **25.00**
90 ❑ May 1959 Cover: 0.10 **NM** value: **25.00**
91 ❑ Jul 1959 Cover: 0.10 **NM** value: **25.00**
92 ❑ Sep 1959 Cover: 0.10 **NM** value: **25.00**
93 ❑ Nov 1959 Cover: 0.10 **NM** value: **25.00**
94 ❑ Jan 1960 Cover: 0.10 **NM** value: **25.00**
95 ❑ Mar 1960 Cover: 0.10 **NM** value: **25.00**
96 ❑ May 1960 Cover: 0.10 **NM** value: **25.00**
97 ❑ Jul 1960 Cover: 0.10 **NM** value: **25.00**
98 ❑ Sep 1960 Cover: 0.10 **NM** value: **25.00**
99 ❑ Nov 1960 Cover: 0.10 **NM** value: **25.00**
100 ❑ Jan 1961 Cover: 0.10 **NM** value: **32.00**
101 ❑ Mar 1961 Cover: 0.10 **NM** value: **15.00**
102 ❑ May 1961 Cover: 0.10 **NM** value: **15.00**
103 ❑ Jul 1961 Cover: 0.10 **NM** value: **15.00**
104 ❑ Sep 1961 Cover: 0.10 **NM** value: **15.00**
105 ❑ Nov 1961 Cover: 0.10 **NM** value: **15.00**
106 ❑ Jan 1962 Cover: 0.10 **NM** value: **15.00**
107 ❑ Mar 1962 Cover: 0.10 **NM** value: **15.00**
108 ❑ May 1962 Cover: 0.10 **NM** value: **15.00**
109 ❑ Jul 1962 Cover: 0.10 **NM** value: **15.00**
110 ❑ Sep 1962 Cover: 0.10 **NM** value: **15.00**
111 ❑ Nov 1962 Cover: 0.10 **NM** value: **15.00**
112 ❑ Jan 1963 Cover: 0.10 **NM** value: **15.00**
Circ: Statement: **173,925**
113 ❑ Mar 1963 Cover: 0.10 **NM** value: **15.00**
Circ: Statement: **173,925**
114 ❑ May 1963 Cover: 0.10 **NM** value: **15.00**
Circ: Statement: **173,925**
115 ❑ Jul 1963 **NM** value: **15.00**
Circ: Statement: **173,925**
116 ❑ Sep 1963 Cover: 0.12 **NM** value: **15.00**
Circ: Statement: **173,925**
117 ❑ Nov 1963 Cover: 0.12 **NM** value: **15.00**
Circ: Statement: **173,925**
118 ❑ Jan 1964 Cover: 0.12 **NM** value: **15.00**
119 ❑ Mar 1964 Cover: 0.12 **NM** value: **15.00**
120 ❑ May 1964 Cover: 0.12 **NM** value: **15.00**
• Has 1963 Statement; avg total paid circ 173,925
121 ❑ Jul 1964 Cover: 0.12 **NM** value: **15.00**
122 ❑ Sep 1964 Cover: 0.12 **NM** value: **15.00**
123 ❑ Oct 1964 Cover: 0.12 **NM** value: **15.00**
124 ❑ Nov 1964 Cover: 0.12 **NM** value: **15.00**
125 ❑ Dec 1964 Cover: 0.12 **NM** value: **15.00**
126 ❑ Jan 1965 Cover: 0.12 **NM** value: **15.00**
Circ: Statement: **219,427**
127 ❑ Mar 1965 Cover: 0.12 **NM** value: **15.00**
Circ: Statement: **219,427**
128 ❑ May 1965 Cover: 0.12 **NM** value: **15.00**
Circ: Statement: **219,427**
129 ❑ Jul 1965 Cover: 0.12 **NM** value: **15.00**
Circ: Statement: **219,427**
130 ❑ Sep 1965 Cover: 0.12 **NM** value: **15.00**
Circ: Statement: **219,427**
131 ❑ Oct 1965 Cover: 0.12 **NM** value: **12.00**
Circ: Statement: **219,427**
132 ❑ Nov 1965 Cover: 0.12 **NM** value: **12.00**
Circ: Statement: **219,427**
133 ❑ Dec 1965 Cover: 0.12 **NM** value: **12.00**
Circ: Statement: **219,427**
134 ❑ Jan 1966 Cover: 0.12 **NM** value: **12.00**
Circ: Statement: **190,217**
135 ❑ Feb 1966 Cover: 0.12 **NM** value: **12.00**
Circ: Statement: **190,217**
136 ❑ Apr 1966 Cover: 0.12 **NM** value: **12.00**
Circ: Statement: **190,217**
137 ❑ May 1966 Cover: 0.12 **NM** value: **12.00**
Circ: Statement: **190,217**
138 ❑ Jun 1966 Cover: 0.12 **NM** value: **12.00**
Circ: Statement: **190,217**
139 ❑ Jul 1966 Cover: 0.12 **NM** value: **12.00**
Circ: Statement: **190,217**
140 ❑ Aug 1966 Cover: 0.12 **NM** value: **12.00**
Circ: Statement: **190,217**
141 ❑ Sep 1966 Cover: 0.12 **NM** value: **12.00**
Circ: Statement: **190,217**
142 ❑ Oct 1966 Cover: 0.12 **NM** value: **12.00**
Circ: Statement: **190,217**
143 ❑ Nov 1966 Cover: 0.12 **NM** value: **12.00**
Circ: Statement: **190,217**
144 ❑ Dec 1966 Cover: 0.12 **NM** value: **12.00**
Circ: Statement: **190,217**
145 ❑ Jan 1967 Cover: 0.12 **NM** value: **12.00**
Circ: Statement: **173,519**
146 ❑ Feb 1967 Cover: 0.12 **NM** value: **12.00**
Circ: Statement: **173,519**
147 ❑ Mar 1967 Cover: 0.12 **NM** value: **12.00**
Circ: Statement: **173,519**
148 ❑ Apr 1967 Cover: 0.12 **NM** value: **12.00**
Circ: Statement: **173,519**
149 ❑ May 1967 Cover: 0.12 **NM** value: **12.00**
Circ: Statement: **173,519**
150 ❑ Jun 1967 Cover: 0.12 **NM** value: **12.00**
Circ: Statement: **173,519**
151 ❑ Jul 1967 Cover: 0.12 **NM** value: **12.00**
Circ: Statement: **173,519**
152 ❑ Aug 1967 Cover: 0.12 **NM** value: **12.00**
Circ: Statement: **173,519**
153 ❑ Sep 1967 Cover: 0.12 **NM** value: **12.00**
Circ: Statement: **173,519** • **CGC:** 3 graded, best 9.4
154 ❑ Oct 1967 Cover: 0.12 **NM** value: **12.00**
Circ: Statement: **173,519**
• New Millie begins
155 ❑ Nov 1967 Cover: 0.12 **NM** value: **10.00**
Circ: Statement: **173,519**
156 ❑ Dec 1967 Cover: 0.12 **NM** value: **10.00**
Circ: Statement: **173,519**
157 ❑ Feb 1968 Cover: 0.12 **NM** value: **10.00**
158 ❑ Apr 1968 Cover: 0.12 **NM** value: **10.00**
159 ❑ Jun 1968 Cover: 0.12 **NM** value: **10.00**
160 ❑ Jul 1968 Cover: 0.12 **NM** value: **10.00**
161 ❑ Aug 1968 Cover: 0.12 **NM** value: **10.00**
162 ❑ Sep 1968 Cover: 0.12 **NM** value: **10.00**
163 ❑ Oct 1968 Cover: 0.12 **NM** value: **10.00**
164 ❑ Nov 1968 Cover: 0.12 **NM** value: **10.00**
165 ❑ Dec 1968 Cover: 0.12 **NM** value: **10.00**
166 ❑ Jan 1969 Cover: 0.12 **NM** value: **10.00**
167 ❑ Feb 1969 Cover: 0.12 **NM** value: **10.00**
168 ❑ Mar 1969 Cover: 0.12 **NM** value: **10.00**
169 ❑ Apr 1969 Cover: 0.12 **NM** value: **10.00**
170 ❑ May 1969 Cover: 0.12 **NM** value: **10.00**
171 ❑ Jun 1969 Cover: 0.12 **NM** value: **10.00**
172 ❑ Jul 1969 Cover: 0.12 **NM** value: **10.00**
173 ❑ Aug 1969 Cover: 0.15 **NM** value: **10.00**
174 ❑ Sep 1969 Cover: 0.15 **NM** value: **10.00**
175 ❑ Oct 1969 Cover: 0.15 **NM** value: **10.00**
176 ❑ Nov 1969 Cover: 0.15 **NM** value: **10.00**
177 ❑ Dec 1969 Cover: 0.15 **NM** value: **10.00**
178 ❑ Jan 1970 Cover: 0.15 **NM** value: **10.00**
179 ❑ Feb 1970 Cover: 0.15 **NM** value: **10.00**
180 ❑ Mar 1970 Cover: 0.15 **NM** value: **10.00**
181 ❑ Apr 1970 Cover: 0.15 **NM** value: **8.50**
182 ❑ May 1970 Cover: 0.15 **NM** value: **8.50**
183 ❑ Jun 1970 Cover: 0.15 **NM** value: **8.50**
184 ❑ Jul 1970 Cover: 0.15 **NM** value: **8.50**
185 ❑ Aug 1970 Cover: 0.15 **NM** value: **8.50**

Other grades: Multiply prices above by **1.5 for Mint • 2/3 for Very Fine • 1/3 for Fine • 1/5 for Very Good • 1/8 for Good**

186 ❑ Oct 1970 Cover: 0.15 **NM** value: **8.50**
187 ❑ Dec 1970 Cover: 0.15 **NM** value: **8.50**
188 ❑ Feb 1970 Cover: 0.15 **NM** value: **8.50**
189 ❑ Apr 1970 Cover: 0.15 **NM** value: **8.50**
190 ❑ Jun 1970 Cover: 0.15 **NM** value: **8.50**
191 ❑ Aug 1970 Cover: 0.15 **NM** value: **8.50**
192 ❑ Oct 1970 Cover: 0.25 **NM** value: **8.50**
193 ❑ Dec 1970 Cover: 0.20 **NM** value: **8.50**
194 ❑ Feb 1971 Cover: 0.20 **NM** value: **8.50**
195 ❑ Apr 1971 Cover: 0.20 **NM** value: **8.50**
196 ❑ Jun 1971 Cover: 0.20 **NM** value: **8.50**
197 ❑ Aug 1971 Cover: 0.20 **NM** value: **8.50**
198 ❑ Cover: 0.20 **NM** value: **8.50**
199 ❑ 1972 Cover: 0.20 **NM** value: **8.50**
200 ❑ 1972 Cover: 0.20 **NM** value: **8.50**
201 ❑ 1972 Cover: 0.20 **NM** value: **8.50**
202 ❑ Cover: 0.20 **NM** value: **8.50**
203 ❑ Aug 1973 Cover: 0.20 **NM** value: **8.50**
204 ❑ Sep 1973 Cover: 0.20 **NM** value: **8.50**
205 ❑ Oct 1973 Cover: 0.20 **NM** value: **8.50**
• **CGC:** 1 graded, best 9.2
206 ❑ Nov 1973 Cover: 0.20 **NM** value: **8.50**
207 ❑ Dec 1973 Cover: 0.20 **NM** value: **8.50**
Anl 1 ❑ ca. 1962 Cover: 0.25 **NM** value: **120.00**
• **CGC:** 2 graded, best 3.5
Anl 2 ❑ ca. 1963 Cover: 0.25 **NM** value: **85.00**
Anl 3 ❑ ca. 1964 Cover: 0.25 **NM** value: **65.00**
Anl 4 ❑ ca. 1965 Cover: 0.25 **NM** value: **65.00**
• **CGC:** 1 graded, best 8.0
Anl 5 ❑ Sep 1966 Cover: 0.25 **NM** value: **65.00**
• **CGC:** 1 graded, best 8.5
Anl 6 ❑ ca. 1967 Cover: 0.25 **NM** value: **45.00**
Anl 7 ❑ ca. 1968 Cover: 0.25 **NM** value: **45.00**
Anl 8 ❑ Sep 1969 Cover: 0.25 **NM** value: **45.00**
Anl 9 ❑ ca. 1970 Cover: 0.25 **NM** value: **45.00**
Anl 10 ❑ ca. 1971 Cover: 0.25 **NM** value: **45.00**

MILTON THE MONSTER AND FEARLESS FLY — Gold Key

1 ❑ ca. 1966 Cover: 0.12 **NM** value: **60.00**
• **CGC:** 1 graded, best 9.6

MINDBENDERS — MBS

1 ❑ Cover: 2.50 **NM** value: **Cover or less**
📖 Freddies Last Dance **A:** Eric Bradbury **W:** Steve Donovan

MINDGAME GALLERY, THE — Mindgame

1 ❑ b&w Cover: 1.95 **NM** value: **Cover or less**
📖 Warwind; This Machine; Magpie **A:** Bernie Mireault; Rick Veitch; Nan Fredman **W:** Stephen R. Bissette; Nan Fredman; Sebastien Hassenger

MIND PROBE — Rip Off

1 ❑ b&w Cover: 3.25 **NM** value: **Cover or less**
📖 Initiation; Ceezed; Omega Chapter **A:** Czar; Dooom; Luis Ramirez **W:** Dooom; Luis Ramirez; Ben Bellot

MINDS' PLAY — Davan

1 ❑ Cover: 2.50 **NM** value: **Cover or less**
📖 Roads to Desire; Alone; Sam Slagg in Quarter Past Midnight **A:** Alastair Duncan; Greg Swanson **W:** Greg Swanson

MINIMUM WAGE — Fantagraphics

This story features Rob Hoffman, a struggling New York City artist who tries to make a living as a porno-mag comic artist. Hoffman is not exactly thrilled with his current occupation, but it pays the bills and puts food in the fridge. Rob has a roommate named Jack who is steadily filling up the apartment with hundreds of semi-collectible books, which creates a strain in the friendship. Rob does have a saving grace, his sex-crazed girlfriend Sylvia, who is anxious to move out of her home which she shares with her brother and mother. Minimum Wage tells of Rob's efforts to try and keep his sanity between wild parties, underground S&M performances, and maintaining a relationship with his tempestuous girlfriend.

The series was created by Bob Fingerman, a heralded creator in the underground comic ranks. Previous efforts include the critically acclaimed White Like She for Dark Horse.

1 ❑ Oct 1995 Cover: 2.95 **NM** value: **Cover or less**
A: Bob Fingerman **W:** Bob Fingerman
2 ❑ Dec 1995 Cover: 2.95 **NM** value: **Cover or less**
A: Bob Fingerman **W:** Bob Fingerman
3 ❑ Mar 1996 Cover: 2.95 **NM** value: **Cover or less**
A: Bob Fingerman **W:** Bob Fingerman
4 ❑ Jun 1996 Cover: 2.95 **NM** value: **Cover or less**
• pin-ups **A:** Bob Fingerman **W:** Bob Fingerman
5 ❑ Nov 1996 Cover: 2.95 **NM** value: **Cover or less**
6 ❑ Mar 1997 Cover: 2.95 **NM** value: **Cover or less**
Circ: Diamd. preorders: **1,862**
7 ❑ Aug 1997 Cover: 2.95 **NM** value: **Cover or less**
8 ❑ Feb 1998 Cover: 2.95 **NM** value: **Cover or less**
9 ❑ Jun 1998 Cover: 2.95 **NM** value: **Cover or less**
10 ❑ Jan 1999 Cover: 2.95 **NM** value: **Cover or less**
Bk 1 ❑ Jul 1995, b&w Cover: 9.95 **NM** value: **Cover or less**
A: Bob Fingerman **W:** Bob Fingerman

MINISTRY OF SPACE — Image

1 ❑ Apr 2001 Cover: 2.95 **NM** value: **Cover or less**
Circ: Diamd. preorders: **30,845** • **CGC:** 5 graded, best 10.0
A: Chris Weston **W:** Warren Ellis

MINOR MIRACLES — DC

1 ❑ Cover: 12.95 **NM** value: **Cover or less**
A: Will Eisner **W:** Will Eisner

MINOTAUR — Labyrinth

1 ❑ Feb 1996, b&w Cover: 2.50 **NM** value: **Cover or less**
2 ❑ Apr 1996, b&w Cover: 2.50 **NM** value: **Cover or less**
3 ❑ Jun 1996, b&w Cover: 2.50 **NM** value: **Cover or less**
cover says Jul, indicia says Jun.
4 ❑ Sep 1996, b&w Cover: 2.50 **NM** value: **Cover or less**
final issue.

MINUTE MAN — Fawcett

1 ❑ Sum 1941 Cover: 0.10 **NM** value: **1500.00**
• **CGC:** 1 graded, best 9.2
2 ❑ Win 1941 Cover: 0.10 **NM** value: **750.00**
3 ❑ Spr 1942 Cover: 0.10 **NM** value: **750.00**
• **CGC:** 1 graded, best 9.6

MINX, THE — DC / Vertigo

1 ❑ Oct 1998 Cover: 2.50 **NM** value: **Cover or less**
Circ: Diamd. preorders: **17,475**
📖 The Chosen, Part 1 **A:** Sean Phillips **W:** Peter Milligan
2 ❑ Nov 1998 Cover: 2.50 **NM** value: **Cover or less**
Circ: Diamd. preorders: **14,179**
📖 The Chosen, Part 2 **A:** Sean Phillips **W:** Peter Milligan
3 ❑ Dec 1998 Cover: 2.50 **NM** value: **Cover or less**
Circ: Diamd. preorders: **13,320**
📖 The Chosen, Part 3 **A:** Sean Phillips **W:** Peter Milligan
4 ❑ Jan 1999 Cover: 2.50 **NM** value: **Cover or less**
Circ: Diamd. preorders: **12,613**
📖 The Monkey Quartet, Part 1 **A:** Sean Phillips **W:** Peter Milligan
5 ❑ Feb 1999 Cover: 2.50 **NM** value: **Cover or less**
Circ: Diamd. preorders: **11,707**
📖 The Monkey Quartet, Part 2, The World Service **A:** Sean Phillips **W:** Peter Milligan
6 ❑ Mar 1999 Cover: 2.50 **NM** value: **Cover or less**
Circ: Diamd. preorders: **11,137**
📖 The Monkey Quartet, Part 3 **A:** Sean Phillips **W:** Peter Milligan
7 ❑ Apr 1999 Cover: 2.50 **NM** value: **Cover or less**
Circ: Diamd. preorders: **10,195**
📖 The Monkey Quartet, Part 4 **A:** Sean Phillips **W:** Peter Milligan
8 ❑ May 1999 Cover: 2.50 **NM** value: **Cover or less**
Circ: Diamd. preorders: **9,747**
📖 Eschatology and the Single Woman **A:** Sean Phillips **W:** Peter Milligan

MIRACLE COMICS — St. John

1 ❑ Feb 1940 Cover: 0.10 **NM** value: **1500.00**
2 ❑ Mar 1940 Cover: 0.10 **NM** value: **750.00**
3 ❑ Apr 1940 Cover: 0.10 **NM** value: **700.00**
4 ❑ Mar 1941 Cover: 0.10 **NM** value: **700.00**

MIRACLEMAN — Eclipse

Comic book super-heroes usually do what they do because they think it makes the world a better place. In their darker moments, however, they come to realize the truth: They're simply defending the status quo. They can stop a criminal but can they stop crime? They might save a person from dying in a plane crash but can they stop death itself?

Miracleman (created by Alan Moore as the return of the existing Marvelman character introduced in the UK) is a hero of a different sort. He really can change the world. He's brought about an age of miracles, put an end to poverty and war.

Continuing from a storyline started in the British comic magazine Warrior, later exploits of Miracleman were written by Neil Gaiman (in his pre-Sandman) days. It exhibits the sort of creativity that marks these two writers as among the best in the field.

1 ❑ Aug 1985 Cover: 0.75 **NM** value: **6.00**
Circ: CapCity orders: **20,600** • **CGC:** 28 graded, best 9.6
📖 A Dream Of Flying **A:** Gary Leach **W:** Alan Moore
2 ❑ Oct 1985 Cover: 0.75 **NM** value: **4.00**
Circ: CapCity orders: **17,325** • **CGC:** 5 graded, best 9.8
📖 Dragons **A:** Gary Leach **W:** Alan Moore
3 ❑ Nov 1985 Cover: 0.75 **NM** value: **4.00**
Circ: CapCity orders: **18,325** • **CGC:** 3 graded, best 9.6
W: Alan Moore
4 ❑ Dec 1985 Cover: 0.75 **NM** value: **4.00**
Circ: CapCity orders: **16,575** • **CGC:** 2 graded, best 9.4
W: Alan Moore
5 ❑ Jan 1986 Cover: 0.95 **NM** value: **4.00**
Circ: CapCity orders: **15,375** • **CGC:** 2 graded, best 9.6
W: Alan Moore
6 ❑ Feb 1986 Cover: 0.95 **NM** value: **4.00**
Circ: CapCity orders: **14,150** • **CGC:** 2 graded, best 9.4
W: Alan Moore
7 ❑ Apr 1986 Cover: 0.95 **NM** value: **4.00**
Circ: CapCity orders: **12,425** • **CGC:** 3 graded, best 9.6
📖 Bodies; Tales of the First Empire: Soul-Stone (back-up) **A:** Chuck Beckum **W:** Alan Moore ★ Death of Gargunza.
8 ❑ Jun 1986 Cover: 0.95 **NM** value: **4.00**
Circ: CapCity orders: **11,950** • **CGC:** 3 graded, best 9.0
W: Alan Moore ★ 1st Appearance of The New Wave.
9 ❑ Jul 1986 Cover: 0.95 **NM** value: **6.00**
Circ: CapCity orders: **12,725** • **CGC:** 6 graded, best 9.6
• birth **W:** Alan Moore
10 ❑ Dec 1986 Cover: 0.95 **NM** value: **6.00**
Circ: CapCity orders: **10,625** • **CGC:** 3 graded, best 9.4
W: Alan Moore
11 ❑ May 1987 Cover: 1.25 **NM** value: **8.00**
Circ: CapCity orders: **9,100** • **CGC:** 7 graded, best 9.8
W: Alan Moore
12 ❑ Sep 1987 Cover: 1.25 **NM** value: **8.00**
Circ: CapCity orders: **9,425** • **CGC:** 11 graded, best 9.8
W: Alan Moore
13 ❑ Nov 1987 Cover: 1.75 **NM** value: **12.00**
Circ: CapCity orders: **8,450** • **CGC:** 17 graded, best 9.8
W: Alan Moore
14 ❑ Apr 1988 Cover: 1.75 **NM** value: **20.00**
Circ: CapCity orders: **8,375** • **CGC:** 8 graded, best 9.6
W: Alan Moore
15 ❑ Nov 1988 Cover: 1.75 **NM** value: **55.00**
Circ: CapCity orders: **7,075** • **CGC:** 47 graded, best 9.8
• Scarce **W:** Alan Moore
16 ❑ Dec 1988 Cover: 1.95 **NM** value: **15.00**
Circ: CapCity orders: **8,000** • **CGC:** 6 graded, best 9.4
📖 Olympus • last Moore **W:** Alan Moore
17 ❑ Jun 1990 Cover: 1.95 **NM** value: **18.00**
Circ: CapCity orders: **7,750** • **CGC:** 2 graded, best 9.6
📖 Miracleman: The Golden Age • 1st Neil Gaiman **A:** Mark Buckingham; Dave McKean(cover); Sam Parsons **W:** Neil Gaiman
18 ❑ Aug 1990 Cover: 2.00 **NM** value: **15.00**
Circ: CapCity orders: **8,000** • **CGC:** 1 graded, best 9.0
📖 Miracleman: The Golden Age; Skin Deep **A:** Mark Buckingham; Dave McKean(cover); Gail Pople; Sam Parsons **W:** Neil Gaiman
19 ❑ Nov 1990 Cover: 2.50 **NM** value: **15.00**
Circ: CapCity orders: **7,950** • **CGC:** 2 graded, best 9.6
cardstock cover. 📖 Miracleman: The Golden Age; Notes From the Underground **A:** Mark Buckingham; Dave McKean(cover) **W:** Neil Gaiman
20 ❑ Mar 1991 Cover: 2.50 **NM** value: **15.00**
Circ: CapCity orders: **712** • **CGC:** 1 graded, best 9.6
cardstock cover. 📖 Miracleman: The Golden Age; Winter's Tale **A:** Mark Buckingham; Dave McKean(cover); Sam Parsons **W:** Neil Gaiman
21 ❑ Jul 1991 Cover: 2.50 **NM** value: **15.00**
Circ: CapCity orders: **6,900** • **CGC:** 2 graded, best 9.2
📖 Miracleman: The Golden Age; Spy Story **A:** Mark Buckingham; Dave McKean(cover); D'Israeli **W:** Neil Gaiman
22 ❑ Aug 1991 Cover: 2.50 **NM** value: **15.00**
Circ: CapCity orders: **7,000** • **CGC:** 6 graded, best 9.8
📖 Miracleman: The Golden Age; Carnival **A:** Mark Buckingham; Dave McKean(cover); D'Israeli **W:** Neil Gaiman
23 ❑ Jun 1992 Cover: 2.50 **NM** value: **17.00**
Circ: CapCity orders: **7,250** • **CGC:** 2 graded, best 9.4
W: Neil Gaiman
24 ❑ Aug 1993 Cover: 2.95 **NM** value: **24.00**
Circ: CapCity orders: **6,400** • **CGC:** 2 graded, best 9.6
• scarcer
3D 1 ❑ Dec 1985 Cover: 2.25 **NM** value: **5.00**
Circ: CapCity orders: **7,700** • **CGC:** 2 graded, best 9.0
• Giant-size. 📖 Miracleman and the Exiled Gods • 3-D Special #1 **A:** Alan Davis **W:** Alan Moore
Bk 1 ❑ Cover: 9.95 **NM** value: **30.00**
• Trade Paperback. • A Dream of Flying **W:** Alan Moore
Bk 1/HC ❑ hardcover Cover: 29.95 **NM** value: **50.00**
Bk 2 ❑ Cover: 12.95 **NM** value: **18.00**
• Trade Paperback. • The Red King Syndrome **W:** Alan Moore
Bk 2/HC ❑ hardcover Cover: 30.95 **NM** value: **35.00**
Bk 3 ❑ Cover: 12.95 **NM** value: **15.00**
• Trade Paperback. • Olympus
Bk 3/HC ❑ hardcover Cover: 30.95 **NM** value: **35.00**
Bk 4 ❑ Cover: 15.95 **NM** value: **16.00**
• Trade Paperback. 📖 Miracleman: The Golden Age • The Golden Age; Collects Miracleman #17-22 **A:** Mark Buckingham; Dave McKean(cover); Sam Parsons; D'Israeli **W:** Neil Gaiman
Bk 4/HC ❑ hardcover Cover: 33.95 **NM** value: **34.00**

MIRACLEMAN: APOCRYPHA — Eclipse

The word "apocrypha" means "writings of doubtful authenticity, not accepted as resulting from revelation or true happenings; not genuine: spurious: counterfeit."

When Eclipse gathered together some of the top talents in the comics industry to work on their own versions of Miracleman, whom Alan Moore had so masterfully explored in the United Kingdom as the return of Marvelman, this title somehow seemed appropriate. In Apocrypha, eleven creative teams are given a shot at telling a story that features what they think would be the perfect Miracleman scenario. The list of creators includes Alex Ross (Marvels), Neil Gaiman (Sandman), Norm Breyfogle (Prime), Stefan Petrucha (The X-Files), and many more. These stories are printed in this three-issue anthology series. A framing story by Neil Gaiman and Mark Buckingham shows Miracleman — a man become like a god — reading them as comic books in order to discover the nature of human aspiration.

1 ❑ Nov 1991 Cover: 2.50 **NM** value: **Cover or less**
Circ: CapCity orders: **7,325**
📖 The Library of Olympus; Miracle Man and the Magic Monsters; Rascal Prince; The Scrapbook; Limbo; Miracleman and the Magic Pen **A:** Norm Breyfogle; Kelley Jones; Mark Buckingham; Stan Woch **W:** James Robinson; Matt Wagner; Steve Moore; Neil Gaiman; Sarah Byam
2 ❑ Jan 1992 Cover: 2.50 **NM** value: **Cover or less**
Circ: CapCity orders: **6,325**
📖 The Library of Olympus; Prodigal; Stray Thoughts; The Janitor **A:** Mark Buckingham; Christopher Schenck; Alan Smith; Pete Williamson; Broderick Macaraeg **W:** Kurt Busiek; Neil Gaiman
3 ❑ Apr 1991 Cover: 2.50 **NM** value: **Cover or less**
Circ: CapCity orders: **5,675**
W: Neil Gaiman
Bk 1 ❑ Cover: 15.95 **NM** value: **Cover or less**
📖 The Library Of Olympus; Miracle Man And The Magic Monsters; The Rascal Prince; The Scrapbook; Limbo; Prodigal; Stray Thoughts; The Janitor; Gospel; Wishing On A Star; A Bright And Sunny Day; • Collects Miracleman: Apocrypha #1-3 **A:** Norm Breyfogle; Matt Wagner; Kelley Jones; Alex Ross; Val Mayerik; Mark Buckingham; Stan

CGC-graded: Multiply prices above by **33 for 9.9 M** • **16 for 9.8 NM/M** • **7 for 9.6 NM+** • **5 for 9.4 NM** • **2.5 for 9.2 NM-** • **1.5 for 9.0 VF/NM**

Woch; Darick Robertson; Alan Smith; Pete Williamson; Broderick Macaraeg **W:** James Robinson; Matt Wagner; Steve Moore; Steven Grant; Dick Foreman; Fred Schiller; Neil Gaiman; Sarah Byam; Stefan Petrucha

MIRACLEMAN FAMILY — Eclipse

1 ❑ May 1988 Cover: 1.95 **NM** value: **2.50**
Circ: CapCity orders: **4,950**
A: Mick Anglo Studios **W:** Mick Anglo Studios ★ Origin of Young Miracleman.

2 ❑ Sep 1988 Cover: 1.95 **NM** value: **2.50**
Circ: CapCity orders: **3,650**
📖 The Shadow Stealers **A:** Mick Anglo Studios **W:** Mick Anglo Studios

MIRACLE SQUAD — Upshot

1 ❑ full color Cover: 2.00 **NM** value: **Cover or less**
Circ: CapCity orders: **5,525**
A: Terry Tidwell **W:** John Wooley

2 ❑ full color Cover: 2.00 **NM** value: **Cover or less**
Circ: CapCity orders: **4,100**
A: Terry Tidwell **W:** John Wooley

3 ❑ b&w Cover: 2.00 **NM** value: **Cover or less**
Circ: CapCity orders: **3,200**
A: Terry Tidwell **W:** John Wooley

4 ❑ b&w Cover: 2.00 **NM** value: **Cover or less**
Circ: CapCity orders: **2,675**
A: Terry Tidwell **W:** John Wooley

MIRACLE SQUAD, THE: BLOOD AND DUST — Apple

1 ❑ Jan 1989, b&w Cover: 1.95 **NM** value: **Cover or less**
📖 The Miracle Squad, Part 1 **A:** Terry Tidwell **W:** John Wooley

2 ❑ Mar 1989, b&w Cover: 1.95 **NM** value: **Cover or less**
A: Terry Tidwell **W:** John Wooley

3 ❑ May 1989, b&w Cover: 1.95 **NM** value: **Cover or less**
A: Terry Tidwell **W:** John Wooley

4 ❑ Jul 1989, b&w Cover: 1.95 **NM** value: **Cover or less**
A: Terry Tidwell **W:** John Wooley

MIRAGE MINI COMICS — Mirage

1 ❑ Cover: 11.95 **NM** value: **Cover or less**
📖 Dead Biker and • 12 mini-comics **A:** Mark Martin; Jim Lawson; Kevin Eastman; Dan Berger; Michael Zulli; Rick Veitch; Peter Laird; Mark Bode; Michael Dooney; Eric Talbot; Steve Bissette; Steve Lavigne; Dean Clarrain; Stephen Murphy **W:** Mark Martin; Jim Lawson; Kevin Eastman; Dan Berger; Michael Zulli; Rick Veitch; Peter Laird; Mark Bode; Michael Dooney; Eric Talbot; Steve Bissette; Steve Lavigne; Dean Clarrain; Stephen Murphy

MIRROR MAN COMIC, THE — Donald F. Peters

21 ❑ **NM** value: **3.00**
📖 Abbie an' Slats **A:** Raeburn VanBuren **W:** Raeburn VanBuren

MIRRORWALKER — Now

1 ❑ Oct 1990 Cover: 2.95 **NM** value: **Cover or less**
Circ: CapCity orders: **2,625**
• semi-fumetti **A:** Barry Daniel Petersen; Erich Schrempp **W:** Marv Wolfman

2 ❑ Cover: 2.95 **NM** value: **Cover or less**
Circ: CapCity orders: **2,000**
A: Barry Daniel Petersen; Erich Schrempp **W:** Marv Wolfman

MIRRORWORLD: RAIN — Netco

0 ❑ Apr 1997 Cover: 3.25 **NM** value: **Cover or less**
Circ: Diamd. preorders: **4,758**
📖 Rain **A:** Fred Harper **W:** Tad Williams

1 ❑ Feb 1997 Cover: 3.25 **NM** value: **Cover or less**
Circ: Diamd. preorders: **6,947**

MISADVENTURES OF BREADMAN AND DOUGHBOY, THE — Hemlock Park

1 ❑ Oct 1999 **NM** value: **1.00**
no cover price.

MISEROTH: AMOK HELL — Northstar

1 ❑ Cover: 4.95 **NM** value: **Cover or less**
📖 The Big Slip Up **A:** Adam McDaniel **W:** Frank Gomez

2 ❑ Cover: 4.95 **NM** value: **Cover or less**
A: Adam McDaniel **W:** Frank Gomez

3 ❑ Cover: 4.95 **NM** value: **Cover or less**
A: Adam McDaniel **W:** Frank Gomez

MISERY — Image

1 ❑ Dec 1995 Cover: 2.95 **NM** value: **Cover or less**
One-shot. 📖 Prometheus Unbound **A:** Brandon Peterson **W:** Brandon Peterson

MISFIT LIT — Fantagraphics

Bk 1❑ Cover: 4.95 **NM** value: **Cover or less**
No issue number. • exhibit catalog

MISS AMERICA (VOL. 1) — Timely

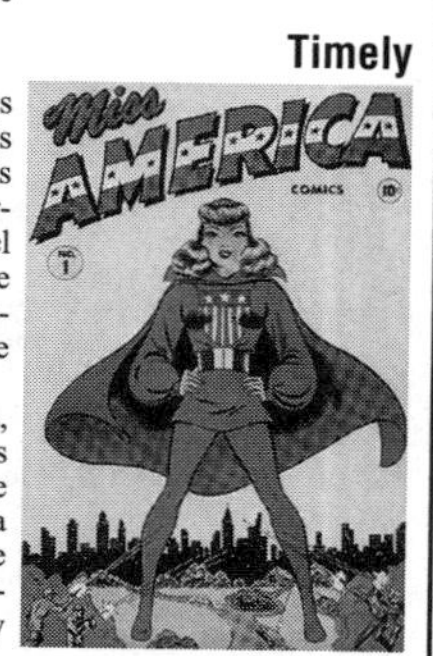

This title began in 1944 as "Miss America Comics." Its title hero is Madeline Frank, a woman who is struck by lightning and gains superpowers. First appearing in Marvel Mystery Comics #49, she fights the Axis powers as a member of The Liberty Legion and later alongside The Invaders.

By the second issue of this series, however, the title has changed its name to Miss Magazine and has gone in a different direction. It becomes a teen romance comic, introducing the characters of Patsy Walker, her boyfriend Buzz Baxter, and rival Hedy Wolfe. These characters became instant hits, attracting a loyal base of female fans. Their success inspired a number of magazines, including Patsy Walker and Patsy and Hedy.

Miss America's numbering can be confusing. The early, text-heavy issues belong to volumes which restart every six issues. The seventh volume — occasionally referred to as the first volume — is the major leg of the series, running more than 90 issues.

1 ❑ ca. 1944 Cover: 0.10 **NM** value: **850.00**
• Title is "Miss America Comics"★ Appearance of Miss America.

2 ❑ Nov 1944 Cover: 0.10 **NM** value: **700.00**
Photo cover. • Title changes to Miss America Magazine. ★ 1st Appearance of Patsy Walker, Hedy Wolfe, Buzz Baxter. ★ Appearance of Miss America.

3 ❑ Dec 1944 Cover: 0.10 **NM** value: **290.00**
4 ❑ Jan 1945 Cover: 0.10 **NM** value: **290.00**
5 ❑ Feb 1945 Cover: 0.10 **NM** value: **290.00**
6 ❑ Mar 1945 Cover: 0.10 **NM** value: **70.00**

MISS AMERICA (VOL. 2) — Timely

1 ❑ Apr 1945 Cover: 0.10 **NM** value: **35.00**
2 ❑ May 1945 Cover: 0.10 **NM** value: **35.00**
📖 Hedy Horns In; Love is No Mistake; Her Delightful Dilemma; Hallow Victory; Romance at the Rapids; Tall Girl; Mystery at Thorn Hill **A:** Blake Gilpin Bowman; Geddes Laird; Marjon Walden; Ruth Berman **W:** Blake Gilpin Bowman; Geddes Laird; Marjon Walden; Ruth Berman
3 ❑ Jun 1945 Cover: 0.10 **NM** value: **35.00**
4 ❑ Jul 1945 Cover: 0.10 **NM** value: **35.00**
5 ❑ Aug 1945 Cover: 0.10 **NM** value: **35.00**
6 ❑ Sep 1945 Cover: 0.10 **NM** value: **35.00**

MISS AMERICA (VOL. 3) — Timely

1 ❑ Oct 1945 Cover: 0.10 **NM** value: **35.00**
• My Date with Van Johnson by Esther Williams
2 ❑ ca. 1945 Cover: 0.10 **NM** value: **35.00**
3 ❑ ca. 1945 Cover: 0.10 **NM** value: **35.00**
4 ❑ Feb 1946 Cover: 0.10 **NM** value: **35.00**
• cover claims "1 Million Circulation"; untitled Patsy Walker story; untitled Betty Blair story
5 ❑ Mar 1946 Cover: 0.10 **NM** value: **35.00**
• untitled Patsy Walker story
6 ❑ Apr 1946 Cover: 0.10 **NM** value: **35.00**
• untitled Patsy Walker story

MISS AMERICA (VOL. 4) — Timely

1 ❑ May 1946 Cover: 0.10 **NM** value: **35.00**
• untitled Patsy Walker story
2 ❑ Jun 1946 Cover: 0.10 **NM** value: **35.00**
3 ❑ Jul 1946 Cover: 0.10 **NM** value: **55.00**
• Elizabeth Taylor photo cover
4 ❑ Aug 1946 Cover: 0.10 **NM** value: **28.00**
5 ❑ Sep 1946 Cover: 0.10 **NM** value: **28.00**
6 ❑ Oct 1946 Cover: 0.10 **NM** value: **28.00**

MISS AMERICA (VOL. 5) — Timely

1 ❑ Nov 1946 Cover: 0.10 **NM** value: **28.00**
2 ❑ Dec 1946 Cover: 0.10 **NM** value: **28.00**
• untitled Patsy Walker Christmas story
3 ❑ Jan 1947 Cover: 0.10 **NM** value: **28.00**
4 ❑ Feb 1947 Cover: 0.10 **NM** value: **28.00**
5 ❑ Mar 1947 Cover: 0.10 **NM** value: **28.00**
6 ❑ Apr 1947 Cover: 0.10 **NM** value: **28.00**

MISS AMERICA (VOL. 6) — Timely

1 ❑ May 1947 Cover: 0.10 **NM** value: **24.00**
2 ❑ Jun 1947 Cover: 0.10 **NM** value: **24.00**
3 ❑ Jul 1947 Cover: 0.10 **NM** value: **24.00**

MISS AMERICA (VOL. 7) — Atlas

1 ❑ Aug 1947 Cover: 0.10 **NM** value: **24.00**
2 ❑ Sep 1947 Cover: 0.10 **NM** value: **24.00**
• **CGC:** 1 graded, best 7.5
• Title changes to Miss America Magazine.
3 ❑ Oct 1947 Cover: 0.10 **NM** value: **24.00**
4 ❑ Nov 1947 Cover: 0.10 **NM** value: **24.00**
• **CGC:** 1 graded, best 7.5
5 ❑ Dec 1947 Cover: 0.10 **NM** value: **24.00**
6 ❑ Jan 1948 Cover: 0.10 **NM** value: **24.00**
7 ❑ Feb 1948 Cover: 0.10 **NM** value: **24.00**
8 ❑ Mar 1948 Cover: 0.10 **NM** value: **24.00**
9 ❑ Apr 1948 Cover: 0.10 **NM** value: **24.00**
📖 Lessons in Love; Patsy's Double Trouble; Seeing is Believing
10 ❑ May 1948 Cover: 0.10 **NM** value: **20.00**
11 ❑ Jun 1948 Cover: 0.10 **NM** value: **20.00**
12 ❑ Jul 1948 Cover: 0.10 **NM** value: **20.00**
📖 She Listened to Love; Patsy's Stolen Heart
13 ❑ Aug 1948 Cover: 0.10 **NM** value: **20.00**
14 ❑ Sep 1948 Cover: 0.10 **NM** value: **20.00**
15 ❑ Oct 1948 Cover: 0.10 **NM** value: **20.00**
16 ❑ Nov 1948 Cover: 0.10 **NM** value: **20.00**
17 ❑ Dec 1948 Cover: 0.10 **NM** value: **20.00**
18 ❑ Jan 1949 Cover: 0.10 **NM** value: **20.00**
19 ❑ Feb 1949 Cover: 0.10 **NM** value: **20.00**
20 ❑ Mar 1949 Cover: 0.10 **NM** value: **20.00**
21 ❑ Apr 1949 Cover: 0.10 **NM** value: **20.00**
22 ❑ May 1949 Cover: 0.10 **NM** value: **20.00**
23 ❑ Jun 1949 Cover: 0.10 **NM** value: **20.00**
24 ❑ Jul 1949 Cover: 0.10 **NM** value: **20.00**
25 ❑ Aug 1949 Cover: 0.10 **NM** value: **16.00**
26 ❑ Sep 1949 Cover: 0.10 **NM** value: **16.00**
27 ❑ Oct 1949 Cover: 0.10 **NM** value: **16.00**
28 ❑ Nov 1949 Cover: 0.10 **NM** value: **16.00**
29 ❑ Dec 1949 Cover: 0.10 **NM** value: **16.00**
30 ❑ Jan 1950 Cover: 0.10 **NM** value: **16.00**
31 ❑ Feb 1950 Cover: 0.10 **NM** value: **16.00**
32 ❑ Mar 1950 Cover: 0.10 **NM** value: **16.00**
33 ❑ May 1950 Cover: 0.10 **NM** value: **16.00**
34 ❑ Jul 1950 Cover: 0.10 **NM** value: **16.00**
35 ❑ Sep 1950 Cover: 0.10 **NM** value: **16.00**
📖 Cheating the Cheaters; Monkey Business
36 ❑ Nov 1950 Cover: 0.10 **NM** value: **16.00**
37 ❑ Jan 1951 Cover: 0.10 **NM** value: **16.00**
38 ❑ Mar 1951 Cover: 0.10 **NM** value: **16.00**
📖 Rumors are Flying
39 ❑ May 1951 Cover: 0.10 **NM** value: **16.00**
40 ❑ Jul 1951 Cover: 0.10 **NM** value: **16.00**
41 ❑ Sep 1951 Cover: 0.10 **NM** value: **16.00**
42 ❑ Nov 1951 Cover: 0.10 **NM** value: **16.00**
43 ❑ Jan 1952 Cover: 0.10 **NM** value: **16.00**
44 ❑ Mar 1952 Cover: 0.10 **NM** value: **16.00**
45 ❑ May 1952 Cover: 0.10 **NM** value: **16.00**
No issue number.
46 ❑ Jul 1952 Cover: 0.10 **NM** value: **16.00**
No issue number. • mislabeled as Vol. 1 with no issue number
47 ❑ Sep 1952 Cover: 0.10 **NM** value: **16.00**
No issue number. • mislabeled as Vol. 1 with no issue number
48 ❑ Nov 1952 Cover: 0.10 **NM** value: **16.00**
No issue number. • mislabeled as Vol. 1 with no issue number
49 ❑ Jan 1953 Cover: 0.10 **NM** value: **16.00**
No issue number. • mislabeled as Vol. 1 with no issue number
50 ❑ Spr 1953 Cover: 0.10 **NM** value: **16.00**
• resumes Vol. 7 numbering
51 ❑ Apr 1953 Cover: 0.10 **NM** value: **16.00**
52 ❑ May 1953 Cover: 0.10 **NM** value: **16.00**
53 ❑ Jun 1953 Cover: 0.10 **NM** value: **16.00**
54 ❑ Jul 1953 Cover: 0.10 **NM** value: **16.00**
55 ❑ Aug 1953 Cover: 0.10 **NM** value: **16.00**
56 ❑ Sep 1953 Cover: 0.10 **NM** value: **16.00**
swimsuit cover.
57 ❑ ca. 1953 Cover: 0.10 **NM** value: **16.00**
58 ❑ ca. 1953 Cover: 0.10 **NM** value: **16.00**
59 ❑ ca. 1954 Cover: 0.10 **NM** value: **16.00**
60 ❑ ca. 1954 Cover: 0.10 **NM** value: **16.00**
61 ❑ ca. 1954 Cover: 0.10 **NM** value: **16.00**
62 ❑ ca. 1954 Cover: 0.10 **NM** value: **16.00**
63 ❑ ca. 1954 Cover: 0.10 **NM** value: **16.00**
64 ❑ ca. 1954 Cover: 0.10 **NM** value: **16.00**
65 ❑ ca. 1954 Cover: 0.10 **NM** value: **16.00**
66 ❑ ca. 1954 Cover: 0.10 **NM** value: **16.00**
67 ❑ ca. 1954 Cover: 0.10 **NM** value: **16.00**
68 ❑ Feb 1955 Cover: 0.10 **NM** value: **16.00**
69 ❑ ca. 1955 Cover: 0.10 **NM** value: **16.00**
70 ❑ ca. 1955 Cover: 0.10 **NM** value: **16.00**
71 ❑ ca. 1955 Cover: 0.10 **NM** value: **16.00**
72 ❑ ca. 1955 Cover: 0.10 **NM** value: **16.00**
73 ❑ ca. 1955 Cover: 0.10 **NM** value: **16.00**
74 ❑ ca. 1955 Cover: 0.10 **NM** value: **16.00**
75 ❑ ca. 1955 Cover: 0.10 **NM** value: **16.00**
76 ❑ Jan 1956 Cover: 0.10 **NM** value: **16.00**
77 ❑ Mar 1956 Cover: 0.10 **NM** value: **16.00**
78 ❑ May 1956 Cover: 0.10 **NM** value: **16.00**
79 ❑ Jul 1956 Cover: 0.10 **NM** value: **16.00**
80 ❑ Sep 1956 Cover: 0.10 **NM** value: **16.00**
81 ❑ Nov 1956 Cover: 0.10 **NM** value: **16.00**
82 ❑ Jan 1957 Cover: 0.10 **NM** value: **16.00**
83 ❑ Mar 1957 Cover: 0.10 **NM** value: **16.00**
84 ❑ May 1957 Cover: 0.10 **NM** value: **16.00**
85 ❑ Jul 1957 Cover: 0.10 **NM** value: **16.00**
86 ❑ Sep 1957 Cover: 0.10 **NM** value: **16.00**
87 ❑ Nov 1957 Cover: 0.10 **NM** value: **16.00**
88 ❑ Jan 1958 Cover: 0.10 **NM** value: **16.00**
89 ❑ Mar 1958 Cover: 0.10 **NM** value: **16.00**
90 ❑ May 1958 Cover: 0.10 **NM** value: **16.00**
91 ❑ Jul 1958 Cover: 0.10 **NM** value: **16.00**
92 ❑ Sep 1958 Cover: 0.10 **NM** value: **16.00**
93 ❑ Nov 1958 Cover: 0.10 **NM** value: **16.00**
final issue.

MISS BEVERLY HILLS OF HOLLYWOOD — DC

1 ❑ Mar 1949 Cover: 0.10 **NM** value: **500.00**
• **CGC:** 1 graded, best 5.0
2 ❑ May 1949 Cover: 0.10 **NM** value: **300.00**
3 ❑ Jul 1949 Cover: 0.10 **NM** value: **300.00**
• **CGC:** 2 graded, best 9.8
4 ❑ Sep 1949 Cover: 0.10 **NM** value: **300.00**
5 ❑ Nov 1949 Cover: 0.10 **NM** value: **300.00**
• **CGC:** 1 graded, best 8.5
6 ❑ Jan 1950 Cover: 0.10 **NM** value: **250.00**
7 ❑ Mar 1950 Cover: 0.10 **NM** value: **250.00**
• **CGC:** 1 graded, best 8.5
8 ❑ May 1950 Cover: 0.10 **NM** value: **250.00**

MISS CAIRO JONES — Croyden

1 ❑ ca. 1944 Cover: 0.10 **NM** value: **150.00**
• **CGC:** 1 graded, best 5.5

MISS FURY (TIMELY) — Timely

In 1941, Miss Fury made her debut as Black Fury. When the debutante put on an African leopardskin costume, she'd fight criminals; the rest of the time, she just looked gorgeous. There were lots of elements to appeal to those looking for stimulating material. Not only was her outfit skin-tight, not only did the socialite appear in her underwear from time to time, but spike heels, bondage, branding irons, and whips accompanied the action.

June "Tarpe" Mills died in 1988, and her strip was not widely circulated, but the comic books presented her dynamic heroine in eye-catching action. Each cover featured her in costume, kicking crooks while swinging onto an already action-packed scene. — Maggie

1 ❑ Win 1942 Cover: 0.10 **NM** value: **3000.00**
2 ❑ Sum 1942 Cover: 0.10 **NM** value: **1500.00**
• **CGC:** 1 graded, best 7.0
3 ❑ Win 1943 Cover: 0.10 **NM** value: **1250.00**
• **CGC:** 2 graded, best 8.5
4 ❑ Sum 1944 Cover: 0.10 **NM** value: **1000.00**

Other grades: Multiply prices above by **1.5 for Mint • 2/3 for Very Fine • 1/3 for Fine • 1/5 for Very Good • 1/8 for Good**

• **CGC:** 2 graded, best 9.0
5 ❑ Fal 1944 Cover: 0.10 **NM** value: **750.00**
6 ❑ Win 1945 Cover: 0.10 **NM** value: **750.00**
• **CGC:** 5 graded, best 9.0
7 ❑ Fal 1945 Cover: 0.10 **NM** value: **700.00**
• **CGC:** 3 graded, best 9.0
8 ❑ Win 1946 Cover: 0.10 **NM** value: **700.00**
• **CGC:** 3 graded, best 8.5

MISS FURY (ADVENTURE) — Adventure

1 ❑ Nov 1991, full color Cover: 2.50 **NM** value: **Cover or less**
📖 From Generation to Generation **A:** Mitch Byrd **W:** Roland Mann
★ Origin of Miss Fury.
1/LE ❑ limited edition. Cover: 4.95 **NM** value: **Cover or less**
2 ❑ Dec 1991 Cover: 2.50 **NM** value: **Cover or less**
A: Mitch Byrd **W:** Roland Mann
3 ❑ Cover: 2.50 **NM** value: **Cover or less**
A: Mitch Byrd **W:** Roland Mann
4 ❑ Cover: 2.50 **NM** value: **Cover or less**
A: Mitch Byrd **W:** Roland Mann

MISS FURY (AVALON) — Avalon

1 ❑ Cover: 2.95 **NM** value: **Cover or less**
A: Tarpe Mills **W:** Tarpe Mills
2 ❑ Cover: 2.95 **NM** value: **Cover or less**
A: Tarpe Mills **W:** Tarpe Mills

MISSING BEINGS SPECIAL — Comics Interview

1 ❑ b&w Cover: 2.25 **NM** value: **Cover or less**
A: Bill Neville; Tom Wimbish **W:** Henry Vogel

MISSION: IMPOSSIBLE (DELL) — Dell

Dell's Mission: Impossible comic book was based on the popular spy-action television series that ran from 1966 to 1973. As anyone who has ever seen an episode of the often-rerun series knows, the Mission: Impossible team is a super-secret group of agents sent out to tackle dangerous, sensitive, or "impossible" missions behind enemy lines. Their success depends on the specialized skills of team members who are, variously, acrobats, weapons experts, masters of disguise, and/or martial artists — in short, having whatever skill is needed to accomplish the assignment.

The comic-book adaptation of sticks closely to the formula of the television show, and the artists struggle to depict the familiar faces of the series stars. The covers often feature photographs taken from the show.

1 ❑ May 1967 Cover: 0.12 **NM** value: **25.00**
2 ❑ Sep 1967 Cover: 0.12 **NM** value: **20.00**
📖 The Lethal List; The Invaders
3 ❑ Dec 1967 Cover: 0.12 **NM** value: **20.00**
4 ❑ Oct 1968 Cover: 0.12 **NM** value: **20.00**
5 ❑ Cover: 0.12 **NM** value: **12.00**

MISSION IMPOSSIBLE (MARVEL) — Marvel

1 ❑ May 1996 Cover: 2.95 **NM** value: **Cover or less**
📖 Through a Mirror Darkly; Should Any of Your Agents... • prequel to movie **A:** Andrew Wildman; Rob Liefeld; Rod Whigham; Pino Rinaldi **C:** Rob Liefeld **W:** Marv Wolfman

MISSIONS IN TIBET — Dimension

1 ❑ Jul 1995 Cover: 2.50 **NM** value: **Cover or less**
A: David Han; Brian Zheng **W:** Brian Zheng; Arthur Schurr

MISS MELODY LANE OF BROADWAY — DC

1 ❑ Feb 1950 Cover: 0.10 **NM** value: **500.00**
• **CGC:** 1 graded, best 6.0
2 ❑ Apr 1950 Cover: 0.10 **NM** value: **300.00**
3 ❑ Jun 1950 Cover: 0.10 **NM** value: **300.00**

MISS PEACH — Dell

1 ❑ Oct 1963 **NM** value: **75.00**
• **CGC:** 1 graded, best 5.5

MISSPENT YOUTHS — Brave New Words

1 ❑ Cover: 2.50 **NM** value: **Cover or less**
📖 Closing Night Attitude **W:** David Lee Ingersoll
2 ❑ Cover: 2.50 **NM** value: **Cover or less**
3 ❑ Jul 1991 Cover: 2.50 **NM** value: **Cover or less**

MISS VICTORY GOLDEN ANNIVERSARY SPECIAL — AC

1 ❑ Nov 1991, full color Cover: 5.00 **NM** value: **Cover or less**
• reprint 1: Miss Victory

MISTER AMERICA — Endeavor

1 ❑ Cover: 2.95 **NM** value: **Cover or less**
2 ❑ Apr 1994 Cover: 2.95 **NM** value: **Cover or less**
A: Mark McCrary **W:** Mark Largent

MR. AND MRS. J. EVIL SCIENTIST — Gold Key

Based on the Hanna-Barbera cartoon, Mr. & Mrs. J. Evil Scientist is a family situation comedy, sort of like the Flintstones with monsters. J. Evil, his wife, and son Junior are green Frankenstein-types, only shorter and without the neck bolts. They're amiable and, unlike The Munsters, do seem to be aware that other people are frightened of them. That doesn't stop them from trying to integrate with society; Junior goes to a normal human school and belongs to the Scouts.

A few other Hanna-Barbera charecters appear in stories with J. Evil and his family in this short-running series, including Touche Turtle and Dum Dum. — JJM

1 ❑ Nov 1963 Cover: 0.12 **NM** value: **75.00**
• **CGC:** 2 graded, best 9.2
2 ❑ ca. 1964 Cover: 0.12 **NM** value: **50.00**
• **CGC:** 1 graded, best 9.0
3 ❑ ca. 1965 Cover: 0.12 **NM** value: **50.00**
• **CGC:** 1 graded, best 7.0
4 ❑ Sep 1966 Cover: 0.12 **NM** value: **50.00**
• **CGC:** 1 graded, best 9.0

MR. AVERAGE — B.S.

1 ❑ Cover: 2.25 **NM** value: **Cover or less**
2 ❑ Cover: 2.25 **NM** value: **Cover or less**
3 ❑ Cover: 2.25 **NM** value: **Cover or less**
📖 Tales from the Rippt

MR. BEAT ADVENTURES — Moordam

1 ❑ Jan 1997, b&w Cover: 2.95 **NM** value: **Cover or less**
📖 Mr. Beat and Bambeano Boy; Mr. Beat Takes a Little Sip; Hey Cats n Chicks; Neato! Mo Comics; Mr. Beat in Slumber Land; The Caf-Fiends; Mr. Beat Visits The Shrink **A:** Chris Yambar **W:** Chris Yambar

MR. BEAT'S BABES AND BONGOS ANNUAL — Moordam

1 ❑ Cover: 2.95 **NM** value: **Cover or less**
📖 Instant Karma!; ...To The destruction of The Spy Girls! **A:** Chris Yambar; Kevin Thomas **W:** Chris Yambar; Kevin Thomas

MR. BEAT'S HOUSE OF BURNING JAZZ LOVE — Moordam

1 ❑ Dec 1997, b&w Cover: 2.95 **NM** value: **Cover or less**

MR. BEAT'S TWO-FISTED ATOMIC ACTION SUPER SPECIAL — Moordam

1 ❑ Sep 1997, b&w Cover: 2.95 **NM** value: **Cover or less**
★ Versus Roswell.

MISTER BLANK — Slave Labor / Amaze Ink

0 ❑ Cover: 2.95 **NM** value: **Cover or less**
A: Christopher J. Hicks **W:** Christopher J. Hicks
1 ❑ May 1997 Cover: 2.95 **NM** value: **Cover or less**
Circ: Diamd. preorders: **1,706**
A: Christopher J. Hicks **W:** Christopher J. Hicks
2 ❑ May 1997 Cover: 2.95 **NM** value: **Cover or less**
A: Christopher J. Hicks **W:** Christopher J. Hicks
3 ❑ Aug 1997 Cover: 2.95 **NM** value: **Cover or less**
A: Christopher J. Hicks **W:** Christopher J. Hicks
4 ❑ Nov 1997 Cover: 2.95 **NM** value: **Cover or less**
A: Christopher J. Hicks **W:** Christopher J. Hicks
5 ❑ Feb 1998 Cover: 2.95 **NM** value: **Cover or less**
A: Christopher J. Hicks **W:** Christopher J. Hicks

MR. CREAM PUFF — Blackthorne

1 ❑ Cover: 1.75 **NM** value: **Cover or less**

MR. DAY & MR. NIGHT — Slave Labor

1 ❑ Apr 1993 Cover: 3.95 **NM** value: **Cover or less**

MR. DISTRICT ATTORNEY — DC

Inspired by the exploits of New York DA Thomas E. Dewey (1902-1971), the award-winning radio show ran from 1939 to 1953 and was enormously popular, in part because the creator-writer-director worked fiercely to keep on top of criminal trends, slang, and other current events. "Mister District Attorney! Champion of the people! Guardian of our fundamental rights to life, liberty, and the pursuit of happiness!" It also had two brief TV runs, one 1951-2 and one 1954-5. The show followed the adventures of a crusading big city DA and his assistant as they go after mobsters, solve murder mysteries, and uphold law and order.

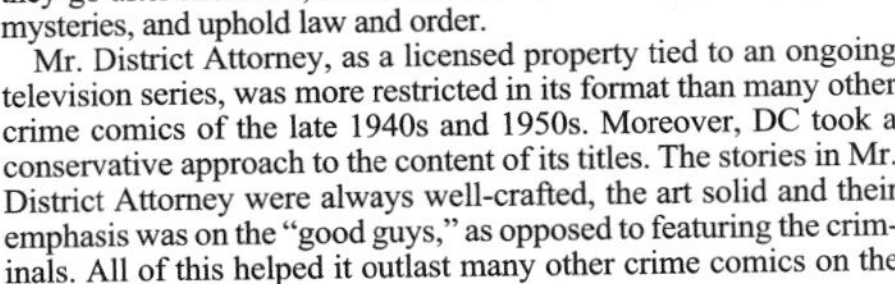

Mr. District Attorney, as a licensed property tied to an ongoing television series, was more restricted in its format than many other crime comics of the late 1940s and 1950s. Moreover, DC took a conservative approach to the content of its titles. The stories in Mr. District Attorney were always well-crafted, the art solid and their emphasis was on the "good guys," as opposed to featuring the criminals. All of this helped it outlast many other crime comics on the newsstands.

1 ❑ Feb 1948 Cover: 0.10 **NM** value: **650.00**
• **CGC:** 1 graded, best 5.0
2 ❑ Apr 1948 Cover: 0.10 **NM** value: **300.00**
• **CGC:** 1 graded, best 9.2
3 ❑ Jun 1948 Cover: 0.10 **NM** value: **210.00**
4 ❑ Aug 1948 Cover: 0.10 **NM** value: **210.00**
5 ❑ Oct 1948 Cover: 0.10 **NM** value: **210.00**
6 ❑ Dec 1948 Cover: 0.10 **NM** value: **160.00**
7 ❑ Feb 1949 Cover: 0.10 **NM** value: **160.00**
8 ❑ Apr 1949 Cover: 0.10 **NM** value: **160.00**
9 ❑ Jun 1949 Cover: 0.10 **NM** value: **160.00**
10 ❑ Aug 1949 Cover: 0.10 **NM** value: **160.00**
11 ❑ Oct 1949 Cover: 0.10 **NM** value: **110.00**
12 ❑ Dec 1949 Cover: 0.10 **NM** value: **110.00**
13 ❑ Feb 1950 Cover: 0.10 **NM** value: **110.00**
14 ❑ Apr 1950 Cover: 0.10 **NM** value: **110.00**
15 ❑ Jun 1950 Cover: 0.10 **NM** value: **110.00**
16 ❑ Aug 1950 Cover: 0.10 **NM** value: **110.00**
17 ❑ Oct 1950 Cover: 0.10 **NM** value: **110.00**
• **CGC:** 1 graded, best 9.2
18 ❑ Dec 1950 Cover: 0.10 **NM** value: **110.00**
19 ❑ Feb 1951 Cover: 0.10 **NM** value: **110.00**
20 ❑ Apr 1951 Cover: 0.10 **NM** value: **110.00**
21 ❑ Jun 1951 Cover: 0.10 **NM** value: **85.00**
22 ❑ Aug 1951 Cover: 0.10 **NM** value: **85.00**
23 ❑ Oct 1951 Cover: 0.10 **NM** value: **85.00**
24 ❑ Dec 1951 Cover: 0.10 **NM** value: **85.00**
25 ❑ Feb 1952 Cover: 0.10 **NM** value: **85.00**
26 ❑ Apr 1952 Cover: 0.10 **NM** value: **85.00**
27 ❑ Jun 1952 Cover: 0.10 **NM** value: **85.00**
28 ❑ Aug 1952 Cover: 0.10 **NM** value: **85.00**
29 ❑ Oct 1952 Cover: 0.10 **NM** value: **85.00**
30 ❑ Dec 1952 Cover: 0.10 **NM** value: **85.00**
31 ❑ Feb 1953 Cover: 0.10 **NM** value: **75.00**
32 ❑ Apr 1953 Cover: 0.10 **NM** value: **75.00**
33 ❑ Jun 1953 Cover: 0.10 **NM** value: **75.00**
34 ❑ Aug 1953 Cover: 0.10 **NM** value: **75.00**
35 ❑ Oct 1953 Cover: 0.10 **NM** value: **75.00**
36 ❑ Dec 1953 Cover: 0.10 **NM** value: **75.00**
37 ❑ Feb 1954 Cover: 0.10 **NM** value: **75.00**
38 ❑ Apr 1954 Cover: 0.10 **NM** value: **75.00**
39 ❑ Jun 1954 Cover: 0.10 **NM** value: **75.00**
40 ❑ Aug 1954 Cover: 0.10 **NM** value: **75.00**
41 ❑ Oct 1954 Cover: 0.10 **NM** value: **60.00**
42 ❑ Dec 1954 Cover: 0.10 **NM** value: **60.00**
43 ❑ Feb 1955 Cover: 0.10 **NM** value: **60.00**
44 ❑ Apr 1955 Cover: 0.10 **NM** value: **60.00**
45 ❑ Jun 1955 Cover: 0.10 **NM** value: **60.00**
46 ❑ Aug 1955 Cover: 0.10 **NM** value: **60.00**
47 ❑ Oct 1955 Cover: 0.10 **NM** value: **60.00**
48 ❑ Dec 1955 Cover: 0.10 **NM** value: **60.00**
49 ❑ Feb 1956 Cover: 0.10 **NM** value: **60.00**
📖 The TV Dragnet; The King of Escapes; Army Lawmen (text story); D.A.-Condemned Man
50 ❑ Apr 1956 Cover: 0.10 **NM** value: **60.00**
51 ❑ Jun 1956 Cover: 0.10 **NM** value: **50.00**
52 ❑ Aug 1956 Cover: 0.10 **NM** value: **50.00**
53 ❑ Oct 1956 Cover: 0.10 **NM** value: **50.00**
54 ❑ Dec 1956 Cover: 0.10 **NM** value: **50.00**
55 ❑ Feb 1957 Cover: 0.10 **NM** value: **50.00**
56 ❑ Apr 1957 Cover: 0.10 **NM** value: **50.00**
57 ❑ Jun 1957 Cover: 0.10 **NM** value: **50.00**
📖 The Underworld Employment Agency; Trailing Crime!; The Case of the Bungling Butler
58 ❑ Aug 1957 Cover: 0.10 **NM** value: **50.00**
59 ❑ Oct 1957 Cover: 0.10 **NM** value: **50.00**
60 ❑ Dec 1957 Cover: 0.10 **NM** value: **50.00**
61 ❑ Feb 1958 Cover: 0.10 **NM** value: **50.00**
62 ❑ Apr 1958 Cover: 0.10 **NM** value: **50.00**
63 ❑ Jun 1958 Cover: 0.10 **NM** value: **50.00**
64 ❑ Aug 1958 Cover: 0.10 **NM** value: **50.00**
65 ❑ Oct 1958 Cover: 0.10 **NM** value: **50.00**
66 ❑ Dec 1958 Cover: 0.10 **NM** value: **50.00**
67 ❑ Feb 1959 Cover: 0.10 **NM** value: **50.00**
final issue.

MR. DOOM — Pied Piper

1 ❑ Cover: 1.95 **NM** value: **Cover or less**

MISTER E — DC

1 ❑ Jun 1991 Cover: 1.75 **NM** value: **2.00**
Circ: CapCity orders: **21,750**
📖 At The End Of Time **A:** John K. Snyder III **W:** K.W. Jeter
2 ❑ Jul 1991 Cover: 1.75 **NM** value: **2.00**
Circ: CapCity orders: **15,200**
A: John K. Snyder III **W:** K.W. Jeter
3 ❑ Aug 1991 Cover: 1.75 **NM** value: **2.00**
Circ: CapCity orders: **14,600**
A: John K. Snyder III **W:** K.W. Jeter
4 ❑ Sep 1991 Cover: 1.75 **NM** value: **2.00**
Circ: CapCity orders: **13,950**
📖 The Power! **A:** John K. Snyder III **W:** K.W. Jeter

MISTER ED, THE TALKING HORSE — Dell

1 ❑ Nov 1962 Cover: 0.12 **NM** value: **100.00**
• **CGC:** 1 graded, best 9.4
2 ❑ Feb 1963 Cover: 0.12 **NM** value: **50.00**
3 ❑ May 1963 Cover: 0.12 **NM** value: **50.00**
4 ❑ Aug 1963 Cover: 0.12 **NM** value: **40.00**
5 ❑ Nov 1963 Cover: 0.12 **NM** value: **40.00**
6 ❑ Feb 1964 Cover: 0.12 **NM** value: **40.00**

MR. FIXITT (APPLE) — Apple

1 ❑ Jan 1989, b&w Cover: 1.95 **NM** value: **Cover or less**
📖 It's The Thought That Counts! **A:** Howard Bender **W:** Howard Bender
2 ❑ Mar 1990 Cover: 2.25 **NM** value: **Cover or less**

MR. FIXITT (HEROIC) — Heroic

1 ❑ b&w Cover: 2.95 **NM** value: **Cover or less**
• trading card

MR. HERO-THE NEWMATIC MAN (1ST SERIES) (NEIL GAIMAN'S...) — Tekno

Neil Gaiman is one of the most wildly imaginative and talented comic-book writers of the 1990s, known for his work on Sandman, Books of Magic, and others. That said, it must be noted that, despite Gaiman's name on this project, what he provided was only the "concept" of Mr. Hero: a steam-driven automaton from another world, programmed to act like a novelty boxing robot from the late 19th century. Mr. Hero (the robot) has fallen into disuse until inherited by a young woman in London and pressed into service as her protector. It falls to the team of James Vance (writer), Ted Slampyak (penciller), and Bob McLeod (inker) to develop Gaiman's high concept, but the gaudy and energetic tekno-style does not always enhance the material's richness.

CGC-graded: Multiply prices above by **33 for 9.9 M** • **16 for 9.8 NM/M** • **7 for 9.6 NM+** • **5 for 9.4 NM** • **2.5 for 9.2 NM-** • **1.5 for 9.0 VF/NM**

1 ❑ Mar 1995 Cover: 1.95 **NM** value: **Cover or less**
Circ: Statement: **83,792** CapCity orders: **37,025**
Toys in the Basement • game piece; trading card **A:** Ted Slampyak **W:** James Vance ★ Origin of Mr. Hero. ★ 1st Appearance of Teknophage, Mr. Hero.
2 ❑ Apr 1995 Cover: 1.95 **NM** value: **Cover or less**
Circ: Statement: **83,792** CapCity orders: **31,425**
• game piece; trading card **A:** Ted Slampyak **W:** James Vance
3 ❑ May 1995 Cover: 1.95 **NM** value: **Cover or less**
Circ: Statement: **83,792** CapCity orders: **25,350**
Cain • game piece; trading card **A:** Ted Slampyak **W:** James Vance
4 ❑ Jun 1995 Cover: 1.95 **NM** value: **Cover or less**
Circ: Statement: **83,792** CapCity orders: **17,825**
• coupon **A:** Ted Slampyak **W:** James Vance
5 ❑ Jul 1995 Cover: 1.95 **NM** value: **Cover or less**
Circ: Statement: **83,792** CapCity orders: **15,700**
Money **A:** Ted Slampyak **W:** James Vance
6 ❑ Aug 1995 Cover: 1.95 **NM** value: **Cover or less**
Circ: Statement: **83,792** CapCity orders: **13,750**
A: Ted Slampyak **W:** James Vance
7 ❑ Sep 1995 Cover: 1.95 **NM** value: **Cover or less**
Circ: Statement: **83,792** CapCity orders: **12,300**
Let's Make a Deal **A:** Ted Slampyak **W:** James Vance
8 ❑ Oct 1995 Cover: 1.95 **NM** value: **Cover or less**
Circ: Statement: **83,792** CapCity orders: **11,275**
A: Ted Slampyak **W:** James Vance
9 ❑ Nov 1995 Cover: 1.95 **NM** value: **Cover or less**
Circ: Statement: **83,792** CapCity orders: **10,775**
A: Ted Slampyak **W:** James Vance
10 ❑ Dec 1995 Cover: 1.95 **NM** value: **Cover or less**
Circ: Statement: **83,792** CapCity orders: **8,825**
A: Ted Slampyak **W:** James Vance
11 ❑ Dec 1995 Cover: 1.95 **NM** value: **Cover or less**
Circ: Statement: **83,792** CapCity orders: **7,125**
A: Ted Slampyak **W:** James Vance
12 ❑ Jan 1996 Cover: 1.95 **NM** value: **2.25**
A: Ted Slampyak **W:** James Vance
13 ❑ Jan 1996 Cover: 2.25 **NM** value: **Cover or less**
• Has 1995 Statement, filed 10/11/95; avg print run 217,773; avg sales 83,664; avg subs 128; avg total paid 83,792; samples 3,931; office use 8,115; max existent 95,838; 56% of run returned **A:** Ted Slampyak **W:** James Vance
14 ❑ Feb 1996 Cover: 2.25 **NM** value: **Cover or less**
A: Ted Slampyak **W:** James Vance
15 ❑ Mar 1996 Cover: 2.25 **NM** value: **Cover or less**
A: Ted Slampyak **W:** James Vance
16 ❑ Apr 1996 Cover: 2.25 **NM** value: **Cover or less**
A: Ted Slampyak **W:** James Vance
17 ❑ May 1996 Cover: 2.25 **NM** value: **Cover or less**
The Big Crossover, Part 3 **A:** Ted Slampyak **W:** James Vance

MR. HERO-THE NEWMATIC MAN (2ND SERIES) (NEIL GAIMAN'S...) Big

1 ❑ Jun 1996 Cover: 2.25 **NM** value: **Cover or less**
The Big Crossover Chapter 10; History; The Big Crossover, Part 10 **A:** Steve Erwin; Ted Slampyak **W:** James Vance; Ron Fortier ★ Death of Mr. Hero.
2 ❑ Jul 1996 Cover: 2.25 **NM** value: **Cover or less**
3 ❑ Aug 1996 Cover: 2.25 **NM** value: **Cover or less**
4 ❑ Sep 1996 Cover: 2.25 **NM** value: **Cover or less**

MR. JIGSAW SPECIAL Ocean

1 ❑ Spr 1988 Cover: 1.75 **NM** value: **2.00**
• blue paper ★ Origin of Mr. Jigsaw.

MR. LIZARD 3-D Now

1 ❑ May 1993 Cover: 3.50 **NM** value: **Cover or less**
• instant Mr. Lizard capsule

MR. LIZARD ANNUAL Now

1 ❑ Sep 1993 Cover: 2.95 **NM** value: **Cover or less**
• Ralph Snart capsule

MR. MAJESTIC DC / Wildstorm

1 ❑ Sep 1999 Cover: 2.50 **NM** value: **Cover or less**
Circ: Diamd. preorders: **27,194**
Cosmology **A:** Ed McGuinness **W:** Joe Casey; Brian Holguin
2 ❑ Oct 1999 Cover: 2.50 **NM** value: **Cover or less**
Circ: Diamd. preorders: **20,055**
Repeating History **A:** Ed McGuinness **W:** Joe Casey; Brian Holguin
3 ❑ Nov 1999 Cover: 2.50 **NM** value: **Cover or less**
Circ: Diamd. preorders: **17,164**
A: Ed McGuinness **W:** Joe Casey; Brian Holguin
4 ❑ Dec 1999 Cover: 2.50 **NM** value: **Cover or less**
Circ: Diamd. preorders: **15,242**
Being & Nothingness **A:** Ed McGuinness **W:** Joe Casey; Brian Holguin
5 ❑ Jan 2000 Cover: 2.50 **NM** value: **Cover or less**
Circ: Diamd. preorders: **13,123**
Jailbreak! **A:** Ed McGuinness **W:** Joe Casey; Brian Holguin
6 ❑ Feb 2000 Cover: 2.50 **NM** value: **Cover or less**
Circ: Diamd. preorders: **13,001**
W: Joe Casey; Brian Holguin
7 ❑ Mar 2000 Cover: 2.50 **NM** value: **Cover or less**
Circ: Diamd. preorders: **11,342**
Univeral Law, Part 1 **W:** Joe Casey; Brian Holguin
8 ❑ Apr 2000 Cover: 2.50 **NM** value: **Cover or less**
Circ: Diamd. preorders: **10,297**
Univeral Law, Part 2 **A:** Eric Canete **W:** Joe Casey; Brian Holguin
9 ❑ May 2000 Cover: 2.50 **NM** value: **Cover or less**
Circ: Diamd. preorders: **9,810**
Univeral Law, Part 3 **A:** Eric Canete; Toby Cypress; Juan Vlasco **W:** Joe Casey; Brian Holguin

MISTER MIRACLE (1ST SERIES) DC

He is the son of Izaya and Avia, the rulers of a world called New Genesis. That world of "New Gods" has long been embroiled in a deadly clash with its sister world, Apokolips. Then, the malevolent Darkseid, ruler of Apokolips proposes a pact: He will trade his own son, Orion, for Izaya's boy — as hostages of peace. When the trade is completed, Darkseid orders the boy to be harshly raised at a military academy on Apokolips. In what is meant to be a cruel joke on the boy's hopeless situation, he is given a name — Scott Free.

Eventually, Scott escapes from Apokolips, coming to Earth via the device known as "the Boom Tube." There, he encounters a dwarf named Oberon, assistant to escape artist Thaddeus Brown, the original Mister Miracle. When Thaddeus is killed, Scott takes on his identity and brings his killer to justice. In later years, Scott will become a member of Justice League International.

1 ❑ Apr 1971 Cover: 0.15 **NM** value: **26.00**
• **CGC:** 21 graded, best 9.4
Murder Missile Trap **A:** Jack Kirby **W:** Jack Kirby ★ 1st Appearance of Oberon, Mister Miracle.
2 ❑ Jun 1971 Cover: 0.15 **NM** value: **16.00**
• **CGC:** 7 graded, best 9.4
X-Pit ★ 1st Appearance of Doctor Bedlam, Granny Goodness.
3 ❑ Aug 1971 Cover: 0.15 **NM** value: **14.00**
• **CGC:** 3 graded, best 9.6
The Paranoid Pill • Boy Commandos reprint ★ Versus Doctor Bedlam. ★ Versus Dr. Bedlam.
4 ❑ Oct 1971 Cover: 0.25 **NM** value: **13.00**
• **CGC:** 1 graded, best 6.0
• Giant-size. The Closing Jaws of Death • Boy Commandos reprint (Detective Comics #82) ★ 1st Appearance of Big Barda, Boy Commandos reprint.
5 ❑ Dec 1971 Cover: 0.25 **NM** value: **13.00**
• **CGC:** 1 graded, best 9.2
• Giant-size. Doctor Vumdabar and His Murder Machine • Boy Commandos reprint (Detective Comics #76)
6 ❑ Feb 1972 Cover: 0.25 **NM** value: **13.00**
• **CGC:** 3 graded, best 9.6
• Giant-size. Funky Flashman • reprints Boy Commandos #1 ★ 1st Appearance of Funky Flashman, Lashina, Female Furies.
7 ❑ Apr 1972 Cover: 0.25 **NM** value: **13.00**
• **CGC:** 6 graded, best 9.8
• Giant-size. Apokolips Traps • reprints Boy Commandos #3
8 ❑ Jun 1972 Cover: 0.25 **NM** value: **13.00**
• **CGC:** 4 graded, best 9.6
• Giant-size. Battle of the ID • Boy Commandos reprint (Detective Comics #64)
9 ❑ Aug 1972 Cover: 0.20 **NM** value: **10.00**
• **CGC:** 1 graded, best 9.8
Himon
10 ❑ Oct 1972 Cover: 0.20 **NM** value: **10.00**
• **CGC:** 1 graded, best 9.2
The Mister Miracle to Be
11 ❑ Dec 1972 Cover: 0.20 **NM** value: **9.00**
• **CGC:** 1 graded, best 9.4
The Greatest Show Off Earth
12 ❑ Feb 1973 Cover: 0.20 **NM** value: **9.00**
• **CGC:** 1 graded, best 9.6
Mystivac
13 ❑ Apr 1973 Cover: 0.20 **NM** value: **9.00**
The Dictator's Dungeon
14 ❑ Jul 1973 Cover: 0.20 **NM** value: **9.00**
The Quick And The Dead! **A:** Jack Kirby **W:** Jack Kirby ★ 1st Appearance of Madame Evil Eye.
15 ❑ Sep 1973 Cover: 0.20 **NM** value: **9.00**
The Secret Gun ★ 1st Appearance of Mister Miracle II (Shilo Norman).
16 ❑ Nov 1973 Cover: 0.20 **NM** value: **8.00**
• **CGC:** 1 graded, best 9.6
Shilo Norman, Super Trouble
17 ❑ Jan 1974 Cover: 0.20 **NM** value: **8.00**
• **CGC:** 3 graded, best 9.4
Murder Lodge
18 ❑ Mar 1974 Cover: 0.20 **NM** value: **8.00**
• **CGC:** 2 graded, best 9.4
Wild Wild Wedding Guests • series goes on hiatus; Wedding of Mister Miracle and Barda
19 ❑ Sep 1977 Cover: 0.35 **NM** value: **5.00**
• **CGC:** 1 graded, best 8.0
20 ❑ Oct 1977 Cover: 0.35 **NM** value: **5.00**
• **CGC:** 1 graded, best 9.0
21 ❑ Dec 1977 Cover: 0.35 **NM** value: **5.00**
22 ❑ Feb 1978 Cover: 0.35 **NM** value: **5.00**
• **CGC:** 1 graded, best 8.0
23 ❑ Apr 1978 Cover: 0.35 **NM** value: **5.00**
24 ❑ Jun 1978 Cover: 0.35 **NM** value: **5.00**
25 ❑ Sep 1978 Cover: 0.35 **NM** value: **5.00**
final issue.
SE 1 ❑ ca. 1987 Cover: 1.25 **NM** value: **3.50**
Circ: CapCity orders: **17,450**

MISTER MIRACLE (2ND SERIES) DC

1 ❑ Jan 1989 Cover: 1.00 **NM** value: **2.50**
Circ: CapCity orders: **24,000**
Be It Ever So Humble **A:** Ian Gibson **W:** J.M. DeMatteis ★ Origin of Mister Miracle. ★ Appearance of Doctor Bedlam, Dr. Bedlam.
2 ❑ Feb 1989 Cover: 1.00 **NM** value: **1.50**
Circ: CapCity orders: **17,750**
3 ❑ Mar 1989 Cover: 1.00 **NM** value: **1.50**
Circ: CapCity orders: **15,500**
4 ❑ Apr 1989 Cover: 1.00 **NM** value: **1.50**
Circ: CapCity orders: **14,450**
5 ❑ Jun 1989 Cover: 1.00 **NM** value: **1.50**
Circ: CapCity orders: **13,500**
6 ❑ Jul 1989 Cover: 1.00 **NM** value: **1.25**
Circ: CapCity orders: **13,100**
7 ❑ Aug 1989 Cover: 1.00 **NM** value: **1.25**
Circ: CapCity orders: **13,150**
8 ❑ Sep 1989 Cover: 1.00 **NM** value: **1.25**
Circ: CapCity orders: **12,150**
9 ❑ Oct 1989 Cover: 1.00 **NM** value: **1.25**
Circ: CapCity orders: **11,800**
★ 1st Appearance of Maxi-Man.
10 ❑ Nov 1989 Cover: 1.00 **NM** value: **1.25**
Circ: CapCity orders: **11,550**
11 ❑ Dec 1989 Cover: 1.00 **NM** value: **1.25**
Circ: CapCity orders: **10,800**
12 ❑ Jan 1990 Cover: 1.00 **NM** value: **1.25**
Circ: CapCity orders: **10,900**
13 ❑ Mar 1990 Cover: 1.00 **NM** value: **1.25**
Circ: CapCity orders: **10,050**
14 ❑ Apr 1990 Cover: 1.00 **NM** value: **1.25**
Circ: CapCity orders: **9,500**
15 ❑ May 1990 Cover: 1.00 **NM** value: **1.25**
Circ: CapCity orders: **9,550**
16 ❑ Jun 1990 Cover: 1.00 **NM** value: **1.25**
Circ: CapCity orders: **9,750**
17 ❑ Jul 1990 Cover: 1.00 **NM** value: **1.25**
Circ: CapCity orders: **9,850**
18 ❑ Aug 1990 Cover: 1.00 **NM** value: **1.25**
Circ: CapCity orders: **9,450**
19 ❑ Sep 1990 Cover: 1.00 **NM** value: **1.25**
Circ: CapCity orders: **9,400**
20 ❑ Oct 1990 Cover: 1.00 **NM** value: **1.25**
Circ: CapCity orders: **9,150**
21 ❑ Nov 1990 Cover: 1.00 **NM** value: **1.25**
Circ: CapCity orders: **9,050**
22 ❑ Dec 1990 Cover: 1.00 **NM** value: **1.25**
Circ: CapCity orders: **9,400**
23 ❑ Jan 1991 Cover: 1.00 **NM** value: **1.25**
Circ: CapCity orders: **8,800**
24 ❑ Feb 1991 Cover: 1.00 **NM** value: **1.25**
Circ: CapCity orders: **8,450**
25 ❑ Mar 1991 Cover: 1.00 **NM** value: **1.25**
Circ: CapCity orders: **8,450**
26 ❑ Apr 1991 Cover: 1.00 **NM** value: **1.25**
Circ: CapCity orders: **7,950**
27 ❑ May 1991 Cover: 1.25 **NM** value: **Cover or less**
Circ: CapCity orders: **8,350**
28 ❑ Jun 1991 Cover: 1.25 **NM** value: **Cover or less**
Circ: CapCity orders: **7,800**
final issue.

MISTER MIRACLE (3RD SERIES) DC

1 ❑ Apr 1996 Cover: 1.95 **NM** value: **Cover or less**
Stone Walls do not a Prison Make... **A:** Steve Crespo **W:** Kevin Dooley
2 ❑ May 1996 Cover: 1.95 **NM** value: **Cover or less**
A: Steve Crespo **W:** Kevin Dooley ★ Versus JLA.
3 ❑ Jun 1996 Cover: 1.95 **NM** value: **Cover or less**
A: Steve Crespo **W:** Kevin Dooley
4 ❑ Jul 1996 Cover: 1.95 **NM** value: **Cover or less**
A: Steve Crespo **W:** Kevin Dooley ★ Versus Black Racer.
5 ❑ Aug 1996 Cover: 1.95 **NM** value: **Cover or less**
A: Steve Crespo **W:** Kevin Dooley
6 ❑ Sep 1996 Cover: 1.95 **NM** value: **Cover or less**
A: Steve Crespo **W:** Kevin Dooley
7 ❑ Oct 1996 Cover: 1.95 **NM** value: **Cover or less**
Freedom is Blind final issue. **A:** Steve Crespo **W:** Kevin Dooley
Bk 1 ❑ Cover: 12.95 **NM** value: **Cover or less**
A: Steve Crespo **W:** Kevin Dooley

MR. MONSTER Dark Horse

1 ❑ Feb 1988 Cover: 1.75 **NM** value: **2.00**
Circ: CapCity orders: **5,875**
Origins, Part 1; The Terror of Trezman! **A:** Michael T. Gilbert; Dave Dorman(cover) **W:** Michael T. Gilbert ★ Origin of Mr. Monster.
2 ❑ Apr 1988 Cover: 1.75 **NM** value: **2.00**
Circ: CapCity orders: **5,700**
Origins, Part 2 **A:** Michael T. Gilbert **W:** Michael T. Gilbert
3 ❑ Jun 1988 Cover: 1.75 **NM** value: **2.00**
Circ: CapCity orders: **5,200**
Origins, Part 3; Doc Stearn **A:** Michael T. Gilbert; Fred Kelly **W:** Michael T. Gilbert; Fred Kelly
4 ❑ Nov 1988 Cover: 1.75 **NM** value: **2.00**
Circ: CapCity orders: **4,925**
Origins, Part 4; Cadavera **A:** Michael T. Gilbert; Mike McCarthy **W:** Michael T. Gilbert; Mike McCarthy; Janet Clark
5 ❑ Mar 1989 Cover: 1.75 **NM** value: **2.00**
Circ: CapCity orders: **4,875**
Origins, Part 5; Monster Boy **A:** Michael T. Gilbert; Bob Supina **W:** Michael T. Gilbert; Bob Supina
6 ❑ Oct 1989 Cover: 1.95 **NM** value: **2.00**
Circ: CapCity orders: **3,550**
Origins, Part 6; The Secret Files of Dr. Drew • has indicia for #5 **A:** Michael T. Gilbert; Jerry Grandienetti **W:** Michael T. Gilbert; Marilyn Mercer
7 ❑ Apr 1990 Cover: 1.95 **NM** value: **2.00**
Circ: CapCity orders: **4,425**
Origins, Part 7; Ghosts Are Dead! **A:** Michael T. Gilbert; Bob Supina **W:** Michael T. Gilbert; Bob Supina
8 ❑ Sep 1990 Cover: 4.95 **NM** value: **5.00**
Circ: CapCity orders: **4,100**
• Giant-size. final issue. **A:** Michael T. Gilbert **W:** Michael T. Gilbert ★ Death of Mr. Monster.

MR. MONSTER ATTACKS! Tundra

1 ❑ Aug 1992 Cover: 3.95 **NM** value: **Cover or less**
2 ❑ Sep 1992 Cover: 3.95 **NM** value: **Cover or less**
Circ: CapCity orders: **2,600**
3 ❑ Oct 1992 Cover: 3.95 **NM** value: **Cover or less**
Circ: CapCity orders: **2,600**

Other grades: Multiply prices above by **1.5 for Mint • 2/3 for Very Fine • 1/3 for Fine • 1/5 for Very Good • 1/8 for Good**

MR. MONSTER PRESENTS (CRACK-A-BOOM!) Caliber

1 ❑ Jun 1997 Cover: 2.95 **NM** value: **Cover or less**
Circ: Diamd. preorders: **4,190**
2 ❑ 1997 Cover: 2.95 **NM** value: **Cover or less**
3 ❑ Sep 1997 Cover: 2.95 **NM** value: **Cover or less**

MR. MONSTER'S GAL FRIDAY...KELLY! Image

1 ❑ Jan 2000 Cover: 3.50 **NM** value: **Cover or less**
Circ: Diamd. preorders: **3,594**
📖 Temporary Insanity; I Married a Monser! **A:** Shawn McManus; Michael T. Gilbert; Trina Robbins; Janet Gilbert; Tom Buss **W:** Shawn McManus; Michael T. Gilbert; Trina Robbins; Janet Gilbert

MR. MONSTER'S HIGH-OCTANE HORROR Eclipse

1 ❑ Aug 1986 Cover: 1.75 **NM** value: **2.00**
Circ: CapCity orders: **6,225**
📖 The Secret Files of Dr. Drew; The Man Who Never Smiled; The Metamorphosis of the Gkmlooms • A.K.A. Super Duper Special #2 **A:** George Evans; Basil Wolverton; Jerry Grandienetti **W:** Basil Wolverton; Jerry Grandienetti
3D 1❑May 1986 Cover: 2.00 **NM** value: **2.50**
• A.K.A. Super Duper Special #1

MR. MONSTER'S HI-SHOCK SCHLOCK Eclipse

1 ❑ Mar 1987 Cover: 1.75 **NM** value: **2.00**
📖 The Flat Man; Frankenstein and the Mummies; Corpses...Coast to Coast; • A.K.A. Super Duper Special #6 **A:** Michael T. Gilbert **W:** Michael T. Gilbert
2 ❑ May 1987 Cover: 1.75 **NM** value: **2.00**
Circ: CapCity orders: **3,275**
• A.K.A. Super Duper Special #7

MR. MONSTER'S HI-VOLTAGE SUPER SCIENCE Eclipse

1 ❑ Jan 1987 Cover: 1.75 **NM** value: **2.00**
Circ: CapCity orders: **3,675**
📖 The Flying Saucer • A.K.A. Super Duper Special #5 **A:** Bob Powell **W:** Bob Powell

MR. MONSTER'S TRIPLE THREAT 3-D 3-D Zone

1 ❑ Cover: 3.95 **NM** value: **Cover or less**
Circ: CapCity orders: **5,450**
No issue number.

MR. MONSTER'S TRUE CRIME Eclipse

1 ❑ Sep 1986 Cover: 1.75 **NM** value: **2.00**
Circ: CapCity orders: **5,575**
📖 Murder, Morphine, & Me!; Demons Dance on Galloway Moor!; A Match for Satan • A.K.A. Super Duper Special #3 **A:** Jack Cole **W:** Jack Cole
2 ❑ Oct 1986 Cover: 1.75 **NM** value: **2.00**
Circ: CapCity orders: **4,400**
📖 Public Enemy #1; Vengeance of the Mounted; $100 Reward • A.K.A. Super Duper Special #4 **A:** Jack Cole **W:** Jack Cole

MR. MONSTER'S WEIRD TALES OF THE FUTURE Eclipse

1 ❑ Cover: 1.75 **NM** value: **2.00**
📖 Brain Bats of Venus; Man From the Moon; Escape to Death; Flight to the Future; Nightmare World • A.K.A. Super Duper Special #8 **A:** Basil Wolverton; Michael T. Gilbert **W:** Basil Wolverton; Michael T. Gilbert

MR. MONSTER VS. GORZILLA Image

1 ❑ Jul 1998 Cover: 2.95 **NM** value: **Cover or less**
Circ: Diamd. preorders: **6,327**
No issue number. One-shot. • red, white, and blue **A:** Ken Bruzenak **W:** Ken Bruzenak

MR. MXYZPTLK (VILLAINS) DC

1 ❑ Feb 1998 Cover: 1.95 **NM** value: **Cover or less**
Circ: Diamd. preorders: **38,699**
• New Year's Evil

MISTER MYSTERY Aragon

It sounds like a whodunit series, doesn't it? But the covers declared, for the first 18 issues, "Tales of horror and suspense" — which provides a far more accurate picture of the contents. This pre-Code series came from a small company that had its imprint on only this and two other series: Mutiny ("Stormy Tales of the Seven Seas") and ("Eerie and Startling Adventures into ...") Weird Tales of the Future. (There were noticeable similarities, however, between the contents of those and, say, those of Weird Mysteries, released under the Gilmore imprint.)

For such a small company, it produced one of the most-recognized covers in the history of the field with its 12th issue: a "hot poker to the eye" cover that is a classic. The company's timing was impeccable, getting more gross as pressures for comics censorship became more intense. — Maggie

1 ❑ Sep 1951 Cover: 0.10 **NM** value: **750.00**
• **CGC:** 2 graded, best 4.5
2 ❑ Nov 1951 Cover: 0.10 **NM** value: **500.00**
• **CGC:** 4 graded, best 9.2
3 ❑ Dec 1951 Cover: 0.10 **NM** value: **500.00**
• **CGC:** 3 graded, best 8.0
4 ❑ Mar 1952 Cover: 0.10 **NM** value: **500.00**
• **CGC:** 4 graded, best 9.2
5 ❑ May 1952 Cover: 0.10 **NM** value: **500.00**
6 ❑ Jul 1952 Cover: 0.10 **NM** value: **500.00**
• **CGC:** 1 graded, best 7.5
7 ❑ Sep 1952 Cover: 0.10 **NM** value: **400.00**
• **CGC:** 2 graded, best 7.0
8 ❑ Nov 1952 Cover: 0.10 **NM** value: **400.00**
• **CGC:** 2 graded, best 9.0
9 ❑ Jan 1953 Cover: 0.10 **NM** value: **400.00**
10 ❑ Mar 1953 Cover: 0.10 **NM** value: **350.00**
• **CGC:** 2 graded, best 9.0
11 ❑ May 1953 Cover: 0.10 **NM** value: **350.00**
• **CGC:** 4 graded, best 8.5
12 ❑ Jul 1953 Cover: 0.10 **NM** value: **350.00**
• **CGC:** 3 graded, best 8.0
13 ❑ Sep 1953 Cover: 0.10 **NM** value: **350.00**
• **CGC:** 1 graded, best 8.0
14 ❑ Nov 1953 Cover: 0.10 **NM** value: **350.00**
• **CGC:** 1 graded, best 8.0
15 ❑ Feb 1954 Cover: 0.10 **NM** value: **350.00**
• **CGC:** 1 graded, best 8.0
16 ❑ Apr 1954 Cover: 0.10 **NM** value: **300.00**
• **CGC:** 1 graded, best 8.5
17 ❑ Jun 1954 Cover: 0.10 **NM** value: **300.00**
• **CGC:** 2 graded, best 9.0
18 ❑ Aug 1954 Cover: 0.10 **NM** value: **300.00**
• **CGC:** 3 graded, best 9.2
19 ❑ Oct 1954 Cover: 0.10 **NM** value: **300.00**
• **CGC:** 1 graded, best 8.0

MR. NATURAL Kitchen Sink

1 ❑ **NM** value: **100.00**
A: Robert Crumb **W:** Robert Crumb
2 ❑ Oct 1971 **NM** value: **60.00**
• **CGC:** 2 graded, best 9.8
A: Robert Crumb **W:** Robert Crumb
3 ❑ Jan 1977 **NM** value: **45.00**
• **CGC:** 2 graded, best 9.4
A: Robert Crumb **W:** Robert Crumb
3-2 ❑ **NM** value: **22.00**
3-3 ❑ **NM** value: **10.00**
3-4 ❑ **NM** value: **4.50**
3-5 ❑ Cover: 1.50 **NM** value: **3.00**
3-6 ❑ **NM** value: **2.50**
3-7 ❑ **NM** value: **2.50**
3-8 ❑ Cover: 2.50 **NM** value: **Cover or less**

MR. NIGHTMARE'S WINTER SPECIAL Moonstone

1 ❑ Dec 1995, b&w Cover: 3.50 **NM** value: **Cover or less**
No issue number.

MR. NIGHTMARE'S WONDERFUL WORLD Moonstone

1 ❑ Jun 1995, b&w Cover: 2.95 **NM** value: **Cover or less**
2 ❑ Aug 1995, b&w Cover: 2.95 **NM** value: **Cover or less**
📖 A Warp Sense of Reality; Evil Man **A:** Bill Halliar; Dave Ulanski **W:** Bill Halliar; Dave Ulanski
3 ❑ Oct 1995, b&w Cover: 2.95 **NM** value: **Cover or less**
4 ❑ Nov 1995, b&w Cover: 2.95 **NM** value: **Cover or less**
📖 Put on Your Party Pants, Part 1
5 ❑ Feb 1996, b&w Cover: 2.95 **NM** value: **Cover or less**
📖 Put on Your Party Pants, Part 2

MISTER PLANET Mr. Planet

1 ❑ b&w Cover: 3.00 **NM** value: **Cover or less**
2 ❑ b&w Cover: 3.00 **NM** value: **Cover or less**

MR. RISK Humor

Owners of the Standard Catalog of Comic Books can feel pretty good about the completeness of the information, when it contains titles like Mr. Risk, an almost unthinkably obscure 1950 two-shot from Ace Magazines. Only two issues saw print: #7 (#1) and #2. Hard to imagine why it didn't catch on — Mr. Risk is "a man of enormous talents, his wealth surpassed only by his courage ... He donates all his fees to worthy, recognized charities. For sheer toughness and brilliance of mind, there is none to compare with the incomparable Mr. Risk!" With unsigned art to match the caliber of writing, Mr. Risk seemed sure to go on to a third, or even a fourth issue — but it was not to be. Readers had to be content with the two hard-hitting exploits of Mr. Risk and his backups in crime-fighting: Kirk Mason the Tough Dick, and "Poke" Bancroft, Special Investigator for the District Attorney.

1 ❑ Cover: 0.10 **NM** value: **40.00**
• No. 7 in Indicia; Continued from All Romances No. 6
2 ❑ Cover: 0.10 **NM** value: **30.00**
📖 The Case of the Psychopathic Lady; The Case of the Jinxed Airline; The Forgotten Chorus Girl; The Trap (text); Seeds of Destruction • Continues in Men Against Crime #3

MISTER SIXX Imagine Nation

1 ❑ Cover: 1.95 **NM** value: **Cover or less**
A: Dennis Francis **W:** Mark Wayne Harris

For up-to-the-week CGC ratios, consult the current issue of **Comics Buyer's Guide**.

MR. T AND THE T-FORCE Now

Mr. T is cleaning up the neighborhood, forcing drug dealers out of business. While they've got guns, he's got his fists, a lot of courage, and a video camera for evidence. He's also got the T-Force: a group of youngsters he has saved from the streets who were told to shape up their lives — or else answer to Mr. T.

Mr. T is a colorful, real-life entertainer who became famous as Rocky's nearly unstoppable opponent in the movie Rocky III, and later as the resident powerhouse on television's A-Team.

Despite promotional appearances by Mr. T at comics conventions the year the series began and a cover by Neal Adams for the first issue, the series really didn't go anywhere and ended in just a few issues.

1 ❑ Jun 1993 Cover: 1.95 **NM** value: **2.50**
Circ: CapCity orders: **21,825**
• trading card **A:** Neal Adams; Continuity Studios **W:** Neal Adams; Peter Stone
1/GO❑ **NM** value: **4.00**
• Gold logo promotional edition. • gold, advance **A:** Neal Adams; Continuity Studios **W:** Neal Adams; Peter Stone
2 ❑ Sep 1993 Cover: 1.95 **NM** value: **2.00**
Circ: CapCity orders: **8,725**
• trading card
3 ❑ Oct 1993 Cover: 1.95 **NM** value: **2.00**
Circ: CapCity orders: **6,650**
• trading card
4 ❑ Nov 1993 Cover: 1.95 **NM** value: **2.00**
Circ: CapCity orders: **4,375**
• trading card
5 ❑ Dec 1993 Cover: 1.95 **NM** value: **2.00**
Circ: CapCity orders: **3,025**
• trading card
6 ❑ Jan 1994 Cover: 1.95 **NM** value: **2.00**
Circ: CapCity orders: **2,175**
• trading card
7 ❑ Feb 1994 Cover: 1.95 **NM** value: **2.00**
• trading card
8 ❑ Mar 1994 Cover: 1.95 **NM** value: **2.00**
• trading card
9 ❑ Apr 1994 Cover: 1.95 **NM** value: **2.00**
cover says Aug, indicia says Apr. • trading card
10 ❑ May 1994 Cover: 1.95 **NM** value: **2.00**
11 ❑ Jun 1994 Cover: 1.95 **NM** value: **2.00**
12 ❑ Jul 1994 Cover: 1.95 **NM** value: **2.00**

MISTER X (VOL. 1) Vortex

Mister X is an angst-ridden underground comic book which has become a cult favorite. Mister X is the architect of Radiant City. A vast metropolis, it was meant to be the perfect city, fulfilling the grand ideas of its creator, but the ideal has never came to pass. Radiant City is now slowly destroying itself from within, with its ruling class mired in decadence and its citizens immersed in perversity and opium addiction.

When building the city, a developer decided to save money by installing low-grade glass in the windows of a skyscraper. That glass eventually shattered, causing the deaths of those below. Mister X, the architect, blames himself for the carnage. Devising a drug which allows him to go completely without sleep, he becomes a private investigator. His goal: to stop the corruption of his dream city.

1 ❑ Jun 1984 Cover: 1.75 **NM** value: **4.00**
A: Gilbert Hernandez; Jaime Hernandez **W:** Gilbert Hernandez; Jaime Hernandez ★ 1st Appearance of Mister X.
2 ❑ Aug 1984 Cover: 1.75 **NM** value: **2.75**
A: Gilbert Hernandez; Jaime Hernandez **W:** Gilbert Hernandez; Jaime Hernandez
3 ❑ Cover: 1.75 **NM** value: **2.75**
A: Gilbert Hernandez; Jaime Hernandez; Mario Hernandez **W:** Gilbert Hernandez; Jaime Hernandez; Mario Hernandez
4 ❑ Cover: 1.75 **NM** value: **2.50**
5 ❑ Cover: 1.75 **NM** value: **2.50**
Circ: CapCity orders: **3,925**
6 ❑ Cover: 1.75 **NM** value: **2.50**
Circ: CapCity orders: **3,625**
📖 The Revenge OF Zamora **A:** Seth **W:** Dean Motter
7 ❑ Cover: 1.75 **NM** value: **2.50**
Circ: CapCity orders: **3,700**
8 ❑ Cover: 1.75 **NM** value: **2.50**
Circ: CapCity orders: **3,800**
📖 The Secret **A:** Seth **W:** Dean Motter
9 ❑ Cover: 1.75 **NM** value: **2.50**
Circ: CapCity orders: **3,600**
10 ❑ Oct 1986 Cover: 1.75 **NM** value: **2.50**
Circ: CapCity orders: **3,025**
C: Bill Sienkiewicz
11 ❑ Cover: 1.75 **NM** value: **2.50**
Circ: CapCity orders: **2,975**
12 ❑ Cover: 1.75 **NM** value: **2.50**
Circ: CapCity orders: **2,875**
13 ❑ Mar 1988 Cover: 1.75 **NM** value: **2.50**
Circ: CapCity orders: **2,875**

CGC-graded: Multiply prices above by **33 for 9.9 M • 16 for 9.8 NM/M • 7 for 9.6 NM+ • 5 for 9.4 NM • 2.5 for 9.2 NM- • 1.5 for 9.0 VF/NM**

14 ❑ Cover: 2.25 **NM** value: **2.50**
Circ: CapCity orders: **2,700**

MISTER X (VOL. 2) — Vortex

1 ❑ b&w Cover: 2.00 **NM** value: **3.00**
📖 Second Comic, Part 1 **A:** Shane Oakley; Brendan McCarthy(cover) **W:** Jeff Morgan

2 ❑ b&w Cover: 2.00 **NM** value: **2.50**
📖 Second Comic, Part 2 **W:** Jeff Morgan

3 ❑ b&w Cover: 2.00 **NM** value: **2.50**
📖 Second Comic, Part 3 **W:** Jeff Morgan

4 ❑ b&w Cover: 2.00 **NM** value: **2.50**
📖 Second Comic, Part 4 **W:** Jeff Morgan

5 ❑ b&w Cover: 2.00 **NM** value: **2.50**
📖 Second Comic, Part 5 **W:** Jeff Morgan

6 ❑ b&w Cover: 2.00 **NM** value: **2.25**
📖 Second Comic, Part 6 **W:** Jeff Morgan

7 ❑ b&w Cover: 2.00 **NM** value: **2.25**
W: Jeff Morgan

8 ❑ b&w Cover: 2.00 **NM** value: **2.25**
W: Jeff Morgan

9 ❑ b&w Cover: 2.00 **NM** value: **2.25**
📖 Dedicated User, Part 1 **A:** D'Israeli **W:** Jeff Morgan

10 ❑ b&w Cover: 2.00 **NM** value: **2.25**
📖 Dedicated User, Part 2 **W:** Jeff Morgan

11 ❑ b&w Cover: 2.00 **NM** value: **2.25**
📖 Dedicated User, Part 3 **W:** Jeff Morgan

12 ❑ b&w Cover: 2.00 **NM** value: **2.50**
📖 Dedicated User, Part 4 **W:** Jeff Morgan

MISTER X (VOL. 3) — Caliber

1 ❑ 1996 Cover: 2.95 **NM** value: **Cover or less**
📖 The Big Picture, Part 1 **A:** Gene Gonzales **W:** Deborah Marks

2 ❑ 1996 Cover: 2.95 **NM** value: **Cover or less**
📖 The Big Picture, Part 2 **A:** Gene Gonzales **W:** Deborah Marks

3 ❑ Sep 1996 Cover: 2.95 **NM** value: **Cover or less**
Circ: Diamd. preorders: **4,709**
📖 The Big Picture, Part 3 **A:** Gene Gonzales **W:** Deborah Marks

4 ❑ Dec 1996 Cover: 2.95 **NM** value: **Cover or less**
Circ: Diamd. preorders: **3,475**
📖 The Big Picture, Part 4 **A:** John Lucas **W:** Deborah Marks

MISTRESS OF BONDAGE — Fantagraphics / Eros

All issues are adults only.

1 ❑ b&w Cover: 2.95 **NM** value: **Cover or less**
2 ❑ b&w Cover: 2.95 **NM** value: **Cover or less**
3 ❑ b&w Cover: 2.95 **NM** value: **Cover or less**

MISTY — Marvel / Star

1 ❑ Dec 1985 Cover: 0.65 **NM** value: **1.00**
Circ: CapCity orders: **3,700**
📖 A Day To Forget **A:** Trina Robbins **W:** Trina Robbins

2 ❑ Jan 1986 Cover: 0.65 **NM** value: **1.00**
Circ: CapCity orders: **2,500**
📖 Ms. Heaventeen is Ms. Understood; The Horseless Horseman of Shady Hollow; A Bad Time **A:** Trina Robbins **W:** Trina Robbins

3 ❑ Feb 1986 Cover: 0.75 **NM** value: **1.00**
Circ: CapCity orders: **2,050**

4 ❑ Mar 1986 Cover: 0.75 **NM** value: **1.00**
Circ: CapCity orders: **1,850**

5 ❑ Apr 1986 Cover: 0.75 **NM** value: **1.00**
Circ: CapCity orders: **1,750**

6 ❑ May 1986 Cover: 0.75 **NM** value: **1.00**
Circ: CapCity orders: **2,150**

MISTY GIRL EXTREME — Fantagraphics / Eros

1 ❑ Jan 1997 Cover: 2.95 **NM** value: **Cover or less**
Circ: Diamd. preorders: **4,703**

2 ❑ Feb 1997 Cover: 2.95 **NM** value: **Cover or less**
Circ: Diamd. preorders: **4,164**

MITES — Continuüm

1 ❑ b&w Cover: 1.25 **NM** value: **1.50**
2 ❑ Cover: 1.75 **NM** value: **Cover or less**

MITZI COMICS — Timely

1 ❑ ca. 1948 Cover: 0.10 **NM** value: **150.00**
• **CGC:** 1 graded, best 2.5

MOBFIRE — DC / Vertigo

1 ❑ Dec 1994 Cover: 2.50 **NM** value: **Cover or less**
Circ: CapCity orders: **12,700**
📖 Guns And Roses **A:** Warren Pleece **W:** Gary Ushaw

2 ❑ Jan 1995 Cover: 2.50 **NM** value: **Cover or less**
Circ: CapCity orders: **8,450**
📖 Petty Magicks **A:** Warren Pleece **W:** Gary Ushaw

3 ❑ Feb 1995 Cover: 2.50 **NM** value: **Cover or less**
Circ: CapCity orders: **7,175**
📖 Blood Fellas **A:** Warren Pleece **W:** Gary Ushaw

4 ❑ Mar 1995 Cover: 2.50 **NM** value: **Cover or less**
Circ: CapCity orders: **6,150**
📖 A Walk Across Rooftops **A:** Warren Pleece **W:** Gary Ushaw

5 ❑ Apr 1995 Cover: 2.50 **NM** value: **Cover or less**
Circ: CapCity orders: **5,475**
📖 Incommunicado **A:** Warren Pleece **W:** Gary Ushaw ★ Appearance of John Constantine.

6 ❑ May 1995 Cover: 2.50 **NM** value: **Cover or less**
Circ: CapCity orders: **5,225**
📖 Terror Firma **A:** Warren Pleece **W:** Gary Ushaw

Ash 1❑ **NM** value: **0.50**
📖 Meet the Family • "Ashcan" preview given away by DC at shows **A:** Warren Pleece **W:** Gary Ushaw

MOBILE POLICE PATLABOR PART 1 — Viz

1 ❑ Jul 1997, b&w Cover: 2.95 **NM** value: **Cover or less**
Circ: Diamd. preorders: **6,919**
A: Masami Yuki **W:** Masami Yuki

2 ❑ Aug 1997, b&w Cover: 2.95 **NM** value: **Cover or less**
Circ: Diamd. preorders: **5,753**
A: Masami Yuki **W:** Masami Yuki

3 ❑ Sep 1997, b&w Cover: 2.95 **NM** value: **Cover or less**
Circ: Diamd. preorders: **5,354**
📖 Mission 1, The Right Staff (such lighthearted folk) **A:** Masami Yuki **W:** Masami Yuki

4 ❑ Oct 1997, b&w Cover: 2.95 **NM** value: **Cover or less**
Circ: Diamd. preorders: **5,188**
A: Masami Yuki **W:** Masami Yuki

5 ❑ Nov 1997, b&w Cover: 2.95 **NM** value: **Cover or less**
Circ: Diamd. preorders: **4,994**
A: Masami Yuki **W:** Masami Yuki

6 ❑ Dec 1997, b&w Cover: 2.95 **NM** value: **Cover or less**
Circ: Diamd. preorders: **4,721**
A: Masami Yuki **W:** Masami Yuki

Bk 1❑ Cover: 15.95 **NM** value: **Cover or less**
• collects Mobile Police Patlabor Part One **A:** Masami Yuki **W:** Masami Yuki

MOBILE POLICE PATLABOR PART 2 — Viz

1 ❑ Jan 1998, b&w Cover: 2.95 **NM** value: **Cover or less**
Circ: Diamd. preorders: **4,895**
A: Masami Yuki **W:** Masami Yuki

2 ❑ Feb 1998, b&w Cover: 2.95 **NM** value: **Cover or less**
Circ: Diamd. preorders: **4,387**
A: Masami Yuki **W:** Masami Yuki

3 ❑ Mar 1998, b&w Cover: 2.95 **NM** value: **Cover or less**
Circ: Diamd. preorders: **4,224**
A: Masami Yuki **W:** Masami Yuki

4 ❑ Apr 1998, b&w Cover: 2.95 **NM** value: **Cover or less**
Circ: Diamd. preorders: **4,219**
A: Masami Yuki **W:** Masami Yuki

5 ❑ May 1998, b&w Cover: 2.95 **NM** value: **Cover or less**
Circ: Diamd. preorders: **3,864**
A: Masami Yuki **W:** Masami Yuki

6 ❑ Jun 1998, b&w Cover: 2.95 **NM** value: **Cover or less**
Circ: Diamd. preorders: **3,856**
A: Masami Yuki **W:** Masami Yuki

Bk 1❑ Nov 1998 Cover: 15.95 **NM** value: **Cover or less**
• collects Part Two

MOBILE SUIT GUNDAM 0079 — Viz

1 ❑ Mar 1999 Cover: 2.95 **NM** value: **Cover or less**
Circ: Diamd. preorders: **6,892**

2 ❑ Apr 1999 Cover: 2.95 **NM** value: **Cover or less**
Circ: Diamd. preorders: **5,297**

3 ❑ May 1999 Cover: 2.95 **NM** value: **Cover or less**
Circ: Diamd. preorders: **4,948**

4 ❑ Jun 1999 Cover: 2.95 **NM** value: **Cover or less**
Circ: Diamd. preorders: **4,427**

5 ❑ Jul 1999 Cover: 2.95 **NM** value: **Cover or less**
Circ: Diamd. preorders: **4,166**

6 ❑ Aug 1999 Cover: 2.95 **NM** value: **Cover or less**
Circ: Diamd. preorders: **3,837**

7 ❑ Sep 1999 Cover: 2.95 **NM** value: **Cover or less**
Circ: Diamd. preorders: **3,646**

8 ❑ Oct 1999 Cover: 2.95 **NM** value: **Cover or less**
Circ: Diamd. preorders: **3,506**

MOBILE SUIT GUNDAM 0083 — Viz

1 ❑ Nov 1999 Cover: 2.95 **NM** value: **4.95**
Circ: CapCity orders: **4,875** Diamd. preorders: **3,464**

2 ❑ Dec 1999 Cover: 2.95 **NM** value: **4.95**
Circ: CapCity orders: **3,200** Diamd. preorders: **3,150**

3 ❑ Jan 2000 Cover: 2.95 **NM** value: **4.95**
Circ: CapCity orders: **3,125** Diamd. preorders: **3,074**

4 ❑ Feb 2000 Cover: 2.95 **NM** value: **4.95**
Circ: CapCity orders: **3,025** Diamd. preorders: **2,875**

5 ❑ Mar 2000 Cover: 2.95 **NM** value: **4.95**
Circ: CapCity orders: **3,075** Diamd. preorders: **2,860**

6 ❑ Apr 2000 Cover: 2.95 **NM** value: **4.95**
Circ: CapCity orders: **3,150**

7 ❑ May 2000 Cover: 2.95 **NM** value: **4.95**
Circ: CapCity orders: **3,350**

8 ❑ Jun 2000 Cover: 2.95 **NM** value: **4.95**
Circ: CapCity orders: **3,450**

9 ❑ Jul 2000 Cover: 2.95 **NM** value: **4.95**
Circ: CapCity orders: **3,425**

10 ❑ Aug 2000 Cover: 2.95 **NM** value: **4.95**
Circ: CapCity orders: **3,325**

11 ❑ Sep 2000 Cover: 2.95 **NM** value: **4.95**
Circ: CapCity orders: **3,250**

12 ❑ Oct 2000 Cover: 2.95 **NM** value: **4.95**
Circ: CapCity orders: **3,175**
📖 La Vie en Rose

13 ❑ Nov 2000 Cover: 2.95 **NM** value: **4.95**
Circ: CapCity orders: **2,925**

MOBILE SUIT GUNDAM WING: GROUND ZERO — Viz

1 ❑ ca. 2000 Cover: 2.95 **NM** value: **Cover or less**
Circ: Diamd. preorders: **10,761**
A: Reku Fuyunagi **W:** Reku Fuyunagi

MOBSTERS AND MONSTERS MAGAZINE — Original Syndicate

1 ❑ Jul 1995 Cover: 3.00 **NM** value: **Cover or less**
📖 The Nine Lives of El Gato, Crime Mangler **A:** Michael Auschenker **W:** Michael Auschenker

MOBY DUCK — Gold Key / Whitman

1 ❑ Oct 1967 Cover: 0.12 **NM** value: **12.00**
2 ❑ Jun 1968 Cover: 0.12 **NM** value: **6.00**
3 ❑ Sep 1968 Cover: 0.15 **NM** value: **5.00**
4 ❑ Dec 1968 Cover: 0.15 **NM** value: **5.00**
5 ❑ Mar 1969 Cover: 0.15 **NM** value: **5.00**
6 ❑ 1969 Cover: 0.15 **NM** value: **3.50**
7 ❑ Oct 1969 Cover: 0.15 **NM** value: **3.50**
8 ❑ Jan 1970 Cover: 0.15 **NM** value: **3.50**
9 ❑ Apr 1970 Cover: 0.15 **NM** value: **3.50**
10 ❑ Jul 1970 Cover: 0.15 **NM** value: **3.50**
11 ❑ Oct 1970 Cover: 0.15 **NM** value: **3.00**
12 ❑ Jan 1974 Cover: 0.20 **NM** value: **3.00**
13 ❑ Apr 1974 Cover: 0.20 **NM** value: **3.00**
14 ❑ Jul 1974 Cover: 0.20 **NM** value: **3.00**
15 ❑ Oct 1974 Cover: 0.25 **NM** value: **3.00**
16 ❑ 1975 Cover: 0.25 **NM** value: **3.00**
17 ❑ 1975 Cover: 0.25 **NM** value: **3.00**
18 ❑ 1975 Cover: 0.25 **NM** value: **3.00**
19 ❑ Aug 1975 Cover: 0.25 **NM** value: **3.00**
20 ❑ Oct 1975 Cover: 0.25 **NM** value: **3.00**
21 ❑ Jan 1976 Cover: 0.25 **NM** value: **2.50**
22 ❑ Apr 1976 Cover: 0.25 **NM** value: **2.50**
23 ❑ Jul 1976 Cover: 0.25 **NM** value: **2.50**
24 ❑ Oct 1976 Cover: 0.30 **NM** value: **2.50**
25 ❑ Jan 1977, four-color Cover: 0.30 **NM** value: **2.50**
📖 Moby's Mysterious Mission; Typhoon Zolinda's Revenge; Undersea Swindle
26 ❑ Apr 1977 Cover: 0.30 **NM** value: **2.50**
27 ❑ Jul 1977 Cover: 0.30 **NM** value: **2.50**
28 ❑ Oct 1977 Cover: 0.30 **NM** value: **2.50**
29 ❑ Jan 1978 Cover: 0.35 **NM** value: **2.50**
30 ❑ Mar 1978 Cover: 0.35 **NM** value: **2.50**

MOD — Kitchen Sink

1 ❑ **NM** value: **4.00**
A: Bob Burden **C:** Bob Burden **W:** Bob Burden ★ 1st Appearance of Adventures in Limbo.

MODEL BY DAY — Rip Off

All issues are adults only.

1 ❑ Jul 1990, b&w Cover: 2.50 **NM** value: **Cover or less**
2 ❑ Oct 1990, b&w Cover: 2.50 **NM** value: **Cover or less**
Bk 1❑ Jul 1994 Cover: 5.95 **NM** value: **Cover or less**
No issue number. • prestige format. • reprints the series with new pin-ups by Joseph Michael Linsner and Dark One

MODELING WITH MILLIE — Marvel

21 ❑ Feb 1963 Cover: 0.12 **NM** value: **60.00**
22 ❑ Apr 1963 Cover: 0.12 **NM** value: **45.00**
• Has 1962 Statement, covering issues from Life With Millie; avg total paid circ 143,476
23 ❑ Jun 1963 Cover: 0.12 **NM** value: **45.00**
24 ❑ Aug 1963 Cover: 0.12 **NM** value: **45.00**
25 ❑ 1963 Cover: 0.12 **NM** value: **45.00**
26 ❑ 1963 Cover: 0.12 **NM** value: **45.00**
27 ❑ Nov 1963 Cover: 0.12 **NM** value: **45.00**
28 ❑ Cover: 0.12 **NM** value: **45.00**
29 ❑ 1964 Cover: 0.12 **NM** value: **45.00**
30 ❑ 1964 Cover: 0.12 **NM** value: **45.00**
31 ❑ 1964 Cover: 0.12 **NM** value: **35.00**
32 ❑ Jul 1964 Cover: 0.12 **NM** value: **35.00**
33 ❑ 1964 Cover: 0.12 **NM** value: **35.00**
34 ❑ 1964 Cover: 0.12 **NM** value: **35.00**
35 ❑ 1964 Cover: 0.12 **NM** value: **35.00**
36 ❑ Dec 1964 Cover: 0.12 **NM** value: **35.00**
37 ❑ Feb 1965 Cover: 0.12 **NM** value: **35.00**
38 ❑ Apr 1965 Cover: 0.12 **NM** value: **35.00**
39 ❑ Jun 1965 Cover: 0.12 **NM** value: **35.00**
40 ❑ 1965 Cover: 0.12 **NM** value: **35.00**
41 ❑ 1965 Cover: 0.12 **NM** value: **28.00**
42 ❑ Oct 1965 Cover: 0.12 **NM** value: **28.00**
43 ❑ Nov 1965 Cover: 0.12 **NM** value: **28.00**
44 ❑ Cover: 0.12 **NM** value: **28.00**
45 ❑ Feb 1966 Cover: 0.12 **NM** value: **28.00**
46 ❑ Apr 1966 Cover: 0.12 **NM** value: **28.00**
47 ❑ Jun 1966 Cover: 0.12 **NM** value: **28.00**
48 ❑ Aug 1966 Cover: 0.12 **NM** value: **28.00**
49 ❑ Sep 1966 Cover: 0.12 **NM** value: **28.00**
50 ❑ Oct 1966 Cover: 0.12 **NM** value: **28.00**
51 ❑ Nov 1966 Cover: 0.12 **NM** value: **28.00**
52 ❑ Dec 1966 Cover: 0.12 **NM** value: **28.00**
53 ❑ Apr 1967 Cover: 0.12 **NM** value: **28.00**
54 ❑ Cover: 0.12 **NM** value: **28.00**

MODERN COMICS — Quality

The title carried the identification "Formerly Military Comics" on its logo for more than two years, but from start (Military Comics #1, Aug 41) to finish (Modern Comics #102, Oct 50) Blackhawk was the focal character. The Blackhawk team (with Blackhawk and his team members Andre, Olaf, Chuck, Hendrickson, Stanislaus, and Chop-Chop) On the other hand, sometimes the focus is on the flying ace and one or another dangerous damsel: Madame Butterfly ("the deadliest of the species"), Tigra ("beautiful and heartless"), Arda Thorn ("gorgeous"), and so on. Much art is outstanding, and Torchy appears in some non-Blackhawk stories. — Maggie

44 ❑ Nov 1945 Cover: 0.10 **NM** value: **450.00**
45 ❑ Jan 1945 Cover: 0.10 **NM** value: **350.00**
46 ❑ Feb 1946 Cover: 0.10 **NM** value: **350.00**
47 ❑ Mar 1946 Cover: 0.10 **NM** value: **350.00**
48 ❑ Apr 1946 Cover: 0.10 **NM** value: **350.00**
49 ❑ May 1946 Cover: 0.10 **NM** value: **350.00**
50 ❑ Jun 1946 Cover: 0.10 **NM** value: **350.00**

Other grades: Multiply prices above by **1.5 for Mint • 2/3 for Very Fine • 1/3 for Fine • 1/5 for Very Good • 1/8 for Good**

51 ❑ Jul 1946 Cover: 0.10 **NM** value: **350.00**
52 ❑ Aug 1946 Cover: 0.10 **NM** value: **350.00**
53 ❑ Sep 1946 Cover: 0.10 **NM** value: **350.00**
54 ❑ Oct 1946 Cover: 0.10 **NM** value: **250.00**
55 ❑ Nov 1946 Cover: 0.10 **NM** value: **250.00**
56 ❑ Dec 1946 Cover: 0.10 **NM** value: **250.00**
57 ❑ Jan 1947 Cover: 0.10 **NM** value: **250.00**
58 ❑ Feb 1947 Cover: 0.10 **NM** value: **200.00**
59 ❑ Mar 1947 Cover: 0.10 **NM** value: **200.00**
60 ❑ Apr 1947 Cover: 0.10 **NM** value: **200.00**
61 ❑ May 1947 Cover: 0.10 **NM** value: **200.00**
62 ❑ Jun 1947 Cover: 0.10 **NM** value: **200.00**
63 ❑ Jul 1947 Cover: 0.10 **NM** value: **200.00**
64 ❑ Aug 1947 Cover: 0.10 **NM** value: **200.00**
65 ❑ Sep 1947 Cover: 0.10 **NM** value: **200.00**
66 ❑ Oct 1947 Cover: 0.10 **NM** value: **200.00**
67 ❑ Nov 1947 Cover: 0.10 **NM** value: **200.00**
68 ❑ Dec 1947 Cover: 0.10 **NM** value: **200.00**
69 ❑ Jan 1948 Cover: 0.10 **NM** value: **200.00**
70 ❑ Feb 1948 Cover: 0.10 **NM** value: **200.00**
71 ❑ Mar 1948 Cover: 0.10 **NM** value: **200.00**
72 ❑ Apr 1948 Cover: 0.10 **NM** value: **200.00**
73 ❑ May 1948 Cover: 0.10 **NM** value: **200.00**
74 ❑ Jun 1948 Cover: 0.10 **NM** value: **200.00**
75 ❑ Jul 1948 Cover: 0.10 **NM** value: **200.00**
76 ❑ Aug 1948 Cover: 0.10 **NM** value: **200.00**
77 ❑ Sep 1948 Cover: 0.10 **NM** value: **200.00**
78 ❑ Oct 1948 Cover: 0.10 **NM** value: **200.00**
79 ❑ Nov 1948 Cover: 0.10 **NM** value: **200.00**
80 ❑ Dec 1948 Cover: 0.10 **NM** value: **200.00**
81 ❑ Jan 1949 Cover: 0.10 **NM** value: **200.00**
82 ❑ Feb 1949 Cover: 0.10 **NM** value: **200.00**
83 ❑ Mar 1949 Cover: 0.10 **NM** value: **200.00**
84 ❑ Apr 1949 Cover: 0.10 **NM** value: **200.00**
85 ❑ May 1949 Cover: 0.10 **NM** value: **200.00**
86 ❑ Jun 1949 Cover: 0.10 **NM** value: **200.00**
87 ❑ Jul 1949 Cover: 0.10 **NM** value: **200.00**
88 ❑ Aug 1949 Cover: 0.10 **NM** value: **200.00**
89 ❑ Sep 1949 Cover: 0.10 **NM** value: **200.00**
90 ❑ Oct 1949 Cover: 0.10 **NM** value: **200.00**
91 ❑ Nov 1949 Cover: 0.10 **NM** value: **200.00**
92 ❑ Dec 1949 Cover: 0.10 **NM** value: **200.00**
93 ❑ Jan 1950 Cover: 0.10 **NM** value: **200.00**
94 ❑ Feb 1950 Cover: 0.10 **NM** value: **200.00**
95 ❑ Mar 1950 Cover: 0.10 **NM** value: **200.00**
96 ❑ Apr 1950 Cover: 0.10 **NM** value: **200.00**
97 ❑ May 1950 Cover: 0.10 **NM** value: **200.00**
98 ❑ Jun 1950 Cover: 0.10 **NM** value: **200.00**
99 ❑ Jul 1950 Cover: 0.10 **NM** value: **200.00**
100 ❑ Aug 1950 Cover: 0.10 **NM** value: **200.00**
101 ❑ Sep 1950 Cover: 0.10 **NM** value: **200.00**
102 ❑ Oct 1950 Cover: 0.10 **NM** value: **200.00**

MODERN GRIMM — Symptom
1 ❑ Dec 1996, b&w Cover: 2.75 **NM** value: **Cover or less**

MODERN LOVE — E.C.
Carrying the cover copy "Real love stories!" the series was an attempt to diversify the E.C. line of comics just before it changed its focus to horror, science fiction, and fantasy. The last issue carried the humorous eight-pager "The Love Story to End All Love Stories" — written and drawn by Al Feldstein as a commentary on the comics industry and with William Gaines and Feldstein as characters. — Maggie

1 ❑ Jun 1949 Cover: 0.10 **NM** value: **450.00**
2 ❑ Aug 1949 Cover: 0.10 **NM** value: **300.00**
3 ❑ Oct 1949 Cover: 0.10 **NM** value: **300.00**
4 ❑ Dec 1949 Cover: 0.10 **NM** value: **400.00**
5 ❑ Feb 1950 Cover: 0.10 **NM** value: **400.00**
6 ❑ Apr 1950 Cover: 0.10 **NM** value: **400.00**
7 ❑ Jun 1950 Cover: 0.10 **NM** value: **300.00**
8 ❑ Aug 1950 Cover: 0.10 **NM** value: **300.00**

MODERN PULP — Special Studio
1 ❑ b&w Cover: 2.75 **NM** value: **Cover or less**
📖 Stealth **A:** Joe Zabel **W:** Joe Zabel

MODERN ROMANS — Fantagraphics / Eros
All issues are adults only.
1 ❑ b&w Cover: 2.25 **NM** value: **Cover or less**
2 ❑ b&w Cover: 2.25 **NM** value: **Cover or less**
3 ❑ b&w Cover: 2.25 **NM** value: **Cover or less**

MODEST PROPOSAL, A — Tome Press
1 ❑ b&w Cover: 2.50 **NM** value: **Cover or less**
2 ❑ b&w Cover: 2.50 **NM** value: **Cover or less**

MODESTY BLAISE — DC
1 ❑ Cover: 19.95 **NM** value: **Cover or less**

MODNIKS, THE — Gold Key
1 ❑ ca. 1967 Cover: 0.15 **NM** value: **8.00**
2 ❑ Cover: 0.15 **NM** value: **4.00**
📖 What's Happening?; Noel Talent: The Most Unkinest Cut; Mini Revolt

Do you have changes or corrections for the **Standard Catalog**? Send your original research to us at
allcomics@krause.com

MOD SQUAD, THE — Dell
The social and political upheavals of the late 1960s were threatening to a lot of people. One way that the media dealt with the threat was to package the "revolution" in a way that assured regular folks that hippies were just like them, only in stranger clothing. As a result, there's the Mod Squad, which was broadcast from 1968 to 1973, featuring a groovy team of three young undercover cops who speak in a television writer's idea of "with-it" slang; each member of the team had had problems with the law at some point. Dell, which seemingly did comic-book adaptations of every television show with more than three viewers during the 1960s, supplied the obligatory four-color artifact.

1 ❑ Jan 1969 Cover: 0.15 **NM** value: **18.00**
• **CGC:** 1 graded, best 7.0
2 ❑ 1969 Cover: 0.15 **NM** value: **10.00**
3 ❑ Oct 1969 Cover: 0.15 **NM** value: **10.00**
📖 Shadow in the Water; Take a Dive!
4 ❑ 1970 Cover: 0.15 **NM** value: **10.00**
5 ❑ 1970 Cover: 0.15 **NM** value: **10.00**
6 ❑ Jul 1970 Cover: 0.15 **NM** value: **8.00**
7 ❑ Jan 1971 Cover: 0.15 **NM** value: **8.00**
8 ❑ Apr 1971 Cover: 0.15 **NM** value: **8.00**
final issue.

MOD WHEELS — Gold Key
This "hip" title from Gold Key is most evocative of the Hot Wheels animated series (1969-1971) and DC comic book (1970-71). Sporting such 1970s accouterments as mutton-chop sideburns and bell-bottom slacks, Wheels and his racing team pals — Lump, Cube, 'Scot, and Bit — take on such evils as unethical drivers and rampaging biker gangs. The dialogue is heavy with the perceived teen slang of the day, and the art is vaguely similar to the "heavy" 1970s style Mike Sekowsky was using on DC's Wonder Woman and Supergirl at the time.

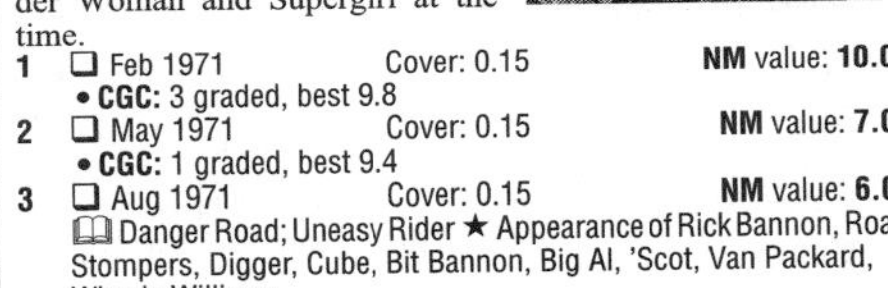

1 ❑ Feb 1971 Cover: 0.15 **NM** value: **10.00**
• **CGC:** 3 graded, best 9.8
2 ❑ May 1971 Cover: 0.15 **NM** value: **7.00**
• **CGC:** 1 graded, best 9.4
3 ❑ Aug 1971 Cover: 0.15 **NM** value: **6.00**
📖 Danger Road; Uneasy Rider ★ Appearance of Rick Bannon, Road Stompers, Digger, Cube, Bit Bannon, Big Al, 'Scot, Van Packard, Wheels Williams.
4 ❑ Nov 1971 Cover: 0.15 **NM** value: **5.00**
5 ❑ Feb 1972 Cover: 0.15 **NM** value: **5.00**
6 ❑ Jun 1972 Cover: 0.15 **NM** value: **5.00**
7 ❑ Jan 1973 Cover: 0.15 **NM** value: **5.00**
8 ❑ Apr 1973 Cover: 0.15 **NM** value: **5.00**
9 ❑ Jul 1973 Cover: 0.20 **NM** value: **5.00**
10 ❑ Oct 1973 Cover: 0.20 **NM** value: **5.00**
11 ❑ Jan 1974 Cover: 0.20 **NM** value: **4.00**
12 ❑ Apr 1974 Cover: 0.20 **NM** value: **4.00**
13 ❑ Jul 1974 Cover: 0.20 **NM** value: **4.00**
14 ❑ Oct 1974 Cover: 0.25 **NM** value: **4.00**
15 ❑ Jan 1975 Cover: 0.25 **NM** value: **4.00**
16 ❑ Apr 1975 Cover: 0.25 **NM** value: **4.00**
17 ❑ Jul 1975 Cover: 0.25 **NM** value: **4.00**
18 ❑ Oct 1976 Cover: 0.25 **NM** value: **4.00**
19 ❑ Jan 1976 Cover: 0.25 **NM** value: **4.00**

MOE & SHMOE COMICS — O.S.
1 ❑ ca. 1948 Cover: 0.10 **NM** value: **50.00**
2 ❑ ca. 1948 Cover: 0.10 **NM** value: **30.00**

MOEBIUS — Marvel / Epic
Bk 1❑ Cover: 9.95 **NM** value: **Cover or less**
Circ: CapCity orders: **2,400**
• Upon a Star **A:** Moebius
Bk 1-2❑ Cover: 9.95 **NM** value: **Cover or less**
Bk 2❑ Cover: 9.95 **NM** value: **Cover or less**
Circ: CapCity orders: **2,850**
• Arzach **A:** Moebius
Bk 3❑ Cover: 12.95 **NM** value: **Cover or less**
Circ: CapCity orders: **3,050**
• Airtight Garage **A:** Moebius
Bk 4❑ Cover: 9.95 **NM** value: **Cover or less**
Circ: CapCity orders: **3,500**
• The Long Tomorrow **A:** Moebius
Bk 5❑ Cover: 9.95 **NM** value: **Cover or less**
Circ: CapCity orders: **3,075**
• The Gardens of Aedena **A:** Moebius
Bk 6❑ Cover: 9.95 **NM** value: **Cover or less**
Circ: CapCity orders: **2,850**
• PhAragonTsia; Pharagonesia **A:** Moebius
Bk 7❑ Cover: 12.95 **NM** value: **Cover or less**
Circ: CapCity orders: **2,450**
• The Goddess **A:** Moebius

MOEBIUS ARZACH — Dark Horse
Bk 1❑ Feb 1996 Cover: 6.95 **NM** value: **Cover or less**
No issue number. • prestige format. • no publication date in indicia; color and b&w; collection of stories **A:** Moebius **W:** Moebius; Jean-Marc Lofficier; Randy Lofficier

MOEBIUS COMICS — Caliber
1 ❑ May 1996 Cover: 2.95 **NM** value: **Cover or less**
📖 The Man from Ciguri; Internal Transfer; Arzaq **A:** Moebius; William Stout **W:** Moebius
2 ❑ Jul 1996 Cover: 2.95 **NM** value: **Cover or less**
A: Moebius **W:** Moebius
3 ❑ Sep 1996 Cover: 2.95 **NM** value: **Cover or less**
Circ: Diamd. preorders: **7,171**
📖 The Arzach; City on Water; Internal Transfer **A:** Moebius **W:** Moebius
4 ❑ Nov 1996 Cover: 2.95 **NM** value: **Cover or less**
Circ: Diamd. preorders: **6,072**
A: Moebius **W:** Moebius
5 ❑ Jan 1997 Cover: 2.95 **NM** value: **Cover or less**
Circ: Diamd. preorders: **4,899**
A: Moebius **W:** Moebius
6 ❑ Mar 1997 Cover: 2.95 **NM** value: **Cover or less**
Circ: Diamd. preorders: **4,439**
A: Moebius **W:** Moebius

MOEBIUS (DARK HORSE) — Dark Horse
Bk 1❑ Cover: 12.95 **NM** value: **Cover or less**
• Horny Goof **A:** Moebius **W:** Moebius

MOEBIUS: EXOTICS — Dark Horse
1 ❑ Cover: 6.95 **NM** value: **Cover or less**
No issue number. One-shot. • prestige format. **A:** Moebius **W:** Moebius

MOEBIUS: H.P.'S ROCK CITY — Dark Horse
1 ❑ Cover: 7.95 **NM** value: **Cover or less**
No issue number. One-shot. • smaller than a normal comic book; squarebound **A:** Moebius **W:** Moebius

MOEBIUS: MADWOMAN OF THE SACRED HEART — Dark Horse
1 ❑ Cover: 12.95 **NM** value: **Cover or less**
A: Moebius **W:** Moebius

MOEBIUS: THE MAN FROM THE CIGURI — Dark Horse
1 ❑ b&w and color Cover: 7.95 **NM** value: **Cover or less**
No issue number. One-shot. • smaller than a normal comic book; squarebound **A:** Moebius **W:** Moebius

MOGOBI DESERT RATS — Studio 91
1 ❑ Jan 1991 Cover: 2.25 **NM** value: **Cover or less**
📖 Waste of the World **A:** Bryant Arnold **W:** Andrew Schaefer

MOJO ACTION COMPANION UNIT, THE — Exclaim
1 ❑ Spr 1997, b&w Cover: 2.75 **NM** value: **Cover or less**

MOJO MECHANICS — Syndicate Publishing
1 ❑ b&w Cover: 2.95 **NM** value: **Cover or less**
2 ❑ Cover: 2.95 **NM** value: **Cover or less**
A: Matt Pasteris **W:** Tait Bergstrom

MOLLY O' DAY — Avon
1 ❑ ca. 1945 Cover: 0.10 **NM** value: **300.00**

MOMENT OF SILENCE — Marvel
1 ❑ ca. 2002 Cover: 3.00 **NM** value: **3.50**
Circ: Diamd. preorders: **111,926**

MONARCHY, THE — WildStorm
1 ❑ Apr 2001 Cover: 2.50 **NM** value: **Cover or less**
Circ: Diamd. preorders: **35,732** • **CGC:** 7 graded, best 9.9
📖 Red Shift **A:** John McCrea **W:** Doselle Young
2 ❑ May 2001 Cover: 2.50 **NM** value: **Cover or less**
Circ: Diamd. preorders: **30,953**
3 ❑ Jun 2001 Cover: 2.50 **NM** value: **Cover or less**
Circ: Diamd. preorders: **30,277**
4 ❑ Jul 2001 Cover: 2.50 **NM** value: **Cover or less**
Circ: Diamd. preorders: **28,010**
5 ❑ Aug 2001 Cover: 2.50 **NM** value: **Cover or less**
Circ: Diamd. preorders: **25,541**

MONDO 3-D — 3-D Zone
1 ❑ Cover: 3.95 **NM** value: **Cover or less**
No issue number.

MONDO BONDO — LCD
1 ❑ Cover: 2.95 **NM** value: **Cover or less**

MONEY TALKS — Slave Labor
1 ❑ Jun 1996 Cover: 3.50 **NM** value: **Cover or less**
📖 Paying the Piper **A:** Shane Simmons **W:** Shane Simmons
2 ❑ Aug 1996 Cover: 2.95 **NM** value: **Cover or less**
📖 Passing the Buck **A:** Shane Simmons **W:** Shane Simmons
3 ❑ Oct 1996 Cover: 2.95 **NM** value: **Cover or less**
📖 Money to Burn **A:** Shane Simmons **W:** Shane Simmons
4 ❑ Dec 1996 Cover: 2.95 **NM** value: **Cover or less**
📖 Heads or Tails **A:** Shane Simmons **W:** Shane Simmons
5 ❑ Feb 1997 Cover: 2.95 **NM** value: **Cover or less**
📖 Dollars and Sense **A:** Shane Simmons **W:** Shane Simmons

MONGREL — Northstar
1/A ❑ Dec 1994 Cover: 3.95 **NM** value: **Cover or less**
📖 Junk Yard Dog **A:** Andrew Kudelka **W:** Ed Dunphy
2 ❑ Cover: 3.95 **NM** value: **Cover or less**
A: Andrew Kudelka **W:** Ed Dunphy

CGC-graded: Multiply prices above by **33 for 9.9 M** • **16 for 9.8 NM/M** • **7 for 9.6 NM+** • **5 for 9.4 NM** • **2.5 for 9.2 NM-** • **1.5 for 9.0 VF/NM**

3 ❑ Cover: 3.95 **NM** value: **Cover or less**
A: Andrew Kudelka **W:** Ed Dunphy

MONICA'S STORY — Alternative

1 ❑ Feb 1999, b&w Cover: 2.95 **NM** value: **3.50**
Circ: Diamd. preorders: **2,359**
No issue number.

MONKEES, THE — Gold Key

A music group created for the comedy TV series, The Monkees (David Jones, Peter Tork, Micky Dolenz, and Mike Nesmith) played in prime time from 1966 to 1968. The fast-paced half-hour stories featured musical numbers and a plot of sorts enhanced by special effects.

Of course, the comic book could provide neither performances of such numbers as "I'm a Believer" nor the feel of the show. Nevertheless, it continued publication for a time after new shows had ended. Now, the "Monkees" name and logo are owned by revival specialist Rhino, and lots of Monkees-associated material is being collected as nostalgia. — Maggie

1 ❑ Mar 1967 Cover: 0.12 **NM** value: **35.00**
• **CGC:** 5 graded, best 8.5
• based on TV series
2 ❑ May 1967 Cover: 0.12 **NM** value: **25.00**
• **CGC:** 3 graded, best 9.4
3 ❑ Jul 1967 Cover: 0.12 **NM** value: **20.00**
• **CGC:** 2 graded, best 9.4
4 ❑ Sep 1967 Cover: 0.12 **NM** value: **16.00**
• **CGC:** 2 graded, best 9.2
5 ❑ Oct 1967 Cover: 0.12 **NM** value: **16.00**
• **CGC:** 1 graded, best 9.4
6 ❑ Nov 1967 Cover: 0.12 **NM** value: **14.00**
• **CGC:** 1 graded, best 9.2
7 ❑ Dec 1967 Cover: 0.12 **NM** value: **14.00**
• **CGC:** 2 graded, best 9.2
8 ❑ Jan 1968 Cover: 0.12 **NM** value: **14.00**
• **CGC:** 1 graded, best 9.2
9 ❑ Feb 1968 Cover: 0.12 **NM** value: **14.00**
• **CGC:** 1 graded, best 9.4
10 ❑ Mar 1968 Cover: 0.12 **NM** value: **14.00**
• **CGC:** 1 graded, best 9.0
11 ❑ May 1968 Cover: 0.12 **NM** value: **10.00**
• **CGC:** 1 graded, best 8.0
12 ❑ Jun 1968 Cover: 0.12 **NM** value: **10.00**
• **CGC:** 1 graded, best 9.2
13 ❑ Jul 1968 Cover: 0.12 **NM** value: **10.00**
14 ❑ Aug 1968 Cover: 0.12 **NM** value: **10.00**
15 ❑ Sep 1968 Cover: 0.12 **NM** value: **10.00**
16 ❑ 1969 Cover: 0.15 **NM** value: **10.00**
17 ❑ 1969 Cover: 0.15 **NM** value: **10.00**

MONKEY & THE BEAR — Avon

1 ❑ Sep 1953 Cover: 0.10 **NM** value: **50.00**
2 ❑ Nov 1953 Cover: 0.10 **NM** value: **30.00**
3 ❑ Jan 1954 Cover: 0.10 **NM** value: **30.00**

MONKEY BUSINESS — Parody

1 ❑ b&w Cover: 2.50 **NM** value: **Cover or less**
2 ❑ Cover: 2.50 **NM** value: **Cover or less**
📖 Rank & Stinky; Mother Goose & Grimm; In The Bleachers; Ernie; Bizarro; It's A Wonderful Life 2 • Ren & Stimpy parody **A:** Bill Maus; John Stinsman; Mike Peters; Bud Grace; Dan Piraro; Nat Gertler; Steve Moore **W:** Bill Maus; John Stinsman; Mike Peters; Bud Grace; Dan Piraro; Nat Gertler; Steve Moore

MONKEYMAN AND O'BRIEN — Dark Horse / Legend

1 ❑ Jul 1996 Cover: 2.95 **NM** value: **3.50**
📖 Attack Of The Shrewmanoid **A:** Arthur Adams **W:** Arthur Adams ★ Versus Shrewmanoid.
2 ❑ Aug 1996 Cover: 2.95 **NM** value: **3.00**
📖 The Invasion Of The Froglodytes! **A:** Arthur Adams **W:** Arthur Adams ★ Versus Froglodytes.
3 ❑ Sep 1996 Cover: 2.95 **NM** value: **Cover or less**
Circ: Diamd. preorders: **29,083**
📖 Into The Terminus final issue. **A:** Arthur Adams **W:** Arthur Adams ★ Appearance of Shrewmanoid. ★ Versus Quash.
Bk 1❑ Jun 1997 Cover: 16.95 **NM** value: **Cover or less**
• collects mini-series and special
SE 1❑ Feb 1996 Cover: 2.95 **NM** value: **Cover or less**
Circ: Diamd. preorders: **5,314**
📖 Who are Monkeyman and O'Brien? **A:** Arthur Adams **W:** Arthur Adams ★ Origin of Monkeyman and O'Brien.

MONKEYSHINES — Ace

1 ❑ Sum 1944 Cover: 0.10 **NM** value: **75.00**
• Marmaduke Monk; Tuffy Bear; Slick Chick
2 ❑ Aut 1944 Cover: 0.10 **NM** value: **40.00**
3 ❑ Win 1944 Cover: 0.10 **NM** value: **30.00**
4 ❑ Spr 1945 Cover: 0.10 **NM** value: **30.00**
5 ❑ Sum 1945 Cover: 0.10 **NM** value: **30.00**
6 ❑ Aut 1945 Cover: 0.10 **NM** value: **30.00**
7 ❑ Win 1945 Cover: 0.10 **NM** value: **30.00**
8 ❑ Spr 1946 Cover: 0.10 **NM** value: **30.00**
9 ❑ Sum 1946 Cover: 0.10 **NM** value: **30.00**
10 ❑ Aut 1946 Cover: 0.10 **NM** value: **30.00**
11 ❑ Win 1946 Cover: 0.10 **NM** value: **30.00**
12 ❑ ca. 1947 Cover: 0.10 **NM** value: **25.00**
13 ❑ Feb 1947 Cover: 0.10 **NM** value: **25.00**
14 ❑ ca. 1947 Cover: 0.10 **NM** value: **25.00**
15 ❑ ca. 1947 Cover: 0.10 **NM** value: **25.00**
16 ❑ ca. 1948 Cover: 0.10 **NM** value: **25.00**
17 ❑ ca. 1948 Cover: 0.10 **NM** value: **25.00**
18 ❑ ca. 1948 Cover: 0.10 **NM** value: **25.00**
19 ❑ Mar 1948 Cover: 0.10 **NM** value: **25.00**
20 ❑ ca. 1948 Cover: 0.10 **NM** value: **25.00**
21 ❑ ca. 1948 Cover: 0.10 **NM** value: **25.00**
22 ❑ ca. 1948 Cover: 0.10 **NM** value: **25.00**
23 ❑ ca. 1949 Cover: 0.10 **NM** value: **25.00**

MONNGA — Daikaiju

1 ❑ Aug 1995 Cover: 3.95 **NM** value: **Cover or less**
📖 Titanic Omega; Leviathan's Crossing; Dimension Fighter; Stray Dogs at the Zoo **A:** Chris Scalf; Hikari Takeda; Jeff Zornow; Naoko Takeda; Wil Glass **W:** Hikari Takeda; Jeff Zornow; Naoko Takeda; Wil Glass; J.D. Lee; Robert Olsen

MONOLITH — Comico

1 ❑ Oct 1991 Cover: 2.50 **NM** value: **Cover or less**
Circ: CapCity orders: **5,125**
📖 Fugue and Variations **A:** Mitch Byrd; Kelley Jones(cover) **W:** Mort Castle
2 ❑ Nov 1991 Cover: 2.50 **NM** value: **Cover or less**
Circ: CapCity orders: **4,725**
A: Mitch Byrd; Kelley Jones(cover) **W:** Mort Castle
3 ❑ Cover: 2.50 **NM** value: **Cover or less**
Circ: CapCity orders: **4,175**
A: Mitch Byrd; Kelley Jones(cover) **W:** Mort Castle

MONOLITH (LAST GASP) — Last Gasp

1 ❑ Cover: 0.50 **NM** value: **3.00**
📖 The Escape from the Dead City; FøX-O; High Adventure with the Contraband Commandos; The Psylicon Psyrcus **A:** Larry Welz; Larry Sutherland; Larry Todd **W:** Larry Welz; Larry Sutherland; Larry Todd

MONROE — Conquest

1 ❑ b&w Cover: 4.95 **NM** value: **Cover or less**
• poster; cards

MONSTER — Fiction House

1 ❑ ca. 1953 Cover: 0.10 **NM** value: **400.00**
• **CGC:** 2 graded, best 9.2
2 ❑ ca. 1953 Cover: 0.10 **NM** value: **300.00**
• **CGC:** 2 graded, best 5.5

MONSTER, THE — Ring

1 ❑ Cover: 2.00 **NM** value: **Cover or less**
A: Derek Ring **W:** Derek Ring

MONSTER BOY — Monster

1 ❑ b&w Cover: 2.25 **NM** value: **2.50**

MONSTER BOY COMICS — Slave Labor

1 ❑ Sep 1997, b&w Cover: 2.95 **NM** value: **Cover or less**
📖 The Collector; Sibling Snacks; Let's Meet the Gang at Monster Boy Comics; Open Wide; Tirez La Langue; A Boy and His Cat; Honko: Another Wacky Adventure **A:** Bob Supina **W:** Bob Supina
2 ❑ Dec 1997, b&w Cover: 2.95 **NM** value: **Cover or less**
A: Bob Supina **W:** Bob Supina
3 ❑ Cover: 2.95 **NM** value: **Cover or less**
A: Bob Supina **W:** Bob Supina

MONSTER (BUTLER & HOGG'S...) — Slave Labor

All issues are adults only.
1 ❑ b&w Cover: 2.95 **NM** value: **Cover or less**
📖 Vampire Love **A:** Chris Hogg **W:** Chris Hogg; Chris Butler

MONSTER CRIME COMICS — Hillman

1 ❑ Oct 1952 Cover: 0.15 **NM** value: **800.00**

MONSTER FIGHTERS INC. — Image

1 ❑ Apr 1999 Cover: 3.50 **NM** value: **Cover or less**
Circ: Diamd. preorders: **11,675**
A: Logan Lubera **W:** J. Torres

MONSTER FIGHTERS INC.: THE BLACK BOOK — Image

1 ❑ Sep 2000 Cover: 3.50 **NM** value: **Cover or less**
Circ: Diamd. preorders: **5,683**
One-shot. **A:** Francis Manapul **W:** J. Torres

MONSTER FIGHTERS INC.: THE GHOSTS OF CHRISTMAS — Image

1 ❑ Dec 1999 Cover: 3.95 **NM** value: **Cover or less**
Circ: Diamd. preorders: **6,390**
One-shot.

MONSTER FRAT HOUSE — Eternity

1 ❑ Oct 1989, b&w Cover: 2.25 **NM** value: **Cover or less**
📖 Night on Wolf Mountain, In the Name of Science **A:** John Grigni; Sandy Carrruthers **W:** Pat O'Connor

MONSTER HUNTERS — Charlton

1 ❑ Aug 1975 Cover: 0.25 **NM** value: **6.00**
• **CGC:** 1 graded, best 9.0
1-2 ❑ **NM** value: **2.50**
• Modern Comics reprint
2 ❑ Oct 1975 Cover: 0.25 **NM** value: **3.50**
📖 The Dictator; A Belief in Vampires; The Wakely Monster; the Key to Magda's Heart (text) • J. Gill story, Marti art credits; Nicola Cuti credits
3 ❑ Dec 1975 Cover: 0.25 **NM** value: **3.00**
4 ❑ Feb 1976 Cover: 0.25 **NM** value: **3.00**
5 ❑ Apr 1976 Cover: 0.30 **NM** value: **3.00**
6 ❑ Jul 1976 Cover: 0.30 **NM** value: **3.00**
📖 The Beast of the Burden; Who Prowls the Night; Dawn at Stonehenge
7 ❑ Sep 1976 Cover: 0.30 **NM** value: **3.00**
8 ❑ Nov 1976 Cover: 0.30 **NM** value: **3.00**
9 ❑ Jan 1977 Cover: 0.30 **NM** value: **3.00**
10 ❑ Oct 1977 Cover: 0.35 **NM** value: **3.00**
11 ❑ Jan 1978 Cover: 0.35 **NM** value: **2.50**
12 ❑ Mar 1978 Cover: 0.35 **NM** value: **2.50**
13 ❑ Apr 1978 Cover: 0.35 **NM** value: **2.50**
14 ❑ May 1978 Cover: 0.35 **NM** value: **2.50**
📖 Giant From The Unknown; The Thing From Below; The Strange Fate Of Captain Fenton **A:** Steve Ditko
15 ❑ Jul 1978 Cover: 0.35 **NM** value: **2.50**
16 ❑ Oct 1978 Cover: 0.35 **NM** value: **2.50**
17 ❑ Dec 1978 Cover: 0.35 **NM** value: **2.50**
18 ❑ Feb 1979 Cover: 0.35 **NM** value: **2.50**
final issue.

MONSTER IN MY POCKET — Harvey

1 ❑ Mar 1991 Cover: 1.25 **NM** value: **1.50**
Circ: CapCity orders: **4,125**
📖 The Convention of Terror **A:** Ernie Colon **W:** Dwayne McDuffie
2 ❑ May 1991 Cover: 1.25 **NM** value: **1.50**
• The Exterminator
3 ❑ Jul 1991 Cover: 1.25 **NM** value: **1.50**
A: Gil Kane
4 ❑ Sep 1991 Cover: 1.25 **NM** value: **1.50**
A: Gil Kane

MONSTER ISLAND — Compass

1 ❑ Nov 1998, b&w Cover: 3.95 **NM** value: **Cover or less**
Circ: Diamd. preorders: **2,205**
wraparound cover. **A:** Graham Nolan **W:** Graham Nolan

MONSTER LOVE — Kitchen Sink

1 ❑ Cover: 2.50 **NM** value: **Cover or less**
📖 I Need to Know You; Monster's Night Out; The One That Got Away; Too Too Too Many Two's; Don't Make Me Wait!; The Mourning After **A:** Scott Deschaine; Bob Donovan **W:** Scott Deschaine

MONSTERMAN — Image

1 ❑ Sep 1997, b&w Cover: 2.95 **NM** value: **Cover or less**
Circ: Diamd. preorders: **4,745**
📖 Curio; The Messenger **A:** Jerry Ordway; Mike Manley **W:** Jerry Ordway; Mike Manley

MONSTER MASSACRE — Atomeka

1 ❑ Cover: 7.95 **NM** value: **Cover or less**
Circ: CapCity orders: **6,150**
No issue number. 📖 The Kingdom of Zitturk; Headcase; Of Ill Omen; Maximum Force

MONSTER MASSACRE SPECIAL — Blackball

1 ❑ Cover: 2.50 **NM** value: **Cover or less**

MONSTER MASTERWORKS — Marvel

Bk 1❑ Cover: 12.95 **NM** value: **Cover or less**
Circ: CapCity orders: **3,000**
A: Steve Ditko; Bill Everett; Jack Kirby

MONSTER MATINEE — Chaos!

1 ❑ Oct 1997 Cover: 2.50 **NM** value: **Cover or less**
Circ: Diamd. preorders: **13,359**
• monster pin-ups; commentary by Forrest J. Ackerman
1/SC❑ Oct 1997 Cover: 2.50 **NM** value: **Cover or less**
alternate logoless cover. • premium edition. • monster pin-ups; commentary by Forrest J. Ackerman
2 ❑ Oct 1997 Cover: 2.50 **NM** value: **Cover or less**
Circ: Diamd. preorders: **11,084**
• monster pin-ups; commentary by Forrest J. Ackerman
3 ❑ Oct 1997 Cover: 2.50 **NM** value: **Cover or less**
Circ: Diamd. preorders: **10,939**
• monster pin-ups; commentary by Forrest J. Ackerman
Bk 1❑ b&w Cover: 7.50 **NM** value: **Cover or less**
• collects pin-ups from the three issues

MONSTER MENACE — Marvel

1 ❑ Dec 1993 Cover: 1.25 **NM** value: **1.50**
Circ: CapCity orders: **9,300**
📖 I Spent Midnight With The Monster On Bald Mountain; The Terror Of Tim Boo Ba; I Fought The Molten Man-Thing! **A:** Steve Ditko **W:** Stan Lee
2 ❑ Jan 1994 Cover: 1.25 **NM** value: **1.50**
Circ: CapCity orders: **5,300**
3 ❑ Feb 1994 Cover: 1.25 **NM** value: **1.50**
Circ: CapCity orders: **4,200**
4 ❑ Mar 1994 Cover: 1.25 **NM** value: **1.50**
Circ: CapCity orders: **3,300**

MONSTERMEN, THE (GARY GIANNI'S...) — Dark Horse

1 ❑ Aug 1999 Cover: 2.95 **NM** value: **Cover or less**
📖 The Skull and the Snowman; Hellboy: Goodbye, Mr. Tod **A:** Mike Mignola; Gary Gianni **W:** Mike Mignola; Gary Gianni

MONSTER POSSE — Adventure

1 ❑ b&w Cover: 2.50 **NM** value: **Cover or less**
A: Greg Boone **W:** Greg Boone
2 ❑ Nov 1992 Cover: 2.50 **NM** value: **Cover or less**
A: Greg Boone **W:** Greg Boone
3 ❑ Cover: 2.50 **NM** value: **Cover or less**
A: Greg Boone **W:** Greg Boone

MONSTERS ATTACK! — Globe

1 ❑ b&w Cover: 2.00 **NM** value: **3.00**
• magazine.

Other grades: Multiply prices above by **1.5 for Mint • 2/3 for Very Fine • 1/3 for Fine • 1/5 for Very Good • 1/8 for Good**

2 ❑ b&w Cover: 2.00 **NM** value: **2.50**
• magazine.
3 ❑ Cover: 2.25 **NM** value: **2.50**
4 ❑ Cover: 2.25 **NM** value: **2.50**
5 ❑ Cover: 2.25 **NM** value: **2.50**
A: Steve Ditko; Alex Toth; Gray Morrow; Gene Colan

MONSTERS FROM OUTER SPACE — Adventure

1 ❑ Dec 1992, b&w Cover: 2.50 **NM** value: **Cover or less**
A: Gary Yap **W:** Will Jacobs; Gerard Jones
2 ❑ b&w Cover: 2.50 **NM** value: **Cover or less**
3 ❑ b&w Cover: 2.50 **NM** value: **Cover or less**

MONSTERS ON THE PROWL — Marvel

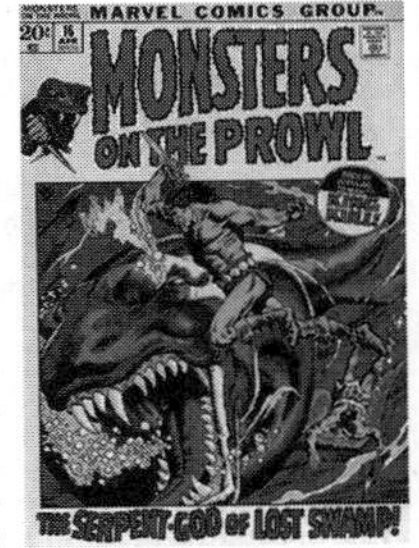

Monsters on the Prowl (originally Chamber of Darkness) combined new material and reprints from Marvel's pre-hero Atlas comics (Strange Tales, Tales of Suspense, etc.), a format that Marvel used in a number of its titles during the early 1970s. The new material included stories featuring Kull, a barbarian swordsman created by Robert E. Howard of Conan the Barbarian fame, adapted by Roy Thomas and exquisitely drawn by John Severin. Other fantasy artists of note, including Barry Windsor-Smith and Ralph Reese, also contributed stories to the short-lived series. The back pages of each issue were filled with Atlas monster stories ("I Challenged Groot...Monster from Planet X!") written by Stan Lee and featuring terrific art from Steve Ditko, Jack Kirby, Dick Ayers, and others.

9 ❑ Feb 1971 Cover: 0.15 **NM** value: **6.00**
• **CGC:** 1 graded, best 9.4
• Title changes to Monsters on the Prowl; Series continued from Chamber of Darkness #8
10 ❑ Apr 1971 Cover: 0.15 **NM** value: **4.00**
11 ❑ Jun 1971 Cover: 0.15 **NM** value: **4.00**
12 ❑ Aug 1971 Cover: 0.15 **NM** value: **4.00**
13 ❑ Oct 1971 Cover: 0.25 **NM** value: **4.00**
• **CGC:** 1 graded, best 9.0
14 ❑ Dec 1971 Cover: 0.25 **NM** value: **4.00**
• **CGC:** 1 graded, best 8.5
15 ❑ Feb 1972 Cover: 0.20 **NM** value: **4.00**
16 ❑ Apr 1972 Cover: 0.20 **NM** value: **6.00**
• **CGC:** 5 graded, best 9.8
📖 Forbidden Swamp; Where Walks the Ghost; Mister Morgan's Monster; • King Kull **A:** John Severin; Marie Severin **W:** Roy Thomas
17 ❑ Jun 1972 Cover: 0.20 **NM** value: **4.00**
18 ❑ Aug 1972 Cover: 0.20 **NM** value: **4.00**
19 ❑ Oct 1972 Cover: 0.20 **NM** value: **4.00**
20 ❑ Dec 1972 Cover: 0.20 **NM** value: **4.00**
📖 Oog Lives Again; The Dangerous Doll; I Made Time Stand Still; Enter The Robot!; Enter The Robot!; **A:** Steve Ditko
21 ❑ Feb 1973 Cover: 0.20 **NM** value: **3.00**
22 ❑ Apr 1973 Cover: 0.20 **NM** value: **3.00**
📖 When the Monster Strikes!; The Wax People; Less Than Human; Trapped in the Room of Shadows
23 ❑ Jun 1973 Cover: 0.20 **NM** value: **3.00**
24 ❑ Aug 1973 Cover: 0.20 **NM** value: **3.00**
25 ❑ Sep 1973 Cover: 0.20 **NM** value: **3.00**
26 ❑ Oct 1973 Cover: 0.20 **NM** value: **3.00**
27 ❑ Nov 1974 Cover: 0.20 **NM** value: **3.00**
28 ❑ Jun 1975 Cover: 0.25 **NM** value: **3.00**
29 ❑ Aug 1975 Cover: 0.25 **NM** value: **3.00**
30 ❑ Oct 1975 Cover: 0.25 **NM** value: **3.00**
final issue.

MONSTERS UNLEASHED — Marvel

1 ❑ Jul 1973, b&w Cover: 0.75 **NM** value: **14.00**
• magazine.
2 ❑ Sep 1973 Cover: 0.75 **NM** value: **10.00**
• Frankenstein
3 ❑ Nov 1973 Cover: 0.75 **NM** value: **9.00**
• Frankenstein, Man-Thing, Son of Satan
4 ❑ Jan 1974 Cover: 0.75 **NM** value: **9.00**
• Frankenstein
5 ❑ Mar 1974 Cover: 0.75 **NM** value: **9.00**
• Frankenstein, Man-Thing
6 ❑ May 1974 Cover: 0.75 **NM** value: **7.00**
• Frankenstein, Werewolf
7 ❑ Jul 1974 Cover: 0.75 **NM** value: **7.00**
• Frankenstein, Werewolf
8 ❑ Sep 1974 Cover: 0.75 **NM** value: **7.00**
• Frankenstein, Man-Thing
9 ❑ Nov 1974 Cover: 0.75 **NM** value: **7.00**
• Frankenstein, Man-Thing, Wendigo
10 ❑ Jan 1975 Cover: 0.75 **NM** value: **7.00**
• Frankenstein, Tigra
11 ❑ Mar 1975 Cover: 0.75 **NM** value: **7.00**
• Gabriel
Anl 1❑ca. 1975 Cover: 1.25 **NM** value: **7.00**

MONSTROSITY — Slap Happy

1 ❑ Oct 1998, b&w Cover: 4.95 **NM** value: **Cover or less**

Statement of Ownership figures are the average number of copies originally sold, as cited by the publisher to the U.S. Postal Service. These estimate **all** sales, in comics shops and on newsstands.

MONTE HALE WESTERN — Fawcett

Monte Hale (1919-) was another singing cowboy, first appearing as a guitar player in The Big Bonanza (1944). Fawcett eventually established an entire line of Western comic books featuring real motion-picture stars such as Tom Mix, Lash LaRue, and Gabby Hayes. Perhaps because of sluggish sales of the Mary Marvel series named for her (and her final cover featuring her in Western garb), Fawcett changed its contents completely and put Hale in the starring role with #29. Cover copy read, "Introducing Monte Hale The Biggest and Boldest Real-Life Cowboy of Them All 6 ft. 5 in.

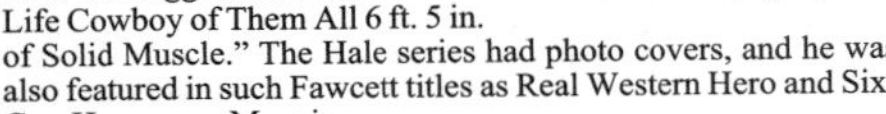

of Solid Muscle." The Hale series had photo covers, and he was also featured in such Fawcett titles as Real Western Hero and Six-Gun Heroes. — Maggie

29 ❑ Oct 1948 Cover: 0.10 **NM** value: **400.00**
30 ❑ Nov 1948 Cover: 0.10 **NM** value: **200.00**
31 ❑ Dec 1948 Cover: 0.10 **NM** value: **150.00**
32 ❑ Jan 1949 Cover: 0.10 **NM** value: **150.00**
33 ❑ Feb 1949 Cover: 0.10 **NM** value: **150.00**
34 ❑ Mar 1949 Cover: 0.10 **NM** value: **150.00**
35 ❑ Apr 1949 Cover: 0.10 **NM** value: **150.00**
36 ❑ May 1949 Cover: 0.10 **NM** value: **150.00**
37 ❑ Jun 1949 Cover: 0.10 **NM** value: **100.00**
38 ❑ Jul 1949 Cover: 0.10 **NM** value: **100.00**
39 ❑ Aug 1949 Cover: 0.10 **NM** value: **100.00**
• **CGC:** 1 graded, best 9.0
40 ❑ Sep 1949 Cover: 0.10 **NM** value: **100.00**
41 ❑ Oct 1949 Cover: 0.10 **NM** value: **100.00**
42 ❑ Nov 1949 Cover: 0.10 **NM** value: **100.00**
43 ❑ Dec 1949 Cover: 0.10 **NM** value: **100.00**
44 ❑ Jan 1950 Cover: 0.10 **NM** value: **100.00**
45 ❑ Feb 1950 Cover: 0.10 **NM** value: **100.00**
46 ❑ Mar 1950 Cover: 0.10 **NM** value: **90.00**
47 ❑ Apr 1950 Cover: 0.10 **NM** value: **90.00**
48 ❑ May 1950 Cover: 0.10 **NM** value: **90.00**
49 ❑ Jun 1950 Cover: 0.10 **NM** value: **90.00**
50 ❑ Jul 1950 Cover: 0.10 **NM** value: **90.00**
51 ❑ Aug 1950 Cover: 0.10 **NM** value: **90.00**
52 ❑ Sep 1950 Cover: 0.10 **NM** value: **90.00**
53 ❑ Oct 1950 Cover: 0.10 **NM** value: **90.00**
54 ❑ Nov 1950 Cover: 0.10 **NM** value: **90.00**
55 ❑ Dec 1950 Cover: 0.10 **NM** value: **90.00**
56 ❑ Jan 1951 Cover: 0.10 **NM** value: **70.00**
57 ❑ Feb 1951 Cover: 0.10 **NM** value: **70.00**
58 ❑ Mar 1951 Cover: 0.10 **NM** value: **70.00**
59 ❑ Apr 1951 Cover: 0.10 **NM** value: **70.00**
60 ❑ May 1951 Cover: 0.10 **NM** value: **70.00**
61 ❑ Jun 1951 Cover: 0.10 **NM** value: **70.00**
62 ❑ Jul 1951 Cover: 0.10 **NM** value: **70.00**
63 ❑ Aug 1951 Cover: 0.10 **NM** value: **70.00**
64 ❑ Sep 1951 Cover: 0.10 **NM** value: **70.00**
65 ❑ Oct 1951 Cover: 0.10 **NM** value: **70.00**
66 ❑ Nov 1951 Cover: 0.10 **NM** value: **70.00**
67 ❑ Dec 1951 Cover: 0.10 **NM** value: **70.00**
68 ❑ Jan 1952 Cover: 0.10 **NM** value: **70.00**
69 ❑ Feb 1952 Cover: 0.10 **NM** value: **70.00**
70 ❑ Mar 1952 Cover: 0.10 **NM** value: **70.00**
71 ❑ Apr 1952 Cover: 0.10 **NM** value: **60.00**
72 ❑ May 1952 Cover: 0.10 **NM** value: **60.00**
73 ❑ Jun 1952 Cover: 0.10 **NM** value: **60.00**
74 ❑ Jul 1952 Cover: 0.10 **NM** value: **60.00**
75 ❑ Aug 1952 Cover: 0.10 **NM** value: **60.00**
76 ❑ Sep 1952 Cover: 0.10 **NM** value: **60.00**
77 ❑ Oct 1952 Cover: 0.10 **NM** value: **60.00**
78 ❑ Nov 1952 Cover: 0.10 **NM** value: **60.00**
79 ❑ ca. 1953 Cover: 0.10 **NM** value: **60.00**
80 ❑ ca. 1953 Cover: 0.10 **NM** value: **60.00**
81 ❑ ca. 1953 Cover: 0.10 **NM** value: **60.00**
82 ❑ Jun 1953 Cover: 0.10 **NM** value: **60.00**
83 ❑ Feb 1955 Cover: 0.10 **NM** value: **60.00**
84 ❑ Apr 1955 Cover: 0.10 **NM** value: **60.00**
85 ❑ ca. 1955 Cover: 0.10 **NM** value: **60.00**
86 ❑ ca. 1955 Cover: 0.10 **NM** value: **60.00**
87 ❑ ca. 1955 Cover: 0.10 **NM** value: **60.00**
88 ❑ ca. 1956 Cover: 0.10 **NM** value: **60.00**

MONTY HALL OF THE U.S. MARINES — Toby

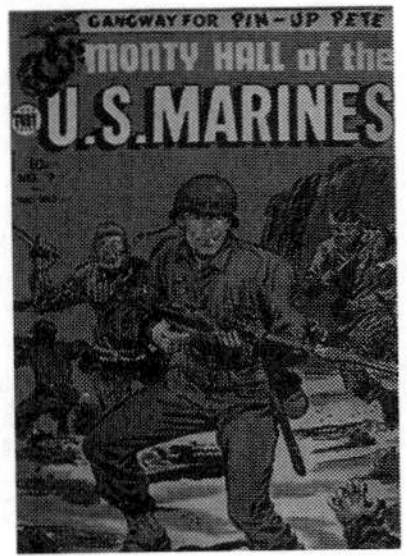

Can there be any greater proof of the ultimate folly and futility of war than the fact that Monty Hall, one of America's most celebrated and decorated war heroes who braved death 100 times for the sake of his country and the honor of the Marine Corps — is today remembered only as the host of the singularly ridiculous game show, "Let's Make a Deal"? Well, back in the days of this title (the Korean War), Monty was a fire-breathing, gun-toting, all-American fighting machine whose life story was the subject of a Hollywood feature film and whose daring exploits filled the pages of 11 action-packed issues of Monty Hall of the U.S. Marines. Behind Door #3 in this brutal, jingoistic pre-Code war comic? Probably a vicious, knife-toting Red Chinese commie and a few hundred of his scheming "yellow" pals. Enjoy.

1 ❑ Aug 1951 Cover: 0.10 **NM** value: **50.00**
2 ❑ Oct 1951 Cover: 0.10 **NM** value: **28.00**
3 ❑ Dec 1951 Cover: 0.10 **NM** value: **20.00**
4 ❑ Feb 1951 Cover: 0.10 **NM** value: **20.00**
5 ❑ Apr 1951 Cover: 0.10 **NM** value: **20.00**
6 ❑ Jun 1951 Cover: 0.10 **NM** value: **20.00**
7 ❑ Aug 1951 Cover: 0.10 **NM** value: **20.00**
8 ❑ Oct 1951 Cover: 0.10 **NM** value: **20.00**
9 ❑ Dec 1951 Cover: 0.10 **NM** value: **20.00**
📖 Feather Fight; The Big Rhubarb; Assignment for Danger;
10 ❑ Feb 1953 Cover: 0.10 **NM** value: **20.00**
11 ❑ Apr 1953 Cover: 0.10 **NM** value: **20.00**

MOON BEAST — Avalon

1 ❑ Cover: 2.95 **NM** value: **Cover or less**
📖 The Night of the Werewolf; The Moon Beast; The Night of the Laughing Wolf **A:** Steve Ditko; Nicholas Alascia **W:** Joe Gill

MOONCHILD — Forbidden Fruit

All issues are adults only.
1 ❑ b&w Cover: 2.95 **NM** value: **Cover or less**
2 ❑ b&w Cover: 2.95 **NM** value: **Cover or less**

MOON CHILD (VOL. 2) — Forbidden Fruit

All issues are adults only.
1 ❑ b&w Cover: 3.50 **NM** value: **Cover or less**
2 ❑ b&w Cover: 3.50 **NM** value: **Cover or less**
3 ❑ b&w Cover: 3.50 **NM** value: **Cover or less**

MOONDOG — Print Mint

1 ❑ Cover: 0.50 **NM** value: **4.00**
A: George Metzger **W:** George Metzger
2 ❑ Cover: 0.50 **NM** value: **3.00**
📖 Moondog; Kaleida Smith **A:** George Metzger **W:** George Metzger

MOONFIGHTING — Harrier

1 ❑ Mar 1988, b&w Cover: 1.95 **NM** value: **2.00**
📖 Air Warfare **A:** John Jackson **W:** Paul Duncan

MOON GIRL — E.C.

The first issue's cover copy said, "Featuring America's newest and most exciting characters in four complete and thrilling episodes!" Drawn by Sheldon Moldoff, it was E.C.'s attempt at creating a sort of super-hero. What happened was a prime example of E.C.'s morphing titles: #2 was simply Moon Girl. With #7 it became Moon Girl Fights Crime! And with #9 it finally angled off 90 degrees to become A Moon, a Girl ... Romance.

E.C. changed gears from the super-heroine Moon Girl to a traditional romance title with cover copy reading, "True stories of young love." The four-issue Pre-Trend experiment then morphed into Weird Fantasy with #13. — Maggie

1 ❑ Fal 1947 Cover: 0.10 **NM** value: **800.00**
• **CGC:** 7 graded, best 7.5
📖 Introducing Moon Girl and the Prince; Invaders from Venus!; Prince Mengu and Moon Girl; Smuggler's Cove!
2 ❑ Win 1947 Cover: 0.10 **NM** value: **425.00**
• **CGC:** 1 graded, best 9.2
📖 The Battle of the Congo!; Old Man Experience; Moon Girl and the Prince; Big Shot(2); Rustlers of Ransom Gap!; The Most Daring Man in the World!
3 ❑ Spr 1948 Cover: 0.10 **NM** value: **340.00**
• **CGC:** 2 graded, best 9.6
📖 Rockets for Riches!; Sky Sabotage!; Fat and Slat in Movieland; Fat and Slat(1); The Spirit of Kokama!; Moon Girl..Wanted for Murder
4 ❑ Sum 1948 Cover: 0.10 **NM** value: **315.00**
• **CGC:** 2 graded, best 7.5
📖 The Challenge of the Cyclops!; Vampire of the Bayous!; Fat and Slat(3); Peace for the Old Countries!
5 ❑ Fal 1948 Cover: 0.10 **NM** value: **725.00**
• **CGC:** 3 graded, best 9.6
📖 Slaves to the Sun!; The Ranch at Barren Acres!; Zombie Terror!; The Corpse with Will-Power • Horror story
6 ❑ Mar 1949 Cover: 0.10 **NM** value: **360.00**
• **CGC:** 5 graded, best 9.4
📖 The Day the World Trembled!; Moon Girl Meets The Buffoon!; Fat and Slat; A Coffin for a Bed (Text Story); The Plunderers From The Past!
7 ❑ May 1949 Cover: 0.10 **NM** value: **360.00**
• **CGC:** 3 graded, best 8.5
📖 The Fiends who fight with fire!; Your Newsdealer- He is your Friend!; The Man who played with the Stars!; The Menace from the Moon!
8 ❑ Sum 1949 Cover: 0.10 **NM** value: **360.00**
• **CGC:** 2 graded, best 7.5
📖 Moon Girl Fights Crime!; Your Newsdealer-He is your friend!; Smashing the Dope Ring; The Witch of the Haunted Hills!
9 ❑ Sep 1949 Cover: 0.10 **NM** value: **465.00**
• **CGC:** 3 graded, best 7.5
📖 I was Jilted and No Desire to Live; I was a flirt; I was a ...Heart Pirate • Title Changes to A Moon, a Girl...Romance!
10 ❑ Nov 1949 Cover: 0.10 **NM** value: **390.00**
• **CGC:** 1 graded, best 3.0
📖 Suspicious of His Intentions!; I was a Wild Girl; Triangle of Love; I Thought I Loved My Boss
11 ❑ Jan 1950 Cover: 0.10 **NM** value: **390.00**
• **CGC:** 1 graded, best 4.5
📖 Hearts along the Ski Trail; Under-Cover Love; My Office Romance; Summer Love
12 ❑ Mar 1950 Cover: 0.10 **NM** value: **485.00**
• **CGC:** 2 graded, best 7.5
📖 Prison Widow; Not Worthy of Love!; Blind to My Real Love!; Rx for Romance • Scarcer; Series continued in Werd Fantasy #13

CGC-graded: Multiply prices above by **33 for 9.9 M • 16 for 9.8 NM/M • 7 for 9.6 NM+ • 5 for 9.4 NM • 2.5 for 9.2 NM- • 1.5 for 9.0 VF/NM**

MOON KNIGHT (1ST SERIES) — Marvel

Marc Spector is a mercenary whose bloodthirsty commander turns on him when he refuses to aid in the execution of innocent civilians. After he's beaten unconscious, Spector's body is dumped in the middle of the desert, where he is left to die. His life is saved, when he discovers an ancient temple of the moon god Khonshu. Mystically healed by powers of the temple, Spector is reborn as a fighter for justice.

To aid in his battles, he cultivates different identities for himself. As Steven Grant, he uses Wall Street wizardry to parlay his savings into a large fortune. Later, he adds the identity of Jake Lockley, a street-smart cabbie who hears everything. Finally, as Moon Knight, he exacts vengeance for the crimes of those who prey on the weak and the innocent.

1 ❑ Nov 1980 Cover: 0.50 **NM** value: **3.50**
• **CGC:** 24 graded, best 9.8
Moon Knight **A:** Bill Sienkiewicz **W:** Doug Moench ★ Origin of Moon Knight.

2 ❑ Dec 1980 Cover: 0.50 **NM** value: **2.50**
The Slasher **A:** Bill Sienkiewicz **W:** Doug Moench

3 ❑ Jan 1981 Cover: 0.50 **NM** value: **2.50**
Circ: Statement: **208,187**
Midnight Means Murder **A:** Bill Sienkiewicz **W:** Doug Moench

4 ❑ Feb 1981 Cover: 0.50 **NM** value: **2.50**
Circ: Statement: **208,187**
A Committee Of Five **A:** Bill Sienkiewicz **W:** Doug Moench

5 ❑ Mar 1981 Cover: 0.50 **NM** value: **2.50**
Circ: Statement: **208,187**
Ghost Story **A:** Bill Sienkiewicz **W:** Doug Moench

6 ❑ Apr 1981 Cover: 0.50 **NM** value: **2.50**
Circ: Statement: **208,187**
White Angels **A:** Bill Sienkiewicz **W:** Doug Moench

7 ❑ May 1981 Cover: 0.50 **NM** value: **2.50**
Circ: Statement: **208,187**
The Moon Kings **A:** Bill Sienkiewicz **W:** Doug Moench

8 ❑ Jun 1981 Cover: 0.50 **NM** value: **2.50**
Circ: Statement: **208,187**
A: Bill Sienkiewicz ★ Versus Moon Kings.

9 ❑ Jul 1981 Cover: 0.50 **NM** value: **2.50**
Circ: Statement: **208,187**
Vengeance In Reprise **A:** Bill Sienkiewicz; Frank Miller **W:** Doug Moench ★ Versus Midnight Man.

10 ❑ Aug 1981 Cover: 0.50 **NM** value: **2.50**
Circ: Statement: **208,187**
Too Many Midnights **A:** Bill Sienkiewicz **W:** Doug Moench ★ Versus Midnight Man.

11 ❑ Sep 1981 Cover: 0.50 **NM** value: **2.50**
Circ: Statement: **208,187**
To Catch A Killer **A:** Bill Sienkiewicz **W:** Doug Moench ★ Versus Creed.

12 ❑ Oct 1981 Cover: 0.50 **NM** value: **2.50**
Circ: Statement: **208,187**
The Nightmare Of Morpheus **A:** Bill Sienkiewicz; Frank Miller **W:** Doug Moench

13 ❑ Nov 1981 Cover: 0.50 **NM** value: **2.50**
Circ: Statement: **208,187**
The Cream Of The Jest **A:** Bill Sienkiewicz; Frank Miller **W:** Doug Moench ★ Appearance of Daredevil.

14 ❑ Dec 1981 Cover: 0.50 **NM** value: **2.50**
Circ: Statement: **208,187**
Stained Glass Scarlet **A:** Bill Sienkiewicz **W:** Doug Moench

15 ❑ Jan 1982 Cover: 0.75 **NM** value: **2.50**
Circ: Statement: **136,262**
Ruling The World From His Basement • direct **A:** Bill Sienkiewicz; Frank Miller **C:** Frank Miller **W:** Doug Moench ★ Appearance of Thing.

16 ❑ Feb 1982 Cover: 0.75 **NM** value: **2.50**
Circ: Statement: **136,262**
Shadows Of The Moon **A:** Denys Cowan; Bill Sienkiewicz(cover) **W:** Jack Harris ★ Versus Blacksmith.

17 ❑ Mar 1982 Cover: 0.75 **NM** value: **2.50**
Circ: Statement: **136,262** • **CGC:** 1 graded, best 9.6
Master Sniper's Legacy! **A:** Bill Sienkiewicz **W:** Doug Moench

18 ❑ Apr 1982 Cover: 0.75 **NM** value: **2.50**
Circ: Statement: **136,262**
A: Bill Sienkiewicz ★ Versus Slayers Elite.

19 ❑ May 1982 Cover: 0.75 **NM** value: **2.50**
Circ: Statement: **136,262** • **CGC:** 1 graded, best 9.8
Assault On Island Strange **A:** Bill Sienkiewicz **W:** Doug Moench ★ Versus Arsenal.

20 ❑ Jun 1982 Cover: 0.75 **NM** value: **2.50**
Circ: Statement: **136,262**
A: Bill Sienkiewicz ★ Versus Arsenal.

21 ❑ Jul 1982 Cover: 0.75 **NM** value: **2.00**
Circ: Statement: **136,262** • **CGC:** 1 graded, best 9.6
The Master Of Night Earth! **A:** Vincente Alcazar; Bill Sienkiewicz(cover) **W:** Doug Moench

22 ❑ Aug 1982 Cover: 0.75 **NM** value: **2.00**
Circ: Statement: **136,262**
The Dream Demon **A:** Bill Sienkiewicz **W:** Doug Moench

23 ❑ Sep 1982 Cover: 0.75 **NM** value: **2.00**
Circ: Statement: **136,262**
A: Bill Sienkiewicz

24 ❑ Oct 1982 Cover: 0.75 **NM** value: **2.00**
Circ: Statement: **136,262**
Scarlet Moonlight **A:** Bill Sienkiewicz **W:** Doug Moench

25 ❑ Nov 1982 Cover: 1.00 **NM** value: **2.50**
Circ: Statement: **136,262** • **CGC:** 1 graded, best 8.0
• double-sized. Black Spectre **A:** Bill Sienkiewicz **W:** Doug Moench

26 ❑ Dec 1982 Cover: 0.75 **NM** value: **2.00**
Circ: Statement: **136,262**
Hit It! **A:** Bill Sienkiewicz **W:** Doug Moench

27 ❑ Jan 1983 Cover: 0.75 **NM** value: **2.00**
Circ: Statement: **87,701**
Cop Killer! **A:** Joe Brozowski; Frank Miller(cover) **W:** Steven Grant

28 ❑ Feb 1983 Cover: 0.75 **NM** value: **2.00**
Circ: Statement: **87,701**
Spirits In The Sand **A:** Bill Sienkiewicz **W:** Doug Moench

29 ❑ Mar 1983 Cover: 0.75 **NM** value: **2.00**
Circ: Statement: **87,701** • **CGC:** 1 graded, best 9.2
Morning Star **A:** Bill Sienkiewicz **W:** Doug Moench

30 ❑ Apr 1983 Cover: 0.75 **NM** value: **2.00**
Circ: Statement: **87,701** • **CGC:** 1 graded, best 6.5
The Moonwraith, Three Sixes, And A Beast **A:** Bill Sienkiewicz **W:** Doug Moench

31 ❑ May 1983 Cover: 0.75 **NM** value: **2.00**
Circ: Statement: **87,701**
A Box Of Music For Savage Studs **A:** Kevin Nowlan; Bill Sienkiewicz(cover) **W:** Doug Moench

32 ❑ Jul 1983 Cover: 0.75 **NM** value: **2.00**
Circ: Statement: **87,701**
When The Music Stops... **A:** Kevin Nowlan; Bill Sienkiewicz(cover) **W:** Doug Moench

33 ❑ Sep 1983 Cover: 0.75 **NM** value: **2.00**
Circ: Statement: **87,701**
Exploding Myths **A:** Kevin Nowlan; Bill Sienkiewicz(cover) **W:** Doug Moench

34 ❑ Nov 1983 Cover: 0.75 **NM** value: **2.00**
Circ: Statement: **87,701**
Primal Scream, Scorecard **A:** Bo Hampton; Richard Howell; Bill Sienkiewicz(cover) **W:** Tony Isabella

35 ❑ Jan 1984 Cover: 1.00 **NM** value: **2.50**
Circ: Statement: **141,197**
• double-sized. Second Wind **A:** Kevin Nowlan; Carl Potts(cover) **W:** Tony Isabella ★ Appearance of X-Men.

36 ❑ Mar 1984 Cover: 0.75 **NM** value: **2.00**
Circ: Statement: **141,197**
Ghosts **A:** Bo Hampton **W:** Alan Zelentz

37 ❑ May 1984 Cover: 0.75 **NM** value: **2.00**
Circ: Statement: **141,197**
Red Sins; Crawley **A:** Bo Hampton; Bill Sienkiewicz **W:** Alan Zelentz

38 ❑ Jul 1984 Cover: 0.75 **NM** value: **2.00**
Circ: Statement: **141,197**
Final Rest **A:** Bo Hampton **W:** Alan Zelentz

MOON KNIGHT (2ND SERIES) — Marvel

1 ❑ Jun 1985 Cover: 1.25 **NM** value: **2.50**
Circ: CapCity orders: **27,900** • **CGC:** 3 graded, best 9.6
• Double-size. Knight Of The Jackal **A:** Chris Warner **W:** Alan Zelentz ★ Origin of Moon Knight.

2 ❑ Aug 1985 Cover: 0.65 **NM** value: **2.00**
Circ: CapCity orders: **20,000**
Deadly Knowledge **A:** Chris Warner **W:** Alan Zelentz

3 ❑ Sep 1985 Cover: 0.65 **NM** value: **2.00**
Circ: CapCity orders: **18,900**

4 ❑ Oct 1985 Cover: 0.65 **NM** value: **2.00**
Circ: CapCity orders: **18,400**
Bluebeard's Castle **A:** Larry Hama; Chris Warner **W:** Alan Zelentz

5 ❑ Nov 1985 Cover: 0.65 **NM** value: **2.00**
Circ: CapCity orders: **17,600**
Debts And Balances **A:** Alan Kupperberg; Chris Warner **W:** Mary Jo Duffy

6 ❑ Dec 1985 Cover: 0.65 **NM** value: **2.00**
Circ: CapCity orders: **15,600**
Painted cover. The Last White Knight **A:** Mark Beachum **W:** James Owsley

MOON KNIGHT (3RD SERIES) — Marvel

1 ❑ Jan 1998 Cover: 2.50 **NM** value: **Cover or less**
Circ: Diamd. preorders: **39,529**
The Resurrection War, Part 1 **A:** Tommy Lee Edwards **W:** Doug Miller

2 ❑ Feb 1998 Cover: 2.50 **NM** value: **Cover or less**
Circ: Diamd. preorders: **29,877**

3 ❑ Mar 1998 Cover: 2.50 **NM** value: **Cover or less**
Circ: Diamd. preorders: **24,235**

4 ❑ Apr 1998 Cover: 2.50 **NM** value: **Cover or less**
Circ: Diamd. preorders: **20,697**

MOON KNIGHT (4TH SERIES) — Marvel

1 ❑ Jan 1999 Cover: 2.99 **NM** value: **Cover or less**
Circ: Diamd. preorders: **31,686**
says Feb on cover, Jan in indicia. Spector of the Past; Hole into Darkness; Extreme Prejudice; Marked man; Stret Sweep; Lab Rat; Deep Black; Unaccounted Hours; Murky Waters; Thicker than Water; The Faith of Lazarus; Leviathans; Umbrella Man; Tattoed Heart **A:** Mark Texeira **W:** Doug Moench

2 ❑ Feb 1999 Cover: 2.99 **NM** value: **Cover or less**
Circ: Diamd. preorders: **28,351**
A: Mark Texeira **W:** Doug Moench

3 ❑ Feb 1999 Cover: 2.99 **NM** value: **Cover or less**
Circ: Diamd. preorders: **27,383**
A: Mark Texeira **W:** Doug Moench

4 ❑ Feb 1999 Cover: 2.99 **NM** value: **Cover or less**
Circ: Diamd. preorders: **26,944**
A: Mark Texeira **W:** Doug Moench

MOON KNIGHT: DIVIDED WE FALL — Marvel

1 ❑ Cover: 4.95 **NM** value: **Cover or less**
Circ: CapCity orders: **7,400**
No issue number. **A:** Denys Cowan **W:** Bruce Jones

MOON KNIGHT SPECIAL — Marvel

1 ❑ Cover: 2.50 **NM** value: **Cover or less**
Circ: CapCity orders: **18,200**
• Shang-Chi

MOON KNIGHT SPECIAL EDITION — Marvel

1 ❑ Nov 1983 Cover: 2.00 **NM** value: **2.50**
• **CGC:** 1 graded, best 9.6
• Reprints from Hulk (magazine). **A:** Bill Sienkiewicz; Joe Rubinstein **W:** Doug Moench

2 ❑ Dec 1983 Cover: 2.00 **NM** value: **2.50**
A: Bill Sienkiewicz

3 ❑ Jan 1984 Cover: 2.00 **NM** value: **2.50**
A: Bill Sienkiewicz

MOON MULLINS (ACG) — ACG

1 ❑ Dec 1947 Cover: 0.10 **NM** value: **80.00**
2 ❑ Feb 1948 Cover: 0.10 **NM** value: **50.00**
3 ❑ Apr 1948 Cover: 0.10 **NM** value: **45.00**
4 ❑ Jun 1948 Cover: 0.10 **NM** value: **45.00**
5 ❑ Aug 1948 Cover: 0.10 **NM** value: **45.00**
6 ❑ Oct 1948 Cover: 0.10 **NM** value: **45.00**

MOON MULLINS (ST. JOHN) — St. John

7 ❑ Dec 1948 Cover: 0.10 **NM** value: **45.00**
8 ❑ Feb 1949 Cover: 0.10 **NM** value: **45.00**

MOONSHADOW — Marvel / Epic

Moonshadow bills itself as "a fairy tale for grown-ups." It's that — and much more.

It begins in 1968, when a naive young hippie named Sheila Bernbaum is spirited across space by a member of the race of beings called "G'L-Doses" (an anagram for "godless"?). The G'L-Doses' sole purpose is to do whatever strikes their whimsy. This G'L-Dose's whimsy is to father a son, which Sheila names "Moonshadow."

Moonshadow grows up as innocent and starry-eyed as his mother has been, having spent his youth reading tales of romance and derring-do. Eventually, the time comes to leave the outer-space "zoo" he's lived in and set off across the universe. His adventures form a haunting story of his fall from innocence and growth into a man: a moving and beautifully illustrated story.

1 ❑ Mar 1985 Cover: 1.50 **NM** value: **3.50**
Circ: CapCity orders: **10,850**
Songs Of Happy Chear **A:** Jon J. Muth **W:** J.M. DeMatteis ★ Origin of Moonshadow.

2 ❑ May 1985 Cover: 1.50 **NM** value: **2.50**
Circ: CapCity orders: **7,850**
A Very Uncomfortable Thing **A:** Jon J. Muth **W:** J.M. DeMatteis

3 ❑ Jul 1985 Cover: 1.50 **NM** value: **2.50**
Circ: CapCity orders: **7,500**
The Crying Of The Wind **A:** Jon J. Muth **W:** J.M. DeMatteis

4 ❑ Sep 1985 Cover: 1.50 **NM** value: **2.00**
Circ: CapCity orders: **6,800**
The Hoofs Of Wrath **A:** Jon J. Muth **W:** J.M. DeMatteis

5 ❑ Nov 1985 Cover: 1.50 **NM** value: **2.00**
Circ: CapCity orders: **6,100**
In A Love Land **A:** Jon J. Muth **W:** J.M. DeMatteis

6 ❑ Jan 1986 Cover: 1.50 **NM** value: **2.00**
Circ: CapCity orders: **5,700**
Through The Window **A:** Kent Williams **W:** J.M. DeMatteis

7 ❑ Apr 1986 Cover: 1.50 **NM** value: **2.00**
Circ: CapCity orders: **5,350**
Counterpane **A:** Jon J. Muth **W:** J.M. DeMatteis

8 ❑ Jun 1986 Cover: 1.50 **NM** value: **2.00**
Circ: CapCity orders: **5,200**
Candles **A:** Jon J. Muth **W:** J.M. DeMatteis

9 ❑ Aug 1986 Cover: 1.50 **NM** value: **2.00**
Circ: CapCity orders: **5,400**
W: J.M. DeMatteis

10 ❑ Oct 1986 Cover: 1.50 **NM** value: **2.00**
Circ: CapCity orders: **5,550**
W: J.M. DeMatteis

11 ❑ Jan 1987 Cover: 1.50 **NM** value: **2.00**
Circ: CapCity orders: **5,700**
Contradictions **A:** Jon J. Muth; George Pratt **W:** J.M. DeMatteis ★ Origin of Moonshadow.

12 ❑ Feb 1987 Cover: 1.75 **NM** value: **2.00**
Circ: CapCity orders: **5,150**
With Joy To Hear final issue. **A:** Jon J. Muth; George Pratt; Kent Williams **W:** J.M. DeMatteis

Bk 1❑ Cover: 18.95 **NM** value: **Cover or less**

MOONSHADOW (VERTIGO) — DC / Vertigo

1 ❑ Sep 1994 Cover: 2.25 **NM** value: **3.00**
Circ: CapCity orders: **15,600**
Songs Of Happy Chear **A:** Jon J. Muth **W:** J.M. DeMatteis ★ Origin of Moonshadow.

2 ❑ Oct 1994 Cover: 2.25 **NM** value: **2.50**
Circ: CapCity orders: **11,150**
A Very Uncomfortable Thing **A:** Jon J. Muth **W:** J.M. DeMatteis

3 ❑ Nov 1994 Cover: 2.25 **NM** value: **2.50**
Circ: CapCity orders: **10,600**
The Crying Of The Wind **A:** Jon J. Muth **W:** J.M. DeMatteis

4 ❑ Dec 1994 Cover: 2.25 **NM** value: **2.50**
Circ: CapCity orders: **10,500**
The Hoofs Of Wrath **A:** Jon J. Muth **W:** J.M. DeMatteis

5 ❑ Jan 1995 Cover: 2.25 **NM** value: **2.50**
Circ: CapCity orders: **10,200**
In A Love Land **A:** Jon J. Muth **W:** J.M. DeMatteis

6 ❑ Feb 1995 Cover: 2.25 **NM** value: **Cover or less**
Circ: CapCity orders: **9,475**
Through The Window **A:** Kent Williams **W:** J.M. DeMatteis

7 ❑ Mar 1995 Cover: 2.25 **NM** value: **Cover or less**

Other grades: Multiply prices above by **1.5 for Mint • 2/3 for Very Fine • 1/3 for Fine • 1/5 for Very Good • 1/8 for Good**

Circ: CapCity orders: **8,725**
📖 Counterpane **A:** Jon J. Muth **W:** J.M. DeMatteis

8 ❑ Apr 1995 Cover: 2.25 **NM** value: **Cover or less**
Circ: CapCity orders: **7,950**
📖 Candles **A:** Jon J. Muth **W:** J.M. DeMatteis

9 ❑ May 1995 Cover: 2.25 **NM** value: **Cover or less**
Circ: CapCity orders: **7,675**
W: J.M. DeMatteis

10 ❑ Jun 1995 Cover: 2.25 **NM** value: **Cover or less**
Circ: CapCity orders: **7,275**
W: J.M. DeMatteis

11 ❑ Jul 1995 Cover: 2.25 **NM** value: **Cover or less**
Circ: CapCity orders: **7,100**
📖 Contradictions **A:** Jon J. Muth; George Pratt **W:** J.M. DeMatteis
★ Origin of Moonshadow.

12 ❑ Aug 1995 Cover: 2.95 **NM** value: **Cover or less**
Circ: CapCity orders: **7,000**
📖 With Joy To Hear final issue. **A:** Jon J. Muth; George Pratt; Kent Williams **W:** J.M. DeMatteis

Bk 1 ❑ Cover: 39.95 **NM** value: **Cover or less**
• The Compleat Moonshadow **A:** Jon J. Muth; George Pratt; Kent Williams **W:** J.M. DeMatteis

MOON SHOT, THE FLIGHT OF APOLLO 12 — Pepper Pike Graphix

1 ❑ Jun 1994 Cover: 2.95 **NM** value: **Cover or less**
One-shot.

MOONSTRUCK — White Wolf

1 ❑ May 1987 Cover: 2.00 **NM** value: **Cover or less**

MOONTRAP — Caliber

1 ❑ b&w Cover: 1.95 **NM** value: **2.00**
A: Gary Kwapisz **W:** Tex Ragsdale

MOONWALKER 3-D — Blackthorne

1 ❑ Cover: 2.50 **NM** value: **Cover or less**
Circ: CapCity orders: **1,875**

MOPSY — St. John

Gladys Parker (1910-1966) created Mopsy in 1939 for daily newspaper syndication, and the stylish urban working girl appeared in panel cartoons until the year before Parker's death. Though the pert and perky brunette was almost invariably portrayed showing off her shapely legs, much of the cartoon's approach was to show things from her viewpoint. That's not to say she didn't have problems with the gents she was with. Nevertheless, she was often shown in control, perhaps best exemplified by the cover of Mopsy #1, in which she speaks simultaneously into two telephone receivers, saying, "Of course you're the only one I love, darling!" — Maggie

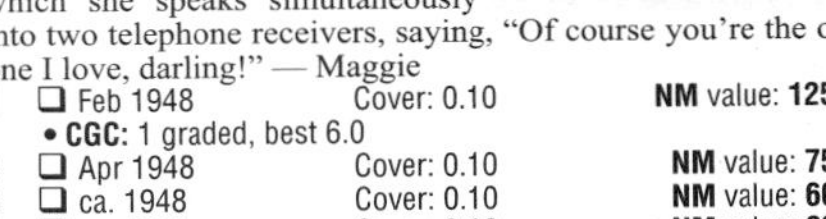

1 ❑ Feb 1948 Cover: 0.10 **NM** value: **125.00**
• **CGC:** 1 graded, best 6.0
2 ❑ Apr 1948 Cover: 0.10 **NM** value: **75.00**
3 ❑ ca. 1948 Cover: 0.10 **NM** value: **60.00**
4 ❑ ca. 1948 Cover: 0.10 **NM** value: **60.00**
5 ❑ ca. 1949 Cover: 0.10 **NM** value: **60.00**
6 ❑ ca. 1949 Cover: 0.10 **NM** value: **60.00**
7 ❑ Sep 1949 Cover: 0.10 **NM** value: **60.00**
8 ❑ Dec 1949 Cover: 0.10 **NM** value: **60.00**
9 ❑ 1950 Cover: 0.10 **NM** value: **60.00**
10 ❑ ca. 1950 Cover: 0.10 **NM** value: **50.00**
11 ❑ ca. 1950 Cover: 0.10 **NM** value: **50.00**
12 ❑ ca. 1950 Cover: 0.10 **NM** value: **50.00**
13 ❑ Nov 1950 Cover: 0.10 **NM** value: **50.00**
14 ❑ ca. 1951 Cover: 0.10 **NM** value: **50.00**
15 ❑ ca. 1951 Cover: 0.10 **NM** value: **50.00**
16 ❑ ca. 1952 Cover: 0.10 **NM** value: **45.00**
17 ❑ ca. 1952 Cover: 0.10 **NM** value: **45.00**
18 ❑ ca. 1953 Cover: 0.10 **NM** value: **45.00**

MORBID ANGEL — London Night

0.5 ❑ Jul 1996 Cover: 3.00 **NM** value: **Cover or less**
A: Everette Hartsoe **W:** Everette Hartsoe

MORBID ANGEL: PENANCE — London Night

1 ❑ Sep 1996 Cover: 3.95 **NM** value: **Cover or less**
Circ: Diamd. preorders: **3,943**
A: Georges Jeanty **W:** Everette Hartsoe; Dominic Dell Aquila

MORBIUS REVISITED — Marvel

1 ❑ Aug 1993 Cover: 1.95 **NM** value: **2.00**
Circ: CapCity orders: **16,700**
• Reprints Fear #27

2 ❑ Sep 1993 Cover: 1.95 **NM** value: **2.00**
Circ: CapCity orders: **11,000**
📖 The Doorway Screaming Into Hell! • Reprints Fear #28 **A:** Frank Robbins **W:** Doug Moench

3 ❑ Oct 1993 Cover: 1.95 **NM** value: **2.00**
Circ: CapCity orders: **8,600**
📖 Through A Helleyes Darkly! • Reprints Fear #29 **A:** Don Heck **W:** Bill Mantlo ★ Appearance of Helleyes, Simon Stroud.

4 ❑ Nov 1993 Cover: 1.95 **NM** value: **2.00**
Circ: CapCity orders: **7,050**
• Reprints Fear #30

5 ❑ Dec 1993 Cover: 1.95 **NM** value: **2.00**
Circ: CapCity orders: **6,700**
• Reprints Fear #31

MORBIUS: THE LIVING VAMPIRE — Marvel

Michael Morbius has it all: He is a brilliant scientist, a Nobel prize-winner, and he is engaged to be married. Then he is struck with an incurable blood disease. Rather than give up, he turns his genius to finding a cure. In a secret laboratory, he tries treatment after treatment but always meets with failure. Finally, a bizarre combination of electroshock coupled with serum taken from vampire bats brings the disease to a standstill. But, in its place, a more terrible disease has taken hold. Michael Morbius has become a sort of "living vampire," required to feed on human blood in order to live.

First appearing in Amazing Spider-Man #101, Morbius now stars in this, his first solo series. Launched as part of The Ghost Rider "Rise of the Midnight Sons" epic, the series begins with Morbius on the verge of developing a serum to cure his vampirism. Then the demon Lilith arranges to add a little something extra to the mixture.

1 ❑ Sep 1992 Cover: 2.75 **NM** value: **Cover or less**
Circ: CapCity orders: **134,400**
• Without poster

1/CS ❑ Sep 1992 Cover: 2.75 **NM** value: **3.00**
📖 Rise of the Midnight Sons, Part 3 **A:** Ron Wagner **W:** Len Kaminski

2 ❑ Oct 1992 Cover: 1.75 **NM** value: **2.00**
Circ: CapCity orders: **66,300**
📖 Welcome to the Jungle **A:** Ron Wagner **W:** Len Kaminski

3 ❑ Nov 1992 Cover: 1.75 **NM** value: **2.00**
Circ: CapCity orders: **65,100**
A: Ron Wagner **W:** Len Kaminski ★ Appearance of Spider-Man.

4 ❑ Dec 1992 Cover: 1.75 **NM** value: **2.00**
Circ: CapCity orders: **58,800**
A: Ron Wagner **W:** Len Kaminski ★ Appearance of Spider-Man.

5 ❑ Jan 1993 Cover: 1.75 **NM** value: **2.00**
Circ: CapCity orders: **48,000**
📖 Here There Be Dragons **A:** Ron Wagner **W:** Len Kaminski ★ 1st Appearance of Basilisk II.

6 ❑ Feb 1993 Cover: 1.75 **NM** value: **Cover or less**
Circ: CapCity orders: **43,300**
📖 Tooth and Nail **A:** Ron Wagner **W:** Len Kaminski

7 ❑ Mar 1993 Cover: 1.75 **NM** value: **Cover or less**
Circ: CapCity orders: **37,700**
📖 Cemetery Dance **A:** Ron Wagner **W:** Len Kaminski

8 ❑ Apr 1993 Cover: 1.75 **NM** value: **Cover or less**
Circ: CapCity orders: **36,300**

9 ❑ May 1993 Cover: 1.75 **NM** value: **Cover or less**
Circ: CapCity orders: **34,100**

10 ❑ Jun 1993 Cover: 1.75 **NM** value: **Cover or less**
Circ: CapCity orders: **31,500**

11 ❑ Jul 1993 Cover: 1.75 **NM** value: **Cover or less**
Circ: CapCity orders: **28,900**

12 ❑ Aug 1993 Cover: 2.95 **NM** value: **Cover or less**
Circ: CapCity orders: **48,800**
Double cover. 📖 Midnight Massacre, Part 4

13 ❑ Sep 1993 Cover: 1.75 **NM** value: **Cover or less**
Circ: CapCity orders: **24,600**

14 ❑ Oct 1993 Cover: 1.75 **NM** value: **Cover or less**
Circ: CapCity orders: **22,100**
A: Ron Wagner **W:** Greg Wright ★ Appearance of Martine, Werewolf by Night, D'Spayre.

15 ❑ Nov 1993 Cover: 1.75 **NM** value: **Cover or less**
Circ: CapCity orders: **20,900**

16 ❑ Dec 1993 Cover: 1.75 **NM** value: **Cover or less**
Circ: CapCity orders: **27,300**
Neon ink/matte finish cover. 📖 Siege of Darkness, Part 4

17 ❑ Jan 1994 Cover: 1.75 **NM** value: **Cover or less**
Circ: Statement: **76,133** CapCity orders: **22,100**
Spot-varnished cover. 📖 Siege of Darkness, Part 13

18 ❑ Feb 1994 Cover: 1.75 **NM** value: **Cover or less**
Circ: Statement: **76,133** CapCity orders: **16,300**

19 ❑ Mar 1994 Cover: 1.75 **NM** value: **Cover or less**
Circ: Statement: **76,133** CapCity orders: **15,650**

20 ❑ Apr 1994 Cover: 1.75 **NM** value: **Cover or less**
Circ: Statement: **76,133** CapCity orders: **14,400**

21 ❑ May 1994 Cover: 1.95 **NM** value: **Cover or less**
Circ: Statement: **76,133** CapCity orders: **13,500**

22 ❑ Jun 1994 Cover: 1.95 **NM** value: **Cover or less**
Circ: Statement: **76,133** CapCity orders: **13,100**

23 ❑ Jul 1994 Cover: 1.95 **NM** value: **Cover or less**
Circ: Statement: **76,133** CapCity orders: **12,250**

24 ❑ Aug 1994 Cover: 1.95 **NM** value: **Cover or less**
Circ: Statement: **76,133** CapCity orders: **11,100**

25 ❑ Sep 1994 Cover: 2.50 **NM** value: **Cover or less**
Circ: Statement: **76,133** CapCity orders: **13,850**
• Giant-size.

26 ❑ Oct 1994 Cover: 1.95 **NM** value: **Cover or less**
Circ: Statement: **76,133** CapCity orders: **10,300**

27 ❑ Nov 1994 Cover: 1.95 **NM** value: **Cover or less**
Circ: Statement: **76,133** CapCity orders: **9,250**

28 ❑ Dec 1994 Cover: 1.95 **NM** value: **Cover or less**
Circ: Statement: **76,133** CapCity orders: **9,000**

29 ❑ Jan 1995 Cover: 1.95 **NM** value: **Cover or less**
Circ: CapCity orders: **8,375**

30 ❑ Feb 1995 Cover: 1.95 **NM** value: **Cover or less**
Circ: CapCity orders: **7,350**

31 ❑ Mar 1995 Cover: 1.95 **NM** value: **Cover or less**
Circ: CapCity orders: **6,350**

32 ❑ Apr 1995 Cover: 1.95 **NM** value: **Cover or less**
Circ: CapCity orders: **5,750**
final issue. • Has 1994 Statement, dated 10/1/94; avg print run 76,758; avg sales 75,375; avg subs 758; avg total paid 76,133; samples 125; office use 500; max existent 77,758; no newsstand sales this year

MORE FETISH — Boneyard

1 ❑ Nov 1993 Cover: 2.95 **NM** value: **Cover or less**
📖 Turning the Worm **A:** Anthony Fanning **W:** Anthony Fanning

MORE FUN COMICS — DC

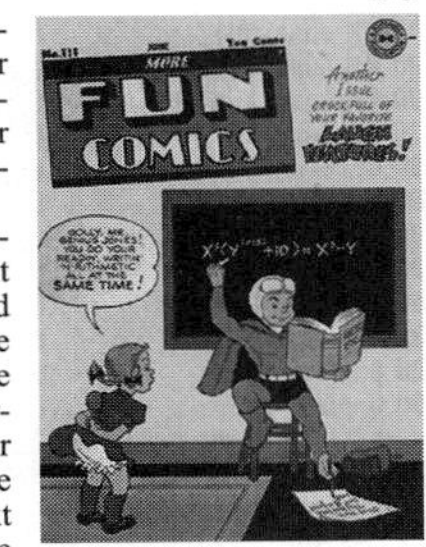

Continuing from New Fun Comics, More Fun began as a humor comic book before it transformed itself into the breeding ground for many of DC's most stalwart super-heroes.

The heroes began with a costumed appearance by Doctor Occult in issue #14. Various Western and other features followed before the undead super-hero The Spectre made his awe-inspiring first appearance with issues #51-52. Doctor Fate and Congo Bill (the future Congorilla) followed in the next few issues, along with Flash clone Johnny Quick in issue #71. Two issues later, DC cloned Marvel's Namor in a more friendly manner when they introduced Aquaman. In the same issue, archer Green Arrow and his boy sidekick Speedy were also introduced.

Issue #101 saw the debut of Superboy in the title. Unfortunately, it was all downhill from there, as super-heroes — and the title — disappeared over the next few years.

7 ❑ Jan 1936 Cover: 0.10 **NM** value: **5500.00**
• Oversized. • Series continued from New Fun Comics #6
8 ❑ Feb 1936 Cover: 0.10 **NM** value: **5500.00**
• Oversized.
9 ❑ Mar 1936 Cover: 0.10 **NM** value: **6500.00**
• **CGC:** 2 graded, best 5.5
• Comic-sized issues begin.
10 ❑ May 1936 Cover: 0.10 **NM** value: **3200.00**
• **CGC:** 1 graded, best 6.5
11 ❑ Jul 1936 Cover: 0.10 **NM** value: **2800.00**
• **CGC:** 3 graded, best 7.5
12 ❑ Aug 1936 Cover: 0.10 **NM** value: **2400.00**
• **CGC:** 1 graded, best 5.0
13 ❑ Sep 1936 Cover: 0.10 **NM** value: **2400.00**
• **CGC:** 1 graded, best 3.0
14 ❑ Oct 1936 Cover: 0.10 **NM** value: **12400.00**
• **CGC:** 2 graded, best 5.5
★ 1st Appearance of on Doctor Occult (in costume).
15 ❑ Nov 1936 Cover: 0.10 **NM** value: **4900.00**
• **CGC:** 1 graded, best 1.5
★ Appearance of Doctor Occult.
16 ❑ Dec 1936 Cover: 0.10 **NM** value: **4900.00**
• **CGC:** 3 graded, best 8.5
★ Appearance of Doctor Occult.
17 ❑ Jan 1937 Cover: 0.10 **NM** value: **4400.00**
• **CGC:** 1 graded, best 2.0
18 ❑ Feb 1937 Cover: 0.10 **NM** value: **2100.00**
19 ❑ Mar 1937 Cover: 0.10 **NM** value: **2100.00**
• **CGC:** 4 graded, best 8.0
20 ❑ May 1937 Cover: 0.10 **NM** value: **2100.00**
• **CGC:** 1 graded, best 1.0
21 ❑ Jun 1937 Cover: 0.10 **NM** value: **1925.00**
22 ❑ Jul 1937 Cover: 0.10 **NM** value: **1925.00**
• **CGC:** 1 graded, best 6.0
23 ❑ Aug 1937 Cover: 0.10 **NM** value: **1925.00**
24 ❑ Sep 1937 Cover: 0.10 **NM** value: **1925.00**
• **CGC:** 1 graded, best 8.5
25 ❑ Oct 1937 Cover: 0.10 **NM** value: **1925.00**
• **CGC:** 1 graded, best 4.0
26 ❑ Nov 1937 Cover: 0.10 **NM** value: **1750.00**
• **CGC:** 1 graded, best 9.4
27 ❑ Dec 1937 Cover: 0.10 **NM** value: **1750.00**
28 ❑ Jan 1938 Cover: 0.10 **NM** value: **1750.00**
• **CGC:** 1 graded, best 9.2
29 ❑ Feb 1938 Cover: 0.10 **NM** value: **1750.00**
• **CGC:** 1 graded, best 9.4
Last humor cover.
30 ❑ Mar 1938 Cover: 0.10 **NM** value: **1600.00**
31 ❑ May 1938 Cover: 0.10 **NM** value: **1600.00**
• **CGC:** 1 graded, best 9.6
32 ❑ Jun 1938 Cover: 0.10 **NM** value: **1600.00**
• **CGC:** 2 graded, best 4.0
33 ❑ Jul 1938 Cover: 0.10 **NM** value: **1600.00**
• **CGC:** 1 graded, best 9.4
34 ❑ Aug 1938 Cover: 0.10 **NM** value: **1600.00**
• **CGC:** 2 graded, best 9.4
35 ❑ Sep 1938 Cover: 0.10 **NM** value: **1600.00**
• **CGC:** 1 graded, best 9.4
36 ❑ Oct 1938 Cover: 0.10 **NM** value: **1600.00**
37 ❑ Nov 1938 Cover: 0.10 **NM** value: **1600.00**
• **CGC:** 1 graded, best .5
38 ❑ Dec 1938 Cover: 0.10 **NM** value: **1600.00**
• **CGC:** 1 graded, best 9.4
39 ❑ Jan 1939 Cover: 0.10 **NM** value: **1600.00**
• **CGC:** 1 graded, best 9.6
40 ❑ Feb 1939 Cover: 0.10 **NM** value: **1600.00**
• **CGC:** 1 graded, best 9.4
41 ❑ Mar 1939 Cover: 0.10 **NM** value: **1300.00**
• **CGC:** 1 graded, best 9.2
42 ❑ Apr 1939 Cover: 0.10 **NM** value: **1300.00**
• **CGC:** 1 graded, best 9.6
43 ❑ May 1939 Cover: 0.10 **NM** value: **1300.00**
44 ❑ Jun 1939 Cover: 0.10 **NM** value: **1300.00**
• **CGC:** 2 graded, best 9.4
45 ❑ Jul 1939 Cover: 0.10 **NM** value: **1300.00**
• **CGC:** 1 graded, best 9.0

CGC-graded: Multiply prices above by **33 for 9.9 M • 16 for 9.8 NM/M • 7 for 9.6 NM+ • 5 for 9.4 NM • 2.5 for 9.2 NM- • 1.5 for 9.0 VF/NM**

46 ❑ Aug 1939 Cover: 0.10 **NM** value: **1185.00**
• **CGC:** 3 graded, best 9.6

47 ❑ Sep 1939 Cover: 0.10 **NM** value: **1185.00**
• **CGC:** 1 graded, best 9.2

48 ❑ Oct 1939 Cover: 0.10 **NM** value: **1185.00**
• **CGC:** 1 graded, best 9.0

49 ❑ Nov 1939 Cover: 0.10 **NM** value: **1185.00**
• **CGC:** 2 graded, best 9.4

50 ❑ Dec 1939 Cover: 0.10 **NM** value: **1185.00**
• **CGC:** 3 graded, best 9.4

51 ❑ Jan 1940 Cover: 0.10 **NM** value: **4900.00**
• **CGC:** 2 graded, best 9.0
★ 1st Appearance of The Spectre (cameo).

52 ❑ Feb 1940 Cover: 0.10 **NM** value: **52000.00**
• **CGC:** 2 graded, best 9.2
Spectre cover. ★ Origin of The Spectre. ★ 1st Appearance of The Spectre (full appearance).

53 ❑ Mar 1940 Cover: 0.10 **NM** value: **34200.00**
• **CGC:** 1 graded, best 9.4
Spectre cover. ★ Origin of The Spectre. ★ 2nd Appearance of The Spectre.

54 ❑ Apr 1940 Cover: 0.10 **NM** value: **9400.00**
• **CGC:** 5 graded, best 9.2
Spectre cover.

55 ❑ May 1940 Cover: 0.10 **NM** value: **12000.00**
• **CGC:** 2 graded, best 9.4
Spectre cover. ★ Origin of Doctor Fate. ★ 1st Appearance of Doctor Fate.

56 ❑ Jun 1940 Cover: 0.10 **NM** value: **4250.00**
• **CGC:** 3 graded, best 9.2
★ 1st Appearance of Congo Bill.

57 ❑ Jul 1940 Cover: 0.10 **NM** value: **3000.00**
• **CGC:** 4 graded, best 9.2

58 ❑ Aug 1940 Cover: 0.10 **NM** value: **3000.00**
• **CGC:** 3 graded, best 9.0

59 ❑ Sep 1940 Cover: 0.10 **NM** value: **3000.00**
• **CGC:** 4 graded, best 9.4

60 ❑ Oct 1940 Cover: 0.10 **NM** value: **3000.00**
• **CGC:** 2 graded, best 7.0
Doctor Fate cover.

61 ❑ Nov 1940 Cover: 0.10 **NM** value: **2425.00**
• **CGC:** 2 graded, best 9.6

62 ❑ Dec 1940 Cover: 0.10 **NM** value: **2425.00**
• **CGC:** 3 graded, best 8.0

63 ❑ Jan 1941 Cover: 0.10 **NM** value: **2425.00**
• **CGC:** 1 graded, best 8.0

64 ❑ Feb 1941 Cover: 0.10 **NM** value: **2425.00**
• **CGC:** 3 graded, best 9.6

65 ❑ Mar 1941 Cover: 0.10 **NM** value: **2600.00**
• **CGC:** 2 graded, best 9.0
Spectre cover.

66 ❑ Apr 1941 Cover: 0.10 **NM** value: **2600.00**
• **CGC:** 1 graded, best 8.5

67 ❑ May 1941 Cover: 0.10 **NM** value: **6600.00**
• **CGC:** 5 graded, best 9.2
★ Origin of Doctor Fate.

68 ❑ Jun 1941 Cover: 0.10 **NM** value: **2050.00**
• **CGC:** 2 graded, best 9.0

69 ❑ Jul 1941 Cover: 0.10 **NM** value: **2050.00**
• **CGC:** 7 graded, best 9.2

70 ❑ Aug 1941 Cover: 0.10 **NM** value: **2050.00**
• **CGC:** 4 graded, best 9.2

71 ❑ Sep 1941 Cover: 0.10 **NM** value: **5650.00**
• **CGC:** 5 graded, best 9.4
★ Origin of Johnny Quick. ★ 1st Appearance of Johnny Quick.

72 ❑ Oct 1941 Cover: 0.10 **NM** value: **1685.00**
• **CGC:** 8 graded, best 9.0

73 ❑ Nov 1941 Cover: 0.10 **NM** value: **11600.00**
• **CGC:** 6 graded, best 9.0
★ Origin of Aquaman. ★ 1st Appearance of Speedy, Green Arrow, Aquaman.

74 ❑ Dec 1941 Cover: 0.10 **NM** value: **2275.00**
• **CGC:** 5 graded, best 9.6
★ 2nd Appearance of Aquaman.

75 ❑ Jan 1942 Cover: 0.10 **NM** value: **1690.00**
• **CGC:** 4 graded, best 9.6

76 ❑ Feb 1942 Cover: 0.10 **NM** value: **1690.00**
• **CGC:** 3 graded, best 9.6

77 ❑ Mar 1942 Cover: 0.10 **NM** value: **1690.00**
• **CGC:** 1 graded, best 9.2

78 ❑ Apr 1942 Cover: 0.10 **NM** value: **1690.00**
• **CGC:** 5 graded, best 9.6

79 ❑ May 1942 Cover: 0.10 **NM** value: **1690.00**
• **CGC:** 2 graded, best 9.6

80 ❑ Jun 1942 Cover: 0.10 **NM** value: **1690.00**
• **CGC:** 2 graded, best 9.4

81 ❑ Jul 1942 Cover: 0.10 **NM** value: **1100.00**
• **CGC:** 3 graded, best 9.0

82 ❑ Aug 1942 Cover: 0.10 **NM** value: **1100.00**
• **CGC:** 2 graded, best 9.6

83 ❑ Sep 1942 Cover: 0.10 **NM** value: **1100.00**
• **CGC:** 3 graded, best 9.2

84 ❑ Oct 1942 Cover: 0.10 **NM** value: **1100.00**
• **CGC:** 1 graded, best 9.6

85 ❑ Nov 1942 Cover: 0.10 **NM** value: **1100.00**
• **CGC:** 5 graded, best 9.4

86 ❑ Dec 1942 Cover: 0.10 **NM** value: **1100.00**
• **CGC:** 2 graded, best 9.2

87 ❑ Jan 1943 Cover: 0.10 **NM** value: **1100.00**
• **CGC:** 4 graded, best 9.8

88 ❑ Feb 1943 Cover: 0.10 **NM** value: **1100.00**
• **CGC:** 3 graded, best 9.6

89 ❑ Mar 1943 Cover: 0.10 **NM** value: **1250.00**
• **CGC:** 1 graded, best 8.0
★ Origin of Green Arrow & Speedy team.

90 ❑ Apr 1943 Cover: 0.10 **NM** value: **900.00**
• **CGC:** 2 graded, best 9.4

91 ❑ May 1943 Cover: 0.10 **NM** value: **900.00**
• **CGC:** 2 graded, best 9.6

92 ❑ Jul 1943 Cover: 0.10 **NM** value: **900.00**
• **CGC:** 4 graded, best 9.4

93 ❑ Sep 1943 Cover: 0.10 **NM** value: **900.00**
• **CGC:** 3 graded, best 9.6

94 ❑ Nov 1943 Cover: 0.10 **NM** value: **900.00**
• **CGC:** 3 graded, best 9.6

95 ❑ Jan 1944 Cover: 0.10 **NM** value: **900.00**
• **CGC:** 3 graded, best 9.2

96 ❑ Mar 1944 Cover: 0.10 **NM** value: **900.00**
• **CGC:** 2 graded, best 9.4

97 ❑ May 1944 Cover: 0.10 **NM** value: **900.00**
• **CGC:** 6 graded, best 9.6

98 ❑ Jul 1944 Cover: 0.10 **NM** value: **900.00**
• **CGC:** 3 graded, best 9.4
• Doctor Fate stories end

99 ❑ Sep 1944 Cover: 0.10 **NM** value: **900.00**
• **CGC:** 5 graded, best 9.4

100 ❑ Nov 1944 Cover: 0.10 **NM** value: **1035.00**
• **CGC:** 8 graded, best 9.4

101 ❑ Jan 1945 Cover: 0.10 **NM** value: **7600.00**
• **CGC:** 11 graded, best 9.0
★ Origin of Superboy. ★ 1st Appearance of Superboy.

102 ❑ Mar 1945 Cover: 0.10 **NM** value: **1285.00**
• **CGC:** 5 graded, best 9.2
★ 2nd Appearance of Superboy.

103 ❑ May 1945 Cover: 0.10 **NM** value: **965.00**
• **CGC:** 2 graded, best 7.0
★ Appearance of Superboy.

104 ❑ Jul 1945 Cover: 0.10 **NM** value: **725.00**
• **CGC:** 1 graded, best 3.0

105 ❑ Sep 1945 Cover: 0.10 **NM** value: **725.00**
• **CGC:** 3 graded, best 8.0

106 ❑ Nov 1945 Cover: 0.10 **NM** value: **620.00**
• **CGC:** 4 graded, best 9.2

107 ❑ Jan 1946 Cover: 0.10 **NM** value: **620.00**
• **CGC:** 2 graded, best 9.4

108 ❑ Mar 1946 Cover: 0.10 **NM** value: **155.00**
• **CGC:** 2 graded, best 8.0
• Humor strips start

109 ❑ Apr 1946 Cover: 0.10 **NM** value: **155.00**
• **CGC:** 1 graded, best 9.4

110 ❑ May 1946 Cover: 0.10 **NM** value: **155.00**
• **CGC:** 1 graded, best 9.4

111 ❑ Jun 1946 Cover: 0.10 **NM** value: **130.00**
• **CGC:** 2 graded, best 9.2
📖 Genius Jones: Jeepers Creepers!; Dover and Clover: A Blue Ribbon Mystery!; Curly's Cafe; Windy; Cabbie Casey; Light Larceny (text story); Rusty; The Gas House Gang; Cunnel Custard **A:** Ben Ballard; Jack Farr **W:** Jack Farr

112 ❑ Jul 1946 Cover: 0.10 **NM** value: **130.00**
• **CGC:** 2 graded, best 8.0

113 ❑ Aug 1946 Cover: 0.10 **NM** value: **130.00**
• **CGC:** 1 graded, best 9.0

114 ❑ Sep 1946 Cover: 0.10 **NM** value: **130.00**
• **CGC:** 2 graded, best 8.5

115 ❑ Oct 1946 Cover: 0.10 **NM** value: **130.00**
• **CGC:** 1 graded, best 7.5

116 ❑ Nov 1946 Cover: 0.10 **NM** value: **130.00**
• **CGC:** 1 graded, best 9.6

117 ❑ Dec 1946 Cover: 0.10 **NM** value: **130.00**

118 ❑ Jan 1947 Cover: 0.10 **NM** value: **130.00**
• **CGC:** 1 graded, best 9.4

119 ❑ Feb 1947 Cover: 0.10 **NM** value: **130.00**
• **CGC:** 1 graded, best 9.8

120 ❑ Mar 1947 Cover: 0.10 **NM** value: **130.00**
• **CGC:** 2 graded, best 9.6

121 ❑ Apr 1947 Cover: 0.10 **NM** value: **105.00**
• **CGC:** 2 graded, best 9.8

122 ❑ May 1947 Cover: 0.10 **NM** value: **105.00**
• **CGC:** 2 graded, best 9.6

123 ❑ Jun 1947 Cover: 0.10 **NM** value: **105.00**

124 ❑ Jul 1947 Cover: 0.10 **NM** value: **105.00**

125 ❑ Aug 1947 Cover: 0.10 **NM** value: **550.00**
• **CGC:** 1 graded, best 9.0
Superman cover.

126 ❑ Sep 1947 Cover: 0.10 **NM** value: **105.00**
• **CGC:** 1 graded, best 7.0

127 ❑ Nov 1947 Cover: 0.10 **NM** value: **210.00**
• **CGC:** 1 graded, best 9.6
final issue. • Scarce

MORE SECRET ORIGINS REPLICA EDITION — DC

1 ❑ Dec 1999 Cover: 4.95 **NM** value: **Cover or less**
Circ: Diamd. preorders: **15,851** • **CGC:** 1 graded, best 9.8
• reprints 80-Page Giant #8. 📖 The Origin of the Justice League!; Birth of the Atom; How Aquaman Got His Powers; The Man from Robin's Past; Origin of Flash's Masked Identity; Story of Superman's Life **A:** Ramona Fradon; Murphy Anderson; Carmine Infantino; Gil Kane; Al Plastino; Joe Giella; Shelly Moldoff; Charles Paris **W:** Bill Finger; Gardner Fox; John Broome; Otto Binder; Robert Bernstein ★ Origin of Superman, The Atom II (Ray Palmer), The Justice League of America, Aquaman.

MORE TALES FROM GIMBLEY — Harrier

1 ❑ Feb 1988 Cover: 1.95 **NM** value: **Cover or less**
📖 A Tale from Gimbley **A:** Paul Grist; Ed Pinsent; Phil Elliot **W:** Phil Elliot

MORE TALES FROM SLEAZE CASTLE — Gratuitous Bunny

1 ❑ **NM** value: **4.00**
📖 Arrival, Part 1; Arrival, Part 2; Arrival, Part 3 **A:** Terry Wiley **W:** Dave Mckinnon

2 ❑ **NM** value: **3.00**
📖 Arrival, Part 4; Arrival, Part 5 **A:** Terry Wiley **W:** Dave Mckinnon

3 ❑ 1990 **NM** value: **3.00**
📖 An Ill Wind **A:** Terry Wiley **W:** Dave Mckinnon

4 ❑ Jan 1991 **NM** value: **3.00**
📖 An Ill Wind; The Adventures of Dweng & Ralph, Part 1; Farewell My Maltese Sleep, Part 1 **A:** Terry Wiley **W:** Dave Mckinnon

5 ❑ Jan 1992 **NM** value: **3.00**
📖 An Ill Wind; The Adventures of Dweng & Ralph, Part 1; Farewell My Maltese Sleep, Part 2 **A:** Terry Wiley **W:** Dave Mckinnon

6 ❑ Jan 1993 **NM** value: **3.00**
📖 An Ill Wind; The Adventures of Dweng & Ralph, Part 1; Farewell My Maltese Sleep, Part 3 **A:** Terry Wiley **W:** Dave Mckinnon

Bk 1 ❑ Cover: 6.99 **NM** value: **Cover or less**
• "Director's Cut"; Collects More Tales From Sleaze Castle #1-3 **A:** Terry Wiley **W:** Dave Mckinnon

Bk 2 ❑ Jan 1995 Cover: 7.99 **NM** value: **Cover or less**
• "Director's Cut"; Collects More Tales From Sleaze Castle #4-6 **A:** Terry Wiley **W:** Dave Mckinnon

MORE THAN MORTAL — Liar

Deirdre, a lowly maid in an Irish church, has strange dreams: she is Brigid the Protector, a wielder of magic and weapons who protects medieval Ireland from demonic invaders. The only one who gives her dreams any credence is Father Colm, a kind priest, who encourages her to explore her dreams and discover their origins. Strangely, he vanishes and is presumed dead by Deirdre, but his advice is enough to send her on a journey to find out what her dreams of the Protector mean.

Writer Sharon Scott and artist Steve Firchow established a fairly solid foundation in the first issue of More Than Mortal, which, apparently, Deirdre is. Questions surround their young Irish heroine, and the reader is compelled to seek the answers along with her. Firchow's art — while a bit on the cheesecake side — moves the story along at a nice pace, but it is his work as a colorist that is particularly striking here.

1 ❑ Jun 1997 Cover: 2.95 **NM** value: **4.00**
Circ: Diamd. preorders: **21,188**
A: Steve Firchow **W:** Sharon Scott

1-2 ❑ Jun 1997 Cover: 2.95 **NM** value: **Cover or less**

2 ❑ Sep 1997 Cover: 2.95 **NM** value: **3.00**
Circ: Diamd. preorders: **17,685**
A: Steve Firchow **W:** Sharon Scott

2/SC ❑ Sep 1997 Cover: 2.95 **NM** value: **Cover or less**
logoless cover.

3 ❑ Dec 1997 Cover: 2.95 **NM** value: **3.00**
Circ: Diamd. preorders: **18,438**
A: Steve Firchow **W:** Sharon Scott

4 ❑ Apr 1998 Cover: 2.95 **NM** value: **3.00**
Circ: Diamd. preorders: **15,898**
A: Steve Firchow **W:** Sharon Scott

5 ❑ Dec 1999 Cover: 2.95 **NM** value: **3.00**
Circ: Diamd. preorders: **13,866**
📖 Famine, Part 1 **A:** Romano **W:** Sharon Scott

6 ❑ Mar 2000 Cover: 2.95 **NM** value: **Cover or less**
Circ: Diamd. preorders: **13,492**
📖 Famine, Part 2 **A:** Romano **W:** Sharon Scott

Bk 1 ❑ Cover: 6.95 **NM** value: **Cover or less**
• Collected Edition #1. • Collects More than Mortal #1-2 **A:** Steve Firchow **W:** Sharon Scott

Dlx 1 ❑ Cover: 14.95 **NM** value: **Cover or less**
• Collects More than Mortal #1-4 **A:** Steve Firchow **W:** Sharon Scott

MORE THAN MORTAL/LADY PENDRAGON — Image

1 ❑ Jun 1999 Cover: 2.50 **NM** value: **Cover or less**
Circ: Diamd. preorders: **26,649**
📖 Good versus Evil **A:** Dan Norton **W:** Matt Hawkins; Matthew Scott; Sharon Scott

1/A ❑ Jun 1999 Cover: 2.50 **NM** value: **3.00**
Circ: Diamd. preorders: **3,212**
alternate cover.

MORE THAN MORTAL: OTHERWORLDS — Image

1 ❑ Jul 1999 Cover: 2.95 **NM** value: **3.00**
Circ: Diamd. preorders: **20,481**
A: Steve Firchow **W:** Brian Holguin

1/A ❑ Jul 1999 Cover: 2.95 **NM** value: **3.00**
alternate cover. **A:** Steve Firchow **W:** Brian Holguin

2 ❑ Aug 1999 Cover: 2.95 **NM** value: **3.00**
Circ: Diamd. preorders: **16,059**
Woman and man kneeling on cover, large figure standing behind. **A:** Steve Firchow **W:** Brian Holguin

2/A ❑ Aug 1999 Cover: 2.95 **NM** value: **3.00**
alternate cover. **A:** Steve Firchow **W:** Brian Holguin

3 ❑ Oct 1999 Cover: 2.95 **NM** value: **3.00**
Circ: Diamd. preorders: **15,365**
Woman holding sword on cover, red top left background. **A:** Steve Firchow **W:** Brian Holguin

3/A ❑ Oct 1999 Cover: 2.95 **NM** value: **3.00**
alternate cover. **A:** Steve Firchow **W:** Brian Holguin

4 ❑ Dec 1999 Cover: 2.95 **NM** value: **3.00**
A: Steve Firchow **W:** Brian Holguin

MORE THAN MORTAL: SAGAS — Liar

1 ❑ Aug 1998 Cover: 2.95 **NM** value: **Cover or less**
Circ: Diamd. preorders: **17,243**
★ Origin of Morlock. ★ 1st Appearance of Morlock.

1/A ❑ Aug 1998 Cover: 2.95 **NM** value: **5.00**
variant cover for New Dimension Comics.

2 ❑ Oct 1998 Cover: 2.95 **NM** value: **Cover or less**
Circ: Diamd. preorders: **14,696**

3 ❑ Dec 1998 Cover: 2.95 **NM** value: **Cover or less**
Circ: Diamd. preorders: **12,381**

MORE THAN MORTAL: TRUTHS & LEGENDS — Liar

1 ❑ Jun 1998 Cover: 2.95 **NM** value: **Cover or less**
Circ: Diamd. preorders: **17,030**

Other grades: Multiply prices above by **1.5 for Mint • 2/3 for Very Fine • 1/3 for Fine • 1/5 for Very Good • 1/8 for Good**

Cover has man with glowing eye at bow of ship. **A:** Steve Firchow **W:** Matthew Scott; Sharon Scott
1/A ❑ Jun 1998 **NM** value: **4.00**
• Variant edition. **A:** Steve Firchow **W:** Matthew Scott; Sharon Scott
1/LE❑ Jun 1998 **NM** value: **5.00**
• Variant edition. **A:** Steve Firchow **W:** Matthew Scott; Sharon Scott
2 ❑ Aug 1998 Cover: 2.95 **NM** value: **Cover or less**
Circ: Diamd. preorders: **14,159**
3 ❑ Oct 1998 Cover: 2.95 **NM** value: **Cover or less**
Circ: Diamd. preorders: **14,666**
4 ❑ Jan 1999 Cover: 2.95 **NM** value: **Cover or less**
Circ: Diamd. preorders: **11,672**
5 ❑ Apr 1999 Cover: 2.95 **NM** value: **Cover or less**
Circ: Diamd. preorders: **11,773**

MORLOCK 2001 — Atlas-Seaboard

1 ❑ Feb 1975 Cover: 0.25 **NM** value: **2.00**
• **CGC:** 1 graded, best 9.4
📖 The Coming Of Morlock! **A:** Al Milgrom **W:** Michael Fleisher ★ Origin of Morlock.
2 ❑ Apr 1975 Cover: 0.25 **NM** value: **1.50**
A: Al Milgrom **W:** Michael Fleisher
3 ❑ Jul 1975 Cover: 0.25 **NM** value: **1.50**
A: Al Milgrom; Steve Ditko; Bernie Wrightson **W:** Michael Fleisher ★ Origin of Midnight Men.

MORNING GLORY — Radio

1 ❑ Nov 1998, b&w Cover: 2.95 **NM** value: **Cover or less**
A: Michael Vega
2 ❑ Dec 1998, b&w Cover: 2.95 **NM** value: **Cover or less**
3 ❑ Jan 1999, b&w Cover: 2.95 **NM** value: **Cover or less**
Circ: Diamd. preorders: **1,230**
5 ❑ May 1999, b&w Cover: 2.95 **NM** value: **Cover or less**
Circ: Diamd. preorders: **1,299**

MORNINGSTAR SPECIAL — Trident

1 ❑ Apr 1990, b&w Cover: 2.50 **NM** value: **Cover or less**
Circ: CapCity orders: **7,850**
📖 The Sword in the Stone **A:** Bill Willingham **W:** Bill Willingham

MORPHOS THE SHAPECHANGER — Dark Horse

1 ❑ Jul 1996 Cover: 4.95 **NM** value: **Cover or less**
No issue number. One-shot. • prestige format. **A:** Burne Hogarth **W:** Burne Hogarth; Harry Hurwitz

MORPHS — Graphxpress

1 ❑ Cover: 2.00 **NM** value: **Cover or less**
2 ❑ Cover: 2.00 **NM** value: **Cover or less**
3 ❑ Cover: 2.00 **NM** value: **Cover or less**
4 ❑ Cover: 2.00 **NM** value: **Cover or less**

MORRIGAN (DIMENSION X) — Dimension X

1 ❑ Aug 1993, b&w Cover: 2.75 **NM** value: **Cover or less**
A: Steve Rittler **W:** Steve Rittler

MORRIGAN (SIRIUS) — Sirius

1 ❑ Jul 1997 Cover: 2.95 **NM** value: **Cover or less**
Circ: Diamd. preorders: **7,126**

MORTAL COIL ASHCAN — Mermaid

Ash 1❑b&w **NM** value: **1.00**
no cover price.

MORTAL KOMBAT — Malibu

Mortal Kombat became legendary as a video game in the arcades, both for its high-tech kung fu fighting animations and for its grisly "finishing scenes," in which the winning player could literally tear apart his hapless opponent. Hugely popular, it was only a matter of time before the characters from Mortal Kombat were adapted into comic-book form. In 1994, Malibu did just that in this six-issue mini-series subtitled "Blood & Thunder."

Here are the world's greatest warriors invited to a deadly duel-to-the-death in Hong Kong. A total of 50 are called, including American film star Johnny Cage, who wants to prove his battle skills are not just Hollywood fiction; Liu Kang, a noble warrior from The Order of Light; Sonya Blade, a blonde American Special Forces operative; and Kano, a fighter from the evil Black Dragon organization. All will battle to the death for the honor of fighting Goro, the multi-armed reigning champion.

1 ❑ Jul 1994 Cover: 2.95 **NM** value: **3.00**
Circ: CapCity orders: **21,525**
📖 A Slow Boat To China • Blood and Thunder **A:** Patrick Rolo **W:** Charles Marshall
1/A ❑ Jul 1994 Cover: 2.95 **NM** value: **3.00**
variant cover (Mortal Kombat logo).
2 ❑ Aug 1994 Cover: 2.95 **NM** value: **3.00**
Circ: CapCity orders: **13,475**
• Blood and Thunder **A:** Patrick Rolo **W:** Charles Marshall
3 ❑ Sep 1994 Cover: 2.95 **NM** value: **3.00**
Circ: CapCity orders: **13,375**
📖 The Art of War • Blood and Thunder **A:** Patrick Rolo **W:** Charles Marshall
4 ❑ Oct 1994 Cover: 2.95 **NM** value: **3.00**
Circ: CapCity orders: **12,400**
• Blood and Thunder **A:** Patrick Rolo **W:** Charles Marshall
5 ❑ Nov 1994 Cover: 2.95 **NM** value: **3.00**
Circ: CapCity orders: **11,600**
• Blood and Thunder **A:** Patrick Rolo **W:** Charles Marshall
6 ❑ Cover: 2.95 **NM** value: **3.00**
Circ: CapCity orders: **10,075**
A: Patrick Rolo **W:** Charles Marshall

MORTAL KOMBAT: BARAKA — Malibu

1 ❑ ca. 1995 Cover: 2.95 **NM** value: **Cover or less**
Circ: CapCity orders: **5,475**

MORTAL KOMBAT: BATTLEWAVE — Malibu

1 ❑ ca. 1995 Cover: 2.95 **NM** value: **3.00**
Circ: CapCity orders: **8,500**
📖 Where The Wild Things Are! **A:** Patrick Rolo **W:** Charles Marshall
2 ❑ ca. 1995 Cover: 2.95 **NM** value: **3.00**
Circ: CapCity orders: **7,150**
A: Patrick Rolo **W:** Charles Marshall
3 ❑ ca. 1995 Cover: 2.95 **NM** value: **3.00**
Circ: CapCity orders: **6,675**
A: Patrick Rolo **W:** Charles Marshall
4 ❑ ca. 1995 Cover: 2.95 **NM** value: **3.00**
Circ: CapCity orders: **5,125**
A: Patrick Rolo **W:** Charles Marshall
5 ❑ ca. 1995 Cover: 2.95 **NM** value: **3.00**
Circ: CapCity orders: **4,950**
A: Patrick Rolo **W:** Charles Marshall
6 ❑ ca. 1995 Cover: 2.95 **NM** value: **3.00**
A: Patrick Rolo **W:** Charles Marshall

MORTAL KOMBAT: GORO, PRINCE OF PAIN — Malibu

1 ❑ Sep 1994 Cover: 2.95 **NM** value: **Cover or less**
Circ: CapCity orders: **13,000**
📖 Stranger in a Strange Land **A:** Roy Burdine **W:** Charles Marshall
2 ❑ Oct 1994 Cover: 2.95 **NM** value: **Cover or less**
Circ: CapCity orders: **10,550**

MORTAL KOMBAT: KITANA & MILEENA — Malibu

1 ❑ ca. 1995 Cover: 2.95 **NM** value: **Cover or less**
Circ: CapCity orders: **9,575**

MORTAL KOMBAT: KUNG LAO — Malibu

1 ❑ ca. 1995 Cover: 2.95 **NM** value: **Cover or less**

MORTAL KOMBAT: RAYDEN & KANO — Malibu

1 ❑ ca. 1995 Cover: 2.95 **NM** value: **Cover or less**
Circ: CapCity orders: **5,125**
2 ❑ ca. 1995 Cover: 2.95 **NM** value: **Cover or less**
Circ: CapCity orders: **6,400**

MORTAL KOMBAT SPECIAL EDITION — Malibu

1 ❑ Nov 1994 Cover: 2.95 **NM** value: **Cover or less**
Circ: CapCity orders: **10,175**
2 ❑ 1994 Cover: 2.95 **NM** value: **Cover or less**

MORTAL KOMBAT U.S. SPECIAL FORCES — Malibu

1 ❑ ca. 1995 Cover: 3.50 **NM** value: **Cover or less**
Circ: CapCity orders: **8,550**
📖 Secret Treasures **A:** Patrick Rolo **W:** Mark Paniccia
2 ❑ ca. 1995 Cover: 3.50 **NM** value: **Cover or less**
Circ: CapCity orders: **7,525**
A: Patrick Rolo **W:** Mark Paniccia

MORTAR MAN — Marshall Comics

1 ❑ May 1993, b&w Cover: 1.95 **NM** value: **Cover or less**
📖 First Boom **A:** Dan Duncan **W:** John Marshall
2 ❑ ca. 1993, b&w Cover: 1.95 **NM** value: **Cover or less**
3 ❑ ca. 1993 Cover: 2.50 **NM** value: **Cover or less**

MORTIE — Magazine Publications

1 ❑ Dec 1952 Cover: 0.10 **NM** value: **50.00**
• **CGC:** 1 graded, best 5.5
2 ❑ Mar 1953 Cover: 0.10 **NM** value: **25.00**
3 ❑ Jun 1953 Cover: 0.10 **NM** value: **25.00**
4 ❑ Sep 1953 Cover: 0.10 **NM** value: **25.00**

MORTIGAN GOTH: IMMORTALIS — Marvel

1 ❑ Sep 1993 Cover: 1.95 **NM** value: **Cover or less**
📖 The Devil's Due, Part 1 **A:** Mark Buckingham **W:** Nicholas Vince ★ Origin of Mortigan Goth.
1/SC❑Sep 1993 Cover: 2.95 **NM** value: **Cover or less**
foil cover. 📖 The Devil's Due, Part 1 **A:** Mark Buckingham **W:** Nicholas Vince
2 ❑ Oct 1993 Cover: 1.95 **NM** value: **Cover or less**
📖 The Devil's Due, Part 2 **A:** Mark Buckingham **W:** Nicholas Vince
3 ❑ Jan 1994 Cover: 1.95 **NM** value: **Cover or less**
📖 The Devil's Due, Part 3 **A:** Mark Buckingham **W:** Nicholas Vince
4 ❑ Mar 1994 Cover: 1.95 **NM** value: **Cover or less**
📖 The Devil's Due, Part 4 **A:** Mark Buckingham **W:** Nicholas Vince

There are two different pricing tiers in the modern comic-book hobby. **The prices seen above** are the prices we have seen **loose copies** of these issues reliably fetch in a variety of environments. Condition alters the price by the fractions seen on the bar on the bottom of left-hand pages of this book. **Comics graded by CGC** usually sell for more. Use the guide on the bottom of right-hand pages of this book to estimate what copies have brought on eBay.

MORT THE DEAD TEENAGER — Marvel

Mort Graves was a loser in life. He was the sort of guy who borrowed his parents' car and doused himself with cologne in order to impress women he had absolutely no chance with. His family and friends weren't exactly stellar achievers either. No, Mort led the depressing life of the average teenager. That is, he did until the day he ran his dad's car into a train while trying to impress the class bombshell. Now he's an equally depressed dead teenager.

Mort is a ghost now, consigned to limbo because hell was full-up with politicians, lawyers, and people who hung up on answering machines — and heaven was closed for repairs. He's been sent back to Earth to haunt his family, but all they care about is whether he's going to want his room back or whether he'll gross out his sister's new boyfriend. It seems that Mort learned the hard way that being dead is like being a teenager: nowhere to go, and it seems like it takes an eternity to get there!

The series was conceived as a potential movie project and, in 2002, it was announced that Quentin Tarantino would co-produce it.

1 ❑ Nov 1992 Cover: 1.75 **NM** value: **Cover or less**
Circ: CapCity orders: **8,000**
📖 Death On The Babylon Express **A:** Gary Hallgren **W:** Larry Hama
2 ❑ Dec 1992 Cover: 1.75 **NM** value: **Cover or less**
Circ: CapCity orders: **4,200**
A: Gary Hallgren **W:** Larry Hama
3 ❑ Jan 1993 Cover: 1.75 **NM** value: **Cover or less**
Circ: CapCity orders: **3,450**
A: Gary Hallgren **W:** Larry Hama
4 ❑ Mar 1993 Cover: 1.75 **NM** value: **Cover or less**
Circ: CapCity orders: **2,600**
A: Gary Hallgren **W:** Larry Hama

MORTY THE DOG (MU) — Mu

1 ❑ b&w Cover: 3.95 **NM** value: **Cover or less**
• digest.
2 ❑ Spr 1991, b&w Cover: 3.95 **NM** value: **Cover or less**
• digest.

MORTY THE DOG (STARHEAD) — Starhead

1 ❑ Cover: 1.75 **NM** value: **2.00**
📖 Bark And Bite!; The Big Break!; The Death Of Morty The Dog **A:** Steve Willis **W:** Steve Willis

MOSAIC — Sirius

1/A ❑ Mar 1999 Cover: 2.95 **NM** value: **Cover or less**
Circ: Diamd. preorders: **6,348**
1/B ❑ Mar 1999 Cover: 2.95 **NM** value: **Cover or less**
alternate cover. • smaller logos
2 ❑ Apr 1999 Cover: 2.95 **NM** value: **Cover or less**
Circ: Diamd. preorders: **3,479**
3 ❑ May 1999 Cover: 2.95 **NM** value: **Cover or less**
Circ: Diamd. preorders: **2,936**
4 ❑ Jun 1999 Cover: 2.95 **NM** value: **Cover or less**
Circ: Diamd. preorders: **2,984**
5 ❑ Jul 1999 Cover: 2.95 **NM** value: **Cover or less**
Circ: Diamd. preorders: **2,987**
Bk 1❑ Jan 2000 Cover: 14.95 **NM** value: **Cover or less**
• Trade Paperback. • collects series

MOSAIC: HELL CITY RIPPER — Sirius

1 ❑ Cover: 2.95 **NM** value: **Cover or less**
A: Kyle Hotz **W:** Kyle Hotz
1/SC❑ Cover: 2.95 **NM** value: **Cover or less**
Alternate cover by Kelley Jones. **A:** Kyle Hotz; Kelley Jones(cover) **W:** Kyle Hotz

MOSES AND THE TEN COMMANDMENTS — Dell

1 ❑ Aug 1957 Cover: 0.10 **NM** value: **75.00**
• **CGC:** 1 graded, best 9.6

MOSTLY WANTED — WildStorm

1 ❑ Jul 2000 Cover: 2.50 **NM** value: **Cover or less**
Circ: Diamd. preorders: **15,208**
A: Roberto Flores **W:** Scott Lobdell
2 ❑ Aug 2000 Cover: 2.50 **NM** value: **Cover or less**
Circ: Diamd. preorders: **11,232**
A: Roberto Flores **W:** Scott Lobdell
3 ❑ Sep 2000 Cover: 2.50 **NM** value: **Cover or less**
Circ: Diamd. preorders: **10,531**
A: Roberto Flores **W:** Scott Lobdell
4 ❑ Nov 2000 Cover: 2.50 **NM** value: **Cover or less**
Circ: Diamd. preorders: **8,950**
A: Roberto Flores **W:** Scott Lobdell

MOTHERLESS CHILD — Kitchen Sink

1 ❑ Cover: 2.95 **NM** value: **Cover or less**
A: Thom Scott III **W:** Thom Scott III

MOTHER'S OATS COMIX — Rip Off

1 ❑ Cover: 0.50 **NM** value: **5.00**
📖 The Doing of Dealer McDope; Bathroom Capers; Ego Trips; A Day in the Life **A:** F. Shrier; Dave Sheridan **W:** F. Shrier; Dave Sheridan
2 ❑ Cover: 0.50 **NM** value: **3.00**
📖 Word Salad; The Vision; The Balloon Sales Man; Dealer Mc Dope Visits Mexico; Bubble Blowers; Madam Olga **A:** F. Shrier **W:** F. Shrier

CGC-graded: Multiply prices above by **33 for 9.9 M • 16 for 9.8 NM/M • 7 for 9.6 NM+ • 5 for 9.4 NM • 2.5 for 9.2 NM- • 1.5 for 9.0 VF/NM**

MOTHER SUPERION — Antarctic

1 ❑ Jul 1997 Cover: 2.95 **NM** value: **Cover or less**
Circ: Diamd. preorders: **9,448**
A: Pat Kelley **W:** Pat Kelley

MOTHER TERESA OF CALCUTTA — Marvel

Catholic missionary Mother Teresa (1910-1997) ran a hospital in the grimmest slums of Calcutta, India, ministering to the lepers, beggars, and orphans of one of the world's most impoverished cities. In the early 1980s, when she was already in her late 1970s, she began to receive world-wide recognition for her work, culminating with her winning the Nobel Peace prize. Mother Teresa of Calcutta is an unusual double-length comic book from Marvel, telling the life story of Mother Teresa from the point of view of a cynical journalist whose hard soul is eventually softened by her gentle goodness.

1 ❑ ca. 1984 Cover: 1.25 **NM** value: **1.50**
A: Father Roy Gasnick; John Tartaglione **W:** David Michelinie

MOTION PICTURE COMICS — Fawcett

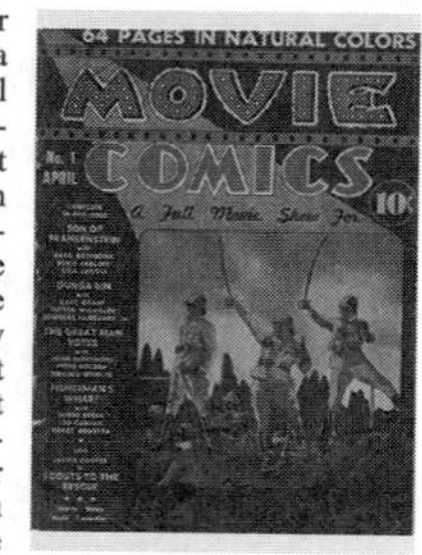

Fawcett Movie Comics changed its name to Motion Picture Comics in 1950, but the concept remained the same: providing comic-book adaptations of popular movies. Motion Picture Comics generally favors war stories and Westerns, including The Vanishing Westerner, Rough Rider of Durango, The Red Badge of Courage, and Code of the Silver Sage. Occasionally a science-fiction title like When Worlds Collide creeps in, as does the odd spy/suspense thriller, like Walk on East Beacon toward the end of the run. Motion Picture Comics all feature photo covers, often taken from the movie theater posters.

101 ❑ Nov 1950 Cover: 0.10 **NM** value: **115.00**
102 ❑ Jan 1951 Cover: 0.10 **NM** value: **80.00**
103 ❑ Mar 1951 Cover: 0.10 **NM** value: **80.00**
104 ❑ May 1951 Cover: 0.10 **NM** value: **80.00**
105 ❑ Jul 1951 Cover: 0.10 **NM** value: **90.00**
106 ❑ Sep 1951 Cover: 0.10 **NM** value: **75.00**
107 ❑ Nov 1951 Cover: 0.10 **NM** value: **75.00**
108 ❑ Jan 1952 Cover: 0.10 **NM** value: **60.00**
109 ❑ Mar 1952 Cover: 0.10 **NM** value: **60.00**
📖 Rough Riders
110 ❑ May 1952 Cover: 0.10 **NM** value: **215.00**
• **CGC:** 2 graded, best 6.0
111 ❑ Jul 1952 Cover: 0.10 **NM** value: **90.00**
112 ❑ Sep 1952 Cover: 0.10 **NM** value: **50.00**
113 ❑ Nov 1952 Cover: 0.10 **NM** value: **40.00**
📖 Walk East on Beacon
114 ❑ Jan 1953 Cover: 0.10 **NM** value: **40.00**

MOTLEY STORIES — Division

1 ❑ b&w Cover: 2.75 **NM** value: **Cover or less**

MOTORBIKE PUPPIES, THE — Dark Zulu Lies

1 ❑ Jun 1992 Cover: 2.50 **NM** value: **Cover or less**
📖 Vengeance Is Mine! **A:** Derek Frost **W:** Nabile Hage ★ 1st Appearance of The Humanals.
2 ❑ Cover: 2.50 **NM** value: **Cover or less**
• Never published?

MOTORHEAD — Dark Horse

1 ❑ Aug 1995 Cover: 2.50 **NM** value: **Cover or less**
Circ: CapCity orders: **7,600**
📖 Hunting Party **A:** Karl Waller **W:** D.G. Chichester ★ Appearance of Predator. ★ Versus Predator.
2 ❑ Sep 1995 Cover: 2.50 **NM** value: **Cover or less**
Circ: CapCity orders: **3,825**
A: Karl Waller **W:** D.G. Chichester
3 ❑ Oct 1995 Cover: 2.50 **NM** value: **Cover or less**
A: Karl Waller **W:** D.G. Chichester
4 ❑ Nov 1995 Cover: 2.50 **NM** value: **Cover or less**
5 ❑ Dec 1995 Cover: 2.50 **NM** value: **Cover or less**
6 ❑ Jan 1996 Cover: 2.50 **NM** value: **Cover or less**
SE 1 ❑ Mar 1994 Cover: 3.95 **NM** value: **Cover or less**
Circ: CapCity orders: **8,650**
📖 Power Play **A:** Karl Waller **W:** D.G. Chichester

MOTORMOUTH — Marvel

1 ❑ Jun 1992 Cover: 1.75 **NM** value: **2.00**
Circ: Statement: **25,040** CapCity orders: **21,000**
★ 1st Appearance of Motormouth.
2 ❑ Jul 1992 Cover: 1.75 **NM** value: **Cover or less**
Circ: Statement: **25,040** CapCity orders: **17,100**
3 ❑ Aug 1992 Cover: 1.75 **NM** value: **Cover or less**
Circ: Statement: **25,040** CapCity orders: **14,700**
• Punisher
4 ❑ Sep 1992 Cover: 1.75 **NM** value: **Cover or less**
Circ: Statement: **25,040** CapCity orders: **15,300**
5 ❑ Oct 1992 Cover: 1.75 **NM** value: **Cover or less**
Circ: Statement: **25,040** CapCity orders: **14,900**
📖 War Zone **A:** Phil Gascoine **W:** Graham Marks ★ Appearance of Punisher.
6 ❑ Nov 1992 Cover: 1.75 **NM** value: **Cover or less**
Circ: Statement: **25,040** CapCity orders: **18,200**
• Title changes to Motormouth & Killpower
7 ❑ Dec 1992 Cover: 1.75 **NM** value: **Cover or less**
Circ: Statement: **25,040** CapCity orders: **13,200**
★ Appearance of Cable.
8 ❑ Jan 1993 Cover: 1.75 **NM** value: **Cover or less**
Circ: CapCity orders: **12,400**
9 ❑ Feb 1993 Cover: 1.75 **NM** value: **Cover or less**
Circ: CapCity orders: **10,700**
📖 MyS-TECH Wars
10 ❑ Apr 1993 Cover: 1.75 **NM** value: **Cover or less**
Circ: CapCity orders: **9,500**
• Has 1992 Statement, filed 10/1/92; avg print run 25,228; avg sales 25,015; avg subs 25; avg total paid 25,040; samples 63; office use 125; max existent 25,228; no newsstand sales
11 ❑ Apr 1993 Cover: 1.75 **NM** value: **Cover or less**
Circ: CapCity orders: **9,400**
12 ❑ May 1993 Cover: 1.75 **NM** value: **Cover or less**
Circ: CapCity orders: **10,100**

MOUNTAIN — Underground

1 ❑ Cover: 0.50 **NM** value: **3.00**
• Flipbook High School Funnies **A:** David Silverberg; Larry Hubble **W:** David Silverberg; Larry Hubble

MOUNTAIN WORLD — Icicle Ridge

1 ❑ b&w Cover: 2.00 **NM** value: **Cover or less**

MOUSE MUSKETEERS (M.G.M.'S...) — Dell

8 ❑ Apr 1957 Cover: 0.10 **NM** value: **35.00**
• Series continued from Two Mouseketeers (M.G.M.'s...) #7
9 ❑ Jul 1957 Cover: 0.10 **NM** value: **30.00**
10 ❑ Oct 1957 Cover: 0.10 **NM** value: **30.00**
11 ❑ Jan 1958 Cover: 0.10 **NM** value: **30.00**
12 ❑ 1958 Cover: 0.10 **NM** value: **30.00**
13 ❑ 1958 Cover: 0.10 **NM** value: **30.00**
14 ❑ Aug 1958 Cover: 0.10 **NM** value: **30.00**
15 ❑ Oct 1958 Cover: 0.10 **NM** value: **30.00**
16 ❑ 1958 Cover: 0.10 **NM** value: **30.00**
17 ❑ Mar 1959 Cover: 0.10 **NM** value: **30.00**
18 ❑ Jun 1959 Cover: 0.10 **NM** value: **30.00**
19 ❑ Sep 1959 Cover: 0.10 **NM** value: **30.00**
20 ❑ Dec 1959 Cover: 0.10 **NM** value: **30.00**
21 ❑ Mar 1960 Cover: 0.10 **NM** value: **30.00**
• Later issues appeared as Dell Four Color #1135, #1175, and #1266

MOUSE ON THE MOON, THE — Dell

1 ❑ Oct 1963 Cover: 0.12 **NM** value: **15.00**

MOVIE LOVE — Famous Funnies

1 ❑ Feb 1950 Cover: 0.10 **NM** value: **100.00**
📖 Mrs. Mike; The Big Wheel. • Dick Powell and Evelyn Keyes photo cover.
2 ❑ Apr 1950 Cover: 0.10 **NM** value: **50.00**
📖 If This be Sin; Indian Scout. • Myrna Loy photo cover.
3 ❑ Jun 1950 Cover: 0.10 **NM** value: **40.00**
📖 Boy From Indiana; Four Days Leave. • Cornell Wilde, Lois Butler, and Lon McCallister photo cover.
4 ❑ Aug 1950 Cover: 0.10 **NM** value: **40.00**
📖 The Torch; Black Jack. • Paulette Goddard photo cover.
5 ❑ Oct 1950 Cover: 0.10 **NM** value: **40.00**
📖 Our Very Own; September Affair. • Farley Granger and Ann Blyth photo cover.
6 ❑ Dec 1950 Cover: 0.10 **NM** value: **40.00**
📖 Two Weeks With Love; Mr. Universe. • Jane Powell and Ricardo Montalban photo cover.
7 ❑ Feb 1951 Cover: 0.10 **NM** value: **40.00**
📖 Let's Dance; 3 Husbands. • Fred Astaire and Betty Hutton photo cover.
8 ❑ Apr 1951 Cover: 0.10 **NM** value: **40.00**
📖 Quebec; New Mexico. • Corrine Calvert photo cover.
9 ❑ Jun 1951 Cover: 0.10 **NM** value: **40.00**
📖 Mating Season; The Redhead and the Cowboy. • Gene Tierney and John Lund photo cover.
10 ❑ Aug 1951 Cover: 0.10 **NM** value: **50.00**
• **CGC:** 1 graded, best 4.0
📖 Dear Brat; Passage West. • Mona Freeman photo cover.
11 ❑ Oct 1951 Cover: 0.10 **NM** value: **35.00**
📖 Pandora and the Flying Dutchman; Crosswinds. • Ava Gardner and James Mason photo cover.
12 ❑ Dec 1951 Cover: 0.10 **NM** value: **35.00**
• **CGC:** 1 graded, best 8.5
📖 That's My Boy; Sherman's Command • Dean Martin and Jerry Lewis photo cover.
13 ❑ Feb 1952 Cover: 0.10 **NM** value: **35.00**
📖 Hong Kong. • Rhonda Fleming and Ronlad Reagan photo cover.
14 ❑ Apr 1952 Cover: 0.10 **NM** value: **35.00**
📖 Just This Once; Singin' in the Rain. • Janet Leigh photo cover.
15 ❑ Jun 1952 Cover: 0.10 **NM** value: **35.00**
📖 The Blazing Forest • John Payne and Susan Morrow photo cover.
16 ❑ Aug 1952 Cover: 0.10 **NM** value: **30.00**
📖 Mutiny. • Mark Stevens and Angela Lansbury photo cover.
17 ❑ Oct 1952 Cover: 0.10 **NM** value: **30.00**
📖 Glory Alley • Ralph Meeker and Leslie Caron photo cover.
18 ❑ Dec 1952 Cover: 0.10 **NM** value: **30.00**
📖 Operation Secret. • Cornel Wilde and Phyllis Thaxter photo cover.
19 ❑ Feb 1953 Cover: 0.10 **NM** value: **30.00**
📖 Prince of Pirates • John Derek photo cover.
20 ❑ Apr 1953 Cover: 0.10 **NM** value: **30.00**
📖 I Love Melvin • Donald O'Connor and Debbie Reynolds photo cover.
21 ❑ Jun 1953 Cover: 0.10 **NM** value: **30.00**
📖 Siren of Bagdad • Paul Henreid and Patricia Medina photo cover.
22 ❑ Aug 1953 Cover: 0.10 **NM** value: **30.00**
📖 Vanquished • John Payne and Coleen Gray photo cover.

MOVIE COMICS — DC

Boasting "A Full Movie Show for 10 Cents," the series began with a cover overline "64 pages in natural colors." Inside that first issue, Editor C. Elbert told readers, "Here it is, boys and girls, the newest idea in Comics and Movie Books — a combination of both, which we believe you will like very much. We hope that it will give you many, many hours of interesting fun and pleasant reading. Movie Comics will present each month, an idea of the outstanding pictures to be shown in your neighborhood theatre so that you will better enjoy them when you see them on the screen. It will also serve as a permanent record of the pictures you have enjoyed, which you can refer to again and again with pleasure and entertainment." Published more than five years before Dell's Four Color Comics featured movie-associated comics, the series offered screened move stills with captions and speech balloons. There were also "cartoons," shorts by Ed Wheelan and Harry Lampert. Films adapted during the series' brief run included Son of Frankenstein, Gunga Din, The Great Man Votes, The Phantom Creeps, In Old Monterey, and Chumps at Oxford. — Maggie

1 ❑ Apr 1939 Cover: 0.10 **NM** value: **3000.00**
2 ❑ May 1939 Cover: 0.10 **NM** value: **2000.00**
3 ❑ Jun 1939 Cover: 0.10 **NM** value: **1500.00**
• **CGC:** 1 graded, best 6.5
4 ❑ Jul 1939 Cover: 0.10 **NM** value: **1200.00**
5 ❑ Aug 1939 Cover: 0.10 **NM** value: **1200.00**
6 ❑ Sep 1939 Cover: 0.10 **NM** value: **1200.00**

MOVIE COMICS (FICTION HOUSE) — Fiction House

1 ❑ Dec 1946 Cover: 0.10 **NM** value: **400.00**
• **CGC:** 2 graded, best 8.0
2 ❑ Mar 1947 Cover: 0.10 **NM** value: **350.00**
3 ❑ Jun 1947 Cover: 0.10 **NM** value: **350.00**
• **CGC:** 1 graded, best 9.0
4 ❑ Sep 1947 Cover: 0.10 **NM** value: **300.00**
• **CGC:** 1 graded, best 7.0

MOVIE STAR NEWS — Pure Imagination

1 ❑ **NM** value: **6.00**
• Bettie Page photos **C:** Dave Stevens

MOVIE THRILLERS — Magazine Enterprises

1 ❑ ca. 1949 Cover: 0.10 **NM** value: **200.00**

MOVING FORTRESS — Forbidden Fruit

Bk 1 ❑ b&w Cover: 8.98 **NM** value: **Cover or less**

MOXI — Lightning

1 ❑ Jul 1996 Cover: 3.00 **NM** value: **Cover or less**
📖 Moxi; Hellina: Heart of Thorns **A:** Paul Abrams; Bill McEvoy **W:** Bill McEvoy; Joseph A. Zyskowski

MOXI'S FRIENDS: BOBBY JOE & NITRO — Lightning

1 ❑ Sep 1996 Cover: 2.75 **NM** value: **Cover or less**

MOXI: STRANGE DAZE — Lightning

1 ❑ Nov 1996, b&w Cover: 3.00 **NM** value: **Cover or less**
Circ: Diamd. preorders: **3,129**

M. REX — Image

1 ❑ Nov 1999 Cover: 2.95 **NM** value: **Cover or less**
Circ: Diamd. preorders: **23,316**
A: Duncan Rouleau **W:** Joe Kelly
1/A ❑ Nov 1999 Cover: 2.95 **NM** value: **Cover or less**
Exclusive cover. • Alternate cover has large figure in background, boy, monkey on waterbike in foreground **A:** Duncan Rouleau **W:** Joe Kelly
2 ❑ Dec 1999 Cover: 2.95 **NM** value: **Cover or less**
Circ: Diamd. preorders: **14,032**
A: Duncan Rouleau **W:** Joe Kelly
ASH 1/A ❑ Jul 1999 Cover: 5.00 **NM** value: **Cover or less**
Circ: Diamd. preorders: **6,205**
Flying car on cover. **A:** Duncan Rouleau **W:** Joe Kelly
ASH 1/B ❑ Jul 1999 Cover: 5.00 **NM** value: **Cover or less**
Blue background on cover. **A:** Duncan Rouleau **W:** Joe Kelly

MS. ANTI-SOCIAL — Helpless Anger

1 ❑ b&w Cover: 1.75 **NM** value: **Cover or less**
No issue number.

MS. CYANIDE & ICE — Black Out

0 ❑ Cover: 2.95 **NM** value: **Cover or less**
Circ: CapCity orders: **3,215**
A: Bill Wylie **W:** John Platt
1 ❑ Cover: 2.95 **NM** value: **Cover or less**
Circ: CapCity orders: **4,325**
• Sly & Furious preview **A:** Mike Leeke **W:** John Platt

MS. FANTASTIC — Conquest

All issues are adults only.

1 ❑ b&w Cover: 2.95 **NM** value: **Cover or less**
2 ❑ b&w Cover: 2.95 **NM** value: **Cover or less**
3 ❑ b&w Cover: 2.95 **NM** value: **Cover or less**
4 ❑ b&w Cover: 2.95 **NM** value: **Cover or less**

MS. FANTASTIC CLASSICS — Conquest

All issues are adults only.

1 ❑ b&w Cover: 2.95 **NM** value: **Cover or less**

Other grades: Multiply prices above by **1.5 for Mint • 2/3 for Very Fine • 1/3 for Fine • 1/5 for Very Good • 1/8 for Good**

MS. FORTUNE — Image

1 ❑ Jan 1998, b&w Cover: 2.95 **NM** value: **Cover or less**
Circ: Diamd. preorders: **5,206**
A: Chris Marrinan **W:** Chris Marrinan

MS. MARVEL — Marvel

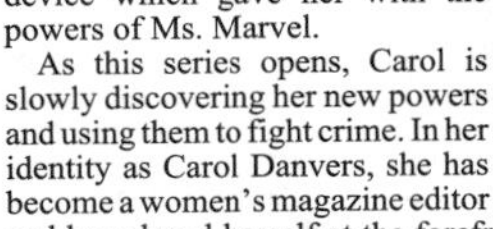

Ms. Marvel is Carol Danvers, a former security chief at NASA, who first appeared in Marvel Super-Heroes #13. Later, she would play a supporting role in the Captain Marvel series, although the events of that series would ultimately cause her to lose her job. Before leaving NASA, however, it seems that she had been unknowingly irradiated by the Kree's Psyche-Magnetron — a device which gave her with the powers of Ms. Marvel.

As this series opens, Carol is slowly discovering her new powers and using them to fight crime. In her identity as Carol Danvers, she has become a women's magazine editor and has placed herself at the forefront of the battle for women's rights. That battle plays a strong role in both the plot and the editorial direction of the Ms. Marvel series.

1 ❑ Jan 1977 Cover: 0.30 **NM** value: **4.00**
• **CGC:** 10 graded, best 9.6
📖 This Woman, This Warrior **A:** John Buscema **W:** Gerry Conway
★ 1st Appearance of Ms. Marvel.
2 ❑ Feb 1977 Cover: 0.30 **NM** value: **3.00**
3 ❑ Mar 1977 Cover: 0.30 **NM** value: **3.00**
4 ❑ Apr 1977 Cover: 0.30 **NM** value: **2.50**
5 ❑ May 1977 Cover: 0.30 **NM** value: **2.50**
★ Appearance of Vision.
6 ❑ Jun 1977 Cover: 0.30 **NM** value: **2.50**
7 ❑ Jul 1977 Cover: 0.30 **NM** value: **2.50**
★ Versus M.O.D.O.K..
8 ❑ Aug 1977 Cover: 0.30 **NM** value: **2.50**
9 ❑ Sep 1977 Cover: 0.30 **NM** value: **2.50**
★ 1st Appearance of Deathbird.
10 ❑ Oct 1977 Cover: 0.30 **NM** value: **2.50**
11 ❑ Nov 1977 Cover: 0.35 **NM** value: **2.00**
12 ❑ Dec 1977 Cover: 0.35 **NM** value: **2.00**
★ Versus Hecate.
13 ❑ Jan 1978 Cover: 0.35 **NM** value: **2.00**
📖 Homecoming
14 ❑ Feb 1978 Cover: 0.35 **NM** value: **2.00**
★ 1st Appearance of Steeplejack II (Maxwell Plumm).
15 ❑ Mar 1978 Cover: 0.35 **NM** value: **2.00**
16 ❑ Apr 1978 Cover: 0.35 **NM** value: **7.50**
• **CGC:** 3 graded, best 9.8
★ 1st Appearance of Mystique (cameo).
17 ❑ May 1978 Cover: 0.35 **NM** value: **4.00**
• **CGC:** 2 graded, best 9.4
18 ❑ Jun 1978 Cover: 0.35 **NM** value: **12.50**
• **CGC:** 14 graded, best 9.6
★ 1st Appearance of Mystique (full appearance).
19 ❑ Aug 1978 Cover: 0.35 **NM** value: **2.50**
★ Appearance of Captain Marvel.
20 ❑ Oct 1978 Cover: 0.35 **NM** value: **2.00**
• New costume
21 ❑ Dec 1978 Cover: 0.35 **NM** value: **2.00**
22 ❑ Feb 1979 Cover: 0.35 **NM** value: **2.00**
23 ❑ Apr 1979 Cover: 0.35 **NM** value: **2.00**
final issue.

MS. MYSTIC (CONTINUITY) — Continuity

1 ❑ Mar 1988 Cover: 2.00 **NM** value: **Cover or less**
Circ: CapCity orders: **4,995**
• reprints Ms. Mystic (Pacific) #1 **A:** Neal Adams ★ Origin of Ms. Mystic.
2 ❑ Jun 1988 Cover: 2.00 **NM** value: **Cover or less**
• reprints Ms. Mystic (Pacific) #2 **A:** Neal Adams
3 ❑ Jan 1989 Cover: 2.00 **NM** value: **Cover or less**
Circ: CapCity orders: **4,075**
A: Neal Adams
4 ❑ May 1989 Cover: 2.00 **NM** value: **Cover or less**
Circ: CapCity orders: **3,300**
A: Neal Adams
5 ❑ Aug 1990 Cover: 2.00 **NM** value: **Cover or less**
Circ: CapCity orders: **3,025**
• Comics Code **C:** Neal Adams
6 ❑ Nov 1990 Cover: 2.00 **NM** value: **Cover or less**
Circ: CapCity orders: **3,050**
• Comics Code **C:** Neal Adams
7 ❑ Aug 1991 Cover: 2.00 **NM** value: **Cover or less**
Circ: CapCity orders: **3,050**
8 ❑ Mar 1992 Cover: 2.00 **NM** value: **Cover or less**
Circ: CapCity orders: **2,500**
9 ❑ May 1992 Cover: 2.00 **NM** value: **Cover or less**
Circ: CapCity orders: **2,475**

MS. MYSTIC DEATHWATCH 2000 — Continuity

1 ❑ May 1993 Cover: 2.50 **NM** value: **Cover or less**
Circ: CapCity orders: **30,300**
Stereo diffusion cover. 📖 Deathwatch 2000, Part 8 **A:** Dwayne Turner; Ernesto Infante **W:** Neal Adams; Peter Stone
2 ❑ Jun 1993 Cover: 2.50 **NM** value: **Cover or less**
Circ: CapCity orders: **22,800**
📖 Deathwatch 2000, Part 12 • trading card
3 ❑ Aug 1993 Cover: 2.50 **NM** value: **Cover or less**
Circ: CapCity orders: **29,075**
📖 Deathwatch 2000, Part 17 • trading card; drops Deathwatch 2000 from indicia **A:** Louis Small Jr. **W:** Neal Adams; Peter Stone

MS. MYSTIC (PACIFIC) — Pacific

She was burned at the stake as a witch because of her ability to mystically heal people. But while her physical body was being burned, she used her powers to inject herself into another dimension. Three-hundred years later, a group of scientists were using a psionic converter to psychically battle an evil environment-destroying corporation. The device bridged the gap between the dimensions and brought Ms. Mystic back to Earth, where she was able to channel earth powers and help the scientists restore nature.

The X-Men's Neal Adams created this series, which lasted for just two issues. It would appear again in other incarnations.

1 ❑ Oct 1982 Cover: 1.00 **NM** value: **1.50**
• **CGC:** 4 graded, best 9.6
• origin **A:** Neal Adams **W:** Neal Adams ★ Origin of Ms. Mystic.
2 ❑ Feb 1984 Cover: 1.50 **NM** value: **Cover or less**
A: Neal Adams **W:** Neal Adams ★ Origin of Ayre, Fyre, Watr, Urth.
★ 1st Appearance of Ayre, Fyre, Watr, Urth 4.

MS. MYSTIC (VOL. 2) — Continuity

1 ❑ Oct 1993 Cover: 2.50 **NM** value: **Cover or less**
Circ: CapCity orders: **12,400**
📖 Rise of Magic **A:** Dwayne Turner **W:** Peter Stone
2 ❑ Nov 1993 Cover: 2.50 **NM** value: **Cover or less**
Circ: CapCity orders: **10,000**
📖 Rise of Magic
3 ❑ Dec 1993 Cover: 2.50 **NM** value: **Cover or less**
Circ: CapCity orders: **8,500**
📖 Rise of Magic
4 ❑ Jan 1994 Cover: 2.50 **NM** value: **Cover or less**
Circ: CapCity orders: **8,075**
📖 Rise of Magic
5 ❑ 1994 Cover: 2.50 **NM** value: **Cover or less**
Circ: CapCity orders: **7,225**
📖 Rise of Magic • Exists?
6 ❑ 1994 Cover: 2.50 **NM** value: **Cover or less**
Circ: CapCity orders: **3,605**
📖 Rise of Magic • Exists?

MS. PMS — Aaaahh!!

1 ❑ Cover: 2.50 **NM** value: **Cover or less**

MS. QUOTED TALES — Chance

1 ❑ Feb 1983 Cover: 1.50 **NM** value: **Cover or less**

MS. TREE — Eclipse

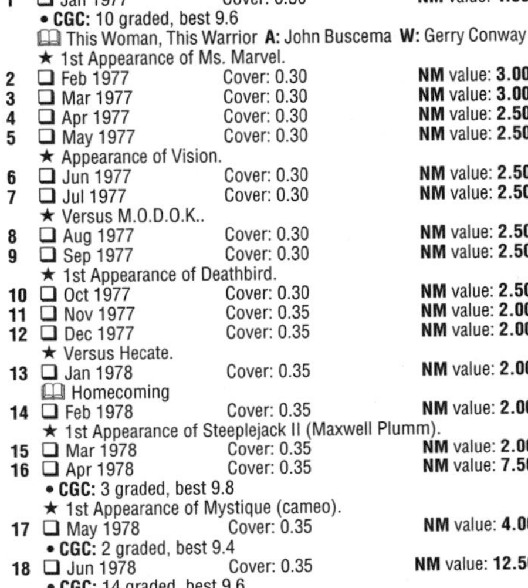

Ms. Tree was a popular detective-adventure comic by Max Collins and Terry Beatty. The Collins-Beatty team produced many works, but Ms. Tree was their best-known creation. A popular crime-novel writer, Max Collins, gave the Ms. Tree stories an edge focusing them on real-life issues such as abortion and child molestation.

The stories were always solidly plotted, and often held surprising twists. Running through three different publishers (Eclipse, Aardvark-Vanaheim, and Renegade), this series lasted fifty issues, with assorted specials and spinoffs.

1 ❑ Apr 1983 Cover: 1.50 **NM** value: **4.00**
• Eclipse publishes **A:** Frank Miller(pin-up)
2 ❑ Jun 1983 Cover: 1.50 **NM** value: **2.75**
A: Frank Miller(pin-up)
3 ❑ Aug 1983 Cover: 1.50 **NM** value: **2.75**
A: Frank Miller(pin-up)
4 ❑ Oct 1983 Cover: 1.50 **NM** value: **2.50**
A: Frank Miller(pin-up)
5 ❑ Nov 1983 Cover: 1.50 **NM** value: **2.50**
6 ❑ Feb 1984 Cover: 1.50 **NM** value: **2.00**
7 ❑ Apr 1984 Cover: 1.50 **NM** value: **2.00**
8 ❑ May 1984 Cover: 1.50 **NM** value: **2.00**
9 ❑ Jul 1984 Cover: 1.75 **NM** value: **2.00**

MS. TREE — Aardvark-Vanaheim

10 ❑ Aug 1984 Cover: 1.70 **NM** value: **2.00**
• Aardvark-Vanaheim begins as publisher
11 ❑ Sep 1984 Cover: 1.70 **NM** value: **2.00**
12 ❑ Oct 1984 Cover: 1.70 **NM** value: **2.00**
13 ❑ Nov 1984 Cover: 1.70 **NM** value: **2.00**
14 ❑ Dec 1984 Cover: 1.70 **NM** value: **2.00**
15 ❑ Jan 1985 Cover: 1.70 **NM** value: **2.00**
16 ❑ Feb 1985 Cover: 1.70 **NM** value: **2.00**
17 ❑ Apr 1985 Cover: 1.70 **NM** value: **2.00**
18 ❑ May 1985 Cover: 1.70 **NM** value: **2.00**

MS. TREE — Renegade

19 ❑ Jun 1985 Cover: 1.70 **NM** value: **2.00**
• Renegade Press begins as publisher
20 ❑ Jul 1985 Cover: 1.70 **NM** value: **2.00**
21 ❑ Sep 1985 Cover: 1.70 **NM** value: **2.00**
22 ❑ Oct 1985 Cover: 1.70 **NM** value: **2.00**
📖 Right to Die, Part 1 • Abortion story **A:** Terry Beatty **W:** Max Allan Collins
23 ❑ Nov 1985 Cover: 1.70 **NM** value: **2.00**
📖 Right to Die, Part 2 • Abortion story
24 ❑ Dec 1985 Cover: 1.70 **NM** value: **2.00**
25 ❑ Jan 1986 Cover: 1.70 **NM** value: **2.00**
26 ❑ Feb 1986 Cover: 1.70 **NM** value: **2.00**
27 ❑ Mar 1986 Cover: 1.70 **NM** value: **2.00**
28 ❑ Apr 1986 Cover: 1.70 **NM** value: **2.00**
29 ❑ May 1986 Cover: 1.70 **NM** value: **2.00**
30 ❑ Jun 1986 Cover: 2.00 **NM** value: **Cover or less**
31 ❑ Jul 1986 Cover: 2.00 **NM** value: **Cover or less**
32 ❑ Sep 1986 Cover: 2.00 **NM** value: **Cover or less**
33 ❑ Oct 1986 Cover: 2.00 **NM** value: **Cover or less**
34 ❑ Nov 1986 Cover: 2.00 **NM** value: **Cover or less**
35 ❑ Dec 1986 Cover: 2.00 **NM** value: **Cover or less**
36 ❑ Feb 1987 Cover: 2.00 **NM** value: **Cover or less**
37 ❑ Mar 1987 Cover: 2.00 **NM** value: **Cover or less**
38 ❑ Apr 1987 Cover: 2.00 **NM** value: **Cover or less**
39 ❑ May 1987 Cover: 2.00 **NM** value: **Cover or less**
40 ❑ Jun 1987 Cover: 2.00 **NM** value: **Cover or less**
41 ❑ Oct 1987 Cover: 2.00 **NM** value: **Cover or less**
42 ❑ Nov 1987 Cover: 2.00 **NM** value: **Cover or less**
43 ❑ Dec 1987 Cover: 2.00 **NM** value: **Cover or less**
44 ❑ Feb 1988 Cover: 2.00 **NM** value: **Cover or less**
45 ❑ Apr 1988 Cover: 2.00 **NM** value: **Cover or less**
• Johnny Dynamite back-up
46 ❑ May 1988 Cover: 2.00 **NM** value: **Cover or less**
47 ❑ Aug 1988 Cover: 2.00 **NM** value: **Cover or less**
48 ❑ Nov 1988 Cover: 2.00 **NM** value: **Cover or less**
49 ❑ May 1989 Cover: 2.00 **NM** value: **Cover or less**
50 ❑ Jul 1989 Cover: 2.75 **NM** value: **Cover or less**
final issue. **A:** Jack Kirby
3D 1❑ Aug 1985 Cover: 2.00 **NM** value: **2.50**
3D 2❑ Jul 1987 Cover: 2.50 **NM** value: **Cover or less**
• Ms. Tree's 1950's Three-Dimensional Crime
Smr 1❑ Aug 1986, b&w Cover: 2.00 **NM** value: **Cover or less**
• Variant edition.

MS. TREE QUARTERLY — DC

1 ❑ Sum 1990 Cover: 3.99 **NM** value: **4.00**
Circ: CapCity orders: **8,250**
📖 Gift of Death; Night Kills; Batman: The Name • Batman, Midnight **A:** Terry Beatty; Graham Nolan; Mike Grell **W:** Max Allan Collins; Denny O'Neil; Ed Gorman
2 ❑ Aut 1990 Cover: 3.95 **NM** value: **4.00**
Circ: CapCity orders: **8,250**
• Butcher
3 ❑ Spr 1991 Cover: 3.95 **NM** value: **4.00**
Circ: CapCity orders: **6,850**
• Butcher
4 ❑ Sum 1991 Cover: 3.95 **NM** value: **4.00**
Circ: CapCity orders: **5,600**
5 ❑ Aut 1991 Cover: 3.95 **NM** value: **4.00**
Circ: CapCity orders: **5,000**
6 ❑ Win 1991 Cover: 3.95 **NM** value: **4.00**
Circ: CapCity orders: **4,850**
7 ❑ Spr 1992 Cover: 3.95 **NM** value: **4.00**
Circ: CapCity orders: **4,300**
📖 The Family Way; Killer's Kiss, Part 2 **A:** Terry Beatty; Rick Burchett **W:** Max Allan Collins; Ed Gorman
8 ❑ Sum 1992 Cover: 3.95 **NM** value: **4.00**
Circ: CapCity orders: **3,900**
9 ❑ Fal 1992 Cover: 3.95 **NM** value: **4.00**
📖 One Mean Mother • Listed as Ms. Tree Special in indicia **A:** Terry Beatty **W:** Max Allan Collins
10 ❑ Win 1992 Cover: 3.50 **NM** value: **Cover or less**
Circ: CapCity orders: **3,900**
final issue.

MS. VICTORY SPECIAL — AC

1 ❑ full color Cover: 1.75 **NM** value: **2.00**
A: Cynthia Martin **W:** Phil White

MUGGSY MOUSE — Magazine Enterprises

1 ❑ ca. 1951 Cover: 0.10 **NM** value: **40.00**
2 ❑ ca. 1951 Cover: 0.10 **NM** value: **35.00**
• **CGC:** 1 graded, best 7.5
3 ❑ ca. 1952 Cover: 0.10 **NM** value: **35.00**
4 ❑ ca. 1953 Cover: 0.10 **NM** value: **30.00**
5 ❑ ca. 1954 Cover: 0.10 **NM** value: **30.00**

MUGGY-DOO BOY CAT — Stanhall

1 ❑ Jul 1953 Cover: 0.10 **NM** value: **35.00**
2 ❑ Sep 1953 Cover: 0.10 **NM** value: **24.00**
3 ❑ Nov 1953 Cover: 0.10 **NM** value: **24.00**
4 ❑ Jan 1954 Cover: 0.10 **NM** value: **24.00**

MUKTUK WOLFSBREATH: HARD-BOILED SHAMAN — DC / Vertigo

1 ❑ Aug 1998 Cover: 2.50 **NM** value: **Cover or less**
Circ: Diamd. preorders: **11,940**
📖 Mommy's Girl **A:** Steve Parkhouse **W:** Terry Laban
2 ❑ Sep 1998 Cover: 2.50 **NM** value: **Cover or less**
Circ: Diamd. preorders: **9,278**
3 ❑ Oct 1998 Cover: 2.50 **NM** value: **Cover or less**
Circ: Diamd. preorders: **8,363**

MULLKON EMPIRE (JOHN JAKES'...) — Tekno

1 ❑ Sep 1995 Cover: 1.95 **NM** value: **Cover or less**
Circ: CapCity orders: **11,725**
A: John Watkiss **W:** Kate Worley
2 ❑ Oct 1995 Cover: 1.95 **NM** value: **Cover or less**
Circ: CapCity orders: **8,700**
A: John Watkiss **W:** Kate Worley
3 ❑ Nov 1995 Cover: 1.95 **NM** value: **Cover or less**
Circ: CapCity orders: **7,525**
A: John Watkiss **W:** Kate Worley
4 ❑ Dec 1995 Cover: 1.95 **NM** value: **Cover or less**
Circ: CapCity orders: **5,675**
A: John Watkiss **W:** Kate Worley
5 ❑ Dec 1995 Cover: 1.95 **NM** value: **Cover or less**
Circ: CapCity orders: **4,250**
A: John Watkiss **W:** Kate Worley
6 ❑ Jan 1996 Cover: 2.25 **NM** value: **Cover or less**
A: John Watkiss **W:** Kate Worley

CGC-graded: Multiply prices above by **33 for 9.9 M • 16 for 9.8 NM/M • 7 for 9.6 NM+ • 5 for 9.4 NM • 2.5 for 9.2 NM- • 1.5 for 9.0 VF/NM**

MULTIVERSE (MICHAEL MOORCOCK'S...) DC / Helix

This twelve-issue maxi-series from DC Comics' science fiction imprint, Helix, brings to the comics form the concepts and characters of one of the most intriguing writers of speculative fiction. Michael Moorcock has had his stories adapted for comics before (Elric, and "Behold the Man" in Unknown Worlds of Science Fiction), but this is the first time he has written specifically for this medium.

Working with artists Walter Simonson, Mark Reeve, and John Ridgway, Moorcock tells three separate, but connected stories featuring his multiverse concept. From a daring riverboat-type gambler testing his skill with the Game of Time; to the pursuit of a brutal murderer in the fog-shrouded streets of London; and to 1000 A.D. and the albino aristocrat, Elric, the reader will recognize familiar names and subjects amid these diverse settings.

1 ❑ Nov 1997 Cover: 2.50 **NM** value: **Cover or less**
Circ: Diamd. preorders: **21,067**
🕮 Moonbeams and Roses, Part 1; The Metaphorical Detective, Part 1; Duke Elric, Part 1 **A:** John Ridgway; Walt Simonson; Mark Reeve **W:** Michael Moorcock

2 ❑ Dec 1997 Cover: 2.50 **NM** value: **Cover or less**
Circ: Diamd. preorders: **16,898**
🕮 Moonbeams and Roses, Part 2; The Metaphorical Detective, Part 2; Duke Elric, Part 2 **A:** John Ridgway; Walt Simonson; Mark Reeve **W:** Michael Moorcock

3 ❑ Jan 1998 Cover: 2.50 **NM** value: **Cover or less**
Circ: Diamd. preorders: **14,688**
🕮 Moonbeams and Roses, Part 3; The Metaphorical Detective, Part 3; Duke Elric, Part 3 **A:** John Ridgway; Walt Simonson; Mark Reeve **W:** Michael Moorcock

4 ❑ Feb 1998 Cover: 2.50 **NM** value: **Cover or less**
Circ: Diamd. preorders: **12,485**
🕮 Moonbeams and Roses, Part 4; The Metaphorical Detective, Part 4; Duke Elric, Part 4 **A:** John Ridgway; Walt Simonson; Mark Reeve **W:** Michael Moorcock

5 ❑ Mar 1998 Cover: 2.50 **NM** value: **Cover or less**
Circ: Diamd. preorders: **10,919**
🕮 Moonbeams and Roses, Part 5; The Metaphorical Detective, Part 5; Duke Elric, Part 5 **A:** John Ridgway; Walt Simonson; Mark Reeve **W:** Michael Moorcock

6 ❑ Apr 1998 Cover: 2.50 **NM** value: **Cover or less**
Circ: Diamd. preorders: **9,637**
A: John Ridgway; Walt Simonson; Mark Reeve **W:** Michael Moorcock

7 ❑ May 1998 Cover: 2.50 **NM** value: **Cover or less**
Circ: Diamd. preorders: **8,964**
A: John Ridgway; Walt Simonson; Mark Reeve **W:** Michael Moorcock

8 ❑ Jun 1998 Cover: 2.50 **NM** value: **Cover or less**
Circ: Diamd. preorders: **8,553**
A: John Ridgway; Walt Simonson; Mark Reeve **W:** Michael Moorcock

9 ❑ Jul 1998 Cover: 2.50 **NM** value: **Cover or less**
Circ: Diamd. preorders: **7,759**
A: John Ridgway; Walt Simonson; Mark Reeve **W:** Michael Moorcock

10 ❑ Aug 1998 Cover: 2.50 **NM** value: **Cover or less**
Circ: Diamd. preorders: **7,351**
A: John Ridgway; Walt Simonson; Mark Reeve **W:** Michael Moorcock

11 ❑ Sep 1998 Cover: 2.50 **NM** value: **Cover or less**
Circ: Diamd. preorders: **6,950**
A: John Ridgway; Walt Simonson; Mark Reeve **W:** Michael Moorcock

12 ❑ Oct 1998 Cover: 2.50 **NM** value: **Cover or less**
Circ: Diamd. preorders: **6,685**
final issue. **A:** John Ridgway; Walt Simonson; Mark Reeve **W:** Michael Moorcock

Bk 1❑ Dec 1999 Cover: 19.95 **NM** value: **Cover or less**
• Collects series **A:** John Ridgway; Walt Simonson; Mark Reeve **W:** Michael Moorcock

MUMMY ARCHIVES, THE Millennium

1 ❑ Jan 1992 Cover: 2.50 **NM** value: **Cover or less**
Circ: CapCity orders: **4,975**
A: Melissa Martin; Darryl Banks; Jim Mooney; Mark Menendez; Robert Lewis **W:** Mark Ellis; Paul Davis; Faye Perozich; Greg Fulton; Mary Anne-Cassata; Terry Collins

MUMMY, THE (MONSTER) Monster

1 ❑ b&w Cover: 1.95 **NM** value: **Cover or less**
A: Scott Beaderstadt **W:** Scott Beaderstadt
2 ❑ b&w Cover: 1.95 **NM** value: **Cover or less**
3 ❑ b&w Cover: 1.95 **NM** value: **Cover or less**
4 ❑ b&w Cover: 1.95 **NM** value: **Cover or less**

MUMMY OR RAMSES THE DAMNED, THE (ANNE RICE'S...) Millennium

1 ❑ ca. 1992 Cover: 5.00 **NM** value: **Cover or less**
Circ: CapCity orders: **15,600** • **CGC:** 2 graded, best 9.2
A: Jim Mooney; Mark Menendez **W:** Anne Rice; Faye Perozich

2 ❑ ca. 1992 Cover: 3.50 **NM** value: **Cover or less**
Circ: CapCity orders: **11,450**
A: Jim Mooney; Mark Menendez **W:** Anne Rice; Faye Perozich

3 ❑ ca. 1992 Cover: 3.50 **NM** value: **Cover or less**
Circ: CapCity orders: **10,350**
A: Jim Mooney; Mark Menendez **W:** Anne Rice; Faye Perozich

4 ❑ ca. 1992 Cover: 3.50 **NM** value: **Cover or less**
Circ: CapCity orders: **9,525**
A: Jim Mooney; Mark Menendez **W:** Anne Rice; Faye Perozich

5 ❑ ca. 1992 Cover: 3.50 **NM** value: **Cover or less**
Circ: CapCity orders: **9,200**
🕮 Celeste Aida **A:** Jim Mooney; Mark Menendez **W:** Anne Rice; Faye Perozich

6 ❑ ca. 1992 Cover: 3.00 **NM** value: **Cover or less**
Circ: CapCity orders: **9,075**
A: Jim Mooney; Mark Menendez **W:** Anne Rice; Faye Perozich

7 ❑ ca. 1992 Cover: 3.00 **NM** value: **Cover or less**
Circ: CapCity orders: **8,600**
🕮 The Queen of the Dead **A:** Jim Mooney; Mark Menendez **W:** Anne Rice; Faye Perozich

8 ❑ ca. 1992 Cover: 3.00 **NM** value: **Cover or less**
Circ: CapCity orders: **8,400**
A: Jim Mooney; Mark Menendez **W:** Anne Rice; Faye Perozich

9 ❑ ca. 1992 Cover: 3.00 **NM** value: **Cover or less**
Circ: CapCity orders: **8,575**
A: Jim Mooney; Mark Menendez **W:** Anne Rice; Faye Perozich

10 ❑ ca. 1992 Cover: 3.00 **NM** value: **Cover or less**
Circ: CapCity orders: **8,400**
A: Jim Mooney; Mark Menendez **W:** Anne Rice; Faye Perozich

11 ❑ ca. 1992 Cover: 3.00 **NM** value: **Cover or less**
Circ: CapCity orders: **8,175**
A: Jim Mooney; Mark Menendez **W:** Anne Rice; Faye Perozich

12 ❑ ca. 1992 Cover: 3.00 **NM** value: **Cover or less**
Circ: CapCity orders: **7,925**
A: Jim Mooney; Mark Menendez **W:** Anne Rice; Faye Perozich

MUMMY'S CURSE, THE Aircel

1 ❑ Nov 1990, b&w Cover: 2.25 **NM** value: **2.50**
2 ❑ Dec 1990, b&w Cover: 2.25 **NM** value: **2.50**
3 ❑ Jan 1991, b&w Cover: 2.25 **NM** value: **2.50**
4 ❑ Feb 1991, b&w Cover: 2.25 **NM** value: **2.50**

MUNDEN'S BAR First

Anl 1❑ Apr 1988 Cover: 2.95 **NM** value: **Cover or less**
Circ: CapCity orders: **5,150**
• prestige format. 🕮 Demolition Drinking II; The Last Vampire; Doppelgangster; Mother's Calling; Big Chief Party Animal **A:** Jerry Ordway; Steve Rude; Brian Bolland; Joe Staton; Steve Moncuse; Matt Feazell **W:** Steve Moncuse; Mike Baron; Del Close; John Ostrander; Walt Lockley ★ Appearance of Fish Police, Anti-Socialman, Clone-zone.

Anl 2❑ Mar 1991 Cover: 5.95 **NM** value: **Cover or less**
• prestige format. ★ Appearance of Omaha the Cat Dancer, Teenage Mutant Ninja Turtles.

MUNSTERS, THE (GOLD KEY) Gold Key

1 ❑ Jan 1965 Cover: 0.12 **NM** value: **100.00**
• **CGC:** 5 graded, best 9.2
Photo cover. 🕮 It's All Fright with Me; Haunted House-Cleaning; Liddle Wolfgang: All Bites are Off; I'm Dancing with Fears in My Eyes

2 ❑ Apr 1965 Cover: 0.12 **NM** value: **65.00**
• **CGC:** 2 graded, best 9.2

3 ❑ Jul 1965 Cover: 0.12 **NM** value: **40.00**
• **CGC:** 2 graded, best 9.0

4 ❑ Oct 1965 Cover: 0.12 **NM** value: **40.00**
• **CGC:** 2 graded, best 9.4

5 ❑ Jan 1966 Cover: 0.12 **NM** value: **40.00**
• **CGC:** 3 graded, best 9.4
back cover pin-up. 🕮 Screams Like Old Times!; All Haunts on Deck; Liddle Wolfgang: I've Got a Secret Panel; Double Feature Creature

6 ❑ Apr 1966 Cover: 0.12 **NM** value: **28.00**
• **CGC:** 3 graded, best 9.2

7 ❑ Jun 1966 Cover: 0.12 **NM** value: **28.00**
• **CGC:** 1 graded, best 9.0

8 ❑ Aug 1966 Cover: 0.12 **NM** value: **28.00**
• **CGC:** 1 graded, best 9.4

9 ❑ Oct 1966 Cover: 0.12 **NM** value: **28.00**
• **CGC:** 2 graded, best 9.4

10 ❑ Dec 1966 Cover: 0.12 **NM** value: **28.00**
• **CGC:** 2 graded, best 9.4

11 ❑ Feb 1967 Cover: 0.12 **NM** value: **24.00**
• **CGC:** 1 graded, best 9.2

12 ❑ Apr 1967 Cover: 0.12 **NM** value: **24.00**
• **CGC:** 1 graded, best 9.4

13 ❑ Jun 1967 Cover: 0.12 **NM** value: **24.00**
• **CGC:** 1 graded, best 7.0

14 ❑ Aug 1967 Cover: 0.12 **NM** value: **24.00**
Photo cover. 🕮 The Shock Heard Round the World; A Bat-Time Story: The Sorcerer's Servant (text piece); Liddle Wolfgang: Spook Talk; Munster of Ceremonies

15 ❑ Nov 1967 Cover: 0.12 **NM** value: **24.00**
• **CGC:** 1 graded, best 9.2

16 ❑ Cover: 0.12 **NM** value: **24.00**

MUNSTERS, THE (TV COMICS) TV Comics

One of the last great sitcoms of black-and-white television, the Munsters became the stars of a second comic book series when TV Comics launched this title at the 1997 San Diego Comic Convention.

The Munsters, who live at 1313 Mockingbird Lane, are (obviously enough) a family of monsters. Herman Munster (the dad) looks just like Frankenstein; Lily (the mom) looks like a female vampire, as does little Eddie Munster; and Grandpa is a dead ringer for an elderly Dracula. In stark contrast, their cousin Marilyn is a blonde, girl-next-door.

Although the family lives in a creepy house decorated in early mausoleum chic, they're really just a fun-loving, all-American family. Herman, for instance, is an affable sort who worries about the sort of boys Marilyn is going out with, while wondering why the neighbors look at them so strangely.

1 ❑ Aug 1997 Cover: 2.95 **NM** value: **3.00**
Circ: Diamd. preorders: **7,231**

2/A ❑ Oct 1997 Cover: 2.95 **NM** value: **3.00**
• blue background

2/B ❑ Oct 1997 Cover: 2.95 **NM** value: **3.00**
Alternate cover (Marilyn). • red background

3 ❑ Dec 1997 Cover: 2.95 **NM** value: **3.00**
4 ❑ Mar 1998 Cover: 2.95 **NM** value: **3.00**
Circ: Diamd. preorders: **2,558**

4/SC❑ Mar 1998 Cover: 2.95 **NM** value: **3.00**
• logoless

SE 1❑ Aug 1997 Cover: 2.95 **NM** value: **3.00**
Circ: Diamd. preorders: **2,420**
• Comic Con 1997 Edition. 🕮 Welcome to the Con • red foil logo **A:** Kelley Jarvis; George Broderick Jr. **W:** Marc Patten

MUPPET BABIES ADVENTURES Harvey

1 ❑ Cover: 1.25 **NM** value: **Cover or less**

MUPPET BABIES BIG BOOK Harvey

1 ❑ Cover: 1.95 **NM** value: **Cover or less**

MUPPET BABIES (HARVEY) Harvey

1 ❑ Jun 1993 Cover: 1.25 **NM** value: **1.50**
2 ❑ Sep 1993 Cover: 1.25 **NM** value: **1.50**
3 ❑ Dec 1993 Cover: 1.50 **NM** value: **Cover or less**
4 ❑ Mar 1994 Cover: 1.50 **NM** value: **Cover or less**
5 ❑ May 1994 Cover: 1.50 **NM** value: **Cover or less**
6 ❑ Aug 1994 Cover: 1.50 **NM** value: **Cover or less**

MUPPET BABIES (STAR/MARVEL) Marvel / Star

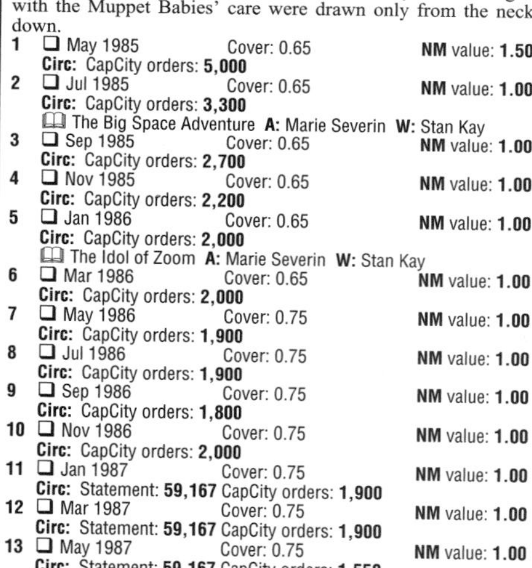

Jim Henson's world famous characters, the Muppets, have been around since the 1970s. In the late 1980s, a new version of the Muppets came to children's television sets on Saturday mornings. The Muppet Babies were toddler versions of Kermit the Frog, Miss Piggy, Fozzy Bear, and the other well-known "adult" Muppets. They proved to be a big hit with children all over the country. Like most successful cartoons or movies, Jim Henson's Muppet Babies sold dolls, play sets, school supplies and most importantly, comic books.

Star Comics, the "kids comics" division of Marvel Comics, acquired the license and published the Babies in a comic series of the same name. Most of the adventures that the Muppet Babies experience are figments of the babies' playful imaginations. In a lovely example of their childlike perspective, any adults charged with the Muppet Babies' care were drawn only from the neck down.

1 ❑ May 1985 Cover: 0.65 **NM** value: **1.50**
Circ: CapCity orders: **5,000**

2 ❑ Jul 1985 Cover: 0.65 **NM** value: **1.00**
Circ: CapCity orders: **3,300**
🕮 The Big Space Adventure **A:** Marie Severin **W:** Stan Kay

3 ❑ Sep 1985 Cover: 0.65 **NM** value: **1.00**
Circ: CapCity orders: **2,700**

4 ❑ Nov 1985 Cover: 0.65 **NM** value: **1.00**
Circ: CapCity orders: **2,200**

5 ❑ Jan 1986 Cover: 0.65 **NM** value: **1.00**
Circ: CapCity orders: **2,000**
🕮 The Idol of Zoom **A:** Marie Severin **W:** Stan Kay

6 ❑ Mar 1986 Cover: 0.65 **NM** value: **1.00**
Circ: CapCity orders: **2,000**

7 ❑ May 1986 Cover: 0.75 **NM** value: **1.00**
Circ: CapCity orders: **1,900**

8 ❑ Jul 1986 Cover: 0.75 **NM** value: **1.00**
Circ: CapCity orders: **1,900**

9 ❑ Sep 1986 Cover: 0.75 **NM** value: **1.00**
Circ: CapCity orders: **1,800**

10 ❑ Nov 1986 Cover: 0.75 **NM** value: **1.00**
Circ: CapCity orders: **2,000**

11 ❑ Jan 1987 Cover: 0.75 **NM** value: **1.00**
Circ: Statement: **59,167** CapCity orders: **1,900**

12 ❑ Mar 1987 Cover: 0.75 **NM** value: **1.00**
Circ: Statement: **59,167** CapCity orders: **1,900**

13 ❑ May 1987 Cover: 0.75 **NM** value: **1.00**
Circ: Statement: **59,167** CapCity orders: **1,550**

14 ❑ Jul 1987 Cover: 1.00 **NM** value: **Cover or less**
Circ: Statement: **59,167** CapCity orders: **1,250**

15 ❑ Sep 1987 Cover: 1.00 **NM** value: **Cover or less**
Circ: Statement: **59,167** CapCity orders: **1,350**
🕮 The Magic Book **A:** Marie Severin **W:** Laura Hitchcock

16 ❑ Nov 1987 Cover: 1.00 **NM** value: **Cover or less**
Circ: Statement: **59,167**

17 ❑ Jan 1988 Cover: 1.00 **NM** value: **Cover or less**
Circ: Statement: **60,350** CapCity orders: **1,250**

18 ❑ Mar 1988 Cover: 1.00 **NM** value: **Cover or less**
Circ: Statement: **60,350** CapCity orders: **1,300**
• Marvel begins as publisher

19 ❑ May 1988 Cover: 1.00 **NM** value: **Cover or less**
Circ: Statement: **60,350** CapCity orders: **1,150**

20 ❑ Jul 1988 Cover: 1.00 **NM** value: **Cover or less**
Circ: Statement: **60,350** CapCity orders: **1,100**

21 ❑ Sep 1988 Cover: 1.00 **NM** value: **Cover or less**
Circ: Statement: **60,350** CapCity orders: **1,100**

22 ❑ Nov 1988 Cover: 1.00 **NM** value: **Cover or less**
Circ: Statement: **60,350** CapCity orders: **1,000**

23 ❑ Jan 1989 Cover: 1.00 **NM** value: **Cover or less**
Circ: CapCity orders: **900**

24 ❑ Mar 1989 Cover: 1.00 **NM** value: **Cover or less**
Circ: CapCity orders: **1,000**

25 ❑ May 1989 Cover: 1.00 **NM** value: **Cover or less**
Circ: CapCity orders: **1,100**

Other grades: Multiply prices above by **1.5 for Mint • 2/3 for Very Fine • 1/3 for Fine • 1/5 for Very Good • 1/8 for Good**

26 ☐ Jul 1989 Cover: 1.00 **NM** value: **Cover or less**
Circ: CapCity orders: **1,050**

MUPPETS TAKE MANHATTAN, THE Marvel / Star

1 ☐ Nov 1984 Cover: 0.60 **NM** value: **1.50**
• Reprints Marvel Super Special #32 **A:** Dean Yeagle **W:** Stan Kay
2 ☐ Dec 1984 Cover: 0.60 **NM** value: **1.50**
• Reprints Marvel Super Special #32
3 ☐ Jan 1985 Cover: 0.60 **NM** value: **1.50**
• Reprints Marvel Super Special #32

MURCIÉLAGA SHE-BAT Heroic

1 ☐ b&w Cover: 1.50 **NM** value: **2.95**
2 ☐ Apr 1993, b&w Cover: 2.95 **NM** value: **Cover or less**
📖 A Lesson in Humility **A:** Dennis Mallonee **W:** Daerick Gr÷ss
3 ☐ Jul 1993, b&w Cover: 2.95 **NM** value: **Cover or less**

MURDER Renegade

1 ☐ Aug 1986 Cover: 2.00 **NM** value: **Cover or less**
📖 The Big Man; Queen of Hairy Flies; **A:** Steve Ditko; Dan Day; Brad W. Foster **W:** Steve Ditko; Rich Margopoulos; Brad W. Foster

MURDER CAN BE FUN Slave Labor

1 ☐ Feb 1996, b&w Cover: 2.95 **NM** value: **4.00**
📖 Hartford Circus Fire; Nashille Train Wreck; Triangle Shirtwaist Fire; Port Chicago Explosion; Great Boston Molasses Flood **A:** Timothy Markin; Scott Saavedra; Dylan Williams; Gabby Gamboa; Garret Izumi **W:** Timothy Markin; Scott Saavedra; Dylan Williams; Gabby Gamboa; Garret Izumi
2 ☐ May 1996, b&w Cover: 2.95 **NM** value: **3.50**
3 ☐ Aug 1996, b&w Cover: 2.95 **NM** value: **3.50**
4 ☐ Nov 1996, b&w Cover: 2.95 **NM** value: **3.50**
5 ☐ May 1997, b&w Cover: 2.95 **NM** value: **3.00**
6 ☐ Jul 1997, b&w Cover: 2.95 **NM** value: **3.00**
7 ☐ Sep 1997, b&w Cover: 2.95 **NM** value: **Cover or less**
8 ☐ Jan 1998, b&w Cover: 2.95 **NM** value: **Cover or less**
9 ☐ Apr 1998, b&w Cover: 2.95 **NM** value: **Cover or less**
10 ☐ Aug 1998, b&w Cover: 2.95 **NM** value: **Cover or less**
11 ☐ Nov 1998, b&w Cover: 2.95 **NM** value: **Cover or less**
12 ☐ Feb 1999, b&w Cover: 2.95 **NM** value: **Cover or less**

MURDER CITY Eternity

1 ☐ b&w Cover: 3.95 **NM** value: **Cover or less**
No issue number. • Minute Movies

MURDER INCORPORATED Fox

1 ☐ Win 1945 Cover: 0.10 **NM** value: **400.00**
• **CGC:** 1 graded, best 7.5
2 ☐ Mar 1948 Cover: 0.10 **NM** value: **300.00**
• **CGC:** 3 graded, best 9.2
3 ☐ May 1948 Cover: 0.10 **NM** value: **175.00**
• **CGC:** 1 graded, best 9.4
4 ☐ Jul 1948 Cover: 0.10 **NM** value: **175.00**
• **CGC:** 1 graded, best 7.5
5 ☐ Sep 1948 Cover: 0.10 **NM** value: **175.00**
6 ☐ Nov 1948 Cover: 0.10 **NM** value: **175.00**
7 ☐ Jan 1949 Cover: 0.10 **NM** value: **150.00**
8 ☐ Feb 1949 Cover: 0.10 **NM** value: **150.00**
9 ☐ Mar 1949 Cover: 0.10 **NM** value: **150.00**

MURDER ME DEAD El Capitán

1 ☐ Aug 2000 Cover: 2.95 **NM** value: **Cover or less**
Circ: Diamd. preorders: **10,354** • **CGC:** 1 graded, best 9.6
A: David Lapham **W:** David Lapham
2 ☐ Oct 2000 Cover: 2.95 **NM** value: **Cover or less**
Circ: Diamd. preorders: **8,247**
A: David Lapham **W:** David Lapham
3 ☐ Dec 2000 Cover: 2.95 **NM** value: **Cover or less**
Circ: Diamd. preorders: **7,924**
A: David Lapham **W:** David Lapham
4 ☐ Feb 2001 Cover: 2.95 **NM** value: **Cover or less**
Circ: Diamd. preorders: **7,824**
A: David Lapham **W:** David Lapham
5 ☐ Apr 2001 Cover: 2.95 **NM** value: **Cover or less**
Circ: Diamd. preorders: **7,576**
A: David Lapham **W:** David Lapham
6 ☐ Jun 2001 Cover: 2.95 **NM** value: **Cover or less**
Circ: Diamd. preorders: **7,206**
A: David Lapham **W:** David Lapham
7 ☐ Jul 2001 Cover: 2.95 **NM** value: **Cover or less**
Circ: Diamd. preorders: **7,684**
A: David Lapham **W:** David Lapham

MURDEROUS GANGSTERS Avon

1 ☐ Jul 1951 Cover: 0.10 **NM** value: **300.00**
• **CGC:** 2 graded, best 9.4
2 ☐ Dec 1951 Cover: 0.10 **NM** value: **200.00**
• **CGC:** 2 graded, best 9.4
3 ☐ ca. 1952 Cover: 0.10 **NM** value: **150.00**
4 ☐ ca. 1952 Cover: 0.10 **NM** value: **150.00**

MUSIC COMICS Personality

2 ☐ full color Cover: 2.95 **NM** value: **Cover or less**
3 ☐ full color Cover: 2.95 **NM** value: **Cover or less**
4 ☐ b&w Cover: 2.50 **NM** value: **Cover or less**

MUSIC COMICS ON TOUR Personality

1 ☐ b&w Cover: 2.95 **NM** value: **Cover or less**
• Beatles

MUTANT BOOK OF THE DEAD, THE Starhead

All issues are adults only.
1 ☐ b&w Cover: 2.50 **NM** value: **Cover or less**

MUTANT CHRONICLES Acclaim / Armada

1 ☐ May 1996 Cover: 2.95 **NM** value: **Cover or less**
cardstock cover. 📖 Golgotha, Part 1; Golgotha • polybagged with Doom Trooper card **A:** David Fabrii; Simon Bisley(cover) **W:** William King
2 ☐ Jun 1996 Cover: 2.95 **NM** value: **Cover or less**
cardstock cover. 📖 Golgotha, Part 2 • polybagged with Doom Trooper card **A:** Simon Bisley(cover)
3 ☐ Jul 1996 Cover: 2.95 **NM** value: **Cover or less**
cardstock cover. 📖 Golgotha, Part 3 • polybagged with Doom Trooper card **A:** Simon Bisley(cover)
4 ☐ Aug 1996 Cover: 2.95 **NM** value: **Cover or less**
cardstock cover. 📖 Golgotha, Part 4 • polybagged with Doom Trooper card **A:** Simon Bisley(cover)
Bk 1 ☐ Dec 1996 Cover: 10.95 **NM** value: **Cover or less**
• Golgotha

MUTANT CHRONICLES SOURCEBOOK Acclaim / Armada

1 ☐ Sep 1996 Cover: 2.95 **NM** value: **Cover or less**
cardstock cover. • polybagged with card

MUTANT MISADVENTURES OF CLOAK & DAGGER, THE Marvel

In this series, Tyrone Johnson and Tandy Bowen returned as Cloak & Dagger. Two teen-age runaways, they received their powers as the result of a brutal experiment at the hands of a Mob chemist. In testing a synthetic drug on the unwilling teens, he inadvertently triggered their latent mutant abilities. Now Tandy (aka Dagger) has become a generator of living light, able to direct that energy at her unfortunate opponents. Conversely, Tyrone (aka Cloak) has become a living portal into another, dark dimension. He is able to teleport by stepping through that dimension, taking others with him if he wishes. He can also enshroud others in his cloak — giving them a taste of the terrible darkness that lies within.

1 ☐ Oct 1988 Cover: 1.25 **NM** value: **2.00**
📖 Blind Salvation! **A:** Daan Lawlis **W:** Terry Austin ★ Appearance of X-Factor.
2 ☐ Dec 1988 Cover: 1.50 **NM** value: **Cover or less**
3 ☐ Feb 1989 Cover: 1.50 **NM** value: **Cover or less**
4 ☐ Apr 1989 Cover: 1.50 **NM** value: **Cover or less**
• Inferno
5 ☐ Jun 1989 Cover: 1.50 **NM** value: **Cover or less**
6 ☐ Aug 1989 Cover: 1.50 **NM** value: **Cover or less**
📖 Agony in Ecstasy **A:** Mike Vosburg **W:** Terry Austin
7 ☐ Oct 1989 Cover: 1.50 **NM** value: **Cover or less**
8 ☐ Dec 1989 Cover: 1.50 **NM** value: **Cover or less**
9 ☐ Jan 1990 Cover: 2.50 **NM** value: **Cover or less**
Circ: Statement: **52,465**
📖 Acts of Vengeance • Avengers; Acts of Vengeance
10 ☐ Feb 1990 Cover: 1.50 **NM** value: **Cover or less**
Circ: Statement: **52,465**
11 ☐ Apr 1990 Cover: 1.50 **NM** value: **Cover or less**
Circ: Statement: **52,465**
📖 The Marked Man! **A:** Mike Vosburg **W:** Terry Austin
12 ☐ Jun 1990 Cover: 1.50 **NM** value: **Cover or less**
Circ: Statement: **52,465**
📖 The Devil You Know **A:** Dave Ross **W:** Terry Kavanagh
13 ☐ Aug 1990 Cover: 1.50 **NM** value: **Cover or less**
Circ: Statement: **52,465**
14 ☐ Oct 1990 Cover: 1.50 **NM** value: **Cover or less**
Circ: Statement: **52,465**
• Title changes to Cloak & Dagger
15 ☐ Dec 1990 Cover: 1.50 **NM** value: **Cover or less**
Circ: Statement: **52,465**
16 ☐ Feb 1991 Cover: 1.50 **NM** value: **Cover or less**
17 ☐ Apr 1991 Cover: 1.50 **NM** value: **Cover or less**
• Spider-Man x-over
18 ☐ Jun 1991 Cover: 1.50 **NM** value: **Cover or less**
📖 Infinity Gauntlet • Spider-Man, Ghost Rider
19 ☐ Aug 1991 Cover: 2.50 **NM** value: **Cover or less**
final issue. ★ Origin of Cloak and Dagger.

MUTANTS AND MISFITS Silverline

1 ☐ full color Cover: 1.95 **NM** value: **2.00**

MUTANTS VS. ULTRAS: FIRST ENCOUNTERS Malibu / Ultraverse

1 ☐ Nov 1995 Cover: 6.95 **NM** value: **Cover or less**
• reprints Prime vs. Hulk, Night Man vs. Wolverine, and Exiles vs. X-Men

Diamond preorders are the estimated number of comics sold, prior to their release, to comics shops in North America by Diamond Comic Distributors, the largest distributor. These figures underreport the actual number of circulating copies by the amount of reorders Diamond took (usually 5-10% again of the preorders) and sales by publishers to newsstand and bookstore distributors. For many independent publishers, Diamond's preorders may be quite close to the actual number of copies in circulation.

MUTANT X (1ST SERIES) Marvel

When X-Factor's leader, Havok, was trapped in an explosion with a space-time device, he was propelled from the regular Marvel universe into an alternate universe, where he is the leader of the Six. This universe has profound differences from Havok's, with a disturbing parallel history and radically altered versions of the regular Marvel characters. The Six is this universe's version of the original X-Men — Havok; his wife, Madelyne Pryor; Brute; Iceman; The Fallen; and Bloodstorm, a vampiric Storm. The Six fight for mutant emancipation, while combating foes such as Nick Fury's S.H.I.E.L.D. terrorists, and the robotic bug, Moot. While Havok tries to come to lead his team as best he can, he secretly searches for a way to return to his own universe.

1 ☐ Oct 1998 Cover: 2.99 **NM** value: **3.00**
Circ: Diamd. preorders: **86,691** • **CGC:** 5 graded, best 9.6
Mutant X, Iceman, Marvel Woman standing on cover. • gatefold summary. 📖 In the End…As in the Beginning! **A:** Andrew Pepoy; Tom Raney; Howard Mackie **W:** Andrew Pepoy; Tom Raney; Howard Mackie
1/A ☐ Oct 1998 Cover: 2.99 **NM** value: **4.00**
• **CGC:** 2 graded, best 9.6
alternate cover. **A:** Andrew Pepoy; Tom Raney; Howard Mackie **W:** Andrew Pepoy; Tom Raney; Howard Mackie
2 ☐ Nov 1998 Cover: 1.99 **NM** value: **2.00**
Circ: Diamd. preorders: **80,059**
• gatefold summary. **A:** Andrew Pepoy; Tom Raney; Howard Mackie **W:** Andrew Pepoy; Tom Raney; Howard Mackie
3 ☐ Dec 1998 Cover: 1.99 **NM** value: **2.00**
Circ: Diamd. preorders: **75,816**
• gatefold summary. 📖 The Pack **A:** Andrew Pepoy; Tom Raney; Howard Mackie **W:** Andrew Pepoy; Tom Raney; Howard Mackie
4 ☐ Jan 1999 Cover: 1.99 **NM** value: **2.00**
Circ: Diamd. preorders: **74,246**
• gatefold summary. **A:** Andrew Pepoy; Tom Raney; Howard Mackie **W:** Andrew Pepoy; Tom Raney; Howard Mackie
5 ☐ Feb 1999 Cover: 1.99 **NM** value: **2.00**
Circ: Diamd. preorders: **70,933**
A: Cary Nord **W:** Howard Mackie ★ Appearance of Havok, Madelyne Pryor, Marvel Woman, Brute.
6 ☐ Mar 1999 Cover: 1.99 **NM** value: **2.00**
Circ: Diamd. preorders: **67,636**
A: Tom Raney **W:** Howard Mackie ★ Appearance of Madelyne Pryor, Man-Spider, Brute.
7 ☐ Apr 1999 Cover: 1.99 **NM** value: **2.00**
Circ: Diamd. preorders: **62,666**
A: Cary Nord **W:** Howard Mackie ★ Appearance of Havok, Man-Spider, Brute, Green Goblin.
8 ☐ May 1999 Cover: 1.99 **NM** value: **2.00**
Circ: Diamd. preorders: **60,293**
📖 The Reign of the Queen **A:** Yancey Labat; Cary Nord **W:** Howard Mackie
9 ☐ Jun 1999 Cover: 1.99 **NM** value: **2.00**
Circ: Diamd. preorders: **59,663**
★ Appearance of Ben Grimm, Havok, Elektra, Mole Man.
10 ☐ Jul 1999 Cover: 1.99 **NM** value: **Cover or less**
Circ: Diamd. preorders: **57,466**
★ Appearance of X-Men, Magneto.
11 ☐ Aug 1999 Cover: 1.99 **NM** value: **Cover or less**
Circ: Diamd. preorders: **56,723**
12 ☐ Sep 1999 Cover: 1.99 **NM** value: **Cover or less**
Circ: Diamd. preorders: **56,800**
13 ☐ Sep 1999 Cover: 1.99 **NM** value: **Cover or less**
Circ: Diamd. preorders: **54,801**
14 ☐ Nov 1999 Cover: 1.99 **NM** value: **Cover or less**
Circ: Diamd. preorders: **52,989**
15 ☐ Dec 1999 Cover: 1.99 **NM** value: **Cover or less**
Circ: Diamd. preorders: **53,413**
16 ☐ Jan 2000 Cover: 1.99 **NM** value: **Cover or less**
Circ: Diamd. preorders: **51,296**
17 ☐ Feb 2000 Cover: 1.99 **NM** value: **Cover or less**
Circ: Diamd. preorders: **48,725**
18 ☐ Mar 2000 Cover: 1.99 **NM** value: **Cover or less**
Circ: Diamd. preorders: **46,422**
19 ☐ Apr 2000 Cover: 1.99 **NM** value: **Cover or less**
Circ: Diamd. preorders: **47,445**
20 ☐ May 2000 Cover: 2.25 **NM** value: **Cover or less**
Circ: Diamd. preorders: **45,805**
21 ☐ Jun 2000 Cover: 2.25 **NM** value: **Cover or less**
Circ: Diamd. preorders: **45,735**
22 ☐ Aug 2000 Cover: 2.25 **NM** value: **Cover or less**
Circ: Diamd. preorders: **45,819**
23 ☐ Sep 2000 Cover: 2.25 **NM** value: **Cover or less**
Circ: Diamd. preorders: **45,678**
24 ☐ Oct 2000 Cover: 2.25 **NM** value: **Cover or less**
Circ: Diamd. preorders: **42,930**
25 ☐ Nov 2000 Cover: 2.25 **NM** value: **Cover or less**
Circ: Diamd. preorders: **43,273**
26 ☐ Dec 2000 Cover: 2.25 **NM** value: **Cover or less**
Circ: Diamd. preorders: **41,939**
📖 Long Day's Journey Through the Night! **A:** Ron Lim **W:** Howard Mackie
27 ☐ Jan 2001 Cover: 2.25 **NM** value: **Cover or less**
Circ: Diamd. preorders: **41,654**
28 ☐ Feb 2001 Cover: 2.25 **NM** value: **Cover or less**
Circ: Diamd. preorders: **41,581**
📖 The Hunted, Part 1 **A:** Ron Lim **W:** Howard Mackie
29 ☐ Mar 2001 Cover: 2.25 **NM** value: **Cover or less**
Circ: Diamd. preorders: **39,188**
📖 Logan's Running **A:** Tom Lyle **W:** Howard Mackie

30 ❑ Apr 2001 Cover: 2.25 **NM** value: **Cover or less**
Circ: Diamd. preorders: **38,503**
📖 Blame Canada! **A:** Ron Lim **W:** Howard Mackie

31 ❑ May 2001 Cover: 2.25 **NM** value: **Cover or less**
Circ: Diamd. preorders: **37,698**
📖 You Say You Want a Resolution? **A:** Ron Lim **W:** Howard Mackie

32 ❑ Jun 2001 Cover: 2.99 **NM** value: **Cover or less**
Circ: Diamd. preorders: **38,565**

Anl 2001 ❑ ca. 2001 Cover: 2.99 **NM** value: **Cover or less**
Circ: Diamd. preorders: **31,538**
📖 The Key **A:** James Fry **W:** Howard Mackie ★ Appearance of Beyonder.

Bk 1 ❑ Cover: 5.99 **NM** value: **Cover or less**
• Collects Issues #1-2 **A:** Tom Raney **W:** Howard Mackie

MUTANT X (2ND SERIES) — Marvel

1 ❑ Oct 2001 Cover: 2.99 **NM** value: **Cover or less**
Circ: Diamd. preorders: **48,924**

MUTANT ZONE — Aircel

1 ❑ Oct 1991, b&w Cover: 2.50 **NM** value: **Cover or less**
📖 Somewhere, Sometime… **A:** Dave Cooper **W:** Dave Cooper

2 ❑ b&w Cover: 2.50 **NM** value: **Cover or less**
A: Dave Cooper **W:** Dave Cooper

3 ❑ b&w Cover: 2.50 **NM** value: **Cover or less**
A: Dave Cooper **W:** Dave Cooper

MUTATIS — Marvel / Epic

1 ❑ ca. 1992 Cover: 2.25 **NM** value: **2.50**
Circ: CapCity orders: **4,200**
A: John Higgins **W:** Andy Lanning; Dan Abnett

2 ❑ ca. 1992 Cover: 2.25 **NM** value: **2.50**
Circ: CapCity orders: **6,100**
A: John Higgins **W:** Andy Lanning; Dan Abnett

3 ❑ ca. 1992 Cover: 2.25 **NM** value: **2.50**
Circ: CapCity orders: **4,000**
A: John Higgins **W:** Andy Lanning; Dan Abnett

MUTATOR — Checker

1 ❑ Sum 1998 Cover: 1.95 **NM** value: **Cover or less**
2 ❑ 1998 Cover: 1.95 **NM** value: **Cover or less**

MUTINY — Aragon

1 ❑ Oct 1954 Cover: 0.10 **NM** value: **125.00**
• **CGC:** 2 graded, best 9.2
2 ❑ Dec 1954 Cover: 0.10 **NM** value: **75.00**
3 ❑ Feb 1955 Cover: 0.10 **NM** value: **75.00**

MUTT & JEFF — DC

Bud Fisher's nutty duo, Mutt and Jeff, have been mainstays on the pages of the Sunday newspaper comic sections since the 1910s. Tall and skinny Mutt, in his cheap suit and hat, is the perpetual fall-guy for the antics of the sawed-off trouble-maker Jeff, who is half Mutt's height even with his trademark top hat on.

Mutt and Jeff have appeared in comic books since the 1930s, including Funnies on Parade, credited as the first comic book published. They had their own title, published by one of the DC companies, All-American Comics, from 1939 into the 1950s, when publishing chores were taken over by humor specialist Harvey Comics.

1 ❑ Sum 1939 Cover: 0.10 **NM** value: **750.00**
• **CGC:** 1 graded, best 4.5
2 ❑ Sum 1940 Cover: 0.10 **NM** value: **385.00**
3 ❑ Sum 1941 Cover: 0.10 **NM** value: **300.00**
4 ❑ Win 1941 Cover: 0.10 **NM** value: **225.00**
5 ❑ Sum 1942 Cover: 0.10 **NM** value: **150.00**
6 ❑ Fal 1942 Cover: 0.10 **NM** value: **130.00**
7 ❑ Win 1942 Cover: 0.10 **NM** value: **130.00**
8 ❑ Mar 1943 Cover: 0.10 **NM** value: **130.00**
9 ❑ May 1943 Cover: 0.10 **NM** value: **130.00**
• **CGC:** 1 graded, best 6.0
10 ❑ Jul 1943 Cover: 0.10 **NM** value: **130.00**
11 ❑ Fal 1943 Cover: 0.10 **NM** value: **100.00**
12 ❑ Win 1943 Cover: 0.10 **NM** value: **100.00**
• **CGC:** 1 graded, best 7.0
13 ❑ Spr 1944 Cover: 0.10 **NM** value: **100.00**
• **CGC:** 1 graded, best 9.2
14 ❑ Sum 1944 Cover: 0.10 **NM** value: **100.00**
15 ❑ Fal 1944 Cover: 0.10 **NM** value: **100.00**
16 ❑ Win 1944 Cover: 0.10 **NM** value: **75.00**
17 ❑ Spr 1945 Cover: 0.10 **NM** value: **75.00**
18 ❑ Sum 1945 Cover: 0.10 **NM** value: **75.00**
19 ❑ Fal 1945 Cover: 0.10 **NM** value: **75.00**
20 ❑ Win 1945 Cover: 0.10 **NM** value: **75.00**
21 ❑ Apr 1946 Cover: 0.10 **NM** value: **60.00**
22 ❑ Jun 1946 Cover: 0.10 **NM** value: **60.00**
• **CGC:** 1 graded, best 5.5
23 ❑ Aug 1946 Cover: 0.10 **NM** value: **60.00**
24 ❑ Oct 1946 Cover: 0.10 **NM** value: **60.00**
25 ❑ Dec 1946 Cover: 0.10 **NM** value: **60.00**
26 ❑ Feb 1947 Cover: 0.10 **NM** value: **60.00**
27 ❑ Apr 1947 Cover: 0.10 **NM** value: **60.00**
28 ❑ Jun 1947 Cover: 0.10 **NM** value: **60.00**
29 ❑ Aug 1947 Cover: 0.10 **NM** value: **60.00**
30 ❑ Oct 1947 Cover: 0.10 **NM** value: **60.00**
31 ❑ Dec 1947 Cover: 0.10 **NM** value: **40.00**
32 ❑ Feb 1948 Cover: 0.10 **NM** value: **40.00**
33 ❑ Apr 1948 Cover: 0.10 **NM** value: **40.00**
34 ❑ Jun 1948 Cover: 0.10 **NM** value: **40.00**
35 ❑ Aug 1948 Cover: 0.10 **NM** value: **40.00**
36 ❑ Oct 1948 Cover: 0.10 **NM** value: **40.00**
37 ❑ Dec 1948 Cover: 0.10 **NM** value: **40.00**
38 ❑ Feb 1949 Cover: 0.10 **NM** value: **40.00**
• **CGC:** 1 graded, best 7.0
39 ❑ Apr 1949 Cover: 0.10 **NM** value: **40.00**
• **CGC:** 1 graded, best 6.0
40 ❑ Jun 1949 Cover: 0.10 **NM** value: **40.00**
41 ❑ Aug 1949 Cover: 0.10 **NM** value: **40.00**
42 ❑ Oct 1949 Cover: 0.10 **NM** value: **40.00**
43 ❑ Dec 1949 Cover: 0.10 **NM** value: **40.00**
44 ❑ Feb 1950 Cover: 0.10 **NM** value: **40.00**
45 ❑ Apr 1950 Cover: 0.10 **NM** value: **40.00**
46 ❑ Jun 1950 Cover: 0.10 **NM** value: **40.00**
47 ❑ Aug 1950 Cover: 0.10 **NM** value: **40.00**
48 ❑ Oct 1950 Cover: 0.10 **NM** value: **40.00**
49 ❑ Dec 1950 Cover: 0.10 **NM** value: **40.00**
• **CGC:** 1 graded, best 7.0
50 ❑ Feb 1951 Cover: 0.10 **NM** value: **40.00**
51 ❑ Apr 1951 Cover: 0.10 **NM** value: **30.00**
52 ❑ Jun 1951 Cover: 0.10 **NM** value: **30.00**
53 ❑ Aug 1951 Cover: 0.10 **NM** value: **30.00**
54 ❑ Oct 1951 Cover: 0.10 **NM** value: **30.00**
55 ❑ Dec 1951 Cover: 0.10 **NM** value: **30.00**
📖 Tame and Wooly (text story) **A:** Bud Fisher **W:** Bud Fisher
56 ❑ Feb 1952 Cover: 0.10 **NM** value: **30.00**
57 ❑ Apr 1952 Cover: 0.10 **NM** value: **30.00**
58 ❑ Jun 1952 Cover: 0.10 **NM** value: **30.00**
59 ❑ Aug 1952 Cover: 0.10 **NM** value: **30.00**
60 ❑ Oct 1952 Cover: 0.10 **NM** value: **30.00**
61 ❑ Dec 1952 Cover: 0.10 **NM** value: **30.00**
62 ❑ Feb 1953 Cover: 0.10 **NM** value: **30.00**
63 ❑ Cover: 0.10 **NM** value: **30.00**
64 ❑ Cover: 0.10 **NM** value: **30.00**
65 ❑ Cover: 0.10 **NM** value: **30.00**
66 ❑ Oct 1953 Cover: 0.10 **NM** value: **30.00**
67 ❑ Dec 1953 Cover: 0.10 **NM** value: **30.00**
68 ❑ Jan 1954 Cover: 0.10 **NM** value: **30.00**
69 ❑ Cover: 0.10 **NM** value: **30.00**
70 ❑ Apr 1954 Cover: 0.10 **NM** value: **30.00**
71 ❑ Jun 1954 Cover: 0.10 **NM** value: **24.00**
72 ❑ Cover: 0.10 **NM** value: **24.00**
73 ❑ Sep 1954 Cover: 0.10 **NM** value: **24.00**
74 ❑ Oct 1954 Cover: 0.10 **NM** value: **24.00**
75 ❑ Dec 1954 Cover: 0.10 **NM** value: **24.00**
76 ❑ Jan 1955 Cover: 0.10 **NM** value: **24.00**
77 ❑ Mar 1955 Cover: 0.10 **NM** value: **24.00**
78 ❑ Apr 1955 Cover: 0.10 **NM** value: **24.00**
79 ❑ Jun 1955 Cover: 0.10 **NM** value: **24.00**
80 ❑ Jul 1955 Cover: 0.10 **NM** value: **24.00**
81 ❑ Sep 1955 Cover: 0.10 **NM** value: **24.00**
82 ❑ Oct 1955 Cover: 0.10 **NM** value: **24.00**
83 ❑ Dec 1955 Cover: 0.10 **NM** value: **24.00**
84 ❑ 1956 Cover: 0.10 **NM** value: **24.00**
85 ❑ Mar 1956 Cover: 0.10 **NM** value: **24.00**
86 ❑ 1956 Cover: 0.10 **NM** value: **24.00**
87 ❑ Jun 1956 Cover: 0.10 **NM** value: **24.00**
• **CGC:** 1 graded, best 9.2
88 ❑ Jul 1956 Cover: 0.10 **NM** value: **24.00**
89 ❑ Sep 1956 Cover: 0.10 **NM** value: **24.00**
90 ❑ 1956 Cover: 0.10 **NM** value: **24.00**
91 ❑ 1957 Cover: 0.10 **NM** value: **18.00**
92 ❑ 1957 Cover: 0.10 **NM** value: **18.00**
93 ❑ Mar 1957 Cover: 0.10 **NM** value: **18.00**
• **CGC:** 1 graded, best 9.0
94 ❑ Apr 1957 Cover: 0.10 **NM** value: **18.00**
95 ❑ May 1957 Cover: 0.10 **NM** value: **18.00**
96 ❑ Jun 1957 Cover: 0.10 **NM** value: **18.00**
97 ❑ Jul 1957 Cover: 0.10 **NM** value: **18.00**
98 ❑ Aug 1957 Cover: 0.10 **NM** value: **18.00**
99 ❑ Sep 1957 Cover: 0.10 **NM** value: **18.00**
100 ❑ Oct 1957 Cover: 0.10 **NM** value: **18.00**
101 ❑ Nov 1957 Cover: 0.10 **NM** value: **15.00**
102 ❑ Dec 1957 Cover: 0.10 **NM** value: **15.00**
103 ❑ Jan 1958 Cover: 0.10 **NM** value: **15.00**

MUTT & JEFF — Dell

104 ❑ 1958 Cover: 0.10 **NM** value: **15.00**
• Dell begins as publisher
105 ❑ 1958 Cover: 0.10 **NM** value: **15.00**
106 ❑ Dec 1958 Cover: 0.10 **NM** value: **15.00**
107 ❑ Jan 1959 Cover: 0.10 **NM** value: **15.00**
108 ❑ Feb 1959 Cover: 0.10 **NM** value: **15.00**
109 ❑ Mar 1959 Cover: 0.10 **NM** value: **15.00**
110 ❑ Apr 1959 Cover: 0.10 **NM** value: **15.00**
111 ❑ May 1959 Cover: 0.10 **NM** value: **15.00**
112 ❑ Jun 1959 Cover: 0.10 **NM** value: **15.00**
113 ❑ 1959 Cover: 0.10 **NM** value: **15.00**
114 ❑ Sep 1959 Cover: 0.10 **NM** value: **15.00**
115 ❑ Oct 1959 Cover: 0.10 **NM** value: **15.00**

MUTT & JEFF — Harvey

116 ❑ Cover: 0.10 **NM** value: **15.00**
• Harvey begins as publisher
117 ❑ 1960 Cover: 0.10 **NM** value: **15.00**
118 ❑ 1960 Cover: 0.10 **NM** value: **15.00**
119 ❑ 1960 Cover: 0.10 **NM** value: **15.00**
120 ❑ Oct 1960 Cover: 0.10 **NM** value: **15.00**
121 ❑ Cover: 0.10 **NM** value: **12.00**
122 ❑ 1961 Cover: 0.10 **NM** value: **12.00**
123 ❑ 1961 Cover: 0.10 **NM** value: **12.00**
124 ❑ 1961 Cover: 0.10 **NM** value: **12.00**
125 ❑ 1961 Cover: 0.10 **NM** value: **12.00**
126 ❑ 1961 Cover: 0.10 **NM** value: **12.00**
127 ❑ Cover: 0.10 **NM** value: **12.00**
128 ❑ 1962 Cover: 0.10 **NM** value: **12.00**
129 ❑ 1962 Cover: 0.10 **NM** value: **12.00**
130 ❑ 1962 **NM** value: **12.00**
131 ❑ 1962 **NM** value: **12.00**
132 ❑ **NM** value: **12.00**
133 ❑ 1963 Cover: 0.12 **NM** value: **12.00**
134 ❑ 1963 Cover: 0.12 **NM** value: **12.00**
135 ❑ 1963 Cover: 0.12 **NM** value: **12.00**
136 ❑ 1963 Cover: 0.12 **NM** value: **12.00**
137 ❑ Cover: 0.12 **NM** value: **12.00**
138 ❑ 1964 Cover: 0.12 **NM** value: **12.00**
139 ❑ 1964 Cover: 0.12 **NM** value: **12.00**
140 ❑ 1964 Cover: 0.12 **NM** value: **12.00**
141 ❑ 1964 Cover: 0.12 **NM** value: **12.00**
142 ❑ 1964 Cover: 0.12 **NM** value: **12.00**
143 ❑ Cover: 0.12 **NM** value: **12.00**
144 ❑ 1965 Cover: 0.12 **NM** value: **12.00**
145 ❑ 1965 Cover: 0.12 **NM** value: **12.00**
146 ❑ 1965 Cover: 0.12 **NM** value: **12.00**
147 ❑ 1965 Cover: 0.12 **NM** value: **12.00**
148 ❑ 1965 Cover: 0.12 **NM** value: **12.00**
final issue.

MUZZLE — Dead Fish

1 ❑ Cover: 1.00 **NM** value: **Cover or less**
Color cover. 📖 Duckman: Hot Bullets for Love; Brian the Human Vacuum **A:** John Graves II **W:** John Graves II

2 ❑ Cover: 1.00 **NM** value: **Cover or less**
📖 Duckman **A:** John Graves II **W:** John Graves II

3 ❑ Cover: 1.00 **NM** value: **Cover or less**
📖 Lil Victim Sally; Duckman: Pickup Lines that Don't Work; Duckman: The Paper of Pathos; **A:** John Graves II **W:** John Graves II

4 ❑ Cover: 1.00 **NM** value: **Cover or less**
📖 Cocoa Marsh & Fran Bumperhumper; 10 Easy Ways to Tell if Your Neighbors Worship Satan; Duckman: Taxi Terror; Cat People on the Moon: Dance of Death!; Brian: The Human Vacuum: The Voice of his People; Things to do on the Subway; Love at First Light **A:** John Graves II **W:** John Graves II

5 ❑ Cover: 1.00 **NM** value: **Cover or less**
📖 Cocoa Marsh & Fran Bumperhumper; The Application Process of Evil!; Preschool Proverbs; Great Historical Rumors **A:** John Graves II **W:** John Graves II

6 ❑ Cover: 1.00 **NM** value: **Cover or less**
📖 Insecure Parent Theater; Great Historical Rumors **A:** John Graves II **W:** John Graves II

MY DIARY — Marvel

1 ❑ Dec 1949 Cover: 0.10 **NM** value: **100.00**
2 ❑ Mar 1950 Cover: 0.10 **NM** value: **100.00**

MY DATE — Hillman

1 ❑ Jul 1947 Cover: 0.10 **NM** value: **250.00**
2 ❑ Sep 1947 Cover: 0.10 **NM** value: **175.00**
3 ❑ Nov 1947 Cover: 0.10 **NM** value: **175.00**
4 ❑ Jan 1948 Cover: 0.10 **NM** value: **175.00**

MY FAVORITE MARTIAN — Gold Key

1 ❑ Jan 1964 Cover: 0.12 **NM** value: **150.00**
• **CGC:** 2 graded, best 9.0
2 ❑ Jul 1964 Cover: 0.12 **NM** value: **75.00**
3 ❑ Feb 1965 Cover: 0.12 **NM** value: **50.00**
• **CGC:** 1 graded, best 9.2
4 ❑ May 1965 Cover: 0.12 **NM** value: **50.00**
5 ❑ Aug 1965 Cover: 0.12 **NM** value: **50.00**
6 ❑ 1966 Cover: 0.12 **NM** value: **50.00**
7 ❑ Apr 1966 Cover: 0.12 **NM** value: **50.00**
8 ❑ Jul 1966 Cover: 0.12 **NM** value: **50.00**
9 ❑ Oct 1966 Cover: 0.12 **NM** value: **50.00**

MY FRIEND IRMA — Marvel

Did you hear the one about the blond fox that got caught in a trap? Yup, she chewed off three legs and was still stuck (ba-dum-bump!). See, I could have been the writer for My Friend Irma, one long blond joke that ran for nearly 50 issues during the early 1950s, except that the actual writer happened to be one Stan Lee and the artist was teen humor genius Dan DeCarlo (of Archie fame). My Friend Irma was based on a popular radio and TV show featuring the adventures of the air-headed Irma and her pals, young "career girls" whose amazing and incurable dumbness was the root of so much hilarity ("Are you girls amateurs?" asks the art instructor. "No," replies Irma, "we're not even related.") In one memorable sequence, Irma actually complained that Stan and Dan were making her too dumb — then ended up walking out with their paychecks. Excelsior!

3 ❑ Jun 1950 Cover: 0.10 **NM** value: **50.00**
4 ❑ Aug 1950 Cover: 0.10 **NM** value: **50.00**
5 ❑ Oct 1950 Cover: 0.10 **NM** value: **50.00**
6 ❑ Dec 1950 Cover: 0.10 **NM** value: **40.00**
7 ❑ Feb 1951 Cover: 0.10 **NM** value: **40.00**
8 ❑ Apr 1951 Cover: 0.10 **NM** value: **40.00**
9 ❑ Jun 1951 Cover: 0.10 **NM** value: **40.00**
10 ❑ Aug 1951 Cover: 0.10 **NM** value: **40.00**
11 ❑ Sep 1951 Cover: 0.10 **NM** value: **25.00**
12 ❑ Oct 1951 Cover: 0.10 **NM** value: **25.00**
13 ❑ Nov 1951 Cover: 0.10 **NM** value: **25.00**
14 ❑ Dec 1951 Cover: 0.10 **NM** value: **25.00**
15 ❑ Jan 1952 Cover: 0.10 **NM** value: **25.00**
16 ❑ Feb 1952 Cover: 0.10 **NM** value: **25.00**
17 ❑ Mar 1952 Cover: 0.10 **NM** value: **25.00**

Other grades: Multiply prices above by **1.5 for Mint • 2/3 for Very Fine • 1/3 for Fine • 1/5 for Very Good • 1/8 for Good**

18 ❑ Apr 1952 Cover: 0.10 **NM** value: **25.00**
19 ❑ May 1952 Cover: 0.10 **NM** value: **25.00**
20 ❑ Jun 1952 Cover: 0.10 **NM** value: **22.00**
21 ❑ Jul 1952 Cover: 0.10 **NM** value: **22.00**
22 ❑ Aug 1952 Cover: 0.10 **NM** value: **22.00**
23 ❑ Sep 1952 Cover: 0.10 **NM** value: **22.00**
24 ❑ Oct 1952 Cover: 0.10 **NM** value: **22.00**
25 ❑ Nov 1952 Cover: 0.10 **NM** value: **22.00**
26 ❑ Dec 1952 Cover: 0.10 **NM** value: **22.00**
27 ❑ Jan 1953 Cover: 0.10 **NM** value: **22.00**
28 ❑ Feb 1953 Cover: 0.10 **NM** value: **22.00**
29 ❑ Mar 1953 Cover: 0.10 **NM** value: **22.00**
30 ❑ Apr 1953 Cover: 0.10 **NM** value: **22.00**
31 ❑ May 1953 Cover: 0.10 **NM** value: **18.00**
32 ❑ Jun 1953 Cover: 0.10 **NM** value: **18.00**
33 ❑ Jul 1953 Cover: 0.10 **NM** value: **18.00**
34 ❑ Aug 1953 Cover: 0.10 **NM** value: **18.00**
35 ❑ Sep 1953 Cover: 0.10 **NM** value: **18.00**
36 ❑ Oct 1953 Cover: 0.10 **NM** value: **18.00**
37 ❑ Nov 1953 Cover: 0.10 **NM** value: **18.00**
38 ❑ Dec 1953 Cover: 0.10 **NM** value: **18.00**
39 ❑ Jan 1954 Cover: 0.10 **NM** value: **18.00**
40 ❑ Feb 1954 Cover: 0.10 **NM** value: **18.00**
41 ❑ Mar 1954 Cover: 0.10 **NM** value: **18.00**
42 ❑ Apr 1954 Cover: 0.10 **NM** value: **18.00**
43 ❑ May 1954 Cover: 0.10 **NM** value: **18.00**
44 ❑ Jun 1954 Cover: 0.10 **NM** value: **18.00**
45 ❑ Jul 1954 Cover: 0.10 **NM** value: **18.00**
46 ❑ Oct 1954 Cover: 0.10 **NM** value: **18.00**
47 ❑ Dec 1954 Cover: 0.10 **NM** value: **18.00**
48 ❑ Feb 1955 Cover: 0.10 **NM** value: **18.00**
final issue. **A:** Dan Decarlo **W:** Stan Lee

MY GIRL PEARL — Atlas

1 ❑ Apr 1955 Cover: 0.10 **NM** value: **100.00**
A: Dan Decarlo **W:** Stan Lee
2 ❑ Jun 1955 Cover: 0.10 **NM** value: **45.00**
3 ❑ Aug 1955 Cover: 0.10 **NM** value: **30.00**
4 ❑ Oct 1955 Cover: 0.10 **NM** value: **30.00**
5 ❑ Jul 1957 Cover: 0.10 **NM** value: **30.00**
6 ❑ Aug 1957 Cover: 0.10 **NM** value: **30.00**
7 ❑ Sep 1957 Cover: 0.10 **NM** value: **25.00**
8 ❑ Aug 1960 Cover: 0.10 **NM** value: **25.00**
9 ❑ Oct 1960 Cover: 0.10 **NM** value: **25.00**
10 ❑ Dec 1960 Cover: 0.10 **NM** value: **25.00**
11 ❑ Feb 1961 Cover: 0.10 **NM** value: **25.00**

MY GREATEST ADVENTURE — DC

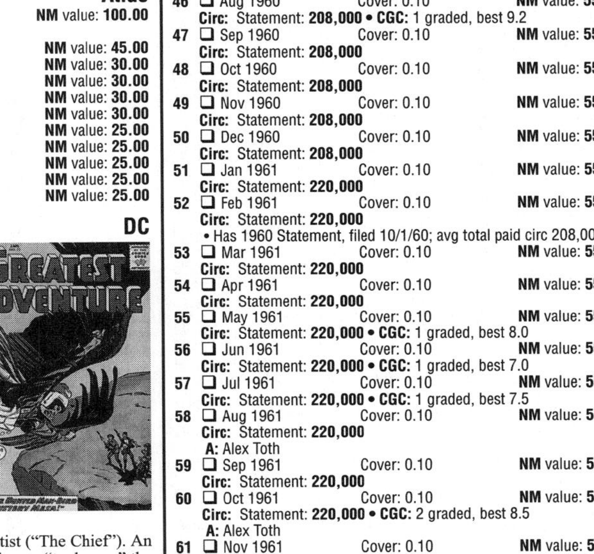
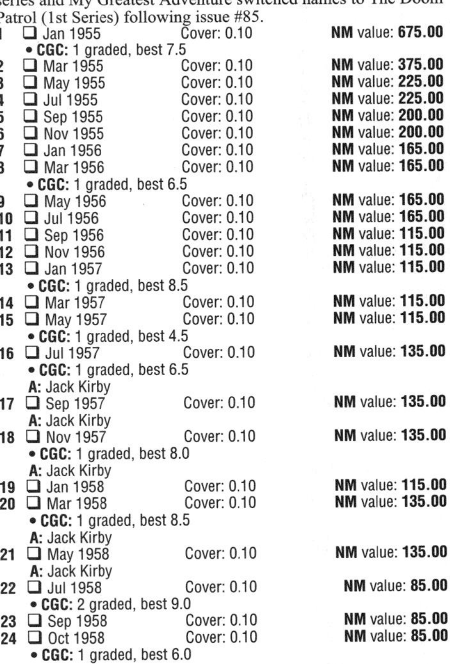

My Greatest Adventure began its life as an adventure series, quickly switching to a science/fantasy-inspired format. For the first 80 issues of its run it turned in a respectable collection of stories, including several issues featuring the art of Jack Kirby and Alex Toth.

Then, issue #80 introduced the world to the strange crew of characters known as The Doom Patrol. This weird team consisted of ex-racer Cliff Steele, now clad in the metal body of Robotman; the stretchable Elasti-Girl; and the mysterious Negative Man. Like Marvel's X-Men, these oddball heroes were led by a wheelchair-bound scientist ("The Chief"). An offbeat and popular team, the Doom Patrol soon "took over" the series and My Greatest Adventure switched names to The Doom Patrol (1st Series) following issue #85.

1 ❑ Jan 1955 Cover: 0.10 **NM** value: **675.00**
• **CGC:** 1 graded, best 7.5
2 ❑ Mar 1955 Cover: 0.10 **NM** value: **375.00**
3 ❑ May 1955 Cover: 0.10 **NM** value: **225.00**
4 ❑ Jul 1955 Cover: 0.10 **NM** value: **225.00**
5 ❑ Sep 1955 Cover: 0.10 **NM** value: **200.00**
6 ❑ Nov 1955 Cover: 0.10 **NM** value: **200.00**
7 ❑ Jan 1956 Cover: 0.10 **NM** value: **165.00**
8 ❑ Mar 1956 Cover: 0.10 **NM** value: **165.00**
• **CGC:** 1 graded, best 6.5
9 ❑ May 1956 Cover: 0.10 **NM** value: **165.00**
10 ❑ Jul 1956 Cover: 0.10 **NM** value: **165.00**
11 ❑ Sep 1956 Cover: 0.10 **NM** value: **115.00**
12 ❑ Nov 1956 Cover: 0.10 **NM** value: **115.00**
13 ❑ Jan 1957 Cover: 0.10 **NM** value: **115.00**
• **CGC:** 1 graded, best 8.5
14 ❑ Mar 1957 Cover: 0.10 **NM** value: **115.00**
15 ❑ May 1957 Cover: 0.10 **NM** value: **115.00**
• **CGC:** 1 graded, best 4.5
16 ❑ Jul 1957 Cover: 0.10 **NM** value: **135.00**
• **CGC:** 1 graded, best 6.5
A: Jack Kirby
17 ❑ Sep 1957 Cover: 0.10 **NM** value: **135.00**
A: Jack Kirby
18 ❑ Nov 1957 Cover: 0.10 **NM** value: **135.00**
• **CGC:** 1 graded, best 8.0
A: Jack Kirby
19 ❑ Jan 1958 Cover: 0.10 **NM** value: **115.00**
20 ❑ Mar 1958 Cover: 0.10 **NM** value: **135.00**
• **CGC:** 1 graded, best 8.5
A: Jack Kirby
21 ❑ May 1958 Cover: 0.10 **NM** value: **135.00**
A: Jack Kirby
22 ❑ Jul 1958 Cover: 0.10 **NM** value: **85.00**
• **CGC:** 2 graded, best 9.0
23 ❑ Sep 1958 Cover: 0.10 **NM** value: **85.00**
24 ❑ Oct 1958 Cover: 0.10 **NM** value: **85.00**
• **CGC:** 1 graded, best 6.0
25 ❑ Nov 1958 Cover: 0.10 **NM** value: **85.00**
• **CGC:** 1 graded, best 9.2
26 ❑ Dec 1958 Cover: 0.10 **NM** value: **85.00**
27 ❑ Jan 1959 Cover: 0.10 **NM** value: **85.00**
28 ❑ Feb 1959 Cover: 0.10 **NM** value: **100.00**
• **CGC:** 1 graded, best 8.5
A: Jack Kirby
29 ❑ Mar 1959 Cover: 0.10 **NM** value: **85.00**
30 ❑ Apr 1959 Cover: 0.10 **NM** value: **85.00**
31 ❑ May 1959 Cover: 0.10 **NM** value: **70.00**
32 ❑ Jun 1959 Cover: 0.10 **NM** value: **70.00**
33 ❑ Jul 1959 Cover: 0.10 **NM** value: **70.00**
34 ❑ Aug 1959 Cover: 0.10 **NM** value: **70.00**
35 ❑ Sep 1959 Cover: 0.10 **NM** value: **70.00**
36 ❑ Oct 1959 Cover: 0.10 **NM** value: **70.00**
• **CGC:** 1 graded, best 2.5
37 ❑ Nov 1959 Cover: 0.10 **NM** value: **70.00**
• **CGC:** 1 graded, best 4.5
38 ❑ Dec 1959 Cover: 0.10 **NM** value: **70.00**
39 ❑ Jan 1960 Cover: 0.10 **NM** value: **70.00**
Circ: Statement: **208,000**
40 ❑ Feb 1960 Cover: 0.10 **NM** value: **70.00**
Circ: Statement: **208,000** • **CGC:** 1 graded, best 9.0
41 ❑ Mar 1960 Cover: 0.10 **NM** value: **55.00**
Circ: Statement: **208,000** • **CGC:** 1 graded, best 9.0
42 ❑ Apr 1960 Cover: 0.10 **NM** value: **55.00**
Circ: Statement: **208,000**
43 ❑ May 1960 Cover: 0.10 **NM** value: **55.00**
Circ: Statement: **208,000**
44 ❑ Jun 1960 Cover: 0.10 **NM** value: **55.00**
Circ: Statement: **208,000**
45 ❑ Jul 1960 Cover: 0.10 **NM** value: **55.00**
Circ: Statement: **208,000**
46 ❑ Aug 1960 Cover: 0.10 **NM** value: **55.00**
Circ: Statement: **208,000** • **CGC:** 1 graded, best 9.2
47 ❑ Sep 1960 Cover: 0.10 **NM** value: **55.00**
Circ: Statement: **208,000**
48 ❑ Oct 1960 Cover: 0.10 **NM** value: **55.00**
Circ: Statement: **208,000**
49 ❑ Nov 1960 Cover: 0.10 **NM** value: **55.00**
Circ: Statement: **208,000**
50 ❑ Dec 1960 Cover: 0.10 **NM** value: **55.00**
Circ: Statement: **208,000**
51 ❑ Jan 1961 Cover: 0.10 **NM** value: **55.00**
Circ: Statement: **220,000**
52 ❑ Feb 1961 Cover: 0.10 **NM** value: **55.00**
Circ: Statement: **220,000**
• Has 1960 Statement, filed 10/1/60; avg total paid circ 208,000
53 ❑ Mar 1961 Cover: 0.10 **NM** value: **55.00**
Circ: Statement: **220,000**
54 ❑ Apr 1961 Cover: 0.10 **NM** value: **55.00**
Circ: Statement: **220,000**
55 ❑ May 1961 Cover: 0.10 **NM** value: **55.00**
Circ: Statement: **220,000** • **CGC:** 1 graded, best 8.0
56 ❑ Jun 1961 Cover: 0.10 **NM** value: **55.00**
Circ: Statement: **220,000** • **CGC:** 1 graded, best 7.0
57 ❑ Jul 1961 Cover: 0.10 **NM** value: **55.00**
Circ: Statement: **220,000** • **CGC:** 1 graded, best 7.5
58 ❑ Aug 1961 Cover: 0.10 **NM** value: **55.00**
Circ: Statement: **220,000**
A: Alex Toth
59 ❑ Sep 1961 Cover: 0.10 **NM** value: **55.00**
Circ: Statement: **220,000**
60 ❑ Oct 1961 Cover: 0.10 **NM** value: **55.00**
Circ: Statement: **220,000** • **CGC:** 2 graded, best 8.5
A: Alex Toth
61 ❑ Nov 1961 Cover: 0.10 **NM** value: **55.00**
Circ: Statement: **220,000**
A: Alex Toth
62 ❑ Dec 1961 Cover: 0.12 **NM** value: **35.00**
Circ: Statement: **220,000**
63 ❑ Jan 1962 Cover: 0.12 **NM** value: **35.00**
Circ: Statement: **175,000**
64 ❑ Feb 1962 Cover: 0.12 **NM** value: **35.00**
Circ: Statement: **175,000**
• Has 1961 Statement, filed 10/1/61; avg total paid circ 220,000
65 ❑ Mar 1962 Cover: 0.12 **NM** value: **35.00**
Circ: Statement: **175,000** • **CGC:** 1 graded, best 9.2
66 ❑ Apr 1962 Cover: 0.12 **NM** value: **35.00**
Circ: Statement: **175,000**
67 ❑ May 1962 Cover: 0.12 **NM** value: **35.00**
Circ: Statement: **175,000** • **CGC:** 2 graded, best 9.4
68 ❑ Jun 1962 Cover: 0.12 **NM** value: **35.00**
Circ: Statement: **175,000**
69 ❑ Jul 1962 Cover: 0.12 **NM** value: **35.00**
Circ: Statement: **175,000**
70 ❑ Aug 1962 Cover: 0.12 **NM** value: **35.00**
Circ: Statement: **175,000** • **CGC:** 1 graded, best 8.5
71 ❑ Sep 1962 Cover: 0.12 **NM** value: **35.00**
Circ: Statement: **175,000** • **CGC:** 2 graded, best 8.5
72 ❑ Oct 1962 Cover: 0.12 **NM** value: **35.00**
Circ: Statement: **175,000** • **CGC:** 1 graded, best 8.0
73 ❑ Nov 1962 Cover: 0.12 **NM** value: **35.00**
Circ: Statement: **175,000**
74 ❑ Dec 1962 Cover: 0.12 **NM** value: **35.00**
Circ: Statement: **175,000** • **CGC:** 2 graded, best 9.0
75 ❑ Jan 1963 Cover: 0.12 **NM** value: **35.00**
• **CGC:** 3 graded, best 9.0
📖 Castaway Cave-Man Of 1950; Bannon vs. The Terrible Titan; Peter Puptent Explorer; Shorty; I Was The Hunted Man-Bird Of Mystery Mesa!
76 ❑ Feb 1963 Cover: 0.12 **NM** value: **35.00**
77 ❑ Mar 1963 Cover: 0.12 **NM** value: **35.00**
A: Alex Toth
78 ❑ Apr 1963 Cover: 0.12 **NM** value: **35.00**
79 ❑ May 1963 Cover: 0.12 **NM** value: **35.00**
80 ❑ Jun 1963 Cover: 0.12 **NM** value: **260.00**
• **CGC:** 13 graded, best 9.6
📖 The Doom Patrol • First Doom Patrol Story★ Origin of The Doom Patrol, Elasti-Girl, Negative Man, Robotman. ★ 1st Appearance of The Doom Patrol.
81 ❑ Aug 1963 Cover: 0.12 **NM** value: **125.00**
• **CGC:** 4 graded, best 9.6
📖 The Nightmare Maker; Listen World… I'm the Missing Link • Doom Patrol story★ Appearance of The Doom Patrol.
82 ❑ Sep 1963 Cover: 0.12 **NM** value: **125.00**
• **CGC:** 4 graded, best 9.0
📖 Three Against the Earth; Hot Cargo to Nowhere • Doom Patrol story★ Appearance of The Doom Patrol.
83 ❑ Nov 1963 Cover: 0.12 **NM** value: **125.00**
• **CGC:** 4 graded, best 9.4
📖 The Night Negative Man Went Berserk; Menace of the Undersea Beanstalk • Doom Patrol story★ Appearance of The Doom Patrol.
84 ❑ Dec 1963 Cover: 0.12 **NM** value: **125.00**
• **CGC:** 2 graded, best 9.6
📖 The Return of General Immortus; Let's Go… Ghost G.I.s! • Doom Patrol story★ Appearance of The Doom Patrol.
85 ❑ Feb 1964 Cover: 0.12 **NM** value: **125.00**
• **CGC:** 2 graded, best 9.6
📖 The Furies from 4,000 Miles Below; The Curse of the Cat's Cradle • Series continued in Doom Patrol (1st Series) #86; Has 1963 Statement, filed 10/1/63; no circ figures published★ Appearance of The Doom Patrol.

MY GREAT LOVE — Fox

1 ❑ Oct 1949 Cover: 0.10 **NM** value: **100.00**
2 ❑ Dec 1949 Cover: 0.10 **NM** value: **50.00**
3 ❑ Feb 1950 Cover: 0.10 **NM** value: **50.00**
4 ❑ Apr 1950 Cover: 0.10 **NM** value: **50.00**

MY INTIMATE AFFAIR — Fox

1 ❑ Mar 1950 Cover: 0.10 **NM** value: **100.00**
2 ❑ May 1950 Cover: 0.10 **NM** value: **50.00**

MY LIFE — Fox

"I am in love with a boy who hardly notices me. Will he think I am very bold if I call him?" For the (1940s-style) answer to this and other burning questions, as well as some gritty, emotionally violent, and downright mean confession-oriented tales of love lost and found, turn to Fox Feature Syndicate's series, My Life.

In its short run, My Life managed to draw the attention of comics censor Frederic Wertham, who cited the series for its indecency and poor family values in his book Seduction of the Innocent. My Life's answer to the above question, by the way, is "I've never known a man who liked to be chased by a girl. Men like to do all the chasing." In like fashion, women who strayed outside the lines by displaying initiative, ability, or emotional sophistication were frequently the villains in these stories.

4 ❑ Sep 1948 Cover: 0.10 **NM** value: **155.00**
📖 I Was a Spoiled Brat • Mentioned in Seduction of the Innocent ("I Was a Spoiled Brat"); Series continued from Meet Corliss Archer #4 **A:** Jack Kamen
5 ❑ Nov 1948 Cover: 0.10 **NM** value: **80.00**
A: Jack Kamen
6 ❑ Jan 1949 Cover: 0.10 **NM** value: **85.00**
A: Jack Kamen
7 ❑ Mar 1949 Cover: 0.10 **NM** value: **85.00**
A: Wally Wood
8 ❑ May 1949 Cover: 0.10 **NM** value: **40.00**
9 ❑ Jul 1949 Cover: 0.10 **NM** value: **40.00**
10 ❑ Sep 1949 Cover: 0.10 **NM** value: **90.00**
A: Wally Wood
11 ❑ Nov 1949 Cover: 0.10 **NM** value: **40.00**
📖 Say A Prayer For Me; Girl From The Tenements; I Sought Revenge;
12 ❑ Jan 1950 Cover: 0.10 **NM** value: **40.00**
13 ❑ Mar 1950 Cover: 0.10 **NM** value: **40.00**
14 ❑ May 1950 Cover: 0.10 **NM** value: **40.00**
15 ❑ Jul 1950 Cover: 0.10 **NM** value: **40.00**
• Final issue?

MY LITTLE MARGIE — Charlton

Margie is the boy-crazed teenage hero of this popular girls' comic, begun in 1954. Each issue collected three to four amusing stories featuring the title character, a story about one of her friends, and an activity page. (coloring page, etc...), and a center spread which featured three to four extra "fashions" created by the comic's fans.

As with many other girls' comics of the day, Charlton solicited contributions from readers of dress designs for Margie to wear. If a dress or costume was selected, the artist would draw Margie actually wearing it. The "clothing designer" was always given credit somewhere on the same page in a caption.

1 ❑ Jul 1954 Cover: 0.10 **NM** value: **125.00**
• **CGC:** 1 graded, best 8.0
2 ❑ Aug 1954 Cover: 0.10 **NM** value: **60.00**
📖 That's The Spirit; Sloop Slip; Collection Day **A:** Chic Stone **W:** Chic Stone
3 ❑ Nov 1954 Cover: 0.10 **NM** value: **35.00**
4 ❑ Cover: 0.10 **NM** value: **35.00**

CGC-graded: Multiply prices above by **33 for 9.9 M** • **16 for 9.8 NM/M** • **7 for 9.6 NM+** • **5 for 9.4 NM** • **2.5 for 9.2 NM-** • **1.5 for 9.0 VF/NM**

5 ❑ ca. 1955 Cover: 0.10 **NM** value: **35.00**
6 ❑ ca. 1955 Cover: 0.10 **NM** value: **32.00**
7 ❑ ca. 1955 Cover: 0.10 **NM** value: **32.00**
8 ❑ ca. 1955 Cover: 0.10 **NM** value: **32.00**
9 ❑ ca. 1955 Cover: 0.10 **NM** value: **32.00**
10 ❑ Cover: 0.10 **NM** value: **32.00**
11 ❑ Cover: 0.10 **NM** value: **26.00**
12 ❑ ca. 1956 Cover: 0.10 **NM** value: **26.00**
13 ❑ ca. 1956 Cover: 0.10 **NM** value: **26.00**
14 ❑ ca. 1956 Cover: 0.10 **NM** value: **26.00**
15 ❑ ca. 1957 Cover: 0.10 **NM** value: **26.00**
16 ❑ ca. 1957 Cover: 0.10 **NM** value: **26.00**
17 ❑ Oct 1957 Cover: 0.10 **NM** value: **26.00**
18 ❑ ca. 1958 Cover: 0.10 **NM** value: **26.00**
19 ❑ ca. 1958 Cover: 0.10 **NM** value: **26.00**
20 ❑ ca. 1958 Cover: 0.25 **NM** value: **45.00**
• Giant-sized issue.
21 ❑ Oct 1958 Cover: 0.10 **NM** value: **20.00**
22 ❑ Cover: 0.10 **NM** value: **20.00**
23 ❑ ca. 1959 Cover: 0.10 **NM** value: **20.00**
24 ❑ ca. 1959 Cover: 0.10 **NM** value: **20.00**
25 ❑ ca. 1959 Cover: 0.10 **NM** value: **20.00**
26 ❑ Cover: 0.10 **NM** value: **20.00**
27 ❑ Cover: 0.10 **NM** value: **20.00**
28 ❑ Mar 1960 Cover: 0.10 **NM** value: **20.00**
29 ❑ ca. 1960 Cover: 0.10 **NM** value: **20.00**
30 ❑ Jun 1960 Cover: 0.10 **NM** value: **20.00**
31 ❑ ca. 1960 Cover: 0.10 **NM** value: **16.00**
32 ❑ Oct 1960 Cover: 0.10 **NM** value: **16.00**
33 ❑ Cover: 0.10 **NM** value: **16.00**
34 ❑ ca. 1961 Cover: 0.10 **NM** value: **16.00**
35 ❑ ca. 1961 Cover: 0.10 **NM** value: **16.00**
36 ❑ ca. 1961 Cover: 0.10 **NM** value: **16.00**
📖 Powerhouse Margie; The Witching Hour; Selected Fashions Of My Little Margie; Hat's Nice; Gag Page; Green Thumb
37 ❑ ca. 1961 Cover: 0.10 **NM** value: **16.00**
38 ❑ Cover: 0.10 **NM** value: **16.00**
39 ❑ ca. 1962 Cover: 0.12 **NM** value: **16.00**
40 ❑ Mar 1962 Cover: 0.12 **NM** value: **12.00**
• **CGC:** 1 graded, best 8.0
41 ❑ ca. 1962 Cover: 0.12 **NM** value: **12.00**
42 ❑ ca. 1962 Cover: 0.12 **NM** value: **12.00**
43 ❑ ca. 1962 Cover: 0.12 **NM** value: **12.00**
44 ❑ Cover: 0.12 **NM** value: **12.00**
45 ❑ Cover: 0.12 **NM** value: **12.00**
46 ❑ ca. 1963 Cover: 0.12 **NM** value: **12.00**
47 ❑ ca. 1963 Cover: 0.12 **NM** value: **12.00**
48 ❑ ca. 1963 Cover: 0.12 **NM** value: **12.00**
49 ❑ ca. 1963 Cover: 0.12 **NM** value: **12.00**
50 ❑ Cover: 0.12 **NM** value: **12.00**
51 ❑ ca. 1964 Cover: 0.12 **NM** value: **8.00**
52 ❑ ca. 1964 Cover: 0.12 **NM** value: **8.00**
53 ❑ ca. 1964 Cover: 0.12 **NM** value: **8.00**
54 ❑ ca. 1964 Cover: 0.12 **NM** value: **40.00**
★ Appearance of Beatles.

MY LITTLE MARGIE'S BOYFRIENDS — Charlton

1 ❑ ca. 1955 Cover: 0.10 **NM** value: **100.00**
2 ❑ ca. 1955 Cover: 0.10 **NM** value: **50.00**
3 ❑ ca. 1956 Cover: 0.10 **NM** value: **50.00**
4 ❑ ca. 1956 Cover: 0.10 **NM** value: **50.00**
5 ❑ ca. 1956 Cover: 0.10 **NM** value: **50.00**
6 ❑ ca. 1956 Cover: 0.10 **NM** value: **40.00**
7 ❑ ca. 1957 Cover: 0.10 **NM** value: **40.00**
8 ❑ ca. 1957 Cover: 0.10 **NM** value: **40.00**
9 ❑ ca. 1957 Cover: 0.10 **NM** value: **40.00**
10 ❑ ca. 1957 Cover: 0.10 **NM** value: **40.00**
11 ❑ ca. 1957 Cover: 0.10 **NM** value: **40.00**

MY LOVE — Marvel

My Love, along with the carbon-copy Our Love Story, was Marvel's attempt to reach the largely untapped, teen-age female audience with a "with-it, sophisticated" love comic book done in the mighty Marvel style that had proven so popular with the Y-chromosome set in the 60s. An unintentionally funny period artifact, My Love is a wonderful example of what nerdy 40-ish men thought would seem "Like, Wow!" to teen-age girls at the tail end of the swinging 1960s. My Love went so far as to employ several top-line Marvel artists like Gene Colan, John Romita, Sr., and John Buscema, as well as to raid the Atlas vaults for the occasional 1950s reprint from the pen of Jack Kirby or Al Williamson. My Love lasted 39 issues, then petered out in the general market contraction of the mid-1970s, which saw the end of romance comics as a genre in the United States.

1 ❑ Sep 1949 Cover: 0.15 **NM** value: **18.00**
📖 A Boy, A Girl, and My Broken Heart; I Dream of Romance; Must I Live Without Love? **A:** John Romita Sr.
2 ❑ Nov 1949 Cover: 0.15 **NM** value: **12.00**
3 ❑ Jan 1950 Cover: 0.15 **NM** value: **10.00**
📖 The Man I Must Not Love! **A:** John Buscema; John Romita Sr. **W:** Stan Lee
4 ❑ Apr 1950 Cover: 0.15 **NM** value: **8.00**
5 ❑ May 1970 Cover: 0.15 **NM** value: **8.00**
6 ❑ Jul 1970 Cover: 0.15 **NM** value: **8.00**
7 ❑ Sep 1970 Cover: 0.15 **NM** value: **8.00**
8 ❑ Nov 1970 Cover: 0.15 **NM** value: **8.00**
9 ❑ Jan 1971 Cover: 0.15 **NM** value: **8.00**
10 ❑ Mar 1971 Cover: 0.15 **NM** value: **6.00**
11 ❑ May 1971 Cover: 0.15 **NM** value: **6.00**
• **CGC:** 1 graded, best 9.4
12 ❑ Jul 1971 Cover: 0.15 **NM** value: **6.00**
13 ❑ Sep 1971 Cover: 0.15 **NM** value: **6.00**
14 ❑ Nov 1971 Cover: 0.15 **NM** value: **6.00**
• **CGC:** 2 graded, best 9.2
15 ❑ Jan 1972 Cover: 0.15 **NM** value: **6.00**
16 ❑ Mar 1972 Cover: 0.15 **NM** value: **6.00**
17 ❑ May 1972 Cover: 0.15 **NM** value: **6.00**
18 ❑ Jul 1972 Cover: 0.15 **NM** value: **6.00**
19 ❑ Sep 1972 Cover: 0.20 **NM** value: **6.00**
20 ❑ Nov 1972 Cover: 0.20 **NM** value: **6.00**
21 ❑ Jan 1973 Cover: 0.20 **NM** value: **4.00**
22 ❑ Mar 1973 Cover: 0.20 **NM** value: **4.00**
23 ❑ May 1973 Cover: 0.20 **NM** value: **4.00**
24 ❑ Jul 1973 Cover: 0.20 **NM** value: **4.00**
25 ❑ Sep 1973 Cover: 0.20 **NM** value: **4.00**
26 ❑ Nov 1973 Cover: 0.20 **NM** value: **4.00**
27 ❑ Jan 1974 Cover: 0.20 **NM** value: **4.00**
28 ❑ May 1974 Cover: 0.20 **NM** value: **4.00**
29 ❑ Jul 1974 Cover: 0.20 **NM** value: **4.00**
30 ❑ Sep 1974 Cover: 0.20 **NM** value: **4.00**
31 ❑ Nov 1974 Cover: 0.20 **NM** value: **4.00**
32 ❑ Jan 1975 Cover: 0.20 **NM** value: **4.00**
33 ❑ Mar 1975 Cover: 0.20 **NM** value: **4.00**
34 ❑ May 1975 Cover: 0.20 **NM** value: **4.00**
35 ❑ 1975 Cover: 0.20 **NM** value: **4.00**
36 ❑ 1975 Cover: 0.20 **NM** value: **4.00**
37 ❑ 1975 Cover: 0.20 **NM** value: **4.00**
38 ❑ 1976 Cover: 0.20 **NM** value: **4.00**
📖 The Man I Must Not Love; I Do...; Big Man On Campus; **A:** John Buscema; John Romita; Jay Scott Piza **W:** Stan Lee
39 ❑ 1976 Cover: 0.20 **NM** value: **4.00**
SE 1 ❑ ca. 1971 Cover: 0.50 **NM** value: **15.00**

MY LOVE AFFAIR — Fox

1 ❑ Jul 1949 Cover: 0.10 **NM** value: **100.00**
2 ❑ Sep 1949 Cover: 0.10 **NM** value: **50.00**
3 ❑ Nov 1949 Cover: 0.10 **NM** value: **50.00**
4 ❑ Jan 1950 Cover: 0.10 **NM** value: **50.00**
5 ❑ Mar 1950 Cover: 0.10 **NM** value: **50.00**
6 ❑ May 1950 Cover: 0.10 **NM** value: **50.00**

MY LOVE STORY (ATLAS) — Atlas

1 ❑ Apr 1956 Cover: 0.10 **NM** value: **75.00**
2 ❑ Jun 1956 Cover: 0.10 **NM** value: **40.00**
3 ❑ Aug 1956 Cover: 0.10 **NM** value: **40.00**
4 ❑ Oct 1956 Cover: 0.10 **NM** value: **40.00**
5 ❑ Dec 1956 Cover: 0.10 **NM** value: **40.00**
6 ❑ Feb 1957 Cover: 0.10 **NM** value: **35.00**
7 ❑ Apr 1957 Cover: 0.10 **NM** value: **35.00**
8 ❑ Jun 1957 Cover: 0.10 **NM** value: **35.00**
9 ❑ Aug 1957 Cover: 0.10 **NM** value: **35.00**

MY LOVE STORY (FOX) — Fox

1 ❑ Sep 1949 Cover: 0.10 **NM** value: **100.00**
2 ❑ Nov 1949 Cover: 0.10 **NM** value: **50.00**
3 ❑ Jan 1950 Cover: 0.10 **NM** value: **50.00**
4 ❑ Mar 1950 Cover: 0.10 **NM** value: **50.00**

MY NAME IS CHAOS — DC

1 ❑ ca. 1992 Cover: 4.95 **NM** value: **5.00**
Circ: CapCity orders: **8,500**
📖 The Song That Laid Waste To The Earth **A:** John Ridgway **W:** Tom Veitch
2 ❑ ca. 1992 Cover: 4.95 **NM** value: **5.00**
Circ: CapCity orders: **5,800**
📖 Metamorphosis and Awakening **A:** John Ridgway **W:** Tom Veitch
3 ❑ ca. 1992 Cover: 4.95 **NM** value: **5.00**
Circ: CapCity orders: **5,000**
📖 I Am Mars **A:** John Ridgway **W:** Tom Veitch
4 ❑ ca. 1992 Cover: 4.95 **NM** value: **5.00**
Circ: CapCity orders: **4,700**
📖 The Power of One **A:** John Ridgway **W:** Tom Veitch

MY NAME IS HOLOCAUST — DC / Milestone

1 ❑ May 1995 Cover: 2.50 **NM** value: **Cover or less**
Circ: CapCity orders: **3,700**
A: Tommy Lee Edwards **W:** Ivan Velez Jr.
2 ❑ Jun 1995 Cover: 2.50 **NM** value: **Cover or less**
Circ: CapCity orders: **2,775**
3 ❑ Jul 1995 Cover: 2.50 **NM** value: **Cover or less**
Circ: CapCity orders: **2,600**
4 ❑ Aug 1995 Cover: 2.50 **NM** value: **Cover or less**
Circ: CapCity orders: **2,500**
5 ❑ Sep 1995 Cover: 2.50 **NM** value: **Cover or less**
Circ: CapCity orders: **2,275**

MY NAME IS MUD — Incognito

1 ❑ Cover: 2.50 **NM** value: **Cover or less**
📖 Incognito **A:** Brian Denham **W:** Brian Denham

MY PERSONAL PROBLEM — Ajax

1 ❑ Nov 1955 Cover: 0.10 **NM** value: **50.00**
2 ❑ ca. 1956 Cover: 0.10 **NM** value: **35.00**
3 ❑ ca. 1956 Cover: 0.10 **NM** value: **35.00**
4 ❑ ca. 1956 Cover: 0.10 **NM** value: **35.00**

MY PRIVATE LIFE — Fox

16 ❑ Feb 1950 Cover: 0.10 **NM** value: **75.00**
17 ❑ Apr 1950 Cover: 0.10 **NM** value: **75.00**

MYRMIDON — Red Hills Productions

1 ❑ Jul 1998, b&w Cover: 2.95 **NM** value: **Cover or less**

MY ROMANCE — Marvel

1 ❑ Sep 1948 Cover: 0.10 **NM** value: **100.00**
2 ❑ Nov 1948 Cover: 0.10 **NM** value: **50.00**
3 ❑ Jan 1949 Cover: 0.10 **NM** value: **50.00**

MY ROMANTIC ADVENTURES — ACG

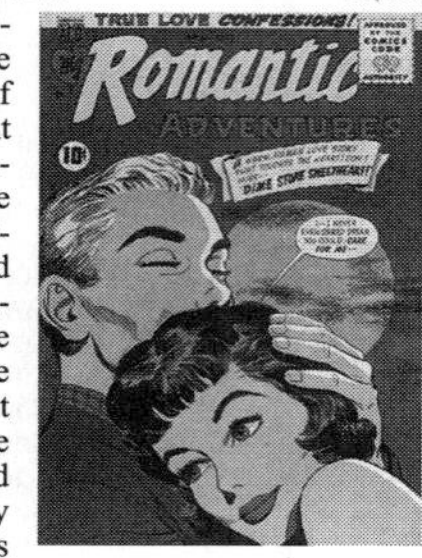

The world of 1950s and 1960s romance comics is one that may be lost to us forever. It was a world of wide-eyed innocence, where pliant young women pined away for dashing, adventurous men, and true love conquered over jealous rivals, personal flaws, family opposition, and harrowing circumstances. The fantasies of chaste, classless romance were rendered in clean lines and rote narrative. By the mid-1950s, the grit and realism of the early romance comics of Simon and Kirby had been burnished to a clean, glossy finish, and the range of products from the different publishers — DC, Charlton, ACG, Marvel — were all stultifyingly similar. My Romantic Adventures fits neatly into this mold, with a tinge of exotic adventure and foreign locales to spice up the usual plot devices.

68 ❑ Aug 1956 Cover: 0.10 **NM** value: **35.00**
69 ❑ Sep 1956 Cover: 0.10 **NM** value: **28.00**
70 ❑ Oct 1956 Cover: 0.10 **NM** value: **28.00**
71 ❑ Nov 1956 Cover: 0.10 **NM** value: **24.00**
72 ❑ Dec 1956 Cover: 0.10 **NM** value: **24.00**
73 ❑ Jan 1957 Cover: 0.10 **NM** value: **24.00**
74 ❑ Feb 1957 Cover: 0.10 **NM** value: **24.00**
75 ❑ Mar 1957 Cover: 0.10 **NM** value: **24.00**
76 ❑ Apr 1957 Cover: 0.10 **NM** value: **24.00**
77 ❑ May 1957 Cover: 0.10 **NM** value: **24.00**
78 ❑ Jun 1957 Cover: 0.10 **NM** value: **24.00**
79 ❑ Jul 1957 Cover: 0.10 **NM** value: **24.00**
80 ❑ Aug 1957 Cover: 0.10 **NM** value: **24.00**
81 ❑ Sep 1957 Cover: 0.10 **NM** value: **20.00**
📖 Dime Store Sweetheart; Romance Rides the Rails; Love of a Counselor; Refugee Romance
82 ❑ Oct 1957 Cover: 0.10 **NM** value: **20.00**
83 ❑ Nov 1957 Cover: 0.10 **NM** value: **20.00**
84 ❑ Dec 1957 Cover: 0.10 **NM** value: **20.00**
85 ❑ Jan 1958 Cover: 0.10 **NM** value: **20.00**
86 ❑ Feb 1958 Cover: 0.10 **NM** value: **20.00**
87 ❑ Mar 1958 Cover: 0.10 **NM** value: **20.00**
88 ❑ Apr 1958 Cover: 0.10 **NM** value: **20.00**
89 ❑ May 1958 Cover: 0.10 **NM** value: **20.00**
90 ❑ Jun 1958 Cover: 0.10 **NM** value: **16.00**
91 ❑ Jul 1958 Cover: 0.10 **NM** value: **16.00**
92 ❑ Aug 1958 Cover: 0.10 **NM** value: **16.00**
93 ❑ Sep 1958 Cover: 0.10 **NM** value: **16.00**
94 ❑ Oct 1958 Cover: 0.10 **NM** value: **16.00**
95 ❑ Nov 1958 Cover: 0.10 **NM** value: **16.00**
96 ❑ Dec 1958 Cover: 0.10 **NM** value: **16.00**
97 ❑ Jan 1959 Cover: 0.10 **NM** value: **16.00**
98 ❑ Feb 1959 Cover: 0.10 **NM** value: **16.00**
99 ❑ Mar 1959 Cover: 0.10 **NM** value: **16.00**
100 ❑ Apr 1959 Cover: 0.10 **NM** value: **12.00**
101 ❑ May 1959 Cover: 0.10 **NM** value: **12.00**
102 ❑ Jun 1959 Cover: 0.10 **NM** value: **12.00**
103 ❑ Jul 1959 Cover: 0.10 **NM** value: **12.00**
104 ❑ Aug 1959 Cover: 0.10 **NM** value: **12.00**
105 ❑ Sep 1959 Cover: 0.10 **NM** value: **12.00**
106 ❑ ca. 1969 Cover: 0.10 **NM** value: **12.00**
107 ❑ ca. 1969 Cover: 0.10 **NM** value: **12.00**
108 ❑ ca. 1960 Cover: 0.10 **NM** value: **12.00**
109 ❑ ca. 1960 Cover: 0.10 **NM** value: **12.00**
110 ❑ ca. 1960 Cover: 0.10 **NM** value: **12.00**
111 ❑ ca. 1960 Cover: 0.10 **NM** value: **10.00**
112 ❑ ca. 1960 Cover: 0.10 **NM** value: **10.00**
113 ❑ ca. 1960 Cover: 0.10 **NM** value: **10.00**
114 ❑ ca. 1960 Cover: 0.10 **NM** value: **10.00**
115 ❑ ca. 1960 Cover: 0.10 **NM** value: **10.00**
116 ❑ Jul 1961 Cover: 0.10 **NM** value: **10.00**
117 ❑ Aug 1961 Cover: 0.10 **NM** value: **10.00**
118 ❑ Sep 1961 Cover: 0.10 **NM** value: **10.00**
119 ❑ Oct 1961 Cover: 0.10 **NM** value: **10.00**
120 ❑ ca. 1961 Cover: 0.10 **NM** value: **10.00**
121 ❑ ca. 1962 Cover: 0.10 **NM** value: **8.00**
122 ❑ ca. 1962 Cover: 0.10 **NM** value: **8.00**
123 ❑ ca. 1962 Cover: 0.10 **NM** value: **8.00**
124 ❑ ca. 1962 Cover: 0.12 **NM** value: **8.00**
125 ❑ ca. 1962 Cover: 0.12 **NM** value: **8.00**
126 ❑ ca. 1962 Cover: 0.12 **NM** value: **8.00**
127 ❑ ca. 1962 Cover: 0.12 **NM** value: **8.00**
128 ❑ ca. 1962 Cover: 0.12 **NM** value: **8.00**
129 ❑ ca. 1963 Cover: 0.12 **NM** value: **8.00**
130 ❑ ca. 1963 Cover: 0.12 **NM** value: **8.00**
131 ❑ ca. 1963 Cover: 0.12 **NM** value: **8.00**
132 ❑ ca. 1963 Cover: 0.12 **NM** value: **8.00**
133 ❑ ca. 1963 Cover: 0.12 **NM** value: **8.00**
134 ❑ ca. 1963 Cover: 0.12 **NM** value: **8.00**
135 ❑ ca. 1963 Cover: 0.12 **NM** value: **8.00**
136 ❑ ca. 1963 Cover: 0.12 **NM** value: **8.00**
137 ❑ ca. 1964 Cover: 0.12 **NM** value: **8.00**
138 ❑ ca. 1964 Cover: 0.12 **NM** value: **8.00**

MY ROMANTIC ADVENTURES? (AVALON) — Avalon

1 ❑ Cover: 2.75 **NM** value: **Cover or less**
📖 Love of a Lunatic!; Cupid is a Horse Named Bertram!; It's Never Too Late to Love!

MYRON MOOSE FUNNIES — Fantagraphics

1 ❑ Cover: 0.50 **NM** value: **1.75**
2 ❑ Cover: 0.50 **NM** value: **1.75**
3 ❑ Cover: 1.75 **NM** value: **Cover or less**

MY SECRET — Superior

1 ❑ Aug 1949 Cover: 0.10 **NM** value: **75.00**

Other grades: Multiply prices above by **1.5 for Mint • 2/3 for Very Fine • 1/3 for Fine • 1/5 for Very Good • 1/8 for Good**

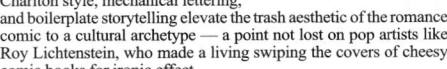

2 ❑ Sep 1949 Cover: 0.10 **NM** value: **35.00**
3 ❑ Oct 1949 Cover: 0.10 **NM** value: **35.00**
• **CGC:** 1 graded, best 7.0

MY SECRET AFFAIR — Fox

1 ❑ Dec 1949 Cover: 0.10 **NM** value: **125.00**
2 ❑ Feb 1950 Cover: 0.10 **NM** value: **100.00**
3 ❑ Apr 1950 Cover: 0.10 **NM** value: **100.00**

MY SECRET LIFE (CHARLTON) — Charlton

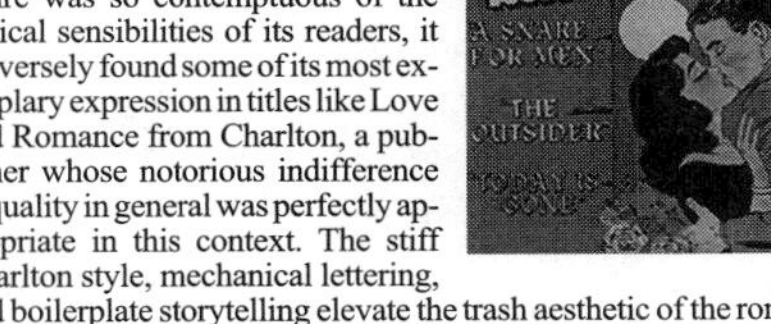

The unworthy scoundrel. The jealous scheming rival. The "unsuitable boy." The meddling mother (-in-law). These are just a few of the time-worn cast of characters to be found in the pages of any love and romance comic published in America from 1955 to 1975. Since the love comics genre was so contemptuous of the critical sensibilities of its readers, it perversely found some of its most exemplary expression in titles like Love and Romance from Charlton, a publisher whose notorious indifference to quality in general was perfectly appropriate in this context. The stiff Charlton style, mechanical lettering, and boilerplate storytelling elevate the trash aesthetic of the romance comic to a cultural archetype — a point not lost on pop artists like Roy Lichtenstein, who made a living swiping the covers of cheesy comic books for ironic effect.

19 ❑ ca. 1957 Cover: 0.10 **NM** value: **12.00**
• Series continued from Young Lovers #18
20 ❑ ca. 1957 Cover: 0.10 **NM** value: **6.00**
21 ❑ ca. 1957 Cover: 0.10 **NM** value: **6.00**
22 ❑ ca. 1958 Cover: 0.10 **NM** value: **6.00**
23 ❑ ca. 1958 Cover: 0.10 **NM** value: **6.00**
24 ❑ ca. 1958 Cover: 0.10 **NM** value: **6.00**
25 ❑ ca. 1958 Cover: 0.10 **NM** value: **6.00**
26 ❑ ca. 1958 Cover: 0.10 **NM** value: **6.00**
27 ❑ ca. 1958 Cover: 0.10 **NM** value: **6.00**
28 ❑ ca. 1958 Cover: 0.10 **NM** value: **6.00**
29 ❑ ca. 1959 Cover: 0.10 **NM** value: **6.00**
30 ❑ ca. 1959 Cover: 0.10 **NM** value: **6.00**
31 ❑ ca. 1959 Cover: 0.10 **NM** value: **4.00**
32 ❑ ca. 1959 Cover: 0.10 **NM** value: **4.00**
33 ❑ Mar 1960 Cover: 0.10 **NM** value: **4.00**
34 ❑ ca. 1960 Cover: 0.10 **NM** value: **4.00**
35 ❑ ca. 1960 Cover: 0.10 **NM** value: **4.00**
36 ❑ Oct 1960 Cover: 0.10 **NM** value: **4.00**
37 ❑ Dec 1960 Cover: 0.10 **NM** value: **4.00**
38 ❑ ca. 1961 Cover: 0.10 **NM** value: **4.00**
39 ❑ ca. 1961 Cover: 0.10 **NM** value: **4.00**
40 ❑ ca. 1961 Cover: 0.10 **NM** value: **4.00**
41 ❑ ca. 1961 Cover: 0.10 **NM** value: **4.00**
42 ❑ ca. 1961 Cover: 0.10 **NM** value: **4.00**
43 ❑ ca. 1962 Cover: 0.10 **NM** value: **4.00**
44 ❑ ca. 1962 Cover: 0.10 **NM** value: **4.00**
45 ❑ ca. 1962 Cover: 0.10 **NM** value: **4.00**
46 ❑ Jul 1962 Cover: 0.12 **NM** value: **4.00**
47 ❑ Sep 1962 Cover: 0.12 **NM** value: **4.00**
• Series continued in Sue & Sally Smith #48

MY SECRET LIFE (FOX) — Fox

22 ❑ Jul 1949 Cover: 0.10 **NM** value: **75.00**
23 ❑ Sep 1949 Cover: 0.10 **NM** value: **75.00**
24 ❑ Nov 1949 Cover: 0.10 **NM** value: **75.00**
25 ❑ Jan 1950 Cover: 0.10 **NM** value: **60.00**
26 ❑ Mar 1950 Cover: 0.10 **NM** value: **60.00**

MY SECRET MARRIAGE — Superior

1 ❑ May 1953 Cover: 0.10 **NM** value: **75.00**
2 ❑ Jul 1953 Cover: 0.10 **NM** value: **40.00**
3 ❑ Sep 1953 Cover: 0.10 **NM** value: **30.00**
4 ❑ Nov 1953 Cover: 0.10 **NM** value: **30.00**
5 ❑ Jan 1954 Cover: 0.10 **NM** value: **30.00**
6 ❑ Mar 1954 Cover: 0.10 **NM** value: **30.00**
7 ❑ May 1954 Cover: 0.10 **NM** value: **30.00**
8 ❑ Jul 1954 Cover: 0.10 **NM** value: **30.00**
• **CGC:** 1 graded, best 7.0
9 ❑ Sep 1954 Cover: 0.10 **NM** value: **30.00**
10 ❑ ca. 1954 Cover: 0.10 **NM** value: **30.00**
11 ❑ ca. 1954 Cover: 0.10 **NM** value: **30.00**
12 ❑ ca. 1955 Cover: 0.10 **NM** value: **30.00**
13 ❑ ca. 1955 Cover: 0.10 **NM** value: **30.00**
14 ❑ ca. 1955 Cover: 0.10 **NM** value: **30.00**
15 ❑ ca. 1955 Cover: 0.10 **NM** value: **30.00**
16 ❑ ca. 1955 Cover: 0.10 **NM** value: **25.00**
17 ❑ ca. 1955 Cover: 0.10 **NM** value: **25.00**
18 ❑ ca. 1955 Cover: 0.10 **NM** value: **25.00**
19 ❑ ca. 1955 Cover: 0.10 **NM** value: **25.00**
20 ❑ ca. 1955 Cover: 0.10 **NM** value: **25.00**
21 ❑ ca. 1956 Cover: 0.10 **NM** value: **25.00**
22 ❑ ca. 1956 Cover: 0.10 **NM** value: **25.00**
23 ❑ ca. 1956 Cover: 0.10 **NM** value: **25.00**
24 ❑ ca. 1956 Cover: 0.10 **NM** value: **25.00**

MY SECRET ROMANCE — Fox

1 ❑ Jan 1950 Cover: 0.10 **NM** value: **100.00**
2 ❑ Mar 1950 Cover: 0.10 **NM** value: **100.00**

MYS-TECH WARS — Marvel

1 ❑ Mar 1993 Cover: 1.75 **NM** value: **Cover or less**
Circ: CapCity orders: **45,900**
📖 Strange Screams Of Death • Virtually all X-Men, Marvel UK characters appear **A:** Bryan Hitch **W:** Dan Abnett
2 ❑ Apr 1993 Cover: 1.75 **NM** value: **Cover or less**
Circ: CapCity orders: **24,100**
• Virtually all X-Men, Marvel UK characters appear **W:** Dan Abnett
3 ❑ May 1993 Cover: 1.75 **NM** value: **Cover or less**
Circ: CapCity orders: **20,400**
📖 Darkness Visible • Virtually all X-Men, Marvel UK characters appear **A:** Bryan Hitch **W:** Dan Abnett
4 ❑ Jun 1993 Cover: 1.75 **NM** value: **Cover or less**
Circ: CapCity orders: **18,200**
• Virtually all X-Men, Marvel UK characters appear **W:** Dan Abnett

MYSTERIES — Superior

1 ❑ May 1953 Cover: 0.10 **NM** value: **300.00**
2 ❑ Jul 1953 Cover: 0.10 **NM** value: **175.00**
• **CGC:** 2 graded, best 8.5
3 ❑ Sep 1953 Cover: 0.10 **NM** value: **150.00**
4 ❑ Nov 1953 Cover: 0.10 **NM** value: **150.00**
• **CGC:** 1 graded, best 8.5
5 ❑ Jan 1954 Cover: 0.10 **NM** value: **150.00**
6 ❑ Mar 1954 Cover: 0.10 **NM** value: **150.00**
7 ❑ May 1954 Cover: 0.10 **NM** value: **150.00**
8 ❑ Jul 1954 Cover: 0.10 **NM** value: **150.00**
• **CGC:** 2 graded, best 8.5
9 ❑ Sep 1954 Cover: 0.10 **NM** value: **150.00**
10 ❑ Nov 1954 Cover: 0.10 **NM** value: **150.00**
• **CGC:** 1 graded, best 8.0
11 ❑ Jan 1955 Cover: 0.10 **NM** value: **150.00**

MYSTERIES OF SCOTLAND YARD — Magazine Enterprises

1 ❑ ca. 1954 Cover: 0.10 **NM** value: **50.00**
• **CGC:** 1 graded, best 8.5
📖 The Stone of the Dying Druid; The Trail of the Killing Kisses; The Case of the Perfect Crime; The Man with The Beast-Like FaceThe Man Who Sold-Death • Reprinted from Manhunt (5 Stories) **A:** Paul Parker **W:** Paul Parker

MYSTERIES OF UNEXPLORED WORLDS — Charlton

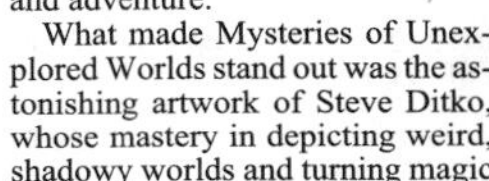

Mysteries of Unexplored Worlds was one of the most successful science-fiction titles of the 1950s and '60s, and was one of the highlights of the Charlton publishing enterprise. The stories were the standard horror and suspense fare found in most similar titles, with shock endings, creepy characters, and a strong undercurrent of pulp-style fantasy and adventure.

What made Mysteries of Unexplored Worlds stand out was the astonishing artwork of Steve Ditko, whose mastery in depicting weird, shadowy worlds and turning magic into a tangible, physical presence on the page was at its absolute peak. Ditko's virtuoso style could gloss over pedestrian storytelling and single-handedly carry the title through most of its early run.

1 ❑ Aug 1956 Cover: 0.10 **NM** value: **185.00**
• **CGC:** 2 graded, best 9.2
2 ❑ Oct 1956 Cover: 0.10 **NM** value: **65.00**
3 ❑ Dec 1956 Cover: 0.10 **NM** value: **100.00**
A: Steve Ditko
4 ❑ Mar 1957 Cover: 0.10 **NM** value: **100.00**
• **CGC:** 1 graded, best 8.5
📖 The Forbidden Room; Valley in the Mist; The Wanderer (text story); Voices From the Dark; At the End of the Road **A:** Steve Ditko
5 ❑ Aug 1957 Cover: 0.10 **NM** value: **135.00**
A: Steve Ditko
6 ❑ Oct 1957 Cover: 0.10 **NM** value: **135.00**
A: Steve Ditko
7 ❑ Feb 1958 Cover: 0.10 **NM** value: **135.00**
• **CGC:** 1 graded, best 7.5
A: Steve Ditko
8 ❑ May 1958 Cover: 0.10 **NM** value: **100.00**
A: Steve Ditko
9 ❑ Aug 1958 Cover: 0.10 **NM** value: **135.00**
• **CGC:** 1 graded, best 4.5
A: Steve Ditko
10 ❑ Nov 1958 Cover: 0.10 **NM** value: **135.00**
A: Steve Ditko
11 ❑ Jan 1959 Cover: 0.10 **NM** value: **110.00**
A: Steve Ditko
12 ❑ Apr 1959 Cover: 0.10 **NM** value: **75.00**
A: Steve Ditko
13 ❑ Jun 1959 Cover: 0.10 **NM** value: **28.00**
14 ❑ 1959 Cover: 0.10 **NM** value: **28.00**
15 ❑ 1959 Cover: 0.10 **NM** value: **28.00**
16 ❑ 1960 Cover: 0.10 **NM** value: **28.00**
17 ❑ 1960 Cover: 0.10 **NM** value: **28.00**
18 ❑ May 1960 Cover: 0.10 **NM** value: **28.00**
19 ❑ Jul 1960 Cover: 0.10 **NM** value: **60.00**
• **CGC:** 1 graded, best 9.2
A: Steve Ditko
20 ❑ Sep 1960 Cover: 0.10 **NM** value: **28.00**
21 ❑ Nov 1960 Cover: 0.10 **NM** value: **60.00**
A: Steve Ditko
22 ❑ Jan 1961 Cover: 0.10 **NM** value: **60.00**
A: Steve Ditko
23 ❑ Mar 1961 Cover: 0.10 **NM** value: **60.00**
A: Steve Ditko
24 ❑ May 1961 Cover: 0.10 **NM** value: **60.00**
A: Steve Ditko
25 ❑ Jul 1961 Cover: 0.10 **NM** value: **20.00**
26 ❑ Sep 1961 Cover: 0.10 **NM** value: **55.00**
A: Steve Ditko
27 ❑ Nov 1961 Cover: 0.10 **NM** value: **20.00**
📖 The Vanishing Point; If You Believe
28 ❑ Jan 1962 Cover: 0.10 **NM** value: **20.00**
29 ❑ Apr 1962 Cover: 0.10 **NM** value: **20.00**
30 ❑ Jun 1962 Cover: 0.12 **NM** value: **20.00**
31 ❑ Aug 1962 Cover: 0.12 **NM** value: **14.00**
32 ❑ Oct 1962 Cover: 0.12 **NM** value: **14.00**
33 ❑ Dec 1962 Cover: 0.12 **NM** value: **14.00**
34 ❑ Feb 1962 Cover: 0.12 **NM** value: **14.00**
35 ❑ Apr 1962 Cover: 0.12 **NM** value: **14.00**
36 ❑ Jun 1962 Cover: 0.12 **NM** value: **14.00**
📖 Dominant Species!; They Can't Be There; Crew; Human Privilege; Day of the Hunter
37 ❑ Aug 1962 Cover: 0.12 **NM** value: **14.00**
38 ❑ Oct 1962 Cover: 0.12 **NM** value: **14.00**
39 ❑ Dec 1962 Cover: 0.12 **NM** value: **14.00**
40 ❑ 1963 Cover: 0.12 **NM** value: **14.00**
41 ❑ May 1963 Cover: 0.12 **NM** value: **10.00**
42 ❑ Jul 1963 Cover: 0.12 **NM** value: **10.00**
43 ❑ Oct 1963 Cover: 0.12 **NM** value: **10.00**
44 ❑ Dec 1963 Cover: 0.12 **NM** value: **10.00**
45 ❑ 1964 Cover: 0.12 **NM** value: **10.00**
46 ❑ May 1964 Cover: 0.12 **NM** value: **22.00**
★ Origin of Son of Vulcan. ★ 1st Appearance of Son of Vulcan.
47 ❑ Jul 1964 Cover: 0.12 **NM** value: **16.00**
★ Appearance of Son of Vulcan.
48 ❑ Sep 1964 Cover: 0.12 **NM** value: **16.00**
• Series continued in Son of Vulcan #49★ Appearance of Son of Vulcan.

MYSTERIOUS ADVENTURES — Story

1 ❑ Mar 1951 Cover: 0.10 **NM** value: **400.00**
• **CGC:** 1 graded, best 9.6
2 ❑ Jun 1951 Cover: 0.10 **NM** value: **200.00**
3 ❑ Aug 1951 Cover: 0.10 **NM** value: **200.00**
4 ❑ Oct 1951 Cover: 0.10 **NM** value: **200.00**
5 ❑ Dec 1951 Cover: 0.10 **NM** value: **200.00**
6 ❑ Feb 1952 Cover: 0.10 **NM** value: **200.00**
• **CGC:** 1 graded, best 9.0
7 ❑ Apr 1952 Cover: 0.10 **NM** value: **200.00**
8 ❑ Jun 1952 Cover: 0.10 **NM** value: **200.00**
9 ❑ Aug 1952 Cover: 0.10 **NM** value: **200.00**
10 ❑ Oct 1952 Cover: 0.10 **NM** value: **200.00**
11 ❑ Dec 1952 Cover: 0.10 **NM** value: **200.00**
12 ❑ Feb 1953 Cover: 0.10 **NM** value: **200.00**
13 ❑ Apr 1953 Cover: 0.10 **NM** value: **200.00**
14 ❑ Jun 1953 Cover: 0.10 **NM** value: **200.00**
• **CGC:** 1 graded, best 8.0
15 ❑ Aug 1953 Cover: 0.10 **NM** value: **200.00**
• **CGC:** 1 graded, best 8.5
16 ❑ Oct 1953 Cover: 0.10 **NM** value: **150.00**
• **CGC:** 1 graded, best 5.0
17 ❑ Dec 1953 Cover: 0.10 **NM** value: **150.00**
• **CGC:** 1 graded, best 6.0
18 ❑ Feb 1954 Cover: 0.10 **NM** value: **150.00**
19 ❑ Apr 1954 Cover: 0.10 **NM** value: **150.00**
• **CGC:** 1 graded, best 5.0
20 ❑ Jun 1954 Cover: 0.10 **NM** value: **150.00**
21 ❑ Aug 1954 Cover: 0.10 **NM** value: **150.00**
• **CGC:** 1 graded, best 8.0
22 ❑ Oct 1954 Cover: 0.10 **NM** value: **150.00**
23 ❑ Dec 1954 Cover: 0.10 **NM** value: **150.00**
• **CGC:** 2 graded, best 9.2
24 ❑ Mar 1955 Cover: 0.10 **NM** value: **150.00**

MYSTERIOUS STORIES — Premier

2 ❑ Dec 1954 Cover: 0.10 **NM** value: **300.00**
3 ❑ Apr 1955 Cover: 0.10 **NM** value: **200.00**
4 ❑ Jun 1955 Cover: 0.10 **NM** value: **200.00**
5 ❑ Aug 1955 Cover: 0.10 **NM** value: **200.00**
6 ❑ Nov 1955 Cover: 0.10 **NM** value: **200.00**
7 ❑ Jan 1956 Cover: 0.10 **NM** value: **200.00**

MYSTERIOUS SUSPENSE — Charlton

1 ❑ Oct 1968 Cover: 0.12 **NM** value: **40.00**
• **CGC:** 2 graded, best 9.0
• Question **A:** Steve Ditko

MYSTERIOUS TRAVELER COMICS — TransWorld

1 ❑ Nov 1948 Cover: 0.10 **NM** value: **500.00**
• **CGC:** 2 graded, best 7.5

MYSTERY COMICS — Wise Publications

1 ❑ ca. 1944 Cover: 0.10 **NM** value: **750.00**
• **CGC:** 2 graded, best 9.0
2 ❑ ca. 1944 Cover: 0.10 **NM** value: **600.00**
• **CGC:** 3 graded, best 9.2
3 ❑ ca. 1944 Cover: 0.10 **NM** value: **550.00**
4 ❑ ca. 1944 Cover: 0.10 **NM** value: **550.00**
• **CGC:** 3 graded, best 9.4

MYSTERY DATE — Lightspeed Press

1 ❑ May 1999, b&w Cover: 2.95 **NM** value: **Cover or less**

The CGC numbers printed in individual listings above represent the **number of copies examined** and given a **Universal** grade by CGC and the **best such copy** graded at press time. For current populations, watch for special ***Comics Buyer's Guide*** issues or check **www.cgccomics.com.**

CGC-graded: Multiply prices above by **33 for 9.9 M • 16 for 9.8 NM/M • 7 for 9.6 NM+ • 5 for 9.4 NM • 2.5 for 9.2 NM- • 1.5 for 9.0 VF/NM**

MYSTERY IN SPACE **DC**

Each issue of this series featured adventures in outer space, many with a twist ending. In one story, a human explorer found aliens dividing up the planets of the solar system in a game. But when he thwarted them, he found out they had all bluffed each other.

The series' most popular feature was the adventures of space ranger Adam Strange, drawn by Carmine Infantino. One of the original space heroes, Strange starred in this series for a good part of its run, and even teamed up with Hawkman for a time in order to restore order on his adopted planet, Rann.

1 ❑ Apr 1951 Cover: 0.10 **NM** value: **2450.00**
• **CGC:** 10 graded, best 8.5
A: Frank Frazetta
2 ❑ Jun 1951 Cover: 0.10 **NM** value: **925.00**
• **CGC:** 4 graded, best 9.2
3 ❑ Aug 1951 Cover: 0.10 **NM** value: **710.00**
• **CGC:** 8 graded, best 9.0
4 ❑ Oct 1951 Cover: 0.10 **NM** value: **590.00**
• **CGC:** 4 graded, best 9.6
5 ❑ Dec 1951 Cover: 0.10 **NM** value: **590.00**
• **CGC:** 2 graded, best 8.5
6 ❑ Feb 1952 Cover: 0.10 **NM** value: **590.00**
• **CGC:** 6 graded, best 9.6
7 ❑ Apr 1952 Cover: 0.10 **NM** value: **590.00**
• **CGC:** 1 graded, best 9.2
8 ❑ Jun 1952 Cover: 0.10 **NM** value: **590.00**
• **CGC:** 2 graded, best 9.0
9 ❑ Aug 1952 Cover: 0.10 **NM** value: **590.00**
• **CGC:** 2 graded, best 9.4
10 ❑ Oct 1952 Cover: 0.10 **NM** value: **590.00**
• **CGC:** 1 graded, best 8.0
11 ❑ Dec 1952 Cover: 0.10 **NM** value: **400.00**
• **CGC:** 1 graded, best 8.5
12 ❑ Feb 1953 Cover: 0.10 **NM** value: **400.00**
• **CGC:** 1 graded, best 4.0
13 ❑ Apr 1953 Cover: 0.10 **NM** value: **400.00**
• **CGC:** 2 graded, best 9.2
14 ❑ Jun 1953 Cover: 0.10 **NM** value: **400.00**
15 ❑ Aug 1953 Cover: 0.10 **NM** value: **400.00**
16 ❑ Oct 1953 Cover: 0.10 **NM** value: **320.00**
• **CGC:** 1 graded, best 7.5
17 ❑ Dec 1953 Cover: 0.10 **NM** value: **320.00**
18 ❑ Feb 1954 Cover: 0.10 **NM** value: **320.00**
• **CGC:** 1 graded, best 5.0
19 ❑ Apr 1954 Cover: 0.10 **NM** value: **320.00**
20 ❑ Jun 1954 Cover: 0.10 **NM** value: **320.00**
21 ❑ Aug 1954 Cover: 0.10 **NM** value: **320.00**
• **CGC:** 1 graded, best 6.5
22 ❑ Oct 1954 Cover: 0.10 **NM** value: **320.00**
• **CGC:** 1 graded, best 9.2
23 ❑ Dec 1954 Cover: 0.10 **NM** value: **320.00**
24 ❑ Feb 1955 Cover: 0.10 **NM** value: **320.00**
25 ❑ Apr 1955 Cover: 0.10 **NM** value: **320.00**
• **CGC:** 1 graded, best 6.0
26 ❑ Jun 1955 Cover: 0.10 **NM** value: **235.00**
27 ❑ Aug 1955 Cover: 0.10 **NM** value: **235.00**
28 ❑ Oct 1955 Cover: 0.10 **NM** value: **235.00**
29 ❑ Dec 1955 Cover: 0.10 **NM** value: **235.00**
30 ❑ Feb 1956 Cover: 0.10 **NM** value: **235.00**
31 ❑ Apr 1956 Cover: 0.10 **NM** value: **235.00**
• **CGC:** 1 graded, best 6.0
32 ❑ Jun 1956 Cover: 0.10 **NM** value: **235.00**
• **CGC:** 1 graded, best 8.0
33 ❑ Aug 1956 Cover: 0.10 **NM** value: **235.00**
34 ❑ Oct 1956 Cover: 0.10 **NM** value: **235.00**
• **CGC:** 1 graded, best 6.5
35 ❑ Dec 1956 Cover: 0.10 **NM** value: **235.00**
• **CGC:** 2 graded, best 6.5
36 ❑ Feb 1957 Cover: 0.10 **NM** value: **235.00**
• **CGC:** 1 graded, best 9.0
37 ❑ Apr 1957 Cover: 0.10 **NM** value: **235.00**
38 ❑ Jun 1957 Cover: 0.10 **NM** value: **235.00**
39 ❑ Aug 1957 Cover: 0.10 **NM** value: **235.00**
40 ❑ Oct 1957 Cover: 0.10 **NM** value: **235.00**
• **CGC:** 4 graded, best 8.5
41 ❑ Dec 1957 Cover: 0.10 **NM** value: **195.00**
42 ❑ Feb 1958 Cover: 0.10 **NM** value: **195.00**
• **CGC:** 3 graded, best 9.0
43 ❑ Apr 1958 Cover: 0.10 **NM** value: **195.00**
• **CGC:** 1 graded, best 8.5
44 ❑ Jun 1958 Cover: 0.10 **NM** value: **195.00**
• **CGC:** 1 graded, best 8.0
45 ❑ Aug 1958 Cover: 0.10 **NM** value: **195.00**
46 ❑ Sep 1958 Cover: 0.10 **NM** value: **195.00**
• **CGC:** 6 graded, best 9.0
47 ❑ Oct 1958 Cover: 0.10 **NM** value: **195.00**
• **CGC:** 1 graded, best 7.0
48 ❑ Dec 1958 Cover: 0.10 **NM** value: **195.00**
• **CGC:** 1 graded, best 7.0
49 ❑ Feb 1959 Cover: 0.10 **NM** value: **195.00**
• **CGC:** 4 graded, best 8.0
50 ❑ Apr 1959 Cover: 0.10 **NM** value: **195.00**
51 ❑ May 1959 Cover: 0.10 **NM** value: **195.00**
• **CGC:** 1 graded, best 9.0
52 ❑ Jun 1959 Cover: 0.10 **NM** value: **195.00**
• **CGC:** 1 graded, best 7.0
53 ❑ Aug 1959 Cover: 0.10 **NM** value: **1250.00**
• **CGC:** 16 graded, best 9.0
• Adam Strange begins **A:** Carmine Infantino
54 ❑ Sep 1959 Cover: 0.10 **NM** value: **440.00**
• **CGC:** 5 graded, best 7.0
A: Carmine Infantino
55 ❑ Nov 1959 Cover: 0.10 **NM** value: **265.00**
• **CGC:** 3 graded, best 7.5
A: Carmine Infantino
56 ❑ Dec 1959 Cover: 0.10 **NM** value: **175.00**
• **CGC:** 1 graded, best 4.0
A: Carmine Infantino
57 ❑ Feb 1960 Cover: 0.10 **NM** value: **175.00**
Circ: Statement: **248,000** • **CGC:** 1 graded, best 3.5
A: Carmine Infantino
58 ❑ Mar 1960 Cover: 0.10 **NM** value: **175.00**
Circ: Statement: **248,000**
A: Carmine Infantino
59 ❑ May 1960 Cover: 0.10 **NM** value: **175.00**
Circ: Statement: **248,000**
A: Carmine Infantino
60 ❑ Jun 1960 Cover: 0.10 **NM** value: **175.00**
Circ: Statement: **248,000**
A: Carmine Infantino
61 ❑ Aug 1960 Cover: 0.10 **NM** value: **120.00**
Circ: Statement: **248,000**
• Later becomes Red Tornado **A:** Carmine Infantino ★ 1st Appearance of Tornado Tyrant.
62 ❑ Sep 1960 Cover: 0.10 **NM** value: **120.00**
Circ: Statement: **248,000**
A: Carmine Infantino
63 ❑ Nov 1960 Cover: 0.10 **NM** value: **120.00**
Circ: Statement: **248,000** • **CGC:** 1 graded, best 7.0
A: Carmine Infantino
64 ❑ Dec 1960 Cover: 0.10 **NM** value: **120.00**
Circ: Statement: **248,000**
A: Carmine Infantino
65 ❑ Feb 1961 Cover: 0.10 **NM** value: **120.00**
Circ: Statement: **240,000**
A: Carmine Infantino
66 ❑ Mar 1961 Cover: 0.10 **NM** value: **120.00**
Circ: Statement: **240,000**
A: Carmine Infantino ★ 1st Appearance of The Star Rovers.
67 ❑ May 1961 Cover: 0.10 **NM** value: **120.00**
Circ: Statement: **240,000** • **CGC:** 2 graded, best 6.0
A: Carmine Infantino
68 ❑ Jun 1961 Cover: 0.10 **NM** value: **120.00**
Circ: Statement: **240,000** • **CGC:** 1 graded, best 9.0
A: Carmine Infantino
69 ❑ Aug 1961 Cover: 0.10 **NM** value: **120.00**
Circ: Statement: **240,000** • **CGC:** 2 graded, best 5.5
A: Carmine Infantino
70 ❑ Sep 1961 Cover: 0.10 **NM** value: **120.00**
Circ: Statement: **240,000** • **CGC:** 1 graded, best 5.0
A: Carmine Infantino
71 ❑ Nov 1961 Cover: 0.10 **NM** value: **120.00**
Circ: Statement: **240,000** • **CGC:** 3 graded, best 9.0
A: Carmine Infantino
72 ❑ Dec 1961 Cover: 0.12 **NM** value: **95.00**
Circ: Statement: **240,000** • **CGC:** 3 graded, best 9.0
A: Carmine Infantino
73 ❑ Feb 1962 Cover: 0.12 **NM** value: **95.00**
Circ: Statement: **190,000** • **CGC:** 4 graded, best 9.4
A: Carmine Infantino
74 ❑ Mar 1962 Cover: 0.12 **NM** value: **95.00**
Circ: Statement: **190,000** • **CGC:** 1 graded, best 6.5
A: Carmine Infantino
75 ❑ May 1962 Cover: 0.12 **NM** value: **140.00**
Circ: Statement: **190,000** • **CGC:** 9 graded, best 9.4
A: Carmine Infantino ★ Appearance of Justice League of America.
76 ❑ Jun 1962 Cover: 0.12 **NM** value: **80.00**
Circ: Statement: **190,000** • **CGC:** 3 graded, best 9.2
A: Carmine Infantino
77 ❑ Aug 1962 Cover: 0.12 **NM** value: **80.00**
Circ: Statement: **190,000** • **CGC:** 3 graded, best 9.4
A: Carmine Infantino
78 ❑ Sep 1962 Cover: 0.12 **NM** value: **80.00**
Circ: Statement: **190,000** • **CGC:** 3 graded, best 9.4
A: Carmine Infantino
79 ❑ Nov 1962 Cover: 0.12 **NM** value: **80.00**
Circ: Statement: **190,000** • **CGC:** 5 graded, best 9.4
A: Carmine Infantino
80 ❑ Dec 1962 Cover: 0.12 **NM** value: **80.00**
Circ: Statement: **190,000** • **CGC:** 4 graded, best 9.6
A: Carmine Infantino
81 ❑ Feb 1963 Cover: 0.12 **NM** value: **60.00**
• **CGC:** 2 graded, best 7.5
• Has 1962 Statement, filed 10/1/62; avg total paid circ 190,000 **A:** Carmine Infantino
82 ❑ Mar 1963 Cover: 0.12 **NM** value: **60.00**
• **CGC:** 3 graded, best 9.4
A: Carmine Infantino
83 ❑ May 1963 Cover: 0.12 **NM** value: **60.00**
• **CGC:** 3 graded, best 9.6
A: Carmine Infantino
84 ❑ Jun 1963 Cover: 0.12 **NM** value: **60.00**
• **CGC:** 2 graded, best 9.4
A: Carmine Infantino
85 ❑ Aug 1963 Cover: 0.12 **NM** value: **60.00**
• **CGC:** 5 graded, best 9.4
A: Carmine Infantino
86 ❑ Sep 1963 Cover: 0.12 **NM** value: **60.00**
• **CGC:** 1 graded, best 9.0
A: Carmine Infantino
87 ❑ Nov 1963 Cover: 0.12 **NM** value: **125.00**
• **CGC:** 9 graded, best 9.2
📖 The Super-Brain of Adam Strange; Amazing thefts of the I.Q. Gang! **A:** Murphy Anderson; Carmine Infantino **W:** Gardner Fox ★ Appearance of Hawkman.
88 ❑ Dec 1963 Cover: 0.12 **NM** value: **90.00**
• **CGC:** 3 graded, best 9.2
📖 The Robot Wraith of Rann; Topsy-Turvy Day in Midway City! **A:** Murphy Anderson; Carmine Infantino **W:** Gardner Fox ★ Appearance of Hawkman.
89 ❑ Feb 1964 Cover: 0.12 **NM** value: **90.00**
• **CGC:** 9 graded, best 9.4
📖 The Super-Motorized Menace!; Siren of the Space Ark • Has 1963 Statement, filed 10/1/63; no circ figures published **A:** Murphy Anderson; Carmine Infantino **W:** Gardner Fox ★ Appearance of Hawkman.
90 ❑ Mar 1964 Cover: 0.12 **NM** value: **90.00**
• **CGC:** 3 graded, best 9.4
📖 Planets in Peril! **A:** Murphy Anderson; Carmine Infantino **W:** Gardner Fox ★ Appearance of Hawkman.
91 ❑ May 1964 Cover: 0.12 **NM** value: **26.00**
• **CGC:** 1 graded, best 9.6
A: Carmine Infantino
92 ❑ Jun 1964 Cover: 0.12 **NM** value: **26.00**
• **CGC:** 1 graded, best 3.5
93 ❑ Aug 1964 Cover: 0.12 **NM** value: **26.00**
• **CGC:** 1 graded, best 4.0
94 ❑ Sep 1964 Cover: 0.12 **NM** value: **26.00**
• **CGC:** 1 graded, best 8.0
95 ❑ Nov 1964 Cover: 0.12 **NM** value: **26.00**
96 ❑ Dec 1964 Cover: 0.12 **NM** value: **26.00**
• **CGC:** 1 graded, best 5.0
97 ❑ Feb 1965 Cover: 0.12 **NM** value: **26.00**
Circ: Statement: **182,376**
98 ❑ Mar 1965 Cover: 0.12 **NM** value: **26.00**
Circ: Statement: **182,376**
• Has 1964 Statement, filed 10/1/64; no circ figures published
99 ❑ May 1965 Cover: 0.12 **NM** value: **26.00**
Circ: Statement: **182,376**
100 ❑ Jun 1965 Cover: 0.12 **NM** value: **26.00**
Circ: Statement: **182,376**
📖 The Death Of Alanna; The Planet Collectors; The Secret Of The Double Agent
101 ❑ Aug 1965 Cover: 0.12 **NM** value: **26.00**
Circ: Statement: **182,376**
102 ❑ Sep 1965 Cover: 0.12 **NM** value: **26.00**
Circ: Statement: **182,376** • **CGC:** 1 graded, best 8.0
103 ❑ Nov 1965 Cover: 0.12 **NM** value: **26.00**
Circ: Statement: **182,376** • **CGC:** 1 graded, best 9.0
104 ❑ Dec 1965 Cover: 0.12 **NM** value: **12.00**
Circ: Statement: **182,376** • **CGC:** 1 graded, best 9.4
105 ❑ Feb 1966 Cover: 0.12 **NM** value: **12.00**
• **CGC:** 1 graded, best 9.2
106 ❑ Mar 1966 Cover: 0.12 **NM** value: **12.00**
• **CGC:** 1 graded, best 9.0
107 ❑ May 1966 Cover: 0.12 **NM** value: **12.00**
• **CGC:** 2 graded, best 9.6
108 ❑ Jun 1966 Cover: 0.12 **NM** value: **12.00**
• **CGC:** 2 graded, best 9.4
109 ❑ Aug 1966 Cover: 0.12 **NM** value: **12.00**
• **CGC:** 1 graded, best 6.0
• Has 1965 Statement, filed 10/1/65 (second statement in year; this one revised to include sales figures); avg print run 312,000; avg sales 181,000; avg subs 1,376; avg total paid 182,376; samples 142; max existent 182,518; 42% of run returned
110 ❑ Sep 1966 Cover: 0.12 **NM** value: **12.00**
• **CGC:** 1 graded, best 9.2
• Original series ends
111 ❑ Sep 1980 Cover: 0.50 **NM** value: **5.00**
• Series begins again
112 ❑ Oct 1980 Cover: 0.50 **NM** value: **5.00**
113 ❑ Nov 1980 Cover: 0.50 **NM** value: **5.00**
114 ❑ Dec 1980 Cover: 0.50 **NM** value: **5.00**
115 ❑ Jan 1981 Cover: 0.50 **NM** value: **5.00**
116 ❑ Feb 1981 Cover: 0.50 **NM** value: **5.00**
• **CGC:** 1 graded, best 9.6
117 ❑ Mar 1981 Cover: 0.50 **NM** value: **5.00**
final issue.

MYSTERY MAN, THE **Slave Labor**

1 ❑ Jul 1988, b&w Cover: 1.75 **NM** value: **Cover or less**
2 ❑ Nov 1988, b&w Cover: 1.75 **NM** value: **Cover or less**

MYSTERY MEN COMICS **Fox**

1 ❑ Aug 1939 Cover: 0.10 **NM** value: **10000.00**
• **CGC:** 1 graded, best 3.5
2 ❑ Sep 1939 Cover: 0.10 **NM** value: **3000.00**
• **CGC:** 3 graded, best 8.5
3 ❑ Oct 1939 Cover: 0.10 **NM** value: **3000.00**
• **CGC:** 3 graded, best 9.4
4 ❑ Nov 1939 Cover: 0.10 **NM** value: **2500.00**
• **CGC:** 1 graded, best 9.0
5 ❑ Dec 1939 Cover: 0.10 **NM** value: **2500.00**
• **CGC:** 1 graded, best 9.0
6 ❑ Jan 1940 Cover: 0.10 **NM** value: **2000.00**
• **CGC:** 5 graded, best 7.0
7 ❑ Feb 1940 Cover: 0.10 **NM** value: **2000.00**
8 ❑ Mar 1940 Cover: 0.10 **NM** value: **2000.00**
• **CGC:** 1 graded, best 7.5
9 ❑ Apr 1940 Cover: 0.10 **NM** value: **1500.00**
10 ❑ May 1940 Cover: 0.10 **NM** value: **1500.00**
11 ❑ Jun 1940 Cover: 0.10 **NM** value: **900.00**
• **CGC:** 1 graded, best 9.0
12 ❑ Jul 1940 Cover: 0.10 **NM** value: **900.00**
13 ❑ Aug 1940 Cover: 0.10 **NM** value: **600.00**
14 ❑ Sep 1940 Cover: 0.10 **NM** value: **500.00**
15 ❑ Oct 1940 Cover: 0.10 **NM** value: **500.00**
16 ❑ Nov 1940 Cover: 0.10 **NM** value: **500.00**
17 ❑ Dec 1940 Cover: 0.10 **NM** value: **500.00**
18 ❑ Jan 1941 Cover: 0.10 **NM** value: **500.00**
19 ❑ Feb 1941 Cover: 0.10 **NM** value: **500.00**
20 ❑ Mar 1941 Cover: 0.10 **NM** value: **450.00**
21 ❑ Apr 1941 Cover: 0.10 **NM** value: **450.00**
• **CGC:** 1 graded, best 4.5

Other grades: Multiply prices above by **1.5 for Mint • 2/3 for Very Fine • 1/3 for Fine • 1/5 for Very Good • 1/8 for Good**

22 ❑ May 1941 Cover: 0.10 **NM** value: **450.00**
23 ❑ Jun 1941 Cover: 0.10 **NM** value: **450.00**
24 ❑ Jul 1941 Cover: 0.10 **NM** value: **450.00**
25 ❑ Aug 1941 Cover: 0.10 **NM** value: **450.00**
26 ❑ Sep 1941 Cover: 0.10 **NM** value: **450.00**
27 ❑ Oct 1941 Cover: 0.10 **NM** value: **450.00**
28 ❑ Nov 1941 Cover: 0.10 **NM** value: **450.00**
29 ❑ Dec 1941 Cover: 0.10 **NM** value: **450.00**
30 ❑ Jan 1942 Cover: 0.10 **NM** value: **450.00**
• **CGC:** 1 graded, best 4.5
31 ❑ Feb 1942 Cover: 0.10 **NM** value: **450.00**

MYSTERY MEN MOVIE ADAPTATION Dark Horse

1 ❑ Jul 1999 Cover: 2.95 **NM** value: **Cover or less**
Circ: Diamd. preorders: **10,329**
A: Chris Mcloughlin **W:** Neil Cuthbert
2 ❑ Aug 1999 Cover: 2.95 **NM** value: **Cover or less**
Circ: Diamd. preorders: **8,786**
A: Chris Mcloughlin **W:** Neil Cuthbert

MYSTERYMEN STORIES Bob Burden Productions

1 ❑ Sum 1996, b&w Cover: 5.00 **NM** value: **Cover or less**
📖 When Stalks The Strangler… • prose story with illustrations **A:** Bob Burden **W:** Bob Burden

MYSTERY PLAY, THE DC / Vertigo

Bk 1❑ Cover: 9.95 **NM** value: **Cover or less**
A: Jon J Muth **W:** Grant Morrison
Bk 1/HC❑ Cover: 19.95 **NM** value: **Cover or less**
hardcover. **A:** Jon J Muth **W:** Grant Morrison

MYSTERY TALES Marvel

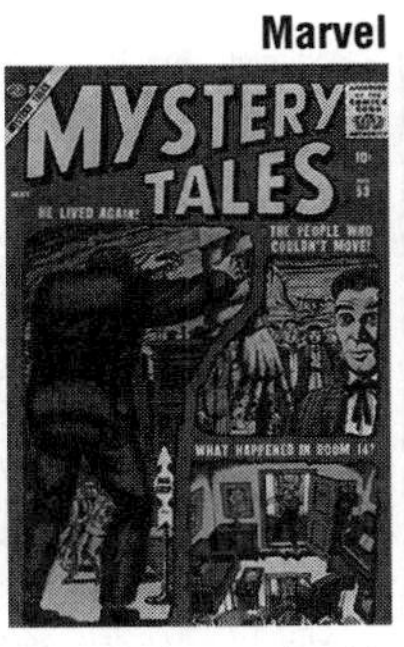

Mystery Tales was one of many titles Atlas hurried to the stands in the wake of the success of E.C.'s "New Trend" horror comics of the early '50s. Early issues featured Atlas' typical heavy-handed mix of gory and gruesome fare, rendered by a roster of talent including Matt Fox, a young Gene Colan, Bill Everett, and the great Joe Maneely. The arrival of the Comics Code banished the buckets of blood, and the focus shifted to tales of suspense and (like the title says) mystery. By 1957, Atlas had hit the skids and cut back on all but a few titles. Mystery Tales did not survive the implosion,
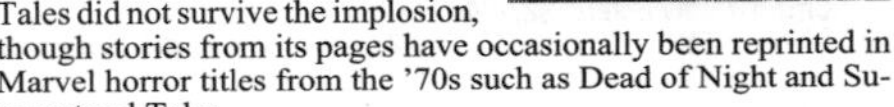
though stories from its pages have occasionally been reprinted in Marvel horror titles from the '70s such as Dead of Night and Supernatural Tales.

1 ❑ Mar 1952 Cover: 0.10 **NM** value: **400.00**
• **CGC:** 7 graded, best 9.0
2 ❑ May 1952 Cover: 0.10 **NM** value: **250.00**
• **CGC:** 1 graded, best 4.0
3 ❑ Jul 1952 Cover: 0.10 **NM** value: **200.00**
4 ❑ Sep 1952 Cover: 0.10 **NM** value: **200.00**
• **CGC:** 1 graded, best 5.0
5 ❑ Nov 1952 Cover: 0.10 **NM** value: **200.00**
• **CGC:** 4 graded, best 8.0
6 ❑ Dec 1952 Cover: 0.10 **NM** value: **185.00**
7 ❑ Jan 1953 Cover: 0.10 **NM** value: **185.00**
8 ❑ Feb 1953 Cover: 0.10 **NM** value: **185.00**
• **CGC:** 2 graded, best 8.5
9 ❑ Mar 1953 Cover: 0.10 **NM** value: **185.00**
• **CGC:** 1 graded, best 6.0
10 ❑ Apr 1953 Cover: 0.10 **NM** value: **185.00**
• **CGC:** 1 graded, best 9.0
11 ❑ May 1953 Cover: 0.10 **NM** value: **150.00**
12 ❑ Jun 1953 Cover: 0.10 **NM** value: **150.00**
13 ❑ Jul 1953 Cover: 0.10 **NM** value: **150.00**
14 ❑ Aug 1953 Cover: 0.10 **NM** value: **150.00**
15 ❑ Sep 1953 Cover: 0.10 **NM** value: **150.00**
• **CGC:** 1 graded, best 7.0
16 ❑ Nov 1953 Cover: 0.10 **NM** value: **150.00**
17 ❑ Jan 1954 Cover: 0.10 **NM** value: **150.00**
• **CGC:** 1 graded, best 8.0
18 ❑ Mar 1954 Cover: 0.10 **NM** value: **150.00**
19 ❑ May 1954 Cover: 0.10 **NM** value: **150.00**
20 ❑ Jul 1954 Cover: 0.10 **NM** value: **150.00**
• **CGC:** 2 graded, best 9.0
21 ❑ Sep 1954 Cover: 0.10 **NM** value: **120.00**
22 ❑ Oct 1954 Cover: 0.10 **NM** value: **120.00**
• **CGC:** 1 graded, best 7.5
23 ❑ Nov 1954 Cover: 0.10 **NM** value: **120.00**
24 ❑ Dec 1954 Cover: 0.10 **NM** value: **120.00**
• **CGC:** 1 graded, best 6.0
25 ❑ Jan 1955 Cover: 0.10 **NM** value: **120.00**
26 ❑ Feb 1955 Cover: 0.10 **NM** value: **120.00**
27 ❑ Mar 1955 Cover: 0.10 **NM** value: **120.00**
28 ❑ Apr 1955 Cover: 0.10 **NM** value: **120.00**
29 ❑ May 1955 Cover: 0.10 **NM** value: **120.00**
30 ❑ Jun 1955 Cover: 0.10 **NM** value: **120.00**
31 ❑ Jul 1955 Cover: 0.10 **NM** value: **90.00**
• **CGC:** 1 graded, best 6.0
32 ❑ Aug 1955 Cover: 0.10 **NM** value: **90.00**
33 ❑ Sep 1955 Cover: 0.10 **NM** value: **90.00**
34 ❑ Oct 1955 Cover: 0.10 **NM** value: **90.00**
35 ❑ Nov 1955 Cover: 0.10 **NM** value: **90.00**
36 ❑ Dec 1955 Cover: 0.10 **NM** value: **90.00**
37 ❑ Jan 1956 Cover: 0.10 **NM** value: **90.00**
38 ❑ Feb 1956 Cover: 0.10 **NM** value: **90.00**
39 ❑ Mar 1956 Cover: 0.10 **NM** value: **90.00**
40 ❑ Apr 1956 Cover: 0.10 **NM** value: **90.00**
41 ❑ May 1956 Cover: 0.10 **NM** value: **65.00**
42 ❑ Jun 1956 Cover: 0.10 **NM** value: **65.00**
43 ❑ Jul 1956 Cover: 0.10 **NM** value: **65.00**
44 ❑ Aug 1956 Cover: 0.10 **NM** value: **65.00**
45 ❑ Sep 1956 Cover: 0.10 **NM** value: **65.00**
46 ❑ Oct 1956 Cover: 0.10 **NM** value: **65.00**
47 ❑ Nov 1956 Cover: 0.10 **NM** value: **65.00**
• **CGC:** 1 graded, best 3.0
48 ❑ Dec 1956 Cover: 0.10 **NM** value: **65.00**
• **CGC:** 2 graded, best 4.0
49 ❑ Jan 1957 Cover: 0.10 **NM** value: **65.00**
50 ❑ Feb 1957 Cover: 0.10 **NM** value: **65.00**
51 ❑ Mar 1957 Cover: 0.10 **NM** value: **65.00**
• **CGC:** 1 graded, best 5.5
52 ❑ Apr 1957 Cover: 0.10 **NM** value: **65.00**
• **CGC:** 2 graded, best 8.5
53 ❑ May 1957 Cover: 0.10 **NM** value: **65.00**
📖 The People who Couldn't Move; That's What You Think; I Died Too Soon; The Hired Hand; The Rainmaker (Text Story); He Lived Again; What happened in Room 14;
54 ❑ Jun 1957 Cover: 0.10 **NM** value: **65.00**

MYSTIC Marvel

1 ❑ Mar 1951 Cover: 0.10 **NM** value: **485.00**
• **CGC:** 4 graded, best 8.5
2 ❑ May 1951 Cover: 0.10 **NM** value: **335.00**
3 ❑ Jul 1951 Cover: 0.10 **NM** value: **235.00**
• **CGC:** 1 graded, best 7.5
4 ❑ Sep 1951 Cover: 0.10 **NM** value: **400.00**
A: Basil Wolverton
5 ❑ Nov 1951 Cover: 0.10 **NM** value: **175.00**
6 ❑ Jan 1952 Cover: 0.10 **NM** value: **400.00**
• **CGC:** 1 graded, best 7.0
📖 The Eye of Doom! **A:** Basil Wolverton
7 ❑ Mar 1952 Cover: 0.10 **NM** value: **175.00**
• **CGC:** 3 graded, best 9.0
8 ❑ May 1952 Cover: 0.10 **NM** value: **135.00**
• **CGC:** 2 graded, best 8.0
9 ❑ Jun 1952 Cover: 0.10 **NM** value: **135.00**
• **CGC:** 1 graded, best 9.0
10 ❑ Jul 1952 Cover: 0.10 **NM** value: **135.00**
• **CGC:** 1 graded, best 9.0
11 ❑ Aug 1952 Cover: 0.10 **NM** value: **135.00**
12 ❑ Sep 1952 Cover: 0.10 **NM** value: **135.00**
13 ❑ Oct 1952 Cover: 0.10 **NM** value: **135.00**
• **CGC:** 1 graded, best 7.0
14 ❑ Nov 1952 Cover: 0.10 **NM** value: **135.00**
• **CGC:** 1 graded, best 8.5
15 ❑ Dec 1952 Cover: 0.10 **NM** value: **135.00**
• **CGC:** 1 graded, best 9.0
16 ❑ Jan 1953 Cover: 0.10 **NM** value: **135.00**
• **CGC:** 1 graded, best 7.5
17 ❑ Feb 1953 Cover: 0.10 **NM** value: **135.00**
• **CGC:** 1 graded, best 5.0
18 ❑ Mar 1953 Cover: 0.10 **NM** value: **135.00**
19 ❑ Apr 1953 Cover: 0.10 **NM** value: **135.00**
20 ❑ May 1953 Cover: 0.10 **NM** value: **135.00**
21 ❑ Jul 1953 Cover: 0.10 **NM** value: **105.00**
22 ❑ Aug 1953 Cover: 0.10 **NM** value: **105.00**
• **CGC:** 1 graded, best 5.0
23 ❑ Sep 1953 Cover: 0.10 **NM** value: **105.00**
• **CGC:** 2 graded, best 8.0
24 ❑ Oct 1953 Cover: 0.10 **NM** value: **105.00**
25 ❑ 1953 Cover: 0.10 **NM** value: **105.00**
26 ❑ Jan 1954 Cover: 0.10 **NM** value: **105.00**
27 ❑ Feb 1954 Cover: 0.10 **NM** value: **105.00**
28 ❑ Mar 1954 Cover: 0.10 **NM** value: **105.00**
• **CGC:** 1 graded, best 9.0
29 ❑ Apr 1954 Cover: 0.10 **NM** value: **105.00**
30 ❑ May 1954 Cover: 0.10 **NM** value: **105.00**
31 ❑ Jun 1954 Cover: 0.10 **NM** value: **85.00**
32 ❑ Jul 1954 Cover: 0.10 **NM** value: **85.00**
• **CGC:** 1 graded, best 8.5
33 ❑ Sep 1954 Cover: 0.10 **NM** value: **85.00**
34 ❑ Nov 1954 Cover: 0.10 **NM** value: **85.00**
• **CGC:** 1 graded, best 7.0
35 ❑ Jan 1955 Cover: 0.10 **NM** value: **85.00**
36 ❑ Mar 1955 Cover: 0.10 **NM** value: **85.00**
📖 The Warning!
37 ❑ May 1955 Cover: 0.10 **NM** value: **70.00**
• **CGC:** 2 graded, best 8.0
• Code-approved issues begin
38 ❑ 1955 Cover: 0.10 **NM** value: **70.00**
39 ❑ 1955 Cover: 0.10 **NM** value: **70.00**
40 ❑ Oct 1955 Cover: 0.10 **NM** value: **70.00**
• **CGC:** 2 graded, best 8.0
41 ❑ Nov 1955 Cover: 0.10 **NM** value: **70.00**
• **CGC:** 1 graded, best 6.5
42 ❑ Dec 1955 Cover: 0.10 **NM** value: **70.00**
43 ❑ Jan 1956 Cover: 0.10 **NM** value: **70.00**
• **CGC:** 1 graded, best 7.5
44 ❑ Feb 1956 Cover: 0.10 **NM** value: **70.00**
45 ❑ Mar 1956 Cover: 0.10 **NM** value: **70.00**
46 ❑ Apr 1956 Cover: 0.10 **NM** value: **70.00**
47 ❑ May 1956 Cover: 0.10 **NM** value: **70.00**
48 ❑ Jun 1956 Cover: 0.10 **NM** value: **70.00**
49 ❑ Jul 1956 Cover: 0.10 **NM** value: **70.00**
50 ❑ Aug 1956 Cover: 0.10 **NM** value: **70.00**
51 ❑ Sep 1956 Cover: 0.10 **NM** value: **70.00**
52 ❑ Oct 1956 Cover: 0.10 **NM** value: **70.00**
• **CGC:** 1 graded, best 9.4
53 ❑ Nov 1956 Cover: 0.10 **NM** value: **70.00**
54 ❑ Dec 1956 Cover: 0.10 **NM** value: **70.00**
• **CGC:** 1 graded, best 8.0
55 ❑ Jan 1957 Cover: 0.10 **NM** value: **70.00**
• **CGC:** 1 graded, best 9.0
56 ❑ Feb 1957 Cover: 0.10 **NM** value: **70.00**
• **CGC:** 1 graded, best 5.5
57 ❑ Mar 1957 Cover: 0.10 **NM** value: **100.00**
• **CGC:** 3 graded, best 9.0
📖 Trapped in the Ant-Hill
58 ❑ Apr 1957 Cover: 0.10 **NM** value: **70.00**
• **CGC:** 1 graded, best 7.5
59 ❑ May 1957 Cover: 0.10 **NM** value: **70.00**
60 ❑ Jun 1957 Cover: 0.10 **NM** value: **70.00**
• **CGC:** 1 graded, best 9.2
61 ❑ Aug 1957 Cover: 0.10 **NM** value: **70.00**
final issue.

MYSTICAL TALES Atlas

1 ❑ Jun 1956 Cover: 0.10 **NM** value: **400.00**
• **CGC:** 2 graded, best 7.0
2 ❑ Aug 1956 Cover: 0.10 **NM** value: **300.00**
3 ❑ Oct 1956 Cover: 0.10 **NM** value: **300.00**
• **CGC:** 1 graded, best 7.0
4 ❑ Dec 1956 Cover: 0.10 **NM** value: **250.00**
• **CGC:** 1 graded, best 7.5
5 ❑ Feb 1957 Cover: 0.10 **NM** value: **250.00**
• **CGC:** 1 graded, best 8.5
6 ❑ Apr 1957 Cover: 0.10 **NM** value: **200.00**
• **CGC:** 1 graded, best 7.5
7 ❑ Jun 1957 Cover: 0.10 **NM** value: **200.00**
• **CGC:** 4 graded, best 9.4

MYSTIC COMICS (1ST SERIES) Timely

1 ❑ Mar 1940 Cover: 0.10 **NM** value: **10000.00**
• **CGC:** 2 graded, best 7.5
2 ❑ Apr 1940 Cover: 0.10 **NM** value: **4000.00**
3 ❑ Jun 1940 Cover: 0.10 **NM** value: **3000.00**
• **CGC:** 1 graded, best 7.5
4 ❑ Jul 1940 Cover: 0.10 **NM** value: **3000.00**
5 ❑ Mar 1941 Cover: 0.10 **NM** value: **3000.00**
• **CGC:** 3 graded, best 9.0
6 ❑ Oct 1941 Cover: 0.10 **NM** value: **3000.00**
• **CGC:** 4 graded, best 8.5
7 ❑ Dec 1941 Cover: 0.10 **NM** value: **3000.00**
• **CGC:** 1 graded, best 6.5
8 ❑ Mar 1942 Cover: 0.10 **NM** value: **2000.00**
• **CGC:** 2 graded, best 7.5
9 ❑ May 1942 Cover: 0.10 **NM** value: **2000.00**
• **CGC:** 3 graded, best 8.5
10 ❑ Aug 1942 Cover: 0.10 **NM** value: **2000.00**
• **CGC:** 2 graded, best 8.0

MYSTIC COMICS (2ND SERIES) Timely

1 ❑ Oct 1944 Cover: 0.10 **NM** value: **2000.00**
• **CGC:** 2 graded, best 5.0
2 ❑ Fal 1944 Cover: 0.10 **NM** value: **1000.00**
• **CGC:** 5 graded, best 8.0
3 ❑ Win 1944 Cover: 0.10 **NM** value: **1000.00**
• **CGC:** 1 graded, best 8.0
4 ❑ Mar 1945 Cover: 0.10 **NM** value: **900.00**
• **CGC:** 2 graded, best 8.0

MYSTIC (CROSSGEN) CrossGen

In the interwoven worlds of the CrossGen universe, Ciress is a world in which magic is involved with daily life.

It's ruled by seven Major Guilds, and the wild Giselle Villard has no interest in magic; nevertheless, she finds a Sigil on her hand and becomes the most powerful Mystic protector on the planet when she interrupts the ceremony of power that was to make her more level-headed sister a master mage.

The spirits from all the Guilds eventually come to reside in Giselle and advise her on her adventures. — Maggie

1❑ Jul 2000 Cover: 2.95 **NM** value: **Cover or less**
Circ: Diamd. preorders: **31,035** • **CGC:** 24 graded, best 9.9
A: Brandon Peterson **W:** Ron Marz
2 ❑ Aug 2000 Cover: 2.95 **NM** value: **Cover or less**
Circ: Diamd. preorders: **24,061** • **CGC:** 1 graded, best 8.5
A: Brandon Peterson **W:** Ron Marz
3 ❑ Sep 2000 Cover: 2.95 **NM** value: **Cover or less**
Circ: Diamd. preorders: **22,734** • **CGC:** 1 graded, best 7.5
A: Brandon Peterson **W:** Ron Marz
4 ❑ Oct 2000 Cover: 2.95 **NM** value: **Cover or less**
Circ: Diamd. preorders: **22,454**
A: Brandon Peterson **W:** Ron Marz
5 ❑ Nov 2000 Cover: 2.95 **NM** value: **Cover or less**
Circ: Diamd. preorders: **22,323**
6 ❑ Dec 2000 Cover: 2.95 **NM** value: **Cover or less**
Circ: Diamd. preorders: **22,277**
7 ❑ Jan 2001 Cover: 2.95 **NM** value: **Cover or less**
Circ: Diamd. preorders: **21,266**
8 ❑ Feb 2001 Cover: 2.95 **NM** value: **Cover or less**
Circ: Diamd. preorders: **20,572**
9 ❑ Mar 2001 Cover: 2.95 **NM** value: **Cover or less**
Circ: Diamd. preorders: **21,894**
10 ❑ Apr 2001 Cover: 2.95 **NM** value: **Cover or less**
Circ: Diamd. preorders: **19,012**
11 ❑ May 2001 Cover: 2.95 **NM** value: **Cover or less**
Circ: Diamd. preorders: **18,777**
12 ❑ Jun 2001 Cover: 2.95 **NM** value: **Cover or less**
Circ: Diamd. preorders: **18,264**
13 ❑ Jul 2001 Cover: 2.95 **NM** value: **Cover or less**
Circ: Diamd. preorders: **18,192**
14 ❑ Aug 2001 Cover: 2.95 **NM** value: **Cover or less**
Circ: Diamd. preorders: **18,621**
15 ❑ Sep 2001 Cover: 2.95 **NM** value: **Cover or less**
16 ❑ Oct 2001 Cover: 2.95 **NM** value: **Cover or less**

CGC-graded: Multiply prices above by **33 for 9.9 M • 16 for 9.8 NM/M • 7 for 9.6 NM+ • 5 for 9.4 NM • 2.5 for 9.2 NM- • 1.5 for 9.0 VF/NM**

17 ❑ Cover: 2.95 NM value: Cover or less
18 ❑ Dec 2001 Cover: 2.95 NM value: Cover or less
19 ❑ Jan 2002 Cover: 2.95 NM value: Cover or less
20 ❑ Feb 2002 Cover: 2.95 NM value: Cover or less
21 ❑ Mar 2002 Cover: 2.95 NM value: Cover or less

MYSTIC EDGE — Antarctic

1 ❑ Oct 1998 Cover: 2.95 NM value: Cover or less
Circ: Diamd. preorders: 6,739
A: Ryan Kinnaird W: Ryan Kinnaird ★ 1st Appearance of Symattra, Risa, Ena, Evron, Kyleen.

MYSTIC TRIGGER, THE — Maelstrom

1 ❑ Cover: 3.25 NM value: Cover or less
• Tales of the Galactic Forces preview A: James Brochey W: James Brochey; Gary Stanley; Marcelo Bravo

MYSTIQUE & SABRETOOTH — Marvel

1 ❑ Dec 1996 Cover: 1.95 NM value: Cover or less
Circ: Direct Market orders: 103,000
📖 Old Sins Cast Long Shadows A: Ariel Olivetti W: Jorge Gonzalez
2 ❑ Jan 1997 Cover: 1.95 NM value: Cover or less
Circ: Direct Market orders: 87,000
📖 Torture A: Ariel Olivetti W: Jorge Gonzalez
3 ❑ Feb 1997 Cover: 1.95 NM value: Cover or less
Circ: Direct Market orders: 71,500
📖 Willing Victims A: Ariel Olivetti W: Jorge Gonzalez
4 ❑ Mar 1997 Cover: 1.95 NM value: Cover or less
Circ: Direct Market orders: 61,750
📖 Dead Ends A: Ariel Olivetti W: Jorge Gonzalez

MYST: THE BOOK OF THE BLACK SHIPS — Dark Horse

0 ❑ ca. 1997 NM value: 1.50
no cover price. • American Entertainment Exclusive Edition. 📖 Passages • based on video game A: Kirk Van Wormer W: Chris Ulm
1 ❑ Aug 1997 Cover: 2.95 NM value: Cover or less
Circ: Diamd. preorders: 8,187
📖 The Joining • based on video game A: Doug Wheatley W: Lovern Kindzierski; Chris Ulm
2 ❑ Sep 1997 Cover: 2.95 NM value: Cover or less
Circ: Diamd. preorders: 6,405
A: Doug Wheatley W: Lovern Kindzierski; Chris Ulm
3 ❑ Oct 1997 Cover: 2.95 NM value: Cover or less
Circ: Diamd. preorders: 6,280
A: Doug Wheatley W: Lovern Kindzierski; Chris Ulm
4 ❑ Nov 1997 Cover: 2.95 NM value: Cover or less
Circ: Diamd. preorders: 6,936
A: Doug Wheatley W: Lovern Kindzierski; Chris Ulm

MYTH — Fygmok

1 ❑ Dec 1996, b&w Cover: 2.95 NM value: Cover or less
wraparound cover.
2 ❑ Feb 1997, b&w Cover: 2.95 NM value: Cover or less

MYTHADVENTURES — Warp

1 ❑ Mar 1984 Cover: 1.50 NM value: 2.00
• Warp publishes
2 ❑ Jun 1984 Cover: 1.50 NM value: Cover or less
3 ❑ Sep 1984 Cover: 1.50 NM value: Cover or less
4 ❑ Dec 1984 Cover: 1.50 NM value: Cover or less
5 ❑ Mar 1985 Cover: 1.50 NM value: Cover or less
6 ❑ Jun 1985 Cover: 1.50 NM value: Cover or less
7 ❑ Sep 1985 Cover: 1.50 NM value: Cover or less
8 ❑ Dec 1985 Cover: 1.50 NM value: Cover or less
A: Phil Foglio W: Phil Foglio; Robert Asprin
9 ❑ Mar 1986 Cover: 1.50 NM value: Cover or less
10 ❑ 1986 Cover: 1.50 NM value: Cover or less
• Apple begins as publisher
11 ❑ 1986 Cover: 1.50 NM value: Cover or less
12 ❑ 1986 Cover: 1.75 NM value: Cover or less
final issue.

MYTH CONCEPTIONS — Apple

1 ❑ Nov 1987 Cover: 1.75 NM value: 2.00
Circ: CapCity orders: 4,600
2 ❑ Jan 1988 Cover: 1.75 NM value: Cover or less
Circ: CapCity orders: 4,075
📖 We're off to be the Wizard A: Ken Mitchroney W: Ken Mitchroney; Beth Mitchroney
3 ❑ Mar 1988 Cover: 1.75 NM value: Cover or less
4 ❑ May 1988 Cover: 1.95 NM value: Cover or less
5 ❑ Jul 1988 Cover: 1.95 NM value: Cover or less
6 ❑ Sep 1988 Cover: 1.95 NM value: Cover or less
7 ❑ Nov 1988 Cover: 1.95 NM value: Cover or less
8 ❑ Jan 1989 Cover: 1.95 NM value: Cover or less

MYTHIC HEROES — Chapterhouse Press

1 ❑ Sep 1996, b&w Cover: 2.50 NM value: Cover or less

MYTH MAKER (ROBERT E. HOWARD'S...) — Cross Plains

1 ❑ Jun 1999 Cover: 6.95 NM value: Cover or less
Circ: Diamd. preorders: 4,257
No issue number.

MYTHOGRAPHY — Bardic Press

1 ❑ Sep 1996 Cover: 3.95 NM value: 4.00
Circ: Diamd. preorders: 9,928
2 ❑ Feb 1997 Cover: 3.95 NM value: 4.00
Circ: Diamd. preorders: 2,952
📖 Oak's Daughter; Mystery Date; Ent' Narcissus Rose; Traitor's Gate; Thirst; Empyrean Tales; Skin Deep Tatoos; The Little Match Girl; The Adventures of Simone & Ajax; Alphabet of Dragons A: Jimmie Robinson; Carla Speed McNeil; Mike Hoffman; Bill Willingham; Andrew Pepoy; Stephen R. Bissette; Michael Cohen; Michael O'Connor; M'Oak; Jim Lowler W: Jimmie Robinson; Carla Speed McNeil; Mike Hoffman; Jerry Beck; Bill Willingham; Andrew Pepoy; Michael Cohen; Matt Levin; Michael O'Connor; M'Oak
3 ❑ Apr 1997 Cover: 3.95 NM value: 4.00
Circ: Diamd. preorders: 4,073
4 ❑ Jun 1997 Cover: 4.25 NM value: Cover or less
5 ❑ Sep 1997 Cover: 4.25 NM value: Cover or less
6 ❑ Nov 1997 Cover: 3.95 NM value: 4.00
• Barr Girls story A: Donna Barr W: Donna Barr
7 ❑ Feb 1998 Cover: 4.25 NM value: Cover or less
📖 One in a Million A: Donna Barr W: Donna Barr
8 ❑ May 1998 Cover: 3.95 NM value: 4.00

MYTHOS — Wonder Comix

1 ❑ Jan 1987 Cover: 1.50 NM value: 2.00
📖 Zakaya! A: Nils Osmar; Tom Christopher W: Nils Osmar
2 ❑ Apr 1987 Cover: 1.50 NM value: 2.00
A: Nils Osmar; Tom Christopher W: Nils Osmar

MYTHOS: THE FINAL TOUR — DC / Vertigo

1 ❑ Dec 1996 Cover: 5.95 NM value: Cover or less
Circ: Diamd. preorders: 19,036
• prestige format. 📖 Shut Heaven A: Gary Amaro W: John Ney Rieber
2 ❑ Jan 1997 Cover: 5.95 NM value: Cover or less
Circ: Diamd. preorders: 13,731
• prestige format. 📖 Uncut A: Peter Snejbjerg W: John Ney Rieber
3 ❑ Feb 1997 Cover: 5.95 NM value: Cover or less
Circ: Diamd. preorders: 12,816
• prestige format. 📖 Salvage A: Teddy Kristiansen; Dean Ormston; Gary Amaro W: John Ney Rieber

MY TRUE LOVE — Fox

66 ❑ Sep 1949 Cover: 0.10 NM value: 100.00
67 ❑ Nov 1949 Cover: 0.10 NM value: 50.00
68 ❑ Jan 1950 Cover: 0.10 NM value: 50.00
69 ❑ Mar 1950 Cover: 0.10 NM value: 50.00

NADESICO — CPM Manga

1 ❑ Jun 1999 Cover: 2.95 NM value: Cover or less
Circ: Diamd. preorders: 6,776
2 ❑ Jul 1999 Cover: 2.95 NM value: Cover or less
Circ: Diamd. preorders: 4,930
3 ❑ Aug 1999 Cover: 2.95 NM value: Cover or less
Circ: Diamd. preorders: 4,288
4 ❑ Sep 1999 Cover: 2.95 NM value: Cover or less
Circ: Diamd. preorders: 3,977
5 ❑ Oct 1999 Cover: 2.95 NM value: Cover or less
Circ: Diamd. preorders: 3,811
6 ❑ Nov 1999 Cover: 2.95 NM value: Cover or less
Circ: Diamd. preorders: 3,600
7 ❑ Dec 1999 Cover: 2.95 NM value: Cover or less
Circ: Diamd. preorders: 3,501
8 ❑ Jan 2000 Cover: 2.95 NM value: Cover or less
Circ: Diamd. preorders: 3,471
9 ❑ Feb 2000 Cover: 2.95 NM value: Cover or less
Circ: Diamd. preorders: 3,224
10 ❑ Mar 2000 Cover: 2.95 NM value: Cover or less
Circ: Diamd. preorders: 3,218
11 ❑ Apr 2000 Cover: 2.95 NM value: Cover or less
Circ: Diamd. preorders: 3,202
12 ❑ May 2000 Cover: 2.95 NM value: Cover or less
Circ: Diamd. preorders: 3,188
13 ❑ Jun 2000 Cover: 2.95 NM value: Cover or less
Circ: Diamd. preorders: 3,166
14 ❑ Jul 2000 Cover: 2.95 NM value: Cover or less
Circ: Diamd. preorders: 3,196
15 ❑ Aug 2000 Cover: 2.95 NM value: Cover or less
Circ: Diamd. preorders: 3,064
16 ❑ Sep 2000 Cover: 2.95 NM value: Cover or less
Circ: Diamd. preorders: 3,027
17 ❑ Oct 2000 Cover: 2.95 NM value: Cover or less
Circ: Diamd. preorders: 2,945
18 ❑ Nov 2000 Cover: 2.95 NM value: Cover or less
Circ: Diamd. preorders: 2,851
19 ❑ Dec 2000 Cover: 2.95 NM value: Cover or less
Circ: Diamd. preorders: 2,748
20 ❑ Jan 2001 Cover: 2.95 NM value: Cover or less
Circ: Diamd. preorders: 2,635
21 ❑ Feb 2001 Cover: 2.95 NM value: Cover or less
Circ: Diamd. preorders: 2,625
22 ❑ Mar 2001 Cover: 2.95 NM value: Cover or less
Circ: Diamd. preorders: 2,576
23 ❑ Apr 2001 Cover: 2.95 NM value: Cover or less
Circ: Diamd. preorders: 2,599
24 ❑ May 2001 Cover: 2.95 NM value: Cover or less
Circ: Diamd. preorders: 2,465
25 ❑ Jun 2001 Cover: 2.95 NM value: Cover or less
Circ: Diamd. preorders: 2,531
26 ❑ Jul 2001 Cover: 2.95 NM value: Cover or less
Circ: Diamd. preorders: 2,499
Bk 1❑ Jun 2000, b&w Cover: 15.95 NM value: Cover or less
• Trade Paperback. A: Kia Asimaya W: Kia Asamiya

NAIVE INTER-DIMENSIONAL COMMANDO KOALAS — Eclipse

1 ❑ Oct 1986, b&w Cover: 1.50 NM value: Cover or less
★ Appearance of Adolescent Radioactive Black Belt Hamsters.

NAKED ANGELS — Eros

1 ❑ 1996 Cover: 2.95 NM value: Cover or less
A: P. Skyler Owens W: P. Skyler Owens
2 ❑ May 1996 Cover: 2.95 NM value: Cover or less
A: P. Skyler Owens W: P. Skyler Owens

NAKED EYE (S.A. KING'S...) — Antarctic

1 ❑ Dec 1994, b&w Cover: 2.75 NM value: Cover or less
A: S.A. King W: S.A. King
2 ❑ Feb 1995, b&w Cover: 2.75 NM value: Cover or less
📖 Manta Ray Country; Crippled Inside; Public Transportation; What's Your Favorite Color?; Sexual Preference; Faces of Death A: S.A. King W: S.A. King
3 ❑ Apr 1995, b&w Cover: 2.75 NM value: Cover or less
📖 Sex, Drugs and E.L.O; Enquiring Mind; Sex, Drugs and E.L.O ...A Conversation A: S.A. King W: S.A. King

'NAM, THE — Marvel

Viet Nam wasn't the sort of place where heroes like G.I. Joe or Sgt. Rock would ever have fit in. It was different in the 'Nam: hard to tell the good guys from the bad guys, or even which side you were playing on.

Marvel's The 'Nam is a war comic for that very different war. Always maintaining a strong sense of story, it nevertheless paints the entire conflict in murky shades of gray, where "good guys" don't always win, and the real losers are often those who weren't doing the fighting.

Although Frank Castle (who would later become The Punisher) made an appearance, The 'Nam was no place for super-heroes. Well-plotted and compelling, this series enjoyed long success in an era where other war comics didn't seem to sell.

1 ❑ Dec 1986 Cover: 0.75 NM value: 3.00
Circ: CapCity orders: 38,300
📖 'Nam: First Patrol A: Michael Golden
1-2 ❑ Dec 1986 Cover: 0.75 NM value: 1.50
2 ❑ Jan 1987 Cover: 0.75 NM value: 2.00
Circ: CapCity orders: 27,500
3 ❑ Feb 1987 Cover: 0.75 NM value: 1.50
Circ: CapCity orders: 27,700
📖 Three Day Pass A: Michael Golden W: Doug Murray
4 ❑ Mar 1987 Cover: 0.75 NM value: 1.50
Circ: CapCity orders: 31,000
5 ❑ Apr 1987 Cover: 0.75 NM value: 1.50
Circ: CapCity orders: 32,100
6 ❑ May 1987 Cover: 0.75 NM value: 1.50
Circ: CapCity orders: 28,900
7 ❑ Jun 1987 Cover: 0.75 NM value: 1.50
Circ: CapCity orders: 27,200
8 ❑ Jul 1987 Cover: 0.75 NM value: 1.50
Circ: CapCity orders: 27,200
9 ❑ Aug 1987 Cover: 0.75 NM value: 1.50
Circ: CapCity orders: 31,500
10 ❑ Sep 1987 Cover: 0.75 NM value: 1.50
Circ: CapCity orders: 33,800
11 ❑ Oct 1987 Cover: 0.75 NM value: 1.50
Circ: CapCity orders: 35,200
12 ❑ Nov 1987 Cover: 0.75 NM value: 1.50
Circ: CapCity orders: 34,800
13 ❑ Dec 1987 Cover: 0.75 NM value: 1.50
Circ: CapCity orders: 33,400
14 ❑ Jan 1988 Cover: 0.75 NM value: 1.50
Circ: CapCity orders: 32,700
15 ❑ Feb 1988 Cover: 0.75 NM value: 1.50
Circ: Statement: 169,655 CapCity orders: 32,900
16 ❑ Mar 1988 Cover: 0.75 NM value: 1.50
Circ: Statement: 169,655 CapCity orders: 33,100
17 ❑ Apr 1988 Cover: 0.75 NM value: 1.50
Circ: Statement: 169,655 CapCity orders: 32,200
18 ❑ May 1988 Cover: 1.25 NM value: 1.50
Circ: Statement: 169,655 CapCity orders: 29,450
19 ❑ Jun 1988 Cover: 1.25 NM value: 1.50
Circ: Statement: 169,655 CapCity orders: 27,200
20 ❑ Jul 1988 Cover: 1.25 NM value: 1.50
Circ: Statement: 169,655 CapCity orders: 25,900
21 ❑ Aug 1988 Cover: 1.25 NM value: 1.50
Circ: Statement: 169,655 CapCity orders: 25,100
22 ❑ Sep 1988 Cover: 1.25 NM value: 1.50
Circ: Statement: 169,655 CapCity orders: 24,800
23 ❑ Oct 1988 Cover: 1.25 NM value: 1.50
Circ: Statement: 169,655 CapCity orders: 24,300
24 ❑ Nov 1988 Cover: 1.25 NM value: 1.50
Circ: Statement: 169,655 CapCity orders: 22,900
25 ❑ Dec 1988 Cover: 1.25 NM value: 1.50
Circ: Statement: 169,655 CapCity orders: 22,600
26 ❑ Jan 1989 Cover: 1.50 NM value: Cover or less
Circ: Statement: 169,655 CapCity orders: 21,100
27 ❑ Feb 1989 Cover: 1.50 NM value: Cover or less
Circ: Statement: 80,000 CapCity orders: 20,200
28 ❑ Mar 1989 Cover: 1.50 NM value: Cover or less
Circ: Statement: 80,000 CapCity orders: 20,100
29 ❑ Apr 1989 Cover: 1.50 NM value: Cover or less
Circ: Statement: 80,000 CapCity orders: 19,700
30 ❑ May 1989 Cover: 1.50 NM value: Cover or less
Circ: Statement: 80,000 CapCity orders: 18,300
31 ❑ Jun 1989 Cover: 1.50 NM value: Cover or less
Circ: Statement: 80,000 CapCity orders: 17,000
• 1988 Statement appears, filed 9/30/1988; avg print run 248,610; shops 163,975; subs 5,680; total paid 169,655; samples 130; office copies 900; max. existent 170,685; 68.2% of run sold
32 ❑ Jul 1989 Cover: 1.50 NM value: Cover or less
Circ: Statement: 80,000 CapCity orders: 17,100
33 ❑ Aug 1989 Cover: 1.50 NM value: Cover or less
Circ: Statement: 80,000 CapCity orders: 16,300

34 ❑ Sep 1989 Cover: 1.50 **NM** value: **Cover or less**
Circ: Statement: **80,000** CapCity orders: **15,550**

35 ❑ Oct 1989 Cover: 1.50 **NM** value: **Cover or less**
Circ: Statement: **80,000** CapCity orders: **15,100**
• Christmas issue ★ Appearance of Bob Hope.

36 ❑ Nov 1989 Cover: 1.50 **NM** value: **Cover or less**
Circ: Statement: **80,000** CapCity orders: **14,600**

37 ❑ Nov 1989 Cover: 1.50 **NM** value: **Cover or less**
Circ: Statement: **80,000** CapCity orders: **14,550**

38 ❑ Dec 1989 Cover: 1.50 **NM** value: **Cover or less**
Circ: Statement: **80,000** CapCity orders: **13,900**

39 ❑ Dec 1989 Cover: 1.50 **NM** value: **Cover or less**
Circ: Statement: **62,755** CapCity orders: **13,150**

40 ❑ Jan 1990 Cover: 1.50 **NM** value: **Cover or less**
Circ: Statement: **62,755** CapCity orders: **13,050**

41 ❑ Feb 1990 Cover: 1.50 **NM** value: **Cover or less**
Circ: Statement: **62,755** CapCity orders: **16,100**

42 ❑ Mar 1990 Cover: 1.50 **NM** value: **Cover or less**
Circ: Statement: **62,755** CapCity orders: **12,150**

43 ❑ Apr 1990 Cover: 1.50 **NM** value: **Cover or less**
Circ: Statement: **62,755** CapCity orders: **11,500**

44 ❑ May 1990 Cover: 1.50 **NM** value: **Cover or less**
Circ: Statement: **62,755** CapCity orders: **11,700**

45 ❑ Jun 1990 Cover: 1.50 **NM** value: **Cover or less**
Circ: Statement: **62,755** CapCity orders: **11,650**

46 ❑ Jul 1990 Cover: 1.50 **NM** value: **Cover or less**
Circ: Statement: **62,755** CapCity orders: **10,850**

47 ❑ Aug 1990 Cover: 1.50 **NM** value: **Cover or less**
Circ: Statement: **62,755** CapCity orders: **11,150**

48 ❑ Sep 1990 Cover: 1.50 **NM** value: **Cover or less**
Circ: Statement: **62,755** CapCity orders: **10,650**

49 ❑ Oct 1990 Cover: 1.50 **NM** value: **Cover or less**
Circ: Statement: **62,755** CapCity orders: **10,200**

50 ❑ Nov 1990 Cover: 1.50 **NM** value: **Cover or less**
Circ: Statement: **62,755** CapCity orders: **10,150**

51 ❑ Dec 1990 Cover: 1.50 **NM** value: **Cover or less**
Circ: CapCity orders: **9,800**

52 ❑ Jan 1991 Cover: 1.50 **NM** value: **2.00**
📖 The Long Sticks, Part 1 ★ Appearance of Frank Castle (Punisher).

52-2❑ Jan 1991 Cover: 1.50 **NM** value: **Cover or less**

53 ❑ Feb 1991 Cover: 1.50 **NM** value: **2.00**
Circ: CapCity orders: **27,700**
📖 The Long Sticks, Part 2 ★ Appearance of Frank Castle (Punisher).

53-2❑ Feb 1991 Cover: 1.50 **NM** value: **Cover or less**

54 ❑ Mar 1991 Cover: 1.50 **NM** value: **Cover or less**
Circ: CapCity orders: **9,900**

55 ❑ Apr 1991 Cover: 1.50 **NM** value: **Cover or less**
Circ: CapCity orders: **10,100**

56 ❑ May 1991 Cover: 1.50 **NM** value: **Cover or less**
Circ: CapCity orders: **10,100**

57 ❑ Jun 1991 Cover: 1.50 **NM** value: **Cover or less**
Circ: CapCity orders: **10,300**

58 ❑ Jul 1991 Cover: 1.50 **NM** value: **Cover or less**
Circ: CapCity orders: **10,450**

59 ❑ Aug 1991 Cover: 1.50 **NM** value: **Cover or less**
Circ: CapCity orders: **10,250**

60 ❑ Sep 1991 Cover: 1.50 **NM** value: **Cover or less**
Circ: CapCity orders: **10,100**

61 ❑ Oct 1991 Cover: 1.50 **NM** value: **Cover or less**
Circ: CapCity orders: **9,850**

62 ❑ Nov 1991 Cover: 1.50 **NM** value: **Cover or less**
Circ: CapCity orders: **9,350**

63 ❑ Dec 1991 Cover: 1.50 **NM** value: **Cover or less**
Circ: Statement: **52,073** CapCity orders: **9,250**

64 ❑ Jan 1992 Cover: 1.50 **NM** value: **Cover or less**
Circ: Statement: **52,073** CapCity orders: **8,900**

65 ❑ Feb 1992 Cover: 1.75 **NM** value: **Cover or less**
Circ: Statement: **52,073** CapCity orders: **8,200**

66 ❑ Mar 1992 Cover: 1.75 **NM** value: **Cover or less**
Circ: Statement: **52,073** CapCity orders: **8,000**

67 ❑ Apr 1992 Cover: 1.75 **NM** value: **2.00**
Circ: Statement: **52,073** CapCity orders: **16,200**
📖 The Punisher First Invades the 'Nam, Part 1 • Punisher

68 ❑ May 1992 Cover: 1.75 **NM** value: **2.00**
Circ: Statement: **52,073** CapCity orders: **17,400**
📖 The Punisher First Invades the 'Nam, Part 2 • Punisher

69 ❑ Jun 1992 Cover: 1.75 **NM** value: **2.00**
Circ: Statement: **52,073** CapCity orders: **18,300**
📖 The Punisher First Invades the 'Nam, Part 3 • Punisher

70 ❑ Jul 1992 Cover: 1.75 **NM** value: **Cover or less**
Circ: Statement: **52,073** CapCity orders: **8,700**
📖 Operation Chicken Lips, Part 1

71 ❑ Aug 1992 Cover: 1.75 **NM** value: **Cover or less**
Circ: Statement: **52,073** CapCity orders: **8,700**
📖 Operation Chicken Lips, Part 2

72 ❑ Sep 1992 Cover: 1.75 **NM** value: **Cover or less**
Circ: Statement: **52,073** CapCity orders: **8,100**
📖 Operation Chicken Lips, Part 3

73 ❑ Oct 1992 Cover: 1.75 **NM** value: **Cover or less**
Circ: Statement: **52,073** CapCity orders: **8,100**
📖 Siege at An Loc, Part 1

74 ❑ Nov 1992 Cover: 1.75 **NM** value: **Cover or less**
Circ: Statement: **52,073** CapCity orders: **7,800**
📖 Siege at An Loc, Part 2

75 ❑ Dec 1992 Cover: 2.25 **NM** value: **Cover or less**
Circ: CapCity orders: **8,000**
• Tells of Mai Lai Massacre from different points of view

76 ❑ Jan 1993 Cover: 1.75 **NM** value: **Cover or less**

77 ❑ Feb 1993 Cover: 1.75 **NM** value: **Cover or less**

78 ❑ Mar 1993 Cover: 1.75 **NM** value: **Cover or less**
• 1992 Statement appears, filed 10/1/1992; avg print run 52,823; shops 50,673; subs 1,400; total paid 52,073; samples 250; office copies 500; max existent 52,823; 98.6% of run sold (title was direct-market only this year)

79 ❑ Apr 1993 Cover: 1.75 **NM** value: **Cover or less**
📖 Beginning of the End, Part 1

80 ❑ May 1993 Cover: 1.75 **NM** value: **Cover or less**
📖 Beginning of the End, Part 2

81 ❑ Jun 1993 Cover: 1.75 **NM** value: **Cover or less**
📖 Beginning of the End, Part 3

82 ❑ Jul 1993 Cover: 1.75 **NM** value: **Cover or less**

83 ❑ Aug 1993 Cover: 1.75 **NM** value: **Cover or less**

84 ❑ Sep 1993 Cover: 1.75 **NM** value: **Cover or less**
final issue. • Told from Vietnamese point of view

Bk 1❑ Sep 1987 Cover: 4.95 **NM** value: **Cover or less**

Bk 2❑ Jan 1988 Cover: 6.95 **NM** value: **Cover or less**

Bk 3❑ May 1988 Cover: 6.95 **NM** value: **Cover or less**

'NAM MAGAZINE, THE — Marvel

1 ❑ Aug 1988, b&w Cover: 2.00 **NM** value: **3.00**
Circ: CapCity orders: **7,250**
📖 First Patrol; Dustoff **A:** Michael Golden **W:** Doug Murray

2 ❑ Sep 1988, b&w Cover: 2.00 **NM** value: **2.50**
Circ: CapCity orders: **5,200**

3 ❑ Oct 1988, b&w Cover: 2.00 **NM** value: **2.50**
Circ: CapCity orders: **4,600**

4 ❑ Nov 1988, b&w Cover: 2.00 **NM** value: **2.50**
Circ: CapCity orders: **3,900**

5 ❑ Dec 1988, b&w Cover: 2.00 **NM** value: **2.50**
Circ: CapCity orders: **3,300**

6 ❑ Dec 1988, b&w Cover: 2.00 **NM** value: **2.50**
Circ: CapCity orders: **2,750**

7 ❑ Jan 1989, b&w Cover: 2.00 **NM** value: **2.50**
Circ: CapCity orders: **2,550**

8 ❑ Feb 1989, b&w Cover: 2.00 **NM** value: **2.50**
Circ: CapCity orders: **2,250**
📖 Notes for the World; Good for the Goose **A:** Wayne Vansant; Geof Isherwood **W:** Doug Murray

9 ❑ Mar 1989, b&w Cover: 2.00 **NM** value: **2.50**
Circ: CapCity orders: **2,300**

10 ❑ Apr 1989, b&w Cover: 2.00 **NM** value: **2.50**
Circ: CapCity orders: **2,150**

NAMELESS, THE — Image

1 ❑ May 1997 Cover: 2.95 **NM** value: **Cover or less**
Circ: Diamd. preorders: **10,386**
A: Phil Hester; Joe Pruet **W:** Phil Hester; Joe Pruet

2 ❑ Jun 1997 Cover: 2.95 **NM** value: **Cover or less**
Circ: Diamd. preorders: **7,793**
A: Phil Hester; Joe Pruet **W:** Phil Hester; Joe Pruet

3 ❑ Jul 1997 Cover: 2.95 **NM** value: **Cover or less**
Circ: Diamd. preorders: **5,826**
A: Phil Hester; Joe Pruet **W:** Phil Hester; Joe Pruet

4 ❑ Aug 1997 Cover: 2.95 **NM** value: **Cover or less**
Circ: Diamd. preorders: **4,985**
A: Phil Hester; Joe Pruet **W:** Phil Hester; Joe Pruet

5 ❑ Sep 1997 Cover: 2.95 **NM** value: **Cover or less**
Circ: Diamd. preorders: **4,371**
A: Phil Hester; Joe Pruet **W:** Phil Hester; Joe Pruet

NAMES OF MAGIC — DC / Vertigo

1 ❑ Feb 2001 Cover: 2.50 **NM** value: **Cover or less**
Circ: Diamd. preorders: **18,133**
📖 Invocation **A:** Richard Case **W:** Dylan Horrocks

2 ❑ Mar 2001 Cover: 2.50 **NM** value: **Cover or less**
Circ: Diamd. preorders: **16,060**
📖 Faith **A:** Richard Case **W:** Dylan Horrocks

3 ❑ Apr 2001 Cover: 2.50 **NM** value: **Cover or less**
Circ: Diamd. preorders: **15,468**
📖 Secrets **A:** Richard Case **W:** Dylan Horrocks

4 ❑ May 2001 Cover: 2.50 **NM** value: **Cover or less**
Circ: Diamd. preorders: **15,235**
📖 Flight **A:** Richard Case **W:** Dylan Horrocks

5 ❑ Jun 2001 Cover: 2.50 **NM** value: **Cover or less**
Circ: Diamd. preorders: **15,336**
A: Richard Case **W:** Dylan Horrocks

NAMORA — Timely

1 ❑ Aug 1948 Cover: 0.10 **NM** value: **1500.00**
• **CGC:** 4 graded, best 9.0

2 ❑ Oct 1948 Cover: 0.10 **NM** value: **1000.00**
• **CGC:** 1 graded, best 8.5

3 ❑ Dec 1948 Cover: 0.10 **NM** value: **1000.00**

NAMOR, THE SUB-MARINER — Marvel

This series begins with the whole world believing that Prince Namor, the Sub-Mariner is dead. Namor, who was making a quiet comeback as the wealthy head of Oracle, Inc., preferred not to dispel that illusion. In his new guise as a corporate head, he instead planned to use sunken treasures of the seas to stop threats to both Atlantis and the environment at large.

Written and pencilled by John Byrne, this series marked a new beginning for The Sub-Mariner. Over the years, the short-tempered monarch has matured somewhat, and this maturity made him a more interesting character than ever before.

1 ❑ Apr 1990 Cover: 1.00 **NM** value: **3.00**
Circ: Statement: **208,975** CapCity orders: **60,500** • **CGC:** 4 graded, best 9.6
📖 Purpose! **A:** John Byrne **W:** John Byrne ★ Origin of Sub-Mariner.

2 ❑ May 1990 Cover: 1.00 **NM** value: **2.00**
Circ: Statement: **208,975** CapCity orders: **42,600**
📖 Eagle's Wing And Lion's Claw! **A:** John Byrne **W:** John Byrne

3 ❑ Jun 1990 Cover: 1.00 **NM** value: **2.00**
Circ: Statement: **208,975** CapCity orders: **39,500**
A: John Byrne

4 ❑ Jul 1990 Cover: 1.00 **NM** value: **2.00**
Circ: Statement: **208,975** CapCity orders: **36,900**
A: John Byrne

5 ❑ Aug 1990 Cover: 1.00 **NM** value: **2.00**
Circ: Statement: **208,975** CapCity orders: **36,000**
A: John Byrne

6 ❑ Sep 1990 Cover: 1.00 **NM** value: **1.75**
Circ: Statement: **208,975** CapCity orders: **34,900**
A: John Byrne

7 ❑ Oct 1990 Cover: 1.00 **NM** value: **1.75**
Circ: Statement: **208,975** CapCity orders: **33,400**
A: John Byrne

8 ❑ Nov 1990 Cover: 1.00 **NM** value: **1.75**
Circ: Statement: **208,975** CapCity orders: **32,700**
A: John Byrne

9 ❑ Dec 1990 Cover: 1.00 **NM** value: **1.75**
Circ: Statement: **208,975** CapCity orders: **32,000**
A: John Byrne

10 ❑ Jan 1991 Cover: 1.00 **NM** value: **1.75**
Circ: Statement: **139,002** CapCity orders: **34,800**
A: John Byrne

11 ❑ Feb 1991 Cover: 1.00 **NM** value: **1.75**
Circ: Statement: **139,002** CapCity orders: **32,500**
A: John Byrne

12 ❑ Mar 1991 Cover: 1.00 **NM** value: **2.00**
Circ: Statement: **139,002** CapCity orders: **32,700**
• Giant-size. • Return of The Invaders **A:** John Byrne ★ Appearance of Human Torch, Captain America.

13 ❑ Apr 1991 Cover: 1.00 **NM** value: **1.50**
Circ: Statement: **139,002** CapCity orders: **30,000**
A: John Byrne

14 ❑ May 1991 Cover: 1.00 **NM** value: **1.50**
Circ: Statement: **139,002** CapCity orders: **30,100**
A: John Byrne

15 ❑ Jun 1991 Cover: 1.00 **NM** value: **1.50**
Circ: Statement: **139,002** CapCity orders: **41,400**
• Has 1990 Statement, filed 10/1/90; avg print run 341,637; avg sales 208,775; avg subs 200; avg total paid 208,975; samples 150; office use 600; max existent 209,725; 39% of run returned **A:** John Byrne

16 ❑ Jul 1991 Cover: 1.00 **NM** value: **1.50**
Circ: Statement: **139,002** CapCity orders: **40,800**
A: John Byrne

17 ❑ Aug 1991 Cover: 1.00 **NM** value: **1.50**
Circ: Statement: **139,002** CapCity orders: **42,300**
A: John Byrne

18 ❑ Sep 1991 Cover: 1.00 **NM** value: **1.50**
Circ: Statement: **139,002** CapCity orders: **32,200**
A: John Byrne

19 ❑ Oct 1991 Cover: 1.00 **NM** value: **1.50**
Circ: Statement: **139,002** CapCity orders: **36,800**
A: John Byrne

20 ❑ Nov 1991 Cover: 1.00 **NM** value: **1.50**
Circ: Statement: **139,002** CapCity orders: **30,200**
A: John Byrne

21 ❑ Dec 1991 Cover: 1.00 **NM** value: **1.50**
Circ: Statement: **139,002** CapCity orders: **30,400**
A: John Byrne

22 ❑ Jan 1992 Cover: 1.00 **NM** value: **1.50**
Circ: CapCity orders: **32,100**
A: John Byrne

23 ❑ Feb 1992 Cover: 1.25 **NM** value: **1.50**
Circ: CapCity orders: **29,700**
• Iron Fist returns **A:** John Byrne ★ Appearance of Wolverine.

24 ❑ Mar 1992 Cover: 1.25 **NM** value: **1.50**
Circ: CapCity orders: **43,200**
• Wolverine; Namor fights Wolverine; Has 1991 Statement, filed 10/1/1991; avg print run 228,258; avg sales 137,752; avg subs 1,250; avg total paid 139,002; samples 125; office use 250; max existent 139,877; 39% of run returned **A:** John Byrne

25 ❑ Apr 1992 Cover: 1.25 **NM** value: **1.50**
Circ: CapCity orders: **27,200**
A: John Byrne ★ Appearance of Wolverine.

26 ❑ May 1992 Cover: 1.25 **NM** value: **2.50**
Circ: CapCity orders: **28,600** • **CGC:** 1 graded, best 9.2
• 1st Jae Lee art **A:** Jae Lee

27 ❑ Jun 1992 Cover: 1.25 **NM** value: **2.00**
Circ: CapCity orders: **27,600**
A: Jae Lee

28 ❑ Jul 1992 Cover: 1.25 **NM** value: **2.00**
Circ: CapCity orders: **28,600**
A: Jae Lee ★ Appearance of Iron Fist.

29 ❑ Aug 1992 Cover: 1.25 **NM** value: **2.50**
Circ: CapCity orders: **29,800**
A: Jae Lee

30 ❑ Sep 1992 Cover: 1.25 **NM** value: **2.50**
Circ: CapCity orders: **27,800**
A: Jae Lee

31 ❑ Oct 1992 Cover: 1.25 **NM** value: **2.50**
Circ: CapCity orders: **26,500**
A: Jae Lee

32 ❑ Nov 1992 Cover: 1.25 **NM** value: **2.50**
Circ: CapCity orders: **25,300**
A: Jae Lee

33 ❑ Dec 1992 Cover: 1.25 **NM** value: **2.00**
Circ: CapCity orders: **23,700**

34 ❑ Jan 1993 Cover: 1.25 **NM** value: **2.00**
Circ: CapCity orders: **23,500**

35 ❑ Feb 1993 Cover: 1.25 **NM** value: **2.00**
Circ: CapCity orders: **24,200**

36 ❑ Mar 1993 Cover: 1.25 **NM** value: **2.00**
Circ: CapCity orders: **23,700**
📖 Killing Time **A:** Jae Lee **W:** Bob Harras

37 ❑ Apr 1993 Cover: 2.00 **NM** value: **Cover or less**
Circ: CapCity orders: **69,700**
foil cover.

38 ❑ May 1993 Cover: 1.25 **NM** value: **1.50**
Circ: CapCity orders: **27,500**

39 ❑ Jun 1993 Cover: 1.25 **NM** value: **1.50**
Circ: CapCity orders: **27,000**

40 ❑ Jul 1993 Cover: 1.25 **NM** value: **1.50**

CGC-graded: Multiply prices above by **33 for 9.9 M • 16 for 9.8 NM/M • 7 for 9.6 NM+ • 5 for 9.4 NM • 2.5 for 9.2 NM- • 1.5 for 9.0 VF/NM**

Circ: CapCity orders: **27,600**
41 ❑ Aug 1993 Cover: 1.25 **NM** value: **1.50**
Circ: CapCity orders: **24,700**
42 ❑ Sep 1993 Cover: 1.25 **NM** value: **1.50**
Circ: CapCity orders: **22,000**
★ Appearance of Stingray.
43 ❑ Oct 1993 Cover: 1.25 **NM** value: **1.50**
Circ: CapCity orders: **19,300**
A: M.C. Wyman **W:** Roy Thomas ★ Appearance of Stingray.
44 ❑ Nov 1993 Cover: 1.25 **NM** value: **1.50**
Circ: CapCity orders: **18,900**
C: Geof Isherwood
45 ❑ Dec 1993 Cover: 1.25 **NM** value: **1.50**
Circ: CapCity orders: **17,200**
C: Geof Isherwood
46 ❑ Jan 1994 Cover: 1.25 **NM** value: **1.50**
Circ: Statement: **52,958** CapCity orders: **15,800**
• Starblast **A:** Geof Isherwood
47 ❑ Feb 1994 Cover: 1.25 **NM** value: **1.50**
Circ: Statement: **52,958** CapCity orders: **15,700**
Starblast, Part 5 • Starblast **A:** Geof Isherwood
48 ❑ Mar 1994 Cover: 1.25 **NM** value: **1.50**
Circ: Statement: **52,958** CapCity orders: **14,450**
Starblast, Part 9 • Starblast **A:** Geof Isherwood
49 ❑ Apr 1994 Cover: 1.25 **NM** value: **1.50**
Circ: Statement: **52,958** CapCity orders: **12,600**
50 ❑ May 1994 Cover: 1.75 **NM** value: **2.25**
Circ: Statement: **52,958**
• Giant-size.
50/SC❑May 1994 Cover: 2.95 **NM** value: **3.00**
Circ: CapCity orders: **24,300**
foil cover. • Giant-size.
51 ❑ Jun 1994 Cover: 1.75 **NM** value: **Cover or less**
Circ: Statement: **52,958** CapCity orders: **14,550**
52 ❑ Jul 1994 Cover: 1.50 **NM** value: **Cover or less**
Circ: Statement: **52,958** CapCity orders: **13,500**
53 ❑ Aug 1994 Cover: 1.50 **NM** value: **Cover or less**
Circ: Statement: **52,958** CapCity orders: **13,100**
54 ❑ Sep 1994 Cover: 1.50 **NM** value: **Cover or less**
Circ: Statement: **52,958** CapCity orders: **12,100**
★ 1st Appearance of Llyron.
55 ❑ Oct 1994 Cover: 1.50 **NM** value: **Cover or less**
Circ: Statement: **52,958** CapCity orders: **10,650**
56 ❑ Nov 1994 Cover: 1.50 **NM** value: **Cover or less**
Circ: Statement: **52,958** CapCity orders: **9,850**
57 ❑ Dec 1994 Cover: 1.50 **NM** value: **Cover or less**
Circ: Statement: **52,958** CapCity orders: **9,600**
58 ❑ Jan 1995 Cover: 1.50 **NM** value: **Cover or less**
Circ: CapCity orders: **8,750**
★ Versus Avengers.
59 ❑ Feb 1995 Cover: 1.95 **NM** value: **Cover or less**
Circ: CapCity orders: **8,125**
60 ❑ Mar 1995 Cover: 1.95 **NM** value: **Cover or less**
Circ: CapCity orders: **7,350**
• Has 1994 Statement, filed 10/1/94; avg print run 53,583; avg sales 52,292; avg subs 667; avg total paid 52,958; samples 125; office use 500; max existent 53,584; no newsstand sales this year
61 ❑ Apr 1995 Cover: 1.50 **NM** value: **Cover or less**
Circ: CapCity orders: **7,475**
Atlantis Rising, Part 1
62 ❑ May 1995 Cover: 1.50 **NM** value: **Cover or less**
Circ: CapCity orders: **7,250**
final issue.
Anl 1❑ca. 1991 Cover: 2.00 **NM** value: **Cover or less**
Circ: CapCity orders: **39,100**
Subterranean Wars, Part 5; The Origin of Namor, the Sub-Mariner; The Potsdam Objective; Day of Reckoning **W:** Scott Lobdell ★ Origin of Namor.
Anl 2❑ca. 1992 Cover: 2.25 **NM** value: **Cover or less**
Circ: CapCity orders: **2,700**
Return of the Defenders, Part 3 • Defenders
Anl 3❑ca. 1993 Cover: 2.95 **NM** value: **Cover or less**
Circ: CapCity orders: **37,600**
Anl 4❑ca. 1994 Cover: 2.95 **NM** value: **Cover or less**
Circ: CapCity orders: **9,650**

NANCY AND SLUGGO (ST. JOHN) — St. John

Feisty young troublemaker Nancy, her hapless pal Sluggo, Aunt Fritzi, and Oona Goosepimple are familiar to readers of Sunday comics pages in newspapers around the world, and were featured in their own Dell comic books periodically during the 1950s and '60s. Ernie Bushmiller's compulsively simple drawing style perfectly matches the silly, kid-oriented humor of Nancy and Sluggo and can sustain interest equally well in a four-panel Sunday strip or an eight-page comic story.

Nancy actually began as part of the Fritzi Ritz newspaper strip cast, taking over the series just a few years after she appeared and delegating Fritzi to a background role. In the comics, the group's gag adventures appeared in United, Tip Top, and Sparkler Comics (which this series picks up the numbering from), among other titles.

121❑ Jun 1955 Cover: 0.10 **NM** value: **18.00**
• Series continued from Sparkler Comics #120
122❑ Jul 1955 Cover: 0.10 **NM** value: **12.00**
123❑ Aug 1955 Cover: 0.10 **NM** value: **12.00**
124❑ Sep 1955 Cover: 0.10 **NM** value: **12.00**
125❑ Oct 1955 Cover: 0.10 **NM** value: **12.00**
126❑ Nov 1955 Cover: 0.10 **NM** value: **12.00**
127❑ Dec 1955 Cover: 0.10 **NM** value: **12.00**
128❑ Jan 1956 Cover: 0.10 **NM** value: **12.00**
129❑ Feb 1956 Cover: 0.10 **NM** value: **12.00**
130❑ Mar 1956 Cover: 0.10 **NM** value: **12.00**
131❑ Apr 1956 Cover: 0.10 **NM** value: **10.00**
132❑ May 1956 Cover: 0.10 **NM** value: **10.00**
133❑ Jun 1956 Cover: 0.10 **NM** value: **10.00**
134❑ Jul 1956 Cover: 0.10 **NM** value: **10.00**
135❑ Aug 1956 Cover: 0.10 **NM** value: **10.00**
136❑ Sep 1956 Cover: 0.10 **NM** value: **10.00**
137❑ Oct 1956 Cover: 0.10 **NM** value: **10.00**
138❑ Nov 1956 Cover: 0.10 **NM** value: **10.00**
139❑ Dec 1956 Cover: 0.10 **NM** value: **10.00**
140❑ Jan 1957 Cover: 0.10 **NM** value: **10.00**
141❑ Feb 1957 Cover: 0.10 **NM** value: **10.00**
142❑ Mar 1957 Cover: 0.10 **NM** value: **10.00**
143❑ Apr 1957 Cover: 0.10 **NM** value: **10.00**
144❑ May 1957 Cover: 0.10 **NM** value: **10.00**
145❑ Jul 1957 Cover: 0.10 **NM** value: **10.00**

NANCY AND SLUGGO (DELL) — Dell

146❑ Sep 1957 Cover: 0.10 **NM** value: **20.00**
• Dell begins as publisher
147❑ Oct 1957 Cover: 0.10 **NM** value: **8.00**
148❑ Nov 1957 Cover: 0.10 **NM** value: **8.00**
149❑ Dec 1957 Cover: 0.10 **NM** value: **8.00**
150❑ Jan 1958 Cover: 0.10 **NM** value: **8.00**
151❑ Feb 1958 Cover: 0.10 **NM** value: **8.00**
152❑ Mar 1958 Cover: 0.10 **NM** value: **8.00**
153❑ Apr 1958 Cover: 0.10 **NM** value: **8.00**
154❑ May 1958 Cover: 0.10 **NM** value: **8.00**
155❑ Jun 1958 Cover: 0.10 **NM** value: **8.00**
156❑ Jul 1958 Cover: 0.10 **NM** value: **8.00**
157❑ Aug 1958 Cover: 0.10 **NM** value: **8.00**
158❑ Sep 1958 Cover: 0.10 **NM** value: **8.00**
159❑ Oct 1958 Cover: 0.10 **NM** value: **8.00**
160❑ Nov 1958 Cover: 0.10 **NM** value: **8.00**
161❑ Dec 1958 Cover: 0.10 **NM** value: **8.00**
162❑ Jan 1959 Cover: 0.10 **NM** value: **8.00**
163❑ Feb 1959 Cover: 0.10 **NM** value: **8.00**
164❑ Mar 1959 Cover: 0.10 **NM** value: **8.00**
165❑ Apr 1959 Cover: 0.10 **NM** value: **8.00**
166❑ May 1959 Cover: 0.10 **NM** value: **8.00**
167❑ Jun 1959 Cover: 0.10 **NM** value: **8.00**
168❑ Jul 1959 Cover: 0.10 **NM** value: **8.00**
169❑ Aug 1959 Cover: 0.10 **NM** value: **8.00**
170❑ Sep 1959 Cover: 0.10 **NM** value: **8.00**
171❑ Oct 1959 Cover: 0.10 **NM** value: **8.00**
172❑ Nov 1959 Cover: 0.10 **NM** value: **8.00**
173❑ Dec 1959 Cover: 0.10 **NM** value: **8.00**
174❑ Jan 1960 Cover: 0.10 **NM** value: **8.00**
175❑ Mar 1960 Cover: 0.10 **NM** value: **8.00**
176❑ May 1960 Cover: 0.10 **NM** value: **8.00**
177❑ Jul 1960 Cover: 0.10 **NM** value: **8.00**
178❑ Sep 1960 Cover: 0.10 **NM** value: **8.00**
179❑ Nov 1960 Cover: 0.10 **NM** value: **8.00**
180❑ Feb 1961 Cover: 0.10 **NM** value: **8.00**
181❑ Apr 1961 Cover: 0.10 **NM** value: **8.00**
182❑ Jun 1961 Cover: 0.10 **NM** value: **8.00**
183❑ Aug 1961 Cover: 0.10 **NM** value: **8.00**
184❑ Oct 1961 Cover: 0.10 **NM** value: **8.00**
185❑ Dec 1961 Cover: 0.10 **NM** value: **8.00**
186❑ Feb 1962 Cover: 0.10 **NM** value: **8.00**
187❑ Apr 1962 Cover: 0.10 **NM** value: **8.00**
• Gold Key begins as publisher

NANCY AND SLUGGO — Gold Key

188❑ 1962 Cover: 0.12 **NM** value: **8.00**
189❑ 1962 Cover: 0.12 **NM** value: **8.00**
190❑ 1963 Cover: 0.12 **NM** value: **8.00**
191❑ Jul 1963 Cover: 0.12 **NM** value: **8.00**
192❑ 1963 Cover: 0.12 **NM** value: **8.00**
It's No Picnic; The Treasure Hunt; Peanuts: Astronomical Error; Caught In The Act; Camp Rollo; Visitor's Day; She Loves Me final issue. • Summer Camp **A:** Ernie Bushmiller **W:** Ernie Bushmiller

NANCY AND SLUGGO TRAVEL TIME — Dell

1 ❑ Sep 1958 Cover: 0.25 **NM** value: **80.00**
• **CGC:** 1 graded, best 9.2

NANCY DREAMS & SCHEMES — Kitchen Sink

Bk 1❑ Cover: 7.95 **NM** value: **Cover or less**

NANCY EATS FOOD — Kitchen Sink

Bk 1❑ Cover: 7.95 **NM** value: **Cover or less**

NANNY AND THE PROFESSOR — Dell

1 ❑ Aug 1970 Cover: 0.15 **NM** value: **14.00**
Photo cover. • based on TV show
2 ❑ Oct 1970 Cover: 0.15 **NM** value: **9.00**

NANOSOUP — Millennium

1 ❑ b&w Cover: 2.95 **NM** value: **Cover or less**
wraparound cover.

NAPOLEON & UNCLE ELBY — Eastern

1 ❑ ca. 1942 Cover: 0.10 **NM** value: **200.00**

NARCOLEPSY DREAMS — Slave Labor

1 ❑ Feb 1995 Cover: 2.95 **NM** value: **Cover or less**
Big; Up and Down Career; Hell Bent, Heaven Sent **A:** Jaime Crespo **W:** Jaime Crespo
2 ❑ Aug 1995 Cover: 2.95 **NM** value: **Cover or less**
1973; Shakeytown; Time; El Brujo; The Big Scam; I Hate Long Goodbyes **A:** Jaime Crespo **W:** Jaime Crespo

NARD N' PAT — Cartoonists' Co-Op Press

1 ❑ b&w Cover: 0.50 **NM** value: **3.00**
A: Jay Lynch

NARRATIVE ILLUSTRATION — E.C.

1 ❑ Sum 1942 **NM** value: **1000.00**
• **CGC:** 2 graded, best 4.5

NASCAR ADVENTURES — Vortex

1 ❑ 1992 Cover: 2.00 **NM** value: **2.95**
regular cover. Welcome Back Fred; Outpost: Apocalypse • Fred Lorenzen **A:** Don Heck; Marat Mychaels **W:** Marat Mychaels; Ben White; Kevin Nash
2 ❑ 1992 Cover: 2.00 **NM** value: **2.50**
• Richard Petty
5 ❑ 1992 Cover: 2.00 **NM** value: **2.50**
• Ernie Irvan
7 ❑ 1992 Cover: 2.00 **NM** value: **2.50**
A: Mark Martin

NASH — Image

1 ❑ Jul 1999 Cover: 2.95 **NM** value: **Cover or less**
Circ: Diamd. preorders: **21,272**
regular cover.
1/A ❑ Jul 1999 Cover: 2.95 **NM** value: **Cover or less**
Circ: Diamd. preorders: **2,418**
Photo cover. Outpost: Apocalypse **A:** Marat Mychaels **W:** Marat Mychaels; Kevin Nash
1/B ❑ Jul 1999 Cover: 2.95 **NM** value: **Cover or less**
no cover price. Outpost: Apocalypse **A:** Marat Mychaels **W:** Marat Mychaels; Kevin Nash
2 ❑ Jul 1999 Cover: 2.95 **NM** value: **Cover or less**
Circ: Diamd. preorders: **14,485**
regular cover. **A:** Marat Mychaels **W:** Marat Mychaels; Kevin Nash
2/A ❑ Jul 1999 Cover: 2.95 **NM** value: **Cover or less**
Photo cover.
Ash 1❑Jul 1999 Cover: 2.50 **NM** value: **Cover or less**
Circ: Diamd. preorders: **15,465**
regular cover. • Preview Book **A:** Marat Mychaels **W:** Kevin Nash
Ash 1/SC❑Jul 1999 Cover: 2.50 **NM** value: **Cover or less**
Photo cover.

NASTI: MONSTER HUNTER — Schism

1 ❑ b&w Cover: 2.50 **NM** value: **Cover or less**
Don't Go Changin'...Just Die! **A:** Mike Pascale **W:** Mike Pascale ★ 1st Appearance of Nasti.
1/Aut❑ Cover: 2.50 **NM** value: **3.00**
Don't Go Changin'...Just Die! **A:** Mike Pascale **W:** Mike Pascale ★ 1st Appearance of Nasti.
2 ❑ b&w Cover: 2.50 **NM** value: **Cover or less**
You Must Be... **A:** Mike Pascale **W:** Mike Pascale
3 ❑ b&w Cover: 2.50 **NM** value: **Cover or less**
Organized Chaos; Bru-Hed: Fast Food for Thought; Bru-Hed: The Brainy Approach; Bru-Hed: Mama! May I?; Bru-Hed: The Build-Up **A:** Mike Pascale **W:** Mike Pascale
Ash 1/LE❑b&w **NM** value: **1.00**
No issue number. no cover price. • preview of upcoming comic book on newsprint **A:** Mike Pascale **W:** Mike Pascale

NATHANIEL DUSK — DC

1 ❑ Feb 1984 Cover: 1.25 **NM** value: **1.50**
Lovers Die At Dusk, Part 1 **A:** Gene Colan **W:** Don McGregor ★ 1st Appearance of Nathaniel Dusk.
2 ❑ Mar 1984 Cover: 1.25 **NM** value: **1.50**
Lovers Die at Dusk, Part 2 **A:** Gene Colan **W:** Don McGregor
3 ❑ Apr 1984 Cover: 1.25 **NM** value: **1.50**
A: Gene Colan **W:** Don McGregor
4 ❑ May 1984 Cover: 1.25 **NM** value: **1.50**
A: Gene Colan **W:** Don McGregor

NATHANIEL DUSK II — DC

1 ❑ Oct 1985 Cover: 2.00 **NM** value: **Cover or less**
Circ: CapCity orders: **6,750**
A: Gene Colan
2 ❑ Nov 1985 Cover: 2.00 **NM** value: **Cover or less**
Circ: CapCity orders: **5,600**
A: Gene Colan
3 ❑ Dec 1985 Cover: 2.00 **NM** value: **Cover or less**
Circ: CapCity orders: **5,050**
A: Gene Colan
4 ❑ Jan 1986 Cover: 2.00 **NM** value: **Cover or less**
Circ: CapCity orders: **4,900**
A: Gene Colan

NATHAN NEVER — Dark Horse

1 ❑ Mar 1999 Cover: 4.95 **NM** value: **Cover or less**
Circ: Diamd. preorders: **6,783**
A: Nicola Mari **W:** Michelle Medda
2 ❑ Apr 1999 Cover: 4.95 **NM** value: **Cover or less**
Circ: Diamd. preorders: **5,401**
A: Nicola Mari **W:** Michelle Medda
3 ❑ May 1999 Cover: 4.95 **NM** value: **Cover or less**
Circ: Diamd. preorders: **4,293**
A: Nicola Mari **W:** Michelle Medda
4 ❑ Jun 1999 Cover: 4.95 **NM** value: **Cover or less**
Circ: Diamd. preorders: **3,967**
A: Nicola Mari **W:** Michelle Medda
5 ❑ Jul 1999 Cover: 4.95 **NM** value: **Cover or less**
Circ: Diamd. preorders: **3,848**
A: Nicola Mari **W:** Michelle Medda
6 ❑ Aug 1999 Cover: 4.95 **NM** value: **Cover or less**
Circ: Diamd. preorders: **3,685**
A: Nicola Mari **W:** Michelle Medda

Other grades: Multiply prices above by **1.5 for Mint • 2/3 for Very Fine • 1/3 for Fine • 1/5 for Very Good • 1/8 for Good**

NATIONAL COMICS — Quality

Begun in 1940, National Comics was published by Quality under its Comic Magazines imprint. Each giant-sized issue packed in a wide variety of features, from gag strips like "Salty Waters" and "Windy Breeze" to crime adventures starring Steve Wood or Sally O'Neil, Policewoman.

National Comics is best remembered today, however, for introducing the comic super-hero Uncle Sam. Looking exactly like the figure in the army recruiting ads, this character had such abilities as super-strength and the power to see into the future. He used these abilities to battle enemies of liberty everywhere, particularly the Axis forces in World War II. Following Quality's demise as a publisher, Uncle Sam would move over to DC where he would eventually become a member of the Freedom Fighters.

2 ❑ Aug 1940 Cover: 0.10 **NM** value: **1650.00**
• **CGC:** 1 graded, best 2.5
A: Will Eisner
3 ❑ Sep 1940 Cover: 0.10 **NM** value: **1200.00**
A: Will Eisner
4 ❑ Oct 1940 Cover: 0.10 **NM** value: **925.00**
• **CGC:** 1 graded, best 4.5
5 ❑ Nov 1940 Cover: 0.10 **NM** value: **1075.00**
• **CGC:** 2 graded, best 7.0
★ Origin of Uncle Sam.
6 ❑ Dec 1940 Cover: 0.10 **NM** value: **940.00**
7 ❑ Jan 1941 Cover: 0.10 **NM** value: **940.00**
• **CGC:** 1 graded, best 5.0
8 ❑ Feb 1941 Cover: 0.10 **NM** value: **940.00**
9 ❑ Mar 1941 Cover: 0.10 **NM** value: **940.00**
• **CGC:** 1 graded, best 7.0
10 ❑ Apr 1941 Cover: 0.10 **NM** value: **940.00**
11 ❑ May 1941 Cover: 0.10 **NM** value: **940.00**
• **CGC:** 1 graded, best 8.5
12 ❑ Jun 1941 Cover: 0.10 **NM** value: **650.00**
13 ❑ Jul 1941 Cover: 0.10 **NM** value: **685.00**
• **CGC:** 1 graded, best 8.5
A: Lou Fine
14 ❑ Aug 1941 Cover: 0.10 **NM** value: **685.00**
A: Lou Fine
15 ❑ Sep 1941 Cover: 0.10 **NM** value: **685.00**
A: Lou Fine
16 ❑ Oct 1941 Cover: 0.10 **NM** value: **685.00**
A: Lou Fine
17 ❑ Nov 1941 Cover: 0.10 **NM** value: **525.00**
• **CGC:** 1 graded, best 6.0
18 ❑ Dec 1941 Cover: 0.10 **NM** value: **760.00**
• **CGC:** 1 graded, best 9.2
Pre-Pearl Harbor Japanese attack cover.
19 ❑ Jan 1942 Cover: 0.10 **NM** value: **525.00**
20 ❑ Feb 1942 Cover: 0.10 **NM** value: **525.00**
21 ❑ Feb 1942 Cover: 0.10 **NM** value: **525.00**
22 ❑ Apr 1942 Cover: 0.10 **NM** value: **525.00**
23 ❑ Jun 1942 Cover: 0.10 **NM** value: **525.00**
• **CGC:** 1 graded, best 7.5
24 ❑ Aug 1942 Cover: 0.10 **NM** value: **365.00**
25 ❑ Oct 1942 Cover: 0.10 **NM** value: **365.00**
26 ❑ Nov 1942 Cover: 0.10 **NM** value: **365.00**
• **CGC:** 2 graded, best 9.6
27 ❑ Dec 1942 Cover: 0.10 **NM** value: **365.00**
• **CGC:** 1 graded, best 9.6
28 ❑ Jan 1943 Cover: 0.10 **NM** value: **365.00**
• **CGC:** 3 graded, best 9.6
29 ❑ Feb 1943 Cover: 0.10 **NM** value: **365.00**
• **CGC:** 1 graded, best 9.6
★ Origin of The Unknown.
30 ❑ Mar 1943 Cover: 0.10 **NM** value: **365.00**
31 ❑ Apr 1943 Cover: 0.10 **NM** value: **320.00**
32 ❑ May 1943 Cover: 0.10 **NM** value: **320.00**
• **CGC:** 2 graded, best 6.0
33 ❑ Jun 1943 Cover: 0.10 **NM** value: **320.00**
• **CGC:** 1 graded, best 6.0
34 ❑ Aug 1943 Cover: 0.10 **NM** value: **320.00**
35 ❑ Sep 1943 Cover: 0.10 **NM** value: **240.00**
36 ❑ Oct 1943 Cover: 0.10 **NM** value: **240.00**
37 ❑ Nov 1943 Cover: 0.10 **NM** value: **240.00**
38 ❑ Jan 1944 Cover: 0.10 **NM** value: **240.00**
39 ❑ Feb 1944 Cover: 0.10 **NM** value: **265.00**
• **CGC:** 1 graded, best 8.5
Hitler cover.
40 ❑ Mar 1944 Cover: 0.10 **NM** value: **160.00**
• **CGC:** 1 graded, best 9.4
41 ❑ Apr 1944 Cover: 0.10 **NM** value: **160.00**
42 ❑ May 1944 Cover: 0.10 **NM** value: **160.00**
• **CGC:** 1 graded, best 9.4
43 ❑ Aug 1944 Cover: 0.10 **NM** value: **160.00**
• **CGC:** 1 graded, best 9.2
44 ❑ Oct 1944 Cover: 0.10 **NM** value: **160.00**
• **CGC:** 1 graded, best 7.0
45 ❑ Dec 1944 Cover: 0.10 **NM** value: **160.00**
46 ❑ Feb 1945 Cover: 0.10 **NM** value: **160.00**
• **CGC:** 1 graded, best 9.0
47 ❑ Apr 1945 Cover: 0.10 **NM** value: **160.00**
48 ❑ Jun 1945 Cover: 0.10 **NM** value: **160.00**
• **CGC:** 1 graded, best 8.0
49 ❑ Aug 1945 Cover: 0.10 **NM** value: **160.00**
50 ❑ Oct 1945 Cover: 0.10 **NM** value: **160.00**
51 ❑ Dec 1945 Cover: 0.10 **NM** value: **210.00**
• **CGC:** 1 graded, best 9.2
• Sally O'Neil, Policewoman
52 ❑ Feb 1946 Cover: 0.10 **NM** value: **110.00**
53 ❑ Apr 1946 Cover: 0.10 **NM** value: **110.00**
• **CGC:** 2 graded, best 9.2
54 ❑ Jun 1946 Cover: 0.10 **NM** value: **110.00**
55 ❑ Aug 1946 Cover: 0.10 **NM** value: **110.00**
56 ❑ Oct 1946 Cover: 0.10 **NM** value: **110.00**
57 ❑ Dec 1946 Cover: 0.10 **NM** value: **110.00**
58 ❑ Feb 1947 Cover: 0.10 **NM** value: **110.00**
59 ❑ Apr 1947 Cover: 0.10 **NM** value: **110.00**
60 ❑ Jun 1947 Cover: 0.10 **NM** value: **110.00**
61 ❑ Aug 1947 Cover: 0.10 **NM** value: **90.00**
62 ❑ Oct 1947 Cover: 0.10 **NM** value: **90.00**
63 ❑ Dec 1947 Cover: 0.10 **NM** value: **90.00**
64 ❑ Feb 1948 Cover: 0.10 **NM** value: **90.00**
65 ❑ Apr 1948 Cover: 0.10 **NM** value: **90.00**
66 ❑ Jun 1948 Cover: 0.10 **NM** value: **90.00**
67 ❑ Aug 1948 Cover: 0.10 **NM** value: **90.00**
68 ❑ Oct 1948 Cover: 0.10 **NM** value: **90.00**
69 ❑ Dec 1948 Cover: 0.10 **NM** value: **90.00**
70 ❑ Feb 1949 Cover: 0.10 **NM** value: **90.00**
71 ❑ Apr 1949 Cover: 0.10 **NM** value: **70.00**
72 ❑ Jun 1949 Cover: 0.10 **NM** value: **70.00**
73 ❑ Aug 1949 Cover: 0.10 **NM** value: **70.00**
74 ❑ Oct 1949 Cover: 0.10 **NM** value: **70.00**
75 ❑ Dec 1949 Cover: 0.10 **NM** value: **70.00**
final issue.

NATIONAL COMICS (2ND SERIES) — DC

1 ❑ May 1999 Cover: 1.99 **NM** value: **2.00**
Circ: Diamd. preorders: **43,377**
📖 Fair Play • Justice Society Returns **A:** Aaron Lopresti **W:** Mark Waid ★ Appearance of Flash, Mr. Terrific.

NATIONAL LAMPOON PRESENTS: FRENCH COMICS (THE KIND MEN LIKE) — National Lampoon

1 ❑ Cover: 2.50 **NM** value: **5.00**

NATION OF SNITCHES, A — DC / Piranha

1 ❑ Cover: 4.95 **NM** value: **Cover or less**
Circ: CapCity orders: **2,100**
No issue number. One-shot.

NATURAL INQUIRER — Fantagraphics

1 ❑ b&w Cover: 2.00 **NM** value: **Cover or less**

NATURAL SELECTION, THE — Atom

1 ❑ Jan 1998, b&w Cover: 2.95 **NM** value: **Cover or less**
2 ❑ Feb 1998, b&w Cover: 2.95 **NM** value: **Cover or less**

NATURE OF THE BEAST — Caliber

1 ❑ b&w Cover: 2.95 **NM** value: **Cover or less**
2 ❑ b&w Cover: 2.95 **NM** value: **Cover or less**

NAUGHTY BITS — Fantagraphics

Alternative cartoonist Roberta Gregory takes on all comers with this daring quarterly. Make no mistake, Naughty Bits can be downright shocking at times. Gregory tackles religion, sex, smut comics, and just about any other controversial topic you can think of. She even takes to task Robert Crumb, grand hero of the underground comix scene, for the role women have played in his books.

For all this, Naughty Bits can be a very funny book. Particularly humorous are the ongoing escapades of "Bitchy Butch," a super-nasty lesbian who takes negative thinking to the extreme. For as much as she tortures other people, it's a riot to watch her contend with dating, disagreeable church services, and other hazards of modern life.

1 ❑ Mar 1991 Cover: 2.00 **NM** value: **7.00**
A: Roberta Gregory **W:** Roberta Gregory
1-2 ❑ Cover: 2.00 **NM** value: **2.50**
2 ❑ 1991 Cover: 2.00 **NM** value: **5.00**
A: Roberta Gregory **W:** Roberta Gregory
3 ❑ Cover: 2.00 **NM** value: **4.00**
A: Roberta Gregory **W:** Roberta Gregory
4 ❑ Cover: 2.00 **NM** value: **3.75**
A: Roberta Gregory **W:** Roberta Gregory
5 ❑ Cover: 2.00 **NM** value: **3.75**
A: Roberta Gregory **W:** Roberta Gregory
6 ❑ Aug 1992 Cover: 2.50 **NM** value: **3.00**
A: Roberta Gregory **W:** Roberta Gregory
7 ❑ Cover: 2.50 **NM** value: **3.00**
A: Roberta Gregory **W:** Roberta Gregory
8 ❑ Cover: 2.50 **NM** value: **3.00**
A: Roberta Gregory **W:** Roberta Gregory
9 ❑ Cover: 2.50 **NM** value: **3.00**
A: Roberta Gregory **W:** Roberta Gregory
10 ❑ Cover: 2.50 **NM** value: **3.00**
A: Roberta Gregory **W:** Roberta Gregory
11 ❑ Jan 1994 Cover: 2.50 **NM** value: **Cover or less**
A: Roberta Gregory **W:** Roberta Gregory
12 ❑ Apr 1994 Cover: 2.50 **NM** value: **Cover or less**
A: Roberta Gregory **W:** Roberta Gregory
13 ❑ Jul 1994 Cover: 2.50 **NM** value: **2.95**
A: Roberta Gregory **W:** Roberta Gregory
14 ❑ Oct 1994 Cover: 2.50 **NM** value: **2.95**
A: Roberta Gregory **W:** Roberta Gregory
15 ❑ Feb 1995 Cover: 2.50 **NM** value: **2.95**
A: Roberta Gregory **W:** Roberta Gregory
16 ❑ Cover: 2.50 **NM** value: **2.95**
A: Roberta Gregory **W:** Roberta Gregory
17 ❑ Cover: 2.50 **NM** value: **2.95**
A: Roberta Gregory **W:** Roberta Gregory
18 ❑ Jan 1996 Cover: 2.95 **NM** value: **Cover or less**
A: Roberta Gregory **W:** Roberta Gregory
19 ❑ Cover: 2.95 **NM** value: **Cover or less**
A: Roberta Gregory **W:** Roberta Gregory
20 ❑ Aug 1996 Cover: 2.95 **NM** value: **Cover or less**
A: Roberta Gregory **W:** Roberta Gregory
21 ❑ Nov 1996 Cover: 2.95 **NM** value: **Cover or less**
Circ: Diamd. preorders: **3,266**
📖 Bitchy Bitch & Bitsy Bitch: Fallout; Bitchy Butch: That Time of the Year; New Hire; Talking to Mom **A:** Marc Campos; Roberta Gregory **W:** Marc Campos; Roberta Gregory
22 ❑ Mar 1997 Cover: 2.95 **NM** value: **Cover or less**
Circ: Diamd. preorders: **2,841**
23 ❑ Jun 1997 Cover: 2.95 **NM** value: **Cover or less**
29 ❑ Jul 1999 Cover: 2.95 **NM** value: **Cover or less**
Circ: Diamd. preorders: **1,924**
Bk 1❑ Cover: 9.95 **NM** value: **Cover or less**
• A Bitch is Born **A:** Roberta Gregory **W:** Roberta Gregory
Bk 2❑ Cover: 9.95 **NM** value: **Cover or less**
• Naughty as She Wants to Be **A:** Roberta Gregory **W:** Roberta Gregory
Bk 3❑ Cover: 9.95 **NM** value: **Cover or less**
• At Work and Play with Bitchy Bitch **A:** Roberta Gregory **W:** Roberta Gregory

NÄU HEADHUNTER — Neotek Iconography

1 ❑ Cover: 2.50 **NM** value: **Cover or less**
A: Cary Polkovitz **W:** Cary Polkovitz

NAUSICAÄ OF THE VALLEY OF WIND PART 1 — Viz

1 ❑ Cover: 3.25 **NM** value: **Cover or less**
Circ: CapCity orders: **4,225**
A: Hayao Miyazaki **W:** Hayao Miyazaki
2 ❑ Cover: 3.25 **NM** value: **Cover or less**
Circ: CapCity orders: **3,425**
A: Hayao Miyazaki **W:** Hayao Miyazaki
3 ❑ Cover: 3.25 **NM** value: **Cover or less**
Circ: CapCity orders: **3,075**
A: Hayao Miyazaki **W:** Hayao Miyazaki
4 ❑ Cover: 3.25 **NM** value: **Cover or less**
A: Hayao Miyazaki **W:** Hayao Miyazaki
5 ❑ Cover: 3.25 **NM** value: **Cover or less**
A: Hayao Miyazaki **W:** Hayao Miyazaki
6 ❑ Cover: 3.25 **NM** value: **Cover or less**
A: Hayao Miyazaki **W:** Hayao Miyazaki
7 ❑ Cover: 3.25 **NM** value: **Cover or less**
A: Hayao Miyazaki **W:** Hayao Miyazaki
Bk 1❑ Cover: 13.95 **NM** value: **Cover or less**
Bk 2❑ Cover: 13.95 **NM** value: **Cover or less**

NAUSICAÄ OF THE VALLEY OF WIND PART 2 — Viz

1 ❑ Cover: 2.95 **NM** value: **Cover or less**
A: Hayao Miyazaki **W:** Hayao Miyazaki
2 ❑ Cover: 2.95 **NM** value: **Cover or less**
A: Hayao Miyazaki **W:** Hayao Miyazaki
3 ❑ Cover: 2.95 **NM** value: **Cover or less**
A: Hayao Miyazaki **W:** Hayao Miyazaki
4 ❑ Cover: 3.25 **NM** value: **Cover or less**
A: Hayao Miyazaki **W:** Hayao Miyazaki
Bk 3❑ Cover: 13.95 **NM** value: **Cover or less**

NAUSICAÄ OF THE VALLEY OF WIND PART 3 — Viz

1 ❑ Cover: 3.95 **NM** value: **Cover or less**
Circ: CapCity orders: **4,075**
A: Hayao Miyazaki **W:** Hayao Miyazaki
2 ❑ Cover: 3.95 **NM** value: **Cover or less**
Circ: CapCity orders: **3,675**
A: Hayao Miyazaki **W:** Hayao Miyazaki
3 ❑ Cover: 3.95 **NM** value: **Cover or less**
Circ: CapCity orders: **3,600**
A: Hayao Miyazaki **W:** Hayao Miyazaki
Bk 4❑ Cover: 13.95 **NM** value: **Cover or less**

NAUSICAÄ OF THE VALLEY OF WIND PART 4 — Viz

1 ❑ Cover: 2.75 **NM** value: **Cover or less**
Circ: CapCity orders: **4,750**
A: Hayao Miyazaki **W:** Hayao Miyazaki
2 ❑ Cover: 2.75 **NM** value: **Cover or less**
Circ: CapCity orders: **4,250**
A: Hayao Miyazaki **W:** Hayao Miyazaki
3 ❑ Cover: 2.75 **NM** value: **Cover or less**
Circ: CapCity orders: **4,050**
A: Hayao Miyazaki **W:** Hayao Miyazaki
4 ❑ Cover: 2.75 **NM** value: **Cover or less**
Circ: CapCity orders: **3,825**
A: Hayao Miyazaki **W:** Hayao Miyazaki
5 ❑ Cover: 2.75 **NM** value: **Cover or less**
Circ: CapCity orders: **3,775**
A: Hayao Miyazaki **W:** Hayao Miyazaki
6 ❑ Cover: 2.75 **NM** value: **Cover or less**
A: Hayao Miyazaki **W:** Hayao Miyazaki
Bk 5❑ May 1995 Cover: 15.95 **NM** value: **Cover or less**

NAUSICAÄ OF THE VALLEY OF WIND PART 5 — Viz

1 ❑ Cover: 2.75 **NM** value: **Cover or less**
A: Hayao Miyazaki **W:** Hayao Miyazaki
2 ❑ Cover: 2.75 **NM** value: **Cover or less**
A: Hayao Miyazaki **W:** Hayao Miyazaki
3 ❑ Cover: 2.75 **NM** value: **Cover or less**
A: Hayao Miyazaki **W:** Hayao Miyazaki
4 ❑ Cover: 2.75 **NM** value: **Cover or less**
A: Hayao Miyazaki **W:** Hayao Miyazaki
5 ❑ Cover: 2.75 **NM** value: **Cover or less**
A: Hayao Miyazaki **W:** Hayao Miyazaki

CGC-graded: Multiply prices above by **33 for 9.9 M • 16 for 9.8 NM/M • 7 for 9.6 NM+ • 5 for 9.4 NM • 2.5 for 9.2 NM- • 1.5 for 9.0 VF/NM**

6 ❑ Cover: 2.75 NM value: Cover or less
A: Hayao Miyazaki W: Hayao Miyazaki
7 ❑ Cover: 2.95 NM value: Cover or less
A: Hayao Miyazaki W: Hayao Miyazaki
8 ❑ Cover: 2.95 NM value: Cover or less
A: Hayao Miyazaki W: Hayao Miyazaki
Bk 6❑ May 1995 Cover: 15.95 NM value: Cover or less
Bk 7❑ Cover: 16.95 NM value: Cover or less

NAUSICAÄ OF THE VALLEY OF WIND PERFECT COLLECTION — Viz

Bk 1❑ Cover: 17.95 NM value: Cover or less
Bk 2❑ Cover: 17.95 NM value: Cover or less
Bk 3❑ Cover: 17.95 NM value: Cover or less
Bk 4❑ Cover: 17.95 NM value: Cover or less

NAUTILUS — Shanda Fantasy Arts

1 ❑ May 1999, b&w Cover: 2.95 NM value: Cover or less

NAVY ACTION — Atlas

1 ❑ Aug 1954 Cover: 0.10 NM value: 50.00
2 ❑ Oct 1954 Cover: 0.10 NM value: 30.00
3 ❑ Dec 1954 Cover: 0.10 NM value: 30.00
4 ❑ Feb 1955 Cover: 0.10 NM value: 30.00
5 ❑ Apr 1955 Cover: 0.10 NM value: 30.00
6 ❑ Jun 1955 Cover: 0.10 NM value: 30.00
7 ❑ Aug 1955 Cover: 0.10 NM value: 30.00
8 ❑ Oct 1955 Cover: 0.10 NM value: 30.00
9 ❑ Dec 1955 Cover: 0.10 NM value: 30.00
10 ❑ Feb 1956 Cover: 0.10 NM value: 30.00
11 ❑ Apr 1956 Cover: 0.10 NM value: 30.00
15 ❑ 1957 Cover: 0.10 NM value: 30.00
16 ❑ 1957 Cover: 0.10 NM value: 30.00
17 ❑ Jun 1957 Cover: 0.10 NM value: 30.00
18 ❑ Aug 1957 Cover: 0.10 NM value: 30.00

NAVY COMBAT — Atlas

Atlas' war comics were infamous for telling readers exactly what they would get inside with such simple titles as Combat, Battle, and its fleet of naval-related comics, including Navy Action, Navy Tales, and this series, Navy Combat.

Featuring cover art by Joe Maneely and interior art by Don Heck, the series featured World War II-related stories starring such colorful characters as "Torpedo" Taylor and "Battleship" Burke in such simply named stories as "Attack by Sea!" and "Salvo!"

The series ran 20 issues between 1955 and 1958. — Brent

1 ❑ Jun 1955 Cover: 0.10 NM value: 200.00
2 ❑ Aug 1955 Cover: 0.10 NM value: 100.00
3 ❑ Oct 1955 Cover: 0.10 NM value: 100.00
4 ❑ Dec 1955 Cover: 0.10 NM value: 100.00
5 ❑ Feb 1956 Cover: 0.10 NM value: 100.00
6 ❑ 1956 Cover: 0.10 NM value: 100.00
7 ❑ 1956 Cover: 0.10 NM value: 100.00
8 ❑ 1956 Cover: 0.10 NM value: 100.00
📖 The Last Torpedo!; Our Fighting Fleet; Evacuation!; On Target!; Trail of the Killer!; The Duel (text) • Torpedo Taylor; Normandy Invasion; Korean War; Aircraft Carrier Bataan
9 ❑ 1956 Cover: 0.10 NM value: 100.00
10 ❑ Cover: 0.10 NM value: 100.00
11 ❑ 1957 Cover: 0.10 NM value: 100.00
12 ❑ 1957 Cover: 0.10 NM value: 100.00
13 ❑ 1957 Cover: 0.10 NM value: 100.00
14 ❑ 1957 Cover: 0.10 NM value: 100.00
15 ❑ Dec 1957 Cover: 0.10 NM value: 100.00
16 ❑ Feb 1958 Cover: 0.10 NM value: 100.00
17 ❑ Apr 1958 Cover: 0.10 NM value: 100.00
18 ❑ Jun 1958 Cover: 0.10 NM value: 100.00
19 ❑ Aug 1958 Cover: 0.10 NM value: 100.00
20 ❑ Oct 1958 Cover: 0.10 NM value: 100.00

NAVY HEROES — Almanac

1 ❑ ca. 1955 Cover: 0.10 NM value: 75.00

NAVY PATROL — Key

1 ❑ May 1955 Cover: 0.10 NM value: 27.50
• CGC: 1 graded, best 5.5

NAVY TALES — Atlas

1 ❑ Jan 1957 Cover: 0.10 NM value: 125.00
2 ❑ Mar 1957 Cover: 0.10 NM value: 80.00
3 ❑ May 1957 Cover: 0.10 NM value: 80.00
4 ❑ Jul 1957 Cover: 0.10 NM value: 80.00

NAVY TASK FORCE — Stanmor

1 ❑ 1954 Cover: 0.10 NM value: 50.00
2 ❑ 1954 Cover: 0.10 NM value: 40.00
3 ❑ 1954 Cover: 0.10 NM value: 40.00
4 ❑ Jun 1955 Cover: 0.10 NM value: 40.00
5 ❑ Aug 1955 Cover: 0.10 NM value: 40.00
6 ❑ Oct 1955 Cover: 0.10 NM value: 40.00
7 ❑ Dec 1956 Cover: 0.10 NM value: 40.00
8 ❑ Apr 1956 Cover: 0.10 NM value: 40.00

NAZRAT — Imperial

1 ❑ Cover: 1.80 NM value: 2.00
A: Jerry Frazee W: Jerry Frazee
2 ❑ Cover: 1.80 NM value: 2.00
A: Jerry Frazee W: Jerry Frazee
3 ❑ Cover: 1.80 NM value: 2.00
A: Jerry Frazee W: Jerry Frazee
4 ❑ Cover: 1.95 NM value: 2.00
A: Jerry Frazee W: Jerry Frazee
5 ❑ Cover: 1.95 NM value: 2.00
A: Jerry Frazee W: Jerry Frazee

NAZZ, THE — DC

1 ❑ Oct 1990 Cover: 4.95 NM value: Cover or less
Circ: CapCity orders: 12,050
📖 Michael's Book A: Bryan Talbot W: Tom Veitch
2 ❑ Nov 1990 Cover: 4.95 NM value: Cover or less
Circ: CapCity orders: 9,300
A: Bryan Talbot
3 ❑ Dec 1990 Cover: 4.95 NM value: Cover or less
Circ: CapCity orders: 8,700
A: Bryan Talbot
4 ❑ Jan 1991 Cover: 4.95 NM value: Cover or less
Circ: CapCity orders: 6,200
A: Bryan Talbot

NBC SATURDAY MORNING COMICS — Harvey

1 ❑ Sep 1991 Cover: 1.25 NM value: 1.50
• Toys "R" Us giveaway. 📖 Wish Kid...Captain Mayhem!; Star Search (activity); Yo Yogi!...Super Duper Snag!; Help Yogi Find Boo-Boo! (activity); Pro Stars...Brazil Nuts; Find the Saved by the Bell Scribbler! (activity); Spacecats...Diamonds are Fur-Ever; Saved by the Bell...Cheer U • Geoffrey Giraffe app

NEAR MYTHS — Rip Off

1 ❑ Jul 1990, b&w Cover: 2.50 NM value: Cover or less
A: Trina Robbins

NEAR TO NOW — Fandom House

1 ❑ b&w Cover: 2.00 NM value: Cover or less
📖 Born to Swallow; Your Sky's the Limit; The Legend of Rick Blue; Sgt. Spacecop; Mission Mars A: Matt Howarth; Debbie Van Dyke; Hal Clement; Jerry Siegel; Scott M.F. Johnson; T. Mtley W: Matt Howarth; Hal Clement; Jerry Siegel; Scott M.F. Johnson; T. Mtley; Dennis Pimple
2 ❑ b&w Cover: 2.00 NM value: Cover or less
A: Matt Howarth W: Matt Howarth

NEAT STUFF — Fantagraphics

Before Peter Bagge's popular comics Hate and Yeah! hit the scene, there was Neat Stuff which featured the model of the dysfunctional American family, the Bradleys. In the Eighties, Bagge chronicled the adventures of this family along with tales of other characters such as The Goon on the Moon, Studs Kirby, Junior, Girly-Girl, and Chuckie Boy.

Fans of underground comics will love Bagge's hard-edged, bitterly truthful observations on everything from the dumbing down of America due to cable television to the cruel tricks kids play on each other for a laugh. Bagge's unique black and white art and intelligent insight into social interaction once again prove that comics have the power to make us laugh while at the same time forcing us to look closer at ourselves.

1 ❑ Cover: 2.50 NM value: 5.00
A: Peter Bagge W: Peter Bagge
1- ❑ NM value: 2.50
1-2 ❑ Cover: 2.50 NM value: Cover or less
2 ❑ Cover: 2.50 NM value: 4.00
A: Peter Bagge W: Peter Bagge
2-2 ❑ Cover: 2.50 NM value: Cover or less
3 ❑ Cover: 2.50 NM value: 3.50
A: Peter Bagge W: Peter Bagge
3-2 ❑ Cover: 2.50 NM value: Cover or less
4 ❑ Cover: 2.50 NM value: 3.00
A: Peter Bagge W: Peter Bagge
4-2 ❑ Cover: 2.50 NM value: Cover or less
5 ❑ Dec 1986 Cover: 2.25 NM value: 2.50
A: Peter Bagge W: Peter Bagge
6 ❑ Apr 1987 Cover: 2.25 NM value: 2.50
• all Bradley issue A: Peter Bagge W: Peter Bagge
7 ❑ Aug 1987 Cover: 2.25 NM value: 2.50
A: Peter Bagge W: Peter Bagge
8 ❑ Dec 1987 Cover: 2.25 NM value: 2.50
A: Peter Bagge W: Peter Bagge
9 ❑ 1988 Cover: 2.50 NM value: Cover or less
A: Peter Bagge W: Peter Bagge
10 ❑ 1988 Cover: 2.50 NM value: Cover or less
A: Peter Bagge W: Peter Bagge
11 ❑ Nov 1988 Cover: 2.50 NM value: Cover or less
A: Peter Bagge W: Peter Bagge
12 ❑ Cover: 2.50 NM value: Cover or less
A: Peter Bagge W: Peter Bagge
13 ❑ Cover: 2.50 NM value: Cover or less
A: Peter Bagge W: Peter Bagge
14 ❑ Cover: 2.50 NM value: Cover or less
A: Peter Bagge W: Peter Bagge
15 ❑ Cover: 2.50 NM value: Cover or less
A: Peter Bagge W: Peter Bagge

NEBBS, THE — Dell

1 ❑ ca. 1945 Cover: 0.10 NM value: 75.00

NECROMANCER — Anarchy

1 ❑ b&w Cover: 3.50 NM value: Cover or less
📖 Strange Eons W: Michael O'Connell
1/Dlx❑ Cover: 3.50 NM value: Cover or less
• Deluxe edition. 📖 Strange Eons W: Michael O'Connell
2 ❑ b&w Cover: 3.50 NM value: Cover or less
W: Michael O'Connell
2/Dlx❑ Cover: 3.50 NM value: Cover or less
• Deluxe edition. W: Michael O'Connell
3 ❑ b&w Cover: 3.50 NM value: Cover or less
📖 Television Snow A: Tomas Sisneros; Drew Hayes W: Michael O'Connell
3/Dlx❑ Cover: 3.50 NM value: Cover or less
• Deluxe edition. 📖 Television Snow A: Tomas Sisneros; Drew Hayes W: Michael O'Connell
4 ❑ b&w Cover: 3.50 NM value: Cover or less
W: Michael O'Connell
4/Dlx❑ Cover: 3.50 NM value: Cover or less
• Deluxe edition. W: Michael O'Connell

NECROMANCER (2ND SERIES) — Anarchy

1 ❑ b&w Cover: 2.50 NM value: Cover or less
2 ❑ b&w Cover: 2.50 NM value: Cover or less
3 ❑ b&w Cover: 2.50 NM value: Cover or less
4 ❑ b&w Cover: 2.50 NM value: Cover or less

NECROPOLIS — Fleetway-Quality

1 ❑ Cover: 2.95 NM value: Cover or less
• Judge Dredd
2 ❑ Cover: 2.95 NM value: Cover or less
• Judge Dredd
3 ❑ Cover: 2.95 NM value: Cover or less
• Judge Dredd
4 ❑ Cover: 2.95 NM value: Cover or less
5 ❑ Cover: 2.95 NM value: Cover or less
6 ❑ Cover: 2.95 NM value: Cover or less
7 ❑ Cover: 2.95 NM value: Cover or less
8 ❑ Cover: 2.95 NM value: Cover or less
9 ❑ Cover: 2.95 NM value: Cover or less

NECROSCOPE — Malibu

1 ❑ Oct 1992 Cover: 2.95 NM value: 3.00
Circ: CapCity orders: 12,375
A: Daerick Grõss Jr. W: Martin Powell
1-2 ❑ Dec 1992 Cover: 2.95 NM value: Cover or less
2 ❑ Dec 1992 Cover: 2.95 NM value: Cover or less
Circ: CapCity orders: 8,675
• bagged with tattoo A: Daerick Grõss Jr. W: Martin Powell
3 ❑ Feb 1993 Cover: 2.95 NM value: Cover or less
Circ: CapCity orders: 8,450
A: Daerick Grõss Jr. W: Martin Powell
4 ❑ Cover: 2.95 NM value: Cover or less
Circ: CapCity orders: 6,825
A: Daerick Grõss Jr. W: Martin Powell
5 ❑ Cover: 2.95 NM value: Cover or less
Circ: CapCity orders: 6,300
A: Daerick Grõss Jr. W: Martin Powell

NECROSCOPE BOOK II: WAMPHYRI — Malibu

1 ❑ Cover: 2.95 NM value: Cover or less
Circ: CapCity orders: 7,125
A: Jon Macy W: Jon Macy
2 ❑ Nov 1994 Cover: 2.95 NM value: Cover or less
Circ: CapCity orders: 5,150
📖 Succulents A: Jon Macy W: Jon Macy
3 ❑ Jan 1994 Cover: 2.95 NM value: Cover or less
Circ: CapCity orders: 3,925
A: Jon Macy W: Jon Macy
4 ❑ Cover: 2.95 NM value: Cover or less
Circ: CapCity orders: 3,475
A: Jon Macy W: Jon Macy
5 ❑ Cover: 2.95 NM value: Cover or less
Circ: CapCity orders: 3,275

NEFARISMO — Eros Comix

5 ❑ May 1995 Cover: 2.95 NM value: Cover or less
A: Jon Macy W: Jon Macy

NEGATION — CrossGen

1 ❑ Jan 2002 Cover: 2.95 NM value: Cover or less
2 ❑ Feb 2002 Cover: 2.95 NM value: Cover or less
3 ❑ Mar 2002 Cover: 2.95 NM value: Cover or less

NEGATIVE BURN — Caliber

1 ❑ ca. 1993, b&w Cover: 2.95 NM value: 4.00
📖 Kilroy is Here; The Flaming Carrot; Mr. Mamoulian; Boneshaker; Matrix 7; The Apparition; Deadaim • Flaming Carrot A: Guy Burwell; Chris Hunter; Tim Bradstreet; Bob Burden; Brian Bolland; Randy Green; Craig Gilmore; Phil Hester; Nathan Massengill W: Bob Burden; Brian Bolland; Phil Hester; Ann Goetz; Charles Moore; James Pruett; Joe Pruett
2 ❑ b&w Cover: 2.95 NM value: 4.00
A: Steve Lieber
3 ❑ b&w Cover: 2.95 NM value: 4.00
★ Appearance of Bone.
4 ❑ b&w Cover: 2.95 NM value: 4.00
5 ❑ b&w Cover: 2.95 NM value: 4.00
6 ❑ b&w Cover: 2.95 NM value: 4.00
7 ❑ b&w Cover: 2.95 NM value: 4.00
8 ❑ b&w Cover: 2.95 NM value: 4.00
9 ❑ b&w Cover: 2.95 NM value: 4.00
W: Alan Moore
10 ❑ b&w Cover: 2.95 NM value: 4.00
W: Alan Moore
11 ❑ b&w Cover: 2.95 NM value: 4.00
A: Donna Barr W: Brian Bolland; Donna Barr; Neil Gaiman
12 ❑ b&w Cover: 2.95 NM value: 4.00
13 ❑ b&w Cover: 3.95 NM value: 6.50
W: Brian Michael Bendis; Alan Moore; Neil Gaiman ★ Appearance of Strangers in Paradise.

Other grades: Multiply prices above by **1.5 for Mint • 2/3 for Very Fine • 1/3 for Fine • 1/5 for Very Good • 1/8 for Good**

14 ❑ b&w Cover: 2.95 **NM** value: **3.95**
15 ❑ b&w Cover: 2.95 **NM** value: **3.95**
📖 Mr. Trianglehead: Canto 5; Mr. Mamoulian: Moving Things About; The Invincible Man; The Lost Laughter, Part 5; Classics Desecrated: The Legend of the Pied Piper; Einstein's Last Case; Bad Vibes in Sucktown **A:** Art Wetherell; Bill Koeb; Brian Bolland; Mark A. Lester; Jim Calafiore; Jeff Nicholson; Ken Lester; Phil Wagstaff **W:** Brian Bolland; Jim Calafiore; Jeff Nicholson; David Jackson; Chris Dowss; Colin Clayton; Dave Louapre; Douglas M. Wheeler
16 ❑ b&w Cover: 2.95 **NM** value: **3.95**
17 ❑ b&w Cover: 2.95 **NM** value: **3.95**
18 ❑ b&w Cover: 2.95 **NM** value: **3.95**
• **CGC:** 2 graded, best 9.4
19 ❑ b&w Cover: 2.95 **NM** value: **3.95**
20 ❑ b&w Cover: 2.95 **NM** value: **3.95**
21 ❑ b&w Cover: 2.95 **NM** value: **3.95**
22 ❑ b&w Cover: 2.95 **NM** value: **3.95**
23 ❑ b&w Cover: 2.95 **NM** value: **3.95**
24 ❑ b&w Cover: 2.95 **NM** value: **3.95**
25 ❑ b&w Cover: 3.95 **NM** value: **Cover or less**
Circ: CapCity orders: **2,155**
26 ❑ b&w Cover: 3.95 **NM** value: **Cover or less**
27 ❑ b&w Cover: 3.95 **NM** value: **Cover or less**
28 ❑ b&w Cover: 3.95 **NM** value: **Cover or less**
• Dusty Star
29 ❑ b&w Cover: 3.95 **NM** value: **Cover or less**
30 ❑ b&w Cover: 3.95 **NM** value: **Cover or less**
31 ❑ b&w Cover: 3.95 **NM** value: **Cover or less**
32 ❑ b&w Cover: 3.95 **NM** value: **Cover or less**
A: Steve Lieber
33 ❑ b&w Cover: 3.95 **NM** value: **Cover or less**
34 ❑ b&w Cover: 3.95 **NM** value: **Cover or less**
35 ❑ b&w Cover: 3.95 **NM** value: **Cover or less**
36 ❑ b&w Cover: 3.95 **NM** value: **Cover or less**
37 ❑ b&w Cover: 3.95 **NM** value: **Cover or less**
📖 Dusty Star: Where the Chips Fall; Mr. Mamoulian: A Really Go • Dusty Star **A:** Andrew Robinson; John McCrea; Edvin Biukovic; Brian Michael Bendis; Michael Avon Oeming; Brian Bolland; P. Craig Russell; David Taylor; Colleen Doran; Mark Ricketts; Phil Hester; Mark Laliberte; Maulwerf Brƒder Design Studio; Maulwerf Brnder Design Studio **W:** John McCrea; Brian Bolland; Warren Ellis; Phil Hester; Bryan J.L. Glass; Darko Macan; Alan Moore; Ian Carney; Joe Pruett; Mark Laliberte; Maulwerf Brƒder Design Studio; Maulwerf Brnder Design Studio; Richard Strauss
38 ❑ Cover: 3.95 **NM** value: **Cover or less**
39 ❑ Cover: 3.95 **NM** value: **Cover or less**
40 ❑ Cover: 3.95 **NM** value: **Cover or less**
41 ❑ Cover: 3.95 **NM** value: **Cover or less**
42 ❑ Cover: 3.95 **NM** value: **Cover or less**
43 ❑ Cover: 3.95 **NM** value: **Cover or less**
44 ❑ Feb 1997 Cover: 3.95 **NM** value: **Cover or less**
Circ: Diamd. preorders: **1,766**
45 ❑ 1997 Cover: 3.95 **NM** value: **Cover or less**
46 ❑ 1997 Cover: 3.95 **NM** value: **Cover or less**
47 ❑ 1997 Cover: 3.95 **NM** value: **Cover or less**
48 ❑ 1997 Cover: 4.95 **NM** value: **Cover or less**
49 ❑ 1997 Cover: 4.95 **NM** value: **Cover or less**
50 ❑ 1997 Cover: 6.95 **NM** value: **Cover or less**
final issue.

NEGRO HEROES — Parents' Magazine Institute

1 ❑ Spr 1947 Cover: 0.10 **NM** value: **500.00**
• **CGC:** 1 graded, best 7.5
2 ❑ ca. 1948 Cover: 0.10 **NM** value: **600.00**

NEGRO ROMANCE — Charlton

1 ❑ Jun 1950 Cover: 0.10 **NM** value: **750.00**
2 ❑ Aug 1950 Cover: 0.10 **NM** value: **600.00**
3 ❑ Oct 1950 Cover: 0.10 **NM** value: **600.00**

NEIL & BUZZ IN SPACE AND TIME — Fantagraphics

1 ❑ Apr 1989, b&w Cover: 2.00 **NM** value: **Cover or less**
A: Henry Mayo **W:** George Alec Effinger

NEIL THE HORSE COMICS AND STORIES — Aardvark-Vanaheim

1 ❑ Feb 1983 Cover: 1.70 **NM** value: **2.50**
2 ❑ Apr 1983 Cover: 1.40 **NM** value: **2.00**
3 ❑ Jun 1983 Cover: 1.40 **NM** value: **2.00**
4 ❑ Aug 1983 Cover: 1.40 **NM** value: **2.00**
5 ❑ Nov 1983 Cover: 1.40 **NM** value: **2.00**
6 ❑ Feb 1984 Cover: 1.70 **NM** value: **2.00**
7 ❑ Apr 1984 Cover: 1.70 **NM** value: **2.00**
8 ❑ Jun 1984 Cover: 1.70 **NM** value: **2.00**
9 ❑ Sep 1984 Cover: 1.70 **NM** value: **2.00**
10 ❑ Dec 1984 Cover: 1.70 **NM** value: **2.00**
11 ❑ Apr 1985 Cover: 2.00 **NM** value: **Cover or less**
• Title changes to Neil the Horse
12 ❑ Jun 1985 Cover: 2.00 **NM** value: **Cover or less**
13 ❑ Dec 1986 Cover: 2.00 **NM** value: **Cover or less**
14 ❑ Jul 1988 Cover: 3.00 **NM** value: **Cover or less**
• giant
15 ❑ Aug 1988 Cover: 3.00 **NM** value: **Cover or less**
• giant

Capital City orders are the actual sales of comic books by Capital City Distribution, once one of the largest U.S. sellers of comics to comics shops. Capital City's share of comics shop sales, while not known exactly, increases from around 10-20% in the mid-1980s to 30-35% in the mid-1990s. Capital City's share of comic books sold on newsstands (most Marvels and DCs) will be less.

NELLIE THE NURSE — Atlas

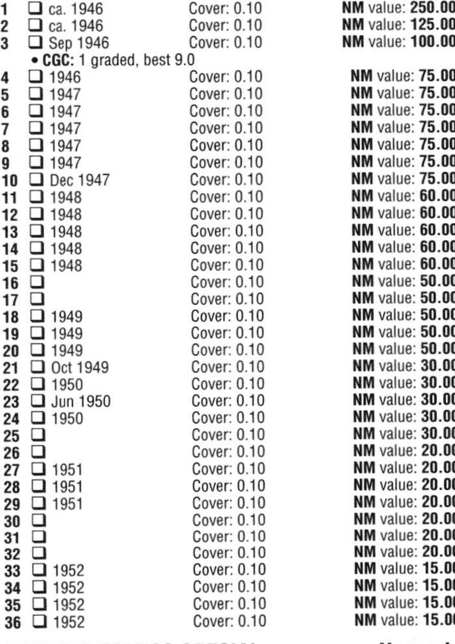

The late 1940s saw the rise of romance comics, silly situation comedy comics, and comics featuring working women.

Nellie the Nurse was a combination of all three. Featuring cheesecake covers featuring Nellie posing like a model in such incongrous settings as the beach and the hospital ward as well as covers with her out on a date or working the ward, Nellie's antics proved popular enough to sustain the series from 1945 to 1952.

The unflappable nurse's stories featured art by Harvey Kurtzman on several issues. — Brent

1 ❑ ca. 1946 Cover: 0.10 **NM** value: **250.00**
2 ❑ ca. 1946 Cover: 0.10 **NM** value: **125.00**
3 ❑ Sep 1946 Cover: 0.10 **NM** value: **100.00**
• **CGC:** 1 graded, best 9.0
4 ❑ 1946 Cover: 0.10 **NM** value: **75.00**
5 ❑ 1947 Cover: 0.10 **NM** value: **75.00**
6 ❑ 1947 Cover: 0.10 **NM** value: **75.00**
7 ❑ 1947 Cover: 0.10 **NM** value: **75.00**
8 ❑ 1947 Cover: 0.10 **NM** value: **75.00**
9 ❑ 1947 Cover: 0.10 **NM** value: **75.00**
10 ❑ Dec 1947 Cover: 0.10 **NM** value: **75.00**
11 ❑ 1948 Cover: 0.10 **NM** value: **60.00**
12 ❑ 1948 Cover: 0.10 **NM** value: **60.00**
13 ❑ 1948 Cover: 0.10 **NM** value: **60.00**
14 ❑ 1948 Cover: 0.10 **NM** value: **60.00**
15 ❑ 1948 Cover: 0.10 **NM** value: **60.00**
16 ❑ Cover: 0.10 **NM** value: **50.00**
17 ❑ Cover: 0.10 **NM** value: **50.00**
18 ❑ 1949 Cover: 0.10 **NM** value: **50.00**
19 ❑ 1949 Cover: 0.10 **NM** value: **50.00**
20 ❑ 1949 Cover: 0.10 **NM** value: **50.00**
21 ❑ Oct 1949 Cover: 0.10 **NM** value: **30.00**
22 ❑ 1950 Cover: 0.10 **NM** value: **30.00**
23 ❑ Jun 1950 Cover: 0.10 **NM** value: **30.00**
24 ❑ 1950 Cover: 0.10 **NM** value: **30.00**
25 ❑ Cover: 0.10 **NM** value: **30.00**
26 ❑ Cover: 0.10 **NM** value: **20.00**
27 ❑ 1951 Cover: 0.10 **NM** value: **20.00**
28 ❑ 1951 Cover: 0.10 **NM** value: **20.00**
29 ❑ 1951 Cover: 0.10 **NM** value: **20.00**
30 ❑ Cover: 0.10 **NM** value: **20.00**
31 ❑ Cover: 0.10 **NM** value: **20.00**
32 ❑ Cover: 0.10 **NM** value: **20.00**
33 ❑ 1952 Cover: 0.10 **NM** value: **15.00**
34 ❑ 1952 Cover: 0.10 **NM** value: **15.00**
35 ❑ 1952 Cover: 0.10 **NM** value: **15.00**
36 ❑ 1952 Cover: 0.10 **NM** value: **15.00**

NEMESIS COMICS SPECIAL — Nemesis

Ash 1❑ **NM** value: **0.50**
• Ashcan promotional edition introducing Ultraman, Frank. 📖 Ultraman: Negative One; Frank: Tail Bone Connects To The Elbow Bone **A:** Denys Cowan; Ernie Colon **W:** D.G. Chichester; Larry Yakata

NEMESISTER — Cheeky Press

1 ❑ Apr 1997, b&w Cover: 2.95 **NM** value: **Cover or less**
cardstock cover. 📖 The Job **A:** Craig Clark **W:** Laura Behary
2 ❑ Jun 1997, b&w Cover: 2.95 **NM** value: **Cover or less**
cardstock cover. 📖 Jesusa! **A:** Craig Clark **W:** Laura Behary
3 ❑ Sep 1997, b&w Cover: 2.95 **NM** value: **Cover or less**
cardstock cover. 📖 Hemi **A:** Craig Clark **W:** Laura Behary
3/Ash❑ **NM** value: **0.50**
• ashcan edition. 📖 Hemi **A:** Craig Clark **W:** Laura Behary
4 ❑ Nov 1997, b&w Cover: 2.95 **NM** value: **Cover or less**
cardstock cover. **A:** Craig Clark **W:** Laura Behary
5 ❑ Cover: 2.95 **NM** value: **Cover or less**
A: Craig Clark **W:** Laura Behary
6 ❑ Cover: 2.95 **NM** value: **Cover or less**
A: Craig Clark **W:** Laura Behary
7 ❑ Cover: 2.95 **NM** value: **Cover or less**
A: Craig Clark **W:** Laura Behary
8 ❑ Cover: 2.95 **NM** value: **Cover or less**
A: Craig Clark **W:** Laura Behary
9 ❑ Cover: 2.95 **NM** value: **Cover or less**
A: Craig Clark **W:** Laura Behary

NEMESIS THE WARLOCK (EAGLE) — Eagle

1 ❑ Sep 1984 Cover: 1.50 **NM** value: **2.00**
2 ❑ Oct 1984 Cover: 1.50 **NM** value: **2.00**
A: Kevin O'Neill **W:** Pat Mills
3 ❑ Nov 1984 Cover: 1.50 **NM** value: **2.00**
4 ❑ Dec 1984 Cover: 1.50 **NM** value: **2.00**
5 ❑ Jan 1984 Cover: 1.50 **NM** value: **2.00**
6 ❑ Feb 1984 Cover: 1.50 **NM** value: **2.00**
7 ❑ Mar 1984 Cover: 1.50 **NM** value: **2.00**
8 ❑ Cover: 1.50 **NM** value: **2.00**

The CGC numbers printed in individual listings above represent the **number of copies examined** and given a **Universal** grade by CGC and the **best such copy** graded at press time. For current populations, watch for special ***Comics Buyer's Guide*** issues or check **www.cgccomics.com.**

NEMESIS THE WARLOCK (FLEETWAY/QUALITY) — Fleetway-Quality

After a four-year absence from American comics, Nemesis the Warlock returned in 1989 to continue his battle against the tyrannical Torquemada. This series continued to reprint Nemesis' later adventures from the British 2000 A.D.

Here we see the crane-headed alien "Warlock" Nemesis some 10 years after he apparently killed Torquemada. In Torquemada's wake, the Terminators on Torquemada's world have begun to mellow a bit and have even forged peace agreements with races that they once would have purged. Still, the ghost of Torquemada continued to loom large, especially when one story placed Torquemada himself in a time loop which wound through the era. This loop was set up by Nemesis' son Thoth in order to punish Torquemada for having killed Thoth's mother. As Torquemada arrived in his future, he was continually burned at the stake as an impostor. In order to stop Thoth, however, Nemesis is forced to rescue his old enemy!

1 ❑ 1989b&w Cover: 1.95 **NM** value: **2.00**
2 ❑ b&w Cover: 1.95 **NM** value: **2.00**
3 ❑ b&w Cover: 1.95 **NM** value: **2.00**
4 ❑ b&w Cover: 1.95 **NM** value: **2.00**
📖 Nemesis the Warlock, Book II **A:** Kevin O'Neill **W:** Pat Mills
5 ❑ b&w Cover: 1.95 **NM** value: **2.00**
6 ❑ b&w Cover: 1.95 **NM** value: **2.00**
7 ❑ b&w Cover: 1.95 **NM** value: **2.00**
8 ❑ b&w Cover: 1.95 **NM** value: **2.00**
9 ❑ b&w Cover: 1.95 **NM** value: **2.00**
📖 The Vengeance Of Thoth **A:** Bryan Talbot **W:** Pat Mills
10 ❑ b&w Cover: 1.95 **NM** value: **2.00**
11 ❑ b&w Cover: 1.95 **NM** value: **2.00**
12 ❑ b&w Cover: 1.95 **NM** value: **2.00**
13 ❑ b&w Cover: 1.95 **NM** value: **2.00**
14 ❑ b&w Cover: 1.95 **NM** value: **2.00**
📖 Torquemada God **A:** Kevin O'Neill **W:** Pat Mills ★ Origin of Torquemada.
15 ❑ b&w Cover: 1.95 **NM** value: **2.00**
16 ❑ b&w Cover: 1.95 **NM** value: **2.00**
17 ❑ b&w Cover: 1.95 **NM** value: **2.00**
18 ❑ b&w Cover: 1.95 **NM** value: **2.00**
19 ❑ b&w Cover: 1.95 **NM** value: **2.00**

NEO — Excalibur

1 ❑ b&w Cover: 1.50 **NM** value: **Cover or less**

NEOMEN — Slave Labor

1 ❑ Oct 1987 Cover: 1.75 **NM** value: **Cover or less**
📖 The Dark Age • no indicia **A:** Frank Cirocco; Gary Winnick **W:** Frank Cirocco; Gary Winnick
2 ❑ Jan 1988 Cover: 1.75 **NM** value: **Cover or less**
A: Frank Cirocco; Gary Winnick **W:** Frank Cirocco; Gary Winnick

NEON CITY — Innovation

1 ❑ b&w Cover: 2.25 **NM** value: **Cover or less**

NEON CITY: AFTER THE FALL — Innovation

1 ❑ b&w Cover: 2.50 **NM** value: **Cover or less**
📖 Fallout **A:** Joseph Dunn **W:** Nick Anastasio

NEON CYBER — Image

1 ❑ Aug 1999 Cover: 2.50 **NM** value: **Cover or less**
Circ: Diamd. preorders: **32,087**
📖 Alliance **A:** Lou Kang **W:** Adrian Tsang
1/SC❑Aug 1999 Cover: 2.50 **NM** value: **5.00**
alternate cover. 📖 Alliance **A:** Lou Kang **W:** Adrian Tsang
2 ❑ Sep 1999 Cover: 2.50 **NM** value: **Cover or less**
Circ: Diamd. preorders: **24,360**
Man facing giant on cover. 📖 Defiance **A:** Lou Kang **W:** Adrian Tsang
2/SC❑Sep 1999 Cover: 2.50 **NM** value: **Cover or less**
alternate cover. 📖 Defiance **A:** Lou Kang **W:** Adrian Tsang
3 ❑ Oct 1999 Cover: 2.50 **NM** value: **Cover or less**
Circ: Diamd. preorders: **20,138**
alternate cover. 📖 Retaliation **A:** Lou Kang **W:** Adrian Tsang
4 ❑ Dec 1999 Cover: 2.50 **NM** value: **Cover or less**
Circ: Diamd. preorders: **20,424**
📖 Betrayal **A:** Lou Kang **W:** Adrian Tsang
5 ❑ Jan 2000 Cover: 2.50 **NM** value: **Cover or less**
Circ: Diamd. preorders: **19,177**
A: Lou Kang **W:** Adrian Tsang
6 ❑ Mar 2000 Cover: 2.50 **NM** value: **Cover or less**
Circ: Diamd. preorders: **19,846**
📖 Ascension **A:** Lou Kang **W:** Adrian Tsang
7 ❑ May 2000 Cover: 2.50 **NM** value: **Cover or less**
Circ: Diamd. preorders: **17,618**
W: Adrian Tsang
8 ❑ Jun 2000 Cover: 2.50 **NM** value: **Cover or less**
Circ: Diamd. preorders: **16,392**
📖 Redemption **A:** Sigmund Torre **W:** Adrian Tsang

NEON GENESIS EVANGELION BOOK 1 — Viz

1/A ❑ Sep 1997 Cover: 2.95 **NM** value: **Cover or less**
Circ: Diamd. preorders: **8,647**
1/B ❑ Sep 1997 Cover: 2.95 **NM** value: **Cover or less**
Circ: Diamd. preorders: **6,092**
• Special collector's edition. • printed in Japanese style (back to front)
2/A ❑ Oct 1997 Cover: 2.95 **NM** value: **Cover or less**
Circ: Diamd. preorders: **7,658**
2/B ❑ Oct 1997 Cover: 2.95 **NM** value: **Cover or less**

CGC-graded: Multiply prices above by **33 for 9.9 M • 16 for 9.8 NM/M • 7 for 9.6 NM+ • 5 for 9.4 NM • 2.5 for 9.2 NM- • 1.5 for 9.0 VF/NM**

Circ: Diamd. preorders: **4,265**
• Special collector's edition. • printed in Japanese style (back to front)
3/A ❑ Nov 1997 Cover: 2.95 **NM** value: **Cover or less**
Circ: Diamd. preorders: **6,725**
3/B ❑ Nov 1997 Cover: 2.95 **NM** value: **Cover or less**
Circ: Diamd. preorders: **4,349**
• Special collector's edition. • printed in Japanese style (back to front)
4/A ❑ Dec 1997 Cover: 2.95 **NM** value: **Cover or less**
Circ: Diamd. preorders: **6,763**
4/B ❑ Dec 1997 Cover: 2.95 **NM** value: **Cover or less**
Circ: Diamd. preorders: **4,995**
• Special collector's edition. • printed in Japanese style (back to front)
5/A ❑ Jan 1998 Cover: 2.95 **NM** value: **Cover or less**
Circ: Diamd. preorders: **6,744**
5/B ❑ Jan 1998 Cover: 2.95 **NM** value: **Cover or less**
Circ: Diamd. preorders: **4,971**
• Special collector's edition. • printed in Japanese style (back to front)
6/A ❑ Feb 1998 Cover: 2.95 **NM** value: **Cover or less**
Circ: Diamd. preorders: **5,942**
6/B ❑ Feb 1998 Cover: 2.95 **NM** value: **Cover or less**
Circ: Diamd. preorders: **4,768**
• Special collector's edition. • printed in Japanese style (back to front)
Bk 1/A ❑ 1998 Cover: 15.95 **NM** value: **Cover or less**
• Trade Paperback.
Bk 1/B ❑ 1998 Cover: 15.95 **NM** value: **Cover or less**
• Special collector's edition. • printed in Japanese style (back to front)
Bk 2/A ❑ Dec 1998 Cover: 15.95 **NM** value: **Cover or less**
• Trade Paperback. • collects Neon Genesis Evangelion Book Two #1-5
Bk 2/B ❑ Dec 1998 Cover: 15.95 **NM** value: **Cover or less**
• Special collector's edition. • printed in Japanese style (back to front)

NEON GENESIS EVANGELION BOOK 2 — Viz

1/A ❑ Mar 1998 Cover: 3.50 **NM** value: **Cover or less**
Circ: Diamd. preorders: **6,631**
1/B ❑ Mar 1998 Cover: 3.50 **NM** value: **Cover or less**
Circ: Diamd. preorders: **5,420**
• Special collector's edition. • printed in Japanese style (back to front)
2/A ❑ Apr 1998 Cover: 3.25 **NM** value: **Cover or less**
Circ: Diamd. preorders: **11,277**
2/B ❑ Apr 1998 Cover: 3.25 **NM** value: **Cover or less**
• Special collector's edition. • printed in Japanese style (back to front)
3/A ❑ May 1998 Cover: 2.95 **NM** value: **Cover or less**
Circ: Diamd. preorders: **10,484**
3/B ❑ May 1998 Cover: 2.95 **NM** value: **Cover or less**
• Special collector's edition. • printed in Japanese style (back to front)
4/A ❑ Jun 1998 Cover: 2.95 **NM** value: **Cover or less**
Circ: Diamd. preorders: **10,322**
4/B ❑ Jun 1998 Cover: 2.95 **NM** value: **Cover or less**
• Special collector's edition. • printed in Japanese style (back to front)
5/A ❑ Jul 1998 Cover: 2.95 **NM** value: **Cover or less**
Circ: Diamd. preorders: **5,046**
5/B ❑ Jul 1998 Cover: 2.95 **NM** value: **Cover or less**
Circ: Diamd. preorders: **4,641**
• Special collector's edition. • printed in Japanese style (back to front)

NEON GENESIS EVANGELION BOOK 3 — Viz

1/A ❑ Aug 1998 Cover: 2.95 **NM** value: **Cover or less**
Circ: Diamd. preorders: **9,791**
1/B ❑ Aug 1998 Cover: 2.95 **NM** value: **Cover or less**
• Special collector's edition. • printed in Japanese style (back to front)
2/A ❑ Sep 1998 Cover: 2.95 **NM** value: **Cover or less**
Circ: Diamd. preorders: **9,403**
2/B ❑ Sep 1998 Cover: 2.95 **NM** value: **Cover or less**
• Special collector's edition. • printed in Japanese style (back to front)
3/A ❑ Oct 1998 Cover: 2.95 **NM** value: **Cover or less**
Circ: Diamd. preorders: **9,484**
3/B ❑ Oct 1998 Cover: 2.95 **NM** value: **Cover or less**
• Special collector's edition. • printed in Japanese style (back to front)
4/A ❑ Nov 1998 Cover: 2.95 **NM** value: **Cover or less**
Circ: Diamd. preorders: **9,272**
4/B ❑ Nov 1998 Cover: 2.95 **NM** value: **Cover or less**
• Special collector's edition. • printed in Japanese style (back to front)
5/A ❑ Dec 1998 Cover: 2.95 **NM** value: **Cover or less**
Circ: Diamd. preorders: **8,884**
5/B ❑ Dec 1998 Cover: 2.95 **NM** value: **Cover or less**
• Special collector's edition. • printed in Japanese style (back to front)
6/A ❑ Jan 1999 Cover: 3.25 **NM** value: **Cover or less**
Circ: Diamd. preorders: **8,936**
6/B ❑ Jan 1999 Cover: 3.25 **NM** value: **Cover or less**
• Special collector's edition. • printed in Japanese style (back to front)

NEON GENESIS EVANGELION BOOK 4 — Viz

1/A ❑ Feb 1999 Cover: 2.95 **NM** value: **Cover or less**
Circ: Diamd. preorders: **9,404**
1/B ❑ Feb 1999 Cover: 2.95 **NM** value: **Cover or less**
• Special collector's edition. • printed in Japanese style (back to front)
2/A ❑ Mar 1999 Cover: 2.95 **NM** value: **Cover or less**
2/B ❑ Mar 1999 Cover: 2.95 **NM** value: **Cover or less**
Circ: Diamd. preorders: **4,264**
• Special collector's edition. • printed in Japanese style (back to front)
3/A ❑ Apr 1999 Cover: 2.95 **NM** value: **Cover or less**
Circ: Diamd. preorders: **8,974**
3/B ❑ Apr 1999 Cover: 2.95 **NM** value: **Cover or less**
• Special collector's edition. • printed in Japanese style (back to front)
4/A ❑ May 1999 Cover: 2.95 **NM** value: **Cover or less**
Circ: Diamd. preorders: **8,826**
4/B ❑ May 1999 Cover: 2.95 **NM** value: **Cover or less**
• Special collector's edition. • printed in Japanese style (back to front)
5/A ❑ Jun 1999 Cover: 2.95 **NM** value: **Cover or less**
Circ: Diamd. preorders: **8,803**
5/B ❑ Jun 1999 Cover: 2.95 **NM** value: **Cover or less**
• Special collector's edition. • printed in Japanese style (back to front)
7 ❑ Jul 1999 Cover: 2.95 **NM** value: **Cover or less**
Circ: Diamd. preorders: **8,351**

NERVE — Nerve

1 ❑ Cover: 1.50 **NM** value: **2.00**
2 ❑ Cover: 1.50 **NM** value: **Cover or less**
3 ❑ Cover: 1.50 **NM** value: **Cover or less**
4 ❑ Cover: 1.50 **NM** value: **Cover or less**
5 ❑ Apr 1987 Cover: 1.50 **NM** value: **Cover or less**
6 ❑ 1987 Cover: 1.50 **NM** value: **Cover or less**
7 ❑ Jul 1987 Cover: 1.50 **NM** value: **Cover or less**
8 ❑ Cover: 4.00 **NM** value: **Cover or less**
• oversize.

NERVOUS REX — Blackthorne

1 ❑ Aug 1985 Cover: 2.00 **NM** value: **Cover or less**
A: William Van Horn W: William Van Horn
2 ❑ Oct 1985 Cover: 2.00 **NM** value: **Cover or less**
A: William Van Horn W: William Van Horn
3 ❑ Dec 1985 Cover: 2.00 **NM** value: **Cover or less**
A: William Van Horn W: William Van Horn
4 ❑ Feb 1986 Cover: 2.00 **NM** value: **Cover or less**
A: William Van Horn W: William Van Horn
5 ❑ Apr 1986 Cover: 2.00 **NM** value: **Cover or less**
A: William Van Horn W: William Van Horn
6 ❑ Jun 1986 Cover: 2.00 **NM** value: **Cover or less**
A: William Van Horn W: William Van Horn
7 ❑ Aug 1986 Cover: 2.00 **NM** value: **Cover or less**
A: William Van Horn W: William Van Horn
8 ❑ Oct 1986 Cover: 2.00 **NM** value: **Cover or less**
A: William Van Horn W: William Van Horn
9 ❑ Dec 1986 Cover: 2.00 **NM** value: **Cover or less**
A: William Van Horn W: William Van Horn
10 ❑ Feb 1987 Cover: 2.00 **NM** value: **Cover or less**
A: William Van Horn W: William Van Horn

NESTROBBER — Blue Sky Blue

1 ❑ Oct 1992, b&w Cover: 1.95 **NM** value: **Cover or less**
📖 Nestrobber; Fast A: Colleen Doran; Maya Sakamoto W: Mary Jo Duffy
2 ❑ Jun 1994, b&w Cover: 1.95 **NM** value: **Cover or less**

NETHERWORLD — Ambition

1 ❑ b&w Cover: 1.50 **NM** value: **Cover or less**

NETHERWORLDS — Adventure

1 ❑ Aug 1988, b&w Cover: 1.95 **NM** value: **Cover or less**
📖 Flame and Darkness A: Gabriel Morrissette W: Mark Ellis

NETMAN — Information Networks

0 ❑ Aug 1992 **NM** value: **0.50**
A: Bradley Gebhart W: Bill Evanow; Bob Sloat

NET PROPHET: TROUBLE ON GARAMOND — Penn & Inc.

Ash 1 ❑ **NM** value: **0.50**
📖 Trouble on Garamond A: Kevin Penn W: Brian & Kevin Penn

NEURO JACK — Big

1 ❑ Aug 1996 Cover: 2.25 **NM** value: **Cover or less**
• all-digital art A: Erika Taguchi; James Chambers W: Erika Taguchi; James Chambers

NEUROMANCER: THE GRAPHIC NOVEL — Marvel / Epic

1 ❑ Cover: 8.95 **NM** value: **Cover or less**
Circ: CapCity orders: **4,150**
A: Bruce Jenson W: Tom De Haven; William Gibson

NEVADA — DC / Vertigo

1 ❑ May 1998 Cover: 2.50 **NM** value: **Cover or less**
Circ: Diamd. preorders: **24,974**
📖 Another Damn Suck-Egg Corpse A: Phil Winslade W: Steve Gerber
2 ❑ Jun 1998 Cover: 2.50 **NM** value: **Cover or less**
Circ: Diamd. preorders: **19,262**
📖 Nibbles A: Phil Winslade W: Steve Gerber
3 ❑ Jul 1998 Cover: 2.50 **NM** value: **Cover or less**
Circ: Diamd. preorders: **17,285**
A: Phil Winslade W: Steve Gerber
4 ❑ Aug 1998 Cover: 2.50 **NM** value: **Cover or less**
Circ: Diamd. preorders: **16,634**
A: Phil Winslade W: Steve Gerber
5 ❑ Sep 1998 Cover: 2.50 **NM** value: **Cover or less**
Circ: Diamd. preorders: **15,215**
A: Phil Winslade W: Steve Gerber
6 ❑ Oct 1998 Cover: 2.50 **NM** value: **Cover or less**
Circ: Diamd. preorders: **14,620**
📖 Existence is Futile A: Phil Winslade W: Steve Gerber
Bk 1 ❑ Cover: 14.95 **NM** value: **Cover or less**
No issue number. • Trade Paperback. • collects mini-series; Collects Nevada #1-6 A: Phil Winslade W: Steve Gerber

NEVERMEN, THE — Dark Horse

1 ❑ May 2000 Cover: 2.95 **NM** value: **Cover or less**
Circ: Diamd. preorders: **10,437** • CGC: 1 graded, best 7.0
A: Guy Davis W: Phil Amara
2 ❑ Jun 2000 Cover: 2.95 **NM** value: **Cover or less**
Circ: Diamd. preorders: **8,566**
📖 Secrets for Dead Men A: Guy Davis W: Phil Amara
3 ❑ Jul 2000 Cover: 2.95 **NM** value: **Cover or less**
Circ: Diamd. preorders: **8,746**
📖 Hello, Goodbye, Good Night A: Guy Davis W: Phil Amara

NEW ADVENTURE COMICS — DC

12 ❑ Jan 1937 Cover: 0.10 **NM** value: **3000.00**
• CGC: 1 graded, best 4.5
13 ❑ Feb 1937 Cover: 0.10 **NM** value: **3000.00**
14 ❑ Mar 1937 Cover: 0.10 **NM** value: **3000.00**
15 ❑ May 1937 Cover: 0.10 **NM** value: **2500.00**
16 ❑ Jun 1937 Cover: 0.10 **NM** value: **2500.00**
• CGC: 1 graded, best 3.5
17 ❑ Jul 1937 Cover: 0.10 **NM** value: **2500.00**
18 ❑ Aug 1937 Cover: 0.10 **NM** value: **2500.00**
19 ❑ Sep 1937 Cover: 0.10 **NM** value: **2500.00**
• CGC: 1 graded, best 8.0
20 ❑ Oct 1937 Cover: 0.10 **NM** value: **2500.00**
21 ❑ Nov 1937 Cover: 0.10 **NM** value: **2500.00**
• CGC: 1 graded, best 2.0
22 ❑ Dec 1937 Cover: 0.10 **NM** value: **2500.00**
23 ❑ Jan 1938 Cover: 0.10 **NM** value: **2000.00**
24 ❑ Feb 1938 Cover: 0.10 **NM** value: **2000.00**
• CGC: 2 graded, best 8.0
25 ❑ Mar 1938 Cover: 0.10 **NM** value: **2000.00**
• CGC: 1 graded, best 4.0
26 ❑ May 1938 Cover: 0.10 **NM** value: **2000.00**
27 ❑ Jun 1938 Cover: 0.10 **NM** value: **2000.00**
28 ❑ Jul 1938 Cover: 0.10 **NM** value: **2000.00**
29 ❑ Aug 1938 Cover: 0.10 **NM** value: **2000.00**
• CGC: 1 graded, best 5.0
30 ❑ Sep 1938 Cover: 0.10 **NM** value: **2000.00**
• CGC: 1 graded, best 6.0
31 ❑ Oct 1938 Cover: 0.10 **NM** value: **2000.00**
• CGC: 4 graded, best 5.5

NEW ADVENTURES OF ABRAHAM LINCOLN, THE — Image

From his quirky Zot! to his absorbing examination of comics as an art form, "Understanding Comics," creator Scott McCloud has presented projects that do not easily fit into standard categories. That is no less true of "The New Adventures of Abraham Lincoln."

This graphic novel is actually a political allegory that presents biting sarcasm of the current American political scene. Lincoln inexplicably arrives in late 20th-century America, reinforcing historical inaccuracies while spouting feel-good slogans that mean nothing. The shallowness of his platform is blissfully accepted by the populace who are willing to make him their leader. When another Abraham Lincoln arrives to challenge the one riding a wave of popularity, McCloud skillfully illustrates the danger of worshiping symbols and ignoring what they represent.

1 ❑ Cover: 19.95 **NM** value: **Cover or less**
A: Scott McCloud W: Scott McCloud

NEW ADVENTURES OF BEAUTY AND THE BEAST (DISNEY'S...) — Disney

1 ❑ Cover: 1.50 **NM** value: **Cover or less**
1/DM ❑ Cover: 2.00 **NM** value: **Cover or less**
2 ❑ Cover: 1.50 **NM** value: **Cover or less**

NEW ADVENTURES OF CHARLIE CHAN — DC

1 ❑ Jun 1958 Cover: 0.10 **NM** value: **500.00**
• CGC: 3 graded, best 6.0
2 ❑ Aug 1958 Cover: 0.10 **NM** value: **250.00**
3 ❑ Oct 1958 Cover: 0.10 **NM** value: **200.00**
4 ❑ Dec 1958 Cover: 0.10 **NM** value: **200.00**
• CGC: 1 graded, best 7.0
5 ❑ Feb 1959 Cover: 0.10 **NM** value: **200.00**
• CGC: 1 graded, best 7.5
6 ❑ Apr 1959 Cover: 0.10 **NM** value: **200.00**
• CGC: 2 graded, best 9.0

NEW ADVENTURES OF CHOLLY AND FLYTRAP, THE: TILL DEATH DO US PART — Marvel / Epic

1 ❑ Dec 1990 Cover: 4.95 **NM** value: **Cover or less**
Circ: CapCity orders: **6,200**
• prestige format. 📖 Till Death Do Us Part; Till Death Do Us Part, Part 1 A: Arthur Suydam W: Arthur Suydam
2 ❑ Jan 1991 Cover: 4.95 **NM** value: **Cover or less**
Circ: CapCity orders: **4,650**
• prestige format. 📖 Till Death Do Us Part, Part 2 A: Arthur Suydam W: Arthur Suydam
3 ❑ Feb 1991 Cover: 4.95 **NM** value: **Cover or less**
Circ: CapCity orders: **3,950**
• prestige format. 📖 Till Death Do Us Part, Part 3 A: Arthur Suydam W: Arthur Suydam

NEW ADVENTURES OF FELIX THE CAT — Felix

1 ❑ Oct 1992 Cover: 1.95 **NM** value: **2.25**
2 ❑ Cover: 1.95 **NM** value: **2.25**
3 ❑ Cover: 1.95 **NM** value: **2.25**
4 ❑ Cover: 1.95 **NM** value: **2.25**
5 ❑ Cover: 1.95 **NM** value: **2.25**
6 ❑ Cover: 1.95 **NM** value: **2.25**
7 ❑ Cover: 1.95 **NM** value: **2.25**
• becomes New Adventures of Felix the Cat and Friends

NEW ADVENTURES OF HUCK FINN, THE — Gold Key

1 ❑ Cover: 0.15 **NM** value: **10.00**
📖 The Curse of Thut

NEW ADVENTURES OF JESUS, THE — Rip Off

1 ❑ Cover: 0.50 **NM** value: **4.50**
📖 Stories from the Good Book; Jesus Gets a Ride; Somebody We all Know Rides Again; Jesus and His Gang on a Hot Day; Jesus to the Movie A: Foolbert Sturgeon W: Foolbert Sturgeon

Other grades: Multiply prices above by **1.5 for Mint • 2/3 for Very Fine • 1/3 for Fine • 1/5 for Very Good • 1/8 for Good**

NEW ADVENTURES OF JUDO JOE, THE — Ace

1 ❑ Mar 1987, b&w Cover: 1.75 **NM** value: **Cover or less**
📖 Streets of Terror; The Championship Bout **A:** Dan Carroll **W:** Joe Gill

NEW ADVENTURES OF PINOCCHIO — Dell

1 ❑ Oct 1962 Cover: 0.12 **NM** value: **50.00**
• **CGC:** 1 graded, best 9.0
2 ❑ 1963 Cover: 0.12 **NM** value: **40.00**
3 ❑ 1963 Cover: 0.12 **NM** value: **40.00**

NEW ADVENTURES OF RICK O'SHAY AND HIPSHOT — Cottonwood

1 ❑ Cover: 4.95 **NM** value: **Cover or less**
2 ❑ Cover: 4.95 **NM** value: **Cover or less**

NEW ADVENTURES OF SHALOMAN — Mark 1

1 ❑ b&w Cover: 1.95 **NM** value: **2.00**
2 ❑ Cover: 2.50 **NM** value: **Cover or less**
3 ❑ Cover: 2.50 **NM** value: **Cover or less**
★ Origin of Shaloman.
4 ❑ b&w Cover: 2.50 **NM** value: **Cover or less**
5 ❑ Cover: 2.95 **NM** value: **Cover or less**
• indicia says #4
8 ❑ b&w Cover: 2.50 **NM** value: **Cover or less**
★ Appearance of Y-Guys.
SE 1 ❑ b&w Cover: 2.50 **NM** value: **Cover or less**

NEW ADVENTURES OF SPEED RACER, THE — Now

0 ❑ Nov 1993 Cover: 3.95 **NM** value: **Cover or less**
Circ: CapCity orders: **6,975**
multi-dimensional cover.
1 ❑ Dec 1993 Cover: 1.95 **NM** value: **Cover or less**
Circ: CapCity orders: **5,225**
📖 The Royal Race **A:** Oscar Gonzalez Loyo **W:** Steven Sullivan
2 ❑ Jan 1994 Cover: 1.95 **NM** value: **Cover or less**
Circ: CapCity orders: **3,775**
3 ❑ Feb 1994 Cover: 1.95 **NM** value: **Cover or less**
Circ: CapCity orders: **3,000**

NEW ADVENTURES OF SUPERBOY, THE — DC

This series witnessed Superboy facing off against a slew of new and imaginative foes, as well as old arch-rival Lex Luthor. During the course of this series, Superboy got both new powers and new parents, as DC played fast and loose with the Kryptonian's established continuity.

"Dial H for Hero," a series that had several homes, ran as a bonus story in issues #28-49. Dial H for Hero featured friends, Christopher King and Victoria Grant, and later Nick Stevens, who become super-heroes by dialing H-E-R-O on hidden dials in their watches. Each time they became different heroes, such as Mr. Muscle, who has super-strength; Miss Hour-Glass, who can speed up or slow down time; and Napalm, who destroys virtually anything by turning into a firebomb.

1 ❑ Jan 1980 Cover: 0.40 **NM** value: **2.00**
• **CGC:** 7 graded, best 9.6
📖 The Most Important Year Of Superboy's Life! **A:** Kurt Schaffenberger **W:** Cary Bates
2 ❑ Feb 1980 Cover: 0.40 **NM** value: **1.50**
• **CGC:** 2 graded, best 9.6
A: Kurt Schaffenberger
3 ❑ Mar 1980 Cover: 0.40 **NM** value: **1.50**
• **CGC:** 1 graded, best 9.0
A: Kurt Schaffenberger
4 ❑ Apr 1980 Cover: 0.40 **NM** value: **1.50**
A: Kurt Schaffenberger
5 ❑ May 1980 Cover: 0.40 **NM** value: **1.50**
A: Kurt Schaffenberger
6 ❑ Jun 1980 Cover: 0.40 **NM** value: **1.50**
A: Kurt Schaffenberger
7 ❑ Jul 1980 Cover: 0.40 **NM** value: **1.50**
• bonus Superman story **A:** Kurt Schaffenberger
8 ❑ Aug 1980 Cover: 0.40 **NM** value: **1.50**
A: Kurt Schaffenberger
9 ❑ Sep 1980 Cover: 0.50 **NM** value: **1.50**
A: Kurt Schaffenberger ★ Versus Phantom Zone villains.
10 ❑ Oct 1980 Cover: 0.50 **NM** value: **1.50**
• Krypto back-up **A:** Kurt Schaffenberger
11 ❑ Nov 1980 Cover: 0.50 **NM** value: **1.50**
• Superbaby back-up **A:** Kurt Schaffenberger
12 ❑ Dec 1980 Cover: 0.50 **NM** value: **1.50**
A: Kurt Schaffenberger
13 ❑ Jan 1981 Cover: 0.50 **NM** value: **1.50**
Circ: Statement: **103,145**
A: Kurt Schaffenberger
14 ❑ Feb 1981 Cover: 0.50 **NM** value: **1.50**
Circ: Statement: **103,145**
A: Kurt Schaffenberger
15 ❑ Mar 1981 Cover: 0.50 **NM** value: **1.50**
Circ: Statement: **103,145**
A: Kurt Schaffenberger
16 ❑ Apr 1981 Cover: 0.50 **NM** value: **1.50**
Circ: Statement: **103,145**
A: Kurt Schaffenberger
17 ❑ May 1981 Cover: 0.50 **NM** value: **1.50**
Circ: Statement: **103,145**
• Krypto back-up **A:** Kurt Schaffenberger
18 ❑ Jun 1981 Cover: 0.50 **NM** value: **1.50**
Circ: Statement: **103,145**
A: Kurt Schaffenberger
19 ❑ Jul 1981 Cover: 0.50 **NM** value: **1.50**
Circ: Statement: **103,145**
A: Kurt Schaffenberger
20 ❑ Aug 1981 Cover: 0.50 **NM** value: **1.50**
Circ: Statement: **103,145**
A: Kurt Schaffenberger
21 ❑ Sep 1981 Cover: 0.50 **NM** value: **1.00**
Circ: Statement: **103,145**
A: Kurt Schaffenberger
22 ❑ Oct 1981 Cover: 0.60 **NM** value: **1.00**
Circ: Statement: **103,145**
A: Kurt Schaffenberger
23 ❑ Nov 1981 Cover: 0.60 **NM** value: **1.00**
Circ: Statement: **103,145**
A: Kurt Schaffenberger
24 ❑ Dec 1981 Cover: 0.60 **NM** value: **1.00**
Circ: Statement: **103,145**
A: Kurt Schaffenberger
25 ❑ Jan 1982 Cover: 0.60 **NM** value: **1.00**
Circ: Statement: **96,323**
A: Kurt Schaffenberger
26 ❑ Feb 1982 Cover: 0.60 **NM** value: **1.00**
Circ: Statement: **96,323**
A: Kurt Schaffenberger
27 ❑ Mar 1982 Cover: 0.60 **NM** value: **1.00**
Circ: Statement: **96,323**
A: Kurt Schaffenberger
28 ❑ Apr 1982 Cover: 0.60 **NM** value: **1.00**
Circ: Statement: **96,323**
A: Kurt Schaffenberger
29 ❑ May 1982 Cover: 0.60 **NM** value: **1.00**
Circ: Statement: **96,323**
• Has 1981 Statement; avg print run 286,761; avg sales 102,992; avg subs 853; avg total paid and max existent 103,145; 63% of run returned **A:** Kurt Schaffenberger
30 ❑ Jun 1982 Cover: 0.60 **NM** value: **1.00**
Circ: Statement: **96,323**
A: Kurt Schaffenberger
31 ❑ Jul 1982 Cover: 0.60 **NM** value: **1.00**
Circ: Statement: **96,323**
A: Kurt Schaffenberger
32 ❑ Aug 1982 Cover: 0.60 **NM** value: **1.00**
Circ: Statement: **96,323**
A: Kurt Schaffenberger
33 ❑ Sep 1982 Cover: 0.60 **NM** value: **1.00**
Circ: Statement: **96,323**
A: Kurt Schaffenberger
34 ❑ Oct 1982 Cover: 0.60 **NM** value: **1.00**
Circ: Statement: **96,323**
📖 Beware The Yellow Peri **A:** Kurt Schaffenberger **W:** Bob Rozakis ★ 1st Appearance of The Yellow Peril.
35 ❑ Nov 1982 Cover: 0.60 **NM** value: **1.00**
Circ: Statement: **96,323**
A: Kurt Schaffenberger
36 ❑ Dec 1982 Cover: 0.60 **NM** value: **1.00**
Circ: Statement: **96,323**
• Dial H for Hero back-up **A:** Kurt Schaffenberger
37 ❑ Jan 1983 Cover: 0.60 **NM** value: **1.00**
Circ: Statement: **80,433**
A: Kurt Schaffenberger
38 ❑ Feb 1983 Cover: 0.60 **NM** value: **1.00**
Circ: Statement: **80,433**
A: Kurt Schaffenberger
39 ❑ Mar 1983 Cover: 0.60 **NM** value: **1.00**
Circ: Statement: **80,433**
A: Kurt Schaffenberger
40 ❑ Apr 1983 Cover: 0.60 **NM** value: **1.00**
Circ: Statement: **80,433**
• Dial H for Hero back-up **A:** Kurt Schaffenberger
41 ❑ May 1983 Cover: 0.60 **NM** value: **1.00**
Circ: Statement: **80,433**
• Has 1982 Statement; avg print run 266,415; avg sales 94,148; avg subs 2,175; avg total paid and max existent 96,323; 62% of run returned **A:** Kurt Schaffenberger **C:** Gil Kane
42 ❑ Jun 1983 Cover: 0.60 **NM** value: **1.00**
Circ: Statement: **80,433**
A: Kurt Schaffenberger **C:** Gil Kane
43 ❑ Jul 1983 Cover: 0.60 **NM** value: **1.00**
Circ: Statement: **80,433**
• Dial H for Hero back-up **A:** Kurt Schaffenberger **C:** Gil Kane
44 ❑ Aug 1983 Cover: 0.60 **NM** value: **1.00**
Circ: Statement: **80,433**
A: Kurt Schaffenberger **C:** Gil Kane
45 ❑ Sep 1983 Cover: 0.60 **NM** value: **1.00**
Circ: Statement: **80,433**
A: Kurt Schaffenberger **C:** Gil Kane ★ 1st Appearance of Sunburst, Sunburst.
46 ❑ Oct 1983 Cover: 0.60 **NM** value: **1.00**
Circ: Statement: **80,433**
A: Kurt Schaffenberger
47 ❑ Nov 1983 Cover: 0.60 **NM** value: **1.00**
Circ: Statement: **80,433**
A: Kurt Schaffenberger
48 ❑ Dec 1983 Cover: 0.75 **NM** value: **1.00**
Circ: Statement: **80,433**
A: Kurt Schaffenberger
49 ❑ Jan 1984 Cover: 0.75 **NM** value: **1.00**
• Dial H for Hero back-up **A:** Kurt Schaffenberger
50 ❑ Feb 1984 Cover: 1.25 **NM** value: **Cover or less**
• Giant-size. **A:** Keith Giffen; Kurt Schaffenberger ★ Appearance of Legion of Super-Heroes.
51 ❑ Mar 1984 Cover: 0.75 **NM** value: **1.00**
A: Kurt Schaffenberger; Frank Miller(cover) **C:** Frank Miller
52 ❑ Apr 1984 Cover: 0.75 **NM** value: **1.00**
A: Kurt Schaffenberger
53 ❑ May 1984 Cover: 0.75 **NM** value: **1.00**
A: Kurt Schaffenberger
54 ❑ Jun 1984 Cover: 0.75 **NM** value: **1.00**
final issue. **A:** Kurt Schaffenberger

NEW ADVENTURES OF TERRY & THE PIRATES — Avalon

1 ❑ ca. 1998 Cover: 2.95 **NM** value: **Cover or less**
Circ: Diamd. preorders: **1,829**
A: Greg Hildebrandt; Tim Hildebrandt **W:** Michael Uslan
2 ❑ Cover: 2.95 **NM** value: **Cover or less**
📖 The Last Garland **A:** Greg Hildebrandt; Tim Hildebrandt **W:** Michael Uslan
3 ❑ Cover: 2.95 **NM** value: **Cover or less**
A: Greg Hildebrandt; Tim Hildebrandt **W:** Michael Uslan
4 ❑ Cover: 2.95 **NM** value: **Cover or less**
A: Greg Hildebrandt; Tim Hildebrandt **W:** Michael Uslan
5 ❑ Cover: 2.95 **NM** value: **Cover or less**
A: Greg Hildebrandt; Tim Hildebrandt **W:** Michael Uslan
6 ❑ Cover: 2.95 **NM** value: **Cover or less**
A: Greg Hildebrandt; Tim Hildebrandt **W:** Michael Uslan

NEW AGE COMICS — Fantagraphics

1 ❑ Cover: 0.35 **NM** value: **1.50**
Circ: CapCity orders: **13,875**
• Independent comics sampler

NEW AMERICA — Eclipse

1 ❑ Nov 1987 Cover: 1.75 **NM** value: **2.00**
Circ: CapCity orders: **7,425**
📖 Baja, Japan **A:** Gary Kwapisz **C:** Tom Yeates **W:** Kim Yale; John Ostrander
2 ❑ Dec 1987 Cover: 1.75 **NM** value: **2.00**
Circ: CapCity orders: **5,975**
3 ❑ Jan 1988 Cover: 1.75 **NM** value: **2.00**
Circ: CapCity orders: **5,450**
C: Tom Yeates
4 ❑ Feb 1988 Cover: 1.75 **NM** value: **2.00**
Circ: CapCity orders: **4,925**

NEW ARCHIES, THE — Archie

1 ❑ Oct 1987 Cover: 0.75 **NM** value: **2.50**
2 ❑ Jan 1988 Cover: 0.75 **NM** value: **1.50**
3 ❑ Feb 1988 Cover: 0.75 **NM** value: **1.50**
4 ❑ Apr 1988 Cover: 0.75 **NM** value: **1.50**
5 ❑ May 1988 Cover: 0.75 **NM** value: **1.50**
6 ❑ Jun 1988 Cover: 0.75 **NM** value: **1.00**
7 ❑ Aug 1988 Cover: 0.75 **NM** value: **1.00**
8 ❑ Sep 1988 Cover: 0.75 **NM** value: **1.00**
9 ❑ Oct 1988 Cover: 0.75 **NM** value: **1.00**
10 ❑ Dec 1988 Cover: 0.75 **NM** value: **1.00**
11 ❑ Jan 1989 Cover: 0.75 **NM** value: **1.00**
12 ❑ Feb 1989 Cover: 0.75 **NM** value: **1.00**
13 ❑ Apr 1989 Cover: 0.75 **NM** value: **1.00**
14 ❑ May 1989 Cover: 0.75 **NM** value: **1.00**
15 ❑ Jun 1989 Cover: 0.95 **NM** value: **1.00**
16 ❑ Aug 1989 Cover: 0.95 **NM** value: **1.00**
17 ❑ Sep 1989 Cover: 0.95 **NM** value: **1.00**
18 ❑ Oct 1989 Cover: 0.95 **NM** value: **1.00**
19 ❑ Dec 1989 Cover: 0.95 **NM** value: **1.00**
20 ❑ Jan 1990 Cover: 1.00 **NM** value: **Cover or less**
21 ❑ Feb 1990 Cover: 1.00 **NM** value: **Cover or less**
📖 Substitute Santa; Pop Tate (activity); Snow War Won!; Shopping Spree Glee; No Beef Beef; A Real Good Skate! **A:** Henry Scarpelli **W:** Mike Pellowski
22 ❑ May 1990 Cover: 1.00 **NM** value: **Cover or less**

NEW BEGINNING — Unicorn

1 ❑ b&w Cover: 1.50 **NM** value: **2.00**
2 ❑ b&w Cover: 1.75 **NM** value: **2.00**
3 ❑ b&w Cover: 1.75 **NM** value: **2.00**

NEW BONDAGE FAIRIES — Eros

1 ❑ Nov 1996 Cover: 2.95 **NM** value: **Cover or less**
Circ: Diamd. preorders: **8,309**
2 ❑ Dec 1996 Cover: 2.95 **NM** value: **Cover or less**
Circ: Diamd. preorders: **7,387**
3 ❑ Jan 1997 Cover: 2.95 **NM** value: **Cover or less**
Circ: Diamd. preorders: **7,080**
4 ❑ Feb 1997 Cover: 2.95 **NM** value: **Cover or less**
Circ: Diamd. preorders: **6,777**
5 ❑ Mar 1997 Cover: 2.95 **NM** value: **Cover or less**
Circ: Diamd. preorders: **6,802**
6 ❑ Apr 1997 Cover: 2.95 **NM** value: **Cover or less**
Circ: Diamd. preorders: **7,259**
7 ❑ May 1997 Cover: 2.95 **NM** value: **Cover or less**
Circ: Diamd. preorders: **7,312**
8 ❑ Jun 1997 Cover: 2.95 **NM** value: **Cover or less**
Circ: Diamd. preorders: **7,256**
9 ❑ Jul 1997 Cover: 2.95 **NM** value: **Cover or less**
Circ: Diamd. preorders: **7,065**
10 ❑ Aug 1997 Cover: 2.95 **NM** value: **Cover or less**
Circ: Diamd. preorders: **7,149**
11 ❑ Sep 1997 Cover: 2.95 **NM** value: **Cover or less**
Circ: Diamd. preorders: **7,193**
12 ❑ Oct 1997 Cover: 2.95 **NM** value: **Cover or less**
Circ: Diamd. preorders: **7,129**

NEW BOOK OF COMICS — DC

1 ❑ Cover: 0.10 **NM** value: **7500.00**
2 ❑ Spr 1938 Cover: 0.10 **NM** value: **4000.00**
• **CGC:** 4 graded, best 7.5

NEWCOMERS ILLUSTRATED — Newcomers

1 ❑ Cover: 2.95 **NM** value: **Cover or less**
📖 Outdoor Guy; Romo and Jolt; Standard Procedure; Dark Guy; Earth War **A:** Arie Van de Graff; James Watson; Joe Percival; Max Fitt; Steve Watson **W:** Arie Van de Graff; James Watson; Joe Percival; Steve Watson; Matt Stumphy

CGC-graded: Multiply prices above by **33 for 9.9 M • 16 for 9.8 NM/M • 7 for 9.6 NM+ • 5 for 9.4 NM • 2.5 for 9.2 NM- • 1.5 for 9.0 VF/NM**

2 ❑ Cover: 2.95 **NM** value: **Cover or less**
3 ❑ Cover: 2.95 **NM** value: **Cover or less**
4 ❑ Cover: 2.95 **NM** value: **Cover or less**
5 ❑ Cover: 2.95 **NM** value: **Cover or less**
6 ❑ Cover: 2.95 **NM** value: **Cover or less**

NEWCOMERS SHOWCASE — Newcomers

1 ❑ Cover: 2.95 **NM** value: **Cover or less**
📖 The I.N.N.Keeper; Chelsea Mascott; Adventures of Kate and Bonnie **A:** Dale Mitchell; Drew Boynton; John Malloy **W:** Dale Mitchell; Drew Boynton; John Malloy

NEW COMICS — DC

1 ❑ Dec 1935 Cover: 0.10 **NM** value: **12000.00**
• **CGC:** 1 graded, best 9.0
2 ❑ Jan 1936 Cover: 0.10 **NM** value: **7500.00**
• **CGC:** 1 graded, best 1.5
3 ❑ Feb 1936 Cover: 0.10 **NM** value: **2500.00**
4 ❑ Mar 1936 Cover: 0.10 **NM** value: **2500.00**
• **CGC:** 1 graded, best 8.0
5 ❑ Jun 1936 Cover: 0.10 **NM** value: **2500.00**
• **CGC:** 1 graded, best 7.0
6 ❑ Jul 1936 Cover: 0.10 **NM** value: **2500.00**
• **CGC:** 1 graded, best 7.5
7 ❑ Aug 1936 Cover: 0.10 **NM** value: **2500.00**
8 ❑ Sep 1936 Cover: 0.10 **NM** value: **2500.00**
9 ❑ Oct 1936 Cover: 0.10 **NM** value: **2500.00**
• **CGC:** 2 graded, best 7.5
10 ❑ Nov 1936 Cover: 0.10 **NM** value: **2500.00**
11 ❑ Dec 1936 Cover: 0.10 **NM** value: **2500.00**
• **CGC:** 1 graded, best 2.5

NEW CREW, THE — Personality

1 ❑ Cover: 2.95 **NM** value: **3.50**
• Patrick Stewart **A:** Kirk Lindo **W:** Stephen Spire III
2 ❑ Cover: 2.95 **NM** value: **3.00**
• Jonathan Frakes
3 ❑ Cover: 2.95 **NM** value: **3.00**
4 ❑ Cover: 2.95 **NM** value: **3.00**
5 ❑ Cover: 2.95 **NM** value: **3.00**
6 ❑ Cover: 2.95 **NM** value: **3.00**
7 ❑ Cover: 2.95 **NM** value: **3.00**
8 ❑ Cover: 2.95 **NM** value: **3.00**
9 ❑ Cover: 2.95 **NM** value: **3.00**
10 ❑ Cover: 2.95 **NM** value: **3.00**

NEW CRIME FILES OF MICHAEL MAUSER, PRIVATE EYE — Apple

1 ❑ b&w Cover: 2.50 **NM** value: **Cover or less**

NEW DNAGENTS, THE — Eclipse

The DNAgents (Surge, Rainbow, Tank, Amber, and Sham) are five super-heroes created by Dr. Harden, a brilliant Russian scientist. Harden was a mole, an undercover spy planted by the Russians years before he was needed, so that he could infiltrate the system. However, when the time came for him to go back and report what he knew, he refused. Harden felt an obligation to his creations, but the head of the super-hero project, Luscious Krell, is a ruthless man corrupted by power. Although the DNAgents each possess miraculous abilities, they were designed as mindless soldiers. However, the world would learn that the DNAgents are not so easily controlled.

One of the unique points about this second version of DNAgents, is that Eclipse priced this series at 75 cents, a cheap price for an independent comic in 1985. The series was printed in color, written by Mark Evanier, drawn by Mitch Schauer, and inked by Willie Blyberg.

1 ❑ Oct 1985 Cover: 0.95 **NM** value: **1.50**
📖 Backstory! **A:** Will Blyberg; Mitch Schauer **W:** Mark Evanier ★ Origin of The DNAgents.
2 ❑ Nov 1985 Cover: 0.95 **NM** value: **1.25**
W: Mark Evanier
3 ❑ Nov 1985 Cover: 0.95 **NM** value: **1.25**
W: Mark Evanier
4 ❑ Dec 1985 Cover: 0.95 **NM** value: **1.00**
Circ: CapCity orders: **9,175**
W: Mark Evanier
5 ❑ Jan 1986 Cover: 0.95 **NM** value: **1.00**
Circ: CapCity orders: **8,350**
W: Mark Evanier
6 ❑ Feb 1986 Cover: 0.95 **NM** value: **1.00**
Circ: CapCity orders: **8,025**
W: Mark Evanier
7 ❑ Apr 1986 Cover: 0.95 **NM** value: **1.00**
Circ: CapCity orders: **7,300**
W: Mark Evanier
8 ❑ Apr 1986 Cover: 0.95 **NM** value: **1.00**
Circ: CapCity orders: **6,875**
W: Mark Evanier
9 ❑ Jun 1986 Cover: 0.95 **NM** value: **1.00**
Circ: CapCity orders: **6,800**
W: Mark Evanier
10 ❑ Jun 1986 Cover: 0.95 **NM** value: **1.00**
Circ: CapCity orders: **6,600**
W: Mark Evanier
11 ❑ Aug 1986 Cover: 0.95 **NM** value: **1.00**
Circ: CapCity orders: **6,550**
W: Mark Evanier
12 ❑ Aug 1986 Cover: 0.95 **NM** value: **1.00**
Circ: CapCity orders: **6,275**
W: Mark Evanier
13 ❑ Oct 1986 Cover: 1.25 **NM** value: **Cover or less**
Circ: CapCity orders: **5,825**
W: Mark Evanier
14 ❑ Nov 1986 Cover: 1.25 **NM** value: **Cover or less**
Circ: CapCity orders: **5,600**
W: Mark Evanier
15 ❑ Dec 1986 Cover: 1.25 **NM** value: **Cover or less**
Circ: CapCity orders: **5,500**
W: Mark Evanier
16 ❑ Jan 1987 Cover: 1.25 **NM** value: **Cover or less**
Circ: CapCity orders: **5,375**
W: Mark Evanier
17 ❑ Mar 1987 Cover: 1.25 **NM** value: **Cover or less**
Circ: CapCity orders: **4,850**
final issue. **W:** Mark Evanier

NEW ENGLAND GOTHIC — Visigoth

1 ❑ Dec 1986 Cover: 2.00 **NM** value: **Cover or less**
A: Tom Brown **W:** James LaPointe

NEW ETERNALS — Marvel

1 ❑ Dec 1999 Cover: 3.99 **NM** value: **Cover or less**
Circ: Diamd. preorders: **24,222**
• no indicia

NEW FANTASTIC FOUR: MONSTERS UNLEASHED — Marvel

Bk 1 ❑ Cover: 5.95 **NM** value: **Cover or less**

NEWFORCE — Image

1 ❑ Jan 1996 Cover: 2.50 **NM** value: **Cover or less**
📖 Extreme Destroyer, Part 8 • polybagged with Kodiak card **A:** Todd Nauck **W:** Rob Liefeld; Eric Stephenson
2 ❑ Feb 1996 Cover: 2.50 **NM** value: **Cover or less**
3 ❑ Mar 1996 Cover: 2.50 **NM** value: **Cover or less**
4 ❑ Apr 1996 Cover: 2.50 **NM** value: **Cover or less**

NEW FRONTIER, THE — Dark Horse

1 ❑ Oct 1992, b&w Cover: 2.75 **NM** value: **Cover or less**
A: Michael Cherkas **W:** Michael Cherkas; John Sabljic
2 ❑ Nov 1992, b&w Cover: 2.75 **NM** value: **Cover or less**
A: Michael Cherkas **W:** Michael Cherkas; John Sabljic
3 ❑ Dec 1992, b&w Cover: 2.75 **NM** value: **Cover or less**
A: Michael Cherkas **W:** Michael Cherkas; John Sabljic
Bk 1 ❑ Jun 1994, b&w Cover: 12.95 **NM** value: **Cover or less**
• collects stories from the series and Heavy Metal **A:** Michael Cherkas **W:** Michael Cherkas; John Sabljic

NEW FRONTIERS — Evolution

1 ❑ b&w Cover: 1.75 **NM** value: **Cover or less**
📖 Devil in Her Heart; Actionmaster: Life Support **A:** Mercy E. Van Vlack; T.J. Glenn **W:** Mike Forrester; Tom & Mary Bierbaum
2 ❑ b&w Cover: 1.95 **NM** value: **Cover or less**
📖 Unspoken Yesterdays; Sticks and Stones and Ancient Bones; **A:** Mercy E. Van Vlack; T.J. Glenn **W:** Mike Forrester; Tom & Mary Bierbaum

NEW FUNNIES (WALTER LANTZ...) — Dell

Dell's long-running New Funnies series was a showcase for many of its funny animal strips, including Felix the Cat, The Brownies, and Walter Lantz's crazy creations such as Woody Woodpecker. Lantz actually got title billing after issue #109.

As the leading funny animal publisher, Dell had access to all the characters from the animation studios and aggressively tied its comic books in with the popularity of cartoon characters. Woody Woodpecker, whose manic motion and trademark giggle are hard to capture on the printed page, was one of the featured characters of the series. Sharing the spotlight in the Walter Lantz issues were Andy Panda and Homer Pigeon.

65 ❑ Jul 1942 Cover: 0.10 **NM** value: **425.00**
• **CGC:** 1 graded, best 6.0
• Series continued from The Funnies #64
66 ❑ Aug 1942 Cover: 0.10 **NM** value: **235.00**
67 ❑ Sep 1942 Cover: 0.10 **NM** value: **235.00**
68 ❑ Oct 1942 Cover: 0.10 **NM** value: **235.00**
69 ❑ Nov 1942 Cover: 0.10 **NM** value: **235.00**
70 ❑ Dec 1942 Cover: 0.10 **NM** value: **235.00**
71 ❑ Jan 1943 Cover: 0.10 **NM** value: **160.00**
72 ❑ Feb 1943 Cover: 0.10 **NM** value: **160.00**
73 ❑ Mar 1943 Cover: 0.10 **NM** value: **160.00**
74 ❑ Apr 1943 Cover: 0.10 **NM** value: **160.00**
75 ❑ May 1943 Cover: 0.10 **NM** value: **160.00**
76 ❑ Jun 1943 Cover: 0.10 **NM** value: **485.00**
• Andy Panda **A:** Carl Barks
77 ❑ Jul 1943 Cover: 0.10 **NM** value: **130.00**
78 ❑ Aug 1943 Cover: 0.10 **NM** value: **130.00**
79 ❑ Sep 1943 Cover: 0.10 **NM** value: **130.00**
• **CGC:** 1 graded, best 7.5
80 ❑ Oct 1943 Cover: 0.10 **NM** value: **130.00**
81 ❑ Nov 1943 Cover: 0.10 **NM** value: **100.00**
82 ❑ Dec 1943 Cover: 0.10 **NM** value: **100.00**
83 ❑ Jan 1944 Cover: 0.10 **NM** value: **100.00**
84 ❑ Feb 1944 Cover: 0.10 **NM** value: **100.00**
85 ❑ Mar 1944 Cover: 0.10 **NM** value: **100.00**
86 ❑ Apr 1944 Cover: 0.10 **NM** value: **100.00**
87 ❑ May 1944 Cover: 0.10 **NM** value: **100.00**
88 ❑ Jun 1944 Cover: 0.10 **NM** value: **100.00**
89 ❑ Jul 1944 Cover: 0.10 **NM** value: **100.00**
90 ❑ Aug 1944 Cover: 0.10 **NM** value: **100.00**
91 ❑ Sep 1944 Cover: 0.10 **NM** value: **65.00**
92 ❑ Oct 1944 Cover: 0.10 **NM** value: **65.00**
93 ❑ Nov 1944 Cover: 0.10 **NM** value: **65.00**
94 ❑ Dec 1944 Cover: 0.10 **NM** value: **65.00**
95 ❑ Jan 1945 Cover: 0.10 **NM** value: **65.00**
96 ❑ Feb 1945 Cover: 0.10 **NM** value: **65.00**
97 ❑ Mar 1945 Cover: 0.10 **NM** value: **65.00**
98 ❑ Apr 1945 Cover: 0.10 **NM** value: **65.00**
99 ❑ May 1945 Cover: 0.10 **NM** value: **65.00**
100 ❑ Jun 1945 Cover: 0.10 **NM** value: **65.00**
101 ❑ Jul 1945 Cover: 0.10 **NM** value: **45.00**
102 ❑ Aug 1945 Cover: 0.10 **NM** value: **45.00**
103 ❑ Sep 1945 Cover: 0.10 **NM** value: **45.00**
104 ❑ Oct 1945 Cover: 0.10 **NM** value: **45.00**
105 ❑ Nov 1945 Cover: 0.10 **NM** value: **45.00**
106 ❑ Dec 1945 Cover: 0.10 **NM** value: **45.00**
107 ❑ Jan 1946 Cover: 0.10 **NM** value: **45.00**
108 ❑ Feb 1946 Cover: 0.10 **NM** value: **45.00**
109 ❑ Mar 1946 Cover: 0.10 **NM** value: **45.00**
110 ❑ Apr 1946 Cover: 0.10 **NM** value: **45.00**
111 ❑ May 1946 Cover: 0.10 **NM** value: **35.00**
112 ❑ Jun 1946 Cover: 0.10 **NM** value: **35.00**
113 ❑ Jul 1946 Cover: 0.10 **NM** value: **35.00**
114 ❑ Aug 1946 Cover: 0.10 **NM** value: **35.00**
115 ❑ Sep 1946 Cover: 0.10 **NM** value: **35.00**
116 ❑ Oct 1946 Cover: 0.10 **NM** value: **35.00**
117 ❑ Nov 1946 Cover: 0.10 **NM** value: **35.00**
118 ❑ Dec 1946 Cover: 0.10 **NM** value: **35.00**
119 ❑ Jan 1947 Cover: 0.10 **NM** value: **35.00**
120 ❑ Feb 1947 Cover: 0.10 **NM** value: **35.00**
121 ❑ Mar 1947 Cover: 0.10 **NM** value: **28.00**
122 ❑ Apr 1947 Cover: 0.10 **NM** value: **28.00**
123 ❑ May 1947 Cover: 0.10 **NM** value: **28.00**
124 ❑ Jun 1947 Cover: 0.10 **NM** value: **28.00**
125 ❑ Jul 1947 Cover: 0.10 **NM** value: **28.00**
126 ❑ Aug 1947 Cover: 0.10 **NM** value: **28.00**
127 ❑ Sep 1947 Cover: 0.10 **NM** value: **28.00**
128 ❑ Oct 1947 Cover: 0.10 **NM** value: **28.00**
129 ❑ Nov 1947 Cover: 0.10 **NM** value: **28.00**
130 ❑ Dec 1947 Cover: 0.10 **NM** value: **28.00**
131 ❑ Jan 1948 Cover: 0.10 **NM** value: **20.00**
132 ❑ Feb 1948 Cover: 0.10 **NM** value: **20.00**
133 ❑ Mar 1948 Cover: 0.10 **NM** value: **20.00**
134 ❑ Apr 1948 Cover: 0.10 **NM** value: **20.00**
135 ❑ May 1948 Cover: 0.10 **NM** value: **20.00**
136 ❑ Jun 1948 Cover: 0.10 **NM** value: **20.00**
137 ❑ Jul 1948 Cover: 0.10 **NM** value: **20.00**
138 ❑ Aug 1948 Cover: 0.10 **NM** value: **20.00**
139 ❑ Sep 1948 Cover: 0.10 **NM** value: **20.00**
140 ❑ Oct 1948 Cover: 0.10 **NM** value: **20.00**
141 ❑ Nov 1948 Cover: 0.10 **NM** value: **20.00**
142 ❑ Dec 1948 Cover: 0.10 **NM** value: **20.00**
143 ❑ Jan 1949 Cover: 0.10 **NM** value: **20.00**
144 ❑ Feb 1949 Cover: 0.10 **NM** value: **20.00**
145 ❑ Mar 1949 Cover: 0.10 **NM** value: **20.00**
146 ❑ Apr 1949 Cover: 0.10 **NM** value: **20.00**
147 ❑ May 1949 Cover: 0.10 **NM** value: **20.00**
148 ❑ Jun 1949 Cover: 0.10 **NM** value: **20.00**
149 ❑ Jul 1949 Cover: 0.10 **NM** value: **20.00**
150 ❑ Aug 1949 Cover: 0.10 **NM** value: **20.00**
151 ❑ Sep 1949 Cover: 0.10 **NM** value: **14.00**
152 ❑ Oct 1949 Cover: 0.10 **NM** value: **14.00**
153 ❑ Nov 1949 Cover: 0.10 **NM** value: **14.00**
154 ❑ Dec 1949 Cover: 0.10 **NM** value: **14.00**
155 ❑ Jan 1950 Cover: 0.10 **NM** value: **14.00**
156 ❑ Feb 1950 Cover: 0.10 **NM** value: **14.00**
157 ❑ Mar 1950 Cover: 0.10 **NM** value: **14.00**
158 ❑ Apr 1950 Cover: 0.10 **NM** value: **14.00**
159 ❑ May 1950 Cover: 0.10 **NM** value: **14.00**
160 ❑ Jun 1950 Cover: 0.10 **NM** value: **14.00**
161 ❑ Jul 1950 Cover: 0.10 **NM** value: **14.00**
162 ❑ Aug 1950 Cover: 0.10 **NM** value: **14.00**
163 ❑ Sep 1950 Cover: 0.10 **NM** value: **14.00**
164 ❑ Oct 1950 Cover: 0.10 **NM** value: **14.00**
165 ❑ Nov 1950 Cover: 0.10 **NM** value: **14.00**
166 ❑ Dec 1950 Cover: 0.10 **NM** value: **14.00**
167 ❑ Jan 1951 Cover: 0.10 **NM** value: **14.00**
168 ❑ Feb 1951 Cover: 0.10 **NM** value: **14.00**
169 ❑ Mar 1951 Cover: 0.10 **NM** value: **14.00**
170 ❑ Apr 1951 Cover: 0.10 **NM** value: **14.00**
171 ❑ May 1951 Cover: 0.10 **NM** value: **12.00**
172 ❑ Jun 1951 Cover: 0.10 **NM** value: **12.00**
173 ❑ Jul 1951 Cover: 0.10 **NM** value: **12.00**
174 ❑ Aug 1951 Cover: 0.10 **NM** value: **12.00**
175 ❑ Sep 1951 Cover: 0.10 **NM** value: **12.00**
176 ❑ Oct 1951 Cover: 0.10 **NM** value: **12.00**
177 ❑ Nov 1951 Cover: 0.10 **NM** value: **12.00**
178 ❑ Dec 1951 Cover: 0.10 **NM** value: **12.00**
179 ❑ Jan 1952 Cover: 0.10 **NM** value: **12.00**
180 ❑ Feb 1952 Cover: 0.10 **NM** value: **12.00**
181 ❑ Mar 1952 Cover: 0.10 **NM** value: **12.00**
182 ❑ Apr 1952 Cover: 0.10 **NM** value: **12.00**
183 ❑ May 1952 Cover: 0.10 **NM** value: **12.00**
184 ❑ Jun 1952 Cover: 0.10 **NM** value: **12.00**
📖 Woody Woodpecker, Andy Panda, Homer Pigeon, Oswald the Rabbit, Happy Hobby **A:** Anahid Dinkjian; Dan Gormley(cover); Irene Little; Lloyd White; Richard Hall; Suzanne Seaborne; Vivie Risto **W:** Charles Hedlinger; Del Connell; Frank Thomas; Mick Dubin; Steve Dubin
185 ❑ Jul 1952 Cover: 0.10 **NM** value: **12.00**
186 ❑ Aug 1952 Cover: 0.10 **NM** value: **12.00**
187 ❑ Sep 1952 Cover: 0.10 **NM** value: **12.00**
188 ❑ Oct 1952 Cover: 0.10 **NM** value: **12.00**
189 ❑ Nov 1952 Cover: 0.10 **NM** value: **12.00**

Other grades: Multiply prices above by **1.5 for Mint • 2/3 for Very Fine • 1/3 for Fine • 1/5 for Very Good • 1/8 for Good**

190 ❑ Dec 1952 Cover: 0.10 **NM** value: **12.00**
191 ❑ Jan 1953 Cover: 0.10 **NM** value: **9.00**
192 ❑ Feb 1953 Cover: 0.10 **NM** value: **9.00**
193 ❑ Mar 1953 Cover: 0.10 **NM** value: **9.00**
194 ❑ Apr 1953 Cover: 0.10 **NM** value: **9.00**
195 ❑ May 1953 Cover: 0.10 **NM** value: **9.00**
196 ❑ Jun 1953 Cover: 0.10 **NM** value: **9.00**
197 ❑ Jul 1953 Cover: 0.10 **NM** value: **9.00**
198 ❑ Aug 1953 Cover: 0.10 **NM** value: **9.00**
199 ❑ Sep 1953 Cover: 0.10 **NM** value: **9.00**
200 ❑ Oct 1953 Cover: 0.10 **NM** value: **9.00**
201 ❑ Nov 1953 Cover: 0.10 **NM** value: **9.00**
202 ❑ Dec 1953 Cover: 0.10 **NM** value: **9.00**
203 ❑ Jan 1954 Cover: 0.10 **NM** value: **9.00**
204 ❑ Feb 1954 Cover: 0.10 **NM** value: **9.00**
205 ❑ Mar 1954 Cover: 0.10 **NM** value: **9.00**
206 ❑ Apr 1954 Cover: 0.10 **NM** value: **9.00**
207 ❑ May 1954 Cover: 0.10 **NM** value: **9.00**
208 ❑ Jun 1954 Cover: 0.10 **NM** value: **9.00**
209 ❑ Jul 1954 Cover: 0.10 **NM** value: **9.00**
210 ❑ Aug 1954 Cover: 0.10 **NM** value: **9.00**
211 ❑ Sep 1954 Cover: 0.10 **NM** value: **9.00**
212 ❑ Oct 1954 Cover: 0.10 **NM** value: **9.00**
213 ❑ Nov 1954 Cover: 0.10 **NM** value: **9.00**
214 ❑ Dec 1954 Cover: 0.10 **NM** value: **9.00**
215 ❑ Jan 1955 Cover: 0.10 **NM** value: **9.00**
216 ❑ Feb 1955 Cover: 0.10 **NM** value: **9.00**
217 ❑ Mar 1955 Cover: 0.10 **NM** value: **9.00**
218 ❑ Apr 1955 Cover: 0.10 **NM** value: **9.00**
219 ❑ May 1955 Cover: 0.10 **NM** value: **9.00**
220 ❑ Jun 1955 Cover: 0.10 **NM** value: **9.00**
221 ❑ Jul 1955 Cover: 0.10 **NM** value: **8.00**
222 ❑ Aug 1955 Cover: 0.10 **NM** value: **8.00**
223 ❑ Sep 1955 Cover: 0.10 **NM** value: **8.00**
224 ❑ Oct 1955 Cover: 0.10 **NM** value: **8.00**
225 ❑ Nov 1955 Cover: 0.10 **NM** value: **8.00**
226 ❑ Dec 1955 Cover: 0.10 **NM** value: **8.00**
227 ❑ Jan 1956 Cover: 0.10 **NM** value: **8.00**
228 ❑ Feb 1956 Cover: 0.10 **NM** value: **8.00**
229 ❑ Mar 1956 Cover: 0.10 **NM** value: **8.00**
230 ❑ Apr 1956 Cover: 0.10 **NM** value: **8.00**
231 ❑ May 1956 Cover: 0.10 **NM** value: **8.00**
232 ❑ Jun 1956 Cover: 0.10 **NM** value: **8.00**
233 ❑ Jul 1956 Cover: 0.10 **NM** value: **8.00**
234 ❑ Aug 1956 Cover: 0.10 **NM** value: **8.00**
235 ❑ Sep 1956 Cover: 0.10 **NM** value: **8.00**
236 ❑ Oct 1956 Cover: 0.10 **NM** value: **8.00**
237 ❑ Nov 1956 Cover: 0.10 **NM** value: **8.00**
238 ❑ Dec 1956 Cover: 0.10 **NM** value: **8.00**
239 ❑ Jan 1957 Cover: 0.10 **NM** value: **8.00**
240 ❑ Feb 1957 Cover: 0.10 **NM** value: **8.00**
241 ❑ Mar 1957 Cover: 0.10 **NM** value: **6.00**
242 ❑ Apr 1957 Cover: 0.10 **NM** value: **6.00**
243 ❑ May 1957 Cover: 0.10 **NM** value: **6.00**
244 ❑ Jun 1957 Cover: 0.10 **NM** value: **6.00**
245 ❑ Jul 1957 Cover: 0.10 **NM** value: **6.00**
246 ❑ Aug 1957 Cover: 0.10 **NM** value: **6.00**
247 ❑ Sep 1957 Cover: 0.10 **NM** value: **6.00**
248 ❑ Oct 1957 Cover: 0.10 **NM** value: **6.00**
249 ❑ Nov 1957 Cover: 0.10 **NM** value: **6.00**
250 ❑ Dec 1957 Cover: 0.10 **NM** value: **6.00**
251 ❑ Jan 1958 Cover: 0.10 **NM** value: **6.00**
252 ❑ Feb 1958 Cover: 0.10 **NM** value: **6.00**
253 ❑ Mar 1958 Cover: 0.10 **NM** value: **6.00**
254 ❑ Apr 1958 Cover: 0.10 **NM** value: **6.00**
255 ❑ May 1958 Cover: 0.10 **NM** value: **6.00**
256 ❑ Jun 1958 Cover: 0.10 **NM** value: **6.00**
257 ❑ Jul 1958 Cover: 0.10 **NM** value: **6.00**
258 ❑ Aug 1958 Cover: 0.10 **NM** value: **6.00**
259 ❑ Sep 1958 Cover: 0.10 **NM** value: **6.00**
260 ❑ Oct 1958 Cover: 0.10 **NM** value: **6.00**
• Series continued in TV Funnies (Walter Lantz...) #261
272 ❑ Oct 1959 Cover: 0.10 **NM** value: **4.00**
• Series continued from TV Funnies (Walter Lantz...) #271)
273 ❑ Nov 1959 Cover: 0.10 **NM** value: **4.00**
274 ❑ Dec 1959 Cover: 0.10 **NM** value: **4.00**
275 ❑ Jan 1960 Cover: 0.10 **NM** value: **4.00**
276 ❑ Mar 1960 Cover: 0.10 **NM** value: **4.00**
277 ❑ May 1960 Cover: 0.10 **NM** value: **4.00**
278 ❑ Jul 1960 Cover: 0.10 **NM** value: **4.00**
279 ❑ Sep 1960 Cover: 0.10 **NM** value: **4.00**
280 ❑ Nov 1960 Cover: 0.10 **NM** value: **4.00**
281 ❑ Feb 1961 Cover: 0.10 **NM** value: **4.00**
282 ❑ Apr 1961 Cover: 0.10 **NM** value: **4.00**
283 ❑ Jun 1961 Cover: 0.10 **NM** value: **4.00**
284 ❑ Aug 1961 Cover: 0.10 **NM** value: **4.00**
285 ❑ Oct 1961 Cover: 0.10 **NM** value: **4.00**
286 ❑ Dec 1961 Cover: 0.10 **NM** value: **4.00**
287 ❑ Feb 1962 Cover: 0.10 **NM** value: **4.00**
288 ❑ Apr 1962 Cover: 0.10 **NM** value: **4.00**
final issue.

Diamond preorders are the estimated number of comics sold, prior to their release, to comics shops in North America by Diamond Comic Distributors, the largest distributor. These figures underreport the actual number of circulating copies by the amount of reorders Diamond took (usually 5-10% again of the preorders) and sales by publishers to newsstand and bookstore distributors. For many independent publishers, Diamond's preorders may be quite close to the actual number of copies in circulation.

NEW GODS, THE (1ST SERIES) DC

On a distant world, the old gods had come into their twilight hour. In dying, two of these old gods gave birth to new worlds: Balduur's atoms became the world of New Genesis, a place of peace and learning; and the warlike world of Apokolips sprung from that which was once a sorceress.

These worlds are populated by the new gods, scientifically advanced and capable of building fantastic cities — or deadly weapons of war. After fighting a deadly clash that devastated both worlds, Apokolips' ruler, Darkseid, offered his son Orion in exchange for New Genesis' ruler Izaya's young boy. These boys were held as hostages for peace between the two worlds. Of course, Darkseid did not really desire peace, but merely time to plot a further strategy. Meanwhile, the boy, dubbed "Scott Free" began a program of rigorous military training on Apokolips; he would later put it to good use as Mister Miracle.

1 ❑ Mar 1971 Cover: 0.15 **NM** value: **35.00**
• **CGC:** 86 graded, best 9.8
📖 In The Beginning • ; **A:** Jack Kirby **W:** Jack Kirby ★ 1st Appearance of Orion, Apokolips, Metron, Kalibak, Highfather, Lightray.
2 ❑ May 1971 Cover: 0.15 **NM** value: **20.00**
• **CGC:** 13 graded, best 9.6
A: Jack Kirby **W:** Jack Kirby ★ 1st Appearance of Deep Six.
3 ❑ Jul 1971 Cover: 0.15 **NM** value: **16.00**
• **CGC:** 7 graded, best 9.6
A: Jack Kirby **W:** Jack Kirby ★ 1st Appearance of Black Racer.
4 ❑ Sep 1971 Cover: 0.25 **NM** value: **14.00**
• **CGC:** 5 graded, best 9.6
• Giant-size. **A:** Jack Kirby **W:** Jack Kirby
5 ❑ Nov 1971 Cover: 0.25 **NM** value: **14.00**
• **CGC:** 2 graded, best 9.6
• Giant-size. **A:** Jack Kirby **W:** Jack Kirby
6 ❑ Jan 1972 Cover: 0.25 **NM** value: **14.00**
• **CGC:** 2 graded, best 9.0
• Giant-size. **A:** Jack Kirby **W:** Jack Kirby ★ 1st Appearance of Fastbak.
7 ❑ Mar 1972 Cover: 0.25 **NM** value: **14.00**
• **CGC:** 3 graded, best 9.4
• Giant-size. **A:** Jack Kirby **W:** Jack Kirby ★ 1st Appearance of Steppenwolf.
8 ❑ May 1972 Cover: 0.25 **NM** value: **10.00**
• **CGC:** 2 graded, best 9.4
• Giant-size. **A:** Jack Kirby **W:** Jack Kirby
9 ❑ Jul 1972 Cover: 0.25 **NM** value: **10.00**
• **CGC:** 1 graded, best 9.6
• Giant-size. **A:** Jack Kirby **W:** Jack Kirby ★ 1st Appearance of Forager.
10 ❑ Sep 1972 Cover: 0.20 **NM** value: **8.00**
A: Jack Kirby **W:** Jack Kirby
11 ❑ Nov 1972 Cover: 0.20 **NM** value: **8.00**
A: Jack Kirby **W:** Jack Kirby
12 ❑ Jul 1977 Cover: 0.35 **NM** value: **4.00**
📖 The Return of the New Gods • Series begins again (1977)
13 ❑ Aug 1977 Cover: 0.35 **NM** value: **4.00**
14 ❑ Oct 1977 Cover: 0.35 **NM** value: **4.00**
15 ❑ Dec 1977 Cover: 0.35 **NM** value: **4.00**
16 ❑ Feb 1978 Cover: 0.35 **NM** value: **4.00**
17 ❑ Apr 1978 Cover: 0.35 **NM** value: **4.00**
18 ❑ Jun 1978 Cover: 0.35 **NM** value: **4.00**
19 ❑ Aug 1978 Cover: 0.35 **NM** value: **4.00**
final issue.
Bk 1 ❑ b&w Cover: 11.95 **NM** value: **Cover or less**
• Jack Kirby's New Gods; collects New Gods **A:** Jack Kirby **W:** Jack Kirby; Mark Evanier

NEW GODS (2ND SERIES) DC

1 ❑ Jun 1984 Cover: 2.00 **NM** value: **Cover or less**
• New Gods (Vol. 1) reprints **A:** Jack Kirby
2 ❑ Jul 1984 Cover: 2.00 **NM** value: **Cover or less**
• New Gods (Vol. 1) reprints **A:** Jack Kirby
3 ❑ Aug 1984 Cover: 2.00 **NM** value: **Cover or less**
• New Gods (Vol. 1) reprints **A:** Jack Kirby
4 ❑ Oct 1984 Cover: 2.00 **NM** value: **Cover or less**
• New Gods (Vol. 1) reprints **A:** Jack Kirby
5 ❑ Nov 1984 Cover: 2.00 **NM** value: **Cover or less**
• New Gods (Vol. 1) reprints **A:** Jack Kirby
6 ❑ Dec 1984 Cover: 2.00 **NM** value: **Cover or less**
• **CGC:** 1 graded, best 9.0
📖 Darkseid and Sons; Even Gods Must Die • reprints New Gods (Vol. 1) #11, plus new stories **A:** Jack Kirby

NEW GODS (3RD SERIES) DC

1 ❑ Feb 1989 Cover: 1.50 **NM** value: **2.25**
Circ: CapCity orders: **21,950** • **CGC:** 1 graded, best 9.6
📖 Hordes **A:** Paris Cullins **W:** Paris Cullins; Mark Evanier
2 ❑ Mar 1989 Cover: 1.50 **NM** value: **2.00**
Circ: CapCity orders: **17,350**
A: Paris Cullins **W:** Paris Cullins; Mark Evanier
3 ❑ Apr 1989 Cover: 1.50 **NM** value: **2.00**
Circ: CapCity orders: **14,650**
A: Paris Cullins **W:** Paris Cullins; Mark Evanier
4 ❑ May 1989 Cover: 1.50 **NM** value: **2.00**
Circ: CapCity orders: **13,750**
A: Paris Cullins **W:** Paris Cullins; Mark Evanier
5 ❑ Jun 1989 Cover: 1.50 **NM** value: **2.00**
Circ: CapCity orders: **13,800**
A: Paris Cullins **W:** Paris Cullins; Mark Evanier
6 ❑ Jul 1989 Cover: 1.50 **NM** value: **Cover or less**
Circ: CapCity orders: **12,900**
A: Paris Cullins **W:** Paris Cullins; Mark Evanier
7 ❑ Aug 1989 Cover: 1.50 **NM** value: **Cover or less**
Circ: CapCity orders: **12,450**
📖 Bloodline, Part 1 **A:** Paris Cullins **W:** Paris Cullins; Mark Evanier
8 ❑ Sep 1989 Cover: 1.50 **NM** value: **Cover or less**
Circ: CapCity orders: **12,050**
📖 Bloodline, Part 2 **A:** Paris Cullins **W:** Paris Cullins; Mark Evanier
9 ❑ Oct 1989 Cover: 1.50 **NM** value: **Cover or less**
Circ: CapCity orders: **11,650**
📖 Bloodline, Part 3 **A:** Paris Cullins **W:** Paris Cullins; Mark Evanier
10 ❑ Nov 1989 Cover: 1.50 **NM** value: **Cover or less**
Circ: CapCity orders: **10,900**
📖 Bloodline, Part 4 **A:** Paris Cullins **W:** Paris Cullins; Mark Evanier
11 ❑ Dec 1989 Cover: 1.50 **NM** value: **Cover or less**
Circ: CapCity orders: **10,450**
📖 Bloodline, Part 5 **A:** Paris Cullins **W:** Paris Cullins; Mark Evanier
12 ❑ Jan 1990 Cover: 1.50 **NM** value: **Cover or less**
Circ: CapCity orders: **10,550**
📖 Bloodline, Part 6 **A:** Paris Cullins **W:** Paris Cullins; Mark Evanier
13 ❑ Feb 1990 Cover: 1.50 **NM** value: **Cover or less**
Circ: CapCity orders: **10,050**
14 ❑ Mar 1990 Cover: 1.50 **NM** value: **Cover or less**
Circ: CapCity orders: **9,750**
15 ❑ Apr 1990 Cover: 1.50 **NM** value: **Cover or less**
Circ: CapCity orders: **9,250**
16 ❑ May 1990 Cover: 1.50 **NM** value: **Cover or less**
Circ: CapCity orders: **9,300**
17 ❑ Jun 1990 Cover: 1.50 **NM** value: **Cover or less**
Circ: CapCity orders: **8,700**
18 ❑ Jul 1990 Cover: 1.50 **NM** value: **Cover or less**
Circ: CapCity orders: **8,400**
19 ❑ Aug 1990 Cover: 1.50 **NM** value: **Cover or less**
Circ: CapCity orders: **8,050**
20 ❑ Sep 1990 Cover: 1.50 **NM** value: **Cover or less**
Circ: CapCity orders: **8,050**
21 ❑ Dec 1990 Cover: 1.50 **NM** value: **Cover or less**
Circ: CapCity orders: **8,100**
22 ❑ Jan 1991 Cover: 1.50 **NM** value: **Cover or less**
Circ: CapCity orders: **8,200**
23 ❑ Feb 1991 Cover: 1.50 **NM** value: **Cover or less**
Circ: CapCity orders: **8,050**
24 ❑ Mar 1991 Cover: 1.50 **NM** value: **Cover or less**
Circ: CapCity orders: **7,800**
25 ❑ Apr 1991 Cover: 1.50 **NM** value: **Cover or less**
Circ: CapCity orders: **7,600**
26 ❑ May 1991 Cover: 1.50 **NM** value: **Cover or less**
Circ: CapCity orders: **7,450**
27 ❑ Jul 1991 Cover: 1.50 **NM** value: **Cover or less**
Circ: CapCity orders: **7,300**
28 ❑ Aug 1991 Cover: 1.50 **NM** value: **Cover or less**
Circ: CapCity orders: **7,050**
final issue.

NEW GODS (4TH SERIES) DC

1 ❑ Oct 1995 Cover: 1.95 **NM** value: **2.00**
Circ: CapCity orders: **23,000**
📖 Attack on the Source! **A:** Luke Ross **W:** Rachel Pollack; Tom Peyer
2 ❑ Nov 1995 Cover: 1.95 **NM** value: **2.00**
3 ❑ Dec 1995 Cover: 1.95 **NM** value: **2.00**
📖 After the Fall **A:** Luke Ross **W:** Rachel Pollack; Tom Peyer
4 ❑ Jan 1996 Cover: 1.95 **NM** value: **2.00**
A: Luke Ross **W:** Rachel Pollack; Tom Peyer
5 ❑ Feb 1996 Cover: 1.95 **NM** value: **2.00**
📖 Descent into Madness! **A:** Luke Ross **W:** Rachel Pollack; Tom Peyer
6 ❑ Mar 1996 Cover: 1.95 **NM** value: **2.00**
📖 Destruction of the Beast! **A:** Luke Ross **W:** Rachel Pollack
7 ❑ Apr 1996 Cover: 1.95 **NM** value: **2.00**
📖 The End of the Gods **A:** Stefano Raffaele **W:** Rachel Pollack
8 ❑ Jun 1996 Cover: 1.95 **NM** value: **2.00**
📖 Sins of the Fathers **A:** Dean Zachary **W:** Rachel Pollack
9 ❑ Jul 1996 Cover: 1.95 **NM** value: **2.00**
10 ❑ Aug 1996 Cover: 1.95 **NM** value: **2.00**
★ Appearance of Superman.
11 ❑ Sep 1996 Cover: 1.95 **NM** value: **2.00**
12 ❑ Nov 1996 Cover: 0.99 **NM** value: **1.00**
Circ: Diamd. preorders: **28,811**
📖 After the Fall **A:** John Byrne **W:** John Byrne
13 ❑ Dec 1996 Cover: 1.95 **NM** value: **2.00**
Circ: Diamd. preorders: **23,125**
📖 Night of the Falling Sky **A:** John Byrne **W:** John Byrne
14 ❑ Jan 1997 Cover: 1.95 **NM** value: **2.00**
Circ: Diamd. preorders: **22,149**
📖 The Gathering Storm! **A:** John Byrne **W:** John Byrne ★ Appearance of Forever People.
15 ❑ Feb 1997 Cover: 1.95 **NM** value: **2.00**
Circ: Diamd. preorders: **20,855**
A: John Byrne; Walt Simonson(cover) **W:** John Byrne

NEW GODS SECRET FILES DC

1 ❑ Sep 1998 Cover: 4.95 **NM** value: **Cover or less**
Circ: Diamd. preorders: **16,210**

NEW GUARDIANS, THE DC

1 ❑ Sep 1988 Cover: 2.00 **NM** value: **Cover or less**
Circ: CapCity orders: **20,850**
• Giant-size. 📖 The New Guardians **A:** Joe Staton **W:** Steve Englehart
2 ❑ Oct 1988 Cover: 1.25 **NM** value: **Cover or less**
Circ: CapCity orders: **16,100**
3 ❑ Nov 1988 Cover: 1.25 **NM** value: **Cover or less**
Circ: CapCity orders: **14,200**
4 ❑ Dec 1988 Cover: 1.25 **NM** value: **Cover or less**
Circ: CapCity orders: **13,000**
5 ❑ Dec 1988 Cover: 1.25 **NM** value: **Cover or less**
Circ: CapCity orders: **11,650**
6 ❑ Jan 1989 Cover: 1.25 **NM** value: **Cover or less**
Circ: CapCity orders: **12,650**
• Invasion!

CGC-graded: Multiply prices above by **33 for 9.9 M • 16 for 9.8 NM/M • 7 for 9.6 NM+ • 5 for 9.4 NM • 2.5 for 9.2 NM- • 1.5 for 9.0 VF/NM**

7 ❑ Feb 1989 Cover: 1.25 **NM** value: **Cover or less**
Circ: CapCity orders: **10,150**
• Invasion!

8 ❑ Apr 1989 Cover: 1.25 **NM** value: **Cover or less**
Circ: CapCity orders: **9,600**

9 ❑ Jun 1989 Cover: 1.25 **NM** value: **Cover or less**
Circ: CapCity orders: **9,050**

10 ❑ Jul 1989 Cover: 1.25 **NM** value: **Cover or less**
Circ: CapCity orders: **7,850**

11 ❑ Aug 1989 Cover: 1.25 **NM** value: **Cover or less**
Circ: CapCity orders: **7,800**

12 ❑ Sep 1989 Cover: 1.25 **NM** value: **Cover or less**
Circ: CapCity orders: **7,550**

NEW HAT — Black Eye

1 ❑ **NM** value: **1.00**

NEW HERO COMICS — Red Spade

1 ❑ b&w **NM** value: **1.00**

NEW HORIZONS — Shanda Fantasy Arts

1 ❑ b&w Cover: 4.95 **NM** value: **Cover or less**
2 ❑ b&w Cover: 4.95 **NM** value: **Cover or less**
3 ❑ b&w Cover: 4.50 **NM** value: **Cover or less**
4 ❑ b&w Cover: 4.50 **NM** value: **Cover or less**
5 ❑ Apr 1999, b&w Cover: 4.50 **NM** value: **Cover or less**

NEW HUMANS, THE (ETERNITY) — Eternity

1 ❑ Dec 1987 Cover: 1.95 **NM** value: **Cover or less**
W: David Lawrence ★ Origin of New Humans.

2 ❑ Jan 1988 Cover: 1.95 **NM** value: **Cover or less**
📖 The Sun Never Sets; The Rovers **A:** Shawn Atkinson; Scott Bieser **W:** David Lawrence; S.A. Bennett

3 ❑ Feb 1988 Cover: 1.95 **NM** value: **Cover or less**
A: Shawn Atkinson **W:** David Lawrence

4 ❑ Mar 1988 Cover: 1.95 **NM** value: **Cover or less**
Nude cover. **A:** Shawn Atkinson **W:** David Lawrence

5 ❑ 1988 Cover: 1.95 **NM** value: **Cover or less**
A: Shawn Atkinson **W:** David Lawrence

6 ❑ 1988 Cover: 1.95 **NM** value: **Cover or less**
A: Shawn Atkinson **W:** David Lawrence

7 ❑ 1988 Cover: 1.95 **NM** value: **Cover or less**
A: Shawn Atkinson **W:** David Lawrence

8 ❑ Sep 1988 Cover: 1.95 **NM** value: **Cover or less**
A: Shawn Atkinson **W:** David Lawrence

9 ❑ 1988 Cover: 1.95 **NM** value: **Cover or less**
A: Shawn Atkinson **W:** David Lawrence

10 ❑ 1989 Cover: 1.95 **NM** value: **Cover or less**
A: Shawn Atkinson **W:** David Lawrence

11 ❑ Cover: 1.95 **NM** value: **Cover or less**
A: Shawn Atkinson **W:** David Lawrence

12 ❑ Mar 1989 Cover: 1.95 **NM** value: **Cover or less**
A: Shawn Atkinson **W:** David Lawrence

13 ❑ Cover: 1.95 **NM** value: **Cover or less**
A: Shawn Atkinson **W:** David Lawrence

14 ❑ Cover: 1.95 **NM** value: **Cover or less**
A: Shawn Atkinson **W:** David Lawrence

15 ❑ Cover: 1.95 **NM** value: **Cover or less**
A: Shawn Atkinson **W:** David Lawrence

16 ❑ Cover: 1.95 **NM** value: **Cover or less**
A: Shawn Atkinson **W:** David Lawrence

17 ❑ Cover: 1.95 **NM** value: **Cover or less**
final issue. **A:** Shawn Atkinson **W:** David Lawrence

Anl 1❑ b&w Cover: 2.95 **NM** value: **Cover or less**
A: Shawn Atkinson **W:** David Lawrence

NEW HUMANS, THE (PIED PIPER) — Pied Piper

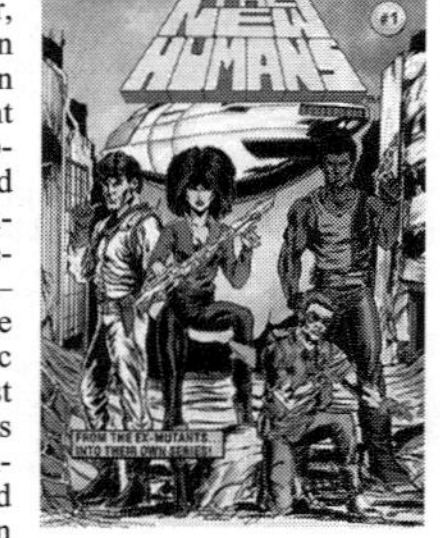

Deep inside a NASA lab, astronauts Kelly Brock, Roger Brunner, Duke Goldberg and Calvin Gordon are placed in suspended animation as part of a short-term experiment for deep-space exploration equipment. But above ground, a swift and sudden nuclear war causes the experiment to go awry. The base is destroyed and everyone is killed — except the four sleepers, who awake 30 years later to a post-apocalyptic nightmare. Now, the explorers must make their way as the only humans in a dangerous world peopled entirely by mutants. Written and drawn by David Lawrence and Ron Lim, this series was a spinoff from Lawrence and Lim's better-known creation, the Ex-Mutants. A second series came from Eclipse.

1 ❑ Jul 1987, b&w Cover: 1.95 **NM** value: **Cover or less**
📖 After the Fire **A:** Ron Lim **W:** David Lawrence ★ Origin of The New Humans.

2 ❑ 1987 Cover: 1.95 **NM** value: **Cover or less**
A: Ron Lim **W:** David Lawrence

3 ❑ 1987 Cover: 1.95 **NM** value: **Cover or less**
A: Ron Lim **W:** David Lawrence

NEW JUSTICE MACHINE, THE — Innovation

1 ❑ Nov 1989 Cover: 1.95 **NM** value: **2.00**
Circ: CapCity orders: **5,100**
📖 Crossroads **A:** Darryl Banks **W:** Mark Ellis; David Lawrence

2 ❑ Jan 1990 Cover: 1.95 **NM** value: **2.00**
Circ: CapCity orders: **4,200**

3 ❑ Mar 1990 Cover: 1.95 **NM** value: **2.00**
Circ: CapCity orders: **4,200**

NEW KIDS ON THE BLOCK, THE: BACKSTAGE PASS — Harvey

1 ❑ ca. 1991 Cover: 1.25 **NM** value: **Cover or less**
📖 Sleepless Knights; A Jordan Knightmare; Two On One; Scared Silly **A:** Ernie Colon **W:** Michael Gallagher

NEW KIDS ON THE BLOCK: CHILLIN' — Harvey

1 ❑ ca. 1990 Cover: 1.25 **NM** value: **1.50**
2 ❑ Jan 1991 Cover: 1.25 **NM** value: **Cover or less**
3 ❑ ca. 1991 Cover: 1.25 **NM** value: **Cover or less**
4 ❑ Apr 1991 Cover: 1.25 **NM** value: **Cover or less**
5 ❑ Jun 1991 Cover: 1.25 **NM** value: **Cover or less**
6 ❑ Oct 1991 Cover: 1.25 **NM** value: **Cover or less**
7 ❑ Dec 1991 Cover: 1.25 **NM** value: **Cover or less**
📖 The Arabian Nightmare **A:** Hy Rosen **W:** Jeff Rovin

NEW KIDS ON THE BLOCK COMIC TOUR '90 — Harvey

1 ❑ ca. 1991 Cover: 1.25 **NM** value: **Cover or less**

NEW KIDS ON THE BLOCK MAGIC SUMMER TOUR — Harvey

1 ❑ ca. 1991 Cover: 1.25 **NM** value: **Cover or less**
Circ: CapCity orders: **2,350**
No issue number.

1/LE❑ ca. 1991 Cover: 3.95 **NM** value: **Cover or less**
Circ: CapCity orders: **2,575**
No issue number. • limited edition.

NEW KIDS ON THE BLOCK, THE: NKOTB — Harvey

1 ❑ Dec 1990 Cover: 1.25 **NM** value: **Cover or less**
Circ: CapCity orders: **5,575**
📖 Vacation Breaks; The World According to Donnie; New News on the Block (text); Double Trouble; Learn to Dance Step by Step with Jordan; …Back to Nature **A:** Ernie Colon; Frank Hill **W:** Angelo Decesare

2 ❑ Jan 1991 Cover: 1.25 **NM** value: **Cover or less**
Circ: CapCity orders: **4,025**

3 ❑ Feb 1991 Cover: 1.25 **NM** value: **Cover or less**
Circ: CapCity orders: **3,825**

4 ❑ Mar 1991 Cover: 1.25 **NM** value: **Cover or less**
Circ: CapCity orders: **2,775**

5 ❑ May 1991 Cover: 1.25 **NM** value: **Cover or less**
Circ: CapCity orders: **2,375**
📖 A Pizza Cake **A:** Neil Grahams **W:** Lisa Trusiani

6 ❑ Jul 1991 Cover: 1.25 **NM** value: **Cover or less**
Circ: CapCity orders: **1,700**
📖 on the Right Track **A:** Neil Grahams **W:** Tom Franco

NEW KIDS ON THE BLOCK STEP BY STEP — Harvey

1 ❑ ca. 1991 Cover: 1.25 **NM** value: **Cover or less**
Circ: CapCity orders: **2,550**
No issue number.

NEW KIDS ON THE BLOCK: VALENTINE GIRL — Harvey

1 ❑ ca. 1991 Cover: 1.25 **NM** value: **Cover or less**
Circ: CapCity orders: **2,525**
No issue number.

NEW LOVE — Fantagraphics

1 ❑ Aug 1996, b&w Cover: 2.95 **NM** value: **Cover or less**
2 ❑ Oct 1996, b&w Cover: 2.95 **NM** value: **Cover or less**
Circ: Diamd. preorders: **6,854**

3 ❑ Mar 1997, b&w Cover: 2.95 **NM** value: **Cover or less**
Circ: Diamd. preorders: **5,649**

4 ❑ Jun 1997, b&w Cover: 2.95 **NM** value: **Cover or less**
Circ: Diamd. preorders: **5,073**

5 ❑ Nov 1997, b&w Cover: 2.95 **NM** value: **Cover or less**
Circ: Diamd. preorders: **4,187**

6 ❑ Dec 1997, b&w Cover: 2.95 **NM** value: **Cover or less**

NEWMAN — Image

1 ❑ Jan 1996 Cover: 2.50 **NM** value: **Cover or less**
📖 Extreme Destroyer, Part 3 • polybagged with card; Extreme Destroyer Part 3 **A:** Manny Clark **W:** Rob Liefeld; Eldon Asp; Eric Stephenson

2 ❑ Feb 1996 Cover: 2.50 **NM** value: **Cover or less**
📖 New Beginnings **A:** Michael Chang **W:** Eldon Asp

3 ❑ Apr 1996 Cover: 2.50 **NM** value: **Cover or less**
4 ❑ Apr 1996 Cover: 2.50 **NM** value: **Cover or less**
📖 Shadowhunt, Part 5 ★ Versus Youngblood.

NEWMEN — Image

1 ❑ Apr 1994 Cover: 1.95 **NM** value: **2.50**
Circ: CapCity orders: **35,950**
A: Jeff Matsuda **W:** Rob Liefeld; Jeff Matsuda; Eric Stephenson

2 ❑ May 1994 Cover: 1.95 **NM** value: **2.25**
Circ: CapCity orders: **28,950**

3 ❑ Jun 1994 Cover: 1.95 **NM** value: **2.25**
Circ: CapCity orders: **27,425**

4 ❑ Jul 1994 Cover: 1.95 **NM** value: **2.25**
Circ: CapCity orders: **24,625**

5 ❑ Aug 1994 Cover: 2.50 **NM** value: **Cover or less**
Circ: CapCity orders: **23,525**

6 ❑ Sep 1994 Cover: 2.50 **NM** value: **Cover or less**
Circ: CapCity orders: **21,400**

7 ❑ Oct 1994 Cover: 2.50 **NM** value: **Cover or less**
Circ: CapCity orders: **20,300**

8 ❑ Nov 1994 Cover: 2.50 **NM** value: **Cover or less**
Circ: CapCity orders: **18,675**

9 ❑ Dec 1994 Cover: 2.50 **NM** value: **Cover or less**
Circ: CapCity orders: **16,500**
• Extreme Sacrifice

10 ❑ Jan 1995 Cover: 2.50 **NM** value: **Cover or less**
Circ: CapCity orders: **19,125**
📖 Extreme Sacrifice, Part 5; Extreme Sacrifice, Part 4

11 ❑ Feb 1995 Cover: 2.50 **NM** value: **Cover or less**
Circ: CapCity orders: **12,725**
📖 Extreme Sacrifice Aftermath • polybagged

11/A❑ Feb 1995 Cover: 2.50 **NM** value: **Cover or less**
alternate cover. 📖 Extreme Sacrifice Aftermath • polybagged

12 ❑ Mar 1995 Cover: 2.50 **NM** value: **Cover or less**
Circ: CapCity orders: **12,275**

13 ❑ Apr 1995 Cover: 2.50 **NM** value: **Cover or less**
Circ: CapCity orders: **11,550**
📖 Dominion, Part 1

14 ❑ May 1995 Cover: 2.50 **NM** value: **Cover or less**
Circ: CapCity orders: **12,050**
📖 Dominion, Part 2

15 ❑ Jun 1995 Cover: 2.50 **NM** value: **Cover or less**
Circ: CapCity orders: **12,000**
• no indicia

16 ❑ Jul 1995 Cover: 2.50 **NM** value: **Cover or less**
Circ: CapCity orders: **11,575**
📖 Dominion, Part 4

16/A❑ Jul 1995 Cover: 2.50 **NM** value: **3.00**
alternate cover. 📖 Dominion, Part 4

17 ❑ Aug 1995 Cover: 2.50 **NM** value: **Cover or less**
Circ: CapCity orders: **10,050**

18 ❑ Sep 1995 Cover: 2.50 **NM** value: **Cover or less**
Circ: CapCity orders: **8,375**

19 ❑ Oct 1995 Cover: 2.50 **NM** value: **Cover or less**
Circ: CapCity orders: **5,650**
📖 Extreme Destroyer

20 ❑ Nov 1995 Cover: 2.50 **NM** value: **Cover or less**
• Babewatch

20/A❑ Nov 1995 Cover: 2.50 **NM** value: **Cover or less**
• Babewatch

21 ❑ Aug 1996 Cover: 2.50 **NM** value: **Cover or less**
22 ❑ Sep 1996 Cover: 2.50 **NM** value: **Cover or less**
Circ: Diamd. preorders: **14,873**

23 ❑ Mar 1997 Cover: 2.50 **NM** value: **Cover or less**
Circ: Diamd. preorders: **9,429**

24 ❑ Apr 1997 Cover: 2.50 **NM** value: **Cover or less**
Circ: Diamd. preorders: **9,466**

25 ❑ May 1997 Cover: 2.50 **NM** value: **Cover or less**
Circ: Diamd. preorders: **9,147**

Bk 1❑ Cover: 12.95 **NM** value: **Cover or less**
• collects issues #1-4

NEW MUTANTS, THE — Marvel

The New Mutants first appeared in Marvel Graphic Novel #4. At that time, Professor Xavier of the Uncanny X-Men had realized that a separate group was needed to train the growing number of young mutants being discovered. This group became the New Mutants.

Originally consisting of Cannonball, Sunspot, Karma, Wolfsbane, and Psyche, the New Mutants quickly added others to its rolls. In the same manner, the original members dropped out for one reason or another.

In issue #87, the New Mutants were revitalized by the introduction of Cable, an militant cyborg who quickly became their leader. Several of the New Mutants declined to become a part of Cable's team, but their ranks were filled with newcomers. Following issue #100, the team started anew as X-Force.

1 ❑ Mar 1983 Cover: 0.60 **NM** value: **2.00**
• **CGC:** 34 graded, best 9.8
📖 Initiation! **A:** Bob McLeod **W:** Chris Claremont

2 ❑ Apr 1983 Cover: 0.60 **NM** value: **2.00**
• **CGC:** 1 graded, best 9.8
📖 Sentinels **A:** Bob McLeod **W:** Chris Claremont ★ Versus Sentinels.

3 ❑ May 1983 Cover: 0.60 **NM** value: **2.00**
📖 Nightmare **A:** Bob McLeod **W:** Chris Claremont ★ Versus Brood.

4 ❑ Jun 1983 Cover: 0.60 **NM** value: **1.50**
📖 Who's Scaring Stevie? **A:** Sal Buscema **W:** Chris Claremont

5 ❑ Jul 1983 Cover: 0.60 **NM** value: **1.50**
📖 Heroes **A:** Sal Buscema **W:** Chris Claremont ★ Appearance of Team America.

6 ❑ Aug 1983 Cover: 0.60 **NM** value: **1.50**
📖 Road Warriors! **A:** Sal Buscema **W:** Chris Claremont ★ Appearance of Team America.

7 ❑ Sep 1983 Cover: 0.60 **NM** value: **1.50**
• **CGC:** 1 graded, best 9.8
📖 Flying Down To Rio! **A:** Sal Buscema **W:** Chris Claremont

8 ❑ Oct 1983 Cover: 0.60 **NM** value: **1.50**
📖 The Road To…Rome? **A:** Bob McLeod **W:** Chris Claremont ★ Origin of Magma. ★ 1st Appearance of Magma.

9 ❑ Nov 1983 Cover: 0.60 **NM** value: **1.50**
📖 Arena **A:** Sal Buscema **W:** Chris Claremont ★ 1st Appearance of Selene.

10 ❑ Dec 1983 Cover: 0.60 **NM** value: **1.50**
📖 Betrayal **A:** Sal Buscema **W:** Chris Claremont ★ 1st Appearance of Magma.

11 ❑ Jan 1984 Cover: 0.60 **NM** value: **1.50**
📖 Magma • Assistant Editor Month **A:** Sal Buscema **W:** Chris Claremont

12 ❑ Feb 1984 Cover: 0.60 **NM** value: **1.50**
• **CGC:** 1 graded, best 9.8
📖 Sunstroke **A:** Sal Buscema **W:** Chris Claremont

13 ❑ Mar 1984 Cover: 0.60 **NM** value: **1.50**
• **CGC:** 1 graded, best 9.8
📖 School Daysze **A:** Sal Buscema **W:** Chris Claremont ★ 1st Appearance of Cypher, Kitty Pryde.

Other grades: Multiply prices above by **1.5 for Mint • 2/3 for Very Fine • 1/3 for Fine • 1/5 for Very Good • 1/8 for Good**

14 ❑ Apr 1984 Cover: 0.60 **NM** value: **1.50**
📖 Do You Believe In Magik? **A:** Sal Buscema **W:** Chris Claremont ★ Appearance of X-Men. ★ Versus Sy'm.

15 ❑ May 1984 Cover: 0.60 **NM** value: **1.50**
• **CGC:** 1 graded, best 9.4
📖 Scaredy Cat! • X-Men **A:** Sal Buscema **W:** Chris Claremont

16 ❑ Jun 1984 Cover: 0.60 **NM** value: **1.50**
★ 1st Appearance of Warpath, Hellions.

17 ❑ Jul 1984 Cover: 0.60 **NM** value: **1.50**
📖 Getaway! • The New Mutants vs. The Hellions **A:** Tom Mandrake; Sal Buscema; Kim Demulder **W:** Chris Claremont

18 ❑ Aug 1984 Cover: 0.60 **NM** value: **1.50**
• **CGC:** 1 graded, best 9.6
📖 Death-Hunt **A:** Bill Sienkiewicz **W:** Chris Claremont ★ 1st Appearance of Warlock (machine).

19 ❑ Sep 1984 Cover: 0.60 **NM** value: **1.50**
📖 Siege **A:** Bill Sienkiewicz **W:** Chris Claremont

20 ❑ Oct 1984 Cover: 0.60 **NM** value: **1.50**
📖 Badlands **A:** Bill Sienkiewicz **W:** Chris Claremont

21 ❑ Nov 1984 Cover: 1.00 **NM** value: **1.50**
• **CGC:** 1 graded, best 9.6
• Double-size. 📖 Slumber Party! **A:** Bill Sienkiewicz **W:** Chris Claremont ★ Origin of Warlock (machine).

22 ❑ Dec 1984 Cover: 0.60 **NM** value: **1.50**
📖 The Shadow Within **A:** Bill Sienkiewicz **W:** Chris Claremont

23 ❑ Jan 1985 Cover: 0.60 **NM** value: **1.50**
A: Bill Sienkiewicz **W:** Chris Claremont ★ Appearance of Cloak & Dagger.

24 ❑ Feb 1985 Cover: 0.60 **NM** value: **1.50**
📖 The Hollow Heart **A:** Bill Sienkiewicz **W:** Chris Claremont ★ Appearance of Cloak & Dagger.

25 ❑ Mar 1985 Cover: 0.60 **NM** value: **2.50**
• **CGC:** 1 graded, best 9.4
A: Bill Sienkiewicz; Bill Sienkiewicz(cover) ★ 1st Appearance of Legion (cameo). ★ Appearance of Cloak & Dagger.

26 ❑ Apr 1985 Cover: 0.65 **NM** value: **2.50**
A: Bill Sienkiewicz; Bill Sienkiewicz(cover) ★ 1st Appearance of Legion (psychic).

27 ❑ May 1985 Cover: 0.65 **NM** value: **2.00**
Circ: CapCity orders: **31,200**
A: Bill Sienkiewicz; Bill Sienkiewicz(cover) ★ Appearance of Legion. ★ Versus Legion.

28 ❑ Jun 1985 Cover: 0.65 **NM** value: **2.00**
Circ: CapCity orders: **28,600** • **CGC:** 1 graded, best 9.8
📖 Soulwar **A:** Bill Sienkiewicz **W:** Chris Claremont ★ Appearance of Legion.

29 ❑ Jul 1985 Cover: 0.65 **NM** value: **2.00**
Circ: CapCity orders: **27,800**
📖 Meanwhile, Back At The Mansion **A:** Bill Sienkiewicz **W:** Chris Claremont ★ 1st Appearance of Guido Carosella (Strong Guy).

30 ❑ Aug 1985 Cover: 0.65 **NM** value: **1.50**
Circ: CapCity orders: **32,600** • **CGC:** 1 graded, best 9.8
📖 Secret Wars II • Secret Wars II **A:** Bill Sienkiewicz **W:** Chris Claremont

31 ❑ Sep 1985 Cover: 0.65 **NM** value: **1.50**
Circ: CapCity orders: **31,900**
📖 Saturday Night Fight! **A:** Bill Sienkiewicz **W:** Chris Claremont

32 ❑ Oct 1985 Cover: 0.65 **NM** value: **1.50**
Circ: CapCity orders: **26,500**

33 ❑ Nov 1985 Cover: 0.65 **NM** value: **1.50**
Circ: CapCity orders: **25,700**
📖 Against All Odds **A:** Steve Leialoha **W:** Chris Claremont

34 ❑ Dec 1985 Cover: 0.65 **NM** value: **1.50**
Circ: CapCity orders: **24,800** • **CGC:** 1 graded, best 9.8
📖 With A Little Bit Of Luck **A:** Steve Leialoha **W:** Chris Claremont

35 ❑ Jan 1986 Cover: 0.75 **NM** value: **1.50**
Circ: Statement: **217,933** CapCity orders: **23,500**
📖 The Times, They Are A' Changin'! • Magneto begins as leader of New Mutants **A:** Bill Sienkiewicz; Mary Wilshire **W:** Chris Claremont ★ Appearance of Magneto.

36 ❑ Feb 1986 Cover: 0.75 **NM** value: **1.50**
Circ: Statement: **217,933** CapCity orders: **30,400**
📖 Secret Wars II • Secret Wars II **A:** Bill Sienkiewicz; Mary Wilshire **C:** Arthur Adams **W:** Chris Claremont

37 ❑ Mar 1986 Cover: 0.75 **NM** value: **1.50**
Circ: Statement: **217,933** CapCity orders: **28,100**
📖 Secret Wars II • Secret Wars II **A:** Bill Sienkiewicz; Mary Wilshire **W:** Chris Claremont

38 ❑ Apr 1986 Cover: 0.75 **NM** value: **1.50**
Circ: Statement: **217,933** CapCity orders: **24,300**
📖 Aftermath **A:** Rick Leonardi **C:** Arthur Adams **W:** Chris Claremont

39 ❑ May 1986 Cover: 0.75 **NM** value: **1.50**
Circ: Statement: **217,933** CapCity orders: **26,700**
📖 Pawns Of The White Queen **A:** Keith Pollard **C:** Arthur Adams **W:** Chris Claremont

40 ❑ Jun 1986 Cover: 0.75 **NM** value: **1.50**
Circ: Statement: **217,933** CapCity orders: **26,400**
★ Appearance of Captain America.

41 ❑ Jul 1986 Cover: 0.75 **NM** value: **1.50**
Circ: Statement: **217,933** CapCity orders: **26,600**

42 ❑ Aug 1986 Cover: 0.75 **NM** value: **1.50**
Circ: Statement: **217,933** CapCity orders: **27,600**

43 ❑ Sep 1986 Cover: 0.75 **NM** value: **1.50**
Circ: Statement: **217,933** CapCity orders: **27,900**

44 ❑ Oct 1986 Cover: 0.75 **NM** value: **1.50**
Circ: Statement: **217,933** CapCity orders: **27,900**
📖 Runaway! **A:** Jackson Guice **W:** Chris Claremont ★ Appearance of Legion.

45 ❑ Nov 1986 Cover: 0.75 **NM** value: **1.50**
Circ: Statement: **217,933** CapCity orders: **28,300**
📖 We Were Only Foolin' **A:** Jackson Guice **W:** Chris Claremont

46 ❑ Dec 1986 Cover: 0.75 **NM** value: **1.50**
Circ: Statement: **217,933** CapCity orders: **31,000**
📖 Mutant Massacre; Bloody Sunday **A:** Jackson Guice **W:** Chris Claremont

47 ❑ Jan 1987 Cover: 0.75 **NM** value: **1.50**
Circ: Statement: **223,667** CapCity orders: **29,500**

48 ❑ Feb 1987 Cover: 0.75 **NM** value: **1.50**
Circ: Statement: **223,667** CapCity orders: **30,300**
📖 Ashes Of The Heart **A:** Jackson Guice **W:** Chris Claremont

49 ❑ Mar 1987 Cover: 0.75 **NM** value: **1.50**
Circ: Statement: **223,667** CapCity orders: **30,700**
📖 Ashes Of The Soul **A:** Bret Blevins **W:** Chris Claremont

50 ❑ Apr 1987 Cover: 1.25 **NM** value: **1.50**
Circ: Statement: **223,667** CapCity orders: **32,800**
• Double-size. 📖 Father's Day! • Professor X returns as headmaster **A:** Jackson Guice **W:** Chris Claremont

51 ❑ May 1987 Cover: 0.75 **NM** value: **1.50**
Circ: Statement: **223,667** CapCity orders: **30,500**
📖 Teacher's Choice **A:** Kevin Nowlan **W:** Chris Claremont ★ Appearance of Star Jammers.

52 ❑ Jun 1987 Cover: 0.75 **NM** value: **1.50**
Circ: Statement: **223,667** CapCity orders: **29,400** • **CGC:** 1 graded, best 9.8

53 ❑ Jul 1987 Cover: 0.75 **NM** value: **1.50**
Circ: Statement: **223,667** CapCity orders: **30,900**

54 ❑ Aug 1987 Cover: 0.75 **NM** value: **1.50**
Circ: Statement: **223,667** CapCity orders: **32,600**

55 ❑ Sep 1987 Cover: 0.75 **NM** value: **1.50**
Circ: Statement: **223,667** CapCity orders: **33,700**
📖 Flying Wild! **A:** Bret Blevins **W:** Louise Simonson

56 ❑ Oct 1987 Cover: 0.75 **NM** value: **1.50**
Circ: Statement: **223,667** CapCity orders: **33,200**
📖 Scavenger Hunt! **A:** June Brigman **W:** Louise Simonson

57 ❑ Nov 1987 Cover: 0.75 **NM** value: **1.50**
Circ: Statement: **223,667** CapCity orders: **34,450**
📖 Birds Of A Feather **A:** Bret Blevins **W:** Louise Simonson

58 ❑ Dec 1987 Cover: 0.75 **NM** value: **1.50**
Circ: Statement: **223,667** CapCity orders: **32,400**
• registration card

59 ❑ Jan 1988 Cover: 0.75 **NM** value: **2.00**
Circ: Statement: **235,180** CapCity orders: **34,800**
📖 Fall of the Mutants • Fall of Mutants

60 ❑ Feb 1988 Cover: 1.25 **NM** value: **2.00**
Circ: Statement: **235,180** CapCity orders: **42,100**
• double-sized. 📖 Fall of the Mutants • Fall of the Mutants **A:** Bret Blevins **W:** Louise Simonson ★ Death of Cypher.

61 ❑ Mar 1988 Cover: 0.75 **NM** value: **2.00**
Circ: Statement: **235,180** CapCity orders: **50,100**
📖 Fall of the Mutants • Fall of the Mutants; new costumes; (conclusion); (conclusion) **A:** Bret Blevins **W:** Louise Simonson

62 ❑ Apr 1988 Cover: 0.75 **NM** value: **1.50**
Circ: Statement: **235,180** CapCity orders: **39,300**
📖 To Build A Fire **A:** Jon J. Muth **W:** Louise Simonson

63 ❑ May 1988 Cover: 1.00 **NM** value: **2.00**
Circ: Statement: **235,180** CapCity orders: **39,900**
★ Appearance of X-Men.

64 ❑ Jun 1988 Cover: 1.00 **NM** value: **1.50**
Circ: Statement: **235,180** CapCity orders: **35,600**
📖 Instant Replay! **A:** Bret Blevins **W:** Louise Simonson

65 ❑ Jul 1988 Cover: 1.00 **NM** value: **1.50**
Circ: Statement: **235,180** CapCity orders: **36,300**

66 ❑ Aug 1988 Cover: 1.00 **NM** value: **1.50**
Circ: Statement: **235,180** CapCity orders: **35,500**

67 ❑ Sep 1988 Cover: 1.00 **NM** value: **1.50**
Circ: Statement: **235,180** CapCity orders: **33,900**
📖 Promise **A:** Bret Blevins **W:** Louise Simonson

68 ❑ Oct 1988 Cover: 1.00 **NM** value: **1.50**
Circ: Statement: **235,180** CapCity orders: **34,800**
📖 Iggusion! **A:** Bret Blevins **W:** Louise Simonson

69 ❑ Nov 1988 Cover: 1.00 **NM** value: **1.50**
Circ: Statement: **235,180** CapCity orders: **34,100**
📖 Bad Company **A:** Bret Blevins **W:** Louise Simonson

70 ❑ Dec 1988 Cover: 1.00 **NM** value: **1.50**
Circ: Statement: **235,180** CapCity orders: **37,500**
• Inferno

71 ❑ Jan 1989 Cover: 1.00 **NM** value: **1.50**
Circ: Statement: **210,335** CapCity orders: **39,300**
📖 Inferno • Inferno★ Origin of N'astirh.

72 ❑ Feb 1989 Cover: 1.00 **NM** value: **1.50**
Circ: Statement: **210,335** CapCity orders: **37,400**
📖 Inferno • Inferno

73 ❑ Mar 1989 Cover: 1.50 **NM** value: **2.00**
Circ: Statement: **210,335** CapCity orders: **38,900**
• Giant-size. • Inferno

74 ❑ Apr 1989 Cover: 1.00 **NM** value: **1.50**
Circ: Statement: **210,335** CapCity orders: **36,200**
📖 The Right Stuff **A:** Bret Blevins **W:** Louise Simonson

75 ❑ May 1989 Cover: 1.00 **NM** value: **1.50**
Circ: Statement: **210,335** CapCity orders: **39,500**

76 ❑ Jun 1989 Cover: 1.00 **NM** value: **1.50**
Circ: Statement: **210,335** CapCity orders: **40,000**
📖 Splash! • Sub-Mariner; X-Terminator appear **A:** Rich Buckler **W:** Louise Simonson ★ Appearance of X-Factor.

77 ❑ Jul 1989 Cover: 1.00 **NM** value: **1.50**
Circ: Statement: **210,335** CapCity orders: **37,400**
📖 Strange! **A:** Rich Buckler **W:** Louise Simonson

78 ❑ Aug 1989 Cover: 1.00 **NM** value: **1.50**
Circ: Statement: **210,335** CapCity orders: **38,900** • **CGC:** 1 graded, best 9.8

79 ❑ Sep 1989 Cover: 1.00 **NM** value: **1.50**
Circ: Statement: **210,335** CapCity orders: **37,000**
📖 Asgard! **A:** Bret Blevins **W:** Louise Simonson

80 ❑ Oct 1989 Cover: 1.00 **NM** value: **1.50**
Circ: Statement: **210,335** CapCity orders: **35,400**
📖 Curse Of The Valkyries **A:** Bret Blevins **W:** Louise Simonson

81 ❑ Nov 1989 Cover: 1.00 **NM** value: **1.50**
Circ: Statement: **210,335** CapCity orders: **33,500**
📖 Faith **A:** Louis Williams **W:** Chris Claremont

82 ❑ Nov 1989 Cover: 1.00 **NM** value: **1.50**
Circ: Statement: **210,335** CapCity orders: **33,700**
📖 The Road To Hel… **A:** Bret Blevins **W:** Louise Simonson

83 ❑ Dec 1989 Cover: 1.00 **NM** value: **1.50**
Circ: Statement: **210,335** CapCity orders: **33,400**
📖 The Quick And The Dead **A:** Bret Blevins **W:** Louise Simonson

84 ❑ Dec 1989 Cover: 1.00 **NM** value: **1.50**
Circ: Statement: **210,335** CapCity orders: **32,900**
📖 Acts of Vengeance • Acts of Vengeance **A:** Terry Shoemaker **W:** Louise Simonson

85 ❑ Jan 1990 Cover: 1.00 **NM** value: **1.50**
Circ: Statement: **182,499** CapCity orders: **33,550**
📖 Acts of Vengeance • Acts of Vengeance **C:** Todd McFarlane

86 ❑ Feb 1990 Cover: 1.00 **NM** value: **4.00**
Circ: Statement: **182,499** CapCity orders: **35,300** • **CGC:** 5 graded, best 9.6
• Acts of Vengeance **C:** Todd McFarlane ★ 1st Appearance of Zero, Cable (cameo).

87 ❑ Mar 1990 Cover: 1.00 **NM** value: **9.00**
Circ: Statement: **182,499** CapCity orders: **34,500** • **CGC:** 112 graded, best 9.8
C: Todd McFarlane ★ 1st Appearance of Stryfe, Cable.

87-2❑ Mar 1990 Cover: 1.00 **NM** value: **2.00**
• 2nd printing (gold) **C:** Todd McFarlane ★ 1st Appearance of Cable.

88 ❑ Apr 1990 Cover: 1.00 **NM** value: **4.00**
Circ: Statement: **182,499** CapCity orders: **35,100** • **CGC:** 2 graded, best 9.8
📖 The Great Escape **A:** Rob Liefeld **C:** Todd McFarlane **W:** Louise Simonson ★ 2nd Appearance of Cable.

89 ❑ May 1990 Cover: 1.00 **NM** value: **3.50**
Circ: Statement: **182,499** CapCity orders: **33,900**
• Has 1989 Statement, filed 11/1/89; avg print run 313,910; avg sales 204,270; avg subs 6,065; avg total paid 210,335; samples 125; office use 600; max existent 211,060; 33% of run returned **C:** Todd McFarlane

90 ❑ Jun 1990 Cover: 1.00 **NM** value: **3.50**
Circ: Statement: **182,499** CapCity orders: **36,900**
★ Appearance of Sabretooth.

91 ❑ Jul 1990 Cover: 1.00 **NM** value: **3.50**
Circ: Statement: **182,499** CapCity orders: **36,300**
★ Appearance of Sabretooth.

92 ❑ Aug 1990 Cover: 1.00 **NM** value: **3.50**
Circ: Statement: **182,499** CapCity orders: **39,600**

93 ❑ Sep 1990 Cover: 1.00 **NM** value: **3.50**
Circ: Statement: **182,499** CapCity orders: **39,300** • **CGC:** 3 graded, best 9.6
C: Todd McFarlane ★ Appearance of Wolverine.

94 ❑ Oct 1990 Cover: 1.00 **NM** value: **3.50**
Circ: Statement: **182,499** CapCity orders: **41,700**
★ Appearance of Wolverine.

95 ❑ Nov 1990 Cover: 1.00 **NM** value: **3.50**
Circ: Statement: **182,499** CapCity orders: **55,200** • **CGC:** 1 graded, best 9.6
📖 X-Tinction Agenda ★ Death of Warlock (machine).

95-2❑ Nov 1990 Cover: 1.00 **NM** value: **2.00**
📖 X-tinction Agenda • 2nd printing (gold)★ Death of Warlock (machine).

96 ❑ Dec 1990 Cover: 1.00 **NM** value: **3.00**
Circ: Statement: **182,499** CapCity orders: **55,500** • **CGC:** 2 graded, best 9.6
📖 X-Tinction Agenda

97 ❑ Jan 1991 Cover: 1.00 **NM** value: **3.00**
Circ: CapCity orders: **64,400** • **CGC:** 6 graded, best 9.8
📖 X-Tinction Agenda

98 ❑ Feb 1991 Cover: 1.00 **NM** value: **5.00**
Circ: CapCity orders: **55,200** • **CGC:** 34 graded, best 9.8
📖 The Beginning Of The End, Part 1 **A:** Rob Liefeld **W:** Rob Liefeld; Fabian Nicieza ★ 1st Appearance of Deadpool, Domino II, Gideon.

99 ❑ Mar 1991 Cover: 1.00 **NM** value: **4.00**
Circ: CapCity orders: **52,800** • **CGC:** 4 graded, best 9.6
📖 The Beginning Of The End, Part 2 • Sunspot leaves team; Has 1990 Statement, filed 10/1/90; avg print run 289,387; avg sales 177,658; avg subs 4,841; avg total paid 182,499; samples 100; office use 600; max existent 183,199; 37% of run returned **A:** Rob Liefeld **W:** Rob Liefeld; Fabian Nicieza ★ 1st Appearance of Feral, Shatterstar (full appearance).

100❑ Apr 1991 Cover: 1.50 **NM** value: **3.50**
Circ: CapCity orders: **102,200** • **CGC:** 36 graded, best 9.8
• Giant-size. 📖 The Beginning Of The End, Part 3 **A:** Rob Liefeld **W:** Rob Liefeld; Fabian Nicieza ★ Origin of Shatterstar. ★ 1st Appearance of X-Force.

100-2❑ Apr 1991 Cover: 1.50 **NM** value: **2.00**
📖 The Beginning Of The End, Part 3 • 2nd printing (gold) **A:** Rob Liefeld **W:** Rob Liefeld; Fabian Nicieza ★ 1st Appearance of X-Force.

100-3❑ Apr 1991 Cover: 1.50 **NM** value: **2.00**
📖 The Beginning Of The End, Part 3 • 3rd printing (silver) **A:** Rob Liefeld **W:** Rob Liefeld; Fabian Nicieza ★ 1st Appearance of X-Force.

Anl 1❑ ca. 1984 Cover: 1.00 **NM** value: **3.00**
📖 The Cosmic Cannonball Caper **A:** Arthur Adams; Bob McLeod **W:** Chris Claremont ★ 1st Appearance of Lila Cheney.

Anl 2❑ Oct 1986 Cover: 1.25 **NM** value: **5.00**
Circ: CapCity orders: **27,900** • **CGC:** 3 graded, best 9.6
★ 1st Appearance of Meggan, Psylocke.

Anl 3❑ ca. 1987 Cover: 1.25 **NM** value: **2.00**
Circ: CapCity orders: **35,600**
★ Appearance of Impossible Man.

Anl 4❑ ca. 1988 Cover: 1.75 **NM** value: **2.00**
📖 Evolutionary War, Part 4

Anl 5❑ ca. 1989 Cover: 2.00 **NM** value: **Cover or less**
📖 Atlantis Attacks, Part 9 • Atlantis Attacks **A:** Rob Liefeld

Anl 6❑ ca. 1990 Cover: 2.00 **NM** value: **2.50**
Circ: CapCity orders: **47,300**
📖 Future Present; Days of Future Present ★ 1st Appearance of Shatterstar (cameo).

Anl 7❑ ca. 1991 Cover: 2.00 **NM** value: **Cover or less**
📖 Kings of Pain; Kings of Pain, Part 1; The Killing Stroke, Part 1; Close Encounters Of The Mutant Kind **A:** Kirk Jarvinen; Guang Yap; Jon Bogdanove **W:** Fabian Nicieza; Judy Bogdanove

Bk 1❑ Dec 1990 Cover: 8.95 **NM** value: **Cover or less**
Circ: CapCity orders: **4,050**
• The Demon Bear Saga

SE 1❑ Dec 1985 Cover: 1.50 **NM** value: **Cover or less**
Circ: CapCity orders: **39,300** • **CGC:** 2 graded, best 9.6
📖 Home Is Where The Heart Is **A:** Arthur Adams **W:** Chris Claremont

Smr 1❑ Cover: 2.95 **NM** value: **Cover or less**
Circ: CapCity orders: **22,300**
• Giant-size.

CGC-graded: Multiply prices above by **33 for 9.9 M • 16 for 9.8 NM/M • 7 for 9.6 NM+ • 5 for 9.4 NM • 2.5 for 9.2 NM- • 1.5 for 9.0 VF/NM**

NEW MUTANTS, THE: TRUTH OR DEATH — Marvel

1 ❑ Nov 1997 Cover: 2.50 **NM** value: **Cover or less**
Circ: Diamd. preorders: **75,142**
• gatefold summary. • original New Mutants travel through time and meet present-day counterparts **A:** Bernard Chang **W:** Ben Raab

2 ❑ Dec 1997 Cover: 2.50 **NM** value: **Cover or less**
Circ: Diamd. preorders: **62,918**
• gatefold summary. **A:** Bernard Chang **W:** Ben Raab

3 ❑ Jan 1998 Cover: 2.50 **NM** value: **Cover or less**
Circ: Diamd. preorders: **57,291**
• gatefold summary. **A:** Bernard Chang **W:** Ben Raab

NEW NIGHT OF THE LIVING DEAD — Fantaco

0 ❑ Cover: 1.95 **NM** value: **2.00**
1 ❑ Cover: 3.95 **NM** value: **Cover or less**
2 ❑ Cover: 3.95 **NM** value: **Cover or less**
3 ❑ Cover: 3.95 **NM** value: **Cover or less**

NEW ORDER, THE — Creative Force

1 ❑ Nov 1994 Cover: 2.95 **NM** value: **Cover or less**
📖 Rage Against the Machine, Part 1 **A:** Jonathan David Moreno **W:** Jonathan David Moreno

NEW PALTZ COMIX — Moods

1 ❑ Cover: 1.25 **NM** value: **1.50**
2 ❑ 1974 Cover: 1.25 **NM** value: **1.50**
• **CGC:** 1 graded, best 9.0
3 ❑ Cover: 1.25 **NM** value: **1.50**
📖 Madhouse; Food; In Spite of Ancient Astronauts; J'nn J'nnzz Manhunter from Marzz: The Rebirth; Astroid; Rot; Old Fruit; Ooops; There's No Race Like Home; Black as Ink; Welcome Traveler **A:** Jeff Bonivert; Michael T. Gilbert; Bob Kessel; Harvey Sobel; Kevin Meek; Mark Roland; Raoul Vezina **W:** Jeff Bonivert; Michael T. Gilbert; Bob Kessel; Kevin Meek; Mark Roland; Raoul Vezina

NEW PARTNERS IN PERIL — Blue Comet

1 ❑ b&w Cover: 2.25 **NM** value: **Cover or less**

NEW POWER STARS, THE — Blue Comet

1 ❑ b&w Cover: 2.00 **NM** value: **Cover or less**

NEW ROMANCES — Standard

5 ❑ May 1951 Cover: 0.10 **NM** value: **35.00**
6 ❑ Jul 1951 Cover: 0.10 **NM** value: **35.00**
7 ❑ Sep 1951 Cover: 0.10 **NM** value: **35.00**
8 ❑ Nov 1951 Cover: 0.10 **NM** value: **35.00**
9 ❑ Jan 1952 Cover: 0.10 **NM** value: **35.00**
10 ❑ Mar 1952 Cover: 0.10 **NM** value: **35.00**
11 ❑ May 1952 Cover: 0.10 **NM** value: **70.00**
• **CGC:** 1 graded, best 9.2
12 ❑ 1952 Cover: 0.10 **NM** value: **35.00**
13 ❑ 1952 Cover: 0.10 **NM** value: **35.00**
14 ❑ Cover: 0.10 **NM** value: **35.00**
15 ❑ Mar 1953 Cover: 0.10 **NM** value: **25.00**
16 ❑ 1953 Cover: 0.10 **NM** value: **25.00**
17 ❑ 1953 Cover: 0.10 **NM** value: **25.00**
18 ❑ Cover: 0.10 **NM** value: **25.00**
19 ❑ Cover: 0.10 **NM** value: **25.00**
20 ❑ 1954 Cover: 0.10 **NM** value: **25.00**
21 ❑ May 1954 Cover: 0.10 **NM** value: **25.00**

NEW SHADOWHAWK, THE — Image

1 ❑ Jun 1995 Cover: 2.50 **NM** value: **Cover or less**
Circ: CapCity orders: **20,475**
📖 Nightmares **A:** Andrew Pepoy **W:** Kurt Busiek
2 ❑ Aug 1995 Cover: 2.50 **NM** value: **Cover or less**
Circ: CapCity orders: **13,000**
📖 Monsters **A:** Andrew Pepoy **W:** Kurt Busiek
3 ❑ Sep 1995 Cover: 2.50 **NM** value: **Cover or less**
Circ: CapCity orders: **10,600**
4 ❑ Nov 1995 Cover: 2.50 **NM** value: **Cover or less**
Circ: CapCity orders: **6,500**
5 ❑ Dec 1995 Cover: 2.50 **NM** value: **Cover or less**
6 ❑ Feb 1996 Cover: 2.50 **NM** value: **Cover or less**
7 ❑ Mar 1996 Cover: 2.50 **NM** value: **Cover or less**

NEW STATESMEN — Fleetway-Quality

1 ❑ Cover: 3.95 **NM** value: **4.00**
Circ: CapCity orders: **7,225**
A: Jim Baikie **W:** John Smith
2 ❑ Cover: 3.95 **NM** value: **4.00**
A: Jim Baikie **W:** John Smith
3 ❑ Cover: 3.95 **NM** value: **4.00**
Circ: CapCity orders: **4,975**
A: Jim Baikie **W:** John Smith
4 ❑ Cover: 3.95 **NM** value: **4.00**
Circ: CapCity orders: **4,450**
A: Jim Baikie **W:** John Smith
5 ❑ Cover: 3.95 **NM** value: **4.00**
Circ: CapCity orders: **3,975**
A: Jim Baikie **W:** John Smith
Bk 1 ❑ Cover: 14.95 **NM** value: **Cover or less**

There are two different pricing tiers in the modern comic-book hobby. **The prices seen above** are the prices we have seen **loose copies** of these issues reliably fetch in a variety of environments. Condition alters the price by the fractions seen on the bar on the bottom of left-hand pages of this book. **Comics graded by CGC** usually sell for more. Use the guide on the bottom of right-hand pages of this book to estimate what copies have brought on eBay.

NEWSTIME — DC
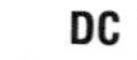

DC released this special "news magazine" as a follow-up to the death of Superman in Superman (2nd Series) #75. It came complete with a suitably stoic letter from the publisher, letters from readers talking about various recent events in Metropolis, music reviews from "local" bands, etc.

Of course, the highlight of the issue is the long "special coverage" of the events leading up to Superman's demise. Newstime obtained reaction statements from both real celebrities (including Shaquille O'Neal, Dan Rather, and William Shatner) and imaginary ones (e.g. Bruce Wayne). In a nice touch, the magazine also contained a raft of ads for everything from WayneTech (Bruce Wayne's corporation) to LexOil (one of Lex Luthor's many holdings).

1 ❑ May 1993 Cover: 2.95 **NM** value: **3.25**
Circ: CapCity orders: **84,600**
No issue number. ★ Death of Superman magazine.

NEWSTRALIA — Innovation

1 ❑ Jul 1989 Cover: 1.75 **NM** value: **2.00**
Circ: CapCity orders: **3,629**
📖 Eyes Of The Overlord! **A:** Tim Truman; Kevin VanHook **W:** Stephen Sullivan
2 ❑ Cover: 1.95 **NM** value: **2.00**
Circ: CapCity orders: **2,475**
3 ❑ Cover: 1.95 **NM** value: **2.25**
Circ: CapCity orders: **2,275**
4 ❑ Cover: 2.25 **NM** value: **Cover or less**
Circ: CapCity orders: **1,850**
5 ❑ b&w Cover: 2.25 **NM** value: **Cover or less**
Circ: CapCity orders: **1,775**

NEW TALENT SHOWCASE — DC

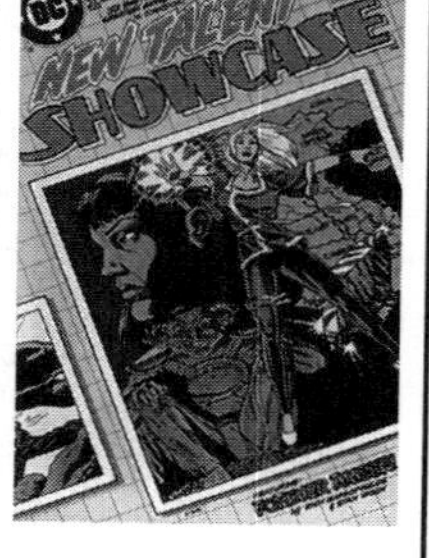

One of the dearest dreams of writers and artists everywhere is "breaking in" to the business. DC's New Talent Showcase provided an avenue for this, and gave recent discoveries a chance to strut their stuff.

It may have oversold the series a bit when it billed the artists and writers featured here as "Tomorrow's Superstars." The stories ranged from average to very good, though probably none will ever be hailed as a classic of the art form. Still, stories like "Forever Amber" by Rich Margopoulos and Stan Woch and "Class of 2064" by Todd Klein and Scott Hampton are enjoyable stories that show a great deal of potential.

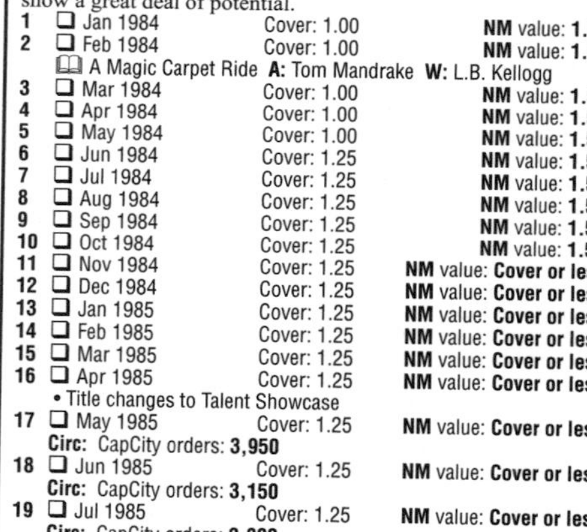

1 ❑ Jan 1984 Cover: 1.00 **NM** value: **1.50**
2 ❑ Feb 1984 Cover: 1.00 **NM** value: **1.50**
📖 A Magic Carpet Ride **A:** Tom Mandrake **W:** L.B. Kellogg
3 ❑ Mar 1984 Cover: 1.00 **NM** value: **1.50**
4 ❑ Apr 1984 Cover: 1.00 **NM** value: **1.50**
5 ❑ May 1984 Cover: 1.00 **NM** value: **1.50**
6 ❑ Jun 1984 Cover: 1.25 **NM** value: **1.50**
7 ❑ Jul 1984 Cover: 1.25 **NM** value: **1.50**
8 ❑ Aug 1984 Cover: 1.25 **NM** value: **1.50**
9 ❑ Sep 1984 Cover: 1.25 **NM** value: **1.50**
10 ❑ Oct 1984 Cover: 1.25 **NM** value: **1.50**
11 ❑ Nov 1984 Cover: 1.25 **NM** value: **Cover or less**
12 ❑ Dec 1984 Cover: 1.25 **NM** value: **Cover or less**
13 ❑ Jan 1985 Cover: 1.25 **NM** value: **Cover or less**
14 ❑ Feb 1985 Cover: 1.25 **NM** value: **Cover or less**
15 ❑ Mar 1985 Cover: 1.25 **NM** value: **Cover or less**
16 ❑ Apr 1985 Cover: 1.25 **NM** value: **Cover or less**
• Title changes to Talent Showcase
17 ❑ May 1985 Cover: 1.25 **NM** value: **Cover or less**
Circ: CapCity orders: **3,950**
18 ❑ Jun 1985 Cover: 1.25 **NM** value: **Cover or less**
Circ: CapCity orders: **3,150**
19 ❑ Jul 1985 Cover: 1.25 **NM** value: **Cover or less**
Circ: CapCity orders: **2,800**

NEW TEEN TITANS, THE (1ST SERIES) — DC

The New Teen Titans first appeared as a preview in DC Comics Presents #26. That issue introduced us to the characters of Cyborg, Raven, and Starfire, who were joined by Robin, Kid Flash, metamorph Changeling (formerly Beast Boy), and various others to form the current team.

Although a later Titans series would seem somewhat ashamed of the "teen" designation, this series used it to good advantage. The team members had lives and families outside of their super-hero identities, inter-team romances came and went, and they dealt with real-world problems such as drugs and runaways. That the team members were teenagers helped make each of these situations ring true to life — although the solid writing of Marv Wolfman deserves a great deal of credit as well.

1 ❑ Nov 1980 Cover: 0.50 **NM** value: **7.50**
• **CGC:** 21 graded, best 9.6
📖 The New Teen Titans **A:** George Pérez; Romeo Tanghal **W:** Marv Wolfman ★ 1st Appearance of Teen Titans.
2 ❑ Dec 1980 Cover: 0.50 **NM** value: **6.00**
• **CGC:** 9 graded, best 9.6
📖 Today...The Terminator **A:** George Pérez; Romeo Tanghal **W:** Marv Wolfman ★ 1st Appearance of Trigon, Wintergreen, Deathstroke the Terminator. ★ Death of The Ravager.
3 ❑ Jan 1981 Cover: 0.50 **NM** value: **3.00**
📖 The Fearsome Five **A:** George Pérez; Frank Chiaramonte **W:** Marv Wolfman ★ 1st Appearance of Shimmer, Gizmo, Mammoth, Fearsome Five, Psimon. ★ Versus Doctor Light. ★ Versus Dr. Light. ★ Versus Docto.
4 ❑ Feb 1981 Cover: 0.50 **NM** value: **3.00**
• **CGC:** 1 graded, best 9.6
📖 Against All Friends **A:** George Pérez **W:** Marv Wolfman ★ Appearance of Justice League.
5 ❑ Mar 1981 Cover: 0.50 **NM** value: **3.00**
📖 Trigon Lives! **A:** Curt Swan; Romeo Tanghal **W:** Marv Wolfman ★ Origin of Raven. ★ 1st Appearance of Trigon.
6 ❑ Apr 1981 Cover: 0.50 **NM** value: **3.00**
📖 Last Kill! **A:** George Pérez **W:** George Pérez; Marv Wolfman ★ Origin of Raven. ★ Versus Trigon.
7 ❑ May 1981 Cover: 0.50 **NM** value: **3.00**
📖 Assault on Titans' Tower **A:** George Pérez; Romeo Tanghal **W:** Marv Wolfman ★ Origin of Cyborg. ★ Versus Fearsome Five.
8 ❑ Jun 1981 Cover: 0.50 **NM** value: **3.00**
• **CGC:** 1 graded, best 9.4
📖 A Day in the Lives... **A:** George Pérez; Romeo Tanghal **W:** George Pérez; Marv Wolfman ★ Origin of Kid Flash.
9 ❑ Jul 1981 Cover: 0.50 **NM** value: **3.00**
• **CGC:** 1 graded, best 9.6
📖 Like Puppets on a String **A:** George Pérez; Romeo Tanghal **W:** Marv Wolfman
10 ❑ Aug 1981 Cover: 0.50 **NM** value: **3.00**
• **CGC:** 6 graded, best 9.6
📖 Promethium: Unbound **A:** George Pérez; Romeo Tanghal **W:** Marv Wolfman ★ Origin of Changeling. ★ Appearance of Deathstroke the Terminator. ★ Versus Terminator.
11 ❑ Sep 1981 Cover: 0.50 **NM** value: **2.00**
📖 When Titans Clash **A:** George Pérez; Romeo Tanghal **W:** Marv Wolfman
12 ❑ Oct 1981 Cover: 0.60 **NM** value: **2.00**
📖 Clash of the Titans **A:** George Pérez; Romeo Tanghal **W:** Marv Wolfman
13 ❑ Nov 1981 Cover: 0.60 **NM** value: **2.00**
📖 Friends and Foes Alike • Doom Patrol; Robotman returns **A:** George Pérez; Romeo Tanghal **W:** Marv Wolfman
14 ❑ Dec 1981 Cover: 0.60 **NM** value: **2.00**
📖 Revolution! • Doom Patrol **A:** George Pérez; Romeo Tanghal **W:** Marv Wolfman ★ 1st Appearance of Houngan, Plasmus.
15 ❑ Jan 1982 Cover: 0.60 **NM** value: **2.00**
• **CGC:** 2 graded, best 9.8
📖 The Brotherhood of Evil Lives Again • Doom Patrol **A:** George Pérez; Romeo Tanghal **W:** Marv Wolfman ★ Versus Brotherhood of Evil.
16 ❑ Feb 1982 Cover: 0.60 **NM** value: **2.00**
📖 Starfire Unleashed!; Captain Carrot and His Amazing Zoo Crew! **A:** George Pérez; Ross Andru; Romeo Tanghal; Scott Shaw **W:** Roy Thomas; Scott; Gerry Conway; Marv Wolfman; Shaw ★ 1st Appearance of Yankee Poodle, Pig-Iron, Fastback, Captain Carrot, Rubberduck, Alley-Kat-Abra.
17 ❑ Mar 1982 Cover: 0.60 **NM** value: **2.00**
📖 The Possessing of Francis Kane **A:** George Pérez; Romeo Tanghal **W:** Marv Wolfman ★ Appearance of Francis Kane.
18 ❑ Apr 1982 Cover: 0.60 **NM** value: **2.00**
📖 A Pretty Girl is Like a-Maladi! **A:** George Pérez; Romeo Tanghal **W:** Marv Wolfman ★ 1st Appearance of Maladi Maranova. ★ Appearance of Starfire (later Red Star).
19 ❑ May 1982 Cover: 0.60 **NM** value: **2.00**
• **CGC:** 2 graded, best 9.6
📖 The Light Fantastic **A:** George Pérez; Romeo Tanghal **W:** Marv Wolfman ★ Appearance of Hawkman.
20 ❑ Jun 1982 Cover: 0.60 **NM** value: **2.00**
📖 Dear Mom and Dad; A Titanic Tale of Titans' Tomfoolery **A:** George Pérez; Romeo Tanghal **W:** Marv Wolfman ★ 1st Appearance of The Disruptor.
21 ❑ Jul 1982 Cover: 0.60 **NM** value: **2.00**
📖 Beware the Wrath of...Brother Blood!; The Night Force **A:** Gene Colan; George Pérez; Romeo Tanghal **W:** Marv Wolfman ★ 1st Appearance of Monitor, Harbinger, Brother Blood, Night Force, Baron Winters. ★ Versus Brother Blood.
22 ❑ Aug 1982 Cover: 0.60 **NM** value: **2.00**
📖 Ashes to Ashes! **A:** George Pérez; Romeo Tanghal **W:** Marv Wolfman ★ Versus Brother Blood.
23 ❑ Sep 1982 Cover: 0.60 **NM** value: **2.00**
• **CGC:** 1 graded, best 9.6
📖 Kidnapped! **A:** George Pérez; Romeo Tanghal **W:** Marv Wolfman ★ 1st Appearance of Blackfire.
24 ❑ Oct 1982 Cover: 0.60 **NM** value: **2.00**
📖 Citadel Strike! **A:** George Pérez; Romeo Tanghal **W:** Marv Wolfman ★ 1st Appearance of X'Hal. ★ Appearance of Omega Men.
25 ❑ Nov 1982 Cover: 0.60 **NM** value: **2.00**
📖 War!; Fate is the Killer • Masters of the Universe preview **A:** George Pérez; Curt Swan; Dave Hunt; Romeo Tanghal **W:** Marv Wolfman; Paul Cleveland; Paul Kupperberg ★ 1st Appearance of Masters of the Universe, Omega Men.
26 ❑ Dec 1982 Cover: 0.60 **NM** value: **2.00**
• **CGC:** 2 graded, best 9.8
📖 Runaways **A:** George Pérez; Romeo Tanghal **W:** Marv Wolfman ★ 1st Appearance of Terra.
27 ❑ Jan 1983 Cover: 0.60 **NM** value: **2.00**
📖 Runaways, Part 2 • Atari Force preview **A:** George Pérez; Romeo Tanghal **W:** Marv Wolfman ★ 1st Appearance of Howard Rondo.
28 ❑ Feb 1983 Cover: 0.60 **NM** value: **2.00**
📖 Terra in the Night **A:** George Pérez; Romeo Tanghal **W:** Marv Wolfman ★ Appearance of Terra. ★ Versus Brotherhood of Evil.

29 ❑ Mar 1983 Cover: 0.60 **NM** value: **2.00**
First Blood! • Return of Speedy **A:** George Pérez; Romeo Tanghal **W:** Marv Wolfman ★ Versus Brotherhood of Evil.
30 ❑ Apr 1983 Cover: 0.60 **NM** value: **2.00**
Nightmare! • Terra joins team **A:** George Pérez; Romeo Tanghal **W:** Marv Wolfman
31 ❑ May 1983 Cover: 0.60 **NM** value: **2.00**
• **CGC:** 2 graded, best 9.6
Inferno! **A:** George Pérez; Romeo Tanghal **W:** Marv Wolfman ★ Versus Brotherhood of Evil.
32 ❑ Jun 1983 Cover: 0.60 **NM** value: **2.00**
• **CGC:** 1 graded, best 9.6
Thunder and Lightning **A:** George Pérez; Romeo Tanghal **W:** Marv Wolfman ★ Origin of Kid Flash. ★ Appearance of Thunder and Lightning.
33 ❑ Jul 1983 Cover: 0.60 **NM** value: **2.00**
Who Killed Trident? **A:** George Pérez; Romeo Tanghal **W:** Marv Wolfman ★ Death of Trident.
34 ❑ Aug 1983 Cover: 0.60 **NM** value: **2.00**
• **CGC:** 1 graded, best 9.6
Endings…and Beginnings! **A:** George Pérez **W:** Marv Wolfman ★ Appearance of Deathstroke the Terminator. ★ Versus Terminator.
35 ❑ Oct 1983 Cover: 0.60 **NM** value: **2.00**
Siege! **A:** George Pérez **W:** Marv Wolfman
36 ❑ Nov 1983 Cover: 0.60 **NM** value: **2.00**
Feedback! **A:** Keith Pollard **W:** Marv Wolfman ★ Appearance of Thunder and Lightning.
37 ❑ Dec 1983 Cover: 0.75 **NM** value: **2.00**
• **CGC:** 1 graded, best 9.8
Lights Out, Everyone! **A:** George Pérez **W:** Marv Wolfman; Mike W. Barr ★ Appearance of Outsiders. ★ Versus Doctor Light. ★ Versus Shimmer. ★ Versus Gizmo. ★ Versus Mammoth. ★ Versus Psimon.
38 ❑ Jan 1984 Cover: 0.75 **NM** value: **2.00**
• **CGC:** 1 graded, best 9.6
Who is Donna Troy? **A:** George Pérez **W:** George Pérez; Marv Wolfman ★ Origin of Wonder Girl.
39 ❑ Feb 1984 Cover: 0.75 **NM** value: **2.50**
• **CGC:** 6 graded, best 9.8
Crossroads • Dick Grayson quits as Robin; Wally West retires as Kid Flash **A:** George Pérez **W:** George Pérez; Marv Wolfman
40 ❑ Mar 1984 Cover: 0.75 **NM** value: **2.00**
Lifeblood! • Series continued in Tales of the Teen Titans #41 **A:** George Pérez **W:** George Pérez; Marv Wolfman
Anl 1❑ca. 1982 Cover: 1.00 **NM** value: **2.00**
• **CGC:** 4 graded, best 9.8
Final Conflict! **A:** George Pérez **W:** Marv Wolfman ★ Appearance of Omega Men.
Anl 2❑ca. 1983 Cover: 1.00 **NM** value: **2.00**
• **CGC:** 1 graded, best 9.8
A: George Pérez ★ 1st Appearance of Lyla (Harbinger), Vigilante. ★ Appearance of Monitor.
Anl 3❑ca. 1984 Cover: 1.25 **NM** value: **2.00**
• **CGC:** 1 graded, best 9.9
The Judas Contract, Part 4 • Published as Teen Titans Annual ★ Death of Terra.

NEW TEEN TITANS, THE (2ND SERIES) DC

1 ❑ Aug 1984 Cover: 1.25 **NM** value: **3.00**
• **CGC:** 27 graded, best 9.8
Shadows in the Dark! **A:** George Pérez **W:** Marv Wolfman
2 ❑ Oct 1984 Cover: 1.25 **NM** value: **2.50**
A: George Pérez **W:** Marv Wolfman ★ Appearance of Trigon.
3 ❑ Nov 1984 Cover: 1.25 **NM** value: **2.50**
A: George Pérez **W:** Marv Wolfman ★ Versus Trigon.
4 ❑ Jan 1985 Cover: 1.25 **NM** value: **2.50**
Torment! **A:** George Pérez **W:** Marv Wolfman ★ Versus Trigon.
5 ❑ Feb 1985 Cover: 1.25 **NM** value: **2.50**
A: George Pérez ★ Versus Trigon.
6 ❑ Mar 1985 Cover: 1.25 **NM** value: **2.00**
7 ❑ Apr 1985 Cover: 1.25 **NM** value: **2.00**
★ Origin of Lilith.
8 ❑ May 1985 Cover: 1.25 **NM** value: **2.00**
Circ: CapCity orders: **28,350**
★ Appearance of Destiny.
9 ❑ Jun 1985 Cover: 1.25 **NM** value: **2.00**
Circ: CapCity orders: **25,950**
★ 1st Appearance of Kole.
10 ❑ Jul 1985 Cover: 1.25 **NM** value: **2.00**
Circ: CapCity orders: **25,100**
11 ❑ Aug 1985 Cover: 1.25 **NM** value: **2.00**
Circ: CapCity orders: **23,450**
12 ❑ Sep 1985 Cover: 1.25 **NM** value: **2.00**
Circ: CapCity orders: **22,450**
Sins of the Past **A:** Stan Woch **W:** Marv Wolfman
13 ❑ Oct 1985 Cover: 1.25 **NM** value: **2.00**
Circ: CapCity orders: **25,450**
Crisis on Infinite Earths • Crisis **A:** Eduardo Barreto **W:** Marv Wolfman
14 ❑ Nov 1985 Cover: 1.25 **NM** value: **2.00**
Circ: CapCity orders: **24,100** • **CGC:** 1 graded, best 9.6
Crisis on Infinite Earths • Crisis
15 ❑ Dec 1985 Cover: 1.50 **NM** value: **2.00**
Circ: CapCity orders: **20,400**
16 ❑ Jan 1986 Cover: 1.50 **NM** value: **2.00**
Circ: CapCity orders: **19,700**
★ Appearance of Omega Men.
17 ❑ Feb 1986 Cover: 1.50 **NM** value: **2.00**
Circ: CapCity orders: **20,600**
• Wedding of Starfire
18 ❑ Mar 1986 Cover: 1.50 **NM** value: **2.00**
Circ: CapCity orders: **19,300**
19 ❑ Apr 1986 Cover: 1.50 **NM** value: **2.00**
Circ: CapCity orders: **18,700**
20 ❑ May 1986 Cover: 1.50 **NM** value: **2.00**
Circ: CapCity orders: **18,000**
• Return of original Titans; Robin II (Jason Todd) joins team
21 ❑ Jun 1986 Cover: 1.50 **NM** value: **Cover or less**
Circ: CapCity orders: **17,800**
★ Appearance of Cheshire.
22 ❑ Jul 1986 Cover: 1.50 **NM** value: **Cover or less**
Circ: CapCity orders: **17,350**
23 ❑ Aug 1986 Cover: 1.50 **NM** value: **Cover or less**
Circ: CapCity orders: **18,850**
★ Versus Hybrids.
24 ❑ Oct 1986 Cover: 1.50 **NM** value: **Cover or less**
Circ: CapCity orders: **18,550**
★ Versus Hybrids.
25 ❑ Nov 1986 Cover: 1.50 **NM** value: **Cover or less**
Circ: CapCity orders: **18,350**
26 ❑ Dec 1986 Cover: 1.50 **NM** value: **Cover or less**
Circ: CapCity orders: **16,950**
27 ❑ Jan 1987 Cover: 1.50 **NM** value: **Cover or less**
Circ: CapCity orders: **17,100**
★ Versus Brotherhood of Evil.
28 ❑ Feb 1987 Cover: 1.50 **NM** value: **Cover or less**
Circ: CapCity orders: **17,550**
★ Versus Brother Blood.
29 ❑ Mar 1987 Cover: 1.50 **NM** value: **Cover or less**
Circ: CapCity orders: **16,300**
★ Versus Brother Blood.
30 ❑ Apr 1987 Cover: 1.50 **NM** value: **Cover or less**
Circ: CapCity orders: **16,000**
★ Versus Brother Blood.
31 ❑ May 1987 Cover: 1.50 **NM** value: **Cover or less**
Circ: CapCity orders: **15,500**
★ Appearance of Superman, Batman. ★ Versus Brother Blood.
32 ❑ Jun 1987 Cover: 1.50 **NM** value: **Cover or less**
Circ: CapCity orders: **15,550**
33 ❑ Jul 1987 Cover: 1.50 **NM** value: **Cover or less**
Circ: CapCity orders: **15,550**
34 ❑ Aug 1987 Cover: 1.50 **NM** value: **Cover or less**
Circ: CapCity orders: **17,200**
★ Versus Hybrid.
35 ❑ Sep 1987 Cover: 1.50 **NM** value: **Cover or less**
Circ: CapCity orders: **17,300**
36 ❑ Oct 1987 Cover: 1.50 **NM** value: **Cover or less**
Circ: CapCity orders: **17,550**
★ Versus Wildebeest.
37 ❑ Nov 1987 Cover: 1.75 **NM** value: **Cover or less**
Circ: CapCity orders: **17,100**
★ Versus Wildebeest.
38 ❑ Dec 1987 Cover: 1.75 **NM** value: **Cover or less**
Circ: CapCity orders: **16,850**
★ Appearance of Infinity Inc.. ★ Versus Ultra-Humanite.
39 ❑ Jan 1988 Cover: 1.75 **NM** value: **Cover or less**
Circ: CapCity orders: **16,450**
40 ❑ Feb 1988 Cover: 1.75 **NM** value: **Cover or less**
Circ: CapCity orders: **16,650**
★ Versus I.Q.. ★ Versus Silver Fog. ★ Versus The Gentleman Ghost.
41 ❑ Mar 1988 Cover: 1.75 **NM** value: **Cover or less**
Circ: CapCity orders: **16,650**
★ Versus Wildebeest.
42 ❑ Apr 1988 Cover: 1.75 **NM** value: **Cover or less**
Circ: CapCity orders: **16,200**
• Brother Blood's child born
43 ❑ May 1988 Cover: 1.75 **NM** value: **Cover or less**
Circ: CapCity orders: **15,850**
• Phobia vs. Raven
44 ❑ Jun 1988 Cover: 1.75 **NM** value: **Cover or less**
Circ: CapCity orders: **14,650**
★ Versus Godiva.
45 ❑ Jul 1988 Cover: 1.75 **NM** value: **Cover or less**
Circ: CapCity orders: **14,350**
★ Appearance of Dial H for Hero.
46 ❑ Aug 1988 Cover: 1.75 **NM** value: **Cover or less**
Circ: CapCity orders: **14,150**
★ Appearance of Dial H for Hero.
47 ❑ Sep 1988 Cover: 1.75 **NM** value: **Cover or less**
Circ: CapCity orders: **13,900**
★ Origin of Titans.
48 ❑ Oct 1988 Cover: 1.75 **NM** value: **Cover or less**
Circ: CapCity orders: **13,600**
★ Versus Red Star.
49 ❑ Nov 1988 Cover: 1.75 **NM** value: **Cover or less**
Circ: CapCity orders: **13,450**
• Series continued in New Titans #50 ★ Versus Red Star.
Anl 1❑ca. 1985 Cover: 2.00 **NM** value: **2.50**
Circ: CapCity orders: **25,050** • **CGC:** 1 graded, best 9.6
★ 1st Appearance of Vanguard. ★ Appearance of Superman. ★ Versus Vanguard.
Anl 2❑Aug 1986 Cover: 2.50 **NM** value: **2.75**
A: John Byrne ★ Origin of Brother Blood. ★ 1st Appearance of Cheshire. ★ Appearance of Doctor Light.
Anl 3❑ca. 1987 Cover: 2.25 **NM** value: **2.50**
Circ: CapCity orders: **16,300**
cover indicates '87 Annual, indicia says '86. ★ 1st Appearance of Godiva, Danny Chase. ★ Appearance of King Faraday.
Anl 4❑ca. 1988 Cover: 2.50 **NM** value: **Cover or less**
Circ: CapCity orders: **13,500**
• Series continues as New Titans Annual; Private Lives

NEW TEEN TITANS ARCHIVES DC

Bk 1❑ Cover: 49.95 **NM** value: **Cover or less**
• Collects DC Comics Presents #26 and New Teen Titans #1-8 **A:** George Pérez **W:** Marv Wolfman
Bk 1/Aut❑ **NM** value: **79.95**
A: George Pérez **W:** Marv Wolfman

NEW TEEN TITANS (GIVEAWAYS AND PROMOS) DC

1 ❑ **NM** value: **1.00**
• Beverage; DC drug issue
2 ❑ **NM** value: **1.00**
• IBM/DC drug issue
3 ❑ Cover: 1.00 **NM** value: **Cover or less**
• Keebler; drug issue **A:** George Pérez; Dave Cockrum
4 ❑ Cover: 1.00 **NM** value: **Cover or less**
• Keebler; drug issue **A:** Dave Cockrum

NEW TEEN TITANS: THE JUDAS CONTRACT DC

Bk 1❑ Dec 1988 Cover: 14.95 **NM** value: **Cover or less**
Circ: CapCity orders: **2,500**
A: George Pérez

NEW TERRYTOONS Dell

1 ❑ Jun 1960 Cover: 0.10 **NM** value: **50.00**
2 ❑ Sep 1960 Cover: 0.10 **NM** value: **25.00**
3 ❑ Dec 1960 Cover: 0.10 **NM** value: **20.00**
4 ❑ Mar 1961 Cover: 0.10 **NM** value: **20.00**
5 ❑ Jun 1961 Cover: 0.12 **NM** value: **20.00**
6 ❑ Sep 1961 Cover: 0.12 **NM** value: **20.00**
7 ❑ Dec 1961 Cover: 0.12 **NM** value: **20.00**
8 ❑ Mar 1962 Cover: 0.12 **NM** value: **20.00**

NEW TERRYTOONS (2ND SERIES) Gold Key

In another adaptation of Paul Terry's animation creations, cartoon blackbirds Heckle and Jeckle are the stars of the show. (Don't let their presence in the logos confuse you — this title is really called New Terrytoons.) The con-artist crows pose as members of many different professions, trying to wrench a dishonest buck — or meal — from their marks. They're not above betraying each other in some of these stories, either.

Back-up features include Silly Sidney, in which a simple elephant is craved by two conniving vultures, and Hashimoto-San, featuring the family of a Japanese mouse. Stories featuring the Honorable Mouse and his arch-enemy, Evil Cat, are hardly politically correct by modern standards, but are often entertaining anyway. — JJM

1 ❑ Oct 1962 Cover: 0.25 **NM** value: **40.00**
• **CGC:** 1 graded, best 7.5
2 ❑ Jan 1963 Cover: 0.25 **NM** value: **26.00**
• **CGC:** 2 graded, best 9.6
3 ❑ Cover: 0.15 **NM** value: **14.00**
4 ❑ Sep 1969 Cover: 0.15 **NM** value: **10.00**
5 ❑ Nov 1970 Cover: 0.15 **NM** value: **10.00**
6 ❑ Jan 1970 Cover: 0.15 **NM** value: **8.00**
7 ❑ Mar 1970 Cover: 0.15 **NM** value: **8.00**
8 ❑ May 1970 Cover: 0.15 **NM** value: **8.00**
9 ❑ Jul 1970 Cover: 0.15 **NM** value: **8.00**
10 ❑ Oct 1970 Cover: 0.15 **NM** value: **8.00**
11 ❑ 1971 Cover: 0.15 **NM** value: **6.00**
12 ❑ 1971 Cover: 0.15 **NM** value: **6.00**
13 ❑ 1971 Cover: 0.15 **NM** value: **6.00**
14 ❑ Nov 1971 Cover: 0.15 **NM** value: **6.00**
15 ❑ Feb 1972 Cover: 0.15 **NM** value: **6.00**
16 ❑ May 1972 Cover: 0.15 **NM** value: **6.00**
17 ❑ Aug 1972 Cover: 0.15 **NM** value: **6.00**
18 ❑ Nov 1972 Cover: 0.15 **NM** value: **6.00**
19 ❑ Feb 1973 Cover: 0.15 **NM** value: **6.00**
20 ❑ May 1973 Cover: 0.15 **NM** value: **6.00**
21 ❑ Jul 1973 Cover: 0.20 **NM** value: **4.00**
22 ❑ 1973 Cover: 0.20 **NM** value: **4.00**
23 ❑ Nov 1973 Cover: 0.20 **NM** value: **4.00**
24 ❑ Jan 1974 Cover: 0.20 **NM** value: **4.00**
25 ❑ Cover: 0.20 **NM** value: **4.00**
26 ❑ Jun 1974 Cover: 0.20 **NM** value: **4.00**
Mud in Your Eye!; The Hot Haiku; The Doughboys
27 ❑ Aug 1974 Cover: 0.25 **NM** value: **4.00**
28 ❑ Oct 1974 Cover: 0.25 **NM** value: **4.00**
29 ❑ Dec 1974 Cover: 0.25 **NM** value: **4.00**
30 ❑ Feb 1975 Cover: 0.25 **NM** value: **4.00**
31 ❑ Apr 1976 Cover: 0.25 **NM** value: **3.00**
32 ❑ Jun 1975 Cover: 0.25 **NM** value: **3.00**
Just Plane Crowded; Show Me Where it Hurts!; The Great Garden Plot!; Trouble Fakers
33 ❑ Aug 1975 Cover: 0.25 **NM** value: **3.00**
34 ❑ Oct 1975 Cover: 0.25 **NM** value: **3.00**
35 ❑ Dec 1975 Cover: 0.25 **NM** value: **3.00**
36 ❑ Feb 1976 Cover: 0.25 **NM** value: **3.00**
37 ❑ Apr 1976 Cover: 0.25 **NM** value: **3.00**
38 ❑ Jun 1976 Cover: 0.25 **NM** value: **3.00**
39 ❑ Aug 1976 Cover: 0.25 **NM** value: **3.00**
40 ❑ Sep 1976 Cover: 0.25 **NM** value: **3.00**
41 ❑ Nov 1976 Cover: 0.30 **NM** value: **2.00**
42 ❑ Jan 1977 Cover: 0.30 **NM** value: **2.00**
43 ❑ Mar 1977 Cover: 0.30 **NM** value: **2.00**
44 ❑ May 1977 Cover: 0.30 **NM** value: **2.00**
45 ❑ Jul 1977 Cover: 0.30 **NM** value: **2.00**
46 ❑ Sep 1977 Cover: 0.30 **NM** value: **2.00**
47 ❑ Nov 1977 Cover: 0.30 **NM** value: **2.00**
48 ❑ Jan 1978 Cover: 0.35 **NM** value: **2.00**
49 ❑ Mar 1978 Cover: 0.35 **NM** value: **2.00**
50 ❑ May 1978 Cover: 0.35 **NM** value: **2.00**
51 ❑ Jul 1979 Cover: 0.35 **NM** value: **2.00**
52 ❑ Sep 1979 Cover: 0.35 **NM** value: **2.00**
53 ❑ Nov 1979 Cover: 0.35 **NM** value: **2.00**
54 ❑ Jan 1979 Cover: 0.35 **NM** value: **2.00**

Do you have changes or corrections for the **Standard Catalog**? Send your original research to us at **allcomics@krause.com**

CGC-graded: Multiply prices above by **33 for 9.9 M • 16 for 9.8 NM/M • 7 for 9.6 NM+ • 5 for 9.4 NM • 2.5 for 9.2 NM- • 1.5 for 9.0 VF/NM**

NEW TITANS, THE — DC

When the Titans, which include Starfire, Nightwing, Cyborg, Changeling, and Aqualad, grew up, this action-packed series changed its name from the New Teen Titans (2nd series) to the New Titans. Adulthood hasn't made things easier; if anything, the bad guys are willing to be more dastardly than ever.

Longtime Titans writer Marv Wolfman continued to script the series in this new incarnation, taking the Titans on far-flung adventures while maintaining the interplay between the members which made the series so interesting.

The direct-market only series had generated controversy from the beginning with a scene of Robin (Nightwing) in bed with Starfire in the first issue and then stirred the pot further when the new title began with yet another origin for Wonder Girl (Donna Troy).

0 ❑ Oct 1994 Cover: 1.95 **NM** value: **2.25**
Circ: CapCity orders: **17,450**
📖 The Changing Order • Impulse, Damage, Terra, Mirage joins team; Series continued in New Titans #115; Nightwing leaves team; Titans get new headquarters **A:** Stephen Jones **W:** Marv Wolfman

50 ❑ Dec 1988 Cover: 1.75 **NM** value: **2.50**
Circ: CapCity orders: **18,750**
📖 Who is Wonder Girl, Part 1 • Series continued from New Teen Titans #49 **A:** George Pérez ★ Origin of Wonder Girl (new origin).

51 ❑ Dec 1988 Cover: 1.75 **NM** value: **2.00**
Circ: CapCity orders: **17,150**
📖 Who is Wonder Girl, Part 2 **A:** George Pérez

52 ❑ Jan 1989 Cover: 1.75 **NM** value: **2.00**
Circ: CapCity orders: **16,785**
📖 Who is Wonder Girl, Part 3 **A:** George Pérez

53 ❑ Feb 1989 Cover: 1.75 **NM** value: **2.00**
Circ: CapCity orders: **18,950**
📖 Who is Wonder Girl, Part 4 **A:** George Pérez

54 ❑ Mar 1989 Cover: 1.75 **NM** value: **2.00**
Circ: CapCity orders: **20,950**
📖 Who is Wonder Girl, Part 5 **A:** George Pérez

55 ❑ Jun 1989 Cover: 1.75 **NM** value: **2.00**
Circ: CapCity orders: **21,400**
📖 Transition **A:** George Pérez **W:** George Pérez; Marv Wolfman ★ 1st Appearance of Troia.

56 ❑ Jul 1989 Cover: 1.75 **NM** value: **2.00**
Circ: CapCity orders: **21,600**
★ Appearance of Gnaark.

57 ❑ Aug 1989 Cover: 1.75 **NM** value: **2.00**
Circ: CapCity orders: **20,800**
A: George Pérez ★ Versus Wildebeest.

58 ❑ Sep 1989 Cover: 1.75 **NM** value: **2.00**
Circ: CapCity orders: **20,850**
A: George Pérez

59 ❑ Oct 1989 Cover: 1.75 **NM** value: **2.00**
Circ: CapCity orders: **24,350**
A: George Pérez ★ Versus Wildebeest.

60 ❑ Nov 1989 Cover: 1.75 **NM** value: **3.00**
Circ: CapCity orders: **51,450**
📖 A Lonely Place of Dying, Part 2 **A:** George Pérez **W:** George Pérez; Marv Wolfman ★ Appearance of Tim Drake.

61 ❑ Dec 1989 Cover: 1.75 **NM** value: **2.50**
Circ: CapCity orders: **57,250**
📖 A Lonely Place of Dying, Part 4 **A:** George Pérez; Tom Grummettt **W:** George Pérez; Marv Wolfman

62 ❑ Jan 1990 Cover: 1.75 **NM** value: **2.00**
Circ: CapCity orders: **22,400**
★ Appearance of Deathstroke the Terminator.

63 ❑ Feb 1990 Cover: 1.75 **NM** value: **2.00**
Circ: CapCity orders: **22,700**
★ Appearance of Deathstroke the Terminator.

64 ❑ Mar 1990 Cover: 1.75 **NM** value: **2.00**
Circ: CapCity orders: **22,600**
★ Appearance of Deathstroke the Terminator.

65 ❑ Apr 1990 Cover: 1.75 **NM** value: **2.00**
Circ: CapCity orders: **25,400**
★ Appearance of Robin III, Deathstroke the Terminator.

66 ❑ May 1990 Cover: 1.75 **NM** value: **2.00**
Circ: CapCity orders: **20,850**
📖 Fatal Attraction **A:** Tom Grummettt **W:** George Pérez; Marv Wolfman

67 ❑ Jul 1990 Cover: 1.75 **NM** value: **2.00**
Circ: CapCity orders: **20,000**
📖 If Looks Could Kill **A:** Tom Grummettt **W:** George Pérez; Marv Wolfman

68 ❑ Jul 1990 Cover: 1.75 **NM** value: **2.00**
Circ: CapCity orders: **20,650**
★ Versus Royal Flush Gang.

69 ❑ Sep 1990 Cover: 1.75 **NM** value: **2.00**
Circ: CapCity orders: **19,950**

70 ❑ Oct 1990 Cover: 1.75 **NM** value: **2.00**
Circ: CapCity orders: **18,600**
★ Appearance of Deathstroke the Terminator.

71 ❑ Nov 1990 Cover: 1.75 **NM** value: **2.00**
Circ: CapCity orders: **19,500**
📖 Titans Hunt; Beginnings... Endings... and New Beginnings **A:** Tom Grummettt **W:** Marv Wolfman

72 ❑ Jan 1991 Cover: 1.75 **NM** value: **2.00**
Circ: CapCity orders: **19,150**
★ Appearance of Deathstroke the Terminator. ★ Death of Golden Eagle.

73 ❑ Feb 1991 Cover: 1.75 **NM** value: **2.00**
Circ: CapCity orders: **18,900**
★ 1st Appearance of Phantasm. ★ Appearance of Deathstroke the Terminator.

74 ❑ Mar 1991 Cover: 1.75 **NM** value: **2.00**
Circ: CapCity orders: **17,850**
★ 1st Appearance of Pantha. ★ Appearance of Deathstroke the Terminator.

75 ❑ Apr 1991 Cover: 1.75 **NM** value: **2.00**
Circ: CapCity orders: **18,050**
★ Appearance of Deathstroke the Terminator.

76 ❑ Jun 1991 Cover: 1.75 **NM** value: **2.00**
Circ: CapCity orders: **18,600**
• destruction of Titans Tower ★ Appearance of Deathstroke the Terminator.

77 ❑ Jul 1991 Cover: 1.75 **NM** value: **2.00**
Circ: CapCity orders: **18,350**
• Cyborg rebuilt ★ Appearance of Deathstroke the Terminator.

78 ❑ Aug 1991 Cover: 1.75 **NM** value: **2.00**
Circ: CapCity orders: **20,250**
★ Appearance of Deathstroke the Terminator.

79 ❑ Sep 1991 Cover: 1.75 **NM** value: **2.00**
Circ: CapCity orders: **20,800**
★ Appearance of Team Titans, Deathstroke the Terminator.

80 ❑ Nov 1991 Cover: 1.75 **NM** value: **Cover or less**
Circ: CapCity orders: **22,050**
★ Appearance of Team Titans.

81 ❑ Dec 1991 Cover: 1.75 **NM** value: **Cover or less**
Circ: CapCity orders: **25,400**
📖 War of the Gods; War of the Gods, Part 23 ★ Appearance of Pariah.

82 ❑ Jan 1992 Cover: 1.75 **NM** value: **Cover or less**
Circ: CapCity orders: **21,750**
📖 The Jericho Gambit, Part 1 **A:** Tom Grummettt **W:** Marv Wolfman

83 ❑ Feb 1992 Cover: 1.75 **NM** value: **Cover or less**
Circ: CapCity orders: **21,950**
📖 The Jericho Gambit, Part 2 **A:** Tom Grummettt **W:** Marv Wolfman ★ Death of Jericho.

84 ❑ Mar 1992 Cover: 1.75 **NM** value: **Cover or less**
Circ: CapCity orders: **21,850**
📖 Titans Hunt; The Jericho Gambit, Part 3 **A:** Tom Grummettt **W:** Marv Wolfman ★ Origin of Phantasm. ★ Death of Raven.

85 ❑ Apr 1992 Cover: 1.75 **NM** value: **Cover or less**
Circ: CapCity orders: **20,100**
• birth of baby Wildebeest ★ Appearance of Team Titans.

86 ❑ May 1992 Cover: 1.75 **NM** value: **Cover or less**
Circ: CapCity orders: **20,900**
• Nightwing vs. Terminator

87 ❑ Jun 1992 Cover: 1.75 **NM** value: **Cover or less**
Circ: CapCity orders: **23,350**
📖 Reflections **A:** Tom Grummettt **W:** Dan Jurgens

88 ❑ Jul 1992 Cover: 1.75 **NM** value: **Cover or less**
Circ: CapCity orders: **22,600**
📖 Bringing Up Baby **A:** Tom Grummettt **W:** Len Wein; Marv Wolfman

89 ❑ Aug 1992 Cover: 1.75 **NM** value: **Cover or less**
Circ: CapCity orders: **24,350**
📖 With Every Little Step We Take **A:** June Brigman **W:** Marv Wolfman

90 ❑ Sep 1992 Cover: 1.75 **NM** value: **Cover or less**
Circ: CapCity orders: **29,300**
📖 Total Chaos, Part 2 **A:** Tom Grummettt **W:** Marv Wolfman

91 ❑ Oct 1992 Cover: 1.75 **NM** value: **Cover or less**
Circ: CapCity orders: **23,550**
📖 Total Chaos, Part 5 **A:** Tom Grummettt **W:** Marv Wolfman ★ Appearance of Phantasm.

92 ❑ Nov 1992 Cover: 1.75 **NM** value: **Cover or less**
Circ: CapCity orders: **22,900**
📖 Total Chaos, Part 8

93 ❑ Dec 1992 Cover: 1.75 **NM** value: **Cover or less**
Circ: CapCity orders: **22,550**
📖 Titans Sell-Out, Part 3 • follow-up to Titans Sell-Out Special

94 ❑ Feb 1993 Cover: 1.75 **NM** value: **Cover or less**
Circ: CapCity orders: **21,050**
covers of #94-96 form triptych.

95 ❑ Mar 1993 Cover: 1.75 **NM** value: **Cover or less**
Circ: CapCity orders: **21,450**
📖 ...Into the Fire **A:** Phil Jimenez **W:** Louise Simonson

96 ❑ Apr 1993 Cover: 1.75 **NM** value: **Cover or less**
Circ: CapCity orders: **21,400**
📖 Patriot Games **A:** Phil Jimenez **W:** Louise Simonson

97 ❑ May 1993 Cover: 1.75 **NM** value: **Cover or less**
Circ: CapCity orders: **20,500**
📖 The Darkening, Part 1 **A:** Tom Grummettt **W:** Marv Wolfman

98 ❑ Jun 1993 Cover: 1.75 **NM** value: **Cover or less**
Circ: CapCity orders: **19,450**
📖 The Darkening, Part 2 **A:** Tom Grummettt **W:** Marv Wolfman

99 ❑ Jul 1993 Cover: 1.75 **NM** value: **Cover or less**
Circ: CapCity orders: **19,700**
📖 The Darkening, Part 3 **A:** Tom Grummettt **W:** Marv Wolfman ★ 1st Appearance of Arsenal.

100 ❑ Aug 1993 Cover: 3.50 **NM** value: **Cover or less**
Circ: CapCity orders: **42,600**
foil cover. • Giant-size. 📖 Something Old, Something New, Something Borrowed, Something Dead • Wedding of Dick Grayson and Koriand'r **A:** Tom Grummettt **W:** Marv Wolfman ★ Versus Evil Raven, pin-ups.

101 ❑ Sep 1993 Cover: 1.75 **NM** value: **Cover or less**
Circ: CapCity orders: **2,000**
📖 Aftermath **A:** Al Vey; Steve George **W:** Marv Wolfman

102 ❑ Oct 1993 Cover: 1.75 **NM** value: **Cover or less**
Circ: CapCity orders: **18,500**

103 ❑ Nov 1993 Cover: 1.75 **NM** value: **Cover or less**
Circ: CapCity orders: **17,750**

104 ❑ Dec 1993 Cover: 1.75 **NM** value: **Cover or less**
Circ: CapCity orders: **17,150**
📖 Terminus!, Part 1 • final fate of Cyborg **A:** Nick Napolitano **W:** Marv Wolfman

105 ❑ Dec 1993 Cover: 1.75 **NM** value: **Cover or less**
Circ: CapCity orders: **15,900**
📖 Terminus!, Part 2 **W:** Marv Wolfman

106 ❑ Jan 1994 Cover: 1.75 **NM** value: **Cover or less**
Circ: CapCity orders: **15,900**
📖 Terminus!, Part 3 **A:** Mark Tenney **W:** Marv Wolfman

107 ❑ Jan 1994 Cover: 1.75 **NM** value: **Cover or less**
Circ: CapCity orders: **14,500**

108 ❑ Feb 1994 Cover: 1.75 **NM** value: **Cover or less**
Circ: CapCity orders: **12,900**

109 ❑ Mar 1994 Cover: 1.75 **NM** value: **Cover or less**
Circ: CapCity orders: **11,950**

110 ❑ May 1994 Cover: 1.75 **NM** value: **Cover or less**
Circ: CapCity orders: **11,650**

111 ❑ Jun 1994 Cover: 1.75 **NM** value: **Cover or less**
Circ: CapCity orders: **11,250**

112 ❑ Jul 1994 Cover: 1.95 **NM** value: **Cover or less**
Circ: CapCity orders: **10,450**

113 ❑ Aug 1994 Cover: 1.95 **NM** value: **Cover or less**
Circ: CapCity orders: **10,700**

114 ❑ Sep 1994 Cover: 1.95 **NM** value: **Cover or less**
Circ: CapCity orders: **10,950**
• new team; Series continued in The New Titans #0

115 ❑ Nov 1994 Cover: 1.95 **NM** value: **Cover or less**
Circ: CapCity orders: **11,900**

116 ❑ Dec 1994 Cover: 1.95 **NM** value: **Cover or less**
• Return of Psimon ★ Appearance of Green Lantern.

117 ❑ Jan 1995 Cover: 1.95 **NM** value: **Cover or less**
Circ: CapCity orders: **12,250**
📖 Psimon Didn't Psay You'd Win **A:** William Rosado **W:** Marv Wolfman ★ Versus Psimon.

118 ❑ Feb 1995 Cover: 1.95 **NM** value: **Cover or less**
Circ: CapCity orders: **10,950**
★ Appearance of Thunder and Lightning.

119 ❑ Mar 1995 Cover: 1.95 **NM** value: **Cover or less**
Circ: CapCity orders: **11,100**
📖 Forever Evil, Part 1 ★ Versus Deathwing.

120 ❑ Apr 1995 Cover: 1.95 **NM** value: **Cover or less**
Circ: CapCity orders: **10,100**
📖 Forever Evil, Part 2 ★ Appearance of Supergirl.

121 ❑ May 1995 Cover: 1.95 **NM** value: **Cover or less**
Circ: CapCity orders: **9,825**

122 ❑ Jun 1995 Cover: 2.25 **NM** value: **Cover or less**
Circ: CapCity orders: **9,700**

123 ❑ Jul 1995 Cover: 2.25 **NM** value: **Cover or less**
Circ: CapCity orders: **9,600**

124 ❑ Aug 1995 Cover: 2.25 **NM** value: **Cover or less**
Circ: CapCity orders: **11,725**
📖 The Siege of The Zi Charam, Part 1

125 ❑ Sep 1995 Cover: 3.50 **NM** value: **Cover or less**
Circ: CapCity orders: **9,875**
• Giant-size. 📖 The Siege of The Zi Charam, Part 5

126 ❑ Oct 1995 Cover: 2.25 **NM** value: **Cover or less**
Circ: CapCity orders: **7,900**
📖 Meltdown

127 ❑ Nov 1995 Cover: 2.25 **NM** value: **Cover or less**
📖 Meltdown

128 ❑ Dec 1995 Cover: 2.25 **NM** value: **Cover or less**
📖 Meltdown

129 ❑ Jan 1996 Cover: 2.25 **NM** value: **Cover or less**
📖 Meltdown

130 ❑ Feb 1996 Cover: 2.25 **NM** value: **Cover or less**
📖 Where Nightmares End! final issue. **A:** William Rosado **W:** Marv Wolfman

Anl 5 ❑ ca. 1989 Cover: 3.50 **NM** value: **Cover or less**
Circ: CapCity orders: **19,700**
• See New Teen Titans Annual for previous issues, Who's Who entries; See New Teen Titans Annual for previous issues; Who's Who entries

Anl 6 ❑ ca. 1990 Cover: 3.50 **NM** value: **Cover or less**
Circ: CapCity orders: **19,750**
📖 Stayfree's World, Chapter 1 • Starfire **A:** Paris Cullins; Curt Swan; Tom Grindberg **W:** Marv Wolfman ★ 1st Appearance of Society of Sin.

Anl 7 ❑ ca. 1991 Cover: 3.50 **NM** value: **Cover or less**
Circ: CapCity orders: **34,150**
📖 Armageddon 2001, Part 10 • Armageddon 2001 ★ Origin of Team Titans. ★ 1st Appearance of Team Titans.

Anl 8 ❑ ca. 1992 Cover: 3.50 **NM** value: **Cover or less**
Circ: CapCity orders: **25,000**
📖 Eclipso: The Darkness Within, Part 14 • Eclipso: The Darkness Within **A:** Phil Jimenez; Curt Swan; Gabriel Morissette **W:** David Cody Weiss; Marv Wolfman

Anl 9 ❑ ca. 1993 Cover: 3.50 **NM** value: **Cover or less**
Circ: CapCity orders: **32,950**
📖 Bloodlines; The Red Hand BluesPaul Witcover, Elizabeth Hand • Bloodlines: Outbreak **A:** Malcolm Davis ★ Origin of Anima. ★ 1st Appearance of Anima.

Anl 10 ❑ ca. 1994 Cover: 3.50 **NM** value: **Cover or less**
Circ: CapCity orders: **10,900**
• Elseworlds

Anl 11 ❑ ca. 1995 Cover: 3.95 **NM** value: **Cover or less**
Circ: CapCity orders: **8,550**
• Year One

NEW TRIUMPH FEATURING NORTHGUARD — Matrix

1 ❑ Cover: 1.50 **NM** value: **1.75**
📖 And Stand on Guard... **A:** Gabriel Morrissette **W:** Mark Shainblum

1-2 ❑ Cover: 1.75 **NM** value: **Cover or less**
2 ❑ Cover: 1.50 **NM** value: **Cover or less**
3 ❑ Cover: 1.50 **NM** value: **Cover or less**
📖 Target Red Target Blue **A:** Gabriel Morrissette **W:** Mark Shainblum

4 ❑ Cover: 1.50 **NM** value: **Cover or less**
5 ❑ Cover: 1.50 **NM** value: **Cover or less**

NEW TWO-FISTED TALES, THE E.C. / Dark Horse

1 ❑ Cover: 4.95 **NM** value: **5.50**

Other grades: Multiply prices above by **1.5 for Mint • 2/3 for Very Fine • 1/3 for Fine • 1/5 for Very Good • 1/8 for Good**

📖 Dustoff; The Crater; Zippo Raid; Raid On Entebbe; Corpse On The Imjin **A:** Wayne Vansant; Rose Lomax; Harvey Kurtzman; Will Eisner; Spain Rodriguez **W:** Wayne Vansant; Don Lomax; Jessica Steinberg

NEW TWO-FISTED TALES, THE (2ND SERIES) — Dark Horse

1 ❑ Oct 1993 Cover: 4.95 **NM** value: **Cover or less**
Circ: CapCity orders: **4,925**
No issue number. 📖 Diversion; Gettysberg; Queen of Cu Chi; War; Hand to Hand

NEW VAMPIRE MIYU (VOL. 1) — Ironcat

Miyu, vampire princess and watcher of the dark, spends her life hunting wandering Shinma, evil gods who take human form in order to wreak havoc on mortals. Aided in her quest only by her mysterious companion, a young man known as Larva, she journeys from town to town pretending to be an ordinary young schoolgirl. In her latest guise, Miyu becomes suspicious of her new substitute teacher; a feeling confirmed when he boldly reveals himself as a Shinma. Surprised by his actions and seemingly innocent nature, Miyu decides to simply wait and see what his true motives are. But can any Shinma ever really be trusted?

This English translation was taken from the original Japanese edition by artist Narumi Kakinouchi, published in 1992 by Akita Publishing.

1 ❑ Sep 1997 Cover: 2.95 **NM** value: **3.00**
Circ: Diamd. preorders: **5,159**
📖 Battle Against the Western Shinmas **A:** Narumi Kakinouchi **W:** Narumi Kakinouchi

2 ❑ Oct 1997 Cover: 2.95 **NM** value: **3.00**
Circ: Diamd. preorders: **4,147**
A: Narumi Kakinouchi **W:** Narumi Kakinouchi

3 ❑ Nov 1997 Cover: 2.95 **NM** value: **3.00**
Circ: Diamd. preorders: **3,992**
A: Narumi Kakinouchi **W:** Narumi Kakinouchi

4 ❑ Dec 1997 Cover: 2.95 **NM** value: **3.00**
Circ: Diamd. preorders: **4,184**
A: Narumi Kakinouchi **W:** Narumi Kakinouchi

5 ❑ Jan 1998 Cover: 2.95 **NM** value: **3.00**
Circ: Diamd. preorders: **4,103**
A: Narumi Kakinouchi **W:** Narumi Kakinouchi

6 ❑ Feb 1998 Cover: 2.95 **NM** value: **3.00**
Circ: Diamd. preorders: **3,991**
A: Narumi Kakinouchi **W:** Narumi Kakinouchi

NEW VAMPIRE MIYU (VOL. 2) — Ironcat

1 ❑ Apr 1998 Cover: 2.95 **NM** value: **Cover or less**
Circ: Diamd. preorders: **4,193**
A: Narumi Kakinouchi **W:** Narumi Kakinouchi

2 ❑ May 1998 Cover: 2.95 **NM** value: **Cover or less**
Circ: Diamd. preorders: **3,839**
A: Narumi Kakinouchi **W:** Narumi Kakinouchi

3 ❑ Jun 1998 Cover: 2.95 **NM** value: **Cover or less**
Circ: Diamd. preorders: **3,797**
A: Narumi Kakinouchi **W:** Narumi Kakinouchi

4 ❑ Jul 1998 Cover: 2.95 **NM** value: **Cover or less**
Circ: Diamd. preorders: **3,518**
A: Narumi Kakinouchi **W:** Narumi Kakinouchi

5 ❑ Aug 1998 Cover: 2.95 **NM** value: **Cover or less**
Circ: Diamd. preorders: **3,274**
A: Narumi Kakinouchi **W:** Narumi Kakinouchi

6 ❑ Sep 1998 Cover: 2.95 **NM** value: **Cover or less**
Circ: Diamd. preorders: **3,210**
A: Narumi Kakinouchi **W:** Narumi Kakinouchi

NEW VAMPIRE MIYU (VOL. 3) — Ironcat

1 ❑ Oct 1998 Cover: 2.95 **NM** value: **Cover or less**
2 ❑ Nov 1998 Cover: 2.95 **NM** value: **Cover or less**
3 ❑ Dec 1998 Cover: 2.95 **NM** value: **Cover or less**
4 ❑ Jan 1999 Cover: 2.95 **NM** value: **Cover or less**
5 ❑ Feb 1999 Cover: 2.95 **NM** value: **Cover or less**
6 ❑ Mar 1999 Cover: 2.95 **NM** value: **Cover or less**
7 ❑ Apr 1999 Cover: 2.95 **NM** value: **Cover or less**

NEW VAMPIRE MIYU (VOL. 4) — Ironcat

1 ❑ May 1999 Cover: 2.95 **NM** value: **Cover or less**
Circ: Diamd. preorders: **3,040**
A: Narumi Kakinouchi **W:** Narumi Kakinouchi

2 ❑ Jun 1999 Cover: 2.95 **NM** value: **Cover or less**
Circ: Diamd. preorders: **2,932**
A: Narumi Kakinouchi **W:** Narumi Kakinouchi

3 ❑ Jul 1999 Cover: 2.95 **NM** value: **Cover or less**
Circ: Diamd. preorders: **2,756**
A: Narumi Kakinouchi **W:** Narumi Kakinouchi

4 ❑ Aug 1999 Cover: 2.95 **NM** value: **Cover or less**
Circ: Diamd. preorders: **2,642**
A: Narumi Kakinouchi **W:** Narumi Kakinouchi

5 ❑ Sep 1999 Cover: 2.95 **NM** value: **Cover or less**
Circ: Diamd. preorders: **2,570**
A: Narumi Kakinouchi **W:** Narumi Kakinouchi

6 ❑ Oct 1999 Cover: 2.95 **NM** value: **Cover or less**
Circ: Diamd. preorders: **2,646**
A: Narumi Kakinouchi **W:** Narumi Kakinouchi

NEW WARRIORS, THE — Marvel

What do you do if you're an aspiring young super-hero in search of a group? Even Marvel Boy was rejected from the Avengers and told to come back when he had more experience. Of course, you can't get that experience unless you join a group.

Conceived by the vigilante Night Thrasher, he soon recruited Nova, Marvel Boy, Speedball, Firestar, and Namorita to join his group. They band together to take on menaces that couldn't be overcome working alone. Together, they are the New Warriors, a young group of super-heroes who makes up with earnestness what they lack in experience.

1 ❑ Jul 1990 Cover: 1.00 **NM** value: **2.00**
Circ: CapCity orders: **36,500** • **CGC:** 3 graded, best 9.4
📖 From The Ground Up! **A:** Mark Bagley **W:** Fabian Nicieza ★ Origin of New Warriors.

1-2 ❑ Jul 1990 Cover: 1.00 **NM** value: **1.50**
📖 From The Ground Up! • 2nd Printing (gold) **A:** Mark Bagley **W:** Fabian Nicieza ★ Origin of New Warriors.

2 ❑ Aug 1990 Cover: 1.00 **NM** value: **1.50**
Circ: CapCity orders: **25,200**
★ Origin of Night Thrasher, Silhouette. ★ 1st Appearance of Silhouette.

3 ❑ Sep 1990 Cover: 1.00 **NM** value: **1.50**
Circ: CapCity orders: **23,600**

4 ❑ Oct 1990 Cover: 1.00 **NM** value: **1.50**
Circ: CapCity orders: **25,200**

5 ❑ Nov 1990 Cover: 1.00 **NM** value: **1.50**
Circ: CapCity orders: **26,400**

6 ❑ Dec 1990 Cover: 1.00 **NM** value: **1.50**
Circ: CapCity orders: **27,100**

7 ❑ Jan 1991 Cover: 1.00 **NM** value: **1.50**
Circ: Statement: **172,858** CapCity orders: **36,400**
• Punisher cameo

8 ❑ Feb 1991 Cover: 1.00 **NM** value: **1.50**
Circ: Statement: **172,858** CapCity orders: **38,300**
★ Origin of Bengal. ★ Appearance of Punisher.

9 ❑ Mar 1991 Cover: 1.00 **NM** value: **1.50**
Circ: Statement: **172,858** CapCity orders: **41,400**
📖 Hard Choices, Part 3 **A:** Mark Bagley **W:** Fabian Nicieza ★ Appearance of Punisher.

10 ❑ Apr 1991 Cover: 1.00 **NM** value: **1.50**
Circ: Statement: **172,858** CapCity orders: **30,900**

11 ❑ May 1991 Cover: 1.00 **NM** value: **1.50**
Circ: Statement: **172,858** CapCity orders: **34,500**
• Wolverine

12 ❑ Jun 1991 Cover: 1.00 **NM** value: **1.50**
Circ: Statement: **172,858** CapCity orders: **36,600**

13 ❑ Jul 1991 Cover: 1.00 **NM** value: **1.50**
Circ: Statement: **172,858** CapCity orders: **36,300**
📖 Forever Yesterday, Part 3 **A:** Mark Bagley **W:** Fabian Nicieza

14 ❑ Aug 1991 Cover: 1.00 **NM** value: **1.50**
Circ: Statement: **172,858** CapCity orders: **42,000**
📖 The Breeze of an Underwater Wind **A:** Mark Bagley **W:** Fabian Nicieza ★ Appearance of Namor, Darkhawk.

15 ❑ Sep 1991 Cover: 1.00 **NM** value: **1.50**
Circ: Statement: **172,858** CapCity orders: **40,800**

16 ❑ Oct 1991 Cover: 1.00 **NM** value: **1.50**
Circ: Statement: **172,858** CapCity orders: **44,400**
📖 Ground War **A:** Mark Bagley **W:** Fabian Nicieza

17 ❑ Nov 1991 Cover: 1.00 **NM** value: **1.50**
Circ: Statement: **172,858** CapCity orders: **46,800**
📖 Spre Winners **A:** Mark Bagley **W:** Fabian Nicieza ★ Appearance of Fantastic Four.

18 ❑ Dec 1991 Cover: 1.00 **NM** value: **1.50**
Circ: Statement: **172,858** CapCity orders: **45,900**
📖 Everything You Always Wanted to know About the Taylor Foundation But Were Afraid to Ask **A:** Mark Bagley **W:** Fabian Nicieza

19 ❑ Jan 1992 Cover: 1.00 **NM** value: **1.50**
Circ: Statement: **231,150** CapCity orders: **47,400**
📖 Sympathy for the Devil **A:** Mark Bagley **W:** Fabian Nicieza

20 ❑ Feb 1992 Cover: 1.25 **NM** value: **1.50**
Circ: Statement: **231,150** CapCity orders: **43,800**
📖 The Breaking Point **A:** Mark Bagley; Hudson; Larry Mahlstedt **W:** Fabian Nicieza

21 ❑ Mar 1992 Cover: 1.25 **NM** value: **1.50**
Circ: Statement: **231,150** CapCity orders: **41,700**
• Has 1991 Statement, filed 10/1/91; avg print run 269,325; avg sales 170,600; avg subs 2,258; avg total paid 172,858; samples 125; office use 250; max existent 173,233; 36% of run returned

22 ❑ Apr 1992 Cover: 1.25 **NM** value: **1.50**
Circ: Statement: **231,150** CapCity orders: **39,600**
📖 Nothing But the Truth, Part 1 **A:** Mark Bagley **W:** Fabian Nicieza

23 ❑ May 1992 Cover: 1.25 **NM** value: **1.50**
Circ: Statement: **231,150** CapCity orders: **39,300**
📖 Nothing But the Truth, Part 2 **A:** Mark Bagley **W:** Fabian Nicieza ★ Origin of Night Thrasher, Silhouette, Chord.

24 ❑ Jun 1992 Cover: 1.25 **NM** value: **1.50**
Circ: Statement: **231,150** CapCity orders: **39,600**
★ Origin of Silhouette, Chord.

25 ❑ Jul 1992 Cover: 2.50 **NM** value: **Cover or less**
Circ: Statement: **231,150** CapCity orders: **54,300**
Die-cut cover. ★ Origin of Chord.

26 ❑ Aug 1992 Cover: 1.25 **NM** value: **Cover or less**
Circ: Statement: **231,150** CapCity orders: **42,700**
📖 The Next Step **A:** Darick Robertson **W:** Fabian Nicieza

27 ❑ Sep 1992 Cover: 1.25 **NM** value: **Cover or less**
Circ: Statement: **231,150** CapCity orders: **47,400**

28 ❑ Oct 1992 Cover: 1.25 **NM** value: **Cover or less**
Circ: Statement: **231,150** CapCity orders: **41,300**
📖 Heavy Turbulence **A:** Darick Robertson **W:** Fabian Nicieza ★ 1st Appearance of Cardinal, Turbo I (Michiko "Mickey" Musashi).

29 ❑ Nov 1992 Cover: 1.25 **NM** value: **Cover or less**
Circ: Statement: **231,150** CapCity orders: **35,100**
📖 World War One: This Land Must Change **A:** Darick Robertson **W:** Fabian Nicieza

30 ❑ Dec 1992 Cover: 1.25 **NM** value: **Cover or less**
Circ: Statement: **231,150** CapCity orders: **33,900**

31 ❑ Jan 1993 Cover: 1.25 **NM** value: **Cover or less**
Circ: CapCity orders: **37,000**
📖 Ruins **A:** Darick Robertson **W:** Fabian Nicieza

32 ❑ Feb 1993 Cover: 1.25 **NM** value: **Cover or less**
Circ: CapCity orders: **34,300**
📖 Forces of Light, Part 1

33 ❑ Mar 1993 Cover: 1.25 **NM** value: **Cover or less**
Circ: CapCity orders: **30,600**
📖 Forces of Light, Part 2 • Has 1992 Statement, filed 10/1/92; avg print run 324,008; avg sales 227,075; avg subs 4,075; avg total paid 231,150; samples 250; office use 500; max existent 231,900; 28% of run returned ★ 1st Appearance of Turbo II (Mike Jeffries).

34 ❑ Apr 1993 Cover: 1.25 **NM** value: **Cover or less**
Circ: CapCity orders: **33,500**
📖 Forces of Light, Part 3

35 ❑ May 1993 Cover: 1.25 **NM** value: **Cover or less**
Circ: CapCity orders: **30,500**
📖 Forces of Light, Part 4

36 ❑ Jun 1993 Cover: 1.25 **NM** value: **Cover or less**
Circ: CapCity orders: **29,700**

37 ❑ Jul 1993 Cover: 1.25 **NM** value: **Cover or less**
Circ: CapCity orders: **29,200**

38 ❑ Aug 1993 Cover: 1.25 **NM** value: **Cover or less**
Circ: CapCity orders: **28,300**

39 ❑ Sep 1993 Cover: 1.25 **NM** value: **Cover or less**
Circ: CapCity orders: **26,700**

40 ❑ Oct 1993 Cover: 1.25 **NM** value: **Cover or less**
Circ: CapCity orders: **34,700**
• Air-Walker appearnce **A:** Darick Robertson **W:** Fabian Nicieza ★ Appearance of Nova, Super Nova, Firelord.

40/SC ❑ Oct 1993 Cover: 2.25 **NM** value: **Cover or less**
Gold foil on cover. **A:** Darick Robertson **W:** Fabian Nicieza ★ Appearance of Nova, Air-Walker, Super Nova, Firelord.

41 ❑ Nov 1993 Cover: 1.25 **NM** value: **Cover or less**
Circ: CapCity orders: **26,200**

42 ❑ Dec 1993 Cover: 1.25 **NM** value: **Cover or less**
Circ: CapCity orders: **25,000**

43 ❑ Jan 1994 Cover: 1.25 **NM** value: **Cover or less**
Circ: Statement: **93,720** CapCity orders: **23,200**

44 ❑ Feb 1994 Cover: 1.25 **NM** value: **Cover or less**
Circ: Statement: **93,720** CapCity orders: **24,000**

45 ❑ Mar 1994 Cover: 1.25 **NM** value: **Cover or less**
Circ: Statement: **93,720** CapCity orders: **30,200**

46 ❑ Apr 1994 Cover: 1.25 **NM** value: **Cover or less**
Circ: Statement: **93,720** CapCity orders: **28,000**

47 ❑ May 1994 Cover: 1.50 **NM** value: **Cover or less**
Circ: Statement: **93,720** CapCity orders: **21,800**
📖 Time and Time Again, Part 1 **A:** Vince Evans; Darick Robertson; John Czop; Kevin Kobas **W:** Fabian Nicieza

48 ❑ Jun 1994 Cover: 1.50 **NM** value: **Cover or less**
Circ: Statement: **93,720** CapCity orders: **21,100**
📖 Time and Time Again, Part 4 **A:** Guy Dorian; Darick Robertson; Richard Pace; John Czop **W:** Fabian Nicieza

49 ❑ Jul 1994 Cover: 1.50 **NM** value: **Cover or less**
Circ: Statement: **93,720** CapCity orders: **22,600**

50 ❑ Aug 1994 Cover: 2.00 **NM** value: **Cover or less**
Circ: Statement: **93,720** CapCity orders: **29,000**
• Giant-size. 📖 Time and Time Again, Part 8

50/SC ❑ Aug 1994 Cover: 2.95 **NM** value: **Cover or less**
Glow-in-the-dark cover. • Giant-size. 📖 Time and Time Again, Part 8

51 ❑ Sep 1994 Cover: 1.50 **NM** value: **Cover or less**
Circ: Statement: **93,720** CapCity orders: **21,250**

52 ❑ Oct 1994 Cover: 1.50 **NM** value: **Cover or less**
Circ: Statement: **93,720** CapCity orders: **19,250**

53 ❑ Nov 1994 Cover: 1.50 **NM** value: **Cover or less**
Circ: Statement: **93,720** CapCity orders: **18,350**

54 ❑ Dec 1994 Cover: 1.50 **NM** value: **Cover or less**
Circ: Statement: **44,083** CapCity orders: **17,600**

55 ❑ Jan 1995 Cover: 1.50 **NM** value: **Cover or less**
Circ: Statement: **44,083** CapCity orders: **15,875**

56 ❑ Feb 1995 Cover: 1.50 **NM** value: **Cover or less**
Circ: Statement: **44,083** CapCity orders: **14,750**

57 ❑ Mar 1995 Cover: 1.50 **NM** value: **Cover or less**
Circ: Statement: **44,083** CapCity orders: **13,200**
• Has 1994 Statement, filed 10/1/94; avg print run 144,333; avg sales 91,877; avg subs 1,843; avg total paid 93,720; samples 125; office use 500; max existent 110,835; 35% of run returned

58 ❑ Apr 1995 Cover: 1.50 **NM** value: **Cover or less**
Circ: Statement: **44,083** CapCity orders: **12,225**

59 ❑ May 1995 Cover: 1.50 **NM** value: **Cover or less**
Circ: Statement: **44,083** CapCity orders: **11,875**

60 ❑ Jun 1995 Cover: 2.50 **NM** value: **Cover or less**
Circ: Statement: **44,083** CapCity orders: **11,800**
• Giant-size.

61 ❑ Jul 1995 Cover: 1.50 **NM** value: **Cover or less**
Circ: Statement: **44,083** CapCity orders: **11,875**
• Maximum Clonage Prologue

62 ❑ Aug 1995 Cover: 1.50 **NM** value: **Cover or less**
Circ: Statement: **44,083**
★ Appearance of Scarlet Spider.

63 ❑ Sep 1995 Cover: 1.50 **NM** value: **Cover or less**
Circ: Statement: **44,083**

64 ❑ Oct 1995 Cover: 1.50 **NM** value: **Cover or less**
Circ: Statement: **44,083**
• return of Night Thrasher and Rage

65 ❑ Nov 1995 Cover: 1.50 **NM** value: **Cover or less**
• return of Namorita

66 ❑ Dec 1995 Cover: 1.50 **NM** value: **Cover or less**
A: Patrick Zircher **W:** Evan Skolnick ★ Appearance of Scarlet Spider, Speedball.

CGC-graded: Multiply prices above by **33 for 9.9 M • 16 for 9.8 NM/M • 7 for 9.6 NM+ • 5 for 9.4 NM • 2.5 for 9.2 NM- • 1.5 for 9.0 VF/NM**

67 ❑ Jan 1996 Cover: 1.50 **NM** value: **Cover or less**
📖 Nightmare in Scarlet, Part 2 • concludes in Web of Scarlet Spider #3; Has 1995 Statement, filed 10/1/95; avg print run 46,527; avg sales 42,850; avg subs 1,233; avg total paid 44,083; samples 750; office use 500; max existent 45,333; little to no newsstand sales this year
68 ❑ Feb 1996 Cover: 1.50 **NM** value: **Cover or less**
📖 Future Shock, Part 1 ★ Appearance of Guardians of the Galaxy.
69 ❑ Mar 1996 Cover: 1.50 **NM** value: **Cover or less**
📖 Future Shock, Part 2 **A:** Patrick Zircher **W:** Evan Skolnick ★ Death of Speedball.
70 ❑ Apr 1996 Cover: 1.50 **NM** value: **Cover or less**
📖 Future Shock, Part 3 **A:** Patrick Zircher **W:** Evan Skolnick
71 ❑ May 1996 Cover: 1.50 **NM** value: **Cover or less**
📖 Future Shock, Part 4
72 ❑ Jun 1996 Cover: 1.50 **NM** value: **Cover or less**
★ Appearance of Avengers.
73 ❑ Jul 1996 Cover: 1.50 **NM** value: **Cover or less**
74 ❑ Aug 1996 Cover: 1.50 **NM** value: **Cover or less**
75 ❑ Sep 1996 Cover: 2.50 **NM** value: **Cover or less**
final issue.
Anl 1❑ca. 1991 Cover: 2.00 **NM** value: **3.00**
Circ: CapCity orders: **52,400**
📖 Kings of Pain; Kings of Pain, Part 2; Night Crawler; Speedball: To Bounce Or Not To Bounce; Firestar **A:** Mark Bagley; Tom Morgan; Marie Severin; Jeff Albrecht; John Calimée **W:** Fabian Nicieza; Dan Slott; Eric Fein; Gary Barnum ★ Origin of Night Thrasher.
Anl 2❑ca. 1992 Cover: 2.25 **NM** value: **Cover or less**
📖 The Hero Killers, Part 4; Days And Nights **A:** Brandon Peterson; Steve Buccellato **W:** Fabian Nicieza
Anl 3❑ca. 1993 Cover: 2.95 **NM** value: **Cover or less**
Circ: CapCity orders: **37,300**
Anl 4❑ca. 1994 Cover: 2.95 **NM** value: **Cover or less**
Circ: CapCity orders: **15,800**
Ash 1❑ Cover: 0.75 **NM** value: **Cover or less**
📖 Team Reflections • "Ashcan" mini-comic **A:** Cathy Colbert **W:** Jim Krueger; Matt Friedman
Bk 1❑ Cover: 12.95 **NM** value: **Cover or less**
• Beginnings

NEW WARRIORS, THE (VOL. 2) Marvel

1 ❑ Oct 1999 Cover: 2.99 **NM** value: **Cover or less**
Circ: Diamd. preorders: **42,274**
📖 One Good Reason **A:** Steve Scott **W:** Jay Faerber
2 ❑ Nov 1999 Cover: 2.99 **NM** value: **Cover or less**
Circ: Diamd. preorders: **36,295**
W: Jay Faerber
3 ❑ Dec 1999 Cover: 2.50 **NM** value: **Cover or less**
Circ: Diamd. preorders: **29,999**
W: Jay Faerber
4 ❑ Jan 2000 Cover: 2.50 **NM** value: **Cover or less**
Circ: Diamd. preorders: **27,042**
W: Jay Faerber
5 ❑ Feb 2000 Cover: 2.50 **NM** value: **Cover or less**
Circ: Diamd. preorders: **26,263**
W: Jay Faerber
6 ❑ Mar 2000 Cover: 2.50 **NM** value: **Cover or less**
Circ: Diamd. preorders: **22,420**
W: Jay Faerber
7 ❑ Apr 2000 Cover: 2.50 **NM** value: **Cover or less**
Circ: Diamd. preorders: **20,317**
W: Jay Faerber
8 ❑ May 2000 Cover: 2.50 **NM** value: **Cover or less**
Circ: Diamd. preorders: **20,396**
📖 Rite of Passage **A:** Jamal Igle **W:** Jay Faerber
9 ❑ Jun 2000 Cover: 2.50 **NM** value: **Cover or less**
Circ: Diamd. preorders: **19,874**
10 ❑ Jul 2000 Cover: 2.50 **NM** value: **Cover or less**
Circ: Diamd. preorders: **18,951**

NEW WAVE, THE Eclipse

High above the earth was a secret space station operated by the U.S. government. Supposedly, the scientists on board were researching energy-mass conversions. In reality, they were investigating the possibilities of reaching alternate universes. Led by a modern-day mad scientist named Cliff Pasternak, it seemed as if they had achieved their goal. Cliff managed to trap a blue-skinned being named Tachyon in a special energy chamber in the station. Other scientists worked to release him, but not before the barrier between worlds was forever shattered. Tachyon was the first, but not the last of this "New Wave" of super-beings.

The New Wave first appeared as a preview in Miracleman #8 and DNAgents #9. It then ran as a 16-page biweekly until 1986's issue #9, when it became a full-sized comic book. By issue #13 in 1987, however, it was all over and the New Wave vanished.

1 ❑ Jun 1986 Cover: 0.50 **NM** value: **2.00**
Circ: CapCity orders: **14,150**
📖 The Man In The Corporate Booth **A:** Lee Weeks **W:** Mindy Newell; Sean Deming
1/A ❑ Cover: 0.50 **NM** value: **2.00**
• misprint
2 ❑ Jul 1986 Cover: 0.50 **NM** value: **1.50**
Circ: CapCity orders: **11,675**
3 ❑ Jul 1986 Cover: 0.50 **NM** value: **1.50**
Circ: CapCity orders: **9,925**
📖 A Space Station Called Hell! **A:** Lee Weeks **W:** Mindy Newell; Sean Deming
4 ❑ Aug 1986 Cover: 0.50 **NM** value: **1.00**
Circ: CapCity orders: **9,550**
5 ❑ Aug 1986 Cover: 0.50 **NM** value: **1.00**
Circ: CapCity orders: **8,650**
6 ❑ Sep 1986 Cover: 0.50 **NM** value: **1.00**
Circ: CapCity orders: **7,975**
7 ❑ Sep 1986 Cover: 0.50 **NM** value: **1.00**
Circ: CapCity orders: **7,800**
8 ❑ Sep 1986 Cover: 0.50 **NM** value: **1.00**
Circ: CapCity orders: **7,625**
9 ❑ Oct 1986 Cover: 1.50 **NM** value: **Cover or less**
Circ: CapCity orders: **7,350**
10 ❑ Nov 1986 Cover: 1.50 **NM** value: **Cover or less**
Circ: CapCity orders: **5,875**
📖 Breach Of Faith **A:** Lee Weeks **W:** Mindy Newell
11 ❑ Dec 1986 Cover: 1.50 **NM** value: **Cover or less**
Circ: CapCity orders: **5,425**
12 ❑ Feb 1987 Cover: 1.50 **NM** value: **Cover or less**
Circ: CapCity orders: **4,550**
13 ❑ Mar 1987 Cover: 1.50 **NM** value: **Cover or less**
Circ: CapCity orders: **4,425**
final issue.

NEW WAVE VERSUS THE VOLUNTEERS, THE Eclipse

1 ❑ Apr 1987 Cover: 2.50 **NM** value: **Cover or less**
Circ: CapCity orders: **3,450**
2 ❑ Jun 1987 Cover: 2.50 **NM** value: **Cover or less**
Circ: CapCity orders: **2,975**
📖 You Can't Fight City Hall

NEW WORLD ORDER Blazer

1 ❑ b&w Cover: 2.50 **NM** value: **3.00**
A: Dan Reed **W:** Dan Reed
2 ❑ b&w Cover: 2.50 **NM** value: **2.75**
A: Dan Reed **W:** Dan Reed
3 ❑ b&w Cover: 2.50 **NM** value: **2.75**
A: Dan Reed **W:** Dan Reed
4 ❑ Aug 1993, b&w Cover: 2.50 **NM** value: **Cover or less**
A: Dan Reed **W:** Dan Reed
5 ❑ Jan 1994, b&w Cover: 2.50 **NM** value: **Cover or less**
A: Dan Reed **W:** Dan Reed
6 ❑ May 1994, b&w Cover: 2.50 **NM** value: **Cover or less**
A: Dan Reed **W:** Dan Reed ★ 1st Appearance of Skinhead.
7 ❑ Aug 1994, b&w Cover: 2.50 **NM** value: **Cover or less**
A: Dan Reed **W:** Dan Reed ★ 1st Appearance of Shining.
8 ❑ Feb 1995, b&w Cover: 2.50 **NM** value: **Cover or less**
A: Dan Reed **W:** Dan Reed

NEW WORLD ORDER (PIG'S EYE) Pig's Eye

1 ❑ Cover: 1.00 **NM** value: **Cover or less**
A: Ryan Clements **W:** Ryan Clements

NEW WORLDS ANTHOLOGY Caliber

1 ❑ Cover: 2.95 **NM** value: **Cover or less**
A: Juan Zanotto **W:** Ricardo Barriero
2 ❑ Jan 1996 Cover: 3.95 **NM** value: **Cover or less**
📖 Mister X, Part 2; Little White Mouse: Dream of the Ghost, Part 1; Mirror Image, Part 2; Beyond the Fringe, Part 2; Antrax, Part 2 **A:** Paul Sizer; Rob Hand; Don Yee; Durwin S. Talon; John B. Ludwick; Theodore Kemtis; D'Israeli **W:** Paul Sizer; Durwin S. Talon; John B. Ludwick; Theodore Kemtis; Rich Rainey; Wilbur R. Webb
3 ❑ Cover: 3.95 **NM** value: **Cover or less**
4 ❑ Cover: 3.95 **NM** value: **Cover or less**
5 ❑ Cover: 3.95 **NM** value: **Cover or less**
6 ❑ Cover: 3.95 **NM** value: **Cover or less**

NEW YORK, THE BIG CITY Kitchen Sink Press

1 ❑ b&w Cover: 13.95 **NM** value: **Cover or less**
A: Will Eisner **W:** Will Eisner

NEW YORK, THE BIG CITY (DC) DC

1 ❑ Cover: 12.95 **NM** value: **Cover or less**
📖 The Treasure of Avenue "C"; Subways; Stoops; Garbage; Street Music; Sentinels; Windows; Walls; The Block **A:** Will Eisner **W:** Will Eisner

NEW YORK CITY OUTLAWS Outlaw

1 ❑ Cover: 2.00 **NM** value: **Cover or less**
2 ❑ Cover: 2.00 **NM** value: **Cover or less**
3 ❑ Cover: 2.00 **NM** value: **Cover or less**
4 ❑ Cover: 2.00 **NM** value: **Cover or less**

NEW YORK WORLD'S FAIR DC

1939❑Apr 1939 Cover: 0.25 **NM** value: **20000.00**
• **CGC:** 6 graded, best 7.0
1940❑ca. 1940 Cover: 0.15 **NM** value: **10000.00**
• **CGC:** 11 graded, best 7.5

NEW YORK: YEAR ZERO Eclipse

1 ❑ Aug 1988 Cover: 2.00 **NM** value: **Cover or less**
A: Juan Zanotto **W:** Ricardo Barriero
2 ❑ Aug 1988 Cover: 2.00 **NM** value: **Cover or less**
A: Juan Zanotto **W:** Ricardo Barriero
3 ❑ Sep 1988 Cover: 2.00 **NM** value: **Cover or less**
A: Juan Zanotto **W:** Ricardo Barriero
4 ❑ Oct 1988 Cover: 2.00 **NM** value: **Cover or less**
A: Juan Zanotto **W:** Ricardo Barriero

NEXT MAN Comico

1 ❑ Mar 1985 Cover: 1.50 **NM** value: **2.00**
Circ: CapCity orders: **3,950**
A: Vince Argondezzi **W:** Roger McKenzie ★ Origin of Next Man. ★ 1st Appearance of Next Man.
2 ❑ Apr 1985 Cover: 1.50 **NM** value: **2.00**
Circ: CapCity orders: **4,275**
📖 American Pie **A:** Vince Argondezzi **W:** Roger McKenzie
3 ❑ Jun 1985 Cover: 1.50 **NM** value: **2.00**
Circ: CapCity orders: **4,375**
4 ❑ Aug 1985 Cover: 1.50 **NM** value: **2.00**
Circ: CapCity orders: **4,300**
5 ❑ Oct 1985 Cover: 1.50 **NM** value: **2.00**
Circ: CapCity orders: **4,775**

NEXT MEN (JOHN BYRNE'S...) Dark Horse

The Next Men are the only survivors of an illegal bio-engineering project. The group consists of Jack, who is incredibly strong; Danny, who can run at phenomenal speed; Bethany, who is both physically and mentally invulnerable; Nathan, who can see through anything; and Jasmine, who has amazing agility. David, a "faded" member of the Next Men, adds a touch of mystery to the plot.

This well-scripted series involves the very human result of an unethical experiment designed to create ideal soldiers. When the Next Men escape from the top-secret biological research facility that they've known as their only home, they find that the real world has little compassion for the human equivalents of lab animals.

0 ❑ Feb 1992 Cover: 2.50 **NM** value: **3.00**
Circ: CapCity orders: **22,325**
📖 Prelude • collects storyline from Dark Horse Presents; Reprints Next Men stories from Dark Horse Presents **A:** John Byrne **W:** John Byrne
1 ❑ Jan 1992 Cover: 2.50 **NM** value: **3.00**
Circ: CapCity orders: **38,100** • **CGC:** 2 graded, best 9.8
Embossed cover (silver logo). 📖 Breakout **A:** John Byrne **W:** John Byrne
1-2 ❑ Jan 1992 Cover: 2.50 **NM** value: **Cover or less**
2 ❑ Mar 1992 Cover: 2.50 **NM** value: **3.00**
Circ: CapCity orders: **31,675** • **CGC:** 1 graded, best 9.4
📖 World View **A:** John Byrne **W:** John Byrne ★ 1st Appearance of Sathanus.
3 ❑ Apr 1992 Cover: 2.50 **NM** value: **Cover or less**
Circ: CapCity orders: **34,000** • **CGC:** 1 graded, best 9.6
📖 Kill Factor **A:** John Byrne **W:** John Byrne
4 ❑ May 1992 Cover: 2.50 **NM** value: **Cover or less**
Circ: CapCity orders: **35,950** • **CGC:** 1 graded, best 9.4
📖 Boneyard **A:** John Byrne **W:** John Byrne
5 ❑ Jun 1992 Cover: 2.50 **NM** value: **Cover or less**
Circ: CapCity orders: **36,750**
📖 Survivor **A:** John Byrne **W:** John Byrne
6 ❑ Jul 1992 Cover: 2.50 **NM** value: **Cover or less**
Circ: CapCity orders: **29,675**
📖 Dominoes **A:** John Byrne **W:** John Byrne
7 ❑ Sep 1992 Cover: 2.50 **NM** value: **Cover or less**
Circ: CapCity orders: **25,650**
📖 Parallel, Part 1 • flipbook with M4 #1 back-up story **A:** John Byrne **W:** John Byrne ★ 1st Appearance of M4.
8 ❑ Oct 1992 Cover: 2.50 **NM** value: **Cover or less**
Circ: CapCity orders: **24,450**
📖 Parallel, Part 2 • flipbook with M4 #2 back-up story **A:** John Byrne **W:** John Byrne
9 ❑ Nov 1992 Cover: 2.50 **NM** value: **Cover or less**
Circ: CapCity orders: **24,425**
📖 Parallel, Part 3 • flipbook with M4 #3 back-up story **A:** John Byrne **W:** John Byrne
10 ❑ Dec 1992 Cover: 2.50 **NM** value: **Cover or less**
Circ: CapCity orders: **23,575**
📖 Parallel, Interlude • flipbook with M4 #4 back-up story **A:** John Byrne **W:** John Byrne
11 ❑ Jan 1993 Cover: 2.50 **NM** value: **Cover or less**
Circ: CapCity orders: **23,800**
📖 Parallel, Part 4 • M4 back-up story **A:** John Byrne **W:** John Byrne
12 ❑ Feb 1993 Cover: 2.50 **NM** value: **Cover or less**
Circ: CapCity orders: **23,800**
📖 Parallel, Part 5 • M4 back-up story **A:** John Byrne **W:** John Byrne
13 ❑ Mar 1993 Cover: 2.50 **NM** value: **Cover or less**
Circ: CapCity orders: **23,025**
📖 Fame, Part 1 • M4 back-up story **A:** John Byrne **W:** John Byrne
14 ❑ Apr 1993 Cover: 2.50 **NM** value: **Cover or less**
Circ: CapCity orders: **21,950**
📖 Fame, Part 2 • M4 back-up story **A:** John Byrne **W:** John Byrne
15 ❑ Jun 1993 Cover: 2.50 **NM** value: **3.00**
Circ: CapCity orders: **19,775**
Photo cover. 📖 Fame, Part 3 • M4 back-up story **A:** John Byrne **W:** John Byrne
16 ❑ Jul 1993 Cover: 2.50 **NM** value: **Cover or less**
Circ: CapCity orders: **18,400**
📖 Fame, Part 4 • M4 back-up story **A:** John Byrne **W:** John Byrne
17 ❑ Aug 1993 Cover: 2.50 **NM** value: **Cover or less**
Circ: CapCity orders: **17,500**
📖 Fame, Part 5 • M4 back-up story **A:** John Byrne; Frank Miller(cover) **C:** Frank Miller **W:** John Byrne
18 ❑ Sep 1993 Cover: 2.50 **NM** value: **Cover or less**
Circ: CapCity orders: **17,300**
📖 Fame, Part 6 • M4 back-up story **A:** John Byrne **W:** John Byrne
19 ❑ Oct 1993 Cover: 2.50 **NM** value: **Cover or less**
Circ: CapCity orders: **21,275**
📖 Faith, Part 1 • M4 back-up story **A:** John Byrne **W:** John Byrne
20 ❑ Nov 1993 Cover: 2.50 **NM** value: **Cover or less**
Circ: CapCity orders: **18,900**
📖 Faith, Part 2 • M4 back-up story **A:** John Byrne **W:** John Byrne
21 ❑ Dec 1993 Cover: 2.50 **NM** value: **Cover or less**
Circ: CapCity orders: **17,475** • **CGC:** 3 graded, best 9.6
📖 Faith, Part 3 • M4 back-up story **A:** John Byrne **W:** John Byrne ★ Appearance of Hellboy.

Other grades: Multiply prices above by **1.5 for Mint • 2/3 for Very Fine • 1/3 for Fine • 1/5 for Very Good • 1/8 for Good**

22 ❑ Jan 1994 Cover: 2.50 **NM** value: **Cover or less**
Circ: CapCity orders: **16,100**
📖 Faith, Part 4 • M4 back-up story **A:** John Byrne **W:** John Byrne
23 ❑ Mar 1994 Cover: 2.50 **NM** value: **Cover or less**
Circ: CapCity orders: **17,125**
📖 Power, Part 1 • M4 back-up story **A:** John Byrne **W:** John Byrne
24 ❑ Apr 1994 Cover: 2.50 **NM** value: **Cover or less**
Circ: CapCity orders: **15,850**
📖 Power, Part 2 • M4 back-up story **A:** John Byrne **W:** John Byrne
25 ❑ May 1994 Cover: 2.50 **NM** value: **Cover or less**
Circ: CapCity orders: **16,275**
📖 Power, Part 3 **A:** John Byrne **W:** John Byrne ★ Appearance of Cutter and Skywise (Elfquest characters).
26 ❑ Jun 1994 Cover: 2.50 **NM** value: **Cover or less**
Circ: CapCity orders: **16,100**
📖 Power, Part 4 **A:** John Byrne **W:** John Byrne
27 ❑ Aug 1994 Cover: 2.50 **NM** value: **Cover or less**
Circ: CapCity orders: **16,300**
📖 Lies, Part 1 **A:** John Byrne **W:** John Byrne
28 ❑ Sep 1994 Cover: 2.50 **NM** value: **Cover or less**
Circ: CapCity orders: **15,075**
📖 Lies, Part 2 **A:** John Byrne **W:** John Byrne
29 ❑ Oct 1994 Cover: 2.50 **NM** value: **Cover or less**
Circ: CapCity orders: **14,625**
📖 Lies, Part 3 **A:** John Byrne **W:** John Byrne
30 ❑ Dec 1994 Cover: 2.50 **NM** value: **Cover or less**
Circ: CapCity orders: **13,800**
📖 Lies, Part 4 • series goes on hiatus **A:** John Byrne **W:** John Byrne
Bk 1❑ May 1995 Cover: 16.95 **NM** value: **Cover or less**
• Power; Collects Next Men (John Byrne's...) #1-6 **A:** John Byrne **W:** John Byrne
Bk 2❑ Dec 1996 Cover: 16.95 **NM** value: **Cover or less**
• Lies; Collects Next Men (John Byrne's...) #7-12 **A:** John Byrne **W:** John Byrne
Bk 3❑ Cover: 16.95 **NM** value: **Cover or less**
📖 Fame • Collects Next Men (John Byrne's...) #13-18 **A:** John Byrne **W:** John Byrne
Bk 4❑ Cover: 14.95 **NM** value: **Cover or less**
📖 Faith • Collects Next Men (John Byrne's...) #19-22 **A:** John Byrne **W:** John Byrne
Bk 5❑ Cover: 16.95 **NM** value: **Cover or less**
📖 Power • Collects Next Men (John Byrne's...) #23-28 **A:** John Byrne **W:** John Byrne

NEXT NEXUS, THE — First

1 ❑ Jan 1989 Cover: 1.95 **NM** value: **2.00**
Circ: CapCity orders: **10,025**
📖 Three Sisters **A:** Steve Rude **W:** Mike Baron
2 ❑ Feb 1989 Cover: 1.95 **NM** value: **2.00**
Circ: CapCity orders: **8,300**
A: Steve Rude **W:** Mike Baron
3 ❑ Mar 1989 Cover: 1.95 **NM** value: **2.00**
Circ: CapCity orders: **7,800**
A: Steve Rude **W:** Mike Baron
4 ❑ Apr 1989 Cover: 1.95 **NM** value: **2.00**
Circ: CapCity orders: **7,975**
A: Steve Rude **W:** Mike Baron
Bk 1❑ Cover: 9.95 **NM** value: **Cover or less**

NEXT WAVE, THE — Overstreet

1 ❑ **NM** value: **2.00**
📖 Rib; Dream Walker; Arcana; Manhattan Project; Tales from the Bog • Sampling of Five Self-Published comics **A:** Rob Clark; Andrew M. Ford; Jenni Gregory; Marcus Lusk; Patricia Breen; T.S. Wells **W:** Rob Clark; Jenni Gregory; Marcus Lusk; T.S. Wells; Gene McDonald; Michael Kelleher

NEXUS: ALIEN JUSTICE — Dark Horse

1 ❑ Dec 1992 Cover: 3.95 **NM** value: **Cover or less**
Circ: CapCity orders: **8,875**
2 ❑ Jan 1993 Cover: 3.95 **NM** value: **Cover or less**
Circ: CapCity orders: **10,350**
3 ❑ Feb 1993 Cover: 3.95 **NM** value: **Cover or less**
Circ: CapCity orders: **9,800**
A: Steve Rude
Bk 1❑ Nov 1996 Cover: 16.95 **NM** value: **Cover or less**

NEXUS LEGENDS — First

Nexus proved to be one of First Comics' most enduring characters. Created by Mike Baron and Steve Rude, this space-bound protector had gone from a little known black-and-white magazine to a graphic novel, then on to a remarkably successful color series. After 55 issues of the latter, First premiered this new title which reprinted Nexus' early color issues with new covers by Steve Rude.

Now, new readers could catch up on this remarkable cast of characters including Judah Maccabee, aka the Hammer of God, wisecracking Dave of Thune, love interest Sundra Peale, a gaggle of floating heads, and of course, the enigmatic Nexus himself.

1 ❑ May 1989 Cover: 1.50 **NM** value: **2.50**
Circ: CapCity orders: **5,450**
A: Steve Rude **W:** Mike Baron
2 ❑ Jun 1989 Cover: 1.50 **NM** value: **2.00**
Circ: CapCity orders: **4,700**
A: Steve Rude **W:** Mike Baron
3 ❑ Jul 1989 Cover: 1.50 **NM** value: **2.00**
Circ: CapCity orders: **4,675**
A: Steve Rude **W:** Mike Baron
4 ❑ Aug 1989 Cover: 1.50 **NM** value: **2.00**
Circ: CapCity orders: **4,400**
A: Steve Rude **W:** Mike Baron
5 ❑ Sep 1989 Cover: 1.50 **NM** value: **2.00**
Circ: CapCity orders: **4,025**
A: Steve Rude **W:** Mike Baron
6 ❑ Oct 1989 Cover: 1.50 **NM** value: **2.00**
Circ: CapCity orders: **3,850**
A: Steve Rude **W:** Mike Baron
7 ❑ Nov 1989 Cover: 1.50 **NM** value: **2.00**
Circ: CapCity orders: **3,725**
A: Steve Rude **W:** Mike Baron
8 ❑ Dec 1989 Cover: 1.50 **NM** value: **2.00**
Circ: CapCity orders: **3,600**
A: Steve Rude **W:** Mike Baron
9 ❑ Jan 1990 Cover: 1.50 **NM** value: **2.00**
Circ: CapCity orders: **3,475**
A: Steve Rude **W:** Mike Baron
10 ❑ Feb 1990 Cover: 1.50 **NM** value: **2.00**
A: Steve Rude **W:** Mike Baron
11 ❑ Mar 1990 Cover: 1.50 **NM** value: **2.00**
Circ: CapCity orders: **3,100**
A: Steve Rude **W:** Mike Baron
12 ❑ Apr 1990 Cover: 1.50 **NM** value: **2.00**
Circ: CapCity orders: **2,750**
A: Steve Rude **W:** Mike Baron
13 ❑ May 1990 Cover: 1.50 **NM** value: **2.00**
Circ: CapCity orders: **2,650**
A: Steve Rude **W:** Mike Baron
14 ❑ Jun 1990 Cover: 1.50 **NM** value: **2.00**
Circ: CapCity orders: **2,575**
A: Steve Rude **W:** Mike Baron
15 ❑ Jul 1990 Cover: 1.50 **NM** value: **2.00**
Circ: CapCity orders: **2,400**
A: Steve Rude **W:** Mike Baron
16 ❑ Aug 1990 Cover: 1.75 **NM** value: **2.00**
Circ: CapCity orders: **2,300**
A: Steve Rude **W:** Mike Baron
17 ❑ Sep 1990 Cover: 1.75 **NM** value: **2.00**
Circ: CapCity orders: **2,200**
A: Steve Rude **W:** Mike Baron
18 ❑ Oct 1990 Cover: 1.95 **NM** value: **2.00**
Circ: CapCity orders: **1,800**
A: Steve Rude **W:** Mike Baron
19 ❑ Nov 1990 Cover: 1.95 **NM** value: **2.00**
Circ: CapCity orders: **1,775**
A: Steve Rude **W:** Mike Baron
20 ❑ Dec 1990 Cover: 1.95 **NM** value: **2.00**
Circ: CapCity orders: **1,650**
A: Steve Rude **W:** Mike Baron
21 ❑ Jan 1991 Cover: 1.95 **NM** value: **2.00**
Circ: CapCity orders: **1,700**
A: Steve Rude **W:** Mike Baron
22 ❑ Feb 1991 Cover: 1.95 **NM** value: **2.00**
Circ: CapCity orders: **1,675**
A: Steve Rude **W:** Mike Baron
23 ❑ Mar 1991 Cover: 1.95 **NM** value: **2.00**
Circ: CapCity orders: **1,575**
final issue. **A:** Steve Rude **W:** Mike Baron

NEXUS MEETS MADMAN — Dark Horse

1 ❑ May 1996 Cover: 2.95 **NM** value: **Cover or less**
No issue number. One-shot. **A:** Steve Rude **W:** Mike Allred; Mike Baron

NEXUS THE LIBERATOR — Dark Horse

1 ❑ Aug 1992 Cover: 2.50 **NM** value: **Cover or less**
Circ: CapCity orders: **15,125**
📖 Walking Dreams **A:** John Calimée **W:** Stefan Petrucha
2 ❑ Sep 1992 Cover: 2.50 **NM** value: **Cover or less**
Circ: CapCity orders: **11,241**
3 ❑ Oct 1992 Cover: 2.50 **NM** value: **Cover or less**
Circ: CapCity orders: **1,041**
4 ❑ Nov 1992 Cover: 2.50 **NM** value: **Cover or less**
Circ: CapCity orders: **10,175**
📖 The Dying of the Light **A:** John Calimée **W:** Stefan Petrucha

NEXUS: THE ORIGIN — Dark Horse

1 ❑ ca. 1995 Cover: 3.95 **NM** value: **Cover or less**
Circ: CapCity orders: **25,875**
No issue number. • ; **A:** Steve Rude ★ Origin of Nexus.

NEXUS: THE WAGES OF SIN — Dark Horse

1 ❑ Mar 1995 Cover: 2.95 **NM** value: **Cover or less**
Circ: CapCity orders: **7,550**
cardstock cover. 📖 The Client **A:** Steve Rude **W:** Mike Baron
2 ❑ Apr 1995 Cover: 2.95 **NM** value: **Cover or less**
Circ: CapCity orders: **6,150**
cardstock cover. **A:** Steve Rude **W:** Mike Baron
3 ❑ May 1995 Cover: 2.95 **NM** value: **Cover or less**
Circ: CapCity orders: **5,900**
cardstock cover. **A:** Steve Rude **W:** Mike Baron
4 ❑ Jun 1995 Cover: 2.95 **NM** value: **Cover or less**
Circ: CapCity orders: **5,975**
A: Steve Rude **W:** Mike Baron

Capital City orders are the actual sales of comic books by Capital City Distribution, once one of the largest U.S. sellers of comics to comics shops. Capital City's share of comics shop sales, while not known exactly, increases from around 10-20% in the mid-1980s to 30-35% in the mid-1990s. Capital City's share of comic books sold on newsstands (most Marvels and DCs) will be less.

NEXUS (VOL. 1) — Capital

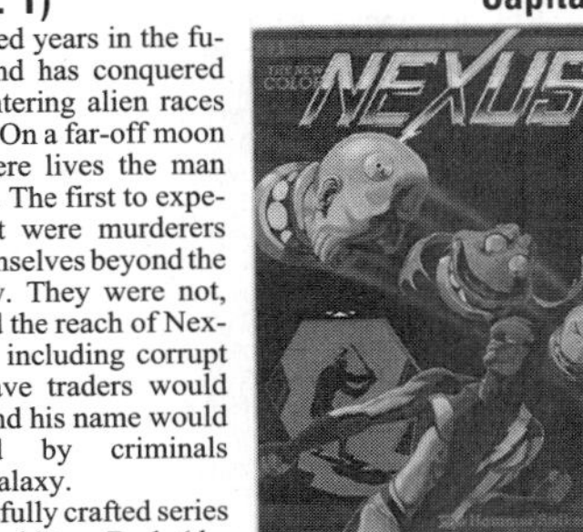

It's five hundred years in the future, and mankind has conquered the stars, encountering alien races without number. On a far-off moon called Ylum, there lives the man known as Nexus. The first to experience his might were murderers who thought themselves beyond the reach of the law. They were not, however, beyond the reach of Nexus. Soon others, including corrupt officials and slave traders would feel his might; and his name would become feared by criminals throughout the galaxy.

Nexus is an artfully crafted series by Mike Baron and Steve Rude (the same team who brought us Badger). In exploring the world of Nexus, you'll travel to distant planets and meet an extraordinary cast of characters, including Mohawk-wearing aliens and the most amusing bunch of decapitated heads you've ever seen.

1 ❑ b&w Cover: 1.95 **NM** value: **18.00**
A: Steve Rude **W:** Mike Baron ★ 1st Appearance of Nexus.
2 ❑ Cover: 1.95 **NM** value: **13.00**
A: Steve Rude **W:** Mike Baron
3 ❑ Oct 1982 Cover: 2.95 **NM** value: **20.00**
A: Steve Rude **W:** Mike Baron

NEXUS (VOL. 2) — Capital

1 ❑ 1983 Cover: 1.50 **NM** value: **4.00**
• **CGC:** 1 graded, best 9.2
• Nexus begins for first time in color; Capital Comics publishes **A:** Steve Rude **W:** Mike Baron
2 ❑ Cover: 1.75 **NM** value: **3.50**
A: Steve Rude **W:** Mike Baron ★ Origin of Nexus.
3 ❑ Cover: 1.75 **NM** value: **3.50**
A: Steve Rude **W:** Mike Baron
4 ❑ Cover: 1.75 **NM** value: **3.50**
A: Steve Rude **W:** Mike Baron
5 ❑ Cover: 1.75 **NM** value: **3.50**
A: Steve Rude **W:** Mike Baron
6 ❑ Cover: 1.75 **NM** value: **3.00**
A: Steve Rude **W:** Mike Baron
7 ❑ Cover: 1.75 **NM** value: **3.00**
• First Comics begins publishing **A:** Steve Rude **W:** Mike Baron
8 ❑ Cover: 1.75 **NM** value: **3.00**
Circ: CapCity orders: **9,300**
A: Steve Rude **W:** Mike Baron
9 ❑ Cover: 1.75 **NM** value: **2.50**
Circ: CapCity orders: **8,675**
📖 Teen Angel **A:** Steve Rude **W:** Mike Baron
10 ❑ Cover: 1.75 **NM** value: **2.25**
Circ: CapCity orders: **8,225**
A: Steve Rude **W:** Mike Baron
11 ❑ Cover: 1.75 **NM** value: **2.25**
Circ: CapCity orders: **8,200**
A: Steve Rude **W:** Mike Baron
12 ❑ Cover: 1.75 **NM** value: **2.25**
Circ: CapCity orders: **8,500**
A: Steve Rude **W:** Mike Baron
13 ❑ Cover: 1.75 **NM** value: **2.25**
Circ: CapCity orders: **7,700**
A: Steve Rude **W:** Mike Baron
14 ❑ Cover: 1.75 **NM** value: **2.25**
Circ: CapCity orders: **6,875**
A: Steve Rude **W:** Mike Baron
15 ❑ Cover: 1.75 **NM** value: **2.25**
Circ: CapCity orders: **6,800**
A: Steve Rude **W:** Mike Baron
16 ❑ Cover: 1.75 **NM** value: **2.25**
Circ: CapCity orders: **6,850**
A: Steve Rude **W:** Mike Baron
17 ❑ Cover: 1.75 **NM** value: **2.25**
Circ: CapCity orders: **6,825**
A: Steve Rude **W:** Mike Baron
18 ❑ Cover: 1.75 **NM** value: **2.25**
Circ: CapCity orders: **6,775**
A: Steve Rude **W:** Mike Baron
19 ❑ Cover: 1.75 **NM** value: **2.25**
Circ: CapCity orders: **6,725**
A: Steve Rude **W:** Mike Baron
20 ❑ Cover: 1.75 **NM** value: **2.25**
Circ: CapCity orders: **6,575**
A: Steve Rude **W:** Mike Baron
21 ❑ Cover: 1.75 **NM** value: **2.25**
Circ: CapCity orders: **6,550**
22 ❑ Cover: 1.75 **NM** value: **2.25**
Circ: CapCity orders: **6,900**
23 ❑ Cover: 1.75 **NM** value: **2.25**
Circ: CapCity orders: **7,100**
24 ❑ Cover: 1.75 **NM** value: **2.25**
Circ: CapCity orders: **7,225**
25 ❑ Cover: 1.75 **NM** value: **2.25**
Circ: CapCity orders: **7,325**
26 ❑ Cover: 1.75 **NM** value: **2.25**
Circ: CapCity orders: **7,375**
27 ❑ Cover: 1.75 **NM** value: **2.25**
Circ: CapCity orders: **7,500**
28 ❑ Cover: 1.75 **NM** value: **2.25**
Circ: CapCity orders: **6,775**
29 ❑ Cover: 1.75 **NM** value: **2.25**
Circ: CapCity orders: **6,750**
30 ❑ Cover: 1.75 **NM** value: **2.25**
Circ: CapCity orders: **6,775**

CGC-graded: Multiply prices above by **33 for 9.9 M** • **16 for 9.8 NM/M** • **7 for 9.6 NM+** • **5 for 9.4 NM** • **2.5 for 9.2 NM-** • **1.5 for 9.0 VF/NM**

31 ❑ Cover: 1.75 **NM** value: **2.00**
Circ: CapCity orders: **6,525**
32 ❑ Cover: 1.75 **NM** value: **2.00**
Circ: CapCity orders: **6,300**
33 ❑ Cover: 1.75 **NM** value: **2.00**
Circ: CapCity orders: **6,700**
34 ❑ Cover: 1.75 **NM** value: **2.00**
Circ: CapCity orders: **6,175**
35 ❑ Cover: 1.75 **NM** value: **2.00**
Circ: CapCity orders: **6,625**
36 ❑ Cover: 1.75 **NM** value: **2.00**
Circ: CapCity orders: **7,050**
37 ❑ Cover: 1.75 **NM** value: **2.00**
Circ: CapCity orders: **6,925**
38 ❑ Cover: 1.75 **NM** value: **2.00**
Circ: CapCity orders: **7,075**
39 ❑ Cover: 1.75 **NM** value: **2.00**
Circ: CapCity orders: **6,800**
40 ❑ Cover: 1.75 **NM** value: **2.00**
Circ: CapCity orders: **6,775**
📖 Possession **A:** Steve Rude **W:** Mike Baron
41 ❑ Cover: 1.75 **NM** value: **2.00**
Circ: CapCity orders: **6,900**
42 ❑ Cover: 1.75 **NM** value: **2.00**
Circ: CapCity orders: **7,225**
43 ❑ Cover: 1.75 **NM** value: **2.00**
Circ: CapCity orders: **6,425**
📖 Portrait Of Death **A:** Steve Rude **W:** Mike Baron
44 ❑ Cover: 1.75 **NM** value: **2.00**
Circ: CapCity orders: **6,700**
45 ❑ Cover: 1.75 **NM** value: **2.00**
Circ: CapCity orders: **6,650**
★ Appearance of Badger.
46 ❑ Cover: 1.75 **NM** value: **2.00**
Circ: CapCity orders: **7,250**
★ Appearance of Badger.
47 ❑ Cover: 1.75 **NM** value: **2.00**
Circ: CapCity orders: **7,175**
★ Appearance of Badger.
48 ❑ Cover: 1.75 **NM** value: **2.00**
Circ: CapCity orders: **7,150**
★ Appearance of Badger.
49 ❑ Cover: 1.75 **NM** value: **2.00**
Circ: CapCity orders: **7,300**
★ Appearance of Badger.
50 ❑ Cover: 1.75 **NM** value: **3.50**
Circ: CapCity orders: **9,150**
• Crossroads ★ Appearance of Badger.
51 ❑ Cover: 1.95 **NM** value: **2.00**
Circ: CapCity orders: **7,250**
52 ❑ Cover: 1.95 **NM** value: **2.00**
Circ: CapCity orders: **7,150**
53 ❑ Cover: 1.95 **NM** value: **2.00**
Circ: CapCity orders: **7,100**
54 ❑ Cover: 1.95 **NM** value: **2.00**
Circ: CapCity orders: **7,100**
55 ❑ Apr 1989 Cover: 1.95 **NM** value: **2.00**
Circ: CapCity orders: **7,300**
56 ❑ May 1989 Cover: 1.95 **NM** value: **2.00**
Circ: CapCity orders: **7,100**
57 ❑ Jun 1989 Cover: 1.95 **NM** value: **2.00**
Circ: CapCity orders: **6,900**
58 ❑ Jul 1989 Cover: 1.95 **NM** value: **2.00**
Circ: CapCity orders: **7,275**
59 ❑ Aug 1989 Cover: 1.95 **NM** value: **2.00**
Circ: CapCity orders: **7,175**
60 ❑ Sep 1989 Cover: 1.95 **NM** value: **2.00**
Circ: CapCity orders: **7,250**
61 ❑ Oct 1989 Cover: 1.95 **NM** value: **2.00**
Circ: CapCity orders: **7,275**
62 ❑ Nov 1989 Cover: 1.95 **NM** value: **2.00**
Circ: CapCity orders: **7,250**
63 ❑ Dec 1989 Cover: 1.95 **NM** value: **2.00**
Circ: CapCity orders: **7,225**
64 ❑ Jan 1990 Cover: 1.95 **NM** value: **2.00**
Circ: CapCity orders: **7,150**
65 ❑ Feb 1990 Cover: 1.95 **NM** value: **2.00**
Circ: CapCity orders: **7,250**
66 ❑ Mar 1990 Cover: 1.95 **NM** value: **2.00**
Circ: CapCity orders: **7,000**
67 ❑ Apr 1990 Cover: 1.95 **NM** value: **2.00**
Circ: CapCity orders: **6,600**
68 ❑ May 1990 Cover: 1.95 **NM** value: **2.00**
Circ: CapCity orders: **6,225**
69 ❑ Jun 1990 Cover: 1.95 **NM** value: **2.00**
Circ: CapCity orders: **6,025**
70 ❑ Jul 1990 Cover: 1.95 **NM** value: **2.00**
Circ: CapCity orders: **6,075**
71 ❑ Aug 1990 Cover: 1.95 **NM** value: **2.00**
Circ: CapCity orders: **5,850**
72 ❑ Sep 1990 Cover: 1.95 **NM** value: **2.00**
Circ: CapCity orders: **6,000**
73 ❑ Oct 1990 Cover: 2.25 **NM** value: **Cover or less**
Circ: CapCity orders: **5,775**
74 ❑ Nov 1990 Cover: 2.25 **NM** value: **Cover or less**
Circ: CapCity orders: **5,725**
75 ❑ Dec 1990 Cover: 2.25 **NM** value: **Cover or less**
Circ: CapCity orders: **6,825**
76 ❑ Jan 1991 Cover: 2.25 **NM** value: **Cover or less**
Circ: CapCity orders: **5,775**
77 ❑ Feb 1991 Cover: 2.25 **NM** value: **Cover or less**
Circ: CapCity orders: **5,750**
78 ❑ Mar 1991 Cover: 2.25 **NM** value: **Cover or less**
Circ: CapCity orders: **5,750**
79 ❑ Apr 1991 Cover: 2.25 **NM** value: **Cover or less**
Circ: CapCity orders: **5,525**
80 ❑ May 1991 Cover: 2.25 **NM** value: **Cover or less**
Circ: CapCity orders: **5,500**
• Final issue of First series

81 ❑ Cover: 3.95 **NM** value: **Cover or less**
📖 Nexus: The Origin • Number not noted in indicia (was retroactive)
82 ❑ Cover: 3.95 **NM** value: **Cover or less**
📖 Nexus: Alien Justice, Part 1 • Nexus: Alien Justice #1; Number not noted in indicia (was retroactive)
83 ❑ Cover: 3.95 **NM** value: **Cover or less**
📖 Nexus: Alien Justice, Part 2 • Nexus: Alien Justice #2; Number not noted in indicia (was retroactive)
84 ❑ Cover: 3.95 **NM** value: **Cover or less**
📖 Nexus: Alien Justice, Part 3 • Nexus: Alien Justice #3; Number not noted in indicia (was retroactive)
85 ❑ **NM** value: **2.95**
📖 Nexus: The Wages of Sin, Part 1 • Nexus: The Wages of Sin #1; Number not noted in indicia (was retroactive)
86 ❑ **NM** value: **2.95**
📖 Nexus: The Wages of Sin, Part 2 • Nexus: The Wages of Sin #2; Number not noted in indicia (was retroactive)
87 ❑ **NM** value: **2.95**
📖 Nexus: The Wages of Sin, Part 3 • Nexus: The Wages of Sin #3; Number not noted in indicia (was retroactive)
88 ❑ **NM** value: **2.95**
📖 Nexus: The Wages of Sin, Part 4 • Nexus: The Wages of Sin #4; Number not noted in indicia (was retroactive)
89 ❑ Jun 1996 Cover: 2.95 **NM** value: **Cover or less**
📖 Executioner's Song, Part 1 **A:** Steve Rude **W:** Mike Baron
90 ❑ Jul 1996 Cover: 2.95 **NM** value: **Cover or less**
📖 Executioner's Song, Part 2 **A:** Steve Rude **W:** Mike Baron
91 ❑ Aug 1996 Cover: 2.95 **NM** value: **Cover or less**
📖 Executioner's Song, Part 3 **A:** Steve Rude **W:** Mike Baron
92 ❑ Sep 1996 Cover: 2.95 **NM** value: **Cover or less**
Circ: Diamd. preorders: **14,180**
📖 Executioner's Song, Part 4 **A:** Steve Rude **W:** Mike Baron
93 ❑ Apr 1997 Cover: 2.95 **NM** value: **Cover or less**
Circ: Diamd. preorders: **15,613**
📖 God Con, Part 1 **A:** Steve Rude **W:** Mike Baron
94 ❑ May 1997 Cover: 2.95 **NM** value: **Cover or less**
Circ: Diamd. preorders: **13,186**
📖 God Con, Part 2 **A:** Steve Rude **W:** Mike Baron
95 ❑ Jul 1997, b&w Cover: 2.95 **NM** value: **Cover or less**
Circ: Diamd. preorders: **14,573**
📖 Nightmare in Blue, Part 1 **A:** Steve Rude **W:** Mike Baron
96 ❑ Aug 1997, b&w Cover: 2.95 **NM** value: **Cover or less**
Circ: Diamd. preorders: **12,879**
📖 Nightmare in Blue, Part 2 **A:** Steve Rude **W:** Mike Baron
97 ❑ Sep 1997, b&w Cover: 2.95 **NM** value: **Cover or less**
Circ: Diamd. preorders: **12,084**
📖 Nightmare in Blue, Part 3 **A:** Steve Rude **W:** Mike Baron
98 ❑ Oct 1997, b&w Cover: 2.95 **NM** value: **Cover or less**
Circ: Diamd. preorders: **11,648**
📖 Nightmare in Blue, Part 4 **A:** Steve Rude **W:** Mike Baron
Bk 1❑ Apr 1993 Cover: 14.95 **NM** value: **Cover or less**
• Trade Paperback. • collects #1-5
Bk 2❑ Aug 1993 Cover: 15.95 **NM** value: **Cover or less**
• Trade Paperback. • collects #6-10

NFL SUPERPRO — Marvel

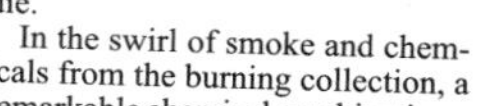

Phil Grayfield was an up-and-coming pro football player when injuries ended his career. He got a second chance at fame when he was hired by Sports Inside as a star field reporter. As a reporter, Grayfield's first assignment was to interview Rudy Custer, the inventor of an experimental football uniform. But Custer was also a football collector — and his collection had piqued the interest of a group of thieves, who robbed Custer, set fire to his home, and tied up Grayfield inside the burning building — leaving him to die.

In the swirl of smoke and chemicals from the burning collection, a remarkable chemical combination occurred — giving the stranded Grayfield enhanced athletic powers and abilities which he used to escape. Now, as NFL SuperPro, he has made it his mission to defend football from the gamblers, extortionists, and racketeers who would corrupt it.

1 ❑ Oct 1991 Cover: 1.00 **NM** value: **Cover or less**
Circ: CapCity orders: **50,100**
📖 You Bet Your Life **A:** Jose Delbo **W:** Fabian Nicieza ★ Origin of NFL SuperPro. ★ Appearance of Spider-Man.
2 ❑ Nov 1991 Cover: 1.00 **NM** value: **Cover or less**
Circ: CapCity orders: **19,900**
📖 The Killer Instinct **A:** Jose Delbo **W:** Fabian Nicieza
3 ❑ Dec 1991 Cover: 1.00 **NM** value: **Cover or less**
Circ: CapCity orders: **17,800**
📖 Time Out **A:** Jose Delbo **W:** Fabian Nicieza
4 ❑ Jan 1992 Cover: 1.00 **NM** value: **Cover or less**
Circ: CapCity orders: **12,800**
5 ❑ Feb 1992 Cover: 1.25 **NM** value: **Cover or less**
Circ: CapCity orders: **10,200**
6 ❑ Mar 1992 Cover: 1.25 **NM** value: **Cover or less**
Circ: CapCity orders: **7,900**
7 ❑ Apr 1992 Cover: 1.25 **NM** value: **Cover or less**
Circ: CapCity orders: **7,100**
8 ❑ May 1992 Cover: 1.25 **NM** value: **Cover or less**
Circ: CapCity orders: **5,900**
• Captain America
9 ❑ Jun 1992 Cover: 1.25 **NM** value: **Cover or less**
Circ: CapCity orders: **5,500**
10 ❑ Jul 1992 Cover: 1.25 **NM** value: **Cover or less**
Circ: CapCity orders: **5,200**
11 ❑ Aug 1992 Cover: 1.25 **NM** value: **Cover or less**
Circ: CapCity orders: **4,850**
📖 Feels Like Team Spirit **A:** Jose Delbo **W:** P.C. Foye
12 ❑ Sep 1992 Cover: 1.25 **NM** value: **Cover or less**
Circ: CapCity orders: **4,000**
final issue.
SE 1❑ Sep 1991 Cover: 2.00 **NM** value: **3.95**
Circ: CapCity orders: **13,500**
• Special collector's edition. 📖 Fourth and Goal to Go **A:** Bob Hall; Jose Delbo; Joe Jusko(cover) **W:** Fabian Nicieza ★ Origin of NFL SuperPro. ★ 1st Appearance of NFL SuperPro.
SE 1-2❑ Sep 1991 Cover: 3.95 **NM** value: **Cover or less**

NICKEL COMICS (DELL) — Dell

1 ❑ ca. 1938 Cover: 0.05 **NM** value: **400.00**

NICKEL COMICS (FAWCETT) — Fawcett

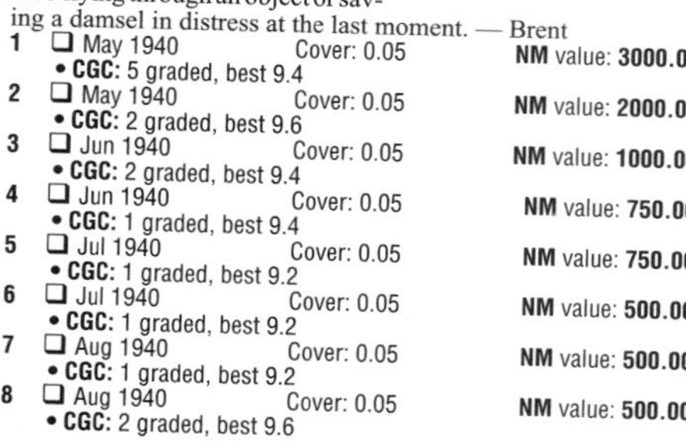

Not to be confused with Dell's one-shot attempt at a half-price comic book and Nationwide's Lucky Star (which sold for a nickel after the first issue), Fawcett trotted out its aptly named Nickel Comics for eight issues in the summer of 1940.

The series, which followed a test ashcan earlier in the year featuring the adventures of Scoop Smith, was the home of Bulletman, a scientist who donned a pointy metal helmet, red shirt and yellow johdpurs and flew around fighting crime. Covers, mostly by C.C. Beck, featured the hero flying through an object or saving a damsel in distress at the last moment. — Brent

1 ❑ May 1940 Cover: 0.05 **NM** value: **3000.00**
• **CGC:** 5 graded, best 9.4
2 ❑ May 1940 Cover: 0.05 **NM** value: **2000.00**
• **CGC:** 2 graded, best 9.6
3 ❑ Jun 1940 Cover: 0.05 **NM** value: **1000.00**
• **CGC:** 2 graded, best 9.4
4 ❑ Jun 1940 Cover: 0.05 **NM** value: **750.00**
• **CGC:** 1 graded, best 9.4
5 ❑ Jul 1940 Cover: 0.05 **NM** value: **750.00**
• **CGC:** 1 graded, best 9.2
6 ❑ Jul 1940 Cover: 0.05 **NM** value: **500.00**
• **CGC:** 1 graded, best 9.2
7 ❑ Aug 1940 Cover: 0.05 **NM** value: **500.00**
• **CGC:** 1 graded, best 9.2
8 ❑ Aug 1940 Cover: 0.05 **NM** value: **500.00**
• **CGC:** 2 graded, best 9.6

NICK FURY, AGENT OF SHIELD (1ST SERIES) — Marvel

Sgt. Fury was a hard-fighting hero of World War II, eventually rising to the rank of colonel. Years later, Nick Fury was recruited by Tony Stark (in Strange Tales #135) to fight a different kind of war. As director of S.H.I.E.L.D. — the Supreme Headquarters International Espionage Law-enforcement Division — Fury now became a sort of James Bond-like super-spy, complete with a bevy of technological gadgets and gizmos.

In his new organization, Fury recruited several of his old war buddies, including Dum-Dum Dugan and Gabe Jones. Together with the dedicated agents of S.H.I.E.L.D., they fight a cloak-and-dagger battle against the threats to world peace.

1 ❑ Jun 1968 Cover: 0.12 **NM** value: **50.00**
📖 Who is Scorpio? **A:** Jim Steranko **W:** Jim Steranko ★ 1st Appearance of Scorpio.
2 ❑ Jul 1968 Cover: 0.12 **NM** value: **32.00**
📖 So Shall Ye Reap Death **A:** Jim Steranko ★ Origin of Centurius. ★ 1st Appearance of Centurius.
3 ❑ Aug 1968 Cover: 0.12 **NM** value: **28.00**
📖 Dark Moon Rise, Hell Hound Kill! **A:** Jim Steranko **W:** Jim Steranko
4 ❑ Sep 1968 Cover: 0.12 **NM** value: **35.00**
📖 And Now It Begins • S.H.I.E.L.D. origin issue ★ Origin of Nick Fury.
5 ❑ Oct 1968 Cover: 0.12 **NM** value: **30.00**
📖 Whatever Happened to Scorpio? **A:** Jim Steranko
6 ❑ Nov 1968 Cover: 0.12 **NM** value: **18.00**
📖 Doom Must Fall! **A:** Frank Springer; Jim Steranko(cover) **W:** Roy Thomas; Archie Goodwin
7 ❑ Dec 1968 Cover: 0.12 **NM** value: **18.00**
📖 Hours of Madness, Day of Death
8 ❑ Jan 1969 Cover: 0.12 **NM** value: **12.00**
📖 Thus Speaks Supremus
9 ❑ Feb 1969 Cover: 0.12 **NM** value: **12.00**
📖 The Name of the Game Is Hate
10 ❑ Mar 1969 Cover: 0.12 **NM** value: **12.00**
📖 Twas the Night Before Christmas
11 ❑ Apr 1969 Cover: 0.12 **NM** value: **12.00**
📖 The First Million Megaton Explosion
12 ❑ May 1969 Cover: 0.12 **NM** value: **13.00**
📖 Hell Hath No Fury!
13 ❑ Jul 1969 Cover: 0.12 **NM** value: **12.00**
📖 The New Super-Patriot!
14 ❑ Aug 1969 Cover: 0.15 **NM** value: **8.00**
📖 Nick Fury – A Day in the Life!
15 ❑ Nov 1969 Cover: 0.15 **NM** value: **35.00**
📖 The Assassination of Nick Fury! ★ 1st Appearance of Bullseye.

Other grades: Multiply prices above by **1.5 for Mint • 2/3 for Very Fine • 1/3 for Fine • 1/5 for Very Good • 1/8 for Good**

16 ❑ Cover: 0.25 **NM** value: **6.00**
• Giant-size. 📖 Find Fury or Die!; The Prize Is Earth!; Sometimes the Good Guys Loose • Reprints from Strange Tales #136-138

17 ❑ Cover: 0.25 **NM** value: **6.00**
• Giant-size. 📖 The Brave Die Hard; The End of HYDRA; Operation: Brain Blast • Reprints from Strange Tales #139-141

18 ❑ Mar 1971 Cover: 0.25 **NM** value: **6.00**
• Giant-size. 📖 Who Strikes at S.H.I.E.L.D.?; To Free a Brain Slave; The Day of the Druid • Reprints from Strange Tales #142-144

NICK FURY, AGENT OF SHIELD (2ND SERIES) Marvel

1 ❑ Dec 1983 Cover: 2.00 **NM** value: **3.00**
wraparound cover. • Reprints from Nick Fury, Agent of SHIELD (1st series)

2 ❑ Jan 1984 Cover: 2.00 **NM** value: **3.00**
• Reprints from Nick Fury, Agent of SHIELD (1st series)

NICK FURY, AGENT OF S.H.I.E.L.D. (3RD SERIES) Marvel

S.H.I.E.L.D. was disbanded in the wake of the Delta Affair (from Nick Fury vs. S.H.I.E.L.D.). Fury, the organization's former director, then led a reclusive life away from the specter of war.

A year later, sinister forces threatened the world again. As much as Fury might have liked to avoid the problem, it quite literally came crashing in on him as he was attacked by Hydra agents in his own home. Fury joined with ex-S.H.I.E.L.D. agents to save the world from a nuclear holocaust.

It became obvious to everyone how desperately an organization like S.H.I.E.L.D. was needed, and the group was reformed under the direction of the United Nations (with a slightly altered meaning for the acronym). Fury had rejoined the war, fighting to keep the world safe from the many forces that threaten it.

1 ❑ Sep 1989 Cover: 1.50 **NM** value: **2.25**
Circ: CapCity orders: **49,200** • **CGC:** 172 graded, best 9.9
📖 The Past Still Haunts **A:** Bob Hall **W:** Bob Harras

2 ❑ Oct 1989 Cover: 1.50 **NM** value: **1.75**
Circ: CapCity orders: **35,200** • **CGC:** 18 graded, best 9.8
📖 A Web With Many Strands • Death's Head **A:** Keith Pollard; Kim Demulder **W:** Bob Harras

3 ❑ Nov 1989 Cover: 1.50 **NM** value: **1.75**
Circ: CapCity orders: **32,200** • **CGC:** 9 graded, best 9.6
📖 In Memory Ever Green • Death's Head **A:** Keith Pollard **W:** Bob Harras

4 ❑ Nov 1989 Cover: 1.50 **NM** value: **Cover or less**
Circ: CapCity orders: **31,500** • **CGC:** 23 graded, best 9.4
📖 Slips Of Memory • Sgt. Fury **A:** Keith Pollard **W:** Bob Harras

5 ❑ Dec 1989 Cover: 1.50 **NM** value: **Cover or less**
Circ: CapCity orders: **28,000** • **CGC:** 16 graded, best 9.6
📖 Memory And Menace! **A:** Keith Pollard **W:** Bob Harras

6 ❑ Dec 1989 Cover: 1.50 **NM** value: **Cover or less**
Circ: CapCity orders: **24,900** • **CGC:** 22 graded, best 9.6
📖 In Final Memory **A:** Keith Pollard **W:** Bob Harras

7 ❑ Jan 1990 Cover: 1.50 **NM** value: **Cover or less**
Circ: Statement: **97,173** CapCity orders: **22,700** • **CGC:** 9 graded, best 9.6
📖 Chaos Serpent, Part 1; The Chaos Serpent, Part 1 **A:** Keith Pollard **W:** D.G. Chichester

8 ❑ Feb 1990 Cover: 1.50 **NM** value: **Cover or less**
Circ: Statement: **97,173** CapCity orders: **21,200** • **CGC:** 3 graded, best 9.6
📖 Chaos Serpent, Part 2; The Chaos Serpent, Part 2

9 ❑ Mar 1990 Cover: 1.50 **NM** value: **Cover or less**
Circ: Statement: **97,173** CapCity orders: **19,500**
📖 Chaos Serpent, Part 3; The Chaos Serpent, Part 3 **A:** Keith Pollard **W:** D.G. Chichester

10 ❑ Apr 1990 Cover: 1.50 **NM** value: **Cover or less**
Circ: Statement: **97,173** CapCity orders: **17,900** • **CGC:** 1 graded, best 8.5
📖 Chaos Serpent, Part 4; The Chaos Serpent, Part 4 **A:** Keith Pollard **W:** D.G. Chichester ★ Appearance of Captain America.

11 ❑ May 1990 Cover: 1.50 **NM** value: **Cover or less**
Circ: Statement: **97,173** CapCity orders: **17,100** • **CGC:** 1 graded, best 9.0
📖 Greetings From Scotland **A:** Cam Kennedy **W:** Alan Grant

12 ❑ Jun 1990 Cover: 1.50 **NM** value: **Cover or less**
Circ: Statement: **97,173** CapCity orders: **16,400** • **CGC:** 4 graded, best 9.4
📖 Hydra Affair; Fears And Obsessions **A:** Michael Bair; Kim Demulder **W:** Bob Harras

13 ❑ Jul 1990 Cover: 1.50 **NM** value: **Cover or less**
Circ: Statement: **97,173** CapCity orders: **16,100** • **CGC:** 2 graded, best 9.4
📖 In Battle Joined! • Return of Yellow Claw **A:** Keith Pollard **W:** Bob Harras

14 ❑ Aug 1990 Cover: 1.50 **NM** value: **Cover or less**
Circ: Statement: **97,173** CapCity orders: **14,800**
📖 Pyrrhic Victory **A:** Keith Pollard; Kim Demulder **W:** Bob Harras

15 ❑ Sep 1990 Cover: 1.50 **NM** value: **Cover or less**
Circ: Statement: **97,173** CapCity orders: **14,900** • **CGC:** 15 graded, best 9.6
📖 Apogee Of Disaster, Part 1 **A:** Bill Jaaska **W:** D.G. Chichester ★ Appearance of Fantastic Four.

16 ❑ Oct 1990 Cover: 1.50 **NM** value: **Cover or less**
Circ: Statement: **97,173** CapCity orders: **14,200**
📖 Apogee Of Disaster, Part 2

17 ❑ Nov 1990 Cover: 1.50 **NM** value: **Cover or less**
Circ: Statement: **97,173** CapCity orders: **13,400**
📖 Apogee Of Disaster, Part 3 **A:** Herb Trimpe **W:** D.G. Chichester

18 ❑ Dec 1990 Cover: 1.50 **NM** value: **Cover or less**
Circ: Statement: **97,173** CapCity orders: **13,100**

19 ❑ Jan 1991 Cover: 1.50 **NM** value: **Cover or less**
Circ: CapCity orders: **12,500**
📖 Downrange Of The End Of The World! **A:** Herb Trimpe **W:** D.G. Chichester

20 ❑ Feb 1991 Cover: 1.50 **NM** value: **Cover or less**
Circ: CapCity orders: **12,900**

21 ❑ Mar 1991 Cover: 1.50 **NM** value: **Cover or less**
Circ: CapCity orders: **11,500**
📖 Der Totenkopf • Baron Strucker revived; Has 1990 Statement, filed 10/1/90; avg print run 97,873; avg sales 96,685; avg subs 488; avg total paid 97,173; samples 100; office use 600; max existent 97,873; no newsstand sales this year **A:** Jackson Guice **W:** D.G. Chichester

22 ❑ Apr 1991 Cover: 1.50 **NM** value: **Cover or less**
Circ: CapCity orders: **11,600**
📖 Pledge Of Allegiance **A:** Jackson Guice **W:** D.G. Chichester

23 ❑ May 1991 Cover: 1.50 **NM** value: **Cover or less**
Circ: CapCity orders: **11,400**
📖 Storm Warning **A:** Jackson Guice **W:** D.G. Chichester

24 ❑ Jun 1991 Cover: 1.50 **NM** value: **Cover or less**
Circ: CapCity orders: **11,800**
📖 The Camouflaged Commemoratives Affair **A:** Norm Dwyer **W:** D.G. Chichester ★ Appearance of Fantastic Four, Captain America.

25 ❑ Jul 1991 Cover: 1.50 **NM** value: **Cover or less**
Circ: CapCity orders: **11,600**

26 ❑ Aug 1991 Cover: 1.50 **NM** value: **Cover or less**
Circ: CapCity orders: **15,000**
📖 The Soldiers Of Anarchy **A:** Jackson Guice **W:** D.G. Chichester ★ Appearance of Fantastic Four, Avengers.

27 ❑ Sep 1991 Cover: 1.50 **NM** value: **2.00**
Circ: CapCity orders: **21,800**
📖 Recruitment Drive **A:** Ernie Stiner **W:** D.G. Chichester ★ Appearance of Wolverine.

28 ❑ Oct 1991 Cover: 1.50 **NM** value: **2.00**
Circ: CapCity orders: **25,800**
📖 Icy Roads **A:** Ernie Stiner **W:** D.G. Chichester ★ Appearance of Wolverine.

29 ❑ Nov 1991 Cover: 1.50 **NM** value: **2.00**
Circ: CapCity orders: **23,400**
📖 The Cold War **A:** Ernie Stiner **W:** D.G. Chichester ★ Appearance of Wolverine.

30 ❑ Dec 1991 Cover: 1.50 **NM** value: **Cover or less**
Circ: CapCity orders: **13,900**
📖 Infinity's Not Forever **A:** Scott Lobdell **W:** D.G. Chichester ★ Appearance of Deathlok.

31 ❑ Jan 1992 Cover: 1.50 **NM** value: **Cover or less**
Circ: Statement: **64,987** CapCity orders: **18,400**
📖 Infinity Is Not Forever After All! **A:** Scott Lobdell **W:** D.G. Chichester ★ Appearance of Deathlok.

32 ❑ Feb 1992 Cover: 1.75 **NM** value: **Cover or less**
Circ: Statement: **64,987** CapCity orders: **12,600**
📖 Formal Wear **A:** Dave Hooper **W:** Scott Lobdell ★ Appearance of Weapon Omega.

33 ❑ Mar 1992 Cover: 1.75 **NM** value: **Cover or less**
Circ: Statement: **64,987** CapCity orders: **11,900**
📖 Man Of Action **A:** M.C. Wyman **W:** Scott Lobdell ★ 1st Appearance of new agents (Psi-Borg, Violence, Knockabout, Ivory).

34 ❑ Apr 1992 Cover: 1.75 **NM** value: **Cover or less**
Circ: Statement: **64,987** CapCity orders: **11,300**
📖 In The Field **A:** M.C. Wyman **W:** Scott Lobdell ★ Versus Hydra. ★ Versus Baron Strucker.

35 ❑ May 1992 Cover: 1.75 **NM** value: **Cover or less**
Circ: Statement: **64,987** CapCity orders: **13,100**
📖 More Men Of Action **A:** M.C. Wyman **W:** Scott Lobdell

36 ❑ Jun 1992 Cover: 1.75 **NM** value: **Cover or less**
Circ: Statement: **64,987** CapCity orders: **10,600**
📖 The Snake Who Came In From The Cold **A:** M.C. Wyman **W:** Scott Lobdell ★ Origin of Constrictor. ★ Appearance of Cage. ★ Versus Constrictor.

37 ❑ Jul 1992 Cover: 1.75 **NM** value: **Cover or less**
Circ: Statement: **64,987** CapCity orders: **10,200**
📖 ...Who Killed The Changelings?! **A:** M.C. Wyman **W:** Scott Lobdell

38 ❑ Aug 1992 Cover: 1.75 **NM** value: **Cover or less**
Circ: Statement: **64,987** CapCity orders: **9,900**
📖 Cold War of Nick Fury, Part 1 **A:** Jerry DeCaire **W:** Eliot Brown; Rob Sharp

39 ❑ Sep 1992 Cover: 1.75 **NM** value: **Cover or less**
Circ: Statement: **64,987** CapCity orders: **8,500**
📖 Cold War of Nick Fury, Part 2 **A:** Don Hudson **W:** Eliot Brown; Rob Sharp

40 ❑ Oct 1992 Cover: 1.75 **NM** value: **Cover or less**
Circ: Statement: **64,987** CapCity orders: **8,600**
📖 Cold War of Nick Fury, Part 3 **A:** Paul Abrams **W:** Scott Lobdell

41 ❑ Nov 1992 Cover: 1.75 **NM** value: **Cover or less**
Circ: Statement: **64,987** CapCity orders: **7,900**
📖 Cold War of Nick Fury, Part 4 **A:** Paul Abrams **W:** Scott Lobdell

42 ❑ Dec 1992 Cover: 1.75 **NM** value: **Cover or less**
Circ: Statement: **64,987** CapCity orders: **7,700**
📖 The Past Recalled **A:** John Heebink **W:** Greg Wright

43 ❑ Jan 1993 Cover: 1.75 **NM** value: **Cover or less**
Circ: CapCity orders: **7,200**
📖 The Dead Zone **A:** John Heebink **W:** Greg Wright

44 ❑ Feb 1993 Cover: 1.75 **NM** value: **Cover or less**
Circ: CapCity orders: **7,800**
📖 Skeletons Reborn **A:** John Heebink **W:** Greg Wright

45 ❑ Mar 1993 Cover: 1.75 **NM** value: **Cover or less**
Circ: CapCity orders: **9,000**
📖 The Treachery Within • Has 1992 Statement, filed 10/1/92; avg print run 66,908; avg sales 64,428; avg subs 558; avg total paid 94,987; samples 250; office use 500; max existent 65,736; 2% of run returned; no newsstand sales this year **A:** John Heebink **W:** Greg Wright

46 ❑ Apr 1993 Cover: 1.75 **NM** value: **Cover or less**
Circ: CapCity orders: **10,900**
📖 Revelations **A:** John Heebink **W:** Greg Wright

47 ❑ May 1993 Cover: 1.75 **NM** value: **Cover or less**
Circ: CapCity orders: **8,900**
📖 Final Retribution! final issue. **A:** Brian Garvey **W:** John Heebink ★ Death of Kate Neville (Nick Fury's Girlfriend).

NICK FURY VS. S.H.I.E.L.D. Marvel

1 ❑ Jun 1988 Cover: 3.50 **NM** value: **4.00**
Circ: CapCity orders: **21,700** • **CGC:** 2 graded, best 9.6
C: Jim Steranko

2 ❑ Jul 1988 Cover: 3.50 **NM** value: **Cover or less**
Circ: CapCity orders: **16,700** • **CGC:** 1 graded, best 9.8
C: Bill Sienkiewicz

3 ❑ Mar 1988 Cover: 3.50 **NM** value: **Cover or less**
Circ: CapCity orders: **17,250** • **CGC:** 1 graded, best 9.8

4 ❑ Sep 1988 Cover: 3.50 **NM** value: **Cover or less**
Circ: CapCity orders: **20,150** • **CGC:** 1 graded, best 9.6

5 ❑ Oct 1988 Cover: 3.50 **NM** value: **Cover or less**
Circ: CapCity orders: **22,150** • **CGC:** 1 graded, best 9.6

6 ❑ Nov 1988 Cover: 3.50 **NM** value: **Cover or less**
Circ: CapCity orders: **23,350** • **CGC:** 1 graded, best 9.8

Bk 1 ❑ Aug 1989 Cover: 15.95 **NM** value: **Cover or less**

NICK HALLIDAY Argo

1 ❑ ca. 1955 Cover: 0.10 **NM** value: **40.00**

NICK HAZARD Harrier

1 ❑ Jan 1988 Cover: 1.95 **NM** value: **Cover or less**
📖 Invaders From Time **A:** Ron Turner **W:** Philip Harbottle

NICKI SHADOW Relentless

0 ❑ Jul 1997 Cover: 1.00 **NM** value: **Cover or less**
📖 In the Way Back **A:** Ted Naifeh **W:** Eric Burnham

1 ❑ Nov 1997 Cover: 2.50 **NM** value: **Cover or less**
A: Ted Naifeh **W:** Eric Burnham

NICK NOYZ AND THE NUISANCE TOUR BOOK Red Bullet

1 ❑ b&w Cover: 2.50 **NM** value: **Cover or less**

NICK RYAN THE SKULL Antarctic

1 ❑ Dec 1994, b&w Cover: 2.75 **NM** value: **Cover or less**
📖 The Next Time I See You **A:** Kevin Miller **W:** David Watkins

2 ❑ Jan 1995, b&w Cover: 2.75 **NM** value: **Cover or less**
📖 Countdown, El Gato Negro • El Gato Negro back-up feature **A:** Kevin Miller; Efrin Molina; Chad Jasper **W:** David Watkins; Efrin Molina

3 ❑ Feb 1995, b&w Cover: 2.75 **NM** value: **Cover or less**
📖 Greener Grass **A:** Mike Christiansen **W:** David Watkins

NIGHT, THE Slave Labor / Amaze Ink

0 ❑ Nov 1995 Cover: 1.50 **NM** value: **Cover or less**
A: Norman Felchle **W:** Dan Vado

NIGHTBIRD Harrier

1 ❑ May 1988, b&w Cover: 1.95 **NM** value: **Cover or less**
📖 Compact of Fire **A:** Cam Smith **W:** Martin Lock

2 ❑ 1988b&w Cover: 1.95 **NM** value: **Cover or less**

NIGHT BREED (CLIVE BARKER'S...) Marvel / Epic

1 ❑ Apr 1990 Cover: 1.95 **NM** value: **3.00**
📖 ...Where The Monsters Go **A:** Jim Baikie **W:** Alan Grant; John Wagner

2 ❑ May 1990 Cover: 1.95 **NM** value: **2.50**
📖 Nightbreed (movie adaptation), Part 2

3 ❑ Jun 1990 Cover: 1.95 **NM** value: **2.50**
📖 Nightbreed (movie adaptation), Part 3

4 ❑ Jul 1990 Cover: 1.95 **NM** value: **2.50**
📖 Nightbreed (movie adaptation), Part 4

5 ❑ Sep 1990 Cover: 2.25 **NM** value: **2.50**

6 ❑ Nov 1990 Cover: 2.25 **NM** value: **2.50**
📖 The Blasphemers, Part 1 **A:** Bret Blevins **W:** D.G. Chichester

7 ❑ Jan 1991 Cover: 2.25 **NM** value: **2.50**

8 ❑ Mar 1991 Cover: 2.25 **NM** value: **2.50**

9 ❑ May 1991 Cover: 2.25 **NM** value: **2.50**

10 ❑ Jul 1991 Cover: 2.25 **NM** value: **2.50**

11 ❑ Sep 1991 Cover: 2.25 **NM** value: **Cover or less**

12 ❑ Nov 1991 Cover: 2.25 **NM** value: **Cover or less**

13 ❑ Jan 1992 Cover: 2.25 **NM** value: **Cover or less**
• Rawhead Rex

14 ❑ Mar 1992 Cover: 2.25 **NM** value: **Cover or less**

15 ❑ May 1992 Cover: 2.25 **NM** value: **Cover or less**

16 ❑ Jun 1992 Cover: 2.25 **NM** value: **Cover or less**

17 ❑ Jul 1992 Cover: 2.25 **NM** value: **Cover or less**

18 ❑ Aug 1992 Cover: 2.25 **NM** value: **Cover or less**
📖 Hunters And Trophies, Part 1

19 ❑ Sep 1992 Cover: 2.25 **NM** value: **Cover or less**
📖 Hunters And Trophies, Part 2

20 ❑ Oct 1992 Cover: 2.50 **NM** value: **Cover or less**
📖 Hunters And Trophies, Part 3 **A:** Tony Harris; Max Douglas **W:** Greg Wright

21 ❑ Nov 1992 Cover: 2.50 **NM** value: **Cover or less**

22 ❑ Dec 1992 Cover: 2.50 **NM** value: **Cover or less**

23 ❑ Jan 1993 Cover: 2.50 **NM** value: **Cover or less**

24 ❑ Feb 1993 Cover: 2.50 **NM** value: **Cover or less**

25 ❑ Mar 1993 Cover: 2.50 **NM** value: **Cover or less**
📖 Revelations final issue. **A:** Phil Hester **W:** Nicholas Vince

NIGHT BRIGADE Wonder Comix

1 ❑ Aug 1987, b&w Cover: 1.95 **NM** value: **Cover or less**
A: Nils Osmar **W:** Nils Osmar

NIGHTCAT Marvel

1 ❑ Apr 1991 Cover: 3.95 **NM** value: **Cover or less**
Circ: CapCity orders: **16,600**
★ Origin of Nightcat.

CGC-graded: Multiply prices above by **33 for 9.9 M • 16 for 9.8 NM/M • 7 for 9.6 NM+ • 5 for 9.4 NM • 2.5 for 9.2 NM- • 1.5 for 9.0 VF/NM**

NIGHT CITY — Thorby

1 ❑ Cover: 2.95 **NM** value: **Cover or less**

NIGHTCRAWLER (1ST SERIES) — Marvel

1 ❑ Nov 1985 Cover: 0.75 **NM** value: **2.00**
Circ: CapCity orders: **38,900**
📖 How Much Is That Boggie In The Window **A:** Dave Cockrum **W:** Dave Cockrum

2 ❑ Dec 1985 Cover: 0.75 **NM** value: **2.00**
Circ: CapCity orders: **33,000**
📖 A Boggie Day In L'un Dun-t'wn **A:** Dave Cockrum **W:** Dave Cockrum

3 ❑ Jan 1986 Cover: 0.75 **NM** value: **2.00**
Circ: CapCity orders: **31,100** • **CGC:** 1 graded, best 9.6
📖 To Bamf Or Not To Bamf! **A:** Dave Cockrum **W:** Dave Cockrum

4 ❑ Feb 1986 Cover: 0.75 **NM** value: **2.00**
Circ: CapCity orders: **31,600**
📖 The Wizard Of Oops! **A:** Dave Cockrum **W:** Dave Cockrum

NIGHTCRAWLER (2ND SERIES) — Marvel

1 ❑ Jan 2002 Cover: 2.50 **NM** value: **Cover or less**
Circ: Diamd. preorders: **49,648**

2 ❑ Feb 2002 Cover: 2.50 **NM** value: **Cover or less**
Circ: Diamd. preorders: **43,837**

3 ❑ Mar 2002 Cover: 2.50 **NM** value: **Cover or less**
Circ: Diamd. preorders: **41,328**

NIGHTCRY — CFD

All issues are adults only.

1 ❑ b&w Cover: 2.75 **NM** value: **3.00**
Circ: CapCity orders: **2,415**
cardstock cover.

2 ❑ b&w Cover: 2.75 **NM** value: **3.00**
Circ: CapCity orders: **3,710**
cardstock cover.

3 ❑ b&w Cover: 2.75 **NM** value: **3.00**
cardstock cover.

4 ❑ b&w Cover: 2.75 **NM** value: **3.00**
cardstock cover.

5 ❑ b&w Cover: 2.75 **NM** value: **3.00**
cardstock cover. 📖 Lycanthropos; Pick-Up #607; The Fall **A:** Hart Fisher; Jason Jewitt; Jeff Crumpler **W:** Hart Fisher; Mike Deodato; Joseph M. Monks

6 ❑ b&w Cover: 2.75 **NM** value: **3.00**
cardstock cover.

NIGHTFALL: THE BLACK CHRONICLES — Homage

1 ❑ Dec 1999 Cover: 2.95 **NM** value: **Cover or less**
Circ: Diamd. preorders: **9,600**
A: Tomm Coker **W:** Tomm Coker; Ford Lytle Gilmore

2 ❑ Jan 2000 Cover: 2.95 **NM** value: **Cover or less**
Circ: Diamd. preorders: **6,865**
A: Tomm Coker **W:** Tomm Coker; Ford Lytle Gilmore

3 ❑ Feb 2000 Cover: 2.95 **NM** value: **Cover or less**
Circ: Diamd. preorders: **5,584**
A: Tomm Coker **W:** Tomm Coker; Ford Lytle Gilmore

NIGHT FORCE — DC

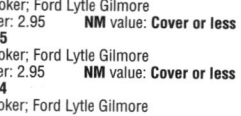

Written by Marv Wolfman and drawn by Gene Colan, the team that brought comic-book fans the Tomb of Dracula, this horror series focused on the evil power of the occult.

The Night Force itself was four characters pulled together by circumstance: the magician Baron Winters, down-on-his-luck reporter Jack Gold, parapsychologist Dr. Donovan Caine, and demonically possessed Vanessa Van Helsing. The story began with Dr. Caine's discovery of Vanessa's hidden demon and Jack Gold's interview with the mysterious Baron. From there, strange happenings conspired to force them together in order to save mankind...

A second series followed in the mid-1990s.

1 ❑ Aug 1982 Cover: 0.60 **NM** value: **2.50**
• **CGC:** 3 graded, best 9.6
📖 The Summoning, Part 1 **A:** Gene Colan **W:** Marv Wolfman ★ 1st Appearance of Night Force.

2 ❑ Sep 1982 Cover: 0.60 **NM** value: **1.50**
📖 The Summoning, Part 2 **A:** Gene Colan **W:** Marv Wolfman

3 ❑ Oct 1982 Cover: 0.60 **NM** value: **1.50**
📖 The Summoning, Part 3 **A:** Gene Colan **W:** Marv Wolfman

4 ❑ Nov 1982 Cover: 0.60 **NM** value: **1.50**
📖 The Summoning, Part 4 **A:** Gene Colan **W:** Marv Wolfman

5 ❑ Dec 1982 Cover: 0.60 **NM** value: **1.50**
📖 The Summoning, Part 5 **A:** Gene Colan **W:** Marv Wolfman

6 ❑ Jan 1983 Cover: 0.60 **NM** value: **1.50**
📖 The Summoning, Part 6 **A:** Gene Colan **W:** Marv Wolfman

7 ❑ Feb 1983 Cover: 0.60 **NM** value: **1.50**
📖 The Summoning, Part 7 **A:** Gene Colan **W:** Marv Wolfman

8 ❑ Mar 1983 Cover: 0.60 **NM** value: **1.50**
📖 The Summoning, Epilogue **A:** Gene Colan **W:** Marv Wolfman

9 ❑ Apr 1983 Cover: 0.60 **NM** value: **1.50**
A: Gene Colan

10 ❑ May 1983 Cover: 0.60 **NM** value: **1.50**
A: Gene Colan

11 ❑ Jun 1983 Cover: 0.60 **NM** value: **1.50**
A: Gene Colan

12 ❑ Jul 1983 Cover: 0.60 **NM** value: **1.50**
A: Gene Colan

13 ❑ Aug 1983 Cover: 0.60 **NM** value: **1.50**
A: Gene Colan

14 ❑ Sep 1983 Cover: 0.60 **NM** value: **1.50**
final issue. **A:** Gene Colan

NIGHT FORCE (2ND SERIES) — DC

1 ❑ Dec 1996 Cover: 2.25 **NM** value: **2.50**
Circ: Diamd. preorders: **25,184**
📖 Millennium, Part 1 **A:** Brent Anderson **W:** Marv Wolfman

2 ❑ Jan 1997 Cover: 2.25 **NM** value: **Cover or less**
Circ: Diamd. preorders: **17,845**
📖 Millennium, Part 2 **A:** Brent Anderson **W:** Marv Wolfman

3 ❑ Feb 1997 Cover: 2.25 **NM** value: **Cover or less**
Circ: Diamd. preorders: **14,372**
📖 Millennium, Part 3 **A:** Brent Anderson **W:** Marv Wolfman

4 ❑ Mar 1997 Cover: 2.25 **NM** value: **Cover or less**
Circ: Diamd. preorders: **11,986**
W: Marv Wolfman

5 ❑ Apr 1997 Cover: 2.25 **NM** value: **Cover or less**
Circ: Diamd. preorders: **10,371**
📖 Dreamers of Dreams, Part 1; Dreamer of Dreams, Part 1 **W:** Marv Wolfman

6 ❑ May 1997 Cover: 2.25 **NM** value: **Cover or less**
Circ: Diamd. preorders: **9,225**
📖 Dreamers of Dreams, Part 2; Dreamer of Dreams, Part 2 **A:** Shawn Martinbrough **W:** Marv Wolfman

7 ❑ Jun 1997 Cover: 2.25 **NM** value: **Cover or less**
Circ: Diamd. preorders: **8,645**
📖 Dreamers of Dreams, Part 3; Dreamer of Dreams, Part 3 **A:** Shawn Martinbrough **W:** Marv Wolfman

8 ❑ Jul 1997 Cover: 2.25 **NM** value: **Cover or less**
Circ: Diamd. preorders: **8,516**
📖 Convergence, Part 2 • continues in Challengers of the Unknown #6 **W:** Marv Wolfman

9 ❑ Aug 1997 Cover: 2.25 **NM** value: **Cover or less**
Circ: Diamd. preorders: **7,205**
📖 The Eleventh Man, Part 1 **W:** Marv Wolfman

10 ❑ Sep 1997 Cover: 2.25 **NM** value: **Cover or less**
Circ: Diamd. preorders: **6,633**
📖 The Eleventh Man, Part 2 **W:** Marv Wolfman

11 ❑ Oct 1997 Cover: 2.25 **NM** value: **Cover or less**
Circ: Diamd. preorders: **6,551**
📖 The Eleventh Man, Part 3 **W:** Marv Wolfman

12 ❑ Nov 1997 Cover: 2.50 **NM** value: **Cover or less**
Circ: Diamd. preorders: **6,232**
📖 The Lady or the Leopard! final issue. **A:** Sergio Cariello **W:** Marv Wolfman

NIGHT GLIDER — Topps

1 ❑ Apr 1993 Cover: 2.95 **NM** value: **Cover or less**
Circ: CapCity orders: **56,475**
📖 She Glides In Beauty, Like The Night **A:** Don Heck; Jack Kirby **W:** Roy Thomas; Gerry Conway

NIGHTHAWK — Marvel

1 ❑ Sep 1998 Cover: 2.99 **NM** value: **Cover or less**
Circ: Diamd. preorders: **21,561**
• gatefold summary. 📖 Pitfall **A:** Richard Case **W:** Jim Krueger

2 ❑ Oct 1998 Cover: 2.99 **NM** value: **Cover or less**
Circ: Diamd. preorders: **17,867**
• gatefold summary. **A:** Richard Case **W:** Jim Krueger

3 ❑ Nov 1998 Cover: 2.99 **NM** value: **Cover or less**
Circ: Diamd. preorders: **16,632**
• gatefold summary. **A:** Richard Case **W:** Jim Krueger

NIGHT LIFE — Strawberry Jam

1 ❑ Cover: 1.50 **NM** value: **Cover or less**
📖 The Kingdom **A:** Ken Hooper; Simon Tristam **W:** Derek McCulloch; Lisabeth Schiller

2 ❑ Cover: 1.50 **NM** value: **Cover or less**
3 ❑ Feb 1987 Cover: 1.50 **NM** value: **Cover or less**
4 ❑ Mar 1987 Cover: 1.50 **NM** value: **Cover or less**
5 ❑ Apr 1987 Cover: 1.50 **NM** value: **Cover or less**
6 ❑ May 1987 Cover: 1.50 **NM** value: **Cover or less**
7 ❑ Cover: 1.50 **NM** value: **Cover or less**
8 ❑ Nov 1991 Cover: 2.50 **NM** value: **Cover or less**

NIGHTLINGER — Gauntlet

1 ❑ b&w Cover: 2.95 **NM** value: **Cover or less**
A: Aldin Baroza **W:** Steven P. Jones

2 ❑ b&w Cover: 2.95 **NM** value: **Cover or less**
A: Aldin Baroza **W:** Steven P. Jones

NIGHT MAN, THE — Malibu / Ultraverse

Not long ago, a strange bolt of energy hit a cable car, causing the riders (known later as The Strangers) to gain super-powers. It also caused the cable car to crash into a sports car, an accident which buried a hunk of steel in the driver's head. That driver was Johnny Domingo, a noted jazz musician, and now, apparently, a dead man.

Shockingly, Johnny "got better." Although the metal was still buried in his skull, his brain somehow worked around it, leaving no ill-effects other than a permanent dilation of his pupils. On the bright side, Johnny found he no longer needed to sleep — and one other thing: he could now hear the thoughts of evil people. As ultra powers go, Johnny had a strange one, but he was determined to use it for good. He became The Night Man, vigilant protector of innocents who watched over the city while others sleep. And as a denizen of the night, he took on some of the darkest, most ghoulish villains in the Malibu Ultraverse.

The series spawned a syndicated television series that can still be found late at night on many independent stations.

1 ❑ Oct 1993 Cover: 2.50 **NM** value: **Cover or less**
Circ: CapCity orders: **40,600**
📖 Rune, Part C • Rune **A:** Barry Windsor-Smith; Darick Robertson **W:** Steve Englehart ★ Origin of The Night Man. ★ 1st Appearance of The Night Man (in costume), Death Mask.

1/LE❑ Cover: 25.00 **NM** value: **Cover or less**
• Ultra-limited edition. 📖 Rune, Part C **A:** Darick Robertson **W:** Steve Englehart ★ Origin of The Night Man. ★ 1st Appearance of The Night Man (in costume), Death Mask.

2 ❑ Nov 1993 Cover: 1.95 **NM** value: **2.00**
Circ: CapCity orders: **22,400**
📖 Mangled **A:** Gene Ha **W:** Steve Englehart ★ 1st Appearance of Mangle.

3 ❑ Dec 1993 Cover: 1.95 **NM** value: **2.00**
Circ: CapCity orders: **21,050**
📖 Break-Thru • Break-Thru **A:** Gene Ha **W:** Gerard Jones; Steve Englehart ★ Appearance of Freex.

4 ❑ Jan 1994 Cover: 1.95 **NM** value: **2.00**
Circ: CapCity orders: **18,075**
📖 Who Is The Night Man? **A:** Kyle Hotz **W:** Steve Englehart ★ Origin of Firearm.

5 ❑ Feb 1994 Cover: 1.95 **NM** value: **2.00**
Circ: CapCity orders: **15,500**
📖 Alone **A:** Kyle Hotz **W:** Steve Englehart

6 ❑ Mar 1994 Cover: 1.95 **NM** value: **Cover or less**
Circ: CapCity orders: **13,800**
W: Steve Englehart

7 ❑ Apr 1994 Cover: 1.95 **NM** value: **Cover or less**
Circ: CapCity orders: **13,125**
W: Steve Englehart

8 ❑ May 1994 Cover: 1.95 **NM** value: **Cover or less**
Circ: CapCity orders: **12,475**
W: Steve Englehart

9 ❑ Jun 1994 Cover: 1.95 **NM** value: **Cover or less**
Circ: CapCity orders: **11,850**
📖 Solitary! **A:** Kyle Hotz **W:** Steve Englehart ★ Death of Teknight I.

10 ❑ Jul 1994 Cover: 1.95 **NM** value: **Cover or less**
Circ: CapCity orders: **10,800**
📖 Chalk **A:** Kyle Hotz **W:** Steve Englehart ★ 1st Appearance of Silver Daggers, Chalk.

11 ❑ Aug 1994 Cover: 1.95 **NM** value: **Cover or less**
Circ: CapCity orders: **9,850**
📖 Turning On **A:** John Dennis; Rick Hoberg(cover) **W:** Steve Englehart ★ 1st Appearance of Teknight II.

12 ❑ Sep 1994 Cover: 1.95 **NM** value: **Cover or less**
Circ: CapCity orders: **9,175**
📖 Hostile Takeover; Hostile Takeover, Part 1 **A:** John Dennis; Kyle Hotz(cover) **W:** Steve Englehart ★ Appearance of The Solution.

13 ❑ Oct 1994 Cover: 1.95 **NM** value: **Cover or less**
Circ: CapCity orders: **8,575**
📖 Life • no indicia **A:** Kyle Hotz; Kirk Van Wormer **W:** Steve Englehart

14 ❑ Nov 1994 Cover: 1.95 **NM** value: **Cover or less**
Circ: CapCity orders: **7,750**
📖 Crossfire! **A:** Dean Zachary; Rick Leonardi(cover) **W:** James Robinson; Steve Englehart ★ Death of Torso.

15 ❑ Dec 1994 Cover: 1.95 **NM** value: **Cover or less**
Circ: CapCity orders: **7,150**
📖 The Night Man Before Christmas **A:** John Dennis **W:** Steve Englehart

16 ❑ Feb 1995 Cover: 3.50 **NM** value: **Cover or less**
Circ: CapCity orders: **6,225**
📖 What's In a Name; Terrible Tuesday; Blind Date; Catharsis, Part 2; A New Game of Death, Part 3 • flipbook with Ultraverse Premiere #11 **A:** David Perrin; Steve Scott; Steve Ellis; Mark Heike; Mike Zeck; Chris Gardner; Mike Miller(cover); Steven Butler(cover) **W:** Buzz Dixon; Hank Kanalz; Len Strazewski; R.A. Jones; Roland Mann; Steve Englehart

17 ❑ Feb 1995 Cover: 2.50 **NM** value: **Cover or less**
Circ: CapCity orders: **5,875**
📖 BloodyFly! **A:** John Dennis; Dean Zachary(cover) **W:** Steve Englehart ★ 1st Appearance of BloodyFly.

18 ❑ Mar 1995 Cover: 2.50 **NM** value: **Cover or less**
Circ: CapCity orders: **5,575**
📖 Sharks! **A:** Dean Zachary; Brian Murray(cover) **W:** Steve Englehart

19 ❑ Apr 1995 Cover: 2.50 **NM** value: **Cover or less**
Circ: CapCity orders: **5,275**
📖 The Edge of Your Seat **A:** Dean Zachary; Keith Conroy(cover) **W:** Steve Englehart ★ Death of Deathmask.

20 ❑ May 1995 Cover: 2.50 **NM** value: **Cover or less**
Circ: CapCity orders: **4,850**
📖 Ashes, Ashes...We All Fall Down **A:** Dean Zachary **W:** Steve Englehart ★ Death of BloodyFly.

21 ❑ Jun 1995 Cover: 2.50 **NM** value: **Cover or less**
Circ: CapCity orders: **4,600**
W: Steve Englehart

22 ❑ Jul 1995 Cover: 2.50 **NM** value: **Cover or less**
W: Steve Englehart ★ Appearance of Loki.

23 ❑ Aug 1995 Cover: 2.50 **NM** value: **Cover or less**
final issue. **W:** Steve Englehart

Anl 1❑ Cover: 3.95 **NM** value: **Cover or less**
Circ: CapCity orders: **6,175**
📖 The Pilgrim Conundrum, Part 1 **A:** Rick Hoberg; Albert Calleros(cover) **W:** Steve Englehart

NIGHT MAN/GAMBIT, THE — Malibu / Ultraverse

1 ❑ Mar 1996 Cover: 1.95 **NM** value: **Cover or less**
📖 Shedding Skin **A:** Dietrich Smith **W:** David Quinn

2 ❑ Apr 1996 Cover: 1.95 **NM** value: **Cover or less**
3 ❑ May 1996 Cover: 1.95 **NM** value: **Cover or less**

NIGHT MAN VS. WOLVERINE — Malibu / Ultraverse

0 ❑ Aug 1995 **NM** value: **5.00**
no cover price.

NIGHT MAN, THE (VOL. 2) — Malibu / Ultraverse

0 ❑ Sep 1995 Cover: 1.50 **NM** value: **Cover or less**

Other grades: Multiply prices above by **1.5 for Mint • 2/3 for Very Fine • 1/3 for Fine • 1/5 for Very Good • 1/8 for Good**

Black September; This Is Black September • Listed as issue #Infinity **A:** Dean Zachary **W:** Steve Englehart
0/A ❑ Sep 1995 Cover: 1.50 **NM** value: **Cover or less**
alternate cover. Black September
1 ❑ Oct 1995 Cover: 1.50 **NM** value: **Cover or less**
The Night's A-shine with Stars **A:** Andrew Wildman **W:** Steve Englehart
2 ❑ Nov 1995 Cover: 1.50 **NM** value: **Cover or less**
3 ❑ Dec 1995 Cover: 1.50 **NM** value: **Cover or less**
★ Versus Lord Pumpkin.
4 ❑ Dec 1995 Cover: 1.50 **NM** value: **Cover or less**
final issue. ★ Versus Lord Pumpkin. ★ Versus Mangle.

NIGHTMARE — Marvel
1 ❑ Dec 1994 Cover: 1.95 **NM** value: **Cover or less**
Circ: CapCity orders: **11,700**
Temptation **A:** Joe Bennett **W:** Ann Nocenti
2 ❑ Jan 1995 Cover: 1.95 **NM** value: **Cover or less**
Circ: CapCity orders: **8,200**
3 ❑ Feb 1995 Cover: 1.95 **NM** value: **Cover or less**
Circ: CapCity orders: **6,250**
4 ❑ Mar 1995 Cover: 1.95 **NM** value: **Cover or less**
Circ: CapCity orders: **4,725**

NIGHTMARE (ALEX NIÑO'S...) — Innovation
1 ❑ Dec 1989 Cover: 1.95 **NM** value: **Cover or less**
Circ: CapCity orders: **4,000**
A: Alex Ni±o **W:** Alex Ni±o

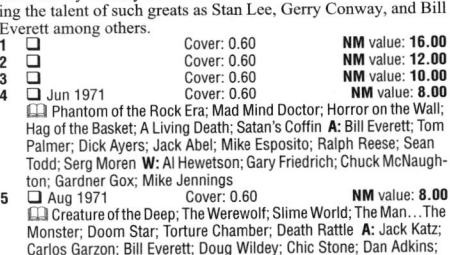

NIGHTMARE (MAGAZINE) — Skywald
Frankenstein's monster is alive and well as part of a freak show in a travelling fair. The Titanic is sinking but not as a result of crashing into an iceberg. A man and woman in search of werewolves discover each other's supernatural secret. And a woman with a fear of roaches learns she has an extraordinary and frightful power. These were only some of the terrifying tales presented in this monthly black-and-white magazine. Each issue included several heart-pounding works, and fans of horror fiction will love reading a wide variety of scary stories featuring the talent of such greats as Stan Lee, Gerry Conway, and Bill Everett among others.

1 ❑ Cover: 0.60 **NM** value: **16.00**
2 ❑ Cover: 0.60 **NM** value: **12.00**
3 ❑ Cover: 0.60 **NM** value: **10.00**
4 ❑ Jun 1971 Cover: 0.60 **NM** value: **8.00**
Phantom of the Rock Era; Mad Mind Doctor; Horror on the Wall; Hag of the Basket; A Living Death; Satan's Coffin **A:** Bill Everett; Tom Palmer; Dick Ayers; Jack Abel; Mike Esposito; Ralph Reese; Sean Todd; Serg Moren **W:** Al Hewetson; Gary Friedrich; Chuck McNaughton; Gardner Gox; Mike Jennings
5 ❑ Aug 1971 Cover: 0.60 **NM** value: **8.00**
Creature of the Deep; The Werewolf; Slime World; The Man...The Monster; Doom Star; Torture Chamber; Death Rattle **A:** Jack Katz; Carlos Garzon; Bill Everett; Doug Wildey; Chic Stone; Dan Adkins; Jack Abel; Ralph Reese; Sean Todd **W:** Chic Stone; Al Hewtson; Alan Asherman; Chuck McNaughton; Kevin Pagan; Len Brown
6 ❑ Cover: 0.60 **NM** value: **8.00**
7 ❑ Jun 1972 Cover: 0.60 **NM** value: **8.00**
The Penitent; Group Jeapordy; The Giant Death Rat; Altar of Blood; A Father's Lament; Artifacts; The Essential Horror **A:** Pablo Marcos; Dennis Fujitake; Amador; Donald Brown; Ferran Sostres; Frank Cueto; Serg Moren **W:** Dennis Fujitake; Donald Brown; Bob Kirschen; Ed Fedory; Howie Anderson; S.F. Starr
8 ❑ Aug 1972 Cover: 0.60 **NM** value: **8.00**
Snow-Bound; Hey Creep: Play the Macabre Waltz; Rot, Robin, Rot; The Tunnels of Horror; Satan's Graveyard; Hung Up; The Sting of Death; The Weird and the Undead **A:** Pablo Marcos; Bruce Jones; Al Hewetson; Dela Rosa; Ferran Sostres; Jim Elder; Chik Stone **W:** Bruce Jones; Al Hewetson; Chik Stone; Ed Fedory; Howie Anderson
9 ❑ 1972 **NM** value: **8.00**
10 ❑ Dec 1972 **NM** value: **8.00**
11 ❑ Feb 1973 **NM** value: **6.00**
12 ❑ Apr 1973 **NM** value: **6.00**
13 ❑ Jun 1973 **NM** value: **6.00**
14 ❑ Aug 1973 **NM** value: **6.00**
15 ❑ Oct 1973 **NM** value: **6.00**
16 ❑ Dec 1973 **NM** value: **6.00**
17 ❑ Feb 1974 **NM** value: **6.00**
18 ❑ Apr 1974 **NM** value: **6.00**
19 ❑ Jun 1974 **NM** value: **6.00**
20 ❑ Aug 1974 **NM** value: **6.00**
21 ❑ Sep 1974 **NM** value: **4.00**
22 ❑ Oct 1974 **NM** value: **4.00**
23 ❑ **NM** value: **4.00**

NIGHTMARE ON ELM STREET, A (FREDDY KRUEGER'S...) — Marvel
1 ❑ Cover: 2.25 **NM** value: **3.00**
Circ: CapCity orders: **12,850**

NIGHTMARE ON ELM STREET : THE BEGINNING — Innovation
1 ❑ Cover: 2.50 **NM** value: **Cover or less**
Circ: CapCity orders: **6,135**
2 ❑ Cover: 2.50 **NM** value: **Cover or less**

NIGHTMARE! (PORTMAN) — Portman
1 ❑ Cover: 0.35 **NM** value: **5.00**
2 ❑ Cover: 0.35 **NM** value: **4.00**
Demon of Slaughter Mansion; Lifeboat; Frankenstein 78; The Madman; Swords of Dragons; The Roaches; Werewolf Tale to End Werewolf Tales **A:** Syd Shores; Bill Everett; Pablo Marcos; Jesus Blasco; John Bescernd; Juan Boix; Ralph Reese **W:** Frank Brunner; Gary Friedrich; Paul Hodge; Stan Lee; Don McGregor; Gerry Conway

NIGHTMARES — Eclipse
1 ❑ Cover: 1.75 **NM** value: **2.00**
Blood on Black Satin, Part 1; The Trespasser, Part 1 **A:** Paul Gulacy **W:** Don McGregor; Doug Moench
2 ❑ Cover: 1.75 **NM** value: **2.00**
Blood on Black Satin, Part 2; The Trespasser, Part 2 **A:** Paul Gulacy **W:** Don McGregor; Doug Moench

NIGHTMARES ON ELM STREET — Innovation

The movie "Nightmare On Elm Street" introduced moviegoers to Freddy, a dead madman who stalked the dreams of Springwood's citizens. Surprisingly popular, it spawned a number of "Elm Street" sequels, and Freddy even hosted a TV horror show.

Innovation's comics title continued the saga of Springwood. It seemed that everyone in this quiet suburban town had their own dirty secret, but the skeletons in their closets were not resting easy. For no matter how well they hid their dirty laundry from their neighbors, they couldn't hide from their own nightmares. And when they dreamed, Freddy was always there.

1 ❑ Sep 1991 Cover: 2.50 **NM** value: **Cover or less**
Circ: CapCity orders: **14,065**
Yours Truly, Freddy Krueger, Part 1 **A:** Tony Harris; Jason Palmer(cover) **W:** Andy Mangels
2 ❑ Cover: 2.50 **NM** value: **Cover or less**
Circ: CapCity orders: **8,480**
Yours Truly, Freddy Krueger, Part 2 **A:** Tony Harris **W:** Andy Mangels
3 ❑ Cover: 2.50 **NM** value: **Cover or less**
Circ: CapCity orders: **7,075**
Loose Ends, Part 1 **W:** Andy Mangels
4 ❑ Cover: 2.50 **NM** value: **Cover or less**
Circ: CapCity orders: **6,735**
Loose Ends, Part 2 **A:** Patrick Rolo **W:** Andy Mangels
5 ❑ Cover: 2.50 **NM** value: **Cover or less**
Circ: CapCity orders: **4,470**
W: Andy Mangels
6 ❑ Cover: 2.50 **NM** value: **Cover or less**
Circ: CapCity orders: **3,920**
W: Andy Mangels

NIGHTMARE (ST. JOHN) — St. John
10 ❑ Dec 1953 Cover: 0.10 **NM** value: **300.00**
• **CGC:** 2 graded, best 9.0
11 ❑ Feb 1954 Cover: 0.10 **NM** value: **250.00**
• **CGC:** 2 graded, best 8.0
12 ❑ Apr 1954 Cover: 0.10 **NM** value: **200.00**
• **CGC:** 2 graded, best 8.5
13 ❑ Aug 1954 Cover: 0.10 **NM** value: **200.00**
• **CGC:** 2 graded, best 8.0

NIGHTMARE THEATER — Chaos!
1 ❑ Nov 1997 Cover: 2.50 **NM** value: **Cover or less**
Circ: Diamd. preorders: **16,127**
One Perfect Night; The Ballad of the Eyeball Dragster; The Monster Hunter's Club; Ticket to Terror, Part 1 • horror anthology **A:** Flint Henry; Bernie Wrightson; Rick Veitch; Anya Martin **W:** Hart Fisher; Anya Martin; Brian Pulido; David Quinn; Joy Mosier
2 ❑ Nov 1997 Cover: 2.50 **NM** value: **Cover or less**
Circ: Diamd. preorders: **15,846**
• horror anthology
3 ❑ Nov 1997 Cover: 2.50 **NM** value: **Cover or less**
Circ: Diamd. preorders: **15,700**
• horror anthology
4 ❑ Nov 1997 Cover: 2.50 **NM** value: **Cover or less**
Circ: Diamd. preorders: **15,722**
• horror anthology

NIGHTMARE WALKER — Boneyard
1 ❑ Jul 1996, b&w Cover: 2.95 **NM** value: **Cover or less**

NIGHTMARK — Alpha Productions
1 ❑ b&w Cover: 2.25 **NM** value: **Cover or less**

NIGHTMARK: BLOOD & HONOR — Alpha
1 ❑ Apr 1994 Cover: 2.50 **NM** value: **Cover or less**
Midnight And Morning Black **A:** Scott Dutton **W:** Christopher Mills
2 ❑ Cover: 2.50 **NM** value: **Cover or less**
3 ❑ Cover: 2.50 **NM** value: **Cover or less**

NIGHTMARK MYSTERY SPECIAL — Alpha
1 ❑ b&w Cover: 2.50 **NM** value: **Cover or less**
The Devil's Brood; Kill Me In The Morning **A:** Steven Butler; DCR **W:** Christopher Mills

NIGHTMASK — Marvel
1 ❑ Nov 1986 Cover: 0.75 **NM** value: **1.00**
Circ: CapCity orders: **31,600**
The Awakening **A:** Tony Salmons **W:** Archie Goodwin ★ Origin of Nightmask.
2 ❑ Dec 1986 Cover: 0.75 **NM** value: **1.00**
Circ: CapCity orders: **21,600**
3 ❑ Jan 1987 Cover: 0.75 **NM** value: **1.00**
Circ: CapCity orders: **18,000**
4 ❑ Feb 1987 Cover: 0.75 **NM** value: **1.00**
Circ: CapCity orders: **17,700**
5 ❑ Mar 1987 Cover: 0.75 **NM** value: **1.00**
Circ: CapCity orders: **16,100**
6 ❑ Apr 1987 Cover: 0.75 **NM** value: **1.00**
Circ: CapCity orders: **14,300**
7 ❑ May 1987 Cover: 0.75 **NM** value: **1.00**
Circ: CapCity orders: **14,200**
8 ❑ Jun 1987 Cover: 0.75 **NM** value: **1.00**
Circ: CapCity orders: **11,700**
9 ❑ Jul 1987 Cover: 0.75 **NM** value: **1.00**
Circ: CapCity orders: **9,800**
10 ❑ Aug 1987 Cover: 0.75 **NM** value: **1.00**
Circ: CapCity orders: **10,300**
11 ❑ Sep 1987 Cover: 0.75 **NM** value: **1.00**
Circ: CapCity orders: **10,000**
12 ❑ Oct 1987 Cover: 0.75 **NM** value: **1.00**
Circ: CapCity orders: **9,000**
final issue.

NIGHT MASTERS — Custom Pic
1 ❑ Cover: 1.50 **NM** value: **Cover or less**
2 ❑ Cover: 1.50 **NM** value: **Cover or less**
3 ❑ Cover: 1.50 **NM** value: **Cover or less**
4 ❑ Cover: 1.50 **NM** value: **Cover or less**
5 ❑ Aug 1986 Cover: 1.50 **NM** value: **Cover or less**
6 ❑ Jan 1987 Cover: 1.50 **NM** value: **Cover or less**
Maximum Metal **A:** Bruce Patnaude **W:** Bruce & DianePatnaude

NIGHT MUSIC — Eclipse
1 ❑ Dec 1984 Cover: 1.75 **NM** value: **2.00**
Breakdown On The Starship Remembrance **A:** P. Craig Russell **W:** P. Craig Russell
2 ❑ Feb 1985 Cover: 1.75 **NM** value: **2.00**
A: P. Craig Russell **W:** P. Craig Russell
3 ❑ Mar 1985 Cover: 1.75 **NM** value: **2.00**
The King's Ankus • Rudyard Kipling adaptation **A:** P. Craig Russell **W:** P. Craig Russell
4 ❑ Dec 1985 Cover: 2.00 **NM** value: **Cover or less**
Pelleas & Mellisande, Part 1 **A:** P. Craig Russell
5 ❑ Dec 1985 Cover: 2.00 **NM** value: **Cover or less**
Pelleas & Mellisande, Part 2 **A:** P. Craig Russell
6 ❑ Cover: 1.75 **NM** value: **2.00**
• Salome **A:** P. Craig Russell
7 ❑ Feb 1988 Cover: 2.00 **NM** value: **Cover or less**
• Red Dog **A:** P. Craig Russell **W:** P. Craig Russell
8 ❑ Cover: 3.95 **NM** value: **Cover or less**
• Arianne and Bluebeard
9 ❑ Cover: 4.95 **NM** value: **Cover or less**
• The Magic Flute **A:** P. Craig Russell
10 ❑ Cover: 4.95 **NM** value: **Cover or less**
• The Magic Flute **A:** P. Craig Russell
11 ❑ Cover: 4.95 **NM** value: **Cover or less**
• The Magic Flute **A:** P. Craig Russell
Bk 1 ❑ Cover: 10.00 **NM** value: **Cover or less**
• Paperback collection **A:** P. Craig Russell **W:** P. Craig Russell

NIGHT NURSE — Marvel
December 1972 marked the start of one of Marvel's periodic attempts to woo female readers, with the premiere of two new series: The Cat and Night Nurse.

Night Nurse was the story of three women who worked as nurses in Metro General hospital. Redhead Christine Palmer was heir to millions, but preferred to work helping people rather than live the life of a debutante. Similar dreams drove her roommates and co-workers Georgia Jenkins and Linda Carter (the nominal star of this series).

The plots were pure soap opera, with the women constantly falling for distinguished surgeons and mysterious (and handsome) patients. For all the romance and plot twists, the series lasted just four issues. Today, it's one of Marvel's great forgotten titles and an in-house joke similar to Forbush Man.

1 ❑ Nov 1972 Cover: 0.20 **NM** value: **42.00**
• **CGC:** 14 graded, best 9.4
The Making of a Nurse! **A:** Win Mortimer **W:** Jean Thomas
2 ❑ Jan 1973 Cover: 0.20 **NM** value: **25.00**
• **CGC:** 2 graded, best 9.0
A: Win Mortimer **W:** Jean Thomas
3 ❑ Mar 1973 Cover: 0.20 **NM** value: **25.00**
• **CGC:** 2 graded, best 9.4
Murder Stalks Ward 8! **A:** Win Mortimer **W:** Jean Thomas
4 ❑ May 1973 Cover: 0.20 **NM** value: **25.00**
• **CGC:** 1 graded, best 6.0
final issue. **A:** Win Mortimer **W:** Jean Thomas

NIGHT OF MYSTERY — Avon
1 ❑ ca. 1953 Cover: 0.10 **NM** value: **200.00**
• **CGC:** 5 graded, best 9.2

NIGHT OF THE LIVING DEAD — Fantaco
0 ❑ b&w Cover: 1.95 **NM** value: **2.00**
1 ❑ b&w Cover: 4.95 **NM** value: **Cover or less**
Circ: CapCity orders: **2,285**
2 ❑ b&w Cover: 4.95 **NM** value: **Cover or less**
Circ: CapCity orders: **4,275**
Zombie Vacation **A:** Rik Rawling **W:** Noel Hannan
3 ❑ b&w Cover: 5.95 **NM** value: **Cover or less**
Circ: CapCity orders: **2,755**

CGC-graded: Multiply prices above by **33 for 9.9 M • 16 for 9.8 NM/M • 7 for 9.6 NM+ • 5 for 9.4 NM • 2.5 for 9.2 NM- • 1.5 for 9.0 VF/NM**

4 ❑ b&w Cover: 5.95 NM value: Cover or less

NIGHT OF THE LIVING DEAD: AFTERMATH Fantaco

1 ❑ Cover: 1.95 NM value: Cover or less

NIGHT OF THE LIVING DEADLINE USA Dark Horse

1 ❑ Apr 1992, b&w Cover: 2.95 NM value: Cover or less

NIGHT OF THE LIVING DEAD: LONDON Fantaco

1 ❑ Cover: 5.95 NM value: Cover or less
Circ: CapCity orders: 4,340
2 ❑ Cover: 5.95 NM value: Cover or less
Bloodline A: Carlos Kastro W: Clive Barker; Steve Niles

NIGHT OF THE LIVING DEAD: PRELUDE Fantaco

1 ❑ b&w Cover: 1.50 NM value: Cover or less

NIGHT RAVEN: HOUSE OF CARDS Marvel

1 ❑ Aug 1991 Cover: 5.95 NM value: Cover or less
Circ: CapCity orders: 1,850
A: David Lloyd W: Jamie Delano

NIGHT RIDER Marvel

1 ❑ Oct 1974 Cover: 0.25 NM value: 5.00
• CGC: 1 graded, best 9.0
• Reprints Ghost Rider (Western) #1
2 ❑ Dec 1974 Cover: 0.25 NM value: 3.50
The Macabre Menace Of The Tarantula! • Reprints Ghost Rider (Western) #2 A: Dick Ayers W: Gary Friedrich
3 ❑ Feb 1975 Cover: 0.25 NM value: 3.50
• Reprints Ghost Rider (Western) #3
4 ❑ Apr 1975 Cover: 0.25 NM value: 3.50
• CGC: 1 graded, best 9.0
• Reprints Ghost Rider (Western) #4
5 ❑ Jun 1975 Cover: 0.25 NM value: 3.50
• CGC: 1 graded, best 8.0
• Reprints Ghost Rider (Western) #5
6 ❑ Aug 1975 Cover: 0.25 NM value: 3.50
• Reprints Ghost Rider (Western) #6

NIGHT'S CHILDREN Fantaco

1 ❑ b&w Cover: 3.50 NM value: Cover or less
2 ❑ b&w Cover: 3.50 NM value: Cover or less
3 ❑ b&w Cover: 3.50 NM value: Cover or less
4 ❑ b&w Cover: 3.50 NM value: Cover or less

NIGHT'S CHILDREN: DOUBLE INDEMNITY Fantaco

1 ❑ b&w Cover: 7.95 NM value: Cover or less

NIGHT'S CHILDREN EROTIC FANTASIES Fantaco

1 ❑ NM value: 4.50

NIGHT'S CHILDREN: EXOTIC FANTASIES Fantaco

1 ❑ b&w Cover: 5.95 NM value: Cover or less

NIGHT'S CHILDREN: FOREPLAY Fantaco

1 ❑ b&w Cover: 4.95 NM value: Cover or less

NIGHT'S CHILDREN: THE VAMPIRE Millennium

1 ❑ Cover: 2.95 NM value: Cover or less
A: Wendy Snow-Lang W: Wendy Snow-Lang
2 ❑ Cover: 2.95 NM value: Cover or less
A: Wendy Snow-Lang W: Wendy Snow-Lang

NIGHT'S CHILDREN: VAMPYR! Fantaco

All issues are adults only.
1 ❑ b&w Cover: 3.50 NM value: Cover or less
2 ❑ b&w Cover: 3.50 NM value: Cover or less
3 ❑ b&w Cover: 3.50 NM value: Cover or less

NIGHTSHADE No Mercy

1 ❑ Aug 1997 Cover: 2.50 NM value: Cover or less
A: Mark Williams W: Mark Williams

NIGHTSHADES London Night

1 ❑ Cover: 2.95 NM value: Cover or less
Hidden Darkness A: Daniel Presedo W: Neal St. Crosse

NIGHTSIDE Marvel

1 ❑ Dec 2001 Cover: 2.99 NM value: Cover or less
Circ: Diamd. preorders: 34,240
2 ❑ Jan 2002 Cover: 2.99 NM value: Cover or less
Circ: Diamd. preorders: 28,389
3 ❑ Feb 2002 Cover: 2.99 NM value: Cover or less
Circ: Diamd. preorders: 25,156
4 ❑ Mar 2002 Cover: 2.99 NM value: Cover or less
Circ: Diamd. preorders: 21,262

NIGHTS INTO DREAMS Archie

1 ❑ Feb 1998 Cover: 1.75 NM value: Cover or less
Circ: Diamd. preorders: 6,718
2 ❑ Mar 1998 Cover: 1.75 NM value: Cover or less
Circ: Diamd. preorders: 4,853
3 ❑ Apr 1998 Cover: 1.75 NM value: Cover or less
Circ: Diamd. preorders: 3,699
4 ❑ Aug 1998 Cover: 1.75 NM value: Cover or less
Circ: Diamd. preorders: 3,016
5 ❑ Sep 1998 Cover: 1.75 NM value: Cover or less
Circ: Diamd. preorders: 2,935
6 ❑ Oct 1998 Cover: 1.75 NM value: Cover or less
Circ: Diamd. preorders: 2,604

NIGHTSTALKERS Marvel

Frank Drake, Hannibal King, and Blade, the Vampire Slayer form the Nightstalkers, were an uneasy team that arose from the Ghost Rider "Rise of the Midnight Sons" crossover series.

The Nightstalkers were uncomfortable not only with each other, but with themselves as well. Blade's mother was killed during his birth by a vampire, and as a result he has some of the powers of the undead. Frank Drake was a descendent of Dracula who devoted his life to killing vampires in the Tomb of Dracula series. Hannibal King used to be a vampire — but now, half-cured by sorcery — he sometimes still found himself lusting after human blood like a former addict. As a team, they waged war against the supernatural forces that turned them into what they themselves despise.

1 ❑ Nov 1992 Cover: 2.75 NM value: Cover or less
Circ: CapCity orders: 114,900
• Missing poster
1/CS❑ Cover: 2.75 NM value: Cover or less
Rise of the Midnight Sons, Part 5 A: Ron Garney W: D.G. Chichester
2 ❑ Dec 1992 Cover: 1.75 NM value: 2.00
Circ: Statement: 147,642 CapCity orders: 44,500
Staking Claim, Part 1 A: Ron Garney W: D.G. Chichester
3 ❑ Jan 1993 Cover: 1.75 NM value: 2.00
Circ: Statement: 147,642 CapCity orders: 39,000
Staking Claim, Part 2 A: Ron Garney W: D.G. Chichester
4 ❑ Feb 1993 Cover: 1.75 NM value: Cover or less
Circ: Statement: 147,642 CapCity orders: 31,300
Staking Claim, Part 3 A: Ron Garney W: D.G. Chichester
5 ❑ Mar 1993 Cover: 1.75 NM value: Cover or less
Circ: Statement: 147,642 CapCity orders: 25,000
Cut to the Bone A: Ron Garney W: D.G. Chichester ★ Appearance of Punisher.
6 ❑ Apr 1993 Cover: 1.75 NM value: Cover or less
Circ: Statement: 147,642 CapCity orders: 23,900
Comes A Pale Rider A: Ron Garney W: D.G. Chichester ★ Appearance of Punisher.
7 ❑ May 1993 Cover: 1.75 NM value: Cover or less
Circ: Statement: 147,642 CapCity orders: 20,800
Ghosts In The Machine A: Ron Garney W: D.G. Chichester ★ Appearance of Ghost Rider.
8 ❑ Jun 1993 Cover: 1.75 NM value: Cover or less
Circ: Statement: 147,642 CapCity orders: 18,100
W: D.G. Chichester ★ Appearance of Ghost Rider.
9 ❑ Jul 1993 Cover: 1.75 NM value: Cover or less
Circ: Statement: 147,642 CapCity orders: 17,600
W: D.G. Chichester
10 ❑ Aug 1993 Cover: 1.75 NM value: 2.25
Circ: Statement: 147,642 CapCity orders: 43,100
Double cover. Midnight Massacre, Part 1 A: Kirk Van Wormer W: D.G. Chichester
11 ❑ Sep 1993 Cover: 1.75 NM value: Cover or less
Circ: Statement: 147,642 CapCity orders: 14,500
A: Kirk Van Wormer W: D.G. Chichester
12 ❑ Oct 1993 Cover: 1.75 NM value: Cover or less
Circ: Statement: 147,642 CapCity orders: 16,500
Gold cover. Portrait of Death Row A: Vince Giarrano; Kirk Van Wormer W: D.G. Chichester ★ Appearance of Row appearance, DOA appearance, Row appearance, DOA appearance.
13 ❑ Nov 1993 Cover: 1.75 NM value: Cover or less
Circ: Statement: 147,642 CapCity orders: 13,850
Short Circuit A: Kirk Van Wormer W: Steven Grant ★ 1st Appearance of Short Circuit.
14 ❑ Dec 1993 Cover: 1.75 NM value: Cover or less
Circ: CapCity orders: 22,800
Neon ink on cover. Siege of Darkness, Part 1 W: Steven Grant
15 ❑ Jan 1994 Cover: 1.75 NM value: Cover or less
Circ: CapCity orders: 17,400
Spot-varnish cover. Siege of Darkness, Part 8 W: Steven Grant
16 ❑ Feb 1994 Cover: 1.75 NM value: Cover or less
Circ: CapCity orders: 11,350
• Has 1993 Statement, filed 10/1/93; avg print run 248,692; avg sales 147,492; avg subs 150; avg total paid circ 147,642; samples 125; office use 500; max existent 148,267; 40% of run returned
17 ❑ Mar 1994 Cover: 1.75 NM value: Cover or less
Circ: CapCity orders: 11,600
18 ❑ Apr 1994 Cover: 1.75 NM value: Cover or less
Circ: CapCity orders: 10,350
All The Threads Unraveled final issue. A: Doug Wheatley W: Frank Lovece

NIGHTSTREETS (ARROW) Arrow

1 ❑ Jul 1986 Cover: 1.50 NM value: 2.50
Mob Rules, Part 1 A: Mark Bloodworth W: Mark Bloodworth ★ 1st Appearance of Mr. Katt.
2 ❑ Oct 1986 Cover: 1.50 NM value: 2.00
A: Mark Bloodworth W: Mark Bloodworth
3 ❑ Jan 1987 Cover: 1.50 NM value: 2.00
A: Mark Bloodworth W: Mark Bloodworth
4 ❑ Apr 1987 Cover: 1.50 NM value: 2.00
A: Mark Bloodworth W: Mark Bloodworth
5 ❑ Jul 1987 Cover: 1.50 NM value: 2.00
A: Mark Bloodworth W: Mark Bloodworth

NIGHTSTREETS (CALIBER) Caliber

Bk 1❑ Cover: 9.95 NM value: Cover or less
• Book 1-2

NIGHT THRASHER Marvel

Dwayne Taylor is the director of the Taylor Foundation, a business left to him by his father. Dwayne is also the vigilante known as Night Thrasher, an armored foe of criminals and head of the New Warriors.

Following a successful try-out in the Night Thrasher: Four Control limited series, Thrash now stars in this ongoing monthly title. Here readers find out more about the man behind the mask, including keeping up on his on-again, off-again relationship with fellow New Warrior Silhouette Chord. We also find out about Bandit — a brother Dwayne never knew he had — and who, jealous of Dwayne's success, threatens to become his greatest enemy.

1 ❑ Aug 1993 Cover: 2.95 NM value: Cover or less
Circ: CapCity orders: 65,500 • CGC: 1 graded, best 9.6
foil cover. ★ Origin of Night Thrasher.
2 ❑ Sep 1993 Cover: 1.75 NM value: Cover or less
Circ: CapCity orders: 28,000
★ 1st Appearance of Tantrum.
3 ❑ Oct 1993 Cover: 1.75 NM value: Cover or less
Circ: CapCity orders: 21,900
A: Javier Saltares W: Fabian Nicieza ★ Appearance of Aardwolf, Silhouette, Tiger Tyger.
4 ❑ Nov 1993 Cover: 1.75 NM value: Cover or less
Circ: CapCity orders: 22,300
5 ❑ Dec 1993 Cover: 1.75 NM value: Cover or less
Circ: CapCity orders: 20,000
6 ❑ Jan 1994 Cover: 1.75 NM value: Cover or less
Circ: CapCity orders: 17,500
7 ❑ Feb 1994 Cover: 1.75 NM value: Cover or less
Circ: CapCity orders: 15,200
Brothers in Arms, Part 1 A: David Boller W: Fabian Nicieza
8 ❑ Mar 1994 Cover: 1.75 NM value: Cover or less
Circ: CapCity orders: 12,650
Brothers in Arms, Part 2
9 ❑ Apr 1994 Cover: 1.75 NM value: Cover or less
Circ: CapCity orders: 11,300
10 ❑ May 1994 Cover: 1.95 NM value: Cover or less
Circ: CapCity orders: 10,600
11 ❑ Jun 1994 Cover: 1.95 NM value: Cover or less
Circ: CapCity orders: 10,750
12 ❑ Jul 1994 Cover: 1.95 NM value: Cover or less
Circ: CapCity orders: 11,400
13 ❑ Aug 1994 Cover: 1.95 NM value: Cover or less
Circ: CapCity orders: 10,100
Lost in the Shadows
14 ❑ Sep 1994 Cover: 1.95 NM value: Cover or less
Circ: CapCity orders: 10,100
Lost in the Shadows
15 ❑ Oct 1994 Cover: 1.95 NM value: Cover or less
Circ: CapCity orders: 9,650
W: Kurt Busiek ★ Versus Hulk.
16 ❑ Nov 1994 Cover: 1.95 NM value: Cover or less
W: Kurt Busiek
17 ❑ Dec 1994 Cover: 1.95 NM value: Cover or less
W: Kurt Busiek
18 ❑ Jan 1995 Cover: 1.95 NM value: Cover or less
Circ: CapCity orders: 7,225
W: Kurt Busiek
19 ❑ Feb 1995 Cover: 1.95 NM value: Cover or less
Circ: CapCity orders: 6,425
20 ❑ Mar 1995 Cover: 1.95 NM value: Cover or less
Circ: CapCity orders: 5,750
Heart of Rage, Part 1 W: Kurt Busiek
21 ❑ Apr 1995 Cover: 1.95 NM value: Cover or less
Circ: CapCity orders: 5,150
Heart of Rage, Part 2 final issue. W: Kurt Busiek

NIGHT THRASHER: FOUR CONTROL Marvel

1 ❑ Oct 1992 Cover: 2.00 NM value: Cover or less
Circ: CapCity orders: 59,700
Strength A: Dave Hoover W: Fabian Nicieza
2 ❑ Nov 1992 Cover: 2.00 NM value: Cover or less
Circ: CapCity orders: 39,800
Money A: Dave Hoover W: Fabian Nicieza
3 ❑ Dec 1992 Cover: 2.00 NM value: Cover or less
Circ: CapCity orders: 34,600
A: Dave Hoover W: Fabian Nicieza
4 ❑ Jan 1993 Cover: 2.00 NM value: Cover or less
Circ: CapCity orders: 31,600
Compassion A: Dave Hoover W: Fabian Nicieza

NIGHT TRIBES DC / Wildstorm

1 ❑ Jul 1999 Cover: 4.95 NM value: Cover or less
Circ: Diamd. preorders: 17,102
No issue number. One-shot. A Gathering of Monsters A: Joyce Chin W: Christopher Golden; Tom Sniegoski

NIGHTVEIL AC

1 ❑ Feb 1984, full color Cover: 1.75 NM value: 2.00
Nightveil; Nightveil: Deathstalk! A: Mark Heike W: Steve Ringgenberg
2 ❑ Cover: 1.75 NM value: 2.00
Circ: CapCity orders: 2,825
3 ❑ Cover: 1.75 NM value: 2.00
Circ: CapCity orders: 3,000
4 ❑ Cover: 1.75 NM value: 2.00
Circ: CapCity orders: 2,525
5 ❑ Cover: 1.75 NM value: 2.00
Circ: CapCity orders: 2,650

Other grades: Multiply prices above by **1.5 for Mint • 2/3 for Very Fine • 1/3 for Fine • 1/5 for Very Good • 1/8 for Good**

6 Cover: 1.75 NM value: 2.00
Circ: CapCity orders: 2,485
7 Mar 1987 Cover: 1.75 NM value: 2.00
Circ: CapCity orders: 2,775
SE 1 Aug 1988 Cover: 1.95 NM value: 2.00
Circ: CapCity orders: 2,175

NIGHTVEIL'S CAULDRON OF HORROR — AC

1 b&w Cover: 2.50 NM value: Cover or less
Nightveil's Cauldron of Horror; The Ghost of Fanciful Hawkins; The Mirror of Isis!; The Thing from the Sea A: Joe Kubert; Bob Powell; Norman Hardy Jr.; Wallace Wood W: Bill Black
2 Cover: 2.95 NM value: Cover or less
3 Sep 1991 Cover: 2.95 NM value: Cover or less

NIGHTVENGER — Axis

Ash 1 May 1994 NM value: 2.00
Circ: CapCity orders: 6,140
A: Joel Thomas W: Joel Thomas; Mike Digesu

NIGHTVISION — Rebel

1 Nov 1996 Cover: 3.00 NM value: Cover or less
Circ: CapCity orders: 3,975 Diamd. preorders: 7,353
A: Hannibal King W: David Quinn
2 1997 Cover: 2.25 NM value: 2.50
A: Hannibal King W: David Quinn
3 1997 Cover: 2.25 NM value: 2.50
Circ: CapCity orders: 2,525
Love Bleeding Pictures A: Hannibal King W: David Quinn
4 1997 Cover: 2.25 NM value: 2.50
A: Hannibal King W: David Quinn
Bk 1 Cover: 14.95 NM value: Cover or less
A: Hannibal King W: David Quinn
Bk 1/LE Cover: 24.95 NM value: Cover or less
A: Hannibal King W: David Quinn

NIGHTVISION: ALL ABOUT EVE — London Night

1 Cover: 3.00 NM value: Cover or less
Expect The Unexpected...Tempest A: Kyle Hotz W: David Quinn

NIGHTVISION (ATOMEKA) — Atomeka

1 b&w Cover: 2.95 NM value: Cover or less
No issue number.

NIGHT VIXEN — ABC Studios

0/A b&w Cover: 3.00 NM value: Cover or less
0/B Cover: 5.00 NM value: Cover or less
• Eurotika Edition.
0/C Cover: 8.00 NM value: Cover or less
• Manga Flux Edition.

NIGHT WALKER — Fleetway-Quality

1 Cover: 2.95 NM value: Cover or less
• Reprints Luke Kirby story from 2000 A.D. A: John Ridgway W: Alan McKenzie
2 Cover: 2.95 NM value: Cover or less
• Reprints Luke Kirby story from 2000 A.D. A: John Ridgway W: Alan McKenzie
3 Cover: 2.95 NM value: Cover or less
• Reprints Luke Kirby story from 2000 A.D. A: John Ridgway W: Alan McKenzie

NIGHT WARRIORS: DARKSTALKERS' REVENGE THE COMIC SERIES — Viz

1 Nov 1998 Cover: 2.95 NM value: Cover or less
Circ: Diamd. preorders: 7,160
2 Dec 1998 Cover: 3.25 NM value: Cover or less
Circ: Diamd. preorders: 5,571
3 Jan 1999 Cover: 2.95 NM value: Cover or less
Circ: Diamd. preorders: 5,400
4 Feb 1999 Cover: 2.95 NM value: Cover or less
Circ: Diamd. preorders: 5,159
5 Mar 1999 Cover: 2.95 NM value: Cover or less
Circ: Diamd. preorders: 4,952
6 Apr 1999 Cover: 2.95 NM value: Cover or less
Circ: Diamd. preorders: 4,778

NIGHTWATCH — Marvel

1 Apr 1994 Cover: 1.50 NM value: Cover or less
★ Appearance of Spider-Man.
1/SC Apr 1994 Cover: 2.95 NM value: Cover or less
Circ: CapCity orders: 38,850
foil cover. ★ Appearance of Spider-Man.
2 May 1994 Cover: 1.50 NM value: Cover or less
Circ: CapCity orders: 18,800
3 Jun 1994 Cover: 1.50 NM value: Cover or less
Circ: CapCity orders: 15,600
Mechamorph A: Al Milgrom; Ron Lim; Keith Williams W: Terry Kavanagh
4 Jul 1994 Cover: 1.50 NM value: Cover or less
Circ: CapCity orders: 15,300
5 Aug 1994 Cover: 1.50 NM value: Cover or less
Circ: CapCity orders: 13,550
6 Sep 1994 Cover: 1.50 NM value: Cover or less
Circ: CapCity orders: 12,050
7 Oct 1994 Cover: 1.50 NM value: Cover or less
Circ: CapCity orders: 9,650
8 Nov 1994 Cover: 1.50 NM value: Cover or less
Circ: CapCity orders: 8,400
9 Dec 1994 Cover: 1.50 NM value: Cover or less
Circ: CapCity orders: 8,100
10 Jan 1995 Cover: 1.50 NM value: Cover or less
Circ: CapCity orders: 6,850
11 Feb 1995 Cover: 1.50 NM value: Cover or less
Circ: CapCity orders: 6,125
12 Mar 1995 Cover: 1.50 NM value: Cover or less
Circ: CapCity orders: 5,325
final issue.

NIGHTWING — DC

Dick Grayson was the original Robin, Batman's teen sidekick. He came under Batman's wing when his family, a group of circus performers, was murdered. Grayson served for years as the Boy Wonder, but eventually tired of living in Batman's shadow. Accordingly, he adopted the new identity of Nightwing and struck out on his own. In the years that followed he would become the leader of The New Teen Titans, as well as a respected crimefighter in his own right.

Comic readers had to wait 13 years for Nightwing to star in this, his first ongoing series. Kicking off in 1996, it follows upon the successful 1995 Nightwing mini-series, and takes Grayson into the one place worse than Gotham — the nearby city of Blndhaven. Founded by German whalers, Blndhaven once proclaimed itself "The Asbestos Capitol of America." Now it's home to gangs, corruption, and a new super-hero named Nightwing.

0.5 NM value: 4.00
• CGC: 6 graded, best 9.4
0.5/Pl NM value: 7.00
• Platinum edition.
1 Oct 1996 Cover: 1.95 NM value: 10.00
• CGC: 49 graded, best 9.9
Child Of Justice A: Scott McDaniel W: Chuck Dixon
2 Nov 1996 Cover: 1.95 NM value: 7.00
Circ: Diamd. preorders: 54,865 • CGC: 7 graded, best 9.8
Gangland Express A: Scott McDaniel W: Chuck Dixon
3 Dec 1996 Cover: 1.95 NM value: 5.00
Circ: Diamd. preorders: 56,676
The Freebooters A: Scott McDaniel W: Chuck Dixon
4 Jan 1997 Cover: 1.95 NM value: 4.50
Circ: Diamd. preorders: 54,323
Lady Be Deadly A: Scott McDaniel W: Chuck Dixon
5 Feb 1997 Cover: 1.95 NM value: 4.50
Circ: Diamd. preorders: 50,511
A: Scott McDaniel W: Chuck Dixon
6 Mar 1997 Cover: 1.95 NM value: 3.50
Circ: Diamd. preorders: 47,978
The Visitor A: Scott McDaniel W: Chuck Dixon
7 Apr 1997 Cover: 1.95 NM value: 3.50
Circ: Diamd. preorders: 44,945
A: Scott McDaniel W: Chuck Dixon
8 May 1997 Cover: 1.95 NM value: 3.50
Circ: Diamd. preorders: 44,219
A: Scott McDaniel W: Chuck Dixon
9 Jun 1997 Cover: 1.95 NM value: 3.50
Circ: Diamd. preorders: 44,608
Die Trying A: Scott McDaniel W: Chuck Dixon
10 Jul 1997 Cover: 1.95 NM value: 3.50
Circ: Diamd. preorders: 43,259
The Neighborhood A: Scott McDaniel W: Chuck Dixon ★ Versus Scarecrow.
11 Aug 1997 Cover: 1.95 NM value: 3.00
Circ: Diamd. preorders: 42,100
Fear Takes Flight A: Scott McDaniel W: Chuck Dixon ★ Versus Scarecrow.
12 Sep 1997 Cover: 1.95 NM value: 3.00
Circ: Diamd. preorders: 41,438
Mutt A: Scott McDaniel W: Chuck Dixon
13 Oct 1997 Cover: 1.95 NM value: 3.00
Circ: Diamd. preorders: 42,493 • CGC: 1 graded, best 9.2
Shadows over Blƒdhaven; Shadows over Blndhaven A: Scott McDaniel W: Chuck Dixon
14 Nov 1997 Cover: 1.95 NM value: 3.00
Circ: Diamd. preorders: 42,269
Dead Meat A: Scott McDaniel W: Chuck Dixon ★ Appearance of Batman.
15 Dec 1997 Cover: 1.95 NM value: 3.00
Circ: Diamd. preorders: 42,733
Face cover. Warriors Two A: Scott McDaniel W: Chuck Dixon ★ Appearance of Batman. ★ Versus Two-Face.
16 Jan 1998 Cover: 1.95 NM value: 2.50
Circ: Diamd. preorders: 42,820
Wheels A: Scott McDaniel W: Chuck Dixon
17 Feb 1998 Cover: 1.95 NM value: 2.50
Circ: Diamd. preorders: 43,563
The Stalking Skies A: Scott McDaniel W: Chuck Dixon
18 Mar 1998 Cover: 1.95 NM value: 2.50
Circ: Diamd. preorders: 42,733
The Hunting Moon A: Scott McDaniel W: Chuck Dixon
19 Apr 1998 Cover: 1.95 NM value: 2.50
Circ: Diamd. preorders: 47,056
Cataclysm, Part 2 • continues in Batman #553 A: Scott McDaniel W: Chuck Dixon
20 May 1998 Cover: 1.95 NM value: 2.50
Circ: Diamd. preorders: 47,712
Cataclysm, Part 11 • continues in Batman #554 A: Scott McDaniel W: Chuck Dixon
21 Jun 1998 Cover: 1.95 NM value: 2.50
Circ: Diamd. preorders: 46,339
A: Scott McDaniel W: Chuck Dixon ★ 1st Appearance of Nitewing. ★ Appearance of Blockbuster.
22 Jul 1998 Cover: 1.95 NM value: 2.50
Circ: Diamd. preorders: 45,317
A: Scott McDaniel W: Chuck Dixon ★ Versus Stallion. ★ Versus Brutale.
23 Aug 1998 Cover: 1.95 NM value: 2.50
Circ: Diamd. preorders: 46,897
Brotherhood of the Fist, Part 4 • concludes in Green Arrow #135 A: Scott McDaniel W: Chuck Dixon ★ Appearance of Lady Shiva.
24 Sep 1998 Cover: 1.99 NM value: 2.00
Circ: Diamd. preorders: 43,913
A: Scott McDaniel W: Chuck Dixon
25 Oct 1998 Cover: 1.99 NM value: 2.00
Circ: Diamd. preorders: 45,858
A: Scott McDaniel W: Chuck Dixon
26 Dec 1998 Cover: 1.99 NM value: 2.00
Circ: Diamd. preorders: 43,753
A: Scott McDaniel W: Chuck Dixon ★ Appearance of Huntress.
27 Jan 1999 Cover: 1.99 NM value: 2.00
Circ: Diamd. preorders: 43,776
A: Scott McDaniel W: Chuck Dixon ★ Appearance of Huntress.
28 Feb 1999 Cover: 1.99 NM value: 2.00
Circ: Diamd. preorders: 43,376
A: Scott McDaniel W: Chuck Dixon ★ 1st Appearance of Torque. ★ Appearance of Huntress.
29 Mar 1999 Cover: 1.99 NM value: 2.00
Circ: Diamd. preorders: 43,742
A: Scott McDaniel W: Chuck Dixon ★ Appearance of Huntress.
30 Apr 1999 Cover: 1.99 NM value: 2.00
Circ: Diamd. preorders: 43,061
A: Scott McDaniel W: Chuck Dixon ★ Appearance of Superman.
31 May 1999 Cover: 1.99 NM value: 2.00
Circ: Diamd. preorders: 42,936
Bad Night in Bludhaven • Dick joins the Bludhaven police force A: Scott McDaniel W: Chuck Dixon
32 Jun 1999 Cover: 1.99 NM value: 2.00
Circ: Diamd. preorders: 44,404
Double Dare A: Scott McDaniel W: Chuck Dixon
33 Jul 1999 Cover: 1.99 NM value: 2.00
Circ: Diamd. preorders: 43,904
Acts of Violence A: Scott McDaniel W: Chuck Dixon
34 Aug 1999 Cover: 1.99 NM value: 2.00
Circ: Diamd. preorders: 44,541
Sister Act A: Scott McDaniel W: Chuck Dixon
35 Sep 1999 Cover: 1.99 NM value: Cover or less
Circ: Diamd. preorders: 45,280
Escape to Blackgate, Part 1 • No Man's Land A: Scott McDaniel W: Chuck Dixon
36 Oct 1999 Cover: 1.99 NM value: Cover or less
Circ: Diamd. preorders: 44,184
Escape to Blackgate, Part 2; Nothing But Time • No Man's Land A: Scott McDaniel W: Chuck Dixon
37 Nov 1999 Cover: 1.99 NM value: Cover or less
Circ: Diamd. preorders: 44,145
Escape to Blackgate, Part 3; Escape from Blackgate • No Man's Land A: Scott McDaniel W: Chuck Dixon
38 Dec 2000 Cover: 1.99 NM value: Cover or less
Circ: Diamd. preorders: 45,953
Ballistic Romance, Part 1 • No Man's Land A: Scott McDaniel W: Chuck Dixon
39 Jan 2000 Cover: 1.99 NM value: Cover or less
Circ: Diamd. preorders: 45,043
Ballistic Romance, Part 2 A: Scott McDaniel W: Chuck Dixon
40 Feb 2000 Cover: 1.99 NM value: Cover or less
Circ: Diamd. preorders: 43,415
The Devil Dies at Dawn A: Scott McDaniel W: Chuck Dixon
41 Mar 2000 Cover: 1.99 NM value: Cover or less
Circ: Diamd. preorders: 43,087
W: Chuck Dixon
42 Apr 2000 Cover: 1.99 NM value: Cover or less
Circ: Diamd. preorders: 40,476
W: Chuck Dixon
43 May 2000 Cover: 1.99 NM value: Cover or less
Circ: Diamd. preorders: 41,047
Improper Angles A: Patrick Zircher; Greg Land W: Chuck Dixon
44 Jun 2000 Cover: 1.99 NM value: Cover or less
Circ: Diamd. preorders: 41,155
The Stalkers A: Patrick Zircher W: Chuck Dixon
45 Jul 2000 Cover: 1.99 NM value: Cover or less
Circ: Diamd. preorders: 42,713
W: Chuck Dixon
46 Aug 2000 Cover: 1.99 NM value: Cover or less
Circ: Diamd. preorders: 42,693
W: Chuck Dixon
47 Sep 2000 Cover: 1.99 NM value: Cover or less
Circ: Diamd. preorders: 41,569
W: Chuck Dixon
48 Oct 2000 Cover: 2.25 NM value: Cover or less
Circ: Diamd. preorders: 39,495
The Sylph, Part 1 A: Greg Land W: Chuck Dixon
49 Nov 2000 Cover: 2.25 NM value: Cover or less
Circ: Diamd. preorders: 39,742
Dangled A: Greg Land W: Chuck Dixon
50 Dec 2000 Cover: 3.50 NM value: Cover or less
Circ: Diamd. preorders: 40,803
Big Guns A: Greg Land W: Chuck Dixon
51 Jan 2001 Cover: 2.25 NM value: Cover or less
Circ: Diamd. preorders: 38,780
Tad A: Kieron Dwyer W: Chuck Dixon
52 Feb 2001 Cover: 2.25 NM value: Cover or less
Circ: Diamd. preorders: 41,029
Modern Romance A: Greg Land W: Chuck Dixon ★ Appearance of Catwoman.
53 Mar 2001 Cover: 2.25 NM value: Cover or less
Circ: Diamd. preorders: 41,645
Officer Down, Part 5 A: Rick Burchett W: Devin Grayson
54 Apr 2001 Cover: 2.25 NM value: Cover or less
Circ: Diamd. preorders: 37,705
In the Middle of the Cold, Cold Night A: Greg Land W: Chuck Dixon
55 May 2001 Cover: 2.25 NM value: Cover or less
Circ: Diamd. preorders: 37,581
Love & Death A: Greg Land W: Chuck Dixon
56 Jun 2001 Cover: 2.25 NM value: Cover or less
Circ: Diamd. preorders: 38,279
Stalked A: Greg Land W: Chuck Dixon
57 Jul 2001 Cover: 2.25 NM value: Cover or less
Circ: Diamd. preorders: 37,868

CGC-graded: Multiply prices above by **33 for 9.9 M • 16 for 9.8 NM/M • 7 for 9.6 NM+ • 5 for 9.4 NM • 2.5 for 9.2 NM- • 1.5 for 9.0 VF/NM**

58 ❑ Aug 2001 Cover: 2.25 **NM** value: **Cover or less**
Circ: Diamd. preorders: **38,745**

59 ❑ Sep 2001 Cover: 2.25 **NM** value: **Cover or less**
Circ: Diamd. preorders: **40,110**

1000000❑Nov 1998 Cover: 1.99 **NM** value: **Cover or less**
Circ: Diamd. preorders: **51,831**
The Anachronism **A:** Scott McDaniel **W:** Chuck Dixon

Anl 1❑ca. 1997 Cover: 3.95 **NM** value: **Cover or less**
Circ: Diamd. preorders: **38,834**
• Pulp Heroes

Bk 1❑ Cover: 14.95 **NM** value: **Cover or less**
• A Knight in Bludhaven; collects issues #1-8

Bk 2❑ Cover: 17.95 **NM** value: **Cover or less**
• Rough Justice; collects issues #9-18

Bk 3❑ Cover: 17.95 **NM** value: **Cover or less**
• Love and Bullets; Collects Nightwing 0.5, 19, 21-22. 24-29 **A:** Scott McDaniel **W:** Chuck Dixon

Bk 4❑ Cover: 19.95 **NM** value: **Cover or less**
• A Darker Shade of Justice; Collects Nightwing #30-39, Secret Files #1 **A:** Scott McDaniel **W:** Chuck Dixon

GS 1❑Dec 2000 Cover: 5.95 **NM** value: **Cover or less**
Circ: Diamd. preorders: **26,453**
Hella **A:** Mike Collins; John Stanisci; Manuel Gutierrez; Sean Parsons; Steve Bird **W:** Chuck Dixon

NIGHTWING: ALFRED'S RETURN — DC

1 ❑ Jul 1995 Cover: 3.50 **NM** value: **Cover or less**
Circ: CapCity orders: **22,025**
One-shot. **A:** Dick Giordano

NIGHTWING AND HUNTRESS — DC

1 ❑ May 1998 Cover: 1.95 **NM** value: **2.00**
Circ: Diamd. preorders: **40,953**
Cosa Nostra, Part 1 **W:** Devin Grayson

2 ❑ Jun 1998 Cover: 1.95 **NM** value: **2.00**
Circ: Diamd. preorders: **38,765**
Cosa Nostra, Part 2 **A:** Bill Sienkiewicz; Greg Land **W:** Devin Grayson

3 ❑ Jul 1998 Cover: 1.95 **NM** value: **2.00**
Circ: Diamd. preorders: **37,402**

4 ❑ Aug 1998 Cover: 1.95 **NM** value: **2.00**
Circ: Diamd. preorders: **39,209**

NIGHTWING (MINI-SERIES) — DC

1 ❑ Sep 1995 Cover: 2.25 **NM** value: **3.50**
Circ: CapCity orders: **28,400** • **CGC:** 3 graded, best 9.6
The Resignation **A:** Greg Land **W:** Denny O'Neil

2 ❑ Oct 1995 Cover: 2.25 **NM** value: **2.50**
Circ: CapCity orders: **19,375** • **CGC:** 1 graded, best 9.0
A: Greg Land **W:** Denny O'Neil

3 ❑ Nov 1995 Cover: 2.25 **NM** value: **2.50**
• **CGC:** 1 graded, best 9.2
A: Greg Land **W:** Denny O'Neil

4 ❑ Dec 1995 Cover: 2.25 **NM** value: **2.50**
• **CGC:** 1 graded, best 9.2
A: Greg Land **W:** Denny O'Neil

Bk 1❑ Cover: 12.95 **NM** value: **Cover or less**
• Ties that Bind; collects mini-series and Nightwing: Alfred's Return **A:** Greg Land **W:** Denny O'Neil

NIGHTWING SECRET FILES — DC

1 ❑ Oct 1999 Cover: 4.95 **NM** value: **Cover or less**
Circ: Diamd. preorders: **30,671**
Taking Wing; Lost Pages: Teen Titans; Day in he Life of Nite-Wing; Blƒdhaven Underground Notes; Nightwings's Romances; Blndhaven Underground Notes • background information on series **A:** Damion Scott; Brian Stelfreeze; Phil Jimenez; Dale Eaglesham; Scott McDaniel; Andy Kuhn; Greg Land; Butch Guice **W:** Eliot Brown; Scott Beatty; Chuck Dixon; Devin Grayson

NIGHTWING: TIES THAT BIND — DC

1 ❑ Cover: 12.95 **NM** value: **Cover or less**
• Collects story from Nightwing: Alfred's Return & Nightwing #1-4 **A:** Dick Giordano; Nick Napolitano; Greg Land; Mike Sellers **W:** Alan Grant; Dennis O'Neil

NIGHTWOLF — Entropy

1 ❑ Cover: 1.50 **NM** value: **Cover or less**
Circ: CapCity orders: **2,375**
King of Spades **A:** Peter Krause **W:** Peter Krause

2 ❑ Cover: 1.50 **NM** value: **Cover or less**
Circ: CapCity orders: **1,800**
A: Peter Krause **W:** Peter Krause

NIGHT ZERO — Fleetway-Quality

1 ❑ b&w Cover: 1.95 **NM** value: **Cover or less**
2 ❑ b&w Cover: 1.95 **NM** value: **Cover or less**
3 ❑ b&w Cover: 1.95 **NM** value: **Cover or less**
A: Kev Hopgood **W:** John Brosnan
4 ❑ b&w Cover: 1.95 **NM** value: **Cover or less**

NIKKI BLADE SUMMER FUN — ABC Studios

All issues are adults only.

1/A ❑ b&w Cover: 3.00 **NM** value: **Cover or less**
1/B ❑ Cover: 3.00 **NM** value: **Cover or less**
solo figure on cover.

NIMROD, THE — Fantagraphics

1 ❑ Jun 1998, b&w Cover: 2.95 **NM** value: **Cover or less**
2 ❑ Aug 1998, b&w Cover: 2.95 **NM** value: **Cover or less**

NINA'S ALL-TIME GREATEST COLLECTORS' ITEM CLASSIC COMICS — Dark Horse

1 ❑ Aug 1992, b&w Cover: 2.25 **NM** value: **2.50**
A Popular Gal; Big Editor Boss-Man; Underground Comix; Ugly Movies In My Head; Deep In The Heart Of Texas **A:** Nina Paley **W:** Nina Paley

NINA'S NEW & IMPROVED ALL-TIME GREATEST COLLECTORS' ITEM CLASSIC COMICS — Dark Horse

1 ❑ Feb 1994, b&w Cover: 2.50 **NM** value: **Cover or less**
The Pet; I Was A Teenage Hairball; Kute Klitty Kartoon; Masochist; The Tragedy Of afrAIDS; Agonisticism **A:** Nina Paley **W:** Nina Paley

NINE LIVES OF FELIX THE CAT — Harvey

1 ❑ Cover: 1.25 **NM** value: **1.50**
Circ: CapCity orders: **4,950**
2 ❑ Cover: 1.25 **NM** value: **1.50**
Circ: CapCity orders: **2,875**
3 ❑ Cover: 1.25 **NM** value: **1.50**
Circ: CapCity orders: **2,275**
4 ❑ Cover: 1.25 **NM** value: **1.50**
5 ❑ Cover: 1.25 **NM** value: **1.50**

NINE LIVES OF LEATHER CAT, THE — Forbidden Fruit

1 ❑ Cover: 3.50 **NM** value: **Cover or less**
★ Origin of Leather Cat. ★ 1st Appearance of Leather Cat.
2 ❑ Cover: 3.50 **NM** value: **Cover or less**
3 ❑ Cover: 3.50 **NM** value: **Cover or less**
4 ❑ Cover: 3.50 **NM** value: **Cover or less**
5 ❑ Cover: 3.50 **NM** value: **Cover or less**
6 ❑ Cover: 3.50 **NM** value: **Cover or less**

NINE RINGS OF WU-TANG, THE — Image

0 ❑ Nov 1999 **NM** value: **2.00**
• Giveaway bundled with Wizard Magazine. **A:** Clayton Henry **W:** Brian Haberlin; Aaron Bullock

1/A ❑ Nov 1999 Cover: 2.95 **NM** value: **Cover or less**
Circ: Diamd. preorders: **29,235**
Woman with bow reclining on cover with jungle cats. **A:** Clayton Henry **W:** Brian Haberlin; Aaron Bullock

1/B ❑ Nov 1999 Cover: 2.95 **NM** value: **Cover or less**
• Tower Records variant **A:** Clayton Henry **W:** Brian Haberlin; Aaron Bullock

2 ❑ Dec 1999 Cover: 2.95 **NM** value: **Cover or less**
Circ: Diamd. preorders: **17,481**
A: Clayton Henry **W:** Brian Haberlin; Aaron Bullock

3 ❑ Feb 2000 Cover: 2.95 **NM** value: **Cover or less**
Circ: Diamd. preorders: **15,334**
A: Clayton Henry **W:** Brian Haberlin; Aaron Bullock

4 ❑ Apr 2000 Cover: 2.95 **NM** value: **Cover or less**
Circ: Diamd. preorders: **15,166**
A: Clayton Henry **W:** Brian Haberlin; Aaron Bullock

5 ❑ Jul 2000 Cover: 2.95 **NM** value: **Cover or less**
Circ: Diamd. preorders: **14,273**
A: Clayton Henry **W:** Aaron Bullock

Bk 1❑ Cover: 19.95 **NM** value: **Cover or less**
• Collects series **A:** Clayton Henry **W:** Aaron Bullock

1984 MAGAZINE — Warren

1 ❑ Jun 1978 Cover: 1.50 **NM** value: **6.00**
2 ❑ Aug 1978 Cover: 1.50 **NM** value: **4.00**
3 ❑ Sep 1978 Cover: 1.50 **NM** value: **4.00**
4 ❑ Oct 1978 Cover: 1.75 **NM** value: **4.00**
5 ❑ Feb 1979 Cover: 1.50 **NM** value: **4.00**
6 ❑ Jun 1979 Cover: 1.50 **NM** value: **4.00**
7 ❑ Aug 1979 Cover: 1.75 **NM** value: **4.00**
8 ❑ Sep 1979 Cover: 1.50 **NM** value: **4.00**
9 ❑ Oct 1979 Cover: 1.75 **NM** value: **4.00**
10 ❑ Dec 1980 Cover: 1.75 **NM** value: **4.00**
• Series continued in 1994 #11

1994 MAGAZINE — Warren

11 ❑ Feb 1980 Cover: 1.75 **NM** value: **3.00**
• Series continued from 1984 #10
12 ❑ Apr 1980 Cover: 1.75 **NM** value: **3.00**
13 ❑ Jun 1980 Cover: 1.75 **NM** value: **3.00**
14 ❑ Aug 1980 Cover: 1.75 **NM** value: **3.00**
15 ❑ Oct 1980 Cover: 1.75 **NM** value: **3.00**
16 ❑ Dec 1980 Cover: 1.95 **NM** value: **3.00**
Telemetry; Sci-Fi Writer; Dog Star; Agony; Doomsday; Starfire Saga; Baby; Fruit **A:** Abel Laxamana; Rudy Nebres; Luis Bermejo; Carlos Gimenez; Delando Niño; Alex Ni±o **W:** Carlos Gimenez; John Ellis Sech; Kevin Duane; Nicola Cuti; Will Richardson
17 ❑ Feb 1981 Cover: 1.95 **NM** value: **3.00**
18 ❑ Apr 1981 Cover: 2.00 **NM** value: **3.00**
Telemetry; Lost Love; Lone Wolf; Mad Planet; Ghita; Starfire Saga **A:** Frank Thorne; Rudy Nebres; Delando Niño; Vic Catan; Alex Ni±o **W:** Frank Thorne; Gerry Boudreau; John Ellis Sech; Will Richardson
19 ❑ Jun 1981 Cover: 2.00 **NM** value: **3.00**
20 ❑ Aug 1981 Cover: 2.00 **NM** value: **3.00**
21 ❑ Oct 1981 Cover: 2.00 **NM** value: **3.00**
Telemetry; Lord Machina; Jacklighter; Love is a Many Tentacled Thing; Ghita; Angel; Mars Bar; Freefall **A:** Frank Thorne; Esteban Maroto; Rudy Nebres; Delando Niño; Redondo Studios; Alex Ni±o **W:** Frank Thorne; Alabaster Redzone; Gerry Boudreau; Will Richardson
22 ❑ Dec 1981 Cover: 2.00 **NM** value: **3.00**
23 ❑ Feb 1982 Cover: 2.00 **NM** value: **3.00**
24 ❑ Apr 1982 Cover: 2.00 **NM** value: **3.00**
25 ❑ Jun 1982 Cover: 2.00 **NM** value: **3.00**
26 ❑ Aug 1982 Cover: 2.00 **NM** value: **3.00**
27 ❑ Oct 1982 Cover: 2.00 **NM** value: **3.00**
28 ❑ Dec 1982 Cover: 2.00 **NM** value: **3.00**
29 ❑ Feb 1983 Cover: 2.25 **NM** value: **3.00**
final issue.

1963 — Image

1 ❑ Apr 1993 Cover: 1.95 **NM** value: **2.00**
Circ: CapCity orders: **149,625**
Mayhem on Mystery Mile • Mystery Incorporated **A:** Dave Gibbons; Rick Veitch **W:** Alan Moore

1/BR❑Apr 1993 **NM** value: **5.00**
• Promotional limited edition. **A:** Dave Gibbons **W:** Alan Moore

1/GO❑Apr 1993 **NM** value: **5.00**
• Gold edition. • Profits donated to cancer research **A:** Dave Gibbons **W:** Alan Moore

1/SI❑ Apr 1993 **NM** value: **5.00**
• silver edition. • Profits donated to cancer research **A:** Dave Gibbons **W:** Alan Moore

2 ❑ May 1993 Cover: 1.95 **NM** value: **2.00**
Circ: CapCity orders: **102,200**
When Wakes The War Beast! • No One Escapes...the Fury **A:** Stephen R. Bissette **W:** Alan Moore

3 ❑ Jun 1993 Cover: 1.95 **NM** value: **2.00**
Circ: CapCity orders: **58,675**
Tales of the Uncanny; Double Deal in Dallas!; The Hypernaut!: It Came From…Higher Space! • Tales of the Uncanny **A:** Rick Veitch; Stephen R. Bissette **W:** Alan Moore

4 ❑ Jul 1993 Cover: 1.95 **NM** value: **2.00**
Circ: CapCity orders: **42,400**
Tales From Beyond; Showdown in the Shimmering Zone!; Flips-ville! • Tales From Beyond; Johnny Beyond **A:** Stephen R. Bissette **W:** Jim Valentino; Alan Moore

5 ❑ Aug 1993 Cover: 1.95 **NM** value: **2.00**
Circ: CapCity orders: **33,300**
Horus, Lord of Light **A:** Rick Veitch **W:** Alan Moore

6 ❑ Oct 1993 Cover: 1.95 **NM** value: **2.00**
Circ: CapCity orders: **28,875**
The Tomorrow Syndicate **W:** Alan Moore

NINETY-NINE GIRLS — Fantagraphics / Eros

All issues are adults only.

1 ❑ b&w Cover: 2.25 **NM** value: **Cover or less**

NINE VOLT — Image

1 ❑ Jul 1997 Cover: 2.50 **NM** value: **Cover or less**
Circ: Diamd. preorders: **44,596**
A: Anthony Chun **W:** Anthony Chun; Cliff Son ★ 1st Appearance of Digit.

1/A ❑ Jul 1997 Cover: 2.50 **NM** value: **Cover or less**
Circ: Diamd. preorders: **16,162**
alternate cover.

2 ❑ Aug 1997 Cover: 2.50 **NM** value: **Cover or less**
Circ: Diamd. preorders: **29,388**
A: Anthony Chun **W:** Anthony Chun; Cliff Son

3 ❑ Sep 1997 Cover: 2.50 **NM** value: **Cover or less**
Circ: Diamd. preorders: **25,988**
A: Anthony Chun **W:** Anthony Chun; Cliff Son

4 ❑ Oct 1997 Cover: 2.50 **NM** value: **Cover or less**
Circ: Diamd. preorders: **25,030**
A: Anthony Chun **W:** Anthony Chun; Cliff Son

NINJA — Eternity

SE 1❑ b&w Cover: 2.25 **NM** value: **Cover or less**

NINJA-BOTS SUPER SPECIAL — Pied Piper

1 ❑ Cover: 1.95 **NM** value: **Cover or less**

NINJA BOY — WildStorm

Ash 1❑ **NM** value: **0.50**
• Ashcan preview; Flip book with Out There Ash #1 **A:** Alé Garza

NINJA ELITE — Adventure

1 ❑ Cover: 1.50 **NM** value: **Cover or less**
7-1/2x8-1/2" version with black-and-white cover. **A:** James Fletcher **W:** Scott Behnke
1-2 ❑ Cover: 1.50 **NM** value: **Cover or less**
2 ❑ Jul 1987 Cover: 1.50 **NM** value: **Cover or less**
3 ❑ 1987 Cover: 1.50 **NM** value: **Cover or less**
4 ❑ Dec 1987 Cover: 1.95 **NM** value: **Cover or less**
5 ❑ Cover: 1.95 **NM** value: **Cover or less**
6 ❑ Cover: 1.95 **NM** value: **Cover or less**
7 ❑ Cover: 1.95 **NM** value: **Cover or less**
8 ❑ Cover: 1.95 **NM** value: **Cover or less**

NINJA FUNNIES — Eternity

1 ❑ Jan 1987 Cover: 1.40 **NM** value: **1.50**
A: Dale W. Berry **W:** Dale W. Berry
2 ❑ Cover: 1.95 **NM** value: **Cover or less**
A: Dale W. Berry **W:** Dale W. Berry
3 ❑ Cover: 1.95 **NM** value: **Cover or less**
A: Dale W. Berry **W:** Dale W. Berry
4 ❑ Cover: 1.95 **NM** value: **Cover or less**
A: Dale W. Berry **W:** Dale W. Berry
5 ❑ Cover: 1.95 **NM** value: **Cover or less**
A: Dale W. Berry **W:** Dale W. Berry

NINJA HIGH SCHOOL — Antarctic

The young ninja, Itchy Koo, is sent to the U.S. in order to convince high school student Jeremy Peeples to marry her. Unfortunately, extra-terrestrial Princess Asrial of the Royal Conglomerate (she reminds everyone of her title and stature frequently, so don't you dare forget it!) has come to Earth for just the same reason. The two girls are left to fight it out at Quagmire High School. Throw in two wacky professors, the "Kenterminator," and a mysterious woman in leather, and you've got a hilarious spoof of Japanese comics, complete with Japanese-style animation and plot.

Artist Ben Dunn never could understand the Japanese comic books he collected, but he remem-

Other grades: Multiply prices above by **1.5 for Mint • 2/3 for Very Fine • 1/3 for Fine • 1/5 for Very Good • 1/8 for Good**

bered one series that featured characters who seemed to be eternally in high school. He called it Ninja High School — and even though he later found out the series' real name, he still couldn't remember it. This is his tribute, so to speak, to one of Japan's best exports.

0 ❑ Jan 1994, b&w Cover: 2.75 **NM** value: **3.00**
Circ: CapCity orders: **3,415**
• Antarctic publishes

0/LE❑ b&w Cover: 2.75 **NM** value: **4.00**
• foil cover edition (500 made).

1 ❑ Cover: 1.50 **NM** value: **7.00**
A: Ben Dunn **W:** Ben Dunn

1-2 ❑ Cover: 1.50 **NM** value: **2.50**

2 ❑ Cover: 1.95 **NM** value: **5.00**
A: Ben Dunn **W:** Ben Dunn

2-2 ❑ **NM** value: **2.00**

3 ❑ Cover: 1.95 **NM** value: **4.00**
A: Ben Dunn **W:** Ben Dunn

3-2 ❑ **NM** value: **2.00**

4 ❑ Cover: 1.95 **NM** value: **4.00**
A: Ben Dunn **W:** Ben Dunn

4-2 ❑ **NM** value: **2.00**

5 ❑ Jun 1988, b&w Cover: 1.95 **NM** value: **4.00**
• Eternity begins publishing **A:** Ben Dunn **W:** Ben Dunn

6 ❑ Cover: 1.95 **NM** value: **3.50**
A: Ben Dunn **W:** Ben Dunn

6-2 ❑ Cover: 1.95 **NM** value: **2.00**

7 ❑ Sep 1988 Cover: 1.95 **NM** value: **3.50**
Ben Dunn's Girls; I Only Have Bobbed for You; Virtua Ninja; Generation NHS; By The Tail; Pack Hunters; Cram'n; Ninja High Crisis; Li'l Asrial **A:** Ben Dunn **W:** Ben Dunn

8 ❑ Dec 1988 Cover: 1.95 **NM** value: **3.50**
A: Ben Dunn **W:** Ben Dunn

9 ❑ Feb 1989 Cover: 1.95 **NM** value: **3.50**
A: Ben Dunn **W:** Ben Dunn

10 ❑ Mar 1989 Cover: 1.95 **NM** value: **3.50**
A: Ben Dunn **W:** Ben Dunn

11 ❑ May 1989 Cover: 1.95 **NM** value: **3.00**
A: Ben Dunn **W:** Ben Dunn

12 ❑ 1989 Cover: 1.95 **NM** value: **3.00**
A: Ben Dunn **W:** Ben Dunn

13 ❑ 1989 Cover: 1.95 **NM** value: **3.00**
A: Ben Dunn **W:** Ben Dunn

14 ❑ 1989 Cover: 1.95 **NM** value: **3.00**
A: Ben Dunn **W:** Ben Dunn

15 ❑ 1989 Cover: 1.95 **NM** value: **3.00**
A: Ben Dunn **W:** Ben Dunn

16 ❑ b&w Cover: 1.95 **NM** value: **2.50**
A: Ben Dunn **W:** Ben Dunn

17 ❑ b&w Cover: 1.95 **NM** value: **2.50**
A: Ben Dunn **W:** Ben Dunn

18 ❑ b&w Cover: 1.95 **NM** value: **2.50**
A: Ben Dunn **W:** Ben Dunn

19 ❑ b&w Cover: 1.95 **NM** value: **2.50**
A: Ben Dunn **W:** Ben Dunn

20 ❑ b&w Cover: 1.95 **NM** value: **2.50**
21 ❑ b&w Cover: 1.95 **NM** value: **2.50**
22 ❑ b&w Cover: 1.95 **NM** value: **2.50**
23 ❑ Cover: 2.25 **NM** value: **Cover or less**
24 ❑ Cover: 2.25 **NM** value: **Cover or less**
25 ❑ Cover: 2.25 **NM** value: **Cover or less**
26 ❑ Cover: 2.25 **NM** value: **Cover or less**
27 ❑ Cover: 2.25 **NM** value: **Cover or less**
28 ❑ Cover: 2.25 **NM** value: **Cover or less**
29 ❑ Cover: 2.25 **NM** value: **Cover or less**
30 ❑ Cover: 2.25 **NM** value: **Cover or less**
31 ❑ 1992 Cover: 2.25 **NM** value: **Cover or less**
32 ❑ 1992b&w Cover: 2.50 **NM** value: **Cover or less**
33 ❑ May 1992, b&w Cover: 2.50 **NM** value: **Cover or less**
34 ❑ b&w Cover: 2.50 **NM** value: **Cover or less**
35 ❑ b&w Cover: 2.50 **NM** value: **Cover or less**
36 ❑ b&w Cover: 2.50 **NM** value: **Cover or less**
37 ❑ b&w Cover: 2.50 **NM** value: **Cover or less**
38 ❑ b&w Cover: 2.50 **NM** value: **Cover or less**
39 ❑ b&w Cover: 2.50 **NM** value: **Cover or less**
Circ: CapCity orders: **2,930**

40 ❑ Jun 1994, b&w Cover: 2.75 **NM** value: **Cover or less**
Circ: CapCity orders: **3,430**
Aftermath **A:** Ben Dunn **W:** Ben Dunn

40/LE❑Jun 1994, b&w Cover: 2.75 **NM** value: **3.00**
• gold foil logo edition (500 made).

41 ❑ Jul 1994, b&w Cover: 2.75 **NM** value: **Cover or less**
Circ: CapCity orders: **3,475**
Enter: The Y-Men **A:** Ben Dunn **W:** Herb Mallette

42 ❑ Sep 1994, b&w Cover: 2.75 **NM** value: **Cover or less**
Circ: CapCity orders: **3,070**
Secrets or Everybody's Got Something to Hide **A:** Ben Dunn **W:** Herb Mallette

43 ❑ Nov 1994, b&w Cover: 2.75 **NM** value: **Cover or less**
Circ: CapCity orders: **2,810**
What Goes Around Comes Around **A:** Ben Dunn **W:** Herb Mallette

44 ❑ Jan 1995, b&w Cover: 2.75 **NM** value: **Cover or less**
Circ: CapCity orders: **2,600**
Boy Meets-Girl...Cobra Meets Mongoose! **A:** Fred Perry **W:** Fred Perry

45 ❑ Mar 1995, b&w Cover: 2.75 **NM** value: **Cover or less**
Grudge-Mismatch **A:** Fred Perry **W:** Fred Perry

46 ❑ May 1995, b&w Cover: 2.75 **NM** value: **Cover or less**
Circ: CapCity orders: **2,610**
The Return of the Giant Monsters, Part 1; Redeemer, Part 1 **A:** Matt Lunsford; Mike Sagara **W:** John Marshall; Kris Overstreet

47 ❑ Jul 1995, b&w Cover: 2.75 **NM** value: **Cover or less**
Circ: CapCity orders: **2,575**
The Return of the Giant Monsters, Part 2; Redeemer, Part 2 **A:** Matt Lunsford; Mike Sagara **W:** John Marshall; Kris Overstreet

48 ❑ Sep 1995, b&w Cover: 2.75 **NM** value: **Cover or less**
The Return of the Giant Monsters, Part 3 **A:** Matt Lunsford **W:** John Marshall

49 ❑ Nov 1995, b&w Cover: 2.75 **NM** value: **Cover or less**

50 ❑ Jan 1996, b&w Cover: 3.95 **NM** value: **Cover or less**
Crossroads; Redeemer; The Incredible Battle of the Iron Sushi Chefs; Smooth Operetta; Street Fighters; Dunne **A:** Ben Dunn; Mike Sagara; David Matsuoka; Joel Christian; Kenichi; Nathan Bonner **W:** Ben Dunn; David Matsuoka; Joel Christian; Kenichi; Kurt Wilcken; Nathan Bonner; Kris Overstreet

51 ❑ Apr 1996, b&w Cover: 2.95 **NM** value: **Cover or less**
Car Wash Freakin' Monster Rally Thing! **A:** Mike Sagara **W:** John Marshall

52 ❑ Jun 1996, b&w Cover: 2.95 **NM** value: **Cover or less**
A: Fred Perry

53 ❑ Sep 1996, b&w Cover: 2.95 **NM** value: **Cover or less**
Circ: Diamd. preorders: **4,694**
A: Fred Perry

54 ❑ Nov 1996, b&w Cover: 2.95 **NM** value: **Cover or less**
Circ: Diamd. preorders: **4,825**
Time Warp, Part 2 **A:** Fred Perry

55 ❑ Jan 1997, b&w Cover: 2.95 **NM** value: **Cover or less**
Circ: Diamd. preorders: **4,678**
Time Warp, Part 4 **A:** Fred Perry

56 ❑ Mar 1997, b&w Cover: 2.95 **NM** value: **Cover or less**
Circ: Diamd. preorders: **4,582**
Time Warp, Part 6

57 ❑ May 1997, b&w Cover: 2.95 **NM** value: **Cover or less**
Circ: Diamd. preorders: **4,670**
Time Warp, Part 8; Redeemer, Part 9 **A:** Rod Espinosa **W:** Kris Overstreet

58 ❑ Aug 1997, b&w Cover: 2.95 **NM** value: **Cover or less**
Circ: Diamd. preorders: **4,692**
Dangerous (Diplomatic) Liasons; We're Off to Outer Space, Part 1 **A:** Duc Tran; Ben Dunn **W:** Ben Dunn; Herb Mallette

59 ❑ Oct 1997, b&w Cover: 2.95 **NM** value: **Cover or less**
Circ: Diamd. preorders: **4,400**
Learning Curves; We're Off to Outer Space, Part 2 **A:** Ben Dunn; Steven Henry **W:** Ben Dunn; Herb Mallette

60 ❑ Dec 1997, b&w Cover: 2.95 **NM** value: **Cover or less**
Circ: Diamd. preorders: **4,311**
Pet Theories **A:** Steven Henry **W:** Herb Mallette

61 ❑ Feb 1998, b&w Cover: 2.95 **NM** value: **Cover or less**
Circ: Diamd. preorders: **3,901**
Humble Pie **A:** Steven Henry **W:** Herb Mallette

62 ❑ Apr 1998, b&w Cover: 2.95 **NM** value: **Cover or less**
Circ: Diamd. preorders: **4,036**
Local Yokels **A:** Rod Espinosa **W:** Herb Mallette

63 ❑ Jun 1998, b&w Cover: 2.95 **NM** value: **Cover or less**
Circ: Diamd. preorders: **3,821**

64 ❑ Aug 1998, b&w Cover: 2.95 **NM** value: **Cover or less**
Circ: Diamd. preorders: **3,479**

65 ❑ Oct 1998, b&w Cover: 2.95 **NM** value: **Cover or less**
Circ: Diamd. preorders: **3,415**
Barring the Unexpected **A:** Rod Espinosa **W:** Herb Mallette

66 ❑ Dec 1998, b&w Cover: 2.95 **NM** value: **Cover or less**
Circ: Diamd. preorders: **3,174**
Wish in a Bottle **A:** Steven Henry **W:** Herb Mallette

67 ❑ Mar 1999, b&w Cover: 2.95 **NM** value: **2.99**
Circ: Diamd. preorders: **3,102**
Crossed Dressed Purposes **A:** Rod Espinosa **W:** Herb Mallette

68 ❑ Apr 1999, b&w Cover: 2.99 **NM** value: **Cover or less**
Circ: Diamd. preorders: **3,214**
Strained Nerves in Paradise **A:** Steven Henry **W:** Herb Mallette

69 ❑ Jun 1999, b&w Cover: 2.99 **NM** value: **Cover or less**
Circ: Diamd. preorders: **3,005**
Prenuptial Aggrievance **A:** Steven Henry **W:** Herb Mallette

3D 1❑Jul 1992 Cover: 3.50 **NM** value: **4.50**
• Trade Paperback.

Bk 1❑ b&w Cover: 6.95 **NM** value: **14.95**
Bk 1-2❑ Cover: 9.95 **NM** value: **Cover or less**
Bk 2❑ Cover: 9.95 **NM** value: **Cover or less**
• Beware of Dog

Bk 3❑ Cover: 9.95 **NM** value: **Cover or less**
• Beans, Steam & Automobiles

Bk 4❑ Cover: 9.95 **NM** value: **Cover or less**
Of Rats and Men

Bk 5❑ Dec 1997 Cover: 14.95 **NM** value: **Cover or less**
• Collects Ninja High School #16-18

Bk 6❑ Jun 1996 Cover: 10.95 **NM** value: **Cover or less**
• Collects Ninja High School #19-21

Bk 7❑ Jul 1995 Cover: 7.95 **NM** value: **Cover or less**
• Collects Ninja High School #22-24

Bk 8❑ Sep 1995 Cover: 7.95 **NM** value: **Cover or less**
• Collects Ninja High School #25-27

Bk 9❑ Dec 1996 Cover: 10.95 **NM** value: **Cover or less**
• Collects Ninja High School #28-31

Bk 10❑Feb 1999 Cover: 10.95 **NM** value: **Cover or less**
• Collects Ninja High School #32-35

Bk 11❑ Cover: 10.95 **NM** value: **Cover or less**
Shades Of Grey • Collects Ninja High School #36-39 **A:** Ben Dunn **W:** Ben Dunn ★ 1st Appearance of Magic Priest (Warrior Nun Areala prototype).

Bk 12❑ Cover: 10.95 **NM** value: **Cover or less**
• Collects Ninja High School #40-43 **A:** Ben Dunn **W:** Ben Dunn; Herb Mallette

Smr 1❑Jun 1999 Cover: 2.99 **NM** value: **Cover or less**
Circ: Diamd. preorders: **2,782**
• Comic-sized. Hell on Wheels • Summer Special (1999) **A:** Jezy Drozd **W:** Jerzy Drozd; Bert Sandel; Tom Root

YB 1❑b&w **NM** value: **6.00**
YB 2❑b&w Cover: 3.25 **NM** value: **4.95**
• 1990 Yearbook.

YB 3❑b&w Cover: 3.75 **NM** value: **4.95**
• 1991 Yearbook.

YB 4❑ Cover: 3.95 **NM** value: **4.95**
• 1992 Yearbook.

YB 5❑Oct 1993, b&w Cover: 3.95 **NM** value: **Cover or less**
• 1993 Yearbook.

YB 6❑Oct 1994, b&w Cover: 3.95 **NM** value: **Cover or less**
• 1994 Yearbook.

YB 7❑Oct 1995, b&w Cover: 3.95 **NM** value: **Cover or less**
cover says Oct 94, indicia says Oct 95. • 1995 Yearbook.

YB 8❑Oct 1996, b&w Cover: 3.95 **NM** value: **Cover or less**
Circ: Diamd. preorders: **3,759**
• 1996 Yearbook.

YB 9/A❑Oct 1997, b&w Cover: 3.95 **NM** value: **Cover or less**
• 1997 Yearbook. Partners in a Strange Relationship; The Quibbler; Flights of Fantasy; Wheats and Creeps; Asrial; Treatman; Wolf of the North Star; Off Your Gourd/Ichi's Birthday; Lady Luck; Ninja Tricks 2; Akaru's Addiction **A:** Cody Pickrodt; Lou Gojira; Phuong-Mai Bui-Quang; Serapio Calm II; Thor Thorvaldson; J.C. Prather; J.J. Sabadoz; John Szalay; Justin Williams; Keiko Szalay; Kyle A. Carrozza; Ben Dunn(cover) **W:** Cody Pickrodt; Lou Gojira; Phuong-Mai Bui-Quang; Serapio Calm II; Thor Thorvaldson; J.C. Prather; J.J. Sabadoz; John Szalay; Justin Williams; Keiko Szalay; Kyle A. Carrozza

YB 9/B❑Oct 1997, b&w Cover: 3.95 **NM** value: **Cover or less**
alternate cover. • 1997 Yearbook. Partners in a Strange Relationship; The Quibbler; Flights of Fantasy; Wheats and Creeps; Asrial; Treatman; Wolf of the North Star; Off Your Gourd/Ichi's Birthday; Lady Luck; Ninja Tricks 2; Akaru's Addiction • Star Trek **A:** Cody Pickrodt; Lou Gojira; Phuong-Mai Bui-Quang; Serapio Calm II; Thor Thorvaldson; J.C. Prather; J.J. Sabadoz; John Szalay; Justin Williams; Keiko Szalay; Kyle A. Carrozza; Fred Perry(cover) **W:** Cody Pickrodt; Lou Gojira; Phuong-Mai Bui-Quang; Serapio Calm II; Thor Thorvaldson; J.C. Prather; J.J. Sabadoz; John Szalay; Justin Williams; Keiko Szalay; Kyle A. Carrozza

YB 10/A❑Oct 1998, b&w Cover: 2.95 **NM** value: **Cover or less**
Circ: Diamd. preorders: **3,492**
• 1998 Yearbook. Five Minutes; Wolf of the North Star 2; Ninja Tricks 4; Gloom, Doom...Broom!; Who's the Champ; Lunchtime; Boy Crazy; Ninja Sunday Funnies **A:** Bryant Velez; Chris Samnee; Jerzy Drozd; John Prather; Lou Gojira; Phuong-Mai Bui-Quang; Ron Murphy; Thor Thorvaldson **W:** Bryant Velez; Chris Samnee; John Prather; Lou Gojira; Phuong-Mai Bui-Quang; Ron Murphy; Thor Thorvaldson; Tom Root

YB 10/B❑Oct 1998, b&w Cover: 2.95 **NM** value: **Cover or less**
"Titanic" themed cover. • 1998 Yearbook. Five Minutes; Wolf of the North Star 2; Ninja Tricks 4; Gloom, Doom...Broom!; Who's the Champ; Lunchtime; Boy Crazy; Ninja Sunday Funnies • Titanic **A:** Bryant Velez; Chris Samnee; Jerzy Drozd; John Prather; Lou Gojira; Phuong-Mai Bui-Quang; Ron Murphy; Thor Thorvaldson **W:** Bryant Velez; Chris Samnee; John Prather; Lou Gojira; Phuong-Mai Bui-Quang; Ron Murphy; Thor Thorvaldson; Tom Root

NINJA HIGH SCHOOL FEATURING SPEED RACER — Eternity / Now

1 ❑ Cover: 2.95 **NM** value: **Cover or less**
2 ❑ Dec 1993 Cover: 2.95 **NM** value: **Cover or less**

NINJA HIGH SCHOOL IN COLOR — Eternity

1 ❑ Jul 1992, full color Cover: 1.95 **NM** value: **2.50**
2 ❑ full color Cover: 1.95 **NM** value: **2.50**
3 ❑ full color Cover: 1.95 **NM** value: **2.50**
4 ❑ full color Cover: 1.95 **NM** value: **2.00**
5 ❑ full color Cover: 1.95 **NM** value: **2.00**
6 ❑ full color Cover: 1.95 **NM** value: **2.00**
7 ❑ full color Cover: 1.95 **NM** value: **2.00**
8 ❑ full color Cover: 1.95 **NM** value: **2.00**
9 ❑ full color Cover: 1.95 **NM** value: **2.00**
10 ❑ full color Cover: 1.95 **NM** value: **2.00**
11 ❑ full color Cover: 1.95 **NM** value: **2.00**
12 ❑ full color Cover: 1.95 **NM** value: **2.00**
13 ❑ full color Cover: 1.95 **NM** value: **2.00**

NINJA HIGH SCHOOL PERFECT MEMORY — Antarctic

1 ❑ b&w Cover: 5.00 **NM** value: **Cover or less**
• sourcebook for series

1-2 ❑ Jun 1996 Cover: 5.95 **NM** value: **Cover or less**

2 ❑ Nov 1993 Cover: 4.95 **NM** value: **5.95**
• 1996 version

2/PL❑Nov 1993 **NM** value: **5.00**
• platinum

NINJA HIGH SCHOOL SPOTLIGHT — Antarctic

1 ❑ Cover: 3.50 **NM** value: **Cover or less**
Penguin Ball; The Unreal Ghosthunters; The H Files; Asrial's New Hobby; Hall's Well; WhatNintendoDidNotWantToDo • Indicia says #29 **A:** Robert DeJesus **W:** Robert DeJesus

2 ❑ Oct 1996 Cover: 2.95 **NM** value: **Cover or less**
Marooned; Cram'n; Balancin the Books **A:** Fred Perry **W:** Fred Perry

3 ❑ Dec 1996 Cover: 3.50 **NM** value: **Cover or less**
Dunn Deal; Fujiko and Her Foo-Foo Bike; Ninja Air Force; Ninja Paradox; Ninja Police; Beach Blanket • Ted Nomura **A:** Ted Nomura **W:** Ted Nomura

4 ❑ May 1999 Cover: 2.99 **NM** value: **Cover or less**
Circ: Diamd. preorders: **2,120**
Flights of Fantasy; • Rod Espinosa; Indicia says #1 **A:** Rod Espinosa **W:** Rod Espinosa

NINJA HIGH SCHOOL SWIMSUIT SPECIAL — Antarctic

1 ❑ Dec 1992 Cover: 2.95 **NM** value: **4.00**
Circ: Diamd. preorders: **2,418**
two different covers. • Gold edition.

2 ❑ Dec 1993 Cover: 2.95 **NM** value: **3.95**
• 1998 Yearbook. • Annual

3 ❑ Dec 1994 Cover: 2.95 **NM** value: **3.95**
• Trade Paperback. • Annual **A:** Pat Kelley; Ryan Kinnaird; Mike Sagara; Fred Perry; Robert DeJesus; Bobee Padilla; Ted Nomura; David Matsuoka; Jochen Weltjens; Phuong-Mai Bui-Quang; Shon Howell; Herb Mallette; Arnie Howell; Masaka; Robert Acosta

4 ❑ Cover: 2.95 **NM** value: **3.95**
• Gold edition.

1996❑Dec 1996, b&w Cover: 2.95 **NM** value: **3.95**
no cover price. • Platinum edition. • pinups **A:** Lazarus Berry; Dean Hsieh; Duc Tran; Ben Dunn; Rod Espinosa; David Hahn; Cayetano Garza Jr.; John Prather; Matt Walker; Michael Vega; R.C. Montesquieu

CGC-graded: Multiply prices above by **33 for 9.9 M • 16 for 9.8 NM/M • 7 for 9.6 NM+ • 5 for 9.4 NM • 2.5 for 9.2 NM- • 1.5 for 9.0 VF/NM**

NINJA HIGH SCHOOL TALKS ABOUT COMIC BOOK PRINTING — Antarctic

1 ❑ full color NM value: 1.00
• giveaway.

NINJA HIGH SCHOOL TALKS ABOUT SEXUALLY TRANSMITTED DISEASES — Antarctic

1 ❑ full color NM value: 2.00
• giveaway.

NINJA HIGH SCHOOL: THE PROM FORMULA — Eternity

1 ❑ full color Cover: 2.95 NM value: Cover or less
Circ: CapCity orders: 3,490
2 ❑ full color Cover: 2.95 NM value: Cover or less
Circ: CapCity orders: 2,370

NINJA HIGH SCHOOL: THE SPECIAL EDITION — Eternity

1 ❑ b&w Cover: 2.25 NM value: 2.50
2 ❑ b&w Cover: 2.25 NM value: 2.50
3 ❑ b&w Cover: 2.25 NM value: 2.50
4 ❑ Cover: 2.25 NM value: 2.50

NINJA HIGH SCHOOL VERSION 2 — Antarctic

1 ❑ Jul 1999 Cover: 2.50 NM value: Cover or less
Circ: Diamd. preorders: 3,353
📖 I's a Family Affair! A: Ben Dunn W: Ben Dunn
2 ❑ Aug 1999 Cover: 2.50 NM value: Cover or less
Circ: Diamd. preorders: 4,068
📖 Decision! Decisions! A: Ben Dunn W: Ben Dunn

NINJAK — Valiant

Colin King, aka Ninjak, is an enforcer in a brutal war between arms merchants. King works for the Weaponeer Organization, arch-enemies with rival arms supplier Webnet. He's a cold, methodical killer, accustomed to living a luxurious lifestyle when not "on duty."

His life changes when he breaks up an arms deal on the docks in Monaco. Meant as a sting against Webnet, he discovers that there is more to this operation than just a few Stinger missiles: Webnet was developing a process called Black Water, which used nanite technology to achieve cold fusion in hydrogen/oxygen molecules.

Soon thereafter, the world seems to go crazy, with Webnet launching a massive retaliation against Weaponeer. Hundreds of people are assassinated, and King flees in a car — which has been rigged to flood its passenger compartment and drown the occupants in Black Water...

0 ❑ Jun 1995 Cover: 2.50 NM value: Cover or less
Circ: CapCity orders: 12,550
📖 Hope & Glory, Part 1 A: Mark Moretti W: Mark Moretti ★ Origin of Doctor Silk, Ninjak.
0/A ❑ Jun 1995 Cover: 2.50 NM value: Cover or less
Circ: CapCity orders: 12,500
cover forms diptych image with #0. 📖 Hope & Glory, Part 2 • #00 A: Mark Moretti W: Mark Moretti ★ Origin of Doctor Silk, Ninjak.
1 ❑ Feb 1994 Cover: 3.50 NM value: Cover or less
Circ: CapCity orders: 104,000 • CGC: 4 graded, best 9.8
chromium cover. 📖 Black Water, Part 1 A: Joe Quesada ★ 1st Appearance of Doctor Silk.
1/GO❑ Feb 1994 Cover: 3.50 NM value: Cover or less
wraparound chromium cover. • Gold edition. 📖 Black Water, Part 1 A: Joe Quesada ★ 1st Appearance of Doctor Silk.
2 ❑ Mar 1994 Cover: 2.25 NM value: Cover or less
Circ: CapCity orders: 48,875
📖 Black Water, Part 2 A: Joe Quesada
3 ❑ Apr 1994 Cover: 2.25 NM value: Cover or less
Circ: CapCity orders: 37,350
A: Joe Quesada
4 ❑ May 1994 Cover: 2.25 NM value: Cover or less
Circ: CapCity orders: 36,750
• trading card
5 ❑ Jun 1994 Cover: 2.25 NM value: Cover or less
Circ: CapCity orders: 30,950
★ Appearance of X-O Manowar.
6 ❑ Aug 1994 Cover: 2.25 NM value: Cover or less
Circ: CapCity orders: 29,875
★ Appearance of X-O Manowar.
7 ❑ Sep 1994 Cover: 2.25 NM value: Cover or less
Circ: CapCity orders: 28,350
8 ❑ Oct 1994 Cover: 2.25 NM value: Cover or less
Circ: CapCity orders: 30,525
📖 The Chaos Effect: Gamma, Part 3 • Chaos Effect
9 ❑ Nov 1994 Cover: 2.25 NM value: Cover or less
Circ: CapCity orders: 24,900
• new uniform
10 ❑ Dec 1994 Cover: 2.25 NM value: Cover or less
Circ: CapCity orders: 21,675
11 ❑ Jan 1995 Cover: 2.25 NM value: Cover or less
Circ: CapCity orders: 19,025
12 ❑ Feb 1995 Cover: 2.25 NM value: Cover or less
Circ: CapCity orders: 17,400
• trading card
13 ❑ Mar 1995 Cover: 2.25 NM value: Cover or less
Circ: CapCity orders: 14,525
• trading card
14 ❑ Apr 1995 Cover: 2.50 NM value: Cover or less
Circ: CapCity orders: 12,750
📖 Cry Wolf; Cry Wolf, Part 1
15 ❑ May 1995 Cover: 2.50 NM value: Cover or less
Circ: CapCity orders: 11,000
📖 Cry Wolf; Cry Wolf, Part 2
16 ❑ Jun 1995 Cover: 2.50 NM value: Cover or less
Circ: CapCity orders: 9,875
📖 Plague
17 ❑ Jul 1995 Cover: 2.50 NM value: Cover or less
Circ: CapCity orders: 9,625
📖 Plague
18 ❑ Jul 1995 Cover: 2.50 NM value: Cover or less
Circ: CapCity orders: 9,600
• Birthquake
19 ❑ Aug 1995 Cover: 2.50 NM value: Cover or less
Circ: CapCity orders: 8,675
20 ❑ Aug 1995 Cover: 2.50 NM value: Cover or less
Circ: CapCity orders: 8,275
21 ❑ Sep 1995 Cover: 2.50 NM value: Cover or less
22 ❑ Sep 1995 Cover: 2.50 NM value: Cover or less
Circ: CapCity orders: 8,200
23 ❑ Oct 1995 Cover: 2.50 NM value: Cover or less
Circ: CapCity orders: 7,725
24 ❑ Oct 1995 Cover: 2.50 NM value: Cover or less
Circ: CapCity orders: 7,725
25 ❑ Nov 1995 Cover: 2.50 NM value: Cover or less
Circ: CapCity orders: 7,275
26 ❑ Nov 1995 Cover: 2.50 NM value: Cover or less
Circ: CapCity orders: 7,250
final issue.
YB 1❑ Cover: 3.95 NM value: Cover or less
Circ: CapCity orders: 18,725
cardstock cover.

NINJAK (VOL. 2) — Acclaim / Valiant

1 ❑ Mar 1997 Cover: 2.50 NM value: Cover or less
Circ: Diamd. preorders: 30,337
📖 I Call on the Power of Ninjak! A: Neil Vokes W: Kurt Busiek ★ Origin of Ninjak. ★ 1st Appearance of Ninjak II.
1/SC❑ Mar 1997 Cover: 2.50 NM value: Cover or less
alternate painted cover. 📖 I Call on the Power of Ninjak! A: Neil Vokes W: Kurt Busiek ★ 1st Appearance of Ninjak II.
2 ❑ Apr 1997 Cover: 2.50 NM value: Cover or less
Circ: Diamd. preorders: 21,486
W: Kurt Busiek
3 ❑ May 1997 Cover: 2.50 NM value: Cover or less
Circ: Diamd. preorders: 16,892
W: Kurt Busiek
4 ❑ Jun 1997 Cover: 2.50 NM value: Cover or less
Circ: Diamd. preorders: 13,014
• real origin of Ninjak W: Kurt Busiek ★ Appearance of Colin King.
5 ❑ Jul 1997 Cover: 2.50 NM value: Cover or less
Circ: Diamd. preorders: 11,798
📖 Dark Dealings A: Pablo Raimondi; Kim Demulder W: Kurt Busiek
6 ❑ Aug 1997 Cover: 2.50 NM value: Cover or less
Circ: Diamd. preorders: 11,442
W: Kurt Busiek ★ Appearance of X-O Manowar.
7 ❑ Sep 1997 Cover: 2.50 NM value: Cover or less
Circ: Diamd. preorders: 10,474
W: Kurt Busiek ★ Appearance of X-O Manowar.
8 ❑ Oct 1997 Cover: 2.50 NM value: Cover or less
Circ: Diamd. preorders: 9,712
W: Kurt Busiek ★ Appearance of Colin King.
9 ❑ Nov 1997 Cover: 2.50 NM value: Cover or less
Circ: Diamd. preorders: 9,095
W: Kurt Busiek
10 ❑ Dec 1997 Cover: 2.50 NM value: Cover or less
Circ: Diamd. preorders: 8,486
W: Kurt Busiek
11 ❑ Jan 1998 Cover: 2.50 NM value: Cover or less
Circ: Diamd. preorders: 7,875
W: Kurt Busiek
12 ❑ Feb 1998 Cover: 2.50 NM value: Cover or less
Circ: Diamd. preorders: 7,321
final issue. W: Kurt Busiek
Ash 1❑ Nov 1996, b&w NM value: 1.00
no cover price. • preview of upcoming series

NINJUTSU, ART OF THE NINJA — Solson

1 ❑ b&w Cover: 2.00 NM value: Cover or less
A: Chuck Wojtkiewicz W: Peter Brody

NINTENDO COMICS SYSTEM — Valiant

1 ❑ Cover: 4.95 NM value: Cover or less
Circ: CapCity orders: 1,700
2 ❑ Cover: 4.95 NM value: Cover or less

NINTENDO COMICS SYSTEM (2ND SERIES) — Valiant

1 ❑ Cover: 1.50 NM value: 2.00
• Game Boy
2 ❑ Cover: 1.50 NM value: 2.00
• Game Boy
3 ❑ Cover: 1.50 NM value: 2.00
• Game Boy
4 ❑ Cover: 1.50 NM value: 2.00
• Game Boy
5 ❑ Cover: 1.50 NM value: 2.00
• Game Boy
6 ❑ Cover: 1.50 NM value: 2.00
• Game Boy
7 ❑ Cover: 1.50 NM value: 2.00
• Zelda
8 ❑ Cover: 1.50 NM value: 2.00
• Super Mario Bros.
9 ❑ Cover: 1.50 NM value: 2.00
• Super Mario Bros.

N.I.O. — Acclaim / Vertigo

1 ❑ Nov 1998 Cover: 2.50 NM value: Cover or less
📖 The Players A: Michael Marts; Omar Banmally W: Evan Skolnick

NIRA X: ANIME — Entity

0 ❑ Jan 1997 Cover: 2.75 NM value: Cover or less
Circ: Diamd. preorders: 2,263

NIRA X: ANNUAL — Express / Entity

1/A ❑ Sep 1996, b&w Cover: 2.75 NM value: Cover or less
• Snowman 1944 preview
1/B ❑ Sep 1996, b&w Cover: 9.95 NM value: Cover or less
• Snowman 1944 preview

NIRA X: CYBERANGEL — Express / Entity

1 ❑ May 1996 Cover: 2.75 NM value: 2.95
Circ: Diamd. preorders: 3,633
📖 New Friends, Old Friends • Gold foil logo A: Bill Maus W: Bill Maus ★ 1st Appearance of Delta-Void, Millennia, Paradoxx, Quid.
1/LE❑ May 1996 Cover: 2.75 NM value: 4.00
• Limited commemorative edition. 📖 New Friends, Old Friends • 3000 printed A: Bill Maus W: Bill Maus ★ 1st Appearance of Delta-Void, Millennia, Paradoxx, Quid.
2 ❑ Jun 1996, b&w Cover: 2.75 NM value: Cover or less
📖 Birth Of The Cyber Angel ★ 1st Appearance of Talon, Vex, Cyberhood, Solace.
3 ❑ Jul 1996, b&w Cover: 2.75 NM value: Cover or less
4 ❑ Aug 1996, b&w Cover: 2.75 NM value: Cover or less
final issue.

NIRA X: CYBERANGEL (3RD SERIES) — Express / Entity

1 ❑ Cover: 2.50 NM value: Cover or less
📖 Eye of the Storm, Part 1

NIRA X: CYBERANGEL – CYNDER: ENDANGERED SPECIES — Express / Entity

1 ❑ Cover: 2.95 NM value: Cover or less
1/LE❑ Cover: 12.95 NM value: Cover or less
cardstock cover. • Commemorative edition. • limited to 1500 copies

NIRA X: CYBERANGEL (MINI-SERIES) — Express / Entity

1 ❑ Dec 1994 Cover: 2.95 NM value: 3.00
Circ: CapCity orders: 5,800
cardstock cover.
2 ❑ Feb 1995 Cover: 2.50 NM value: Cover or less
Circ: CapCity orders: 3,035
3 ❑ Apr 1995 Cover: 2.50 NM value: Cover or less
Circ: CapCity orders: 3,895
4 ❑ Jun 1995 Cover: 2.50 NM value: Cover or less
Circ: CapCity orders: 3,275
Ash 1❑ Sum 1994, b&w NM value: 1.00
no cover price.

NIRA X: EXODUS — Avatar / Entity

1 ❑ Oct 1997 Cover: 3.00 NM value: Cover or less
A: Bill Maus W: Bill Maus

NIRA X: HEATWAVE — Express / Entity

1 ❑ Jul 1995 Cover: 3.75 NM value: Cover or less
enhanced wraparound cover.
2 ❑ Aug 1995 Cover: 2.50 NM value: Cover or less
3 ❑ Sep 1995 Cover: 2.50 NM value: Cover or less

NIRA X: SOUL SKURGE — Express / Entity

1 ❑ Nov 1996, b&w Cover: 2.75 NM value: Cover or less
Circ: Diamd. preorders: 3,059

NOAH'S ARK — Barbour

1 ❑ Cover: 0.49 NM value: 2.00
A: Al Hartley W: Al Hartley

NOBLE ARMOUR HALBERDER (JOHN AND JASON WALTRIP'S...) — Academy

1 ❑ Jan 1997 Cover: 2.95 NM value: Cover or less
📖 Knight Vision A: Jason Waltrip; John Waltrip W: Jason Waltrip; John Waltrip

NOBODY — Oni Press

1 ❑ Nov 1998 Cover: 2.95 NM value: 3.00
Circ: Diamd. preorders: 3,157
A: Charles Adlard W: Alex Amado; Sharon Cho
2 ❑ Dec 1998 Cover: 2.95 NM value: 3.00
Circ: Diamd. preorders: 2,666
A: Charles Adlard W: Alex Amado; Sharon Cho
3 ❑ Jan 1999 Cover: 2.95 NM value: 3.00
Circ: Diamd. preorders: 2,455
A: Charles Adlard W: Alex Amado; Sharon Cho
4 ❑ Feb 1999 Cover: 2.95 NM value: 3.00
Circ: Diamd. preorders: 2,218
A: Charles Adlard W: Alex Amado; Sharon Cho

NO BUSINESS LIKE SHOW BUSINESS — 3-D Zone

1 ❑ b&w Cover: 2.50 NM value: Cover or less
• not 3-D

NOCTURNAL EMISSIONS — Vortex

All issues are adults only.
1 ❑ b&w Cover: 2.50 NM value: Cover or less

Other grades: Multiply prices above by **1.5 for Mint • 2/3 for Very Fine • 1/3 for Fine • 1/5 for Very Good • 1/8 for Good**

NOCTURNALS, THE — Malibu / Bravura

1 ☐ Jan 1995 Cover: 2.95 **NM value: 3.50**
Circ: CapCity orders: **9,600**
Black Planet **A:** Dan Brereton **W:** Dan Brereton ★ 1st Appearance of The Nocturnals.
2 ☐ Feb 1995 Cover: 2.95 **NM value: 3.00**
Circ: CapCity orders: **6,975**
A: Dan Brereton **W:** Dan Brereton
3 ☐ Apr 1995 Cover: 2.95 **NM value: 3.00**
Circ: CapCity orders: **6,200**
A: Dan Brereton **W:** Dan Brereton
4 ☐ Apr 1995 Cover: 2.95 **NM value: 3.00**
Circ: CapCity orders: **6,200**
A: Dan Brereton **W:** Dan Brereton
5 ☐ Jun 1995 Cover: 2.95 **NM value: 3.00**
Circ: CapCity orders: **6,125**
A: Dan Brereton **W:** Dan Brereton
6 ☐ Aug 1995 Cover: 2.95 **NM value: 3.00**
A: Dan Brereton **W:** Dan Brereton
Bk 1 ☐ Oct 1998 Cover: 19.95 **NM value: Cover or less**
No issue number. • Trade Paperback. • "Black Planet"; collects Malibu/Bravura mini-series **A:** Dan Brereton **W:** Dan Brereton

NOCTURNALS: TROLL BRIDGE — Oni Press

1 ☐ Oct 2000 Cover: 4.95 **NM value: Cover or less**
Circ: Diamd. preorders: **6,896**
No issue number. One-shot. • b&w and orange **A:** Eric Jones; Adam Warren; Kieron Dwyer; Arthur Adams; Steve Purcell; Dan Brereton; Jay Stephens; Ted Naifeh; Stephen DeStefano; John Heebink; Jill Thompson; Stan Sakai; Bruce Timm; Joyce Chin **C:** Dan Brereton **W:** Dan Brereton

NOCTURNALS, THE: WITCHING HOUR — Dark Horse

1 ☐ May 1998 Cover: 4.95 **NM value: Cover or less**
Circ: Diamd. preorders: **7,322**
No issue number. One-shot. **A:** Dan Brereton **W:** Dan Brereton

NOCTURNE (AIRCEL) — Aircel

1 ☐ b&w Cover: 2.50 **NM value: Cover or less**
A: Angel de Mioche **W:** Angel de Mioche
2 ☐ b&w Cover: 2.50 **NM value: Cover or less**
A: Angel de Mioche **W:** Angel de Mioche
3 ☐ Aug 1991, b&w Cover: 2.50 **NM value: Cover or less**
A: Angel de Mioche **W:** Angel de Mioche

NOCTURNE (MARVEL) — Marvel

1 ☐ Jun 1995 Cover: 1.50 **NM value: Cover or less**
Circ: CapCity orders: **10,650**
2 ☐ Jul 1995 Cover: 1.50 **NM value: Cover or less**
Through the Looking Glass • indicia says Sep 95 **A:** José Fonteriz **W:** Dan Abnett
3 ☐ Aug 1995 Cover: 1.50 **NM value: Cover or less**
4 ☐ Sep 1995 Cover: 1.50 **NM value: Cover or less**

NODWICK — Henchman Publishing

Presenting humorous modern-day human foibles in a medieval setting, Nodwick is a full-length comic book based upon the characters created for both Dragon Magazine and Dungeon Magazine by cartoonist Aaron Williams. The embodiment of the blue-collar work ethic, the title character, Nodwick, is a henchman who toils with few complaints, and for little reward. Written with tongue firmly planted in cheek, Nodwick often blurs the lines between traditional fantasy genres and current day situations by using modern euphemisms for the sake of parody. Though often spoofing the characters and settings developed for Dungeons and Dragons, Williams' goofy reverence for the game and the lifestyle of its players has endeared him to fans of the popular role-playing game.

1 ☐ Feb 2000, b&w Cover: 2.95 **NM value: Cover or less**
Circ: Diamd. preorders: **1,854**
A: Aaron Williams **W:** Aaron Williams
2 ☐ Mar 2000, b&w Cover: 2.95 **NM value: Cover or less**
The Great Grave Robbery **A:** Aaron Williams **W:** Aaron Williams
3 ☐ b&w Cover: 2.95 **NM value: Cover or less**
A: Aaron Williams **W:** Aaron Williams
4 ☐ Aug 2000, b&w Cover: 2.95 **NM value: Cover or less**
The Tides of War **A:** Aaron Williams **W:** Aaron Williams
5 ☐ Oct 2000, b&w Cover: 2.95 **NM value: Cover or less**
Circ: Diamd. preorders: **2,060**
The Thirteenth Edition **A:** Aaron Williams **W:** Aaron Williams

NO ESCAPE — Marvel

1 ☐ Jun 1994 Cover: 1.50 **NM value: Cover or less**
A: Mike Harris **W:** Roger Salick
2 ☐ Jul 1994 Cover: 1.50 **NM value: Cover or less**
A: Mike Harris **W:** Roger Salick
3 ☐ Aug 1994 Cover: 1.50 **NM value: Cover or less**
Circ: CapCity orders: **2,550**
A: Mike Harris **W:** Roger Salick

NOG THE PROTECTOR OF THE PYRAMIDES — Onli Studios

1 ☐ Cover: 2.00 **NM value: Cover or less**
No issue number.

NO GUTS OR GLORY — Fantaco

1 ☐ b&w Cover: 2.95 **NM value: Cover or less**
A: Kevin Eastman

NO HONOR — Image

1 ☐ Feb 2001 Cover: 2.50 **NM value: Cover or less**
Circ: Diamd. preorders: **37,118** • **CGC:** 4 graded, best 9.8
A: Clayton Crain **W:** Fiona Kai Avery
2 ☐ Mar 2001 Cover: 2.50 **NM value: Cover or less**
Circ: Diamd. preorders: **24,557**
A: Clayton Crain **W:** Fiona Kai Avery
3 ☐ Apr 2001 Cover: 2.50 **NM value: Cover or less**
Circ: Diamd. preorders: **23,902**
A: Clayton Crain **W:** Fiona Kai Avery

NO HOPE — Slave Labor

1 ☐ Apr 1993 Cover: 2.95 **NM value: Cover or less**
Life Is...; The Great Experiment or a Dangerous Idea; Drowning in a Sea of Boredom; Lunchbreak; Another Friday Night; You're Killing Me You F*ck **A:** Jeff Levine **W:** Jeff Levine
1-2 ☐ Feb 1995 Cover: 2.95 **NM value: Cover or less**
2 ☐ Aug 1993 Cover: 2.95 **NM value: Cover or less**
My Train Story; Wednesday; Hate My Life; Johnny Bored's Talk Show Report; No Bullsh*t Ever; **A:** Jeff Levine **W:** Jeff Levine
2-2 ☐ Apr 1994 Cover: 2.95 **NM value: Cover or less**
3 ☐ Nov 1993 Cover: 2.95 **NM value: Cover or less**
A: Jeff Levine **W:** Jeff Levine
3-2 ☐ Apr 1994 Cover: 2.95 **NM value: Cover or less**
4 ☐ Feb 1994 Cover: 2.95 **NM value: Cover or less**
Greetings Loser; A Short Walk Later; The Next Day; Ladies and Gentlemen Meet Mr. Sun; ...And You Think Your Life Sucks Now.; Nothin' to Do; Bad Luck Boy; A Close Call; A Christmas Story; Ladies and Gentlemen Meet Mr. Sun; ...And You Think Your Life Su **A:** Jeff Levine **W:** Jeff Levine
4-2 ☐ Oct 1994 Cover: 2.95 **NM value: Cover or less**
5 ☐ Jun 1994 Cover: 2.95 **NM value: Cover or less**
Fun?; Ladies and Gentlemen Meet Mr. Sun, Part 2; Dreaming of a Better World; What the Hell; Vacation **A:** Jeff Levine **W:** Jeff Levine
6 ☐ Sep 1994 Cover: 2.95 **NM value: Cover or less**
The Dresser; For the Losers; Darkness; Weird Hair Nightmare; White Night; ...And the Days Go By Like Broken Records; The Rock **A:** Jeff Levine **W:** Jeff Levine
7 ☐ Jan 1995 Cover: 2.95 **NM value: Cover or less**
Freedom; Starship Earth; Centuries End; Today is the First Day of the Rest of Your Life; I Felt Something; Public Transportation **A:** Jeff Levine **W:** Jeff Levine
8 ☐ Apr 1995 Cover: 2.95 **NM value: Cover or less**
San Francisco; Happy Birthday to Me; Outside **A:** Jeff Levine **W:** Jeff Levine
9 ☐ Jul 1995 Cover: 2.95 **NM value: Cover or less**
Honesty is a Scary Thing; Ed Has No Brain; Sally Considers Buying a Gun; Bad Childhood Memory #357; Walking, Thinking and Remembering (text story); I Guess Everything's Okay **A:** Jeff Levine **W:** Jeff Levine

NOID IN 3-D, THE — Blackthorne

1 ☐ Cover: 2.50 **NM value: Cover or less**
2 ☐ Cover: 2.50 **NM value: Cover or less**

NOIR (ALPHA) — Alpha

1 ☐ Win 1994 Cover: 3.95 **NM value: Cover or less**
• text & comics

NOIR (CREATIVE FORCE) — Creative Force

1 ☐ Apr 1995 Cover: 4.95 **NM value: Cover or less**

NO JUSTICE, NO PIECE! — Head Press

1 ☐ Oct 1997, b&w Cover: 2.95 **NM value: Cover or less**
• benefit anthology for CBLDF
2 ☐ Jul 1998, b&w Cover: 2.95 **NM value: Cover or less**
• benefit anthology for CBLDF

NOLAN RYAN — Celebrity

1 ☐ Cover: 2.95 **NM value: Cover or less**

NOLAN RYAN'S 7 NO-HITTERS — Revolutionary

1 ☐ Aug 1993, b&w Cover: 2.95 **NM value: Cover or less**

NOMAD — Marvel

Jack Monroe is Nomad. As a boy, he was injected with a derivative of the Super Soldier Serum which created Captain America. For a while, he wore the mask of Bucky, Captain America's sidekick, but he became increasingly unstable, and was eventually placed in cryogenic sleep. He reappeared in Captain America #282 as Nomad, a costumed vigilante. However, his vigilante tendencies caused the government to take a harsh view of him, and he was forced to drop out of sight.

In Nomad, Monroe becomes truly worthy of that name. A reluctant "father" to a baby he calls Bucky, he wandered across America, displaying an uncanny ability to find trouble wherever he went.

1 ☐ May 1992 Cover: 2.00 **NM value: 2.50**
Circ: Statement: **117,217** CapCity orders: **75,600**
gatefold cover. The Favor Banker **A:** S. Clarke Hawbaker **W:** Fabian Nicieza
2 ☐ Jun 1992 Cover: 1.75 **NM value: Cover or less**
Circ: Statement: **117,217** CapCity orders: **43,500**
Roadkill **A:** S. Clarke Hawbaker **W:** Fabian Nicieza
3 ☐ Jul 1992 Cover: 1.75 **NM value: Cover or less**
Circ: Statement: **117,217** CapCity orders: **43,200**
Agents Of Questionable Ethics • Nomad vs. U.S.Agent **A:** S. Clarke Hawbaker **W:** Fabian Nicieza
4 ☐ Aug 1992 Cover: 1.75 **NM value: Cover or less**
Circ: Statement: **117,217** CapCity orders: **45,400**
Dead Man's Hand, Part 2; Neon Knights **A:** Patrick Olliffe **W:** Fabian Nicieza
5 ☐ Sep 1992 Cover: 1.75 **NM value: Cover or less**
Circ: Statement: **117,217** CapCity orders: **36,900**
Dead Man's Hand, Part 5 **A:** Patrick Olliffe **W:** Fabian Nicieza
6 ☐ Oct 1992 Cover: 1.75 **NM value: Cover or less**
Circ: Statement: **117,217** CapCity orders: **34,200**
Dead Man's Hand, Part 8 **A:** Patrick Olliffe **W:** Fabian Nicieza
7 ☐ Nov 1992 Cover: 1.75 **NM value: Cover or less**
Circ: Statement: **117,217** CapCity orders: **36,900**
Infinity War; Airport Security • Infinity War **A:** Mike Harris; S. Clarke Hawbaker **W:** Fabian Nicieza
8 ☐ Dec 1992 Cover: 1.75 **NM value: Cover or less**
Circ: Statement: **117,217** CapCity orders: **28,900**
City of Angels • L.A riots
9 ☐ Jan 1993 Cover: 1.75 **NM value: Cover or less**
Circ: CapCity orders: **28,700**
10 ☐ Feb 1993 Cover: 1.75 **NM value: Cover or less**
Circ: CapCity orders: **24,000**
Raw Deals **A:** Patrick Olliffe **W:** Fabian Nicieza ★ Appearance of Red Wolf.
11 ☐ Mar 1993 Cover: 1.75 **NM value: Cover or less**
Circ: CapCity orders: **22,200**
Criss Cross • Has 1992 Statement, filed 10/1/92; avg print run 179,283; avg sales 117,142; avg subs 75; avg total paid 117,217; samples 104; office use 208; max existent 117,529; 34% of run returned **A:** Rick Mays **W:** Fabian Nicieza
12 ☐ Apr 1993 Cover: 1.75 **NM value: Cover or less**
Circ: CapCity orders: **20,100**
Hidden In View, Part 1 **A:** Patrick Olliffe **W:** Fabian Nicieza ★ Appearance of Hate-Monger.
13 ☐ May 1993 Cover: 1.75 **NM value: Cover or less**
Circ: CapCity orders: **18,900**
Hidden In View, Part 2; If It Weren't For Love **A:** Patrick Olliffe **W:** Fabian Nicieza ★ Appearance of Hate-Monger.
14 ☐ Jun 1993 Cover: 1.75 **NM value: Cover or less**
Circ: CapCity orders: **16,900**
Hidden In View, Part 3 **A:** Rick Mays **W:** Fabian Nicieza ★ Appearance of Hate-Monger.
15 ☐ Jul 1993 Cover: 1.75 **NM value: Cover or less**
Circ: CapCity orders: **15,400**
Hidden In View, Part 4 **A:** Patrick Olliffe **W:** Fabian Nicieza ★ Appearance of Hate-Monger.
16 ☐ Aug 1993 Cover: 1.75 **NM value: Cover or less**
Circ: CapCity orders: **16,600**
Honor Among Thieves **A:** Art Nichols **W:** Fabian Nicieza ★ Appearance of Gambit.
17 ☐ Sep 1993 Cover: 1.75 **NM value: Cover or less**
Circ: CapCity orders: **13,300**
18 ☐ Oct 1993 Cover: 1.75 **NM value: Cover or less**
Circ: CapCity orders: **12,800**
The Faustus Affair, Part 1 **A:** Rick Mays **W:** Fabian Nicieza ★ Appearance of Dr. Faustus.
19 ☐ Nov 1993 Cover: 1.75 **NM value: Cover or less**
Circ: CapCity orders: **11,750**
The Faustus Affair, Part 3
20 ☐ Dec 1993 Cover: 1.75 **NM value: Cover or less**
Circ: CapCity orders: **11,650**
21 ☐ Jan 1994 Cover: 1.75 **NM value: Cover or less**
Circ: CapCity orders: **10,250**
★ Appearance of Man-Thing.
22 ☐ Feb 1994 Cover: 1.75 **NM value: Cover or less**
Circ: CapCity orders: **10,000**
American Dreamers, Part 1
23 ☐ Mar 1994 Cover: 1.75 **NM value: Cover or less**
Circ: CapCity orders: **9,000**
American Dreamers, Part 2
24 ☐ Apr 1994 Cover: 1.75 **NM value: Cover or less**
Circ: CapCity orders: **8,250**
American Dreamers, Part 3 **A:** Pete Garcia **W:** Fabian Nicieza
25 ☐ May 1994 Cover: 1.75 **NM value: Cover or less**
Circ: CapCity orders: **8,550**
American Dreamers, Part 4 final issue. **A:** Pete Garcia **W:** Fabian Nicieza

NOMAD (LTD. SERIES) — Marvel

1 ☐ Nov 1990 Cover: 1.50 **NM value: 2.00**
Circ: CapCity orders: **33,800**
The Big Fall Apart **A:** James W. Fry III III **W:** Fabian Nicieza
2 ☐ Dec 1990 Cover: 1.50 **NM value: 2.00**
Circ: CapCity orders: **24,200**
The Wild Horses **A:** James W. Fry III III **W:** Fabian Nicieza ★ Origin of Nomad.
3 ☐ Mar 1991 Cover: 1.50 **NM value: 2.00**
Circ: CapCity orders: **23,600**
Cool Cats and Cry Babies **A:** James W. Fry III III **W:** Fabian Nicieza
4 ☐ Feb 1991 Cover: 1.50 **NM value: 2.00**
Circ: CapCity orders: **25,500**
Melting Fire with Ice **A:** James W. Fry III III **W:** Fabian Nicieza

NOMAN — Tower

1 ☐ Nov 1966 Cover: 0.25 **NM value: 30.00**
• **CGC:** 4 graded, best 9.6
A: Wally Wood

CGC-graded: Multiply prices above by **33 for 9.9 M** • **16 for 9.8 NM/M** • **7 for 9.6 NM+** • **5 for 9.4 NM** • **2.5 for 9.2 NM-** • **1.5 for 9.0 VF/NM**

2 ❑ Mar 1967 Cover: 0.25 **NM** value: **22.00**
• **CGC:** 2 graded, best 9.4
A: Wally Wood

NO MAN'S LAND — Tundra

1 ❑ Cover: 14.95 **NM** value: **Cover or less**
A: George Pratt

NON — Red Ink

1 ❑ Cover: 3.00 **NM** value: **Cover or less**
📖 You can be Poor; I Am a Pineaple Pt. 1; Affirmative; I Am a Pineaple Pt. 2; Funtyme; Subway Religion; Gone; Once Upon a Bug's Life; Yet Again; Long Distance; Misery; Neruda; Hole Hearted Love; Madman Dans Guide to the Internet; Punk Rockrocketboy **A:** Jordan Crane; Larry Stone; Ted May **W:** Jordan Crane; Larry Stone; Ted May
2 ❑ Cover: 3.00 **NM** value: **Cover or less**
3 ❑ Cover: 3.00 **NM** value: **Cover or less**

NO NEED FOR TENCHI! PART 1 — Viz

1 ❑ Cover: 2.95 **NM** value: **Cover or less**
2 ❑ Cover: 2.95 **NM** value: **Cover or less**
3 ❑ Cover: 2.95 **NM** value: **Cover or less**
4 ❑ Cover: 2.95 **NM** value: **Cover or less**
5 ❑ Cover: 2.95 **NM** value: **Cover or less**
6 ❑ Cover: 2.95 **NM** value: **Cover or less**
7 ❑ Cover: 2.95 **NM** value: **Cover or less**

NO NEED FOR TENCHI! PART 2 — Viz

This is the black-and-white comic book adaptation of Hitoshi Okuda's hit comedy anime series. The story picks up where Tenchi Muyo! and No Need For Tenchi! left off with Tales of Tenchi #8.

Tenchi is plagued by girls! After releasing the demon and space pirate Ryoko from his grandfather's shrine, his life was never the same. Princess Ayeka came after Ryoko with her little sister Sasami. Minagi, a clone of Ryoko, attacked the group but later developed amnesia. They discovered that she was created by an alien warrior named Yakage who failed to steal Tenchi's sword but did manage to kidnap Ayeka. Now, Ayeka needs rescuing and who better to do it than Tenchi?

1 ❑ Cover: 2.95 **NM** value: **Cover or less**
2 ❑ Cover: 2.95 **NM** value: **Cover or less**
3 ❑ Cover: 2.95 **NM** value: **Cover or less**
4 ❑ Cover: 2.95 **NM** value: **Cover or less**
5 ❑ Cover: 2.95 **NM** value: **Cover or less**
6 ❑ Cover: 2.95 **NM** value: **Cover or less**
7 ❑ Cover: 2.95 **NM** value: **Cover or less**

NO NEED FOR TENCHI! PART 3 — Viz

1 ❑ Jun 1996 Cover: 2.95 **NM** value: **Cover or less**
Circ: Diamd. preorders: **6,911**
2 ❑ Jul 1996 Cover: 2.95 **NM** value: **Cover or less**
Circ: Diamd. preorders: **6,571**
3 ❑ Aug 1996 Cover: 2.95 **NM** value: **Cover or less**
Circ: Diamd. preorders: **6,580**
4 ❑ Sep 1996 Cover: 2.95 **NM** value: **Cover or less**
Circ: Diamd. preorders: **6,612**
5 ❑ Oct 1996 Cover: 2.95 **NM** value: **Cover or less**
Circ: Diamd. preorders: **6,662**
6 ❑ Nov 1996 Cover: 2.95 **NM** value: **Cover or less**
Circ: Diamd. preorders: **6,500**
Bk 3❑ Cover: 15.95 **NM** value: **Cover or less**
📖 Magical Girl Pretty Sammy

NO NEED FOR TENCHI! PART 4 — Viz

1 ❑ Dec 1997 Cover: 2.95 **NM** value: **Cover or less**
Circ: Diamd. preorders: **6,869**
2 ❑ Jan 1998 Cover: 2.95 **NM** value: **Cover or less**
Circ: Diamd. preorders: **6,392**
3 ❑ Feb 1998 Cover: 2.95 **NM** value: **Cover or less**
Circ: Diamd. preorders: **5,995**
4 ❑ Mar 1998 Cover: 2.95 **NM** value: **Cover or less**
Circ: Diamd. preorders: **6,089**
5 ❑ Apr 1998 Cover: 2.95 **NM** value: **Cover or less**
Circ: Diamd. preorders: **6,172**
6 ❑ May 1998 Cover: 2.95 **NM** value: **Cover or less**
Circ: Diamd. preorders: **5,857**
Bk 4❑ Dec 1998 Cover: 15.95 **NM** value: **Cover or less**
• Samurai Space Opera

NO NEED FOR TENCHI! PART 5 — Viz

1 ❑ Jun 1998 Cover: 3.25 **NM** value: **Cover or less**
Circ: Diamd. preorders: **6,272**
A: Hitoshi Okyda **W:** Hitoshi Okyda
2 ❑ Jul 1998 Cover: 2.95 **NM** value: **Cover or less**
Circ: Diamd. preorders: **5,760**
A: Hitoshi Okyda **W:** Hitoshi Okyda
3 ❑ Aug 1998 Cover: 2.95 **NM** value: **Cover or less**
Circ: Diamd. preorders: **5,527**
A: Hitoshi Okyda **W:** Hitoshi Okyda
4 ❑ Sep 1998 Cover: 2.95 **NM** value: **Cover or less**
Circ: Diamd. preorders: **5,511**
A: Hitoshi Okyda **W:** Hitoshi Okyda
5 ❑ Oct 1998 Cover: 2.95 **NM** value: **Cover or less**
Circ: Diamd. preorders: **5,462**

NO NEED FOR TENCHI! PART 6 — Viz

1 ❑ Nov 1998 Cover: 3.25 **NM** value: **Cover or less**
Circ: Diamd. preorders: **5,639**
2 ❑ Dec 1998 Cover: 2.95 **NM** value: **Cover or less**
Circ: Diamd. preorders: **5,349**
3 ❑ Jan 1999 Cover: 3.25 **NM** value: **Cover or less**
Circ: Diamd. preorders: **5,381**
4 ❑ Feb 1999 Cover: 3.25 **NM** value: **Cover or less**
Circ: Diamd. preorders: **5,177**
5 ❑ Mar 1999 Cover: 3.25 **NM** value: **Cover or less**
Circ: Diamd. preorders: **5,244**

NO NEED FOR TENCHI! PART 7 — Viz

1 ❑ Apr 1999 Cover: 2.95 **NM** value: **Cover or less**
Circ: Diamd. preorders: **5,577**
2 ❑ May 1999 Cover: 2.95 **NM** value: **Cover or less**
Circ: Diamd. preorders: **5,281**
3 ❑ Jun 1999 Cover: 2.95 **NM** value: **Cover or less**
Circ: Diamd. preorders: **5,229**
4 ❑ Jul 1999 Cover: 2.95 **NM** value: **Cover or less**
Circ: Diamd. preorders: **5,151**
5 ❑ Aug 1999 Cover: 2.95 **NM** value: **Cover or less**
Circ: Diamd. preorders: **5,060**
6 ❑ Sep 1999 Cover: 2.95 **NM** value: **Cover or less**
Circ: Diamd. preorders: **4,892**

NO NEED FOR TENCHI! PART 8 — Viz

1 ❑ Oct 1999 Cover: 3.25 **NM** value: **Cover or less**
Circ: Diamd. preorders: **5,314**

NO NINJA MAN — Custom Pic

1 ❑ Cover: 1.50 **NM** value: **Cover or less**
A: Bruce Patnaude **W:** Paul Leader
1-2 ❑ Cover: 1.50 **NM** value: **Cover or less**

NO NO UFO — Antarctic / Venus

All issues are adults only.

1 ❑ Aug 1996 Cover: 2.95 **NM** value: **Cover or less**
Circ: Diamd. preorders: **1,940**
📖 Male Domain Earth **A:** Det Arumon **W:** Det Arumon
2 ❑ May 1997, b&w Cover: 2.95 **NM** value: **Cover or less**
📖 Mad Sisters Temple of Sex, Part 1; Male Domain Earth Part 2; Refuel **A:** Det Arumon **W:** Det Arumon
3 ❑ Sep 1997, b&w Cover: 2.95 **NM** value: **Cover or less**
📖 Mad Sisters Temple of Sex, Part 2; Male Domain Earth Part 3; Storbirds Part 1 **A:** Det Arumon **W:** Det Arumon
4 ❑ May 1998, b&w Cover: 2.95 **NM** value: **Cover or less**
📖 Mad Sisters Temple of Sex, Part 3 **A:** Det Arumon **W:** Det Arumon

NO PROFIT FOR THE WISE — CFD

1 ❑ Jul 1996, b&w Cover: 2.95 **NM** value: **Cover or less**
No issue number.

NORB — Mu

1 ❑ Jan 1992 Cover: 8.95 **NM** value: **Cover or less**

NORMALMAN — Aardvark-Vanaheim

The best series to come out from Renegade "came in the divorce." When Deni Loubert took the titles she'd been publishing for Dave Sim's Aardvark-Vanaheim to start Renegade, Jim Valentino's normalman (that's right, no capital letter) had already distinguished itself as a hysterical parody of everything in comics.

The title character is the son of an accountant who mistakenly thought his planet was going to explode and launched his child into space. Now, normalman is the only normal person on Levram, a planet of super-powered characters.

Once Valentino gets going, nothing is sacred, as issues parody everything from E.C. comics to characters in kids' comics. (Mickey Money, anyone?) One issue even finds Fred Hembeck shooting ads for Hostess starring Cutey Bunny!

Later joining the "comics establishment" as one of Marvel's better creators and a founding member of Image, Valentino here sends it up mercilessly. — JJM

1 ❑ Jan 1984 Cover: 1.70 **NM** value: **2.50**
📖 Not a Dream; Not a Hoax; Not an Imaginary Tale • Aardvark-Vanaheim publishes **A:** Jim Valentino **W:** Jim Valentino
2 ❑ Apr 1984 Cover: 1.70 **NM** value: **2.00**
📖 ...And One Shall Slay Him! **A:** Jim Valentino **W:** Jim Valentino
★ Origin of Normalman.
3 ❑ Jun 1984 Cover: 1.70 **NM** value: **2.00**
📖 The Pope of Pain **A:** Jim Valentino **W:** Jim Valentino
4 ❑ Aug 1984 Cover: 1.70 **NM** value: **2.00**
📖 Crisis on Earth-Twinkey **A:** Jim Valentino **W:** Jim Valentino
5 ❑ Oct 1984 Cover: 1.70 **NM** value: **2.00**
A: Jim Valentino **W:** Jim Valentino
6 ❑ Dec 1984 Cover: 2.00 **NM** value: **Cover or less**
📖 Normalman, P.I. **A:** Jim Valentino **W:** Jim Valentino
7 ❑ Feb 1985 Cover: 2.00 **NM** value: **Cover or less**
Circ: CapCity orders: **2,800**
📖 Who Killed Sgt. Fluffy This Time? **A:** Jim Valentino **W:** Jim Valentino
8 ❑ Apr 1985 Cover: 2.00 **NM** value: **Cover or less**
Circ: CapCity orders: **2,850**
📖 Misery in Space **A:** Jim Valentino **W:** Jim Valentino

NORMALMAN — Renegade

9 ❑ Jun 1985 Cover: 2.00 **NM** value: **Cover or less**
Circ: CapCity orders: **3,150**
📖 Normalman Has Gaul • Renegade begins as publisher **A:** Jim Valentino **W:** Jim Valentino
10 ❑ Aug 1985, full color Cover: 2.00 **NM** value: **Cover or less**
Circ: CapCity orders: **2,875**
📖 Normalman for President **A:** Jim Valentino **W:** Jim Valentino
11 ❑ Oct 1985, full color Cover: 2.00 **NM** value: **Cover or less**
Circ: CapCity orders: **2,475**
📖 Bet On It **A:** Jim Valentino **W:** Jim Valentino
12 ❑ Dec 1985, full color Cover: 2.00 **NM** value: **Cover or less**
Circ: CapCity orders: **2,800**
📖 Love Stinks **A:** Jim Valentino **W:** Jim Valentino
3D 1❑ Cover: 2.25 **NM** value: **2.50**
• Double-size. **A:** Jim Valentino **W:** Jim Valentino

NORMALMAN 3-D — Renegade

1 ❑ Feb 1986 Cover: 2.25 **NM** value: **Cover or less**
A: Jim Valentino

NORMALMAN-MEGATON MAN SPECIAL — Image

1 ❑ Aug 1994 Cover: 2.50 **NM** value: **Cover or less**
Circ: CapCity orders: **9,325**
A: Jim Valentino; Donald Simpson **W:** Jim Valentino; Bob Burden; Donald Simpson; Larry Marder ★ Appearance of Flaming Carrot, Mr. Spook.

NORMALMAN THE NOVEL — Slave Labor

Bk 1❑ Apr 1987 Cover: 12.95 **NM** value: **Cover or less**
• Valentino **A:** Jim Valentino

NORTHERN'S HEMISPHERE — Northern's Hemisphere

5 ❑ b&w Cover: 2.49 **NM** value: **Cover or less**
6 ❑ b&w Cover: 2.49 **NM** value: **Cover or less**
7 ❑ b&w Cover: 2.49 **NM** value: **Cover or less**

NORTHERN'S HEMISPHERE UNDISGUISED — Northern's Hemisphere

1 ❑ Cover: 2.50 **NM** value: **Cover or less**

NORTHGUARD: THE MANDES CONCLUSION — Caliber

1 ❑ Sep 1989, b&w Cover: 2.50 **NM** value: **Cover or less**
A: Gabriel Morrissette **W:** Mark Shainblum
2 ❑ Oct 1989, b&w Cover: 2.50 **NM** value: **Cover or less**
A: Gabriel Morrissette **W:** Mark Shainblum
3 ❑ Nov 1989, b&w Cover: 2.50 **NM** value: **Cover or less**
A: Gabriel Morrissette **W:** Mark Shainblum

NORTHSTAR — Marvel

1 ❑ Apr 1994 Cover: 1.75 **NM** value: **2.00**
Circ: CapCity orders: **22,300**
📖 Fast And Loose! **A:** Dario Carrasco Jr. **W:** Simon Furman
2 ❑ May 1994 Cover: 1.75 **NM** value: **2.00**
Circ: CapCity orders: **15,650**
📖 Fast and Furious! **A:** Dario Carrasco Jr. **W:** Simon Furman
3 ❑ Jun 1994 Cover: 1.75 **NM** value: **2.00**
Circ: CapCity orders: **14,050**
📖 Quick And The Dead! **A:** Dario Carrasco Jr. **W:** Simon Furman
4 ❑ Jul 1994 Cover: 1.75 **NM** value: **2.00**
Circ: CapCity orders: **12,750**
📖 Running on Empty! **A:** Dario Carrasco Jr. **W:** Simon Furman

NORTHSTAR PRESENTS — Northstar

1 ❑ Oct 1994 Cover: 2.50 **NM** value: **Cover or less**
Circ: CapCity orders: **6,715**
📖 Zeigeist; Blood Rape of the Lust Ghouls **A:** James O'Bar **W:** David J. Schow; James O'Bar
2 ❑ Cover: 2.50 **NM** value: **Cover or less**

NORTHWEST CARTOON COOKERY — Starhead

1 ❑ b&w Cover: 2.75 **NM** value: **Cover or less**
• recipes from Pacific Northwest cartoonists **A:** R.L. Crabb; Joe Sacco; J.R. Williams; Jim Woodring; Roberta Gregory; Pat Moriarty; Ellen Forney; Donna Barr; Holly Tuttle; Jim Blanchard; Mark Zingarelli; Shary Flenniken; Cat Kinney; Dennis Eichhorn; Michael Dougan **W:** R.L. Crabb; Joe Sacco; J.R. Williams; Jim Woodring; Roberta Gregory; Pat Moriarty; Ellen Forney; Donna Barr; Holly Tuttle; Jim Blanchard; Mark Zingarelli; Shary Flenniken; Cat Kinney; Dennis Eichhorn; Michael Dougan

NORTHWEST MOUNTIES — St. John

1 ❑ Oct 1948 Cover: 0.10 **NM** value: **300.00**
• **CGC:** 1 graded, best 7.0
2 ❑ Jan 1949 Cover: 0.10 **NM** value: **250.00**
3 ❑ Apr 1949 Cover: 0.10 **NM** value: **250.00**
• **CGC:** 3 graded, best 9.0
4 ❑ Jul 1949 Cover: 0.10 **NM** value: **250.00**

NOSFERATU (CALIBER) — Tome Press

1 ❑ Jul 1991, b&w Cover: 2.95 **NM** value: **Cover or less**
Circ: CapCity orders: **3,555**
📖 A Symphony of Shadows **A:** Ken Holewczynski **W:** Rafael Nieves
2 ❑ Jul 1991, b&w Cover: 2.95 **NM** value: **Cover or less**
Circ: CapCity orders: **2,980**
📖 A Symphony of Shadows **A:** Ken Holewczynski **W:** Rafael Nieves
Bk 1❑ Mar 1995 Cover: 3.95 **NM** value: **Cover or less**
• Deluxe edition. 📖 A Symphony of Shadows • collects series **A:** Ken Holewczynski **W:** Rafael Nieves

NOSFERATU (DARK HORSE) — Dark Horse

1 ❑ Mar 1991, b&w Cover: 3.95 **NM** value: **Cover or less**
A: Phillipe Druillet **W:** Phillipe Druillet

NOSFERATU, PLAGUE OF TERROR — Millennium

1 ❑ b&w Cover: 2.50 **NM** value: **Cover or less**
Circ: CapCity orders: **5,000**
• duotone **A:** Richard Pace **W:** Richard Pace; Mark Ellis
2 ❑ b&w Cover: 2.50 **NM** value: **Cover or less**
Circ: CapCity orders: **3,325**
• duotone **A:** Richard Pace **W:** Richard Pace; Mark Ellis

Other grades: Multiply prices above by **1.5 for Mint • 2/3 for Very Fine • 1/3 for Fine • 1/5 for Very Good • 1/8 for Good**

3 ❑ b&w Cover: 2.50 **NM** value: **Cover or less**
Circ: CapCity orders: **3,175**
• duotone **A:** Richard Pace **W:** Richard Pace; Mark Ellis
4 ❑ b&w Cover: 2.50 **NM** value: **Cover or less**
Circ: CapCity orders: **3,225**
📖 Cathedral Sinister • duotone **A:** Richard Pace **W:** Richard Pace; Mark Ellis

NOSFERATU: THE DEATH MASS Antarctic / Venus

All issues are adults only.
1 ❑ Dec 1997, b&w Cover: 2.95 **NM** value: **Cover or less**
A: Holden Morris **W:** Holden Morris
2 ❑ Jan 1998, b&w Cover: 2.95 **NM** value: **Cover or less**
A: Holden Morris **W:** Holden Morris
3 ❑ Feb 1998, b&w Cover: 2.95 **NM** value: **Cover or less**
A: Holden Morris **W:** Holden Morris
4 ❑ Mar 1998, b&w Cover: 2.95 **NM** value: **Cover or less**
A: Holden Morris **W:** Holden Morris

NOSTALGIC MAD, THE E.C.

1 ❑ **NM** value: **5.00**
2 ❑ **NM** value: **4.00**
📖 Hah! Noon!; Sound Effects!; Ping Pong!; Bat Boy and Rubin! **A:** Bill Elder; Wally Wood; Jack Davis **W:** Bill Elder; Wally Wood; Jack Davis

NOSTRADAMUS CHRONICLES, THE: 1559-1821 Tome / Venus

1 ❑ Cover: 2.95 **NM** value: **Cover or less**
A: Donald Marquez **W:** Donald Marquez

NOT APPROVED CRIME Avalon

1 ❑ Cover: 2.95 **NM** value: **Cover or less**
📖 The Loot; H Is for Heroin; Deep Death; What Would You Do? **A:** Pete Morisi

NOT BRAND ECHH Marvel

Not Brand Echh was part of Marvel's expansion in 1967, a boom time for the comic-book industry. Feeling confident in itself, Marvel decided the time was right to have some fun.

The title was a takeoff on the old advertising icon of inferior "Brand X" products. Not Brand Echh promised to bring readers the finest in humor and entertainment, done up in the madcap Marvel style. Nothing was sacred here: Marvel heroes and villains were routinely lampooned, along with Pogo, Peanuts, and of course, the "Brand Echh" competition at DC.

Although it would be canceled a little over a year and a half later, Not Brand Echh left at least one enduring legacy: the stove pot-wearing super-hero Forbush Man. This incredibly incompetent super-hero became a fixture on letters columns and in Marvel bullpen gags for many years to come.

1 ❑ Aug 1967 Cover: 0.12 **NM** value: **16.00**
• **CGC:** 12 graded, best 9.6
📖 The Silver Burper; Too-Gone Kid: The Fastest Gums in the West!; The Human Scorch Versus The Sunk-Mariner; Sgt. Furious and his Hostile Commandos: A Day of Blunder! **A:** Bill Everett; Jack Kirby; John Severin; Ross Andru **W:** Gary Friedrich; Roy Thomas; Stan Lee ★ 1st Appearance of Forbush Man (on cover).
2 ❑ Sep 1967 Cover: 0.12 **NM** value: **10.00**
• **CGC:** 1 graded, best 9.4
3 ❑ Oct 1967 Cover: 0.12 **NM** value: **9.00**
• **CGC:** 1 graded, best 8.0
📖 Captain America Vs. The Revengers! ★ Origin of Charlie America, Sore, Bulk.
4 ❑ Nov 1967 Cover: 0.12 **NM** value: **9.00**
5 ❑ Dec 1967 Cover: 0.12 **NM** value: **9.00**
📖 The Ever-Lovin' Thung vs. The Inedible Bulk! ★ Origin of Forbush Man. ★ 1st Appearance of Forbush Man (full appearance).
6 ❑ Feb 1968 Cover: 0.12 **NM** value: **8.00**
• **CGC:** 2 graded, best 9.4
7 ❑ Apr 1968 Cover: 0.12 **NM** value: **8.00**
• **CGC:** 5 graded, best 9.4
★ Origin of Stupor-Man, Fantastical Four.
8 ❑ Jun 1968 Cover: 0.12 **NM** value: **8.00**
• **CGC:** 2 graded, best 9.4
9 ❑ Aug 1968 Cover: 0.25 **NM** value: **10.00**
• **CGC:** 1 graded, best 9.2
• Giant-size.
10 ❑ Oct 1968 Cover: 0.25 **NM** value: **10.00**
• **CGC:** 2 graded, best 9.0
• Giant-size.
11 ❑ Dec 1968 Cover: 0.25 **NM** value: **10.00**
• **CGC:** 1 graded, best 9.0
• Giant-size.
12 ❑ Feb 1969 Cover: 0.25 **NM** value: **10.00**
• **CGC:** 1 graded, best 9.2
• Giant-size. 📖 Comiclot; Blechhman; The Unhuman Beans; Fuzz Frighten Of the Unhuman; Good Ol' Charlie Blecch; Howlers; Revengers; My Search For True Love!; Frankenstein Sicksty-Nine **A:** Marie Severin; Schlitz **W:** Roy Thomas; Schlitz
13 ❑ Apr 1969 Cover: 0.25 **NM** value: **10.00**
• **CGC:** 1 graded, best 9.6
• Giant-size. final issue.

(NOT ONLY) THE BEST OF WONDER WART-HOG Print Mint

1 ❑ Cover: 0.50 **NM** value: **5.00**
2 ❑ Cover: 0.50 **NM** value: **4.00**
3 ❑ Cover: 0.50 **NM** value: **4.00**
📖 The Wird Ones!; The Year They Blew Christmas; Wonder Wart-Hog and the Comet Insurance Man; Wonder Wart-Hog Opens a Concession Stand; Wonder Wart-Hog Builds a Dream Car; Wonder Wart-Hog Meets the Internation Order of Bomb-Flinging Fiends; The Name Game **A:** Gilbert Shelton **W:** Gilbert Shelton

NOT QUITE DEAD Rip Off

1 ❑ Mar 1993, b&w Cover: 2.95 **NM** value: **Cover or less**
A: Gilbert Shelton **W:** Gilbert Shelton
1-2 ❑ Cover: 2.95 **NM** value: **Cover or less**
2 ❑ b&w Cover: 2.95 **NM** value: **Cover or less**
A: Gilbert Shelton **W:** Gilbert Shelton
3 ❑ Cover: 2.95 **NM** value: **Cover or less**
A: Gilbert Shelton **W:** Gilbert Shelton
4 ❑ Cover: 2.95 **NM** value: **Cover or less**
A: Gilbert Shelton **W:** Gilbert Shelton

NOVA (1ST SERIES) Marvel

This series introduced us to Richard Rider, a young man who was given extraordinary powers by a dying "Nova Centurion." Originally from the planet Xandar, these Nova Centurions acted as protectors of the galaxy. Having been deputized by the dying alien, Richard found himself with the ability to fly, incredible strength, and a degree of invulnerability. Although inexperienced, he was determined to use these powers to the best of his ability.

After the conclusion of this series, Nova made an ill-fated appearance in ROM #24 where he lost his powers. As it turned out, the ability to use them had merely been submerged in his subconscious. This was revealed to Richard by Night Thrasher in New Warriors #1, when Night Thrasher dropped him off a building, literally scaring Ryder into regaining the power of flight.

1 ❑ Sep 1976 Cover: 0.30 **NM** value: **4.00**
• **CGC:** 37 graded, best 9.8
A: John Buscema; Joe Sinnott **W:** Marv Wolfman ★ Origin of Nova I (Richard Ryder). ★ 1st Appearance of Nova I (Richard Ryder).
2 ❑ Oct 1976 Cover: 0.30 **NM** value: **2.50**
📖 The First Night Of...Condor! **A:** John Buscema; Joe Sinnott **W:** Marv Wolfman ★ 1st Appearance of Powerhouse.
3 ❑ Nov 1976 Cover: 0.30 **NM** value: **2.00**
★ 1st Appearance of Diamondhead.
4 ❑ Dec 1976 Cover: 0.30 **NM** value: **2.00**
5 ❑ Jan 1977 Cover: 0.30 **NM** value: **2.00**
6 ❑ Feb 1977 Cover: 0.30 **NM** value: **2.00**
★ 1st Appearance of The Sphinx.
7 ❑ Mar 1977 Cover: 0.30 **NM** value: **2.00**
★ Origin of The Sphinx.
8 ❑ Apr 1977 Cover: 0.30 **NM** value: **2.00**
9 ❑ May 1977 Cover: 0.30 **NM** value: **2.00**
10 ❑ Jun 1977 Cover: 0.30 **NM** value: **2.00**
11 ❑ Jul 1977 Cover: 0.30 **NM** value: **2.00**
12 ❑ Aug 1977 Cover: 0.30 **NM** value: **1.50**
• **CGC:** 1 graded, best 9.4
★ Appearance of Spider-Man.
13 ❑ Sep 1977 Cover: 0.30 **NM** value: **1.50**
★ 1st Appearance of Crimebuster.
14 ❑ Oct 1977 Cover: 0.30 **NM** value: **1.50**
15 ❑ Nov 1977 Cover: 0.35 **NM** value: **1.50**
16 ❑ Dec 1977 Cover: 0.35 **NM** value: **1.50**
• **CGC:** 1 graded, best 9.4
★ Versus Yellow Claw.
17 ❑ Jan 1978 Cover: 0.35 **NM** value: **1.50**
18 ❑ Mar 1978 Cover: 0.35 **NM** value: **1.50**
19 ❑ May 1978 Cover: 0.35 **NM** value: **1.50**
★ Origin of Blackout I (Marcus Daniels). ★ 1st Appearance of Blackout I (Marcus Daniels).
20 ❑ Jul 1978 Cover: 0.35 **NM** value: **1.50**
21 ❑ Sep 1978 Cover: 0.35 **NM** value: **1.50**
• Only appears as Harris Moore ★ 1st Appearance of Harris Moore (Comet).
22 ❑ Nov 1978 Cover: 0.35 **NM** value: **1.50**
★ Origin of Comet (Harris Moore). ★ 1st Appearance of Comet (Harris Moore).
23 ❑ Jan 1979 Cover: 0.35 **NM** value: **1.50**
24 ❑ Mar 1979 Cover: 0.35 **NM** value: **1.50**
★ Origin of Crimebuster.
25 ❑ May 1979 Cover: 0.40 **NM** value: **1.50**
final issue.

NOVA (2ND SERIES) Marvel

1 ❑ Jan 1994 Cover: 2.25 **NM** value: **Cover or less**
Circ: Statement: **51,692** CapCity orders: **42,200**
📖 Meavy Mettle **A:** Chris Marrinan **W:** Fabian Nicieza
1/SC ❑ Jan 1994 Cover: 2.95 **NM** value: **Cover or less**
Special cover. 📖 Meavy Mettle **A:** Chris Marrinan **W:** Fabian Nicieza
2 ❑ Feb 1994 Cover: 1.75 **NM** value: **2.00**
Circ: Statement: **51,692** CapCity orders: **22,375**
3 ❑ Mar 1994 Cover: 1.75 **NM** value: **Cover or less**
Circ: Statement: **51,692** CapCity orders: **18,850**
4 ❑ Apr 1994 Cover: 1.75 **NM** value: **Cover or less**
Circ: Statement: **51,692** CapCity orders: **15,700**
5 ❑ May 1994 Cover: 1.95 **NM** value: **Cover or less**
Circ: Statement: **51,692** CapCity orders: **14,200**
6 ❑ Jun 1994 Cover: 1.95 **NM** value: **Cover or less**
Circ: Statement: **51,692** CapCity orders: **13,950**
7 ❑ Jul 1994 Cover: 1.95 **NM** value: **Cover or less**
Circ: Statement: **51,692** CapCity orders: **14,000**
📖 Time and Time Again, Part 6
8 ❑ Aug 1994 Cover: 1.95 **NM** value: **Cover or less**
Circ: Statement: **51,692** CapCity orders: **12,800**
9 ❑ Sep 1994 Cover: 1.95 **NM** value: **Cover or less**
Circ: Statement: **51,692** CapCity orders: **12,550**
10 ❑ Oct 1994 Cover: 1.95 **NM** value: **Cover or less**
Circ: Statement: **51,692** CapCity orders: **11,800**
11 ❑ Nov 1994 Cover: 1.95 **NM** value: **Cover or less**
Circ: Statement: **51,692** CapCity orders: **10,750**
★ Versus new Fantastic Four.
12 ❑ Dec 1994 Cover: 1.95 **NM** value: **Cover or less**
Circ: Statement: **51,692** CapCity orders: **10,050**
13 ❑ Jan 1995 Cover: 1.95 **NM** value: **Cover or less**
Circ: CapCity orders: **9,650**
14 ❑ Feb 1995 Cover: 1.95 **NM** value: **Cover or less**
Circ: CapCity orders: **8,500**
15 ❑ Mar 1995 Cover: 1.95 **NM** value: **Cover or less**
Circ: CapCity orders: **7,675**
• Has 1994 Statement, filed 10/1/94; avg print run 83,592; avg sales 325; avg subs 51,692; avg total paid 51,692; samples 125; office use 500; max existent 52,317; 37% of run returned
16 ❑ Apr 1995 Cover: 1.95 **NM** value: **Cover or less**
Circ: CapCity orders: **7,275**
17 ❑ May 1995 Cover: 1.95 **NM** value: **Cover or less**
Circ: CapCity orders: **6,925**
18 ❑ Jun 1995 Cover: 1.95 **NM** value: **Cover or less**
Circ: CapCity orders: **7,125**
final issue.

NOVA (3RD SERIES) Marvel

1 ❑ May 1999 Cover: 2.99 **NM** value: **Cover or less**
Circ: Diamd. preorders: **41,417**
wraparound cover. 📖 Starting Over **A:** Erik Larsen; Joe Bennett **W:** Erik Larsen
2 ❑ Jun 1999 Cover: 1.99 **NM** value: **Cover or less**
Circ: Diamd. preorders: **37,751**
A: Erik Larsen **W:** Erik Larsen ★ Appearance of Captain America, Namorita regains human. ★ Versus Diamondhead.
3 ❑ Jul 1999 Cover: 1.99 **NM** value: **Cover or less**
Circ: Diamd. preorders: **29,754**
A: Erik Larsen **W:** Erik Larsen ★ Appearance of Sphinx. ★ Versus Quintronic Man.
4 ❑ Aug 1999 Cover: 1.99 **NM** value: **Cover or less**
Circ: Diamd. preorders: **29,535**
A: Erik Larsen **W:** Erik Larsen ★ Appearance of Fantastic Four.
5 ❑ Sep 1999 Cover: 1.99 **NM** value: **Cover or less**
Circ: Diamd. preorders: **28,416**
W: Erik Larsen
6 ❑ Oct 1999 Cover: 1.99 **NM** value: **Cover or less**
Circ: Diamd. preorders: **25,656**
📖 The Dying Game **A:** Joe Bennett **W:** Erik Larsen
7 ❑ Nov 1999 Cover: 1.99 **NM** value: **Cover or less**
Circ: Diamd. preorders: **23,836**

NOVA HUNTER Ryal

1 ❑ Cover: 2.50 **NM** value: **Cover or less**
A: Max Nichols **W:** Robert Schaeffer
1/Aut ❑ Cover: 4.00 **NM** value: **Cover or less**
A: Max Nichols **W:** Robert Schaeffer

NOW COMICS PREVIEW Now

1 ❑ **NM** value: **1.00**
★ 1st Appearance of Thunderstar, Valor, Vector, Syphons, Ralph Snart.

NOW HEPESVILLE Caliber

1 ❑ b&w Cover: 3.50 **NM** value: **Cover or less**
One-shot.

NOWHERESVILLE Caliber

1 ❑ b&w Cover: 3.50 **NM** value: **Cover or less**

NOWHERESVILLE: DEATH BY STARLIGHT Caliber

1 ❑ b&w Cover: 2.95 **NM** value: **Cover or less**
A: Mark Ricketts **W:** Mark Ricketts
2 ❑ b&w Cover: 2.95 **NM** value: **Cover or less**
A: Mark Ricketts **W:** Mark Ricketts
3 ❑ b&w Cover: 2.95 **NM** value: **Cover or less**
• flip book with Wordsmith #7 back-up **A:** Mark Ricketts **W:** Mark Ricketts
4 ❑ Cover: 2.95 **NM** value: **Cover or less**
A: Mark Ricketts **W:** Mark Ricketts

NOW, ON A MORE SERIOUS NOTE... Dawn

1 ❑ Sum 1994, b&w **NM** value: **2.00**
no cover price.

NOW WE ARE SICK Dreamhaven

1 ❑ Cover: 11.95 **NM** value: **Cover or less**
A: Gahan Wilson; Andy Smith; Clive Barker **W:** Stephen Jones; Galad Elf; Harry Adam Knight; John Grant; Kim Newman; Neil Gaiman; Richard Hill; Robert Bloch; Terry Pratchett

NOW WHAT?! Now

1 ❑ Cover: 0.50 **NM** value: **3.00**
2 ❑ Cover: 0.50 **NM** value: **2.00**
3 ❑ Cover: 0.50 **NM** value: **2.00**
4 ❑ Cover: 0.50 **NM** value: **2.00**
5 ❑ Cover: 0.50 **NM** value: **2.00**
6 ❑ Cover: 0.50 **NM** value: **2.00**
7 ❑ Cover: 0.50 **NM** value: **2.00**
8 ❑ Cover: 0.50 **NM** value: **2.00**
9 ❑ Cover: 0.50 **NM** value: **2.00**
10 ❑ Cover: 0.50 **NM** value: **2.00**
11 ❑ Cover: 0.50 **NM** value: **2.00**

NTH MAN, THE ULTIMATE NINJA Marvel

1 ❑ Aug 1989 Cover: 1.00 **NM** value: **Cover or less**
Circ: CapCity orders: **29,200**
📖 Recall **A:** Ron Wagner **W:** Larry Hama

CGC-graded: Multiply prices above by **33 for 9.9 M • 16 for 9.8 NM/M • 7 for 9.6 NM+ • 5 for 9.4 NM • 2.5 for 9.2 NM- • 1.5 for 9.0 VF/NM**

2 ❑ Sep 1989 Cover: 1.00 **NM** value: **Cover or less**
Circ: CapCity orders: **20,500**
3 ❑ Oct 1989 Cover: 1.00 **NM** value: **Cover or less**
Circ: CapCity orders: **18,700**
4 ❑ Nov 1989 Cover: 1.00 **NM** value: **Cover or less**
Circ: CapCity orders: **18,200**
5 ❑ Nov 1989 Cover: 1.00 **NM** value: **Cover or less**
Circ: CapCity orders: **18,700**
6 ❑ Dec 1989 Cover: 1.00 **NM** value: **Cover or less**
Circ: CapCity orders: **17,400**
7 ❑ Dec 1989 Cover: 1.00 **NM** value: **Cover or less**
Circ: CapCity orders: **16,200**
8 ❑ Jan 1990 Cover: 1.00 **NM** value: **Cover or less**
Circ: CapCity orders: **15,500**
A: Dale Keown
9 ❑ Feb 1990 Cover: 1.00 **NM** value: **Cover or less**
Circ: CapCity orders: **14,300**
10 ❑ Mar 1990 Cover: 1.00 **NM** value: **Cover or less**
Circ: CapCity orders: **13,100**
11 ❑ Apr 1990 Cover: 1.00 **NM** value: **Cover or less**
Circ: CapCity orders: **12,100**
12 ❑ May 1990 Cover: 1.00 **NM** value: **Cover or less**
Circ: CapCity orders: **12,200**
13 ❑ Jun 1990 Cover: 1.00 **NM** value: **Cover or less**
Circ: CapCity orders: **11,400**
14 ❑ Jul 1990 Cover: 1.00 **NM** value: **Cover or less**
Circ: CapCity orders: **11,300**
15 ❑ Aug 1990 Cover: 1.00 **NM** value: **Cover or less**
Circ: CapCity orders: **10,700**
16 ❑ Sep 1990 Cover: 1.00 **NM** value: **Cover or less**
Circ: CapCity orders: **10,400**

NUANCE — Magnetic Ink

1 ❑ b&w Cover: 2.75 **NM** value: **Cover or less**
2 ❑ b&w Cover: 2.75 **NM** value: **Cover or less**
3 ❑ b&w Cover: 2.75 **NM** value: **Cover or less**

NUCLEAR WAR! — NEC

1 ❑ Cover: 3.50 **NM** value: **Cover or less**
2 ❑ Nov 2000 Cover: 3.50 **NM** value: **Cover or less**
📖 Give me Shelter, Part 2 **A:** Ron Ledwell **W:** Ron Ledwell

NUKLA — Dell

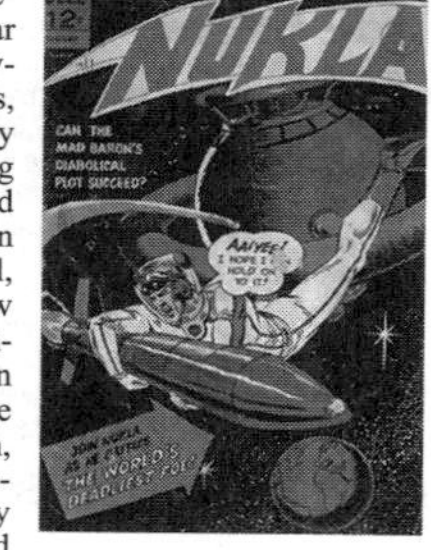

Nukla is one of the slew of nuclear-powered super-heroes to appear in the mid-Sixties to the mid-Seventies. Nukla was Matthew Gibbs, a U-2 pilot, who was atomized by an atomic blast. Instead of killing him, however, the blast transformed him, giving him the ability to turn into Nukla, the Nuclear Man. Still, a job's a job, and Gibbs used his new abilities in the service of his government. He was still a pilot, but when he transformed into Nukla he gained invisibility, super-strength, nuclear blasts, and the ability to become immaterial. Best yet, any damage done to Gibbs was healed during his transformations.

Nukla was called on to fight cold-war enemies, such as Baron Von Zee (your basic megalomaniacal would-be dictator). The series encompassed a variety of different genres, including superhero, hard science fiction, undercover government espionage, and cold-war adventure. Though highly entertaining, it lasted just four issues.

1 ❑ Oct 1965 Cover: 0.12 **NM** value: **12.00**
• **CGC:** 2 graded, best 9.6
📖 The City In Space ★ Origin of Nukla. ★ 1st Appearance of Nukla.
2 ❑ Mar 1966 Cover: 0.12 **NM** value: **8.00**
3 ❑ Jun 1966 Cover: 0.12 **NM** value: **6.00**
4 ❑ Sep 1966 Cover: 0.12 **NM** value: **10.00**
A: Steve Ditko

NULL PATROL — Escape Velocity

1 ❑ Cover: 1.50 **NM** value: **Cover or less**
2 ❑ Cover: 1.50 **NM** value: **Cover or less**
📖 Fuel Endeavors **A:** Kirk Durfey **W:** Brett Frymire

NUMIDIAN FORCE — Kamite

4 ❑ Cover: 2.00 **NM** value: **Cover or less**

NURSE BETSY CRANE — Charlton

Considering how much play the medical soap opera theme gets elsewhere in popular culture, it is interesting that comic books have not mined this vein with much conviction. Nurse Betsy Crane, a product of Charlton comics, is one of the few examples. Betsy Crane is (surprise!) a kind-hearted nurse with a knack for picking really cute, really troubled patients. The medical setting allows for an element of Gothic atmosphere and mystery in addition to the usual romance comics histrionics. Also, since Nurse Crane is the titular heroine of the strip, her presence provides continuity, if not genuine character development, that other romance books lack by virtue of the usual anthology format. Dick Giordano, who subsequently went on to become an artist and editor at DC, applied his eye-pleasing style to the covers and stories of this book.

12 ❑ 1961 **NM** value: **10.00**
13 ❑ 1961 **NM** value: **8.00**
14 ❑ **NM** value: **8.00**
15 ❑ **NM** value: **8.00**
16 ❑ Cover: 0.12 **NM** value: **8.00**
17 ❑ Cover: 0.12 **NM** value: **8.00**
18 ❑ May 1962 Cover: 0.12 **NM** value: **8.00**
19 ❑ Jun 1962 Cover: 0.12 **NM** value: **8.00**
20 ❑ Jul 1962 Cover: 0.12 **NM** value: **8.00**
21 ❑ Aug 1962 Cover: 0.12 **NM** value: **6.00**
22 ❑ Sep 1962 Cover: 0.12 **NM** value: **6.00**
23 ❑ Cover: 0.12 **NM** value: **6.00**
24 ❑ Cover: 0.12 **NM** value: **6.00**
25 ❑ Cover: 0.12 **NM** value: **6.00**
26 ❑ Cover: 0.12 **NM** value: **6.00**
27 ❑ Mar 1964 Cover: 0.12 **NM** value: **6.00**
final issue.

NURSERY RHYMES — Ziff-Davis

10 ❑ ca. 1951 Cover: 0.10 **NM** value: **75.00**

NURTURE THE DEVIL — Fantagraphics

2 ❑ Jul 1994, b&w Cover: 2.50 **NM** value: **Cover or less**
3 ❑ Dec 1994, b&w Cover: 2.50 **NM** value: **Cover or less**

NUT RUNNERS — Rip Off

1 ❑ Sep 1991, b&w Cover: 2.50 **NM** value: **Cover or less**
2 ❑ Jan 1992, b&w Cover: 2.50 **NM** value: **Cover or less**

NUTS! — Premiere

1 ❑ Mar 1954 Cover: 0.10 **NM** value: **150.00**
2 ❑ May 1954 Cover: 0.10 **NM** value: **100.00**
• **CGC:** 1 graded, best 9.0
3 ❑ Jul 1954 Cover: 0.10 **NM** value: **100.00**
4 ❑ Sep 1954 Cover: 0.10 **NM** value: **100.00**
5 ❑ Nov 1954 Cover: 0.10 **NM** value: **100.00**

NUTS & BOTS — Excel Graphics

1 ❑ Aug 1998, b&w Cover: 3.95 **NM** value: **Cover or less**
• magazine.

NUTTY COMICS (FAWCETT) — Fawcett

1 ❑ Win 1946 Cover: 0.10 **NM** value: **100.00**

NUTTY COMICS (HARVEY) — Harvey

4 ❑ 1946 Cover: 0.10 **NM** value: **50.00**
5 ❑ 1946 Cover: 0.10 **NM** value: **40.00**
6 ❑ Feb 1947 Cover: 0.10 **NM** value: **40.00**
7 ❑ Apr 1947 Cover: 0.10 **NM** value: **40.00**
8 ❑ Jul 1947 Cover: 0.10 **NM** value: **40.00**

NUTTY LIFE — Fox

2 ❑ 1947 Cover: 0.10 **NM** value: **60.00**

NYGHT SCHOOL — Brainstorm

All issues are adults only.
2 ❑ b&w Cover: 2.95 **NM** value: **Cover or less**

NYOKA THE JUNGLE GIRL — Fawcett

Prior to becoming the star of this third major jungle title (behind Jungle Comics and Sheena, Queen of the Jungle), Nyoka was the centerpiece of a number of movie serials. She was the daughter of one Dr. Meredith (later anthropologist Henry Gordon) who moved to Africa to avoid being confused with his evil twin brother "Slick." Like Tarzan before her, she learned the ways of the jungle from the natives and soon became a white-skinned adventuress in her own right. Her comics appearances portrayed her in shorts and a low-cut blouse accented by a knife and revolver. Although meant as a girl's adventure, Nyoka (and her somewhat skimpy outfits) no doubt also appealed to a sizeable male readership. Nevertheless, it was her quick wits, self-reliance, and occasional use of a solid right hook that made her more than just another leotard-clad damsel in distress.

3 ❑ Spr 1946 Cover: 0.10 **NM** value: **235.00**
4 ❑ Fal 1946 Cover: 0.10 **NM** value: **175.00**
• **CGC:** 1 graded, best 9.2
5 ❑ Mar 1947 Cover: 0.10 **NM** value: **175.00**
6 ❑ Apr 1947 Cover: 0.10 **NM** value: **145.00**
7 ❑ May 1947 Cover: 0.10 **NM** value: **145.00**
• **CGC:** 1 graded, best 7.5
8 ❑ Jun 1947 Cover: 0.10 **NM** value: **145.00**
9 ❑ Jul 1947 Cover: 0.10 **NM** value: **145.00**
10 ❑ Aug 1947 Cover: 0.10 **NM** value: **145.00**
• **CGC:** 1 graded, best 7.5
11 ❑ Sep 1947 Cover: 0.10 **NM** value: **110.00**
• **CGC:** 1 graded, best 9.0
12 ❑ Oct 1947 Cover: 0.10 **NM** value: **110.00**
13 ❑ Nov 1947 Cover: 0.10 **NM** value: **110.00**
• **CGC:** 1 graded, best 8.0
14 ❑ Dec 1947 Cover: 0.10 **NM** value: **110.00**
• **CGC:** 1 graded, best 9.4
15 ❑ Jan 1948 Cover: 0.10 **NM** value: **110.00**
16 ❑ Feb 1948 Cover: 0.10 **NM** value: **110.00**
17 ❑ Mar 1948 Cover: 0.10 **NM** value: **110.00**
• **CGC:** 1 graded, best 7.5
18 ❑ Apr 1948 Cover: 0.10 **NM** value: **110.00**
19 ❑ May 1948 Cover: 0.10 **NM** value: **110.00**
• **CGC:** 1 graded, best 7.0
20 ❑ Jun 1948 Cover: 0.10 **NM** value: **110.00**
• **CGC:** 1 graded, best 8.5
21 ❑ Jul 1948 Cover: 0.10 **NM** value: **85.00**
22 ❑ Aug 1948 Cover: 0.10 **NM** value: **85.00**
23 ❑ Sep 1948 Cover: 0.10 **NM** value: **85.00**
24 ❑ Oct 1948 Cover: 0.10 **NM** value: **85.00**
25 ❑ Nov 1948 Cover: 0.10 **NM** value: **85.00**
26 ❑ Dec 1948 Cover: 0.10 **NM** value: **85.00**
• **CGC:** 1 graded, best 9.0
27 ❑ Jan 1949 Cover: 0.10 **NM** value: **85.00**
28 ❑ Feb 1949 Cover: 0.10 **NM** value: **85.00**
📖 The Human Statues of the Jungle; The Legendary Jungle Bird; The Weakling (text story); Colonel Corn and Korny Kobb: Job Hunters; Persistent Paul: Hang it All!; Egbert the Explorer: Tramp Steamer
29 ❑ Mar 1949 Cover: 0.10 **NM** value: **85.00**
30 ❑ Apr 1949 Cover: 0.10 **NM** value: **85.00**
31 ❑ May 1949 Cover: 0.10 **NM** value: **65.00**
32 ❑ Jun 1949 Cover: 0.10 **NM** value: **65.00**
33 ❑ Jul 1949 Cover: 0.10 **NM** value: **65.00**
34 ❑ Aug 1949 Cover: 0.10 **NM** value: **65.00**
35 ❑ Sep 1949 Cover: 0.10 **NM** value: **65.00**
• **CGC:** 1 graded, best 7.5
36 ❑ Oct 1949 Cover: 0.10 **NM** value: **65.00**
• **CGC:** 1 graded, best 8.5
37 ❑ Nov 1949 Cover: 0.10 **NM** value: **65.00**
38 ❑ Dec 1949 Cover: 0.10 **NM** value: **65.00**
39 ❑ Jan 1950 Cover: 0.10 **NM** value: **65.00**
40 ❑ Feb 1950 Cover: 0.10 **NM** value: **65.00**
41 ❑ Mar 1950 Cover: 0.10 **NM** value: **52.00**
42 ❑ Apr 1950 Cover: 0.10 **NM** value: **52.00**
43 ❑ May 1950 Cover: 0.10 **NM** value: **52.00**
44 ❑ Jun 1950 Cover: 0.10 **NM** value: **52.00**
45 ❑ Jul 1950 Cover: 0.10 **NM** value: **52.00**
46 ❑ Aug 1950 Cover: 0.10 **NM** value: **52.00**
47 ❑ Sep 1950 Cover: 0.10 **NM** value: **52.00**
48 ❑ Oct 1950 Cover: 0.10 **NM** value: **52.00**
49 ❑ Nov 1950 Cover: 0.10 **NM** value: **52.00**
50 ❑ Dec 1950 Cover: 0.10 **NM** value: **52.00**
51 ❑ Jan 1951 Cover: 0.10 **NM** value: **42.00**
52 ❑ Feb 1951 Cover: 0.10 **NM** value: **42.00**
53 ❑ Mar 1951 Cover: 0.10 **NM** value: **42.00**
54 ❑ Apr 1951 Cover: 0.10 **NM** value: **42.00**
55 ❑ May 1951 Cover: 0.10 **NM** value: **42.00**
56 ❑ Jun 1951 Cover: 0.10 **NM** value: **42.00**
57 ❑ Jul 1951 Cover: 0.10 **NM** value: **42.00**
58 ❑ Aug 1951 Cover: 0.10 **NM** value: **42.00**
59 ❑ Sep 1951 Cover: 0.10 **NM** value: **42.00**
60 ❑ Oct 1951 Cover: 0.10 **NM** value: **42.00**
61 ❑ Nov 1951 Cover: 0.10 **NM** value: **38.00**
62 ❑ Dec 1951 Cover: 0.10 **NM** value: **38.00**
63 ❑ Jan 1952 Cover: 0.10 **NM** value: **38.00**
64 ❑ Feb 1952 Cover: 0.10 **NM** value: **38.00**
65 ❑ Mar 1952 Cover: 0.10 **NM** value: **38.00**
66 ❑ Apr 1952 Cover: 0.10 **NM** value: **38.00**
67 ❑ May 1952 Cover: 0.10 **NM** value: **38.00**
68 ❑ Jun 1952 Cover: 0.10 **NM** value: **38.00**
69 ❑ Jul 1952 Cover: 0.10 **NM** value: **38.00**
70 ❑ Aug 1952 Cover: 0.10 **NM** value: **38.00**
71 ❑ Sep 1952 Cover: 0.10 **NM** value: **38.00**
72 ❑ Oct 1952 Cover: 0.10 **NM** value: **38.00**
73 ❑ Nov 1952 Cover: 0.10 **NM** value: **38.00**
74 ❑ Dec 1953 Cover: 0.10 **NM** value: **38.00**
75 ❑ Jan 1953 Cover: 0.10 **NM** value: **38.00**
76 ❑ Apr 1953 Cover: 0.10 **NM** value: **38.00**
77 ❑ Jun 1953 Cover: 0.10 **NM** value: **38.00**
final issue.

OAKY DOAKS — Eastern Color

1 ❑ Jul 1942 Cover: 0.10 **NM** value: **250.00**

OBERGEIST: RAGNAROK HIGHWAY — Image

1 ❑ May 2001 Cover: 2.95 **NM** value: **Cover or less**
Circ: Diamd. preorders: **20,452** • **CGC:** 4 graded, best 9.8
📖 Playing Pinochle with Dead Folks **A:** Tony Harris **W:** Dan Jolley
2 ❑ Jun 2001 Cover: 2.95 **NM** value: **Cover or less**
Circ: Diamd. preorders: **16,626**
A: Tony Harris **W:** Dan Jolley
3 ❑ Jul 2001 Cover: 2.95 **NM** value: **Cover or less**
Circ: Diamd. preorders: **16,193**
A: Tony Harris **W:** Dan Jolley
4 ❑ Aug 2001 Cover: 2.95 **NM** value: **Cover or less**
Circ: Diamd. preorders: **16,284**
A: Tony Harris **W:** Dan Jolley
5 ❑ Sep 2001 Cover: 2.95 **NM** value: **Cover or less**
Circ: Diamd. preorders: **14,882**
A: Tony Harris **W:** Dan Jolley
6 ❑ Oct 2001 Cover: 2.95 **NM** value: **Cover or less**
Circ: Diamd. preorders: **13,771**
A: Tony Harris **W:** Dan Jolley

OBIE — Store

1 ❑ ca. 1953 Cover: 0.06 **NM** value: **20.00**

OBJECTIVE FIVE — Image

1 ❑ Jul 2000 Cover: 2.95 **NM** value: **Cover or less**
Circ: Diamd. preorders: **18,997**
📖 Index Case **A:** Luke Lizalde **W:** Glenn Kaino; Kevin Hoffer
2 ❑ Aug 2000 Cover: 2.95 **NM** value: **Cover or less**
Circ: Diamd. preorders: **13,386**
A: Luke Lizalde **W:** Kevin Hoffler
3 ❑ Sep 2000 Cover: 2.95 **NM** value: **Cover or less**
Circ: Diamd. preorders: **11,522**
📖 Airborne **A:** Luke Lizalde **W:** Kevin Hoffler; RJ Gamayo
4 ❑ Nov 2000 Cover: 2.95 **NM** value: **Cover or less**
Circ: Diamd. preorders: **10,061**
📖 Reunion **A:** Luke Lizalde **W:** Kevin Hoffler
5 ❑ Dec 2000 Cover: 2.95 **NM** value: **Cover or less**
Circ: Diamd. preorders: **9,623**

Other grades: Multiply prices above by **1.5 for Mint • 2/3 for Very Fine • 1/3 for Fine • 1/5 for Very Good • 1/8 for Good**

📖 Point of No Return **A:** Luke Lizalde **W:** Kevin Hoffler; Todd Samovitz
6 ❑ Jan 2001 Cover: 2.95 **NM** value: **Cover or less**
Circ: Diamd. preorders: **9,105**
📖 Digging in China **A:** Luke Lizalde **W:** Kevin Hoffer; Todd Samovitz

OBLIVION — Comico
1 ❑ Jan 1996 Cover: 2.50 **NM** value: **Cover or less**
Circ: CapCity orders: **5,975**
A: Andrew Dimitt **W:** Jack Herman
2 ❑ Mar 1996 Cover: 2.50 **NM** value: **Cover or less**
Circ: CapCity orders: **2,735**
A: Andrew Dimitt **W:** Jack Herman
3 ❑ May 1996 Cover: 2.95 **NM** value: **Cover or less**
Circ: CapCity orders: **2,010**
A: Andrew Dimitt **W:** Jack Herman

OBLIVION CITY — Slave Labor
1 ❑ Mar 1991, b&w Cover: 2.50 **NM** value: **Cover or less**
2 ❑ May 1991, b&w Cover: 2.50 **NM** value: **Cover or less**
3 ❑ Jun 1991, b&w Cover: 2.50 **NM** value: **Cover or less**
4 ❑ Jun 1991, b&w Cover: 2.50 **NM** value: **Cover or less**
5 ❑ Sep 1991, b&w Cover: 2.50 **NM** value: **Cover or less**
6 ❑ Jan 1992, b&w Cover: 2.50 **NM** value: **Cover or less**
7 ❑ Apr 1992 Cover: 2.95 **NM** value: **Cover or less**
8 ❑ May 1992 Cover: 2.95 **NM** value: **Cover or less**
9 ❑ Jun 1992 Cover: 3.95 **NM** value: **Cover or less**

OBNOXIO THE CLOWN — Marvel
This one-shot comic featured Obnoxio, the decrepit, cigar-smoking, alcoholic clown from Crazy magazine. The Uncanny X-Men's Professor Xavier hires him to entertain at Kitty Pryde's birthday party, but things don't turn out the way they should. An intruder sets off the X-Men's alarms and Obnoxio gets caught in the midst of it all. As a result, the clown ends up fighting the X-Men with seltzer water and sneezing powder. In the end, Professor Xavier catches the real intruder-an ice cream man gone bad.

Obnoxio closes his show by thwarting a crime gang when he's called in for jury duty. Despite his good deed for the day, we doubt the X-Men are going to be inviting him back soon.

The issue doesn't always work, but some funny back-up features help make the sale.

1 ❑ Apr 1983 Cover: 0.60 **NM** value: **2.00**
• **CGC:** 2 graded, best 9.6
📖 Something Slimey This Way Comes! • X-Men **A:** Alan Kupperberg **W:** Alan Kupperberg

OCCULT FILES OF DR. SPEKTOR, THE — Gold Key
Attempting to cash in on the horror comic anthology format that had proven so popular at DC and Marvel, Gold Key (which had earlier had success with Twilight Zone) trotted out its own horror host in the form of Dr. Spektor, a supernatural researcher who opened his files of the strange and bizarre as the basis for the series' stories.

In addition to the standard horror stories, the series ran a couple of unused Doctor Solar, Man of the Atom tales. The first 24 issues, produced between 1973 and 1977, had painted covers, while a final issue, #25, was produced in 1982. — Brent

1 ❑ Apr 1973 Cover: 0.20 **NM** value: **12.00**
2 ❑ Jun 1973 Cover: 0.20 **NM** value: **6.00**
3 ❑ Aug 1973 Cover: 0.20 **NM** value: **4.00**
4 ❑ Oct 1973 Cover: 0.20 **NM** value: **4.00**
5 ❑ Dec 1973 Cover: 0.20 **NM** value: **4.00**
6 ❑ Feb 1974 Cover: 0.20 **NM** value: **3.00**
7 ❑ Apr 1974 Cover: 0.20 **NM** value: **3.00**
8 ❑ Jun 1974 Cover: 0.20 **NM** value: **3.00**
9 ❑ Aug 1974 Cover: 0.25 **NM** value: **3.00**
📖 She Who Serves The Dark Gods; The Pit
10 ❑ Oct 1974 Cover: 0.25 **NM** value: **3.00**
11 ❑ Dec 1974 Cover: 0.25 **NM** value: **3.00**
12 ❑ Feb 1975 Cover: 0.25 **NM** value: **3.00**
13 ❑ Apr 1975 Cover: 0.25 **NM** value: **3.00**
14 ❑ Jun 1975 Cover: 0.25 **NM** value: **3.00**
15 ❑ Aug 1975 Cover: 0.25 **NM** value: **3.00**
16 ❑ Oct 1975 Cover: 0.25 **NM** value: **3.00**
17 ❑ Dec 1975 Cover: 0.25 **NM** value: **3.00**
18 ❑ Feb 1976 Cover: 0.25 **NM** value: **3.00**
19 ❑ Apr 1976 Cover: 0.25 **NM** value: **3.00**
20 ❑ Jun 1976 Cover: 0.25 **NM** value: **3.00**
21 ❑ Aug 1976 Cover: 0.25 **NM** value: **2.00**
22 ❑ Oct 1976 Cover: 0.30 **NM** value: **2.00**
23 ❑ Dec 1977 Cover: 0.30 **NM** value: **2.00**
24 ❑ Feb 1977 Cover: 0.30 **NM** value: **2.00**
25 ❑ May 1982 **NM** value: **2.00**

OCCULT LAFF-PARADE — Print Mint
1 ❑ Cover: 0.50 **NM** value: **3.00**
📖 Death is Love; Fingernail of Fear; Bayooh Blooze; Telephone Booth to Nirvana; Teddy Meets the Kootcha Bug; Bud Tuttle and Commander Jesus **A:** Jay Kinney; Justin; Kim Deitch; Larry Todd; Ned Sonntag; Rory Hayes and Rick Griffin **W:** Jay Kinney; Justin; Kim Deitch; Larry Todd; Ned Sonntag; Rory Hayes and Rick Griffin

OCEAN COMICS — Ocean
1 ❑ b&w Cover: 1.75 **NM** value: **Cover or less**

OCELOT, THE — Eros
1 ❑ Cover: 2.75 **NM** value: **Cover or less**
2 ❑ Cover: 2.75 **NM** value: **Cover or less**
3 ❑ Cover: 2.75 **NM** value: **Cover or less**

OCTOBER YEN — Antarctic
1 ❑ Jul 1996, b&w Cover: 3.50 **NM** value: **Cover or less**
A: Brandon Graham **W:** Brandon Graham
2 ❑ Sep 1996, b&w Cover: 2.95 **NM** value: **Cover or less**
A: Brandon Graham **W:** Brandon Graham
3 ❑ Nov 1996, b&w Cover: 2.95 **NM** value: **Cover or less**
A: Brandon Graham **W:** Brandon Graham

OCTOBRIANA — Revolution
1 ❑ Cover: 2.95 **NM** value: **3.50**
📖 The Octobriana Files, Part 1; Return of Octobriana, Part 1 **A:** Adrian Bamforth; Blake O'Farrell **W:** John A. Short; Stuart Taylor
2 ❑ Cover: 2.95 **NM** value: **Cover or less**
3 ❑ Cover: 2.95 **NM** value: **Cover or less**
4 ❑ Cover: 2.95 **NM** value: **Cover or less**
5 ❑ Cover: 2.95 **NM** value: **Cover or less**

OCTOBRIANA: FILLING IN THE BLANKS — Artful Salamander
1 ❑ Win 1998, b&w Cover: 2.95 **NM** value: **Cover or less**

ODD ADVENTURE-ZINE, THE — Zamboni Press
1 ❑ Cover: 2.95 **NM** value: **Cover or less**
2 ❑ Apr 1997 Cover: 2.95 **NM** value: **Cover or less**
3 ❑ Jul 1997 Cover: 2.95 **NM** value: **Cover or less**
4 ❑ Dec 1997 Cover: 2.95 **NM** value: **Cover or less**

ODDJOB — Slave Labor
1 ❑ Spr 1999, b&w Cover: 2.95 **NM** value: **Cover or less**
Circ: Diamd. preorders: **2,003**
📖 Death by Gummi **A:** Ian Smith; Tyson Smith **W:** Ian Smith; Tyson Smith

OFFCASTES — Marvel / Epic
1 ❑ Cover: 2.50 **NM** value: **Cover or less**
Circ: CapCity orders: **16,400**
Embossed cover. **A:** Mike Vosburg **W:** Mike Vosburg
2 ❑ Cover: 1.95 **NM** value: **Cover or less**
Circ: CapCity orders: **7,900**
A: Mike Vosburg **W:** Mike Vosburg
3 ❑ Cover: 1.95 **NM** value: **Cover or less**
Circ: CapCity orders: **5,800**
A: Mike Vosburg **W:** Mike Vosburg

OFFERINGS — Cry for Dawn
All issues are adults only.
1 ❑ b&w Cover: 2.75 **NM** value: **Cover or less**
2 ❑ b&w Cover: 2.50 **NM** value: **Cover or less**

OFFICIAL BUZ SAWYER — Pioneer
1 ❑ Aug 1988, b&w Cover: 2.00 **NM** value: **Cover or less**
A: Roy Crane
2 ❑ Sep 1988, b&w Cover: 2.00 **NM** value: **Cover or less**
A: Roy Crane
3 ❑ Oct 1988, b&w Cover: 2.00 **NM** value: **Cover or less**
A: Roy Crane
4 ❑ Nov 1988, b&w Cover: 2.00 **NM** value: **Cover or less**
A: Roy Crane
5 ❑ Dec 1988, b&w Cover: 2.00 **NM** value: **Cover or less**
A: Roy Crane

OFFICIAL HANDBOOK OF THE CONAN UNIVERSE — Marvel
1 ❑ Cover: 1.25 **NM** value: **1.50**
Circ: CapCity orders: **8,300**
2 ❑ Cover: 1.25 **NM** value: **Cover or less**
No issue number. • no price; sold with Conan Saga #75

OFFICIAL HANDBOOK OF THE MARVEL UNIVERSE (VOL. 1) — Marvel
Not a comics series but involving huge amounts of comics art and work by Marvel's staff, the Official Handbook of the Marvel Universe sought to detail every Marvel character, from the Abomination to Zzzax. Issues #1-12 covered living heroes, followed by two issues covering characters who were (at least then) dead or inactive, and one on weapons and paraphernalia.

Covers depicted characters inside and fused (if a bit unevenly) to make a giant poster. Clearly tapping an area of great collector interest, Marvel went back to the well with a updated Deluxe editions, followed by the Master Edition, which is not comic-book sized but is actually designed for three-ring binders (so later updates could be made). The success of this title also inspired DC's Who's Who series. — JJM

1 ❑ Jan 1983 Cover: 1.00 **NM** value: **2.00**
• **CGC:** 1 graded, best 9.4
• Abomination to Avengers Quinjet
2 ❑ Feb 1983 Cover: 1.00 **NM** value: **2.00**
• Baron Mordo to The Collective Man
3 ❑ Mar 1983 Cover: 1.00 **NM** value: **2.00**
• The Collector to Dracula
4 ❑ Apr 1983 Cover: 1.00 **NM** value: **2.00**
• Dragon Man to Gypsy Moth
5 ❑ May 1983 Cover: 1.00 **NM** value: **2.00**
• Hangman to Juggernaut
6 ❑ Jun 1983 Cover: 1.00 **NM** value: **2.00**
• Kang to Man-Bull
7 ❑ Jul 1983 Cover: 1.00 **NM** value: **2.00**
• Mandarin to Mystique
8 ❑ Aug 1983 Cover: 1.00 **NM** value: **2.00**
• Namorita to Pyro
9 ❑ Sep 1983 Cover: 1.00 **NM** value: **2.00**
• Quasar to She-Hulk
10 ❑ Oct 1983 Cover: 1.00 **NM** value: **2.00**
• Shi'ar to Sub-Mariner
11 ❑ Nov 1983 Cover: 1.00 **NM** value: **2.00**
• Subterraneans to Ursa Major
12 ❑ Dec 1983 Cover: 1.00 **NM** value: **2.00**
• Valkyrie to Zzzax
13 ❑ Feb 1984 Cover: 1.00 **NM** value: **2.00**
• Book of the Dead: Air-Walker to Man-Wolf
14 ❑ Mar 1984 Cover: 1.00 **NM** value: **2.00**
• Book of the Dead: Marvel Boy to Zuras
15 ❑ May 1984 Cover: 1.00 **NM** value: **2.00**
• Weapons, Hardware, and Paraphernalia

OFFICIAL HANDBOOK OF THE MARVEL UNIVERSE (VOL. 2) — Marvel
1 ❑ Dec 1985 Cover: 1.50 **NM** value: **2.00**
Circ: CapCity orders: **40,100**
• Abomination to Batroc's Brigade
2 ❑ Jan 1986 Cover: 1.50 **NM** value: **2.00**
Circ: CapCity orders: **32,700**
• Beast to Clea
3 ❑ Feb 1986 Cover: 1.50 **NM** value: **2.00**
Circ: CapCity orders: **33,400**
• Cloak to Doctor Octopus
4 ❑ Mar 1986 Cover: 1.50 **NM** value: **2.00**
Circ: CapCity orders: **31,400**
• Doctor Strange to Galactus
5 ❑ Apr 1986 Cover: 1.50 **NM** value: **2.00**
Circ: CapCity orders: **32,200**
• Gardener to Hulk
6 ❑ May 1986 Cover: 1.50 **NM** value: **2.00**
Circ: CapCity orders: **31,900**
• Human Torch to Ka-Zar
7 ❑ Jun 1986 Cover: 1.50 **NM** value: **2.00**
Circ: CapCity orders: **33,600**
• Khoryphos to Magneto
8 ❑ Jul 1986 Cover: 1.50 **NM** value: **2.00**
Circ: CapCity orders: **32,300**
• Magus to Mole Man
9 ❑ Aug 1986 Cover: 1.50 **NM** value: **2.00**
Circ: CapCity orders: **32,900**
• Molecule Man to Owl
10 ❑ Sep 1986 Cover: 1.50 **NM** value: **2.00**
Circ: CapCity orders: **32,100**
• Paladin to The Rhino
11 ❑ Oct 1986 Cover: 1.50 **NM** value: **2.00**
Circ: CapCity orders: **31,500**
• Richard Rider to Sidewinder
12 ❑ Nov 1986 Cover: 1.50 **NM** value: **2.00**
Circ: CapCity orders: **32,500**
• Sif to Sunspot
13 ❑ Dec 1986 Cover: 1.50 **NM** value: **2.00**
Circ: CapCity orders: **31,800**
• Super-Adaptoid to Umar
14 ❑ Jan 1987 Cover: 1.50 **NM** value: **2.00**
Circ: CapCity orders: **30,600**
• Unicorn to Wolverine
15 ❑ Mar 1987 Cover: 1.50 **NM** value: **2.00**
Circ: CapCity orders: **33,000**
• Wonder Man to Zzzax and Alien Races
16 ❑ Jun 1987 Cover: 1.50 **NM** value: **2.00**
Circ: CapCity orders: **27,700**
• Book of the Dead: Air-Walker to Death-Stalker
17 ❑ Aug 1987 Cover: 1.50 **NM** value: **2.00**
Circ: CapCity orders: **28,500**
• Book of the Dead: Destiny to Hobgoblin
18 ❑ Oct 1987 Cover: 1.50 **NM** value: **2.00**
Circ: CapCity orders: **29,000**
• Book of the Dead: Hyperion to Nighthawk; Book of the Dead: Hyperion II to Nighthawk II
19 ❑ Dec 1987 Cover: 1.50 **NM** value: **2.00**
Circ: CapCity orders: **26,700**
• Book of the Dead: Nuke to Obadiah Stane
20 ❑ Feb 1988 Cover: 1.50 **NM** value: **2.00**
Circ: CapCity orders: **26,900**
• Book of the Dead: Stick to Zuras
Bk 1 ❑ Jan 1987 Cover: 6.95 **NM** value: **Cover or less**
Bk 2 ❑ Mar 1987 Cover: 6.95 **NM** value: **Cover or less**
Bk 3 ❑ May 1987 Cover: 6.95 **NM** value: **Cover or less**
Bk 4 ❑ Jul 1987 Cover: 6.95 **NM** value: **Cover or less**
Bk 5 ❑ Sep 1987 Cover: 6.95 **NM** value: **Cover or less**
Bk 6 ❑ Nov 1987 Cover: 6.95 **NM** value: **Cover or less**
Bk 7 ❑ Jan 1988 Cover: 6.95 **NM** value: **Cover or less**
Bk 8 ❑ Mar 1988 Cover: 6.95 **NM** value: **Cover or less**
Bk 9 ❑ May 1988 Cover: 6.95 **NM** value: **Cover or less**
Bk 10 ❑ Jul 1988 Cover: 6.95 **NM** value: **Cover or less**

OFFICIAL HANDBOOK OF THE MARVEL UNIVERSE (VOL. 3) — Marvel
1 ❑ Jul 1989 Cover: 1.50 **NM** value: **2.00**
Circ: CapCity orders: **29,600**
• Adversary to Chameleon

CGC-graded: Multiply prices above by **33 for 9.9 M • 16 for 9.8 NM/M • 7 for 9.6 NM+ • 5 for 9.4 NM • 2.5 for 9.2 NM- • 1.5 for 9.0 VF/NM**

2 ❑ Aug 1989 Cover: 1.50 **NM** value: **2.00**
Circ: CapCity orders: **27,100**
• Champion of the Universe to Ecstasy

3 ❑ Sep 1989 Cover: 1.50 **NM** value: **2.00**
Circ: CapCity orders: **27,100**
• Eon to Hulk

4 ❑ Oct 1989 Cover: 1.50 **NM** value: **2.00**
Circ: CapCity orders: **28,200**
• Human Torch I to Manikin

5 ❑ Nov 1989 Cover: 1.50 **NM** value: **2.00**
Circ: CapCity orders: **29,700**
• Marauders to Power Princess

6 ❑ Nov 1989 Cover: 1.50 **NM** value: **2.00**
Circ: CapCity orders: **31,800**
• Prowler to Serpent Society

7 ❑ Dec 1989 Cover: 1.50 **NM** value: **2.00**
Circ: CapCity orders: **31,700**
• Set to Tyrak

8 ❑ Dec 1989 Cover: 1.50 **NM** value: **2.00**
Circ: CapCity orders: **30,100**
• U-Man to Madelyne Pryor

OFFICIAL HANDBOOK OF THE MARVEL UNIVERSE MASTER EDITION — Marvel

1 ❑ Dec 1990 Cover: 3.95 **NM** value: **4.50**
Circ: CapCity orders: **23,240**
• Three-hole punched looseleaf format

2 ❑ Jan 1991 Cover: 3.95 **NM** value: **4.50**
Circ: CapCity orders: **19,700**

3 ❑ Feb 1991 Cover: 3.95 **NM** value: **4.50**
Circ: CapCity orders: **20,260**

4 ❑ Mar 1991 Cover: 3.95 **NM** value: **4.50**
Circ: CapCity orders: **19,480**

5 ❑ Apr 1991 Cover: 3.95 **NM** value: **4.50**
Circ: CapCity orders: **17,100**

6 ❑ May 1991 Cover: 3.95 **NM** value: **Cover or less**
Circ: CapCity orders: **16,400**

7 ❑ Jun 1991 Cover: 3.95 **NM** value: **Cover or less**
Circ: CapCity orders: **16,040**

8 ❑ Jul 1991 Cover: 3.95 **NM** value: **Cover or less**
Circ: CapCity orders: **15,580**

9 ❑ Aug 1991 Cover: 3.95 **NM** value: **Cover or less**
Circ: CapCity orders: **13,990**

10 ❑ Sep 1991 Cover: 3.95 **NM** value: **Cover or less**
Circ: CapCity orders: **14,020**

11 ❑ Oct 1991 Cover: 3.95 **NM** value: **Cover or less**
Circ: CapCity orders: **13,900**

12 ❑ Nov 1991 Cover: 4.50 **NM** value: **Cover or less**
Circ: CapCity orders: **13,460**

13 ❑ Dec 1991 Cover: 4.50 **NM** value: **Cover or less**
Circ: CapCity orders: **12,820**

14 ❑ Jan 1992 Cover: 4.50 **NM** value: **Cover or less**
Circ: CapCity orders: **12,440**

15 ❑ Feb 1992 Cover: 4.50 **NM** value: **Cover or less**
Circ: CapCity orders: **11,540**

16 ❑ Mar 1992 Cover: 4.50 **NM** value: **Cover or less**
Circ: CapCity orders: **10,580**

17 ❑ Apr 1992 Cover: 4.50 **NM** value: **Cover or less**
Circ: CapCity orders: **9,960**

18 ❑ May 1992 Cover: 4.50 **NM** value: **Cover or less**
Circ: CapCity orders: **9,640**

19 ❑ Jun 1992 Cover: 4.50 **NM** value: **Cover or less**
Circ: CapCity orders: **9,440**

20 ❑ Jul 1992 Cover: 4.50 **NM** value: **Cover or less**
Circ: CapCity orders: **8,340**

21 ❑ Aug 1992 Cover: 4.50 **NM** value: **Cover or less**
Circ: CapCity orders: **8,060**

22 ❑ Sep 1992 Cover: 4.50 **NM** value: **Cover or less**
Circ: CapCity orders: **7,480**

23 ❑ Oct 1992 Cover: 4.50 **NM** value: **Cover or less**
Circ: CapCity orders: **6,740**

24 ❑ Nov 1992 Cover: 4.50 **NM** value: **Cover or less**
Circ: CapCity orders: **7,800**

25 ❑ Dec 1992 Cover: 4.50 **NM** value: **Cover or less**
Circ: CapCity orders: **7,580**

26 ❑ Jan 1993 Cover: 4.50 **NM** value: **Cover or less**
Circ: CapCity orders: **7,140**

27 ❑ Feb 1993 Cover: 4.50 **NM** value: **Cover or less**
Circ: CapCity orders: **6,900**

28 ❑ Mar 1993 Cover: 4.95 **NM** value: **Cover or less**
Circ: CapCity orders: **6,840**

29 ❑ Apr 1993 Cover: 4.95 **NM** value: **Cover or less**
Circ: CapCity orders: **7,100**

30 ❑ May 1993 Cover: 4.95 **NM** value: **Cover or less**
Circ: CapCity orders: **7,000**

31 ❑ Jun 1993 Cover: 4.95 **NM** value: **Cover or less**
Circ: CapCity orders: **6,560**

32 ❑ Jul 1993 Cover: 4.95 **NM** value: **Cover or less**
Circ: CapCity orders: **6,520**

33 ❑ Aug 1993 Cover: 4.95 **NM** value: **Cover or less**
Circ: CapCity orders: **6,520**

34 ❑ Sep 1993 Cover: 4.95 **NM** value: **Cover or less**
Circ: CapCity orders: **6,040**

35 ❑ Oct 1993 Cover: 4.95 **NM** value: **Cover or less**
Circ: CapCity orders: **5,840**
A: Keith Pollard ★ Appearance of Hellstrom, Lilith, Spider-Man 2099, Beyonder, Omega Red, Avengers West Coast.

36 ❑ Nov 1993 Cover: 4.95 **NM** value: **Cover or less**
Circ: CapCity orders: **5,440**
final issue.

OFFICIAL HOW TO DRAW G.I. JOE — Blackthorne

1 ❑ Nov 1987 Cover: 2.00 **NM** value: **Cover or less**
2 ❑ Jan 1988 Cover: 2.00 **NM** value: **Cover or less**

OFFICIAL HOW TO DRAW ROBOTECH — Blackthorne

1 ❑ Feb 1987 Cover: 2.00 **NM** value: **Cover or less**
2 ❑ Mar 1987 Cover: 2.00 **NM** value: **Cover or less**
3 ❑ Apr 1987 Cover: 2.00 **NM** value: **Cover or less**
4 ❑ May 1987 Cover: 2.00 **NM** value: **Cover or less**
5 ❑ Jun 1987 Cover: 2.00 **NM** value: **Cover or less**
6 ❑ Jul 1987 Cover: 2.00 **NM** value: **Cover or less**
7 ❑ Aug 1987 Cover: 2.00 **NM** value: **Cover or less**
8 ❑ Sep 1987 Cover: 2.00 **NM** value: **Cover or less**
9 ❑ Oct 1987 Cover: 2.00 **NM** value: **Cover or less**
10 ❑ Nov 1987 Cover: 2.00 **NM** value: **Cover or less**
11 ❑ Dec 1987 Cover: 2.00 **NM** value: **Cover or less**
12 ❑ Jan 1988 Cover: 2.00 **NM** value: **Cover or less**
13 ❑ Feb 1988 Cover: 2.00 **NM** value: **Cover or less**
14 ❑ Mar 1988 Cover: 2.00 **NM** value: **Cover or less**

OFFICIAL HOW TO DRAW TRANSFORMERS — Blackthorne

1 ❑ Sep 1987 Cover: 2.00 **NM** value: **Cover or less**
2 ❑ Nov 1987 Cover: 2.00 **NM** value: **Cover or less**
3 ❑ Jan 1988 Cover: 2.00 **NM** value: **Cover or less**
4 ❑ Mar 1988 Cover: 2.00 **NM** value: **Cover or less**

OFFICIAL JOHNNY HAZARD — Pioneer

1 ❑ Aug 1988, b&w Cover: 2.00 **NM** value: **Cover or less**
• strips

OFFICIAL JUNGLE JIM — Pioneer

1 ❑ Jun 1988, b&w Cover: 2.00 **NM** value: **Cover or less**
A: Alex Raymond
2 ❑ Jul 1988, b&w Cover: 2.00 **NM** value: **Cover or less**
A: Alex Raymond
3 ❑ Aug 1988, b&w Cover: 2.00 **NM** value: **Cover or less**
A: Alex Raymond
4 ❑ Sep 1988, b&w Cover: 2.00 **NM** value: **Cover or less**
A: Alex Raymond
5 ❑ Oct 1988, b&w Cover: 2.00 **NM** value: **Cover or less**
A: Alex Raymond
6 ❑ Nov 1988, b&w Cover: 2.00 **NM** value: **Cover or less**
A: Alex Raymond
7 ❑ Dec 1988, b&w Cover: 2.00 **NM** value: **Cover or less**
A: Alex Raymond
8 ❑ Jan 1989, b&w Cover: 2.00 **NM** value: **Cover or less**
A: Alex Raymond
9 ❑ Feb 1989, b&w Cover: 2.00 **NM** value: **Cover or less**
A: Alex Raymond
10 ❑ Apr 1989 Cover: 2.50 **NM** value: **Cover or less**
11 ❑ Apr 1989 Cover: 2.50 **NM** value: **Cover or less**
12 ❑ Cover: 2.50 **NM** value: **Cover or less**
13 ❑ Cover: 2.50 **NM** value: **Cover or less**
14 ❑ Cover: 2.50 **NM** value: **Cover or less**
15 ❑ Cover: 2.50 **NM** value: **Cover or less**
16 ❑ Cover: 2.50 **NM** value: **Cover or less**
Anl 1 ❑ Jan 1989, b&w Cover: 3.95 **NM** value: **Cover or less**
A: Alex Raymond

OFFICIAL MANDRAKE — Pioneer

1 ❑ Jun 1988, b&w Cover: 2.00 **NM** value: **Cover or less**
2 ❑ Jul 1988, b&w Cover: 2.00 **NM** value: **Cover or less**
3 ❑ Aug 1988, b&w Cover: 2.00 **NM** value: **Cover or less**
4 ❑ Sep 1988, b&w Cover: 2.00 **NM** value: **Cover or less**
5 ❑ Oct 1988, b&w Cover: 2.00 **NM** value: **Cover or less**
6 ❑ Nov 1988, b&w Cover: 2.00 **NM** value: **Cover or less**
7 ❑ Dec 1988, b&w Cover: 2.00 **NM** value: **Cover or less**
8 ❑ Jan 1989, b&w Cover: 2.00 **NM** value: **Cover or less**
9 ❑ Feb 1989, b&w Cover: 2.00 **NM** value: **Cover or less**
10 ❑ Apr 1989 Cover: 2.50 **NM** value: **Cover or less**
11 ❑ Apr 1989 Cover: 2.50 **NM** value: **Cover or less**
12 ❑ Cover: 2.50 **NM** value: **Cover or less**
13 ❑ Cover: 2.50 **NM** value: **Cover or less**
14 ❑ Cover: 2.50 **NM** value: **Cover or less**
15 ❑ Cover: 2.50 **NM** value: **Cover or less**

OFFICIAL MODESTY BLAISE, THE — Pioneer

1 ❑ Jul 1988, b&w Cover: 2.00 **NM** value: **Cover or less**
2 ❑ Aug 1988, b&w Cover: 2.00 **NM** value: **Cover or less**
3 ❑ Sep 1988, b&w Cover: 2.00 **NM** value: **Cover or less**
4 ❑ Oct 1988, b&w Cover: 2.00 **NM** value: **Cover or less**
5 ❑ Nov 1988, b&w Cover: 2.00 **NM** value: **Cover or less**
6 ❑ Dec 1988, b&w Cover: 2.00 **NM** value: **Cover or less**
7 ❑ Dec 1988, b&w Cover: 2.00 **NM** value: **Cover or less**
8 ❑ Jan 1989, b&w Cover: 2.00 **NM** value: **Cover or less**
Anl 1 ❑ Dec 1988, b&w Cover: 4.95 **NM** value: **Cover or less**
★ Origin of Modesty.

OFFICIAL PRINCE VALIANT, THE — Pioneer

1 ❑ b&w Cover: 2.00 **NM** value: **Cover or less**
• Hal Foster **A:** Hal Foster
2 ❑ b&w Cover: 2.00 **NM** value: **Cover or less**
• Hal Foster **A:** Hal Foster
3 ❑ Aug 1988, b&w Cover: 2.00 **NM** value: **Cover or less**
• Hal Foster **A:** Hal Foster
4 ❑ Sep 1988, b&w Cover: 2.00 **NM** value: **Cover or less**
• Hal Foster **A:** Hal Foster
5 ❑ Oct 1988, b&w Cover: 2.00 **NM** value: **Cover or less**
• Hal Foster **A:** Hal Foster
6 ❑ Oct 1988, b&w Cover: 2.00 **NM** value: **Cover or less**
• Hal Foster **A:** Hal Foster
7 ❑ Nov 1988 Cover: 2.00 **NM** value: **Cover or less**
• Foster **A:** Hal Foster **C:** Mike Grell
8 ❑ Dec 1988 Cover: 2.00 **NM** value: **Cover or less**
• Foster **A:** Hal Foster **C:** Mike Grell
9 ❑ Jan 1989 Cover: 2.00 **NM** value: **Cover or less**
• Foster **A:** Hal Foster
10 ❑ Feb 1989 Cover: 2.50 **NM** value: **Cover or less**
11 ❑ Mar 1989 Cover: 2.50 **NM** value: **Cover or less**
12 ❑ Apr 1989 Cover: 2.50 **NM** value: **Cover or less**
13 ❑ Cover: 2.50 **NM** value: **Cover or less**
14 ❑ Cover: 2.50 **NM** value: **Cover or less**
15 ❑ Cover: 2.50 **NM** value: **Cover or less**
16 ❑ Cover: 2.50 **NM** value: **Cover or less**
17 ❑ Cover: 2.50 **NM** value: **Cover or less**
18 ❑ Cover: 2.50 **NM** value: **Cover or less**
Anl 1 ❑ Win 1988, b&w Cover: 3.95 **NM** value: **Cover or less**
• Hal Foster **A:** Hal Foster
KS 1 ❑ Apr 1989, b&w Cover: 3.95 **NM** value: **Cover or less**
• Foster **A:** Hal Foster

OFFICIAL PRINCE VALIANT MONTHLY — Pioneer

1 ❑ Jun 1989, b&w Cover: 3.95 **NM** value: **Cover or less**

OFFICIAL RIP KIRBY — Pioneer

1 ❑ Aug 1988, b&w Cover: 2.00 **NM** value: **Cover or less**
A: Alex Raymond
2 ❑ Sep 1988, b&w Cover: 2.00 **NM** value: **Cover or less**
A: Alex Raymond
3 ❑ Oct 1988, b&w Cover: 2.00 **NM** value: **Cover or less**
A: Alex Raymond
4 ❑ Nov 1988, b&w Cover: 2.00 **NM** value: **Cover or less**
A: Alex Raymond **C:** John Bolton
5 ❑ Dec 1988, b&w Cover: 2.00 **NM** value: **Cover or less**
A: Alex Raymond
6 ❑ Jan 1989, b&w Cover: 2.00 **NM** value: **Cover or less**
A: Alex Raymond

OFFICIAL SECRET AGENT, THE — Pioneer

The Official Secret Agent was one of a collection of "official" reprints of famous newspaper strips published by Pioneer Comics. (Others in the series included The Official Modesty Blaise, The Official Rip Hunter, and The Official Prince Valiant.)

Secret Agent has a history stretching over 50 years. Its star is Phil Corrigan, a G-Man known variously as Secret Agent X-9 and Secret Agent Corrigan. In his newspaper comics adventures, begun as Secret Agent X-9 by artist Alex Raymond and scripter Dashiell Hammett, he ranged the world, taking on smugglers, communist saboteurs, and even a machine gun-toting grandmother a la Ma Barker. In many ways, Secret Agent can be considered a prototype for the later James Bond.

The newspaper strips reprinted here were created by Al Williamson and Archie Goodwin, a creative team known also for their Star Wars newspaper strips.

1 ❑ Jun 1988, b&w Cover: 2.00 **NM** value: **Cover or less**
A: Al Williamson
2 ❑ Jul 1988, b&w Cover: 2.00 **NM** value: **Cover or less**
A: Al Williamson
3 ❑ Aug 1988, b&w Cover: 2.00 **NM** value: **Cover or less**
A: Al Williamson
4 ❑ Sep 1988, b&w Cover: 2.00 **NM** value: **Cover or less**
A: Al Williamson
5 ❑ Oct 1988, b&w Cover: 2.00 **NM** value: **Cover or less**
A: Al Williamson
6 ❑ Nov 1988, b&w Cover: 2.00 **NM** value: **Cover or less**
A: Al Williamson
7 ❑ Dec 1988, b&w Cover: 2.00 **NM** value: **Cover or less**
A: Al Williamson

OFFICIAL, AUTHORIZED ZEN INTERGALACTIC NINJA SOURCEBOOK — Express / Entity

1 ❑ b&w Cover: 3.50 **NM** value: **Cover or less**
1-2 ❑ Cover: 3.50 **NM** value: **Cover or less**
• 94 revised edition.

OFFWORLD — Graphic Image

1 ❑ Cover: 3.95 **NM** value: **Cover or less**
📖 Return Post; The Neighborhood; He Wonders, As he Cuts his Way; Tribute; The Thief; There are no Dragons; The Toll **A:** Michael W. Kaluta; Barb Armata; Justin Leiter; Laura Freeman; Lurene Haines; Nathan Massengill; Neil Geigeles; Tony Williams **W:** Nat Gertler; Franklin Delano Carr; Geoffrey Notkin; Michael Markopoulos; Oriana Whitney Damascus; Rick Wilber

OF MIND AND SOUL — Rage

1 ❑ b&w Cover: 2.25 **NM** value: **Cover or less**

OF MYTHS AND MEN — Blackthorne

1 ❑ b&w Cover: 1.75 **NM** value: **Cover or less**
2 ❑ Mar 1987, b&w Cover: 1.75 **NM** value: **Cover or less**

OGENKI CLINIC — Akita

1 ❑ Sep 1997 Cover: 3.95 **NM** value: **Cover or less**
Circ: Diamd. preorders: **3,717**
A: Haruka I'nui **W:** Haruka I'nui
2 ❑ Oct 1997 Cover: 3.95 **NM** value: **Cover or less**
A: Haruka I'nui **W:** Haruka I'nui
3 ❑ Nov 1997 Cover: 4.50 **NM** value: **Cover or less**
A: Haruka I'nui **W:** Haruka I'nui
4 ❑ Dec 1997 Cover: 4.50 **NM** value: **Cover or less**
A: Haruka I'nui **W:** Haruka I'nui
5 ❑ Jan 1998 Cover: 4.50 **NM** value: **Cover or less**
Circ: Diamd. preorders: **2,892**
A: Haruka I'nui **W:** Haruka I'nui
6 ❑ Feb 1998 Cover: 4.50 **NM** value: **Cover or less**
Circ: Diamd. preorders: **2,542**
A: Haruka I'nui **W:** Haruka I'nui

OGENKI CLINIC (VOL. 2) — Akita

1 ❑ Mar 1998 Cover: 3.95 **NM** value: **Cover or less**
A: Haruka I'nui **W:** Haruka I'nui

2 ❑ Apr 1998 Cover: 3.95 **NM** value: **Cover or less**
Circ: Diamd. preorders: **2,625**
A: Haruka I'nui **W:** Haruka I'nui

3 ❑ May 1998 Cover: 3.95 **NM** value: **Cover or less**
A: Haruka I'nui **W:** Haruka I'nui

4 ❑ Jun 1998 Cover: 3.95 **NM** value: **Cover or less**
Circ: Diamd. preorders: **2,623**
A: Haruka I'nui **W:** Haruka I'nui

5 ❑ Jul 1998 Cover: 3.95 **NM** value: **Cover or less**
Circ: Diamd. preorders: **2,537**
A: Haruka I'nui **W:** Haruka I'nui

6 ❑ Aug 1998 Cover: 3.95 **NM** value: **Cover or less**
Circ: Diamd. preorders: **2,339**
A: Haruka I'nui **W:** Haruka I'nui

OGENKI CLINIC (VOL. 3) — Sexy Fruit

1 ❑ Sep 1998 Cover: 3.95 **NM** value: **Cover or less**
Circ: Diamd. preorders: **2,196**
📖 Medical Record #33, Sex=Death?!?; Medical Record #34, New Year Sex Party!; Medical Record #35, The Ultimate Lingerie Maniac! • Antonio Honduras translation **A:** Haruka I'nui **W:** Haruka I'nui ★ Appearance of Detective Pochi, Detective Sorikomi, Iko, Landlord, Diane.

2 ❑ Oct 1998 Cover: 3.95 **NM** value: **Cover or less**
Circ: Diamd. preorders: **2,264**
A: Haruka I'nui **W:** Haruka I'nui

3 ❑ Nov 1998 Cover: 3.95 **NM** value: **Cover or less**
Circ: Diamd. preorders: **2,201**
A: Haruka I'nui **W:** Haruka I'nui

4 ❑ Dec 1998 Cover: 3.95 **NM** value: **Cover or less**
Circ: Diamd. preorders: **2,275**
A: Haruka I'nui **W:** Haruka I'nui

5 ❑ Jan 1999 Cover: 3.95 **NM** value: **Cover or less**
Circ: Diamd. preorders: **2,066**
A: Haruka I'nui **W:** Haruka I'nui

6 ❑ Feb 1999 Cover: 3.95 **NM** value: **Cover or less**
Circ: Diamd. preorders: **1,994**
A: Haruka I'nui **W:** Haruka I'nui

7 ❑ Mar 1999 Cover: 3.95 **NM** value: **Cover or less**
Circ: Diamd. preorders: **2,018**
A: Haruka I'nui **W:** Haruka I'nui

OGENKI CLINIC (VOL. 4) — Sexy Fruit

1 ❑ Apr 1999 Cover: 2.95 **NM** value: **Cover or less**
Circ: Diamd. preorders: **2,082**
A: Haruka I'nui **W:** Haruka I'nui

2 ❑ May 1999 Cover: 2.95 **NM** value: **Cover or less**
Circ: Diamd. preorders: **2,006**
A: Haruka I'nui **W:** Haruka I'nui

3 ❑ Jun 1999 Cover: 2.95 **NM** value: **Cover or less**
Circ: Diamd. preorders: **2,038**
A: Haruka I'nui **W:** Haruka I'nui

4 ❑ Jul 1999 Cover: 2.95 **NM** value: **Cover or less**
Circ: Diamd. preorders: **2,029**
📖 Medical record # 54 **A:** Haruka I'nui **W:** Haruka I'nui

5 ❑ Aug 1999 Cover: 2.95 **NM** value: **Cover or less**
Circ: Diamd. preorders: **1,915**
A: Haruka I'nui **W:** Haruka I'nui

6 ❑ Sep 1999 Cover: 2.95 **NM** value: **Cover or less**
A: Haruka I'nui **W:** Haruka I'nui

OGENKI CLINIC (VOL. 5) — Sexy Fruit

1 ❑ Oct 1999 Cover: 2.95 **NM** value: **Cover or less**
📖 Medical Record #62: Romance or Raunch?; Medical Record #63: Otenki Clinic!! **A:** Haruka I'nui **W:** Haruka I'nui

2 ❑ Nov 1999 Cover: 2.95 **NM** value: **Cover or less**
A: Haruka I'nui **W:** Haruka I'nui

3 ❑ Dec 1999 Cover: 2.95 **NM** value: **Cover or less**
A: Haruka I'nui **W:** Haruka I'nui

4 ❑ Jan 2000 Cover: 2.95 **NM** value: **Cover or less**
Circ: Diamd. preorders: **1,809**
A: Haruka I'nui **W:** Haruka I'nui

5 ❑ Feb 2000 Cover: 2.95 **NM** value: **Cover or less**
Circ: Diamd. preorders: **1,753**
A: Haruka I'nui **W:** Haruka I'nui

6 ❑ Mar 2000 Cover: 2.95 **NM** value: **Cover or less**
A: Haruka I'nui **W:** Haruka I'nui

7 ❑ Apr 2000 Cover: 2.95 **NM** value: **Cover or less**
A: Haruka I'nui **W:** Haruka I'nui

OGENKI CLINIC (VOL. 6) — Sexy Fruit

1 ❑ May 2000 Cover: 2.95 **NM** value: **Cover or less**
A: Haruka I'nui **W:** Haruka I'nui

2 ❑ Jun 2000 Cover: 2.95 **NM** value: **Cover or less**
A: Haruka I'nui **W:** Haruka I'nui

3 ❑ Jul 2000 Cover: 2.95 **NM** value: **Cover or less**
A: Haruka I'nui **W:** Haruka I'nui

4 ❑ Aug 2000 Cover: 2.95 **NM** value: **Cover or less**
A: Haruka I'nui **W:** Haruka I'nui

5 ❑ Sep 2000 Cover: 2.95 **NM** value: **Cover or less**
A: Haruka I'nui **W:** Haruka I'nui

6 ❑ Oct 2000 Cover: 2.95 **NM** value: **Cover or less**
A: Haruka I'nui **W:** Haruka I'nui

OGRE — Black Diamond

1 ❑ Jan 1994 Cover: 2.95 **NM** value: **Cover or less**
Circ: CapCity orders: **3,335**
★ 1st Appearance of Ogre, Barnacle Bill, Felony.

2 ❑ Mar 1994 Cover: 2.95 **NM** value: **Cover or less**

3 ❑ May 1994 Cover: 2.95 **NM** value: **Cover or less**

4 ❑ Jul 1994 Cover: 2.95 **NM** value: **Cover or less**

OGRE SLAYER — Viz

Bk 1 ❑ b&w Cover: 15.95 **NM** value: **Cover or less**
• Japanese

O.G. WHIZ — Gold Key

The former owner of the Tinkletoy Company was, to put it mildly, a little senile. One day, he wandered into a reception room to read the huge stack of ancient magazines, and traded control of the company to a boy in exchange for a shoeshine box.

The boy, O.G. Whiz, had suddenly come to realize every child's dream: owning his own toy company, complete with all the toys he could ever desire, a squadron of yes-men who tell him his every idea was brilliant, and a dutiful secretary who made sure not to allow any visitors when he was in the middle of his afternoon conference with "Mr. Snooze" — doing sleep research. The only fly in the ointment was the embittered son of the original president, who held a deep resentment for the two-foot-tall tyke who had suddenly become his boss.

1 ❑ Feb 1971 Cover: 0.15 **NM** value: **25.00**

2 ❑ May 1971 Cover: 0.15 **NM** value: **15.00**

3 ❑ Aug 1971 Cover: 0.15 **NM** value: **10.00**

4 ❑ Nov 1971 Cover: 0.15 **NM** value: **10.00**

5 ❑ Feb 1972 Cover: 0.15 **NM** value: **10.00**

6 ❑ May 1972 Cover: 0.15 **NM** value: **10.00**
• Final issue of original run (1972)

7 ❑ May 1978 Cover: 0.15 **NM** value: **3.00**
• Series begins again (1978)

8 ❑ Jul 1978 Cover: 0.15 **NM** value: **3.00**

9 ❑ Sep 1978 Cover: 0.15 **NM** value: **3.00**
★ Appearance of Tubby.

10 ❑ Nov 1978 Cover: 0.15 **NM** value: **3.00**

11 ❑ Jan 1979 Cover: 0.15 **NM** value: **3.00**
📖 Stop that Mirror; Testy Testers; The Great Marble Swindle; The Toy Spies final issue.

OH. — B Publications

1 ❑ Cover: 2.95 **NM** value: **Cover or less**

2 ❑ Cover: 2.95 **NM** value: **Cover or less**

3 ❑ Cover: 2.95 **NM** value: **Cover or less**

4 ❑ Cover: 2.95 **NM** value: **Cover or less**

5 ❑ Cover: 2.95 **NM** value: **Cover or less**

6 ❑ Cover: 2.95 **NM** value: **Cover or less**

7 ❑ Cover: 2.95 **NM** value: **Cover or less**

8 ❑ Cover: 2.95 **NM** value: **Cover or less**
• Immola and the Luna Legion

OH BROTHER! — Stanhall

1 ❑ ca. 1953 Cover: 0.10 **NM** value: **40.00**

2 ❑ ca. 1953 Cover: 0.10 **NM** value: **25.00**

3 ❑ ca. 1953 Cover: 0.10 **NM** value: **25.00**

4 ❑ ca. 1953 Cover: 0.10 **NM** value: **25.00**

5 ❑ ca. 1953 Cover: 0.10 **NM** value: **25.00**

OHM'S LAW — Imperial

1 ❑ full color Cover: 2.25 **NM** value: **Cover or less**
📖 Books of the Jihad Saga, Part 1 **A:** Demetrios Moyles **W:** Chris Brinkman ★ 1st Appearance of Black Hurrikan, Drakkus, Ohm.

2 ❑ b&w Cover: 1.95 **NM** value: **Cover or less**
• Black and White **A:** Demetrios Moyles **W:** Chris Brinkman

3 ❑ b&w Cover: 1.95 **NM** value: **Cover or less**
• Published out of sequence; Black and white **A:** Demetrios Moyles **W:** Chris Brinkman

OH MY GODDESS! — Dark Horse

Keiichi Morisato meant to order takeout but, instead, he got a live-in goddess, Belldandy. Romance soon blossoms between the two, but the course of love is too slow for Belldandy's older sister, Urd, who seeks to hasten the process. She is banished to Earth for meddling, much to Keiichi's dismay.

Soon, Belldandy and Urd are involved in Keiichi's school life, and, while many of his friends celebrate his new, beautiful companions, others are not as pleased about Belldandy's special bond to Keiichi.

Suave, rich freshman Toshi wants Belldandy for himself, and his rules of conquest fool even Keiichi about his intentions. Toshi's cousin Sayoko wants Keiichi and was interrupted in her pursuit, when Belldandy arrived. Now she's ready to do anything to get rid of Belldandy — even to make a deal with a demon.

1 ❑ Aug 1994 Cover: 2.50 **NM** value: **5.00**
Circ: CapCity orders: **6,550**
📖 The Wish **A:** Kosuke Fujishima **W:** Kosuke Fujishima ★ 1st Appearance of Otaki, Belldandy, Tamiya, Keiichi Morisato.

2 ❑ Sep 1994 Cover: 2.50 **NM** value: **3.00**
Circ: CapCity orders: **5,275**
📖 Sexy Sister **A:** Kosuke Fujishima **W:** Kosuke Fujishima ★ 1st Appearance of Urd. ★ 2nd Appearance of Belldandy, Keiichi Morisato.

3 ❑ Oct 1994 Cover: 2.50 **NM** value: **3.00**
Circ: CapCity orders: **5,050**

Creator Key
W = Writer • A = Artist • C = Cover Artist

📖 Belldandy's Narrow Escape **A:** Kosuke Fujishima **W:** Kosuke Fujishima ★ 1st Appearance of Sayoko Aoshima, Nekomi Motor Club, Toshiyuki Aoshima. ★ 2nd Appearance of Otaki. ★ 2nd Appearance of Urd. ★ 2nd Appearance of Tamiya.

4 ❑ Nov 1994 Cover: 2.50 **NM** value: **3.00**
Circ: CapCity orders: **5,325**
📖 The CD from Hell **A:** Kosuke Fujishima **W:** Kosuke Fujishima ★ 1st Appearance of Mara, Urd, Tamiya.

5 ❑ Dec 1994 Cover: 2.50 **NM** value: **3.00**
Circ: CapCity orders: **5,425**
📖 Mara Strikes Back!! **A:** Kosuke Fujishima **W:** Kosuke Fujishima ★ 2nd Appearance of Sayoko Aoshima. ★ 2nd Appearance of Sayoko Aoshima. ★ 2nd Appearance of Mara. ★ 2nd Appearance of Mara. ★ Appearance of Urd.

6 ❑ Jan 1995 Cover: 2.50 **NM** value: **3.00**
Circ: CapCity orders: **5,200**
📖 The Scales of Love **A:** Kosuke Fujishima **W:** Kosuke Fujishima ★ 1st Appearance of Super-Deformed (SD) Urd. ★ Appearance of Urd, Sayoko Aoshima, Mara.

Bk 1 ❑ b&w Cover: 12.95 **NM** value: **Cover or less**
• 1-555-GODDESS; collects Oh My Goddess! Part I #1-3 and Oh My Goddess! Part II #3-5 **A:** Kosuke Fujishima **W:** Kosuke Fujishima

OH MY GODDESS! PART II — Dark Horse

1 ❑ Feb 1995 Cover: 2.50 **NM** value: **3.00**
Circ: CapCity orders: **5,450**
📖 Bugs **A:** Kosuke Fujishima **W:** Kosuke Fujishima ★ 1st Appearance of Skuld. ★ Appearance of Urd.

2 ❑ Mar 1995 Cover: 2.50 **NM** value: **3.00**
Circ: CapCity orders: **5,125**
📖 A Singular Sensation **A:** Kosuke Fujishima **W:** Kosuke Fujishima ★ 2nd Appearance of Skuld. ★ 2nd Appearance of Skuld. ★ Appearance of Urd.

3 ❑ Apr 1995 Cover: 2.50 **NM** value: **2.75**
Circ: CapCity orders: **5,175**
📖 Turkey with all the Trimmings... • Oh My Cartoonist! follow-up story **A:** Kosuke Fujishima **W:** Kosuke Fujishima ★ Appearance of Otaki, Urd, Sayoko Aoshima, Tamiya.

4 ❑ May 1995 Cover: 2.50 **NM** value: **2.75**
Circ: CapCity orders: **5,200**
📖 Life's Just a Game of "Sugoroku Roulette" **A:** Kosuke Fujishima **W:** Kosuke Fujishima ★ 1st Appearance of Megumi Morisato. ★ Appearance of Otaki, Urd, Sayoko Aoshima, Tamiya.

5 ❑ Jun 1995 Cover: 2.50 **NM** value: **2.75**
Circ: CapCity orders: **5,450**
📖 Final Exam **A:** Kosuke Fujishima **W:** Kosuke Fujishima ★ Appearance of Otaki, Urd, Sayoko Aoshima, Tamiya.

6 ❑ Jul 1995 Cover: 2.50 **NM** value: **2.75**
Circ: CapCity orders: **5,575**
📖 The Secret's Out **A:** Kosuke Fujishima **W:** Kosuke Fujishima ★ 1st Appearance of Parapsychology Research club, S&M club. ★ 2nd Appearance of Toshiyuki Aoshima. ★ Appearance of Urd, Sayoko Aoshima.

7 ❑ Aug 1995 Cover: 2.95 **NM** value: **3.00**
Circ: CapCity orders: **5,200**
📖 Go-Kart Go **A:** Kosuke Fujishima **W:** Kosuke Fujishima ★ Appearance of Otaki, Urd, Tamiya, Toshiyuki Aoshima.

8 ❑ Sep 1995 Cover: 2.95 **NM** value: **3.00**
Circ: CapCity orders: **4,700**
📖 What a Miracle • The Adventures of Mini-Urd story **A:** Kosuke Fujishima **W:** Kosuke Fujishima ★ 2nd Appearance of SD Urd. ★ 2nd Appearance of Megumi Morisato. ★ Appearance of Otaki, Urd, Tamiya, Toshiyuki Aoshima.

Bk 2 ❑ Oct 1997, b&w Cover: 12.95 **NM** value: **Cover or less**
• Love Potion No. 9 **A:** Kosuke Fujishima **W:** Kosuke Fujishima

OH MY GODDESS! PART III — Dark Horse / Manga

1 ❑ Nov 1995 Cover: 2.95 **NM** value: **3.00**
Cover reads "Oh My Goddess Special". 📖 On a Wing and a Prayer **A:** Kosuke Fujishima **W:** Kosuke Fujishima ★ Appearance of Otaki, Urd, Tamiya.

2 ❑ Dec 1995 Cover: 2.95 **NM** value: **3.00**
Cover reads "Oh My Goddess Special". 📖 Love Potion #9 **A:** Kosuke Fujishima **W:** Kosuke Fujishima ★ Appearance of Otaki, Urd, Tamiya.

3 ❑ Jan 1996 Cover: 2.95 **NM** value: **3.00**
Cover reads "Oh My Goddess Special". 📖 Sympathy for the Devil **A:** Kosuke Fujishima **W:** Kosuke Fujishima ★ Appearance of Otaki, Urd, SD Urd, Mara, Megumi Morisato.

4 ❑ Feb 1996 Cover: 2.95 **NM** value: **3.00**
Cover reads "Oh My Goddess Special". 📖 Mystical Engine **A:** Kosuke Fujishima **W:** Kosuke Fujishima ★ Appearance of Otaki, Urd, Tamiya, Toshiyuki Aoshima.

5 ❑ Mar 1996 Cover: 2.95 **NM** value: **3.00**
Cover reads "Oh My Goddess Special". 📖 Valentine Rhapsody **A:** Kosuke Fujishima **W:** Kosuke Fujishima ★ Origin of Sudaru. ★ 1st Appearance of Sudaru. ★ Appearance of Urd, Mara.

6 ❑ Apr 1996 Cover: 2.95 **NM** value: **3.00**
Cover reads "Oh My Goddess! 1 of 6". 📖 Terrible Master Urd, Part 1, Urd Goes Berserk! **A:** Kosuke Fujishima **W:** Kosuke Fujishima ★ 1st Appearance of Mao Za Haxon. ★ Appearance of Mara.

7 ❑ May 1996 Cover: 2.95 **NM** value: **3.00**
Cover reads "Oh My Goddess! 2 of 6". 📖 Terrible Master Urd, Part 2, Urd's Terrible Master **A:** Kosuke Fujishima **W:** Kosuke Fujishima ★ 2nd Appearance of Mao Za Haxon (possessing Urd). ★ Appearance of Mara.

8 ❑ Jun 1996 Cover: 2.95 **NM** value: **3.00**
Cover reads "Oh My Goddess! 3 of 6". 📖 Terrible Master Urd, Part 3, The Ultimate Destruction Program **A:** Kosuke Fujishima **W:** Kosuke Fujishima ★ Appearance of Mao Za Haxon, SD Urd, Sayoko Aoshima, Mara.

9 ❑ Jul 1996 Cover: 2.95 **NM** value: **3.00**
Cover reads "Oh My Goddess! 4 of 6". 📖 Terrible Master Urd, Part 4, Urd Calls Forth the Beast **A:** Kosuke Fujishima **W:** Kosuke Fujishima ★ 1st Appearance of Fenrir, Midgard Serpent. ★ Appearance of Mao Za Haxon, Mara.

CGC-graded: Multiply prices above by **33 for 9.9 M • 16 for 9.8 NM/M • 7 for 9.6 NM+ • 5 for 9.4 NM • 2.5 for 9.2 NM- • 1.5 for 9.0 VF/NM**

10 ❑ Aug 1996 Cover: 2.95 **NM** value: **3.00**
Cover reads "Oh My Goddess, part 5 of 6". 📖 Terrible Master Urd, part 5, The Secret of the Lord of Terror **A:** Kosuke Fujishima; Kosuke FujishimaMa **W:** Kosuke Fujishima; Kosuke FujishimaMa ★ 2nd Appearance of Fenrir. ★ 2nd Appearance of Fenrir.

11 ❑ Sep 1996 Cover: 2.95 **NM** value: **3.00**
Circ: Diamd. preorders: **12,662**
Cover reads "Oh My Goddess! 6 of 6". 📖 Terrible Master Urd, Part 6, Confession **A:** Kosuke Fujishima **W:** Kosuke Fujishima ★ 2nd Appearance of Universal Superstring. ★ Appearance of Mao Za Haxon.

Bk 3❑ May 1998, b&w Cover: 12.95 **NM** value: **Cover or less**
• Sympathy for the Devil **A:** Kosuke Fujishima **W:** Kosuke Fujishima

Bk 4❑ Apr 1999, b&w Cover: 13.95 **NM** value: **Cover or less**
• Terrible Master Urd; collects Oh My Goddess! Part III #6-11 **A:** Kosuke Fujishima **W:** Kosuke Fujishima

OH MY GODDESS! PART IV Dark Horse / Manga

1 ❑ Dec 1996 Cover: 2.95 **NM** value: **Cover or less**
Circ: Diamd. preorders: **14,561**
Cover reads "Oh My Goddess Special". 📖 Robot Wars **A:** Kosuke Fujishima **W:** Kosuke Fujishima ★ Appearance of Otaki, Tamiya, Megumi Morisato.

2 ❑ Jan 1997 Cover: 2.95 **NM** value: **Cover or less**
Circ: Diamd. preorders: **13,396**
Cover reads " Oh My Goddess! 1 of 3". 📖 The Trials of Morisato, Part 1 **A:** Kosuke Fujishima **W:** Kosuke Fujishima ★ 1st Appearance of Yuki Gomorrah, SD Belldandy.

3 ❑ Feb 1997 Cover: 2.95 **NM** value: **Cover or less**
Circ: Diamd. preorders: **12,251**
Cover reads " Oh My Goddess! 2 of 3". 📖 The Trials of Morisato, Part 2, Urd's Fantastic Adventure **A:** Kosuke Fujishima **W:** Kosuke Fujishima ★ 1st Appearance of Shohei Yoshida. ★ 2nd Appearance of SD Belldandy.

4 ❑ Mar 1997 Cover: 2.95 **NM** value: **Cover or less**
Circ: Diamd. preorders: **12,342**
Cover reads " Oh My Goddess! 3 of 3". 📖 The Trials of Morisato, Part 3, Belldandy's Tempestuous Heart **A:** Kosuke Fujishima **W:** Kosuke Fujishima

5 ❑ Apr 1997 Cover: 2.95 **NM** value: **Cover or less**
Circ: Diamd. preorders: **13,491**
Cover reads " Oh My Goddess Special". 📖 The Queen of Vengeance **A:** Kosuke Fujishima **W:** Kosuke Fujishima ★ Appearance of Sayoko Aoshima.

6 ❑ May 1997 Cover: 2.95 **NM** value: **Cover or less**
Circ: Diamd. preorders: **13,385**
Cover reads " Oh My Goddess! 1 of 3". 📖 Mara Strikes Back, Part 1, Mister Unhappy **A:** Kosuke Fujishima **W:** Kosuke Fujishima

7 ❑ Jun 1997 Cover: 2.95 **NM** value: **Cover or less**
Circ: Diamd. preorders: **12,542**
Cover reads " Oh My Go. 📖 Mara Strikes Back, Part 2, Thank You **A:** Kosuke Fujishima **W:** Kosuke Fujishima ★ Origin of Mini-Banpei RX. ★ 1st Appearance of Mini-Banpei RX. ★ 2nd Appearance of Senbei the Genie. ★ Appearance of Mara.

8 ❑ Jul 1997 Cover: 2.95 **NM** value: **Cover or less**
Circ: Diamd. preorders: **12,061**
Cover reads " Oh My Goddess! 3 of 3". 📖 Mara Strikes Back, Part 3, Good-bye and Hello **A:** Kosuke Fujishima **W:** Kosuke Fujishima ★ 1st Appearance of SD Mara. ★ 2nd Appearance of Mini-Banpei RX.

Bk 5❑ Nov 1999 Cover: 13.95 **NM** value: **Cover or less**
📖 The Queen of Vengeance **A:** Kosuke Fujishima **W:** Kosuke Fujishima

Bk 6❑ Apr 2000 Cover: 14.95 **NM** value: **Cover or less**
📖 Mara Strikes Back **A:** Kosuke Fujishima **W:** Kosuke Fujishima

OH MY GODDESS! PART V Dark Horse / Manga

1 ❑ Sep 1997 Cover: 2.95 **NM** value: **Cover or less**
Circ: Diamd. preorders: **13,258**
Cover reads " Oh My Goddess Special". 📖 The Forgotten Promise **A:** Kosuke Fujishima **W:** Kosuke Fujishima ★ Appearance of Otaki, Tamiya, Nekomi Tech Motor Club.

2 ❑ Oct 1997 Cover: 2.95 **NM** value: **Cover or less**
Circ: Diamd. preorders: **13,437**
Cover reads " Oh My Goddess Special". 📖 The Lunchbox of Love **A:** Kosuke Fujishima **W:** Kosuke Fujishima ★ 2nd Appearance of Sora Hasegawa. ★ 2nd Appearance of Sora Hasegawa. ★ Appearance of Tamiya, Mini-Banpei RX, Toshiyuki Aoshima.

3 ❑ Nov 1997 Cover: 3.95 **NM** value: **Cover or less**
Circ: Diamd. preorders: **13,187**
Cover reads " Oh My Goddess Special". 📖 Meet Me by the Seashore **A:** Kosuke Fujishima **W:** Kosuke Fujishima ★ Appearance of Mini-Banpei RX.

4 ❑ Dec 1997 Cover: 3.95 **NM** value: **Cover or less**
Circ: Diamd. preorders: **12,796**
Cover reads " Oh My Goddess Special". 📖 You're So Bad **A:** Kosuke Fujishima **W:** Kosuke Fujishima ★ Appearance of SD Urd, SD Belldandy.

5 ❑ Jan 1998 Cover: 2.95 **NM** value: **Cover or less**
Circ: Diamd. preorders: **13,265**
Cover reads " Oh My Goddess! 1 of 2". 📖 Ninja Master, Part 1 **A:** Kosuke Fujishima **W:** Kosuke Fujishima ★ 1st Appearance of Kodama. ★ Appearance of Mini-Banpei RX, Mara.

6 ❑ Feb 1998 Cover: 3.95 **NM** value: **Cover or less**
Circ: Diamd. preorders: **12,312**
Cover reads " Oh My Goddess! 2 of 2. 📖 Ninja Master, Part 2; The Law of the Ninja • Alan Gleason and Toren Smith translation **A:** Kosuke Fujishima **W:** Kosuke Fujishima ★ 1st Appearance of Hikari. ★ 2nd Appearance of Kodama.

7 ❑ Mar 1998 Cover: 3.95 **NM** value: **Cover or less**
Circ: Diamd. preorders: **13,114**
Cover reads " Oh My Goddess! 1 of 2". 📖 Miss Keiichi, Part 1; Together for Never **A:** Kosuke Fujishima **W:** Kosuke Fujishima ★ Appearance of Mini-Banpei RX, Megumi Morisato.

8 ❑ Apr 1998 Cover: 2.95 **NM** value: **Cover or less**
Circ: Diamd. preorders: **13,116**
Cover reads " Oh My Goddess! 2 of 2". 📖 Miss Keiichi, Part 2; Jealous Love **A:** Kosuke Fujishima **W:** Kosuke Fujishima ★ 1st Appearance of Troubadour.

9 ❑ May 1998 Cover: 3.50 **NM** value: **Cover or less**
📖 It's Lonely at the Top **A:** Kosuke Fujishima **W:** Kosuke Fujishima

10 ❑ Jun 1998 Cover: 3.50 **NM** value: **3.95**
Circ: Diamd. preorders: **12,535**
Cover reads " Oh My Goddess! One-Shot". 📖 Fallen Angel **A:** Kosuke Fujishima **W:** Kosuke Fujishima ★ 1st Appearance of Garm, Shiho Sakakibara. ★ Appearance of Mini-Banpei RX.

11 ❑ Jul 1998 Cover: 3.95 **NM** value: **Cover or less**
Circ: Diamd. preorders: **12,263**
Cover reads " Oh My Goddess! One-Shot". 📖 Play the Game **A:** Kosuke Fujishima **W:** Kosuke Fujishima ★ 1st Appearance of Nekomi Tech Softball Club. ★ Appearance of Tamiya, Sora Hasegawa, Megumi Morisato.

12 ❑ Aug 1998 Cover: 3.95 **NM** value: **Cover or less**
Circ: Diamd. preorders: **12,404**
Cover reads " Oh My Goddess! One-Shot". 📖 Sorrow/ Fear Not **A:** Kosuke Fujishima **W:** Kosuke Fujishima ★ Appearance of Megumi Morisato.

Bk 7❑ Oct 2000 Cover: 13.95 **NM** value: **Cover or less**
📖 Ninja Master **A:** Kosuke Fujishima **W:** Kosuke Fujishima

Bk 8❑ Feb 2001 Cover: 16.95 **NM** value: **Cover or less**
📖 Miss Keichi **A:** Kosuke Fujishima **W:** Kosuke Fujishima

OH MY GODDESS! PART VI Dark Horse / Manga

1 ❑ Oct 1998 Cover: 3.50 **NM** value: **Cover or less**
Circ: Diamd. preorders: **12,325**
📖 The Devil in Miss Urd, Part 1 **A:** Kosuke Fujishima **W:** Kosuke Fujishima

2 ❑ Dec 1998 Cover: 2.95 **NM** value: **Cover or less**
Circ: Diamd. preorders: **12,128**
📖 The Devil in Miss Urd, Part 2 **A:** Kosuke Fujishima **W:** Kosuke Fujishima

3 ❑ Jan 1999 Cover: 2.95 **NM** value: **Cover or less**
Circ: Diamd. preorders: **11,987**
📖 The Devil in Miss Urd, Part 3 **A:** Kosuke Fujishima **W:** Kosuke Fujishima

4 ❑ Feb 1999 Cover: 2.95 **NM** value: **Cover or less**
Circ: Diamd. preorders: **11,650**
📖 The Devil in Miss Urd, Part 4 **A:** Kosuke Fujishima **W:** Kosuke Fujishima

5 ❑ Mar 1999 Cover: 2.95 **NM** value: **Cover or less**
Circ: Diamd. preorders: **11,835**
📖 The Devil in Miss Urd, Part 5 **A:** Kosuke Fujishima **W:** Kosuke Fujishima

6 ❑ Apr 1999 Cover: 2.95 **NM** value: **Cover or less**
Circ: Diamd. preorders: **12,505**
📖 Super Urd **A:** Kosuke Fujishima **W:** Kosuke Fujishima

OH MY GODDESS! PART VII Dark Horse / Manga

1 ❑ May 1999 Cover: 2.95 **NM** value: **Cover or less**
Circ: Diamd. preorders: **12,839**
📖 The Fourth Goddess, Part 1 **A:** Kosuke Fujishima **W:** Kosuke Fujishima

2 ❑ Jun 1999 Cover: 2.95 **NM** value: **Cover or less**
Circ: Diamd. preorders: **12,259**
📖 The Fourth Goddess, Part 2 **A:** Kosuke Fujishima **W:** Kosuke Fujishima

3 ❑ Jul 1999 Cover: 2.95 **NM** value: **Cover or less**
Circ: Diamd. preorders: **12,482**
📖 The Fourth Goddess, Part 3 **A:** Kosuke Fujishima **W:** Kosuke Fujishima

4 ❑ Aug 1999 Cover: 3.50 **NM** value: **Cover or less**
Circ: Diamd. preorders: **12,261**
📖 The Fourth Goddess, Part 4 **A:** Kosuke Fujishima **W:** Kosuke Fujishima

5 ❑ Sep 1999 Cover: 3.50 **NM** value: **Cover or less**
Circ: Diamd. preorders: **12,024**
📖 The Fourth Goddess, Part 5 **A:** Kosuke Fujishima **W:** Kosuke Fujishima

6 ❑ Oct 1999 Cover: 3.50 **NM** value: **Cover or less**
Circ: Diamd. preorders: **12,490**
📖 The Fourth Goddess, Part 6 **A:** Kosuke Fujishima **W:** Kosuke Fujishima

7 ❑ Nov 1999 Cover: 3.50 **NM** value: **Cover or less**
Circ: Diamd. preorders: **12,134**
📖 The Fourth Goddess, Part 7 **A:** Kosuke Fujishima **W:** Kosuke Fujishima

8 ❑ Dec 1999 Cover: 2.95 **NM** value: **Cover or less**
Circ: Diamd. preorders: **11,922**
📖 The Fourth Goddess, Part 8 **A:** Kosuke Fujishima **W:** Kosuke Fujishima

OH MY GODDESS! PART VIII Dark Horse / Manga

1 ❑ Jan 2000 Cover: 3.50 **NM** value: **Cover or less**
Circ: Diamd. preorders: **12,148**
A: Kosuke Fujishima **W:** Kosuke Fujishima

2 ❑ Feb 2000 Cover: 3.50 **NM** value: **Cover or less**
Circ: Diamd. preorders: **11,241**
A: Kosuke Fujishima **W:** Kosuke Fujishima

3 ❑ Mar 2000 Cover: 3.50 **NM** value: **Cover or less**
Circ: Diamd. preorders: **11,541**
A: Kosuke Fujishima **W:** Kosuke Fujishima

4 ❑ Apr 2000 Cover: 3.50 **NM** value: **Cover or less**
📖 Hail to the Chief, Part 1 **A:** Kosuke Fujishima **W:** Kosuke Fujishima

5 ❑ May 2000 Cover: 3.50 **NM** value: **Cover or less**
📖 Hail to the Chief, Part 2 **A:** Kosuke Fujishima **W:** Kosuke Fujishima

6 ❑ Jun 2000 Cover: 3.50 **NM** value: **Cover or less**
📖 Hail to the Chief, Part 3 **A:** Kosuke Fujishima **W:** Kosuke Fujishima

OH MY GODDESS! PART IX Dark Horse / Manga

1 ❑ Jul 2000 Cover: 3.50 **NM** value: **Cover or less**
Circ: Diamd. preorders: **11,540**
📖 Pretty in Scarlet **A:** Kosuke Fujishima **W:** Kosuke Fujishima

2 ❑ Aug 2000 Cover: 3.50 **NM** value: **Cover or less**
Circ: Diamd. preorders: **10,880**
📖 The Goddess's Apprentice **A:** Kosuke Fujishima **W:** Kosuke Fujishima

3 ❑ Sep 2000 Cover: 3.50 **NM** value: **Cover or less**
Circ: Diamd. preorders: **11,233**
📖 Queen Sayoko, Part 1 **A:** Kosuke Fujishima **W:** Kosuke Fujishima

4 ❑ Oct 2000 Cover: 3.50 **NM** value: **Cover or less**
Circ: Diamd. preorders: **10,820**
📖 Queen Sayoko, Part 2 **A:** Kosuke Fujishima **W:** Kosuke Fujishima

5 ❑ Nov 2000 Cover: 3.50 **NM** value: **Cover or less**
Circ: Diamd. preorders: **10,799**
📖 Queen Sayoko, Part 3 **A:** Kosuke Fujishima **W:** Kosuke Fujishima

6 ❑ Dec 2000 Cover: 3.50 **NM** value: **Cover or less**
📖 Queen Sayoko, Part 4 **A:** Kosuke Fujishima **W:** Kosuke Fujishima

7 ❑ Jan 2001 Cover: 3.50 **NM** value: **Cover or less**
Circ: Diamd. preorders: **10,227**
📖 Queen Sayoko, Part 5 **A:** Kosuke Fujishima **W:** Kosuke Fujishima

OH MY GODDESS! PART X Dark Horse / Manga

1 ❑ Feb 2001 Cover: 3.50 **NM** value: **Cover or less**
Circ: Diamd. preorders: **10,372**
A: Kosuke Fujishima **W:** Kosuke Fujishima

2 ❑ Mar 2001 Cover: 3.50 **NM** value: **Cover or less**
Circ: Diamd. preorders: **10,104**
A: Kosuke Fujishima **W:** Kosuke Fujishima

3 ❑ Apr 2001 Cover: 3.50 **NM** value: **Cover or less**
Circ: Diamd. preorders: **10,154**
📖 Another Me **A:** Kosuke Fujishima **W:** Kosuke Fujishima

OH MY GODDESS!: ADVENTURES OF THE MINI-GODDESSES Dark Horse / Manga

1 ❑ May 2000 Cover: 9.95 **NM** value: **Cover or less**
A: Kosuke Fujishima **W:** Kosuke Fujishima

OH MY GOTH Sirius / Dog Star

The Goth movement, in which young people dress in black, listen to depressing music, and attempt to be pessimistic about life, takes gentle ribbing from one of its own in this title. Voltaire, who began this book to promote his music, commits what might be the ultimate sin in the Goth lifestyle: He doesn't take it seriously. For instance, a Goth musician describes himself thus: "I am Vlad the Impaler. I am 200 years old. I lurk in my dark lair where I seek the blood of hapless victims." But when aliens can't understand him and subject his speech to their Universal Translator, it comes out: "I am Bernie Weinstein. I am 17 1/2 years old. I live in my mother's basement where I drink cheap red wine, when I can get it."

Unfortunately, while Voltaire's use of an Old English typeface for lettering may be appropriate, it is hard to read in large doses.

1 ❑ 1998 Cover: 2.95 **NM** value: **Cover or less**
A: Voltaire **W:** Voltaire

2 ❑ Oct 1998 Cover: 2.95 **NM** value: **Cover or less**
Circ: Diamd. preorders: **1,743**

3 ❑ Jan 1999 Cover: 2.95 **NM** value: **Cover or less**
Circ: Diamd. preorders: **1,667**

4 ❑ Apr 1999 Cover: 2.95 **NM** value: **Cover or less**
Circ: Diamd. preorders: **1,521**

OH MY GOTH: HUMANS SUCK! Sirius

1 ❑ Jun 2000, b&w Cover: 2.95 **NM** value: **Cover or less**
Circ: Diamd. preorders: **3,451**
📖 Dragon Con or Bust!

2 ❑ Aug 2000, b&w Cover: 2.95 **NM** value: **Cover or less**
Circ: Diamd. preorders: **2,346**
📖 The Stupid Voyage of Sinbad

OINK: HEAVEN'S BUTCHER Kitchen Sink

1 ❑ Dec 1995 Cover: 4.95 **NM** value: **Cover or less**
A: John Muller **W:** John Muller

2 ❑ Feb 1996 Cover: 4.95 **NM** value: **Cover or less**
A: John Muller **W:** John Muller

3 ❑ Apr 1996 Cover: 4.95 **NM** value: **Cover or less**
A: John Muller **W:** John Muller

Bk 1❑ Jan 1997 Cover: 19.95 **NM** value: **Cover or less**
• collects mini-series

OJ'S BIG BUST OUT Boneyard

1 ❑ Mar 1995, b&w Cover: 2.95 **NM** value: **3.50**
A: Nelson Danielson **W:** Hart Fisher

OKAY COMICS United Feature

1 ❑ Jul 1940 Cover: 0.10 **NM** value: **200.00**
• **CGC:** 5 graded, best 9.0
• Captain and the Kids strip reprints **A:** Rudolph Dirks **W:** Rudolph Dirks

OKLAHOMA KID Ajax

1 ❑ Jun 1957 Cover: 0.10 **NM** value: **75.00**
2 ❑ Sep 1958 Cover: 0.10 **NM** value: **40.00**
3 ❑ Dec 1958 Cover: 0.10 **NM** value: **40.00**
4 ❑ Mar 1958 Cover: 0.10 **NM** value: **40.00**

OKTANE Dark Horse

1 ❑ Aug 1995 Cover: 2.50 **NM** value: **Cover or less**
Circ: CapCity orders: **4,925**
📖 Kicks On Route 66 **A:** Gene Ha **W:** Gerard Jones

2 ❑ Sep 1995 Cover: 2.50 **NM** value: **Cover or less**
Circ: CapCity orders: **3,050**
A: Gene Ha **W:** Gerard Jones

Other grades: Multiply prices above by **1.5 for Mint • 2/3 for Very Fine • 1/3 for Fine • 1/5 for Very Good • 1/8 for Good**

3 ❑ Oct 1995 Cover: 2.50 **NM** value: **Cover or less**
A: Gene Ha **W:** Gerard Jones

4 ❑ Nov 1995 Cover: 2.50 **NM** value: **Cover or less**
final issue. **A:** Gene Ha **W:** Gerard Jones

Bk 1❑ Jan 1997 Cover: 12.95 **NM** value: **Cover or less**

OLDBLOOD — Parody Press

1 ❑ Cover: 2.50 **NM** value: **Cover or less**
A: Rus Sever **W:** Don Chin

1-2 ❑ Cover: 2.50 **NM** value: **Cover or less**

OLYMPIANS, THE — Marvel / Epic

1 ❑ Cover: 3.95 **NM** value: **Cover or less**
Circ: CapCity orders: **7,800**
📖 It's Not The End Of The World **A:** Gary Chaloner; Todd McFarlane(cover) **W:** Stephen Jewell

2 ❑ Cover: 3.95 **NM** value: **Cover or less**
Circ: CapCity orders: **5,300**
A: Gary Chaloner **W:** Stephen Jewell

OMAC — DC

Technology has a long and nasty history of progressing far faster than man's ability to use it wisely. In Jack Kirby's vision of the future, technologies such as genetics and robotics give powerful tools to those who want to do the devil's work. To keep things in line, the World Peace Organization has been founded — a non-partisan group of troubleshooters whose faces are cosmetically blanked to hide their racial origins. A secret agent organization of sorts, they infiltrate groups that are using technology to evil ends. Their point man is a powerhouse called Omac: One Man Army Corps. Omac is linked via a sigil on his chest to an orbiting satellite called "Brother Eye." He receives his incredible powers through that link, as well as information he needs to complete his missions.

This original series lasted only eight issues, but Omac lasted far longer, including appearances in Kamandi and Warlord, and a four-issue remake by John Byrne.

1 ❑ Oct 1974 Cover: 0.20 **NM** value: **5.00**
• **CGC:** 9 graded, best 9.4
📖 Build-A-Friend; Brother Eye and Buddy Blank **A:** Jack Kirby **W:** Jack Kirby ★ Origin of Omac. ★ 1st Appearance of Omac.

2 ❑ Dec 1974 Cover: 0.20 **NM** value: **3.50**
A: Jack Kirby ★ Versus Mr. Big.

3 ❑ Feb 1975 Cover: 0.20 **NM** value: **3.00**
• **CGC:** 1 graded, best 9.0
A: Jack Kirby

4 ❑ Apr 1975 Cover: 0.20 **NM** value: **3.00**
• **CGC:** 1 graded, best 9.4
A: Jack Kirby

5 ❑ Jun 1975 Cover: 0.25 **NM** value: **3.00**
• **CGC:** 2 graded, best 9.4
A: Jack Kirby **W:** Jack Kirby

6 ❑ Aug 1975 Cover: 0.25 **NM** value: **2.50**
A: Jack Kirby

7 ❑ Oct 1975 Cover: 0.25 **NM** value: **2.50**
A: Jack Kirby

8 ❑ Dec 1975 Cover: 0.25 **NM** value: **2.50**
A: Jack Kirby **C:** Joe Kubert

OMAC: ONE MAN ARMY CORPS — DC

1 ❑ b&w Cover: 3.95 **NM** value: **Cover or less**
Circ: CapCity orders: **28,250**
• prestige format. **A:** John Byrne **W:** John Byrne

2 ❑ b&w Cover: 3.95 **NM** value: **Cover or less**
• prestige format. **A:** John Byrne **W:** John Byrne

3 ❑ b&w Cover: 3.95 **NM** value: **Cover or less**
Circ: CapCity orders: **18,500**
• prestige format. 📖 Mein Kampf **A:** John Byrne **W:** John Byrne

4 ❑ b&w Cover: 3.95 **NM** value: **Cover or less**
Circ: CapCity orders: **15,200**
• prestige format. **A:** John Byrne **W:** John Byrne

OMAHA: CAT DANCER — Steeldragon

1 ❑ **NM** value: **12.00**

1/Ash❑ **NM** value: **3.00**
• preview

1-2 ❑ Cover: 1.75 **NM** value: **4.00**

2 ❑ Cover: 1.75 **NM** value: **8.00**

OMAHA THE CAT DANCER (KITCHEN SINK) — Kitchen Sink

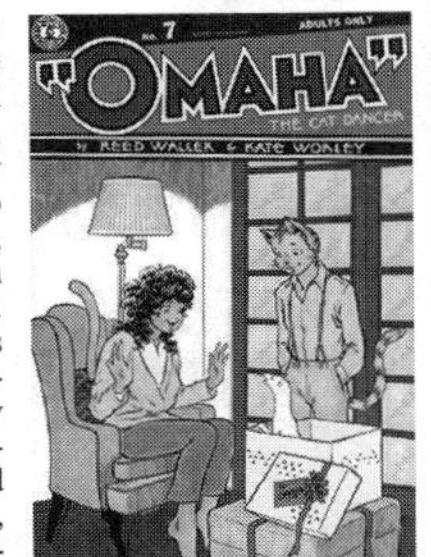

This cult favorite moves anthropomorphism into the realm of the erotic. The result is a sort of X-rated animal soap opera. It stars Omaha, an exotic dancer and cat with a very human female body. Omaha is (to say the least) a very sensual being, and she cavorts her way through many an adventure, in bed and out.

First appearing in a amateur press association magazine called Vootie, Omaha stunned readers by bringing sex into the realm of "funny animal" stories. She soon gained a loyal following among readers, however, and following a full-length premiere in Bizarre Sex #9, she made the leap into her own comic title.

The series started at Steeldragon, moved to Kitchen Sink, and finally landed at Fantagraphics, which restarted the numbering and reprinted several of the Kitchen Sink issues. But after only four issues of the second series, creators Reed Waller and Kate Worley split up, bringing Omaha's adventures to a premature end.

0 ❑ Cover: 2.50 **NM** value: **4.00**
• Reprints early Omaha stories from Vootie, Bizarre Sex #9 **A:** Reed Waller **W:** Kate Worley ★ 1st Appearance of Omaha the Cat Dancer.

1 ❑ Oct 1986 Cover: 2.00 **NM** value: **10.00**
A: Reed Waller **W:** Kate Worley

1-2 ❑ Cover: 2.00 **NM** value: **4.00**

1-3 ❑ Cover: 2.50 **NM** value: **3.00**

2 ❑ Oct 1986 Cover: 2.00 **NM** value: **5.00**
A: Reed Waller **W:** Kate Worley

3 ❑ Oct 1986 Cover: 2.00 **NM** value: **4.00**
A: Reed Waller **W:** Kate Worley

4 ❑ Jan 1987 Cover: 2.00 **NM** value: **4.00**
A: Reed Waller **W:** Kate Worley

5 ❑ Mar 1987 Cover: 2.00 **NM** value: **4.00**
A: Reed Waller **W:** Kate Worley

6 ❑ May 1987 Cover: 2.00 **NM** value: **3.00**
A: Reed Waller **W:** Kate Worley

7 ❑ Jul 1987 Cover: 2.00 **NM** value: **3.00**
A: Reed Waller **W:** Kate Worley

8 ❑ Oct 1987 Cover: 2.00 **NM** value: **3.00**
A: Reed Waller **W:** Kate Worley

9 ❑ Feb 1988 Cover: 2.00 **NM** value: **3.00**
A: Reed Waller **W:** Kate Worley

10 ❑ May 1988 Cover: 2.00 **NM** value: **3.00**
A: Reed Waller **W:** Kate Worley

11 ❑ Dec 1988 Cover: 2.00 **NM** value: **3.00**
A: Reed Waller **W:** Kate Worley

12 ❑ 1989 Cover: 2.00 **NM** value: **3.00**
A: Reed Waller **W:** Kate Worley

12-2❑ Cover: 2.95 **NM** value: **Cover or less**

13 ❑ Sep 1989 Cover: 2.00 **NM** value: **3.00**
A: Reed Waller **W:** Kate Worley

13-2❑ Cover: 2.95 **NM** value: **Cover or less**

14 ❑ Mar 1990 Cover: 2.50 **NM** value: **3.00**
• Wendel back-up **A:** Reed Waller **W:** Kate Worley

15 ❑ Jan 1991 Cover: 2.50 **NM** value: **3.00**
A: Reed Waller **W:** Kate Worley

16 ❑ Nov 1991 Cover: 2.50 **NM** value: **2.95**
Circ: CapCity orders: **4,200**
A: Reed Waller **W:** Kate Worley

17 ❑ Feb 1992 Cover: 2.50 **NM** value: **2.95**
Circ: CapCity orders: **3,515**
A: Reed Waller **W:** Kate Worley

18 ❑ Jan 1993 Cover: 2.95 **NM** value: **Cover or less**
Circ: CapCity orders: **3,730**
A: Reed Waller **W:** Kate Worley

19 ❑ Jun 1993 Cover: 2.95 **NM** value: **Cover or less**
Circ: CapCity orders: **3,700**
A: Reed Waller **W:** Kate Worley

20 ❑ Cover: 2.95 **NM** value: **Cover or less**
Circ: CapCity orders: **3,760**
• Final Kitchen Sink issue **A:** Reed Waller **W:** Kate Worley

Bk 1❑ Cover: 12.95 **NM** value: **15.95**
• Collects Omaha the Cat Dancer #1-5 **A:** Reed Waller **W:** Kate Worley

Bk 2❑ Cover: 15.95 **NM** value: **Cover or less**
• Collects Omaha the Cat Dancer #6-10 **A:** Reed Waller **W:** Kate Worley

Bk 3❑ Cover: 14.95 **NM** value: **15.95**
• Collects Omaha the Cat Dancer #11-15 **A:** Reed Waller **W:** Kate Worley

Bk 4❑ Cover: 15.95 **NM** value: **Cover or less**
• Collects Omaha the Cat Dancer #16-20 **A:** Reed Waller **W:** Kate Worley

OMAHA THE CAT DANCER (FANTAGRAPHICS) — Fantagraphics

1 ❑ Jul 1994 Cover: 2.50 **NM** value: **3.00**
A: Reed Waller **W:** Kate Worley

2 ❑ Aug 1994 Cover: 2.50 **NM** value: **3.00**
A: Reed Waller **W:** Kate Worley

3 ❑ Nov 1994 Cover: 2.50 **NM** value: **3.00**
A: Reed Waller **W:** Kate Worley

4 ❑ Feb 1995 Cover: 2.50 **NM** value: **3.00**
A: Reed Waller **W:** Kate Worley

O'MALLEY AND THE ALLEY CATS — Gold Key

1 ❑ Apr 1971 Cover: 0.15 **NM** value: **8.00**
2 ❑ Jul 1971 Cover: 0.15 **NM** value: **6.00**
3 ❑ Jul 1972 Cover: 0.15 **NM** value: **6.00**
4 ❑ Oct 1972 Cover: 0.15 **NM** value: **4.00**
5 ❑ Jan 1973 Cover: 0.15 **NM** value: **4.00**
6 ❑ Apr 1973 Cover: 0.15 **NM** value: **4.00**
7 ❑ Jul 1973 Cover: 0.20 **NM** value: **4.00**
8 ❑ Oct 1973 Cover: 0.20 **NM** value: **4.00**
9 ❑ Jan 1974 Cover: 0.20 **NM** value: **4.00**

OMAR LENNYX — Magnecom

1 ❑ b&w Cover: 2.95 **NM** value: **Cover or less**
📖 Blood Seekers

OMEGA ELITE — Blackthorne

1 ❑ b&w Cover: 3.50 **NM** value: **Cover or less**
Circ: CapCity orders: **450**

OMEGA FORCE — Entity

1 ❑ Cover: 2.50 **NM** value: **Cover or less**
★ 1st Appearance of Archetype, Flashback (Entity), The Drakon, Omega Force, Karad the Godslayer, The Earon Raider, Dual.

OMEGA FORCE II — Entity

1 ❑ Cover: 2.75 **NM** value: **Cover or less**
wraparound cover. 📖 Dark Secret **A:** Jonah Cagley **W:** Michael Cagley

2 ❑ Cover: 2.75 **NM** value: **Cover or less**
A: Jonah Cagley **W:** Michael Cagley

3 ❑ Cover: 2.75 **NM** value: **Cover or less**
A: Jonah Cagley **W:** Michael Cagley

OMEGA FORCE (SOUTH STAR) — South Star

1 ❑ Aug 1992 Cover: 2.00 **NM** value: **Cover or less**
A: Robert Alvord **W:** Robert Alvord

OMEGA KNIGHTS — Underground

1 ❑ Cover: 2.00 **NM** value: **Cover or less**
2 ❑ Cover: 2.00 **NM** value: **Cover or less**
3 ❑ Cover: 2.00 **NM** value: **Cover or less**
4 ❑ Cover: 2.00 **NM** value: **Cover or less**
5 ❑ Cover: 2.00 **NM** value: **Cover or less**
📖 Sundance, Part 1 **A:** Dave Marcus **W:** Michael Connaery

6 ❑ Oct 1992 Cover: 2.00 **NM** value: **Cover or less**
📖 Sundance, Part 2 **A:** Dave Marcus **W:** Michael Connaery

OMEGA MAN — Omega 7

0 ❑ Cover: 3.00 **NM** value: **Cover or less**

1 ❑ b&w Cover: 4.00 **NM** value: **Cover or less**
• Simpson trial; no indicia

Ash 1❑full color **NM** value: **1.00**
No issue number. no cover price. • no indicia; sideways format

OMEGA MEN, THE — DC

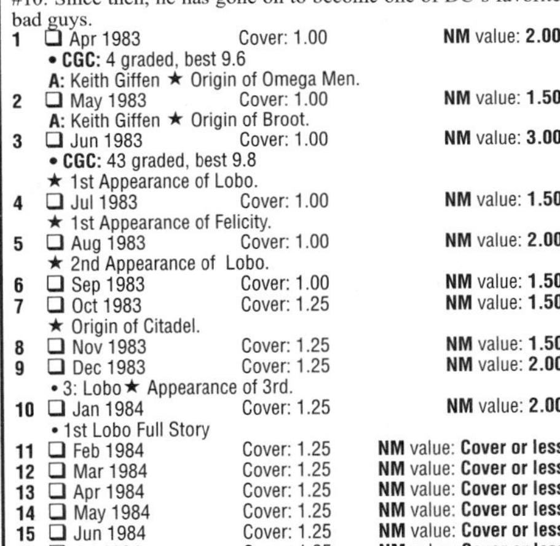

In the far-away Vegan system, the alien dictatorship called the Citadel has achieved near-complete domination. In doing so, the occupation forces rounded up 100 of the world's leaders — the Omega Men — and subjected them to "special" care.

But, led by Primus, a powerful psychic and former king, the Omega Men have escaped. Now, they must travel from the remotest worlds of the Vegan system, sowing the seeds of freedom and gathering a force of freedom fighters to win back their worlds.

In addition to its epic storyline, Omega Men is famous for its introduction of the bloodthirsty character Lobo. First appearing in Omega Men #3, Lobo is featured in his first full story in Omega Men #10. Since then, he has gone on to become one of DC's favorite bad guys.

1 ❑ Apr 1983 Cover: 1.00 **NM** value: **2.00**
• **CGC:** 4 graded, best 9.6
A: Keith Giffen ★ Origin of Omega Men.

2 ❑ May 1983 Cover: 1.00 **NM** value: **1.50**
A: Keith Giffen ★ Origin of Broot.

3 ❑ Jun 1983 Cover: 1.00 **NM** value: **3.00**
• **CGC:** 43 graded, best 9.8
★ 1st Appearance of Lobo.

4 ❑ Jul 1983 Cover: 1.00 **NM** value: **1.50**
★ 1st Appearance of Felicity.

5 ❑ Aug 1983 Cover: 1.00 **NM** value: **2.00**
★ 2nd Appearance of Lobo.

6 ❑ Sep 1983 Cover: 1.00 **NM** value: **1.50**

7 ❑ Oct 1983 Cover: 1.25 **NM** value: **1.50**
★ Origin of Citadel.

8 ❑ Nov 1983 Cover: 1.25 **NM** value: **1.50**

9 ❑ Dec 1983 Cover: 1.25 **NM** value: **2.00**
• 3: Lobo★ Appearance of 3rd.

10 ❑ Jan 1984 Cover: 1.25 **NM** value: **2.00**
• 1st Lobo Full Story

11 ❑ Feb 1984 Cover: 1.25 **NM** value: **Cover or less**
12 ❑ Mar 1984 Cover: 1.25 **NM** value: **Cover or less**
13 ❑ Apr 1984 Cover: 1.25 **NM** value: **Cover or less**
14 ❑ May 1984 Cover: 1.25 **NM** value: **Cover or less**
15 ❑ Jun 1984 Cover: 1.25 **NM** value: **Cover or less**
16 ❑ Jul 1984 Cover: 1.25 **NM** value: **Cover or less**
17 ❑ Aug 1984 Cover: 1.25 **NM** value: **Cover or less**
18 ❑ Sep 1984 Cover: 1.25 **NM** value: **Cover or less**
19 ❑ Oct 1984 Cover: 1.25 **NM** value: **Cover or less**
★ Appearance of Lobo.

20 ❑ Nov 1984 Cover: 1.25 **NM** value: **2.00**
★ Appearance of Lobo.

21 ❑ Dec 1984 Cover: 1.25 **NM** value: **Cover or less**
22 ❑ Jan 1985 Cover: 1.25 **NM** value: **Cover or less**
23 ❑ Feb 1985 Cover: 1.25 **NM** value: **Cover or less**
24 ❑ Mar 1985 Cover: 1.25 **NM** value: **Cover or less**
25 ❑ Apr 1985 Cover: 1.25 **NM** value: **Cover or less**
26 ❑ May 1985 Cover: 1.25 **NM** value: **Cover or less**
Circ: CapCity orders: **7,700**
★ 1st Appearance of Elu.

27 ❑ Jun 1985 Cover: 1.25 **NM** value: **Cover or less**
Circ: CapCity orders: **7,350**

28 ❑ Jul 1985 Cover: 1.25 **NM** value: **Cover or less**
Circ: CapCity orders: **7,150**

29 ❑ Aug 1985 Cover: 1.25 **NM** value: **Cover or less**
Circ: CapCity orders: **7,300**

30 ❑ Sep 1985 Cover: 1.25 **NM** value: **Cover or less**
Circ: CapCity orders: **7,000**

31 ❑ Oct 1985 Cover: 1.50 **NM** value: **Cover or less**
Circ: CapCity orders: **8,400**
📖 Crisis On Infinite Earths • Crisis

32 ❑ Nov 1985 Cover: 1.25 **NM** value: **Cover or less**
Circ: CapCity orders: **6,750**

CGC-graded: Multiply prices above by **33 for 9.9 M • 16 for 9.8 NM/M • 7 for 9.6 NM+ • 5 for 9.4 NM • 2.5 for 9.2 NM- • 1.5 for 9.0 VF/NM**

33 ❑ Dec 1985 Cover: 1.25 **NM** value: **Cover or less**
Circ: CapCity orders: **6,400**
34 ❑ Jan 1986 Cover: 1.25 **NM** value: **Cover or less**
Circ: CapCity orders: **9,300**
35 ❑ Feb 1986 Cover: 1.25 **NM** value: **Cover or less**
Circ: CapCity orders: **8,900**
36 ❑ Mar 1986 Cover: 1.25 **NM** value: **Cover or less**
Circ: CapCity orders: **6,850**
37 ❑ Apr 1986 Cover: 1.25 **NM** value: **Cover or less**
Circ: CapCity orders: **6,650**
★ Appearance of Lobo.
38 ❑ May 1986 Cover: 1.25 **NM** value: **Cover or less**
Circ: CapCity orders: **7,100**
Anl 1❑ca. 1984 Cover: 1.50 **NM** value: **2.00**
Anl 2❑ca. 1985 Cover: 1.50 **NM** value: **1.75**
Circ: CapCity orders: **6,750**
★ Origin of Primus.

OMEGA THE UNKNOWN — Marvel

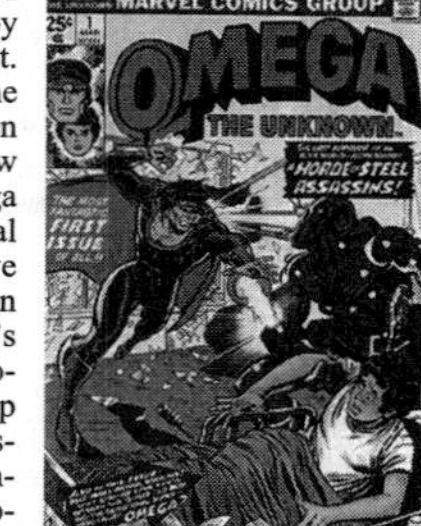

This 1970s series takes the old formula of super-hero with boy sidekick and gives it a novel twist. The title character, Omega, is the creation of the Protar, an alien mechanoid race. The Protar foresaw their own death and created Omega as a prototype for a line of artificial humanoids who would survive them. Omega eventually arrives on Earth, hotly pursued by his race's old enemies. After at least temporarily defeating them, he winds up being drawn to a boy, James-Michael Starling. [Spoiler Warning: This gives away plot developments.] The shocked boy knows only that he and Omega share a sympathetic bond. Little could he know that he is actually the final "model" of the Protar's artificial humanoids.

This series ended on a tragic note in #10 with Omega being shot dead. James-Michael eventually learns his full origin in The Defenders #76 and commits suicide in the following issue.

1 ❑ Mar 1976 Cover: 0.25 **NM** value: **4.00**
• **CGC:** 2 graded, best 9.2
A: Jim Mooney **W:** Mary Skrenes; Steve Gerber ★ 1st Appearance of James-Michael Starling (Omega the Unknown's counterpart), Omega the Unknown.
2 ❑ May 1976 Cover: 0.25 **NM** value: **2.50**
★ Appearance of Hulk.
3 ❑ Jul 1976 Cover: 0.25 **NM** value: **2.00**
4 ❑ Sep 1976 Cover: 0.30 **NM** value: **2.00**
5 ❑ Nov 1976 Cover: 0.30 **NM** value: **2.00**
6 ❑ Jan 1977 Cover: 0.30 **NM** value: **2.00**
7 ❑ Mar 1977 Cover: 0.30 **NM** value: **2.00**
8 ❑ May 1977 Cover: 0.30 **NM** value: **2.00**
★ 1st Appearance of Foolkiller II (Greg Salinger)-cameo.
9 ❑ Jul 1977 Cover: 0.30 **NM** value: **3.00**
★ 1st Appearance of Foolkiller II (Greg Salinger)-full.
10 ❑ Oct 1977 Cover: 0.30 **NM** value: **2.00**
final issue. ★ Death of Omega the Unknown.

OMEN, THE (CHAOS) — Chaos!

1 ❑ May 1998 Cover: 2.95 **NM** value: **Cover or less**
Circ: Diamd. preorders: **26,446**
W: Brian Pulido
2 ❑ Jun 1998 Cover: 2.95 **NM** value: **Cover or less**
Circ: Diamd. preorders: **16,778**
W: Brian Pulido
3 ❑ Jul 1998 Cover: 2.95 **NM** value: **Cover or less**
Circ: Diamd. preorders: **16,847**
W: Brian Pulido
4 ❑ Aug 1998 Cover: 2.95 **NM** value: **Cover or less**
Circ: Diamd. preorders: **15,920**
W: Brian Pulido
5 ❑ Sep 1998 Cover: 2.95 **NM** value: **Cover or less**
Circ: Diamd. preorders: **15,153**
W: Brian Pulido
Bk 1❑ Cover: 12.95 **NM** value: **Cover or less**
• Collect The Omen #1-5 **W:** Brian Pulido

OMEN (NORTHSTAR) — Northstar

1 ❑ b&w Cover: 2.00 **NM** value: **Cover or less**
2 ❑ b&w Cover: 2.00 **NM** value: **Cover or less**

OMEN, THE: SAVE THE CHOSEN PREVIEW — Chaos!

1 ❑ Sep 1997 Cover: 2.50 **NM** value: **Cover or less**
No issue number. • preview of upcoming series

OMEN, THE: VEXED — Chaos!

1 ❑ Oct 1998 Cover: 2.95 **NM** value: **Cover or less**
Circ: Diamd. preorders: **13,361**

OMICRON: ASTONISHING ADVENTURES ON OTHER WORLDS — Pyramid

1 ❑ b&w Cover: 2.25 **NM** value: **Cover or less**
• flexi-disc
2 ❑ Sep 1987, b&w Cover: 2.25 **NM** value: **Cover or less**
🕮 Andromeda Space Cadet: Criss-Cross Confusion; Alexus of Vertigo: Duel; Dimension Z: Minds' Eyes: Impressions o Kevin Stuart • flexi-disc **A:** Mark Paniccia; Marc Lampert **W:** Rick McCollum; John Brewer; Paula Robinson

OMNIBUS: MODERN PERVERSITY — Blackbird

1 ❑ b&w Cover: 3.25 **NM** value: **Cover or less**
No issue number. • squarebound

OMNI COMIX — Omni

1 ❑ Mar 1995 Cover: 2.95 **NM** value: **4.00**
Circ: CapCity orders: **4,730**
• magazine. 🕮 High Guard; Mission to Mars • Mar '95 issue of Omni inserted **A:** Andrew Robinson; Bob Wiacek; Dave Elliot; Mark Texeira; Paris Cullens **W:** George Caragonne; Tom Thornton
2 ❑ Apr 1995 Cover: 3.95 **NM** value: **4.00**
insert in Apr. '95 issue of Omni with Omni Comix #2 cover. • magazine.
3 ❑ Oct 1995 Cover: 4.95 **NM** value: **Cover or less**
Circ: CapCity orders: **2,065**
• magazine. • T.H.U.N.D.E.R. Agents story

OMNI MEN — Blackthorne

1 ❑ Apr 1989, b&w Cover: 3.50 **NM** value: **Cover or less**
Circ: CapCity orders: **3,600**

ON A PALE HORSE — Innovation

1 ❑ Cover: 4.95 **NM** value: **Cover or less**
Circ: CapCity orders: **5,375**
2 ❑ Cover: 4.95 **NM** value: **Cover or less**
Circ: CapCity orders: **5,665**
3 ❑ Cover: 4.95 **NM** value: **Cover or less**
Circ: CapCity orders: **4,970**
4 ❑ Cover: 4.95 **NM** value: **Cover or less**
Circ: CapCity orders: **4,270**
5 ❑ Dec 1993 Cover: 4.95 **NM** value: **Cover or less**
Circ: CapCity orders: **3,805**

ONCE UPON A TIME IN THE FUTURE — Platinum

1 ❑ Cover: 9.95 **NM** value: **Cover or less**

ONE, THE — Marvel / Epic

1 ❑ Jul 1985 Cover: 1.50 **NM** value: **2.00**
Circ: CapCity orders: **12,250**
🕮 The Big Sleep **A:** Brent Anderson; Rick Veitch **W:** Rick Veitch
2 ❑ Sep 1985 Cover: 1.50 **NM** value: **2.00**
Circ: CapCity orders: **8,850**
A: Brent Anderson; Rick Veitch **W:** Rick Veitch
3 ❑ Nov 1985 Cover: 1.50 **NM** value: **2.00**
Circ: CapCity orders: **7,100**
A: Brent Anderson; Rick Veitch **W:** Rick Veitch
4 ❑ Jan 1986 Cover: 1.50 **NM** value: **2.00**
Circ: CapCity orders: **6,550**
A: Brent Anderson; Rick Veitch **W:** Rick Veitch
5 ❑ Mar 1986 Cover: 1.50 **NM** value: **2.00**
Circ: CapCity orders: **6,200**
A: Brent Anderson; Rick Veitch **W:** Rick Veitch
6 ❑ May 1986 Cover: 1.50 **NM** value: **2.00**
Circ: CapCity orders: **6,250**
A: Brent Anderson; Rick Veitch **W:** Rick Veitch
Bk 1❑ b&w Cover: 14.95 **NM** value: **Cover or less**

ONE-ARM SWORDSMAN — Dr. Leung's

1 ❑ Cover: 1.80 **NM** value: **Cover or less**
Circ: CapCity orders: **2,025**
2 ❑ Cover: 1.80 **NM** value: **Cover or less**
Circ: CapCity orders: **1,400**
3 ❑ Cover: 1.80 **NM** value: **Cover or less**
Circ: CapCity orders: **800**
4 ❑ Cover: 1.80 **NM** value: **Cover or less**
5 ❑ Cover: 1.80 **NM** value: **Cover or less**
6 ❑ Cover: 1.80 **NM** value: **Cover or less**
7 ❑ Cover: 1.80 **NM** value: **Cover or less**

ONE BIG HAPPY — NBM

Bk 1❑ b&w Cover: 9.95 **NM** value: **Cover or less**
• strip collection

ONE-FISTED TALES — Slave Labor

All issues are adults only.

1 ❑ May 1990, b&w Cover: 2.50 **NM** value: **3.00**
• brown paper wrapper
1-2 ❑ Nov 1990 Cover: 2.50 **NM** value: **Cover or less**
2 ❑ Sep 1990, b&w Cover: 2.50 **NM** value: **3.00**
• brown paper wrapper (some wrappers printed red in error)
2-2 ❑ Apr 1993 Cover: 2.95 **NM** value: **Cover or less**
3 ❑ Feb 1991, b&w Cover: 2.50 **NM** value: **Cover or less**
Cherry cover and story. • brown paper wrapper
3-2 ❑ Apr 1993 Cover: 2.95 **NM** value: **Cover or less**
3-3 ❑ Aug 1993 Cover: 2.95 **NM** value: **Cover or less**
4 ❑ Jun 1991, b&w Cover: 2.50 **NM** value: **Cover or less**
A: Evan Dorkin **C:** Evan Dorkin
4-2 ❑ Jan 1992 Cover: 2.50 **NM** value: **2.95**
4-3 ❑ Aug 1993 Cover: 2.95 **NM** value: **Cover or less**
5 ❑ Sep 1991, b&w Cover: 3.95 **NM** value: **Cover or less**
5-2 ❑ Feb 1992 Cover: 2.95 **NM** value: **Cover or less**
6 ❑ Apr 1992 Cover: 2.95 **NM** value: **Cover or less**
7 ❑ Sep 1992, b&w Cover: 2.95 **NM** value: **Cover or less**
8 ❑ Mar 1993, b&w Cover: 2.95 **NM** value: **Cover or less**
9 ❑ Oct 1993, b&w Cover: 2.95 **NM** value: **Cover or less**
10 ❑ Feb 1994, b&w Cover: 2.95 **NM** value: **Cover or less**
11 ❑ Aug 1994, b&w Cover: 2.95 **NM** value: **Cover or less**
Bk 1❑ Sep 1993 Cover: 12.95 **NM** value: **Cover or less**
• Hot Works: The Best of One-Fisted Tales

ONE HUNDRED AND ONE DALMATIANS (WALT DISNEY'S...) — Disney

1 ❑ Cover: 2.50 **NM** value: **Cover or less**

100 BULLETS — DC / Vertigo

1 ❑ Aug 1999 Cover: 2.50 **NM** value: **4.50**
Circ: Diamd. preorders: **17,328**
2 ❑ Sep 1999 Cover: 2.50 **NM** value: **3.50**
Circ: Diamd. preorders: **15,895**
3 ❑ Oct 1999 Cover: 2.50 **NM** value: **3.50**
Circ: Diamd. preorders: **15,383**
4 ❑ Nov 1999 Cover: 2.50 **NM** value: **3.00**
Circ: Diamd. preorders: **14,470**
🕮 Shot, Water Back, Part 1 **A:** Eduardo Risso **W:** Brian Azzarello
5 ❑ Dec 1999 Cover: 2.50 **NM** value: **3.00**
Circ: Diamd. preorders: **14,456**
🕮 Shot, Water Back, Part 2 **A:** Eduardo Risso **W:** Brian Azzarello
6 ❑ Jan 2000 Cover: 2.50 **NM** value: **Cover or less**
Circ: Diamd. preorders: **13,291**
🕮 Short Con, Long Odds, Part 1 **A:** Eduardo Risso **W:** Brian Azzarello
7 ❑ Feb 2000 Cover: 2.50 **NM** value: **Cover or less**
Circ: Diamd. preorders: **12,734**
🕮 Short Con, Long Odds, Part 2 **A:** Eduardo Risso **W:** Brian Azzarello
8 ❑ Mar 2000 Cover: 2.50 **NM** value: **Cover or less**
Circ: Diamd. preorders: **12,464**
9 ❑ Apr 2000 Cover: 2.50 **NM** value: **Cover or less**
Circ: Diamd. preorders: **11,644**
🕮 The Right Ear, Left in the Cold, Part 1 **A:** Eduardo Risso **W:** Brian Azzarello
10 ❑ May 2000 Cover: 2.50 **NM** value: **Cover or less**
Circ: Diamd. preorders: **12,078**
🕮 The Right Ear, Left in the Cold, Part 2 **A:** Eduardo Risso **W:** Brian Azzarello
11 ❑ Jun 2000 Cover: 2.50 **NM** value: **Cover or less**
Circ: Diamd. preorders: **12,532**
🕮 Heartbreak, Sunnyside Up **A:** Eduardo Risso **W:** Brian Azzarello
12 ❑ Jul 2000 Cover: 2.50 **NM** value: **Cover or less**
Circ: Diamd. preorders: **13,082**
13 ❑ Aug 2000 Cover: 2.50 **NM** value: **Cover or less**
Circ: Diamd. preorders: **14,037**
14 ❑ Sep 2000 Cover: 2.50 **NM** value: **Cover or less**
Circ: Diamd. preorders: **14,441**
15 ❑ Oct 2000 Cover: 2.50 **NM** value: **Cover or less**
Circ: Diamd. preorders: **14,419**
🕮 Hang Up on the Hang Low, Part 1 **A:** Eduardo Risso **W:** Brian Azzarello
16 ❑ Nov 2000 Cover: 2.50 **NM** value: **Cover or less**
Circ: Diamd. preorders: **15,090**
🕮 Hang Up on the Hang Low, Part 2 **A:** Eduardo Risso **W:** Brian Azzarello
17 ❑ Dec 2000 Cover: 2.50 **NM** value: **Cover or less**
Circ: Diamd. preorders: **15,792**
🕮 Hang Up on the Hang Low, Part 3 **A:** Eduardo Risso **W:** Brian Azzarello
18 ❑ Jan 2001 Cover: 2.50 **NM** value: **Cover or less**
Circ: Diamd. preorders: **15,663**
🕮 Hang Up on the Hang Low, Part 4 **A:** Eduardo Risso **W:** Brian Azzarello
19 ❑ Feb 2001 Cover: 2.50 **NM** value: **Cover or less**
Circ: Diamd. preorders: **15,659**
🕮 Epilogue for a Road Dog **A:** Eduardo Risso **W:** Brian Azzarello
20 ❑ Mar 2001 Cover: 2.50 **NM** value: **Cover or less**
Circ: Diamd. preorders: **15,695**
🕮 The Mimic **A:** Eduardo Risso **W:** Brian Azzarello
21 ❑ Apr 2001 Cover: 2.50 **NM** value: **Cover or less**
Circ: Diamd. preorders: **16,048**
🕮 Selfish & Out to Sea, Part 1 **A:** Eduardo Risso **W:** Brian Azzarello
22 ❑ May 2001 Cover: 2.50 **NM** value: **Cover or less**
Circ: Diamd. preorders: **16,420**
🕮 Selfish & Out to Sea, Part 2 **A:** Eduardo Risso **W:** Brian Azzarello
23 ❑ Jun 2001 Cover: 2.50 **NM** value: **Cover or less**
Circ: Diamd. preorders: **16,622**
🕮 Red Prince Blues, Part 1 **A:** Eduardo Risso **W:** Brian Azzarello
24 ❑ Jul 2001 Cover: 2.50 **NM** value: **Cover or less**
Circ: Diamd. preorders: **17,379**
25 ❑ Aug 2001 Cover: 2.50 **NM** value: **Cover or less**
Circ: Diamd. preorders: **19,417**
26 ❑ Sep 2001 Cover: 2.50 **NM** value: **Cover or less**
Bk 1❑ Cover: 14.95 **NM** value: **Cover or less**
• Split Second Chance; Collects 100 Bullets #6-14 **A:** Eduardo Risso **W:** Brian Azzarello

100 DEGREES IN THE SHADE — Fantagraphics / Eros

All issues are adults only.

1 ❑ b&w Cover: 2.50 **NM** value: **Cover or less**
2 ❑ b&w Cover: 2.50 **NM** value: **Cover or less**
3 ❑ b&w Cover: 2.50 **NM** value: **Cover or less**
4 ❑ b&w Cover: 2.50 **NM** value: **Cover or less**

100 GREATEST MARVELS OF ALL TIME — Marvel

1 ❑ Dec 2001 Cover: 7.50 **NM** value: **Cover or less**
Circ: Diamd. preorders: **14,587**
cardstock cover. • reprints Uncanny X-Men #141, Fantastic Four (Vol. 1) #48, Amazing Spider-Man (Vol. 1) #1, Daredevil #181
2 ❑ Dec 2001 Cover: 7.50 **NM** value: **Cover or less**
Circ: Diamd. preorders: **14,057**
cardstock cover. • reprints Avengers (Vol. 1) #1, Uncanny X-Men #350, Amazing Spider-Man (Vol. 1) #122, Captain America #109
3 ❑ Dec 2001 Cover: 7.50 **NM** value: **Cover or less**
Circ: Diamd. preorders: **13,951**
cardstock cover. • reprints Incredible Hulk #181, X-Men #25, Amazing Spider-Man (Vol. 1) #33, Spider-Man #1
4 ❑ Dec 2001 Cover: 7.50 **NM** value: **Cover or less**
Circ: Diamd. preorders: **13,932**
cardstock cover. • reprints Incredible Hulk (Vol. 1) #1, Ultimate X-Men #1, Daredevil #227, Wolverine #75
5 ❑ Dec 2001 Cover: 7.50 **NM** value: **Cover or less**
Circ: Diamd. preorders: **14,011**
cardstock cover. • reprints Ultimate Spider-Man #1, X-Men (1st series) #1, Avengers (Vol. 1) #4, Amazing Spider-Man (Vol. 1) #121
6 ❑ Dec 2001 Cover: 3.50 **NM** value: **Cover or less**
Circ: Diamd. preorders: **19,560**
cardstock cover. • reprints X-Men (2nd series) #1
7 ❑ Dec 2001 Cover: 3.50 **NM** value: **Cover or less**
Circ: Diamd. preorders: **16,373**
• reprints Giant-Size X-Men #1

Other grades: Multiply prices above by **1.5 for Mint • 2/3 for Very Fine • 1/3 for Fine • 1/5 for Very Good • 1/8 for Good**

8 ❑ Dec 2001 Cover: 3.50 **NM** value: **Cover or less**
Circ: Diamd. preorders: **16,181**
cardstock cover. • reprints X-Men (1st series) #137
9 ❑ Dec 2001 Cover: 3.50 **NM** value: **Cover or less**
Circ: Diamd. preorders: **16,168**
• reprints Fantastic Four (Vol. 1) #1
10 ❑ Dec 2001 Cover: 3.50 **NM** value: **Cover or less**
Circ: Diamd. preorders: **15,832**
• reprints Amazing Fantasy #15

101 OTHER USES FOR A CONDOM — Apple
1 ❑ Cover: 4.95 **NM** value: **Cover or less**

101 WAYS TO END THE CLONE SAGA — Marvel
1 ❑ Jan 1997 Cover: 2.50 **NM** value: **Cover or less**
Circ: Diamd. preorders: **31,684**
One-shot.

100 PAGES OF COMICS — Dell
1 ❑ ca. 1937 **NM** value: **1100.00**

100% TRUE? — DC / Paradox Press
1 ❑ Sum 1996, b&w Cover: 3.50 **NM** value: **Cover or less**
• magazine. • excerpts from The Big Books of Death, Conspiracies, Weirdos, and Freaks
2 ❑ Win 1997, b&w Cover: 3.50 **NM** value: **Cover or less**
Circ: Diamd. preorders: **4,127**
• magazine. • excerpts from The Big Books of Death, Conspiracies, Weirdos, and Freaks; Winter, 1996 issue

ONE MILE UP — Eclipse
1 ❑ b&w Cover: 2.50 **NM** value: **Cover or less**
A: Shepherd Hendrix **W:** Fred Schiller
2 ❑ Cover: 2.50 **NM** value: **Cover or less**

ONE MILLENNIUM — Hunter Productions
1 ❑ b&w Cover: 2.50 **NM** value: **Cover or less**
2 ❑ b&w Cover: 2.50 **NM** value: **Cover or less**
3 ❑ b&w Cover: 2.50 **NM** value: **Cover or less**
4 ❑ b&w Cover: 2.50 **NM** value: **Cover or less**
5 ❑ b&w Cover: 2.50 **NM** value: **Cover or less**

ONE MILLION YEARS AGO — St. John

Joe Kubert and Norman Maurer's One Million Years Ago was a groundbreaking comic, although it was little recognized as such. Kubert and Maurer put themselves into the comic book to introduce readers to the various stories, all set in the world as it might have been at the dawn of mankind.

This comic featured three different stories, the first of which introduced Tor, Kubert's legendary caveman. Tor was more than an adventure hero. His exploits were used to illustrate the dawning of conscience and morality in a world dominated quite literally by the law of the jungle. Kubert even went so far as to break the fourth wall at certain points in the story to point out the nature of the conflicts taking place. The other main features in this title were the improbable caveman comedy "The Wizard of Ugghh" and fantasy/adventure "Danny Dreams." With issue #2, the comic book would be retitled "3-D Comics," ushering in a short-lived fad.

1 ❑ Cover: 0.10 **NM** value: **100.00**
📖 Tor; Wizard of Ugghh; Danny Dreams • Series continued in 3-D Comics #2 **A:** Joe Kubert **W:** Norman Maurer ★ 1st Appearance of Tor.

ONE (PACIFIC) — Pacific
1 ❑ b&w Cover: 3.00 **NM** value: **Cover or less**
• 1st Pacific title

ONE-POUND GOSPEL — Viz
1 ❑ Cover: 3.50 **NM** value: **Cover or less**
2 ❑ Cover: 3.50 **NM** value: **Cover or less**
3 ❑ Cover: 2.95 **NM** value: **Cover or less**
4 ❑ Cover: 2.95 **NM** value: **Cover or less**
Bk 1❑ b&w **NM** value: **16.95**
• Trade Paperback.
Bk 2❑ Cover: 16.95 **NM** value: **Cover or less**
Bk 3❑ Cover: 15.95 **NM** value: **Cover or less**
• Hungry for Victory
Bk 4❑ Cover: 15.95 **NM** value: **Cover or less**
📖 Knuckle Sandwich

ONE-POUND GOSPEL ROUND 2 — Viz
1 ❑ Jan 1997 Cover: 2.95 **NM** value: **Cover or less**
Circ: Diamd. preorders: **3,717**
A: Rumiko Takahashi **W:** Rumiko Takahashi
2 ❑ Feb 1997 Cover: 2.95 **NM** value: **Cover or less**
Circ: Diamd. preorders: **3,545**
A: Rumiko Takahashi **W:** Rumiko Takahashi
3 ❑ Mar 1997 Cover: 2.95 **NM** value: **Cover or less**
Circ: Diamd. preorders: **3,374**
A: Rumiko Takahashi **W:** Rumiko Takahashi
4 ❑ 1997 Cover: 2.95 **NM** value: **Cover or less**
A: Rumiko Takahashi **W:** Rumiko Takahashi
5 ❑ 1997 Cover: 2.95 **NM** value: **Cover or less**
A: Rumiko Takahashi **W:** Rumiko Takahashi
6 ❑ 1997 Cover: 2.95 **NM** value: **Cover or less**
📖 The Fallen Lamb, Part 2 **A:** Rumiko Takahashi **W:** Rumiko Takahashi

ONE-SHOT PARODY — Milky Way
1 ❑ Cover: 1.50 **NM** value: **Cover or less**
• X-Men

ONE-SHOT WESTERN — Caliber
1 ❑ b&w Cover: 2.50 **NM** value: **Cover or less**
Circ: CapCity orders: **2,050**

1111 — Crusade
1 ❑ Oct 1996, b&w Cover: 2.95 **NM** value: **Cover or less**
Circ: Diamd. preorders: **16,152**
No issue number. One-shot. • prose story with facing page illustrations; illustrated story **A:** Bernie Wrightson **W:** Joy Mosier-Dubinsky

1,001 NIGHTS OF BACCHUS, THE — Dark Horse
1 ❑ May 1993, b&w Cover: 3.95 **NM** value: **4.50**
Circ: CapCity orders: **2,500**
No issue number. One-shot. 📖 Up All Night With Sheherezade; Oh King, it has Come to my Ears That...; Hearkening and Obedience; One for the Road, O Auspicious King The Send for the Wazir) **A:** Eddie Campbell; Wes Kublick; Steve Stamatiadis; Dylan Horrocks; Gilgamesh **W:** Eddie Campbell

...ONE TO GO — Äardwolf
1 ❑ Cover: 2.50 **NM** value: **Cover or less**
📖 The Poet; What They Don't Know...; Don't Blame Me; Bru-Hed: Divine Intervention; Bru-Hed: Road Vengeance **A:** Paty Cockrum; Mike Pascale **W:** Mike Pascale; Clifford Meth; Dave Sonnett

ONE TRICK RIP OFF, THE — Dark Horse
Bk 1❑ May 1997, b&w Cover: 12.95 **NM** value: **Cover or less**
• collects story from Dark Horse Presents #101-112 **A:** Paul Pope **W:** Paul Pope

ONI — Dark Horse
1 ❑ Feb 2001 Cover: 2.99 **NM** value: **Cover or less**
A: Sunny Lee **W:** David Land
2 ❑ Feb 2001 Cover: 2.99 **NM** value: **Cover or less**
A: Sunny Lee **W:** David Land
3 ❑ Feb 2001 Cover: 2.99 **NM** value: **Cover or less**
A: Sunny Lee **W:** David Land

ONI DOUBLE FEATURE — Oni Press

Gen Xer's are featured prominently in this anthology flip book from Oni Press. "The Secret Broadcast" focuses on a trio of would-be anarchists that run a pirate radio station to free the airwaves from trashy radio programs. Of course, the FCC takes a dim view of unlicensed broadcasts, no matter what the motivation.

Independent film maker and comic fan, Kevin Smith, known for the movies Clerks, Mallrats, and Chasing Amy, brings two characters from Clerks, to the comic pages. Jay and his alter ego, Silent Bob are the main characters in "Walt Flanagan's Dog," a viciously funny story illustrated by Matt Wagner (Mage). Crude, vulgar, and oblivious to everything including their complete lack of potential, Jay and Silent Bob are definitely not role models as they pass time loitering, antagonizing service workers, and selling dope. It's not much of a life, but the resulting story is hilarious.

Later stories in the series included Paul Dini's Jingle Belle, Shannon Wheeler's Too Much Coffee Man, Judd Winick's Frumpy the Clown, and Stan Sakai's Usagi Yojimbo.

1 ❑ Jan 1998 Cover: 2.95 **NM** value: **6.00**
Circ: Diamd. preorders: **12,059**
• Flip-book. 📖 Jay & Silent Bob: Walt Flanagan's Dog; Secret Broadcast; Milk 'n' Cheese: Dental Hi-Jinx • Jay & Silent Bob, Milk & Cheese, Secret Broadcast **A:** Matt Wagner; Evan Dorkin; Arnold Pander; Jacob Pander **W:** Evan Dorkin; Arnold Pander; Jacob Pander; Kevin Smith ★ 1st Appearance of Silent Bob, Jay.
1-2 ❑ Mar 1998 Cover: 2.95 **NM** value: **Cover or less**
Circ: Diamd. preorders: **3,141**
2 ❑ Feb 1998 Cover: 2.95 **NM** value: **4.00**
Circ: Diamd. preorders: **7,322**
• Too Much Coffee Man, Car Crash, Secret Broadcast
3 ❑ Mar 1998 Cover: 2.95 **NM** value: **3.50**
Circ: Diamd. preorders: **6,323**
• Frumpy the Clown, Bacon, Car Crash
4 ❑ Apr 1998 Cover: 2.95 **NM** value: **3.50**
Circ: Diamd. preorders: **8,183**
• Bacon, A River in Egypt, Cheetahman **C:** Bill Sienkiewicz
5 ❑ May 1998 Cover: 2.95 **NM** value: **3.50**
Circ: Diamd. preorders: **6,876**
6 ❑ Jun 1998 Cover: 2.95 **NM** value: **4.00**
Circ: Diamd. preorders: **13,089**
📖 Only the End of the World Again, Part 1 • Only The End of the World Again, Zombie Kid **A:** Troy Nixey **W:** P. Craig Russell; Neil Gaiman
7 ❑ Jul 1998 Cover: 2.95 **NM** value: **Cover or less**
Circ: Diamd. preorders: **8,807**
8 ❑ Aug 1998 Cover: 2.95 **NM** value: **Cover or less**
Circ: Diamd. preorders: **9,289**
• Only The End of the World Again, Satchel of Weltschmerz, Pip & Norton
9 ❑ Oct 1998 Cover: 2.95 **NM** value: **Cover or less**
Circ: Diamd. preorders: **6,929**
10 ❑ Nov 1998 Cover: 2.95 **NM** value: **Cover or less**
Circ: Diamd. preorders: **5,740**
• Sam & Max, Drive-By, Road Trip
11 ❑ Feb 1999 Cover: 2.95 **NM** value: **Cover or less**
Circ: Diamd. preorders: **4,926**
• Usagi Yojimbo, Blue Monday, Drive-By
12 ❑ May 1999 Cover: 2.95 **NM** value: **Cover or less**
Circ: Diamd. preorders: **23,547**
• The Harpooner, Bluntman & Chronic, The Honor Rollers

ONIGAMI — Antarctic
1 ❑ Apr 1998 Cover: 2.95 **NM** value: **Cover or less**
Circ: Diamd. preorders: **3,000**
📖 In the Shadow of Every Crime **A:** Michel Lacombe **W:** Michel Lacombe
2 ❑ Jun 1998 Cover: 2.95 **NM** value: **Cover or less**
📖 The Beginning of Parting **A:** Michel Lacombe **W:** Michel Lacombe
3 ❑ Jul 1998 Cover: 2.95 **NM** value: **Cover or less**
📖 Revenge at an Unexpected Place **A:** Michel Lacombe **W:** Michel Lacombe

ONLY THE END OF THE WORLD AGAIN — Oni
1 ❑ Cover: 6.95 **NM** value: **Cover or less**
A: Troy Nixey **W:** P. Craig Russell; Neil Gaiman

ON OUR BUTTS — Aeon
1 ❑ Apr 1995 Cover: 2.95 **NM** value: **Cover or less**

ON RAVEN'S WINGS — Boneyard
1 ❑ Cover: 2.95 **NM** value: **Cover or less**
A: Garry Way **W:** Garry Way
2 ❑ Sep 1994 Cover: 2.95 **NM** value: **Cover or less**
A: Garry Way **W:** Garry Way

ONSLAUGHT: EPILOGUE — Marvel
1 ❑ Feb 1997 Cover: 2.95 **NM** value: **Cover or less**
Circ: Direct Market orders: **123,000**
One-shot. 📖 Prisoner M-13 **A:** Randy Green **W:** Larry Hama ★ 1st Appearance of Nina.

ONSLAUGHT: MARVEL — Marvel
1 ❑ Oct 1996 Cover: 3.95 **NM** value: **6.00**
Circ: Direct Market orders: **11,000** • **CGC:** 1 graded, best 9.6
wraparound cover. 📖 With Great Power... **A:** Adam Kubert; Dan Green(inks) **W:** Scott Lobdell; Mark Waid ★ Appearance of di.

ONSLAUGHT: X-MEN — Marvel
1 ❑ Aug 1996 Cover: 3.95 **NM** value: **5.00**
wraparound cover. 📖 Traitor to the Cause • set-up for Onslaught crossover in Marvel titles **A:** Adam Kubert; Dan Green(inks) **W:** Scott Lobdell; Mark Waid
1/SC❑ Cover: 3.95 **NM** value: **8.00**
variant cover. 📖 Traitor to the Cause **A:** Adam Kubert; Dan Green(inks) **W:** Scott Lobdell; Mark Waid

ON THE AIR — National Broadcasting Company
1 ❑ ca. 1947 **NM** value: **175.00**
• **CGC:** 1 graded, best 8.0

ON THE BUS — Slave Labor
1 ❑ Aug 1994 Cover: 2.95 **NM** value: **Cover or less**
📖 The Overland Route **A:** F. Andrew Taylor **W:** F. Andrew Taylor

ON THE SPOT — Fawcett
1 ❑ Fal 1948 Cover: 0.10 **NM** value: **250.00**
• **CGC:** 1 graded, best 8.0

ONYX OVERLORD — Marvel / Epic
1 ❑ Oct 1992 Cover: 2.75 **NM** value: **Cover or less**
Circ: CapCity orders: **5,800**
📖 The Onyx Overlord, Log 1 **A:** Jerry Bingham; Moebius **W:** Moebius; R.J.M. Lofficier
2 ❑ Nov 1992 Cover: 2.75 **NM** value: **Cover or less**
Circ: CapCity orders: **4,200**
📖 The Onyx Overlord, Log 2 **A:** Jerry Bingham **W:** Moebius; R.J.M. Lofficier
3 ❑ Dec 1992 Cover: 2.75 **NM** value: **Cover or less**
Circ: CapCity orders: **3,500**
📖 The Onyx Overlord, Log 3 **A:** Jerry Bingham **W:** Moebius; R.J.M. Lofficier
4 ❑ Jan 1993 Cover: 2.75 **NM** value: **Cover or less**
Circ: CapCity orders: **3,350**
📖 The Onyx Overlord, Log 4 **A:** Jerry Bingham **W:** Moebius; R.J.M. Lofficier

OOMBAH, JUNGLE MOON MAN — Strawberry Jam
1 ❑ b&w Cover: 2.50 **NM** value: **Cover or less**

OPEN SEASON — Renegade

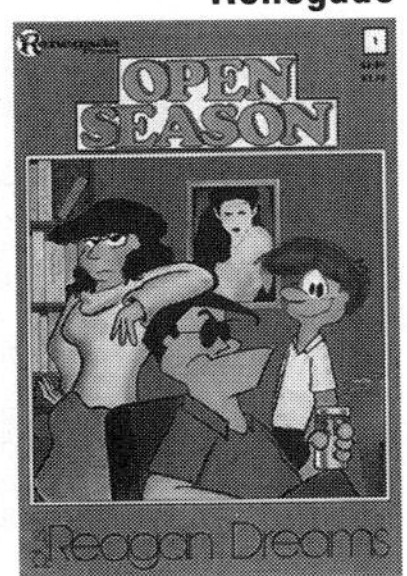

Years before "slice-of-life" series would become popular among alternative cartoonists (who all-too-often would provide slices of lives no one would want to know much about), Jim Bricker provided an excellent example in Open Season.

Hapless Joe moves in with Robin, a straight-talking reporter, and Cliff, a drunkard much resembling Bloom County's Steve Dallas. That makes it sitcom city, as the three find that sharing space isn't the bargain they bargained for.

But there are also thoughtful and memorable pieces, such as Joe's gut-wrenching recollection of a high-school dance. There was even a limited stage production of Open Season, and the comics programs from it turn up now and again. — JJM

CGC-graded: Multiply prices above by **33 for 9.9 M** • **16 for 9.8 NM/M** • **7 for 9.6 NM+** • **5 for 9.4 NM** • **2.5 for 9.2 NM-** • **1.5 for 9.0 VF/NM**

1 ❑ 1987, b&w Cover: 2.00 NM value: Cover or less
2 ❑ 1987, b&w Cover: 2.00 NM value: Cover or less
3 ❑ 1987, b&w Cover: 2.00 NM value: Cover or less
4 ❑ Oct 1987, b&w Cover: 2.00 NM value: Cover or less
5 ❑ Dec 1987, b&w Cover: 2.00 NM value: Cover or less
6 ❑ Apr 1988, b&w Cover: 2.00 NM value: Cover or less
• black issue
7 ❑ b&w Cover: 2.00 NM value: Cover or less

OPEN SORE FUNNIES — Home-Made Euthanasia

1 ❑ Cover: 1.25 NM value: Cover or less

OPEN SPACE — Marvel

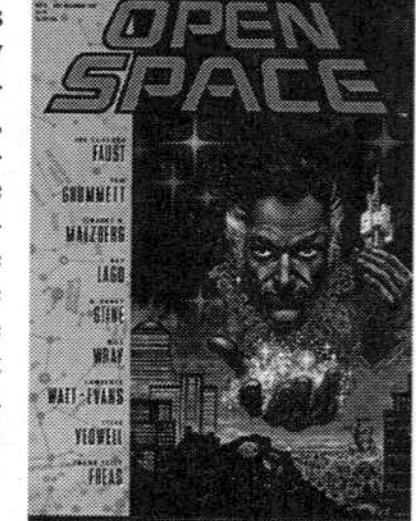

Open Space is a collection of stories told by some of science-fiction's best writers, loosely tied together by an overarching plot. The plot concerns the release of the Smoots drive, a device which ingeniously circumvents the ultimate speed limit: the speed of light. With the cheap, easy-to-manufacture Smoots drive, the stars become open to everyone. The only problem is that Astranet (the company that created it) doesn't want it released until they can find a way to properly capitalize on it. As far as Astranet is concerned, let humanity rot until then.

But that wasn't good enough for inventor Drake Etchison. He arranged to steal a prototype of the drive and give it to wild card Jack Brody. Jack succeeded in demonstrating the drive to an incredulous world. Meanwhile, Drake was tracked down and murdered — but not before he succeeded in transmitting the plans to a hacker bulletin board. Now, at last, humanity has access to the open space...

The series only lasted four issues, but, if the fifth issue had been published it would have had two events of note: Alex Ross' first professional work and a story by CBG editor Maggie Thompson.

1 ❑ Dec 1989 Cover: 4.95 NM value: Cover or less
Circ: CapCity orders: 10,050
📖 Handshake; The Land Of Nod; Frontiers A: Steve Yeowell; Tom Grummettt; Ray Lago W: Kurt Busiek; Barry Malzberg; Joe Clifford Faust; Lawrence Watt-Evans
2 ❑ Apr 1990 Cover: 4.95 NM value: Cover or less
Circ: CapCity orders: 7,200
3 ❑ Jun 1990 Cover: 4.95 NM value: Cover or less
Circ: CapCity orders: 5,300
📖 There Ain't No Such Thing As A Free Launch!; Dear Jenny; Home is a Hard Place; Fix-It Man A: Norm Breyfogle; Donald Simpson; John Garcia; Patrick Olliffe W: Dana Kramer-Rolls; L. Neil Smith; Matthew J. Costello; Will Shetterly
4 ❑ Aug 1990 Cover: 4.95 NM value: Cover or less
Circ: CapCity orders: 4,800

OPERA — Eclipse

Bk 1❑ Cover: 19.95 NM value: Cover or less
A: P. Craig Russell

OPERATION: KANSAS CITY — Motion

1 ❑ Win 1993, b&w Cover: 2.50 NM value: Cover or less
• Breakneck Blvd. Preview

OPERATION: KNIGHTSTRIKE — Image

1 ❑ May 1995 Cover: 2.50 NM value: Cover or less
Circ: CapCity orders: 29,450 • CGC: 1 graded, best 9.6
A: Richard Horie W: Brian Witten
1/A ❑ May 1995 Cover: 2.50 NM value: Cover or less
2 ❑ Jun 1995 Cover: 2.50 NM value: Cover or less
Circ: CapCity orders: 20,575
A: Richard Horie W: Brian Witten
2/A ❑ Jun 1995 Cover: 2.50 NM value: Cover or less
3 ❑ Jul 1995 Cover: 2.50 NM value: Cover or less
Circ: CapCity orders: 19,475
A: Richard Horie W: Brian Witten ★ Appearance of Bloodstrike.

OPERATION PERIL — American Comics Group

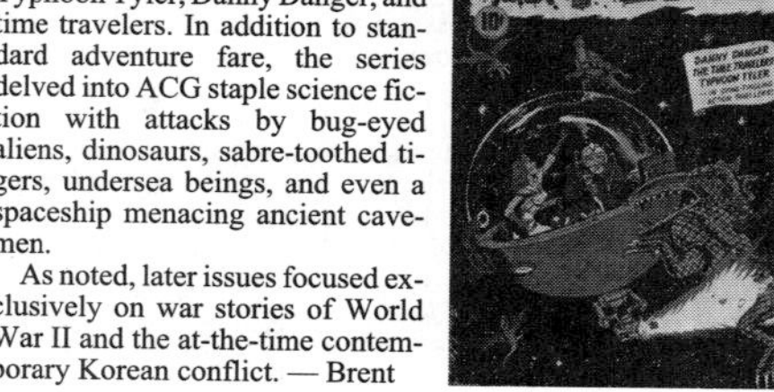

Later subtitled, "G.I.'s in Deadly Combat," Operation Peril began as an adventure anthology featuring Typhoon Tyler, Danny Danger, and time travelers. In addition to standard adventure fare, the series delved into ACG staple science fiction with attacks by bug-eyed aliens, dinosaurs, sabre-toothed tigers, undersea beings, and even a spaceship menacing ancient cavemen.

As noted, later issues focused exclusively on war stories of World War II and the at-the-time contemporary Korean conflict. — Brent

1 ❑ Oct 1950 Cover: 0.10 NM value: 275.00
• CGC: 1 graded, best 9.0
2 ❑ Dec 1950 Cover: 0.10 NM value: 250.00
3 ❑ Feb 1951 Cover: 0.10 NM value: 225.00
4 ❑ Apr 1951 Cover: 0.10 NM value: 225.00
5 ❑ Jun 1951 Cover: 0.10 NM value: 200.00
• CGC: 1 graded, best 7.0
6 ❑ Aug 1951 Cover: 0.10 NM value: 200.00
• CGC: 1 graded, best 9.2
7 ❑ Oct 1951 Cover: 0.10 NM value: 150.00
8 ❑ Dec 1951 Cover: 0.10 NM value: 150.00
9 ❑ Mar 1952 Cover: 0.10 NM value: 150.00
10 ❑ May 1952 Cover: 0.10 NM value: 125.00
11 ❑ Jul 1952 Cover: 0.10 NM value: 125.00
12 ❑ Sep 1952 Cover: 0.10 NM value: 125.00
13 ❑ Nov 1952 Cover: 0.10 NM value: 100.00
14 ❑ Jan 1953 Cover: 0.10 NM value: 100.00
15 ❑ Mar 1953 Cover: 0.10 NM value: 100.00
16 ❑ May 1953 Cover: 0.10 NM value: 100.00

OPERATION: STORMBREAKER — Acclaim / Valiant

1 ❑ Aug 1997 Cover: 3.95 NM value: Cover or less
Circ: Diamd. preorders: 17,534
One-shot. cover says Jul, indicia says Aug. ★ 1st Appearance of Doctor Tomorrow, Bravado, Nemesis, Sgt. Turok.

OPERATIVE: SCORPIO — Blackthorne

1 ❑ Jan 1989, b&w Cover: 3.50 NM value: Cover or less

OPTIC NERVE — Drawn & Quarterly

1 ❑ Cover: 2.95 NM value: 5.00
Circ: CapCity orders: 2,160
2 ❑ Cover: 2.95 NM value: 3.00
3 ❑ Cover: 2.95 NM value: 3.00
4 ❑ Mar 1997 Cover: 2.95 NM value: 3.00
Circ: Diamd. preorders: 6,150
5 ❑ Feb 1998 Cover: 2.95 NM value: 3.00
Circ: Diamd. preorders: 5,662
6 ❑ Jan 1999 Cover: 2.95 NM value: 3.00
Circ: Diamd. preorders: 5,727
7 ❑ Jun 2000 Cover: 2.95 NM value: 3.00
Circ: Diamd. preorders: 6,572
• Mini-Comic

OPUS — Fantagraphics

Bk 1❑ Cover: 39.95 NM value: Cover or less

ORA — Son of a Treebob Studios

1 ❑ Mar 1999, b&w Cover: 2.95 NM value: Cover or less

ORACLE — Oracle

1 ❑ b&w NM value: 3.00
A: George Pérez

ORACLE – A TRESPASSERS MYSTERY — Amazing Montage

1 ❑ b&w Cover: 4.95 NM value: Cover or less
No issue number.

ORACLE PRESENTS — Oracle

1 ❑ b&w NM value: 3.00
• reprint of Oracle #1 A: George Pérez
2 ❑ Aug 1986, b&w Cover: 1.00 NM value: 3.00
• Critter Corps

ORBIT — Eclipse

1 ❑ Cover: 4.95 NM value: Cover or less
📖 Nothing for Nothing; Ginny Sweethips' Flying Circus; Fermi and Frost A: John Bolton; Brent Anderson; Mark Pacella C: Dave Stevens W: Brent Anderson; Fred Burke; Frederik Pohl; Isaac Asimov; Leslie Clague; Neal Barrett Jr.; Steve Niles
2 ❑ Cover: 4.95 NM value: Cover or less
A: Brent Anderson
3 ❑ Cover: 4.95 NM value: Cover or less
Circ: CapCity orders: 2,975
📖 The Lost Garden of Enid Blyton, Beatrix Potter, Lucy Atwell and the Rest of the Lads of the 32nd Parachute Regiment; The Last Question; The End of Life as We Know It A: John Bolton; Tom Yeates; John Estes W: Tom Yeates; Don Thompson; Fred Burke; Garry Kilworth; Isaac Asimov; Lucius Shepard

ORB MAGAZINE — Orb

1 ❑ Cover: 1.25 NM value: Cover or less
2 ❑ Cover: 1.25 NM value: Cover or less
3 ❑ Cover: 1.25 NM value: Cover or less
📖 Lepers; Half-Life; Cheezy-Nuggets; Super-Student; The Lone Guardian Strikes; Escape The Truth; Karkass; A Shroud of Tattered Grey!; The Rescue of Raniff the Fair A: Jim Craig; Gene Day; Ronn Sutton; Alex Emond; John Allison; Matt Rust; Paul McCusker; Richard Robertson; Dan Archambault; Ken Syeacy; Paul Savard; Rob McIntyre W: Ken Steacy; Gene Day; Steve Skeates; Alex Emond; John Allison; Mary Skrenes; Matt Rust; Paul Mc Cusker; Richard Robertson; T.Casey Brennan

ORGY BOUND — Fantagraphics

Bk 1❑ Mar 1996, b&w Cover: 14.95 NM value: Cover or less
• collects cartoons A: Daniel Clowes

ORIENTAL HEROES — Jademan

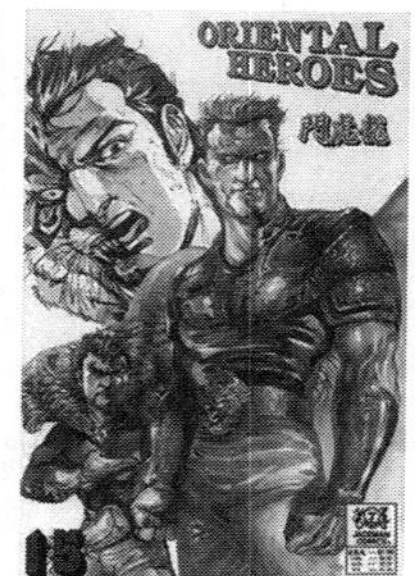

Jademan Comics struck again with Oriental Heroes — another in its line of martial arts, action/adventure comics. Unfortunately, a convoluted storyline coupled with careless art and lettering made new reader acquisition a difficult proposition.

Oriental Heroes tells the story of a century's old struggle between the forces of Red and White Sect — two of Asia's most powerful Kung Fu armies. Within each particular organization breeds an additional battle — the age-old sin of ambition. As each member of Red and White Sect's hierarchy achieves another level of Kung Fu, his quest for power grows proportionately. But as history has proven, there can be only one leader and that person will be the strongest.

While the soap opera style plot may be intimidating for some, the illustrations revolving around the story's fight sequences are beautifully mastered. With each particular combat move named and explained within the story, it's almost as if the reader can learn the art of Kung Fu just by studying the title.

1 ❑ Aug 1988 Cover: 1.95 NM value: Cover or less
Circ: CapCity orders: 7,625
A: Tony Wong W: Mike Baron
2 ❑ Sep 1988 Cover: 1.95 NM value: Cover or less
Circ: CapCity orders: 3,450
A: Tony Wong W: Mike Baron
3 ❑ Oct 1988 Cover: 1.95 NM value: Cover or less
Circ: CapCity orders: 3,275
A: Tony Wong W: Mike Baron
4 ❑ Nov 1988 Cover: 1.95 NM value: Cover or less
Circ: CapCity orders: 3,175
A: Tony Wong W: Mike Baron
5 ❑ Dec 1988 Cover: 1.95 NM value: Cover or less
Circ: CapCity orders: 3,425
A: Tony Wong W: Mike Baron
6 ❑ Jan 1989 Cover: 1.95 NM value: Cover or less
Circ: CapCity orders: 3,425
A: Tony Wong W: Mike Baron
7 ❑ Feb 1989 Cover: 1.95 NM value: Cover or less
Circ: CapCity orders: 3,225
A: Tony Wong W: Mike Baron
8 ❑ Mar 1989 Cover: 1.95 NM value: Cover or less
Circ: CapCity orders: 2,950
A: Tony Wong W: Mike Baron
9 ❑ Apr 1989 Cover: 1.95 NM value: Cover or less
Circ: CapCity orders: 3,000
A: Tony Wong W: Mike Baron
10 ❑ May 1989 Cover: 1.95 NM value: Cover or less
Circ: CapCity orders: 3,000
A: Tony Wong W: Mike Baron
11 ❑ Jun 1989 Cover: 1.95 NM value: Cover or less
Circ: CapCity orders: 2,600
A: Tony Wong W: Mike Baron
12 ❑ Jul 1989 Cover: 1.95 NM value: Cover or less
Circ: CapCity orders: 2,400
A: Tony Wong W: Mike Baron
13 ❑ Aug 1989 Cover: 1.95 NM value: Cover or less
Circ: CapCity orders: 2,600
A: Tony Wong W: Mike Baron
14 ❑ Sep 1989 Cover: 1.95 NM value: Cover or less
Circ: CapCity orders: 2,600
A: Tony Wong W: Mike Baron
15 ❑ Oct 1989 Cover: 1.95 NM value: Cover or less
Circ: CapCity orders: 2,600
A: Tony Wong W: Mike Baron
16 ❑ Nov 1989 Cover: 1.95 NM value: Cover or less
Circ: CapCity orders: 2,400
A: Tony Wong W: Mike Baron
17 ❑ Dec 1989 Cover: 1.95 NM value: Cover or less
Circ: CapCity orders: 2,400
A: Tony Wong W: Mike Baron
18 ❑ Jan 1990 Cover: 1.95 NM value: Cover or less
Circ: CapCity orders: 2,400
A: Tony Wong W: Mike Baron
19 ❑ Feb 1990 Cover: 1.95 NM value: Cover or less
Circ: CapCity orders: 2,200
A: Tony Wong W: Mike Baron
20 ❑ Mar 1990 Cover: 1.95 NM value: Cover or less
Circ: CapCity orders: 2,200
A: Tony Wong W: Mike Baron
21 ❑ Apr 1990 Cover: 1.95 NM value: Cover or less
Circ: CapCity orders: 2,200
A: Tony Wong W: Mike Baron
22 ❑ May 1990 Cover: 1.95 NM value: Cover or less
Circ: CapCity orders: 2,200
A: Tony Wong W: Mike Baron
23 ❑ Jun 1990 Cover: 1.95 NM value: Cover or less
Circ: CapCity orders: 2,000
A: Tony Wong W: Mike Baron
24 ❑ Jul 1990 Cover: 1.95 NM value: Cover or less
Circ: CapCity orders: 2,000
A: Tony Wong W: Mike Baron
25 ❑ Aug 1990 Cover: 1.95 NM value: Cover or less
Circ: CapCity orders: 2,000
A: Tony Wong W: Mike Baron
26 ❑ Sep 1990 Cover: 1.95 NM value: Cover or less
Circ: CapCity orders: 2,000
A: Tony Wong W: Mike Baron
27 ❑ Oct 1990 Cover: 1.95 NM value: Cover or less
Circ: CapCity orders: 2,000
A: Tony Wong W: Mike Baron
28 ❑ Nov 1990 Cover: 1.95 NM value: Cover or less
Circ: CapCity orders: 2,000
A: Tony Wong W: Mike Baron
29 ❑ Dec 1990 Cover: 1.95 NM value: Cover or less
Circ: CapCity orders: 2,000
A: Tony Wong W: Mike Baron
30 ❑ Jan 1991 Cover: 1.95 NM value: Cover or less
Circ: CapCity orders: 2,000
A: Tony Wong W: Mike Baron
31 ❑ Feb 1991 Cover: 1.95 NM value: Cover or less
Circ: CapCity orders: 2,000
A: Tony Wong W: Mike Baron
32 ❑ Mar 1991 Cover: 1.95 NM value: Cover or less
Circ: CapCity orders: 2,000
A: Tony Wong W: Mike Baron
33 ❑ Apr 1991 Cover: 1.95 NM value: Cover or less
Circ: CapCity orders: 2,000
A: Tony Wong W: Mike Baron

34 ❑ May 1991 Cover: 1.95 **NM** value: **Cover or less**
Circ: CapCity orders: **2,000**
A: Tony Wong **W:** Mike Baron
35 ❑ Jun 1991 Cover: 1.95 **NM** value: **Cover or less**
Circ: CapCity orders: **2,000**
A: Tony Wong **W:** Mike Baron
36 ❑ Jul 1991 Cover: 1.95 **NM** value: **Cover or less**
Circ: CapCity orders: **1,800**
A: Tony Wong **W:** Mike Baron
37 ❑ Aug 1991 Cover: 1.95 **NM** value: **Cover or less**
Circ: CapCity orders: **1,800**
A: Tony Wong **W:** Mike Baron
38 ❑ Sep 1991 Cover: 1.95 **NM** value: **Cover or less**
Circ: CapCity orders: **1,800**
A: Tony Wong **W:** Mike Baron
39 ❑ Oct 1991 Cover: 1.95 **NM** value: **Cover or less**
Circ: CapCity orders: **1,800**
A: Tony Wong **W:** Mike Baron
40 ❑ Nov 1991 Cover: 1.95 **NM** value: **Cover or less**
Circ: CapCity orders: **1,800**
A: Tony Wong **W:** Mike Baron
41 ❑ Dec 1991 Cover: 1.95 **NM** value: **Cover or less**
Circ: CapCity orders: **1,800**
A: Tony Wong **W:** Mike Baron
42 ❑ Jan 1992 Cover: 1.95 **NM** value: **Cover or less**
Circ: CapCity orders: **2,025**
A: Tony Wong **W:** Mike Baron

ORIGINAL ASTRO BOY, THE — Now

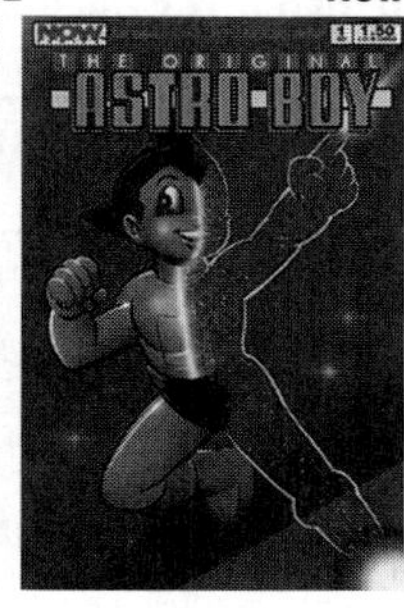

Astro-Boy, the child-sized robot with the heart of gold, was one of the first generation of Japanese anime characters to gain popularity in the United States, debuting (along with Speed Racer) in 1964. It is no exaggeration to say that Astro-Boy enjoys superstar status in the Japanese comic world, and was a natural to help lead the first wave of manga titles to see print in the U.S. in the late 1980s. Now Comics gave Astro-Boy a well-packaged showcase, with colorful, open, kid-friendly art and storytelling from writer Michael Dimpsey, and illustrators Ken Steacy and Rodney Dunn.

Astro-Boy inhabits a future world where robots are common, but treated as second-class citizens. Created as a child-surrogate by a slightly megalomaniacal mad scientist, Astro-Boy has the innocence of a little boy but the powers of a fighting machine.

1 ❑ Sep 1987 Cover: 1.50 **NM** value: **2.00**
Circ: CapCity orders: **5,775**
A: Ken Steacy **W:** Mike Dimpsey ★ Origin of Astro Boy.
2 ❑ Oct 1987 Cover: 1.50 **NM** value: **Cover or less**
Circ: CapCity orders: **4,300**
3 ❑ Nov 1987 Cover: 1.75 **NM** value: **Cover or less**
Circ: CapCity orders: **5,175**
4 ❑ Dec 1987 Cover: 1.75 **NM** value: **Cover or less**
Circ: CapCity orders: **5,850**
5 ❑ Jan 1988 Cover: 1.75 **NM** value: **Cover or less**
Circ: CapCity orders: **6,150**
6 ❑ Feb 1988 Cover: 1.75 **NM** value: **Cover or less**
Circ: CapCity orders: **5,650**
7 ❑ Mar 1988 Cover: 1.75 **NM** value: **Cover or less**
Circ: CapCity orders: **4,650**
8 ❑ Apr 1988 Cover: 1.75 **NM** value: **Cover or less**
Circ: CapCity orders: **3,975**
9 ❑ May 1988 Cover: 1.75 **NM** value: **Cover or less**
Circ: CapCity orders: **3,775**
10 ❑ Jun 1988 Cover: 1.75 **NM** value: **Cover or less**
Circ: CapCity orders: **3,250**
11 ❑ Aug 1988 Cover: 1.75 **NM** value: **Cover or less**
Circ: CapCity orders: **2,850**
12 ❑ Sep 1988 Cover: 1.75 **NM** value: **Cover or less**
Circ: CapCity orders: **2,750**
13 ❑ Oct 1988 Cover: 1.75 **NM** value: **Cover or less**
Circ: CapCity orders: **2,600**
14 ❑ Nov 1988 Cover: 1.75 **NM** value: **Cover or less**
Circ: CapCity orders: **2,400**
15 ❑ Jan 1989 Cover: 1.75 **NM** value: **Cover or less**
Circ: CapCity orders: **2,100**
16 ❑ Feb 1989 Cover: 1.75 **NM** value: **Cover or less**
17 ❑ Mar 1989 Cover: 1.75 **NM** value: **Cover or less**
18 ❑ Apr 1989 Cover: 1.75 **NM** value: **Cover or less**
19 ❑ May 1989 Cover: 1.75 **NM** value: **Cover or less**
20 ❑ Jun 1989 Cover: 1.75 **NM** value: **Cover or less**
final issue.

ORIGINAL BLACK CAT, THE — Recollections

1 ❑ Cover: 2.00 **NM** value: **Cover or less**
2 ❑ Mar 1989 Cover: 2.00 **NM** value: **Cover or less**
C: Murphy Anderson ★ 1st Appearance of Kit.
3 ❑ Sep 1990 Cover: 2.00 **NM** value: **Cover or less**
4 ❑ Jun 1991 Cover: 2.00 **NM** value: **Cover or less**
5 ❑ Jul 1991 Cover: 2.00 **NM** value: **Cover or less**
6 ❑ Aug 1991 Cover: 2.00 **NM** value: **Cover or less**
• reprints first Black Cat story from Pocket Comics #1
7 ❑ Nov 1991 Cover: 2.00 **NM** value: **Cover or less**
8 ❑ Cover: 2.00 **NM** value: **Cover or less**
• Title changes to Black Cat for one issue only
9 ❑ Cover: 2.00 **NM** value: **Cover or less**
• Title reverts to Original Black Cat
10 ❑ Cover: 1.00 **NM** value: **Cover or less**
• Title changes to Black Cat Comics for final issue

ORIGINAL BOY: DAY OF ATONEMENT — Omega 7

1 ❑ **NM** value: **1.95**
No issue number. no cover price. • no indicia; events deal with Million Man March on Washington **A:** Johnnie Johnson **W:** Alonzo Washington

ORIGINAL CREW, THE — Personality

1 ❑ Cover: 2.95 **NM** value: **3.00**
• William Shatner **A:** Aldrin Aw **W:** Stephen Spire III
2 ❑ Cover: 2.95 **NM** value: **3.00**
• Leonard Nimoy
3 ❑ Cover: 2.95 **NM** value: **3.00**
• DeForest Kelley
4 ❑ Cover: 2.95 **NM** value: **Cover or less**
5 ❑ Cover: 2.95 **NM** value: **Cover or less**
6 ❑ Cover: 2.95 **NM** value: **Cover or less**
7 ❑ Cover: 2.95 **NM** value: **Cover or less**
8 ❑ Cover: 2.95 **NM** value: **Cover or less**
9 ❑ Cover: 2.95 **NM** value: **Cover or less**
• Bruce Hyde
10 ❑ Cover: 2.95 **NM** value: **Cover or less**

ORIGINAL DICK TRACY, THE — Gladstone

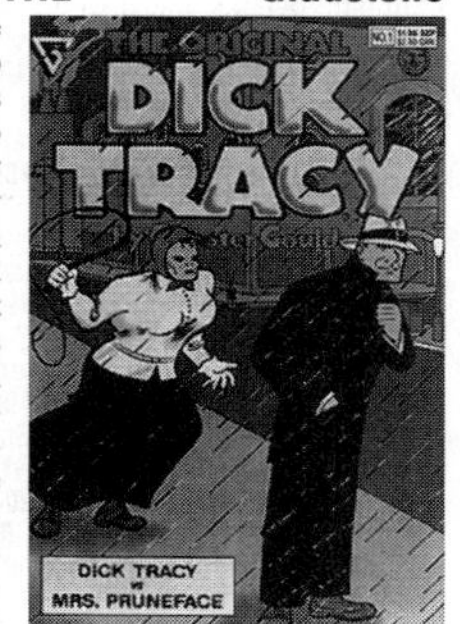

Chester Gould's famous police detective with the razor-sharp chin returns to the comics in this series from Gladstone. Also present is Gould's customary practice of pointing out the 2-way wrist radio and other elements in the story with tiny arrows and type, as though the reader might not realize their significance. This is a 64-page book that reprints an entire storyline from the newspaper comic strip. This comic features all the macabre and bizarre villains like Pruneface, Itchy, Gargles and his unlikely named allies as well as friends like Tess Trueheart, Pat Patton, and Sam Catchem. It gives readers, too young to have read the original adventures, the opportunity to experience the brutal, often violent world of Dick Tracy.

1 ❑ Sep 1990 Cover: 1.95 **NM** value: **2.00**
Circ: CapCity orders: **7,300**
📖 Dick Tracy vs. Mrs. Pruneface • Mrs. Pruneface **A:** Chester Gould **W:** Chester Gould
2 ❑ Nov 1990 Cover: 1.95 **NM** value: **2.00**
Circ: CapCity orders: **6,650**
• Influence **A:** Chester Gould **W:** Chester Gould
3 ❑ Jan 1991 Cover: 2.00 **NM** value: **Cover or less**
Circ: CapCity orders: **7,950**
📖 Dick Tracy Exterminates the Extortioner • Gargles **A:** Chester Gould **W:** Chester Gould
4 ❑ Mar 1991 Cover: 2.00 **NM** value: **Cover or less**
Circ: CapCity orders: **5,800**
📖 Dick Tracy Confronts Itchy Oliver • Itchy **A:** Chester Gould **W:** Chester Gould
5 ❑ May 1991 Cover: 2.00 **NM** value: **Cover or less**
Circ: CapCity orders: **4,350**
📖 Dick Tracy Rubs Shoulders • Shoulders **A:** Chester Gould **W:** Chester Gould

ORIGINAL DICK TRACY COMIC ALBUM — Gladstone

Bk 1 ❑ Jul 1990 Cover: 5.95 **NM** value: **Cover or less**
• Mumbles
Bk 2 ❑ Sep 1990 Cover: 5.95 **NM** value: **Cover or less**
★ Origin of wrist radio.
Bk 3 ❑ Jan 1991 Cover: 5.95 **NM** value: **Cover or less**
• Mole

ORIGINAL DOCTOR SOLAR, MAN OF THE ATOM, THE — Valiant

1 ❑ Apr 1995 Cover: 2.95 **NM** value: **Cover or less**
Circ: CapCity orders: **6,400**

ORIGINAL E-MAN — First

1 ❑ Oct 1985 Cover: 1.75 **NM** value: **2.00**
Circ: Statement: **16,206** CapCity orders: **4,500**
2 ❑ Nov 1985 Cover: 1.75 **NM** value: **2.00**
Circ: Statement: **16,206** CapCity orders: **3,725**
3 ❑ Dec 1985 Cover: 1.75 **NM** value: **2.00**
Circ: Statement: **16,206** CapCity orders: **3,525**
4 ❑ Jan 1986 Cover: 1.75 **NM** value: **2.00**
Circ: CapCity orders: **3,350**
5 ❑ Feb 1986 Cover: 1.75 **NM** value: **2.00**
Circ: CapCity orders: **3,125**
6 ❑ Mar 1986 Cover: 1.75 **NM** value: **2.00**
Circ: CapCity orders: **2,950**
7 ❑ Apr 1986 Cover: 2.00 **NM** value: **Cover or less**
Circ: CapCity orders: **2,950**

ORIGINAL GHOST RIDER, THE — Marvel

1 ❑ Jul 1992 Cover: 1.75 **NM** value: **2.00**
Circ: CapCity orders: **27,900**
★ Origin of Ghost Rider.
2 ❑ Aug 1992 Cover: 1.75 **NM** value: **2.00**
Circ: CapCity orders: **18,500**
📖 Angels from Hell **A:** Mike Ploog **W:** Gary Friedrich ★ Origin of Ghost Rider.
3 ❑ Sep 1992 Cover: 1.75 **NM** value: **2.00**
Circ: CapCity orders: **18,700**
4 ❑ Oct 1992 Cover: 1.75 **NM** value: **2.00**
Circ: CapCity orders: **17,100**
📖 The Hordes of Hell; Phantom Rider: The End of the Line **A:** Dick Ayers; Mike Ploog; Jim Mooney **W:** Gary Friedrich; Dan Slott
5 ❑ Nov 1992 Cover: 1.75 **NM** value: **2.00**
Circ: CapCity orders: **14,400**
📖 The Snakes Crawl at Night... **A:** Tom Sutton **W:** Gary Friedrich
6 ❑ Dec 1992 Cover: 1.75 **NM** value: **2.00**
Circ: CapCity orders: **12,800**
7 ❑ Jan 1993 Cover: 1.75 **NM** value: **2.00**
Circ: CapCity orders: **11,200**
8 ❑ Feb 1993 Cover: 1.75 **NM** value: **2.00**
Circ: CapCity orders: **11,100**
9 ❑ Mar 1993 Cover: 1.75 **NM** value: **2.00**
Circ: CapCity orders: **9,700**
10 ❑ Apr 1993 Cover: 1.75 **NM** value: **2.00**
Circ: CapCity orders: **10,500**
11 ❑ May 1993 Cover: 1.75 **NM** value: **2.00**
Circ: CapCity orders: **9,600**
📖 Wheels On Fire **A:** Jim Mooney **W:** Gary Friedrich
12 ❑ Jun 1993 Cover: 1.75 **NM** value: **2.00**
Circ: CapCity orders: **9,100**
13 ❑ Jul 1993 Cover: 1.75 **NM** value: **2.00**
Circ: CapCity orders: **9,700**
14 ❑ Aug 1993 Cover: 1.75 **NM** value: **2.00**
Circ: CapCity orders: **8,100**
15 ❑ Sep 1993 Cover: 1.75 **NM** value: **2.00**
Circ: CapCity orders: **6,550**
📖 ...And Lose His Own Soul! **A:** Jim Mooney **W:** Tony Isabella
16 ❑ Oct 1993 Cover: 1.75 **NM** value: **2.00**
Circ: CapCity orders: **6,500**
📖 Satan Himself! **A:** Jim Mooney **W:** Tony Isabella ★ 1st Appearance of Inferno. ★ Appearance of Roxanne.
17 ❑ Nov 1993 Cover: 1.75 **NM** value: **2.00**
Circ: CapCity orders: **5,500**
18 ❑ Dec 1993 Cover: 1.75 **NM** value: **2.00**
Circ: CapCity orders: **5,500**
📖 The Desolation Run! **A:** Sal Buscema **W:** Tony Isabella ★ Appearance of Hulk.
19 ❑ Jan 1994 Cover: 1.75 **NM** value: **2.00**
Circ: CapCity orders: **4,600**
• Reprints Marvel Two-In-One #8
20 ❑ Feb 1994 Cover: 1.75 **NM** value: **2.00**
Circ: CapCity orders: **4,450**
📖 Phantom of the Killer Skies **A:** Frank Robbins **W:** Tony Isabella

ORIGINAL GHOST RIDER RIDES AGAIN, THE — Marvel

1 ❑ Jul 1991 Cover: 1.50 **NM** value: **2.50**
Circ: CapCity orders: **43,200**
📖 The Curse Of Jonathan Blaze! • Reprinted from Ghost Rider #68 **A:** Bob Budiansky **W:** Roger Stern ★ Origin of Ghost Rider.
2 ❑ Aug 1991 Cover: 1.50 **NM** value: **2.00**
Circ: CapCity orders: **33,600**
3 ❑ Sep 1991 Cover: 1.50 **NM** value: **2.00**
Circ: CapCity orders: **34,200**
📖 Temptations; Tears of a Clown **A:** Bob Budiansky **W:** Roger Stern
4 ❑ Oct 1991 Cover: 1.50 **NM** value: **2.00**
Circ: CapCity orders: **33,000**
5 ❑ Nov 1991 Cover: 1.50 **NM** value: **2.00**
Circ: CapCity orders: **28,800**
6 ❑ Dec 1991 Cover: 1.50 **NM** value: **1.75**
Circ: CapCity orders: **25,400**
7 ❑ Jan 1992 Cover: 1.50 **NM** value: **1.75**
Circ: CapCity orders: **21,400**

ORIGINAL MAGNUS ROBOT FIGHTER, THE — Valiant

1 ❑ Apr 1992 Cover: 2.95 **NM** value: **Cover or less**
Circ: CapCity orders: **6,600**
cardstock cover. 📖 Operation Disguise • Reprints Magnus, Robot Fighter 4000 A.D. #2 **A:** Russ Manning **W:** Russ Manning

ORIGINAL MAN — Omega 7

1 ❑ Cover: 3.50 **NM** value: **Cover or less**
Circ: CapCity orders: **6,950**

ORIGINAL MAN: THE MOST POWERFUL MAN IN THE UNIVERSE — Omega 7

1 ❑ Cover: 1.95 **NM** value: **Cover or less**
📖 Payback! • Darkforce #0 as flip-side support story **A:** Tony Jappa **W:** Alonzo Washington

ORIGINAL MYSTERYMEN PRESENTS (BOB BURDEN'S...) — Dark Horse

1 ❑ Jul 1999 Cover: 2.95 **NM** value: **Cover or less**
📖 Who Are the Mysterymen? **A:** Stephen Sadowski **W:** Bob Burden
2 ❑ Aug 1999 Cover: 2.95 **NM** value: **Cover or less**
📖 The Amazing Disc Man **A:** Stephen Sadowski **W:** Bob Burden
3 ❑ Sep 1999 Cover: 2.95 **NM** value: **Cover or less**
A: Chris Mcloughlin **W:** Bob Burden
4 ❑ Oct 1999 Cover: 3.50 **NM** value: **Cover or less**

ORIGINAL SAD SACK — Recollections

1 ❑ b&w Cover: 2.00 **NM** value: **Cover or less**
A: George Baker

ORIGINAL SHIELD — Archie

1 ❑ Apr 1984 Cover: 0.75 **NM** value: **1.00**
2 ❑ Jun 1984 Cover: 0.75 **NM** value: **1.00**
3 ❑ Aug 1984 Cover: 0.75 **NM** value: **1.00**
4 ❑ Oct 1984 Cover: 0.75 **NM** value: **1.00**

ORIGINAL SIN, THE — Thwack! Pow!

1 ❑ Cover: 1.00 **NM** value: **Cover or less**
A: Garth Haslam **W:** Garth Haslam
2 ❑ Cover: 1.00 **NM** value: **Cover or less**
A: Garth Haslam **W:** Garth Haslam

CGC-graded: Multiply prices above by **33 for 9.9 M • 16 for 9.8 NM/M • 7 for 9.6 NM+ • 5 for 9.4 NM • 2.5 for 9.2 NM- • 1.5 for 9.0 VF/NM**

3 ❑ Cover: 1.00 **NM** value: **Cover or less**
A: Garth Haslam **W:** Garth Haslam

ORIGINAL SINS — Avalon
1 ❑ Cover: 2.95 **NM** value: **Cover or less**
📖 Silo **A:** James O'Barr **W:** James O'Barr

ORIGINAL STREET FIGHTER, THE — Alpha
1 ❑ b&w Cover: 2.50 **NM** value: **Cover or less**
📖 The Wheelman; The Lion & The Lady: The Inn At Journey's End **A:** Gary Kato **W:** Ron Fortier

ORIGINAL TOM CORBETT, THE — Eternity
1 ❑ b&w Cover: 2.95 **NM** value: **Cover or less**
• Reprinted from Field Enterprises strips Tom Corbett, Space Cadet **A:** Ray Bailey **W:** Ray Bailey
2 ❑ b&w Cover: 2.95 **NM** value: **Cover or less**
• Reprinted from Field Enterprises strips Tom Corbett, Space Cadet **A:** Ray Bailey **W:** Ray Bailey
3 ❑ b&w Cover: 2.95 **NM** value: **Cover or less**
• Reprinted from Field Enterprises strips Tom Corbett, Space Cadet **A:** Ray Bailey **W:** Ray Bailey
4 ❑ b&w Cover: 2.95 **NM** value: **Cover or less**
• Reprinted from Field Enterprises strips Tom Corbett, Space Cadet **A:** Ray Bailey **W:** Ray Bailey
5 ❑ b&w Cover: 2.95 **NM** value: **Cover or less**
• Reprinted from Field Enterprises strips Tom Corbett, Space Cadet **A:** Ray Bailey **W:** Ray Bailey
6 ❑ Cover: 2.95 **NM** value: **Cover or less**
• Reprinted from Field Enterprises strips Tom Corbett, Space Cadet **A:** Ray Bailey **W:** Ray Bailey
7 ❑ Cover: 2.95 **NM** value: **Cover or less**
• Reprinted from Field Enterprises strips Tom Corbett, Space Cadet **A:** Ray Bailey **W:** Ray Bailey
8 ❑ Cover: 2.95 **NM** value: **Cover or less**
• Reprinted from Field Enterprises strips Tom Corbett, Space Cadet **A:** Ray Bailey **W:** Ray Bailey
9 ❑ Cover: 2.95 **NM** value: **Cover or less**
• Reprinted from Field Enterprises strips Tom Corbett, Space Cadet **A:** Ray Bailey **W:** Ray Bailey
10 ❑ Cover: 2.95 **NM** value: **Cover or less**
• Reprinted from Field Enterprises strips Tom Corbett, Space Cadet **A:** Ray Bailey **W:** Ray Bailey

ORIGINAL TUROK, SON OF STONE, THE — Valiant
1 ❑ Apr 1995 Cover: 2.95 **NM** value: **Cover or less**
Circ: CapCity orders: **6,800**
cardstock cover.
2 ❑ May 1995 Cover: 2.95 **NM** value: **Cover or less**
Circ: CapCity orders: **4,800**
cardstock cover. 📖 The Cliff Men; Terror of the Bog final issue. • Reprints of Turok, Son of Stone #24, #33

ORIGINAL TZU, THE: SPIRITS OF DEATH — Murim
1 ❑ Dec 1997, b&w Cover: 2.95 **NM** value: **Cover or less**
• reprints manga series

ORIGIN OF GALACTUS — Marvel
1 ❑ Feb 1996 Cover: 2.50 **NM** value: **Cover or less**
No issue number. • reprints Super-Villain Classics #1 **A:** Jack Kirby **W:** Stan Lee ★ Origin of Galactus.

ORIGIN OF THE DEFIANT UNIVERSE, THE — Defiant
1 ❑ Feb 1994 Cover: 1.50 **NM** value: **Cover or less**
Circ: CapCity orders: **14,200**
A: The Defiant Creative Crew **W:** Jim Shooter ★ Origin of the Defiant Universe.

ORIGINS OF MARVEL COMICS — Marvel
Bk 1❑ Cover: 6.95 **NM** value: **25.00**
• Trade Paperback. • (Fireside)
Bk 1/HC❑ Cover: 10.95 **NM** value: **40.00**
hardcover. • first edition. • (Fireside)

ORION — Dark Horse
1 ❑ Feb 1993, b&w Cover: 3.95 **NM** value: **Cover or less**
Circ: CapCity orders: **5,300**
• manga **A:** Masamune Shirow **W:** Masamune Shirow
2 ❑ Mar 1993, b&w Cover: 2.50 **NM** value: **2.95**
Circ: CapCity orders: **3,575**
• manga **A:** Masamune Shirow **W:** Masamune Shirow
3 ❑ Apr 1993, b&w Cover: 2.50 **NM** value: **2.95**
Circ: CapCity orders: **4,000**
• manga **A:** Masamune Shirow **W:** Masamune Shirow
4 ❑ May 1993, b&w Cover: 2.50 **NM** value: **2.95**
Circ: CapCity orders: **4,650**
• manga **A:** Masamune Shirow **W:** Masamune Shirow
5 ❑ Jun 1993, b&w Cover: 2.95 **NM** value: **Cover or less**
Circ: CapCity orders: **4,375**
• manga **A:** Masamune Shirow **W:** Masamune Shirow
6 ❑ Jul 1993 Cover: 3.95 **NM** value: **Cover or less**
Circ: CapCity orders: **4,100**
A: Masamune Shirow **W:** Masamune Shirow
Bk 1❑ Cover: 15.95 **NM** value: **Cover or less**
A: Masamune Shirow **W:** Masamune Shirow
Bk 1-2❑ Dec 1995 Cover: 17.95 **NM** value: **Cover or less**

The CGC numbers printed in individual listings above represent the **number of copies examined** and given a **Universal** grade by CGC and the **best such copy** graded at press time. For current populations, watch for special ***Comics Buyer's Guide*** issues or check **www.cgccomics.com.**

ORION (DC) — DC
The New Gods — Orion, Lightray, Mister Miracle, and company — have been part of the DC universe since the early 1970s, when Jack Kirby unleashed them on unsuspecting comic-book readers.

Following on the heels of writer and artist John Byrne's excellent 20-issue Fourth World (Jack Kirby's...) series, writer and artist Walter Simonson launched Orion. It focused more particularly on the adventures of the alleged son of Darkseid, the despotic ruler of Apokolips whose pursuit of the ultimate power — the Anti-Life Equation — continued in this series and brought him into conflict with the title character, the greatest warrior of New Genesis. Simonson's work here matches the greatness of his run on Thor in the 1980s. Readers are not only treated to this comics industry legend's exquisite pencils and inks on the main feature, but also the gorgeous line work of such luminaries as Frank Miller (Batman: The Dark Knight, 300) and Dave Gibbons (Watchmen, Give Me Liberty) on the "Tales of the New Gods" backup feature.

1 ❑ Jun 2000 Cover: 2.50 **NM** value: **Cover or less**
Circ: Diamd. preorders: **27,034**
📖 O Beautiful for Spacious Skies… **A:** Walt Simonson **W:** Walt Simonson
2 ❑ Jul 2000 Cover: 2.50 **NM** value: **Cover or less**
Circ: Diamd. preorders: **21,691**
A: Walt Simonson **W:** Walt Simonson
3 ❑ Aug 2000 Cover: 2.50 **NM** value: **Cover or less**
Circ: Diamd. preorders: **23,696**
A: Walt Simonson **W:** Walt Simonson
4 ❑ Sep 2000 Cover: 2.50 **NM** value: **Cover or less**
Circ: Diamd. preorders: **21,204**
📖 Above the Fruited Plain… **A:** Walt Simonson **W:** Walt Simonson
5 ❑ Oct 2000 Cover: 2.50 **NM** value: **Cover or less**
Circ: Diamd. preorders: **19,331**
📖 Day of Wrath **A:** Walt Simonson **W:** Walt Simonson
6 ❑ Nov 2000 Cover: 2.50 **NM** value: **Cover or less**
Circ: Diamd. preorders: **18,227**
📖 The King is Dead…Long Live the King!; Tales of the New Gods: The Perfect Servant **A:** Erik Larsen; Walt Simonson **W:** Walt Simonson; Eric Stephenson
7 ❑ Dec 2000 Cover: 2.50 **NM** value: **Cover or less**
Circ: Diamd. preorders: **17,460**
📖 Tough Love! **A:** Walt Simonson **W:** Walt Simonson
8 ❑ Jan 2001 Cover: 2.50 **NM** value: **Cover or less**
Circ: Diamd. preorders: **16,898**
📖 The Righteous Treacheries of Desaad! Or Orion Rules! **A:** Walt Simonson **W:** Walt Simonson
9 ❑ Feb 2001 Cover: 2.50 **NM** value: **Cover or less**
Circ: Diamd. preorders: **16,099**
📖 The Electro Death of Honor! **A:** Walt Simonson **W:** Walt Simonson
10 ❑ Mar 2001 Cover: 2.50 **NM** value: **Cover or less**
Circ: Diamd. preorders: **15,437**
📖 Sirius Business! Or Dog is God Spelled Backwards! **A:** Walt Simonson **W:** Walt Simonson
11 ❑ Apr 2001 Cover: 2.50 **NM** value: **Cover or less**
Circ: Diamd. preorders: **14,876**
📖 Orion Rules! **A:** Walt Simonson **W:** Walt Simonson
12 ❑ May 2001 Cover: 2.50 **NM** value: **Cover or less**
Circ: Diamd. preorders: **14,883**
📖 Legends of Apokolips **A:** Walt Simonson **W:** Walt Simonson
13 ❑ Jun 2001 Cover: 2.50 **NM** value: **Cover or less**
Circ: Diamd. preorders: **16,434**
14 ❑ Jul 2001 Cover: 2.50 **NM** value: **Cover or less**
Circ: Diamd. preorders: **15,781**
15 ❑ Aug 2001 Cover: 2.50 **NM** value: **Cover or less**
Circ: Diamd. preorders: **15,323**
16 ❑ Sep 2001 Cover: 2.50 **NM** value: **Cover or less**
Circ: Diamd. preorders: **15,454**
Bk 1❑ Cover: 12.95 **NM** value: **Cover or less**
• The Gates of Apokolips; Collects Orion (DC) #1-5 **A:** Walt Simonson **W:** Walt Simonson

ORLAK REDUX — Caliber
1 ❑ b&w Cover: 3.95 **NM** value: **Cover or less**

OSBORN JOURNALS — Marvel
1 ❑ Feb 1997 Cover: 2.95 **NM** value: **Cover or less**
Circ: Direct Market orders: **36,000**
One-shot. 📖 Spider-man: The Osborn Journals • summation of Clone Saga and return of Norman Osborn as Green Goblin **A:** Kyle Hotz **W:** Glenn Greenberg

OSCAR COMICS — Marvel
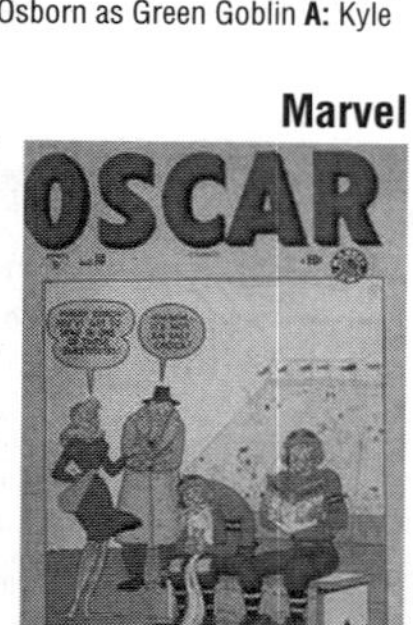

Continuing the numbering of Funny Tunes, the first three issues of Oscar Comics carry #24, #25, and #26, respectively, on their covers, although it is blacked out on the third issue with a #3 added below. A second printing, with no blacked-out number, was also produced.

The typical teen-age comedy featured a dark-haired crewcut teenage boy who was smitten with Kitty, a statuesque blonde who was prominently featured on the covers of each issue.

For the final two issues of the run, the series was retitled Awful Oscar and changed direction to focus on the mischevious antics of a younger red-headed child. — Brent

1 ❑ Spr 1947 Cover: 0.10 **NM** value: **125.00**
2 ❑ Sum 1947 Cover: 0.10 **NM** value: **100.00**
3 ❑ Fal 1947 Cover: 0.10 **NM** value: **100.00**
4 ❑ Win 1947 Cover: 0.10 **NM** value: **80.00**
5 ❑ Jun 1948 Cover: 0.10 **NM** value: **80.00**
6 ❑ Aug 1948 Cover: 0.10 **NM** value: **80.00**
7 ❑ Oct 1948 Cover: 0.10 **NM** value: **60.00**
8 ❑ Dec 1948 Cover: 0.10 **NM** value: **60.00**
9 ❑ Feb 1949 Cover: 0.10 **NM** value: **60.00**
10 ❑ Apr 1949 Cover: 0.10 **NM** value: **60.00**

OTHELLO — Tome
1 ❑ b&w Cover: 3.50 **NM** value: **Cover or less**
No issue number.

OTHER BIG THING (COLIN UPTON'S...) — Fantagraphics
1 ❑ b&w Cover: 2.75 **NM** value: **Cover or less**
A: Colin Upton **W:** Colin Upton
2 ❑ Cover: 2.25 **NM** value: **Cover or less**
3 ❑ Cover: 2.25 **NM** value: **Cover or less**
4 ❑ Jul 1992 Cover: 2.50 **NM** value: **Cover or less**

OTHERS, THE (CORMAC) — Cormac
1 ❑ Cover: 1.50 **NM** value: **Cover or less**

OTHERS, THE (IMAGE) — Image
0 ❑ Mar 1995 Cover: 1.00 **NM** value: **Cover or less**
Circ: CapCity orders: **16,225**
📖 Opening Shots, Part 1; Opening Shots, Part 2; The Descent, Part 3 **A:** Jim Valentino; Patrick Blaine; Chance Wolf **W:** Jim Valentino; Tom Sniegoski
1 ❑ Apr 1995 Cover: 2.50 **NM** value: **Cover or less**
Circ: CapCity orders: **15,075 • CGC:** 1 graded, best 9.6
📖 The Mighty Fallen **A:** Jim Valentino; Patrick Blaine **W:** Tom Sniegoski
2 ❑ May 1995 Cover: 2.50 **NM** value: **Cover or less**
Circ: CapCity orders: **10,825**
3 ❑ Jul 1995 Cover: 2.50 **NM** value: **Cover or less**
Circ: CapCity orders: **9,750**
4 ❑ Cover: 2.50 **NM** value: **Cover or less**

OTIS GOES HOLLYWOOD — Dark Horse
1 ❑ Apr 1997, b&w Cover: 2.95 **NM** value: **Cover or less**
Circ: Diamd. preorders: **3,848**
A: Bob Fingerman **W:** Bob Fingerman
2 ❑ May 1997, b&w Cover: 2.95 **NM** value: **Cover or less**
A: Bob Fingerman **W:** Bob Fingerman

OTTO SPACE! — Manifest Destiny
1 ❑ Cover: 2.00 **NM** value: **Cover or less**
2 ❑ Cover: 2.00 **NM** value: **Cover or less**
📖 Otto Space!; Revolt 3000 **A:** Dave Sim; Jim Keean; Ruth Keegan **W:** Dave Sim; Jim Keean; Ruth Keegan

OUR ARMY AT WAR — DC
One of the longest-running war comics of all time, Our Army At War enjoyed a continuous, 25-year run from 1952 to 1977. During that time, it brought countless tales of courage, cowardice, and irony — set primarily in World War II.

The highlight of this series was the first appearance of hard-bitten Sgt. Rock in issue #81. Rock, who starred in the remaining run of the series, was DC's premier war hero. He was a hero of unflagging bravery who was tough enough to handle any situation, but who knew the costs of war only too well.

Our Army At War was also notable for its introduction of Enemy Ace in issue #151. Remarkably, the hero in this case was a German pilot in World War I. Nevertheless, he was a man of extreme honor and courage, and was useful in showing that the real enemy is war itself.

1 ❑ Aug 1952 Cover: 0.10 **NM** value: **1250.00**
• **CGC:** 1 graded, best 4.0
2 ❑ Sep 1952 Cover: 0.10 **NM** value: **600.00**
• **CGC:** 1 graded, best 5.0
3 ❑ Oct 1952 Cover: 0.10 **NM** value: **475.00**
4 ❑ Nov 1952 Cover: 0.10 **NM** value: **475.00**
• **CGC:** 2 graded, best 4.5
5 ❑ Dec 1952 Cover: 0.10 **NM** value: **350.00**
6 ❑ Jan 1953 Cover: 0.10 **NM** value: **350.00**
7 ❑ Feb 1953 Cover: 0.10 **NM** value: **350.00**
8 ❑ Mar 1953 Cover: 0.10 **NM** value: **350.00**
9 ❑ Apr 1953 Cover: 0.10 **NM** value: **350.00**
10 ❑ May 1953 Cover: 0.10 **NM** value: **350.00**
11 ❑ Jun 1953 Cover: 0.10 **NM** value: **290.00**
• **CGC:** 1 graded, best 7.0
12 ❑ Jul 1953 Cover: 0.10 **NM** value: **245.00**
13 ❑ Aug 1953 Cover: 0.10 **NM** value: **290.00**
A: Bernie Krigstein
14 ❑ Sep 1953 Cover: 0.10 **NM** value: **245.00**
15 ❑ Oct 1953 Cover: 0.10 **NM** value: **245.00**
16 ❑ Nov 1953 Cover: 0.10 **NM** value: **200.00**
17 ❑ Dec 1953 Cover: 0.10 **NM** value: **200.00**
18 ❑ Jan 1954 Cover: 0.10 **NM** value: **200.00**
• **CGC:** 1 graded, best 7.0
19 ❑ Feb 1954 Cover: 0.10 **NM** value: **200.00**

Other grades: Multiply prices above by **1.5 for Mint • 2/3 for Very Fine • 1/3 for Fine • 1/5 for Very Good • 1/8 for Good**

20 ❑ Mar 1954 Cover: 0.10 **NM** value: **200.00**
21 ❑ Apr 1954 Cover: 0.10 **NM** value: **150.00**
22 ❑ May 1954 Cover: 0.10 **NM** value: **150.00**
• **CGC:** 1 graded, best 7.5
23 ❑ Jun 1954 Cover: 0.10 **NM** value: **150.00**
24 ❑ Jul 1954 Cover: 0.10 **NM** value: **150.00**
25 ❑ Aug 1954 Cover: 0.10 **NM** value: **150.00**
26 ❑ Sep 1954 Cover: 0.10 **NM** value: **150.00**
27 ❑ Oct 1954 Cover: 0.10 **NM** value: **150.00**
• **CGC:** 1 graded, best 2.5
28 ❑ Nov 1954 Cover: 0.10 **NM** value: **150.00**
29 ❑ Dec 1954 Cover: 0.10 **NM** value: **150.00**
30 ❑ Jan 1955 Cover: 0.10 **NM** value: **150.00**
31 ❑ Feb 1955 Cover: 0.10 **NM** value: **150.00**
32 ❑ Mar 1955 Cover: 0.10 **NM** value: **125.00**
33 ❑ Apr 1955 Cover: 0.10 **NM** value: **125.00**
34 ❑ May 1955 Cover: 0.10 **NM** value: **125.00**
35 ❑ Jun 1955 Cover: 0.10 **NM** value: **125.00**
36 ❑ Jul 1955 Cover: 0.10 **NM** value: **125.00**
37 ❑ Aug 1955 Cover: 0.10 **NM** value: **125.00**
38 ❑ Sep 1955 Cover: 0.10 **NM** value: **125.00**
39 ❑ Oct 1955 Cover: 0.10 **NM** value: **125.00**
40 ❑ Nov 1955 Cover: 0.10 **NM** value: **125.00**
41 ❑ Dec 1955 Cover: 0.10 **NM** value: **95.00**
42 ❑ Jan 1956 Cover: 0.10 **NM** value: **95.00**
• **CGC:** 1 graded, best 8.0
43 ❑ Feb 1956 Cover: 0.10 **NM** value: **95.00**
• **CGC:** 1 graded, best 8.5
44 ❑ Mar 1956 Cover: 0.10 **NM** value: **95.00**
45 ❑ Apr 1956 Cover: 0.10 **NM** value: **95.00**
46 ❑ May 1956 Cover: 0.10 **NM** value: **95.00**
47 ❑ Jun 1956 Cover: 0.10 **NM** value: **95.00**
48 ❑ Jul 1956 Cover: 0.10 **NM** value: **95.00**
49 ❑ Aug 1956 Cover: 0.10 **NM** value: **95.00**
50 ❑ Sep 1956 Cover: 0.10 **NM** value: **95.00**
51 ❑ Oct 1956 Cover: 0.10 **NM** value: **80.00**
52 ❑ Nov 1956 Cover: 0.10 **NM** value: **80.00**
53 ❑ Dec 1956 Cover: 0.10 **NM** value: **80.00**
54 ❑ Jan 1957 Cover: 0.10 **NM** value: **80.00**
55 ❑ Feb 1957 Cover: 0.10 **NM** value: **80.00**
56 ❑ Mar 1957 Cover: 0.10 **NM** value: **80.00**
• **CGC:** 1 graded, best 9.4
57 ❑ Apr 1957 Cover: 0.10 **NM** value: **80.00**
• **CGC:** 1 graded, best 1.0
58 ❑ May 1957 Cover: 0.10 **NM** value: **80.00**
59 ❑ Jun 1957 Cover: 0.10 **NM** value: **80.00**
60 ❑ Jul 1957 Cover: 0.10 **NM** value: **80.00**
• **CGC:** 1 graded, best 4.0
61 ❑ Aug 1957 Cover: 0.10 **NM** value: **75.00**
62 ❑ Sep 1957 Cover: 0.10 **NM** value: **75.00**
63 ❑ Oct 1957 Cover: 0.10 **NM** value: **75.00**
64 ❑ Nov 1957 Cover: 0.10 **NM** value: **75.00**
65 ❑ Dec 1957 Cover: 0.10 **NM** value: **75.00**
66 ❑ Jan 1958 Cover: 0.10 **NM** value: **75.00**
67 ❑ Feb 1958 Cover: 0.10 **NM** value: **75.00**
68 ❑ Mar 1958 Cover: 0.10 **NM** value: **75.00**
69 ❑ Apr 1958 Cover: 0.10 **NM** value: **75.00**
70 ❑ May 1958 Cover: 0.10 **NM** value: **75.00**
71 ❑ Jun 1958 Cover: 0.10 **NM** value: **60.00**
72 ❑ Jul 1958 Cover: 0.10 **NM** value: **60.00**
73 ❑ Aug 1958 Cover: 0.10 **NM** value: **60.00**
• **CGC:** 1 graded, best 8.5
74 ❑ Sep 1958 Cover: 0.10 **NM** value: **60.00**
75 ❑ Oct 1958 Cover: 0.10 **NM** value: **60.00**
76 ❑ Nov 1958 Cover: 0.10 **NM** value: **60.00**
77 ❑ Dec 1958 Cover: 0.10 **NM** value: **60.00**
78 ❑ Jan 1959 Cover: 0.10 **NM** value: **60.00**
79 ❑ Feb 1959 Cover: 0.10 **NM** value: **60.00**
80 ❑ Mar 1959 Cover: 0.10 **NM** value: **60.00**
81 ❑ Apr 1959 Cover: 0.10 **NM** value: **2200.00**
• **CGC:** 3 graded, best 8.0
📖 The Rock of Easy Co.!; Fighting Footsteps; The Liberators; Umbrella Pilot; No Pocket for Easy; The Unsafe Safe **A:** Joe Kubert; Ross Andru; Russ Heath; Jack Abel **W:** Bob Haney; Robert Kanigher ★ 1st Appearance of Sgt. Rock.
82 ❑ May 1959 Cover: 0.10 **NM** value: **550.00**
• **CGC:** 1 graded, best 8.0
★ 2nd Appearance of Sgt. Rock. ★ 2nd Appearance of Sgt. Rock.
83 ❑ Jun 1959 Cover: 0.10 **NM** value: **900.00**
• **CGC:** 6 graded, best 7.0
• 1st Kubert Sgt. Rock **A:** Joe Kubert ★ 1st Appearance of Easy Company.
84 ❑ Jul 1959 Cover: 0.10 **NM** value: **200.00**
85 ❑ Aug 1959 Cover: 0.10 **NM** value: **240.00**
★ Origin of The Ice Cream Soldier. ★ 1st Appearance of The Ice Cream Soldier.
86 ❑ Sep 1959 Cover: 0.10 **NM** value: **200.00**
87 ❑ Oct 1959 Cover: 0.10 **NM** value: **200.00**
• **CGC:** 1 graded, best 7.0
88 ❑ Nov 1959 Cover: 0.10 **NM** value: **200.00**
89 ❑ Dec 1959 Cover: 0.10 **NM** value: **200.00**
90 ❑ Jan 1960 Cover: 0.10 **NM** value: **200.00**
Circ: Statement: **172,000** • **CGC:** 1 graded, best 7.0
91 ❑ Feb 1960 Cover: 0.10 **NM** value: **500.00**
Circ: Statement: **172,000** • **CGC:** 3 graded, best 8.5
• 1st full-length Sgt. Rock story; All-Rock issue
92 ❑ Mar 1960 Cover: 0.10 **NM** value: **125.00**
Circ: Statement: **172,000**
93 ❑ Apr 1960 Cover: 0.10 **NM** value: **125.00**
Circ: Statement: **172,000**
94 ❑ May 1960 Cover: 0.10 **NM** value: **125.00**
Circ: Statement: **172,000**
95 ❑ Jun 1960 Cover: 0.10 **NM** value: **125.00**
Circ: Statement: **172,000**
96 ❑ Jul 1960 Cover: 0.10 **NM** value: **125.00**
Circ: Statement: **172,000**
97 ❑ Aug 1960 Cover: 0.10 **NM** value: **125.00**
Circ: Statement: **172,000**
98 ❑ Sep 1960 Cover: 0.10 **NM** value: **125.00**
Circ: Statement: **172,000**
99 ❑ Oct 1960 Cover: 0.10 **NM** value: **125.00**
Circ: Statement: **172,000**
100 ❑ Nov 1960 Cover: 0.10 **NM** value: **125.00**
Circ: Statement: **172,000**
101 ❑ Dec 1960 Cover: 0.10 **NM** value: **75.00**
Circ: Statement: **172,000**
102 ❑ Jan 1961 Cover: 0.10 **NM** value: **75.00**
103 ❑ Feb 1961 Cover: 0.10 **NM** value: **75.00**
104 ❑ Mar 1961 Cover: 0.10 **NM** value: **75.00**
105 ❑ Apr 1961 Cover: 0.10 **NM** value: **75.00**
106 ❑ May 1961 Cover: 0.10 **NM** value: **75.00**
107 ❑ Jun 1961 Cover: 0.10 **NM** value: **75.00**
108 ❑ Jul 1961 Cover: 0.10 **NM** value: **75.00**
109 ❑ Aug 1961 Cover: 0.10 **NM** value: **75.00**
110 ❑ Sep 1961 Cover: 0.10 **NM** value: **75.00**
111 ❑ Oct 1961 Cover: 0.10 **NM** value: **60.00**
112 ❑ Nov 1961 Cover: 0.10 **NM** value: **60.00**
• **CGC:** 1 graded, best 2.0
113 ❑ Dec 1961 Cover: 0.12 **NM** value: **60.00**
114 ❑ Jan 1962 Cover: 0.12 **NM** value: **60.00**
115 ❑ Feb 1962 Cover: 0.12 **NM** value: **60.00**
116 ❑ Mar 1962 Cover: 0.12 **NM** value: **60.00**
117 ❑ Apr 1962 Cover: 0.12 **NM** value: **60.00**
118 ❑ May 1962 Cover: 0.12 **NM** value: **60.00**
119 ❑ Jun 1962 Cover: 0.12 **NM** value: **60.00**
120 ❑ Jul 1962 Cover: 0.12 **NM** value: **60.00**
121 ❑ Aug 1962 Cover: 0.12 **NM** value: **48.00**
122 ❑ Sep 1962 Cover: 0.12 **NM** value: **48.00**
• **CGC:** 1 graded, best 4.0
123 ❑ Oct 1962 Cover: 0.12 **NM** value: **48.00**
• **CGC:** 1 graded, best 6.5
124 ❑ Nov 1962 Cover: 0.12 **NM** value: **48.00**
125 ❑ Dec 1962 Cover: 0.12 **NM** value: **48.00**
126 ❑ Jan 1963 Cover: 0.12 **NM** value: **48.00**
• **CGC:** 1 graded, best 8.5
127 ❑ Feb 1963 Cover: 0.12 **NM** value: **48.00**
• **CGC:** 1 graded, best 8.5
128 ❑ Mar 1963 Cover: 0.12 **NM** value: **185.00**
• **CGC:** 2 graded, best 7.0
★ Origin of Sgt. Rock.
129 ❑ Apr 1963 Cover: 0.12 **NM** value: **45.00**
130 ❑ May 1963 Cover: 0.12 **NM** value: **45.00**
131 ❑ Jun 1963 Cover: 0.12 **NM** value: **35.00**
132 ❑ Jul 1963 Cover: 0.12 **NM** value: **35.00**
• **CGC:** 1 graded, best 6.5
133 ❑ Aug 1963 Cover: 0.12 **NM** value: **35.00**
134 ❑ Sep 1963 Cover: 0.12 **NM** value: **35.00**
135 ❑ Oct 1963 Cover: 0.12 **NM** value: **35.00**
136 ❑ Nov 1963 Cover: 0.12 **NM** value: **35.00**
137 ❑ Dec 1963 Cover: 0.12 **NM** value: **35.00**
📖 Too Many Sergeants
138 ❑ Jan 1964 Cover: 0.12 **NM** value: **35.00**
139 ❑ Feb 1964 Cover: 0.12 **NM** value: **35.00**
140 ❑ Mar 1964 Cover: 0.12 **NM** value: **35.00**
141 ❑ Apr 1964 Cover: 0.12 **NM** value: **35.00**
142 ❑ May 1964 Cover: 0.12 **NM** value: **35.00**
143 ❑ Jun 1964 Cover: 0.12 **NM** value: **35.00**
• **CGC:** 2 graded, best 9.4
144 ❑ Jul 1964 Cover: 0.12 **NM** value: **35.00**
145 ❑ Aug 1964 Cover: 0.12 **NM** value: **35.00**
• **CGC:** 1 graded, best 9.2
146 ❑ Sep 1964 Cover: 0.12 **NM** value: **35.00**
147 ❑ Oct 1964 Cover: 0.12 **NM** value: **35.00**
148 ❑ Nov 1964 Cover: 0.12 **NM** value: **35.00**
149 ❑ Dec 1964 Cover: 0.12 **NM** value: **35.00**
150 ❑ Jan 1965 Cover: 0.12 **NM** value: **35.00**
Circ: Statement: **270,100**
151 ❑ Feb 1965 Cover: 0.12 **NM** value: **240.00**
Circ: Statement: **270,100** • **CGC:** 6 graded, best 9.0
A: Joe Kubert ★ 1st Appearance of Enemy Ace.
152 ❑ Mar 1965 Cover: 0.12 **NM** value: **20.00**
Circ: Statement: **270,100** • **CGC:** 1 graded, best 8.0
153 ❑ Apr 1965 Cover: 0.12 **NM** value: **100.00**
Circ: Statement: **270,100** • **CGC:** 2 graded, best 9.2
★ 2nd Appearance of Enemy Ace.
154 ❑ May 1965 Cover: 0.12 **NM** value: **18.00**
Circ: Statement: **270,100** • **CGC:** 1 graded, best 7.5
155 ❑ Jun 1965 Cover: 0.12 **NM** value: **45.00**
Circ: Statement: **270,100** • **CGC:** 1 graded, best 6.5
📖 No Stripes for Me!; Fokker Fury! **A:** Joe Kubert ★ 3rd Appearance of Enemy Ace (next appearance is in Showcase #57).
156 ❑ Jul 1965 Cover: 0.12 **NM** value: **18.00**
Circ: Statement: **270,100** • **CGC:** 1 graded, best 9.0
157 ❑ Aug 1965 Cover: 0.12 **NM** value: **18.00**
Circ: Statement: **270,100**
📖 Nothin's Ever Lost in War!; Spotter on the Spot!; ★ Appearance of Enemy Ace.
158 ❑ Sep 1965 Cover: 0.12 **NM** value: **28.00**
Circ: Statement: **270,100**
★ 1st Appearance of Iron Major.
159 ❑ Oct 1965 Cover: 0.12 **NM** value: **18.00**
Circ: Statement: **270,100**
📖 The Blind Gun!; The Silent Piper!
160 ❑ Nov 1965 Cover: 0.12 **NM** value: **18.00**
Circ: Statement: **270,100**
📖 What's the Color of Your Blood?
161 ❑ Dec 1965 Cover: 0.12 **NM** value: **18.00**
Circ: Statement: **270,100**
162 ❑ Jan 1966 Cover: 0.12 **NM** value: **18.00**
Circ: Statement: **243,906** • **CGC:** 1 graded, best 9.0
★ Appearance of Viking Prince.
163 ❑ Feb 1966 Cover: 0.12 **NM** value: **18.00**
Circ: Statement: **243,906** • **CGC:** 1 graded, best 9.2
★ Appearance of Viking Prince.
164 ❑ Feb 1966 Cover: 0.25 **NM** value: **40.00**
Circ: Statement: **243,906** • **CGC:** 2 graded, best 9.6
• Giant-size (80-Page Giant #G-19).
165 ❑ Mar 1966 Cover: 0.12 **NM** value: **18.00**
Circ: Statement: **243,906** • **CGC:** 1 graded, best 9.2
★ Versus Iron Major.
166 ❑ Apr 1966 Cover: 0.12 **NM** value: **18.00**
Circ: Statement: **243,906** • **CGC:** 2 graded, best 9.2
167 ❑ May 1966 Cover: 0.12 **NM** value: **18.00**
Circ: Statement: **243,906** • **CGC:** 1 graded, best 8.5
168 ❑ Jun 1966 Cover: 0.12 **NM** value: **18.00**
Circ: Statement: **243,906** • **CGC:** 1 graded, best 8.5
169 ❑ Jul 1966 Cover: 0.12 **NM** value: **18.00**
Circ: Statement: **243,906** • **CGC:** 1 graded, best 8.5
170 ❑ Aug 1966 Cover: 0.12 **NM** value: **18.00**
Circ: Statement: **243,906** • **CGC:** 2 graded, best 9.4
171 ❑ Sep 1966 Cover: 0.12 **NM** value: **16.00**
Circ: Statement: **243,906**
172 ❑ Oct 1966 Cover: 0.12 **NM** value: **16.00**
Circ: Statement: **243,906**
173 ❑ Nov 1966 Cover: 0.12 **NM** value: **16.00**
Circ: Statement: **243,906** • **CGC:** 2 graded, best 9.6
174 ❑ Dec 1966 Cover: 0.12 **NM** value: **16.00**
Circ: Statement: **243,906**
175 ❑ Jan 1967 Cover: 0.12 **NM** value: **16.00**
Circ: Statement: **196,500** • **CGC:** 1 graded, best 9.6
176 ❑ Feb 1967 Cover: 0.12 **NM** value: **16.00**
Circ: Statement: **196,500**
177 ❑ Feb 1967 Cover: 0.25 **NM** value: **35.00**
Circ: Statement: **196,500** • **CGC:** 1 graded, best 9.8
• Giant-size (80-Page Giant #G-32).
178 ❑ Mar 1967 Cover: 0.12 **NM** value: **16.00**
Circ: Statement: **196,500** • **CGC:** 1 graded, best 9.4
179 ❑ Apr 1967 Cover: 0.12 **NM** value: **16.00**
Circ: Statement: **196,500** • **CGC:** 1 graded, best 9.0
180 ❑ May 1967 Cover: 0.12 **NM** value: **16.00**
Circ: Statement: **196,500** • **CGC:** 2 graded, best 9.4
181 ❑ Jun 1967 Cover: 0.12 **NM** value: **16.00**
Circ: Statement: **196,500** • **CGC:** 1 graded, best 9.4
182 ❑ Jul 1967 Cover: 0.12 **NM** value: **20.00**
Circ: Statement: **196,500**
A: Neal Adams
183 ❑ Aug 1967 Cover: 0.12 **NM** value: **20.00**
Circ: Statement: **196,500**
A: Neal Adams
184 ❑ Sep 1967 Cover: 0.12 **NM** value: **14.00**
Circ: Statement: **196,500**
185 ❑ Oct 1967 Cover: 0.12 **NM** value: **14.00**
Circ: Statement: **196,500**
186 ❑ Nov 1967 Cover: 0.12 **NM** value: **20.00**
Circ: Statement: **196,500**
A: Neal Adams
187 ❑ Dec 1967 Cover: 0.12 **NM** value: **14.00**
Circ: Statement: **196,500**
188 ❑ Jan 1968 Cover: 0.12 **NM** value: **14.00**
189 ❑ Feb 1968 Cover: 0.12 **NM** value: **14.00**
• **CGC:** 1 graded, best 8.5
190 ❑ Feb 1968 Cover: 0.25 **NM** value: **14.00**
• **CGC:** 2 graded, best 9.2
191 ❑ Mar 1968 Cover: 0.12 **NM** value: **12.00**
192 ❑ Apr 1968 Cover: 0.12 **NM** value: **12.00**
193 ❑ May 1968 Cover: 0.12 **NM** value: **12.00**
194 ❑ Jun 1968 Cover: 0.12 **NM** value: **12.00**
• **CGC:** 1 graded, best 9.6
★ 1st Appearance of Unit 3 (kid guerrillas).
195 ❑ Jul 1968 Cover: 0.12 **NM** value: **12.00**
196 ❑ Aug 1968 Cover: 0.12 **NM** value: **12.00**
• **CGC:** 1 graded, best 8.5
📖 Stop the War I Want to Get Off
197 ❑ Sep 1968 Cover: 0.12 **NM** value: **12.00**
• **CGC:** 1 graded, best 9.6
198 ❑ Oct 1968 Cover: 0.12 **NM** value: **12.00**
199 ❑ Nov 1968 Cover: 0.12 **NM** value: **12.00**
200 ❑ Dec 1968 Cover: 0.12 **NM** value: **18.00**
• **CGC:** 1 graded, best 9.0
• 200th issue
201 ❑ Jan 1969 Cover: 0.12 **NM** value: **8.00**
• **CGC:** 1 graded, best 5.5
202 ❑ Feb 1969 Cover: 0.12 **NM** value: **8.00**
203 ❑ Feb 1969 Cover: 0.25 **NM** value: **20.00**
• **CGC:** 2 graded, best 9.2
• Giant-size.
204 ❑ Mar 1969 Cover: 0.12 **NM** value: **8.00**
205 ❑ Apr 1969 Cover: 0.12 **NM** value: **8.00**
206 ❑ May 1969 Cover: 0.12 **NM** value: **8.00**
• **CGC:** 1 graded, best 9.2
207 ❑ Jun 1969 Cover: 0.12 **NM** value: **8.00**
• **CGC:** 1 graded, best 9.0
208 ❑ Jul 1969 Cover: 0.15 **NM** value: **8.00**
• **CGC:** 1 graded, best 9.4
209 ❑ Aug 1969 Cover: 0.15 **NM** value: **8.00**
210 ❑ Sep 1969 Cover: 0.15 **NM** value: **8.00**
• **CGC:** 2 graded, best 9.6
211 ❑ Oct 1969 Cover: 0.15 **NM** value: **7.00**
212 ❑ Nov 1969 Cover: 0.15 **NM** value: **7.00**
213 ❑ Dec 1969 Cover: 0.15 **NM** value: **7.00**
214 ❑ Jan 1970 Cover: 0.15 **NM** value: **7.00**
• **CGC:** 1 graded, best 9.0
215 ❑ Feb 1970 Cover: 0.15 **NM** value: **7.00**
216 ❑ Feb 1970 Cover: 0.15 **NM** value: **15.00**
• **CGC:** 2 graded, best 9.4
• Giant-size (80-Page Giant #G-80).
217 ❑ Mar 1970 Cover: 0.15 **NM** value: **7.00**
• **CGC:** 2 graded, best 9.6
218 ❑ Apr 1970 Cover: 0.15 **NM** value: **7.00**
• **CGC:** 1 graded, best 9.4
219 ❑ May 1970 Cover: 0.15 **NM** value: **7.00**
• **CGC:** 1 graded, best 9.4
220 ❑ Jun 1970 Cover: 0.15 **NM** value: **7.00**
• **CGC:** 1 graded, best 9.6
221 ❑ Jul 1970 Cover: 0.15 **NM** value: **6.00**
• **CGC:** 1 graded, best 9.4

CGC-graded: Multiply prices above by **33 for 9.9 M • 16 for 9.8 NM/M • 7 for 9.6 NM+ • 5 for 9.4 NM • 2.5 for 9.2 NM- • 1.5 for 9.0 VF/NM**

222 ❑ Aug 1970 Cover: 0.15 **NM** value: **6.00**
223 ❑ Sep 1970 Cover: 0.15 **NM** value: **6.00**
224 ❑ Oct 1970 Cover: 0.15 **NM** value: **6.00**
225 ❑ Nov 1970 Cover: 0.15 **NM** value: **6.00**
226 ❑ Dec 1970 Cover: 0.15 **NM** value: **6.00**
227 ❑ Jan 1971 Cover: 0.15 **NM** value: **6.00**
228 ❑ Feb 1971 Cover: 0.15 **NM** value: **6.00**
229 ❑ Mar 1971 Cover: 0.25 **NM** value: **7.00**
• **CGC:** 1 graded, best 9.0
• Giant-size.
230 ❑ Mar 1971 Cover: 0.15 **NM** value: **6.00**
• **CGC:** 1 graded, best 9.4
231 ❑ Apr 1971 Cover: 0.15 **NM** value: **6.00**
• **CGC:** 1 graded, best 9.0
232 ❑ May 1971 Cover: 0.15 **NM** value: **6.00**
📖 Three Men In A Tub; Q-Boat Of World War I; Buck Taylor: You Can't Fool Me!
233 ❑ Jun 1971 Cover: 0.15 **NM** value: **6.00**
• **CGC:** 2 graded, best 9.4
234 ❑ Jul 1971 Cover: 0.15 **NM** value: **6.00**
235 ❑ Aug 1971 Cover: 0.25 **NM** value: **6.00**
236 ❑ Sep 1971 Cover: 0.25 **NM** value: **6.00**
• **CGC:** 1 graded, best 9.0
237 ❑ Oct 1971 Cover: 0.25 **NM** value: **6.00**
• **CGC:** 2 graded, best 9.4
238 ❑ Nov 1971 Cover: 0.25 **NM** value: **6.00**
239 ❑ Dec 1971 Cover: 0.25 **NM** value: **6.00**
240 ❑ Jan 1972 Cover: 0.25 **NM** value: **6.00**
Circ: Statement: **161,881**
241 ❑ Feb 1972 Cover: 0.25 **NM** value: **6.00**
Circ: Statement: **161,881**
242 ❑ Feb 1972 Cover: 0.50 **NM** value: **10.00**
Circ: Statement: **161,881** • **CGC:** 3 graded, best 9.0
wraparound cover. • a.k.a. DC 100-Page Super Spectacular #DC-9
C: Joe Kubert
243 ❑ Mar 1972 Cover: 0.25 **NM** value: **6.00**
Circ: Statement: **161,881** • **CGC:** 1 graded, best 8.0
📖 24 Hour Pass!; Visit To A Small War!; Rita, A Truck!; Blazing Battle Stations
244 ❑ Apr 1972 Cover: 0.25 **NM** value: **6.00**
Circ: Statement: **161,881**
245 ❑ May 1972 Cover: 0.25 **NM** value: **6.00**
Circ: Statement: **161,881**
246 ❑ Jun 1972 Cover: 0.25 **NM** value: **6.00**
Circ: Statement: **161,881** • **CGC:** 1 graded, best 9.4
247 ❑ Jul 1972 Cover: 0.20 **NM** value: **6.00**
Circ: Statement: **161,881**
248 ❑ Aug 1972 Cover: 0.20 **NM** value: **6.00**
Circ: Statement: **161,881**
249 ❑ Sep 1972 Cover: 0.20 **NM** value: **6.00**
Circ: Statement: **161,881**
250 ❑ Oct 1972 Cover: 0.20 **NM** value: **5.00**
Circ: Statement: **161,881**
251 ❑ Nov 1972 Cover: 0.20 **NM** value: **5.00**
Circ: Statement: **161,881**
252 ❑ Dec 1972 Cover: 0.20 **NM** value: **5.00**
Circ: Statement: **161,881**
253 ❑ Jan 1973 Cover: 0.20 **NM** value: **5.00**
Circ: Statement: **163,221**
254 ❑ Feb 1973 Cover: 0.20 **NM** value: **5.00**
Circ: Statement: **163,221**
255 ❑ Mar 1973 Cover: 0.20 **NM** value: **5.00**
Circ: Statement: **163,221**
256 ❑ Apr 1973 Cover: 0.20 **NM** value: **5.00**
Circ: Statement: **163,221**
257 ❑ Jun 1973 Cover: 0.20 **NM** value: **5.00**
Circ: Statement: **163,221**
258 ❑ Jul 1973 Cover: 0.20 **NM** value: **5.00**
Circ: Statement: **163,221**
259 ❑ Aug 1973 Cover: 0.20 **NM** value: **5.00**
Circ: Statement: **163,221**
260 ❑ Sep 1973 Cover: 0.20 **NM** value: **5.00**
Circ: Statement: **163,221**
261 ❑ Oct 1973 Cover: 0.20 **NM** value: **5.00**
Circ: Statement: **163,221**
262 ❑ Nov 1973 Cover: 0.20 **NM** value: **5.00**
Circ: Statement: **163,221**
263 ❑ Dec 1973 Cover: 0.20 **NM** value: **5.00**
Circ: Statement: **163,221**
264 ❑ Jan 1974 Cover: 0.20 **NM** value: **5.00**
Circ: Statement: **178,134**
265 ❑ Feb 1974 Cover: 0.20 **NM** value: **5.00**
Circ: Statement: **178,134**
266 ❑ Mar 1974 Cover: 0.20 **NM** value: **5.00**
Circ: Statement: **178,134**
267 ❑ Apr 1974 Cover: 0.20 **NM** value: **5.00**
Circ: Statement: **178,134**
268 ❑ May 1974 Cover: 0.20 **NM** value: **5.00**
Circ: Statement: **178,134**
269 ❑ Jun 1974 Cover: 0.60 **NM** value: **5.00**
Circ: Statement: **178,134**
270 ❑ Jul 1974 Cover: 0.20 **NM** value: **5.00**
Circ: Statement: **178,134**
271 ❑ Aug 1974 Cover: 0.20 **NM** value: **5.00**
Circ: Statement: **178,134**
272 ❑ Sep 1974 Cover: 0.20 **NM** value: **5.00**
Circ: Statement: **178,134**
273 ❑ Oct 1974 Cover: 0.20 **NM** value: **5.00**
Circ: Statement: **178,134**
274 ❑ Nov 1974 Cover: 0.20 **NM** value: **5.00**
Circ: Statement: **178,134**
275 ❑ Dec 1974 Cover: 0.60 **NM** value: **5.00**
Circ: Statement: **178,134** • **CGC:** 1 graded, best 9.2
276 ❑ Jan 1975 Cover: 0.25 **NM** value: **5.00**
Circ: Statement: **191,000**
277 ❑ Feb 1975 Cover: 0.25 **NM** value: **5.00**
Circ: Statement: **191,000**
278 ❑ Mar 1975 Cover: 0.25 **NM** value: **5.00**
Circ: Statement: **191,000**
279 ❑ Apr 1975 Cover: 0.25 **NM** value: **5.00**
Circ: Statement: **191,000**
280 ❑ May 1975 Cover: 0.25 **NM** value: **5.00**
Circ: Statement: **191,000**
281 ❑ Jun 1975 Cover: 0.25 **NM** value: **5.00**
Circ: Statement: **191,000**
282 ❑ Jul 1975 Cover: 0.25 **NM** value: **5.00**
Circ: Statement: **191,000**
283 ❑ Aug 1975 Cover: 0.25 **NM** value: **5.00**
Circ: Statement: **191,000** • **CGC:** 1 graded, best 9.2
284 ❑ Sep 1975 Cover: 0.25 **NM** value: **5.00**
Circ: Statement: **191,000**
285 ❑ Oct 1975 Cover: 0.25 **NM** value: **5.00**
Circ: Statement: **191,000**
286 ❑ Nov 1975 Cover: 0.25 **NM** value: **5.00**
Circ: Statement: **191,000**
287 ❑ Dec 1975 Cover: 0.25 **NM** value: **5.00**
Circ: Statement: **191,000**
288 ❑ Jan 1976 Cover: 0.25 **NM** value: **5.00**
Circ: Statement: **152,000**
289 ❑ Feb 1976 Cover: 0.25 **NM** value: **5.00**
Circ: Statement: **152,000**
290 ❑ Mar 1976 Cover: 0.30 **NM** value: **5.00**
Circ: Statement: **152,000**
291 ❑ Apr 1976 Cover: 0.30 **NM** value: **5.00**
Circ: Statement: **152,000**
292 ❑ May 1976 Cover: 0.30 **NM** value: **5.00**
Circ: Statement: **152,000**
293 ❑ Jun 1976 Cover: 0.30 **NM** value: **5.00**
Circ: Statement: **152,000**
294 ❑ Jul 1976 Cover: 0.30 **NM** value: **5.00**
Circ: Statement: **152,000** • **CGC:** 1 graded, best 8.0
295 ❑ Aug 1976 Cover: 0.30 **NM** value: **5.00**
Circ: Statement: **152,000**
296 ❑ Sep 1976 Cover: 0.30 **NM** value: **5.00**
Circ: Statement: **152,000**
297 ❑ Oct 1976 Cover: 0.30 **NM** value: **5.00**
Circ: Statement: **152,000**
298 ❑ Nov 1976 Cover: 0.30 **NM** value: **5.00**
Circ: Statement: **152,000**
299 ❑ Dec 1976 Cover: 0.30 **NM** value: **5.00**
Circ: Statement: **152,000**
300 ❑ Jan 1977 Cover: 0.30 **NM** value: **5.00**
Circ: Statement: **137,403**
301 ❑ Feb 1977 Cover: 0.30 **NM** value: **5.00**
Circ: Statement: **137,403**
final issue. • Series is continued as "Sgt. Rock"

OUR CANCER YEAR — Four Walls Eight Windows

1 ❑ Cover: 17.95 **NM** value: **Cover or less**
A: Frank Stack **W:** Joyce Brabner; Harvey Pekar

OUR FIGHTING FORCES — DC

This exciting war comic from the Fifties, Sixties, and Seventies launched many memorable heroes, including Captain Hunter and his Hellcats, and the Unknown Soldier.

However, the real star of this series was The Losers, a squad of hard-fighting soldiers who never gave up — no matter how hopeless the situation. The team consisted of Gunner, Sarge, Johnny Cloud, and their leader, the indomitable Captain Storm.

As a series, Our Fighting Forces gave time to all aspects of the military, from the army infantryman to the ace pilot. The feature stories of Our Fighting Forces hailed the merits of camaraderie, courage, and loyalty, as did the true exploits of U.S. fighting forces and bonus stories printed in each issue.

1 ❑ Oct 1954 Cover: 0.10 **NM** value: **750.00**
• **CGC:** 3 graded, best 7.0
2 ❑ Dec 1954 Cover: 0.10 **NM** value: **350.00**
• **CGC:** 2 graded, best 7.0
3 ❑ Feb 1955 Cover: 0.10 **NM** value: **300.00**
4 ❑ Apr 1955 Cover: 0.10 **NM** value: **235.00**
• **CGC:** 1 graded, best 5.5
5 ❑ Jun 1955 Cover: 0.10 **NM** value: **235.00**
6 ❑ Aug 1955 Cover: 0.10 **NM** value: **200.00**
• **CGC:** 1 graded, best 6.5
7 ❑ Oct 1955 Cover: 0.10 **NM** value: **200.00**
8 ❑ Dec 1955 Cover: 0.10 **NM** value: **200.00**
9 ❑ Feb 1956 Cover: 0.10 **NM** value: **200.00**
• **CGC:** 1 graded, best 7.0
10 ❑ Apr 1956 Cover: 0.10 **NM** value: **225.00**
A: Wally Wood
11 ❑ Jul 1956 Cover: 0.10 **NM** value: **140.00**
12 ❑ Aug 1956 Cover: 0.10 **NM** value: **140.00**
13 ❑ Sep 1956 Cover: 0.10 **NM** value: **140.00**
14 ❑ Oct 1956 Cover: 0.10 **NM** value: **140.00**
15 ❑ Nov 1956 Cover: 0.10 **NM** value: **140.00**
16 ❑ Dec 1956 Cover: 0.10 **NM** value: **125.00**
17 ❑ Jan 1957 Cover: 0.10 **NM** value: **125.00**
18 ❑ Feb 1957 Cover: 0.10 **NM** value: **125.00**
19 ❑ Mar 1957 Cover: 0.10 **NM** value: **125.00**
20 ❑ Apr 1957 Cover: 0.10 **NM** value: **125.00**
21 ❑ May 1957 Cover: 0.10 **NM** value: **95.00**
22 ❑ Jun 1957 Cover: 0.10 **NM** value: **95.00**
23 ❑ Jul 1957 Cover: 0.10 **NM** value: **95.00**
24 ❑ Aug 1957 Cover: 0.10 **NM** value: **95.00**
25 ❑ Sep 1957 Cover: 0.10 **NM** value: **95.00**
26 ❑ Oct 1957 Cover: 0.10 **NM** value: **95.00**
27 ❑ Nov 1957 Cover: 0.10 **NM** value: **95.00**
28 ❑ Dec 1957 Cover: 0.10 **NM** value: **95.00**
29 ❑ Jan 1958 Cover: 0.10 **NM** value: **95.00**
30 ❑ Feb 1958 Cover: 0.10 **NM** value: **95.00**
31 ❑ Mar 1958 Cover: 0.10 **NM** value: **80.00**
32 ❑ Apr 1958 Cover: 0.10 **NM** value: **80.00**
33 ❑ May 1958 Cover: 0.10 **NM** value: **80.00**
34 ❑ Jun 1958 Cover: 0.10 **NM** value: **80.00**
35 ❑ Jul 1958 Cover: 0.10 **NM** value: **80.00**
36 ❑ Aug 1958 Cover: 0.10 **NM** value: **80.00**
37 ❑ Sep 1958 Cover: 0.10 **NM** value: **80.00**
38 ❑ Oct 1958 Cover: 0.10 **NM** value: **80.00**
39 ❑ Nov 1958 Cover: 0.10 **NM** value: **80.00**
40 ❑ Dec 1958 Cover: 0.10 **NM** value: **80.00**
41 ❑ Jan 1959 Cover: 0.10 **NM** value: **100.00**
• Unknown Soldier prototype
42 ❑ Feb 1959 Cover: 0.10 **NM** value: **75.00**
43 ❑ Mar 1959 Cover: 0.10 **NM** value: **75.00**
44 ❑ Apr 1959 Cover: 0.10 **NM** value: **75.00**
45 ❑ May 1959 Cover: 0.10 **NM** value: **260.00**
★ 1st Appearance of Gunner & Sarge.
46 ❑ Jun 1959 Cover: 0.10 **NM** value: **100.00**
47 ❑ Jul 1959 Cover: 0.10 **NM** value: **85.00**
48 ❑ Aug 1959 Cover: 0.10 **NM** value: **65.00**
49 ❑ Sep 1959 Cover: 0.10 **NM** value: **65.00**
50 ❑ Oct 1959 Cover: 0.10 **NM** value: **65.00**
51 ❑ Nov 1959 Cover: 0.10 **NM** value: **38.00**
52 ❑ Dec 1959 Cover: 0.10 **NM** value: **38.00**
53 ❑ Feb 1960 Cover: 0.10 **NM** value: **38.00**
Circ: Statement: **175,000**
54 ❑ Apr 1960 Cover: 0.10 **NM** value: **38.00**
Circ: Statement: **175,000**
55 ❑ Jun 1960 Cover: 0.10 **NM** value: **38.00**
Circ: Statement: **175,000**
56 ❑ Aug 1960 Cover: 0.10 **NM** value: **38.00**
Circ: Statement: **175,000**
57 ❑ Oct 1960 Cover: 0.10 **NM** value: **38.00**
Circ: Statement: **175,000**
58 ❑ Dec 1960 Cover: 0.10 **NM** value: **38.00**
Circ: Statement: **175,000** • **CGC:** 1 graded, best 8.0
59 ❑ Feb 1961 Cover: 0.10 **NM** value: **38.00**
Circ: Statement: **210,000**
60 ❑ Apr 1961 Cover: 0.10 **NM** value: **38.00**
Circ: Statement: **210,000**
• Has 1960 Statement, filed 10/1/60; avg total paid circ 175,000
61 ❑ Jun 1961 Cover: 0.10 **NM** value: **30.00**
Circ: Statement: **210,000**
62 ❑ Aug 1961 Cover: 0.10 **NM** value: **30.00**
Circ: Statement: **210,000**
63 ❑ Oct 1961 Cover: 0.10 **NM** value: **30.00**
Circ: Statement: **210,000**
64 ❑ Dec 1961 Cover: 0.10 **NM** value: **30.00**
Circ: Statement: **210,000**
65 ❑ Jan 1962 Cover: 0.12 **NM** value: **20.00**
66 ❑ Feb 1962 Cover: 0.12 **NM** value: **20.00**
67 ❑ Apr 1962 Cover: 0.12 **NM** value: **20.00**
68 ❑ Jun 1962 Cover: 0.12 **NM** value: **20.00**
69 ❑ Jul 1962 Cover: 0.12 **NM** value: **20.00**
70 ❑ Aug 1962 Cover: 0.12 **NM** value: **20.00**
71 ❑ Oct 1962 Cover: 0.12 **NM** value: **16.00**
72 ❑ Nov 1962 Cover: 0.12 **NM** value: **16.00**
73 ❑ Jan 1963 Cover: 0.12 **NM** value: **16.00**
74 ❑ Feb 1963 Cover: 0.12 **NM** value: **16.00**
75 ❑ Apr 1963 Cover: 0.12 **NM** value: **16.00**
• **CGC:** 1 graded, best 9.2
76 ❑ Jun 1963 Cover: 0.12 **NM** value: **16.00**
77 ❑ Jul 1963 Cover: 0.12 **NM** value: **16.00**
78 ❑ Aug 1963 Cover: 0.12 **NM** value: **16.00**
79 ❑ Oct 1963 Cover: 0.12 **NM** value: **16.00**
• **CGC:** 1 graded, best 6.0
80 ❑ Nov 1963 Cover: 0.12 **NM** value: **16.00**
81 ❑ Jan 1964 Cover: 0.12 **NM** value: **10.00**
82 ❑ Feb 1964 Cover: 0.12 **NM** value: **10.00**
• Has 1963 Statement, filed 10/1/63; no circ figures published
83 ❑ Apr 1964 Cover: 0.12 **NM** value: **10.00**
84 ❑ May 1964 Cover: 0.12 **NM** value: **10.00**
• Gunner & Sarge
85 ❑ Jul 1964 Cover: 0.12 **NM** value: **10.00**
86 ❑ Aug 1964 Cover: 0.12 **NM** value: **10.00**
87 ❑ Oct 1964 Cover: 0.12 **NM** value: **10.00**
88 ❑ Nov 1964 Cover: 0.12 **NM** value: **10.00**
89 ❑ Jan 1965 Cover: 0.12 **NM** value: **10.00**
90 ❑ Feb 1965 Cover: 0.12 **NM** value: **10.00**
91 ❑ Apr 1965 Cover: 0.12 **NM** value: **7.00**
• Has 1964 Statement, filed 10/1/64; no circ figures published
92 ❑ May 1965 Cover: 0.12 **NM** value: **7.00**
93 ❑ Jul 1965 Cover: 0.12 **NM** value: **7.00**
94 ❑ Aug 1965 Cover: 0.12 **NM** value: **7.00**
• **CGC:** 1 graded, best 9.4
95 ❑ Oct 1965 Cover: 0.12 **NM** value: **7.00**
96 ❑ Nov 1965 Cover: 0.12 **NM** value: **7.00**
97 ❑ Dec 1965 Cover: 0.12 **NM** value: **7.00**
98 ❑ Jan 1966 Cover: 0.12 **NM** value: **7.00**
Circ: Statement: **207,885**
99 ❑ Feb 1966 Cover: 0.12 **NM** value: **7.00**
Circ: Statement: **207,885**
★ 1st Appearance of Captain Phil Hunter.
100 ❑ Apr 1966 Cover: 0.12 **NM** value: **6.00**
Circ: Statement: **207,885**
📖 Death Also Stalks The Hunter!; The Thunderbolts; If We Miss-You Die!; ★ Appearance of Captain Hunter.
101 ❑ Jun 1966 Cover: 0.12 **NM** value: **6.00**
Circ: Statement: **207,885**
102 ❑ Aug 1966 Cover: 0.12 **NM** value: **6.00**
Circ: Statement: **207,885**
103 ❑ Oct 1966 Cover: 0.12 **NM** value: **6.00**
Circ: Statement: **207,885**
104 ❑ Dec 1966 Cover: 0.12 **NM** value: **6.00**
Circ: Statement: **207,885**

Other grades: Multiply prices above by **1.5 for Mint • 2/3 for Very Fine • 1/3 for Fine • 1/5 for Very Good • 1/8 for Good**

105 ❑ Feb 1967 Cover: 0.12 **NM** value: **6.00**
Circ: Statement: **152,200**
106 ❑ Apr 1967 Cover: 0.12 **NM** value: **6.00**
Circ: Statement: **152,200**
★ 1st Appearance of Ben Hunter, Hunter's Hellcats.
107 ❑ Jul 1967 Cover: 0.12 **NM** value: **6.00**
Circ: Statement: **152,200**
108 ❑ Aug 1967 Cover: 0.12 **NM** value: **6.00**
Circ: Statement: **152,200**
★ Appearance of Lt. Hunter's Hellcats.
109 ❑ Oct 1967 Cover: 0.12 **NM** value: **6.00**
Circ: Statement: **152,200**
110 ❑ Dec 1967 Cover: 0.12 **NM** value: **6.00**
Circ: Statement: **152,200**
111 ❑ Feb 1968 Cover: 0.12 **NM** value: **6.00**
112 ❑ Apr 1968 Cover: 0.12 **NM** value: **6.00**
113 ❑ Jul 1968 Cover: 0.12 **NM** value: **6.00**
114 ❑ Aug 1968 Cover: 0.12 **NM** value: **6.00**
115 ❑ Sep 1968 Cover: 0.12 **NM** value: **6.00**
• **CGC:** 1 graded, best 8.5
116 ❑ Nov 1968 Cover: 0.12 **NM** value: **6.00**
117 ❑ Jan 1969 Cover: 0.12 **NM** value: **6.00**
118 ❑ Mar 1969 Cover: 0.12 **NM** value: **6.00**
★ Appearance of Lt. Hunter's Hellcats.
119 ❑ May 1969 Cover: 0.12 **NM** value: **6.00**
• **CGC:** 1 graded, best 6.5
120 ❑ Jul 1969 Cover: 0.15 **NM** value: **6.00**
121 ❑ Sep 1969 Cover: 0.15 **NM** value: **5.00**
• **CGC:** 1 graded, best 9.0
★ 1st Appearance of Heller.
122 ❑ Nov 1969 Cover: 0.15 **NM** value: **5.00**
• **CGC:** 1 graded, best 8.5
123 ❑ Jan 1970 Cover: 0.15 **NM** value: **5.00**
• **CGC:** 2 graded, best 9.4
• Losers series begins
124 ❑ Mar 1970 Cover: 0.15 **NM** value: **5.00**
125 ❑ May 1970 Cover: 0.15 **NM** value: **5.00**
• **CGC:** 1 graded, best 9.2
126 ❑ Jul 1970 Cover: 0.15 **NM** value: **5.00**
127 ❑ Sep 1970 Cover: 0.15 **NM** value: **5.00**
📖 Angels over Hell's Corner; Private Buck's Army!; U.S.S. Stevens: Dragonfly • Losers **A:** Ross Andru; Mike Esposito **W:** Robert Kanigher
128 ❑ Nov 1970 Cover: 0.15 **NM** value: **5.00**
129 ❑ Jan 1971 Cover: 0.15 **NM** value: **5.00**
130 ❑ Mar 1971 Cover: 0.15 **NM** value: **5.00**
131 ❑ May 1971 Cover: 0.15 **NM** value: **5.00**
• **CGC:** 1 graded, best 9.2
132 ❑ Jul 1971 Cover: 0.15 **NM** value: **5.00**
• Losers
133 ❑ Sep 1971 Cover: 0.25 **NM** value: **5.00**
134 ❑ Nov 1971 Cover: 0.25 **NM** value: **5.00**
135 ❑ Jan 1972 Cover: 0.25 **NM** value: **5.00**
Circ: Statement: **164,142**
136 ❑ Mar 1972 Cover: 0.25 **NM** value: **5.00**
Circ: Statement: **164,142** • **CGC:** 1 graded, best 9.4
137 ❑ May 1972 Cover: 0.25 **NM** value: **5.00**
Circ: Statement: **164,142**
• Giant-size. 📖 God Of The Losers!; Frogman Jinx!; Dive Bombers Of Midway; A Fort Called Lucky!; Three Bullets; Battle Beat • Losers
138 ❑ Jul 1972 Cover: 0.20 **NM** value: **5.00**
Circ: Statement: **164,142**
139 ❑ Sep 1972 Cover: 0.20 **NM** value: **5.00**
Circ: Statement: **164,142**
140 ❑ Nov 1972 Cover: 0.20 **NM** value: **5.00**
Circ: Statement: **164,142**
141 ❑ Jan 1973 Cover: 0.20 **NM** value: **5.00**
Circ: Statement: **147,968**
142 ❑ Mar 1973 Cover: 0.20 **NM** value: **5.00**
Circ: Statement: **147,968**
• Has 1972 Statement; avg total paid circ 164,142
143 ❑ May 1973 Cover: 0.20 **NM** value: **5.00**
Circ: Statement: **147,968**
144 ❑ Jul 1973 Cover: 0.20 **NM** value: **5.00**
Circ: Statement: **147,968**
145 ❑ Sep 1973 Cover: 0.20 **NM** value: **5.00**
Circ: Statement: **147,968**
146 ❑ Nov 1973 Cover: 0.20 **NM** value: **5.00**
Circ: Statement: **147,968**
147 ❑ Jan 1974 Cover: 0.20 **NM** value: **5.00**
Circ: Statement: **161,417**
148 ❑ Mar 1974 Cover: 0.20 **NM** value: **5.00**
Circ: Statement: **161,417**
149 ❑ May 1974 Cover: 0.20 **NM** value: **5.00**
Circ: Statement: **161,417**
150 ❑ Jul 1974 Cover: 0.20 **NM** value: **5.00**
Circ: Statement: **161,417**
• Has 1973 Statement; avg total paid circ 147,968
151 ❑ Sep 1974 Cover: 0.20 **NM** value: **4.00**
Circ: Statement: **161,417**
📖 Kill Me With Wagner • Losers
152 ❑ Nov 1974 Cover: 0.20 **NM** value: **4.00**
Circ: Statement: **161,417**
📖 A Small Place in Hell • Losers
153 ❑ Feb 1975 Cover: 0.25 **NM** value: **4.00**
Circ: Statement: **148,000** • **CGC:** 1 graded, best 8.0
📖 Devastator vs. Big Max • Losers
154 ❑ Apr 1975 Cover: 0.25 **NM** value: **4.00**
Circ: Statement: **148,000**
📖 Bushido • Losers **A:** Jack Kirby
155 ❑ May 1975 Cover: 0.25 **NM** value: **4.00**
Circ: Statement: **148,000**
📖 The Partisans • Losers; Has 1974 Statement; avg total paid circ 161,417
156 ❑ Jun 1975 Cover: 0.25 **NM** value: **4.00**
Circ: Statement: **148,000**
📖 Good-Bye Broadway, Hello Death • Losers
157 ❑ Jul 1975 Cover: 0.25 **NM** value: **4.00**
Circ: Statement: **148,000**
• Losers
158 ❑ Aug 1975 Cover: 0.25 **NM** value: **4.00**
Circ: Statement: **148,000**
• Losers **A:** Jack Kirby
159 ❑ Sep 1975 Cover: 0.25 **NM** value: **4.00**
Circ: Statement: **148,000**
📖 Mile-A-Minute Jones • Losers **A:** Jack Kirby
160 ❑ Oct 1975 Cover: 0.25 **NM** value: **4.00**
Circ: Statement: **148,000** • **CGC:** 1 graded, best 8.0
📖 Ivan • Losers **A:** Jack Kirby
161 ❑ Nov 1975 Cover: 0.25 **NM** value: **4.00**
Circ: Statement: **148,000**
• Losers
162 ❑ Dec 1975 Cover: 0.25 **NM** value: **4.00**
Circ: Statement: **148,000**
📖 Gung-Ho • Losers **A:** Jack Kirby
163 ❑ Jan 1976 Cover: 0.25 **NM** value: **4.00**
Circ: Statement: **112,000**
164 ❑ Feb 1976 Cover: 0.25 **NM** value: **4.00**
Circ: Statement: **112,000**
165 ❑ Mar 1976 Cover: 0.25 **NM** value: **4.00**
Circ: Statement: **112,000**
166 ❑ Apr 1976 Cover: 0.25 **NM** value: **4.00**
Circ: Statement: **112,000**
167 ❑ Jun 1976 Cover: 0.30 **NM** value: **4.00**
Circ: Statement: **112,000**
168 ❑ Aug 1976 Cover: 0.30 **NM** value: **4.00**
Circ: Statement: **112,000**
169 ❑ Oct 1976 Cover: 0.30 **NM** value: **4.00**
Circ: Statement: **112,000**
170 ❑ Dec 1976 Cover: 0.30 **NM** value: **4.00**
Circ: Statement: **112,000**
171 ❑ Feb 1977 Cover: 0.30 **NM** value: **4.00**
Circ: Statement: **114,226**
172 ❑ Apr 1977 Cover: 0.30 **NM** value: **4.00**
Circ: Statement: **114,226**
173 ❑ Jun 1977 Cover: 0.30 **NM** value: **4.00**
Circ: Statement: **114,226**
• Has 1976 Statement; avg total paid circ 112,000
174 ❑ Aug 1977 Cover: 0.35 **NM** value: **4.00**
Circ: Statement: **114,226**
175 ❑ Oct 1977 Cover: 0.35 **NM** value: **4.00**
Circ: Statement: **114,226**
176 ❑ Dec 1977 Cover: 0.35 **NM** value: **4.00**
Circ: Statement: **114,226**
177 ❑ Feb 1978 Cover: 0.35 **NM** value: **4.00**
178 ❑ Apr 1978 Cover: 0.35 **NM** value: **4.00**
179 ❑ Jun 1978 Cover: 0.35 **NM** value: **4.00**
• Has 1977 Statement; avg total paid circ 114,226
180 ❑ Aug 1978 Cover: 0.35 **NM** value: **4.00**
181 ❑ Oct 1978 Cover: 0.35 **NM** value: **4.00**
• **CGC:** 2 graded, best 9.4
final issue.

OUR FLAG COMICS — Ace

1 ❑ Aug 1941 Cover: 0.10 **NM** value: **1800.00**
• **CGC:** 1 graded, best 5.0
2 ❑ Oct 1941 Cover: 0.10 **NM** value: **1000.00**
• **CGC:** 1 graded, best .5
3 ❑ Dec 1941 Cover: 0.10 **NM** value: **800.00**
• **CGC:** 1 graded, best 6.5
4 ❑ Feb 1942 Cover: 0.10 **NM** value: **800.00**
5 ❑ Apr 1942 Cover: 0.10 **NM** value: **800.00**
• **CGC:** 1 graded, best 4.0

OUR GANG WITH TOM & JERRY — Dell

Our Gang Comics was launched by Dell in the early 1940s and adapted the wildly popular kiddie comedy that had been featured in movie shorts since the early days of film. The adventures of Buckwheat, Spanky, Froggy, and the rest were told by a young Walt Kelly, whose later work on the strip Pogo enshrined him as one of the finest cartoonists of the century. Kelly's fine style and uncanny knack for loopy logic helped animate a kids' comedy adventure series; his stories pioneered both equality of sexes and equality of races in comics plot and art. The series also sometimes featured non-Donald Duck stories by Carl Barks: Barney Bear, Benny Burro, and Happy Hound. It wasn't long before the animated movie duo of Tom Cat and Jerry Mouse (who were at that time beating out Warner Brothers and Disney cartoons in the Oscar awards for best animated films) took over the cover and then the title. They eventually took over the series completely. In fact, #58 and #59 had no Our Gang story.

1 ❑ Sep 1942 Cover: 0.10 **NM** value: **585.00**
2 ❑ Nov 1942 Cover: 0.10 **NM** value: **325.00**
3 ❑ Jan 1943 Cover: 0.10 **NM** value: **180.00**
4 ❑ Mar 1943 Cover: 0.10 **NM** value: **180.00**
5 ❑ May 1943 Cover: 0.10 **NM** value: **180.00**
6 ❑ Jul 1943 Cover: 0.10 **NM** value: **185.00**
7 ❑ Sep 1943 Cover: 0.10 **NM** value: **125.00**
8 ❑ Nov 1943 Cover: 0.10 **NM** value: **165.00**
• Benny Burro features begin **A:** Carl Barks
9 ❑ Jan 1944 Cover: 0.10 **NM** value: **150.00**
• Happy Hound; Benny Burro **A:** Carl Barks
10 ❑ Mar 1944 Cover: 0.10 **NM** value: **150.00**
• Benny Burro **A:** Carl Barks
11 ❑ May 1944 Cover: 0.10 **NM** value: **140.00**
• Barney Bear and Benny Burro; Happy Hound **A:** Carl Barks
12 ❑ Jul 1944 Cover: 0.10 **NM** value: **125.00**
• Barney Bear and Benny Burro **A:** Carl Barks
13 ❑ Sep 1944 Cover: 0.10 **NM** value: **125.00**
• Barney Bear and Benny Burro **A:** Carl Barks
14 ❑ Nov 1944 Cover: 0.10 **NM** value: **125.00**
• Barney Bear and Benny Burro **A:** Carl Barks
15 ❑ Jan 1945 Cover: 0.10 **NM** value: **125.00**
• Barney Bear and Benny Burro **A:** Carl Barks
16 ❑ Mar 1945 Cover: 0.10 **NM** value: **125.00**
• Barney Bear and Benny Burro **A:** Carl Barks
17 ❑ May 1945 Cover: 0.10 **NM** value: **125.00**
• Barney Bear and Benny Burro **A:** Carl Barks
18 ❑ Jul 1945 Cover: 0.10 **NM** value: **125.00**
• Barney Bear and Benny Burro **A:** Carl Barks
19 ❑ Sep 1945 Cover: 0.10 **NM** value: **125.00**
• Barney Bear and Benny Burro **A:** Carl Barks
20 ❑ Nov 1945 Cover: 0.10 **NM** value: **125.00**
• Barney Bear and Benny Burro **A:** Carl Barks
21 ❑ Jan 1946 Cover: 0.10 **NM** value: **110.00**
• Barney Bear and Benny Burro **A:** Carl Barks
22 ❑ Mar 1946 Cover: 0.10 **NM** value: **110.00**
• Barney Bear and Benny Burro **A:** Carl Barks
23 ❑ May 1946 Cover: 0.10 **NM** value: **110.00**
• Barney Bear and Benny Burro **A:** Carl Barks
24 ❑ Jul 1946 Cover: 0.10 **NM** value: **110.00**
• Barney Bear and Benny Burro **A:** Carl Barks
25 ❑ Aug 1946 Cover: 0.10 **NM** value: **110.00**
• Barney Bear and Benny Burro **A:** Carl Barks
26 ❑ Sep 1946 Cover: 0.10 **NM** value: **110.00**
• Barney Bear and Benny Burro **A:** Carl Barks
27 ❑ Oct 1946 Cover: 0.10 **NM** value: **110.00**
• Barney Bear and Benny Burro **A:** Carl Barks
28 ❑ Nov 1946 Cover: 0.10 **NM** value: **110.00**
• Barney Bear and Benny Burro **A:** Carl Barks
29 ❑ Dec 1946 Cover: 0.10 **NM** value: **110.00**
• Barney Bear and Benny Burro **A:** Carl Barks
30 ❑ Jan 1947 Cover: 0.10 **NM** value: **110.00**
• Barney Bear and Benny Burro **A:** Carl Barks
31 ❑ Feb 1947 Cover: 0.10 **NM** value: **85.00**
• Barney Bear and Benny Burro **A:** Carl Barks
32 ❑ Mar 1947 Cover: 0.10 **NM** value: **85.00**
• Barney Bear and Benny Burro **A:** Carl Barks
33 ❑ Apr 1947 Cover: 0.10 **NM** value: **85.00**
• Barney Bear and Benny Burro **A:** Carl Barks
34 ❑ May 1947 Cover: 0.10 **NM** value: **85.00**
• Barney Bear and Benny Burro **A:** Carl Barks
35 ❑ Jun 1947 Cover: 0.10 **NM** value: **85.00**
• Barney Bear and Benny Burro **A:** Carl Barks
36 ❑ Jul 1947 Cover: 0.10 **NM** value: **85.00**
• Barney Bear and Benny Burro **A:** Carl Barks
37 ❑ Aug 1947 Cover: 0.10 **NM** value: **45.00**
38 ❑ Sep 1947 Cover: 0.10 **NM** value: **45.00**
39 ❑ Oct 1947 Cover: 0.10 **NM** value: **45.00**
40 ❑ Nov 1947 Cover: 0.10 **NM** value: **45.00**
41 ❑ Dec 1947 Cover: 0.10 **NM** value: **30.00**
42 ❑ Jan 1948 Cover: 0.10 **NM** value: **30.00**
• Tom & Jerry; Our Gang; Wuff the Prairie Dog; Saturday Night (text story); Barney the Bear and Benny Burro
43 ❑ Feb 1948 Cover: 0.10 **NM** value: **30.00**
44 ❑ Mar 1948 Cover: 0.10 **NM** value: **30.00**
45 ❑ Apr 1948 Cover: 0.10 **NM** value: **30.00**
46 ❑ May 1948 Cover: 0.10 **NM** value: **30.00**
47 ❑ Jun 1948 Cover: 0.10 **NM** value: **30.00**
48 ❑ Jul 1948 Cover: 0.10 **NM** value: **30.00**
49 ❑ Aug 1948 Cover: 0.10 **NM** value: **30.00**
50 ❑ Sep 1948 Cover: 0.10 **NM** value: **30.00**
51 ❑ Oct 1948 Cover: 0.10 **NM** value: **25.00**
52 ❑ Nov 1948 Cover: 0.10 **NM** value: **25.00**
53 ❑ Dec 1948 Cover: 0.10 **NM** value: **25.00**
54 ❑ Jan 1949 Cover: 0.10 **NM** value: **25.00**
55 ❑ Feb 1949 Cover: 0.10 **NM** value: **25.00**
56 ❑ Mar 1949 Cover: 0.10 **NM** value: **25.00**
57 ❑ Apr 1949 Cover: 0.10 **NM** value: **25.00**
58 ❑ May 1949 Cover: 0.10 **NM** value: **25.00**
59 ❑ Jun 1949 Cover: 0.10 **NM** value: **25.00**

OUR LOVE — Marvel

1 ❑ Sep 1949 Cover: 0.10 **NM** value: **75.00**
2 ❑ Jan 1950 Cover: 0.10 **NM** value: **50.00**

OUR LOVE STORY — Marvel

In the late 1960s, Marvel branched out from its niche as the leading super-hero comic publisher to start new titles in mystery, Westerns, humor, and romance. Our Love Story was a product of this period and an effort to use the then-formidable cultural power of the "mighty Marvel style" to breathe life into the most conventional and turgid comics genre — love and romance, which by the late 1960s was completely played out and encrusted in cliches.

Our Love Story was nothing if not stylish, with up-to-the-minute romance stories told in the breezy Marvel fashion and illustrated by bullpen luminaries like John Romita, Gene Colan, and Vince Colletta. The high-water mark of the series is the impossibly scarce issue #5, featuring the classic story "My Heart Broke...in Hollywood," Jim Steranko's tour de force kiss-off to Marvel and comic-book work in general.

1 ❑ Oct 1969 Cover: 0.15 **NM** value: **15.00**
📖 ...But Oh, My Lonely Nights!; Why Did I Lose You, My Love?; We Dare Not Marry! **A:** John Romita
2 ❑ Dec 1969 Cover: 0.15 **NM** value: **8.00**
3 ❑ Feb 1970 Cover: 0.15 **NM** value: **8.00**
4 ❑ Apr 1970 Cover: 0.15 **NM** value: **8.00**
5 ❑ Jun 1970 Cover: 0.15 **NM** value: **18.00**
• **CGC:** 5 graded, best 9.0
A: Jim Steranko
6 ❑ Aug 1970 Cover: 0.15 **NM** value: **5.00**
• **CGC:** 1 graded, best 9.2

CGC-graded: Multiply prices above by **33 for 9.9 M • 16 for 9.8 NM/M • 7 for 9.6 NM+ • 5 for 9.4 NM • 2.5 for 9.2 NM- • 1.5 for 9.0 VF/NM**

7 ❑ Oct 1970 Cover: 0.15 **NM** value: **5.00**
8 ❑ Dec 1970 Cover: 0.15 **NM** value: **5.00**
• **CGC:** 2 graded, best 9.4
9 ❑ Feb 1971 Cover: 0.15 **NM** value: **5.00**
10 ❑ Apr 1971 Cover: 0.15 **NM** value: **5.00**
11 ❑ Jun 1971 Cover: 0.15 **NM** value: **4.00**
• **CGC:** 1 graded, best 9.2
12 ❑ Aug 1971 Cover: 0.15 **NM** value: **4.00**
13 ❑ Oct 1971 Cover: 0.15 **NM** value: **4.00**
• **CGC:** 1 graded, best 9.2
14 ❑ Dec 1971 Cover: 0.20 **NM** value: **4.00**
15 ❑ Feb 1972 Cover: 0.20 **NM** value: **4.00**
16 ❑ Apr 1972 Cover: 0.20 **NM** value: **4.00**
17 ❑ Jun 1972 Cover: 0.20 **NM** value: **4.00**
18 ❑ Aug 1972 Cover: 0.20 **NM** value: **4.00**
19 ❑ Oct 1972 Cover: 0.20 **NM** value: **4.00**
20 ❑ Dec 1972 Cover: 0.20 **NM** value: **4.00**
21 ❑ Feb 1973 Cover: 0.20 **NM** value: **3.00**
22 ❑ Apr 1973 Cover: 0.20 **NM** value: **3.00**
23 ❑ Jun 1973 Cover: 0.20 **NM** value: **3.00**
24 ❑ Aug 1973 Cover: 0.20 **NM** value: **3.00**
25 ❑ Oct 1973 Cover: 0.20 **NM** value: **3.00**
26 ❑ Dec 1973 Cover: 0.20 **NM** value: **3.00**
27 ❑ Feb 1974 Cover: 0.20 **NM** value: **3.00**
28 ❑ Jun 1974 Cover: 0.25 **NM** value: **3.00**
29 ❑ Aug 1974 Cover: 0.25 **NM** value: **3.00**
30 ❑ Oct 1974 Cover: 0.25 **NM** value: **3.00**
31 ❑ Dec 1974 Cover: 0.25 **NM** value: **3.00**
32 ❑ Feb 1975 Cover: 0.25 **NM** value: **3.00**
33 ❑ Apr 1975 Cover: 0.25 **NM** value: **3.00**
34 ❑ Jun 1975 Cover: 0.25 **NM** value: **3.00**
35 ❑ Aug 1975 Cover: 0.25 **NM** value: **3.00**
36 ❑ Oct 1975 Cover: 0.25 **NM** value: **3.00**
37 ❑ Dec 1975 Cover: 0.25 **NM** value: **3.00**
38 ❑ Feb 1976 Cover: 0.30 **NM** value: **3.00**
final issue.

OUR SECRET — Superior

4 ❑ Nov 1949 Cover: 0.10 **NM** value: **125.00**
5 ❑ Jan 1950 Cover: 0.10 **NM** value: **75.00**
6 ❑ Feb 1950 Cover: 0.10 **NM** value: **75.00**
7 ❑ Apr 1950 Cover: 0.10 **NM** value: **75.00**
8 ❑ Jun 1950 Cover: 0.10 **NM** value: **60.00**

OUTBREED 999 — Blackout

Matt Chaney — subject 999 — escapes from a prison where he and his fellow convicts were experimented on like laboratory rats. In some cases, the experiments created mindless super-soldiers, like Chaney's friend Mickey McBride. But in Chaney's case, a normal man now has a demonic right arm that spells trouble for those who would recapture him. It's sort of "The Fugitive" meets "The Terminator."

It wasn't a bad start for Blackout Comics, one of many new publishers to come from the glut of the early 1990s. But Blackout followed Outbreed 999 with the launch of Hari Kari and Lady Vampre, mindless titles engineered to ride the mid-1990s wave of Bad Girl comics — and soon it was known for little else.

1 ❑ May 1994 Cover: 2.95 **NM** value: **Cover or less**
Circ: CapCity orders: **3,725**
A: Bob Berry **W:** Bruce Schoengood
2 ❑ Jul 1994 Cover: 2.95 **NM** value: **Cover or less**
W: Bruce Schoengood
3 ❑ Aug 1994 Cover: 2.95 **NM** value: **Cover or less**
W: Bruce Schoengood
4 ❑ Cover: 2.95 **NM** value: **Cover or less**
W: Bruce Schoengood
5 ❑ Cover: 2.95 **NM** value: **Cover or less**
W: Bruce Schoengood

OUTCAST, THE — Acclaim / Valiant

1 ❑ Dec 1995 Cover: 2.50 **NM** value: **Cover or less**
Circ: CapCity orders: **6,900**
One-shot. 🕮 Here and Now **A:** Norm Breyfogle **W:** Jesse Berdinka

OUTCASTS — DC

1 ❑ Oct 1987 Cover: 1.75 **NM** value: **Cover or less**
Circ: CapCity orders: **21,750**
A: Cam Kennedy; Steve Montano **W:** Alan Grant; John Wagner ★ 1st Appearance of Kaine Salinger, Outcasts.
2 ❑ Nov 1987 Cover: 1.75 **NM** value: **Cover or less**
Circ: CapCity orders: **18,150**
A: Cam Kennedy; Steve Montano **W:** Alan Grant; John Wagner
3 ❑ Dec 1987 Cover: 1.75 **NM** value: **Cover or less**
Circ: CapCity orders: **14,750**
A: Cam Kennedy; Steve Montano **W:** Alan Grant; John Wagner
4 ❑ Jan 1988 Cover: 1.75 **NM** value: **Cover or less**
Circ: CapCity orders: **13,150**
A: Cam Kennedy; Steve Montano **W:** Alan Grant; John Wagner
5 ❑ Feb 1988 Cover: 1.75 **NM** value: **Cover or less**
Circ: CapCity orders: **12,050**
A: Cam Kennedy; Steve Montano **W:** Alan Grant; John Wagner
6 ❑ Mar 1988 Cover: 1.75 **NM** value: **Cover or less**
Circ: CapCity orders: **11,600**
A: Cam Kennedy; Steve Montano **W:** Alan Grant; John Wagner
7 ❑ Apr 1988 Cover: 1.75 **NM** value: **Cover or less**
Circ: CapCity orders: **10,250**
A: Cam Kennedy; Steve Montano **W:** Alan Grant; John Wagner ★ Death of Kaine Salinger.
8 ❑ May 1988 Cover: 1.75 **NM** value: **Cover or less**
Circ: CapCity orders: **8,950**
A: Cam Kennedy; Steve Montano **W:** Alan Grant; John Wagner
9 ❑ Jun 1988 Cover: 1.75 **NM** value: **Cover or less**
Circ: CapCity orders: **8,150**
A: Cam Kennedy; Steve Montano **W:** Alan Grant; John Wagner
10 ❑ Jul 1988 Cover: 1.75 **NM** value: **Cover or less**
Circ: CapCity orders: **7,750**
A: Cam Kennedy; Steve Montano **W:** Alan Grant; John Wagner
11 ❑ Aug 1988 Cover: 1.75 **NM** value: **Cover or less**
Circ: CapCity orders: **7,600**
A: Cam Kennedy; Steve Montano **W:** Alan Grant; John Wagner
12 ❑ Sep 1988 Cover: 1.75 **NM** value: **Cover or less**
Circ: CapCity orders: **7,050**
🕮 The Last Outcast final issue. **A:** Cam Kennedy; Steve Montano **W:** Alan Grant; John Wagner

OUTER EDGE — Innovation

1 ❑ b&w Cover: 2.50 **NM** value: **Cover or less**

OUTER LIMITS, THE — Dell

The Outer Limits was an intelligent and thought-provoking science-fiction television show of the 1960s, featuring half-hour dramas of future societies, alien invasions, and supernatural occurrences, usually in the form of fables with shock endings to drive home the point. The format was similar to The Twilight Zone, but with a harder science-fiction edge. It inspired many imitators and a series revival in the mid-1990s.

Dell published comic-book adaptations of the series from 1964-1969. The stories were either based on the original television screenplays or stuck very close to their style, and the artwork was typical of Dell's no-nonsense approach to television and movie-inspired comics, which they cranked out by the carload from the 1940s through the 1970s.

1 ❑ Jan 1964 Cover: 0.12 **NM** value: **55.00**
• **CGC:** 1 graded, best 6.0
2 ❑ Apr 1964 Cover: 0.12 **NM** value: **30.00**
🕮 The Boy Who Saved the World!
3 ❑ Jul 1964 Cover: 0.12 **NM** value: **24.00**
🕮 They Landed First; Beyond Human Range!; End to the Nightmare
4 ❑ Dec 1964 Cover: 0.12 **NM** value: **20.00**
5 ❑ Jan 1965 Cover: 0.12 **NM** value: **20.00**
6 ❑ Apr 1965 Cover: 0.12 **NM** value: **20.00**
🕮 The Mystery Moon; When Disasters Strike; The Aliens Attack
7 ❑ Jul 1965 Cover: 0.12 **NM** value: **20.00**
🕮 The Space Change; Strange Masquerade; The Strike
8 ❑ Dec 1965 Cover: 0.12 **NM** value: **20.00**
• **CGC:** 1 graded, best 9.0
9 ❑ Jul 1966 Cover: 0.12 **NM** value: **20.00**
🕮 Death From the Depths!; Sea Creature Attack; Battle Below!
10 ❑ Oct 1966 Cover: 0.12 **NM** value: **20.00**
🕮 Journey into the Earth; Ancient Worlds; Living Legends
11 ❑ Jan 1967 Cover: 0.12 **NM** value: **10.00**
🕮 The Prehistoric Peril; Mutations! Giants!; The Aliens Attack!
12 ❑ Apr 1967 Cover: 0.12 **NM** value: **10.00**
• **CGC:** 1 graded, best 9.2
13 ❑ May 1967 Cover: 0.12 **NM** value: **10.00**
14 ❑ Jul 1967 Cover: 0.12 **NM** value: **10.00**
🕮 Mother and Child; Martian Stimulators, Inc.; The Voice From Out There!
15 ❑ Sep 1967 Cover: 0.12 **NM** value: **10.00**
16 ❑ 1968 Cover: 0.12 **NM** value: **10.00**
17 ❑ Oct 1968 Cover: 0.12 **NM** value: **10.00**
🕮 Battleground of Monsters
18 ❑ Oct 1969 Cover: 0.15 **NM** value: **10.00**
final issue.

OUTER SPACE — Charlton

By 1968, the brief flourishing of quality that Charlton Comics enjoyed under the enlightened editorship of Dick Giordano (who had by then departed for a solid career at DC) had come to a close and the publisher was back up to its old tricks of repackaging mediocre stories, amateurish artwork, and mechanical lettering in anthology titles. Outer Space actually turned out to be a one-shot, but it may have originally been intended as a relaunch of Charlton's relatively successful science-fiction book Outer Space from the late 1950s. The single 1968 issue highlights the prodigious talents of Steve Ditko in a jaunty alien invasion tale called "The Third Planet."

17 ❑ May 1958 Cover: 0.10 **NM** value: **30.00**
18 ❑ Aug 1958 Cover: 0.10 **NM** value: **50.00**
A: Steve Ditko
19 ❑ Oct 1958 Cover: 0.10 **NM** value: **50.00**
• **CGC:** 1 graded, best 9.6
A: Steve Ditko
20 ❑ Dec 1958 Cover: 0.10 **NM** value: **50.00**
• **CGC:** 1 graded, best 9.6
A: Steve Ditko
21 ❑ Mar 1959 Cover: 0.10 **NM** value: **30.00**
• **CGC:** 1 graded, best 9.4
A: Steve Ditko
22 ❑ May 1959 Cover: 0.10 **NM** value: **30.00**
A: Steve Ditko
23 ❑ Aug 1959 Cover: 0.10 **NM** value: **30.00**
A: Steve Ditko
24 ❑ Oct 1959 Cover: 0.10 **NM** value: **30.00**
• **CGC:** 1 graded, best 9.4
A: Steve Ditko
25 ❑ Dec 1959 Cover: 0.10 **NM** value: **30.00**
A: Steve Ditko

OUTER SPACE BABES, THE (VOL. 3) — Silhouette

1 ❑ Cover: 2.95 **NM** value: **Cover or less**
Circ: CapCity orders: **4,070**
🕮 Dear Dad…; Big Guns **A:** Matt Thompson; Uriel Caton **W:** C.J. Henderson

OUT FOR BLOOD — Dark Horse

1 ❑ Sep 1999 Cover: 2.95 **NM** value: **Cover or less**
Circ: Diamd. preorders: **5,316**
A: Paul Erskine **W:** Steven Grant; Michael Part
2 ❑ Oct 1999 Cover: 2.95 **NM** value: **Cover or less**
Circ: Diamd. preorders: **4,254**
A: Paul Erskine **W:** Steven Grant; Michael Part
3 ❑ Nov 1999 Cover: 2.95 **NM** value: **Cover or less**
Circ: Diamd. preorders: **3,877**
A: Paul Erskine **W:** Steven Grant; Michael Part
4 ❑ Dec 1999 Cover: 2.95 **NM** value: **Cover or less**
Circ: Diamd. preorders: **3,354**
A: Paul Erskine **W:** Steven Grant; Michael Part

OUTLANDER — Malibu

1 ❑ 1987 Cover: 1.95 **NM** value: **Cover or less**
2 ❑ 1987 Cover: 1.95 **NM** value: **Cover or less**
3 ❑ Dec 1987, b&w Cover: 1.95 **NM** value: **Cover or less**
4 ❑ Jan 1988 Cover: 1.95 **NM** value: **Cover or less**
5 ❑ Mar 1988 Cover: 1.95 **NM** value: **Cover or less**
6 ❑ 1988 Cover: 1.95 **NM** value: **Cover or less**
7 ❑ 1988 Cover: 1.95 **NM** value: **Cover or less**

OUTLANDERS — Dark Horse

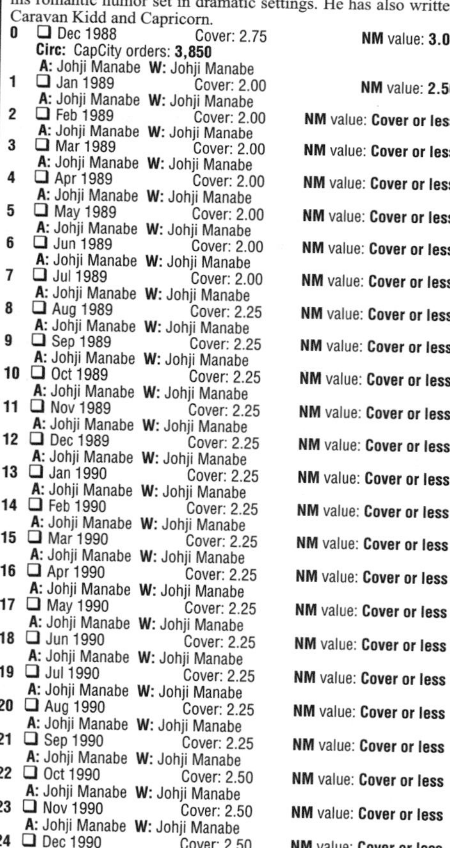

The great Santovasku Empire has returned to the sacred planet of its origin on a pilgrimage, led by the Princess Kahm, heir to the empire. To its horror, the planet has been populated by non-Santovasku vermin. Preparations for the extermination of this repulsive species begin immediately.

Across the galaxy, aliens have invaded Earth! Tetsuya is going to get the scoop on the front lines, no matter what the government says. Best of all, the aliens are led by this fabulous babe! A few extra pictures for himself certainly can't hurt...until she looks his way. Now if he survives long enough to ask her out, he may just be the key to peace between their races.

Johji Manabe is a Japanese manga artist and writer known for his romantic humor set in dramatic settings. He has also written Caravan Kidd and Capricorn.

0 ❑ Dec 1988 Cover: 2.75 **NM** value: **3.00**
Circ: CapCity orders: **3,850**
A: Johji Manabe **W:** Johji Manabe
1 ❑ Jan 1989 Cover: 2.00 **NM** value: **2.50**
A: Johji Manabe **W:** Johji Manabe
2 ❑ Feb 1989 Cover: 2.00 **NM** value: **Cover or less**
A: Johji Manabe **W:** Johji Manabe
3 ❑ Mar 1989 Cover: 2.00 **NM** value: **Cover or less**
A: Johji Manabe **W:** Johji Manabe
4 ❑ Apr 1989 Cover: 2.00 **NM** value: **Cover or less**
A: Johji Manabe **W:** Johji Manabe
5 ❑ May 1989 Cover: 2.00 **NM** value: **Cover or less**
A: Johji Manabe **W:** Johji Manabe
6 ❑ Jun 1989 Cover: 2.00 **NM** value: **Cover or less**
A: Johji Manabe **W:** Johji Manabe
7 ❑ Jul 1989 Cover: 2.00 **NM** value: **Cover or less**
A: Johji Manabe **W:** Johji Manabe
8 ❑ Aug 1989 Cover: 2.25 **NM** value: **Cover or less**
A: Johji Manabe **W:** Johji Manabe
9 ❑ Sep 1989 Cover: 2.25 **NM** value: **Cover or less**
A: Johji Manabe **W:** Johji Manabe
10 ❑ Oct 1989 Cover: 2.25 **NM** value: **Cover or less**
A: Johji Manabe **W:** Johji Manabe
11 ❑ Nov 1989 Cover: 2.25 **NM** value: **Cover or less**
A: Johji Manabe **W:** Johji Manabe
12 ❑ Dec 1989 Cover: 2.25 **NM** value: **Cover or less**
A: Johji Manabe **W:** Johji Manabe
13 ❑ Jan 1990 Cover: 2.25 **NM** value: **Cover or less**
A: Johji Manabe **W:** Johji Manabe
14 ❑ Feb 1990 Cover: 2.25 **NM** value: **Cover or less**
A: Johji Manabe **W:** Johji Manabe
15 ❑ Mar 1990 Cover: 2.25 **NM** value: **Cover or less**
A: Johji Manabe **W:** Johji Manabe
16 ❑ Apr 1990 Cover: 2.25 **NM** value: **Cover or less**
A: Johji Manabe **W:** Johji Manabe
17 ❑ May 1990 Cover: 2.25 **NM** value: **Cover or less**
A: Johji Manabe **W:** Johji Manabe
18 ❑ Jun 1990 Cover: 2.25 **NM** value: **Cover or less**
A: Johji Manabe **W:** Johji Manabe
19 ❑ Jul 1990 Cover: 2.25 **NM** value: **Cover or less**
A: Johji Manabe **W:** Johji Manabe
20 ❑ Aug 1990 Cover: 2.25 **NM** value: **Cover or less**
A: Johji Manabe **W:** Johji Manabe
21 ❑ Sep 1990 Cover: 2.25 **NM** value: **Cover or less**
A: Johji Manabe **W:** Johji Manabe
22 ❑ Oct 1990 Cover: 2.50 **NM** value: **Cover or less**
A: Johji Manabe **W:** Johji Manabe
23 ❑ Nov 1990 Cover: 2.50 **NM** value: **Cover or less**
A: Johji Manabe **W:** Johji Manabe
24 ❑ Dec 1990 Cover: 2.50 **NM** value: **Cover or less**
A: Johji Manabe **W:** Johji Manabe
25 ❑ Jan 1991 Cover: 2.50 **NM** value: **Cover or less**
A: Johji Manabe **W:** Johji Manabe
26 ❑ Feb 1991 Cover: 2.50 **NM** value: **Cover or less**
A: Johji Manabe **W:** Johji Manabe

Other grades: Multiply prices above by **1.5 for Mint • 2/3 for Very Fine • 1/3 for Fine • 1/5 for Very Good • 1/8 for Good**

27 ❑ Mar 1991 Cover: 2.95 NM value: Cover or less
• Giant-size special. A: Johji Manabe W: Johji Manabe
28 ❑ Apr 1991 Cover: 2.50 NM value: Cover or less
A: Johji Manabe W: Johji Manabe
29 ❑ May 1991 Cover: 2.50 NM value: Cover or less
A: Johji Manabe W: Johji Manabe
30 ❑ Jun 1991 Cover: 2.50 NM value: Cover or less
A: Johji Manabe W: Johji Manabe
31 ❑ Jul 1991 Cover: 2.50 NM value: Cover or less
A: Johji Manabe W: Johji Manabe
32 ❑ Aug 1991 Cover: 2.50 NM value: Cover or less
A: Johji Manabe W: Johji Manabe
33 ❑ Sep 1991 Cover: 2.50 NM value: Cover or less
final issue. A: Johji Manabe W: Johji Manabe
Bk 1❑ Cover: 10.95 NM value: 13.95
• Book 1-2 reprint A: Johji Manabe W: Johji Manabe
Bk 2❑ Cover: 13.95 NM value: Cover or less
A: Johji Manabe W: Johji Manabe
Bk 3❑ Cover: 13.95 NM value: Cover or less
A: Johji Manabe W: Johji Manabe
Bk 4❑ Cover: 12.95 NM value: Cover or less
A: Johji Manabe W: Johji Manabe
Bk 5❑ Cover: 14.95 NM value: Cover or less
A: Johji Manabe W: Johji Manabe
Bk 6❑ Jul 1999 Cover: 14.95 NM value: Cover or less
SE 1❑ b&w Cover: 2.50 NM value: Cover or less
• manga; Epilogue A: Johji Manabe W: Johji Manabe

OUTLANDERS EPILOGUE — Dark Horse

1 ❑ Mar 1994, b&w Cover: 2.50 NM value: Cover or less
No issue number.

OUTLAW FIGHTERS — Atlas

1 ❑ Aug 1954 Cover: 0.10 NM value: 90.00
2 ❑ Oct 1954 Cover: 0.10 NM value: 50.00
3 ❑ Dec 1954 Cover: 0.10 NM value: 50.00
4 ❑ Feb 1955 Cover: 0.10 NM value: 50.00
5 ❑ Apr 1955 Cover: 0.10 NM value: 50.00

OUTLAW KID, THE (1ST SERIES) — Marvel

To most people, Lance Temple appears to be just a mild-mannered rancher in the Old West. Bound by an oath he made to his father, who was blinded in a gunfight, Lance is sworn to shun all violence, no matter the circumstances.

But Lance is not the type of man to easily look the other way when he sees an injustice. Not wanting to break his oath, he finds a less apparent way to defend his family and friends. As the Outlaw Kid, a mysterious masked vigilante, he protects the Wild West from rustlers, bank robbers, and other outlaws.

Other Western heroes had appearances in this title, including the Black Rider. Like Lance, Doc Masters has sworn an oath of non-violence, but he also often finds it necessary to trade his medical kit for a mask and a set of six-guns.

1 ❑ Sep 1954 Cover: 0.10 NM value: 140.00
• CGC: 1 graded, best 9.4
★ Origin of Outlaw Kid.
2 ❑ Nov 1954 Cover: 0.10 NM value: 80.00
📖 The Fast Gun; Redman's Revenge; The Trap (text); Black Rider...The Challenge!; Fury at Echo Pass! A: Syd Shores; Doug Wildey
3 ❑ Jan 1955 Cover: 0.10 NM value: 65.00
4 ❑ Mar 1955 Cover: 0.10 NM value: 65.00
5 ❑ May 1955 Cover: 0.10 NM value: 65.00
• CGC: 1 graded, best 9.4
6 ❑ Jul 1955 Cover: 0.10 NM value: 65.00
• CGC: 1 graded, best 9.4
7 ❑ Sep 1955 Cover: 0.10 NM value: 65.00
• CGC: 1 graded, best 9.4
8 ❑ Nov 1955 Cover: 0.10 NM value: 65.00
9 ❑ Jan 1956 Cover: 0.10 NM value: 65.00
10 ❑ Mar 1956 Cover: 0.10 NM value: 65.00
• CGC: 1 graded, best 9.4
11 ❑ May 1956 Cover: 0.10 NM value: 45.00
12 ❑ Jul 1956 Cover: 0.10 NM value: 45.00
13 ❑ Sep 1956 Cover: 0.10 NM value: 45.00
14 ❑ Nov 1956 Cover: 0.10 NM value: 45.00
15 ❑ Jan 1957 Cover: 0.10 NM value: 45.00
16 ❑ Mar 1957 Cover: 0.10 NM value: 45.00
17 ❑ May 1957 Cover: 0.10 NM value: 45.00
18 ❑ Jul 1957 Cover: 0.10 NM value: 45.00
19 ❑ Sep 1957 Cover: 0.10 NM value: 45.00

OUTLAW KID, THE (2ND SERIES) — Marvel

1 ❑ Aug 1970 Cover: 0.15 NM value: 12.00
📖 Hostage!; Breakthrough!; The Silver Holster; Showdown! A: Doug Wldey W: Doug Wildey
2 ❑ Oct 1970 Cover: 0.15 NM value: 6.00
3 ❑ Dec 1970 Cover: 0.15 NM value: 3.50
4 ❑ Feb 1971 Cover: 0.15 NM value: 2.50
5 ❑ Apr 1971 Cover: 0.15 NM value: 2.50
6 ❑ Jun 1971 Cover: 0.15 NM value: 2.50
7 ❑ Aug 1971 Cover: 0.15 NM value: 2.50
8 ❑ Oct 1971 Cover: 0.15 NM value: 2.50
• Giant-size.
9 ❑ Dec 1971 Cover: 0.20 NM value: 3.00
10 ❑ Jun 1972 Cover: 0.20 NM value: 2.00
• series goes on hiatus ★ Origin of Outlaw Kid.
11 ❑ Aug 1972 Cover: 0.20 NM value: 2.00
12 ❑ Oct 1972 Cover: 0.20 NM value: 2.00
13 ❑ Dec 1972 Cover: 0.20 NM value: 2.00
14 ❑ Feb 1973 Cover: 0.20 NM value: 2.00
15 ❑ Apr 1973 Cover: 0.20 NM value: 2.00
16 ❑ Jun 1973 Cover: 0.20 NM value: 2.00
17 ❑ Aug 1973 Cover: 0.20 NM value: 2.00
18 ❑ Oct 1973 Cover: 0.20 NM value: 2.00
19 ❑ Dec 1973 Cover: 0.20 NM value: 2.00
20 ❑ Feb 1974 Cover: 0.20 NM value: 2.00
21 ❑ Apr 1974 Cover: 0.20 NM value: 2.00
22 ❑ Jun 1974 Cover: 0.20 NM value: 2.00
23 ❑ Aug 1974 Cover: 0.20 NM value: 2.00
24 ❑ Oct 1974 Cover: 0.20 NM value: 2.00
25 ❑ Dec 1974 Cover: 0.20 NM value: 2.00
26 ❑ Feb 1975 Cover: 0.20 NM value: 2.00
27 ❑ Apr 1975 Cover: 0.25 NM value: 2.00
★ Origin of Outlaw Kid.
28 ❑ Jun 1975 Cover: 0.25 NM value: 2.00
29 ❑ Aug 1975 Cover: 0.25 NM value: 2.00
30 ❑ Oct 1975 Cover: 0.25 NM value: 2.00

OUTLAW NATION (VERTIGO) — DC / Vertigo

1 ❑ Nov 2000 Cover: 2.50 NM value: Cover or less
Circ: Diamd. preorders: 25,527
📖 The End A: Goran Sudzuka W: Jamie Delano
2 ❑ Dec 2000 Cover: 2.50 NM value: Cover or less
Circ: Diamd. preorders: 19,351
📖 Does God Look Down? A: Goran Sudzuka W: Jamie Delano
3 ❑ Jan 2001 Cover: 2.50 NM value: Cover or less
Circ: Diamd. preorders: 18,430
📖 Too Much Force A: Goran Sudzuka W: Jamie Delano
4 ❑ Feb 2001 Cover: 2.50 NM value: Cover or less
Circ: Diamd. preorders: 18,968
📖 Careless Love A: Goran Sudzuka W: Jamie Delano
5 ❑ Mar 2001 Cover: 2.50 NM value: Cover or less
Circ: Diamd. preorders: 14,386
A: Goran Sudzuka W: Jamie Delano
6 ❑ Apr 2001 Cover: 2.50 NM value: Cover or less
Circ: Diamd. preorders: 13,555
📖 Two More Dead in Texas A: Goran Sudzuka W: Jamie Delano
7 ❑ May 2001 Cover: 2.50 NM value: Cover or less
Circ: Diamd. preorders: 12,831
📖 Distant Cousins A: Goran Sudzuka W: Jamie Delano
8 ❑ Jun 2001 Cover: 2.50 NM value: Cover or less
Circ: Diamd. preorders: 12,593
9 ❑ Jul 2001 Cover: 2.50 NM value: Cover or less
Circ: Diamd. preorders: 12,284
10 ❑ Aug 2001 Cover: 2.50 NM value: Cover or less
Circ: Diamd. preorders: 12,124
11 ❑ Sep 2001 Cover: 2.50 NM value: Cover or less
Circ: Diamd. preorders: 12,369

OUTLAW NATION (VOL. 2) — Boneyard

1 ❑ Cover: 4.95 NM value: Cover or less
📖 Werewulf; Shake That Dirt Out of Your Hair, Annie Rayne; Dead Man Walking; I Am The American Dream A: Vaughn Schultz; Kyle Holtz; Guy Burwell; Damon Threet W: Michael Ryan; Wayne Allen Sallee; Bill Yukich; David Quinn
1/PL❑ NM value: 5.00
Tim Bradstreet cover. 📖 Werewulf; Shake That Dirt Out of Your Hair, Annie Rayne; Dead Man Walking; I Am The American Dream A: Vaughn Schultz; Kyle Holtz; Guy Burwell; Damon Threet W: Michael Ryan; Wayne Allen Sallee; Bill Yukich; David Quinn

OUTLAW OVERDRIVE — Blue Comet

1 ❑ Cover: 2.95 NM value: Cover or less
• Red Edition. 📖 Lethal Oversight A: Manny W: Mark Hettergott
★ Appearance of Deathrow.

OUTLAWS, THE (DC) — DC

1 ❑ Sep 1991 Cover: 1.95 NM value: 2.00
Circ: CapCity orders: 17,850
📖 The Wheel A: Luke McDonnell W: Michael Jan Friedman
2 ❑ Oct 1991 Cover: 1.95 NM value: 2.00
Circ: CapCity orders: 12,000
3 ❑ Nov 1991 Cover: 1.95 NM value: 2.00
Circ: CapCity orders: 9,800
4 ❑ Dec 1991 Cover: 1.95 NM value: 2.00
Circ: CapCity orders: 8,900
5 ❑ Jan 1992 Cover: 1.95 NM value: 2.00
Circ: CapCity orders: 7,550
6 ❑ Feb 1992 Cover: 1.95 NM value: 2.00
Circ: CapCity orders: 6,450
7 ❑ Mar 1992 Cover: 1.95 NM value: 2.00
Circ: CapCity orders: 5,200
8 ❑ Apr 1992 Cover: 1.95 NM value: 2.00
Circ: CapCity orders: 5,200
final issue.

OUTLAWS (D.S.) — D.S.

1 ❑ Feb 1948 Cover: 0.10 NM value: 250.00
2 ❑ Apr 1948 Cover: 0.10 NM value: 250.00
3 ❑ Jun 1948 Cover: 0.10 NM value: 125.00
4 ❑ Aug 1948 Cover: 0.10 NM value: 125.00
5 ❑ Oct 1948 Cover: 0.10 NM value: 125.00
6 ❑ Dec 1948 Cover: 0.10 NM value: 100.00
7 ❑ Feb 1949 Cover: 0.10 NM value: 200.00
8 ❑ Apr 1949 Cover: 0.10 NM value: 200.00
9 ❑ Jun 1949 Cover: 0.10 NM value: 200.00
• CGC: 2 graded, best 7.0

📖 indicates **Story Title** or **Storyline** information.
★ indicates **Character Appearance** information.
W = Writer • A = Artist • C = Cover Artist

OUTLAWS OF THE WEST — Charlton

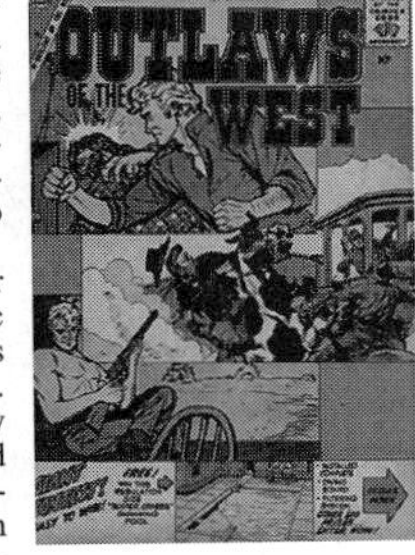

After World War II, the popularity of super-heroes declined for a while, opening the door for a wide variety of genre-comics. Western, horror, and mystery comics all enjoyed their time in the spotlight, until the resurgence of the super-hero phenomenon in the 1960s and 70s.

But these theme titles were never completely gone, as this comic book, published from the late 1950s to the late 1970s, attempts to prove. Unfortunately, the series lacks any central characters or continuity, and the individual stories are not particularly memorable or original. Given the title, readers might expect stories — fictional or fact — about notorious cowboy criminals. Instead, the recurring plot seems to involve basically nice guys who end up on the wrong side of the law by accident or circumstance. These reluctant outlaws usually see the error of their ways, often helping to bring their former partners to justice.

11 ❑ 1957 Cover: 0.10 NM value: 20.00
• Continues from Cody of the Pony Express #10
12 ❑ ca. 1957 Cover: 0.10 NM value: 12.00
13 ❑ ca. 1958 Cover: 0.10 NM value: 12.00
14 ❑ ca. 1958 Cover: 0.10 NM value: 12.00
15 ❑ Jun 1958 Cover: 0.10 NM value: 12.00
16 ❑ Sep 1958 Cover: 0.10 NM value: 12.00
17 ❑ Nov 1958 Cover: 0.10 NM value: 12.00
18 ❑ ca. 1959 Cover: 0.10 NM value: 12.00
19 ❑ Apr 1959 Cover: 0.10 NM value: 12.00
20 ❑ ca. 1959 Cover: 0.10 NM value: 12.00
21 ❑ ca. 1959 Cover: 0.10 NM value: 8.00
📖 The Right-of-Way War; Big Shot; Smokey Valley; Salvation (text); The Haunted Trail! A: Ram
22 ❑ ca. 1959 Cover: 0.10 NM value: 8.00
23 ❑ ca. 1960 Cover: 0.10 NM value: 8.00
24 ❑ Mar 1960 Cover: 0.10 NM value: 8.00
25 ❑ May 1960 Cover: 0.10 NM value: 8.00
26 ❑ Jul 1960 Cover: 0.10 NM value: 8.00
27 ❑ Sep 1960 Cover: 0.10 NM value: 8.00
28 ❑ Nov 1960 Cover: 0.10 NM value: 8.00
29 ❑ Jan 1961 Cover: 0.10 NM value: 8.00
30 ❑ Mar 1961 Cover: 0.10 NM value: 8.00
31 ❑ May 1961 Cover: 0.10 NM value: 5.00
32 ❑ Jul 1961 Cover: 0.10 NM value: 5.00
33 ❑ Sep 1961 Cover: 0.10 NM value: 5.00
34 ❑ Nov 1961 Cover: 0.10 NM value: 5.00
35 ❑ Jan 1962 Cover: 0.10 NM value: 5.00
36 ❑ Apr 1962 Cover: 0.10 NM value: 5.00
37 ❑ Jun 1962 Cover: 0.12 NM value: 5.00
38 ❑ Aug 1962 Cover: 0.12 NM value: 5.00
39 ❑ Oct 1962 Cover: 0.12 NM value: 5.00
40 ❑ Dec 1962 Cover: 0.12 NM value: 5.00
41 ❑ Feb 1963 Cover: 0.12 NM value: 5.00
42 ❑ Apr 1963 Cover: 0.12 NM value: 5.00
43 ❑ Jun 1963 Cover: 0.12 NM value: 5.00
44 ❑ Aug 1963 Cover: 0.12 NM value: 5.00
45 ❑ Oct 1963 Cover: 0.12 NM value: 5.00
46 ❑ Dec 1963 Cover: 0.12 NM value: 5.00
47 ❑ Feb 1964 Cover: 0.12 NM value: 5.00
Circ: Statement: 24,071
48 ❑ 1964 Cover: 0.12 NM value: 5.00
Circ: Statement: 24,071
49 ❑ 1964 Cover: 0.12 NM value: 5.00
Circ: Statement: 24,071
50 ❑ Oct 1964 Cover: 0.12 NM value: 5.00
Circ: Statement: 24,071
51 ❑ 1964 Cover: 0.12 NM value: 4.00
Circ: Statement: 24,071
52 ❑ 1965 Cover: 0.12 NM value: 4.00
Circ: Statement: 126,012
53 ❑ May 1965 Cover: 0.12 NM value: 4.00
Circ: Statement: 126,012
• Has 1964 Statement, filed 9/30/1964; avg print run 88,601; avg sales 24,065; avg subs 6; avg total paid 24,071; samples 25; max existent 24,096; 73% of run returned; (ALERT: Error is suspected in these figures; sales are far lower than the next year's, and the return ratio is high for the era.)
54 ❑ Jul 1965 Cover: 0.12 NM value: 4.00
Circ: Statement: 126,012
55 ❑ Sep 1965 Cover: 0.12 NM value: 4.00
Circ: Statement: 126,012
56 ❑ 1965 Cover: 0.12 NM value: 4.00
Circ: Statement: 126,012
57 ❑ 1966 Cover: 0.12 NM value: 4.00
Circ: Statement: 124,813
58 ❑ May 1966 Cover: 0.12 NM value: 4.00
Circ: Statement: 124,813
59 ❑ Jul 1966 Cover: 0.12 NM value: 4.00
Circ: Statement: 124,813
60 ❑ Sep 1966 Cover: 0.12 NM value: 4.00
Circ: Statement: 124,813
61 ❑ Nov 1966 Cover: 0.12 NM value: 3.00
Circ: Statement: 124,813
62 ❑ Jan 1967 Cover: 0.12 NM value: 3.00
Circ: Statement: 118,313
63 ❑ Mar 1967 Cover: 0.12 NM value: 3.00
Circ: Statement: 118,313
64 ❑ May 1967 Cover: 0.12 NM value: 3.00
Circ: Statement: 118,313
65 ❑ Jul 1967 Cover: 0.12 NM value: 3.00
Circ: Statement: 118,313
66 ❑ Sep 1967 Cover: 0.12 NM value: 3.00
Circ: Statement: 118,313

CGC-graded: Multiply prices above by **33 for 9.9 M • 16 for 9.8 NM/M • 7 for 9.6 NM+ • 5 for 9.4 NM • 2.5 for 9.2 NM- • 1.5 for 9.0 VF/NM**

67 ❑ Nov 1967 Cover: 0.12 **NM** value: **3.00**
Circ: Statement: **118,313**
68 ❑ 1968 Cover: 0.12 **NM** value: **3.00**
69 ❑ 1968 Cover: 0.12 **NM** value: **3.00**
70 ❑ Jul 1968 Cover: 0.12 **NM** value: **3.00**
71 ❑ Sep 1968 Cover: 0.12 **NM** value: **2.00**
72 ❑ Nov 1968 Cover: 0.12 **NM** value: **2.00**
73 ❑ Jan 1969 Cover: 0.12 **NM** value: **2.00**
74 ❑ Mar 1969 Cover: 0.12 **NM** value: **2.00**
75 ❑ May 1969 Cover: 0.12 **NM** value: **2.00**
76 ❑ Jul 1969 Cover: 0.15 **NM** value: **2.00**
77 ❑ Sep 1969 Cover: 0.15 **NM** value: **2.00**
78 ❑ Nov 1969 Cover: 0.15 **NM** value: **2.00**
79 ❑ Jan 1970 Cover: 0.15 **NM** value: **2.00**
80 ❑ Mar 1970 Cover: 0.15 **NM** value: **2.00**
81 ❑ May 1970 Cover: 0.15 **NM** value: **2.00**
82 ❑ Jul 1979 Cover: 0.40 **NM** value: **2.00**
83 ❑ Aug 1979 Cover: 0.40 **NM** value: **2.00**
84 ❑ Oct 1979 Cover: 0.40 **NM** value: **2.00**
📖 The Outlaw!; Apprentice Badman; The One that Got Away; The Owlhooter **A:** Rocke Mastroserio
85 ❑ Nov 1979 Cover: 0.40 **NM** value: **2.00**
86 ❑ Jan 1980 Cover: 0.40 **NM** value: **2.00**
87 ❑ Mar 1980 Cover: 0.40 **NM** value: **2.00**
88 ❑ Apr 1980 Cover: 0.40 **NM** value: **2.00**

OUTLAWS (STAR) — Star

10 ❑ May 1952 Cover: 0.10 **NM** value: **150.00**
• **CGC:** 2 graded, best 9.4
11 ❑ Cover: 0.10 **NM** value: **125.00**
12 ❑ Cover: 0.10 **NM** value: **125.00**
13 ❑ Cover: 0.10 **NM** value: **125.00**
14 ❑ Cover: 0.10 **NM** value: **125.00**

OUT OF THE NIGHT — American Comics Group

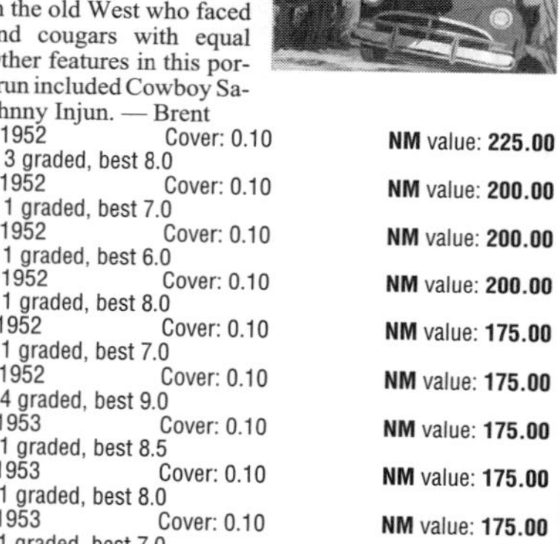

Out of the Night joined ACG's other horror titles of the 1950s with its lurid covers featuring vampires, mummies, ghouls, skeletons, and other horrific creatures for its first 17 issues, until it was retitled The Hooded Horseman for #18-27. The series ran at the height of the horror comics boom of the 1950s from 1952 to 1956 and featured art by Al Williamson and Ogden Whitney.

The Hooded Horseman portion of the run featured a red-masked adventurer in the old West who faced Indians and cougars with equal aplomb. Other features in this portion of the run included Cowboy Sahib and Johnny Injun. — Brent

1 ❑ Feb 1952 Cover: 0.10 **NM** value: **225.00**
• **CGC:** 3 graded, best 8.0
2 ❑ Apr 1952 Cover: 0.10 **NM** value: **200.00**
• **CGC:** 1 graded, best 7.0
3 ❑ Jun 1952 Cover: 0.10 **NM** value: **200.00**
• **CGC:** 1 graded, best 6.0
4 ❑ Aug 1952 Cover: 0.10 **NM** value: **200.00**
• **CGC:** 1 graded, best 8.0
5 ❑ Oct 1952 Cover: 0.10 **NM** value: **175.00**
• **CGC:** 1 graded, best 7.0
6 ❑ Dec 1952 Cover: 0.10 **NM** value: **175.00**
• **CGC:** 4 graded, best 9.0
7 ❑ Feb 1953 Cover: 0.10 **NM** value: **175.00**
• **CGC:** 1 graded, best 8.5
8 ❑ Apr 1953 Cover: 0.10 **NM** value: **175.00**
• **CGC:** 1 graded, best 8.0
9 ❑ Jun 1953 Cover: 0.10 **NM** value: **175.00**
• **CGC:** 1 graded, best 7.0
10 ❑ Aug 1953 Cover: 0.10 **NM** value: **150.00**
11 ❑ Oct 1953 Cover: 0.10 **NM** value: **150.00**
12 ❑ Dec 1953 Cover: 0.10 **NM** value: **150.00**
13 ❑ Feb 1954 Cover: 0.10 **NM** value: **140.00**
14 ❑ Apr 1954 Cover: 0.10 **NM** value: **140.00**
• **CGC:** 1 graded, best 3.5
15 ❑ Jun 1954 Cover: 0.10 **NM** value: **140.00**
16 ❑ Aug 1954 Cover: 0.10 **NM** value: **130.00**
17 ❑ Oct 1954 Cover: 0.10 **NM** value: **130.00**

OUT OF THE SHADOWS — Standard

5 ❑ Jul 1952 Cover: 0.10 **NM** value: **475.00**
• **CGC:** 4 graded, best 9.0
6 ❑ Oct 1952 Cover: 0.10 **NM** value: **300.00**
7 ❑ Jan 1953 Cover: 0.10 **NM** value: **250.00**
8 ❑ Apr 1953 Cover: 0.10 **NM** value: **250.00**
• **CGC:** 6 graded, best 9.2
9 ❑ Jul 1953 Cover: 0.10 **NM** value: **250.00**
10 ❑ Oct 1953 Cover: 0.10 **NM** value: **200.00**
11 ❑ Jan 1954 Cover: 0.10 **NM** value: **200.00**
12 ❑ Apr 1954 Cover: 0.10 **NM** value: **200.00**
13 ❑ Jul 1954 Cover: 0.10 **NM** value: **175.00**
14 ❑ Oct 1954 Cover: 0.10 **NM** value: **175.00**

OUT OF THE VORTEX (COMICS' GREATEST WORLD...) — Dark Horse

1 ❑ Oct 1993 Cover: 2.00 **NM** value: **Cover or less**
Circ: CapCity orders: **21,200**
Foil embossed cover. 📖 From The Maelstrom **A:** Damon Willis **W:** John Ostrander
2 ❑ Nov 1993 Cover: 2.00 **NM** value: **Cover or less**
Circ: CapCity orders: **12,900**
A: Damon Willis **W:** John Ostrander
3 ❑ Dec 1993 Cover: 2.00 **NM** value: **Cover or less**
Circ: CapCity orders: **12,125**
📖 The Final Seeker **A:** Damon Willis **W:** John Ostrander
4 ❑ Jan 1994 Cover: 2.00 **NM** value: **Cover or less**
Circ: CapCity orders: **9,775**
5 ❑ Feb 1994 Cover: 2.00 **NM** value: **Cover or less**
Circ: CapCity orders: **8,255**
📖 Deep Six Death **A:** Pete McDonnell **W:** Neal Barrett Jr. ★ Appearance of Grace.
6 ❑ Mar 1994 Cover: 2.00 **NM** value: **Cover or less**
Circ: CapCity orders: **7,800**
★ Appearance of Hero Zero.
7 ❑ Apr 1994 Cover: 2.00 **NM** value: **Cover or less**
Circ: CapCity orders: **7,300**
📖 The Seventh **A:** Damon Willis **W:** Neal Barrett Jr.
8 ❑ May 1994 Cover: 2.00 **NM** value: **Cover or less**
Circ: CapCity orders: **7,125**
📖 Trapped in the Vortex **A:** Damon Willis **W:** Neal Barrett Jr.
9 ❑ Jun 1994 Cover: 2.00 **NM** value: **Cover or less**
Circ: CapCity orders: **6,425**
10 ❑ Jul 1994 Cover: 2.00 **NM** value: **Cover or less**
Circ: CapCity orders: **5,975**
★ Appearance of Division 13.
11 ❑ Sep 1994 Cover: 2.50 **NM** value: **Cover or less**
Circ: CapCity orders: **4,875**
12 ❑ Oct 1994 Cover: 2.50 **NM** value: **Cover or less**
Circ: CapCity orders: **4,650**
final issue.

OUT OF THIS WORLD (CHARLTON) — Charlton

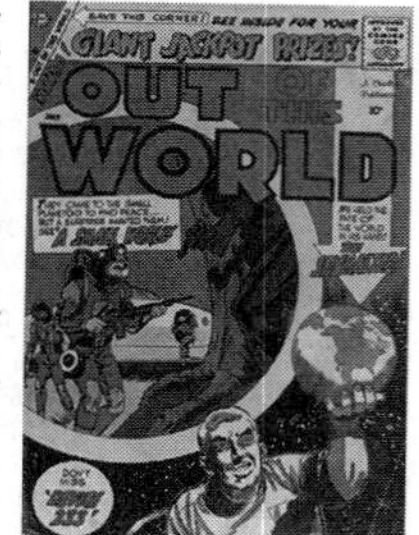

The period immediately following the imposition of the Comics Code and the collapse of quality-conscious publishers like E.C. was the heyday of pulp science-fiction comics. Charlton's Out of This World was not conspicuously worse than its competition from ACG, DC, and Atlas. Often featuring the imaginative artwork of Steve Ditko or the strong storytelling style of Paul Reinman, Out of This World offered tales of space adventures in the style of science-fiction writers such as Jack Williamson and Edmund Hamilton. Charlton generally favored the out-and-out action tale to the snap-endings, monsters, or hard-science approaches of its competitors, and appeared to be after younger or less discriminating readers.

1 ❑ Oct 1956 Cover: 0.10 **NM** value: **85.00**
2 ❑ Jan 1957 Cover: 0.10 **NM** value: **45.00**
3 ❑ Apr 1957 Cover: 0.10 **NM** value: **60.00**
A: Steve Ditko
4 ❑ Jul 1957 Cover: 0.10 **NM** value: **60.00**
• **CGC:** 1 graded, best 9.0
A: Steve Ditko
5 ❑ Oct 1957 Cover: 0.10 **NM** value: **60.00**
A: Steve Ditko
6 ❑ Dec 1957 Cover: 0.10 **NM** value: **60.00**
• **CGC:** 2 graded, best 9.2
A: Steve Ditko
7 ❑ Feb 1958 Cover: 0.10 **NM** value: **65.00**
A: Steve Ditko
8 ❑ May 1958 Cover: 0.10 **NM** value: **60.00**
A: Steve Ditko
9 ❑ Aug 1958 Cover: 0.10 **NM** value: **60.00**
A: Steve Ditko
10 ❑ Oct 1958 Cover: 0.10 **NM** value: **60.00**
• **CGC:** 1 graded, best 8.0
A: Steve Ditko
11 ❑ Jan 1959 Cover: 0.10 **NM** value: **55.00**
A: Steve Ditko
12 ❑ Mar 1959 Cover: 0.10 **NM** value: **55.00**
A: Steve Ditko
13 ❑ May 1959 Cover: 0.10 **NM** value: **20.00**
14 ❑ Aug 1959 Cover: 0.10 **NM** value: **20.00**
📖 A Small World; Device 233; Fire Dog; Dream On; Drop 43298A (text story); The Spymaster
15 ❑ Oct 1959 Cover: 0.10 **NM** value: **20.00**
📖 A Planet to Remember; Xondu the Eternal; Mystery Button; Top Secret (text); The Remarkable Mr. Ramsay
16 ❑ Dec 1959 Cover: 0.10 **NM** value: **55.00**
final issue. **A:** Steve Ditko

OUT OF THIS WORLD (ETERNITY) — Eternity

1 ❑ b&w Cover: 3.50 **NM** value: **Cover or less**
📖 Ransom-One Million Decimars!; World of the Monster Brain; Radium Monsters; Kenton of the Star Patrol…Monster Men of Space; The Survivors; The Man Who Owned the Earth; Ten Thousand Years Old • Reprints stories from Strange Worlds #9, Strange Planets #16, Tomb of Terror #6, and Weird Tales of the Future #1 **A:** Everett Kintsler

OUTPOSTS — Blackthorne

1 ❑ Jun 1997 Cover: 1.25 **NM** value: **1.50**
📖 The Darkling Chronicles; Mad 7 **A:** Chris Miller; Dante Fuget **W:** Mark Wayne Harris

Capital City orders are the actual sales of comic books by Capital City Distribution, once one of the largest U.S. sellers of comics to comics shops. Capital City's share of comics shop sales, while not known exactly, increases from around 10-20% in the mid-1980s to 30-35% in the mid-1990s. Capital City's share of comic books sold on newsstands (most Marvels and DCs) will be less.

OUTSIDERS, THE (1ST SERIES) — DC

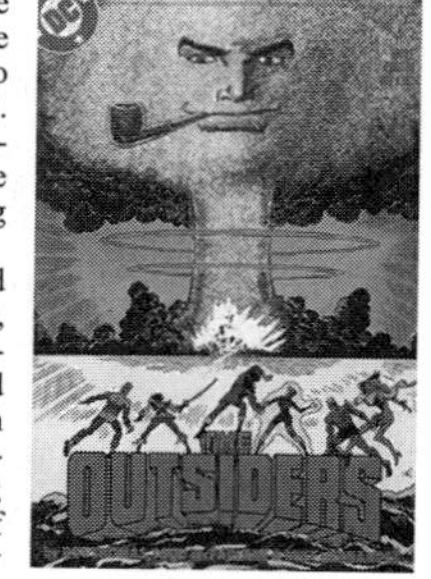

Having co-starred with The Caped Crusader in Batman and the Outsiders, this offbeat super-hero team got its own title in late 1985. In contrast to their illustrious comrades in the Justice League, these heroes were more well-meaning than world-saving.

The Outsiders' roster included Katanna, a swordswoman; Looker, a psychic; Black Lightning, an athletic hero with electrically based powers; Metamorpho, who can change his body to any element; Halo, who can fly and fire force blasts; and leader Geo-Force, a prince of Markovia who also has the ability to control objects using earth-based powers. This series still finds them in a loose collaboration with Batman, although by now they are operating largely independently.

1 ❑ Nov 1985 Cover: 1.25 **NM** value: **2.00**
Circ: CapCity orders: **19,450**
W: Mike W. Barr
2 ❑ Dec 1985 Cover: 1.50 **NM** value: **Cover or less**
Circ: CapCity orders: **13,700**
W: Mike W. Barr ★ Versus Nuclear Family.
3 ❑ Jan 1986 Cover: 1.50 **NM** value: **Cover or less**
Circ: CapCity orders: **13,150**
W: Mike W. Barr ★ Versus Force of July.
4 ❑ Feb 1986 Cover: 1.50 **NM** value: **Cover or less**
Circ: CapCity orders: **13,200**
W: Mike W. Barr
5 ❑ Mar 1986 Cover: 1.50 **NM** value: **Cover or less**
Circ: CapCity orders: **11,800**
• Christmas Carol story **W:** Mike W. Barr
6 ❑ Apr 1986 Cover: 1.50 **NM** value: **Cover or less**
Circ: CapCity orders: **11,000**
W: Mike W. Barr ★ Versus Duke of Oil.
7 ❑ May 1986 Cover: 1.50 **NM** value: **Cover or less**
Circ: CapCity orders: **10,250**
W: Mike W. Barr ★ Versus Duke of Oil.
8 ❑ Jun 1986 Cover: 1.50 **NM** value: **Cover or less**
Circ: CapCity orders: **9,850**
A: Jan Duursema **W:** Mike W. Barr
9 ❑ Jul 1986 Cover: 1.50 **NM** value: **Cover or less**
Circ: CapCity orders: **9,450**
W: Mike W. Barr
10 ❑ Aug 1986 Cover: 1.50 **NM** value: **Cover or less**
Circ: CapCity orders: **9,400**
W: Mike W. Barr
11 ❑ Sep 1986 Cover: 1.50 **NM** value: **Cover or less**
Circ: CapCity orders: **9,150**
W: Mike W. Barr
12 ❑ Oct 1986 Cover: 1.50 **NM** value: **Cover or less**
Circ: CapCity orders: **9,300**
W: Mike W. Barr
13 ❑ Nov 1986 Cover: 1.50 **NM** value: **Cover or less**
Circ: CapCity orders: **9,500**
W: Mike W. Barr
14 ❑ Dec 1986 Cover: 1.50 **NM** value: **Cover or less**
Circ: CapCity orders: **8,850**
W: Mike W. Barr
15 ❑ Jan 1987 Cover: 1.50 **NM** value: **Cover or less**
Circ: CapCity orders: **8,800**
W: Mike W. Barr
16 ❑ Feb 1987 Cover: 1.50 **NM** value: **Cover or less**
Circ: CapCity orders: **8,550**
W: Mike W. Barr
17 ❑ Mar 1987 Cover: 1.50 **NM** value: **Cover or less**
Circ: CapCity orders: **9,150**
• Batman returns **W:** Mike W. Barr
18 ❑ Apr 1987 Cover: 1.50 **NM** value: **Cover or less**
Circ: CapCity orders: **9,600**
W: Mike W. Barr ★ Versus Eclipso.
19 ❑ May 1987 Cover: 1.50 **NM** value: **Cover or less**
Circ: CapCity orders: **8,950**
W: Mike W. Barr
20 ❑ Jun 1987 Cover: 1.50 **NM** value: **Cover or less**
Circ: CapCity orders: **8,350**
W: Mike W. Barr
21 ❑ Jul 1987 Cover: 1.50 **NM** value: **Cover or less**
Circ: CapCity orders: **8,450**
W: Mike W. Barr
22 ❑ Aug 1987 Cover: 1.50 **NM** value: **Cover or less**
Circ: CapCity orders: **9,050**
• EC parody back-up **W:** Mike W. Barr
23 ❑ Sep 1987 Cover: 1.50 **NM** value: **Cover or less**
Circ: CapCity orders: **8,900**
W: Mike W. Barr
24 ❑ Oct 1987 Cover: 1.50 **NM** value: **Cover or less**
Circ: CapCity orders: **9,150**
W: Mike W. Barr
25 ❑ Nov 1987 Cover: 1.50 **NM** value: **Cover or less**
Circ: CapCity orders: **9,000**
W: Mike W. Barr
26 ❑ Dec 1987 Cover: 1.50 **NM** value: **Cover or less**
Circ: CapCity orders: **8,550**
W: Mike W. Barr
27 ❑ Jan 1988 Cover: 1.50 **NM** value: **Cover or less**
Circ: CapCity orders: **13,350**
• Millennium **W:** Mike W. Barr
28 ❑ Feb 1988 Cover: 1.50 **NM** value: **Cover or less**
Circ: CapCity orders: **13,800**
• Millennium **W:** Mike W. Barr

Anl 1❑ Cover: 2.50 **NM** value: **Cover or less**
Circ: CapCity orders: **10,050**
W: Mike W. Barr

SE 1❑ Cover: 1.50 **NM** value: **Cover or less**
Circ: CapCity orders: **10,750**
📖 From Here To Infinity • Crossover continued in Infinity Inc. SE #1 **A:** Chuck Patton **W:** Mike W. Barr ★ Appearance of Infinity, Inc..

OUTSIDERS (2ND SERIES) — DC

0 ❑ Oct 1994 Cover: 1.95 **NM** value: **2.50**
Circ: CapCity orders: **14,400**
📖 From The Ashes • New team begins **A:** Paul Pelletier **W:** Mike W. Barr

1/A ❑ Nov 1993 Cover: 1.75 **NM** value: **2.50**
Circ: CapCity orders: **19,350**
📖 Blood & Ashes • Alpha version **A:** Paul Pelletier **W:** Mike W. Barr

1/B ❑ Nov 1993 Cover: 1.75 **NM** value: **2.50**
Circ: CapCity orders: **19,300**
• Omega version **A:** Paul Pelletier **W:** Mike W. Barr

2 ❑ Dec 1993 Cover: 1.75 **NM** value: **2.00**
Circ: CapCity orders: **12,500**
A: Paul Pelletier **W:** Mike W. Barr

3 ❑ Jan 1994 Cover: 1.75 **NM** value: **2.00**
Circ: CapCity orders: **11,750**
A: Paul Pelletier **W:** Mike W. Barr ★ Appearance of Eradicator.

4 ❑ Feb 1994 Cover: 1.75 **NM** value: **2.00**
Circ: CapCity orders: **12,600**
📖 Storming the Palace **A:** Paul Pelletier **W:** Mike W. Barr

5 ❑ Mar 1994 Cover: 1.75 **NM** value: **2.00**
Circ: CapCity orders: **10,450**

6 ❑ Apr 1994 Cover: 1.75 **NM** value: **2.00**
Circ: CapCity orders: **9,250**

7 ❑ May 1994 Cover: 1.75 **NM** value: **2.00**
Circ: CapCity orders: **9,500**

8 ❑ Jun 1994 Cover: 1.75 **NM** value: **2.00**
Circ: CapCity orders: **9,800**
📖 Shadows of Knight **A:** Jim Aparo **W:** Mike W. Barr ★ Appearance of Batman (Azrael).

9 ❑ Jul 1994 Cover: 1.75 **NM** value: **2.00**
Circ: CapCity orders: **8,650**

10 ❑ Aug 1994 Cover: 1.95 **NM** value: **2.00**
Circ: CapCity orders: **8,150**
📖 Final Blood, Part 1

11 ❑ Sep 1994 Cover: 1.95 **NM** value: **2.00**
Circ: CapCity orders: **9,550**
📖 Final Blood, Part 2; Zero Hour

12 ❑ Nov 1994 Cover: 1.95 **NM** value: **2.00**
Circ: CapCity orders: **8,250**

13 ❑ Dec 1994 Cover: 1.95 **NM** value: **2.00**
Circ: CapCity orders: **8,450**
★ Appearance of Superman.

14 ❑ Jan 1995 Cover: 1.95 **NM** value: **2.00**
Circ: CapCity orders: **8,300**
📖 Proving Ground! **A:** Paul Pelletier **W:** Mike W. Barr

15 ❑ Feb 1995 Cover: 1.95 **NM** value: **2.00**
Circ: CapCity orders: **7,575**

16 ❑ Mar 1995 Cover: 1.95 **NM** value: **2.00**
Circ: CapCity orders: **7,100**

17 ❑ Apr 1995 Cover: 1.95 **NM** value: **2.00**
Circ: CapCity orders: **6,975**

18 ❑ May 1995 Cover: 1.95 **NM** value: **2.00**
Circ: CapCity orders: **6,425**

19 ❑ Jun 1995 Cover: 2.25 **NM** value: **Cover or less**
Circ: CapCity orders: **6,225**

20 ❑ Jul 1995 Cover: 2.25 **NM** value: **Cover or less**
Circ: CapCity orders: **6,175**

21 ❑ Aug 1995 Cover: 2.25 **NM** value: **Cover or less**
Circ: CapCity orders: **6,225**

22 ❑ Sep 1995 Cover: 2.25 **NM** value: **Cover or less**
Circ: CapCity orders: **5,725**

23 ❑ Oct 1995 Cover: 2.25 **NM** value: **Cover or less**
Circ: CapCity orders: **4,750**

24 ❑ Nov 1995 Cover: 2.25 **NM** value: **Cover or less**
final issue.

OUT THERE — WildStorm

Ash 1❑ ca. 2001 **NM** value: **0.50**
• Ashcan preview; Flip book with Ninja Boy Ash 1 **A:** Humberto Ramos

OVERKILL: WITCHBLADE/ALIENS/DARKNESS/PREDATOR — Image

1 ❑ Dec 2000 Cover: 5.95 **NM** value: **Cover or less**
Circ: Diamd. preorders: **34,778**
A: Brian Ching; Clarence Lansang; Joe Benitez **W:** Paul Jenkins

2 ❑ Mar 2001 Cover: 5.95 **NM** value: **Cover or less**
Circ: Diamd. preorders: **25,231**
A: Brian Ching; Clarence Lansang; Joe Benitez **W:** Paul Jenkins

OVERLOAD MAGAZINE — Eclipse

1 ❑ Apr 1987, b&w Cover: 1.50 **NM** value: **Cover or less**

OVERMEN, THE — Excel

1 ❑ Cover: 2.95 **NM** value: **Cover or less**
A: Daniel Patrick Rice; John Warren **W:** John Warren

OVER THE EDGE — Marvel

1 ❑ Nov 1995 Cover: 0.99 **NM** value: **1.25**
📖 ...And Fear Will Follow! • Daredevil **A:** Robert Brown **W:** Ralph Macchio

2 ❑ Dec 1995 Cover: 0.99 **NM** value: **1.00**
A: Robert Brown **W:** Mark Gruenwald ★ Appearance of Doctor Strange.

3 ❑ Jan 1996 Cover: 0.99 **NM** value: **1.00**
• Hulk

4 ❑ Feb 1996 Cover: 0.99 **NM** value: **1.00**
• Ghost Rider

5 ❑ Mar 1996 Cover: 0.99 **NM** value: **1.00**
📖 Magdelena Black And Red • Punisher **A:** Scott Kolins; Jeff Johnson; Stephen Jones **W:** Ivan Velez Jr.

6 ❑ Apr 1996 Cover: 0.99 **NM** value: **1.00**
📖 Of Kings...And Bight, Shiny Things • Daredevil and Black Panther **A:** Robert Brown **W:** Ralph Macchio

7 ❑ May 1996 Cover: 0.99 **NM** value: **1.00**
• Doctor Strange vs. Nightmare

8 ❑ Jun 1996 Cover: 0.99 **NM** value: **1.00**
• Elektra

9 ❑ Jul 1996 Cover: 0.99 **NM** value: **1.00**
• Ghost Rider, John Blaze

10 ❑ Aug 1996 Cover: 0.99 **NM** value: **1.00**
final issue. • Daredevil

OVERTURE — All American

1 ❑ b&w Cover: 2.25 **NM** value: **Cover or less**

2 ❑ Apr 1990, b&w Cover: 2.25 **NM** value: **Cover or less**
📖 Hot to Trot Sky!; Spunik the Space Man; Stranger in the Skite **A:** George Broderick **W:** Alan Sissom; Dan Tyree; David Lawrence

OWL, THE — Gold Key

1 ❑ Apr 1967 Cover: 0.10 **NM** value: **50.00**
• **CGC:** 1 graded, best 9.6

2 ❑ **NM** value: **40.00**

OWLHOOTS — Kitchen Sink

1 ❑ two-color Cover: 2.50 **NM** value: **Cover or less**
2 ❑ two-color Cover: 2.50 **NM** value: **Cover or less**

OX COW O' WAR — Spoof

1 ❑ b&w Cover: 2.95 **NM** value: **Cover or less**
• parody

OZ — Caliber

0 ❑ Cover: 2.95 **NM** value: **4.00**
Circ: CapCity orders: **2,600**
📖 Mayhem in Munchkinland! **A:** Bill Bryan **W:** Ralph Griffith; Stuart Kerr

1 ❑ Cover: 2.95 **NM** value: **6.00**
Circ: CapCity orders: **4,485**

2 ❑ Cover: 2.95 **NM** value: **4.00**
Circ: CapCity orders: **3,375**

3 ❑ Cover: 2.95 **NM** value: **4.00**
4 ❑ Cover: 2.95 **NM** value: **4.00**
5 ❑ Cover: 2.95 **NM** value: **3.50**
6 ❑ Cover: 2.95 **NM** value: **3.50**
Circ: CapCity orders: **3,080**

7 ❑ Cover: 2.95 **NM** value: **3.50**
Circ: CapCity orders: **2,850**

8 ❑ Cover: 2.95 **NM** value: **3.50**
Circ: CapCity orders: **2,630**

9 ❑ Cover: 2.95 **NM** value: **3.50**
Circ: CapCity orders: **2,715**

10 ❑ Cover: 2.95 **NM** value: **3.50**
Circ: CapCity orders: **2,540**

11 ❑ Cover: 2.95 **NM** value: **3.00**
12 ❑ Cover: 2.95 **NM** value: **3.00**
13 ❑ Cover: 2.95 **NM** value: **3.00**
14 ❑ Cover: 2.95 **NM** value: **3.00**
15 ❑ 1996 Cover: 2.95 **NM** value: **3.00**
16 ❑ 1996 Cover: 2.95 **NM** value: **3.00**
17 ❑ Sep 1996 Cover: 2.95 **NM** value: **3.00**
Circ: Diamd. preorders: **3,228**
📖 Peace be so Fragile **A:** Tim Holtrop **W:** Ralph Griffith; Stuart Kerr

18 ❑ Nov 1996 Cover: 2.95 **NM** value: **Cover or less**
Circ: Diamd. preorders: **3,070**

19 ❑ Jan 1997 Cover: 2.95 **NM** value: **Cover or less**
Circ: Diamd. preorders: **2,674**

20 ❑ Mar 1997 Cover: 2.95 **NM** value: **Cover or less**
Circ: Diamd. preorders: **2,488**

21 ❑ 1997 Cover: 2.95 **NM** value: **Cover or less**
22 ❑ 1997 Cover: 2.95 **NM** value: **Cover or less**

OZARK IKE — Standard

Ozark Ike was a poor man's Li'l Abner which ran from 1948 to 1952. The plots were simple, playing off the naivete and straight-forward thinking of the stereotypical hillbilly.

Covers often featured Ike playing some sport while his blonde girlfriend posed seductively nearby.

The series, by Ray Gotto, made one appearance in Dell's Four Color series before Standard took over publication, starting the series inexplicably with #11, no doubt picking up the numbering from some other defunct series to avoid postal regulations. Issue numbers run to #25, but only 15 issues were really published. — Brent

11 ❑ ca. 1948 Cover: 0.10 **NM** value: **50.00**
12 ❑ ca. 1949 Cover: 0.10 **NM** value: **50.00**
13 ❑ ca. 1949 Cover: 0.10 **NM** value: **50.00**
14 ❑ ca. 1949 Cover: 0.10 **NM** value: **50.00**
15 ❑ ca. 1949 Cover: 0.10 **NM** value: **50.00**
16 ❑ ca. 1949 Cover: 0.10 **NM** value: **40.00**
17 ❑ ca. 1950 Cover: 0.10 **NM** value: **40.00**
18 ❑ ca. 1950 Cover: 0.10 **NM** value: **40.00**
19 ❑ ca. 1950 Cover: 0.10 **NM** value: **40.00**
20 ❑ ca. 1950 Cover: 0.10 **NM** value: **40.00**
21 ❑ ca. 1951 Cover: 0.10 **NM** value: **35.00**
22 ❑ ca. 1951 Cover: 0.10 **NM** value: **35.00**
23 ❑ ca. 1951 Cover: 0.10 **NM** value: **35.00**
24 ❑ ca. 1951 Cover: 0.10 **NM** value: **35.00**
25 ❑ ca. 1952 Cover: 0.10 **NM** value: **35.00**

OZ COLLECTION (BILL BRYAN'S...) — Arrow

1 ❑ Cover: 2.95 **NM** value: **Cover or less**
A: Bill Bryan **W:** Bill Bryan

OZ: DAEMONSTORM — Caliber

1 ❑ b&w Cover: 3.95 **NM** value: **Cover or less**
No issue number. One-shot. • intracompany crossover

OZ: ROMANCE IN RAGS — Caliber

1 ❑ b&w Cover: 2.95 **NM** value: **Cover or less**
2 ❑ b&w Cover: 2.95 **NM** value: **Cover or less**
3 ❑ b&w Cover: 2.95 **NM** value: **Cover or less**

OZ SPECIAL: FREEDOM FIGHTERS — Caliber

1 ❑ b&w Cover: 2.95 **NM** value: **Cover or less**

OZ SPECIAL: LION — Caliber

1 ❑ b&w Cover: 2.95 **NM** value: **Cover or less**
Circ: CapCity orders: **2,020**
• continues in Oz Special: Tin Man

OZ SPECIAL: SCARECROW — Caliber

1 ❑ b&w Cover: 2.95 **NM** value: **Cover or less**
Circ: CapCity orders: **2,035**
• continues in Oz Special: Lion **A:** Daniel Preece **W:** Ralph Griffith; Stuart Kerr

OZ SPECIAL: TIN MAN — Caliber

1 ❑ b&w Cover: 2.95 **NM** value: **Cover or less**
• continues in Oz Special: Freedom Fighters

OZ SQUAD (1ST SERIES) — Brave New Words

1 ❑ Oct 1991 Cover: 2.50 **NM** value: **3.00**
2 ❑ Jan 1992 Cover: 2.50 **NM** value: **Cover or less**
3 ❑ Cover: 2.50 **NM** value: **Cover or less**
4 ❑ Cover: 2.50 **NM** value: **Cover or less**

OZ SQUAD (2ND SERIES) — Patchwork Press

1 ❑ Cover: 2.50 **NM** value: **3.00**
2 ❑ Cover: 2.50 **NM** value: **Cover or less**
3 ❑ Cover: 2.50 **NM** value: **Cover or less**
4 ❑ Cover: 2.75 **NM** value: **Cover or less**
5 ❑ Cover: 2.75 **NM** value: **Cover or less**
6 ❑ Cover: 2.95 **NM** value: **Cover or less**
7 ❑ Aug 1995 Cover: 2.75 **NM** value: **Cover or less**
8 ❑ Oct 1995 Cover: 2.75 **NM** value: **Cover or less**
9 ❑ Dec 1995 Cover: 2.75 **NM** value: **Cover or less**
★ Origin of Tin Man.

10 ❑ Cover: 2.75 **NM** value: **Cover or less**
★ Origin of Tin Man.

OZ: STRAW & SORCERY — Caliber

1 ❑ Mar 1997, b&w Cover: 2.95 **NM** value: **Cover or less**
Circ: Diamd. preorders: **2,470**
A: Bill Bryan **W:** Ralph Griffith; Stuart Kerr

2 ❑ 1997b&w Cover: 2.95 **NM** value: **Cover or less**
A: Bill Bryan **W:** Ralph Griffith; Stuart Kerr

3 ❑ 1997b&w Cover: 2.95 **NM** value: **Cover or less**
A: Bill Bryan **W:** Ralph Griffith; Stuart Kerr

OZ-WONDERLAND WARS — DC

1 ❑ Jan 1986 Cover: 2.00 **NM** value: **2.50**
Circ: CapCity orders: **6,100**

2 ❑ Feb 1986 Cover: 2.00 **NM** value: **2.50**
Circ: CapCity orders: **5,400**
★ Appearance of Hoppy the Marvel Bunny.

3 ❑ Mar 1986 Cover: 2.00 **NM** value: **2.50**
Circ: CapCity orders: **5,350**

OZZIE AND BABS — Fawcett

1 ❑ Dec 1947 Cover: 0.10 **NM** value: **50.00**
• **CGC:** 1 graded, best 7.5

2 ❑ Spr 1948 Cover: 0.10 **NM** value: **25.00**
3 ❑ Sum 1948 Cover: 0.10 **NM** value: **20.00**
4 ❑ Sep 1948 Cover: 0.10 **NM** value: **20.00**
5 ❑ Oct 1948 Cover: 0.10 **NM** value: **20.00**
6 ❑ Nov 1948 Cover: 0.10 **NM** value: **20.00**
7 ❑ Dec 1948 Cover: 0.10 **NM** value: **20.00**
8 ❑ Jan 1949 Cover: 0.10 **NM** value: **20.00**
9 ❑ Feb 1949 Cover: 0.10 **NM** value: **20.00**
10 ❑ Mar 1949 Cover: 0.10 **NM** value: **15.00**
11 ❑ Apr 1949 Cover: 0.10 **NM** value: **15.00**
• **CGC:** 1 graded, best 8.5

12 ❑ May 1949 Cover: 0.10 **NM** value: **15.00**
13 ❑ Jun 1949 Cover: 0.10 **NM** value: **15.00**

OZZY OSBOURNE — Rock-It Comics

1 ❑ Cover: 4.95 **NM** value: **6.00**
Circ: CapCity orders: **4,725**

PACIFIC PRESENTS — Pacific

1 ❑ Oct 1982 Cover: 1.00 **NM** value: **4.00**
• **CGC:** 5 graded, best 9.6
📖 Rocketeer Chapter 3; Missing Man Meets Quen Bee • Rocketeer; Missing Man **A:** Steve Ditko; Dave Stevens **W:** Dave Stevens. Steve Ditko

2 ❑ Apr 1983 Cover: 1.00 **NM** value: **3.00**
• **CGC:** 4 graded, best 9.6
📖 Rocketeer Chapter 4; The Missing Man Meets The Payne Family • Rocketeer; Missing Man **A:** Steve Ditko; Dave Stevens **W:** Dave Stevens. Steve Ditko

3 ❑ Mar 1984 Cover: 1.50 **NM** value: **Cover or less**

CGC-graded: Multiply prices above by **33 for 9.9 M • 16 for 9.8 NM/M • 7 for 9.6 NM+ • 5 for 9.4 NM • 2.5 for 9.2 NM- • 1.5 for 9.0 VF/NM**

E. Erie Smith and Walter Weary: When Ya Gotta Go-Ya Gotta Go...; The Missing Man: Am I Maro, Roma, or Raem?; Vanity: Scoop! • Missing Man **A:** Steve Ditko; Will Meugniot; Tim Conrad **W:** Steve Ditko; Will Meugniot; Tim Conrad; Robin Snyder
4 ❑ Jun 1984 Cover: 1.50 **NM** value: **Cover or less**

PAC (PRETER-HUMAN ASSAULT CORPS) — Artifacts
1 ❑ Oct 1993 Cover: 1.95 **NM** value: **Cover or less**
Circ: CapCity orders: **6,125**
A: Frederic Cooper **W:** Frederic Cooper

PACT, THE — Image
1 ❑ Feb 1994 Cover: 1.95 **NM** value: **Cover or less**
Circ: CapCity orders: **35,750**
Nowhere To Run, Nowhere To Hide **A:** Jim Valentino; Walter McDaniel **W:** Jim Valentino; Len Senecal
2 ❑ Apr 1994 Cover: 1.95 **NM** value: **Cover or less**
Circ: CapCity orders: **24,100**
Welcome To The Big Leagues **A:** Jim Valentino; Walter McDaniel **W:** Jim Valentino; Len Senecal ★ Appearance of Youngblood.
3 ❑ Jun 1994 Cover: 1.95 **NM** value: **Cover or less**
Circ: CapCity orders: **20,750**
final issue. ★ 1st Appearance of Atrocity.

PAGEANT OF COMICS — St. John
1 ❑ Sep 1947 Cover: 0.10 **NM** value: **50.00**
2 ❑ Oct 1947 Cover: 0.10 **NM** value: **50.00**

PAGERS COMICS ANTHOLOGY — No Talent
1 ❑ Spr 1997 Cover: 2.50 **NM** value: **Cover or less**
2 ❑ Sum 1997 Cover: 2.50 **NM** value: **Cover or less**
3 ❑ Fal 1997 Cover: 2.50 **NM** value: **Cover or less**
4 ❑ Win 1997 Cover: 2.50 **NM** value: **Cover or less**
5 ❑ Spr 1998 Cover: 2.50 **NM** value: **Cover or less**
6 ❑ Sum 1998 Cover: 2.50 **NM** value: **Cover or less**

PAINKILLER JANE — Event
0 ❑ Nov 1998 Cover: 3.95 **NM** value: **Cover or less**
Circ: Diamd. preorders: **15,650**
Jane's Addiction **A:** Amanda Conner **W:** Joe Quesada; Jimmy Palmiotti ★ Origin of Painkiller Jane.
0/LE❑ Cover: 39.95 **NM** value: **Cover or less**
★ Origin of Painkiller Jane.
1 ❑ Jun 1997 Cover: 2.95 **NM** value: **3.00**
Circ: Diamd. preorders: **17,257**
wraparound cover. **A:** Rick Leonardi; Joe Quesada(cover) **W:** Brian Augustyn; Mark Waid
1/A ❑ Jun 1997 Cover: 2.95 **NM** value: **3.00**
Circ: Diamd. preorders: **13,787**
variant cover. **A:** Rick Leonardi **W:** Brian Augustyn; Mark Waid
1/B ❑ Jun 1997 Cover: 25.00 **NM** value: **Cover or less**
• Red foil **A:** Rick Leonardi; Joe Quesada(cover) **W:** Brian Augustyn; Mark Waid
2 ❑ Jul 1997 Cover: 2.95 **NM** value: **3.00**
Circ: Diamd. preorders: **14,040**
Standard cover. Dead in the Water • Jane in sunglasses close-up **A:** Rick Leonardi; Joe Quesada(cover) **W:** Brian Augustyn; Mark Waid
2/A ❑ Jul 1997 Cover: 2.95 **NM** value: **3.00**
Circ: Diamd. preorders: **11,091**
variant cover. Dead in the Water • Jane running **A:** Rick Leonardi **W:** Brian Augustyn; Mark Waid
3 ❑ Aug 1997 Cover: 2.95 **NM** value: **3.00**
Circ: Diamd. preorders: **12,422**
A: Rick Leonardi; Joe Quesada(cover) **W:** Brian Augustyn; Mark Waid
3/A ❑ Aug 1997 Cover: 2.95 **NM** value: **3.00**
Circ: Diamd. preorders: **9,501**
variant cover. **A:** Rick Leonardi **W:** Brian Augustyn; Mark Waid
4 ❑ Sep 1997 Cover: 2.95 **NM** value: **3.00**
Circ: Diamd. preorders: **11,755**
A Place Too Bright For Dying **A:** Rick Leonardi; Joe Quesada(cover) **W:** Brian Augustyn; Mark Waid
4/A ❑ Sep 1997 Cover: 2.95 **NM** value: **3.00**
Circ: Diamd. preorders: **8,965**
variant cover. A Place Too Bright For Dying **A:** Rick Leonardi **W:** Brian Augustyn; Mark Waid
5 ❑ Oct 1997 Cover: 2.95 **NM** value: **3.00**
Circ: Diamd. preorders: **17,180**
A: Rick Leonardi; Joe Quesada(cover) **W:** Brian Augustyn; Mark Waid
5/A ❑ 1997 Cover: 2.95 **NM** value: **3.00**
variant cover. **A:** Rick Leonardi **W:** Brian Augustyn; Mark Waid

PAINKILLER JANE/DARKCHYLDE — Event
0 ❑ Cover: 10.00 **NM** value: **Cover or less**
• European Preview book
0/AUT❑ Cover: 29.95 **NM** value: **Cover or less**
• European Preview book
1 ❑ Oct 1998 Cover: 2.95 **NM** value: **3.00**
Circ: Diamd. preorders: **28,717** • **CGC:** 1 graded, best 9.4
Lost in a Dream **A:** J.G. Jones **W:** Brian Augustyn; Randy Queen
1/A ❑ Oct 1998 Cover: 29.95 **NM** value: **Cover or less**
Lost in a Dream **A:** J.G. Jones **W:** Brian Augustyn
1/B ❑ Oct 1998 Cover: 6.95 **NM** value: **Cover or less**
DFE alternate cover. Lost in a Dream **A:** J.G. Jones **W:** Brian Augustyn
1/C ❑ Oct 1998 Cover: 39.95 **NM** value: **Cover or less**
Lost in a Dream **A:** J.G. Jones **W:** Brian Augustyn
Ash 1❑ Jul 1998 **NM** value: **5.00**
• DF Exclusive; Sketches **A:** J.G. Jones **W:** Brian Augustyn; Randy Queen

PAINKILLER JANE/HELLBOY — Event
1 ❑ Aug 1998 Cover: 2.95 **NM** value: **Cover or less**
Circ: Diamd. preorders: **21,830**
1/LE❑ Aug 1998 Cover: 29.95 **NM** value: **Cover or less**

PAINKILLER JANE VS. THE DARKNESS: STRIPPER — Event
1 ❑ Apr 1997 Cover: 2.95 **NM** value: **Cover or less**
Circ: Diamd. preorders: **20,730**
four alternate covers. **A:** Amanda Conner **W:** Garth Ennis
1/A ❑ Apr 1997 Cover: 2.95 **NM** value: **3.00**
Circ: Diamd. preorders: **18,864**
Jane facing forward, shooting on cover.
1/B❑ Apr 1997 Cover: 2.95 **NM** value: **3.00**
Circ: Diamd. preorders: **16,434**
1/C ❑ Apr 1997 Cover: 2.95 **NM** value: **3.00**
Circ: Diamd. preorders: **15,489**
C: Greg Hildebrandt(cover)
1/LE❑ Apr 1997 Cover: 20.00 **NM** value: **Cover or less**
A: Amanda Conner **W:** Garth Ennis

PAINTBALL UNIVERSE 2000 — Splattoons
1 ❑ Cover: 2.95 **NM** value: **Cover or less**

PAJAMA CHRONICLES — Blackthorne
1 ❑ Cover: 1.75 **NM** value: **Cover or less**

PAKKINS' LAND — Caliber / Tapestry
0 ❑ Jun 1997 Cover: 1.95 **NM** value: **Cover or less**
A: Gary Shipman **W:** Gary Shipman; Rhoda Shipman
1 ❑ Oct 1996 Cover: 2.95 **NM** value: **Cover or less**
A: Gary Shipman **W:** Gary Shipman; Rhoda Shipman
2 ❑ Dec 1996 Cover: 2.95 **NM** value: **Cover or less**
A: Gary Shipman **W:** Gary Shipman; Rhoda Shipman
3 ❑ Feb 1997 Cover: 2.95 **NM** value: **Cover or less**
A: Gary Shipman **W:** Gary Shipman; Rhoda Shipman
4 ❑ May 1997 Cover: 2.95 **NM** value: **Cover or less**
A: Gary Shipman **W:** Gary Shipman; Rhoda Shipman
5 ❑ Jun 1997 Cover: 2.95 **NM** value: **Cover or less**
A: Gary Shipman **W:** Gary Shipman; Rhoda Shipman
6 ❑ Jul 1997 Cover: 2.95 **NM** value: **Cover or less**
A: Gary Shipman **W:** Gary Shipman; Rhoda Shipman

PAKKINS' LAND: FORGOTTEN DREAMS — Caliber / Tapestry
1 ❑ Apr 1998 Cover: 2.95 **NM** value: **Cover or less**
A: Gary Shipman **W:** Gary Shipman; Rhoda Shipman
2 ❑ Cover: 2.95 **NM** value: **Cover or less**
A: Gary Shipman **W:** Gary Shipman; Rhoda Shipman
3 ❑ Cover: 2.95 **NM** value: **Cover or less**
A: Gary Shipman **W:** Gary Shipman; Rhoda Shipman
4 ❑ Mar 2000 Cover: 2.95 **NM** value: **Cover or less**
Circ: Diamd. preorders: **1,686**
• published by Image **A:** Gary Shipman **W:** Gary Shipman; Rhoda Shipman

PAKKINS' LAND: QUEST FOR KINGS — Caliber / Tapestry
1 ❑ Aug 1997 Cover: 2.95 **NM** value: **Cover or less**
Quest for Kings **A:** Gary Shipman **W:** Gary Shipman; Rhoda Shipman
1/A ❑ Aug 1997 Cover: 2.95 **NM** value: **Cover or less**
2 ❑ Sep 1997 Cover: 2.95 **NM** value: **Cover or less**
A: Gary Shipman **W:** Gary Shipman; Rhoda Shipman
2/A ❑ Aug 1997 Cover: 2.95 **NM** value: **Cover or less**
alternate cover. **C:** Jeff Smith
3 ❑ Nov 1997 Cover: 2.95 **NM** value: **Cover or less**
A: Gary Shipman **W:** Gary Shipman; Rhoda Shipman
4 ❑ Dec 1997 Cover: 2.95 **NM** value: **Cover or less**
A: Gary Shipman **W:** Gary Shipman; Rhoda Shipman
5 ❑ Jan 1998 Cover: 2.95 **NM** value: **Cover or less**
A: Gary Shipman **W:** Gary Shipman; Rhoda Shipman
6 ❑ Mar 1998 Cover: 2.95 **NM** value: **Cover or less**
A: Gary Shipman **W:** Gary Shipman; Rhoda Shipman
Bk 1❑ Cover: 2.95 **NM** value: **Cover or less**
• Collects Pakkins' Land #1-6 **A:** Gary Shipman **W:** Gary Shipman; Rhoda Shipman

PALATINE, THE — Gryphon Rampant
1 ❑ Cover: 2.50 **NM** value: **Cover or less**
A: Lawrence "Fryphon" Klimecki **W:** Lawrence "Fryphon" Klimecki
2 ❑ Oct 1994 Cover: 2.50 **NM** value: **Cover or less**
The Consort of Perun **A:** Lawrence "Fryphon" Klimecki **W:** Lawrence "Fryphon" Klimecki

PALESTINE — Fantagraphics
1 ❑ b&w Cover: 2.50 **NM** value: **Cover or less**
2 ❑ b&w Cover: 2.50 **NM** value: **Cover or less**
3 ❑ b&w Cover: 2.50 **NM** value: **Cover or less**
4 ❑ b&w Cover: 2.95 **NM** value: **Cover or less**
5 ❑ Cover: 2.50 **NM** value: **Cover or less**
6 ❑ Cover: 2.50 **NM** value: **Cover or less**
7 ❑ Sep 1994 Cover: 2.95 **NM** value: **Cover or less**
9 ❑ Oct 1995, b&w Cover: 2.95 **NM** value: **Cover or less**

PAL-YAT-CHEE — Adhesive
1 ❑ b&w Cover: 2.50 **NM** value: **Cover or less**

PAMELA ANDERSON UNCOVERED — Pop
1 ❑ Cover: 2.95 **NM** value: **Cover or less**
Thinking About Pamela Anderson **A:** Matt Thompson **W:** Ray Dawn Odilon

PANDA KHAN SPECIAL — Abacus
1 ❑ b&w Cover: 3.00 **NM** value: **Cover or less**

PANDEMONIUM — Chaos!
1 ❑ Sep 1998 Cover: 2.95 **NM** value: **Cover or less**
Circ: Diamd. preorders: **16,143**

PANDORA PILL, THE — Acid Rain
1 ❑ Cover: 2.50 **NM** value: **Cover or less**
A: Mark Paniccia **W:** Mark Paniccia

PANIC — E.C.
E.C.'s Mad had been running for more than a year when Panic, edited by Al Feldstein, began. The first issue was banned in Boston because, it was claimed, its version of "The Night before Christmas" showed Santa Claus "in a pagan manner." Classic E.C. artists Jack Davis, Will Elder, Feldstein, Jack Kamen, Joe Orlando, and Wally Wood provided art for the stories which definitely followed in Mad's footsteps, occasionally surpassing their predecessor.

The final issue carried the seal of the Comics Magazine Association of America. — Maggie

1 ❑ Mar 1954 Cover: 0.10 **NM** value: **150.00**
• **CGC:** 4 graded, best 9.6
2 ❑ May 1954 Cover: 0.10 **NM** value: **75.00**
• **CGC:** 3 graded, best 9.4
3 ❑ Jul 1954 Cover: 0.10 **NM** value: **50.00**
• **CGC:** 4 graded, best 9.8
4 ❑ Sep 1954 Cover: 0.10 **NM** value: **50.00**
• **CGC:** 3 graded, best 9.6
5 ❑ Nov 1954 Cover: 0.10 **NM** value: **50.00**
• **CGC:** 3 graded, best 9.6
6 ❑ Jan 1955 Cover: 0.10 **NM** value: **50.00**
• **CGC:** 6 graded, best 9.8
7 ❑ Mar 1955 Cover: 0.10 **NM** value: **50.00**
• **CGC:** 5 graded, best 9.8
8 ❑ May 1955 Cover: 0.10 **NM** value: **50.00**
• **CGC:** 6 graded, best 9.8
9 ❑ Jul 1955 Cover: 0.10 **NM** value: **50.00**
• **CGC:** 5 graded, best 9.0
10 ❑ Sep 1955 Cover: 0.10 **NM** value: **50.00**
• **CGC:** 7 graded, best 9.6
11 ❑ Nov 1955 Cover: 0.10 **NM** value: **50.00**
• **CGC:** 2 graded, best 9.4
12 ❑ Jan 1956 Cover: 0.10 **NM** value: **100.00**
• **CGC:** 5 graded, best 9.2
final issue. • Low distribution

PANIC (RCP) — Gemstone
1 ❑ Mar 1997 Cover: 2.50 **NM** value: **Cover or less**
Circ: Statement: **5,376** Diamd. preorders: **5,203**
• Reprints Panic (EC) #1
2 ❑ Jun 1997 Cover: 2.50 **NM** value: **Cover or less**
Circ: Statement: **5,376** Diamd. preorders: **4,414**
African Scream; The Lady or the Tiger?; Breakfast with the Fershlugginers; Come Back Little Street Car!; • Reprints Panic (EC) #2
3 ❑ Sep 1997 Cover: 2.50 **NM** value: **Cover or less**
Circ: Statement: **5,376** Diamd. preorders: **4,463**
• Reprints Panic (EC) #3
4 ❑ Dec 1997 Cover: 2.50 **NM** value: **Cover or less**
Circ: Diamd. preorders: **4,288**
• Reprints Panic (EC) #4; Has 1997 Statement (filed very early in run); avg total paid circ 5,376
5 ❑ Mar 1998 Cover: 2.50 **NM** value: **Cover or less**
Circ: Diamd. preorders: **3,888**
Tick Dracy; Baseball Jargon; Golf Match!; Footbal Terms!; Basketball!; Spots Before Your Eyes!; You Too Can Hook a Zillionaire! • Reprints Panic (EC) #5 **A:** Joe Orlando; Bill Elder; Wally Wood; Jack Davis **W:** Joe Orlando; Bill Elder; Wally Wood; Jack Davis
6 ❑ Jun 1998 Cover: 2.50 **NM** value: **Cover or less**
Circ: Diamd. preorders: **4,042**
The Phansom; Executive Seat; Comic Strip Advertising Dept.; Popular Mecpanics • Reprints Panic (EC) #6 **A:** Joe Orlando; Bill Elder; Wally Wood; Jack Davis **W:** Joe Orlando; Bill Elder; Wally Wood; Jack Davis
7 ❑ Sep 1998 Cover: 2.50 **NM** value: **Cover or less**
Circ: Diamd. preorders: **3,632**
Mel Padooka; You Axed for It!; Travel Posters; Them There Those • Reprints Panic (EC) #7 **A:** Joe Orlando; Bill Elder; Wally Wood; Jack Davis **W:** Joe Orlando; Bill Elder; Wally Wood; Jack Davis
8 ❑ Dec 1998 Cover: 2.50 **NM** value: **Cover or less**
Circ: Diamd. preorders: **3,464**
Irving Oops; Carmen; Old Under Paints; Gone with the Widow • Reprints Panic (EC) #8 **A:** Joe Orlando; Bill Elder; Wally Wood; Jack Davis **W:** Joe Orlando; Bill Elder; Wally Wood; Jack Davis
9 ❑ Mar 1999 Cover: 2.50 **NM** value: **Cover or less**
Circ: Diamd. preorders: **3,300**
10 ❑ Jun 1999 Cover: 2.50 **NM** value: **Cover or less**
Circ: Diamd. preorders: **3,251**
11 ❑ Sep 1999 Cover: 2.50 **NM** value: **Cover or less**
Circ: Diamd. preorders: **3,100**
12 ❑ Dec 1999 Cover: 2.50 **NM** value: **Cover or less**
Circ: Diamd. preorders: **3,036**
Anl 1❑ Cover: 10.95 **NM** value: **Cover or less**
• Collects issues #1-4
Anl 2❑ Cover: 10.95 **NM** value: **Cover or less**
Tick Dracy; Baseball Jargon; Golf Match!; Footbal Terms!; Basketball!; Spot • Collects issues #5-8 **A:** Joe Orlando; Bill Elder; Wally Wood; Jack Davis **W:** Joe Orlando; Bill Elder; Wally Wood; Jack Davis

PANTERA — Malibu / Rock-It
1 ❑ Aug 1994 Cover: 3.95 **NM** value: **4.00**
• magazine.

PANTHA: HAUNTED PASSION — Harris / Rock-It
1 ❑ Cover: 2.95 **NM** value: **Cover or less**
Circ: Diamd. preorders: **11,076**
Re-Birth; Family Ties **A:** Auraleon **W:** Auraleon

Other grades: Multiply prices above by **1.5 for Mint • 2/3 for Very Fine • 1/3 for Fine • 1/5 for Very Good • 1/8 for Good**

PANTHEON: ANCIENT HISTORY — Lone Star
1 ❑ Aug 1999 Cover: 3.95 **NM** value: **Cover or less**
A: Bobby Diaz **W:** Bill Willingham

PANTHEON (ARCHER) — Archer Books & Games
1 ❑ Oct 1995, b&w Cover: 2.95 **NM** value: **Cover or less**

PANTHEON (LONE STAR) — Lone Star Press
1 ❑ May 1998 Cover: 2.95 **NM** value: **Cover or less**
• **CGC:** 1 graded, best 9.8
📖 Comrades in Arms **A:** Mike Leeke **W:** Bill Willingham
2 ❑ Jul 1998 Cover: 2.95 **NM** value: **Cover or less**
📖 Glory Days **A:** Mike Leeke **W:** Bill Willingham
3 ❑ Sep 1998 Cover: 2.95 **NM** value: **Cover or less**
📖 Welcome to the Machine **A:** Mike Leeke **W:** Bill Willingham
4 ❑ Jan 1999 Cover: 2.95 **NM** value: **Cover or less**
📖 The Final Cut **A:** Mike Leeke **W:** Bill Willingham
5 ❑ Jul 1999 Cover: 2.95 **NM** value: **Cover or less**
Circ: Diamd. preorders: **1,696**
📖 Under Pressure **A:** Brian Hagan; Mike Leeke **W:** Bill Willingham
6 ❑ Aug 1999 Cover: 2.95 **NM** value: **Cover or less**
📖 Who Knows **A:** Brian Hagan; Mike Leeke; Derec Aucoin **W:** Bill Willingham

PAPER CINEMA — Grey Blossom Sequentials
1 ❑ 1998
2 ❑ 1998
3 ❑ Dec 1998 Cover: 3.55 **NM** value: **Cover or less**

PAPER DOLLS FROM THE CALIFORNIA GIRLS — Eclipse
1 ❑ Cover: 5.95 **NM** value: **Cover or less**
• paper dolls

PAPER TALES — CLG Comics
1 ❑ Sum 1993, b&w Cover: 2.50 **NM** value: **Cover or less**
2 ❑ Sum 1994, b&w Cover: 2.50 **NM** value: **Cover or less**

PARA-COPS — Excel
1 ❑ Cover: 2.95 **NM** value: **Cover or less**
A: Mark McElligott **W:** Fred Archer III; Marc McElligott

PARADAX — Vortex
1 ❑ Cover: 1.75 **NM** value: **Cover or less**
Circ: CapCity orders: **2,650**
📖 Paradax the Insane People; Mirkin the Mystic: The Importance of Being Mirkin; Roaring's Rantings: Rudcliff & Williams in Blithe Horizons; Ruff and Reddy **A:** Brendan McCarthy; Tony Riot **W:** Pete Miligan
2 ❑ Aug 1987 Cover: 1.75 **NM** value: **Cover or less**
Circ: CapCity orders: **1,475**

PARADIGM — Gauntlet
1 ❑ Cover: 2.95 **NM** value: **Cover or less**
Circ: CapCity orders: **7,900**
📖 Starts with a Bang **A:** Georges Jeanty **W:** Brent Carpenter; Reginald Chaney

PARADISE X: THE HERALDS — Marvel
1 ❑ Dec 2001 Cover: 3.50 **NM** value: **Cover or less**
Circ: Diamd. preorders: **46,831** • **CGC:** 1 graded, best 9.8
2 ❑ Jan 2002 Cover: 3.50 **NM** value: **Cover or less**
Circ: Diamd. preorders: **43,964**
3 ❑ Feb 2002 Cover: 3.50 **NM** value: **Cover or less**
Circ: Diamd. preorders: **41,774**

PARADOX PROJECT: GENESIS — Paradox Project
1 ❑ Dec 1998, b&w Cover: 2.95 **NM** value: **Cover or less**

PARAGON: DARK APOCALYPSE — AC
1 ❑ Cover: 2.95 **NM** value: **Cover or less**
Circ: CapCity orders: **2,675**
2 ❑ Cover: 2.95 **NM** value: **Cover or less**
3 ❑ Cover: 2.95 **NM** value: **Cover or less**
4 ❑ Cover: 2.95 **NM** value: **Cover or less**

PARALLAX: EMERALD NIGHT — DC
1 ❑ Nov 1996 Cover: 2.95 **NM** value: **Cover or less**
Circ: Diamd. preorders: **71,405**
📖 The Final Night • Final Night **A:** Mike McKone **W:** Ron Marz ★ Death of Cyborg Superman.

PARAMOUNT ANIMATED COMICS — Harvey
Published by Harvey from 1953 to 1956, this short-lived series began as Harvey Hits #60 and #62 before starting as its own title with #3.

Featuring the comic-book adventures of several animated characters put on film by Paramount, the early issues featured Katnip the cat, Herman the Mouse, and Baby Huey, the Baby Giant, an overgrown duckling clad in a diaper and bonnet with a baby's outlook on life but the strength of an army. The series was the first appearance of Huey in a Harvey title and he quickly took over the series before beginning his own title in the late 1950s. — Brent

3 ❑ Jun 1953 Cover: 0.10 **NM** value: **150.00**
• **CGC:** 1 graded, best 7.0
4 ❑ Aug 1953 Cover: 0.10 **NM** value: **125.00**
5 ❑ Oct 1953 Cover: 0.10 **NM** value: **100.00**
6 ❑ Dec 1953 Cover: 0.10 **NM** value: **100.00**
7 ❑ Feb 1954 Cover: 0.10 **NM** value: **100.00**
8 ❑ Apr 1954 Cover: 0.10 **NM** value: **75.00**
9 ❑ Jun 1954 Cover: 0.10 **NM** value: **75.00**
10 ❑ Aug 1954 Cover: 0.10 **NM** value: **75.00**
11 ❑ Oct 1954 Cover: 0.10 **NM** value: **75.00**
12 ❑ Dec 1954 Cover: 0.10 **NM** value: **75.00**
13 ❑ Feb 1955 Cover: 0.10 **NM** value: **50.00**
14 ❑ Apr 1955 Cover: 0.10 **NM** value: **50.00**
15 ❑ Jun 1955 Cover: 0.10 **NM** value: **50.00**
16 ❑ Aug 1955 Cover: 0.10 **NM** value: **50.00**
17 ❑ Oct 1955 Cover: 0.10 **NM** value: **50.00**
18 ❑ Dec 1955 Cover: 0.10 **NM** value: **50.00**
19 ❑ Feb 1956 Cover: 0.10 **NM** value: **50.00**
20 ❑ Apr 1956 Cover: 0.10 **NM** value: **50.00**
21 ❑ Jun 1956 Cover: 0.10 **NM** value: **50.00**
22 ❑ Aug 1956 Cover: 0.10 **NM** value: **50.00**

PARANOIA (ADVENTURE) — Adventure
1 ❑ Oct 1991, full color Cover: 2.95 **NM** value: **Cover or less**
Circ: CapCity orders: **5,550**
2 ❑ Dec 1991, full color Cover: 2.95 **NM** value: **Cover or less**
Circ: CapCity orders: **3,150**
A: Kipper **W:** Paul O'Connor
3 ❑ Feb 1992, full color Cover: 2.95 **NM** value: **Cover or less**
Circ: CapCity orders: **3,140**
4 ❑ Apr 1992, full color Cover: 2.95 **NM** value: **Cover or less**
Circ: CapCity orders: **2,880**
5 ❑ Jun 1992, full color Cover: 2.95 **NM** value: **Cover or less**
6 ❑ Aug 1992, full color Cover: 2.95 **NM** value: **Cover or less**
A: Hector **W:** Paul O'Connor

PARANOIA (CO. & SONS) — Co. & Sons
1 ❑ Cover: 0.50 **NM** value: **4.00**
📖 Tales from the Ogre's Tower; The Hunter; Passengers; Love Story; Sea Hag **A:** Larry Todd; Michael Smith; Patricia Moodian **W:** Charles Dallas; Larry Todd; Michael Smith; Patricia Moodian; Damon Knight; S. Goodyear

PARAPHERNALIA — Graphitti
1 ❑ Cover: 2.00 **NM** value: **Cover or less**
• Ordering Catalogue

PARASYTE — Mixx
Bk 1❑ Cover: 11.95 **NM** value: **Cover or less**

PARA TROOP — Comics Conspiracy
0 ❑ Cover: 3.95 **NM** value: **Cover or less**
1 ❑ Cover: 2.95 **NM** value: **Cover or less**
📖 So Much Left Unsaid **A:** Jay Naylor **W:** Doug Miers
2 ❑ Cover: 2.95 **NM** value: **Cover or less**
3 ❑ Oct 1998 Cover: 2.95 **NM** value: **Cover or less**
4 ❑ Dec 1998 Cover: 2.95 **NM** value: **Cover or less**
5 ❑ Feb 1999 Cover: 2.95 **NM** value: **Cover or less**
Ash 1❑ Cover: 2.95 **NM** value: **Cover or less**
• ashcan edition.

PARDNERS — Cottonwood Graphics
1 ❑ b&w Cover: 7.95 **NM** value: **Cover or less**
A: Stan Lynde **C:** Stan Lynde
2 ❑ b&w Cover: 7.95 **NM** value: **Cover or less**
A: Stan Lynde **C:** Stan Lynde

PARIS THE MAN OF PLASTER — Harrier
1 ❑ May 1987 Cover: 1.95 **NM** value: **Cover or less**
📖 Paris the Man of Plaster; Temptation; Mr. Day and Mr. Night **A:** Glenn Dakin; Phil Elliott **W:** Glenn Dakin
2 ❑ 1987 Cover: 1.95 **NM** value: **Cover or less**
3 ❑ 1987 Cover: 1.95 **NM** value: **Cover or less**
4 ❑ 1987 Cover: 1.95 **NM** value: **Cover or less**
5 ❑ 1987 Cover: 1.95 **NM** value: **Cover or less**
6 ❑ 1987 Cover: 1.95 **NM** value: **Cover or less**

PARO-DEE — Parody
1 ❑ b&w Cover: 2.50 **NM** value: **Cover or less**
📖 The Conscientious ø-Men: Sheep of Fools!; Sam Sundae; The Moral of the Story; We Saw the Thing From Heck!; The Flim -Flam Artist; The Truest Kind of Love!; ...With Liberty and Justice for All; The Greatest Super-Hero of All **A:** Kathleen Webb; Sandy Carruthers; Kerry Gammill; Frank Fosco; Ashton Brown; Jr.; Kevin Frank; Mark Brayer **W:** Kathleen Webb; Kevin Frank; Brian Bunink; Jose Ponce; Nate Butler; Rob Bradford; Vic Emert

PARODY PRESS ANNUAL SWIMSUIT SPECIAL '93 — Parody Press
1 ❑ Aug 1993 Cover: 2.50 **NM** value: **Cover or less**
A: Bill Maus **W:** Bill Maus

PAROLE BREAKERS — Avon
1 ❑ ca. 1951 Cover: 0.10 **NM** value: **300.00**
• **CGC:** 1 graded, best 7.5
2 ❑ ca. 1952 Cover: 0.10 **NM** value: **200.00**
• **CGC:** 1 graded, best 8.0
3 ❑ ca. 1952 Cover: 0.10 **NM** value: **200.00**

PARTICLE DREAMS — Fantagraphics
1 ❑ Oct 1986 Cover: 2.25 **NM** value: **Cover or less**
2 ❑ Jan 1987 Cover: 2.25 **NM** value: **Cover or less**
3 ❑ Apr 1987 Cover: 2.25 **NM** value: **Cover or less**
📖 This Fear of Gods; Make-Up Paper; Sacred Ground; First Neighbor **A:** Matt Howarth; W.E. Rittenhouse **W:** Matt Howarth; W.E. Rittenhouse
4 ❑ Jun 1987 Cover: 2.25 **NM** value: **Cover or less**
5 ❑ 1987 Cover: 2.25 **NM** value: **Cover or less**
6 ❑ 1987 Cover: 2.25 **NM** value: **Cover or less**

PARTNERS IN PANDEMONIUM — Caliber
1 ❑ b&w Cover: 2.50 **NM** value: **Cover or less**
2 ❑ b&w Cover: 2.50 **NM** value: **Cover or less**
3 ❑ b&w Cover: 2.50 **NM** value: **Cover or less**

PARTRIDGE FAMILY, THE — Charlton
One of the "grooviest" comic-book titles ever created, The Partridge Family is a must-have for fans of the make-believe band and 1970s nostalgists alike. Each issue has a new adventure starring the members of America's favorite singing family (even though the family in question was created by a television casting director). Their show ran from 1970 to 1974, with Shirley Jones (1934-) as a widowed mom of a family of singers.

Unusual for comics of the time, The Partridge Family typically has only a few panels per page. The extra room is used for lots and lots of starry-eyed close-ups of each of the Partridge family members, especially heart-throbs David Cassidy (1950-) and Susan Dey (1952-). Issues also reprinted the lyrics to Partridge Family songs, so that fans could sing along with their records or 8-track tapes.

1 ❑ Mar 1971 Cover: 0.15 **NM** value: **20.00**
2 ❑ May 1971 Cover: 0.15 **NM** value: **10.00**
3 ❑ Jul 1971 Cover: 0.15 **NM** value: **9.00**
4 ❑ Sep 1971 Cover: 0.15 **NM** value: **9.00**
5 ❑ Sum 1971 Cover: 0.25 **NM** value: **12.00**
• Giant-size.
6 ❑ ca. 1971 Cover: 0.20 **NM** value: **7.00**
7 ❑ Feb 1972 Cover: 0.20 **NM** value: **7.00**
8 ❑ Mar 1972 Cover: 0.20 **NM** value: **7.00**
9 ❑ Apr 1972 Cover: 0.20 **NM** value: **7.00**
10 ❑ May 1972 Cover: 0.20 **NM** value: **7.00**
11 ❑ Aug 1972 Cover: 0.20 **NM** value: **7.00**
12 ❑ Sep 1972 Cover: 0.20 **NM** value: **7.00**
13 ❑ Nov 1972 Cover: 0.20 **NM** value: **7.00**
14 ❑ Dec 1973 Cover: 0.20 **NM** value: **7.00**
15 ❑ Jan 1973 Cover: 0.20 **NM** value: **6.00**
16 ❑ ca. 1973 Cover: 0.20 **NM** value: **6.00**
17 ❑ ca. 1973 Cover: 0.20 **NM** value: **6.00**
18 ❑ ca. 1973 Cover: 0.20 **NM** value: **6.00**
19 ❑ Jul 1973 Cover: 0.20 **NM** value: **6.00**
20 ❑ Sep 1973 Cover: 0.20 **NM** value: **6.00**
21 ❑ ca. 1973 Cover: 0.20 **NM** value: **6.00**
📖 The Kid Who Knew Too Much; Yankee Doodle Danny final issue. **A:** Don Sherwood **W:** Don Sherwood

PARTS OF A HOLE — Caliber
1 ❑ b&w Cover: 2.50 **NM** value: **Cover or less**
No issue number.

PARTS UNKNOWN — Eclipse
1 ❑ Aug 1995, b&w Cover: 2.50 **NM** value: **Cover or less**
Circ: CapCity orders: **4,475**
2 ❑ Mar 1995, b&w Cover: 2.50 **NM** value: **Cover or less**
3 ❑ Jun 1995, b&w Cover: 2.50 **NM** value: **Cover or less**
4 ❑ Oct 1995, b&w Cover: 2.50 **NM** value: **Cover or less**

PARTS UNKNOWN: DARK INTENTIONS — Knight Press
0 ❑ Aug 1995 Cover: 2.95 **NM** value: **Cover or less**
A: Brad Gorby **W:** Beau Smith
1 ❑ Mar 1995 Cover: 2.95 **NM** value: **Cover or less**
A: Brad Gorby **W:** Beau Smith
2 ❑ Jun 1995 Cover: 2.95 **NM** value: **Cover or less**
A: Brad Gorby **W:** Beau Smith
3 ❑ Oct 1995 Cover: 2.95 **NM** value: **Cover or less**
A: Brad Gorby **W:** Beau Smith
4 ❑ 1995 Cover: 2.95 **NM** value: **Cover or less**
A: Brad Gorby **W:** Beau Smith

PARTS UNKNOWN: HOSTILE TAKEOVER — Image
1 ❑ Jun 2000 Cover: 2.95 **NM** value: **Cover or less**
Circ: Diamd. preorders: **3,521**
A: Brad Gorby **W:** Beau Smith
1/Ash❑Jun 2000 Cover: 4.95 **NM** value: **Cover or less**
• Preview edition. **A:** Brad Gorby **W:** Beau Smith
2 ❑ Jul 2000 Cover: 2.95 **NM** value: **Cover or less**
Circ: Diamd. preorders: **2,842**
A: Brad Gorby **W:** Beau Smith
2/Ash❑Jul 2000 Cover: 4.95 **NM** value: **Cover or less**
• Preview edition. **A:** Brad Gorby **W:** Beau Smith
3 ❑ Aug 2000 Cover: 2.95 **NM** value: **Cover or less**
Circ: Diamd. preorders: **2,263**
A: Brad Gorby **W:** Beau Smith
3/Ash❑Aug 2000 Cover: 4.95 **NM** value: **Cover or less**
• Preview edition. **A:** Brad Gorby **W:** Beau Smith
4 ❑ Sep 2000 Cover: 2.95 **NM** value: **Cover or less**
Circ: Diamd. preorders: **2,436**
A: Brad Gorby **W:** Beau Smith
4/Ash❑Sep 2000 Cover: 4.95 **NM** value: **Cover or less**
• Preview edition. **A:** Brad Gorby **W:** Beau Smith

PARTS UNKNOWN II: THE NEXT INVASION — Eclipse
1 ❑ Dec 1993, b&w Cover: 2.95 **NM** value: **Cover or less**
Circ: CapCity orders: **2,100**

PASSOVER — Maximum
1 ❑ Dec 1996 Cover: 2.99 **NM** value: **Cover or less**
Circ: Diamd. preorders: **16,273**
📖 Passover **A:** Eric Cannon; Livesay; Sean Parsons **W:** Jeff Rebner; Robert Napton; Matt Hawkins

CGC-graded: Multiply prices above by **33 for 9.9 M • 16 for 9.8 NM/M • 7 for 9.6 NM+ • 5 for 9.4 NM • 2.5 for 9.2 NM- • 1.5 for 9.0 VF/NM**

PAT BOONE — DC

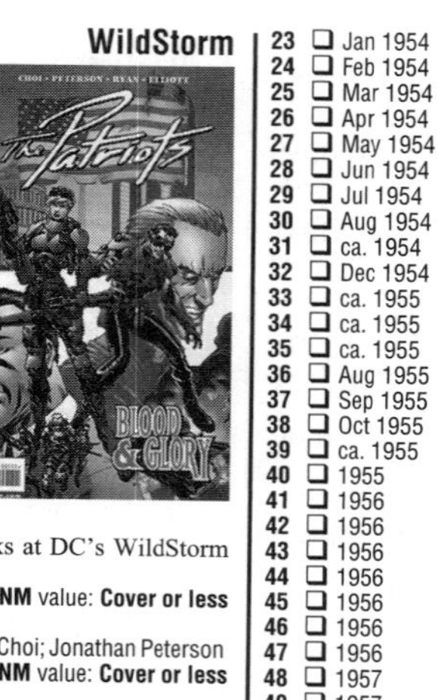

Pat Boone (1934-) was a regular singer on Arthur Godfrey's TV show in 1949 and had become a teen idol even before he began starring in movies of the day. His comic-book series was an oddity, looking more like a teen fan magazine than a comic book. With photo covers and no Comics Code seal, the series clearly aimed for that fan audience. Covers display, in addition to color photos of Boone, black-and-white photos of other popular singers of the day (Jimmie Rodgers, "Kookie" Byrnes, Fabian, Connie Francis, etc.), and regular features include Fan Clubs U.S.A., Record Round-up, TV Topics, and cartoons. And, of course, there are features on Boone himself, such as a preview of his latest picture (Journey to the Center of the Earth). — Maggie

1 ❑ Sep 1959 Cover: 0.10 **NM** value: **200.00**
• **CGC:** 2 graded, best 8.5
2 ❑ Nov 1959 Cover: 0.10 **NM** value: **150.00**
• **CGC:** 1 graded, best 7.0
3 ❑ Jan 1960 Cover: 0.10 **NM** value: **150.00**
• **CGC:** 2 graded, best 9.0
4 ❑ Mar 1960 Cover: 0.10 **NM** value: **150.00**
5 ❑ May 1960 Cover: 0.10 **NM** value: **150.00**

PATCHES — Rural Home / Orbit

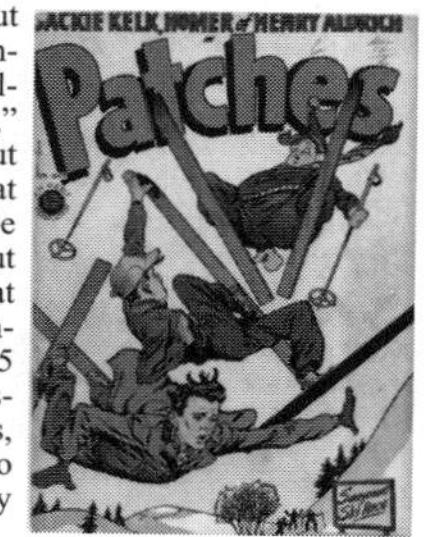

Looking for an oddball Boy Scout item that's difficult to hunt for on-line? Try Patches. What are good filter terms? "Patches," "Boy Scout," and "comic book" come to mind, but even taken as a unit, the hits that come up will almost invariably be one form or another of a Boy Scout patch, not the comic-book title that ran from 1945 to 1947. And Ella Cinders (a comic strip that ran from 1925 to 1961) eventually married a mysterious adventurer named Patches, but this comic book has nothing to do with him, either. This is a tricky title to collect.

The comic book featured the slim, dark-haired boy Patches and his hefty pal Tubby and promoted the Boy Scouts of America. To top off the oddities, many issues featured celebrities of the day, some of them major (Danny Kaye, Hopalong Cassidy), some of them sidekick types (Jackie Kelk, Smiley Burnette, Senator Claghorn). Good luck in tracking this one down. — Maggie

1 ❑ Mar 1945 Cover: 0.10 **NM** value: **300.00**
2 ❑ ca. 1946 Cover: 0.10 **NM** value: **125.00**
3 ❑ Jul 1946 Cover: 0.10 **NM** value: **100.00**
4 ❑ Sep 1946 Cover: 0.10 **NM** value: **100.00**
5 ❑ Nov 1946 Cover: 0.10 **NM** value: **100.00**
6 ❑ Feb 1947 Cover: 0.10 **NM** value: **100.00**
7 ❑ Apr 1947 Cover: 0.10 **NM** value: **100.00**
8 ❑ Jun 1947 Cover: 0.10 **NM** value: **75.00**
9 ❑ Aug 1947 Cover: 0.10 **NM** value: **75.00**
10 ❑ Oct 1947 Cover: 0.10 **NM** value: **75.00**
11 ❑ Dec 1947 Cover: 0.10 **NM** value: **75.00**

PATER CONTRARIUS — Robot

1 ❑ Cover: 2.00 **NM** value: **Cover or less**
📖 A Lunchtime Story

PATHWAYS TO FANTASY — Pacific

1 ❑ Jul 1984 Cover: 1.50 **NM** value: **2.00**
• **CGC:** 1 graded, best 9.0
📖 Stalking **A:** John Bolton; Barry Windsor-Smith; Jeff Jones; April Campbell **W:** Bruce Jones

PATRICK RABBIT — Fragments West

1 ❑ Sum 1988 Cover: 2.00 **NM** value: **Cover or less**
2 ❑ Cover: 2.00 **NM** value: **Cover or less**
3 ❑ Cover: 2.00 **NM** value: **Cover or less**
4 ❑ Cover: 2.00 **NM** value: **Cover or less**
5 ❑ Cover: 2.00 **NM** value: **Cover or less**
6 ❑ Cover: 2.00 **NM** value: **Cover or less**
7 ❑ Cover: 2.00 **NM** value: **Cover or less**

PATRICK STEWART — Celebrity

1 ❑ Cover: 2.95 **NM** value: **Cover or less**

PATRICK STEWART VS. WILLIAM SHATNER — Celebrity

1 ❑ b&w Cover: 5.95 **NM** value: **Cover or less**
Circ: CapCity orders: **2,795**

Capital City orders are the actual sales of comic books by Capital City Distribution, once one of the largest U.S. sellers of comics to comics shops. Capital City's share of comics shop sales, while not known exactly, increases from around 10-20% in the mid-1980s to 30-35% in the mid-1990s. Capital City's share of comic books sold on newsstands (most Marvels and DCs) will be less.

PATRIOTS, THE — WildStorm

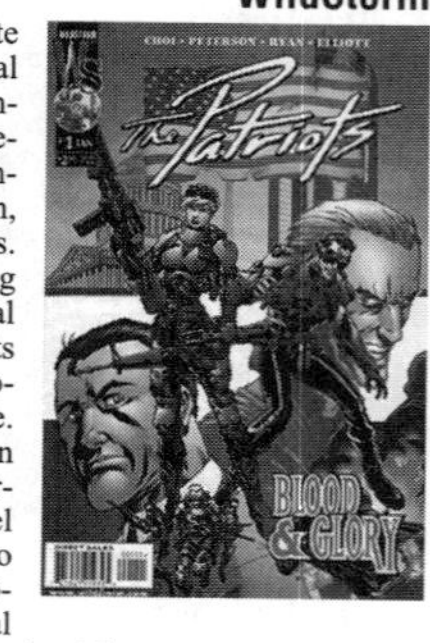

The WildStorm universe's elite force of super-agents, International Operations, needs to do housecleaning, so they get pretty-boy FBI recruit Zach Donovan and his tough-as-nails partner, Rocky Boorman, to wrap up their unsolved cases. Since IO's purpose is pretty dealing with paranormal threats to national security, it's dollars to doughnuts that Donovan and Boorman are going to be up to their ears in trouble. This series from writers Brandon Choi (Gen13) and Jonathan Peterson (Strikeback!) and artist Michael Ryan (Grifter) is like a John Woo flick: action on every page! Explosions! Chases! And, hey, political intrigue, too! A fun package from the folks at DC's WildStorm imprint.

1 ❑ Jan 2000 Cover: 2.50 **NM** value: **Cover or less**
Circ: Diamd. preorders: **17,587**
📖 Induction **A:** Michael Ryan **W:** Brandon Choi; Jonathan Peterson
2 ❑ Feb 2000 Cover: 2.50 **NM** value: **Cover or less**
Circ: Diamd. preorders: **14,105**
A: Michael Ryan **W:** Brandon Choi; Jonathan Peterson
3 ❑ Mar 2000 Cover: 2.50 **NM** value: **Cover or less**
Circ: Diamd. preorders: **10,807**
A: Michael Ryan **W:** Brandon Choi; Jonathan Peterson
4 ❑ Apr 2000 Cover: 2.50 **NM** value: **Cover or less**
Circ: Diamd. preorders: **8,174**
📖 Rebirth **A:** Michael Ryan **W:** Brandon Choi; Jonathan Peterson
5 ❑ May 2000 Cover: 2.50 **NM** value: **Cover or less**
Circ: Diamd. preorders: **7,218**
📖 Rocky Road **A:** Michael Ryan **W:** Brandon Choi; Jonathan Peterson
6 ❑ Jun 2000 Cover: 2.50 **NM** value: **Cover or less**
Circ: Diamd. preorders: **6,633**
A: Michael Ryan
7 ❑ Jul 2000 Cover: 2.50 **NM** value: **Cover or less**
Circ: Diamd. preorders: **6,241**
A: Michael Ryan
8 ❑ Aug 2000 Cover: 2.50 **NM** value: **Cover or less**
Circ: Diamd. preorders: **6,011**
A: Michael Ryan
9 ❑ Sep 2000 Cover: 2.50 **NM** value: **Cover or less**
Circ: Diamd. preorders: **5,641**
📖 Judgement Day; Judgement Day, Part 1 **A:** Michael Ryan **W:** Jonathan Peterson
10 ❑ Oct 2000 Cover: 2.50 **NM** value: **Cover or less**
Circ: Diamd. preorders: **5,117**
📖 Judgement Day, Part 2 **A:** Michael Ryan **W:** Jonathan Peterson

PAT SAVAGE: THE WOMAN OF BRONZE — Millennium

1 ❑ Oct 1992 Cover: 2.50 **NM** value: **Cover or less**
Circ: CapCity orders: **9,475**
No issue number. 📖 Family Blood

PATSY AND HEDY — Marvel

Patsy Walker and her rival Hedy Wolfe are the stars of this "Good Girl Art" series. Running throughout the 1950s and '60s, it features the two in a more-or-less endless catfight, disagreeing on virtually everything. Nevertheless, the two are friends deep down. Sort of.

One of the more unusual features of this series is the non-stop outfit and hairdo changes that all its characters seem to go through. This comes from the title's practice (taken from Bill Woggon's pioneering work on Katy Keene) of letting readers submit their own ideas for dresses and hair styles, giving the readers credit when they were used (e.g., "Patsy's a Park Avenue pinup in her perky suit by: Inez Colon, N.Y.C., N.Y.").

When her carefree young adult days were over, Patsy Walker will one day become the super-hero known as Hellcat, one of The Defenders.

1 ❑ Feb 1952 Cover: 0.10 **NM** value: **125.00**
2 ❑ Apr 1952 Cover: 0.10 **NM** value: **65.00**
3 ❑ May 1952 Cover: 0.10 **NM** value: **45.00**
4 ❑ Jun 1952 Cover: 0.10 **NM** value: **45.00**
5 ❑ Jul 1952 Cover: 0.10 **NM** value: **45.00**
6 ❑ Aug 1952 Cover: 0.10 **NM** value: **45.00**
7 ❑ Sep 1952 Cover: 0.10 **NM** value: **45.00**
8 ❑ Oct 1952 Cover: 0.10 **NM** value: **45.00**
9 ❑ Nov 1952 Cover: 0.10 **NM** value: **45.00**
10 ❑ Dec 1952 Cover: 0.10 **NM** value: **45.00**
11 ❑ Jan 1953 Cover: 0.10 **NM** value: **30.00**
12 ❑ Feb 1953 Cover: 0.10 **NM** value: **30.00**
13 ❑ Mar 1953 Cover: 0.10 **NM** value: **30.00**
14 ❑ Apr 1953 Cover: 0.10 **NM** value: **30.00**
15 ❑ May 1953 Cover: 0.10 **NM** value: **30.00**
16 ❑ Jun 1953 Cover: 0.10 **NM** value: **30.00**
17 ❑ Jul 1953 Cover: 0.10 **NM** value: **30.00**
18 ❑ Aug 1953 Cover: 0.10 **NM** value: **30.00**
19 ❑ Sep 1953 Cover: 0.10 **NM** value: **30.00**
20 ❑ Oct 1953 Cover: 0.10 **NM** value: **30.00**
21 ❑ Nov 1953 Cover: 0.10 **NM** value: **24.00**
22 ❑ Dec 1953 Cover: 0.10 **NM** value: **24.00**
23 ❑ Jan 1954 Cover: 0.10 **NM** value: **24.00**
24 ❑ Feb 1954 Cover: 0.10 **NM** value: **24.00**
25 ❑ Mar 1954 Cover: 0.10 **NM** value: **24.00**
26 ❑ Apr 1954 Cover: 0.10 **NM** value: **24.00**
27 ❑ May 1954 Cover: 0.10 **NM** value: **24.00**
28 ❑ Jun 1954 Cover: 0.10 **NM** value: **24.00**
29 ❑ Jul 1954 Cover: 0.10 **NM** value: **24.00**
30 ❑ Aug 1954 Cover: 0.10 **NM** value: **24.00**
31 ❑ ca. 1954 Cover: 0.10 **NM** value: **22.00**
32 ❑ Dec 1954 Cover: 0.10 **NM** value: **22.00**
33 ❑ ca. 1955 Cover: 0.10 **NM** value: **22.00**
34 ❑ ca. 1955 Cover: 0.10 **NM** value: **22.00**
35 ❑ ca. 1955 Cover: 0.10 **NM** value: **22.00**
36 ❑ Aug 1955 Cover: 0.10 **NM** value: **22.00**
37 ❑ Sep 1955 Cover: 0.10 **NM** value: **22.00**
38 ❑ Oct 1955 Cover: 0.10 **NM** value: **22.00**
39 ❑ ca. 1955 Cover: 0.10 **NM** value: **22.00**
40 ❑ 1955 Cover: 0.10 **NM** value: **22.00**
41 ❑ 1956 Cover: 0.10 **NM** value: **22.00**
42 ❑ 1956 Cover: 0.10 **NM** value: **22.00**
43 ❑ 1956 Cover: 0.10 **NM** value: **22.00**
44 ❑ 1956 Cover: 0.10 **NM** value: **22.00**
45 ❑ 1956 Cover: 0.10 **NM** value: **22.00**
46 ❑ 1956 Cover: 0.10 **NM** value: **22.00**
47 ❑ 1956 Cover: 0.10 **NM** value: **22.00**
48 ❑ 1957 Cover: 0.10 **NM** value: **22.00**
49 ❑ 1957 Cover: 0.10 **NM** value: **22.00**
50 ❑ 1957 Cover: 0.10 **NM** value: **22.00**
51 ❑ 1957 Cover: 0.10 **NM** value: **14.00**
52 ❑ 1957 Cover: 0.10 **NM** value: **14.00**
53 ❑ 1957 Cover: 0.10 **NM** value: **14.00**
54 ❑ 1957 Cover: 0.10 **NM** value: **14.00**
55 ❑ 1957 Cover: 0.10 **NM** value: **14.00**
56 ❑ Feb 1958 Cover: 0.10 **NM** value: **14.00**
57 ❑ Apr 1958 Cover: 0.10 **NM** value: **14.00**
58 ❑ Jun 1958 Cover: 0.10 **NM** value: **14.00**
59 ❑ Aug 1958 Cover: 0.10 **NM** value: **14.00**
60 ❑ Oct 1958 Cover: 0.10 **NM** value: **14.00**
61 ❑ Dec 1958 Cover: 0.10 **NM** value: **10.00**
62 ❑ Feb 1959 Cover: 0.10 **NM** value: **10.00**
63 ❑ Apr 1959 Cover: 0.10 **NM** value: **10.00**
64 ❑ Jun 1959 Cover: 0.10 **NM** value: **10.00**
65 ❑ Aug 1959 Cover: 0.10 **NM** value: **10.00**
66 ❑ Oct 1959 Cover: 0.10 **NM** value: **10.00**
67 ❑ Dec 1959 Cover: 0.10 **NM** value: **10.00**
68 ❑ Feb 1960 Cover: 0.10 **NM** value: **10.00**
69 ❑ Apr 1960 Cover: 0.10 **NM** value: **10.00**
70 ❑ Jun 1960 Cover: 0.10 **NM** value: **10.00**
71 ❑ Aug 1960 Cover: 0.10 **NM** value: **10.00**
72 ❑ Oct 1960 Cover: 0.10 **NM** value: **10.00**
73 ❑ Dec 1960 Cover: 0.10 **NM** value: **10.00**
74 ❑ Feb 1961 Cover: 0.10 **NM** value: **10.00**
75 ❑ Apr 1961 Cover: 0.10 **NM** value: **10.00**
76 ❑ Jun 1961 Cover: 0.10 **NM** value: **10.00**
77 ❑ Aug 1961 Cover: 0.10 **NM** value: **10.00**
78 ❑ Oct 1961 Cover: 0.10 **NM** value: **10.00**
79 ❑ Dec 1961 Cover: 0.10 **NM** value: **10.00**
80 ❑ Feb 1962 Cover: 0.12 **NM** value: **10.00**
Circ: Statement: **139,855**
81 ❑ Apr 1962 Cover: 0.12 **NM** value: **10.00**
Circ: Statement: **139,855**
82 ❑ Jun 1962 Cover: 0.12 **NM** value: **10.00**
Circ: Statement: **139,855**
83 ❑ Aug 1962 Cover: 0.12 **NM** value: **10.00**
Circ: Statement: **139,855**
84 ❑ Oct 1962 Cover: 0.12 **NM** value: **10.00**
Circ: Statement: **139,855**
85 ❑ Dec 1962 Cover: 0.12 **NM** value: **10.00**
Circ: Statement: **139,855**
86 ❑ Feb 1963 Cover: 0.12 **NM** value: **10.00**
87 ❑ Apr 1963 Cover: 0.12 **NM** value: **10.00**
• Has 1962 Statement; avg total paid circ 139,855
88 ❑ Jun 1963 Cover: 0.12 **NM** value: **10.00**
89 ❑ Aug 1963 Cover: 0.12 **NM** value: **10.00**
90 ❑ Oct 1963 Cover: 0.12 **NM** value: **10.00**
91 ❑ Dec 1963 Cover: 0.12 **NM** value: **9.00**
92 ❑ Feb 1964 Cover: 0.12 **NM** value: **9.00**
93 ❑ Apr 1964 Cover: 0.12 **NM** value: **9.00**
94 ❑ Jun 1964 Cover: 0.12 **NM** value: **9.00**
95 ❑ Aug 1964 Cover: 0.12 **NM** value: **9.00**
96 ❑ Oct 1964 Cover: 0.12 **NM** value: **9.00**
97 ❑ Dec 1964 Cover: 0.12 **NM** value: **9.00**
98 ❑ Feb 1965 Cover: 0.12 **NM** value: **9.00**
99 ❑ Apr 1965 Cover: 0.12 **NM** value: **9.00**
100 ❑ Jun 1965 Cover: 0.12 **NM** value: **9.00**
101 ❑ Aug 1965 Cover: 0.12 **NM** value: **9.00**
102 ❑ Oct 1965 Cover: 0.12 **NM** value: **9.00**
103 ❑ Dec 1965 Cover: 0.12 **NM** value: **9.00**
104 ❑ Feb 1966 Cover: 0.12 **NM** value: **9.00**
105 ❑ Apr 1966 Cover: 0.12 **NM** value: **9.00**
106 ❑ Jun 1966 Cover: 0.12 **NM** value: **9.00**
107 ❑ Aug 1966 Cover: 0.12 **NM** value: **9.00**
108 ❑ Oct 1966 Cover: 0.12 **NM** value: **9.00**
109 ❑ Dec 1966 Cover: 0.12 **NM** value: **9.00**
110 ❑ Feb 1967 Cover: 0.12 **NM** value: **9.00**
final issue.
Anl 1 ❑ ca. 1963 Cover: 0.15 **NM** value: **50.00**

PATSY & HER PALS — Atlas

1 ❑ May 1953 Cover: 0.10 **NM** value: **125.00**
2 ❑ Jul 1953 Cover: 0.10 **NM** value: **75.00**
3 ❑ Sep 1953 Cover: 0.10 **NM** value: **75.00**
4 ❑ Nov 1953 Cover: 0.10 **NM** value: **75.00**
5 ❑ Jan 1954 Cover: 0.10 **NM** value: **60.00**
6 ❑ Mar 1954 Cover: 0.10 **NM** value: **60.00**
7 ❑ May 1954 Cover: 0.10 **NM** value: **60.00**
8 ❑ Jul 1954 Cover: 0.10 **NM** value: **60.00**

Other grades: Multiply prices above by **1.5 for Mint • 2/3 for Very Fine • 1/3 for Fine • 1/5 for Very Good • 1/8 for Good**

9 ❑ 1954 Cover: 0.10 **NM** value: **60.00**
10 ❑ Cover: 0.10 **NM** value: **55.00**
11 ❑ 1955 Cover: 0.10 **NM** value: **55.00**
12 ❑ 1955 Cover: 0.10 **NM** value: **55.00**
13 ❑ 1955 Cover: 0.10 **NM** value: **55.00**
14 ❑ 1955 Cover: 0.10 **NM** value: **55.00**
15 ❑ 1955 Cover: 0.10 **NM** value: **55.00**
16 ❑ Cover: 0.10 **NM** value: **50.00**
17 ❑ Cover: 0.10 **NM** value: **50.00**
18 ❑ 1956 Cover: 0.10 **NM** value: **50.00**
19 ❑ 1956 Cover: 0.10 **NM** value: **50.00**
20 ❑ 1956 Cover: 0.10 **NM** value: **45.00**
21 ❑ 1956 Cover: 0.10 **NM** value: **45.00**
22 ❑ 1956 Cover: 0.10 **NM** value: **45.00**
23 ❑ Cover: 0.10 **NM** value: **45.00**
24 ❑ Cover: 0.10 **NM** value: **45.00**
25 ❑ Cover: 0.10 **NM** value: **45.00**
26 ❑ 1957 Cover: 0.10 **NM** value: **40.00**
27 ❑ 1957 Cover: 0.10 **NM** value: **40.00**
28 ❑ 1957 Cover: 0.10 **NM** value: **40.00**
29 ❑ 1957 Cover: 0.10 **NM** value: **40.00**

PATSY WALKER — Marvel

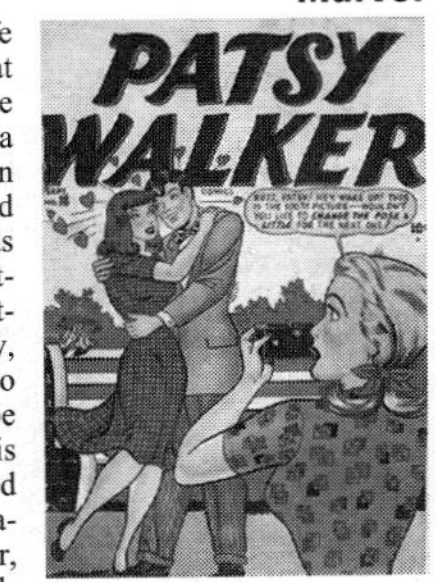

Patsy Walker and Hedy Wolfe are the stars of the series aimed at teen girls. Patsy, the redhead, is the quintessential "Miss Popularity," a fact that causes no end of friction between her and raven-haired Hedy. As a result, Hedy spends most of her time trying to steal Patsy's spotlight or beat time with Patsy's many admirers. In one story, Hedy steals Patsy's homework so that she will get in trouble and be disqualified as class queen. Hedy is appointed in her stead and is pleased to be photographed for the local paper. In the end, the joke is on her, when the harried editors accidentally swap headline photos between the winners of the class queen contest and the adjoining story on the local pet show.

A immediate favorite when it was launched in 1945, this title lasted for two decades. Patsy Walker also appeared in Miss America, Patsy and Hedy — and much later — as the super-hero Hellcat in The Defenders.

1 ❑ Sum 1945 Cover: 0.10 **NM** value: **400.00**
2 ❑ Fal 1945 Cover: 0.10 **NM** value: **175.00**
3 ❑ Feb 1946 Cover: 0.10 **NM** value: **125.00**
4 ❑ Apr 1946 Cover: 0.10 **NM** value: **125.00**
5 ❑ Jun 1946 Cover: 0.10 **NM** value: **125.00**
6 ❑ Aug 1946 Cover: 0.10 **NM** value: **125.00**
7 ❑ Oct 1946 Cover: 0.10 **NM** value: **125.00**
• **CGC:** 1 graded, best 7.0
8 ❑ Dec 1946 Cover: 0.10 **NM** value: **125.00**
• **CGC:** 2 graded, best 9.4
9 ❑ Feb 1947 Cover: 0.10 **NM** value: **125.00**
10 ❑ Apr 1947 Cover: 0.10 **NM** value: **125.00**
• **CGC:** 1 graded, best 7.0
11 ❑ Jun 1947 Cover: 0.10 **NM** value: **70.00**
12 ❑ Aug 1947 Cover: 0.10 **NM** value: **70.00**
13 ❑ Oct 1947 Cover: 0.10 **NM** value: **80.00**
A: Harvey Kurtzman
14 ❑ Dec 1947 Cover: 0.10 **NM** value: **80.00**
A: Harvey Kurtzman
15 ❑ Mar 1948 Cover: 0.10 **NM** value: **70.00**
• **CGC:** 1 graded, best 8.5
16 ❑ May 1948 Cover: 0.10 **NM** value: **70.00**
17 ❑ Jul 1948 Cover: 0.10 **NM** value: **80.00**
A: Harvey Kurtzman
18 ❑ Sep 1948 Cover: 0.10 **NM** value: **70.00**
📖 You Can't Stop Pop!; Her Peculiar Personality!; Mickey's Tragic Tale!; Georgie: What's in a Game?; Cindy: Well Bowl Me Over!; Patsy Walker: Parley-Vous Too?
19 ❑ Nov 1948 Cover: 0.10 **NM** value: **80.00**
A: Harvey Kurtzman
20 ❑ Jan 1949 Cover: 0.10 **NM** value: **80.00**
A: Harvey Kurtzman
21 ❑ Mar 1949 Cover: 0.10 **NM** value: **80.00**
A: Harvey Kurtzman
22 ❑ May 1949 Cover: 0.10 **NM** value: **80.00**
A: Harvey Kurtzman
23 ❑ Jul 1949 Cover: 0.10 **NM** value: **55.00**
24 ❑ Sep 1949 Cover: 0.10 **NM** value: **55.00**
25 ❑ Nov 1949 Cover: 0.10 **NM** value: **80.00**
A: Harvey Kurtzman
26 ❑ Jan 1950 Cover: 0.10 **NM** value: **55.00**
27 ❑ Mar 1950 Cover: 0.10 **NM** value: **55.00**
28 ❑ May 1950 Cover: 0.10 **NM** value: **55.00**
29 ❑ Jul 1950 Cover: 0.10 **NM** value: **55.00**
30 ❑ Sep 1950 Cover: 0.10 **NM** value: **70.00**
A: Harvey Kurtzman
31 ❑ Nov 1950 Cover: 0.10 **NM** value: **30.00**
32 ❑ Jan 1951 Cover: 0.10 **NM** value: **30.00**
33 ❑ Mar 1951 Cover: 0.10 **NM** value: **30.00**
34 ❑ May 1951 Cover: 0.10 **NM** value: **30.00**
35 ❑ Jul 1951 Cover: 0.10 **NM** value: **30.00**
36 ❑ Sep 1951 Cover: 0.10 **NM** value: **30.00**
37 ❑ Nov 1951 Cover: 0.10 **NM** value: **30.00**
38 ❑ Jan 1952 Cover: 0.10 **NM** value: **30.00**
39 ❑ Mar 1952 Cover: 0.10 **NM** value: **30.00**
40 ❑ May 1952 Cover: 0.10 **NM** value: **30.00**
41 ❑ Jul 1952 Cover: 0.10 **NM** value: **30.00**
42 ❑ Sep 1952 Cover: 0.10 **NM** value: **25.00**
43 ❑ Nov 1952 Cover: 0.10 **NM** value: **25.00**
44 ❑ Jan 1953 Cover: 0.10 **NM** value: **25.00**
45 ❑ Mar 1953 Cover: 0.10 **NM** value: **25.00**
46 ❑ May 1953 Cover: 0.10 **NM** value: **25.00**
47 ❑ Jul 1953 Cover: 0.10 **NM** value: **25.00**
48 ❑ Sep 1953 Cover: 0.10 **NM** value: **25.00**
49 ❑ Nov 1953 Cover: 0.10 **NM** value: **25.00**
50 ❑ Jan 1954 Cover: 0.10 **NM** value: **25.00**
51 ❑ Mar 1954 Cover: 0.10 **NM** value: **22.00**
52 ❑ May 1954 Cover: 0.10 **NM** value: **22.00**
53 ❑ Jul 1954 Cover: 0.10 **NM** value: **22.00**
54 ❑ Sep 1954 Cover: 0.10 **NM** value: **22.00**
55 ❑ Nov 1954 Cover: 0.10 **NM** value: **22.00**
56 ❑ Jan 1955 Cover: 0.10 **NM** value: **22.00**
57 ❑ Mar 1955 Cover: 0.10 **NM** value: **22.00**
58 ❑ May 1955 Cover: 0.10 **NM** value: **22.00**
59 ❑ Jul 1955 Cover: 0.10 **NM** value: **22.00**
60 ❑ 1955 Cover: 0.10 **NM** value: **22.00**
61 ❑ 1955 Cover: 0.10 **NM** value: **16.00**
62 ❑ Jan 1956 Cover: 0.10 **NM** value: **16.00**
63 ❑ Apr 1956 Cover: 0.10 **NM** value: **16.00**
64 ❑ Jun 1956 Cover: 0.10 **NM** value: **16.00**
65 ❑ ca. 1956 Cover: 0.10 **NM** value: **16.00**
66 ❑ ca. 1956 Cover: 0.10 **NM** value: **16.00**
67 ❑ Nov 1956 Cover: 0.10 **NM** value: **16.00**
68 ❑ Cover: 0.10 **NM** value: **16.00**
69 ❑ ca. 1957 Cover: 0.10 **NM** value: **16.00**
70 ❑ ca. 1957 Cover: 0.10 **NM** value: **16.00**
71 ❑ ca. 1957 Cover: 0.10 **NM** value: **16.00**
72 ❑ Sep 1957 Cover: 0.10 **NM** value: **16.00**
73 ❑ ca. 1957 Cover: 0.10 **NM** value: **16.00**
74 ❑ Cover: 0.10 **NM** value: **16.00**
75 ❑ Feb 1958 Cover: 0.10 **NM** value: **16.00**
76 ❑ Apr 1958 Cover: 0.10 **NM** value: **16.00**
77 ❑ Jun 1958 Cover: 0.10 **NM** value: **16.00**
78 ❑ Aug 1958 Cover: 0.10 **NM** value: **16.00**
79 ❑ Oct 1958 Cover: 0.10 **NM** value: **16.00**
80 ❑ Dec 1958 Cover: 0.10 **NM** value: **16.00**
81 ❑ Feb 1959 Cover: 0.10 **NM** value: **13.00**
82 ❑ Apr 1959 Cover: 0.10 **NM** value: **13.00**
83 ❑ Jun 1959 Cover: 0.10 **NM** value: **13.00**
84 ❑ Aug 1959 Cover: 0.10 **NM** value: **13.00**
85 ❑ Oct 1959 Cover: 0.10 **NM** value: **13.00**
86 ❑ Dec 1959 Cover: 0.10 **NM** value: **13.00**
87 ❑ Feb 1960 Cover: 0.10 **NM** value: **13.00**
88 ❑ Apr 1960 Cover: 0.10 **NM** value: **13.00**
89 ❑ Jun 1960 Cover: 0.10 **NM** value: **13.00**
90 ❑ Aug 1960 Cover: 0.10 **NM** value: **13.00**
91 ❑ Oct 1960 Cover: 0.10 **NM** value: **13.00**
92 ❑ Dec 1960 Cover: 0.10 **NM** value: **13.00**
93 ❑ Feb 1961 Cover: 0.10 **NM** value: **13.00**
94 ❑ Apr 1961 Cover: 0.10 **NM** value: **13.00**
95 ❑ Jun 1961 Cover: 0.10 **NM** value: **13.00**
96 ❑ Aug 1961 Cover: 0.10 **NM** value: **13.00**
97 ❑ Oct 1961 Cover: 0.10 **NM** value: **13.00**
98 ❑ Dec 1961 Cover: 0.10 **NM** value: **13.00**
99 ❑ Feb 1962 Cover: 0.12 **NM** value: **13.00**
100 ❑ Apr 1962 Cover: 0.12 **NM** value: **13.00**
101 ❑ Jun 1962 Cover: 0.12 **NM** value: **10.00**
102 ❑ Aug 1962 Cover: 0.12 **NM** value: **10.00**
103 ❑ Oct 1962 Cover: 0.12 **NM** value: **10.00**
104 ❑ Dec 1962 Cover: 0.12 **NM** value: **10.00**
105 ❑ Feb 1963 Cover: 0.12 **NM** value: **10.00**
106 ❑ Apr 1963 Cover: 0.12 **NM** value: **10.00**
107 ❑ ca. 1963 Cover: 0.12 **NM** value: **10.00**
108 ❑ ca. 1963 Cover: 0.12 **NM** value: **10.00**
109 ❑ ca. 1963 Cover: 0.12 **NM** value: **10.00**
110 ❑ Oct 1963 Cover: 0.12 **NM** value: **10.00**
111 ❑ Nov 1963 Cover: 0.12 **NM** value: **10.00**
112 ❑ Dec 1963 Cover: 0.12 **NM** value: **10.00**
113 ❑ Feb 1964 Cover: 0.12 **NM** value: **10.00**
114 ❑ Apr 1964 Cover: 0.12 **NM** value: **10.00**
115 ❑ Jun 1964 Cover: 0.12 **NM** value: **10.00**
116 ❑ Aug 1964 Cover: 0.12 **NM** value: **10.00**
117 ❑ Oct 1964 Cover: 0.12 **NM** value: **10.00**
118 ❑ Dec 1964 Cover: 0.10 **NM** value: **10.00**
119 ❑ Feb 1965 Cover: 0.10 **NM** value: **10.00**
120 ❑ Apr 1965 Cover: 0.10 **NM** value: **10.00**
121 ❑ Jun 1965 Cover: 0.10 **NM** value: **10.00**
122 ❑ Aug 1965 Cover: 0.10 **NM** value: **10.00**
123 ❑ Oct 1965 Cover: 0.10 **NM** value: **10.00**
124 ❑ Dec 1965 Cover: 0.10 **NM** value: **10.00**
final issue.
SE 1 ❑ ca. 1966 Cover: 0.25 **NM** value: **45.00**
• **CGC:** 1 graded, best 8.5
• Fashion Parade special

PAT THE BRAT — Archie

Think of Dennis the Menace. Hank Ketcham's panel cartoon made its debut in 1951 and featured the adventures of a basically nice little blond 5-year-old whose activities lead to others' consternation most usually because he doesn't understand the consequences of what he's doing. He's a good kid. And his adventures were so endearing that the character became a monumental, long-lasting success and brought countless awards to Ketcham.

Now think of Pat the Brat. He's about 5, but he's got black hair. His father smokes a cigar, not a pipe. And Pat is, yes, a brat, hitting girls, painting on the wall, sawing a violin. It's heartwarming to think that the attempt to rip off Dennis without grasping the character's essential sweetness failed so utterly, compared to its inspiration. — Maggie

1 ❑ Sum 1955 Cover: 0.10 **NM** value: **40.00**
2 ❑ Fal 1955 Cover: 0.10 **NM** value: **30.00**
3 ❑ Win 1955 Cover: 0.10 **NM** value: **30.00**
4 ❑ Spr 1956 Cover: 0.10 **NM** value: **30.00**
15 ❑ Jul 1956 Cover: 0.10 **NM** value: **20.00**
16 ❑ Sep 1956 Cover: 0.10 **NM** value: **20.00**
17 ❑ Nov 1956 Cover: 0.10 **NM** value: **20.00**
18 ❑ Jan 1957 Cover: 0.10 **NM** value: **20.00**
19 ❑ Mar 1957 Cover: 0.10 **NM** value: **20.00**
20 ❑ May 1957 Cover: 0.10 **NM** value: **15.00**
21 ❑ Jul 1957 Cover: 0.10 **NM** value: **15.00**
22 ❑ Sep 1957 Cover: 0.10 **NM** value: **15.00**
23 ❑ Nov 1957 Cover: 0.10 **NM** value: **10.00**
24 ❑ Jan 1958 Cover: 0.10 **NM** value: **10.00**
25 ❑ Mar 1958 Cover: 0.10 **NM** value: **10.00**
26 ❑ May 1958 Cover: 0.10 **NM** value: **10.00**
27 ❑ Jul 1958 Cover: 0.10 **NM** value: **10.00**
28 ❑ Sep 1958 Cover: 0.10 **NM** value: **8.00**
29 ❑ Nov 1958 Cover: 0.10 **NM** value: **8.00**
30 ❑ Jan 1959 Cover: 0.10 **NM** value: **8.00**
31 ❑ Mar 1959 Cover: 0.10 **NM** value: **8.00**
32 ❑ May 1959 Cover: 0.10 **NM** value: **8.00**
33 ❑ Jul 1959 Cover: 0.10 **NM** value: **8.00**

PATTY CAKE — Permanent Press

1 ❑ Cover: 2.95 **NM** value: **Cover or less**
2 ❑ Cover: 2.95 **NM** value: **Cover or less**
3 ❑ Cover: 2.95 **NM** value: **Cover or less**
4 ❑ Cover: 2.95 **NM** value: **Cover or less**
5 ❑ Cover: 2.95 **NM** value: **Cover or less**
6 ❑ Cover: 2.95 **NM** value: **Cover or less**
7 ❑ Cover: 2.95 **NM** value: **Cover or less**
8 ❑ Cover: 2.95 **NM** value: **Cover or less**
9 ❑ Cover: 2.95 **NM** value: **Cover or less**

PATTY CAKE (2ND SERIES) — Caliber / Tapestry

1 ❑ ca. 1996, b&w Cover: 2.95 **NM** value: **Cover or less**
📖 Another Patty Cake Tour; Baby Broken Bones; Dog; Come Meet the Cast of TV's Curious Cavern; The Babysitter's Here
2 ❑ ca. 1997, b&w Cover: 2.95 **NM** value: **Cover or less**
📖 From the Heart; Help Birdy Get the Worm!!; Show Time; In the Swing; The Great Fallo; Daydream; Snow
3 ❑ ca. 1997, b&w Cover: 2.95 **NM** value: **Cover or less**
📖 Fright Night; The Weasels; That's What It's All About; Dutch Treats; Field of Daydreams
HS 1 ❑ b&w Cover: 2.95 **NM** value: **Cover or less**
📖 A Patty-Cake Christmas

PATTY CAKE & FRIENDS — Slave Labor

1 ❑ Nov 1997, b&w Cover: 2.95 **NM** value: **Cover or less**
📖 The Boob Tube; The Naked Truth; Weenie Pops; Coldwater Comfort; It's Payback Time; Ride
2 ❑ Dec 1997, b&w Cover: 2.95 **NM** value: **Cover or less**
📖 A Hard Lesson; Smell-Check; Darn Those Chimps; Who's Sorry Now?; Smoke Signals; Halls of Learning
3 ❑ Jan 1998, b&w Cover: 2.95 **NM** value: **Cover or less**
📖 Told Ya So!; A Big Help; Guilty; Bubble Bath Theatre; Gross
4 ❑ Feb 1998, b&w Cover: 2.95 **NM** value: **Cover or less**
📖 Road Food; I Dare Ya; It's About Time; Scorned; It's All in the Telling
5 ❑ Mar 1998, b&w Cover: 2.95 **NM** value: **Cover or less**
6 ❑ Apr 1998, b&w Cover: 2.95 **NM** value: **Cover or less**
7 ❑ May 1998 Cover: 2.95 **NM** value: **Cover or less**
📖 You Get What You Pay For **A:** Scott Roberts **W:** Scott Roberts
8 ❑ Jun 1998 Cover: 2.95 **NM** value: **Cover or less**
📖 Now You See It, Now You Don't **A:** Scott Roberts **W:** Scott Roberts
9 ❑ Aug 1998 Cover: 2.95 **NM** value: **Cover or less**
📖 Short Trip; How to Write Your Own Way-Cool Sci-Fi Script; Choices; Mask of the Fanmagazine **A:** Scott Roberts **W:** Scott Roberts
10 ❑ Sep 1998 Cover: 2.95 **NM** value: **Cover or less**
📖 Anybody Can Make a Mistake; Zip the Fox (text story) **A:** Scott Roberts **W:** Scott Roberts
11 ❑ Nov 1998 Cover: 2.95 **NM** value: **Cover or less**
📖 It's a Fad, Fad, Fad, Fad World; The Girl With the Funny Mags; Birdy: You Don't Say; Bad Moon Rising; Takin' Care of Business; Patty Cake Looks at Life From Her Unique Perspective **A:** Scott Roberts **W:** Scott Roberts
12 ❑ Cover: 2.95 **NM** value: **Cover or less**
📖 On With the Show; The Big Day; **A:** Scott Roberts **W:** Scott Roberts
SE 1 ❑ Oct 1997 Cover: 3.95 **NM** value: **Cover or less**
No issue number. 📖 Here There Be Monsters **A:** Scott Roberts **W:** Scott Roberts

PATTY CAKE & FRIENDS (VOL. 2) — Slave Labor

1 ❑ Nov 2000, b&w Cover: 4.95 **NM** value: **Cover or less**
cardstock cover. 📖 Early to Rise; For Art's Sake; Why Hothead Totally Rules!; Strange Bedfellows **A:** Scott Roberts **W:** Scott Roberts

PATTY POWERS — Atlas

4 ❑ 1955 Cover: 0.10 **NM** value: **50.00**
5 ❑ 1956 Cover: 0.10 **NM** value: **30.00**
6 ❑ 1956 Cover: 0.10 **NM** value: **30.00**
7 ❑ 1956 Cover: 0.10 **NM** value: **30.00**

The CGC numbers printed in individual listings above represent the **number of copies examined** and given a **Universal** grade by CGC and the **best such copy** graded at press time. For current populations, watch for special ***Comics Buyer's Guide*** issues or check **www.cgccomics.com.**

CGC-graded: Multiply prices above by **33 for 9.9 M • 16 for 9.8 NM/M • 7 for 9.6 NM+ • 5 for 9.4 NM • 2.5 for 9.2 NM- • 1.5 for 9.0 VF/NM**

PAUL TERRY'S COMICS — St. John

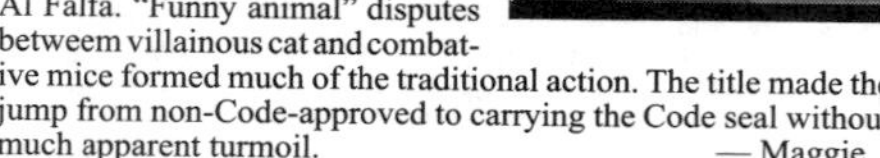

This is one of those transition titles, coming out of Terry-Toons Comics and going on to Adventures of Mighty Mouse, which soon moved to Dell. The cover design on many issues is, oddly enough, reminiscent of cover designs for the Dell Our Gang Comics of the 1940s, emphasizing a "strip of film" in the design. Issues of Paul Terry's Comics featured the stable of "performers" seen in the Terrytoons theatrical cartoons from Paul Terry: Mighty Mouse, Heckle and Jeckle, Gandy Goose, and bearded Farmer Al Falfa. "Funny animal" disputes betweem villainous cat and combative mice formed much of the traditional action. The title made the jump from non-Code-approved to carrying the Code seal without much apparent turmoil. — Maggie

85 ❑ 1951 Cover: 0.10 **NM** value: **40.00**
86 ❑ 1951 Cover: 0.10 **NM** value: **35.00**
87 ❑ 1951 Cover: 0.10 **NM** value: **35.00**
88 ❑ 1951 Cover: 0.10 **NM** value: **35.00**
89 ❑ Cover: 0.10 **NM** value: **35.00**
90 ❑ Cover: 0.10 **NM** value: **35.00**
91 ❑ 1952 Cover: 0.10 **NM** value: **25.00**
92 ❑ May 1952 Cover: 0.10 **NM** value: **25.00**
93 ❑ 1952 Cover: 0.10 **NM** value: **25.00**
94 ❑ 1952 Cover: 0.10 **NM** value: **25.00**
95 ❑ 1952 Cover: 0.10 **NM** value: **25.00**
96 ❑ 1952 Cover: 0.10 **NM** value: **25.00**
97 ❑ Jan 1953 Cover: 0.10 **NM** value: **20.00**
98 ❑ Feb 1953 Cover: 0.10 **NM** value: **20.00**
99 ❑ Mar 1953 Cover: 0.10 **NM** value: **20.00**
100 ❑ Apr 1953 Cover: 0.10 **NM** value: **20.00**
101 ❑ May 1953 Cover: 0.10 **NM** value: **20.00**
102 ❑ Jun 1953 Cover: 0.10 **NM** value: **20.00**
103 ❑ Jul 1953 Cover: 0.10 **NM** value: **20.00**
104 ❑ Aug 1953 Cover: 0.10 **NM** value: **20.00**
105 ❑ Sep 1953 Cover: 0.10 **NM** value: **20.00**
106 ❑ Oct 1953 Cover: 0.10 **NM** value: **15.00**
107 ❑ Nov 1953 Cover: 0.10 **NM** value: **15.00**
108 ❑ Dec 1953 Cover: 0.10 **NM** value: **15.00**
109 ❑ Jan 1954 Cover: 0.10 **NM** value: **15.00**
110 ❑ Feb 1954 Cover: 0.10 **NM** value: **15.00**
111 ❑ Mar 1954 Cover: 0.10 **NM** value: **15.00**
112 ❑ Apr 1954 Cover: 0.10 **NM** value: **15.00**
113 ❑ May 1954 Cover: 0.10 **NM** value: **15.00**
114 ❑ Jun 1954 Cover: 0.10 **NM** value: **15.00**
115 ❑ Jul 1954 Cover: 0.10 **NM** value: **15.00**
116 ❑ Aug 1954 Cover: 0.10 **NM** value: **15.00**
117 ❑ Sep 1954 Cover: 0.10 **NM** value: **15.00**
118 ❑ Oct 1954 Cover: 0.10 **NM** value: **15.00**
119 ❑ Nov 1954 Cover: 0.10 **NM** value: **15.00**
120 ❑ Dec 1954 Cover: 0.10 **NM** value: **15.00**
121 ❑ Jan 1955 Cover: 0.10 **NM** value: **10.00**
122 ❑ Feb 1955 Cover: 0.10 **NM** value: **10.00**
123 ❑ Mar 1955 Cover: 0.10 **NM** value: **10.00**
124 ❑ Apr 1955 Cover: 0.10 **NM** value: **10.00**
125 ❑ May 1955 Cover: 0.10 **NM** value: **10.00**

PAUL THE SAMURAI — New England

1 ❑ Jul 1992 Cover: 2.75 **NM** value: **4.00**
Circ: CapCity orders: **4,655**
📖 The Decline and Fall of the Tailfin Empire!! **A:** Dave Garcia **W:** Clay Griffith
2 ❑ Sep 1992 Cover: 2.75 **NM** value: **3.00**
3 ❑ Nov 1992 Cover: 2.75 **NM** value: **6.00**
• Scarcer
4 ❑ Jan 1993 Cover: 2.75 **NM** value: **4.00**
5 ❑ Mar 1993 Cover: 2.75 **NM** value: **Cover or less**
6 ❑ May 1993 Cover: 2.75 **NM** value: **Cover or less**
7 ❑ Jul 1993 Cover: 2.75 **NM** value: **Cover or less**
8 ❑ Sep 1993 Cover: 2.75 **NM** value: **Cover or less**
9 ❑ Nov 1993 Cover: 2.75 **NM** value: **Cover or less**
★ Appearance of The Tick.
10 ❑ Cover: 2.75 **NM** value: **Cover or less**
★ Appearance of The Tick.
Bk 1 ❑ Cover: 7.50 **NM** value: **Cover or less**
• Collects Paul the Samurai #1-4
Bk 2 ❑ Cover: 5.00 **NM** value: **Cover or less**
• Collects Paul the Samurai #5-8

PAUL THE SAMURAI (MINI-SERIES) — NEC

1 ❑ Cover: 2.25 **NM** value: **3.50**
📖 Boiler Men: Boiler Menace! **A:** Dave Garcia **W:** Ben Edlund ★ Appearance of The Tick.
2 ❑ Cover: 2.75 **NM** value: **3.00**
📖 Revolt! **A:** Dave Garcia **W:** Dave Garcia; Ben Edlund; Monica Sharp
3 ❑ Cover: 2.75 **NM** value: **3.00**
Bk 1 ❑ Cover: 8.95 **NM** value: **Cover or less**
• Collected Paul the Samurai

PAWNEE BILL — Story

1 ❑ Feb 1951 Cover: 0.10 **NM** value: **100.00**
2 ❑ May 1951 Cover: 0.10 **NM** value: **75.00**
3 ❑ Jul 1951 Cover: 0.10 **NM** value: **75.00**

PAYNE — Dream Catcher Press

1 ❑ Sep 1995, b&w Cover: 2.50 **NM** value: **Cover or less**

PAY-OFF — D.S.

1 ❑ Jul 1948 Cover: 0.10 **NM** value: **150.00**
2 ❑ Sep 1948 Cover: 0.10 **NM** value: **100.00**
3 ❑ Nov 1948 Cover: 0.10 **NM** value: **75.00**
4 ❑ Jan 1949 Cover: 0.10 **NM** value: **75.00**
5 ❑ Mar 1949 Cover: 0.10 **NM** value: **75.00**

P. CITY PARADE — Horse

1 ❑ Nov 1996, b&w Cover: 4.95 **NM** value: **5.00**
Circ: Diamd. preorders: **4,534**
No issue number. • oversized collection of THB-related stories and other material. 📖 The Theme; P. City Paradeessay; THB Excerpts; Megagangsters; P. city Parody (Comic Book)

PEACEMAKER, THE — Charlton

1 ❑ Mar 1967 Cover: 0.12 **NM** value: **12.00**
2 ❑ May 1967 Cover: 0.12 **NM** value: **8.00**
• Fightin' 5 back-up story
3 ❑ Jul 1967 Cover: 0.12 **NM** value: **8.00**
📖 The Survivors; The Fightin' 5
4 ❑ Sep 1967 Cover: 0.12 **NM** value: **10.00**
★ Origin of The Peacemaker.
5 ❑ Nov 1967 Cover: 0.12 **NM** value: **8.00**

PEACEMAKER (MINI-SERIES) — DC

1 ❑ Jan 1988 Cover: 1.25 **NM** value: **1.50**
Circ: CapCity orders: **25,950**
📖 A Breach Of The Peace! **A:** Tod Smith **W:** Paul Kupperberg
2 ❑ Feb 1988 Cover: 1.25 **NM** value: **1.50**
Circ: CapCity orders: **18,900**
📖 The Wages Of Tzin **A:** Tod Smith **W:** Paul Kupperberg
3 ❑ Mar 1988 Cover: 1.25 **NM** value: **1.50**
Circ: CapCity orders: **17,400**
4 ❑ Apr 1988 Cover: 1.25 **NM** value: **1.50**
Circ: CapCity orders: **13,900**

PEACEMAKERS — Kinetic

1 ❑ Cover: 2.50 **NM** value: **Cover or less**
📖 And Then There Was One **A:** Tony Santini **W:** Luciano Santini

PEACE PARTY — Blue Corn

1 ❑ Cover: 2.95 **NM** value: **Cover or less**
📖 Beginnings **A:** Rob Schmidt; Ron Fattoruso **W:** Rob Schmidt

PEACE POSSE — Mellon Bank

1 ❑ Cover: 2.95 **NM** value: **Cover or less**
📖 The End of the Violence Begins with Me! **A:** Reggie Byers **W:** Reggie Byers

PEANUT BUTTER AND JEREMY — Alternative

1 ❑ Aug 2000, b&w Cover: 2.95 **NM** value: **Cover or less**
No issue number. **A:** James Kochalka **W:** James Kochalka

PEANUTS (DELL) — Dell

Charles Schulz (1922-2000) was a magazine cartoonist who developed one of the biggest success stories in newspaper strips. Peanuts began in seven newspapers in 1950 and grew to an incredible powerhouse of entertainment, including TV specials, movies, and a musical.

Like many other comic strips, Peanuts provided filler material to anthology comics including Tip Top Comics, United Comics, Tip Topper, and Fritzi Ritz.

However, Dell gave the strip its own comic-book home, and Schulz drew special covers for the issues. Although Schulz refused to give up creation of the newspaper strip, he had help on the comic-book, with Jim Sasseville providing much of the new work found in free-standing stories structured in comic-book format. — Maggie

1 ❑ ca. 1954 Cover: 0.10 **NM** value: **150.00**
4 ❑ Feb 1960 Cover: 0.10 **NM** value: **75.00**
• **CGC:** 2 graded, best 9.2
5 ❑ May 1960 Cover: 0.10 **NM** value: **75.00**
• **CGC:** 1 graded, best 9.4
6 ❑ Aug 1960 Cover: 0.10 **NM** value: **75.00**
• **CGC:** 1 graded, best 9.2
7 ❑ Nov 1960 Cover: 0.10 **NM** value: **60.00**
8 ❑ Feb 1961 Cover: 0.15 **NM** value: **60.00**
9 ❑ May 1961 Cover: 0.15 **NM** value: **60.00**
10 ❑ Aug 1961 Cover: 0.10 **NM** value: **50.00**
11 ❑ Nov 1961 Cover: 0.15 **NM** value: **50.00**
• **CGC:** 1 graded, best 9.0
12 ❑ Feb 1962 Cover: 0.15 **NM** value: **50.00**
13 ❑ May 1962 Cover: 0.15 **NM** value: **50.00**

PEANUTS (GOLD KEY) — Gold Key

1 ❑ May 1963 Cover: 0.12 **NM** value: **125.00**
2 ❑ Aug 1963 Cover: 0.12 **NM** value: **75.00**
3 ❑ Nov 1963 Cover: 0.12 **NM** value: **75.00**
4 ❑ Feb 1964 Cover: 0.12 **NM** value: **75.00**

PEASANT AND THE DEVIL, THE — Fantagraphics

1 ❑ **NM** value: **2.95**
📖 Death's Messengers; Frau Trude; The Peasant and the Devil; The Louse and the Flea **W:** Caitlan Masley; Graham Worden; Tim Pickstone

Statement of Ownership figures are the average number of copies originally sold, as cited by the publisher to the U.S. Postal Service. These estimate **all** sales, in comics shops and on newsstands.

PEBBLES AND BAMM-BAMM — Charlton

Pebbles and Bamm-Bamm are the children, respectively, of Fred and Wilma Flintstone and Barney and Betty Rubble. During the original Flintstones TV series of the 1960s, they were introduced as very young children to add an element of domesticity to the increasingly outlandish exploits of Fred and the Barney. In the early 1970s, Hanna-Barbera launched a new Flintstones series aimed at younger viewers, aging the kids to their teen years and giving them a supporting cast. As voiced by Sally Struthers, bubbly redhead Pebbles inherited her father's knack for getting into trouble, while the amiable — if dim — Bamm-Bamm often saved the day with his strength.

Charlton generated new stories featuring the kids and their friends, following in lock-step with the series' animated sitcom beginnings. In one story, a prince comes to town and mistakes Pebbles, the queen of a parade for Fred's lodge, for royalty. "Your father is a Pooh-Bah? My father is only a king!"

1 ❑ Jan 1972 Cover: 0.20 **NM** value: **18.00**
2 ❑ Mar 1972 Cover: 0.20 **NM** value: **12.00**
3 ❑ May 1972 Cover: 0.20 **NM** value: **9.00**
📖 Without All That…What?; A-Haunting-We-Will-Go; Bedrock Beauty Contest; The Lunch Crunch; Puttin' on the Dawg
4 ❑ Jul 1972 Cover: 0.20 **NM** value: **9.00**
5 ❑ Aug 1972 Cover: 0.20 **NM** value: **9.00**
6 ❑ Sep 1972 Cover: 0.20 **NM** value: **7.00**
7 ❑ Oct 1972 Cover: 0.20 **NM** value: **7.00**
📖 The Weaker Sex?; My Unfair Lady; First Flight (text); Shleprock's Great Day • No credits in issue
8 ❑ Nov 1972 Cover: 0.20 **NM** value: **7.00**
9 ❑ Cover: 0.20 **NM** value: **7.00**
10 ❑ ca. 1973 Cover: 0.20 **NM** value: **7.00**
11 ❑ ca. 1973 Cover: 0.20 **NM** value: **5.00**
12 ❑ ca. 1973 Cover: 0.20 **NM** value: **5.00**
13 ❑ ca. 1973 Cover: 0.20 **NM** value: **5.00**
14 ❑ ca. 1973 Cover: 0.20 **NM** value: **5.00**
15 ❑ Aug 1973 Cover: 0.20 **NM** value: **5.00**
16 ❑ Oct 1973 Cover: 0.20 **NM** value: **5.00**
17 ❑ Nov 1973 Cover: 0.20 **NM** value: **5.00**
18 ❑ Jan 1974 Cover: 0.20 **NM** value: **5.00**
19 ❑ Feb 1974 Cover: 0.20 **NM** value: **5.00**
📖 End of the World; The Early Riser; The Big Beanstalk; Foiled; Jo-Jo the Strong Boy; Diluted Soup; The Assist
20 ❑ Jun 1974 Cover: 0.25 **NM** value: **5.00**
21 ❑ Aug 1974 Cover: 0.25 **NM** value: **4.00**
22 ❑ Nov 1974 Cover: 0.25 **NM** value: **4.00**
23 ❑ Jan 1975 Cover: 0.25 **NM** value: **4.00**
24 ❑ Feb 1975 Cover: 0.25 **NM** value: **4.00**
25 ❑ Mar 1975 Cover: 0.25 **NM** value: **4.00**
26 ❑ ca. 1975 Cover: 0.25 **NM** value: **4.00**
27 ❑ ca. 1975 Cover: 0.25 **NM** value: **4.00**
28 ❑ ca. 1975 Cover: 0.25 **NM** value: **4.00**
29 ❑ ca. 1975 Cover: 0.25 **NM** value: **4.00**
30 ❑ Dec 1975 Cover: 0.25 **NM** value: **4.00**
31 ❑ Feb 1976 Cover: 0.25 **NM** value: **3.00**
32 ❑ Apr 1976 Cover: 0.25 **NM** value: **3.00**
33 ❑ Jun 1976 Cover: 0.25 **NM** value: **3.00**
34 ❑ Aug 1976 Cover: 0.30 **NM** value: **3.00**
📖 The Bank Robbers; The Hiding Place; The Heiress • No credits listed
35 ❑ Oct 1976 Cover: 0.30 **NM** value: **3.00**
36 ❑ Dec 1976 Cover: 0.30 **NM** value: **3.00**
📖 Costume Caper; Rocky Rob Hits Bedrock; A Girl's Goal; Not So Nice • No credits listed

PEBBLES & BAMM-BAMM (HARVEY) — Harvey

1 ❑ Nov 1993 Cover: 1.50 **NM** value: **Cover or less**
2 ❑ Jan 1994 Cover: 1.50 **NM** value: **Cover or less**
📖 Mugged in the Museum; King for a Day; A Fine Time; Numbers Never Lie
3 ❑ Mar 1994 Cover: 1.50 **NM** value: **Cover or less**
📖 Fabian's Fate; Scarlet Pimple Face; Plant Panic; Contest Catastrophes
Smr 1 ❑ Cover: 2.25 **NM** value: **Cover or less**
• first edition.

PEDESTRIAN VULGARITY — Fantagraphics

1 ❑ b&w Cover: 2.50 **NM** value: **Cover or less**

PEDRO — Fox

1 ❑ **NM** value: **150.00**
2 ❑ **NM** value: **100.00**

PEEK-A-BOO 3-D — 3-D Zone

1 ❑ Cover: 3.95 **NM** value: **Cover or less**
No issue number. **A:** Bill Ward

PEEPSHOW — Drawn & Quarterly

1 ❑ Cover: 2.50 **NM** value: **Cover or less**
2 ❑ Cover: 2.50 **NM** value: **Cover or less**
3 ❑ Cover: 2.50 **NM** value: **Cover or less**
4 ❑ Cover: 2.50 **NM** value: **Cover or less**
5 ❑ Oct 1993 Cover: 2.95 **NM** value: **Cover or less**
6 ❑ Apr 1994 Cover: 2.95 **NM** value: **Cover or less**
7 ❑ Cover: 2.95 **NM** value: **Cover or less**
8 ❑ Cover: 2.95 **NM** value: **Cover or less**
9 ❑ Cover: 2.95 **NM** value: **Cover or less**

Other grades: Multiply prices above by **1.5 for Mint • 2/3 for Very Fine • 1/3 for Fine • 1/5 for Very Good • 1/8 for Good**

PEEP SHOW (KITCHEN SINK) — Kitchen Sink

Bk 1 ❑ b&w Cover: 10.95 **NM** value: **Cover or less**
A: Joe Matt **W:** Joe Matt

PELLESTAR — Eternity

1 ❑ Sep 1987 Cover: 1.95 **NM** value: **Cover or less**
A: Richard Case **W:** Steve Palmer
2 ❑ Cover: 1.95 **NM** value: **Cover or less**
A: Richard Case **W:** Steve Palmer

PENDRAGON (AIRCEL) — Aircel

All issues are adults only.
1 ❑ Nov 1991, b&w Cover: 2.95 **NM** value: **Cover or less**
2 ❑ Dec 1991, b&w Cover: 2.95 **NM** value: **Cover or less**

PENDULUM — Adventure

1 ❑ b&w Cover: 2.50 **NM** value: **Cover or less**
2 ❑ b&w Cover: 2.50 **NM** value: **Cover or less**
3 ❑ b&w Cover: 2.50 **NM** value: **Cover or less**
4 ❑ b&w Cover: 2.50 **NM** value: **Cover or less**

PENDULUM'S ILLUSTRATED STORIES — Pendulum

1 ❑ Cover: 4.95 **NM** value: **Cover or less**
Circ: CapCity orders: **2,975**
No apparent cover price. • Moby Dick **A:** Alex Ni±o **W:** Herman Melville
2 ❑ Cover: 4.95 **NM** value: **Cover or less**
• Treasure Island
3 ❑ Cover: 4.95 **NM** value: **Cover or less**
• Doctor Jekyll; Dr. Jekyll
4 ❑ Cover: 4.95 **NM** value: **Cover or less**
• 20, 000 Leagues Under the Sea
5 ❑ Cover: 4.95 **NM** value: **Cover or less**
• Midsummer Night's Dream
6 ❑ Cover: 4.95 **NM** value: **Cover or less**
• Christmas Carol

PENGUIN & PENCILGUIN — Fragments West

1 ❑ Jan 1987 Cover: 2.00 **NM** value: **Cover or less**
📖 Shoguin; Aladguin and 1001 Flavors; Friends **A:** Phil Yeh **W:** Phil Yeh; Leigh Rubin
2 ❑ Feb 1987 Cover: 2.00 **NM** value: **Cover or less**
3 ❑ Mar 1987 Cover: 2.00 **NM** value: **Cover or less**
4 ❑ Apr 1987 Cover: 2.00 **NM** value: **Cover or less**
5 ❑ May 1987 Cover: 2.00 **NM** value: **Cover or less**
6 ❑ Jun 1987 Cover: 2.00 **NM** value: **Cover or less**

PENGUIN BROS. — Labyrinth Studios

1 ❑ Cover: 2.50 **NM** value: **Cover or less**
A: Josh Blaylock **W:** Josh Blaylock
2 ❑ Cover: 2.50 **NM** value: **Cover or less**

PENNY — Avon

Penny was created by Harry Haenigsen (1900-1990) for the Herald Tribune Syndicate in 1943 and ran in newspapers until 1970. She was one of the first "bobby-soxers" in comics, a harbinger of the teen culture that would dominate the latter half of the century. To modern readers, young Penelope Mildred Pringle seems like just another happy-go-lucky teen character. At the time of her introduction, however, she was a revelation. She was constantly on the phone to her friend Judy, hanging out with the tall basketball player Steeple, or otherwise bound up in an endless round of teen concerns. Avon introduced her in the first issue as "the slickest chick of 'em all," later as "America's teen-age sweetheart."

1 ❑ ca. 1947 Cover: 0.10 **NM** value: **55.00**
📖 Penny's Pop!; Penny and Our Bill • Creator's Biography included **A:** Harry Haenigsen **W:** Harry Haenigsen
2 ❑ ca. 1948 Cover: 0.10 **NM** value: **30.00**
A: Harry Haenigsen **W:** Harry Haenigsen
3 ❑ ca. 1948 Cover: 0.10 **NM** value: **30.00**
A: Harry Haenigsen **W:** Harry Haenigsen
4 ❑ ca. 1949 Cover: 0.10 **NM** value: **30.00**
A: Harry Haenigsen **W:** Harry Haenigsen
5 ❑ ca. 1949 Cover: 0.10 **NM** value: **30.00**
A: Harry Haenigsen **W:** Harry Haenigsen
6 ❑ ca. 1949 Cover: 0.10 **NM** value: **35.00**
final issue. **A:** Harry Haenigsen **W:** Harry Haenigsen

PENNY CENTURY — Fantagraphics

1 ❑ Dec 1997, b&w Cover: 2.95 **NM** value: **Cover or less**
Circ: Diamd. preorders: **6,902**
2 ❑ Mar 1998, b&w Cover: 2.95 **NM** value: **Cover or less**
Circ: Diamd. preorders: **5,552**
3 ❑ Sep 1998, b&w Cover: 2.95 **NM** value: **Cover or less**
Circ: Diamd. preorders: **5,609**
4 ❑ Jan 1999, b&w Cover: 2.95 **NM** value: **Cover or less**
Circ: Diamd. preorders: **4,924**
5 ❑ Jun 1999, b&w Cover: 2.95 **NM** value: **Cover or less**
Circ: Diamd. preorders: **4,843**
6 ❑ Nov 1999, b&w Cover: 2.95 **NM** value: **Cover or less**
Circ: Diamd. preorders: **4,829**
7 ❑ Jul 2000, b&w Cover: 2.95 **NM** value: **Cover or less**
Circ: Diamd. preorders: **4,626**

PENTACLE: THE SIGN OF THE FIVE — Eternity

1 ❑ Feb 1991 Cover: 2.25 **NM** value: **Cover or less**
A: John Ross **W:** Lowell Cunningham
2 ❑ 1991 Cover: 2.25 **NM** value: **Cover or less**
A: John Ross **W:** Lowell Cunningham
3 ❑ 1991 Cover: 2.25 **NM** value: **Cover or less**
A: John Ross **W:** Lowell Cunningham
4 ❑ 1991 Cover: 2.25 **NM** value: **Cover or less**
A: John Ross **W:** Lowell Cunningham

PENTHOUSE COMIX — Penthouse International

Penthouse Magazine is both famous and infamous as one of the leading adult magazines published throughout the world. In 1994, they launched Penthouse Comix, combining two great strengths: a love for the naked female form, and stories featuring work from top artists such as Boris Vallejo, Arthur Suydam, and Mark Texeira.

From vampire-hunting prostitutes to action-adventure stories in the nude, Penthouse Comix is a storehouse for adult comic entertainment. Each issue contained six to seven stories that had been written and/or drawn by many different creators. Art was uniformly excellent, but the stories sometimes suffered from an emphasis more on prurience than on plot.

This was also the site of a reprint of Larry Niven's "Man of Steel, Woman of Kleenex" short story illustrated by Curt Swan and carrying the notice that the characters in no way, shape, or form resembled their DC counterparts.

1 ❑ Jun 1994 Cover: 4.95 **NM** value: **8.00**
Circ: CapCity orders: **8,555**
1-2 ❑ Cover: 4.95 **NM** value: **Cover or less**
2 ❑ Jul 1994 Cover: 4.95 **NM** value: **Cover or less**
Circ: CapCity orders: **6,040**
3 ❑ Sep 1994 Cover: 4.95 **NM** value: **Cover or less**
Circ: CapCity orders: **9,790**
4 ❑ Nov 1994 Cover: 4.95 **NM** value: **Cover or less**
Circ: CapCity orders: **10,850**
5 ❑ Jan 1995 Cover: 4.95 **NM** value: **Cover or less**
Circ: CapCity orders: **11,500**
📖 Man of Steel, Woman of Kleenex **C:** Larry Niven
6 ❑ Mar 1995 Cover: 4.95 **NM** value: **Cover or less**
Circ: CapCity orders: **7,725**
• Comic size. 📖 Young Captain Adventure; Action Figures, Part 1; Libby and the Lost World, Part 6; Doctor Dare and the Spear of Destiny, Part 6; Backlash, Part 5; Bethlehem Steele, Part 5; Hot Stories, Part 3 **A:** Wayne Hawkes **W:** Mark McClellan
6/A ❑ Mar 1995 Cover: 4.95 **NM** value: **Cover or less**
• Magazine size.
7 ❑ May 1995 Cover: 4.95 **NM** value: **Cover or less**
Circ: CapCity orders: **6,875**
• Comic size.
7/A ❑ May 1995 Cover: 4.95 **NM** value: **Cover or less**
• Magazine size.
8 ❑ Jul 1995 Cover: 4.95 **NM** value: **Cover or less**
9 ❑ Sep 1995 Cover: 4.95 **NM** value: **Cover or less**
10 ❑ Nov 1995 Cover: 4.95 **NM** value: **Cover or less**
11 ❑ Jan 1996 Cover: 4.95 **NM** value: **Cover or less**
12 ❑ Mar 1996 Cover: 4.95 **NM** value: **Cover or less**
• second anniversary issue.
13 ❑ May 1996 Cover: 4.95 **NM** value: **Cover or less**
14 ❑ Jul 1996 Cover: 4.95 **NM** value: **Cover or less**
15 ❑ Sep 1996 Cover: 4.95 **NM** value: **Cover or less**
📖 Denz
16 ❑ Oct 1996 Cover: 4.95 **NM** value: **Cover or less**
17 ❑ Nov 1996 Cover: 4.95 **NM** value: **Cover or less**
• reprints Manara's Hidden Camera
18 ❑ Dec 1996 Cover: 4.95 **NM** value: **Cover or less**
19 ❑ Jan 1997 Cover: 4.95 **NM** value: **Cover or less**
20 ❑ Feb 1997 Cover: 4.95 **NM** value: **Cover or less**
21 ❑ Apr 1997 Cover: 4.95 **NM** value: **Cover or less**
22 ❑ May 1997 Cover: 4.95 **NM** value: **Cover or less**
23 ❑ Jun 1997 Cover: 4.95 **NM** value: **Cover or less**
24 ❑ Jul 1997 Cover: 4.95 **NM** value: **Cover or less**
25 ❑ Sep 1997 Cover: 4.95 **NM** value: **Cover or less**
• Sweet Chastity reprints begin
26 ❑ Oct 1997 Cover: 4.95 **NM** value: **Cover or less**
27 ❑ Nov 1997 Cover: 4.95 **NM** value: **Cover or less**
28 ❑ Jan 1998 Cover: 4.95 **NM** value: **Cover or less**
29 ❑ Feb 1998 Cover: 4.95 **NM** value: **Cover or less**
30 ❑ Apr 1998 Cover: 4.95 **NM** value: **Cover or less**
31 ❑ May 1998 Cover: 4.95 **NM** value: **Cover or less**
32 ❑ Jun 1998 Cover: 4.95 **NM** value: **Cover or less**
33 ❑ Jul 1998 Cover: 4.95 **NM** value: **Cover or less**
final issue.

PENTHOUSE MAX — Penthouse International

1 ❑ Jul 1996 Cover: 4.95 **NM** value: **Cover or less**
2 ❑ Nov 1996 Cover: 4.95 **NM** value: **Cover or less**
3 ❑ Spr 1997 Cover: 4.95 **NM** value: **Cover or less**

PEOPLE ARE PHONY — Siegel and Simon

1 ❑ Cover: 0.75 **NM** value: **4.00**
📖 Will Rogers Tonight; Raw Fun!; Blackwall Sigel: Qaalude to War!; The Mechanical Age!; Never Mime!; Interview with French Milton **A:** Barry Siegel; Bruce Simon **W:** Barry Siegel; Bruce Simon

PEOPLE'S COMICS, THE — Golden Gate

1 ❑ Sep 1972 Cover: 0.50 **NM** value: **4.00**
• **CGC:** 1 graded, best 9.4
📖 On the Street with Shuman the Human; The Confessions of Robert Crumb; Patricia Pig in Patricia Stays At Home; Fritz the Cat: Superstar; **A:** Robert Crumb **W:** Robert Crumb

PEP — Archie

Most readers know Pep as the home of Archie, Jughead, Veronica, Betty, and the rest of the Archies. Indeed, these delightful teens inhabited the majority of Pep's issues, following their introduction in #22.

What is less well-known to the world at large is that Pep started out as a super-hero title, featuring the first appearances of The Shield, The Comet, and many others. The early days of this series even included an appearance by the decidedly un-Archie-like Madam Satan.

Even after Archie's introduction (as a filler in an issue cover-featuring super-heroes fighting a Nazi
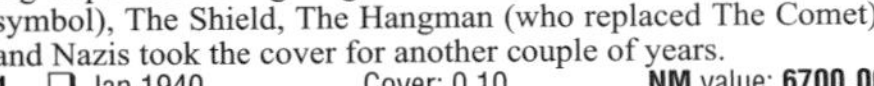
symbol), The Shield, The Hangman (who replaced The Comet), and Nazis took the cover for another couple of years.

1 ❑ Jan 1940 Cover: 0.10 **NM** value: **6700.00**
★ Origin of The Queen of Diamonds, The Comet. ★ 1st Appearance of The Shield I.
2 ❑ Feb 1940 Cover: 0.10 **NM** value: **1750.00**
• **CGC:** 1 graded, best 5.0
★ Origin of The Rocket.
3 ❑ Apr 1940 Cover: 0.10 **NM** value: **1300.00**
4 ❑ May 1940 Cover: 0.10 **NM** value: **1000.00**
• **CGC:** 3 graded, best 7.0
• Wizard cameo
5 ❑ Jun 1940 Cover: 0.10 **NM** value: **1000.00**
• Wizard cameo
6 ❑ Jul 1940 Cover: 0.10 **NM** value: **775.00**
• **CGC:** 1 graded, best 7.5
7 ❑ Aug 1940 Cover: 0.10 **NM** value: **750.00**
• **CGC:** 1 graded, best 8.0
8 ❑ Sep 1940 Cover: 0.10 **NM** value: **750.00**
• **CGC:** 1 graded, best 8.0
9 ❑ Nov 1940 Cover: 0.10 **NM** value: **750.00**
• **CGC:** 1 graded, best 4.0
10 ❑ Dec 1940 Cover: 0.10 **NM** value: **750.00**
• **CGC:** 1 graded, best 7.0
11 ❑ Jan 1941 Cover: 0.10 **NM** value: **750.00**
★ 1st Appearance of Dusty (Shield I's sidekick).
12 ❑ Feb 1941 Cover: 0.10 **NM** value: **875.00**
★ Origin of Fireball. ★ 1st Appearance of Fireball.
13 ❑ Mar 1941 Cover: 0.10 **NM** value: **650.00**
14 ❑ Apr 1941 Cover: 0.10 **NM** value: **650.00**
15 ❑ May 1941 Cover: 0.10 **NM** value: **650.00**
16 ❑ Jun 1941 Cover: 0.10 **NM** value: **950.00**
• **CGC:** 3 graded, best 8.0
★ Origin of Madam Satan.
17 ❑ Jul 1941 Cover: 0.10 **NM** value: **2600.00**
★ 1st Appearance of The Hangman. ★ Death of The Comet.
18 ❑ Aug 1941 Cover: 0.10 **NM** value: **550.00**
19 ❑ Sep 1941 Cover: 0.10 **NM** value: **550.00**
20 ❑ Oct 1941 Cover: 0.10 **NM** value: **550.00**
21 ❑ Nov 1941 Cover: 0.10 **NM** value: **550.00**
22 ❑ Dec 1941 Cover: 0.10 **NM** value: **10000.00**
• **CGC:** 1 graded, best 2.5
• Betty; Jughead ★ 1st Appearance of Betty. ★ 1st Appearance of Archie, Jughead.
23 ❑ Jan 1942 Cover: 0.10 **NM** value: **1100.00**
24 ❑ Feb 1942 Cover: 0.10 **NM** value: **900.00**
25 ❑ Mar 1942 Cover: 0.10 **NM** value: **900.00**
26 ❑ Apr 1942 Cover: 0.10 **NM** value: **1400.00**
• **CGC:** 1 graded, best 5.5
★ 1st Appearance of Veronica Lodge.
27 ❑ May 1942 Cover: 0.10 **NM** value: **725.00**
• **CGC:** 2 graded, best 5.0
28 ❑ Jun 1942 Cover: 0.10 **NM** value: **725.00**
• **CGC:** 1 graded, best 3.5
29 ❑ Jul 1942 Cover: 0.10 **NM** value: **725.00**
30 ❑ Aug 1942 Cover: 0.10 **NM** value: **725.00**
★ 1st Appearance of Mrs. Grundy.
31 ❑ Sep 1942 Cover: 0.10 **NM** value: **575.00**
• **CGC:** 1 graded, best 8.0
32 ❑ Oct 1942 Cover: 0.10 **NM** value: **575.00**
• **CGC:** 1 graded, best 8.5
33 ❑ Nov 1942 Cover: 0.10 **NM** value: **575.00**
34 ❑ Dec 1942 Cover: 0.10 **NM** value: **575.00**
• **CGC:** 1 graded, best 4.5
35 ❑ Jan 1943 Cover: 0.10 **NM** value: **575.00**
36 ❑ Feb 1943 Cover: 0.10 **NM** value: **1000.00**
• **CGC:** 1 graded, best 1.0
Archie cover.
37 ❑ Mar 1943 Cover: 0.10 **NM** value: **400.00**
38 ❑ Apr 1943 Cover: 0.10 **NM** value: **400.00**
39 ❑ May 1943 Cover: 0.10 **NM** value: **400.00**
40 ❑ Jul 1943 Cover: 0.10 **NM** value: **400.00**
41 ❑ Aug 1943 Cover: 0.10 **NM** value: **225.00**
42 ❑ Sep 1943 Cover: 0.10 **NM** value: **225.00**
43 ❑ Oct 1943 Cover: 0.10 **NM** value: **225.00**
44 ❑ Dec 1943 Cover: 0.10 **NM** value: **225.00**
45 ❑ Jan 1944 Cover: 0.10 **NM** value: **225.00**
46 ❑ Feb 1944 Cover: 0.10 **NM** value: **225.00**
47 ❑ Mar 1944 Cover: 0.10 **NM** value: **225.00**
48 ❑ May 1944 Cover: 0.10 **NM** value: **275.00**
• Black Hood begins
49 ❑ Jun 1944 Cover: 0.10 **NM** value: **225.00**
50 ❑ Sep 1944 Cover: 0.10 **NM** value: **225.00**
51 ❑ Dec 1944 Cover: 0.10 **NM** value: **180.00**
52 ❑ Mar 1945 Cover: 0.10 **NM** value: **180.00**
53 ❑ Jun 1945 Cover: 0.10 **NM** value: **180.00**
54 ❑ Sep 1945 Cover: 0.10 **NM** value: **180.00**
• **CGC:** 1 graded, best 9.6
55 ❑ Dec 1945 Cover: 0.10 **NM** value: **180.00**

CGC-graded: Multiply prices above by **33 for 9.9 M • 16 for 9.8 NM/M • 7 for 9.6 NM+ • 5 for 9.4 NM • 2.5 for 9.2 NM- • 1.5 for 9.0 VF/NM**

56 ❑ Mar 1946 Cover: 0.10 **NM** value: **175.00**
57 ❑ Jun 1946 Cover: 0.10 **NM** value: **175.00**
58 ❑ Sep 1946 Cover: 0.10 **NM** value: **175.00**
59 ❑ Dec 1946 Cover: 0.10 **NM** value: **175.00**
60 ❑ Mar 1947 Cover: 0.10 **NM** value: **175.00**
• **CGC:** 1 graded, best 8.0
• Katy Keene begins
61 ❑ May 1947 Cover: 0.10 **NM** value: **135.00**
62 ❑ Jul 1947 Cover: 0.10 **NM** value: **135.00**
63 ❑ Sep 1947 Cover: 0.10 **NM** value: **135.00**
64 ❑ Nov 1947 Cover: 0.10 **NM** value: **135.00**
65 ❑ Jan 1948 Cover: 0.10 **NM** value: **135.00**
• **CGC:** 1 graded, best 7.0
66 ❑ Feb 1948 Cover: 0.10 **NM** value: **95.00**
67 ❑ May 1948 Cover: 0.10 **NM** value: **95.00**
68 ❑ Jul 1948 Cover: 0.10 **NM** value: **95.00**
69 ❑ Sep 1948 Cover: 0.10 **NM** value: **95.00**
70 ❑ Nov 1948 Cover: 0.10 **NM** value: **95.00**
71 ❑ Jan 1949 Cover: 0.10 **NM** value: **80.00**
72 ❑ Mar 1949 Cover: 0.10 **NM** value: **80.00**
73 ❑ May 1949 Cover: 0.10 **NM** value: **80.00**
74 ❑ Jul 1949 Cover: 0.10 **NM** value: **80.00**
75 ❑ Sep 1949 Cover: 0.10 **NM** value: **80.00**
76 ❑ Nov 1949 Cover: 0.10 **NM** value: **80.00**
77 ❑ Jan 1950 Cover: 0.10 **NM** value: **80.00**
78 ❑ Mar 1950 Cover: 0.10 **NM** value: **80.00**
79 ❑ May 1950 Cover: 0.10 **NM** value: **80.00**
80 ❑ Jul 1950 Cover: 0.10 **NM** value: **80.00**
81 ❑ Sep 1950 Cover: 0.10 **NM** value: **60.00**
82 ❑ Nov 1950 Cover: 0.10 **NM** value: **60.00**
• **CGC:** 1 graded, best 7.5
83 ❑ Jan 1951 Cover: 0.10 **NM** value: **60.00**
84 ❑ Mar 1951 Cover: 0.10 **NM** value: **60.00**
85 ❑ May 1951 Cover: 0.10 **NM** value: **60.00**
86 ❑ Jul 1951 Cover: 0.10 **NM** value: **60.00**
87 ❑ Sep 1951 Cover: 0.10 **NM** value: **60.00**
88 ❑ Nov 1951 Cover: 0.10 **NM** value: **60.00**
89 ❑ Jan 1952 Cover: 0.10 **NM** value: **60.00**
• **CGC:** 1 graded, best 9.2
90 ❑ Mar 1952 Cover: 0.10 **NM** value: **60.00**
91 ❑ May 1952 Cover: 0.10 **NM** value: **60.00**
92 ❑ Jul 1952 Cover: 0.10 **NM** value: **60.00**
93 ❑ Sep 1952 Cover: 0.10 **NM** value: **60.00**
94 ❑ Nov 1952 Cover: 0.10 **NM** value: **60.00**
95 ❑ Jan 1953 Cover: 0.10 **NM** value: **60.00**
96 ❑ Mar 1953 Cover: 0.10 **NM** value: **60.00**
97 ❑ May 1953 Cover: 0.10 **NM** value: **60.00**
98 ❑ Jul 1953 Cover: 0.10 **NM** value: **60.00**
99 ❑ Sep 1953 Cover: 0.10 **NM** value: **60.00**
100 ❑ Nov 1953 Cover: 0.10 **NM** value: **85.00**
• 100th anniversary issue.
101 ❑ Jan 1954 Cover: 0.10 **NM** value: **40.00**
102 ❑ Mar 1954 Cover: 0.10 **NM** value: **40.00**
103 ❑ May 1954 Cover: 0.10 **NM** value: **40.00**
104 ❑ Jul 1954 Cover: 0.10 **NM** value: **40.00**
105 ❑ Sep 1954 Cover: 0.10 **NM** value: **40.00**
106 ❑ Nov 1954 Cover: 0.10 **NM** value: **40.00**
107 ❑ Jan 1955 Cover: 0.10 **NM** value: **40.00**
108 ❑ Mar 1955 Cover: 0.10 **NM** value: **40.00**
109 ❑ May 1955 Cover: 0.10 **NM** value: **40.00**
110 ❑ Jul 1955 Cover: 0.10 **NM** value: **40.00**
111 ❑ Sep 1955 Cover: 0.10 **NM** value: **28.00**
112 ❑ Nov 1955 Cover: 0.10 **NM** value: **28.00**
113 ❑ Jan 1956 Cover: 0.10 **NM** value: **28.00**
114 ❑ Mar 1956 Cover: 0.10 **NM** value: **28.00**
115 ❑ May 1956 Cover: 0.10 **NM** value: **28.00**
116 ❑ Jul 1956 Cover: 0.10 **NM** value: **28.00**
117 ❑ Sep 1956 Cover: 0.10 **NM** value: **28.00**
118 ❑ Nov 1956 Cover: 0.10 **NM** value: **28.00**
119 ❑ Jan 1957 Cover: 0.10 **NM** value: **28.00**
120 ❑ Mar 1957 Cover: 0.10 **NM** value: **28.00**
121 ❑ May 1957 Cover: 0.10 **NM** value: **23.00**
122 ❑ Jul 1957 Cover: 0.10 **NM** value: **23.00**
123 ❑ Sep 1957 Cover: 0.10 **NM** value: **23.00**
124 ❑ Nov 1957 Cover: 0.10 **NM** value: **23.00**
125 ❑ Jan 1958 Cover: 0.10 **NM** value: **23.00**
126 ❑ Mar 1958 Cover: 0.10 **NM** value: **23.00**
127 ❑ May 1958 Cover: 0.10 **NM** value: **23.00**
128 ❑ Jul 1958 Cover: 0.10 **NM** value: **23.00**
129 ❑ Sep 1958 Cover: 0.10 **NM** value: **23.00**
130 ❑ Nov 1958 Cover: 0.10 **NM** value: **23.00**
131 ❑ Feb 1959 Cover: 0.10 **NM** value: **19.00**
132 ❑ Apr 1959 Cover: 0.10 **NM** value: **19.00**
133 ❑ Jun 1959 Cover: 0.10 **NM** value: **19.00**
134 ❑ Aug 1959 Cover: 0.10 **NM** value: **19.00**
135 ❑ Oct 1959 Cover: 0.10 **NM** value: **19.00**
136 ❑ Dec 1959 Cover: 0.10 **NM** value: **19.00**
137 ❑ ca. 1960 Cover: 0.10 **NM** value: **19.00**
138 ❑ ca. 1960 Cover: 0.10 **NM** value: **19.00**
Circ: Statement: **269,504**
139 ❑ ca. 1960 Cover: 0.10 **NM** value: **19.00**
Circ: Statement: **269,504**
140 ❑ ca. 1960 Cover: 0.10 **NM** value: **19.00**
Circ: Statement: **269,504**
141 ❑ ca. 1960 Cover: 0.10 **NM** value: **15.00**
Circ: Statement: **269,504**
142 ❑ ca. 1960 Cover: 0.10 **NM** value: **15.00**
Circ: Statement: **269,504**
143 ❑ ca. 1960 Cover: 0.10 **NM** value: **15.00**
Circ: Statement: **269,504**
144 ❑ Jan 1961 Cover: 0.10 **NM** value: **15.00**
Circ: Statement: **250,317**
145 ❑ Mar 1961 Cover: 0.10 **NM** value: **15.00**
Circ: Statement: **250,317**
146 ❑ May 1961 Cover: 0.10 **NM** value: **15.00**
Circ: Statement: **250,317**
147 ❑ Jun 1961 Cover: 0.10 **NM** value: **15.00**
Circ: Statement: **250,317**
148 ❑ Aug 1961 Cover: 0.10 **NM** value: **15.00**
Circ: Statement: **250,317**
149 ❑ Sep 1961 Cover: 0.10 **NM** value: **15.00**
Circ: Statement: **250,317**
150 ❑ Oct 1961 Cover: 0.10 **NM** value: **15.00**
Circ: Statement: **250,317**
★ Appearance of Jaguar.
151 ❑ ca. 1961 Cover: 0.10 **NM** value: **15.00**
Circ: Statement: **250,317**
★ Appearance of The Fly.
152 ❑ Jan 1962 Cover: 0.12 **NM** value: **15.00**
Circ: Statement: **246,491**
★ Appearance of Jaguar.
153 ❑ Mar 1962 Cover: 0.12 **NM** value: **15.00**
Circ: Statement: **246,491**
★ Appearance of Fly Girl.
154 ❑ May 1962 Cover: 0.12 **NM** value: **15.00**
Circ: Statement: **246,491**
★ Appearance of The Fly.
155 ❑ Jun 1962 Cover: 0.12 **NM** value: **15.00**
Circ: Statement: **246,491**
★ Appearance of Fly Girl.
156 ❑ Aug 1962 Cover: 0.12 **NM** value: **15.00**
Circ: Statement: **246,491**
★ Appearance of Fly Girl.
157 ❑ Sep 1962 Cover: 0.12 **NM** value: **15.00**
Circ: Statement: **246,491**
★ 1st Appearance of Kree-Nal. ★ Appearance of Jaguar.
158 ❑ Oct 1962 Cover: 0.12 **NM** value: **15.00**
Circ: Statement: **246,491**
★ Appearance of Fly Girl.
159 ❑ ca. 1962 Cover: 0.12 **NM** value: **15.00**
Circ: Statement: **246,491**
★ Appearance of Jaguar.
160 ❑ Jan 1963 Cover: 0.12 **NM** value: **15.00**
Circ: Statement: **252,621**
★ Appearance of The Fly.
161 ❑ Mar 1963 Cover: 0.12 **NM** value: **7.00**
Circ: Statement: **252,621**
162 ❑ May 1963 Cover: 0.12 **NM** value: **7.00**
Circ: Statement: **252,621**
163 ❑ Jun 1963 Cover: 0.12 **NM** value: **7.00**
Circ: Statement: **252,621**
164 ❑ Aug 1963 Cover: 0.12 **NM** value: **7.00**
Circ: Statement: **252,621**
165 ❑ Sep 1963 Cover: 0.12 **NM** value: **7.00**
Circ: Statement: **252,621**
166 ❑ Oct 1963 Cover: 0.12 **NM** value: **7.00**
Circ: Statement: **252,621**
167 ❑ ca. 1963 Cover: 0.12 **NM** value: **7.00**
Circ: Statement: **252,621**
168 ❑ Jan 1964 Cover: 0.12 **NM** value: **7.00**
Circ: Statement: **258,904**
169 ❑ Mar 1964 Cover: 0.12 **NM** value: **7.00**
Circ: Statement: **258,904**
170 ❑ May 1964 Cover: 0.12 **NM** value: **7.00**
Circ: Statement: **258,904**
171 ❑ Jun 1964 Cover: 0.12 **NM** value: **7.00**
Circ: Statement: **258,904**
172 ❑ Aug 1964 Cover: 0.12 **NM** value: **7.00**
Circ: Statement: **258,904**
173 ❑ Sep 1964 Cover: 0.12 **NM** value: **7.00**
Circ: Statement: **258,904**
174 ❑ Oct 1964 Cover: 0.12 **NM** value: **7.00**
Circ: Statement: **258,904**
175 ❑ Nov 1964 Cover: 0.12 **NM** value: **7.00**
Circ: Statement: **258,904**
176 ❑ Dec 1964 Cover: 0.12 **NM** value: **7.00**
Circ: Statement: **258,904**
177 ❑ Jan 1965 Cover: 0.12 **NM** value: **7.00**
Circ: Statement: **220,010**
178 ❑ Feb 1965 Cover: 0.12 **NM** value: **6.00**
Circ: Statement: **220,010**
179 ❑ Mar 1965 Cover: 0.12 **NM** value: **6.00**
Circ: Statement: **220,010**
180 ❑ Apr 1965 Cover: 0.12 **NM** value: **6.00**
Circ: Statement: **220,010**
181 ❑ May 1965 Cover: 0.12 **NM** value: **6.00**
Circ: Statement: **220,010**
182 ❑ Jun 1965 Cover: 0.12 **NM** value: **6.00**
Circ: Statement: **220,010**
183 ❑ Jul 1965 Cover: 0.12 **NM** value: **6.00**
Circ: Statement: **220,010**
184 ❑ Aug 1965 Cover: 0.12 **NM** value: **6.00**
Circ: Statement: **220,010**
185 ❑ Sep 1965 Cover: 0.12 **NM** value: **6.00**
Circ: Statement: **220,010**
186 ❑ Oct 1965 Cover: 0.12 **NM** value: **6.00**
Circ: Statement: **220,010**
187 ❑ Nov 1965 Cover: 0.12 **NM** value: **6.00**
Circ: Statement: **220,010**
188 ❑ Dec 1965 Cover: 0.12 **NM** value: **6.00**
Circ: Statement: **220,010**
189 ❑ Jan 1966 Cover: 0.12 **NM** value: **6.00**
Circ: Statement: **248,718**
190 ❑ Feb 1966 Cover: 0.12 **NM** value: **6.00**
Circ: Statement: **248,718**
191 ❑ Mar 1966 Cover: 0.12 **NM** value: **6.00**
Circ: Statement: **248,718**
📖 The Wind-Up; Getting Things Done; Wet Paint; The Gossip Column
192 ❑ Apr 1966 Cover: 0.12 **NM** value: **6.00**
Circ: Statement: **248,718**
193 ❑ May 1966 Cover: 0.12 **NM** value: **6.00**
Circ: Statement: **248,718**
194 ❑ Jun 1966 Cover: 0.12 **NM** value: **6.00**
Circ: Statement: **248,718**
195 ❑ Jul 1966 Cover: 0.12 **NM** value: **6.00**
Circ: Statement: **248,718**
196 ❑ Aug 1966 Cover: 0.12 **NM** value: **6.00**
Circ: Statement: **248,718**
197 ❑ Sep 1966 Cover: 0.12 **NM** value: **6.00**
Circ: Statement: **248,718**
198 ❑ Oct 1966 Cover: 0.12 **NM** value: **6.00**
Circ: Statement: **248,718**
199 ❑ Nov 1966 Cover: 0.12 **NM** value: **6.00**
Circ: Statement: **248,718**
200 ❑ Dec 1966 Cover: 0.12 **NM** value: **6.00**
Circ: Statement: **248,718**
201 ❑ Jan 1967 Cover: 0.12 **NM** value: **5.00**
Circ: Statement: **242,821**
202 ❑ Feb 1967 Cover: 0.12 **NM** value: **5.00**
Circ: Statement: **242,821**
203 ❑ Mar 1967 Cover: 0.12 **NM** value: **5.00**
Circ: Statement: **242,821**
204 ❑ Apr 1967 Cover: 0.12 **NM** value: **5.00**
Circ: Statement: **242,821**
205 ❑ May 1967 Cover: 0.12 **NM** value: **5.00**
Circ: Statement: **242,821**
206 ❑ Jun 1967 Cover: 0.12 **NM** value: **5.00**
Circ: Statement: **242,821**
207 ❑ Jul 1967 Cover: 0.12 **NM** value: **5.00**
Circ: Statement: **242,821**
208 ❑ Aug 1967 Cover: 0.12 **NM** value: **5.00**
Circ: Statement: **242,821**
209 ❑ Sep 1967 Cover: 0.12 **NM** value: **5.00**
Circ: Statement: **242,821**
210 ❑ Oct 1967 Cover: 0.12 **NM** value: **5.00**
Circ: Statement: **242,821**
211 ❑ Nov 1967 Cover: 0.12 **NM** value: **5.00**
Circ: Statement: **242,821**
212 ❑ Dec 1967 Cover: 0.12 **NM** value: **5.00**
Circ: Statement: **242,821**
213 ❑ Jan 1968 Cover: 0.12 **NM** value: **5.00**
Circ: Statement: **292,572**
214 ❑ Feb 1968 Cover: 0.12 **NM** value: **5.00**
Circ: Statement: **292,572**
215 ❑ Mar 1968 Cover: 0.12 **NM** value: **5.00**
Circ: Statement: **292,572**
216 ❑ Apr 1968 Cover: 0.12 **NM** value: **5.00**
Circ: Statement: **292,572**
217 ❑ May 1968 Cover: 0.12 **NM** value: **5.00**
Circ: Statement: **292,572**
218 ❑ Jun 1968 Cover: 0.12 **NM** value: **5.00**
Circ: Statement: **292,572**
219 ❑ Jul 1968 Cover: 0.12 **NM** value: **5.00**
Circ: Statement: **292,572**
220 ❑ Aug 1968 Cover: 0.12 **NM** value: **5.00**
Circ: Statement: **292,572**
221 ❑ Sep 1968 Cover: 0.12 **NM** value: **4.00**
Circ: Statement: **292,572**
222 ❑ Oct 1968 Cover: 0.12 **NM** value: **4.00**
Circ: Statement: **292,572**
223 ❑ Nov 1968 Cover: 0.12 **NM** value: **4.00**
Circ: Statement: **292,572**
224 ❑ Dec 1968 Cover: 0.12 **NM** value: **4.00**
Circ: Statement: **292,572**
225 ❑ Jan 1969 Cover: 0.12 **NM** value: **4.00**
226 ❑ Feb 1969 Cover: 0.12 **NM** value: **4.00**
227 ❑ Mar 1969 Cover: 0.12 **NM** value: **4.00**
228 ❑ Apr 1969 Cover: 0.12 **NM** value: **4.00**
229 ❑ May 1969 Cover: 0.12 **NM** value: **4.00**
230 ❑ Jun 1969 Cover: 0.12 **NM** value: **4.00**
231 ❑ Jul 1969 Cover: 0.15 **NM** value: **4.00**
232 ❑ Aug 1969 Cover: 0.15 **NM** value: **3.50**
233 ❑ Sep 1969 Cover: 0.15 **NM** value: **3.50**
234 ❑ Oct 1969 Cover: 0.15 **NM** value: **3.50**
235 ❑ Nov 1969 Cover: 0.15 **NM** value: **3.50**
236 ❑ Dec 1969 Cover: 0.15 **NM** value: **3.50**
237 ❑ Jan 1970 Cover: 0.15 **NM** value: **3.50**
238 ❑ Feb 1970 Cover: 0.15 **NM** value: **3.50**
239 ❑ Mar 1970 Cover: 0.15 **NM** value: **3.50**
240 ❑ Apr 1970 Cover: 0.15 **NM** value: **3.50**
241 ❑ May 1970 Cover: 0.15 **NM** value: **3.50**
242 ❑ Jun 1970 Cover: 0.15 **NM** value: **3.50**
243 ❑ Jul 1970 Cover: 0.15 **NM** value: **3.50**
244 ❑ Aug 1970 Cover: 0.15 **NM** value: **3.50**
245 ❑ Sep 1970 Cover: 0.15 **NM** value: **3.50**
246 ❑ Oct 1970 Cover: 0.15 **NM** value: **3.50**
247 ❑ Nov 1970 Cover: 0.15 **NM** value: **3.50**
248 ❑ Dec 1970 Cover: 0.15 **NM** value: **3.50**
249 ❑ Jan 1971 Cover: 0.15 **NM** value: **3.50**
250 ❑ Feb 1971 Cover: 0.15 **NM** value: **3.50**
251 ❑ Mar 1971 Cover: 0.15 **NM** value: **1.75**
252 ❑ Apr 1971 Cover: 0.15 **NM** value: **1.75**
253 ❑ May 1971 Cover: 0.15 **NM** value: **1.75**
254 ❑ Jun 1971 Cover: 0.15 **NM** value: **1.75**
255 ❑ Jul 1971 Cover: 0.15 **NM** value: **1.75**
256 ❑ Aug 1971 Cover: 0.15 **NM** value: **1.75**
257 ❑ Sep 1971 Cover: 0.15 **NM** value: **1.75**
258 ❑ Oct 1971 Cover: 0.15 **NM** value: **1.75**
259 ❑ Nov 1971 Cover: 0.15 **NM** value: **1.75**
260 ❑ Dec 1971 Cover: 0.15 **NM** value: **1.75**
261 ❑ Jan 1972 Cover: 0.15 **NM** value: **1.75**
Circ: Statement: **231,963**
262 ❑ Feb 1972 Cover: 0.15 **NM** value: **1.75**
Circ: Statement: **231,963**
263 ❑ Mar 1972 Cover: 0.15 **NM** value: **1.75**
Circ: Statement: **231,963**
264 ❑ Apr 1972 Cover: 0.15 **NM** value: **1.75**
Circ: Statement: **231,963**
265 ❑ May 1972 Cover: 0.20 **NM** value: **1.75**
Circ: Statement: **231,963**
266 ❑ Jun 1972 Cover: 0.20 **NM** value: **1.75**
Circ: Statement: **231,963**
267 ❑ Jul 1972 Cover: 0.20 **NM** value: **1.75**
Circ: Statement: **231,963**

Other grades: Multiply prices above by **1.5 for Mint • 2/3 for Very Fine • 1/3 for Fine • 1/5 for Very Good • 1/8 for Good**

268 ❑ Aug 1972 Cover: 0.20 NM value: 1.75
Circ: Statement: 231,963
269 ❑ Sep 1972 Cover: 0.20 NM value: 1.75
Circ: Statement: 231,963
270 ❑ Oct 1972 Cover: 0.20 NM value: 1.75
Circ: Statement: 231,963
271 ❑ Nov 1972 Cover: 0.20 NM value: 1.75
Circ: Statement: 231,963
272 ❑ Dec 1972 Cover: 0.20 NM value: 1.75
Circ: Statement: 231,963
273 ❑ Jan 1973 Cover: 0.20 NM value: 1.75
Circ: Statement: 206,109
274 ❑ Feb 1973 Cover: 0.20 NM value: 1.75
Circ: Statement: 206,109
275 ❑ Mar 1973 Cover: 0.20 NM value: 1.75
Circ: Statement: 206,109
276 ❑ Apr 1973 Cover: 0.20 NM value: 1.75
Circ: Statement: 206,109
277 ❑ May 1973 Cover: 0.20 NM value: 1.75
Circ: Statement: 206,109
278 ❑ Jun 1973 Cover: 0.20 NM value: 1.75
Circ: Statement: 206,109
279 ❑ Jul 1973 Cover: 0.20 NM value: 1.75
Circ: Statement: 206,109
280 ❑ Aug 1973 Cover: 0.20 NM value: 1.75
Circ: Statement: 206,109
281 ❑ Sep 1973 Cover: 0.20 NM value: 1.50
Circ: Statement: 206,109
282 ❑ Oct 1973 Cover: 0.20 NM value: 1.50
Circ: Statement: 206,109
283 ❑ Nov 1973 Cover: 0.20 NM value: 1.50
Circ: Statement: 206,109
284 ❑ Dec 1973 Cover: 0.20 NM value: 1.50
Circ: Statement: 206,109
285 ❑ Jan 1974 Cover: 0.20 NM value: 1.50
Circ: Statement: 193,289
286 ❑ Feb 1974 Cover: 0.20 NM value: 1.50
Circ: Statement: 193,289
287 ❑ Mar 1974 Cover: 0.20 NM value: 1.50
Circ: Statement: 193,289
288 ❑ Apr 1974 Cover: 0.25 NM value: 1.50
Circ: Statement: 193,289
289 ❑ May 1974 Cover: 0.25 NM value: 1.50
Circ: Statement: 193,289
290 ❑ Jun 1974 Cover: 0.25 NM value: 1.50
Circ: Statement: 193,289
291 ❑ Jul 1974 Cover: 0.25 NM value: 1.50
Circ: Statement: 193,289
292 ❑ Aug 1974 Cover: 0.25 NM value: 1.50
Circ: Statement: 193,289
293 ❑ Sep 1974 Cover: 0.25 NM value: 1.50
Circ: Statement: 193,289
294 ❑ Oct 1974 Cover: 0.25 NM value: 1.50
Circ: Statement: 193,289
295 ❑ Nov 1974 Cover: 0.25 NM value: 1.50
Circ: Statement: 193,289
296 ❑ Dec 1974 Cover: 0.25 NM value: 1.50
Circ: Statement: 193,289
297 ❑ Jan 1975 Cover: 0.25 NM value: 1.50
Circ: Statement: 142,807
298 ❑ Feb 1975 Cover: 0.25 NM value: 1.50
Circ: Statement: 142,807
299 ❑ Mar 1975 Cover: 0.25 NM value: 1.50
Circ: Statement: 142,807
300 ❑ Apr 1975 Cover: 0.25 NM value: 1.50
Circ: Statement: 142,807
301 ❑ May 1975 Cover: 0.25 NM value: 1.25
Circ: Statement: 142,807
302 ❑ Jun 1975 Cover: 0.25 NM value: 1.25
Circ: Statement: 142,807
303 ❑ Jul 1975 Cover: 0.25 NM value: 1.25
Circ: Statement: 142,807
304 ❑ Aug 1975 Cover: 0.25 NM value: 1.25
Circ: Statement: 142,807
305 ❑ Sep 1975 Cover: 0.25 NM value: 1.25
Circ: Statement: 142,807
306 ❑ Oct 1975 Cover: 0.25 NM value: 1.25
Circ: Statement: 142,807
307 ❑ Nov 1975 Cover: 0.25 NM value: 1.25
Circ: Statement: 142,807
308 ❑ Dec 1975 Cover: 0.25 NM value: 1.25
Circ: Statement: 142,807
309 ❑ Jan 1976 Cover: 0.25 NM value: 1.25
Circ: Statement: 132,352
310 ❑ Feb 1976 Cover: 0.30 NM value: 1.25
Circ: Statement: 132,352
311 ❑ Mar 1976 Cover: 0.30 NM value: 1.25
Circ: Statement: 132,352
312 ❑ Apr 1976 Cover: 0.30 NM value: 1.25
Circ: Statement: 132,352
313 ❑ May 1976 Cover: 0.30 NM value: 1.25
Circ: Statement: 132,352
314 ❑ Jun 1976 Cover: 0.30 NM value: 1.25
Circ: Statement: 132,352
315 ❑ Jul 1976 Cover: 0.30 NM value: 1.25
Circ: Statement: 132,352
316 ❑ Aug 1976 Cover: 0.30 NM value: 1.25
Circ: Statement: 132,352
317 ❑ Sep 1976 Cover: 0.30 NM value: 1.25
Circ: Statement: 132,352
318 ❑ Oct 1976 Cover: 0.30 NM value: 1.25
Circ: Statement: 132,352
319 ❑ Nov 1976 Cover: 0.30 NM value: 1.25
Circ: Statement: 132,352
320 ❑ Dec 1976 Cover: 0.30 NM value: 1.25
Circ: Statement: 132,352
321 ❑ Jan 1977 Cover: 0.30 NM value: 1.25
Circ: Statement: 124,462
322 ❑ Feb 1977 Cover: 0.30 NM value: 1.25
Circ: Statement: 124,462
323 ❑ Mar 1977 Cover: 0.30 NM value: 1.25
Circ: Statement: 124,462
324 ❑ Apr 1977 Cover: 0.30 NM value: 1.25
Circ: Statement: 124,462
325 ❑ May 1977 Cover: 0.30 NM value: 1.25
Circ: Statement: 124,462
326 ❑ Jun 1977 Cover: 0.35 NM value: 1.25
Circ: Statement: 124,462
327 ❑ Jul 1977 Cover: 0.35 NM value: 1.25
Circ: Statement: 124,462
328 ❑ Aug 1977 Cover: 0.35 NM value: 1.25
Circ: Statement: 124,462
329 ❑ Sep 1977 Cover: 0.35 NM value: 1.25
Circ: Statement: 124,462
330 ❑ Oct 1977 Cover: 0.35 NM value: 1.25
Circ: Statement: 124,462
331 ❑ Nov 1977 Cover: 0.35 NM value: 1.25
Circ: Statement: 124,462
332 ❑ Dec 1977 Cover: 0.35 NM value: 1.25
Circ: Statement: 124,462
333 ❑ Jan 1978 Cover: 0.35 NM value: 1.25
Circ: Statement: 108,806
334 ❑ Feb 1978 Cover: 0.35 NM value: 1.25
Circ: Statement: 108,806
335 ❑ Mar 1978 Cover: 0.35 NM value: 1.25
Circ: Statement: 108,806
336 ❑ Apr 1978 Cover: 0.35 NM value: 1.25
Circ: Statement: 108,806
337 ❑ May 1978 Cover: 0.35 NM value: 1.25
Circ: Statement: 108,806
338 ❑ Jun 1978 Cover: 0.35 NM value: 1.25
Circ: Statement: 108,806
339 ❑ Jul 1978 Cover: 0.35 NM value: 1.25
Circ: Statement: 108,806
340 ❑ Aug 1978 Cover: 0.35 NM value: 1.25
Circ: Statement: 108,806
341 ❑ Sep 1978 Cover: 0.35 NM value: 1.25
Circ: Statement: 108,806
342 ❑ Oct 1978 Cover: 0.35 NM value: 1.25
Circ: Statement: 108,806
343 ❑ Nov 1978 Cover: 0.35 NM value: 1.25
Circ: Statement: 108,806
344 ❑ Dec 1978 Cover: 0.35 NM value: 1.25
Circ: Statement: 108,806
345 ❑ Jan 1979 Cover: 0.35 NM value: 1.25
Circ: Statement: 100,827
346 ❑ Feb 1979 Cover: 0.35 NM value: 1.25
Circ: Statement: 100,827
347 ❑ Mar 1979 Cover: 0.35 NM value: 1.25
Circ: Statement: 100,827
348 ❑ Apr 1979 Cover: 0.40 NM value: 1.25
Circ: Statement: 100,827
349 ❑ May 1979 Cover: 0.40 NM value: 1.25
Circ: Statement: 100,827
350 ❑ Jun 1979 Cover: 0.40 NM value: 1.25
Circ: Statement: 100,827
351 ❑ Jul 1979 Cover: 0.40 NM value: 1.25
Circ: Statement: 100,827
352 ❑ Aug 1979 Cover: 0.40 NM value: 1.25
Circ: Statement: 100,827
353 ❑ Sep 1979 Cover: 0.40 NM value: 1.25
Circ: Statement: 100,827
354 ❑ Oct 1979 Cover: 0.40 NM value: 1.25
Circ: Statement: 100,827
355 ❑ Nov 1979 Cover: 0.40 NM value: 1.25
Circ: Statement: 100,827
356 ❑ Dec 1979 Cover: 0.40 NM value: 1.25
Circ: Statement: 100,827
357 ❑ Jan 1980 Cover: 0.40 NM value: 1.25
358 ❑ Feb 1980 Cover: 0.40 NM value: 1.25
359 ❑ Mar 1980 Cover: 0.40 NM value: 1.25
360 ❑ Apr 1980 Cover: 0.40 NM value: 1.25
361 ❑ May 1980 Cover: 0.40 NM value: 1.25
362 ❑ Jun 1980 Cover: 0.40 NM value: 1.25
363 ❑ Jul 1980 Cover: 0.40 NM value: 1.25
364 ❑ Aug 1980 Cover: 0.50 NM value: 1.25
365 ❑ ca. 1980 Cover: 0.50 NM value: 1.25
366 ❑ ca. 1980 Cover: 0.50 NM value: 1.25
367 ❑ ca. 1980 Cover: 0.50 NM value: 1.25
368 ❑ Cover: 0.50 NM value: 1.25
369 ❑ ca. 1981 Cover: 0.50 NM value: 1.25
370 ❑ ca. 1981 Cover: 0.50 NM value: 1.00
371 ❑ ca. 1981 Cover: 0.50 NM value: 1.00
372 ❑ ca. 1981 Cover: 0.50 NM value: 1.00
373 ❑ ca. 1981 Cover: 0.50 NM value: 1.00
374 ❑ ca. 1981 Cover: 0.50 NM value: 1.00
375 ❑ ca. 1981 Cover: 0.50 NM value: 1.00
376 ❑ ca. 1981 Cover: 0.50 NM value: 1.00
377 ❑ ca. 1981 Cover: 0.50 NM value: 1.00
378 ❑ ca. 1981 Cover: 0.50 NM value: 1.00
379 ❑ ca. 1981 Cover: 0.50 NM value: 1.00
380 ❑ NM value: 1.00
381 ❑ ca. 1982 Cover: 0.60 NM value: 1.00
382 ❑ ca. 1982 Cover: 0.60 NM value: 1.00
383 ❑ Apr 1982 Cover: 0.60 NM value: 1.00
384 ❑ Cover: 0.60 NM value: 1.00
385 ❑ Cover: 0.60 NM value: 1.00
386 ❑ Cover: 0.60 NM value: 1.00
Circ: Statement: 61,226
387 ❑ Cover: 0.60 NM value: 1.00
Circ: Statement: 61,226
388 ❑ Cover: 0.60 NM value: 1.00
Circ: Statement: 61,226
389 ❑ ca. 1983 Cover: 0.60 NM value: 1.00
Circ: Statement: 61,226
390 ❑ ca. 1983 Cover: 0.60 NM value: 1.00
Circ: Statement: 61,226
391 ❑ Nov 1983 Cover: 0.60 NM value: 1.00
Circ: Statement: 61,226
392 ❑ Jan 1984 Cover: 0.60 NM value: 1.00
Circ: Statement: 55,078
393 ❑ Mar 1984 Cover: 0.60 NM value: 1.00
Circ: Statement: 55,078
394 ❑ May 1984 Cover: 0.60 NM value: 1.00
Circ: Statement: 55,078
395 ❑ Jul 1984 Cover: 0.60 NM value: 1.00
Circ: Statement: 55,078
396 ❑ Sep 1984 Cover: 0.60 NM value: 1.00
Circ: Statement: 55,078
397 ❑ Nov 1984 Cover: 0.60 NM value: 1.00
Circ: Statement: 55,078
398 ❑ Jan 1985 Cover: 0.60 NM value: 1.00
Circ: Statement: 55,164
399 ❑ Mar 1985 Cover: 0.65 NM value: 1.00
Circ: Statement: 55,164
400 ❑ May 1985 Cover: 0.65 NM value: 1.00
Circ: Statement: 55,164
401 ❑ Jul 1985 Cover: 0.65 NM value: 1.00
Circ: Statement: 55,164
402 ❑ Sep 1985 Cover: 0.65 NM value: 1.00
Circ: Statement: 55,164
403 ❑ Nov 1985 Cover: 0.65 NM value: 1.00
Circ: Statement: 55,164
404 ❑ Jan 1986 Cover: 0.65 NM value: 1.00
405 ❑ Mar 1986 Cover: 0.65 NM value: 1.00
406 ❑ May 1986 Cover: 0.65 NM value: 1.00
407 ❑ Jul 1986 Cover: 0.75 NM value: 1.00
408 ❑ Sep 1986 Cover: 0.75 NM value: 1.00
409 ❑ Nov 1986 Cover: 0.75 NM value: 1.00
410 ❑ Jan 1987 Cover: 0.75 NM value: 1.00
411 ❑ Mar 1987 Cover: 0.75 NM value: 1.00
final issue.

PERAZIM — Antarctic

1 ❑ Sep 1996, b&w Cover: 2.95 NM value: Cover or less
A: Patrick R. Kelley W: Patrick R. Kelley
2 ❑ Cover: 2.95 NM value: Cover or less
A: Patrick R. Kelley W: Patrick R. Kelley
3 ❑ Cover: 2.95 NM value: Cover or less
A: Patrick R. Kelley W: Patrick R. Kelley

PERCEVAN: THE THREE STARS OF INGAAR — Fantasy Flight

1 ❑ Cover: 8.95 NM value: Cover or less

PEREGRINE, THE — Alliance

1 ❑ Apr 1994, b&w Cover: 2.50 NM value: Cover or less
2 ❑ Aug 1994, b&w Cover: 2.50 NM value: Cover or less

PERFECT LOVE — Ziff-Davis

1 ❑ Aug 1951 Cover: 0.10 NM value: 125.00
2 ❑ Oct 1951 Cover: 0.10 NM value: 100.00
3 ❑ Win 1951 Cover: 0.10 NM value: 100.00
• CGC: 2 graded, best 9.6
4 ❑ ca. 1952 Cover: 0.10 NM value: 100.00
5 ❑ ca. 1952 Cover: 0.10 NM value: 75.00
6 ❑ ca. 1952 Cover: 0.10 NM value: 75.00
7 ❑ Aug 1952 Cover: 0.10 NM value: 75.00
8 ❑ Fal 1952 Cover: 0.10 NM value: 75.00
9 ❑ ca. 1953 Cover: 0.10 NM value: 75.00
10 ❑ Dec 1953 Cover: 0.10 NM value: 75.00

PERFECT CRIME — Cross

Hot dog! Now readers will be set for the caper of a lifetime! They've found a comic book that'll tell them how to do it: The Perfect Crime. Wups! How many of the would-be criminals picking up a copy noticed the line over the top of the logo: "True Facts! How Police Smash"—and then the title, "The Perfect Crime"? Darn. Sometimes, a notice even appeared on the cover, beginning, "The crusade against crime and murder!" And covers feature one crook or another about to get his comeuppance, whether from another crook or from the police. "It's bullets outside or burn!" "It's curtains!" "No! No! Maxie! Don't hit me again!" Ongoing featured character is Steve Duncan, starring in such stories as "The Fatal Mistake" and "Murder Mountain." — Maggie

1 ❑ Oct 1949 Cover: 0.10 NM value: 225.00
• CGC: 1 graded, best 9.2
2 ❑ Apr 1950 Cover: 0.10 NM value: 125.00
3 ❑ Jun 1950 Cover: 0.10 NM value: 125.00
4 ❑ Aug 1950 Cover: 0.10 NM value: 125.00
• CGC: 1 graded, best 7.5
5 ❑ Oct 1950 Cover: 0.10 NM value: 125.00
6 ❑ Nov 1950 Cover: 0.10 NM value: 125.00
7 ❑ Dec 1950 Cover: 0.10 NM value: 125.00
• CGC: 1 graded, best 7.0
8 ❑ Jan 1951 Cover: 0.10 NM value: 125.00
9 ❑ Feb 1951 Cover: 0.10 NM value: 125.00
10 ❑ Mar 1951 Cover: 0.10 NM value: 100.00
11 ❑ Apr 1951 Cover: 0.10 NM value: 100.00
12 ❑ May 1951 Cover: 0.10 NM value: 100.00
13 ❑ Jun 1951 Cover: 0.10 NM value: 100.00
14 ❑ Jul 1951 Cover: 0.10 NM value: 100.00
15 ❑ Aug 1951 Cover: 0.10 NM value: 100.00
16 ❑ Sep 1951 Cover: 0.10 NM value: 100.00
17 ❑ Oct 1951 Cover: 0.10 NM value: 100.00

CGC-graded: Multiply prices above by **33 for 9.9 M • 16 for 9.8 NM/M • 7 for 9.6 NM+ • 5 for 9.4 NM • 2.5 for 9.2 NM- • 1.5 for 9.0 VF/NM**

18 ❑ Nov 1951 Cover: 0.10 **NM** value: **100.00**
19 ❑ Dec 1951 Cover: 0.10 **NM** value: **100.00**
20 ❑ Jan 1952 Cover: 0.10 **NM** value: **75.00**
21 ❑ Feb 1952 Cover: 0.10 **NM** value: **75.00**
22 ❑ Mar 1952 Cover: 0.10 **NM** value: **75.00**
23 ❑ Apr 1952 Cover: 0.10 **NM** value: **75.00**
24 ❑ May 1952 Cover: 0.10 **NM** value: **75.00**
25 ❑ Jun 1952 Cover: 0.10 **NM** value: **75.00**
26 ❑ Jul 1952 Cover: 0.10 **NM** value: **75.00**
27 ❑ Aug 1952 Cover: 0.10 **NM** value: **75.00**
• **CGC:** 1 graded, best 6.0
28 ❑ Sep 1952 Cover: 0.10 **NM** value: **75.00**
• **CGC:** 1 graded, best 3.0
29 ❑ Oct 1952 Cover: 0.10 **NM** value: **75.00**
30 ❑ Nov 1952 Cover: 0.10 **NM** value: **75.00**
31 ❑ Jan 1953 Cover: 0.10 **NM** value: **75.00**
32 ❑ Mar 1953 Cover: 0.10 **NM** value: **75.00**
33 ❑ May 1953 Cover: 0.10 **NM** value: **75.00**

PERG — Lightning

1 ❑ Oct 1993 Cover: 3.50 **NM** value: **Cover or less**
Circ: CapCity orders: **7,975**
📖 Origin of Perg • Glow-in the dark flip book **A:** Karl Kerschl **W:** Joseph A. Zyskowski ★ Appearance of Dreadwolf.
1/GO❑Oct 1993 Cover: 3.50 **NM** value: **Cover or less**
• Gold edition.
1/PL❑ Oct 1993 Cover: 2.50 **NM** value: **Cover or less**
• Platinum edition. 📖 Origin of Perg **A:** Karl Kerschl **W:** Joseph A. Zyskowski
1/SC❑Oct 1993 Cover: 3.50 **NM** value: **Cover or less**
glow cover.
2 ❑ Nov 1993 Cover: 2.95 **NM** value: **Cover or less**
Circ: CapCity orders: **5,500**
W: Joseph A. Zyskowski ★ Appearance of Dreadwolf.
2/PL❑ Nov 1993 Cover: 2.95 **NM** value: **Cover or less**
• Platinum edition. • platinum **W:** Joseph A. Zyskowski
3 ❑ Dec 1993 Cover: 2.95 **NM** value: **Cover or less**
Circ: CapCity orders: **5,475**
W: Joseph A. Zyskowski
3/PL❑ Dec 1993 Cover: 2.50 **NM** value: **Cover or less**
• Platinum edition. **W:** Joseph A. Zyskowski
4 ❑ Jan 1994 Cover: 2.95 **NM** value: **Cover or less**
Circ: CapCity orders: **5,300**
W: Joseph A. Zyskowski ★ Origin of Perg.
4/PL❑ Jan 1994 Cover: 2.95 **NM** value: **Cover or less**
• Platinum edition. • platinum **W:** Joseph A. Zyskowski
5 ❑ Feb 1994 Cover: 2.95 **NM** value: **Cover or less**
Circ: CapCity orders: **4,075**
W: Joseph A. Zyskowski
6 ❑ Mar 1994 Cover: 2.95 **NM** value: **Cover or less**
Circ: CapCity orders: **3,150** • **CGC:** 2 graded, best 9.6
W: Joseph A. Zyskowski
7 ❑ Apr 1994 Cover: 2.95 **NM** value: **Cover or less**
Circ: CapCity orders: **2,675**
W: Joseph A. Zyskowski
8 ❑ May 1994 Cover: 2.95 **NM** value: **Cover or less**
Circ: CapCity orders: **2,650**
final issue. **W:** Joseph A. Zyskowski

PERIPHERY — Arch-Type

1 ❑ Cover: 2.95 **NM** value: **Cover or less**
📖 The Trashman; Lore: Imperfect Gentleman; Dead Man's Date; Hacker Boy; Quack Duck of Doom: The Devil Wears Suspenders, Part 1; Dead Dolls; The Half Life Chronicles, The Gravedigger's Prelude **A:** Brian LaFramboise; Giorgio Giunta; Jan Hachigian; Jason Whitley; The Brothers Grinn; Travis Hanson **W:** Andrew Dabb; Jack Feerick; Jen Hachigian; Mare Fleury; Michael Triggs; Scott Ekelaert

PERRAMUS: ESCAPE FROM THE PAST — Fantagraphics

1 ❑ b&w Cover: 3.50 **NM** value: **Cover or less**
2 ❑ b&w Cover: 3.50 **NM** value: **Cover or less**
3 ❑ b&w Cover: 3.50 **NM** value: **Cover or less**
4 ❑ b&w Cover: 3.50 **NM** value: **Cover or less**

PERRY — Lightning

1 ❑ Oct 1997 Cover: 2.95 **NM** value: **Cover or less**
A: Mike Kelleher **W:** Mike Kelleher; Toby Mays

PERSONALITY CLASSICS — Personality

1 ❑ Cover: 2.95 **NM** value: **Cover or less**
• John Wayne
2 ❑ Cover: 2.95 **NM** value: **Cover or less**
• Marilyn Monroe
3 ❑ Cover: 2.95 **NM** value: **Cover or less**
4 ❑ Cover: 2.95 **NM** value: **Cover or less**

PERSONALITY COMICS PRESENTS — Personality

1 ❑ 1991 Cover: 2.50 **NM** value: **Cover or less**
• Paulina Porizkova
2 ❑ Apr 1991 Cover: 2.50 **NM** value: **Cover or less**
• Traci Lords
3 ❑ 1991 Cover: 2.50 **NM** value: **Cover or less**
• Arnold Schwarzenegger
4 ❑ 1991 Cover: 2.50 **NM** value: **Cover or less**
• Christina Applegate
5 ❑ 1991 Cover: 2.95 **NM** value: **Cover or less**
• Patrick Swayze, Demi Moore
6 ❑ 1991 Cover: 2.95 **NM** value: **Cover or less**
• Michael Jordan
7 ❑ Cover: 2.95 **NM** value: **Cover or less**
• Samantha Fox
8 ❑ Cover: 2.95 **NM** value: **Cover or less**
• Bettie Page, Jennifer Connelly
9 ❑ Cover: 2.95 **NM** value: **Cover or less**
• Kim Basinger, Michael Keaton
10 ❑ Cover: 2.95 **NM** value: **Cover or less**
• Gloria Estefan

11 ❑ Cover: 2.95 **NM** value: **Cover or less**
12 ❑ Cover: 2.95 **NM** value: **Cover or less**
13 ❑ Cover: 2.95 **NM** value: **Cover or less**
14 ❑ Cover: 2.95 **NM** value: **Cover or less**
15 ❑ Cover: 2.95 **NM** value: **Cover or less**
16 ❑ Cover: 2.95 **NM** value: **Cover or less**
17 ❑ Cover: 2.95 **NM** value: **Cover or less**
18 ❑ Cover: 2.95 **NM** value: **Cover or less**

PERSONAL LOVE — Famous Funnies

Although the title is Personal Love, the covers displayed public love — in the form of loving publicity photos of famous film personalities. Kathryn Grayson and Mario Lanza, Robert Walker and Joanne Dru, Esther Williams and Howard Keel, Gene Tierney and Glenn Ford, Yvonne DeCarlo and Rock Hudson, Susan Hayward and Gregory Peck, Rhonda Fleming and Fernando Lamas, and Marlon Brando and Jean Simmons are only a few of the celebrities who necked on Personal Love's covers.

The performers (the Brando and Simmons, for example, is from Desiree) have nothing to do with the stories inside (in that case, "Save My Love," Wrong Kind of Girl,“ and "A Lady in Love“). Nevertheless, the issues do offer collectible photo covers, which hikes the value of some. — Maggie

1 ❑ Jan 1950 Cover: 0.10 **NM** value: **100.00**
2 ❑ Mar 1950 Cover: 0.10 **NM** value: **50.00**
3 ❑ May 1950 Cover: 0.10 **NM** value: **50.00**
4 ❑ Jul 1950 Cover: 0.10 **NM** value: **50.00**
5 ❑ Sep 1950 Cover: 0.10 **NM** value: **50.00**
6 ❑ Nov 1950 Cover: 0.10 **NM** value: **50.00**
7 ❑ Jan 1951 Cover: 0.10 **NM** value: **50.00**
8 ❑ Mar 1951 Cover: 0.10 **NM** value: **50.00**
9 ❑ May 1951 Cover: 0.10 **NM** value: **50.00**
10 ❑ Jul 1951 Cover: 0.10 **NM** value: **50.00**
11 ❑ Sep 1951 Cover: 0.10 **NM** value: **50.00**
12 ❑ Nov 1951 Cover: 0.10 **NM** value: **50.00**
13 ❑ Jan 1952 Cover: 0.10 **NM** value: **50.00**
14 ❑ Mar 1952 Cover: 0.10 **NM** value: **50.00**
15 ❑ May 1952 Cover: 0.10 **NM** value: **50.00**
16 ❑ Jul 1952 Cover: 0.10 **NM** value: **50.00**
17 ❑ Sep 1952 Cover: 0.10 **NM** value: **50.00**
18 ❑ Nov 1952 Cover: 0.10 **NM** value: **50.00**
19 ❑ Jan 1953 Cover: 0.10 **NM** value: **50.00**
20 ❑ Mar 1953 Cover: 0.10 **NM** value: **45.00**
21 ❑ May 1953 Cover: 0.10 **NM** value: **45.00**
22 ❑ Jul 1953 Cover: 0.10 **NM** value: **45.00**
23 ❑ Sep 1953 Cover: 0.10 **NM** value: **45.00**
24 ❑ Nov 1953 Cover: 0.10 **NM** value: **45.00**
25 ❑ Jan 1954 Cover: 0.10 **NM** value: **45.00**
26 ❑ Apr 1954 Cover: 0.10 **NM** value: **45.00**
27 ❑ Jun 1954 Cover: 0.10 **NM** value: **45.00**
28 ❑ Aug 1954 Cover: 0.10 **NM** value: **45.00**
29 ❑ Oct 1954 Cover: 0.10 **NM** value: **45.00**
30 ❑ Dec 1954 Cover: 0.10 **NM** value: **45.00**
31 ❑ Feb 1955 Cover: 0.10 **NM** value: **45.00**
32 ❑ Apr 1955 Cover: 0.10 **NM** value: **45.00**
• **CGC:** 2 graded, best 9.2
33 ❑ Jun 1955 Cover: 0.10 **NM** value: **45.00**

PEST — Pest Comics

1 ❑ Cover: 1.95 **NM** value: **Cover or less**
A: Dave Fox; Tim Price **W:** Dave Fox; Tim Price
2 ❑ Cover: 1.95 **NM** value: **Cover or less**
A: Dave Fox; Tim Price **W:** Dave Fox; Tim Price
3 ❑ Cover: 1.95 **NM** value: **Cover or less**
A: Dave Fox; Tim Price **W:** Dave Fox; Tim Price
4 ❑ Cover: 1.95 **NM** value: **Cover or less**
📖 Pipi Soiledstockings; Bargirl; Chameleon Kids; Superpoop **A:** Dave Fox; Tim Price **W:** Dave Fox; Tim Price
5 ❑ Cover: 1.95 **NM** value: **Cover or less**
📖 Bargirl Returns; Party Pigs at Pigstock; Tom Scummie and the Station Wagon Family; The Tale of Bundleturds **A:** Dave Fox; Tim Price **W:** Dave Fox; Tim Price
6 ❑ b&w Cover: 1.85 **NM** value: **1.95**
📖 The Puke-O the Clown Story; Sky Cow; The Chameleon Kids; Poop Finster **A:** Dave Fox; Tim Price **W:** Dave Fox; Tim Price
7 ❑ Cover: 1.95 **NM** value: **Cover or less**
📖 Fart-Force; Babushka; Atomic Newtie **A:** Dave Fox; Tim Price **W:** Dave Fox; Tim Price

PET — Eros

1 ❑ May 1997 Cover: 2.95 **NM** value: **Cover or less**
A: Tayyar Ozkan **W:** Tayyar Ozkan

PETER AND THE WOLF — NBM

1 ❑ Cover: 15.95 **NM** value: **Cover or less**
hardcover adaptation of Prokofiev's symphony.

Capital City orders are the actual sales of comic books by Capital City Distribution, once one of the largest U.S. sellers of comics to comics shops. Capital City's share of comics shop sales, while not known exactly, increases from around 10-20% in the mid-1980s to 30-35% in the mid-1990s. Capital City's share of comic books sold on newsstands (most Marvels and DCs) will be less.

PETER CANNON-THUNDERBOLT — DC

Richard Cannon and his wife were aid workers in Tibet during the time of the Communist takeover. As Americans, their lives were in danger from the Communists, so Richard took refuge with his pregnant wife in a monastery. Richard's wife died in giving birth to their son Peter, and Richard died soon afterward from an illness. The boy was raised by the monks who thought he might be the reincarnation of their protector and hero Varja. As it turned out, the monks may have been right.

They trained Peter to use his body and mind to perfection. This combination turned Peter into the swift and powerful Thunderbolt. Now living in London, he is a reluctant hero, but one who conquers his fears in order to save the day.

Originally a Charlton character, Thunderbolt made the transition to DC along with Captain Atom, The Question, and Blue Beetle in Crisis on Infinite Earths #6.

1 ❑ Sep 1992 Cover: 1.25 **NM** value: **1.50**
Circ: CapCity orders: **22,450**
📖 Rebirth **A:** Mike Collins **W:** Mike Collins ★ Origin of Thunderbolt.
2 ❑ Oct 1992 Cover: 1.25 **NM** value: **1.50**
Circ: CapCity orders: **12,400**
3 ❑ Nov 1992 Cover: 1.25 **NM** value: **1.50**
Circ: CapCity orders: **10,600**
4 ❑ Dec 1992 Cover: 1.25 **NM** value: **Cover or less**
Circ: CapCity orders: **8,450**
5 ❑ Jan 1993 Cover: 1.25 **NM** value: **Cover or less**
Circ: CapCity orders: **7,100**
6 ❑ Feb 1993 Cover: 1.25 **NM** value: **Cover or less**
Circ: CapCity orders: **6,250**
7 ❑ Mar 1993 Cover: 1.25 **NM** value: **Cover or less**
Circ: CapCity orders: **5,700**
8 ❑ Apr 1993 Cover: 1.25 **NM** value: **Cover or less**
Circ: CapCity orders: **6,450**
9 ❑ May 1993 Cover: 1.50 **NM** value: **Cover or less**
Circ: CapCity orders: **5,300**
10 ❑ May 1993 Cover: 1.50 **NM** value: **Cover or less**
Circ: CapCity orders: **4,875**
11 ❑ Jul 1993 Cover: 1.50 **NM** value: **Cover or less**
Circ: CapCity orders: **4,300**
12 ❑ Aug 1993 Cover: 1.50 **NM** value: **Cover or less**
Circ: CapCity orders: **4,700**
final issue.

PETER COTTONTAIL — Key

1 ❑ Jan 1954 Cover: 0.10 **NM** value: **50.00**
2 ❑ Mar 1954 Cover: 0.10 **NM** value: **35.00**

PETER KOCK — Fantagraphics / Eros

All issues are adults only.

1 ❑ 1994b&w Cover: 3.50 **NM** value: **Cover or less**
2 ❑ 1994b&w Cover: 2.75 **NM** value: **Cover or less**
3 ❑ 1994b&w Cover: 2.75 **NM** value: **Cover or less**
4 ❑ May 1994, b&w Cover: 2.75 **NM** value: **Cover or less**
5 ❑ Jul 1994, b&w Cover: 2.75 **NM** value: **Cover or less**
6 ❑ Aug 1994, b&w Cover: 2.75 **NM** value: **Cover or less**

PETER PAN AND THE WARLORDS OF OZ — Hand of Doom

1 ❑ Cover: 2.95 **NM** value: **Cover or less**
A: Al Hubbard **W:** Don Christensen

PETER PAN & THE WARLORDS OF OZ: DEAD HEAD WATER — Hand of Doom

1 ❑ Cover: 2.95 **NM** value: **Cover or less**
A: Rob Hand **W:** Rob Hand

PETER PANDA — DC

1 ❑ Aug 1953 Cover: 0.10 **NM** value: **300.00**
2 ❑ Oct 1953 Cover: 0.10 **NM** value: **150.00**
3 ❑ Dec 1953 Cover: 0.10 **NM** value: **150.00**
4 ❑ Feb 1954 Cover: 0.10 **NM** value: **125.00**
5 ❑ Apr 1954 Cover: 0.10 **NM** value: **125.00**
6 ❑ Jun 1954 Cover: 0.10 **NM** value: **125.00**
7 ❑ Aug 1954 Cover: 0.10 **NM** value: **125.00**
8 ❑ Oct 1954 Cover: 0.10 **NM** value: **125.00**
9 ❑ Dec 1954 Cover: 0.10 **NM** value: **125.00**
10 ❑ Feb 1954 Cover: 0.10 **NM** value: **125.00**
11 ❑ Apr 1954 Cover: 0.10 **NM** value: **100.00**
12 ❑ Jun 1954 Cover: 0.10 **NM** value: **100.00**
13 ❑ Aug 1955 Cover: 0.10 **NM** value: **100.00**
14 ❑ Oct 1955 Cover: 0.10 **NM** value: **100.00**
15 ❑ Jan 1956 Cover: 0.10 **NM** value: **100.00**
16 ❑ Mar 1956 Cover: 0.10 **NM** value: **100.00**
17 ❑ May 1956 Cover: 0.10 **NM** value: **100.00**
18 ❑ Jul 1956 Cover: 0.10 **NM** value: **100.00**
19 ❑ Sep 1956 Cover: 0.10 **NM** value: **100.00**
20 ❑ Nov 1956 Cover: 0.10 **NM** value: **75.00**
21 ❑ Jan 1957 Cover: 0.10 **NM** value: **75.00**
22 ❑ Mar 1957 Cover: 0.10 **NM** value: **75.00**
23 ❑ May 1957 Cover: 0.10 **NM** value: **75.00**
24 ❑ Jul 1957 Cover: 0.10 **NM** value: **75.00**
25 ❑ Sep 1957 Cover: 0.10 **NM** value: **75.00**
26 ❑ Nov 1957 Cover: 0.10 **NM** value: **75.00**
27 ❑ Jan 1958 Cover: 0.10 **NM** value: **75.00**
28 ❑ Mar 1958 Cover: 0.10 **NM** value: **75.00**
29 ❑ May 1958 Cover: 0.10 **NM** value: **75.00**
30 ❑ Jul 1958 Cover: 0.10 **NM** value: **75.00**
31 ❑ Sep 1958 Cover: 0.10 **NM** value: **75.00**

PETER PAN (GOLD KEY) — Gold Key

1 ❑ Sep 1969 Cover: 0.15 **NM** value: **20.00**
• 10086-909
2 ❑ Cover: 0.15 **NM** value: **12.00**

PETER PAN: RETURN TO NEVER-NEVER LAND — Adventure

1 ❑ full color Cover: 2.50 **NM** value: **Cover or less**
Circ: CapCity orders: **2,310**
2 ❑ full color Cover: 2.50 **NM** value: **Cover or less**
Circ: CapCity orders: **2,100**

PETER PAN (WALT DISNEY'S...) — Disney

1 ❑ Cover: 5.95 **NM** value: **Cover or less**
• prestige format. 📖 Peter Pan; The Pirate Plot **A:** Al Hubbard **W:** Don Christenson

PETER PARKER: SPIDER-MAN — Marvel

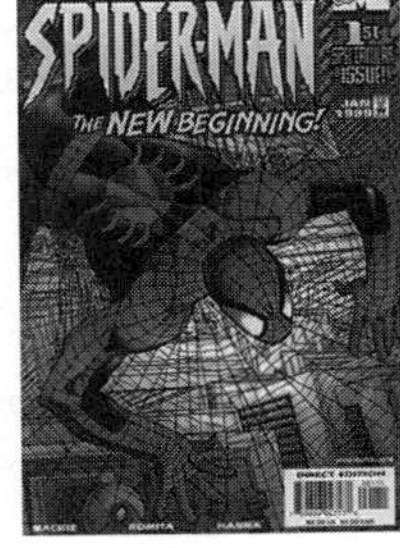

In the wake of the much-heralded relaunches of such titles as Avengers and Fantastic Four, Marvel rebooted its main "Spider-verse" titles with The Amazing Spider-Man (Vol. 2) and Peter Parker, Spider-Man.

With the first issue, writer Howard Mackie (Ghost Rider) and artist John Romita, Jr. (Iron Man) do much to return Spidey to his former glory. Peter Parker's life is once again made difficult by the juggling of a multitude of responsibilities as the dutiful nephew of his ever-ailing Aunt May; as the devoted husband of his jet-setting, supermodel wife, Mary Jane Watson-Parker; as the determined photographer for The Daily Bugle; as the distracted employee of a scientific research facility; and as the dedicated super-hero...your friendly, neighborhood Spider-Man. "Duty and responsibility" has long been the theme of the Spider-Man. While our hero got a bit lost for awhile among the clones and the alien symbiotes, this title restored him to his proper place in the Marvel universe.

1 ❑ Jan 1999 Cover: 2.99 **NM** value: **Cover or less**
Circ: Statement: **110,875** Diamd. preorders: **115,545** • **CGC:** 8 graded, best 9.8
wraparound cover. 📖 Power Without Responsibility! **A:** John Romita Jr. **W:** Howard Mackie ★ Versus Scorpion.
1/A ❑ Jan 1999 Cover: 2.99 **NM** value: **Cover or less**
• **CGC:** 8 graded, best 9.8
sunburst variant cover. 📖 Power Without Responsibility! **A:** John Romita Jr. **W:** Howard Mackie
1/Aut ❑ Jan 1999 Cover: 35.00 **NM** value: **Cover or less**
📖 Power Without Responsibility! **A:** John Romita Jr. **W:** Howard Mackie
1/SC ❑ Jan 1999 Cover: 6.95 **NM** value: **Cover or less**
• **CGC:** 6 graded, best 9.8
DFE alternate cover. 📖 Power Without Responsibility! **A:** John Romita Jr. **W:** Howard Mackie
2/A ❑ Feb 1999 Cover: 1.99 **NM** value: **2.00**
Circ: Statement: **110,875** Diamd. preorders: **96,489**
Cover A. **A:** John Romita Jr. **W:** Howard Mackie ★ Appearance of Tocketts, Thor.
2/B ❑ Feb 1999 Cover: 1.99 **NM** value: **2.00**
Cover B by Arthur Suydam. **A:** John Romita Jr. **W:** Howard Mackie ★ Appearance of Tocketts, Thor.
3 ❑ Mar 1999 Cover: 1.99 **NM** value: **2.00**
Circ: Statement: **110,875** Diamd. preorders: **78,485**
• Continued from Amazing Spider-Man #3 **A:** John Romita Jr. **W:** Howard Mackie ★ Appearance of Shadrac, Iceman, Mary Jane. ★ Versus Shadrac.
4 ❑ Apr 1999 Cover: 1.99 **NM** value: **2.00**
Circ: Statement: **110,875** Diamd. preorders: **73,534**
A: John Romita Jr. **W:** Howard Mackie ★ Appearance of Marrow.
5 ❑ May 1999 Cover: 1.99 **NM** value: **2.00**
Circ: Statement: **110,875** Diamd. preorders: **70,600**
★ Appearance of Black Cat. ★ Versus Spider-Woman.
6 ❑ Jun 1999 Cover: 1.99 **NM** value: **Cover or less**
Circ: Statement: **110,875** Diamd. preorders: **69,001**
★ Versus Kingpin. ★ Versus Bullseye.
7 ❑ Jul 1999 Cover: 1.99 **NM** value: **Cover or less**
Circ: Statement: **110,875** Diamd. preorders: **66,116**
★ Appearance of Blade.
8 ❑ Aug 1999 Cover: 1.99 **NM** value: **Cover or less**
Circ: Statement: **110,875** Diamd. preorders: **64,891**
★ Appearance of Kingpin, Blade, Morbius.
9 ❑ Sep 1999 Cover: 1.99 **NM** value: **Cover or less**
Circ: Diamd. preorders: **65,337**
★ Versus Venom.
10 ❑ Oct 1999 Cover: 1.99 **NM** value: **Cover or less**
Circ: Diamd. preorders: **61,140**
★ Versus Venom.
11 ❑ Nov 1999 Cover: 1.99 **NM** value: **Cover or less**
Circ: Diamd. preorders: **60,824**
📖 Eighth Day, Part 3 • continues in Juggernaut #1; Has 1999 Statement, filed 10/1/99; avg print run 188,067; avg sales 107,818; avg subs 3,057; avg total paid 110,875; samples 5,228; office use 125; max existent 116,228; 41% of run returned
12 ❑ Dec 1999 Cover: 2.99 **NM** value: **Cover or less**
Circ: Diamd. preorders: **59,514**
📖 Return Of The Sinister Six!
13 ❑ Jan 2000 Cover: 2.25 **NM** value: **Cover or less**
Circ: Diamd. preorders: **58,030**
14 ❑ Feb 2000 Cover: 2.25 **NM** value: **Cover or less**
Circ: Diamd. preorders: **60,571**
15 ❑ Mar 2000 Cover: 2.25 **NM** value: **Cover or less**
Circ: Diamd. preorders: **54,318**
16 ❑ Apr 2000 Cover: 2.25 **NM** value: **Cover or less**
Circ: Diamd. preorders: **51,473**
17 ❑ May 2000 Cover: 2.25 **NM** value: **Cover or less**
Circ: Diamd. preorders: **51,579**
18 ❑ Jun 2000 Cover: 2.25 **NM** value: **Cover or less**
Circ: Diamd. preorders: **50,688**
19 ❑ Jul 2000 Cover: 2.25 **NM** value: **Cover or less**
Circ: Diamd. preorders: **49,906**
20 ❑ Aug 2000 Cover: 2.25 **NM** value: **Cover or less**
Circ: Diamd. preorders: **51,310**
21 ❑ Sep 2000 Cover: 2.25 **NM** value: **Cover or less**
Circ: Diamd. preorders: **49,748**
📖 A Day in the Life **A:** Mark Buckingham **W:** Paul Jenkins
22 ❑ Oct 2000 Cover: 2.25 **NM** value: **Cover or less**
Circ: Statement: **73,264** Diamd. preorders: **46,904**
23 ❑ Nov 2000 Cover: 2.25 **NM** value: **Cover or less**
Circ: Statement: **73,264** Diamd. preorders: **46,914**
📖 Read 'em and Weep **A:** Mark Buckingham **W:** Paul Jenkins
24 ❑ Dec 2000 Cover: 2.25 **NM** value: **Cover or less**
Circ: Statement: **73,264** Diamd. preorders: **47,722**
25 ❑ Jan 2001 Cover: 2.25 **NM** value: **Cover or less**
Circ: Statement: **73,264** Diamd. preorders: **49,717** • **CGC:** 4 graded, best 9.6
26 ❑ Feb 2001 Cover: 2.25 **NM** value: **Cover or less**
Circ: Statement: **73,264** Diamd. preorders: **46,446**
📖 Police Story **A:** Joe Bennett **W:** Paul Jenkins
27 ❑ Mar 2001 Cover: 2.25 **NM** value: **Cover or less**
Circ: Statement: **73,264** Diamd. preorders: **45,964**
📖 Getting Ahead **A:** Mark Buckingham **W:** Paul Jenkins ★ Appearance of Mendel Stromm.
28 ❑ Apr 2001 Cover: 2.25 **NM** value: **Cover or less**
Circ: Statement: **73,264** Diamd. preorders: **45,495** • **CGC:** 1 graded, best 9.6
📖 Field of Dream **A:** Mark Buckingham **W:** Paul Jenkins ★ Appearance of Mendel Stromm.
29 ❑ May 2001 Cover: 2.25 **NM** value: **Cover or less**
Circ: Statement: **73,264** Diamd. preorders: **46,042** • **CGC:** 1 graded, best 9.6
📖 Destinations • continues in Amazing Spider-Man Annual 2001 **A:** Charles Adlard **W:** Paul Jenkins
30 ❑ Jun 2001 Cover: 2.25 **NM** value: **Cover or less**
Circ: Statement: **73,264** Diamd. preorders: **51,610** • **CGC:** 1 graded, best 9.4
31 ❑ Jul 2001 Cover: 2.25 **NM** value: **Cover or less**
Circ: Statement: **73,264** Diamd. preorders: **52,285**
32 ❑ Aug 2001 Cover: 2.25 **NM** value: **Cover or less**
Circ: Statement: **73,264** Diamd. preorders: **54,850**
33 ❑ Sep 2001 Cover: 2.25 **NM** value: **Cover or less**
Circ: Statement: **73,264** Diamd. preorders: **58,400**
34 ❑ Oct 2001 Cover: 2.25 **NM** value: **Cover or less**
Circ: Diamd. preorders: **58,947**
1st printing.
35 ❑ Nov 2001 Cover: 2.25 **NM** value: **Cover or less**
Circ: Diamd. preorders: **56,088**
36 ❑ Dec 2001 Cover: 2.25 **NM** value: **Cover or less**
Circ: Diamd. preorders: **53,805**
37 ❑ Jan 2002 Cover: 2.25 **NM** value: **Cover or less**
Circ: Diamd. preorders: **53,718**
38 ❑ Feb 2002 Cover: 2.25 **NM** value: **Cover or less**
Circ: Diamd. preorders: **53,064**
• Has 2001 Statement, filed 10/1/2001; avg print run 116,950; avg sales 69,700; avg subs 3,564; avg total paid 73,264; samples 600; max existent 73,864; 37% of run returned
39 ❑ Mar 2002 Cover: 2.25 **NM** value: **Cover or less**
Circ: Diamd. preorders: **51,929**
Anl 1998 ❑ ca. 1998 Cover: 2.99 **NM** value: **Cover or less**
Circ: Diamd. preorders: **38,133**
• gatefold summary. 📖 The Night They Killed Big Bear... • Peter Parker: Spider-Man/Elektra '98 **A:** Joyce Chen **W:** John Morelli
Anl 1999 ❑ Aug 1999 Cover: 3.50 **NM** value: **Cover or less**
Circ: Diamd. preorders: **42,638**
★ Appearance of Man-Thing.

PETER PORKCHOPS — DC

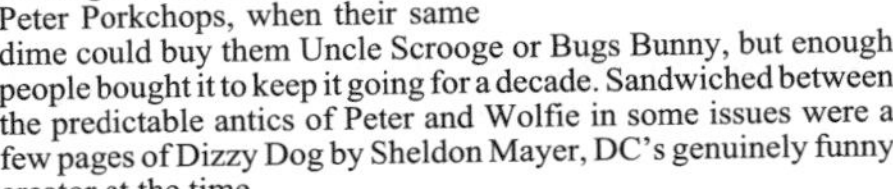

DC was the preeminent publisher of super-hero comics from the 1940s, but, when super-heroes went out of favor toward the end of the decade, staffers had to cast around in the territory of funny animal comics, among other genres, to maintain their readership. Some of their efforts, like Fox and the Crow, were quite successful. Then there were series like Peter Porkchops, an uncomfortable hodgepodge of Porky Pig and Donald Duck that pitted the cagey pig Peter Porkchops against hapless rival Wolfie Wolf. It's hard to imagine that kids would opt for Peter Porkchops, when their same dime could buy them Uncle Scrooge or Bugs Bunny, but enough people bought it to keep it going for a decade. Sandwiched between the predictable antics of Peter and Wolfie in some issues were a few pages of Dizzy Dog by Sheldon Mayer, DC's genuinely funny creator at the time.

1 ❑ Nov 1949 Cover: 0.10 **NM** value: **165.00**
2 ❑ Jan 1950 Cover: 0.10 **NM** value: **85.00**
3 ❑ Mar 1950 Cover: 0.10 **NM** value: **60.00**
4 ❑ May 1950 Cover: 0.10 **NM** value: **60.00**
5 ❑ Jul 1950 Cover: 0.10 **NM** value: **60.00**
6 ❑ Sep 1950 Cover: 0.10 **NM** value: **50.00**
7 ❑ Nov 1950 Cover: 0.10 **NM** value: **50.00**
8 ❑ Feb 1951 Cover: 0.10 **NM** value: **50.00**
9 ❑ Apr 1951 Cover: 0.10 **NM** value: **50.00**
10 ❑ Jun 1951 Cover: 0.10 **NM** value: **50.00**
11 ❑ Aug 1951 Cover: 0.10 **NM** value: **45.00**
12 ❑ Oct 1951 Cover: 0.10 **NM** value: **45.00**
13 ❑ Dec 1951 Cover: 0.10 **NM** value: **45.00**
• **CGC:** 1 graded, best 9.2
14 ❑ Feb 1952 Cover: 0.10 **NM** value: **45.00**
• **CGC:** 1 graded, best 9.4
15 ❑ Apr 1952 Cover: 0.10 **NM** value: **45.00**
16 ❑ Jun 1952 Cover: 0.10 **NM** value: **45.00**
17 ❑ Aug 1952 Cover: 0.10 **NM** value: **45.00**
18 ❑ Oct 1952 Cover: 0.10 **NM** value: **45.00**
19 ❑ Dec 1952 Cover: 0.10 **NM** value: **45.00**
20 ❑ Feb 1953 Cover: 0.10 **NM** value: **45.00**
21 ❑ Apr 1953 Cover: 0.10 **NM** value: **40.00**
22 ❑ Jun 1953 Cover: 0.10 **NM** value: **40.00**
23 ❑ Aug 1953 Cover: 0.10 **NM** value: **40.00**
24 ❑ Oct 1953 Cover: 0.10 **NM** value: **40.00**
25 ❑ Dec 1953 Cover: 0.10 **NM** value: **40.00**
26 ❑ Feb 1954 Cover: 0.10 **NM** value: **40.00**
27 ❑ Apr 1954 Cover: 0.10 **NM** value: **40.00**
28 ❑ Jun 1954 Cover: 0.10 **NM** value: **40.00**
29 ❑ Aug 1954 Cover: 0.10 **NM** value: **40.00**
30 ❑ Oct 1954 Cover: 0.10 **NM** value: **40.00**
31 ❑ Sep 1954 Cover: 0.10 **NM** value: **32.00**
32 ❑ Cover: 0.10 **NM** value: **32.00**
33 ❑ Cover: 0.10 **NM** value: **32.00**
34 ❑ ca. 1955 Cover: 0.10 **NM** value: **32.00**
35 ❑ 1955 Cover: 0.10 **NM** value: **32.00**
36 ❑ 1955 Cover: 0.10 **NM** value: **32.00**
37 ❑ 1955 Cover: 0.10 **NM** value: **32.00**
38 ❑ 1955 Cover: 0.10 **NM** value: **32.00**
39 ❑ 1955 Cover: 0.10 **NM** value: **32.00**
40 ❑ Cover: 0.10 **NM** value: **32.00**
41 ❑ 1956 Cover: 0.10 **NM** value: **25.00**
42 ❑ 1956 Cover: 0.10 **NM** value: **25.00**
43 ❑ 1956 Cover: 0.10 **NM** value: **25.00**
44 ❑ 1956 Cover: 0.10 **NM** value: **25.00**
45 ❑ 1956 Cover: 0.10 **NM** value: **25.00**
46 ❑ Nov 1956 Cover: 0.10 **NM** value: **25.00**
📖 Putting on the Dog (text story); Dizzy Dog; Peter Porkchops: Be Kind to your Neighbor Day; The Grass is Greener (text story) **A:** Sheldon Mayer **W:** Sheldon Mayer
47 ❑ Jan 1957 Cover: 0.10 **NM** value: **25.00**
48 ❑ Mar 1957 Cover: 0.10 **NM** value: **25.00**
49 ❑ May 1957 Cover: 0.10 **NM** value: **25.00**
50 ❑ Jul 1957 Cover: 0.10 **NM** value: **25.00**
51 ❑ Aug 1957 Cover: 0.10 **NM** value: **20.00**
52 ❑ Cover: 0.10 **NM** value: **20.00**
53 ❑ Cover: 0.10 **NM** value: **20.00**
54 ❑ Cover: 0.10 **NM** value: **20.00**
55 ❑ Cover: 0.10 **NM** value: **20.00**
56 ❑ 1959 Cover: 0.10 **NM** value: **20.00**
57 ❑ 1959 Cover: 0.10 **NM** value: **20.00**
58 ❑ Nov 1959 Cover: 0.10 **NM** value: **20.00**
59 ❑ Feb 1960 Cover: 0.10 **NM** value: **20.00**
60 ❑ May 1960 Cover: 0.10 **NM** value: **20.00**
61 ❑ ca. 1960 Cover: 0.10 **NM** value: **18.00**
62 ❑ Dec 1960 Cover: 0.10 **NM** value: **18.00**
final issue.

PETER PORKER, THE SPECTACULAR SPIDER-HAM — Marvel / Star

Marvel Comics' children's comic-book line, Star Comics, published these spoof stories which made fun of one of the biggest heroes in the Marvel Universe. Peter Porker, The Spectacular Spider-Ham, is a fun-filled series based on the popular character Spider-Man.

The comic book adapted most of the supporting characters from the regular series using animals. For instance, J. Jonah Jameson is J. Jonah Jackal in the spoof; Doctor Doom is Duck Doom.

As a side-note, the letterer on the series is Rick Parker, who went on to do more humor series for Marvel, including Beavis and Butthead.

This lighthearted series began its run in 1985.

1 ❑ May 1985 Cover: 0.65 **NM** value: **1.00**
Circ: Statement: **62,570** CapCity orders: **6,700**
📖 The Mysterious Island Of Ducktor Doom! **A:** Mark Armstrong **W:** Steve Skeates ★ 1st Appearance of Spider-Ham, J. Jonah Jackal, Peter Porker, Duck Doom.
2 ❑ Jul 1985 Cover: 0.65 **NM** value: **1.00**
Circ: Statement: **62,570** CapCity orders: **6,500**
3 ❑ Sep 1985 Cover: 0.65 **NM** value: **1.00**
Circ: Statement: **62,570** CapCity orders: **5,800**
4 ❑ Nov 1985 Cover: 0.65 **NM** value: **1.00**
Circ: Statement: **62,570** CapCity orders: **4,800**
5 ❑ Jan 1986 Cover: 0.65 **NM** value: **1.00**
Circ: CapCity orders: **3,200**
6 ❑ Mar 1986 Cover: 0.65 **NM** value: **1.00**
Circ: CapCity orders: **3,550**
7 ❑ May 1986 Cover: 0.75 **NM** value: **1.00**
Circ: CapCity orders: **3,700**
8 ❑ Jul 1986 Cover: 0.75 **NM** value: **1.00**
Circ: CapCity orders: **3,750**
9 ❑ Aug 1986 Cover: 0.75 **NM** value: **1.00**
Circ: CapCity orders: **3,250**
10 ❑ Sep 1986 Cover: 0.75 **NM** value: **1.00**
Circ: CapCity orders: **3,300**
11 ❑ Oct 1986 Cover: 0.75 **NM** value: **1.00**
Circ: CapCity orders: **3,700**
12 ❑ Nov 1986 Cover: 0.75 **NM** value: **1.00**
Circ: CapCity orders: **3,500**

CGC-graded: Multiply prices above by **33 for 9.9 M • 16 for 9.8 NM/M • 7 for 9.6 NM+ • 5 for 9.4 NM • 2.5 for 9.2 NM- • 1.5 for 9.0 VF/NM**

13 ❑ Jan 1987 Cover: 0.75 **NM** value: **1.00**
Circ: CapCity orders: **3,650**

14 ❑ Mar 1987 Cover: 0.75 **NM** value: **1.00**
Circ: CapCity orders: **3,600**

15 ❑ May 1987 Cover: 0.75 **NM** value: **1.00**
Circ: CapCity orders: **3,100**

16 ❑ Jul 1987 Cover: 1.00 **NM** value: **Cover or less**
Circ: CapCity orders: **2,800**

17 ❑ Sep 1987 Cover: 1.00 **NM** value: **Cover or less**
Circ: CapCity orders: **2,950**
final issue.

PETER RABBIT 3-D — Eternity

1 ❑ Cover: 2.95 **NM** value: **Cover or less**
• Reprints from Peter Rabbit (Avon) stories **A:** Harrison Cady **W:** Harrison Cady

PETER RABBIT (AVON) — Avon

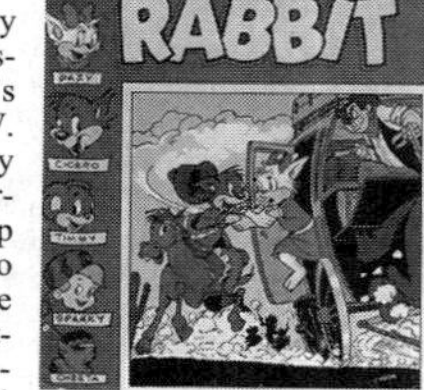

The children's nature books by Thornton W. Burgess (1874-1965), starting with Old Mother West Wind in 1910, introduced such characters as Peter Rabbit, Sammy Jay, and Jerry Muskrat. The illustrator of many of his children's books about the characters was W. Harrison Cady (1877-1970). Cady then adapted the Peter Rabbit character for use in Sunday comic-strip form, and the strip ran from 1920 to 1956. The portly bunny bore little resemblance to either Beatrix Potter's character (who'd first appeared in 1901), Howard R. Garis' Uncle Wiggily (also 1910), or Joel Chandler Harris' Bre'r Rabbit (1877). Cady's Peter Rabbit is a sweet, good-natured, funny-animal character. Forgotten kingdoms, haunted houses, and distant planets are all possible settings for his wacky antics.

Peter Rabbit comics also feature a variety of backup characters, including Cicero, the trouble-making alley cat, and his inevitable mouse sidekick Timmy, and Sparky and Cheetah, a cowboy-and-Indian kid duo who romp around the Old West in 'coonskin caps and war paint.

1 ❑ ca. 1947 Cover: 0.10 **NM** value: **150.00**
A: Harrison Cady **W:** Harrison Cady

2 ❑ Cover: 0.10 **NM** value: **90.00**
A: Harrison Cady **W:** Harrison Cady

3 ❑ Cover: 0.10 **NM** value: **70.00**
A: Harrison Cady **W:** Harrison Cady

4 ❑ Cover: 0.10 **NM** value: **70.00**
• **CGC:** 1 graded, best 7.5
A: Harrison Cady **W:** Harrison Cady

5 ❑ Cover: 0.10 **NM** value: **70.00**
A: Harrison Cady **W:** Harrison Cady

6 ❑ Sep 1949 Cover: 0.10 **NM** value: **70.00**
• Last Cady issue **A:** Harrison Cady **W:** Harrison Cady

7 ❑ ca. 1950 Cover: 0.10 **NM** value: **20.00**
8 ❑ Cover: 0.10 **NM** value: **20.00**
9 ❑ Cover: 0.10 **NM** value: **20.00**
10 ❑ Aug 1951 Cover: 0.10 **NM** value: **20.00**
11 ❑ Cover: 0.10 **NM** value: **14.00**
12 ❑ 1952 Cover: 0.10 **NM** value: **14.00**
13 ❑ 1952 Cover: 0.10 **NM** value: **14.00**
14 ❑ 1952 Cover: 0.10 **NM** value: **14.00**
15 ❑ Cover: 0.10 **NM** value: **14.00**
📖 The Strange Planet; The Bankers; The Leaper; The Gold Diggers **A:** Carin
16 ❑ 1953 Cover: 0.10 **NM** value: **14.00**
17 ❑ 1953 Cover: 0.10 **NM** value: **14.00**
18 ❑ 1953 Cover: 0.10 **NM** value: **14.00**
19 ❑ 1953 Cover: 0.10 **NM** value: **14.00**
20 ❑ Cover: 0.10 **NM** value: **14.00**
21 ❑ 1954 Cover: 0.10 **NM** value: **10.00**
22 ❑ 1954 Cover: 0.10 **NM** value: **10.00**
23 ❑ 1954 Cover: 0.10 **NM** value: **10.00**
24 ❑ Sep 1954 Cover: 0.10 **NM** value: **10.00**
25 ❑ Nov 1954 Cover: 0.10 **NM** value: **10.00**
26 ❑ 1955 Cover: 0.10 **NM** value: **10.00**
27 ❑ 1955 Cover: 0.10 **NM** value: **10.00**
28 ❑ 1955 Cover: 0.10 **NM** value: **10.00**
29 ❑ 1955 Cover: 0.10 **NM** value: **10.00**
30 ❑ Cover: 0.10 **NM** value: **10.00**
31 ❑ 1956 Cover: 0.10 **NM** value: **10.00**
32 ❑ 1956 Cover: 0.10 **NM** value: **10.00**
33 ❑ 1956 Cover: 0.10 **NM** value: **10.00**
34 ❑ Sep 1956 Cover: 0.10 **NM** value: **10.00**
final issue.

PETER RABBIT (ETERNITY) — Eternity

Bk 1❑ Cover: 9.95 **NM** value: **Cover or less**
• strip reprints

PETER THE LITTLE PEST — Marvel

1 ❑ Nov 1969 Cover: 0.15 **NM** value: **18.00**
• **CGC:** 2 graded, best 9.0
📖 Peter the Little Pest; Little Pixie ★ 1st Appearance of Peter, The Little Pest, Little Pixie.

2 ❑ Jan 1970 Cover: 0.15 **NM** value: **14.00**
• **CGC:** 1 graded, best 8.5

3 ❑ Mar 1970 Cover: 0.15 **NM** value: **14.00**
• **CGC:** 1 graded, best 9.0

4 ❑ May 1970 Cover: 0.15 **NM** value: **14.00**
• titled Petey

For up-to-the-week CGC ratios, consult the current issue of **Comics Buyer's Guide.**

PETE THE P.O.'D POSTAL WORKER — Sharkbait

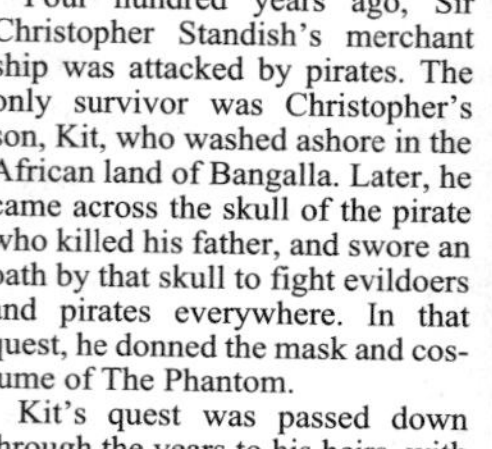

This cheerful paean to mayhem and mail delivery comes from the same folks who brought you the books Nice Guys Don't Get Laid and Hunting for Lawyers as well as The Adventures of Liberal Man. It's the saga of Pete, a hard-working letter carrier who deals with the daily stresses that come with unending reams of mail, dog attacks, nasty coworkers, and all the other little joys that are part of the U.S. Mail "Team" in his own unique way.

So, Pete prepares himself for the day by getting his knobby knees into his postal worker shorts, donning his jaunty mailman's cap, and stuffing his bag full of every deadly weapon he can find. Then, with a glazedly nervous expression permanently affixed to his face, he goes out to deliver the mail...and nothing...repeat, nothing is going to get in his way!

1 ❑ Oct 1997 Cover: 2.95 **NM** value: **3.50**
Circ: Diamd. preorders: **4,434**

2 ❑ Jan 1998 Cover: 2.95 **NM** value: **3.00**
3 ❑ Mar 1998 Cover: 2.95 **NM** value: **3.00**
4 ❑ Jun 1998 Cover: 2.95 **NM** value: **3.00**
Circ: Diamd. preorders: **3,054**

5 ❑ Aug 1998 Cover: 2.95 **NM** value: **3.00**
Circ: Diamd. preorders: **2,398**
• in England

6 ❑ Oct 1998 Cover: 2.95 **NM** value: **Cover or less**
Circ: Diamd. preorders: **2,300**

7 ❑ Jan 1999 Cover: 2.95 **NM** value: **Cover or less**
Circ: Diamd. preorders: **2,088**
★ Versus Teddy Cougar.

8 ❑ Apr 1999 Cover: 2.95 **NM** value: **Cover or less**
Circ: Diamd. preorders: **1,830**
📖 Postman on Elm Street, Part 2 **A:** Pete Garcia **W:** Marcus Pierce Jr ★ Versus Teddy Cougar.

9 ❑ Jun 1999 Cover: 2.95 **NM** value: **Cover or less**
Circ: Diamd. preorders: **1,803**
• on Jerry Ringer Show

10 ❑ Aug 1999 Cover: 2.95 **NM** value: **Cover or less**
★ Versus Y2K.

PETTICOAT JUNCTION — Dell

1 ❑ Oct 1964 Cover: 0.12 **NM** value: **35.00**
• **CGC:** 1 graded, best 9.2

2 ❑ Jan 1965 Cover: 0.12 **NM** value: **25.00**
• **CGC:** 1 graded, best 9.4

3 ❑ Apr 1965 Cover: 0.12 **NM** value: **25.00**
• **CGC:** 1 graded, best 7.5

4 ❑ Jul 1965 Cover: 0.12 **NM** value: **25.00**
• **CGC:** 1 graded, best 9.2

5 ❑ Oct 1965 Cover: 0.12 **NM** value: **25.00**
• **CGC:** 1 graded, best 7.5

PETWORKS VS. WILDK.A.T.S. — Parody Press

1 ❑ Cover: 2.50 **NM** value: **Cover or less**
📖 Night of the Undead Customers **A:** Tatsuya Ishida **W:** Don Chin

PHAEDRA — Express / Entity

1 ❑ Sep 1994, b&w Cover: 2.95 **NM** value: **Cover or less**
No issue number. cardstock cover. • third in series of Entity illustrated novellas with Zen Intergalactic Ninja

PHAGE: SHADOWDEATH (NEIL GAIMAN'S...) — Big

1 ❑ Jun 1996 Cover: 2.25 **NM** value: **Cover or less**
📖 Insurrection!; The Big Crossover, Part 8 **A:** David Pugh **W:** Bryan Talbot

2 ❑ Aug 1996 Cover: 2.25 **NM** value: **Cover or less**
A: David Pugh **W:** Bryan Talbot

3 ❑ Sep 1996 Cover: 2.25 **NM** value: **Cover or less**
A: David Pugh **W:** Bryan Talbot

4 ❑ Sep 1996 Cover: 2.25 **NM** value: **Cover or less**
A: David Pugh **W:** Bryan Talbot

5 ❑ Oct 1996 Cover: 2.25 **NM** value: **Cover or less**
A: David Pugh **W:** Bryan Talbot

6 ❑ Nov 1996 Cover: 2.25 **NM** value: **Cover or less**
Circ: Diamd. preorders: **8,019**
A: David Pugh **W:** Bryan Talbot

PHANTACEA: PHASE ONE — Mcpherson

1 ❑ Cover: 1.50 **NM** value: **5.00**

PHANTASMAGORIA — Tome Press

1 ❑ b&w Cover: 2.50 **NM** value: **Cover or less**

PHANTASY AGAINST HUNGER — Tiger

1 ❑ Cover: 1.50 **NM** value: **2.00**
A: Arthur Adams; Bill Sienkiewicz; Joe Orlando; Gene Colan; Brent Anderson; John Romita

The prices seen above do not represent the highest possible prices seen in online auctions, but rather the prices we have seen these issues reliably fetch in a variety of environments (storefront retail, mail order, auction and convention).

PHANTOM, THE (1ST SERIES) — Gold Key

Four hundred years ago, Sir Christopher Standish's merchant ship was attacked by pirates. The only survivor was Christopher's son, Kit, who washed ashore in the African land of Bangalla. Later, he came across the skull of the pirate who killed his father, and swore an oath by that skull to fight evildoers and pirates everywhere. In that quest, he donned the mask and costume of The Phantom.

Kit's quest was passed down through the years to his heirs, with a male in each generation taking up the mask. The Phantom of the modern day is actually the 21st person to wear the mask, but to natives, he is simply the man who would not die — the "Ghost-Who-Walks."

A longtime pulp hero, the Phantom made the transition to comic books with this series. During its run, it moved between publishers Gold Key and King Features Syndicate before finally settling in as a Charlton publication.

1 ❑ Nov 1962 Cover: 0.12 **NM** value: **90.00**
• **CGC:** 2 graded, best 9.0
• Gold Key publishes

2 ❑ Feb 1963 Cover: 0.12 **NM** value: **55.00**
3 ❑ May 1963 Cover: 0.12 **NM** value: **36.00**
4 ❑ Aug 1963 Cover: 0.12 **NM** value: **36.00**
5 ❑ Nov 1963 Cover: 0.12 **NM** value: **36.00**
6 ❑ Feb 1964 Cover: 0.12 **NM** value: **36.00**
Circ: Statement: **236,028**

7 ❑ May 1964 Cover: 0.12 **NM** value: **36.00**
Circ: Statement: **236,028**

8 ❑ Aug 1964 Cover: 0.12 **NM** value: **36.00**
Circ: Statement: **236,028**

9 ❑ Nov 1964 Cover: 0.12 **NM** value: **36.00**
Circ: Statement: **236,028**

10 ❑ Feb 1965 Cover: 0.12 **NM** value: **36.00**
Circ: Statement: **229,890**

11 ❑ Apr 1965 Cover: 0.12 **NM** value: **28.00**
Circ: Statement: **229,890**
• Has 1964 Statement, filed 9/28/64; avg print run 365,194; avg sales 235,500; avg subs 528; avg total paid 236,028; samples 601; max existent 236,629; 36% of run returned

12 ❑ Jun 1965 Cover: 0.12 **NM** value: **28.00**
Circ: Statement: **229,890**

13 ❑ Aug 1965 Cover: 0.12 **NM** value: **28.00**
Circ: Statement: **229,890**

14 ❑ Oct 1965 Cover: 0.12 **NM** value: **28.00**
Circ: Statement: **229,890**

15 ❑ Dec 1965 Cover: 0.12 **NM** value: **28.00**
Circ: Statement: **229,890**

16 ❑ Apr 1966 Cover: 0.12 **NM** value: **28.00**
Circ: Statement: **221,141**
• Has 1965 Statement, filed 9/28/65; avg print run 387,461; avg sales 228,600; avg subs 1,290; avg total paid 229,890; samples 843; max existent 230,733; 41% of run returned

17 ❑ Jul 1966 Cover: 0.12 **NM** value: **28.00**
Circ: Statement: **221,141**

18 ❑ Sep 1966 Cover: 0.12 **NM** value: **32.00**
Circ: Statement: **221,141**
• King Features Syndicate begins publishing

19 ❑ Nov 1966 Cover: 0.12 **NM** value: **24.00**
Circ: Statement: **221,141**

20 ❑ Jan 1967 Cover: 0.12 **NM** value: **24.00**
21 ❑ Mar 1967 Cover: 0.12 **NM** value: **24.00**
22 ❑ May 1967 Cover: 0.12 **NM** value: **24.00**
• **CGC:** 1 graded, best 9.4
• Has 1966 Statement, filed 12/20/66 (Alert: Late in year); avg print run 386,252; avg sales 220,750; avg subs 391; avg total paid and max existent 221,141; 43% of run returned

23 ❑ Jul 1967 Cover: 0.12 **NM** value: **24.00**
24 ❑ Aug 1967 Cover: 0.12 **NM** value: **24.00**
25 ❑ Sep 1967 Cover: 0.12 **NM** value: **24.00**
• **CGC:** 5 graded, best 9.6

26 ❑ Oct 1967 Cover: 0.12 **NM** value: **24.00**
27 ❑ Nov 1967 Cover: 0.12 **NM** value: **24.00**
28 ❑ Dec 1967 Cover: 0.12 **NM** value: **24.00**
30 ❑ Feb 1969 Cover: 0.12 **NM** value: **15.00**
Circ: Statement: **199,045**
• Charlton begins publishing (no issue #29)

31 ❑ Apr 1969 Cover: 0.12 **NM** value: **15.00**
Circ: Statement: **199,045**

32 ❑ Jun 1969 Cover: 0.12 **NM** value: **15.00**
Circ: Statement: **199,045**
• Has 1968 Statement; avg print run 325,000; avg subs 125; no other circ figures published

33 ❑ Aug 1969 Cover: 0.12 **NM** value: **15.00**
Circ: Statement: **199,045**
📖 The Jungle People; The Phantom's Death; **A:** Pat Boyette; Nicholas Alascia **W:** Dick Wood

34 ❑ Oct 1969 Cover: 0.15 **NM** value: **15.00**
Circ: Statement: **199,045**

35 ❑ Dec 1969 Cover: 0.15 **NM** value: **15.00**
Circ: Statement: **199,045**

36 ❑ Feb 1970 Cover: 0.15 **NM** value: **15.00**
Circ: Statement: **160,120**

37 ❑ Apr 1970 Cover: 0.15 **NM** value: **15.00**
Circ: Statement: **160,120**
• Has 1969 Statement, filed 9/30/69; avg print run 300,000; avg sales 199,000; avg subs 45; avg total paid 199,045; samples 125; max existent 199,170; 34% of run returned

38 ❑ Jun 1970 Cover: 0.15 **NM** value: **15.00**
Circ: Statement: **160,120**

39 ❑ Aug 1970 Cover: 0.15 **NM** value: **15.00**

Other grades: Multiply prices above by **1.5 for Mint • 2/3 for Very Fine • 1/3 for Fine • 1/5 for Very Good • 1/8 for Good**

Circ: Statement: **160,120**
40 ❑ Oct 1970 Cover: 0.15 **NM** value: **15.00**
Circ: Statement: **160,120**
41 ❑ Dec 1970 Cover: 0.15 **NM** value: **12.00**
Circ: Statement: **160,120**
42 ❑ Feb 1971 Cover: 0.15 **NM** value: **12.00**
Circ: Statement: **150,150**
43 ❑ Apr 1971 Cover: 0.15 **NM** value: **12.00**
Circ: Statement: **150,150**
44 ❑ Jun 1971 Cover: 0.15 **NM** value: **12.00**
Circ: Statement: **150,150**
• Has 1970 Statement, filed 9/30/70; avg print run 242,000; avg sales 160,000; avg subs 120; avg total paid 160,120; samples 300; max existent 160,420; 34% of run returned
45 ❑ Aug 1971 Cover: 0.15 **NM** value: **12.00**
Circ: Statement: **150,150**
46 ❑ Oct 1971 Cover: 0.20 **NM** value: **12.00**
Circ: Statement: **150,150**
★ 1st Appearance of Piranha.
47 ❑ Dec 1971 Cover: 0.20 **NM** value: **12.00**
Circ: Statement: **150,150**
48 ❑ Feb 1972 Cover: 0.20 **NM** value: **12.00**
Circ: Statement: **125,122**
49 ❑ Apr 1972 Cover: 0.20 **NM** value: **12.00**
Circ: Statement: **125,122**
• Has 1971 Statement; avg print run 220,000; avg sales 150,000; avg subs 150; avg total paid 150,150
50 ❑ Jun 1972 Cover: 0.20 **NM** value: **12.00**
Circ: Statement: **125,122**
51 ❑ Aug 1972 Cover: 0.20 **NM** value: **12.00**
Circ: Statement: **125,122**
52 ❑ Oct 1972 Cover: 0.20 **NM** value: **12.00**
Circ: Statement: **125,122**
53 ❑ Nov 1972 Cover: 0.20 **NM** value: **12.00**
Circ: Statement: **125,122**
54 ❑ Feb 1973 Cover: 0.20 **NM** value: **12.00**
Circ: Statement: **130,123**
55 ❑ Apr 1973 Cover: 0.20 **NM** value: **12.00**
Circ: Statement: **130,123**
56 ❑ Jun 1973 Cover: 0.20 **NM** value: **12.00**
Circ: Statement: **130,123**
• Has 1972 Statement; avg total paid circ 125,122
57 ❑ ca. 1973 Cover: 0.20 **NM** value: **12.00**
Circ: Statement: **130,123**
58 ❑ 1973 Cover: 0.20 **NM** value: **12.00**
Circ: Statement: **130,123**
59 ❑ 1974 **NM** value: **12.00**
Circ: Statement: **105,212**
60 ❑ Jun 1974 Cover: 0.25 **NM** value: **9.00**
Circ: Statement: **105,212**
• Has 1973 Statement; avg total paid circ 130,123
61 ❑ Sep 1974 Cover: 0.25 **NM** value: **9.00**
Circ: Statement: **105,212**
62 ❑ Nov 1974 Cover: 0.25 **NM** value: **9.00**
Circ: Statement: **105,212**
63 ❑ Jan 1975 Cover: 0.25 **NM** value: **9.00**
Circ: Statement: **88,360**
64 ❑ Mar 1975 Cover: 0.25 **NM** value: **9.00**
Circ: Statement: **88,360**
65 ❑ Jun 1975 Cover: 0.25 **NM** value: **9.00**
Circ: Statement: **88,360**
• Has 1974 Statement; avg total paid circ 105,212
66 ❑ Aug 1975 Cover: 0.25 **NM** value: **9.00**
Circ: Statement: **88,360**
67 ❑ Oct 1975 Cover: 0.25 **NM** value: **9.00**
Circ: Statement: **88,360**
68 ❑ Dec 1975 Cover: 0.25 **NM** value: **9.00**
Circ: Statement: **88,360**
69 ❑ Feb 1976 Cover: 0.25 **NM** value: **9.00**
📖 The Shining City
70 ❑ Apr 1976 Cover: 0.25 **NM** value: **9.00**
71 ❑ Jul 1976 Cover: 0.25 **NM** value: **7.00**
72 ❑ Aug 1976 Cover: 0.25 **NM** value: **7.00**
73 ❑ Oct 1976 Cover: 0.25 **NM** value: **7.00**
74 ❑ Jan 1977 Cover: 0.30 **NM** value: **7.00**
final issue.

PHANTOM 2040 — Marvel

1 ❑ May 1995 Cover: 1.50 **NM** value: **Cover or less**
Circ: CapCity orders: **8,100**
📖 Generation Unto Generation **A:** Steve Ditko **W:** Peter Quinones ★ Origin of Phantom 2040. ★ 1st Appearance of Phantom 2040.
2 ❑ Jun 1995 Cover: 1.50 **NM** value: **Cover or less**
Circ: CapCity orders: **5,800**
A: Steve Ditko **W:** Peter Quinones
3 ❑ Jul 1995 Cover: 1.50 **NM** value: **Cover or less**
Circ: CapCity orders: **4,700**
• Poster **A:** Steve Ditko **W:** Peter Quinones
4 ❑ Aug 1995 Cover: 1.50 **NM** value: **Cover or less**
Circ: CapCity orders: **4,000**
• Poster **A:** Steve Ditko **W:** Peter Quinones

PHANTOM, THE (2ND SERIES) — DC

1 ❑ May 1988 Cover: 1.25 **NM** value: **2.00**
Circ: CapCity orders: **22,000**
📖 Guns **A:** Luke McDonnell **W:** Mark Verheiden ★ Origin of Phantom.
2 ❑ Jun 1988 Cover: 1.25 **NM** value: **2.00**
Circ: CapCity orders: **15,600**
3 ❑ Jul 1988 Cover: 1.25 **NM** value: **2.00**
Circ: CapCity orders: **14,350**
4 ❑ Aug 1988 Cover: 1.25 **NM** value: **2.00**
Circ: CapCity orders: **14,050**

PHANTOM, THE (3RD SERIES) — DC

1 ❑ May 1989 Cover: 1.50 **NM** value: **2.00**
Circ: CapCity orders: **21,050**
2 ❑ Jun 1989 Cover: 1.50 **NM** value: **Cover or less**
Circ: CapCity orders: **15,000**
3 ❑ Jul 1989 Cover: 1.50 **NM** value: **Cover or less**
Circ: CapCity orders: **13,400**
4 ❑ Aug 1989 Cover: 1.50 **NM** value: **Cover or less**
Circ: CapCity orders: **13,050**
5 ❑ Sep 1989 Cover: 1.50 **NM** value: **Cover or less**
Circ: CapCity orders: **12,800**
6 ❑ Oct 1989 Cover: 1.50 **NM** value: **Cover or less**
Circ: CapCity orders: **12,500**
7 ❑ Nov 1989 Cover: 1.50 **NM** value: **Cover or less**
Circ: CapCity orders: **11,750**
8 ❑ Dec 1989 Cover: 1.50 **NM** value: **Cover or less**
Circ: CapCity orders: **10,900**
9 ❑ Jan 1989 Cover: 1.50 **NM** value: **Cover or less**
Circ: CapCity orders: **10,200**
10 ❑ Feb 1989 Cover: 1.50 **NM** value: **Cover or less**
Circ: CapCity orders: **9,450**
11 ❑ Mar 1990 Cover: 1.50 **NM** value: **Cover or less**
Circ: CapCity orders: **9,450**
12 ❑ Apr 1990 Cover: 1.50 **NM** value: **Cover or less**
Circ: CapCity orders: **8,650**
13 ❑ May 1990 Cover: 1.50 **NM** value: **Cover or less**
Circ: CapCity orders: **8,550**
final issue.

PHANTOM, THE (4TH SERIES) — Wolf

0/LE❑ Cover: 3.50 **NM** value: **Cover or less**
• limited edition subscribers' issue.
1 ❑ 1992 Cover: 0.99 **NM** value: **2.50**
2 ❑ 1992 Cover: 0.99 **NM** value: **2.25**
3 ❑ 1992 Cover: 0.99 **NM** value: **2.25**
4 ❑ 1992 Cover: 0.99 **NM** value: **2.25**
5 ❑ 1992 Cover: 0.99 **NM** value: **2.25**
6 ❑ 1992 Cover: 0.99 **NM** value: **2.25**
7 ❑ 1992 Cover: 0.99 **NM** value: **1.95**
8 ❑ 1992 Cover: 0.99 **NM** value: **1.95**

PHANTOM FORCE — Image

Phantom Force consists of a group of seemingly randomly assembled super-heroes, including kung-fu fighter Gin Seng, cosmic-powered swordsman Apocalypse (no relation to the X-Factor villain), and the mysterious woman named Probe.

Phantom Force first appeared in Last of the Viking Heroes #4, part of Jack Kirby's Genesis West line of independent comics. This title came about as a result of Mike Thibodeux' display of unpublished Kirby pencil sketches to Image co-founder Rob Liefeld. Thibodeux had co-created Phantom Force with Kirby and was looking for a publisher. The Image crew, great admirers of Kirby's, quickly agreed to help out. This title appeared in 1993 as one of Kirby's last completely pencilled stories and featured inks and colors by virtually everyone at Image. Sadly, Kirby died in 1994, before the story could really develop.

0 ❑ Mar 1994 Cover: 2.50 **NM** value: **Cover or less**
Circ: CapCity orders: **13,435**
A: Jack Kirby; Michael Thibodeaux **W:** Jack Kirby; Michael Thibodeaux; Richard French
1 ❑ Dec 1993 Cover: 2.50 **NM** value: **Cover or less**
Circ: CapCity orders: **58,875**
📖 Phantom Force **A:** Jack Kirby; Rob Liefeld **W:** Jack Kirby; Michael Thibodeaux; Richard French
2 ❑ Apr 1994 Cover: 3.50 **NM** value: **Cover or less**
Circ: CapCity orders: **23,425**
📖 Plan B
3 ❑ May 1994 Cover: 2.50 **NM** value: **Cover or less**
Circ: CapCity orders: **11,645**
4 ❑ Jun 1994 Cover: 2.50 **NM** value: **Cover or less**
Circ: CapCity orders: **9,600**
5 ❑ Jul 1994 Cover: 2.50 **NM** value: **Cover or less**
Circ: CapCity orders: **7,165**
📖 Calm Before the Storm
6 ❑ Aug 1994 Cover: 2.50 **NM** value: **Cover or less**
Circ: CapCity orders: **6,325**
📖 Omnisword
7 ❑ Sep 1994 Cover: 2.50 **NM** value: **Cover or less**
Circ: CapCity orders: **4,880**
8 ❑ Oct 1994 Cover: 2.50 **NM** value: **Cover or less**
Circ: CapCity orders: **4,215**
📖 Attainment of the Omnisword
Ash 1❑ Cover: 2.50 **NM** value: **Cover or less**
• ashcan

PHANTOM FORCE (GENESIS WEST) — Genesis West

0 ❑ Cover: 2.50 **NM** value: **Cover or less**
W: Jack Kirby

PHANTOM GUARD — Image

1 ❑ Oct 1997 Cover: 2.50 **NM** value: **Cover or less**
Circ: Diamd. preorders: **24,720**
A: Saleem Crawford **W:** Sean Ruffner
1/A ❑ Oct 1997 Cover: 2.50 **NM** value: **Cover or less**
alternate cover (white background).
2 ❑ Oct 1997 Cover: 2.50 **NM** value: **Cover or less**
Circ: Diamd. preorders: **20,027**
A: Saleem Crawford **W:** Sean Ruffner
3 ❑ Dec 1997 Cover: 2.50 **NM** value: **Cover or less**
Circ: Diamd. preorders: **19,391**
A: Saleem Crawford **W:** Sean Ruffner

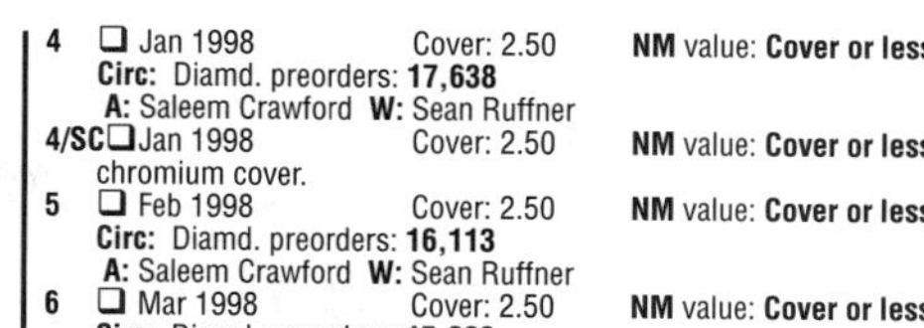

4 ❑ Jan 1998 Cover: 2.50 **NM** value: **Cover or less**
Circ: Diamd. preorders: **17,638**
A: Saleem Crawford **W:** Sean Ruffner
4/SC❑Jan 1998 Cover: 2.50 **NM** value: **Cover or less**
chromium cover.
5 ❑ Feb 1998 Cover: 2.50 **NM** value: **Cover or less**
Circ: Diamd. preorders: **16,113**
A: Saleem Crawford **W:** Sean Ruffner
6 ❑ Mar 1998 Cover: 2.50 **NM** value: **Cover or less**
Circ: Diamd. preorders: **15,999**
A: Saleem Crawford **W:** Sean Ruffner

PHANTOM LADY (1ST SERIES) — Fox

Sandra Knight made her debut in Police Comics #1, where she fended off two gunmen who were planning to kidnap her father, a senator.

Neither the gunmen nor her father saw clearly who had done the deed, attributing it to a "phantom lady" at Sandra's whispered suggestion. Eventually, she donned a miniscule swimsuit, green cape, and put a black light projector on her wrist. Rather than simply creating funky colors on psychedelic posters, this black light could blind her enemies by casting them and their surroundings into deep darkness.

When she couldn't distract them with that light, Knight distracted them with her skimpy costume, which got skimpier and filmier over the years, especially under the able pencils of Matt Baker. In the 1970s, Knight became a member of The Freedom Fighters. — Brent

13 ❑ Aug 1947 Cover: 0.10 **NM** value: **3000.00**
• **CGC:** 3 graded, best 9.0
14 ❑ Oct 1947 Cover: 0.10 **NM** value: **2000.00**
• **CGC:** 6 graded, best 9.0
15 ❑ Dec 1947 Cover: 0.10 **NM** value: **2000.00**
• **CGC:** 7 graded, best 9.2
16 ❑ Feb 1948 Cover: 0.10 **NM** value: **2000.00**
• **CGC:** 5 graded, best 9.4
17 ❑ Apr 1948 Cover: 0.10 **NM** value: **2000.00**
• **CGC:** 7 graded, best 9.0
18 ❑ Jun 1948 Cover: 0.10 **NM** value: **1200.00**
• **CGC:** 3 graded, best 9.4
19 ❑ Aug 1948 Cover: 0.10 **NM** value: **1200.00**
• **CGC:** 2 graded, best 9.0
20 ❑ Oct 1948 Cover: 0.10 **NM** value: **1200.00**
• **CGC:** 1 graded, best 8.5
21 ❑ Dec 1948 Cover: 0.10 **NM** value: **1000.00**
• **CGC:** 1 graded, best 7.0
22 ❑ Feb 1949 Cover: 0.10 **NM** value: **1000.00**
• **CGC:** 1 graded, best 8.0
23 ❑ Apr 1949 Cover: 0.10 **NM** value: **1000.00**
• **CGC:** 4 graded, best 9.2

PHANTOM LADY — Verotik

1 ❑ Cover: 9.95 **NM** value: **Cover or less**
No issue number. • squarebound; Golden Age reprints

PHANTOM OF FEAR CITY — Claypool

1 ❑ May 1993 Cover: 2.50 **NM** value: **Cover or less**
Circ: CapCity orders: **2,350**
2 ❑ Jul 1993 Cover: 2.50 **NM** value: **Cover or less**
📖 Incarnation! **A:** Matt Haley **W:** Steve Englehart
3 ❑ Aug 1993 Cover: 2.50 **NM** value: **Cover or less**
4 ❑ Oct 1993 Cover: 2.50 **NM** value: **Cover or less**
5 ❑ Nov 1993 Cover: 2.50 **NM** value: **Cover or less**
6 ❑ Jan 1994 Cover: 2.50 **NM** value: **Cover or less**
7 ❑ 1994 Cover: 2.50 **NM** value: **Cover or less**
8 ❑ Jul 1994 Cover: 2.50 **NM** value: **Cover or less**
9 ❑ Sep 1994 Cover: 2.50 **NM** value: **Cover or less**
10 ❑ Nov 1994 Cover: 2.50 **NM** value: **Cover or less**
11 ❑ Feb 1995 Cover: 2.50 **NM** value: **Cover or less**
12 ❑ May 1995 Cover: 2.50 **NM** value: **Cover or less**
final issue.

PHANTOM OF THE OPERA (ETERNITY) — Eternity

1 ❑ b&w Cover: 1.95 **NM** value: **2.00**

PHANTOM OF THE OPERA (INNOVATION) — Innovation

1 ❑ Dec 1991 Cover: 6.95 **NM** value: **Cover or less**

PHANTOM QUEST CORP. — Pioneer

1 ❑ Mar 1997, b&w Cover: 2.95 **NM** value: **Cover or less**
Circ: Diamd. preorders: **3,488**
wraparound cover.

PHANTOM STRANGER, THE (1ST SERIES) — DC

The mystical being known as The Phantom Stranger (who would often refer to himself simply as "a stranger") was a man dressed in black (or dark blue) with a blue opera cape and dark fedora that shadowed much of his features.

In this 1950s series, The Stranger would appear to those in deep despair or in some sort of supernatural danger, and either offer them advice, which they could heed or not at their own risk; or summon other supernatural beings to help in the struggle.

The Stranger's origins nor the full extent of his powers have never been revealed. — Brent

1 ❑ Aug 1952 Cover: 0.10 **NM** value: **900.00**
• **CGC:** 5 graded, best 8.0
2 ❑ Oct 1952 Cover: 0.10 **NM** value: **500.00**
3 ❑ Dec 1952 Cover: 0.10 **NM** value: **425.00**
• **CGC:** 2 graded, best 9.0

CGC-graded: Multiply prices above by **33 for 9.9 M • 16 for 9.8 NM/M • 7 for 9.6 NM+ • 5 for 9.4 NM • 2.5 for 9.2 NM- • 1.5 for 9.0 VF/NM**

4 ❑ Feb 1953 Cover: 0.10 **NM** value: **425.00**
5 ❑ Apr 1953 Cover: 0.10 **NM** value: **425.00**
6 ❑ Jun 1953 Cover: 0.10 **NM** value: **425.00**
• **CGC:** 3 graded, best 9.0

PHANTOM STRANGER, THE (2ND SERIES) DC

The Phantom Stranger is a mysterious figure who appears out of nowhere to help save innocents from evil forces. To accomplish his goal, he employs a variety of mystical powers, then disappears as suddenly as he first arrived.

This second Phantom Stranger series brought him out of the shadows and into the Silver Age. He served as the headliner in this collection of supernatural tales which included backup stories featuring Mark Merlin, a modern day sorcerer; and Doctor Thirteen, a "ghost-breaker" who specialized in solving mysteries while proving that the ghosts who seemed to be behind things were in fact frauds; and Deadman, the spirit of an assassinated circus aerialist who can inhabit other people's bodies in order to fight for good.

1 ❑ May 1969 Cover: 0.12 **NM** value: **50.00**
• **CGC:** 12 graded, best 9.6
📖 When Ghosts Walk!; Dr. 13, The Hermit's Ghost Dog!; Defeat the Dragon Curse…or Die! **A:** Bill Draut **W:** Mike Friedrich ★ Appearance of Doctor 13.
2 ❑ Aug 1969 Cover: 0.15 **NM** value: **20.00**
• **CGC:** 2 graded, best 9.2
★ Appearance of Doctor 13.
3 ❑ Oct 1969 Cover: 0.15 **NM** value: **20.00**
• **CGC:** 2 graded, best 9.2
★ Appearance of Doctor 13.
4 ❑ Dec 1969 Cover: 0.15 **NM** value: **24.00**
• **CGC:** 1 graded, best 8.5
A: Neal Adams ★ 1st Appearance of Tala. ★ Appearance of Doctor 13.
5 ❑ Feb 1970 Cover: 0.15 **NM** value: **12.00**
• **CGC:** 2 graded, best 9.4
★ Appearance of Doctor 13.
6 ❑ Apr 1970 Cover: 0.15 **NM** value: **12.00**
• **CGC:** 1 graded, best 9.2
★ Appearance of Doctor 13.
7 ❑ Jun 1970 Cover: 0.15 **NM** value: **12.00**
• **CGC:** 2 graded, best 9.4
★ Appearance of Doctor 13.
8 ❑ Aug 1970 Cover: 0.15 **NM** value: **10.00**
• **CGC:** 2 graded, best 9.2
★ Appearance of Doctor 13.
9 ❑ Oct 1970 Cover: 0.15 **NM** value: **10.00**
• **CGC:** 3 graded, best 9.2
★ Appearance of Doctor 13.
10 ❑ Dec 1970 Cover: 0.15 **NM** value: **10.00**
• **CGC:** 2 graded, best 9.0
★ Appearance of Doctor 13.
11 ❑ Feb 1971 Cover: 0.15 **NM** value: **10.00**
• **CGC:** 1 graded, best 9.6
12 ❑ Apr 1971 Cover: 0.15 **NM** value: **8.00**
• **CGC:** 2 graded, best 9.2
★ Appearance of Doctor 13.
13 ❑ Jun 1971 Cover: 0.15 **NM** value: **8.00**
• **CGC:** 1 graded, best 9.4
★ Appearance of Doctor 13.
14 ❑ Aug 1971 Cover: 0.15 **NM** value: **8.00**
• **CGC:** 1 graded, best 9.4
★ Appearance of Doctor 13.
15 ❑ Oct 1971 Cover: 0.25 **NM** value: **8.00**
• Giant-size. ★ Appearance of Doctor 13.
16 ❑ Dec 1971 Cover: 0.25 **NM** value: **8.00**
• Giant-size. 📖 Image In Wax **A:** Jim Aparo **W:** Len Wein ★ Appearance of Doctor 13, Mark Merlin.
17 ❑ Feb 1972 Cover: 0.25 **NM** value: **8.00**
Circ: Statement: **155,641** • **CGC:** 1 graded, best 9.4
• Giant-size. ★ Appearance of Doctor 13.
18 ❑ Apr 1972 Cover: 0.25 **NM** value: **8.00**
Circ: Statement: **155,641** • **CGC:** 3 graded, best 9.6
• Giant-size. ★ 1st Appearance of Cassandra Craft. ★ Appearance of Doctor 13, Mark Merlin.
19 ❑ Jun 1972 Cover: 0.25 **NM** value: **8.00**
Circ: Statement: **155,641** • **CGC:** 1 graded, best 8.5
• Giant-size. ★ Appearance of Doctor 13, Mark Merlin.
20 ❑ Aug 1972 Cover: 0.20 **NM** value: **8.00**
Circ: Statement: **155,641** • **CGC:** 1 graded, best 9.6
21 ❑ Oct 1972 Cover: 0.20 **NM** value: **6.00**
Circ: Statement: **155,641**
★ Appearance of Doctor 13.
22 ❑ Dec 1972 Cover: 0.20 **NM** value: **6.00**
Circ: Statement: **155,641**
★ Appearance of Doctor 13.
23 ❑ Feb 1973 Cover: 0.20 **NM** value: **6.00**
Circ: Statement: **149,760**
★ 1st Appearance of The Spawn of Frankenstein.
24 ❑ Apr 1973 Cover: 0.20 **NM** value: **6.00**
Circ: Statement: **149,760**
★ Appearance of The Spawn of Frankenstein.
25 ❑ Jul 1973 Cover: 0.20 **NM** value: **6.00**
Circ: Statement: **149,760**
• Has 1972 Statement; avg total paid circ 155,641 ★ Appearance of The Spawn of Frankenstein.
26 ❑ Sep 1973 Cover: 0.20 **NM** value: **6.00**
Circ: Statement: **149,760** • **CGC:** 1 graded, best 9.6
★ Appearance of Doctor 13, The Spawn of Frankenstein.
27 ❑ Nov 1973 Cover: 0.20 **NM** value: **6.00**
Circ: Statement: **149,760**
★ Appearance of The Spawn of Frankenstein.
28 ❑ Jan 1974 Cover: 0.20 **NM** value: **6.00**
Circ: Statement: **147,710**
★ Appearance of The Spawn of Frankenstein.
29 ❑ Mar 1974 Cover: 0.20 **NM** value: **6.00**
Circ: Statement: **147,710**
★ Appearance of The Spawn of Frankenstein.
30 ❑ May 1974 Cover: 0.20 **NM** value: **6.00**
Circ: Statement: **147,710** • **CGC:** 1 graded, best 9.4
• Has 1973 Statement, filed 10/1/73; avg print run 301,500; avg sales 149,273; avg subs 487; avg total paid 149,760; samples 100; office use 1,296; max existent 151,156; 50% of run returned ★ Appearance of The Spawn of Frankenstein.
31 ❑ Jul 1974 Cover: 0.20 **NM** value: **6.00**
Circ: Statement: **147,710**
★ Appearance of Black Orchid.
32 ❑ Sep 1974 Cover: 0.20 **NM** value: **6.00**
Circ: Statement: **147,710**
★ Appearance of Black Orchid.
33 ❑ Nov 1974 Cover: 0.20 **NM** value: **6.00**
Circ: Statement: **147,710**
★ Appearance of Deadman.
34 ❑ Jan 1975 Cover: 0.20 **NM** value: **6.00**
• **CGC:** 1 graded, best 8.5
★ Appearance of Black Orchid, Doctor 13.
35 ❑ Mar 1975 Cover: 0.25 **NM** value: **6.00**
★ Appearance of Black Orchid.
36 ❑ May 1975 Cover: 0.25 **NM** value: **6.00**
★ Appearance of Black Orchid.
37 ❑ Jul 1975 Cover: 0.25 **NM** value: **6.00**
• Has 1974 Statement; avg total paid circ 147,710
38 ❑ Sep 1975 Cover: 0.25 **NM** value: **6.00**
★ Appearance of Black Orchid.
39 ❑ Nov 1975 Cover: 0.25 **NM** value: **6.00**
★ Appearance of Deadman.
40 ❑ Jan 1976 Cover: 0.25 **NM** value: **6.00**
★ Appearance of Deadman.
41 ❑ Mar 1976 Cover: 0.25 **NM** value: **6.00**
final issue. ★ Appearance of Deadman.

PHANTOM STRANGER, THE (MINI-SERIES) DC

1 ❑ Oct 1987 Cover: 0.75 **NM** value: **3.00**
Circ: CapCity orders: **29,950**
📖 The Heart Of A Stranger **A:** Mike Mignola **W:** Paul Kupperberg
2 ❑ Nov 1987 Cover: 0.75 **NM** value: **2.50**
Circ: CapCity orders: **24,100**
3 ❑ Dec 1987 Cover: 0.75 **NM** value: **2.50**
Circ: CapCity orders: **21,200**
4 ❑ Jan 1988 Cover: 0.75 **NM** value: **2.50**
Circ: CapCity orders: **19,850**

PHANTOM, THE: THE GHOST WHO WALKS (LEE FALK'S...) Marvel

1 ❑ Feb 1995 Cover: 2.95 **NM** value: **Cover or less**
Circ: CapCity orders: **10,450**
cardstock cover. **A:** Glenn Lumsden **W:** Dave DeVries
2 ❑ Mar 1995 Cover: 2.95 **NM** value: **Cover or less**
Circ: CapCity orders: **7,025**
cardstock cover. 📖 Heart or Darkness **A:** Glenn Lumsden **W:** Dave DeVries
3 ❑ Apr 1995 Cover: 2.95 **NM** value: **Cover or less**
Circ: CapCity orders: **6,450**
cardstock cover. **A:** Glenn Lumsden **W:** Dave DeVries

PHANTOM WITCH DOCTOR Avon

1 ❑ ca. 1952 Cover: 0.10 **NM** value: **300.00**
• **CGC:** 2 graded, best 8.0

PHANTOM ZONE, THE DC

1 ❑ Jan 1982 Cover: 0.60 **NM** value: **1.50**
• **CGC:** 1 graded, best 8.0
📖 The Haunting of Charlie Kweskill! **A:** Gene Colan **W:** Steve Gerber
2 ❑ Feb 1982 Cover: 0.60 **NM** value: **1.25**
A: Gene Colan **W:** Steve Gerber
3 ❑ Mar 1982 Cover: 0.60 **NM** value: **1.25**
A: Gene Colan **W:** Steve Gerber
4 ❑ Apr 1982 Cover: 0.60 **NM** value: **1.25**
A: Gene Colan **W:** Steve Gerber

PHASE ONE Victory

1 ❑ Oct 1986 Cover: 1.50 **NM** value: **Cover or less**
📖 Death has a Face! **A:** Robert Durham **W:** Robert Durham
2 ❑ Cover: 1.50 **NM** value: **Cover or less**
3 ❑ Cover: 1.50 **NM** value: **Cover or less**
4 ❑ Cover: 1.50 **NM** value: **Cover or less**
5 ❑ Cover: 1.50 **NM** value: **Cover or less**

PHATWARS Bon

1 ❑ Cover: 2.00 **NM** value: **Cover or less**

PHAZE Eclipse

1 ❑ Apr 1988 Cover: 2.25 **NM** value: **Cover or less**
Circ: CapCity orders: **6,300**
📖 One Of Those Days **A:** Rafael Kayanan **C:** Bill Sienkiewicz **W:** Fred Burke
2 ❑ Oct 1988 Cover: 2.25 **NM** value: **Cover or less**
Circ: CapCity orders: **4,025**
C: Paul Gulacy

PHENOMERAMA Caliber

1 ❑ Cover: 2.95 **NM** value: **Cover or less**
📖 Monkey Vato; Lifetimes; Serg; Wolfbrow **A:** C. Scott Morse **W:** C. Scott Morse

PHIGMENTS Amazing

1 ❑ b&w Cover: 1.95 **NM** value: **Cover or less**
A: Evan Dorkin; Jim Fern **W:** Alan Rowlands
2 ❑ Cover: 1.95 **NM** value: **Cover or less**

PHILBERT DESANEX' DREAMS Rip Off

1 ❑ b&w Cover: 2.95 **NM** value: **Cover or less**

PHILISTINE, THE One-Shot

1 ❑ Sep 1993, b&w Cover: 2.50 **NM** value: **Cover or less**
📖 Into the Limelight **A:** Mike Zittel **W:** Michael Mongillo
2 ❑ Apr 1994, b&w Cover: 2.50 **NM** value: **Cover or less**
3 ❑ Sep 1994, b&w Cover: 2.50 **NM** value: **Cover or less**
4 ❑ Cover: 2.50 **NM** value: **Cover or less**
5 ❑ Cover: 2.50 **NM** value: **Cover or less**
6 ❑ Cover: 2.50 **NM** value: **Cover or less**

PHIL RIZZUTO, BASEBALL HERO Fawcett

1 ❑ ca. 1951 Cover: 0.10 **NM** value: **500.00**
• **CGC:** 2 graded, best 9.0

PHINEUS: MAGICIAN FOR HIRE Piffle

1 ❑ Cover: 2.95 **NM** value: **Cover or less**
📖 Largo the Dread; Gil the Walking Dead or Vampires Suck **A:** Barry Linck **W:** Barry Linck

PHOBOS Flashpoint

1 ❑ Jan 1994 Cover: 2.50 **NM** value: **Cover or less**

PHOEBE: ANGEL IN BLACK Angel

1 ❑ Cover: 2.95 **NM** value: **Cover or less**
📖 City of the Spirits **A:** Nirut Chamsuwan **W:** Lois Sanborn

PHOENIX Atlas-Seaboard

1 ❑ Mar 1975 Cover: 0.25 **NM** value: **2.00**
• **CGC:** 2 graded, best 9.6
📖 From The Ashes **A:** Sal Amendola **W:** Jeff Rovin ★ Origin of Phoenix (Atlas character).
2 ❑ Jun 1975 Cover: 0.25 **NM** value: **2.00**
📖 And the Sea Ran Red! **A:** Sal Amendola **W:** Gabriel Levy
3 ❑ Oct 1975 Cover: 0.25 **NM** value: **2.00**
4 ❑ 1975 Cover: 0.25 **NM** value: **2.00**

PHOENIX RESTAURANT Fandom House

1 ❑ b&w Cover: 3.50 **NM** value: **Cover or less**

PHOENIX RESURRECTION, THE: AFTERMATH Malibu / Ultraverse

1 ❑ Jan 1996 Cover: 3.95 **NM** value: **Cover or less**
📖 Aftermath • continues in Foxfire #1 **A:** Jeff Lafferty; John Royle; John Cleary; Pino Rinaldi **W:** Dan Abnett; Ian Edginton

PHOENIX RESURRECTION, THE: GENESIS Malibu / Ultraverse

1 ❑ Dec 1995 Cover: 3.95 **NM** value: **Cover or less**
wraparound cover. • Giant-size. 📖 Genesis • continues in The Phoenix Resurrection: Revelations; Phoenix force returns **A:** Greg Luzniak; Darick Robertson; Rob Haynes; Mark Pacella **W:** Dan Abnett; Ian Edginton
2 ❑ Cover: 3.95 **NM** value: **Cover or less**
📖 Red Shift Mantra **A:** Chuck Wojtkiewicz **W:** Ian Edginton

PHOENIX RESURRECTION, THE: RED SHIFT Malibu / Ultraverse

0 ❑ Mar 1996 Cover: 1.95 **NM** value: **2.50**
• collects the seven flipbook chapters plus one new chapter
0/LE ❑ Dec 1995 **NM** value: **2.50**
no cover price. • American Entertainment Edition.

PHOENIX RESURRECTION, THE: REVELATIONS Malibu / Ultraverse

1 ❑ Dec 1995 Cover: 3.95 **NM** value: **Cover or less**
wraparound cover. 📖 Revelations • continues in The Phoenix Resurrection: Aftermath **A:** Kevin West; Rick Leonardi; John Royle; Randy Green **W:** Dan Abnett; Ian Edginton

PHOENIX SQUARE Slave Labor

1 ❑ Aug 1997, b&w Cover: 2.95 **NM** value: **Cover or less**
A: Paul Barlow **W:** Paul Barlow
2 ❑ Nov 1997 Cover: 2.95 **NM** value: **Cover or less**
A: Paul Barlow **W:** Paul Barlow

PHOENIX: THE UNTOLD STORY Marvel

In the classic "Dark Phoenix Saga" (roughly, X-Men Vol. 1, #129-137), Chris Claremont, John Byrne, and Terry Austin put a beloved character through the wringer — and created one of the greatest editorial controversy ever to emerge from behind the scenes.

Earlier, Jean Grey, as Marvel Girl, had bonded with the Phoenix Force, a source of unearthly power, to become the X-Man Phoenix. Losing control of her powers (with a little help from Mastermind), Jean goes mad and consumes an alien star system with her powers. In retaliation, the alien Shi'ar hunt her down — and then the story really gets interesting. Claremont had intended to cure Jean of her curse, where Editor-in-Chief Jim Shooter had demanded she pay for her crimes. Shooter won, and a new ending to X-Men #137 was created — along with a comics legend.

Here, by popular demand, #137 is reprinted with the original ending. There's also an eligthening round-table with all the creators and Shooter, including an exchange that foreshadows, for those who read between the lines, the later return of Jean in X-Factor. — JJM

Other grades: Multiply prices above by **1.5 for Mint • 2/3 for Very Fine • 1/3 for Fine • 1/5 for Very Good • 1/8 for Good**

1 ❑ Apr 1984 Cover: 2.00 **NM** value: **8.00**
• **CGC:** 8 graded, best 9.6
📖 The Fate Of The Phoenix • X-Men #137 with unpublished alternate ending **A:** John Byrne **W:** Chris Claremont

PHONY PAGES, THE (TERRY BEATTY'S...) Renegade

1 ❑ Cover: 2.00 **NM** value: **Cover or less**
📖 The Blue Kid; Muton Chop; Gnutty Gnat; Little Nimoy in Slumberland; Terry and the Pie Fights; Nick Nostril; Angel (Himself) Clare; Henri; Prince Valium; Dondy the Dead; Beatle Baily; It Couldn't be Worse; Popstar • Parody of Famous Comic Strips **A:** Terry Beatty **W:** Terry Beatty
2 ❑ Cover: 2.00 **NM** value: **Cover or less**
📖 Chaplain America; Capt. Mortal; The A • Parody of Famous Comic Books **A:** Terry Beatty **W:** Terry Beatty

PICNIC PARTY Dell

6 ❑ ca. 1955 Cover: 0.25 **NM** value: **150.00**
• **CGC:** 1 graded, best 9.0
7 ❑ Jun 1956 Cover: 0.25 **NM** value: **150.00**
• **CGC:** 1 graded, best 9.0

PICTORIAL CONFESSIONS St. John

1 ❑ Sep 1949 Cover: 0.10 **NM** value: **200.00**
• **CGC:** 1 graded, best 9.2
2 ❑ Oct 1949 Cover: 0.10 **NM** value: **125.00**
3 ❑ Nov 1949 Cover: 0.10 **NM** value: **100.00**

PICTORIAL LOVE STORIES Charlton

22 ❑ 1949 Cover: 0.10 **NM** value: **150.00**
23 ❑ 1949 Cover: 0.10 **NM** value: **150.00**
24 ❑ 1950 Cover: 0.10 **NM** value: **150.00**
25 ❑ 1950 Cover: 0.10 **NM** value: **150.00**
26 ❑ 1950 Cover: 0.10 **NM** value: **150.00**

PICTORIAL ROMANCES St. John

It started as Pictorial Confessions, which indicated something of a sleazy take on romance; that continued, as the name changed. For most of its run, Pictorial Romances features on its covers comic-book panels of the stories inside, and most of those stories have as their basic plot element nasty, duplicitous women. Oh, they're gorgeous women, but few of them are to be trusted. They're lying to their parents about running around with men. They're pledging lifelong fidelity to one guy while engaged to another. They're scheming to take away another woman's husband. "But," thinks a Matt Baker woman in #9, for example, "it's so hard to doublecross someone who's in love with you!"

With #17, it boasts of "3 full-length comics in 1" and goes to giant size for a quarter. — Maggie

4 ❑ Jan 1950 Cover: 0.10 **NM** value: **200.00**
5 ❑ Jan 1951 Cover: 0.10 **NM** value: **175.00**
6 ❑ Mar 1951 Cover: 0.10 **NM** value: **175.00**
7 ❑ May 1951 Cover: 0.10 **NM** value: **175.00**
8 ❑ Jul 1951 Cover: 0.10 **NM** value: **175.00**
9 ❑ Sep 1951 Cover: 0.10 **NM** value: **175.00**
10 ❑ Nov 1951 Cover: 0.10 **NM** value: **175.00**
11 ❑ Jan 1952 Cover: 0.10 **NM** value: **150.00**
12 ❑ Mar 1952 Cover: 0.10 **NM** value: **150.00**
• **CGC:** 1 graded, best 7.5
13 ❑ May 1952 Cover: 0.10 **NM** value: **150.00**
14 ❑ Jul 1952 Cover: 0.10 **NM** value: **150.00**
15 ❑ Sep 1952 Cover: 0.10 **NM** value: **150.00**
16 ❑ Nov 1952 Cover: 0.10 **NM** value: **125.00**
• **CGC:** 1 graded, best 8.5
17 ❑ Jan 1953 Cover: 0.25 **NM** value: **125.00**
• giant-size
18 ❑ Mar 1953 Cover: 0.25 **NM** value: **125.00**
• giant-size
19 ❑ May 1953 Cover: 0.25 **NM** value: **125.00**
• giant-size
20 ❑ Jul 1953 Cover: 0.25 **NM** value: **125.00**
• giant-size
21 ❑ Sep 1953 Cover: 0.25 **NM** value: **125.00**
22 ❑ Nov 1953 Cover: 0.25 **NM** value: **125.00**
23 ❑ Jan 1954 Cover: 0.25 **NM** value: **125.00**
24 ❑ Mar 1954 Cover: 0.25 **NM** value: **125.00**

PICTURE NEWS News in Color and Action

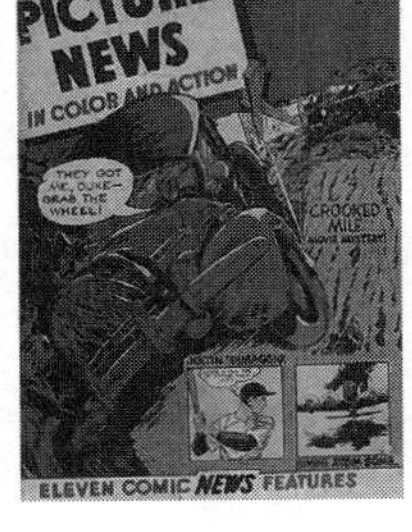

Picture News featured comic-book stories based on actual news events of the day. In fact, since the series begin a year after the end of World War II, several issues feature atomic bomb-related stories. Designed to educate and entertain, Picture News also presented stories based on the lives and experiences of celebrities in the news, such as Frank Sinatra, Perry Como, June Allyson, and Jackie Robinson. Issue #10, the series' last, introduced the fictional Dick Quick, Ace Reporter, an effort to place in the stories a young person with whom readers could identify.

1 ❑ Jan 1946 Cover: 0.10 **NM** value: **120.00**
• **CGC:** 1 graded, best 8.0
2 ❑ Feb 1946 Cover: 0.10 **NM** value: **100.00**
• **CGC:** 1 graded, best 4.0
3 ❑ Mar 1946 Cover: 0.10 **NM** value: **80.00**
4 ❑ Apr 1946 Cover: 0.10 **NM** value: **95.00**
• **CGC:** 1 graded, best 9.0
5 ❑ May 1946 Cover: 0.10 **NM** value: **60.00**
• **CGC:** 1 graded, best 9.2
6 ❑ Jun 1946 Cover: 0.10 **NM** value: **60.00**
7 ❑ Aug 1946 Cover: 0.10 **NM** value: **60.00**
8 ❑ Sep 1946 Cover: 0.10 **NM** value: **60.00**
9 ❑ Nov 1946 Cover: 0.10 **NM** value: **60.00**
10 ❑ Jan 1947 Cover: 0.10 **NM** value: **60.00**
📖 Dick Quick, Ace Reporter: Boy Reporter; Fi **A:** Bernie Krigstein; Kwarst; Milt Gross **W:** Milt Gross

PICTURE PARADE Gilberton

1 ❑ Sep 1953 Cover: 0.10 **NM** value: **100.00**
2 ❑ Oct 1953 Cover: 0.10 **NM** value: **75.00**
3 ❑ Nov 1953 Cover: 0.10 **NM** value: **75.00**
4 ❑ Dec 1953 Cover: 0.10 **NM** value: **75.00**
• Continues as Picture Progress

PICTURE PROGRESS Gilberton

Gilberton had met with great success in publishing comic books with an educational slant, even if most copies of its Classics Illustrated line served primarily as crib notes or substitutes for reading the actual classic novels assigned to students in schools. In the mid-1950s, the company tried a new title in which more general topics were covered. The first issue of Picture Parade carried an atom bomb cover (with the bomb in the background, a boy and his dog in the foreground), and the title soon evolved to Picture Progress. Topics were specified on the cover by the second volume. These included flight, the flag, a review of 1954 news, primitive man, and Christopher Columbus. — Maggie

1st Series
5 ❑ Jan 1954 Cover: 0.10 **NM** value: **35.00**
6 ❑ Feb 1954 Cover: 0.10 **NM** value: **35.00**
7 ❑ Mar 1954 Cover: 0.10 **NM** value: **35.00**
8 ❑ Apr 1954 Cover: 0.10 **NM** value: **35.00**
9 ❑ May 1954 Cover: 0.10 **NM** value: **35.00**
2nd Series
1 ❑ Sep 1954 Cover: 0.10 **NM** value: **35.00**
2 ❑ Oct 1954 Cover: 0.10 **NM** value: **35.00**
3 ❑ Nov 1954 Cover: 0.10 **NM** value: **35.00**
4 ❑ Dec 1954 Cover: 0.10 **NM** value: **35.00**
5 ❑ Jan 1955 Cover: 0.10 **NM** value: **35.00**
6 ❑ Feb 1955 Cover: 0.10 **NM** value: **35.00**
7 ❑ Mar 1955 Cover: 0.10 **NM** value: **35.00**
8 ❑ Apr 1955 Cover: 0.10 **NM** value: **35.00**
9 ❑ May 1955 Cover: 0.10 **NM** value: **35.00**

PICTURE STORIES FROM AMERICAN HISTORY E.C.

One of the early series from E.C., it featured such people as Christopher Columbus, Sir Walter Raleigh, and Benjamin Franklin; such peoples as the Aztecs; such communities as Jamestown; and such events as the French and Indian War and the first shots of the revolution. Almost all of the art was by Allen Simon. — Maggie

1 ❑ ca. 1946 Cover: 0.10 **NM** value: **125.00**
• **CGC:** 2 graded, best 9.4
Discovery and exploration.
2 ❑ ca. 1946 Cover: 0.10 **NM** value: **100.00**
• **CGC:** 2 graded, best 9.6
• Colonization and independence
3 ❑ Spr 1947 Cover: 0.15 **NM** value: **100.00**
• **CGC:** 5 graded, best 9.6
• Economic growth of our nation
4 ❑ ca. 1947 Cover: 0.15 **NM** value: **100.00**
• **CGC:** 2 graded, best 9.0

PICTURE STORIES FROM SCIENCE E.C.

One of the earliest series from E.C., the two issues featured such topics as bacteria, blood, and water. Virtually all the art was by Don Cameron. — Maggie

1 ❑ Spr 1947 Cover: 0.10 **NM** value: **65.00**
• **CGC:** 4 graded, best 9.2
• Understanding Air and Water **A:** Don Cameron **W:** Morris Nelson Sachs
2 ❑ Fal 1947 Cover: 0.10 **NM** value: **45.00**
• **CGC:** 2 graded, best 9.2

To find the median price offered on eBay at press time for pre-1990 **CGC-graded comics**, multiply by:

9.9 (M): **33**	8.5 (VF+): **1.25**
9.8(NM/M): **16**	8.0 (VF): **0.85**
9.6 (NM+): **7**	7.5 (VF-): **0.6**
9.4 (NM): **5**	7.0 (F/VF): **0.5**
9.2 (NM-): **2.5**	6.5 (F+): **0.4**
9.0 (VF/NM): **1.5**	6.0 (F-): **0.33**

These are median prices of all CGC comics auctioned on eBay; prices for individual issues will vary.

PICTURE STORIES FROM THE BIBLE E.C.

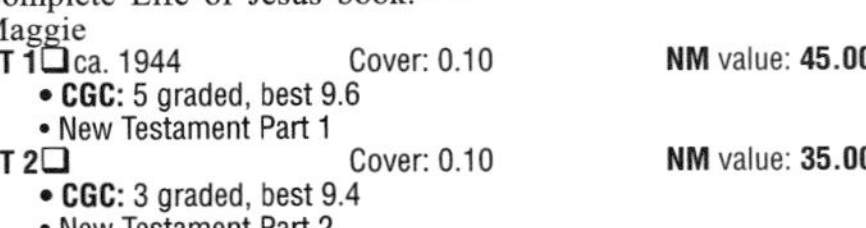

This series started the company that became the most highly collected simply from the publisher imprint. First released by the National (DC and AA) company in 1942 and 1943, the material was diverted into publication in another imprint, founded by M.C. Gaines: "E.C." The letters initially stood for "Educational Comics." Almost all of the art was by Don Cameron.

Originally published as a series of individual comics, the various books of the Bible were then collected into Old Testament and New Testament editions as well as a Complete Life of Jesus book. — Maggie

NT 1❑ ca. 1944 Cover: 0.10 **NM** value: **45.00**
• **CGC:** 5 graded, best 9.6
• New Testament Part 1
NT 2❑ Cover: 0.10 **NM** value: **35.00**
• **CGC:** 3 graded, best 9.4
• New Testament Part 2
NT 3❑ Cover: 0.10 **NM** value: **35.00**
• **CGC:** 2 graded, best 9.8
📖 The Story of Peter, Paul and Other Disciples in the Formation of the Early Christian Church • New Testament Part 3 **A:** Don Cameron **W:** Edward L. Wertheim
OT 1❑ ca. 1943 Cover: 0.10 **NM** value: **85.00**
• **CGC:** 3 graded, best 9.6
• Old Testament Part 1
OT 2❑ ca. 1943 Cover: 0.10 **NM** value: **70.00**
• **CGC:** 3 graded, best 9.0
• Old Testament Part 2
OT 3❑ Cover: 0.10 **NM** value: **70.00**
• **CGC:** 3 graded, best 9.8
• Old Testament Part 3
OT 4❑ Cover: 0.10 **NM** value: **70.00**
• **CGC:** 3 graded, best 9.2
• Old Testament Part 4
OTBK 1❑ ca. 1943 Cover: 0.50 **NM** value: **150.00**
• Old Testament Hardcover collection-1943 edition.
OTBK 1-2❑ ca. 1943 Cover: 0.50 **NM** value: **120.00**
• Old Testament Hardcover collection-1945 edition.

PICTURE STORIES FROM WORLD HISTORY E.C.

Another early title from E.C., the series covered events in early Babylon, China, Greece, and Europe. Most of the art was by Harley M. Griffiths. — Maggie

1 ❑ Spr 1947 Cover: 0.15 **NM** value: **200.00**
• **CGC:** 3 graded, best 9.0
2 ❑ Sum 1947 Cover: 0.10 **NM** value: **150.00**
• **CGC:** 4 graded, best 9.6

PICTURE TAKER, THE Slave Labor

1 ❑ Jan 1998, b&w Cover: 2.95 **NM** value: **Cover or less**
📖 The Picture Taker **A:** Mike Worley **W:** Phil Hester

PIE Wow Cool

1 ❑ b&w Cover: 2.95 **NM** value: **Cover or less**

PIECE OF STEAK, A Tome Press

1 ❑ b&w Cover: 2.50 **NM** value: **Cover or less**
A: Ron McCain **W:** Jack London

PIECES 5th Panel

1 ❑ Apr 1997, b&w Cover: 1.95 **NM** value: **2.50**
📖 Too Much **A:** Todd Richards **W:** Todd Richards
2 ❑ Jul 1997, b&w Cover: 1.95 **NM** value: **2.50**
A: Todd Richards **W:** Todd Richards
3 ❑ Cover: 2.50 **NM** value: **Cover or less**
A: Todd Richards **W:** Todd Richards

PIED PIPER GRAPHIC ALBUM Pied Piper

1 ❑ Cover: 6.95 **NM** value: **Cover or less**
• Hero Alliance • Issue 2 never published.
3 ❑ Cover: 6.95 **NM** value: **Cover or less**
• Beast Warriors

PIED PIPER OF HAMELIN Tome Press

1 ❑ b&w Cover: 2.95 **NM** value: **Cover or less**

PIGEONMAN Above & Beyond

1 ❑ Cover: 2.95 **NM** value: **Cover or less**
A: Peter Noga Jr. **W:** Peter Noga Jr.

PIGEON-MAN, THE BIRD-BRAIN Ferry Tail Studio

1 ❑ Apr 1993, b&w Cover: 2.50 **NM** value: **Cover or less**

PIGHEAD Williamson

1 ❑ b&w Cover: 2.95 **NM** value: **Cover or less**

PILGRIM'S PROGRESS, THE Marvel / Nelson

1 ❑ Cover: 9.99 **NM** value: **Cover or less**
• adaptation

PINEAPPLE ARMY Viz

1 ❑ Dec 1988 Cover: 1.75 **NM** value: **Cover or less**
A: Naoki Urasawa **W:** Kazuya Kudo
2 ❑ Dec 1988 Cover: 1.75 **NM** value: **Cover or less**
A: Naoki Urasawa **W:** Kazuya Kudo
3 ❑ Jan 1989 Cover: 1.75 **NM** value: **Cover or less**
A: Naoki Urasawa **W:** Kazuya Kudo

CGC-graded: Multiply prices above by **33 for 9.9 M • 16 for 9.8 NM/M • 7 for 9.6 NM+ • 5 for 9.4 NM • 2.5 for 9.2 NM- • 1.5 for 9.0 VF/NM**

4 ❑ Jan 1989 Cover: 1.75 **NM** value: **Cover or less**
A: Naoki Urasawa **W:** Kazuya Kudo
5 ❑ Feb 1989 Cover: 1.75 **NM** value: **Cover or less**
A: Naoki Urasawa **W:** Kazuya Kudo
6 ❑ Feb 1989 Cover: 1.75 **NM** value: **Cover or less**
A: Naoki Urasawa **W:** Kazuya Kudo
7 ❑ Mar 1989 Cover: 1.75 **NM** value: **Cover or less**
A: Naoki Urasawa **W:** Kazuya Kudo
8 ❑ Mar 1989 Cover: 1.75 **NM** value: **Cover or less**
📖 A Bouquet of Flowers **A:** Naoki Urasawa **W:** Kazuya Kudo
9 ❑ Apr 1989 Cover: 1.75 **NM** value: **Cover or less**
A: Naoki Urasawa **W:** Kazuya Kudo
10 ❑ Apr 1989 Cover: 1.75 **NM** value: **Cover or less**
Bk 1❑ Cover: 16.95 **NM** value: **Cover or less**

PINHEAD — Marvel / Epic

1 ❑ Dec 1993 Cover: 2.95 **NM** value: **Cover or less**
Circ: CapCity orders: **18,100**
Embossed foil cover. 📖 The Devil You Know **A:** Dario Carrasco Jr. **W:** D.G. Chichester
2 ❑ Jan 1994 Cover: 2.50 **NM** value: **Cover or less**
Circ: CapCity orders: **8,700**
3 ❑ Feb 1994 Cover: 2.50 **NM** value: **Cover or less**
Circ: CapCity orders: **7,400**
4 ❑ Mar 1994 Cover: 2.50 **NM** value: **Cover or less**
Circ: CapCity orders: **6,400**
5 ❑ Apr 1994 Cover: 2.50 **NM** value: **Cover or less**
Circ: CapCity orders: **5,100**
6 ❑ May 1994 Cover: 2.50 **NM** value: **Cover or less**
Circ: CapCity orders: **4,600**
final issue.

PINHEAD & FOODINI — Fawcett

1 ❑ Jul 1951 Cover: 0.10 **NM** value: **250.00**
2 ❑ Sep 1951 Cover: 0.10 **NM** value: **125.00**
3 ❑ Nov 1951 Cover: 0.10 **NM** value: **125.00**
4 ❑ Jan 1952 Cover: 0.10 **NM** value: **100.00**

PINHEAD VS. MARSHAL LAW: LAW IN HELL — Marvel / Epic

1 ❑ Nov 1993 Cover: 2.95 **NM** value: **Cover or less**
Circ: CapCity orders: **13,000**
foil cover.
2 ❑ Dec 1993 Cover: 2.95 **NM** value: **Cover or less**
Circ: CapCity orders: **10,550**
foil cover.

PINK DUST — Kitchen Sink

1 ❑ Aug 1998 Cover: 3.50 **NM** value: **Cover or less**
Circ: Diamd. preorders: **8,427**
No issue number.

PINK FLOYD — Personality

1 ❑ b&w Cover: 2.95 **NM** value: **Cover or less**
2 ❑ b&w Cover: 2.95 **NM** value: **Cover or less**

PINK FLOYD EXPERIENCE — Revolutionary

1 ❑ Jun 1991, b&w Cover: 2.50 **NM** value: **Cover or less**
2 ❑ Aug 1991, b&w Cover: 2.50 **NM** value: **Cover or less**
3 ❑ Oct 1991, b&w Cover: 2.50 **NM** value: **Cover or less**
4 ❑ Dec 1991, b&w Cover: 2.50 **NM** value: **Cover or less**
5 ❑ Feb 1992, b&w Cover: 2.50 **NM** value: **Cover or less**

PINK PANTHER, THE (GOLD KEY) — Gold Key

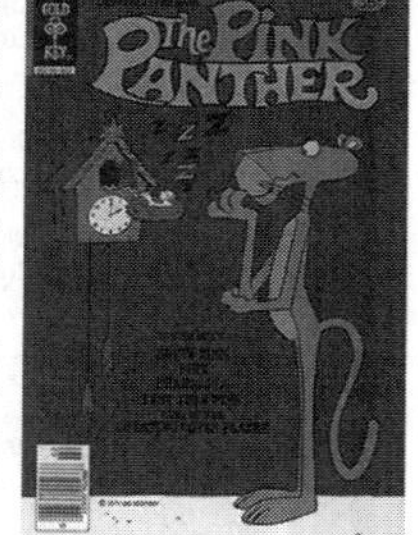

Comics characters have sprung from strange places, but The Pink Panther is the only case where one came from the title credits of a series of movies. Friz Freleng first animated the cool cat for the opening sequences for the film adventures of bumbling French detective Jacques Clouseau, with Saturday-morning cartoons coming later.

And, naturally, comic books, from Gold Key. Here, unlike in the original cartoons, the Pink Panther talks — and usually he's talking about becoming famous or getting a free meal. Much of the humor in this series comes from Pinky trying to "help out" his big-nosed co-stars, with disastrous results.

The sparkling highlights of this series, however, are the clever back-up stories starring The Inspector (who'd get his own short-run spin-off series). While he's not in France as in the cartoons, The Inspector drives The Commissioner to distraction with his many bungled adventures (all titled, "The Case of" this or that).
— JJM

1 ❑ Apr 1971 Cover: 0.15 **NM** value: **18.00**
2 ❑ Jul 1971 Cover: 0.15 **NM** value: **10.00**
3 ❑ Oct 1971 Cover: 0.15 **NM** value: **8.00**
4 ❑ Jan 1972 Cover: 0.15 **NM** value: **8.00**
5 ❑ Mar 1972 Cover: 0.15 **NM** value: **8.00**
6 ❑ May 1972 Cover: 0.15 **NM** value: **6.00**
7 ❑ Jul 1972 Cover: 0.15 **NM** value: **6.00**
8 ❑ Sep 1972 Cover: 0.15 **NM** value: **6.00**
9 ❑ Nov 1972 Cover: 0.15 **NM** value: **6.00**
10 ❑ Jan 1973 Cover: 0.15 **NM** value: **6.00**
11 ❑ Mar 1973 Cover: 0.15 **NM** value: **5.00**
12 ❑ May 1973 Cover: 0.15 **NM** value: **5.00**
13 ❑ Jul 1973 Cover: 0.15 **NM** value: **5.00**
14 ❑ Sep 1973 Cover: 0.20 **NM** value: **5.00**
15 ❑ Oct 1973 Cover: 0.20 **NM** value: **5.00**
16 ❑ Nov 1973 Cover: 0.20 **NM** value: **5.00**
17 ❑ Jan 1974 Cover: 0.20 **NM** value: **5.00**
18 ❑ Mar 1974 Cover: 0.20 **NM** value: **5.00**
19 ❑ May 1974 Cover: 0.20 **NM** value: **5.00**
20 ❑ Jul 1974 Cover: 0.25 **NM** value: **5.00**
21 ❑ Sep 1974 Cover: 0.25 **NM** value: **3.00**
22 ❑ Oct 1974 Cover: 0.25 **NM** value: **3.00**
23 ❑ Nov 1974 Cover: 0.25 **NM** value: **3.00**
24 ❑ Jan 1975 Cover: 0.25 **NM** value: **3.00**
25 ❑ Mar 1975 Cover: 0.25 **NM** value: **3.00**
26 ❑ May 1975 Cover: 0.25 **NM** value: **3.00**
27 ❑ Jul 1975 Cover: 0.25 **NM** value: **3.00**
28 ❑ Sep 1975 Cover: 0.25 **NM** value: **3.00**
29 ❑ Oct 1975 Cover: 0.25 **NM** value: **3.00**
30 ❑ Nov 1975 Cover: 0.25 **NM** value: **3.00**
31 ❑ Jan 1976 Cover: 0.25 **NM** value: **3.00**
32 ❑ Mar 1976 Cover: 0.25 **NM** value: **3.00**
33 ❑ Apr 1976 Cover: 0.25 **NM** value: **3.00**
34 ❑ May 1976 Cover: 0.25 **NM** value: **3.00**
35 ❑ Jun 1976 Cover: 0.25 **NM** value: **3.00**
36 ❑ Jul 1976 Cover: 0.25 **NM** value: **3.00**
37 ❑ Sep 1976 Cover: 0.30 **NM** value: **3.00**
38 ❑ Oct 1976 Cover: 0.30 **NM** value: **3.00**
39 ❑ Nov 1976 Cover: 0.30 **NM** value: **3.00**
40 ❑ Jan 1977 Cover: 0.30 **NM** value: **3.00**
41 ❑ Mar 1977 Cover: 0.30 **NM** value: **2.00**
42 ❑ Apr 1977 Cover: 0.30 **NM** value: **2.00**
43 ❑ May 1977 Cover: 0.30 **NM** value: **2.00**
44 ❑ Jun 1977 Cover: 0.30 **NM** value: **2.00**
45 ❑ Jul 1977 Cover: 0.30 **NM** value: **2.00**
46 ❑ Sep 1977 Cover: 0.30 **NM** value: **2.00**
47 ❑ Oct 1977 Cover: 0.30 **NM** value: **2.00**
48 ❑ Nov 1977 Cover: 0.30 **NM** value: **2.00**
49 ❑ Jan 1978 Cover: 0.35 **NM** value: **2.00**
50 ❑ Mar 1978 Cover: 0.35 **NM** value: **2.00**
51 ❑ Apr 1978 Cover: 0.35 **NM** value: **2.00**
52 ❑ May 1978 Cover: 0.35 **NM** value: **2.00**
53 ❑ Jun 1978 Cover: 0.35 **NM** value: **2.00**
54 ❑ Jul 1978 Cover: 0.35 **NM** value: **2.00**
55 ❑ Aug 1978 Cover: 0.35 **NM** value: **2.00**
56 ❑ Sep 1978 Cover: 0.35 **NM** value: **2.00**
57 ❑ Oct 1978 Cover: 0.35 **NM** value: **2.00**
58 ❑ Nov 1978 Cover: 0.35 **NM** value: **2.00**
59 ❑ Dec 1978 Cover: 0.35 **NM** value: **2.00**
60 ❑ Jan 1979 Cover: 0.35 **NM** value: **2.00**
61 ❑ Feb 1979 Cover: 0.35 **NM** value: **2.00**
📖 Batty Pink; Pink Shangri-La; Test Tube Pink; Cheating Chess Player
62 ❑ Mar 1979 Cover: 0.35 **NM** value: **2.00**
63 ❑ Apr 1979 Cover: 0.40 **NM** value: **2.00**
64 ❑ May 1979 Cover: 0.40 **NM** value: **2.00**
65 ❑ Jun 1979 Cover: 0.40 **NM** value: **2.00**
66 ❑ Jul 1979 Cover: 0.40 **NM** value: **2.00**
67 ❑ Aug 1979 Cover: 0.40 **NM** value: **2.00**
68 ❑ Sep 1979 Cover: 0.40 **NM** value: **2.00**
69 ❑ Oct 1979 Cover: 0.40 **NM** value: **2.00**
70 ❑ Nov 1979 Cover: 0.40 **NM** value: **2.00**
71 ❑ Dec 1979 Cover: 0.40 **NM** value: **2.00**
72 ❑ Jan 1980 Cover: 0.40 **NM** value: **2.00**
73 ❑ Feb 1980 Cover: 0.40 **NM** value: **2.00**
74 ❑ ca. 1980 Cover: 0.40 **NM** value: **2.00**
75 ❑ Aug 1980 Cover: 0.40 **NM** value: **2.00**
76 ❑ ca. 1981 Cover: 0.40 **NM** value: **2.00**
77 ❑ ca. 1981 Cover: 0.40 **NM** value: **2.00**
78 ❑ ca. 1981 Cover: 0.40 **NM** value: **2.00**
79 ❑ ca. 1981 Cover: 0.40 **NM** value: **2.00**
80 ❑ Cover: 0.40 **NM** value: **2.00**
81 ❑ Feb 1982 Cover: 0.60 **NM** value: **2.00**
82 ❑ Cover: 0.60 **NM** value: **2.00**
📖 Pink Tester
83 ❑ Cover: 0.60 **NM** value: **2.00**
84 ❑ Cover: 0.60 **NM** value: **2.00**
85 ❑ Cover: 0.60 **NM** value: **2.00**
86 ❑ Cover: 0.60 **NM** value: **2.00**
87 ❑ ca. 1984 Cover: 0.60 **NM** value: **2.00**

PINK PANTHER (HARVEY) — Harvey

1 ❑ Nov 1993 Cover: 1.50 **NM** value: **Cover or less**
2 ❑ Dec 1993 Cover: 1.50 **NM** value: **Cover or less**
📖 Pink Contestant; Pink Ventriloquism; Case of: the Cat Burglar; Pink Hostage
3 ❑ Jan 1994 Cover: 1.50 **NM** value: **Cover or less**
📖 Pink Chemistry; Pink Volcano; Pink Bodyguard; Casper the Friendly Ghost
4 ❑ Feb 1994 Cover: 1.50 **NM** value: **Cover or less**
📖 Pink Reporter; Pink Palm; Case of: The Crime, Inc. Caper; Pink Volunteer
5 ❑ Mar 1994 Cover: 1.50 **NM** value: **Cover or less**
📖 Pink Christmas
6 ❑ Apr 1994 Cover: 1.50 **NM** value: **Cover or less**
7 ❑ May 1994 Cover: 1.50 **NM** value: **Cover or less**
8 ❑ Jun 1994 Cover: 1.50 **NM** value: **Cover or less**
9 ❑ Jul 1994 Cover: 1.50 **NM** value: **Cover or less**
SS 1❑ ca. 1993 Cover: 2.25 **NM** value: **Cover or less**
• Super Special

There are two different pricing tiers in the modern comic-book hobby. **The prices seen above** are the prices we have seen **loose copies** of these issues reliably fetch in a variety of environments. Condition alters the price by the fractions seen on the bar on the bottom of left-hand pages of this book. **Comics graded by CGC** usually sell for more. Use the guide on the bottom of right-hand pages of this book to estimate what copies have brought on eBay.

PINKY AND THE BRAIN — DC

The misadventures of a super-smart lab mouse whose only goal is to take over the world and his brainless assistant with a Cockney accent began as part of the Animaniacs animated series. When the popular segment spun off into its own series in 1996, DC followed suit with an ongoing series.

Much like the animated series, the comics series poked fun at various popular trends and pop culture icons, including Ed Wood movies, Orson Welles (the apparent inspiration for The Brain), and even such fellow DC characters as Batman. The duo's speech patterns were even captured by the writers, including Pinky's one-word exclamation, "Narf!" — Brent

1 ❑ Jul 1996 Cover: 1.75 **NM** value: **2.50**
• based on animated series
2 ❑ Aug 1996 Cover: 1.75 **NM** value: **2.00**
📖 Excalibrain; Little Big Brain **A:** Walter Carzon **W:** David Cody Weiss; Bobbi JG Weiss; Jesse Leon McCann
3 ❑ Sep 1996 Cover: 1.75 **NM** value: **2.00**
📖 Verminator
4 ❑ Oct 1996 Cover: 1.75 **NM** value: **Cover or less**
📖 Pink O' The Irish; Caged Heat • Oz parody **A:** Walter Carzon; Mike DeCarlo **W:** David Cody Weiss; Bobbi JG Weiss; Dan Slott; Dana Kurtin
5 ❑ Nov 1996 Cover: 1.75 **NM** value: **Cover or less**
Circ: Diamd. preorders: **12,308**
📖 Oil's Well that Ends Well • Western parody issue **A:** Walter Carzon; Mike DeCarlo **W:** David Cody Weiss; Bobbi JG Weiss
6 ❑ Dec 1996 Cover: 1.75 **NM** value: **Cover or less**
Circ: Diamd. preorders: **12,098**
Photo cover. 📖 Plan Brain from Outer Space • Ed Wood parody issue **A:** Walter Carzon; Mike DeCarlo **W:** Jesse Leon McCann
7 ❑ Jan 1997 Cover: 1.75 **NM** value: **Cover or less**
Circ: Diamd. preorders: **11,040**
📖 Faust Things Faust; Clan of the Cave Mice • Faust parody **A:** Walter Carzon **W:** Jess Leon McCann
8 ❑ Feb 1997 Cover: 1.75 **NM** value: **Cover or less**
Circ: Diamd. preorders: **10,538**
📖 Mission: Impinkable
9 ❑ Mar 1997 Cover: 1.75 **NM** value: **Cover or less**
Circ: Diamd. preorders: **9,912**
📖 The Mouse who Would be King; Kappa Delta Rodent **A:** Walter Carzon **W:** Jesse Leon McCann; Shaun McLaughlin
10 ❑ Apr 1997 Cover: 1.75 **NM** value: **Cover or less**
Circ: Diamd. preorders: **9,433**
11 ❑ May 1997 Cover: 1.75 **NM** value: **Cover or less**
Circ: Diamd. preorders: **9,662**
• Fantasia parody
12 ❑ Jun 1997 Cover: 1.75 **NM** value: **Cover or less**
Circ: Diamd. preorders: **9,600**
• surfing parody
13 ❑ Jul 1997 Cover: 1.75 **NM** value: **Cover or less**
Circ: Diamd. preorders: **9,018**
📖 Ali-Brain and the Forty Thieves
14 ❑ Aug 1997 Cover: 1.75 **NM** value: **Cover or less**
Circ: Diamd. preorders: **8,853**
📖 Brainlet
15 ❑ Sep 1997 Cover: 1.75 **NM** value: **Cover or less**
Circ: Diamd. preorders: **8,551**
• Bikers
16 ❑ Oct 1997 Cover: 1.75 **NM** value: **Cover or less**
Circ: Diamd. preorders: **8,645**
📖 Verminator 2
17 ❑ Nov 1997 Cover: 1.75 **NM** value: **Cover or less**
Circ: Diamd. preorders: **8,367**
📖 Pinkenstein **A:** Walter Carzon **W:** Jesse Leon McCann
18 ❑ Dec 1997 Cover: 1.95 **NM** value: **Cover or less**
Circ: Diamd. preorders: **8,255**
📖 Braintech; Brinky 1/2 • Manga parody **A:** Walter Carzon **W:** Jesse Leon McCann
19 ❑ Jan 1998 Cover: 1.95 **NM** value: **Cover or less**
Circ: Diamd. preorders: **7,926**
• Brain plays Santa
20 ❑ Feb 1998 Cover: 1.95 **NM** value: **Cover or less**
Circ: Diamd. preorders: **7,716**
📖 Mice in Pink
21 ❑ Mar 1998 Cover: 1.95 **NM** value: **Cover or less**
Circ: Diamd. preorders: **7,352**
📖 Fantastic Voyage to the Bottom of the President's Brain; Acme Valley PTA **A:** Walter Carzon; Horacio Saavedra **W:** Jesse Leon McCann
22 ❑ May 1998 Cover: 1.95 **NM** value: **Cover or less**
Circ: Diamd. preorders: **7,063**
📖 The Mouse in the Iron Mask
23 ❑ Jun 1998 Cover: 1.95 **NM** value: **Cover or less**
Circ: Diamd. preorders: **7,364**
Jaws parody cover.
24 ❑ Jul 1998 Cover: 1.95 **NM** value: **Cover or less**
Circ: Diamd. preorders: **7,031**
📖 El Cerebro; Pinky Mon Amour • Zorro parody **A:** Walter Carzon; Pablo Zamboni **W:** Jesse Leon McCann
25 ❑ Aug 1998 Cover: 1.95 **NM** value: **Cover or less**
Circ: Diamd. preorders: **7,237**
📖 The Dark Pinky Returns
26 ❑ Oct 1998 Cover: 1.99 **NM** value: **Cover or less**
Circ: Diamd. preorders: **6,553**
• Demi Moore parody issue
27 ❑ Nov 1998 Cover: 1.99 **NM** value: **Cover or less**
Circ: Diamd. preorders: **6,579**

Other grades: Multiply prices above by **1.5 for Mint • 2/3 for Very Fine • 1/3 for Fine • 1/5 for Very Good • 1/8 for Good**

HS 1 ☐ Jan 1996 Cover: 1.50 **NM** value: **Cover or less**
• Giant-size.

PINOCCHIO AND THE EMPEROR OF THE NIGHT — Marvel

1 ☐ Mar 1988 Cover: 1.25 **NM** value: **Cover or less**
A: Ben Brown **W:** Sid Jacobson

PINOCCHIO SPECIAL (WALT DISNEY'S...) — Gladstone

1 ☐ Mar 1990 Cover: 1.00 **NM** value: **1.50**
Circ: CapCity orders: **5,550**
A: Walt Kelly

PINT-SIZED X-BABIES — Marvel

1 ☐ Aug 1998 Cover: 2.99 **NM** value: **Cover or less**
Circ: Diamd. preorders: **34,664**
One-shot. • gatefold summary. ★ Versus Li'l Bad Guys.

PIONEER PICTURE STORIES — Street & Smith

1 ☐ Dec 1941 Cover: 0.10 **NM** value: **125.00**
2 ☐ Mar 1942 Cover: 0.10 **NM** value: **60.00**
3 ☐ Jun 1942 Cover: 0.10 **NM** value: **60.00**
4 ☐ Sep 1942 Cover: 0.10 **NM** value: **50.00**
5 ☐ Dec 1942 Cover: 0.10 **NM** value: **50.00**
6 ☐ Mar 1943 Cover: 0.10 **NM** value: **50.00**
7 ☐ Jun 1943 Cover: 0.10 **NM** value: **50.00**
8 ☐ Sep 1943 Cover: 0.10 **NM** value: **50.00**
• **CGC:** 1 graded, best 9.2
9 ☐ Dec 1943 Cover: 0.10 **NM** value: **50.00**

PIPSQUEAK PAPERS (WALLACE WOOD'S...) — Fantagraphics / Eros

All issues are adults only.
1 ☐ b&w Cover: 2.75 **NM** value: **Cover or less**

PIRACY (E.C.) — E.C.

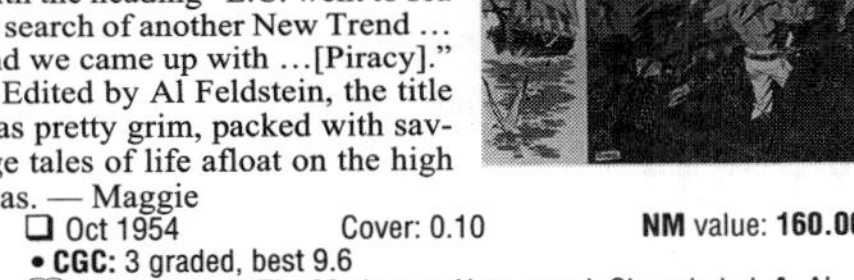

This E.C. title carried the above-the-title words, "Sagas of the sea, ships, plunder and ..." and is considered to have come before E.C.'s "New Direction" line of Comics Code-approved comics, though the last three issues carried the Code seal. House ads for the title featured Wally Wood caricatures of the E.C. staff, dressed as pirates, with the heading "E.C. went to sea in search of another New Trend ... and we came up with ...[Piracy]."

Edited by Al Feldstein, the title was pretty grim, packed with savage tales of life afloat on the high seas. — Maggie

1 ☐ Oct 1954 Cover: 0.10 **NM** value: **160.00**
• **CGC:** 3 graded, best 9.6
📖 The Privateer; The Mutineers; Harpooned; Shanghaied **A:** Al Williamson
2 ☐ Dec 1954 Cover: 0.10 **NM** value: **115.00**
• **CGC:** 2 graded, best 9.8
📖 Sea Food; Kismet; The Shell Game; A Fitting End **A:** Al Williamson
3 ☐ Feb 1955 Cover: 0.10 **NM** value: **85.00**
• **CGC:** 3 graded, best 9.6
📖 Blackbeard; U-Boat; Mouse Trap; Slave Ship
4 ☐ Apr 1955 Cover: 0.10 **NM** value: **85.00**
• **CGC:** 2 graded, best 9.4
📖 Pirate Master; The King's Buccaneer (text story); By the Book; The Sheba; Inheritance; **A:** George Evans; Bernie Krigstein; Reed Crandall; Graham Ingels **W:** George Evans; Bernie Krigstein; Reed Crandall; Graham Ingels
5 ☐ Jun 1955 Cover: 0.10 **NM** value: **85.00**
• **CGC:** 3 graded, best 9.2
📖 Jean Lafitte; Rag Doll; Salvage; The Keg • Comics Code approved
6 ☐ Aug 1955 Cover: 0.10 **NM** value: **85.00**
• **CGC:** 3 graded, best 9.8
📖 Fit for a King; The Skipper; Fur Crazy; Solitary • Comics Code approved
7 ☐ Oct 1955 Cover: 0.10 **NM** value: **85.00**
• **CGC:** 2 graded, best 9.2
📖 Partners; Up the River; John's Reward; Temptation final issue. • Comics Code approved

PIRACY (RCP) — Gemstone

1 ☐ Mar 1998 Cover: 2.50 **NM** value: **Cover or less**
Circ: Diamd. preorders: **5,263**
📖 The Privateer; The Mutineers; Harpooned; The Challenge (text); Shanghaied **A:** Wally Wood; Angelo Torres; Reed Crandall; Jack Davis **W:** Al Williamson; Wally Wood; Reed Crandall; Jack Davis
2 ☐ Apr 1998 Cover: 2.50 **NM** value: **Cover or less**
Circ: Diamd. preorders: **4,446**
📖 Sea Food; Kismet; Loblolly Boy (text); The Shell Game; A Fitting End **A:** Wally Wood; Angelo Torres; Reed Crandall; Jack Davis **W:** Al Williamson; Wally Wood; Reed Crandall; Jack Davis
3 ☐ May 1998 Cover: 2.50 **NM** value: **Cover or less**
Circ: Diamd. preorders: **4,203**
📖 Blackbeard; U-Boat; The Beast (text); Mouse Trap; Slave Ship **A:** George Evans; Bernie Krigstein; Reed Crandall; Graham Ingels **W:** George Evans; Bernie Krigstein; Reed Crandall; Graham Ingels
4 ☐ Jun 1998 Cover: 2.50 **NM** value: **Cover or less**
Circ: Diamd. preorders: **4,630**
📖 Pirate Master; The King's Buccaneer (text story); By the Book; The Sheba; Inheritance; **A:** George Evans; Bernie Krigstein; Reed Crandall; Graham Ingels **W:** George Evans; Bernie Krigstein; Reed Crandall; Graham Ingels
5 ☐ Jul 1998 Cover: 2.50 **NM** value: **Cover or less**
Circ: Diamd. preorders: **4,411**
📖 Jean Lafitte; Rag Doll; Salvage; Breakers on the Shore (text); The Keg **A:** George Evans; Bernie Krigstein; Reed Crandall; Graham Ingels **W:** George Evans; Bernie Krigstein; Reed Crandall; Graham Ingels
6 ☐ Aug 1998 Cover: 2.50 **NM** value: **Cover or less**
Circ: Diamd. preorders: **4,401**
📖 Fit for a King; The Skipper; Fur Crazy; Breakers on the Shore (text); Sailor for Queen Bees (text); Solitary **A:** George Evans; Reed Crandall; Jack Davis; Graham Ingels **W:** George Evans; Reed Crandall; Jack Davis; Graham Ingels
7 ☐ Sep 1998 Cover: 2.50 **NM** value: **Cover or less**
Circ: Diamd. preorders: **4,199**
📖 Partners; Prologue (text); Up the River; John's Reward; Temptation **A:** George Evans; Bernie Krigstein; Reed Crandall; Graham Ingels **W:** George Evans; Bernie Krigstein; Reed Crandall; Graham Ingels
Bk 1 ☐ Cover: 10.95 **NM** value: **Cover or less**
Bk 2 ☐ Cover: 7.95 **NM** value: **Cover or less**
📖 Jean Lafitte; Rag Doll; Salvage; Breakers on the Shore (text); The Keg; Fit for a King; The Skipper; Fur Crazy; Sailor for Queen Bees (text); Solitary; Partners; Prologue (text); Up the River; John's Reward; Temptation • Collects issues 5-7 **A:** George Evans; Bernie Krigstein; Reed Crandall; Jack Davis; Graham Ingels

PIRANHA IS LOOSE! — Special Studio

1 ☐ b&w Cover: 2.75 **NM** value: **Cover or less**
2 ☐ b&w Cover: 2.75 **NM** value: **Cover or less**

PIRATE CORP$! (2ND SERIES) — Slave Labor

1 ☐ Jun 1989 Cover: 1.75 **NM** value: **2.50**
A: Evan Dorkin **W:** Evan Dorkin
1-2 ☐ Aug 1993 Cover: 2.50 **NM** value: **Cover or less**
2 ☐ Sep 1989 Cover: 1.75 **NM** value: **2.50**
A: Evan Dorkin **W:** Evan Dorkin
2-2 ☐ Feb 1993 Cover: 2.50 **NM** value: **Cover or less**
3 ☐ Feb 1991 Cover: 2.50 **NM** value: **Cover or less**
A: Evan Dorkin **W:** Evan Dorkin
3-2 ☐ Feb 1993 Cover: 2.50 **NM** value: **Cover or less**
4 ☐ Apr 1992 Cover: 2.50 **NM** value: **Cover or less**
A: Evan Dorkin **W:** Evan Dorkin
4-2 ☐ Sep 1993 Cover: 2.50 **NM** value: **Cover or less**
5 ☐ Dec 1992 Cover: 2.50 **NM** value: **Cover or less**
A: Evan Dorkin **W:** Evan Dorkin
5-2 ☐ Apr 1994 Cover: 2.50 **NM** value: **Cover or less**
SE 1 ☐ Mar 1989, b&w Cover: 1.95 **NM** value: **Cover or less**
has Futurama ad on back cover. **A:** Evan Dorkin **W:** Evan Dorkin
SE 1-2 ☐ Aug 1993 Cover: 2.95 **NM** value: **Cover or less**

PIRATE CORPS — Eternity

1 ☐ Cover: 1.95 **NM** value: **2.50**
Circ: CapCity orders: **2,125**
A: Evan Dorkin **W:** Evan Dorkin
2 ☐ Cover: 1.95 **NM** value: **2.50**
A: Evan Dorkin **W:** Evan Dorkin
3 ☐ Dec 1987 Cover: 1.95 **NM** value: **2.50**
A: Evan Dorkin **W:** Evan Dorkin
4 ☐ Feb 1988 Cover: 1.95 **NM** value: **2.50**
Circ: CapCity orders: **1,475**
A: Evan Dorkin **W:** Evan Dorkin

PIRATE CORP$: THE BLUNDER YEARS — Slave Labor

Bk 1 ☐ Jul 1993 Cover: 4.50 **NM** value: **Cover or less**
• Pirate Corp$: The Blunder Years Book 1; reprints Eternity issues #1 and 2 **A:** Evan Dorkin **W:** Evan Dorkin
Bk 2 ☐ Jul 1993 Cover: 4.50 **NM** value: **Cover or less**
• Pirate Corp$: The Blunder Years Book 2; reprints Eternity issues #3 and 4 **A:** Evan Dorkin **W:** Evan Dorkin

PIRATE QUEEN, THE — Comax

All issues are adults only.
1 ☐ b&w Cover: 2.95 **NM** value: **3.00**
📖 Lost City Of Gold **A:** Butch Burcham **W:** Butch Burcham

PIRATES COMICS — Hillman

1 ☐ Feb 1950 Cover: 0.10 **NM** value: **150.00**
• **CGC:** 2 graded, best 9.2
2 ☐ May 1950 Cover: 0.10 **NM** value: **100.00**
3 ☐ Jul 1950 Cover: 0.10 **NM** value: **100.00**
• **CGC:** 1 graded, best 6.0
4 ☐ Sep 1950 Cover: 0.10 **NM** value: **100.00**

PIRATES OF DARK WATER, THE — Marvel

1 ☐ Nov 1991 Cover: 1.00 **NM** value: **Cover or less**
Circ: CapCity orders: **12,900**
2 ☐ Dec 1991 Cover: 1.00 **NM** value: **Cover or less**
Circ: CapCity orders: **8,300**
3 ☐ Jan 1992 Cover: 1.00 **NM** value: **Cover or less**
Circ: CapCity orders: **6,800**
4 ☐ Feb 1992 Cover: 1.25 **NM** value: **Cover or less**
Circ: CapCity orders: **5,800**
5 ☐ Mar 1992 Cover: 1.25 **NM** value: **Cover or less**
Circ: CapCity orders: **4,800**
6 ☐ Apr 1992 Cover: 1.25 **NM** value: **Cover or less**
Circ: CapCity orders: **3,900**
7 ☐ May 1992 Cover: 1.25 **NM** value: **Cover or less**
Circ: CapCity orders: **3,700**
8 ☐ Jun 1992 Cover: 1.25 **NM** value: **Cover or less**
Circ: CapCity orders: **3,800**
9 ☐ Jul 1992 Cover: 1.25 **NM** value: **Cover or less**
Circ: CapCity orders: **3,400**
final issue.

P.I.'S, THE: MICHAEL MAUSER AND MS. TREE — First

1 ☐ Jan 1985 Cover: 1.25 **NM** value: **1.50**
📖 The Odd Couple • Ms. Tree, E-Man **A:** Mike Grell; Joe Staton **W:** Max Allan Collins
2 ☐ Mar 1985 Cover: 1.25 **NM** value: **1.50**
A: Joe Staton **W:** Max Allan Collins
3 ☐ May 1985 Cover: 1.25 **NM** value: **1.50**
A: Joe Staton **W:** Max Allan Collins

PISTOLERO — Eternity

1 ☐ b&w Cover: 3.95 **NM** value: **Cover or less**
No issue number. One-shot.

PI: THE BOOK OF ANTS — Artisan Entertainment

1 ☐ b&w Cover: 2.95 **NM** value: **Cover or less**
No issue number. • based on movie

PITT — Image

Pitt was Dale Keown's first work for Image. Its star is a huge creature named Pitt, who shares his consciousness with an energy being named Jereb. Pitt was created by a splicing of human and Creed genes to become a deadly killing machine. Now, the very forces that created him have deemed him a traitor. Pitt fled to Earth where he must save not only himself, but a small child named Timmy from the galactic bruisers that want to kill them both.

After a popular trading-card series was produced based on the property, Keown eventually took the title out on its own.

0.5 ☐ Cover: 1.50 **NM** value: **Cover or less**
Circ: CapCity orders: **33,250**
📖 Lupe: A Nice Girl Like You... **A:** Dale Keown **W:** Dale Keown
1 ☐ Jan 1993 Cover: 1.95 **NM** value: **Cover or less**
Circ: CapCity orders: **172,725** • **CGC:** 31 graded, best 10.0
📖 Fight & Flight! **A:** Dale Keown **W:** Dale Keown ★ 1st Appearance of Pitt.
1/GO ☐ Jan 1993 Cover: 1.95 **NM** value: **Cover or less**
• Gold edition.
2 ☐ Jul 1993 Cover: 1.95 **NM** value: **Cover or less**
Circ: CapCity orders: **147,200** • **CGC:** 1 graded, best 9.4
📖 Dead Or Alive **A:** Dale Keown **W:** Dale Keown
3 ☐ Feb 1994 Cover: 1.95 **NM** value: **Cover or less**
Circ: CapCity orders: **140,350**
A: Dale Keown **W:** Dale Keown
4 ☐ Apr 1994 Cover: 1.95 **NM** value: **Cover or less**
Circ: CapCity orders: **153,350**
A: Dale Keown **W:** Dale Keown
5 ☐ Jun 1994 Cover: 1.95 **NM** value: **Cover or less**
Circ: CapCity orders: **67,650**
A: Dale Keown **W:** Dale Keown
6 ☐ Sep 1994 Cover: 1.95 **NM** value: **Cover or less**
Circ: CapCity orders: **59,950**
A: Dale Keown **W:** Dale Keown
7 ☐ Dec 1994 Cover: 1.95 **NM** value: **Cover or less**
Circ: CapCity orders: **48,725**
A: Dale Keown **W:** Dale Keown
8 ☐ Apr 1994 Cover: 1.95 **NM** value: **Cover or less**
Circ: CapCity orders: **41,625**
A: Dale Keown **W:** Dale Keown
9 ☐ Aug 1995 Cover: 1.95 **NM** value: **Cover or less**
Circ: CapCity orders: **39,525**
A: Dale Keown **W:** Dale Keown
10 ☐ 1996 Cover: 1.95 **NM** value: **Cover or less**
Circ: CapCity orders: **41,400**
A: Dale Keown **W:** Dale Keown
11 ☐ 1996 Cover: 1.95 **NM** value: **Cover or less**
A: Dale Keown **W:** Dale Keown
12 ☐ Dec 1996 Cover: 1.95 **NM** value: **Cover or less**
Circ: Diamd. preorders: **52,698**
A: Dale Keown **W:** Dale Keown
13 ☐ Mar 1997 Cover: 1.95 **NM** value: **Cover or less**
Circ: Diamd. preorders: **48,072**
A: Dale Keown **W:** Dale Keown
14 ☐ Jun 1997 Cover: 2.50 **NM** value: **Cover or less**
Circ: Diamd. preorders: **44,959**
A: Dale Keown **W:** Dale Keown
15 ☐ Sep 1997 Cover: 2.50 **NM** value: **Cover or less**
Circ: Diamd. preorders: **41,090**
A: Dale Keown **W:** Dale Keown
16 ☐ Dec 1997 Cover: 2.50 **NM** value: **Cover or less**
Circ: Diamd. preorders: **39,636**
A: Dale Keown **W:** Dale Keown
17 ☐ Mar 1998 Cover: 2.50 **NM** value: **Cover or less**
Circ: Diamd. preorders: **34,810**
A: Dale Keown **W:** Dale Keown
18 ☐ Jun 1998 Cover: 2.50 **NM** value: **Cover or less**
Circ: Diamd. preorders: **33,095**
A: Dale Keown **W:** Dale Keown
19 ☐ Sep 1998 Cover: 2.50 **NM** value: **Cover or less**
Circ: Diamd. preorders: **29,742**
A: Dale Keown **W:** Dale Keown
Bk 1 ☐ Cover: 9.95 **NM** value: **Cover or less**
A: Dale Keown **W:** Dale Keown

PITT, THE — Marvel

1 ☐ Cover: 3.25 **NM** value: **Cover or less**
Circ: CapCity orders: **28,000**
A: Sal Buscema; John Byrne **W:** John Byrne; Mark Gruenwald

PIXIES — Magazine Enterprises

1 ☐ Win 1946 Cover: 0.10 **NM** value: **40.00**
2 ☐ Spr 1947 Cover: 0.10 **NM** value: **25.00**
3 ☐ Sum 1947 Cover: 0.10 **NM** value: **25.00**
4 ☐ Fal 1947 Cover: 0.10 **NM** value: **25.00**
5 ☐ Win 1947 Cover: 0.10 **NM** value: **25.00**

CGC-graded: Multiply prices above by **33 for 9.9 M • 16 for 9.8 NM/M • 7 for 9.6 NM+ • 5 for 9.4 NM • 2.5 for 9.2 NM- • 1.5 for 9.0 VF/NM**

PIXY JUNKET — Viz

1 ❑ b&w Cover: 2.75 **NM** value: **Cover or less**
Circ: CapCity orders: **3,525**
A: Pure **W:** Pure
2 ❑ b&w Cover: 2.75 **NM** value: **Cover or less**
Circ: CapCity orders: **2,775**
A: Pure **W:** Pure
3 ❑ b&w Cover: 2.75 **NM** value: **Cover or less**
A: Pure **W:** Pure
4 ❑ b&w Cover: 2.75 **NM** value: **Cover or less**
A: Pure **W:** Pure
5 ❑ b&w Cover: 2.75 **NM** value: **Cover or less**
Circ: CapCity orders: **2,450**
A: Pure **W:** Pure
6 ❑ b&w Cover: 2.75 **NM** value: **Cover or less**
Circ: CapCity orders: **2,450**
A: Pure **W:** Pure
Bk 1❑ b&w Cover: 15.95 **NM** value: **Cover or less**

P.J. WARLOCK — Eclipse

1 ❑ Nov 1986, b&w Cover: 2.00 **NM** value: **Cover or less**
A: Bill Schorr **W:** Bill Schorr
2 ❑ Jan 1987, b&w Cover: 2.00 **NM** value: **Cover or less**
A: Bill Schorr **W:** Bill Schorr
3 ❑ Mar 1987, b&w Cover: 2.00 **NM** value: **Cover or less**
A: Bill Schorr **W:** Bill Schorr

PLACES THAT ARE GONE — Aeon

1 ❑ Jul 1994 Cover: 2.75 **NM** value: **Cover or less**
2 ❑ Aug 1994 Cover: 2.75 **NM** value: **Cover or less**

PLAGUE — Tome Press

1 ❑ b&w Cover: 2.95 **NM** value: **Cover or less**

PLAN 9 FROM OUTER SPACE — Eternity

1 ❑ b&w Cover: 4.95 **NM** value: **Cover or less**
A: Stan Timmons; Bruce McCorkindale **W:** John Wooley
1-2 ❑ Cover: 5.95 **NM** value: **Cover or less**

PLAN 9 FROM OUTER SPACE: THIRTY YEARS LATER — Eternity

1 ❑ Jan 1991, b&w Cover: 2.50 **NM** value: **Cover or less**
A: Gary Dumm; Joe Zabel; Greg Budgett **W:** John Wooley
2 ❑ b&w Cover: 2.50 **NM** value: **Cover or less**
A: Gary Dumm; Joe Zabel; Greg Budgett **W:** John Wooley
3 ❑ b&w Cover: 2.50 **NM** value: **Cover or less**
A: Gary Dumm; Joe Zabel; Greg Budgett **W:** John Wooley

PLANET 29 — Caliber

1 ❑ b&w Cover: 2.50 **NM** value: **Cover or less**
2 ❑ b&w Cover: 2.50 **NM** value: **Cover or less**

PLANETARY — DC / Wildstorm

Planetary is a mysterious world-wide corporation that investigates the strange, the unusual, and the weird.

This series follows three members of the Planetary team. The Drummer is a Bohemian hippie whose very body is a natural anti-surveillance device; Jakita Wagner, who exhibits super speed, amazing eyesight, and a spectacular jump-suited figure; and the white-haired Elijah Snow, a man much older than he looks, who uses his power of heat subtraction to dissipate deadly nerve gas or simply chill out a room.

From islands filled with strangely familiar Japanese-style monsters, and cities haunted by dead cops, to run-ins with pulp-fiction bronze doctors, the Planetary team explores, as the publisher describes it, "the strange and beautiful things beneath the skin of the world we know."

1 ❑ Apr 1999 Cover: 2.50 **NM** value: **3.00**
Circ: Diamd. preorders: **37,650 • CGC:** 28 graded, best 9.8
A: John Cassaday **W:** Warren Ellis
2 ❑ May 1999 Cover: 2.50 **NM** value: **3.00**
Circ: Diamd. preorders: **30,889**
📖 Island **A:** John Cassaday **W:** Warren Ellis
3 ❑ Jun 1999 Cover: 2.50 **NM** value: **3.00**
Circ: Diamd. preorders: **33,264**
📖 Dead Gunfighters **A:** John Cassaday **W:** Warren Ellis
4 ❑ Jul 1999 Cover: 2.50 **NM** value: **Cover or less**
Circ: Diamd. preorders: **33,201 • CGC:** 2 graded, best 9.8
📖 Strange Harbours **A:** John Cassaday **W:** Warren Ellis
5 ❑ Sep 1999 Cover: 2.50 **NM** value: **Cover or less**
Circ: Diamd. preorders: **33,415 • CGC:** 1 graded, best 9.6
📖 The Good Doctor **A:** John Cassaday **W:** Warren Ellis
6 ❑ Nov 1999 Cover: 2.50 **NM** value: **Cover or less**
Circ: Diamd. preorders: **34,305**
A: John Cassaday **W:** Warren Ellis
7 ❑ Jan 2000 Cover: 2.50 **NM** value: **Cover or less**
Circ: Diamd. preorders: **33,532**
📖 To be in England, in the Summertime **A:** John Cassaday **W:** Warren Ellis
8 ❑ Feb 2000 Cover: 2.50 **NM** value: **Cover or less**
Circ: Diamd. preorders: **32,892**
A: John Cassaday **W:** Warren Ellis
9 ❑ Apr 2000 Cover: 2.50 **NM** value: **Cover or less**
Circ: Diamd. preorders: **30,274**
A: John Cassaday **W:** Warren Ellis
10 ❑ 2000 Cover: 2.50 **NM** value: **Cover or less**
Circ: Diamd. preorders: **31,679**
A: John Cassaday **W:** Warren Ellis
11 ❑ Sep 2000 Cover: 2.50 **NM** value: **Cover or less**
Circ: Diamd. preorders: **33,585 • CGC:** 1 graded, best 9.6
📖 Cold World **A:** John Cassaday **W:** Warren Ellis
12 ❑ Jan 2001 Cover: 2.50 **NM** value: **Cover or less**
Circ: Diamd. preorders: **35,295 • CGC:** 1 graded, best 9.6
📖 Memory Cloud **A:** John Cassaday **W:** Warren Ellis
13 ❑ Feb 2001 Cover: 2.50 **NM** value: **Cover or less**
Circ: Diamd. preorders: **36,848**
📖 Century **A:** John Cassaday **W:** Warren Ellis
14 ❑ Jun 2001 Cover: 2.50 **NM** value: **Cover or less**
Circ: Diamd. preorders: **36,859**
📖 Zero Point **A:** John Cassaday **W:** Warren Ellis
Bk 1❑ Cover: 2.50 **NM** value: **14.95**
• All Over the World and Other Stories; Collects Planetary #1-6, Planetary Preview **A:** John Cassaday **W:** Warren Ellis
Bk 1/HC❑ Cover: 24.95 **NM** value: **Cover or less**
• Hardcover edition. • All Over the World and Other Stories; Collects Planetary #1-6 **A:** John Cassaday **W:** Warren Ellis
Bk 2/HC❑ Cover: 24.95 **NM** value: **Cover or less**
• Hardcover edition. • The Fourth Man **A:** John Cassaday **W:** Warren Ellis

PLANET COMICS — Fiction House

Planet Comics, published by Fiction House, was the first all-science-fiction comic-book title to appear in the United States. The first issue came out in 1940 and employed the same general style and storytelling flavor of the "space opera," science-fiction pulp magazines, complete with space cowboys, bug-eyed monsters, and star pirates. Early issues benefited from the high craftsmanship of Will Eisner and his studio, including Lou Fine. Planet Comics followed the winning formula of other Fiction House comics like Jumbo Comics and Jungle Comics by prominently featuring scantily-clad women in distress on the covers and throughout the stories. Planet wrapped up its run in the early 1950s after being singled out for its alleged lewdness in anticomics propaganda like Seduction of the Innocent and Parade of Pleasure.

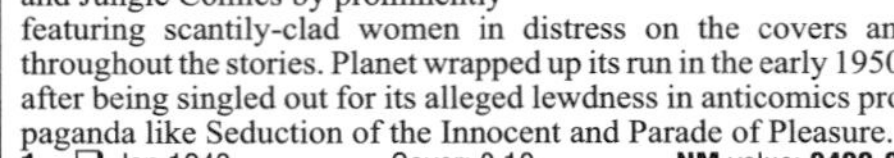

1 ❑ Jan 1940 Cover: 0.10 **NM** value: **9400.00**
• **CGC:** 5 graded, best 9.2
A: Will Eisner; Lou Fine
2 ❑ Feb 1940 Cover: 0.10 **NM** value: **3500.00**
• **CGC:** 2 graded, best 5.0
3 ❑ Mar 1940 Cover: 0.10 **NM** value: **2450.00**
• **CGC:** 3 graded, best 9.0
4 ❑ Apr 1940 Cover: 0.10 **NM** value: **1950.00**
• **CGC:** 2 graded, best 7.0
5 ❑ May 1940 Cover: 0.10 **NM** value: **1950.00**
6 ❑ Jun 1940 Cover: 0.10 **NM** value: **1675.00**
• **CGC:** 1 graded, best 7.5

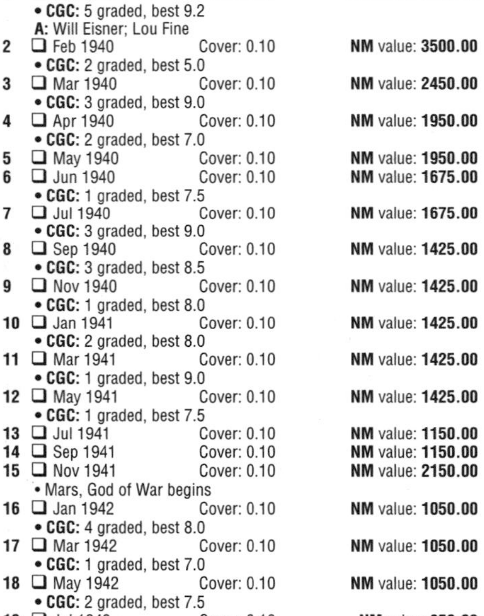

7 ❑ Jul 1940 Cover: 0.10 **NM** value: **1675.00**
• **CGC:** 3 graded, best 9.0
8 ❑ Sep 1940 Cover: 0.10 **NM** value: **1425.00**
• **CGC:** 3 graded, best 8.5
9 ❑ Nov 1940 Cover: 0.10 **NM** value: **1425.00**
• **CGC:** 1 graded, best 8.0
10 ❑ Jan 1941 Cover: 0.10 **NM** value: **1425.00**
• **CGC:** 2 graded, best 8.0
11 ❑ Mar 1941 Cover: 0.10 **NM** value: **1425.00**
• **CGC:** 1 graded, best 9.0
12 ❑ May 1941 Cover: 0.10 **NM** value: **1425.00**
• **CGC:** 1 graded, best 7.5
13 ❑ Jul 1941 Cover: 0.10 **NM** value: **1150.00**
14 ❑ Sep 1941 Cover: 0.10 **NM** value: **1150.00**
15 ❑ Nov 1941 Cover: 0.10 **NM** value: **2150.00**
• Mars, God of War begins
16 ❑ Jan 1942 Cover: 0.10 **NM** value: **1050.00**
• **CGC:** 4 graded, best 8.0
17 ❑ Mar 1942 Cover: 0.10 **NM** value: **1050.00**
• **CGC:** 1 graded, best 7.0
18 ❑ May 1942 Cover: 0.10 **NM** value: **1050.00**
• **CGC:** 2 graded, best 7.5

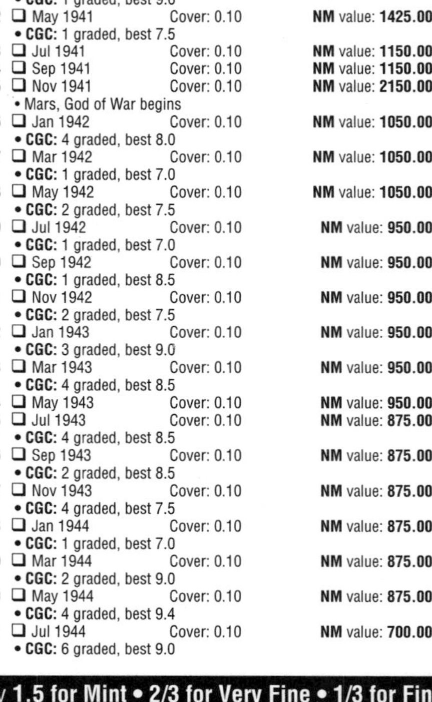

19 ❑ Jul 1942 Cover: 0.10 **NM** value: **950.00**
• **CGC:** 1 graded, best 7.0
20 ❑ Sep 1942 Cover: 0.10 **NM** value: **950.00**
• **CGC:** 1 graded, best 8.5
21 ❑ Nov 1942 Cover: 0.10 **NM** value: **950.00**
• **CGC:** 2 graded, best 7.5
22 ❑ Jan 1943 Cover: 0.10 **NM** value: **950.00**
• **CGC:** 3 graded, best 9.0
23 ❑ Mar 1943 Cover: 0.10 **NM** value: **950.00**
• **CGC:** 4 graded, best 8.5
24 ❑ May 1943 Cover: 0.10 **NM** value: **950.00**
25 ❑ Jul 1943 Cover: 0.10 **NM** value: **875.00**
• **CGC:** 4 graded, best 8.5
26 ❑ Sep 1943 Cover: 0.10 **NM** value: **875.00**
• **CGC:** 2 graded, best 8.5
27 ❑ Nov 1943 Cover: 0.10 **NM** value: **875.00**
• **CGC:** 4 graded, best 7.5
28 ❑ Jan 1944 Cover: 0.10 **NM** value: **875.00**
• **CGC:** 1 graded, best 7.0
29 ❑ Mar 1944 Cover: 0.10 **NM** value: **875.00**
• **CGC:** 2 graded, best 9.0
30 ❑ May 1944 Cover: 0.10 **NM** value: **875.00**
• **CGC:** 4 graded, best 9.4
31 ❑ Jul 1944 Cover: 0.10 **NM** value: **700.00**
• **CGC:** 6 graded, best 9.0

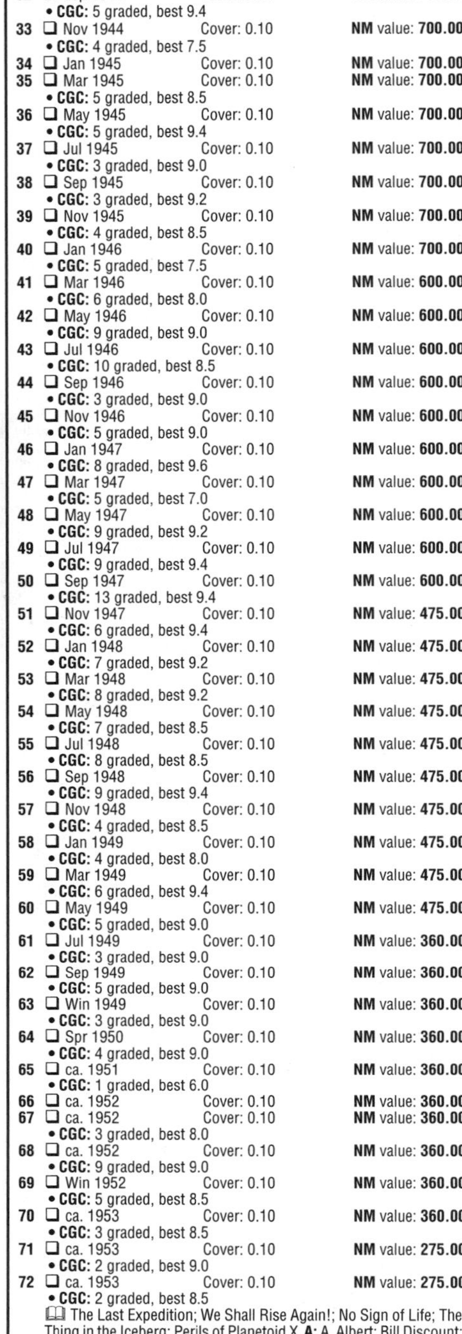

32 ❑ Sep 1944 Cover: 0.10 **NM** value: **700.00**
• **CGC:** 5 graded, best 9.4
33 ❑ Nov 1944 Cover: 0.10 **NM** value: **700.00**
• **CGC:** 4 graded, best 7.5
34 ❑ Jan 1945 Cover: 0.10 **NM** value: **700.00**
35 ❑ Mar 1945 Cover: 0.10 **NM** value: **700.00**
• **CGC:** 5 graded, best 8.5
36 ❑ May 1945 Cover: 0.10 **NM** value: **700.00**
• **CGC:** 5 graded, best 9.4
37 ❑ Jul 1945 Cover: 0.10 **NM** value: **700.00**
• **CGC:** 3 graded, best 9.0
38 ❑ Sep 1945 Cover: 0.10 **NM** value: **700.00**
• **CGC:** 3 graded, best 9.2
39 ❑ Nov 1945 Cover: 0.10 **NM** value: **700.00**
• **CGC:** 4 graded, best 8.5
40 ❑ Jan 1946 Cover: 0.10 **NM** value: **700.00**
• **CGC:** 5 graded, best 7.5
41 ❑ Mar 1946 Cover: 0.10 **NM** value: **600.00**
• **CGC:** 6 graded, best 8.0
42 ❑ May 1946 Cover: 0.10 **NM** value: **600.00**
• **CGC:** 9 graded, best 9.0
43 ❑ Jul 1946 Cover: 0.10 **NM** value: **600.00**
• **CGC:** 10 graded, best 8.5
44 ❑ Sep 1946 Cover: 0.10 **NM** value: **600.00**
• **CGC:** 3 graded, best 9.0
45 ❑ Nov 1946 Cover: 0.10 **NM** value: **600.00**
• **CGC:** 5 graded, best 9.0
46 ❑ Jan 1947 Cover: 0.10 **NM** value: **600.00**
• **CGC:** 8 graded, best 9.6
47 ❑ Mar 1947 Cover: 0.10 **NM** value: **600.00**
• **CGC:** 5 graded, best 7.0
48 ❑ May 1947 Cover: 0.10 **NM** value: **600.00**
• **CGC:** 9 graded, best 9.2
49 ❑ Jul 1947 Cover: 0.10 **NM** value: **600.00**
• **CGC:** 9 graded, best 9.4
50 ❑ Sep 1947 Cover: 0.10 **NM** value: **600.00**
• **CGC:** 13 graded, best 9.4
51 ❑ Nov 1947 Cover: 0.10 **NM** value: **475.00**
• **CGC:** 6 graded, best 9.4
52 ❑ Jan 1948 Cover: 0.10 **NM** value: **475.00**
• **CGC:** 7 graded, best 9.2
53 ❑ Mar 1948 Cover: 0.10 **NM** value: **475.00**
• **CGC:** 8 graded, best 9.2
54 ❑ May 1948 Cover: 0.10 **NM** value: **475.00**
• **CGC:** 7 graded, best 8.5
55 ❑ Jul 1948 Cover: 0.10 **NM** value: **475.00**
• **CGC:** 8 graded, best 8.5
56 ❑ Sep 1948 Cover: 0.10 **NM** value: **475.00**
• **CGC:** 9 graded, best 9.4
57 ❑ Nov 1948 Cover: 0.10 **NM** value: **475.00**
• **CGC:** 4 graded, best 8.5
58 ❑ Jan 1949 Cover: 0.10 **NM** value: **475.00**
• **CGC:** 4 graded, best 8.0
59 ❑ Mar 1949 Cover: 0.10 **NM** value: **475.00**
• **CGC:** 6 graded, best 9.4
60 ❑ May 1949 Cover: 0.10 **NM** value: **475.00**
• **CGC:** 5 graded, best 9.0
61 ❑ Jul 1949 Cover: 0.10 **NM** value: **360.00**
• **CGC:** 3 graded, best 9.0
62 ❑ Sep 1949 Cover: 0.10 **NM** value: **360.00**
• **CGC:** 5 graded, best 9.0
63 ❑ Win 1949 Cover: 0.10 **NM** value: **360.00**
• **CGC:** 3 graded, best 9.0
64 ❑ Spr 1950 Cover: 0.10 **NM** value: **360.00**
• **CGC:** 4 graded, best 9.0
65 ❑ ca. 1951 Cover: 0.10 **NM** value: **360.00**
• **CGC:** 1 graded, best 6.0
66 ❑ ca. 1952 Cover: 0.10 **NM** value: **360.00**
67 ❑ ca. 1952 Cover: 0.10 **NM** value: **360.00**
• **CGC:** 3 graded, best 8.0
68 ❑ ca. 1952 Cover: 0.10 **NM** value: **360.00**
• **CGC:** 9 graded, best 9.0
69 ❑ Win 1952 Cover: 0.10 **NM** value: **360.00**
• **CGC:** 5 graded, best 8.5
70 ❑ ca. 1953 Cover: 0.10 **NM** value: **360.00**
• **CGC:** 3 graded, best 8.5
71 ❑ ca. 1953 Cover: 0.10 **NM** value: **275.00**
• **CGC:** 2 graded, best 9.0
72 ❑ ca. 1953 Cover: 0.10 **NM** value: **275.00**
• **CGC:** 2 graded, best 8.5
📖 The Last Expedition; We Shall Rise Again!; No Sign of Life; The Thing in the Iceberg; Perils of Planetoid X **A:** A. Albert; Bill Discount; Bitt Benuhs; Jack; Johnny Bell; Vic
73 ❑ Win 1953 Cover: 0.10 **NM** value: **275.00**
• **CGC:** 3 graded, best 7.0
final issue.

PLANET COMICS (A-LIST) — A-List

1 ❑ Spr 1997 Cover: 2.95 **NM** value: **Cover or less**
2 ❑ Fal 1997 Cover: 2.95 **NM** value: **Cover or less**
📖 Flint Baker; Auro Lord of Jupiter; The Red Comet; Captain Nelson Cole

PLANET COMICS (BLACKTHORNE) — Blackthorne

1 ❑ Apr 1988 Cover: 2.00 **NM** value: **Cover or less**
Circ: CapCity orders: **4,950**
📖 Hunt Bowman in The Lost World; Flamingo; Secret Circle **A:** Ken Hooper; Rico Rival; Adrian Moro **C:** Dan Spiegle **W:** Bruce Jones
2 ❑ Jun 1988 Cover: 2.00 **NM** value: **Cover or less**
Circ: CapCity orders: **3,550**
📖 Hunt Bowman of the Lost World; Flamingo; Secret Circle **A:** Ken Hooper; Rico Rival; Adrian Moro **C:** William Stout **W:** Bruce Jones
3 ❑ Aug 1988 Cover: 2.00 **NM** value: **Cover or less**
Circ: CapCity orders: **2,000**
C: William Stout

PLANET OF GEEKS — Starhead

All issues are adults only.

1 ❑ b&w Cover: 2.75 **NM** value: **Cover or less**

Other grades: Multiply prices above by **1.5 for Mint • 2/3 for Very Fine • 1/3 for Fine • 1/5 for Very Good • 1/8 for Good**

PLANET OF TERROR (BASIL WOLVERTON'S...) — Dark Horse

1 ❑ Jul 1987 Cover: 1.75 **NM value: 2.00**
Planet of Terror; End of the World; Devil Birds **A:** Basil Wolverton **W:** Basil Wolverton

PLANET OF THE APES (1ST SERIES) — Marvel

Marvel's black-and-white magazine line expanded in 1974 with the licensing of the blockbuster Planet of the Apes franchise.

The series began by adapting the first film, which had featured a group of astronauts, led by Charlton Heston, reviving from a centuries-long sleep to find that they had crash-landed on a desert planet.

Based on the Pierre Boule novel, the original film spawned a series of spin-offs, including one in which the apes came to our Earth. The comics magazine expanded on the events of those films with original stories of its own. — Brent

1 ❑ Aug 1974, b&w Cover: 1.00 **NM value: 10.00**
Special "split-cover". • magazine. Beneath • adapts first movie plus new story **A:** Kent Burles **W:** Charles Marshall

1-2 ❑ Cover: 2.50 **NM value: 5.00**

2 ❑ Oct 1974, b&w Cover: 1.00 **NM value: 5.00**
• magazine. • adapts first movie plus new story

3 ❑ Dec 1974, b&w Cover: 1.00 **NM value: 5.00**
• magazine. • adapts first movie plus new stories

4 ❑ Jan 1975, b&w Cover: 1.00 **NM value: 5.00**
• magazine. • adapts first movie plus new stories

5 ❑ Feb 1975, b&w Cover: 1.00 **NM value: 5.00**
• magazine. • adapts first movie plus new stories

6 ❑ Mar 1975, b&w Cover: 1.00 **NM value: 5.00**
• magazine. • concludes first movie adaptations plus new stories

7 ❑ Apr 1975, b&w Cover: 1.00 **NM value: 4.00**
• magazine. Beneath the Planet of the Apes

8 ❑ May 1975, b&w Cover: 1.00 **NM value: 4.00**
• magazine. Beneath the Planet of the Apes

9 ❑ Jun 1975 Cover: 1.00 **NM value: 4.00**
Kingdom of the Apes; Beneath the Planet of the Apes, Part 3

10 ❑ Jul 1975 Cover: 1.00 **NM value: 4.00**
Kingdom of the Apes; Beneath the Planet of the Apes, Part 4

11 ❑ Aug 1975 Cover: 1.00 **NM value: 4.00**
Kingdom of the Apes; Beneath the Planet of the Apes, Part 5

12 ❑ Sep 1975 Cover: 1.00 **NM value: 4.00**
Escape from the Planet of the Apes, Part 1

13 ❑ Aug 1975 Cover: 1.00 **NM value: 4.00**
Escape from the Planet of the Apes, Part 2

14 ❑ Nov 1975 Cover: 0.75 **NM value: 4.00**
Escape from the Planet of the Apes, Part 3

15 ❑ Dec 1975 Cover: 0.75 **NM value: 4.00**
Escape from the Planet of the Apes, Part 4

16 ❑ Jan 1976 Cover: 0.75 **NM value: 4.00**
Escape from the Planet of the Apes, Part 5 ★ Death of Zira. ★ Death of Cornelius.

17 ❑ Feb 1976 Cover: 0.75 **NM value: 4.00**
Conquest of the Planet of the Apes, Part 1

18 ❑ Mar 1976 Cover: 0.75 **NM value: 4.00**
Conquest of the Planet of the Apes, Part 2

19 ❑ Apr 1976, b&w Cover: 0.75 **NM value: 4.00**
• magazine.

20 ❑ May 1976, b&w Cover: 0.75 **NM value: 4.00**
• magazine.

21 ❑ Jun 1976, b&w Cover: 0.75 **NM value: 4.00**
• magazine.

22 ❑ Jul 1976, b&w Cover: 0.75 **NM value: 4.00**
• magazine.

23 ❑ Aug 1976, b&w Cover: 0.75 **NM value: 4.00**
• magazine. Battle for the Planet of the Apes

24 ❑ Sep 1976, b&w Cover: 0.75 **NM value: 4.00**
• magazine. Battle for the Planet of the Apes

25 ❑ Oct 1976, b&w Cover: 0.75 **NM value: 4.00**
• magazine. Battle for the Planet of the Apes

26 ❑ Nov 1976, b&w Cover: 0.75 **NM value: 4.00**
• magazine. Battle for the Planet of the Apes

27 ❑ Dec 1976, b&w Cover: 0.75 **NM value: 4.00**
• magazine. Battle for the Planet of the Apes

28 ❑ Jan 1977, b&w Cover: 0.75 **NM value: 4.00**
• magazine. Battle for the Planet of the Apes

29 ❑ Feb 1977, b&w Cover: 0.75 **NM value: 4.00**
• magazine. Battle for the Planet of the Apes

Anl 1❑ Cover: 3.50 **NM value: 4.00**

PLANET OF THE APES (2ND SERIES) — Adventure

1 ❑ Apr 1990 Cover: 2.50 **NM value: 4.00**
extra cover in pink, yellow, or green. Beneath **A:** Kent Burles **W:** Charles Marshall

1/LE❑ Apr 1990 Cover: 5.00 **NM value: Cover or less**
Beneath • limited **A:** Kent Burles **W:** Charles Marshall

1-2 ❑ Cover: 2.50 **NM value: Cover or less**

2 ❑ Jun 1990 Cover: 3.50 **NM value: Cover or less**
Escape! **A:** Kent Burles **W:** Charles Marshall

3 ❑ Jul 1990 Cover: 3.50 **NM value: Cover or less**
Conquest **A:** Kent Burles **W:** Charles Marshall

4 ❑ Aug 1990 Cover: 2.50 **NM value: 3.00**
A: Kent Burles **W:** Charles Marshall

5 ❑ Sep 1990 Cover: 2.50 **NM value: 3.00**
Loss **A:** Kent Burles **W:** Charles Marshall

6 ❑ Oct 1990 Cover: 2.50 **NM value: 3.00**
Welcome to Ape City **A:** Kent Burles **W:** Charles Marshall

7 ❑ Nov 1990 Cover: 2.50 **NM value: 3.00**
A: Kent Burles **W:** Charles Marshall

8 ❑ Dec 1990 Cover: 2.50 **NM value: 3.00**
• Christmas **A:** Kent Burles **W:** Charles Marshall

9 ❑ Jan 1991 Cover: 2.50 **NM value: 3.00**
Changes **A:** Kent Burles **W:** Charles Marshall

10 ❑ Mar 1991 Cover: 2.50 **NM value: 3.00**
Return to the Forbidden City **A:** Kent Burles **W:** Charles Marshall

11 ❑ Apr 1991 Cover: 2.50 **NM value: Cover or less**
Warriors **A:** Kent Burles **W:** Charles Marshall

12 ❑ May 1991 Cover: 2.50 **NM value: Cover or less**
Bells • Wedding of Alexander and Coure **A:** M.C. Wyman **W:** Charles Marshall

13 ❑ Jun 1991 Cover: 2.50 **NM value: Cover or less**
A: M.C. Wyman **W:** Charles Marshall

14 ❑ Jul 1991 Cover: 2.50 **NM value: Cover or less**
Countdown Zero, Part 1 **A:** M.C. Wyman **W:** Charles Marshall

15 ❑ Aug 1991 Cover: 2.50 **NM value: Cover or less**
Countdown Zero, Part 2 **A:** M.C. Wyman **W:** Charles Marshall

16 ❑ Sep 1991 Cover: 2.50 **NM value: Cover or less**
Countdown Zero, Part 3 **A:** M.C. Wyman **W:** Charles Marshall

17 ❑ Oct 1991 Cover: 2.50 **NM value: Cover or less**
Countdown Zero, Part 4 **A:** M.C. Wyman **W:** Charles Marshall

18 ❑ Nov 1991 Cover: 2.50 **NM value: Cover or less**
Gorillas in the Mist **A:** M.C. Wyman **W:** Charles Marshall

19 ❑ Dec 1991 Cover: 2.50 **NM value: Cover or less**
Quitting Time **A:** M.C. Wyman **W:** Charles Marshall

20 ❑ Jan 1992 Cover: 2.50 **NM value: Cover or less**
Cowboys and Simians **A:** M.C. Wyman **W:** Charles Marshall

21 ❑ Feb 1992 Cover: 2.50 **NM value: Cover or less**
The Terror Beneath **A:** M.C. Wyman **W:** Charles Marshall

22 ❑ Apr 1992 Cover: 2.50 **NM value: Cover or less**
The Land of No Escape • sequel to Conquest of the Planet of the Apes **A:** M.C. Wyman **W:** Charles Marshall

23 ❑ May 1992 Cover: 2.50 **NM value: Cover or less**
Final Conquest **A:** M.C. Wyman **W:** Charles Marshall

24 ❑ Jul 1992 Cover: 2.50 **NM value: Cover or less**
Last Battle **A:** M.C. Wyman **W:** Charles Marshall

Anl 1❑ b&w Cover: 3.50 **NM value: Cover or less**
A Day on the Planet of the Apes **A:** James Tucker; Greg Cravens **W:** Charles Marshall

PLANET OF THE APES: BLOOD OF THE APES — Adventure

1 ❑ Nov 1991, b&w Cover: 2.50 **NM value: Cover or less**
A: Darren Goodheart **W:** Roland Mann

2 ❑ Dec 1991, b&w Cover: 2.50 **NM value: Cover or less**
A: Darren Goodheart **W:** Roland Mann

3 ❑ Jan 1992, b&w Cover: 2.50 **NM value: Cover or less**
A: Darren Goodheart **W:** Roland Mann

4 ❑ Feb 1992, b&w Cover: 2.50 **NM value: Cover or less**
A: Darren Goodheart **W:** Roland Mann

PLANET OF THE APES: FORBIDDEN ZONE — Adventure

1 ❑ Cover: 2.50 **NM value: Cover or less**

2 ❑ Cover: 2.50 **NM value: Cover or less**

3 ❑ Cover: 2.50 **NM value: Cover or less**

4 ❑ Cover: 2.50 **NM value: Cover or less**

PLANET OF THE APES MOVIE ADAPTATION — Adventure

Bk 1❑ Cover: 9.95 **NM value: Cover or less**
• reprints Marvel movie adaptation

PLANET OF THE APES: SINS OF THE FATHER — Adventure

1 ❑ Mar 1992, b&w Cover: 2.50 **NM value: Cover or less**
A: Mitch Byrd **W:** Mike Valerio

PLANET OF THE APES: URCHAK'S FOLLY — Adventure

1 ❑ Jan 1991, b&w Cover: 2.50 **NM value: Cover or less**
The Valley **A:** Gary Chaloner **W:** Gary Chaloner

2 ❑ Feb 1991, b&w Cover: 2.50 **NM value: Cover or less**
The Bridge **A:** Gary Chaloner **W:** Gary Chaloner

3 ❑ Mar 1991, b&w Cover: 2.50 **NM value: Cover or less**
The Savages **A:** Gary Chaloner **W:** Gary Chaloner

4 ❑ Apr 1991, b&w Cover: 2.50 **NM value: Cover or less**
The War **A:** Gary Chaloner **W:** Gary Chaloner

PLANET OF VAMPIRES — Atlas-Seaboard

1 ❑ Apr 1975 Cover: 0.25 **NM value: 2.00**
• **CGC:** 1 graded, best 8.5
The Long Road Home! **A:** Pat Broderick **C:** Neal Adams **W:** Larry Hama

2 ❑ Jul 1975 Cover: 0.25 **NM value: 1.50**
C: Neal Adams

3 ❑ Jul 1975 Cover: 0.25 **NM value: 1.50**
• **CGC:** 1 graded, best 9.4

PLANET PATROL — Edge / Seaboard

1 ❑ Cover: 2.95 **NM value: Cover or less**
Signal in Space; The Girl from Astroid Six; Enter the Finch **A:** Bruce David **W:** Bruce David

PLANET RACERS — Zeromayo Studios

Bk 1❑ Dec 1997, b&w Cover: 14.95 **NM value: Cover or less**

Bk 2❑ Aug 1998, b&w Cover: 7.95 **NM value: Cover or less**

PLANET TERRY — Marvel / Star

Planet Terry is a humorous adventure series for kids. It stars Terry, a boy born aboard a space "life ship," floating alone across the reaches of space. The ship fed him, comforted him, and taught him all the important things he'd need to know in order to make it through life ("Never wear a tie without a shirt. Never attempt to juggle five bowling balls." And so on...). Still, Terry was all alone, left with nothing but a bracelet with his name on it and a picture frame inscribed "To Terry, Love Mom and Dad."

Terry spent his young life searching for his lost parents. One day, he discovered an old miner named Diggs who told him of a starship captain who had lost his baby in a freak accident that left the baby floating alone in the starship's life ship. Finally, Terry had the clue he had sought for so long. Joined by his friends Robota the robot and Omnus the crocodile-like creature, he was on his way to finding his long-lost parents.

1 ❑ Apr 1984 Cover: 0.65 **NM value: 1.00**
The Search; A Clue; Some Answers; Malt Shop Menace; **A:** Warren Kremer **W:** Lennie Herman; Lenny Herman ★ Origin of Planet Terry. ★ 1st Appearance of Planet Terry.

2 ❑ May 1984 Cover: 0.65 **NM value: 1.00**
Circ: CapCity orders: **4,300**

3 ❑ Jun 1984 Cover: 0.65 **NM value: 1.00**
Circ: CapCity orders: **3,800**

4 ❑ Jul 1984 Cover: 0.65 **NM value: 1.00**
Circ: CapCity orders: **3,200**

5 ❑ Aug 1984 Cover: 0.65 **NM value: 1.00**
Circ: CapCity orders: **2,900**

6 ❑ Sep 1984 Cover: 0.65 **NM value: 1.00**
Circ: CapCity orders: **2,800**

7 ❑ Oct 1984 Cover: 0.65 **NM value: 1.00**
Circ: CapCity orders: **2,100**

8 ❑ Nov 1984 Cover: 0.65 **NM value: 1.00**
Circ: CapCity orders: **2,100**

9 ❑ Dec 1984 Cover: 0.65 **NM value: 1.00**
Circ: CapCity orders: **1,700**

10 ❑ Jan 1985 Cover: 0.65 **NM value: 1.00**
Circ: CapCity orders: **1,500**

11 ❑ Feb 1985 Cover: 0.65 **NM value: 1.00**
Circ: CapCity orders: **1,600**

12 ❑ Mar 1985 Cover: 0.65 **NM value: 1.00**
Circ: CapCity orders: **1,500**
final issue.

PLANET-X — Eternity

1 ❑ b&w Cover: 2.50 **NM value: Cover or less**

PLANET X REPRINT COMIC — Planet X

1 ❑ **NM value: 2.00**
no cover price. • reprints adaptation of The Man from Planet X

PLASM — Defiant

0 ❑ **NM value: 1.00**
• bound in Diamond Previews

PLASMA BABY — Caliber

1 ❑ b&w Cover: 2.50 **NM value: Cover or less**

2 ❑ b&w Cover: 2.50 **NM value: Cover or less**
★ Appearance of George Bush.

3 ❑ b&w Cover: 2.50 **NM value: Cover or less**

PLASMER — Marvel

Doctor Oonagh Mullarky had long been a pivotal, if unrecognized character in the Marvel UK universe. She was a scientist in the employ of MyS-TECH who was responsible for many of their plots, as well as for the creation of Killpower (her son, with super-powers he got as a result of her experiments). Mullarky got her turn in the spotlight when she managed to split herself into separate good and bad beings. The bad one got a wilder haircut, and the good one became Plasmer, a super-hero.

This lighthearted mini-series is most notable for the distinctly unamusing battle it helped launch between Marvel and Defiant. To wit: Defiant had planned to name their first series "Plasm," but Marvel sued them because Plasmer was in production and they felt the names were too close. Defiant relented and renamed their title "Warriors of Plasm," but this was not enough to pacify Marvel, who continued with the suit and eventually lost.

1 ❑ Nov 1993 Cover: 2.50 **NM value: Cover or less**
Circ: CapCity orders: **19,400**
Within You...Without You! • four trading cards **A:** Pascual Ferry **W:** Glenn Dakin ★ Origin of Plasmer. ★ 1st Appearance of Plasmer.

2 ❑ Dec 1993 Cover: 1.95 **NM value: Cover or less**
Circ: CapCity orders: **8,900**
London Calling

3 ❑ Jan 1994 Cover: 1.95 **NM value: Cover or less**
Circ: CapCity orders: **6,900**
Masters Of War! **A:** Pascual Ferry **W:** Glenn Dakin

CGC-graded: Multiply prices above by **33 for 9.9 M • 16 for 9.8 NM/M • 7 for 9.6 NM+ • 5 for 9.4 NM • 2.5 for 9.2 NM- • 1.5 for 9.0 VF/NM**

4 ❑ Feb 1994 Cover: 1.95 **NM** value: **Cover or less**
Circ: CapCity orders: **5,000**

PLASTIC FORKS — Marvel / Epic

1 ❑ ca. 1990 Cover: 4.95 **NM** value: **Cover or less**
Circ: CapCity orders: **8,000**
📖 Trauma Humane **A:** Ted McKeever **W:** Ted McKeever

2 ❑ ca. 1990 Cover: 4.95 **NM** value: **Cover or less**
Circ: CapCity orders: **6,900**
📖 Gravity's Angel **A:** Ted McKeever **W:** Ted McKeever

3 ❑ ca. 1990 Cover: 4.95 **NM** value: **Cover or less**
Circ: CapCity orders: **6,000**
📖 Ritual Bride **A:** Ted McKeever **W:** Ted McKeever

4 ❑ ca. 1990 Cover: 4.95 **NM** value: **Cover or less**
Circ: CapCity orders: **5,250**
A: Ted McKeever **W:** Ted McKeever

5 ❑ ca. 1990 Cover: 4.95 **NM** value: **Cover or less**
Circ: CapCity orders: **4,750**
A: Ted McKeever **W:** Ted McKeever

PLASTIC LITTLE — CPM

1 ❑ Aug 1997 Cover: 2.95 **NM** value: **Cover or less**
Circ: Diamd. preorders: **5,959**
📖 Prologue: Gentaro Koshigaya; Chapter 1, Tita Mu Koshigaya • Laura Jackson and Yoko Kobayashi translation **A:** Satoshi Urushihara **W:** Satoshi Urushihara ★ Origin of Captain Tita Mu Koshigaya. ★ 1st Appearance of Tita Mu Koshigay, Mei Lin Jones, Joshua Balboa, Tita Mu Koshigaya, Roger Rogers.

2 ❑ Sep 1997 Cover: 2.95 **NM** value: **Cover or less**
Circ: Diamd. preorders: **5,449**
📖 Chapter 2, Joshua L. Balboa • Laura Jackson and Yoko Kobayashi translation **A:** Satoshi Urushihara **W:** Satoshi Urushihara ★ 2nd Appearance of Mikail Diagleff. ★ 2nd Appearance of Joshua Balbo. ★ 2nd Appearance of Mei Lin Jones. ★ 2nd Appearance of Joshua Balboa. ★ 2nd Appearance of Tita Mu Koshigaya. ★ 2nd Appearance of Roger Rogers.

3 ❑ Oct 1997 Cover: 2.95 **NM** value: **Cover or less**
Circ: Diamd. preorders: **5,103**
📖 Chapter 3, Mei Lin Jones • Laura Jackson and Yoko Kobayashi translation **A:** Satoshi Urushihara **W:** Satoshi Urushihara

4 ❑ Nov 1997 Cover: 2.95 **NM** value: **Cover or less**
Circ: Diamd. preorders: **5,562**
📖 Chapter 4, Roger Rogers • Laura Jackson and Yoko Kobayashi translation **A:** Satoshi Urushihara **W:** Satoshi Urushihara

5 ❑ Dec 1997 Cover: 2.95 **NM** value: **Cover or less**
Circ: Diamd. preorders: **5,337**
📖 Chapter 5, Mikail Diagleff • Laura Jackson and Yoko Kobayashi translation **A:** Satoshi Urushihara **W:** Satoshi Urushihara

Bk 1 ❑ Jul 1998 Cover: 15.95 **NM** value: **Cover or less**
📖 Captain's Log • Captain's Log; collects Plastic Little #1-5; Laura Jackson and Yoko Kobayashi translation **A:** Satoshi Urushihara **W:** Satoshi Urushihara

PLASTIC MAN ARCHIVES — DC

1 ❑ Cover: 49.95 **NM** value: **Cover or less**
• Collects Police Comics #1-20 **A:** Jack Cole **W:** Jack Cole ★ Origin of Plastic Man.

2 ❑ Cover: 49.95 **NM** value: **Cover or less**
• Collects Plastic Man #1, Police Comics #21-30 **A:** Jack Cole **W:** Jack Cole

PLASTIC MAN (COMIC MAGAZINES) — Comic Magazines

Imaginative covers and stories by creator Jack Cole make this solo series stand out from the pack.

Plastic Man was originally gangster Eel O'Brian who, while on a robbery at a chemical plant, was doused with acid, and crawled away into the countryside where a group of monks took him in. Discovering that he had the ability to bend and stretch his body into any shape, O'Brian resolved to reform and fight on the side of the law for a change. With his sidekick, Woozy Winks, who was impervious to harm (making it a bit of a stretch to imagine him in mortal danger), Plas took on some of the strangest criminals of all.

The Cole covers of this series show many of the weird forms that Plastic Man could take on. In the 1960s, DC attempted to revive the character, but without Cole at the helm, the revival was short-lived. — Brent

1 ❑ Sum 1943 Cover: 0.10 **NM** value: **3200.00**
• **CGC:** 4 graded, best 9.2
📖 The Game of Death; Now You see It, Now You Don't; Willie McGoon, Dope; go West, Young Plastic Man, Go West • Published by Vital Publications **A:** Jack Cole **W:** Jack Cole

2 ❑ Feb 1944 Cover: 0.10 **NM** value: **1300.00**
• **CGC:** 3 graded, best 8.5

3 ❑ Spr 1946 Cover: 0.10 **NM** value: **800.00**
• **CGC:** 2 graded, best 8.5
• 1st issue published by Quality Comics

4 ❑ Sum 1946 Cover: 0.10 **NM** value: **700.00**
• **CGC:** 1 graded, best 9.0

5 ❑ Fal 1946 Cover: 0.10 **NM** value: **565.00**

6 ❑ Win 1946 Cover: 0.10 **NM** value: **450.00**
• **CGC:** 2 graded, best 8.0

7 ❑ Spr 1947 Cover: 0.10 **NM** value: **450.00**
• **CGC:** 2 graded, best 8.0

8 ❑ Sum 1947 Cover: 0.10 **NM** value: **450.00**
• **CGC:** 2 graded, best 7.0

9 ❑ Fal 1947 Cover: 0.10 **NM** value: **450.00**
• **CGC:** 2 graded, best 8.5

10 ❑ Win 1947 Cover: 0.10 **NM** value: **450.00**
• **CGC:** 3 graded, best 9.0

11 ❑ Spr 1948 Cover: 0.10 **NM** value: **375.00**
• **CGC:** 1 graded, best 3.0

12 ❑ Jul 1948 Cover: 0.10 **NM** value: **375.00**

13 ❑ Sep 1948 Cover: 0.10 **NM** value: **375.00**
• **CGC:** 1 graded, best 6.0

14 ❑ Nov 1948 Cover: 0.10 **NM** value: **375.00**
• **CGC:** 1 graded, best 6.0

15 ❑ Jan 1949 Cover: 0.10 **NM** value: **375.00**
• **CGC:** 1 graded, best 6.5

16 ❑ Mar 1949 Cover: 0.10 **NM** value: **375.00**
• **CGC:** 1 graded, best 6.0

17 ❑ May 1949 Cover: 0.10 **NM** value: **375.00**
• **CGC:** 2 graded, best 9.0

18 ❑ Jul 1949 Cover: 0.10 **NM** value: **375.00**
• **CGC:** 1 graded, best 7.0

19 ❑ Sep 1949 Cover: 0.10 **NM** value: **375.00**

20 ❑ Nov 1949 Cover: 0.10 **NM** value: **375.00**

21 ❑ Jan 1950 Cover: 0.10 **NM** value: **310.00**

22 ❑ Mar 1950 Cover: 0.10 **NM** value: **310.00**

23 ❑ May 1950 Cover: 0.10 **NM** value: **310.00**
• **CGC:** 1 graded, best 8.0

24 ❑ Jul 1950 Cover: 0.10 **NM** value: **310.00**

25 ❑ Sep 1950 Cover: 0.10 **NM** value: **310.00**

26 ❑ Nov 1950 Cover: 0.10 **NM** value: **310.00**
• **CGC:** 1 graded, best 8.5

27 ❑ Jan 1951 Cover: 0.10 **NM** value: **310.00**
• **CGC:** 1 graded, best 9.0

28 ❑ Mar 1951 Cover: 0.10 **NM** value: **310.00**

29 ❑ May 1951 Cover: 0.10 **NM** value: **310.00**
• **CGC:** 1 graded, best 8.0

30 ❑ Jul 1951 Cover: 0.10 **NM** value: **310.00**

31 ❑ Sep 1951 Cover: 0.10 **NM** value: **240.00**

32 ❑ Nov 1951 Cover: 0.10 **NM** value: **240.00**

33 ❑ Jan 1952 Cover: 0.10 **NM** value: **240.00**
• **CGC:** 1 graded, best 8.0

34 ❑ Mar 1952 Cover: 0.10 **NM** value: **240.00**

35 ❑ May 1952 Cover: 0.10 **NM** value: **240.00**

36 ❑ Jul 1952 Cover: 0.10 **NM** value: **240.00**
• **CGC:** 1 graded, best 6.5

37 ❑ Sep 1952 Cover: 0.10 **NM** value: **240.00**

38 ❑ Nov 1952 Cover: 0.10 **NM** value: **240.00**

39 ❑ Jan 1953 Cover: 0.10 **NM** value: **240.00**

40 ❑ Mar 1953 Cover: 0.10 **NM** value: **240.00**
• **CGC:** 1 graded, best 5.0

41 ❑ May 1953 Cover: 0.10 **NM** value: **200.00**
• **CGC:** 1 graded, best 6.0

42 ❑ Jul 1953 Cover: 0.10 **NM** value: **200.00**
• **CGC:** 1 graded, best 4.5

43 ❑ Nov 1953 Cover: 0.10 **NM** value: **200.00**

44 ❑ Jan 1954 Cover: 0.10 **NM** value: **200.00**

45 ❑ Mar 1954 Cover: 0.10 **NM** value: **200.00**

46 ❑ May 1954 Cover: 0.10 **NM** value: **200.00**

47 ❑ Jul 1954 Cover: 0.10 **NM** value: **200.00**

48 ❑ Sep 1954 Cover: 0.10 **NM** value: **200.00**

49 ❑ Nov 1954 Cover: 0.10 **NM** value: **200.00**
• **CGC:** 1 graded, best 4.0

50 ❑ Dec 1954 Cover: 0.10 **NM** value: **200.00**

51 ❑ Jan 1955 Cover: 0.10 **NM** value: **165.00**

52 ❑ Feb 1955 Cover: 0.10 **NM** value: **165.00**

53 ❑ Apr 1955 Cover: 0.10 **NM** value: **165.00**

54 ❑ Jun 1955 Cover: 0.10 **NM** value: **165.00**
• **CGC:** 1 graded, best 9.2

55 ❑ Oct 1955 Cover: 0.10 **NM** value: **165.00**
• **CGC:** 1 graded, best 7.5

56 ❑ Nov 1955 Cover: 0.10 **NM** value: **165.00**
• **CGC:** 1 graded, best 7.0

57 ❑ Dec 1955 Cover: 0.10 **NM** value: **165.00**
• **CGC:** 1 graded, best 9.0

58 ❑ Jan 1956 Cover: 0.10 **NM** value: **165.00**
• **CGC:** 2 graded, best 9.2
📖 The Overlord of Crime; Wildfire (text); Woozy

59 ❑ Feb 1956 Cover: 0.10 **NM** value: **165.00**

60 ❑ Mar 1956 Cover: 0.10 **NM** value: **165.00**

61 ❑ Apr 1956 Cover: 0.10 **NM** value: **165.00**

62 ❑ May 1956 Cover: 0.10 **NM** value: **165.00**

63 ❑ Jul 1956 Cover: 0.10 **NM** value: **165.00**

64 ❑ Nov 1956 Cover: 0.10 **NM** value: **165.00**
• **CGC:** 1 graded, best 9.0

PLASTIC MAN (DC) — DC

1 ❑ Dec 1966 Cover: 0.12 **NM** value: **45.00**
• **CGC:** 19 graded, best 9.8
📖 The Dirty Devices of Dr. Dome **A:** Gil Kane **W:** Arnold Drake ★ Origin of Plastic Man.

2 ❑ Feb 1967 Cover: 0.12 **NM** value: **25.00**
• **CGC:** 4 graded, best 9.2

3 ❑ Apr 1967 Cover: 0.12 **NM** value: **20.00**
• **CGC:** 3 graded, best 9.6
📖 The Biggest Wheel In Town

4 ❑ Jun 1967 Cover: 0.12 **NM** value: **20.00**
• **CGC:** 3 graded, best 9.6

5 ❑ Aug 1967 Cover: 0.12 **NM** value: **20.00**
• **CGC:** 2 graded, best 9.4

6 ❑ Oct 1967 Cover: 0.12 **NM** value: **14.00**
• **CGC:** 1 graded, best 9.4

7 ❑ Dec 1967 Cover: 0.12 **NM** value: **14.00**
• **CGC:** 1 graded, best 9.0
📖 Plastic Man's Fantastic Old Man! ★ Appearance of Plas' father (Plastic Man 1), Woozy Winks.

8 ❑ Feb 1968 Cover: 0.12 **NM** value: **14.00**

9 ❑ Apr 1968 Cover: 0.12 **NM** value: **14.00**
• **CGC:** 1 graded, best 9.0

10 ❑ Jun 1968 Cover: 0.12 **NM** value: **14.00**
• **CGC:** 1 graded, best 9.6
• series goes on hiatus until 1976

11 ❑ Mar 1976 Cover: 0.25 **NM** value: **4.00**
• **CGC:** 3 graded, best 9.6
• Series begins again: 1976

12 ❑ May 1976 Cover: 0.30 **NM** value: **4.00**
• **CGC:** 1 graded, best 9.6

13 ❑ Jul 1976 Cover: 0.30 **NM** value: **4.00**
• **CGC:** 2 graded, best 9.4

14 ❑ Sep 1976 Cover: 0.30 **NM** value: **4.00**
• **CGC:** 2 graded, best 9.6

15 ❑ Nov 1976 Cover: 0.30 **NM** value: **4.00**
• **CGC:** 1 graded, best 9.6

16 ❑ Mar 1977 Cover: 0.30 **NM** value: **4.00**
• **CGC:** 1 graded, best 9.8

17 ❑ May 1977 Cover: 0.30 **NM** value: **4.00**
• **CGC:** 1 graded, best 9.4

18 ❑ Jul 1977 Cover: 0.35 **NM** value: **4.00**
• **CGC:** 1 graded, best 9.6

19 ❑ Sep 1977 Cover: 0.35 **NM** value: **4.00**
• **CGC:** 1 graded, best 9.4

20 ❑ Nov 1977 Cover: 0.35 **NM** value: **4.00**
final issue.

PLASTIC MAN (MINI-SERIES) — DC

1 ❑ Nov 1988 Cover: 1.00 **NM** value: **1.25**
Circ: CapCity orders: **17,800**
A: Hilary Barta **W:** Phil Foglio ★ Origin of Plastic Man.

2 ❑ Dec 1988 Cover: 1.00 **NM** value: **1.25**
Circ: CapCity orders: **13,350**
A: Hilary Barta **W:** Phil Foglio

3 ❑ Jan 1989 Cover: 1.00 **NM** value: **1.25**
Circ: CapCity orders: **13,050**
A: Hilary Barta **W:** Phil Foglio

4 ❑ Feb 1989 Cover: 1.00 **NM** value: **1.25**
Circ: CapCity orders: **11,600**
A: Hilary Barta **W:** Phil Foglio

PLASTIC MAN SPECIAL — DC

1 ❑ Aug 1999 Cover: 3.95 **NM** value: **Cover or less**
Circ: Diamd. preorders: **22,345**
📖 Plastic Fantastic; Plastic Facts; The Secreted Origin of Woozy Winks; The Age of Crisis on Infinite Clones Saga **A:** Aaron Lopresti; Rick Burchett; Richard Pace; Dev Madan **W:** Ty Templeton ★ Origin of Woozy Winks.

PLASTRON CAFÉ — Mirage

1 ❑ Dec 1992 Cover: 2.25 **NM** value: **Cover or less**
Circ: CapCity orders: **4,550**
📖 North by Downeast; Old Times; SirenSong; The Origin of Guzzi LeMans **A:** Jim Lawson; Kevin Eastman; Peter Laird; Michael Dooney **W:** Jim Lawson; Rick Veitch; Peter Laird; Michael Dooney

2 ❑ Feb 1993 Cover: 2.25 **NM** value: **Cover or less**
Circ: CapCity orders: **2,900**

3 ❑ May 1993 Cover: 2.25 **NM** value: **Cover or less**
Circ: CapCity orders: **2,700**
📖 Alien Fire; North by Downeast; Spaced; Tales of Altered Earth **A:** Eric Vincent; Kevin Eastman; Rick Veitch; A.C. Farley; Anthony Smith; Mary Kelleher; Tom Stazer **W:** Eric Vincent; Kevin Eastman; Rick Veitch; A.C. Farley; Anthony Smith; Mary Kelleher; Tom Stazer

4 ❑ Jul 1993 Cover: 2.25 **NM** value: **Cover or less**
📖 Spaced; North by Downeast Part IV; Alien Fire; Bioneers **A:** Eric Vincent; Kevin Eastman; Rick Veitch; A.C. Farley; Anthony Smith; Mary Kelleher; Tom Stazer **W:** Eric Vincent; Kevin Eastman; Rick Veitch; A.C. Farley; Anthony Smith; Mary Kelleher; Tom Stazer

PLATINUM.44 — Comax

All issues are adults only.

1 ❑ b&w Cover: 2.95 **NM** value: **Cover or less**

PLATINUM GRIT — Dead Numbat

1 ❑ Cover: 3.50 **NM** value: **Cover or less**

2 ❑ Cover: 3.50 **NM** value: **Cover or less**

3 ❑ Cover: 3.50 **NM** value: **Cover or less**

4 ❑ Cover: 3.50 **NM** value: **Cover or less**

5 ❑ Cover: 3.50 **NM** value: **Cover or less**

6 ❑ Cover: 3.50 **NM** value: **Cover or less**
📖 Throw That Old Thing Away Grandma; Spanky the Monkey: Spittin' Toothpaste; Hallelujia and All that Jazz; In the Ghetto **A:** Fil Barlow; Tim Danko; Tonia Walden; Trudy Cooper **W:** Fil Barlow; Tim Danko; Tonia Walden; Trudy Cooper

PLAYBEAR — Fantagraphics / Eros

1 ❑ Cover: 2.95 **NM** value: **Cover or less**
A: Fellx **W:** Fellx

2 ❑ Cover: 2.95 **NM** value: **Cover or less**
A: Fellx **W:** Fellx

3 ❑ Aug 1995 Cover: 2.95 **NM** value: **Cover or less**
📖 Lil & Jill **A:** Fellx **W:** Fellx

PLAYFUL LITTLE AUDREY — Harvey

Little Audrey is a mischievous child in the time-honored tradition of Little Lulu. When Paramount's Famous Studio realized that it could keep more of the profits if it stopped licensing Lulu and replaced her with a similar character, right down to the short red dress.

Smarter than her playmates, including Melvin, Audrey often engages in practical jokes on kids and adults alike. The themes of the stories are simplistic and easily identifiable by the younger readers that the series was aimed at. After a successful series of theatrical shorts, the character was also featured on TV. — Brent

Other grades: Multiply prices above by **1.5 for Mint • 2/3 for Very Fine • 1/3 for Fine • 1/5 for Very Good • 1/8 for Good**

1 ❑ Jun 1957 Cover: 0.10 **NM** value: **90.00**
• **CGC:** 1 graded, best 6.5
2 ❑ Aug 1957 Cover: 0.10 **NM** value: **50.00**
3 ❑ Oct 1957 Cover: 0.10 **NM** value: **35.00**
4 ❑ Dec 1957 Cover: 0.10 **NM** value: **35.00**
5 ❑ Feb 1958 Cover: 0.10 **NM** value: **35.00**
6 ❑ Apr 1958 Cover: 0.10 **NM** value: **24.00**
7 ❑ ca. 1958 Cover: 0.10 **NM** value: **24.00**
8 ❑ ca. 1958 Cover: 0.10 **NM** value: **24.00**
9 ❑ ca. 1958 Cover: 0.10 **NM** value: **24.00**
10 ❑ Jan 1959 Cover: 0.10 **NM** value: **24.00**
11 ❑ Mar 1959 Cover: 0.10 **NM** value: **15.00**
12 ❑ May 1959 Cover: 0.10 **NM** value: **15.00**
13 ❑ Jul 1959 Cover: 0.10 **NM** value: **15.00**
14 ❑ Sep 1959 Cover: 0.10 **NM** value: **15.00**
15 ❑ Nov 1959 Cover: 0.10 **NM** value: **15.00**
16 ❑ Jan 1960 Cover: 0.10 **NM** value: **15.00**
17 ❑ Mar 1960 Cover: 0.10 **NM** value: **15.00**
18 ❑ May 1960 Cover: 0.10 **NM** value: **15.00**
19 ❑ Jul 1960 Cover: 0.10 **NM** value: **15.00**
20 ❑ Sep 1960 Cover: 0.10 **NM** value: **15.00**
21 ❑ Oct 1960 Cover: 0.10 **NM** value: **15.00**
22 ❑ Nov 1960 Cover: 0.10 **NM** value: **12.00**
23 ❑ Dec 1960 Cover: 0.10 **NM** value: **12.00**
24 ❑ Jan 1961 Cover: 0.10 **NM** value: **12.00**
25 ❑ Feb 1961 Cover: 0.10 **NM** value: **12.00**
26 ❑ Mar 1961 Cover: 0.10 **NM** value: **12.00**
27 ❑ Apr 1961 Cover: 0.10 **NM** value: **12.00**
28 ❑ May 1961 Cover: 0.10 **NM** value: **12.00**
29 ❑ Jun 1961 Cover: 0.10 **NM** value: **12.00**
30 ❑ Jul 1961 Cover: 0.10 **NM** value: **12.00**
31 ❑ Aug 1961 Cover: 0.10 **NM** value: **12.00**
32 ❑ Sep 1961 Cover: 0.10 **NM** value: **12.00**
33 ❑ Oct 1961 Cover: 0.10 **NM** value: **12.00**
34 ❑ Nov 1961 Cover: 0.10 **NM** value: **12.00**
35 ❑ Dec 1961 Cover: 0.10 **NM** value: **12.00**
36 ❑ Jan 1962 Cover: 0.12 **NM** value: **12.00**
37 ❑ Feb 1962 Cover: 0.12 **NM** value: **12.00**
38 ❑ Mar 1962 Cover: 0.12 **NM** value: **12.00**
39 ❑ Apr 1962 Cover: 0.12 **NM** value: **12.00**
40 ❑ Jun 1962 Cover: 0.12 **NM** value: **12.00**
41 ❑ Aug 1962 Cover: 0.12 **NM** value: **10.00**
42 ❑ Oct 1962 Cover: 0.12 **NM** value: **10.00**
43 ❑ Dec 1962 Cover: 0.12 **NM** value: **10.00**
44 ❑ Feb 1963 Cover: 0.12 **NM** value: **10.00**
45 ❑ Apr 1963 Cover: 0.12 **NM** value: **10.00**
46 ❑ Jun 1963 Cover: 0.12 **NM** value: **10.00**
47 ❑ Aug 1963 Cover: 0.12 **NM** value: **10.00**
48 ❑ Oct 1963 Cover: 0.12 **NM** value: **10.00**
49 ❑ Dec 1963 Cover: 0.12 **NM** value: **10.00**
50 ❑ Feb 1964 Cover: 0.12 **NM** value: **10.00**
51 ❑ Apr 1964 Cover: 0.12 **NM** value: **8.00**
52 ❑ Jun 1964 Cover: 0.12 **NM** value: **8.00**
53 ❑ Aug 1964 Cover: 0.12 **NM** value: **8.00**
54 ❑ Oct 1964 Cover: 0.12 **NM** value: **8.00**
55 ❑ Dec 1964 Cover: 0.12 **NM** value: **8.00**
56 ❑ Feb 1965 Cover: 0.12 **NM** value: **8.00**
57 ❑ Apr 1965 Cover: 0.12 **NM** value: **8.00**
58 ❑ Jun 1965 Cover: 0.12 **NM** value: **8.00**
59 ❑ Aug 1965 Cover: 0.12 **NM** value: **8.00**
60 ❑ Oct 1965 Cover: 0.12 **NM** value: **8.00**
61 ❑ Dec 1965 Cover: 0.12 **NM** value: **5.00**
62 ❑ Feb 1966 Cover: 0.12 **NM** value: **5.00**
63 ❑ Apr 1966 Cover: 0.12 **NM** value: **5.00**
64 ❑ Jun 1966 Cover: 0.12 **NM** value: **5.00**
65 ❑ Aug 1966 Cover: 0.12 **NM** value: **5.00**
66 ❑ Oct 1966 Cover: 0.12 **NM** value: **5.00**
67 ❑ Dec 1966 Cover: 0.12 **NM** value: **5.00**
68 ❑ Feb 1967 Cover: 0.12 **NM** value: **5.00**
69 ❑ Apr 1967 Cover: 0.12 **NM** value: **5.00**
70 ❑ Jun 1967 Cover: 0.12 **NM** value: **5.00**
71 ❑ Aug 1967 Cover: 0.12 **NM** value: **5.00**
72 ❑ Oct 1967 Cover: 0.12 **NM** value: **5.00**
73 ❑ Dec 1967 Cover: 0.12 **NM** value: **5.00**
74 ❑ Feb 1968 Cover: 0.12 **NM** value: **5.00**
75 ❑ Apr 1968 Cover: 0.12 **NM** value: **5.00**
76 ❑ Jun 1968 Cover: 0.12 **NM** value: **5.00**
77 ❑ Aug 1968 Cover: 0.12 **NM** value: **5.00**
78 ❑ Oct 1968 Cover: 0.12 **NM** value: **5.00**
79 ❑ Dec 1968 Cover: 0.12 **NM** value: **5.00**
80 ❑ Feb 1969 Cover: 0.12 **NM** value: **5.00**
81 ❑ Apr 1969 Cover: 0.12 **NM** value: **3.00**
82 ❑ May 1969 Cover: 0.12 **NM** value: **3.00**
83 ❑ Jun 1969 Cover: 0.12 **NM** value: **3.00**
84 ❑ Sep 1969 Cover: 0.15 **NM** value: **3.00**
85 ❑ Nov 1969 Cover: 0.15 **NM** value: **3.00**
86 ❑ Jan 1970 Cover: 0.15 **NM** value: **3.00**
87 ❑ Mar 1970 Cover: 0.15 **NM** value: **3.00**
88 ❑ May 1970 Cover: 0.15 **NM** value: **3.00**
89 ❑ Jul 1970 Cover: 0.15 **NM** value: **3.00**
90 ❑ Sep 1970 Cover: 0.15 **NM** value: **3.00**
91 ❑ Oct 1970 Cover: 0.15 **NM** value: **3.00**
92 ❑ Nov 1970 Cover: 0.15 **NM** value: **3.00**
93 ❑ Jan 1971 Cover: 0.15 **NM** value: **3.00**
94 ❑ Mar 1971 Cover: 0.15 **NM** value: **3.00**
95 ❑ May 1971 Cover: 0.15 **NM** value: **3.00**
96 ❑ Jul 1971 Cover: 0.15 **NM** value: **3.00**
97 ❑ Sep 1971 Cover: 0.15 **NM** value: **3.00**
98 ❑ Oct 1971 Cover: 0.15 **NM** value: **3.00**
99 ❑ Cover: 0.15 **NM** value: **3.00**
📖 It's Pop Who Pays; Super Duper; Smartly Dressed; The Soda Contest (text); The Two Kittens (text); Going All Out!
100 ❑ Mar 1972 Cover: 0.25 **NM** value: **4.00**
• Giant-size.
101 ❑ May 1972 Cover: 0.25 **NM** value: **4.00**
• Giant-size.
102 ❑ Jul 1972 Cover: 0.25 **NM** value: **4.00**
• Giant-size.
103 ❑ Sep 1972 Cover: 0.25 **NM** value: **4.00**
• Giant-size.
104 ❑ Nov 1972 Cover: 0.20 **NM** value: **3.00**
105 ❑ Jan 1973 Cover: 0.20 **NM** value: **3.00**
Circ: Statement: **119,058**
106 ❑ Mar 1973 Cover: 0.20 **NM** value: **3.00**
Circ: Statement: **119,058**
107 ❑ May 1973 Cover: 0.20 **NM** value: **3.00**
Circ: Statement: **119,058**
108 ❑ Jul 1973 Cover: 0.20 **NM** value: **3.00**
Circ: Statement: **119,058**
109 ❑ Sep 1973 Cover: 0.20 **NM** value: **3.00**
Circ: Statement: **119,058**
110 ❑ Nov 1973 Cover: 0.20 **NM** value: **3.00**
Circ: Statement: **119,058**
111 ❑ Aug 1974 Cover: 0.25 **NM** value: **3.00**
Circ: Statement: **138,800**
• Has 1973 Statement; avg total paid circ 119,058
112 ❑ Oct 1974 Cover: 0.25 **NM** value: **3.00**
Circ: Statement: **138,800**
113 ❑ Dec 1974 Cover: 0.25 **NM** value: **3.00**
Circ: Statement: **138,800**
114 ❑ Feb 1975 Cover: 0.25 **NM** value: **3.00**
115 ❑ Apr 1975 Cover: 0.25 **NM** value: **3.00**
116 ❑ Jun 1975 Cover: 0.25 **NM** value: **3.00**
• Has 1974 Statement; avg total paid circ 138,800
117 ❑ Aug 1975 Cover: 0.25 **NM** value: **3.00**
118 ❑ Oct 1975 Cover: 0.25 **NM** value: **3.00**
119 ❑ Dec 1975 Cover: 0.25 **NM** value: **3.00**
120 ❑ Feb 1976 Cover: 0.25 **NM** value: **3.00**
121 ❑ Apr 1976 Cover: 0.25 **NM** value: **3.00**

PLAYGROUND — Caliber

1 ❑ b&w Cover: 2.50 **NM** value: **Cover or less**

PLAYGROUNDS — Fantagraphics

1 ❑ b&w Cover: 2.00 **NM** value: **Cover or less**

PLEASURE & PASSION (ALAZAR'S...) — Brainstorm

1 ❑ Oct 1997 Cover: 2.95 **NM** value: **Cover or less**
A: Alazar **W:** Alazar

PLEASURE BOUND — Eros

1 ❑ Feb 1996 Cover: 2.95 **NM** value: **Cover or less**
A: Pretorius **W:** Pretorius

PLOP! — DC

Offbeat humor and spoofs were a major genre of the Seventies, with comics companies trying to match the success of E.C.'s Mad magazine. Marvel dominated the pack numerically, saturating the field with a score of titles such as Arrgh! and Spoof. DC published few by comparison, but what they did publish was more often funny.

Plop! was a good example of this. Its humor was decidedly droll, but by drawing on the talents of Mad's own Sergio Aragones, it managed to remain consistently humorous. Aragones stayed with this magazine for almost the entire 24-issue run, sharing the spotlight with other creators such as Bernie Wrightson, and later going on to become an Eighties phenomenon with his Conan the Barbarian satire, "Groo the Wanderer."

1 ❑ Oct 1973 Cover: 0.20 **NM** value: **8.00**
• **CGC:** 14 graded, best 9.8
A: Sergio Aragonés; Bernie Wrightson **C:** Basil Wolverton
2 ❑ Dec 1973 Cover: 0.20 **NM** value: **6.00**
• **CGC:** 1 graded, best 9.6
A: Sergio Aragonés
3 ❑ Feb 1974, four-color Cover: 0.20 **NM** value: **6.00**
• **CGC:** 3 graded, best 9.8
A: Sergio Aragonés
4 ❑ Apr 1974 Cover: 0.20 **NM** value: **6.00**
• **CGC:** 2 graded, best 9.4
📖 Welcome to the Monster Convention; Now and Then; A Perfectly Crazy Crime; The Last Laugh **A:** Sergio Aragonés; Basil Wolverton; Frank Robbins **W:** Steve Skeates
5 ❑ Jun 1974 Cover: 0.20 **NM** value: **6.00**
A: Sergio Aragonés
6 ❑ Aug 1974 Cover: 0.20 **NM** value: **5.00**
A: Sergio Aragonés
7 ❑ Oct 1974 Cover: 0.20 **NM** value: **5.00**
A: Sergio Aragonés
8 ❑ Dec 1974 Cover: 0.20 **NM** value: **5.00**
A: Sergio Aragonés
9 ❑ Feb 1975 Cover: 0.25 **NM** value: **5.00**
Circ: Statement: **157,000**
📖 Temple Of Ikka-Ka-Ka; Super Plops; Historical Plops; Prescription Plops; The Killer Kind; People Plops, Plop Drop; Prison Plop; A Nose To Remember; Gourmet Plops; Monster Plops **A:** Sergio Aragonés; Basil Wolverton; Frank Robbins **W:** Steve Skeates
10 ❑ Mar 1975 Cover: 0.25 **NM** value: **5.00**
Circ: Statement: **157,000**
📖 Androklutz and the Lion; A Change of Diet!; The Secret Origin of Grooble Man **A:** Sergio Aragonés; Basil Wolverton; Dave Manak; Ric Estrada **W:** Joe Orlando; Steve Skeates; Coram Nobis; E. Nelson Bridwell; John Jacobson
11 ❑ Apr 1975 Cover: 0.25 **NM** value: **4.00**
Circ: Statement: **157,000**
A: Sergio Aragonés
12 ❑ May 1975 Cover: 0.25 **NM** value: **4.00**
Circ: Statement: **157,000**
A: Sergio Aragonés
13 ❑ Jun 1975 Cover: 0.25 **NM** value: **4.00**
Circ: Statement: **157,000**
A: Sergio Aragonés
14 ❑ Jul 1975 Cover: 0.25 **NM** value: **4.00**
Circ: Statement: **157,000**
A: Sergio Aragonés
15 ❑ Aug 1975 Cover: 0.25 **NM** value: **4.00**
Circ: Statement: **157,000**
A: Sergio Aragonés
16 ❑ Sep 1975 Cover: 0.25 **NM** value: **4.00**
Circ: Statement: **157,000**
A: Sergio Aragonés
17 ❑ Oct 1975 Cover: 0.25 **NM** value: **4.00**
Circ: Statement: **157,000**
A: Sergio Aragonés
18 ❑ Dec 1975 Cover: 0.25 **NM** value: **4.00**
Circ: Statement: **157,000**
A: Sergio Aragonés
19 ❑ Feb 1976 Cover: 0.25 **NM** value: **4.00**
A: Sergio Aragonés
20 ❑ Apr 1976 Cover: 0.25 **NM** value: **4.00**
A: Sergio Aragonés
21 ❑ Jun 1976 Cover: 0.50 **NM** value: **6.00**
• Giant-size. **A:** Sergio Aragonés
22 ❑ Aug 1976 Cover: 0.50 **NM** value: **6.00**
• Giant-size. **A:** Sergio Aragonés
23 ❑ Oct 1976 Cover: 0.50 **NM** value: **4.00**
• **CGC:** 1 graded, best 9.4
• Giant-size. • Wally Wood's Lord of the Rings parody
24 ❑ Dec 1976 Cover: 0.50 **NM** value: **6.00**
• Giant-size. **A:** Sergio Aragonés

PMS BOOK, THE — Ivory Tower

1 ❑ Cover: 3.50 **NM** value: **Cover or less**
📖 ms **A:** Florence Schlotts **W:** Florence Schlotts
1-2 ❑ Cover: 3.50 **NM** value: **Cover or less**
1-3 ❑ Cover: 3.50 **NM** value: **Cover or less**
1-4 ❑ Cover: 3.50 **NM** value: **Cover or less**
1-5 ❑ Cover: 3.50 **NM** value: **Cover or less**
1-6 ❑ Cover: 3.50 **NM** value: **Cover or less**
1-7 ❑ Cover: 3.50 **NM** value: **Cover or less**

POCAHONTAS (DISNEY'S...) — Marvel

1 ❑ Jul 1995 Cover: 4.95 **NM** value: **Cover or less**
Circ: CapCity orders: **7,175**
• prestige format one-shot

POCKET COMICS — Harvey

1 ❑ Aug 1941 Cover: 0.10 **NM** value: **450.00**
2 ❑ Sep 1941 Cover: 0.10 **NM** value: **300.00**
3 ❑ Nov 1941 Cover: 0.10 **NM** value: **225.00**
4 ❑ Jan 1942 Cover: 0.10 **NM** value: **225.00**

POE — Cheese

Jason Asala's saga of Edgar Allan Poe follows the famous writer of dark tales of terror on a personal quest. While still recovering from the death of his young wife, Poe is visited by an angel who tells him he may yet be reunited with his wife, but only if he defeats 12 earthly demons. Numerous friends and acquaintances join him on this mission as he is haunted by dreams of his lost Lenore.

Normally published as a black-and-white book, the series' one special gives a look at Poe's world through muted earth tones that are a good match for the style of the storytelling. It also offers the opportunity to see other artists such as Rick Geary and Joseph Linsner lend their work to this unique character's story.

1 ❑ Sep 1996 Cover: 2.00 **NM** value: **2.50**
2 ❑ Oct 1996 Cover: 2.00 **NM** value: **2.50**
3 ❑ Nov 1996 Cover: 2.00 **NM** value: **2.50**
4 ❑ Dec 1996 Cover: 2.00 **NM** value: **2.50**
📖 The Lords of Brass, Part 1
5 ❑ Feb 1997 Cover: 2.00 **NM** value: **2.50**
📖 The Lords of Brass, Part 2
6 ❑ Apr 1997 Cover: 2.00 **NM** value: **2.50**
📖 A Rough Night at Mad Meg's Tavern
7 ❑ Cover: 2.50 **NM** value: **Cover or less**
8 ❑ Cover: 2.50 **NM** value: **Cover or less**
9 ❑ Cover: 2.50 **NM** value: **Cover or less**
10 ❑ Cover: 2.50 **NM** value: **Cover or less**
11 ❑ Cover: 2.50 **NM** value: **Cover or less**
Bk 1 ❑ Cover: 14.95 **NM** value: **Cover or less**

POEMS FOR THE DEAD — Boneyard

Bk 1 ❑ Mar 1995, b&w Cover: 10.95 **NM** value: **Cover or less**

POEM TOONS (VAUGHN BODÉ'S...) — Tundra

Bk 1 ❑ Cover: 7.95 **NM** value: **Cover or less**
A: Vaughn Bodé

POETS PROSPER: RHYME & REVELRY — Tome

1 ❑ Cover: 3.50 **NM** value: **Cover or less**

POE (VOL. 2) — Sirius

1 ❑ Oct 1997 Cover: 2.50 **NM** value: **Cover or less**
Circ: Diamd. preorders: **3,815**
2 ❑ Nov 1997 Cover: 2.50 **NM** value: **Cover or less**
3 ❑ Dec 1997 Cover: 2.50 **NM** value: **Cover or less**
4 ❑ Jan 1998 Cover: 2.50 **NM** value: **Cover or less**
5 ❑ Feb 1998 Cover: 2.50 **NM** value: **Cover or less**
6 ❑ Mar 1998 Cover: 2.50 **NM** value: **Cover or less**
7 ❑ May 1998 Cover: 2.50 **NM** value: **Cover or less**
8 ❑ Jun 1998 Cover: 2.50 **NM** value: **Cover or less**
9 ❑ Jul 1998 Cover: 2.50 **NM** value: **Cover or less**
10 ❑ Aug 1998 Cover: 2.50 **NM** value: **Cover or less**
11 ❑ Sep 1998 Cover: 2.50 **NM** value: **Cover or less**

CGC-graded: Multiply prices above by **33 for 9.9 M • 16 for 9.8 NM/M • 7 for 9.6 NM+ • 5 for 9.4 NM • 2.5 for 9.2 NM- • 1.5 for 9.0 VF/NM**

12 ❑ Oct 1998 Cover: 2.50 **NM** value: **Cover or less**
13 ❑ Nov 1998 Cover: 2.50 **NM** value: **Cover or less**
14 ❑ Jan 1999 Cover: 2.50 **NM** value: **Cover or less**
Circ: Diamd. preorders: **1,215**
15 ❑ Feb 1999 Cover: 2.50 **NM** value: **Cover or less**
Circ: Diamd. preorders: **1,175**
16 ❑ Mar 1999 Cover: 2.50 **NM** value: **Cover or less**
17 ❑ Apr 1999 Cover: 2.50 **NM** value: **Cover or less**
Circ: Diamd. preorders: **1,210**
18 ❑ Aug 1999 Cover: 2.50 **NM** value: **Cover or less**
19 ❑ Cover: 2.50 **NM** value: **Cover or less**
📖 The Balloon Hoax, A Tale of Science, Part 1
20 ❑ Cover: 2.50 **NM** value: **Cover or less**
📖 The Balloon Hoax, A Tale of Science, Part 2; Mad Meg in Fire and Ice, Part 1
21 ❑ Jan 2000 Cover: 2.95 **NM** value: **Cover or less**
📖 The Balloon Hoax, A Tale of Science, Part 3; Mad Meg in Fire and Ice, Part 2 **A:** Rick Geary; Jason Asala **W:** Jason Asala
22 ❑ Mar 2000 Cover: 2.95 **NM** value: **Cover or less**
📖 The Balloon Hoax, A Tale of Science, Part 4; Mad Meg in Fire and Ice, Part 3 **A:** Rick Geary; Jason Asala
23 ❑ May 2000 Cover: 2.95 **NM** value: **Cover or less**
📖 The Balloon Hoax, A Tale of Science, Part 5; Mad Meg in Fire and Ice, Part 4 **A:** Rick Geary; Jason Asala
24 ❑ Jul 2000 Cover: 2.95 **NM** value: **Cover or less**
📖 The Balloon Hoax, A Tale of Science, Part 6; Mad Meg in Fire and Ice, Part 5 **A:** Rick Geary; Jason Asala
SE 1❑ Dec 1998 Cover: 2.95 **NM** value: **Cover or less**
• Color Special **A:** Rick Geary; Joseph Michael Linsner; David Yurkovich; Jason Asala **W:** Rick Geary; Joseph Michael Linsner; David Yurkovich; Jason Asala

POGO PARADE — Dell

1 ❑ Sep 1953 Cover: 0.10 **NM** value: **350.00**
• **CGC:** 3 graded, best 9.6

POGO POSSUM — Dell

Walt Kelly's character of the swamp-dwelling opossum, introduced in Animal Comics #1, had his own series, as well, begun after Animal Comics had folded and after Kelly's characters had been running in the nation's newspapers as a daily comic strip. Kelly had softened the look of his characters by the time of this comic-book series.

While many of the plot lines in these issues derived from the sorts of antics that appeared in Kelly's strips, none of the stories here were actually strip reprints. — Maggie

1 ❑ Oct 1949 Cover: 0.10 **NM** value: **260.00**
• **CGC:** 1 graded, best 9.2
A: Walt Kelly **W:** Walt Kelly
2 ❑ Apr 1950 Cover: 0.10 **NM** value: **175.00**
A: Walt Kelly **W:** Walt Kelly
3 ❑ Aug 1950 Cover: 0.10 **NM** value: **130.00**
A: Walt Kelly **W:** Walt Kelly
4 ❑ Feb 1951 Cover: 0.10 **NM** value: **130.00**
A: Walt Kelly **W:** Walt Kelly
5 ❑ May 1951 Cover: 0.10 **NM** value: **130.00**
A: Walt Kelly **W:** Walt Kelly
6 ❑ Jul 1951 Cover: 0.10 **NM** value: **110.00**
A: Walt Kelly **W:** Walt Kelly
7 ❑ Oct 1951 Cover: 0.10 **NM** value: **110.00**
A: Walt Kelly **W:** Walt Kelly
8 ❑ Jan 1952 Cover: 0.10 **NM** value: **110.00**
• **CGC:** 2 graded, best 8.5
• Copyright switches from Western to Walt Kelly **A:** Walt Kelly **W:** Walt Kelly
9 ❑ Apr 1952 Cover: 0.15 **NM** value: **125.00**
A: Walt Kelly **W:** Walt Kelly
10 ❑ Jul 1952 Cover: 0.15 **NM** value: **125.00**
A: Walt Kelly **W:** Walt Kelly
11 ❑ Jan 1953 Cover: 0.15 **NM** value: **125.00**
• **CGC:** 1 graded, best 6.5
A: Walt Kelly **W:** Walt Kelly
12 ❑ Apr 1953 Cover: 0.15 **NM** value: **125.00**
• **CGC:** 1 graded, best 7.0
A: Walt Kelly **W:** Walt Kelly
13 ❑ Jul 1953 Cover: 0.15 **NM** value: **125.00**
A: Walt Kelly **W:** Walt Kelly
14 ❑ Oct 1953 Cover: 0.10 **NM** value: **100.00**
A: Walt Kelly **W:** Walt Kelly
15 ❑ Jan 1954 Cover: 0.10 **NM** value: **100.00**
• **CGC:** 1 graded, best 7.0
A: Walt Kelly **W:** Walt Kelly
16 ❑ Apr 1954 Cover: 0.10 **NM** value: **100.00**
• **CGC:** 3 graded, best 9.0
• Contains reprint from 10/47 Animal Comics **A:** Walt Kelly **W:** Walt Kelly

POINT-BLANK — Eclipse

1 ❑ b&w Cover: 2.95 **NM** value: **Cover or less**
2 ❑ b&w Cover: 2.95 **NM** value: **Cover or less**

The CGC numbers printed in individual listings above represent the **number of copies examined** and given a **Universal** grade by CGC and the **best such copy** graded at press time. For current populations, watch for special ***Comics Buyer's Guide*** issues or check **www.cgccomics.com.**

POISON ELVES (MULEHIDE) — Mulehide

Poison Elves is a wonderful series by Drew Hayes about an elf who's bad right down to the bone.

The "hero," is an assassin named Lusiphur who, although he's an elf, bears no relationship to the fanciful creatures most elf comics portray. He drinks, he swears like a sailor, and his greatest joy in life is to lay waste to an enemy with excruciating slowness.

One might have thought this would make for an unsympathetic, unpopular comic. Instead, it's made Poison Elves (formerly I, Lusiphur) into a modern cult classic.

8 ❑ Cover: 2.50 **NM** value: **25.00**
• magazine-sized. • Series continued from I, Lusiphur #7 **A:** Drew Hayes **W:** Drew Hayes
9 ❑ Cover: 2.50 **NM** value: **22.00**
• magazine-sized. **A:** Drew Hayes **W:** Drew Hayes
10 ❑ Cover: 2.50 **NM** value: **22.00**
• magazine-sized. **A:** Drew Hayes **W:** Drew Hayes
11 ❑ Cover: 2.50 **NM** value: **20.00**
A: Drew Hayes **W:** Drew Hayes
12 ❑ Oct 1993 Cover: 2.50 **NM** value: **20.00**
A: Drew Hayes **W:** Drew Hayes
13 ❑ Dec 1993 Cover: 2.50 **NM** value: **20.00**
📖 Desert of the Third Sin, Part 1 **A:** Drew Hayes **W:** Drew Hayes
14 ❑ Feb 1994 Cover: 2.50 **NM** value: **20.00**
📖 Desert of the Third Sin, Part 2 **A:** Drew Hayes **W:** Drew Hayes
15 ❑ Apr 1994 Cover: 2.50 **NM** value: **20.00**
• Scarcer **A:** Drew Hayes **W:** Drew Hayes
15-2❑ Cover: 2.50 **NM** value: **4.00**
A: Drew Hayes **W:** Drew Hayes
16 ❑ Jun 1994 Cover: 2.50 **NM** value: **16.00**
A: Drew Hayes **W:** Drew Hayes
17 ❑ Cover: 2.50 **NM** value: **16.00**
A: Drew Hayes **W:** Drew Hayes
17-2❑ Cover: 2.50 **NM** value: **5.00**
A: Drew Hayes **W:** Drew Hayes
18 ❑ Cover: 2.50 **NM** value: **10.00**
A: Drew Hayes **W:** Drew Hayes
19 ❑ Cover: 2.50 **NM** value: **10.00**
A: Drew Hayes **W:** Drew Hayes
20 ❑ Cover: 2.50 **NM** value: **10.00**
final issue. **A:** Drew Hayes **W:** Drew Hayes
Bk 1❑ b&w Cover: 14.95 **NM** value: **Cover or less**
• Requiem for an Elf; collects #1-6
Bk 2❑ b&w Cover: 14.95 **NM** value: **Cover or less**
• Traumatic Dogs; collects #7-12
Bk 3❑ Apr 1997 Cover: 14.95 **NM** value: **Cover or less**
• Desert of the Third Sin; collects #13-16 from Mulehide
Bk 4❑ Jan 1998 Cover: 4.95 **NM** value: **Cover or less**
• Patrons; collects #19 and 20 from Mulehide
Dlx 1❑ ca. 2001 Cover: 34.95 **NM** value: **Cover or less**
• Poison Elves: The Mulehide Years

POISON ELVES (SIRIUS) — Sirius

1 ❑ May 1995 Cover: 2.50 **NM** value: **8.00**
Circ: CapCity orders: **6,870**
A: Drew Hayes **W:** Drew Hayes
1-2 ❑ Cover: 2.50 **NM** value: **Cover or less**
2 ❑ Jun 1995 Cover: 2.50 **NM** value: **5.00**
Circ: CapCity orders: **5,225**
A: Drew Hayes **W:** Drew Hayes
3 ❑ Jul 1995 Cover: 2.50 **NM** value: **5.00**
Circ: CapCity orders: **4,875**
A: Drew Hayes **W:** Drew Hayes
4 ❑ Aug 1995 Cover: 2.50 **NM** value: **4.00**
Circ: CapCity orders: **5,275**
A: Drew Hayes **W:** Drew Hayes
5 ❑ 1995 Cover: 2.50 **NM** value: **4.00**
Circ: CapCity orders: **5,570**
A: Drew Hayes **W:** Drew Hayes
6 ❑ 1995 Cover: 2.50 **NM** value: **4.00**
A: Drew Hayes **W:** Drew Hayes
7 ❑ 1995 Cover: 2.50 **NM** value: **3.00**
A: Drew Hayes **W:** Drew Hayes
8 ❑ 1996 Cover: 2.50 **NM** value: **3.00**
A: Drew Hayes **W:** Drew Hayes
9 ❑ 1996 Cover: 2.50 **NM** value: **3.00**
A: Drew Hayes **W:** Drew Hayes
10 ❑ 1996 Cover: 2.50 **NM** value: **3.00**
A: Drew Hayes **W:** Drew Hayes
11 ❑ 1996 Cover: 2.50 **NM** value: **Cover or less**
A: Drew Hayes **W:** Drew Hayes
12 ❑ 1996 Cover: 2.50 **NM** value: **Cover or less**
A: Drew Hayes **W:** Drew Hayes
13 ❑ 1996 Cover: 2.50 **NM** value: **Cover or less**
📖 Desert Of The Third Sin, Part 1 **A:** Drew Hayes **W:** Drew Hayes
14 ❑ 1996 Cover: 2.50 **NM** value: **Cover or less**
📖 Desert Of The Third Sin, Part 2 **A:** Drew Hayes **W:** Drew Hayes
15 ❑ 1996 Cover: 2.50 **NM** value: **Cover or less**
A: Drew Hayes **W:** Drew Hayes
16 ❑ Sep 1996 Cover: 2.50 **NM** value: **Cover or less**
Circ: Diamd. preorders: **15,699**
A: Drew Hayes **W:** Drew Hayes
17 ❑ Oct 1996 Cover: 2.50 **NM** value: **Cover or less**
Circ: Diamd. preorders: **15,711**
A: Drew Hayes **W:** Drew Hayes
18 ❑ Nov 1996 Cover: 2.50 **NM** value: **Cover or less**
Circ: Diamd. preorders: **14,911**
A: Drew Hayes **W:** Drew Hayes
19 ❑ Dec 1996 Cover: 2.50 **NM** value: **Cover or less**
Circ: Diamd. preorders: **14,502**
A: Drew Hayes **W:** Drew Hayes
20 ❑ Jan 1997 Cover: 2.50 **NM** value: **Cover or less**
Circ: Diamd. preorders: **13,737**
A: Drew Hayes **W:** Drew Hayes
21 ❑ Feb 1997 Cover: 2.50 **NM** value: **Cover or less**
Circ: Diamd. preorders: **13,074**
A: Drew Hayes **W:** Drew Hayes
22 ❑ Mar 1997 Cover: 2.50 **NM** value: **Cover or less**
Circ: Diamd. preorders: **12,791**
23 ❑ Apr 1997 Cover: 2.50 **NM** value: **Cover or less**
Circ: Diamd. preorders: **13,175**
24 ❑ May 1997 Cover: 2.50 **NM** value: **Cover or less**
Circ: Diamd. preorders: **12,946**
25 ❑ Jul 1997 Cover: 2.95 **NM** value: **Cover or less**
Circ: Diamd. preorders: **12,868**
26 ❑ Aug 1997 Cover: 2.50 **NM** value: **Cover or less**
Circ: Diamd. preorders: **12,158**
27 ❑ Sep 1997 Cover: 2.50 **NM** value: **Cover or less**
Circ: Diamd. preorders: **11,839**
28 ❑ Oct 1997 Cover: 2.50 **NM** value: **Cover or less**
Circ: Diamd. preorders: **11,524**
29 ❑ Nov 1997 Cover: 2.50 **NM** value: **Cover or less**
Circ: Diamd. preorders: **10,865**
30 ❑ Dec 1997 Cover: 2.50 **NM** value: **Cover or less**
Circ: Diamd. preorders: **10,774**
31 ❑ Jan 1998 Cover: 2.50 **NM** value: **Cover or less**
Circ: Diamd. preorders: **10,561**
32 ❑ Feb 1998 Cover: 2.50 **NM** value: **Cover or less**
Circ: Diamd. preorders: **9,859**
33 ❑ Mar 1998 Cover: 2.50 **NM** value: **Cover or less**
Circ: Diamd. preorders: **9,745**
34 ❑ Apr 1998 Cover: 2.50 **NM** value: **Cover or less**
Circ: Diamd. preorders: **10,246**
35 ❑ May 1998 Cover: 2.50 **NM** value: **Cover or less**
Circ: Diamd. preorders: **9,611**
36 ❑ Jun 1998 Cover: 2.50 **NM** value: **Cover or less**
Circ: Diamd. preorders: **9,673**
37 ❑ Jul 1998 Cover: 2.50 **NM** value: **Cover or less**
Circ: Diamd. preorders: **9,107**
38 ❑ Aug 1998 Cover: 2.50 **NM** value: **Cover or less**
Circ: Diamd. preorders: **8,737**
39 ❑ Sep 1998 Cover: 2.50 **NM** value: **Cover or less**
Circ: Diamd. preorders: **8,722**
40 ❑ Oct 1998 Cover: 2.50 **NM** value: **Cover or less**
Circ: Diamd. preorders: **8,723**
41 ❑ Nov 1998 Cover: 2.50 **NM** value: **Cover or less**
Circ: Diamd. preorders: **8,668**
42 ❑ Dec 1998 Cover: 2.50 **NM** value: **Cover or less**
Circ: Diamd. preorders: **8,476**
43 ❑ Jan 1999 Cover: 2.50 **NM** value: **Cover or less**
Circ: Diamd. preorders: **8,393**
44 ❑ Feb 1999 Cover: 2.50 **NM** value: **Cover or less**
Circ: Diamd. preorders: **8,256**
45 ❑ Mar 1999 Cover: 2.50 **NM** value: **Cover or less**
Circ: Diamd. preorders: **8,104**
46 ❑ Jun 1999 Cover: 2.95 **NM** value: **Cover or less**
Circ: Diamd. preorders: **7,800**
47 ❑ Jul 1999 Cover: 2.50 **NM** value: **Cover or less**
Circ: Diamd. preorders: **7,369**
48 ❑ Aug 1999 Cover: 2.50 **NM** value: **Cover or less**
Circ: Diamd. preorders: **7,753**
49 ❑ Sep 1999 Cover: 2.50 **NM** value: **Cover or less**
Circ: Diamd. preorders: **7,530**
50 ❑ Oct 1999 Cover: 2.50 **NM** value: **Cover or less**
Circ: Diamd. preorders: **7,987**
51 ❑ Nov 1999 Cover: 2.50 **NM** value: **Cover or less**
Circ: Diamd. preorders: **7,414**
52 ❑ Dec 1999 Cover: 2.50 **NM** value: **Cover or less**
Circ: Diamd. preorders: **7,264**
53 ❑ Jan 2000 Cover: 2.95 **NM** value: **Cover or less**
Circ: Diamd. preorders: **7,152**
54 ❑ Feb 2000 Cover: 2.95 **NM** value: **Cover or less**
Circ: Diamd. preorders: **6,861**
55 ❑ Mar 2000 Cover: 2.95 **NM** value: **Cover or less**
Circ: Diamd. preorders: **7,009**
56 ❑ Apr 2000 Cover: 2.95 **NM** value: **Cover or less**
Circ: Diamd. preorders: **6,871**
57 ❑ May 2000 Cover: 2.95 **NM** value: **Cover or less**
Circ: Diamd. preorders: **6,946**
58 ❑ Jun 2000 Cover: 2.95 **NM** value: **Cover or less**
Circ: Diamd. preorders: **7,058**
59 ❑ Jul 2000 Cover: 2.95 **NM** value: **Cover or less**
Circ: Diamd. preorders: **6,927**
60 ❑ Aug 2000 Cover: 2.95 **NM** value: **Cover or less**
Circ: Diamd. preorders: **6,594**
61 ❑ Sep 2000 Cover: 2.95 **NM** value: **Cover or less**
Circ: Diamd. preorders: **6,782**
📖 All the Beautiful People or: Bad Doin's at Knuckledown Lonesome
62 ❑ Nov 2000 Cover: 2.95 **NM** value: **Cover or less**
Circ: Diamd. preorders: **6,530**
📖 The Hunt
63 ❑ Jan 2001 Cover: 2.95 **NM** value: **Cover or less**
Circ: Diamd. preorders: **6,276**
64 ❑ Mar 2001 Cover: 2.95 **NM** value: **Cover or less**
Circ: Diamd. preorders: **6,142**
65 ❑ May 2001 Cover: 2.95 **NM** value: **Cover or less**
Circ: Diamd. preorders: **6,200**
66 ❑ Jul 2001 Cover: 2.95 **NM** value: **Cover or less**
Circ: Diamd. preorders: **6,465**
Bk 5❑ Nov 1998, b&w Cover: 14.95 **NM** value: **Cover or less**
• Trade Paperback. 📖 Sanctuary
Bk 6❑ Cover: 14.95 **NM** value: **Cover or less**
• Guild War
SE 1❑ Dec 1998 Cover: 2.95 **NM** value: **3.00**

Other grades: Multiply prices above by **1.5 for Mint • 2/3 for Very Fine • 1/3 for Fine • 1/5 for Very Good • 1/8 for Good**

Circ: Diamd. preorders: **9,549**
• Color Special

Bk 7 ❑ Cover: 19.95 **NM** value: **Cover or less**
• Salvation

POIZON London Night

0 ❑ Cover: 3.00 **NM** value: **Cover or less**
A: Georges Jeanty **W:** Everette Hartsoe

0/Nude ❑ **NM** value: **3.50**
A: Georges Jeanty **W:** Everette Hartsoe

0.5 ❑ Cover: 3.00 **NM** value: **Cover or less**
Circ: CapCity orders: **6,400**
A: Georges Jeanty **W:** Everette Hartsoe

1 ❑ Feb 1996 Cover: 3.00 **NM** value: **Cover or less**
A: Georges Jeanty **W:** Everette Hartsoe

1/A ❑ Cover: 15.00 **NM** value: **Cover or less**
• Green Death edition. **A:** Georges Jeanty **W:** Everette Hartsoe

1/Nude ❑ Cover: 5.95 **NM** value: **Cover or less**
A: Georges Jeanty **W:** Everette Hartsoe

2 ❑ Apr 1996 Cover: 3.00 **NM** value: **Cover or less**
📖 Lost Child **A:** Georges Jeanty **W:** Everette Hartsoe

3 ❑ Jun 1996 Cover: 3.00 **NM** value: **Cover or less**
A: Georges Jeanty **W:** Everette Hartsoe

POKÉMON ADVENTURES Viz

1 ❑ Sep 1999 Cover: 5.95 **NM** value: **Cover or less**
Circ: Diamd. preorders: **20,604**
📖 Mysterious Mew • Mysterious Mew

2 ❑ Oct 1999 Cover: 5.95 **NM** value: **Cover or less**
Circ: Diamd. preorders: **15,337**
📖 Wanted: Pikachu • Wanted: Pikachu

3 ❑ Nov 1999 Cover: 5.95 **NM** value: **Cover or less**

4 ❑ Dec 1999 Cover: 5.95 **NM** value: **Cover or less**
Circ: Diamd. preorders: **9,740**

5 ❑ Jan 2000 Cover: 5.95 **NM** value: **Cover or less**
Circ: Diamd. preorders: **7,687**
📖 The Gastly Ghosts

POKÉMON PART 2 Viz

1 ❑ Mar 1999 Cover: 3.25 **NM** value: **Cover or less**
Circ: Diamd. preorders: **26,846**
📖 Pikachu Shocks Back **A:** Toshiro Ono **W:** Toshiro Ono

2 ❑ Apr 1999 Cover: 3.25 **NM** value: **Cover or less**
Circ: Diamd. preorders: **28,611**
A: Toshiro Ono **W:** Toshiro Ono

3 ❑ May 1999 Cover: 3.25 **NM** value: **Cover or less**
Circ: Diamd. preorders: **34,407**
A: Toshiro Ono **W:** Toshiro Ono

4 ❑ Jun 1999 Cover: 2.95 **NM** value: **Cover or less**
Circ: Diamd. preorders: **40,233**
A: Toshiro Ono **W:** Toshiro Ono

POKÉMON PART 3 Viz

1 ❑ Jul 1999 Cover: 3.50 **NM** value: **Cover or less**
Circ: Diamd. preorders: **41,302**

2 ❑ Aug 1999 Cover: 3.50 **NM** value: **Cover or less**
Circ: Diamd. preorders: **34,520**

3 ❑ Sep 1999 Cover: 3.50 **NM** value: **Cover or less**
Circ: Diamd. preorders: **30,270**

4 ❑ Oct 1999 Cover: 3.50 **NM** value: **Cover or less**
Circ: Diamd. preorders: **32,419**

POKÉMON: THE ELECTRIC TALE OF PIKACHU Viz

Published by Viz Comics, this origin story of a wildly popular manga series doesn't come across as one big advertisement for the video games, movies, and comics that comprise the Pokemon phenomenon.

Pikachu, a mouse that generates electricity, is discovered happily destroying the wiring of aspiring Pokemon master Ash Ketchum's home. Through a series of encounters with a mean rival and a flock of vicious birds, Ash learns to treat Pikachu with respect, and in turn earns a valuable friend.

Created by Toshihiro Ono, translated by William Flanagan and rewritten by Annette Roman, the series smoothly explains the highly structured Pokemon world, making it an invaluable primer for adults trying to figure out what on earth the kids are going on about. Ono's art has the clean energy of traditional manga.

Despite low initial orders from comics shops caught unaware by 1999's Pokemon-crazy world, #1 of this series went through more than a dozen printings and sold more than 1 million copies in the mass market. There's no discernable difference in value between the printings.

1 ❑ Nov 1998 Cover: 3.25 **NM** value: **Cover or less**
Circ: Diamd. preorders: **9,321**
📖 Pikachu, I See You! **A:** Toshihiro Ono **W:** Toshihiro Ono ★ 1st Appearance of Pikachu.

1-2 ❑ Cover: 3.25 **NM** value: **Cover or less**

1-3 ❑ Mar 1999 Cover: 3.25 **NM** value: **Cover or less**
Circ: Diamd. preorders: **6,872**

2 ❑ Dec 1998 Cover: 3.25 **NM** value: **Cover or less**
Circ: Diamd. preorders: **9,210**
A: Toshihiro Ono **W:** Toshihiro Ono

2-2 ❑ Cover: 3.25 **NM** value: **Cover or less**
Circ: Diamd. preorders: **2,673**

3 ❑ Jan 1999 Cover: 3.25 **NM** value: **Cover or less**
Circ: Diamd. preorders: **14,097**
A: Toshihiro Ono **W:** Toshihiro Ono

4 ❑ Feb 1999 Cover: 3.25 **NM** value: **Cover or less**
Circ: Diamd. preorders: **18,374**
A: Toshihiro Ono **W:** Toshihiro Ono

POLICE ACADEMY Marvel

1 ❑ Oct 1989 Cover: 1.00 **NM** value: **Cover or less**
Circ: CapCity orders: **6,700**

2 ❑ Nov 1989 Cover: 1.00 **NM** value: **Cover or less**
Circ: CapCity orders: **4,650**
📖 The Beast from 2 1/2 Fathoms; The Cookoo Commandant **A:** Howie Post **W:** Angelo Decesare

3 ❑ Dec 1989 Cover: 1.00 **NM** value: **Cover or less**
Circ: CapCity orders: **3,700**

4 ❑ Jan 1990 Cover: 1.00 **NM** value: **Cover or less**
Circ: CapCity orders: **2,800**

5 ❑ Feb 1990 Cover: 1.00 **NM** value: **Cover or less**
Circ: CapCity orders: **3,350**

6 ❑ Mar 1990 Cover: 1.00 **NM** value: **Cover or less**
Circ: CapCity orders: **2,300**

POLICE ACTION Atlas-Seaboard

1 ❑ Feb 1975 Cover: 0.25 **NM** value: **2.00**
A: Mike Sekowsky **W:** Jack Younger

2 ❑ Apr 1975 Cover: 0.25 **NM** value: **1.50**

3 ❑ Jun 1975 Cover: 0.25 **NM** value: **1.50**

POLICE AGAINST CRIME Premiere

1 ❑ Apr 1954 Cover: 0.10 **NM** value: **150.00**
2 ❑ Jun 1954 Cover: 0.10 **NM** value: **75.00**
3 ❑ Aug 1954 Cover: 0.10 **NM** value: **50.00**
4 ❑ Oct 1954 Cover: 0.10 **NM** value: **50.00**
5 ❑ Dec 1954 Cover: 0.10 **NM** value: **50.00**
6 ❑ Feb 1955 Cover: 0.10 **NM** value: **50.00**
7 ❑ Apr 1955 Cover: 0.10 **NM** value: **50.00**
8 ❑ Jun 1955 Cover: 0.10 **NM** value: **50.00**
9 ❑ Aug 1955 Cover: 0.10 **NM** value: **50.00**

POLICE BADGE #479 Atlas

5 ❑ Sep 1955 Cover: 0.10 **NM** value: **75.00**

POLICE COMICS Comic Magazines

Premiering in the fall of 1941, Police Comics featured few police, but lots of crimefighting super-heroes. First and most famous was Plastic Man, who debuted in Police Comics #1. This stretchable super-hero was not only great for visual gag appeal, but would later become the prototype for DC's Elongated Man and Elastic Lad, as well as Marvel's Mister Fantastic (leader of the Fantastic Four). Also appearing in the first issue was future Nazi-fighter Firebrand, the explosive Human Bomb, and the mysterious Phantom Lady (all later members of The Freedom Fighters).

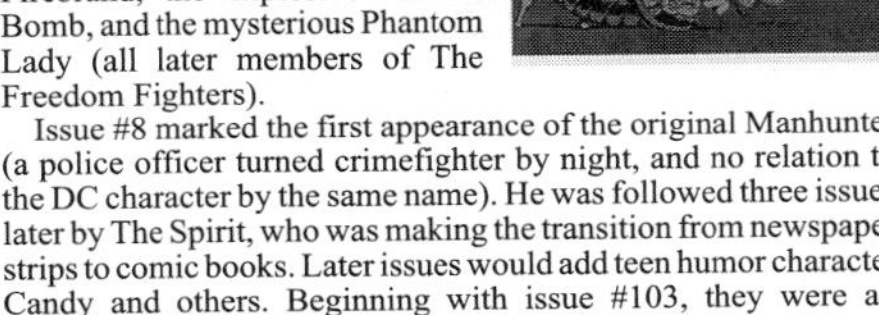

Issue #8 marked the first appearance of the original Manhunter (a police officer turned crimefighter by night, and no relation to the DC character by the same name). He was followed three issues later by The Spirit, who was making the transition from newspaper strips to comic books. Later issues would add teen humor character Candy and others. Beginning with issue #103, they were all dropped and Police Comics became a regular crime comic.

1 ❑ Aug 1941 Cover: 0.10 **NM** value: **6000.00**
• **CGC:** 3 graded, best 9.2
★ Origin of Plastic Man. ★ 1st Appearance of Plastic Man, The Mouthpiece, Firebrand, Phantom Lady, The Human Bomb.

2 ❑ Sep 1941 Cover: 0.10 **NM** value: **2250.00**
• **CGC:** 2 graded, best 8.5

3 ❑ Oct 1941 Cover: 0.10 **NM** value: **1700.00**
• **CGC:** 1 graded, best 4.0

4 ❑ Nov 1941 Cover: 0.10 **NM** value: **1450.00**
5 ❑ Dec 1941 Cover: 0.10 **NM** value: **1450.00**
6 ❑ Jan 1942 Cover: 0.10 **NM** value: **1350.00**
7 ❑ Feb 1942 Cover: 0.10 **NM** value: **1350.00**
8 ❑ Mar 1942 Cover: 0.10 **NM** value: **1500.00**
• **CGC:** 2 graded, best 7.0
★ Origin of Manhunter (Daniel Richards). ★ 1st Appearance of Manhunter (Daniel Richards).

9 ❑ May 1942 Cover: 0.10 **NM** value: **1100.00**
10 ❑ Jul 1942 Cover: 0.10 **NM** value: **1100.00**
11 ❑ Sep 1942 Cover: 0.10 **NM** value: **1750.00**
• **CGC:** 4 graded, best 9.2
• Reprints Spirit story from The Spirit #1 **A:** Will Eisner **W:** Will Eisner ★ Origin of The Spirit. ★ 1st Appearance of The Spirit (in comic books).

12 ❑ Oct 1942 Cover: 0.10 **NM** value: **985.00**
13 ❑ Nov 1942 Cover: 0.10 **NM** value: **985.00**
★ 1st Appearance of Woozy Winks.

14 ❑ Dec 1942 Cover: 0.10 **NM** value: **725.00**
15 ❑ Jan 1943 Cover: 0.10 **NM** value: **725.00**
• **CGC:** 1 graded, best 8.0

16 ❑ Feb 1943 Cover: 0.10 **NM** value: **725.00**
• **CGC:** 1 graded, best 6.5

17 ❑ Mar 1943 Cover: 0.10 **NM** value: **725.00**
• **CGC:** 1 graded, best 9.0

18 ❑ Apr 1943 Cover: 0.10 **NM** value: **725.00**
19 ❑ May 1943 Cover: 0.10 **NM** value: **725.00**
• **CGC:** 1 graded, best 6.0

20 ❑ Jul 1943 Cover: 0.10 **NM** value: **725.00**
• **CGC:** 2 graded, best 7.5

21 ❑ Aug 1943 Cover: 0.10 **NM** value: **575.00**
• **CGC:** 1 graded, best 9.4
📖 Plastic Man: The Menace of Serpina **A:** Jack Cole **W:** Jack Cole

22 ❑ Sep 1943 Cover: 0.10 **NM** value: **575.00**
• **CGC:** 1 graded, best 8.0
📖 Plastic Man: The Eyes Have It! **A:** Jack Cole **W:** Jack Cole

23 ❑ Oct 1943 Cover: 0.10 **NM** value: **500.00**
📖 Plastic Man: The Ghost Train **A:** Jack Cole **W:** Jack Cole

24 ❑ Nov 1943 Cover: 0.10 **NM** value: **500.00**
• **CGC:** 1 graded, best 7.5
📖 Plastic Man: The Hundred Plastic Men **A:** Jack Cole **W:** Jack Cole

25 ❑ Dec 1943 Cover: 0.10 **NM** value: **500.00**
📖 Plastic Man: The Rare Edition Murders **A:** Jack Cole **W:** Jack Cole

26 ❑ Jan 1944 Cover: 0.10 **NM** value: **500.00**
• **CGC:** 1 graded, best 9.0
📖 Plastic Man: Body, Mind and Soul **A:** Jack Cole **W:** Jack Cole

27 ❑ Feb 1944 Cover: 0.10 **NM** value: **500.00**
• **CGC:** 1 graded, best 5.0
📖 Plastic Man: Woozy Winks, Juror **A:** Jack Cole **W:** Jack Cole

28 ❑ Mar 1944 Cover: 0.10 **NM** value: **500.00**
• **CGC:** 3 graded, best 9.0
📖 Plastic Man: The Movie **A:** Jack Cole **W:** Jack Cole

29 ❑ Apr 1944 Cover: 0.10 **NM** value: **500.00**
• **CGC:** 2 graded, best 8.5
📖 Plastic Man: Death in Derlin's Castle **A:** Jack Cole **W:** Jack Cole

30 ❑ May 1944 Cover: 0.10 **NM** value: **500.00**
• **CGC:** 2 graded, best 8.5
📖 Plastic Man: Blinky Winks and Gooie Louie **A:** Jack Cole **W:** Jack Cole

31 ❑ Jun 1944 Cover: 0.10 **NM** value: **375.00**
• **CGC:** 2 graded, best 8.5

32 ❑ Jul 1944 Cover: 0.10 **NM** value: **375.00**
33 ❑ Aug 1944 Cover: 0.10 **NM** value: **375.00**
• **CGC:** 2 graded, best 8.0

34 ❑ Sep 1944 Cover: 0.10 **NM** value: **375.00**
• **CGC:** 1 graded, best 8.0

35 ❑ Oct 1944 Cover: 0.10 **NM** value: **375.00**
• **CGC:** 4 graded, best 9.2

36 ❑ Nov 1944 Cover: 0.10 **NM** value: **375.00**
• **CGC:** 1 graded, best 8.0

37 ❑ Dec 1944 Cover: 0.10 **NM** value: **375.00**
• **CGC:** 1 graded, best 9.0

38 ❑ Jan 1945 Cover: 0.10 **NM** value: **375.00**
• **CGC:** 3 graded, best 9.0

39 ❑ Feb 1945 Cover: 0.10 **NM** value: **375.00**
• **CGC:** 1 graded, best 9.8

40 ❑ Mar 1945 Cover: 0.10 **NM** value: **375.00**
• **CGC:** 1 graded, best 8.0

41 ❑ Apr 1945 Cover: 0.10 **NM** value: **315.00**
• **CGC:** 2 graded, best 9.6
A: Will Eisner

42 ❑ May 1945 Cover: 0.10 **NM** value: **315.00**
• **CGC:** 1 graded, best 9.6
A: Will Eisner

43 ❑ Jun 1945 Cover: 0.10 **NM** value: **315.00**
• **CGC:** 2 graded, best 9.0
A: Lou Fine

44 ❑ Jul 1945 Cover: 0.10 **NM** value: **260.00**
• **CGC:** 1 graded, best 9.6

45 ❑ Aug 1945 Cover: 0.10 **NM** value: **260.00**
• **CGC:** 1 graded, best 9.0

46 ❑ Sep 1945 Cover: 0.10 **NM** value: **260.00**
• **CGC:** 2 graded, best 9.4

47 ❑ Oct 1945 Cover: 0.10 **NM** value: **260.00**
• **CGC:** 1 graded, best 5.0

48 ❑ Nov 1945 Cover: 0.10 **NM** value: **260.00**
49 ❑ Dec 1945 Cover: 0.10 **NM** value: **260.00**
50 ❑ Jan 1946 Cover: 0.10 **NM** value: **260.00**
• **CGC:** 1 graded, best 7.0

51 ❑ Feb 1946 Cover: 0.10 **NM** value: **195.00**
• **CGC:** 1 graded, best 9.2

52 ❑ Mar 1946 Cover: 0.10 **NM** value: **195.00**
• **CGC:** 1 graded, best 7.5

53 ❑ Apr 1946 Cover: 0.10 **NM** value: **195.00**
54 ❑ May 1946 Cover: 0.10 **NM** value: **195.00**
• **CGC:** 2 graded, best 9.2

55 ❑ Jun 1946 Cover: 0.10 **NM** value: **195.00**
56 ❑ Jul 1946 Cover: 0.10 **NM** value: **195.00**
• **CGC:** 1 graded, best 9.6

57 ❑ Aug 1946 Cover: 0.10 **NM** value: **195.00**
58 ❑ Sep 1946 Cover: 0.10 **NM** value: **195.00**
• **CGC:** 1 graded, best 7.0

59 ❑ Oct 1946 Cover: 0.10 **NM** value: **195.00**
60 ❑ Nov 1946 Cover: 0.10 **NM** value: **195.00**
• **CGC:** 1 graded, best 9.4

61 ❑ Dec 1946 Cover: 0.10 **NM** value: **175.00**
• **CGC:** 1 graded, best 5.0

62 ❑ Jan 1947 Cover: 0.10 **NM** value: **175.00**
63 ❑ Feb 1947 Cover: 0.10 **NM** value: **175.00**
64 ❑ Mar 1947 Cover: 0.10 **NM** value: **175.00**
65 ❑ Apr 1947 Cover: 0.10 **NM** value: **175.00**
66 ❑ May 1947 Cover: 0.10 **NM** value: **175.00**
• **CGC:** 1 graded, best 9.2

67 ❑ Jun 1947 Cover: 0.10 **NM** value: **175.00**
68 ❑ Jul 1947 Cover: 0.10 **NM** value: **175.00**
• **CGC:** 1 graded, best 8.0

69 ❑ Aug 1947 Cover: 0.10 **NM** value: **175.00**
70 ❑ Sep 1947 Cover: 0.10 **NM** value: **175.00**
• **CGC:** 1 graded, best 9.4

71 ❑ Oct 1947 Cover: 0.10 **NM** value: **160.00**
72 ❑ Nov 1947 Cover: 0.10 **NM** value: **160.00**
• **CGC:** 1 graded, best 9.6

73 ❑ Dec 1947 Cover: 0.10 **NM** value: **160.00**
74 ❑ Jan 1948 Cover: 0.10 **NM** value: **160.00**
75 ❑ Feb 1948 Cover: 0.10 **NM** value: **160.00**
• **CGC:** 2 graded, best 6.5

76 ❑ Mar 1948 Cover: 0.10 **NM** value: **160.00**
• **CGC:** 1 graded, best 9.2

77 ❑ Apr 1948 Cover: 0.10 **NM** value: **160.00**
78 ❑ May 1948 Cover: 0.10 **NM** value: **160.00**
• **CGC:** 1 graded, best 9.0

CGC-graded: Multiply prices above by **33 for 9.9 M • 16 for 9.8 NM/M • 7 for 9.6 NM+ • 5 for 9.4 NM • 2.5 for 9.2 NM- • 1.5 for 9.0 VF/NM**

79 ❑ Jun 1948 Cover: 0.10 **NM** value: **160.00**
80 ❑ Jul 1948 Cover: 0.10 **NM** value: **160.00**
• **CGC:** 1 graded, best 8.5
81 ❑ Aug 1948 Cover: 0.10 **NM** value: **145.00**
82 ❑ Sep 1948 Cover: 0.10 **NM** value: **145.00**
83 ❑ Oct 1948 Cover: 0.10 **NM** value: **145.00**
84 ❑ Nov 1948 Cover: 0.10 **NM** value: **145.00**
85 ❑ Dec 1948 Cover: 0.10 **NM** value: **145.00**
86 ❑ Jan 1949 Cover: 0.10 **NM** value: **145.00**
• **CGC:** 1 graded, best 7.5
87 ❑ Feb 1949 Cover: 0.10 **NM** value: **145.00**
88 ❑ Mar 1949 Cover: 0.10 **NM** value: **145.00**
• **CGC:** 1 graded, best 9.4
89 ❑ Apr 1949 Cover: 0.10 **NM** value: **145.00**
90 ❑ May 1949 Cover: 0.10 **NM** value: **145.00**
• **CGC:** 2 graded, best 2.5
91 ❑ Jun 1949 Cover: 0.10 **NM** value: **145.00**
• **CGC:** 1 graded, best 3.0
92 ❑ Jul 1949 Cover: 0.10 **NM** value: **145.00**
• **CGC:** 1 graded, best 9.4
93 ❑ Aug 1949 Cover: 0.10 **NM** value: **145.00**
94 ❑ Sep 1949 Cover: 0.10 **NM** value: **225.00**
A: Will Eisner
95 ❑ Oct 1949 Cover: 0.10 **NM** value: **225.00**
A: Will Eisner
96 ❑ Nov 1949 Cover: 0.10 **NM** value: **225.00**
• **CGC:** 1 graded, best 9.4
A: Will Eisner
97 ❑ Dec 1949 Cover: 0.10 **NM** value: **225.00**
A: Will Eisner
98 ❑ Feb 1950 Cover: 0.10 **NM** value: **225.00**
A: Will Eisner
99 ❑ Apr 1950 Cover: 0.10 **NM** value: **225.00**
A: Will Eisner
100 ❑ Jun 1950 Cover: 0.10 **NM** value: **225.00**
• **CGC:** 1 graded, best 8.5
A: Will Eisner
101 ❑ Aug 1950 Cover: 0.10 **NM** value: **225.00**
A: Will Eisner
102 ❑ Oct 1950 Cover: 0.10 **NM** value: **225.00**
A: Will Eisner
103 ❑ Dec 1950 Cover: 0.10 **NM** value: **140.00**
• New format begins★ 1st Appearance of Ken Shannon.
104 ❑ Feb 1951 Cover: 0.10 **NM** value: **110.00**
105 ❑ Apr 1951 Cover: 0.10 **NM** value: **110.00**
106 ❑ Jun 1951 Cover: 0.10 **NM** value: **110.00**
107 ❑ Aug 1951 Cover: 0.10 **NM** value: **110.00**
108 ❑ Oct 1951 Cover: 0.10 **NM** value: **110.00**
109 ❑ Nov 1951 Cover: 0.10 **NM** value: **110.00**
110 ❑ Dec 1951 Cover: 0.10 **NM** value: **110.00**
111 ❑ Jan 1952 Cover: 0.10 **NM** value: **110.00**
112 ❑ Feb 1952 Cover: 0.10 **NM** value: **110.00**
• **CGC:** 1 graded, best 8.5
113 ❑ Mar 1952 Cover: 0.10 **NM** value: **110.00**
114 ❑ Apr 1952 Cover: 0.10 **NM** value: **110.00**
115 ❑ May 1952 Cover: 0.10 **NM** value: **110.00**
116 ❑ Jun 1952 Cover: 0.10 **NM** value: **110.00**
117 ❑ Jul 1952 Cover: 0.10 **NM** value: **110.00**
118 ❑ Aug 1952 Cover: 0.10 **NM** value: **110.00**
119 ❑ Sep 1952 Cover: 0.10 **NM** value: **110.00**
120 ❑ Oct 1952 Cover: 0.10 **NM** value: **110.00**
121 ❑ Nov 1952 Cover: 0.10 **NM** value: **110.00**
122 ❑ Dec 1952 Cover: 0.10 **NM** value: **110.00**
123 ❑ Jan 1953 Cover: 0.10 **NM** value: **110.00**
124 ❑ Feb 1953 Cover: 0.10 **NM** value: **110.00**
125 ❑ Apr 1953 Cover: 0.10 **NM** value: **110.00**
126 ❑ Jun 1953 Cover: 0.10 **NM** value: **110.00**
127 ❑ Oct 1953 Cover: 0.10 **NM** value: **110.00**
final issue.

POLICE LINE-UP — Avon

1 ❑ ca. 1951 Cover: 0.10 **NM** value: **275.00**
2 ❑ ca. 1951 Cover: 0.10 **NM** value: **200.00**
3 ❑ ca. 1952 Cover: 0.10 **NM** value: **125.00**
4 ❑ ca. 1952 Cover: 0.10 **NM** value: **125.00**

POLICE TRAP — Mainline

1 ❑ Sep 1954 Cover: 0.10 **NM** value: **200.00**
• **CGC:** 1 graded, best 7.5
2 ❑ Nov 1954 Cover: 0.10 **NM** value: **100.00**
3 ❑ Dec 1954 Cover: 0.10 **NM** value: **100.00**
4 ❑ Feb 1955 Cover: 0.10 **NM** value: **100.00**

POLICE TRAP (CHARLTON) — Charlton

5 ❑ Jul 1955 Cover: 0.10 **NM** value: **100.00**
6 ❑ Sep 1955 Cover: 0.10 **NM** value: **100.00**

POLIS — Brave New Words

1 ❑ b&w Cover: 2.50 **NM** value: **Cover or less**
A: Al Bigley **W:** Ed Fuqua
2 ❑ b&w Cover: 2.50 **NM** value: **Cover or less**
A: Al Bigley **W:** Ed Fuqua

POLLY AND HER PALS — Eternity

1 ❑ Oct 1990, b&w Cover: 2.95 **NM** value: **Cover or less**
• strip reprints
2 ❑ 1990b&w Cover: 2.95 **NM** value: **Cover or less**
• strip reprints
3 ❑ 1991b&w Cover: 2.95 **NM** value: **Cover or less**
• strip reprints
4 ❑ 1991b&w Cover: 2.95 **NM** value: **Cover or less**
• strip reprints
5 ❑ 1991b&w Cover: 2.95 **NM** value: **Cover or less**
• strip reprints

POLLY PIGTAILS — Parents' Magazine Institute

Parents Magazine Institute was famous for its series of comics aimed at specific groups, including Calling All Boys, Calling All Girls, and one that was aimed at both groups, Calling All Kids. In the case of Polly Pigtails, the publisher hedged its bet adding the subtitle, "The Magazine for Girls," although it was doubtful that any self-respecting boy would pick up a title that featured photo covers of — what else? — a pig-tailed little girl engaging in typically feminine activities. The series ran from 1946 to 1949. — Brent

1 ❑ Jan 1946 Cover: 0.15 **NM** value: **75.00**
2 ❑ Feb 1946 Cover: 0.15 **NM** value: **35.00**
3 ❑ Apr 1946 Cover: 0.15 **NM** value: **30.00**
4 ❑ May 1946 Cover: 0.15 **NM** value: **30.00**
5 ❑ Jun 1946 Cover: 0.15 **NM** value: **30.00**
6 ❑ Jul 1946 Cover: 0.15 **NM** value: **25.00**
7 ❑ Aug 1946 Cover: 0.15 **NM** value: **25.00**
8 ❑ Sep 1946 Cover: 0.15 **NM** value: **25.00**
9 ❑ Oct 1946 Cover: 0.15 **NM** value: **25.00**
10 ❑ Nov 1946 Cover: 0.15 **NM** value: **25.00**
11 ❑ Dec 1946 Cover: 0.15 **NM** value: **25.00**
12 ❑ Jan 1947 Cover: 0.15 **NM** value: **25.00**
13 ❑ Feb 1947 Cover: 0.15 **NM** value: **25.00**
14 ❑ Mar 1947 Cover: 0.15 **NM** value: **25.00**
15 ❑ Apr 1947 Cover: 0.15 **NM** value: **25.00**
16 ❑ May 1947 Cover: 0.15 **NM** value: **25.00**
17 ❑ Jun 1947 Cover: 0.15 **NM** value: **25.00**
18 ❑ Jul 1947 Cover: 0.15 **NM** value: **25.00**
19 ❑ Aug 1947 Cover: 0.15 **NM** value: **25.00**
20 ❑ Sep 1947 Cover: 0.15 **NM** value: **25.00**
21 ❑ Oct 1947 Cover: 0.15 **NM** value: **20.00**
22 ❑ Nov 1947 Cover: 0.15 **NM** value: **20.00**
23 ❑ Dec 1947 Cover: 0.15 **NM** value: **20.00**
24 ❑ Jan 1948 Cover: 0.15 **NM** value: **20.00**
25 ❑ Feb 1948 Cover: 0.15 **NM** value: **20.00**
26 ❑ Mar 1948 Cover: 0.15 **NM** value: **20.00**
27 ❑ Apr 1948 Cover: 0.15 **NM** value: **20.00**
28 ❑ May 1948 Cover: 0.15 **NM** value: **20.00**
29 ❑ Jun 1948 Cover: 0.15 **NM** value: **20.00**
30 ❑ Jul 1948 Cover: 0.15 **NM** value: **20.00**
31 ❑ Aug 1948 Cover: 0.15 **NM** value: **15.00**
32 ❑ Sep 1948 Cover: 0.15 **NM** value: **15.00**
33 ❑ Oct 1948 Cover: 0.15 **NM** value: **15.00**
34 ❑ Nov 1948 Cover: 0.15 **NM** value: **15.00**
35 ❑ Dec 1948 Cover: 0.15 **NM** value: **15.00**
36 ❑ Jan 1949 Cover: 0.15 **NM** value: **15.00**
37 ❑ Feb 1949 Cover: 0.15 **NM** value: **15.00**
38 ❑ Mar 1949 Cover: 0.15 **NM** value: **15.00**
39 ❑ Apr 1949 Cover: 0.15 **NM** value: **15.00**
40 ❑ May 1949 Cover: 0.15 **NM** value: **15.00**
41 ❑ Jun 1949 Cover: 0.15 **NM** value: **15.00**
42 ❑ Aug 1949 Cover: 0.15 **NM** value: **15.00**
43 ❑ Oct 1949 Cover: 0.15 **NM** value: **15.00**

POOT — Fantagraphics

1 ❑ Win 1997 Cover: 2.95 **NM** value: **Cover or less**
2 ❑ Spr 1998 Cover: 2.95 **NM** value: **Cover or less**
3 ❑ Sum 1998 Cover: 2.95 **NM** value: **Cover or less**
4 ❑ Win 1998 Cover: 3.95 **NM** value: **Cover or less**

POPCORN! — Discovery

1 ❑ b&w Cover: 3.95 **NM** value: **Cover or less**
No issue number. cardstock cover. **A:** Scott Deschaine; Bob Donovan **W:** Scott Deschaine

POPCORN PIMPS — Fantagraphics

1 ❑ Jun 1996, b&w Cover: 8.95 **NM** value: **Cover or less**
No issue number. • squarebound

POPEYE — Dell

E.C. Segar's Popeye the Sailor is one of the classic comics characters of the century and an enduring favorite for more than 70 years. The crusty sailor with the outsized forearms and taste for spinach first appeared in Segar's Thimble Theatre newspaper strip, along with his familiar cast of characters including his sweetheart Olive Oyl, nemesis Bluto, sidekick Wimpy, and many others. Popeye has appeared in comic books since 1937 and his adventures have been carried in titles published by David McKay, Dell, King, Charlton, Gold Key, Whitman, and Ocean. The template for Popeye's success — a goofy blend of humor and adventure, fuelled by unforgettable characters and bizarre dialogue — is almost failure-proof, and comics publishers have been using it to delight young fans to the present day.

1 ❑ Feb 1948 Cover: 0.10 **NM** value: **125.00**
• **CGC:** 4 graded, best 9.0
2 ❑ May 1948 Cover: 0.10 **NM** value: **85.00**
3 ❑ Aug 1948 Cover: 0.10 **NM** value: **60.00**
4 ❑ Nov 1948 Cover: 0.10 **NM** value: **60.00**
5 ❑ Feb 1949 Cover: 0.10 **NM** value: **60.00**
6 ❑ Apr 1949 Cover: 0.10 **NM** value: **48.00**
7 ❑ Jun 1949 Cover: 0.10 **NM** value: **48.00**
• **CGC:** 1 graded, best 5.5
8 ❑ Aug 1949 Cover: 0.10 **NM** value: **48.00**
9 ❑ Oct 1949 Cover: 0.10 **NM** value: **48.00**
10 ❑ Dec 1949 Cover: 0.10 **NM** value: **48.00**
11 ❑ Feb 1950 Cover: 0.10 **NM** value: **40.00**
12 ❑ Apr 1950 Cover: 0.10 **NM** value: **40.00**
13 ❑ Jun 1950 Cover: 0.10 **NM** value: **40.00**
14 ❑ Oct 1950 Cover: 0.10 **NM** value: **40.00**
15 ❑ Jan 1951 Cover: 0.10 **NM** value: **40.00**
16 ❑ Apr 1951 Cover: 0.10 **NM** value: **40.00**
17 ❑ Jul 1951 Cover: 0.10 **NM** value: **40.00**
18 ❑ Oct 1951 Cover: 0.10 **NM** value: **40.00**
19 ❑ Jan 1952 Cover: 0.10 **NM** value: **40.00**
• **CGC:** 1 graded, best 8.5
20 ❑ Apr 1952 Cover: 0.10 **NM** value: **40.00**
21 ❑ Jul 1952 Cover: 0.10 **NM** value: **32.00**
22 ❑ Oct 1952 Cover: 0.10 **NM** value: **32.00**
23 ❑ Jan 1953 Cover: 0.10 **NM** value: **32.00**
24 ❑ Apr 1953 Cover: 0.10 **NM** value: **32.00**
25 ❑ Jul 1953 Cover: 0.10 **NM** value: **32.00**
26 ❑ Oct 1953 Cover: 0.10 **NM** value: **32.00**
27 ❑ Jan 1954 Cover: 0.10 **NM** value: **32.00**
28 ❑ Apr 1954 Cover: 0.10 **NM** value: **32.00**
29 ❑ Jul 1954 Cover: 0.10 **NM** value: **32.00**
30 ❑ Oct 1954 Cover: 0.10 **NM** value: **32.00**
31 ❑ Jan 1955 Cover: 0.10 **NM** value: **28.00**
32 ❑ Apr 1955 Cover: 0.10 **NM** value: **28.00**
33 ❑ Jul 1955 Cover: 0.10 **NM** value: **28.00**
34 ❑ Oct 1955 Cover: 0.10 **NM** value: **28.00**
• **CGC:** 1 graded, best 8.5
35 ❑ Jan 1956 Cover: 0.10 **NM** value: **28.00**
36 ❑ Apr 1956 Cover: 0.10 **NM** value: **28.00**
37 ❑ Jul 1956 Cover: 0.10 **NM** value: **28.00**
38 ❑ Oct 1956 Cover: 0.10 **NM** value: **28.00**
39 ❑ Jan 1957 Cover: 0.10 **NM** value: **28.00**
40 ❑ Apr 1957 Cover: 0.10 **NM** value: **28.00**
41 ❑ Jul 1957 Cover: 0.10 **NM** value: **28.00**
42 ❑ Oct 1957 Cover: 0.10 **NM** value: **28.00**
43 ❑ Jan 1958 Cover: 0.10 **NM** value: **28.00**
44 ❑ Apr 1958 Cover: 0.10 **NM** value: **28.00**
45 ❑ Jul 1958 Cover: 0.10 **NM** value: **28.00**
46 ❑ Oct 1958 Cover: 0.10 **NM** value: **28.00**
47 ❑ Jan 1959 Cover: 0.10 **NM** value: **28.00**
• **CGC:** 1 graded, best 6.0
48 ❑ Apr 1959 Cover: 0.10 **NM** value: **28.00**
• Has 1958 Statement, filed 10/1/1958; no sales figures published
49 ❑ Jul 1959 Cover: 0.10 **NM** value: **28.00**
• Dell publishes
50 ❑ Oct 1959 Cover: 0.10 **NM** value: **28.00**
• Dell publishes
51 ❑ Jan 1960 Cover: 0.10 **NM** value: **24.00**
52 ❑ Mar 1960 Cover: 0.10 **NM** value: **24.00**
53 ❑ May 1960 Cover: 0.10 **NM** value: **24.00**
54 ❑ Jul 1960 Cover: 0.10 **NM** value: **24.00**
55 ❑ Jun 1960 Cover: 0.15 **NM** value: **24.00**
56 ❑ 1960 Cover: 0.15 **NM** value: **24.00**
57 ❑ 1961 Cover: 0.15 **NM** value: **24.00**
58 ❑ Apr 1961 Cover: 0.15 **NM** value: **24.00**
59 ❑ Jun 1961 Cover: 0.15 **NM** value: **24.00**
60 ❑ Aug 1961 Cover: 0.15 **NM** value: **24.00**
61 ❑ Oct 1961 Cover: 0.15 **NM** value: **24.00**
62 ❑ Dec 1961 Cover: 0.15 **NM** value: **24.00**
63 ❑ Jan 1962 Cover: 0.15 **NM** value: **24.00**
64 ❑ Apr 1962 Cover: 0.15 **NM** value: **24.00**
65 ❑ Jul 1962 Cover: 0.15 **NM** value: **24.00**
66 ❑ Oct 1962 Cover: 0.25 **NM** value: **20.00**
• **CGC:** 3 graded, best 8.0
67 ❑ Jan 1963 Cover: 0.25 **NM** value: **20.00**
68 ❑ May 1963 Cover: 0.12 **NM** value: **20.00**
• Has 1962 Statement; only reports subscription sales; avg subs 2,030
69 ❑ Jul 1963 Cover: 0.12 **NM** value: **20.00**
70 ❑ Nov 1963 Cover: 0.12 **NM** value: **20.00**
71 ❑ Jan 1964 Cover: 0.12 **NM** value: **20.00**
72 ❑ Apr 1964 Cover: 0.12 **NM** value: **20.00**
73 ❑ Jul 1964 Cover: 0.12 **NM** value: **20.00**
74 ❑ Nov 1964 Cover: 0.12 **NM** value: **20.00**
75 ❑ Feb 1965 Cover: 0.12 **NM** value: **20.00**
76 ❑ May 1965 Cover: 0.12 **NM** value: **20.00**
77 ❑ Aug 1965 Cover: 0.12 **NM** value: **20.00**
78 ❑ Nov 1965 Cover: 0.12 **NM** value: **20.00**
79 ❑ Feb 1966 Cover: 0.12 **NM** value: **20.00**
80 ❑ May 1966 Cover: 0.12 **NM** value: **20.00**
81 ❑ Aug 1966 Cover: 0.12 **NM** value: **16.00**
82 ❑ Oct 1966 Cover: 0.12 **NM** value: **16.00**
83 ❑ Dec 1966 Cover: 0.12 **NM** value: **16.00**
84 ❑ Feb 1967 Cover: 0.12 **NM** value: **16.00**
85 ❑ Apr 1967 Cover: 0.12 **NM** value: **16.00**
86 ❑ Jun 1967 Cover: 0.12 **NM** value: **16.00**
87 ❑ Jul 1967 Cover: 0.12 **NM** value: **16.00**
88 ❑ Aug 1967 Cover: 0.12 **NM** value: **16.00**
89 ❑ Sep 1967 Cover: 0.12 **NM** value: **16.00**
90 ❑ Oct 1967 Cover: 0.12 **NM** value: **16.00**
91 ❑ Nov 1967 Cover: 0.12 **NM** value: **16.00**
92 ❑ Dec 1967 Cover: 0.12 **NM** value: **16.00**
94 ❑ Feb 1969 Cover: 0.12 **NM** value: **12.00**
95 ❑ Apr 1969 Cover: 0.12 **NM** value: **12.00**
96 ❑ Jun 1969 Cover: 0.12 **NM** value: **12.00**
97 ❑ Aug 1969 Cover: 0.15 **NM** value: **12.00**
98 ❑ Oct 1969 Cover: 0.15 **NM** value: **12.00**
99 ❑ Dec 1969 Cover: 0.15 **NM** value: **12.00**
100 ❑ Feb 1970 Cover: 0.15 **NM** value: **12.00**
101 ❑ Apr 1970 Cover: 0.15 **NM** value: **8.00**
102 ❑ Jun 1970 Cover: 0.15 **NM** value: **8.00**
103 ❑ Aug 1970 Cover: 0.15 **NM** value: **8.00**
104 ❑ Oct 1970 Cover: 0.15 **NM** value: **8.00**
105 ❑ Dec 1970 Cover: 0.15 **NM** value: **8.00**

Other grades: Multiply prices above by **1.5 for Mint • 2/3 for Very Fine • 1/3 for Fine • 1/5 for Very Good • 1/8 for Good**

106❑ Feb 1971 Cover: 0.15 **NM** value: **8.00**
Stop the Oil; Granny's Birthday!; Sea Hag!; Some Smiles (text); Wimpy: Missing Clue; Snuffy's Secret Spot; Junior Smith: Not a Sign of Fish; The Monsker Hunt **A:** George Wildman(cover) ★ Appearance of Sea Hag, Brutus, Junior Smith, Wimpy, Swee' Pea, Granny, Snuffy Smith, Pappy, Olive Oyl, Ma Smith.
107❑ Apr 1971 Cover: 0.15 **NM** value: **8.00**
108❑ Jun 1971 Cover: 0.15 **NM** value: **8.00**
109❑ Aug 1971 Cover: 0.15 **NM** value: **8.00**
110❑ Oct 1971 Cover: 0.20 **NM** value: **8.00**
111❑ Dec 1971 Cover: 0.20 **NM** value: **8.00**
112❑ Jan 1972 Cover: 0.20 **NM** value: **8.00**
113❑ Mar 1972 Cover: 0.20 **NM** value: **8.00**
114❑ May 1972 Cover: 0.20 **NM** value: **8.00**
115❑ Jul 1972 Cover: 0.20 **NM** value: **8.00**
116❑ Sep 1972 Cover: 0.20 **NM** value: **8.00**
117❑ Nov 1972 Cover: 0.20 **NM** value: **8.00**
118❑ Feb 1973 Cover: 0.20 **NM** value: **8.00**
119❑ Apr 1973 Cover: 0.20 **NM** value: **8.00**
120❑ Jun 1973 Cover: 0.20 **NM** value: **8.00**
121❑ Aug 1973 Cover: 0.20 **NM** value: **5.00**
122❑ Oct 1973 Cover: 0.20 **NM** value: **5.00**
123❑ Nov 1973 Cover: 0.20 **NM** value: **5.00**
124❑ ca. 1974 Cover: 0.25 **NM** value: **5.00**
125❑ Sep 1974 Cover: 0.25 **NM** value: **5.00**
126❑ Dec 1974 Cover: 0.25 **NM** value: **5.00**
127❑ Feb 1975 Cover: 0.25 **NM** value: **5.00**
128❑ Apr 1975 Cover: 0.25 **NM** value: **5.00**
129❑ Jun 1975 Cover: 0.25 **NM** value: **5.00**
130❑ Aug 1975 Cover: 0.25 **NM** value: **5.00**
131❑ Oct 1975 Cover: 0.25 **NM** value: **5.00**
• **CGC:** 1 graded, best 8.5
132❑ **NM** value: **5.00**
133❑ **NM** value: **5.00**
134❑ ca. 1976 Cover: 0.35 **NM** value: **5.00**
135❑ ca. 1976 Cover: 0.35 **NM** value: **5.00**
136❑ ca. 1976 Cover: 0.35 **NM** value: **5.00**
137❑ ca. 1976 Cover: 0.35 **NM** value: **5.00**
138❑ Jan 1977 Cover: 0.35 **NM** value: **5.00**
139❑ May 1978 Cover: 0.35 **NM** value: **5.00**
140❑ Jul 1978 Cover: 0.35 **NM** value: **5.00**
141❑ Sep 1978 Cover: 0.35 **NM** value: **3.00**
142❑ Nov 1978 Cover: 0.35 **NM** value: **3.00**
143❑ Jan 1979 Cover: 0.35 **NM** value: **3.00**
144❑ Mar 1979 Cover: 0.35 **NM** value: **3.00**
145❑ Apr 1979 Cover: 0.40 **NM** value: **3.00**
146❑ May 1979 Cover: 0.40 **NM** value: **3.00**
147❑ Jun 1979 Cover: 0.40 **NM** value: **3.00**
148❑ Jul 1979 Cover: 0.40 **NM** value: **3.00**
149❑ Aug 1979 Cover: 0.40 **NM** value: **3.00**
150❑ Cover: 0.40 **NM** value: **3.00**
151❑ Cover: 0.40 **NM** value: **3.00**
• Gold Key publishes
152❑ Cover: 0.40 **NM** value: **3.00**
153❑ Cover: 0.40 **NM** value: **3.00**
154❑ 1980 Cover: 0.40 **NM** value: **3.00**
155❑ 1980 Cover: 0.40 **NM** value: **3.00**
156❑ Mar 1980 Cover: 0.40 **NM** value: **3.00**
157❑ 1980 Cover: 0.40 **NM** value: **3.00**
158❑ Sep 1980 Cover: 0.40 **NM** value: **3.00**
159❑ Cover: 0.40 **NM** value: **3.00**
162❑ 1981 Cover: 0.50 **NM** value: **3.00**
163❑ 1981 Cover: 0.50 **NM** value: **3.00**
164❑ 1981 Cover: 0.50 **NM** value: **3.00**
165❑ 1981 Cover: 0.50 **NM** value: **3.00**
166❑ **NM** value: **3.00**
167❑ **NM** value: **3.00**
168❑ **NM** value: **3.00**
169❑ **NM** value: **3.00**
170❑ Cover: 0.60 **NM** value: **3.00**
171❑ ca. 1984 Cover: 0.60 **NM** value: **3.00**
SE 1❑ **NM** value: **2.00**
• Bold Detergent giveaway. • Reprints issue #94;

POPEYE (EDUCATIONAL SERIES) Charlton

E 1 ❑ ca. 1972 **NM** value: **4.00**
• Health Careers
E 2 ❑ ca. 1972 **NM** value: **4.00**
• Environmental Careers
E 3 ❑ ca. 1972 **NM** value: **4.00**
• Communications and Media Careers
E 4 ❑ ca. 1972 **NM** value: **4.00**
• Transportation Careers
E 5 ❑ ca. 1972 **NM** value: **4.00**
• Construction Careers
E 6 ❑ ca. 1972 **NM** value: **4.00**
• Consumer and Homemaking Careers
E 7 ❑ ca. 1972 **NM** value: **4.00**
• Manufacturing Careers
E 8 ❑ ca. 1972 **NM** value: **4.00**
• Hospitality and Recreation Careers
E 9 ❑ ca. 1972 **NM** value: **4.00**
• Marketing and Distribution Careers
E 10❑ ca. 1972 **NM** value: **4.00**
• Business and Office Careers
E 11❑ ca. 1972 **NM** value: **4.00**
• Public Services Careers
E 12❑ ca. 1972 **NM** value: **4.00**
• Personal Service Careers
E 13❑ ca. 1972 **NM** value: **4.00**
• Marine Science Careers
E 14❑ ca. 1972 **NM** value: **4.00**
• Fine Arts and Humanities Careers
E 15❑ ca. 1972 **NM** value: **4.00**
final issue. • Agri-Business-Natural Resources Careers

POPEYE (HARVEY) Harvey

1 ❑ Cover: 1.50 **NM** value: **Cover or less**
2 ❑ Cover: 1.50 **NM** value: **Cover or less**
3 ❑ Mar 1994 Cover: 1.50 **NM** value: **Cover or less**
4 ❑ 1994 Cover: 1.50 **NM** value: **Cover or less**
5 ❑ Jun 1994 Cover: 1.50 **NM** value: **Cover or less**
6 ❑ Jul 1994 Cover: 1.50 **NM** value: **Cover or less**
Smr 1❑ Cover: 2.25 **NM** value: **Cover or less**

POPEYE SPECIAL Ocean

1 ❑ Sum 1987 Cover: 1.75 **NM** value: **2.00**
Circ: CapCity orders: **5,625**
Borned to the Sea **A:** Ben Dunn **W:** Ron Portier ★ Origin of Popeye.
2 ❑ Sep 1988 Cover: 2.00 **NM** value: **Cover or less**
Circ: CapCity orders: **4,675**
Double Trouble Down Under **A:** Ben Dunn **W:** Ron Portier

POP LIFE Fantagraphics

1 ❑ Oct 1998 Cover: 3.95 **NM** value: **Cover or less**
Circ: Diamd. preorders: **2,749**
Naked Girls, Part 1; Park Life; Miles from Home, Part 1 **A:** Wilfred Santiago; Ho Che Anderson **W:** Ho Che Anderson
2 ❑ Mar 1999 Cover: 3.95 **NM** value: **Cover or less**
Circ: Diamd. preorders: **1,864**

POPPLES Marvel / Star

1 ❑ Dec 1986 Cover: 0.75 **NM** value: **1.00**
Circ: CapCity orders: **5,200**
Pop Goes the Spy **A:** John Costanza **W:** Stan Kay
2 ❑ Feb 1987 Cover: 0.75 **NM** value: **1.00**
Circ: CapCity orders: **2,850**
3 ❑ Apr 1987 Cover: 0.75 **NM** value: **1.00**
Circ: CapCity orders: **1,800**
4 ❑ Jun 1987 Cover: 1.00 **NM** value: **Cover or less**
Circ: CapCity orders: **1,150**

POPPO OF THE POPCORN THEATRE Fuller

1 ❑ Oct 1955 Cover: 0.10 **NM** value: **25.00**
A: Charles Biro **W:** Charles Biro
2 ❑ Nov 1955 Cover: 0.10 **NM** value: **15.00**
A: Charles Biro **W:** Charles Biro
3 ❑ Nov 1955 Cover: 0.10 **NM** value: **12.00**
A: Charles Biro **W:** Charles Biro
4 ❑ Nov 1955 Cover: 0.10 **NM** value: **12.00**
It's Snow Mystery; Cool Characters; Spoofing Spooks; Fit to be Tied **A:** Charles Biro **W:** Charles Biro
5 ❑ Nov 1955 Cover: 0.10 **NM** value: **12.00**
A: Charles Biro **W:** Charles Biro
6 ❑ Dec 1955 Cover: 0.10 **NM** value: **10.00**
A: Charles Biro **W:** Charles Biro
7 ❑ Dec 1955 Cover: 0.10 **NM** value: **10.00**
A: Charles Biro **W:** Charles Biro
8 ❑ Dec 1955 Cover: 0.10 **NM** value: **10.00**
A: Charles Biro **W:** Charles Biro
9 ❑ Dec 1955 Cover: 0.10 **NM** value: **10.00**
A: Charles Biro **W:** Charles Biro
10 ❑ Dec 1955 Cover: 0.10 **NM** value: **10.00**
A: Charles Biro **W:** Charles Biro
11 ❑ Jan 1956 Cover: 0.10 **NM** value: **10.00**
A: Charles Biro **W:** Charles Biro
12 ❑ Jan 1956 Cover: 0.10 **NM** value: **10.00**
A: Charles Biro **W:** Charles Biro
13 ❑ Jan 1956 Cover: 0.10 **NM** value: **10.00**
• Final issue? **A:** Charles Biro **W:** Charles Biro

POPULAR COMICS Dell

Popular Comics was one of the first comic book titles published, first appearing on newsstands in 1936. At that time, comics reprinted complete stories from several weeks' worth of Sunday strips, which featured better art and storytelling than was to be found in the few original comic-book series of the day. Such classic comic-strip characters as Dick Tracy, Terry and the Pirates, Smilin' Jack, Felix the Cat, Little Orphan Annie, and Mutt and Jeff were reprinted in the pages of Popular Comics for the benefit of readers who did not get them in their regular papers, or who had missed episodes in the often-complicated plots of these series.

Popular stuck with this format into the 1940s, introducing a few original characters such as Supermind along the way. Popular presented comics of all genres, from adventure to gag strips, true crime to funny animals, in six eight-page chunks in each issue.

1 ❑ Feb 1936 Cover: 0.10 **NM** value: **3400.00**
• **CGC:** 2 graded, best 2.0
★ 1st Appearance of Dick Tracy (in a comic book).
2 ❑ Mar 1936 Cover: 0.10 **NM** value: **1150.00**
3 ❑ Apr 1936 Cover: 0.10 **NM** value: **900.00**
4 ❑ May 1936 Cover: 0.10 **NM** value: **750.00**
5 ❑ Jun 1936 Cover: 0.10 **NM** value: **700.00**
★ Appearance of Tom Mix.
6 ❑ Jul 1936 Cover: 0.10 **NM** value: **560.00**
7 ❑ Aug 1936 Cover: 0.10 **NM** value: **560.00**
• **CGC:** 1 graded, best 4.0
8 ❑ Sep 1936 Cover: 0.10 **NM** value: **525.00**
• **CGC:** 1 graded, best 4.0
9 ❑ Oct 1936 Cover: 0.10 **NM** value: **525.00**
• **CGC:** 1 graded, best 4.0
10 ❑ Nov 1936 Cover: 0.10 **NM** value: **525.00**
11 ❑ Dec 1936 Cover: 0.10 **NM** value: **425.00**
• **CGC:** 1 graded, best 7.5
12 ❑ Jan 1937 Cover: 0.10 **NM** value: **425.00**
13 ❑ Feb 1937 Cover: 0.10 **NM** value: **425.00**
• **CGC:** 1 graded, best 3.0
14 ❑ Mar 1937 Cover: 0.10 **NM** value: **425.00**
15 ❑ Apr 1937 Cover: 0.10 **NM** value: **425.00**
16 ❑ May 1937 Cover: 0.10 **NM** value: **375.00**
17 ❑ Jun 1937 Cover: 0.10 **NM** value: **375.00**
18 ❑ Jul 1937 Cover: 0.10 **NM** value: **375.00**
19 ❑ Aug 1937 Cover: 0.10 **NM** value: **375.00**
• **CGC:** 1 graded, best 4.0
20 ❑ Sep 1937 Cover: 0.10 **NM** value: **375.00**
• **CGC:** 1 graded, best .5
21 ❑ Oct 1937 Cover: 0.10 **NM** value: **315.00**
22 ❑ Nov 1937 Cover: 0.10 **NM** value: **315.00**
• **CGC:** 1 graded, best 7.0
23 ❑ Dec 1937 Cover: 0.10 **NM** value: **315.00**
24 ❑ Jan 1938 Cover: 0.10 **NM** value: **315.00**
25 ❑ Feb 1938 Cover: 0.10 **NM** value: **315.00**
26 ❑ Mar 1938 Cover: 0.10 **NM** value: **315.00**
27 ❑ Apr 1938 Cover: 0.10 **NM** value: **315.00**
28 ❑ May 1938 Cover: 0.10 **NM** value: **315.00**
29 ❑ Jun 1938 Cover: 0.10 **NM** value: **315.00**
30 ❑ Jul 1938 Cover: 0.10 **NM** value: **315.00**
31 ❑ Aug 1938 Cover: 0.10 **NM** value: **285.00**
32 ❑ Sep 1938 Cover: 0.10 **NM** value: **285.00**
33 ❑ Oct 1938 Cover: 0.10 **NM** value: **285.00**
34 ❑ Nov 1938 Cover: 0.10 **NM** value: **285.00**
35 ❑ Dec 1938 Cover: 0.10 **NM** value: **285.00**
36 ❑ Jan 1939 Cover: 0.10 **NM** value: **285.00**
37 ❑ Feb 1939 Cover: 0.10 **NM** value: **285.00**
38 ❑ Apr 1939 Cover: 0.10 **NM** value: **285.00**
39 ❑ May 1939 Cover: 0.10 **NM** value: **285.00**
40 ❑ Jun 1939 Cover: 0.10 **NM** value: **285.00**
41 ❑ Jul 1939 Cover: 0.10 **NM** value: **225.00**
42 ❑ Aug 1939 Cover: 0.10 **NM** value: **225.00**
43 ❑ Sep 1939 Cover: 0.10 **NM** value: **225.00**
44 ❑ Oct 1939 Cover: 0.10 **NM** value: **225.00**
• **CGC:** 1 graded, best 7.5
45 ❑ Nov 1939 Cover: 0.10 **NM** value: **225.00**
46 ❑ Dec 1939 Cover: 0.10 **NM** value: **280.00**
★ Origin of Martan, the Marvel Man. ★ 1st Appearance of Martan, the Marvel Man.
47 ❑ Jan 1940 Cover: 0.10 **NM** value: **225.00**
48 ❑ Feb 1940 Cover: 0.10 **NM** value: **225.00**
49 ❑ Mar 1940 Cover: 0.10 **NM** value: **225.00**
50 ❑ Apr 1940 Cover: 0.10 **NM** value: **225.00**
51 ❑ May 1940 Cover: 0.10 **NM** value: **190.00**
★ Origin of The Voice. ★ 1st Appearance of The Voice.
52 ❑ Jun 1940 Cover: 0.10 **NM** value: **190.00**
• **CGC:** 1 graded, best 9.4
53 ❑ Jul 1940 Cover: 0.10 **NM** value: **190.00**
54 ❑ Aug 1940 Cover: 0.10 **NM** value: **190.00**
• **CGC:** 1 graded, best 8.0
55 ❑ Sep 1940 Cover: 0.10 **NM** value: **190.00**
• **CGC:** 1 graded, best 7.5
56 ❑ Oct 1940 Cover: 0.10 **NM** value: **190.00**
57 ❑ Nov 1940 Cover: 0.10 **NM** value: **190.00**
58 ❑ Dec 1940 Cover: 0.10 **NM** value: **190.00**
59 ❑ Jan 1941 Cover: 0.10 **NM** value: **190.00**
60 ❑ Feb 1941 Cover: 0.10 **NM** value: **190.00**
★ Origin of Professor Supermind and Son. ★ 1st Appearance of Professor Supermind and Son.
61 ❑ Mar 1941 Cover: 0.10 **NM** value: **145.00**
62 ❑ Apr 1941 Cover: 0.10 **NM** value: **145.00**
• **CGC:** 1 graded, best 9.6
63 ❑ May 1941 Cover: 0.10 **NM** value: **145.00**
64 ❑ Jun 1941 Cover: 0.10 **NM** value: **145.00**
65 ❑ Jul 1941 Cover: 0.10 **NM** value: **145.00**
66 ❑ Aug 1941 Cover: 0.10 **NM** value: **145.00**
67 ❑ Sep 1941 Cover: 0.10 **NM** value: **145.00**
• **CGC:** 2 graded, best 9.4
68 ❑ Oct 1941 Cover: 0.10 **NM** value: **145.00**
• **CGC:** 1 graded, best 9.4
69 ❑ Nov 1941 Cover: 0.10 **NM** value: **145.00**
70 ❑ Dec 1941 Cover: 0.10 **NM** value: **145.00**
71 ❑ Jan 1942 Cover: 0.10 **NM** value: **145.00**
• **CGC:** 1 graded, best 9.0
72 ❑ Feb 1942 Cover: 0.10 **NM** value: **125.00**
73 ❑ Mar 1942 Cover: 0.10 **NM** value: **125.00**
74 ❑ Apr 1942 Cover: 0.10 **NM** value: **125.00**
75 ❑ May 1942 Cover: 0.10 **NM** value: **125.00**
76 ❑ Jun 1942 Cover: 0.10 **NM** value: **175.00**
★ Appearance of Captain Midnight.
77 ❑ Jul 1942 Cover: 0.10 **NM** value: **175.00**
• **CGC:** 1 graded, best 9.0
★ Appearance of Captain Midnight.
78 ❑ Aug 1942 Cover: 0.10 **NM** value: **175.00**
★ Appearance of Captain Midnight.
79 ❑ Sep 1942 Cover: 0.10 **NM** value: **125.00**
• **CGC:** 1 graded, best 9.2
80 ❑ Oct 1942 Cover: 0.10 **NM** value: **125.00**
81 ❑ Nov 1942 Cover: 0.10 **NM** value: **120.00**
82 ❑ Dec 1942 Cover: 0.10 **NM** value: **120.00**
83 ❑ Jan 1943 Cover: 0.10 **NM** value: **120.00**
84 ❑ Feb 1943 Cover: 0.10 **NM** value: **120.00**
85 ❑ Mar 1943 Cover: 0.10 **NM** value: **120.00**
• **CGC:** 1 graded, best 7.0
86 ❑ Apr 1943 Cover: 0.10 **NM** value: **120.00**
87 ❑ May 1943 Cover: 0.10 **NM** value: **120.00**
88 ❑ Jun 1943 Cover: 0.10 **NM** value: **120.00**
89 ❑ Jul 1943 Cover: 0.10 **NM** value: **120.00**
90 ❑ Aug 1943 Cover: 0.10 **NM** value: **120.00**
91 ❑ Sep 1943 Cover: 0.10 **NM** value: **100.00**
92 ❑ Oct 1943 Cover: 0.10 **NM** value: **100.00**
93 ❑ Nov 1943 Cover: 0.10 **NM** value: **100.00**
94 ❑ Dec 1943 Cover: 0.10 **NM** value: **100.00**
95 ❑ Jan 1944 Cover: 0.10 **NM** value: **100.00**

CGC-graded: Multiply prices above by **33 for 9.9 M • 16 for 9.8 NM/M • 7 for 9.6 NM+ • 5 for 9.4 NM • 2.5 for 9.2 NM- • 1.5 for 9.0 VF/NM**

96 ❑ Feb 1944 Cover: 0.10 **NM** value: **100.00**
97 ❑ Mar 1944 Cover: 0.10 **NM** value: **100.00**
98 ❑ Apr 1944 Cover: 0.10 **NM** value: **100.00**
99 ❑ May 1944 Cover: 0.10 **NM** value: **100.00**
100 ❑ Jun 1944 Cover: 0.10 **NM** value: **100.00**
101 ❑ Jul 1944 Cover: 0.10 **NM** value: **75.00**
102 ❑ Aug 1944 Cover: 0.10 **NM** value: **75.00**
103 ❑ Sep 1944 Cover: 0.10 **NM** value: **75.00**
104 ❑ Oct 1944 Cover: 0.10 **NM** value: **75.00**
105 ❑ Nov 1944 Cover: 0.10 **NM** value: **75.00**
106 ❑ Dec 1944 Cover: 0.10 **NM** value: **75.00**
107 ❑ Jan 1945 Cover: 0.10 **NM** value: **75.00**
108 ❑ Feb 1945 Cover: 0.10 **NM** value: **75.00**
109 ❑ Mar 1945 Cover: 0.10 **NM** value: **75.00**
• **CGC:** 1 graded, best 9.4
110 ❑ Apr 1945 Cover: 0.10 **NM** value: **75.00**
111 ❑ May 1945 Cover: 0.10 **NM** value: **68.00**
112 ❑ Jun 1945 Cover: 0.10 **NM** value: **68.00**
113 ❑ Jul 1945 Cover: 0.10 **NM** value: **68.00**
War bonds cover. 📖 Smilin' Jack; Terry And The Pirates; Doctor Bobbs; The Flop Family; Felix The Cat; Gasoline Alley; Polly And Her Pals; Smokey Stover **A:** Milton Caniff; Bill Holman; Cliff Sterrett; Pat Sullivan; Phillips Lord **W:** Milton Caniff; Bill Holman; Cliff Sterrett; Pat Sullivan; Phillips Lord
114 ❑ Aug 1945 Cover: 0.10 **NM** value: **68.00**
115 ❑ Sep 1945 Cover: 0.10 **NM** value: **68.00**
116 ❑ Oct 1945 Cover: 0.10 **NM** value: **68.00**
117 ❑ Nov 1945 Cover: 0.10 **NM** value: **68.00**
118 ❑ Dec 1945 Cover: 0.10 **NM** value: **68.00**
• **CGC:** 1 graded, best 9.2
119 ❑ Jan 1946 Cover: 0.10 **NM** value: **68.00**
120 ❑ Feb 1946 Cover: 0.10 **NM** value: **68.00**
• **CGC:** 1 graded, best 9.6
121 ❑ Mar 1946 Cover: 0.10 **NM** value: **62.00**
122 ❑ Apr 1946 Cover: 0.10 **NM** value: **62.00**
123 ❑ May 1946 Cover: 0.10 **NM** value: **62.00**
124 ❑ Jun 1946 Cover: 0.10 **NM** value: **62.00**
125 ❑ Jul 1946 Cover: 0.10 **NM** value: **62.00**
126 ❑ Aug 1946 Cover: 0.10 **NM** value: **62.00**
127 ❑ Sep 1946 Cover: 0.10 **NM** value: **62.00**
128 ❑ Oct 1946 Cover: 0.10 **NM** value: **62.00**
129 ❑ Nov 1946 Cover: 0.10 **NM** value: **62.00**
• **CGC:** 1 graded, best 9.6
130 ❑ Dec 1946 Cover: 0.10 **NM** value: **62.00**
131 ❑ Jan 1947 Cover: 0.10 **NM** value: **55.00**
132 ❑ Feb 1947 Cover: 0.10 **NM** value: **55.00**
📖 Felix the Cat; Smilin' Jack; Smokey Stover; Terry and the Pirates; Gang Busters; The Big Squeeze (text story); Gasoline Alley; The Gumps **A:** Milton Caniff; Bill Holman; Pat Sullivan; Zack Mosley **W:** Milton Caniff; Bill Holman; Pat Sullivan; Zack Mosley
133 ❑ Mar 1947 Cover: 0.10 **NM** value: **55.00**
134 ❑ Apr 1947 Cover: 0.10 **NM** value: **55.00**
135 ❑ May 1947 Cover: 0.10 **NM** value: **55.00**
136 ❑ Jun 1947 Cover: 0.10 **NM** value: **55.00**
137 ❑ Jul 1947 Cover: 0.10 **NM** value: **55.00**
138 ❑ Aug 1947 Cover: 0.10 **NM** value: **55.00**
139 ❑ Sep 1947 Cover: 0.10 **NM** value: **55.00**
140 ❑ Oct 1947 Cover: 0.10 **NM** value: **55.00**
141 ❑ Nov 1947 Cover: 0.10 **NM** value: **55.00**
• **CGC:** 1 graded, best 9.0
142 ❑ Jan 1948 Cover: 0.10 **NM** value: **55.00**
143 ❑ Mar 1948 Cover: 0.10 **NM** value: **55.00**
144 ❑ May 1948 Cover: 0.10 **NM** value: **55.00**
145 ❑ Jul 1948 Cover: 0.10 **NM** value: **55.00**
final issue.

POPULAR ROMANCE — Better

5 ❑ ca. 1950 Cover: 0.10 **NM** value: **60.00**
6 ❑ ca. 1950 Cover: 0.10 **NM** value: **40.00**
7 ❑ ca. 1950 Cover: 0.10 **NM** value: **40.00**
8 ❑ ca. 1950 Cover: 0.10 **NM** value: **40.00**
9 ❑ ca. 1950 Cover: 0.10 **NM** value: **40.00**
10 ❑ ca. 1950 Cover: 0.10 **NM** value: **40.00**
11 ❑ ca. 1951 Cover: 0.10 **NM** value: **40.00**
12 ❑ ca. 1951 Cover: 0.10 **NM** value: **40.00**
13 ❑ ca. 1951 Cover: 0.10 **NM** value: **40.00**
14 ❑ ca. 1951 Cover: 0.10 **NM** value: **40.00**
15 ❑ ca. 1952 Cover: 0.10 **NM** value: **40.00**
16 ❑ ca. 1952 Cover: 0.10 **NM** value: **30.00**
17 ❑ ca. 1952 Cover: 0.10 **NM** value: **30.00**
18 ❑ ca. 1952 Cover: 0.10 **NM** value: **30.00**
19 ❑ ca. 1952 Cover: 0.10 **NM** value: **30.00**
20 ❑ ca. 1952 Cover: 0.10 **NM** value: **30.00**
21 ❑ ca. 1953 Cover: 0.10 **NM** value: **30.00**
22 ❑ ca. 1953 Cover: 0.10 **NM** value: **30.00**
23 ❑ ca. 1953 Cover: 0.10 **NM** value: **30.00**
24 ❑ ca. 1953 Cover: 0.10 **NM** value: **30.00**
25 ❑ ca. 1953 Cover: 0.10 **NM** value: **30.00**
26 ❑ ca. 1953 Cover: 0.10 **NM** value: **30.00**
27 ❑ ca. 1954 Cover: 0.10 **NM** value: **30.00**
28 ❑ ca. 1954 Cover: 0.10 **NM** value: **30.00**
29 ❑ ca. 1954 Cover: 0.10 **NM** value: **30.00**

Capital City orders are the actual sales of comic books by Capital City Distribution, once one of the largest U.S. sellers of comics to comics shops. Capital City's share of comics shop sales, while not known exactly, increases from around 10-20% in the mid-1980s to 30-35% in the mid-1990s. Capital City's share of comic books sold on newsstands (most Marvels and DCs) will be less.

POPULAR TEENAGERS — Star

The series started as School Day Romances, then had cover copy reading "School-Day Romances of Teen-Agers," and then evolved still further with the odd cover logo "POPular TEEN-AGERS." Many of the covers were cluttered, and some featured photos of movie stars in addition to pin-up-type poses of young women. (By the way, considering the complaints some make about shapely women portrayed in skin-tight outfits in comics today, it's interesting to note how many comics of the early 1950s featured the same thing, even when ostensibly aimed at a female readership.)

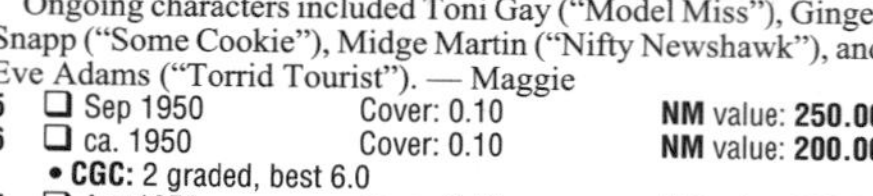

Ongoing characters included Toni Gay ("Model Miss"), Ginger Snapp ("Some Cookie"), Midge Martin ("Nifty Newshawk"), and Eve Adams ("Torrid Tourist"). — Maggie

5 ❑ Sep 1950 Cover: 0.10 **NM** value: **250.00**
6 ❑ ca. 1950 Cover: 0.10 **NM** value: **200.00**
• **CGC:** 2 graded, best 6.0
7 ❑ Apr 1951 Cover: 0.10 **NM** value: **200.00**
8 ❑ Jul 1951 Cover: 0.10 **NM** value: **200.00**
9 ❑ Oct 1951 Cover: 0.10 **NM** value: **200.00**
10 ❑ Jan 1952 Cover: 0.10 **NM** value: **150.00**
11 ❑ Apr 1952 Cover: 0.10 **NM** value: **150.00**
12 ❑ Jul 1952 Cover: 0.10 **NM** value: **150.00**
13 ❑ Oct 1952 Cover: 0.10 **NM** value: **150.00**
14 ❑ Jan 1953 Cover: 0.10 **NM** value: **150.00**
15 ❑ Apr 1953 Cover: 0.10 **NM** value: **150.00**
16 ❑ Jul 1953 Cover: 0.10 **NM** value: **100.00**
17 ❑ Oct 1953 Cover: 0.10 **NM** value: **100.00**
18 ❑ Jan 1954 Cover: 0.10 **NM** value: **100.00**
19 ❑ Apr 1954 Cover: 0.10 **NM** value: **100.00**
20 ❑ May 1954 Cover: 0.10 **NM** value: **100.00**
21 ❑ Jul 1954 Cover: 0.10 **NM** value: **100.00**
22 ❑ Sep 1954 Cover: 0.10 **NM** value: **100.00**
23 ❑ Oct 1954 Cover: 0.10 **NM** value: **100.00**
• **CGC:** 1 graded, best 5.0

PORK KNIGHT: THIS LITTLE PIGGY — Silver Snail

1 ❑ Cover: 1.70 **NM** value: **2.00**
📖 Pork Knight **A:** Rob Walton **W:** Rob Walton

PORKY PIG (DELL) — Dell

Stammering swine Porky Pig was a mainstay of the Warner Bros. stable of cartoon characters, which also included Bugs Bunny, Daffy Duck, Tweety, and others. Porky's adventures in print appeared in Porky Pig, early issues of which were actually part of Dell's catchall Four Color Comics.

Frequently paired with Daffy or Bugs, Porky usually appears as a sensible everyman (or everypig) figure in this title, generally trying to stay out of trouble — though occasionally his ambition gets the better of him. Supporting characters include Petunia, his girlfriend from the cartoons, and his nephew, blue beret-wearing Cicero.

25 ❑ Nov 1952 Cover: 0.10 **NM** value: **12.00**
26 ❑ Jan 1953 Cover: 0.10 **NM** value: **12.00**
27 ❑ Mar 1953 Cover: 0.10 **NM** value: **12.00**
28 ❑ May 1953 Cover: 0.10 **NM** value: **12.00**
29 ❑ Jul 1953 Cover: 0.10 **NM** value: **12.00**
30 ❑ Sep 1953 Cover: 0.10 **NM** value: **12.00**
31 ❑ Nov 1953 Cover: 0.10 **NM** value: **9.00**
32 ❑ Jan 1954 Cover: 0.10 **NM** value: **9.00**
33 ❑ Mar 1954 Cover: 0.10 **NM** value: **9.00**
34 ❑ May 1954 Cover: 0.10 **NM** value: **9.00**
35 ❑ Jul 1954 Cover: 0.10 **NM** value: **9.00**
36 ❑ Sep 1954 Cover: 0.10 **NM** value: **9.00**
37 ❑ Nov 1954 Cover: 0.10 **NM** value: **9.00**
38 ❑ Jan 1955 Cover: 0.10 **NM** value: **9.00**
39 ❑ Mar 1955 Cover: 0.10 **NM** value: **9.00**
40 ❑ May 1955 Cover: 0.10 **NM** value: **9.00**
41 ❑ Jul 1955 Cover: 0.10 **NM** value: **9.00**
42 ❑ Sep 1955 Cover: 0.10 **NM** value: **9.00**
43 ❑ Nov 1955 Cover: 0.10 **NM** value: **9.00**
44 ❑ Jan 1956 Cover: 0.10 **NM** value: **9.00**
45 ❑ Mar 1956 Cover: 0.10 **NM** value: **9.00**
46 ❑ May 1956 Cover: 0.10 **NM** value: **9.00**
47 ❑ Jul 1956 Cover: 0.10 **NM** value: **9.00**
48 ❑ Sep 1956 Cover: 0.10 **NM** value: **9.00**
49 ❑ Nov 1956 Cover: 0.10 **NM** value: **9.00**
50 ❑ Jan 1957 Cover: 0.10 **NM** value: **9.00**
51 ❑ Mar 1957 Cover: 0.10 **NM** value: **7.00**
52 ❑ May 1957 Cover: 0.10 **NM** value: **7.00**
53 ❑ Jul 1957 Cover: 0.10 **NM** value: **7.00**
54 ❑ Sep 1957 Cover: 0.10 **NM** value: **7.00**
55 ❑ Nov 1957 Cover: 0.10 **NM** value: **7.00**
56 ❑ Jan 1958 Cover: 0.10 **NM** value: **7.00**
57 ❑ Mar 1958 Cover: 0.10 **NM** value: **7.00**
58 ❑ May 1958 Cover: 0.10 **NM** value: **7.00**
59 ❑ Jul 1958 Cover: 0.10 **NM** value: **7.00**
60 ❑ Sep 1958 Cover: 0.10 **NM** value: **7.00**
61 ❑ Nov 1958 Cover: 0.10 **NM** value: **7.00**
62 ❑ Jan 1959 Cover: 0.10 **NM** value: **7.00**
63 ❑ Mar 1959 Cover: 0.10 **NM** value: **7.00**
64 ❑ May 1959 Cover: 0.10 **NM** value: **7.00**
65 ❑ Jul 1959 Cover: 0.10 **NM** value: **7.00**
66 ❑ Sep 1959 Cover: 0.10 **NM** value: **7.00**
67 ❑ Nov 1959 Cover: 0.10 **NM** value: **7.00**
68 ❑ Jan 1960 Cover: 0.10 **NM** value: **7.00**
69 ❑ Mar 1960 Cover: 0.10 **NM** value: **7.00**
70 ❑ May 1960 Cover: 0.10 **NM** value: **7.00**
71 ❑ Jul 1960 Cover: 0.10 **NM** value: **6.00**
72 ❑ Sep 1960 Cover: 0.10 **NM** value: **6.00**
73 ❑ Nov 1960 Cover: 0.10 **NM** value: **6.00**
74 ❑ Jan 1961 Cover: 0.10 **NM** value: **6.00**
75 ❑ Mar 1961 Cover: 0.10 **NM** value: **6.00**
76 ❑ May 1961 Cover: 0.10 **NM** value: **6.00**
77 ❑ Jul 1961 Cover: 0.10 **NM** value: **6.00**
78 ❑ Sep 1961 Cover: 0.10 **NM** value: **6.00**
79 ❑ Nov 1961 Cover: 0.10 **NM** value: **6.00**
80 ❑ Jan 1962 Cover: 0.10 **NM** value: **6.00**
81 ❑ Mar 1962 Cover: 0.10 **NM** value: **6.00**

PORKY PIG (GOLD KEY) — Gold Key

1 ❑ Jan 1965 Cover: 0.12 **NM** value: **30.00**
2 ❑ May 1965 Cover: 0.12 **NM** value: **14.00**
3 ❑ Aug 1965 Cover: 0.12 **NM** value: **12.00**
4 ❑ Nov 1965 Cover: 0.12 **NM** value: **12.00**
5 ❑ Mar 1966 Cover: 0.12 **NM** value: **12.00**
Circ: Statement: **261,850**
6 ❑ Jun 1966 Cover: 0.12 **NM** value: **8.00**
Circ: Statement: **261,850**
7 ❑ Jul 1966 Cover: 0.12 **NM** value: **8.00**
Circ: Statement: **261,850**
8 ❑ Sep 1966 Cover: 0.12 **NM** value: **8.00**
Circ: Statement: **261,850**
9 ❑ Nov 1966 Cover: 0.12 **NM** value: **8.00**
Circ: Statement: **261,850**
10 ❑ Jan 1967 Cover: 0.12 **NM** value: **8.00**
Circ: Statement: **241,735**
11 ❑ Mar 1967 Cover: 0.12 **NM** value: **5.00**
Circ: Statement: **241,735**
12 ❑ May 1967 Cover: 0.12 **NM** value: **5.00**
Circ: Statement: **241,735**
13 ❑ Jul 1967 Cover: 0.12 **NM** value: **5.00**
Circ: Statement: **241,735**
14 ❑ Sep 1967 Cover: 0.12 **NM** value: **5.00**
Circ: Statement: **241,735**
15 ❑ Nov 1967 Cover: 0.12 **NM** value: **5.00**
Circ: Statement: **241,735**
16 ❑ Jan 1968 Cover: 0.12 **NM** value: **5.00**
17 ❑ ca. 1968 Cover: 0.12 **NM** value: **5.00**
18 ❑ Jun 1968 Cover: 0.12 **NM** value: **5.00**
19 ❑ Aug 1968 Cover: 0.15 **NM** value: **5.00**
20 ❑ Oct 1968 Cover: 0.15 **NM** value: **5.00**
21 ❑ Dec 1968 Cover: 0.15 **NM** value: **4.00**
22 ❑ Feb 1969 Cover: 0.15 **NM** value: **4.00**
23 ❑ Apr 1969 Cover: 0.15 **NM** value: **4.00**
24 ❑ Jun 1969 Cover: 0.15 **NM** value: **4.00**
25 ❑ Aug 1969 Cover: 0.15 **NM** value: **4.00**
26 ❑ Oct 1969 Cover: 0.15 **NM** value: **4.00**
27 ❑ Dec 1969 Cover: 0.15 **NM** value: **4.00**
28 ❑ Feb 1970 Cover: 0.15 **NM** value: **4.00**
29 ❑ Apr 1970 Cover: 0.15 **NM** value: **4.00**
30 ❑ Jun 1970 Cover: 0.15 **NM** value: **4.00**
31 ❑ Aug 1970 Cover: 0.15 **NM** value: **3.00**
32 ❑ Oct 1970 Cover: 0.15 **NM** value: **3.00**
33 ❑ Dec 1970 Cover: 0.15 **NM** value: **3.00**
34 ❑ Feb 1971 Cover: 0.15 **NM** value: **3.00**
35 ❑ Apr 1971 Cover: 0.15 **NM** value: **3.00**
36 ❑ Jun 1971 Cover: 0.15 **NM** value: **3.00**
37 ❑ Aug 1971 Cover: 0.15 **NM** value: **3.00**
38 ❑ Oct 1971 Cover: 0.15 **NM** value: **3.00**
39 ❑ Dec 1971 Cover: 0.15 **NM** value: **3.00**
40 ❑ Feb 1972 Cover: 0.15 **NM** value: **3.00**
41 ❑ Apr 1972 Cover: 0.15 **NM** value: **3.00**
42 ❑ Jun 1972 Cover: 0.15 **NM** value: **3.00**
43 ❑ Aug 1972 Cover: 0.15 **NM** value: **3.00**
• **CGC:** 9 graded, best 9.6
44 ❑ Oct 1972 Cover: 0.15 **NM** value: **3.00**
45 ❑ Dec 1972 Cover: 0.15 **NM** value: **3.00**
46 ❑ Feb 1973 Cover: 0.15 **NM** value: **3.00**
• **CGC:** 18 graded, best 9.8
47 ❑ Apr 1973 Cover: 0.15 **NM** value: **3.00**
48 ❑ Jun 1973 Cover: 0.20 **NM** value: **3.00**
49 ❑ Aug 1973 Cover: 0.20 **NM** value: **3.00**
50 ❑ Oct 1973 Cover: 0.20 **NM** value: **3.00**
51 ❑ Dec 1973 Cover: 0.20 **NM** value: **2.00**
52 ❑ Feb 1974 Cover: 0.20 **NM** value: **2.00**
53 ❑ Apr 1974 Cover: 0.20 **NM** value: **2.00**
54 ❑ Jun 1974 Cover: 0.20 **NM** value: **2.00**
55 ❑ Aug 1974 Cover: 0.25 **NM** value: **2.00**
56 ❑ Oct 1974 Cover: 0.25 **NM** value: **2.00**
57 ❑ Dec 1974 Cover: 0.25 **NM** value: **2.00**
58 ❑ Feb 1975 Cover: 0.25 **NM** value: **2.00**
59 ❑ Apr 1975 Cover: 0.25 **NM** value: **2.00**
60 ❑ Jun 1975 Cover: 0.25 **NM** value: **2.00**
61 ❑ Aug 1975 Cover: 0.25 **NM** value: **2.00**
62 ❑ Sep 1975 Cover: 0.25 **NM** value: **2.00**
63 ❑ Oct 1975 Cover: 0.25 **NM** value: **2.00**
64 ❑ Nov 1975 Cover: 0.25 **NM** value: **2.00**
65 ❑ Dec 1975 Cover: 0.25 **NM** value: **2.00**
66 ❑ Apr 1976 Cover: 0.25 **NM** value: **2.00**
67 ❑ Jun 1976 Cover: 0.25 **NM** value: **2.00**
68 ❑ Jul 1976 Cover: 0.25 **NM** value: **2.00**
69 ❑ Aug 1976 Cover: 0.25 **NM** value: **2.00**
70 ❑ Sep 1976 Cover: 0.30 **NM** value: **2.00**
71 ❑ Nov 1976 Cover: 0.30 **NM** value: **2.00**
72 ❑ Jan 1977 Cover: 0.30 **NM** value: **2.00**
73 ❑ Mar 1977 Cover: 0.30 **NM** value: **2.00**
74 ❑ May 1977 Cover: 0.30 **NM** value: **2.00**
75 ❑ Jul 1977 Cover: 0.30 **NM** value: **2.00**

Other grades: Multiply prices above by **1.5 for Mint • 2/3 for Very Fine • 1/3 for Fine • 1/5 for Very Good • 1/8 for Good**

76 ❑ Aug 1977 Cover: 0.30 **NM** value: **2.00**
77 ❑ Sep 1977 Cover: 0.30 **NM** value: **2.00**
78 ❑ Nov 1977 Cover: 0.30 **NM** value: **2.00**
79 ❑ Jan 1978 Cover: 0.35 **NM** value: **2.00**
80 ❑ Mar 1978 Cover: 0.35 **NM** value: **2.00**
81 ❑ May 1978 Cover: 0.35 **NM** value: **2.00**
82 ❑ Jul 1978 Cover: 0.35 **NM** value: **2.00**
83 ❑ Aug 1978 Cover: 0.35 **NM** value: **2.00**
84 ❑ Sep 1978 Cover: 0.35 **NM** value: **2.00**
85 ❑ Oct 1978 Cover: 0.35 **NM** value: **2.00**
86 ❑ Nov 1978 Cover: 0.35 **NM** value: **2.00**
87 ❑ Jan 1979 Cover: 0.35 **NM** value: **2.00**
88 ❑ Mar 1979 Cover: 0.35 **NM** value: **2.00**
89 ❑ May 1979 Cover: 0.40 **NM** value: **2.00**
90 ❑ Jul 1979 Cover: 0.40 **NM** value: **2.00**
91 ❑ Sep 1979 Cover: 0.40 **NM** value: **2.00**
92 ❑ Nov 1979 Cover: 0.40 **NM** value: **2.00**
93 ❑ Jan 1980 Cover: 0.40 **NM** value: **2.00**
94 ❑ Mar 1980 Cover: 0.40 **NM** value: **2.00**
95 ❑ May 1980 Cover: 0.40 **NM** value: **2.00**
96 ❑ Jul 1980 Cover: 0.40 **NM** value: **2.00**
97 ❑ Sep 1980 Cover: 0.40 **NM** value: **2.00**
98 ❑ Nov 1980 Cover: 0.40 **NM** value: **2.00**
99 ❑ Jan 1981 Cover: 0.40 **NM** value: **2.00**
100 ❑ Mar 1981 Cover: 0.50 **NM** value: **2.00**
101 ❑ ca. 1981 Cover: 0.50 **NM** value: **2.00**
102 ❑ Sep 1981 Cover: 0.50 **NM** value: **2.00**
Pied Piper Porky; The Mysterious Mountain; A Piggy Tale; Fixit Fiasco; Tweety and Sylvester: Down in the Dumps; The Salt Shaker Mystery
103 ❑ Nov 1981 Cover: 0.50 **NM** value: **2.00**
104 ❑ Feb 1982 Cover: 0.60 **NM** value: **2.00**
The Furry Frog; Hotel Hassle; The Treasure of Castaway Island;
105 ❑ Apr 1982 Cover: 0.60 **NM** value: **2.00**
106 ❑ Cover: 0.60 **NM** value: **2.00**
107 ❑ Cover: 0.60 **NM** value: **2.00**
108 ❑ Cover: 0.60 **NM** value: **2.00**
109 ❑ ca. 1984 Cover: 0.60 **NM** value: **2.00**

PORNOTOPIA — Radio
1 ❑ Aug 1999 Cover: 2.95 **NM** value: **Cover or less**

PORT — Silverwolf
1 ❑ b&w Cover: 1.50 **NM** value: **Cover or less**
The Egg **A:** Phil Hester **W:** Kris Silver
2 ❑ b&w Cover: 1.50 **NM** value: **Cover or less**
A: Phil Hester **W:** Kris Silver

PORTABLE LOWLIFE — Aeon
1 ❑ Jul 1993 Cover: 4.95 **NM** value: **Cover or less**
No issue number. • prestige format.

PORTALS OF ELONDAR — Storybook Press
1 ❑ Jul 1996, b&w Cover: 2.95 **NM** value: **Cover or less**

PORTFOLIOS PREVIEW — Delta
Ash 1❑ **NM** value: **1.00**
• Reckshop; Skulker; Frost Fire **A:** Joe Bernardo; Mark Henry; Terrance Griep Jr. **W:** Joe Bernardo; Mark Henry; Terrance Griep Jr.

PORTIA PRINZ OF THE GLAMAZONS — Eclipse
1 ❑ Dec 1986, b&w Cover: 2.00 **NM** value: **Cover or less**
2 ❑ Feb 1987, b&w Cover: 2.00 **NM** value: **Cover or less**
3 ❑ Apr 1987, b&w Cover: 2.00 **NM** value: **Cover or less**
4 ❑ Jun 1987, b&w Cover: 2.00 **NM** value: **Cover or less**
5 ❑ Aug 1987, b&w Cover: 2.00 **NM** value: **Cover or less**
6 ❑ Oct 1987, b&w Cover: 2.00 **NM** value: **Cover or less**

PORTRAIT OF A YOUNG MAN AS A CARTOONIST — Hammer & Anvil Press
1 ❑ Oct 1996 Cover: 2.95 **NM** value: **Cover or less**
2 ❑ Dec 1996 Cover: 2.95 **NM** value: **Cover or less**
3 ❑ Feb 1997 Cover: 2.95 **NM** value: **Cover or less**
4 ❑ Apr 1997 Cover: 2.95 **NM** value: **Cover or less**
5 ❑ Jun 1997 Cover: 2.95 **NM** value: **Cover or less**
6 ❑ Aug 1997 Cover: 2.95 **NM** value: **Cover or less**
7 ❑ Oct 1997 Cover: 2.95 **NM** value: **Cover or less**
8 ❑ Jan 1998 Cover: 2.95 **NM** value: **Cover or less**

POSSIBLEMAN — Blackthorne
1 ❑ Jan 1987 Cover: 1.75 **NM** value: **Cover or less**
Revenge of the Zit Queen **A:** William Van Horn **W:** William Van Horn
2 ❑ Apr 1987 Cover: 1.75 **NM** value: **Cover or less**
Possibleman Met the Tapioca Terror **A:** William Van Horn **W:** William Van Horn

POST APOCALYPSE — Slave Labor
1 ❑ Dec 1994 Cover: 2.95 **NM** value: **Cover or less**

(POST-ATOMIC) CYBORG GERBILS — Trigon
1 ❑ Aug 1986 Cover: 2.50 **NM** value: **Cover or less**
My Darkness Consumes… **A:** John Jackson **W:** Brian P. Cuffe

POST BROTHERS — Rip Off
19 ❑ Apr 1991, b&w Cover: 2.00 **NM** value: **2.50**
• Series continued from Those Annoying Post Brothers #18
20 ❑ Jun 1991, b&w Cover: 2.50 **NM** value: **Cover or less**
21 ❑ Aug 1991, b&w Cover: 2.50 **NM** value: **Cover or less**
22 ❑ Oct 1991, b&w Cover: 2.50 **NM** value: **Cover or less**
23 ❑ Oct 1991, b&w Cover: 2.50 **NM** value: **Cover or less**
24 ❑ Dec 1991, b&w Cover: 2.50 **NM** value: **Cover or less**
25 ❑ Feb 1992, b&w Cover: 2.50 **NM** value: **Cover or less**
26 ❑ Apr 1992, b&w Cover: 2.50 **NM** value: **Cover or less**
27 ❑ Jun 1992, b&w Cover: 2.50 **NM** value: **Cover or less**
28 ❑ Aug 1992, b&w Cover: 2.50 **NM** value: **Cover or less**
29 ❑ Oct 1992, b&w Cover: 2.50 **NM** value: **Cover or less**
30 ❑ Dec 1992, b&w Cover: 2.50 **NM** value: **Cover or less**
31 ❑ Feb 1993, b&w Cover: 2.50 **NM** value: **Cover or less**
32 ❑ Apr 1993, b&w Cover: 2.50 **NM** value: **Cover or less**
33 ❑ Jun 1993, b&w Cover: 2.50 **NM** value: **Cover or less**
Distorion for All • Listed as "Those Annoying Post Brothers" **A:** Matt Howarth **W:** Matt Howarth
34 ❑ Aug 1993, b&w Cover: 2.50 **NM** value: **Cover or less**
35 ❑ Oct 1993, b&w Cover: 2.50 **NM** value: **Cover or less**
36 ❑ Dec 1993, b&w Cover: 2.50 **NM** value: **Cover or less**
37 ❑ Feb 1994, b&w Cover: 2.50 **NM** value: **Cover or less**
38 ❑ Apr 1994, b&w Cover: 2.50 **NM** value: **Cover or less**
• series continues as Those Annoying Post Bros.

POTENTIAL — Slave Labor
1 ❑ Mar 1998, b&w Cover: 3.50 **NM** value: **Cover or less**
• magazine-sized. Unit One: The Cell **A:** Ariel Schrag **W:** Ariel Schrag
2 ❑ Cover: 3.50 **NM** value: **Cover or less**
A: Ariel Schrag **W:** Ariel Schrag
3 ❑ Sep 1998 Cover: 4.95 **NM** value: **Cover or less**
Unit Three: Mechanisms of Evolution **A:** Ariel Schrag **W:** Ariel Schrag
4 ❑ Feb 1999 Cover: 3.50 **NM** value: **Cover or less**
Unit Four: Plants Form and Function **A:** Ariel Schrag **W:** Ariel Schrag

POUND, THE — Radio Comix
1 ❑ Mar 2000, b&w Cover: 2.95 **NM** value: **Cover or less**

POWDER BURN — Antarctic
1 ❑ Mar 1999, b&w Cover: 2.99 **NM** value: **Cover or less**
Circ: Diamd. preorders: **2,335**
A: Nathan Lumm **W:** Nathan Lumm
1/A ❑ Mar 1999, b&w Cover: 2.99 **NM** value: **Cover or less**
wraparound cover. **A:** Nathan Lumm **W:** Nathan Lumm
1/CS❑ Mar 1999 Cover: 5.99 **NM** value: **Cover or less**
• Collector's Set **A:** Nathan Lumm **W:** Nathan Lumm

POWER, THE — Aircel
1 ❑ Mar 1991, b&w Cover: 2.25 **NM** value: **Cover or less**
The Power, Part 1; the Power **A:** Dave Cooper **W:** Barry Blair; Dave Cooper
2 ❑ Apr 1991, b&w Cover: 2.25 **NM** value: **Cover or less**
The Power, Part 2 **A:** Dave Cooper **W:** Barry Blair; Dave Cooper
3 ❑ May 1991, b&w Cover: 2.25 **NM** value: **Cover or less**
The Power, Part 3 **A:** Dave Cooper **W:** Barry Blair; Dave Cooper
4 ❑ Jun 1991, b&w Cover: 2.25 **NM** value: **Cover or less**
The Power, Part 4 **A:** Dave Cooper **W:** Barry Blair; Dave Cooper

POWER & GLORY — Bravura / Malibu
Howard Chaykin rose to prominence with American Flagg, his creator-owned series from First Comics. Other credits include remakes of Batman and The Shadow, as well as independent series such as Midnight Men. In 1994, Malibu Comics published Chaykin's newest creator-owned series, Power & Glory, under its Bravura imprint.

Power & Glory is about a dirty government agency that experiments with humans in order to find a hero that is, "Superman with an American flag on his chest, a guy who makes Captain America look like a wimp." The problem is that the man they choose looks good as a super-hero but can't fight his way out of a paper bag. The person who trains the subject actually ends up doing the dirty work.

1LE ❑ Mar 1999 **NM** value: **3.00**
serigraph cover.
1/A ❑ Feb 1994 Cover: 2.50 **NM** value: **Cover or less**
Circ: CapCity orders: **21,450**
Alternate cover (marked). **A:** Howard Chaykin **W:** Howard Chaykin
1/B ❑ Feb 1994 Cover: 2.50 **NM** value: **Cover or less**
Alternate cover (marked). **A:** Howard Chaykin **W:** Howard Chaykin
1/LE❑ Feb 1994 **NM** value: **2.50**
serigraph cover.
1/SC❑ Feb 1994 **NM** value: **3.00**
• blue foil
2 ❑ Mar 1994 Cover: 2.50 **NM** value: **Cover or less**
Circ: CapCity orders: **15,525**
A: Howard Chaykin **W:** Howard Chaykin
3 ❑ Apr 1994 Cover: 2.50 **NM** value: **Cover or less**
Circ: CapCity orders: **16,025**
A: Howard Chaykin **W:** Howard Chaykin
4 ❑ May 1994 Cover: 2.50 **NM** value: **Cover or less**
Circ: CapCity orders: **16,575**
A: Howard Chaykin **W:** Howard Chaykin
Bk 1❑ Cover: 12.95 **NM** value: **Cover or less**
• Reprints Power & Glory #1-4 **A:** Howard Chaykin **W:** Howard Chaykin
WS 1❑ Dec 1994 Cover: 2.95 **NM** value: **Cover or less**
Circ: CapCity orders: **7,525**
• Giant-size. • Winter Special #1 **A:** Howard Chaykin **W:** Howard Chaykin

POWER BRIGADE — Moving Target / Malibu
1 ❑ Cover: 1.75 **NM** value: **Cover or less**
A: David Toledo **W:** David Toledo

POWER COMICS (ECLIPSE) — Eclipse
1 ❑ Mar 1988, b&w Cover: 2.00 **NM** value: **Cover or less**
Powerbolt; Invasion of the Robots **A:** Dave Gibbons; Brian Bolland **W:** Don Avenall; Norman Worker
2 ❑ May 1988, b&w Cover: 2.00 **NM** value: **Cover or less**
The All-Africa Wrestling Championship; The return of Dr. Crime **A:** Dave Gibbons; Brian Bolland **W:** Don Avenall; Norman Worker
3 ❑ Jul 1988, b&w Cover: 2.00 **NM** value: **Cover or less**
A: Dave Gibbons; Brian Bolland
4 ❑ Sep 1988, b&w Cover: 2.00 **NM** value: **Cover or less**
A: Dave Gibbons; Brian Bolland

POWER COMICS (HOLYOKE) — Holyoke
1 ❑ ca. 1944 Cover: 0.10 **NM** value: **1000.00**
• **CGC:** 4 graded, best 8.5
2 ❑ ca. 1944 Cover: 0.10 **NM** value: **900.00**
• **CGC:** 6 graded, best 9.4
3 ❑ ca. 1944 Cover: 0.10 **NM** value: **900.00**
• **CGC:** 6 graded, best 9.4
4 ❑ ca. 1945 Cover: 0.10 **NM** value: **900.00**
• **CGC:** 8 graded, best 9.2

POWER COMICS (POWER) — Power
1 ❑ Aug 1977 Cover: 2.00 **NM** value: **Cover or less**
• 1st Dave Sim aardvark; 1st Dave Sims aardvark ★ Origin of Nightwitch.
1-2 ❑ Cover: 2.00 **NM** value: **Cover or less**
2 ❑ Sep 1977 Cover: 2.00 **NM** value: **Cover or less**
A: Mike Gustovich ★ Origin of Cobalt Blue. ★ 1st Appearance of Cobalt Blue.
3 ❑ Oct 1977 Cover: 2.00 **NM** value: **Cover or less**
Who Serves the Gentle Lady?
4 ❑ Nov 1977 Cover: 2.00 **NM** value: **Cover or less**
5 ❑ Dec 1977 Cover: 2.00 **NM** value: **Cover or less**
A: Mike Gustovich **W:** Joe Zabel

POWER DEFENSE — Miller
1 ❑ b&w Cover: 2.50 **NM** value: **Cover or less**

POWER FACTOR (1ST SERIES) — Wonder
1 ❑ May 1986 Cover: 1.95 **NM** value: **Cover or less**
Circ: CapCity orders: **5,650**
• Wonder Color Publisher
2 ❑ Jun 1986 Cover: 1.95 **NM** value: **Cover or less**
Circ: CapCity orders: **2,725**
• Pied Piper Publisher **W:** Kevin Juaire

POWER FACTOR (2ND SERIES) — Innovation
1 ❑ Oct 1990 Cover: 1.95 **NM** value: **Cover or less**
Circ: CapCity orders: **4,175**
A Factor of One **A:** Tom Lyle; Doug Hazelwood **W:** Kevin Juaire
2 ❑ Dec 1990 Cover: 2.25 **NM** value: **Cover or less**
Circ: CapCity orders: **2,165**
W: Kevin Juaire
3 ❑ Feb 1991 Cover: 2.25 **NM** value: **Cover or less**
Circ: CapCity orders: **1,500**
W: Kevin Juaire
SE 1❑ Jan 1991 Cover: 2.75 **NM** value: **Cover or less**
Circ: CapCity orders: **2,900**
Who Runs This Town, Anyway? **A:** Scott Clark **W:** Kevin Juaire

POWER GIRL — DC
1 ❑ Jun 1988 Cover: 1.00 **NM** value: **Cover or less**
Circ: CapCity orders: **18,550**
Threads! **A:** Rick Hoberg **W:** Paul Kupperberg
2 ❑ Jul 1988 Cover: 1.00 **NM** value: **Cover or less**
Circ: CapCity orders: **14,600**
A: Rick Hoberg **W:** Paul Kupperberg
3 ❑ Aug 1988 Cover: 1.00 **NM** value: **Cover or less**
Circ: CapCity orders: **14,200**
A: Rick Hoberg **W:** Paul Kupperberg
4 ❑ Sep 1988 Cover: 1.00 **NM** value: **Cover or less**
Circ: CapCity orders: **14,500**
A: Rick Hoberg **W:** Paul Kupperberg

POWERHOUSE PEPPER COMICS — Timely
1 ❑ ca. 1943 Cover: 0.10 **NM** value: **1250.00**
• **CGC:** 3 graded, best 9.0
2 ❑ Spr 1948 Cover: 0.10 **NM** value: **750.00**
• **CGC:** 2 graded, best 7.5
3 ❑ Jul 1948 Cover: 0.10 **NM** value: **750.00**
4 ❑ Sep 1948 Cover: 0.10 **NM** value: **750.00**
• **CGC:** 1 graded, best 8.0
5 ❑ Nov 1948 Cover: 0.10 **NM** value: **750.00**
• **CGC:** 1 graded, best 7.5

POWER LINE — Marvel / Epic
1 ❑ May 1988 Cover: 1.25 **NM** value: **1.50**
Circ: CapCity orders: **19,650**
A: Dave Ross; Bill Sienkiewicz(cover) **W:** D.G. Chichester; Margaret Clark
2 ❑ Jul 1988 Cover: 1.25 **NM** value: **1.50**
Circ: CapCity orders: **14,850**
3 ❑ Sep 1988 Cover: 1.25 **NM** value: **1.50**
Circ: CapCity orders: **11,600**
4 ❑ Nov 1988 Cover: 1.50 **NM** value: **Cover or less**
Circ: CapCity orders: **9,600**
5 ❑ Jan 1989 Cover: 1.50 **NM** value: **Cover or less**
Circ: CapCity orders: **8,400**
6 ❑ Mar 1989 Cover: 1.50 **NM** value: **Cover or less**
Circ: CapCity orders: **7,400**
7 ❑ May 1989 Cover: 1.50 **NM** value: **Cover or less**
Circ: CapCity orders: **6,650**
Hidden Cargo **A:** Gray Morrow **W:** D.G. Chichester; Margaret Clark
8 ❑ Jul 1989 Cover: 1.50 **NM** value: **Cover or less**
Circ: CapCity orders: **5,950**

POWER LORDS — DC
1 ❑ Dec 1983 Cover: 1.00 **NM** value: **Cover or less**
To The Victor…The Universe! **A:** Mark Texeira **W:** Michael Fleisher ★ Origin of Power Lords. ★ 1st Appearance of Power Lords.

CGC-graded: Multiply prices above by **33 for 9.9 M • 16 for 9.8 NM/M • 7 for 9.6 NM+ • 5 for 9.4 NM • 2.5 for 9.2 NM- • 1.5 for 9.0 VF/NM**

2 ❑ Jan 1984 Cover: 1.00 **NM** value: **Cover or less**
📖 The Dimension Of Doom! **A:** Mark Texeira **W:** Michael Fleisher
3 ❑ Feb 1985 Cover: 1.00 **NM** value: **Cover or less**
📖 All Hail Arkus, Lord Of The Universe **A:** Mark Texeira **W:** Michael Fleisher

POWER MAN & IRON FIST — Marvel

Beginning its life as Hero for Hire, this series introduced Luke Cage, the bulletproof, freelance super-hero. When Cage adopted the name Power Man, the series changed to follow suit, switching with issue #17. With the introduction of Cage's partner, Iron Fist, it changed names again, becoming Power Man & Iron Fist.

Together, the two heroes ran "Heroes for Hire," an agency which sold their services to people in need. The agency suffered dramatic success, then dramatic failure-ending in the apparent death of Iron Fist in issue #125. Cage, who was blamed for the death, was forced to go into hiding. He eventually reappeared in the pages of the Punisher, and later in a new series, Cage. And, of course, Iron Fist got better.

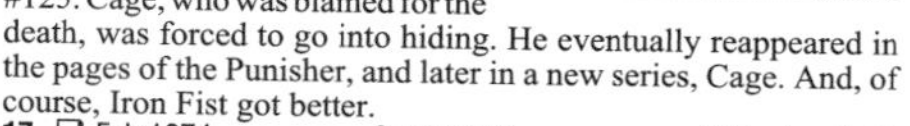

17 ❑ Feb 1974 Cover: 0.20 **NM** value: **5.00**
• **CGC:** 1 graded, best 9.0
• Title continued from "Hero For Hire" **A:** George Tuska ★ Appearance of Iron Man.
18 ❑ Apr 1974 Cover: 0.20 **NM** value: **3.00**
19 ❑ Jun 1974 Cover: 0.25 **NM** value: **3.00**
• **CGC:** 1 graded, best 9.4
20 ❑ Aug 1974 Cover: 0.25 **NM** value: **3.00**
21 ❑ Oct 1974 Cover: 0.25 **NM** value: **2.50**
★ Versus Power Man.
22 ❑ Dec 1974 Cover: 0.25 **NM** value: **2.50**
23 ❑ Feb 1975 Cover: 0.25 **NM** value: **2.50**
24 ❑ Apr 1975 Cover: 0.25 **NM** value: **2.50**
★ 1st Appearance of Black Goliath. ★ Versus Circus of Crime.
25 ❑ Jun 1975 Cover: 0.25 **NM** value: **2.50**
★ Versus Circus of Crime.
26 ❑ Aug 1975 Cover: 0.25 **NM** value: **2.50**
27 ❑ Oct 1975 Cover: 0.25 **NM** value: **2.50**
A: George Pérez
28 ❑ Dec 1975 Cover: 0.25 **NM** value: **2.50**
29 ❑ Feb 1976 Cover: 0.25 **NM** value: **2.50**
30 ❑ Apr 1976 Cover: 0.25 **NM** value: **2.50**
31 ❑ May 1976 Cover: 0.25 **NM** value: **2.50**
A: Neal Adams
32 ❑ Jun 1976 Cover: 0.25 **NM** value: **2.00**
33 ❑ Jul 1976 Cover: 0.25 **NM** value: **2.00**
34 ❑ Aug 1976 Cover: 0.25 **NM** value: **2.00**
35 ❑ Sep 1976 Cover: 0.30 **NM** value: **2.00**
36 ❑ Oct 1976 Cover: 0.30 **NM** value: **2.00**
37 ❑ Nov 1976 Cover: 0.30 **NM** value: **2.00**
★ 1st Appearance of Chemistro II (Archibald "Arch" Morton).
38 ❑ Dec 1976 Cover: 0.30 **NM** value: **2.00**
39 ❑ Jan 1977 Cover: 0.30 **NM** value: **2.00**
40 ❑ Feb 1977 Cover: 0.30 **NM** value: **2.00**
41 ❑ Mar 1977 Cover: 0.30 **NM** value: **2.00**
★ 1st Appearance of Thunderbolt (William Carver as...).
42 ❑ Apr 1977 Cover: 0.30 **NM** value: **2.00**
43 ❑ May 1977 Cover: 0.30 **NM** value: **2.00**
44 ❑ Jun 1977 Cover: 0.30 **NM** value: **2.00**
45 ❑ Jul 1977 Cover: 0.30 **NM** value: **2.00**
A: Jim Starlin ★ Appearance of Mace.
46 ❑ Aug 1977 Cover: 0.30 **NM** value: **2.00**
A: George Tuska ★ 1st Appearance of Zzax.
47 ❑ Oct 1977 Cover: 0.30 **NM** value: **2.00**
A: Barry Windsor-Smith ★ Appearance of Iron Fist.
48 ❑ Dec 1977 Cover: 0.35 **NM** value: **2.00**
• **CGC:** 1 graded, best 8.0
A: John Byrne ★ 1st Appearance of Power Man and Iron Fist.
49 ❑ Feb 1978 Cover: 0.35 **NM** value: **2.00**
• series continues as Power Man & Iron Fist **A:** John Byrne ★ Appearance of Iron Fist.
50 ❑ Apr 1978 Cover: 0.35 **NM** value: **2.00**
• **CGC:** 1 graded, best 9.2
A: John Byrne
51 ❑ Jun 1978 Cover: 0.35 **NM** value: **1.50**
52 ❑ Aug 1978 Cover: 0.35 **NM** value: **1.50**
53 ❑ Oct 1978 Cover: 0.35 **NM** value: **1.50**
★ Origin of Nightshade.
54 ❑ Dec 1978 Cover: 0.35 **NM** value: **1.50**
★ Origin of Iron Fist.
55 ❑ Feb 1979 Cover: 0.35 **NM** value: **1.50**
56 ❑ Apr 1979 Cover: 0.35 **NM** value: **1.50**
★ Origin of Señor Suerte II (Jaime Garcia). ★ 1st Appearance of Señor Suerte II (Jaime Garcia).
57 ❑ Jun 1979 Cover: 0.40 **NM** value: **2.50**
• **CGC:** 4 graded, best 9.8
★ Appearance of X-Men.
58 ❑ Aug 1979 Cover: 0.40 **NM** value: **1.50**
★ 1st Appearance of El Aguila.
59 ❑ Oct 1979 Cover: 0.40 **NM** value: **1.50**
A: Bob Layton
60 ❑ Dec 1979 Cover: 0.40 **NM** value: **1.50**
A: Bob Layton
61 ❑ Feb 1980 Cover: 0.40 **NM** value: **1.00**
Circ: Statement: **107,231**
A: Bob Layton
62 ❑ Apr 1980 Cover: 0.40 **NM** value: **1.00**
Circ: Statement: **107,231**
A: Bob Layton ★ Death of Thunderbolt.
63 ❑ Jun 1980 Cover: 0.40 **NM** value: **1.00**
Circ: Statement: **107,231**
A: Bob Layton
64 ❑ Aug 1980 Cover: 0.40 **NM** value: **1.00**
Circ: Statement: **107,231**
A: Bob Layton
65 ❑ Oct 1980 Cover: 0.50 **NM** value: **1.00**
Circ: Statement: **107,231**
A: Bob Layton ★ Versus El Aguila.
66 ❑ Dec 1980 Cover: 0.50 **NM** value: **12.00**
Circ: Statement: **107,231** • **CGC:** 12 graded, best 9.6
A: Frank Miller(cover) **C:** Frank Miller ★ 2nd Appearance of Sabretooth. ★ 2nd Appearance of Sabretooth.
67 ❑ Feb 1981 Cover: 0.50 **NM** value: **1.00**
Circ: Statement: **106,168**
A: Frank Miller(cover)
68 ❑ Apr 1981 Cover: 0.50 **NM** value: **1.00**
Circ: Statement: **106,168**
• Has 1980 Statement; avg print run 232,798; avg sales 105,414; avg subs 1,817; avg total paid 107,231 **A:** Frank Miller **C:** Frank Miller
69 ❑ May 1981 Cover: 0.50 **NM** value: **1.00**
Circ: Statement: **106,168**
70 ❑ Jun 1981 Cover: 0.50 **NM** value: **1.00**
Circ: Statement: **106,168**
A: Frank Miller(cover) **C:** Frank Miller ★ Origin of Colleen Wing.
71 ❑ Jul 1981 Cover: 0.50 **NM** value: **1.00**
Circ: Statement: **106,168**
A: Frank Miller(cover) **C:** Frank Miller
72 ❑ Aug 1981 Cover: 0.50 **NM** value: **1.00**
Circ: Statement: **106,168**
A: Frank Miller(cover) **C:** Frank Miller
73 ❑ Sep 1981 Cover: 0.50 **NM** value: **1.00**
Circ: Statement: **106,168**
A: Frank Miller(cover) **C:** Frank Miller ★ Appearance of ROM.
74 ❑ Oct 1981 Cover: 0.50 **NM** value: **1.00**
Circ: Statement: **106,168**
C: Frank Miller
75 ❑ Nov 1981 Cover: 0.75 **NM** value: **1.00**
Circ: Statement: **106,168**
• origins
76 ❑ Dec 1981 Cover: 0.50 **NM** value: **1.00**
Circ: Statement: **106,168**
A: Frank Miller
77 ❑ Jan 1982 Cover: 0.60 **NM** value: **1.00**
Circ: Statement: **118,020**
★ Appearance of Daredevil.
78 ❑ Feb 1982 Cover: 0.60 **NM** value: **6.00**
Circ: Statement: **118,020** • **CGC:** 4 graded, best 9.6
★ Appearance of Sabretooth. ★ Versus El Aguila.
79 ❑ Mar 1982 Cover: 0.60 **NM** value: **1.00**
Circ: Statement: **118,020**
80 ❑ Apr 1982 Cover: 0.60 **NM** value: **1.00**
Circ: Statement: **118,020**
• Has 1981 Statement; avg print run 239,079; avg sales 103,899; avg subs 2,269; avg total paid 106,168 **A:** Frank Miller(cover) ★ Versus Montenegro.
81 ❑ May 1982 Cover: 0.60 **NM** value: **1.00**
Circ: Statement: **118,020**
82 ❑ Jun 1982 Cover: 0.60 **NM** value: **1.00**
Circ: Statement: **118,020**
83 ❑ Jul 1982 Cover: 0.60 **NM** value: **1.00**
Circ: Statement: **118,020**
84 ❑ Aug 1982 Cover: 0.60 **NM** value: **5.00**
Circ: Statement: **118,020** • **CGC:** 13 graded, best 9.8
★ Appearance of Sabretooth.
85 ❑ Sep 1982 Cover: 0.60 **NM** value: **1.00**
Circ: Statement: **118,020**
86 ❑ Oct 1982 Cover: 0.60 **NM** value: **1.00**
Circ: Statement: **118,020**
★ Appearance of Moon Knight.
87 ❑ Nov 1982 Cover: 0.60 **NM** value: **1.00**
Circ: Statement: **118,020**
★ Appearance of Moon Knight.
88 ❑ Dec 1982 Cover: 0.60 **NM** value: **1.00**
Circ: Statement: **118,020**
89 ❑ Jan 1983 Cover: 0.60 **NM** value: **1.00**
Circ: Statement: **116,561**
90 ❑ Feb 1983 Cover: 0.60 **NM** value: **1.00**
Circ: Statement: **116,561**
W: Kurt Busiek ★ Appearance of Unus the Untouchable. ★ Versus Unus.
91 ❑ Mar 1983 Cover: 0.60 **NM** value: **1.00**
Circ: Statement: **116,561**
92 ❑ Apr 1983 Cover: 0.60 **NM** value: **1.00**
Circ: Statement: **116,561**
• Has 1982 Statement; avg print run 240,942; avg sales 115,371; avg subs 2,649; avg total paid 118,020 **W:** Kurt Busiek ★ 1st Appearance of Eel II (Edward Lavell). ★ Versus Hammerhead.
93 ❑ May 1983 Cover: 0.60 **NM** value: **1.00**
Circ: Statement: **116,561**
W: Kurt Busiek ★ Versus Chemistro.
94 ❑ Jun 1983 Cover: 0.60 **NM** value: **1.00**
Circ: Statement: **116,561**
W: Kurt Busiek ★ 1st Appearance of Chemistro III (Calvin Carr).
95 ❑ Jul 1983 Cover: 0.60 **NM** value: **1.00**
Circ: Statement: **116,561**
W: Kurt Busiek
96 ❑ Aug 1983 Cover: 0.60 **NM** value: **1.00**
Circ: Statement: **116,561**
W: Kurt Busiek ★ Versus Chemistro.
97 ❑ Sep 1983 Cover: 0.60 **NM** value: **1.00**
Circ: Statement: **116,561**
W: Kurt Busiek ★ Versus Fera.
98 ❑ Oct 1983 Cover: 0.60 **NM** value: **1.00**
Circ: Statement: **116,561**
W: Kurt Busiek
99 ❑ Nov 1983 Cover: 0.60 **NM** value: **1.00**
Circ: Statement: **116,561**
W: Kurt Busiek ★ Versus Fera.
100 ❑ Dec 1983 Cover: 1.00 **NM** value: **Cover or less**
Circ: Statement: **116,561**
• Giant-size. **W:** Kurt Busiek ★ Versus Khan.
101 ❑ Jan 1984 Cover: 0.60 **NM** value: **1.00**
Circ: Statement: **115,734**
102 ❑ Feb 1984 Cover: 0.60 **NM** value: **1.00**
Circ: Statement: **115,734**
W: Kurt Busiek
103 ❑ Mar 1984 Cover: 0.60 **NM** value: **1.00**
Circ: Statement: **115,734**
104 ❑ Apr 1984 Cover: 0.60 **NM** value: **1.00**
Circ: Statement: **115,734**
105 ❑ May 1984 Cover: 0.60 **NM** value: **1.00**
Circ: Statement: **115,734**
W: Kurt Busiek
106 ❑ Jun 1984 Cover: 0.60 **NM** value: **1.00**
Circ: Statement: **115,734**
107 ❑ Jul 1984 Cover: 0.60 **NM** value: **1.00**
Circ: Statement: **115,734**
108 ❑ Aug 1984 Cover: 0.60 **NM** value: **1.00**
Circ: Statement: **115,734**
109 ❑ Sep 1984 Cover: 0.60 **NM** value: **1.00**
Circ: Statement: **115,734**
★ Versus Reaper.
110 ❑ Oct 1984 Cover: 0.60 **NM** value: **1.00**
Circ: Statement: **115,734**
111 ❑ Nov 1984 Cover: 0.60 **NM** value: **1.00**
Circ: Statement: **115,734**
112 ❑ Dec 1984 Cover: 0.60 **NM** value: **1.00**
Circ: Statement: **115,734**
113 ❑ Jan 1985 Cover: 0.60 **NM** value: **1.00**
Circ: Statement: **102,109**
★ Death of Solarr.
114 ❑ Feb 1985 Cover: 0.60 **NM** value: **1.00**
Circ: Statement: **102,109**
115 ❑ Mar 1985 Cover: 0.60 **NM** value: **1.00**
Circ: Statement: **102,109**
116 ❑ Apr 1985 Cover: 0.65 **NM** value: **1.00**
Circ: Statement: **102,109**
117 ❑ May 1985 Cover: 0.65 **NM** value: **1.00**
Circ: Statement: **102,109** CapCity orders: **6,500**
118 ❑ Jul 1985 Cover: 0.65 **NM** value: **1.00**
Circ: Statement: **102,109** CapCity orders: **6,800**
119 ❑ Sep 1985 Cover: 0.65 **NM** value: **1.00**
Circ: Statement: **102,109** CapCity orders: **7,000**
120 ❑ Nov 1985 Cover: 0.65 **NM** value: **1.00**
Circ: Statement: **102,109** CapCity orders: **7,100**
121 ❑ Jan 1986 Cover: 0.65 **NM** value: **1.00**
Circ: CapCity orders: **15,000**
• Secret Wars II
122 ❑ Mar 1986 Cover: 0.75 **NM** value: **1.00**
Circ: CapCity orders: **9,400**
123 ❑ May 1986 Cover: 0.75 **NM** value: **1.00**
Circ: CapCity orders: **8,400**
124 ❑ Jul 1986 Cover: 0.75 **NM** value: **1.00**
Circ: CapCity orders: **8,300**
125 ❑ Sep 1986 Cover: 1.25 **NM** value: **2.50**
Circ: CapCity orders: **9,200**
★ Death of Iron Fist (H'yithri double).
Anl 1 ❑ Jan 1976 Cover: 0.50 **NM** value: **3.50**
• **CGC:** 2 graded, best 7.0
GS 1 ❑ ca. 1975 Cover: 0.50 **NM** value: **4.00**

POWER OF IRON MAN, THE — Marvel

Bk 1 ❑ Cover: 6.95 **NM** value: **Cover or less**

POWER OF PRIME — Malibu / Ultraverse

1 ❑ Jul 1995 Cover: 2.50 **NM** value: **Cover or less**
📖 Primal Mysteries • story continues in Prime #25 and #26 **A:** Mark Pacella **W:** Gerard Jones; Len Strazewski ★ Origin of Prime.
2 ❑ Aug 1995 Cover: 2.50 **NM** value: **Cover or less**
A: Mark Pacella **W:** Gerard Jones; Len Strazewski ★ Origin of Prime.
3 ❑ Sep 1995 Cover: 2.50 **NM** value: **Cover or less**
A: Mark Pacella **W:** Gerard Jones; Len Strazewski ★ Origin of Prime.
4 ❑ Nov 1995 Cover: 2.50 **NM** value: **Cover or less**
A: Mark Pacella **W:** Gerard Jones; Len Strazewski ★ Origin of Prime.

POWER OF SHAZAM, THE — DC

In 1995, Jerry Ordway brought the character of Shazam back into the mainstream DC universe with his award-winning Power of Shazam graphic novel. As the monthly series begins, it has been four years since the homeless orphan Billy Batson first learned the magic word that would turn him into the World's Mightiest Mortal. During this time, he's been trying to make it through school while living by himself, and periodically saving the world.

When Batson was given the role of Captain Marvel by the old wizard Shazam on the Rock of Eternity, it was considered a sacred duty. But now, Billy's having a hard time holding his many lives together.

As the series progressed, Cap was joined by his sister Mary and fellow orphan Freddy Freeman, who initially took on the mantle of Captain Marvel Jr. until he realized that he couldn't even say his own name, so shortened it to CM3.

1 ❑ Mar 1995 Cover: 1.50 **NM** value: **3.00**

Other grades: Multiply prices above by **1.5 for Mint • 2/3 for Very Fine • 1/3 for Fine • 1/5 for Very Good • 1/8 for Good**

Circ: CapCity orders: **25,050** • **CGC:** 6 graded, best 9.8
📖 Things Change **A:** Peter Krause; Mike Manley **W:** Jerry Ordway

2 ❑ Apr 1995 Cover: 1.50 **NM** value: **2.00**
Circ: CapCity orders: **17,550**
W: Jerry Ordway ★ Versus Arson Fiend.

3 ❑ May 1995 Cover: 1.75 **NM** value: **2.00**
Circ: CapCity orders: **15,500**
W: Jerry Ordway

4 ❑ Jun 1995 Cover: 1.75 **NM** value: **2.00**
Circ: CapCity orders: **15,575**
📖 Family Values • Return of Mary Marvel, Tawky Tawny **A:** Peter Krause **W:** Jerry Ordway

5 ❑ Jul 1995 Cover: 1.75 **NM** value: **2.00**
Circ: CapCity orders: **14,400**
W: Jerry Ordway

6 ❑ Aug 1995 Cover: 1.75 **NM** value: **2.00**
Circ: CapCity orders: **13,150**
• Return of Captain Nazi; Freddy Freeman and grandfather injured **W:** Jerry Ordway

7 ❑ Sep 1995 Cover: 1.75 **NM** value: **2.00**
Circ: CapCity orders: **12,250**
• Return of Captain Marvel Jr. **W:** Jerry Ordway

8 ❑ Oct 1995 Cover: 1.75 **NM** value: **2.00**
Circ: CapCity orders: **10,175**
A: Curt Swan **W:** Jerry Ordway ★ Appearance of Minuteman, Bulletman, Spy Smasher.

9 ❑ Nov 1995 Cover: 1.75 **NM** value: **2.00**
W: Jerry Ordway

10 ❑ Dec 1995 Cover: 1.75 **NM** value: **2.00**
W: Jerry Ordway ★ Origin of Satanus, Blaze, Black Adam, Rock of Eternity, Shazam.

11 ❑ Jan 1996 Cover: 1.75 **NM** value: **Cover or less**
• Return of Ibis; Return of Uncle Marvel; Return of Marvel Family; Return of Ibis, Uncle Marvel, Marvel Family **W:** Jerry Ordway ★ Appearance of Bulletman.

12 ❑ Feb 1996 Cover: 1.75 **NM** value: **Cover or less**
📖 End Game **A:** Peter Krause **W:** Jerry Ordway ★ Origin of Seven Deadly Foes of Man.

13 ❑ Mar 1996 Cover: 1.75 **NM** value: **Cover or less**
📖 The Worm Turns **A:** Peter Krause **W:** Jerry Ordway

14 ❑ Apr 1996 Cover: 1.75 **NM** value: **Cover or less**
📖 Chain Lightning • Captain Marvel Jr. solo story **A:** Gil Kane **W:** Jerry Ordway ★ 1st Appearance of Chain Lightning.

15 ❑ Jun 1996 Cover: 1.75 **NM** value: **Cover or less**
W: Jerry Ordway

16 ❑ Jul 1996 Cover: 1.75 **NM** value: **Cover or less**
W: Jerry Ordway

17 ❑ Aug 1996 Cover: 1.75 **NM** value: **Cover or less**
W: Jerry Ordway

18 ❑ Sep 1996 Cover: 1.75 **NM** value: **Cover or less**
W: Jerry Ordway

19 ❑ Oct 1996 Cover: 1.75 **NM** value: **Cover or less**
📖 The Wall • Captain Marvel Jr. vs. Captain Nazi **A:** Gil Kane; Joe Staton **W:** Jerry Ordway ★ Appearance of Minuteman.

20 ❑ Nov 1996 Cover: 1.75 **NM** value: **Cover or less**
Circ: Diamd. preorders: **31,221**
📖 Shelter from the Storm • Final Night **A:** Peter Krause **W:** Jerry Ordway ★ Appearance of Superman.

21 ❑ Dec 1996 Cover: 1.75 **NM** value: **Cover or less**
Circ: Diamd. preorders: **24,197**
📖 The Big Rubout! **A:** Peter Krause **W:** Jerry Ordway ★ Appearance of Plastic Man.

22 ❑ Jan 1997 Cover: 1.75 **NM** value: **Cover or less**
Circ: Diamd. preorders: **26,209**
📖 Of Shadows and Fog… **A:** Peter Krause **W:** Jerry Ordway ★ Appearance of Batman.

23 ❑ Feb 1997 Cover: 1.75 **NM** value: **Cover or less**
Circ: Diamd. preorders: **22,834**
📖 Child of the Atom **A:** Peter Krause **W:** Jerry Ordway ★ Versus Mr. Atom.

24 ❑ Mar 1997 Cover: 1.75 **NM** value: **Cover or less**
Circ: Diamd. preorders: **22,209**
📖 The Trail of the Scorpion **A:** Peter Krause **W:** Jerry Ordway ★ Appearance of C.C. Batson, Baron Blitzkrieg, Spy Smasher.

25 ❑ Apr 1997 Cover: 1.75 **NM** value: **Cover or less**
Circ: Diamd. preorders: **21,102**
• C.C. Batson as Captain Marvel ★ Versus Ibac.

26 ❑ May 1997 Cover: 1.75 **NM** value: **Cover or less**
Circ: Diamd. preorders: **20,796**
• Shazam attempts to set time right again

27 ❑ Jun 1997 Cover: 1.75 **NM** value: **Cover or less**
Circ: Diamd. preorders: **21,687**
• time is restored to proper course ★ Appearance of Waverider.

28 ❑ Jul 1997 Cover: 1.75 **NM** value: **Cover or less**
Circ: Diamd. preorders: **20,931**

29 ❑ Aug 1997 Cover: 1.75 **NM** value: **Cover or less**
Circ: Diamd. preorders: **20,866**
★ Appearance of Hoppy the Marvel Bunny.

30 ❑ Sep 1997 Cover: 1.75 **NM** value: **Cover or less**
Circ: Diamd. preorders: **20,051**
• Mary receives new costume ★ Versus Mr. Finish.

31 ❑ Oct 1997 Cover: 1.75 **NM** value: **1.95**
Circ: Diamd. preorders: **22,639**
• Genesis; Billy and Mary reveal their identities to the Bromfields

32 ❑ Nov 1997 Cover: 1.95 **NM** value: **Cover or less**
Circ: Diamd. preorders: **19,737**
★ 1st Appearance of Windshear.

33 ❑ Dec 1997 Cover: 1.95 **NM** value: **Cover or less**
Circ: Diamd. preorders: **19,920**
Face cover. **A:** Peter Krause **W:** Jerry Ordway

34 ❑ Jan 1998 Cover: 1.95 **NM** value: **Cover or less**
Circ: Diamd. preorders: **19,191**
📖 With Friends Like These… **A:** Peter Krause **W:** Jerry Ordway ★ Appearance of Gangbuster.

35 ❑ Feb 1998 Cover: 1.95 **NM** value: **Cover or less**
Circ: Diamd. preorders: **25,792**
📖 Lightning and Stars, Part 2 • continues in Starman #40 ★ Appearance of Starman.

36 ❑ Mar 1998 Cover: 1.95 **NM** value: **Cover or less**
Circ: Diamd. preorders: **25,048**
📖 Lightning and Stars, Part 4 ★ Appearance of Starman.

37 ❑ Apr 1998 Cover: 1.95 **NM** value: **Cover or less**
Circ: Diamd. preorders: **18,212**
📖 CM3 • CM3 vs. Doctor Morpheus; CM3 vs. Dr. Morpheus **A:** Mike Manley **W:** Jerry Ordway

38 ❑ May 1998 Cover: 1.95 **NM** value: **Cover or less**
Circ: Diamd. preorders: **19,586**
📖 The Monster Society of Evil!, Part 1

39 ❑ Jun 1998 Cover: 1.95 **NM** value: **Cover or less**
Circ: Diamd. preorders: **19,601**
📖 The Monster Society of Evil!, Part 2

40 ❑ Jul 1998 Cover: 1.95 **NM** value: **Cover or less**
Circ: Diamd. preorders: **17,978**
📖 The Monster Society of Evil!, Part 3

41 ❑ Aug 1998 Cover: 1.95 **NM** value: **Cover or less**
Circ: Diamd. preorders: **19,525**
📖 The Monster Society of Evil!, Part 4 ★ Death of Mr. Mind.

42 ❑ Sep 1998 Cover: 2.50 **NM** value: **Cover or less**
Circ: Diamd. preorders: **18,395**
★ Appearance of Chain Lightning.

43 ❑ Oct 1998 Cover: 2.50 **NM** value: **Cover or less**
Circ: Diamd. preorders: **17,652**
• kids on life support

44 ❑ Dec 1998 Cover: 2.50 **NM** value: **Cover or less**
Circ: Diamd. preorders: **16,817**
★ Appearance of Black Adam, Thunder.

45 ❑ Jan 1999 Cover: 2.50 **NM** value: **Cover or less**
Circ: Diamd. preorders: **18,421**
★ Appearance of Justice League of America.

46 ❑ Feb 1999 Cover: 2.50 **NM** value: **Cover or less**
Circ: Diamd. preorders: **18,112**
A: Jerry Ordway **W:** Jerry Ordway ★ Appearance of Superman, Black Adam. ★ Versus Superman.

47 ❑ Mar 1999 Cover: 2.50 **NM** value: **Cover or less**
Circ: Diamd. preorders: **17,297**
final issue. **A:** Jerry Ordway **W:** Jerry Ordway ★ Appearance of Black Adam.

1000000 ❑ Nov 1998 Cover: 2.50 **NM** value: **Cover or less**
Circ: Diamd. preorders: **27,224**
📖 Between the Rock and a Hot Place **A:** Jerry Ordway **W:** Jerry Ordway

Anl 1 ❑ ca. 1996 Cover: 2.95 **NM** value: **Cover or less**
📖 Legends of the Dead Earth; True Believers • 1996; Legends of the Dead Earth **A:** Mike Manley **W:** Jerry Ordway

Bk 1 ❑ Cover: 9.95 **NM** value: **Cover or less**
A: Jerry Ordway **W:** Jerry Ordway

Bk 1/HC ❑ Cover: 19.95 **NM** value: **Cover or less**
Circ: CapCity orders: **4,960**
• Hardcover edition. **A:** Jerry Ordway **W:** Jerry Ordway

POWER OF STRONG MAN — AC

1 ❑ b&w Cover: 2.50 **NM** value: **Cover or less**

POWER OF THE ATOM — DC

At the end of his adventure in Sword of the Atom, Palmer escaped the police in South America by beaming himself through a phone line. This old trick, which he hadn't tried in several years, went horribly awry. He literally burst through the phone at his old residence in America, but his costume vanished, and he was only able to reach the height of three feet before losing control of his power. He theorized that the new technology of microwave transmission had altered his structure as he beamed through the international communications satellite.

As bad as this was, an altered physical structure and the loss of his powers were not Palmer's only problems. His wife had left him just as he left for South America, and currently believed him to be dead; the house he had once owned with her had been sold; and now his old "friends" at the CIA had learned that he was back in town, and were anxious to renew their acquaintance with the new Atom.

1 ❑ Aug 1988 Cover: 1.00 **NM** value: **Cover or less**
Circ: CapCity orders: **18,700**
📖 Home Is The Hero **A:** Dwayne Turner **W:** Roger Stern

2 ❑ Sep 1988 Cover: 1.00 **NM** value: **Cover or less**
Circ: CapCity orders: **14,850**

3 ❑ Oct 1988 Cover: 1.00 **NM** value: **Cover or less**
Circ: CapCity orders: **14,350**
★ Versus Strobe.

4 ❑ Nov 1988 Cover: 1.00 **NM** value: **Cover or less**
Circ: CapCity orders: **14,800**
• Bonus Book #8

5 ❑ Dec 1988 Cover: 1.00 **NM** value: **Cover or less**
Circ: CapCity orders: **14,100**
★ Appearance of Elongated Man.

6 ❑ Win 1988 Cover: 1.00 **NM** value: **Cover or less**
Circ: CapCity orders: **13,150**
★ Versus Chronos.

7 ❑ Hol 1988 Cover: 1.00 **NM** value: **Cover or less**
Circ: CapCity orders: **14,700**
• Invasion!

8 ❑ Jan 1989 Cover: 1.00 **NM** value: **Cover or less**
Circ: CapCity orders: **13,200**
• Invasion!

9 ❑ Feb 1989 Cover: 1.00 **NM** value: **Cover or less**
Circ: CapCity orders: **12,150**
★ Appearance of Justice League International.

10 ❑ Mar 1989 Cover: 1.00 **NM** value: **Cover or less**
Circ: CapCity orders: **11,300**
★ Versus Humbug.

11 ❑ Apr 1989 Cover: 1.00 **NM** value: **Cover or less**
Circ: CapCity orders: **11,200**

12 ❑ May 1989 Cover: 1.00 **NM** value: **Cover or less**
Circ: CapCity orders: **11,200**

13 ❑ Jun 1989 Cover: 1.00 **NM** value: **Cover or less**
Circ: CapCity orders: **10,950**

14 ❑ Jul 1989 Cover: 1.00 **NM** value: **Cover or less**
Circ: CapCity orders: **10,750**
★ Versus Humbug.

15 ❑ Aug 1989 Cover: 1.00 **NM** value: **Cover or less**
Circ: CapCity orders: **10,350**

16 ❑ Sep 1989 Cover: 1.00 **NM** value: **Cover or less**
Circ: CapCity orders: **10,150**

17 ❑ Oct 1989 Cover: 1.00 **NM** value: **Cover or less**
Circ: CapCity orders: **9,700**

18 ❑ Nov 1989 Cover: 1.00 **NM** value: **Cover or less**
Circ: CapCity orders: **9,400**

POWER PACHYDERMS — Marvel

1 ❑ ca. 1988 Cover: 1.25 **NM** value: **Cover or less**
Circ: CapCity orders: **14,600**
• one-shot parody **A:** Adam Blaustein **W:** Roger Stern

POWER PACK — Marvel

Dr. Jim Powers was a scientist who was on the verge of making an extraordinary breakthrough — a working matter/anti-matter engine. But his discovery was of interest to more people than he knew: The Z'Nrx, an alien race, hoped to steal the secrets from him to power their own galactic warships. And another had landed on Earth, hoping to warn him.

In desperation, the alien who had come to warn Powers bestowed his abilities on Powers' four children. With their newfound talents, they helped beat back the alien attack. Now the four Powers children fight as Power Pack, Marvel's youngest super-group.

A valiant attempt to create a super-hero series for children, Power Pack did manage to win some fervent supporters, even if it never really found acceptance with Marvel's main audience.

1 ❑ Aug 1984 Cover: 1.00 **NM** value: **2.00**
• **CGC:** 1 graded, best 9.0
• Giant-size. ★ Origin of Mass Master, Power Pack, Lightspeed. ★ 1st Appearance of Mass Master, Power Pack, Lightspeed. ★ Versus Snarks.

2 ❑ Sep 1984 Cover: 0.60 **NM** value: **1.50**
3 ❑ Oct 1984 Cover: 0.60 **NM** value: **1.00**
4 ❑ Nov 1984 Cover: 0.60 **NM** value: **1.00**
5 ❑ Dec 1984 Cover: 0.60 **NM** value: **1.00**
6 ❑ Jan 1985 Cover: 0.60 **NM** value: **1.00**
★ Appearance of Spider-Man.

7 ❑ Feb 1985 Cover: 0.60 **NM** value: **1.00**
★ Appearance of Cloak & Dagger.

8 ❑ Mar 1985 Cover: 0.60 **NM** value: **1.00**
★ Appearance of Cloak & Dagger.

9 ❑ Apr 1985 Cover: 0.65 **NM** value: **1.00**
A: Brent Anderson

10 ❑ May 1985 Cover: 0.65 **NM** value: **1.00**
Circ: CapCity orders: **14,000**
A: Brent Anderson

11 ❑ Jun 1985 Cover: 0.65 **NM** value: **1.00**
Circ: CapCity orders: **13,000**

12 ❑ Jul 1985 Cover: 0.65 **NM** value: **1.00**
Circ: CapCity orders: **16,300**
★ Appearance of X-Men.

13 ❑ Aug 1985 Cover: 0.65 **NM** value: **1.00**
Circ: CapCity orders: **11,800**
A: Brent Anderson

14 ❑ Sep 1985 Cover: 0.65 **NM** value: **1.00**
Circ: CapCity orders: **11,400**

15 ❑ Oct 1985 Cover: 0.65 **NM** value: **1.00**
Circ: CapCity orders: **12,800**

16 ❑ Nov 1985 Cover: 0.65 **NM** value: **1.00**
Circ: CapCity orders: **12,200**
★ 1st Appearance of Kofi.

17 ❑ Dec 1985 Cover: 0.65 **NM** value: **1.00**
Circ: CapCity orders: **12,500**

18 ❑ Jan 1986 Cover: 0.65 **NM** value: **1.00**
Circ: Statement: **121,761** CapCity orders: **19,100**
📖 Secret Wars II • Secret Wars II **A:** Brent Anderson

19 ❑ Feb 1986 Cover: 1.25 **NM** value: **1.50**
Circ: Statement: **121,761** CapCity orders: **17,100**
• Giant-size. **A:** Brent Anderson ★ Appearance of Wolverine.

20 ❑ Mar 1986 Cover: 0.75 **NM** value: **1.00**
Circ: Statement: **121,761** CapCity orders: **16,100**
★ Appearance of New Mutants.

21 ❑ Apr 1986 Cover: 0.75 **NM** value: **1.00**
Circ: Statement: **121,761** CapCity orders: **16,300**
A: Brent Anderson

22 ❑ May 1986 Cover: 0.75 **NM** value: **1.00**
Circ: Statement: **121,761** CapCity orders: **15,400**

23 ❑ Jun 1986 Cover: 0.75 **NM** value: **1.00**
Circ: Statement: **121,761** CapCity orders: **15,700**

24 ❑ Jul 1986 Cover: 0.75 **NM** value: **1.00**
Circ: Statement: **121,761** CapCity orders: **14,300**

25 ❑ Aug 1986 Cover: 1.25 **NM** value: **Cover or less**
Circ: Statement: **121,761** CapCity orders: **15,200**

26 ❑ Oct 1986 Cover: 1.00 **NM** value: **Cover or less**
Circ: Statement: **121,761** CapCity orders: **14,900**
★ Appearance of Cloak & Dagger.

CGC-graded: Multiply prices above by **33 for 9.9 M • 16 for 9.8 NM/M • 7 for 9.6 NM+ • 5 for 9.4 NM • 2.5 for 9.2 NM- • 1.5 for 9.0 VF/NM**

27 ❑ Dec 1986 Cover: 1.00 **NM** value: **1.50**
Circ: Statement: **121,761** CapCity orders: **24,100**
📖 Mutant Massacre • Mutant Massacre ★ Appearance of Wolverine, Sabretooth.

28 ❑ Feb 1987 Cover: 1.00 **NM** value: **Cover or less**
Circ: Statement: **103,150** CapCity orders: **17,300**
★ Appearance of Fantastic Four, Avengers.

29 ❑ Apr 1987 Cover: 1.00 **NM** value: **Cover or less**
Circ: Statement: **103,150** CapCity orders: **20,500**
• Giant-size. ★ Appearance of Hobgoblin, Spider-Man.

30 ❑ Jun 1987 Cover: 1.00 **NM** value: **Cover or less**
Circ: Statement: **103,150** CapCity orders: **17,900**

31 ❑ Aug 1987 Cover: 1.00 **NM** value: **Cover or less**
Circ: Statement: **103,150** CapCity orders: **16,900**
★ 1st Appearance of Trash.

32 ❑ Oct 1987 Cover: 1.00 **NM** value: **Cover or less**
Circ: Statement: **103,150** CapCity orders: **17,400**

33 ❑ Nov 1987 Cover: 1.00 **NM** value: **Cover or less**
Circ: Statement: **103,150** CapCity orders: **16,900**

34 ❑ Jan 1988 Cover: 1.00 **NM** value: **Cover or less**
Circ: Statement: **76,100** CapCity orders: **15,100**

35 ❑ Feb 1988 Cover: 1.00 **NM** value: **Cover or less**
Circ: Statement: **76,100** CapCity orders: **21,200**
• Fall of Mutants

36 ❑ Apr 1988 Cover: 1.00 **NM** value: **Cover or less**
Circ: Statement: **76,100** CapCity orders: **16,700**

37 ❑ May 1988 Cover: 1.00 **NM** value: **Cover or less**
Circ: Statement: **76,100** CapCity orders: **15,450**

38 ❑ Jul 1988 Cover: 1.00 **NM** value: **Cover or less**
Circ: Statement: **76,100** CapCity orders: **15,150**

39 ❑ Aug 1988 Cover: 1.25 **NM** value: **Cover or less**
Circ: Statement: **76,100** CapCity orders: **15,000**

40 ❑ Sep 1988 Cover: 1.25 **NM** value: **Cover or less**
Circ: Statement: **76,100** CapCity orders: **15,400**

41 ❑ Nov 1988 Cover: 1.25 **NM** value: **Cover or less**
Circ: Statement: **76,100** CapCity orders: **13,200**

42 ❑ Dec 1988 Cover: 1.25 **NM** value: **Cover or less**
Circ: Statement: **76,100** CapCity orders: **19,000**
📖 Inferno; Revenge of the Boogy Man, Part 1 • Inferno

43 ❑ Jan 1989 Cover: 1.50 **NM** value: **Cover or less**
Circ: CapCity orders: **19,700**
📖 Revenge of the Boogy Man, Part 2 • Inferno

44 ❑ Mar 1989 Cover: 1.50 **NM** value: **Cover or less**
Circ: CapCity orders: **19,600**
📖 Revenge of the Boogy Man, Part 3 • Inferno

45 ❑ Apr 1989 Cover: 1.50 **NM** value: **Cover or less**
Circ: CapCity orders: **14,300**
📖 Revenge of the Boogy Man

46 ❑ May 1989 Cover: 1.50 **NM** value: **Cover or less**
Circ: CapCity orders: **18,000**
★ Appearance of Punisher.

47 ❑ Jul 1989 Cover: 1.50 **NM** value: **Cover or less**
Circ: CapCity orders: **13,700**

48 ❑ Sep 1989 Cover: 1.50 **NM** value: **Cover or less**
Circ: CapCity orders: **13,700**

49 ❑ Oct 1989 Cover: 1.50 **NM** value: **Cover or less**
Circ: CapCity orders: **12,400**

50 ❑ Nov 1989 Cover: 1.95 **NM** value: **2.00**
Circ: CapCity orders: **12,400**
• Giant-size.

51 ❑ Dec 1989 Cover: 1.50 **NM** value: **Cover or less**
Circ: CapCity orders: **11,200**
★ 1st Appearance of Numinus.

52 ❑ Dec 1989 Cover: 1.50 **NM** value: **Cover or less**
Circ: CapCity orders: **11,050**

53 ❑ Jan 1990 Cover: 1.50 **NM** value: **Cover or less**
Circ: CapCity orders: **15,400**
📖 Acts of Vengeance • Acts of Vengeance

54 ❑ Feb 1990 Cover: 1.50 **NM** value: **Cover or less**
Circ: CapCity orders: **10,900**

55 ❑ Apr 1990 Cover: 1.50 **NM** value: **Cover or less**
Circ: CapCity orders: **10,950**

56 ❑ Jun 1990 Cover: 1.50 **NM** value: **Cover or less**
Circ: CapCity orders: **10,750**

57 ❑ Jul 1990 Cover: 1.50 **NM** value: **Cover or less**
Circ: CapCity orders: **10,500**

58 ❑ Sep 1990 Cover: 1.50 **NM** value: **Cover or less**
Circ: CapCity orders: **10,050**
• Galactus

59 ❑ Oct 1990 Cover: 1.50 **NM** value: **Cover or less**
Circ: CapCity orders: **9,600**

60 ❑ Nov 1990 Cover: 1.50 **NM** value: **Cover or less**
Circ: CapCity orders: **9,500**

61 ❑ Dec 1990 Cover: 1.50 **NM** value: **Cover or less**
Circ: CapCity orders: **9,300**

62 ❑ Jan 1991 Cover: 1.50 **NM** value: **2.00**
Circ: CapCity orders: **9,100**
final issue.

Bk 1❑ Cover: 7.95 **NM** value: **Cover or less**
Circ: CapCity orders: **1,900**
• Power Pack Origin Album ★ Origin of Power Pack.

HS 1❑Feb 1992 Cover: 2.25 **NM** value: **2.50**
Circ: CapCity orders: **8,800**
• magazine-sized. 📖 Small Changes; Aaw, Christmas! **A:** Alexander Morrissey; June Brigman **W:** Louise Simonson; Dan Slott

POWER PACK (VOL. 2) — Marvel

1 ❑ Aug 2000 Cover: 2.99 **NM** value: **Cover or less**
Circ: Diamd. preorders: **18,586**
📖 Power Re-Play **A:** Colleen Doran **W:** SC Bury

POWER PLAYS (AC) — AC

1 ❑ b&w Cover: 1.75 **NM** value: **Cover or less**
2 ❑ Fal 1985, b&w Cover: 1.75 **NM** value: **Cover or less**

POWER PLAYS (EXTRAVA-GANDT) — Extrava-Gandt

1 ❑ b&w Cover: 2.00 **NM** value: **Cover or less**
2 ❑ Cover: 2.00 **NM** value: **Cover or less**
3 ❑ b&w Cover: 2.00 **NM** value: **Cover or less**

POWERPUFF GIRLS, THE — DC

When Townsville is threatened by the wicked plans of the evil Mojo Jojo or other evildoers, Bubbles, Blossom, and Buttercup — the amazing, super-powered Powerpuff Girls — fly into action...under the guidance of Professor Utonium, of course!

Both the animated series and the comic-book series contain pure, unadulterated action, but they also contain humor that appeals to older viewers and readers. Creator Craig McCracken's cute li'l super-toons are a part of the Cartoon Network's incredibly popular lineup.

1 ❑ May 2000 Cover: 1.99 **NM** value: **8.50**
Circ: Diamd. preorders: **14,561** • **CGC:** 13 graded, best 9.8
📖 Squirrelly Burly **A:** Phil Moy **W:** Jennifer Moore; Sean Carolan

2 ❑ Jun 2000 Cover: 1.99 **NM** value: **4.50**
Circ: Diamd. preorders: **10,089**
A: Phil Moy **W:** Jennifer Moore; Sean Carolan

3 ❑ Jul 2000 Cover: 1.99 **NM** value: **4.00**
Circ: Diamd. preorders: **10,316**
A: Phil Moy **W:** Jennifer Moore; Sean Carolan

4 ❑ Aug 2000 Cover: 1.99 **NM** value: **3.00**
Circ: Diamd. preorders: **11,372**

5 ❑ Sep 2000 Cover: 1.99 **NM** value: **2.50**
Circ: Diamd. preorders: **11,269**
📖 Holy Molar! **A:** Phil Moy **W:** Jennifer Moore; Sean Carolan

6 ❑ Oct 2000 Cover: 1.99 **NM** value: **Cover or less**
Circ: Diamd. preorders: **10,527**
📖 Dial "M" for Mojo **A:** Riocardo Garcia Fuentes **W:** John Rozum

7 ❑ Nov 2000 Cover: 1.99 **NM** value: **Cover or less**
Circ: Diamd. preorders: **11,119**
📖 Remote Controller **A:** Mike Manley **W:** Chuck Kim

8 ❑ Dec 2000 Cover: 1.99 **NM** value: **Cover or less**
Circ: Diamd. preorders: **11,390**
📖 Mayor, May I? **A:** Phil Moy **W:** Jennifer Moore; Sean Carolan

9 ❑ Jan 2001 Cover: 1.99 **NM** value: **Cover or less**
Circ: Diamd. preorders: **11,727**
📖 Creature at Large! **A:** Cynthia Morrow **W:** Chris Savino

10 ❑ Feb 2001 Cover: 1.99 **NM** value: **Cover or less**
Circ: Diamd. preorders: **11,318**
📖 Rogue Clowns **A:** Ricardo Garcia Fuentes **W:** Abby Denson

11 ❑ Mar 2001 Cover: 1.99 **NM** value: **Cover or less**
Circ: Diamd. preorders: **10,406**

12 ❑ Apr 2001 Cover: 1.99 **NM** value: **Cover or less**
Circ: Diamd. preorders: **10,200**
📖 Snow Day **A:** Ricardo Garcia Fuentes **W:** Abby Denson

13 ❑ May 2001 Cover: 1.99 **NM** value: **Cover or less**
Circ: Diamd. preorders: **10,215**
📖 Paranoid Puffs **A:** Cindy Morrow **W:** Bobbi JG Weiss

14 ❑ Jun 2001 Cover: 1.99 **NM** value: **Cover or less**
Circ: Diamd. preorders: **10,293**

15 ❑ Jul 2001 Cover: 1.99 **NM** value: **Cover or less**
Circ: Diamd. preorders: **10,382**

16 ❑ Aug 2001 Cover: 1.99 **NM** value: **Cover or less**
Circ: Diamd. preorders: **10,757**

17 ❑ Sep 2001 Cover: 1.99 **NM** value: **Cover or less**
Circ: Diamd. preorders: **11,225**

POWERPUFF GIRLS DOUBLE WHAMMY, THE — DC

1 ❑ Dec 2000 Cover: 3.95 **NM** value: **5.00**
Circ: Diamd. preorders: **6,564**
📖 Squirrelly Burly • Collects stories from Powerpuff Girls #1-2, Dexter's Laboratory #7 **A:** Phil Moy **W:** Jenifer Moore; Sean Carolan

POWER RANGERS TURBO: INTO THE FIRE — Acclaim

1 ❑ Cover: 4.50 **NM** value: **Cover or less**
📖 Into The Fire; 90 Miles Per Horror; Too Much Golf **A:** Ron Lim; John Herbert; Rusty Haller **W:** Clay & Susan Griffith; Dan Slott; Robert L. Washington III

POWER RANGERS ZEO — Image

1 ❑ Sep 1996 Cover: 2.50 **NM** value: **Cover or less**
Circ: Diamd. preorders: **19,435**
📖 With Friends Like These... **A:** Todd Nauck **W:** Tom & Mary Bierbaum

2 ❑ Oct 1996 Cover: 2.50 **NM** value: **Cover or less**
Circ: Diamd. preorders: **12,630**

> There are two different pricing tiers in the modern comic-book hobby. **The prices seen above** are the prices we have seen **loose copies** of these issues reliably fetch in a variety of environments. Condition alters the price by the fractions seen on the bar on the bottom of left-hand pages of this book. **Comics graded by CGC** usually sell for more. Use the guide on the bottom of right-hand pages of this book to estimate what copies have brought on eBay.

POWERS — Image

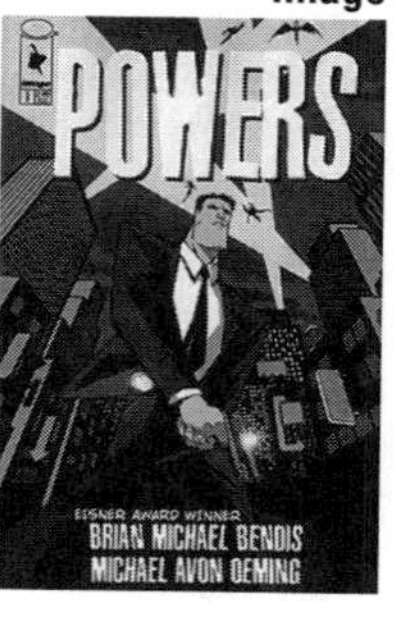

Brian Michael Bendis teamed with artist Michael Avon Oeming to bring out this refreshing and original take on crime fiction, mixed with a sprinkling of super-heroes. The protagonist is Detective Walker, as hardboiled as they come. He is called to the scene of a hostage situation by a man locked in his apartment with a little girl and a rocket strapped to his back. And why did this nutcase call for Walker, whom he'd never met?

Because word on the street was that Walker was soft on crooks with powers.

When the rocket-case gets sent up the river, babysitting duties fall to Walker. As if his day weren't going badly enough, he soon finds he's got a new partner — and a new case: the murder of a female super-hero.

Fast-paced, brilliantly dialogued, and surprisingly approachable, Powers is Bendis at his best. Oeming's artwork works beautifully with it, giving a sort of "Superman Adventures" style to what otherwise would be a cop noir drama.

1 ❑ Apr 2000 Cover: 2.95 **NM** value: **5.00**
Circ: Diamd. preorders: **14,200** • **CGC:** 51 graded, best 9.8
A: Michael Avon Oeming **W:** Brian Michael Bendis

2 ❑ May 2000 Cover: 2.95 **NM** value: **8.00**
Circ: Diamd. preorders: **9,279** • **CGC:** 9 graded, best 9.6
A: Michael Avon Oeming **W:** Brian Michael Bendis

3 ❑ Jun 2000 Cover: 2.95 **NM** value: **4.00**
Circ: Diamd. preorders: **11,938** • **CGC:** 5 graded, best 9.8
• #1 in indicia **A:** Michael Avon Oeming **W:** Brian Michael Bendis

4 ❑ Aug 2000 Cover: 2.95 **NM** value: **3.50**
Circ: Diamd. preorders: **14,049** • **CGC:** 1 graded, best 9.8
A: Michael Avon Oeming **W:** Brian Michael Bendis

5 ❑ Sep 2000 Cover: 2.95 **NM** value: **Cover or less**
Circ: Diamd. preorders: **15,731**
A: Michael Avon Oeming **W:** Brian Michael Bendis

6 ❑ Oct 2000 Cover: 2.95 **NM** value: **Cover or less**
Circ: Diamd. preorders: **17,326**
A: Michael Avon Oeming **W:** Brian Michael Bendis

7 ❑ Nov 2000 Cover: 2.95 **NM** value: **Cover or less**
Circ: Diamd. preorders: **23,666** • **CGC:** 1 graded, best 9.8
A: Michael Avon Oeming **W:** Brian Michael Bendis

8 ❑ Dec 2001 Cover: 2.95 **NM** value: **Cover or less**
Circ: Diamd. preorders: **23,434**
A: Michael Avon Oeming **W:** Brian Michael Bendis

9 ❑ Jan 2001 Cover: 2.95 **NM** value: **Cover or less**
Circ: Diamd. preorders: **22,831** • **CGC:** 1 graded, best 9.6
A: Michael Avon Oeming **W:** Brian Michael Bendis

10 ❑ Mar 2001 Cover: 2.95 **NM** value: **Cover or less**
Circ: Diamd. preorders: **25,120**
A: Michael Avon Oeming **W:** Brian Michael Bendis

11 ❑ Apr 2001 Cover: 2.95 **NM** value: **Cover or less**
Circ: Diamd. preorders: **27,048** • **CGC:** 1 graded, best 9.8
A: Michael Avon Oeming **W:** Brian Michael Bendis

12 ❑ May 2001 Cover: 2.95 **NM** value: **Cover or less**
Circ: Diamd. preorders: **27,589** • **CGC:** 1 graded, best 9.8
A: Michael Avon Oeming **W:** Brian Michael Bendis

13 ❑ Jun 2001 Cover: 2.95 **NM** value: **Cover or less**
Circ: Diamd. preorders: **28,879**
A: Michael Avon Oeming **W:** Brian Michael Bendis

14 ❑ Jul 2001 Cover: 2.95 **NM** value: **Cover or less**
Circ: Diamd. preorders: **30,153**
A: Michael Avon Oeming **W:** Brian Michael Bendis

Bk 1❑ Cover: 21.95 **NM** value: **Cover or less**
• Who Killed Retro Girl?; Collects series **A:** Michael Avon Oeming **W:** Brian Michael Bendis

POWERS COLORING/ACTIVITY BOOK — Image

1 ❑ Feb 2001 Cover: 1.50 **NM** value: **Cover or less**
Circ: Diamd. preorders: **14,091**
A: Michael Avon Oeming **W:** Brian Michael Bendis

POWERS THAT BE — Broadway

Jim Shooter came to fame as a comic-book writer at Marvel Comics in the mid to late Seventies. He has worked on most of the more popular Marvel characters. He worked his way up to editor and then to editor in chief. In the late 1980s, Shooter left Marvel to pursue his dream of running his own company, founding Valiant Comics which published X-O Manowar, Bloodshot and many others.

After internal struggles at Valiant, he left to form Defiant, releasing a number of worthwhile titles such as Warriors of Plasm before that company fell victim to the industry shakeout of 1993-1994. Shooter then struck a deal with Broadway Video to create a line of comics: Broadway Comics. Their first title, Powers That Be, debuted in 1995 and introduced two super-heroes: Star Seed and Fatale. Fatale is a woman who can absorb energy from anyone she touches. Star Seed is a super-powered caped hero who is strong enough to catch cars in midair.

1 ❑ Nov 1995 Cover: 2.50 **NM** value: **Cover or less**

Other grades: Multiply prices above by **1.5 for Mint • 2/3 for Very Fine • 1/3 for Fine • 1/5 for Very Good • 1/8 for Good**

Because I Can • Fatale and Star Seed; 1st comic from Broadway Comics **A:** Andrew Wendel **W:** Joe James; Jim Shooter; Janet Jackson; Pauline Weiss ★ 1st Appearance of Fatale, Star Seed.

2 ❑ Dec 1995 Cover: 2.50 **NM** value: **Cover or less**
• Star Seed

2/Ash❑Sep 1995, b&w **NM** value: **1.00**
• giveaway preview edition. • Star Seed

3 ❑ Jan 1996 Cover: 2.50 **NM** value: **Cover or less**
• Star Seed

3/Ash❑Oct 1995, b&w **NM** value: **1.00**
• giveaway preview edition. • Star Seed

4 ❑ Feb 1996 Cover: 2.50 **NM** value: **Cover or less**
• Star Seed

5 ❑ Apr 1996 Cover: 2.50 **NM** value: **Cover or less**
• Star Seed★ 1st Appearance of Marnie. ★ Versus Gina and Charlotte.

6 ❑ May 1996 Cover: 2.95 **NM** value: **Cover or less**
• Star Seed★ 1st Appearance of Ajax.

7 ❑ Jul 1996 Cover: 2.95 **NM** value: **Cover or less**
• Title changes to Star Seed

8 ❑ 1996 Cover: 2.95 **NM** value: **Cover or less**

9 ❑ Oct 1996 Cover: 2.95 **NM** value: **Cover or less**

PRAIRIE MOON AND OTHER STORIES Dark Horse

1 ❑ b&w Cover: 2.25 **NM** value: **Cover or less**
No issue number. • Rick Geary **A:** Rick Geary **W:** Rick Geary

PREACHER DC / Vertigo

Somewhere up in Heaven, things have gone wrong. A being has escaped its confinement — a being called Genesis whose powers might someday grow to rival those of the Almighty Himself. It sped toward Earth where it sought out a human soul with which to bond. In doing so, it hoped to gain the awareness which would enable it to unleash its unmeasurable powers. Genesis chose the body of Justin Custer, a small-town Texas preacher who was having his own crisis of faith. Genesis struck him in the midst of his sermon, inhabiting his body, and sending out waves of energy which incinerated the entire congregation.

This was the beginning of Justin's odyssey, a "road trip" of sorts in which he would be accompanied by a psychotic ex-lover, an Irish vampire, and the Saint of Killers. It's a weird saga set in the shadowlands between Heaven and Hell, brought to life by writer Garth (Hellblazer) Ennis and artist Steve Dillon.

1 ❑ Apr 1995 Cover: 2.95 **NM** value: **10.00**
Circ: CapCity orders: **17,600** • **CGC:** 50 graded, best 9.8
A: Steve Dillon; Glenn Fabry(cover) **W:** Garth Ennis ★ 1st Appearance of Jesse Custer.

2 ❑ May 1995 Cover: 2.50 **NM** value: **5.00**
Circ: CapCity orders: **12,900** • **CGC:** 5 graded, best 9.6
A: Steve Dillon; Glenn Fabry(cover) **W:** Garth Ennis ★ 1st Appearance of The Saint of Killers.

3 ❑ Jun 1995 Cover: 2.50 **NM** value: **4.00**
Circ: CapCity orders: **11,925** • **CGC:** 2 graded, best 9.6
A: Steve Dillon; Glenn Fabry(cover) **W:** Garth Ennis

4 ❑ Jul 1995 Cover: 2.50 **NM** value: **4.00**
Circ: CapCity orders: **12,625** • **CGC:** 1 graded, best 9.6
A: Steve Dillon; Glenn Fabry(cover) **W:** Garth Ennis

5 ❑ Aug 1995 Cover: 2.50 **NM** value: **4.00**
Circ: CapCity orders: **13,650** • **CGC:** 1 graded, best 9.0
A: Steve Dillon; Glenn Fabry(cover) **W:** Garth Ennis

6 ❑ Sep 1995 Cover: 2.50 **NM** value: **3.50**
Circ: CapCity orders: **13,325** • **CGC:** 1 graded, best 9.4
A: Steve Dillon; Glenn Fabry(cover) **W:** Garth Ennis

7 ❑ Oct 1995 Cover: 2.50 **NM** value: **3.50**
Circ: CapCity orders: **12,175**
A: Steve Dillon; Glenn Fabry(cover) **W:** Garth Ennis

8 ❑ Nov 1995 Cover: 2.50 **NM** value: **3.50**
All in the Family, Part 1 **A:** Steve Dillon; Glenn Fabry(cover) **W:** Garth Ennis

9 ❑ Dec 1995 Cover: 2.50 **NM** value: **3.50**
All in the Family, Part 2 **A:** Steve Dillon; Glenn Fabry(cover) **W:** Garth Ennis

10 ❑ Jan 1996 Cover: 2.50 **NM** value: **3.50**
All in the Family, Part 3 **A:** Steve Dillon; Glenn Fabry(cover) **W:** Garth Ennis

11 ❑ Feb 1996 Cover: 2.50 **NM** value: **3.00**
All in the Family, Part 4 **A:** Steve Dillon; Glenn Fabry(cover) **W:** Garth Ennis

12 ❑ Mar 1996 Cover: 2.50 **NM** value: **3.00**
All in the Family, Part 5 **A:** Steve Dillon; Glenn Fabry(cover) **W:** Garth Ennis

13 ❑ Apr 1996 Cover: 2.50 **NM** value: **3.00**
Hunters, Part 1 **A:** Steve Dillon **W:** Garth Ennis

14 ❑ Jun 1996 Cover: 2.50 **NM** value: **3.00**
Hunters, Part 2 **A:** Steve Dillon **W:** Garth Ennis

15 ❑ Jul 1996 Cover: 2.50 **NM** value: **3.00**
Hunters, Part 3 **A:** Steve Dillon **W:** Garth Ennis

16 ❑ Aug 1996 Cover: 2.50 **NM** value: **Cover or less**
Hunters, Part 4 **A:** Steve Dillon **W:** Garth Ennis

17 ❑ Sep 1996 Cover: 2.50 **NM** value: **Cover or less**
• **CGC:** 1 graded, best 9.2
Hunters, Part 5 **A:** Steve Dillon **W:** Garth Ennis

18 ❑ Oct 1996 Cover: 2.50 **NM** value: **Cover or less**
Texas and the Spaceman **A:** Steve Dillon; Glenn Fabry(cover) **W:** Garth Ennis

19 ❑ Nov 1996 Cover: 2.50 **NM** value: **Cover or less**
Circ: Diamd. preorders: **50,568**
Crusaders, Part 1 **A:** Steve Dillon; Glenn Fabry(cover) **W:** Garth Ennis

20 ❑ Dec 1996 Cover: 2.50 **NM** value: **Cover or less**
Circ: Diamd. preorders: **51,201**
Crusaders, Part 2 **A:** Steve Dillon; Glenn Fabry(cover) **W:** Garth Ennis

21 ❑ Jan 1997 Cover: 2.50 **NM** value: **Cover or less**
Circ: Diamd. preorders: **49,918**
Crusaders, Part 3 **A:** Steve Dillon; Glenn Fabry(cover) **W:** Garth Ennis

22 ❑ Feb 1997 Cover: 2.50 **NM** value: **Cover or less**
Circ: Diamd. preorders: **49,834**
Crusaders, Part 4 **A:** Steve Dillon; Glenn Fabry(cover) **W:** Garth Ennis

23 ❑ Mar 1997 Cover: 2.50 **NM** value: **Cover or less**
Circ: Diamd. preorders: **49,236**
Crusaders, Part 5 **A:** Steve Dillon; Glenn Fabry(cover) **W:** Garth Ennis

24 ❑ Apr 1997 Cover: 2.50 **NM** value: **Cover or less**
Circ: Diamd. preorders: **48,358**
Crusaders, Part 6 **A:** Steve Dillon; Glenn Fabry(cover) **W:** Garth Ennis

25 ❑ May 1997 Cover: 2.50 **NM** value: **Cover or less**
Circ: Diamd. preorders: **49,532**
A: Steve Dillon; Glenn Fabry(cover) **W:** Garth Ennis ★ Origin of Cassidy.

26 ❑ Jun 1997 Cover: 2.50 **NM** value: **Cover or less**
Circ: Diamd. preorders: **47,721**
To the Streets of Manhattan I Wandered Away **A:** Steve Dillon; Glenn Fabry(cover) **W:** Garth Ennis ★ Origin of Cassidy.

27 ❑ Jul 1997 Cover: 2.50 **NM** value: **Cover or less**
Circ: Diamd. preorders: **45,720**
Gunchicks **A:** Steve Dillon; Glenn Fabry(cover) **W:** Garth Ennis

28 ❑ Aug 1997 Cover: 2.50 **NM** value: **Cover or less**
Circ: Diamd. preorders: **45,691**
Rumors of War **A:** Steve Dillon; Glenn Fabry(cover) **W:** Garth Ennis

29 ❑ Sep 1997 Cover: 2.50 **NM** value: **Cover or less**
Circ: Diamd. preorders: **45,027**
A: Steve Dillon; Glenn Fabry(cover) **W:** Garth Ennis ★ Appearance of You-Know-Who.

30 ❑ Oct 1997 Cover: 2.50 **NM** value: **Cover or less**
Circ: Diamd. preorders: **45,865**
A: Steve Dillon; Glenn Fabry(cover) **W:** Garth Ennis ★ Appearance of You-Know-Who.

31 ❑ Nov 1997 Cover: 2.50 **NM** value: **Cover or less**
Circ: Diamd. preorders: **45,819**
A: Steve Dillon; Glenn Fabry(cover) **W:** Garth Ennis

32 ❑ Dec 1997 Cover: 2.50 **NM** value: **Cover or less**
Circ: Diamd. preorders: **45,260**
Snakes in the Grass **A:** Steve Dillon; Glenn Fabry(cover) **W:** Garth Ennis

33 ❑ Jan 1998 Cover: 2.50 **NM** value: **Cover or less**
Circ: Diamd. preorders: **45,473**
A: Steve Dillon; Glenn Fabry(cover) **W:** Garth Ennis

34 ❑ Feb 1998 Cover: 2.50 **NM** value: **Cover or less**
Circ: Diamd. preorders: **44,816**
War in the Sun, Part 1 **A:** Steve Dillon; Glenn Fabry(cover) **W:** Garth Ennis

35 ❑ Mar 1998 Cover: 2.50 **NM** value: **Cover or less**
Circ: Diamd. preorders: **43,790**
War in the Sun, Part 2 **A:** Steve Dillon; Glenn Fabry(cover) **W:** Garth Ennis

36 ❑ Apr 1998 Cover: 2.50 **NM** value: **Cover or less**
Circ: Diamd. preorders: **42,319**
War in the Sun, Part 3 **A:** Steve Dillon; Glenn Fabry(cover) **W:** Garth Ennis

37 ❑ May 1998 Cover: 2.50 **NM** value: **Cover or less**
Circ: Diamd. preorders: **43,148**
War in the Sun, Part 4 **A:** Steve Dillon; Glenn Fabry(cover) **W:** Garth Ennis

38 ❑ Jun 1998 Cover: 2.50 **NM** value: **Cover or less**
Circ: Diamd. preorders: **44,443**
A: Steve Dillon; Glenn Fabry(cover) **W:** Garth Ennis ★ Appearance of You-Know-Who.

39 ❑ Jul 1998 Cover: 2.50 **NM** value: **Cover or less**
Circ: Diamd. preorders: **42,707**
• Jesse loses an eye; Starr loses a leg **A:** Steve Dillon; Glenn Fabry(cover) **W:** Garth Ennis

40 ❑ Aug 1998 Cover: 2.50 **NM** value: **Cover or less**
Circ: Diamd. preorders: **42,956**
A: Steve Dillon; Glenn Fabry(cover) **W:** Garth Ennis

41 ❑ Sep 1998 Cover: 2.50 **NM** value: **Cover or less**
Circ: Diamd. preorders: **41,380**
• six months later; Jesse becomes sheriff of Salvation, Texas **A:** Steve Dillon; Glenn Fabry(cover) **W:** Garth Ennis

42 ❑ Oct 1998 Cover: 2.50 **NM** value: **Cover or less**
Circ: Diamd. preorders: **40,956**
A: Steve Dillon; Glenn Fabry(cover) **W:** Garth Ennis ★ 1st Appearance of Odin Quincannon.

43 ❑ Nov 1998 Cover: 2.50 **NM** value: **Cover or less**
Circ: Diamd. preorders: **41,119**
• Jesse's mother's story **A:** Steve Dillon; Glenn Fabry(cover) **W:** Garth Ennis

44 ❑ Dec 1998 Cover: 2.50 **NM** value: **Cover or less**
Circ: Diamd. preorders: **41,004**
A: Steve Dillon; Glenn Fabry(cover) **W:** Garth Ennis

45 ❑ Jan 1999 Cover: 2.50 **NM** value: **Cover or less**
Circ: Diamd. preorders: **40,596**
Southern Cross **A:** Steve Dillon; Glenn Fabry(cover) **W:** Garth Ennis

46 ❑ Feb 1999 Cover: 2.50 **NM** value: **Cover or less**
Circ: Diamd. preorders: **40,119**
White Mischief **A:** Steve Dillon; Glenn Fabry(cover) **W:** Garth Ennis

47 ❑ Mar 1999 Cover: 2.50 **NM** value: **Cover or less**
Circ: Diamd. preorders: **40,297**
Jesse Get Your Gun **A:** Steve Dillon; Glenn Fabry(cover) **W:** Garth Ennis

48 ❑ Apr 1999 Cover: 2.50 **NM** value: **Cover or less**
Circ: Diamd. preorders: **39,543**
Salvation **A:** Steve Dillon; Glenn Fabry(cover) **W:** Garth Ennis ★ Death of Odin Quincannon.

49 ❑ May 1999 Cover: 2.50 **NM** value: **Cover or less**
Circ: Diamd. preorders: **40,344**
First Contact **A:** Steve Dillon; Glenn Fabry(cover) **W:** Garth Ennis

50 ❑ Jun 1999 Cover: 3.75 **NM** value: **Cover or less**
Circ: Diamd. preorders: **44,435**
• Giant-size. The Land of Bad Things **A:** Tim Bradstreet; John McCrea; Doug Mahnke; Steve Dillon; Jim Lee; Joe Quesada; Glenn Fabry(cover); Jimmy Palmiotti; Kieron Swyer **W:** Garth Ennis

51 ❑ Jul 1999 Cover: 2.50 **NM** value: **Cover or less**
Circ: Diamd. preorders: **41,383**
Freedom's Just Another Word for Nothing Left to Lose • 100 Bullets preview **A:** Steve Dillon; Glenn Fabry(cover) **W:** Garth Ennis

52 ❑ Aug 1999 Cover: 2.50 **NM** value: **Cover or less**
Circ: Diamd. preorders: **41,102**
Even Hitgirls get the Blues **A:** Steve Dillon; Glenn Fabry(cover) **W:** Garth Ennis

53 ❑ Sep 1999 Cover: 2.50 **NM** value: **Cover or less**
Circ: Diamd. preorders: **41,938**
Too Dumb for New York City and Too Ugly for L.A. **A:** Steve Dillon; Glenn Fabry(cover) **W:** Garth Ennis

54 ❑ Oct 1999 Cover: 2.50 **NM** value: **Cover or less**
Circ: Diamd. preorders: **40,888**
A: Steve Dillon; Glenn Fabry(cover) **W:** Garth Ennis

55 ❑ Nov 1999 Cover: 2.50 **NM** value: **Cover or less**
Circ: Diamd. preorders: **40,184**
Harbinger **A:** Steve Dillon; Glenn Fabry(cover) **W:** Garth Ennis

56 ❑ Dec 1999 Cover: 2.50 **NM** value: **Cover or less**
Circ: Diamd. preorders: **41,240**
A: Steve Dillon; Glenn Fabry(cover) **W:** Garth Ennis

57 ❑ Jan 2000 Cover: 2.50 **NM** value: **Cover or less**
Circ: Diamd. preorders: **39,888**
Of the Irish in America **A:** Steve Dillon; Glenn Fabry(cover) **W:** Garth Ennis

58 ❑ Feb 2000 Cover: 2.50 **NM** value: **Cover or less**
Circ: Diamd. preorders: **39,411**
Dot the I's and Cross the T's **A:** Steve Dillon; Glenn Fabry(cover) **W:** Garth Ennis

59 ❑ Mar 2000 Cover: 2.50 **NM** value: **Cover or less**
Circ: Diamd. preorders: **39,508**
Alamo, Part 1 **A:** Steve Dillon; Glenn Fabry(cover) **W:** Garth Ennis

60 ❑ Apr 2000 Cover: 2.50 **NM** value: **Cover or less**
Circ: Diamd. preorders: **37,946**
Alamo, Part 2 **A:** Steve Dillon; Glenn Fabry(cover) **W:** Garth Ennis

61 ❑ May 2000 Cover: 2.50 **NM** value: **Cover or less**
Circ: Diamd. preorders: **39,251**
Alamo, Part 3 **A:** Steve Dillon; Glenn Fabry(cover) **W:** Garth Ennis

62 ❑ Jun 2000 Cover: 2.50 **NM** value: **Cover or less**
Circ: Diamd. preorders: **39,971**
Alamo, Part 4 **A:** Steve Dillon; Glenn Fabry(cover) **W:** Garth Ennis

63 ❑ Jul 2000 Cover: 2.50 **NM** value: **Cover or less**
Circ: Diamd. preorders: **40,199**
Alamo, Part 5 **A:** Steve Dillon; Glenn Fabry(cover) **W:** Garth Ennis

64 ❑ Aug 2000 Cover: 2.50 **NM** value: **Cover or less**
Circ: Diamd. preorders: **41,290**
Alamo, Part 6 **A:** Steve Dillon; Glenn Fabry(cover) **W:** Garth Ennis

65 ❑ Sep 2000 Cover: 2.50 **NM** value: **Cover or less**
Circ: Diamd. preorders: **42,205**
Alamo, Part 7 **A:** Steve Dillon; Glenn Fabry(cover) **W:** Garth Ennis

66 ❑ Oct 2000 Cover: 3.75 **NM** value: **Cover or less**
Circ: Diamd. preorders: **43,327**
• Giant-size. A Hell of a Vision final issue. **A:** Steve Dillon; Glenn Fabry(cover) **W:** Garth Ennis

Bk 1❑ Cover: 14.95 **NM** value: **Cover or less**
Gone to Texas • collects issues #1-7 **A:** Steve Dillon; Glenn Fabry(cover) **W:** Garth Ennis

Bk 2❑ Cover: 14.95 **NM** value: **Cover or less**
Until the End of the World • collects issues #8-17 **A:** Steve Dillon; Glenn Fabry(cover) **W:** Garth Ennis

Bk 3❑ Cover: 14.95 **NM** value: **Cover or less**
Proud Americans • collects issues #18-26 **A:** Steve Dillon; Glenn Fabry(cover) **W:** Garth Ennis

Bk 4❑ Cover: 14.95 **NM** value: **Cover or less**
I Built My Dream Around You • Ancient History; collects Preacher Specials Saint of Killers; The Good Old Boys; and The Story of You-Know-Who **A:** Steve Dillon; Glenn Fabry(cover) **W:** Garth Ennis

Bk 5❑ Cover: 14.95 **NM** value: **Cover or less**
War in the Sun • collects #34-40 and Special: One Man's War **A:** Steve Dillon; Glenn Fabry(cover) **W:** Garth Ennis

Bk 6❑ Cover: 14.95 **NM** value: **Cover or less**
War in the Sun • Collects issues #34-40 **A:** Steve Dillon; Glenn Fabry(cover) **W:** Garth Ennis

Bk 7❑ Cover: 14.95 **NM** value: **Cover or less**
Salvation • collects #41-50 **A:** Steve Dillon; Glenn Fabry(cover) **W:** Garth Ennis

Bk 8❑ **NM** value: **14.95**
A: Steve Dillon; Glenn Fabry(cover) **W:** Garth Ennis

Bk 9❑ Cover: 17.95 **NM** value: **Cover or less**
Alamo • Collects #59-66 **A:** Steve Dillon; Glenn Fabry(cover) **W:** Garth Ennis

PREACHER: DEAD OR ALIVE DC / Vertigo

1 ❑ Cover: 29.95 **NM** value: **Cover or less**
A: Glenn Fabry **W:** Garth Ennis

PREACHER SPECIAL: CASSIDY: BLOOD & WHISKEY DC / Vertigo

1 ❑ Feb 1998 Cover: 5.95 **NM** value: **Cover or less**
Circ: Diamd. preorders: **38,667**
One-shot. • prestige format.

CGC-graded: Multiply prices above by **33 for 9.9 M** • **16 for 9.8 NM/M** • **7 for 9.6 NM+** • **5 for 9.4 NM** • **2.5 for 9.2 NM-** • **1.5 for 9.0 VF/NM**

PREACHER SPECIAL: ONE MAN'S WAR — DC / Vertigo

1 ❑ Mar 1998 Cover: 4.95 NM value: 5.00
Circ: Diamd. preorders: 38,870
A: Peter Snejbjerg W: Garth Ennis ★ Origin of Starr.

PREACHER SPECIAL: SAINT OF KILLERS — DC / Vertigo

1 ❑ Aug 1996 Cover: 2.50 NM value: 4.00
• CGC: 3 graded, best 9.8
A: Steve Pugh W: Garth Ennis
2 ❑ Sep 1996 Cover: 2.50 NM value: 3.50
A: Steve Pugh W: Garth Ennis
3 ❑ Oct 1996 Cover: 2.50 NM value: 3.00
A: Steve Pugh W: Garth Ennis
4 ❑ Nov 1996 Cover: 2.50 NM value: 3.00
Circ: Diamd. preorders: 48,239
A: Steve Pugh W: Garth Ennis
Bk 1❑ Cover: 14.95 NM value: Cover or less
Ancient History • Collects issues #1-4 and Preacher Special: The Story of You-Know-Who A: Steve Pugh W: Garth Ennis

PREACHER SPECIAL: TALL IN THE SADDLE — DC / Vertigo

1 ❑ Feb 2000 Cover: 5.95 NM value: Cover or less
Circ: Diamd. preorders: 35,203

PREACHER SPECIAL: THE GOOD OLD BOYS — DC / Vertigo

1 ❑ Aug 1997 Cover: 4.95 NM value: Cover or less
Circ: Diamd. preorders: 42,123
One-shot. ★ Appearance of Jody, T.C..

PREACHER SPECIAL: THE STORY OF YOU-KNOW-WHO — DC / Vertigo

1 ❑ Dec 1996 Cover: 4.95 NM value: Cover or less
Circ: Diamd. preorders: 49,745 • CGC: 1 graded, best 9.6
One-shot. A: Richard Case W: Garth Ennis ★ Origin of You-Know-Who.

PRECIOUS METAL — Arts Industria

All issues are adults only.
1 ❑ b&w Cover: 2.50 NM value: Cover or less

PREDATOR — Dark Horse

In the movie "Predator," a single one of these alien hunters virtually annihilated a South American druglord's army, as well as the special forces team sent to destroy it. Only the team's leader, Dutch Schaeffer survived.

The Predators are drawn to heat and battle, so it was only natural that they be attracted to the jungle battles surrounding the Medellin drug cartel. When violence flares up again, Dutch's brother, a New York City cop, jumps at the chance to investigate. To his terror, he discovers that not only has a Predator returned, but he's not alone this time.

And meanwhile, back in New York, Schaeffer's partner puts on the helmet of a slain Predator — and sees the sky, blanketed with the Predators' otherwise invisible ships!

1 ❑ Jun 1989, full color Cover: 2.25 NM value: 5.00
Circ: CapCity orders: 16,225 • CGC: 7 graded, best 9.6
A: Chris Warner W: Mark Verheiden
1-2 ❑ Cover: 2.25 NM value: 2.50
2 ❑ Sep 1989 Cover: 2.25 NM value: 3.50
Circ: CapCity orders: 15,250
A: Chris Warner W: Mark Verheiden
3 ❑ Dec 1989 Cover: 2.25 NM value: 3.00
Circ: CapCity orders: 16,525
A: Ron Randall; Chris Warner W: Mark Verheiden
4 ❑ Mar 1990 Cover: 2.25 NM value: 3.00
Circ: CapCity orders: 20,550
A: Chris Warner W: Mark Verheiden
Bk 1❑ Cover: 12.95 NM value: Cover or less
Circ: CapCity orders: 4,300
• Concrete Jungle A: Chris Warner W: Mark Verheiden
Bk 1-2❑ Cover: 14.95 NM value: Cover or less
Bk 1-3❑Apr 1996 Cover: 14.95 NM value: Cover or less

PREDATOR 2 — Dark Horse

1 ❑ Feb 1991 Cover: 2.50 NM value: 3.00
Photo cover. A: Dan Barry W: Franz Henkel
2 ❑ Jun 1991 Cover: 2.50 NM value: 3.00
Photo cover. A: Dan Barry W: Franz Henkel

PREDATOR: BAD BLOOD — Dark Horse

1 ❑ Dec 1993 Cover: 2.50 NM value: Cover or less
Circ: CapCity orders: 23,075
A: Derek Thompson W: Evan Dorkin
2 ❑ Feb 1994 Cover: 2.50 NM value: Cover or less
Circ: CapCity orders: 17,050
A: Derek Thompson W: Evan Dorkin
3 ❑ May 1994 Cover: 2.50 NM value: Cover or less
Circ: CapCity orders: 15,475
A: Derek Thompson W: Evan Dorkin
4 ❑ Jun 1994 Cover: 2.50 NM value: Cover or less
Circ: CapCity orders: 14,150
A: Derek Thompson W: Evan Dorkin

PREDATOR: BIG GAME — Dark Horse

1 ❑ Mar 1991 Cover: 2.50 NM value: Cover or less
Circ: CapCity orders: 53,900
• trading cards A: Evan Dorkin W: John Arcudi
2 ❑ Apr 1991 Cover: 2.50 NM value: Cover or less
Circ: CapCity orders: 47,175
no trading cards despite cover advisory. A: Evan Dorkin W: John Arcudi
3 ❑ May 1991 Cover: 2.50 NM value: Cover or less
Circ: CapCity orders: 42,425
• trading cards A: Evan Dorkin W: John Arcudi
4 ❑ Jun 1991 Cover: 2.50 NM value: Cover or less
Circ: CapCity orders: 44,400
A: Evan Dorkin W: John Arcudi
Bk 1❑ Cover: 14.95 NM value: Cover or less
• collects mini-series A: Evan Dorkin W: John Arcudi
Bk 1-2❑Apr 1996 Cover: 14.95 NM value: Cover or less

PREDATOR: CAPTIVE — Dark Horse

1 ❑ Apr 1998 Cover: 2.95 NM value: Cover or less
Circ: Diamd. preorders: 14,142
No issue number. One-shot. A: Dean Ormston W: Gordon Rennie

PREDATOR: COLD WAR — Dark Horse

1 ❑ Sep 1991 Cover: 2.50 NM value: Cover or less
Circ: CapCity orders: 56,050
A: Ron Randall W: Mark Verheiden
2 ❑ Oct 1991 Cover: 2.50 NM value: Cover or less
Circ: CapCity orders: 43,400
A: Ron Randall W: Mark Verheiden
3 ❑ Nov 1991 Cover: 2.50 NM value: Cover or less
Circ: CapCity orders: 41,775
A: Ron Randall W: Mark Verheiden
4 ❑ Dec 1991 Cover: 2.50 NM value: Cover or less
Circ: CapCity orders: 37,475
A: Ron Randall W: Mark Verheiden
Bk 1❑ Cover: 13.95 NM value: Cover or less
• Trade Paperback. • Collects Predator: Cold War #1-4 A: Ron Randall W: Mark Verheiden

PREDATOR: DARK RIVER — Dark Horse

1 ❑ Jul 1996 Cover: 2.95 NM value: Cover or less
A: Ron Randall W: Mark Verheiden
2 ❑ Aug 1996 Cover: 2.95 NM value: Cover or less
A: Ron Randall W: Mark Verheiden
3 ❑ Sep 1996 Cover: 2.95 NM value: Cover or less
Circ: Diamd. preorders: 23,836
A: Ron Randall W: Mark Verheiden
4 ❑ Oct 1996 Cover: 2.95 NM value: Cover or less
Circ: Diamd. preorders: 22,243
A: Ron Randall W: Mark Verheiden

PREDATOR: HELL & HOT WATER — Dark Horse

1 ❑ Apr 1997 Cover: 2.95 NM value: Cover or less
Circ: Diamd. preorders: 22,344
• uninked pencils A: Gene Colan W: Mark Schultz
2 ❑ May 1997 Cover: 2.95 NM value: Cover or less
Circ: Diamd. preorders: 18,230
• uninked pencils A: Gene Colan W: Mark Schultz
3 ❑ Jun 1997 Cover: 2.95 NM value: Cover or less
Circ: Diamd. preorders: 17,580
• uninked pencils A: Gene Colan W: Mark Schultz

PREDATOR: HELL COME A WALKIN' — Dark Horse

1 ❑ Feb 1998 Cover: 2.95 NM value: Cover or less
Circ: Diamd. preorders: 15,030
• Predator in Civil War A: Dean Ormston W: Nancy Collins
2 ❑ Mar 1998 Cover: 2.95 NM value: Cover or less
Circ: Diamd. preorders: 13,619
• Predator in Civil War A: Dean Ormston W: Nancy Collins

PREDATOR: HOMEWORLD — Dark Horse

1 ❑ Mar 1999 Cover: 2.95 NM value: Cover or less
Circ: Diamd. preorders: 12,602
A: Toby Cypress W: Kate Worley; James Vance
2 ❑ Apr 1999 Cover: 2.95 NM value: Cover or less
Circ: Diamd. preorders: 11,446
A: Toby Cypress W: Kate Worley; James Vance
3 ❑ May 1999 Cover: 2.95 NM value: Cover or less
Circ: Diamd. preorders: 10,905
A: Toby Cypress W: Kate Worley; James Vance
4 ❑ Jun 1999 Cover: 2.95 NM value: Cover or less
Circ: Diamd. preorders: 10,707
A: Toby Cypress W: Kate Worley; James Vance

PREDATOR: INVADERS FROM THE FOURTH DIMENSION — Dark Horse

1 ❑ Jul 1994 Cover: 3.95 NM value: Cover or less
Circ: CapCity orders: 11,600
No issue number. One-shot. A: Jim Somerville W: Jerry Prosser

PREDATOR: JUNGLE TALES — Dark Horse

1 ❑ Mar 1995 Cover: 2.95 NM value: Cover or less
Circ: CapCity orders: 10,450
No issue number. Predator: Rite of Passage; Predator: The Pride at Nghasa • collects Predator: Rite of Passage from DHC #1 and 2; Predator: The Pride of Nghasa from DHC #10-12 A: Rick Leonardi; Enrique Alcatena W: Chuck Dixon; Ian Edginton

PREDATOR: KINDRED — Dark Horse

1 ❑ Dec 1996 Cover: 2.50 NM value: Cover or less
Circ: Diamd. preorders: 23,823
Kindred, Part 1 A: Brian O'Connell W: Scott Tolson; Jason R. Lamb
2 ❑ Jan 1997 Cover: 2.50 NM value: Cover or less
Circ: Diamd. preorders: 20,483
Kindred, Part 2 A: Roger Petersen W: Scott Tolson; Jason R. Lamb
3 ❑ Feb 1997 Cover: 2.50 NM value: Cover or less
Circ: Diamd. preorders: 18,602
Kindred, Part 3 A: Roger Petersen W: Scott Tolson; Jason R. Lamb
4 ❑ Mar 1997 Cover: 2.50 NM value: Cover or less
Circ: Diamd. preorders: 17,607
A: Roger Petersen W: Scott Tolson; Jason R. Lamb
Bk 1❑ Dec 1997 Cover: 14.95 NM value: Cover or less

PREDATOR: NEMESIS — Dark Horse

1 ❑ Dec 1997 Cover: 2.95 NM value: Cover or less
Circ: Diamd. preorders: 16,002
Predator Nemesis, Part 1 A: Colin MacNeil W: Gordon Rennie
2 ❑ Jan 1998 Cover: 2.95 NM value: Cover or less
Circ: Diamd. preorders: 14,619
A: Colin MacNeil W: Gordon Rennie

PREDATOR: PRIMAL — Dark Horse

1 ❑ Jul 1997 Cover: 2.95 NM value: Cover or less
Circ: Diamd. preorders: 18,044
• Predator vs. bears A: Scott Kolins W: Kevin J. Anderson
2 ❑ Aug 1997 Cover: 2.95 NM value: Cover or less
Circ: Diamd. preorders: 16,006
• Predator vs. bears A: Scott Kolins W: Kevin J. Anderson

PREDATOR: RACE WAR — Dark Horse

0 ❑ Apr 1993 Cover: 2.50 NM value: Cover or less
Circ: CapCity orders: 34,875
A: Jordan Raskin W: Andrew Vachss; Randy Stradley
1 ❑ Feb 1993 Cover: 2.50 NM value: Cover or less
Circ: CapCity orders: 40,300
A: Jordan Raskin W: Andrew Vachss; Randy Stradley
2 ❑ Mar 1993 Cover: 2.50 NM value: Cover or less
Circ: CapCity orders: 31,375
A: Jordan Raskin W: Andrew Vachss; Randy Stradley
3 ❑ Aug 1993 Cover: 2.50 NM value: Cover or less
Circ: CapCity orders: 29,400
A: Jordan Raskin W: Andrew Vachss; Randy Stradley
4 ❑ Oct 1993 Cover: 2.50 NM value: Cover or less
Circ: CapCity orders: 24,750
A: Lauchland Pelle W: Andrew Vachss; Randy Stradley
Bk 1❑ Aug 1995 Cover: 17.95 NM value: Cover or less
• Collects Predator: Race War #0-4 A: Lauchland Pelle W: Andrew Vachss; Randy Stradley

PREDATOR: STRANGE ROUX — Dark Horse

1 ❑ Nov 1996 Cover: 2.95 NM value: Cover or less
Circ: Diamd. preorders: 24,216
No issue number. One-shot. • recipe for Strange Roux in back A: Mitch Byrd W: Brian McDonald

PREDATOR: THE BLOODY SANDS OF TIME — Dark Horse

1 ❑ Feb 1992 Cover: 2.50 NM value: 2.75
Circ: CapCity orders: 40,625
• Predator in WW I A: Dan Barry; Chris Warner W: Dan Barry
2 ❑ Feb 1992 Cover: 2.50 NM value: 2.75
Circ: CapCity orders: 32,675
• Predator in WW I

PREDATOR VERSUS JUDGE DREDD — Dark Horse / Egmont

1 ❑ Oct 1997 Cover: 2.50 NM value: Cover or less
Circ: Diamd. preorders: 25,013
A: Enrique Alcatena; Brian Bolland(cover) W: John Wagner
2 ❑ Nov 1997 Cover: 2.50 NM value: Cover or less
Circ: Diamd. preorders: 20,649
A: Enrique Alcatena W: John Wagner
3 ❑ Dec 1997 Cover: 2.50 NM value: Cover or less
Circ: Diamd. preorders: 19,318
A: Enrique Alcatena W: John Wagner
Bk 1❑ Nov 1998 Cover: 9.95 NM value: Cover or less
• Trade Paperback. • collects mini-series

PREDATOR VS. MAGNUS ROBOT FIGHTER — Dark Horse / Valiant

1 ❑ Nov 1992 Cover: 2.95 NM value: 3.00
Circ: CapCity orders: 102,925
Sport A: Lee Weeks W: Jim Shooter; John Ostrander
1/PL❑ Nov 1992 NM value: 4.00
• Platinum promotional edition. Sport A: Lee Weeks W: Jim Shooter; John Ostrander
2 ❑ Dec 1992 Cover: 2.95 NM value: 3.00
Circ: CapCity orders: 58,100
Spoils • trading cards A: Lee Weeks C: Barry Windsor-Smith W: Jim Shooter; John Ostrander

PREDATOR: XENOGENESIS — Dark Horse

1 ❑ Aug 1999 Cover: 2.95 NM value: Cover or less
Circ: Diamd. preorders: 13,056
A: Mel Rubi W: Ian Edginton
2 ❑ Sep 1999 Cover: 2.95 NM value: Cover or less
Circ: Diamd. preorders: 11,253
A: Mel Rubi W: Ian Edginton
3 ❑ Oct 1999 Cover: 2.95 NM value: Cover or less
Circ: Diamd. preorders: 11,177
A: Mel Rubi W: Ian Edginton
4 ❑ Nov 1999 Cover: 2.95 NM value: Cover or less
Circ: Diamd. preorders: 10,611
A: Mel Rubi W: Ian Edginton

PREMIERE — Diversity

1 ❑ Cover: 2.75 NM value: Cover or less
Kolmec the Savage: When a Stranger Calls, Part 1 • 1500 printed

1/GO ☐ Cover: 10.00 **NM value: Cover or less**
• Gold limited edition (175 printed). 📖 Kolmec the Savage: When a Stranger Calls, Part 1

1/LE ☐ Cover: 5.00 **NM value: Cover or less**
• Limited edition (175 printed). 📖 Kolmec the Savage: When a Stranger Calls, Part 1

2 ☐ Cover: 2.75 **NM value: Cover or less**
📖 Kolmec the Savage: When a Stranger Calls, Part 2; Lifer: Guilty as Sin, Part 2; Alpha Korps **A:** Tony Lopez **W:** Tony Lopez

PREMIERE GRAPHIC NOVELS — Innovation

Bk 1 ☐ Cover: 5.95 **NM value: Cover or less**
• Sherlock Holmes

PRESERVATION OF OBSCURITY, THE — Lump of Squid

1 ☐ Cover: 2.75 **NM value: Cover or less**
2 ☐ Cover: 2.75 **NM value: Cover or less**

PRESSED TONGUE (DAVE COOPER'S...) — Fantagraphics

All issues are adults only.

1 ☐ b&w Cover: 2.95 **NM value: Cover or less**
3 ☐ Dec 1994, b&w Cover: 2.95 **NM value: Cover or less**

PRESTO KID, THE — AC

1 ☐ b&w Cover: 2.50 **NM value: Cover or less**

PRE-TEEN DIRTY-GENE KUNG-FU KANGAROOS — Blackthorne

1 ☐ Aug 1986 Cover: 1.50 **NM value: 2.00**
★ Appearance of TMNT.
2 ☐ Nov 1986 Cover: 1.50 **NM value: 2.00**
3 ☐ 1987 Cover: 1.75 **NM value: 2.00**

PREY — Monster

1 ☐ b&w Cover: 2.25 **NM value: Cover or less**
2 ☐ b&w Cover: 2.25 **NM value: Cover or less**
3 ☐ b&w Cover: 2.25 **NM value: Cover or less**

PREY FOR US SINNERS — Fantaco

1 ☐ Cover: 4.95 **NM value: Cover or less**
No issue number. **A:** Omaha Perez **W:** Franz Henkel

PREZ — DC

This campy commentary on early Seventies events and culture, written by Joe Simon, imagines a U.S. with a teen-age president elected, as a result of lowering the voting age to 18, in 1971. Evil anti-environmental businessman, Mr. Smiley, sees in the youth vote a chance to sponsor and influence a malleable young candidate. He quickly finds Prez who wins a place in the U.S. Senate together with several other young youth-elected senators. In short time, the senators lower the required age of the president from 35 to 18. Prez, running on the new Flower Party ticket, sweeps the youth vote and becomes the first teen-age president.

By this time, Prez, through the help of American Indian chief, Eagle Free, has seen through Mr. Smiley's machinations. He sets up a young, multi-cultural cabinet and sets about making historic achievements during his time in office. Mr. Smiley is no longer smiling though, and Prez faces more challenges than simple inexperience...

1 ☐ Sep 1973 Cover: 0.20 **NM value: 8.00**
• **CGC:** 2 graded, best 9.4
📖 Oh Say Does That Star Spangled Banner Yet Wave?
2 ☐ Nov 1973 Cover: 0.20 **NM value: 4.00**
3 ☐ Jan 1974 Cover: 0.20 **NM value: 4.00**
4 ☐ Mar 1974 Cover: 0.20 **NM value: 4.00**

PRIDE & JOY — DC / Vertigo

1 ☐ Jul 1997 Cover: 2.50 **NM value: Cover or less**
Circ: Diamd. preorders: **35,508**
A: John Higgins **W:** Garth Ennis
2 ☐ Aug 1997 Cover: 2.50 **NM value: Cover or less**
Circ: Diamd. preorders: **28,664**
A: John Higgins **W:** Garth Ennis
3 ☐ Sep 1997 Cover: 2.50 **NM value: Cover or less**
Circ: Diamd. preorders: **26,775**
A: John Higgins **W:** Garth Ennis
4 ☐ Oct 1997 Cover: 2.50 **NM value: Cover or less**
Circ: Diamd. preorders: **25,319**
A: John Higgins **W:** Garth Ennis

PRIDE OF THE YANKEES — Magazine Enterprises

1 ☐ ca. 1949 Cover: 0.10 **NM value: 350.00**
No issue number. Photo cover. • based on life of Lou Gehrig

PRIEST — Maximum

1 ☐ Aug 1996 Cover: 2.99 **NM value: Cover or less**
A: Mark Pajarillo **W:** Rob Liefeld; Robert Napton ★ 1st Appearance of Priest.
2 ☐ Sep 1996 Cover: 2.99 **NM value: Cover or less**
Circ: Diamd. preorders: **16,480**
A: Mark Pajarillo **W:** Rob Liefeld; Robert Napton
3 ☐ Oct 1996 Cover: 2.99 **NM value: Cover or less**
Circ: Diamd. preorders: **13,400**
A: Mark Pajarillo **W:** Rob Liefeld; Robert Napton

PRIMAL — Dark Horse

1 ☐ Cover: 2.50 **NM value: Cover or less**
Circ: CapCity orders: **5,525**
A: Lionel Talaro **W:** Clive Barker; D.G. Chichester; Erik Saltzgaber
2 ☐ Cover: 2.50 **NM value: Cover or less**
Circ: CapCity orders: **3,900**

PRIMAL FORCE — DC

0 ☐ Oct 1994 Cover: 1.95 **NM value: 2.25**
Circ: CapCity orders: **22,050**
📖 The Call **A:** Ken Hooper **W:** Steven Seagle ★ Origin of Primal Force. ★ 1st Appearance of Primal Force.
1 ☐ Nov 1994 Cover: 1.95 **NM value: 2.25**
Circ: CapCity orders: **18,850**
📖 Water Signs **A:** Ken Hooper **W:** Steven Seagle ★ Origin of the Leymen.
2 ☐ Dec 1994 Cover: 1.95 **NM value: Cover or less**
Circ: CapCity orders: **14,050**
3 ☐ Jan 1995 Cover: 1.95 **NM value: Cover or less**
Circ: CapCity orders: **12,750**
📖 Histories **A:** Ken Hooper; Christopher Schenck **W:** Steven Seagle
4 ☐ Feb 1995 Cover: 1.95 **NM value: Cover or less**
Circ: CapCity orders: **10,050**
5 ☐ Mar 1995 Cover: 1.95 **NM value: Cover or less**
Circ: CapCity orders: **8,300**
6 ☐ Apr 1995 Cover: 1.95 **NM value: Cover or less**
Circ: CapCity orders: **7,025**
7 ☐ May 1995 Cover: 1.95 **NM value: Cover or less**
Circ: CapCity orders: **7,125**
8 ☐ Jun 1995 Cover: 2.25 **NM value: Cover or less**
Circ: CapCity orders: **6,025**
9 ☐ Jul 1995 Cover: 2.25 **NM value: Cover or less**
Circ: CapCity orders: **5,675**
10 ☐ Aug 1995 Cover: 2.25 **NM value: Cover or less**
Circ: CapCity orders: **5,750**
11 ☐ Sep 1995 Cover: 2.25 **NM value: Cover or less**
Circ: CapCity orders: **5,150**
12 ☐ Oct 1995 Cover: 2.25 **NM value: Cover or less**
Circ: CapCity orders: **4,225**
13 ☐ Nov 1995 Cover: 2.25 **NM value: Cover or less**
📖 Underworld Unleashed • Underworld Unleashed ★ Appearance of Lord Satanus.
14 ☐ Dec 1995 Cover: 2.25 **NM value: Cover or less**
final issue.

PRIMAL RAGE — Sirius

1 ☐ Aug 1996, b&w Cover: 2.50 **NM value: 2.95**
A: Kevin Rasel **W:** Chris Knowles
2 ☐ Oct 1996, b&w Cover: 2.50 **NM value: 2.95**
Circ: Diamd. preorders: **5,804**
3 ☐ Dec 1996, b&w Cover: 2.50 **NM value: 2.95**
Circ: Diamd. preorders: **4,361**
4 ☐ Feb 1997, b&w Cover: 2.50 **NM value: 2.95**

PRIME/CAPTAIN AMERICA — Malibu / Ultraverse

1 ☐ Mar 1996 Cover: 3.95 **NM value: Cover or less**

PRIME CUTS — Fantagraphics

1 ☐ Jan 1987 Cover: 3.50 **NM value: Cover or less**
2 ☐ Mar 1987 Cover: 3.50 **NM value: Cover or less**
3 ☐ May 1987 Cover: 3.50 **NM value: Cover or less**
4 ☐ 1987 Cover: 3.50 **NM value: Cover or less**
5 ☐ 1987 Cover: 3.50 **NM value: Cover or less**
6 ☐ 1987 Cover: 3.50 **NM value: Cover or less**
7 ☐ 1988 Cover: 3.95 **NM value: Cover or less**
8 ☐ Apr 1988 Cover: 3.95 **NM value: Cover or less**
9 ☐ 1988 Cover: 3.95 **NM value: Cover or less**
10 ☐ 1988 Cover: 3.95 **NM value: Cover or less**

PRIME CUTS (MIKE DEODATO'S...) — Caliber

1 ☐ Cover: 2.95 **NM value: Cover or less**
📖 Jack; Lycanthropos; Djinns **A:** Mike Deodato Jr. **W:** Mike Deodato Sr.; Julio E. Braz

PRIMER — Comico

1 ☐ b&w Cover: 1.50 **NM value: 6.00**
• **CGC:** 1 graded, best 9.2
★ 1st Appearance of Slaughterman, Skrog, Az.
2 ☐ 1982 Cover: 1.50 **NM value: 65.00**
• **CGC:** 80 graded, best 9.8
📖 My Brother's Keeper?; Judas Kiss **A:** Matt Wagner; Andrew Murphy; Jim Alderman **W:** Matt Wagner; Andrew Murphy; Jim Alderman ★ 1st Appearance of Argent, Grendel I (Hunter Rose).
3 ☐ Cover: 1.50 **NM value: 5.00**
4 ☐ b&w Cover: 1.50 **NM value: 5.00**
• **CGC:** 1 graded, best 8.0
📖 Victor; The Power; Max, the Imperial Wizard; Extinction; Hexakeras **A:** Larry Nadolsky; Barb Armata; Andrew Murphy; Bill Anderson; Francis J. Mao; Ron Kasman **W:** Larry Nadolsky; Barb Armata; Andrew Murphy; Bill Anderson; Bernie Armata; Francis Mao ★ 1st Appearance of Firebringer, Laserman.
5 ☐ 1983 Cover: 1.50 **NM value: 20.00**
• **CGC:** 3 graded, best 9.2
• 1st professional art by Sam Kieth **A:** Sam Kieth ★ 1st Appearance of The Maxx (original).
6 ☐ Cover: 1.50 **NM value: 6.00**
W: Chuck Dixon ★ 1st Appearance of Evangeline.

PRIMER (VOL. 2) — Comico

1 ☐ May 1996 Cover: 2.95 **NM value: Cover or less**
📖 Lady Bathory: The Assassin's Song **A:** Andrew Kudelka; Vincent Proce **W:** Brian Azzarello; Ed Dunphy

PRIME SLIME TALES — Mirage

1 ☐ Cover: 1.50 **NM value: Cover or less**
📖 Slime after Slime • Published By Mirage Studio **A:** Tony Basilicato; Rowen Basilicato **W:** Tony Basilicato; Rowen Basilicato
2 ☐ Cover: 1.50 **NM value: Cover or less**
📖 Having the Slime of Their Lives... • Published By Mirage Studio **A:** Tony Basilicato; Rowen Basilicato **W:** Tony Basilicato; Rowen Basilicato
3 ☐ Nov 1986 Cover: 1.50 **NM value: Cover or less**
Circ: CapCity orders: **1,700**
📖 Roach Wars • Published By Now Comics **A:** Tony Basilicato; Rowen Basilicato **W:** Tony Basilicato; Rowen Basilicato
4 ☐ Jan 1987 Cover: 1.50 **NM value: Cover or less**
• Published By Now Comics **A:** Tony Basilicato; Rowen Basilicato **W:** Tony Basilicato; Rowen Basilicato

PRIME VS. THE INCREDIBLE HULK — Malibu

0 ☐ Jul 1995 **NM value: 5.00**
no cover price.

PRIME (VOL. 1) — Malibu / Ultraverse

Prime is one of the strangest superheroes ever created. By all exterior appearances, he's a brawny powerhouse bristling with super-human strength. But the truth is that inside him, literally, is a little boy named Kevin.

Prime was the result of a series of gruesome genetic experiments near the start of the 1980s. The idea was to implant fast-mutating genes into babies, with the hopes of turning the children into super-soldiers. Unfortunately, this usually resulted in death — except for Kevin.

Now a junior high school student, Kevin has the ability to "grow" super-human bodies around him, including costumes made of living cells. These bodies are unstable, however, and when they expire, Kevin literally discards them like a second skin.

One of Malibu's more successful later creations, Prime got to costar with Spider-Man once Marvel bought Malibu.

0.5 ☐ **NM value: 2.50**
• Wizard promotional edition. **W:** Gerard Jones; Len Strazewski
1 ☐ Jun 1993 Cover: 1.95 **NM value: 3.00**
Circ: CapCity orders: **55,150**
📖 The King Of Beasts • Ultraverse **A:** Joel Thomas **W:** Gerard Jones; Len Strazewski ★ 1st Appearance of Prime, Doctor Gross.
1/Hol ☐ **NM value: 5.00**
• Holographic promotional edition. 📖 The King Of Beasts **W:** Gerard Jones; Len Strazewski ★ 1st Appearance of Prime, Doctor Gross.
1/LE ☐ Jun 1993 Cover: 1.95 **NM value: 3.00**
$1.95 on cover. • "Ultra-Limited" edition. 📖 The King Of Beasts • foil stamped **W:** Gerard Jones; Len Strazewski ★ 1st Appearance of Prime, Doctor Gross.
2 ☐ Jul 1993 Cover: 1.95 **NM value: 2.00**
Circ: CapCity orders: **20,925**
• Ultraverse; trading card **W:** Gerard Jones; Len Strazewski
3 ☐ Aug 1993 Cover: 1.95 **NM value: 2.00**
Circ: CapCity orders: **19,150**
📖 Dead Again...And Again **A:** Norm Breyfogle **W:** Gerard Jones; Len Strazewski ★ Origin of Prime.
4 ☐ Sep 1993 Cover: 1.95 **NM value: 2.00**
Circ: CapCity orders: **22,725**
two different covers. **W:** Gerard Jones; Len Strazewski ★ 1st Appearance of Maxi-Man. ★ Appearance of Prototype II (Jimmy Ruiz). ★ Versus Prototype.
5 ☐ Oct 1993 Cover: 2.50 **NM value: Cover or less**
Circ: CapCity orders: **31,625**
📖 Rune, Part B • Rune **A:** Barry Windsor-Smith **W:** Gerard Jones; Len Strazewski
6 ☐ Nov 1993 Cover: 1.95 **NM value: 2.00**
Circ: CapCity orders: **24,450**
W: Gerard Jones; Len Strazewski
7 ☐ Dec 1993 Cover: 1.95 **NM value: 2.00**
Circ: CapCity orders: **24,275**
📖 Break-Thru • Break-Thru **W:** Gerard Jones; Len Strazewski
8 ☐ Jan 1994 Cover: 1.95 **NM value: Cover or less**
Circ: CapCity orders: **21,425**
📖 The Return Of Doctor Gross **A:** Norm Breyfogle **W:** Gerard Jones; Len Strazewski ★ Origin of Freex. ★ Appearance of Mantra.
9 ☐ Feb 1994 Cover: 1.95 **NM value: Cover or less**
Circ: CapCity orders: **18,425**
📖 Atomic Lies! **A:** Norm Breyfogle **W:** Gerard Jones; Len Strazewski
10 ☐ Mar 1994 Cover: 1.95 **NM value: Cover or less**
Circ: CapCity orders: **17,275**
📖 The Men From The Boys **A:** Norm Breyfogle **W:** Gerard Jones; Len Strazewski ★ Appearance of Firearm.
11 ☐ Apr 1994 Cover: 1.95 **NM value: Cover or less**
Circ: CapCity orders: **17,075**
📖 Heroes Of Sunset Strip **A:** Norm Breyfogle **W:** Gerard Jones; Len Strazewski
12 ☐ May 1994 Cover: 3.50 **NM value: Cover or less**
Circ: CapCity orders: **18,825**
• flip-book with Ultraverse Premiere #3 **W:** Gerard Jones; Len Strazewski
13 ☐ Jul 1994 Cover: 2.95 **NM value: Cover or less**
Circ: CapCity orders: **17,875**
two different covers. 📖 Double Dangerous • Freex preview **A:** Scott Kolins; Darick Robertson **W:** Gerard Jones; Len Strazewski
13/A ☐ Cover: 1.95 **NM value: Cover or less**
variant cover. 📖 Double Dangerous **A:** Scott Kolins; Darick Robertson; Norm Breyfogle(cover) **W:** Gerard Jones; Len Strazewski
14 ☐ Sep 1994 Cover: 1.95 **NM value: Cover or less**
Circ: CapCity orders: **15,125**
📖 Age of Rebellion **A:** Darick Robertson **W:** Gerard Jones; Len Strazewski ★ 1st Appearance of Papa VeritT.
15 ☐ Oct 1994 Cover: 1.95 **NM value: Cover or less**
Circ: CapCity orders: **14,450**
📖 House of Horrors **A:** George Pérez **W:** Gerard Jones; Len Strazewski

CGC-graded: Multiply prices above by **33 for 9.9 M** • **16 for 9.8 NM/M** • **7 for 9.6 NM+** • **5 for 9.4 NM** • **2.5 for 9.2 NM-** • **1.5 for 9.0 VF/NM**

16 ❑ Nov 1994 Cover: 1.95 **NM** value: **Cover or less**
Circ: CapCity orders: **12,825**
📖 Up Against the Wall! **A:** Joel Thomas **W:** Gerard Jones; Len Strazewski ★ 1st Appearance of TurboCharge.

17 ❑ Dec 1994 Cover: 1.95 **NM** value: **Cover or less**
Circ: CapCity orders: **12,675**
📖 Hungry for Heroes **A:** John Statema **W:** Gerard Jones; Len Strazewski

18 ❑ Dec 1994 Cover: 1.95 **NM** value: **Cover or less**
Circ: CapCity orders: **11,125**
📖 One-Two Punch **A:** Kirk Jarvinen; David Williams **W:** Gerard Jones; Len Strazewski

19 ❑ Jan 1995 Cover: 1.95 **NM** value: **Cover or less**
Circ: CapCity orders: **9,975**
📖 Prime Season **A:** Tim Hamilton; Dave Cockrum; Brian Murray(cover) **W:** Gerard Jones; Len Strazewski

20 ❑ Mar 1995 Cover: 2.50 **NM** value: **Cover or less**
Circ: CapCity orders: **7,975**
📖 Cupid's Arrow **A:** Greg Luzniak; Brian Murray(cover) **W:** Gerard Jones; Len Strazewski ★ 1st Appearance of Phade.

21 ❑ Apr 1995 Cover: 2.50 **NM** value: **Cover or less**
Circ: CapCity orders: **7,225**
📖 A Hero Dies! **A:** Joe Staton; Brian Murray(cover) **W:** Gerard Jones; Len Strazewski ★ Appearance of Chelsea Clinton.

22 ❑ May 1995 Cover: 2.50 **NM** value: **Cover or less**
Circ: CapCity orders: **6,725**
📖 Getting Weird **A:** Joel Thomas; Mark Pacella(cover) **W:** Gerard Jones; Len Strazewski

23 ❑ Jun 1995 Cover: 2.50 **NM** value: **Cover or less**
Circ: CapCity orders: **6,425**

24 ❑ Jun 1995 Cover: 2.50 **NM** value: **Cover or less**
Circ: CapCity orders: **6,400**

25 ❑ Jul 1995 Cover: 2.50 **NM** value: **Cover or less**
• continued from Power of Prime #1 ★ Origin of Prime.

26 ❑ Aug 1995 Cover: 2.50 **NM** value: **Cover or less**
• continues in Power of Prime #2 ★ Origin of Prime.

Anl 1 ❑ Oct 1994 Cover: 3.95 **NM** value: **Cover or less**
Circ: CapCity orders: **13,150**
📖 Gross and Disgusting, Part 1 • Prime: Gross and Disgusting **A:** Norm Breyfogle; Boris Vallejo(cover) **C:** Boris Vallejo **W:** Gerard Jones; Len Strazewski ★ 1st Appearance of new Prime. ★ Appearance of Hardcase.

Ash 1 ❑ Cover: 0.75 **NM** value: **1.00**
• ashcan edition. **A:** Norm Breyfogle; Boris Vallejo(cover) **W:** Gerard Jones; Len Strazewski

Bk 1 ❑ Cover: 9.95 **NM** value: **Cover or less**
• Prime Time trade paperback; Collects Prime #1-4 **W:** Gerard Jones; Len Strazewski

PRIME (VOL. 2) — Malibu / Ultraverse

0 ❑ Sep 1995 Cover: 1.50 **NM** value: **Cover or less**
• Black September; #Infinity **A:** Kevin West **W:** Gerard Jones; Len Strazewski ★ Appearance of Spider-Man.

0/A ❑ Sep 1995 Cover: 1.50 **NM** value: **Cover or less**
alternate cover. • Black September ★ Appearance of Spider-Man.

1 ❑ Oct 1995 Cover: 1.50 **NM** value: **Cover or less**
📖 A Matter of Soul • Spider-Prime **A:** Kevin West **W:** Gerard Jones; Len Strazewski ★ Appearance of Lizard.

2 ❑ Nov 1995 Cover: 1.50 **NM** value: **Cover or less**
A: Kevin West **W:** Gerard Jones; Len Strazewski

3 ❑ Dec 1995 Cover: 1.50 **NM** value: **Cover or less**
A: Kevin West **W:** Gerard Jones; Len Strazewski

4 ❑ Jan 1996 Cover: 1.50 **NM** value: **Cover or less**
Circ: Diamd. preorders: **11,676**
• Kevin rejoins Prime body **A:** Kevin West **W:** Gerard Jones; Len Strazewski

5 ❑ Feb 1996 Cover: 1.50 **NM** value: **Cover or less**
A: Kevin West **W:** Gerard Jones; Len Strazewski

6 ❑ Mar 1996 Cover: 1.50 **NM** value: **Cover or less**
A: Kevin West **W:** Gerard Jones; Len Strazewski ★ Appearance of Solitaire.

7 ❑ Apr 1996 Cover: 1.50 **NM** value: **Cover or less**
A: Kevin West **W:** Gerard Jones; Len Strazewski

8 ❑ May 1996 Cover: 1.50 **NM** value: **Cover or less**
A: Kevin West **W:** Gerard Jones; Len Strazewski

9 ❑ Jun 1996 Cover: 1.50 **NM** value: **Cover or less**
A: Kevin West **W:** Gerard Jones; Len Strazewski

10 ❑ Jul 1996 Cover: 1.50 **NM** value: **Cover or less**
A: Kevin West **C:** Humberto Ramos **W:** Gerard Jones; Len Strazewski

11 ❑ Aug 1996 Cover: 1.50 **NM** value: **Cover or less**
A: Kevin West **C:** Humberto Ramos **W:** Gerard Jones; Len Strazewski

12 ❑ Sep 1996 Cover: 1.50 **NM** value: **Cover or less**
Circ: Diamd. preorders: **13,340**
A: Kevin West **C:** Humberto Ramos **W:** Gerard Jones; Len Strazewski

13 ❑ Oct 1996 Cover: 1.50 **NM** value: **Cover or less**
Circ: Diamd. preorders: **12,396**
A: Kevin West **C:** Humberto Ramos **W:** Gerard Jones; Len Strazewski

14 ❑ Nov 1996 Cover: 1.50 **NM** value: **Cover or less**
Circ: Diamd. preorders: **10,778**
📖 Monster Mash **A:** Al Rio **C:** Humberto Ramos **W:** Dan Shaheen

15 ❑ Dec 1996 Cover: 1.50 **NM** value: **Cover or less**
final issue. ★ Versus Lord Pumpkin.

PRIMITIVE CRETIN — Fantagraphics

Bk 1 ❑ May 1996, b&w Cover: 8.95 **NM** value: **Cover or less**
• oversized tpb.

PRIMITIVES — Sparetime Studios

1 ❑ Jan 1995, b&w Cover: 2.50 **NM** value: **Cover or less**
A: Larry Merrill; Steve Campbell **W:** Steve Campbell ★ Origin of Primitives. ★ 1st Appearance of Primitives.

2 ❑ May 1995, b&w Cover: 2.50 **NM** value: **Cover or less**

3 ❑ Oct 1995, b&w Cover: 2.50 **NM** value: **Cover or less**

PRIMORTALS ORIGINS (LEONARD NIMOY'S...) — Tekno

1 ❑ Jun 1995 Cover: 2.25 **NM** value: **Cover or less**
A: Scot Eaton **W:** James Chambers; Leonard Nimoy ★ Origin of the Primortals.

2 ❑ Cover: 2.25 **NM** value: **Cover or less**
A: Scot Eaton **W:** James Chambers; Leonard Nimoy ★ Origin of the Primortals.

PRIMORTALS (VOL. 1) (LEONARD NIMOY'S...) — Tekno

In the early issues of this series by celebrity comics publisher Tekno, two plots proceed in parallel. On Earth, signals have been received from space indicating that intelligent life is out there. Meanwhile, in space, it is revealed that various Earth animals, including dinosaurs, have been previously harvested from Earth and have evolved into intelligent beings — and are on their way home.

Some fans questioned the association of some Tekno titles with the celebrities whose names they bore, but according to Lawrence Watt-Evans, who worked on the title, the use of Leonard Nimoy's name on this comic was fully appropriate. Not only did Nimoy provide its concept, he said, but the Star Trek actor and director critiqued the plots and the scripts.

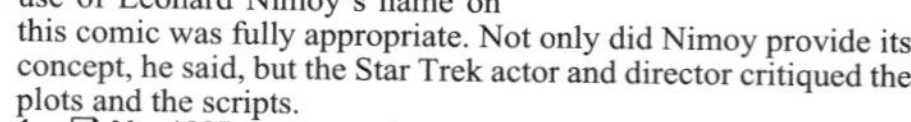

1 ❑ Mar 1995 Cover: 1.95 **NM** value: **Cover or less**
Circ: CapCity orders: **37,600**
📖 Escape to Earth **A:** Scot Eaton **W:** Kate Worley

2 ❑ Apr 1995 Cover: 1.95 **NM** value: **Cover or less**
Circ: CapCity orders: **31,625**

3 ❑ May 1995 Cover: 1.95 **NM** value: **Cover or less**
Circ: CapCity orders: **26,350**
📖 The Approaching Storm **A:** Mike Barreiro **W:** Christopher Mills

4 ❑ Jun 1995 Cover: 1.95 **NM** value: **Cover or less**
Circ: CapCity orders: **19,200**

5 ❑ Jul 1995 Cover: 1.95 **NM** value: **Cover or less**
Circ: CapCity orders: **17,025**

6 ❑ Aug 1995 Cover: 1.95 **NM** value: **Cover or less**
Circ: CapCity orders: **15,100**

7 ❑ Sep 1995 Cover: 1.95 **NM** value: **Cover or less**
Circ: CapCity orders: **13,100**

8 ❑ Oct 1995 Cover: 1.95 **NM** value: **Cover or less**
Circ: CapCity orders: **12,175**

9 ❑ Nov 1995 Cover: 1.95 **NM** value: **Cover or less**
Circ: CapCity orders: **11,525**

10 ❑ Dec 1995 Cover: 1.95 **NM** value: **Cover or less**
Circ: CapCity orders: **9,700**

11 ❑ Dec 1995 Cover: 1.95 **NM** value: **Cover or less**
Circ: CapCity orders: **7,750**

12 ❑ Jan 1996 Cover: 2.25 **NM** value: **Cover or less**
Circ: CapCity orders: **5,725**

13 ❑ Mar 1996 Cover: 2.25 **NM** value: **Cover or less**

14 ❑ Apr 1996 Cover: 2.25 **NM** value: **Cover or less**

15 ❑ May 1996 Cover: 2.25 **NM** value: **Cover or less**
final issue.

16 ❑ Cover: 2.25 **NM** value: **Cover or less**
final issue.

PRIMORTALS (VOL. 2) (LEONARD NIMOY'S...) — Big

0 ❑ Jun 1996 Cover: 2.25 **NM** value: **Cover or less**
📖 The Big Crossover, Part 9; Cross Country: World in Flames **A:** Scot Eaton **W:** James Chambers

1 ❑ Jul 1996 Cover: 2.25 **NM** value: **Cover or less**
2 ❑ Aug 1996 Cover: 2.25 **NM** value: **Cover or less**
3 ❑ Sep 1996 Cover: 2.25 **NM** value: **Cover or less**
4 ❑ Oct 1996 Cover: 2.25 **NM** value: **Cover or less**
5 ❑ Nov 1996 Cover: 2.25 **NM** value: **Cover or less**
6 ❑ Dec 1996 Cover: 2.25 **NM** value: **Cover or less**
7 ❑ Jan 1997 Cover: 2.25 **NM** value: **Cover or less**
final issue.

PRIMUS — Charlton

1 ❑ Feb 1972 Cover: 0.20 **NM** value: **7.00**
2 ❑ 1972 Cover: 0.20 **NM** value: **4.00**
3 ❑ 1972 Cover: 0.20 **NM** value: **4.00**
4 ❑ Jun 1972 Cover: 0.20 **NM** value: **4.00**
5 ❑ 1972 Cover: 0.20 **NM** value: **3.00**
6 ❑ 1972 Cover: 0.20 **NM** value: **3.00**
7 ❑ Oct 1972 Cover: 0.20 **NM** value: **3.00**

PRINCE: ALTER EGO — DC/Piranha Music

1 ❑ Dec 1991 Cover: 2.00 **NM** value: **Cover or less**
Circ: CapCity orders: **5,200**
C: Brian Bolland

CGC price ratios appearing on the bottom of right-hand pages are for pre-1990 comic books "slabbed" by Comics Guaranty Corp.

They represent the median price offered on eBay above our printed prices for comics in each grade. These are only a guide; individual prices vary by interest in the issue and the number of CGC-graded copies on the market.

For up-to-the-week CGC ratios, consult the current issue of **Comics Buyer's Guide.**

PRINCE AND THE NEW POWER GENERATION: THREE CHAINS OF GOLD — DC / Piranha

Pop icon Prince stars in this fantasy/adventure tale. It begins when Prince and his latest band, the New Power Generation, tour Erech, a country located "somewhere in the Middle East." Prince's raunchy brand of funk brings scandal and controversy to that country, but it also wins him the admiration of Princess Mayte. Mayte spends a charmed afternoon with Prince, giving him a golden chain as a mark of affection.

Erech's leader had planned to step down and hand over rule of the kingdom to Mayte. Angry at being passed over, her brother Tammuz slays the leader in order to seize power. But to finish the job, he needs to possess the three chains of gold which together designated the kingdom's rightful ruler, one of which now hangs from Prince's neck...

Mayte was based on a dancer in Prince's act, whom he later married. Do you really have to guess what unpronounceable symbol the three chains in this story form when put together?

1 ❑ Cover: 3.50 **NM** value: **Cover or less**
No issue number. **A:** Steve Carr; Deryl Skelton; David Williams **W:** Dwayne McDuffie

PRINCE AND THE PAUPER — Dell

1 ❑ Jul 1962 Cover: 0.15 **NM** value: **15.00**
• 01-654-207

PRINCE AND THE PAUPER, THE (DISNEY'S...) — Disney

1 ❑ Cover: 5.95 **NM** value: **Cover or less**
• squarebound **A:** Sergio Asteriti **W:** Scott Saavedra

PRINCE NAMOR, THE SUB-MARINER — Marvel

1 ❑ Sep 1984 Cover: 0.75 **NM** value: **1.50**
A: Bob Budiansky **W:** J.M. DeMatteis

2 ❑ Oct 1984 Cover: 0.75 **NM** value: **1.50**
A: Bob Budiansky **W:** J.M. DeMatteis

3 ❑ Nov 1984 Cover: 0.75 **NM** value: **1.50**
A: Bob Budiansky **W:** J.M. DeMatteis

4 ❑ Dec 1984 Cover: 0.75 **NM** value: **1.50**
📖 The Road Not Taken! **A:** Bob Budiansky **W:** J.M. DeMatteis

PRINCE NIGHTMARE — Aaaargh!

1 ❑ Cover: 2.95 **NM** value: **Cover or less**

PRINCESS KARANAM AND THE DJINN OF THE GREEN JUG — Mu Press

1 ❑ b&w Cover: 2.50 **NM** value: **Cover or less**
No issue number.

PRINCESS PRINCE — CPM Manga

1 ❑ Oct 2000 Cover: 2.95 **NM** value: **Cover or less**
Circ: Diamd. preorders: **3,156**
A: Tomoko Taniguhi **W:** Tomo Taniguhi

1/A ❑ Oct 2000 Cover: 2.95 **NM** value: **Cover or less**
alternate wraparound cover. **A:** Tomoko Taniguhi **W:** Tomo Taniguhi

2 ❑ Nov 2000 Cover: 2.95 **NM** value: **Cover or less**
Circ: Diamd. preorders: **1,967**
A: Tomoko Taniguhi **W:** Tomo Taniguhi

3 ❑ Dec 2000 Cover: 2.95 **NM** value: **Cover or less**
Circ: Diamd. preorders: **1,745**
A: Tomoko Taniguhi **W:** Tomo Taniguhi

4 ❑ Jan 2001 Cover: 2.95 **NM** value: **Cover or less**
Circ: Diamd. preorders: **1,678**
A: Tomoko Taniguhi **W:** Tomo Taniguhi

5 ❑ Feb 2001 Cover: 2.95 **NM** value: **Cover or less**
Circ: Diamd. preorders: **1,638**
A: Tomoko Taniguhi **W:** Tomo Taniguhi

6 ❑ Mar 2001 Cover: 2.95 **NM** value: **Cover or less**
Circ: Diamd. preorders: **1,595**
A: Tomoko Taniguhi **W:** Tomo Taniguhi

7 ❑ Apr 2001 Cover: 2.95 **NM** value: **Cover or less**
Circ: Diamd. preorders: **1,588**
A: Tomoko Taniguhi **W:** Tomo Taniguhi

8 ❑ May 2001 Cover: 2.95 **NM** value: **Cover or less**
Circ: Diamd. preorders: **1,529**
A: Tomoko Taniguhi **W:** Tomo Taniguhi

9 ❑ Jun 2001 Cover: 2.95 **NM** value: **Cover or less**
Circ: Diamd. preorders: **1,551**
A: Tomoko Taniguhi **W:** Tomo Taniguhi

10 ❑ Jul 2001 Cover: 2.95 **NM** value: **Cover or less**
Circ: Diamd. preorders: **1,562**
A: Tomoko Taniguhi **W:** Tomo Taniguhi

PRINCESS SALLY — Archie

1 ❑ Apr 1995 Cover: 1.50 **NM** value: **Cover or less**
2 ❑ May 1995 Cover: 1.50 **NM** value: **Cover or less**
3 ❑ Jun 1995 Cover: 1.50 **NM** value: **Cover or less**

PRINCE VALIANT (MARVEL) — Marvel

1 ❑ Dec 1994 Cover: 3.95 **NM** value: **Cover or less**
Circ: CapCity orders: **10,950**
cardstock cover. 📖 The Sword in the Stone **A:** John Ridgway **W:** Charles Vess; Elaine Lee

2 ❑ Jan 1995 Cover: 3.95 **NM** value: **Cover or less**
Circ: CapCity orders: **6,450**
cardstock cover. **A:** John Ridgway **W:** Charles Vess; Elaine Lee

Other grades: Multiply prices above by **1.5 for Mint • 2/3 for Very Fine • 1/3 for Fine • 1/5 for Very Good • 1/8 for Good**

3 ❑ Feb 1995 Cover: 3.95 **NM** value: **Cover or less**
Circ: CapCity orders: **5,750**
cardstock cover. **A:** John Ridgway **W:** Charles Vess; Elaine Lee
4 ❑ Mar 1995 Cover: 3.95 **NM** value: **Cover or less**
Circ: CapCity orders: **5,600**
cardstock cover.

PRINCE VALIANT MONTHLY — Pioneer
1 ❑ b&w Cover: 4.95 **NM** value: **Cover or less**
2 ❑ b&w Cover: 4.95 **NM** value: **Cover or less**
3 ❑ b&w Cover: 4.95 **NM** value: **Cover or less**
4 ❑ b&w Cover: 4.95 **NM** value: **Cover or less**

PRINCE VANDAL — Triumphant
1 ❑ Cover: 2.50 **NM** value: **Cover or less**
Circ: CapCity orders: **6,850**
📖 Interference • Unleashed! **A:** Jason Vega **W:** John Riley
2 ❑ Cover: 2.50 **NM** value: **Cover or less**
Circ: CapCity orders: **4,730**
• Unleashed! **A:** Jason Vega **W:** John Riley
3 ❑ Cover: 2.50 **NM** value: **Cover or less**
Circ: CapCity orders: **3,750**
A: Jason Vega **W:** John Riley
4 ❑ Cover: 2.50 **NM** value: **Cover or less**
Circ: CapCity orders: **3,320**
A: Jason Vega **W:** John Riley
5 ❑ Cover: 2.50 **NM** value: **Cover or less**
Circ: CapCity orders: **2,575**
A: Jason Vega **W:** John Riley
6 ❑ Cover: 2.50 **NM** value: **Cover or less**
Circ: CapCity orders: **2,127**
A: Jason Vega **W:** John Riley

PRIORITY: WHITE HEAT — AC
1 ❑ Mar 1987 Cover: 1.75 **NM** value: **Cover or less**
Circ: CapCity orders: **3,825**
📖 The Blitz of vengeance!: Two Riddles to Recife **A:** Don Secrease **W:** Ed Stehlin
2 ❑ Cover: 1.75 **NM** value: **Cover or less**
Circ: CapCity orders: **2,725**

PRISON BREAK — Realistic Comics
1 ❑ Sep 1951 Cover: 0.10 **NM** value: **300.00**
• **CGC:** 1 graded, best 7.0
2 ❑ Dec 1951 Cover: 0.10 **NM** value: **200.00**
• **CGC:** 1 graded, best 3.5
3 ❑ Mar 1952 Cover: 0.10 **NM** value: **200.00**
• **CGC:** 1 graded, best 7.5
4 ❑ Jun 1952 Cover: 0.10 **NM** value: **200.00**
5 ❑ Sep 1952 Cover: 0.10 **NM** value: **200.00**

PRISONER, THE — DC

If you were fortunate enough to catch The Prisoner on BBC television or on its A&E re-runs in the States, you already know that it was a remarkable series — possibly the finest television series ever. In its 18 episodes, it told the story of a secret agent (possibly Frank Drake from the old Secret Agent Man series) who wanted out. Instead, he was kidnapped and taken to a strange island town called simply, "The Village." There, identities were replaced by numbers — and the agent was subjected to endless mind games in an effort to gain information from him (we never find out which side wants the information). However, the agent, now known only as "Number Six" resisted all attempts to break him, eventually fulfilling a promise not only to escape, but to destroy the Village. Afterward, he simply disappeared.

This series serves as the "official" sequel to The Prisoner. It begins years later, as another British intelligence officer discovers the whereabouts of the now-abandoned Village...

In lieu of numbers, the series' individual issues were denoted by letters, a, b, c, and d.

1 ❑ Dec 1988 Cover: 3.50 **NM** value: **4.00**
Circ: CapCity orders: **23,550**
📖 Arrival • a **A:** Dave Hornung; Mark Askwith **W:** Dean Motter
2 ❑ Jan 1989 Cover: 3.50 **NM** value: **4.00**
Circ: CapCity orders: **18,200**
📖 By Hook Or By Crook • b **A:** Dave Hornung; Mark Askwith **W:** Dean Motter
3 ❑ Jan 1989 Cover: 3.50 **NM** value: **4.00**
Circ: CapCity orders: **17,850**
📖 Confrontation • c **A:** Dave Hornung; Mark Askwith **W:** Dean Motter
4 ❑ Feb 1989 Cover: 3.50 **NM** value: **4.00**
Circ: CapCity orders: **18,200**
📖 Departure • d **A:** Dave Hornung; Mark Askwith **W:** Dean Motter
Bk 1❑ Cover: 19.95 **NM** value: **Cover or less**
📖 Arrival; By Hook Or By Crook; Confrontation; Departure • Collects The Prisoner #1-4 **A:** Dave Hornung; Mark Askwith **W:** Dean Motter
Bk 1-2❑ Cover: 19.95 **NM** value: **Cover or less**

PRISONER OF CHILLON — Tome Press
1 ❑ b&w Cover: 2.95 **NM** value: **Cover or less**

PRISONOPOLIS — Mediawarp
1 ❑ Feb 1997, b&w Cover: 2.75 **NM** value: **Cover or less**
2 ❑ Apr 1997, b&w Cover: 2.75 **NM** value: **Cover or less**

PRISON RIOT — Avon
1 ❑ ca. 1952 Cover: 0.10 **NM** value: **200.00**
• **CGC:** 1 graded, best 9.0

PRIVATE BEACH: FUN AND PERILS IN THE TRUDYVERSE — Antarctic
1 ❑ Jan 1995, b&w Cover: 2.75 **NM** value: **Cover or less**
A: David Hahn **W:** David Hahn
2 ❑ Mar 1995, b&w Cover: 2.75 **NM** value: **Cover or less**
A: David Hahn **W:** David Hahn
3 ❑ May 1995, b&w Cover: 2.75 **NM** value: **Cover or less**
A: David Hahn **W:** David Hahn

PRIVATE COMMISSIONS (GRAY MORROW'S...) — Forbidden Fruit
All issues are adults only.
1 ❑ b&w Cover: 2.95 **NM** value: **Cover or less**
2 ❑ b&w Cover: 2.95 **NM** value: **Cover or less**

PRIVATEERS — Vanguard
1 ❑ Cover: 1.50 **NM** value: **Cover or less**
2 ❑ Cover: 1.50 **NM** value: **Cover or less**
Circ: CapCity orders: **1,700**

PRIVATE EYE — Atlas
1 ❑ Jan 1951 Cover: 0.10 **NM** value: **150.00**
• **CGC:** 1 graded, best 8.5
2 ❑ Mar 1951 Cover: 0.10 **NM** value: **75.00**
3 ❑ May 1951 Cover: 0.10 **NM** value: **75.00**
4 ❑ Jul 1951 Cover: 0.10 **NM** value: **60.00**
5 ❑ Sep 1951 Cover: 0.10 **NM** value: **60.00**
6 ❑ Nov 1951 Cover: 0.10 **NM** value: **60.00**
7 ❑ Jan 1952 Cover: 0.10 **NM** value: **60.00**
8 ❑ Mar 1952 Cover: 0.10 **NM** value: **60.00**

PRIVATE EYES — Eternity
1 ❑ Sep 1988, b&w Cover: 1.95 **NM** value: **Cover or less**
• Saint reprints
2 ❑ Nov 1988, b&w Cover: 1.95 **NM** value: **Cover or less**
• Saint reprints
3 ❑ Jan 1989, b&w Cover: 1.95 **NM** value: **Cover or less**
• Saint reprints
4 ❑ May 1989 Cover: 2.95 **NM** value: **Cover or less**
5 ❑ Aug 1989 Cover: 3.50 **NM** value: **Cover or less**
6 ❑ Cover: 3.95 **NM** value: **Cover or less**

PRIVATE FILES OF THE SHADOW — DC
1 ❑ Cover: 19.95 **NM** value: **Cover or less**
Circ: CapCity orders: **2,900**
hardcover. **A:** Michael W. Kaluta

PRIZE COMICS — Feature

Prize Comics was the flagship title of Prize Publications during the Golden Age. It featured the usual anthology of super-heroes, adventure strips, jungle action stories, aviation and spy tales, and humor. The main hero features of the book were The Black Owl, later succeeded by his sons, Yank and Doodle, and The Green Lama, who made his first appearance in Prize Comics #7. One of the best loved and remembered characters from the pages of Prize was Frankenstein, a goofy-humor version of Dr. Frankenstein's famous monster, but capable of a wide and powerful storytelling range. The artwork and stories improved steadily, and Prize often featured art that was a step above the crude work of many of the lesser Golden Age publishers. In 1948, Prize became Prize Western Comics and turned to adaptations of movie Westerns, including Streets of Laredo, Roughshod, and Gunsmoke Justice.

1 ❑ Mar 1940 Cover: 0.10 **NM** value: **1550.00**
• **CGC:** 1 graded, best .5
2 ❑ Apr 1940 Cover: 0.10 **NM** value: **775.00**
3 ❑ May 1940 Cover: 0.10 **NM** value: **600.00**
4 ❑ Jun 1940 Cover: 0.10 **NM** value: **600.00**
5 ❑ Jul 1940 Cover: 0.10 **NM** value: **600.00**
6 ❑ Aug 1940 Cover: 0.10 **NM** value: **525.00**
7 ❑ Dec 1940 Cover: 0.10 **NM** value: **1100.00**
• **CGC:** 1 graded, best 2.0
★ 1st Appearance of The Green Lama.
8 ❑ Jan 1941 Cover: 0.10 **NM** value: **575.00**
9 ❑ Feb 1941 Cover: 0.10 **NM** value: **575.00**
• **CGC:** 1 graded, best 8.0
10 ❑ May 1941 Cover: 0.10 **NM** value: **500.00**
11 ❑ Jun 1941 Cover: 0.10 **NM** value: **500.00**
12 ❑ Jul 1941 Cover: 0.10 **NM** value: **500.00**
13 ❑ Aug 1941 Cover: 0.10 **NM** value: **540.00**
★ Origin of Yank and Doodle. ★ 1st Appearance of Yank and Doodle.
14 ❑ Sep 1941 Cover: 0.10 **NM** value: **440.00**
15 ❑ Oct 1941 Cover: 0.10 **NM** value: **440.00**
• **CGC:** 1 graded, best 9.4
16 ❑ Nov 1941 Cover: 0.10 **NM** value: **440.00**
• **CGC:** 1 graded, best 9.2
17 ❑ Dec 1941 Cover: 0.10 **NM** value: **440.00**
18 ❑ Jan 1942 Cover: 0.10 **NM** value: **440.00**
19 ❑ Feb 1942 Cover: 0.10 **NM** value: **440.00**
20 ❑ Mar 1942 Cover: 0.10 **NM** value: **440.00**
21 ❑ May 1942 Cover: 0.10 **NM** value: **340.00**
22 ❑ Jul 1942 Cover: 0.10 **NM** value: **340.00**
23 ❑ Sep 1942 Cover: 0.10 **NM** value: **340.00**
24 ❑ Oct 1942 Cover: 0.10 **NM** value: **340.00**
25 ❑ Nov 1942 Cover: 0.10 **NM** value: **275.00**
26 ❑ Dec 1942 Cover: 0.10 **NM** value: **275.00**
27 ❑ Jan 1943 Cover: 0.10 **NM** value: **275.00**
28 ❑ Feb 1943 Cover: 0.10 **NM** value: **275.00**
29 ❑ Mar 1943 Cover: 0.10 **NM** value: **275.00**
30 ❑ Apr 1943 Cover: 0.10 **NM** value: **275.00**
31 ❑ Jun 1943 Cover: 0.10 **NM** value: **210.00**
32 ❑ Jul 1943 Cover: 0.10 **NM** value: **210.00**
33 ❑ Aug 1943 Cover: 0.10 **NM** value: **210.00**
34 ❑ Sep 1943 Cover: 0.10 **NM** value: **210.00**
35 ❑ Oct 1943 Cover: 0.10 **NM** value: **210.00**
• **CGC:** 1 graded, best 6.5
36 ❑ Nov 1943 Cover: 0.10 **NM** value: **155.00**
37 ❑ Dec 1943 Cover: 0.10 **NM** value: **155.00**
38 ❑ Jan 1944 Cover: 0.10 **NM** value: **155.00**
39 ❑ Feb 1944 Cover: 0.10 **NM** value: **155.00**
40 ❑ Mar 1944 Cover: 0.10 **NM** value: **155.00**
41 ❑ Apr 1944 Cover: 0.10 **NM** value: **125.00**
42 ❑ Jun 1944 Cover: 0.10 **NM** value: **125.00**
43 ❑ Jul 1944 Cover: 0.10 **NM** value: **125.00**
44 ❑ Aug 1944 Cover: 0.10 **NM** value: **125.00**
45 ❑ Sep 1944 Cover: 0.10 **NM** value: **125.00**
46 ❑ Oct 1944 Cover: 0.10 **NM** value: **100.00**
47 ❑ Nov 1944 Cover: 0.10 **NM** value: **100.00**
48 ❑ Dec 1944 Cover: 0.10 **NM** value: **100.00**
49 ❑ Jan 1945 Cover: 0.10 **NM** value: **100.00**
• **CGC:** 1 graded, best 9.2
50 ❑ Feb 1945 Cover: 0.10 **NM** value: **100.00**
51 ❑ Mar 1945 Cover: 0.10 **NM** value: **75.00**
• **CGC:** 1 graded, best 8.0
52 ❑ Apr 1945 Cover: 0.10 **NM** value: **75.00**
53 ❑ May 1945 Cover: 0.10 **NM** value: **75.00**
• **CGC:** 1 graded, best 9.2
54 ❑ Jul 1945 Cover: 0.10 **NM** value: **75.00**
📖 Boom Boom Brannigan; Frankenstein and His Own Story of His Childhood; An Inside Job (text story); Zar King of Beasts; Yank and Doodle; Caveman Frolics; Sir Prize **W:** Clem Colbert
55 ❑ Sep 1945 Cover: 0.10 **NM** value: **75.00**
56 ❑ Nov 1945 Cover: 0.10 **NM** value: **75.00**
57 ❑ Jan 1946 Cover: 0.10 **NM** value: **75.00**
58 ❑ Mar 1946 Cover: 0.10 **NM** value: **75.00**
59 ❑ May 1946 Cover: 0.10 **NM** value: **75.00**
60 ❑ Jul 1946 Cover: 0.10 **NM** value: **75.00**
61 ❑ Sep 1946 Cover: 0.10 **NM** value: **60.00**
62 ❑ Nov 1946 Cover: 0.10 **NM** value: **60.00**
63 ❑ Mar 1947 Cover: 0.10 **NM** value: **60.00**
64 ❑ Jun 1947 Cover: 0.10 **NM** value: **60.00**
65 ❑ Aug 1947 Cover: 0.10 **NM** value: **60.00**
66 ❑ Oct 1947 Cover: 0.10 **NM** value: **60.00**
📖 Swami Rhiva-Stay 'way from My Dough; Frankenstein; Jason; The Iron Man; Comeback (Text Story); Charlie CrowThe Switched Suitcase
67 ❑ Dec 1947 Cover: 0.10 **NM** value: **60.00**
68 ❑ Feb 1948 Cover: 0.10 **NM** value: **60.00**
• Series continued in Prize Comics Western #69

PRIZE COMICS WESTERN — Feature
69 ❑ May 1948 Cover: 0.10 **NM** value: **100.00**
70 ❑ Jul 1948 Cover: 0.10 **NM** value: **90.00**
• **CGC:** 1 graded, best 9.4
71 ❑ Sep 1948 Cover: 0.10 **NM** value: **90.00**
• **CGC:** 1 graded, best 9.2
72 ❑ Nov 1948 Cover: 0.10 **NM** value: **90.00**
73 ❑ Jan 1949 Cover: 0.10 **NM** value: **90.00**
74 ❑ Mar 1949 Cover: 0.10 **NM** value: **90.00**
75 ❑ May 1949 Cover: 0.10 **NM** value: **90.00**
76 ❑ Jul 1949 Cover: 0.10 **NM** value: **90.00**
77 ❑ Sep 1949 Cover: 0.10 **NM** value: **90.00**
78 ❑ Nov 1949 Cover: 0.10 **NM** value: **90.00**
79 ❑ Jan 1950 Cover: 0.10 **NM** value: **90.00**
80 ❑ Mar 1950 Cover: 0.10 **NM** value: **90.00**
81 ❑ May 1950 Cover: 0.10 **NM** value: **90.00**
82 ❑ Jul 1950 Cover: 0.10 **NM** value: **90.00**
83 ❑ Sep 1950 Cover: 0.10 **NM** value: **90.00**
84 ❑ Nov 1950 Cover: 0.10 **NM** value: **90.00**
85 ❑ Jan 1951 Cover: 0.10 **NM** value: **90.00**
86 ❑ Mar 1951 Cover: 0.10 **NM** value: **90.00**
87 ❑ May 1951 Cover: 0.10 **NM** value: **90.00**
88 ❑ Jul 1951 Cover: 0.10 **NM** value: **90.00**
89 ❑ Sep 1951 Cover: 0.10 **NM** value: **90.00**
90 ❑ Nov 1951 Cover: 0.10 **NM** value: **90.00**
91 ❑ Jan 1952 Cover: 0.10 **NM** value: **80.00**
92 ❑ Mar 1952 Cover: 0.10 **NM** value: **80.00**
93 ❑ May 1952 Cover: 0.10 **NM** value: **80.00**
94 ❑ Jul 1952 Cover: 0.10 **NM** value: **80.00**
95 ❑ Sep 1952 Cover: 0.10 **NM** value: **80.00**
96 ❑ Nov 1952 Cover: 0.10 **NM** value: **80.00**
97 ❑ Jan 1953 Cover: 0.10 **NM** value: **80.00**
98 ❑ Mar 1953 Cover: 0.10 **NM** value: **80.00**
99 ❑ May 1953 Cover: 0.10 **NM** value: **80.00**
100 ❑ Jul 1953 Cover: 0.10 **NM** value: **80.00**
101 ❑ Sep 1953 Cover: 0.10 **NM** value: **80.00**
102 ❑ Nov 1953 Cover: 0.10 **NM** value: **80.00**
103 ❑ Jan 1954 Cover: 0.10 **NM** value: **80.00**
104 ❑ Mar 1954 Cover: 0.10 **NM** value: **80.00**
105 ❑ May 1954 Cover: 0.10 **NM** value: **80.00**
106 ❑ 1954 Cover: 0.10 **NM** value: **80.00**
107 ❑ 1954 Cover: 0.10 **NM** value: **80.00**
108 ❑ Cover: 0.10 **NM** value: **80.00**
109 ❑ 1955 Cover: 0.10 **NM** value: **80.00**
110 ❑ 1955 Cover: 0.10 **NM** value: **80.00**
111 ❑ 1955 Cover: 0.10 **NM** value: **80.00**
112 ❑ 1955 Cover: 0.10 **NM** value: **80.00**
113 ❑ 1955 Cover: 0.10 **NM** value: **125.00**
114 ❑ Cover: 0.10 **NM** value: **80.00**
115 ❑ Cover: 0.10 **NM** value: **80.00**
116 ❑ 1956 Cover: 0.10 **NM** value: **80.00**

117 ❑ 1956 Cover: 0.10 **NM** value: **80.00**
118 ❑ 1956 Cover: 0.10 **NM** value: **80.00**
119 ❑ Nov 1956 Cover: 0.10 **NM** value: **80.00**

PRIZE MYSTERY — Key

1 ❑ May 1955 Cover: 0.10 **NM** value: **75.00**
2 ❑ Jul 1955 Cover: 0.10 **NM** value: **50.00**
3 ❑ Sep 1955 Cover: 0.10 **NM** value: **50.00**

PRO ACTION MAGAZINE (VOL. 2) — Marvel / NFL Properties

1 ❑ Jul 1994 Cover: 2.95 **NM** value: **Cover or less**
2 ❑ Sep 1994 Cover: 2.95 **NM** value: **Cover or less**
3 ❑ Nov 1994 Cover: 2.95 **NM** value: **Cover or less**
• magazine with bound-in Spider-Man comic book.

PROBE — Imperial

1 ❑ Cover: 1.80 **NM** value: **2.00**
Earth Case **A:** Frank Turner **W:** Frank Turner
2 ❑ Cover: 1.95 **NM** value: **2.00**
3 ❑ Cover: 1.95 **NM** value: **2.00**

PROF. COFFIN — Charlton

19 ❑ Oct 1985 Cover: 0.75 **NM** value: **2.00**
The Midnight Philosopher; Weave Me a Web; The Doll; Last Kind **A:** Joe Staton; Jack Abel; Wayne Howard **W:** Nicola Cutii; Wayne Howard
20 ❑ Dec 1985 Cover: 0.75 **NM** value: **2.00**
21 ❑ Feb 1986 Cover: 0.75 **NM** value: **2.00**
The Midnight Philosopher: The Fortune teller; Game Preserve; Malfunction; Lost in Transit **A:** Tom Sutton; Joe Staton; Wayne Howard **W:** Nicola Cutii

PROFESSIONAL, THE: GOLGO 13 — Viz

1 ❑ full color Cover: 4.95 **NM** value: **Cover or less**
Circ: CapCity orders: **4,600**
• Japanese
2 ❑ full color Cover: 4.95 **NM** value: **Cover or less**
Circ: CapCity orders: **2,900**
• Japanese
3 ❑ full color Cover: 4.95 **NM** value: **Cover or less**
Circ: CapCity orders: **2,925**
• Japanese

PROFESSOR OM — Innovation

1 ❑ May 1990 Cover: 2.50 **NM** value: **Cover or less**
Circ: CapCity orders: **1,650**
W: Power

PROFESSOR XAVIER AND THE X-MEN — Marvel

Introduced in 1995, this series had a twin appeal. First, it was one of Marvel's new line of 99-cent comics, a bargain at a time when the average comic price had climbed over $2. Second, it gave readers a contemporary look at the earliest adventures of the mutant group X-Men.

This series is a retelling of the events that took place in the original Lee/Kirby X-Men comic of the '60s, featuring new scripts and art. Recreating the original X-Men (1st Series) issue by issue, the new series used a wide roster of creators, who took the old stories and redid them in a '90s style.

1 ❑ Nov 1995 Cover: 0.99 **NM** value: **1.50**
Trial by Fire! • retells origin of team and first mission **A:** Jan Duursema **W:** Fred Schiller
2 ❑ Dec 1995 Cover: 0.99 **NM** value: **1.50**
• retells first Vanisher story **A:** Jan Duursema **W:** Fred Schiller ★ Appearance of Vanisher.
3 ❑ Jan 1996 Cover: 0.99 **NM** value: **1.50**
• retells first Blob story
4 ❑ Feb 1996 Cover: 0.99 **NM** value: **1.25**
• retells first meeting with Brotherhood of Evil Mutants
5 ❑ Mar 1996 Cover: 0.99 **NM** value: **1.25**
The Brotherhood • retells first meeting with Brotherhood of Evil Mutants **A:** Steve Ellis **W:** Fred Schiller
6 ❑ Apr 1996 Cover: 0.99 **NM** value: **1.25**
Fallen Angel **A:** Jorge Gonzalez **W:** Fred Schiller
7 ❑ May 1996 Cover: 0.99 **NM** value: **1.25**
• Sub-Mariner vs. Magneto
8 ❑ Jun 1996 Cover: 0.99 **NM** value: **1.25**
9 ❑ Jul 1996 Cover: 0.99 **NM** value: **1.25**
10 ❑ Aug 1996 Cover: 0.99 **NM** value: **1.25**
★ Versus Avengers.
11 ❑ Sep 1996 Cover: 0.99 **NM** value: **1.00**
★ Appearance of Ka-Zar.
12 ❑ Oct 1996 Cover: 0.99 **NM** value: **1.00**
★ Versus Juggernaut.
13 ❑ Nov 1996 Cover: 0.99 **NM** value: **1.00**
Circ: Direct Market orders: **41,250**
★ Versus Juggernaut.
14 ❑ Dec 1996 Cover: 0.99 **NM** value: **1.00**
Circ: Direct Market orders: **40,000**
Living Dangerously **A:** Eric Battle **W:** Jorge Gonzalez
15 ❑ Jan 1997 Cover: 0.99 **NM** value: **1.00**
Circ: Direct Market orders: **37,000**
Dangerous Convictions **A:** Nick Gnazzo **W:** Jorge Gonzalez ★ Versus Magneto. ★ Versus Stranger.
16 ❑ Feb 1997 Cover: 0.99 **NM** value: **1.00**
Circ: Direct Market orders: **34,000**
Enter the Sentinels **A:** Anthony Castrillo; Nick Gnazzo **W:** Jorge Gonzalez ★ Versus Sentinels.
17 ❑ Mar 1997 Cover: 0.99 **NM** value: **1.00**
Circ: Direct Market orders: **32,000**
Probes **A:** Chris Batista **W:** Jorge Gonzalez
18 ❑ Apr 1997 Cover: 0.99 **NM** value: **1.00**
Circ: Direct Market orders: **30,500**
Final Sanction final issue. **A:** Chris Batista **W:** Jorge Gonzalez ★ Versus Sentinels.

PROFOLIO — Alchemy

1 ❑ b&w Cover: 1.50 **NM** value: **Cover or less**
2 ❑ Cover: 2.50 **NM** value: **Cover or less**
• some color
3 ❑ b&w Cover: 2.50 **NM** value: **Cover or less**

PROFOLIO (VOL. 3) — Alchemy

1 ❑ Cover: 5.95 **NM** value: **Cover or less**

PROGENY — Caliber

1 ❑ b&w Cover: 4.95 **NM** value: **Cover or less**
No issue number.

PROGRAM ERROR: BATTLEBOT — Phantasy

1 ❑ Cover: 2.00 **NM** value: **Cover or less**

PROJECT, THE — DC / Paradox Press

1 ❑ ca. 1997, b&w Cover: 5.95 **NM** value: **Cover or less**
• digest. • short story collection
2 ❑ ca. 1997, b&w Cover: 5.95 **NM** value: **Cover or less**
• digest. • short story collection

PROJECT A-KO — Malibu

1 ❑ Mar 1994 Cover: 2.95 **NM** value: **Cover or less**
Circ: CapCity orders: **7,475**
It Came Form A-Ko Space **A:** Ben Dunn **W:** Tim Eldred
2 ❑ Mar 1994 Cover: 2.95 **NM** value: **Cover or less**
Circ: CapCity orders: **7,000**
The Rivals **A:** Ben Dunn **W:** Tim Eldred
3 ❑ May 1994 Cover: 2.95 **NM** value: **Cover or less**
Circ: CapCity orders: **5,025**
Dual Duel **A:** Ben Dunn **W:** Tim Eldred
4 ❑ Jun 1994 Cover: 2.95 **NM** value: **Cover or less**
Circ: CapCity orders: **5,000**
Hit And Rum **A:** Ben Dunn **W:** Tim Eldred
Bk 1 ❑ Mar 1995 Cover: 12.95 **NM** value: **Cover or less**
It Came Form A-Ko Space; The Rivals; Dual Duel; Hit And Rum • collects Malibu mini-series; Collects Project A-Ko #1-4 **A:** Ben Dunn **W:** Tim Eldred

PROJECT A-KO 2 — CPM

1 ❑ Apr 1995 Cover: 2.95 **NM** value: **Cover or less**
Circ: CapCity orders: **3,840**
The Plot Of The Daitokuji Financial Group! **A:** Tim Eldred **W:** Tim Eldred
2 ❑ Jun 1995 Cover: 2.95 **NM** value: **Cover or less**
Circ: CapCity orders: **2,980**
Off The Ground **A:** Tim Eldred **W:** Tim Eldred
3 ❑ Aug 1995 Cover: 2.95 **NM** value: **Cover or less**
Circ: CapCity orders: **2,470**
Like Father, Like Daughter **A:** Tim Eldred **W:** Tim Eldred
Bk 1 ❑ Cover: 12.95 **NM** value: **Cover or less**
The Plot Of The Daitokuji Financial Group!; Off The Ground; Like Father, Like Daughter **A:** Tim Eldred **W:** Tim Eldred

PROJECT A-KO VERSUS — CPM

1 ❑ Oct 1995 Cover: 2.95 **NM** value: **Cover or less**
Project A-Ko Versus the Universe **A:** Tim Eldred **W:** Tim Eldred
2 ❑ Dec 1995 Cover: 2.95 **NM** value: **Cover or less**
A: Tim Eldred; Studio Go! **W:** Tim Eldred
3 ❑ Feb 1996 Cover: 2.95 **NM** value: **Cover or less**
A: Tim Eldred **W:** Tim Eldred
4 ❑ Apr 1996 Cover: 2.95 **NM** value: **Cover or less**
A: Tim Eldred **W:** Tim Eldred
5 ❑ Jun 1996 Cover: 2.95 **NM** value: **Cover or less**
final issue. **A:** Tim Eldred **W:** Tim Eldred

PROJECT: DARK MATTER — Dimm Comics

1 ❑ Apr 1996, b&w Cover: 2.50 **NM** value: **Cover or less**
Project: Dark Matter; Fishbone **A:** Jon Morris; Ron Cornett **W:** Jon Morris; Anthony Gardaux
2 ❑ Jun 1996, b&w Cover: 2.50 **NM** value: **Cover or less**
cardstock cover.
3 ❑ b&w Cover: 2.50 **NM** value: **Cover or less**
cardstock cover.
4 ❑ Sep 1997, b&w Cover: 2.50 **NM** value: **Cover or less**
Bk 1 ❑ May 1997 Cover: 3.50 **NM** value: **Cover or less**
• John Morris' Fishbone; collects stories from Project: Dark Matter

PROJECT: GENERATION — Truth

1 ❑ Jun 2000 **NM** value: **1.00**
• Distributed at San Diego Comic-Con

PROJECT: HERO — Vanguard

1 ❑ Aug 1987 Cover: 1.50 **NM** value: **Cover or less**
2 ❑ Cover: 1.50 **NM** value: **Cover or less**

PROJECT SEX — Fantagraphics / Eros

All issues are adults only.
1 ❑ b&w Cover: 2.50 **NM** value: **Cover or less**

PROJECT X — Kitchen Sink

1 ❑ Cover: 4.95 **NM** value: **Cover or less**
No issue number. • Eastman/Bisley; bagged Thump'n Guts; poster; trading card

PROMETHEA — DC / America's Best Comics

In fifth century Egypt, a young girl named Promethea was taken to Immateria, the world of myth and fiction. Growing up in the world where all dreams and stories come from, she would wander from time to time into the imagination of writers in our world whose enthusiasm for the character would project her onto themselves or others. In 1999, young Sophie Bangs began her term paper on the ever-appearing character and discovered Promethea's last host. Now a new Promethea flies above the streets of the city. And her enemies, gained over the ages, are not happy to see her back.

1 ❑ Aug 1999 Cover: 3.50 **NM** value: **Cover or less**
Circ: Diamd. preorders: **56,325** • **CGC:** 2 graded, best 9.8
Promethea: The Radiant, Heavenly City **A:** J.H. Williams III **W:** Alan Moore ★ Origin of Promethea.
2 ❑ Sep 1999 Cover: 2.95 **NM** value: **Cover or less**
Circ: Diamd. preorders: **42,266** • **CGC:** 1 graded, best 9.6
The Judgment of Solomon **A:** J.H. Williams III **W:** Alan Moore
3 ❑ Oct 1999 Cover: 2.95 **NM** value: **Cover or less**
Circ: Diamd. preorders: **38,482** • **CGC:** 1 graded, best 9.6
Misty Magicians **A:** J.H. Williams III **W:** Alan Moore
4 ❑ Nov 1999 Cover: 2.95 **NM** value: **Cover or less**
Circ: Diamd. preorders: **35,850** • **CGC:** 1 graded, best 9.6
A Faerie Romance **A:** J.H. Williams III **W:** Alan Moore
5 ❑ Dec 1999 Cover: 2.95 **NM** value: **Cover or less**
Circ: Diamd. preorders: **34,910**
A: J.H. Williams III **W:** Alan Moore
6 ❑ Mar 2000 Cover: 2.95 **NM** value: **Cover or less**
Circ: Diamd. preorders: **29,812**
The 5 Swell Guys: Firefight on 5th Avenue! **A:** J.H. Williams III **W:** Alan Moore
7 ❑ Apr 2000 Cover: 2.95 **NM** value: **Cover or less**
Circ: Diamd. preorders: **27,768**
Rocks and Hard Places **A:** J.H. Williams III **W:** Alan Moore
8 ❑ May 2000 Cover: 2.95 **NM** value: **Cover or less**
Circ: Diamd. preorders: **27,001**
W: Alan Moore
9 ❑ Sep 2000 Cover: 2.95 **NM** value: **Cover or less**
Circ: Diamd. preorders: **26,637**
W: Alan Moore
10 ❑ Oct 2000 Cover: 2.95 **NM** value: **Cover or less**
Circ: Diamd. preorders: **24,965** • **CGC:** 1 graded, best 9.4
Sex, Stars & Serpents **A:** J.H. Williams III **W:** Alan Moore
11 ❑ Dec 2000 Cover: 2.95 **NM** value: **Cover or less**
Circ: Diamd. preorders: **25,367**
Promethea Under Attack! **A:** J.H. Williams III; Mick Gray **W:** Alan Moore
12 ❑ Feb 2001 Cover: 2.95 **NM** value: **Cover or less**
Circ: Diamd. preorders: **25,565**
A: J.H. Williams III **W:** Alan Moore
13 ❑ Apr 2001 Cover: 2.95 **NM** value: **Cover or less**
Circ: Diamd. preorders: **24,532**
The Fields we Know **A:** J.H. Williams III **W:** Alan Moore
Bk 1/HC ❑ Cover: 24.95 **NM** value: **Cover or less**
hardcover. **A:** J.H. Williams III; Mick Gray **W:** Alan Moore

PROMETHEUS' GIFT — Cat-Head

1 ❑ b&w Cover: 2.25 **NM** value: **Cover or less**
No issue number.

PROMETHEUS (VILLAINS) — DC

1 ❑ Feb 1998 Cover: 1.95 **NM** value: **Cover or less**
Circ: Diamd. preorders: **48,047**
• New Year's Evil

PROMISE — Viz

1 ❑ b&w Cover: 5.95 **NM** value: **Cover or less**
Circ: CapCity orders: **2,250**
No issue number. • squarebound

PROPELLERMAN — Dark Horse

1 ❑ ca. 1993 Cover: 2.95 **NM** value: **Cover or less**
Circ: CapCity orders: **11,800**
A: Matthias Schultheiss **W:** Matthias Schultheiss
2 ❑ ca. 1993 Cover: 2.95 **NM** value: **Cover or less**
Circ: CapCity orders: **7,875**
A: Matthias Schultheiss **W:** Matthias Schultheiss
3 ❑ ca. 1993 Cover: 2.95 **NM** value: **Cover or less**
Circ: CapCity orders: **6,250**
A: Matthias Schultheiss **W:** Matthias Schultheiss
4 ❑ ca. 1993 Cover: 2.95 **NM** value: **Cover or less**
Circ: CapCity orders: **5,125**
A: Matthias Schultheiss **W:** Matthias Schultheiss
5 ❑ ca. 1994 Cover: 2.95 **NM** value: **Cover or less**
Circ: CapCity orders: **5,050**
A: Matthias Schultheiss **W:** Matthias Schultheiss
6 ❑ ca. 1994 Cover: 2.95 **NM** value: **Cover or less**
Circ: CapCity orders: **4,425**
A: Matthias Schultheiss **W:** Matthias Schultheiss
7 ❑ ca. 1994 Cover: 2.95 **NM** value: **Cover or less**
Circ: CapCity orders: **3,900**
A: Matthias Schultheiss **W:** Matthias Schultheiss
8 ❑ ca. 1994 Cover: 2.95 **NM** value: **Cover or less**
Circ: CapCity orders: **3,675**
A: Matthias Schultheiss **W:** Matthias Schultheiss

PROPHECY OF THE SOUL SORCERER — Arcane

1 ❑ May 1999 Cover: 2.95 **NM** value: **Cover or less**
Circ: Diamd. preorders: **4,818**

2 ❑ Jun 1999 Cover: 2.95 **NM** value: **Cover or less**
Circ: Diamd. preorders: **3,936**
3 ❑ Jul 1999 Cover: 2.95 **NM** value: **Cover or less**
Circ: Diamd. preorders: **3,579**
Ash 1❑Oct 1998 Cover: 1.99 **NM** value: **2.00**

PROPHECY OF THE SOUL SORCERER PREVIEW ISSUE — Arcane

1 ❑ Cover: 1.99 **NM** value: **2.00**

PROPHECY OF THE SOUL SORCERER (VOL. 2) — Arcane

1 ❑ Mar 2000 Cover: 2.95 **NM** value: **Cover or less**
Circ: Diamd. preorders: **2,925**
2 ❑ Apr 2000 Cover: 2.95 **NM** value: **Cover or less**
Circ: Diamd. preorders: **2,681**
3 ❑ May 2000 Cover: 2.95 **NM** value: **Cover or less**
Circ: Diamd. preorders: **2,599**
Today, Tomorrow and Yesterday, Part 1 **A:** Patrick Blaine **W:** Eric Dean Seaton

PROPHET — Image

More than 50 years ago, Jonathan Prophet's father died for bringing the Word of God to the people in Nazi Germany. With his father gone, Jonathan became responsible for his mother and his younger brother. Needing money to support them, he allowed himself to be subjected to experiments conducted by scientists in the employ of the Nazis. These experiments were part of a plan to create a super-human. As a result, the preacher's son became a super-powerful warrior.

After all the painful tests he went through to become Prophet, the biggest one was yet to come. Hitler desired the fruits of his experiment, but the kindly scientist who "created" him resisted, placing Jonathan Prophet in a cryogenic chamber where he slept for 50 years before being discovered by Youngblood in Youngblood #2. Now, while trying to adjust to this new world, he continues to fight evil in his own, rather direct style.

0 ❑ Jul 1994 Cover: 2.50 **NM** value: **3.00**
0/A ❑ Jul 1994 Cover: 2.50 **NM** value: **3.00**
• San Diego Comic-Con edition.
1 ❑ Oct 1993 Cover: 2.50 **NM** value: **3.00**
Circ: CapCity orders: **106,875**
A: Dan Panosian **W:** Rob Liefeld ★ Origin of Prophet.
1/GO❑Oct 1993 **NM** value: **3.00**
• Gold edition.
2 ❑ Nov 1993 Cover: 1.95 **NM** value: **2.50**
Circ: CapCity orders: **65,275**
A: Frank Miller(cover)
3 ❑ Jan 1994 Cover: 1.95 **NM** value: **2.50**
Circ: CapCity orders: **51,275**
4 ❑ Feb 1994 Cover: 1.95 **NM** value: **2.50**
Circ: CapCity orders: **43,075**
4/SC❑Feb 1994 Cover: 1.95 **NM** value: **3.00**
• **CGC:** 1 graded, best 9.6
Variant cover by Platt. **A:** Stephen Platt(cover) **C:** Stephen Platt
5 ❑ Apr 1994 Cover: 1.95 **NM** value: **2.50**
Circ: CapCity orders: **40,550**
A: Stephen Platt
6 ❑ Jun 1994 Cover: 1.95 **NM** value: **2.50**
Circ: CapCity orders: **37,375**
A: Stephen Platt
7 ❑ Sep 1994 Cover: 2.50 **NM** value: **Cover or less**
Circ: CapCity orders: **42,400**
A: Stephen Platt
8 ❑ Nov 1994 Cover: 2.50 **NM** value: **Cover or less**
Circ: CapCity orders: **35,525**
War Games part 2
9 ❑ Dec 1994 Cover: 2.50 **NM** value: **Cover or less**
Circ: CapCity orders: **31,800**
10 ❑ Jan 1995 Cover: 2.50 **NM** value: **Cover or less**
Circ: CapCity orders: **28,825**
Extreme Sacrifice, Part 7; Extreme Sacrifice, Part 6
Bk 1❑ Cover: 12.95 **NM** value: **Cover or less**
• collects issues #1-7

PROPHET BABEWATCH — Image

1 ❑ Dec 1995 Cover: 2.50 **NM** value: **Cover or less**
cover says #1. • indicia says #2

PROPHET/CABLE — Maximum

1 ❑ Jan 1997 Cover: 3.50 **NM** value: **Cover or less**
Circ: Diamd. preorders: **42,945**
• crossover with Marvel **A:** Mark Pajarillo; Paul Scott **W:** Rob Liefeld; Robert Napton
2 ❑ Mar 1997 Cover: 3.50 **NM** value: **Cover or less**
Circ: Diamd. preorders: **37,326**
cover says #1, indicia says #2. • crossover with Marvel **A:** Mark Pajarillo; Paul Scott **W:** Rob Liefeld; Robert Napton

PROPHET/CHAPEL: SUPER SOLDIERS — Image

1/A ❑ May 1996 Cover: 2.50 **NM** value: **Cover or less**
1/B ❑ May 1996 Cover: 2.50 **NM** value: **Cover or less**
alternate cover (b&w).
2 ❑ Jun 1996 Cover: 2.50 **NM** value: **Cover or less**

PROPHET (VOL. 2) — Image

1/A ❑ Aug 1995 Cover: 3.50 **NM** value: **Cover or less**
Circ: CapCity orders: **37,825**
C: Boris Vallejo
1/B ❑ Aug 1995 Cover: 3.50 **NM** value: **Cover or less**
1/C ❑ Aug 1995 Cover: 3.50 **NM** value: **Cover or less**
enhanced wraparound cover.
2/A ❑ Sep 1995 Cover: 2.50 **NM** value: **Cover or less**
Circ: CapCity orders: **21,375**
C: Frank Miller
2/B ❑ Sep 1995 Cover: 2.50 **NM** value: **Cover or less**
alternate cover.
3 ❑ Nov 1995 Cover: 2.50 **NM** value: **Cover or less**
4 ❑ Feb 1996 Cover: 2.50 **NM** value: **Cover or less**
★ Appearance of NewMen.
5 ❑ Feb 1996 Cover: 2.50 **NM** value: **Cover or less**
6 ❑ Apr 1996 Cover: 2.50 **NM** value: **Cover or less**
7 ❑ May 1996 Cover: 2.50 **NM** value: **Cover or less**
★ Appearance of Youngblood.
8 ❑ Jul 1996 Cover: 2.50 **NM** value: **Cover or less**
Anl 1/A❑Sep 1995 Cover: 2.50 **NM** value: **Cover or less**
Circ: CapCity orders: **21,625**
• polybagged with PowerCardz
Anl 1/B❑Sep 1995 Cover: 2.50 **NM** value: **Cover or less**
• polybagged with PowerCardz

PROPHET (VOL. 3) — Awesome

1 ❑ Mar 2000 Cover: 2.99 **NM** value: **Cover or less**
Flip cover (McFarlane cover on back side). **A:** Chad Walker; Eric Walker; Todd McFarlane(cover) **W:** Rob Liefeld; Robert Napton
1/A ❑ Mar 2000 Cover: 2.99 **NM** value: **Cover or less**
• Red background, woman standing with sword, large man in background **A:** Chad Walker; Eric Walker **W:** Rob Liefeld; Robert Napton

PROPOSITION PLAYER — DC / Vertigo

1 ❑ Dec 1999 Cover: 2.50 **NM** value: **Cover or less**
Circ: Diamd. preorders: **11,926**
A New Player or the Truth About Cat and Dog Owners! **A:** Bill Willingham; Paul Guinan **W:** Bill Willingham
2 ❑ Jan 2000 Cover: 2.50 **NM** value: **Cover or less**
Circ: Diamd. preorders: **9,826**
High Stakes Game, or The Man Who Could Bullsh*t his Way Out of Trouble, Twice (But not Thrice) **A:** Paul Guinan **W:** Bill Willingham
3 ❑ Feb 2000 Cover: 2.50 **NM** value: **Cover or less**
Circ: Diamd. preorders: **9,714**
A: Paul Guinan **W:** Bill Willingham
4 ❑ Mar 2000 Cover: 2.50 **NM** value: **Cover or less**
Circ: Diamd. preorders: **7,998**
A: Paul Guinan **W:** Bill Willingham
5 ❑ Apr 2000 Cover: 2.50 **NM** value: **Cover or less**
Circ: Diamd. preorders: **7,609**
Full House or No Way to Treat a Lady **A:** Paul Guinan **W:** Bill Willingham
6 ❑ May 2000 Cover: 2.50 **NM** value: **Cover or less**
Circ: Diamd. preorders: **7,571**
Stacking the Deck or A Clean Well-Lit Place **A:** Paul Guinan **W:** Bill Willingham

PROTECTORS HANDBOOK — Malibu

1 ❑ Cover: 2.50 **NM** value: **Cover or less**
Circ: CapCity orders: **4,150**

PROTECTORS, THE (MALIBU) — Malibu

1 ❑ Sep 1992 Cover: 1.95 **NM** value: **Cover or less**
Split cover (in various colors). When Heroes Gather **A:** Thomas Derenick **W:** R.A. Jones ★ Origin of Protectors.
1/CS❑Sep 1992 Cover: 2.50 **NM** value: **Cover or less**
Circ: CapCity orders: **14,825**
• with poster and wrapper ★ Origin of Protectors.
2 ❑ Oct 1992 Cover: 2.50 **NM** value: **Cover or less**
Circ: CapCity orders: **10,975**
• with poster
3 ❑ Nov 1992 Cover: 2.50 **NM** value: **Cover or less**
Circ: CapCity orders: **10,425**
4 ❑ Dec 1992 Cover: 2.50 **NM** value: **Cover or less**
Circ: CapCity orders: **12,850**
5/A ❑ Jan 1993 Cover: 2.50 **NM** value: **Cover or less**
Circ: CapCity orders: **11,250**
• bullet hole; bagged
5/B ❑ Jan 1993 Cover: 2.95 **NM** value: **Cover or less**
Embossed cover. • bullet hole
5/C ❑ Jan 1993 Cover: 4.50 **NM** value: **Cover or less**
Die-cut cover. • bullet hole
6 ❑ Feb 1993 Cover: 2.50 **NM** value: **Cover or less**
6/CS❑Feb 1993 Cover: 2.50 **NM** value: **Cover or less**
Circ: CapCity orders: **11,000**
• with poster
7 ❑ Mar 1993 Cover: 2.50 **NM** value: **Cover or less**
Circ: CapCity orders: **9,625**
Prelude To Chaos **A:** Thomas Derenick **W:** R.A. Jones
8 ❑ Apr 1993 Cover: 2.50 **NM** value: **Cover or less**
Circ: CapCity orders: **9,350**
9 ❑ May 1993 Cover: 2.50 **NM** value: **Cover or less**
Circ: CapCity orders: **8,575**
10 ❑ Jun 1993 Cover: 2.50 **NM** value: **Cover or less**
Circ: CapCity orders: **7,175**
11 ❑ Jul 1993 Cover: 2.50 **NM** value: **Cover or less**
Circ: CapCity orders: **6,150**
12 ❑ Aug 1993 Cover: 2.50 **NM** value: **Cover or less**
Circ: CapCity orders: **5,475**
13 ❑ Sep 1993 Cover: 2.25 **NM** value: **Cover or less**
Circ: CapCity orders: **7,725**
• Genesis
14 ❑ Oct 1993 Cover: 2.25 **NM** value: **Cover or less**
Circ: CapCity orders: **7,700**
15 ❑ Nov 1993 Cover: 2.25 **NM** value: **Cover or less**
Circ: CapCity orders: **5,625**
16 ❑ Dec 1993 Cover: 2.25 **NM** value: **Cover or less**
Circ: CapCity orders: **4,625**
17 ❑ Jan 1994 Cover: 2.25 **NM** value: **Cover or less**
Circ: CapCity orders: **4,025**
18 ❑ Feb 1994 Cover: 2.25 **NM** value: **Cover or less**
Circ: CapCity orders: **3,500**
19 ❑ Mar 1994 Cover: 2.50 **NM** value: **Cover or less**
Circ: CapCity orders: **3,100**
• Genesis
20 ❑ Cover: 2.50 **NM** value: **Cover or less**
Circ: CapCity orders: **2,975**
final issue.

PROTECTORS, THE (NEW YORK) — New York

1 ❑ Cover: 1.70 **NM** value: **Cover or less**
2 ❑ Cover: 1.70 **NM** value: **Cover or less**

PROTHEUS (MIKE DEODATO'S...) — Caliber

1 ❑ Cover: 2.95 **NM** value: **Cover or less**
Leo Protheus and the Last Defense **A:** Mike Deodato Jr. **W:** Mike Deodato Jr.
2 ❑ Cover: 2.95 **NM** value: **Cover or less**
A: Mike Deodato Jr. **W:** Mike Deodato Jr.

PROTISTA CHRONICLES, THE — Xulu

1 ❑ **NM** value: **2.00**
no cover price.

PROTOTYKES HOLIDAY SPECIAL/HERO ILLUSTRATED HOLIDAY SPECIAL — Dark Horse

1 ❑ **NM** value: **1.00**
2 ❑ **NM** value: **1.00**
Clause and Effect **A:** John Byrne **W:** John Byrne

PROTOTYPE — Malibu / Ultraverse

Bob Campbell used to have a job as Ultra-Tech's version of Iron Man. Clad in a powerful suit of high-tech "Prototype" armor, he was the company's showpiece. For a time he was Ultra-Tech's pride and joy — until an airshow duel gone tragically wrong sheared his right arm off. A bionic replacement was fashioned for him, but his days wearing the Prototype armor were over.

Years later, a new Prototype armor was created, less bulky and more powerful than the original. Only this time, the person inside the armor was really nothing more than an overgrown kid, genetically altered to "match" the armor. The armor is interfaced directly with the kid's brain — and when the strain of this becomes too intense, they feed the kid drugs to ease the pain. Young and inexperienced, this new Prototype is about to get crash-tested...

0 ❑ Aug 1994 Cover: 2.50 **NM** value: **Cover or less**
Circ: CapCity orders: **10,600**
First...and Foremost; Buena Sera, Mrs. Campbell; Prototype Re-engineering; Prototype No More • Reprints origin story from Malibu Sun plus new story **A:** Gordon Purcell **W:** Len Strazewski; Tom Mason ★ Origin of Prototype I (Bob Campbell).
1 ❑ Aug 1993 Cover: 1.95 **NM** value: **2.50**
Circ: CapCity orders: **33,075**
Budget Cuts • Ultraverse; 1st appear **A:** David Ammerman **W:** Len Strazewski; Tom Mason ★ 1st Appearance of Prototype II (Jimmy Ruiz), Prototype I (Bob Campbell), Glare, Veil.
1/Hol❑ Cover: 1.95 **NM** value: **5.00**
• Hologram cover limited edition. Budget Cuts • hologram **A:** David Ammerman **W:** Len Strazewski; Tom Mason ★ 1st Appearance of Prototype II (Jimmy Ruiz), Prototype I (Bob Campbell), Glare, Veil.
2 ❑ Sep 1993 Cover: 1.95 **NM** value: **Cover or less**
Circ: CapCity orders: **23,000**
Games Of Death **A:** David Ammerman **W:** Len Strazewski; Tom Mason ★ 1st Appearance of Backstabber. ★ Appearance of Prime.
3 ❑ Oct 1993 Cover: 2.50 **NM** value: **Cover or less**
Circ: CapCity orders: **29,775**
• Giant-size. Rune, Part F • Rune **A:** Barry Windsor-Smith; David Ammerman **W:** Len Strazewski; Tom Mason
4 ❑ Nov 1993 Cover: 1.95 **NM** value: **Cover or less**
Circ: CapCity orders: **22,400**
Wrathful Moon **A:** David Ammerman **W:** Len Strazewski; Tom Mason ★ 1st Appearance of Wrath.
5 ❑ Dec 1993 Cover: 1.95 **NM** value: **Cover or less**
Circ: CapCity orders: **22,175**
Break-Thru • Break-Thru; Continued in Strangers #7 **A:** Roger Robinson **W:** Len Strazewski; Steve Englehart; Tom Mason ★ Appearance of Strangers.
6 ❑ Jan 1994 Cover: 1.95 **NM** value: **Cover or less**
Circ: CapCity orders: **17,325**
★ 1st Appearance of Arena.
7 ❑ Feb 1994 Cover: 1.95 **NM** value: **Cover or less**
Circ: CapCity orders: **14,650**
8 ❑ Mar 1994 Cover: 1.95 **NM** value: **Cover or less**
Circ: CapCity orders: **12,875**
9 ❑ Apr 1994 Cover: 1.95 **NM** value: **Cover or less**
Circ: CapCity orders: **12,050**
10 ❑ May 1994 Cover: 1.95 **NM** value: **Cover or less**
Circ: CapCity orders: **11,150**
11 ❑ Jun 1994 Cover: 1.95 **NM** value: **Cover or less**
Circ: CapCity orders: **10,400**
I'm on Fire **W:** Len Strazewski; Tom Mason
12 ❑ Jul 1994 Cover: 1.95 **NM** value: **Cover or less**
Circ: CapCity orders: **9,300**
Assault on the Dark Tower **W:** Len Strazewski; Tom Mason
13 ❑ Aug 1994 Cover: 3.50 **NM** value: **Cover or less**
Hostile Takeover; A Firm Hand; Days of Summer Glory; Design for Living; The Eye Has It; Candid Pixx • flipbook with Ultraverse Premiere #6 **A:** Dean Zachary; Brian O'Connell; Brock Hor Jr.; Kris

CGC-graded: Multiply prices above by **33 for 9.9 M • 16 for 9.8 NM/M • 7 for 9.6 NM+ • 5 for 9.4 NM • 2.5 for 9.2 NM- • 1.5 for 9.0 VF/NM**

Renkewitz; Roger Robinson(cover) **W:** Kurt Busiek; Mark Paniccia; Gerard Jones; Len Strazewski; Tom Mason

14 ❑ Oct 1994 Cover: 1.95 **NM** value: **Cover or less**
Circ: CapCity orders: **6,800**
📖 Bent, Folded, Spindled and Mutilated **A:** Roger Robinson; Aaron Lopresti(cover) **W:** Len Strazewski

15 ❑ Nov 1994 Cover: 1.95 **NM** value: **Cover or less**
Circ: CapCity orders: **6,075**
📖 Burning Commitment **A:** Dean Zachary; Roger Robinson(cover) **W:** Len Strazewski

16 ❑ Dec 1994 Cover: 1.95 **NM** value: **Cover or less**
Circ: CapCity orders: **5,600**
📖 Driven to Kill **A:** Dean Zachary **W:** Len Strazewski ★ 1st Appearance of Wild Popes.

17 ❑ Jan 1995 Cover: 1.95 **NM** value: **Cover or less**
Circ: CapCity orders: **4,600**
📖 On the Trail of the Techuza **A:** George Dove; Keith Conroy(cover) **W:** Len Strazewski

18 ❑ Feb 1995 Cover: 2.50 **NM** value: **Cover or less**
Circ: CapCity orders: **4,475**
📖 Friendly Fire **A:** Paul Abrams; Keith Conroy(cover) **W:** R.A. Jones

GS 1❑ca. 1994 Cover: 2.50 **NM** value: **Cover or less**
Circ: CapCity orders: **8,050**
• Giant-Size edition. 📖 Hostile Takeover, Part 4 **A:** Roger Robinson; Steve Ellis **W:** Len Strazewski

PROWLER (ECLIPSE) — Eclipse

1 ❑ Jul 1987 Cover: 1.75 **NM** value: **Cover or less**
Circ: CapCity orders: **6,825**
📖 Blood And Magic **A:** John K. Snyder III **W:** Tim Truman ★ 1st Appearance of Prowler.

2 ❑ Aug 1987 Cover: 1.75 **NM** value: **Cover or less**
Circ: CapCity orders: **5,325**

3 ❑ Sep 1987 Cover: 1.75 **NM** value: **Cover or less**
Circ: CapCity orders: **4,825**

4 ❑ Oct 1987 Cover: 1.75 **NM** value: **Cover or less**
Circ: CapCity orders: **4,800**

PROWLER IN "WHITE ZOMBIE", THE — Eclipse

1 ❑ Oct 1988, b&w Cover: 2.00 **NM** value: **Cover or less**
📖 White Zombie **A:** Gerald Forton; Graham Nolan **W:** Michael Price

PROWLER (MARVEL) — Marvel

1 ❑ Nov 1994 Cover: 1.75 **NM** value: **Cover or less**
Circ: CapCity orders: **14,550**
📖 Approaching Dust **A:** Bill Reinhold **W:** Carl Potts

2 ❑ Dec 1994 Cover: 1.75 **NM** value: **Cover or less**
Circ: CapCity orders: **9,550**
A: Bill Reinhold **W:** Carl Potts

3 ❑ Jan 1995 Cover: 1.75 **NM** value: **Cover or less**
Circ: CapCity orders: **7,400**
A: Bill Reinhold **W:** Carl Potts

4 ❑ Feb 1995 Cover: 1.75 **NM** value: **Cover or less**
Circ: CapCity orders: **5,975**
A: Bill Reinhold **W:** Carl Potts

PRO WRESTLING'S TRUE FACTS — Dan Pettiglio

1 ❑ Apr 1994, b&w Cover: 2.95 **NM** value: **Cover or less**
No issue number.

PRUDENCE & CAUTION — Defiant

1 ❑ May 1994 Cover: 3.25 **NM** value: **Cover or less**
Circ: CapCity orders: **16,200**
• Double-size. 📖 A' Hunting We Will GO • English and Spanish versions **A:** Jim Fern **W:** Chris Claremont

2 ❑ Jun 1994 Cover: 2.50 **NM** value: **Cover or less**
Circ: CapCity orders: **9,575**
A: Jim Fern **W:** Chris Claremont

3 ❑ Jul 1994 Cover: 2.50 **NM** value: **Cover or less**
Circ: CapCity orders: **7,450**
A: Jim Fern **W:** Chris Claremont

4 ❑ Aug 1994 Cover: 2.50 **NM** value: **Cover or less**
Circ: CapCity orders: **6,050**
A: Jim Fern **W:** Chris Claremont

5 ❑ Sep 1994 Cover: 2.50 **NM** value: **Cover or less**
Circ: CapCity orders: **4,875**
A: Jim Fern **W:** Chris Claremont

6 ❑ Oct 1994 Cover: 2.50 **NM** value: **Cover or less**
final issue. **A:** Jim Fern **W:** Chris Claremont

PRYDE & WISDOM — Marvel

1 ❑ Sep 1996 Cover: 1.95 **NM** value: **Cover or less**
📖 Mystery School **A:** Terry Dodson; Karl Story **W:** Warren Ellis

2 ❑ Oct 1996 Cover: 1.95 **NM** value: **Cover or less**
A: Terry Dodson **W:** Warren Ellis

3 ❑ Nov 1996 Cover: 1.95 **NM** value: **Cover or less**
📖 Mystery Train final issue. **A:** Aaron Lopresti; Terry Dodson **W:** Warren Ellis

PSI-FORCE — Marvel

Emmett Proudhawk worked for the CIA searching for people with "special abilities." As a person with an especially high ESP quotient, the job seemed to suit him well. One day, Emmett's own abilities manifested themselves, giving him the power to mentally "push" people to do his bidding. Proudhawk also learned that someone had stolen the list of potential "specials" he had compiled — and now these people were disappearing.

To protect them, Proudhawk quit the agency and began collecting the youngsters from his list who had recently experienced sudden increases in their powers. He saved five such youngsters, but incurred the wrath of the KGB in saving the fifth, a healer named Anastasia. When an assassin finally caught up with Proudhawk, the five youngsters used their powers to bring Proudhawk back in a spiritual form. On their own, these children were vulnerable, but together they became unbreakable.

1 ❑ Nov 1986 Cover: 0.75 **NM** value: **1.00**
Circ: CapCity orders: **35,600**
📖 Hour Of The Wolf! **A:** Mark Texeira **W:** Steve Perry

2 ❑ Dec 1986 Cover: 0.75 **NM** value: **1.00**
Circ: CapCity orders: **24,200**

3 ❑ Jan 1987 Cover: 0.75 **NM** value: **1.00**
Circ: CapCity orders: **19,800**

4 ❑ Feb 1987 Cover: 0.75 **NM** value: **1.00**
Circ: CapCity orders: **20,200**

5 ❑ Mar 1987 Cover: 0.75 **NM** value: **1.00**
Circ: CapCity orders: **19,100**

6 ❑ Apr 1987 Cover: 0.75 **NM** value: **1.00**
Circ: CapCity orders: **17,800**

7 ❑ May 1987 Cover: 0.75 **NM** value: **1.00**
Circ: CapCity orders: **14,900**

8 ❑ Jun 1987 Cover: 0.75 **NM** value: **1.00**
Circ: CapCity orders: **13,700**

9 ❑ Jul 1987 Cover: 0.75 **NM** value: **1.00**
Circ: CapCity orders: **12,400**

10 ❑ Aug 1987 Cover: 0.75 **NM** value: **1.00**
Circ: CapCity orders: **12,500**

11 ❑ Sep 1987 Cover: 0.75 **NM** value: **1.00**
Circ: CapCity orders: **11,900**

12 ❑ Oct 1987 Cover: 0.75 **NM** value: **1.00**
Circ: CapCity orders: **11,100**

13 ❑ Nov 1987 Cover: 0.75 **NM** value: **1.00**
Circ: CapCity orders: **11,300**

14 ❑ Dec 1987 Cover: 0.75 **NM** value: **1.00**
Circ: CapCity orders: **10,500**

15 ❑ Jan 1988 Cover: 0.75 **NM** value: **1.00**
Circ: CapCity orders: **11,100**

16 ❑ Feb 1988 Cover: 0.75 **NM** value: **1.00**
Circ: CapCity orders: **11,300**

17 ❑ Mar 1988 Cover: 0.75 **NM** value: **1.00**
Circ: CapCity orders: **11,600**

18 ❑ Apr 1988 Cover: 0.75 **NM** value: **1.00**
Circ: CapCity orders: **11,700**

19 ❑ May 1988 Cover: 1.25 **NM** value: **Cover or less**
Circ: CapCity orders: **12,100**

20 ❑ Jun 1988 Cover: 1.25 **NM** value: **Cover or less**
Circ: CapCity orders: **10,800**

21 ❑ Jul 1988 Cover: 1.25 **NM** value: **Cover or less**
Circ: CapCity orders: **10,900**

22 ❑ Aug 1988 Cover: 1.25 **NM** value: **Cover or less**
Circ: CapCity orders: **11,300**

23 ❑ Sep 1988 Cover: 1.25 **NM** value: **Cover or less**
Circ: CapCity orders: **11,500**

24 ❑ Oct 1988 Cover: 1.25 **NM** value: **Cover or less**
Circ: CapCity orders: **11,100**

25 ❑ Nov 1988 Cover: 1.25 **NM** value: **Cover or less**
Circ: CapCity orders: **10,600**

26 ❑ Dec 1988 Cover: 1.50 **NM** value: **Cover or less**
Circ: CapCity orders: **10,300**

27 ❑ Jan 1989 Cover: 1.50 **NM** value: **Cover or less**
Circ: CapCity orders: **9,600**

28 ❑ Feb 1989 Cover: 1.50 **NM** value: **Cover or less**
Circ: CapCity orders: **8,800**

29 ❑ Mar 1989 Cover: 1.50 **NM** value: **Cover or less**
Circ: CapCity orders: **8,700**

30 ❑ Apr 1989 Cover: 1.50 **NM** value: **Cover or less**
Circ: CapCity orders: **8,600**

31 ❑ May 1989 Cover: 1.50 **NM** value: **Cover or less**
Circ: CapCity orders: **8,200**

32 ❑ Jun 1989 Cover: 1.50 **NM** value: **Cover or less**
Circ: CapCity orders: **8,250**
final issue.

Anl 1❑ca. 1987 Cover: 1.25 **NM** value: **Cover or less**
Circ: CapCity orders: **11,300**

PSI-JUDGE ANDERSON — Fleetway-Quality

1 ❑ Cover: 1.95 **NM** value: **2.00**
📖 Revenge **A:** Brett Ewins **W:** Alan Grant; T.B. Grover

2 ❑ Cover: 1.95 **NM** value: **2.00**
3 ❑ Cover: 1.95 **NM** value: **2.00**
4 ❑ Cover: 1.95 **NM** value: **2.00**
5 ❑ Cover: 1.95 **NM** value: **2.00**
6 ❑ Cover: 1.95 **NM** value: **2.00**
7 ❑ Cover: 1.95 **NM** value: **2.00**
8 ❑ Cover: 1.95 **NM** value: **2.00**
9 ❑ Cover: 1.95 **NM** value: **2.00**
10 ❑ Cover: 1.95 **NM** value: **2.00**
11 ❑ Cover: 1.95 **NM** value: **2.00**
12 ❑ Cover: 1.95 **NM** value: **2.00**
13 ❑ Cover: 1.95 **NM** value: **2.00**
14 ❑ Cover: 1.95 **NM** value: **2.00**
15 ❑ Cover: 1.95 **NM** value: **2.00**
final issue.

PSI-JUDGE ANDERSON: ENGRAMS — Fleetway-Quality

1 ❑ b&w Cover: 1.95 **NM** value: **Cover or less**
Circ: CapCity orders: **3,100**
📖 Anderson, Psi Division: Engram **A:** David Roach **W:** Alan Grant

2 ❑ b&w Cover: 1.95 **NM** value: **Cover or less**
📖 Anderson, Psi Division: Engram

PSI-JUDGE ANDERSON: PSIFILES — Fleetway-Quality

1 ❑ Cover: 2.95 **NM** value: **Cover or less**

PSI-LORDS — Valiant

1 ❑ Sep 1994 Cover: 3.50 **NM** value: **Cover or less**
chromium wrap-around cover. 📖 Postcard From Olympus • Valiant Vision **A:** Mike Leeke **W:** Antony J.L. Bedard

1/GO❑Sep 1994 Cover: 3.50 **NM** value: **5.00**
no cover price. • Gold edition. 📖 Postcard From Olympus **A:** Mike Leeke **W:** Antony J.L. Bedard

2 ❑ Oct 1994 Cover: 2.25 **NM** value: **Cover or less**
• Valiant Vision

3 ❑ Nov 1994 Cover: 2.25 **NM** value: **Cover or less**
📖 The Chaos Effect: Epsilon, Part 3 • Valiant Vision; Chaos Effect

4 ❑ Dec 1994 Cover: 2.25 **NM** value: **Cover or less**
Circ: CapCity orders: **12,475**

5 ❑ Jan 1995 Cover: 2.25 **NM** value: **Cover or less**
Circ: CapCity orders: **10,525**

6 ❑ Feb 1995 Cover: 2.25 **NM** value: **Cover or less**
Circ: CapCity orders: **9,525**
📖 Infection, Part 1

7 ❑ Mar 1995 Cover: 2.25 **NM** value: **Cover or less**
Circ: CapCity orders: **7,925**
📖 Infection, Part 2

8 ❑ Apr 1995 Cover: 2.25 **NM** value: **Cover or less**
Circ: CapCity orders: **7,025**
★ Versus Destroyer.

9 ❑ May 1995 Cover: 2.25 **NM** value: **Cover or less**
Circ: CapCity orders: **5,950**

10 ❑ Jun 1995 Cover: 2.25 **NM** value: **Cover or less**
Circ: CapCity orders: **5,150**
final issue.

PSYBA-RATS, THE — DC

1 ❑ Apr 1995 Cover: 2.50 **NM** value: **Cover or less**
Circ: CapCity orders: **9,275**
📖 They Byte **A:** Michal Dutkiewicz; A.J. Kent **W:** Chuck Dixon ★ Death of Channelman.

2 ❑ May 1995 Cover: 1.50 **NM** value: **2.50**
Circ: CapCity orders: **6,300**

3 ❑ Jun 1995 Cover: 1.50 **NM** value: **2.50**
Circ: CapCity orders: **5,250**

PSYCHO, THE — DC

1 ❑ Sep 1991 Cover: 4.95 **NM** value: **Cover or less**
Circ: CapCity orders: **15,750**
A: Dan Brereton **W:** James D. Hudnall

2 ❑ Oct 1991 Cover: 4.95 **NM** value: **Cover or less**
Circ: CapCity orders: **11,700**
A: Dan Brereton **W:** James D. Hudnall

3 ❑ Dec 1991 Cover: 4.95 **NM** value: **Cover or less**
Circ: CapCity orders: **10,800**
A: Dan Brereton **W:** James D. Hudnall

PSYCHO (ALFRED HITCHCOCK'S...) — Innovation

1 ❑ Cover: 2.50 **NM** value: **Cover or less**
Circ: CapCity orders: **5,895**
A: Felipe Echevarria **W:** Matt Thompson; Felipe Echevarria

2 ❑ Cover: 2.50 **NM** value: **Cover or less**
Circ: CapCity orders: **3,815**

3 ❑ Cover: 2.50 **NM** value: **Cover or less**
Circ: CapCity orders: **2,835**

PSYCHOANALYSIS — E.C.

There were six E.C. titles in its "New Direction," cover-bannered as "an entirely novel and unique reading experience." The cover of each had a frame with the title on top and an identifying icon down the left side. The "New Direction" was one designed to accommodate the Comics Magazine of America's new Comics Code, though the first issue of each did not carry the Code stamp, and all but one lasted for five issues. The six titles were: Aces High, Extra!, Impact, MD, Valor — and Psychoanalysis, the title that lasted only four issues.

Above Psychoanalysis' title was the line "People Searching for Peace of Mind through ..." and the stories — all drawn by Jack Kamen — followed the psychoanalysis, by the same analyst, of Freddy Carter, Ellen Lyman, and Mark Stone. All were cured by series' end. (Whew!) — Maggie

1 ❑ Mar 1955 Cover: 0.10 **NM** value: **100.00**
• **CGC:** 1 graded, best 9.6
📖 Freddy Carter; Ellen Lyman; The Man From Vienna (text story); Mark Stone **A:** Jack Kamen **W:** Jack Kamen

2 ❑ May 1955 Cover: 0.10 **NM** value: **85.00**
• **CGC:** 1 graded, best 8.5
📖 Freddy Carter; Ellen Lyman; Your Doodles Give You Away (text story); Mark Stone **A:** Jack Kamen **W:** Jack Kamen

3 ❑ Jul 1955 Cover: 0.10 **NM** value: **85.00**
• **CGC:** 1 graded, best 8.5
📖 Freddy Carter; Ellen Lyman; Your Life is In Your Dreams (text story); Mark Stone **A:** Jack Kamen **W:** Jack Kamen

4 ❑ Sep 1955 Cover: 0.10 **NM** value: **85.00**
• **CGC:** 1 graded, best 9.6
📖 Freddy Carter; Mark Stone; A Fifth Dimension? (text story) **A:** Jack Kamen **W:** Jack Kamen

PSYCHOANALYSIS (GEMSTONE) — Gemstone

1 ❑ Aug 1999 Cover: 2.50 **NM** value: **Cover or less**
Circ: Diamd. preorders: **3,257**
📖 Freddy Carter; Ellen Lyman; The Man From Vienna (text story); Mark Stone **A:** Jack Kamen **W:** Jack Kamen

2 ❑ Sep 1999 Cover: 2.50 **NM** value: **Cover or less**
Circ: Diamd. preorders: **2,932**

Other grades: Multiply prices above by **1.5 for Mint • 2/3 for Very Fine • 1/3 for Fine • 1/5 for Very Good • 1/8 for Good**

Freddy Carter; Ellen Lyman; Your Doodles Give You Away (text story); Mark Stone **A:** Jack Kamen **W:** Jack Kamen

3 ❑ Oct 1999 Cover: 2.50 **NM** value: **Cover or less**
Circ: Diamd. preorders: **2,920**
Freddy Carter; Ellen Lyman; Your Life is In Your Dreams (text story); Mark Stone **A:** Jack Kamen **W:** Jack Kamen

4 ❑ Nov 1999 Cover: 2.50 **NM** value: **Cover or less**
Circ: Diamd. preorders: **2,736**
Freddy Carter; Mark Stone; A Fifth Dimension? (text story) **A:** Jack Kamen **W:** Jack Kamen

Anl 1❑ Cover: 10.95 **NM** value: **Cover or less**
• Collects series **A:** Jack Kamen **W:** Jack Kamen

PSYCHOBLAST — First

1 ❑ Nov 1987 Cover: 1.75 **NM** value: **Cover or less**
Circ: CapCity orders: **7,475**
Coming Back **A:** Robb Phipps **W:** Steven Grant ★ 1st Appearance of Psychoblast.

2 ❑ Dec 1987 Cover: 1.75 **NM** value: **Cover or less**
Circ: CapCity orders: **5,350**
A: Robb Phipps **W:** Steven Grant

3 ❑ Jan 1988 Cover: 1.75 **NM** value: **Cover or less**
Circ: CapCity orders: **5,100**
Forever Yours! **A:** Robb Phipps **W:** Steven Grant

4 ❑ Feb 1988 Cover: 1.75 **NM** value: **Cover or less**
Circ: CapCity orders: **4,900**
A: Robb Phipps **W:** Steven Grant

5 ❑ Mar 1988 Cover: 1.75 **NM** value: **Cover or less**
Circ: CapCity orders: **4,875**
A: Robb Phipps **W:** Steven Grant

6 ❑ Apr 1988 Cover: 1.75 **NM** value: **Cover or less**
Circ: CapCity orders: **4,500**
A: Robb Phipps **W:** Steven Grant

7 ❑ May 1988 Cover: 1.75 **NM** value: **Cover or less**
Circ: CapCity orders: **4,150**
A: Robb Phipps **W:** Steven Grant

8 ❑ Jun 1988 Cover: 1.75 **NM** value: **Cover or less**
Circ: CapCity orders: **3,625**
A: Robb Phipps **W:** Steven Grant

9 ❑ Jul 1988 Cover: 1.75 **NM** value: **Cover or less**
Circ: CapCity orders: **3,650**
final issue. **A:** Robb Phipps **W:** Steven Grant

PSYCHO KILLERS — Comic Zone

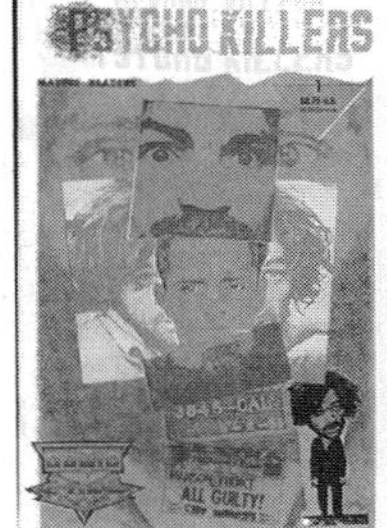

Comics have seen some scary monsters over the years, but none more frightening than the real-life monsters depicted in this series. Comic Zone's Psycho Killers series delves into the backgrounds and crimes of some of the most infamous serial killers and mass murderers the world has ever seen. Included are bios on "Helter Skelter" murderer Charles Manson, "Son of Sam" killer David Berkowitz, and the infamous Ed Gein — a psychotic whose house was decorated with bits of his victims' bodies. The stories of these and many others are told in all their heinous detail — from their almost universally unhappy childhoods to their crimes, trials, and sentencing.

In a move that proves life is indeed stranger than fiction, sales of the 11th volume of this series (The Hillside Strangler) was suspended following a lawsuit one of the stranglers filed against Eclipse Comics for "unauthorized use of his story" in its True Crime trading cards.

1 ❑ b&w Cover: 2.75 **NM** value: **4.00**
• Charles Manson

1-2 ❑ Cover: 2.95 **NM** value: **3.00**

2 ❑ b&w Cover: 2.75 **NM** value: **3.50**
• David Berkowitz ("The Son of Sam")

2-2 ❑ Cover: 2.95 **NM** value: **3.00**

3 ❑ b&w Cover: 2.75 **NM** value: **3.50**
• Ed Gein

3-2 ❑ Cover: 2.95 **NM** value: **Cover or less**

4 ❑ Cover: 2.95 **NM** value: **Cover or less**
• Henry Lee Lucas

5 ❑ Cover: 2.95 **NM** value: **3.25**
• Jeffrey Dahmer

6 ❑ Cover: 2.95 **NM** value: **Cover or less**
• Richard Ramirez ("The Nightstalker") **A:** Stan Timmons; Derek Brown; Jim Brozman **W:** Jack Herman; Karen Herman

7 ❑ Cover: 2.95 **NM** value: **Cover or less**
• Judias Buenoano

8 ❑ Cover: 2.95 **NM** value: **Cover or less**
• John Wayne Gacy **A:** Stan Timmons; John Wayne Gacy(cover) **W:** Jack Herman; Karen Herman

9 ❑ Cover: 2.95 **NM** value: **Cover or less**
• Ted Bundy

10 ❑ Cover: 2.95 **NM** value: **Cover or less**
• Dean Corll ("The Candy Man")

11 ❑ Cover: 2.95 **NM** value: **3.50**
• The Hillside Strangler; A lawsuit was filed and resulted in this book being taken off the market

12 ❑ Cover: 2.95 **NM** value: **Cover or less**
• The Boston Strangler

13 ❑ Cover: 2.95 **NM** value: **Cover or less**
• Andrei Chikatilo

14 ❑ Cover: 2.95 **NM** value: **Cover or less**
• Aileen Wuornos **A:** Dan O'Connor **W:** Jack Herman; Karen Herman

15 ❑ Cover: 2.95 **NM** value: **Cover or less**
• Charles Starkweather **A:** Stan Timmons **W:** Jack Herman; Karen Herman

PSYCHO KILLERS PMS SPECIAL — Zone

1 ❑ Cover: 2.95 **NM** value: **3.25**
A: J. Adam J. Walters **W:** Jack Herman; Karen Herman

PSYCHO (MAGAZINE) — Skywald

Perhaps best-known for its liberal use of properties from defunct publishers, Skywald was an independent publisher in the early 1970s, when the stands were dominated by Marvel, DC, Archie, Harvey, Charlton, and Gold Key.

Trying to eke out a portion of the newsstand space, Skywald published such titles as Blazing Six-Guns, The Bravados, and the horror magazine Psycho.

The Heap, a shambling muck monster first introduced in Airboy Comics, appeared in the second issue of this short-lived series. — Brent

1 ❑ ca. 1971 Cover: 0.50 **NM** value: **20.00**
2 ❑ ca. 1971 Cover: 0.50 **NM** value: **12.00**
3 ❑ ca. 1971 Cover: 0.50 **NM** value: **10.00**
4 ❑ Sep 1971 Cover: 0.50 **NM** value: **8.00**
5 ❑ **NM** value: **8.00**
6 ❑ May 1972 Cover: 0.60 **NM** value: **8.00**
7 ❑ Jul 1972 Cover: 0.60 **NM** value: **8.00**
8 ❑ Sep 1972 Cover: 0.60 **NM** value: **8.00**
9 ❑ Nov 1972 Cover: 0.60 **NM** value: **8.00**
10 ❑ Jan 1973 Cover: 0.60 **NM** value: **8.00**
11 ❑ Mar 1973 Cover: 0.60 **NM** value: **6.00**
12 ❑ May 1973 Cover: 0.60 **NM** value: **6.00**
13 ❑ Jul 1973 **NM** value: **6.00**
14 ❑ Sep 1973 Cover: 0.75 **NM** value: **6.00**
15 ❑ Nov 1973 Cover: 0.75 **NM** value: **6.00**
16 ❑ Jan 1974 Cover: 0.75 **NM** value: **6.00**
17 ❑ Mar 1974 Cover: 0.75 **NM** value: **6.00**
18 ❑ May 1974 Cover: 0.75 **NM** value: **6.00**
19 ❑ Jul 1974 Cover: 0.75 **NM** value: **6.00**
20 ❑ Sep 1974 Cover: 0.75 **NM** value: **6.00**
21 ❑ Nov 1974 Cover: 0.75 **NM** value: **5.00**
23 ❑ Jan 1975 Cover: 0.75 **NM** value: **5.00**
24 ❑ Mar 1975 Cover: 0.75 **NM** value: **5.00**

PSYCHOMAN — Revolutionary

1 ❑ Cover: 2.50 **NM** value: **Cover or less**
A: Steven S. Crompton **W:** Patrick McCray; Todd Loren ★ Origin of Psychoman. ★ 1st Appearance of Psychoman.

PSYCHONAUT — Fantagraphics

1 ❑ Mar 1996, b&w Cover: 3.95 **NM** value: **Cover or less**
3 ❑ b&w Cover: 3.50 **NM** value: **Cover or less**
• flipbook with The Pursuers

PSYCHONAUTS — Marvel / Epic

1 ❑ Cover: 4.95 **NM** value: **Cover or less**
Circ: CapCity orders: **4,900**
A: Yasuo Yazaki **W:** Alan Grant; Tony Luke

2 ❑ Cover: 4.95 **NM** value: **Cover or less**
Circ: CapCity orders: **3,400**
A: Yasuo Yazaki **W:** Alan Grant; Tony Luke

3 ❑ Cover: 4.95 **NM** value: **Cover or less**
A: Yasuo Yazaki **W:** Alan Grant; Tony Luke

4 ❑ Cover: 4.95 **NM** value: **Cover or less**
Circ: CapCity orders: **2,100**
A: Yasuo Yazaki **W:** Alan Grant; Tony Luke

PSYCHO-PATH — Venusian / Epic

1 ❑ **NM** value: **2.00**
Gang Bang, Part 2

2 ❑ Sep 1990 Cover: 2.00 **NM** value: **Cover or less**
Gang Bang, Part 2 **A:** Darryl Cobbs **W:** Benny Gugliotti

PSYCHOTIC ADVENTURES ILLUSTRATED — Last Gasp / Epic

1 ❑ Cover: 0.50 **NM** value: **3.00**
The Book of Zee; The Dreamer; The Underground Artist **A:** Charles Dallas **W:** Charles Dallas; S. Goodyear

2 ❑ Cover: 0.50 **NM** value: **3.00**

3 ❑ Cover: 0.50 **NM** value: **3.00**
The Wreck of the Ship John B.; Women of the Wood; The Death of Doctor Dark **A:** Charles Dallas; Larry S. Todd **W:** Charles Dallas; Larry S. Todd

PSYENCE FICTION — Abaculus

0.5 ❑ Sum 1998, b&w Cover: 0.99 **NM** value: **1.00**
• Ashcan preview edition. Truth & Bone, Part 1; The Fallen **A:** Dave Morris; Ian Richardson **W:** Dan Abnett; Rik Hoskin

1 ❑ Cover: 2.95 **NM** value: **Cover or less**
Truth & Bone, Part 1; The Fallen **A:** Dave Morris; Ian Richardson **W:** Dan Abnett; Rik Hoskin

PSYLOCKE & ARCHANGEL: CRIMSON DAWN — Marvel

1 ❑ Aug 1997 Cover: 2.50 **NM** value: **Cover or less**
Circ: Diamd. preorders: **72,235**
gatefold cover. • gatefold summary. **A:** Salvador Larroca **W:** Ben Raab

2 ❑ Sep 1997 Cover: 2.50 **NM** value: **Cover or less**
Circ: Diamd. preorders: **59,729**
• gatefold summary. **A:** Salvador Larroca **W:** Ben Raab

3 ❑ Oct 1997 Cover: 2.50 **NM** value: **Cover or less**
Circ: Diamd. preorders: **59,684**
• gatefold summary. **A:** Salvador Larroca **W:** Ben Raab

4 ❑ Nov 1997 Cover: 2.50 **NM** value: **Cover or less**
Circ: Diamd. preorders: **61,090**
• gatefold summary. **A:** Salvador Larroca **W:** Ben Raab

PT 109 — K.K.

1 ❑ Cover: 0.12 **NM** value: **12.00**
• Based on the movie PT 109

PTERANOMAN — Kitchen Sink

1 ❑ Aug 1990 Cover: 2.00 **NM** value: **Cover or less**
• Donald Simpson **A:** Donald Simpson **W:** Donald Simpson

PUBLIC ENEMIES — D.S.

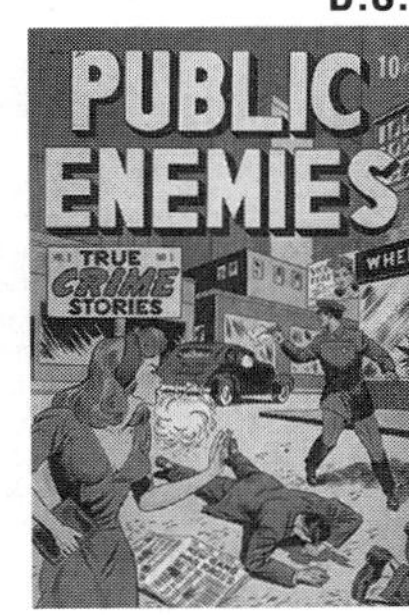

These classic tales of crime and the stupidity of criminals are sprinkled with warnings to the reader on how to be aware of swindles, cons, and various other dangerous situations.

A few humorous oddities are thrown in to keep the reader from getting too depressed, such as the man who was hitchhiking and was picked up by his own stolen car.

The stories are based on true criminals and where they went wrong, from being too smartly dressed to killing a policeman in cold blood.

1 ❑ ca. 1948 Cover: 0.10 **NM** value: **100.00**
• **CGC:** 1 graded, best 8.5
Man With a Gun!; Watch Out for these Swindles; Gang War; Little Alex (text); Criminal Oddities; Dressed to Kill; Hi-Lights; Siege; Sidelights; You Don't Kill a Cop! **A:** Art Gates; Al Melean **W:** Art Gates; Al Melean

2 ❑ ca. 1948 Cover: 0.10 **NM** value: **90.00**
3 ❑ ca. 1948 Cover: 0.10 **NM** value: **60.00**
4 ❑ ca. 1948 Cover: 0.10 **NM** value: **60.00**
5 ❑ ca. 1948 Cover: 0.10 **NM** value: **60.00**
6 ❑ Jan 1949 Cover: 0.10 **NM** value: **50.00**
• **CGC:** 1 graded, best 7.0
7 ❑ Mar 1949 Cover: 0.10 **NM** value: **50.00**

PUBLIC ENEMIES (ETERNITY) — Eternity

1 ❑ b&w Cover: 3.95 **NM** value: **Cover or less**
2 ❑ b&w Cover: 3.95 **NM** value: **Cover or less**

PUDGY PIG — Charlton

1 ❑ Sep 1958 Cover: 0.10 **NM** value: **20.00**
2 ❑ Nov 1958 Cover: 0.10 **NM** value: **20.00**

PUKE & EXPLODE — Northstar

1 ❑ Cover: 2.50 **NM** value: **Cover or less**
2 ❑ Cover: 2.50 **NM** value: **Cover or less**

PULP ACTION — Avalon

1 ❑ Cover: 2.95 **NM** value: **Cover or less**
A: Vernon V. Greene **W:** Vernon V. Greene

2 ❑ Cover: 2.95 **NM** value: **Cover or less**
3 ❑ Cover: 2.95 **NM** value: **Cover or less**
4 ❑ Cover: 2.95 **NM** value: **Cover or less**
5 ❑ Cover: 2.95 **NM** value: **Cover or less**
Remember Me?; One Lone Man **A:** Sanho Kim

6 ❑ Cover: 2.95 **NM** value: **Cover or less**
Safe Behind Bars **A:** Vernon V. Greene **W:** Vernon V. Greene

7 ❑ Cover: 2.95 **NM** value: **Cover or less**
8 ❑ Cover: 2.95 **NM** value: **Cover or less**
Any Stranger; Grim Reaper's Wax Museum **A:** Steve Ditko; Nicholas Alascia; Vernon V. Greene **W:** Vernon V. Greene

PULP DREAMS — Fantagraphics / Eros

All issues are adults only.

1 ❑ b&w Cover: 2.50 **NM** value: **Cover or less**

PULP FANTASTIC — DC / Vertigo

1 ❑ Feb 2000 Cover: 2.50 **NM** value: **Cover or less**
Circ: Diamd. preorders: **12,666**
The Father **A:** Rick Buchett **W:** Howard Chaykin; Davis Tischman

2 ❑ Mar 2000 Cover: 2.50 **NM** value: **Cover or less**
Circ: Diamd. preorders: **9,543**
The Son **A:** Rick Buchett **W:** Howard Chaykin; Davis Tischman

3 ❑ Apr 2000 Cover: 2.50 **NM** value: **Cover or less**
Circ: Diamd. preorders: **8,481**
And the Holy S*it **A:** Rick Buchett **W:** Howard Chaykin; Davis Tischman

PULP FICTION — A List

1 ❑ Spr 1997, b&w Cover: 2.50 **NM** value: **Cover or less**
Circ: Diamd. preorders: **4,500**
The Hawk; The vengeful Corpse; Marry in Haste! (text story); The Ol' Skipper; Serafina...Serafina; Ginger Snap • reprints Golden Age material **A:** Bob Kane; Will Eisner; Jack Kirby; Rod Roche **W:** Bob Kane; Will Eisner; Jack Kirby; Rod Roche; Arthur Wallace; Brenda Starr

2 ❑ Fal 1997, b&w Cover: 2.50 **NM** value: **Cover or less**
• reprints Golden Age material

3 ❑ Win 1997, b&w Cover: 2.50 **NM** value: **Cover or less**
• reprints Golden Age material

4 ❑ Cover: 2.95 **NM** value: **Cover or less**
5 ❑ Cover: 2.95 **NM** value: **Cover or less**
Spencer Steel; Wine, Women and-Sign!; Tugboat Tessie **A:** Dennis Colebrook; E.J. Crescent; Lee Stoken **W:** Dennis Colebrook; E.J. Crescent; Lee Stoken

6 ❑ Cover: 2.95 **NM** value: **Cover or less**

CGC-graded: Multiply prices above by **33 for 9.9 M • 16 for 9.8 NM/M • 7 for 9.6 NM+ • 5 for 9.4 NM • 2.5 for 9.2 NM- • 1.5 for 9.0 VF/NM**

PULP FICTION LIBRARY: MYSTERY IN SPACE DC

1 ❑ Dec 1999 Cover: 19.95 **NM** value: **Cover or less**
📖 Rocket Lanes of Tomorrow; Mr. Fu • Reprints stories from Action Comics, Mystery in Space, etc. **A:** Howard Sherman; Dick Sprang; Jack Kirby; Fra; Virgil Finlay **W:** Bruce Jones; Jerry Siegel; Len Wein; Arnold Drake; Dave Wood; Edmund Hamilton; Gardner Fox; Gerry Conway; John Broome; Larry Niven; Manly Wade Wellman; Otto Binder; Robert Kanigher; Robert Starr; Sid Gerson

PULP (VOL. 1) Viz

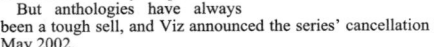

One of the largest comic books anyone's attempted to saddle-stitch — that is, package with staples rather than with squarebinding — Pulp regularly offered issues in excess of 120 pages. Billed as "manga for grownups," Pulp offered a sizable portal into the world of Japanese comics.

Stories of crime, adventure, and espionage using a wide variety of appealing art styles appear in this series' various volumes, dispelling notions that manga is nothing but big-eyed characters fighting giant robots amid a flurry of speed lines.

But anthologies have always been a tough sell, and Viz announced the series' cancellation in May 2002.

1 ❑ Dec 1997 Cover: 5.95 **NM** value: **Cover or less**
Circ: Diamd. preorders: **10,206**
Volume 2
1 ❑ Jan 1998 Cover: 5.95 **NM** value: **Cover or less**
Circ: Diamd. preorders: **8,032**
2 ❑ Feb 1998 Cover: 5.95 **NM** value: **Cover or less**
3 ❑ Mar 1998 Cover: 5.95 **NM** value: **Cover or less**
4 ❑ Apr 1998 Cover: 5.95 **NM** value: **Cover or less**
5 ❑ May 1998 Cover: 5.95 **NM** value: **Cover or less**
6 ❑ Jun 1998 Cover: 5.95 **NM** value: **Cover or less**
7 ❑ Jul 1998 Cover: 5.95 **NM** value: **Cover or less**
8 ❑ Aug 1998 Cover: 5.95 **NM** value: **Cover or less**
9 ❑ Sep 1998 Cover: 5.95 **NM** value: **Cover or less**
📖 Dance Till Tomorrow, Part 16; Dance Till Tomorrow, Part 17; Black & White, Part 12; Voyeur, Part 4; Heartbroken Angels, Part 10; Strain, Part 10; Banana Fish, Part 10 **A:** Taiyo Matsumoto; Ryoichi Ikegami; Akimi Yoshida; Hideo Yamamoto; Masahiko Kikuni; Naoki Yamamoto **W:** Taiyo Matsumoto; Akimi Yoshida; Hideo Yamamoto; Masahiko Kikuni; Naoki Yamamoto; Buronson
10 ❑ Oct 1998 Cover: 5.95 **NM** value: **Cover or less**
11 ❑ Nov 1998 Cover: 5.95 **NM** value: **Cover or less**
Circ: Diamd. preorders: **5,081**
12 ❑ Dec 1998 Cover: 5.95 **NM** value: **Cover or less**
Volume 3
1 ❑ Jan 1999 Cover: 5.95 **NM** value: **Cover or less**
📖 Strain, Part 14; Voyeurs, Inc.: Case One, Part 3; Banana Fish, Part 14; Dance till Tomorrow, Part 22; Black & White, Part 16 **A:** Taiyo Matsumoto; Ryoichi Ikegami; Akimi Yoshida; Hideo Yamamoto; Masahiko Kikuni; Naoki Yamamoto **W:** Taiyo Matsumoto; Akimi Yoshida; Hideo Yamamoto; Masahiko Kikuni; Naoki Yamamoto; Buronson
2 ❑ Feb 1999 Cover: 5.95 **NM** value: **Cover or less**
3 ❑ Mar 1999 Cover: 5.95 **NM** value: **Cover or less**
4 ❑ Apr 1999 Cover: 5.95 **NM** value: **Cover or less**
5 ❑ May 1999 Cover: 5.95 **NM** value: **Cover or less**
6 ❑ Jun 1999 Cover: 5.95 **NM** value: **Cover or less**
7 ❑ Jul 1999 Cover: 5.95 **NM** value: **Cover or less**
8 ❑ Aug 1999 Cover: 5.95 **NM** value: **Cover or less**
9 ❑ Sep 1999 Cover: 5.95 **NM** value: **Cover or less**
10 ❑ Oct 1999 Cover: 5.95 **NM** value: **Cover or less**
11 ❑ Nov 1999 Cover: 5.95 **NM** value: **Cover or less**
12 ❑ Dec 1999 Cover: 5.95 **NM** value: **Cover or less**
Volume 4
1 ❑ Jan 2000 Cover: 5.95 **NM** value: **Cover or less**
2 ❑ Feb 2000 Cover: 5.95 **NM** value: **Cover or less**
3 ❑ Mar 2000 Cover: 5.95 **NM** value: **Cover or less**
4 ❑ Apr 2000 Cover: 5.95 **NM** value: **Cover or less**
5 ❑ May 2000 Cover: 5.95 **NM** value: **Cover or less**
6 ❑ Jun 2000 Cover: 5.95 **NM** value: **Cover or less**

PULP WESTERN Avalon

1 ❑ Cover: 2.95 **NM** value: **Cover or less**

PULSE, THE Blackjack

1 ❑ Jun 1997, b&w **NM** value: **2.00**
no cover price. 📖 Lab Rat 7; Project: Gotterdammerung; Cuda and Spitfyre; C.o.r.p.s.e. Grinders; Dark Siders; Blackjack **A:** Daryl Thompson; Felix Toussaint; Jeremy Pellegrin; Josh Williams; Scott Klauder **W:** Daryl Thompson; James Blair; John Kostelny; Sean Herbert; William Blair

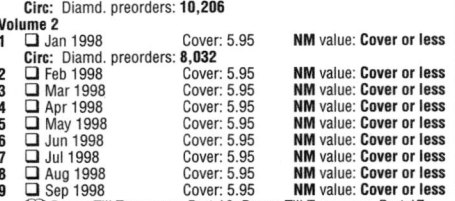

To find the median price offered on eBay at press time for pre-1990 **CGC-graded comics**, multiply by:

9.9 (M): **33**	8.5 (VF+): **1.25**
9.8(NM/M): **16**	8.0 (VF): **0.85**
9.6 (NM+): **7**	7.5 (VF-): **0.6**
9.4 (NM): **5**	7.0 (F/VF): **0.5**
9.2 (NM-): **2.5**	6.5 (F+): **0.4**
9.0 (VF/NM): **1.5**	6.0 (F-): **0.33**

These are median prices of all CGC comics auctioned on eBay; prices for individual issues will vary.

PUMA BLUES, THE Aardvark One

In Puma Blues, Steven Murphy and Michael Zulli deliver one of the first truly "environmental" comic-book series. But its place in comics history comes from the events surrounding the title.

The title was the only comic book by another creator published by Aardvark-Vanaheim President Dave Sim following the split-up that sent many titles to Renegade Press with ex-wife Deni Loubert. When Sim self-distributed his Cerebus: High Society trade paperback, a major comics distributor retaliated by threatening to drop the poorer-selling Puma Blues. A major controversy played out in the comics press, with Murphy and Zulli caught in the middle. The parties worked things out, but the attendant publicity evidently didn't drive many new readers to the title. — JJM

1 ❑ Jun 1986 Cover: 2.00 **NM** value: **Cover or less**
• 10, 000 copies printed; Aardvark One International Publisher **A:** Michael Zulli **W:** Stephen Murphy
1-2 ❑ Cover: 1.70 **NM** value: **2.00**
2 ❑ Sep 1986 Cover: 1.70 **NM** value: **2.00**
• 10, 000 copies printed
3 ❑ Dec 1986 Cover: 1.70 **NM** value: **2.00**
• 19, 000 copies printed
4 ❑ Feb 1987 Cover: 1.70 **NM** value: **Cover or less**
• 13, 000 copies printed
5 ❑ Mar 1987 Cover: 1.70 **NM** value: **Cover or less**
• 13, 000 copies printed
6 ❑ Apr 1987 Cover: 1.70 **NM** value: **Cover or less**
• 13, 000 copies printed
7 ❑ May 1987 Cover: 1.70 **NM** value: **Cover or less**
• 12, 000 copies printed
8 ❑ May 1987 Cover: 1.70 **NM** value: **Cover or less**
9 ❑ Jul 1987 Cover: 1.70 **NM** value: **Cover or less**
10 ❑ Aug 1987 Cover: 1.70 **NM** value: **Cover or less**
11 ❑ Sep 1987 Cover: 1.70 **NM** value: **Cover or less**
12 ❑ Oct 1987 Cover: 1.70 **NM** value: **Cover or less**
13 ❑ Nov 1987 Cover: 1.70 **NM** value: **Cover or less**
14 ❑ Dec 1987 Cover: 1.70 **NM** value: **Cover or less**
15 ❑ Jan 1988 Cover: 1.70 **NM** value: **Cover or less**
16 ❑ Feb 1988 Cover: 1.70 **NM** value: **Cover or less**
17 ❑ Mar 1988 Cover: 1.70 **NM** value: **Cover or less**
18 ❑ Apr 1988 Cover: 1.70 **NM** value: **Cover or less**
• self-published
19 ❑ 1988 Cover: 1.70 **NM** value: **Cover or less**
• self-published
20 ❑ 1988 Cover: 1.70 **NM** value: **Cover or less**
• self-published **W:** Alan Moore
21 ❑ 1988b&w Cover: 1.70 **NM** value: **Cover or less**
• Mirage Studio Publisher
22 ❑ 1988b&w Cover: 1.70 **NM** value: **Cover or less**
23 ❑ b&w Cover: 1.70 **NM** value: **Cover or less**
Bk 1❑ Cover: 10.95 **NM** value: **Cover or less**
• Sense of Doubt
Bk 2❑ Cover: 10.95 **NM** value: **Cover or less**
• Watch that Man

PUMMELER Parody Press

1 ❑ b&w Cover: 2.95 **NM** value: **Cover or less**
Foil embossed cover. • Punisher parody

PUMMELER $2099 Parody Press

1 ❑ Cover: 2.95 **NM** value: **Cover or less**
Gold Trimmed Foil Cover. **A:** Thad Rhodes III **W:** Ross Turner

PUMPKINHEAD: THE RITES OF EXORCISM Dark Horse

1 ❑ ca. 1992 Cover: 2.50 **NM** value: **Cover or less**
Circ: CapCity orders: **3,950**
A: Shawn McManus; Jim McDermott **W:** Gary Gerani
2 ❑ ca. 1992 Cover: 2.50 **NM** value: **Cover or less**
Circ: CapCity orders: **5,900**
A: Shawn McManus; Jim McDermott **W:** Gary Gerani; Mark Patrick Carducci
3 ❑ ca. 1992 Cover: 2.50 **NM** value: **Cover or less**
4 ❑ ca. 1992 Cover: 2.50 **NM** value: **Cover or less**

PUNCH & JUDY Hillman

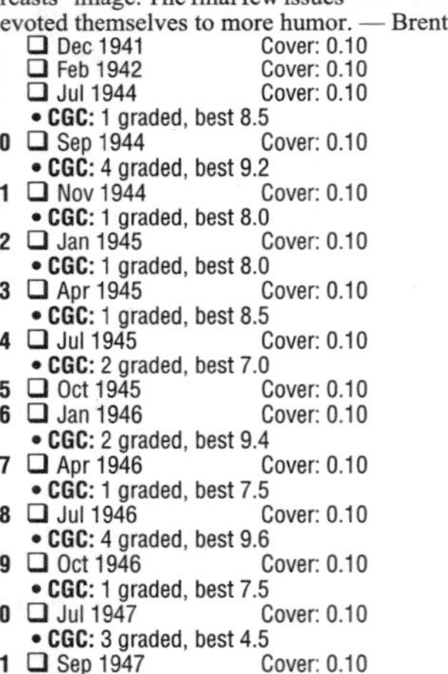

Although Punch and Judy shows are more familiar to those growing up in the United Kingdom (and for a different view of those entertainments, check out Neil Gaiman's Mr. Punch), that didn't stop Hillman from producing its own comic book based on the hot-tempered Punch puppet.

The anthology kids' title was introduced with the cover copy on the first issue "Comics to Tickle Children" and "The funniest show on earth!!" — not to mention "New! Cute! Fun-show for kiddies." While Punch is a mischievous puppet, however, Judy is a sweet little blonde girl, occasionally taken aback by the antics of her outrageous friend.

There were other continuing characters in the mix, including a pig, monkeys, and, note, even a Jack Kirby feature, "Earl the Rich Rabbit." — Maggie

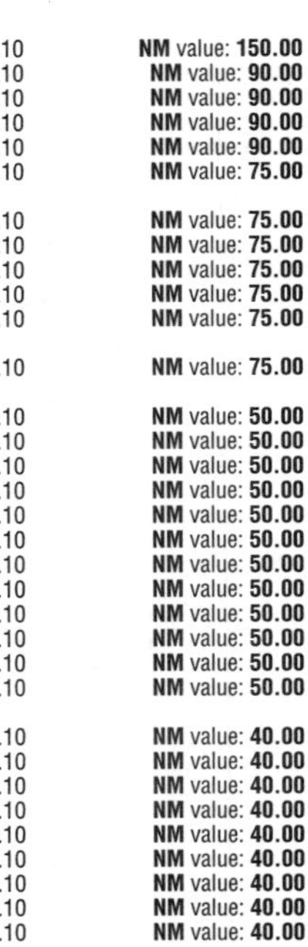

Volume 1
1 ❑ ca. 1944 Cover: 0.10 **NM** value: **150.00**
2 ❑ Fal 1944 Cover: 0.10 **NM** value: **90.00**
3 ❑ Win 1944 Cover: 0.10 **NM** value: **90.00**
4 ❑ Fal 1945 Cover: 0.10 **NM** value: **90.00**
5 ❑ Dec 1945 Cover: 0.10 **NM** value: **90.00**
6 ❑ Jan 1946 Cover: 0.10 **NM** value: **75.00**
• **CGC:** 1 graded, best 9.0
7 ❑ Feb 1946 Cover: 0.10 **NM** value: **75.00**
8 ❑ Mar 1946 Cover: 0.10 **NM** value: **75.00**
9 ❑ Apr 1946 Cover: 0.10 **NM** value: **75.00**
10 ❑ May 1946 Cover: 0.10 **NM** value: **75.00**
11 ❑ Jun 1946 Cover: 0.10 **NM** value: **75.00**
• **CGC:** 1 graded, best 9.0
12 ❑ Jul 1946 Cover: 0.10 **NM** value: **75.00**
Volume 2
1 ❑ Aug 1949 Cover: 0.10 **NM** value: **50.00**
2 ❑ Sep 1949 Cover: 0.10 **NM** value: **50.00**
3 ❑ Oct 1949 Cover: 0.10 **NM** value: **50.00**
4 ❑ Nov 1949 Cover: 0.10 **NM** value: **50.00**
5 ❑ Dec 1949 Cover: 0.10 **NM** value: **50.00**
6 ❑ Jan 1950 Cover: 0.10 **NM** value: **50.00**
7 ❑ Feb 1950 Cover: 0.10 **NM** value: **50.00**
8 ❑ Mar 1950 Cover: 0.10 **NM** value: **50.00**
9 ❑ Apr 1950 Cover: 0.10 **NM** value: **50.00**
10 ❑ May 1950 Cover: 0.10 **NM** value: **50.00**
11 ❑ Jun 1950 Cover: 0.10 **NM** value: **50.00**
12 ❑ Jul 1950 Cover: 0.10 **NM** value: **50.00**
Volume 3
1 ❑ Apr 1951 Cover: 0.10 **NM** value: **40.00**
2 ❑ May 1951 Cover: 0.10 **NM** value: **40.00**
3 ❑ Jun 1951 Cover: 0.10 **NM** value: **40.00**
4 ❑ Jul 1951 Cover: 0.10 **NM** value: **40.00**
5 ❑ Aug 1951 Cover: 0.10 **NM** value: **40.00**
6 ❑ Sep 1951 Cover: 0.10 **NM** value: **40.00**
7 ❑ Oct 1951 Cover: 0.10 **NM** value: **40.00**
8 ❑ Nov 1951 Cover: 0.10 **NM** value: **40.00**
9 ❑ Dec 191 Cover: 0.10 **NM** value: **40.00**

PUNCH COMICS Harry A. Chesler

Starting out as an anthology title with stories featuring Mr. "E", Carnival, Unholy "3", Hale the Magician, Captain Glory, Kitty Kelly, Captain Courage, and Sky Chief, Punch Comics quickly morphed into a crime and horror title with humorous bits thrown in.

The cover of #12 is especially well-known with criminals and lawmen shooting it out around a gigantic human skull with a dead gunman hanging out of one of the eyesockets. The cover of #20 is also highly collectible, with its "bare breasts" image. The final few issues devoted themselves to more humor. — Brent

1 ❑ Dec 1941 Cover: 0.10 **NM** value: **750.00**
2 ❑ Feb 1942 Cover: 0.10 **NM** value: **600.00**
9 ❑ Jul 1944 Cover: 0.10 **NM** value: **600.00**
• **CGC:** 1 graded, best 8.5
10 ❑ Sep 1944 Cover: 0.10 **NM** value: **600.00**
• **CGC:** 4 graded, best 9.2
11 ❑ Nov 1944 Cover: 0.10 **NM** value: **600.00**
• **CGC:** 1 graded, best 8.0
12 ❑ Jan 1945 Cover: 0.10 **NM** value: **600.00**
• **CGC:** 1 graded, best 8.0
13 ❑ Apr 1945 Cover: 0.10 **NM** value: **500.00**
• **CGC:** 1 graded, best 8.5
14 ❑ Jul 1945 Cover: 0.10 **NM** value: **500.00**
• **CGC:** 2 graded, best 7.0
15 ❑ Oct 1945 Cover: 0.10 **NM** value: **500.00**
16 ❑ Jan 1946 Cover: 0.10 **NM** value: **500.00**
• **CGC:** 2 graded, best 9.4
17 ❑ Apr 1946 Cover: 0.10 **NM** value: **500.00**
• **CGC:** 1 graded, best 7.5
18 ❑ Jul 1946 Cover: 0.10 **NM** value: **400.00**
• **CGC:** 4 graded, best 9.6
19 ❑ Oct 1946 Cover: 0.10 **NM** value: **400.00**
• **CGC:** 1 graded, best 7.5
20 ❑ Jul 1947 Cover: 0.10 **NM** value: **400.00**
• **CGC:** 3 graded, best 4.5
21 ❑ Sep 1947 Cover: 0.10 **NM** value: **400.00**
• **CGC:** 1 graded, best 9.0
22 ❑ Nov 1947 Cover: 0.10 **NM** value: **400.00**
23 ❑ Jan 1948 Cover: 0.10 **NM** value: **400.00**

PUNISHER (1ST SERIES) Marvel

Having first appeared in Amazing Spider-Man #129, Frank Castle, the Punisher, got his own title at last with the premiere of this limited series.

The action begins when Castle is sentenced to serve out a long term in the Rykers Island maximum security facility. As can be expected, he makes no friends among his fellow inmates, and the resulting violence threatens to tear the prison apart. When Castle stops a jailbreak, the warden recruits him into a secret organization which allows him to what he does best: punish criminals.

There was a significant run on early issues of this series in 1986, prompting Marvel to launch an on-

Other grades: Multiply prices above by **1.5 for Mint • 2/3 for Very Fine • 1/3 for Fine • 1/5 for Very Good • 1/8 for Good**

going series for the character. This is also one of the few memorable five-issue limited series; most publishers have gone for an even number.

1 ❑ Jan 1986 Cover: 1.25 **NM value: 8.00**
Circ: CapCity orders: **22,600** • **CGC:** 42 graded, best 9.8
• Double-size.

2 ❑ Feb 1986 Cover: 0.75 **NM value: 5.00**
Circ: CapCity orders: **20,100** • **CGC:** 5 graded, best 9.6
Back To The War **A:** Mike Zeck **W:** Steven Grant

3 ❑ Mar 1986 Cover: 0.75 **NM value: 4.00**
Circ: CapCity orders: **21,300** • **CGC:** 11 graded, best 9.6
Slaughterday **A:** Mike Zeck **W:** Steven Grant

4 ❑ Apr 1986 Cover: 0.75 **NM value: 4.00**
Circ: CapCity orders: **25,000** • **CGC:** 5 graded, best 9.6
Final Solution, Part 1 **A:** Mike Zeck **W:** Steven Grant

5 ❑ May 1986 Cover: 0.75 **NM value: 4.00**
Circ: CapCity orders: **26,600** • **CGC:** 1 graded, best 9.2
Final Solution, Part 2 **A:** Mike Zeck **W:** Steven Grant

Bk 1 ❑ Cover: 7.95 **NM value: Cover or less**

PUNISHER, THE (2ND SERIES) Marvel

This first ongoing series for Marvel's most ruthless vigilante fleshes out Frank Castle's character. Well, perhaps "flesh" isn't the right word; actually, "blood and guts" tends to better describe the grim-and-gritty adventures the Punisher sends himself on. But the title does give the Punisher a support system in Microchip, a computer genius, and a fine foil in the villlain Jigsaw.

Early issues are better than later ones, when the character was spread across three titles, and later issues find Frank Castle completely replaced as the Punisher by a female vigilante. After this series' cancellation, Castle returns to the role in Punisher 3rd Series — castas a mob boss, strangely enough, by John Ostrander. — JJM

1 ❑ Jul 1987 Cover: 0.75 **NM value: 4.00**
Circ: CapCity orders: **62,500** • **CGC:** 49 graded, best 9.8

2 ❑ Aug 1987 Cover: 0.75 **NM value: 3.00**
Circ: CapCity orders: **49,400** • **CGC:** 8 graded, best 9.8
Bolivia **A:** Klaus Janson **W:** Mike Baron

3 ❑ Oct 1987 Cover: 0.75 **NM value: 2.50**
Circ: CapCity orders: **54,200**
The Devil Came From Kansas! **A:** Klaus Janson **W:** Mike Baron

4 ❑ Nov 1987 Cover: 0.75 **NM value: 2.00**
Circ: CapCity orders: **48,300**

5 ❑ Jan 1988 Cover: 0.75 **NM value: 2.00**
Circ: CapCity orders: **40,700**

6 ❑ Feb 1988 Cover: 0.75 **NM value: 2.00**
Circ: CapCity orders: **38,400**

7 ❑ Mar 1988 Cover: 0.75 **NM value: 2.00**
Circ: CapCity orders: **38,600**

8 ❑ May 1988 Cover: 1.00 **NM value: 2.00**
Circ: CapCity orders: **33,500**
A: Whilce Portacio

9 ❑ Jun 1988 Cover: 1.00 **NM value: 2.00**
Circ: CapCity orders: **31,400** • **CGC:** 4 graded, best 9.6
A: Whilce Portacio

10 ❑ Aug 1988 Cover: 1.00 **NM value: 3.00**
Circ: CapCity orders: **32,700** • **CGC:** 16 graded, best 9.8
A: Whilce Portacio ★ Appearance of Daredevil.

11 ❑ Sep 1988 Cover: 1.00 **NM value: 2.00**
Circ: CapCity orders: **31,300**
A: Whilce Portacio

12 ❑ Oct 1988 Cover: 1.00 **NM value: 2.00**
Circ: CapCity orders: **32,800**
A: Whilce Portacio

13 ❑ Nov 1988 Cover: 1.00 **NM value: 2.00**
Circ: CapCity orders: **34,200**
A: Whilce Portacio

14 ❑ Dec 1988 Cover: 1.00 **NM value: 2.00**
Circ: CapCity orders: **35,000**
A: Whilce Portacio ★ Appearance of Kingpin.

15 ❑ Jan 1989 Cover: 1.00 **NM value: 2.00**
Circ: Statement: **184,265** CapCity orders: **33,900**
To Topple The Kingpin **A:** Whilce Portacio **W:** Mike Baron ★ Appearance of Kingpin.

16 ❑ Feb 1989 Cover: 1.00 **NM value: 2.00**
Circ: Statement: **184,265** CapCity orders: **34,600**
Escalation **A:** Whilce Portacio **W:** Mike Baron ★ Appearance of Kingpin.

17 ❑ Mar 1989 Cover: 1.00 **NM value: 2.00**
Circ: Statement: **184,265** CapCity orders: **35,700**
A: Whilce Portacio **W:** Mike Baron

18 ❑ Apr 1989 Cover: 1.00 **NM value: 2.00**
Circ: Statement: **184,265** CapCity orders: **38,600**
A: Whilce Portacio **W:** Mike Baron ★ Versus Kingpin.

19 ❑ May 1989 Cover: 1.00 **NM value: 2.00**
Circ: Statement: **184,265** CapCity orders: **36,100**
The Spider **A:** Larry Stroman **W:** Mike Baron

20 ❑ Jun 1989 Cover: 1.00 **NM value: 2.00**
Circ: Statement: **184,265** CapCity orders: **36,900**
Bad Tip **A:** Shea Anton Pensa **W:** Mike Baron

21 ❑ Jul 1989 Cover: 1.00 **NM value: 2.00**
Circ: Statement: **184,265** CapCity orders: **37,700**
The Boxer **A:** Erik Larsen **W:** Mike Baron

22 ❑ Aug 1989 Cover: 1.00 **NM value: 2.00**
Circ: Statement: **184,265** CapCity orders: **39,900**
Ninja Training Camp **A:** Erik Larsen **W:** Mike Baron

23 ❑ Sep 1989 Cover: 1.00 **NM value: 2.00**
Circ: Statement: **184,265** CapCity orders: **39,700**
Capture The Flag **A:** Erik Larsen **W:** Mike Baron

24 ❑ Oct 1989 Cover: 1.00 **NM value: 2.00**
Circ: Statement: **184,265** CapCity orders: **42,000**
Land Of The Eternal Sun **A:** Erik Larsen **W:** Mike Baron ★ 1st Appearance of Shadowmasters.

25 ❑ Nov 1989 Cover: 1.75 **NM value: 2.00**
Circ: Statement: **184,265** CapCity orders: **42,900**
• Giant-sized. Sunset In Kansas **A:** Erik Larsen **W:** Mike Baron ★ Appearance of Shadowmasters.

26 ❑ Nov 1989 Cover: 1.00 **NM value: 2.00**
Circ: Statement: **184,265** CapCity orders: **46,200**
The Whistle Blower **A:** Russ Heath **W:** Mike Baron

27 ❑ Dec 1989 Cover: 1.00 **NM value: 2.00**
Circ: Statement: **184,265** CapCity orders: **46,800**

28 ❑ Dec 1989 Cover: 1.00 **NM value: 2.00**
Circ: Statement: **184,265** CapCity orders: **49,600**
Acts of Vengeance • Acts of Vengeance **W:** Mike Baron

29 ❑ Jan 1990 Cover: 1.00 **NM value: 2.00**
Circ: Statement: **227,766** CapCity orders: **52,200**
Acts of Vengeance • Acts of Vengeance **A:** Bill Reinhold **W:** Mike Baron

30 ❑ Feb 1990 Cover: 1.00 **NM value: 2.00**
Circ: Statement: **227,766**
Confession **A:** Bill Reinhold **W:** Mike Baron

31 ❑ Mar 1990 Cover: 1.00 **NM value: 2.00**
Circ: Statement: **227,766** CapCity orders: **48,300**
Crankin' **A:** Bill Reinhold **W:** Mike Baron

32 ❑ Apr 1990 Cover: 1.00 **NM value: 2.00**
Circ: Statement: **227,766** CapCity orders: **46,500**
Speedy Solution **A:** Bill Reinhold **W:** Mike Baron

33 ❑ May 1990 Cover: 1.00 **NM value: 2.00**
Circ: Statement: **227,766** CapCity orders: **47,400**
Reaver Fever **A:** Bill Reinhold **W:** Mike Baron

34 ❑ Jun 1990 Cover: 1.00 **NM value: 2.00**
Circ: Statement: **227,766** CapCity orders: **46,800**
Exo-Skeleton • Has 1989 Statement, filed 11/1/89; avg print run 287,180; avg sales 179,665; avg subs 4,600; avg total paid 184,265; samples 150; office use 600; max existent 185,015; 36% of run returned **A:** Bill Reinhold **W:** Mike Baron

35 ❑ Jul 1990 Cover: 1.00 **NM value: 2.00**
Circ: Statement: **227,766** CapCity orders: **46,500**
Jigsaw Puzzle, Part 1 • Jigsaw Puzzle **A:** Bill Reinhold **W:** Mike Baron

36 ❑ Aug 1990 Cover: 1.00 **NM value: 2.00**
Circ: Statement: **227,766** CapCity orders: **45,600**
Jigsaw Puzzle, Part 2 • Jigsaw Puzzle **A:** Mark Texeira **W:** Mike Baron

37 ❑ Aug 1990 Cover: 1.00 **NM value: 2.00**
Circ: Statement: **227,766** CapCity orders: **45,300**
Jigsaw Puzzle, Part 3 • Jigsaw Puzzle **A:** Mark Texeira **W:** Mike Baron

38 ❑ Sep 1990 Cover: 1.00 **NM value: 2.00**
Circ: Statement: **227,766** CapCity orders: **45,300**
Jigsaw Puzzle, Part 4 • Jigsaw Puzzle **A:** Bill Reinhold **W:** Mike Baron

39 ❑ Sep 1990 Cover: 1.00 **NM value: 2.00**
Circ: Statement: **227,766** CapCity orders: **44,700**
Jigsaw Puzzle, Part 5 • Jigsaw Puzzle **A:** Jack Slamn **W:** Mike Baron

40 ❑ Oct 1990 Cover: 1.00 **NM value: 2.00**
Circ: Statement: **227,766** CapCity orders: **44,400**
Jigsaw Puzzle, Part 6 • Jigsaw Puzzle **A:** Bill Reinhold **W:** Mike Baron

41 ❑ Oct 1990 Cover: 1.00 **NM value: 1.50**
Circ: Statement: **227,766** CapCity orders: **44,400**
Should A Gentleman Offer A Tiparillo To A Lady? **A:** Bill Reinhold **W:** Mike Baron

42 ❑ Nov 1990 Cover: 1.00 **NM value: 1.50**
Circ: Statement: **227,766** CapCity orders: **42,600**
The Punisher In St. Paradine's **A:** Mark Texeira **W:** Mike Baron

43 ❑ Dec 1990 Cover: 1.00 **NM value: 1.50**
Circ: Statement: **227,766** CapCity orders: **42,600**
Border Run **A:** Bill Reinhold **W:** Mike Baron

44 ❑ Jan 1991 Cover: 1.00 **NM value: 1.50**
Circ: CapCity orders: **42,900**
Flag Burner **A:** Neil Hanson **W:** Mike Baron

45 ❑ Feb 1991 Cover: 1.00 **NM value: 1.50**
Circ: CapCity orders: **41,700**
One Way Fare **A:** Tod Smith **W:** Chuck Dixon

46 ❑ Mar 1991 Cover: 1.00 **NM value: 1.50**
Circ: CapCity orders: **38,700**
Cold Cache • Has 1990 Statement, filed 10/1/90; avg print run 330,375; avg sales 222,858; avg subs 4,908; avg total paid 227,766; samples 150; office use 600; max existent 228,516; 31% of run returned **A:** Hugh Haynes **W:** Mike Baron

47 ❑ Apr 1991 Cover: 1.00 **NM value: 1.50**
Circ: CapCity orders: **37,800**
The Brattle Gun, Part 1 **A:** Hugh Haynes **W:** Mike Baron

48 ❑ May 1991 Cover: 1.00 **NM value: 1.50**
Circ: CapCity orders: **39,300**
The Brattle Gun, Part 2 **A:** Hugh Haynes **W:** Mike Baron

49 ❑ Jun 1991 Cover: 1.00 **NM value: 1.50**
Circ: CapCity orders: **39,600**
Death Below Zero **A:** Ron Wagner **W:** Chuck Dixon

50 ❑ Jul 1991 Cover: 1.50 **NM value: 2.00**
Circ: CapCity orders: **48,300**
• double-sized. Bark Like A Dog; Yo Yo **A:** Hugh Haynes; Roderick Delgado **W:** Marc McLaurin; Mike Baron

51 ❑ Aug 1991 Cover: 1.00 **NM value: 1.50**
Circ: CapCity orders: **43,200**
Golden Buddha

52 ❑ Sep 1991 Cover: 1.00 **NM value: 1.50**
Circ: CapCity orders: **43,500**
Lupe **A:** Paul Guinan **W:** Mike Baron

53 ❑ Oct 1991 Cover: 1.00 **NM value: 1.50**
Circ: CapCity orders: **53,400**
Final Days, Part 1 **A:** Hugh Haynes **W:** Mike Baron

54 ❑ Nov 1991 Cover: 1.00 **NM value: 1.50**
Circ: CapCity orders: **49,600**
Final Days, Part 2 **A:** Hugh Haynes **W:** Mike Baron

55 ❑ Nov 1991 Cover: 1.00 **NM value: 1.50**
Circ: CapCity orders: **49,200**
Final Days, Part 3 **A:** Hugh Haynes **W:** Mike Baron

56 ❑ Dec 1991 Cover: 1.00 **NM value: 1.50**
Circ: CapCity orders: **50,700**
Final Days, Part 4 **A:** Hugh Haynes **W:** Mike Baron

57 ❑ Dec 1991 Cover: 1.00 **NM value: 2.00**
Circ: CapCity orders: **79,200**
photo cover with paper overlay. Final Days, Part 5 **A:** Hugh Haynes **W:** Mike Baron

58 ❑ Jan 1992 Cover: 1.00 **NM value: 1.50**
Circ: CapCity orders: **50,400**
Final Days, Part 6 **A:** Hugh Haynes **W:** Mike Baron

59 ❑ Jan 1992 Cover: 1.00 **NM value: 1.50**
Circ: CapCity orders: **50,400**
Final Days, Part 7 • Punisher becomes black **A:** Hugh Haynes **W:** Mike Baron

60 ❑ Feb 1992 Cover: 1.25 **NM value: 1.50**
Circ: CapCity orders: **57,900**
Escape from New York **A:** Val Mayerik **W:** Marc McLaurin; Mike Baron ★ Appearance of Luke Cage.

61 ❑ Mar 1992 Cover: 1.25 **NM value: 1.50**
Circ: CapCity orders: **55,200**
Crackdown **A:** Val Mayerik **W:** Marc McLaurin; Mike Baron ★ Appearance of Luke Cage.

62 ❑ Apr 1992 Cover: 1.25 **NM value: 1.50**
Circ: CapCity orders: **50,700**
Fade to White • Punisher becomes white again **A:** Val Mayerik **W:** Marc McLaurin; Mike Baron

63 ❑ May 1992 Cover: 1.25 **NM value: Cover or less**
Circ: CapCity orders: **47,400**
The Big Check-Out **A:** Tod Smith **W:** Chuck Dixon

64 ❑ 1992 Cover: 1.25 **NM value: Cover or less**
Circ: CapCity orders: **48,600**
Eurohit, Part 1 **A:** Dougie Braithwaite **W:** Andy Lanning; Dan Abnett

65 ❑ 1992 Cover: 1.25 **NM value: Cover or less**
Circ: CapCity orders: **46,500**
Eurohit, Part 2 **A:** Dougie Braithwaite **W:** Andy Lanning; Dan Abnett

66 ❑ 1992 Cover: 1.25 **NM value: Cover or less**
Circ: CapCity orders: **46,500**
Eurohit, Part 3 **A:** Dougie Braithwaite **W:** Andy Lanning; Dan Abnett

67 ❑ 1992 Cover: 1.25 **NM value: Cover or less**
Circ: CapCity orders: **45,500**
Eurohit, Part 4 **A:** Dougie Braithwaite **W:** Andy Lanning; Dan Abnett

68 ❑ 1992 Cover: 1.25 **NM value: Cover or less**
Circ: CapCity orders: **45,900**
Eurohit, Part 5 **A:** Dougie Braithwaite **W:** Andy Lanning; Dan Abnett

69 ❑ 1992 Cover: 1.25 **NM value: Cover or less**
Circ: CapCity orders: **39,300**
Eurohit, Part 6 **A:** Dougie Braithwaite **W:** Andy Lanning; Dan Abnett

70 ❑ 1992 Cover: 1.25 **NM value: Cover or less**
Circ: CapCity orders: **39,600**
Eurohit, Part 7 **A:** Dougie Braithwaite **W:** Andy Lanning; Dan Abnett

71 ❑ Oct 1992 Cover: 1.25 **NM value: Cover or less**
Circ: CapCity orders: **36,600**
Loose Ends **A:** Dougie Braithwaite **W:** Andy Lanning; Dan Abnett

72 ❑ Nov 1992 Cover: 1.25 **NM value: Cover or less**
Circ: CapCity orders: **33,700**
Life During Wartime **A:** Dougie Braithwaite **W:** Andy Lanning; Dan Abnett

73 ❑ Dec 1992 Cover: 1.25 **NM value: Cover or less**
Circ: Statement: **215,600** CapCity orders: **32,100**
Police Action, Part 1 **A:** Dougie Braithwaite **W:** Andy Lanning; Dan Abnett

74 ❑ Jan 1993 Cover: 1.25 **NM value: Cover or less**
Circ: Statement: **215,600** CapCity orders: **30,700**
Police Action, Part 2 **A:** Dougie Braithwaite **W:** Andy Lanning; Dan Abnett

75 ❑ Feb 1993 Cover: 2.75 **NM value: Cover or less**
Circ: Statement: **215,600** • **CGC:** 1 graded, best 9.6
Embossed cover. Police Action, Part 3 **A:** Dougie Braithwaite **W:** Andy Lanning; Dan Abnett

76 ❑ Mar 1993 Cover: 1.25 **NM value: 1.50**
Circ: Statement: **215,600**
Lava **A:** Larry Stroman **W:** Mike Baron

77 ❑ Apr 1993 Cover: 1.25 **NM value: 1.50**
Circ: Statement: **215,600** CapCity orders: **30,600**
Survival, Part 1

78 ❑ May 1993 Cover: 1.25 **NM value: 1.50**
Circ: Statement: **215,600** CapCity orders: **29,400**
Survival, Part 2 **A:** Val Mayerik **W:** Roger Salick

79 ❑ Jun 1993 Cover: 1.25 **NM value: 1.50**
Circ: Statement: **215,600** CapCity orders: **29,700**
Survival, Part 3

80 ❑ Jul 1993 Cover: 1.25 **NM value: 1.50**
Circ: Statement: **215,600** CapCity orders: **29,100**
Last Confession **A:** Dave Hooper **W:** Steven Grant

81 ❑ Aug 1993 Cover: 1.25 **NM value: Cover or less**
Circ: Statement: **215,600** CapCity orders: **29,250**
Bodies Of Evidence **A:** Hoang Nguyen **W:** Steven Grant

82 ❑ Sep 1993 Cover: 1.25 **NM value: Cover or less**
Circ: Statement: **215,600** CapCity orders: **26,700**
Firefight, Part 1

83 ❑ Oct 1993 Cover: 1.25 **NM value: Cover or less**
Circ: Statement: **215,600** CapCity orders: **25,500**
Firefight, Part 2 **A:** Hugh Haynes **W:** Andy Lanning; Dan Abnett

84 ❑ Nov 1993 Cover: 1.25 **NM value: Cover or less**
Circ: Statement: **215,600** CapCity orders: **25,450**
Firefight, Part 3

85 ❑ Dec 1993 Cover: 1.25 **NM value: Cover or less**

CGC-graded: Multiply prices above by **33 for 9.9 M • 16 for 9.8 NM/M • 7 for 9.6 NM+ • 5 for 9.4 NM • 2.5 for 9.2 NM- • 1.5 for 9.0 VF/NM**

Circ: Statement: **106,800** CapCity orders: **24,400**
📖 Suicide Run Prelude **A:** Hugh Haynes **W:** Steven Grant

86 ❑ Jan 1994 Cover: 2.95 **NM** value: **Cover or less**
Circ: Statement: **106,800** CapCity orders: **26,500 • CGC:** 1 graded, best 9.8
• Giant-size. 📖 Suicide Run, Part 3

87 ❑ Feb 1994 Cover: 1.25 **NM** value: **Cover or less**
Circ: Statement: **106,800** CapCity orders: **26,400**
📖 Suicide Run, Part 6 • Has 1993 Statement, filed 10/1/93; avg print run 302,000; avg sales 203,533; avg subs 12,067; avg total paid 215,600; samples 125; office use 500; max existent 216,225; 28% of run returned **A:** Hugh Haynes **W:** Steven Grant

88 ❑ Mar 1994 Cover: 1.25 **NM** value: **Cover or less**
Circ: Statement: **106,800** CapCity orders: **30,200**
📖 Suicide Run, Part 9

89 ❑ Apr 1994 Cover: 1.25 **NM** value: **Cover or less**
Circ: Statement: **106,800** CapCity orders: **21,850**
📖 Fortress: Miami, Part 1

90 ❑ May 1994 Cover: 1.50 **NM** value: **Cover or less**
Circ: Statement: **106,800** CapCity orders: **20,800**
📖 Fortress: Miami, Part 2

91 ❑ Jun 1994 Cover: 1.50 **NM** value: **Cover or less**
Circ: Statement: **106,800** CapCity orders: **20,100**
📖 Fortress: Miami, Part 3 **A:** Russ Heath **W:** Chuck Dixon

92 ❑ Jul 1994 Cover: 1.50 **NM** value: **Cover or less**
Circ: Statement: **106,800** CapCity orders: **19,800**
📖 Fortress: Miami, Part 4 **A:** Russ Heath **W:** Chuck Dixon

93 ❑ Aug 1994 Cover: 1.50 **NM** value: **Cover or less**
Circ: Statement: **106,800** CapCity orders: **17,700**

94 ❑ Sep 1994 Cover: 1.50 **NM** value: **Cover or less**
Circ: Statement: **106,800** CapCity orders: **16,000**
📖 No Rules, Part 1

95 ❑ Oct 1994 Cover: 1.50 **NM** value: **Cover or less**
Circ: Statement: **106,800** CapCity orders: **15,150**
📖 No Rules, Part 2

96 ❑ Nov 1994 Cover: 1.50 **NM** value: **Cover or less**
Circ: Statement: **106,800** CapCity orders: **13,950**
📖 Raving Beauty **A:** Isaac M. Del Rivero **W:** Richard Rainey

97 ❑ Dec 1994 Cover: 1.50 **NM** value: **Cover or less**
Circ: CapCity orders: **14,100**
📖 The Devil's Secret Name **A:** Rod Whigham **W:** Chuck Dixon

98 ❑ Jan 1995 Cover: 1.50 **NM** value: **Cover or less**
Circ: CapCity orders: **12,875**

99 ❑ Feb 1995 Cover: 1.50 **NM** value: **Cover or less**
Circ: CapCity orders: **12,825**

100 ❑ Mar 1995 Cover: 2.95 **NM** value: **Cover or less**
• Giant-size. 📖 The Cage! • Has 1994 Statement, filed 10/1/94; avg print run 173,183; avg sales 104,850; avg subs 1,950; avg total paid 106,800; samples 125; office use 500; max existent 107,425; 38% of run returned **A:** Rod Whigham **W:** Chuck Dixon

100/SC ❑ Mar 1995 Cover: 3.95 **NM** value: **Cover or less**
Circ: CapCity orders: **16,325**
foil cover. • Giant-size. 📖 The Cage! **A:** Rod Whigham **W:** Chuck Dixon

101 ❑ Apr 1995 Cover: 1.50 **NM** value: **Cover or less**
Circ: CapCity orders: **11,700**

102 ❑ May 1995 Cover: 1.50 **NM** value: **Cover or less**
Circ: CapCity orders: **11,325**

103 ❑ Jun 1995 Cover: 1.50 **NM** value: **Cover or less**
Circ: CapCity orders: **13,425**
📖 Countdown, Part 1 (4) **A:** Rod Whigham **W:** Chuck Dixon

104 ❑ Jul 1995 Cover: 1.50 **NM** value: **Cover or less**
Circ: CapCity orders: **13,500**
📖 Countdown, Part 4 (1) final issue.

Anl 1 ❑ ca. 1988 Cover: 1.75 **NM** value: **3.50**
Circ: CapCity orders: **34,800**
📖 Evolutionary War, Part 2 **A:** Mark Texeira **W:** Mike Baron

Anl 2 ❑ ca. 1989 Cover: 2.00 **NM** value: **2.50**
Circ: CapCity orders: **50,400**
📖 Atlantis Attacks, Part 5 • Atlantis Attacks **A:** Mark Bagley; Bill Reinhold; Jim Lee; Tod Smith **W:** Mike Baron; Peter Sanderson; Roger Salick ★ Appearance of Moon Knight. ★ Versus Moon Knight.

Anl 3 ❑ ca. 1990 Cover: 2.00 **NM** value: **2.50**
Circ: CapCity orders: **50,600**
📖 Lifeform; Lifeform, Part 1 **A:** Mark Texeira; Neil Hansen; Lee Sullivan **W:** Greg Wright; Mike Baron; Roger Salick

Anl 4 ❑ ca. 1991 Cover: 2.00 **NM** value: **Cover or less**
Circ: CapCity orders: **44,200**
📖 Von Strucker Gambit; The Von Strucker Gambit **A:** Jim Lee; John Herbert **W:** Greg Wright; D.G. Chichester

Anl 5 ❑ ca. 1992 Cover: 2.25 **NM** value: **Cover or less**
Circ: CapCity orders: **41,400**
📖 The System Bytes, Part 1 • System Bytes **A:** Vince Evans; Val Mayerik; Steven Butler; Art Nichols **W:** George Caragonne; Bob Tokar; Peter David; Roger Salick

Anl 6 ❑ 1993 Cover: 2.95 **NM** value: **Cover or less**
Circ: CapCity orders: **23,100**
📖 Death Metal; Preacher; Tracers • 1993 Annual; Polybagged **A:** Dave Hoover **W:** Pat Mills

Anl 7 ❑ ca. 1994 Cover: 2.95 **NM** value: **Cover or less**
Circ: CapCity orders: **11,050**

PUNISHER (3RD SERIES) Marvel

1 ❑ Nov 1995 Cover: 2.95 **NM** value: **Cover or less**
foil cover. 📖 Condemned **A:** Tom Lyle **W:** John Ostrander

2 ❑ Dec 1995 Cover: 1.95 **NM** value: **Cover or less**
A: Tom Lyle **W:** John Ostrander ★ Appearance of Hatchetman.

3 ❑ Dec 1995 Cover: 1.95 **NM** value: **Cover or less**
W: John Ostrander

4 ❑ Feb 1996 Cover: 1.95 **NM** value: **Cover or less**
W: John Ostrander ★ Appearance of Daredevil. ★ Versus Jigsaw.

5 ❑ Mar 1996 Cover: 1.95 **NM** value: **Cover or less**
📖 Firepower! **A:** Pat Broderick **W:** John Ostrander

6 ❑ Apr 1996 Cover: 1.95 **NM** value: **Cover or less**
📖 Hostage to the Devil **A:** Pat Broderick **W:** John Ostrander

7 ❑ May 1996 Cover: 1.95 **NM** value: **Cover or less**
W: John Ostrander

8 ❑ Jun 1996 Cover: 1.95 **NM** value: **Cover or less**
W: John Ostrander

9 ❑ Jul 1996 Cover: 1.95 **NM** value: **Cover or less**
W: John Ostrander

10 ❑ Aug 1996 Cover: 1.95 **NM** value: **Cover or less**
W: John Ostrander ★ Versus Jigsaw.

11 ❑ Sep 1996 Cover: 1.95 **NM** value: **Cover or less**
📖 Onslaught: Impact 2 • S.H.I.E.L.D. helicarrier crashes **W:** John Ostrander

12 ❑ Oct 1996 Cover: 1.95 **NM** value: **Cover or less**
📖 Total X-Tinction, Part 1 **W:** John Ostrander ★ Versus X-Cutioner.

13 ❑ Nov 1996 Cover: 1.95 **NM** value: **Cover or less**
Circ: Direct Market orders: **30,500**
📖 Total X-Tinction, Part 2 **W:** John Ostrander ★ Versus X-Cutioner.

14 ❑ Dec 1996 Cover: 1.95 **NM** value: **Cover or less**
Circ: Direct Market orders: **31,250**
📖 Total X-Tinction, Part 3 **A:** Darick Robertson **W:** John Ostrander ★ Versus X-Cutioner.

15 ❑ Jan 1997 Cover: 1.95 **NM** value: **Cover or less**
Circ: Direct Market orders: **30,750**
📖 Total X-Tinction, Part 4 **A:** Tom Lyle **W:** John Ostrander ★ Versus X-Cutioner.

16 ❑ Feb 1997 Cover: 1.50 **NM** value: **Cover or less**
Circ: Direct Market orders: **29,500**
📖 Total X-Tinction, Part 5 **A:** Tom Lyle **W:** John Ostrander ★ Versus X-Cutioner.

17 ❑ Mar 1997 Cover: 1.95 **NM** value: **Cover or less**
Circ: Direct Market orders: **27,750**
📖 Dead Man Walking **A:** Tom Lyle **W:** John Ostrander

18 ❑ Apr 1997 Cover: 1.95 **NM** value: **Cover or less**
Circ: Direct Market orders: **26,250**
📖 Double Cross final issue. **A:** Tom Lyle **W:** John Ostrander

PUNISHER, THE (4TH SERIES) Marvel

1 ❑ Nov 1998 Cover: 2.99 **NM** value: **3.00**
Circ: Diamd. preorders: **57,588 • CGC:** 7 graded, best 9.6
• gatefold summary. 📖 Purgatory, Part 1 **A:** Bernie Wrightson **W:** Christopher Golden; Tom Sniegoski

1/SC ❑ Nov 1998 Cover: 6.95 **NM** value: **Cover or less**
• **CGC:** 1 graded, best 9.0
DFE alternate cover. 📖 Purgatory, Part 1 **A:** Bernie Wrightson **W:** Christopher Golden; Tom Sniegoski

2 ❑ Dec 1998 Cover: 2.99 **NM** value: **Cover or less**
Circ: Diamd. preorders: **43,368 • CGC:** 1 graded, best 9.4
• gatefold summary. 📖 Purgatory, Part 2 **A:** Bernie Wrightson; Joe Jusko(cover) **W:** Christopher Golden; Tom Sniegoski

3 ❑ Jan 1999 Cover: 2.99 **NM** value: **Cover or less**
Circ: Diamd. preorders: **46,080 • CGC:** 1 graded, best 9.6
📖 Purgatory, Part 3 **A:** Bernie Wrightson; Joe Jusko(cover) **W:** Christopher Golden; Tom Sniegoski

4 ❑ Feb 1999 Cover: 2.99 **NM** value: **Cover or less**
Circ: Diamd. preorders: **47,284 • CGC:** 1 graded, best 9.8
📖 Purgatory, Part 4 **A:** Bernie Wrightson; Joe Jusko(cover) **W:** Christopher Golden; Tom Sniegoski ★ Appearance of Oliver.

PUNISHER (5TH SERIES) Marvel

At one time the Punisher had three on-going monthly titles, The Punisher, The Punisher War Journal and The Punisher War Zone, as well as myriad specials and crossovers. The character was practically a sub-imprint. But over-exposure eventually accomplished what the mob could not and the Punisher was gone. After a strange attempt to revitalize the vigilante via a quasi-religious direction [The Punisher (4th Series)], failed in 1999, Marvel called upon Garth Ennis and Steve Dillon of Preacher fame to breathe new life into the Punisher franchise.

Utilizing the amalgam of brutal violence and absurd characters often found in Preacher, Ennis took a back-to-basics approach. Frank Castle is a lone, fierce killing machine with a price on his head from Mafia queen, Ma Gnucci, whose encounters with the Punisher mirror those of Herr Starr in Preacher. Additionally three Punisher admirers attempt to emulate him. Payback, a blue-collar killer whose targets are big business types; Elite, an upper class snob who kills those who would lower his property values, and The Holy, a priest who absolves the sinners who confess to him with a very extreme penance. However this trio's hero worship does not impress Frank Castle.

1 ❑ Apr 2000 Cover: 2.99 **NM** value: **4.00**
Circ: Diamd. preorders: **71,551 • CGC:** 44 graded, best 9.8
📖 Welcome Back, Frank **A:** Steve Dillon **W:** Garth Ennis

1/SC ❑ Apr 2000 Cover: 2.99 **NM** value: **8.50**
• **CGC:** 31 graded, best 9.8
White background on cover. 📖 Welcome Back, Frank **A:** Steve Dillon **W:** Garth Ennis

2 ❑ May 2000 Cover: 2.99 **NM** value: **3.50**
Circ: Diamd. preorders: **67,364 • CGC:** 2 graded, best 9.8
📖 Badaboom, Badabing **A:** Steve Dillon **W:** Garth Ennis

2/SC ❑ May 2000 Cover: 2.99 **NM** value: **6.00**
• **CGC:** 11 graded, best 9.8
White background on cover. 📖 Badaboom, Badabing **A:** Steve Dillon **W:** Garth Ennis

3 ❑ Jun 2000 Cover: 2.99 **NM** value: **3.50**
Circ: Diamd. preorders: **68,964 • CGC:** 4 graded, best 9.9
• Polybagged with Marvel Knights/Marvel Boy Genesis Edition. 📖 The Devil by the Horns **A:** Steve Dillon **W:** Garth Ennis

4 ❑ Jul 2000 Cover: 2.99 **NM** value: **3.00**
Circ: Diamd. preorders: **71,452**
📖 Wild Kingdom **A:** Steve Dillon **W:** Garth Ennis

5 ❑ Aug 2000 Cover: 2.99 **NM** value: **3.00**
Circ: Diamd. preorders: **73,524**
📖 Even Worse Things **A:** Steve Dillon **W:** Garth Ennis

6 ❑ Sep 2000 Cover: 2.99 **NM** value: **Cover or less**
Circ: Diamd. preorders: **73,252**
📖 Spit Out of Luck **A:** Steve Dillon **W:** Garth Ennis

7 ❑ Oct 2000 Cover: 2.99 **NM** value: **Cover or less**
Circ: Diamd. preorders: **68,655**
📖 Bring Out Your Dead **A:** Steve Dillon **W:** Garth Ennis

8 ❑ Nov 2000 Cover: 2.99 **NM** value: **Cover or less**
Circ: Diamd. preorders: **68,493**
📖 Desperate Measures **A:** Steve Dillon **W:** Garth Ennis ★ 1st Appearance of The Russian.

9 ❑ Dec 2000 Cover: 2.99 **NM** value: **Cover or less**
Circ: Diamd. preorders: **67,737**
📖 From Russia with Love **A:** Steve Dillon **W:** Garth Ennis

10 ❑ Jan 2001 Cover: 2.99 **NM** value: **Cover or less**
Circ: Diamd. preorders: **67,473 • CGC:** 1 graded, best 9.6
📖 Glutton for Punishment **A:** Steve Dillon **W:** Garth Ennis

11 ❑ Feb 2001 Cover: 2.99 **NM** value: **Cover or less**
Circ: Diamd. preorders: **66,325**
📖 Any Which Way You Can **A:** Steve Dillon **W:** Garth Ennis ★ 1st Appearance of The Vigilante Squad. ★ Death of The Russian.

12 ❑ Mar 2001 Cover: 2.99 **NM** value: **Cover or less**
Circ: Diamd. preorders: **65,278 • CGC:** 1 graded, best 9.6
📖 Go Frank Go **A:** Steve Dillon **W:** Garth Ennis ★ Death of Ma Gnucci.

Bk 1 ❑ Jun 2000 Cover: 5.95 **NM** value: **Cover or less**
• Collected Edition #1. • Collects Punisher (5th Series) #1-2 **A:** Steve Dillon **W:** Garth Ennis

PUNISHER, THE: A MAN NAMED FRANK Marvel

1 ❑ Jun 1994 Cover: 6.95 **NM** value: **Cover or less**
Circ: CapCity orders: **7,500**
No issue number. One-shot.

PUNISHER: AN EYE FOR AN EYE Marvel

Bk 1 ❑ Cover: 9.95 **NM** value: **Cover or less**
Circ: CapCity orders: **3,700**

PUNISHER ANNIVERSARY MAGAZINE, THE Marvel

1 ❑ Cover: 4.95 **NM** value: **Cover or less**

PUNISHER ARMORY, THE Marvel

1 ❑ Jul 1990 Cover: 1.50 **NM** value: **2.00**
Circ: CapCity orders: **43,100 • CGC:** 1 graded, best 9.2
• weapons **A:** Eliot Brown **W:** Eliot Brown

2 ❑ Jun 1991 Cover: 1.75 **NM** value: **2.00**
Circ: CapCity orders: **41,200**
A: Eliot Brown **W:** Eliot Brown

3 ❑ 1991 Cover: 1.75 **NM** value: **2.00**
Circ: CapCity orders: **39,400**
A: Eliot Brown **W:** Eliot Brown

4 ❑ Cover: 2.00 **NM** value: **Cover or less**
A: Eliot Brown **W:** Eliot Brown

5 ❑ 1992 Cover: 2.00 **NM** value: **Cover or less**
A: Eliot Brown **W:** Eliot Brown

6 ❑ Cover: 2.00 **NM** value: **Cover or less**
Circ: CapCity orders: **22,100**
A: Eliot Brown **W:** Eliot Brown

7 ❑ 1993 Cover: 2.00 **NM** value: **Cover or less**
Circ: CapCity orders: **19,800**
A: Eliot Brown **W:** Eliot Brown

8 ❑ 1993 Cover: 2.00 **NM** value: **Cover or less**
Circ: CapCity orders: **15,250**
A: Eliot Brown **W:** Eliot Brown

9 ❑ Cover: 2.00 **NM** value: **Cover or less**
Circ: CapCity orders: **11,100**
A: Eliot Brown **W:** Eliot Brown

10 ❑ Nov 1994 Cover: 2.00 **NM** value: **Cover or less**
Circ: CapCity orders: **8,750**
A: Eliot Brown **W:** Eliot Brown

PUNISHER: ASSASSIN'S GUILD Marvel

Bk 1 ❑ Cover: 6.95 **NM** value: **Cover or less**

PUNISHER BACK TO SCHOOL SPECIAL Marvel

1 ❑ Nov 1992 Cover: 2.95 **NM** value: **3.50**
📖 The Sinner; Mott Haven 10454; Child's Play; Back to School • 1992 **A:** John Ridgway; Walter McDaniel; Alex Morrissey; Mark Nelson **W:** Chuck Dixon; Barry Dutter; Mike Kanterovich; Tom Brevoort

2 ❑ Cover: 2.95 **NM** value: **3.00**
Circ: CapCity orders: **25,300**
📖 No Pain • 1993 **A:** Hoang Nguyen; Ernie Stiner; Bill Sienkiewicz(cover) **W:** Mike Lackey

3 ❑ Oct 1994 Cover: 2.95 **NM** value: **3.00**
Circ: CapCity orders: **8,950**
• 1994

PUNISHER/BATMAN: DEADLY KNIGHTS Marvel

1 ❑ Oct 1994 Cover: 4.95 **NM** value: **Cover or less**
Circ: CapCity orders: **49,150** Diamd. preorders: **2,903**
No issue number. **A:** John Romita; Klaus Janson; Jr. **W:** Chuck Dixon

PUNISHER/BLACK WIDOW: SPINNING DOOMSDAY'S WEB Marvel

1 ❑ Cover: 9.95 **NM** value: **Cover or less**

PUNISHER: BLOODLINES Marvel

1 ❑ ca. 1991 Cover: 5.95 **NM** value: **Cover or less**
Circ: CapCity orders: **23,550**
No issue number. • prestige format. **A:** Dave Cockrum **W:** Gerry Conway

PUNISHER, THE: BLOOD ON THE MOORS Marvel

1 ❑ Cover: 16.95 **NM** value: **Cover or less**
Circ: CapCity orders: **5,750**

Other grades: Multiply prices above by **1.5 for Mint • 2/3 for Very Fine • 1/3 for Fine • 1/5 for Very Good • 1/8 for Good**

PUNISHER BOOK ONE — Marvel

Bk 1 ❑ Cover: 9.95 **NM** value: **Cover or less**

PUNISHER, THE: CIRCLE OF BLOOD — Marvel

Bk 1 ❑ Cover: 7.95 **NM** value: **Cover or less**

PUNISHER: DIE HARD IN THE BIG EASY — Marvel

1 ❑ ca. 1992 Cover: 4.95 **NM** value: **Cover or less**
No issue number. • prestige format one-shot

PUNISHER, THE: EMPTY QUARTER — Marvel

1 ❑ Nov 1994 Cover: 6.95 **NM** value: **Cover or less**
No issue number. • prestige format one-shot

PUNISHER: G-FORCE — Marvel

1 ❑ ca. 1992 Cover: 4.95 **NM** value: **Cover or less**
Circ: CapCity orders: **26,750**
No issue number. One-shot. squarebound with cardstock cover.
A: Hugh Haynes **W:** Mike Baron

PUNISHER HOLIDAY SPECIAL — Marvel

1 ❑ Jan 1993 Cover: 2.95 **NM** value: **3.00**
Circ: CapCity orders: **29,100 • CGC:** 1 graded, best 9.8
foil cover.
2 ❑ 1994 Cover: 2.95 **NM** value: **3.00**
Circ: CapCity orders: **13,900**
📖 The Killing Season **A:** J.J. Birch **W:** George Caragonne; Eric Fein
3 ❑ Jan 1995 Cover: 2.95 **NM** value: **3.00**

PUNISHER: INTRUDER — Marvel

1 ❑ Cover: 9.95 **NM** value: **Cover or less**
Circ: CapCity orders: **1,650**
1/HC ❑ Cover: 14.95 **NM** value: **Cover or less**

PUNISHER INVADES THE 'NAM: FINAL INVASION — Marvel

1 ❑ Feb 1994 Cover: 6.95 **NM** value: **Cover or less**
No issue number.

PUNISHER KILLS THE MARVEL UNIVERSE — Marvel

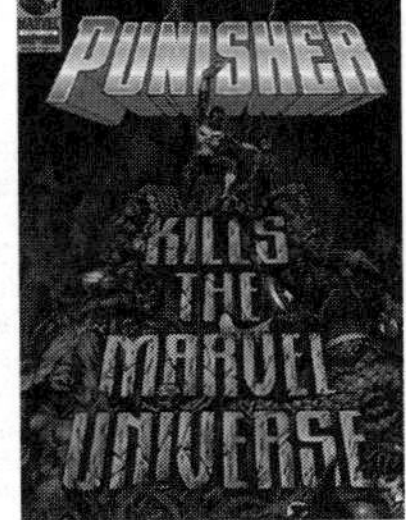

This alternate-universe one-shot poses an interesting question: "What if the Punisher hunted superheroes with the same ferocity that he hunts criminals?"

The chilling story began when Frank Castle's family was killed by the crossfire as The X-Men and The Avengers battled aliens in Central Park. When Castle, a policeman, arrived on the scene, the superhumans could only make feeble apologies for not clearing the park before blasting it to shreds with their struggle. Castle responded by drawing his gun and cutting down the X-Men's Cyclops and Jubilee.

Sentenced to life in prison, Castle was freed by a group of humans who had suffered similar tragedies due to the struggles of superhumans. Now calling himself The Punisher, Castle carried out a cunning, methodical revenge on those he believes stole his family from him.

Initially overlooked, the success of Garth Ennis' The Punisher (5th series) brought about a reprint of this one-shot.

1 ❑ Nov 1995 Cover: 5.95 **NM** value: **25.00**
Circ: Direct Market orders: **16,526 • CGC:** 25 graded, best 9.9
A: Dougie Braithwaite **W:** Garth Ennis
36893 ❑ Mar 2000 Cover: 5.95 **NM** value: **Cover or less**
• **CGC:** 1 graded, best 9.8

PUNISHER, THE: KINGDOM GONE — Marvel

1 ❑ Cover: 16.95 **NM** value: **Cover or less**
Circ: CapCity orders: **9,400**
A: Jorge Zaffino **W:** Chuck Dixon

PUNISHER MAGAZINE, THE — Marvel

1 ❑ Sep 1989, b&w Cover: 2.25 **NM** value: **3.00**
Circ: CapCity orders: **10,450**
• Reprints Punisher (Ltd. Series) #1 in black & white
2 ❑ Oct 1989, b&w Cover: 2.25 **NM** value: **2.50**
Circ: CapCity orders: **9,150**
• Reprints Punisher (Ltd. Series) #2-3 in black & white
3 ❑ Nov 1989, b&w Cover: 2.25 **NM** value: **2.50**
• Reprints Punisher (Ltd. Series) #4-5 in black & white
4 ❑ Dec 1989, b&w Cover: 2.25 **NM** value: **2.50**
• Reprints Punisher #1-2 in black & white
5 ❑ Dec 1989, b&w Cover: 2.25 **NM** value: **2.50**
• Reprints Punisher #3-4 in black & white
6 ❑ Jan 1990, b&w Cover: 2.25 **NM** value: **2.50**
📖 Garbage; Wild Rose • Reprints Punisher #5-6 in black & white
A: David Ross; Joe Jusko(cover) **W:** Mike Baron
7 ❑ Feb 1990, b&w Cover: 2.25 **NM** value: **2.50**
• Reprints Punisher #7-8 in black & white
8 ❑ Mar 1990, b&w Cover: 2.25 **NM** value: **2.50**
9 ❑ Apr 1990, b&w Cover: 2.25 **NM** value: **2.50**
10 ❑ May 1990, b&w Cover: 2.25 **NM** value: **2.50**
11 ❑ Jun 1990, b&w Cover: 2.25 **NM** value: **2.50**
12 ❑ Jul 1990, b&w Cover: 2.25 **NM** value: **2.50**
13 ❑ Aug 1990, b&w Cover: 2.25 **NM** value: **2.50**
14 ❑ Sep 1990, b&w Cover: 2.25 **NM** value: **2.50**
• Reprints Punisher War Journal #1-2
15 ❑ Oct 1990, b&w Cover: 2.25 **NM** value: **2.50**
16 ❑ Nov 1990, b&w Cover: 2.25 **NM** value: **2.50**

PUNISHER MEETS ARCHIE, THE — Marvel

It's the crossover they said could never happen. The Punisher, Marvel's grim 'n' gritty vigilante, was on the track of a villain who had escaped to Riverdale, all-American town and home to Archie Andrews. The villain, a two-bit mobster named "Red" Fever was a virtual double for Archie, causing no end of trouble for all involved. Eventually The Punisher gets his man, Archie gets out of trouble, and Riverdale reverts to its old self. Next stop for the Punisher: Gotham City (for the Batman/Punisher: Lake of Fire crossover).

This improbable crossover is really a remarkable piece of work, largely because of the talents of writer Batton Lash (Wolff & Byrd, Counselors of the Macabre). All the characters stay true to themselves and to their genres while at the same time joining up to tell what from the Punisher's perspective is a gritty manhunt, and what from the Archie side is another wacky adventure.

This special was punished both as "Archie Meets the Punisher" and a die-cut "Punisher Meets Archie" with identical contents.

1 ❑ Aug 1994 Cover: 3.95 **NM** value: **4.00**
• **CGC:** 3 graded, best 9.4
enhanced cover. **W:** Batton Lash
1/SC ❑ Aug 1994 Cover: 3.95 **NM** value: **4.50**
Circ: CapCity orders: **25,850**
Die-cut cover. **W:** Batton Lash

PUNISHER MOVIE SPECIAL, THE — Marvel

1 ❑ Jun 1990 Cover: 5.95 **NM** value: **Cover or less**
Circ: CapCity orders: **23,900**
No issue number. **A:** Brent Anderson **W:** Carl Potts

PUNISHER, THE: NO ESCAPE — Marvel

1 ❑ Cover: 4.95 **NM** value: **Cover or less**
Circ: CapCity orders: **32,700**
No issue number. • prestige format. **A:** Tod Smith **W:** Greg Wright

PUNISHER, THE: ORIGIN MICRO CHIP — Marvel

1 ❑ Jul 1993 Cover: 1.75 **NM** value: **2.00**
Circ: CapCity orders: **31,000**
📖 Over The Edge **A:** Louis Williams **W:** Carl Potts; Mike Baron ★ Origin of Micro Chip.
2 ❑ Aug 1993 Cover: 1.75 **NM** value: **2.00**
Circ: CapCity orders: **25,800**

PUNISHER/PAINKILLER JANE — Marvel

1 ❑ Jan 2001 Cover: 3.50 **NM** value: **Cover or less**
Circ: Diamd. preorders: **47,500**
One-shot. cardstock cover. 📖 Lovesick **A:** Joe Jusko; Dave Ross **W:** Garth Ennis

PUNISHER: P.O.V. — Marvel

1 ❑ ca. 1991 Cover: 4.95 **NM** value: **5.00**
Circ: CapCity orders: **40,700 • CGC:** 5 graded, best 9.8
📖 Foresight **A:** Bernie Wrightson; Basil Wolverton **W:** Jim Starlin
2 ❑ ca. 1991 Cover: 4.95 **NM** value: **5.00**
Circ: CapCity orders: **34,350**
📖 Extro-Spection **A:** Bernie Wrightson; Basil Wolverton **W:** Jim Starlin
3 ❑ ca. 1991 Cover: 4.95 **NM** value: **5.00**
Circ: CapCity orders: **32,050**
📖 Intro-Spection **A:** Bernie Wrightson; Basil Wolverton **W:** Jim Starlin
4 ❑ ca. 1991 Cover: 4.95 **NM** value: **5.00**
Circ: CapCity orders: **30,950**
📖 Hindsight **A:** Bernie Wrightson; Basil Wolverton **W:** Jim Starlin

PUNISHER, THE: RETURN TO BIG NOTHING — Marvel

1 ❑ Cover: 12.95 **NM** value: **Cover or less**
published in hardcover as an Epic Graphic Novel.
1/HC ❑ Cover: 16.95 **NM** value: **Cover or less**
published in hardcover as an Epic Graphic Novel.

PUNISHER SUMMER SPECIAL — Marvel

1 ❑ Aug 1991 Cover: 2.95 **NM** value: **3.00**
Circ: CapCity orders: **42,500**
2 ❑ Aug 1992 Cover: 2.95 **NM** value: **3.00**
📖 Rough Cut; High Risk; The Local **A:** Flint Henry; Mike McKone; John Hinklenton **W:** Chuck Dixon; Pat Mills
3 ❑ 1993 Cover: 2.50 **NM** value: **Cover or less**
📖 Dead Man Coming Through; Faster, Faster; Idyll **A:** Brian Stelfreeze; Joe Phillips; Tony Harris **W:** Chuck Dixon; Steven Grant; Pat Mills; Tony Skinner
4 ❑ Jul 1994 Cover: 2.95 **NM** value: **Cover or less**
Circ: CapCity orders: **12,100**
📖 Soiled Legacy; Killing An Afternoon **A:** Greg Luzniak; Alberto Saichann **W:** Don Lomax; Chuck Dixon

PUNISHER: THE GHOSTS OF INNOCENTS — Marvel

1 ❑ ca. 1993 Cover: 5.95 **NM** value: **Cover or less**
A: Tom Grindberg **W:** Jim Starlin
2 ❑ ca. 1993 Cover: 5.95 **NM** value: **Cover or less**
Circ: CapCity orders: **16,200**
A: Tom Grindberg **W:** Jim Starlin

PUNISHER: THE PRIZE — Marvel

1 ❑ ca. 1990 Cover: 4.95 **NM** value: **Cover or less**
Circ: CapCity orders: **23,700**
No issue number. • prestige format. **A:** Mike Harris **W:** C.J. Henderson

PUNISHER 2099 — Marvel

Jake Gallows is a cop in a world where crime is just a matter of business. Police protection is paid for (and is cut off if you don't pay) just like your electricity bill. Criminals, when they are caught, can charge the fine for murder to their major credit card and walk away. Just business.

But it became more than business for Jake when a madman, named Kron Stone, and his followers gunned down Jake's family right in front of him. Kron was captured, but because he was the son of Tyler Stone, of the Alchemax Corporation, he was fined lightly and let free.

When Jake recovered from the wounds he had received in the attack, he decided that business as usual wasn't good enough any more. Borrowing a page from the Punisher of a century ago, he began a whole new career...as the Punisher of 2099.

1 ❑ Feb 1993 Cover: 1.75 **NM** value: **Cover or less**
Circ: Statement: **313,908** CapCity orders: **217,200**
foil cover. 📖 Deadly Genesis **A:** Tom Morgan **W:** Pat Mills; Tony Skinner ★ Origin of Punisher 2099. ★ 1st Appearance of Punisher 2099.
2 ❑ Mar 1993 Cover: 1.25 **NM** value: **Cover or less**
Circ: Statement: **313,908** CapCity orders: **100,200**
📖 The Morning After **A:** Tom Morgan **W:** Pat Mills; Tony Skinner ★ 1st Appearance of Fearmaster.
3 ❑ Apr 1993 Cover: 1.25 **NM** value: **Cover or less**
Circ: Statement: **313,908** CapCity orders: **81,300**
4 ❑ May 1993 Cover: 1.25 **NM** value: **Cover or less**
Circ: Statement: **313,908** CapCity orders: **69,800**
📖 Heroes Day **A:** Tom Morgan **W:** Pat Mills; Tony Skinner
5 ❑ Jun 1993 Cover: 1.25 **NM** value: **Cover or less**
Circ: Statement: **313,908** CapCity orders: **61,800**
📖 Punishment Hotel **A:** Tom Morgan **W:** Pat Mills; Tony Skinner
6 ❑ Jul 1993 Cover: 1.25 **NM** value: **Cover or less**
Circ: Statement: **313,908** CapCity orders: **54,300**
7 ❑ Aug 1993 Cover: 1.25 **NM** value: **Cover or less**
Circ: Statement: **313,908** CapCity orders: **50,400**
📖 Love 'n' Bullets, Part 1
8 ❑ Sep 1993 Cover: 1.25 **NM** value: **Cover or less**
Circ: Statement: **313,908** CapCity orders: **42,800**
📖 Love 'n' Bullets, Part 2
9 ❑ Oct 1993 Cover: 1.25 **NM** value: **Cover or less**
Circ: Statement: **120,615** CapCity orders: **38,300**
📖 Love 'n' Bullets, Part 3 **A:** Tom Morgan **W:** Pat Mills; Tony Skinner ★ Death of Kerry Dowen.
10 ❑ Nov 1993 Cover: 1.25 **NM** value: **Cover or less**
Circ: Statement: **120,615** CapCity orders: **36,000**
11 ❑ Dec 1993 Cover: 1.25 **NM** value: **Cover or less**
Circ: Statement: **120,615** CapCity orders: **32,800**
12 ❑ Jan 1994 Cover: 1.25 **NM** value: **Cover or less**
Circ: Statement: **120,615** CapCity orders: **29,600**
• Has 1993 Statement, filed 10/1/93 (Alert: Filed very early in series, figures high as a result); avg print run 407,958; avg sales 310,575; avg subs 3,333; avg total paid 313,908; samples 125; office use 500; max existent 314,533; 23% of run returned
13 ❑ Feb 1994 Cover: 1.25 **NM** value: **Cover or less**
Circ: Statement: **120,615** CapCity orders: **40,200**
📖 Fall of the Hammer, Part 5
14 ❑ Mar 1994 Cover: 1.25 **NM** value: **Cover or less**
Circ: Statement: **120,615** CapCity orders: **25,350**
15 ❑ Apr 1994 Cover: 1.25 **NM** value: **Cover or less**
Circ: Statement: **120,615** CapCity orders: **23,000**
16 ❑ May 1994 Cover: 1.50 **NM** value: **Cover or less**
Circ: Statement: **120,615** CapCity orders: **22,700**
17 ❑ Jun 1994 Cover: 1.50 **NM** value: **Cover or less**
Circ: Statement: **120,615** CapCity orders: **21,300**
18 ❑ Jul 1994 Cover: 1.50 **NM** value: **Cover or less**
Circ: Statement: **120,615** CapCity orders: **20,250**
19 ❑ Aug 1994 Cover: 1.50 **NM** value: **Cover or less**
Circ: Statement: **120,615** CapCity orders: **18,800**
20 ❑ Sep 1994 Cover: 1.50 **NM** value: **Cover or less**
Circ: Statement: **120,615** CapCity orders: **16,700**
21 ❑ Oct 1994 Cover: 1.50 **NM** value: **Cover or less**
Circ: CapCity orders: **15,350**
📖 Punisher Versus Punisher! **A:** Simon Coleby **W:** Pat Mills; Tony Skinner
22 ❑ Nov 1994 Cover: 1.50 **NM** value: **Cover or less**
Circ: CapCity orders: **13,950**
23 ❑ Dec 1994 Cover: 1.50 **NM** value: **Cover or less**
Circ: CapCity orders: **13,550**
24 ❑ Jan 1995 Cover: 1.50 **NM** value: **Cover or less**
Circ: CapCity orders: **12,725**
25 ❑ Feb 1995 Cover: 2.25 **NM** value: **Cover or less**
25/SC ❑ Feb 1995 Cover: 2.95 **NM** value: **Cover or less**
Circ: CapCity orders: **13,800**
Embossed cover. 📖 Crazed
26 ❑ Mar 1995 Cover: 1.50 **NM** value: **Cover or less**
Circ: CapCity orders: **10,700**
27 ❑ Apr 1995 Cover: 1.50 **NM** value: **Cover or less**
Circ: CapCity orders: **9,850**
• Has 1994 Statement, filed 10/1/94; avg print run 171,767; avg sales 117,648; avg subs 2,967; avg total paid 120,615; samples 125; office use 500; max existent 121,240; 29% of run returned
28 ❑ May 1995 Cover: 1.95 **NM** value: **Cover or less**
Circ: CapCity orders: **12,850**
29 ❑ Jun 1995 Cover: 1.95 **NM** value: **Cover or less**
Circ: CapCity orders: **10,725**

CGC-graded: Multiply prices above by **33 for 9.9 M • 16 for 9.8 NM/M • 7 for 9.6 NM+ • 5 for 9.4 NM • 2.5 for 9.2 NM- • 1.5 for 9.0 VF/NM**

30 ❑ Jul 1995 Cover: 1.95 **NM** value: **Cover or less**
Circ: CapCity orders: **9,650**

31 ❑ Aug 1995 Cover: 1.95 **NM** value: **Cover or less**

32 ❑ Sep 1995 Cover: 1.95 **NM** value: **Cover or less**

33 ❑ Oct 1995 Cover: 1.95 **NM** value: **Cover or less**

34 ❑ Nov 1995 Cover: 1.95 **NM** value: **Cover or less**
final issue. • continues in 2099 A.D. Apocalypse #1

PUNISHER VS. DAREDEVIL — Marvel

1 ❑ Jun 2000 Cover: 3.50 **NM** value: **Cover or less**
Child's Play; Good Guys Wear Red; The Bully **A:** John Romita Jr.; Frank Miller; Klaus Janson **W:** Frank Miller; Ann Nocenti; Roger McKenzie

PUNISHER WAR JOURNAL, THE — Marvel

Frank Castle, The Punisher, considers himself to be fighting a war. His war is upon the criminals, the drug dealers, and others who prey upon the innocent. In his war, The Punisher plans his attacks, then strikes without mercy. He takes no prisoners.

Punisher War Journal was introduced following the success of "Punisher," Marvel's monthly series. "War Journal" has a harder edge than the monthly series, bringing a more realistic feel to Marvel's most popular vigilante.

It borrows its title from The Punisher's record-keeping device which he often begins with "War Journal Entry #..."

This title and its similarly named companion, The Punisher: War Zone, were part of Marvel's over-saturation of the genre and both faded into oblivion, along with the main title, in the mid-1990s.

1 ❑ Nov 1988 Cover: 1.50 **NM** value: **2.00**
Circ: CapCity orders: **61,000 • CGC:** 17 graded, best 9.9
A Eye for an Eye, Part 1 **A:** Jim Lee **W:** Carl Potts ★ Origin of Punisher.

2 ❑ Dec 1988 Cover: 1.50 **NM** value: **Cover or less**
Circ: CapCity orders: **43,100**
A Eye for an Eye, Part 2 **A:** Jim Lee **W:** Carl Potts ★ Appearance of Daredevil.

3 ❑ Feb 1989 Cover: 1.50 **NM** value: **Cover or less**
Circ: CapCity orders: **40,800**
A Eye for an Eye, Part 3 **A:** Carl Potts; Jim Lee **W:** Carl Potts ★ Appearance of Daredevil.

4 ❑ Mar 1989 Cover: 1.50 **NM** value: **Cover or less**
Circ: CapCity orders: **39,000**
A: Jim Lee

5 ❑ May 1989 Cover: 1.50 **NM** value: **Cover or less**
Circ: CapCity orders: **37,300**
Crucible **A:** Jim Lee **W:** Carl Potts

6 ❑ Jun 1989 Cover: 1.50 **NM** value: **Cover or less**
Circ: CapCity orders: **55,300 • CGC:** 31 graded, best 9.8
A: Jim Lee ★ Appearance of Wolverine.

7 ❑ Jul 1989 Cover: 1.50 **NM** value: **Cover or less**
Circ: CapCity orders: **54,000 • CGC:** 23 graded, best 9.8
Endangered Species **A:** Jim Lee **W:** Carl Potts ★ Appearance of Wolverine.

8 ❑ Sep 1989 Cover: 1.50 **NM** value: **Cover or less**
Circ: CapCity orders: **41,700**
A: Jim Lee

9 ❑ Oct 1989 Cover: 1.50 **NM** value: **Cover or less**
Circ: CapCity orders: **44,400**
Guilt Trip **A:** Jim Lee **W:** Carl Potts

10 ❑ Nov 1989 Cover: 1.50 **NM** value: **Cover or less**
Circ: CapCity orders: **44,800**
Second Shot **A:** Jim Lee **W:** Carl Potts

11 ❑ Dec 1989 Cover: 1.50 **NM** value: **Cover or less**
Circ: CapCity orders: **46,200**
Shock Treatment **A:** Jim Lee **W:** Carl Potts

12 ❑ Dec 1989 Cover: 1.50 **NM** value: **Cover or less**
Circ: CapCity orders: **49,200**
Acts of Vengeance • Acts of Vengeance **A:** Jim Lee **W:** Carl Potts

13 ❑ Dec 1989 Cover: 1.50 **NM** value: **Cover or less**
Circ: CapCity orders: **49,600**
Acts of Vengeance • Acts of Vengeance **A:** Jim Lee **W:** Carl Potts

14 ❑ Jan 1990 Cover: 1.50 **NM** value: **Cover or less**
Circ: CapCity orders: **53,100 • CGC:** 2 graded, best 9.6
Blind Faith **A:** Russ Heath **W:** Carl Potts ★ Appearance of Spider-Man.

15 ❑ Feb 1990 Cover: 1.50 **NM** value: **Cover or less**
Circ: CapCity orders: **54,000 • CGC:** 1 graded, best 9.4
Headlines! **A:** Russ Heath **W:** Carl Potts ★ Appearance of Spider-Man.

16 ❑ Mar 1990 Cover: 1.50 **NM** value: **Cover or less**
Circ: CapCity orders: **47,600**
Panhandle **A:** Neil Hansen **W:** Mike Baron

17 ❑ Apr 1990 Cover: 1.50 **NM** value: **Cover or less**
Circ: CapCity orders: **46,600**
Topical Trouble **A:** Jim Lee **W:** Carl Potts

18 ❑ May 1990 Cover: 1.50 **NM** value: **Cover or less**
Circ: CapCity orders: **47,400**
Kahuna **A:** Jim Lee **W:** Carl Potts

19 ❑ Jun 1990 Cover: 1.50 **NM** value: **Cover or less**
Circ: CapCity orders: **46,200**
Trauma In Paradise **A:** Jim Lee **W:** Carl Potts

20 ❑ Jul 1990 Cover: 1.50 **NM** value: **Cover or less**
Circ: CapCity orders: **45,800**
The Debt **A:** Tod Smith **W:** Carl Potts

21 ❑ Aug 1990 Cover: 1.50 **NM** value: **Cover or less**
Circ: CapCity orders: **45,000**
Deep Water **A:** Tod Smith **W:** Carl Potts

22 ❑ Sep 1990 Cover: 1.50 **NM** value: **Cover or less**
Circ: CapCity orders: **43,600**
Snowstorm **A:** Tod Smith **W:** Carl Potts

23 ❑ Oct 1990 Cover: 1.75 **NM** value: **Cover or less**
Circ: CapCity orders: **42,800**
Firepower Among The Ruins, Part 1 **A:** Tod Smith **W:** Carl Potts

24 ❑ Nov 1990 Cover: 1.75 **NM** value: **Cover or less**
Circ: CapCity orders: **41,000**
Firepower Among The Ruins, Part 2 **A:** Tod Smith **W:** Carl Potts

25 ❑ Dec 1990 Cover: 1.75 **NM** value: **Cover or less**
Circ: CapCity orders: **41,200**
Sicilian Saga, Part 1 **A:** Mark Texeira **W:** Mike Baron

26 ❑ Jan 1991 Cover: 1.75 **NM** value: **Cover or less**
Circ: CapCity orders: **40,200**
Sicilian Saga, Part 2 **A:** Mark Texeira **W:** Mike Baron

27 ❑ Feb 1991 Cover: 1.75 **NM** value: **Cover or less**
Circ: CapCity orders: **39,200**
Sicilian Saga, Part 3 **A:** Mark Texeira **W:** Mike Baron

28 ❑ Mar 1991 Cover: 1.75 **NM** value: **Cover or less**
Circ: CapCity orders: **36,600**
Meat **A:** Mark Texeira **W:** Mike Baron

29 ❑ Apr 1991 Cover: 1.75 **NM** value: **Cover or less**
Circ: CapCity orders: **53,700**
Crash And Burn **A:** Mark Texeira **W:** Mike Baron ★ Appearance of Ghost Rider.

30 ❑ May 1991 Cover: 1.75 **NM** value: **Cover or less**
Circ: CapCity orders: **54,600**
Spin Cycle **A:** Mark Texeira **W:** Mike Baron ★ Appearance of Ghost Rider.

31 ❑ Jun 1991 Cover: 1.75 **NM** value: **Cover or less**
Circ: CapCity orders: **38,400**
Painted cover. Pipeline **A:** Andy Kubert **W:** Mike Baron

32 ❑ Jul 1991 Cover: 1.75 **NM** value: **Cover or less**
Circ: CapCity orders: **39,900**
Blow Out **A:** Ron Wagner **W:** Mike Baron

33 ❑ Aug 1991 Cover: 1.75 **NM** value: **Cover or less**
Circ: CapCity orders: **41,700**
Fire In The Hole **A:** Ron Wagner **W:** Mike Baron

34 ❑ Sep 1991 Cover: 1.75 **NM** value: **Cover or less**
Circ: CapCity orders: **42,300**
Blackout **A:** Ron Wagner **W:** Mike Baron

35 ❑ Oct 1991 Cover: 1.75 **NM** value: **Cover or less**
Circ: CapCity orders: **41,100**
Motivation **A:** Ron Wagner **W:** Mike Baron

36 ❑ Nov 1991 Cover: 1.75 **NM** value: **Cover or less**
Circ: CapCity orders: **40,200**
Photo cover. Let Them Eat Cake **A:** Steven Butler **W:** Mike Baron

37 ❑ Dec 1991 Cover: 1.75 **NM** value: **Cover or less**
Circ: CapCity orders: **40,800**
Controversy **A:** Mike Harris(cover)

38 ❑ Jan 1992 Cover: 1.75 **NM** value: **Cover or less**
Circ: CapCity orders: **40,000**
Terminal Velocity **A:** Ron Wagner **W:** Chuck Dixon

39 ❑ Feb 1992 Cover: 1.75 **NM** value: **Cover or less**
Circ: CapCity orders: **36,500**
Slay Ride **A:** Ron Wagner **W:** Mike Baron

40 ❑ Mar 1992 Cover: 1.75 **NM** value: **Cover or less**
Circ: CapCity orders: **39,000**
Good Money After Bad **A:** Steven Butler **W:** Chuck Dixon

41 ❑ Apr 1992 Cover: 1.75 **NM** value: **Cover or less**
Circ: CapCity orders: **33,100**
Armageddon Express **A:** Gary Kwapisz **W:** Chuck Dixon

42 ❑ May 1992 Cover: 1.75 **NM** value: **Cover or less**
Circ: CapCity orders: **33,700**
Ten To One **A:** Todd Fox **W:** Chuck Dixon

43 ❑ Jun 1992 Cover: 1.75 **NM** value: **Cover or less**
Circ: CapCity orders: **35,500**
Adirondack Haunts **A:** Val Mayerik **W:** Richard Rainey

44 ❑ Jul 1992 Cover: 1.75 **NM** value: **Cover or less**
Circ: CapCity orders: **34,100 • CGC:** 1 graded, best 9.0
Home Sweet Home **A:** Val Mayerik **W:** Chuck Dixon

45 ❑ Aug 1992 Cover: 1.75 **NM** value: **Cover or less**
Circ: CapCity orders: **38,700**
Dead Man's Hand, Part 3 **A:** John Herbert **W:** Chuck Dixon

46 ❑ Sep 1992 Cover: 1.75 **NM** value: **Cover or less**
Circ: CapCity orders: **33,600**
Dead Man's Hand, Part 6 **A:** John Hebert **W:** Chuck Dixon

47 ❑ Oct 1992 Cover: 1.75 **NM** value: **Cover or less**
Circ: CapCity orders: **31,500**
Dead Man's Hand, Part 9

48 ❑ Nov 1992 Cover: 1.75 **NM** value: **Cover or less**
Circ: CapCity orders: **28,500**
Walk Through Fire, Part 1 **A:** Todd Fox **W:** Chuck Dixon

49 ❑ Dec 1992 Cover: 1.75 **NM** value: **Cover or less**
Circ: Statement: **138,566** CapCity orders: **27,300**
Walk Through Fire, Part 2 **A:** Todd Fox **W:** Chuck Dixon

50 ❑ Jan 1993 Cover: 2.95 **NM** value: **Cover or less**
Circ: Statement: **138,566** CapCity orders: **66,800**
Embossed cover. Payback!, Part 1 • Punisher 2099 Preview **A:** Mark Texeira; Tom Morgan; Shawn McManus **W:** Chuck Dixon; Steven Grant; Pat Mills; Tony Skinner ★ 1st Appearance of Punisher 2099.

51 ❑ Feb 1993 Cover: 1.75 **NM** value: **Cover or less**
Circ: Statement: **138,566** CapCity orders: **27,100**
Payback!, Part 2 **A:** Todd Fox **W:** Chuck Dixon

52 ❑ Mar 1993 Cover: 1.75 **NM** value: **Cover or less**
Circ: Statement: **138,566** CapCity orders: **24,900**
Heart of Ice **A:** Gary Kwapisz **W:** Chuck Dixon

53 ❑ Apr 1993 Cover: 1.75 **NM** value: **Cover or less**
Circ: Statement: **138,566** CapCity orders: **25,900**
Heart Of Stone **A:** Gary Kwapisz **W:** Chuck Dixon

54 ❑ May 1993 Cover: 1.75 **NM** value: **Cover or less**
Circ: Statement: **138,566** CapCity orders: **25,100**
Surface Thrill **A:** Gary Kwapisz **W:** Chuck Dixon

55 ❑ Jun 1993 Cover: 1.75 **NM** value: **Cover or less**
Circ: Statement: **138,566** CapCity orders: **24,700**
Conviction, Part 3 **A:** Gary Kwapisz **W:** Chuck Dixon

56 ❑ Jul 1993 Cover: 1.75 **NM** value: **Cover or less**
Circ: Statement: **138,566** CapCity orders: **24,300**
24 Hours of Power! **A:** Gary Kwapisz **W:** Chuck Dixon

57 ❑ Aug 1993 Cover: 1.75 **NM** value: **Cover or less**
Circ: Statement: **138,566** CapCity orders: **25,000**
Blood Money **A:** Gary Kwapisz **W:** Chuck Dixon ★ Appearance of Ghost Rider, Daredevil.

58 ❑ Sep 1993 Cover: 1.75 **NM** value: **Cover or less**
Circ: Statement: **138,566** CapCity orders: **22,500**
Hideout, Part 6 ★ Appearance of Ghost Rider, Daredevil.

59 ❑ Oct 1993 Cover: 1.75 **NM** value: **Cover or less**
Circ: Statement: **138,566** CapCity orders: **20,200**
The House That Hate Built **A:** Gary Kwapisz **W:** Chuck Dixon ★ Appearance of Max.

60 ❑ Nov 1993 Cover: 1.75 **NM** value: **Cover or less**
Circ: Statement: **138,566** CapCity orders: **19,000**
★ Appearance of Cage.

61 ❑ Dec 1993 Cover: 2.95 **NM** value: **Cover or less**
Circ: Statement: **86,433** CapCity orders: **22,100**
Embossed foil cover. • Giant-size. Suicide Run, Part 1

62 ❑ Jan 1994 Cover: 1.75 **NM** value: **Cover or less**
Circ: Statement: **86,433** CapCity orders: **20,800**
Suicide Run, Part 4 **A:** Gary Kwapisz **W:** Chuck Dixon

63 ❑ Feb 1994 Cover: 1.75 **NM** value: **Cover or less**
Circ: Statement: **86,433** CapCity orders: **20,650**
Suicide Run, Part 7 • Has 1993 Statement, filed 10/1/93; avg print run 179,101; avg sales 136,774; avg subs 1,792; avg total paid 138,566; samples 125; office use 500; max existent 139,191; 22% of run returned **A:** Gary Kwapisz **W:** Chuck Dixon

64 ❑ Mar 1994 Cover: 2.25 **NM** value: **Cover or less**
regular cover. Suicide Run, Part 10 **A:** Gary Kwapisz **W:** Chuck Dixon

64/SC ❑ Mar 1994 Cover: 2.95 **NM** value: **Cover or less**
Circ: Statement: **86,433** CapCity orders: **32,200**
Die-cut cover. Suicide Run, Part 10 **A:** Gary Kwapisz **W:** Chuck Dixon

65 ❑ Apr 1994 Cover: 1.75 **NM** value: **Cover or less**
Pariah, Part 1 **A:** Hugh Haynes **W:** Steven Grant

66 ❑ May 1994 Cover: 1.75 **NM** value: **1.95**
Circ: Statement: **86,433** CapCity orders: **17,400**
Pariah, Part 2 **A:** Brent Anderson

67 ❑ Jun 1994 Cover: 1.95 **NM** value: **Cover or less**
Circ: Statement: **86,433** CapCity orders: **16,950**
Pariah, Part 3; Trouble, Part 1 **A:** Hugh Haynes; Elman Brown **W:** Steven Grant

68 ❑ Jul 1994 Cover: 1.95 **NM** value: **Cover or less**
Circ: Statement: **86,433** CapCity orders: **16,800**
Pariah, Part 4; Trouble, Part 2 **A:** Hugh Haynes; Kevin Kobasic; Elman Brown **W:** Steven Grant

69 ❑ Aug 1994 Cover: 1.95 **NM** value: **Cover or less**
Circ: Statement: **86,433** CapCity orders: **15,350**
Pariah, Part 5

70 ❑ Sep 1994 Cover: 1.95 **NM** value: **Cover or less**
Circ: Statement: **86,433** CapCity orders: **14,500**

71 ❑ Oct 1994 Cover: 1.95 **NM** value: **Cover or less**
Circ: Statement: **86,433** CapCity orders: **12,700**
Last Entry, Part 1 **A:** Hugh Haynes **W:** Steven Grant

72 ❑ Nov 1994 Cover: 1.95 **NM** value: **Cover or less**
Circ: Statement: **86,433** CapCity orders: **12,150**
Last Entry, Part 2 **A:** Mel Rubi **W:** Steven Grant

73 ❑ Dec 1994 Cover: 1.95 **NM** value: **Cover or less**
Circ: CapCity orders: **12,650**
Last Entry, Part 3 **A:** Mel Rubi **W:** Steven Grant

74 ❑ Jan 1995 Cover: 1.95 **NM** value: **Cover or less**
Circ: CapCity orders: **10,950**
Last Entry, Part 4

75 ❑ Feb 1995 Cover: 2.50 **NM** value: **Cover or less**
Circ: CapCity orders: **12,975**
• Giant-size. Last Entry, Part 5 **A:** Hugh Haynes **W:** Chuck Dixon; Steven Grant

76 ❑ Mar 1995 Cover: 1.95 **NM** value: **Cover or less**
Circ: CapCity orders: **11,125**
First Entry, Part 1 • New Punisher (Lynn Michaels) begins; Has 1994 Statement, filed 10/1/94; avg print run 87,058; avg sales 85,483; avg subs 950; avg total paid 86,433; samples 125; office use 500; max existent 87,058; no newsstand sales this year **A:** Mel Rubi **W:** Chuck Dixon

77 ❑ Apr 1995 Cover: 1.95 **NM** value: **Cover or less**
Circ: CapCity orders: **9,725**

78 ❑ May 1995 Cover: 1.95 **NM** value: **Cover or less**
Circ: CapCity orders: **9,625**

79 ❑ Jun 1995 Cover: 1.95 **NM** value: **Cover or less**
Circ: CapCity orders: **11,575**
Countdown, Part 2 (3) **A:** Doug Wheatley **W:** Chuck Dixon ★ Death of Microchip.

80 ❑ Jul 1995 Cover: 1.95 **NM** value: **Cover or less**
Circ: CapCity orders: **12,625**
Countdown, Part 5 (0) final issue. ★ Death of Stone Cold.

Bk 1 ❑ Cover: 9.95 **NM** value: **Cover or less**
Eye for an Eye • Collects issues #1-3 **A:** Jim Lee **W:** Carl Potts ★ Origin of Punisher. ★ Appearance of Daredevil.

PUNISHER, THE: WAR ZONE — Marvel

1 ❑ Mar 1992 Cover: 2.25 **NM** value: **Cover or less**
Circ: CapCity orders: **175,200 • CGC:** 13 graded, best 9.9
Die-cut cover. Only the Dead Know Brooklyn **A:** John Romita Jr. **W:** Chuck Dixon

2 ❑ Apr 1992 Cover: 1.75 **NM** value: **Cover or less**
Circ: CapCity orders: **78,300**
Blood in the Water **A:** John Romita Jr. **W:** Chuck Dixon

3 ❑ May 1992 Cover: 1.75 **NM** value: **Cover or less**
Circ: CapCity orders: **69,900**
The Frame **A:** John Romita Jr. **W:** Chuck Dixon

4 ❑ Jun 1992 Cover: 1.75 **NM** value: **Cover or less**
Circ: CapCity orders: **67,200**
Closer to the Frame **A:** John Romita Jr. **W:** Chuck Dixon

5 ❑ Jul 1992 Cover: 1.75 **NM** value: **Cover or less**
Circ: CapCity orders: **64,500**
Feeding Frenzy **A:** John Romita Jr. **W:** Chuck Dixon

6 ❑ Aug 1992 Cover: 1.75 **NM** value: **Cover or less**

Other grades: Multiply prices above by **1.5 for Mint • 2/3 for Very Fine • 1/3 for Fine • 1/5 for Very Good • 1/8 for Good**

Circ: CapCity orders: **63,000**
🕮 The Carrion Eaters **A:** John Romita Jr. **W:** Chuck Dixon
7 ❑ Sep 1992 Cover: 1.75 **NM** value: **Cover or less**
Circ: CapCity orders: **52,200**
🕮 Mugger's Picnic **A:** John Romita Jr. **W:** Chuck Dixon
8 ❑ Oct 1992 Cover: 1.75 **NM** value: **Cover or less**
Circ: CapCity orders: **46,800**
🕮 The Hunting Ground **A:** John Romita Jr. **W:** Chuck Dixon
9 ❑ Nov 1992 Cover: 1.75 **NM** value: **Cover or less**
Circ: CapCity orders: **44,700**
🕮 Goners **A:** Mike Harris **W:** Chuck Dixon
10 ❑ Dec 1992 Cover: 1.75 **NM** value: **Cover or less**
Circ: CapCity orders: **40,500**
🕮 Tight Spot **A:** Mike Harris **W:** Chuck Dixon
11 ❑ Jan 1993 Cover: 1.75 **NM** value: **Cover or less**
Circ: CapCity orders: **38,700**
🕮 In a Deadly Place **A:** Mike Harris **W:** Chuck Dixon
12 ❑ Feb 1993 Cover: 1.75 **NM** value: **Cover or less**
Circ: CapCity orders: **36,400**
🕮 Psychoville, Part 1 **A:** Mike McKone **W:** Andy Lanning; Dan Abnett
13 ❑ Mar 1993 Cover: 1.75 **NM** value: **Cover or less**
Circ: CapCity orders: **34,100**
🕮 Psychoville, Part 2 **A:** Mike McKone **W:** Andy Lanning; Dan Abnett
14 ❑ Apr 1992 Cover: 1.75 **NM** value: **Cover or less**
Circ: CapCity orders: **33,900**
🕮 Psychoville, Part 3 **A:** Mike McKone **W:** Andy Lanning; Dan Abnett
15 ❑ May 1993 Cover: 1.75 **NM** value: **Cover or less**
Circ: CapCity orders: **32,200**
🕮 Psychoville, Part 4 **A:** Mike McKone **W:** Andy Lanning; Dan Abnett
16 ❑ Jun 1993 Cover: 1.75 **NM** value: **Cover or less**
Circ: CapCity orders: **32,400**
🕮 Psychoville, Part 5 **A:** Mike McKone **W:** Andy Lanning; Dan Abnett
17 ❑ Jul 1993 Cover: 1.75 **NM** value: **Cover or less**
Circ: CapCity orders: **30,000**
🕮 The Jericho Syndrome, Part 1 **A:** Hugh Haynes **W:** Andy Lanning; Dan Abnett
18 ❑ Aug 1993 Cover: 1.75 **NM** value: **Cover or less**
Circ: CapCity orders: **29,000**
🕮 The Jericho Syndrome, Part 2 **A:** Hugh Haynes **W:** Andy Lanning; Dan Abnett
19 ❑ Sep 1993 Cover: 1.75 **NM** value: **Cover or less**
Circ: CapCity orders: **28,600**
🕮 The Jericho Syndrome, Part 3 **A:** Hugh Haynes **W:** Andy Lanning; Dan Abnett ★ Appearance of Wolverine.
20 ❑ Oct 1993 Cover: 1.75 **NM** value: **Cover or less**
Circ: CapCity orders: **25,100**
🕮 Numbah One Boom Boom **A:** Hoang Nguyen **W:** Larry Hama
21 ❑ Nov 1993 Cover: 1.75 **NM** value: **Cover or less**
Circ: CapCity orders: **23,750**
🕮 2 Mean 2 Die! **A:** Hoang Nguyen **W:** Larry Hama
22 ❑ Dec 1993 Cover: 1.75 **NM** value: **Cover or less**
Circ: CapCity orders: **22,100**
🕮 Taking Tiger Mountain **A:** Hoang Nguyen **W:** Larry Hama
23 ❑ Jan 1994 Cover: 2.95 **NM** value: **Cover or less**
Circ: CapCity orders: **23,800**
Embossed foil cover. • Giant-size. 🕮 Suicide Run, Part 2 **A:** Val Mayerik **W:** Roger Salick ★ Death of Rapido.
24 ❑ Feb 1994 Cover: 1.75 **NM** value: **Cover or less**
Circ: CapCity orders: **22,400**
🕮 Suicide Run, Part 5 **A:** John Buscema; Val Mayerik **W:** Larry Hama
25 ❑ Mar 1994 Cover: 2.25 **NM** value: **Cover or less**
Circ: CapCity orders: **25,550**
🕮 Suicide Run, Part 8 **A:** John Buscema; Val Mayerik **W:** Larry Hama
26 ❑ Apr 1994 Cover: 1.75 **NM** value: **Cover or less**
Circ: CapCity orders: **19,200**
🕮 Conan with a Gun, Part 1 **A:** John Buscema **W:** Chuck Dixon
27 ❑ May 1994 Cover: 1.95 **NM** value: **Cover or less**
Circ: CapCity orders: **18,250**
🕮 Conan with a Gun, Part 2
28 ❑ Jun 1994 Cover: 1.95 **NM** value: **Cover or less**
Circ: CapCity orders: **17,750**
🕮 Conan with a Gun, Part 3 **A:** John Buscema **W:** Chuck Dixon
29 ❑ Jul 1994 Cover: 1.95 **NM** value: **Cover or less**
Circ: CapCity orders: **17,500**
🕮 Conan with a Gun, Part 4 **A:** John Buscema **W:** Chuck Dixon
30 ❑ Aug 1994 Cover: 1.95 **NM** value: **Cover or less**
Circ: CapCity orders: **15,700**
🕮 Conan with a Gun, Part 5
31 ❑ Sep 1994 Cover: 1.95 **NM** value: **Cover or less**
Circ: CapCity orders: **14,850**
🕮 River of Blood; River of Blood, Part 1
32 ❑ Oct 1994 Cover: 1.95 **NM** value: **Cover or less**
Circ: CapCity orders: **13,800**
🕮 River of Blood; River of Blood, Part 2
33 ❑ Nov 1994 Cover: 1.95 **NM** value: **Cover or less**
Circ: CapCity orders: **13,150**
🕮 River of Blood, Part 3 **A:** Joe Kubert **W:** Chuck Dixon
34 ❑ Dec 1994 Cover: 1.95 **NM** value: **Cover or less**
Circ: CapCity orders: **12,300**
🕮 River of Blood, Part 4 **A:** Joe Kubert **W:** Chuck Dixon
35 ❑ Jan 1995 Cover: 1.95 **NM** value: **Cover or less**
Circ: CapCity orders: **11,350**
🕮 River of Blood, Part 5
36 ❑ Feb 1995 Cover: 1.95 **NM** value: **Cover or less**
Circ: CapCity orders: **11,100**
🕮 River of Blood, Part 6
37 ❑ Mar 1995 Cover: 1.95 **NM** value: **Cover or less**
Circ: CapCity orders: **11,150**
A: Mark Texeira **W:** Chuck Dixon ★ Origin of Max (The Punisher's dog).
38 ❑ Apr 1995 Cover: 1.95 **NM** value: **Cover or less**
Circ: CapCity orders: **9,800**
🕮 Dark Judgment, Part 1 **A:** John Hebert **W:** Steven Grant
39 ❑ May 1995 Cover: 1.95 **NM** value: **Cover or less**
Circ: CapCity orders: **9,450**
🕮 Dark Judgment, Part 2
40 ❑ Jun 1995 Cover: 1.95 **NM** value: **Cover or less**
Circ: CapCity orders: **10,000**
🕮 Dark Judgment, Part 3 **A:** John Herbert **W:** Steven Grant
41 ❑ Jul 1995 Cover: 1.95 **NM** value: **Cover or less**
Circ: CapCity orders: **120,550**
🕮 Countdown, Part 3 (2) final issue.
Anl 1❑ca. 1993 Cover: 2.95 **NM** value: **Cover or less**
Circ: CapCity orders: **37,000**
• card
Anl 2❑ca. 1994 Cover: 2.95 **NM** value: **Cover or less**
Circ: CapCity orders: **11,900**
🕮 Hurt So Good; Second Chance; Domino Theory **A:** Dale Eaglesham; Dave Ross; Alberto Saichann **W:** Ralph Macchio; Chuck Dixon; Steven Grant ★ Death of Roc.

PUNISHER/WOLVERINE AFRICAN SAGA — Marvel

1 ❑ Cover: 5.95 **NM** value: **Cover or less**
Circ: CapCity orders: **15,400**
No issue number.

PUNISHER, THE: YEAR ONE — Marvel

1 ❑ Dec 1994 Cover: 2.50 **NM** value: **Cover or less**
Circ: CapCity orders: **17,800**
🕮 Family Business **A:** Dale Eaglesham **W:** Andy Lanning; Dan Abnett ★ Origin of the Punisher.
2 ❑ Jan 1995 Cover: 2.50 **NM** value: **Cover or less**
Circ: CapCity orders: **12,450**
A: Dale Eaglesham **W:** Andy Lanning; Dan Abnett ★ Origin of the Punisher.
3 ❑ Feb 1995 Cover: 2.50 **NM** value: **Cover or less**
Circ: CapCity orders: **11,400**
A: Dale Eaglesham **W:** Andy Lanning; Dan Abnett ★ Origin of the Punisher.
4 ❑ Mar 1995 Cover: 2.50 **NM** value: **Cover or less**
Circ: CapCity orders: **10,250**
🕮 Fire With Fire **A:** Dale Eaglesham **W:** Andy Lanning; Dan Abnett ★ Origin of the Punisher.

PUNX — Acclaim / Valiant

1 ❑ Nov 1995 Cover: 2.50 **NM** value: **Cover or less**
Circ: CapCity orders: **10,025**
🕮 Street Smarrts **A:** Keith Giffen **W:** Keith Giffen
2 ❑ Dec 1995 Cover: 2.50 **NM** value: **Cover or less**
Circ: CapCity orders: **6,800**
A: Keith Giffen **W:** Keith Giffen
3 ❑ Jan 1996 Cover: 2.50 **NM** value: **Cover or less**
Circ: CapCity orders: **5,250**
A: Keith Giffen **W:** Keith Giffen

PUNX (MANGA) SPECIAL — Acclaim / Valiant

1 ❑ Mar 1996 Cover: 2.50 **NM** value: **Cover or less**
No issue number. • to be read from back to front

PUPPET COMICS — George W. Dougherty

1 ❑ Spr 1946 Cover: 0.10 **NM** value: **75.00**
2 ❑ Sum 1946 Cover: 0.10 **NM** value: **75.00**

PUPPET MASTER — Eternity

1 ❑ full color Cover: 2.50 **NM** value: **Cover or less**
Circ: CapCity orders: **5,010**
A: Glenn Lumsden **W:** Dave DeVries
2 ❑ full color Cover: 2.50 **NM** value: **Cover or less**
Circ: CapCity orders: **2,990**
A: Glenn Lumsden **W:** Dave DeVries
3 ❑ full color Cover: 2.50 **NM** value: **Cover or less**
Circ: CapCity orders: **2,660**
A: Glenn Lumsden **W:** Dave DeVries
4 ❑ full color Cover: 2.50 **NM** value: **Cover or less**
Circ: CapCity orders: **2,380**
A: Glenn Lumsden **W:** Dave DeVries

PUPPET MASTER: CHILDREN OF THE PUPPET MASTER — Eternity

1 ❑ full color Cover: 2.50 **NM** value: **Cover or less**
Circ: CapCity orders: **1,770**
2 ❑ full color Cover: 2.50 **NM** value: **Cover or less**
Circ: CapCity orders: **1,710**
Bk 1❑ Sep 1991, full color Cover: 4.95 **NM** value: **Cover or less**

PUPPY ACTION! — Northstar

1 ❑ Cover: 2.50 **NM** value: **Cover or less**
A: Michael Pearlstein **W:** Michael Pearlstein

PURE IMAGES — Pure Imagination

1 ❑ Cover: 2.50 **NM** value: **Cover or less**
• some color **A:** Joe Simon; Jack Kirby; C.C. Beck
2 ❑ Cover: 2.50 **NM** value: **Cover or less**
• some color **A:** Joe Simon; Jack Kirby
3 ❑ Cover: 2.50 **NM** value: **Cover or less**
• monsters; some color
4 ❑ Cover: 2.50 **NM** value: **Cover or less**
• monsters; some color

Statement of Ownership figures are the average number of copies originally sold, as cited by the publisher to the U.S. Postal Service. These estimate **all** sales, in comics shops and on newsstands.

PURGATORI — Chaos

Chaos! Comics' vampire from Hell gets her own monthly series and the body count is bound to be high. Purgatori, once an Egyptian slave named Sakkara, is now a vampire that feeds on the blood of fallen angels. To slake her thirst she turns to the ruins of Manhattan, which has become a magnet for fallen angels. She stalks them through the wreckage of our world even as vampire hunters and more powerful supernatural foes hunt her. With such eerie companions as Blattidae, queen of cockroaches, at her side, Manhattan is becoming a terrifyingly bloody place to be....

0.5 ❑ Dec 2000 Cover: 2.95 **NM** value: **Cover or less**
Circ: Diamd. preorders: **13,504** • **CGC:** 4 graded, best 9.8
A: Al Rio **W:** Steven Grant
1 ❑ Oct 1998 Cover: 2.95 **NM** value: **3.00**
Circ: Diamd. preorders: **31,977**
🕮 Revelations **A:** Al Rio **W:** David Quinn
2 ❑ Nov 1998 Cover: 2.95 **NM** value: **Cover or less**
Circ: Diamd. preorders: **25,953**
A: Al Rio **W:** David Quinn ★ Versus Lady Death.
3 ❑ Dec 1998 Cover: 2.95 **NM** value: **Cover or less**
Circ: Diamd. preorders: **24,034**
A: Al Rio **W:** David Quinn
4 ❑ Jan 1999 Cover: 2.95 **NM** value: **Cover or less**
Circ: Diamd. preorders: **22,923**
A: Al Rio **W:** David Quinn
5 ❑ Feb 1999 Cover: 2.95 **NM** value: **Cover or less**
Circ: Diamd. preorders: **21,751**
🕮 Karmilla **A:** Al Rio **W:** David Quinn
6 ❑ Mar 1999 Cover: 2.95 **NM** value: **Cover or less**
Circ: Diamd. preorders: **19,742**
🕮 Jade **A:** Al Rio **W:** David Quinn
7 ❑ Apr 1999 Cover: 2.95 **NM** value: **Cover or less**
Circ: Diamd. preorders: **19,093**
🕮 Blood Finale! **A:** Al Rio **W:** David Quinn ★ Versus Dracula.
Ash 1❑ **NM** value: **3.00**
No issue number. no cover price. • ashcan preview
Bk 1❑ Cover: 5.95 **NM** value: **Cover or less**
• Collected Edition #1. • collects #1 and #2
Bk 2❑ Cover: 5.95 **NM** value: **Cover or less**
• Collected Edition #2. • collects #3 and #4
Bk 3❑ Jul 2000 Cover: 5.95 **NM** value: **Cover or less**
• Collected Edition #3. • collects #5 and #6
Bk 4❑ Aug 2000 Cover: 5.95 **NM** value: **Cover or less**
• Collected Edition #4, collects #7 and Dracula Gambit.

PURGATORI: EMPIRE — Chaos

1 ❑ May 2000 Cover: 2.95 **NM** value: **Cover or less**
Circ: Diamd. preorders: **18,366**
🕮 Reign of Blood **A:** Ken Lashley **W:** Len Kaminski
2 ❑ Jun 2000 Cover: 2.95 **NM** value: **Cover or less**
Circ: Diamd. preorders: **16,205**
A: Ken Lashley **W:** Len Kaminski
3 ❑ Jul 2000 Cover: 2.95 **NM** value: **Cover or less**
Circ: Diamd. preorders: **15,234**
A: Ken Lashley **W:** Len Kaminski

PURGATORI: GODDESS RISING — Chaos!

1 ❑ Jul 1999 Cover: 2.95 **NM** value: **Cover or less**
Circ: Diamd. preorders: **20,225**
2 ❑ Aug 1999 Cover: 2.95 **NM** value: **Cover or less**
Circ: Diamd. preorders: **18,274**
A: Mike Deodato Jr. **W:** Mark Andreyko
3 ❑ Sep 1999 Cover: 2.95 **NM** value: **Cover or less**
Circ: Diamd. preorders: **17,598**
4 ❑ Dec 1999 Cover: 2.95 **NM** value: **Cover or less**
Circ: Diamd. preorders: **16,994**

PURGATORI: THE DRACULA GAMBIT — Chaos!

1 ❑ Aug 1997 Cover: 2.95 **NM** value: **Cover or less**
Circ: Diamd. preorders: **37,081**
1/SC❑Aug 1997 **NM** value: **3.00**
no cover price. • Centennial Premium Edition.

PURGATORI: THE DRACULA GAMBIT SKETCHBOOK — Chaos!

1 ❑ Jul 1997 Cover: 2.95 **NM** value: **Cover or less**
Circ: Diamd. preorders: **13,519**
No issue number. • b&w preliminary sketches

PURGATORI: THE VAMPIRES MYTH — Chaos!

-1 ❑ Aug 1996 Cover: 1.50 **NM** value: **Cover or less**
A: Jim Balent **W:** Brian Pulido
1 ❑ Aug 1996 Cover: 3.50 **NM** value: **Cover or less**
• **CGC:** 27 graded, best 10.0
• Red foil embossed **A:** Jim Balent **W:** Brian Pulido
1/LE❑ Aug 1996 **NM** value: **5.00**
• **CGC:** 1 graded, best 9.8
wraparound acetate cover. • premium edition. • limited to 10, 000 copies
1/SC❑Oct 1996 Cover: 3.50 **NM** value: **8.00**
• **CGC:** 1 graded, best 9.8
• "Krome" edition (color). **A:** Jim Balent **W:** Brian Pulido
2 ❑ Oct 1996 Cover: 2.95 **NM** value: **3.00**
Circ: Diamd. preorders: **47,539**
A: Jim Balent **W:** Brian Pulido
3 ❑ Dec 1996 Cover: 2.95 **NM** value: **Cover or less**

CGC-graded: Multiply prices above by **33 for 9.9 M** • **16 for 9.8 NM/M** • **7 for 9.6 NM+** • **5 for 9.4 NM** • **2.5 for 9.2 NM-** • **1.5 for 9.0 VF/NM**

Circ: Diamd. preorders: **44,414**
A: Jim Balent **W:** Brian Pulido

4 ❑ Feb 1997 Cover: 2.95 **NM** value: **Cover or less**
A: Jim Balent **W:** Brian Pulido

5 ❑ Apr 1997 Cover: 2.95 **NM** value: **Cover or less**
A: Jim Balent **W:** Brian Pulido

6 ❑ Jun 1997 Cover: 2.95 **NM** value: **Cover or less**
A: Jim Balent **W:** Brian Pulido

Bk 1❑ Cover: 12.95 **NM** value: **Cover or less**
A: Jim Balent **W:** Brian Pulido

PURGATORY USA — Slave Labor

1 ❑ Mar 1989, b&w Cover: 1.75 **NM** value: **2.00**
📖 Welcome to Maynardville; Chicken; The rain; A Minor Altercation • Ed Brubaker's first published work **A:** Ed Brubaker **W:** Ed Brubaker

PURGE — Ania

0 ❑ Cover: 1.95 **NM** value: **Cover or less**
📖 Purification Agenda **A:** Bill Hobbs **W:** Roosevelt Pitt Jr.

1 ❑ Aug 1993 Cover: 1.95 **NM** value: **Cover or less**
📖 Codeblock, Part 1 **A:** Bill Hobbs **W:** Roosevelt Pitt Jr.

PURGE (AMARA) — Amara

0 ❑ Cover: 1.50 **NM** value: **Cover or less**
• Preview edition. **A:** Rob Haynes **W:** David Self; Rob Haynes; Roosevelt Pitt Jr.

PURPLE CLAW — Toby

1 ❑ Jan 1953 Cover: 0.10 **NM** value: **200.00**

2 ❑ Mar 1953 Cover: 0.10 **NM** value: **150.00**
• **CGC:** 1 graded, best 7.0

3 ❑ May 1953 Cover: 0.10 **NM** value: **150.00**

PURPLE CLAW MYSTERIES — AC

1 ❑ b&w Cover: 2.95 **NM** value: **Cover or less**

PURR — Blue Eyed Dog

1 ❑ Cover: 5.00 **NM** value: **8.00**
📖 Harry Clarke; Angel with a Gun; World of Hope, World of Fear; Sirius; Metropol **A:** Ted McKeever; Dix; Lydia Lunch; Simon Henwood

PUSSYCAT — Marvel

1 ❑ ca. 1968, b&w Cover: 0.35 **NM** value: **150.00**
• magazine. **A:** Bill Ward; Wally Wood

Q-LOC — Chiasmus

1 ❑ Aug 1994 Cover: 2.50 **NM** value: **Cover or less**

QUACK! — Star*Reach

An anthology from Star*Reach, Quack represents an early attempt to break independent comics creators into the comics-shop scene. Issues #3-5 notably feature The Beavers, a humor strip by Dave Sim, who would later go on to create the long-running Cerebus the Aardvark for Aardvark-Vanaheim.

Other creators contributing to the series include Mad cartoonist (and later Groo creator) Sergio Aragones, Michael T. Gilbert, Steve Leialoha, Scott Shaw! (still spelled with an exclamation point), and Dave Stevens, who would go on to create The Rocketeer.

1 ❑ Jul 1976, b&w Cover: 1.25 **NM** value: **2.50**
📖 Duckaneer; The Wraith!; You-All Gibbon; E.Z. Wolf: Smokey Mountain High; On the Skids, Duckula; Kosmo Cat: The Case of the Purloined Periodicals **A:** Alan Kupperberg; Ted Richards; Frank Brunner; Howard Chaykin; Michael T. Gilbert; Steve Leialoha; Dave Stevens; Mark Evanier; Scott Shaw **W:** Ted Richards; Frank Brunner; Howard Chaykin; Michael T. Gilbert; Mark Evanier; Scott Shaw

2 ❑ Jan 1977 Cover: 1.25 **NM** value: **2.50**
📖 Newton the Rabbit Wonder!; The Cure; Be True to Your School; On the Skids!: A Day at the Rat Race; Tales of the Oregon Bobcat; You-All Gibbon: The Incredible Edible Invasion of Earth!; A Job Well Done **A:** Alan Kupperberg; Sergio Aragonés; Michael T. Gilbert; Steve Leialoha; Dot Bucher; Ken Macklin; Scott Shaw; Steve Skeates **W:** Alan Kupperberg; Sergio Aragonés; Michael T. Gilbert; Steve Leialoha; Dot Bucher; Ken Macklin; Scott Shaw; Steve Skeates

3 ❑ Apr 1977 Cover: 1.25 **NM** value: **2.50**
📖 The Beavers; The Wraith: Duck Death; Wolfjack: The Case of the Missing Quack; You-All Gibbon: On the Trail of Pigfoot the Awful Boar!; Deserter; The Rabbit Wonder Meets the Barbarian Bunny **A:** Dave Sim; Ted Richards; Michael T. Gilbert; Steve Leialoha; Ken Macklin; Scott Shaw **W:** Dave Sim; Ted Richards; Michael T. Gilbert; Steve Leialoha; Ken Macklin; Scott Shaw

4 ❑ Jun 1977 Cover: 1.25 **NM** value: **2.50**
📖 Home on the Range, Rabbit!; The Beavers; On the Skids!: Into the Breach; Tales of the Oregon Bobcat: Bounce on the Wild Side!; Inspector Mulenberry; The Wraith: The Fall of the House of Silver **A:** Dave Sim; Alan Kupperberg; Michael T. Gilbert; Steve Leialoha; Dot Bucher **W:** Dave Sim; Alan Kupperberg; Michael T. Gilbert; Steve Leialoha; Dot Bucher

5 ❑ Sep 1977 Cover: 1.25 **NM** value: **2.50**
📖 The Reality Wraith; Tales of the Oregon Bobcat: At Last, Long Love!; The Beavers; Planet of the Ducks **A:** Dave Sim; Michael T. Gilbert; Steve Leialoha; Dot Bucher; Ken Macklin **W:** Dave Sim; Michael T. Gilbert; Steve Leialoha; Dot Bucher; Ken Macklin

6 ❑ Dec 1977 Cover: 1.25 **NM** value: **2.50**
📖 The Quark: Son of Quack; Into the Motherlode!; Duckaneer; The Fleet Foot Foogle!; The Wraith: Fear **A:** Larry Gonick; Ted Richards; Frank Brunner; Gilbert Shelton; Michael T. Gilbert; J. Michael Leonard; Steve Leialoha; Lee Marrs; Scott Shaw **W:** Larry Gonick; Ted Richards; Frank Brunner; Michael T. Gilbert; J. Michael Leonard; Steve Leialoha; Lee Marrs; Scott Shaw

QUADRANT — Quadrant

All issues are adults only.

1 ❑ ca. 1983 Cover: 1.95 **NM** value: **Cover or less**
A: Peter Hsu **W:** Peter Hsu

2 ❑ ca. 1984 Cover: 1.95 **NM** value: **Cover or less**
A: Peter Hsu **W:** Peter Hsu

3 ❑ ca. 1984 Cover: 1.95 **NM** value: **Cover or less**
A: Peter Hsu **W:** Peter Hsu

4 ❑ ca. 1985 Cover: 1.95 **NM** value: **Cover or less**
A: Peter Hsu **W:** Peter Hsu

5 ❑ ca. 1985 Cover: 1.95 **NM** value: **Cover or less**
A: Peter Hsu **W:** Peter Hsu

6 ❑ ca. 1985 Cover: 1.95 **NM** value: **Cover or less**
no cover date. **A:** Peter Hsu **W:** Peter Hsu

7 ❑ ca. 1986 Cover: 1.95 **NM** value: **Cover or less**
A: Peter Hsu **W:** Peter Hsu

8 ❑ ca. 1986, b&w Cover: 1.95 **NM** value: **Cover or less**
A: Peter Hsu **W:** Peter Hsu

Bk 1❑ b&w Cover: 19.95 **NM** value: **Cover or less**
📖 Travesty; Goddess • Collects Quadrant #1-8 plus new stories **A:** Peter Hsu **W:** Peter Hsu

QUADRO GANG, THE — Nonsense Unlimited

1 ❑ b&w Cover: 1.25 **NM** value: **Cover or less**

QUAGMIRE — Kitchen Sink

All issues are adults only.

1 ❑ Sum 1970, b&w Cover: 0.50 **NM** value: **3.00**

QUAGMIRE U.S.A. — Antarctic

1 ❑ Mar 1994, b&w Cover: 2.75 **NM** value: **Cover or less**

2 ❑ May 1994, b&w Cover: 2.75 **NM** value: **Cover or less**

3 ❑ Jul 1994, b&w Cover: 2.75 **NM** value: **Cover or less**

QUALITY SPECIAL — Fleetway-Quality

1 ❑ Cover: 1.50 **NM** value: **2.00**
• Strontium Dog

2 ❑ Cover: 1.50 **NM** value: **2.00**
• Midnight Surfer

QUANTUM & WOODY — Acclaim / Valiant

Eric and Woody have known each other since childhood. Despite their differences, they became friends, partly because their fathers worked together in a research facility. When their fathers were mysteriously killed, Eric and Woody discovered high-tech gauntlets, which, when slipped onto their arms, would not come off. These gauntlets can access an electromagnetic containment field, but unless Eric and Woody connect with each others' gauntlets once a day, they will be transformed from matter to energy.

In part, this title deals with the issue of friendship between two people with incompatible personalities. Eric, who calls himself Quantum, is serious and self-absorbed, while Woody, who calls himself...Woody, is flippant and superficial. Though it sounds like standard super-hero fare, this title uses flashbacks and humorous and sarcastic banter to set itself apart.

In the spirit of Spawn, an issue #34 was published out of sequence, with the missing issues promised, but never delivered.

0/AE❑ **NM** value: **3.00**
• American Entertainment exclusive

1 ❑ Jun 1997 Cover: 2.50 **NM** value: **Cover or less**
Circ: Diamd. preorders: **13,795**
📖 Klang **A:** Mark D. Bright **W:** Christopher Priest

1/A ❑ Jun 1997 Cover: 2.50 **NM** value: **Cover or less**
Painted cover. 📖 Klang **A:** Mark D. Bright **W:** Christopher Priest

2 ❑ Jul 1997 Cover: 2.50 **NM** value: **Cover or less**
Circ: Diamd. preorders: **10,416**

3 ❑ Aug 1997 Cover: 2.50 **NM** value: **Cover or less**
Circ: Diamd. preorders: **9,691**
★ 1st Appearance of The Goat.

4 ❑ Sep 1997 Cover: 2.50 **NM** value: **Cover or less**
Circ: Diamd. preorders: **9,802**

5 ❑ Oct 1997 Cover: 2.50 **NM** value: **Cover or less**
Circ: Diamd. preorders: **9,741**
📖 Bad Haircut at Table Six **W:** Christopher Priest

6 ❑ Nov 1997 Cover: 2.50 **NM** value: **Cover or less**
Circ: Diamd. preorders: **9,706**

7 ❑ Dec 1997 Cover: 2.50 **NM** value: **Cover or less**
Circ: Diamd. preorders: **9,818**

8 ❑ Jan 1998 Cover: 2.50 **NM** value: **Cover or less**
Circ: Diamd. preorders: **10,240**

9 ❑ Feb 1998 Cover: 2.50 **NM** value: **Cover or less**
Circ: Diamd. preorders: **10,297**
★ Appearance of Troublemakers.

10 ❑ Mar 1998 Cover: 2.50 **NM** value: **Cover or less**
Circ: Diamd. preorders: **10,123**

11 ❑ Apr 1998 Cover: 2.50 **NM** value: **Cover or less**
Circ: Diamd. preorders: **10,122**

12 ❑ Jan 1998 Cover: 2.50 **NM** value: **Cover or less**
Circ: Diamd. preorders: **10,035**
no cover date. • indicia says Jan

13 ❑ Feb 1998 Cover: 2.50 **NM** value: **Cover or less**
Circ: Diamd. preorders: **10,060**
no cover date. • indicia says Feb

14 ❑ Mar 1998 Cover: 2.50 **NM** value: **Cover or less**
Circ: Diamd. preorders: **10,749**

15 ❑ Apr 1998 Cover: 2.50 **NM** value: **Cover or less**
Circ: Diamd. preorders: **11,532**

16 ❑ May 1998 Cover: 2.50 **NM** value: **Cover or less**
Circ: Diamd. preorders: **11,052**

17 ❑ Jun 1998 Cover: 2.50 **NM** value: **Cover or less**
Circ: Diamd. preorders: **10,916**
final issue.

Ash 1❑ Feb 1997 **NM** value: **1.00**
no cover price. • b&w preview of series

Bk 1❑ Cover: 7.95 **NM** value: **Cover or less**
• Collects Quantum & Woody #1-4

Bk 2❑ Cover: 7.95 **NM** value: **Cover or less**
• Kiss Your Ass Goodbye

Bk 3❑ Cover: 7.95 **NM** value: **Cover or less**
• Holy S-Word! We're Cancelled!!

QUANTUM CREEP — Parody Press

1 ❑ b&w Cover: 2.50 **NM** value: **Cover or less**
A: Ted Slampyak **W:** Nat Gertler

QUANTUM LEAP — Innovation

Quantum Leap was a popular television show of the early '90s. It starred Dr. Sam Beckett, head of Project Quantum Leap. The goal of the project was to produce a method of time travel, with Beckett theorizing that time travel might be possible within the span of one's own lifetime.The project was under the threat of losing its funding unless it showed quick results. In desperation, Beckett risked all and stepped into the untested time travel apparatus.

As it turned out, Beckett was right — but not in the way he expected. He now "leaps" randomly in time, winding up in the bodies of different people at various times throughout the last half-century. Beckett must help these people overcome some life difficulty before an unknown force causes him to leap into a different time, place, and identity. His only help in his travels is Al, the project observer who appears as a computer-generated hologram. Somehow, Al must aid Beckett in finding his way back to his own time.

1 ❑ Sep 1991 Cover: 2.50 **NM** value: **6.00**
Circ: CapCity orders: **10,355**
📖 First There Was A Mountain, Then There Was No Mountain, Then There Was **A:** Mark Jones **W:** George Broderick Jr. ★ Origin of Doctor Sam Beckett (Quantum Leap). ★ 1st Appearance of Doctor Sam Beckett (Quantum Leap).

2 ❑ Dec 1991 Cover: 2.50 **NM** value: **5.00**
Circ: CapCity orders: **7,490**

3 ❑ Mar 1992 Cover: 2.50 **NM** value: **5.00**
Circ: CapCity orders: **6,435**
• Sam as Santa

4 ❑ Apr 1992 Cover: 2.50 **NM** value: **5.00**
Circ: CapCity orders: **6,730**
📖 The 50,000 Quest • Sam on game show **A:** Andy Price; Mark Jones **W:** Steven Dorfman

5 ❑ May 1992 Cover: 2.50 **NM** value: **5.00**
Circ: CapCity orders: **6,220**
Superman theme cover. 📖 Seeing is Believing **A:** Rob Davis **W:** Terry Collins

6 ❑ Sep 1992 Cover: 2.50 **NM** value: **4.00**
Circ: CapCity orders: **5,735**
📖 A Tale of Two Cindys **A:** Andy Price **W:** George Broderick; Becky Broderick

7 ❑ Oct 1992 Cover: 2.50 **NM** value: **4.00**
Circ: CapCity orders: **5,125**
📖 Lives on the Fringe **A:** Dan Day; Dave Day **W:** Charles Marshall

8 ❑ Dec 1992 Cover: 2.50 **NM** value: **4.00**
Circ: CapCity orders: **4,975**
📖 Getaway **A:** Mike Deodato Sr. **W:** Bill Spangler

9 ❑ Feb 1993 Cover: 2.50 **NM** value: **4.00**
Circ: CapCity orders: **4,500**
📖 Up Against a Stonewall **A:** Mike Deodato Sr. **W:** Andy Mangels

10 ❑ Apr 1993 Cover: 2.50 **NM** value: **3.00**
Circ: CapCity orders: **4,450**
📖 Too Funny for Words **A:** John Garcia **W:** Peter Quinones

11 ❑ May 1993 Cover: 2.50 **NM** value: **3.00**
Circ: CapCity orders: **4,870**
📖 For the Good of the Nation **A:** Mike Deodato Sr. **W:** Bruce Scalet

12 ❑ Jun 1993 Cover: 2.50 **NM** value: **3.00**
Circ: CapCity orders: **4,685**
📖 Waiting… **A:** Mike Deodato Sr. **W:** Scott Rockwell

13 ❑ Aug 1993 Cover: 2.95 **NM** value: **3.00**
foil-enhanced cardstock cover. 📖 One Giant Leap • Time and Space Special #1 **A:** Luke Ross **W:** Christine Elaine Hantzopulos

Anl 1❑ Cover: 2.95 **NM** value: **3.00**

SE 1❑ Oct 1992 Cover: 2.50 **NM** value: **3.00**
Circ: CapCity orders: **5,340**
📖 First There Was A Mountain, Then There Was No Mountain, Then There Was • reprints #1 **A:** Mark Jones **W:** George Broderick Jr.

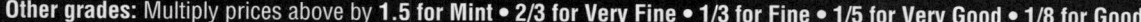

The CGC numbers printed in individual listings above represent the **number of copies examined** and given a **Universal** grade by CGC and the **best such copy** graded at press time. For current populations, watch for special ***Comics Buyer's Guide*** issues or check **www.cgccomics.com.**

Other grades: Multiply prices above by **1.5 for Mint • 2/3 for Very Fine • 1/3 for Fine • 1/5 for Very Good • 1/8 for Good**

QUASAR — Marvel

The first Marvel Boy was Robert Grayson, the son of a famous rocket scientist. Robert wore the alien bracelets known as quantum-bands to gain the ability both to fly and to generate powerful solar blasts. Once a hero of the Golden Age, his Silver Age appearance in Fantastic Four #164 spelled his demise, as his quantum bands' energy went out of control and engulfed him. All that remained were the bands themselves.

They were taken into custody by S.H.I.E.L.D. and were about to be captured by A.I.M. agents when a young S.H.I.E.L.D. agent, Wendell Vaughn, grabbed them instead, gaining the powers of the original Marvel Boy, as well the power to shape the energies of the bands into physical objects. Thus Wendell Vaughn became the second Marvel Boy, later known as Quasar.

Never counted among even the second-rate Marvel characters, Quasar is remembered mostly for giving Marvel a fairly long series beginning with Q.

1 ❑ Oct 1989 Cover: 1.00 **NM** value: **1.50**
Circ: CapCity orders: **33,100**
📖 The Price of Power! **A:** Paul Ryan; Danny Bulanadi **W:** Mark Gruenwald ★ Origin of Quasar.

2 ❑ Nov 1989 Cover: 1.00 **NM** value: **Cover or less**
Circ: CapCity orders: **24,600**

3 ❑ Nov 1989 Cover: 1.00 **NM** value: **Cover or less**
Circ: CapCity orders: **20,700**

4 ❑ Dec 1989 Cover: 1.00 **NM** value: **Cover or less**
Circ: CapCity orders: **18,400**
★ Origin of Quantum.

5 ❑ Dec 1989 Cover: 1.00 **NM** value: **Cover or less**
Circ: CapCity orders: **21,100**
📖 Acts of Vengeance, Part 10 • Acts of Vengeance ★ Versus Absorbing Man.

6 ❑ Jan 1990 Cover: 1.00 **NM** value: **Cover or less**
Circ: Statement: **119,985** CapCity orders: **21,400**
📖 Acts of Vengeance, Part 19 • Acts of Vengeance ★ Appearance of Venom. ★ Versus Red Ghost. ★ Versus Living Laser. ★ Versus Venom.

7 ❑ Feb 1990 Cover: 1.00 **NM** value: **Cover or less**
Circ: Statement: **119,985** CapCity orders: **20,900**
• Spider-Man has cosmic powers ★ Appearance of Spider-Man.

8 ❑ Mar 1990 Cover: 1.00 **NM** value: **Cover or less**
Circ: Statement: **119,985** CapCity orders: **18,800**

9 ❑ Apr 1990 Cover: 1.00 **NM** value: **Cover or less**
Circ: Statement: **119,985** CapCity orders: **18,100**
★ 1st Appearance of Captain Atlas.

10 ❑ May 1990 Cover: 1.00 **NM** value: **Cover or less**
Circ: Statement: **119,985** CapCity orders: **18,100**
★ Origin of Captain Atlas.

11 ❑ Jun 1990 Cover: 1.00 **NM** value: **Cover or less**
Circ: Statement: **119,985** CapCity orders: **19,200**
• Phoenix

12 ❑ Jul 1990 Cover: 1.00 **NM** value: **Cover or less**
Circ: Statement: **119,985** CapCity orders: **17,000**

13 ❑ Aug 1990 Cover: 1.00 **NM** value: **Cover or less**
Circ: Statement: **119,985** CapCity orders: **16,200**

14 ❑ Sep 1990 Cover: 1.00 **NM** value: **Cover or less**
Circ: Statement: **119,985** CapCity orders: **17,300**
C: Todd McFarlane

15 ❑ Oct 1990 Cover: 1.00 **NM** value: **Cover or less**
Circ: Statement: **119,985** CapCity orders: **15,700**

16 ❑ Nov 1990 Cover: 1.50 **NM** value: **Cover or less**
Circ: Statement: **119,985** CapCity orders: **16,000**

17 ❑ Dec 1990 Cover: 1.00 **NM** value: **Cover or less**
Circ: Statement: **119,985**

18 ❑ Jan 1991 Cover: 1.50 **NM** value: **Cover or less**

19 ❑ Feb 1991 Cover: 1.00 **NM** value: **Cover or less**
★ 1st Appearance of Starlight.

20 ❑ Mar 1991 Cover: 1.00 **NM** value: **Cover or less**
• Fantastic Four

21 ❑ Apr 1991 Cover: 1.00 **NM** value: **Cover or less**

22 ❑ May 1991 Cover: 1.00 **NM** value: **Cover or less**

23 ❑ Jun 1991 Cover: 1.00 **NM** value: **Cover or less**
★ Appearance of Ghost Rider.

24 ❑ Jul 1991 Cover: 1.00 **NM** value: **Cover or less**
★ 1st Appearance of Infinity (physical).

25 ❑ Aug 1991 Cover: 1.00 **NM** value: **Cover or less**
• new costume

26 ❑ Sep 1991 Cover: 1.00 **NM** value: **Cover or less**
📖 Infinity Gauntlet • Infinity Gauntlet

27 ❑ Oct 1991 Cover: 1.00 **NM** value: **Cover or less**
📖 Infinity Gauntlet • Infinity Gauntlet ★ 1st Appearance of Epoch.

28 ❑ Nov 1991 Cover: 1.00 **NM** value: **Cover or less**
Circ: CapCity orders: **20,200**

29 ❑ Dec 1991 Cover: 1.00 **NM** value: **Cover or less**
Circ: CapCity orders: **19,900**

30 ❑ Jan 1992 Cover: 1.00 **NM** value: **Cover or less**
Circ: Statement: **88,295** CapCity orders: **18,900**

31 ❑ Feb 1992 Cover: 1.25 **NM** value: **Cover or less**
Circ: Statement: **88,295** CapCity orders: **19,200**
• New Universe ★ Appearance of D.P.7.

32 ❑ Mar 1992 Cover: 1.25 **NM** value: **Cover or less**
Circ: Statement: **88,295** CapCity orders: **27,600**
📖 Operation: Galactic Storm, Part 3 • Galactic Storm ★ 1st Appearance of Korath the Pursuer. ★ Appearance of Imperial Guard, Starfox.

33 ❑ Apr 1992 Cover: 1.25 **NM** value: **Cover or less**
Circ: Statement: **88,295** CapCity orders: **24,600**
📖 Operation: Galactic Storm, Part 10 • Galactic Storm

34 ❑ May 1992 Cover: 1.25 **NM** value: **Cover or less**
Circ: Statement: **88,295** CapCity orders: **26,700**
📖 Operation: Galactic Storm, Part 17 • Galactic Storm **A:** Rurik Tyler **W:** Mark Gruenwald ★ Appearance of Binary.

35 ❑ Jun 1992 Cover: 1.25 **NM** value: **Cover or less**
Circ: Statement: **88,295** CapCity orders: **22,500**
📖 Operation: Galactic Storm aftermath • Galactic Storm **A:** Greg Capullo **W:** Mark Gruenwald

36 ❑ Jul 1992 Cover: 1.25 **NM** value: **Cover or less**
Circ: Statement: **88,295** CapCity orders: **23,200**
★ Appearance of Her, Makkari. ★ Versus Souleater.

37 ❑ Aug 1992 Cover: 1.25 **NM** value: **Cover or less**
Circ: Statement: **88,295** CapCity orders: **35,400**

38 ❑ Sep 1992 Cover: 1.25 **NM** value: **Cover or less**
Circ: Statement: **88,295** CapCity orders: **34,500**
📖 Infinity War • Infinity War

39 ❑ Oct 1992 Cover: 1.25 **NM** value: **Cover or less**
Circ: Statement: **88,295** CapCity orders: **30,000**
📖 Infinity War • Infinity War

40 ❑ Nov 1992 Cover: 1.25 **NM** value: **Cover or less**
Circ: Statement: **88,295** CapCity orders: **27,000**
📖 Infinity War • Infinity War

41 ❑ Dec 1992 Cover: 1.25 **NM** value: **Cover or less**
Circ: Statement: **88,295** CapCity orders: **19,400**
★ 1st Appearance of Kismet.

42 ❑ Jan 1993 Cover: 1.25 **NM** value: **Cover or less**
Circ: Statement: **77,069** CapCity orders: **18,400**

43 ❑ Feb 1993 Cover: 1.25 **NM** value: **Cover or less**
Circ: Statement: **77,069** CapCity orders: **18,100**
• Has 1992 Statement, filed 10/1/92; avg print run 89,842; avg sales 86,953; avg subs 1,342; avg total paid 88,295; no newsstand sales this year

44 ❑ Mar 1993 Cover: 1.25 **NM** value: **Cover or less**
Circ: Statement: **77,069** CapCity orders: **17,100**

45 ❑ Apr 1993 Cover: 1.25 **NM** value: **Cover or less**
Circ: Statement: **77,069** CapCity orders: **171,000**

46 ❑ May 1993 Cover: 1.25 **NM** value: **Cover or less**
Circ: Statement: **77,069** CapCity orders: **16,800**

47 ❑ Jun 1993 Cover: 1.25 **NM** value: **1.75**
Circ: Statement: **77,069** CapCity orders: **15,600**
★ 1st Appearance of Thunderstrike.

48 ❑ Jul 1993 Cover: 1.25 **NM** value: **Cover or less**
Circ: Statement: **77,069** CapCity orders: **16,600**

49 ❑ Aug 1993 Cover: 1.25 **NM** value: **Cover or less**
Circ: Statement: **77,069** CapCity orders: **15,400**

50 ❑ Sep 1993 Cover: 2.95 **NM** value: **Cover or less**
Circ: Statement: **77,069** CapCity orders: **24,600**
Holo-grafix cover. • Giant-size. 📖 Horizon Of Holes **A:** Andy Smith **W:** Mark Gruenwald ★ Appearance of Silver Surfer.

51 ❑ Oct 1993 Cover: 1.25 **NM** value: **Cover or less**
Circ: Statement: **77,069** CapCity orders: **14,500**
📖 The Conservation of Angular Momentum **A:** John Heebink **W:** Mark Gruenwald ★ Appearance of Squadron Supreme, Anglemen.

52 ❑ Nov 1993 Cover: 1.25 **NM** value: **Cover or less**
Circ: Statement: **77,069** CapCity orders: **13,600**

53 ❑ Dec 1993 Cover: 1.25 **NM** value: **Cover or less**
Circ: Statement: **77,069** CapCity orders: **13,750**

54 ❑ Jan 1994 Cover: 1.25 **NM** value: **Cover or less**
Circ: CapCity orders: **13,100**

55 ❑ Feb 1994 Cover: 1.25 **NM** value: **Cover or less**
Circ: CapCity orders: **12,650**
📖 Starblast, Part 6 • Has 1993 Statement, filed 10/1/93; avg print run 81,213; avg sales 75,994; avg subs 1,075; avg total paid 77,069; samples 125; office use 500; no newsstand sales this year

56 ❑ Mar 1994 Cover: 1.25 **NM** value: **Cover or less**
Circ: CapCity orders: **11,950**
📖 Starblast, Part 10

57 ❑ Apr 1994 Cover: 1.25 **NM** value: **Cover or less**
Circ: CapCity orders: **10,600**

58 ❑ May 1994 Cover: 1.25 **NM** value: **Cover or less**
Circ: CapCity orders: **10,100**

59 ❑ Jun 1994 Cover: 1.25 **NM** value: **Cover or less**
Circ: CapCity orders: **9,850**

60 ❑ Jul 1994 Cover: 1.25 **NM** value: **Cover or less**
Circ: CapCity orders: **10,500**
final issue.

SE 1 ❑ Mar 1992 Cover: 1.25 **NM** value: **Cover or less**
• reprints Quasar #32

SE 2 ❑ Apr 1992 Cover: 1.25 **NM** value: **Cover or less**
Circ: CapCity orders: **4,500**
• reprints Quasar #33

SE 3 ❑ May 1992 Cover: 1.25 **NM** value: **Cover or less**
• reprints Quasar #34

QUEEN & COUNTRY — Oni

1 ❑ Mar 2001 Cover: 2.95 **NM** value: **Cover or less**
Circ: Diamd. preorders: **9,144** • **CGC:** 3 graded, best 9.6
A: Steve Rolston **W:** Greg Rucka

QUEEN OF THE DAMNED (ANNE RICE'S...) — Innovation

1 ❑ ca. 1991 Cover: 2.50 **NM** value: **Cover or less**
Circ: CapCity orders: **15,765**
📖 On the Road to the Vampire Lestat **A:** Scott Multer **W:** Anne Rice; Cynthy J. Wood

2 ❑ ca. 1992 Cover: 2.50 **NM** value: **Cover or less**
Circ: CapCity orders: **10,080**
A: Scott Multer **W:** Anne Rice; Cynthy J. Wood

3 ❑ ca. 1992 Cover: 2.50 **NM** value: **Cover or less**
Circ: CapCity orders: **7,275**
A: Scott Multer **W:** Anne Rice; Cynthy J. Wood

4 ❑ ca. 1992 Cover: 2.50 **NM** value: **Cover or less**
Circ: CapCity orders: **6,095**
A: Scott Multer **W:** Anne Rice; Cynthy J. Wood

5 ❑ ca. 1992 Cover: 2.50 **NM** value: **Cover or less**
Circ: CapCity orders: **5,715**
A: Scott Multer **W:** Anne Rice; Cynthy J. Wood

6 ❑ ca. 1993 Cover: 2.50 **NM** value: **Cover or less**
Circ: CapCity orders: **7,430**
📖 All Hallow's Eve, Part 1 **A:** Scott Multer **W:** Anne Rice; Cynthy J. Wood

7 ❑ ca. 1993 Cover: 2.50 **NM** value: **Cover or less**
Circ: CapCity orders: **5,900**
📖 All Hallow's Eve, Part 2 **A:** Scott Multer **W:** Anne Rice; Cynthy J. Wood

8 ❑ Jul 1993 Cover: 2.50 **NM** value: **Cover or less**
Circ: CapCity orders: **5,370**
A: Scott Multer **W:** Anne Rice; Cynthy J. Wood

9 ❑ Sep 1993 Cover: 2.50 **NM** value: **Cover or less**
Circ: CapCity orders: **5,590**
A: Scott Multer **W:** Anne Rice; Cynthy J. Wood

10 ❑ Nov 1993 Cover: 2.50 **NM** value: **Cover or less**
Circ: CapCity orders: **5,655**
A: Scott Multer **W:** Anne Rice; Cynthy J. Wood

11 ❑ Dec 1993 Cover: 2.50 **NM** value: **Cover or less**
Circ: CapCity orders: **5,170**
A: Scott Multer **W:** Anne Rice; Cynthy J. Wood

12 ❑ Jan 1994 Cover: 2.50 **NM** value: **Cover or less**
Circ: CapCity orders: **5,220**
A: Scott Multer **W:** Anne Rice; Cynthy J. Wood

QUEEN OF THE WEST, DALE EVANS — Dell

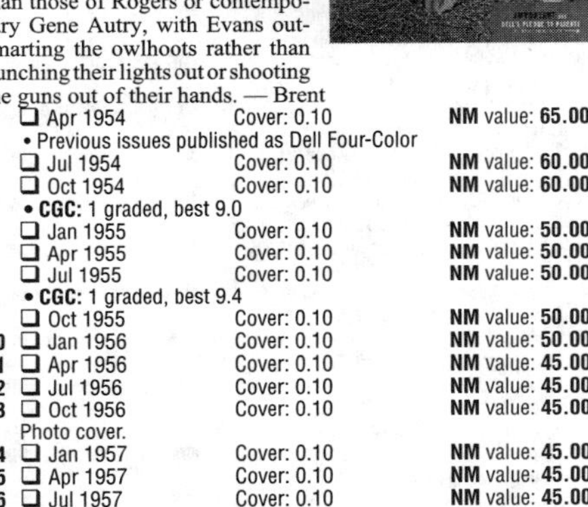

Perhaps best-known as the wife of King of the Cowboys, Roy Rogers, Dale Evans has had two comics series in her career, one from DC and this slightly longer one from Dell.

Begun in 1953 with appearances in Dell Four Color, Evans' adventures were set in a more modern West, where she could ride her horse Buttercup while the comic relief followed along in a Jeep.

The stories were a bit less violent than those of Rogers or contemporary Gene Autry, with Evans outsmarting the owlhoots rather than punching their lights out or shooting the guns out of their hands. — Brent

3 ❑ Apr 1954 Cover: 0.10 **NM** value: **65.00**
• Previous issues published as Dell Four-Color

4 ❑ Jul 1954 Cover: 0.10 **NM** value: **60.00**

5 ❑ Oct 1954 Cover: 0.10 **NM** value: **60.00**
• **CGC:** 1 graded, best 9.0

6 ❑ Jan 1955 Cover: 0.10 **NM** value: **50.00**

7 ❑ Apr 1955 Cover: 0.10 **NM** value: **50.00**

8 ❑ Jul 1955 Cover: 0.10 **NM** value: **50.00**
• **CGC:** 1 graded, best 9.4

9 ❑ Oct 1955 Cover: 0.10 **NM** value: **50.00**

10 ❑ Jan 1956 Cover: 0.10 **NM** value: **50.00**

11 ❑ Apr 1956 Cover: 0.10 **NM** value: **45.00**

12 ❑ Jul 1956 Cover: 0.10 **NM** value: **45.00**

13 ❑ Oct 1956 Cover: 0.10 **NM** value: **45.00**
Photo cover.

14 ❑ Jan 1957 Cover: 0.10 **NM** value: **45.00**

15 ❑ Apr 1957 Cover: 0.10 **NM** value: **45.00**

16 ❑ Jul 1957 Cover: 0.10 **NM** value: **45.00**

17 ❑ Oct 1957 Cover: 0.10 **NM** value: **45.00**

18 ❑ Jan 1958 Cover: 0.10 **NM** value: **45.00**
• **CGC:** 1 graded, best 9.2

19 ❑ Apr 1958 Cover: 0.10 **NM** value: **45.00**

20 ❑ Jul 1958 Cover: 0.10 **NM** value: **45.00**
• **CGC:** 1 graded, best 8.0

21 ❑ Oct 1958 Cover: 0.10 **NM** value: **45.00**

22 ❑ Jan 1959 Cover: 0.10 **NM** value: **45.00**

QUEEN'S GREATEST HITS — Revolutionary

1 ❑ Nov 1993, b&w Cover: 2.50 **NM** value: **Cover or less**

QUEST FOR CAMELOT — DC

1 ❑ Jul 1998 Cover: 4.95 **NM** value: **Cover or less**
Circ: Diamd. preorders: **5,445**

QUEST FOR DREAMS LOST — Literacy Volunteers

1 ❑ ca. 1987, b&w Cover: 2.00 **NM** value: **Cover or less**
📖 The Quest for Dreams Lost; Teenage Mutant Ninja Turtles; The Silent Invasion; Eb'nn the Raven; Have Time, Will Travel; Tales from the Aniverse; Keepsake of a Crime-fighter (text); Home Is a Four Letter Word; Trollords • The Realm story **A:** Jim Lawson; Ken Holewczynski; Mike Parobeck; Guy Davis; Michael Cherkas; Rob Davis; Paul Fricke; Susan Van Camp **W:** Jim Lawson; Ken Holewczynski; Kevin Eastman; Scott Beaderstadt; Peter Laird; Randy Zimmerman; Susan Van Camp; Clay Washburn; Larry Hancock; Len Strazewski; Mike Dimpsey; Stuart Kerr ★ Appearance of J.B. Space, Falterous, Reacto Man, Eb'nn the Raven, Trollords, Teenage Mutant Ninja Turtles.

> **Diamond** preorders are the estimated number of comics sold, prior to their release, to comics shops in North America by Diamond Comic Distributors, the largest distributor. These figures underreport the actual number of circulating copies by the amount of reorders Diamond took (usually 5-10% again of the preorders) and sales by publishers to newsstand and bookstore distributors. For many independent publishers, Diamond's preorders may be quite close to the actual number of copies in circulation.

CGC-graded: Multiply prices above by **33 for 9.9 M • 16 for 9.8 NM/M • 7 for 9.6 NM+ • 5 for 9.4 NM • 2.5 for 9.2 NM- • 1.5 for 9.0 VF/NM**

QUESTION, THE — DC

Vic Sage could turn himself into the faceless Question by simply donning a mask and unleashing the adhesive gas to attach it. To criminals, the effect was like being attacked by a faceless enemy.

However, by the time of this series begins, too many people knew his secret identity, forcing Sage to give it up and flee to South America. But Sage soon realizes he needs his "identity" as the Question.

Originally a Charlton character, he came to DC as part of its Crisis on Infinite Earths. The Question converted to a quarterly format at the conclusion of this series, allowing DC the rare opportunity to have an alliterative series title beginning with Q.

1 ❑ Feb 1987 Cover: 1.50 **NM** value: **2.00**
Circ: CapCity orders: **17,850**
Painted cover. 📖 The Bad News **A:** Denys Cowan; Bill Sienkiewicz(cover) **W:** Denny O'Neil
2 ❑ Mar 1987 Cover: 1.50 **NM** value: **1.75**
Circ: CapCity orders: **13,550**
3 ❑ Apr 1987 Cover: 1.50 **NM** value: **1.75**
Circ: CapCity orders: **13,650**
4 ❑ May 1987 Cover: 1.50 **NM** value: **Cover or less**
Circ: CapCity orders: **113,250**
5 ❑ Jun 1987 Cover: 1.50 **NM** value: **Cover or less**
Circ: CapCity orders: **13,850**
6 ❑ Jul 1987 Cover: 1.50 **NM** value: **Cover or less**
Circ: CapCity orders: **13,400**
7 ❑ Aug 1987 Cover: 1.50 **NM** value: **Cover or less**
Circ: CapCity orders: **14,200**
8 ❑ Sep 1987 Cover: 1.50 **NM** value: **Cover or less**
Circ: CapCity orders: **15,000**
9 ❑ Oct 1987 Cover: 1.50 **NM** value: **Cover or less**
Circ: CapCity orders: **14,750**
10 ❑ Nov 1987 Cover: 1.50 **NM** value: **Cover or less**
Circ: CapCity orders: **14,050**
11 ❑ Dec 1987 Cover: 1.50 **NM** value: **Cover or less**
Circ: CapCity orders: **13,000**
12 ❑ Jan 1988 Cover: 1.50 **NM** value: **Cover or less**
Circ: CapCity orders: **12,800**
13 ❑ Feb 1988 Cover: 1.75 **NM** value: **Cover or less**
Circ: CapCity orders: **12,350**
14 ❑ Mar 1988 Cover: 1.75 **NM** value: **Cover or less**
Circ: CapCity orders: **12,050**
15 ❑ Apr 1988 Cover: 1.75 **NM** value: **Cover or less**
Circ: CapCity orders: **11,500**
16 ❑ May 1988 Cover: 1.75 **NM** value: **Cover or less**
Circ: CapCity orders: **10,700**
17 ❑ Jun 1988 Cover: 1.75 **NM** value: **Cover or less**
Circ: CapCity orders: **11,550**
• Rorschach, Green Arrow
18 ❑ Jul 1988 Cover: 1.75 **NM** value: **Cover or less**
Circ: CapCity orders: **13,900**
• Green Arrow
19 ❑ Aug 1988 Cover: 1.75 **NM** value: **Cover or less**
Circ: CapCity orders: **10,800**
20 ❑ Oct 1988 Cover: 1.75 **NM** value: **Cover or less**
Circ: CapCity orders: **11,050**
21 ❑ Nov 1988 Cover: 1.75 **NM** value: **Cover or less**
Circ: CapCity orders: **11,050**
22 ❑ Dec 1988 Cover: 1.75 **NM** value: **Cover or less**
Circ: CapCity orders: **10,650**
23 ❑ Win 1988 Cover: 1.75 **NM** value: **Cover or less**
Circ: CapCity orders: **10,750**
24 ❑ Jan 1989 Cover: 1.75 **NM** value: **Cover or less**
Circ: CapCity orders: **10,650**
25 ❑ Feb 1989 Cover: 1.75 **NM** value: **Cover or less**
Circ: CapCity orders: **10,750**
26 ❑ Mar 1989 Cover: 1.75 **NM** value: **Cover or less**
Circ: CapCity orders: **10,050**
★ Appearance of Riddler.
27 ❑ Jun 1989 Cover: 1.75 **NM** value: **Cover or less**
Circ: CapCity orders: **10,450**
28 ❑ Jul 1989 Cover: 1.75 **NM** value: **Cover or less**
Circ: CapCity orders: **10,450**
29 ❑ Aug 1989 Cover: 1.75 **NM** value: **Cover or less**
Circ: CapCity orders: **10,500**
30 ❑ Sep 1989 Cover: 1.75 **NM** value: **Cover or less**
Circ: CapCity orders: **10,800**
31 ❑ Oct 1989 Cover: 1.75 **NM** value: **Cover or less**
Circ: CapCity orders: **10,350**
32 ❑ Nov 1989 Cover: 1.75 **NM** value: **Cover or less**
Circ: CapCity orders: **10,350**
33 ❑ Dec 1989 Cover: 1.75 **NM** value: **Cover or less**
Circ: CapCity orders: **10,500**
34 ❑ Jan 1990 Cover: 1.75 **NM** value: **Cover or less**
Circ: CapCity orders: **10,150**
35 ❑ Mar 1990 Cover: 1.75 **NM** value: **Cover or less**
Circ: CapCity orders: **9,850**
36 ❑ Apr 1990 Cover: 1.75 **NM** value: **Cover or less**
Circ: CapCity orders: **10,100**
final issue.
Anl 1❑ca. 1988 Cover: 2.50 **NM** value: **Cover or less**
Circ: CapCity orders: **19,850**
• Batman, Green Arrow
Anl 2❑ca. 1989 Cover: 3.50 **NM** value: **Cover or less**
Circ: CapCity orders: **16,200**
• Green Arrow

QUESTION QUARTERLY, THE — DC

1 ❑ Aut 1990 Cover: 2.50 **NM** value: **Cover or less**
Circ: CapCity orders: **12,550**
📖 Any Man's Death **A:** Denys Cowan **W:** Denny O'Neil
2 ❑ Sum 1991 Cover: 2.50 **NM** value: **Cover or less**
Circ: CapCity orders: **9,300**
📖 Gomorrah Homecoming **A:** Denys Cowan **W:** Denny O'Neil
3 ❑ Aut 1991 Cover: 2.50 **NM** value: **Cover or less**
Circ: CapCity orders: **8,500**
A: Denys Cowan **W:** Denny O'Neil
4 ❑ Win 1991 Cover: 2.95 **NM** value: **Cover or less**
Circ: CapCity orders: **6,900**
A: Denys Cowan
5 ❑ Spr 1992 Cover: 2.95 **NM** value: **Cover or less**
Circ: CapCity orders: **6,300**
📖 Outrage final issue. **A:** Shea Anton Pensa; Mark Badger; Denys Cowan; Mike Manley; Kelley Puckett; Mike Baron; Mike Gold **W:** Mike Mignola; Joe Quesada; Denny O'Neil; Jan Harpes

QUESTION RETURNS, THE — DC

1 ❑ Feb 1997 Cover: 3.50 **NM** value: **Cover or less**
Circ: Diamd. preorders: **20,152**
One-shot.

QUEST OF THE TIGER WOMAN, THE — Millennium

1 ❑ Cover: 2.95 **NM** value: **Cover or less**
📖 The Sky Devil **A:** Donald Marquez **W:** Donald Marquez

QUEST PRESENTS — Quest

1 ❑ Jul 1983 Cover: 1.00 **NM** value: **1.50**
A: Jay Disbrow
2 ❑ Sep 1983 Cover: 1.25 **NM** value: **1.50**
A: Jay Disbrow
3 ❑ Nov 1983 Cover: 1.50 **NM** value: **Cover or less**
A: Jay Disbrow

QUESTPROBE — Marvel

Scott Adams was a pioneer of the computer game in the early 1980s, taking gamers from desert islands to haunted houses with his ingenious series of adventure games. With personal computers becoming commonplace in the homes of many a comic book reader, Marvel tried its luck with this new form of entertainment, creating the Questprobe series in cooperation with Adams.

The Questprobe computer adventure games featured such prominent Marvel characters as Spider-Man and the Incredible Hulk. As a marketing tool, Marvel also published Questprobe comic books that were related to, but did not provide the answers for, the adventure games.

Unfortunately, both the comics and the games were poorly distributed, and probably very few people who got one ever saw the other.

1 ❑ Aug 1984 Cover: 0.75 **NM** value: **1.50**
• Hulk **A:** John Romita ★ Origin of Chief Examiner. ★ 1st Appearance of Chief Examiner.
2 ❑ Jan 1985 Cover: 0.75 **NM** value: **1.50**
📖 Mysterio Times Two! • Spider-Man **A:** Al Milgrom; Jim Mooney **W:** Al Milgrom
3 ❑ Nov 1985 Cover: 0.75 **NM** value: **1.50**
Circ: CapCity orders: **9,600**
• Human Torch; Thing

QUICK DRAW MCGRAW (CHARLTON) — Charlton

1 ❑ Nov 1970 Cover: 0.15 **NM** value: **10.00**
2 ❑ Jan 1971 Cover: 0.15 **NM** value: **7.00**
3 ❑ Mar 1971 Cover: 0.15 **NM** value: **5.00**
4 ❑ May 1971 Cover: 0.15 **NM** value: **5.00**
5 ❑ Jul 1971 Cover: 0.15 **NM** value: **5.00**
6 ❑ Sep 1971 Cover: 0.15 **NM** value: **4.00**
7 ❑ Nov 1971 Cover: 0.15 **NM** value: **4.00**
8 ❑ Jan 1972 Cover: 0.15 **NM** value: **4.00**

QUICK DRAW MCGRAW (DELL) — Dell

2 ❑ Apr 1960 Cover: 0.10 **NM** value: **15.00**
3 ❑ Jul 1960 Cover: 0.10 **NM** value: **10.00**
4 ❑ Oct 1960 Cover: 0.10 **NM** value: **10.00**
• **CGC:** 1 graded, best 9.0
5 ❑ Jan 1961 Cover: 0.10 **NM** value: **10.00**
• **CGC:** 1 graded, best 7.0
6 ❑ Apr 1961 Cover: 0.12 **NM** value: **10.00**
7 ❑ Jul 1961 Cover: 0.12 **NM** value: **10.00**
8 ❑ Oct 1961 Cover: 0.12 **NM** value: **8.00**
9 ❑ Jan 1962 Cover: 0.12 **NM** value: **8.00**
• **CGC:** 1 graded, best 8.5
10 ❑ Apr 1962 Cover: 0.12 **NM** value: **8.00**
11 ❑ Jul 1962 **NM** value: **8.00**
12 ❑ Oct 1962 **NM** value: **8.00**
• **CGC:** 2 graded, best 9.6
13 ❑ Feb 1963 **NM** value: **6.00**
• **CGC:** 4 graded, best 9.0
14 ❑ ca. 1963 Cover: 0.12 **NM** value: **6.00**
15 ❑ Cover: 0.15 **NM** value: **10.00**

QUICKEN FORBIDDEN — Cryptic Press

1 ❑ ca. 1996, b&w Cover: 2.95 **NM** value: **3.25**
2 ❑ ca. 1996, b&w Cover: 2.95 **NM** value: **3.00**
3 ❑ ca. 1997, b&w Cover: 2.95 **NM** value: **3.00**
4 ❑ ca. 1997, b&w Cover: 2.95 **NM** value: **3.00**
5 ❑ ca. 1998, b&w Cover: 2.95 **NM** value: **3.00**
6 ❑ ca. 1998, b&w Cover: 2.95 **NM** value: **3.00**
7 ❑ ca. 1999, b&w Cover: 2.95 **NM** value: **3.00**
8 ❑ ca. 1999, b&w Cover: 2.95 **NM** value: **3.00**
9 ❑ ca. 2000, b&w Cover: 2.95 **NM** value: **3.00**
📖 Anxiety Disorder, Part 1 **A:** John Green **W:** Dave Roman
10 ❑ ca. 2000 Cover: 2.95 **NM** value: **Cover or less**

QUICKSILVER — Marvel

1 ❑ Nov 1997 Cover: 2.99 **NM** value: **Cover or less**
Circ: Diamd. preorders: **57,087**
wraparound cover. • gatefold summary. 📖 The Beast in Me **A:** Rob Haynes; Casey Jones **W:** Tom Peyer
2 ❑ Dec 1997 Cover: 1.99 **NM** value: **Cover or less**
Circ: Diamd. preorders: **51,275**
• gatefold summary.
3 ❑ Jan 1998 Cover: 1.99 **NM** value: **Cover or less**
Circ: Diamd. preorders: **37,964**
• gatefold summary.
4 ❑ Feb 1998 Cover: 1.99 **NM** value: **Cover or less**
Circ: Diamd. preorders: **33,382**
• gatefold summary.
5 ❑ Mar 1998 Cover: 1.99 **NM** value: **Cover or less**
Circ: Diamd. preorders: **27,919**
• gatefold summary.
6 ❑ Apr 1998 Cover: 1.99 **NM** value: **Cover or less**
Circ: Diamd. preorders: **24,424**
• gatefold summary. ★ Appearance of Inhumans.
7 ❑ May 1998 Cover: 1.99 **NM** value: **Cover or less**
Circ: Diamd. preorders: **23,332**
• gatefold summary. ★ Appearance of Black Knight.
8 ❑ Jun 1998 Cover: 1.99 **NM** value: **Cover or less**
Circ: Diamd. preorders: **22,659**
• gatefold summary. • in Savage Land
9 ❑ Jul 1998 Cover: 1.99 **NM** value: **Cover or less**
Circ: Diamd. preorders: **20,844**
• gatefold summary.
10 ❑ Aug 1998 Cover: 1.99 **NM** value: **Cover or less**
Circ: Diamd. preorders: **36,540**
• gatefold summary. 📖 Live Kree or Die, Part 3 • concludes in Avengers #7
11 ❑ Sep 1998 Cover: 1.99 **NM** value: **Cover or less**
Circ: Diamd. preorders: **21,752**
• gatefold summary. 📖 The Siege of Wundagore, Part 2 ★ Appearance of Heroes for Hire.
12 ❑ Oct 1998 Cover: 2.99 **NM** value: **Cover or less**
Circ: Diamd. preorders: **22,404**
• double-sized. 📖 The siege of Wundagore, Part 4 ★ Versus Exodus.
13 ❑ Nov 1998 Cover: 1.99 **NM** value: **Cover or less**
Circ: Diamd. preorders: **20,459**
• gatefold summary.

QUINCY LOOKS INTO HIS FUTURE — General Electric

1 ❑ **NM** value: **2.00**
No issue number. • giveaway. • King Features strip

QUIT YOUR JOB — Alternative

1 ❑ b&w Cover: 6.95 **NM** value: **Cover or less**
No issue number.

QUIVERS — Caliber

1 ❑ ca. 1991, b&w Cover: 2.95 **NM** value: **Cover or less**
Circ: CapCity orders: **2,880**
A: Brian Michael Bendis **W:** Brian Michael Bendis
2 ❑ ca. 1991, b&w Cover: 2.95 **NM** value: **Cover or less**

Q-UNIT — Harris

1 ❑ Cover: 2.95 **NM** value: **Cover or less**
• trading card; Polybagged with "layered reality cybercard" **A:** Karl Altstaetter **W:** Robert Napton; Karl Altstaetter ★ 1st Appearance of Q-Unit.

RABBIT — Sharkbait

1 ❑ Cover: 2.50 **NM** value: **Cover or less**
📖 The Serpent's Agenda, Part 1 **A:** David Hedgecock **W:** David Hedgecock

RABID — Fantaco

1 ❑ Cover: 5.95 **NM** value: **Cover or less**
No issue number.

RABID ANIMAL KOMIX — Krankin' Komix

1 ❑ Cover: 2.95 **NM** value: **Cover or less**
📖 Another Day, Another 12-Pack **A:** Mike Hersh **W:** Mike Hersh
2 ❑ Cover: 2.95 **NM** value: **Cover or less**
📖 Laff Riot **A:** Mike Hersh **W:** Mike Hersh

RABID RACHEL — Miller

1 ❑ b&w Cover: 2.00 **NM** value: **Cover or less**

RACE AGAINST TIME — Dark Angel

1 ❑ Jun 1997 Cover: 2.50 **NM** value: **Cover or less**
2 ❑ Aug 1997 Cover: 2.50 **NM** value: **Cover or less**

RACE FOR THE MOON — Harvey

1 ❑ Mar 1958 Cover: 0.10 **NM** value: **100.00**
2 ❑ Sep 1958 Cover: 0.10 **NM** value: **100.00**
• **CGC:** 1 graded, best 8.0
3 ❑ Nov 1958 Cover: 0.10 **NM** value: **100.00**

RACE OF SCORPIONS — Dark Horse

1 ❑ Jul 1991, b&w Cover: 2.25 **NM** value: **Cover or less**
📖 The Big Lizards **A:** Leopoldo Durañona **W:** Leopoldo Durañona
2 ❑ Aug 1991 Cover: 2.50 **NM** value: **Cover or less**
A: Leopoldo Durañona **W:** Leopoldo Durañona

Other grades: Multiply prices above by **1.5 for Mint • 2/3 for Very Fine • 1/3 for Fine • 1/5 for Very Good • 1/8 for Good**

3 ❑ Sep 1992 Cover: 2.50 **NM** value: **Cover or less**
A: Leopoldo Durañona **W:** Leopoldo Durañona
4 ❑ Oct 1991 Cover: 2.50 **NM** value: **Cover or less**
A: Leopoldo Durañona **W:** Leopoldo Durañona

RACE OF SCORPIONS (MINI-SERIES) Dark Horse
1 ❑ Mar 1990, b&w Cover: 4.50 **NM** value: **Cover or less**
A: Leopoldo Dura±ona **W:** Leopoldo Dura±ona
2 ❑ Sep 1990, b&w Cover: 4.95 **NM** value: **Cover or less**
A: Leopoldo Dura±ona **W:** Leopoldo Dura±ona

RACER X Now
1 ❑ Sep 1988 Cover: 1.75 **NM** value: **2.00**
Circ: CapCity orders: **5,900**
2 ❑ Oct 1988 Cover: 1.75 **NM** value: **Cover or less**
Circ: CapCity orders: **4,200**
3 ❑ Nov 1988 Cover: 1.75 **NM** value: **Cover or less**
Circ: CapCity orders: **3,700**
4 ❑ Jan 1989 Cover: 1.75 **NM** value: **Cover or less**
Circ: CapCity orders: **3,150**
5 ❑ Feb 1989 Cover: 1.75 **NM** value: **Cover or less**
Circ: CapCity orders: **3,050**
6 ❑ Mar 1989 Cover: 1.75 **NM** value: **Cover or less**
Circ: CapCity orders: **3,000**
7 ❑ Apr 1989 Cover: 1.75 **NM** value: **Cover or less**
Circ: CapCity orders: **2,750**
8 ❑ May 1989 Cover: 1.75 **NM** value: **Cover or less**
Circ: CapCity orders: **2,625**
• Comics Code
9 ❑ Jun 1989 Cover: 1.75 **NM** value: **Cover or less**
Circ: CapCity orders: **2,650**
• Comics Code
10 ❑ Jul 1989 Cover: 1.75 **NM** value: **Cover or less**
Circ: CapCity orders: **2,500**
• Comics Code
11 ❑ Aug 1989 Cover: 1.75 **NM** value: **Cover or less**
Circ: CapCity orders: **2,275**
• Comics Code

RACER X (VOL. 2) Now
1 ❑ Sep 1989 Cover: 1.75 **NM** value: **2.00**
Circ: CapCity orders: **2,700**
W: Chuck Dixon
2 ❑ Oct 1989 Cover: 1.75 **NM** value: **Cover or less**
Circ: CapCity orders: **2,325**
📖 Death Drives a rented Car! **A:** Todd Fox; Enrique Villagran **W:** Chuck Dixon
3 ❑ Nov 1989 Cover: 1.75 **NM** value: **Cover or less**
Circ: CapCity orders: **2,350**
W: Chuck Dixon
4 ❑ Dec 1989 Cover: 1.75 **NM** value: **Cover or less**
Circ: CapCity orders: **2,350**
W: Chuck Dixon
5 ❑ Jan 1990 Cover: 1.75 **NM** value: **Cover or less**
Circ: CapCity orders: **2,225**
W: Chuck Dixon
6 ❑ Feb 1990 Cover: 1.75 **NM** value: **Cover or less**
Circ: CapCity orders: **2,125**
W: Chuck Dixon
7 ❑ Mar 1990 Cover: 1.75 **NM** value: **Cover or less**
Circ: CapCity orders: **2,175**
W: Chuck Dixon
8 ❑ Apr 1990 Cover: 1.75 **NM** value: **Cover or less**
Circ: CapCity orders: **2,025**
W: Chuck Dixon
9 ❑ May 1990 Cover: 1.75 **NM** value: **Cover or less**
Circ: CapCity orders: **2,000**
W: Chuck Dixon
10 ❑ Jun 1990 Cover: 1.75 **NM** value: **Cover or less**
Circ: CapCity orders: **1,825**
W: Chuck Dixon

RACER X (3RD SERIES) WildStorm
Rex Racer needed to prove to his father that he was the best. He left his family and journeyed to the kingdom of Kapetapek at the invitation of its leader Prince Kabala. Yet, terrorists are determined to take over the small nation and only Rex can discover the secret of the Treasure of Kapetapek.

Based on the character from the Speed Racer cartoons, this mini-series gives readers some background on Speed Racer's long lost brother. It also covers the events which lead up to his striking out on his own and becoming the mysterious driver constantly challenging Speed and his friends as Racer X.

1 ❑ Oct 2000 Cover: 2.95 **NM** value: **Cover or less**
Circ: Diamd. preorders: **17,749**
📖 The Prince **A:** Jo Chen **W:** Tommy Yune
2 ❑ Nov 2000 Cover: 2.95 **NM** value: **Cover or less**
Circ: Diamd. preorders: **14,732**
📖 The ProtTgT **A:** Jo Chen **W:** Tommy Yune
3 ❑ Dec 2000 Cover: 2.95 **NM** value: **Cover or less**
Circ: Diamd. preorders: **13,895**
📖 The Mark of Death **A:** Jo Chen **W:** Tommy Yune

RACER X PREMIERE Now
1 ❑ Aug 1988 Cover: 3.50 **NM** value: **Cover or less**
Circ: CapCity orders: **5,300**
No issue number.

RACK & PAIN Dark Horse
1 ❑ Mar 1994 Cover: 2.50 **NM** value: **Cover or less**
Circ: CapCity orders: **6,550**
📖 Death & Deception • Dark Horse **A:** Leonardo Jimenez **W:** Brian Pulido
2 ❑ Apr 1994 Cover: 2.50 **NM** value: **Cover or less**
Circ: CapCity orders: **3,975**
A: Leonardo Jimenez **W:** Brian Pulido
3 ❑ May 1994 Cover: 2.50 **NM** value: **Cover or less**
Circ: CapCity orders: **3,375**
📖 Why the Gods Kill **A:** Leonardo Jimenez **W:** Brian Pulido
4 ❑ Jun 1994 Cover: 2.50 **NM** value: **Cover or less**
Circ: CapCity orders: **3,075**
A: Leonardo Jimenez **W:** Brian Pulido

RACK & PAIN: KILLERS Chaos
1 ❑ 1996 Cover: 2.95 **NM** value: **Cover or less**
📖 Death & Deception • Chaos **A:** Leonardo Jimenez **W:** Brian Pulido
2 ❑ 1996 Cover: 2.95 **NM** value: **Cover or less**
Circ: Diamd. preorders: **14,166**
A: Leonardo Jimenez **W:** Brian Pulido
3 ❑ 1996 Cover: 2.95 **NM** value: **Cover or less**
Circ: Diamd. preorders: **11,048**
A: Leonardo Jimenez **W:** Brian Pulido
4 ❑ 1996 Cover: 2.95 **NM** value: **Cover or less**
Circ: Diamd. preorders: **9,048**
A: Leonardo Jimenez **W:** Brian Pulido

RACKET SQUAD IN ACTION Charlton
1 ❑ May 1952 Cover: 0.10 **NM** value: **200.00**
2 ❑ Jul 1952 Cover: 0.10 **NM** value: **125.00**
3 ❑ Sep 1952 Cover: 0.10 **NM** value: **125.00**
4 ❑ Nov 1952 Cover: 0.10 **NM** value: **125.00**
5 ❑ Jan 1953 Cover: 0.10 **NM** value: **125.00**
6 ❑ Mar 1953 Cover: 0.10 **NM** value: **100.00**
7 ❑ May 1953 Cover: 0.10 **NM** value: **100.00**
8 ❑ Jul 1953 Cover: 0.10 **NM** value: **100.00**
9 ❑ Sep 1953 Cover: 0.10 **NM** value: **100.00**
10 ❑ Nov 1953 Cover: 0.10 **NM** value: **100.00**
11 ❑ Jan 1954 Cover: 0.10 **NM** value: **100.00**
• **CGC:** 2 graded, best 9.2
12 ❑ Aug 1954 Cover: 0.10 **NM** value: **100.00**
• **CGC:** 11 graded, best 8.5
13 ❑ Oct 1954 Cover: 0.10 **NM** value: **90.00**
• **CGC:** 5 graded, best 9.0
14 ❑ Jan 1955 Cover: 0.10 **NM** value: **90.00**
• **CGC:** 1 graded, best 9.0
15 ❑ Mar 1955 Cover: 0.10 **NM** value: **90.00**
16 ❑ May 1955 Cover: 0.10 **NM** value: **90.00**
17 ❑ Jul 1955 Cover: 0.10 **NM** value: **90.00**
18 ❑ Sep 1955 Cover: 0.10 **NM** value: **90.00**
19 ❑ Nov 1955 Cover: 0.10 **NM** value: **90.00**
20 ❑ Feb 1956 Cover: 0.10 **NM** value: **75.00**
21 ❑ May 1956 Cover: 0.10 **NM** value: **75.00**
22 ❑ Aug 1956 Cover: 0.10 **NM** value: **75.00**
23 ❑ Nov 1956 Cover: 0.10 **NM** value: **75.00**
24 ❑ Feb 1957 Cover: 0.10 **NM** value: **75.00**
25 ❑ May 1957 Cover: 0.10 **NM** value: **50.00**
26 ❑ Aug 1957 Cover: 0.10 **NM** value: **50.00**
27 ❑ Nov 1957 Cover: 0.10 **NM** value: **50.00**
28 ❑ Jan 1957 Cover: 0.10 **NM** value: **50.00**
29 ❑ Mar 1958 Cover: 0.10 **NM** value: **50.00**

RADICAL DREAMER Blackball
One of the stranger experiments in comics is Radical Dreamer, several issues of which fold out into giant comics posters. Not just foldouts or inserts — the entire issue!

In 3040, Max Wrighter discovered an alien technology which he transformed into the Dream Network — the "DreamNet." The network connected directly into its users' minds, promising them entertainment and education. The E-CO company that bought Wrighter's technology, however, had other plans.

In 3054, they hooked a madman up to the DreamNet. The nature of his illness allowed him to become the first "Radical Dreamer," one whose very consciousness left his body and wandered the Net. His madness entered the minds of the users, instantly killing 10% of the DreamNet subscribers. To stop the madness, Wrighter was forced to try to become a Radical Dreamer himself, leaving his body behind and floating madly in a world of dreams.

0 ❑ May 1994 Cover: 1.99 **NM** value: **2.50**
📖 Dreams Cannot Die! • poster comic **A:** Mark Wheatley **W:** Mark Wheatley
1 ❑ Jun 1994 Cover: 1.99 **NM** value: **2.00**
Circ: CapCity orders: **3,250**
📖 Dreamnet Mainline • poster comic **A:** Mark Wheatley **W:** Mark Wheatley
2 ❑ Jul 1994 Cover: 1.99 **NM** value: **2.95**
• poster comic **A:** Mark Wheatley **W:** Mark Wheatley
3 ❑ Sep 1994 Cover: 1.99 **NM** value: **2.50**
• poster comic **A:** Mark Wheatley **W:** Mark Wheatley
4 ❑ Nov 1994 Cover: 2.50 **NM** value: **Cover or less**
• foldout comic on cardstock **A:** Mark Wheatley **W:** Mark Wheatley

RADICAL DREAMER (VOL. 2) Mark's Giant Economy Size
1 ❑ Jun 1995, b&w Cover: 2.95 **NM** value: **Cover or less**
2 ❑ Jul 1995, b&w Cover: 2.95 **NM** value: **Cover or less**
3 ❑ Aug 1995, b&w Cover: 2.95 **NM** value: **Cover or less**
4 ❑ Sep 1995, b&w Cover: 2.95 **NM** value: **Cover or less**
5 ❑ Dec 1995, b&w Cover: 2.95 **NM** value: **Cover or less**

RADIOACTIVE MAN Bongo

Radioactive Man is best known as comic-book character Bart Simpson's favorite super-hero. Radioactive Man was the archetypical silly comic-book character, accidentally caught in a radiation bomb test which should have killed him. Instead it left him with super-powers and a lightning bolt-shaped piece of shrapnel permanently embedded in his skull. (He desperately attempts to hide this under a hat in his civilian identity as Claude Kane III.)

In the fictional world of the Simpsons, Radioactive Man is a long-running comic book. This real life mini-series consists of six issues from the fictional run of Radioactive Man. Issue #1 of the mini-series "reprints" the shocking origin of Radioactive Man from the fictional Radioactive Man #1; the second issue covers Radioactive Man #88 from the Silver Age; and so on until the final issue, showing Radioactive Man in the "laughingly contemporary Polybagged Age."

1 ❑ Cover: 2.95 **NM** value: **4.00**
Circ: CapCity orders: **38,700** • **CGC:** 1 graded, best 4.0
glow cover. 📖 The Origin Of Radioactive Man **A:** Bill Morrison **W:** Steve Vance ★ Origin of Radioactive Man.
88 ❑ Cover: 1.95 **NM** value: **2.50**
Circ: CapCity orders: **30,500**
📖 The Molten Menace Of Magmom The Lava Man • 2nd issue **A:** Bill Morrison **W:** Steve Vance
216 ❑ Cover: 1.95 **NM** value: **2.25**
Circ: CapCity orders: **30,175**
📖 See No Evil, Hear No Evil • 3rd issue **A:** Bill Morrison **W:** Steve Vance
412 ❑ Cover: 2.25 **NM** value: **Cover or less**
Circ: CapCity orders: **26,475**
📖 In Ze Clutches of Doctor Crab! • 4th issue **A:** Bill Morrison **W:** Steve Vance
679 ❑ Cover: 2.25 **NM** value: **Cover or less**
Circ: CapCity orders: **20,850**
• 5th issue **A:** Bill Morrison **W:** Steve Vance
1000 ❑ Jan 1995 Cover: 2.25 **NM** value: **Cover or less**
Circ: CapCity orders: **19,050**
📖 In his own Image • 6th issue **A:** Steve Vance **W:** Steve Vance

RADIOACTIVE MAN 80 PAGE COLOSSAL Bongo
1 ❑ ca. 1995 Cover: 4.95 **NM** value: **Cover or less**
Circ: CapCity orders: **8,525** • **CGC:** 1 graded, best 9.2
📖 To Betroth a Foe; Radioactive Man, Teen Idol; The 1,001 Faces of Radioactive Ape; Gloria Grand, Radioactive Girl; The Radioactive Man of 1995; Inside the Containment Dome; the Origin of Glowy; How to Draw Radioactive Man **A:** Bill Morrison; Phil Ortiz; Christian Roman; David Silverman; Scott Shaw; Sharon Bridgeman; Stephanie Gladden **W:** Bill Morrison; David Silverman; Scott Shaw; Kayre Morrison; Terry Delegeane

RADIOACTIVE MAN (VOL. 2) Bongo
1 ❑ Cover: 2.50 **NM** value: **Cover or less**
#100 on cover.

RADIO BOY Eclipse
1 ❑ b&w Cover: 1.50 **NM** value: **Cover or less**

RADREX Bullet
1 ❑ Cover: 2.25 **NM** value: **Cover or less**
A: Greg Boone **W:** Greg Boone

RAGAMUFFINS Eclipse
1 ❑ Jan 1985 Cover: 1.75 **NM** value: **2.00**
A: Gene Colan

RAGE Anarchy Bridgeworks
1 ❑ Cover: 2.95 **NM** value: **Cover or less**
📖 Enemy of the People **A:** Daniel Presedo **W:** Vinson Watson

RAGGEDY ANN AND ANDY (1ST SERIES) Dell
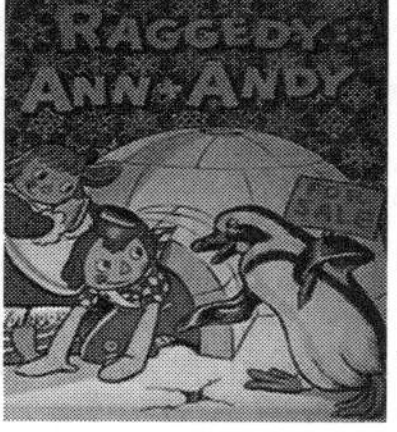

Though apparently not hotly collected these days, except by collectors of Raggedy Ann material in general, this series was one of the very best ever aimed at preteens. With contributors brought together by Editor Oskar Lebeck and with the focus on the Raggedys (whose outspoken driving force was love), the anthology title featured such additional delights as Billy and Bonnie Bee, Dan Noonan's Egbert Elephant and His Friends, and Walt Kelly's Animal Mother Goose.

Created by Johnny Gruelle (1880-1938) in 1918, Raggedy Ann was enormously popular, and Dell's series brought much of the cast of Gruelle's works to comic-book format. Lebeck later added such features as children's book adaptations before a creator shift changed the cover feature to John Stanley's creation, Peterkin Pottle. In those stories, fat little Peterkin daydreams elab-

CGC-graded: Multiply prices above by **33** for **9.9 M** • **16** for **9.8 NM/M** • **7** for **9.6 NM+** • **5** for **9.4 NM** • **2.5** for **9.2 NM-** • **1.5** for **9.0 VF/NM**

orate fantasies in which he is the hero. At that point, Stanley also created Raggedys stories that bore little resemblance to the warm fantasies of his predecessors. — Maggie

1 ❑ Jun 1946 Cover: 0.10 **NM** value: **180.00**
• **CGC:** 1 graded, best 9.4
2 ❑ Jul 1946 Cover: 0.10 **NM** value: **125.00**
• **CGC:** 1 graded, best 9.0
3 ❑ Aug 1946 Cover: 0.10 **NM** value: **125.00**
4 ❑ Sep 1946 Cover: 0.10 **NM** value: **125.00**
5 ❑ Oct 1946 Cover: 0.10 **NM** value: **100.00**
6 ❑ Nov 1946 Cover: 0.10 **NM** value: **100.00**
7 ❑ Dec 1946 Cover: 0.10 **NM** value: **100.00**
8 ❑ Jan 1947 Cover: 0.10 **NM** value: **100.00**
9 ❑ Feb 1947 Cover: 0.10 **NM** value: **100.00**
10 ❑ Mar 1947 Cover: 0.10 **NM** value: **75.00**
11 ❑ Apr 1947 Cover: 0.10 **NM** value: **75.00**
12 ❑ May 1947 Cover: 0.10 **NM** value: **75.00**
13 ❑ Jun 1947 Cover: 0.10 **NM** value: **75.00**
14 ❑ Jul 1947 Cover: 0.10 **NM** value: **75.00**
15 ❑ Aug 1947 Cover: 0.10 **NM** value: **75.00**
16 ❑ Sep 1947 Cover: 0.10 **NM** value: **60.00**
17 ❑ Oct 1947 Cover: 0.10 **NM** value: **60.00**
18 ❑ Nov 1947 Cover: 0.10 **NM** value: **60.00**
19 ❑ Dec 1947 Cover: 0.10 **NM** value: **60.00**
• **CGC:** 1 graded, best 8.5
20 ❑ Jan 1948 Cover: 0.10 **NM** value: **50.00**
21 ❑ Feb 1948 Cover: 0.10 **NM** value: **50.00**
22 ❑ Mar 1948 Cover: 0.10 **NM** value: **50.00**
23 ❑ Apr 1948 Cover: 0.10 **NM** value: **50.00**
24 ❑ May 1948 Cover: 0.10 **NM** value: **50.00**
25 ❑ Jun 1948 Cover: 0.10 **NM** value: **50.00**
26 ❑ Jul 1948 Cover: 0.10 **NM** value: **50.00**
27 ❑ Aug 1948 Cover: 0.10 **NM** value: **50.00**
28 ❑ Sep 1948 Cover: 0.10 **NM** value: **50.00**

RAGGEDY ANN AND ANDY (2ND SERIES) Dell

1 ❑ Oct 1964 Cover: 0.12 **NM** value: **35.00**
2 ❑ Cover: 0.12 **NM** value: **20.00**
3 ❑ Cover: 0.12 **NM** value: **20.00**

RAGGEDY ANN AND ANDY (3RD SERIES) Gold Key

1 ❑ Dec 1971 Cover: 0.15 **NM** value: **5.00**
2 ❑ Mar 1972 Cover: 0.15 **NM** value: **3.50**
🕮 Follow that Carpet; Snowed in; Homesick; The Haunted House
3 ❑ Dec 1972 Cover: 0.15 **NM** value: **3.50**
4 ❑ Cover: 0.15 **NM** value: **3.50**
5 ❑ Cover: 0.15 **NM** value: **3.50**
6 ❑ Cover: 0.15 **NM** value: **3.50**

RAGGEDYMAN Cult

1 ❑ b&w Cover: 2.50 **NM** value: **Cover or less**
A: Anthony Jon Hicks **W:** T.M. Lowe
1/SC❑ b&w Cover: 2.75 **NM** value: **Cover or less**
Prism cover. **A:** Anthony Jon Hicks **W:** T.M. Lowe
2 ❑ b&w Cover: 2.50 **NM** value: **Cover or less**
🕮 Corporate Entity, Part 1 **A:** Anthony Jon Hicks **W:** T.M. Lowe
3 ❑ b&w Cover: 2.50 **NM** value: **Cover or less**
🕮 Corporate Entity, Part 2 **A:** Anthony Jon Hicks **W:** T.M. Lowe
4 ❑ b&w Cover: 2.50 **NM** value: **Cover or less**
🕮 Corporate Entity, Part 3 **A:** Anthony Jon Hicks; Bryan Talbot(cover) **W:** T.M. Lowe
5 ❑ Jul 1993, b&w Cover: 2.50 **NM** value: **Cover or less**
A: Anthony Jon Hicks **W:** T.M. Lowe
6 ❑ **NM** value: **2.50**
A: Anthony Jon Hicks **W:** T.M. Lowe

RAGING ANGELS Classic Hippie

1 ❑ b&w Cover: 2.50 **NM** value: **Cover or less**

RAGMAN DC

Ragman is Rory Regan, a Vietnam veteran who runs a pawn shop by day, but becomes a crimefighter by night.

In the original telling of his origin, Rory's father discovered $2 million in mob cash stuffed inside a mattress someone had pawned at his store. Before he could enjoy the fruits of this discovery, the "owner" came to reclaim it.

Rory arrives on the scene and attempts to rescue his father from the gangsters, who had been torturing him with live electrical waires. Unfortunately, Rory was grounded, so when he touched his father, the electricity surged through them all, leaving everyone dead except for Rory. Rory then discovers a suit of rags his father had thrown together as a costume, and decides to strike back at the mobsters.

1 ❑ Sep 1976 Cover: 0.30 **NM** value: **5.00**
• **CGC:** 10 graded, best 9.6
🕮 Origin Of The Tatterdemalion **A:** Redondo Studio; Joe Kubert **W:** Robert Kanigher ★ Origin of Ragman. ★ 1st Appearance of Ragman.
2 ❑ Nov 1976 Cover: 0.30 **NM** value: **3.00**
• **CGC:** 1 graded, best 9.8
A: Redondo Studio; Joe Kubert **W:** Robert Kanigher
3 ❑ Jan 1977 Cover: 0.30 **NM** value: **3.00**
A: Joe Kubert; The Redondo Studio **W:** Robert Kanigher
4 ❑ Mar 1977 Cover: 0.30 **NM** value: **3.00**
A: Joe Kubert; The Redondo Studio **W:** Robert Kanigher
5 ❑ Jul 1977 Cover: 0.30 **NM** value: **3.00**
A: Joe Kubert; The Redondo Studio **W:** Robert Kanigher

RAGMAN: CRY OF THE DEAD DC

1 ❑ Aug 1993 Cover: 1.75 **NM** value: **2.00**
Circ: CapCity orders: **20,150**
A: Gabriel Morrissette **W:** Elaine Lee
2 ❑ Sep 1993 Cover: 1.75 **NM** value: **Cover or less**
Circ: CapCity orders: **13,600**
🕮 Child's Play **A:** Gabriel Morrissette **W:** Elaine Lee
3 ❑ Oct 1993 Cover: 1.75 **NM** value: **Cover or less**
Circ: CapCity orders: **10,600**
🕮 Mange Moun! **A:** Gabriel Morrissette **W:** Elaine Lee
4 ❑ Nov 1993 Cover: 1.75 **NM** value: **Cover or less**
Circ: CapCity orders: **9,300**
🕮 Blood Sacrifice **A:** Gabriel Morrissette **W:** Elaine Lee
5 ❑ Dec 1993 Cover: 1.75 **NM** value: **Cover or less**
Circ: CapCity orders: **8,050**
A: Gabriel Morrissette **W:** Elaine Lee
6 ❑ Jan 1994 Cover: 1.75 **NM** value: **Cover or less**
Circ: CapCity orders: **7,250**
🕮 Cheval Blanc! **A:** Gabriel Morrissette **W:** Elaine Lee

RAGMAN (MINI-SERIES) DC

1 ❑ Oct 1991 Cover: 1.50 **NM** value: **2.00**
Circ: CapCity orders: **41,700** • **CGC:** 1 graded, best 9.6
🕮 Bones Of The Defenseless **A:** Pat Broderick **W:** Keith Giffen; Robert Loren Flemming
2 ❑ Nov 1991 Cover: 1.50 **NM** value: **2.00**
Circ: CapCity orders: **27,100**
🕮 A Ragged Revenge **A:** Pat Broderick **W:** Robert Loren Flemming
3 ❑ Dec 1991 Cover: 1.50 **NM** value: **2.00**
Circ: CapCity orders: **25,750**
4 ❑ Jan 1992 Cover: 1.50 **NM** value: **2.00**
Circ: CapCity orders: **25,400**
5 ❑ Feb 1992 Cover: 1.50 **NM** value: **2.00**
Circ: CapCity orders: **21,300**
6 ❑ Mar 1992 Cover: 1.25 **NM** value: **2.00**
Circ: CapCity orders: **20,100**
7 ❑ Apr 1992 Cover: 1.25 **NM** value: **2.00**
Circ: CapCity orders: **18,100**
🕮 The Summit **A:** Keith Giffen; Pat Broderick; Romeo Tanghal **W:** Keith Giffen; Robert Loren Flemming
8 ❑ May 1992 Cover: 1.25 **NM** value: **2.00**
Circ: CapCity orders: **17,900**
final issue.

RAGMOP Planet Lucy

1 ❑ Cover: 2.75 **NM** value: **Cover or less**
1-2 ❑ Dec 1995 Cover: 3.10 **NM** value: **Cover or less**
2 ❑ Cover: 2.75 **NM** value: **Cover or less**
2-2 ❑ Dec 1995 Cover: 2.95 **NM** value: **Cover or less**
3 ❑ Oct 1995 Cover: 2.95 **NM** value: **Cover or less**
4 ❑ Dec 1995 Cover: 2.95 **NM** value: **Cover or less**
5 ❑ Feb 1996 Cover: 2.95 **NM** value: **Cover or less**
6 ❑ Apr 1996 Cover: 2.95 **NM** value: **Cover or less**
7 ❑ Jun 1996 Cover: 2.95 **NM** value: **Cover or less**

RAGMOP (VOL. 2) Image

1 ❑ Sep 1997, b&w Cover: 2.95 **NM** value: **Cover or less**
Circ: Diamd. preorders: **5,645**
• synopsis of first series **A:** Rob Walton **W:** Rob Walton ★ Origin of Thrill Kitten.
2 ❑ Nov 1997, b&w Cover: 2.95 **NM** value: **Cover or less**
Circ: Diamd. preorders: **3,828**
A: Rob Walton **W:** Rob Walton
3 ❑ Feb 1998 Cover: 2.95 **NM** value: **Cover or less**
Circ: Diamd. preorders: **3,684**
A: Rob Walton **W:** Rob Walton

RAGNAROK GUY Sun

1 ❑ Cover: 2.50 **NM** value: **Cover or less**
A: Tsuguo Okazaki **W:** Tsuguo Okazaki

RAGS RABBIT Harvey

11 ❑ Jun 1957 Cover: 0.10 **NM** value: **25.00**
12 ❑ Aug 1957 Cover: 0.10 **NM** value: **20.00**
13 ❑ Oct 1957 Cover: 0.10 **NM** value: **20.00**
14 ❑ Dec 1957 Cover: 0.10 **NM** value: **20.00**
15 ❑ 1952 Cover: 0.10 **NM** value: **20.00**
16 ❑ 1953 Cover: 0.10 **NM** value: **20.00**
17 ❑ 1953 Cover: 0.10 **NM** value: **20.00**
18 ❑ 1954 Cover: 0.10 **NM** value: **20.00**

RAHRWL Northstar

1 ❑ Cover: 2.25 **NM** value: **2.50**
• Limited edition original print (1988). 32 pages. 500 copies produced. **A:** Ragne Naess **W:** Ragne Naess
1-2 ❑ Cover: 2.25 **NM** value: **Cover or less**

RAI Valiant

Rai's story began in 1992 when Project Rising Spirit succeeded in infusing a human with "The Blood of Heroes." This was a special synthetic blood composed of microscopic nano-machines. Rising Spirit had infused this into a subject codenamed Bloodshot, and the nano-machines gave him incredible speed, agility, an accelerated healing factor, and a strange ability to control machines.

Following Bloodshot's death in the year 2028, others would try to control the Blood of Heroes. Still, its secrets would become lost until 3216 when Japanese anarchists were rebelling against their island's all-powerful master computer. To stop them, the computer created the Rais in the image of Bloodshot. The Rai's put down the rebellion and obtained the blood, which they stored in a secure vault. There it lay until 4002, when the last Rai, Takao Konishi, would infuse himself with it to become a hero.

0 ❑ Nov 1992 Cover: 2.25 **NM** value: **Cover or less**
Circ: CapCity orders: **29,650** • **CGC:** 11 graded, best 10.0
🕮 The Blood Of Heroes • series continues as Rai and the Future Force; Foretells future of Valiant Universe **A:** David Lapham **W:** Bob Layton ★ Origin of Rai. ★ 1st Appearance of Bloodshot, Rai (new).
1 ❑ Mar 1992 Cover: 1.95 **NM** value: **Cover or less**
Circ: CapCity orders: **11,900** • **CGC:** 5 graded, best 9.8
🕮 Invasion, Part 2 • Flip-book with Magnus Robot Fighter (Valiant) #5 **A:** Paul Creddick **W:** Jim Shooter
2 ❑ Apr 1992 Cover: 1.95 **NM** value: **Cover or less**
Circ: CapCity orders: **8,600**
3 ❑ May 1992 Cover: 1.95 **NM** value: **Cover or less**
Circ: CapCity orders: **8,000** • **CGC:** 4 graded, best 9.6
4 ❑ Jun 1992 Cover: 1.95 **NM** value: **Cover or less**
Circ: CapCity orders: **8,000** • **CGC:** 4 graded, best 9.6
• Scarcer
5 ❑ Jul 1992 Cover: 2.25 **NM** value: **Cover or less**
Circ: CapCity orders: **9,000**
6 ❑ Aug 1992 Cover: 2.25 **NM** value: **Cover or less**
Circ: CapCity orders: **26,300**
🕮 Unity, Part 7 • Unity **A:** Sal Velluto; Joe St. Pierre **C:** Frank Miller **W:** David Michelinie
7 ❑ Sep 1992 Cover: 2.25 **NM** value: **Cover or less**
Circ: CapCity orders: **30,200**
🕮 Unity, Part 15 • Unity **C:** Walt Simonson ★ Death of Rai (original).
8 ❑ Oct 1992 Cover: 2.25 **NM** value: **Cover or less**
Circ: CapCity orders: **15,900**
• Unity epilogue; Series continued in Rai and the Future Force #9
25 ❑ Oct 1994 Cover: 2.25 **NM** value: **Cover or less**
Circ: CapCity orders: **15,750**
• Series continued from Rai and the Future Force #24
26 ❑ Nov 1994 Cover: 2.25 **NM** value: **Cover or less**
Circ: CapCity orders: **21,050**
🕮 The Chaos Effect: Epsilon, Part 3 • Chaos Effect **A:** Dave Ross **W:** Antony J.L. Bedard
27 ❑ Dec 1994 Cover: 2.25 **NM** value: **Cover or less**
Circ: CapCity orders: **13,275**
28 ❑ Jan 1995 Cover: 2.25 **NM** value: **Cover or less**
Circ: CapCity orders: **11,750**
29 ❑ Feb 1995 Cover: 2.25 **NM** value: **Cover or less**
Circ: CapCity orders: **10,825**
30 ❑ Mar 1995 Cover: 2.25 **NM** value: **Cover or less**
Circ: CapCity orders: **9,375**
31 ❑ Apr 1995 Cover: 2.25 **NM** value: **Cover or less**
Circ: CapCity orders: **8,475**
🕮 Bad Penny; Bad Penny, Part 1
32 ❑ May 1995 Cover: 2.25 **NM** value: **Cover or less**
Circ: CapCity orders: **7,525**
🕮 Bad Penny; Bad Penny, Part 2
33 ❑ Jun 1995 Cover: 2.25 **NM** value: **Cover or less**
Circ: CapCity orders: **6,575**
final issue.

RAI AND THE FUTURE FORCE Valiant

9 ❑ May 1993 Cover: 2.50 **NM** value: **Cover or less**
Circ: CapCity orders: **169,500** • **CGC:** 1 graded, best 9.2
• Series continued from Rai #8 ★ Appearance of X-O Commando, Eternal Warrior, Magnus.
9/GO❑ May 1993 **NM** value: **3.50**
• Gold
9/LE❑ May 1993 Cover: 2.50 **NM** value: **3.00**
• Series continued from Rai #8
10 ❑ Jun 1993 Cover: 2.25 **NM** value: **Cover or less**
Circ: CapCity orders: **87,700**
🕮 The Death of Japan **A:** Sean Chen **W:** John Ostrander
11 ❑ Jul 1993 Cover: 2.25 **NM** value: **Cover or less**
Circ: CapCity orders: **91,100**
12 ❑ Aug 1993 Cover: 2.25 **NM** value: **Cover or less**
Circ: CapCity orders: **73,000**
13 ❑ Sep 1993 Cover: 2.25 **NM** value: **Cover or less**
Circ: CapCity orders: **59,300**
14 ❑ Oct 1993 Cover: 2.25 **NM** value: **Cover or less**
Circ: CapCity orders: **47,200**
★ Appearance of X-O Manowar armor.
15 ❑ Nov 1993 Cover: 2.25 **NM** value: **Cover or less**
Circ: CapCity orders: **41,175**
🕮 The Battle For South Am, Part 1
16 ❑ Dec 1993 Cover: 2.25 **NM** value: **Cover or less**
Circ: CapCity orders: **36,725**
17 ❑ Jan 1994 Cover: 2.25 **NM** value: **Cover or less**
Circ: CapCity orders: **31,100**
18 ❑ Feb 1994 Cover: 2.25 **NM** value: **Cover or less**
Circ: CapCity orders: **27,800**
19 ❑ Mar 1994 Cover: 2.25 **NM** value: **Cover or less**
Circ: CapCity orders: **22,450**
20 ❑ Apr 1994 Cover: 2.25 **NM** value: **Cover or less**
Circ: CapCity orders: **19,700**
• Spylocke revealed as spider-alien
21 ❑ May 1994 Cover: 2.25 **NM** value: **Cover or less**
Circ: CapCity orders: **25,300**
• trading card; series continues as Rai
22 ❑ Jun 1994 Cover: 2.25 **NM** value: **Cover or less**
Circ: CapCity orders: **18,625**
★ Death of Rai.
23 ❑ Aug 1994 Cover: 2.25 **NM** value: **Cover or less**
Circ: CapCity orders: **17,175**
24 ❑ Sep 1994 Cover: 2.25 **NM** value: **Cover or less**
Circ: CapCity orders: **16,825**
• new Rai; Series continued in Rai #25

RAI COMPANION Valiant

1 ❑ **NM** value: **1.00**
no cover price.

Other grades: Multiply prices above by **1.5 for Mint • 2/3 for Very Fine • 1/3 for Fine • 1/5 for Very Good • 1/8 for Good**

RAIDERS OF THE LOST ARK — Marvel

1 ❑ Sep 1981 Cover: 0.50 **NM** value: **2.00**
• **CGC:** 5 graded, best 9.6
A: John Buscema; Klaus Janson **W:** Walt Simonson

2 ❑ Oct 1981 Cover: 0.50 **NM** value: **2.00**
A: John Buscema; Klaus Janson **W:** Walt Simonson

3 ❑ Nov 1981 Cover: 0.50 **NM** value: **2.00**
A: John Buscema; Klaus Janson **W:** Walt Simonson

RAIDER 3000 — Gauntlet

1 ❑ b&w Cover: 2.95 **NM** value: **Cover or less**
🕮 Lethal Enforcement! **A:** Andrew James Kent **W:** Andrew James Kent

2 ❑ b&w Cover: 2.95 **NM** value: **Cover or less**
A: Andrew James Kent **W:** Andrew James Kent

RAIN — Tundra

1 ❑ Cover: 1.95 **NM** value: **Cover or less**
🕮 Moments In The Rain • Introduction by Stephen R. Bissette **A:** Rolf Stark **W:** Rolf Stark

2 ❑ Cover: 1.95 **NM** value: **Cover or less**
A: Rolf Stark **W:** Rolf Stark

3 ❑ Cover: 1.95 **NM** value: **Cover or less**
A: Rolf Stark **W:** Rolf Stark

4 ❑ Cover: 1.95 **NM** value: **Cover or less**
A: Rolf Stark **W:** Rolf Stark

5 ❑ Cover: 1.95 **NM** value: **Cover or less**
A: Rolf Stark **W:** Rolf Stark

6 ❑ Cover: 1.95 **NM** value: **Cover or less**
A: Rolf Stark **W:** Rolf Stark

RAINBOW BRITE AND THE STAR STEALER — DC

1 ❑ ca. 1985 Cover: 0.75 **NM** value: **1.00**
🕮 Rainbow Brite and the Star Stealer • Official movie adaption **A:** Jose Delbo; Willie Vander **W:** Bob Rozakis; Howard Cohen

RAK — Rak Graphics

1 ❑ b&w Cover: 5.00 **NM** value: **Cover or less**

RAKEHELL — Draculina

1 ❑ Cover: 2.50 **NM** value: **Cover or less**
A: Michael Shuter **W:** Michael Shuter

RALFY ROACH — Bugged Out

1 ❑ Jun 1993 Cover: 2.95 **NM** value: **Cover or less**
No issue number.

RALPH KINER, HOME RUN KING — Fawcett

1 ❑ ca. 1950 Cover: 0.10 **NM** value: **250.00**
• **CGC:** 3 graded, best 7.5

RALPH SNART ADVENTURES (VOL. 1) — Now

Ralph Snart is a man who has become completely fed up with modern society. After one of the worst days he has ever had, Snart makes a decision to go insane and to create his own adventures in his head. While locked in a padded cell, his "other self" goes on incredibly zany adventures.

In this three-issue mini-series, Snart becomes a space-freighter pilot, among other things. When the "other self" realizes that this conjured story is way too dull, he decides to dump his cargo and head straight for the nearest party world. The problem lies in the fact that the cargo is actually a gigantic space alien that wants to have Ralph for lunch. Snart spends the entire story trying to figure out how to defeat the monster, which he ultimately does, making him a hero...in his own mind.

This mini-series kicked off a plethora of Ralph Snart Adventures titles which would follow in the years to come.

1 ❑ Jun 1986 Cover: 1.00 **NM** value: **3.00**
A: Marc Hansen **W:** Marc Hansen ★ Origin of Ralph Snart. ★ 1st Appearance of Ralph Snart.

2 ❑ Jul 1986 Cover: 1.00 **NM** value: **2.00**
A: Marc Hansen **W:** Marc Hansen

3 ❑ Aug 1986 Cover: 1.00 **NM** value: **2.00**
A: Marc Hansen **W:** Marc Hansen

RALPH SNART ADVENTURES (VOL. 2) — Now

1 ❑ Nov 1986 Cover: 1.25 **NM** value: **2.00**
🕮 Ralph Snart: Derelict Bum! **A:** Marc Hansen **W:** Marc Hansen

2 ❑ Dec 1986 Cover: 1.25 **NM** value: **1.50**
A: Marc Hansen **W:** Marc Hansen

3 ❑ Jan 1987 Cover: 1.50 **NM** value: **Cover or less**
A: Marc Hansen **W:** Marc Hansen

4 ❑ Feb 1987 Cover: 1.50 **NM** value: **Cover or less**
A: Marc Hansen **W:** Marc Hansen

5 ❑ Mar 1987 Cover: 1.50 **NM** value: **Cover or less**
A: Marc Hansen **W:** Marc Hansen

6 ❑ Apr 1987 Cover: 1.50 **NM** value: **Cover or less**
A: Marc Hansen **W:** Marc Hansen

7 ❑ May 1987 Cover: 1.50 **NM** value: **Cover or less**
A: Marc Hansen **W:** Marc Hansen

8 ❑ Jun 1987 Cover: 1.50 **NM** value: **Cover or less**
A: Marc Hansen **W:** Marc Hansen

9 ❑ Jul 1987 Cover: 1.50 **NM** value: **Cover or less**
A: Marc Hansen **W:** Marc Hansen

RALPH SNART ADVENTURES (VOL. 3) — Now

1 ❑ Sep 1988 Cover: 1.75 **NM** value: **Cover or less**
Circ: CapCity orders: **1,625**
A: Marc Hansen **W:** Marc Hansen

1/3D ❑ Nov 1992 Cover: 2.95 **NM** value: **Cover or less**
• bagged with no cards **A:** Marc Hansen **W:** Marc Hansen

1/CS ❑ Nov 1992 Cover: 3.50 **NM** value: **Cover or less**
• 3-D. • bagged with 12 cards **A:** Marc Hansen **W:** Marc Hansen

2 ❑ Oct 1988 Cover: 1.75 **NM** value: **Cover or less**
Circ: CapCity orders: **1,475**
A: Marc Hansen **W:** Marc Hansen

3 ❑ Nov 1988 Cover: 1.75 **NM** value: **Cover or less**
Circ: CapCity orders: **1,575**
A: Marc Hansen **W:** Marc Hansen

4 ❑ Jan 1989 Cover: 1.75 **NM** value: **Cover or less**
Circ: CapCity orders: **1,600**
A: Marc Hansen **W:** Marc Hansen

5 ❑ Feb 1989 Cover: 1.75 **NM** value: **Cover or less**
Circ: CapCity orders: **1,700**
A: Marc Hansen **W:** Marc Hansen

6 ❑ Mar 1989 Cover: 1.75 **NM** value: **Cover or less**
Circ: CapCity orders: **1,875**
A: Marc Hansen **W:** Marc Hansen

7 ❑ Apr 1989 Cover: 1.75 **NM** value: **Cover or less**
Circ: CapCity orders: **1,875**
A: Marc Hansen **W:** Marc Hansen

8 ❑ May 1989 Cover: 1.75 **NM** value: **Cover or less**
Circ: CapCity orders: **1,925**
A: Marc Hansen **W:** Marc Hansen

9 ❑ Jun 1989 Cover: 1.75 **NM** value: **Cover or less**
Circ: CapCity orders: **2,150**
A: Marc Hansen **W:** Marc Hansen

10 ❑ Jul 1989 Cover: 1.75 **NM** value: **Cover or less**
Circ: CapCity orders: **2,325**
A: Marc Hansen **W:** Marc Hansen

11 ❑ Aug 1989 Cover: 1.75 **NM** value: **Cover or less**
Circ: CapCity orders: **2,200**
A: Marc Hansen **W:** Marc Hansen

12 ❑ Sep 1989 Cover: 1.75 **NM** value: **Cover or less**
Circ: CapCity orders: **2,325**
A: Marc Hansen **W:** Marc Hansen

13 ❑ Oct 1989 Cover: 1.75 **NM** value: **Cover or less**
Circ: CapCity orders: **2,375**
A: Marc Hansen **W:** Marc Hansen

14 ❑ Nov 1989 Cover: 1.75 **NM** value: **Cover or less**
Circ: CapCity orders: **2,575**
A: Marc Hansen **W:** Marc Hansen

15 ❑ Dec 1989 Cover: 1.75 **NM** value: **Cover or less**
Circ: CapCity orders: **2,600**
A: Marc Hansen **W:** Marc Hansen

16 ❑ Jan 1990 Cover: 1.75 **NM** value: **Cover or less**
Circ: CapCity orders: **2,600**
A: Marc Hansen **W:** Marc Hansen

17 ❑ Feb 1990 Cover: 1.75 **NM** value: **Cover or less**
Circ: CapCity orders: **2,675**
A: Marc Hansen **W:** Marc Hansen

18 ❑ Mar 1990 Cover: 1.75 **NM** value: **Cover or less**
Circ: CapCity orders: **2,750**
A: Marc Hansen **W:** Marc Hansen

19 ❑ Apr 1990 Cover: 1.75 **NM** value: **Cover or less**
Circ: CapCity orders: **2,775**
A: Marc Hansen **W:** Marc Hansen

20 ❑ May 1990 Cover: 1.75 **NM** value: **Cover or less**
Circ: CapCity orders: **2,800**
A: Marc Hansen **W:** Marc Hansen

21 ❑ Jun 1990 Cover: 1.75 **NM** value: **Cover or less**
Circ: CapCity orders: **2,675**
A: Marc Hansen **W:** Marc Hansen

22 ❑ Jul 1990 Cover: 1.75 **NM** value: **Cover or less**
Circ: CapCity orders: **2,800**
A: Marc Hansen **W:** Marc Hansen

23 ❑ Aug 1990 Cover: 1.75 **NM** value: **Cover or less**
Circ: CapCity orders: **2,775**
cover says May, indicia says Aug. **A:** Marc Hansen **W:** Marc Hansen

24 ❑ Sep 1990 Cover: 2.95 **NM** value: **Cover or less**
Circ: CapCity orders: **2,525**
• prestige format. 🕮 Three-Dimensional Ralph Snart • with glasses **A:** Marc Hansen **W:** Marc Hansen

25 ❑ Oct 1990 Cover: 1.75 **NM** value: **Cover or less**
Circ: CapCity orders: **2,750**
• The Early Years **A:** Marc Hansen **W:** Marc Hansen

26 ❑ Nov 1990 Cover: 1.75 **NM** value: **Cover or less**
Circ: CapCity orders: **2,700**
A: Marc Hansen **W:** Marc Hansen

Bk 1 ❑ Oct 1992 Cover: 7.95 **NM** value: **Cover or less**
• Trade Paperback. **A:** Marc Hansen **W:** Marc Hansen

Bk 2 ❑ Dec 1992 Cover: 7.95 **NM** value: **Cover or less**
• Trade Paperback. **A:** Marc Hansen **W:** Marc Hansen

RALPH SNART ADVENTURES (VOL. 4) — Now

1 ❑ May 1992 Cover: 2.50 **NM** value: **Cover or less**
2 ❑ Jun 1992 Cover: 2.50 **NM** value: **Cover or less**
3 ❑ Jul 1992 Cover: 2.50 **NM** value: **Cover or less**

RALPH SNART ADVENTURES (VOL. 5) — Now

1 ❑ Jul 1993 Cover: 2.50 **NM** value: **Cover or less**
2 ❑ Aug 1993 Cover: 2.50 **NM** value: **Cover or less**
3 ❑ Sep 1993 Cover: 2.50 **NM** value: **Cover or less**
4 ❑ Oct 1993 Cover: 2.50 **NM** value: **Cover or less**
5 ❑ Nov 1993 Cover: 2.50 **NM** value: **Cover or less**

RALPH SNART: THE LOST ISSUES — Now

1 ❑ Apr 1993 Cover: 2.50 **NM** value: **Cover or less**
2 ❑ May 1993 Cover: 2.50 **NM** value: **Cover or less**
3 ❑ Jun 1993 Cover: 2.50 **NM** value: **Cover or less**

RAMAR OF THE JUNGLE — Charlton

1 ❑ 1954 Cover: 0.10 **NM** value: **150.00**
2 ❑ 1955 Cover: 0.10 **NM** value: **100.00**
3 ❑ 1956 Cover: 0.10 **NM** value: **100.00**
4 ❑ 1956 Cover: 0.10 **NM** value: **100.00**
5 ❑ 1956 Cover: 0.10 **NM** value: **100.00**

RAMBA — Eros

1 ❑ **NM** value: **2.95**
2 ❑ **NM** value: **2.95**
3 ❑ **NM** value: **2.95**
4 ❑ **NM** value: **2.95**
5 ❑ **NM** value: **2.95**
6 ❑ **NM** value: **2.95**
7 ❑ **NM** value: **2.95**
8 ❑ Jun 1993 Cover: 2.95 **NM** value: **Cover or less**
🕮 A Deadly Shock **A:** Mauro Laurenti **W:** Rosano Rossi

RAMBLIN' DAWG — Edge

1 ❑ Jul 1994 Cover: 2.95 **NM** value: **Cover or less**

RAMBO — Blackthorne

1 ❑ Oct 1988, b&w Cover: 2.00 **NM** value: **Cover or less**

RAMBO III — Blackthorne

1 ❑ Cover: 2.00 **NM** value: **Cover or less**
A: Charlie Baldorado **W:** Bruce Jones

3D 1 ❑ Cover: 2.50 **NM** value: **Cover or less**
Circ: CapCity orders: **1,600**
A: Charlie Baldorado **W:** Bruce Jones

RAMM — Megaton

1 ❑ May 1987 Cover: 1.50 **NM** value: **Cover or less**
🕮 Rammifications **A:** Chris Ecker **W:** Lee A. Dolezal

2 ❑ Cover: 1.50 **NM** value: **Cover or less**

RAMPAGING HULK — Marvel

In an effort to capitalize on the popularity of The Incredible Hulk, which had achieved much greatness during Peter David's 12-year tenure as writer, Marvel launched this second Hulk title in 1998, with writer Glenn Greenberg and artist Rick Leonardi at the helm. Essentially an "Untold Tales" series, The Rampaging Hulk was set in the early years of the Green Goliath's career, when he was still in his savage, "Hulk smash" state of mind. An interesting idea with all the major supporting players of the day — General "Thunderbolt" Ross, Betty Ross Talbot, and Major Glenn Talbot — in place, but Marvel's financial woes, as well as the generally depressed condition of the comic-book marketplace, forced the cancellation of this promising new series with its seventh issue.

1 ❑ Aug 1998, b&w Cover: 1.99 **NM** value: **Cover or less**
Circ: Diamd. preorders: **64,259** • **CGC:** 1 graded, best 9.6
• Giant-size.

2 ❑ Sep 1998 Cover: 1.99 **NM** value: **Cover or less**
Circ: Diamd. preorders: **60,585**
• gatefold summary. ★ Origin of Ravage. ★ 1st Appearance of Ravage.

2/A ❑ Sep 1998 Cover: 1.99 **NM** value: **Cover or less**
variant cover. • gatefold summary.

3 ❑ Oct 1998 Cover: 1.99 **NM** value: **Cover or less**
Circ: Diamd. preorders: **42,324**
• gatefold summary. ★ Versus Ravage.

4 ❑ Nov 1998 Cover: 1.99 **NM** value: **Cover or less**
Circ: Diamd. preorders: **38,715**
• gatefold summary.

5 ❑ Dec 1998 Cover: 1.99 **NM** value: **Cover or less**
Circ: Diamd. preorders: **33,236**
• gatefold summary. ★ Versus Fantastic Four.

6 ❑ Jan 1999 Cover: 1.99 **NM** value: **Cover or less**
Circ: Diamd. preorders: **28,210**
• gatefold summary. final issue. ★ Versus Puma.

RAMPAGING HULK (MAGAZINE) — Marvel

1 ❑ Jan 1977, b&w Cover: 1.00 **NM** value: **6.50**
🕮 The Krylorian Conspiracy; Bloodstone • Bloodstone back-up **A:** Rick Leonardi; Denys Cowan **W:** Glenn Greenberg

2 ❑ Apr 1977 Cover: 1.00 **NM** value: **7.50**
🕮 And Then … the X-Men; Bloodstone: Scream, the Shrike! • Bloodstone back-up **A:** Alfredo Alcala; Walt Simonson **W:** Doug Moench ★ Origin of the X-Men.

3 ❑ Jun 1977 Cover: 1.00 **NM** value: **3.50**
🕮 The Monster and The Metal Master; Bloodstone: And There Shall Come Death! • Bloodstone/Iron Man back-up story **A:** Alfredo Alcala; Walt Simonson **W:** Doug Moench; John Warner

4 ❑ Aug 1977 Cover: 1.00 **NM** value: **3.50**
🕮 The Other Side of Night; Bloodstone: Return from Oblivion • Bloodstone/Iron Man back-up story ★ 1st Appearance of Exo-Mind.

5 ❑ Oct 1977 Cover: 1.00 **NM** value: **3.50**
🕮 Lo, The Sub-Mariner Strikes; Bloodstone: Suite Fear • Bloodstone back-up **A:** Keith Pollard; Alfredo Alcala **W:** Doug Moench ★ Appearance of Sub-Mariner.

6 ❑ Dec 1977 Cover: 1.00 **NM** value: **3.00**
🕮 And All the Sea With Monsters; Bloodstone: Suite Fear • Bloodstone back-up

7 ❑ Feb 1978 Cover: 1.00 **NM** value: **3.00**
🕮 Night of the Wraith; Man-Thing: Beyond the Great Divide • Man-Thing back-up **A:** Keith Pollard; Jim Mooney **W:** Doug Moench ★ Appearance of Man-Thing.

8 ❑ Apr 1978 Cover: 1.00 **NM** value: **3.00**

CGC-graded: Multiply prices above by **33 for 9.9 M • 16 for 9.8 NM/M • 7 for 9.6 NM+ • 5 for 9.4 NM • 2.5 for 9.2 NM- • 1.5 for 9.0 VF/NM**

A Gathering of Doom; Bloodstone: Earth Shall Have a New Master • Bloodstone back-up **A:** Herb Trimpe; Alfredo Alcala **W:** Doug Moench ★ Appearance of Avengers.
9 ❑ Jun 1978 Cover: 1.00 **NM** value: **3.00**
To Avenge the Earth; Shanna: The Wrath of Raga-Shah • Shanna back-up
10 ❑ Cover: 1.00 **NM** value: **3.00**
Thunder at Dawn; The Runaway and the Rescuer • Color issue; renamed The Hulk!; has Bill Bixby interview

RANA 7 — NGNG
1 ❑ Cover: 2.95 **NM** value: **Cover or less**
2 ❑ Cover: 2.95 **NM** value: **Cover or less**
3 ❑ Cover: 2.95 **NM** value: **Cover or less**
4 ❑ Cover: 2.95 **NM** value: **Cover or less**

RANA 7: WARRIORS OF VENGEANCE — NGNG Studios
1 ❑ Dec 1995 Cover: 2.50 **NM** value: **Cover or less**
Warriors of Vengeance, Part 1 **A:** Ovi Hondru **W:** Glen Sica
2 ❑ Mar 1996 Cover: 2.50 **NM** value: **Cover or less**
Warriors of Vengeance, Part 2 **A:** Ovi Hondru **W:** Glen Sica

RANGE BUSTERS — Charlton
8 ❑ May 1955 Cover: 0.10 **NM** value: **50.00**
9 ❑ Jul 1955 Cover: 0.10 **NM** value: **30.00**
10 ❑ Sep 1955 Cover: 0.10 **NM** value: **30.00**

RANGELAND LOVE — Atlas
1 ❑ Dec 1949 Cover: 0.10 **NM** value: **100.00**
2 ❑ Mar 1950 Cover: 0.10 **NM** value: **100.00**

RANGE ROMANCES — Quality
1 ❑ Dec 1949 Cover: 0.10 **NM** value: **150.00**
2 ❑ Feb 1950 Cover: 0.10 **NM** value: **150.00**
3 ❑ Apr 1950 Cover: 0.10 **NM** value: **100.00**
4 ❑ Jun 1950 Cover: 0.10 **NM** value: **100.00**
5 ❑ Aug 1950 Cover: 0.10 **NM** value: **100.00**

RANGERS COMICS — Fiction House
1 ❑ Oct 1941 Cover: 0.10 **NM** value: **1500.00**
• **CGC:** 4 graded, best 9.6
2 ❑ Dec 1941 Cover: 0.10 **NM** value: **600.00**
3 ❑ Feb 1942 Cover: 0.10 **NM** value: **500.00**
• **CGC:** 2 graded, best 8.0
4 ❑ Apr 1942 Cover: 0.10 **NM** value: **400.00**
• **CGC:** 1 graded, best 9.2
5 ❑ Jun 1942 Cover: 0.10 **NM** value: **400.00**
6 ❑ Aug 1942 Cover: 0.10 **NM** value: **350.00**
7 ❑ Oct 1942 Cover: 0.10 **NM** value: **350.00**
• **CGC:** 1 graded, best 8.5
8 ❑ Dec 1942 Cover: 0.10 **NM** value: **350.00**
• **CGC:** 1 graded, best 7.0
9 ❑ Feb 1943 Cover: 0.10 **NM** value: **350.00**
• **CGC:** 2 graded, best 9.0
10 ❑ Apr 1943 Cover: 0.10 **NM** value: **350.00**
• **CGC:** 1 graded, best 5.5
11 ❑ Jun 1943 Cover: 0.10 **NM** value: **350.00**
• **CGC:** 1 graded, best 6.5
12 ❑ Aug 1943 Cover: 0.10 **NM** value: **350.00**
• **CGC:** 1 graded, best 7.5
13 ❑ Oct 1943 Cover: 0.10 **NM** value: **300.00**
14 ❑ Dec 1943 Cover: 0.10 **NM** value: **300.00**
• **CGC:** 1 graded, best 8.5
15 ❑ Feb 1944 Cover: 0.10 **NM** value: **300.00**
16 ❑ Apr 1944 Cover: 0.10 **NM** value: **300.00**
17 ❑ Jun 1944 Cover: 0.10 **NM** value: **300.00**
18 ❑ Aug 1944 Cover: 0.10 **NM** value: **300.00**
19 ❑ Oct 1944 Cover: 0.10 **NM** value: **300.00**
20 ❑ Dec 1944 Cover: 0.10 **NM** value: **250.00**
21 ❑ Feb 1945 Cover: 0.10 **NM** value: **250.00**
• **CGC:** 3 graded, best 8.0
22 ❑ Apr 1945 Cover: 0.10 **NM** value: **250.00**
23 ❑ Jun 1945 Cover: 0.10 **NM** value: **250.00**
24 ❑ Aug 1945 Cover: 0.10 **NM** value: **250.00**
• **CGC:** 1 graded, best 8.5
25 ❑ Oct 1945 Cover: 0.10 **NM** value: **200.00**
26 ❑ Dec 1945 Cover: 0.10 **NM** value: **200.00**
27 ❑ Feb 1946 Cover: 0.10 **NM** value: **200.00**
28 ❑ Apr 1946 Cover: 0.10 **NM** value: **200.00**
• **CGC:** 1 graded, best 7.0
29 ❑ Jun 1946 Cover: 0.10 **NM** value: **200.00**
• **CGC:** 1 graded, best 9.0
30 ❑ Aug 1946 Cover: 0.10 **NM** value: **150.00**
• **CGC:** 1 graded, best 8.0
31 ❑ Oct 1946 Cover: 0.10 **NM** value: **150.00**
• **CGC:** 2 graded, best 9.2
32 ❑ Dec 1946 Cover: 0.10 **NM** value: **150.00**
• **CGC:** 2 graded, best 8.0
33 ❑ Feb 1947 Cover: 0.10 **NM** value: **150.00**
• **CGC:** 1 graded, best 9.2
34 ❑ Apr 1947 Cover: 0.10 **NM** value: **150.00**
35 ❑ Jun 1947 Cover: 0.10 **NM** value: **150.00**
• **CGC:** 2 graded, best 8.5
36 ❑ Aug 1947 Cover: 0.10 **NM** value: **150.00**
• **CGC:** 3 graded, best 9.2
37 ❑ Oct 1947 Cover: 0.10 **NM** value: **150.00**
• **CGC:** 2 graded, best 7.5
38 ❑ Dec 1947 Cover: 0.10 **NM** value: **150.00**
• **CGC:** 2 graded, best 8.5
39 ❑ Feb 1948 Cover: 0.10 **NM** value: **150.00**
• **CGC:** 2 graded, best 9.0
40 ❑ Apr 1948 Cover: 0.10 **NM** value: **100.00**
• **CGC:** 1 graded, best 8.5
41 ❑ Jun 1948 Cover: 0.10 **NM** value: **100.00**
• **CGC:** 1 graded, best 9.4
42 ❑ Aug 1948 Cover: 0.10 **NM** value: **100.00**
• **CGC:** 1 graded, best 9.0
43 ❑ Oct 1948 Cover: 0.10 **NM** value: **100.00**
44 ❑ Dec 1948 Cover: 0.10 **NM** value: **100.00**
45 ❑ Feb 1949 Cover: 0.10 **NM** value: **100.00**
46 ❑ Apr 1949 Cover: 0.10 **NM** value: **100.00**
47 ❑ Jun 1949 Cover: 0.10 **NM** value: **100.00**
48 ❑ Aug 1949 Cover: 0.10 **NM** value: **100.00**
49 ❑ Oct 1949 Cover: 0.10 **NM** value: **100.00**
• **CGC:** 1 graded, best 9.2
50 ❑ Dec 1949 Cover: 0.10 **NM** value: **100.00**
51 ❑ Feb 1950 Cover: 0.10 **NM** value: **100.00**
52 ❑ Apr 1950 Cover: 0.10 **NM** value: **100.00**
53 ❑ Jun 1950 Cover: 0.10 **NM** value: **100.00**
54 ❑ Aug 1950 Cover: 0.10 **NM** value: **100.00**
55 ❑ Oct 1950 Cover: 0.10 **NM** value: **100.00**
56 ❑ Dec 1950 Cover: 0.10 **NM** value: **100.00**
57 ❑ Feb 1951 Cover: 0.10 **NM** value: **100.00**
58 ❑ Apr 1951 Cover: 0.10 **NM** value: **100.00**
• **CGC:** 1 graded, best 7.5
59 ❑ Jun 1951 Cover: 0.10 **NM** value: **100.00**
60 ❑ Aug 1951 Cover: 0.10 **NM** value: **75.00**
61 ❑ Oct 1951 Cover: 0.10 **NM** value: **75.00**
62 ❑ Dec 1951 Cover: 0.10 **NM** value: **75.00**
63 ❑ Feb 1952 Cover: 0.10 **NM** value: **75.00**
64 ❑ Apr 1952 Cover: 0.10 **NM** value: **75.00**
65 ❑ Jun 1952 Cover: 0.10 **NM** value: **75.00**
• **CGC:** 2 graded, best 9.2
66 ❑ Aug 1952 Cover: 0.10 **NM** value: **75.00**
67 ❑ Oct 1952 Cover: 0.10 **NM** value: **75.00**
68 ❑ Fal 1952 Cover: 0.10 **NM** value: **75.00**
69 ❑ Win 1952 Cover: 0.10 **NM** value: **75.00**
• **CGC:** 1 graded, best 6.5

RANK & STINKY — Parody Press
1 ❑ b&w Cover: 2.50 **NM** value: **Cover or less**
A: Bill Maus **W:** Don Chin; Nat Gertler
1-2 ❑ Cover: 2.50 **NM** value: **Cover or less**
• Rank & Stinky Eencore Eedition. **A:** Bill Maus **W:** Don Chin; Nat Gertler
SE 1 ❑ b&w Cover: 2.75 **NM** value: **Cover or less**

RANMA 1/2 — Viz
When Ranma Saotome and his father, Genma, don't listen to their guide's warning about the cursed training ground of Ten Thousand Lakes, they learn that the curse is all too real. When doused with cold water, Ranma becomes a chesty young woman and Genma turns into a panda. Hot water reverses the effect-but only until the next time.

So begins a hilarious romp of mistaken identity and gender-bending when Ranma learns that his father has engaged him to a daughter of his friend Soun Tendo in order to carry on the Tendo Martial Arts School. Katsumi and Nabiki don't like the idea, until they decide that tomboy Akane can have him!

Rumiko Takahashi is widely renowned both in Japan and the United States for her brilliant storytelling skills in manga and anime. She has also written Lum Urusei-Yatsura and Mermaid Forest.

1 ❑ ca. 1991 Cover: 4.95 **NM** value: **25.00**
Circ: CapCity orders: **3,675** • **CGC:** 4 graded, best 9.8
Here's Ranma; Ranma's Secret • Comic in color **A:** Rumiko Takahashi **W:** Rumiko Takahashi ★ 1st Appearance of Kasumi Tendo, Nabiki, and Soun Tendo.
2 ❑ ca. 1991 Cover: 4.95 **NM** value: **10.00**
Circ: CapCity orders: **3,100** • **CGC:** 1 graded, best 9.4
I Hate Men; Never, Never, Never **A:** Rumiko Takahashi **W:** Rumiko Takahashi ★ 2nd Appearance of Kasumi Tendo, and Ranma Saotome (as girl).
3 ❑ ca. 1991 Cover: 4.95 **NM** value: **8.00**
• **CGC:** 1 graded, best 9.6
To the Tree-Borne Kettle-Girl; Body and Soul **A:** Rumiko Takahashi **W:** Rumiko Takahashi
4 ❑ ca. 1991 Cover: 2.95 **NM** value: **6.00**
Circ: CapCity orders: **3,075**
You'll Understand Soon Enough; Because There's a Girl He Likes • Comics become B&W **A:** Rumiko Takahashi **W:** Rumiko Takahashi ★ 2nd Appearance of Dr. Tofu, Tatewaki Kuno, Ranma Saotome, Nabiki Tendo, and Akane Tendo.
5 ❑ ca. 1991 Cover: 2.95 **NM** value: **6.00**
Circ: CapCity orders: **3,075**
You're Cute When You Smile; The Hunter **A:** Rumiko Takahashi **W:** Rumiko Takahashi ★ Appearance of Ranma Saotome.
6 ❑ ca. 1991 Cover: 2.95 **NM** value: **5.00**
Circ: CapCity orders: **3,225**
Bread Feud; Showdown **A:** Rumiko Takahashi **W:** Rumiko Takahashi ★ Origin of Ryoga Hibiki. ★ 2nd Appearance of Ryoga Hibiki. ★ Appearance of Kasumi Tendo, Ranma Saotome, Nabiki Tendo, and Akane Tendo.
7 ❑ ca. 1991 Cover: 2.95 **NM** value: **5.00**
Circ: CapCity orders: **3,350**
A Bad Cut; Who Says You're Cute **A:** Rumiko Takahashi **W:** Rumiko Takahashi ★ Appearance of Ranma Saotome, Ryoga Hibiki, and Akane Tendo.

RANMA 1/2 PART 2 — Viz
1 ❑ Jan 1992 Cover: 2.95 **NM** value: **7.00**
Circ: CapCity orders: **4,025**
The Transformation of Ryoga; He's Got a Beef **A:** Rumiko Takahashi **W:** Rumiko Takahashi ★ 1st Appearance of Ranma Saotome. ★ Appearance of Genma Saotome, and Ryoga Hibiki.
2 ❑ Feb 1992 Cover: 2.95 **NM** value: **5.00**
Circ: CapCity orders: **3,800**
Kodachi, the Black Rose; The Love of the Black Rose **A:** Rumiko Takahashi **W:** Rumiko Takahashi
3 ❑ Mar 1992 Cover: 2.95 **NM** value: **4.00**
Circ: CapCity orders: **3,750**
Take Care of My Sister; I'll See That You Lose **A:** Rumiko Takahashi **W:** Rumiko Takahashi ★ Appearance of Akane Tendo.
4 ❑ Apr 1992 Cover: 2.95 **NM** value: **4.00**
Circ: CapCity orders: **3,875**
Hot Competition; I Give Up **A:** Rumiko Takahashi **W:** Rumiko Takahashi
5 ❑ May 1992 Cover: 2.95 **NM** value: **4.00**
Circ: CapCity orders: **3,800**
Darling Charlotte; A Kiss in the Rink **A:** Rumiko Takahashi **W:** Rumiko Takahashi ★ 1st Appearance of Azusa Shiratori. ★ Appearance of P-chan, Akane Tendo.
6 ❑ Jun 1992 Cover: 2.95 **NM** value: **3.50**
Circ: CapCity orders: **4,025**
Lips at a Loss; Lips at War **A:** Rumiko Takahashi **W:** Rumiko Takahashi
7 ❑ Jul 1992 Cover: 2.95 **NM** value: **3.50**
Circ: CapCity orders: **3,850**
I'll Never Let Go; Burning the Bridges **A:** Rumiko Takahashi **W:** Rumiko Takahashi
8 ❑ Aug 1992 Cover: 2.95 **NM** value: **3.50**
Circ: CapCity orders: **3,900**
Ryoga Explodes!; The Waters of Love **A:** Rumiko Takahashi **W:** Rumiko Takahashi ★ 1st Appearance of Shampoo.
9 ❑ Sep 1992 Cover: 2.95 **NM** value: **3.50**
Circ: CapCity orders: **4,000**
Kiss of Death; You I Love **A:** Rumiko Takahashi **W:** Rumiko Takahashi ★ Origin of Shampoo. ★ 2nd Appearance of Shampoo.
10 ❑ Oct 1992 Cover: 2.95 **NM** value: **3.50**
Circ: CapCity orders: **3,925**
Akane Gets Shampooed; Shampoo Cleans Up **A:** Rumiko Takahashi **W:** Rumiko Takahashi
11 ❑ Nov 1992 Cover: 2.75 **NM** value: **3.50**
Circ: CapCity orders: **3,825**
Formula #911; Bie Liao (Goodbye) **A:** Rumiko Takahashi **W:** Rumiko Takahashi

RANMA 1/2 PART 3 — Viz
1 ❑ Dec 1992 Cover: 2.75ñ **NM** value: **3.00**
Circ: CapCity orders: **4,750**
Looking for a Weak Spot; Weak Spot – Found! **A:** Rumiko Takahashi **W:** Rumiko Takahashi ★ 1st Appearance of Hikaru Gosunkugi. ★ Appearance of Akane Tendo.
2 ❑ Jan 1993 Cover: 2.75 **NM** value: **3.00**
Circ: CapCity orders: **4,175**
Cat Hell; Cat-Fu **A:** Rumiko Takahashi **W:** Rumiko Takahashi ★ 2nd Appearance of Hikaru Gosunkugi. ★ Appearance of Tatewaki Kuno.
3 ❑ Feb 1993 Cover: 2.75 **NM** value: **3.00**
Circ: CapCity orders: **4,100**
You'd Have Kissed Anybody?; Shampoo Rides Again **A:** Rumiko Takahashi **W:** Rumiko Takahashi ★ Appearance of Dr. Tofu, Tatewaki Kuno, Gosunkugi, Ryouga Hibiki, Genma Saotome, and Akane Tendo.
4 ❑ Mar 1993 Cover: 2.75 **NM** value: **3.00**
Circ: CapCity orders: **4,275**
Attack of the Wild Mousse; The Martial Arts Magic Show **A:** Rumiko Takahashi **W:** Rumiko Takahashi
5 ❑ Apr 1993 Cover: 2.75 **NM** value: **3.00**
Circ: CapCity orders: **4,625**
Cat's Tongue Got You?; The Phoenix Pill **A:** Rumiko Takahashi **W:** Rumiko Takahashi ★ 2nd Appearance of Mousse.
6 ❑ May 1993 Cover: 2.75 **NM** value: **3.00**
Circ: CapCity orders: **5,075**
All's Fair at the Fair; War of the Melons **A:** Rumiko Takahashi **W:** Rumiko Takahashi ★ Appearance of Soun Tendo.
7 ❑ Jun 1993 Cover: 2.75 **NM** value: **3.00**
Circ: CapCity orders: **5,450**
Naval Engagement; Kitten of the Sea **A:** Rumiko Takahashi **W:** Rumiko Takahashi ★ Appearance of Akane Tendo, and Cologne.
8 ❑ Jul 1993 Cover: 2.75 **NM** value: **3.00**
Circ: CapCity orders: **5,325**
Care to Join Me?; Training Meals **A:** Rumiko Takahashi **W:** Rumiko Takahashi
9 ❑ Aug 1993 Cover: 2.75 **NM** value: **3.00**
Circ: CapCity orders: **5,475**
The Breaking Point; The Immortal Man **A:** Rumiko Takahashi **W:** Rumiko Takahashi ★ Appearance of Ryoga Hibiki, Akane Tendo, and Cologne.
10 ❑ Sep 1993 Cover: 2.75 **NM** value: **3.00**
Circ: CapCity orders: **5,400**
Fast Break; The Way of Tea **A:** Rumiko Takahashi **W:** Rumiko Takahashi ★ Appearance of Ryoga Hibiki, Akane Tendo, and Cologne.
11 ❑ Oct 1993 Cover: 2.75 **NM** value: **3.00**
Circ: CapCity orders: **5,500**
Meet Miss Satsuki; Proposal Accepted **A:** Rumiko Takahashi **W:** Rumiko Takahashi ★ 2nd Appearance of Sentaro. ★ Appearance of Akane Tendo.
12 ❑ Nov 1993 Cover: 2.75 **NM** value: **3.00**
Circ: CapCity orders: **5,425**
It's Fast or It's Free; Eyes on the Prize **A:** Rumiko Takahashi **W:** Rumiko Takahashi ★ Appearance of Kasumi Tendo, P-chan, Tatewaki Kuno, Soun Tendo, and Akane Tendo.
13 ❑ Dec 1993 Cover: 2.75 **NM** value: **3.00**
Circ: CapCity orders: **5,350**
Noodles, Anyone?; I Won't Eat It! **A:** Rumiko Takahashi **W:** Rumiko Takahashi ★ Appearance of Tatewaki Kuno, Shampoo, Akane Tendo, and Cologne.

RANMA 1/2 PART 4 — Viz
1 ❑ Jan 1994 Cover: 2.75 **NM** value: **3.00**
Circ: CapCity orders: **5,400**

Other grades: Multiply prices above by **1.5 for Mint • 2/3 for Very Fine • 1/3 for Fine • 1/5 for Very Good • 1/8 for Good**

📖 The Evil Wakes; He's Something Else **A:** Rumiko Takahashi **W:** Rumiko Takahashi ★ 1st Appearance of Happosai, Soun Tendo, Genma Saotome, Akane Tendo.
2 ❑ Feb 1994 Cover: 2.75 **NM** value: **3.00**
Circ: CapCity orders: **5,050**
📖 Bathhouse Battle; Moonlight Serenade **A:** Rumiko Takahashi **W:** Rumiko Takahashi ★ Appearance of Kasumi Tendo.
3 ❑ Mar 1994 Cover: 2.75 **NM** value: **3.00**
Circ: CapCity orders: **5,150**
📖 The Wrath of Happosai; The Scent of a Woman **A:** Rumiko Takahashi **W:** Rumiko Takahashi ★ Appearance of Kasumi Tendo.
4 ❑ Apr 1994 Cover: 2.75 **NM** value: **3.00**
Circ: CapCity orders: **5,000**
📖 Fathers Know Best; Instant Spring **A:** Rumiko Takahashi **W:** Rumiko Takahashi ★ Appearance of Happosai, and Akane Tendo.
5 ❑ May 1994 Cover: 2.75 **NM** value: **3.00**
Circ: CapCity orders: **5,025**
📖 No Need for Ranma; The Destroyer Strikes **A:** Rumiko Takahashi **W:** Rumiko Takahashi ★ Appearance of Soun Tendo, and Shampoo.
6 ❑ Jun 1994 Cover: 2.75 **NM** value: **3.00**
Circ: CapCity orders: **5,225**
📖 Just One More Kiss; Wherefore Art Thou, Romeo? **A:** Rumiko Takahashi **W:** Rumiko Takahashi ★ 2nd Appearance of Dojo Destroyer.★ Appearance of Shampoo.
7 ❑ Jul 1994 Cover: 2.75 **NM** value: **3.00**
Circ: CapCity orders: **5,325**
📖 Romeo? Romeo? Romeo?; Not Your Typical Juliet **A:** Rumiko Takahashi **W:** Rumiko Takahashi ★ Appearance of Akane Tendo.
8 ❑ Aug 1994 Cover: 2.75 **NM** value: **3.00**
Circ: CapCity orders: **5,000**
📖 A Kiss to the Victor; Quest for the Hidden Spring **A:** Rumiko Takahashi **W:** Rumiko Takahashi ★ Appearance of Tatewaki Kuno, Hikaru Gosunkugi, Soun Tendo, Genma Saotome, and Akane Tendo.
9 ❑ Sep 1994 Cover: 2.75 **NM** value: **3.00**
Circ: CapCity orders: **4,725**
📖 The Trouble with Girls' Locker Rooms; From the Spring, Springs a Message **A:** Rumiko Takahashi **W:** Rumiko Takahashi ★ Appearance of Kasumi Tendo, P-chan, Happosai, Ryoga Hibiki, and Akane Tendo.
10 ❑ Oct 1994 Cover: 2.75 **NM** value: **3.00**
📖 The Way the Cookie Crumbles; Negative Feelings **A:** Rumiko Takahashi **W:** Rumiko Takahashi ★ Appearance of Kodachi Kuno.
11 ❑ Nov 1994 Cover: 2.75 **NM** value: **3.00**
📖 Take Me Out to the Bathtub; …I Ate the Whole Thing **A:** Rumiko Takahashi **W:** Rumiko Takahashi ★ Appearance of Kodachi Kuno, Kasumi Tendo, Genma Saotome, and Akane Tendo.

RANMA 1/2 PART 5 — Viz

1 ❑ Dec 1994 Cover: 2.75 **NM** value: **3.00**
📖 Okonomiyaki Means "I Love You"; Saucy Reply **A:** Rumiko Takahashi **W:** Rumiko Takahashi ★ 1st Appearance of Ukyo Kuonji.
2 ❑ Jan 1995 Cover: 2.95 **NM** value: **3.00**
📖 Ukyo's Secret; Ryoga vs. Ukyo **A:** Rumiko Takahashi **W:** Rumiko Takahashi ★ Appearance of Genma Saotome, Akane Tendo.
3 ❑ Feb 1995 Cover: 2.95 **NM** value: **3.00**
📖 Love Letters in the Sauce; Ryoga's What!? **A:** Rumiko Takahashi **W:** Rumiko Takahashi ★ Appearance of Ukyo Kuonji, and Akane Tendo.
4 ❑ Mar 1995 Cover: 2.95 **NM** value: **3.00**
📖 At Long Last…The Date!; Happosai Days Are Here Again **A:** Rumiko Takahashi **W:** Rumiko Takahashi ★ Appearance of Kasumi Tendo, Ukyo Kuonji, Soun Tendo, Ryoga Hibiki, and Akane Tendo.
5 ❑ Apr 1995 Cover: 2.95 **NM** value: **3.00**
📖 One Moment to Love; I Won't Fall in Love! **A:** Rumiko Takahashi **W:** Rumiko Takahashi ★ Appearance of Shampoo.
6 ❑ May 1995 Cover: 2.95 **NM** value: **3.00**
📖 The Abduction of…Akane?; Duck, Ranma, Duck! **A:** Rumiko Takahashi **W:** Rumiko Takahashi ★ 1st Appearance of Mousse (as duck). ★ Appearance of Kasumi Tendo, Shampoo, Mousse, and Akane Tendo.
7 ❑ Jun 1995 Cover: 2.95 **NM** value: **3.00**
📖 Akane Becomes a Duck; Fowl Play **A:** Rumiko Takahashi **W:** Rumiko Takahashi
8 ❑ Jul 1995 Cover: 2.95 **NM** value: **3.00**
📖 The Happiest Mousse; Tsubasa Kurenai Busts Loose! **A:** Rumiko Takahashi **W:** Rumiko Takahashi
9 ❑ Aug 1995 Cover: 2.95 **NM** value: **3.00**
📖 Lunchtime Lunacy; The Perfect Match **A:** Rumiko Takahashi **W:** Rumiko Takahashi ★ 2nd Appearance of Tsubasa Kurenai. ★ Appearance of Ukyo Kuonji.
10 ❑ Sep 1995 Cover: 2.95 **NM** value: **3.00**
Circ: Diamd. preorders: **12,758**
📖 Ryoga, Come Home; Oh, Brother! **A:** Rumiko Takahashi **W:** Rumiko Takahashi ★ Appearance of Kasumi Tendo.
11 ❑ Oct 1995 Cover: 2.75 **NM** value: **3.00**
Circ: Diamd. preorders: **12,868**
📖 Get Lost, Yoiko!; The Ultimate Technique **A:** Rumiko Takahashi **W:** Rumiko Takahashi ★ 2nd Appearance of Checkers Hibiki. ★ Appearance of Ryouga Hibiki.
12 ❑ Nov 1995 Cover: 2.75 **NM** value: **3.00**
Circ: Diamd. preorders: **12,674**
📖 Get The Secret Scroll!; The Fire-Burst of Terror! **A:** Rumiko Takahashi **W:** Rumiko Takahashi

RANMA 1/2 PART 6 — Viz

1 ❑ Dec 1996 Cover: 2.95 **NM** value: **Cover or less**
Circ: Diamd. preorders: **13,298**
📖 Embraceable You; Hold Me Close **A:** Rumiko Takahashi **W:** Rumiko Takahashi ★ Appearance of Tatewaki Kuno, Shampoo, and Akane Tendo.
2 ❑ Jan 1997 Cover: 2.95 **NM** value: **Cover or less**
Circ: Diamd. preorders: **12,568**
📖 Akane's Power-Up!; Super Badminton **A:** Rumiko Takahashi **W:** Rumiko Takahashi
3 ❑ Feb 1997 Cover: 2.95 **NM** value: **Cover or less**
Circ: Diamd. preorders: **11,825**
📖 Serious Side Effects; The Return of the Principal **A:** Rumiko Takahashi **W:** Rumiko Takahashi
4 ❑ Mar 1997 Cover: 2.95 **NM** value: **Cover or less**
Circ: Diamd. preorders: **11,822**
📖 Journey into the Principal's Office; The Principal of the Thing **A:** Rumiko Takahashi **W:** Rumiko Takahashi ★ 2nd Appearance of Principal Kuno. ★ Appearance of Tatewaki Kuno, and Akane Tendo.
5 ❑ Apr 1997 Cover: 2.95 **NM** value: **Cover or less**
Circ: Diamd. preorders: **12,056**
📖 One Hairy Day; Shear Folly **A:** Rumiko Takahashi **W:** Rumiko Takahashi ★ Appearance of Tatewaki Kuno, Principal Kuno, and Akane Tendo.
6 ❑ May 1997 Cover: 2.95 **NM** value: **Cover or less**
Circ: Diamd. preorders: **11,456**
📖 Gonna Make You Tardy!; The Soap of Happiness **A:** Rumiko Takahashi **W:** Rumiko Takahashi
7 ❑ Jun 1997 Cover: 2.95 **NM** value: **Cover or less**
Circ: Diamd. preorders: **11,516**
📖 Cupids, Draw Back Your Bow; Don't Follow Me **A:** Rumiko Takahashi **W:** Rumiko Takahashi ★ Appearance of Ryoga Hibiki.
8 ❑ Jul 1997 Cover: 2.95 **NM** value: **Cover or less**
Circ: Diamd. preorders: **11,567**
A: Rumiko Takahashi **W:** Rumiko Takahashi
9 ❑ Aug 1997 Cover: 2.95 **NM** value: **Cover or less**
Circ: Diamd. preorders: **11,401**
📖 The Legendary Moxibustion of Evil; The World's Weakest Man **A:** Rumiko Takahashi **W:** Rumiko Takahashi ★ Appearance of Happosai, Soun Tendo, Genma Saotome, and Akane Tendo.
10 ❑ Sep 1997 Cover: 2.95 **NM** value: **Cover or less**
Circ: Diamd. preorders: **11,179**
📖 Weak for Life?; The Valley of Moxibustion **A:** Rumiko Takahashi **W:** Rumiko Takahashi ★ Appearance of Mousse, and Cologne.
11 ❑ Oct 1997 Cover: 2.95 **NM** value: **Cover or less**
Circ: Diamd. preorders: **11,642**
📖 Training in the Spiral of Hell; The Inflammable Man **A:** Rumiko Takahashi **W:** Rumiko Takahashi ★ Appearance of Ukyo Kuonji, Genma Saotome, Ryoga Hibiki, Akane Tendo, and Cologne.
12 ❑ Nov 1997 Cover: 2.95 **NM** value: **Cover or less**
Circ: Diamd. preorders: **11,475**
📖 The Roar of Heaven; The Great Rematch **A:** Rumiko Takahashi **W:** Rumiko Takahashi ★ Appearance of Ukyo Kuonji, Happosai, Genma Saotome, Ryoga Hibiki, Akane Tendo, and Cologne.
13 ❑ Dec 1997 Cover: 2.95 **NM** value: **Cover or less**
Circ: Diamd. preorders: **11,317**
📖 St. Happosai; Burn, Happy, Burn! **A:** Rumiko Takahashi **W:** Rumiko Takahashi ★ Appearance of Happosai, Genma Saotome, Akane Tendo, and Cologne.
14 ❑ Jan 1998 Cover: 2.95 **NM** value: **Cover or less**
Circ: Diamd. preorders: **11,134**
📖 The Paper Chase; Ranma Reborn **A:** Rumiko Takahashi **W:** Rumiko Takahashi ★ Appearance of Ukyo Kuonji, Ryoga Hibiki, and Cologne.

RANMA 1/2 PART 7 — Viz

1 ❑ Feb 1998 Cover: 2.95 **NM** value: **Cover or less**
Circ: Diamd. preorders: **10,901**
📖 Who Will Bell the Cat?; Kitty Takes a Bride **A:** Rumiko Takahashi **W:** Rumiko Takahashi ★ Appearance of Akane Tendo.
2 ❑ Mar 1998 Cover: 2.95 **NM** value: **Cover or less**
Circ: Diamd. preorders: **10,978**
📖 Swim Like a Hammer; Courage Under Water **A:** Rumiko Takahashi **W:** Rumiko Takahashi
3 ❑ Apr 1998 Cover: 2.95 **NM** value: **Cover or less**
Circ: Diamd. preorders: **11,053**
📖 Step Outside!; The Mark of the Gods **A:** Rumiko Takahashi **W:** Rumiko Takahashi
4 ❑ May 1998 Cover: 2.95 **NM** value: **Cover or less**
Circ: Diamd. preorders: **10,675**
A: Rumiko Takahashi **W:** Rumiko Takahashi
5 ❑ Jun 1998 Cover: 2.95 **NM** value: **Cover or less**
Circ: Diamd. preorders: **10,841**
A: Rumiko Takahashi **W:** Rumiko Takahashi
6 ❑ Jul 1998 Cover: 2.95 **NM** value: **Cover or less**
Circ: Diamd. preorders: **10,259**
A: Rumiko Takahashi **W:** Rumiko Takahashi
7 ❑ Aug 1998 Cover: 2.95 **NM** value: **Cover or less**
Circ: Diamd. preorders: **10,078**
A: Rumiko Takahashi **W:** Rumiko Takahashi
8 ❑ Sep 1998 Cover: 2.95 **NM** value: **Cover or less**
Circ: Diamd. preorders: **9,861**
A: Rumiko Takahashi **W:** Rumiko Takahashi
9 ❑ Oct 1998 Cover: 2.95 **NM** value: **Cover or less**
Circ: Diamd. preorders: **10,032**
A: Rumiko Takahashi **W:** Rumiko Takahashi
10 ❑ Nov 1998 Cover: 2.95 **NM** value: **Cover or less**
Circ: Diamd. preorders: **9,922**
A: Rumiko Takahashi **W:** Rumiko Takahashi
11 ❑ Dec 1998 Cover: 2.95 **NM** value: **Cover or less**
Circ: Diamd. preorders: **9,540**
A: Rumiko Takahashi **W:** Rumiko Takahashi
12 ❑ Jan 1999 Cover: 2.95 **NM** value: **Cover or less**
Circ: Diamd. preorders: **9,575**
A: Rumiko Takahashi **W:** Rumiko Takahashi
13 ❑ Feb 1999 Cover: 2.95 **NM** value: **Cover or less**
Circ: Diamd. preorders: **9,271**
A: Rumiko Takahashi **W:** Rumiko Takahashi
14 ❑ Mar 1999 Cover: 2.95 **NM** value: **Cover or less**
Circ: Diamd. preorders: **9,385**
A: Rumiko Takahashi **W:** Rumiko Takahashi

RANMA 1/2 PART 8 — Viz

1 ❑ Apr 1999 Cover: 2.95 **NM** value: **Cover or less**
Circ: Diamd. preorders: **10,049**
📖 Kung Fu Stew **A:** Rumiko Takahashi **W:** Rumiko Takahashi
2 ❑ May 1999 Cover: 2.95 **NM** value: **Cover or less**
Circ: Diamd. preorders: **9,616**
A: Rumiko Takahashi **W:** Rumiko Takahashi
3 ❑ Jun 1999 Cover: 2.95 **NM** value: **Cover or less**
Circ: Diamd. preorders: **9,497**
A: Rumiko Takahashi **W:** Rumiko Takahashi
4 ❑ Jul 1999 Cover: 2.95 **NM** value: **Cover or less**
Circ: Diamd. preorders: **9,554**
A: Rumiko Takahashi **W:** Rumiko Takahashi
5 ❑ Aug 1999 Cover: 2.95 **NM** value: **Cover or less**
Circ: Diamd. preorders: **9,309**
A: Rumiko Takahashi **W:** Rumiko Takahashi
7 ❑ Sep 1999 Cover: 2.95 **NM** value: **Cover or less**
Circ: Diamd. preorders: **9,268**
A: Rumiko Takahashi **W:** Rumiko Takahashi

RANMA 1/2 PART 9 — Viz

1 ❑ May 2000 Cover: 2.95 **NM** value: **Cover or less**
Circ: Diamd. preorders: **8,543**
📖 Melonhead **A:** Rumiko Takahashi **W:** Rumiko Takahashi

RANMA 1/2 (COLLECTIONS) — Viz

Bk 1❑ Cover: 16.95 **NM** value: **Cover or less**
A: Rumiko Takahashi **W:** Rumiko Takahashi
Bk 1-2❑b&w **NM** value: **16.95**
• Trade Paperback. **A:** Rumiko Takahashi **W:** Rumiko Takahashi
Bk 2❑ Jun 1994 Cover: 15.95 **NM** value: **Cover or less**
A: Rumiko Takahashi **W:** Rumiko Takahashi
Bk 3❑ Aug 1994 Cover: 15.95 **NM** value: **Cover or less**
A: Rumiko Takahashi **W:** Rumiko Takahashi
Bk 4❑ Cover: 15.95 **NM** value: **Cover or less**
A: Rumiko Takahashi **W:** Rumiko Takahashi
Bk 5❑ Cover: 15.95 **NM** value: **Cover or less**
A: Rumiko Takahashi **W:** Rumiko Takahashi
Bk 6❑ Cover: 15.95 **NM** value: **Cover or less**
A: Rumiko Takahashi **W:** Rumiko Takahashi
Bk 7❑ Cover: 15.95 **NM** value: **Cover or less**
A: Rumiko Takahashi **W:** Rumiko Takahashi
Bk 8❑ Cover: 15.95 **NM** value: **Cover or less**
A: Rumiko Takahashi **W:** Rumiko Takahashi
Bk 9❑ Cover: 15.95 **NM** value: **Cover or less**
A: Rumiko Takahashi **W:** Rumiko Takahashi
Bk 10❑Dec 1997 Cover: 15.95 **NM** value: **Cover or less**
A: Rumiko Takahashi **W:** Rumiko Takahashi
Bk 11❑Jun 1998 Cover: 15.95 **NM** value: **Cover or less**
A: Rumiko Takahashi **W:** Rumiko Takahashi

RANT — Boneyard

1 ❑ Nov 1994, b&w Cover: 2.95 **NM** value: **Cover or less**
A: Jeff Jones **W:** Jonathan Larsen
2 ❑ Feb 1995, b&w Cover: 2.95 **NM** value: **Cover or less**
A: Jeff Jones
3 ❑ Cover: 2.95 **NM** value: **Cover or less**
A: Jeff Jones
Ash 1❑ **NM** value: **2.50**
Ashcan version of issue #1. Black and white cover. **A:** Jeff Jones

RAPHAEL TEENAGE MUTANT NINJA TURTLE — Mirage

1 ❑ Nov 1987 Cover: 1.50 **NM** value: **2.00**
• Oversized.
1-2 ❑ Cover: 1.50 **NM** value: **Cover or less**

RAPTORS — NBM

Bk 1❑ Oct 1999 Cover: 10.95 **NM** value: **Cover or less**

RARE BREED — Chrysalis Studios

1 ❑ Nov 1995 Cover: 2.50 **NM** value: **Cover or less**
A: Zoe Rochelle **W:** Zoe Rochelle ★ 1st Appearance of The Ravager, Ammo, Buffalo Soldier, Swede, Ambush.
2 ❑ Mar 1996 Cover: 2.50 **NM** value: **Cover or less**
A: Zoe Rochelle **W:** Zoe Rochelle

RASCALS IN PARADISE — Dark Horse

1 ❑ Aug 1994 Cover: 3.95 **NM** value: **4.00**
Circ: CapCity orders: **7,200**
• magazine. **A:** Jim Silke **W:** Jim Silke
2 ❑ Oct 1994 Cover: 3.95 **NM** value: **4.00**
Circ: CapCity orders: **5,325**
• magazine. **A:** Jim Silke **W:** Jim Silke
3 ❑ Dec 1994 Cover: 3.95 **NM** value: **4.00**
Circ: CapCity orders: **6,675**
• magazine. final issue. **A:** Jim Silke **W:** Jim Silke
Bk 1❑ Nov 1995 Cover: 16.95 **NM** value: **Cover or less**

RAT BASTARD — Crucial

1 ❑ Jun 1997 Cover: 1.95 **NM** value: **2.50**
Circ: Diamd. preorders: **3,470**
📖 Fix for a King **A:** Cliff Galbraith **W:** Cliff Galbraith
1/Ash❑Jun 1997 Cover: 1.95 **NM** value: **2.50**
• Black and white ashcan edition. 📖 Fix for a King **A:** Cliff Galbraith **W:** Cliff Galbraith
2 ❑ Nov 1997 Cover: 1.95 **NM** value: **2.00**
📖 Fix for a King
3 ❑ Apr 1998 Cover: 1.95 **NM** value: **2.00**
Circ: Diamd. preorders: **2,406**
📖 Fix for a King
4 ❑ Jul 1998 Cover: 1.95 **NM** value: **2.00**
Circ: Diamd. preorders: **2,228**
📖 Fix for a King
5 ❑ Oct 1998 Cover: 1.95 **NM** value: **Cover or less**
Circ: Diamd. preorders: **2,169**
📖 Vengeance Day
6 ❑ Jul 1999 Cover: 1.95 **NM** value: **Cover or less**
Circ: Diamd. preorders: **1,789**
📖 Vengeance Day

RATED X — Aircel

All issues are adults only.
1 ❑ Apr 1991, b&w Cover: 2.95 **NM** value: **Cover or less**
📖 The Non-Entity
2 ❑ b&w Cover: 2.95 **NM** value: **Cover or less**
3 ❑ b&w Cover: 2.95 **NM** value: **Cover or less**
SE 1❑ b&w Cover: 2.95 **NM** value: **Cover or less**

CGC-graded: Multiply prices above by **33 for 9.9 M • 16 for 9.8 NM/M • 7 for 9.6 NM+ • 5 for 9.4 NM • 2.5 for 9.2 NM- • 1.5 for 9.0 VF/NM**

RAT FINK COMICS — World of Fandom

1 ❑ b&w Cover: 2.50 **NM** value: **Cover or less**
2 ❑ b&w Cover: 2.50 **NM** value: **Cover or less**
3 ❑ b&w Cover: 2.50 **NM** value: **Cover or less**

RAT FINK COMIX (ED "BIG DADDY" ROTH'S...) — Starhead

1 ❑ Cover: 2.00 **NM** value: **Cover or less**
Life with Rat F **A:** R.K. Sloan **W:** Ed Roth; Franco

RATFOO — Spit Wad

1 ❑ Sep 1997, b&w Cover: 2.95 **NM** value: **Cover or less**

RAT PREVIEW (JUSTIN HAMPTON'S...) — Aeon / Backbone Press

1 ❑ May 1997, b&w **NM** value: **1.00**
no cover price. • ashcan-sized.

RATS! — Slave Labor

1 ❑ Aug 1992, b&w Cover: 2.50 **NM** value: **Cover or less**

RAVAGE 2099 — Marvel

When Stan Lee, long away from regular comics work, created a character for Marvel's line of future comics, the company proudly trumpeted the event. Unfortunately, Ravage 2099 proved to be one of the weak links of a weak line.

Paul-Phillip Ravage, a rising young star of the corporate world, was convinced that his company was a force for good. When Paul-Phillip reported evidence of corruption to his superiors, he went from being a corporate asset to a liability. Accordingly, he was marked for elimination.

Escaping the assassination attempt, Ravage is forced to fight against the very forces he had once controlled. In doing so, Paul-Phillip, the company man is reborn as the renegade named Ravage — a name he is determined his former corporation will never forget.

1 ❑ Dec 1992 Cover: 1.75 **NM** value: **Cover or less**
Circ: CapCity orders: **155,100**
Metallic ink cover. **A:** Paul Ryan **W:** Stan Lee
2 ❑ Jan 1993 Cover: 1.25 **NM** value: **Cover or less**
Circ: CapCity orders: **83,400**
The Madness Unleashed **A:** Paul Ryan **W:** Stan Lee
3 ❑ Feb 1993 Cover: 1.25 **NM** value: **Cover or less**
Circ: CapCity orders: **73,200**
Horror in Hellrock **A:** Paul Ryan **W:** Stan Lee
4 ❑ Mar 1993 Cover: 1.25 **NM** value: **Cover or less**
Circ: CapCity orders: **54,300**
The Mark of the Mutroid **A:** Paul Ryan **W:** Stan Lee
5 ❑ Apr 1993 Cover: 1.25 **NM** value: **Cover or less**
Circ: CapCity orders: **51,100**
6 ❑ May 1993 Cover: 1.25 **NM** value: **Cover or less**
Circ: CapCity orders: **42,700**
7 ❑ Jun 1993 Cover: 1.25 **NM** value: **Cover or less**
Circ: CapCity orders: **39,000**
8 ❑ Jul 1993 Cover: 1.25 **NM** value: **Cover or less**
Circ: CapCity orders: **35,600**
9 ❑ Aug 1993 Cover: 1.25 **NM** value: **Cover or less**
Circ: CapCity orders: **32,000**
10 ❑ Sep 1993 Cover: 1.25 **NM** value: **Cover or less**
Circ: CapCity orders: **32,000**
11 ❑ Oct 1993 Cover: 1.25 **NM** value: **Cover or less**
Circ: CapCity orders: **24,700**
The Stigmata Effect **A:** Grant Miehm **W:** Pat Mills; Tony Skinner
12 ❑ Nov 1993 Cover: 1.25 **NM** value: **Cover or less**
Circ: CapCity orders: **23,200**
13 ❑ Dec 1993 Cover: 1.25 **NM** value: **Cover or less**
Circ: CapCity orders: **21,200**
14 ❑ Jan 1994 Cover: 1.25 **NM** value: **Cover or less**
Circ: Statement: **78,382** CapCity orders: **19,000**
15 ❑ Feb 1994 Cover: 1.25 **NM** value: **Cover or less**
Circ: Statement: **78,382** CapCity orders: **32,600**
Fall of the Hammer, Part 2
16 ❑ Mar 1994 Cover: 1.25 **NM** value: **Cover or less**
Circ: Statement: **78,382** CapCity orders: **16,350**
17 ❑ Apr 1994 Cover: 1.25 **NM** value: **Cover or less**
Circ: Statement: **78,382** CapCity orders: **15,400**
18 ❑ May 1994 Cover: 1.25 **NM** value: **Cover or less**
Circ: Statement: **78,382** CapCity orders: **15,150**
19 ❑ Jun 1994 Cover: 1.50 **NM** value: **Cover or less**
Circ: Statement: **78,382** CapCity orders: **14,150**
20 ❑ Jul 1994 Cover: 1.50 **NM** value: **Cover or less**
Circ: Statement: **78,382** CapCity orders: **13,150**
21 ❑ Aug 1994 Cover: 1.50 **NM** value: **Cover or less**
Circ: Statement: **78,382** CapCity orders: **11,850**
22 ❑ Sep 1994 Cover: 1.50 **NM** value: **Cover or less**
Circ: Statement: **78,382** CapCity orders: **10,700**
23 ❑ Oct 1994 Cover: 1.50 **NM** value: **Cover or less**
Circ: Statement: **78,382** CapCity orders: **1,000**
24 ❑ Nov 1994 Cover: 1.50 **NM** value: **Cover or less**
Circ: Statement: **78,382** CapCity orders: **9,400**
25 ❑ Dec 1994 Cover: 2.25 **NM** value: **Cover or less**
25/SC❑ Dec 1994 Cover: 2.95 **NM** value: **Cover or less**
Circ: Statement: **78,382** CapCity orders: **10,650**
enhanced cover.
26 ❑ Jan 1995 Cover: 1.50 **NM** value: **Cover or less**
Circ: CapCity orders: **8,125**
27 ❑ Feb 1995 Cover: 1.50 **NM** value: **Cover or less**
Circ: CapCity orders: **7,375**
28 ❑ Mar 1995 Cover: 1.50 **NM** value: **Cover or less**
Circ: CapCity orders: **6,750**
29 ❑ Apr 1995 Cover: 1.50 **NM** value: **Cover or less**
Circ: CapCity orders: **6,200**
• Has 1994 Statement, filed 10/1/94; avg print run 125,351; avg sales 77,324; avg subs 1,058; avg total paid 78,382; samples 125; office use 500; max existent 79,007; 38% of run returned
30 ❑ May 1995 Cover: 1.50 **NM** value: **Cover or less**
Circ: CapCity orders: **7,025**
31 ❑ Jun 1995 Cover: 1.95 **NM** value: **Cover or less**
Circ: CapCity orders: **7,025**
32 ❑ Jul 1995 Cover: 1.95 **NM** value: **Cover or less**
Circ: CapCity orders: **6,350**
33 ❑ Aug 1995 Cover: 1.95 **NM** value: **Cover or less**
Circ: CapCity orders: **6,200**
final issue.

RAVEN, THE — Malan Classical Enterprises

1 ❑ b&w Cover: 4.95 **NM** value: **Cover or less**
No issue number. **A:** Gustave Dore

RAVEN — Renaissance

1 ❑ Sep 1993 Cover: 2.50 **NM** value: **Cover or less**
A: Craig Enslin **W:** Michael Pederson ★ 1st Appearance of Raven, Ian Macauley.
2 ❑ Nov 1993 Cover: 2.50 **NM** value: **Cover or less**
A: Craig Enslin **W:** Michael Pederson
3 ❑ Apr 1994 Cover: 2.50 **NM** value: **Cover or less**
A: Craig Enslin **W:** Michael Pederson
4 ❑ Aug 1994 Cover: 2.75 **NM** value: **Cover or less**
A: Craig Enslin **W:** Michael Pederson

RAVEN CHRONICLES — Caliber

1 ❑ Jul 1995, b&w Cover: 2.95 **NM** value: **Cover or less**
Circ: CapCity orders: **2,985**
Prelude; The Bloodfire **A:** Craig Brasfield **W:** Eric Jackson; Gary Reed
2 ❑ b&w Cover: 2.95 **NM** value: **Cover or less**
3 ❑ b&w Cover: 2.95 **NM** value: **Cover or less**
4 ❑ b&w Cover: 2.95 **NM** value: **Cover or less**

RAVENS AND RAINBOWS — Pacific

1 ❑ Dec 1983 Cover: 1.50 **NM** value: **Cover or less**
Union; Bias; Home; Spirit of '76 **A:** Jeff Jones **W:** Jeff Jones

RAVENWIND — Pariah

1 ❑ Jun 1996, b&w Cover: 2.50 **NM** value: **Cover or less**

RAVER — Malibu

1 ❑ Apr 1993 Cover: 2.95 **NM** value: **Cover or less**
Circ: CapCity orders: **20,000**
foil cover. **A:** Dan Day **W:** Walter Koenig ★ 1st Appearance of Raver.
2 ❑ Cover: 1.95 **NM** value: **Cover or less**
Circ: CapCity orders: **7,300**
W: Walter Koenig
3 ❑ Cover: 1.95 **NM** value: **Cover or less**
Circ: CapCity orders: **6,225**
W: Walter Koenig

RAWHIDE KID — Marvel

Johnny Bart was the nephew of retired Texas Ranger Ben Bart. Ben was widely known as a fast gun, and he taught Johnny how to shoot. The boy practiced and practiced until even Ben had to admit that the boy had learned to shoot faster than him.

One day, a drifter named Hawk Brown decided to make a name for himself by calling out Ben Bart. In a fair fight, Hawk wouldn't have stood a chance, but he had his men distract Ben just as the time came to draw. Hawk's sixguns roared, and Ben was cut down. Johnny learned of the treachery and swore to avenge his uncle. He took on Hawk and shot the guns out of his hands. After that, he left to make his way in the world as a gunslinger, The Rawhide Kid. One day, The Kid was forced to kill a man in Laramie who called him out and drew first. Although it was a matter of self-defense, The Kid was branded an outlaw and spent the rest of his life on the run.

1 ❑ Mar 1955 Cover: 0.10 **NM** value: **600.00**
• **CGC:** 3 graded, best 7.0
2 ❑ May 1955 Cover: 0.10 **NM** value: **275.00**
3 ❑ Jul 1955 Cover: 0.10 **NM** value: **165.00**
4 ❑ Sep 1955 Cover: 0.10 **NM** value: **165.00**
5 ❑ Nov 1955 Cover: 0.10 **NM** value: **165.00**
6 ❑ Jan 1956 Cover: 0.10 **NM** value: **130.00**
7 ❑ Mar 1956 Cover: 0.10 **NM** value: **130.00**
8 ❑ May 1956 Cover: 0.10 **NM** value: **130.00**
9 ❑ Jul 1956 Cover: 0.10 **NM** value: **130.00**
10 ❑ Sep 1956 Cover: 0.10 **NM** value: **130.00**
11 ❑ Nov 1956 Cover: 0.10 **NM** value: **100.00**
12 ❑ Jan 1957 Cover: 0.10 **NM** value: **100.00**
13 ❑ Mar 1957 Cover: 0.10 **NM** value: **100.00**
14 ❑ May 1957 Cover: 0.10 **NM** value: **100.00**
15 ❑ Jul 1957 Cover: 0.10 **NM** value: **100.00**
16 ❑ Sep 1957 Cover: 0.10 **NM** value: **100.00**
• series goes on hiatus
17 ❑ Aug 1960 Cover: 0.10 **NM** value: **300.00**
• **CGC:** 3 graded, best 8.0
Beware, the Rawhide Kid; Stagecoach to Shotgun Gap; When the Outlaw Kid Turned Outlaw • Origin of Rawhide Kid **A:** Jack Kirby ★ Origin of Rawhide Kid.
18 ❑ Oct 1960 Cover: 0.10 **NM** value: **80.00**
At the Mercy of Wolf Waco; A Legend is Born
19 ❑ Dec 1960 Cover: 0.10 **NM** value: **80.00**
Gun Duel In Trigger Gap
20 ❑ Feb 1961 Cover: 0.10 **NM** value: **80.00**
Circ: Statement: **150,162** • **CGC:** 1 graded, best 8.5
Shoot-Out with Blackjack Borden
21 ❑ Apr 1961 Cover: 0.10 **NM** value: **75.00**
Circ: Statement: **150,162**
The Gunmen of Sundon City
22 ❑ Jun 1961 Cover: 0.10 **NM** value: **75.00**
Circ: Statement: **150,162** • **CGC:** 1 graded, best 9.0
Beware, the Terrible Totem
23 ❑ Aug 1961 Cover: 0.10 **NM** value: **165.00**
Circ: Statement: **150,162**
Origin of the Rawhide Kid; No Place to Hide **A:** Jack Kirby ★ Origin of Rawhide Kid.
24 ❑ Oct 1961 Cover: 0.10 **NM** value: **75.00**
Circ: Statement: **150,162**
Showdown in Silver City; Gunman's Gamble
25 ❑ Dec 1961 Cover: 0.10 **NM** value: **75.00**
Circ: Statement: **150,162**
The Bat Strikes; The Twister; Those Who Live By The Gun
26 ❑ Feb 1962 Cover: 0.10 **NM** value: **75.00**
• **CGC:** 1 graded, best 8.0
Trapped By The Bounty Hunter; Shoot-Out in Scragg's Saloon; The Bullet-Proof Man
27 ❑ Apr 1962 Cover: 0.12 **NM** value: **75.00**
When Six-Guns Roar; The Girl, The Gunmen, and The Apaches; The Mna Who Caught The Kid
28 ❑ Jun 1962 Cover: 0.12 **NM** value: **75.00**
Doom in The Desert; The Guns of Jasker Jelko; When a Gunslinger Gets Mad • Has 1961 Statement; avg total paid circ 150,162
29 ❑ Aug 1962 Cover: 0.12 **NM** value: **75.00**
The Trail of Apache Joe; The Little Man Laughs Last; The Fallen Hero
30 ❑ Oct 1962 Cover: 0.12 **NM** value: **75.00**
When the Kid Went Wild; Showdown With The Crow Magnum Gang; Riot in Railtown
31 ❑ Dec 1962 Cover: 0.12 **NM** value: **60.00**
32 ❑ Feb 1963 Cover: 0.12 **NM** value: **60.00**
Circ: Statement: **194,390** • **CGC:** 1 graded, best 8.0
33 ❑ Apr 1963 Cover: 0.12 **NM** value: **60.00**
Circ: Statement: **194,390**
34 ❑ Jun 1963 Cover: 0.12 **NM** value: **60.00**
Circ: Statement: **194,390** • **CGC:** 1 graded, best 7.0
35 ❑ Aug 1963 Cover: 0.12 **NM** value: **60.00**
Circ: Statement: **194,390**
36 ❑ Oct 1963 Cover: 0.12 **NM** value: **55.00**
Circ: Statement: **194,390**
37 ❑ Dec 1963 Cover: 0.12 **NM** value: **55.00**
Circ: Statement: **194,390**
38 ❑ Feb 1964 Cover: 0.12 **NM** value: **55.00**
Circ: Statement: **187,190**
39 ❑ Apr 1964 Cover: 0.12 **NM** value: **55.00**
Circ: Statement: **187,190**
40 ❑ Jun 1964 Cover: 0.12 **NM** value: **55.00**
Circ: Statement: **187,190**
• Has 1963 Statement; avg total paid circ 194,390★ Appearance of Two-Gun Kid.
41 ❑ Aug 1964 Cover: 0.12 **NM** value: **55.00**
Circ: Statement: **187,190** • **CGC:** 1 graded, best 3.0
42 ❑ Oct 1964 Cover: 0.12 **NM** value: **55.00**
Circ: Statement: **187,190**
43 ❑ Dec 1964 Cover: 0.12 **NM** value: **55.00**
Circ: Statement: **187,190**
44 ❑ Feb 1965 Cover: 0.12 **NM** value: **55.00**
Circ: Statement: **192,540**
45 ❑ Apr 1965 Cover: 0.12 **NM** value: **85.00**
Circ: Statement: **192,540** • **CGC:** 2 graded, best 7.5
• Has 1964 Statement, filed 10/1/64; avg print run 315,200; avg sales 187,100; avg subs 90; avg total paid 187,190; samples 125; max existent 187,315; 41% of run returned **A:** Jack Kirby ★ Origin of Rawhide Kid.
46 ❑ Jun 1965 Cover: 0.12 **NM** value: **55.00**
Circ: Statement: **192,540**
47 ❑ Aug 1965 Cover: 0.12 **NM** value: **30.00**
Circ: Statement: **192,540**
48 ❑ Oct 1965 Cover: 0.12 **NM** value: **30.00**
Circ: Statement: **192,540**
★ Versus Marko the Manhunter.
49 ❑ Dec 1965 Cover: 0.12 **NM** value: **30.00**
Circ: Statement: **192,540**
★ Versus Masquerader.
50 ❑ Feb 1966 Cover: 0.12 **NM** value: **30.00**
Circ: Statement: **202,823**
★ Appearance of Kid Colt. ★ Versus Masquerader.
51 ❑ Apr 1966 Cover: 0.12 **NM** value: **30.00**
Circ: Statement: **202,823**
• Has 1965 Statement, filed 10/1/65; avg print run 330,461; avg sales 192,435; avg subs 105; avg total paid 192,540; samples 60; max existent 192,600; 42% of run returned★ Versus Aztecs.
52 ❑ Jun 1966 Cover: 0.12 **NM** value: **30.00**
Circ: Statement: **202,823**
53 ❑ Aug 1966 Cover: 0.12 **NM** value: **30.00**
Circ: Statement: **202,823** • **CGC:** 1 graded, best 9.2
54 ❑ Oct 1966 Cover: 0.12 **NM** value: **30.00**
Circ: Statement: **202,823**
55 ❑ Dec 1966 Cover: 0.12 **NM** value: **30.00**
Circ: Statement: **202,823**
★ Versus Plunderers.
56 ❑ Feb 1967 Cover: 0.12 **NM** value: **30.00**
Circ: Statement: **205,221** • **CGC:** 3 graded, best 9.4
★ Versus Peacemaker.
57 ❑ Apr 1967 Cover: 0.12 **NM** value: **30.00**
Circ: Statement: **205,221**

•Has 1966 Statement, filed 10/1/66; avg print run 338,851; avg sales 202,638X; avg subs 185; avg total paid 202,823; samples 60; max existent 202,883; 40% of run returned ★ Versus Enforcerers (not Spider-Man villains).

58 ❑ Jun 1967 Cover: 0.12 **NM** value: **30.00**
Circ: Statement: **205,221**

59 ❑ Aug 1967 Cover: 0.12 **NM** value: **30.00**
Circ: Statement: **205,221**
★ Versus Drako.

60 ❑ Oct 1967 Cover: 0.12 **NM** value: **30.00**
Circ: Statement: **205,221** • **CGC:** 1 graded, best 9.4

61 ❑ Dec 1967 Cover: 0.12 **NM** value: **22.00**
Circ: Statement: **205,221**
★ Appearance of Wild Bill Hickock, Calamity Jane.

62 ❑ Feb 1968 Cover: 0.12 **NM** value: **22.00**
Circ: Statement: **216,045** • **CGC:** 1 graded, best 9.4
★ Versus Drako.

63 ❑ Apr 1968 Cover: 0.12 **NM** value: **22.00**
Circ: Statement: **216,045**
•Has 1967 Statement, filed 10/1/67; avg print run 339,640; avg sales 205,021; avg subs 200; avg total paid 205,221; samples 95; max existent 205,316; 40% of run returned

64 ❑ Jun 1968 Cover: 0.12 **NM** value: **22.00**
Circ: Statement: **216,045**
• Kid Colt back-up

65 ❑ Aug 1968 Cover: 0.12 **NM** value: **22.00**
Circ: Statement: **216,045**

66 ❑ Oct 1968 Cover: 0.12 **NM** value: **22.00**
Circ: Statement: **216,045**
• Two-Gun Kid back-up

67 ❑ Dec 1968 Cover: 0.12 **NM** value: **22.00**
Circ: Statement: **216,045**

68 ❑ Feb 1969 Cover: 0.12 **NM** value: **22.00**
Circ: Statement: **204,896**
★ Versus Cougar.

69 ❑ Apr 1969 Cover: 0.12 **NM** value: **22.00**
Circ: Statement: **204,896**
•Has 1968 Statement, filed 10/1/68; avg print run 320,400; avg sales 215,875; avg subs 170; avg total paid 216,045; samples 400; max existent 216,445; 32% of run returned

70 ❑ Jun 1969 Cover: 0.12 **NM** value: **22.00**
Circ: Statement: **204,896**

71 ❑ Aug 1969 Cover: 0.15 **NM** value: **14.00**
Circ: Statement: **204,896**

72 ❑ Oct 1969 Cover: 0.15 **NM** value: **14.00**
Circ: Statement: **204,896**

73 ❑ Dec 1969 Cover: 0.15 **NM** value: **14.00**
Circ: Statement: **204,896** • **CGC:** 2 graded, best 7.5

74 ❑ Feb 1970 Cover: 0.15 **NM** value: **14.00**
75 ❑ Apr 1970 Cover: 0.15 **NM** value: **14.00**
•Has 1969 Statement, filed 10/1/69; avg print run 339,123; avg sales 204,748; avg subs 148; avg total paid 204,896; samples 110; max existent 205,006; 37% of run returned

76 ❑ May 1970 Cover: 0.15 **NM** value: **14.00**
77 ❑ Jun 1970 Cover: 0.15 **NM** value: **14.00**
78 ❑ Jul 1970 Cover: 0.15 **NM** value: **14.00**
79 ❑ Aug 1970 Cover: 0.15 **NM** value: **14.00**
80 ❑ Oct 1970 Cover: 0.15 **NM** value: **14.00**
81 ❑ Nov 1970 Cover: 0.15 **NM** value: **14.00**
📖 Range War **A:** Larry Lieber **W:** Larry Lieber

82 ❑ Dec 1970 Cover: 0.15 **NM** value: **14.00**
83 ❑ Jan 1971 Cover: 0.15 **NM** value: **14.00**
Circ: Statement: **193,624**

84 ❑ Feb 1971 Cover: 0.15 **NM** value: **14.00**
Circ: Statement: **193,624**

85 ❑ Mar 1971 Cover: 0.15 **NM** value: **14.00**
Circ: Statement: **193,624**

86 ❑ Apr 1971 Cover: 0.15 **NM** value: **14.00**
Circ: Statement: **193,624**
A: Jack Kirby ★ Origin of Rawhide Kid.

87 ❑ May 1971 Cover: 0.15 **NM** value: **10.00**
Circ: Statement: **193,624**

88 ❑ Jun 1971 Cover: 0.15 **NM** value: **10.00**
Circ: Statement: **193,624**

89 ❑ Jul 1971 Cover: 0.15 **NM** value: **10.00**
Circ: Statement: **193,624**

90 ❑ Aug 1971 Cover: 0.15 **NM** value: **10.00**
Circ: Statement: **193,624**

91 ❑ Sep 1971 Cover: 0.15 **NM** value: **10.00**
Circ: Statement: **193,624**

92 ❑ Oct 1971 Cover: 0.25 **NM** value: **10.00**
Circ: Statement: **193,624**

93 ❑ Nov 1971 Cover: 0.25 **NM** value: **10.00**
Circ: Statement: **193,624**

94 ❑ Dec 1971 Cover: 0.20 **NM** value: **10.00**
Circ: Statement: **193,624**

95 ❑ Jan 1972 Cover: 0.20 **NM** value: **10.00**
96 ❑ Feb 1972 Cover: 0.20 **NM** value: **10.00**
97 ❑ Mar 1972 Cover: 0.25 **NM** value: **10.00**
98 ❑ Apr 1972 Cover: 0.25 **NM** value: **10.00**
99 ❑ May 1972 Cover: 0.20 **NM** value: **10.00**
•Has 1971 Statement, filed 9/23/71; avg print run 316,844; avg sales 193,444; avg subs 180; avg total paid 193,624; samples 110; max existent 193,734; 39% of run returned

100 ❑ Jun 1972 Cover: 0.20 **NM** value: **14.00**
★ Origin of Rawhide Kid.

101 ❑ Jul 1972 Cover: 0.20 **NM** value: **7.00**
102 ❑ Aug 1972 Cover: 0.20 **NM** value: **7.00**
103 ❑ Sep 1972 Cover: 0.20 **NM** value: **7.00**
104 ❑ Oct 1972 Cover: 0.20 **NM** value: **7.00**
105 ❑ Nov 1972 Cover: 0.20 **NM** value: **7.00**
106 ❑ Dec 1972 Cover: 0.20 **NM** value: **7.00**
107 ❑ Jan 1973 Cover: 0.20 **NM** value: **7.00**
Circ: Statement: **138,720**

108 ❑ Feb 1973 Cover: 0.20 **NM** value: **7.00**
Circ: Statement: **138,720**

109 ❑ Mar 1973 Cover: 0.20 **NM** value: **7.00**
Circ: Statement: **138,720**

110 ❑ Apr 1973 Cover: 0.20 **NM** value: **7.00**
Circ: Statement: **138,720**

111 ❑ May 1973 Cover: 0.20 **NM** value: **7.00**
Circ: Statement: **138,720**

112 ❑ Jun 1973 Cover: 0.20 **NM** value: **7.00**
Circ: Statement: **138,720**

113 ❑ Jul 1973 Cover: 0.20 **NM** value: **7.00**
Circ: Statement: **138,720**

114 ❑ Aug 1973 Cover: 0.20 **NM** value: **7.00**
Circ: Statement: **138,720**

115 ❑ Sep 1973 Cover: 0.20 **NM** value: **7.00**
Circ: Statement: **138,720**

116 ❑ Oct 1973 Cover: 0.20 **NM** value: **6.00**
Circ: Statement: **138,720**

117 ❑ Nov 1973 Cover: 0.20 **NM** value: **6.00**
Circ: Statement: **138,720**

118 ❑ Jan 1974 Cover: 0.20 **NM** value: **6.00**
Circ: Statement: **151,165**

119 ❑ Mar 1974 Cover: 0.20 **NM** value: **6.00**
Circ: Statement: **151,165**

120 ❑ May 1974 Cover: 0.20 **NM** value: **6.00**
Circ: Statement: **151,165**
• Has 1973 Statement; avg total paid circ 138,720

121 ❑ Jul 1974 Cover: 0.25 **NM** value: **6.00**
Circ: Statement: **151,165**
• reprints

122 ❑ Sep 1974 Cover: 0.25 **NM** value: **6.00**
Circ: Statement: **151,165**
• reprints

123 ❑ Nov 1974 Cover: 0.25 **NM** value: **6.00**
Circ: Statement: **151,165**
• reprints

124 ❑ Jan 1975 Cover: 0.25 **NM** value: **6.00**
Circ: Statement: **143,972**
• reprints

125 ❑ Mar 1975 Cover: 0.25 **NM** value: **6.00**
Circ: Statement: **143,972**
• reprints

126 ❑ May 1975 Cover: 0.25 **NM** value: **6.00**
Circ: Statement: **143,972**
• reprints; Has 1974 Statement; avg total paid circ 151,165

127 ❑ Jul 1975 Cover: 0.25 **NM** value: **6.00**
Circ: Statement: **143,972**
• reprints

128 ❑ Sep 1975 Cover: 0.25 **NM** value: **6.00**
Circ: Statement: **143,972**
• reprints

129 ❑ Oct 1975 Cover: 0.25 **NM** value: **6.00**
Circ: Statement: **143,972**
• reprints

130 ❑ Nov 1975 Cover: 0.25 **NM** value: **6.00**
Circ: Statement: **143,972**
• reprints

131 ❑ Jan 1976 Cover: 0.25 **NM** value: **6.00**
• reprints

132 ❑ Mar 1976 Cover: 0.25 **NM** value: **6.00**
• reprints

133 ❑ May 1976 Cover: 0.25 **NM** value: **6.00**
• reprints

134 ❑ Jul 1976 Cover: 0.25 **NM** value: **6.00**
• reprints

135 ❑ Sep 1976 Cover: 0.30 **NM** value: **6.00**
• reprints

136 ❑ Nov 1976 Cover: 0.30 **NM** value: **6.00**
• reprints

137 ❑ Jan 1977 Cover: 0.30 **NM** value: **6.00**
Circ: Statement: **98,978**
• reprints

138 ❑ Mar 1977 Cover: 0.30 **NM** value: **6.00**
Circ: Statement: **98,978**
• reprints

139 ❑ May 1977 Cover: 0.30 **NM** value: **6.00**
Circ: Statement: **98,978**
• reprints

140 ❑ Jul 1977 Cover: 0.30 **NM** value: **6.00**
Circ: Statement: **98,978**
• reprints

141 ❑ Sep 1977 Cover: 0.30 **NM** value: **6.00**
Circ: Statement: **98,978**
• reprints

142 ❑ Nov 1977 Cover: 0.30 **NM** value: **6.00**
Circ: Statement: **98,978**
• reprints

143 ❑ Jan 1978 Cover: 0.35 **NM** value: **6.00**
Circ: Statement: **89,414**
• reprints

144 ❑ Mar 1978 Cover: 0.35 **NM** value: **6.00**
Circ: Statement: **89,414**
• reprints

145 ❑ May 1978 Cover: 0.35 **NM** value: **6.00**
Circ: Statement: **89,414**
• reprints; Has 1977 Statement, filed 9/20/77; avg print run 253,484; avg sales 98,748; avg subs 230; avg total paid 98,978; samples 75; office use 750; max existent 99,803; 61% of run returned

146 ❑ Jul 1978 Cover: 0.35 **NM** value: **6.00**
Circ: Statement: **89,414**
• reprints

147 ❑ Sep 1978 Cover: 0.35 **NM** value: **6.00**
Circ: Statement: **89,414**
• reprints

148 ❑ Nov 1978 Cover: 0.35 **NM** value: **6.00**
Circ: Statement: **89,414**
• reprints

149 ❑ Jan 1979 Cover: 0.35 **NM** value: **6.00**
• reprints

150 ❑ Mar 1979 Cover: 0.35 **NM** value: **6.00**
• reprints

151 ❑ May 1979 Cover: 0.35 **NM** value: **6.00**
• reprints; Has 1978 Statement, filed 9/25/78; avg print run 239,506; avg sales 89,207; avg subs 207; avg total paid 89,414; samples 175; office use 810; max existent 90,399; 62% of run returned

SE 1 ❑ Sep 1971 Cover: 0.25 **NM** value: **12.00**

RAWHIDE KID (LTD. SERIES) Marvel

1 ❑ Aug 1985 Cover: 0.75 **NM** value: **1.50**
Circ: CapCity orders: **8,300**
📖 The Living Legend **A:** John Byrne; Herb Trimpe; John Severin **W:** Bill Mantlo ★ Origin of Rawhide Kid.

2 ❑ Sep 1985 Cover: 0.75 **NM** value: **1.50**
Circ: CapCity orders: **6,800**
📖 The Not-so-Wild-West **A:** John Byrne; Herb Trimpe; John Severin **W:** Bill Mantlo

3 ❑ Oct 1985 Cover: 0.75 **NM** value: **1.50**
Circ: CapCity orders: **7,100**
A: John Byrne; Herb Trimpe; John Severin **W:** Bill Mantlo

4 ❑ Nov 1985 Cover: 0.75 **NM** value: **1.50**
Circ: CapCity orders: **7,000**
A: John Byrne; Herb Trimpe; John Severin **W:** Bill Mantlo

RAW MEDIA ILLUSTRATED ABC Studios

1 ❑ May 1998 Cover: 3.25 **NM** value: **Cover or less**
wet T-shirt cover.

1/Nude ❑ May 1998 Cover: 3.25 **NM** value: **Cover or less**
nude photo cover.

RAW MEDIA MAGS Rebel

All issues are adults only.

1 ❑ b&w Cover: 5.00 **NM** value: **Cover or less**
Circ: CapCity orders: **3,340**

2 ❑ b&w Cover: 5.00 **NM** value: **Cover or less**
3 ❑ b&w Cover: 5.00 **NM** value: **Cover or less**
4 ❑ May 1994, b&w Cover: 5.00 **NM** value: **Cover or less**

RAW PERIPHERY Slave Labor

All issues are adults only.

1 ❑ b&w Cover: 2.95 **NM** value: **Cover or less**
📖 Dear Reader; Jazebel's Virtue; The Watchman; Dreamlogic **A:** James Roberger; Omaga Pérez **W:** Ann Nocenti; Richard Hell; Robert Hunter; Omaha Pérez

RAY, THE DC

0 ❑ Oct 1994 Cover: 1.95 **NM** value: **2.25**
Circ: CapCity orders: **19,150**
📖 Missing **A:** Howard Porter **W:** Christopher Priest ★ Origin of The Ray II (Ray Terrill).

1 ❑ May 1994 Cover: 1.75 **NM** value: **2.25**
Circ: CapCity orders: **26,300** • **CGC:** 1 graded, best 9.0
📖 Rebirth **A:** Howard Porter **W:** Christopher Priest

1/SC ❑ May 1994 Cover: 2.95 **NM** value: **3.00**
foil cover. 📖 Rebirth **A:** Howard Porter **W:** Christopher Priest

2 ❑ Jun 1994 Cover: 1.75 **NM** value: **2.00**
Circ: CapCity orders: **17,700**
📖 Juice **A:** Howard Porter **W:** Christopher Priest ★ Origin of The Ray II (Ray Terrill).

3 ❑ Jul 1994 Cover: 1.75 **NM** value: **2.00**
Circ: CapCity orders: **15,100**

4 ❑ Aug 1994 Cover: 1.95 **NM** value: **2.00**
Circ: CapCity orders: **14,350**

5 ❑ Sep 1994 Cover: 1.95 **NM** value: **2.00**
Circ: CapCity orders: **13,700**

6 ❑ Nov 1994 Cover: 1.95 **NM** value: **2.00**
Circ: CapCity orders: **19,150**

7 ❑ Dec 1994 Cover: 1.95 **NM** value: **2.00**
Circ: CapCity orders: **11,800**
★ Appearance of Black Canary.

8 ❑ Jan 1995 Cover: 1.95 **NM** value: **2.00**
Circ: CapCity orders: **12,000**
📖 The Main Man **A:** Howard Porter **W:** Christopher Priest ★ Versus Lobo.

9 ❑ Feb 1995 Cover: 1.95 **NM** value: **2.00**
Circ: CapCity orders: **10,825**

10 ❑ Mar 1995 Cover: 1.95 **NM** value: **2.00**
Circ: CapCity orders: **9,800**

11 ❑ Apr 1995 Cover: 1.95 **NM** value: **2.00**
Circ: CapCity orders: **9,225**

12 ❑ May 1995 Cover: 1.95 **NM** value: **2.00**
Circ: CapCity orders: **8,850**

13 ❑ Jun 1995 Cover: 2.25 **NM** value: **Cover or less**
Circ: CapCity orders: **8,725**

14 ❑ Jul 1995 Cover: 2.25 **NM** value: **Cover or less**
Circ: CapCity orders: **8,325**

15 ❑ Aug 1995 Cover: 2.25 **NM** value: **Cover or less**
Circ: CapCity orders: **8,550**
★ Versus Deathmasque.

16 ❑ Sep 1995 Cover: 2.25 **NM** value: **Cover or less**
Circ: CapCity orders: **7,800**

17 ❑ Oct 1995 Cover: 2.25 **NM** value: **Cover or less**
Circ: CapCity orders: **6,300**

18 ❑ Nov 1995 Cover: 2.25 **NM** value: **Cover or less**
📖 Underworld Unleashed • Underworld Unleashed

19 ❑ Dec 1995 Cover: 2.25 **NM** value: **Cover or less**
📖 Underworld Unleashed • Underworld Unleashed

20 ❑ Jan 1996 Cover: 2.25 **NM** value: **Cover or less**
📖 The Tide **A:** Jason Armstrong **W:** Christopher Priest ★ Appearance of Golden Age Black Condor.

21 ❑ Feb 1996 Cover: 2.25 **NM** value: **Cover or less**
📖 It **A:** Jason Armstrong **W:** Christopher Priest ★ Versus Black Condor.

22 ❑ Mar 1996 Cover: 2.25 **NM** value: **Cover or less**
📖 Masks **A:** Jason Armstrong **W:** Christopher Priest

23 ❑ May 1996 Cover: 2.25 **NM** value: **Cover or less**
24 ❑ Jun 1996 Cover: 2.25 **NM** value: **Cover or less**
25 ❑ Jul 1996 Cover: 3.50 **NM** value: **Cover or less**
📖 Time and Tempest!, Part 1 • Ray in the future ★ Appearance of Bart Allen, Triumph.

CGC-graded: Multiply prices above by **33 for 9.9 M • 16 for 9.8 NM/M • 7 for 9.6 NM+ • 5 for 9.4 NM • 2.5 for 9.2 NM- • 1.5 for 9.0 VF/NM**

26 ❑ Aug 1996 Cover: 2.25 **NM** value: **Cover or less**
📖 Time and Tempest!, Part 2 • continued from events in JLA Annual #10
27 ❑ Sep 1996 Cover: 2.25 **NM** value: **Cover or less**
📖 Time and Tempest!, Part 3
28 ❑ Oct 1996 Cover: 2.25 **NM** value: **Cover or less**
📖 Disclosure final issue. • secrets of both Ray's pasts revealed **A:** Jason Armstrong **W:** Christopher Priest ★ Origin of Joshua.
Anl 1❑ca. 1995 Cover: 3.95 **NM** value: **Cover or less**
Circ: CapCity orders: **7,900**

RAY BRADBURY COMICS — Topps

1 ❑ Feb 1993 Cover: 2.95 **NM** value: **3.50**
Circ: CapCity orders: **19,150**
📖 Dinosaurs **W:** Al Williamson; Richard Corben; Garces
2 ❑ Apr 1993 Cover: 2.95 **NM** value: **3.50**
Circ: CapCity orders: **12,525**
📖 Horror **A:** Matt Wagner; Harvey Kurtzman **W:** Matt Wagner; Harvey Kurtzman; Sean Phillips; Jack Davis
3 ❑ Jun 1993 Cover: 2.95 **NM** value: **3.50**
Circ: CapCity orders: **12,275**
📖 Dinosaurs **W:** Mike Kucharski; Wayne Barlowe
4 ❑ Aug 1993 Cover: 2.95 **NM** value: **3.50**
Circ: CapCity orders: **7,475**
📖 Alien Terror **A:** Ron Wilber; Dave McKean **W:** Mike Mignola; James Van Hise
5 ❑ Oct 1993 Cover: 2.95 **NM** value: **3.50**
Circ: CapCity orders: **5,175**
• Final issue (#6 canceled) **A:** John Van Fleet **W:** Jon J. Muth; John Ney Rieber; Ross MacDonald
SE 1❑ca. 1994 Cover: 2.95 **NM** value: **3.50**
📖 The Illustrated Man • Illustrated Man **A:** Michael Lark **W:** Guy Davis; P. Craig Russell; Jack Kamen

RAY BRADBURY COMICS: MARTIAN CHRONICLES — Topps

1 ❑ Jun 1994 Cover: 2.50 **NM** value: **3.25**
Circ: CapCity orders: **4,725**
📖 The Off Season; Kaleidoscope **A:** Dell Barras **W:** Howard Simpson; James Van Hise

RAY BRADBURY COMICS: TRILOGY OF TERROR — Topps

1 ❑ May 1994 Cover: 2.50 **NM** value: **3.25**
Circ: CapCity orders: **5,275**
A: Wally Wood

RAY, THE (MINI-SERIES) — DC

Ray Terrill's father, the original Ray, was exposed to a light bomb that not only gave him his super-human powers but also changed his genetic make-up. When he saw that his son had inherited his powers, Ray's father sent him to live with a foster family, and told him exposure to sunlight would kill him. For 18 years, Ray lived in complete darkness and was privately tutored in a home with permanently darkened windows.

Luckily, an emergency forced Ray to realize his long-hidden powers, which he now uses, much as his father did, in the eternal battle against evil.

In addition to reviving the Golden Age Ray, this mini-series is notable as the professional debut of artist Joe Quesada, later the editor in chief at Marvel.

1 ❑ Feb 1992 Cover: 1.00 **NM** value: **4.00**
Circ: CapCity orders: **24,300**
📖 Grander than Fire **A:** Joe Quesada **W:** Jack Harris ★ Origin of The Ray II (Ray Terrill).
2 ❑ Mar 1992 Cover: 1.00 **NM** value: **3.00**
Circ: CapCity orders: **14,500**
A: Joe Quesada **W:** Jack Harris
3 ❑ Apr 1992 Cover: 1.00 **NM** value: **2.00**
Circ: CapCity orders: **11,250**
A: Joe Quesada **W:** Jack Harris
4 ❑ May 1992 Cover: 1.00 **NM** value: **2.00**
Circ: CapCity orders: **12,350**
A: Joe Quesada **W:** Jack Harris
5 ❑ Jun 1992 Cover: 1.00 **NM** value: **2.00**
Circ: CapCity orders: **12,850**
📖 Emerson Must Die **A:** Joe Quesada **W:** Jack Harris
6 ❑ Jul 1992 Cover: 1.00 **NM** value: **2.00**
Circ: CapCity orders: **12,650**
A: Joe Quesada **W:** Jack Harris
Bk 1❑ Cover: 9.95 **NM** value: **Cover or less**
• In A Blaze Of Power **A:** Joe Quesada **W:** Jack Harris
Bk 1-2❑ Cover: 12.95 **NM** value: **Cover or less**

RAY-MOND — Deep-Sea

1 ❑ Cover: 2.95 **NM** value: **Cover or less**
2 ❑ Cover: 2.95 **NM** value: **Cover or less**

RAYNE — Sheet Happies

1 ❑ Jul 1995, b&w Cover: 2.50 **NM** value: **Cover or less**
2 ❑ Apr 1996, b&w Cover: 2.50 **NM** value: **Cover or less**
cover says Mar, indicia says Apr.
3 ❑ Aug 1996, b&w Cover: 2.50 **NM** value: **Cover or less**
4 ❑ Jul 1997, b&w Cover: 2.95 **NM** value: **Cover or less**

RAZOR — London Night

Razor is Nicole Symone Mitchell, daughter of the infamous Frank Mitchell. Frank Mitchell owned the city's cops, but he stepped over the line — and wound up dead. He was killed in a so-called robbery arranged by rival Roman Von Drake. Mitchell's younger daughter, Jackie, was kidnapped, and never heard from again. Nicole, the eldest, was found lying beside her dead father. She spent the next several years in intensive psychiatric care.

Apparently, the cure didn't take. Now, as Razor, she's getting even. Wielding a pair of claw-like razors, she's out to avenge her father's killer, and tearing up anyone who gets in her way-even her long lost sister!

Razor is an action-packed series, although often brutal and shockingly violent. There are also the occasional "nude" covers, almost a London Night trademark.

0 ❑ Cover: 3.00 **NM** value: **Cover or less**
Circ: CapCity orders: **6,985**
📖 Torture **A:** Slick **W:** Jude Millien
0/A ❑ Cover: 3.95 **NM** value: **4.00**
• Direct Market edition.
0-2 ❑ **NM** value: **3.00**
0.5 ❑ **NM** value: **3.00**
• Promotional giveaway. ★ 1st Appearance of Poizon.
1 ❑ Aug 1992 Cover: 2.50 **NM** value: **4.00**
📖 The Suffering **A:** Everette Hartsoe **W:** Everette Hartsoe
1-2 ❑ Cover: 3.00 **NM** value: **Cover or less**
2 ❑ Cover: 2.50 **NM** value: **3.00**
A: James O'Barr(cover)
2/PL❑ **NM** value: **4.00**
• Platinum edition. **A:** James O'Barr(cover)
2/SC❑ Cover: 3.95 **NM** value: **5.00**
A: James O'Barr(cover)
3 ❑ Cover: 2.50 **NM** value: **3.00**
3/CS❑ **NM** value: **4.00**
4 ❑ Cover: 2.50 **NM** value: **3.00**
4/PL❑ **NM** value: **4.00**
5 ❑ **NM** value: **3.00**
A: Joseph Michael Linsner(cover)
5/PL❑ **NM** value: **4.00**
• Platinum edition. **A:** Joseph Michael Linsner(cover)
6 ❑ **NM** value: **3.00**
7 ❑ **NM** value: **3.00**
8 ❑ Cover: 2.95 **NM** value: **3.00**
9 ❑ **NM** value: **3.00**
10 ❑ Cover: 3.00 **NM** value: **Cover or less**
Circ: CapCity orders: **4,105**
★ Origin of Stryke.
11 ❑ Sep 1994, b&w Cover: 3.00 **NM** value: **Cover or less**
Circ: CapCity orders: **4,360**
12 ❑ b&w Cover: 3.00 **NM** value: **Cover or less**
• Series continued in Razor Uncut #13
Anl 1❑ca. 1993 Cover: 2.95 **NM** value: **20.00**
• **CGC:** 5 graded, best 9.0
★ 1st Appearance of Shi.
Anl 1/GO❑ Cover: 2.95 **NM** value: **25.00**
• Gold limited edition. ★ 1st Appearance of Shi.
Anl 2❑b&w Cover: 3.00 **NM** value: **3.50**

RAZOR & SHI SPECIAL — London Night

1 ❑ **NM** value: **3.00**
Circ: CapCity orders: **13,455**
• Crossover with Crusade
1/PL❑ **NM** value: **4.00**
• Platinum edition.

RAZOR ARCHIVES — London Night

1 ❑ May 1997 Cover: 3.95 **NM** value: **Cover or less**
Circ: Diamd. preorders: **4,529**
📖 Angel in Black **A:** Everette Hartsoe **W:** Everette Hartsoe
2 ❑ Jun 1997 Cover: 5.00 **NM** value: **Cover or less**
Circ: Diamd. preorders: **4,132**
📖 Angel in Black **A:** Richard Pollard **W:** Everette Hartsoe
3 ❑ Cover: 5.00 **NM** value: **Cover or less**
W: Everette Hartsoe
4 ❑ Jul 1997 Cover: 5.00 **NM** value: **Cover or less**
A: Jude Millien; Eric Johns **W:** Everette Hartsoe

RAZOR: BURN — London Night

1 ❑ Cover: 3.00 **NM** value: **Cover or less**
Circ: CapCity orders: **11,505**
A: Everette Hartsoe **W:** Everette Hartsoe
2 ❑ Cover: 3.00 **NM** value: **Cover or less**
A: Everette Hartsoe **W:** Everette Hartsoe
3 ❑ Cover: 3.00 **NM** value: **Cover or less**
Circ: CapCity orders: **9,800**
A: Everette Hartsoe **W:** Everette Hartsoe
4 ❑ Cover: 3.00 **NM** value: **Cover or less**
Circ: CapCity orders: **9,695**
A: Everette Hartsoe **W:** Everette Hartsoe

RAZOR/CRY NO MORE — London Night

1 ❑ Cover: 3.95 **NM** value: **Cover or less**
No issue number. **A:** Richard Pollard **W:** Everette Hartsoe

RAZOR: DARK ANGEL/FINAL NAIL — London Night

1 ❑ Cover: 3.00 **NM** value: **Cover or less**
Circ: CapCity orders: **3,360**

RAZORGUTS — Monster

1 ❑ b&w Cover: 2.25 **NM** value: **Cover or less**
A: Francisco Solano Lopez **W:** Barreir
2 ❑ Feb 1992, b&w Cover: 2.25 **NM** value: **Cover or less**
A: Francisco Solano Lopez **W:** Barreir
3 ❑ b&w Cover: 2.25 **NM** value: **Cover or less**
4 ❑ b&w Cover: 2.25 **NM** value: **Cover or less**

RAZORLINE: THE FIRST CUT — Marvel

1 ❑ Cover: 0.75 **NM** value: **1.00**
Circ: CapCity orders: **36,300**
📖 Have You Heard The One About Felon Bale? • sampler; Previews Hokum & Hex, Hyperkind, Saint Sinner, and Ectokid **A:** Anthony Williams; Max Douglas **W:** Elaine Lee; Frank Lovece

RAZOR/MORBID ANGEL — London Night

1 ❑ Aug 1996 Cover: 3.00 **NM** value: **Cover or less**
2 ❑ Nov 1996 Cover: 3.00 **NM** value: **Cover or less**
Circ: Diamd. preorders: **10,584**
3 ❑ Dec 1996 Cover: 3.00 **NM** value: **Cover or less**
Circ: Diamd. preorders: **9,192**
A: Albert Kolaso **W:** Everette Hartsoe

RAZOR'S EDGE — Innovation

1 ❑ b&w Cover: 2.50 **NM** value: **Cover or less**

RAZOR: THE SUFFERING — London Night

1 ❑ Cover: 3.00 **NM** value: **Cover or less**
Circ: CapCity orders: **4,255**
1/A ❑ Cover: 3.00 **NM** value: **Cover or less**
Circ: CapCity orders: **5,680**
• "Director's Cut"
2 ❑ Cover: 3.00 **NM** value: **Cover or less**
Circ: CapCity orders: **3,450**
2/A ❑ Cover: 3.00 **NM** value: **Cover or less**
• "Director's Cut"
3 ❑ Cover: 3.00 **NM** value: **Cover or less**
Circ: CapCity orders: **4,025**
Bk 1❑ Cover: 12.95 **NM** value: **Cover or less**
• Collects Razor: The Suffering #1-3

RAZOR: TORTURE — London Night

0 ❑ Dec 1995 Cover: 3.95 **NM** value: **Cover or less**
• **CGC:** 3 graded, best 9.8
enhanced wraparound cover. • polybagged with card and catalog
1 ❑ 1996 Cover: 3.00 **NM** value: **Cover or less**
1/SC❑1996 **NM** value: **3.00**
alternate cover with no cover price.
2 ❑ 1996 Cover: 3.00 **NM** value: **Cover or less**
2/SC❑1996 **NM** value: **3.00**
no cover price.
3 ❑ Apr 1996 Cover: 3.00 **NM** value: **Cover or less**

RAZOR: UNCUT — London Night

13 ❑ 1995 Cover: 3.00 **NM** value: **Cover or less**
Circ: CapCity orders: **7,040**
• Series continued from Razor #12
14 ❑ 1995 Cover: 3.00 **NM** value: **Cover or less**
Circ: CapCity orders: **7,750**
15 ❑ 1995 Cover: 3.00 **NM** value: **Cover or less**
Circ: CapCity orders: **7,515**
16 ❑ 1995 Cover: 3.00 **NM** value: **Cover or less**
Circ: CapCity orders: **7,650**
17 ❑ 1995 Cover: 3.00 **NM** value: **Cover or less**
18 ❑ Dec 1995 Cover: 3.00 **NM** value: **Cover or less**
19 ❑ 1995 Cover: 3.00 **NM** value: **Cover or less**
20 ❑ 1995b&w Cover: 3.00 **NM** value: **Cover or less**
21 ❑ May 1996, b&w Cover: 3.00 **NM** value: **Cover or less**
22 ❑ 1996b&w Cover: 3.00 **NM** value: **Cover or less**
23 ❑ 1996 Cover: 3.00 **NM** value: **Cover or less**
24 ❑ 1996 Cover: 3.00 **NM** value: **Cover or less**
25 ❑ 1996 Cover: 3.00 **NM** value: **Cover or less**
26 ❑ Sep 1996 Cover: 3.00 **NM** value: **Cover or less**
Circ: Diamd. preorders: **11,085**
27 ❑ Oct 1996 Cover: 3.00 **NM** value: **Cover or less**
Circ: Diamd. preorders: **10,908**
28 ❑ Oct 1996 Cover: 3.00 **NM** value: **Cover or less**
Circ: Diamd. preorders: **10,845**
29 ❑ Nov 1996 Cover: 3.00 **NM** value: **Cover or less**
Circ: Diamd. preorders: **10,193**
30 ❑ Dec 1996 Cover: 3.00 **NM** value: **Cover or less**
Circ: Diamd. preorders: **9,353**
31 ❑ Jan 1997 Cover: 3.00 **NM** value: **Cover or less**
Circ: Diamd. preorders: **8,471**
32 ❑ Feb 1997 Cover: 3.00 **NM** value: **Cover or less**
Circ: Diamd. preorders: **8,888**
33 ❑ Feb 1997 Cover: 3.00 **NM** value: **Cover or less**
Circ: Diamd. preorders: **7,646**
34 ❑ Mar 1997 Cover: 3.00 **NM** value: **Cover or less**
Circ: Diamd. preorders: **7,697**
35 ❑ Apr 1997 Cover: 3.00 **NM** value: **Cover or less**
Circ: Diamd. preorders: **7,382**
36 ❑ May 1997 Cover: 3.00 **NM** value: **Cover or less**
Circ: Diamd. preorders: **7,631**
37 ❑ Jun 1997 Cover: 3.00 **NM** value: **Cover or less**
Circ: Diamd. preorders: **6,740**
38 ❑ Jul 1997 Cover: 3.00 **NM** value: **Cover or less**
Circ: Diamd. preorders: **6,434**
39 ❑ Aug 1997 Cover: 3.00 **NM** value: **Cover or less**
Circ: Diamd. preorders: **6,434**
40 ❑ Sep 1997 Cover: 3.00 **NM** value: **Cover or less**
Circ: Diamd. preorders: **5,852**
41 ❑ Oct 1997 Cover: 3.00 **NM** value: **Cover or less**
Circ: Diamd. preorders: **5,880**
42 ❑ Nov 1997 Cover: 3.00 **NM** value: **Cover or less**
Circ: Diamd. preorders: **5,564**
43 ❑ Dec 1997 Cover: 3.00 **NM** value: **Cover or less**
Circ: Diamd. preorders: **5,221**

44 ❑ 1998 Cover: 3.00 **NM** value: **Cover or less**
Circ: Diamd. preorders: **4,345**
45 ❑ 1998 Cover: 3.00 **NM** value: **Cover or less**
Circ: Diamd. preorders: **4,830**
46 ❑ 1998 Cover: 3.00 **NM** value: **Cover or less**
Circ: Diamd. preorders: **4,354**
47 ❑ 1998 Cover: 3.00 **NM** value: **Cover or less**
Circ: Diamd. preorders: **4,323**
48 ❑ 1998 Cover: 3.00 **NM** value: **Cover or less**
49 ❑ 1998 Cover: 3.00 **NM** value: **Cover or less**
50 ❑ 1999 Cover: 3.00 **NM** value: **Cover or less**
Circ: Diamd. preorders: **4,465**
51 ❑ Mar 1999 Cover: 3.00 **NM** value: **Cover or less**
Circ: Diamd. preorders: **2,439**

RAZOR (VOL. 2) — London Night

1 ❑ Oct 1996 Cover: 3.95 **NM** value: **Cover or less**
Circ: Diamd. preorders: **24,197**
2 ❑ Nov 1996 Cover: 3.00 **NM** value: **Cover or less**
Circ: Diamd. preorders: **13,413**
3 ❑ Dec 1996 Cover: 3.00 **NM** value: **Cover or less**
Circ: Diamd. preorders: **11,742**
4 ❑ Mar 1997 Cover: 3.00 **NM** value: **Cover or less**
5 ❑ Apr 1997 Cover: 3.00 **NM** value: **Cover or less**
Circ: Diamd. preorders: **8,694**
6 ❑ May 1997 Cover: 3.00 **NM** value: **Cover or less**
Circ: Diamd. preorders: **8,019**
A: Albert Holaso **W:** David Quinn
7 ❑ Jun 1997 Cover: 3.00 **NM** value: **Cover or less**
Circ: Diamd. preorders: **7,862**
📖 Money for Hire final issue. **A:** Shawn Atkinson **W:** Roger Brown

RAZOR/WARRIOR NUN AREALA-FAITH — London Night

1 ❑ May 1996 Cover: 3.95 **NM** value: **Cover or less**
No issue number. • one-shot crossover with Antarctic **A:** Jude Millien **W:** Jude Millien

RAZORWIRE — 5th Panel

1 ❑ Jun 1996, b&w Cover: 1.50 **NM** value: **Cover or less**
📖 All Parts Being Equal, Run Amok, Pieces, Bite **A:** Kevin Leen; Todd Richards; David Witt **W:** Todd Richards; David Witt; Nora Callahan
2 ❑ Jul 1997, b&w Cover: 1.95 **NM** value: **Cover or less**
📖 Bite 2; All Parts Being Equal Part 2; Run Amok Part 2; They Call me Ball Breaker Part 2 **A:** Kevin Leen; Todd Richards; David Witt **W:** Todd Richards; David Witt; Nora Callahan

REACTION: THE ULTIMATE MAN — Studio Archein

1 ❑ Cover: 2.95 **NM** value: **Cover or less**
No issue number.

REACTO-MAN — B-Movie

1 ❑ Cover: 1.50 **NM** value: **Cover or less**
📖 Shock Value **A:** Ken Holewczynski **W:** Ken Holewczynski
2 ❑ Cover: 1.50 **NM** value: **Cover or less**
A: Ken Holewczynski **W:** Ken Holewczynski
3 ❑ Cover: 1.50 **NM** value: **Cover or less**
A: Ken Holewczynski **W:** Ken Holewczynski ★ 1st Appearance of Warhead.

REACTOR GIRL — Tragedy Strikes

1 ❑ b&w Cover: 2.50 **NM** value: **Cover or less**
2 ❑ Cover: 2.95 **NM** value: **Cover or less**
3 ❑ Cover: 2.95 **NM** value: **Cover or less**
4 ❑ Cover: 2.95 **NM** value: **Cover or less**
5 ❑ Cover: 2.95 **NM** value: **Cover or less**

READ MY LIPS! — Malibu

Bk 1❑ Cover: 6.95 **NM** value: **Cover or less**
No issue number. • political humor

REAGAN'S RAIDERS — Solson

1 ❑ Cover: 2.00 **NM** value: **Cover or less**
A: Rich Buckler
2 ❑ Cover: 2.00 **NM** value: **Cover or less**
A: Rich Buckler
3 ❑ Cover: 2.00 **NM** value: **Cover or less**
A: Rich Buckler

REAL ADVENTURE COMICS — Gilmore

1 ❑ Apr 1955 Cover: 0.10 **NM** value: **25.00**

REAL ADVENTURES OF JONNY QUEST, THE — Dark Horse

TV cartoon hero Jonny Quest doesn't spend his time playing video games or hanging out at the mall: most of the time, he's traveling the world and helping his father investigate mysterious crimes. He's not alone-his friend Hadji and his clever dog Bandit help thwart criminals and get Jonny of out tight binds. Jonny now even has a female sidekick, Jessie, who just happens to be clever enough with computers that she can hack into a rogue's system and decrypt stolen files.

The comic book series follows the tone of the revamped 1990s cartoon show faithfully, including its emphasis on appreciating diversity and cross-cultural understanding.

1 ❑ Sep 1996 Cover: 2.95 **NM** value: **3.00**
📖 Net of Chaos, Part 1 • based on 1996 animated series **A:** Francisco Solano Lopez **W:** Kate Worley
2 ❑ Oct 1996 Cover: 2.95 **NM** value: **Cover or less**
Circ: Diamd. preorders: **12,322**
📖 Net of Chaos, Part 2 **A:** Francisco Solano Lopez **W:** Kate Worley
3 ❑ Nov 1996 Cover: 2.95 **NM** value: **Cover or less**
Circ: Diamd. preorders: **9,624**
4 ❑ Dec 1996 Cover: 2.95 **NM** value: **Cover or less**
Circ: Diamd. preorders: **8,038**
5 ❑ Jan 1997 Cover: 2.95 **NM** value: **Cover or less**
Circ: Diamd. preorders: **6,796**
6 ❑ Feb 1997 Cover: 2.95 **NM** value: **Cover or less**
Circ: Diamd. preorders: **6,170**
7 ❑ Mar 1997 Cover: 2.95 **NM** value: **Cover or less**
Circ: Diamd. preorders: **5,411**
8 ❑ May 1997 Cover: 2.95 **NM** value: **Cover or less**
Circ: Diamd. preorders: **5,494**
9 ❑ Jun 1997 Cover: 2.95 **NM** value: **Cover or less**
Circ: Diamd. preorders: **5,216**
10 ❑ Jul 1997 Cover: 2.95 **NM** value: **Cover or less**
Circ: Diamd. preorders: **4,928**
11 ❑ Aug 1997 Cover: 2.95 **NM** value: **Cover or less**
Circ: Diamd. preorders: **4,680**
12 ❑ Sep 1997 Cover: 2.95 **NM** value: **Cover or less**
Circ: Diamd. preorders: **4,460**
final issue.

REAL CLUE CRIME STORIES — Hillman

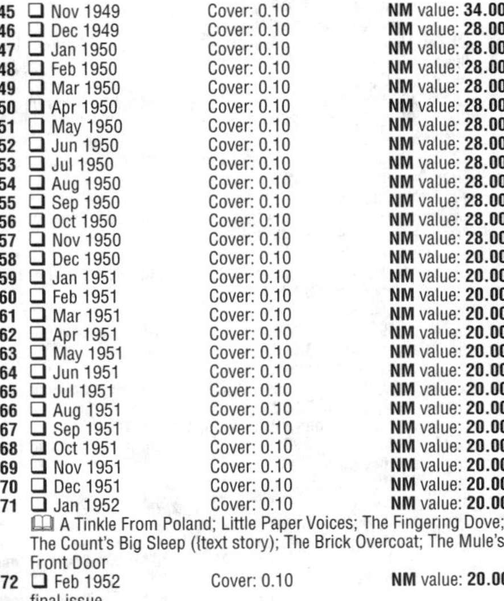

The slogan of this crime and detective series is "Commit a crime, and the world is made of glass."

Formerly known as Clue Comics, Real Clue Crime Stories served up rather standard crime-story fare from 1947 up until just before the Comics Code came along. Like its sister title Crime Detective, Real Clue Crime stories featured assorted gangsters, robbers, and murderers who were inevitably brought down by the long arm of the law.

For variety, Real Clue Crime Stories also included a handful of period pieces, set in exotic locations and times such as the old Spanish West.

1 ❑ Jan 1943 Cover: 0.10 **NM** value: **275.00**
• **CGC:** 1 graded, best 8.5
• Series continued from Clue Comics **A:** Joe Simon; Jack Kirby
2 ❑ Feb 1943 Cover: 0.10 **NM** value: **200.00**
📖 The Dummies Died Screaming; Terrible Whyos; Gang Doctor; Wyatt Earpp's Bluff • Gun Master **A:** Joe Simon; Jack Kirby
3 ❑ Mar 1943 Cover: 0.10 **NM** value: **200.00**
📖 Get Me The Golden Gun; Let Me Plan Your Murder • Gun Master **A:** Joe Simon; Jack Kirby
4 ❑ Jun 1943 Cover: 0.10 **NM** value: **200.00**
📖 Mr. Reed Waddell; Gang War; The Mad White God of Palm Island **A:** Joe Simon; Jack Kirby
5 ❑ Sep 1943 Cover: 0.10 **NM** value: **55.00**
• **CGC:** 1 graded, best 9.4
6 ❑ Dec 1943 Cover: 0.10 **NM** value: **55.00**
7 ❑ Mar 1944 Cover: 0.10 **NM** value: **55.00**
8 ❑ Fal 1944 Cover: 0.10 **NM** value: **55.00**
9 ❑ Win 1944 Cover: 0.10 **NM** value: **55.00**
10 ❑ Oct 1946 Cover: 0.10 **NM** value: **45.00**
• **CGC:** 1 graded, best 9.6
11 ❑ Dec 1946 Cover: 0.10 **NM** value: **45.00**
12 ❑ Feb 1947 Cover: 0.10 **NM** value: **45.00**
• **CGC:** 1 graded, best 9.0
13 ❑ Mar 1947 Cover: 0.10 **NM** value: **45.00**
14 ❑ Apr 1947 Cover: 0.10 **NM** value: **45.00**
15 ❑ May 1947 Cover: 0.10 **NM** value: **45.00**
16 ❑ Jun 1947 Cover: 0.10 **NM** value: **45.00**
17 ❑ Jul 1947 Cover: 0.10 **NM** value: **45.00**
18 ❑ Aug 1947 Cover: 0.10 **NM** value: **45.00**
• Cited in Seduction of the Innocent as story representing anti-Semitic stereotypes
19 ❑ Sep 1947 Cover: 0.10 **NM** value: **45.00**
20 ❑ Oct 1947 Cover: 0.10 **NM** value: **45.00**
21 ❑ Nov 1947 Cover: 0.10 **NM** value: **45.00**
22 ❑ Dec 1947 Cover: 0.10 **NM** value: **40.00**
23 ❑ Jan 1948 Cover: 0.10 **NM** value: **40.00**
24 ❑ Feb 1948 Cover: 0.10 **NM** value: **40.00**
25 ❑ Mar 1948 Cover: 0.10 **NM** value: **40.00**
26 ❑ Apr 1948 Cover: 0.10 **NM** value: **40.00**
27 ❑ May 1948 Cover: 0.10 **NM** value: **40.00**
28 ❑ Jun 1948 Cover: 0.10 **NM** value: **40.00**
29 ❑ Jul 1948 Cover: 0.10 **NM** value: **40.00**
30 ❑ Aug 1948 Cover: 0.10 **NM** value: **40.00**
31 ❑ Sep 1948 Cover: 0.10 **NM** value: **40.00**
32 ❑ Oct 1948 Cover: 0.10 **NM** value: **40.00**
33 ❑ Nov 1948 Cover: 0.10 **NM** value: **40.00**
34 ❑ Dec 1948 Cover: 0.10 **NM** value: **34.00**
35 ❑ Jan 1949 Cover: 0.10 **NM** value: **34.00**
36 ❑ Feb 1949 Cover: 0.10 **NM** value: **34.00**
37 ❑ Mar 1949 Cover: 0.10 **NM** value: **34.00**
38 ❑ Apr 1949 Cover: 0.10 **NM** value: **34.00**
39 ❑ May 1949 Cover: 0.10 **NM** value: **34.00**
40 ❑ Jun 1949 Cover: 0.10 **NM** value: **34.00**
📖 The Rat Loves to Bump; The Weapon of Da Vinci; Willie the Weeper; The Nickel Nurser; The Books are Closed (Text Story); Maestro McCoy; The Murder Rock; Gas Tank Killer; The Hard-Working Gun;
41 ❑ Jul 1949 Cover: 0.10 **NM** value: **34.00**
42 ❑ Aug 1949 Cover: 0.10 **NM** value: **34.00**
43 ❑ Sep 1949 Cover: 0.10 **NM** value: **34.00**
44 ❑ Oct 1949 Cover: 0.10 **NM** value: **34.00**
45 ❑ Nov 1949 Cover: 0.10 **NM** value: **34.00**
46 ❑ Dec 1949 Cover: 0.10 **NM** value: **28.00**
47 ❑ Jan 1950 Cover: 0.10 **NM** value: **28.00**
48 ❑ Feb 1950 Cover: 0.10 **NM** value: **28.00**
49 ❑ Mar 1950 Cover: 0.10 **NM** value: **28.00**
50 ❑ Apr 1950 Cover: 0.10 **NM** value: **28.00**
51 ❑ May 1950 Cover: 0.10 **NM** value: **28.00**
52 ❑ Jun 1950 Cover: 0.10 **NM** value: **28.00**
53 ❑ Jul 1950 Cover: 0.10 **NM** value: **28.00**
54 ❑ Aug 1950 Cover: 0.10 **NM** value: **28.00**
55 ❑ Sep 1950 Cover: 0.10 **NM** value: **28.00**
56 ❑ Oct 1950 Cover: 0.10 **NM** value: **28.00**
57 ❑ Nov 1950 Cover: 0.10 **NM** value: **28.00**
58 ❑ Dec 1950 Cover: 0.10 **NM** value: **20.00**
59 ❑ Jan 1951 Cover: 0.10 **NM** value: **20.00**
60 ❑ Feb 1951 Cover: 0.10 **NM** value: **20.00**
61 ❑ Mar 1951 Cover: 0.10 **NM** value: **20.00**
62 ❑ Apr 1951 Cover: 0.10 **NM** value: **20.00**
63 ❑ May 1951 Cover: 0.10 **NM** value: **20.00**
64 ❑ Jun 1951 Cover: 0.10 **NM** value: **20.00**
65 ❑ Jul 1951 Cover: 0.10 **NM** value: **20.00**
66 ❑ Aug 1951 Cover: 0.10 **NM** value: **20.00**
67 ❑ Sep 1951 Cover: 0.10 **NM** value: **20.00**
68 ❑ Oct 1951 Cover: 0.10 **NM** value: **20.00**
69 ❑ Nov 1951 Cover: 0.10 **NM** value: **20.00**
70 ❑ Dec 1951 Cover: 0.10 **NM** value: **20.00**
71 ❑ Jan 1952 Cover: 0.10 **NM** value: **20.00**
📖 A Tinkle From Poland; Little Paper Voices; The Fingering Dove; The Count's Big Sleep ((text story); The Brick Overcoat; The Mule's Front Door
72 ❑ Feb 1952 Cover: 0.10 **NM** value: **20.00**
final issue.

REAL DEAL MAGAZINE — Real Deal

5 ❑ b&w Cover: 2.00 **NM** value: **Cover or less**
• magazine.

REAL EXPERIENCES — Atlas

25 ❑ ca. 1950 Cover: 0.10 **NM** value: **35.00**

REAL FACT COMICS — DC

1 ❑ Mar 1946 Cover: 0.10 **NM** value: **500.00**
• **CGC:** 3 graded, best 8.5
2 ❑ May 1946 Cover: 0.10 **NM** value: **400.00**
• **CGC:** 1 graded, best 9.2
3 ❑ Jul 1946 Cover: 0.10 **NM** value: **400.00**
• **CGC:** 2 graded, best 9.6
4 ❑ Sep 1946 Cover: 0.10 **NM** value: **400.00**
• **CGC:** 2 graded, best 9.6
5 ❑ Nov 1946 Cover: 0.10 **NM** value: **375.00**
• **CGC:** 6 graded, best 9.4
6 ❑ Jan 1947 Cover: 0.10 **NM** value: **375.00**
• **CGC:** 3 graded, best 9.4
7 ❑ Mar 1947 Cover: 0.10 **NM** value: **375.00**
• **CGC:** 2 graded, best 9.0
8 ❑ May 1947 Cover: 0.10 **NM** value: **375.00**
• **CGC:** 3 graded, best 9.4
9 ❑ Jul 1947 Cover: 0.10 **NM** value: **375.00**
10 ❑ Sep 1947 Cover: 0.10 **NM** value: **350.00**
• **CGC:** 1 graded, best 9.6
11 ❑ Nov 1947 Cover: 0.10 **NM** value: **350.00**
• **CGC:** 3 graded, best 8.5
12 ❑ Jan 1948 Cover: 0.10 **NM** value: **350.00**
• **CGC:** 1 graded, best 9.0
13 ❑ Mar 1948 Cover: 0.10 **NM** value: **350.00**
14 ❑ May 1948 Cover: 0.10 **NM** value: **300.00**
15 ❑ Jul 1948 Cover: 0.10 **NM** value: **300.00**
• **CGC:** 2 graded, best 8.5
16 ❑ Sep 1948 Cover: 0.10 **NM** value: **250.00**
17 ❑ Nov 1948 Cover: 0.10 **NM** value: **250.00**
18 ❑ Jan 1949 Cover: 0.10 **NM** value: **250.00**
19 ❑ Mar 1949 Cover: 0.10 **NM** value: **250.00**
• **CGC:** 1 graded, best 9.6
20 ❑ May 1949 Cover: 0.10 **NM** value: **200.00**
21 ❑ Jul 1949 Cover: 0.10 **NM** value: **200.00**

REAL FUNNIES — Nedor

1 ❑ Jan 1943 Cover: 0.10 **NM** value: **250.00**
2 ❑ Mar 1943 Cover: 0.10 **NM** value: **125.00**
3 ❑ Jun 1943 Cover: 0.10 **NM** value: **125.00**

REAL GHOSTBUSTERS SUMMER SPECIAL — Now

1 ❑ Sum 1993 Cover: 2.95 **NM** value: **Cover or less**
No issue number.

REAL GHOSTBUSTERS, THE (VOL. 1) — Now

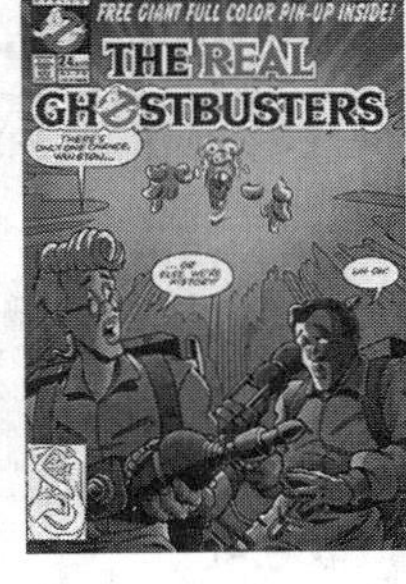

The movie Ghostbusters, starring Bill Murray, Dan Ackroyd, Rick Moranis, and others, was one of the more enjoyable films of 1984. Parapsychologists who decided to form the astral equivalent of an exterminator service, the Ghostbusters answered the call whenever anyone's house, castle, or office building was haunted.

Inevitably, the film was made into a cartoon series. "The Real Ghostbusters" added the standard comic relief character in Slimer, a pudgy ghost who'd get his own comic book. There was already an unrelated cartoon called Ghostbusters, explaining the need to identify this version as "Real."

1 ❑ Aug 1988 Cover: 1.75 **NM** value: **2.00**

CGC-graded: Multiply prices above by **33 for 9.9 M • 16 for 9.8 NM/M • 7 for 9.6 NM+ • 5 for 9.4 NM • 2.5 for 9.2 NM- • 1.5 for 9.0 VF/NM**

Circ: CapCity orders: **4,450**
• Ghostbusters movie adaptation **W:** James Van Hise

2 ❑ Sep 1988 Cover: 1.75 **NM** value: **Cover or less**
Circ: CapCity orders: **3,525**
W: James Van Hise

3 ❑ Oct 1988 Cover: 1.75 **NM** value: **Cover or less**
Circ: CapCity orders: **2,200**
W: James Van Hise

4 ❑ Nov 1988 Cover: 1.75 **NM** value: **Cover or less**
Circ: CapCity orders: **3,200**
W: James Van Hise

5 ❑ Jan 1989 Cover: 1.75 **NM** value: **Cover or less**
Circ: CapCity orders: **3,275**
W: James Van Hise

6 ❑ Feb 1989 Cover: 1.75 **NM** value: **Cover or less**
Circ: CapCity orders: **3,675**
W: James Van Hise

7 ❑ Mar 1989 Cover: 1.75 **NM** value: **Cover or less**
Circ: CapCity orders: **3,650**
A: John Tobias **W:** James Van Hise

8 ❑ Apr 1989 Cover: 1.75 **NM** value: **Cover or less**
Circ: CapCity orders: **3,500**
📖 Toad Island **A:** John Tobias **W:** James Van Hise

9 ❑ May 1989 Cover: 1.75 **NM** value: **Cover or less**
Circ: CapCity orders: **3,300**
W: James Van Hise

10 ❑ Jun 1989 Cover: 1.75 **NM** value: **Cover or less**
Circ: CapCity orders: **3,250**
W: James Van Hise

11 ❑ Jul 1989 Cover: 1.75 **NM** value: **Cover or less**
W: James Van Hise

12 ❑ Aug 1989 Cover: 1.75 **NM** value: **Cover or less**
Circ: CapCity orders: **3,275**
W: James Van Hise

13 ❑ Sep 1989 Cover: 1.75 **NM** value: **Cover or less**
Circ: CapCity orders: **3,025**
W: James Van Hise

14 ❑ Oct 1989 Cover: 1.75 **NM** value: **Cover or less**
Circ: CapCity orders: **2,875**
W: James Van Hise

15 ❑ Nov 1989 Cover: 1.75 **NM** value: **Cover or less**
Circ: CapCity orders: **2,850**
W: James Van Hise

16 ❑ Dec 1989 Cover: 1.75 **NM** value: **Cover or less**
Circ: CapCity orders: **3,250**
W: James Van Hise

17 ❑ Jan 1990 Cover: 1.75 **NM** value: **Cover or less**
Circ: CapCity orders: **3,025**
W: James Van Hise

18 ❑ Feb 1990 Cover: 1.75 **NM** value: **Cover or less**
Circ: CapCity orders: **2,775**
W: James Van Hise

19 ❑ Mar 1990 Cover: 1.75 **NM** value: **Cover or less**
Circ: CapCity orders: **2,775**
W: James Van Hise

20 ❑ Apr 1990 Cover: 1.75 **NM** value: **Cover or less**
Circ: CapCity orders: **2,725**
📖 ...At the Earth's Core! **A:** Phil Hester **W:** James Van Hise

21 ❑ May 1990 Cover: 1.75 **NM** value: **Cover or less**
Circ: CapCity orders: **2,450**
📖 Ecto-X!; The Spooked Suit!; Neanderthal Nightmare! **A:** Phil Elliott; Anthony Williams; Andy Lanning **W:** Phil Elliott; Andrew Brenner; John Carnell

22 ❑ Jun 1990 Cover: 1.75 **NM** value: **Cover or less**
Circ: CapCity orders: **2,275**
W: James Van Hise

23 ❑ Jul 1990 Cover: 1.75 **NM** value: **Cover or less**
Circ: CapCity orders: **2,250**
W: James Van Hise

24 ❑ Aug 1990 Cover: 1.75 **NM** value: **Cover or less**
Circ: CapCity orders: **2,050**
📖 Carnival **A:** Neil Graham **W:** James Van Hise

25 ❑ Sep 1990 Cover: 1.75 **NM** value: **Cover or less**
Circ: CapCity orders: **2,075**
W: James Van Hise

26 ❑ Oct 1990 Cover: 1.75 **NM** value: **Cover or less**
Circ: CapCity orders: **1,950**
W: James Van Hise

27 ❑ Nov 1990 Cover: 1.75 **NM** value: **Cover or less**
Circ: CapCity orders: **1,875**
📖 The Last Voyage of the Lady Anne **A:** Neil Graham **W:** James Van Hise

28 ❑ Dec 1990 Cover: 1.75 **NM** value: **Cover or less**
Circ: CapCity orders: **1,750**
• Final issue? **W:** James Van Hise

3D 1❑ Cover: 2.95 **NM** value: **Cover or less**
• gatefold summary. 📖 Slimer's Unbirthday; It's Slimer!; Cooking With Slimer; Singing the Slime Blues **A:** Phil Elliott; Bambos; Jerry Salinas; Mark Bralin **W:** Bambos; Joe Carnell; Larry Parr; Shannon McCutcheon

REAL GHOSTBUSTERS (VOL. 2) — Now

1 ❑ Nov 1991 Cover: 1.75 **NM** value: **Cover or less**
1/3D❑ Oct 1991 Cover: 2.95 **NM** value: **Cover or less**
• polybagged; w/glasses
2 ❑ Dec 1991 Cover: 1.75 **NM** value: **Cover or less**
Circ: CapCity orders: **1,500**
3 ❑ Jan 1992 Cover: 1.75 **NM** value: **Cover or less**
4 ❑ Feb 1992 Cover: 1.75 **NM** value: **Cover or less**
Anl 1992❑ Mar 1992 Cover: 1.00 **NM** value: **Cover or less**
Anl 1993❑ Dec 1992 Cover: 2.95 **NM** value: **Cover or less**
• 3-D.

REAL GIRL — Fantagraphics

All issues are adults only.

1 ❑ b&w Cover: 2.50 **NM** value: **Cover or less**
2 ❑ b&w Cover: 2.50 **NM** value: **Cover or less**
3 ❑ b&w Cover: 2.95 **NM** value: **Cover or less**
4 ❑ b&w Cover: 2.95 **NM** value: **Cover or less**
5 ❑ b&w Cover: 3.50 **NM** value: **Cover or less**
6 ❑ b&w Cover: 3.50 **NM** value: **Cover or less**
7 ❑ Aug 1994, b&w Cover: 3.50 **NM** value: **Cover or less**

REAL HEROES — Parents' Magazine Institute

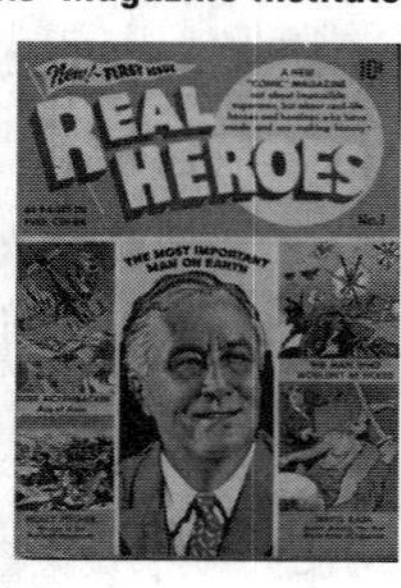

During World War II and the years following, great effort was expended to increase morale and national loyalty. In a time of great challenge, it was crucial to provide heroic role models. Usually this meant world leaders and other public figures, like Franklin Delano Roosevelt, Winston Churchill, and Lou Gehrig — but it was also important to remind people that even ordinary folks just like themselves could perform deeds of heroism and courage.

The Parents' Magazine Institute published 16 issues of Real Heroes between 1941 and 1946, each with several stories about men and women doing extraordinary things. Every kind of hero was featured: famous explorers and adventurers, contemporary and historical soldiers and world leaders, record-setting sports figures, even stage and screen celebrities. Scattered among the stories of the more famous people, tales of 'Everyday Heroes' were spotlighted. Even animals got a few pages of fame.

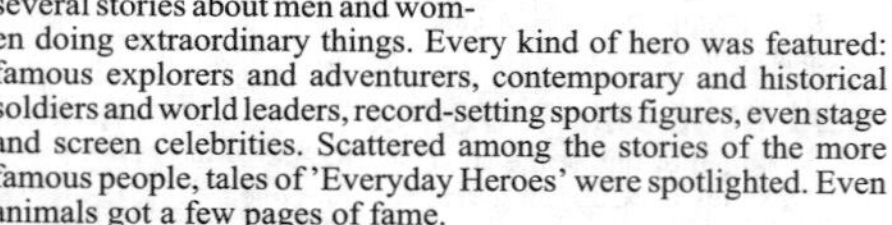

1 ❑ Sep 1941 Cover: 0.10 **NM** value: **125.00**
• **CGC:** 2 graded, best 7.0
2 ❑ 1941 Cover: 0.10 **NM** value: **75.00**
3 ❑ 1942 Cover: 0.10 **NM** value: **60.00**
📖 John Paul Jones; Gellert; The Avenger; Toussant Louverture; Everyday Hero; Real Heroes' Quiz; Sitting Bull; Real heroes' Hall of Fame; Eddie Foy; Snatched From Death; Girl in Command; Glenn Cunningham; Super-Strategist
4 ❑ 1942 Cover: 0.10 **NM** value: **60.00**
5 ❑ 1942 Cover: 0.10 **NM** value: **60.00**
6 ❑ 1942 Cover: 0.10 **NM** value: **90.00**
• Lou Gehrig feature
7 ❑ Nov 1942 Cover: 0.10 **NM** value: **45.00**
• **CGC:** 1 graded, best 9.4
8 ❑ Jan 1943 Cover: 0.10 **NM** value: **45.00**
9 ❑ Mar 1943 Cover: 0.10 **NM** value: **45.00**
10 ❑ May 1943 Cover: 0.10 **NM** value: **45.00**
11 ❑ Jul 1943 Cover: 0.10 **NM** value: **40.00**
• **CGC:** 1 graded, best 9.6
12 ❑ ca. 1943 Cover: 0.10 **NM** value: **40.00**
13 ❑ Mar 1946 Cover: 0.10 **NM** value: **40.00**
14 ❑ May 1946 Cover: 0.10 **NM** value: **40.00**
15 ❑ Aug 1946 Cover: 0.10 **NM** value: **40.00**
• **CGC:** 1 graded, best 9.6
16 ❑ Oct 1946 Cover: 0.10 **NM** value: **40.00**

REALISTIC ROMANCES — Realistic Comics

1 ❑ ca. 1951 Cover: 0.10 **NM** value: **125.00**
2 ❑ ca. 1951 Cover: 0.10 **NM** value: **50.00**
3 ❑ ca. 1951 Cover: 0.10 **NM** value: **50.00**
4 ❑ ca. 1952 Cover: 0.10 **NM** value: **50.00**
5 ❑ ca. 1952 Cover: 0.10 **NM** value: **45.00**
6 ❑ ca. 1952 Cover: 0.10 **NM** value: **45.00**
7 ❑ ca. 1952 Cover: 0.10 **NM** value: **45.00**
8 ❑ ca. 1952 Cover: 0.10 **NM** value: **45.00**
15 ❑ ca. 1954 Cover: 0.10 **NM** value: **45.00**
16 ❑ ca. 1954 Cover: 0.10 **NM** value: **45.00**
17 ❑ ca. 1954 Cover: 0.10 **NM** value: **45.00**

REAL LIFE — Fantagraphics

1 ❑ b&w Cover: 2.50 **NM** value: **Cover or less**

REAL LIFE COMICS — Standard

Comic books ordinarily feature the implausible — not surprising, considering that the art form is genuinely suited to depictions of the incredible. But it's not limited to super-heroes or science-fiction, as this title from Standard so effectively demonstrated.

Real Life Comics features tales of heroes that don't wear colorful costumes, but rather army fatigues, buckskins, a coat and tie, or medieval armor. Culling stories from history, this title portrays characters from a myriad of occupations. Stories about everyone from soldiers of the Korean War, to King Louis XI of France, to frontiersman John Colter, to the heroics of everyday people, can be found in this title.

1 ❑ Sep 1941 Cover: 0.10 **NM** value: **300.00**
2 ❑ Nov 1941 Cover: 0.10 **NM** value: **120.00**
3 ❑ Jan 1942 Cover: 0.10 **NM** value: **200.00**
• **CGC:** 3 graded, best 7.5
Hitler cover.
4 ❑ Mar 1942 Cover: 0.10 **NM** value: **85.00**
5 ❑ May 1942 Cover: 0.10 **NM** value: **85.00**
6 ❑ Jul 1942 Cover: 0.10 **NM** value: **75.00**
📖 The United States Navy; Lieutenant Boyd D. Wagner; Japan: The Rise of Yellow Fascism; General U.S. Grant; John Poe: Soldier of Fortune; Peter The Great; The Fighting Admiral (Text Story); Wild Bill Hickok; Black Beard The Pirate; Titan of the North **A:** Charles M. Quinlan; Maurice Gutwirth **W:** Charles M. Quinlan; Maurice Gutwirth; Charles Stoddard
7 ❑ Sep 1942 Cover: 0.10 **NM** value: **75.00**
8 ❑ Nov 1942 Cover: 0.10 **NM** value: **75.00**
9 ❑ Jan 1943 Cover: 0.10 **NM** value: **75.00**
10 ❑ Mar 1943 Cover: 0.10 **NM** value: **75.00**
11 ❑ May 1943 Cover: 0.10 **NM** value: **60.00**
12 ❑ Jul 1943 Cover: 0.10 **NM** value: **60.00**
13 ❑ Sep 1943 Cover: 0.10 **NM** value: **60.00**
14 ❑ Nov 1943 Cover: 0.10 **NM** value: **60.00**
15 ❑ Jan 1944 Cover: 0.10 **NM** value: **60.00**
16 ❑ Mar 1944 Cover: 0.10 **NM** value: **60.00**
17 ❑ May 1944 Cover: 0.10 **NM** value: **60.00**
• **CGC:** 1 graded, best 6.5
18 ❑ Jul 1944 Cover: 0.10 **NM** value: **60.00**
19 ❑ Sep 1944 Cover: 0.10 **NM** value: **60.00**
20 ❑ Nov 1944 Cover: 0.10 **NM** value: **60.00**
• **CGC:** 1 graded, best 7.5
21 ❑ Jan 1945 Cover: 0.10 **NM** value: **45.00**
22 ❑ Mar 1945 Cover: 0.10 **NM** value: **45.00**
23 ❑ May 1945 Cover: 0.10 **NM** value: **45.00**
24 ❑ Jul 1945 Cover: 0.10 **NM** value: **75.00**
• Babe Ruth **A:** Alex Schomburg(cover)
25 ❑ Sep 1945 Cover: 0.10 **NM** value: **45.00**
26 ❑ Nov 1945 Cover: 0.10 **NM** value: **45.00**
27 ❑ Jan 1946 Cover: 0.10 **NM** value: **65.00**
A: Alex Schomburg(cover)
28 ❑ Feb 1946 Cover: 0.10 **NM** value: **45.00**
29 ❑ Mar 1946 Cover: 0.10 **NM** value: **45.00**
30 ❑ Apr 1946 Cover: 0.10 **NM** value: **45.00**
31 ❑ May 1946 Cover: 0.10 **NM** value: **35.00**
32 ❑ Jun 1946 Cover: 0.10 **NM** value: **35.00**
33 ❑ Jul 1946 Cover: 0.10 **NM** value: **35.00**
34 ❑ Aug 1946 Cover: 0.10 **NM** value: **35.00**
35 ❑ Sep 1946 Cover: 0.10 **NM** value: **35.00**
36 ❑ Nov 1946 Cover: 0.10 **NM** value: **35.00**
37 ❑ Jan 1947 Cover: 0.10 **NM** value: **35.00**
38 ❑ Mar 1947 Cover: 0.10 **NM** value: **35.00**
39 ❑ May 1947 Cover: 0.10 **NM** value: **35.00**
40 ❑ Jul 1947 Cover: 0.10 **NM** value: **35.00**
41 ❑ Sep 1947 Cover: 0.10 **NM** value: **30.00**
42 ❑ Nov 1947 Cover: 0.10 **NM** value: **30.00**
43 ❑ Jan 1948 Cover: 0.10 **NM** value: **30.00**
44 ❑ Apr 1948 Cover: 0.10 **NM** value: **30.00**
45 ❑ Jul 1948 Cover: 0.10 **NM** value: **30.00**
46 ❑ Oct 1948 Cover: 0.10 **NM** value: **30.00**
47 ❑ Jan 1949 Cover: 0.10 **NM** value: **30.00**
48 ❑ Apr 1949 Cover: 0.10 **NM** value: **30.00**
49 ❑ Jul 1949 Cover: 0.10 **NM** value: **30.00**
50 ❑ Oct 1949 Cover: 0.10 **NM** value: **125.00**
A: Frank Frazetta
51 ❑ Jan 1950 Cover: 0.10 **NM** value: **24.00**
52 ❑ Apr 1950 Cover: 0.10 **NM** value: **145.00**
• **CGC:** 1 graded, best 9.0
A: Frank Frazetta
53 ❑ Jul 1950 Cover: 0.10 **NM** value: **24.00**
54 ❑ Oct 1950 Cover: 0.10 **NM** value: **24.00**
55 ❑ Jan 1951 Cover: 0.10 **NM** value: **24.00**
56 ❑ Apr 1951 Cover: 0.10 **NM** value: **24.00**
57 ❑ 1951 Cover: 0.10 **NM** value: **24.00**
58 ❑ 1952 Cover: 0.10 **NM** value: **24.00**
📖 Jim Reavis: Arizona's Bogus Baron; Trail Drives; Action Over Korea; Basutoland Buckaroo (text story); Raveneau De Lussan; Story of Iron and Steel; Bonus Rookie... **A:** Bill Elder; Moreira **W:** John Severin; Ruben; Chuck Stanley
59 ❑ Sep 1952 Cover: 0.10 **NM** value: **24.00**
📖 Battle Orphan; Louis XI: The Spider King; Race Against Death; Table Top Railroaders; Our Solar System; Forger's Tracks; Death on the Plains final issue.

REAL LIFE SECRETS — Ace

1 ❑ ca. 1949 Cover: 0.10 **NM** value: **75.00**

REALLY FANTASTIC ALIEN SEX FRENZY (CYNTHIA PETAL'S...) — Fantagraphics / Eros

All issues are adults only.

1 ❑ b&w Cover: 3.95 **NM** value: **Cover or less**

REALM BOOK, THE — Caliber

Bk 1❑ b&w Cover: 9.95 **NM** value: **Cover or less**
Bk 2❑ b&w Cover: 9.95 **NM** value: **Cover or less**
Bk 3❑ b&w Cover: 9.95 **NM** value: **Cover or less**
Bk 4❑ b&w Cover: 12.95 **NM** value: **Cover or less**

REALM HANDBOOK, THE — Caliber

1 ❑ Cover: 2.95 **NM** value: **Cover or less**

REALM OF THE DEAD — Caliber

1 ❑ Cover: 2.95 **NM** value: **Cover or less**
2 ❑ Cover: 2.95 **NM** value: **Cover or less**
3 ❑ Cover: 2.95 **NM** value: **Cover or less**

REALM, THE (VOL. 1) — Arrow

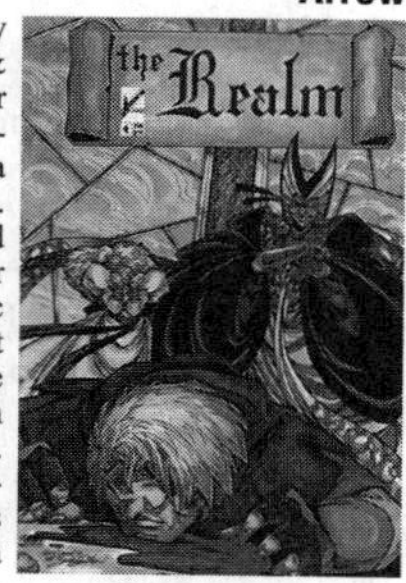

This title was inspired, no doubt, by such fantasy games as Dungeons & Dragons. The story begins when four University of Michigan students travel to a cabin in the Upper Peninsula for a week of rest and relaxation. When they arrive, however, they find themselves transported to another world. In this fantastic place, magic is real, and elves and other races fight against evil on a mythic scale. The college kids become adventurers in this new realm of sword and sorcery.

The Realm was a modestly successful independent fantasy series drawn by Guy Davis. It spawned a

Other grades: Multiply prices above by **1.5 for Mint • 2/3 for Very Fine • 1/3 for Fine • 1/5 for Very Good • 1/8 for Good**

follow-up series at Caliber, as well as a spinoff starring Silverfawn, an Elfin heroine of the series. It is probably most notable for #4's introduction of Deadworld, a zombie-filled nightmare where the dead fight with the living for control of the land.

1 ❑ Cover: 1.50 **NM** value: **3.00**
A: Guy Davis; Ralph Griffith **W:** Stuart Kerr
2 ❑ Cover: 1.50 **NM** value: **2.00**
• repeats indicia for #1 **A:** Guy Davis; Ralph Griffith **W:** Stuart Kerr
3 ❑ Cover: 1.50 **NM** value: **2.00**
A: Guy Davis; Ralph Griffith **W:** Stuart Kerr
4 ❑ Sep 1986 Cover: 1.50 **NM** value: **4.00**
📖 Of Damsels and Darklords; It's a Small World; Black Sabbath **A:** Vincent Locke; Guy Davis; Ralph Griffith **W:** Stuart Kerr ★ 1st Appearance of Deadworld.
5 ❑ Cover: 1.50 **NM** value: **1.75**
A: Guy Davis; Ralph Griffith **W:** Stuart Kerr
6 ❑ Cover: 1.50 **NM** value: **1.75**
A: Guy Davis; Ralph Griffith **W:** Stuart Kerr
7 ❑ Cover: 1.50 **NM** value: **1.75**
A: Guy Davis; Ralph Griffith **W:** Stuart Kerr
8 ❑ Cover: 1.50 **NM** value: **1.75**
A: Guy Davis; Ralph Griffith **W:** Stuart Kerr
9 ❑ Cover: 1.50 **NM** value: **1.75**
A: Guy Davis; Ralph Griffith **W:** Stuart Kerr
10 ❑ Cover: 1.50 **NM** value: **1.75**
A: Guy Davis; Ralph Griffith **W:** Stuart Kerr
11 ❑ Cover: 1.50 **NM** value: **1.75**
📖 A Night on the Town **A:** Guy Davis **W:** Ralph Griffith; Stuart Kerr
12 ❑ Cover: 1.50 **NM** value: **1.75**
A: Guy Davis; Ralph Griffith **W:** Stuart Kerr
13 ❑ Cover: 1.95 **NM** value: **Cover or less**
14 ❑ Feb 1989, b&w Cover: 1.95 **NM** value: **Cover or less**
15 ❑ Apr 1989, b&w Cover: 1.95 **NM** value: **Cover or less**
16 ❑ May 1989, b&w Cover: 1.95 **NM** value: **2.50**
17 ❑ Cover: 2.50 **NM** value: **Cover or less**
18 ❑ Cover: 2.50 **NM** value: **Cover or less**
19 ❑ Cover: 2.50 **NM** value: **Cover or less**
• no publication date
20 ❑ Dec 1990 Cover: 2.50 **NM** value: **Cover or less**
📖 Demonstorm
21 ❑ Cover: 2.50 **NM** value: **Cover or less**
📖 Demonstorm • no publication date
Bk 1❑ Cover: 4.95 **NM** value: **Cover or less**

REALM, THE (VOL. 2) — Caliber

1 ❑ b&w Cover: 2.95 **NM** value: **Cover or less**
A: Brian Michael Bendis; Donald Marquez **W:** Brent Truax
2 ❑ b&w Cover: 2.95 **NM** value: **Cover or less**
3 ❑ b&w Cover: 2.95 **NM** value: **Cover or less**
4 ❑ b&w Cover: 2.95 **NM** value: **Cover or less**
5 ❑ b&w Cover: 2.95 **NM** value: **Cover or less**
6 ❑ b&w Cover: 2.95 **NM** value: **Cover or less**
7 ❑ b&w Cover: 2.95 **NM** value: **Cover or less**
8 ❑ b&w Cover: 2.95 **NM** value: **Cover or less**
9 ❑ b&w Cover: 2.95 **NM** value: **Cover or less**
10 ❑ b&w Cover: 2.95 **NM** value: **Cover or less**
11 ❑ b&w Cover: 2.95 **NM** value: **Cover or less**
12 ❑ b&w Cover: 2.95 **NM** value: **Cover or less**
13 ❑ b&w Cover: 2.95 **NM** value: **Cover or less**

REAL SCHMUCK — Starhead

1 ❑ b&w Cover: 2.95 **NM** value: **Cover or less**
📖 Near Death Of A Mail-Man; First Date; Fuss On The Bus; Hot Foot; Iron Denny; Make My Night; Real Lies; Stuck In A Dog Town; The Dollar; The Sharing **A:** R.L. Crabb; J.R. Williams; Jim Woodring; Pat Moriarty; Gene Fama; Jim Blanchard; Mario Hernandez; Danny Hellman; Ryder Windham; Sam Henderson; Drew Friedman(cover) **W:** Dennis Eichhorn

REAL SCREEN COMICS — DC

Though Tito and his Burrito occupied the top of the cover, and Flippity and Flop were featured inside, as well, it was DC's Fox and Crow who took the cover throughout the run of this funny-animal title. The conniving Crow is ever aiming to be more cunning than the agreeable Fox, whose less-aggressive stance often pays off in stories by Jim Davis (no relation to the creator of Garfield).

Fox and Crow originated as Columbia Studios cartoon characters, starting with "The Fox and the Grapes," created by Frank Tashlin (1913-1972). So the title "Real Screen Comics" was justifiable. The basic concept of the relatively amiable Fox dealing with the attacks of the Crow was successfully played in endless variation in the comic-book series. — Maggie

1 ❑ Spr 1945 Cover: 0.10 **NM** value: **450.00**
• **CGC:** 1 graded, best 7.0
2 ❑ Sum 1945 Cover: 0.10 **NM** value: **250.00**
3 ❑ Fal 1945 Cover: 0.10 **NM** value: **200.00**
4 ❑ Win 1945 Cover: 0.10 **NM** value: **200.00**
• **CGC:** 1 graded, best 5.5
5 ❑ Apr 1946 Cover: 0.10 **NM** value: **200.00**
6 ❑ Jun 1946 Cover: 0.10 **NM** value: **200.00**
7 ❑ Aug 1946 Cover: 0.10 **NM** value: **150.00**
8 ❑ Oct 1946 Cover: 0.10 **NM** value: **150.00**
9 ❑ Dec 1946 Cover: 0.10 **NM** value: **150.00**
10 ❑ Feb 1947 Cover: 0.10 **NM** value: **150.00**
11 ❑ Apr 1947 Cover: 0.10 **NM** value: **125.00**
12 ❑ Jun 1947 Cover: 0.10 **NM** value: **125.00**
13 ❑ Aug 1947 Cover: 0.10 **NM** value: **125.00**
14 ❑ Oct 1947 Cover: 0.10 **NM** value: **125.00**
15 ❑ Dec 1947 Cover: 0.10 **NM** value: **125.00**
16 ❑ Feb 1948 Cover: 0.10 **NM** value: **125.00**
17 ❑ Apr 1948 Cover: 0.10 **NM** value: **125.00**
18 ❑ Jun 1948 Cover: 0.10 **NM** value: **125.00**
19 ❑ Aug 1948 Cover: 0.10 **NM** value: **125.00**
20 ❑ Oct 1948 Cover: 0.10 **NM** value: **100.00**
21 ❑ Dec 1948 Cover: 0.10 **NM** value: **100.00**
22 ❑ Feb 1949 Cover: 0.10 **NM** value: **100.00**
23 ❑ Apr 1949 Cover: 0.10 **NM** value: **100.00**
24 ❑ Jun 1949 Cover: 0.10 **NM** value: **100.00**
25 ❑ Aug 1949 Cover: 0.10 **NM** value: **100.00**
26 ❑ Oct 1949 Cover: 0.10 **NM** value: **100.00**
27 ❑ Dec 1949 Cover: 0.10 **NM** value: **100.00**
28 ❑ Feb 1950 Cover: 0.10 **NM** value: **100.00**
29 ❑ Apr 1950 Cover: 0.10 **NM** value: **100.00**
30 ❑ Jun 1950 Cover: 0.10 **NM** value: **80.00**
31 ❑ Aug 1950 Cover: 0.10 **NM** value: **80.00**
32 ❑ Oct 1950 Cover: 0.10 **NM** value: **80.00**
33 ❑ Dec 1950 Cover: 0.10 **NM** value: **80.00**
34 ❑ Feb 1951 Cover: 0.10 **NM** value: **80.00**
35 ❑ Apr 1951 Cover: 0.10 **NM** value: **80.00**
36 ❑ Jun 1951 Cover: 0.10 **NM** value: **80.00**
37 ❑ Aug 1951 Cover: 0.10 **NM** value: **80.00**
38 ❑ Oct 1951 Cover: 0.10 **NM** value: **80.00**
39 ❑ Dec 1951 Cover: 0.10 **NM** value: **80.00**
40 ❑ Feb 1952 Cover: 0.10 **NM** value: **70.00**
41 ❑ Apr 1951 Cover: 0.10 **NM** value: **70.00**
42 ❑ Jun 1951 Cover: 0.10 **NM** value: **70.00**
43 ❑ Aug 1951 Cover: 0.10 **NM** value: **70.00**
44 ❑ Oct 1951 Cover: 0.10 **NM** value: **70.00**
45 ❑ Dec 1951 Cover: 0.10 **NM** value: **70.00**
• **CGC:** 1 graded, best 9.4
46 ❑ Jan 1952 Cover: 0.10 **NM** value: **70.00**
47 ❑ Feb 1952 Cover: 0.10 **NM** value: **70.00**
48 ❑ Mar 1952 Cover: 0.10 **NM** value: **70.00**
49 ❑ Apr 1952 Cover: 0.10 **NM** value: **70.00**
50 ❑ May 1952 Cover: 0.10 **NM** value: **50.00**
51 ❑ Jun 1952 Cover: 0.10 **NM** value: **50.00**
52 ❑ Jul 1952 Cover: 0.10 **NM** value: **50.00**
• **CGC:** 1 graded, best 9.2
53 ❑ Aug 1952 Cover: 0.10 **NM** value: **50.00**
54 ❑ Sep 1952 Cover: 0.10 **NM** value: **50.00**
55 ❑ Oct 1952 Cover: 0.10 **NM** value: **50.00**
56 ❑ Nov 1952 Cover: 0.10 **NM** value: **50.00**
57 ❑ Dec 1952 Cover: 0.10 **NM** value: **50.00**
58 ❑ Jan 1953 Cover: 0.10 **NM** value: **50.00**
59 ❑ Feb 1953 Cover: 0.10 **NM** value: **50.00**
60 ❑ Mar 1953 Cover: 0.10 **NM** value: **40.00**
61 ❑ Apr 1953 Cover: 0.10 **NM** value: **40.00**
62 ❑ May 1953 Cover: 0.10 **NM** value: **40.00**
63 ❑ Jun 1953 Cover: 0.10 **NM** value: **40.00**
64 ❑ Jul 1953 Cover: 0.10 **NM** value: **40.00**
65 ❑ Aug 1953 Cover: 0.10 **NM** value: **40.00**
66 ❑ Sep 1953 Cover: 0.10 **NM** value: **40.00**
67 ❑ Oct 1953 Cover: 0.10 **NM** value: **40.00**
68 ❑ Nov 1953 Cover: 0.10 **NM** value: **40.00**
69 ❑ Dec 1953 Cover: 0.10 **NM** value: **40.00**
70 ❑ Jan 1954 Cover: 0.10 **NM** value: **35.00**
71 ❑ Feb 1954 Cover: 0.10 **NM** value: **35.00**
72 ❑ Mar 1954 Cover: 0.10 **NM** value: **35.00**
73 ❑ Apr 1954 Cover: 0.10 **NM** value: **35.00**
74 ❑ May 1954 Cover: 0.10 **NM** value: **35.00**
75 ❑ Jun 1954 Cover: 0.10 **NM** value: **35.00**
76 ❑ Jul 1954 Cover: 0.10 **NM** value: **35.00**
77 ❑ Aug 1954 Cover: 0.10 **NM** value: **35.00**
78 ❑ Sep 1954 Cover: 0.10 **NM** value: **35.00**
79 ❑ Oct 1954 Cover: 0.10 **NM** value: **35.00**
80 ❑ Nov 1954 Cover: 0.10 **NM** value: **35.00**
81 ❑ Dec 1954 Cover: 0.10 **NM** value: **35.00**
82 ❑ Jan 1955 Cover: 0.10 **NM** value: **35.00**
83 ❑ Feb 1955 Cover: 0.10 **NM** value: **35.00**
84 ❑ Mar 1955 Cover: 0.10 **NM** value: **35.00**
85 ❑ Apr 1955 Cover: 0.10 **NM** value: **35.00**
86 ❑ May 1955 Cover: 0.10 **NM** value: **35.00**
87 ❑ Jun 1955 Cover: 0.10 **NM** value: **35.00**
88 ❑ Jul 1955 Cover: 0.10 **NM** value: **35.00**
89 ❑ Aug 1955 Cover: 0.10 **NM** value: **35.00**
90 ❑ Sep 1955 Cover: 0.10 **NM** value: **35.00**
91 ❑ Oct 1955 Cover: 0.10 **NM** value: **35.00**
92 ❑ Nov 1955 Cover: 0.10 **NM** value: **35.00**
93 ❑ Dec 1955 Cover: 0.10 **NM** value: **35.00**
94 ❑ Jan 1956 Cover: 0.10 **NM** value: **35.00**
95 ❑ Feb 1956 Cover: 0.10 **NM** value: **35.00**
96 ❑ Mar 1956 Cover: 0.10 **NM** value: **35.00**
97 ❑ Apr 1956 Cover: 0.10 **NM** value: **35.00**
98 ❑ May 1956 Cover: 0.10 **NM** value: **35.00**
99 ❑ Jun 1956 Cover: 0.10 **NM** value: **35.00**
100 ❑ Jul 1956 Cover: 0.10 **NM** value: **25.00**
101 ❑ Aug 1956 Cover: 0.10 **NM** value: **25.00**
102 ❑ Sep 1956 Cover: 0.10 **NM** value: **25.00**
103 ❑ Oct 1956 Cover: 0.10 **NM** value: **25.00**
104 ❑ Nov 1956 Cover: 0.10 **NM** value: **25.00**
105 ❑ Dec 1956 Cover: 0.10 **NM** value: **25.00**
106 ❑ Jan 1957 Cover: 0.10 **NM** value: **25.00**
107 ❑ Feb 1957 Cover: 0.10 **NM** value: **25.00**
108 ❑ Mar 1957 Cover: 0.10 **NM** value: **25.00**
109 ❑ Apr 1957 Cover: 0.10 **NM** value: **25.00**
110 ❑ May 1957 Cover: 0.10 **NM** value: **20.00**
111 ❑ Jun 1957 Cover: 0.10 **NM** value: **20.00**
112 ❑ Jul 1957 Cover: 0.10 **NM** value: **20.00**
113 ❑ Aug 1957 Cover: 0.10 **NM** value: **20.00**
114 ❑ Sep 1957 Cover: 0.10 **NM** value: **20.00**
115 ❑ Oct 1957 Cover: 0.10 **NM** value: **20.00**
116 ❑ Nov 1957 Cover: 0.10 **NM** value: **20.00**
117 ❑ Dec 1957 Cover: 0.10 **NM** value: **20.00**
118 ❑ Jan 1958 Cover: 0.10 **NM** value: **20.00**
119 ❑ Feb 1958 Cover: 0.10 **NM** value: **20.00**
120 ❑ Mar 1958 Cover: 0.10 **NM** value: **20.00**
121 ❑ Apr 1958 Cover: 0.10 **NM** value: **20.00**
122 ❑ Jun 1958 Cover: 0.10 **NM** value: **20.00**
123 ❑ Aug 1958 Cover: 0.10 **NM** value: **20.00**
124 ❑ Oct 1958 Cover: 0.10 **NM** value: **20.00**
125 ❑ Dec 1958 Cover: 0.10 **NM** value: **20.00**
126 ❑ Feb 1958 Cover: 0.10 **NM** value: **20.00**
127 ❑ Apr 1958 Cover: 0.10 **NM** value: **20.00**
128 ❑ Jun 1958 Cover: 0.10 **NM** value: **20.00**

REAL SMUT — Fantagraphics / Eros

All issues are adults only.

1 ❑ b&w Cover: 2.50 **NM** value: **Cover or less**
2 ❑ b&w Cover: 2.50 **NM** value: **Cover or less**
3 ❑ b&w Cover: 2.50 **NM** value: **Cover or less**
4 ❑ b&w Cover: 2.75 **NM** value: **Cover or less**
5 ❑ b&w Cover: 2.75 **NM** value: **Cover or less**
6 ❑ b&w Cover: 2.50 **NM** value: **Cover or less**

REAL SPORTS COMICS — Hillman

1 ❑ Oct 1948 Cover: 0.10 **NM** value: **250.00**
• **CGC:** 1 graded, best 7.0

REAL STUFF — Fantagraphics

All issues are adults only.

1 ❑ b&w Cover: 2.00 **NM** value: **3.00**
W: Dennis Eichhorn
2 ❑ b&w Cover: 2.00 **NM** value: **2.75**
W: Dennis Eichhorn
3 ❑ b&w Cover: 2.25 **NM** value: **2.50**
W: Dennis Eichhorn
4 ❑ b&w Cover: 2.25 **NM** value: **2.50**
📖 Death Of A Junkie; Our Thing; All Forked Up; Was My Face Red; I Had A Dream; Eleanor's Habit **A:** J.R. Williams; Jaime Hernandez; Pat Moriarty; Holly Tuttle; Jim Blanchard; Mark Zingarelli; Rantz Hoseley; Sean Hurley **W:** Dennis Eichhorn
5 ❑ b&w Cover: 2.25 **NM** value: **2.50**
W: Dennis Eichhorn
6 ❑ b&w Cover: 2.25 **NM** value: **2.50**
W: Dennis Eichhorn
7 ❑ b&w Cover: 2.25 **NM** value: **2.50**
W: Dennis Eichhorn
8 ❑ b&w Cover: 2.25 **NM** value: **2.50**
W: Dennis Eichhorn
9 ❑ b&w Cover: 2.25 **NM** value: **2.50**
W: Dennis Eichhorn
10 ❑ b&w Cover: 2.95 **NM** value: **Cover or less**
W: Dennis Eichhorn
11 ❑ b&w Cover: 2.50 **NM** value: **Cover or less**
W: Dennis Eichhorn
12 ❑ b&w Cover: 2.50 **NM** value: **Cover or less**
📖 The Surprise; Flashback; Ed's Uncle's Temper; Five Rays of the Sun; Timing **A:** J.R. Williams; Pat Moriarty; Pete Friedrich **W:** Dennis Eichhorn
13 ❑ b&w Cover: 2.50 **NM** value: **Cover or less**
W: Dennis Eichhorn
14 ❑ b&w Cover: 2.50 **NM** value: **Cover or less**
W: Dennis Eichhorn
15 ❑ b&w Cover: 2.50 **NM** value: **Cover or less**
W: Dennis Eichhorn
16 ❑ b&w Cover: 2.50 **NM** value: **Cover or less**
W: Dennis Eichhorn
17 ❑ b&w Cover: 2.50 **NM** value: **Cover or less**
W: Dennis Eichhorn
18 ❑ Cover: 2.50 **NM** value: **Cover or less**
W: Dennis Eichhorn
19 ❑ Jul 1994, b&w Cover: 2.50 **NM** value: **Cover or less**
W: Dennis Eichhorn
20 ❑ Oct 1994, b&w Cover: 2.95 **NM** value: **Cover or less**
W: Dennis Eichhorn

REAL WAR STORIES — Eclipse

1 ❑ Cover: 2.00 **NM** value: **Cover or less**
Circ: CapCity orders: **7,525**
📖 The Elite of the Fleet; Tapestries Part1, False Note; Alternate Service; The Decision; A Long Time Ago & Today **A:** Tom Yeates; Brian Bolland; Stan Woch; Stephen R. Bissette; Steve Leialoha; John Totleben; Mark Farmer; Marl Johnson; Rebecca Huntington **C:** Bill Sienkiewicz **W:** Joyce Brabner; Alan Moore; Denny O'Neil; Lou Ann Merkle; Mike W. Barr; W.D. Ehrhart
2 ❑ Cover: 4.95 **NM** value: **Cover or less**
A: Bill Sienkiewicz

REAL WEIRD WAR — Avalon

1 ❑ Cover: 2.95 **NM** value: **Cover or less**
"Real Weird War" on cover. 📖 The Last Kamikaze; Theatre of Fear **A:** Sanho Kim **W:** Sanho Kim

REAL WEIRD WEST — Avalon

1 ❑ Cover: 2.95 **NM** value: **Cover or less**
📖 Water, Water, Everywhere; Valley of Death; Raise the Devil! Well, Hello Dolly **A:** Jim Aparo; Warren Sattler; Paul Kirchner **W:** Warren Sattler; Paul Kirchner; Norm Dipluhm

REAL WESTERN HERO — Fawcett

70 ❑ Sep 1948 Cover: 0.10 **NM** value: **250.00**
• **CGC:** 1 graded, best 9.0
71 ❑ Oct 1948 Cover: 0.10 **NM** value: **150.00**
• **CGC:** 1 graded, best 7.0
72 ❑ Nov 1948 Cover: 0.10 **NM** value: **150.00**
73 ❑ Dec 1948 Cover: 0.10 **NM** value: **150.00**
74 ❑ Jan 1949 Cover: 0.10 **NM** value: **150.00**
75 ❑ Feb 1949 Cover: 0.10 **NM** value: **150.00**

REAL WEST ROMANCES — Crestwood

1 ❑ Apr 1949 Cover: 0.10 **NM** value: **150.00**
2 ❑ Jul 1949 Cover: 0.10 **NM** value: **75.00**
3 ❑ Aug 1949 Cover: 0.10 **NM** value: **75.00**

CGC-graded: Multiply prices above by **33 for 9.9 M • 16 for 9.8 NM/M • 7 for 9.6 NM+ • 5 for 9.4 NM • 2.5 for 9.2 NM- • 1.5 for 9.0 VF/NM**

4 ❑ Oct 1949 Cover: 0.10 **NM** value: **75.00**
• **CGC:** 1 graded, best 7.5
5 ❑ Dec 1950 Cover: 0.10 **NM** value: **50.00**
6 ❑ Feb 1950 Cover: 0.10 **NM** value: **50.00**

REALWORLDS: JUSTICE LEAGUE OF AMERICA — DC

1 ❑ Jul 2000 Cover: 5.95 **NM** value: **Cover or less**
Circ: Diamd. preorders: **21,827**
📖 The Return of the Justice League **A:** Glenn Barr **W:** J.M. DeMatteis

REALWORLDS: WONDER WOMAN — DC

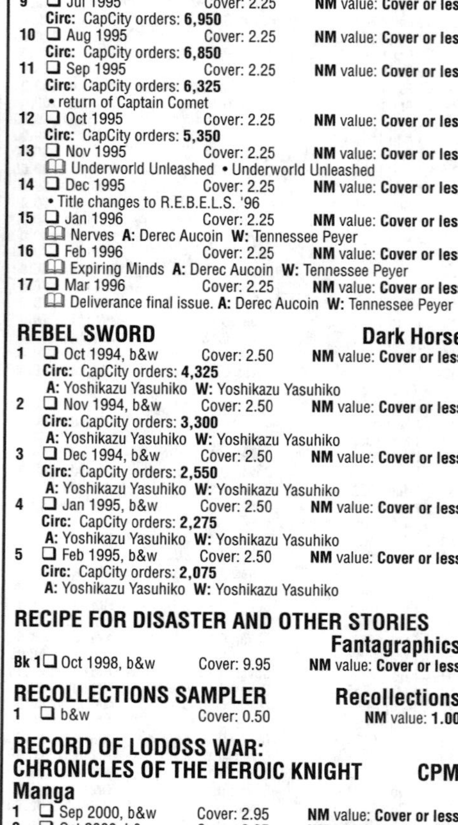

Much like how the Elseworlds imprint separates the publisher's more popular stable of heroes from mainstream continuity, DC Comics' Realworlds books tell stories of ordinary people whose real lives and real ambitions intersect with familiar iconic figures from the DC universe, inspiring them to a level worthy of hero status.

In this one-shot, actress Brenda Kelly portrays the post-World War II silver screen version of Wonder Woman. America adores her as a symbol of all that is good and right. But when a politician bent on ridding Hollywood of the communist element (much like McCarthy's Red Scare of the 1950s) begins targeting his baseless allegations toward her friends and loved ones, the actress is forced to pull her fictional persona into the real world in order to make a stand for what is just.

1 ❑ Jun 2000 Cover: 5.95 **NM** value: **Cover or less**
Circ: Diamd. preorders: **14,556**
📖 Wonder Woman versus the Red Menace! **A:** Salgood Sam **W:** Glen Hanson; Allan Neuwirth

RE-ANIMATOR (AIRCEL) — Aircel

1 ❑ full color Cover: 2.95 **NM** value: **Cover or less**
Circ: CapCity orders: **4,300**
2 ❑ full color Cover: 2.95 **NM** value: **Cover or less**
Circ: CapCity orders: **2,620**
3 ❑ full color Cover: 2.95 **NM** value: **Cover or less**

RE-ANIMATOR: DAWN OF THE RE-ANIMATOR — Adventure

1 ❑ b&w Cover: 2.50 **NM** value: **Cover or less**
📖 Dead and Buried **A:** Jose Malaga **W:** Bill Spangler
2 ❑ Apr 1992 Cover: 2.95 **NM** value: **Cover or less**
📖 Creatures of the Night **A:** Jose Malaga **W:** Bill Spangler
3 ❑ May 1992 Cover: 2.50 **NM** value: **Cover or less**
📖 The Dead in Their Masquerade **A:** Jose Malaga **W:** Bill Spangler
4 ❑ Cover: 2.50 **NM** value: **Cover or less**
A: Jose Malaga **W:** Bill Spangler

RE-ANIMATOR (ETERNITY) — Eternity

Bk 1 ❑ Cover: 4.95 **NM** value: **Cover or less**
• pb stories; not comics

RE-ANIMATOR IN FULL COLOR — Adventure

1 ❑ Nov 1991 Cover: 2.95 **NM** value: **Cover or less**
A: Christopher Jones **W:** Steven Philip Jones
2 ❑ Cover: 2.95 **NM** value: **Cover or less**
A: Christopher Jones **W:** Steven Philip Jones
3 ❑ Apr 1992 Cover: 2.95 **NM** value: **Cover or less**
A: Christopher Jones **W:** Steven Philip Jones

R.E.B.E.L.S. — DC

Once they were known as L.E.G.I.O.N., the Licensed Extra-Governmental Interstellar Operatives Network. Led by Vril Dox II, their number included Stealth, Phase, Strata, and the infamous Lobo. These super-powered heroes were the core of a force of peacekeepers that maintained order on countless worlds — for a price.

Then the cloned Yril Dox managed to seize control of L.E.G.I.O.N.'s military operations and brainwash the rank and file. Vril and his core teammates were forced to flee for their lives. Now they are R.E.B.E.L.S. (periods included for tradition's sake, we imagine), and must fight their own colleagues for survival.

0 ❑ Oct 1994 Cover: 1.95 **NM** value: **Cover or less**
Circ: CapCity orders: **21,750**
📖 Less Than Zero • story continued from L.E.G.I.O.N. '94 #70 **A:** Arnie Jorgensen **W:** Tennessee Peyer ★ Origin of Yril Dox, L.E.G.I.O.N., Vril Dox II.
1 ❑ Nov 1994 Cover: 1.95 **NM** value: **Cover or less**
Circ: CapCity orders: **18,150**
📖 Escape To Nowhere **A:** Arnie Jorgensen **W:** Tennessee Peyer
2 ❑ Dec 1994 Cover: 1.95 **NM** value: **Cover or less**
Circ: CapCity orders: **13,800**
3 ❑ Jan 1995 Cover: 1.95 **NM** value: **Cover or less**
Circ: CapCity orders: **12,200**
📖 Brains **A:** Derec Aucoin **W:** Tennessee Peyer
4 ❑ Feb 1995 Cover: 1.95 **NM** value: **Cover or less**
Circ: CapCity orders: **10,900**
5 ❑ Mar 1995 Cover: 1.95 **NM** value: **Cover or less**
Circ: CapCity orders: **9,400**
6 ❑ Apr 1995 Cover: 1.95 **NM** value: **Cover or less**
Circ: CapCity orders: **8,200**
7 ❑ May 1995 Cover: 1.95 **NM** value: **Cover or less**
Circ: CapCity orders: **7,750**
8 ❑ Jun 1995 Cover: 2.25 **NM** value: **Cover or less**
Circ: CapCity orders: **7,325**
9 ❑ Jul 1995 Cover: 2.25 **NM** value: **Cover or less**
Circ: CapCity orders: **6,950**
10 ❑ Aug 1995 Cover: 2.25 **NM** value: **Cover or less**
Circ: CapCity orders: **6,850**
11 ❑ Sep 1995 Cover: 2.25 **NM** value: **Cover or less**
Circ: CapCity orders: **6,325**
• return of Captain Comet
12 ❑ Oct 1995 Cover: 2.25 **NM** value: **Cover or less**
Circ: CapCity orders: **5,350**
13 ❑ Nov 1995 Cover: 2.25 **NM** value: **Cover or less**
📖 Underworld Unleashed • Underworld Unleashed
14 ❑ Dec 1995 Cover: 2.25 **NM** value: **Cover or less**
• Title changes to R.E.B.E.L.S. '96
15 ❑ Jan 1996 Cover: 2.25 **NM** value: **Cover or less**
📖 Nerves **A:** Derec Aucoin **W:** Tennessee Peyer
16 ❑ Feb 1996 Cover: 2.25 **NM** value: **Cover or less**
📖 Expiring Minds **A:** Derec Aucoin **W:** Tennessee Peyer
17 ❑ Mar 1996 Cover: 2.25 **NM** value: **Cover or less**
📖 Deliverance final issue. **A:** Derec Aucoin **W:** Tennessee Peyer

REBEL SWORD — Dark Horse

1 ❑ Oct 1994, b&w Cover: 2.50 **NM** value: **Cover or less**
Circ: CapCity orders: **4,325**
A: Yoshikazu Yasuhiko **W:** Yoshikazu Yasuhiko
2 ❑ Nov 1994, b&w Cover: 2.50 **NM** value: **Cover or less**
Circ: CapCity orders: **3,300**
A: Yoshikazu Yasuhiko **W:** Yoshikazu Yasuhiko
3 ❑ Dec 1994, b&w Cover: 2.50 **NM** value: **Cover or less**
Circ: CapCity orders: **2,550**
A: Yoshikazu Yasuhiko **W:** Yoshikazu Yasuhiko
4 ❑ Jan 1995, b&w Cover: 2.50 **NM** value: **Cover or less**
Circ: CapCity orders: **2,275**
A: Yoshikazu Yasuhiko **W:** Yoshikazu Yasuhiko
5 ❑ Feb 1995, b&w Cover: 2.50 **NM** value: **Cover or less**
Circ: CapCity orders: **2,075**
A: Yoshikazu Yasuhiko **W:** Yoshikazu Yasuhiko

RECIPE FOR DISASTER AND OTHER STORIES — Fantagraphics

Bk 1 ❑ Oct 1998, b&w Cover: 9.95 **NM** value: **Cover or less**

RECOLLECTIONS SAMPLER — Recollections

1 ❑ b&w Cover: 0.50 **NM** value: **1.00**

RECORD OF LODOSS WAR: CHRONICLES OF THE HEROIC KNIGHT — CPM Manga

1 ❑ Sep 2000, b&w Cover: 2.95 **NM** value: **Cover or less**
2 ❑ Oct 2000, b&w Cover: 2.95 **NM** value: **Cover or less**
3 ❑ Nov 2000 Cover: 2.95 **NM** value: **Cover or less**
4 ❑ Dec 2000 Cover: 2.95 **NM** value: **Cover or less**
5 ❑ Jan 2001 Cover: 2.95 **NM** value: **Cover or less**
6 ❑ Feb 2001 Cover: 2.95 **NM** value: **Cover or less**
7 ❑ Mar 2001 Cover: 2.95 **NM** value: **Cover or less**
8 ❑ Apr 2001 Cover: 2.95 **NM** value: **Cover or less**
9 ❑ May 2001 Cover: 2.95 **NM** value: **Cover or less**
10 ❑ Jun 2001 Cover: 2.95 **NM** value: **Cover or less**
11 ❑ Jul 2001 Cover: 2.95 **NM** value: **Cover or less**

RECORD OF LODOSS WAR: THE GREY WITCH — CPM

An elf, a priest, a dwarf warrior, and a young, hot-tempered fighter find themselves thrown together when darkness descends on the island of Lodoss. Suddenly, goblins have become bold, attacking travelers and villages in broad daylight.

In a Tolkien-esque land of wizards, witches, and trolls, the little band of adventurers must rise to the challenge presented by the Grey Witch. The heroes must overcome their differences and unite in the face of evil, if they are going to survive the onslaught from Ashram and the witch's other deadly minions.

This successful Central Park Manga mini-series is the first Lodoss War story ever written by Ryo Mizuno, creator of the entire Lodoss War universe, and shows how the saga began.

1 ❑ Nov 1998 Cover: 2.95 **NM** value: **Cover or less**
wraparound cover. **A:** Yoshihiko Ochi **W:** Ryo Mizuno
2 ❑ Dec 1998 Cover: 2.95 **NM** value: **Cover or less**
3 ❑ Jan 1999 Cover: 2.95 **NM** value: **Cover or less**
wraparound cover.
4 ❑ Feb 1999 Cover: 2.95 **NM** value: **Cover or less**
5 ❑ Mar 1999 Cover: 2.95 **NM** value: **Cover or less**
6 ❑ Apr 1999 Cover: 2.95 **NM** value: **Cover or less**
7 ❑ May 1999 Cover: 2.95 **NM** value: **Cover or less**
8 ❑ Jun 1999 Cover: 2.95 **NM** value: **Cover or less**
9 ❑ Jul 1999 Cover: 2.95 **NM** value: **Cover or less**
10 ❑ Aug 1999 Cover: 2.95 **NM** value: **Cover or less**
11 ❑ Sep 1999 Cover: 2.95 **NM** value: **Cover or less**
12 ❑ Oct 1999 Cover: 2.95 **NM** value: **Cover or less**
13 ❑ Nov 1999 Cover: 2.95 **NM** value: **Cover or less**
14 ❑ Dec 1999 Cover: 2.95 **NM** value: **Cover or less**
15 ❑ Jan 2000 Cover: 2.95 **NM** value: **Cover or less**
16 ❑ Feb 2000 Cover: 2.95 **NM** value: **Cover or less**
17 ❑ Mar 2000 Cover: 2.95 **NM** value: **Cover or less**
18 ❑ Apr 2000 Cover: 2.95 **NM** value: **Cover or less**
19 ❑ May 2000 Cover: 2.95 **NM** value: **Cover or less**
20 ❑ Jun 2000 Cover: 2.95 **NM** value: **Cover or less**
21 ❑ Jul 2000 Cover: 2.95 **NM** value: **Cover or less**
22 ❑ Aug 2000 Cover: 2.95 **NM** value: **Cover or less**
Bk 1 ❑ b&w Cover: 15.95 **NM** value: **Cover or less**
• Trade Paperback.
Bk 2 ❑ Sep 2000, b&w Cover: 15.95 **NM** value: **Cover or less**
• Trade Paperback. • collects 11-15

RECORD OF LODOSS WAR: THE LADY OF PHARIS — CPM

1 ❑ Cover: 2.95 **NM** value: **Cover or less**
2 ❑ Cover: 2.95 **NM** value: **Cover or less**
3 ❑ Cover: 2.95 **NM** value: **Cover or less**
4 ❑ Cover: 2.95 **NM** value: **Cover or less**
5 ❑ Cover: 2.95 **NM** value: **Cover or less**
6 ❑ Cover: 2.95 **NM** value: **Cover or less**
7 ❑ Cover: 2.95 **NM** value: **Cover or less**
8 ❑ Cover: 2.95 **NM** value: **Cover or less**

RECTUM ERRRECTUM — Boneyard

1 ❑ Cover: 3.95 **NM** value: **Cover or less**
📖 Catamite's Anal RevengeThe Penile Colony **A:** Eric Gnoeff **W:** Eric Gnoeff

RED ARROW — P.L. Publishing

1 ❑ May 1951 Cover: 0.10 **NM** value: **50.00**
2 ❑ Aug 1951 Cover: 0.10 **NM** value: **45.00**
3 ❑ Oct 1951 Cover: 0.10 **NM** value: **45.00**

REDBLADE — Dark Horse

1 ❑ Cover: 2.50 **NM** value: **Cover or less**
Circ: CapCity orders: **7,325**
gatefold cover. 📖 The Death Factory **A:** Vince Giarrano **W:** Vince Giarrano
2 ❑ Cover: 2.50 **NM** value: **Cover or less**
Circ: CapCity orders: **4,475**
3 ❑ Cover: 2.50 **NM** value: **Cover or less**
Circ: CapCity orders: **4,275**

RED CIRCLE — Rural Home

1 ❑ Jan 1945 Cover: 0.10 **NM** value: **250.00**
• **CGC:** 1 graded, best 7.5
2 ❑ Feb 1945 Cover: 0.10 **NM** value: **125.00**
3 ❑ Mar 1945 Cover: 0.10 **NM** value: **65.00**
• **CGC:** 1 graded, best 5.5
4 ❑ Apr 1945 Cover: 0.10 **NM** value: **65.00**

RED CIRCLE SORCERY — Red Circle

6 ❑ Apr 1974 Cover: 0.25 **NM** value: **1.50**
• **CGC:** 1 graded, best 9.6
• Series continued from Chilling Adventures in Sorcery #5
7 ❑ Jun 1974 Cover: 0.25 **NM** value: **1.50**
8 ❑ Aug 1974 Cover: 0.25 **NM** value: **1.50**
📖 The Highwayman's Escape; Die in the name of the Law!; Poltergeists; Enough to Raise the Dead; The Man Who Tried to Kill Death **A:** Gray Morrow; Frank Thorne; Carlos Pino **W:** Don Glut; Don Karr; Marv Channing
9 ❑ Oct 1974 Cover: 0.25 **NM** value: **1.50**
10 ❑ Dec 1974 Cover: 0.25 **NM** value: **1.50**
11 ❑ Feb 1975 Cover: 0.25 **NM** value: **1.50**

REDDEVIL — AC

1 ❑ b&w and red Cover: 2.95 **NM** value: **Cover or less**
📖 Clutches of the Claws Part 1; Claw • no indicia **A:** Dick Ayers; Jack Cole **W:** Jack Cole; Bill Black

RED DIARIES, THE — Caliber

1 ❑ Cover: 3.95 **NM** value: **Cover or less**
2 ❑ Cover: 3.95 **NM** value: **Cover or less**
3 ❑ Cover: 3.95 **NM** value: **Cover or less**
4 ❑ Cover: 3.95 **NM** value: **Cover or less**

RED DRAGON — Comico

1 ❑ Jun 1996 Cover: 2.95 **NM** value: **Cover or less**

RED DRAGON COMICS (1ST SERIES) — Street & Smith

Red Dragon began as the series titled Trail Blazers, and, even when it became Red Dragon Comics, the character who would soon take over the cover didn't appear. Instead, #5 put Captain Jack Commando and his pals in combat with Nazis. However, with #6, The Red Dragon introduces himself, announcing, "I, the Red Dragon, conjure up the ancient and forbidden magic of Tibet in my fight against the bestial Jap!" And he gets right to work. Featured in Super-Magician, as well, Red Dragon is notable for outstanding Edd Cartier art, with Robert Powell's similar style continuing the attractive feature.

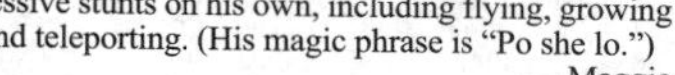

Bob Reed ends up with a team of sidekicks including Ching Foo, Gnorman the Gnome, and the dragon Komodo and can handle a number of impressive stunts on his own, including flying, growing and shrinking, and teleporting. (His magic phrase is "Po she lo.")

— Maggie

Other grades: Multiply prices above by **1.5 for Mint • 2/3 for Very Fine • 1/3 for Fine • 1/5 for Very Good • 1/8 for Good**

5 ❑ Jan 1943 Cover: 0.10 **NM** value: **900.00**
• **CGC:** 1 graded, best 5.0
6 ❑ Mar 1943 Cover: 0.10 **NM** value: **1500.00**
• **CGC:** 1 graded, best 9.6
7 ❑ Jul 1943 Cover: 0.10 **NM** value: **1000.00**
• **CGC:** 3 graded, best 9.4
8 ❑ Oct 1943 Cover: 0.10 **NM** value: **500.00**
• **CGC:** 1 graded, best 3.0
9 ❑ Jan 1944 Cover: 0.10 **NM** value: **500.00**
• **CGC:** 2 graded, best 9.0

RED DRAGON COMICS (2ND SERIES) Street & Smith

1 ❑ Nov 1947 Cover: 0.10 **NM** value: **700.00**
• **CGC:** 2 graded, best 8.0
2 ❑ Feb 1948 Cover: 0.10 **NM** value: **500.00**
• **CGC:** 1 graded, best 8.0
3 ❑ May 1948 Cover: 0.10 **NM** value: **400.00**
• **CGC:** 3 graded, best 9.0
4 ❑ Aug 1948 Cover: 0.10 **NM** value: **350.00**
5 ❑ Oct 1948 Cover: 0.10 **NM** value: **350.00**
6 ❑ Jan 1949 Cover: 0.10 **NM** value: **350.00**
• **CGC:** 1 graded, best 7.0
7 ❑ May 1949 Cover: 0.10 **NM** value: **350.00**

REDEEMER, THE Images & Realities

1 ❑ Cover: 2.95 **NM** value: **Cover or less**
A: Dale McNeal **W:** Dale McNeal

REDEEMERS, THE Antarctic

1 ❑ Dec 1997, b&w Cover: 2.95 **NM** value: **Cover or less**
Circ: Diamd. preorders: **4,526**
📖 Phatasms **A:** Ben Dunn **W:** Herb Malette

RED FLANNEL SQUIRREL, THE Sirius

1 ❑ Oct 1997, b&w Cover: 2.95 **NM** value: **Cover or less**
📖 David Quinn **A:** Oct-97 **W:** Kristen Perry

REDFOX Harrier

1 ❑ Jan 1986 Cover: 1.75 **NM** value: **4.00**
📖 Treasure Of Pthud • Harrier publishes **A:** Fox **W:** Fox; Mike Lewis ★ 1st Appearance of Redfox.
1-2 ❑ Cover: 1.75 **NM** value: **Cover or less**
2 ❑ Mar 1986 Cover: 1.75 **NM** value: **3.00**
3 ❑ May 1986 Cover: 1.75 **NM** value: **2.50**
4 ❑ Jul 1986 Cover: 1.75 **NM** value: **Cover or less**
5 ❑ Sep 1986 Cover: 1.75 **NM** value: **Cover or less**
6 ❑ Nov 1986 Cover: 1.75 **NM** value: **Cover or less**
📖 The Captain's Story; White Lies **A:** Fox; Dave Harwood **W:** Fox; Cat Leslie
7 ❑ Jan 1987 Cover: 1.75 **NM** value: **Cover or less**
8 ❑ Mar 1987 Cover: 1.75 **NM** value: **Cover or less**
📖 White Company **A:** Fox; Dave Harwood **W:** Fox; Chris Bell
9 ❑ May 1987 Cover: 1.75 **NM** value: **Cover or less**
📖 Welcom to the Darkside **A:** Fox; Dave Harwood **W:** Fox; Chris Bell
10 ❑ Jul 1987 Cover: 2.00 **NM** value: **Cover or less**
📖 Never Forever • Last Harrier issue **A:** Fox; Dave Harwood **W:** Fox; Chris Bell
11 ❑ Sep 1987 Cover: 2.00 **NM** value: **Cover or less**
📖 Life After Death • Valkyrie begins publishing **A:** Fox; Dave Harwood **W:** Fox; Chris Bell
12 ❑ Nov 1987 Cover: 2.00 **NM** value: **Cover or less**
📖 Requiem; Cantata **A:** Fox; Dave Harwood **W:** Fox; Chris Bell
13 ❑ Jan 1988 Cover: 2.00 **NM** value: **Cover or less**
📖 Thorns **A:** Fox; Tony O'Donnell **W:** Fox; Chris Bell
14 ❑ Mar 1988 Cover: 2.00 **NM** value: **Cover or less**
📖 White Waves **A:** Matthew Meadows **W:** Fox; Chris Bell
15 ❑ May 1988 Cover: 2.00 **NM** value: **Cover or less**
📖 To Market, To Market... • Luther Arkwright cameo **A:** Fox; Tony O'Donnell **W:** Chris Bell
16 ❑ Jun 1988 Cover: 2.00 **NM** value: **Cover or less**
📖 Road to Mulhaarn **A:** Fox; Dave Harwood **W:** Chris Bell
17 ❑ Aug 1988 Cover: 2.00 **NM** value: **Cover or less**
📖 Raid on Pthud: A Bespoke Fantasy **A:** Fox **W:** Fox; Chris Bell
18 ❑ Oct 1988 Cover: 2.00 **NM** value: **Cover or less**
📖 Lyssa the Axe...Csárdás; Lyssa the Axe...Csárdás **A:** Fox **W:** Chris Bell
19 ❑ Feb 1989 Cover: 2.00 **NM** value: **Cover or less**
A: Fox **W:** Fox; Chris Bell
20 ❑ Jun 1989 Cover: 2.00 **NM** value: **Cover or less**
📖 Fragments final issue. **A:** Fox; SMS **W:** Chris Bell; Neil Gaiman
Bk 1❑ Cover: 6.95 **NM** value: **7.00**
📖 Fair Exchange; Tower Of The Sorcerer • Reprints Redfox #1-4 **A:** Fox; Brian Bolland(cover) **W:** Martin Lock ★ 1st Appearance of Redfox.

RED-HEADED BOMBSHELL: BRENDA STARR, REPORTER Eternity

Bk 1❑ Cover: 12.95 **NM** value: **Cover or less**
• strip reprints

RED HEAT Blackthorne

1 ❑ Jul 1988, b&w Cover: 2.00 **NM** value: **Cover or less**
A: Abel Laxamana **W:** Jhn Stephenson
1/3D❑Jul 1988 Cover: 2.50 **NM** value: **Cover or less**
Circ: CapCity orders: **1,025**
A: Abel Laxamana **W:** Jhn Stephenson

RED ICEBERG Impact

1 ❑ 1960 **NM** value: **300.00**
• **CGC:** 2 graded, best 9.0

RED MASK Magazine Enterprises

42 ❑ Jun 1954 Cover: 0.10 **NM** value: **150.00**
43 ❑ Aug 1954 Cover: 0.10 **NM** value: **125.00**
44 ❑ Sep 1954 Cover: 0.10 **NM** value: **100.00**
45 ❑ Oct 1954 Cover: 0.10 **NM** value: **100.00**
46 ❑ Dec 1954 Cover: 0.10 **NM** value: **100.00**
47 ❑ Jan 1955 Cover: 0.10 **NM** value: **100.00**
48 ❑ Mar 1955 Cover: 0.10 **NM** value: **100.00**
49 ❑ May 1955 Cover: 0.10 **NM** value: **100.00**
50 ❑ Jul 1955 Cover: 0.10 **NM** value: **100.00**
51 ❑ Sep 1955 Cover: 0.10 **NM** value: **100.00**
52 ❑ Mar 1955 Cover: 0.10 **NM** value: **100.00**
53 ❑ May 1956 Cover: 0.10 **NM** value: **100.00**

REDMASK OF THE RIO GRANDE AC

1 ❑ full color Cover: 2.95 **NM** value: **Cover or less**
2 ❑ Cover: 2.95 **NM** value: **Cover or less**
3 ❑ Cover: 2.95 **NM** value: **Cover or less**
• 3-D effects

RED MOON Millennium

1 ❑ Mar 1995, b&w Cover: 2.95 **NM** value: **Cover or less**
Circ: CapCity orders: **1,830**
📖 The Tale of Terror; Lycanthropos **A:** Deodato Filho; John Bolton(cover); Rich Sunchy **W:** Deodato Borges; Faye Perozich
2 ❑ Cover: 2.95 **NM** value: **Cover or less**

RED PLANET PIONEER Inesco

1 ❑ Cover: 2.95 **NM** value: **Cover or less**

RED RABBIT Dearfield

1 ❑ 1947 Cover: 0.10 **NM** value: **75.00**
2 ❑ 1947 Cover: 0.10 **NM** value: **75.00**
3 ❑ 1947 Cover: 0.10 **NM** value: **60.00**
4 ❑ 1947 Cover: 0.10 **NM** value: **60.00**
5 ❑ 1948 Cover: 0.10 **NM** value: **60.00**
6 ❑ 1948 Cover: 0.10 **NM** value: **60.00**
7 ❑ 1948 Cover: 0.10 **NM** value: **60.00**
8 ❑ 1948 Cover: 0.10 **NM** value: **60.00**
9 ❑ 1949 Cover: 0.10 **NM** value: **60.00**
10 ❑ 1949 Cover: 0.10 **NM** value: **35.00**
11 ❑ Jul 1949 Cover: 0.10 **NM** value: **35.00**
12 ❑ 1949 Cover: 0.10 **NM** value: **35.00**
13 ❑ 1950 Cover: 0.10 **NM** value: **35.00**
14 ❑ 1950 Cover: 0.10 **NM** value: **35.00**
15 ❑ 1950 Cover: 0.10 **NM** value: **35.00**
16 ❑ 1950 Cover: 0.10 **NM** value: **30.00**
17 ❑ Oct 1950 Cover: 0.10 **NM** value: **30.00**
18 ❑ Jan 1951 Cover: 0.10 **NM** value: **30.00**
19 ❑ 1951 Cover: 0.10 **NM** value: **30.00**
20 ❑ 1951 Cover: 0.10 **NM** value: **30.00**
21 ❑ Aug 1951 Cover: 0.10 **NM** value: **30.00**
22 ❑ Oct 1951 Cover: 0.10 **NM** value: **30.00**

RED RAVEN COMICS Timely

1 ❑ Aug 1940 Cover: 0.10 **NM** value: **10000.00**

RED RAZORS: A DREDDWORLD ADVENTURE Fleetway-Quality

1 ❑ Cover: 2.95 **NM** value: **Cover or less**
📖 Red Razors; Strange Cases **A:** Dean Ormston **W:** David Stone
2 ❑ Cover: 2.95 **NM** value: **Cover or less**
3 ❑ Cover: 2.95 **NM** value: **Cover or less**

RED REVOLUTION, THE Caliber / Tome

1 ❑ b&w Cover: 2.95 **NM** value: **Cover or less**

RED ROCKET 7 Dark Horse / Legend

1 ❑ Aug 1997 Cover: 3.95 **NM** value: **Cover or less**
Circ: Diamd. preorders: **16,516**
2 ❑ Sep 1997 Cover: 3.95 **NM** value: **Cover or less**
Circ: Diamd. preorders: **13,420**
3 ❑ Oct 1997 Cover: 3.95 **NM** value: **Cover or less**
Circ: Diamd. preorders: **12,048**
4 ❑ Nov 1997 Cover: 3.95 **NM** value: **Cover or less**
Circ: Diamd. preorders: **10,820**
5 ❑ Jan 1998 Cover: 3.95 **NM** value: **Cover or less**
Circ: Diamd. preorders: **9,836**
6 ❑ Mar 1998 Cover: 3.95 **NM** value: **Cover or less**
Circ: Diamd. preorders: **9,457**
📖 All Apologies **A:** Mike Allred **W:** Mike Allred
7 ❑ Jun 1998 Cover: 3.95 **NM** value: **Cover or less**
Circ: Diamd. preorders: **9,336**

RED RYDER COMICS Dell

Dell's Red Ryder Comics, featuring Fred Harman's intrepid frontier lawman and his sidekick Little Beaver, was one of the most successful and long-running comic strip adaptations. The early issues reprinted Red Ryder Sunday strips along with other classic adventure-hero serials such as Captain Easy and Alley Oop. Eventually, talented writer/artist Harmon began producing original material for the 52-page issues — generally three to four stories per month.

Red Ryder is a tough-as-nails cowboy matching wits and bullets with the typical array of frontier bad-guys, including cattle rustlers, crooked politicians, Mexican banditos, and stagecoach robbers. His no-nonsense approach was lightened up by the comic relief of Little Beaver, a feisty Indian kid.

1 ❑ Sep 1940 Cover: 0.10 **NM** value: **1800.00**
• **CGC:** 1 graded, best 1.5
A: Fred Harman **W:** Fred Harman
3 ❑ Aug 1941 Cover: 0.10 **NM** value: **850.00**
A: Fred Harman **W:** Fred Harman
4 ❑ Oct 1941 Cover: 0.10 **NM** value: **450.00**
• **CGC:** 1 graded, best 8.0
A: Fred Harman **W:** Fred Harman
5 ❑ Dec 1941 Cover: 0.10 **NM** value: **450.00**
A: Fred Harman **W:** Fred Harman
6 ❑ Apr 1942 Cover: 0.10 **NM** value: **350.00**
A: Fred Harman **W:** Fred Harman
7 ❑ Jun 1942 Cover: 0.10 **NM** value: **300.00**
A: Fred Harman **W:** Fred Harman
8 ❑ Aug 1942 Cover: 0.10 **NM** value: **300.00**
A: Fred Harman **W:** Fred Harman
9 ❑ Oct 1942 Cover: 0.10 **NM** value: **300.00**
A: Fred Harman **W:** Fred Harman
10 ❑ Dec 1942 Cover: 0.10 **NM** value: **300.00**
A: Fred Harman **W:** Fred Harman
11 ❑ Feb 1943 Cover: 0.10 **NM** value: **240.00**
A: Fred Harman **W:** Fred Harman
12 ❑ Apr 1943 Cover: 0.10 **NM** value: **240.00**
• **CGC:** 1 graded, best 7.5
A: Fred Harman **W:** Fred Harman
13 ❑ Jun 1943 Cover: 0.10 **NM** value: **240.00**
A: Fred Harman **W:** Fred Harman
14 ❑ Jul 1943 Cover: 0.10 **NM** value: **240.00**
A: Fred Harman **W:** Fred Harman
15 ❑ Sep 1943 Cover: 0.10 **NM** value: **240.00**
A: Fred Harman **W:** Fred Harman
16 ❑ Nov 1943 Cover: 0.10 **NM** value: **240.00**
A: Fred Harman **W:** Fred Harman
17 ❑ Jan 1944 Cover: 0.10 **NM** value: **240.00**
A: Fred Harman **W:** Fred Harman
18 ❑ Mar 1944 Cover: 0.10 **NM** value: **240.00**
A: Fred Harman **W:** Fred Harman
19 ❑ May 1944 Cover: 0.10 **NM** value: **240.00**
A: Fred Harman **W:** Fred Harman
20 ❑ Jul 1944 Cover: 0.10 **NM** value: **240.00**
A: Fred Harman **W:** Fred Harman
21 ❑ Sep 1944 Cover: 0.10 **NM** value: **165.00**
A: Fred Harman **W:** Fred Harman
22 ❑ Nov 1944 Cover: 0.10 **NM** value: **165.00**
• **CGC:** 1 graded, best 8.5
A: Fred Harman **W:** Fred Harman
23 ❑ Jan 1945 Cover: 0.10 **NM** value: **165.00**
A: Fred Harman **W:** Fred Harman
24 ❑ Mar 1945 Cover: 0.10 **NM** value: **165.00**
A: Fred Harman **W:** Fred Harman
25 ❑ May 1945 Cover: 0.10 **NM** value: **165.00**
A: Fred Harman **W:** Fred Harman
26 ❑ Jul 1945 Cover: 0.10 **NM** value: **165.00**
A: Fred Harman **W:** Fred Harman
27 ❑ Sep 1945 Cover: 0.10 **NM** value: **165.00**
A: Fred Harman **W:** Fred Harman
28 ❑ Nov 1945 Cover: 0.10 **NM** value: **165.00**
A: Fred Harman **W:** Fred Harman
29 ❑ Dec 1945 Cover: 0.10 **NM** value: **165.00**
• **CGC:** 1 graded, best 9.2
A: Fred Harman **W:** Fred Harman
30 ❑ Jan 1946 Cover: 0.10 **NM** value: **165.00**
A: Fred Harman **W:** Fred Harman
31 ❑ Feb 1946 Cover: 0.10 **NM** value: **105.00**
A: Fred Harman **W:** Fred Harman
32 ❑ Mar 1946 Cover: 0.10 **NM** value: **105.00**
A: Fred Harman **W:** Fred Harman
33 ❑ Apr 1946 Cover: 0.10 **NM** value: **105.00**
A: Fred Harman **W:** Fred Harman
34 ❑ May 1946 Cover: 0.10 **NM** value: **105.00**
A: Fred Harman **W:** Fred Harman
35 ❑ Jun 1946 Cover: 0.10 **NM** value: **105.00**
A: Fred Harman **W:** Fred Harman
36 ❑ Jul 1946 Cover: 0.10 **NM** value: **105.00**
A: Fred Harman **W:** Fred Harman
37 ❑ Aug 1946 Cover: 0.10 **NM** value: **105.00**
• **CGC:** 1 graded, best 9.4
A: Fred Harman **W:** Fred Harman
38 ❑ Sep 1946 Cover: 0.10 **NM** value: **105.00**
A: Fred Harman **W:** Fred Harman
39 ❑ Oct 1946 Cover: 0.10 **NM** value: **105.00**
A: Fred Harman **W:** Fred Harman
40 ❑ Nov 1946 Cover: 0.10 **NM** value: **105.00**
A: Fred Harman **W:** Fred Harman
41 ❑ Dec 1946 Cover: 0.10 **NM** value: **85.00**
A: Fred Harman **W:** Fred Harman
42 ❑ Jan 1947 Cover: 0.10 **NM** value: **85.00**
A: Fred Harman **W:** Fred Harman
43 ❑ Feb 1947 Cover: 0.10 **NM** value: **85.00**
A: Fred Harman **W:** Fred Harman
44 ❑ Mar 1947 Cover: 0.10 **NM** value: **85.00**
A: Fred Harman **W:** Fred Harman
45 ❑ Apr 1947 Cover: 0.10 **NM** value: **85.00**
A: Fred Harman **W:** Fred Harman
46 ❑ May 1947 Cover: 0.10 **NM** value: **85.00**
A: Fred Harman **W:** Fred Harman
47 ❑ Jun 1947 Cover: 0.10 **NM** value: **85.00**
A: Fred Harman **W:** Fred Harman
48 ❑ Jul 1947 Cover: 0.10 **NM** value: **85.00**
A: Fred Harman **W:** Fred Harman
49 ❑ Aug 1947 Cover: 0.10 **NM** value: **85.00**
A: Fred Harman **W:** Fred Harman
50 ❑ Sep 1947 Cover: 0.10 **NM** value: **85.00**
A: Fred Harman **W:** Fred Harman
51 ❑ Oct 1947 Cover: 0.10 **NM** value: **64.00**
A: Fred Harman **W:** Fred Harman
52 ❑ Nov 1947 Cover: 0.10 **NM** value: **64.00**
A: Fred Harman **W:** Fred Harman
53 ❑ Dec 1947 Cover: 0.10 **NM** value: **64.00**
A: Fred Harman **W:** Fred Harman
54 ❑ Jan 1948 Cover: 0.10 **NM** value: **64.00**
A: Fred Harman **W:** Fred Harman
55 ❑ Feb 1948 Cover: 0.10 **NM** value: **64.00**
A: Fred Harman **W:** Fred Harman

CGC-graded: Multiply prices above by **33 for 9.9 M • 16 for 9.8 NM/M • 7 for 9.6 NM+ • 5 for 9.4 NM • 2.5 for 9.2 NM- • 1.5 for 9.0 VF/NM**

56 ☐ Mar 1948 Cover: 0.10 **NM** value: **64.00**
A: Fred Harman **W:** Fred Harman

57 ☐ Apr 1948 Cover: 0.10 **NM** value: **64.00**
A: Fred Harman **W:** Fred Harman

58 ☐ May 1948 Cover: 0.10 **NM** value: **64.00**
A: Fred Harman **W:** Fred Harman

59 ☐ Jun 1948 Cover: 0.10 **NM** value: **64.00**
A: Fred Harman **W:** Fred Harman

60 ☐ Jul 1948 Cover: 0.10 **NM** value: **64.00**
A: Fred Harman **W:** Fred Harman

61 ☐ Aug 1948 Cover: 0.10 **NM** value: **50.00**
A: Fred Harman **W:** Fred Harman

62 ☐ Sep 1948 Cover: 0.10 **NM** value: **50.00**
A: Fred Harman **W:** Fred Harman

63 ☐ Oct 1948 Cover: 0.10 **NM** value: **50.00**
A: Fred Harman **W:** Fred Harman

64 ☐ Nov 1948 Cover: 0.10 **NM** value: **50.00**
A: Fred Harman **W:** Fred Harman

65 ☐ Dec 1948 Cover: 0.10 **NM** value: **50.00**
• **CGC:** 1 graded, best 8.0
A: Fred Harman **W:** Fred Harman

66 ☐ Jan 1949 Cover: 0.10 **NM** value: **50.00**
A: Fred Harman **W:** Fred Harman

67 ☐ Feb 1949 Cover: 0.10 **NM** value: **50.00**
A: Fred Harman **W:** Fred Harman

68 ☐ Mar 1949 Cover: 0.10 **NM** value: **50.00**
A: Fred Harman **W:** Fred Harman

69 ☐ Apr 1949 Cover: 0.10 **NM** value: **50.00**
A: Fred Harman **W:** Fred Harman

70 ☐ May 1949 Cover: 0.10 **NM** value: **50.00**
A: Fred Harman **W:** Fred Harman

71 ☐ Jun 1949 Cover: 0.10 **NM** value: **42.00**
A: Fred Harman **W:** Fred Harman

72 ☐ Jul 1949 Cover: 0.10 **NM** value: **42.00**
A: Fred Harman **W:** Fred Harman

73 ☐ Aug 1949 Cover: 0.10 **NM** value: **42.00**
A: Fred Harman **W:** Fred Harman

74 ☐ Sep 1949 Cover: 0.10 **NM** value: **42.00**
A: Fred Harman **W:** Fred Harman

75 ☐ Oct 1949 Cover: 0.10 **NM** value: **42.00**
A: Fred Harman **W:** Fred Harman

76 ☐ Nov 1949 Cover: 0.10 **NM** value: **42.00**
A: Fred Harman **W:** Fred Harman

77 ☐ Dec 1949 Cover: 0.10 **NM** value: **42.00**
A: Fred Harman **W:** Fred Harman

78 ☐ Jan 1950 Cover: 0.10 **NM** value: **42.00**
79 ☐ Feb 1950 Cover: 0.10 **NM** value: **42.00**
80 ☐ Mar 1950 Cover: 0.10 **NM** value: **42.00**
81 ☐ Apr 1950 Cover: 0.10 **NM** value: **36.00**
82 ☐ May 1950 Cover: 0.10 **NM** value: **36.00**
83 ☐ Jun 1950 Cover: 0.10 **NM** value: **36.00**
84 ☐ Jul 1950 Cover: 0.10 **NM** value: **36.00**
85 ☐ Aug 1950 Cover: 0.10 **NM** value: **36.00**
86 ☐ Sep 1950 Cover: 0.10 **NM** value: **36.00**
87 ☐ Oct 1950 Cover: 0.10 **NM** value: **36.00**
88 ☐ Nov 1950 Cover: 0.10 **NM** value: **36.00**
89 ☐ Dec 1950 Cover: 0.10 **NM** value: **36.00**
90 ☐ Jan 1951 Cover: 0.10 **NM** value: **36.00**
91 ☐ Feb 1951 Cover: 0.10 **NM** value: **26.00**
92 ☐ Mar 1951 Cover: 0.10 **NM** value: **26.00**
93 ☐ Apr 1951 Cover: 0.10 **NM** value: **26.00**
94 ☐ May 1951 Cover: 0.10 **NM** value: **26.00**
95 ☐ Jun 1951 Cover: 0.10 **NM** value: **26.00**
96 ☐ Jul 1951 Cover: 0.10 **NM** value: **26.00**
97 ☐ Aug 1951 Cover: 0.10 **NM** value: **26.00**
98 ☐ Sep 1951 Cover: 0.10 **NM** value: **26.00**
99 ☐ Oct 1951 Cover: 0.10 **NM** value: **26.00**
100 ☐ Nov 1951 Cover: 0.10 **NM** value: **26.00**
101 ☐ Dec 1951 Cover: 0.10 **NM** value: **24.00**
102 ☐ Jan 1952 Cover: 0.10 **NM** value: **24.00**
103 ☐ Feb 1952 Cover: 0.10 **NM** value: **24.00**
104 ☐ Mar 1952 Cover: 0.10 **NM** value: **24.00**
105 ☐ Apr 1952 Cover: 0.10 **NM** value: **24.00**
106 ☐ May 1952 Cover: 0.10 **NM** value: **24.00**
107 ☐ Jun 1952 Cover: 0.10 **NM** value: **24.00**
• **CGC:** 1 graded, best 9.6

108 ☐ Jul 1952 Cover: 0.10 **NM** value: **24.00**
• **CGC:** 1 graded, best 9.4

109 ☐ Aug 1952 Cover: 0.10 **NM** value: **24.00**
• **CGC:** 1 graded, best 9.4

110 ☐ Sep 1952 Cover: 0.10 **NM** value: **24.00**
• **CGC:** 1 graded, best 9.4

111 ☐ Oct 1952 Cover: 0.10 **NM** value: **20.00**
• **CGC:** 1 graded, best 9.4

112 ☐ Nov 1952 Cover: 0.10 **NM** value: **20.00**
113 ☐ Dec 1952 Cover: 0.10 **NM** value: **20.00**
114 ☐ Jan 1953 Cover: 0.10 **NM** value: **20.00**
115 ☐ Feb 1953 Cover: 0.10 **NM** value: **20.00**
116 ☐ Mar 1953 Cover: 0.10 **NM** value: **20.00**
Little Beaver; Auntie Duchess; **A:** Fred Harman **W:** Fred Harman

117 ☐ Apr 1953 Cover: 0.10 **NM** value: **20.00**
• **CGC:** 2 graded, best 9.8

118 ☐ May 1953 Cover: 0.10 **NM** value: **20.00**
• **CGC:** 1 graded, best 9.6

119 ☐ Jun 1953 Cover: 0.10 **NM** value: **20.00**
• **CGC:** 1 graded, best 9.8

120 ☐ Jul 1953 Cover: 0.10 **NM** value: **20.00**
121 ☐ Aug 1953 Cover: 0.10 **NM** value: **18.00**
122 ☐ Sep 1953 Cover: 0.10 **NM** value: **18.00**
123 ☐ Oct 1953 Cover: 0.10 **NM** value: **18.00**
124 ☐ Nov 1953 Cover: 0.10 **NM** value: **18.00**
125 ☐ Dec 1953 Cover: 0.10 **NM** value: **18.00**
126 ☐ Jan 1954 Cover: 0.10 **NM** value: **18.00**
127 ☐ Feb 1954 Cover: 0.10 **NM** value: **18.00**
128 ☐ Mar 1954 Cover: 0.10 **NM** value: **18.00**
129 ☐ Apr 1954 Cover: 0.10 **NM** value: **18.00**
130 ☐ May 1954 Cover: 0.10 **NM** value: **18.00**
131 ☐ Jun 1954 Cover: 0.10 **NM** value: **15.00**
132 ☐ Jul 1954 Cover: 0.10 **NM** value: **15.00**
133 ☐ Aug 1954 Cover: 0.10 **NM** value: **15.00**
134 ☐ Sep 1954 Cover: 0.10 **NM** value: **15.00**
135 ☐ Oct 1954 Cover: 0.10 **NM** value: **15.00**
136 ☐ Nov 1954 Cover: 0.10 **NM** value: **15.00**
137 ☐ Dec 1954 Cover: 0.10 **NM** value: **15.00**
138 ☐ Jan 1955 Cover: 0.10 **NM** value: **15.00**
• **CGC:** 2 graded, best 8.0

139 ☐ Feb 1955 Cover: 0.10 **NM** value: **15.00**
140 ☐ Mar 1955 Cover: 0.10 **NM** value: **15.00**
141 ☐ Apr 1955 Cover: 0.10 **NM** value: **14.00**
142 ☐ May 1955 Cover: 0.10 **NM** value: **14.00**
• **CGC:** 1 graded, best 9.2

143 ☐ Jun 1955 Cover: 0.10 **NM** value: **14.00**
144 ☐ Jul 1955 Cover: 0.10 **NM** value: **14.00**
145 ☐ Oct 1955 Cover: 0.10 **NM** value: **14.00**
146 ☐ Jan 1956 Cover: 0.10 **NM** value: **14.00**
147 ☐ Apr 1956 Cover: 0.10 **NM** value: **14.00**
148 ☐ Jul 1956 Cover: 0.10 **NM** value: **14.00**
149 ☐ Oct 1956 Cover: 0.10 **NM** value: **14.00**
150 ☐ Jan 1957 Cover: 0.10 **NM** value: **14.00**
151 ☐ Apr 1957 Cover: 0.10 **NM** value: **14.00**
final issue.

RED SEAL COMICS — Harry A. Chesler

14 ☐ Oct 1945 Cover: 0.10 **NM** value: **600.00**
15 ☐ Jan 1946 Cover: 0.10 **NM** value: **400.00**
• **CGC:** 1 graded, best 9.2

16 ☐ Apr 1946 Cover: 0.10 **NM** value: **400.00**
17 ☐ Jul 1946 Cover: 0.10 **NM** value: **350.00**
• **CGC:** 1 graded, best 9.4

18 ☐ Oct 1946 Cover: 0.10 **NM** value: **350.00**
• **CGC:** 2 graded, best 8.0

19 ☐ Jun 1947 Cover: 0.10 **NM** value: **350.00**
• **CGC:** 2 graded, best 9.4

20 ☐ Aug 1947 Cover: 0.10 **NM** value: **300.00**
21 ☐ Oct 1947 Cover: 0.10 **NM** value: **300.00**
22 ☐ Dec 1947 Cover: 0.10 **NM** value: **300.00**
• **CGC:** 1 graded, best 7.5

RED SHETLAND — Graphxpress

1 ☐ Cover: 2.00 **NM** value: **Cover or less**
2 ☐ Cover: 2.00 **NM** value: **Cover or less**
3 ☐ Cover: 2.00 **NM** value: **Cover or less**
4 ☐ Cover: 2.00 **NM** value: **Cover or less**
5 ☐ Cover: 2.50 **NM** value: **Cover or less**
6 ☐ Cover: 2.50 **NM** value: **Cover or less**
7 ☐ Cover: 2.50 **NM** value: **Cover or less**
8 ☐ Cover: 2.50 **NM** value: **Cover or less**
9 ☐ Cover: 3.50 **NM** value: **Cover or less**

REDSKIN — Youthful

1 ☐ Sep 1950 Cover: 0.10 **NM** value: **100.00**
2 ☐ Dec 1950 Cover: 0.10 **NM** value: **50.00**
3 ☐ Feb 1951 Cover: 0.10 **NM** value: **50.00**
4 ☐ May 1951 Cover: 0.10 **NM** value: **50.00**
5 ☐ Jul 1951 Cover: 0.10 **NM** value: **50.00**
6 ☐ Sep 1951 Cover: 0.10 **NM** value: **50.00**
7 ☐ Nov 1951 Cover: 0.10 **NM** value: **45.00**
8 ☐ Feb 1952 Cover: 0.10 **NM** value: **45.00**
9 ☐ Apr 1952 Cover: 0.10 **NM** value: **45.00**
10 ☐ Jun 1952 Cover: 0.10 **NM** value: **45.00**
11 ☐ Aug 1952 Cover: 0.10 **NM** value: **45.00**
12 ☐ Oct 1952 Cover: 0.10 **NM** value: **45.00**

RED SONJA: A DEATH IN SCARLET — Cross Plains

1 ☐ Sep 1999 Cover: 2.95 **NM** value: **Cover or less**
Circ: Diamd. preorders: **8,088**
A: Steve Lightle **W:** Steve Lightle; Roy Thomas

RED SONJA IN 3-D — Blackthorne

1 ☐ Cover: 2.50 **NM** value: **Cover or less**
Circ: CapCity orders: **1,700**

RED SONJA: SCAVENGER HUNT — Marvel

1 ☐ Dec 1995 Cover: 2.95 **NM** value: **Cover or less**
One-shot. **A:** Alexander Jubran; Ken Lashley; Daniel Horn; Harry Candelario; Joe Pimentel; R. Micheletti **W:** Glenn Herdling

RED SONJA: THE MOVIE — Marvel

1 ☐ Nov 1985 Cover: 0.75 **NM** value: **1.25**
Circ: CapCity orders: **6,000**
Into the Realm of Darkness! **A:** Mary Wilshire **W:** Mary Wilshire; Louise Simonson

2 ☐ Dec 1985 Cover: 0.75 **NM** value: **1.25**
Circ: CapCity orders: **4,900**
A: Mary Wilshire **W:** Mary Wilshire; Louise Simonson

RED SONJA (VOL. 1) — Marvel

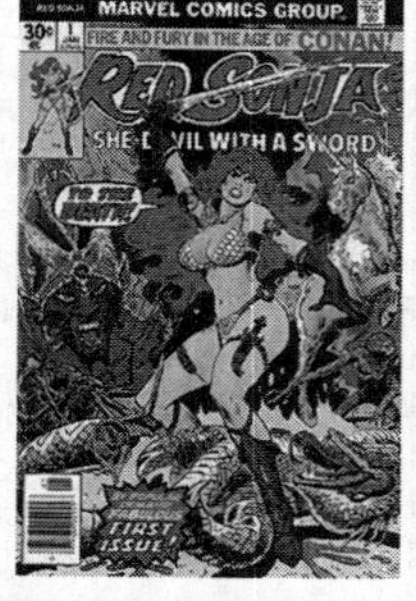

A flame-tressed warrior of legend, she is called Red Sonja. As a girl, she lived a quiet life with her brother and parents, until the day that soldiers came to take away her brother to serve in a tyrant's army. When her parents resisted, the soldiers slew her family and raped Sonja. In the wake of the attack, she was visited by an apparition-a goddess who offered Sonja strength equal to any man or woman. The condition of this offer was that Sonja could never give herself to a man who had not first bested her in a fair fight.

From that offbeat origin came one of the best characters of the genre, and a welcome counterpoint to the musclebound men who dominate it. Red Sonja first appeared in Conan the Barbarian #23, then went on to a solo stint in Marvel Feature (1st Series). Her adventures continue in this series, which is also notable for its reception upon release: There was a run on the first issue, one of the earliest examples of speculation on a new comic book.

1 ☐ Nov 1976 Cover: 0.30 **NM** value: **3.00**
• **CGC:** 14 graded, best 9.8
A: Frank Thorne ★ Origin of Red Sonja.

2 ☐ Jan 1977 Cover: 0.30 **NM** value: **2.00**
• **CGC:** 1 graded, best 9.6
A: Frank Thorne

3 ☐ May 1977 Cover: 0.30 **NM** value: **2.00**
• **CGC:** 2 graded, best 9.8
The Games of Gita **A:** Frank Thorne **W:** Roy Thomas; Clara Noto

4 ☐ Jul 1977 Cover: 0.30 **NM** value: **2.00**
• **CGC:** 1 graded, best 9.6
The Lake of the Unknownb **A:** Frank Thorne **W:** Roy Thomas; Clara Noto

5 ☐ Sep 1977 Cover: 0.30 **NM** value: **2.00**
Master Of The Bells! **A:** Frank Thorne **W:** Roy Thomas; Clara Noto

6 ☐ Nov 1977 Cover: 0.35 **NM** value: **1.50**
The Singing Tower **A:** Frank Thorne **W:** Wendy Pini; Roy Thomas; Clara Noto

7 ☐ Jan 1978 Cover: 0.35 **NM** value: **1.50**
Throne of Blood! **A:** Frank Thorne **W:** Roy Thomas; Clara Noto

8 ☐ Mar 1978 Cover: 0.35 **NM** value: **1.50**
Vengeance of the Golden Circle **A:** Frank Thorne **W:** Roy Thomas; Clara Noto

9 ☐ May 1978 Cover: 0.35 **NM** value: **1.50**
Chariot of the Fire Stallions **A:** Frank Thorne **W:** Roy Thomas; Clara Noto

10 ☐ Jul 1978 Cover: 0.35 **NM** value: **1.50**
Red Lace **A:** Frank Thorne **W:** Roy Thomas; Clara Noto

11 ☐ Sep 1978 Cover: 0.35 **NM** value: **1.50**
Sightless in a Strage Land! **A:** Frank Thorne **W:** Roy Thomas; Clara Noto

12 ☐ Nov 1978 Cover: 0.35 **NM** value: **1.50**
13 ☐ Jan 1979 Cover: 0.35 **NM** value: **1.50**
14 ☐ Mar 1979 Cover: 0.35 **NM** value: **1.50**
15 ☐ May 1979 Cover: 0.40 **NM** value: **1.50**

RED SONJA (VOL. 2) — Marvel

1 ☐ Feb 1983 Cover: 0.60 **NM** value: **1.00**
• **CGC:** 2 graded, best 9.8
The Blood That Binds! **A:** Alan Kupperberg; Tony DeZuniga; Ernie Colon; Mel Candido **W:** Roy Thomas; Christine Mark

2 ☐ Mar 1983 Cover: 0.60 **NM** value: **1.00**

RED SONJA (VOL. 3) — Marvel

1 ☐ Aug 1983 Cover: 1.00 **NM** value: **1.50**
While Lovers Embrace- Demons Feed! • giant **A:** Dave Simons **W:** Tom DeFalco

2 ☐ Oct 1983 Cover: 1.00 **NM** value: **1.50**
Blood Debt • giant **A:** Mary Wilshire **W:** Tom DeFalco

3 ☐ Dec 1983 Cover: 1.00 **NM** value: **1.50**
• giant

4 ☐ Feb 1984 Cover: 1.00 **NM** value: **1.50**
• giant

5 ☐ Jan 1985 Cover: 0.60 **NM** value: **1.50**
Circ: Statement: **167,734**
The Armies Of The Inland Sea **A:** Pat Broderick **W:** Bill Mantlo

6 ☐ Feb 1985 Cover: 0.60 **NM** value: **1.50**
Circ: Statement: **167,734**
The Endless Swamp! **A:** Pat Broderick **W:** Bill Mantlo

7 ☐ Mar 1985 Cover: 0.60 **NM** value: **1.50**
Circ: Statement: **167,734**
Harvest! **A:** Rudy Nebres **W:** Bill Mantlo

8 ☐ Apr 1985 Cover: 0.65 **NM** value: **1.50**
Circ: Statement: **167,734**

9 ☐ May 1985 Cover: 0.65 **NM** value: **1.50**
Circ: Statement: **167,734** CapCity orders: **7,000**
The Queen Of Hearts! **A:** Mary Wilshire **W:** Louise Simonson

10 ☐ Aug 1985 Cover: 0.65 **NM** value: **1.50**
Circ: Statement: **167,734** CapCity orders: **6,600**
Strangers! **A:** Mary Wilshire **W:** Louise Simonson

11 ☐ Nov 1985 Cover: 0.65 **NM** value: **1.50**
Circ: Statement: **167,734** CapCity orders: **6,600**
Buried Alive **A:** Mary Wilshire **W:** Louise Simonson

12 ☐ Feb 1986 Cover: 0.75 **NM** value: **1.50**
Circ: CapCity orders: **6,200**
Descent! **A:** Mary Wilshire **W:** Louise Simonson

13 ☐ Cover: 0.75 **NM** value: **1.50**
Circ: CapCity orders: **6,300**
The Demon's Tooth final issue. **A:** Mary Wilshire **W:** Louise Simonson

RED STAR, THE — Image

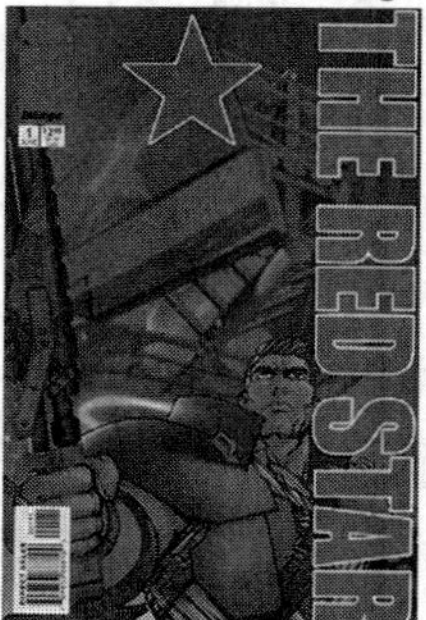

Blending the worlds of fantasy and science fiction into a visually stunning package, The Red Star is a comic book like no other. The title's visuals incorporate stunning 3-D computer models and coloring effects to create imagery unmatched by the industry's standard super-hero fare.

Presented as a flashback, the story follows the aftermath that ensues with the collapse of the Red Fleet — a Soviet like military power — at the hands of the evil sorcerer Imbohl. Even its futuristic crafts and weaponry (powered by the Warkasters, a class of military sorcerers) is no match for

Other grades: Multiply prices above by **1.5 for Mint • 2/3 for Very Fine • 1/3 for Fine • 1/5 for Very Good • 1/8 for Good**

this master of the dark arts. Set against this turmoil is the all too human story of Maya Antare (a Sorceress Major and member of the Warkaster) who is struggling to find her husband, Marcus, allegedly lost while leading a frontal assault against the enemy.

1 ❑ Jun 2000 Cover: 2.95 **NM** value: **3.50**
Circ: Diamd. preorders: **29,519** • **CGC:** 27 graded, best 9.8
A: Christian Gossett **W:** Christian Gossett

2 ❑ Jul 2000 Cover: 2.95 **NM** value: **3.00**
Circ: Diamd. preorders: **18,754** • **CGC:** 14 graded, best 9.9
A: Christian Gossett **W:** Christian Gossett

3 ❑ Oct 2000 Cover: 2.95 **NM** value: **Cover or less**
Circ: Diamd. preorders: **19,985** • **CGC:** 1 graded, best 9.4
A: Christian Gossett **W:** Christian Gossett

4 ❑ Jan 2001 Cover: 2.95 **NM** value: **Cover or less**
Circ: Diamd. preorders: **22,077** • **CGC:** 2 graded, best 9.4
A: Christian Gossett; A.D. Coulter **W:** Christian Gossett; Bradley James Kayl

5 ❑ Feb 2001 Cover: 2.95 **NM** value: **Cover or less**
Circ: Diamd. preorders: **23,048** • **CGC:** 1 graded, best 9.6
A: Christian Gossett; A.D. Coulter **W:** Christian Gossett; Bradley James Kayl

RED TORNADO — DC

1 ❑ Jul 1985 Cover: 0.75 **NM** value: **1.00**
📖 Storm Warning **A:** Carmine Infantino **W:** Kurt Busiek

2 ❑ Aug 1985 Cover: 0.75 **NM** value: **1.00**
📖 Shattered **A:** Carmine Infantino **W:** Kurt Busiek

3 ❑ Sep 1985 Cover: 0.75 **NM** value: **1.00**
📖 The Eye of the Storm **A:** Carmine Infantino **W:** Kurt Busiek

4 ❑ Oct 1985 Cover: 0.75 **NM** value: **1.00**
📖 Ghost in the Machine **A:** Carmine Infantino **W:** Kurt Busiek

RED WARRIOR — Atlas

1 ❑ Jan 1951 Cover: 0.10 **NM** value: **100.00**
2 ❑ Mar 1951 Cover: 0.10 **NM** value: **50.00**
3 ❑ May 1951 Cover: 0.10 **NM** value: **40.00**
4 ❑ Jul 1951 Cover: 0.10 **NM** value: **40.00**
5 ❑ Sep 1951 Cover: 0.10 **NM** value: **40.00**
6 ❑ Nov 1951 Cover: 0.10 **NM** value: **40.00**

RED WOLF — Marvel

Billed as the first Native American super-hero to appear in comics, Red Wolf debuted in Avengers #80 as an embittered young Indian radical bent on stopping the exploitation of his people and their reservation lands by unscrupulous businessmen. When he next appeared in Marvel Spotlight (Vol. 1) #1, the scene had shifted to the Old West, with the Red Wolf there actually the ancestor of the original character.

It's this Old West Red Wolf who won his own title in the early 1970s, with solid art by veteran pen Syd Shores and writing by Golden Age pro Gardner Fox. The title was a low-key effort, and Marvel probably enjoyed more public relations benefits from the title than sales.

1 ❑ May 1972 Cover: 0.20 **NM** value: **4.00**
• **CGC:** 3 graded, best 9.6
★ 1st Appearance of Red Wolf, Lobo (Marvel).

2 ❑ Jul 1972 Cover: 0.20 **NM** value: **2.00**
• **CGC:** 1 graded, best 9.6

3 ❑ Sep 1972 Cover: 0.20 **NM** value: **2.00**
4 ❑ Nov 1972 Cover: 0.20 **NM** value: **2.00**
★ Versus Man-Bear.
5 ❑ Jan 1973 Cover: 0.20 **NM** value: **2.00**
6 ❑ Mar 1973 Cover: 0.20 **NM** value: **2.00**
7 ❑ May 1973 Cover: 0.20 **NM** value: **2.00**
8 ❑ Jul 1973 Cover: 0.20 **NM** value: **2.00**
9 ❑ Sep 1973 Cover: 0.20 **NM** value: **2.00**
final issue.

REESE'S PIECES — Eclipse

1 ❑ ca. 1986 Cover: 1.75 **NM** value: **Cover or less**
Circ: CapCity orders: **3,550**

2 ❑ ca. 1986 Cover: 1.75 **NM** value: **Cover or less**
Circ: CapCity orders: **3,350**

REFORM SCHOOL GIRL — Realistic Comics

1 ❑ ca. 1951 Cover: 0.10 **NM** value: **1000.00**
• **CGC:** 1 graded, best 5.5

RE:GEX — Awesome

0 ❑ Dec 1998 Cover: 2.50 **NM** value: **Cover or less**
Circ: Diamd. preorders: **21,085**
📖 Re:Gex • Woman with swords standing over figures **A:** Rob Liefeld **W:** Jeph Loeb; Rob Liefeld

0/A ❑ Jan 1999 Cover: 2.50 **NM** value: **Cover or less**
📖 Re:Gex • Man with swords standing over figures **A:** Rob Liefeld **W:** Jeph Loeb; Rob Liefeld

1 ❑ 1998 Cover: 2.50 **NM** value: **Cover or less**
Circ: Diamd. preorders: **41,278**
A: Rob Liefeld **W:** Jeph Loeb; Rob Liefeld

1/A ❑ Cover: 2.50 **NM** value: **Cover or less**
Two women with swords on cover. • White background **A:** Rob Liefeld **W:** Jeph Loeb; Rob Liefeld

REGGIE AND ME — Archie

19 ❑ Aug 1966 Cover: 0.12 **NM** value: **10.00**
• Series continued from Reggie #18
20 ❑ Oct 1966 Cover: 0.12 **NM** value: **8.00**
21 ❑ Dec 1966 Cover: 0.12 **NM** value: **6.00**
22 ❑ Feb 1967 Cover: 0.12 **NM** value: **6.00**
23 ❑ Apr 1967 Cover: 0.12 **NM** value: **6.00**
24 ❑ Jun 1967 Cover: 0.12 **NM** value: **6.00**
25 ❑ Aug 1967 Cover: 0.12 **NM** value: **6.00**
26 ❑ Nov 1967 Cover: 0.12 **NM** value: **5.00**
27 ❑ Jan 1968 Cover: 0.12 **NM** value: **5.00**
28 ❑ Mar 1968 Cover: 0.12 **NM** value: **5.00**
29 ❑ May 1968 Cover: 0.12 **NM** value: **5.00**
📖 Seat of the Trouble; The Best Policy; Suit Yourself; Li'l Jinx: Food for Thought; Ski Scamps
30 ❑ Jul 1968 Cover: 0.12 **NM** value: **5.00**
31 ❑ Sep 1968 Cover: 0.12 **NM** value: **3.00**
32 ❑ Nov 1968 Cover: 0.12 **NM** value: **3.00**
33 ❑ Jan 1969 Cover: 0.12 **NM** value: **3.00**
Circ: Statement: **276,275**
34 ❑ Mar 1969 Cover: 0.12 **NM** value: **3.00**
Circ: Statement: **276,275**
35 ❑ May 1969 Cover: 0.12 **NM** value: **3.00**
Circ: Statement: **276,275**
36 ❑ Jul 1969 Cover: 0.15 **NM** value: **3.00**
Circ: Statement: **276,275**
37 ❑ Sep 1969 Cover: 0.15 **NM** value: **3.00**
Circ: Statement: **276,275**
38 ❑ Nov 1969 Cover: 0.15 **NM** value: **3.00**
Circ: Statement: **276,275**
39 ❑ Jan 1970 Cover: 0.15 **NM** value: **3.00**
Circ: Statement: **250,904**
40 ❑ Mar 1970 Cover: 0.15 **NM** value: **3.00**
Circ: Statement: **250,904**
41 ❑ May 1970 Cover: 0.15 **NM** value: **3.00**
Circ: Statement: **250,904**
42 ❑ Jul 1970 Cover: 0.15 **NM** value: **3.00**
Circ: Statement: **250,904**
43 ❑ Sep 1970 Cover: 0.15 **NM** value: **3.00**
Circ: Statement: **250,904**
44 ❑ Oct 1970 Cover: 0.15 **NM** value: **3.00**
Circ: Statement: **250,904**
45 ❑ Nov 1970 Cover: 0.15 **NM** value: **3.00**
Circ: Statement: **250,904**
46 ❑ Jan 1971 Cover: 0.15 **NM** value: **3.00**
Circ: Statement: **256,551**
47 ❑ Mar 1971 Cover: 0.15 **NM** value: **3.00**
Circ: Statement: **256,551**
48 ❑ May 1971 Cover: 0.15 **NM** value: **3.00**
Circ: Statement: **256,551**
49 ❑ Jul 1971 Cover: 0.15 **NM** value: **3.00**
Circ: Statement: **256,551**
50 ❑ Sep 1971 Cover: 0.25 **NM** value: **3.00**
Circ: Statement: **256,551**
51 ❑ Oct 1971 Cover: 0.25 **NM** value: **2.00**
Circ: Statement: **256,551**
52 ❑ Nov 1971 Cover: 0.25 **NM** value: **2.00**
Circ: Statement: **256,551**
53 ❑ Jan 1972 Cover: 0.25 **NM** value: **2.00**
Circ: Statement: **187,688**
54 ❑ Mar 1972 Cover: 0.25 **NM** value: **2.00**
Circ: Statement: **187,688**
55 ❑ May 1972 Cover: 0.25 **NM** value: **2.00**
Circ: Statement: **187,688**
56 ❑ Jul 1972 Cover: 0.25 **NM** value: **2.00**
Circ: Statement: **187,688**
57 ❑ Sep 1972 Cover: 0.25 **NM** value: **2.00**
Circ: Statement: **187,688**
58 ❑ Oct 1972 Cover: 0.25 **NM** value: **2.00**
Circ: Statement: **187,688**
59 ❑ Nov 1972 Cover: 0.25 **NM** value: **2.00**
Circ: Statement: **187,688**
60 ❑ Feb 1973 Cover: 0.25 **NM** value: **2.00**
Circ: Statement: **165,279**
61 ❑ Apr 1973 Cover: 0.25 **NM** value: **2.00**
Circ: Statement: **165,279**
62 ❑ May 1973 Cover: 0.25 **NM** value: **2.00**
Circ: Statement: **165,279**
• Has 1972 Statement; avg total paid circ 187,688
63 ❑ Jul 1973 Cover: 0.25 **NM** value: **2.00**
Circ: Statement: **165,279**
64 ❑ Aug 1973 Cover: 0.25 **NM** value: **2.00**
Circ: Statement: **165,279**
65 ❑ Sep 1973 Cover: 0.25 **NM** value: **2.00**
Circ: Statement: **165,279**
66 ❑ Oct 1973 Cover: 0.25 **NM** value: **2.00**
Circ: Statement: **165,279**
67 ❑ Dec 1973 Cover: 0.25 **NM** value: **2.00**
Circ: Statement: **165,279**
68 ❑ Jan 1974 Cover: 0.25 **NM** value: **2.00**
Circ: Statement: **172,305**
69 ❑ Mar 1974 Cover: 0.25 **NM** value: **2.00**
Circ: Statement: **172,305**
• Has 1973 Statement; avg total paid circ 165,279
70 ❑ May 1974 Cover: 0.25 **NM** value: **2.00**
Circ: Statement: **172,305**
71 ❑ Jul 1974 Cover: 0.25 **NM** value: **2.00**
Circ: Statement: **172,305**
72 ❑ Aug 1974 Cover: 0.25 **NM** value: **2.00**
Circ: Statement: **172,305**
73 ❑ Sep 1974 Cover: 0.25 **NM** value: **2.00**
Circ: Statement: **172,305**
74 ❑ Oct 1974 Cover: 0.25 **NM** value: **2.00**
Circ: Statement: **172,305**
75 ❑ Dec 1974 Cover: 0.25 **NM** value: **2.00**
Circ: Statement: **172,305**
76 ❑ Jan 1975 Cover: 0.25 **NM** value: **2.00**
Circ: Statement: **141,118**
77 ❑ Mar 1975 Cover: 0.25 **NM** value: **2.00**
Circ: Statement: **141,118**
78 ❑ May 1975 Cover: 0.25 **NM** value: **2.00**
Circ: Statement: **141,118**
• Has 1974 Statement; avg total paid circ 172,305
79 ❑ Jul 1975 Cover: 0.25 **NM** value: **2.00**
Circ: Statement: **141,118**
80 ❑ Aug 1975 Cover: 0.25 **NM** value: **2.00**
Circ: Statement: **141,118**
81 ❑ Sep 1975 Cover: 0.25 **NM** value: **1.50**
Circ: Statement: **141,118**
82 ❑ Oct 1975 Cover: 0.25 **NM** value: **1.50**
Circ: Statement: **141,118**
83 ❑ Dec 1975 Cover: 0.25 **NM** value: **1.50**
Circ: Statement: **141,118**
84 ❑ Jan 1976 Cover: 0.25 **NM** value: **1.50**
Circ: Statement: **121,460**
85 ❑ Mar 1976 Cover: 0.30 **NM** value: **1.50**
Circ: Statement: **121,460**
86 ❑ Apr 1976 Cover: 0.30 **NM** value: **1.50**
Circ: Statement: **121,460**
87 ❑ May 1976 Cover: 0.30 **NM** value: **1.50**
Circ: Statement: **121,460**
88 ❑ Jul 1976 Cover: 0.30 **NM** value: **1.50**
Circ: Statement: **121,460**
89 ❑ Aug 1976 Cover: 0.30 **NM** value: **1.50**
Circ: Statement: **121,460**
90 ❑ Sep 1976 Cover: 0.30 **NM** value: **1.50**
Circ: Statement: **121,460**
91 ❑ Oct 1976 Cover: 0.30 **NM** value: **1.50**
Circ: Statement: **121,460**
92 ❑ Dec 1976 Cover: 0.30 **NM** value: **1.50**
Circ: Statement: **121,460**
93 ❑ Jan 1977 Cover: 0.30 **NM** value: **1.50**
Circ: Statement: **117,620**
94 ❑ Mar 1977 Cover: 0.30 **NM** value: **1.50**
Circ: Statement: **117,620**
95 ❑ Apr 1977 Cover: 0.30 **NM** value: **1.50**
Circ: Statement: **117,620**
• Has 1976 Statement; avg total paid circ 121,460
96 ❑ May 1977 Cover: 0.30 **NM** value: **1.50**
Circ: Statement: **117,620**
97 ❑ Jul 1977 Cover: 0.35 **NM** value: **1.50**
Circ: Statement: **117,620**
98 ❑ Aug 1977 Cover: 0.35 **NM** value: **1.50**
Circ: Statement: **117,620**
99 ❑ Sep 1977 Cover: 0.35 **NM** value: **1.50**
Circ: Statement: **117,620**
100 ❑ Oct 1977 Cover: 0.35 **NM** value: **1.50**
Circ: Statement: **117,620**
101 ❑ Dec 1977 Cover: 0.35 **NM** value: **1.00**
Circ: Statement: **117,620**
102 ❑ Jan 1978 Cover: 0.35 **NM** value: **1.00**
Circ: Statement: **97,828**
103 ❑ Mar 1978 Cover: 0.35 **NM** value: **1.00**
Circ: Statement: **97,828**
104 ❑ Apr 1978 Cover: 0.35 **NM** value: **1.00**
Circ: Statement: **97,828**
• Has 1977 Statement; avg total paid circ 117,620
105 ❑ May 1978 Cover: 0.35 **NM** value: **1.00**
Circ: Statement: **97,828**
106 ❑ Jul 1978 Cover: 0.35 **NM** value: **1.00**
Circ: Statement: **97,828**
107 ❑ Aug 1978 Cover: 0.35 **NM** value: **1.00**
Circ: Statement: **97,828**
108 ❑ Sep 1978 Cover: 0.35 **NM** value: **1.00**
Circ: Statement: **97,828**
109 ❑ Oct 1978 Cover: 0.35 **NM** value: **1.00**
Circ: Statement: **97,828**
110 ❑ Dec 1978 Cover: 0.35 **NM** value: **1.00**
Circ: Statement: **97,828**
111 ❑ Jan 1979 Cover: 0.35 **NM** value: **1.00**
Circ: Statement: **92,684**
112 ❑ Mar 1979 Cover: 0.35 **NM** value: **1.00**
Circ: Statement: **92,684**
113 ❑ Apr 1979 Cover: 0.40 **NM** value: **1.00**
Circ: Statement: **92,684**
• Has 1978 Statement, filed 10/1/78; avg print run 271,762; avg sales 97,818; avg subs 10; avg total paid 97,828; samples 0; office use 300; max existent 98,128; 64% of run returned
114 ❑ May 1979 Cover: 0.40 **NM** value: **1.00**
Circ: Statement: **92,684**
115 ❑ Jul 1979 Cover: 0.40 **NM** value: **1.00**
Circ: Statement: **92,684**
116 ❑ Aug 1979 Cover: 0.40 **NM** value: **1.00**
Circ: Statement: **92,684**
117 ❑ Sep 1979 Cover: 0.40 **NM** value: **1.00**
Circ: Statement: **92,684**
118 ❑ Oct 1979 Cover: 0.40 **NM** value: **1.00**
Circ: Statement: **92,684**
119 ❑ Dec 1979 Cover: 0.40 **NM** value: **1.00**
Circ: Statement: **92,684**
120 ❑ Jan 1980 Cover: 0.40 **NM** value: **1.00**
121 ❑ Mar 1980 Cover: 0.40 **NM** value: **1.00**
122 ❑ Apr 1980 Cover: 0.40 **NM** value: **1.00**
• Has 1979 Statement, filed 10/1/79; avg print run 261,354; avg sales 92,617; avg subs 67; avg total paid 92,684; samples 0; office use 300; max existent 92,984; 64% of run returned
123 ❑ May 1980 Cover: 0.40 **NM** value: **1.00**
124 ❑ Jul 1980 Cover: 0.40 **NM** value: **1.00**
125 ❑ Sep 1980 Cover: 0.50 **NM** value: **1.00**
126 ❑ Oct 1980 Cover: 0.50 **NM** value: **1.00**
final issue.

REGGIE'S REVENGE — Archie

1 ❑ Spr 1994 Cover: 2.00 **NM** value: **Cover or less**
2 ❑ Fal 1994 Cover: 2.00 **NM** value: **Cover or less**
3 ❑ Spr 1995 Cover: 2.00 **NM** value: **Cover or less**

REGGIE'S WISE GUY JOKES — Archie

1 ❑ Aug 1968 Cover: 0.12 **NM** value: **8.00**
• **CGC:** 1 graded, best 6.0
📖 Motor Matter; Wet Set; Fan Elan; F
2 ❑ Oct 1968 Cover: 0.12 **NM** value: **5.00**

CGC-graded: Multiply prices above by **33 for 9.9 M • 16 for 9.8 NM/M • 7 for 9.6 NM+ • 5 for 9.4 NM • 2.5 for 9.2 NM- • 1.5 for 9.0 VF/NM**

3 ❑ Dec 1968 Cover: 0.12 **NM** value: **4.00**
Romantic Antic; Bumped; Swing Thing; Switch Pitch; Custom School Desks!; Speed Deed; Pitchitch; Meal Deal; Good News; Image Maker; Jinx: List Less; Skate Strait; Heave Peeve; Loud Crowd; Mark Lark; Flat Scat; Repeat Performance; Swap Flop; Idle Idol
4 ❑ Feb 1969 Cover: 0.12 **NM** value: **3.00**
Circ: Statement: **222,732**
5 ❑ Apr 1969 Cover: 0.25 **NM** value: **3.00**
Circ: Statement: **222,732**
6 ❑ Jun 1969 Cover: 0.25 **NM** value: **2.00**
Circ: Statement: **222,732**
7 ❑ Aug 1969 Cover: 0.25 **NM** value: **2.00**
Circ: Statement: **222,732**
8 ❑ Oct 1969 Cover: 0.25 **NM** value: **2.00**
Circ: Statement: **222,732**
9 ❑ Dec 1969 Cover: 0.25 **NM** value: **2.00**
Circ: Statement: **222,732**
10 ❑ Feb 1970 Cover: 0.25 **NM** value: **2.00**
Circ: Statement: **194,601**
11 ❑ Apr 1970 Cover: 0.25 **NM** value: **1.00**
Circ: Statement: **194,601**
12 ❑ Jun 1970 Cover: 0.25 **NM** value: **1.00**
Circ: Statement: **194,601**
• Has 1969 Statement, filed 10/1/69; avg print run 412,949; avg sales 221,905; avg subs 827; avg total paid 222,732; samples 0; max existent 222,732; 46% of run returned
13 ❑ Aug 1970 Cover: 0.25 **NM** value: **1.00**
Circ: Statement: **194,601**
14 ❑ Oct 1970 Cover: 0.25 **NM** value: **1.00**
Circ: Statement: **194,601**
15 ❑ Dec 1970 Cover: 0.25 **NM** value: **1.00**
Circ: Statement: **194,601**
16 ❑ Jan 1971 Cover: 0.25 **NM** value: **1.00**
Circ: Statement: **174,467**
17 ❑ May 1971 Cover: 0.25 **NM** value: **1.00**
Circ: Statement: **174,467**
• Has 1970 Statement, filed 10/1/70; avg print run 372,784; avg sales 194,601; avg subs 0; avg total paid 194,601; samples 0; max existent 194,601; 48% of run returned
18 ❑ Aug 1971 Cover: 0.25 **NM** value: **1.00**
Circ: Statement: **174,467**
19 ❑ Oct 1971 Cover: 0.25 **NM** value: **1.00**
Circ: Statement: **174,467**
20 ❑ Jan 1972 Cover: 0.25 **NM** value: **1.00**
Circ: Statement: **164,712**
21 ❑ May 1972 Cover: 0.25 **NM** value: **1.00**
Circ: Statement: **164,712**
• Has 1971 Statement, filed 10/1/71; avg print run 362,581; avg sales 174,467; avg subs 0; avg total paid 174,467; samples 0; max existent 174,467; 52% of run returned
22 ❑ Aug 1972 Cover: 0.25 **NM** value: **1.00**
Circ: Statement: **164,712**
23 ❑ Oct 1972 Cover: 0.25 **NM** value: **1.00**
Circ: Statement: **164,712**
24 ❑ Jan 1973 Cover: 0.25 **NM** value: **1.00**
Circ: Statement: **149,760**
25 ❑ May 1973 Cover: 0.25 **NM** value: **1.00**
Circ: Statement: **149,760**
• Has 1972 Statement; avg total paid circ 164,712
26 ❑ Aug 1973 Cover: 0.25 **NM** value: **1.00**
Circ: Statement: **149,760**
27 ❑ Oct 1973 Cover: 0.25 **NM** value: **1.00**
Circ: Statement: **149,760**
28 ❑ Jan 1974 Cover: 0.25 **NM** value: **1.00**
Circ: Statement: **146,866**
29 ❑ May 1974 Cover: 0.25 **NM** value: **1.00**
Circ: Statement: **146,866**
• Has 1973 Statement; avg total paid circ 149,760
30 ❑ Aug 1974 Cover: 0.25 **NM** value: **1.00**
Circ: Statement: **146,866**
31 ❑ Oct 1974 Cover: 0.25 **NM** value: **1.00**
Circ: Statement: **146,866**
32 ❑ Jan 1975 Cover: 0.25 **NM** value: **1.00**
Circ: Statement: **122,176**
33 ❑ May 1975 Cover: 0.25 **NM** value: **1.00**
Circ: Statement: **122,176**
• Has 1974 Statement; avg total paid circ 146,866
34 ❑ Aug 1975 Cover: 0.25 **NM** value: **1.00**
Circ: Statement: **122,176**
35 ❑ Oct 1975 Cover: 0.25 **NM** value: **1.00**
Circ: Statement: **122,176**
36 ❑ Jan 1976 Cover: 0.25 **NM** value: **1.00**
Circ: Statement: **109,664**
37 ❑ May 1976 Cover: 0.30 **NM** value: **1.00**
Circ: Statement: **109,664**
38 ❑ Aug 1976 Cover: 0.30 **NM** value: **1.00**
Circ: Statement: **109,664**
39 ❑ Oct 1976 Cover: 0.30 **NM** value: **1.00**
Circ: Statement: **109,664**
40 ❑ Jan 1977 Cover: 0.30 **NM** value: **1.00**
Circ: Statement: **107,844**
41 ❑ May 1977 Cover: 0.30 **NM** value: **1.00**
Circ: Statement: **107,844**
• Has 1976 Statement; avg total paid circ 109,664
42 ❑ Aug 1977 Cover: 0.35 **NM** value: **1.00**
Circ: Statement: **107,844**
43 ❑ Oct 1977 Cover: 0.35 **NM** value: **1.00**
Circ: Statement: **107,844**
44 ❑ Jan 1978 Cover: 0.35 **NM** value: **1.00**
45 ❑ May 1978 Cover: 0.35 **NM** value: **1.00**
• Has 1977 Statement; avg total paid circ 107,844
46 ❑ Aug 1978 Cover: 0.35 **NM** value: **1.00**
47 ❑ Oct 1978 Cover: 0.35 **NM** value: **1.00**
48 ❑ Jan 1979 Cover: 0.35 **NM** value: **1.00**
49 ❑ May 1979 Cover: 0.40 **NM** value: **1.00**
50 ❑ Aug 1979 Cover: 0.40 **NM** value: **1.00**
51 ❑ Oct 1979 Cover: 0.40 **NM** value: **1.00**
52 ❑ Jan 1980 Cover: 0.40 **NM** value: **1.00**
53 ❑ May 1980 Cover: 0.40 **NM** value: **1.00**
54 ❑ Aug 1980 Cover: 0.50 **NM** value: **1.00**
55 ❑ Oct 1980 Cover: 0.50 **NM** value: **1.00**
56 ❑ Jan 1981 Cover: 0.50 **NM** value: **1.00**
57 ❑ May 1981 Cover: 0.50 **NM** value: **1.00**
58 ❑ Aug 1981 Cover: 0.50 **NM** value: **1.00**
59 ❑ Oct 1981 Cover: 0.50 **NM** value: **1.00**
60 ❑ Jan 1982 Cover: 0.60 **NM** value: **1.00**
final issue.

REGISTRY OF DEATH — Kitchen Sink
1 ❑ Nov 1996 Cover: 15.95 **NM** value: **Cover or less**
No issue number. • oversized tpb.

REGULATORS — Image
1 ❑ Jun 1995 Cover: 2.50 **NM** value: **Cover or less**
Circ: CapCity orders: **20,325**
A Touch Of Scandal **A:** Ron Randall; Dan Davis(inks) **W:** Kurt Busiek
2 ❑ Jul 1995 Cover: 2.50 **NM** value: **Cover or less**
Circ: CapCity orders: **14,375**
A: Ron Randall; Dan Davis(inks) **W:** Kurt Busiek ★ Appearance of Vortex.
3 ❑ Aug 1995 Cover: 2.50 **NM** value: **Cover or less**
Circ: CapCity orders: **9,975**
A: Ron Randall; Dan Davis(inks) **W:** Kurt Busiek
4 ❑ Cover: 2.50 **NM** value: **Cover or less**
A: Ron Randall; Dan Davis(inks) **W:** Kurt Busiek

REID FLEMING — Boswell
1 ❑ **NM** value: **10.00**
★ 1st Appearance of Reid Fleming.
1-2 ❑ **NM** value: **4.00**

REID FLEMING, WORLD'S TOUGHEST MILKMAN — Eclipse

First published in 1980, Reid Fleming is a long-running cult hit lasting almost two decades with less than a dozen issues to its credit. The star is an ornery milkman who delights in dumping milk in customers' fish tanks and drinking on the job. His real joy, however, comes from battling his boss, Mr. Crabbe. The ornery Fleming crashes milk trucks with alarming frequency, assaults everyone in sight, and manages to stay employed only through the use of blackmail and other dirty tricks.

It's tempting to compare Reid to Pete the P.O.'d Postal Worker, since both are case studies in labor relations gone wrong. But Pete actually likes his job — any homicides he may commit while doing it are purely incidental.

1 ❑ Oct 1986 Cover: 2.00 **NM** value: **8.00**
Rogue to Riches; A Day Like Any Other; Monday Morning **A:** David Boswell **W:** David Boswell
1-2 ❑ Cover: 2.00 **NM** value: **4.00**
1-3 ❑ Cover: 2.00 **NM** value: **3.00**
1-4 ❑ Cover: 2.00 **NM** value: **3.00**
1-5 ❑ Cover: 2.00 **NM** value: **2.50**
1-6 ❑ Cover: 2.95 **NM** value: **Cover or less**
2 ❑ Mar 1987 Cover: 2.00 **NM** value: **4.00**
• **CGC:** 1 graded, best 9.4
Rogue to Riches **A:** David Boswell **W:** David Boswell
2-2 ❑ Cover: 2.00 **NM** value: **Cover or less**
• **CGC:** 1 graded, best 9.4
2-3 ❑ Mar 1989 Cover: 2.00 **NM** value: **Cover or less**
• **CGC:** 1 graded, best 9.4
3 ❑ Dec 1988 Cover: 2.00 **NM** value: **3.00**
Rogue to Riches **A:** David Boswell **W:** David Boswell
4 ❑ Nov 1989 Cover: 2.00 **NM** value: **3.00**
Rogue to Riches **A:** David Boswell **W:** David Boswell
5 ❑ Nov 1990 Cover: 2.00 **NM** value: **3.00**
Rogue to Riches **A:** David Boswell **W:** David Boswell
6 ❑ **NM** value: **2.00**
A: David Boswell **W:** David Boswell
7 ❑ Jan 1997 Cover: 2.95 **NM** value: **Cover or less**
Circ: Diamd. preorders: **4,536**
Another Dawn **A:** David Boswell **W:** David Boswell
8 ❑ Aug 1997 Cover: 2.95 **NM** value: **Cover or less**
Circ: Diamd. preorders: **4,580**
Another Dawn **A:** David Boswell **W:** David Boswell
9 ❑ Apr 1998 Cover: 2.95 **NM** value: **Cover or less**
Another Dawn **A:** David Boswell **W:** David Boswell

REIGN OF THE DRAGONLORD — Eternity
1 ❑ Oct 1986 Cover: 1.80 **NM** value: **Cover or less**
A: Kevin Farrell **W:** C. J. Henderson
2 ❑ Cover: 1.80 **NM** value: **Cover or less**
A: Kevin Farrell **W:** C. J. Henderson

REIKI WARRIORS — Revolutionary
1 ❑ Aug 1993, b&w Cover: 2.95 **NM** value: **Cover or less**
Never a Good Time to Die; Guilt by Association **A:** Duncan Rouleau **W:** Eric Dinehart; Spike Steffenhagen

REINVENTING COMICS — DC/Paradox
1 ❑ ca. 2000 Cover: 22.95 **NM** value: **Cover or less**
A: Scott McCloud **W:** Scott McCloud

RELATIVE HEROES — DC
1 ❑ Mar 2000 Cover: 2.50 **NM** value: **Cover or less**
Circ: Diamd. preorders: **18,556**
A: Yvel Guichet **W:** Devin Grayson
2 ❑ Apr 2000 Cover: 2.50 **NM** value: **Cover or less**
Circ: Diamd. preorders: **13,258**
A: Yvel Guichet **W:** Devin Grayson
3 ❑ May 2000 Cover: 2.50 **NM** value: **Cover or less**
Circ: Diamd. preorders: **11,506**
Free Lunch **A:** Yvel Guichet **W:** Devin Grayson
4 ❑ Jun 2000 Cover: 2.50 **NM** value: **Cover or less**
Circ: Diamd. preorders: **9,906**
Visibility **A:** Yvel Guichet **W:** Devin Grayson
5 ❑ Jul 2000 Cover: 2.50 **NM** value: **Cover or less**
Circ: Diamd. preorders: **9,420**
A: Yvel Guichet **W:** Devin Grayson
6 ❑ Aug 2000 Cover: 2.50 **NM** value: **Cover or less**
Circ: Diamd. preorders: **9,117**
A: Yvel Guichet **W:** Devin Grayson

RELENTLESS PURSUIT — Slave Labor
1 ❑ Jan 1989, b&w Cover: 1.75 **NM** value: **Cover or less**
2 ❑ May 1989, b&w Cover: 1.75 **NM** value: **Cover or less**
The Battle of White Bird Canyon **A:** Jeff Kear **W:** Jeff Kear
3 ❑ Sep 1989, b&w Cover: 2.95 **NM** value: **Cover or less**
The Nez Perce Flight **A:** Jeff Kear **W:** Jeff Kear
4 ❑ Jan 1990, b&w Cover: 3.95 **NM** value: **Cover or less**

REMARKABLE WORLDS OF PHINEAS B. FUDDLE, THE — DC/Paradox
1 ❑ Jul 2000 Cover: 5.95 **NM** value: **Cover or less**
Circ: Diamd. preorders: **7,257**
A: Erez Yakin **W:** Boaz Yakin
2 ❑ Aug 2000 Cover: 5.95 **NM** value: **Cover or less**
Circ: Diamd. preorders: **5,712**
A: Erez Yakin **W:** Boaz Yakin
3 ❑ Sep 2000 Cover: 5.95 **NM** value: **Cover or less**
Circ: Diamd. preorders: **5,555**
A: Erez Yakin **W:** Boaz Yakin
4 ❑ Oct 2000 Cover: 5.95 **NM** value: **Cover or less**
Circ: Diamd. preorders: **5,585**
A: Erez Yakin **W:** Boaz Yakin

REMEMBER PEARL HARBOR — Street & Smith
1 ❑ ca. 1942 Cover: 0.10 **NM** value: **350.00**
• **CGC:** 1 graded, best 5.0

REN & STIMPY SHOW — Marvel
Ren Hoek is a depraved Chihuahua. Stimpy is an extremely stupid cat. Together, they're the hip, bizarre, and hilarious sensation known as Ren and Stimpy.

Marvel adapted this title from the immensely popular animated cartoon series seen on Nickelodeon and MTV. From Ren and Stimpy turning to a life of crime after Stimpy can't resist stealing the litter box of his dreams — to Ren offering bribes to readers who vote him in as president — Marvel did a terrific job of capturing the offbeat humor of the animated series. Fans of the series will also find such favorites as "Log for Girls" and "The Adventures of Powdered Toast Man." If that weren't enough, the premiere issue came with one of two scratch 'n' sniff "air foulers" enclosed, reportedly smelling either of wet Chihuahua or kitty litter box.

1/A ❑ Dec 1992 Cover: 2.25 **NM** value: **2.50**
Circ: CapCity orders: **54,000** • **CGC:** 1 graded, best 9.0
• Ren scratch&sniff card
1/B ❑ Dec 1992 Cover: 2.25 **NM** value: **2.50**
• **CGC:** 1 graded, best 9.0
• Stimpy scratch&sniff card
1-2 ❑ Cover: 2.25 **NM** value: **Cover or less**
1-3 ❑ Cover: 2.25 **NM** value: **Cover or less**
2 ❑ Jan 1993 Cover: 1.75 **NM** value: **2.00**
Circ: Statement: **258,000** CapCity orders: **27,900** • **CGC:** 3 graded, best 9.4
A: Mike Kazaleh **W:** Dan Slott
2-2 ❑ Cover: 1.75 **NM** value: **Cover or less**
3 ❑ Feb 1993 Cover: 1.75 **NM** value: **2.00**
Circ: Statement: **258,000** CapCity orders: **33,000**
A: Mike Kazaleh **W:** Dan Slott
3-2 ❑ Cover: 1.75 **NM** value: **Cover or less**
4 ❑ Mar 1993 Cover: 1.75 **NM** value: **2.00**
Circ: Statement: **258,000** CapCity orders: **34,800**
A: Mike Kazaleh **W:** Dan Slott ★ Appearance of Muddy Mudskipper.
5 ❑ Apr 1993 Cover: 1.75 **NM** value: **2.00**
Circ: Statement: **258,000** CapCity orders: **40,500**
The Croco-Men From Planet Zed! • in space **A:** Mike Kazaleh **W:** Dan Slott
6 ❑ May 1993 Cover: 1.75 **NM** value: **Cover or less**
Circ: Statement: **258,000** CapCity orders: **82,200**
Clash Of Titans: Break-Fest Of Champions **A:** Mike Kazaleh **W:** Dan Slott ★ Appearance of Spider-Man.
7 ❑ Jun 1993 Cover: 1.75 **NM** value: **Cover or less**
Circ: Statement: **258,000** CapCity orders: **54,300**
Kid Stimpy • Kid Stimpy **A:** Mike Kazaleh **W:** Dan Slott
8 ❑ Jul 1993 Cover: 1.75 **NM** value: **Cover or less**
Circ: Statement: **258,000** CapCity orders: **56,100**
The Maltese Stimpy • Maltese Stimpy **A:** Mike Kazaleh **W:** Dan Slott
9 ❑ Aug 1993 Cover: 1.75 **NM** value: **Cover or less**
Circ: Statement: **258,000** CapCity orders: **56,100**
Wakka Makka Ho'k, Mekka Stimpy Ho!; Wakka Makka Hodk, Mekka Stimpy Ho! **A:** Mike Kazaleh **W:** Dan Slott
10 ❑ Sep 1993 Cover: 1.75 **NM** value: **Cover or less**

Other grades: Multiply prices above by **1.5 for Mint • 2/3 for Very Fine • 1/3 for Fine • 1/5 for Very Good • 1/8 for Good**

Circ: Statement: **258,000** CapCity orders: **54,300**
📖 Bug Out **A:** Mike Kazaleh **W:** Dan Slott
11 ❑ Oct 1993 Cover: 1.75 **NM value: Cover or less**
Circ: Statement: **258,000** CapCity orders: **51,900**
📖 Ren's Peaceful Place **A:** Mike Kazaleh **W:** Dan Slott
12 ❑ Nov 1993 Cover: 1.75 **NM value: Cover or less**
Circ: Statement: **258,000** CapCity orders: **47,600**
• Stimpy cloned
13 ❑ Dec 1993 Cover: 1.75 **NM value: Cover or less**
Circ: Statement: **258,000** CapCity orders: **45,700**
📖 Eencredeebly Pathetic Excuse For A Halloween Eesue! • Halloween issue **A:** Mike Kazaleh **W:** Dan Slott
14 ❑ Jan 1994 Cover: 1.75 **NM value: Cover or less**
Circ: Statement: **205,442** CapCity orders: **38,200**
📖 Mars Needs Velcro **A:** Ken Mitchroney **W:** Sholly Fisch
15 ❑ Feb 1994 Cover: 1.75 **NM value: Cover or less**
Circ: Statement: **205,442** CapCity orders: **34,900**
📖 Black Mail, White Christmas, Green Moulah • Christmas issue **A:** Mike Kazaleh **W:** Dan Slott
16 ❑ Mar 1994 Cover: 1.75 **NM value: Cover or less**
Circ: Statement: **205,442** CapCity orders: **30,750**
📖 The King And We! • Elvis parody **A:** Ken Mitchroney **W:** Steven Boyett
17 ❑ Apr 1994 Cover: 1.75 **NM value: Cover or less**
Circ: Statement: **205,442** CapCity orders: **29,200**
18 ❑ May 1994 Cover: 1.95 **NM value: Cover or less**
Circ: Statement: **205,442** CapCity orders: **29,100**
• Powdered Toast Man
19 ❑ Jun 1994 Cover: 1.95 **NM value: Cover or less**
Circ: Statement: **205,442** CapCity orders: **29,000**
📖 Minimalist Issue **A:** Mike Kazaleh **W:** Dan Slott
20 ❑ Jul 1994 Cover: 1.95 **NM value: Cover or less**
Circ: Statement: **205,442** CapCity orders: **28,750**
📖 Late Night With Muddy Mudskipper **A:** Mike Kazaleh **W:** Barry Dutter ★ Appearance of Muddy Mudskipper.
21 ❑ Aug 1994 Cover: 1.95 **NM value: Cover or less**
Circ: Statement: **205,442** CapCity orders: **27,750**
22 ❑ Sep 1994 Cover: 1.95 **NM value: Cover or less**
Circ: Statement: **205,442** CapCity orders: **25,250**
23 ❑ Oct 1994 Cover: 1.95 **NM value: Cover or less**
Circ: Statement: **205,442** CapCity orders: **22,050**
• wrestling
24 ❑ Nov 1994 Cover: 1.95 **NM value: Cover or less**
Circ: Statement: **205,442** CapCity orders: **19,850**
📖 Box Tops • box top collecting **A:** Ken Mitchroney **W:** Barry Dutter
25 ❑ Dec 1994 Cover: 1.95 **NM value: Cover or less**
📖 Obedience School **A:** Ken Mitchroney **W:** Barry Dutter ★ Versus Dogzilla.
25/SC❑ Dec 1994 Cover: 2.95 **NM value: Cover or less**
Circ: Statement: **205,442** CapCity orders: **19,500**
enhanced cover.
26 ❑ Jan 1995 Cover: 1.95 **NM value: Cover or less**
Circ: Statement: **89,419** CapCity orders: **17,150**
★ Appearance of Sven Hoek.
27 ❑ Feb 1995 Cover: 1.95 **NM value: Cover or less**
Circ: Statement: **89,419** CapCity orders: **15,675**
📖 Raiders of the Lost Yak
28 ❑ Mar 1995 Cover: 1.95 **NM value: Cover or less**
Circ: Statement: **89,419** CapCity orders: **14,000**
📖 Bath Time • Has 1994 Statement, filed 10/1/94; avg print run 353,025; avg sales 202,667; avg subs 2,775; avg total paid 205,442; samples 125; office use 500; max existent 206,067; 42% of run returned **A:** Mike Kazaleh **W:** Barry Dutter ★ Appearance of Filthy the monkey.
29 ❑ Apr 1995 Cover: 1.95 **NM value: Cover or less**
Circ: Statement: **89,419** CapCity orders: **12,925**
📖 Sherlock Ho'k; Sherlock Hodk **A:** Ken Mitchroney **W:** Scott Benson
30 ❑ May 1995 Cover: 1.95 **NM value: Cover or less**
Circ: Statement: **89,419** CapCity orders: **12,125**
• Ren's birthday
31 ❑ Jun 1995 Cover: 1.95 **NM value: Cover or less**
Circ: Statement: **89,419** CapCity orders: **11,575**
📖 From Vienna With Love
32 ❑ Jul 1995 Cover: 1.95 **NM value: Cover or less**
Circ: Statement: **89,419** CapCity orders: **10,725**
33 ❑ Aug 1995 Cover: 1.95 **NM value: Cover or less**
Circ: Statement: **89,419** CapCity orders: **10,200**
34 ❑ Sep 1995 Cover: 1.95 **NM value: Cover or less**
Circ: Statement: **89,419**
35 ❑ Oct 1995 Cover: 1.95 **NM value: Cover or less**
Circ: Statement: **89,419**
36 ❑ Nov 1995 Cover: 1.95 **NM value: Cover or less**
Circ: Statement: **89,419**
37 ❑ Dec 1995 Cover: 1.95 **NM value: Cover or less**
Circ: Statement: **89,419**
• aliens **A:** Gary Fields **W:** Terry Collins
38 ❑ Jan 1996 Cover: 1.95 **NM value: Cover or less**
• Has 1995 Statement, filed 10/1/95; avg print run 217,015; avg sales 87,603; avg subs 1,816; avg total paid 89,419; samples 750; office use 500; max existent 90,669; 58% of run returned
39 ❑ Feb 1996 Cover: 1.95 **NM value: Cover or less**
40 ❑ Mar 1996 Cover: 1.95 **NM value: Cover or less**
41 ❑ Apr 1996 Cover: 1.95 **NM value: Cover or less**
📖 Stockboy Ren; It's a Joyful Life **A:** Gary Fields; Matt Maley **W:** Barry Dutter; Terry Collins
42 ❑ May 1996 Cover: 1.95 **NM value: Cover or less**
43 ❑ Jun 1996 Cover: 1.95 **NM value: Cover or less**
44 ❑ Jul 1996 Cover: 1.95 **NM value: Cover or less**
final issue.
Bk 1❑ Cover: 12.95 **NM value: Cover or less**
• Tastes Like Chicken!; Collects Ren & Stimpy Show #5-8 **A:** Mike Kazaleh; Ken Mitchroney **W:** Dan Slott
Bk 2❑ Jan 1995 Cover: 12.95 **NM value: Cover or less**
• Seeck Leetle Monkeys; collects The Ren & Stimpy Show #17-20
HS 1❑ Feb 1995 Cover: 2.95 **NM value: Cover or less**
No issue number.
SE 1❑ Jul 1994 Cover: 2.95 **NM value: Cover or less**
Circ: CapCity orders: **23,000**
SE 2❑ Oct 1994 Cover: 2.95 **NM value: 3.00**
📖 Want Ads; Quarterback Sneaks; Lost Action Hero; Clean-Up Crusaders • Summer Jobs **A:** Ken Mitchroney; Stephanie Gladden **W:** Steven Boyett

REN & STIMPY SHOW, THE: RADIO DAZE Marvel
1 ❑ Nov 1995 Cover: 1.95 **NM value: Cover or less**
• based on audio release of same name

REN & STIMPY SHOW SPECIAL, THE: AROUND THE WORLD IN A DAZE Marvel
1 ❑ Jan 1996 Cover: 2.95 **NM value: Cover or less**
No issue number. One-shot.

REN & STIMPY SHOW SPECIAL: EENTERACTIVE Marvel
1 ❑ Jul 1995 Cover: 2.95 **NM value: Cover or less**
No issue number.

REN & STIMPY SHOW SPECIAL: FOUR SWERKS Marvel
1 ❑ Jan 1995 Cover: 2.95 **NM value: Cover or less**
Circ: CapCity orders: **11,500**
No issue number.

REN & STIMPY SHOW SPECIAL: POWDERED TOAST MAN Marvel
1 ❑ Apr 1994 Cover: 2.95 **NM value: 3.00**
Circ: CapCity orders: **32,650** • **CGC:** 2 graded, best 9.9
📖 Leave Everything To Me! • Powdered Toast Man **A:** Ty Templeton **W:** Dan Slott

REN & STIMPY SHOW SPECIAL: POWDERED TOASTMAN'S CEREAL Marvel
1 ❑ Apr 1995 Cover: 2.95 **NM value: Cover or less**
Circ: CapCity orders: **8,475**
No issue number.

REN & STIMPY SHOW SPECIAL: SPORTS Marvel
1 ❑ Oct 1995 Cover: 2.95 **NM value: Cover or less**
No issue number.

RENEGADE, THE Rip Off
All issues are adults only.
1 ❑ Aug 1991, b&w Cover: 2.50 **NM value: Cover or less**

RENEGADE!, THE (MAGNECOM) Magnecom
1 ❑ Dec 1993 Cover: 2.95 **NM value: Cover or less**
📖 Night Slayer **A:** Sterling Clark **W:** Sterling Clark

RENEGADE RABBIT Printed Matter
1 ❑ Cover: 1.75 **NM value: Cover or less**
📖 The Good, The Bad-and The Furry **A:** Craig Miller **W:** Craig Miller
2 ❑ Cover: 1.75 **NM value: Cover or less**
A: Craig Miller **W:** Craig Miller
3 ❑ Cover: 1.75 **NM value: Cover or less**
A: Craig Miller **W:** Craig Miller
4 ❑ Cover: 1.75 **NM value: Cover or less**
A: Craig Miller **W:** Craig Miller
5 ❑ Cover: 1.50 **NM value: 1.75**
• Cerebus parody **A:** Craig Miller **W:** Craig Miller

RENEGADE ROMANCE Renegade
1 ❑ b&w Cover: 3.50 **NM value: Cover or less**
2 ❑ b&w Cover: 3.50 **NM value: Cover or less**

RENEGADES, THE Age of Heroes
1 ❑ Cover: 1.00 **NM value: Cover or less**
2 ❑ Cover: 1.00 **NM value: Cover or less**

RENEGADES OF JUSTICE, THE Blue Masque
1 ❑ b&w Cover: 2.50 **NM value: Cover or less**
2 ❑ b&w Cover: 2.50 **NM value: Cover or less**

RENFIELD Caliber
1 ❑ Cover: 2.95 **NM value: Cover or less**
📖 The Patient **A:** Galen Showman **W:** Kyle Garrettt
1/LE❑ Cover: 5.95 **NM value: Cover or less**
• Limited "special edition" with second cover. 📖 The Patient **A:** Galen Showman **W:** Kyle Garrettt
2 ❑ Cover: 2.95 **NM value: Cover or less**
3 ❑ Cover: 2.95 **NM value: Cover or less**
Ash 1❑ b&w **NM value: 1.00**
No issue number. no cover price.

RENNIN COMICS (JIM CHADWICK'S...) Restless Muse
1 ❑ Sum 1997, b&w Cover: 2.95 **NM value: Cover or less**

Diamond preorders are the estimated number of comics sold, prior to their release, to comics shops in North America by Diamond Comic Distributors, the largest distributor. These figures underreport the actual number of circulating copies by the amount of reorders Diamond took (usually 5-10% again of the preorders) and sales by publishers to newsstand and bookstore distributors. For many independent publishers, Diamond's preorders may be quite close to the actual number of copies in circulation.

REPLACEMENT GOD, THE Slave Labor / Amaze Ink

This is the story of a young man named Knute, who has been chosen as the "Replacement God." Not only is this a lot for him to take in, it's a politically touchy situation, as the Replacement God is prophesied to topple the kingdom.

Thus, King Ursus and his Political Advisor arrest Knute, but he manages to escape their dungeon. Along the way, Knute meets a girl named Anne and becomes smitten with her. For his part, Knute has been informed of the prophecy but does not believe that he is in fact the Replacement God.

The Replacement God is a comedic, black-and-white series created by Zander Cannon and published by Amaze Ink, a division of Slave Labor Graphics. Its creator, Zander Cannon, is also known for his work on the Tick spinoff series, Chainsaw Vigilante, from NEC Press.

1 ❑ Jun 1995 Cover: 2.95 **NM value: 6.00**
📖 Freedom **A:** Zander Cannon **W:** Zander Cannon
1-2 ❑ Dec 1995 Cover: 2.95 **NM value: 3.00**
2 ❑ Sep 1995 Cover: 2.95 **NM value: 3.50**
📖 I of Knute **A:** Zander Cannon **W:** Zander Cannon
3 ❑ Dec 1995 Cover: 2.95 **NM value: 3.00**
📖 Bravery **A:** Zander Cannon **W:** Zander Cannon
4 ❑ Apr 1996 Cover: 2.95 **NM value: Cover or less**
A: Zander Cannon **W:** Zander Cannon
5 ❑ Jul 1996 Cover: 2.95 **NM value: Cover or less**
A: Zander Cannon **W:** Zander Cannon
6 ❑ Sep 1996 Cover: 2.95 **NM value: Cover or less**
Circ: Diamd. preorders: **3,058**
A: Zander Cannon **W:** Zander Cannon
7 ❑ Dec 1996 Cover: 2.95 **NM value: Cover or less**
Circ: Diamd. preorders: **2,623**
A: Zander Cannon **W:** Zander Cannon
8 ❑ Cover: 2.95 **NM value: Cover or less**
A: Zander Cannon **W:** Zander Cannon
Bk 1❑ Cover: 19.95 **NM value: Cover or less**
• Collects The Replacement God #1-8 **A:** Zander Cannon **W:** Zander Cannon

REPLACEMENT GOD Handicraft
6 ❑ Dec 1998 Cover: 6.95 **NM value: Cover or less**

REPLACEMENT GOD AND OTHER STORIES, THE Image
1 ❑ May 1997, b&w Cover: 2.95 **NM value: Cover or less**
• flip-book with Knute's Escapes back-up **A:** Zander Cannon **W:** Zander Cannon
2 ❑ Jul 1997, b&w Cover: 2.95 **NM value: Cover or less**
Circ: Diamd. preorders: **5,590**
• flip-book with Harris Thermidor back-up **A:** Zander Cannon **W:** Zander Cannon
3 ❑ Sep 1997, b&w Cover: 2.95 **NM value: Cover or less**
Circ: Diamd. preorders: **5,131**
📖 Replacement God; Knute's Escapes; Myth & Legend • flip-book with Knute's Escapes back-up **A:** Zander Cannon **W:** Zander Cannon
4 ❑ Nov 1997, b&w Cover: 2.95 **NM value: Cover or less**
Circ: Diamd. preorders: **4,352**
📖 Replacement God; Knute's Escapes • flip-book with Knute's Escapes back-up **A:** Zander Cannon **W:** Zander Cannon
5 ❑ Jan 1998, b&w Cover: 2.95 **NM value: Cover or less**
Circ: Diamd. preorders: **3,771**
📖 Replacement God; Knute's Escapes • flip-book with Knute's Escapes back-up **A:** Zander Cannon **W:** Zander Cannon

REPORTER Reporter
1 ❑ Cover: 3.00 **NM value: Cover or less**

REPTILICUS Charlton
1 ❑ Aug 1961 Cover: 0.10 **NM value: 150.00**
2 ❑ Oct 1961 Cover: 0.10 **NM value: 75.00**

REPTISAURUS Charlton
3 ❑ Jan 1962 Cover: 0.10 **NM value: 50.00**
• **CGC:** 3 graded, best 9.0
4 ❑ Apr 1962 Cover: 0.12 **NM value: 50.00**
• **CGC:** 5 graded, best 9.2
5 ❑ Jun 1962 Cover: 0.12 **NM value: 50.00**
6 ❑ Aug 1962 Cover: 0.12 **NM value: 50.00**
7 ❑ Oct 1962 Cover: 0.12 **NM value: 50.00**
• **CGC:** 1 graded, best 9.2
8 ❑ Dec 1962 Cover: 0.12 **NM value: 50.00**
• **CGC:** 1 graded, best 8.5
SE 1❑ Sum 1963 **NM value: 50.00**
• **CGC:** 1 graded, best 9.2

REQUIEM FOR DRACULA Marvel
1 ❑ Cover: 2.00 **NM value: Cover or less**
📖 Batwings Over Transylvania! • Reprints Tomb of Dracula #69, 70 **A:** Gene Colan **W:** Marv Wolfman

RESCUEMAN Best
1 ❑ b&w Cover: 2.95 **NM value: Cover or less**

RESCUERS DOWN UNDER, THE (DISNEY'S...) Disney
1 ❑ Cover: 2.95 **NM value: Cover or less**
A: Hector Saavedra; Paul Barbero **W:** William Rotsler

CGC-graded: Multiply prices above by **33 for 9.9 M** • **16 for 9.8 NM/M** • **7 for 9.6 NM+** • **5 for 9.4 NM** • **2.5 for 9.2 NM-** • **1.5 for 9.0 VF/NM**

RESIDENT EVIL — Image

Usually comics adaptations of video games are a cause for trepidation, with the comic book doing little to build on the thin characters and plots used in most games. The magazine-sided Resident Evil, on the other hand, is genuinely intriguing, although it's hard to say whether it's because the game itself is a richer source of material or because the adaptation is done to a higher standard.

Genetic researchers develop the "T-Virus," which gives those affected increased strength and aggression, but at the same time causes their minds and bodies to decay, turning them into bloodthirsty zombies. The early animal experiments were sabotaged, deliberately exposing the researchers themselves to the virus. Now, it's broken loose in a city, leaving the police with a hopeless quest to contain the disease — and zombies!

1 ❑ Mar 1998 Cover: 4.95 **NM** value: **5.50**
S.T.A.R.S. Files; Who Are These Guys?; Dangerous Secrets; Raccoon City-R.I.P. **A:** Carlos D'Anda; Ryan Odagawa; Lee Bermejo **W:** Kris Oprisko; Ted Adams

2 ❑ Jun 1998 Cover: 4.95 **NM** value: **5.00**
A New Chapter of Evil; Mutant Menagerie; Lock Down **A:** Carlos D'Anda; Lee Bermejo **W:** Kris Oprisko; Ted Adams

3 ❑ Sep 1998 Cover: 4.95 **NM** value: **5.00**
Wolf Hunt; Danger Island; Dead Air; The Resident Evil Files **A:** Carlos D'Anda; Ryan Odagawa; Lee Bermejo **W:** Kris Oprisko; Ted Adams

4 ❑ Dec 1998 Cover: 4.95 **NM** value: **5.00**

5 ❑ Feb 1999 Cover: 4.95 **NM** value: **5.00**
Circ: Diamd. preorders: **10,776**

Bk 1 ❑ Dec 1999 Cover: 14.95 **NM** value: **Cover or less**
• Collects series **A:** Carlos D'Anda; Ryan Odagawa; Lee Bermejo **W:** Kris Oprisko; Ted Adams

RESIDENT EVIL: FIRE AND ICE — WildStorm

1 ❑ Dec 2000 Cover: 2.50 **NM** value: **Cover or less**
Circ: Diamd. preorders: **13,886**
A: Lee Bermejo **W:** Kris Oprisko; Ted Adams

2 ❑ Jan 2001 Cover: 2.50 **NM** value: **Cover or less**
Circ: Diamd. preorders: **9,660**
A: Lee Bermejo **W:** Kris Oprisko; Ted Adams

3 ❑ Feb 2001 Cover: 2.50 **NM** value: **Cover or less**
Circ: Diamd. preorders: **8,270**
A: Lee Bermejo **W:** Kris Oprisko; Ted Adams

4 ❑ May 2001 Cover: 2.50 **NM** value: **Cover or less**
Circ: Diamd. preorders: **7,355**
A: Lee Bermejo **W:** Kris Oprisko; Ted Adams

RESTAURANT AT THE END OF THE UNIVERSE, THE — DC

1 ❑ 1994 Cover: 6.95 **NM** value: **Cover or less**
Circ: CapCity orders: **5,850**
• prestige format. **A:** Steve Leialoha; Rich Larson(cover); Steve Fastner(cover) **W:** Douglas Adams; John Carnell

2 ❑ 1994 Cover: 6.95 **NM** value: **Cover or less**
Circ: CapCity orders: **4,575**
• prestige format. **A:** Steve Leialoha **W:** Douglas Adams; John Carnell

3 ❑ 1994 Cover: 6.95 **NM** value: **Cover or less**
Circ: CapCity orders: **4,150**
• prestige format. final issue. **A:** Steve Leialoha **W:** Douglas Adams; John Carnell

RESURRECTION MAN — DC

Former lawyer Mitchell Shelley found himself in an interesting situation. Wandering the country with a severe case of amnesia, he would rediscover bits and pieces of his past, while also learning that every time he was killed he would return to life with a new superpower, one designed to prevent him from dying in that manner again.

Eventually, Shelley came up against Vandal Savage and learned that he wasn't just a former lawyer who had been experimented on by a government agency, but that he was actually the Immortal Man, a hero who had faced Savage many times over the centuries and who was thought to have perished in the Crisis on Infinite Earths. — Brent

1 ❑ May 1997 Cover: 2.50 **NM** value: **3.00**
Circ: Diamd. preorders: **31,691** • **CGC:** 2 graded, best 9.8
Lenticular disc on cover.

2 ❑ Jun 1997 Cover: 2.50 **NM** value: **Cover or less**
Circ: Diamd. preorders: **22,015** • **CGC:** 1 graded, best 9.6
★ Appearance of Justice League of America.

3 ❑ Jul 1997 Cover: 2.50 **NM** value: **Cover or less**
Circ: Diamd. preorders: **22,433**

4 ❑ Aug 1997 Cover: 2.50 **NM** value: **Cover or less**
Circ: Diamd. preorders: **23,822**

5 ❑ Sep 1997 Cover: 2.50 **NM** value: **Cover or less**
Circ: Diamd. preorders: **22,922**

6 ❑ Oct 1997 Cover: 2.50 **NM** value: **Cover or less**
Circ: Diamd. preorders: **23,448**
• Genesis; Resurrection Man powerless

7 ❑ Nov 1997 Cover: 2.50 **NM** value: **Cover or less**
Circ: Diamd. preorders: **20,939**
Gotham D.O.A. **A:** Butch Guice; Tom Grindberg **W:** Andy Lanning; Dan Abnett ★ Appearance of Batman.

8 ❑ Dec 1997 Cover: 2.50 **NM** value: **Cover or less**
Circ: Diamd. preorders: **21,462**
Face cover. Tricks or Treats **A:** Butch Guice **W:** Andy Lanning; Dan Abnett

9 ❑ Jan 1998 Cover: 2.50 **NM** value: **Cover or less**
Circ: Diamd. preorders: **21,922**
★ Appearance of Hitman.

10 ❑ Feb 1998 Cover: 2.50 **NM** value: **Cover or less**
Circ: Diamd. preorders: **21,750**
★ Appearance of Hitman.

11 ❑ Mar 1998 Cover: 2.50 **NM** value: **Cover or less**
Circ: Diamd. preorders: **19,902**
Origin of the Species, Part 1 **A:** Butch Guice **W:** Andy Lanning; Dan Abnett ★ Origin of Resurrection Man.

12 ❑ Apr 1998 Cover: 2.50 **NM** value: **Cover or less**
Circ: Diamd. preorders: **18,973**

13 ❑ May 1998 Cover: 2.50 **NM** value: **Cover or less**
Circ: Diamd. preorders: **18,917**

14 ❑ Jun 1998 Cover: 2.50 **NM** value: **Cover or less**
Circ: Diamd. preorders: **18,778**

15 ❑ Jul 1998 Cover: 2.50 **NM** value: **Cover or less**
Circ: Diamd. preorders: **17,637**

16 ❑ Aug 1998 Cover: 2.50 **NM** value: **Cover or less**
Circ: Diamd. preorders: **22,050**
★ Appearance of Supergirl.

17 ❑ Sep 1998 Cover: 2.50 **NM** value: **Cover or less**
Circ: Diamd. preorders: **20,352**
★ Appearance of Supergirl.

18 ❑ Oct 1998 Cover: 2.50 **NM** value: **Cover or less**
Circ: Diamd. preorders: **16,718**
★ Appearance of Deadman, Phantom Stranger.

19 ❑ Dec 1998 Cover: 2.50 **NM** value: **Cover or less**
Circ: Diamd. preorders: **16,056**

20 ❑ Jan 1999 Cover: 2.50 **NM** value: **Cover or less**
Circ: Diamd. preorders: **15,730**

21 ❑ Feb 1999 Cover: 2.50 **NM** value: **Cover or less**
Circ: Diamd. preorders: **16,826**
A: Jackson Guice **W:** Andy Lanning; Dan Abnett ★ Appearance of Justice League of America. ★ Versus Major Force.

22 ❑ Mar 1999 Cover: 2.50 **NM** value: **Cover or less**
Circ: Diamd. preorders: **15,548**
A: Jackson Guice **W:** Andy Lanning; Dan Abnett

23 ❑ Apr 1999 Cover: 2.50 **NM** value: **Cover or less**
Circ: Diamd. preorders: **15,410**
• Mitch as a woman **A:** Jackson Guice **W:** Andy Lanning; Dan Abnett

24 ❑ May 1999 Cover: 2.50 **NM** value: **Cover or less**
Circ: Diamd. preorders: **14,942**
Forgotten but not Gone **A:** Jackson Guice **W:** Andy Lanning; Dan Abnett ★ Appearance of Animal Man, Ray, Cave Carson, Ballistic, Vandal Savage, Vigilante.

25 ❑ Jun 1999 Cover: 2.50 **NM** value: **Cover or less**
Circ: Diamd. preorders: **16,042**
Millennium then **A:** Jackson Guice; Paul Ryan **W:** Andy Lanning; Dan Abnett ★ Appearance of Forgotten Heroes.

26 ❑ Jul 1999 Cover: 2.50 **NM** value: **Cover or less**
Circ: Diamd. preorders: **15,870**
Millennium Now! **A:** Anthony Williams **W:** Andy Lanning; Dan Abnett ★ Appearance of Immortal Man.

27 ❑ Aug 1999 Cover: 2.50 **NM** value: **Cover or less**
Circ: Diamd. preorders: **15,104**
The Ends of the Earth **A:** Jackson Guice **W:** Andy Lanning; Dan Abnett ★ Death of Immortal Man.

1000000 ❑ Nov 1998 Cover: 2.50 **NM** value: **Cover or less**
Circ: Diamd. preorders: **27,404**
A Handful of Dust **A:** Jackson Guice **W:** Andy Lanning; Dan Abnett

RETALIATOR, THE — Eclipse

1 ❑ b&w Cover: 2.50 **NM** value: **Cover or less**
Circ: CapCity orders: **4,300**
Avenging Angel **A:** Tom Simonton **W:** Valarie Jones

2 ❑ b&w Cover: 2.50 **NM** value: **Cover or less**
My Little Sunshine **A:** Tom Simonton **W:** Valarie Jones

3 ❑ b&w Cover: 2.50 **NM** value: **Cover or less**
A: Tom Simonton **W:** Valarie Jones

4 ❑ b&w Cover: 2.50 **NM** value: **Cover or less**
A: Tom Simonton **W:** Valarie Jones

5 ❑ Cover: 2.50 **NM** value: **Cover or less**
A: Tom Simonton **W:** Valarie Jones

RETIEF — Adventure

1 ❑ b&w Cover: 2.25 **NM** value: **Cover or less**
2 ❑ b&w Cover: 2.25 **NM** value: **Cover or less**
3 ❑ b&w Cover: 2.25 **NM** value: **Cover or less**
4 ❑ b&w Cover: 2.25 **NM** value: **Cover or less**
5 ❑ b&w Cover: 2.25 **NM** value: **Cover or less**
6 ❑ b&w Cover: 2.25 **NM** value: **Cover or less**
Bk 1 ❑ b&w Cover: 14.95 **NM** value: **Cover or less**

RETIEF AND THE WARLORDS — Adventure

1 ❑ b&w Cover: 2.50 **NM** value: **Cover or less**
2 ❑ b&w Cover: 2.50 **NM** value: **Cover or less**
3 ❑ b&w Cover: 2.50 **NM** value: **Cover or less**
4 ❑ b&w Cover: 2.50 **NM** value: **Cover or less**

RETIEF: DIPLOMATIC IMMUNITY — Adventure

1 ❑ b&w Cover: 2.50 **NM** value: **Cover or less**
2 ❑ b&w Cover: 2.50 **NM** value: **Cover or less**

RETIEF: GRIME AND PUNISHMENT — Adventure

1 ❑ Nov 1991, b&w Cover: 2.50 **NM** value: **Cover or less**
Grime and Punishment **A:** Darren Goodhart **W:** Keith Laumer

RETIEF (KEITH LAUMER'S...) — Mad Dog

Space is large and its people varied: different governments, different worlds, different problems. The humans of Earth's colonies have always tried to smooth out the rough diplomatic patches with their neighbors, but sometimes they have to do more than talk. That's where Jaime Retief gets called in. His hands-on style of diplomacy gets answers and results, no matter what world he's sent to or who he has to work with.

Here, Denis Fujitake and Jan Strnad here take (John) Keith Laumer's interstellar diplomatic troubleshooter and portray him in a manner very faithful to the original stories, published by Adventure.

1 ❑ Apr 1987 Cover: 2.00 **NM** value: **Cover or less**
Policy **A:** Dennis Fujitake **W:** Dennis Fujitake; Jan Strnad; Keith Laumer

2 ❑ Jun 1987 Cover: 2.00 **NM** value: **Cover or less**
3 ❑ Aug 1987 Cover: 2.00 **NM** value: **Cover or less**
4 ❑ Oct 1987 Cover: 2.00 **NM** value: **Cover or less**
5 ❑ Jan 1988 Cover: 2.00 **NM** value: **Cover or less**
6 ❑ Mar 1988 Cover: 2.00 **NM** value: **Cover or less**

RETIEF OF THE C.D.T. — Mad Dog

1 ❑ b&w Cover: 2.00 **NM** value: **Cover or less**

RETIEF: THE GARBAGE INVASION — Adventure

1 ❑ b&w Cover: 2.50 **NM** value: **Cover or less**

RETIEF: THE GIANT KILLER — Adventure

1 ❑ b&w Cover: 2.50 **NM** value: **Cover or less**

RETRO 50'S COMIX — Edge

1 ❑ b&w Cover: 2.95 **NM** value: **Cover or less**
2 ❑ b&w Cover: 2.95 **NM** value: **Cover or less**
3 ❑ b&w Cover: 3.50 **NM** value: **Cover or less**
• free fly

RETRO COMICS — AC

0 ❑ b&w Cover: 5.95 **NM** value: **Cover or less**
cardstock cover. • Cat-Man

1 ❑ b&w Cover: 5.95 **NM** value: **Cover or less**
cardstock cover. • Fighting Yank

2 ❑ b&w Cover: 5.95 **NM** value: **Cover or less**
cardstock cover. • Miss Victory

3 ❑ Cover: 5.95 **NM** value: **Cover or less**
The League of the Rotting Dead; Hog Wild!; The Skyway Bandits! • Original Cat-Man and Kitten **A:** Mark Heike; Brad Gorby; Bill Black **W:** Mark Heike; Bill Black

RETRO-DEAD — Blazer

1 ❑ Nov 1995, b&w Cover: 2.95 **NM** value: **Cover or less**
A: Dan Reed **W:** Dan Reed

RETROGRADE — Eternity

1 ❑ Cover: 1.95 **NM** value: **Cover or less**
2 ❑ Cover: 1.95 **NM** value: **Cover or less**
3 ❑ Cover: 1.95 **NM** value: **Cover or less**

RETURN OF DISNEY'S ALADDIN, THE — Disney

1 ❑ Cover: 1.50 **NM** value: **Cover or less**
More Arabian Nights, Part 1 **A:** The Jaime Diaz Studio **W:** John Blair Moore

2 ❑ Cover: 1.50 **NM** value: **Cover or less**
More Arabian Nights, Part 2 **A:** The Jaime Diaz Studio **W:** John Blair Moore

RETURN OF GIRL SQUAD X — Fantaco

1 ❑ Cover: 4.95 **NM** value: **Cover or less**
No issue number.

RETURN OF GORGO — Charlton

2 ❑ Sum 1963 Cover: 0.10 **NM** value: **75.00**
3 ❑ Fal 1964 Cover: 0.12 **NM** value: **75.00**
• **CGC:** 1 graded, best 9.2

RETURN OF HAPPY THE CLOWN, THE — Caliber

1 ❑ b&w Cover: 3.50 **NM** value: **Cover or less**
A: Troy Boyle **W:** Gary Francis

2 ❑ b&w Cover: 2.95 **NM** value: **Cover or less**
A: Troy Boyle **W:** Gary Francis

RETURN OF HERBIE, THE — Avalon

1 ❑ b&w Cover: 2.50 **NM** value: **Cover or less**
• reprints and new story (originally scheduled for Dark Horse's Herbie #3)

RETURN OF KONGA — Charlton

1 ❑ ca. 1962 **NM** value: **50.00**
• **CGC:** 1 graded, best 8.0

RETURN OF LUM URUSEI*YATSURA, THE — Viz

1 ❑ Oct 1994, b&w Cover: 2.95 **NM** value: **3.00**
Circ: CapCity orders: **4,400**
A: Rumiko Takahashi **W:** Rumiko Takahashi

2 ❑ Nov 1994, b&w Cover: 2.75 **NM** value: **3.00**
Circ: CapCity orders: **3,575**
A: Rumiko Takahashi **W:** Rumiko Takahashi

3 ❑ Dec 1994, b&w Cover: 2.75 **NM** value: **3.00**
Circ: CapCity orders: **3,225**
A: Rumiko Takahashi **W:** Rumiko Takahashi

Other grades: Multiply prices above by **1.5 for Mint • 2/3 for Very Fine • 1/3 for Fine • 1/5 for Very Good • 1/8 for Good**

4 ❑ Jan 1995, b&w Cover: 2.95 **NM** value: **3.00**
Circ: CapCity orders: **3,125**
A: Rumiko Takahashi **W:** Rumiko Takahashi
5 ❑ Feb 1995, b&w Cover: 2.95 **NM** value: **3.00**
Circ: CapCity orders: **3,050**
A: Rumiko Takahashi **W:** Rumiko Takahashi
6 ❑ Mar 1995, b&w Cover: 2.95 **NM** value: **3.00**
Circ: CapCity orders: **2,950**
A: Rumiko Takahashi **W:** Rumiko Takahashi
Bk 1❑ Cover: 15.95 **NM** value: **Cover or less**

RETURN OF LUM URUSEI*YATSURA, PART 2, THE — Viz

1 ❑ Apr 1995, b&w Cover: 2.75 **NM** value: **3.00**
Circ: CapCity orders: **3,025**
2 ❑ May 1995, b&w Cover: 2.75 **NM** value: **3.00**
Circ: CapCity orders: **2,625**
3 ❑ Jun 1995, b&w Cover: 2.75 **NM** value: **3.00**
4 ❑ Jul 1995, b&w Cover: 2.75 **NM** value: **3.00**
5 ❑ Aug 1995, b&w Cover: 2.75 **NM** value: **3.00**
6 ❑ Sep 1995, b&w Cover: 2.75 **NM** value: **3.00**
7 ❑ Oct 1995, b&w Cover: 2.75 **NM** value: **3.00**
8 ❑ Nov 1995, b&w Cover: 2.75 **NM** value: **3.00**
9 ❑ Dec 1995, b&w Cover: 2.75 **NM** value: **3.00**
10 ❑ Jan 1996, b&w Cover: 2.75 **NM** value: **3.00**
11 ❑ Feb 1996, b&w Cover: 2.75 **NM** value: **3.00**
12 ❑ Mar 1996, b&w Cover: 2.75 **NM** value: **3.00**
13 ❑ Apr 1996, b&w Cover: 2.75 **NM** value: **3.00**
Bk 2❑ Cover: 15.95 **NM** value: **Cover or less**
• Lum in the Sun
Bk 3❑ Cover: 15.95 **NM** value: **Cover or less**
• Sweet Revenge
Bk 4❑ Cover: 15.95 **NM** value: **Cover or less**
📖 Trouble Times Ten

RETURN OF LUM URUSEI*YATSURA, PART 3, THE — Viz

1 ❑ May 1996, b&w Cover: 2.95 **NM** value: **Cover or less**
A: Rumiko Takahashi **W:** Rumiko Takahashi
2 ❑ Jun 1996, b&w Cover: 2.95 **NM** value: **Cover or less**
A: Rumiko Takahashi **W:** Rumiko Takahashi
3 ❑ Jul 1996, b&w Cover: 2.95 **NM** value: **Cover or less**
A: Rumiko Takahashi **W:** Rumiko Takahashi
4 ❑ Aug 1996, b&w Cover: 2.95 **NM** value: **Cover or less**
A: Rumiko Takahashi **W:** Rumiko Takahashi
5 ❑ Sep 1996, b&w Cover: 2.95 **NM** value: **Cover or less**
Circ: Diamd. preorders: **5,631**
A: Rumiko Takahashi **W:** Rumiko Takahashi
6 ❑ Oct 1996, b&w Cover: 2.95 **NM** value: **Cover or less**
Circ: Diamd. preorders: **5,510**
A: Rumiko Takahashi **W:** Rumiko Takahashi
7 ❑ Nov 1996, b&w Cover: 2.95 **NM** value: **Cover or less**
Circ: Diamd. preorders: **5,381**
A: Rumiko Takahashi **W:** Rumiko Takahashi
8 ❑ Dec 1996, b&w Cover: 2.95 **NM** value: **Cover or less**
Circ: Diamd. preorders: **5,220**
A: Rumiko Takahashi **W:** Rumiko Takahashi
9 ❑ Jan 1997, b&w Cover: 2.95 **NM** value: **Cover or less**
Circ: Diamd. preorders: **5,051**
10 ❑ Feb 1997, b&w Cover: 2.95 **NM** value: **Cover or less**
Circ: Diamd. preorders: **4,440**
11 ❑ Mar 1997, b&w Cover: 2.95 **NM** value: **Cover or less**
Circ: Diamd. preorders: **4,618**
Bk 5❑ Cover: 15.95 **NM** value: **Cover or less**
• Feudal Furor
Bk 6❑ Cover: 15.95 **NM** value: **Cover or less**
• Creature Features

RETURN OF LUM URUSEI*YATSURA, PART 4, THE — Viz

1 ❑ Apr 1997, b&w Cover: 2.95 **NM** value: **Cover or less**
Circ: Diamd. preorders: **4,915**
2 ❑ May 1997, b&w Cover: 2.95 **NM** value: **Cover or less**
Circ: Diamd. preorders: **4,594**
3 ❑ Jun 1997, b&w Cover: 2.95 **NM** value: **Cover or less**
Circ: Diamd. preorders: **4,423**
4 ❑ Jul 1997, b&w Cover: 2.95 **NM** value: **Cover or less**
Circ: Diamd. preorders: **4,330**
5 ❑ Aug 1997, b&w Cover: 2.95 **NM** value: **Cover or less**
Circ: Diamd. preorders: **4,242**
6 ❑ Sep 1997, b&w Cover: 2.95 **NM** value: **Cover or less**
Circ: Diamd. preorders: **4,322**
7 ❑ Oct 1997, b&w Cover: 2.95 **NM** value: **Cover or less**
Circ: Diamd. preorders: **3,917**
8 ❑ Nov 1997, b&w Cover: 2.95 **NM** value: **Cover or less**
Circ: Diamd. preorders: **3,990**
9 ❑ Dec 1997, b&w Cover: 2.95 **NM** value: **Cover or less**
Circ: Diamd. preorders: **3,953**
10 ❑ Jan 1998, b&w Cover: 2.95 **NM** value: **Cover or less**
Circ: Diamd. preorders: **3,889**
11 ❑ Feb 1998, b&w Cover: 2.95 **NM** value: **Cover or less**
Circ: Diamd. preorders: **3,871**
Bk 7❑ May 1998 Cover: 15.95 **NM** value: **Cover or less**
• For Better or Curse
Bk 8❑ Nov 1998 Cover: 15.95 **NM** value: **Cover or less**
• Ran Attacks!

RETURN OF MEGATON MAN, THE — Kitchen Sink

1 ❑ Jul 1988 Cover: 2.00 **NM** value: **2.50**
Circ: CapCity orders: **4,750**
📖 Returns! **A:** Donald Simpson **W:** Donald Simpson
2 ❑ Cover: 2.00 **NM** value: **2.50**
Circ: CapCity orders: **3,550**
📖 Revamp Relive!!! **A:** Donald Simpson **W:** Donald Simpson
3 ❑ Cover: 2.00 **NM** value: **2.50**
Circ: CapCity orders: **3,850**
📖 Reborn-Redeemed! **A:** Donald Simpson **W:** Donald Simpson

RETURN OF TARZAN, THE (EDGAR RICE BURROUGHS'...) — Dark Horse

A frightened child runs into his village sounding an alarm about a white man. During the African slave trade years, this is a call to arms. Amazingly, this "white man" is treated as a long-time family member and not as an enemy. When children begin asking questions about the stranger, it's an ideal situation for telling stories. The children quickly learn that the waziri is none other than Tarzan. One imagines the children leaning closer to the storyteller as she recalls Tarzan's adventures. As day becomes night, she speaks about Tarzan's battles with monsters, holding a child's attention merely on the breath of her words. Shadows of campfire flames are dancing across her face when speaking about Tarzan's great love, Jane Porter. Close your eyes and see the Lord of Apes adventures unfold along the lines of Tales of Brave Ulysses.

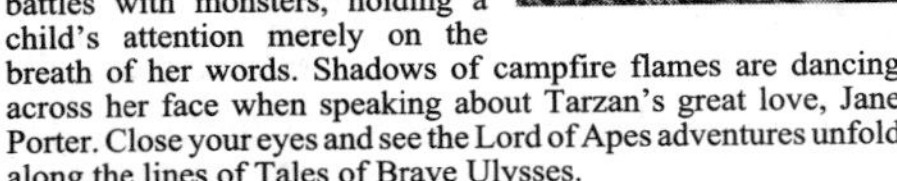

1 ❑ Apr 1997 Cover: 2.95 **NM** value: **Cover or less**
Circ: Diamd. preorders: **11,406**
• adapts Burroughs novel **A:** Tom Yeates **W:** Tom Yeates
2 ❑ May 1997 Cover: 2.95 **NM** value: **Cover or less**
Circ: Diamd. preorders: **10,252**
• adapts Burroughs novel **A:** Tom Yeates **W:** Tom Yeates
3 ❑ Jun 1997 Cover: 2.95 **NM** value: **Cover or less**
Circ: Diamd. preorders: **9,850**
• back cover has reproductions of New Story Magazine covers. • adapts Burroughs novel **A:** Tom Yeates **W:** Tom Yeates

RETURN OF THE OUTLAW — Toby

1 ❑ ca. 1953 Cover: 0.10 **NM** value: **60.00**
2 ❑ ca. 1953 Cover: 0.10 **NM** value: **35.00**
3 ❑ ca. 1953 Cover: 0.10 **NM** value: **35.00**
4 ❑ ca. 1953 Cover: 0.10 **NM** value: **35.00**
5 ❑ ca. 1954 Cover: 0.10 **NM** value: **35.00**
6 ❑ ca. 1954 Cover: 0.10 **NM** value: **35.00**
7 ❑ ca. 1954 Cover: 0.10 **NM** value: **35.00**
8 ❑ ca. 1954 Cover: 0.10 **NM** value: **35.00**
9 ❑ ca. 1955 Cover: 0.10 **NM** value: **35.00**
10 ❑ ca. 1955 Cover: 0.10 **NM** value: **30.00**
11 ❑ ca. 1955 Cover: 0.10 **NM** value: **30.00**

RETURN OF THE SKYMAN — Ace

1 ❑ Sep 1987 Cover: 1.75 **NM** value: **Cover or less**
A: Steve Ditko

RETURN OF VALKYRIE, THE — Eclipse

1 ❑ Cover: 9.95 **NM** value: **Cover or less**
📖 The Heap; On Wings of Death; The Wolf and the Phoenix; Misery Loves Company; Assault on Villa Miserio; Misery Takes a Holiday; Airboy one Through Five **A:** Will Blyberg; Tim Truman; Tom Yeates; Stan Woch **W:** Tim Truman; Chuck Dixon

RETURN TO JURASSIC PARK — Topps

1 ❑ Apr 1995 Cover: 2.50 **NM** value: **Cover or less**
Circ: CapCity orders: **5,900**
📖 No Man's Land **A:** Joe Staton **W:** Steve Englehart
2 ❑ May 1995 Cover: 2.50 **NM** value: **Cover or less**
Circ: CapCity orders: **4,475**
3 ❑ Jun 1995 Cover: 2.95 **NM** value: **Cover or less**
Circ: CapCity orders: **4,225**
📖 No Wimps Land **A:** Joe Staton
4 ❑ Jul 1995 Cover: 2.95 **NM** value: **Cover or less**
Circ: CapCity orders: **4,050**
A: Joe Staton
5 ❑ Aug 1995 Cover: 2.95 **NM** value: **Cover or less**
Circ: CapCity orders: **3,375**
6 ❑ Sep 1995 Cover: 2.95 **NM** value: **Cover or less**
Circ: CapCity orders: **3,000**
7 ❑ Nov 1995 Cover: 2.95 **NM** value: **Cover or less**
📖 Inquiring Minds, Part 1
8 ❑ Jan 1996 Cover: 2.95 **NM** value: **Cover or less**
📖 Inquiring Minds, Part 2
9 ❑ Cover: 2.95 **NM** value: **Cover or less**

RETURN TO THE AMALGAM AGE OF COMICS: THE DC COMICS COLLECTION — DC

Bk 1❑ Cover: 12.95 **NM** value: **Cover or less**
• collects DC's six Amalgam titles from early 1997 **A:** Adam Pollina; Dave Gibbons; Oscar Jimenez; Val Semeiks; Ty Templeton; Rodolfo DaMaggio **W:** Dave Gibbons; Larry Hama; Ty Templeton; Peter Milligan; Alan Grant; Christopher Priest; Mark Waid

RETURN TO THE EVE — Monolith

1 ❑ Cover: 2.50 **NM** value: **Cover or less**
📖 The Hanging Garden **A:** Holden Morris **W:** Holden & Shelley Morris

REVEALING ROMANCES — Ace

1 ❑ Sep 1949 Cover: 0.10 **NM** value: **50.00**
2 ❑ Nov 1949 Cover: 0.10 **NM** value: **30.00**
3 ❑ Jan 1950 Cover: 0.10 **NM** value: **25.00**
4 ❑ Mar 1950 Cover: 0.10 **NM** value: **25.00**
5 ❑ May 1950 Cover: 0.10 **NM** value: **25.00**
6 ❑ Jul 1950 Cover: 0.10 **NM** value: **25.00**

REVELATIONS (CLIVE BARKER'S...) — Eclipse

1 ❑ Cover: 7.95 **NM** value: **Cover or less**
A: Lionel Talaro **W:** Clive Barker; Steve Niles

REVELATIONS (DARK HORSE) — Dark Horse

1/Ash❑ Mar 1995 **NM** value: **1.00**
A: Matt Haley **W:** Keith Giffen

REVELATIONS (GOLDEN REALM) — Golden Realm Unlimited

1 ❑ Cover: 2.75 **NM** value: **Cover or less**

REVELATION: THE COMIC BOOK — Draw Near Art Studios

1 ❑ b&w Cover: 3.50 **NM** value: **Cover or less**
no cover price. • based on Book of Revelation
2 ❑ b&w Cover: 3.50 **NM** value: **Cover or less**
• based on Book of Revelation
3 ❑ b&w Cover: 3.50 **NM** value: **Cover or less**
• based on Book of Revelation
4 ❑ b&w Cover: 3.50 **NM** value: **Cover or less**
• based on Book of Revelation

REVELRY IN HELL — Fantagraphics / Eros

All issues are adults only.
1 ❑ b&w Cover: 2.50 **NM** value: **Cover or less**

REVENGE OF THE OIL SLICK DUCKS — Canew Ideas

1 ❑ Cover: 1.00 **NM** value: **Cover or less**

REVENGE OF THE PROWLER — Eclipse

1 ❑ Feb 1988 Cover: 1.75 **NM** value: **2.00**
Circ: CapCity orders: **4,675**
📖 Slow Burn **A:** John K. Snyder III **W:** Tim Truman
2 ❑ Mar 1988 Cover: 2.50 **NM** value: **Cover or less**
Circ: CapCity orders: **3,950**
📖 Search and Destroy **A:** John K. Snyder III **W:** Tim Truman
3 ❑ Apr 1988 Cover: 1.95 **NM** value: **2.00**
Circ: CapCity orders: **3,700**
📖 If I Should Die Before I Wake, Part 1 **A:** John K. Snyder III **W:** Tim Truman
4 ❑ Jun 1988 Cover: 1.95 **NM** value: **2.00**
Circ: CapCity orders: **3,350**
📖 If I Should Die Before I Wake, Part 2 **A:** John K. Snyder III **W:** Tim Truman

REVENGERS, THE — Continuity

Jack is a young guy snatched from his everyday life during an alien invasion of Earth and transformed into a gleaming metallic titan: Armor. Aboard the alien mother-ship, he is pitted against another superbeing, Silver Streak, for the amusement of his captors. Can the two adversaries join forces, escape, and save the Earth from the invaders?

The Revengers was written and drawn by Neal Adams, the revolutionary illustrator who was one of the biggest names in comics during the late 1960s. By 1985, when he produced this title for Continuity, the comics world had caught up to Adams and his once groundbreaking style seemed familiar. By 1994, with Continuity experiencing shipping delays worse than those of any other comics publisher of its size, Adams returned once more to commercial art.

1 ❑ Sep 1985 Cover: 2.00 **NM** value: **Cover or less**
• Revengers Featuring Armor and Silver Streak, The **A:** Neal Adams; Will Junkutz **W:** Neal Adams
2 ❑ Jun 1986 Cover: 2.00 **NM** value: **Cover or less**
• Revengers Featuring Megalith **A:** Neal Adams **W:** Neal Adams
3 ❑ Feb 1987 Cover: 2.00 **NM** value: **Cover or less**
SE 1❑ Nov 1993 Cover: 4.95 **NM** value: **Cover or less**
A: Larry Stroman **W:** Neal Adams; Elliot Maggin; Peter Stone

REVENGERS FEATURING MEGALITH — Continuity

1 ❑ Apr 1985 Cover: 2.00 **NM** value: **Cover or less**
• newsstand
1/DM❑ Apr 1985 Cover: 2.00 **NM** value: **Cover or less**
2 ❑ Sep 1985 Cover: 2.00 **NM** value: **Cover or less**
3 ❑ Nov 1986 Cover: 2.00 **NM** value: **Cover or less**
4 ❑ Mar 1988 Cover: 2.00 **NM** value: **Cover or less**
Circ: CapCity orders: **3,975**
5 ❑ Mar 1988 Cover: 2.00 **NM** value: **Cover or less**
Circ: CapCity orders: **3,650**
6 ❑ Mar 1988 Cover: 2.00 **NM** value: **Cover or less**
Circ: CapCity orders: **2,975**

REVENGERS: HYBRIDS SPECIAL — Continuity

1 ❑ Jul 1992 Cover: 4.95 **NM** value: **Cover or less**
Circ: CapCity orders: **7,425**
• continues in Hybrids: The Origin #2

REVEREND ABLACK: ADVENTURES OF THE ANTICHRIST — Creativeforce Designs

1 ❑ Cover: 2.50 **NM** value: **Cover or less**
2 ❑ Jul 1996, b&w Cover: 2.50 **NM** value: **Cover or less**

The prices seen above do not represent the highest possible prices seen in online auctions, but rather the prices we have seen these issues reliably fetch in a variety of environments (storefront retail, mail order, auction and convention).

CGC-graded: Multiply prices above by **33 for 9.9 M • 16 for 9.8 NM/M • 7 for 9.6 NM+ • 5 for 9.4 NM • 2.5 for 9.2 NM- • 1.5 for 9.0 VF/NM**

REVOLVER — Fleetway-Quality

Revolver was a short-lived but well-regarded anthology series, published in Britain and repackaged for the North American market.

Revolver aimed beyond the science-fiction territory that Fleetway plumbed with its 2000 A.D. series, striving toward more eclectic stories. Standouts included the psychedelic Rogan Gosh and Grant Morrison's deconstruction of Dan Dare (a space hero who figured prominently in the early issues of 2000 A.D.). Other regular features of Revolver included Paul Neary and Steve Parkhouse's Happenstance and Kismet, as well as Charles Shaar Murphy and Floyd Hughes' Purple Days, a homage to the late Jimi Hendrix.

Morrison's Dan Dare would later appear in the pages of Crisis.

1 ❑ Cover: 2.50 **NM** value: **Cover or less**
Circ: CapCity orders: **2,750**
★ Origin of Dan Dare.
2 ❑ Cover: 2.50 **NM** value: **Cover or less**
Circ: CapCity orders: **1,800**
3 ❑ Cover: 2.50 **NM** value: **Cover or less**
4 ❑ Cover: 2.50 **NM** value: **Cover or less**
5 ❑ Cover: 2.50 **NM** value: **Cover or less**
🕮 Purple Days; Happenstance & Kismet; Circular Motion; Dare; Dire Streets; The Greatest; Pinhead Nation **W:** Grant Morrison; Peter Milligan
6 ❑ Cover: 2.50 **NM** value: **Cover or less**
7 ❑ Cover: 2.50 **NM** value: **Cover or less**
🕮 Purple Days; Happenstance & Kismet; The Secret Garden; Dare; All Around the World; Did I? Did I? Did I in my own Self Shine?; Zen & The Art of Shopping; 51 Stars; Evolve **W:** Grant Morrison; Peter Milligan

REVOLVER (ROBIN SNYDER'S...) — Renegade

1 ❑ Nov 1985 Cover: 1.70 **NM** value: **2.00**
🕮 Star Guide; Cookie for the Bear; Marshal of the Zodiac: Loser Take All; The Planet Zog; Starlad; Seek Not the Idol of Death • Sci-Fi Adventure **A:** Henry Boltinoff; Tom Mandrake; Steve Ditko **W:** Henry Boltinoff; Jack C. Harris; Rich Margopoulos
2 ❑ Dec 1985 Cover: 1.70 **NM** value: **2.00**
• Sci-Fi Adventure
3 ❑ Jan 1986 Cover: 1.70 **NM** value: **2.00**
🕮 The Expert; Marshal of the Zodiac: The Icarus Assigment; Marsa Flemming, Rocketeeress • Sci-Fi Adventure **A:** Tom Mandrake; Steve Ditko **W:** Steve Ditko; Rich Margopoulos
4 ❑ Feb 1986 Cover: 1.70 **NM** value: **2.00**
• Fantastic Fables
5 ❑ Mar 1986 Cover: 1.70 **NM** value: **2.00**
• Fantastic Fables
6 ❑ Apr 1986 Cover: 1.70 **NM** value: **2.00**
• Fantastic Fables
7 ❑ May 1986 Cover: 1.70 **NM** value: **2.00**
🕮 Ditko's World: Static
8 ❑ Jun 1986 Cover: 1.70 **NM** value: **2.00**
🕮 Ditko's World: Static
9 ❑ Jul 1986 Cover: 1.70 **NM** value: **2.00**
🕮 Ditko's World: Static
10 ❑ Aug 1986 Cover: 1.70 **NM** value: **2.00**
• Murder
11 ❑ Sep 1986 Cover: 1.70 **NM** value: **2.00**
• Murder
12 ❑ Oct 1986 Cover: 1.70 **NM** value: **2.00**
• Murder
Anl 1❑ca. 1986, b&w Cover: 2.00 **NM** value: **Cover or less**
C: Alex Toth

REVOLVING DOORS — Blackthorne

1 ❑ Oct 1986 Cover: 1.75 **NM** value: **Cover or less**
A: Chris Miller **W:** Chris Miller
2 ❑ Cover: 1.75 **NM** value: **Cover or less**
A: Chris Miller **W:** Chris Miller
3 ❑ Cover: 1.75 **NM** value: **Cover or less**
A: Chris Miller **W:** Chris Miller

REX ALLEN — Dell

2 ❑ Sep 1951 Cover: 0.10 **NM** value: **75.00**
3 ❑ Dec 1951 Cover: 0.10 **NM** value: **50.00**
4 ❑ Mar 1952 Cover: 0.10 **NM** value: **50.00**
5 ❑ Jun 1952 Cover: 0.10 **NM** value: **50.00**
• **CGC:** 1 graded, best 9.2
6 ❑ Sep 1952 Cover: 0.10 **NM** value: **50.00**
7 ❑ Dec 1952 Cover: 0.10 **NM** value: **50.00**
• **CGC:** 1 graded, best 9.0
8 ❑ Mar 1953 Cover: 0.10 **NM** value: **50.00**
9 ❑ Jun 1953 Cover: 0.10 **NM** value: **50.00**
10 ❑ Sep 1953 Cover: 0.10 **NM** value: **40.00**
11 ❑ Dec 1953 Cover: 0.10 **NM** value: **40.00**
12 ❑ Mar 1954 Cover: 0.10 **NM** value: **40.00**
• **CGC:** 1 graded, best 9.0
13 ❑ Jun 1954 Cover: 0.10 **NM** value: **40.00**
14 ❑ Sep 1954 Cover: 0.10 **NM** value: **40.00**
15 ❑ Dec 1954 Cover: 0.10 **NM** value: **40.00**
16 ❑ Mar 1955 Cover: 0.10 **NM** value: **35.00**
17 ❑ Jun 1955 Cover: 0.10 **NM** value: **35.00**
18 ❑ Sep 1955 Cover: 0.10 **NM** value: **35.00**
19 ❑ Dec 1955 Cover: 0.10 **NM** value: **35.00**
20 ❑ Mar 1956 Cover: 0.10 **NM** value: **30.00**
21 ❑ Jun 1956 Cover: 0.10 **NM** value: **30.00**
22 ❑ Sep 1956 Cover: 0.10 **NM** value: **30.00**
• **CGC:** 1 graded, best 9.0
23 ❑ Dec 1956 Cover: 0.10 **NM** value: **30.00**
24 ❑ Mar 1957 Cover: 0.10 **NM** value: **30.00**

REX DEXTER OF MARS — Fox

1 ❑ Fal 1940 Cover: 0.10 **NM** value: **1500.00**
• **CGC:** 1 graded, best 8.0

REX HELLWIG — Black Cat

1 ❑ Cover: 2.95 **NM** value: **Cover or less**
🕮 The Start is a Good Place to Begin **A:** Stewart McKenny **W:** Travis Burch

REX MORGAN, M.D. — Argo

1 ❑ Dec 1950 Cover: 0.10 **NM** value: **75.00**
2 ❑ Feb 1950 Cover: 0.10 **NM** value: **50.00**
3 ❑ Apr 1950 Cover: 0.10 **NM** value: **50.00**

RHAJ — Mu

1 ❑ b&w Cover: 2.00 **NM** value: **Cover or less**
2 ❑ b&w Cover: 2.00 **NM** value: **Cover or less**
3 ❑ b&w Cover: 2.00 **NM** value: **Cover or less**
4 ❑ Cover: 2.25 **NM** value: **Cover or less**

RHANES OF TERROR, THE — Buffalo Nickel

1 ❑ Oct 1999 Cover: 2.99 **NM** value: **Cover or less**
A: Darius Johnson **W:** Darius Johnson; Fred Archer
2 ❑ Cover: 2.99 **NM** value: **Cover or less**
A: Darius Johnson **W:** Darius Johnson; Fred Archer
3 ❑ Cover: 2.99 **NM** value: **Cover or less**
A: Darius Johnson **W:** Darius Johnson; Fred Archer
4 ❑ Cover: 2.99 **NM** value: **Cover or less**
A: Darius Johnson **W:** Darius Johnson; Fred Archer

RHUDIPRRT, PRINCE OF FUR — Mu

When Warren Schafer was alive, the only creature he really cared for was his cat, Delilah. When he died, he asked to be with her. The goddess Ilura, known as Bast on Earth, granted him his wish. Cats are reborn as intelligent humanoids on the planet Rherau. Ilura places Warren's mind into the witless body of Prince Rhudiprrt, youngest of the ruling family of Thrallmar. Warren/Rhudiprrt discovers that life isn't easy in this new world. With his knowledge from Earth and the help of Ilura, Rhudiprrt will be instrumental in restoring peace to Rherau.

An imaginative story written by Dwight Decker and drawn by Teri Wood (Wandering Star), Rhudiprrt is a favorite in the furry fan community.

1 ❑ b&w Cover: 2.00 **NM** value: **Cover or less**
2 ❑ b&w Cover: 2.00 **NM** value: **Cover or less**
3 ❑ Cover: 2.25 **NM** value: **Cover or less**
4 ❑ Nov 1990 Cover: 2.50 **NM** value: **Cover or less**
5 ❑ Jun 1991 Cover: 2.25 **NM** value: **2.50**
6 ❑ Nov 1991 Cover: 2.50 **NM** value: **Cover or less**
7 ❑ b&w Cover: 2.50 **NM** value: **Cover or less**
8 ❑ Jan 1994 Cover: 2.50 **NM** value: **Cover or less**

RIB — Dilemma

1 ❑ Apr 1996, b&w Cover: 1.95 **NM** value: **Cover or less**

RIBIT! — Comico

1 ❑ Cover: 1.95 **NM** value: **Cover or less**
Circ: CapCity orders: **5,100**
A: Frank Thorne **W:** Frank Thorne
2 ❑ Cover: 1.95 **NM** value: **Cover or less**
Circ: CapCity orders: **3,600**
A: Frank Thorne **W:** Frank Thorne
3 ❑ Cover: 1.95 **NM** value: **Cover or less**
Circ: CapCity orders: **3,550**
A: Frank Thorne **W:** Frank Thorne
4 ❑ Cover: 1.95 **NM** value: **Cover or less**
Circ: CapCity orders: **3,550**
A: Frank Thorne **W:** Frank Thorne

RICHARD DRAGON, KUNG-FU FIGHTER — DC

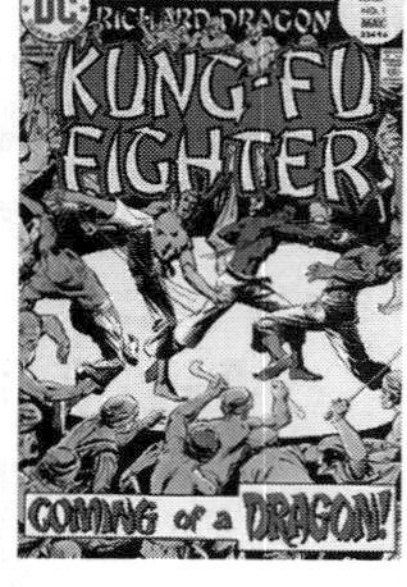

As a young man, Richard Dragon came to a temple in Kyoto to rob it of a precious statue. The temple's teacher (sensei) confronted the young man and prevented the theft. But the sensei sensed a spark of goodness in Richard and invited him to become his student.

In time, Richard and another student named Benjamin became masters of the martial arts. When the day came for them to leave the temple, they were recruited by the organization known as G.O.O.D. ("It's not important what the letters stand for.") That organization sent these two kung-fu fighters on a variety of missions across the globe: battling slavers, criminals, and other such villains.

Richard Dragon, Kung-Fu Fighter was originally adapted from Jim Dennis' novel, "Dragon's Fists."

1 ❑ Apr 1975 Cover: 0.25 **NM** value: **3.00**
• **CGC:** 7 graded, best 9.6
🕮 Coming Of A Dragon! **A:** Leopoldo Dura±ona **W:** Jim Dennis ★ Origin of Richard Dragon, Kung Fu Fighter. ★ 1st Appearance of Richard Dragon, Kung Fu Fighter.
2 ❑ Jul 1975 Cover: 0.25 **NM** value: **2.00**
A: Jim Starlin
3 ❑ Sep 1975 Cover: 0.25 **NM** value: **2.00**
🕮 Claws of the Dragon
4 ❑ Nov 1975 Cover: 0.25 **NM** value: **2.00**
5 ❑ Jan 1976 Cover: 0.25 **NM** value: **2.00**
6 ❑ Mar 1976 Cover: 0.25 **NM** value: **2.00**
7 ❑ Apr 1976 Cover: 0.30 **NM** value: **2.00**
8 ❑ May 1976 Cover: 0.30 **NM** value: **2.00**
9 ❑ Jun 1976 Cover: 0.30 **NM** value: **2.00**
10 ❑ Jul 1976 Cover: 0.30 **NM** value: **2.00**
11 ❑ Sep 1976 Cover: 0.30 **NM** value: **1.50**
12 ❑ Nov 1976 Cover: 0.30 **NM** value: **1.50**
13 ❑ Feb 1977 Cover: 0.30 **NM** value: **1.50**
14 ❑ Apr 1977 Cover: 0.30 **NM** value: **1.50**
15 ❑ Jun 1977 Cover: 0.30 **NM** value: **1.50**
16 ❑ Aug 1977 Cover: 0.35 **NM** value: **1.50**
17 ❑ Oct 1977 Cover: 0.35 **NM** value: **1.50**
18 ❑ Nov 1977 Cover: 0.35 **NM** value: **1.50**
final issue.

RICHARD SPECK — Boneyard

1 ❑ Mar 1993 Cover: 2.75 **NM** value: **Cover or less**
A: Ralph Horsely **W:** Wayne Allen Sallee

RICHIE RICH (1ST SERIES) — Harvey

With his big red bow tie, top coat, and blond hair parted down the middle (turn-of-the-century style), Richie Rich became one of the world's most recognizable comic-book characters.

Richie is a "poor little rich boy," with enough cash to give Scrooge McDuck a run for his money, yet with all the same problems and turmoils as any eight-year-old kid. (Yeah, right! But anyway...)

Richie began as a supporting character in Little Dot, but Harvey could tell it had hit on a successful formula and spun Richie off into his own book. Eventually, he would star in more than 30 titles, digests, specials, and annuals as the flagship character of Harvey's comic book line.

If there's a failing in Harvey worse than its obsession with certain characters and plotlines, it's in the anonymity its creators worked under. Most other publishers had been crediting creators for years while the Richie Rich titles continued to simply magically appear, at least judging from the lack of attribution.

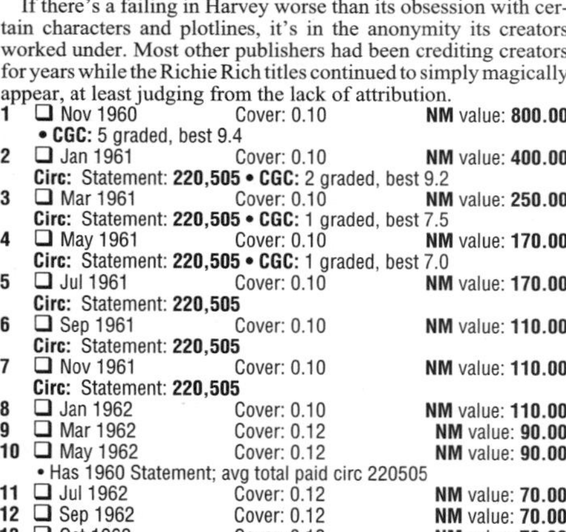

1 ❑ Nov 1960 Cover: 0.10 **NM** value: **800.00**
• **CGC:** 5 graded, best 9.4
2 ❑ Jan 1961 Cover: 0.10 **NM** value: **400.00**
Circ: Statement: **220,505** • **CGC:** 2 graded, best 9.2
3 ❑ Mar 1961 Cover: 0.10 **NM** value: **250.00**
Circ: Statement: **220,505** • **CGC:** 1 graded, best 7.5
4 ❑ May 1961 Cover: 0.10 **NM** value: **170.00**
Circ: Statement: **220,505** • **CGC:** 1 graded, best 7.0
5 ❑ Jul 1961 Cover: 0.10 **NM** value: **170.00**
Circ: Statement: **220,505**
6 ❑ Sep 1961 Cover: 0.10 **NM** value: **110.00**
Circ: Statement: **220,505**
7 ❑ Nov 1961 Cover: 0.10 **NM** value: **110.00**
Circ: Statement: **220,505**
8 ❑ Jan 1962 Cover: 0.10 **NM** value: **110.00**
9 ❑ Mar 1962 Cover: 0.12 **NM** value: **90.00**
10 ❑ May 1962 Cover: 0.12 **NM** value: **90.00**
• Has 1960 Statement; avg total paid circ 220505
11 ❑ Jul 1962 Cover: 0.12 **NM** value: **70.00**
12 ❑ Sep 1962 Cover: 0.12 **NM** value: **70.00**
13 ❑ Oct 1962 Cover: 0.12 **NM** value: **70.00**
14 ❑ Nov 1962 Cover: 0.12 **NM** value: **70.00**
15 ❑ Jan 1963 Cover: 0.12 **NM** value: **70.00**
16 ❑ Mar 1963 Cover: 0.12 **NM** value: **52.00**
17 ❑ May 1963 Cover: 0.12 **NM** value: **52.00**
18 ❑ Jul 1963 Cover: 0.12 **NM** value: **52.00**
19 ❑ Sep 1963 Cover: 0.12 **NM** value: **52.00**
20 ❑ Nov 1963 Cover: 0.12 **NM** value: **52.00**
21 ❑ Jan 1964 Cover: 0.12 **NM** value: **35.00**
22 ❑ Mar 1964 Cover: 0.12 **NM** value: **35.00**
23 ❑ May 1964 Cover: 0.12 **NM** value: **35.00**
• Has 1963 Statement, filed 10/1/63; no circ figures published
24 ❑ Jul 1964 Cover: 0.12 **NM** value: **35.00**
25 ❑ Sep 1964 Cover: 0.12 **NM** value: **35.00**
26 ❑ Oct 1964 Cover: 0.12 **NM** value: **35.00**
27 ❑ Nov 1964 Cover: 0.12 **NM** value: **35.00**
28 ❑ Dec 1964 Cover: 0.12 **NM** value: **35.00**
29 ❑ Jan 1965 Cover: 0.12 **NM** value: **35.00**
30 ❑ Feb 1965 Cover: 0.12 **NM** value: **35.00**
31 ❑ Mar 1965 Cover: 0.12 **NM** value: **22.00**
32 ❑ Apr 1965 Cover: 0.12 **NM** value: **22.00**
33 ❑ May 1965 Cover: 0.12 **NM** value: **22.00**
34 ❑ Jun 1965 Cover: 0.12 **NM** value: **22.00**
• Has 1964 Statement, filed 10/1/64; no circ figures published
35 ❑ Jul 1965 Cover: 0.12 **NM** value: **22.00**
36 ❑ Aug 1965 Cover: 0.12 **NM** value: **22.00**
37 ❑ Sep 1965 Cover: 0.12 **NM** value: **22.00**
38 ❑ Oct 1965 Cover: 0.12 **NM** value: **22.00**
39 ❑ Nov 1965 Cover: 0.12 **NM** value: **22.00**
40 ❑ Dec 1965 Cover: 0.12 **NM** value: **22.00**
41 ❑ Jan 1966 Cover: 0.12 **NM** value: **14.00**
42 ❑ Feb 1966 Cover: 0.12 **NM** value: **14.00**
43 ❑ Mar 1966 Cover: 0.12 **NM** value: **14.00**

Other grades: Multiply prices above by **1.5 for Mint • 2/3 for Very Fine • 1/3 for Fine • 1/5 for Very Good • 1/8 for Good**

44 ❑ Apr 1966 Cover: 0.12 **NM** value: **14.00**
45 ❑ May 1966 Cover: 0.12 **NM** value: **14.00**
• Has 1965 Statement, filed 10/1/65; no circ figures published
46 ❑ Jun 1966 Cover: 0.12 **NM** value: **14.00**
47 ❑ Jul 1966 Cover: 0.12 **NM** value: **14.00**
48 ❑ Aug 1966 Cover: 0.12 **NM** value: **14.00**
49 ❑ Sep 1966 Cover: 0.12 **NM** value: **14.00**
50 ❑ Oct 1966 Cover: 0.12 **NM** value: **10.00**
51 ❑ Nov 1966 Cover: 0.12 **NM** value: **10.00**
52 ❑ Dec 1966 Cover: 0.12 **NM** value: **10.00**
53 ❑ Jan 1967 Cover: 0.12 **NM** value: **10.00**
54 ❑ Feb 1967 Cover: 0.12 **NM** value: **10.00**
55 ❑ Mar 1967 Cover: 0.12 **NM** value: **10.00**
56 ❑ Apr 1967 Cover: 0.12 **NM** value: **10.00**
57 ❑ May 1967 Cover: 0.12 **NM** value: **10.00**
• Has 1966 Statement; no circ figures published
58 ❑ Jun 1967 Cover: 0.12 **NM** value: **10.00**
59 ❑ Jul 1967 Cover: 0.12 **NM** value: **10.00**
60 ❑ Aug 1967 Cover: 0.12 **NM** value: **10.00**
61 ❑ Sep 1967 Cover: 0.12 **NM** value: **7.00**
62 ❑ Oct 1967 Cover: 0.12 **NM** value: **7.00**
📖 Richie Rich: Disappearance; Richie Rich: The Reappearance; Cadbury: The Butler of Youth; The Littlest Fox (text story); Engine Trouble (text story); Cadbury: Oh, Baby!
63 ❑ Nov 1967 Cover: 0.12 **NM** value: **7.00**
64 ❑ Dec 1967 Cover: 0.12 **NM** value: **7.00**
65 ❑ Jan 1968 Cover: 0.12 **NM** value: **7.00**
66 ❑ Feb 1968 Cover: 0.12 **NM** value: **7.00**
67 ❑ Mar 1968 Cover: 0.12 **NM** value: **7.00**
68 ❑ Apr 1968 Cover: 0.12 **NM** value: **7.00**
69 ❑ May 1968 Cover: 0.12 **NM** value: **7.00**
70 ❑ Jun 1968 Cover: 0.12 **NM** value: **7.00**
• Has 1967 Statement; no circ figures published
71 ❑ Jul 1968 Cover: 0.12 **NM** value: **5.00**
72 ❑ Aug 1968 Cover: 0.12 **NM** value: **5.00**
73 ❑ Sep 1968 Cover: 0.12 **NM** value: **5.00**
74 ❑ Oct 1968 Cover: 0.12 **NM** value: **5.00**
75 ❑ Nov 1968 Cover: 0.12 **NM** value: **5.00**
76 ❑ Dec 1968 Cover: 0.12 **NM** value: **5.00**
77 ❑ Jan 1969 Cover: 0.12 **NM** value: **5.00**
78 ❑ Feb 1969 Cover: 0.12 **NM** value: **5.00**
79 ❑ Mar 1969 Cover: 0.12 **NM** value: **5.00**
80 ❑ Apr 1969 Cover: 0.12 **NM** value: **5.00**
81 ❑ May 1969 Cover: 0.12 **NM** value: **5.00**
• Has 1968 Statement; no circ figures published
82 ❑ Jun 1969 Cover: 0.12 **NM** value: **5.00**
83 ❑ Jul 1969 Cover: 0.12 **NM** value: **5.00**
84 ❑ Aug 1969 Cover: 0.15 **NM** value: **5.00**
85 ❑ Sep 1969 Cover: 0.15 **NM** value: **5.00**
86 ❑ Oct 1969 Cover: 0.15 **NM** value: **5.00**
87 ❑ Nov 1969 Cover: 0.15 **NM** value: **5.00**
88 ❑ Dec 1969 Cover: 0.15 **NM** value: **5.00**
89 ❑ Jan 1970 Cover: 0.15 **NM** value: **5.00**
90 ❑ Feb 1970 Cover: 0.15 **NM** value: **5.00**
91 ❑ Mar 1970 Cover: 0.15 **NM** value: **5.00**
92 ❑ Apr 1970 Cover: 0.15 **NM** value: **5.00**
93 ❑ May 1970 Cover: 0.15 **NM** value: **5.00**
• Has 1969 Statement; no circ figures published
94 ❑ Jun 1970 Cover: 0.15 **NM** value: **5.00**
95 ❑ Jul 1970 Cover: 0.15 **NM** value: **5.00**
96 ❑ Aug 1970 Cover: 0.15 **NM** value: **5.00**
97 ❑ Sep 1970 Cover: 0.15 **NM** value: **5.00**
98 ❑ Oct 1970 Cover: 0.15 **NM** value: **5.00**
99 ❑ Nov 1970 Cover: 0.15 **NM** value: **5.00**
100 ❑ Dec 1970 Cover: 0.15 **NM** value: **5.00**
101 ❑ Jan 1971 Cover: 0.15 **NM** value: **3.00**
Circ: Statement: **273,698**
102 ❑ Feb 1971 Cover: 0.15 **NM** value: **3.00**
Circ: Statement: **273,698**
103 ❑ Mar 1971 Cover: 0.15 **NM** value: **3.00**
Circ: Statement: **273,698**
104 ❑ Apr 1971 Cover: 0.15 **NM** value: **3.00**
Circ: Statement: **273,698**
105 ❑ May 1971 Cover: 0.15 **NM** value: **3.00**
Circ: Statement: **273,698**
• Has 1970 Statement; no circ figures published
106 ❑ Jun 1971 Cover: 0.15 **NM** value: **3.00**
Circ: Statement: **273,698**
107 ❑ Jul 1971 Cover: 0.15 **NM** value: **3.00**
Circ: Statement: **273,698** • **CGC:** 1 graded, best 9.0
108 ❑ Aug 1971 Cover: 0.15 **NM** value: **3.00**
Circ: Statement: **273,698**
109 ❑ Sep 1971 Cover: 0.15 **NM** value: **3.00**
Circ: Statement: **273,698**
110 ❑ Oct 1971 Cover: 0.15 **NM** value: **3.00**
Circ: Statement: **273,698**
111 ❑ Nov 1971 Cover: 0.15 **NM** value: **3.00**
Circ: Statement: **273,698**
112 ❑ Jan 1972 **NM** value: **3.00**
Circ: Statement: **251,833**
113 ❑ Mar 1972 Cover: 0.25 **NM** value: **3.00**
Circ: Statement: **251,833**
114 ❑ May 1972 Cover: 0.25 **NM** value: **3.00**
Circ: Statement: **251,833** • **CGC:** 1 graded, best 9.0
• Has 1971 Statement, filed 10/1/71; avg print run 552,612; avg sales 273,644; avg subs 54; avg total paid 273,698; samples 345; max existent 274,043; 50% of run returned
115 ❑ Jul 1972 Cover: 0.25 **NM** value: **3.00**
Circ: Statement: **251,833**
116 ❑ Sep 1972 Cover: 0.25 **NM** value: **3.00**
Circ: Statement: **251,833**
117 ❑ Nov 1972 Cover: 0.20 **NM** value: **3.00**
Circ: Statement: **251,833**
118 ❑ Jan 1973 Cover: 0.20 **NM** value: **3.00**
Circ: Statement: **210,352**
119 ❑ Mar 1973 Cover: 0.20 **NM** value: **3.00**
Circ: Statement: **210,352**
120 ❑ May 1973 Cover: 0.20 **NM** value: **3.00**
Circ: Statement: **210,352**
121 ❑ Jul 1973 Cover: 0.20 **NM** value: **3.00**
Circ: Statement: **210,352**
• Has 1972 Statement; avg print run 466,687; avg sales 251,833; no subscription copies; avg total paid 251,833; samples 345; max existent 252,178; 46% of run returned
122 ❑ Sep 1973 Cover: 0.20 **NM** value: **3.00**
Circ: Statement: **210,352**
📖 Movie Music!; All Fur a Coat!; One Picture is Worth a Thousand Hollers; The Bread Line (text story); Clickomaniac
123 ❑ Nov 1973 Cover: 0.20 **NM** value: **3.00**
Circ: Statement: **210,352**
124 ❑ Jan 1974 Cover: 0.20 **NM** value: **3.00**
Circ: Statement: **210,352**
125 ❑ Mar 1974 Cover: 0.20 **NM** value: **3.00**
Circ: Statement: **210,352**
126 ❑ May 1974 Cover: 0.25 **NM** value: **3.00**
Circ: Statement: **210,352**
• Has 1973 Statement; avg print run 442,616; avg sales 210,840; avg subs 15; avg total paid 210,855; samples 345; max existent 211,200; 52% of run returned
127 ❑ Jul 1974 Cover: 0.25 **NM** value: **3.00**
Circ: Statement: **210,352**
128 ❑ Sep 1974 Cover: 0.25 **NM** value: **3.00**
Circ: Statement: **210,352**
129 ❑ Nov 1974 Cover: 0.25 **NM** value: **3.00**
Circ: Statement: **210,352**
130 ❑ Jan 1975 Cover: 0.25 **NM** value: **3.00**
Circ: Statement: **150,125**
131 ❑ Mar 1975 Cover: 0.25 **NM** value: **3.00**
Circ: Statement: **150,125**
132 ❑ May 1975 Cover: 0.25 **NM** value: **3.00**
Circ: Statement: **150,125**
• Has 1974 Statement; avg print run 354,204; avg sales 210,337; avg subs 15; avg total paid 210,352; samples 345; max existent 210,697; 41% of run returned
133 ❑ Jul 1975 Cover: 0.25 **NM** value: **3.00**
Circ: Statement: **150,125**
134 ❑ Sep 1975 Cover: 0.25 **NM** value: **3.00**
Circ: Statement: **150,125**
135 ❑ Oct 1975 Cover: 0.25 **NM** value: **3.00**
Circ: Statement: **150,125**
136 ❑ Nov 1975 Cover: 0.25 **NM** value: **3.00**
Circ: Statement: **150,125**
137 ❑ Dec 1975 Cover: 0.25 **NM** value: **3.00**
Circ: Statement: **150,125**
138 ❑ Jan 1976 Cover: 0.25 **NM** value: **3.00**
139 ❑ Feb 1976 Cover: 0.25 **NM** value: **3.00**
140 ❑ Mar 1976 Cover: 0.25 **NM** value: **3.00**
141 ❑ Apr 1976 Cover: 0.25 **NM** value: **3.00**
142 ❑ May 1976 Cover: 0.25 **NM** value: **3.00**
143 ❑ Jun 1976 Cover: 0.25 **NM** value: **3.00**
144 ❑ Jul 1976 Cover: 0.25 **NM** value: **3.00**
• Has 1975 Statement; avg print run 344,325; avg sales 150,115; avg subs 15; avg total paid 150,130; samples 345; max existent 150,475; 56% of run returned
145 ❑ Aug 1976 Cover: 0.25 **NM** value: **3.00**
146 ❑ Sep 1976 Cover: 0.25 **NM** value: **3.00**
147 ❑ Oct 1976 Cover: 0.30 **NM** value: **3.00**
148 ❑ Nov 1976 Cover: 0.30 **NM** value: **3.00**
149 ❑ Dec 1976 Cover: 0.30 **NM** value: **3.00**
150 ❑ Jan 1977 Cover: 0.30 **NM** value: **3.00**
151 ❑ Feb 1977 Cover: 0.30 **NM** value: **2.00**
152 ❑ Mar 1977 Cover: 0.30 **NM** value: **2.00**
153 ❑ Apr 1977 Cover: 0.30 **NM** value: **2.00**
154 ❑ May 1977 Cover: 0.30 **NM** value: **2.00**
155 ❑ Jun 1977 Cover: 0.30 **NM** value: **2.00**
156 ❑ Jul 1977 Cover: 0.30 **NM** value: **2.00**
157 ❑ Aug 1977 Cover: 0.30 **NM** value: **2.00**
158 ❑ Sep 1977 Cover: 0.30 **NM** value: **2.00**
159 ❑ Oct 1977 Cover: 0.35 **NM** value: **2.00**
160 ❑ Nov 1977 Cover: 0.35 **NM** value: **2.00**
161 ❑ Dec 1977 Cover: 0.35 **NM** value: **2.00**
162 ❑ Jan 1978 Cover: 0.35 **NM** value: **2.00**
163 ❑ Feb 1978 Cover: 0.35 **NM** value: **2.00**
164 ❑ Mar 1978 Cover: 0.35 **NM** value: **2.00**
165 ❑ Apr 1978 Cover: 0.35 **NM** value: **2.00**
166 ❑ May 1978 Cover: 0.35 **NM** value: **2.00**
167 ❑ Jun 1978 Cover: 0.35 **NM** value: **2.00**
168 ❑ Jul 1978 Cover: 0.35 **NM** value: **2.00**
169 ❑ Aug 1978 Cover: 0.35 **NM** value: **2.00**
170 ❑ Sep 1978 Cover: 0.35 **NM** value: **2.00**
171 ❑ Oct 1978 Cover: 0.35 **NM** value: **2.00**
172 ❑ Nov 1978 Cover: 0.35 **NM** value: **2.00**
173 ❑ Dec 1978 Cover: 0.35 **NM** value: **2.00**
174 ❑ Jan 1979 Cover: 0.35 **NM** value: **2.00**
175 ❑ Feb 1979 Cover: 0.35 **NM** value: **2.00**
176 ❑ Mar 1979 Cover: 0.35 **NM** value: **2.00**
177 ❑ Apr 1979 Cover: 0.35 **NM** value: **2.00**
178 ❑ May 1979 Cover: 0.35 **NM** value: **2.00**
179 ❑ Jun 1979 Cover: 0.35 **NM** value: **2.00**
180 ❑ Jul 1979 Cover: 0.35 **NM** value: **2.00**
181 ❑ Aug 1979 Cover: 0.35 **NM** value: **2.00**
182 ❑ Sep 1979 Cover: 0.40 **NM** value: **2.00**
183 ❑ Oct 1979 Cover: 0.40 **NM** value: **2.00**
184 ❑ Nov 1979 Cover: 0.40 **NM** value: **2.00**
185 ❑ Dec 1979 Cover: 0.40 **NM** value: **2.00**
186 ❑ Jan 1980 Cover: 0.40 **NM** value: **2.00**
187 ❑ Feb 1980 Cover: 0.40 **NM** value: **2.00**
188 ❑ Mar 1980 Cover: 0.40 **NM** value: **2.00**
189 ❑ Apr 1980 Cover: 0.40 **NM** value: **2.00**
190 ❑ May 1980 Cover: 0.40 **NM** value: **2.00**
191 ❑ Jun 1980 Cover: 0.40 **NM** value: **2.00**
192 ❑ Jul 1980 Cover: 0.40 **NM** value: **2.00**
193 ❑ Aug 1980 Cover: 0.40 **NM** value: **2.00**
194 ❑ Sep 1980 **NM** value: **2.00**
195 ❑ Oct 1980 Cover: 0.50 **NM** value: **2.00**
196 ❑ Nov 1980 Cover: 0.50 **NM** value: **2.00**
197 ❑ Dec 1980 Cover: 0.50 **NM** value: **2.00**
198 ❑ Jan 1981 Cover: 0.50 **NM** value: **2.00**
199 ❑ Feb 1981 Cover: 0.50 **NM** value: **2.00**
200 ❑ Mar 1981 Cover: 0.50 **NM** value: **2.00**
201 ❑ Apr 1981 Cover: 0.50 **NM** value: **1.25**
202 ❑ May 1981 Cover: 0.50 **NM** value: **1.25**
203 ❑ Jun 1981 Cover: 0.50 **NM** value: **1.25**
204 ❑ Jul 1981 Cover: 0.50 **NM** value: **1.25**
205 ❑ Aug 1981 Cover: 0.50 **NM** value: **1.25**
206 ❑ Sep 1981 Cover: 0.50 **NM** value: **1.25**
207 ❑ Oct 1981 Cover: 0.50 **NM** value: **1.25**
208 ❑ Nov 1981 Cover: 0.50 **NM** value: **1.25**
209 ❑ Dec 1981 Cover: 0.50 **NM** value: **1.25**
210 ❑ Jan 1982 **NM** value: **1.25**
211 ❑ Feb 1982 **NM** value: **1.25**
212 ❑ Mar 1982 Cover: 0.60 **NM** value: **1.25**
213 ❑ Apr 1982 Cover: 0.60 **NM** value: **1.25**
214 ❑ May 1982 Cover: 0.60 **NM** value: **1.25**
215 ❑ Jun 1982 Cover: 0.60 **NM** value: **1.25**
216 ❑ Jul 1982 Cover: 0.60 **NM** value: **1.25**
217 ❑ Aug 1982 Cover: 0.60 **NM** value: **1.25**
218 ❑ Oct 1982 Cover: 0.60 **NM** value: **1.25**
219 ❑ Oct 1986 Cover: 0.75 **NM** value: **1.25**
220 ❑ Nov 1986 Cover: 0.75 **NM** value: **1.25**
221 ❑ Dec 1986 Cover: 0.75 **NM** value: **1.25**
222 ❑ Jan 1987 Cover: 0.75 **NM** value: **1.25**
223 ❑ Feb 1987 Cover: 0.75 **NM** value: **1.25**
224 ❑ Mar 1987 Cover: 0.75 **NM** value: **1.25**
225 ❑ Apr 1987 Cover: 0.75 **NM** value: **1.25**
226 ❑ May 1987 Cover: 0.75 **NM** value: **1.25**
227 ❑ Jun 1987 Cover: 0.75 **NM** value: **1.25**
228 ❑ Jul 1987 Cover: 0.75 **NM** value: **1.25**
229 ❑ Aug 1987 Cover: 0.75 **NM** value: **1.25**
230 ❑ Sep 1987 Cover: 0.75 **NM** value: **1.25**
231 ❑ Nov 1987 Cover: 0.75 **NM** value: **1.25**
232 ❑ 1988 **NM** value: **1.25**
233 ❑ Apr 1988 Cover: 1.00 **NM** value: **1.25**
234 ❑ Jun 1988 Cover: 1.00 **NM** value: **1.25**
235 ❑ Aug 1988 Cover: 1.00 **NM** value: **1.25**
236 ❑ 1988 Cover: 1.00 **NM** value: **1.25**
237 ❑ 1989 Cover: 1.00 **NM** value: **1.25**
238 ❑ 1989 Cover: 1.00 **NM** value: **1.25**
239 ❑ Jul 1989 Cover: 1.00 **NM** value: **1.25**
240 ❑ Sep 1989 Cover: 1.00 **NM** value: **1.25**
241 ❑ Oct 1989 Cover: 1.00 **NM** value: **1.25**
242 ❑ Dec 1989 Cover: 1.00 **NM** value: **1.25**
243 ❑ Feb 1990 Cover: 1.00 **NM** value: **1.25**
244 ❑ Mar 1990 Cover: 1.00 **NM** value: **1.25**
245 ❑ Apr 1990 Cover: 1.00 **NM** value: **1.25**
246 ❑ May 1990 Cover: 1.00 **NM** value: **1.25**
247 ❑ Jun 1990 Cover: 0.10 **NM** value: **1.25**
248 ❑ Jul 1990 Cover: 0.10 **NM** value: **1.25**
249 ❑ Aug 1990 Cover: 0.10 **NM** value: **1.25**
250 ❑ Sep 1990 Cover: 0.10 **NM** value: **1.25**
251 ❑ Oct 1990 Cover: 0.10 **NM** value: **1.25**
252 ❑ Nov 1990 Cover: 0.10 **NM** value: **1.25**
253 ❑ Dec 1990 Cover: 0.10 **NM** value: **1.25**
254 ❑ Jan 1991 Cover: 0.10 **NM** value: **1.25**
final issue.

RICHIE RICH (2ND SERIES) — Harvey

1 ❑ Mar 1991 Cover: 1.25 **NM** value: **5.00**
2 ❑ May 1991 Cover: 1.25 **NM** value: **3.00**
Circ: CapCity orders: **1,450**
3 ❑ Jul 1991 Cover: 1.25 **NM** value: **1.50**
Circ: CapCity orders: **1,100**
4 ❑ Sep 1991 Cover: 1.25 **NM** value: **1.50**
Circ: CapCity orders: **1,100**
5 ❑ Nov 1991 Cover: 1.25 **NM** value: **1.50**
6 ❑ Jan 1992 Cover: 1.25 **NM** value: **1.50**
7 ❑ Mar 1992 Cover: 1.25 **NM** value: **1.50**
8 ❑ May 1992 Cover: 1.25 **NM** value: **1.50**
9 ❑ Jul 1992 Cover: 1.25 **NM** value: **1.50**
10 ❑ Sep 1992 Cover: 1.25 **NM** value: **1.50**
11 ❑ Nov 1992 Cover: 1.25 **NM** value: **Cover or less**
📖 The $1,000,000 Pool Party; Reggie; As You Love it!; Pee Wee and the Witch's House; Irona: Responsive Robot **A:** Ernie Colon; Ben Brown
12 ❑ Jan 1993 Cover: 1.25 **NM** value: **Cover or less**
13 ❑ Mar 1993 Cover: 1.25 **NM** value: **Cover or less**
14 ❑ May 1993 Cover: 1.25 **NM** value: **Cover or less**
15 ❑ Jul 1993 Cover: 1.25 **NM** value: **Cover or less**
16 ❑ Sep 1993 Cover: 1.50 **NM** value: **Cover or less**
17 ❑ Nov 1993 Cover: 1.50 **NM** value: **Cover or less**
18 ❑ Jan 1994 Cover: 1.50 **NM** value: **Cover or less**
19 ❑ Feb 1994 Cover: 1.50 **NM** value: **Cover or less**
20 ❑ Mar 1994 Cover: 1.50 **NM** value: **Cover or less**
21 ❑ Apr 1994 Cover: 1.50 **NM** value: **Cover or less**
22 ❑ May 1994 Cover: 1.50 **NM** value: **Cover or less**
23 ❑ Jun 1994 Cover: 1.50 **NM** value: **Cover or less**
24 ❑ Jul 1994 Cover: 1.50 **NM** value: **Cover or less**
25 ❑ Aug 1994 Cover: 1.50 **NM** value: **Cover or less**
26 ❑ Sep 1994 Cover: 1.50 **NM** value: **Cover or less**
27 ❑ Oct 1994 Cover: 1.50 **NM** value: **Cover or less**
28 ❑ Nov 1994 Cover: 1.50 **NM** value: **Cover or less**

RICHIE RICH ADVENTURE DIGEST MAGAZINE — Harvey

1 ❑ May 1992 Cover: 1.75 **NM** value: **2.00**
2 ❑ Feb 1993 Cover: 1.75 **NM** value: **Cover or less**
3 ❑ Jun 1993 Cover: 1.75 **NM** value: **Cover or less**
4 ❑ Oct 1993 Cover: 1.75 **NM** value: **Cover or less**
5 ❑ Feb 1994 Cover: 1.75 **NM** value: **Cover or less**
6 ❑ Jun 1994 Cover: 1.75 **NM** value: **Cover or less**

RICHIE RICH AND BILLY BELLHOPS — Harvey

1 ❑ Oct 1977 Cover: 0.50 **NM** value: **5.00**

CGC-graded: Multiply prices above by **33 for 9.9 M** • **16 for 9.8 NM/M** • **7 for 9.6 NM+** • **5 for 9.4 NM** • **2.5 for 9.2 NM-** • **1.5 for 9.0 VF/NM**

RICHIE RICH AND CADBURY — Harvey

1 ❑ Oct 1977 Cover: 0.50 NM value: 15.00
• CGC: 1 graded, best 9.2
2 ❑ Sep 1978 Cover: 0.50 NM value: 10.00
3 ❑ Oct 1978 Cover: 0.50 NM value: 10.00
4 ❑ Cover: 0.50 NM value: 10.00
5 ❑ 1979 Cover: 0.50 NM value: 10.00
6 ❑ 1979 Cover: 0.50 NM value: 10.00
7 ❑ May 1979 Cover: 0.50 NM value: 10.00
8 ❑ 1979 Cover: 0.50 NM value: 10.00
9 ❑ 1979 Cover: 0.50 NM value: 10.00
10 ❑ Cover: 0.50 NM value: 10.00
11 ❑ 1980 Cover: 0.40 NM value: 5.00
12 ❑ 1980 Cover: 0.40 NM value: 5.00
13 ❑ 1980 Cover: 0.40 NM value: 4.00
14 ❑ 1980 Cover: 0.50 NM value: 4.00
15 ❑ Cover: 0.50 NM value: 4.00
16 ❑ 1981 Cover: 0.50 NM value: 4.00
17 ❑ 1981 Cover: 0.50 NM value: 4.00
18 ❑ Aug 1981 Cover: 0.50 NM value: 4.00
19 ❑ 1981 NM value: 4.00
20 ❑ Cover: 0.50 NM value: 3.00
21 ❑ NM value: 3.00
22 ❑ May 1982 Cover: 0.60 NM value: 3.00
23 ❑ Jul 1982 Cover: 0.60 NM value: 3.00
24 ❑ Jul 1990 Cover: 1.00 NM value: 3.00
25 ❑ Sep 1990 Cover: 1.00 NM value: 3.00
26 ❑ Oct 1990 Cover: 1.00 NM value: 3.00
27 ❑ Nov 1990 Cover: 1.00 NM value: 3.00
28 ❑ Dec 1990 Cover: 1.00 NM value: 3.00
29 ❑ Jan 1991 Cover: 1.00 NM value: 3.00

RICHIE RICH & CASPER — Harvey

1 ❑ Aug 1974 Cover: 0.25 NM value: 12.00
• CGC: 2 graded, best 9.2
2 ❑ Oct 1974 Cover: 0.25 NM value: 6.00
• CGC: 1 graded, best 9.0
3 ❑ Dec 1974 Cover: 0.25 NM value: 4.00
4 ❑ Feb 1975 Cover: 0.25 NM value: 4.00
5 ❑ Apr 1975 Cover: 0.25 NM value: 4.00
6 ❑ Jun 1975 Cover: 0.25 NM value: 3.00
7 ❑ Aug 1975 Cover: 0.25 NM value: 3.00
8 ❑ Oct 1975 Cover: 0.25 NM value: 3.00
9 ❑ Dec 1975 Cover: 0.25 NM value: 3.00
10 ❑ Feb 1976 Cover: 0.25 NM value: 3.00
11 ❑ Apr 1976 Cover: 0.25 NM value: 2.00
12 ❑ Jun 1976 Cover: 0.25 NM value: 2.00
13 ❑ Aug 1976 Cover: 0.25 NM value: 2.00
14 ❑ Oct 1976 Cover: 0.30 NM value: 2.00
📖 Heads I Win, Tails You Lose
15 ❑ Dec 1977 Cover: 0.30 NM value: 2.00
16 ❑ Feb 1977 Cover: 0.30 NM value: 2.00
17 ❑ Apr 1977 Cover: 0.30 NM value: 2.00
18 ❑ Jun 1977 Cover: 0.30 NM value: 2.00
19 ❑ Aug 1977 Cover: 0.30 NM value: 2.00
📖 Vacation; Come on to My House; Rich Ghosts; Work Like a Demon
20 ❑ Oct 1977 Cover: 0.35 NM value: 2.00
21 ❑ Dec 1977 Cover: 0.35 NM value: 2.00
22 ❑ Feb 1978 Cover: 0.35 NM value: 2.00
23 ❑ Apr 1978 Cover: 0.35 NM value: 2.00
24 ❑ Jul 1978 Cover: 0.35 NM value: 2.00
25 ❑ Sep 1978 Cover: 0.35 NM value: 2.00
26 ❑ Nov 1978 Cover: 0.35 NM value: 2.00
27 ❑ 1979 Cover: 0.35 NM value: 2.00
28 ❑ 1979 Cover: 0.35 NM value: 2.00
29 ❑ 1979 Cover: 0.35 NM value: 2.00
30 ❑ 1979 NM value: 2.00
31 ❑ 1979 NM value: 2.00
32 ❑ 1980 NM value: 2.00
33 ❑ 1980 NM value: 2.00
34 ❑ Jun 1980 Cover: 0.40 NM value: 2.00
35 ❑ 1980 NM value: 2.00
36 ❑ 1980 NM value: 2.00
37 ❑ 1980 NM value: 2.00
38 ❑ Mar 1981 Cover: 0.50 NM value: 2.00
39 ❑ 1981 Cover: 0.50 NM value: 2.00
40 ❑ Sep 1981 Cover: 0.50 NM value: 2.00
41 ❑ 1981 NM value: 2.00
42 ❑ 1982 NM value: 2.00
43 ❑ 1982 NM value: 2.00
44 ❑ 1982 Cover: 0.60 NM value: 2.00
45 ❑ Sep 1982 Cover: 0.60 NM value: 2.00

RICHIE RICH AND CASPER IN 3-D — Blackthorne

1/A ❑ Cover: 2.50 NM value: Cover or less
Circ: CapCity orders: 1,775
1/B ❑ Cover: 2.50 NM value: Cover or less
• Spanish; Burger King

RICHIE RICH & DOLLAR, THE DOG — Harvey

1 ❑ Sep 1977 Cover: 0.50 NM value: 5.00
📖 The Run-Away; Dog-Napped; Dressy Doggie; Canine Caper; Shadowed; The Dotted ClothLittle Lotta; Dot•Land; Uncle Touchy;
2 ❑ Cover: 0.50 NM value: 3.00
3 ❑ 1978 Cover: 0.50 NM value: 2.00
4 ❑ 1978 Cover: 0.50 NM value: 2.00
5 ❑ 1978 Cover: 0.50 NM value: 2.00
6 ❑ Cover: 0.50 NM value: 1.50
7 ❑ Apr 1979 Cover: 0.50 NM value: 1.50
8 ❑ Jun 1979 Cover: 0.50 NM value: 1.50
9 ❑ 1979 Cover: 0.50 NM value: 1.50
10 ❑ 1979 Cover: 0.50 NM value: 1.50
11 ❑ Cover: 0.40 NM value: 1.50
12 ❑ 1980 Cover: 0.40 NM value: 1.50
13 ❑ 1980 Cover: 0.40 NM value: 1.50
14 ❑ 1980 Cover: 0.40 NM value: 1.50
15 ❑ 1980 Cover: 0.50 NM value: 1.50
16 ❑ Cover: 0.50 NM value: 1.50
17 ❑ 1981 Cover: 0.50 NM value: 1.50
18 ❑ May 1981 Cover: 0.50 NM value: 1.50
19 ❑ 1981 Cover: 0.50 NM value: 1.50
20 ❑ Cover: 0.50 NM value: 1.50
21 ❑ Cover: 0.60 NM value: 1.50
22 ❑ 1982 Cover: 0.60 NM value: 1.50
23 ❑ Jun 1982 Cover: 0.60 NM value: 1.50
24 ❑ Aug 1982 Cover: 0.60 NM value: 1.50

RICHIE RICH AND DOT — Harvey

1 ❑ ca. 1974 Cover: 0.25 NM value: 20.00

RICHIE RICH AND GLORIA — Harvey

1 ❑ Sep 1977 Cover: 0.50 NM value: 10.00
2 ❑ 1978 Cover: 0.50 NM value: 8.00
3 ❑ Aug 1978 Cover: 0.50 NM value: 8.00
4 ❑ Oct 1978 Cover: 0.50 NM value: 8.00
5 ❑ Cover: 0.50 NM value: 8.00
6 ❑ 1979 Cover: 0.50 NM value: 8.00
7 ❑ 1979 Cover: 0.50 NM value: 8.00
8 ❑ 1979 Cover: 0.50 NM value: 8.00
9 ❑ 1979 Cover: 0.50 NM value: 8.00
10 ❑ Cover: 0.50 NM value: 8.00
11 ❑ Cover: 0.50 NM value: 5.00
12 ❑ Cover: 0.40 NM value: 5.00
13 ❑ 1980 Cover: 0.40 NM value: 5.00
14 ❑ 1980 Cover: 0.40 NM value: 5.00
15 ❑ 1980 Cover: 0.40 NM value: 5.00
16 ❑ 1980 Cover: 0.50 NM value: 5.00
17 ❑ Cover: 0.50 NM value: 5.00
18 ❑ Mar 1981 Cover: 0.50 NM value: 5.00
19 ❑ Jun 1981 Cover: 0.50 NM value: 5.00
20 ❑ Aug 1981 Cover: 0.50 NM value: 4.00
21 ❑ Oct 1981 Cover: 0.50 NM value: 4.00
22 ❑ Cover: 0.60 NM value: 4.00
23 ❑ Mar 1982 Cover: 0.60 NM value: 4.00
24 ❑ 1982 Cover: 0.60 NM value: 4.00
25 ❑ Sep 1982 Cover: 0.60 NM value: 4.00

RICHIE RICH AND HIS GIRLFRIENDS — Harvey

1 ❑ Apr 1979 Cover: 0.50 NM value: 10.00
2 ❑ Cover: 0.50 NM value: 8.00
3 ❑ Cover: 0.40 NM value: 8.00
4 ❑ 1980 Cover: 0.40 NM value: 8.00
5 ❑ 1980 Cover: 0.40 NM value: 8.00
6 ❑ Oct 1980 Cover: 0.50 NM value: 8.00
7 ❑ Cover: 0.50 NM value: 8.00
8 ❑ Cover: 0.50 NM value: 8.00
9 ❑ 1981 Cover: 0.50 NM value: 8.00
10 ❑ 1981 Cover: 0.50 NM value: 8.00
11 ❑ 1981 Cover: 0.50 NM value: 5.00
12 ❑ Dec 1981 Cover: 0.50 NM value: 5.00
13 ❑ 1982 NM value: 5.00
14 ❑ 1982 NM value: 5.00
15 ❑ 1982 Cover: 0.60 NM value: 5.00
16 ❑ Dec 1982 Cover: 0.60 NM value: 5.00

RICHIE RICH AND HIS MEAN COUSIN REGGIE — Harvey

1 ❑ Apr 1979 Cover: 0.50 NM value: 10.00
2 ❑ 1979 Cover: 0.50 NM value: 5.00
3 ❑ Jan 1980 Cover: 0.40 NM value: 5.00

RICHIE RICH & JACKIE JOKERS — Harvey

1 ❑ Nov 1973 Cover: 0.25 NM value: 18.00
• CGC: 2 graded, best 9.4
2 ❑ Jan 1974 Cover: 0.25 NM value: 10.00
3 ❑ Mar 1974 Cover: 0.25 NM value: 6.00
4 ❑ May 1974 Cover: 0.25 NM value: 6.00
5 ❑ Jul 1974 Cover: 0.25 NM value: 6.00
6 ❑ Sep 1974 Cover: 0.25 NM value: 4.00
7 ❑ Nov 1974 Cover: 0.25 NM value: 4.00
8 ❑ Jan 1975 Cover: 0.25 NM value: 4.00
9 ❑ Mar 1975 Cover: 0.25 NM value: 4.00
10 ❑ May 1975 Cover: 0.25 NM value: 4.00
11 ❑ Sep 1975 Cover: 0.25 NM value: 3.00
12 ❑ Nov 1975 Cover: 0.25 NM value: 3.00
13 ❑ Jan 1976 Cover: 0.25 NM value: 3.00
14 ❑ Mar 1976 Cover: 0.25 NM value: 3.00
15 ❑ May 1976 Cover: 0.25 NM value: 3.00
16 ❑ Jul 1976 Cover: 0.25 NM value: 3.00
17 ❑ Sep 1976 Cover: 0.25 NM value: 3.00
18 ❑ Nov 1976 Cover: 0.30 NM value: 3.00
19 ❑ Jan 1977 Cover: 0.30 NM value: 3.00
📖 Proud to Be; WelcomeJack Kotduh; Everybody's Going Ape • Welcome Back Kotter parody
20 ❑ Apr 1977 Cover: 0.30 NM value: 3.00
21 ❑ Jun 1977 Cover: 0.30 NM value: 3.00
22 ❑ Aug 1977 Cover: 0.30 NM value: 3.00
23 ❑ Oct 1977 Cover: 0.35 NM value: 3.00
24 ❑ Dec 1977 Cover: 0.35 NM value: 3.00
25 ❑ Feb 1978 Cover: 0.35 NM value: 3.00
26 ❑ Apr 1978 Cover: 0.35 NM value: 3.00
27 ❑ Jun 1978 Cover: 0.35 NM value: 3.00
28 ❑ Aug 1978 Cover: 0.35 NM value: 3.00
29 ❑ Oct 1978 Cover: 0.35 NM value: 3.00
30 ❑ Feb 1979 Cover: 0.35 NM value: 3.00
31 ❑ Apr 1979 Cover: 0.35 NM value: 2.00
32 ❑ Jun 1979 Cover: 0.35 NM value: 2.00
33 ❑ Aug 1979 Cover: 0.35 NM value: 2.00
34 ❑ Oct 1979 Cover: 0.40 NM value: 2.00
35 ❑ Dec 1979 Cover: 0.40 NM value: 2.00
36 ❑ Feb 1980 Cover: 0.40 NM value: 2.00
37 ❑ Apr 1980 Cover: 0.40 NM value: 2.00
38 ❑ Jul 1980 Cover: 0.40 NM value: 2.00
39 ❑ Sep 1980 Cover: 0.50 NM value: 2.00
40 ❑ Nov 1980 Cover: 0.50 NM value: 2.00
41 ❑ Jan 1981 Cover: 0.50 NM value: 2.00
42 ❑ Apr 1981 Cover: 0.50 NM value: 2.00
43 ❑ Jun 1981 Cover: 0.50 NM value: 2.00
44 ❑ Aug 1981 Cover: 0.50 NM value: 2.00
45 ❑ Nov 1981 Cover: 0.50 NM value: 2.00
46 ❑ Feb 1982 Cover: 0.60 NM value: 2.00
47 ❑ May 1982 Cover: 0.60 NM value: 2.00
48 ❑ Dec 1982 Cover: 0.60 NM value: 2.00

RICHIE RICH AND PROFESSOR KEENBEAN — Harvey

1 ❑ Sep 1990 Cover: 1.00 NM value: Cover or less
2 ❑ Nov 1990 Cover: 1.00 NM value: Cover or less

RICHIE RICH AND THE NEW KIDS ON THE BLOCK — Harvey

1 ❑ Feb 1991 Cover: 1.25 NM value: 1.50
Circ: CapCity orders: 2,850

RICHIE RICH AND TIMMY TIME — Harvey

1 ❑ ca. 1977 Cover: 0.50 NM value: 8.00

RICHIE RICH BANK BOOKS — Harvey

1 ❑ Oct 1972 Cover: 0.20 NM value: 24.00
2 ❑ Dec 1972 Cover: 0.20 NM value: 10.00
3 ❑ Feb 1973 Cover: 0.20 NM value: 6.00
4 ❑ Apr 1973 Cover: 0.20 NM value: 6.00
5 ❑ Jun 1973 Cover: 0.20 NM value: 6.00
6 ❑ Aug 1973 Cover: 0.20 NM value: 4.00
7 ❑ Oct 1973 Cover: 0.20 NM value: 4.00
8 ❑ Dec 1973 Cover: 0.20 NM value: 4.00
9 ❑ Feb 1974 Cover: 0.20 NM value: 4.00
10 ❑ Apr 1974 Cover: 0.20 NM value: 4.00
11 ❑ Jun 1974 Cover: 0.25 NM value: 3.00
12 ❑ Aug 1974 Cover: 0.25 NM value: 3.00
13 ❑ Oct 1974 Cover: 0.25 NM value: 3.00
14 ❑ Dec 1974 Cover: 0.25 NM value: 3.00
15 ❑ Feb 1975 Cover: 0.25 NM value: 3.00
16 ❑ Apr 1975 Cover: 0.25 NM value: 3.00
17 ❑ Jun 1975 Cover: 0.25 NM value: 3.00
18 ❑ Aug 1975 Cover: 0.25 NM value: 3.00
19 ❑ Oct 1975 Cover: 0.25 NM value: 3.00
20 ❑ Dec 1975 Cover: 0.25 NM value: 3.00
21 ❑ Feb 1976 Cover: 0.25 NM value: 2.00
22 ❑ Apr 1976 Cover: 0.25 NM value: 2.00
23 ❑ Jun 1976 Cover: 0.25 NM value: 2.00
24 ❑ Aug 1976 Cover: 0.25 NM value: 2.00
25 ❑ Oct 1976 Cover: 0.30 NM value: 2.00
26 ❑ Dec 1976 Cover: 0.30 NM value: 2.00
27 ❑ Feb 1977 Cover: 0.30 NM value: 2.00
28 ❑ Apr 1977 Cover: 0.30 NM value: 2.00
29 ❑ Jun 1977 Cover: 0.30 NM value: 2.00
30 ❑ Aug 1977 Cover: 0.30 NM value: 2.00
31 ❑ Sep 1977 Cover: 0.30 NM value: 2.00
32 ❑ Nov 1977 Cover: 0.35 NM value: 2.00
33 ❑ Jan 1978 Cover: 0.35 NM value: 2.00
34 ❑ Mar 1978 Cover: 0.35 NM value: 2.00
📖 The Genius of Long Ago; Fast Fortune; Tennis, Anyone?
35 ❑ May 1978 Cover: 0.35 NM value: 2.00
36 ❑ Aug 1978 Cover: 0.35 NM value: 2.00
37 ❑ Oct 1978 Cover: 0.35 NM value: 2.00
38 ❑ Jan 1979 Cover: 0.35 NM value: 2.00
39 ❑ Mar 1979 Cover: 0.35 NM value: 2.00
40 ❑ May 1979 Cover: 0.35 NM value: 2.00
41 ❑ Jul 1979 Cover: 0.35 NM value: 2.00
42 ❑ 1979 Cover: 0.40 NM value: 2.00
43 ❑ 1979 Cover: 0.40 NM value: 2.00
44 ❑ Dec 1979 Cover: 0.40 NM value: 2.00
45 ❑ Mar 1980 Cover: 0.40 NM value: 2.00
46 ❑ May 1980 Cover: 0.40 NM value: 2.00
47 ❑ Aug 1980 Cover: 0.40 NM value: 2.00
48 ❑ Oct 1980 Cover: 0.50 NM value: 2.00
49 ❑ Nov 1980 Cover: 0.50 NM value: 2.00
50 ❑ 1981 Cover: 0.50 NM value: 2.00
51 ❑ Apr 1981 Cover: 0.50 NM value: 2.00
52 ❑ Jun 1981 Cover: 0.50 NM value: 2.00
53 ❑ Aug 1981 Cover: 0.50 NM value: 2.00
54 ❑ Oct 1981 Cover: 0.50 NM value: 2.00
55 ❑ 1981 Cover: 0.50 NM value: 2.00
56 ❑ 1982 NM value: 2.00
57 ❑ 1982 NM value: 2.00
58 ❑ Jul 1982 Cover: 0.60 NM value: 2.00
59 ❑ Sep 1982 Cover: 0.60 NM value: 2.00

RICHIE RICH BEST OF THE YEARS — Harvey

1 ❑ ca. 1977 NM value: 10.00
2 ❑ ca. 1978 NM value: 6.00
3 ❑ ca. 1979 NM value: 6.00
4 ❑ ca. 1979 NM value: 6.00
5 ❑ ca. 1980 NM value: 6.00
6 ❑ ca. 1980 NM value: 6.00

RICHIE RICH BIG BOOK (VOL. 2) — Harvey

1 ❑ Nov 1992 Cover: 1.95 NM value: Cover or less
📖 Keep It Cool; Always Courteous; Little Dot: The Perfectionist; Little Lotta: Spurtin' Sports; Hard to Hide Part 1; Foolong the Fooler; Decoration Daze;
2 ❑ May 1993 Cover: 1.95 NM value: Cover or less

RICHIE RICH BIG BUCKS — Harvey

1 ❑ Apr 1991 Cover: 1.25 NM value: 2.00
Circ: CapCity orders: 1,900
2 ❑ Jun 1991 Cover: 1.25 NM value: Cover or less
Circ: CapCity orders: 1,100
3 ❑ Aug 1991 Cover: 1.25 NM value: Cover or less

Other grades: Multiply prices above by **1.5 for Mint • 2/3 for Very Fine • 1/3 for Fine • 1/5 for Very Good • 1/8 for Good**

4 ❑ 1991 Cover: 1.25 **NM** value: **Cover or less**
5 ❑ 1991 Cover: 1.25 **NM** value: **Cover or less**
6 ❑ 1992 Cover: 1.25 **NM** value: **Cover or less**
7 ❑ 1992 Cover: 1.25 **NM** value: **Cover or less**
8 ❑ 1992 Cover: 1.25 **NM** value: **Cover or less**

RICHIE RICH BILLIONS — Harvey

1 ❑ Oct 1974 **NM** value: **12.00**
• **CGC:** 1 graded, best 7.0
2 ❑ 1974 **NM** value: **7.00**
3 ❑ 1975 Cover: 0.35 **NM** value: **6.00**
4 ❑ 1975 Cover: 0.35 **NM** value: **5.00**
5 ❑ 1975 Cover: 0.35 **NM** value: **5.00**
6 ❑ 1975 Cover: 0.35 **NM** value: **4.00**
7 ❑ 1975 Cover: 0.35 **NM** value: **4.00**
8 ❑ 1976 Cover: 0.35 **NM** value: **4.00**
9 ❑ 1976 Cover: 0.35 **NM** value: **4.00**
10 ❑ 1976 Cover: 0.35 **NM** value: **4.00**
11 ❑ 1976 Cover: 0.35 **NM** value: **3.00**
12 ❑ Sep 1976 Cover: 0.35 **NM** value: **3.00**
13 ❑ 1976 **NM** value: **3.00**
14 ❑ 1977 **NM** value: **3.00**
15 ❑ 1977 **NM** value: **3.00**
16 ❑ 1977 **NM** value: **3.00**
17 ❑ 1977 **NM** value: **3.00**
18 ❑ 1977 **NM** value: **3.00**
19 ❑ Oct 1977 Cover: 0.50 **NM** value: **3.00**
20 ❑ 1977 Cover: 0.50 **NM** value: **3.00**
21 ❑ 1978 Cover: 0.50 **NM** value: **3.00**
22 ❑ 1978 Cover: 0.50 **NM** value: **3.00**
23 ❑ May 1978 Cover: 0.50 **NM** value: **3.00**
📖 Secrets; Guardian Butler; The Gourmet Chef!; Mayda's Plot; Ali Oops!; Haunted House
24 ❑ Jul 1978 Cover: 0.50 **NM** value: **3.00**
25 ❑ Sep 1978 Cover: 0.50 **NM** value: **3.00**
26 ❑ Nov 1978 Cover: 0.50 **NM** value: **3.00**
27 ❑ 1979 Cover: 0.50 **NM** value: **3.00**
28 ❑ Feb 1979 Cover: 0.50 **NM** value: **3.00**
29 ❑ Apr 1979 Cover: 0.50 **NM** value: **3.00**
30 ❑ Jun 1979 Cover: 0.50 **NM** value: **3.00**
31 ❑ 1979 Cover: 0.50 **NM** value: **2.00**
📖 Looking Out for Irona; Robot's Helper; The Microbe Ray; Swallowed Up; Dangerous Voyage; Ghostly Guarded Secret; Cadbury's Secret; Two Good to be True
32 ❑ 1979 Cover: 0.50 **NM** value: **2.00**
33 ❑ 1980 Cover: 0.50 **NM** value: **2.00**
34 ❑ 1980 **NM** value: **2.00**
35 ❑ 1980 **NM** value: **2.00**
36 ❑ 1980 **NM** value: **2.00**
37 ❑ 1980 **NM** value: **2.00**
38 ❑ Dec 1980 Cover: 0.50 **NM** value: **2.00**
39 ❑ Feb 1981 Cover: 0.50 **NM** value: **2.00**
40 ❑ Apr 1981 Cover: 0.50 **NM** value: **2.00**
41 ❑ 1981 Cover: 0.50 **NM** value: **2.00**
42 ❑ 1981 Cover: 0.50 **NM** value: **2.00**
43 ❑ 1981 Cover: 0.50 **NM** value: **2.00**
44 ❑ 1981 **NM** value: **2.00**
45 ❑ 1982 Cover: 0.60 **NM** value: **2.00**
46 ❑ May 1982 Cover: 0.60 **NM** value: **2.00**
47 ❑ 1982 **NM** value: **2.00**
48 ❑ 1982 **NM** value: **2.00**

RICHIE RICH CASH — Harvey

1 ❑ Sep 1974 Cover: 0.25 **NM** value: **10.00**
2 ❑ Nov 1974 Cover: 0.25 **NM** value: **6.00**
3 ❑ Jan 1975 Cover: 0.25 **NM** value: **4.00**
4 ❑ Mar 1975 Cover: 0.25 **NM** value: **4.00**
5 ❑ May 1975 Cover: 0.25 **NM** value: **4.00**
• **CGC:** 1 graded, best 9.0
6 ❑ Jul 1975 Cover: 0.25 **NM** value: **4.00**
7 ❑ Sep 1975 Cover: 0.25 **NM** value: **4.00**
8 ❑ Nov 1975 Cover: 0.25 **NM** value: **4.00**
9 ❑ Jan 1976 Cover: 0.25 **NM** value: **4.00**
10 ❑ Mar 1976 Cover: 0.25 **NM** value: **4.00**
11 ❑ 1976 Cover: 0.25 **NM** value: **3.00**
12 ❑ 1976 Cover: 0.25 **NM** value: **3.00**
13 ❑ Aug 1976 Cover: 0.25 **NM** value: **3.00**
14 ❑ Oct 1976 Cover: 0.30 **NM** value: **3.00**
15 ❑ Dec 1976 Cover: 0.30 **NM** value: **3.00**
16 ❑ Feb 1977 Cover: 0.30 **NM** value: **3.00**
17 ❑ Apr 1977 Cover: 0.30 **NM** value: **3.00**
18 ❑ Jun 1977 Cover: 0.30 **NM** value: **3.00**
19 ❑ Aug 1977 Cover: 0.30 **NM** value: **3.00**
20 ❑ 1977 Cover: 0.35 **NM** value: **3.00**
21 ❑ 1977 Cover: 0.35 **NM** value: **3.00**
22 ❑ Mar 1978 Cover: 0.35 **NM** value: **3.00**
23 ❑ May 1978 Cover: 0.35 **NM** value: **3.00**
📖 The World's Strangest Crook; Goddess of Puh-Lenty!; Little Dot: The Retirement of Uncle Cash (text story); Cadbury: Wildlife Appreciator
24 ❑ Jul 1978 Cover: 0.35 **NM** value: **3.00**
25 ❑ Sep 1978 Cover: 0.35 **NM** value: **3.00**
26 ❑ Dec 1978 Cover: 0.35 **NM** value: **3.00**
27 ❑ 1979 Cover: 0.35 **NM** value: **3.00**
28 ❑ 1979 Cover: 0.35 **NM** value: **3.00**
29 ❑ 1979 Cover: 0.35 **NM** value: **3.00**
30 ❑ 1979 Cover: 0.35 **NM** value: **3.00**
31 ❑ Sep 1979 Cover: 0.35 **NM** value: **2.00**
32 ❑ 1979 Cover: 0.40 **NM** value: **2.00**
33 ❑ 1980 Cover: 0.40 **NM** value: **2.00**
34 ❑ 1980 Cover: 0.40 **NM** value: **2.00**
35 ❑ Jun 1980 Cover: 0.40 **NM** value: **2.00**
36 ❑ Sep 1980 Cover: 0.50 **NM** value: **2.00**
37 ❑ Nov 1980 Cover: 0.50 **NM** value: **2.00**
38 ❑ Jan 1981 Cover: 0.50 **NM** value: **2.00**
39 ❑ Mar 1981 Cover: 0.50 **NM** value: **2.00**
40 ❑ May 1981 Cover: 0.50 **NM** value: **2.00**
41 ❑ Jul 1981 Cover: 0.50 **NM** value: **2.00**
42 ❑ Sep 1981 Cover: 0.50 **NM** value: **2.00**
43 ❑ Nov 1981 Cover: 0.50 **NM** value: **2.00**
44 ❑ 1982 **NM** value: **2.00**
45 ❑ Apr 1982 Cover: 0.60 **NM** value: **2.00**
46 ❑ Jun 1982 Cover: 0.60 **NM** value: **2.00**
47 ❑ Aug 1982 Cover: 0.60 **NM** value: **2.00**

RICHIE RICH CASH MONEY — Harvey

1 ❑ ca. 1992 Cover: 1.25 **NM** value: **1.50**
2 ❑ ca. 1992 Cover: 1.25 **NM** value: **1.50**

RICHIE RICH DIAMONDS — Harvey

1 ❑ Aug 1972 Cover: 0.25 **NM** value: **15.00**
• **CGC:** 1 graded, best 9.0
2 ❑ Oct 1972 Cover: 0.20 **NM** value: **9.00**
3 ❑ Dec 1972 Cover: 0.20 **NM** value: **7.00**
4 ❑ Feb 1973 Cover: 0.20 **NM** value: **7.00**
5 ❑ Apr 1973 Cover: 0.20 **NM** value: **7.00**
• **CGC:** 1 graded, best 9.4
6 ❑ Jun 1973 Cover: 0.20 **NM** value: **5.00**
7 ❑ Aug 1973 Cover: 0.20 **NM** value: **5.00**
8 ❑ Oct 1973 Cover: 0.20 **NM** value: **5.00**
9 ❑ Dec 1973 Cover: 0.20 **NM** value: **5.00**
10 ❑ Feb 1974 Cover: 0.20 **NM** value: **5.00**
11 ❑ Apr 1974 Cover: 0.20 **NM** value: **4.00**
12 ❑ Jun 1974 Cover: 0.25 **NM** value: **4.00**
13 ❑ Aug 1974 Cover: 0.25 **NM** value: **4.00**
14 ❑ Oct 1974 Cover: 0.25 **NM** value: **4.00**
15 ❑ Dec 1974 Cover: 0.25 **NM** value: **4.00**
16 ❑ Feb 1975 Cover: 0.25 **NM** value: **4.00**
17 ❑ Apr 1975 Cover: 0.25 **NM** value: **4.00**
18 ❑ Jun 1975 Cover: 0.25 **NM** value: **4.00**
19 ❑ Aug 1975 Cover: 0.25 **NM** value: **4.00**
20 ❑ Oct 1975 Cover: 0.25 **NM** value: **4.00**
21 ❑ Dec 1975 Cover: 0.25 **NM** value: **4.00**
22 ❑ Feb 1976 Cover: 0.25 **NM** value: **4.00**
23 ❑ Apr 1976 Cover: 0.35 **NM** value: **4.00**
📖 The Luckiest Kid; All that Glitters; A Born Loser; Bad Actor; The Jewelry Guard; Reggie: Around the World Rascal; Little Dot: Dot Luck
24 ❑ Jun 1976 Cover: 0.35 **NM** value: **4.00**
25 ❑ Aug 1976 Cover: 0.35 **NM** value: **4.00**
26 ❑ Oct 1976 Cover: 0.40 **NM** value: **4.00**
📖 The Mood Diamond; The Mood For a Million; The Idol Rich; Jealousy; Cadbury the Perfect Butler; The Amazing Ray; Surprise Package;
27 ❑ Dec 1976 Cover: 0.40 **NM** value: **4.00**
28 ❑ Feb 1977 Cover: 0.40 **NM** value: **4.00**
29 ❑ Mar 1977 Cover: 0.40 **NM** value: **4.00**
30 ❑ May 1977 Cover: 0.40 **NM** value: **4.00**
31 ❑ Jul 1977 **NM** value: **3.00**
32 ❑ Sep 1977 **NM** value: **3.00**
33 ❑ Nov 1977 **NM** value: **3.00**
34 ❑ Jan 1978 **NM** value: **3.00**
35 ❑ Mar 1978 **NM** value: **3.00**
36 ❑ May 1978 **NM** value: **3.00**
37 ❑ Jul 1978 Cover: 0.50 **NM** value: **3.00**
38 ❑ Sep 1978 Cover: 0.50 **NM** value: **3.00**
39 ❑ Nov 1978 Cover: 0.50 **NM** value: **3.00**
40 ❑ Jan 1979 Cover: 0.50 **NM** value: **3.00**
41 ❑ Mar 1979 Cover: 0.50 **NM** value: **2.00**
42 ❑ May 1979 Cover: 0.50 **NM** value: **2.00**
43 ❑ 1979 Cover: 0.50 **NM** value: **2.00**
44 ❑ 1979 Cover: 0.50 **NM** value: **2.00**
45 ❑ Cover: 0.50 **NM** value: **2.00**
46 ❑ 1980 **NM** value: **2.00**
47 ❑ 1980 **NM** value: **2.00**
48 ❑ 1980 **NM** value: **2.00**
49 ❑ 1980 Cover: 0.50 **NM** value: **2.00**
50 ❑ Nov 1980 Cover: 0.50 **NM** value: **2.00**
51 ❑ 1981 Cover: 0.50 **NM** value: **2.00**
52 ❑ 1981 Cover: 0.50 **NM** value: **2.00**
53 ❑ 1981 Cover: 0.50 **NM** value: **2.00**
54 ❑ 1981 Cover: 0.50 **NM** value: **2.00**
55 ❑ Nov 1981 Cover: 0.50 **NM** value: **2.00**
56 ❑ 1982 Cover: 0.50 **NM** value: **2.00**
57 ❑ 1982 **NM** value: **2.00**
58 ❑ Jun 1982 Cover: 0.60 **NM** value: **2.00**
59 ❑ Aug 1982 Cover: 0.60 **NM** value: **2.00**

RICHIE RICH DIGEST MAGAZINE — Harvey

1 ❑ Oct 1986 Cover: 1.25 **NM** value: **4.00**
2 ❑ Nov 1986 Cover: 1.25 **NM** value: **3.00**
3 ❑ Dec 1986 Cover: 1.25 **NM** value: **3.00**
4 ❑ Jan 1987 Cover: 1.25 **NM** value: **3.00**
5 ❑ Feb 1987 Cover: 1.25 **NM** value: **3.00**
6 ❑ Mar 1987 Cover: 1.75 **NM** value: **3.00**
7 ❑ Apr 1987 Cover: 1.75 **NM** value: **3.00**
8 ❑ Cover: 1.75 **NM** value: **3.00**
9 ❑ Cover: 1.75 **NM** value: **3.00**
10 ❑ Cover: 1.75 **NM** value: **3.00**
11 ❑ Cover: 1.75 **NM** value: **2.00**
12 ❑ Cover: 1.75 **NM** value: **2.00**
13 ❑ Cover: 1.75 **NM** value: **2.00**
14 ❑ Cover: 1.75 **NM** value: **2.00**
15 ❑ Cover: 1.75 **NM** value: **2.00**
16 ❑ Cover: 1.75 **NM** value: **2.00**
17 ❑ Cover: 1.75 **NM** value: **2.00**
18 ❑ Cover: 1.75 **NM** value: **2.00**
19 ❑ Cover: 1.75 **NM** value: **2.00**
20 ❑ Apr 1990 Cover: 1.75 **NM** value: **2.00**
📖 Kops 'n' Krooks Special
21 ❑ Jun 1990 Cover: 1.75 **NM** value: **2.00**
22 ❑ Aug 1990 Cover: 1.75 **NM** value: **2.00**
23 ❑ 1990 Cover: 1.75 **NM** value: **2.00**
24 ❑ 1990 Cover: 1.75 **NM** value: **2.00**
25 ❑ Cover: 1.75 **NM** value: **2.00**
26 ❑ Cover: 1.75 **NM** value: **2.00**
27 ❑ Cover: 1.75 **NM** value: **2.00**
28 ❑ 1991 Cover: 1.75 **NM** value: **2.00**
29 ❑ May 1991 Cover: 1.75 **NM** value: **2.00**
30 ❑ 1991 Cover: 1.75 **NM** value: **2.00**
31 ❑ Cover: 1.75 **NM** value: **2.00**
32 ❑ Cover: 1.75 **NM** value: **2.00**
33 ❑ Feb 1992 Cover: 1.75 **NM** value: **2.00**
34 ❑ Jun 1992 Cover: 1.75 **NM** value: **2.00**
35 ❑ Sep 1992 Cover: 1.75 **NM** value: **2.00**
36 ❑ Jan 1993 Cover: 1.75 **NM** value: **2.00**
37 ❑ May 1993 Cover: 1.75 **NM** value: **2.00**
38 ❑ Sep 1993 Cover: 1.75 **NM** value: **2.00**
39 ❑ Cover: 1.75 **NM** value: **2.00**
40 ❑ Cover: 1.75 **NM** value: **2.00**
41 ❑ Jul 1994 Cover: 1.75 **NM** value: **2.00**
42 ❑ Oct 1994 Cover: 1.75 **NM** value: **2.00**

RICHIE RICH DIGEST STORIES — Harvey

1 ❑ **NM** value: **10.00**
2 ❑ Cover: 0.75 **NM** value: **5.00**
3 ❑ **NM** value: **5.00**
4 ❑ **NM** value: **5.00**
5 ❑ **NM** value: **5.00**
6 ❑ **NM** value: **5.00**
7 ❑ **NM** value: **5.00**
8 ❑ **NM** value: **5.00**
9 ❑ **NM** value: **5.00**
10 ❑ **NM** value: **5.00**
11 ❑ **NM** value: **3.00**
12 ❑ **NM** value: **3.00**
13 ❑ **NM** value: **3.00**
14 ❑ **NM** value: **3.00**
15 ❑ **NM** value: **3.00**
16 ❑ **NM** value: **3.00**
17 ❑ **NM** value: **3.00**

RICHIE RICH DIGEST WINNERS — Harvey

1 ❑ **NM** value: **10.00**
2 ❑ **NM** value: **5.00**
3 ❑ **NM** value: **5.00**
4 ❑ **NM** value: **5.00**
5 ❑ **NM** value: **5.00**

RICHIE RICH DOLLARS & CENTS — Harvey

OK, so there are all these Richie Rich spin-off titles; Dollars and Cents, Bankbooks, Profits, Diamonds, Gems, Gold & Silver, ad infinitum, ad nauseum. Harvey was frequently had a dozen titles a month for everyone's favorite preteen plutocrat back in the 1970s. And, you're thinking, there's no way whatsoever to tell between them, right?

Well, there is, sort of. While the choice of stories to go into each appears to have been completely unconnected with the series title, it does appear that Harvey's artists took a look at the title they were working on when designing cover gags. Most issues of Dollar$ and ¢ents depict greenbacks, not diamonds — which were generally all that was found in gags on the covers of Gems and Diamonds. Gold & Silver depicted, well, gold and silver jokes.

No biggie, but you could look at these anonymous-looking covers for 20 years without noticing it. We did ... — JJM

1 ❑ Aug 1963 Cover: 0.25 **NM** value: **85.00**
2 ❑ Cover: 0.25 **NM** value: **45.00**
3 ❑ Cover: 0.25 **NM** value: **24.00**
4 ❑ Cover: 0.25 **NM** value: **24.00**
5 ❑ Cover: 0.25 **NM** value: **24.00**
6 ❑ Cover: 0.25 **NM** value: **16.00**
7 ❑ Cover: 0.25 **NM** value: **16.00**
8 ❑ Cover: 0.25 **NM** value: **16.00**
9 ❑ Cover: 0.25 **NM** value: **16.00**
10 ❑ Cover: 0.25 **NM** value: **16.00**
11 ❑ Cover: 0.25 **NM** value: **12.00**
12 ❑ Cover: 0.25 **NM** value: **12.00**
13 ❑ Cover: 0.25 **NM** value: **12.00**
14 ❑ Aug 1966 Cover: 0.25 **NM** value: **12.00**
15 ❑ Oct 1966 Cover: 0.25 **NM** value: **12.00**
16 ❑ Dec 1966 Cover: 0.25 **NM** value: **12.00**
17 ❑ Feb 1967 Cover: 0.25 **NM** value: **12.00**
18 ❑ Apr 1967 Cover: 0.25 **NM** value: **12.00**
19 ❑ Jun 1967 Cover: 0.25 **NM** value: **12.00**
20 ❑ Oct 1967 Cover: 0.25 **NM** value: **12.00**
21 ❑ Dec 1967 Cover: 0.25 **NM** value: **9.00**
22 ❑ Feb 1968 Cover: 0.25 **NM** value: **9.00**
23 ❑ Apr 1968 Cover: 0.25 **NM** value: **9.00**
24 ❑ Jun 1968 Cover: 0.25 **NM** value: **9.00**
25 ❑ Aug 1968 Cover: 0.25 **NM** value: **9.00**
26 ❑ Oct 1968 Cover: 0.25 **NM** value: **9.00**
27 ❑ Dec 1968 Cover: 0.25 **NM** value: **9.00**
28 ❑ Feb 1969 Cover: 0.25 **NM** value: **9.00**
29 ❑ Apr 1969 Cover: 0.25 **NM** value: **9.00**
30 ❑ May 1969 Cover: 0.25 **NM** value: **9.00**
31 ❑ Jul 1969 Cover: 0.25 **NM** value: **7.00**
32 ❑ Sep 1969 Cover: 0.25 **NM** value: **7.00**
33 ❑ Nov 1969 Cover: 0.25 **NM** value: **7.00**
34 ❑ Jan 1970 Cover: 0.25 **NM** value: **7.00**
35 ❑ Mar 1970 Cover: 0.25 **NM** value: **7.00**
36 ❑ May 1970 Cover: 0.25 **NM** value: **7.00**
37 ❑ Jul 1970 Cover: 0.25 **NM** value: **7.00**
38 ❑ Sep 1970 Cover: 0.25 **NM** value: **7.00**

CGC-graded: Multiply prices above by **33 for 9.9 M • 16 for 9.8 NM/M • 7 for 9.6 NM+ • 5 for 9.4 NM • 2.5 for 9.2 NM- • 1.5 for 9.0 VF/NM**

39 ❑ Nov 1970 Cover: 0.25 **NM** value: **7.00**
40 ❑ Jan 1971 Cover: 0.25 **NM** value: **7.00**
41 ❑ Mar 1971 Cover: 0.25 **NM** value: **5.00**
42 ❑ May 1971 Cover: 0.25 **NM** value: **5.00**
43 ❑ Jul 1971 Cover: 0.25 **NM** value: **5.00**
44 ❑ Sep 1971 Cover: 0.25 **NM** value: **5.00**
45 ❑ Nov 1971 Cover: 0.25 **NM** value: **5.00**
46 ❑ Jan 1972 Cover: 0.25 **NM** value: **5.00**
47 ❑ Mar 1972 Cover: 0.25 **NM** value: **5.00**
48 ❑ May 1972 Cover: 0.25 **NM** value: **5.00**
49 ❑ Jun 1972 Cover: 0.25 **NM** value: **5.00**
50 ❑ Aug 1972 Cover: 0.25 **NM** value: **5.00**
51 ❑ Oct 1972 Cover: 0.25 **NM** value: **4.00**
52 ❑ Dec 1972 Cover: 0.25 **NM** value: **4.00**
53 ❑ Feb 1973 Cover: 0.25 **NM** value: **4.00**
54 ❑ Apr 1973 Cover: 0.25 **NM** value: **4.00**
55 ❑ Jun 1973 Cover: 0.25 **NM** value: **4.00**
56 ❑ Aug 1973 Cover: 0.25 **NM** value: **4.00**
57 ❑ Oct 1973 Cover: 0.25 **NM** value: **4.00**
58 ❑ Dec 1973 Cover: 0.25 **NM** value: **4.00**
59 ❑ Feb 1974 Cover: 0.25 **NM** value: **4.00**
60 ❑ Apr 1974 Cover: 0.25 **NM** value: **4.00**
61 ❑ Jun 1974 Cover: 0.25 **NM** value: **2.50**
62 ❑ Aug 1974 Cover: 0.25 **NM** value: **2.50**
63 ❑ Oct 1974 Cover: 0.25 **NM** value: **2.50**
64 ❑ Dec 1974 Cover: 0.25 **NM** value: **2.50**
65 ❑ Feb 1975 Cover: 0.25 **NM** value: **2.50**
66 ❑ Apr 1975 Cover: 0.25 **NM** value: **2.50**
67 ❑ Jun 1975 Cover: 0.25 **NM** value: **2.50**
68 ❑ Aug 1975 Cover: 0.25 **NM** value: **2.50**
69 ❑ Oct 1975 Cover: 0.25 **NM** value: **2.50**
70 ❑ Dec 1975 Cover: 0.25 **NM** value: **2.50**
71 ❑ Feb 1976 Cover: 0.25 **NM** value: **2.00**
72 ❑ Apr 1976 Cover: 0.35 **NM** value: **2.00**
73 ❑ Jun 1976 Cover: 0.35 **NM** value: **2.00**
74 ❑ Aug 1976 Cover: 0.35 **NM** value: **2.00**
📖 Crook Watchers; Dollar Allowance; Real Fun Business; Richie Rich and the Instant Uglies!; Little Lotta: The Ample Camper; Irona: Replacement Robot; Reggie: Like Now!
75 ❑ Sep 1976 Cover: 0.35 **NM** value: **2.00**
76 ❑ Nov 1976 Cover: 0.40 **NM** value: **2.00**
77 ❑ Jan 1977 Cover: 0.40 **NM** value: **2.00**
78 ❑ Mar 1977 Cover: 0.40 **NM** value: **2.00**
79 ❑ May 1977 Cover: 0.40 **NM** value: **2.00**
80 ❑ Jul 1977 Cover: 0.40 **NM** value: **2.00**
81 ❑ Sep 1977 Cover: 0.50 **NM** value: **2.00**
82 ❑ Oct 1977 Cover: 0.50 **NM** value: **2.00**
83 ❑ Dec 1977 Cover: 0.50 **NM** value: **2.00**
84 ❑ Feb 1978 Cover: 0.50 **NM** value: **2.00**
85 ❑ Apr 1978 Cover: 0.50 **NM** value: **2.00**
86 ❑ Jun 1978 Cover: 0.50 **NM** value: **2.00**
87 ❑ Aug 1978 Cover: 0.50 **NM** value: **2.00**
88 ❑ Oct 1978 Cover: 0.50 **NM** value: **2.00**
89 ❑ Cover: 0.50 **NM** value: **2.00**
90 ❑ 1979 Cover: 0.50 **NM** value: **2.00**
91 ❑ 1979 Cover: 0.50 **NM** value: **1.25**
92 ❑ 1979 Cover: 0.50 **NM** value: **1.25**
93 ❑ 1979 Cover: 0.50 **NM** value: **1.25**
94 ❑ 1979 Cover: 0.50 **NM** value: **1.25**
95 ❑ Cover: 0.40 **NM** value: **1.25**
96 ❑ Apr 1980 Cover: 0.40 **NM** value: **1.25**
97 ❑ 1980 Cover: 0.40 **NM** value: **1.25**
98 ❑ Sep 1980 Cover: 0.50 **NM** value: **1.25**
99 ❑ Nov 1980 Cover: 0.50 **NM** value: **1.25**
100 ❑ Jan 1981 Cover: 0.50 **NM** value: **1.25**
101 ❑ Mar 1981 Cover: 0.50 **NM** value: **1.25**
102 ❑ May 1981 Cover: 0.50 **NM** value: **1.25**
103 ❑ 1981 Cover: 0.50 **NM** value: **1.25**
104 ❑ 1981 Cover: 0.50 **NM** value: **1.25**
105 ❑ 1981 Cover: 0.50 **NM** value: **1.25**
106 ❑ 1982 **NM** value: **1.25**
107 ❑ Apr 1982 Cover: 0.60 **NM** value: **1.25**
108 ❑ Jun 1982 Cover: 0.60 **NM** value: **1.25**
109 ❑ Aug 1982 Cover: 0.60 **NM** value: **1.25**
final issue.

RICHIE RICH FORTUNES — Harvey

1 ❑ Sep 1971 Cover: 0.25 **NM** value: **25.00**
• **CGC:** 1 graded, best 9.0
2 ❑ Nov 1971 Cover: 0.25 **NM** value: **10.00**
3 ❑ Jan 1972 Cover: 0.25 **NM** value: **7.00**
4 ❑ Mar 1972 Cover: 0.25 **NM** value: **7.00**
5 ❑ May 1972 Cover: 0.25 **NM** value: **7.00**
6 ❑ Jul 1972 Cover: 0.25 **NM** value: **5.00**
7 ❑ Sep 1972 Cover: 0.25 **NM** value: **5.00**
8 ❑ Jan 1973 Cover: 0.25 **NM** value: **5.00**
9 ❑ Mar 1973 Cover: 0.25 **NM** value: **5.00**
10 ❑ May 1973 Cover: 0.25 **NM** value: **5.00**
• **CGC:** 1 graded, best 9.0
11 ❑ Jul 1973 Cover: 0.25 **NM** value: **4.00**
12 ❑ Sep 1973 Cover: 0.25 **NM** value: **4.00**
13 ❑ Nov 1973 Cover: 0.25 **NM** value: **4.00**
14 ❑ Jan 1974 Cover: 0.25 **NM** value: **4.00**
15 ❑ Mar 1974 Cover: 0.25 **NM** value: **4.00**
• **CGC:** 1 graded, best 9.4
16 ❑ May 1974 Cover: 0.25 **NM** value: **4.00**
17 ❑ Jul 1974 Cover: 0.25 **NM** value: **4.00**
18 ❑ Sep 1974 Cover: 0.25 **NM** value: **4.00**
19 ❑ Nov 1974 Cover: 0.25 **NM** value: **4.00**
20 ❑ Jan 1975 Cover: 0.25 **NM** value: **4.00**
21 ❑ Mar 1975 Cover: 0.25 **NM** value: **3.00**
22 ❑ May 1975 Cover: 0.25 **NM** value: **3.00**
23 ❑ Jul 1975 Cover: 0.25 **NM** value: **3.00**
24 ❑ Sep 1975 Cover: 0.25 **NM** value: **3.00**
25 ❑ Nov 1975 Cover: 0.25 **NM** value: **3.00**
26 ❑ Jan 1976 Cover: 0.25 **NM** value: **3.00**
27 ❑ Mar 1976 Cover: 0.25 **NM** value: **3.00**
28 ❑ May 1976 Cover: 0.25 **NM** value: **3.00**
29 ❑ Jul 1976 Cover: 0.25 **NM** value: **3.00**
30 ❑ Sep 1976 Cover: 0.25 **NM** value: **3.00**
31 ❑ Nov 1976 Cover: 0.30 **NM** value: **3.00**
32 ❑ Jan 1977 Cover: 0.30 **NM** value: **3.00**
33 ❑ Mar 1977 Cover: 0.30 **NM** value: **3.00**
34 ❑ May 1977 Cover: 0.30 **NM** value: **3.00**
35 ❑ Jul 1977 Cover: 0.30 **NM** value: **3.00**
36 ❑ Sep 1977 Cover: 0.30 **NM** value: **3.00**
37 ❑ Nov 1977 Cover: 0.35 **NM** value: **3.00**
38 ❑ Jan 1978 Cover: 0.35 **NM** value: **3.00**
📖 The Tickle Bee-Hickle; Skidaddle!; Mayda Munny: The Papers; Little Dot: The Signs
39 ❑ Mar 1978 Cover: 0.35 **NM** value: **3.00**
40 ❑ May 1978 Cover: 0.35 **NM** value: **3.00**
41 ❑ Jul 1978 Cover: 0.35 **NM** value: **2.00**
42 ❑ Sep 1978 Cover: 0.35 **NM** value: **2.00**
43 ❑ Dec 1978 Cover: 0.35 **NM** value: **2.00**
44 ❑ Feb 1979 Cover: 0.35 **NM** value: **2.00**
45 ❑ Apr 1979 Cover: 0.35 **NM** value: **2.00**
46 ❑ Jun 1979 Cover: 0.35 **NM** value: **2.00**
47 ❑ Aug 1979 Cover: 0.35 **NM** value: **2.00**
48 ❑ Oct 1979 Cover: 0.40 **NM** value: **2.00**
49 ❑ Dec 1979 Cover: 0.40 **NM** value: **2.00**
50 ❑ Mar 1980 Cover: 0.40 **NM** value: **2.00**
51 ❑ May 1980 Cover: 0.40 **NM** value: **2.00**
52 ❑ Aug 1980 Cover: 0.40 **NM** value: **2.00**
53 ❑ Oct 1980 Cover: 0.50 **NM** value: **2.00**
54 ❑ Nov 1980 Cover: 0.50 **NM** value: **2.00**
55 ❑ Mar 1981 Cover: 0.50 **NM** value: **2.00**
56 ❑ May 1981 Cover: 0.50 **NM** value: **2.00**
57 ❑ Jul 1981 Cover: 0.50 **NM** value: **2.00**
58 ❑ Sep 1981 Cover: 0.50 **NM** value: **2.00**
59 ❑ Nov 1981 Cover: 0.50 **NM** value: **2.00**
60 ❑ Jan 1982 Cover: 0.60 **NM** value: **2.00**
61 ❑ Mar 1982 Cover: 0.60 **NM** value: **2.00**
62 ❑ Jun 1982 Cover: 0.60 **NM** value: **2.00**
63 ❑ Aug 1982 Cover: 0.60 **NM** value: **2.00**

RICHIE RICH GEMS — Harvey

1 ❑ Sep 1974 Cover: 0.25 **NM** value: **10.00**
• 1st Appearance of Professor Keenbean and Professor Inventos.
2 ❑ Nov 1974 Cover: 0.25 **NM** value: **6.00**
3 ❑ Jan 1975 Cover: 0.25 **NM** value: **4.00**
4 ❑ Mar 1975 Cover: 0.25 **NM** value: **4.00**
5 ❑ May 1975 Cover: 0.25 **NM** value: **4.00**
6 ❑ Jul 1975 Cover: 0.25 **NM** value: **3.00**
7 ❑ Sep 1975 Cover: 0.25 **NM** value: **3.00**
8 ❑ Nov 1975 Cover: 0.25 **NM** value: **3.00**
9 ❑ Jan 1976 Cover: 0.25 **NM** value: **3.00**
10 ❑ Mar 1976 Cover: 0.25 **NM** value: **3.00**
11 ❑ May 1976 Cover: 0.25 **NM** value: **2.00**
📖 The Big Jewel Movement!; The Exercising Machine; Mayda Munny: The Richie Attractor; The Big Diamond Counting Adventure (text story); Penny Van Dough: Baby Power
12 ❑ Jul 1976 Cover: 0.25 **NM** value: **2.00**
13 ❑ Sep 1976 Cover: 0.25 **NM** value: **2.00**
14 ❑ Nov 1976 Cover: 0.30 **NM** value: **2.00**
15 ❑ Jan 1977 Cover: 0.30 **NM** value: **2.00**
16 ❑ Mar 1977 Cover: 0.30 **NM** value: **2.00**
17 ❑ May 1977 Cover: 0.30 **NM** value: **2.00**
18 ❑ Jul 1977 Cover: 0.30 **NM** value: **2.00**
19 ❑ Sep 1977 Cover: 0.30 **NM** value: **2.00**
20 ❑ Nov 1977 Cover: 0.35 **NM** value: **2.00**
21 ❑ Jan 1978 Cover: 0.35 **NM** value: **2.00**
22 ❑ Mar 1978 Cover: 0.35 **NM** value: **2.00**
23 ❑ 1978 Cover: 0.35 **NM** value: **2.00**
24 ❑ Nov 1978 Cover: 0.35 **NM** value: **2.00**
25 ❑ Jan 1979 Cover: 0.35 **NM** value: **2.00**
26 ❑ Jul 1979 Cover: 0.35 **NM** value: **2.00**
27 ❑ Sep 1979 Cover: 0.40 **NM** value: **2.00**
28 ❑ 1979 Cover: 0.40 **NM** value: **2.00**
29 ❑ Feb 1980 Cover: 0.40 **NM** value: **2.00**
30 ❑ 1980 Cover: 0.40 **NM** value: **2.00**
31 ❑ Jul 1980 Cover: 0.40 **NM** value: **2.00**
32 ❑ Sep 1980 Cover: 0.50 **NM** value: **2.00**
33 ❑ Nov 1980 Cover: 0.50 **NM** value: **2.00**
34 ❑ Jan 1981 Cover: 0.50 **NM** value: **2.00**
35 ❑ Mar 1981 Cover: 0.50 **NM** value: **2.00**
36 ❑ May 1981 Cover: 0.50 **NM** value: **2.00**
37 ❑ Aug 1981 Cover: 0.50 **NM** value: **2.00**
38 ❑ Oct 1981 Cover: 0.50 **NM** value: **2.00**
39 ❑ Dec 1981 Cover: 0.50 **NM** value: **2.00**
40 ❑ Feb 1982 Cover: 0.60 **NM** value: **2.00**
41 ❑ Apr 1982 Cover: 0.60 **NM** value: **2.00**
42 ❑ 1982 Cover: 0.60 **NM** value: **2.00**
43 ❑ Sep 1982 Cover: 0.60 **NM** value: **2.00**

RICHIE RICH GIANT SIZE — Harvey

1 ❑ Cover: 2.25 **NM** value: **Cover or less**
2 ❑ Cover: 2.25 **NM** value: **Cover or less**
3 ❑ Cover: 2.25 **NM** value: **Cover or less**
4 ❑ Cover: 2.25 **NM** value: **Cover or less**

RICHIE RICH GOLD AND SILVER — Harvey

1 ❑ Sep 1975 Cover: 0.35 **NM** value: **10.00**
• **CGC:** 1 graded, best 9.2
2 ❑ 1975 Cover: 0.35 **NM** value: **6.00**
3 ❑ 1976 Cover: 0.35 **NM** value: **4.00**
4 ❑ 1976 Cover: 0.35 **NM** value: **4.00**
5 ❑ 1976 Cover: 0.35 **NM** value: **4.00**
6 ❑ 1976 Cover: 0.35 **NM** value: **3.00**
7 ❑ Aug 1976 Cover: 0.35 **NM** value: **3.00**
8 ❑ Oct 1976 Cover: 0.40 **NM** value: **3.00**
📖 The Sneezer; Super Prankster; The Trespasser Discourager; Mum's the Word!; Uncle Tuckaway; Little Dot:Cool It, Baby; Little Lotta: Caught in the Act!
9 ❑ Dec 1976 Cover: 0.40 **NM** value: **3.00**
10 ❑ Feb 1977 Cover: 0.40 **NM** value: **3.00**
11 ❑ 1977 Cover: 0.40 **NM** value: **2.00**
12 ❑ 1977 Cover: 0.40 **NM** value: **2.00**
13 ❑ Jul 1977 Cover: 0.40 **NM** value: **2.00**
14 ❑ Sep 1977 Cover: 0.50 **NM** value: **2.00**
15 ❑ Nov 1977 Cover: 0.50 **NM** value: **2.00**
16 ❑ Jan 1978 Cover: 0.50 **NM** value: **2.00**
17 ❑ Mar 1978 Cover: 0.50 **NM** value: **2.00**
18 ❑ May 1978 Cover: 0.50 **NM** value: **2.00**
19 ❑ Jul 1978 Cover: 0.50 **NM** value: **2.00**
20 ❑ Sep 1978 Cover: 0.50 **NM** value: **2.00**
21 ❑ Nov 1978 Cover: 0.50 **NM** value: **2.00**
22 ❑ Jan 1979 Cover: 0.50 **NM** value: **2.00**
23 ❑ Mar 1979 Cover: 0.50 **NM** value: **2.00**
24 ❑ May 1979 Cover: 0.50 **NM** value: **2.00**
25 ❑ Jul 1979 Cover: 0.50 **NM** value: **2.00**
26 ❑ Sep 1979 Cover: 0.50 **NM** value: **2.00**
27 ❑ Cover: 0.50 **NM** value: **2.00**
28 ❑ Cover: 0.40 **NM** value: **2.00**
29 ❑ Cover: 0.40 **NM** value: **2.00**
30 ❑ Cover: 0.40 **NM** value: **2.00**
31 ❑ Cover: 0.50 **NM** value: **2.00**
32 ❑ Cover: 0.50 **NM** value: **2.00**
33 ❑ Cover: 0.50 **NM** value: **2.00**
34 ❑ Cover: 0.50 **NM** value: **2.00**
35 ❑ Cover: 0.50 **NM** value: **2.00**
36 ❑ Cover: 0.50 **NM** value: **2.00**
37 ❑ Cover: 0.50 **NM** value: **2.00**
38 ❑ Cover: 0.50 **NM** value: **2.00**
39 ❑ 1982 Cover: 0.60 **NM** value: **2.00**
40 ❑ May 1982 Cover: 0.60 **NM** value: **2.00**
41 ❑ 1982 Cover: 0.60 **NM** value: **2.00**
42 ❑ Oct 1982 Cover: 0.60 **NM** value: **2.00**

RICHIE RICH GOLD NUGGETS DIGEST MAGAZINE — Harvey

1 ❑ Cover: 1.75 **NM** value: **2.00**
2 ❑ Cover: 1.75 **NM** value: **2.00**
3 ❑ Apr 1991 Cover: 1.75 **NM** value: **2.00**
4 ❑ Cover: 1.75 **NM** value: **2.00**

RICHIE RICH HOLIDAY DIGEST — Harvey

1 ❑ **NM** value: **3.00**
2 ❑ **NM** value: **2.00**
3 ❑ **NM** value: **2.00**
4 ❑ **NM** value: **2.00**
5 ❑ **NM** value: **2.00**

RICHIE RICH INVENTIONS — Harvey

1 ❑ Oct 1977 Cover: 0.50 **NM** value: **10.00**
★ Appear
2 ❑ Cover: 0.50 **NM** value: **6.00**
3 ❑ Cover: 0.50 **NM** value: **6.00**
4 ❑ Cover: 0.50 **NM** value: **6.00**
5 ❑ Cover: 0.50 **NM** value: **6.00**
6 ❑ Cover: 0.50 **NM** value: **6.00**
7 ❑ Cover: 0.50 **NM** value: **6.00**
8 ❑ Cover: 0.50 **NM** value: **6.00**
9 ❑ Cover: 0.50 **NM** value: **6.00**
10 ❑ Cover: 0.50 **NM** value: **6.00**
11 ❑ Cover: 0.50 **NM** value: **4.00**
12 ❑ Cover: 0.50 **NM** value: **4.00**
13 ❑ Cover: 0.50 **NM** value: **4.00**
14 ❑ Cover: 0.50 **NM** value: **4.00**
15 ❑ Cover: 0.50 **NM** value: **4.00**
16 ❑ Cover: 0.50 **NM** value: **4.00**
17 ❑ Cover: 0.50 **NM** value: **4.00**
18 ❑ Apr 1981 Cover: 0.50 **NM** value: **4.00**
19 ❑ Jun 1981 Cover: 0.50 **NM** value: **4.00**
20 ❑ Aug 1981 Cover: 0.50 **NM** value: **3.00**
21 ❑ Oct 1981 Cover: 0.50 **NM** value: **3.00**
22 ❑ Feb 1981 Cover: 0.60 **NM** value: **3.00**
23 ❑ Apr 1982 Cover: 0.60 **NM** value: **3.00**
24 ❑ Jun 1982 Cover: 0.60 **NM** value: **3.00**
25 ❑ Aug 1982 Cover: 0.60 **NM** value: **3.00**
26 ❑ Oct 1982 Cover: 0.60 **NM** value: **3.00**

RICHIE RICH JACKPOTS — Harvey

1 ❑ Oct 1972 Cover: 0.20 **NM** value: **30.00**
• **CGC:** 2 graded, best 9.6
2 ❑ Dec 1972 Cover: 0.20 **NM** value: **12.00**
3 ❑ Feb 1973 Cover: 0.20 **NM** value: **8.00**
4 ❑ Apr 1973 Cover: 0.20 **NM** value: **8.00**
5 ❑ Jun 1973 Cover: 0.20 **NM** value: **8.00**
6 ❑ Aug 1973 Cover: 0.20 **NM** value: **6.00**
7 ❑ Oct 1973 Cover: 0.20 **NM** value: **6.00**
8 ❑ Dec 1973 Cover: 0.20 **NM** value: **6.00**
9 ❑ Feb 1974 Cover: 0.20 **NM** value: **4.00**
10 ❑ Apr 1974 Cover: 0.20 **NM** value: **4.00**
11 ❑ Jun 1974 Cover: 0.25 **NM** value: **4.00**
12 ❑ Aug 1974 Cover: 0.25 **NM** value: **4.00**
13 ❑ Oct 1974 Cover: 0.25 **NM** value: **4.00**
14 ❑ Dec 1974 Cover: 0.25 **NM** value: **4.00**
15 ❑ Feb 1975 Cover: 0.25 **NM** value: **4.00**
16 ❑ Apr 1975 Cover: 0.25 **NM** value: **4.00**
17 ❑ Jun 1975 Cover: 0.25 **NM** value: **4.00**
18 ❑ Aug 1975 Cover: 0.25 **NM** value: **4.00**
19 ❑ Oct 1975 Cover: 0.25 **NM** value: **4.00**
20 ❑ Dec 1975 Cover: 0.25 **NM** value: **4.00**
21 ❑ Feb 1976 Cover: 0.25 **NM** value: **3.00**
22 ❑ Apr 1976 Cover: 0.25 **NM** value: **3.00**
📖 Through the Mists of Time; Mayda Munny: The Bad Actor; At Home With Richie Rich (text story); Irona: Menace, Anyone?
23 ❑ Jun 1976 Cover: 0.25 **NM** value: **3.00**
24 ❑ Aug 1976 Cover: 0.25 **NM** value: **3.00**
25 ❑ Oct 1976 Cover: 0.30 **NM** value: **3.00**

Other grades: Multiply prices above by **1.5 for Mint • 2/3 for Very Fine • 1/3 for Fine • 1/5 for Very Good • 1/8 for Good**

26 ❑ Dec 1976 Cover: 0.30 **NM** value: **3.00**
27 ❑ Feb 1977 Cover: 0.30 **NM** value: **3.00**
28 ❑ Apr 1977 Cover: 0.30 **NM** value: **3.00**
29 ❑ Jun 1977 Cover: 0.30 **NM** value: **3.00**
30 ❑ Aug 1977 **NM** value: **3.00**
31 ❑ Oct 1977 **NM** value: **3.00**
32 ❑ Dec 1977 Cover: 0.35 **NM** value: **3.00**
33 ❑ Feb 1978 Cover: 0.35 **NM** value: **3.00**
34 ❑ Apr 1978 Cover: 0.35 **NM** value: **3.00**
35 ❑ Jun 1978 Cover: 0.35 **NM** value: **3.00**
36 ❑ Aug 1978 Cover: 0.35 **NM** value: **3.00**
37 ❑ Oct 1978 Cover: 0.35 **NM** value: **3.00**
38 ❑ Dec 1978 Cover: 0.35 **NM** value: **3.00**
39 ❑ Feb 1979 Cover: 0.35 **NM** value: **3.00**
40 ❑ Apr 1979 Cover: 0.35 **NM** value: **3.00**
41 ❑ Jun 1979 Cover: 0.50 **NM** value: **2.00**
42 ❑ Aug 1979 Cover: 0.50 **NM** value: **2.00**
43 ❑ Oct 1979 Cover: 0.50 **NM** value: **2.00**
44 ❑ 1980 **NM** value: **2.00**
45 ❑ Apr 1980 Cover: 0.50 **NM** value: **2.00**
46 ❑ Jun 1980 Cover: 0.50 **NM** value: **2.00**
47 ❑ Aug 1980 Cover: 0.50 **NM** value: **2.00**
48 ❑ Oct 1980 Cover: 0.50 **NM** value: **2.00**
49 ❑ Dec 1980 Cover: 0.50 **NM** value: **2.00**
50 ❑ Feb 1981 Cover: 0.50 **NM** value: **2.00**
51 ❑ Apr 1981 Cover: 0.50 **NM** value: **2.00**
52 ❑ Jun 1981 Cover: 0.50 **NM** value: **2.00**
53 ❑ Aug 1981 Cover: 0.50 **NM** value: **2.00**
54 ❑ Oct 1981 Cover: 0.50 **NM** value: **2.00**
55 ❑ 1982 Cover: 0.60 **NM** value: **2.00**
56 ❑ Apr 1982 Cover: 0.60 **NM** value: **2.00**
57 ❑ Jun 1982 Cover: 0.60 **NM** value: **2.00**
58 ❑ Aug 1982 Cover: 0.60 **NM** value: **2.00**

RICHIE RICH MILLION DOLLAR DIGEST Harvey

1 ❑ Nov 1986 Cover: 1.25 **NM** value: **5.00**
2 ❑ Jan 1987 Cover: 1.25 **NM** value: **3.00**
3 ❑ Mar 1987 Cover: 1.25 **NM** value: **3.00**
4 ❑ May 1987 Cover: 1.25 **NM** value: **3.00**
5 ❑ Jul 1987 Cover: 1.25 **NM** value: **3.00**
6 ❑ Sep 1987 Cover: 1.25 **NM** value: **3.00**
7 ❑ Nov 1987 Cover: 1.75 **NM** value: **3.00**
8 ❑ 1988 Cover: 1.75 **NM** value: **3.00**
9 ❑ 1988 Cover: 1.75 **NM** value: **3.00**
10 ❑ 1988 Cover: 1.75 **NM** value: **3.00**
11 ❑ Cover: 1.75 **NM** value: **2.00**
12 ❑ 1989 Cover: 1.75 **NM** value: **2.00**
13 ❑ Aug 1989 Cover: 1.75 **NM** value: **2.00**
14 ❑ 1989 Cover: 1.75 **NM** value: **2.00**
15 ❑ Cover: 1.75 **NM** value: **2.00**
16 ❑ 1990 Cover: 1.75 **NM** value: **2.00**
17 ❑ 1990 Cover: 1.75 **NM** value: **2.00**
18 ❑ 1990 Cover: 1.75 **NM** value: **2.00**
19 ❑ Cover: 1.75 **NM** value: **2.00**
20 ❑ 1991 Cover: 1.75 **NM** value: **2.00**
21 ❑ 1991 Cover: 1.75 **NM** value: **2.00**
22 ❑ Aug 1991 Cover: 1.75 **NM** value: **2.00**
23 ❑ Cover: 1.75 **NM** value: **2.00**
24 ❑ 1992 Cover: 1.75 **NM** value: **2.00**
25 ❑ 1992 Cover: 1.75 **NM** value: **2.00**
26 ❑ Jul 1992 Cover: 1.75 **NM** value: **2.00**
27 ❑ Nov 1992 Cover: 1.75 **NM** value: **2.00**
28 ❑ Mar 1993 Cover: 1.75 **NM** value: **2.00**
29 ❑ Jul 1993 Cover: 1.75 **NM** value: **2.00**
30 ❑ Nov 1993 Cover: 1.75 **NM** value: **2.00**
31 ❑ Mar 1994 Cover: 1.75 **NM** value: **2.00**
32 ❑ May 1994 Cover: 1.75 **NM** value: **2.00**
33 ❑ Aug 1994 Cover: 1.75 **NM** value: **2.00**
34 ❑ Nov 1994 Cover: 1.75 **NM** value: **2.00**

RICHIE RICH MILLIONS Harvey

1 ❑ Sep 1961 Cover: 0.25 **NM** value: **90.00**
2 ❑ Sep 1962 Cover: 0.25 **NM** value: **50.00**
3 ❑ Dec 1962 Cover: 0.25 **NM** value: **35.00**
4 ❑ Mar 1963 Cover: 0.25 **NM** value: **28.00**
5 ❑ Jun 1963 Cover: 0.25 **NM** value: **28.00**
6 ❑ Sep 1963 Cover: 0.25 **NM** value: **20.00**
7 ❑ Dec 1963 Cover: 0.25 **NM** value: **20.00**
8 ❑ Mar 1964 Cover: 0.25 **NM** value: **16.00**
9 ❑ Jun 1964 Cover: 0.25 **NM** value: **16.00**
10 ❑ Sep 1964 Cover: 0.25 **NM** value: **16.00**
11 ❑ Dec 1964 Cover: 0.25 **NM** value: **13.00**
12 ❑ Mar 1965 Cover: 0.25 **NM** value: **13.00**
Suspicion; Desperate Customers; Greymoor Castle; Little Dot and Uncle Honker; Brownie's Honor (text story); Pretty Boy (text story); The Right Shape; The Molehill Mountain; Sailor Be Where; The Cowgirl; The Winner (text story); The Riddle (text story); It
13 ❑ Jun 1965 Cover: 0.25 **NM** value: **13.00**
14 ❑ Sep 1965 Cover: 0.25 **NM** value: **13.00**
15 ❑ Dec 1965 Cover: 0.25 **NM** value: **13.00**
16 ❑ Mar 1966 Cover: 0.25 **NM** value: **13.00**
17 ❑ May 1966 Cover: 0.25 **NM** value: **13.00**
18 ❑ Jul 1966 Cover: 0.25 **NM** value: **13.00**
19 ❑ Sep 1966 Cover: 0.25 **NM** value: **13.00**
20 ❑ Oct 1966 Cover: 0.25 **NM** value: **13.00**
21 ❑ Jan 1967 Cover: 0.25 **NM** value: **9.00**
22 ❑ Mar 1967 Cover: 0.25 **NM** value: **9.00**
Richie Rich: The Hideout; Richie Rich: The Dungeon; Richie Rich: The Fantastic Surprise; Little Dot: Uncle Branes Defe
23 ❑ Jun 1967 Cover: 0.25 **NM** value: **9.00**
24 ❑ Aug 1967 Cover: 0.25 **NM** value: **9.00**
25 ❑ Oct 1967 Cover: 0.25 **NM** value: **9.00**
26 ❑ Dec 1967 Cover: 0.25 **NM** value: **9.00**
27 ❑ Feb 1968 Cover: 0.25 **NM** value: **9.00**
28 ❑ Apr 1968 Cover: 0.25 **NM** value: **9.00**
29 ❑ Jun 1968 Cover: 0.25 **NM** value: **9.00**
30 ❑ Aug 1968 Cover: 0.25 **NM** value: **9.00**
31 ❑ Oct 1968 Cover: 0.25 **NM** value: **7.00**
32 ❑ Dec 1968 Cover: 0.25 **NM** value: **7.00**
33 ❑ Feb 1969 Cover: 0.25 **NM** value: **7.00**
34 ❑ Apr 1969 Cover: 0.25 **NM** value: **7.00**
35 ❑ May 1969 Cover: 0.25 **NM** value: **7.00**
36 ❑ Jul 1969 Cover: 0.25 **NM** value: **7.00**
37 ❑ Sep 1969 Cover: 0.25 **NM** value: **7.00**
38 ❑ Nov 1969 Cover: 0.25 **NM** value: **7.00**
39 ❑ Jan 1970 Cover: 0.25 **NM** value: **7.00**
40 ❑ Mar 1970 Cover: 0.25 **NM** value: **7.00**
41 ❑ May 1970 Cover: 0.25 **NM** value: **5.00**
42 ❑ Jul 1970 Cover: 0.25 **NM** value: **5.00**
43 ❑ Sep 1970 Cover: 0.25 **NM** value: **5.00**
44 ❑ Nov 1970 Cover: 0.25 **NM** value: **5.00**
45 ❑ Jan 1971 Cover: 0.25 **NM** value: **5.00**
46 ❑ Mar 1971 Cover: 0.25 **NM** value: **5.00**
47 ❑ May 1971 Cover: 0.25 **NM** value: **5.00**
48 ❑ Jul 1971 Cover: 0.25 **NM** value: **5.00**
49 ❑ Sep 1971 Cover: 0.25 **NM** value: **5.00**
50 ❑ Nov 1971 Cover: 0.25 **NM** value: **5.00**
51 ❑ Jan 1972 Cover: 0.25 **NM** value: **4.00**
52 ❑ Mar 1972 Cover: 0.25 **NM** value: **4.00**
53 ❑ May 1972 Cover: 0.25 **NM** value: **4.00**
54 ❑ Jul 1972 Cover: 0.25 **NM** value: **4.00**
55 ❑ Sep 1972 Cover: 0.25 **NM** value: **4.00**
56 ❑ Nov 1972 Cover: 0.25 **NM** value: **4.00**
57 ❑ Jan 1973 Cover: 0.25 **NM** value: **4.00**
58 ❑ Mar 1973 Cover: 0.25 **NM** value: **4.00**
59 ❑ May 1973 Cover: 0.25 **NM** value: **4.00**
60 ❑ Jul 1973 Cover: 0.25 **NM** value: **4.00**
61 ❑ Sep 1973 Cover: 0.25 **NM** value: **3.00**
62 ❑ Nov 1973 Cover: 0.25 **NM** value: **3.00**
63 ❑ Jan 1974 Cover: 0.25 **NM** value: **3.00**
64 ❑ Mar 1974 Cover: 0.25 **NM** value: **3.00**
65 ❑ May 1974 Cover: 0.25 **NM** value: **3.00**
66 ❑ Jul 1974 Cover: 0.25 **NM** value: **3.00**
67 ❑ Sep 1974 Cover: 0.25 **NM** value: **3.00**
68 ❑ Nov 1974 Cover: 0.25 **NM** value: **3.00**
69 ❑ Jan 1975 Cover: 0.25 **NM** value: **3.00**
70 ❑ Mar 1975 Cover: 0.25 **NM** value: **3.00**
71 ❑ May 1975 Cover: 0.25 **NM** value: **3.00**
72 ❑ Jul 1975 Cover: 0.25 **NM** value: **3.00**
73 ❑ Sep 1975 Cover: 0.25 **NM** value: **3.00**
74 ❑ Nov 1975 Cover: 0.25 **NM** value: **3.00**
75 ❑ Jan 1976 Cover: 0.25 **NM** value: **3.00**
76 ❑ Mar 1976 Cover: 0.25 **NM** value: **3.00**
77 ❑ May 1976 Cover: 0.25 **NM** value: **3.00**
78 ❑ Jul 1976 Cover: 0.25 **NM** value: **3.00**
79 ❑ Sep 1976 Cover: 0.25 **NM** value: **3.00**
80 ❑ Nov 1976 Cover: 0.30 **NM** value: **3.00**
81 ❑ Jan 1977 Cover: 0.30 **NM** value: **2.50**
82 ❑ Mar 1977 Cover: 0.30 **NM** value: **2.50**
83 ❑ May 1977 Cover: 0.30 **NM** value: **2.50**
84 ❑ Jul 1977 Cover: 0.30 **NM** value: **2.50**
85 ❑ Sep 1977 Cover: 0.50 **NM** value: **2.50**
86 ❑ Nov 1977 Cover: 0.50 **NM** value: **2.50**
87 ❑ Jan 1978 Cover: 0.50 **NM** value: **2.50**
88 ❑ Mar 1978 Cover: 0.50 **NM** value: **2.50**
The Butler Did It; Chairdog of the Board; The Quick Stopper; A Better Way; Little Lotta: The Monsters; Little Dot Meets Uncle Whammy
89 ❑ May 1978 Cover: 0.50 **NM** value: **2.50**
90 ❑ Aug 1978 Cover: 0.50 **NM** value: **2.50**
91 ❑ Oct 1978 Cover: 0.50 **NM** value: **2.00**
92 ❑ Dec 1978 Cover: 0.50 **NM** value: **2.00**
93 ❑ Feb 1979 Cover: 0.50 **NM** value: **2.00**
94 ❑ Apr 1979 Cover: 0.50 **NM** value: **2.00**
95 ❑ Jun 1979 Cover: 0.50 **NM** value: **2.00**
96 ❑ Aug 1979 Cover: 0.50 **NM** value: **2.00**
97 ❑ Oct 1979 Cover: 0.50 **NM** value: **2.00**
98 ❑ Dec 1979 Cover: 0.40 **NM** value: **2.00**
99 ❑ Mar 1980 Cover: 0.40 **NM** value: **2.00**
100 ❑ May 1980 Cover: 0.40 **NM** value: **2.00**
101 ❑ Aug 1980 Cover: 0.40 **NM** value: **1.50**
102 ❑ Oct 1980 Cover: 0.50 **NM** value: **1.50**
103 ❑ Dec 1981 Cover: 0.50 **NM** value: **1.50**
104 ❑ Feb 1981 Cover: 0.50 **NM** value: **1.50**
105 ❑ Apr 1981 Cover: 0.50 **NM** value: **1.50**
106 ❑ Jun 1981 Cover: 0.50 **NM** value: **1.50**
107 ❑ Aug 1981 Cover: 0.50 **NM** value: **1.50**
108 ❑ Oct 1981 Cover: 0.50 **NM** value: **1.50**
109 ❑ 1981 Cover: 0.50 **NM** value: **1.50**
110 ❑ Apr 1982 Cover: 0.60 **NM** value: **1.50**
111 ❑ Jun 1982 Cover: 0.60 **NM** value: **1.00**
112 ❑ Aug 1982 Cover: 0.60 **NM** value: **1.00**
113 ❑ Oct 1982 Cover: 0.60 **NM** value: **1.00**
final issue.

RICHIE RICH MONEY WORLD Harvey

1 ❑ Sep 1972 Cover: 0.20 **NM** value: **30.00**
• **CGC:** 2 graded, best 9.4
2 ❑ Nov 1972 Cover: 0.20 **NM** value: **12.00**
3 ❑ Jan 1973 Cover: 0.20 **NM** value: **10.00**
4 ❑ Mar 1973 Cover: 0.20 **NM** value: **8.00**
5 ❑ May 1973 Cover: 0.20 **NM** value: **8.00**
6 ❑ Jul 1973 Cover: 0.20 **NM** value: **6.00**
7 ❑ Sep 1973 Cover: 0.20 **NM** value: **6.00**
8 ❑ Nov 1973 Cover: 0.20 **NM** value: **6.00**
9 ❑ Jan 1974 Cover: 0.20 **NM** value: **6.00**
10 ❑ Mar 1974 Cover: 0.20 **NM** value: **6.00**
11 ❑ May 1974 Cover: 0.20 **NM** value: **4.00**
12 ❑ Jul 1974 Cover: 0.25 **NM** value: **4.00**
13 ❑ Sep 1974 Cover: 0.25 **NM** value: **4.00**
14 ❑ Nov 1974 Cover: 0.25 **NM** value: **4.00**
15 ❑ Jan 1975 Cover: 0.25 **NM** value: **4.00**
16 ❑ Mar 1975 Cover: 0.25 **NM** value: **4.00**
17 ❑ May 1975 Cover: 0.25 **NM** value: **4.00**
18 ❑ Jul 1975 Cover: 0.25 **NM** value: **4.00**
19 ❑ Sep 1975 Cover: 0.25 **NM** value: **4.00**
20 ❑ Nov 1975 Cover: 0.25 **NM** value: **4.00**
21 ❑ Jan 1976 Cover: 0.25 **NM** value: **3.00**
22 ❑ Mar 1976 Cover: 0.25 **NM** value: **3.00**
23 ❑ May 1976 Cover: 0.25 **NM** value: **3.00**
24 ❑ Jul 1976 Cover: 0.25 **NM** value: **3.00**
25 ❑ Sep 1976 Cover: 0.25 **NM** value: **3.00**
26 ❑ Nov 1976 Cover: 0.30 **NM** value: **3.00**
27 ❑ Jan 1977 Cover: 0.30 **NM** value: **3.00**
28 ❑ Mar 1977 Cover: 0.30 **NM** value: **3.00**
29 ❑ May 1977 Cover: 0.30 **NM** value: **3.00**
30 ❑ Jul 1977 Cover: 0.30 **NM** value: **3.00**
31 ❑ Sep 1977 Cover: 0.30 **NM** value: **2.00**
32 ❑ Nov 1977 Cover: 0.30 **NM** value: **2.00**
33 ❑ Jan 1978 Cover: 0.35 **NM** value: **2.00**
34 ❑ Mar 1978 Cover: 0.35 **NM** value: **2.00**
The All Situation Suit!; Pierre's Masterpiece; The Erroneous Irona; The Withdraw-All
35 ❑ May 1978 Cover: 0.35 **NM** value: **2.00**
36 ❑ Aug 1978 Cover: 0.35 **NM** value: **2.00**
37 ❑ Oct 1978 Cover: 0.35 **NM** value: **2.00**
38 ❑ Jan 1979 Cover: 0.35 **NM** value: **2.00**
39 ❑ Mar 1979 Cover: 0.35 **NM** value: **2.00**
40 ❑ Jun 1979 Cover: 0.35 **NM** value: **2.00**
41 ❑ Aug 1979 Cover: 0.35 **NM** value: **2.00**
42 ❑ Sep 1979 Cover: 0.40 **NM** value: **2.00**
43 ❑ Nov 1979 Cover: 0.40 **NM** value: **2.00**
44 ❑ Jan 1980 Cover: 0.40 **NM** value: **2.00**
45 ❑ Apr 1980 Cover: 0.40 **NM** value: **2.00**
46 ❑ Jun 1980 Cover: 0.40 **NM** value: **2.00**
47 ❑ Sep 1980 Cover: 0.50 **NM** value: **2.00**
48 ❑ Oct 1980 Cover: 0.50 **NM** value: **2.00**
49 ❑ Dec 1980 Cover: 0.50 **NM** value: **2.00**
50 ❑ Feb 1981 Cover: 0.50 **NM** value: **2.00**
51 ❑ Apr 1981 Cover: 0.50 **NM** value: **2.00**
52 ❑ Jun 1981 Cover: 0.50 **NM** value: **2.00**
53 ❑ Aug 1981 Cover: 0.50 **NM** value: **2.00**
54 ❑ Oct 1981 Cover: 0.50 **NM** value: **2.00**
55 ❑ Mar 1982 Cover: 0.60 **NM** value: **2.00**
56 ❑ 1982 Cover: 0.60 **NM** value: **2.00**
57 ❑ 1982 Cover: 0.60 **NM** value: **2.00**
58 ❑ 1982 Cover: 0.60 **NM** value: **2.00**
59 ❑ Sep 1982 Cover: 0.60 **NM** value: **2.00**

RICHIE RICH MONEY WORLD DIGEST Harvey

1 ❑ Apr 1991 Cover: 1.75 **NM** value: **2.00**
2 ❑ Dec 1991 Cover: 1.75 **NM** value: **Cover or less**
3 ❑ Apr 1992 Cover: 1.75 **NM** value: **Cover or less**
4 ❑ Aug 1992 Cover: 1.75 **NM** value: **Cover or less**
5 ❑ Dec 1992 Cover: 1.75 **NM** value: **Cover or less**
6 ❑ Apr 1993 Cover: 1.75 **NM** value: **Cover or less**
7 ❑ Aug 1993 Cover: 1.75 **NM** value: **Cover or less**
8 ❑ Dec 1993 Cover: 1.75 **NM** value: **Cover or less**

RICHIE RICH (MOVIE ADAPTATION) Marvel

After decades as a kids' comic book, Richie Rich made it to the big screen in early 1995. The movie starred Home Alone's Macauley Culkin as Richie, son of Richard and Regina Rich, the two richest people in the world. Richie had everything a kid could ask for and more: devoted parents, a personal staff, and his own amusement park. Unfortunately, his life of privilege had a way of isolating him from other kids his own age, making for some lonely times when his parents had to travel.

This one-shot movie adaptation retains the charm and cartoon art style of Harvey's Richie Rich comics — even if Cadbury was the only character in the movie who closely resembled his comics inspiration. It's also ironic to find it at Marvel, which in the 1980s failed in an attempt to buy Harvey and created its own Harvey, basically, in the Star imprint. (Complete with Royal Roy, A Prince of A Boy!)

1 ❑ Feb 1995 Cover: 2.95 **NM** value: **Cover or less**

RICHIE RICH PROFITS Harvey

1 ❑ Oct 1974 Cover: 0.25 **NM** value: **25.00**
• **CGC:** 1 graded, best 7.5
2 ❑ Dec 1974 Cover: 0.25 **NM** value: **15.00**
3 ❑ Feb 1975 Cover: 0.25 **NM** value: **15.00**
4 ❑ Apr 1975 Cover: 0.25 **NM** value: **10.00**
5 ❑ Jun 1975 Cover: 0.25 **NM** value: **10.00**
6 ❑ Aug 1975 Cover: 0.25 **NM** value: **10.00**
7 ❑ Oct 1975 Cover: 0.25 **NM** value: **10.00**
8 ❑ Dec 1975 Cover: 0.25 **NM** value: **10.00**
9 ❑ Feb 1976 Cover: 0.25 **NM** value: **10.00**
10 ❑ Apr 1976 Cover: 0.25 **NM** value: **10.00**
11 ❑ Jun 1976 Cover: 0.25 **NM** value: **8.00**
12 ❑ Aug 1976 Cover: 0.25 **NM** value: **8.00**
13 ❑ Oct 1976 Cover: 0.30 **NM** value: **8.00**
14 ❑ Dec 1976 Cover: 0.30 **NM** value: **8.00**
15 ❑ Feb 1977 Cover: 0.30 **NM** value: **8.00**
16 ❑ Apr 1977 Cover: 0.30 **NM** value: **8.00**
17 ❑ Jun 1977 Cover: 0.30 **NM** value: **8.00**
18 ❑ Aug 1977 Cover: 0.30 **NM** value: **8.00**
19 ❑ Oct 1977 Cover: 0.35 **NM** value: **8.00**
20 ❑ Dec 1977 Cover: 0.35 **NM** value: **6.00**
21 ❑ Feb 1978 Cover: 0.35 **NM** value: **6.00**
22 ❑ Apr 1978 Cover: 0.35 **NM** value: **6.00**

CGC-graded: Multiply prices above by **33 for 9.9 M • 16 for 9.8 NM/M • 7 for 9.6 NM+ • 5 for 9.4 NM • 2.5 for 9.2 NM- • 1.5 for 9.0 VF/NM**

23 ❑ Jun 1978 Cover: 0.35 **NM** value: **6.00**
24 ❑ 1978 Cover: 0.35 **NM** value: **6.00**
25 ❑ 1978 Cover: 0.35 **NM** value: **6.00**
26 ❑ Jan 1979 Cover: 0.35 **NM** value: **6.00**
27 ❑ 1979 Cover: 0.35 **NM** value: **6.00**
28 ❑ 1979 Cover: 0.35 **NM** value: **6.00**
29 ❑ 1979 Cover: 0.35 **NM** value: **6.00**
30 ❑ 1979 Cover: 0.30 **NM** value: **5.00**
31 ❑ Oct 1979 Cover: 0.40 **NM** value: **5.00**
32 ❑ Dec 1979 Cover: 0.40 **NM** value: **5.00**
33 ❑ Feb 1980 Cover: 0.40 **NM** value: **5.00**
34 ❑ Apr 1980 Cover: 0.40 **NM** value: **5.00**
35 ❑ Jul 1980 Cover: 0.40 **NM** value: **5.00**
36 ❑ Sep 1980 Cover: 0.50 **NM** value: **5.00**
37 ❑ Nov 1980 Cover: 0.50 **NM** value: **5.00**
38 ❑ Jan 1981 Cover: 0.50 **NM** value: **5.00**
39 ❑ Mar 1981 Cover: 0.50 **NM** value: **5.00**
40 ❑ May 1981 Cover: 0.50 **NM** value: **4.00**
41 ❑ Jul 1981 Cover: 0.50 **NM** value: **4.00**
42 ❑ Sep 1981 Cover: 0.50 **NM** value: **4.00**
43 ❑ Nov 1981 Cover: 0.50 **NM** value: **4.00**
44 ❑ Feb 1982 Cover: 0.60 **NM** value: **4.00**
45 ❑ Apr 1982 Cover: 0.60 **NM** value: **4.00**
46 ❑ Jun 1982 Cover: 0.60 **NM** value: **4.00**
47 ❑ Sep 1982 Cover: 0.60 **NM** value: **4.00**

RICHIE RICH RELICS — Harvey

1 ❑ Jan 1988 Cover: 1.00 **NM** value: **2.50**
• **CGC:** 2 graded, best 9.2
2 ❑ May 1988 Cover: 1.00 **NM** value: **2.50**
3 ❑ Sep 1988 Cover: 1.00 **NM** value: **2.50**
4 ❑ Jan 1989 Cover: 1.00 **NM** value: **2.50**

RICHIE RICH RICHES — Harvey

1 ❑ Jul 1972 Cover: 0.25 **NM** value: **28.00**
2 ❑ Sep 1972 Cover: 0.25 **NM** value: **13.00**
3 ❑ Nov 1972 Cover: 0.20 **NM** value: **8.00**
4 ❑ Jan 1973 Cover: 0.20 **NM** value: **8.00**
5 ❑ Mar 1973 Cover: 0.20 **NM** value: **8.00**
6 ❑ May 1973 Cover: 0.20 **NM** value: **5.00**
7 ❑ Jul 1973 Cover: 0.20 **NM** value: **5.00**
8 ❑ Sep 1973 Cover: 0.20 **NM** value: **5.00**
9 ❑ Nov 1973 Cover: 0.20 **NM** value: **5.00**
10 ❑ Jan 1974 Cover: 0.20 **NM** value: **5.00**
11 ❑ Mar 1974 Cover: 0.20 **NM** value: **4.00**
12 ❑ May 1974 Cover: 0.25 **NM** value: **4.00**
13 ❑ Jul 1974 Cover: 0.25 **NM** value: **4.00**
14 ❑ Sep 1974 Cover: 0.25 **NM** value: **4.00**
15 ❑ Nov 1974 Cover: 0.25 **NM** value: **4.00**
16 ❑ Jan 1975 Cover: 0.25 **NM** value: **4.00**
17 ❑ Mar 1975 Cover: 0.25 **NM** value: **4.00**
18 ❑ May 1975 Cover: 0.25 **NM** value: **4.00**
📖 President Richie; The State Visit; The Almost Perfect Driver; Nurse Jenny: The Sensitive Crook
19 ❑ Jul 1975 Cover: 0.25 **NM** value: **4.00**
20 ❑ Sep 1975 Cover: 0.25 **NM** value: **4.00**
21 ❑ Nov 1975 Cover: 0.25 **NM** value: **3.00**
22 ❑ Jan 1976 Cover: 0.25 **NM** value: **3.00**
23 ❑ Mar 1976 Cover: 0.25 **NM** value: **3.00**
24 ❑ May 1976 Cover: 0.25 **NM** value: **3.00**
25 ❑ Jul 1976 Cover: 0.25 **NM** value: **3.00**
26 ❑ Sep 1976 Cover: 0.30 **NM** value: **3.00**
27 ❑ Nov 1976 Cover: 0.30 **NM** value: **3.00**
28 ❑ Jan 1977 Cover: 0.30 **NM** value: **3.00**
29 ❑ Mar 1977 Cover: 0.30 **NM** value: **3.00**
30 ❑ May 1977 Cover: 0.30 **NM** value: **3.00**
31 ❑ Jul 1977 Cover: 0.30 **NM** value: **2.00**
32 ❑ Sep 1977 Cover: 0.30 **NM** value: **2.00**
33 ❑ Nov 1977 Cover: 0.35 **NM** value: **2.00**
34 ❑ Jan 1978 Cover: 0.35 **NM** value: **2.00**
35 ❑ Mar 1978 Cover: 0.35 **NM** value: **2.00**
36 ❑ May 1978 Cover: 0.35 **NM** value: **2.00**
37 ❑ Jul 1978 Cover: 0.35 **NM** value: **2.00**
38 ❑ Oct 1978 Cover: 0.35 **NM** value: **2.00**
39 ❑ Dec 1978 Cover: 0.35 **NM** value: **2.00**
40 ❑ Feb 1979 Cover: 0.35 **NM** value: **2.00**
41 ❑ Apr 1979 Cover: 0.50 **NM** value: **2.00**
42 ❑ Jun 1979 Cover: 0.50 **NM** value: **2.00**
43 ❑ Aug 1979 Cover: 0.50 **NM** value: **2.00**
44 ❑ Oct 1979 Cover: 0.50 **NM** value: **2.00**
45 ❑ Dec 1979 Cover: 0.50 **NM** value: **2.00**
46 ❑ Feb 1980 Cover: 0.40 **NM** value: **2.00**
47 ❑ May 1980 Cover: 0.40 **NM** value: **2.00**
48 ❑ Aug 1980 Cover: 0.40 **NM** value: **2.00**
49 ❑ Oct 1980 Cover: 0.50 **NM** value: **2.00**
50 ❑ Dec 1980 Cover: 0.50 **NM** value: **2.00**
51 ❑ Feb 1981 Cover: 0.50 **NM** value: **2.00**
52 ❑ Apr 1981 Cover: 0.50 **NM** value: **2.00**
53 ❑ Jun 1981 Cover: 0.50 **NM** value: **2.00**
📖 Withering Heist; Bungling Burglar; Crook Watchers; Little Lotta; Chef Pierre; Replacement Robot
54 ❑ Aug 1981 Cover: 0.50 **NM** value: **2.00**
55 ❑ 1981 Cover: 0.50 **NM** value: **2.00**
56 ❑ 1981 Cover: 0.50 **NM** value: **2.00**

RICHIE RICH SUCCESS STORIES — Harvey

1 ❑ Nov 1964 Cover: 0.25 **NM** value: **100.00**
• **CGC:** 1 graded, best 8.0
2 ❑ Feb 1965 Cover: 0.25 **NM** value: **45.00**
3 ❑ May 1965 Cover: 0.25 **NM** value: **35.00**
4 ❑ Aug 1965 Cover: 0.25 **NM** value: **28.00**
5 ❑ Nov 1965 Cover: 0.25 **NM** value: **28.00**
6 ❑ Feb 1966 Cover: 0.25 **NM** value: **28.00**
📖 Of Parties and Pirates; The Double Doublecross; The Disappearing Butler; Butler Build-Up; The Funny Lady; Gift for Dad; The Race; Big Date (text story); Cat-Nipped (text story); For Gloria's Sake
7 ❑ May 1966 Cover: 0.25 **NM** value: **20.00**
• **CGC:** 1 graded, best 9.4
8 ❑ Jul 1966 Cover: 0.25 **NM** value: **20.00**
9 ❑ Aug 1966 Cover: 0.25 **NM** value: **20.00**
10 ❑ Oct 1966 Cover: 0.25 **NM** value: **20.00**
11 ❑ Dec 1966 Cover: 0.25 **NM** value: **14.00**
12 ❑ Feb 1967 Cover: 0.25 **NM** value: **14.00**
13 ❑ Apr 1967 Cover: 0.25 **NM** value: **14.00**
14 ❑ Jun 1967 Cover: 0.25 **NM** value: **14.00**
15 ❑ Aug 1967 Cover: 0.25 **NM** value: **14.00**
16 ❑ Nov 1967 Cover: 0.25 **NM** value: **14.00**
17 ❑ Jan 1968 Cover: 0.25 **NM** value: **14.00**
18 ❑ Mar 1968 Cover: 0.25 **NM** value: **14.00**
19 ❑ May 1968 Cover: 0.25 **NM** value: **14.00**
20 ❑ Jul 1968 Cover: 0.25 **NM** value: **14.00**
21 ❑ Sep 1968 Cover: 0.25 **NM** value: **10.00**
22 ❑ Nov 1968 Cover: 0.25 **NM** value: **10.00**
23 ❑ Jan 1969 Cover: 0.25 **NM** value: **10.00**
24 ❑ Mar 1969 Cover: 0.25 **NM** value: **10.00**
25 ❑ Apr 1969 Cover: 0.25 **NM** value: **10.00**
26 ❑ Jun 1969 Cover: 0.25 **NM** value: **10.00**
27 ❑ Aug 1969 Cover: 0.25 **NM** value: **10.00**
28 ❑ Oct 1969 Cover: 0.25 **NM** value: **10.00**
29 ❑ Dec 1969 Cover: 0.25 **NM** value: **10.00**
30 ❑ Feb 1970 Cover: 0.25 **NM** value: **10.00**
31 ❑ Apr 1970 Cover: 0.25 **NM** value: **8.00**
32 ❑ Jun 1970 Cover: 0.25 **NM** value: **8.00**
33 ❑ Aug 1970 Cover: 0.25 **NM** value: **8.00**
34 ❑ Oct 1970 Cover: 0.25 **NM** value: **8.00**
35 ❑ Dec 1970 Cover: 0.25 **NM** value: **8.00**
36 ❑ Feb 1971 Cover: 0.25 **NM** value: **8.00**
37 ❑ Apr 1971 Cover: 0.25 **NM** value: **8.00**
38 ❑ Jun 1971 Cover: 0.25 **NM** value: **8.00**
39 ❑ Aug 1971 Cover: 0.25 **NM** value: **8.00**
40 ❑ Oct 1971 Cover: 0.25 **NM** value: **8.00**
41 ❑ Dec 1971 Cover: 0.25 **NM** value: **5.00**
42 ❑ Feb 1972 Cover: 0.25 **NM** value: **5.00**
43 ❑ Apr 1972 Cover: 0.25 **NM** value: **5.00**
44 ❑ Jun 1972 Cover: 0.25 **NM** value: **5.00**
45 ❑ Aug 1972 Cover: 0.25 **NM** value: **5.00**
46 ❑ Oct 1972 Cover: 0.25 **NM** value: **5.00**
47 ❑ Dec 1972 Cover: 0.25 **NM** value: **5.00**
48 ❑ Feb 1973 Cover: 0.25 **NM** value: **5.00**
49 ❑ Apr 1973 Cover: 0.25 **NM** value: **5.00**
50 ❑ Jun 1973 Cover: 0.25 **NM** value: **5.00**
51 ❑ Aug 1973 Cover: 0.25 **NM** value: **5.00**
52 ❑ Oct 1973 Cover: 0.25 **NM** value: **5.00**
53 ❑ Dec 1973 Cover: 0.25 **NM** value: **5.00**
54 ❑ Feb 1974 Cover: 0.25 **NM** value: **5.00**
55 ❑ Apr 1974 Cover: 0.25 **NM** value: **5.00**
56 ❑ Jun 1974 Cover: 0.25 **NM** value: **5.00**
57 ❑ Aug 1974 Cover: 0.25 **NM** value: **5.00**
58 ❑ Oct 1974 Cover: 0.25 **NM** value: **5.00**
59 ❑ Dec 1974 Cover: 0.25 **NM** value: **5.00**
60 ❑ Feb 1975 Cover: 0.25 **NM** value: **5.00**
61 ❑ Apr 1975 Cover: 0.25 **NM** value: **5.00**
62 ❑ Jun 1975 Cover: 0.25 **NM** value: **5.00**
63 ❑ Aug 1975 Cover: 0.25 **NM** value: **5.00**
64 ❑ Oct 1975 Cover: 0.25 **NM** value: **5.00**
65 ❑ Dec 1975 Cover: 0.25 **NM** value: **5.00**
66 ❑ Feb 1976 Cover: 0.25 **NM** value: **5.00**
67 ❑ Apr 1976 Cover: 0.35 **NM** value: **5.00**
68 ❑ Jun 1976 Cover: 0.35 **NM** value: **5.00**
69 ❑ Aug 1976 Cover: 0.35 **NM** value: **5.00**
70 ❑ Oct 1976 Cover: 0.40 **NM** value: **5.00**
📖 The Iron Will; Backfire!; Bascomb: Smaller and Smaller; Nurse Jenny: TheImprover; Old Hup; Reggie Can't Lose; The Chicken Kid (text story); Reggie Gets a Move On
71 ❑ Dec 1976 Cover: 0.40 **NM** value: **3.00**
72 ❑ Feb 1977 Cover: 0.40 **NM** value: **3.00**
73 ❑ Mar 1977 Cover: 0.40 **NM** value: **3.00**
74 ❑ May 1977 Cover: 0.40 **NM** value: **3.00**
75 ❑ Jul 1977 Cover: 0.40 **NM** value: **3.00**
76 ❑ Sep 1977 Cover: 0.50 **NM** value: **3.00**
77 ❑ Oct 1977 Cover: 0.50 **NM** value: **3.00**
78 ❑ Dec 1977 Cover: 0.50 **NM** value: **3.00**
79 ❑ Feb 1978 Cover: 0.50 **NM** value: **3.00**
80 ❑ Apr 1978 Cover: 0.50 **NM** value: **3.00**
81 ❑ Jun 1978 Cover: 0.50 **NM** value: **3.00**
82 ❑ Aug 1978 Cover: 0.50 **NM** value: **3.00**
83 ❑ Oct 1978 Cover: 0.50 **NM** value: **3.00**
84 ❑ Dec 1978 Cover: 0.50 **NM** value: **3.00**
85 ❑ Jan 1979 Cover: 0.50 **NM** value: **3.00**
86 ❑ Mar 1979 Cover: 0.50 **NM** value: **3.00**
87 ❑ May 1979 Cover: 0.50 **NM** value: **3.00**
88 ❑ Jul 1979 Cover: 0.50 **NM** value: **3.00**
89 ❑ Sep 1979 Cover: 0.50 **NM** value: **3.00**
90 ❑ Nov 1979 Cover: 0.50 **NM** value: **3.00**
91 ❑ Jan 1980 Cover: 0.40 **NM** value: **3.00**
92 ❑ Apr 1980 Cover: 0.40 **NM** value: **3.00**
93 ❑ Jun 1980 Cover: 0.40 **NM** value: **3.00**
94 ❑ Sep 1980 Cover: 0.50 **NM** value: **3.00**
95 ❑ Nov 1980 Cover: 0.50 **NM** value: **3.00**
96 ❑ Jan 1981 Cover: 0.50 **NM** value: **3.00**
97 ❑ Mar 1981 Cover: 0.50 **NM** value: **3.00**
98 ❑ May 1981 Cover: 0.50 **NM** value: **3.00**
99 ❑ Jul 1981 Cover: 0.50 **NM** value: **3.00**
100 ❑ Sep 1981 Cover: 0.50 **NM** value: **3.00**
101 ❑ Dec 1981 Cover: 0.50 **NM** value: **2.00**
102 ❑ Feb 1982 Cover: 0.60 **NM** value: **2.00**
103 ❑ May 1982 Cover: 0.60 **NM** value: **2.00**
104 ❑ Jul 1982 Cover: 0.60 **NM** value: **2.00**
105 ❑ Sep 1982 Cover: 0.60 **NM** value: **2.00**

RICHIE RICH VACATION DIGEST — Harvey

1992 ❑ Oct 1992 Cover: 1.75 **NM** value: **Cover or less**
#1 on cover.
1993 ❑ Oct 1993 Cover: 1.75 **NM** value: **Cover or less**
#1 on cover.

RICHIE RICH VACATIONS DIGEST — Harvey

1 ❑ Oct 1980 Cover: 0.95 **NM** value: **10.00**
2 ❑ Dec 1980 Cover: 0.95 **NM** value: **5.00**
3 ❑ Feb 1981 Cover: 0.95 **NM** value: **5.00**
4 ❑ Apr 1981 Cover: 0.95 **NM** value: **5.00**
5 ❑ Jun 1981 Cover: 0.95 **NM** value: **5.00**
6 ❑ Aug 1981 Cover: 0.95 **NM** value: **5.00**
7 ❑ Oct 1981 Cover: 0.95 **NM** value: **5.00**
8 ❑ Dec 1981 Cover: 0.95 **NM** value: **5.00**

RICHIE RICH VAULTS OF MYSTERY — Harvey

1 ❑ Nov 1974 Cover: 0.25 **NM** value: **10.00**
• **CGC:** 1 graded, best 9.2
2 ❑ Jan 1975 Cover: 0.25 **NM** value: **7.00**
3 ❑ Mar 1975 Cover: 0.25 **NM** value: **5.00**
4 ❑ May 1975 Cover: 0.25 **NM** value: **5.00**
5 ❑ Jul 1975 Cover: 0.25 **NM** value: **5.00**
6 ❑ Sep 1975 Cover: 0.25 **NM** value: **4.00**
7 ❑ Nov 1975 Cover: 0.25 **NM** value: **4.00**
8 ❑ Jan 1976 Cover: 0.25 **NM** value: **4.00**
9 ❑ Mar 1976 Cover: 0.25 **NM** value: **4.00**
10 ❑ May 1976 Cover: 0.25 **NM** value: **4.00**
11 ❑ Jul 1976 Cover: 0.25 **NM** value: **3.00**
12 ❑ Sep 1976 Cover: 0.25 **NM** value: **3.00**
📖 The Mini-Mansion Caper; The Wacky Weather Machine; Cadbury: Jolly Good Hunting
13 ❑ Nov 1976 Cover: 0.30 **NM** value: **3.00**
📖 The Seance at Spectro Castle; The Vengeance of the Spirits; The Diary Talks; Too Many Friends; Boy, That's Rich!
14 ❑ Jan 1977 Cover: 0.30 **NM** value: **3.00**
15 ❑ Mar 1977 Cover: 0.30 **NM** value: **3.00**
16 ❑ May 1977 Cover: 0.30 **NM** value: **3.00**
17 ❑ Jul 1977 Cover: 0.30 **NM** value: **3.00**
18 ❑ Sep 1977 Cover: 0.30 **NM** value: **3.00**
📖 The Voice in the Vault; Richie Rich Meets Sokrates Monopoles; Little Lotta: A Weighty Problem
19 ❑ Nov 1977 Cover: 0.35 **NM** value: **3.00**
20 ❑ Jan 1978 Cover: 0.35 **NM** value: **3.00**
21 ❑ Mar 1978 Cover: 0.35 **NM** value: **2.00**
22 ❑ May 1978 Cover: 0.35 **NM** value: **2.00**
23 ❑ Jul 1978 Cover: 0.35 **NM** value: **2.00**
24 ❑ Sep 1978 Cover: 0.35 **NM** value: **2.00**
25 ❑ Nov 1978 Cover: 0.35 **NM** value: **2.00**
26 ❑ Jan 1979 Cover: 0.35 **NM** value: **2.00**
27 ❑ Mar 1979 Cover: 0.35 **NM** value: **2.00**
28 ❑ May 1979 Cover: 0.35 **NM** value: **2.00**
29 ❑ Jul 1979 Cover: 0.35 **NM** value: **2.00**
30 ❑ Sep 1979 Cover: 0.35 **NM** value: **2.00**
31 ❑ Nov 1979 Cover: 0.40 **NM** value: **2.00**
32 ❑ Jan 1980 Cover: 0.40 **NM** value: **2.00**
33 ❑ Apr 1980 Cover: 0.40 **NM** value: **2.00**
34 ❑ Jun 1980 Cover: 0.40 **NM** value: **2.00**
35 ❑ Aug 1980 Cover: 0.40 **NM** value: **2.00**
36 ❑ Oct 1980 Cover: 0.50 **NM** value: **2.00**
37 ❑ Dec 1980 Cover: 0.50 **NM** value: **2.00**
38 ❑ Feb 1981 Cover: 0.50 **NM** value: **2.00**
39 ❑ Apr 1981 Cover: 0.50 **NM** value: **2.00**
40 ❑ Jun 1981 Cover: 0.50 **NM** value: **2.00**
41 ❑ 1981 **NM** value: **2.00**
42 ❑ 1981 **NM** value: **2.00**
43 ❑ 1981 **NM** value: **2.00**
44 ❑ 1982 Cover: 0.60 **NM** value: **2.00**
45 ❑ 1982 Cover: 0.60 **NM** value: **2.00**
46 ❑ 1982 Cover: 0.60 **NM** value: **2.00**
47 ❑ Sep 1982 Cover: 0.60 **NM** value: **2.00**

RICHIE RICH ZILLIONZ — Harvey

1 ❑ Oct 1976 Cover: 0.50 **NM** value: **12.00**
• **CGC:** 2 graded, best 9.6
2 ❑ 1979 Cover: 0.50 **NM** value: **6.00**
3 ❑ 1977 Cover: 0.50 **NM** value: **4.00**
4 ❑ 1977 Cover: 0.50 **NM** value: **4.00**
5 ❑ Aug 1977 Cover: 0.50 **NM** value: **4.00**
6 ❑ Oct 1977 Cover: 0.50 **NM** value: **3.00**
7 ❑ Dec 1977 Cover: 0.50 **NM** value: **3.00**
8 ❑ Feb 1978 Cover: 0.50 **NM** value: **3.00**
9 ❑ Apr 1978 Cover: 0.50 **NM** value: **3.00**
📖 The Big Money Gun; Wealth Woes; Test Pie-Lot; A Bad Blast-Off!; The Darker Side of Nowhere; Little Dot: Animals in the Area; The Robot Quarterback (text story); Little Lotta: Tired all the Time
10 ❑ Jul 1978 Cover: 0.50 **NM** value: **3.00**
11 ❑ Sep 1978 Cover: 0.50 **NM** value: **2.00**
12 ❑ Nov 1978 Cover: 0.50 **NM** value: **2.00**
13 ❑ Jan 1979 Cover: 0.50 **NM** value: **2.00**
14 ❑ Mar 1979 Cover: 0.50 **NM** value: **2.00**
15 ❑ May 1979 Cover: 0.50 **NM** value: **2.00**
16 ❑ Jul 1979 Cover: 0.50 **NM** value: **2.00**
17 ❑ Sep 1979 Cover: 0.50 **NM** value: **2.00**
18 ❑ Nov 1979 Cover: 0.50 **NM** value: **2.00**
19 ❑ Jan 1980 Cover: 0.40 **NM** value: **2.00**
20 ❑ Mar 1980 Cover: 0.40 **NM** value: **2.00**
21 ❑ May 1980 Cover: 0.40 **NM** value: **2.00**
22 ❑ 1980 Cover: 0.40 **NM** value: **2.00**
23 ❑ Oct 1980 Cover: 0.50 **NM** value: **2.00**
24 ❑ 1980 Cover: 0.50 **NM** value: **2.00**
25 ❑ 1981 Cover: 0.50 **NM** value: **2.00**
26 ❑ 1981 Cover: 0.50 **NM** value: **2.00**
27 ❑ 1981 Cover: 0.50 **NM** value: **2.00**
28 ❑ 1981 Cover: 0.50 **NM** value: **2.00**
29 ❑ 1981 Cover: 0.50 **NM** value: **2.00**
30 ❑ 1982 **NM** value: **2.00**
31 ❑ 1982 Cover: 0.60 **NM** value: **2.00**
32 ❑ 1982 Cover: 0.60 **NM** value: **2.00**
33 ❑ Sep 1982 Cover: 0.60 **NM** value: **2.00**

RICKY — Standard

5 ❑ ca. 1953 Cover: 0.10 **NM** value: **20.00**

Other grades: Multiply prices above by **1.5 for Mint • 2/3 for Very Fine • 1/3 for Fine • 1/5 for Very Good • 1/8 for Good**

RIDER — Ajax

1 ❑ Mar 1957 Cover: 0.10 **NM** value: **75.00**
2 ❑ Jun 1957 Cover: 0.10 **NM** value: **40.00**
3 ❑ Aug 1957 Cover: 0.10 **NM** value: **40.00**
4 ❑ Oct 1957 Cover: 0.10 **NM** value: **40.00**
5 ❑ Dec 1957 Cover: 0.10 **NM** value: **40.00**

RIFLEMAN, THE — Dell

2 ❑ Jan 1960 Cover: 0.10 **NM** value: **150.00**
• **CGC:** 2 graded, best 9.4
3 ❑ Apr 1960 Cover: 0.10 **NM** value: **150.00**
4 ❑ Jul 1960 Cover: 0.10 **NM** value: **150.00**
5 ❑ Oct 1960 Cover: 0.10 **NM** value: **100.00**
6 ❑ Jan 1961 Cover: 0.10 **NM** value: **100.00**
• **CGC:** 1 graded, best 9.2
7 ❑ Jun 1961 Cover: 0.15 **NM** value: **100.00**
• **CGC:** 1 graded, best 9.2
8 ❑ Sep 1961 Cover: 0.15 **NM** value: **100.00**
• **CGC:** 1 graded, best 9.2
9 ❑ Dec 1961 Cover: 0.15 **NM** value: **100.00**
10 ❑ Jan 1962 Cover: 0.15 **NM** value: **100.00**
11 ❑ Apr 1962 Cover: 0.15 **NM** value: **75.00**
12 ❑ Jul 1962 Cover: 0.15 **NM** value: **75.00**
13 ❑ Nov 1962 Cover: 0.12 **NM** value: **75.00**
14 ❑ Feb 1963 Cover: 0.12 **NM** value: **75.00**
15 ❑ May 1963 Cover: 0.12 **NM** value: **75.00**
16 ❑ Aug 1963 Cover: 0.12 **NM** value: **75.00**
17 ❑ Nov 1963 Cover: 0.12 **NM** value: **75.00**
18 ❑ Apr 1964 Cover: 0.12 **NM** value: **75.00**
19 ❑ Jul 1964 Cover: 0.12 **NM** value: **75.00**
20 ❑ Oct 1964 Cover: 0.12 **NM** value: **75.00**

RIMA, THE JUNGLE GIRL — DC

Deep in the jungles of Venezuela, there is a secret place that even the local Indians fear to enter. This place is said to be the domain of a witch, who can change form between woman and beast at will.

Abel, a refugee from a Venezuelan revolution comes upon this place and meets the mysterious woman known as Rima. Bitten by a bushmaster snake, Abel is nursed back to health by Rima and her grandfather, and becomes the first man in an age to know her true story.

Although short-lived as a series, Rima, the Jungle Girl, with art by Nestor Redondo, was easily one of the most intriguing of the various jungle titles at the time. However, for those whose tastes ran far from the wilds, the series also included an ongoing backup story featuring the Space Voyagers.

1 ❑ May 1974 Cover: 0.20 **NM** value: **3.00**
• **CGC:** 9 graded, best 9.6
📖 Spirit Of The Woods ★ Origin of Rima, the Jungle Girl.
2 ❑ Jul 1974 Cover: 0.20 **NM** value: **2.00**
📖 Flight From Eden **A:** Nestor Redondo; Joe Kubert(cover); Alex Ni±o **W:** Robert Kanigher ★ Origin of Rima, the Jungle Girl.
3 ❑ Sep 1974 Cover: 0.20 **NM** value: **2.00**
📖 Rio Lama; Space Voyagers: The Hot Spot **A:** Nestor Redondo; Joe Kubert(cover); Alex Ni±o **W:** Robert Kanigher ★ Origin of Rima, the Jungle Girl.
4 ❑ Nov 1974 Cover: 0.20 **NM** value: **2.00**
📖 The Flaming Forest ★ Origin of Rima, the Jungle Girl.
5 ❑ Jan 1975 Cover: 0.20 **NM** value: **2.00**
6 ❑ Mar 1975 Cover: 0.25 **NM** value: **2.00**
7 ❑ May 1975 Cover: 0.25 **NM** value: **2.00**
final issue.

RIME OF THE ANCIENT MARINER (ECLIPSE) — Eclipse

Bk 1❑ Cover: 9.95 **NM** value: **Cover or less**
• paperback
Bk 1/LE❑ Cover: 15.95 **NM** value: **Cover or less**
• Revised edition.

RIME OF THE ANCIENT MARINER, THE (TOME) — Tome Press

1 ❑ b&w Cover: 3.95 **NM** value: **Cover or less**
No issue number. **A:** Gustav Dore

RIMSHOT — Rip Off

All issues are adults only.
1 ❑ Jun 1990, b&w Cover: 2.00 **NM** value: **Cover or less**
2 ❑ Feb 1991, b&w Cover: 2.00 **NM** value: **Cover or less**
3 ❑ Jul 1991, b&w Cover: 2.50 **NM** value: **Cover or less**

RING OF BRIGHT WATER — Dell

1 ❑ Cover: 0.15 **NM** value: **7.00**

RING OF ROSES — Dark Horse

1 ❑ b&w Cover: 2.50 **NM** value: **Cover or less**
A: John Watkiss **W:** Das Petrou
2 ❑ b&w Cover: 2.50 **NM** value: **Cover or less**
3 ❑ b&w Cover: 2.50 **NM** value: **Cover or less**
4 ❑ b&w Cover: 2.50 **NM** value: **Cover or less**

RING OF THE NIBELUNG, THE — DC

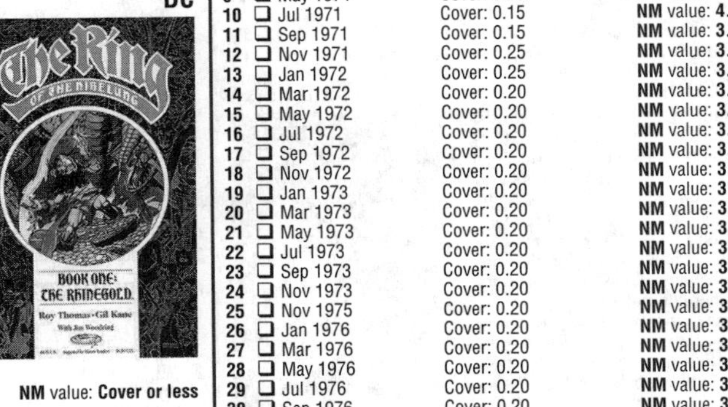

Roy Thomas and Gil Kane made an early attempt to boil Wagner's operatic Ring of the Nibelung saga in 1989 with this four-issue series.

Each prestige format issue was devoted to adapting one chapter of the four-part magnum opus that begins with a troll's theft of the Rhinegold from the gods, moves on to the trials of Siegfried and his slaying of a dragon, and ends with the Twilight of the Gods.

While it's obvious that Thomas had a limited amount of space to work with, he used it to the best of his ability and Kane's art is lush and rich and ideally suited to the story. — Brent

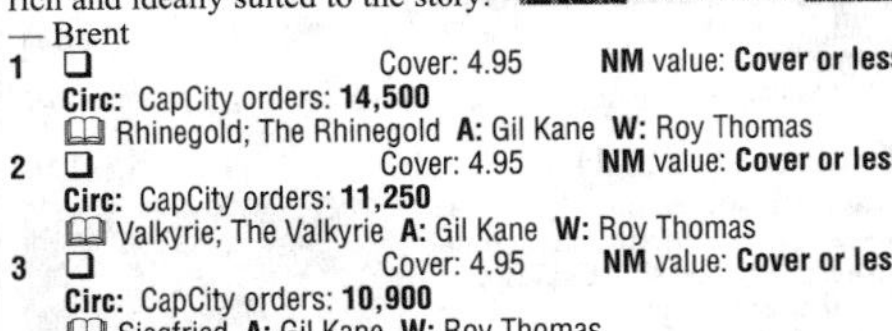

1 ❑ Cover: 4.95 **NM** value: **Cover or less**
Circ: CapCity orders: **14,500**
📖 Rhinegold; The Rhinegold **A:** Gil Kane **W:** Roy Thomas
2 ❑ Cover: 4.95 **NM** value: **Cover or less**
Circ: CapCity orders: **11,250**
📖 Valkyrie; The Valkyrie **A:** Gil Kane **W:** Roy Thomas
3 ❑ Cover: 4.95 **NM** value: **Cover or less**
Circ: CapCity orders: **10,900**
📖 Siegfried **A:** Gil Kane **W:** Roy Thomas
4 ❑ Cover: 4.95 **NM** value: **Cover or less**
Circ: CapCity orders: **10,800**
📖 Twilight of Gods **A:** Gil Kane **W:** Roy Thomas
Bk 1❑ Cover: 19.95 **NM** value: **Cover or less**
Circ: CapCity orders: **1,600**

RING OF THE NIBELUNG, THE (DARK HORSE) — Dark Horse

Learning from DC's example, Dark Horse gave P. Craig Russell plenty of room when he began his adaptation of Wagner's Ring saga.

Each four-issue mini-series in the overall series is devoted to a separate opera in the cycle, beginning here with Das Rhinegold. Russell's work, which he had been longing to do for years, netted him an Eisner Award in 2001 and Dark Horse began collecting the individual issues in separate trade paperbacks in 2002. Until each and every word, action, and nuance from Wagner is put into comics form, this is the definitive adaptation. — Brent

1 ❑ Feb 2000 Cover: 2.95 **NM** value: **Cover or less**
Circ: Diamd. preorders: **10,498**
📖 The Rape of the Gold **A:** P. Craig Russell **W:** P. Craig Russell
2 ❑ Mar 2000 Cover: 2.95 **NM** value: **Cover or less**
Circ: Diamd. preorders: **9,183**
A: P. Craig Russell **W:** P. Craig Russell
3 ❑ Apr 2000 Cover: 2.95 **NM** value: **Cover or less**
Circ: Diamd. preorders: **9,153**
A: P. Craig Russell **W:** P. Craig Russell
4 ❑ May 2000 Cover: 2.95 **NM** value: **Cover or less**
Circ: Diamd. preorders: **9,037**
📖 The First Murder **A:** P. Craig Russell **W:** P. Craig Russell

RING OF THE NIBELUNG, THE (VOL. 2) — Dark Horse

1 ❑ Aug 2000 Cover: 2.95 **NM** value: **Cover or less**
Circ: Diamd. preorders: **9,059**
📖 The Valkyrie **A:** P. Craig Russell **W:** P. Craig Russell
2 ❑ Sep 2000 Cover: 2.95 **NM** value: **Cover or less**
Circ: Diamd. preorders: **8,673**
📖 The Valkyrie **A:** P. Craig Russell **W:** P. Craig Russell
3 ❑ Oct 2000 Cover: 2.99 **NM** value: **Cover or less**
Circ: Diamd. preorders: **8,279**
📖 The Valkyrie **A:** P. Craig Russell **W:** P. Craig Russell

RING OF THE NIBELUNG, THE (VOL. 3) — Dark Horse

1 ❑ Dec 2000 Cover: 2.99 **NM** value: **Cover or less**
Circ: Diamd. preorders: **8,365**
📖 Siegfried **A:** P. Craig Russell **W:** P. Craig Russell
2 ❑ Jan 2001 Cover: 2.99 **NM** value: **Cover or less**
Circ: Diamd. preorders: **7,827**
📖 Siegfried **A:** P. Craig Russell **W:** P. Craig Russell
3 ❑ Feb 2001 Cover: 2.99 **NM** value: **Cover or less**
Circ: Diamd. preorders: **7,777**
📖 Siegfried **A:** P. Craig Russell **W:** P. Craig Russell

RINGO KID, THE — Marvel

1 ❑ Jan 1970 Cover: 0.15 **NM** value: **8.00**
• **CGC:** 1 graded, best 9.0
📖 The Hostage; Stranger in Town; One Must Die! • Reprint from Ringo Kid Western **A:** Al Williamson **W:** Stan Lee
2 ❑ Mar 1970 Cover: 0.15 **NM** value: **5.00**
📖 The Sheriff's Star!; Deadly Ambush **A:** John Severin
3 ❑ May 1970 Cover: 0.15 **NM** value: **4.00**
4 ❑ Jul 1970 Cover: 0.15 **NM** value: **4.00**
5 ❑ Sep 1970 Cover: 0.15 **NM** value: **4.00**
6 ❑ Nov 1970 Cover: 0.15 **NM** value: **4.00**
7 ❑ Jan 1971 Cover: 0.15 **NM** value: **4.00**
8 ❑ Mar 1971 Cover: 0.15 **NM** value: **4.00**
9 ❑ May 1971 Cover: 0.15 **NM** value: **4.00**
10 ❑ Jul 1971 Cover: 0.15 **NM** value: **4.00**
11 ❑ Sep 1971 Cover: 0.15 **NM** value: **3.00**
12 ❑ Nov 1971 Cover: 0.25 **NM** value: **3.00**
13 ❑ Jan 1972 Cover: 0.25 **NM** value: **3.00**
14 ❑ Mar 1972 Cover: 0.20 **NM** value: **3.00**
15 ❑ May 1972 Cover: 0.20 **NM** value: **3.00**
16 ❑ Jul 1972 Cover: 0.20 **NM** value: **3.00**
17 ❑ Sep 1972 Cover: 0.20 **NM** value: **3.00**
18 ❑ Nov 1972 Cover: 0.20 **NM** value: **3.00**
19 ❑ Jan 1973 Cover: 0.20 **NM** value: **3.00**
20 ❑ Mar 1973 Cover: 0.20 **NM** value: **3.00**
21 ❑ May 1973 Cover: 0.20 **NM** value: **3.00**
22 ❑ Jul 1973 Cover: 0.20 **NM** value: **3.00**
23 ❑ Sep 1973 Cover: 0.20 **NM** value: **3.00**
24 ❑ Nov 1973 Cover: 0.20 **NM** value: **3.00**
25 ❑ Nov 1975 Cover: 0.20 **NM** value: **3.00**
26 ❑ Jan 1976 Cover: 0.20 **NM** value: **3.00**
27 ❑ Mar 1976 Cover: 0.20 **NM** value: **3.00**
28 ❑ May 1976 Cover: 0.20 **NM** value: **3.00**
29 ❑ Jul 1976 Cover: 0.20 **NM** value: **3.00**
30 ❑ Sep 1976 Cover: 0.20 **NM** value: **3.00**
final issue.

RINGO KID WESTERN, THE — Marvel

The Ringo Kid is a Western hero loner of the "good guys wear black" school, roaming the plains of the desert Southwest in the frontier days with his faithful horse Arab. Ringo had a knack for getting ambushed by the bad guys, but his fast wits and faster six-guns helped him out of trouble every time.

Ringo Kid was one of the mainstays of the Atlas (later Marvel) Western comics, which also included Two-Gun Kid, Black Rider, and Outlaw Kid. Ringo benefited from some excellent artwork courtesy of master illustrators John Severin and Al Williamson. Many of the Ringo Kid stories from the 1950s were later reprinted in a second Ringo Kid series from Marvel during the early 1970s.

1 ❑ Aug 1954 Cover: 0.10 **NM** value: **175.00**
• **CGC:** 1 graded, best 6.5
★ Origin of The Ringo Kid.
2 ❑ Oct 1954 Cover: 0.10 **NM** value: **90.00**
3 ❑ Dec 1954 Cover: 0.10 **NM** value: **60.00**
4 ❑ Feb 1955 Cover: 0.10 **NM** value: **48.00**
5 ❑ Apr 1955 Cover: 0.10 **NM** value: **48.00**
6 ❑ Jun 1955 Cover: 0.10 **NM** value: **42.00**
7 ❑ Aug 1955 Cover: 0.10 **NM** value: **42.00**
8 ❑ Oct 1955 Cover: 0.10 **NM** value: **42.00**
9 ❑ Dec 1955 Cover: 0.10 **NM** value: **42.00**
📖 Man Trap!; Deadly Ambush!; Prairie Schooner (text story); The Sheriff's Star! **A:** John Severin
10 ❑ Feb 1956 Cover: 0.10 **NM** value: **42.00**
11 ❑ Apr 1956 Cover: 0.10 **NM** value: **36.00**
12 ❑ Jun 1956 Cover: 0.10 **NM** value: **36.00**
13 ❑ Aug 1956 Cover: 0.10 **NM** value: **36.00**
14 ❑ Oct 1956 Cover: 0.10 **NM** value: **36.00**
15 ❑ Dec 1956 Cover: 0.10 **NM** value: **36.00**
16 ❑ Feb 1957 Cover: 0.10 **NM** value: **36.00**
17 ❑ Apr 1957 Cover: 0.10 **NM** value: **36.00**
18 ❑ Jun 1957 Cover: 0.10 **NM** value: **36.00**
19 ❑ Jul 1957 Cover: 0.10 **NM** value: **36.00**
20 ❑ Aug 1957 Cover: 0.10 **NM** value: **36.00**
21 ❑ Sep 1957 Cover: 0.10 **NM** value: **36.00**
final issue.

RIN TIN TIN — Dell

4 ❑ Mar 1954 Cover: 0.10 **NM** value: **50.00**
5 ❑ Jun 1954 Cover: 0.10 **NM** value: **50.00**
6 ❑ Sep 1954 Cover: 0.10 **NM** value: **50.00**
7 ❑ Dec 1954 Cover: 0.10 **NM** value: **50.00**
8 ❑ Mar 1955 Cover: 0.10 **NM** value: **50.00**
9 ❑ Jun 1955 Cover: 0.10 **NM** value: **50.00**
10 ❑ Sep 1956 Cover: 0.10 **NM** value: **50.00**
11 ❑ Dec 1956 Cover: 0.10 **NM** value: **40.00**
12 ❑ Mar 1956 Cover: 0.10 **NM** value: **40.00**
13 ❑ Jun 1956 Cover: 0.10 **NM** value: **40.00**
14 ❑ Aug 1956 Cover: 0.10 **NM** value: **40.00**
15 ❑ Sep 1956 Cover: 0.10 **NM** value: **40.00**
16 ❑ Nov 1956 Cover: 0.10 **NM** value: **40.00**
17 ❑ Feb 1956 Cover: 0.10 **NM** value: **40.00**
18 ❑ Apr 1957 Cover: 0.10 **NM** value: **40.00**
19 ❑ Jun 1957 Cover: 0.10 **NM** value: **40.00**
20 ❑ Sep 1957 Cover: 0.10 **NM** value: **40.00**
21 ❑ Nov 1957 Cover: 0.10 **NM** value: **35.00**
22 ❑ Jan 1958 Cover: 0.10 **NM** value: **35.00**
23 ❑ Mar 1958 Cover: 0.10 **NM** value: **35.00**
24 ❑ Apr 1958 Cover: 0.10 **NM** value: **35.00**
• **CGC:** 1 graded, best 7.5
25 ❑ Jun 1958 Cover: 0.10 **NM** value: **35.00**
26 ❑ Aug 1958 Cover: 0.10 **NM** value: **35.00**
27 ❑ Oct 1958 Cover: 0.10 **NM** value: **35.00**
28 ❑ Nov 1958 Cover: 0.10 **NM** value: **35.00**
29 ❑ Feb 1959 Cover: 0.10 **NM** value: **35.00**
30 ❑ May 1959 Cover: 0.10 **NM** value: **35.00**
31 ❑ Aug 1959 Cover: 0.10 **NM** value: **35.00**
32 ❑ Nov 1959 Cover: 0.10 **NM** value: **35.00**
33 ❑ Feb 1960 Cover: 0.10 **NM** value: **35.00**
34 ❑ May 1960 Cover: 0.10 **NM** value: **35.00**
35 ❑ Aug 1960 Cover: 0.10 **NM** value: **35.00**
36 ❑ Nov 1960 Cover: 0.10 **NM** value: **35.00**
37 ❑ 1961 **NM** value: **35.00**

CGC-graded: Multiply prices above by **33 for 9.9 M • 16 for 9.8 NM/M • 7 for 9.6 NM+ • 5 for 9.4 NM • 2.5 for 9.2 NM- • 1.5 for 9.0 VF/NM**

38 ❑ Jul 1961 Cover: 0.15 **NM** value: **35.00**

RIN TIN TIN & RUSTY — Gold Key

1 ❑ Nov 1963 Cover: 0.12 **NM** value: **50.00**

RIO AT BAY — Dark Horse

Doug Wildey is one of the most notable, if often unrecognized, illustrators in comics. Before creating Rio, he did a comic version of The Saint, ghosted strips for Steve Canyon, and served a three-year stint on Marvel's The Outlaw Kid. His most popular creation, however, was Jonny Quest, developed for both comics and TV.

Drawing from his experience at Marvel, Wildey created Rio, a western rifleman who stars in this two-issue mini-series. Here Rio must defend a young miner who made the mistake of winning a family heirloom from the mining company owner's son in a game of poker. The owner's son was a bad loser, however, and sent gunmen to kill the boy and reclaim what he had lost.

1 ❑ Aug 1992 Cover: 2.95 **NM** value: **Cover or less**
📖 Hot Lead For Jonny Hardluck **A:** Doug Wildey **W:** Doug Wildey

2 ❑ Aug 1992 Cover: 2.95 **NM** value: **Cover or less**
A: Doug Wildey **W:** Doug Wildey

Bk 1❑ Cover: 6.95 **NM** value: **Cover or less**
• Softcover edition. • Collects Rio at Bay #1-2 **A:** Doug Wildey

RIO GRAPHIC NOVEL — Comico

1 ❑ May 1987 Cover: 8.95 **NM** value: **Cover or less**
Circ: CapCity orders: **1,336**

RIO KID — Eternity

1 ❑ b&w Cover: 2.50 **NM** value: **Cover or less**
2 ❑ b&w Cover: 2.50 **NM** value: **Cover or less**
3 ❑ b&w Cover: 2.50 **NM** value: **Cover or less**

RION 2990 — Rion

1 ❑ b&w Cover: 1.50 **NM** value: **Cover or less**
📖 Despair **A:** Ryan Brown **W:** Doug Bramer
2 ❑ b&w Cover: 1.50 **NM** value: **Cover or less**
3 ❑ Cover: 1.50 **NM** value: **Cover or less**
4 ❑ Cover: 1.50 **NM** value: **Cover or less**

RIO RIDES AGAIN — Marvel

Bk 1❑ Cover: 9.95 **NM** value: **Cover or less**
Circ: CapCity orders: **1,400**

RIO RITA — AC / Paragon

Bk 1❑ Cover: 6.95 **NM** value: **Cover or less**
• Reprints Golden Age stories

RIOT — Atlas

1 ❑ Apr 1954 Cover: 0.10 **NM** value: **200.00**
2 ❑ Jun 1954 Cover: 0.10 **NM** value: **150.00**
3 ❑ Aug 1954 Cover: 0.10 **NM** value: **150.00**
4 ❑ Feb 1956 Cover: 0.10 **NM** value: **150.00**
5 ❑ Apr 1956 Cover: 0.10 **NM** value: **150.00**
6 ❑ Jun 1956 Cover: 0.10 **NM** value: **150.00**

RIOT, ACT 1 — Viz

1 ❑ Oct 1995 Cover: 2.75 **NM** value: **Cover or less**
2 ❑ Nov 1995 Cover: 2.75 **NM** value: **Cover or less**
3 ❑ Dec 1995 Cover: 2.75 **NM** value: **Cover or less**
4 ❑ Jan 1996 Cover: 2.95 **NM** value: **Cover or less**
5 ❑ Feb 1996 Cover: 2.95 **NM** value: **Cover or less**
6 ❑ Mar 1996 Cover: 2.95 **NM** value: **Cover or less**
Bk 1❑ Cover: 15.95 **NM** value: **Cover or less**

RIOT, ACT 2 — Viz

1 ❑ Apr 1996 Cover: 2.95 **NM** value: **Cover or less**
2 ❑ May 1996 Cover: 2.95 **NM** value: **Cover or less**
3 ❑ Jun 1996 Cover: 2.95 **NM** value: **Cover or less**
4 ❑ Jul 1996 Cover: 2.95 **NM** value: **Cover or less**
5 ❑ Aug 1996 Cover: 2.95 **NM** value: **Cover or less**
6 ❑ Sep 1996 Cover: 2.95 **NM** value: **Cover or less**
Circ: Diamd. preorders: **5,306**
7 ❑ Oct 1996 Cover: 2.95 **NM** value: **Cover or less**
Circ: Diamd. preorders: **5,223**
Bk 1❑ Cover: 15.95 **NM** value: **Cover or less**

RIOT GEAR — Triumphant

1 ❑ Sep 1993 Cover: 2.50 **NM** value: **Cover or less**
Circ: CapCity orders: **6,300**
A: Fred Harper **W:** John Riley

1/Ash❑Sep 1993 Cover: 2.50 **NM** value: **Cover or less**
• Ashcan edition (color). 📖 Escape **A:** Fred Harper **W:** John Riley

2 ❑ Oct 1993 Cover: 2.50 **NM** value: **Cover or less**
Circ: CapCity orders: **4,170**
A: Fred Harper **W:** John Riley

3 ❑ Nov 1993 Cover: 2.50 **NM** value: **Cover or less**
Circ: CapCity orders: **6,185**
A: Fred Harper **W:** John Riley

4 ❑ Dec 1993 Cover: 2.50 **NM** value: **Cover or less**
Circ: CapCity orders: **7,400**
• Unleashed! **A:** Fred Harper **W:** John Riley ★ Death of Captain Tich.

5 ❑ Jan 1994 Cover: 2.50 **NM** value: **Cover or less**
Circ: CapCity orders: **4,075**
📖 Retribution **A:** Fred Harper **W:** John Riley

6 ❑ Feb 1994 Cover: 2.50 **NM** value: **Cover or less**
Circ: CapCity orders: **3,560**
📖 Retribution **A:** Fred Harper **W:** John Riley

7 ❑ Mar 1994 Cover: 2.50 **NM** value: **Cover or less**
Circ: CapCity orders: **2,730**
A: Fred Harper **W:** John Riley

8 ❑ Apr 1994 Cover: 2.50 **NM** value: **Cover or less**
Circ: CapCity orders: **2,288**
📖 One Last Exit **A:** Fred Harper **W:** John Riley

9 ❑ May 1994 Cover: 2.50 **NM** value: **Cover or less**
A: Fred Harper **W:** John Riley

10 ❑ Jun 1994 Cover: 2.50 **NM** value: **Cover or less**
A: Fred Harper **W:** John Riley

11 ❑ Jul 1994 Cover: 2.50 **NM** value: **Cover or less**
• Final issue? **A:** Fred Harper **W:** John Riley

Ash 1❑full color Cover: 2.50 **NM** value: **Cover or less**
• ashcan

RIOT GEAR: VIOLENT PAST — Triumphant

1 ❑ Feb 1994 Cover: 2.50 **NM** value: **Cover or less**
Circ: CapCity orders: **3,605**
A: Andrew Walls **W:** John Riley

2 ❑ Feb 1994 Cover: 2.50 **NM** value: **Cover or less**
Circ: CapCity orders: **3,295**
• 14,000 printed **A:** Andrew Walls; Fred Harper(cover) **W:** John Riley

RIPCLAW (VOL. 1) — Image

Robert Bearclaw, also known as Ripclaw, is an American Indian super-hero affiliated with Cyberforce. This fearsome character has little trouble finding trouble on his own, as this limited series proves.

When not on the team, Bearclaw tries to lead a peaceful life on the. That, of course, is an impossibility. The first story arc involves a rare mystical stone that empowers the holder with enormous powers. When in the right hands, the stone can perform wondrous tasks. When in the wrong hands, the stone can be warped into a dreadful weapon. Ripclaw is asked to recover the magic rock, which he agrees to do. The task puts him in competition with Doonongaes, a demon lord who also seeks the stone's power.

0.5 ❑ **NM** value: **2.00**
• Wizard promotional edition. **A:** Brandon Peterson **W:** Eric Silvestri

0.5/GO❑ **NM** value: **2.50**
• Gold edition. **A:** Brandon Peterson **W:** Eric Silvestri

1 ❑ Apr 1995 Cover: 2.50 **NM** value: **Cover or less**
Circ: CapCity orders: **39,475**
A: Brandon Peterson **W:** Eric Silvestri

2 ❑ Jun 1995 Cover: 2.50 **NM** value: **Cover or less**
Circ: CapCity orders: **28,825**
A: Brandon Peterson **W:** Eric Silvestri

3 ❑ Jul 1995 Cover: 2.50 **NM** value: **Cover or less**
Circ: CapCity orders: **26,900**
A: Brandon Peterson **W:** Eric Silvestri

4 ❑ Aug 1995 Cover: 2.50 **NM** value: **Cover or less**
Circ: CapCity orders: **25,925**
A: Brandon Peterson **W:** Eric Silvestri

RIPCLAW (VOL. 2) — Image

1 ❑ Dec 1995 Cover: 2.50 **NM** value: **Cover or less**
Circ: CapCity orders: **17,725**
A: Anthony Winn **W:** Brian Haberlin; David Wohl

2 ❑ Jan 1996 Cover: 2.50 **NM** value: **Cover or less**
A: Anthony Winn **W:** Brian Haberlin; David Wohl

3 ❑ Feb 1996 Cover: 2.50 **NM** value: **Cover or less**
A: Anthony Winn **W:** Brian Haberlin; David Wohl

4 ❑ Mar 1996 Cover: 2.50 **NM** value: **Cover or less**
A: Anthony Winn **W:** Brian Haberlin; David Wohl

5 ❑ Apr 1996 Cover: 2.50 **NM** value: **Cover or less**
A: Anthony Winn **W:** Brian Haberlin; David Wohl

6 ❑ Jun 1996 Cover: 2.50 **NM** value: **Cover or less**
A: Anthony Winn **W:** Brian Haberlin; David Wohl

SE 1❑ Oct 1995 Cover: 2.50 **NM** value: **Cover or less**
Circ: CapCity orders: **27,400**
• Special Edition #1. **A:** Jordan Raskin **W:** Brian Holguin; David Wohl; Marc Silverstri

R.I.P. COMICS MODULE — TSR

1 ❑ Cover: 2.95 **NM** value: **Cover or less**
Circ: CapCity orders: **4,224**

2 ❑ Cover: 2.95 **NM** value: **Cover or less**
Circ: CapCity orders: **3,100**

3 ❑ Cover: 2.95 **NM** value: **Cover or less**
Circ: CapCity orders: **2,400**

4 ❑ Cover: 2.95 **NM** value: **Cover or less**
Circ: CapCity orders: **2,250**

5 ❑ Cover: 2.95 **NM** value: **Cover or less**
Circ: CapCity orders: **1,920**
• Brasher

6 ❑ Cover: 2.95 **NM** value: **Cover or less**
Circ: CapCity orders: **1,920**
• Brasher

7 ❑ Cover: 2.95 **NM** value: **Cover or less**
Circ: CapCity orders: **1,920**
• Brasher

8 ❑ Cover: 2.95 **NM** value: **Cover or less**
Circ: CapCity orders: **1,728**
• Brasher

R.I.P.D. — Dark Horse

1 ❑ Oct 1999 Cover: 2.95 **NM** value: **Cover or less**
Circ: Diamd. preorders: **6,843**
A: Lucas Marangon **W:** Peter M. Lenkov

2 ❑ Nov 1999 Cover: 2.95 **NM** value: **Cover or less**
Circ: Diamd. preorders: **5,107**
A: Lucas Marangon **W:** Peter M. Lenkov

3 ❑ Dec 1999 Cover: 2.95 **NM** value: **Cover or less**
Circ: Diamd. preorders: **4,312**
A: Lucas Marangon **W:** Peter M. Lenkov

4 ❑ Jan 2000 Cover: 2.95 **NM** value: **Cover or less**
Circ: Diamd. preorders: **4,175**
A: Lucas Marangon **W:** Peter M. Lenkov

RIPFIRE — Malibu

0 ❑ Jan 1995 Cover: 2.50 **NM** value: **Cover or less**
Circ: CapCity orders: **6,200**
📖 Genesis **A:** Darick Robertson **W:** Darick Robertson

RIP HUNTER...TIME MASTER — DC

Rip Hunter was the leader of a foursome of daring adventurers. While others would explore space or the hidden worlds under the sea, Rip and his crew would solve mysteries in time.

Rip's team consisted of himself, Bonnie Baxter, her little brother Corky, and their friend Jeff Smith. (Similar line-ups were used in both the Fantastic Four and the Sea Devils.) This crew would travel back in time in their globe-shaped time sphere to solve historical mysteries and save the present day by setting some event in motion in the distant past.

Rip Hunter debuted in Showcase #21 and was featured in several other issues of that series before getting his own title in 1961. This title ran some 29 issues before concluding in 1965.

An updated version of the team was introduced in the early 1990s mini-series Time Masters.

1 ❑ Mar 1961 Cover: 0.12 **NM** value: **325.00**
Circ: Statement: **215,000** • **CGC:** 10 graded, best 8.5

2 ❑ May 1961 Cover: 0.12 **NM** value: **125.00**
Circ: Statement: **215,000** • **CGC:** 3 graded, best 8.5

3 ❑ Jul 1961 Cover: 0.12 **NM** value: **100.00**
Circ: Statement: **215,000** • **CGC:** 4 graded, best 9.4

4 ❑ Sep 1961 Cover: 0.12 **NM** value: **85.00**
Circ: Statement: **215,000** • **CGC:** 3 graded, best 9.2

5 ❑ Nov 1961 Cover: 0.12 **NM** value: **85.00**
Circ: Statement: **215,000** • **CGC:** 3 graded, best 9.0

6 ❑ Jan 1962 Cover: 0.12 **NM** value: **75.00**
Circ: Statement: **195,000** • **CGC:** 4 graded, best 8.5
A: Alex Toth

7 ❑ Mar 1962 Cover: 0.12 **NM** value: **75.00**
Circ: Statement: **195,000** • **CGC:** 2 graded, best 9.2
• Has 1961 Statement, filed 10/1/61; avg total paid circ 215,000 **A:** Alex Toth

8 ❑ May 1962 Cover: 0.12 **NM** value: **60.00**
Circ: Statement: **195,000** • **CGC:** 3 graded, best 9.0

9 ❑ Jul 1962 Cover: 0.12 **NM** value: **60.00**
Circ: Statement: **195,000** • **CGC:** 3 graded, best 9.2

10 ❑ Sep 1962 Cover: 0.12 **NM** value: **60.00**
Circ: Statement: **195,000** • **CGC:** 4 graded, best 9.2

11 ❑ Nov 1962 Cover: 0.12 **NM** value: **60.00**
Circ: Statement: **195,000** • **CGC:** 2 graded, best 9.0

12 ❑ Jan 1963 Cover: 0.12 **NM** value: **60.00**
• **CGC:** 1 graded, best 9.0

13 ❑ Mar 1963 Cover: 0.12 **NM** value: **60.00**
• **CGC:** 1 graded, best 9.2
• Has 1962 Statement, filed 10/1/62; avg total paid circ 195,000

14 ❑ May 1963 Cover: 0.12 **NM** value: **60.00**
• **CGC:** 5 graded, best 9.2

15 ❑ Jul 1963 Cover: 0.12 **NM** value: **60.00**
• **CGC:** 2 graded, best 9.4

16 ❑ Sep 1963 Cover: 0.12 **NM** value: **50.00**
• **CGC:** 3 graded, best 9.4

17 ❑ Nov 1963 Cover: 0.12 **NM** value: **50.00**
• **CGC:** 2 graded, best 9.2

18 ❑ Jan 1964 Cover: 0.12 **NM** value: **50.00**
Circ: Statement: **197,398** • **CGC:** 1 graded, best 9.4

19 ❑ Mar 1964 Cover: 0.12 **NM** value: **50.00**
Circ: Statement: **197,398**
📖 Cleopatra's Deadly Trap; Rip Caesar-Conqueror of Egypt; The Time Journal; Caesar's Forgotten Foe • Has 1963 Statement, filed 10/1/63; no circ figures published **W:** Jack E. Miller

20 ❑ May 1964 Cover: 0.12 **NM** value: **50.00**
Circ: Statement: **197,398** • **CGC:** 1 graded, best 8.0

21 ❑ Jul 1964 Cover: 0.12 **NM** value: **42.00**
Circ: Statement: **197,398** • **CGC:** 2 graded, best 9.2

22 ❑ Sep 1964 Cover: 0.12 **NM** value: **42.00**
Circ: Statement: **197,398** • **CGC:** 1 graded, best 6.0

23 ❑ Nov 1964 Cover: 0.12 **NM** value: **42.00**
Circ: Statement: **197,398** • **CGC:** 2 graded, best 8.0

24 ❑ Jan 1965 Cover: 0.12 **NM** value: **42.00**
• **CGC:** 1 graded, best 8.5

25 ❑ Mar 1965 Cover: 0.12 **NM** value: **42.00**
• **CGC:** 1 graded, best 9.2
• Has 1964 Statement, filed 10/1/64; avg print run 313,000; avg sales 197,000; avg subs 398; avg total paid 197,398; samples 387; max existent 197,785; 37% of run returned

26 ❑ May 1965 Cover: 0.12 **NM** value: **35.00**
• **CGC:** 1 graded, best 9.2
📖 Bring Back The Cosmic Key

27 ❑ Jul 1965 Cover: 0.12 **NM** value: **35.00**
• **CGC:** 2 graded, best 9.0

28 ❑ Sep 1965 Cover: 0.12 **NM** value: **35.00**
• **CGC:** 1 graded, best 9.2

29 ❑ Nov 1965 Cover: 0.12 **NM** value: **35.00**
• **CGC:** 1 graded, best 6.0
final issue.

RIP IN TIME — Fantagor

1 ❑ b&w Cover: 1.50 **NM** value: **2.00**
A: Richard Corben **W:** Richard Corben; Bruce Jones
2 ❑ b&w Cover: 1.50 **NM** value: **2.00**
Rip in Time; Going Home **A:** Richard Corben **W:** Richard Corben; Bruce Jones
3 ❑ b&w Cover: 1.50 **NM** value: **2.00**
Rip in Time; The Secret of Zokma **A:** Richard Corben **W:** Richard Corben; Bruce Jones
4 ❑ b&w Cover: 1.50 **NM** value: **2.00**
Rip in Time **A:** Richard Corben **W:** Richard Corben; Bruce Jones
5 ❑ b&w Cover: 1.50 **NM** value: **2.00**
Rip in Time; The Awakening **A:** Richard Corben **W:** Richard Corben; Bruce Jones

RIPLEY'S BELIEVE IT OR NOT! — Gold Key

For generations, Ripley's Believe It or Not! told tales of the bizarre and uncanny, but which "were absolutely true — believe it or not!" In doing so, Ripley has introduced readers to everything from child prodigies who composed masterpieces before they turned 12 to great islands built by people throwing pebbles into the water over a period of several generations.

In this series, previously entitled "True War Stories," the writers tended to stretch the bounds of credibility. Readers who do not dispute the existence of spirits may have trouble believing these thrilling tales of ghost ships, hauntings, and other supernatural phenomena.

4 ❑ Apr 1967 Cover: 0.12 **NM** value: **26.00**
• Series continued from "Ripley's Believe it Or Not True War Stories"
5 ❑ Jun 1967 Cover: 0.12 **NM** value: **16.00**
The Last Kamikaze; The General Was a Spy (text story); Miracle of the Marne; Hand to Hand; Dead Man's Ambush; The Balloon Buster
6 ❑ Aug 1967 Cover: 0.12 **NM** value: **16.00**
Testimony of the Ghost; The Forbes Tragedy (text story); The Haunted Villa; The Phantom Navigator; Hounds of Death
7 ❑ Nov 1967 Cover: 0.12 **NM** value: **16.00**
The Golem; The Berbalang Ghouls (text story); The Vampire; The Werewolves of Poligny; The Devil's Steed
8 ❑ Feb 1968 Cover: 0.12 **NM** value: **16.00**
The Black Spectre; The Floating Coffin (text story); The Phantom in White; Appointment at Ticonderoga; Death Comes Knocking
9 ❑ May 1968 Cover: 0.12 **NM** value: **16.00**
10 ❑ Aug 1968 Cover: 0.15 **NM** value: **16.00**
The Ravens of Doom; The Thing at Loch Ness (text story); The Vampire of the Schloss; The Demon in the Glass Cage; The Shadow Men
11 ❑ Nov 1968 Cover: 0.15 **NM** value: **12.00**
Death Comes Riding; The Ballerina's Last Dance (text story); Phantom Hands of Vengeance; The Ghost Warriors; The Crystal Skull of Doom • 10208-811
12 ❑ Feb 1969 Cover: 0.15 **NM** value: **12.00**
The Strangling Oak; The Spectres of Goodwin Sands (text story); Death's Spectral Hand; The Ghostly Horseman; The Headless Ghost of Halley Hollow
13 ❑ Apr 1969 Cover: 0.15 **NM** value: **12.00**
The Curse of the Four; Haunted by Death (text story); The Gray Angel; The Treasure of the Ghost Queen; The Phantom Pallbearers
14 ❑ Jun 1969 Cover: 0.15 **NM** value: **12.00**
The Demon of Beachy-Head; Return of the Monsters (text story); The Horror of Lincoln's Inn; The Foxes of Doom; The Monster of Croglin Grange
15 ❑ Aug 1969 Cover: 0.15 **NM** value: **12.00**
The Curse of the Shroud; Half a Ghost (text story); Herne the Hunter; Armies of the Doomed; The Headless Conquistador
16 ❑ Oct 1969 Cover: 0.15 **NM** value: **10.00**
17 ❑ Dec 1969 Cover: 0.15 **NM** value: **10.00**
The Doom Flower; The Mystic Mine (text story); The Man Who Walked on Air!; The Curse of Humble Lee; Spawn of the Wolf Pack;
18 ❑ Feb 1970 Cover: 0.15 **NM** value: **10.00**
The Headless Huntsman; The Phantom German (text story); The Ghost's Vendetta; The Spectacled Warriors; The Devil's Violin
19 ❑ Apr 1970 Cover: 0.15 **NM** value: **10.00**
The Sea Hags; Satan Walks the Streets (text story); Demon-Wizard; The Devil-Eyed Cat; The Lurking Monster
20 ❑ Jun 1970 Cover: 0.15 **NM** value: **10.00**
The Living Dead; The Creeping Plague (text story); The Boy with the Fiery Eyes; The Psychic Detective; Curse of the Blind Idol
21 ❑ Aug 1970 Cover: 0.15 **NM** value: **8.00**
• **CGC:** 1 graded, best 9.6
My Lady Death; The Haunted Highway (text story); The Living Phantom; The Ghost Drums of Rathmoy; Voyage to Doom!
22 ❑ Oct 1970 Cover: 0.15 **NM** value: **8.00**
23 ❑ Dec 1970 Cover: 0.15 **NM** value: **8.00**
24 ❑ Feb 1971 Cover: 0.15 **NM** value: **8.00**
Circ: Statement: **236,459**
25 ❑ Apr 1971 Cover: 0.15 **NM** value: **8.00**
Circ: Statement: **236,459**
26 ❑ Jun 1971 Cover: 0.15 **NM** value: **8.00**
Circ: Statement: **236,459**
Wedding of the Demons!; Spawn of Hades (text story); The Moth-men; The Horns of Lucifer; The Dracula of Monteros
27 ❑ Aug 1971 Cover: 0.15 **NM** value: **8.00**
Circ: Statement: **236,459**
Satan's Apprentice; Death Calls a Warning (text story); Guardian of the Tomb; The Curse of the House of Mara; Three Ghostly Kisses
28 ❑ Sep 1971 Cover: 0.15 **NM** value: **8.00**
Circ: Statement: **236,459**
29 ❑ Oct 1971 Cover: 0.15 **NM** value: **8.00**
Circ: Statement: **236,459**
30 ❑ Dec 1971 Cover: 0.15 **NM** value: **8.00**
Circ: Statement: **236,459**
31 ❑ Feb 1972 Cover: 0.15 **NM** value: **5.00**
• Has 1971 Statement; avg print run 334,807; avg total paid 236,459
32 ❑ Apr 1972 Cover: 0.15 **NM** value: **5.00**
33 ❑ Jun 1972 Cover: 0.15 **NM** value: **5.00**
The Witch Dolls of Locheen; The Red Ribbon of Death (text story); The Restless Spirit; The White Bull Ghost of the Calgary Rodeo; Curse of the Black Monk
34 ❑ Aug 1972 Cover: 0.15 **NM** value: **5.00**
The Surprise Party; The Ghost Hunter (text story); But No One Knocked; The Ghost of Spire Church; The Unholy Summons • 90208-208
35 ❑ Sep 1972 Cover: 0.15 **NM** value: **5.00**
36 ❑ Oct 1972 Cover: 0.15 **NM** value: **5.00**
37 ❑ Dec 1972 Cover: 0.15 **NM** value: **5.00**
The Ruby Ring; To the Gallows (text story); The Stone Angels; Face at the Window; Green Eyes • 90208-212
38 ❑ Feb 1973 Cover: 0.15 **NM** value: **5.00**
39 ❑ Apr 1973 Cover: 0.15 **NM** value: **5.50**
40 ❑ Jun 1973 Cover: 0.20 **NM** value: **5.00**
41 ❑ Aug 1973 Cover: 0.20 **NM** value: **5.00**
42 ❑ Sep 1973 Cover: 0.20 **NM** value: **5.00**
43 ❑ Oct 1973 Cover: 0.20 **NM** value: **5.00**
44 ❑ Dec 1973 Cover: 0.20 **NM** value: **5.00**
45 ❑ Feb 1974 Cover: 0.20 **NM** value: **5.00**
46 ❑ Apr 1974 Cover: 0.20 **NM** value: **5.00**
47 ❑ Jun 1974 Cover: 0.20 **NM** value: **5.00**
48 ❑ Aug 1974 Cover: 0.25 **NM** value: **5.00**
Dance to Eternity; Train to Zurich!; The Guide; Cry Fake!
49 ❑ Sep 1974 Cover: 0.25 **NM** value: **5.00**
50 ❑ Oct 1974 Cover: 0.25 **NM** value: **5.00**
51 ❑ Dec 1974 Cover: 0.25 **NM** value: **4.00**
52 ❑ Feb 1975 Cover: 0.25 **NM** value: **4.00**
53 ❑ Apr 1975 Cover: 0.25 **NM** value: **4.00**
54 ❑ Jun 1975 Cover: 0.25 **NM** value: **4.00**
55 ❑ Jul 1975 Cover: 0.25 **NM** value: **4.00**
56 ❑ Aug 1975 Cover: 0.25 **NM** value: **4.00**
57 ❑ Sep 1975 Cover: 0.25 **NM** value: **4.00**
58 ❑ Oct 1975 Cover: 0.25 **NM** value: **4.00**
59 ❑ Dec 1975 Cover: 0.25 **NM** value: **4.00**
60 ❑ Feb 1976 Cover: 0.25 **NM** value: **4.00**
61 ❑ Apr 1976 Cover: 0.25 **NM** value: **4.00**
62 ❑ Jun 1976 Cover: 0.25 **NM** value: **4.00**
63 ❑ Jul 1976 Cover: 0.25 **NM** value: **4.00**
64 ❑ Aug 1976 Cover: 0.25 **NM** value: **4.00**
65 ❑ Oct 1976 Cover: 0.30 **NM** value: **4.00**
An Affair Of Honor; Horse Thief; Faces In The Deep; Watery Visions
66 ❑ Dec 1976 Cover: 0.30 **NM** value: **4.00**
67 ❑ Jan 1977 Cover: 0.30 **NM** value: **4.00**
68 ❑ Feb 1977 Cover: 0.30 **NM** value: **4.00**
69 ❑ Apr 1977 Cover: 0.30 **NM** value: **4.00**
70 ❑ Jun 1977 Cover: 0.30 **NM** value: **4.00**
71 ❑ Jul 1977 Cover: 0.30 **NM** value: **3.00**
72 ❑ Aug 1977 Cover: 0.30 **NM** value: **3.00**
73 ❑ Oct 1977 Cover: 0.30 **NM** value: **3.00**
74 ❑ Dec 1977 Cover: 0.50 **NM** value: **5.00**
75 ❑ Jan 1978 Cover: 0.35 **NM** value: **3.00**
76 ❑ Feb 1978 Cover: 0.35 **NM** value: **3.00**
77 ❑ Apr 1978 Cover: 0.50 **NM** value: **3.00**
78 ❑ Jun 1978 Cover: 0.50 **NM** value: **3.00**
79 ❑ Jul 1978 Cover: 0.50 **NM** value: **3.00**
80 ❑ Aug 1978 Cover: 0.50 **NM** value: **3.00**
81 ❑ Sep 1978 Cover: 0.50 **NM** value: **3.00**
82 ❑ Oct 1978 Cover: 0.50 **NM** value: **3.00**
83 ❑ Nov 1978 Cover: 0.50 **NM** value: **3.00**
84 ❑ Dec 1978 Cover: 0.35 **NM** value: **3.00**
85 ❑ Jan 1979 Cover: 0.35 **NM** value: **3.00**
86 ❑ Feb 1979 Cover: 0.35 **NM** value: **3.00**
The Born-Again Queen; Who Goes There?; The Welcoming Spirit; Time for Justice;
87 ❑ Apr 1979 Cover: 0.40 **NM** value: **3.00**
88 ❑ May 1979 Cover: 0.40 **NM** value: **3.00**
89 ❑ Jul 1979 Cover: 0.40 **NM** value: **3.00**
90 ❑ Aug 1979 Cover: 0.40 **NM** value: **3.00**
The Face of Guilt; The Iron Cage; The Power to See Beyond; Hound of Death
91 ❑ Sep 1979 Cover: 0.40 **NM** value: **3.00**
92 ❑ Oct 1979 Cover: 0.40 **NM** value: **3.00**
93 ❑ Nov 1979 Cover: 0.40 **NM** value: **3.00**
94 ❑ Feb 1980 Cover: 0.40 **NM** value: **3.00**
final issue.

RIPLEY'S BELIEVE IT OR NOT!: BEAUTY & GROOMING — Schanes

1 ❑ Cover: 2.50 **NM** value: **Cover or less**

RIPLEY'S BELIEVE IT OR NOT!: CHILD PRODIGIES — Schanes

1 ❑ Cover: 2.50 **NM** value: **Cover or less**

RIPLEY'S BELIEVE IT OR NOT!: CRUELTY — Schanes Products

1 ❑ Jun 1993, b&w Cover: 2.50 **NM** value: **Cover or less**
says Crime & Murder on cover. • reprints newspaper cartoons
2 ❑ Jun 1993, b&w Cover: 2.50 **NM** value: **Cover or less**
says Crime & Murder on cover. • reprints newspaper cartoons

RIPLEY'S BELIEVE IT OR NOT!: FAIRY TALES & LITERATURE — Schanes

1 ❑ Cover: 2.50 **NM** value: **Cover or less**

RIPLEY'S BELIEVE IT OR NOT!: FEATS OF WONDER — Schanes

1 ❑ Cover: 2.50 **NM** value: **Cover or less**

RIPLEY'S BELIEVE IT OR NOT MAGAZINE — Harvey

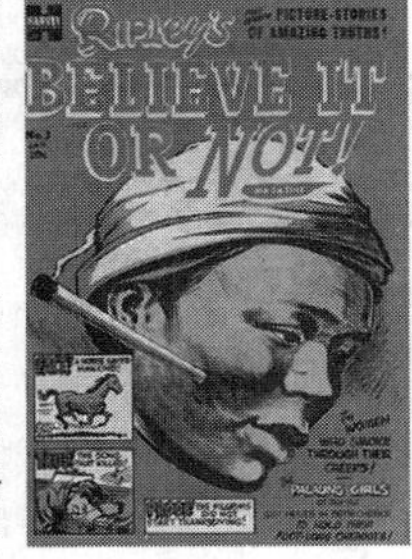

Published in 1953, this Harvey publication was the first time Ripley's Believe It or Not! was featured in a regular comic book. A fixture of newspaper strips and paperback books, comics were a perfect medium for this collection of uncanny facts from around the world.

In the four issues of this series, readers learned of how blood extracted from a horse led to a cure for tetanus, the real story behind the first Thanksgiving celebration, and how another turkey sparked a gold rush in Ontario, Canada. Some of these stories were set in traditional comic strip format, whereas others were simply large panels reprinted from Sunday newspapers where they ran originally. A collection of optical illusions and other interesting miscellania rounded out each issue.

1 ❑ Sep 1953 Cover: 0.10 **NM** value: **60.00**
• **CGC:** 1 graded, best 7.5
2 ❑ Nov 1953 Cover: 0.10 **NM** value: **45.00**
3 ❑ Jan 1954 Cover: 0.10 **NM** value: **40.00**
4 ❑ Mar 1954 Cover: 0.10 **NM** value: **40.00**
final issue.

RIPLEY'S BELIEVE IT OR NOT!: SPORTS FEATS — Schanes Products

1 ❑ Jun 1993, b&w Cover: 2.50 **NM** value: **Cover or less**
• reprints newspaper cartoons

RIPLEY'S BELIEVE IT OR NOT!: STRANGE DEATHS — Schanes Products

1 ❑ Jun 1993, b&w Cover: 2.50 **NM** value: **Cover or less**
• reprints newspaper cartoons

RIPLEY'S BELIEVE IT OR NOT TRUE WAR STORIES — Gold Key

1 ❑ ca. 1966 Cover: 0.12 **NM** value: **24.00**
The Red Knight of Germany; The Incredible Sea Hunt of Sub E-11; The Lost Battalion • #3 in overall series; Continued in Ripley's Believe It or Not #4

RIP OFF COMIX — Rip Off

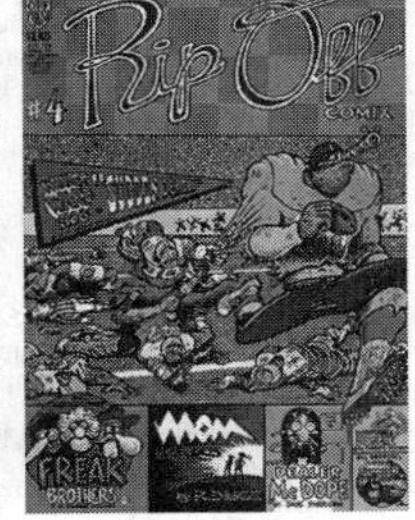

In a classic salute to everything that is '70s, Rip Off Comix collects several stories — humorous, entertaining and just plain out there — from some of the best-known creators of underground comics. Dave Sheridan, Bill Griffith, and Gilbert Shelton are just a few of the artists lending their characters and unique style of storytelling to this black-and-white compilation.

What make the stories in this title of particular interest to unsuspecting readers are not the striking similarities they share with other mainstream titles, but rather the dated jokes and subject matter that creep into each story's narrative. Abundant references to Nixon, the oil crisis, and such cultural phenomena as New Wave, Pepsi Cola, and the cult classic Alien make for an open window to a time gone but not forgotten.

1 ❑ Cover: 0.75 **NM** value: **20.00**
2 ❑ Cover: 1.50 **NM** value: **12.00**
3 ❑ Cover: 1.50 **NM** value: **8.00**
4 ❑ Nov 1978 Cover: 1.50 **NM** value: **6.00**
Kangaroo Court; Freak Brothers: the 4th Freak Brother!; Noo Yawkah; The Redneck; Mom Squad Meets Dr. Krull; Dealer McDope Does the Snowshovel Shuffle; Doorman's Doggie; Wonder Wart-Hog: Sudden Death! **A:** Ted Richards; Gilbert Shelton; Foolbert Sturgeon; Dave Sheridan; Joel Beck; Bill Griffith; R.Diggs **W:** Ted Richards; Gilbert Shelton; Dave Sheridan; Joel Beck; Bill Griffith; R.Diggs
5 ❑ Sep 1979 Cover: 2.00 **NM** value: **5.00**
Think Eighties; Freak Brothers: Take Out...; The Bill Bland Show; Mom Squad and the Space Pirates!; Time Twisted Tales; Wonder Wart-Hog and the Superheroes School; Let's Welcome Out the Seventies!; Forty Year Old Hippie **A:** Ted Richards; Gilbert Shelton; Foolbert Sturgeon; Dave Sheridan; Joel Beck; Bill Griffith; R.Diggs **W:** Ted Richards; Gilbert Shelton; Foolbert Sturgeon; Dave Sheridan; Joel Beck; Bill Griffith; R.Diggs
6 ❑ Mar 1980 Cover: 2.00 **NM** value: **5.00**
The Adventures of Fat Freddy's Cat; Freak Brothers: Death of Fat Freddy; Philbert Desanex' 100,000th; Motoring Tips **A:** Gilbert Shelton **W:** Gilbert Shelton
6-2 ❑ Jan 1980 Cover: 1.50 **NM** value: **2.50**
The Adventures of Fat Freddy's Cat; Freak Brothers: Death of Fat Freddy; Philbert Desanex' 100,000th; Motoring Tips • 2nd printing (1980) **A:** Gilbert Shelton **W:** Gilbert Shelton
7 ❑ Nov 1980 Cover: 1.50 **NM** value: **5.00**
8 ❑ May 1981 Cover: 2.00 **NM** value: **4.00**
• 1981
9 ❑ Sep 1981 Cover: 2.00 **NM** value: **4.00**
• 1981
10 ❑ Mar 1982 Cover: 2.00 **NM** value: **4.00**
11 ❑ Oct 1982 Cover: 2.95 **NM** value: **3.00**
12 ❑ Apr 1983 Cover: 2.95 **NM** value: **3.00**
13 ❑ Cover: 2.95 **NM** value: **3.00**
14 ❑ Apr 1987 Cover: 2.95 **NM** value: **3.00**
15 ❑ Jul 1987 Cover: 2.95 **NM** value: **3.00**

CGC-graded: Multiply prices above by **33 for 9.9 M • 16 for 9.8 NM/M • 7 for 9.6 NM+ • 5 for 9.4 NM • 2.5 for 9.2 NM- • 1.5 for 9.0 VF/NM**

16 ❑ Oct 1987 Cover: 2.95 **NM** value: **3.00**
17 ❑ Jan 1988 Cover: 2.95 **NM** value: **3.00**
18 ❑ Apr 1988 Cover: 2.95 **NM** value: **3.00**
19 ❑ Jul 1988 Cover: 2.95 **NM** value: **3.00**
20 ❑ Oct 1988 Cover: 2.95 **NM** value: **3.00**
21 ❑ Jan 1989 Cover: 3.50 **NM** value: **Cover or less**
• 20th Anniversary.
22 ❑ Apr 1989 Cover: 2.95 **NM** value: **3.00**
23 ❑ Jul 1989 Cover: 2.95 **NM** value: **3.00**
24 ❑ Oct 1989 Cover: 3.25 **NM** value: **Cover or less**
• San Diego Con
25 ❑ Jan 1990 Cover: 3.25 **NM** value: **Cover or less**
26 ❑ Apr 1990 Cover: 3.25 **NM** value: **Cover or less**
27 ❑ Jul 1990 Cover: 3.25 **NM** value: **3.95**
28 ❑ Oct 1990 Cover: 3.50 **NM** value: **Cover or less**
29 ❑ Jan 1991 Cover: 3.50 **NM** value: **Cover or less**
30 ❑ Apr 1991 Cover: 3.50 **NM** value: **Cover or less**
31 ❑ Mar 1992 Cover: 3.50 **NM** value: **Cover or less**
Bk 1❑ **NM** value: **10.00**

RIPPER — Aircel

1 ❑ Cover: 2.50 **NM** value: **Cover or less**
A: Barry Blair **W:** Barry Blair ★ Origin of Ripper. ★ 1st Appearance of Ripper.
2 ❑ Cover: 2.50 **NM** value: **Cover or less**
A: Barry Blair **W:** Barry Blair
3 ❑ Cover: 2.50 **NM** value: **Cover or less**
A: Barry Blair **W:** Barry Blair
4 ❑ Cover: 2.50 **NM** value: **Cover or less**
A: Barry Blair **W:** Barry Blair
5 ❑ Cover: 2.50 **NM** value: **Cover or less**
6 ❑ Cover: 2.50 **NM** value: **Cover or less**

RIPPER LEGACY, THE — Caliber

1 ❑ Cover: 2.95 **NM** value: **Cover or less**
A: Mark Bloodworth **W:** Jim Alexander
2 ❑ Cover: 2.95 **NM** value: **Cover or less**
A: Mark Bloodworth **W:** Jim Alexander
3 ❑ Cover: 2.95 **NM** value: **Cover or less**
A: Mark Bloodworth **W:** Jim Alexander

RIPTIDE — Image

1 ❑ Sep 1995 Cover: 2.50 **NM** value: **Cover or less**
Circ: CapCity orders: **20,575**
📖 Ugly Little Dreams **A:** Andy Park **W:** Eric Stephenson
2 ❑ Oct 1995 Cover: 2.50 **NM** value: **Cover or less**
Circ: CapCity orders: **10,875**
A: Andy Park **W:** Eric Stephenson

RISE OF APOCALYPSE — Marvel

1 ❑ Oct 1996 Cover: 1.95 **NM** value: **Cover or less**
wraparound cover. 📖 Hammer & Chisel **A:** Adam Pollina **W:** Terry Kavanagh; James Felder ★ Origin of Apocalypse.
2 ❑ Nov 1996 Cover: 1.95 **NM** value: **Cover or less**
wraparound cover. **A:** Adam Pollina **W:** Terry Kavanagh; James Felder ★ Origin of Apocalypse.
3 ❑ Dec 1996 Cover: 1.95 **NM** value: **Cover or less**
wraparound cover. 📖 Face of the Gods **A:** Adam Pollina **W:** Terry Kavanagh; James Felder ★ Origin of Apocalypse.
4 ❑ Jan 1997 Cover: 1.95 **NM** value: **Cover or less**
wraparound cover. final issue. **A:** Adam Pollina **W:** Terry Kavanagh; James Felder ★ Origin of Apocalypse.

RISE OF THE MIDNIGHT SONS — Marvel

Bk 1❑ Cover: 19.95 **NM** value: **Cover or less**

RISING STARS — Image

In this series, J. Michael Straczynski, creator of the popular Babylon 5 television series, asks the difficult questions about a world with superpowered beings. How would they learn to cope with their powers? How would they really interact with each other? And how would the rest of society cope with these powerful beings suddenly in their midst?

For example, Pyro has the power to control flames. As he grows up, even other superpowered children fear his abilities. Later, he finds himself ostracized and turns to a life of entertaining and petty crime. Soon, the patriotic super-hero named Flagg — a childhood acquaintance who has gone "corporate" — is hunting down Pyro.

In the tradition of Astro City and Watchmen, Rising Stars follows the life of these and other heroes in a realistic, character-driven story which explores the world of costumed super-heroes as they might exist in the "real world."

0 ❑ Apr 2000 Cover: 2.50 **NM** value: **8.00**
Circ: Diamd. preorders: **34,365 • CGC:** 1 graded, best 9.6
• Wizard promotional edition. **A:** Keu Cha; Kue Cha **W:** J. Michael Straczynski
0/GO❑1999 **NM** value: **20.00**
• Gold logo variant from Wizard promotion **A:** Keu Cha; Kue Cha **W:** J. Michael Straczynski
1 ❑ Aug 1999 Cover: 2.50 **NM** value: **3.50**
Circ: Diamd. preorders: **95,551 • CGC:** 37 graded, best 9.8
• Standard edition. • Team standing over coffin **A:** Keu Cha; Kue Cha **W:** J. Michael Straczynski
1/A ❑ Aug 1999 Cover: 2.50 **NM** value: **15.00**
• Holofoil edition.
1/B ❑ Aug 1999 Cover: 2.50 **NM** value: **20.00**
chromium cover.
1/C ❑ Aug 1999 Cover: 2.50 **NM** value: **12.50**
• Gold "Monster Edition". • Team with burning figure kneeling in foreground
1/D ❑ Aug 1999 Cover: 2.50 **NM** value: **12.50**
• Gold "Monster Edition". • Children running to house
1/E ❑ Aug 1999 Cover: 2.50 **NM** value: **12.50**
• Gold "Monster Edition". • Battle scene with blonde woman in foreground
1/F ❑ Aug 1999 Cover: 2.50 **NM** value: **12.50**
• Gold "Monster Edition". • Team standing over coffin
1/G ❑ Aug 1999 Cover: 2.50 **NM** value: **5.00**
• **CGC:** 22 graded, best 9.8
• Another Universe/Wizard World variant (boy standing in foreground looking at large glowing sphere, Wizard World/AU markings)
1/H ❑ Aug 1999 Cover: 2.50 **NM** value: **5.00**
• No "Monster Edition" logo. • Battle scene with blonde woman in foreground
2 ❑ Oct 1999 Cover: 2.50 **NM** value: **Cover or less**
Circ: Diamd. preorders: **51,618 • CGC:** 13 graded, best 9.8
A: Keu Cha; Kue Cha **W:** J. Michael Straczynski
2/A ❑ Dec 1999 Cover: 2.50 **NM** value: **5.00**
• **CGC:** 8 graded, best 9.8
Dymamic Forces variant cover. **A:** Ken Lashley; Christian Zanier
2/B ❑ Dec 1999 Cover: 2.50 **NM** value: **10.00**
• **CGC:** 2 graded, best 9.8
Dymamic Forces gold variant cover (Dynamic Forces seal on cover).
3 ❑ Dec 1999 Cover: 2.50 **NM** value: **Cover or less**
Circ: Diamd. preorders: **51,589 • CGC:** 5 graded, best 9.8
A: Ken Lashley; Christian Zanier **W:** J. Michael Straczynski
4 ❑ 2000 Cover: 2.50 **NM** value: **Cover or less**
Circ: Diamd. preorders: **53,181 • CGC:** 1 graded, best 9.6
A: Ken Lashley; Christian Zanier **W:** J. Michael Straczynski
5 ❑ Mar 2000 Cover: 2.50 **NM** value: **Cover or less**
Circ: Diamd. preorders: **47,527 • CGC:** 1 graded, best 9.6
📖 The World Between **A:** Ken Lashley; Christian Zanier **W:** J. Michael Straczynski
6 ❑ Apr 2000 Cover: 2.50 **NM** value: **Cover or less**
Circ: Diamd. preorders: **47,266**
A: Ken Lashley; Christian Zanier **W:** J. Michael Straczynski
7 ❑ May 2000 Cover: 2.50 **NM** value: **Cover or less**
Circ: Diamd. preorders: **47,698 • CGC:** 3 graded, best 9.8
A: Ken Lashley; Christian Zanier **W:** J. Michael Straczynski
8 ❑ 2000 Cover: 2.50 **NM** value: **Cover or less**
Circ: Diamd. preorders: **48,128**
A: Ken Lashley; Christian Zanier **W:** J. Michael Straczynski
9 ❑ Aug 2000 Cover: 2.50 **NM** value: **Cover or less**
Circ: Diamd. preorders: **50,738 • CGC:** 3 graded, best 9.6
📖 Choices Made **A:** Ken Lashley; Christian Zanier **W:** J. Michael Straczynski
10 ❑ Oct 2000 Cover: 2.50 **NM** value: **Cover or less**
Circ: Diamd. preorders: **49,520**
📖 Reversals of Fortune **A:** Ken Lashley; Christian Zanier **W:** J. Michael Straczynski
11 ❑ Nov 2000 Cover: 2.50 **NM** value: **Cover or less**
Circ: Diamd. preorders: **51,086**
📖 What Goes Around… **A:** Ken Lashley; Christian Zanier **W:** J. Michael Straczynski
12 ❑ Jan 2001 Cover: 2.50 **NM** value: **Cover or less**
Circ: Diamd. preorders: **52,898 • CGC:** 2 graded, best 9.8
📖 A, B, C, and D **A:** Ken Lashley **W:** J. Michael Straczynski
13 ❑ Mar 2001 Cover: 2.50 **NM** value: **Cover or less**
Circ: Diamd. preorders: **51,123**
📖 Stalingrad **A:** Christian Zanier **W:** J. Michael Straczynski
14 ❑ May 2001 Cover: 2.50 **NM** value: **Cover or less**
Circ: Diamd. preorders: **51,900**
📖 Things Change **A:** Stuart Immonen **W:** J. Michael Straczynski
Ash 1❑Oct 2000 Cover: 2.95 **NM** value: **6.00**
Circ: Diamd. preorders: **17,346**
📖 Variations & Midnight Thoughts • Convention Exclusive preview **A:** Keu Cha; Kue Cha **W:** J. Michael Straczynski
ASH 1/A❑Mar 1999 Cover: 5.00 **NM** value: **Cover or less**
Circ: Diamd. preorders: **32,027**
• Prelude edition. **A:** Keu Cha **W:** J. Michael Straczynski
Bk 1❑ Cover: 19.95 **NM** value: **Cover or less**
• Born in Fire; Collects Rising Stars #1-8 **A:** Keu Cha **W:** J. Michael Straczynski

RIVERDALE HIGH — Archie

1 ❑ Aug 1990 Cover: 1.00 **NM** value: **1.50**
2 ❑ Oct 1990 Cover: 1.00 **NM** value: **Cover or less**
3 ❑ Dec 1990 Cover: 1.00 **NM** value: **Cover or less**
4 ❑ Feb 1990 Cover: 1.00 **NM** value: **Cover or less**
5 ❑ Apr 1990 Cover: 1.00 **NM** value: **Cover or less**

RIVETS — Argo

1 ❑ Jan 1956 Cover: 0.10 **NM** value: **30.00**
2 ❑ Mar 1956 Cover: 0.10 **NM** value: **20.00**
3 ❑ May 1956 Cover: 0.10 **NM** value: **20.00**

RIVETS & RUBY — Radio

1 ❑ Feb 1998 Cover: 2.95 **NM** value: **Cover or less**
2 ❑ Apr 1998 Cover: 2.95 **NM** value: **Cover or less**
3 ❑ Jul 1998 Cover: 2.95 **NM** value: **Cover or less**
4 ❑ Cover: 2.95 **NM** value: **Cover or less**

RIVIT — Blackthorne

1 ❑ Cover: 1.75 **NM** value: **Cover or less**
📖 A Rivit in Time: Saves None!!!; Bare Bones; Not the First Dte; Hip **A:** Richard Johnson; Alice Clausen; Clayt Moore; Jim McDivit; John Dooley; Leiulf Clausen; Marilyn Draving; Marvin Nelson; Michael Kelley; William Clausen **W:** Leiulf Clausen; William Clausen

ROACHMILL (BLACKTHORNE) — Blackthorne

1 ❑ Dec 1986 Cover: 1.75 **NM** value: **2.00**
A: Tom McWeeney; Rich Hedden **W:** Tom McWeeney; Rich Hedden
2 ❑ Feb 1987 Cover: 1.75 **NM** value: **2.00**
3 ❑ Apr 1987 Cover: 1.75 **NM** value: **2.00**
4 ❑ Jun 1987 Cover: 1.75 **NM** value: **2.00**
5 ❑ Sep 1987 Cover: 1.75 **NM** value: **2.00**
6 ❑ Oct 1987 Cover: 1.75 **NM** value: **2.00**
Circ: CapCity orders: **1,550**

ROACHMILL (DARK HORSE) — Dark Horse

1 ❑ May 1988 Cover: 1.75 **NM** value: **Cover or less**
A: Tom McWeeney; Rich Hedden **W:** Tom McWeeney; Rich Hedden
2 ❑ Jun 1988 Cover: 1.75 **NM** value: **Cover or less**
A: Tom McWeeney; Rich Hedden **W:** Tom McWeeney; Rich Hedden
3 ❑ Sep 1988 Cover: 1.75 **NM** value: **Cover or less**
A: Tom McWeeney; Rich Hedden **W:** Tom McWeeney; Rich Hedden
4 ❑ Nov 1988 Cover: 1.75 **NM** value: **Cover or less**
A: Tom McWeeney; Rich Hedden **W:** Tom McWeeney; Rich Hedden
5 ❑ Apr 1989 Cover: 1.75 **NM** value: **Cover or less**
📖 Hot Sex **A:** Tom McWeeney; Rich Hedden **W:** Tom McWeeney; Rich Hedden
6 ❑ Jun 1989 Cover: 1.75 **NM** value: **Cover or less**
A: Tom McWeeney; Rich Hedden **W:** Tom McWeeney; Rich Hedden
7 ❑ Oct 1989 Cover: 1.75 **NM** value: **Cover or less**
A: Tom McWeeney; Rich Hedden **W:** Tom McWeeney; Rich Hedden
8 ❑ Jan 1990 Cover: 1.75 **NM** value: **Cover or less**
• indicia says Jan 89; a misprint **A:** Tom McWeeney; Rich Hedden **W:** Tom McWeeney; Rich Hedden
9 ❑ Apr 1990 Cover: 1.95 **NM** value: **Cover or less**
📖 The Hunt for Miss October **A:** Tom McWeeney; Rich Hedden **W:** Tom McWeeney; Rich Hedden
10 ❑ Dec 1990 Cover: 1.95 **NM** value: **Cover or less**
final issue. • trading cards **A:** Tom McWeeney; Rich Hedden **W:** Tom McWeeney; Rich Hedden
Bk 1❑ b&w Cover: 5.95 **NM** value: **Cover or less**
• Trade Paperback. 📖 Framed **A:** Tom McWeeney; Rich Hedden **W:** Tom McWeeney; Rich Hedden
Bk 2❑ b&w Cover: 6.95 **NM** value: **Cover or less**
📖 The greatest Stories Ever Told **A:** Tom McWeeney; Rich Hedden **W:** Tom McWeeney; Rich Hedden

ROADKILL — Lighthouse

1 ❑ b&w Cover: 2.00 **NM** value: **Cover or less**
2 ❑ b&w Cover: 2.00 **NM** value: **Cover or less**

ROADKILL: A CHRONICLE OF THE DEADWORLD — Caliber

1 ❑ Cover: 2.95 **NM** value: **Cover or less**
No issue number. • text **A:** David Dorman **W:** Del Stone Jr.

ROAD TRIP — Oni

1 ❑ Aug 2000, b&w Cover: 2.95 **NM** value: **Cover or less**
Circ: Diamd. preorders: **3,041**
No issue number. • collects story from Oni Double Feature #9 and #10 **A:** Judd Winick **W:** Judd Winick

ROADWAYS — Cult Press

1 ❑ May 1994, b&w Cover: 2.75 **NM** value: **Cover or less**
📖 The Road to Nowhere **A:** Steve Lieber; Ted Slampyak **W:** Jeffrey Lang
2 ❑ Jun 1994, b&w Cover: 2.75 **NM** value: **Cover or less**
A: Steve Lieber; Ted Slampyak **W:** Jeffrey Lang
3 ❑ Cover: 2.75 **NM** value: **Cover or less**
A: Steve Lieber; Ted Slampyak **W:** Jeffrey Lang
4 ❑ Cover: 2.75 **NM** value: **Cover or less**
A: Steve Lieber; Ted Slampyak **W:** Jeffrey Lang

ROARIN' RICK'S RARE BIT FIENDS — King Hell

1 ❑ Jul 1994 Cover: 2.95 **NM** value: **Cover or less**
2 ❑ Aug 1994 Cover: 2.95 **NM** value: **Cover or less**
3 ❑ Sep 1994 Cover: 2.95 **NM** value: **Cover or less**
4 ❑ Oct 1994 Cover: 2.95 **NM** value: **Cover or less**
5 ❑ Nov 1994 Cover: 2.95 **NM** value: **Cover or less**
6 ❑ Dec 1994 Cover: 2.95 **NM** value: **Cover or less**
7 ❑ Jan 1995 Cover: 2.95 **NM** value: **Cover or less**

ROBBIN' $3000 — Parody

1 ❑ b&w Cover: 2.50 **NM** value: **Cover or less**
A: Marl Lewis **W:** Lyle Dodd

ROB HANES — WCG

1 ❑ Jan 1991, b&w Cover: 2.50 **NM** value: **Cover or less**
📖 The Care Package **A:** Randy Reynaldo **W:** Randy Reynaldo

ROB HANES ADVENTURES — WCG

1 ❑ Oct 2000 Cover: 2.50 **NM** value: **Cover or less**
📖 Where in the World is Rob Hanes? **A:** Randy Reynaldo **W:** Randy Reynaldo

ROBIN — DC

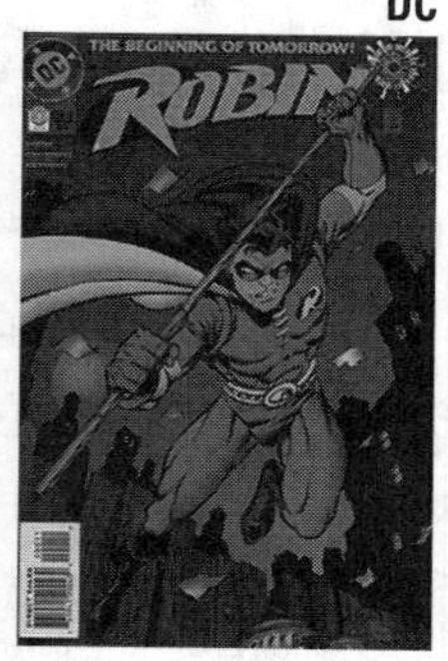

After starring in numerous mini-series (the Robin mini-series, Robin II, and Robin III: Cry of the Huntress) Batman's sidekick finally got an ongoing title of his own.

The title character, Timothy Drake, is the third Robin. The original, Dick Grayson, had become Nightwing; his successor, Jason Todd was killed by The Joker. Drake is a teenager who battles the normal troubles of schoolwork and girlfriends when not swinging into action as a super-hero. When Batman was incapacitated during the Knightfall saga, Robin was forced to partner with Azrael, then Nightwing, as they in turn assumed the identity of Batman. Throughout the chaos, however, it became clear that this Robin is more than capable of holding his own. Later, after a plague and an earthquake in Gotham City, Drake was relocated to a private school nearby.

0 ❑ Oct 1994 Cover: 1.50 **NM** value: **2.00**
Circ: CapCity orders: **44,750**
W: Chuck Dixon ★ Origin of Robin I (Dick Grayson), Robin III (Timothy Drake), Robin II (Jason Todd).

1 ❑ Nov 1993 Cover: 1.50 **NM** value: **2.50**
• **CGC:** 6 graded, best 9.6
📖 Outcast **A:** Tom Grummettt **W:** Chuck Dixon ★ 1st Appearance of Shotgun Smith.

1/SC❑Nov 1993 Cover: 2.95 **NM** value: **3.50**
Circ: CapCity orders: **87,100 • CGC:** 1 graded, best 9.8
Embossed cover. **W:** Chuck Dixon

2 ❑ Jan 1994 Cover: 1.50 **NM** value: **2.00**
Circ: CapCity orders: **42,900**
W: Chuck Dixon

3 ❑ Feb 1994 Cover: 1.50 **NM** value: **2.00**
Circ: CapCity orders: **37,500**
A: Tom Grummettt **W:** Chuck Dixon

4 ❑ Mar 1994 Cover: 1.50 **NM** value: **2.00**
Circ: CapCity orders: **35,600**
📖 Clueless **W:** Chuck Dixon ★ Appearance of Spoiler.

5 ❑ Apr 1994 Cover: 1.50 **NM** value: **2.00**
Circ: CapCity orders: **34,350**
W: Chuck Dixon

6 ❑ May 1994 Cover: 1.50 **NM** value: **2.00**
Circ: CapCity orders: **32,800**
W: Chuck Dixon ★ Appearance of Huntress.

7 ❑ Jun 1994 Cover: 1.50 **NM** value: **2.00**
Circ: CapCity orders: **45,650**
📖 KnightQuest Conclusion **W:** Chuck Dixon

8 ❑ Jul 1994 Cover: 1.50 **NM** value: **2.00**
Circ: CapCity orders: **43,250**
📖 KnightsEnd, Part 5 **W:** Chuck Dixon

9 ❑ Aug 1994 Cover: 1.50 **NM** value: **2.00**
Circ: CapCity orders: **41,350**
📖 KnightsEnd Aftermath; KnightsEnd Aftermath, Part 1 **W:** Chuck Dixon

10 ❑ Sep 1994 Cover: 1.50 **NM** value: **2.00**
Circ: CapCity orders: **36,050**
• Zero Hour; Tim Drake Robin teams with Dick Grayson Robin **W:** Chuck Dixon

11 ❑ Nov 1994 Cover: 1.50 **NM** value: **1.75**
Circ: CapCity orders: **35,200**
📖 Prodigal, Part 4 **W:** Chuck Dixon

12 ❑ Dec 1994 Cover: 1.50 **NM** value: **1.75**
Circ: CapCity orders: **34,650**
📖 Prodigal, Part 8 **W:** Chuck Dixon

13 ❑ Jan 1995 Cover: 1.50 **NM** value: **1.75**
Circ: CapCity orders: **32,850**
📖 Prodigal Conclusion **W:** Chuck Dixon

14 ❑ Feb 1995 Cover: 1.50 **NM** value: **1.75**
📖 Troika, Part 4 **W:** Chuck Dixon

14/SC❑Feb 1995 Cover: 2.50 **NM** value: **Cover or less**
Circ: CapCity orders: **40,225**
enhanced cardstock cover. 📖 Troika, Part 4 **W:** Chuck Dixon

15 ❑ Mar 1995 Cover: 1.50 **NM** value: **1.75**
Circ: CapCity orders: **30,425**
W: Chuck Dixon

16 ❑ Apr 1995 Cover: 1.50 **NM** value: **1.75**
Circ: CapCity orders: **28,800**
📖 All Fall Down **A:** Paul Jimenez **W:** Chuck Dixon

17 ❑ Jun 1995 Cover: 1.95 **NM** value: **2.00**
Circ: CapCity orders: **27,225**
A: Steve Lieber **W:** Chuck Dixon

18 ❑ Jul 1995 Cover: 1.95 **NM** value: **2.00**
Circ: CapCity orders: **25,500**
W: Chuck Dixon

19 ❑ Aug 1995 Cover: 1.95 **NM** value: **2.00**
Circ: CapCity orders: **26,200**
W: Chuck Dixon ★ Versus Ulysses.

20 ❑ Sep 1995 Cover: 1.95 **NM** value: **2.00**
Circ: CapCity orders: **24,150**
W: Chuck Dixon ★ Versus Ulysses.

21 ❑ Oct 1995 Cover: 1.95 **NM** value: **2.00**
Circ: CapCity orders: **20,175**
• Ninja camp **W:** Chuck Dixon

22 ❑ Nov 1995 Cover: 1.95 **NM** value: **2.00**
• Ninja camp **W:** Chuck Dixon

23 ❑ Dec 1995 Cover: 1.95 **NM** value: **2.00**
• Underworld Unleashed **W:** Chuck Dixon ★ Versus Killer Moth a.k.a. Charaxes.

24 ❑ Jan 1996 Cover: 1.95 **NM** value: **2.00**
• Underworld Unleashed **W:** Chuck Dixon ★ Versus Killer Moth a.k.a. Charaxes.

25 ❑ Feb 1996 Cover: 1.95 **NM** value: **2.00**
📖 Sophomore Lethal • anti-guns issue **A:** Mike Wieringo **W:** Chuck Dixon

26 ❑ Mar 1996 Cover: 1.95 **NM** value: **2.00**
📖 The Hard Lessons **A:** Mike Wieringo **W:** Chuck Dixon

27 ❑ Mar 1996 Cover: 1.95 **NM** value: **2.00**
📖 Contagion, Part 3 **W:** Chuck Dixon

28 ❑ Apr 1996 Cover: 1.95 **NM** value: **2.00**
📖 Contagion, Part 11 **A:** Mike Wieringo **W:** Chuck Dixon

29 ❑ May 1996 Cover: 1.95 **NM** value: **2.00**
W: Chuck Dixon

30 ❑ Jun 1996 Cover: 1.95 **NM** value: **2.00**
W: Chuck Dixon

31 ❑ Jul 1996 Cover: 1.95 **NM** value: **2.00**
W: Chuck Dixon ★ Appearance of Wildcat.

32 ❑ Aug 1996 Cover: 1.95 **NM** value: **2.00**
📖 Legacy, Part 3 **W:** Chuck Dixon

33 ❑ Sep 1996 Cover: 1.95 **NM** value: **2.00**
📖 Legacy, Part 7 **W:** Chuck Dixon

34 ❑ Oct 1996 Cover: 1.95 **NM** value: **2.00**
📖 Situations and Comedies • self-contained story **A:** Jennifer Graves **W:** Chuck Dixon

35 ❑ Nov 1996 Cover: 1.95 **NM** value: **2.00**
Circ: Diamd. preorders: **55,116**
📖 Iced! • Final Night **A:** Staz Johnson **W:** Chuck Dixon ★ Appearance of Spoiler.

36 ❑ Dec 1996 Cover: 1.95 **NM** value: **2.00**
Circ: Diamd. preorders: **51,229**
📖 War Toy Story **A:** Staz Johnson **W:** Chuck Dixon ★ Versus Toyman. ★ Versus Ulysses.

37 ❑ Jan 1997 Cover: 1.95 **NM** value: **2.00**
Circ: Diamd. preorders: **48,542**
📖 Who Dies With the Most Toys… **A:** Staz Johnson **W:** Chuck Dixon ★ Versus Toyman. ★ Versus Ulysses.

38 ❑ Feb 1997 Cover: 1.95 **NM** value: **2.00**
Circ: Diamd. preorders: **46,514**
A: Staz Johnson **W:** Chuck Dixon

39 ❑ Mar 1997 Cover: 1.95 **NM** value: **2.00**
Circ: Diamd. preorders: **44,349**
📖 Gotaway Gone **A:** Staz Johnson **W:** Chuck Dixon

40 ❑ Apr 1997 Cover: 1.95 **NM** value: **Cover or less**
Circ: Diamd. preorders: **42,066**
W: Chuck Dixon

41 ❑ May 1997 Cover: 1.95 **NM** value: **Cover or less**
Circ: Diamd. preorders: **40,928**
W: Chuck Dixon

42 ❑ Jun 1997 Cover: 1.95 **NM** value: **Cover or less**
Circ: Diamd. preorders: **40,395**
W: Chuck Dixon

43 ❑ Jul 1997 Cover: 1.95 **NM** value: **Cover or less**
Circ: Diamd. preorders: **40,237**
W: Chuck Dixon

44 ❑ Aug 1997 Cover: 1.95 **NM** value: **Cover or less**
Circ: Diamd. preorders: **39,789**
W: Chuck Dixon ★ Appearance of Spoiler.

45 ❑ Sep 1997 Cover: 1.95 **NM** value: **Cover or less**
Circ: Diamd. preorders: **38,174**
• self-contained story **W:** Chuck Dixon

46 ❑ Oct 1997 Cover: 1.95 **NM** value: **Cover or less**
Circ: Diamd. preorders: **39,906**
• self-contained story **W:** Chuck Dixon

47 ❑ Nov 1997 Cover: 1.95 **NM** value: **Cover or less**
Circ: Diamd. preorders: **37,199**
📖 Warchild **A:** Eduardo Barreto **W:** Chuck Dixon ★ Appearance of Nightwing, Batman. ★ Versus Ulysses.

48 ❑ Dec 1997 Cover: 1.95 **NM** value: **Cover or less**
Circ: Diamd. preorders: **37,286**
Face cover. 📖 Mission Creep **A:** Eduardo Barreto **W:** Chuck Dixon

49 ❑ Jan 1998 Cover: 1.95 **NM** value: **Cover or less**
Circ: Diamd. preorders: **36,884**
W: Chuck Dixon ★ Appearance of King Snake.

50 ❑ Feb 1998 Cover: 2.95 **NM** value: **Cover or less**
Circ: Diamd. preorders: **38,557**
• Giant-size. 📖 Faster, Faster! **A:** Staz Johnson **W:** Chuck Dixon ★ Appearance of King Snake, Lady Shiva.

51 ❑ Mar 1998 Cover: 1.95 **NM** value: **Cover or less**
Circ: Diamd. preorders: **35,620**
📖 Kiss and Kill **A:** Staz Johnson **W:** Chuck Dixon

52 ❑ Apr 1998 Cover: 1.95 **NM** value: **Cover or less**
Circ: Diamd. preorders: **40,792**
📖 Cataclysm, Part 7 • continues in Batman: Blackgate-Isle of Men #1 **W:** Chuck Dixon

53 ❑ May 1998 Cover: 1.95 **NM** value: **Cover or less**
Circ: Diamd. preorders: **41,474**
📖 Cataclysm Conclusion **W:** Chuck Dixon

54 ❑ Jun 1998 Cover: 1.95 **NM** value: **Cover or less**
Circ: Diamd. preorders: **38,369**
• Aftershock **W:** Chuck Dixon ★ Appearance of Spoiler.

55 ❑ Jul 1998 Cover: 1.95 **NM** value: **Cover or less**
Circ: Diamd. preorders: **41,056**
📖 Brotherhood of the Fist, Part 3 • continues in Nightwing #23 **W:** Chuck Dixon

56 ❑ Aug 1998 Cover: 1.95 **NM** value: **Cover or less**
Circ: Diamd. preorders: **38,357**
• Tim breaks up with Ariana **W:** Chuck Dixon ★ Appearance of Spoiler.

57 ❑ Sep 1998 Cover: 1.99 **NM** value: **Cover or less**
Circ: Diamd. preorders: **36,339**
• Spoiler and Robin date **W:** Chuck Dixon

58 ❑ Oct 1998 Cover: 1.99 **NM** value: **Cover or less**
Circ: Diamd. preorders: **36,026**
W: Chuck Dixon ★ Versus Steeljacket.

59 ❑ Dec 1998 Cover: 1.99 **NM** value: **Cover or less**
Circ: Diamd. preorders: **34,604**
W: Chuck Dixon ★ Versus Steeljacket.

60 ❑ Jan 1999 Cover: 1.99 **NM** value: **Cover or less**
Circ: Diamd. preorders: **34,196**
W: Chuck Dixon

61 ❑ Feb 1999 Cover: 1.99 **NM** value: **Cover or less**
Circ: Diamd. preorders: **33,280**
A: Staz Johnson **W:** Chuck Dixon

62 ❑ Mar 1999 Cover: 1.99 **NM** value: **Cover or less**
Circ: Diamd. preorders: **33,830**
• Tim relocates to Keystone City **A:** Staz Johnson **W:** Chuck Dixon ★ Appearance of Flash III (Wally West).

63 ❑ Apr 1999 Cover: 1.99 **NM** value: **Cover or less**
Circ: Diamd. preorders: **33,272**
A: Staz Johnson **W:** Chuck Dixon ★ Appearance of Riddler, Superman, Flash III (Wally West), Captain Boomerang.

64 ❑ May 1999 Cover: 1.99 **NM** value: **Cover or less**
Circ: Diamd. preorders: **33,333**
📖 Stop Me If You've Heard This One **A:** Staz Johnson **W:** Chuck Dixon ★ Appearance of Flash III (Wally West). ★ Versus Riddler. ★ Versus Captain Boomerang.

65 ❑ Jun 1999 Cover: 1.99 **NM** value: **Cover or less**
Circ: Diamd. preorders: **34,521**
📖 A Blessed Event • Spoiler's child is born **A:** Will Rosado **W:** Chuck Dixon

66 ❑ Jul 1999 Cover: 1.99 **NM** value: **Cover or less**
Circ: Diamd. preorders: **33,913**
• Tim returns to Gotham **W:** Chuck Dixon

67 ❑ Aug 1999 Cover: 1.99 **NM** value: **Cover or less**
Circ: Diamd. preorders: **36,281**
📖 Way Dark • No Man's Land **A:** Staz Johnson **W:** Chuck Dixon ★ Appearance of Nightwing.

68 ❑ Sep 1999 Cover: 1.99 **NM** value: **Cover or less**
Circ: Diamd. preorders: **35,693**
📖 War Beneath the Streets! Part 1 • No Man's Land **A:** Staz Johnson **W:** Chuck Dixon ★ Versus Ratcatcher.

69 ❑ Oct 1999 Cover: 1.99 **NM** value: **Cover or less**
Circ: Diamd. preorders: **34,869**
📖 War Beneath the Streets! Part 2 • No Man's Land **A:** Staz Johnson **W:** Chuck Dixon ★ Versus Ratcatcher.

70 ❑ Nov 1999 Cover: 1.99 **NM** value: **Cover or less**
Circ: Diamd. preorders: **35,219**
W: Chuck Dixon

71 ❑ Dec 1999 Cover: 1.99 **NM** value: **Cover or less**
Circ: Diamd. preorders: **36,268**
📖 The Lizard King **A:** Staz Johnson **W:** Chuck Dixon

72 ❑ Jan 2000 Cover: 1.99 **NM** value: **Cover or less**
Circ: Diamd. preorders: **35,022**
📖 Stand on Grand Avenue **A:** Gordon Purcell **W:** Chuck Dixon

73 ❑ Feb 2000 Cover: 1.99 **NM** value: **Cover or less**
Circ: Diamd. preorders: **36,940**
W: Chuck Dixon

74 ❑ Mar 2000 Cover: 1.99 **NM** value: **Cover or less**
Circ: Diamd. preorders: **33,253**
W: Chuck Dixon

75 ❑ Apr 2000 Cover: 2.95 **NM** value: **Cover or less**
Circ: Diamd. preorders: **32,315**
• Giant-size. 📖 Thrashed **A:** Pete Woods **W:** Chuck Dixon

76 ❑ May 2000 Cover: 1.99 **NM** value: **Cover or less**
Circ: Diamd. preorders: **32,072**
📖 Wings over Brentwood **A:** Pete Woods **W:** Chuck Dixon

77 ❑ Jun 2000 Cover: 1.99 **NM** value: **Cover or less**
Circ: Diamd. preorders: **31,926**
A: Pete Woods **W:** Chuck Dixon

78 ❑ Jul 2000 Cover: 2.25 **NM** value: **Cover or less**
Circ: Diamd. preorders: **31,620**
A: Pete Woods **W:** Chuck Dixon

79 ❑ Aug 2000 Cover: 2.25 **NM** value: **Cover or less**
Circ: Diamd. preorders: **31,747**
A: Pete Woods **W:** Chuck Dixon

80 ❑ Sep 2000 Cover: 2.25 **NM** value: **Cover or less**
Circ: Diamd. preorders: **31,261**
📖 The Girl **A:** Pete Woods **W:** Chuck Dixon

81 ❑ Oct 2000 Cover: 2.25 **NM** value: **Cover or less**
Circ: Diamd. preorders: **29,269**
📖 The Obtuse Conundrum **A:** Marcos Martin **W:** Chuck Dixon

82 ❑ Nov 2000 Cover: 2.25 **NM** value: **Cover or less**
Circ: Diamd. preorders: **29,332**
📖 The New Kid **A:** Pete Woods **W:** Chuck Dixon

83 ❑ Dec 2000 Cover: 2.25 **NM** value: **Cover or less**
Circ: Diamd. preorders: **28,707**
📖 Wrong Place, Wrong Time **A:** Pete Woods **W:** Chuck Dixon

84 ❑ Jan 2001 Cover: 2.25 **NM** value: **Cover or less**
Circ: Diamd. preorders: **28,594**
📖 UnFathomable **A:** Pete Woods **W:** Chuck Dixon

85 ❑ Feb 2001 Cover: 2.25 **NM** value: **Cover or less**
Circ: Diamd. preorders: **31,665**
📖 Fool's Errand **A:** Pete Woods **W:** Chuck Dixon ★ Appearance of Joker.

86 ❑ Mar 2001 Cover: 2.25 **NM** value: **Cover or less**
Circ: Diamd. preorders: **34,096**
📖 Officer Down, Part 2 **A:** Arnold Pander; Jacob Pander **W:** Ed Brubaker

87 ❑ Apr 2001 Cover: 2.25 **NM** value: **Cover or less**
Circ: Diamd. preorders: **28,041 • CGC:** 1 graded, best 9.6
📖 Secrets Revealed **A:** Pete Woods **W:** Chuck Dixon

88 ❑ May 2001 Cover: 2.25 **NM** value: **Cover or less**
Circ: Diamd. preorders: **28,075**
📖 Secrets & Lies **A:** Scott Beatty **W:** Chuck Dixon

89 ❑ Jun 2001 Cover: 2.25 **NM** value: **Cover or less**
Circ: Diamd. preorders: **28,780**

90 ❑ Jul 2001 Cover: 2.25 **NM** value: **Cover or less**
Circ: Diamd. preorders: **28,764**

91 ❑ Aug 2001 Cover: 2.25 **NM** value: **Cover or less**
Circ: Diamd. preorders: **29,125**

92 ❑ Sep 2001 Cover: 2.25 **NM** value: **Cover or less**
Circ: Diamd. preorders: **30,179**

1000000❑Nov 1998 Cover: 1.99 **NM** value: **Cover or less**
Circ: Diamd. preorders: **42,842**
📖 Dark Planet **A:** Stan Woch; Staz Johnson **W:** Chuck Dixon ★ Appearance of Robin the Toy Wonder.

Anl 3❑ca. 1994 Cover: 2.95 **NM** value: **Cover or less**
Circ: CapCity orders: **27,750**
• Elseworlds

Anl 4❑ca. 1995 Cover: 2.95 **NM** value: **3.95**
• Year One

Anl 5❑ca. 1996 Cover: 2.95 **NM** value: **Cover or less**
• Legends of the Dead Earth

Anl 6❑ca. 1997 Cover: 3.95 **NM** value: **Cover or less**
Circ: Diamd. preorders: **33,794**
• Pulp Heroes

Bk 1❑ Cover: 12.95 **NM** value: **Cover or less**
• Flying Solo trade paperback; Reprints Robin #1-6, Showcase '94 #5-6 **A:** Phil Jimenez; Tom Grummett **W:** Chuck Dixon

GS 1❑Sep 2000 Cover: 5.95 **NM** value: **Cover or less**
Circ: Diamd. preorders: **21,738**
• Eighty Page Giant. 📖 Nature's Bride: A Tale of Robin and Marital Bliss **A:** Diego Barreto **W:** Chuck Dixon

ROBIN/ARGENT DOUBLE-SHOT DC

1 ❑ Feb 1998 Cover: 1.95 **NM** value: **Cover or less**
Circ: Diamd. preorders: **30,098**

CGC-graded: Multiply prices above by **33 for 9.9 M • 16 for 9.8 NM/M • 7 for 9.6 NM+ • 5 for 9.4 NM • 2.5 for 9.2 NM- • 1.5 for 9.0 VF/NM**

ROBIN HOOD (CHARLTON) — Charlton

28 ❑ Apr 1956 Cover: 0.10 **NM** value: **40.00**
• Series continued from Danger & Adventure #27
29 ❑ 1956 Cover: 0.10 **NM** value: **35.00**
30 ❑ 1956 Cover: 0.10 **NM** value: **35.00**
31 ❑ 1956 Cover: 0.10 **NM** value: **30.00**
32 ❑ 1957 Cover: 0.10 **NM** value: **30.00**
33 ❑ 1957 Cover: 0.10 **NM** value: **30.00**
34 ❑ 1957 Cover: 0.10 **NM** value: **30.00**
35 ❑ 1957 Cover: 0.10 **NM** value: **30.00**
🕮 The Rival of a King; Golden Revenge; The Conquered Rise; A Boar for a Feast
36 ❑ 1958 Cover: 0.10 **NM** value: **30.00**
37 ❑ May 1958 Cover: 0.10 **NM** value: **30.00**
38 ❑ Aug 1958 Cover: 0.10 **NM** value: **45.00**
final issue.

ROBIN HOOD (DELL) — Dell

1 ❑ ca. 1963 Cover: 0.12 **NM** value: **20.00**

ROBIN HOOD (ECLIPSE) — Eclipse

1 ❑ ca. 1991 Cover: 2.50 **NM** value: **Cover or less**
Circ: CapCity orders: **13,675**
A: Tim Truman **W:** Valarie Jones
2 ❑ ca. 1991 Cover: 2.50 **NM** value: **Cover or less**
Circ: CapCity orders: **8,175**
A: Tim Truman **W:** Valarie Jones
3 ❑ ca. 1991 Cover: 2.50 **NM** value: **Cover or less**
Circ: CapCity orders: **6,325**
A: Tim Truman **W:** Valarie Jones

ROBIN HOOD (ETERNITY) — Eternity

1 ❑ Aug 1989, b&w Cover: 2.25 **NM** value: **Cover or less**
A: Stan Timmons **W:** Martin Powell
2 ❑ b&w Cover: 2.25 **NM** value: **Cover or less**
A: Stan Timmons **W:** Martin Powell
3 ❑ b&w Cover: 2.25 **NM** value: **Cover or less**
A: Stan Timmons **W:** Martin Powell
4 ❑ b&w Cover: 2.25 **NM** value: **Cover or less**
A: Stan Timmons **W:** Martin Powell
Bk 1❑ Cover: 9.95 **NM** value: **Cover or less**

ROBIN HOOD (MAGAZINE ENTERPRISES) — Magazine Enterprises

52 ❑ Nov 1955 Cover: 0.10 **NM** value: **100.00**
53 ❑ 1956 Cover: 0.10 **NM** value: **90.00**
3 ❑ 1956 Cover: 0.10 **NM** value: **90.00**
4 ❑ 1956 Cover: 0.10 **NM** value: **90.00**
5 ❑ 1957 Cover: 0.10 **NM** value: **90.00**
6 ❑ Jun 1957 Cover: 0.10 **NM** value: **90.00**

ROBIN HOOD TALES (DC) — DC

7 ❑ Feb 1957 Cover: 0.10 **NM** value: **250.00**
8 ❑ Apr 1957 Cover: 0.10 **NM** value: **200.00**
• **CGC:** 2 graded, best 9.4
9 ❑ Jun 1957 Cover: 0.10 **NM** value: **200.00**
10 ❑ Aug 1958 Cover: 0.10 **NM** value: **200.00**
11 ❑ Oct 1958 Cover: 0.10 **NM** value: **150.00**
• **CGC:** 1 graded, best 6.5
12 ❑ Dec 1958 Cover: 0.10 **NM** value: **150.00**
13 ❑ Feb 1958 Cover: 0.10 **NM** value: **150.00**
14 ❑ Apr 1958 Cover: 0.10 **NM** value: **150.00**

ROBIN HOOD TALES (QUALITY) — Quality

1 ❑ Feb 1956 Cover: 0.10 **NM** value: **175.00**
• **CGC:** 2 graded, best 8.0
2 ❑ Apr 1956 Cover: 0.10 **NM** value: **145.00**
3 ❑ Jun 1956 Cover: 0.10 **NM** value: **145.00**
4 ❑ Aug 1956 Cover: 0.10 **NM** value: **145.00**
• **CGC:** 2 graded, best 8.5
5 ❑ Oct 1956 Cover: 0.10 **NM** value: **145.00**
• **CGC:** 1 graded, best 8.5
6 ❑ Dec 1956 Cover: 0.10 **NM** value: **145.00**
• **CGC:** 1 graded, best 8.5

ROBIN II — DC

The Joker is on the loose, and with Batman out of town, it falls to Robin to stop him before he destroys Gotham. This second Robin limited series begins with The Joker once again breaking out of Arkham Asylum. Then, with the help of a captured computer genius, The Joker breaks into the city's computers, infecting them with a cleverly written virus. Unless the city pays his ransom, he threatens to shut it down.

As remarkable for its marketing as for its story, this series appeared in a blitz of publicity. Each issue came with up to five different covers, many of which featured special holograms. In addition, DC packaged the various editions together in a number of regular and deluxe "Collectors Edition" sets. All this special packaging spurred the desired buying frenzy, with many collectors eagerly snatching up all the different permutations.

1 ❑ Oct 1991 Cover: 1.00 **NM** value: **Cover or less**
Circ: CapCity orders: **322,250** • **CGC:** 1 graded, best 9.4
• newsstand; no hologram **A:** P. Craig Russell **W:** Byron Preiss
1/A ❑ Oct 1991 Cover: 1.50 **NM** value: **1.75**
• Robin Hologram; Joker in straight jacket **A:** P. Craig Russell **W:** Byron Preiss
1/B ❑ Oct 1991 Cover: 1.50 **NM** value: **1.75**
Joker Holding cover. • Robin Hologram **A:** P. Craig Russell **W:** Byron Preiss
1/C ❑ Oct 1991 Cover: 1.50 **NM** value: **1.75**
Batman cover. • Robin Hologram **A:** P. Craig Russell **W:** Byron Preiss
1/CS❑Oct 1991 Cover: 10.00 **NM** value: **Cover or less**
set of all covers. • extra hologram
1/D ❑ Oct 1991 Cover: 1.50 **NM** value: **1.75**
Joker Standing cover. • Robin Hologram **A:** P. Craig Russell **W:** Byron Preiss
2 ❑ Nov 1991 Cover: 1.00 **NM** value: **Cover or less**
Circ: CapCity orders: **170,600**
Normal cover. • newsstand; no hologram
2/A ❑ Nov 1991 Cover: 1.50 **NM** value: **1.75**
Joker w/mallet cover. • Batman Hologram
2/B ❑ Nov 1991 Cover: 1.50 **NM** value: **1.75**
Joker w/dart board cover. • Batman Hologram
2/C ❑ Nov 1991 Cover: 1.00 **NM** value: **1.75**
Joker w/dagger cover. • Batman Hologram
2/CS❑Nov 1991 Cover: 8.00 **NM** value: **9.00**
3 ❑ Nov 1991 Cover: 1.00 **NM** value: **Cover or less**
Circ: CapCity orders: **140,100**
Normal cover. • newsstand; no hologram
3/A ❑ Nov 1991 Cover: 1.50 **NM** value: **Cover or less**
Robin Swinging cover. • Joker Hologram
3/B ❑ Nov 1991 Cover: 1.50 **NM** value: **Cover or less**
• Joker Hologram; Robin perched
3/CS❑Nov 1991 Cover: 6.00 **NM** value: **Cover or less**
4 ❑ Dec 1991 Cover: 1.00 **NM** value: **Cover or less**
Circ: CapCity orders: **106,850**
Normal cover. • newsstand, no hologram
4/A ❑ Dec 1991 Cover: 1.50 **NM** value: **Cover or less**
• Bat signal hologram
4/CS❑Dec 1991 Cover: 4.00 **NM** value: **4.25**
Dlx 1❑ Cover: 30.00 **NM** value: **Cover or less**
• boxed with hologram cards (limited to 25, 000); Deluxe set; Contains all issues and variations in bookshelf binder

ROBIN III: CRY OF THE HUNTRESS — DC

1 ❑ Dec 1992 Cover: 1.25 **NM** value: **Cover or less**
🕮 Cry of the Huntress, Part 1 • newsstand **A:** Tom Lyle **W:** Chuck Dixon
1/SC❑Dec 1992 Cover: 2.50 **NM** value: **Cover or less**
Circ: CapCity orders: **98,350**
moving cover.
2 ❑ Jan 1993 Cover: 1.25 **NM** value: **Cover or less**
🕮 Cry of the Huntress, Part 2 • newsstand **A:** Tom Lyle **W:** Chuck Dixon
2/SC❑Jan 1993 Cover: 2.50 **NM** value: **Cover or less**
Circ: CapCity orders: **65,250**
moving cover.
3 ❑ Jan 1993 Cover: 1.25 **NM** value: **Cover or less**
🕮 Cry of the Huntress, Part 3 • newsstand **A:** Tom Lyle **W:** Chuck Dixon
3/SC❑Jan 1993 Cover: 2.50 **NM** value: **Cover or less**
Circ: CapCity orders: **62,900**
moving cover.
4 ❑ Feb 1993 Cover: 1.25 **NM** value: **Cover or less**
🕮 Cry of the Huntress, Part 4 • newsstand **A:** Tom Lyle **W:** Chuck Dixon
4/SC❑Feb 1993 Cover: 2.50 **NM** value: **Cover or less**
Circ: CapCity orders: **56,600**
moving cover.
5 ❑ Feb 1993 Cover: 1.25 **NM** value: **Cover or less**
🕮 Cry of the Huntress, Part 5 • newsstand **A:** Tom Lyle **W:** Chuck Dixon
5/SC❑Feb 1993 Cover: 2.50 **NM** value: **Cover or less**
Circ: CapCity orders: **56,250**
moving cover.
6 ❑ Mar 1993 Cover: 1.25 **NM** value: **Cover or less**
🕮 Cry of the Huntress, Part 6 • newsstand **A:** Tom Lyle **W:** Chuck Dixon
6/SC❑Mar 1993 Cover: 2.50 **NM** value: **Cover or less**
Circ: CapCity orders: **54,900**
moving cover.

ROBIN (MINI-SERIES) — DC

Timothy Drake is Robin, filling the gap left by the death of Jason Todd, who died in Batman #428. Although Timothy has served since as Batman's sidekick, he gets his wings as a legitimate crime-fighter in his own right in this five-part series.

Written by Chuck Dixon, the Robin limited series pitted the Boy Wonder against Sir Edmund Dorrance, a high-class heroin dealer who was moving on to grander designs. Sir Edmund had acquired a sample of plague toxin left over from Hitler's wartime laboratories. He planned to release the toxin into the air of Gotham City, and come back later to cash in on the destruction. Now, without Batman to help him, Robin had to save Gotham City.

1 ❑ Jan 1991 Cover: 1.00 **NM** value: **3.00**
Circ: CapCity orders: **103,300**
🕮 Big Bad World • poster **A:** Tom Lyle **W:** Chuck Dixon ★ 1st Appearance of King Snake.
1-2 ❑ Jan 1991 Cover: 1.00 **NM** value: **1.50**
1-3 ❑ Cover: 1.00 **NM** value: **1.50**
2 ❑ Feb 1991 Cover: 1.00 **NM** value: **2.50**
Circ: CapCity orders: **74,250**
A: Tom Lyle **W:** Chuck Dixon
2-2 ❑ Feb 1991 Cover: 1.00 **NM** value: **1.50**
3 ❑ Mar 1991 Cover: 1.00 **NM** value: **2.00**
Circ: CapCity orders: **100,700**
A: Tom Lyle **W:** Chuck Dixon
4 ❑ Apr 1991 Cover: 1.00 **NM** value: **2.00**
Circ: CapCity orders: **111,300**
A: Tom Lyle **W:** Chuck Dixon ★ Versus Lady Shiva.
5 ❑ May 1991 Cover: 1.00 **NM** value: **2.00**
Circ: CapCity orders: **110,350**
A: Tom Lyle **W:** Chuck Dixon ★ Versus King Shark.
Anl 1❑ca. 1992 Cover: 2.50 **NM** value: **Cover or less**
Circ: CapCity orders: **42,800**
🕮 Eclipso: The Darkness Within, Part 12 • Eclipso **A:** Tom Lyle **W:** Alan Grant; John Wagner
Anl 2❑ca. 1993 Cover: 2.50 **NM** value: **Cover or less**
Circ: CapCity orders: **29,800**
🕮 Bloodlines • Bloodlines ★ 1st Appearance of Razorsharp.
Bk 1❑ Jul 1991 Cover: 4.95 **NM** value: **Cover or less**
• A Hero Reborn; collects mini-series and Batman #455-457

ROBIN PLUS — DC

1 ❑ Dec 1996 Cover: 2.95 **NM** value: **Cover or less**
Circ: Diamd. preorders: **48,947**
🕮 Dashing Through the Storm **A:** John Royle **W:** Brian Augustyn; Mark Waid ★ Appearance of Impulse.
2 ❑ Dec 1997 Cover: 2.95 **NM** value: **Cover or less**
Circ: Diamd. preorders: **27,140**
• continues in Scare Tactics #10★ Appearance of Fang.

ROBIN RED AND THE LUTINS — Ace

1 ❑ Nov 1986 Cover: 1.75 **NM** value: **Cover or less**
A: Pat Boyette **W:** Pat Boyette
2 ❑ Cover: 1.75 **NM** value: **Cover or less**
A: Pat Boyette **W:** Pat Boyette

ROBIN 3000 — DC

1 ❑ ca. 1992 Cover: 4.95 **NM** value: **Cover or less**
Circ: CapCity orders: **38,350**
A: P. Craig Russell **W:** Byron Preiss
2 ❑ ca. 1992 Cover: 4.95 **NM** value: **Cover or less**
Circ: CapCity orders: **34,000**
A: P. Craig Russell **W:** Byron Preiss

ROBIN: YEAR ONE — DC

1 ❑ Dec 2000 Cover: 4.95 **NM** value: **Cover or less**
Circ: Diamd. preorders: **27,414**
A: Scott Beatty **W:** Chuck Dixon
2 ❑ Jan 2001 Cover: 4.95 **NM** value: **Cover or less**
Circ: Diamd. preorders: **25,325**
A: Scott Beatty **W:** Chuck Dixon
3 ❑ Feb 2001 Cover: 4.95 **NM** value: **Cover or less**
Circ: Diamd. preorders: **25,240**
A: Scott Beatty **W:** Chuck Dixon
4 ❑ Mar 2001 Cover: 4.95 **NM** value: **Cover or less**
Circ: Diamd. preorders: **25,528**
A: Scott Beatty **W:** Chuck Dixon

ROBOCOP 2 — Marvel

1 ❑ Aug 1990 Cover: 1.00 **NM** value: **1.50**
Circ: CapCity orders: **16,900**
🕮 Kid's Stuff • comic book **A:** Mark Bagley **W:** Alan Grant
2 ❑ Sep 1990 Cover: 1.00 **NM** value: **1.50**
Circ: CapCity orders: **14,600**
• comic book **A:** Mark Bagley **W:** Alan Grant
3 ❑ Sep 1990 Cover: 1.00 **NM** value: **1.50**
Circ: CapCity orders: **14,300**
• comic book **A:** Mark Bagley **W:** Alan Grant
Bk 1❑ ca. 1990 Cover: 4.95 **NM** value: **Cover or less**
• prestige format. • Collects Robocop 2 1-3 **A:** Mark Bagley **W:** Alan Grant

ROBOCOP 2 (MAGAZINE) — Marvel

1 ❑ Aug 1990, b&w Cover: 2.25 **NM** value: **2.50**
• magazine.

ROBOCOP 3 — Dark Horse

1 ❑ Jul 1993 Cover: 2.50 **NM** value: **Cover or less**
Circ: CapCity orders: **9,250**
A: Hoang Nguyen **W:** Steven Grant
2 ❑ Sep 1993 Cover: 2.50 **NM** value: **Cover or less**
Circ: CapCity orders: **7,450**
A: Hoang Nguyen **W:** Steven Grant
3 ❑ Nov 1993 Cover: 2.50 **NM** value: **Cover or less**
Circ: CapCity orders: **5,575**
A: Hoang Nguyen **W:** Steven Grant

ROBOCOP (MAGAZINE) — Marvel

1 ❑ Oct 1987 Cover: 2.00 **NM** value: **2.50**
A: Alan Kupperberg; Javier Saltares **W:** Bob Harras; Ed Neumeier; Michael Miner

ROBOCOP (MARVEL) — Marvel

1 ❑ Mar 1990 Cover: 1.50 **NM** value: **3.00**
Circ: CapCity orders: **40,600** • **CGC:** 6 graded, best 9.8
🕮 Kombat Zone **A:** Lee Sullivan **W:** Alan Grant
2 ❑ Apr 1990 Cover: 1.50 **NM** value: **2.00**
Circ: CapCity orders: **24,500**
3 ❑ May 1990 Cover: 1.50 **NM** value: **Cover or less**
Circ: CapCity orders: **24,500** • **CGC:** 2 graded, best 9.6
🕮 Dreamerama **A:** Lee Sullivan **W:** Alan Grant
4 ❑ Jun 1990 Cover: 1.50 **NM** value: **Cover or less**
Circ: CapCity orders: **27,600**
5 ❑ Jul 1990 Cover: 1.50 **NM** value: **Cover or less**
Circ: CapCity orders: **26,200**
6 ❑ Aug 1990 Cover: 1.50 **NM** value: **Cover or less**
Circ: CapCity orders: **24,700**
7 ❑ Sep 1990 Cover: 1.50 **NM** value: **Cover or less**
Circ: CapCity orders: **22,700**

Other grades: Multiply prices above by **1.5 for Mint • 2/3 for Very Fine • 1/3 for Fine • 1/5 for Very Good • 1/8 for Good**

8 ❑ Oct 1990 Cover: 1.50 **NM** value: **Cover or less**
Circ: CapCity orders: **21,200**
9 ❑ Nov 1990 Cover: 1.50 **NM** value: **Cover or less**
Circ: CapCity orders: **18,600**
10 ❑ Dec 1990 Cover: 1.50 **NM** value: **Cover or less**
Circ: CapCity orders: **16,900**
11 ❑ Jan 1991 Cover: 1.50 **NM** value: **Cover or less**
Circ: CapCity orders: **15,200**
12 ❑ Feb 1991 Cover: 1.50 **NM** value: **Cover or less**
Circ: CapCity orders: **13,700**
13 ❑ Mar 1991 Cover: 1.50 **NM** value: **Cover or less**
Circ: CapCity orders: **12,000**
14 ❑ Apr 1991 Cover: 1.50 **NM** value: **Cover or less**
Circ: CapCity orders: **10,600**
15 ❑ May 1991 Cover: 1.50 **NM** value: **Cover or less**
Circ: CapCity orders: **10,200**
16 ❑ Jun 1991 Cover: 1.50 **NM** value: **Cover or less**
Circ: CapCity orders: **9,800**
17 ❑ Jul 1991 Cover: 1.50 **NM** value: **Cover or less**
Circ: CapCity orders: **9,500**
18 ❑ Aug 1991 Cover: 1.50 **NM** value: **Cover or less**
Circ: CapCity orders: **9,200**
19 ❑ Sep 1991 Cover: 1.50 **NM** value: **Cover or less**
Circ: CapCity orders: **8,900**
20 ❑ Oct 1991 Cover: 1.50 **NM** value: **Cover or less**
Circ: CapCity orders: **8,700**
21 ❑ Nov 1991 Cover: 1.50 **NM** value: **Cover or less**
Circ: CapCity orders: **8,200**
22 ❑ Dec 1991 Cover: 1.50 **NM** value: **Cover or less**
Circ: CapCity orders: **8,000**
23 ❑ Jan 1992 Cover: 1.50 **NM** value: **Cover or less**
Circ: CapCity orders: **7,600**
final issue.

ROBOCOP: MORTAL COILS — Dark Horse

1 ❑ Sep 1993 Cover: 2.50 **NM** value: **Cover or less**
Circ: CapCity orders: **9,050**
A: Nick Gnazzo **W:** Steven Grant
2 ❑ Oct 1993 Cover: 2.50 **NM** value: **Cover or less**
Circ: CapCity orders: **6,400**
A: Nick Gnazzo **W:** Steven Grant
3 ❑ Nov 1993 Cover: 2.50 **NM** value: **Cover or less**
Circ: CapCity orders: **5,725**
4 ❑ Dec 1993 Cover: 2.50 **NM** value: **Cover or less**
Circ: CapCity orders: **5,200**

ROBOCOP (MOVIE ADAPTATION) — Marvel

1 ❑ Jul 1990 Cover: 4.95 **NM** value: **Cover or less**
Circ: CapCity orders: **9,000**
• prestige format.

ROBOCOP: PRIME SUSPECT — Dark Horse

1 ❑ Oct 1992 Cover: 2.50 **NM** value: **Cover or less**
Circ: CapCity orders: **24,000**
A: John Paul Leon **W:** John Arcudi
2 ❑ Nov 1992 Cover: 2.50 **NM** value: **Cover or less**
Circ: CapCity orders: **16,800**
A: John Paul Leon **W:** John Arcudi
3 ❑ Dec 1992 Cover: 2.50 **NM** value: **Cover or less**
Circ: CapCity orders: **15,425**
A: John Paul Leon **W:** John Arcudi
4 ❑ Jan 1993 Cover: 2.50 **NM** value: **Cover or less**
Circ: CapCity orders: **13,725**
A: John Paul Leon **W:** John Arcudi

ROBOCOP: ROULETTE — Dark Horse

1 ❑ Dec 1993 Cover: 2.50 **NM** value: **Cover or less**
Circ: CapCity orders: **7,175**
A: Mitch Byrd **W:** John Arcudi
2 ❑ Jan 1994 Cover: 2.50 **NM** value: **Cover or less**
Circ: CapCity orders: **5,075**
A: Mitch Byrd **W:** John Arcudi
3 ❑ Feb 1994 Cover: 2.50 **NM** value: **Cover or less**
Circ: CapCity orders: **4,700**
A: Mitch Byrd **W:** John Arcudi
4 ❑ Mar 1994 Cover: 2.50 **NM** value: **Cover or less**
Circ: CapCity orders: **4,700**
A: Mitch Byrd **W:** John Arcudi

ROBOCOP VERSUS THE TERMINATOR — Dark Horse

1 ❑ ca. 1992 Cover: 2.50 **NM** value: **3.00**
Circ: CapCity orders: **88,325** • **CGC:** 1 graded, best 9.4
A: Walt Simonson **W:** Frank Miller
1/PL❑ ca. 1992 **NM** value: **4.00**
• Platinum promotional edition. **A:** Walt Simonson **W:** Frank Miller
2 ❑ ca. 1992 Cover: 2.50 **NM** value: **Cover or less**
Circ: CapCity orders: **54,875**
📖 Includes Terminator cut-out **A:** Walt Simonson **W:** Frank Miller
3 ❑ ca. 1992 Cover: 2.50 **NM** value: **Cover or less**
Circ: CapCity orders: **45,525**
A: Walt Simonson **W:** Frank Miller
4 ❑ ca. 1992 Cover: 2.50 **NM** value: **Cover or less**
Circ: CapCity orders: **48,175**
A: Walt Simonson **W:** Frank Miller

ROBO-HUNTER — Eagle

1 ❑ Cover: 1.00 **NM** value: **1.50**
A: Ian Gibson; Jose Ferrer **W:** John Wagner
2 ❑ Cover: 1.00 **NM** value: **1.25**
📖 Robo-Hunter; Harlem Heroes **A:** Dave Gibbons; Ian Gibson **W:** John Wagner; Tom Tully
3 ❑ Cover: 1.00 **NM** value: **1.25**
📖 Robo-Hunter; Harlem Heroes **A:** Dave Gibbons; Ian Gibson **W:** John Wagner; Tom Tully
4 ❑ Cover: 1.00 **NM** value: **1.25**
📖 Robo-Hunter; Harlem Heroes **A:** Dave Gibbons; Ian Gibson **W:** John Wagner; Tom Tully
5 ❑ Cover: 1.00 **NM** value: **1.25**
📖 Robo-Hunter **A:** Ian Gibson **W:** John Wagner

ROBOTECH — Antarctic

Teen angst and daydreams seem to be the order of the day in this Robotech series set against a military backdrop in the not-too-distant future of 2007. It's "Beverly Hills 90210" with fighter jets and rockets!

While Ted Nomura's script is somewhat pedestrian, his artwork — due in great part to the coloring — is gorgeous and certainly brings this anime-inspired comic book to life. Readers will need to be familiar with the Robotech saga in order to fully appreciate this series, because little effort is made to introduce the characters and their motivations to the audience. Still, if doe-eyed manga girls are to your liking, this is probably right up your alley.

1 ❑ Mar 1997 Cover: 2.95 **NM** value: **Cover or less**
Circ: Diamd. preorders: **10,679**
📖 Megastorm, Part 1 **A:** Ben Dunn **W:** Fred Perry
2 ❑ May 1997 Cover: 2.95 **NM** value: **Cover or less**
Circ: Diamd. preorders: **8,101**
📖 Megastorm, Part 2 **A:** Ben Dunn **W:** Fred Perry
3 ❑ Jul 1997 Cover: 2.95 **NM** value: **Cover or less**
Circ: Diamd. preorders: **8,854**
📖 Megastorm, Part 3 **A:** Ben Dunn **W:** Fred Perry
4 ❑ Sep 1997 Cover: 2.95 **NM** value: **Cover or less**
Circ: Diamd. preorders: **8,937**
📖 Rolling Thunder, Part 1 **A:** Fred Perry **W:** Fred Perry
5 ❑ Nov 1997 Cover: 2.95 **NM** value: **Cover or less**
Circ: Diamd. preorders: **8,221**
📖 Rolling Thunder, Part 2 **A:** Fred Perry **W:** Fred Perry
6 ❑ Jan 1998 Cover: 2.95 **NM** value: **Cover or less**
Circ: Diamd. preorders: **7,352**
📖 Rolling Thunder, Part 3 **A:** Fred Perry **W:** Fred Perry
7 ❑ Mar 1998 Cover: 2.95 **NM** value: **Cover or less**
Circ: Diamd. preorders: **6,567**
📖 Rolling Thunder, Part 4 **A:** Fred Perry **W:** Fred Perry
8 ❑ May 1998 Cover: 2.95 **NM** value: **Cover or less**
Circ: Diamd. preorders: **6,263**
📖 Variants, Part 1 **A:** Ted Nomura **W:** Ted Nomura
9 ❑ Jul 1998 Cover: 2.95 **NM** value: **Cover or less**
Circ: Diamd. preorders: **5,903**
📖 Variants, Part 2 **A:** Ted Nomura **W:** Ted Nomura
10 ❑ Sep 1998 Cover: 2.95 **NM** value: **Cover or less**
Circ: Diamd. preorders: **5,358**
📖 Variants, Part 3 **A:** Ted Nomura **W:** Ted Nomura
11 ❑ Nov 1998 Cover: 2.95 **NM** value: **Cover or less**
Circ: Diamd. preorders: **5,038**
📖 Variants, Part 4 **A:** Ted Nomura **W:** Ted Nomura
Anl 1❑ Apr 1998, b&w Cover: 2.95 **NM** value: **Cover or less**
Circ: Diamd. preorders: **5,938**
📖 The First Person; Shop Talk or Why You Should Never Ride Without a Helmet **A:** Lester O'Brien Jr.; Thor Badendyck **W:** Thor Badendyck; Curtis Allen

ROBOTECH: AMAZON WORLD-ESCAPE FROM PRAXIS — Academy

1 ❑ Dec 1994 Cover: 2.95 **NM** value: **Cover or less**
A: John Waltrip **W:** Jason Waltrip

ROBOTECH: CLASS REUNION — Antarctic

1 ❑ Dec 1998, b&w Cover: 3.95 **NM** value: **Cover or less**
Circ: Diamd. preorders: **4,190**
A: Greg Lane **W:** Greg Lane

ROBOTECH: CLONE — Academy

0 ❑ Cover: 2.95 **NM** value: **Cover or less**
Circ: CapCity orders: **3,380**
1 ❑ Cover: 2.95 **NM** value: **Cover or less**
Circ: CapCity orders: **2,095**
📖 The Dialect Of Duality, Part 2 **A:** Tavisha Wolfgarth **W:** Rosearik Rikki
2 ❑ Cover: 2.95 **NM** value: **Cover or less**
3 ❑ Cover: 2.95 **NM** value: **Cover or less**
4 ❑ Cover: 2.95 **NM** value: **Cover or less**
5 ❑ Cover: 2.95 **NM** value: **Cover or less**
SE 1❑ Cover: 3.50 **NM** value: **Cover or less**

ROBOTECH: COVERT-OPS — Antarctic

1 ❑ Aug 1998, b&w Cover: 2.95 **NM** value: **Cover or less**
Circ: Diamd. preorders: **4,993**
A: Greg Lane **W:** Greg Lane
2 ❑ Sep 1998, b&w Cover: 2.95 **NM** value: **Cover or less**
Circ: Diamd. preorders: **4,579**
A: Greg Lane **W:** Greg Lane

ROBOTECH: CYBER WORLD-SECRETS OF HAYDON IV — Academy

1 ❑ Cover: 2.95 **NM** value: **Cover or less**
A: John Waltrip **W:** Jason Waltrip

ROBOTECH DEFENDERS — DC

1 ❑ Jan 1985 Cover: 0.75 **NM** value: **2.00**
Circ: CapCity orders: **6,775**
📖 The Gathering **A:** Murphy Anderson; Judith Hunt **W:** Andy Helfer
2 ❑ Apr 1985 Cover: 0.75 **NM** value: **2.00**
• three-issue series was finished in two issues **A:** Murphy Anderson

ROBOTECH: ESCAPE — Antarctic

1 ❑ May 1998, b&w Cover: 2.95 **NM** value: **Cover or less**
Circ: Diamd. preorders: **6,133**
A: Jean-Sebastien Duberger **W:** Asylum Khan

ROBOTECH: FINAL FIRE — Antarctic

1 ❑ Dec 1998, b&w Cover: 2.95 **NM** value: **Cover or less**
Circ: Diamd. preorders: **4,398**
A: Lee Duhig **W:** Lee Duhig

ROBOTECH: FIREWALKERS — Eternity

1 ❑ Cover: 2.50 **NM** value: **Cover or less**
Circ: CapCity orders: **4,080**
A: Tim Eldred **W:** Bill Spangler

ROBOTECH GENESIS — Eternity

1 ❑ full color Cover: 2.50 **NM** value: **Cover or less**
Circ: CapCity orders: **4,780**
• trading cards
1/LE❑ Cover: 5.95 **NM** value: **Cover or less**
• limited
2 ❑ Cover: 2.50 **NM** value: **Cover or less**
Circ: CapCity orders: **3,600**
3 ❑ Cover: 2.50 **NM** value: **Cover or less**
Circ: CapCity orders: **3,590**
4 ❑ Cover: 2.50 **NM** value: **Cover or less**
Circ: CapCity orders: **3,625**
• trading cards
5 ❑ Cover: 2.50 **NM** value: **Cover or less**
Circ: CapCity orders: **3,475**
• trading cards
6 ❑ Cover: 2.50 **NM** value: **Cover or less**
Circ: CapCity orders: **3,350**

ROBOTECH II: INVID WORLD, ASSAULT ON OPTERA — Academy

1 ❑ Oct 1994 Cover: 2.95 **NM** value: **Cover or less**
A: John Waltrip **W:** Jason Waltrip

ROBOTECH II: THE SENTINELS — Eternity

1 ❑ Nov 1988 Cover: 1.95 **NM** value: **3.50**
📖 A New Threat **A:** Jason Waltrip **W:** Chris Ulm; Tom Mason
1-2 ❑ Cover: 1.95 **NM** value: **2.00**
2 ❑ Dec 1988 Cover: 1.95 **NM** value: **2.50**
3 ❑ Jan 1989 Cover: 1.95 **NM** value: **2.50**
3-2 ❑ Feb 1989 Cover: 1.95 **NM** value: **2.00**
4 ❑ Mar 1989 Cover: 1.95 **NM** value: **2.25**
5 ❑ Apr 1989 Cover: 1.95 **NM** value: **2.25**
6 ❑ May 1989 Cover: 1.95 **NM** value: **2.00**
7 ❑ Jun 1989 Cover: 1.95 **NM** value: **2.00**
8 ❑ Jul 1989 Cover: 1.95 **NM** value: **2.00**
9 ❑ Sep 1989 Cover: 1.95 **NM** value: **2.00**
10 ❑ Oct 1989 Cover: 1.95 **NM** value: **2.00**
11 ❑ Oct 1989 Cover: 1.95 **NM** value: **2.00**
12 ❑ Nov 1989 Cover: 1.95 **NM** value: **2.00**
13 ❑ Dec 1989 Cover: 1.95 **NM** value: **2.00**
14 ❑ Jan 1990 Cover: 1.95 **NM** value: **2.00**
15 ❑ Cover: 1.95 **NM** value: **2.00**
16 ❑ Apr 1990 Cover: 1.95 **NM** value: **Cover or less**
final issue.
Bk 1/HC❑ Cover: 19.95 **NM** value: **Cover or less**
hardcover.
Bk 2/HC❑ Cover: 19.95 **NM** value: **Cover or less**
hardcover.

ROBOTECH II: THE SENTINELS-A NEW BEGINNING — Eternity

Bk 1❑ Cover: 9.95 **NM** value: **Cover or less**

ROBOTECH II: THE SENTINELS BOOK II — Eternity

1 ❑ May 1990 Cover: 2.25 **NM** value: **Cover or less**
A: Jason Waltrip **W:** Chris Ulm; Tom Mason
2 ❑ Cover: 2.25 **NM** value: **Cover or less**
A: Jason Waltrip **W:** Chris Ulm; Tom Mason
3 ❑ Cover: 2.25 **NM** value: **Cover or less**
A: Jason Waltrip **W:** Chris Ulm; Tom Mason
4 ❑ Cover: 2.25 **NM** value: **Cover or less**
A: Jason Waltrip **W:** Chris Ulm; Tom Mason
5 ❑ 1991 Cover: 2.25 **NM** value: **Cover or less**
A: Jason Waltrip **W:** Chris Ulm; Tom Mason
6 ❑ 1991 Cover: 2.25 **NM** value: **Cover or less**
A: Jason Waltrip **W:** Chris Ulm; Tom Mason
7 ❑ 1991 Cover: 2.25 **NM** value: **Cover or less**
A: Jason Waltrip **W:** Chris Ulm; Tom Mason
8 ❑ 1991 Cover: 2.25 **NM** value: **Cover or less**
A: Jason Waltrip **W:** Chris Ulm; Tom Mason
9 ❑ 1991 Cover: 2.25 **NM** value: **Cover or less**
A: Jason Waltrip **W:** Chris Ulm; Tom Mason
10 ❑ 1991 Cover: 2.25 **NM** value: **Cover or less**
A: Jason Waltrip **W:** Chris Ulm; Tom Mason
11 ❑ Cover: 2.25 **NM** value: **Cover or less**
A: Jason Waltrip **W:** Chris Ulm; Tom Mason
12 ❑ Cover: 2.50 **NM** value: **Cover or less**
Circ: CapCity orders: **3,450**
A: Jason Waltrip **W:** Chris Ulm; Tom Mason
13 ❑ Mar 1992 Cover: 2.50 **NM** value: **Cover or less**
Circ: CapCity orders: **3,120**
A: Jason Waltrip **W:** Chris Ulm; Tom Mason
14 ❑ Cover: 2.50 **NM** value: **Cover or less**
Circ: CapCity orders: **3,450**
A: Jason Waltrip **W:** Chris Ulm; Tom Mason
15 ❑ Cover: 2.50 **NM** value: **Cover or less**
Circ: CapCity orders: **3,390**
A: Jason Waltrip **W:** Chris Ulm; Tom Mason
16 ❑ Cover: 2.50 **NM** value: **Cover or less**
Circ: CapCity orders: **3,210**
A: Jason Waltrip **W:** Chris Ulm; Tom Mason

CGC-graded: Multiply prices above by **33 for 9.9 M • 16 for 9.8 NM/M • 7 for 9.6 NM+ • 5 for 9.4 NM • 2.5 for 9.2 NM- • 1.5 for 9.0 VF/NM**

17 ❑ Cover: 2.50 **NM** value: **Cover or less**
Circ: CapCity orders: **3,550**
A: Jason Waltrip **W:** Chris Ulm; Tom Mason
18 ❑ Cover: 2.50 **NM** value: **Cover or less**
Circ: CapCity orders: **3,300**
A: Jason Waltrip **W:** Chris Ulm; Tom Mason
19 ❑ Cover: 2.50 **NM** value: **Cover or less**
Circ: CapCity orders: **3,440**
A: Jason Waltrip **W:** Chris Ulm; Tom Mason
20 ❑ Cover: 2.50 **NM** value: **Cover or less**
Circ: CapCity orders: **3,180**
A: Jason Waltrip **W:** Chris Ulm; Tom Mason

ROBOTECH II: THE SENTINELS BOOK III Eternity
1 ❑ Cover: 2.50 **NM** value: **Cover or less**
Circ: CapCity orders: **3,500**
2 ❑ Cover: 2.50 **NM** value: **Cover or less**
Circ: CapCity orders: **2,750**
3 ❑ Cover: 2.50 **NM** value: **Cover or less**
4 ❑ Cover: 2.50 **NM** value: **Cover or less**
5 ❑ Cover: 2.50 **NM** value: **Cover or less**
Circ: CapCity orders: **2,440**
6 ❑ Cover: 2.50 **NM** value: **Cover or less**
Circ: CapCity orders: **2,250**

ROBOTECH II: THE SENTINELS BOOK IVAcademy
1 ❑ Cover: 2.95 **NM** value: **Cover or less**
A: John & Jason Waltrip **W:** John & Jason Waltrip
2 ❑ Cover: 2.95 **NM** value: **Cover or less**
A: John & Jason Waltrip **W:** John & Jason Waltrip
3 ❑ Cover: 2.95 **NM** value: **Cover or less**
A: John & Jason Waltrip **W:** John & Jason Waltrip
4 ❑ Cover: 2.95 **NM** value: **Cover or less**
A: John & Jason Waltrip **W:** John & Jason Waltrip
5 ❑ Cover: 2.95 **NM** value: **Cover or less**
A: John & Jason Waltrip **W:** John & Jason Waltrip
6 ❑ May 1996 Cover: 2.95 **NM** value: **Cover or less**
📖 Clockwork of Doom! **A:** John & Jason Waltrip **W:** John & Jason Waltrip

ROBOTECH II: THE SENTINELS CYBERPIRATES Eternity
1 ❑ Cover: 2.25 **NM** value: **Cover or less**
2 ❑ Cover: 2.25 **NM** value: **Cover or less**
3 ❑ Cover: 2.25 **NM** value: **Cover or less**
4 ❑ Cover: 2.25 **NM** value: **Cover or less**

ROBOTECH II: THE SENTINELS SCRIPT BOOK Eternity
1 ❑ b&w Cover: 9.95 **NM** value: **Cover or less**

ROBOTECH II: THE SENTINELS SPECIAL Eternity
1 ❑ Apr 1989 Cover: 1.95 **NM** value: **Cover or less**
A: Jason Waltrip **W:** Chris Ulm; Tom Mason
2 ❑ Cover: 1.95 **NM** value: **Cover or less**
A: Jason Waltrip **W:** Chris Ulm; Tom Mason

ROBOTECH II: THE SENTINELS SWIMSUIT SPECTACULAR Eternity
1 ❑ Cover: 2.95 **NM** value: **Cover or less**

ROBOTECH II: THE SENTINELS: THE ILLUSTRATED HANDBOOK Eternity
1 ❑ Cover: 2.50 **NM** value: **Cover or less**
2 ❑ Cover: 2.50 **NM** value: **Cover or less**
3 ❑ Cover: 2.50 **NM** value: **Cover or less**

ROBOTECH II: THE SENTINELS THE MALCONTENT UPRISINGS Eternity

ROBOTECH II: THE SENTINELS: THE UNTOLD STORY Eternity
1 ❑ b&w Cover: 2.50 **NM** value: **Cover or less**

ROBOTECH II: THE SENTINELS WEDDING SPECIAL Eternity
1 ❑ Apr 1989 Cover: 1.95 **NM** value: **2.00**

ROBOTECH IN 3-D Comico
1 ❑ Jul 1985 Cover: 2.50 **NM** value: **Cover or less**
Circ: CapCity orders: **5,975**

ROBOTECH: INVID WAR Eternity
1 ❑ May 1992, b&w Cover: 2.50 **NM** value: **Cover or less**
Circ: CapCity orders: **5,180**
A: Tim Eldred **W:** Tim Eldred; Bill Spangler
2 ❑ b&w Cover: 2.50 **NM** value: **Cover or less**
3 ❑ b&w Cover: 2.50 **NM** value: **Cover or less**
Circ: CapCity orders: **3,930**
4 ❑ b&w Cover: 2.50 **NM** value: **Cover or less**
Circ: CapCity orders: **3,870**
5 ❑ b&w Cover: 2.50 **NM** value: **Cover or less**
Circ: CapCity orders: **3,550**
6 ❑ b&w Cover: 2.50 **NM** value: **Cover or less**
7 ❑ b&w Cover: 2.50 **NM** value: **Cover or less**
Circ: CapCity orders: **4,150**
8 ❑ b&w Cover: 2.50 **NM** value: **Cover or less**
Circ: CapCity orders: **3,650**
9 ❑ b&w Cover: 2.50 **NM** value: **Cover or less**
Circ: CapCity orders: **3,440**
10 ❑ b&w Cover: 1.25 **NM** value: **Cover or less**
Circ: CapCity orders: **3,400**
11 ❑ b&w Cover: 1.25 **NM** value: **Cover or less**
Circ: CapCity orders: **3,480**
12 ❑ b&w Cover: 1.25 **NM** value: **Cover or less**
Circ: CapCity orders: **3,200**
13 ❑ b&w Cover: 1.25 **NM** value: **Cover or less**
Circ: CapCity orders: **3,170**
14 ❑ Cover: 2.50 **NM** value: **Cover or less**
Circ: CapCity orders: **3,120**
15 ❑ Cover: 2.50 **NM** value: **Cover or less**
16 ❑ Cover: 2.50 **NM** value: **Cover or less**
Circ: CapCity orders: **2,700**
17 ❑ Cover: 2.50 **NM** value: **Cover or less**
18 ❑ Cover: 2.50 **NM** value: **Cover or less**

ROBOTECH: INVID WAR AFTERMATH Eternity
1 ❑ b&w Cover: 2.50 **NM** value: **Cover or less**
Circ: CapCity orders: **3,240**
A: Bruce Lewis; David Lanphear **W:** Bruce Lewis; David Lanphear
2 ❑ b&w Cover: 2.50 **NM** value: **Cover or less**
Circ: CapCity orders: **2,440**

ROBOTECH MASTERS Comico
1 ❑ Jul 1985 Cover: 2.50 **NM** value: **Cover or less**
Circ: CapCity orders: **6,700 • CGC:** 1 graded, best 9.6
📖 False Start **A:** Neil D. Vokes **W:** Mike Baron
2 ❑ Sep 1985 Cover: 1.50 **NM** value: **Cover or less**
Circ: CapCity orders: **8,625**
A: Neil D. Vokes **W:** Mike Baron
3 ❑ Nov 1985 Cover: 1.50 **NM** value: **Cover or less**
Circ: CapCity orders: **9,825**
📖 Volunteers! **A:** Neil D. Vokes **W:** Mike Baron
4 ❑ Nov 1985 Cover: 1.50 **NM** value: **Cover or less**
Circ: CapCity orders: **9,525**
5 ❑ Cover: 1.50 **NM** value: **Cover or less**
Circ: CapCity orders: **8,000**
6 ❑ 1986 Cover: 1.50 **NM** value: **Cover or less**
Circ: CapCity orders: **7,600**
7 ❑ 1986 Cover: 1.50 **NM** value: **Cover or less**
Circ: CapCity orders: **6,850**
8 ❑ 1986 Cover: 1.50 **NM** value: **Cover or less**
Circ: CapCity orders: **6,900**
9 ❑ 1986 Cover: 1.50 **NM** value: **Cover or less**
Circ: CapCity orders: **7,125**
10 ❑ Aug 1986 Cover: 1.50 **NM** value: **Cover or less**
Circ: CapCity orders: **6,150**
11 ❑ Cover: 1.50 **NM** value: **Cover or less**
Circ: CapCity orders: **7,500**
12 ❑ Cover: 1.50 **NM** value: **Cover or less**
Circ: CapCity orders: **7,950**
13 ❑ Cover: 1.50 **NM** value: **Cover or less**
Circ: CapCity orders: **7,275**
14 ❑ 1987 Cover: 1.50 **NM** value: **Cover or less**
Circ: CapCity orders: **6,225**
15 ❑ 1987 Cover: 1.50 **NM** value: **Cover or less**
Circ: CapCity orders: **6,050**
16 ❑ 1987 Cover: 1.50 **NM** value: **Cover or less**
Circ: CapCity orders: **5,875**
17 ❑ 1987 Cover: 1.50 **NM** value: **Cover or less**
Circ: CapCity orders: **5,775**
18 ❑ 1987 Cover: 1.50 **NM** value: **Cover or less**
Circ: CapCity orders: **5,225**
19 ❑ 1987 Cover: 1.50 **NM** value: **Cover or less**
Circ: CapCity orders: **5,250**
20 ❑ 1987 Cover: 1.50 **NM** value: **Cover or less**
Circ: CapCity orders: **5,250**
21 ❑ Cover: 1.50 **NM** value: **Cover or less**
Circ: CapCity orders: **4,550**
22 ❑ Cover: 1.50 **NM** value: **Cover or less**
Circ: CapCity orders: **4,225**
23 ❑ 1988 Cover: 1.50 **NM** value: **Cover or less**
Circ: CapCity orders: **4,075**

ROBOTECH: MECHANGEL Academy
1 ❑ Cover: 2.95 **NM** value: **Cover or less**
A: William Jang **W:** Bill Spangler
2 ❑ Cover: 2.95 **NM** value: **Cover or less**
A: William Jang **W:** Bill Spangler
3 ❑ Cover: 2.95 **NM** value: **Cover or less**
📖 War in the Wastelands **A:** William Jang **W:** Bill Spangler ★ Origin of Mechangel.

ROBOTECH: MEGASTORM Antarctic
1 ❑ Aug 1998 Cover: 7.95 **NM** value: **Cover or less**
wraparound cover.

ROBOTECH: RETURN TO MACROSS Eternity
1 ❑ Mar 1993, b&w Cover: 2.50 **NM** value: **3.00**
Circ: CapCity orders: **5,940**
A: Mujib Rahiman **W:** Bill Spangler
2 ❑ b&w Cover: 2.50 **NM** value: **Cover or less**
Circ: CapCity orders: **3,980**
3 ❑ b&w Cover: 2.50 **NM** value: **Cover or less**
Circ: CapCity orders: **3,650**
4 ❑ b&w Cover: 2.50 **NM** value: **Cover or less**
Circ: CapCity orders: **3,510**
5 ❑ b&w Cover: 2.50 **NM** value: **Cover or less**
Circ: CapCity orders: **3,210**
6 ❑ b&w Cover: 2.50 **NM** value: **Cover or less**
Circ: CapCity orders: **2,850**
7 ❑ b&w Cover: 2.50 **NM** value: **Cover or less**
Circ: CapCity orders: **2,780**
8 ❑ b&w Cover: 2.50 **NM** value: **Cover or less**
Circ: CapCity orders: **2,490**
9 ❑ b&w Cover: 2.50 **NM** value: **Cover or less**
Circ: CapCity orders: **2,250**
10 ❑ Jan 1994, b&w Cover: 2.50 **NM** value: **Cover or less**
Circ: CapCity orders: **2,380**
11 ❑ Cover: 2.50 **NM** value: **Cover or less**

ROBOTECH: RETURN TO MACROSS Academy
12 ❑ Cover: 2.50 **NM** value: **Cover or less**
• First Academy comics issue.
13 ❑ Cover: 2.50 **NM** value: **Cover or less**
14 ❑ Cover: 2.50 **NM** value: **Cover or less**
15 ❑ Cover: 2.50 **NM** value: **Cover or less**
16 ❑ Cover: 2.50 **NM** value: **Cover or less**
17 ❑ Cover: 2.50 **NM** value: **Cover or less**
18 ❑ Cover: 2.50 **NM** value: **Cover or less**
19 ❑ Cover: 2.50 **NM** value: **Cover or less**
20 ❑ Cover: 2.50 **NM** value: **Cover or less**
21 ❑ Cover: 2.50 **NM** value: **Cover or less**
22 ❑ Cover: 2.50 **NM** value: **Cover or less**
23 ❑ Cover: 2.50 **NM** value: **Cover or less**
24 ❑ Cover: 2.50 **NM** value: **Cover or less**
25 ❑ Cover: 2.50 **NM** value: **Cover or less**
26 ❑ Cover: 2.95 **NM** value: **Cover or less**
27 ❑ Cover: 2.95 **NM** value: **Cover or less**
28 ❑ Cover: 2.95 **NM** value: **Cover or less**
29 ❑ Cover: 2.95 **NM** value: **Cover or less**
30 ❑ Cover: 2.95 **NM** value: **Cover or less**
31 ❑ Cover: 2.95 **NM** value: **Cover or less**
32 ❑ May 1996 Cover: 2.95 **NM** value: **Cover or less**
A: Dusty Griffin **W:** Robert W. Gibson
33 ❑ Cover: 2.50 **NM** value: **Cover or less**
34 ❑ Cover: 2.50 **NM** value: **Cover or less**
35 ❑ Cover: 2.50 **NM** value: **Cover or less**
36 ❑ Cover: 2.50 **NM** value: **Cover or less**
37 ❑ Cover: 2.50 **NM** value: **Cover or less**

ROBOTECH: SENTINELS – RUBICON Antarctic
1 ❑ Jun 1998, b&w Cover: 2.95 **NM** value: **Cover or less**
📖 A Sort of Homecoming **A:** Vithoon Kamchareon **W:** Alan Nepomuceno
2 ❑ Cover: 2.95 **NM** value: **Cover or less**
A: Vithoon Kamchareon **W:** Alan Nepomuceno
3 ❑ Cover: 2.95 **NM** value: **Cover or less**
A: Vithoon Kamchareon **W:** Alan Nepomuceno
4 ❑ Cover: 2.95 **NM** value: **Cover or less**
A: Vithoon Kamchareon **W:** Alan Nepomuceno
5 ❑ Cover: 2.95 **NM** value: **Cover or less**
A: Vithoon Kamchareon **W:** Alan Nepomuceno
6 ❑ Cover: 2.95 **NM** value: **Cover or less**
A: Vithoon Kamchareon **W:** Alan Nepomuceno
7 ❑ Cover: 2.95 **NM** value: **Cover or less**
A: Vithoon Kamchareon **W:** Alan Nepomuceno

ROBOTECH SPECIAL Comico
1 ❑ May 1988 Cover: 2.50 **NM** value: **Cover or less**
Circ: CapCity orders: **5,875**
★ Origin of Dana Sterling.

ROBOTECH THE GRAPHIC NOVEL Comico
1 ❑ Cover: 5.95 **NM** value: **Cover or less**
Circ: CapCity orders: **900**

ROBOTECH: THE MACROSS SAGA Comico
When an alien spaceship crashed on Macross Island, it had a profound effect upon humanity. Suddenly shocked into realizing that they were not alone in the universe, the various races of man agreed to cease their fighting, and band together instead. They built upon the technology found in the wrecked spaceship, calling it "Robotech." Using the products of that technology, they formed the Robotech Defenders, an Earth defense force.

Many years later, Robotech would face its greatest challenge, when it encounters the Zentraedi, a warlike alien race. Hopelessly outnumbered by the Zentraedi warships, the Robotech warriors must somehow beat the odds if Earth is to survive.

1 ❑ Cover: 15.00 **NM** value: **Cover or less**
• "Macross" this issue
2 ❑ 1985 Cover: 1.50 **NM** value: **4.00**
Circ: CapCity orders: **4,825**
• Title changes to Robotech: The Macross Saga
3 ❑ 1985 Cover: 1.50 **NM** value: **3.00**
Circ: CapCity orders: **7,425**
4 ❑ 1985 Cover: 1.50 **NM** value: **3.00**
Circ: CapCity orders: **8,875**
5 ❑ 1985 Cover: 1.50 **NM** value: **3.00**
Circ: CapCity orders: **8,700**
6 ❑ Sep 1985 Cover: 1.50 **NM** value: **2.00**
Circ: CapCity orders: **8,875**
7 ❑ Nov 1985 Cover: 1.50 **NM** value: **2.00**
Circ: CapCity orders: **9,750**
8 ❑ Cover: 1.50 **NM** value: **2.00**
Circ: CapCity orders: **10,400**
9 ❑ 1986 Cover: 1.50 **NM** value: **2.00**
Circ: CapCity orders: **8,375**
10 ❑ 1986 Cover: 1.50 **NM** value: **2.00**
Circ: CapCity orders: **7,725**
11 ❑ 1986 Cover: 1.50 **NM** value: **2.00**
Circ: CapCity orders: **7,350**
12 ❑ 1986 Cover: 1.50 **NM** value: **2.00**
Circ: CapCity orders: **7,475**
13 ❑ 1986 Cover: 1.50 **NM** value: **2.00**
Circ: CapCity orders: **6,625**
14 ❑ 1986 Cover: 1.50 **NM** value: **2.00**
Circ: CapCity orders: **8,075**

Other grades: Multiply prices above by **1.5 for Mint • 2/3 for Very Fine • 1/3 for Fine • 1/5 for Very Good • 1/8 for Good**

15 ❑ 1986 Cover: 1.50 **NM** value: **2.00**
Circ: CapCity orders: **8,100**

16 ❑ 1986 Cover: 1.50 **NM** value: **2.00**
Circ: CapCity orders: **7,950**

17 ❑ 1986 Cover: 1.50 **NM** value: **2.00**
Circ: CapCity orders: **6,800**

18 ❑ Cover: 1.50 **NM** value: **2.00**
Circ: CapCity orders: **6,625**

19 ❑ Cover: 1.50 **NM** value: **2.00**
Circ: CapCity orders: **6,350**

20 ❑ Cover: 1.50 **NM** value: **2.00**
Circ: CapCity orders: **6,375**

21 ❑ Cover: 1.50 **NM** value: **2.00**
Circ: CapCity orders: **5,900**

22 ❑ 1987 Cover: 1.50 **NM** value: **2.00**
Circ: CapCity orders: **5,725**

23 ❑ 1987 Cover: 1.50 **NM** value: **2.00**
Circ: CapCity orders: **5,875**

24 ❑ 1987 Cover: 1.50 **NM** value: **2.00**
Circ: CapCity orders: **5,650**

25 ❑ 1987 Cover: 1.50 **NM** value: **2.00**
Circ: CapCity orders: **4,775**

26 ❑ 1987 Cover: 1.75 **NM** value: **2.00**
Circ: CapCity orders: **4,800**

27 ❑ 1987 Cover: 1.75 **NM** value: **2.00**
Circ: CapCity orders: **4,575**

28 ❑ Cover: 1.75 **NM** value: **2.00**
Circ: CapCity orders: **4,600**

29 ❑ Cover: 1.75 **NM** value: **2.00**
Circ: CapCity orders: **4,250**

30 ❑ Cover: 1.75 **NM** value: **2.00**
Circ: CapCity orders: **4,400**

31 ❑ Cover: 1.75 **NM** value: **2.00**
Circ: CapCity orders: **4,200**

32 ❑ Cover: 1.75 **NM** value: **2.00**
Circ: CapCity orders: **4,275**

33 ❑ 1988 Cover: 1.75 **NM** value: **2.00**
Circ: CapCity orders: **4,125**

34 ❑ 1988 Cover: 1.75 **NM** value: **2.00**
Circ: CapCity orders: **4,450**

35 ❑ Cover: 1.75 **NM** value: **2.00**
Circ: CapCity orders: **4,350**

36 ❑ 1989 Cover: 1.95 **NM** value: **2.00**
Circ: CapCity orders: **4,400**
final issue.

ROBOTECH: THE NEW GENERATION — Comico

1 ❑ Jul 1985 Cover: 2.50 **NM** value: **Cover or less**
📖 The Invid Invasion **A:** Reggie Byers **W:** Carl Macek

2 ❑ Sep 1985 Cover: 1.50 **NM** value: **Cover or less**
Circ: CapCity orders: **8,950**
📖 The Lost City **A:** Dave Johnson **W:** Kack Herman

3 ❑ 1985 Cover: 1.50 **NM** value: **Cover or less**
Circ: CapCity orders: **9,800**

4 ❑ 1985 Cover: 1.50 **NM** value: **Cover or less**
Circ: CapCity orders: **10,300**

5 ❑ Jan 1986 Cover: 1.50 **NM** value: **Cover or less**
Circ: CapCity orders: **7,975**

6 ❑ Mar 1986 Cover: 1.50 **NM** value: **Cover or less**
Circ: CapCity orders: **7,375**

7 ❑ 1986 Cover: 1.50 **NM** value: **Cover or less**
Circ: CapCity orders: **7,050**

8 ❑ 1986 Cover: 1.50 **NM** value: **Cover or less**
Circ: CapCity orders: **7,100**

9 ❑ Jul 1986 Cover: 1.50 **NM** value: **Cover or less**
Circ: CapCity orders: **7,150**

10 ❑ Cover: 1.50 **NM** value: **Cover or less**
Circ: CapCity orders: **6,875**

11 ❑ Cover: 1.50 **NM** value: **Cover or less**
Circ: CapCity orders: **7,675**

12 ❑ Cover: 1.50 **NM** value: **Cover or less**
Circ: CapCity orders: **7,975**

13 ❑ Cover: 1.50 **NM** value: **Cover or less**
Circ: CapCity orders: **6,250**

14 ❑ Cover: 1.50 **NM** value: **Cover or less**
Circ: CapCity orders: **6,225**

15 ❑ 1987 Cover: 1.50 **NM** value: **Cover or less**
Circ: CapCity orders: **5,800**

16 ❑ 1987 Cover: 1.50 **NM** value: **Cover or less**
Circ: CapCity orders: **5,875**

17 ❑ 1987 Cover: 1.50 **NM** value: **Cover or less**
Circ: CapCity orders: **5,850**

18 ❑ 1987 Cover: 1.50 **NM** value: **Cover or less**
Circ: CapCity orders: **5,225**

19 ❑ 1987 Cover: 1.50 **NM** value: **Cover or less**
Circ: CapCity orders: **5,325**

20 ❑ Cover: 1.50 **NM** value: **Cover or less**
Circ: CapCity orders: **5,225**

21 ❑ Cover: 1.50 **NM** value: **Cover or less**
Circ: CapCity orders: **4,625**

22 ❑ Cover: 1.75 **NM** value: **Cover or less**
Circ: CapCity orders: **4,500**

23 ❑ Cover: 1.75 **NM** value: **Cover or less**
Circ: CapCity orders: **4,150**

24 ❑ Cover: 1.75 **NM** value: **Cover or less**
Circ: CapCity orders: **4,125**

25 ❑ 1988 Cover: 1.75 **NM** value: **Cover or less**
Circ: CapCity orders: **3,925**
• last

ROBOTECH: VERMILION — Antarctic

1 ❑ Aug 1997 Cover: 2.95 **NM** value: **Cover or less**
Circ: Diamd. preorders: **8,252**
A: Duc Tran **W:** Duc Tran

2 ❑ Oct 1997 Cover: 2.95 **NM** value: **Cover or less**
Circ: Diamd. preorders: **7,394**
A: Duc Tran **W:** Duc Tran

3 ❑ Dec 1997 Cover: 2.95 **NM** value: **Cover or less**
Circ: Diamd. preorders: **6,606**
A: Duc Tran **W:** Duc Tran; Alistar Syme

4 ❑ Feb 1997 Cover: 2.95 **NM** value: **Cover or less**
Circ: Diamd. preorders: **5,603**
A: Duc Tran **W:** Duc Tran; Alistar Syme

ROBOTECH WARRIORS — Academy

1 ❑ Feb 1995 Cover: 2.95 **NM** value: **Cover or less**
Circ: CapCity orders: **2,105**
A: Byron Penaranda **W:** Bill Spangler

ROBOTECH: WINGS OF GIBRALTAR — Antarctic

1 ❑ Aug 1998 Cover: 2.95 **NM** value: **Cover or less**
Circ: Diamd. preorders: **5,034**
A: Lee Duhig **W:** Lee Duhig

2 ❑ Sep 1998 Cover: 2.95 **NM** value: **Cover or less**
Circ: Diamd. preorders: **4,530**
A: Lee Duhig **W:** Lee Duhig

ROBOTIX — Marvel

1 ❑ Feb 1986 Cover: 0.75 **NM** value: **1.00**
📖 A World In Chaos **A:** Herb Trimpe **W:** Herb Trimpe ★ 1st Appearance of The Terrokors, The Protectons.

ROBOTMEN OF THE LOST PLANET — Avon

1 ❑ ca. 1952 Cover: 0.10 **NM** value: **850.00**
• **CGC:** 2 graded, best 9.0

ROBO WARRIORS — CFW

1 ❑ Cover: 1.75 **NM** value: **Cover or less**
★ 1st Appearance of Reiki. ★ Appearance of Sifu.

2 ❑ Cover: 1.95 **NM** value: **Cover or less**
• 0: Citation; Origin of Citation

3 ❑ Cover: 1.95 **NM** value: **Cover or less**
★ 1st Appearance of She-Bat. ★ Appearance of Soliloquy Jones, Soldiers of Reiki.

4 ❑ Cover: 1.95 **NM** value: **Cover or less**

5 ❑ Cover: 1.95 **NM** value: **Cover or less**

6 ❑ Cover: 1.95 **NM** value: **Cover or less**

7 ❑ Cover: 1.95 **NM** value: **Cover or less**
★ 1st Appearance of Mr. Slimey.

8 ❑ Cover: 1.95 **NM** value: **Cover or less**
• Reiki becomes Mister No

ROBYN OF SHERWOOD — Caliber

1 ❑ Mar 1998, b&w Cover: 2.95 **NM** value: **Cover or less**
Circ: Diamd. preorders: **3,724**

ROCKERS — Rip Off

All issues are adults only.

1 ❑ Jul 1988, b&w Cover: 2.00 **NM** value: **Cover or less**

2 ❑ Oct 1988, b&w Cover: 2.00 **NM** value: **Cover or less**
📖 A Night of Spinning Stars, Pink Elephants and the Midnite Man; Kick Me; Vintage Rockers **A:** R.L. Crabb; Steve Lafler **W:** R.L. Crabb; Steve Lafler

3 ❑ Jan 1989, b&w Cover: 2.00 **NM** value: **Cover or less**
📖 Confessions; Mister Rectumy; Vintage Rockers; The Cure **A:** R.L. Crabb; George Parsons **W:** R.L. Crabb; George Parsons

4 ❑ Feb 1989, b&w Cover: 2.00 **NM** value: **Cover or less**

5 ❑ May 1989, b&w Cover: 2.00 **NM** value: **Cover or less**

6 ❑ Jun 1989, b&w Cover: 2.00 **NM** value: **Cover or less**

7 ❑ Sep 1989, b&w Cover: 2.00 **NM** value: **Cover or less**

8 ❑ Feb 1990, b&w Cover: 2.00 **NM** value: **Cover or less**

ROCKET COMICS — Hillman

1 ❑ Mar 1940 Cover: 0.10 **NM** value: **2000.00**
• **CGC:** 3 graded, best 8.0

2 ❑ Apr 1940 Cover: 0.10 **NM** value: **1000.00**

3 ❑ May 1940 Cover: 0.10 **NM** value: **1000.00**

ROCKETEER 3-D COMIC, THE — Disney

1 ❑ Jun 1991 Cover: 5.00 **NM** value: **Cover or less**
Circ: CapCity orders: **3,075**
No issue number. • with audiotape; Based on The Rocketeer movie
A: Neal Adams **W:** Neal Adams

ROCKETEER ADVENTURE MAGAZINE, THE — Comico

1 ❑ Jul 1988 Cover: 2.00 **NM** value: **5.00**
Circ: CapCity orders: **17,275** • **CGC:** 3 graded, best 9.6
📖 Cliff's New York Adventure; Brucilla The Muscle Galactic girl Guide • Comico publishes **A:** Michael W. Kaluta; Charles Vess; Dave Stevens; Elaine Lee **W:** Michael W. Kaluta; Dave Stevens; Elaine Lee

2 ❑ Jul 1989 Cover: 2.75 **NM** value: **3.50**
Circ: CapCity orders: **15,050**
📖 Nightmare at Large; Sitting Duck **A:** Michael W. Kaluta; Dave Stevens; Elaine Lee **W:** Michael W. Kaluta; Dave Stevens; Elaine Lee

3 ❑ Jan 1995 Cover: 2.95 **NM** value: **3.00**
Circ: CapCity orders: **7,600** • **CGC:** 1 graded, best 9.6
📖 Death Stalks The Midway • Dark Horse publishes **A:** Dave Stevens **W:** Dave Stevens

Bk 1❑ Sep 1996 Cover: 9.95 **NM** value: **Cover or less**
• collects The Rocketeer Adventure Magazine #1-3 (#1 and #2 originally published by Comico). • Cliff's New York Adventure

ROCKETEER SPECIAL EDITION, THE — Eclipse

1 ❑ Nov 1984 Cover: 1.50 **NM** value: **Cover or less**
• **CGC:** 6 graded, best 9.8
A: Dave Stevens **W:** Dave Stevens

ROCKETEER, THE: THE OFFICIAL MOVIE ADAPTATION — Disney

This remarkably faithful movie adaptation does a wonderful job of capturing both the whimsy and nostalgia of the Disney movie, as well as the magic of Dave Stevens' Rocketeer character.

The story begins when pilot Cliff Secord is testing a new airplane at a small airfield in 1938. Suddenly, the peace is shattered by a car roaring across the field, pursued by another car filled with FBI agents. The gangsters in the first vehicle crash into a hangar, but one escapes and manages to hide something in the hangar before being captured. Cliff and his mechanic discovered the device — an experimental jet-pack — and Cliff learned to use it to fly through the air like a rocket. Dubbed "The Rocketeer," he soon winds up tangling with gangsters, the FBI, and a secret Nazi conspiracy. It's all high-flying fun, and a terrifically enjoyable tale, beautifully drawn by Russ Heath.

1 ❑ 1991 Cover: 2.95 **NM** value: **Cover or less**
Circ: CapCity orders: **10,650**
No issue number. no cover date. • stapled **A:** Russ Heath **C:** Dave Stevens **W:** Peter David

1/DM❑ 1991 Cover: 5.95 **NM** value: **Cover or less**
Circ: CapCity orders: **12,050**
No issue number. no cover date. • squarebound **A:** Russ Heath **C:** Dave Stevens **W:** Peter David

ROCKET KELLY — Fox

0 ❑ ca. 1944 Cover: 0.10 **NM** value: **200.00**

1 ❑ Fal 1945 Cover: 0.10 **NM** value: **200.00**

2 ❑ Win 1945 Cover: 0.10 **NM** value: **175.00**

3 ❑ Jun 1946 Cover: 0.10 **NM** value: **150.00**

4 ❑ Aug 1946 Cover: 0.10 **NM** value: **150.00**

5 ❑ Oct 1946 Cover: 0.10 **NM** value: **150.00**

ROCKETMAN — AC

1 ❑ **NM** value: **5.95**

Ash 1❑ Cover: 5.95 **NM** value: **Cover or less**

Ash 2❑ Cover: 5.95 **NM** value: **Cover or less**

ROCKETMAN: KING OF THE ROCKET MEN — Innovation

1 ❑ Cover: 2.50 **NM** value: **Cover or less**
Circ: CapCity orders: **6,510**
A: Christopher Moeller **W:** Christopher Moeller

2 ❑ Cover: 2.50 **NM** value: **Cover or less**
Circ: CapCity orders: **4,220**
A: Christopher Moeller **W:** Christopher Moeller

3 ❑ Cover: 2.50 **NM** value: **Cover or less**
Circ: CapCity orders: **4,170**
A: Christopher Moeller **W:** Christopher Moeller

4 ❑ Cover: 2.50 **NM** value: **Cover or less**
Circ: CapCity orders: **3,630**
A: Christopher Moeller **W:** Christopher Moeller

Bk 1❑ Cover: 8.95 **NM** value: **Cover or less**

ROCKET RACCOON — Marvel

1 ❑ May 1985 Cover: 0.75 **NM** value: **1.00**
Circ: CapCity orders: **13,700**
📖 Animal Crackers **A:** Mike Mignola **W:** Bill Mantlo

2 ❑ Jun 1985 Cover: 0.75 **NM** value: **1.00**
Circ: CapCity orders: **11,100**
A: Mike Mignola **W:** Bill Mantlo

3 ❑ Jul 1985 Cover: 0.75 **NM** value: **1.00**
Circ: CapCity orders: **10,800**
A: Mike Mignola **W:** Bill Mantlo

4 ❑ Aug 1985 Cover: 0.75 **NM** value: **1.00**
Circ: CapCity orders: **10,700**
A: Mike Mignola **W:** Bill Mantlo

ROCKET RANGER — Adventure

In an alternate world where the Nazis succeeded in conquering nearly every country except for the United States, only one brave man can turn the tide for freedom: Rocket Ranger!

Based on the videogame of the same name, this short-lived series detailed the jet-packed adventures of the title character, Tom Cory, (also known as Rocket Ranger) as he fought to end the ever-expanding grasp of the Third Reich. From the battlefields of Eastern Europe to the Nazi "lunarium mines" on the surface of the moon, Rocket Ranger epitomized the feel of the 1940s movie serials from which the videogame was originally inspired. Enthusiasts of the original videogame as well as fans of the similarly themed comic book and subsequent motion picture, The Rocketeer, will love this comic's often B-movie tone.

1 ❑ Sep 1991, full color Cover: 2.95 **NM** value: **Cover or less**
Circ: CapCity orders: **3,280**

2 ❑ Dec 1991, b&w Cover: 2.95 **NM** value: **Cover or less**

3 ❑ 1992b&w Cover: 2.95 **NM** value: **Cover or less**

CGC-graded: Multiply prices above by **33 for 9.9 M • 16 for 9.8 NM/M • 7 for 9.6 NM+ • 5 for 9.4 NM • 2.5 for 9.2 NM- • 1.5 for 9.0 VF/NM**

4 ❑ 1992b&w Cover: 2.95 NM value: Cover or less
5 ❑ Jul 1992, b&w Cover: 2.95 NM value: Cover or less
📖 Arrested! A: Khato W: Roland Mann
6 ❑ Cover: 2.95 NM value: Cover or less

ROCKET SHIP X — Fox

1 ❑ Sep 1951 Cover: 0.10 NM value: 500.00

ROCKET TO THE MOON — Avon

1 ❑ ca. 1951 Cover: 0.10 NM value: 800.00
• CGC: 9 graded, best 8.0

ROCK FANTASY — Rock Fantasy

1 ❑ Cover: 3.00 NM value: Cover or less
• Pink Floyd
2 ❑ Cover: 3.00 NM value: Cover or less
• Rolling Stones
3 ❑ Cover: 3.00 NM value: Cover or less
• Led Zeppelin
4 ❑ Cover: 3.00 NM value: Cover or less
• New Kids on the Block; Stevie Nicks
5 ❑ Cover: 3.00 NM value: Cover or less
• Guns 'n Roses
6 ❑ Cover: 3.00 NM value: Cover or less
• Monstrosities of Rock
7 ❑ Cover: 3.00 NM value: Cover or less
• The Sex Pistols
8 ❑ Cover: 3.00 NM value: Cover or less
• Alice Cooper
9 ❑ Cover: 3.00 NM value: Cover or less
• Van Halen
10 ❑ Cover: 3.00 NM value: Cover or less
• Kiss
11 ❑ Cover: 3.00 NM value: Cover or less
• Jimi Hendrix
12 ❑ Cover: 3.00 NM value: Cover or less
• Def Leppard
13 ❑ Cover: 3.00 NM value: Cover or less
• David Bowie
14 ❑ Cover: 3.00 NM value: Cover or less
• The Doors
15 ❑ Cover: 3.00 NM value: Cover or less
• Pink Floyd II
16 ❑ Cover: 5.00 NM value: Cover or less
• Double-size. • The Great Gig in the Sky
17 ❑ Cover: 3.00 NM value: Cover or less
📖 Send me An Angel • Rock Vixens A: Jerry Tinor W: Jerry Tinor

ROCKHEADS — Solson

1 ❑ Cover: 1.95 NM value: Cover or less
A: Rich Sawyer W: Phil Clarke

ROCKIN' BONES — New England

1 ❑ b&w Cover: 2.75 NM value: Cover or less
2 ❑ b&w Cover: 2.75 NM value: Cover or less
3 ❑ b&w Cover: 2.75 NM value: Cover or less
HS 1❑ Cover: 2.75 NM value: Cover or less
• Xmas Special

ROCKINFREAKAPOTAMUS PRESENTS THE RED HOT CHILI PEPPERS ILLUSTRATED LYRICS — Telltale Publications

1 ❑ Jul 1997, b&w Cover: 3.95 NM value: Cover or less
No issue number. • magazine-sized.

ROCKMEEZ, THE — Jzink Comics

1 ❑ Cover: 2.50 NM value: Cover or less
2 ❑ Nov 1992 Cover: 2.50 NM value: Cover or less
3 ❑ Cover: 2.50 NM value: Cover or less
4 ❑ Cover: 2.50 NM value: Cover or less

ROCK 'N' ROLL: A CARTOON HISTORY — Revolutionary

Bk 1❑ Jul 1999 Cover: 14.95 NM value: Cover or less
• The Sixties

ROCK 'N' ROLL COMICS — Revolutionary

From The Beatles to Public Enemy, Rock 'n' Roll Comics presented the unauthorized biographies of the most important names in music, in comics form. Its "tell-it-like-it-is" style extended into the political realm as well, crying out for a stop to censorship and taking hard shots at Tipper Gore and the PMRC (the Parent's Music Resource Center — an organization which promoted warning labels for albums containing "offensive" lyrics).

Reading several of these issues in a row quickly reveals the cookie-cutter sameness of the basic story (one teen gets a guitar, another hates music lessons, one can sing, they form a band, have drug and alcohol problems, etc.) and the art is journeyman at best, with likenesses of the actual band members a rarity.

1 ❑ Jun 1989 Cover: 1.50 NM value: 8.00
• CGC: 4 graded, best 9.6
• Guns 'N' Roses
1-2 ❑ Jul 1989 Cover: 1.50 NM value: 6.00
1-3 ❑ Aug 1989 Cover: 1.95 NM value: 2.00
1-4 ❑ Sep 1989 Cover: 1.95 NM value: 2.00
1-5 ❑ Oct 1989 Cover: 1.95 NM value: 2.00
1-6 ❑ Nov 1989 Cover: 1.95 NM value: 2.00
1-7 ❑ Dec 1989 Cover: 1.95 NM value: 2.00
2 ❑ Aug 1989 Cover: 1.50 NM value: 5.00
• Metallica
2-2 ❑ Sep 1989 Cover: 1.95 NM value: 3.00
2-3 ❑ Sep 1989 Cover: 1.95 NM value: 2.00
2-4 ❑ Sep 1989 Cover: 1.95 NM value: 2.00
2-5 ❑ Sep 1989 Cover: 1.95 NM value: 2.00
2-6 ❑ full color Cover: 1.50 NM value: 2.00
3 ❑ Sep 1989 Cover: 1.95 NM value: 15.00
• Bon Jovi; Banned by Great Southern Co.; Rare
3-2 ❑ Oct 1989 Cover: 1.95 NM value: Cover or less
4 ❑ Oct 1989 Cover: 1.95 NM value: 60.00
• Motley Crue; Banned by Great Southern Co.; 15,000 copies burned by Great Southern
4-2 ❑ Oct 1989 Cover: 1.95 NM value: 4.00
• 2nd printing (no Ace Backwords); Banned by Great Southern Co.
5 ❑ Nov 1989 Cover: 1.95 NM value: 2.50
• Def Leppard
5-2 ❑ Nov 1989 Cover: 1.95 NM value: Cover or less
6 ❑ Dec 1989 Cover: 1.95 NM value: 3.00
• Rolling Stones
6-2 ❑ Jan 1990 Cover: 1.95 NM value: Cover or less
6-3 ❑ Jan 1990 Cover: 1.95 NM value: Cover or less
6-4 ❑ Feb 1990 Cover: 1.95 NM value: Cover or less
7 ❑ Jan 1990 Cover: 1.95 NM value: 2.50
• The Who
7-2 ❑ Feb 1990 Cover: 1.95 NM value: Cover or less
7-3 ❑ Mar 1990 Cover: 1.95 NM value: Cover or less
8 ❑ Feb 1990 Cover: 1.50 NM value: 2.00
• Skid Row; Never published: banned by injunction from Great Southern Company
9 ❑ Mar 1990 Cover: 1.95 NM value: 6.00
• CGC: 1 graded, best 9.2
• Kiss
9-2 ❑ Apr 1990 Cover: 1.95 NM value: 2.00
9-3 ❑ May 1990 Cover: 1.95 NM value: 2.00
10 ❑ Apr 1990 Cover: 1.95 NM value: 2.50
• CGC: 1 graded, best 9.8
Two different versions printed, one with Whitesnake on cover, one with Warrant. • Warrant, Whitesnake
10-2❑ May 1990 Cover: 1.95 NM value: Cover or less
11 ❑ May 1990 Cover: 1.95 NM value: 2.50
• Aerosmith
12 ❑ Jun 1990 Cover: 1.95 NM value: 3.00
• New Kids on the Block
12-2❑ Aug 1990 Cover: 1.95 NM value: Cover or less
13 ❑ Jul 1990 Cover: 1.95 NM value: 2.50
• Led Zeppelin
14 ❑ Aug 1990 Cover: 1.95 NM value: 2.50
• Sex Pistols
15 ❑ Sep 1990, full color Cover: 1.95 NM value: 2.50
• Poison W: Todd Loren
16 ❑ Oct 1990, full color Cover: 1.95 NM value: 2.50
• Van Halen
17 ❑ Nov 1990, full color Cover: 1.95 NM value: 4.00
Circ: CapCity orders: 5,700
• Madonna
18 ❑ Dec 1990 Cover: 1.95 NM value: 2.50
Circ: CapCity orders: 5,625
• Alice Cooper; Full color
19 ❑ Apr 1991, b&w Cover: 2.50 NM value: Cover or less
Circ: CapCity orders: 3,700
📖 Fight For The Right To Fight; 2 Live Crew, 1 Brave Mother; The New Censorship; The World According To Jesse Helms • Public Enemy, 2 Live Crew A: Stuart Immonen; Mark Erickson; Tom Luth W: Todd Loren
20 ❑ Apr 1991, b&w Cover: 2.50 NM value: Cover or less
Circ: CapCity orders: 3,425
• Queensryche
21 ❑ Jan 1991, b&w Cover: 2.50 NM value: Cover or less
Circ: CapCity orders: 4,650
• Prince
22 ❑ Feb 1991, full color Cover: 2.50 NM value: Cover or less
Circ: CapCity orders: 5,100
• AC/DC
23 ❑ Mar 1991, b&w Cover: 2.50 NM value: Cover or less
Circ: CapCity orders: 4,050
• Living Colour
24 ❑ Mar 1991 Cover: 2.50 NM value: Cover or less
Circ: CapCity orders: 4,225
• Anthrax b&w
25 ❑ May 1991, b&w Cover: 2.50 NM value: Cover or less
Circ: CapCity orders: 3,850
• ZZ Top
26 ❑ May 1991 Cover: 2.50 NM value: Cover or less
Circ: CapCity orders: 4,250
• Doors
27 ❑ Jun 1991 Cover: 2.50 NM value: Cover or less
• Doors
28 ❑ Jun 1991 Cover: 2.50 NM value: Cover or less
• Ozzy Osbourne; Black Sabbath
29 ❑ Jul 1991 Cover: 2.50 NM value: Cover or less
• Ozzy Osbourne; Black Sabbath
30 ❑ Jul 1991 Cover: 2.50 NM value: Cover or less
📖 The Cure • The Cure
31 ❑ Aug 1991 Cover: 2.50 NM value: Cover or less
📖 A New Ice Age • Vanilla Ice A: Greg Fox W: Jay Allen Sanford
32 ❑ Aug 1991 Cover: 2.50 NM value: Cover or less
• Frank Zappa
33 ❑ Sep 1991 Cover: 2.50 NM value: Cover or less
• Guns 'N' Roses II
34 ❑ Sep 1991 Cover: 2.50 NM value: Cover or less
• Black Crowes
35 ❑ Oct 1991 Cover: 2.50 NM value: Cover or less
• R.E.M.
36 ❑ Oct 1991 Cover: 2.50 NM value: Cover or less
• Michael Jackson
37 ❑ Nov 1991 Cover: 2.50 NM value: Cover or less
• Ice-T
38 ❑ Nov 1991 Cover: 2.50 NM value: Cover or less
• Rod Stewart
39 ❑ Dec 1991 Cover: 2.50 NM value: Cover or less
• The Fall of the New Kids
40 ❑ Dec 1991 Cover: 2.50 NM value: Cover or less
• NWA; Ice Cube
41 ❑ Jan 1992 Cover: 2.50 NM value: Cover or less
• Paula Abdul
42 ❑ Jan 1992 Cover: 2.50 NM value: Cover or less
• Metallica II
43 ❑ Feb 1992 Cover: 2.50 NM value: Cover or less
• Guns N' Roses: Tales from the Tour
44 ❑ Feb 1992 Cover: 2.50 NM value: Cover or less
• Scorpions
45 ❑ Mar 1992 Cover: 2.50 NM value: Cover or less
• Grateful Dead
46 ❑ Apr 1992 Cover: 2.50 NM value: Cover or less
• Grateful Dead II
47 ❑ May 1992 Cover: 2.50 NM value: Cover or less
• Grateful Dead III
48 ❑ Jun 1992 Cover: 2.50 NM value: Cover or less
• Queen
49 ❑ Jul 1992 Cover: 2.50 NM value: Cover or less
• Rush
50 ❑ Aug 1992 Cover: 2.50 NM value: Cover or less
• Bob Dylan
51 ❑ Sep 1992 Cover: 2.50 NM value: Cover or less
• Bob Dylan II
52 ❑ Oct 1992 Cover: 2.50 NM value: Cover or less
• Bob Dylan III
53 ❑ Nov 1992 Cover: 2.50 NM value: Cover or less
• Bruce Springsteen
54 ❑ Dec 1992 Cover: 2.50 NM value: Cover or less
• U2
55 ❑ Jan 1993 Cover: 2.50 NM value: Cover or less
• U2 II
56 ❑ Feb 1993 Cover: 2.50 NM value: Cover or less
• David Bowie
57 ❑ Mar 1993 Cover: 2.50 NM value: Cover or less
• Aerosmith
58 ❑ Apr 1993 Cover: 2.50 NM value: Cover or less
• Kate Bush
59 ❑ May 1993 Cover: 2.50 NM value: Cover or less
• Eric Clapton
60 ❑ Jun 1993 Cover: 2.50 NM value: Cover or less
• Genesis
61 ❑ Jul 1993 Cover: 2.50 NM value: Cover or less
• Yes
62 ❑ Aug 1993 Cover: 2.50 NM value: Cover or less
• Elton John
63 ❑ Sep 1993 Cover: 2.50 NM value: Cover or less
• Janis Joplin
64 ❑ Oct 1993 Cover: 2.50 NM value: Cover or less
• '60s San Francisco
65 ❑ Nov 1993 Cover: 2.50 NM value: Cover or less
• Sci-Fi Space Rockers

ROCK N' ROLL COMICS MAGAZINE — Revolutionary

1 ❑ NM value: 2.95
2 ❑ NM value: 2.95
3 ❑ NM value: 2.95
4 ❑ NM value: 2.95
5 ❑ Oct 1990 Cover: 2.95 NM value: Cover or less
📖 Rock This Way!; Satisfaction • Aerosmith/Rolling Stones A: Andy Kuhn; Greg Fox W: Dean Hsieh; Todd Loren

ROCKOLA — Mirage

1 ❑ Cover: 1.50 NM value: Cover or less

ROCKO'S MODERN LIFE — Marvel

1 ❑ Jun 1994 Cover: 1.95 NM value: Cover or less
Circ: CapCity orders: 15,100
📖 Dental Hyjinks; This is a Test! • TV cartoon A: Darren Auck W: John Lewandowski
2 ❑ Jul 1994 Cover: 1.95 NM value: Cover or less
Circ: CapCity orders: 8,600
3 ❑ Aug 1994 Cover: 1.95 NM value: Cover or less
Circ: CapCity orders: 7,100
4 ❑ Sep 1994 Cover: 1.95 NM value: Cover or less
Circ: CapCity orders: 6,450
5 ❑ Oct 1994 Cover: 1.95 NM value: Cover or less
Circ: CapCity orders: 5,250
6 ❑ Nov 1994 Cover: 1.95 NM value: Cover or less
Circ: CapCity orders: 4,600
7 ❑ Dec 1994 Cover: 1.95 NM value: Cover or less
Circ: CapCity orders: 4,000

ROCKY AND HIS FIENDISH FRIENDS — Gold Key

1 ❑ Oct 1962 Cover: 0.12 NM value: 200.00
• CGC: 5 graded, best 9.6
2 ❑ Dec 1962 Cover: 0.12 NM value: 150.00
• CGC: 3 graded, best 9.6
3 ❑ Mar 1963 Cover: 0.12 NM value: 150.00
• CGC: 4 graded, best 9.4
4 ❑ Jun 1963 Cover: 0.12 NM value: 100.00
• CGC: 1 graded, best 9.4
5 ❑ Sep 1963 Cover: 0.12 NM value: 100.00
• CGC: 1 graded, best 7.0

Other grades: Multiply prices above by 1.5 for Mint • 2/3 for Very Fine • 1/3 for Fine • 1/5 for Very Good • 1/8 for Good

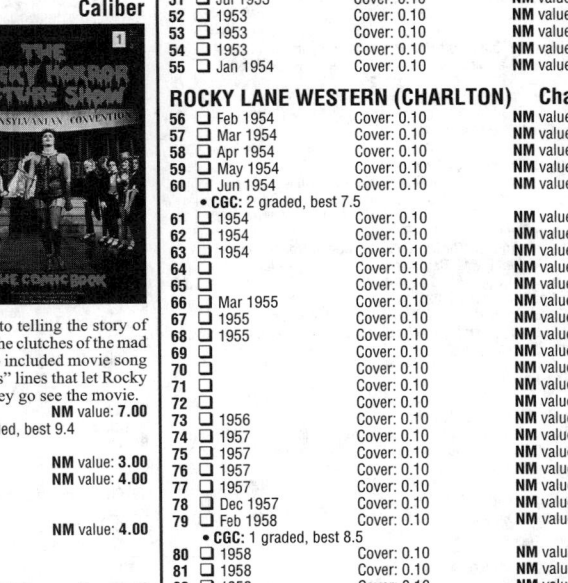

ROCKY HORROR PICTURE SHOW, THE: THE COMIC BOOK — Caliber

The Rocky Horror Picture Show is the ultimate cult movie. Produced on a shoestring budget, its combination of schmaltz, sex, and song proved infectious. Fifteen years after its release the movie was still going strong, playing to packed audiences at midnight showings. The trick is that nobody really goes to see the movie — they go to see the show: the parade of costumed moviegoers who perform routines, sass back at the actors onscreen, and do the "Time Warp" dance in the aisles.

In honor of the film's 15th anniversary, Caliber released a three-part comic adaptation in 1990. In addition to telling the story of normal couple Brad and Janet who fall into the clutches of the mad (and transvestite) Dr. Frank-n-Furter, it also included movie song lyrics, interviews with the stars, and "chorus" lines that let Rocky "virgins" know what the routine is when they go see the movie.

1 ❑ Jul 1990, full color — Cover: 2.95 — **NM** value: **7.00**
Circ: CapCity orders: **17,100** • **CGC:** 1 graded, best 9.4
A: Kevin VanHook **W:** Kevin VanHook
1-2 ❑ — Cover: 2.95 — **NM** value: **3.00**
2 ❑ Aug 1990, full color — Cover: 2.95 — **NM** value: **4.00**
Circ: CapCity orders: **12,200**
A: Kevin VanHook **W:** Kevin VanHook
3 ❑ Sep 1990, full color — Cover: 2.95 — **NM** value: **4.00**
Circ: CapCity orders: **11,875**
A: Kevin VanHook **W:** Kevin VanHook

ROCKY LANE WESTERN (FAWCETT) — Fawcett

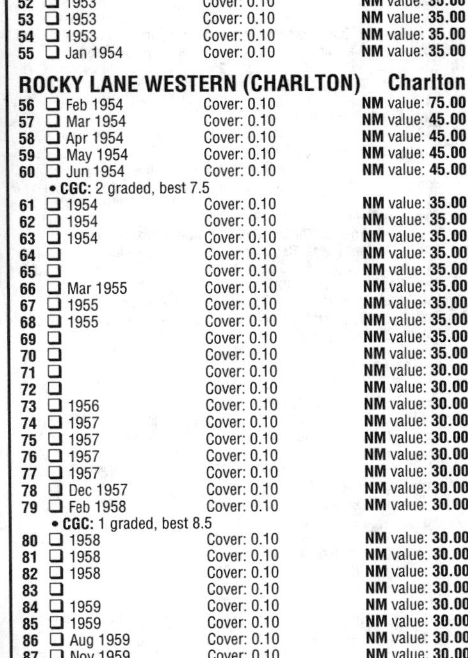

Rocky Lane, like Tom Mix, Monte Hale, Lash LaRue, and Gabby Hayes, was a star of cowboy movies whom Fawcett licensed into an ongoing comic-book series. Films of Allan ("Rocky") Lane (1904-1973)traditionally opened with a shot of him riding his horse, Black Jack, and crediting them both. (The credit for his horse, by the way, extended to the cover of his comic-book series.)

Fans of the Republic serial star were promised "rip-snorting thrillers" or "exciting adventures" in the comics. Who among faithful readers of the series could have predicted that, only two years after the end of his comic-book existence, he'd be providing the voice of the horse "Mister Ed" for that TV sitcom? — Maggie

#	Date	Cover	NM value
1	❑ May 1949	Cover: 0.10	**NM** value: **450.00**
2	❑ Jun 1949	Cover: 0.10	**NM** value: **175.00**
3	❑ Jul 1949	Cover: 0.10	**NM** value: **125.00**
4	❑ Aug 1949	Cover: 0.10	**NM** value: **125.00**
5	❑ Sep 1949	Cover: 0.10	**NM** value: **125.00**
6	❑ Oct 1949	Cover: 0.10	**NM** value: **125.00**
7	❑ Nov 1949	Cover: 0.10	**NM** value: **125.00**
8	❑ Dec 1949	Cover: 0.10	**NM** value: **125.00**
9	❑ Jan 1950	Cover: 0.10	**NM** value: **125.00**
10	❑ Feb 1950	Cover: 0.10	**NM** value: **75.00**
11	❑ Mar 1950	Cover: 0.10	**NM** value: **75.00**
12	❑ Apr 1950	Cover: 0.10	**NM** value: **75.00**
13	❑ May 1950	Cover: 0.10	**NM** value: **75.00**
14	❑ Jun 1950	Cover: 0.10	**NM** value: **75.00**
15	❑ Jul 1950	Cover: 0.10	**NM** value: **75.00**
16	❑ Aug 1950	Cover: 0.10	**NM** value: **75.00**
17	❑ Sep 1950	Cover: 0.10	**NM** value: **75.00**
18	❑ Oct 1950	Cover: 0.10	**NM** value: **75.00**
19	❑ Nov 1950	Cover: 0.10	**NM** value: **75.00**
20	❑ Dec 1950	Cover: 0.10	**NM** value: **55.00**
21	❑ Jan 1951	Cover: 0.10	**NM** value: **55.00**
22	❑ Feb 1951	Cover: 0.10	**NM** value: **55.00**
23	❑ Mar 1951	Cover: 0.10	**NM** value: **55.00**
24	❑ Apr 1951	Cover: 0.10	**NM** value: **55.00**
25	❑ May 1951	Cover: 0.10	**NM** value: **55.00**
26	❑ Jun 1951	Cover: 0.10	**NM** value: **55.00**
27	❑ Jul 1951	Cover: 0.10	**NM** value: **55.00**
28	❑ Aug 1951	Cover: 0.10	**NM** value: **55.00**
29	❑ Sep 1951	Cover: 0.10	**NM** value: **55.00**
30	❑ Oct 1951	Cover: 0.10	**NM** value: **55.00**
31	❑ Nov 1951	Cover: 0.10	**NM** value: **55.00**
32	❑ Dec 1951	Cover: 0.10	**NM** value: **55.00**
33	❑ Jan 1952	Cover: 0.10	**NM** value: **55.00**
34	❑ Feb 1952	Cover: 0.10	**NM** value: **55.00**
35	❑ Mar 1952	Cover: 0.10	**NM** value: **55.00**
36	❑ Apr 1952	Cover: 0.10	**NM** value: **40.00**
37	❑ May 1952	Cover: 0.10	**NM** value: **40.00**
38	❑ Jun 1952	Cover: 0.10	**NM** value: **40.00**
39	❑ Jul 1952	Cover: 0.10	**NM** value: **40.00**
40	❑ Aug 1952	Cover: 0.10	**NM** value: **40.00**
41	❑ Sep 1952	Cover: 0.10	**NM** value: **40.00**
42	❑ Oct 1952	Cover: 0.10	**NM** value: **40.00**
43	❑ Nov 1957	Cover: 0.10	**NM** value: **40.00**
44	❑ Dec 1952	Cover: 0.10	**NM** value: **40.00**
45	❑ Jan 1953	Cover: 0.10	**NM** value: **40.00**
46	❑ Feb 1953	Cover: 0.10	**NM** value: **35.00**
47	❑ Mar 1953	Cover: 0.10	**NM** value: **35.00**
48	❑ Apr 1953	Cover: 0.10	**NM** value: **35.00**
49	❑ May 1953	Cover: 0.10	**NM** value: **35.00**
50	❑ Jun 1953	Cover: 0.10	**NM** value: **35.00**
51	❑ Jul 1953	Cover: 0.10	**NM** value: **35.00**
52	❑ 1953	Cover: 0.10	**NM** value: **35.00**
53	❑ 1953	Cover: 0.10	**NM** value: **35.00**
54	❑ 1953	Cover: 0.10	**NM** value: **35.00**
55	❑ Jan 1954	Cover: 0.10	**NM** value: **35.00**

ROCKY LANE WESTERN (CHARLTON) — Charlton

#	Date	Cover	NM value
56	❑ Feb 1954	Cover: 0.10	**NM** value: **75.00**
57	❑ Mar 1954	Cover: 0.10	**NM** value: **45.00**
58	❑ Apr 1954	Cover: 0.10	**NM** value: **45.00**
59	❑ May 1954	Cover: 0.10	**NM** value: **45.00**
60	❑ Jun 1954	Cover: 0.10	**NM** value: **45.00**
	• **CGC:** 2 graded, best 7.5		
61	❑ 1954	Cover: 0.10	**NM** value: **35.00**
62	❑ 1954	Cover: 0.10	**NM** value: **35.00**
63	❑ 1954	Cover: 0.10	**NM** value: **35.00**
64	❑	Cover: 0.10	**NM** value: **35.00**
65	❑	Cover: 0.10	**NM** value: **35.00**
66	❑ Mar 1955	Cover: 0.10	**NM** value: **35.00**
67	❑ 1955	Cover: 0.10	**NM** value: **35.00**
68	❑ 1955	Cover: 0.10	**NM** value: **35.00**
69	❑	Cover: 0.10	**NM** value: **35.00**
70	❑	Cover: 0.10	**NM** value: **35.00**
71	❑	Cover: 0.10	**NM** value: **30.00**
72	❑	Cover: 0.10	**NM** value: **30.00**
73	❑ 1956	Cover: 0.10	**NM** value: **30.00**
74	❑ 1957	Cover: 0.10	**NM** value: **30.00**
75	❑ 1957	Cover: 0.10	**NM** value: **30.00**
76	❑ 1957	Cover: 0.10	**NM** value: **30.00**
77	❑ 1957	Cover: 0.10	**NM** value: **30.00**
78	❑ Dec 1957	Cover: 0.10	**NM** value: **30.00**
79	❑ Feb 1958	Cover: 0.10	**NM** value: **30.00**
	• **CGC:** 1 graded, best 8.5		
80	❑ 1958	Cover: 0.10	**NM** value: **30.00**
81	❑ 1958	Cover: 0.10	**NM** value: **30.00**
82	❑ 1958	Cover: 0.10	**NM** value: **30.00**
83	❑	Cover: 0.10	**NM** value: **30.00**
84	❑ 1959	Cover: 0.10	**NM** value: **30.00**
85	❑ 1959	Cover: 0.10	**NM** value: **30.00**
86	❑ Aug 1959	Cover: 0.10	**NM** value: **30.00**
87	❑ Nov 1959	Cover: 0.10	**NM** value: **30.00**

ROCKY LANE WESTERN (AC) — AC

1 ❑ b&w — Cover: 2.50 — **NM** value: **Cover or less**
2 ❑ b&w — Cover: 5.95 — **NM** value: **Cover or less**
Anl 1❑b&w — Cover: 2.95 — **NM** value: **Cover or less**

ROD CAMERON WESTERN — Fawcett

#	Date	Cover	NM value
1	❑ Feb 1950	Cover: 0.10	**NM** value: **310.00**
2	❑ Apr 1950	Cover: 0.10	**NM** value: **175.00**
3	❑ Jun 1950	Cover: 0.10	**NM** value: **150.00**
4	❑ Aug 1950	Cover: 0.10	**NM** value: **150.00**
5	❑ Oct 1950	Cover: 0.10	**NM** value: **150.00**
6	❑ Dec 1950	Cover: 0.10	**NM** value: **150.00**
7	❑ Feb 1951	Cover: 0.10	**NM** value: **150.00**
8	❑ Apr 1951	Cover: 0.10	**NM** value: **150.00**
9	❑ Jun 1951	Cover: 0.10	**NM** value: **150.00**
10	❑ Aug 1951	Cover: 0.10	**NM** value: **150.00**
11	❑ Oct 1951	Cover: 0.10	**NM** value: **100.00**
12	❑ Dec 1951	Cover: 0.10	**NM** value: **100.00**
13	❑ Feb 1952	Cover: 0.10	**NM** value: **100.00**
14	❑ Apr 1952	Cover: 0.10	**NM** value: **100.00**
15	❑ Jun 1952	Cover: 0.10	**NM** value: **100.00**
16	❑ Aug 1952	Cover: 0.10	**NM** value: **100.00**
17	❑ Oct 1952	Cover: 0.10	**NM** value: **100.00**
18	❑ Dec 1952	Cover: 0.10	**NM** value: **100.00**
19	❑ Feb 1953	Cover: 0.10	**NM** value: **100.00**
20	❑ Apr 1953	Cover: 0.10	**NM** value: **100.00**

ROEL — Sirius

1 ❑ Feb 1997, b&w — Cover: 2.95 — **NM** value: **Cover or less**
Circ: Diamd. preorders: **12,936**
One-shot. cardstock cover. **A:** Roel **W:** Roel

ROGAN GOSH — DC / Vertigo

1 ❑ — Cover: 6.95 — **NM** value: **Cover or less**
No issue number.

ROGER DODGER — Standard

5 ❑ ca. 1952 — Cover: 0.10 — **NM** value: **25.00**

ROGER FNORD — Rip Off

All issues are adults only.

1 ❑ Apr 1992, b&w — Cover: 2.50 — **NM** value: **Cover or less**

ROGER RABBIT — Disney

The film "Who Framed Roger Rabbit?" was a monumental success for Disney. This remarkable movie deftly combined a live-action detective thriller on the same screen with animated cartoon characters. In 1990, Disney comics followed up the film with a new Roger Rabbit comic book series.

Ever since Eddie Valiant made a name for himself as a detective, by capturing Judge Doom in the movie, he has been too busy to help Roger in the many adventures for the comic series. In the first issue, Eddie paired Roger up with an old friend, Rick Flint. Together, the odd twosome go on one wacky adventure after another.

Most of the characters from the film find their way into the series. Among them, the reader will find Jessica Rabbit, Roger's sexy wife; Benny the Cab; and Baby Herman; although, obviously none of the Warner Bros. characters (and few of the traditional Disney characters) pop up.

1 ❑ Jun 1990 — Cover: 1.50 — **NM** value: **3.50**
Circ: CapCity orders: **12,700**
📖 The Trouble with Toons!; Good Neighbor Roger **A:** Rick Hoberg; Dave Simons; Bill Langley **W:** Doug Rice; Kate Worley ★ 1st Appearance of Dick Flint.
2 ❑ Jul 1990 — Cover: 1.50 — **NM** value: **2.50**
Circ: CapCity orders: **8,350**
📖 The Color of Trouble!; Gym Dandy **A:** Rick Hoberg; Bill Langley **W:** Doug Rice; Kate Worley
3 ❑ Aug 1990 — Cover: 1.50 — **NM** value: **2.50**
Circ: CapCity orders: **8,450**
📖 Rollercoaster Rabbit; Roller Coaster Riot; 20,000 Leaks Under the Sink **A:** Rick Hoberg; Bill Langley **W:** Doug Rice; Kate Worley
4 ❑ Sep 1990 — Cover: 1.50 — **NM** value: **2.50**
Circ: CapCity orders: **8,450**
📖 Little China in Big Trouble; Cotton-Tailspin **A:** Bill Langley; Cosmé Quartieri **W:** Doug Rice; Kate Worley
5 ❑ Oct 1990 — Cover: 1.50 — **NM** value: **2.50**
Circ: CapCity orders: **9,300**
📖 Justifiable Hamicide!; Nuts 'n' Volts **A:** Bill Langley; Cosmé Quartieri **W:** Doug Rice; Kate Worley
6 ❑ Nov 1990 — Cover: 1.50 — **NM** value: **2.00**
Circ: CapCity orders: **8,850**
📖 Taxi Turmoil; The Candy Cane Mutiny **A:** Bill Langley; Cosmé Quartieri **W:** Doug Rice; Kate Worley
7 ❑ Dec 1990 — Cover: 1.50 — **NM** value: **2.00**
Circ: CapCity orders: **8,550**
📖 Djinn Game; Dial M for Roger **A:** Bill Langley; Cosmé Quartieri **W:** Doug Rice; Kate Worley
8 ❑ Jan 1991 — Cover: 1.50 — **NM** value: **2.00**
Circ: CapCity orders: **8,600**
📖 The Spies of Life; Top Bun **A:** Jose Marzan Jr.; Bill Langley; Cosmé Quartieri **W:** Doug Rice; Kate Worley
9 ❑ Feb 1991 — Cover: 1.50 — **NM** value: **2.00**
Circ: CapCity orders: **8,000**
10 ❑ Mar 1991 — Cover: 1.50 — **NM** value: **2.00**
Circ: CapCity orders: **7,700**
11 ❑ Apr 1991 — Cover: 1.50 — **NM** value: **Cover or less**
Circ: CapCity orders: **7,100**
12 ❑ May 1991 — Cover: 1.50 — **NM** value: **Cover or less**
Circ: CapCity orders: **6,500**
13 ❑ Jun 1991 — Cover: 1.50 — **NM** value: **Cover or less**
Circ: CapCity orders: **5,800**
📖 Stork Raving Mad!; Hare Apparent **A:** Sparky Moore; Bill Langley; Doug Rice **W:** Doug Rice; Martin Pasko
14 ❑ Jul 1991 — Cover: 1.50 — **NM** value: **Cover or less**
Circ: CapCity orders: **1,700**
15 ❑ Aug 1991 — Cover: 1.50 — **NM** value: **Cover or less**
Circ: CapCity orders: **5,650**
16 ❑ Sep 1991 — Cover: 1.50 — **NM** value: **Cover or less**
Circ: CapCity orders: **5,550**
17 ❑ Oct 1991 — Cover: 1.50 — **NM** value: **Cover or less**
Circ: CapCity orders: **5,450**
18 ❑ Nov 1991 — Cover: 1.50 — **NM** value: **Cover or less**
Circ: CapCity orders: **5,250**
final issue.
SE 1❑ — Cover: 3.50 — **NM** value: **Cover or less**
No issue number. 📖 Who Framed Rick Flint?

ROGER RABBIT IN 3-D — Disney

1 ❑ — Cover: 2.50 — **NM** value: **Cover or less**
• with glasses; 3-D Zone reprints

ROGER RABBIT'S TOONTOWN — Disney

1 ❑ Aug 1991 — Cover: 1.50 — **NM** value: **Cover or less**
Circ: CapCity orders: **9,600**
📖 Well, You Name It!; Baby Herman: Shopping Spree; The Dreaded Flying Pizzas; Jessica Rabbit: Beauty on the Spot **A:** Bill Fugate; Cosme Quartieri; John Costanza **W:** John Blair Moore; Jack Enyart; Tom Yakutis
2 ❑ Sep 1991 — Cover: 1.50 — **NM** value: **Cover or less**
Circ: CapCity orders: **6,200**
• Winsor McCay tribute
3 ❑ Oct 1991 — Cover: 1.50 — **NM** value: **Cover or less**
Circ: CapCity orders: **5,550**
4 ❑ Nov 1991 — Cover: 1.50 — **NM** value: **Cover or less**
Circ: CapCity orders: **5,100**
★ 1st Appearance of Winnie Weasel.
5 ❑ Dec 1991 — Cover: 1.50 — **NM** value: **Cover or less**
Circ: CapCity orders: **4,650**
• Weasels solo story

ROGER WILCO — Adventure

1 ❑ full color — Cover: 2.95 — **NM** value: **Cover or less**
Circ: CapCity orders: **2,950**
2 ❑ Apr 1992, b&w — Cover: 2.95 — **NM** value: **Cover or less**
📖 Death to the Deltaur **A:** Andrew Walls; Craig A. Taillefer **W:** Paul O'Connor

ROG-2000 — Pacific

1 ❑ — Cover: 2.00 — **NM** value: **Cover or less**
Circ: CapCity orders: **2,350**
A: John Byrne

ROGUE BATTLEBOOK — Marvel

1 ❑ — Cover: 3.99 — **NM** value: **Cover or less**

CGC-graded: Multiply prices above by **33 for 9.9 M • 16 for 9.8 NM/M • 7 for 9.6 NM+ • 5 for 9.4 NM • 2.5 for 9.2 NM- • 1.5 for 9.0 VF/NM**

ROGUE (MARVEL) — Marvel

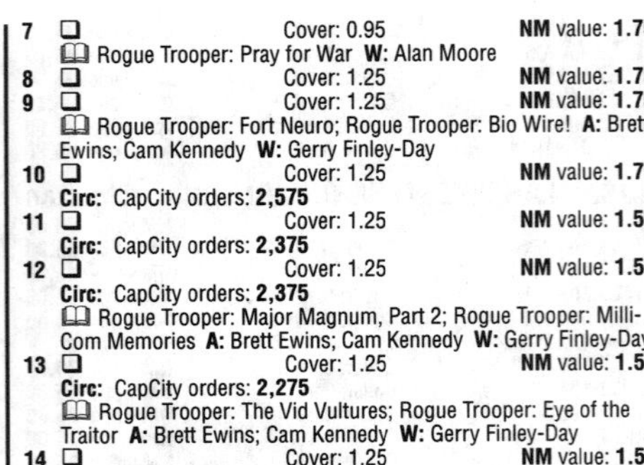

As an X-Man, pitting your life against evil madmen to protect a society that fears and despises you isn't a dream life. If you're the mutant Southern belle known only as Rogue, it's a lonely life as well. "Gifted" with the ability to steal another person's memories, energy, and powers by contact with her skin, Rogue is the consummate outsider, never feeling the touch of another.

Rogue's curse has filled her life with regret: the robbing of Ms. Marvel's powers, the inability to hold Gambit, the man she loves. Even her first kiss ended in tragedy, with her sweetheart, Cody, being placed into a permanent coma after touching her lips.

In this series, a love from Gambit's past steals Cody's body to settle a score with the Thieves Guild in New Orleans. Rogue's shot at redemption has arrived.

1 ❑ Jan 1995 Cover: 2.95 **NM** value: **Cover or less**
Circ: CapCity orders: **79,225** • **CGC:** 1 graded, best 9.6
enhanced cover. **A:** Mike Wieringo **W:** Howard Mackie

2 ❑ Feb 1995 Cover: 2.95 **NM** value: **Cover or less**
Circ: CapCity orders: **63,825** • **CGC:** 1 graded, best 9.6
enhanced cover. **A:** Mike Wieringo **W:** Howard Mackie

3 ❑ Mar 1995 Cover: 2.95 **NM** value: **Cover or less**
Circ: CapCity orders: **55,625**
enhanced cover. 📖 The Gauntlet **A:** Mike Wieringo **W:** Howard Mackie

4 ❑ Apr 1995 Cover: 2.95 **NM** value: **Cover or less**
Circ: CapCity orders: **53,325**
enhanced cover. **A:** Mike Wieringo **W:** Howard Mackie

Bk 1 ❑ Cover: 12.95 **NM** value: **Cover or less**
• Collects Rogue #1-4 **A:** Mike Wieringo **W:** Howard Mackie

ROGUE (MONSTER) — Monster

1 ❑ b&w Cover: 1.95 **NM** value: **Cover or less**

ROGUE SATELLITE COMICS — Slave Labor

1 ❑ Aug 1996, b&w Cover: 2.95 **NM** value: **Cover or less**
2 ❑ b&w Cover: 2.95 **NM** value: **Cover or less**
3 ❑ Mar 1997, b&w Cover: 2.95 **NM** value: **Cover or less**
SE 1 ❑ b&w Cover: 2.95 **NM** value: **Cover or less**
No issue number. ★ Appearance of Flaming Carrot.

ROGUES GALLERY — DC

1 ❑ Cover: 3.50 **NM** value: **Cover or less**
One-shot. • pin-ups **A:** Matt Wagner; Bill Sienkiewicz; Rebecca Guay; John K. Snyder III; Ray Lago; John Van Fleet; Cliff Nielsen; D. Alexander Gregory; John Hanley; Tom Taggart(cover)

ROGUES, THE (VILLAINS) — DC

1 ❑ Feb 1998 Cover: 1.95 **NM** value: **Cover or less**
• New Year's Evil

ROGUE TROOPER (1ST SERIES) — Fleetway-Quality

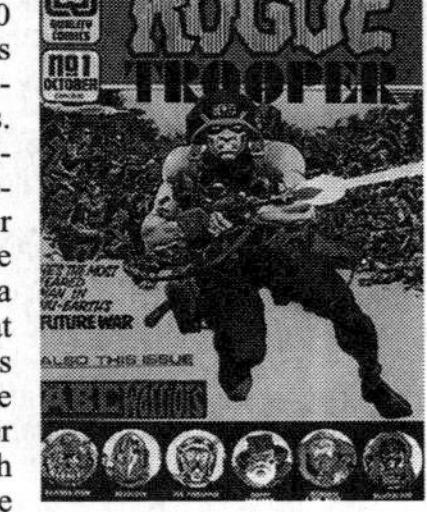

This series reprinted for the American market Rogue Trooper's adventures from the British 2000 A.D., along with backup features starring the A.B.C. Warriors, Chopper, and other 2000 A.D. favorites.

Rogue Trooper a genetically-engineered soldier called Friday. Designed as part of a squad to fight for the Southers in their war against the "Norts" on Nu Earth, he fell into a disastrous "quartz massacre" that killed his comrades. Their minds live on, however, as bio-chips in the backpack, gun, helmet, and other equipment he carries. Through them, he is able to control each piece of equipment remotely.

The trooper went rogue when betrayed by a traitorous general, and has since only sporadically fought for the Southers. Mainly, he strives to stay alive in a world which seems to be one large battleground.

1 ❑ Cover: 0.75 **NM** value: **2.00**
📖 Rogue Trooper; Rogue Trooper: Tower of Death; Rogue Trooper: Crystal Nightmare!; Rogue Trooper: Clash in Doomsday Valley; ABC Warriors **A:** Dave Gibbons **W:** Gerry Finley-Day; Pat Mills

2 ❑ Cover: 0.75 **NM** value: **2.00**
📖 Rogue Trooper: Moving Target; Rogue Trooper: Triple Cross; ABC Warriors: The Retreat From Volgow! **A:** Dave Gibbons; Art McCarthy; Colin Wilson **W:** Gerry Finley-Day; Pat Mills

3 ❑ Cover: 0.75 **NM** value: **2.00**
📖 Rogue Trooper: The Decapitators; Rogue Trooper: The Rookies; Rogue Trooper: Blue Moon; Rogue Trooper: Termination Trap; ABC Warriors **A:** Dave Gibbons; Mike McMahon; Colin Wilson **W:** Gerry Finley-Day; Pat Mills

4 ❑ Cover: 0.75 **NM** value: **2.00**
📖 Rogue Trooper: Eraser Evaders!; Rogue Trooper: War of Nerves; Rogue Trooper: Surrender!; ABC Warriors **A:** Mike McMahon; Colin Wilson **W:** Gerry Finley-Day; Pat Mills

5 ❑ Cover: 0.75 **NM** value: **2.00**
📖 Rogue Trooper: Menace of the Dream Weavers; Rogue Trooper: Bagman Blues; ABC Warriors **A:** Dave Gibbons; Brett Ewins; Eric Bradbury; Kevin O'Neill **W:** Gerry Finley-Day; Pat Mills

6 ❑ Cover: 1.50 **NM** value: **1.75**

7 ❑ Cover: 0.95 **NM** value: **1.75**
📖 Rogue Trooper: Pray for War **W:** Alan Moore

8 ❑ Cover: 1.25 **NM** value: **1.75**

9 ❑ Cover: 1.25 **NM** value: **1.75**
📖 Rogue Trooper: Fort Neuro; Rogue Trooper: Bio Wire! **A:** Brett Ewins; Cam Kennedy **W:** Gerry Finley-Day

10 ❑ Cover: 1.25 **NM** value: **1.75**
Circ: CapCity orders: **2,575**

11 ❑ Cover: 1.25 **NM** value: **1.50**
Circ: CapCity orders: **2,375**

12 ❑ Cover: 1.25 **NM** value: **1.50**
Circ: CapCity orders: **2,375**
📖 Rogue Trooper: Major Magnum, Part 2; Rogue Trooper: Milli-Com Memories **A:** Brett Ewins; Cam Kennedy **W:** Gerry Finley-Day

13 ❑ Cover: 1.25 **NM** value: **1.50**
Circ: CapCity orders: **2,275**
📖 Rogue Trooper: The Vid Vultures; Rogue Trooper: Eye of the Traitor **A:** Brett Ewins; Cam Kennedy **W:** Gerry Finley-Day

14 ❑ Cover: 1.25 **NM** value: **1.50**
Circ: CapCity orders: **2,025**
📖 Rogue Trooper: Eye of the Traitor; Rogue Trooper: Mega-Minefield; Rogue Trooper: Nort by Nortwest **A:** Jose Ortiz; Cam Kennedy; Boluda **W:** Peter Milligan; Gerry Finley-Day

15 ❑ Cover: 1.25 **NM** value: **1.50**
Circ: CapCity orders: **1,900**

16 ❑ Cover: 1.25 **NM** value: **1.50**
Circ: CapCity orders: **1,875**
📖 Rogue Trooper: You Only Die Twice; Rogue Trooper: Message From Milli-Com; Rogue Trooper: The Gasbah **A:** Cam Kennedy **W:** Gerry Finley-Day

17 ❑ Cover: 1.25 **NM** value: **1.50**
Circ: CapCity orders: **1,750**
📖 Rogue Trooper: Rank and Vile! **A:** Cam Kennedy **W:** Gerry Finley-Day

18 ❑ Cover: 1.25 **NM** value: **1.50**
Circ: CapCity orders: **1,650**
📖 Rogue Trooper: Death Valley! **A:** Cam Kennedy **W:** Gerry Finley-Day

19 ❑ Cover: 1.25 **NM** value: **1.50**
📖 Rogue Trooper: To the Ends of Nu Earth; Rogue Trooper: Return of a Hero? **A:** Cam Kennedy **W:** Gerry Finley-Day

20 ❑ Cover: 1.50 **NM** value: **Cover or less**
Circ: CapCity orders: **1,600**

21 ❑ Cover: 1.50 **NM** value: **Cover or less**
Circ: CapCity orders: **1,600**
• double issue #21/22

23 ❑ Cover: 1.50 **NM** value: **Cover or less**
Circ: CapCity orders: **1,625**
• double issue #23/24

25 ❑ Cover: 1.50 **NM** value: **Cover or less**
Circ: CapCity orders: **1,575**

26 ❑ Cover: 1.50 **NM** value: **Cover or less**

27 ❑ Cover: 1.50 **NM** value: **Cover or less**
Circ: CapCity orders: **1,550**

28 ❑ Cover: 1.50 **NM** value: **Cover or less**
Circ: CapCity orders: **1,500**

29 ❑ Cover: 1.50 **NM** value: **Cover or less**
Circ: CapCity orders: **1,475**

30 ❑ Cover: 1.50 **NM** value: **1.75**
Circ: CapCity orders: **1,500**
📖 Rogue Trooper: Testing, Testing…; Tyranny Rex; ABC Warriors; Tharg's Future Shocks **A:** Steve Dillon **W:** John Smith; Simon Geller; Steve McManus

31 ❑ Cover: 1.50 **NM** value: **1.75**
Circ: CapCity orders: **1,500**

32 ❑ Cover: 1.50 **NM** value: **1.75**
Circ: CapCity orders: **1,425**
📖 Rogue Trooper: Hit One; Thirst; Chopper: Soul on Fire; A.B.C. Warriors **A:** Steve Dillon **W:** Simon Geller

33 ❑ Cover: 1.50 **NM** value: **1.75**
Circ: CapCity orders: **1,375**

34 ❑ Cover: 1.50 **NM** value: **1.75**
Circ: CapCity orders: **1,375**
📖 Rogue Trooper: Hit One; Chopper: Soul on Fire; ABC Warriors **A:** Simon Bisley **W:** Pat Mills

35 ❑ Cover: 1.50 **NM** value: **1.75**
Circ: CapCity orders: **1,400**
📖 Rogue Trooper: Hit One; Chopper: Soul on Fire; Tharg's Future Shocks; Ace Trucking Co **A:** Massimo Belardinelli; Steve Dillon; Colin MacNeil **W:** Alan Grant; John Wagner; Simon Geller; T.B. Grover

36 ❑ Cover: 1.50 **NM** value: **1.75**
Circ: CapCity orders: **1,400**
📖 Rogue Trooper: The Hit Parade; Ace Trucking Co.: Last Lug to Abbo Dabbo; Time Twisters **A:** Massimo Belardinelli; Steve Dillon **W:** Alan Grant; Simon Geller; T.B. Grover

37 ❑ Cover: 1.50 **NM** value: **1.75**
Circ: CapCity orders: **1,375**

38 ❑ Cover: 1.50 **NM** value: **1.75**
Circ: CapCity orders: **1,350**
📖 Rogue Trooper: Hit Two; Rogue Trooper: Hit Three; Ace Trucking Co.: Joobaloo! **A:** Massimo Belardinelli; Steve Dillon **W:** Alan Grant; Simon Geller; T.B. Grover

39 ❑ Cover: 1.75 **NM** value: **Cover or less**
Circ: CapCity orders: **1,325**

40 ❑ Cover: 1.75 **NM** value: **Cover or less**
Circ: CapCity orders: **1,275**

41 ❑ Cover: 1.75 **NM** value: **Cover or less**
Circ: CapCity orders: **1,175**

42 ❑ Cover: 1.75 **NM** value: **Cover or less**
Circ: CapCity orders: **1,150**

43 ❑ Cover: 1.75 **NM** value: **Cover or less**
Circ: CapCity orders: **1,175**

44 ❑ Cover: 1.75 **NM** value: **Cover or less**
📖 Rogue Trooper: Nu Earth Flashback; Visible Man; Ace Trucking Co: The Kloistar Run **A:** Massimo Belardinelli; Steve Dillon; Kevin Walker; Montero **W:** John Smith; Alan Grant; Pat Mills; T.B. Grover

45 ❑ Cover: 1.75 **NM** value: **Cover or less**
Circ: CapCity orders: **1,100**
📖 Rogue Trooper: Nu Earth Flashback; Strontium Dog: Tales From the Doghouse; Ace Trucking Co.: Stoop Coop Soup **A:** Massimo Belardinelli; Simon Jacob **W:** Alan Grant; Hilary Robinson; T.B. Grover

46 ❑ Cover: 1.75 **NM** value: **Cover or less**

47 ❑ Cover: 1.75 **NM** value: **Cover or less**
Circ: CapCity orders: **1,125**

48 ❑ Cover: 1.75 **NM** value: **Cover or less**
Circ: CapCity orders: **1,125**
📖 Rogue Trooper; Ace Trucking Co.: On the Dangle; Tharg's Future Shocks: Termination Explanation **A:** Robin Smith; Carlos Ezquerra **W:** Alan Grant; Ian Rogan

49 ❑ Cover: 1.75 **NM** value: **Cover or less**
Circ: CapCity orders: **1,125**

ROGUE TROOPER (2ND SERIES) — Fleetway-Quality

1 ❑ Cover: 2.95 **NM** value: **Cover or less**
Circ: CapCity orders: **7,575**
★ Origin of Rogue Trooper.

2 ❑ Cover: 2.95 **NM** value: **Cover or less**
Circ: CapCity orders: **6,075**

3 ❑ Cover: 2.95 **NM** value: **Cover or less**
Circ: CapCity orders: **4,500**

4 ❑ Cover: 2.95 **NM** value: **Cover or less**
Circ: CapCity orders: **4,425**

5 ❑ Cover: 2.95 **NM** value: **Cover or less**
Circ: CapCity orders: **4,300**

6 ❑ Cover: 2.95 **NM** value: **Cover or less**
Circ: CapCity orders: **3,875**

7 ❑ Cover: 2.95 **NM** value: **Cover or less**
Circ: CapCity orders: **4,200**

8 ❑ Cover: 2.95 **NM** value: **Cover or less**
Circ: CapCity orders: **3,300**
📖 Apocalypse Dreadnought Part 6-10 **A:** Ron Smith **W:** Michael Fleisher

9 ❑ Cover: 2.95 **NM** value: **Cover or less**
Circ: CapCity orders: **2,925**

ROJA FUSION — Antarctic

1 ❑ Apr 1995 Cover: 2.95 **NM** value: **Cover or less**
A: Tyrone Ford **W:** Tyrone Ford

ROLAND: DAYS OF WRATH — Terra Major

1 ❑ Jul 1999 Cover: 2.95 **NM** value: **Cover or less**

ROLLERCOASTER — Fantagraphics

1 ❑ Sep 1996, b&w Cover: 3.95 **NM** value: **Cover or less**
cardstock cover. • magazine.

ROLLERCOASTERS SPECIAL EDITION — Blue Comet

1 ❑ Cover: 1.80 **NM** value: **2.00**

ROLLING STONES — Personality

1 ❑ b&w Cover: 2.95 **NM** value: **Cover or less**
2 ❑ b&w Cover: 2.95 **NM** value: **Cover or less**
3 ❑ b&w Cover: 2.95 **NM** value: **Cover or less**

ROLLING STONES: VOODOO LOUNGE — Marvel / Marvel Music

1 ❑ Cover: 6.95 **NM** value: **Cover or less**
No issue number. • prestige format one-shot **A:** Dave McKean **W:** Dave McKean

ROLY POLY COMICS — Green Publications

1 ❑ ca. 1945 Cover: 0.10 **NM** value: **200.00**
10 ❑ Jan 1946 Cover: 0.10 **NM** value: **200.00**
• **CGC:** 1 graded, best 7.0
11 ❑ Feb 1946 Cover: 0.10 **NM** value: **125.00**
12 ❑ Mar 1946 Cover: 0.10 **NM** value: **125.00**
• **CGC:** 1 graded, best 9.0
13 ❑ Apr 1946 Cover: 0.10 **NM** value: **125.00**
14 ❑ May 1946 Cover: 0.10 **NM** value: **125.00**
• **CGC:** 1 graded, best 7.5

ROM — Marvel

Marvel had a number of titles based on toys in the late 1970s and early 1980s, but the story of Rom has to be the strangest. Based on a robot-like figure from Parker Brothers, Rom had a suitably computer-sounding name (the abbreviation for Read-Only Memory just then coming into general knowledge). The toy died a quick death on the shelves — but the comics title went on for years, with many readers completely oblivious to its origin!

As for Rom's origin, he's from Galador, a planet which, when threatened by the Dire Wraiths, created cyborg warriors known as Spaceknights. Rom is one, and he travels to earth to banish the shape-shifting Wraiths to Limbo.

Inexplicably, several Marvel creators took Rom and his story seriously enough to incorporate it into their own titles. Chris Claremont, who had shown a weakness for hard-luck cases by bringing Team America into the New Mutants, brought the Dire Wraiths into Uncanny X-Men. And a series simply called Spaceknights would follow nearly two decades after the launch and failure of the Rom toy! — JJM

1 ❑ Dec 1979 Cover: 0.40 **NM** value: **2.00**
• **CGC:** 6 graded, best 9.6

Other grades: Multiply prices above by **1.5 for Mint** • **2/3 for Very Fine** • **1/3 for Fine** • **1/5 for Very Good** • **1/8 for Good**

📖 Arrival! **A:** Sal Buscema **W:** Bill Mantlo ★ Origin of ROM. ★ 1st Appearance of ROM.
2 ❑ Jan 1980 Cover: 0.40 **NM** value: **2.00**
A: Sal Buscema; Frank Miller(cover) **C:** Frank Miller
3 ❑ Feb 1980 Cover: 0.40 **NM** value: **2.00**
A: Sal Buscema; Frank Miller(cover) **C:** Frank Miller ★ 1st Appearance of Firefall.
4 ❑ Mar 1980 Cover: 0.40 **NM** value: **1.50**
A: Sal Buscema
5 ❑ Apr 1980 Cover: 0.40 **NM** value: **1.50**
A: Sal Buscema
6 ❑ May 1990 Cover: 0.40 **NM** value: **1.50**
A: Sal Buscema
7 ❑ Jun 1990 Cover: 0.40 **NM** value: **1.50**
A: Sal Buscema
8 ❑ Jul 1990 Cover: 0.40 **NM** value: **1.50**
📖 Deathwing! **A:** Sal Buscema **W:** Bill Mantlo
9 ❑ Aug 1990 Cover: 0.40 **NM** value: **1.50**
📖 The Stalker In The Night! **A:** Sal Buscema **W:** Bill Mantlo
10 ❑ Sep 1990 Cover: 0.50 **NM** value: **1.50**
📖 Warrior Over Washington **A:** Sal Buscema **W:** Bill Mantlo
11 ❑ Oct 1990 Cover: 0.50 **NM** value: **1.25**
A: Sal Buscema
12 ❑ Nov 1990 Cover: 0.50 **NM** value: **1.25**
A: Sal Buscema
13 ❑ Dec 1980 Cover: 0.50 **NM** value: **1.25**
A: Sal Buscema
14 ❑ Jan 1981 Cover: 0.50 **NM** value: **1.25**
Circ: Statement: **147,000**
📖 Ultimate Android **A:** Sal Buscema **W:** Bill Mantlo
15 ❑ Feb 1981 Cover: 0.50 **NM** value: **1.25**
Circ: Statement: **147,000**
A: Sal Buscema
16 ❑ Mar 1981 Cover: 0.50 **NM** value: **1.25**
Circ: Statement: **147,000**
A: Sal Buscema
17 ❑ Apr 1981 Cover: 0.50 **NM** value: **1.50**
Circ: Statement: **147,000** • **CGC:** 3 graded, best 9.8
📖 Hybrid! **A:** Sal Buscema; Frank Miller(cover) **W:** Bill Mantlo ★ Appearance of X-Men.
18 ❑ May 1981 Cover: 0.50 **NM** value: **1.50**
Circ: Statement: **147,000** • **CGC:** 1 graded, best 9.6
A: Sal Buscema; Frank Miller(cover) ★ Appearance of X-Men.
19 ❑ Jun 1981 Cover: 0.50 **NM** value: **1.25**
Circ: Statement: **147,000**
A: Sal Buscema; Joe Sinnott ★ Appearance of X-Men.
20 ❑ Jul 1981 Cover: 0.50 **NM** value: **1.25**
Circ: Statement: **147,000**
📖 Mindgames **A:** Sal Buscema; Joe Sinnott **W:** Bill Mantlo
21 ❑ Aug 1981 Cover: 0.50 **NM** value: **1.25**
Circ: Statement: **147,000**
📖 Move Over Rom- There's A New Hero In Town! **A:** Sal Buscema; Joe Sinnott **W:** Bill Mantlo
22 ❑ Sep 1981 Cover: 0.50 **NM** value: **1.25**
Circ: Statement: **147,000**
A: Sal Buscema; Joe Sinnott
23 ❑ Oct 1981 Cover: 0.50 **NM** value: **1.25**
Circ: Statement: **147,000**
A: Sal Buscema; Joe Sinnott ★ Appearance of Power Man.
24 ❑ Nov 1981 Cover: 0.50 **NM** value: **1.50**
Circ: Statement: **147,000**
A: Sal Buscema; Joe Sinnott ★ Death of Crimebuster. ★ Death of Powerhouse. ★ Death of Nova-Prime. ★ Death of Comet (Harris Moore). ★ Death of Protector.
25 ❑ Dec 1981 Cover: 0.75 **NM** value: **1.50**
Circ: Statement: **147,000**
• Giant-size. **A:** Sal Buscema; Joe Sinnott
26 ❑ Jan 1982 Cover: 0.60 **NM** value: **1.25**
27 ❑ Feb 1982 Cover: 0.60 **NM** value: **1.25**
28 ❑ Mar 1982 Cover: 0.60 **NM** value: **1.25**
29 ❑ Apr 1982 Cover: 0.60 **NM** value: **1.25**
30 ❑ May 1982 Cover: 0.60 **NM** value: **1.25**
31 ❑ Jun 1982 Cover: 0.60 **NM** value: **1.25**
32 ❑ Jul 1982 Cover: 0.60 **NM** value: **1.25**
33 ❑ Aug 1982 Cover: 0.60 **NM** value: **1.25**
34 ❑ Sep 1982 Cover: 0.60 **NM** value: **1.25**
35 ❑ Oct 1982 Cover: 0.60 **NM** value: **1.25**
36 ❑ Nov 1982 Cover: 0.60 **NM** value: **1.25**
37 ❑ Dec 1982 Cover: 0.60 **NM** value: **1.25**
38 ❑ Jan 1983 Cover: 0.60 **NM** value: **1.25**
Circ: Statement: **160,741**
39 ❑ Feb 1983 Cover: 0.60 **NM** value: **1.25**
Circ: Statement: **160,741**
40 ❑ Mar 1983 Cover: 0.60 **NM** value: **1.25**
Circ: Statement: **160,741**
41 ❑ Apr 1983 Cover: 0.60 **NM** value: **1.25**
Circ: Statement: **160,741**
42 ❑ May 1983 Cover: 0.60 **NM** value: **1.25**
Circ: Statement: **160,741**
43 ❑ Jun 1983 Cover: 0.60 **NM** value: **1.25**
Circ: Statement: **160,741**
44 ❑ Jul 1983 Cover: 0.60 **NM** value: **1.25**
Circ: Statement: **160,741**
★ 1st Appearance of Devastator II.
45 ❑ Aug 1983 Cover: 0.60 **NM** value: **1.25**
Circ: Statement: **160,741**
46 ❑ Sep 1983 Cover: 0.60 **NM** value: **1.25**
Circ: Statement: **160,741**
47 ❑ Oct 1983 Cover: 0.60 **NM** value: **1.25**
Circ: Statement: **160,741**
48 ❑ Nov 1983 Cover: 0.60 **NM** value: **1.25**
Circ: Statement: **160,741**
49 ❑ Dec 1983 Cover: 0.60 **NM** value: **1.25**
Circ: Statement: **160,741**
50 ❑ Jan 1984 Cover: 1.00 **NM** value: **1.25**
Circ: Statement: **162,090**
• double-sized. 📖 Extraterrestrials! **A:** Sal Buscema **W:** Bill Mantlo ★ Appearance of Skrulls. ★ Death of Torpedo.
51 ❑ Feb 1984 Cover: 0.60 **NM** value: **1.25**
Circ: Statement: **162,090**
52 ❑ Mar 1984 Cover: 0.60 **NM** value: **1.25**
Circ: Statement: **162,090**
53 ❑ Apr 1984 Cover: 0.60 **NM** value: **1.25**
Circ: Statement: **162,090**
54 ❑ May 1984 Cover: 0.60 **NM** value: **1.25**
Circ: Statement: **162,090**
• Has 1983 Statement, filed 10/3/1993; avg print run 327,803; avg sales 153,445; avg subs 7,296; avg total paid 160,741; samples 794; office use 948; max existent 162,483; 50% of run returned
55 ❑ Jun 1984 Cover: 0.60 **NM** value: **1.25**
Circ: Statement: **162,090**
56 ❑ Jul 1984 Cover: 0.60 **NM** value: **1.25**
Circ: Statement: **162,090**
★ Appearance of Alpha Flight.
57 ❑ Aug 1984 Cover: 0.60 **NM** value: **1.25**
Circ: Statement: **162,090**
★ Appearance of Alpha Flight.
58 ❑ Sep 1984 Cover: 0.60 **NM** value: **1.25**
Circ: Statement: **162,090**
• Dire Wraiths
59 ❑ Oct 1984 Cover: 0.60 **NM** value: **1.25**
Circ: Statement: **162,090**
A: Steve Ditko
60 ❑ Nov 1984 Cover: 0.60 **NM** value: **1.25**
Circ: Statement: **162,090**
A: Steve Ditko
61 ❑ Dec 1984 Cover: 0.60 **NM** value: **1.25**
Circ: Statement: **162,090**
A: Steve Ditko
62 ❑ Jan 1985 Cover: 0.60 **NM** value: **1.25**
A: Steve Ditko
63 ❑ Feb 1985 Cover: 0.60 **NM** value: **1.25**
A: Steve Ditko
64 ❑ Mar 1985 Cover: 0.60 **NM** value: **1.25**
65 ❑ Apr 1985 Cover: 0.65 **NM** value: **1.25**
66 ❑ May 1985 Cover: 0.65 **NM** value: **1.25**
Circ: CapCity orders: **13,000**
• Has 1984 Statement, filed 9/28/94; avg print run 320,919; avg sales 155,587; avg subs 6,503; avg total paid 162,090; samples 140; office use 2,652; max existent 164,882; 49% of run returned
67 ❑ Jun 1985 Cover: 0.65 **NM** value: **1.25**
Circ: CapCity orders: **11,500**
68 ❑ Jul 1985 Cover: 0.65 **NM** value: **1.25**
Circ: CapCity orders: **11,400**
69 ❑ Aug 1985 Cover: 0.65 **NM** value: **1.25**
Circ: CapCity orders: **10,900**
70 ❑ Sep 1985 Cover: 0.65 **NM** value: **1.25**
Circ: CapCity orders: **10,500**
71 ❑ Oct 1985 Cover: 0.65 **NM** value: **1.25**
Circ: CapCity orders: **9,900**
★ Death of The Unseen.
72 ❑ Nov 1985 Cover: 0.65 **NM** value: **1.25**
Circ: CapCity orders: **17,400**
📖 Secret Wars II • Secret Wars II
73 ❑ Dec 1985 Cover: 0.75 **NM** value: **1.25**
Circ: CapCity orders: **9,100**
74 ❑ Jan 1986 Cover: 0.75 **NM** value: **1.25**
Circ: CapCity orders: **8,900**
★ Death of Seeker.
75 ❑ Feb 1986 Cover: 0.75 **NM** value: **1.25**
Circ: CapCity orders: **10,600**
★ Death of Trapper. ★ Death of Scanner.
Anl 1❑ca. 1982 Cover: 1.00 **NM** value: **1.50**
• Stardust
Anl 2❑ca. 1983 Cover: 1.00 **NM** value: **1.25**
Anl 3❑ca. 1984 Cover: 1.00 **NM** value: **1.50**
★ Appearance of New Mutants.
Anl 4❑ca. 1985 Cover: 1.25 **NM** value: **Cover or less**
Circ: CapCity orders: **9,700**
★ Appearance of Gladiator. ★ Death of Pulsar.

ROMANCE & CONFESSION STORIES St. John
1 ❑ ca. 1949 Cover: 0.25 **NM** value: **300.00**

ROMANCER Moonstone
1 ❑ Dec 1996, b&w Cover: 2.95 **NM** value: **Cover or less**
No issue number.

ROMANCES OF NURSE HELEN GRANT, THE Atlas
1 ❑ Aug 1957 Cover: 0.10 **NM** value: **35.00**

ROMANCES OF THE WEST Marvel
1 ❑ Nov 1949 Cover: 0.10 **NM** value: **150.00**
2 ❑ ca. 1950 Cover: 0.10 **NM** value: **100.00**

ROMANCE TALES Marvel
7 ❑ Oct 1949 Cover: 0.10 **NM** value: **75.00**
8 ❑ Jan 1950 Cover: 0.10 **NM** value: **50.00**
9 ❑ Apr 1950 Cover: 0.10 **NM** value: **50.00**

ROMANCE TRAIL DC
1 ❑ Jul 1949 Cover: 0.10 **NM** value: **500.00**
• **CGC:** 1 graded, best 7.5
2 ❑ Sep 1949 Cover: 0.10 **NM** value: **200.00**
3 ❑ Nov 1949 Cover: 0.10 **NM** value: **200.00**
• **CGC:** 1 graded, best 9.4
4 ❑ Jan 1950 Cover: 0.10 **NM** value: **200.00**
5 ❑ Mar 1950 Cover: 0.10 **NM** value: **150.00**
6 ❑ May 1950 Cover: 0.10 **NM** value: **150.00**

ROMANTIC ADVENTURES ACG

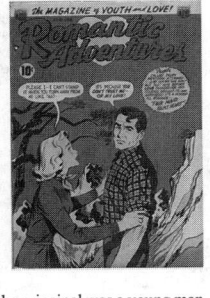

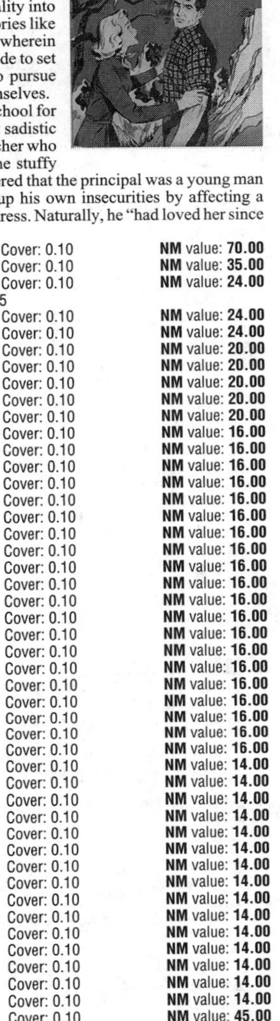

ACG's long-running "Romantic Adventures" was by most respects a cookie-cutter affair, full of love-struck damsels trying to catch the eye of the Man They Love. Even then, Ogden Whitney (creator of Herbie) occasionally appeared to throw his off-kilter personality into the mix. The result were stories like "We Had to be Practical!" wherein two lower-class lovers decide to set their own feelings aside to pursue wealthier matches for themselves.

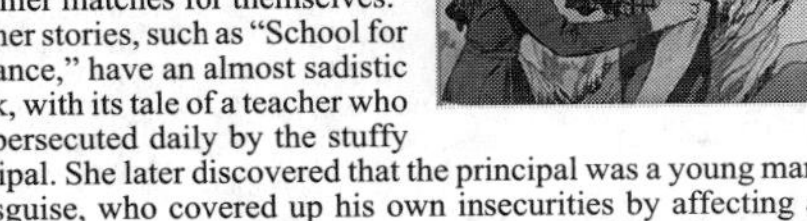

Other stories, such as "School for Romance," have an almost sadistic streak, with its tale of a teacher who was persecuted daily by the stuffy principal. She later discovered that the principal was a young man in disguise, who covered up his own insecurities by affecting a harsh attitude and style of dress. Naturally, he "had loved her since he first laid eyes on her."

1 ❑ Mar 1949 Cover: 0.10 **NM** value: **70.00**
2 ❑ May 1949 Cover: 0.10 **NM** value: **35.00**
3 ❑ Jul 1949 Cover: 0.10 **NM** value: **24.00**
• **CGC:** 1 graded, best 7.5
4 ❑ Sep 1949 Cover: 0.10 **NM** value: **24.00**
5 ❑ Nov 1949 Cover: 0.10 **NM** value: **24.00**
6 ❑ Jan 1950 Cover: 0.10 **NM** value: **20.00**
7 ❑ Mar 1950 Cover: 0.10 **NM** value: **20.00**
8 ❑ May 1950 Cover: 0.10 **NM** value: **20.00**
9 ❑ Jul 1950 Cover: 0.10 **NM** value: **20.00**
10 ❑ Sep 1950 Cover: 0.10 **NM** value: **20.00**
11 ❑ Nov 1950 Cover: 0.10 **NM** value: **16.00**
12 ❑ Jan 1951 Cover: 0.10 **NM** value: **16.00**
13 ❑ Mar 1951 Cover: 0.10 **NM** value: **16.00**
14 ❑ May 1951 Cover: 0.10 **NM** value: **16.00**
15 ❑ Jul 1951 Cover: 0.10 **NM** value: **16.00**
16 ❑ Sep 1951 Cover: 0.10 **NM** value: **16.00**
17 ❑ Nov 1951 Cover: 0.10 **NM** value: **16.00**
18 ❑ Jan 1952 Cover: 0.10 **NM** value: **16.00**
19 ❑ Mar 1952 Cover: 0.10 **NM** value: **16.00**
20 ❑ Apr 1952 Cover: 0.10 **NM** value: **16.00**
21 ❑ May 1952 Cover: 0.10 **NM** value: **16.00**
22 ❑ Jun 1952 Cover: 0.10 **NM** value: **16.00**
23 ❑ Jul 1952 Cover: 0.10 **NM** value: **16.00**
24 ❑ Aug 1952 Cover: 0.10 **NM** value: **16.00**
25 ❑ Sep 1952 Cover: 0.10 **NM** value: **16.00**
26 ❑ Oct 1952 Cover: 0.10 **NM** value: **16.00**
27 ❑ Nov 1952 Cover: 0.10 **NM** value: **16.00**
28 ❑ Dec 1952 Cover: 0.10 **NM** value: **16.00**
29 ❑ Jan 1953 Cover: 0.10 **NM** value: **16.00**
30 ❑ Feb 1953 Cover: 0.10 **NM** value: **16.00**
31 ❑ Mar 1953 Cover: 0.10 **NM** value: **14.00**
32 ❑ Apr 1953 Cover: 0.10 **NM** value: **14.00**
33 ❑ May 1953 Cover: 0.10 **NM** value: **14.00**
34 ❑ Jun 1953 Cover: 0.10 **NM** value: **14.00**
35 ❑ Jul 1953 Cover: 0.10 **NM** value: **14.00**
36 ❑ Aug 1953 Cover: 0.10 **NM** value: **14.00**
37 ❑ Sep 1953 Cover: 0.10 **NM** value: **14.00**
38 ❑ Oct 1953 Cover: 0.10 **NM** value: **14.00**
39 ❑ Nov 1953 Cover: 0.10 **NM** value: **14.00**
40 ❑ Dec 1953 Cover: 0.10 **NM** value: **14.00**
41 ❑ Jan 1954 Cover: 0.10 **NM** value: **14.00**
42 ❑ Feb 1954 Cover: 0.10 **NM** value: **14.00**
43 ❑ Mar 1954 Cover: 0.10 **NM** value: **14.00**
44 ❑ Apr 1954 Cover: 0.10 **NM** value: **14.00**
45 ❑ May 1954 Cover: 0.10 **NM** value: **14.00**
46 ❑ Jun 1954 Cover: 0.10 **NM** value: **45.00**
• 3-D.
47 ❑ Jul 1954 Cover: 0.10 **NM** value: **45.00**
• 3-D.
48 ❑ Aug 1954 Cover: 0.10 **NM** value: **45.00**
• 3-D.
49 ❑ Sep 1954 Cover: 0.10 **NM** value: **14.00**
50 ❑ Oct 1954 Cover: 0.10 **NM** value: **14.00**
• **CGC:** 1 graded, best 3.0
51 ❑ Dec 1954 Cover: 0.10 **NM** value: **12.00**
52 ❑ Feb 1955 Cover: 0.10 **NM** value: **12.00**
53 ❑ 1955 Cover: 0.10 **NM** value: **12.00**
54 ❑ 1955 Cover: 0.10 **NM** value: **12.00**
55 ❑ 1955 Cover: 0.10 **NM** value: **12.00**
56 ❑ 1955 Cover: 0.10 **NM** value: **12.00**
57 ❑ 1955 Cover: 0.10 **NM** value: **12.00**
58 ❑ 1955 Cover: 0.10 **NM** value: **12.00**
59 ❑ 1955 Cover: 0.10 **NM** value: **12.00**
60 ❑ 1956 Cover: 0.10 **NM** value: **12.00**
61 ❑ 1956 Cover: 0.10 **NM** value: **12.00**
62 ❑ 1956 Cover: 0.10 **NM** value: **12.00**
63 ❑ 1956 Cover: 0.10 **NM** value: **12.00**
64 ❑ 1956 Cover: 0.10 **NM** value: **12.00**
65 ❑ 1956 Cover: 0.10 **NM** value: **12.00**
66 ❑ 1956 Cover: 0.10 **NM** value: **12.00**
67 ❑ 1956 Cover: 0.10 **NM** value: **12.00**
📖 We Had to be Practical!; School for Romance!; Miss Bag-of-Bones (text story); Country Girl Kisses! • Series continued in My Romantic Adventures #68 **A:** Ogden Whitney

ROMANTIC CONFESSIONS Hillman
Volume 1
1 ❑ Oct 1949 Cover: 0.10 **NM** value: **100.00**
• **CGC:** 1 graded, best 9.6
2 ❑ Nov 1949 Cover: 0.10 **NM** value: **50.00**
3 ❑ Dec 1949 Cover: 0.10 **NM** value: **40.00**
4 ❑ Jan 1950 Cover: 0.10 **NM** value: **40.00**
5 ❑ Feb 1950 Cover: 0.10 **NM** value: **40.00**

CGC-graded: Multiply prices above by **33 for 9.9 M • 16 for 9.8 NM/M • 7 for 9.6 NM+ • 5 for 9.4 NM • 2.5 for 9.2 NM- • 1.5 for 9.0 VF/NM**

6 ❑ Mar 1950 Cover: 0.10 **NM** value: **40.00**
7 ❑ Apr 1950 Cover: 0.10 **NM** value: **40.00**
8 ❑ May 1950 Cover: 0.10 **NM** value: **40.00**
9 ❑ Jun 1950 Cover: 0.10 **NM** value: **40.00**
10 ❑ 1950 Cover: 0.10 **NM** value: **40.00**
11 ❑ 1950 Cover: 0.10 **NM** value: **40.00**
12 ❑ 1950 Cover: 0.10 **NM** value: **40.00**

Volume 2

1 ❑ 1951 Cover: 0.10 **NM** value: **50.00**
2 ❑ 1951 Cover: 0.10 **NM** value: **50.00**
3 ❑ Aug 1951 Cover: 0.10 **NM** value: **50.00**
4 ❑ Oct 1951 Cover: 0.10 **NM** value: **50.00**
5 ❑ Dec 1951 Cover: 0.10 **NM** value: **50.00**
6 ❑ Feb 1952 Cover: 0.10 **NM** value: **50.00**
7 ❑ Apr 1952 Cover: 0.10 **NM** value: **50.00**
8 ❑ Jun 1952 Cover: 0.10 **NM** value: **50.00**
9 ❑ Aug 1952 Cover: 0.10 **NM** value: **35.00**
10 ❑ Oct 1952 Cover: 0.10 **NM** value: **35.00**
11 ❑ Dec 1952 Cover: 0.10 **NM** value: **35.00**
12 ❑ Feb 1953 Cover: 0.10 **NM** value: **35.00**

ROMANTIC HEARTS — Story

Volume 1

1 ❑ Mar 1951 Cover: 0.10 **NM** value: **75.00**
2 ❑ Jun 1951 Cover: 0.10 **NM** value: **40.00**
3 ❑ Aug 1951 Cover: 0.10 **NM** value: **35.00**
A: Bernie Krigstein
4 ❑ Oct 1951 Cover: 0.10 **NM** value: **35.00**
5 ❑ Dec 1951 Cover: 0.10 **NM** value: **35.00**
6 ❑ Feb 1952 Cover: 0.10 **NM** value: **35.00**
7 ❑ Apr 1952 Cover: 0.10 **NM** value: **35.00**
8 ❑ Jun 1952 Cover: 0.10 **NM** value: **35.00**
9 ❑ Aug 1952 Cover: 0.10 **NM** value: **35.00**
10 ❑ Oct 1952 Cover: 0.10 **NM** value: **35.00**

Volume 2

1 ❑ Jul 1953 Cover: 0.10 **NM** value: **50.00**
2 ❑ Sep 1953 Cover: 0.10 **NM** value: **30.00**
3 ❑ Nov 1953 Cover: 0.10 **NM** value: **25.00**
4 ❑ Jan 1954 Cover: 0.10 **NM** value: **25.00**
5 ❑ Mar 1954 Cover: 0.10 **NM** value: **25.00**
6 ❑ May 1954 Cover: 0.10 **NM** value: **25.00**
7 ❑ Jul 1954 Cover: 0.10 **NM** value: **25.00**
8 ❑ Sep 1954 Cover: 0.10 **NM** value: **25.00**
9 ❑ Nov 1954 Cover: 0.10 **NM** value: **25.00**
10 ❑ Jan 1955 Cover: 0.10 **NM** value: **25.00**
11 ❑ Mar 1955 Cover: 0.10 **NM** value: **25.00**
12 ❑ May 1955 Cover: 0.10 **NM** value: **25.00**

ROMANTIC LOVE — Avon

1 ❑ Sep 1949 Cover: 0.10 **NM** value: **175.00**
2 ❑ Nov 1949 Cover: 0.10 **NM** value: **100.00**
3 ❑ Jan 1950 Cover: 0.10 **NM** value: **100.00**
4 ❑ 1950 Cover: 0.10 **NM** value: **100.00**
📖 Nobody Will Ever Know!; Detour to Love; Teardrops From my Heart!; Don't Lie to me My Love
5 ❑ 1950 Cover: 0.10 **NM** value: **100.00**
📖 Love Me Always, Darling!; Innocence was My Angle; With Evil in Your Heart; Afraid to Love!
6 ❑ 1950 Cover: 0.10 **NM** value: **100.00**
7 ❑ 1950 Cover: 0.10 **NM** value: **100.00**
📖 I Craved Excitement; Dangerous Woman; Bride of Fear; Nightmare Romance
8 ❑ 1950 Cover: 0.10 **NM** value: **100.00**
📖 I Knew About Men; No Cure for Love; Driven by Desire; Bride Without Love
9 ❑ 1951 Cover: 0.10 **NM** value: **100.00**
10 ❑ 1951 Cover: 0.10 **NM** value: **100.00**
📖 I'll Make Him Mine; Loveless Marraige; Trapped inot Marraige; Love is Like Hate
11 ❑ ca. 1952 Cover: 0.10 **NM** value: **100.00**
📖 I Married You Didn't I?; Phantom Husband; Love Thief; The Honeymoon is Over
12 ❑ ca. 1952 Cover: 0.10 **NM** value: **100.00**
13 ❑ ca. 1952 Cover: 0.10 **NM** value: **100.00**
📖 My Shameful Secret; Stage Crazy; Search for Happiness; I was a Profiteer
20 ❑ Mar 1954 Cover: 0.10 **NM** value: **100.00**
21 ❑ May 1954 Cover: 0.10 **NM** value: **100.00**
22 ❑ Jul 1954 Cover: 0.10 **NM** value: **100.00**
23 ❑ Sep 1954 Cover: 0.10 **NM** value: **100.00**

ROMANTIC MARRIAGE — Ziff-Davis

1 ❑ Nov 1950 Cover: 0.10 **NM** value: **150.00**
2 ❑ Jan 1951 Cover: 0.10 **NM** value: **100.00**
📖 The Two Sides of Love; In Sickness and in Health; Mother's Boy
3 ❑ Mar 1951 Cover: 0.10 **NM** value: **75.00**
4 ❑ May 1951 Cover: 0.10 **NM** value: **75.00**
5 ❑ Jul 1951 Cover: 0.10 **NM** value: **75.00**
6 ❑ Sep 1951 Cover: 0.10 **NM** value: **75.00**
7 ❑ Nov 1951 Cover: 0.10 **NM** value: **75.00**
8 ❑ Dec 1951 Cover: 0.10 **NM** value: **75.00**
9 ❑ Jan 1951 Cover: 0.10 **NM** value: **75.00**
10 ❑ Feb 1952 Cover: 0.10 **NM** value: **75.00**
11 ❑ Mar 1952 Cover: 0.10 **NM** value: **50.00**
12 ❑ Apr 1952 Cover: 0.10 **NM** value: **50.00**
13 ❑ May 1952 Cover: 0.10 **NM** value: **50.00**
• **CGC:** 1 graded, best 8.0
14 ❑ Jun 1952 Cover: 0.10 **NM** value: **50.00**
📖 I Married in Haste; Ruthless Ambition; The Road to Heartbreak
15 ❑ Jul 1952 Cover: 0.10 **NM** value: **50.00**
16 ❑ Aug 1952 Cover: 0.10 **NM** value: **50.00**
17 ❑ Sep 1952 Cover: 0.10 **NM** value: **50.00**
18 ❑ Cover: 0.10 **NM** value: **50.00**
19 ❑ Cover: 0.10 **NM** value: **50.00**
20 ❑ Cover: 0.10 **NM** value: **45.00**
21 ❑ Cover: 0.10 **NM** value: **45.00**
22 ❑ Cover: 0.10 **NM** value: **45.00**
23 ❑ Cover: 0.10 **NM** value: **45.00**
24 ❑ Cover: 0.10 **NM** value: **45.00**

ROMANTIC PICTURE NOVELETTES — Magazine Enterprises

1 ❑ ca. 1946 Cover: 0.10 **NM** value: **125.00**
• **CGC:** 1 graded, best 7.5

ROMANTIC SECRETS (1ST SERIES) — Fawcett

1 ❑ Sep 1949 Cover: 0.10 **NM** value: **100.00**
2 ❑ Nov 1949 Cover: 0.10 **NM** value: **50.00**
3 ❑ Jan 1950 Cover: 0.10 **NM** value: **50.00**
4 ❑ Feb 1950 Cover: 0.10 **NM** value: **50.00**
5 ❑ Apr 1950 Cover: 0.10 **NM** value: **50.00**
6 ❑ May 1950 Cover: 0.10 **NM** value: **50.00**
7 ❑ Jun 1950 Cover: 0.10 **NM** value: **50.00**
8 ❑ Jul 1950 Cover: 0.10 **NM** value: **50.00**
📖 Empty Dreams; The Man I Love; Conflict; Restless Heart
9 ❑ Aug 1950 Cover: 0.10 **NM** value: **50.00**
10 ❑ Sep 1950 Cover: 0.10 **NM** value: **50.00**
11 ❑ Oct 1950 Cover: 0.10 **NM** value: **40.00**
12 ❑ Nov 1950 Cover: 0.10 **NM** value: **40.00**
13 ❑ Dec 1950 Cover: 0.10 **NM** value: **40.00**
14 ❑ Jan 1951 Cover: 0.10 **NM** value: **40.00**
15 ❑ Feb 1951 Cover: 0.10 **NM** value: **40.00**
16 ❑ Mar 1951 Cover: 0.10 **NM** value: **40.00**
17 ❑ Apr 1951 Cover: 0.10 **NM** value: **40.00**
18 ❑ May 1951 Cover: 0.10 **NM** value: **40.00**
19 ❑ Jun 1951 Cover: 0.10 **NM** value: **40.00**
20 ❑ Jul 1951 Cover: 0.10 **NM** value: **35.00**
21 ❑ Aug 1951 Cover: 0.10 **NM** value: **35.00**
22 ❑ Sep 1951 Cover: 0.10 **NM** value: **35.00**
23 ❑ Oct 1951 Cover: 0.10 **NM** value: **35.00**
24 ❑ Nov 1951 Cover: 0.10 **NM** value: **35.00**
25 ❑ Dec 1951 Cover: 0.10 **NM** value: **35.00**
26 ❑ Jan 1952 Cover: 0.10 **NM** value: **35.00**
27 ❑ Feb 1952 Cover: 0.10 **NM** value: **35.00**
28 ❑ Mar 1952 Cover: 0.10 **NM** value: **35.00**
29 ❑ Apr 1952 Cover: 0.10 **NM** value: **35.00**
30 ❑ May 1952 Cover: 0.10 **NM** value: **30.00**
31 ❑ Jun 1952 Cover: 0.10 **NM** value: **30.00**
32 ❑ Jul 1952 Cover: 0.10 **NM** value: **30.00**
33 ❑ Aug 1952 Cover: 0.10 **NM** value: **30.00**
34 ❑ Sep 1952 Cover: 0.10 **NM** value: **30.00**
35 ❑ Oct 1952 Cover: 0.10 **NM** value: **30.00**
36 ❑ Nov 1952 Cover: 0.10 **NM** value: **30.00**
37 ❑ Dec 1952 Cover: 0.10 **NM** value: **30.00**
38 ❑ Jan 1952 Cover: 0.10 **NM** value: **30.00**
39 ❑ Feb 1953 Cover: 0.10 **NM** value: **30.00**

ROMANTIC SECRETS (2ND SERIES) — Charlton

5 ❑ Oct 1955 Cover: 0.10 **NM** value: **45.00**
• Series continued from "Negro Romances"
6 ❑ Cover: 0.10 **NM** value: **22.00**
7 ❑ Cover: 0.10 **NM** value: **22.00**
8 ❑ 1956 Cover: 0.10 **NM** value: **22.00**
9 ❑ Cover: 0.10 **NM** value: **22.00**
10 ❑ Cover: 0.10 **NM** value: **22.00**
11 ❑ Jun 1957 Cover: 0.10 **NM** value: **12.00**
12 ❑ Cover: 0.10 **NM** value: **12.00**
13 ❑ Cover: 0.10 **NM** value: **12.00**
14 ❑ Cover: 0.10 **NM** value: **12.00**
15 ❑ 1958 Cover: 0.10 **NM** value: **12.00**
16 ❑ Cover: 0.10 **NM** value: **12.00**
17 ❑ Cover: 0.10 **NM** value: **12.00**
18 ❑ Cover: 0.10 **NM** value: **12.00**
19 ❑ 1959 Cover: 0.10 **NM** value: **12.00**
20 ❑ 1959 Cover: 0.10 **NM** value: **12.00**
21 ❑ 1959 Cover: 0.10 **NM** value: **8.00**
22 ❑ 1959 Cover: 0.10 **NM** value: **8.00**
23 ❑ Cover: 0.10 **NM** value: **8.00**
24 ❑ Cover: 0.10 **NM** value: **8.00**
25 ❑ Mar 1960 Cover: 0.10 **NM** value: **8.00**
26 ❑ 1960 Cover: 0.10 **NM** value: **8.00**
27 ❑ 1960 Cover: 0.10 **NM** value: **8.00**
28 ❑ Cover: 0.10 **NM** value: **8.00**
29 ❑ Cover: 0.10 **NM** value: **8.00**
30 ❑ Cover: 0.10 **NM** value: **8.00**
31 ❑ Cover: 0.10 **NM** value: **6.00**
32 ❑ 1961 Cover: 0.10 **NM** value: **6.00**
33 ❑ Jun 1961 Cover: 0.10 **NM** value: **6.00**
34 ❑ 1961 Cover: 0.10 **NM** value: **6.00**
35 ❑ 1961 Cover: 0.10 **NM** value: **6.00**
36 ❑ Cover: 0.10 **NM** value: **6.00**
37 ❑ Feb 1962 Cover: 0.10 **NM** value: **6.00**
38 ❑ May 1962 Cover: 0.12 **NM** value: **6.00**
39 ❑ Jul 1962 Cover: 0.12 **NM** value: **6.00**
40 ❑ Sep 1962 Cover: 0.12 **NM** value: **6.00**
41 ❑ Nov 1962 Cover: 0.12 **NM** value: **6.00**
42 ❑ Cover: 0.12 **NM** value: **6.00**
43 ❑ Cover: 0.12 **NM** value: **6.00**
44 ❑ 1963 Cover: 0.12 **NM** value: **6.00**
45 ❑ 1963 Cover: 0.12 **NM** value: **6.00**
46 ❑ 1963 Cover: 0.12 **NM** value: **6.00**
47 ❑ 1963 Cover: 0.12 **NM** value: **6.00**
48 ❑ 1963 Cover: 0.12 **NM** value: **6.00**
49 ❑ Cover: 0.12 **NM** value: **6.00**
50 ❑ Cover: 0.12 **NM** value: **6.00**
51 ❑ Cover: 0.12 **NM** value: **6.00**
52 ❑ 1964 Cover: 0.12 **NM** value: **6.00**
final issue.

ROMANTIC STORY — Charlton

For many publishers whose creators found more fertile creative ground in more fantastic comics, romance comics may have been seen strictly as a revenue generator. Romance comics were regarded as the comics complement to the relationship magazines women were already reading, combining the topics of unrequited love and heartbreak.

In Romantic Story, Fawcett — and then Charlton — hits most of the standard romance comics themes. Not that it didn't try to help its readers out: #51 cover-featured a contest sponsored by TWA, offering trips for two to Disneyland and New York City. Finding the date was the reader's problem.

Charlton brought its typical shipping schedule to this series, with little uniformity in the release dates.

1 ❑ Nov 1949 Cover: 0.10 **NM** value: **65.00**
2 ❑ Jan 1950 Cover: 0.10 **NM** value: **40.00**
3 ❑ Mar 1950 Cover: 0.10 **NM** value: **30.00**
4 ❑ May 1950 Cover: 0.10 **NM** value: **20.00**
5 ❑ Jul 1950 Cover: 0.10 **NM** value: **20.00**
6 ❑ Sep 1950 Cover: 0.10 **NM** value: **20.00**
7 ❑ Nov 1950 Cover: 0.10 **NM** value: **20.00**
8 ❑ Jan 1951 Cover: 0.10 **NM** value: **20.00**
9 ❑ Mar 1951 Cover: 0.10 **NM** value: **20.00**
10 ❑ May 1951 Cover: 0.10 **NM** value: **14.00**
11 ❑ Jul 1951 Cover: 0.10 **NM** value: **14.00**
12 ❑ Sep 1951 Cover: 0.10 **NM** value: **14.00**
13 ❑ Nov 1951 Cover: 0.10 **NM** value: **14.00**
14 ❑ Jan 1952 Cover: 0.10 **NM** value: **14.00**
15 ❑ Mar 1952 Cover: 0.10 **NM** value: **14.00**
16 ❑ May 1952 Cover: 0.10 **NM** value: **14.00**
17 ❑ Jul 1952 Cover: 0.10 **NM** value: **14.00**
18 ❑ Sep 1952 Cover: 0.10 **NM** value: **14.00**
19 ❑ Nov 1952 Cover: 0.10 **NM** value: **14.00**
20 ❑ Jan 1953 Cover: 0.10 **NM** value: **14.00**
21 ❑ Mar 1953 Cover: 0.10 **NM** value: **14.00**
22 ❑ May 1953 Cover: 0.10 **NM** value: **14.00**
• Last Fawcett issue
23 ❑ May 1954 Cover: 0.10 **NM** value: **12.00**
• Charlton begins as publisher
24 ❑ Jul 1954 Cover: 0.10 **NM** value: **12.00**
25 ❑ Aug 1954 Cover: 0.10 **NM** value: **12.00**
26 ❑ Sep 1954 Cover: 0.10 **NM** value: **12.00**
📖 Letter to a Soldier; Second Fiddle; Teasing; Masquerade In White
• Feature on actress Barbara Hale
27 ❑ ca. 1954 Cover: 0.10 **NM** value: **12.00**
28 ❑ ca. 1955 Cover: 0.10 **NM** value: **12.00**
29 ❑ Cover: 0.10 **NM** value: **12.00**
30 ❑ Cover: 0.10 **NM** value: **12.00**
31 ❑ Cover: 0.10 **NM** value: **12.00**
32 ❑ Cover: 0.10 **NM** value: **12.00**
33 ❑ Cover: 0.10 **NM** value: **12.00**
34 ❑ Cover: 0.10 **NM** value: **12.00**
35 ❑ Cover: 0.10 **NM** value: **12.00**
36 ❑ Cover: 0.10 **NM** value: **12.00**
37 ❑ Cover: 0.10 **NM** value: **12.00**
38 ❑ Cover: 0.10 **NM** value: **12.00**
39 ❑ Mar 1958 Cover: 0.10 **NM** value: **12.00**
• Giant size.
40 ❑ Cover: 0.10 **NM** value: **12.00**
41 ❑ Cover: 0.10 **NM** value: **10.00**
42 ❑ Cover: 0.10 **NM** value: **10.00**
43 ❑ Cover: 0.10 **NM** value: **10.00**
44 ❑ Cover: 0.10 **NM** value: **10.00**
45 ❑ Cover: 0.10 **NM** value: **10.00**
46 ❑ Cover: 0.10 **NM** value: **10.00**
47 ❑ Cover: 0.10 **NM** value: **10.00**
48 ❑ Cover: 0.10 **NM** value: **10.00**
49 ❑ Cover: 0.10 **NM** value: **10.00**
50 ❑ Cover: 0.10 **NM** value: **10.00**
51 ❑ Mar 1960 Cover: 0.10 **NM** value: **10.00**
📖 Gypsy Holiday; End of a Dream • Has TWA contest
52 ❑ Cover: 0.10 **NM** value: **10.00**
53 ❑ Feb 1961 Cover: 0.10 **NM** value: **10.00**
54 ❑ Apr 1961 Cover: 0.10 **NM** value: **10.00**
55 ❑ Jun 1961 Cover: 0.10 **NM** value: **10.00**
56 ❑ Aug 1961 Cover: 0.10 **NM** value: **10.00**
57 ❑ Oct 1961 Cover: 0.10 **NM** value: **10.00**
58 ❑ Dec 1961 Cover: 0.10 **NM** value: **10.00**
• **CGC:** 2 graded, best 9.4
59 ❑ 1962 Cover: 0.12 **NM** value: **10.00**
60 ❑ 1962 Cover: 0.12 **NM** value: **10.00**
61 ❑ 1962 Cover: 0.12 **NM** value: **8.00**
62 ❑ Sep 1962 Cover: 0.12 **NM** value: **8.00**
63 ❑ Nov 1962 Cover: 0.12 **NM** value: **8.00**
64 ❑ Jan 1963 Cover: 0.12 **NM** value: **8.00**
65 ❑ Mar 1963 Cover: 0.12 **NM** value: **8.00**
66 ❑ May 1963 Cover: 0.12 **NM** value: **8.00**
67 ❑ Jul 1963 Cover: 0.12 **NM** value: **8.00**
68 ❑ Sep 1963 Cover: 0.12 **NM** value: **8.00**
69 ❑ Nov 1963 Cover: 0.12 **NM** value: **8.00**
70 ❑ Jan 1964 Cover: 0.12 **NM** value: **8.00**
71 ❑ Mar 1964 Cover: 0.12 **NM** value: **8.00**
72 ❑ 1964 Cover: 0.12 **NM** value: **8.00**
73 ❑ Sep 1964 Cover: 0.12 **NM** value: **8.00**
📖 The Meaning of Love; Let Love Wait; Martha Marsden Meditates (text); Jealous Sister; Roam No More **A:** Nicholas Alascia
74 ❑ Nov 1964 Cover: 0.12 **NM** value: **8.00**
75 ❑ 1965 Cover: 0.12 **NM** value: **8.00**
Circ: Statement: **140,528**

Other grades: Multiply prices above by **1.5 for Mint • 2/3 for Very Fine • 1/3 for Fine • 1/5 for Very Good • 1/8 for Good**

76 ❑ 1965 Cover: 0.12 **NM** value: **8.00**
Circ: Statement: **140,528**
77 ❑ Jul 1965 Cover: 0.12 **NM** value: **8.00**
Circ: Statement: **140,528**
78 ❑ Sep 1965 Cover: 0.12 **NM** value: **8.00**
Circ: Statement: **140,528**
79 ❑ Nov 1965 Cover: 0.12 **NM** value: **8.00**
Circ: Statement: **140,528**
80 ❑ Jan 1966 Cover: 0.12 **NM** value: **8.00**
81 ❑ Mar 1966 Cover: 0.12 **NM** value: **5.00**
82 ❑ May 1966 Cover: 0.12 **NM** value: **5.00**
83 ❑ Jul 1966 Cover: 0.12 **NM** value: **5.00**
84 ❑ Sep 1966 Cover: 0.12 **NM** value: **5.00**
85 ❑ Nov 1966 Cover: 0.12 **NM** value: **5.00**
86 ❑ Jan 1967 Cover: 0.12 **NM** value: **5.00**
Circ: Statement: **134,018**
87 ❑ Mar 1967 Cover: 0.12 **NM** value: **5.00**
Circ: Statement: **134,018**
88 ❑ Jun 1967 Cover: 0.12 **NM** value: **5.00**
Circ: Statement: **134,018**
89 ❑ Aug 1967 Cover: 0.12 **NM** value: **5.00**
Circ: Statement: **134,018**
90 ❑ Oct 1967 Cover: 0.12 **NM** value: **5.00**
Circ: Statement: **134,018**
91 ❑ 1967 Cover: 0.12 **NM** value: **5.00**
Circ: Statement: **134,018**
92 ❑ 1968 Cover: 0.12 **NM** value: **5.00**
93 ❑ 1968 Cover: 0.12 **NM** value: **5.00**
94 ❑ Jul 1968 Cover: 0.12 **NM** value: **5.00**
95 ❑ 1968 Cover: 0.12 **NM** value: **5.00**
96 ❑ 1968 Cover: 0.12 **NM** value: **5.00**
97 ❑ Nov 1968 Cover: 0.12 **NM** value: **5.00**
98 ❑ Jan 1969 Cover: 0.12 **NM** value: **5.00**
99 ❑ 1969 Cover: 0.12 **NM** value: **5.00**
100 ❑ 1969 Cover: 0.12 **NM** value: **5.00**
101 ❑ 1969 Cover: 0.12 **NM** value: **5.00**
102 ❑ Cover: 0.12 **NM** value: **5.00**
103 ❑ Cover: 0.12 **NM** value: **5.00**
104 ❑ Cover: 0.12 **NM** value: **5.00**
105 ❑ 1970 Cover: 0.12 **NM** value: **5.00**
106 ❑ 1970 Cover: 0.12 **NM** value: **5.00**
107 ❑ 1970 Cover: 0.12 **NM** value: **5.00**
108 ❑ Cover: 0.12 **NM** value: **5.00**
109 ❑ Cover: 0.12 **NM** value: **5.00**
110 ❑ Cover: 0.12 **NM** value: **5.00**
111 ❑ 1971 Cover: 0.12 **NM** value: **5.00**
112 ❑ 1971 Cover: 0.12 **NM** value: **5.00**
113 ❑ 1971 Cover: 0.12 **NM** value: **5.00**
114 ❑ 1971 Cover: 0.12 **NM** value: **5.00**
115 ❑ Cover: 0.12 **NM** value: **5.00**
116 ❑ Cover: 0.12 **NM** value: **5.00**
117 ❑ 1972 Cover: 0.12 **NM** value: **5.00**
Circ: Statement: **110,028**
118 ❑ 1972 Cover: 0.12 **NM** value: **5.00**
Circ: Statement: **110,028**
119 ❑ Jun 1972 Cover: 0.12 **NM** value: **5.00**
Circ: Statement: **110,028**
120 ❑ Jul 1972 Cover: 0.12 **NM** value: **5.00**
Circ: Statement: **110,028**
121 ❑ Aug 1972 Cover: 0.12 **NM** value: **5.00**
Circ: Statement: **110,028**
122 ❑ Sep 1972 Cover: 0.12 **NM** value: **5.00**
Circ: Statement: **110,028**
123 ❑ 1972 Cover: 0.12 **NM** value: **5.00**
Circ: Statement: **110,028**
124 ❑ 1972 Cover: 0.12 **NM** value: **5.00**
Circ: Statement: **110,028**
125 ❑ Cover: 0.12 **NM** value: **5.00**
126 ❑ 1973 Cover: 0.12 **NM** value: **5.00**
127 ❑ May 1973 Cover: 0.12 **NM** value: **5.00**
• Has 1971 Statement; avg total paid circ 110,028
128 ❑ 1973 Cover: 0.12 **NM** value: **5.00**
129 ❑ 1973 Cover: 0.12 **NM** value: **5.00**
130 ❑ Nov 1973 Cover: 0.12 **NM** value: **5.00**

ROMANTIC TAILS — Head Press
1 ❑ Aug 1998, b&w Cover: 2.95 **NM** value: **Cover or less**

RONALD MCDONALD — Charlton
1 ❑ Sep 1970 Cover: 0.15 **NM** value: **30.00**
• **CGC:** 1 graded, best 9.0
2 ❑ Nov 1970 Cover: 0.15 **NM** value: **20.00**
3 ❑ Jan 1971 Cover: 0.15 **NM** value: **20.00**
• **CGC:** 1 graded, best .5
4 ❑ Mar 1971 Cover: 0.15 **NM** value: **20.00**

RONIN — DC
"If you intend to die, you can do anything." So went the slogan for Frank Miller's renowned series for DC, which did more than any other title to kick off the wave of ninja-clones in comics.

Centuries ago, a young samurai pledged his life to his master, Lord Ozaki, wielder of the Bloodsword, a mystical blade stolen from the demon Agat. When Ozaki was killed by Agat, the young ronin (a samurai with no master) sought vengeance. The Bloodsword had the power to slay Agat only if it had been used to slay an innocent — so to complete his quest, the ronin plunged the blade through his own heart, spearing the demon as well. But as he died, the demon uttered one final curse...

Now, the bio-engineered Aquarius Complex sprawls over the ruins of New York City. Within, an armless kid named Billy melds cybernetically with a living computer and dreams about an ancient ronin. When the complex is attacked, Billy realizes that he is part of an old conflict which had never truly ended...

1 ❑ Jul 1983 Cover: 2.50 **NM** value: **5.00**
• **CGC:** 9 graded, best 9.8
A: Frank Miller **W:** Frank Miller
2 ❑ Sep 1983 Cover: 2.50 **NM** value: **4.00**
• **CGC:** 4 graded, best 9.8
A: Frank Miller **W:** Frank Miller
3 ❑ Nov 1983 Cover: 2.50 **NM** value: **4.00**
A: Frank Miller **W:** Frank Miller
4 ❑ Jan 1984 Cover: 2.50 **NM** value: **4.00**
A: Frank Miller **W:** Frank Miller
5 ❑ Jan 1984 Cover: 2.50 **NM** value: **4.00**
A: Frank Miller **W:** Frank Miller
6 ❑ Aug 1984 Cover: 2.50 **NM** value: **6.00**
• Scarcer **A:** Frank Miller **W:** Frank Miller
Bk 1 ❑ Cover: 16.95 **NM** value: **Cover or less**
• Collects Ronin #1-6 **A:** Frank Miller **W:** Frank Miller

ROOK, THE — Harris
1 ❑ Jun 1995 Cover: 2.95 **NM** value: **Cover or less**
Circ: CapCity orders: **9,475**
No issue number. 📖 Fist Full of Chaos **A:** Kirk Van Wormer **W:** Tom Sniegoski
2 ❑ 1995 Cover: 2.95 **NM** value: **Cover or less**
Circ: CapCity orders: **5,750**
📖 The Good, The Bad and The Chaotic **A:** Kirk Van Wormer **W:** Tom Sniegoski

ROOK MAGAZINE, THE — Warren
1 ❑ Oct 1979 Cover: 1.75 **NM** value: **4.00**
2 ❑ Feb 1980 Cover: 1.75 **NM** value: **2.50**
📖 The Man Whom Time Forgot; Day Before Tomorrow; Yesterday, the Final Day; The Land of Nowhen **A:** Luis Bermejo **W:** Bill Dubay; Budd Lewis
3 ❑ Jun 1980 Cover: 2.00 **NM** value: **2.50**
4 ❑ Aug 1980 Cover: 2.00 **NM** value: **2.50**
5 ❑ Oct 1980 Cover: 2.00 **NM** value: **2.50**
6 ❑ Dec 1980 Cover: 2.00 **NM** value: **2.50**
7 ❑ Feb 1981 Cover: 2.00 **NM** value: **2.50**
8 ❑ Apr 1981 Cover: 2.00 **NM** value: **2.50**
9 ❑ Jun 1981 Cover: 2.00 **NM** value: **2.50**
10 ❑ Aug 1981 Cover: 2.00 **NM** value: **2.50**
11 ❑ Oct 1981 Cover: 2.00 **NM** value: **Cover or less**
12 ❑ Dec 1981 Cover: 2.00 **NM** value: **Cover or less**
13 ❑ Feb 1982 Cover: 2.00 **NM** value: **Cover or less**
14 ❑ Apr 1982 Cover: 2.00 **NM** value: **Cover or less**

ROOTER — Custom
1 ❑ Aug 1996 Cover: 2.95 **NM** value: **Cover or less**
📖 Sweatin' Bullets
2 ❑ Dec 1996 Cover: 2.95 **NM** value: **Cover or less**
📖 Big Bad Beaver
3 ❑ Feb 1997 Cover: 2.95 **NM** value: **Cover or less**
📖 The Big Izzy
4 ❑ May 1997 Cover: 2.95 **NM** value: **Cover or less**
📖 Da Voodoo Blues
5 ❑ Jul 1997 Cover: 2.95 **NM** value: **Cover or less**
6 ❑ Oct 1997 Cover: 2.95 **NM** value: **Cover or less**

ROOTER (VOL. 2) — Custom
1 ❑ b&w Cover: 2.95 **NM** value: **Cover or less**
📖 Da Voodoo Blues

ROOTS OF THE OPPRESSOR — Northstar
1 ❑ b&w Cover: 2.95 **NM** value: **Cover or less**

ROOTS OF THE SWAMP THING — DC
1 ❑ Jul 1986 Cover: 2.00 **NM** value: **Cover or less**
Circ: CapCity orders: **7,650**
A: Bernie Wrightson **W:** Len Wein
2 ❑ Aug 1986 Cover: 2.00 **NM** value: **Cover or less**
Circ: CapCity orders: **6,950**
A: Bernie Wrightson **W:** Len Wein
3 ❑ Sep 1986 Cover: 2.00 **NM** value: **Cover or less**
Circ: CapCity orders: **6,900**
📖 The Last of the Ravenwind Witches; A Clockwork Horror; Night Prowler • reprints Swamp Thing #5 and #6 and House of Mystery #191 **A:** Bernie Wrightson **W:** Len Wein
4 ❑ Oct 1986 Cover: 2.00 **NM** value: **Cover or less**
Circ: CapCity orders: **7,400**
📖 Night of the Bat; The Lurker in Tunnel 13!; He Who Laughs Last ... • reprints Swamp Thing #7 and #8 and House of Mystery #221 **A:** Bernie Wrightson **W:** Len Wein ★ Appearance of Batman.
5 ❑ Nov 1986 Cover: 2.00 **NM** value: **Cover or less**
Circ: CapCity orders: **6,900**
📖 The Stalker From Beyond; The Man Who Would Not Die; Swamp Thing • reprints Swamp Thing #9 and #10 and House of Mystery #92; Reprints stories from Swamp Thing #9, #10, House of Mystery #92 **A:** Bernie Wrightson **W:** Len Wein ★ Origin of Swamp Thing.

ROSCOE! THE DAWG, ACE DETECTIVE — Renegade
1 ❑ Jul 1987, b&w Cover: 2.00 **NM** value: **Cover or less**
2 ❑ Oct 1987, b&w Cover: 2.00 **NM** value: **Cover or less**
3 ❑ Nov 1987, b&w Cover: 2.00 **NM** value: **Cover or less**
4 ❑ Jan 1988, b&w Cover: 2.00 **NM** value: **Cover or less**

ROSE — Hero
1 ❑ Cover: 3.50 **NM** value: **Cover or less**
2 ❑ Cover: 2.95 **NM** value: **Cover or less**
3 ❑ Cover: 3.95 **NM** value: **Cover or less**
4 ❑ Cover: 3.95 **NM** value: **Cover or less**
5 ❑ Dec 1993 Cover: 2.95 **NM** value: **Cover or less**

ROSE & GUNN — Bishop
3 ❑ May 1995, b&w Cover: 2.95 **NM** value: **Cover or less**
4 ❑ Jun 1995, b&w Cover: 2.95 **NM** value: **Cover or less**
5 ❑ Aug 1995, b&w Cover: 2.95 **NM** value: **Cover or less**

ROSE & GUNN CREATOR'S CHOICE — Bishop
1 ❑ Sep 1995, b&w Cover: 2.95 **NM** value: **Cover or less**

ROSWELL: LITTLE GREEN MAN — Bongo
1 ❑ ca. 1996 Cover: 2.95 **NM** value: **3.50**
Circ: Diamd. preorders: **14,276**
📖 The Untold Story **A:** Bill Morrison **W:** Bill Morrison
2 ❑ ca. 1996 Cover: 2.95 **NM** value: **3.00**
Circ: Diamd. preorders: **10,102**
A: Bill Morrison **W:** Bill Morrison
3 ❑ ca. 1996 Cover: 2.95 **NM** value: **3.00**
Circ: Diamd. preorders: **7,939**
A: Bill Morrison **W:** Bill Morrison ★ Versus Professor Von Sphinkter.
4 ❑ ca. 1997 Cover: 2.95 **NM** value: **3.00**
Circ: Diamd. preorders: **6,375**
A: Bill Morrison **W:** Bill Morrison ★ Death of Shorty George.
5 ❑ ca. 1998 Cover: 2.95 **NM** value: **3.00**
Circ: Diamd. preorders: **5,503**
A: Bill Morrison **W:** Bill Morrison
6 ❑ ca. 1999 Cover: 2.95 **NM** value: **3.00**
Circ: Diamd. preorders: **3,954**
A: Bill Morrison **W:** Bill Morrison
Bk 1 ❑ Cover: 12.95 **NM** value: **Cover or less**
• Roswell Walks Among Us; collects back-up Roswell stories from Simpsons Comics and first three issues of ongoing series **A:** Bill Morrison **W:** Bill Morrison

ROUGH RAIDERS — Blue Comet
1 ❑ Cover: 1.80 **NM** value: **2.00**
2 ❑ Cover: 1.80 **NM** value: **2.00**
3 ❑ Cover: 1.80 **NM** value: **2.00**
Anl 1 ❑ Cover: 2.50 **NM** value: **Cover or less**

ROULETTE — Caliber
1 ❑ b&w Cover: 2.50 **NM** value: **Cover or less**

ROUNDUP — D.S.
1 ❑ Jul 1948 Cover: 0.10 **NM** value: **150.00**
• **CGC:** 1 graded, best 9.2
2 ❑ Sep 1948 Cover: 0.10 **NM** value: **100.00**
3 ❑ Nov 1948 Cover: 0.10 **NM** value: **100.00**
4 ❑ Jan 1949 Cover: 0.10 **NM** value: **100.00**
• **CGC:** 1 graded, best 7.5
5 ❑ Mar 1949 Cover: 0.10 **NM** value: **100.00**

ROVERS, THE — Malibu
1 ❑ Sep 1987 Cover: 1.95 **NM** value: **Cover or less**
📖 I Don't Like Mondays **A:** Scott Bieser **W:** S.A. Bennett
2 ❑ 1987 Cover: 1.95 **NM** value: **Cover or less**
A: Scott Bieser **W:** S.A. Bennett
3 ❑ 1987 Cover: 1.95 **NM** value: **Cover or less**
A: Scott Bieser **W:** S.A. Bennett
4 ❑ 1988 Cover: 1.95 **NM** value: **Cover or less**
A: Scott Bieser **W:** S.A. Bennett
5 ❑ 1988 Cover: 1.95 **NM** value: **Cover or less**
A: Scott Bieser **W:** S.A. Bennett
6 ❑ 1988b&w Cover: 1.95 **NM** value: **Cover or less**
7 ❑ 1988b&w Cover: 1.95 **NM** value: **Cover or less**

ROYAL ROY — Marvel / Star
1 ❑ May 1985 Cover: 0.65 **NM** value: **1.00**
Circ: CapCity orders: **5,000**
📖 The Mystery Of The Missing Crown **A:** Warren Kremer **W:** Lennie Herman; Lenny Herman ★ 1st Appearance of Royal Roy.
2 ❑ Jul 1985 Cover: 0.65 **NM** value: **1.00**
Circ: CapCity orders: **3,300**
3 ❑ Sep 1985 Cover: 0.65 **NM** value: **1.00**
Circ: CapCity orders: **2,500**
4 ❑ Nov 1985 Cover: 0.65 **NM** value: **1.00**
Circ: CapCity orders: **1,900**
5 ❑ Jan 1986 Cover: 0.65 **NM** value: **1.00**
Circ: CapCity orders: **1,500**
6 ❑ Mar 1986 Cover: 0.65 **NM** value: **1.00**
Circ: CapCity orders: **1,400**
final issue.

ROY CAMPANELLA, BASEBALL HERO — Fawcett
1 ❑ ca. 1950 Cover: 0.10 **NM** value: **500.00**
• **CGC:** 1 graded, best 7.0

ROY ROGERS COMICS — Dell
The legendary star of cowboy musicals left his mark on the four-color world of comics with these modern-day Wild West tales. As the daring deputy of Pronghorn (among other occupations), Roy's life was one exciting adventure after another, dealing with everything from stampeding buffaloes to stopping range wars. Of course, getting out of his many scraps would be a lot more difficult without his two "sidekicks." Roy's faithful horse, Trigger, and his courageous dog, Bullet, are always at his side, no matter the danger. So saddle up and get ready for some fun, courtesy of Roy Rogers, King of the Cowboys.

1 ❑ Jan 1948 Cover: 0.10 **NM** value: **700.00**
• **CGC:** 6 graded, best 8.0

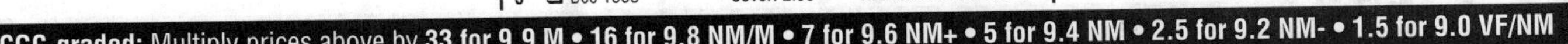
CGC-graded: Multiply prices above by **33 for 9.9 M • 16 for 9.8 NM/M • 7 for 9.6 NM+ • 5 for 9.4 NM • 2.5 for 9.2 NM- • 1.5 for 9.0 VF/NM**

2 ❑ Feb 1948 Cover: 0.10 **NM** value: **300.00**
3 ❑ Mar 1948 Cover: 0.10 **NM** value: **215.00**
4 ❑ Apr 1948 Cover: 0.10 **NM** value: **215.00**
5 ❑ May 1948 Cover: 0.10 **NM** value: **215.00**
• **CGC:** 1 graded, best 9.6
6 ❑ Jun 1948 Cover: 0.10 **NM** value: **150.00**
7 ❑ Jul 1948 Cover: 0.10 **NM** value: **150.00**
• **CGC:** 1 graded, best 9.4
8 ❑ Aug 1948 Cover: 0.10 **NM** value: **150.00**
9 ❑ Sep 1948 Cover: 0.10 **NM** value: **150.00**
• **CGC:** 1 graded, best 4.0
10 ❑ Oct 1948 Cover: 0.10 **NM** value: **150.00**
• **CGC:** 1 graded, best 4.5
11 ❑ Nov 1948 Cover: 0.10 **NM** value: **115.00**
• **CGC:** 1 graded, best 7.5
12 ❑ Dec 1948 Cover: 0.10 **NM** value: **115.00**
• **CGC:** 1 graded, best 4.0
13 ❑ Jan 1949 Cover: 0.10 **NM** value: **115.00**
14 ❑ Feb 1949 Cover: 0.10 **NM** value: **115.00**
15 ❑ Mar 1949 Cover: 0.10 **NM** value: **115.00**
16 ❑ Apr 1949 Cover: 0.10 **NM** value: **115.00**
17 ❑ May 1949 Cover: 0.10 **NM** value: **115.00**
• **CGC:** 1 graded, best 9.0
18 ❑ Jun 1949 Cover: 0.10 **NM** value: **115.00**
• **CGC:** 1 graded, best 7.0
19 ❑ Jul 1949 Cover: 0.10 **NM** value: **115.00**
20 ❑ Aug 1949 Cover: 0.10 **NM** value: **115.00**
21 ❑ Sep 1949 Cover: 0.10 **NM** value: **95.00**
• **CGC:** 2 graded, best 9.0
22 ❑ Oct 1949 Cover: 0.10 **NM** value: **95.00**
• **CGC:** 1 graded, best 6.5
23 ❑ Nov 1949 Cover: 0.10 **NM** value: **95.00**
• **CGC:** 1 graded, best 7.0
24 ❑ Dec 1949 Cover: 0.10 **NM** value: **95.00**
25 ❑ Jan 1950 Cover: 0.10 **NM** value: **95.00**
• **CGC:** 1 graded, best 9.2
26 ❑ Feb 1950 Cover: 0.10 **NM** value: **95.00**
27 ❑ Mar 1950 Cover: 0.10 **NM** value: **95.00**
28 ❑ Apr 1950 Cover: 0.10 **NM** value: **95.00**
• **CGC:** 1 graded, best 8.5
29 ❑ May 1950 Cover: 0.10 **NM** value: **95.00**
30 ❑ Jun 1950 Cover: 0.10 **NM** value: **95.00**
• **CGC:** 1 graded, best 8.0
31 ❑ Jul 1950 Cover: 0.10 **NM** value: **80.00**
32 ❑ Aug 1950 Cover: 0.10 **NM** value: **80.00**
33 ❑ Sep 1950 Cover: 0.10 **NM** value: **80.00**
34 ❑ Oct 1950 Cover: 0.10 **NM** value: **80.00**
35 ❑ Nov 1950 Cover: 0.10 **NM** value: **80.00**
36 ❑ Dec 1950 Cover: 0.10 **NM** value: **80.00**
37 ❑ Jan 1951 Cover: 0.10 **NM** value: **80.00**
38 ❑ Feb 1951 Cover: 0.10 **NM** value: **80.00**
• **CGC:** 1 graded, best 9.4
39 ❑ Mar 1951 Cover: 0.10 **NM** value: **80.00**
40 ❑ Apr 1951 Cover: 0.10 **NM** value: **80.00**
41 ❑ May 1951 Cover: 0.10 **NM** value: **60.00**
42 ❑ Jun 1951 Cover: 0.10 **NM** value: **60.00**
43 ❑ Jul 1951 Cover: 0.10 **NM** value: **60.00**
44 ❑ Aug 1951 Cover: 0.10 **NM** value: **60.00**
45 ❑ Sep 1951 Cover: 0.10 **NM** value: **60.00**
46 ❑ Oct 1951 Cover: 0.10 **NM** value: **60.00**
47 ❑ Nov 1951 Cover: 0.10 **NM** value: **60.00**
48 ❑ Dec 1951 Cover: 0.10 **NM** value: **60.00**
• **CGC:** 1 graded, best 9.2
49 ❑ Jan 1952 Cover: 0.10 **NM** value: **60.00**
50 ❑ Feb 1952 Cover: 0.10 **NM** value: **60.00**
51 ❑ Mar 1952 Cover: 0.10 **NM** value: **50.00**
52 ❑ Apr 1952 Cover: 0.10 **NM** value: **50.00**
53 ❑ May 1952 Cover: 0.10 **NM** value: **50.00**
54 ❑ Jun 1952 Cover: 0.10 **NM** value: **50.00**
55 ❑ Jul 1952 Cover: 0.10 **NM** value: **50.00**
56 ❑ Aug 1952 Cover: 0.10 **NM** value: **50.00**
57 ❑ Sep 1952 Cover: 0.10 **NM** value: **50.00**
58 ❑ Oct 1952 Cover: 0.10 **NM** value: **50.00**
59 ❑ Nov 1952 Cover: 0.10 **NM** value: **50.00**
60 ❑ Dec 1952 Cover: 0.10 **NM** value: **50.00**
61 ❑ Jan 1953 Cover: 0.10 **NM** value: **40.00**
62 ❑ Feb 1953 Cover: 0.10 **NM** value: **40.00**
• **CGC:** 2 graded, best 9.2
63 ❑ Mar 1953 Cover: 0.10 **NM** value: **40.00**
• **CGC:** 1 graded, best 9.4
64 ❑ Apr 1953 Cover: 0.10 **NM** value: **40.00**
65 ❑ May 1953 Cover: 0.10 **NM** value: **40.00**
66 ❑ Jun 1953 Cover: 0.10 **NM** value: **40.00**
67 ❑ Jul 1953 Cover: 0.10 **NM** value: **40.00**
• **CGC:** 1 graded, best 9.6
68 ❑ Aug 1953 Cover: 0.10 **NM** value: **40.00**
📖 Rifles at Piute Wells; The Missing Splinters; Bullet Guards a Friend; Prairie Ghost (text story); Chuckwagon Charley's Tales;
69 ❑ Sep 1953 Cover: 0.10 **NM** value: **40.00**
70 ❑ Oct 1953 Cover: 0.10 **NM** value: **40.00**
• **CGC:** 1 graded, best 8.5
71 ❑ Nov 1953 Cover: 0.10 **NM** value: **40.00**
72 ❑ Dec 1953 Cover: 0.10 **NM** value: **40.00**
• **CGC:** 1 graded, best 9.6
73 ❑ Jan 1954 Cover: 0.10 **NM** value: **40.00**
74 ❑ Feb 1954 Cover: 0.10 **NM** value: **40.00**
• **CGC:** 1 graded, best 9.0
75 ❑ Mar 1954 Cover: 0.10 **NM** value: **40.00**
76 ❑ Apr 1954 Cover: 0.10 **NM** value: **40.00**
77 ❑ May 1954 Cover: 0.10 **NM** value: **40.00**
78 ❑ Jun 1954 Cover: 0.10 **NM** value: **40.00**
• **CGC:** 1 graded, best 9.6
79 ❑ Jul 1954 Cover: 0.10 **NM** value: **40.00**
• **CGC:** 1 graded, best 9.6
80 ❑ Aug 1954 Cover: 0.10 **NM** value: **40.00**
81 ❑ Sep 1954 Cover: 0.10 **NM** value: **35.00**
• **CGC:** 1 graded, best 9.0
82 ❑ Oct 1954 Cover: 0.10 **NM** value: **35.00**
83 ❑ Nov 1954 Cover: 0.10 **NM** value: **35.00**
84 ❑ Dec 1954 Cover: 0.10 **NM** value: **35.00**
85 ❑ Jan 1955 Cover: 0.10 **NM** value: **35.00**
• **CGC:** 1 graded, best 9.2
86 ❑ Feb 1955 Cover: 0.10 **NM** value: **35.00**
87 ❑ Mar 1955 Cover: 0.10 **NM** value: **35.00**
• **CGC:** 1 graded, best 9.4
88 ❑ Apr 1955 Cover: 0.10 **NM** value: **35.00**
• **CGC:** 2 graded, best 9.4
89 ❑ May 1955 Cover: 0.10 **NM** value: **35.00**
• **CGC:** 1 graded, best 9.2
90 ❑ Jun 1955 Cover: 0.10 **NM** value: **35.00**
91 ❑ Jul 1955 Cover: 0.10 **NM** value: **35.00**
92 ❑ Aug 1955 Cover: 0.10 **NM** value: **35.00**
93 ❑ Sep 1955 Cover: 0.10 **NM** value: **35.00**
94 ❑ Oct 1955 Cover: 0.10 **NM** value: **35.00**
• **CGC:** 1 graded, best 9.4
95 ❑ Nov 1955 Cover: 0.10 **NM** value: **35.00**
• **CGC:** 1 graded, best 9.4
96 ❑ Dec 1955 Cover: 0.10 **NM** value: **35.00**
• **CGC:** 1 graded, best 9.6
97 ❑ Jan 1956 Cover: 0.10 **NM** value: **35.00**
• **CGC:** 1 graded, best 9.2
98 ❑ Feb 1956 Cover: 0.10 **NM** value: **35.00**
• **CGC:** 1 graded, best 9.6
99 ❑ Mar 1956 Cover: 0.10 **NM** value: **35.00**
100 ❑ Apr 1956 Cover: 0.10 **NM** value: **35.00**
• **CGC:** 1 graded, best 9.4
101 ❑ May 1956 Cover: 0.10 **NM** value: **30.00**
102 ❑ Jun 1956 Cover: 0.10 **NM** value: **30.00**
103 ❑ Jul 1956 Cover: 0.10 **NM** value: **30.00**
• **CGC:** 1 graded, best 9.2
104 ❑ Aug 1956 Cover: 0.10 **NM** value: **30.00**
105 ❑ Sep 1956 Cover: 0.10 **NM** value: **30.00**
106 ❑ Oct 1956 Cover: 0.10 **NM** value: **30.00**
107 ❑ Nov 1956 Cover: 0.10 **NM** value: **30.00**
108 ❑ Dec 1956 Cover: 0.10 **NM** value: **30.00**
109 ❑ Jan 1957 Cover: 0.10 **NM** value: **30.00**
110 ❑ Feb 1957 Cover: 0.10 **NM** value: **30.00**
111 ❑ Mar 1957 Cover: 0.10 **NM** value: **30.00**
112 ❑ Apr 1957 Cover: 0.10 **NM** value: **30.00**
113 ❑ May 1957 Cover: 0.10 **NM** value: **30.00**
114 ❑ Jun 1957 Cover: 0.10 **NM** value: **30.00**
115 ❑ Jul 1957 Cover: 0.10 **NM** value: **30.00**
116 ❑ Aug 1957 Cover: 0.10 **NM** value: **30.00**
117 ❑ Sep 1957 Cover: 0.10 **NM** value: **30.00**
118 ❑ Oct 1957 Cover: 0.10 **NM** value: **30.00**
119 ❑ Nov 1957 Cover: 0.10 **NM** value: **30.00**
120 ❑ Dec 1957 Cover: 0.10 **NM** value: **30.00**
121 ❑ Jan 1958 Cover: 0.10 **NM** value: **30.00**
122 ❑ Feb 1958 Cover: 0.10 **NM** value: **30.00**
123 ❑ Mar 1958 Cover: 0.10 **NM** value: **30.00**
124 ❑ Apr 1958 Cover: 0.10 **NM** value: **30.00**
125 ❑ May 1958 Cover: 0.10 **NM** value: **30.00**
126 ❑ Jun 1958 Cover: 0.10 **NM** value: **30.00**
127 ❑ Jul 1958 Cover: 0.10 **NM** value: **30.00**
128 ❑ Sep 1958 Cover: 0.10 **NM** value: **30.00**
129 ❑ Nov 1958 Cover: 0.10 **NM** value: **30.00**
130 ❑ Jan 1959 Cover: 0.10 **NM** value: **30.00**
131 ❑ Mar 1959 Cover: 0.10 **NM** value: **30.00**
• **CGC:** 1 graded, best 9.4
132 ❑ Jul 1959 Cover: 0.10 **NM** value: **30.00**
133 ❑ Sep 1959 Cover: 0.10 **NM** value: **30.00**
• **CGC:** 1 graded, best 9.2
134 ❑ Nov 1959 Cover: 0.10 **NM** value: **30.00**
• **CGC:** 1 graded, best 9.4
135 ❑ Jan 1960 Cover: 0.10 **NM** value: **30.00**
136 ❑ Mar 1960 Cover: 0.10 **NM** value: **30.00**
137 ❑ May 1960 Cover: 0.10 **NM** value: **30.00**
138 ❑ Jul 1960 Cover: 0.10 **NM** value: **30.00**
139 ❑ Sep 1960 Cover: 0.10 **NM** value: **30.00**
140 ❑ Nov 1960 Cover: 0.10 **NM** value: **30.00**
141 ❑ Jan 1961 Cover: 0.10 **NM** value: **30.00**
142 ❑ Mar 1961 Cover: 0.10 **NM** value: **30.00**
• **CGC:** 1 graded, best 9.0
143 ❑ May 1961 Cover: 0.10 **NM** value: **30.00**
144 ❑ Jul 1961 Cover: 0.10 **NM** value: **30.00**
145 ❑ Sep 1961 Cover: 0.10 **NM** value: **30.00**
final issue.

ROY ROGERS: TRAIL OF ROBIN HOOD — AC
Bk 1 ❑ Cover: 12.00 **NM** value: **Cover or less**
• photo album; color and b&w

ROY ROGERS WESTERN — AC
1 ❑ b&w Cover: 4.95 **NM** value: **Cover or less**
📖 Roy Rogers: The Vengeance Trail; Dale Evans: The Old Cowboy; Roy Rogers: The Land Grabber **A:** Russ Manning **W:** Bill Black

ROY ROGERS WESTERN CLASSICS — AC
1 ❑ Cover: 2.95 **NM** value: **Cover or less**
• some color
2 ❑ Cover: 2.95 **NM** value: **Cover or less**
• some color
3 ❑ Cover: 3.95 **NM** value: **Cover or less**
• some color
4 ❑ Cover: 3.95 **NM** value: **Cover or less**
• some color
5 ❑ Cover: 2.95 **NM** value: **Cover or less**
• photos

RUBBER BLANKET — Rubber Blanket
1 ❑ b&w Cover: 5.75 **NM** value: **Cover or less**
2 ❑ Cover: 7.75 **NM** value: **Cover or less**
3 ❑ Cover: 7.95 **NM** value: **Cover or less**

RUBBER DUCK — Print Mint
1 ❑ Cover: 0.50 **NM** value: **3.00**
2 ❑ Cover: 0.50 **NM** value: **3.00**
📖 Hi Ho Platinum Away; Shishka-Bob the Wunda Hoss; Shit List **A:** Michael J. and Robbie Landeros **W:** Michael J. and Robbie Landeros

RUBES REVUE, THE — Fragments West
1 ❑ b&w Cover: 2.00 **NM** value: **Cover or less**

RUBY SHAFT'S TALES OF THE UNEXPURGATED — Fantagraphics / Eros
All issues are adults only.
1 ❑ b&w Cover: 2.50 **NM** value: **Cover or less**

RUCK BUD WEBSTER AND HIS SCREECHING COMMANDOS — Pyramid
1 ❑ b&w Cover: 1.60 **NM** value: **Cover or less**

RUDE AWAKENING — Dennis Mcmillan
1 ❑ Apr 1996, b&w Cover: 12.95 **NM** value: **Cover or less**

RUDOLPH THE RED-NOSED REINDEER — DC
1 ❑ Cover: 1.00 **NM** value: **15.00**
No issue number. • treasury-sized.

RUDOLPH THE RED-NOSED REINDEER ANNUAL — DC
Originally appearing in promotional comics from Montgomery Ward, the "most famous reindeer of all" appeared in a series of yearly one-shots published by DC from 1951 to 1962.

Written and drawn by Shelly Mayer, the stories often featured Rudolph getting into trouble in the off-season, usually with the aid of his pal, Grover Gopher.

After a series of additional misadventures, Rudolph would eventually save the day and return to Santa's workshop just in time to help with the Christmas rush. In addition to the delightful stories, each issue was rounded out with puzzle and activity pages. In the mid-1970s, many of the stories were reprinted in a series of over-sized treasury editions. — Brent

1950 ❑ Dec 1950 Cover: 0.10 **NM** value: **100.00**
1951 ❑ Dec 1951 Cover: 0.10 **NM** value: **80.00**
1952 ❑ Dec 1952 Cover: 0.10 **NM** value: **70.00**
1953 ❑ Dec 1953 Cover: 0.10 **NM** value: **70.00**
1954 ❑ Dec 1954 Cover: 0.10 **NM** value: **55.00**
1955 ❑ Dec 1955 Cover: 0.10 **NM** value: **55.00**
1956 ❑ Win 1956 Cover: 0.10 **NM** value: **55.00**
1957 ❑ Win 1957 Cover: 0.10 **NM** value: **45.00**
1958 ❑ Fal 1958 Cover: 0.10 **NM** value: **45.00**
1959 ❑ Win 1959 Cover: 0.10 **NM** value: **45.00**
• 1958-1959
1960 ❑ Win 1960 Cover: 0.10 **NM** value: **45.00**
1961 ❑ Win 1961 Cover: 0.10 **NM** value: **45.00**
• **CGC:** 1 graded, best 4.5
1962 ❑ Win 1962 Cover: 0.25 **NM** value: **70.00**
• **CGC:** 2 graded, best 8.0

RUGGED ACTION — Atlas
1 ❑ Dec 1954 Cover: 0.10 **NM** value: **100.00**
• **CGC:** 1 graded, best 8.0
2 ❑ Feb 1955 Cover: 0.10 **NM** value: **50.00**
3 ❑ Apr 1955 Cover: 0.10 **NM** value: **50.00**
4 ❑ Jun 1955 Cover: 0.10 **NM** value: **50.00**

RUGRATS COMIC ADVENTURES — Nickelodeon Magazines
1 ❑ 1997 Cover: 2.95 **NM** value: **3.50**
2 ❑ 1997 Cover: 2.95 **NM** value: **3.00**
3 ❑ 1998 Cover: 2.95 **NM** value: **3.00**
4 ❑ 1998 Cover: 2.95 **NM** value: **3.00**
5 ❑ 1998 Cover: 2.95 **NM** value: **3.00**
6 ❑ 1998 Cover: 2.95 **NM** value: **3.00**
7 ❑ 1998 Cover: 2.95 **NM** value: **3.00**
8 ❑ Jun 1998 Cover: 2.95 **NM** value: **3.00**
no cover price. • magazine.
9 ❑ 1998 Cover: 2.95 **NM** value: **3.00**
10 ❑ Aug 1998 Cover: 2.95 **NM** value: **3.00**
no cover price. • magazine.

RUGRATS COMIC ADVENTURES (VOL. 2) — Nickelodeon Magazines
1 ❑ Sep 1998 Cover: 2.95 **NM** value: **3.00**
no cover price. • magazine. 📖 Tales from the Crib!; Most Valuable Baby; Chocolate Chew Circle; Monster in the Basement

RUINS — Marvel
1 ❑ Aug 1995 Cover: 4.95 **NM** value: **Cover or less**
Circ: CapCity orders: **24,000**
Acetate cover overlaying cardstock inner cover. 📖 Men On Fire **A:** Cliff Nielsen; Terese Nielsen **W:** Warren Ellis
2 ❑ Sep 1995 Cover: 4.95 **NM** value: **Cover or less**
Acetate cover overlaying cardstock inner cover. 📖 Women In Flight **A:** Christopher Moeller; Cliff Nielsen; Terese Nelson **W:** Warren Ellis

Other grades: Multiply prices above by **1.5 for Mint • 2/3 for Very Fine • 1/3 for Fine • 1/5 for Very Good • 1/8 for Good**

RULAH JUNGLE GODDESS — Fox

17 ❑ Aug 1948 Cover: 0.10 **NM** value: **800.00**
• **CGC:** 2 graded, best 9.0
18 ❑ Sep 1948 Cover: 0.10 **NM** value: **600.00**
• **CGC:** 2 graded, best 8.0
19 ❑ Oct 1948 Cover: 0.10 **NM** value: **500.00**
• **CGC:** 2 graded, best 9.0
20 ❑ Nov 1948 Cover: 0.10 **NM** value: **500.00**
• **CGC:** 1 graded, best 8.0
21 ❑ Dec 1948 Cover: 0.10 **NM** value: **500.00**
• **CGC:** 1 graded, best 7.5
22 ❑ Jan 1949 Cover: 0.10 **NM** value: **500.00**
23 ❑ Feb 1949 Cover: 0.10 **NM** value: **400.00**
24 ❑ Mar 1949 Cover: 0.10 **NM** value: **400.00**
25 ❑ Apr 1949 Cover: 0.10 **NM** value: **400.00**
• **CGC:** 1 graded, best 8.0
26 ❑ May 1949 Cover: 0.10 **NM** value: **400.00**
• **CGC:** 1 graded, best 7.0
27 ❑ Jun 1949 Cover: 0.10 **NM** value: **400.00**

RUMBLE GIRLS: SILKY WARRIOR TANSIE — Image

1 ❑ Apr 2000 Cover: 3.50 **NM** value: **Cover or less**
Circ: Diamd. preorders: **5,889**
A: Lea Hernandez **W:** Lea Hernandez
2 ❑ Jun 2000 Cover: 3.50 **NM** value: **Cover or less**
Circ: Diamd. preorders: **3,411**
🕮 Speed! Candy! **A:** Lea Hernandez **W:** Lea Hernandez
3 ❑ Jul 2000 Cover: 3.50 **NM** value: **Cover or less**
Circ: Diamd. preorders: **3,162**
🕮 Sugar and Wax **A:** Lea Hernandez **W:** Lea Hernandez
4 ❑ Aug 2000 Cover: 3.50 **NM** value: **Cover or less**
Circ: Diamd. preorders: **2,753**
🕮 Sapphire Bullets **A:** Lea Hernandez **W:** Lea Hernandez
5 ❑ Nov 2000 Cover: 3.50 **NM** value: **Cover or less**
Circ: Diamd. preorders: **2,980**
🕮 It's Not Romantic **A:** Lea Hernandez **W:** Lea Hernandez
6 ❑ Jan 2001 Cover: 3.50 **NM** value: **Cover or less**
Circ: Diamd. preorders: **2,871**
🕮 Boy, Girl, Boy, Girl **A:** Lea Hernandez **W:** Lea Hernandez

RUMIC THEATER — Viz

Bk 1❑ b&w Cover: 15.95 **NM** value: **Cover or less**
Bk 2❑ Feb 1998, b&w Cover: 16.95 **NM** value: **Cover or less**

RUMIC WORLD — Viz

1 ❑ b&w Cover: 3.25 **NM** value: **Cover or less**
• Fire Tripper
2 ❑ b&w Cover: 3.50 **NM** value: **Cover or less**
• Laughing Target
Bk 1❑ Feb 1993, b&w Cover: 14.95 **NM** value: **Cover or less**

RUMIC WORLD TRILOGY — Viz

Bk 1❑ b&w Cover: 15.95 **NM** value: **Cover or less**
Bk 2❑ b&w Cover: 15.95 **NM** value: **Cover or less**
Bk 3❑ b&w Cover: 15.95 **NM** value: **Cover or less**

RUMMAGE $2099 — Parody Press

1 ❑ Cover: 2.95 **NM** value: **Cover or less**
foil cover. 🕮 Spirits of Whispers of the Dark Miniseries of Vengeance, Part 2 **A:** Bob Hanon **W:** Ross Turner

RUNAWAY-A KNOWN ASSOCIATES MYSTERY — Known Associates

1 ❑ b&w Cover: 2.50 **NM** value: **Cover or less**
No issue number. One-shot.

RUNE — Malibu / Ultraverse

One of Malibu's last major launches before being gobbled up by Marvel, this series by Barry Windsor-Smith depicts Erik Johnson, a boy plagued by dreams of an otherworldly vampire named Rune who's out to kill him. Then, one night, his dream comes crashing through his bedroom window.

Erik's parents hear the commotion and rush into their son's room only to have the demon, with its horrible fangs, kill Erik's father. It's then that Erik discovers some sort of power within himself — one which sends the demon crashing into a pole some 15 miles away.

Immediately, a cover-up begins, with both the demon and Erik's family spirited away to secret facilities. There, they discover that the horror has just begun...

0 ❑ Jan 1994 **NM** value: **3.00**
no cover price. • Promotional edition (from redeeming coupons in early Ultraverse comics). **A:** Barry Windsor-Smith **W:** Barry Windsor-Smith; Chris Ulm
1 ❑ Jan 1994 Cover: 1.95 **NM** value: **2.00**
Circ: CapCity orders: **40,925**
A: Barry Windsor-Smith **W:** Barry Windsor-Smith; Chris Ulm
1/SC❑Jan 1994 Cover: 1.95 **NM** value: **2.00**
• Foil limited edition. • silver foil logo **A:** Barry Windsor-Smith **W:** Barry Windsor-Smith; Chris Ulm
2 ❑ Feb 1994 Cover: 1.95 **NM** value: **Cover or less**
Circ: CapCity orders: **24,075**
🕮 The Source **A:** Barry Windsor-Smith **W:** Barry Windsor-Smith; Chris Ulm
3 ❑ Mar 1994 Cover: 3.50 **NM** value: **Cover or less**
Circ: CapCity orders: **24,725**
🕮 The Spoils Of War; Ripfire; Warstrike; Elven; Blue Prints • Flip-book with Ultraverse Premiere #1 **A:** Barry Windsor-Smith; Greg Luzniak; Hoang Nguyen; Darick Robertson; Alex Bialy **W:** Barry Windsor-Smith; Darick Robertson; Chris Ulm; Dan Danko; Len Strazewski ★ 1st Appearance of Ripfire, Elven.
4 ❑ Jun 1994 Cover: 1.95 **NM** value: **Cover or less**
Circ: CapCity orders: **19,900**
5 ❑ Sep 1994 Cover: 1.95 **NM** value: **Cover or less**
Circ: CapCity orders: **18,775**
🕮 Gemini **A:** Barry Windsor-Smith **W:** Barry Windsor-Smith; Chris Ulm
6 ❑ Dec 1994 Cover: 1.95 **NM** value: **Cover or less**
Circ: CapCity orders: **17,800**
A: Barry Windsor-Smith **W:** Barry Windsor-Smith; Chris Ulm
7 ❑ Feb 1995 Cover: 1.95 **NM** value: **Cover or less**
Circ: CapCity orders: **11,350**
🕮 Rise of the Gods, Part 1 **A:** Javier Saltares **W:** Chris Ulm
8 ❑ Feb 1995 Cover: 1.95 **NM** value: **Cover or less**
Circ: CapCity orders: **10,250**
🕮 Rise of the Gods, Part 2 **A:** Richard Pace; Craig Babiar **W:** Chris Ulm
9 ❑ Apr 1995 Cover: 1.95 **NM** value: **Cover or less**
Circ: CapCity orders: **9,325**
🕮 Rise of the Gods, Part 3 **A:** Jeff Moore; Keith Conroy; Barry Windsor-Smith(cover) **W:** Chris Ulm ★ Death of Sybil. ★ Death of Master Oshi. ★ Death of Tantalus.
Bk 1❑ Cover: 12.95 **NM** value: **Cover or less**
• Trade Paperback. • Reprints Rune #1-5 **W:** Barry Windsor-Smith; Chris Ulm
GS 1❑ Cover: 2.50 **NM** value: **Cover or less**
Circ: CapCity orders: **12,650**
• Giant-size Rune #1. **A:** Barry Windsor-Smith; John Floyd **W:** Barry Windsor-Smith; Chris Ulm ★ Origin of Rune. ★ 1st Appearance of Sybil, Master Oshi, Tantalus. ★ Death of El Gato.

RUNE: HEARTS OF DARKNESS — Malibu

1 ❑ Sep 1996 Cover: 1.50 **NM** value: **Cover or less**
Circ: Diamd. preorders: **14,980**
• Flip-book.
2 ❑ Oct 1996 Cover: 1.50 **NM** value: **Cover or less**
Circ: Diamd. preorders: **12,425**
• Flip-book.
3 ❑ Nov 1996 Cover: 1.50 **NM** value: **Cover or less**
Circ: Diamd. preorders: **11,594**
• Flip-book.

RUNE/SILVER SURFER — Marvel

1 ❑ Apr 1995 Cover: 2.95 **NM** value: **3.00**
Circ: CapCity orders: **13,025**
• newsstand edition. 🕮 Into Infinity • crossover **A:** Henry Flint; Barry Windsor-Smith(cover) **W:** Chris Ulm; Dan Danko
1/DM❑Apr 1995 Cover: 5.95 **NM** value: **6.00**
Circ: CapCity orders: **6,300**
• Direct Market edition. • crossover; Squarebound with glossier paper

RUNE VS. VENOM — Malibu / Ultraverse

1 ❑ Dec 1995 Cover: 3.95 **NM** value: **Cover or less**
🕮 Rune-Venom **A:** Greg Luzniak; Gabriel Gecko; Mark Pacella **W:** Chris Ulm

RUNE (VOL. 2) — Malibu / Ultraverse

0 ❑ Sep 1995 Cover: 1.50 **NM** value: **Cover or less**
black cover. 🕮 Curse Of Rune: Day For Night • Black September; Rune #¦ (Infinity) **A:** Kyle Hotz **W:** Len Kaminski
0/SC❑Sep 1995 Cover: 1.50 **NM** value: **2.00**
alternate cover. 🕮 Curse Of Rune: Day For Night • Rune #¦ (Infinity) **A:** Kyle Hotz **W:** Len Kaminski
1 ❑ Oct 1995 Cover: 1.50 **NM** value: **Cover or less**
A: Kyle Hotz **W:** Len Kaminski ★ Appearance of Gemini, Adam Warlock, Annihilus.
2 ❑ Nov 1995 Cover: 1.50 **NM** value: **Cover or less**
🕮 The Quality of Mercy **A:** Kyle Hotz **W:** Len Kaminski
3 ❑ Dec 1995 Cover: 1.50 **NM** value: **Cover or less**
🕮 Tooth and Claw **A:** Steve Ellis **W:** Len Kaminski
4 ❑ Jan 1996 Cover: 1.50 **NM** value: **Cover or less**
5 ❑ Feb 1996 Cover: 1.50 **NM** value: **Cover or less**
6 ❑ Mar 1996 Cover: 1.50 **NM** value: **Cover or less**
7 ❑ Apr 1996 Cover: 1.50 **NM** value: **Cover or less**
final issue.

RUNE/WRATH — Malibu / Ultraverse

1 ❑ **NM** value: **1.00**
• gold foil ashcan

RUSE — CrossGen

Set in the CrossGen universe, Ruse's early issues did not display the CrossGen Sigil but introduced a fantasy element to the seeming Victorian world of detection, although obviously on a different world than Earth. Detective Simon Archard is a brilliant sleuth in the mold of Sherlock Holmes whose seeming assistant, Emma Bishop, has special powers and is playing some sort of fantasy game.

Written by Mark Waid and drawn by Butch Guice, the series immediately plunged the detecting pair into life-threatening controversy.

— Maggie

1 ❑ Nov 2001 Cover: 2.95 **NM** value: **Cover or less**
• **CGC:** 2 graded, best 9.8
2 ❑ Dec 2001 Cover: 2.95 **NM** value: **Cover or less**
3 ❑ Jan 2002 Cover: 2.95 **NM** value: **Cover or less**
4 ❑ Feb 2002 Cover: 2.95 **NM** value: **Cover or less**
5 ❑ Mar 2002 Cover: 2.95 **NM** value: **Cover or less**

RUSH LIMBAUGH MUST DIE — Boneyard

All issues are adults only.

1 ❑ Nov 1993, b&w Cover: 3.95 **NM** value: **5.00**
No issue number.

RUST — Now

1 ❑ Jul 1987 Cover: 1.50 **NM** value: **2.00**
2 ❑ Aug 1987 Cover: 1.50 **NM** value: **2.00**
3 ❑ Sep 1987 Cover: 1.50 **NM** value: **2.00**
4 ❑ Nov 1987 Cover: 1.75 **NM** value: **2.00**
Circ: CapCity orders: **1,850**
5 ❑ Dec 1987 Cover: 1.75 **NM** value: **2.00**
Circ: CapCity orders: **1,900**
6 ❑ Jan 1988 Cover: 1.50 **NM** value: **2.00**
Circ: CapCity orders: **1,950**
7 ❑ Feb 1988 Cover: 1.75 **NM** value: **2.00**
Circ: CapCity orders: **1,775**
8 ❑ Mar 1988 Cover: 1.50 **NM** value: **2.00**
Circ: CapCity orders: **1,650**
9 ❑ Apr 1988 Cover: 1.75 **NM** value: **2.00**
Circ: CapCity orders: **1,500**
10 ❑ May 1988 Cover: 1.75 **NM** value: **2.00**
Circ: CapCity orders: **1,450**
11 ❑ Jul 1988 Cover: 1.75 **NM** value: **2.00**
Circ: CapCity orders: **1,350**
12 ❑ Aug 1988 Cover: 1.75 **NM** value: **2.00**
Circ: CapCity orders: **1,250**
• Terminator preview
13 ❑ Sep 1988 Cover: 1.75 **NM** value: **2.00**
Circ: CapCity orders: **1,225**

RUST (2ND SERIES) — Now

1 ❑ Feb 1989 Cover: 1.75 **NM** value: **2.00**
Circ: CapCity orders: **1,775**
2 ❑ Mar 1989 Cover: 1.75 **NM** value: **2.00**
Circ: CapCity orders: **1,525**
3 ❑ Apr 1989 Cover: 1.75 **NM** value: **2.00**
Circ: CapCity orders: **1,625**
4 ❑ May 1989 Cover: 1.75 **NM** value: **2.00**
Circ: CapCity orders: **1,975**
5 ❑ Jun 1989 Cover: 1.75 **NM** value: **2.00**
Circ: CapCity orders: **1,975**
6 ❑ Aug 1989 Cover: 1.75 **NM** value: **2.00**
Circ: CapCity orders: **1,950**
7 ❑ Sep 1989 Cover: 1.75 **NM** value: **2.00**
Circ: CapCity orders: **2,000**

RUST (3RD SERIES) — Adventure

1 ❑ Apr 1992, full color Cover: 2.95 **NM** value: **Cover or less**
Circ: CapCity orders: **6,730**
• Adventure Comics **A:** Phil Hester **W:** Steve Miller ★ Origin of Rust.
1/LE❑ Apr 1992 Cover: 4.95 **NM** value: **Cover or less**
cardstock cover. • limited edition. • rust-colored foil logo
2 ❑ Jun 1992 Cover: 2.95 **NM** value: **Cover or less**
Circ: CapCity orders: **3,650**
A: Phil Hester **W:** Steve Miller
3 ❑ Aug 1992, full color Cover: 2.95 **NM** value: **Cover or less**
Circ: CapCity orders: **3,210**
🕮 Sandblasting **A:** Phil Hester **W:** Steve Miller
4 ❑ Sep 1992 Cover: 2.95 **NM** value: **Cover or less**
🕮 Recycled **A:** Phil Hester **W:** Steve Miller

RUST (4TH SERIES) — Caliber

1 ❑ Cover: 2.95 **NM** value: **Cover or less**
🕮 Hazing Part 1 **A:** Mike Huddleston **W:** Steve Miller
2 ❑ Cover: 2.95 **NM** value: **Cover or less**
🕮 Hazing Part 2 **A:** Mike Huddleston **W:** Steve Miller

RUSTY — Marvel

Rusty was another in the stable of nearly interchangeable teen-age humor comics published by Marvel in the 1940s and 1950s (others included Mitzi and the long-lived Millie the Model).

Redheaded heartthrob Rusty spends her days planning how to manipulate her boyfriends and foil her jealous female rivals while contriving to appear in all manner of slinky dresses and lingerie. Events are punctuated by madcap sub-Archie-caliber humor and goofy artwork solidly in the teen comic genre.

Every so often, readers would find a treat in the back pages, with a short Hey Look! feature by Mad-man Harvey Kurtzman or a bit of inspired looniness from the pen of Basil Wolverton.

12 ❑ ca. 1947 Cover: 0.10 **NM** value: **55.00**
13 ❑ ca. 1947 Cover: 0.10 **NM** value: **40.00**
14 ❑ ca. 1947 Cover: 0.10 **NM** value: **60.00**
A: Harvey Kurtzman; Basil Wolverton
15 ❑ ca. 1947 Cover: 0.10 **NM** value: **48.00**
A: Harvey Kurtzman
16 ❑ ca. 1948 Cover: 0.10 **NM** value: **48.00**
A: Harvey Kurtzman
17 ❑ ca. 1948 Cover: 0.10 **NM** value: **48.00**
A: Harvey Kurtzman
18 ❑ ca. 1948 Cover: 0.10 **NM** value: **30.00**
19 ❑ ca. 1948 Cover: 0.10 **NM** value: **30.00**

CGC-graded: Multiply prices above by **33 for 9.9 M • 16 for 9.8 NM/M • 7 for 9.6 NM+ • 5 for 9.4 NM • 2.5 for 9.2 NM- • 1.5 for 9.0 VF/NM**

20 ❑ ca. 1949 Cover: 0.10 **NM** value: **55.00**
A: Harvey Kurtzman
21 ❑ ca. 1949 Cover: 0.10 **NM** value: **60.00**
A: Harvey Kurtzman
22 ❑ ca. 1949 Cover: 0.10 **NM** value: **60.00**
final issue. **A:** Harvey Kurtzman

RUSTY, BOY DETECTIVE — Lev Gleason

1 ❑ Mar 1955 Cover: 0.10 **NM** value: **50.00**
2 ❑ May 1955 Cover: 0.10 **NM** value: **30.00**
3 ❑ Jul 1955 Cover: 0.10 **NM** value: **30.00**
4 ❑ Sep 1955 Cover: 0.10 **NM** value: **30.00**
5 ❑ Nov 1955 Cover: 0.10 **NM** value: **30.00**

SAARI — P.L. Publishing

1 ❑ Nov 1951 Cover: 0.10 **NM** value: **350.00**
• **CGC:** 1 graded, best 8.0

SABAN POWERHOUSE — Acclaim

1 ❑ ca. 1997 Cover: 4.50 **NM** value: **Cover or less**
• digest. • Power Rangers Turbo, Masked Rider, Samurai Pizza Cats; no indicia
2 ❑ ca. 1997 Cover: 4.50 **NM** value: **Cover or less**
• digest. • Power Rangers Turbo, Masked Rider, Samurai Pizza Cats, BettleBorgs

SABAN PRESENTS POWER RANGERS TURBO VS. BEETLEBORGS METALLIX — Acclaim

1 ❑ ca. 1997 Cover: 4.50 **NM** value: **Cover or less**
No issue number. • digest.

SABER TIGER — Viz

1 ❑ b&w Cover: 12.95 **NM** value: **Cover or less**
No issue number.

SABINA — Eros

1 ❑ Cover: 2.95 **NM** value: **Cover or less**
A: Paul Naring **W:** Martin Lock
2 ❑ Cover: 2.95 **NM** value: **Cover or less**
A: Paul Naring **W:** Martin Lock
3 ❑ Cover: 2.95 **NM** value: **Cover or less**
A: Paul Naring **W:** Martin Lock
4 ❑ Cover: 2.95 **NM** value: **Cover or less**
A: Paul Naring **W:** Martin Lock
5 ❑ Cover: 2.95 **NM** value: **Cover or less**
A: Paul Naring **W:** Martin Lock
6 ❑ Cover: 2.95 **NM** value: **Cover or less**
A: Paul Naring **W:** Martin Lock
7 ❑ Jul 1996 Cover: 2.95 **NM** value: **Cover or less**
📖 The Rivals **A:** Paul Naring **W:** Martin Lock

SABLE — First

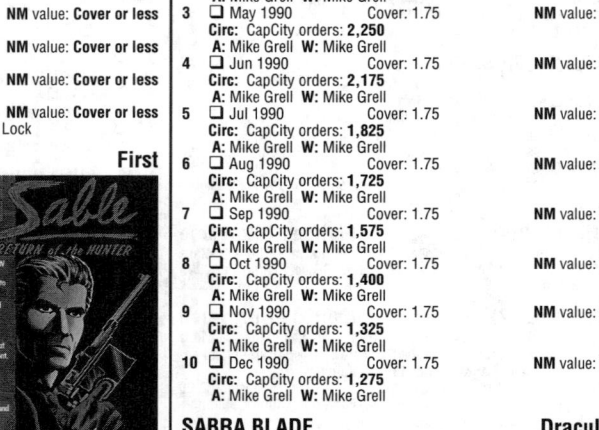

Although the name has changed from Jon Sable, Freelance to simply Sable (in part to reflect a short-lived TV-series by that name), the action remains the same. Mike Grell's noble mercenary still brings a sense of adventure to each issue, fighting for money and justice from the jungles of Vietnam to the human jungle of New York City. Along the way, this series handles such issues as AIDS with a striking sensitivity.

Sable also has another identity: children's book author B.B. Flemm. The secret of Sable's double life is known only to to his editor, Eden Kendall. Although this "secret identity" rarely causes Sable much trouble, it does make for an interesting contrast with his violent persona as Sable the freelance paladin.

This second Sable series features new creative team Marv Wolfman and Bill Jaaska.

1 ❑ Mar 1988 Cover: 1.75 **NM** value: **2.00**
Circ: CapCity orders: **10,150**
📖 Resting Place **A:** Bill Jaaska **W:** Marv Wolfman
2 ❑ Apr 1988 Cover: 1.75 **NM** value: **2.00**
Circ: CapCity orders: **6,675**
3 ❑ May 1988 Cover: 1.75 **NM** value: **2.00**
Circ: CapCity orders: **7,150**
4 ❑ Jun 1988 Cover: 1.75 **NM** value: **2.00**
Circ: CapCity orders: **6,650**
5 ❑ Jul 1988 Cover: 1.75 **NM** value: **2.00**
Circ: CapCity orders: **6,675**
📖 Fatal Mistakes **A:** Denys Cowan **W:** Marv Wolfman
6 ❑ Aug 1988 Cover: 1.75 **NM** value: **2.00**
Circ: CapCity orders: **6,625**
📖 ...Painful To Get As Well As Keep **A:** Bill Jaaska **W:** Marv Wolfman
7 ❑ Sep 1988 Cover: 1.75 **NM** value: **2.00**
Circ: CapCity orders: **6,425**
📖 ...Into The Toxic Wasteland **A:** Bill Jaaska **W:** Marv Wolfman
8 ❑ Oct 1988 Cover: 1.95 **NM** value: **2.00**
Circ: CapCity orders: **5,925**
9 ❑ Nov 1988 Cover: 1.95 **NM** value: **2.00**
Circ: CapCity orders: **5,475**
📖 Into The Heart Of Darkness **A:** Bill Jaaska **W:** Marv Wolfman
10 ❑ Dec 1988 Cover: 1.95 **NM** value: **2.00**
Circ: CapCity orders: **5,500**
11 ❑ Jan 1989 Cover: 1.95 **NM** value: **2.00**
Circ: CapCity orders: **5,150**
📖 Word Of Honor **A:** Tristan Schane **W:** Roger Salick
12 ❑ Feb 1989 Cover: 1.95 **NM** value: **2.00**
Circ: CapCity orders: **4,950**
13 ❑ Mar 1989 Cover: 1.95 **NM** value: **2.00**
Circ: CapCity orders: **4,975**
14 ❑ Apr 1989 Cover: 1.95 **NM** value: **2.00**
Circ: CapCity orders: **4,950**
📖 And The Creatures Were Stirring **A:** Bill Jaaska **W:** Cherie Wilkerson; Marv Wolfman
15 ❑ May 1989 Cover: 1.95 **NM** value: **2.00**
Circ: CapCity orders: **4,700**
📖 Art In The Blood, Part 1 **A:** Bill Jaaska **W:** Cherie Wilkerson; Marv Wolfman
16 ❑ Jun 1989 Cover: 1.95 **NM** value: **2.00**
Circ: CapCity orders: **4,600**
📖 Art In The Blood, Part 2 **A:** Bill Jaaska **W:** Cherie Wilkerson; Marv Wolfman
17 ❑ Jul 1989 Cover: 1.95 **NM** value: **2.00**
Circ: CapCity orders: **4,550**
18 ❑ Aug 1989 Cover: 1.95 **NM** value: **2.00**
Circ: CapCity orders: **4,650**
19 ❑ Sep 1989 Cover: 1.95 **NM** value: **2.00**
Circ: CapCity orders: **4,525**
20 ❑ Oct 1989 Cover: 1.95 **NM** value: **2.00**
Circ: CapCity orders: **4,625**
21 ❑ Nov 1989 Cover: 1.95 **NM** value: **2.00**
Circ: CapCity orders: **4,525**
22 ❑ Dec 1989 Cover: 1.95 **NM** value: **2.00**
Circ: CapCity orders: **4,550**
23 ❑ Jan 1990 Cover: 1.95 **NM** value: **2.00**
Circ: CapCity orders: **4,450**
24 ❑ Feb 1990 Cover: 1.95 **NM** value: **2.00**
Circ: CapCity orders: **4,175**
25 ❑ Mar 1990 Cover: 1.95 **NM** value: **2.00**
Circ: CapCity orders: **4,300**
26 ❑ Apr 1990 Cover: 1.95 **NM** value: **2.00**
Circ: CapCity orders: **4,200**
27 ❑ May 1990 Cover: 1.95 **NM** value: **2.00**
Circ: CapCity orders: **3,975**

SABLE (MIKE GRELL'S...) — First

1 ❑ Mar 1990 Cover: 1.75 **NM** value: **2.00**
Circ: CapCity orders: **2,850**
📖 The Iron Monster • Reprints Jon Sable, Freelance #1 **A:** Mike Grell **W:** Mike Grell
2 ❑ Apr 1990 Cover: 1.75 **NM** value: **2.00**
Circ: CapCity orders: **2,500**
A: Mike Grell **W:** Mike Grell
3 ❑ May 1990 Cover: 1.75 **NM** value: **2.00**
Circ: CapCity orders: **2,250**
A: Mike Grell **W:** Mike Grell
4 ❑ Jun 1990 Cover: 1.75 **NM** value: **2.00**
Circ: CapCity orders: **2,175**
A: Mike Grell **W:** Mike Grell
5 ❑ Jul 1990 Cover: 1.75 **NM** value: **2.00**
Circ: CapCity orders: **1,825**
A: Mike Grell **W:** Mike Grell
6 ❑ Aug 1990 Cover: 1.75 **NM** value: **2.00**
Circ: CapCity orders: **1,725**
A: Mike Grell **W:** Mike Grell
7 ❑ Sep 1990 Cover: 1.75 **NM** value: **2.00**
Circ: CapCity orders: **1,575**
A: Mike Grell **W:** Mike Grell
8 ❑ Oct 1990 Cover: 1.75 **NM** value: **2.00**
Circ: CapCity orders: **1,400**
A: Mike Grell **W:** Mike Grell
9 ❑ Nov 1990 Cover: 1.75 **NM** value: **2.00**
Circ: CapCity orders: **1,325**
A: Mike Grell **W:** Mike Grell
10 ❑ Dec 1990 Cover: 1.75 **NM** value: **2.00**
Circ: CapCity orders: **1,275**
A: Mike Grell **W:** Mike Grell

SABRA BLADE — Draculina

1 ❑ Dec 1994, b&w Cover: 2.50 **NM** value: **Cover or less**
1/SC❑ Dec 1994, b&w Cover: 2.50 **NM** value: **Cover or less**
alternate two-color cover.

SABRE — Eclipse

A remarkable comic by Paul Gulacy and Don McGregor, Sabre is the tale of the struggle for freedom in a world gone mad. The Eclipse series continues the story they began in Eclipse Graphic Album #1, regarded to be the first direct-sale graphic novel.

Sabre's future is not a nice place in which to live. The world is ravaged by multiple energy crises and a nine-year drought. A biological weapon has been inadvertently released into the atmosphere. Nuclear spillage had rendered the entire states of Oklahoma, Wisconsin, and Rhode Island inhabitable. As terrorism and violence destroyed the last vestiges of the "civilized world," the government retreated to a central fortress.

Now led by a cyborg called the Overseer, what's left of authority leads with an iron fist. But even then, there are still those, led by a poetic renegade named Sabre, who dare to fight back.

1 ❑ Aug 1982 Cover: 1.00 **NM** value: **2.50**
📖 Slow Fade Of An Endangered Species **A:** Paul Gulacy **W:** Don McGregor ★ 1st Appearance of Sabre.
2 ❑ Oct 1982 Cover: 1.00 **NM** value: **2.00**
📖 Slow Fade Of An Endangered Species **A:** Paul Gulacy **W:** Don McGregor
3 ❑ Dec 1982 Cover: 1.00 **NM** value: **2.00**
📖 Exploitation Of Everything Dear, Part 1 **A:** Paul Gulacy **W:** Don McGregor
4 ❑ Mar 1983 Cover: 1.50 **NM** value: **2.00**
📖 Exploitation Of Everything Dear, Part 2 **A:** Billy Graham **W:** Don McGregor
5 ❑ Jul 1983 Cover: 1.50 **NM** value: **2.00**
📖 Exploitation Of Everything Dear, Part 3 **A:** Billy Graham **W:** Don McGregor
6 ❑ Oct 1983 Cover: 1.50 **NM** value: **2.00**
📖 Exploitation Of Everything Dear, Part 4 **A:** Billy Graham **W:** Don McGregor
7 ❑ Dec 1983 Cover: 1.50 **NM** value: **2.00**
📖 Exploitation Of Everything Dear, Part 5 **A:** Billy Graham **W:** Don McGregor
8 ❑ Feb 1984 Cover: 1.50 **NM** value: **2.00**
📖 Exploitation Of Everything Dear, Part 6 **A:** Billy Graham **W:** Don McGregor
9 ❑ Apr 1984 Cover: 1.50 **NM** value: **2.00**
📖 Exploitation Of Everything Dear, Part 7 **A:** Billy Graham **W:** Don McGregor
10 ❑ Jun 1984 Cover: 1.50 **NM** value: **1.75**
📖 The Decadence Indoctrination, Part 1 **A:** José Ortiz **W:** Don McGregor
11 ❑ Aug 1984 Cover: 1.75 **NM** value: **Cover or less**
📖 The Decadence Indoctrination, Part 2 **A:** José Ortiz **W:** Don McGregor
12 ❑ Jan 1985 Cover: 1.75 **NM** value: **Cover or less**
📖 The Decadence Indoctrination, Part 3 **A:** José Ortiz **W:** Don McGregor
13 ❑ Apr 1985 Cover: 1.75 **NM** value: **Cover or less**
📖 The Decadence Indoctrination, Part 4 **A:** José Ortiz **W:** Don McGregor
14 ❑ Aug 1985 Cover: 2.00 **NM** value: **Cover or less**
📖 The Decadence Indoctrination, Part 5 **A:** José Ortiz **W:** Don McGregor
Bk 1❑ Cover: 6.95 **NM** value: **Cover or less**
• 10th anniversary edition trade paperback.
Bk 1/LE❑ Cover: 24.95 **NM** value: **Cover or less**
• 10th anniversary edition special.
Bk 2❑ b&w Cover: 12.95 **NM** value: **Cover or less**
• 20th anniversary edition.

SABRE: 20TH ANNIVERSARY EDITION — Image

1 ❑ Cover: 12.95 **NM** value: **Cover or less**
A: Paul Gulacy **W:** Don McGregor

SABRETOOTH — Marvel

1 ❑ Aug 1993 Cover: 2.95 **NM** value: **3.00**
Circ: CapCity orders: **162,500** • **CGC:** 22 graded, best 9.9
Die-cut cover. 📖 Home Is The Hunter **A:** Mark Texeira **W:** Larry Hama
2 ❑ Sep 1993 Cover: 2.95 **NM** value: **3.00**
Circ: CapCity orders: **90,000** • **CGC:** 1 graded, best 9.6
A: Mark Texeira **W:** Larry Hama
3 ❑ Oct 1993 Cover: 2.95 **NM** value: **3.00**
Circ: CapCity orders: **75,300** • **CGC:** 1 graded, best 9.8
cardstock cover. 📖 City Of Light, City Of Night! **A:** Mark Texeira **W:** Larry Hama ★ Appearance of Mystique.
4 ❑ Nov 1993 Cover: 2.95 **NM** value: **3.00**
Circ: CapCity orders: **76,500** • **CGC:** 5 graded, best 9.6
Bk 1❑ Cover: 12.95 **NM** value: **Cover or less**
• Collects Sabretooth #1-4
SE 1❑ Jan 1995 Cover: 4.95 **NM** value: **Cover or less**
• **CGC:** 10 graded, best 9.9
One-shot. enhanced wraparound cover. • Special edition. 📖 In the Red Zone **A:** Gary Frank **W:** Fabian Nicieza

SABRETOOTH CLASSIC — Marvel

1 ❑ May 1994 Cover: 1.50 **NM** value: **2.00**
Circ: Statement: **40,898**
• reprints Power Man & Iron Fist #66
2 ❑ Jun 1994 Cover: 1.50 **NM** value: **Cover or less**
Circ: Statement: **40,898**
📖 Slasher • reprints Power Man & Iron Fist #78 **A:** Kerry Gammill **W:** Mary Jo Duffy
3 ❑ Jul 1994 Cover: 1.50 **NM** value: **Cover or less**
Circ: Statement: **40,898**
• reprints Power Man & Iron Fist #84
4 ❑ Aug 1994 Cover: 1.50 **NM** value: **Cover or less**
Circ: Statement: **40,898**
• reprints Peter Parker; The Spectacular Spider-Man #116; reprints Peter Parker, The Spectacular Spider-Man #116
5 ❑ Sep 1994 Cover: 1.50 **NM** value: **Cover or less**
Circ: Statement: **40,898**
• reprints Peter Parker; The Spectacular Spider-Man #119; reprints Peter Parker, The Spectacular Spider-Man #119
6 ❑ Oct 1994 Cover: 1.50 **NM** value: **Cover or less**
Circ: Statement: **40,898**
• reprints X-Factor #10
7 ❑ Nov 1994 Cover: 1.50 **NM** value: **Cover or less**
Circ: Statement: **40,898**
• reprints The Mighty Thor #374
8 ❑ Dec 1994 Cover: 1.50 **NM** value: **Cover or less**
Circ: Statement: **40,898**
• reprints Power Pack #27
9 ❑ Jan 1995 Cover: 1.50 **NM** value: **Cover or less**
• reprints Uncanny X-Men #212
10 ❑ Feb 1995 Cover: 1.50 **NM** value: **Cover or less**
• reprints Uncanny X-Men #213
11 ❑ Mar 1995 Cover: 1.50 **NM** value: **Cover or less**
Circ: CapCity orders: **5,175**
• reprints Daredevil #238
12 ❑ Apr 1995 Cover: 1.50 **NM** value: **Cover or less**
Circ: CapCity orders: **5,125**
• reprints back-up stories from Classic X-Men #10 and Marvel Super-Heroes (no issue given); Has 1994 Statement, filed 10/1/94; avg print run 66,758; avg sales 40,723; avg subs 175; avg total paid 40,898; samples 125; office use 500; max existent 41,523; 38% of run returned

Other grades: Multiply prices above by **1.5 for Mint • 2/3 for Very Fine • 1/3 for Fine • 1/5 for Very Good • 1/8 for Good**

13 ❑ May 1995 Cover: 1.50 **NM** value: **Cover or less**
Circ: CapCity orders: **4,450**
• reprints Uncanny X-Men #219

14 ❑ Jun 1995 Cover: 1.50 **NM** value: **Cover or less**
Circ: CapCity orders: **4,375**
• reprints Uncanny X-Men #221

15 ❑ Jul 1995 Cover: 1.50 **NM** value: **Cover or less**
Circ: CapCity orders: **3,925**
• reprints Uncanny X-Men #222

SABRINA — Archie

1 ❑ May 1997 Cover: 1.50 **NM** value: **2.50**
Circ: Diamd. preorders: **7,931**
📖 The Cleopatra Chronicles, Part 1; Queen of Denial; Show News Is New News (text); Sabrina's Bewitching Style; Picky Eater **A:** Dan Decarlo **W:** Bill Golliher; Dan Parent

2 ❑ Jun 1997 Cover: 1.50 **NM** value: **2.00**
Circ: Diamd. preorders: **7,047**
📖 The Cleopatra Chronicles, Part 2

3 ❑ Jul 1997 Cover: 1.50 **NM** value: **2.00**
Circ: Diamd. preorders: **6,621**
📖 The Cleopatra Chronicles, Part 3

4 ❑ Aug 1997 Cover: 1.50 **NM** value: **Cover or less**
Circ: Diamd. preorders: **6,382**

5 ❑ Sep 1997 Cover: 1.50 **NM** value: **Cover or less**
Circ: Diamd. preorders: **6,778**

6 ❑ Oct 1997 Cover: 1.50 **NM** value: **Cover or less**
Circ: Diamd. preorders: **6,986**

7 ❑ Nov 1997 Cover: 1.50 **NM** value: **Cover or less**
Circ: Diamd. preorders: **7,008**

8 ❑ Dec 1997 Cover: 1.50 **NM** value: **Cover or less**
Circ: Diamd. preorders: **6,797**

9 ❑ Jan 1998 Cover: 1.75 **NM** value: **Cover or less**
Circ: Diamd. preorders: **7,135**

10 ❑ Feb 1998 Cover: 1.75 **NM** value: **Cover or less**
Circ: Diamd. preorders: **7,208**

11 ❑ Mar 1998 Cover: 1.75 **NM** value: **Cover or less**
Circ: Diamd. preorders: **6,858**

12 ❑ Apr 1998 Cover: 1.75 **NM** value: **Cover or less**
Circ: Diamd. preorders: **6,857**

13 ❑ May 1998 Cover: 1.75 **NM** value: **Cover or less**
Circ: Diamd. preorders: **6,270**

14 ❑ Jun 1998 Cover: 1.75 **NM** value: **Cover or less**
Circ: Diamd. preorders: **6,264**

15 ❑ Jul 1998 Cover: 1.75 **NM** value: **Cover or less**
Circ: Diamd. preorders: **6,469**

16 ❑ Aug 1998 Cover: 1.75 **NM** value: **Cover or less**
Circ: Diamd. preorders: **6,138**

17 ❑ Sep 1998 Cover: 1.75 **NM** value: **Cover or less**
Circ: Diamd. preorders: **6,703**
★ Appearance of Josie & the Pussycats.

18 ❑ Oct 1998 Cover: 1.75 **NM** value: **Cover or less**
Circ: Diamd. preorders: **6,079**

19 ❑ Nov 1998 Cover: 1.75 **NM** value: **Cover or less**
Circ: Diamd. preorders: **5,736**
Photo cover. • back to the '60s **A:** Dan Decarlo **W:** Bill Golliher; Dan Parent

20 ❑ Dec 1998 Cover: 1.75 **NM** value: **Cover or less**
Circ: Diamd. preorders: **5,920**

21 ❑ Jan 1999 Cover: 1.75 **NM** value: **Cover or less**
Circ: Diamd. preorders: **5,992**

22 ❑ Feb 1999 Cover: 1.75 **NM** value: **Cover or less**
Circ: Diamd. preorders: **5,759**

23 ❑ Mar 1999 Cover: 1.75 **NM** value: **Cover or less**
Circ: Diamd. preorders: **5,606**

24 ❑ Apr 1999 Cover: 1.79 **NM** value: **Cover or less**
Circ: Diamd. preorders: **5,434**

25 ❑ May 1999 Cover: 1.79 **NM** value: **Cover or less**
Circ: Diamd. preorders: **5,356**

26 ❑ Jun 1999 Cover: 1.79 **NM** value: **Cover or less**
Circ: Diamd. preorders: **5,066**

27 ❑ Jul 1999 Cover: 1.79 **NM** value: **Cover or less**
Circ: Diamd. preorders: **5,224**

28 ❑ Aug 1999 Cover: 1.79 **NM** value: **Cover or less**
Circ: Diamd. preorders: **6,045**
• continues in Sonic Super Special #10 ★ Appearance of Sonic.

29 ❑ Sep 1999 Cover: 1.79 **NM** value: **Cover or less**
Circ: Diamd. preorders: **5,498**

30 ❑ Oct 1999 Cover: 1.79 **NM** value: **Cover or less**
Circ: Diamd. preorders: **5,059**

31 ❑ Nov 1999 Cover: 1.79 **NM** value: **Cover or less**
Circ: Diamd. preorders: **4,823**

SABRINA (VOL. 2) — Archie

1 ❑ Jan 2000 Cover: 1.99 **NM** value: **Cover or less**
Circ: Diamd. preorders: **5,782**
• based on the animated series

2 ❑ Feb 2000 Cover: 1.99 **NM** value: **Cover or less**
Circ: Diamd. preorders: **5,180**

3 ❑ Mar 2000 Cover: 1.99 **NM** value: **Cover or less**
Circ: Diamd. preorders: **4,893**

4 ❑ Apr 2000 Cover: 1.99 **NM** value: **Cover or less**
Circ: Diamd. preorders: **4,414**

5 ❑ May 2000 Cover: 1.99 **NM** value: **Cover or less**
Circ: Diamd. preorders: **3,914**

6 ❑ Jun 2000 Cover: 1.99 **NM** value: **Cover or less**
Circ: Diamd. preorders: **3,830**

7 ❑ Jul 2000 Cover: 1.99 **NM** value: **Cover or less**
Circ: Diamd. preorders: **3,729**

8 ❑ Aug 2000 Cover: 1.99 **NM** value: **Cover or less**
Circ: Diamd. preorders: **3,818**

9 ❑ Sep 2000 Cover: 1.99 **NM** value: **Cover or less**
Circ: Diamd. preorders: **3,972**

10 ❑ Oct 2000 Cover: 1.99 **NM** value: **Cover or less**
Circ: Diamd. preorders: **3,735**

11 ❑ Nov 2000 Cover: 1.99 **NM** value: **Cover or less**
Circ: Diamd. preorders: **3,452**

12 ❑ Dec 2000 Cover: 1.99 **NM** value: **Cover or less**
Circ: Diamd. preorders: **3,457**

13 ❑ Jan 2001 Cover: 1.99 **NM** value: **Cover or less**
Circ: Diamd. preorders: **3,367**

14 ❑ Feb 2001 Cover: 1.99 **NM** value: **Cover or less**
Circ: Diamd. preorders: **3,336**

15 ❑ Mar 2001 Cover: 1.99 **NM** value: **Cover or less**
Circ: Diamd. preorders: **3,193**

16 ❑ Apr 2001 Cover: 1.99 **NM** value: **Cover or less**
Circ: Diamd. preorders: **3,069**

17 ❑ May 2001 Cover: 1.99 **NM** value: **Cover or less**
Circ: Diamd. preorders: **3,058**

18 ❑ Jun 2001 Cover: 1.99 **NM** value: **Cover or less**
Circ: Diamd. preorders: **2,959**

19 ❑ Jul 2001 Cover: 1.99 **NM** value: **Cover or less**
Circ: Diamd. preorders: **3,120**

20 ❑ Aug 2001 Cover: 1.99 **NM** value: **Cover or less**
Circ: Diamd. preorders: **3,098**

21 ❑ Sep 2001 Cover: 1.99 **NM** value: **Cover or less**
Circ: Diamd. preorders: **3,357**

22 ❑ Oct 2001 Cover: 1.99 **NM** value: **Cover or less**
Circ: Diamd. preorders: **3,302**

SABRINA THE TEENAGE WITCH — Archie

Sabrina first appeared as a supporting character in Archie comics. She had a little something extra, however, that the rest of Archie's pals didn't: she's a witch, complete with magical powers — an unusual addition to a cast that defined wholesome comics. But she's a wholesome witch. Here, in her own title, she has her own supporting cast, featuring her cranky old Aunt Hilda and her goofball boyfriend Harvey. Of course, Sabrina just wants to live a normal teenage life, and the problems of keeping her magical powers a secret is what sets the stage for most of her adventures.

The character of Sabrina gained much wider recognition when she became the star of a popular ABC sitcom in the 1990s, with Melissa Joan Hart in the lead role.

1 ❑ Apr 1971 Cover: 0.25 **NM** value: **45.00**
• **CGC:** 3 graded, best 9.4
• Giant-size.

2 ❑ Jul 1971 Cover: 0.25 **NM** value: **20.00**
• Giant-size.

3 ❑ Sep 1971 Cover: 0.25 **NM** value: **12.00**
• **CGC:** 1 graded, best 9.0
• Giant-size.

4 ❑ Dec 1971 Cover: 0.25 **NM** value: **12.00**
• Giant-size.

5 ❑ Feb 1972 Cover: 0.25 **NM** value: **12.00**
• Giant-size.

6 ❑ Jun 1972 Cover: 0.25 **NM** value: **10.00**
• Giant-size.

7 ❑ Aug 1972 Cover: 0.25 **NM** value: **10.00**
• Giant-size.

8 ❑ Sep 1972 Cover: 0.25 **NM** value: **10.00**
• Giant-size.

9 ❑ Oct 1972 Cover: 0.25 **NM** value: **10.00**
• Giant-size.

10 ❑ Feb 1973 Cover: 0.25 **NM** value: **10.00**
• Giant-size.

11 ❑ Apr 1973 Cover: 0.25 **NM** value: **8.00**
• Giant-size.

12 ❑ Jun 1973 Cover: 0.25 **NM** value: **8.00**
• Giant-size.

13 ❑ Aug 1973 Cover: 0.25 **NM** value: **8.00**
• Giant-size.

14 ❑ Sep 1973 Cover: 0.25 **NM** value: **8.00**
• Giant-size.

15 ❑ Oct 1973 Cover: 0.25 **NM** value: **8.00**
• Giant-size.

16 ❑ Dec 1973 Cover: 0.25 **NM** value: **8.00**
• Giant-size.

17 ❑ Feb 1974 Cover: 0.25 **NM** value: **8.00**
Circ: Statement: **144,041**
• Giant-size.

18 ❑ Apr 1974 Cover: 0.25 **NM** value: **6.00**
Circ: Statement: **144,041**

19 ❑ Jun 1974 Cover: 0.25 **NM** value: **6.00**
Circ: Statement: **144,041**

20 ❑ Aug 1974 Cover: 0.25 **NM** value: **6.00**
Circ: Statement: **144,041**

21 ❑ Sep 1974 Cover: 0.25 **NM** value: **5.00**
Circ: Statement: **144,041**

22 ❑ Oct 1974 Cover: 0.25 **NM** value: **5.00**
Circ: Statement: **144,041**

23 ❑ Feb 1975 Cover: 0.25 **NM** value: **5.00**
Circ: Statement: **129,791**

24 ❑ Apr 1975 Cover: 0.25 **NM** value: **5.00**
Circ: Statement: **129,791**

25 ❑ Jun 1975 Cover: 0.25 **NM** value: **5.00**
Circ: Statement: **129,791**
• Has 1974 Statement; avg total paid circ 144,041

26 ❑ Aug 1975 Cover: 0.25 **NM** value: **5.00**
Circ: Statement: **129,791**

27 ❑ Sep 1975 Cover: 0.25 **NM** value: **5.00**
Circ: Statement: **129,791**

28 ❑ Oct 1975 Cover: 0.25 **NM** value: **5.00**
Circ: Statement: **129,791**

29 ❑ Dec 1975 Cover: 0.25 **NM** value: **5.00**
Circ: Statement: **129,791**

30 ❑ Feb 1976 Cover: 0.30 **NM** value: **5.00**
Circ: Statement: **107,825**

31 ❑ Apr 1976 Cover: 0.30 **NM** value: **4.00**
Circ: Statement: **107,825**

32 ❑ Jun 1976 Cover: 0.30 **NM** value: **4.00**
Circ: Statement: **107,825**

33 ❑ Aug 1976 Cover: 0.30 **NM** value: **4.00**
Circ: Statement: **107,825**

34 ❑ Sep 1976 Cover: 0.30 **NM** value: **4.00**
Circ: Statement: **107,825**

35 ❑ Oct 1976 Cover: 0.30 **NM** value: **4.00**
Circ: Statement: **107,825**
📖 An Emotion Potion; Li'l Jinx…It Adds Up!; Have a Happy; Spell Spiel; Zap Flap; The Good Samaritan; Glorified Ride; Guest Work ★ Appearance of Betty, Ethel, Jughead, Veronica.

36 ❑ Dec 1977 Cover: 0.30 **NM** value: **4.00**
Circ: Statement: **107,825**

37 ❑ Feb 1977 Cover: 0.30 **NM** value: **4.00**
Circ: Statement: **108,092**

38 ❑ May 1977 Cover: 0.30 **NM** value: **4.00**
Circ: Statement: **108,092**
• Has 1976 Statement; avg total paid circ 107,825

39 ❑ Jun 1977 Cover: 0.35 **NM** value: **4.00**
Circ: Statement: **108,092**

40 ❑ Aug 1977 Cover: 0.35 **NM** value: **4.00**
Circ: Statement: **108,092**

41 ❑ Sep 1977 Cover: 0.35 **NM** value: **4.00**
Circ: Statement: **108,092**

42 ❑ Oct 1977 Cover: 0.35 **NM** value: **4.00**
Circ: Statement: **108,092**

43 ❑ Dec 1977 Cover: 0.35 **NM** value: **4.00**
Circ: Statement: **108,092**

44 ❑ Feb 1978 Cover: 0.35 **NM** value: **4.00**

45 ❑ May 1978 Cover: 0.35 **NM** value: **4.00**
• Has 1977 Statement; avg total paid circ 108,092

46 ❑ Jun 1978 Cover: 0.35 **NM** value: **4.00**

47 ❑ Aug 1978 Cover: 0.35 **NM** value: **4.00**

48 ❑ Sep 1978 Cover: 0.35 **NM** value: **4.00**

49 ❑ Oct 1978 Cover: 0.35 **NM** value: **4.00**

50 ❑ Dec 1978 Cover: 0.35 **NM** value: **4.00**

51 ❑ Feb 1979 Cover: 0.35 **NM** value: **3.00**
Circ: Statement: **97,445**

52 ❑ May 1979 Cover: 0.40 **NM** value: **3.00**
Circ: Statement: **97,445**

53 ❑ Jun 1979 Cover: 0.40 **NM** value: **3.00**
Circ: Statement: **97,445**

54 ❑ Aug 1979 Cover: 0.40 **NM** value: **3.00**
Circ: Statement: **97,445**

55 ❑ Sep 1979 Cover: 0.40 **NM** value: **3.00**
Circ: Statement: **97,445**

56 ❑ Oct 1979 Cover: 0.40 **NM** value: **3.00**
Circ: Statement: **97,445**

57 ❑ Dec 1979 Cover: 0.40 **NM** value: **3.00**
Circ: Statement: **97,445**

58 ❑ Feb 1980 Cover: 0.40 **NM** value: **3.00**
Circ: Statement: **84,389**

59 ❑ Apr 1980 Cover: 0.40 **NM** value: **3.00**
Circ: Statement: **84,389**
• Has 1979 Statement, filed 10/1/79; avg print run 261,019; avg sales 97,332; avg subs 113; avg total paid 97,445; office use 300; max existent 97,745; 63% of run returned

60 ❑ Jun 1980 Cover: 0.40 **NM** value: **3.00**
Circ: Statement: **84,389**

61 ❑ Aug 1980 Cover: 0.50 **NM** value: **2.00**
Circ: Statement: **84,389**

62 ❑ Sep 1980 Cover: 0.50 **NM** value: **2.00**
Circ: Statement: **84,389**

63 ❑ Oct 1980 Cover: 0.50 **NM** value: **2.00**
Circ: Statement: **84,389**

64 ❑ Dec 1980 Cover: 0.50 **NM** value: **2.00**
Circ: Statement: **84,389**

65 ❑ Feb 1981 Cover: 0.50 **NM** value: **2.00**
Circ: Statement: **74,005**

66 ❑ Apr 1981 Cover: 0.50 **NM** value: **2.00**
Circ: Statement: **74,005**
• Has 1980 Statement, filed 10/1/80; avg print run 242,398; avg sales 84,362; avg subs 27; avg total paid 84,389; office use 300; max existent 84,689; 65% of run returned

67 ❑ Jun 1981 Cover: 0.50 **NM** value: **2.00**
Circ: Statement: **74,005**

68 ❑ Aug 1981 Cover: 0.50 **NM** value: **2.00**
Circ: Statement: **74,005**

69 ❑ Oct 1981 Cover: 0.50 **NM** value: **2.00**
Circ: Statement: **74,005**

70 ❑ Dec 1981 Cover: 0.50 **NM** value: **2.00**
Circ: Statement: **74,005**

71 ❑ Feb 1982 Cover: 0.60 **NM** value: **2.00**

72 ❑ Apr 1982 Cover: 0.60 **NM** value: **2.00**
• Has 1981 Statement, filed 10/1/81; avg print run 221,199; avg sales 73,959; avg subs 46; avg total paid 74,005; office use 300; max existent 74,305; 66% of run returned

73 ❑ Jun 1982 Cover: 0.60 **NM** value: **2.00**

74 ❑ Aug 1982 Cover: 0.60 **NM** value: **2.00**

75 ❑ Oct 1982 Cover: 0.60 **NM** value: **2.00**

76 ❑ Dec 1982 Cover: 0.60 **NM** value: **2.00**

77 ❑ Feb 1983 Cover: 0.60 **NM** value: **2.00**

HS 1 ❑ ca. 1993 Cover: 2.00 **NM** value: **Cover or less**
• "Sabrina's Halloween Spoook-Tacular"

HS 2 ❑ ca. 1994 Cover: 2.00 **NM** value: **Cover or less**

HS 3 ❑ ca. 1995 Cover: 2.00 **NM** value: **Cover or less**

SABRINA THE TEENAGE WITCH (2ND SERIES) — Archie

1 ❑ Cover: 2.00 **NM** value: **Cover or less**
One-shot.

CGC-graded: Multiply prices above by **33 for 9.9 M • 16 for 9.8 NM/M • 7 for 9.6 NM+ • 5 for 9.4 NM • 2.5 for 9.2 NM- • 1.5 for 9.0 VF/NM**

SACHS & VIOLENS — Marvel / Epic

Juanita Jean Sachs ("J.J." to her friends) is a fiery Latina who makes her living as a model for adult magazines. Ernie "Violens" Schultz is her photographer, a former photojournalist from the jungle wars.

J.J.'s friend Wendy was also involved in the adult entertainment industry and thought she was onto a promising job in a softcore movie. Instead, she became the victim of a "snuff film" — a movie where people are actually killed at the end. Those responsible for dumping her body got involved in an auto accident, exposing Wendy's mutilated body and pictures of the slaying. The police unable to come up with leads, J.J. decides to investigate using her own unique industry connections. Ernie, like an aging Rambo, has no choice but to aid her using his cache of heavy weaponry (which he kept for just such emergencies)!

1 ❑ Nov 1993 Cover: 2.75 **NM** value: **3.00**
Circ: CapCity orders: **18,400**
Embossed cover. 📖 Sachs and the Single Girl, Part 1 **A:** George Pérez **W:** Peter David

1/PL ❑ Nov 1993 **NM** value: **3.00**
Embossed cover. • Platinum promotional edition. 📖 Sachs and the Single Girl, Part 1 **A:** George Pérez **W:** Peter David

2 ❑ May 1994 Cover: 2.25 **NM value: Cover or less**
Circ: CapCity orders: **17,400** • **CGC:** 1 graded, best 9.0
📖 Sachs and the Single Girl, Part 2 **A:** George Pérez **W:** Peter David

3 ❑ Jun 1994 Cover: 2.25 **NM value: Cover or less**
Circ: CapCity orders: **15,550** • **CGC:** 1 graded, best 9.4
📖 Sachs and the Single Girl, Part 3 • Sex, nudity **A:** George Pérez **W:** Peter David

4 ❑ Jul 1994 Cover: 2.25 **NM value: Cover or less**
Circ: CapCity orders: **13,800** • **CGC:** 1 graded, best 9.2
📖 Sachs and the Single Girl, Part 4 **A:** George Pérez **W:** Peter David

SACRIFICED TREES — Mansion / Epic

1 ❑ Cover: 3.00 **NM value: Cover or less**
📖 Zakiriah: The Raven Sleeps Tonight **A:** Edwind Nieves **W:** David Watkins

SADDLE JUSTICE — E.C.

The title began life as the bigfoot series The Happy Houlihans. As the E.C. line shifted and adapted to find its spot in the marketplace, it kept the numbering but radically changed title and contents of its later-designated "Pre-Trend" titles.

Covers on Saddle Justice were by E.C.-stars-to-be Johnny Craig (dynamic cowboy scenes) and Graham Ingels (beautiful women in Western action). For some reason, the heading "True and Terrific" appeared over the title; there were stories on such historical figures as Sam Bass and Belle Starr. After six issues, it shifted gears (or changed horses) slightly, taking the title Saddle Romances. — Maggie

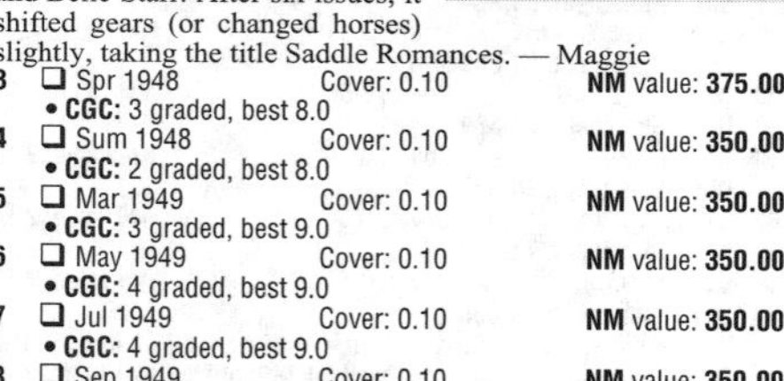

3 ❑ Spr 1948 Cover: 0.10 **NM** value: **375.00**
• **CGC:** 3 graded, best 8.0
4 ❑ Sum 1948 Cover: 0.10 **NM** value: **350.00**
• **CGC:** 2 graded, best 8.0
5 ❑ Mar 1949 Cover: 0.10 **NM** value: **350.00**
• **CGC:** 3 graded, best 9.0
6 ❑ May 1949 Cover: 0.10 **NM** value: **350.00**
• **CGC:** 4 graded, best 9.0
7 ❑ Jul 1949 Cover: 0.10 **NM** value: **350.00**
• **CGC:** 4 graded, best 9.0
8 ❑ Sep 1949 Cover: 0.10 **NM** value: **350.00**
• **CGC:** 4 graded, best 9.0

SADDLE ROMANCES — E.C.

The Pre-Trend E.C. title continued the numbering from Saddle Justice with stories like "A Reno Dance-Hall Hostess!" itself a variant on the E.C. "Dance-Hall Racket" in Crime Patrol #10. The title finally morphed into Weird Science with #12. — Maggie

9 ❑ Nov 1949 Cover: 0.10 **NM** value: **350.00**
• **CGC:** 3 graded, best 7.5
10 ❑ Jan 1950 Cover: 0.10 **NM** value: **350.00**
• **CGC:** 3 graded, best 7.5
11 ❑ Mar 1950 Cover: 0.10 **NM** value: **350.00**
• **CGC:** 1 graded, best 7.0

Diamond preorders are the estimated number of comics sold, prior to their release, to comics shops in North America by Diamond Comic Distributors, the largest distributor. These figures underreport the actual number of circulating copies by the amount of reorders Diamond took (usually 5-10% again of the preorders) and sales by publishers to newsstand and bookstore distributors. For many independent publishers, Diamond's preorders may be quite close to the actual number of copies in circulation.

SAD SACK — Harvey

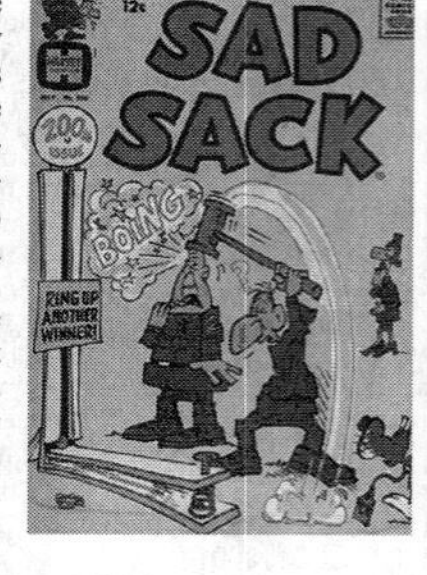

Originally created by George Baker (1915-1975) for the May 1942 issue of the servicemen's weekly "Yank," Sad Sack was the proverbial loser who seemed woefully out of place in the Army. Following the war, Sad Sack (and his creator) were released into civilian life, an adjustment that, actually, provided even more topics for the character who defined a type that exists to this day — but the gags were, of necessity, cleaner. Harvey Comics introduced a Sad Sack comic book in 1949 and in 1951 put Sad Sack back in the military, where he became a fan favorite — and Jerry Lewis starred in a film based on the material in 1957.

A virtual comrade to Beetle Bailey, he shares the former's ability to mess up any task and to create havoc out of the simplest assignment. He can be differentiated in that he is slightly less lazy but a great deal more gloomily pathetic.

This long-running series by Fred Rhoads continued until 1982, with a brief revival a decade later.

Versions of issues with "Complimentary Copy" printed on their covers by Harvey are known to exist from the 1950s.

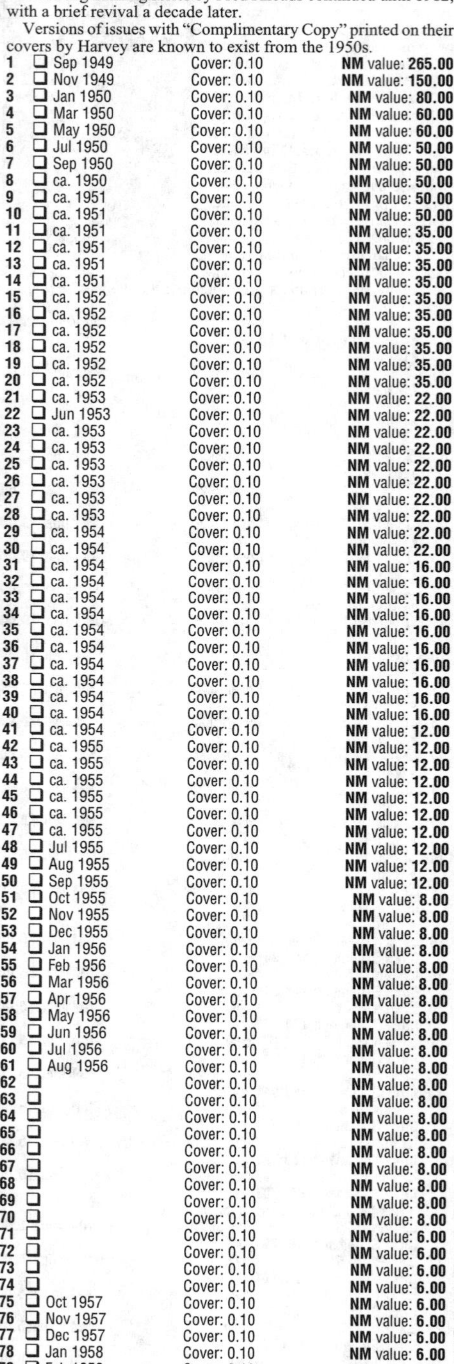

1 ❑ Sep 1949 Cover: 0.10 **NM** value: **265.00**
2 ❑ Nov 1949 Cover: 0.10 **NM** value: **150.00**
3 ❑ Jan 1950 Cover: 0.10 **NM** value: **80.00**
4 ❑ Mar 1950 Cover: 0.10 **NM** value: **60.00**
5 ❑ May 1950 Cover: 0.10 **NM** value: **60.00**
6 ❑ Jul 1950 Cover: 0.10 **NM** value: **50.00**
7 ❑ Sep 1950 Cover: 0.10 **NM** value: **50.00**
8 ❑ ca. 1950 Cover: 0.10 **NM** value: **50.00**
9 ❑ ca. 1951 Cover: 0.10 **NM** value: **50.00**
10 ❑ ca. 1951 Cover: 0.10 **NM** value: **50.00**
11 ❑ ca. 1951 Cover: 0.10 **NM** value: **35.00**
12 ❑ ca. 1951 Cover: 0.10 **NM** value: **35.00**
13 ❑ ca. 1951 Cover: 0.10 **NM** value: **35.00**
14 ❑ ca. 1951 Cover: 0.10 **NM** value: **35.00**
15 ❑ ca. 1952 Cover: 0.10 **NM** value: **35.00**
16 ❑ ca. 1952 Cover: 0.10 **NM** value: **35.00**
17 ❑ ca. 1952 Cover: 0.10 **NM** value: **35.00**
18 ❑ ca. 1952 Cover: 0.10 **NM** value: **35.00**
19 ❑ ca. 1952 Cover: 0.10 **NM** value: **35.00**
20 ❑ ca. 1952 Cover: 0.10 **NM** value: **35.00**
21 ❑ ca. 1953 Cover: 0.10 **NM** value: **22.00**
22 ❑ Jun 1953 Cover: 0.10 **NM** value: **22.00**
23 ❑ ca. 1953 Cover: 0.10 **NM** value: **22.00**
24 ❑ ca. 1953 Cover: 0.10 **NM** value: **22.00**
25 ❑ ca. 1953 Cover: 0.10 **NM** value: **22.00**
26 ❑ ca. 1953 Cover: 0.10 **NM** value: **22.00**
27 ❑ ca. 1953 Cover: 0.10 **NM** value: **22.00**
28 ❑ ca. 1953 Cover: 0.10 **NM** value: **22.00**
29 ❑ ca. 1954 Cover: 0.10 **NM** value: **22.00**
30 ❑ ca. 1954 Cover: 0.10 **NM** value: **22.00**
31 ❑ ca. 1954 Cover: 0.10 **NM** value: **16.00**
32 ❑ ca. 1954 Cover: 0.10 **NM** value: **16.00**
33 ❑ ca. 1954 Cover: 0.10 **NM** value: **16.00**
34 ❑ ca. 1954 Cover: 0.10 **NM** value: **16.00**
35 ❑ ca. 1954 Cover: 0.10 **NM** value: **16.00**
36 ❑ ca. 1954 Cover: 0.10 **NM** value: **16.00**
37 ❑ ca. 1954 Cover: 0.10 **NM** value: **16.00**
38 ❑ ca. 1954 Cover: 0.10 **NM** value: **16.00**
39 ❑ ca. 1954 Cover: 0.10 **NM** value: **16.00**
40 ❑ ca. 1954 Cover: 0.10 **NM** value: **16.00**
41 ❑ ca. 1954 Cover: 0.10 **NM** value: **12.00**
42 ❑ ca. 1955 Cover: 0.10 **NM** value: **12.00**
43 ❑ ca. 1955 Cover: 0.10 **NM** value: **12.00**
44 ❑ ca. 1955 Cover: 0.10 **NM** value: **12.00**
45 ❑ ca. 1955 Cover: 0.10 **NM** value: **12.00**
46 ❑ ca. 1955 Cover: 0.10 **NM** value: **12.00**
47 ❑ ca. 1955 Cover: 0.10 **NM** value: **12.00**
48 ❑ Jul 1955 Cover: 0.10 **NM** value: **12.00**
49 ❑ Aug 1955 Cover: 0.10 **NM** value: **12.00**
50 ❑ Sep 1955 Cover: 0.10 **NM** value: **12.00**
51 ❑ Oct 1955 Cover: 0.10 **NM** value: **8.00**
52 ❑ Nov 1955 Cover: 0.10 **NM** value: **8.00**
53 ❑ Dec 1955 Cover: 0.10 **NM** value: **8.00**
54 ❑ Jan 1956 Cover: 0.10 **NM** value: **8.00**
55 ❑ Feb 1956 Cover: 0.10 **NM** value: **8.00**
56 ❑ Mar 1956 Cover: 0.10 **NM** value: **8.00**
57 ❑ Apr 1956 Cover: 0.10 **NM** value: **8.00**
58 ❑ May 1956 Cover: 0.10 **NM** value: **8.00**
59 ❑ Jun 1956 Cover: 0.10 **NM** value: **8.00**
60 ❑ Jul 1956 Cover: 0.10 **NM** value: **8.00**
61 ❑ Aug 1956 Cover: 0.10 **NM** value: **8.00**
62 ❑ Cover: 0.10 **NM** value: **8.00**
63 ❑ Cover: 0.10 **NM** value: **8.00**
64 ❑ Cover: 0.10 **NM** value: **8.00**
65 ❑ Cover: 0.10 **NM** value: **8.00**
66 ❑ Cover: 0.10 **NM** value: **8.00**
67 ❑ Cover: 0.10 **NM** value: **8.00**
68 ❑ Cover: 0.10 **NM** value: **8.00**
69 ❑ Cover: 0.10 **NM** value: **8.00**
70 ❑ Cover: 0.10 **NM** value: **8.00**
71 ❑ Cover: 0.10 **NM** value: **6.00**
72 ❑ Cover: 0.10 **NM** value: **6.00**
73 ❑ Cover: 0.10 **NM** value: **6.00**
74 ❑ Cover: 0.10 **NM** value: **6.00**
75 ❑ Oct 1957 Cover: 0.10 **NM** value: **6.00**
76 ❑ Nov 1957 Cover: 0.10 **NM** value: **6.00**
77 ❑ Dec 1957 Cover: 0.10 **NM** value: **6.00**
78 ❑ Jan 1958 Cover: 0.10 **NM** value: **6.00**
79 ❑ Feb 1958 Cover: 0.10 **NM** value: **6.00**
80 ❑ Cover: 0.10 **NM** value: **6.00**
81 ❑ Cover: 0.10 **NM** value: **6.00**
82 ❑ Cover: 0.10 **NM** value: **6.00**
83 ❑ Cover: 0.10 **NM** value: **6.00**
84 ❑ Cover: 0.10 **NM** value: **6.00**
85 ❑ Cover: 0.10 **NM** value: **6.00**
86 ❑ Cover: 0.10 **NM** value: **6.00**
87 ❑ Cover: 0.10 **NM** value: **6.00**
88 ❑ Cover: 0.10 **NM** value: **6.00**
89 ❑ Cover: 0.10 **NM** value: **6.00**
90 ❑ Cover: 0.10 **NM** value: **6.00**
91 ❑ Cover: 0.10 **NM** value: **4.00**
92 ❑ Cover: 0.10 **NM** value: **4.00**
93 ❑ May 1961 Cover: 0.10 **NM** value: **4.00**
94 ❑ Jun 1961 Cover: 0.10 **NM** value: **4.00**
95 ❑ Jul 1961 Cover: 0.10 **NM** value: **4.00**
96 ❑ Aug 1961 Cover: 0.10 **NM** value: **4.00**
97 ❑ Sep 1961 Cover: 0.10 **NM** value: **4.00**
98 ❑ Oct 1961 Cover: 0.10 **NM** value: **4.00**
99 ❑ Nov 1961 Cover: 0.10 **NM** value: **4.00**
100 ❑ Dec 1961 Cover: 0.10 **NM** value: **4.00**
101 ❑ Jan 1962 Cover: 0.10 **NM** value: **2.50**
102 ❑ Feb 1962 Cover: 0.10 **NM** value: **2.50**
103 ❑ Mar 1962 Cover: 0.10 **NM** value: **2.50**
104 ❑ Apr 1962 Cover: 0.10 **NM** value: **2.50**
105 ❑ May 1962 Cover: 0.10 **NM** value: **2.50**
106 ❑ Jun 1962 Cover: 0.10 **NM** value: **2.50**
107 ❑ Jul 1962 Cover: 0.10 **NM** value: **2.50**
108 ❑ Aug 1962 Cover: 0.10 **NM** value: **2.50**
109 ❑ Sep 1962 Cover: 0.10 **NM** value: **2.50**
110 ❑ Oct 1962 Cover: 0.10 **NM** value: **2.50**
111 ❑ Nov 1962 Cover: 0.10 **NM** value: **2.50**
112 ❑ Dec 1962 Cover: 0.10 **NM** value: **2.50**
113 ❑ Jan 1963 Cover: 0.10 **NM** value: **2.50**
114 ❑ Feb 1963 Cover: 0.10 **NM** value: **2.50**
115 ❑ Mar 1963 Cover: 0.10 **NM** value: **2.50**
116 ❑ Apr 1963 Cover: 0.10 **NM** value: **2.50**
117 ❑ May 1963 Cover: 0.10 **NM** value: **2.50**
118 ❑ Jun 1963 Cover: 0.10 **NM** value: **2.50**
119 ❑ Jul 1963 Cover: 0.10 **NM** value: **2.50**
120 ❑ Aug 1963 Cover: 0.10 **NM** value: **2.50**
121 ❑ Sep 1963 Cover: 0.10 **NM** value: **2.50**
122 ❑ Oct 1963 **NM** value: **2.50**
123 ❑ Nov 1963 **NM** value: **2.50**
124 ❑ Dec 1963 **NM** value: **2.50**
125 ❑ Jan 1962 **NM** value: **2.50**
126 ❑ Feb 1962 Cover: 0.12 **NM** value: **2.50**
127 ❑ Mar 1962 Cover: 0.12 **NM** value: **2.50**
128 ❑ Apr 1962 Cover: 0.12 **NM** value: **2.50**
129 ❑ May 1962 Cover: 0.12 **NM** value: **2.50**
130 ❑ Jun 1962 Cover: 0.12 **NM** value: **2.50**
131 ❑ Jul 1962 Cover: 0.12 **NM** value: **2.50**
132 ❑ Aug 1962 Cover: 0.12 **NM** value: **2.50**
133 ❑ Sep 1962 Cover: 0.12 **NM** value: **2.50**
📖 Relaxation; Anything for a Change; The Touch; The Line-Up; The Try Out; Tune Up; The Opening; Timing
134 ❑ Oct 1962 Cover: 0.12 **NM** value: **2.50**
135 ❑ Nov 1962 Cover: 0.12 **NM** value: **2.50**
136 ❑ Dec 1962 Cover: 0.12 **NM** value: **2.50**
137 ❑ Jan 1963 Cover: 0.12 **NM** value: **2.50**
138 ❑ Feb 1963 Cover: 0.12 **NM** value: **2.50**
139 ❑ Mar 1963 Cover: 0.12 **NM** value: **2.50**
140 ❑ Apr 1963 Cover: 0.12 **NM** value: **2.50**
141 ❑ May 1963 Cover: 0.12 **NM** value: **2.50**
142 ❑ Jun 1963 Cover: 0.12 **NM** value: **2.50**
143 ❑ Jul 1963 Cover: 0.12 **NM** value: **2.50**
144 ❑ Aug 1963 Cover: 0.12 **NM** value: **2.50**
145 ❑ Sep 1963 Cover: 0.12 **NM** value: **2.50**
146 ❑ Oct 1963 Cover: 0.12 **NM** value: **2.50**
147 ❑ Nov 1963 Cover: 0.12 **NM** value: **2.50**
148 ❑ Dec 1963 Cover: 0.12 **NM** value: **2.50**
149 ❑ Jan 1964 Cover: 0.12 **NM** value: **2.50**
150 ❑ Feb 1964 Cover: 0.12 **NM** value: **2.50**
151 ❑ Mar 1964 Cover: 0.12 **NM** value: **2.00**
152 ❑ Apr 1964 Cover: 0.12 **NM** value: **2.00**
153 ❑ May 1964 Cover: 0.12 **NM** value: **2.00**
154 ❑ Jun 1964 Cover: 0.12 **NM** value: **2.00**
155 ❑ Jul 1964 Cover: 0.12 **NM** value: **2.00**
156 ❑ Aug 1964 Cover: 0.12 **NM** value: **2.00**
157 ❑ Sep 1964 Cover: 0.12 **NM** value: **2.00**
158 ❑ Oct 1964 Cover: 0.12 **NM** value: **2.00**
159 ❑ Nov 1964 Cover: 0.12 **NM** value: **2.00**
160 ❑ Dec 1964 Cover: 0.12 **NM** value: **2.00**
161 ❑ Jan 1965 Cover: 0.12 **NM** value: **2.00**
162 ❑ Feb 1965 Cover: 0.12 **NM** value: **2.00**
163 ❑ Mar 1965 Cover: 0.12 **NM** value: **2.00**
164 ❑ Apr 1965 Cover: 0.12 **NM** value: **2.00**
165 ❑ May 1965 Cover: 0.12 **NM** value: **2.00**
166 ❑ Jun 1965 Cover: 0.12 **NM** value: **2.00**
167 ❑ Jul 1965 Cover: 0.12 **NM** value: **2.00**
168 ❑ Aug 1965 Cover: 0.12 **NM** value: **2.00**
169 ❑ Sep 1965 Cover: 0.12 **NM** value: **2.00**
170 ❑ Oct 1965 Cover: 0.12 **NM** value: **2.00**
171 ❑ Nov 1965 Cover: 0.12 **NM** value: **2.00**
172 ❑ Dec 1965 Cover: 0.12 **NM** value: **2.00**
173 ❑ Jan 1966 Cover: 0.12 **NM** value: **2.00**
Circ: Statement: **204,253**
174 ❑ Feb 1966 Cover: 0.12 **NM** value: **2.00**
Circ: Statement: **204,253**
175 ❑ Mar 1966 Cover: 0.12 **NM** value: **2.00**
Circ: Statement: **204,253**
176 ❑ Apr 1966 Cover: 0.12 **NM** value: **2.00**
Circ: Statement: **204,253**
177 ❑ May 1966 Cover: 0.12 **NM** value: **2.00**
Circ: Statement: **204,253**
178 ❑ Jun 1966 Cover: 0.12 **NM** value: **2.00**
Circ: Statement: **204,253**
179 ❑ Jul 1966 Cover: 0.12 **NM** value: **2.00**
Circ: Statement: **204,253**

Other grades: Multiply prices above by **1.5 for Mint • 2/3 for Very Fine • 1/3 for Fine • 1/5 for Very Good • 1/8 for Good**

180 ❑ Aug 1966 Cover: 0.12 **NM** value: **2.00**
Circ: Statement: **204,253**
181 ❑ Sep 1966 Cover: 0.12 **NM** value: **2.00**
Circ: Statement: **204,253**
182 ❑ Oct 1966 Cover: 0.12 **NM** value: **2.00**
Circ: Statement: **204,253**
183 ❑ Nov 1966 Cover: 0.12 **NM** value: **2.00**
Circ: Statement: **204,253**
184 ❑ Dec 1966 Cover: 0.12 **NM** value: **2.00**
Circ: Statement: **204,253**
185 ❑ Jan 1967 Cover: 0.12 **NM** value: **2.00**
Circ: Statement: **192,213**
186 ❑ Feb 1967 Cover: 0.12 **NM** value: **2.00**
Circ: Statement: **192,213**
187 ❑ Mar 1967 Cover: 0.12 **NM** value: **2.00**
Circ: Statement: **192,213**
188 ❑ Apr 1967 Cover: 0.12 **NM** value: **2.00**
Circ: Statement: **192,213**
189 ❑ May 1967 Cover: 0.12 **NM** value: **2.00**
Circ: Statement: **192,213**
• Has 1966 Statement; avg print run 401,892; avg sales 204,218; avg subs 35; avg total paid 204,253; samples 345; max existent 204,598; 49% of run returned
190 ❑ Jun 1967 Cover: 0.12 **NM** value: **2.00**
Circ: Statement: **192,213**
191 ❑ Jul 1967 Cover: 0.12 **NM** value: **2.00**
Circ: Statement: **192,213**
192 ❑ Aug 1967 Cover: 0.12 **NM** value: **2.00**
Circ: Statement: **192,213**
193 ❑ Sep 1967 Cover: 0.12 **NM** value: **2.00**
Circ: Statement: **192,213**
194 ❑ Oct 1967 Cover: 0.12 **NM** value: **2.00**
Circ: Statement: **192,213**
195 ❑ Nov 1967 Cover: 0.12 **NM** value: **2.00**
Circ: Statement: **192,213**
196 ❑ Dec 1967 Cover: 0.12 **NM** value: **2.00**
Circ: Statement: **192,213**
197 ❑ 1968 Cover: 0.12 **NM** value: **2.00**
198 ❑ 1968 Cover: 0.12 **NM** value: **2.00**
199 ❑ 1968 Cover: 0.12 **NM** value: **2.00**
200 ❑ Jul 1968 Cover: 0.12 **NM** value: **2.00**
📖 Alert Army; Chain of Events; Play War; Quick Trip; Sneak Attack; Grudge; Bad Night (text); Foul Up **A:** George Baker(cover)
201 ❑ 1968 Cover: 0.12 **NM** value: **1.50**
202 ❑ 1968 Cover: 0.12 **NM** value: **1.50**
203 ❑ 1968 Cover: 0.12 **NM** value: **1.50**
204 ❑ Jan 1969 Cover: 0.12 **NM** value: **1.50**
205 ❑ 1969 Cover: 0.12 **NM** value: **1.50**
206 ❑ 1969 Cover: 0.12 **NM** value: **1.50**
207 ❑ 1969 Cover: 0.12 **NM** value: **1.50**
208 ❑ 1969 Cover: 0.15 **NM** value: **1.50**
209 ❑ 1969 Cover: 0.15 **NM** value: **1.50**
210 ❑ Nov 1969 Cover: 0.15 **NM** value: **1.50**
211 ❑ 1970 Cover: 0.15 **NM** value: **1.50**
Circ: Statement: **202,783**
212 ❑ 1970 Cover: 0.15 **NM** value: **1.50**
Circ: Statement: **202,783**
213 ❑ 1970 Cover: 0.15 **NM** value: **1.50**
Circ: Statement: **202,783**
214 ❑ 1970 Cover: 0.15 **NM** value: **1.50**
Circ: Statement: **202,783**
215 ❑ 1970 Cover: 0.15 **NM** value: **1.50**
Circ: Statement: **202,783**
216 ❑ 1970 Cover: 0.15 **NM** value: **1.50**
Circ: Statement: **202,783**
217 ❑ 1970 Cover: 0.15 **NM** value: **1.50**
Circ: Statement: **202,783**
218 ❑ Jan 1971 Cover: 0.15 **NM** value: **1.50**
219 ❑ Mar 1971 Cover: 0.15 **NM** value: **1.50**
📖 Cloud 9; Get a Load of This!; Planning Ahead; Spread It; Sunk; Relaxation; Tables Turned (text); Pipe Dream **A:** George Baker(cover)
220 ❑ May 1971 Cover: 0.15 **NM** value: **1.50**
221 ❑ Jul 1971 Cover: 0.15 **NM** value: **1.50**
• Has 1970 Statement, filed 10/1/70; avg print run 386,078; avg sales 202,729; avg subs 54; avg total paid 202,783; max existent 202,783; 48% of run returned
222 ❑ Sep 1971 Cover: 0.15 **NM** value: **1.50**
223 ❑ Nov 1971 Cover: 0.25 **NM** value: **2.50**
224 ❑ Jan 1972 Cover: 0.25 **NM** value: **2.50**
225 ❑ Mar 1972 Cover: 0.25 **NM** value: **2.50**
226 ❑ May 1972 Cover: 0.25 **NM** value: **2.50**
227 ❑ Jul 1972 Cover: 0.25 **NM** value: **2.50**
228 ❑ Sep 1972 Cover: 0.25 **NM** value: **2.50**
229 ❑ Nov 1972 Cover: 0.20 **NM** value: **1.50**
230 ❑ Jan 1973 Cover: 0.20 **NM** value: **1.50**
Circ: Statement: **149,634**
231 ❑ Mar 1973 Cover: 0.20 **NM** value: **1.50**
Circ: Statement: **149,634**
232 ❑ May 1973 Cover: 0.20 **NM** value: **1.50**
Circ: Statement: **149,634**
233 ❑ Jul 1973 Cover: 0.20 **NM** value: **1.50**
Circ: Statement: **149,634**
234 ❑ Sep 1973 Cover: 0.20 **NM** value: **1.50**
Circ: Statement: **149,634**
235 ❑ Nov 1973 Cover: 0.20 **NM** value: **1.50**
Circ: Statement: **149,634**
236 ❑ Jan 1974 Cover: 0.20 **NM** value: **1.50**
Circ: Statement: **147,877**
237 ❑ Mar 1974 Cover: 0.20 **NM** value: **1.50**
Circ: Statement: **147,877**
238 ❑ May 1974 Cover: 0.25 **NM** value: **1.50**
Circ: Statement: **147,877**
• Has 1973 Statement, filed 10/1/73; avg print run 343,216; avg sales 149,619; avg subs 15; avg total paid 149,634; samples 345; max existent 149,979; 56% of run returned
239 ❑ Jul 1974 Cover: 0.25 **NM** value: **1.50**
Circ: Statement: **147,877**
240 ❑ Sep 1974 Cover: 0.25 **NM** value: **1.50**
Circ: Statement: **147,877**
241 ❑ Nov 1974 Cover: 0.25 **NM** value: **1.50**
Circ: Statement: **147,877**
242 ❑ Jan 1975 Cover: 0.25 **NM** value: **1.50**
Circ: Statement: **112,404**
243 ❑ Mar 1975 Cover: 0.25 **NM** value: **1.50**
Circ: Statement: **112,404**
244 ❑ May 1975 Cover: 0.25 **NM** value: **1.50**
Circ: Statement: **112,404**
• Has 1974 Statement, filed 10/1/74; avg print run 264,470; avg sales 148,983; avg subs 15; avg total paid 147,877; samples 345; max existent 149,343; 44% of run returned
245 ❑ Jul 1975 Cover: 0.25 **NM** value: **1.50**
Circ: Statement: **112,404**
246 ❑ Sep 1975 Cover: 0.25 **NM** value: **1.50**
Circ: Statement: **112,404**
247 ❑ Nov 1975 Cover: 0.25 **NM** value: **1.50**
Circ: Statement: **112,404**
248 ❑ Jan 1976 Cover: 0.25 **NM** value: **1.50**
249 ❑ Mar 1976 Cover: 0.25 **NM** value: **1.50**
250 ❑ May 1976 Cover: 0.25 **NM** value: **1.50**
251 ❑ Jul 1976 Cover: 0.25 **NM** value: **1.50**
252 ❑ Sep 1976 Cover: 0.25 **NM** value: **1.50**
253 ❑ Nov 1976 Cover: 0.30 **NM** value: **1.50**
254 ❑ Jan 1977 Cover: 0.30 **NM** value: **1.50**
255 ❑ Mar 1977 Cover: 0.30 **NM** value: **1.50**
256 ❑ May 1977 Cover: 0.30 **NM** value: **1.50**
257 ❑ Jul 1977 Cover: 0.30 **NM** value: **1.50**
258 ❑ Sep 1977 Cover: 0.30 **NM** value: **1.50**
259 ❑ Nov 1977 Cover: 0.35 **NM** value: **1.50**
📖 Close Call; Bullseye; Strange Doings; Hazardous Duty; Too Much Help (text); Western Love Story **A:** George Baker(cover)
260 ❑ Jan 1978 Cover: 0.35 **NM** value: **1.50**
261 ❑ Mar 1978 Cover: 0.35 **NM** value: **1.50**
262 ❑ May 1978 Cover: 0.35 **NM** value: **1.50**
263 ❑ Jul 1978 Cover: 0.35 **NM** value: **1.50**
264 ❑ Sep 1978 Cover: 0.35 **NM** value: **1.50**
265 ❑ Nov 1978 Cover: 0.35 **NM** value: **1.50**
266 ❑ Jan 1979 Cover: 0.35 **NM** value: **1.50**
267 ❑ Mar 1979 Cover: 0.35 **NM** value: **1.50**
268 ❑ May 1979 Cover: 0.35 **NM** value: **1.50**
269 ❑ Jul 1979 Cover: 0.35 **NM** value: **1.50**
270 ❑ Sep 1979 Cover: 0.40 **NM** value: **1.50**
271 ❑ Nov 1979 Cover: 0.40 **NM** value: **1.50**
272 ❑ Jan 1980 Cover: 0.40 **NM** value: **1.50**
273 ❑ Mar 1980 Cover: 0.40 **NM** value: **1.50**
274 ❑ May 1980 Cover: 0.40 **NM** value: **1.50**
275 ❑ Jul 1980 Cover: 0.40 **NM** value: **1.50**
276 ❑ Sep 1980 Cover: 0.50 **NM** value: **1.50**
277 ❑ Nov 1980 Cover: 0.50 **NM** value: **1.50**
278 ❑ Jan 1981 Cover: 0.50 **NM** value: **1.50**
279 ❑ Mar 1981 Cover: 0.50 **NM** value: **1.50**
280 ❑ May 1981 Cover: 0.50 **NM** value: **1.50**
281 ❑ Jul 1981 Cover: 0.50 **NM** value: **1.50**
282 ❑ Sep 1981 Cover: 0.50 **NM** value: **1.50**
283 ❑ Nov 1981 Cover: 0.50 **NM** value: **1.50**
284 ❑ Jan 1982 Cover: 0.60 **NM** value: **1.50**
285 ❑ Mar 1982 Cover: 0.60 **NM** value: **1.50**
286 ❑ May 1982 Cover: 0.60 **NM** value: **1.50**
287 ❑ Jul 1982 Cover: 0.60 **NM** value: **1.50**
288 ❑ ca. 1992 Cover: 2.75 **NM** value: **Cover or less**
289 ❑ ca. 1992 Cover: 2.75 **NM** value: **Cover or less**
290 ❑ ca. 1992, b&w Cover: 1.00 **NM** value: **1.50**
291 ❑ ca. 1993 Cover: 1.00 **NM** value: **1.50**
292 ❑ ca. 1993 Cover: 1.00 **NM** value: **1.50**
293 ❑ ca. 1993 Cover: 1.00 **NM** value: **1.50**
final issue.

SAD SACK & THE SARGE — Harvey

Sad Sack and Beetle Bailey are the best-known military humor strip of postwar America, with Sack providing one of the most enduring characters in Harvey's publishing enterprise. Created during World War II by George Baker, the goofy buck private and his hard-nosed drill sergeant, Sarge, headed up a cast of service stereotypes whose broad satire of barracks life struck a familiar chord with returning servicemen after World War II. Sad Sack's brand of humor was universal enough to seem current and topical with new generations of GIs through the 1950s, 1960s, and into the 1970s. Sad Sack and the Sarge, drawn by Fred Rhoads, is a spinoff of the original Sad Sack Harvey title, focusing on Sarge, his dog, the General, the camp cook, and Sad Sack's sweetheart, Sadie Sack.

1 ❑ Sep 1957 Cover: 0.10 **NM** value: **80.00**
2 ❑ Nov 1957 Cover: 0.10 **NM** value: **45.00**
3 ❑ Jan 1958 Cover: 0.10 **NM** value: **30.00**
4 ❑ Mar 1958 Cover: 0.10 **NM** value: **30.00**
5 ❑ 1958 Cover: 0.10 **NM** value: **30.00**
6 ❑ Jun 1958 Cover: 0.10 **NM** value: **20.00**
7 ❑ 1958 Cover: 0.10 **NM** value: **20.00**
8 ❑ 1958 Cover: 0.10 **NM** value: **20.00**
9 ❑ Oct 1958 Cover: 0.10 **NM** value: **20.00**
10 ❑ Dec 1958 Cover: 0.10 **NM** value: **20.00**
11 ❑ Feb 1959 Cover: 0.10 **NM** value: **16.00**
12 ❑ Apr 1959 Cover: 0.10 **NM** value: **16.00**
13 ❑ Jun 1959 Cover: 0.10 **NM** value: **16.00**
14 ❑ Aug 1959 Cover: 0.10 **NM** value: **16.00**
15 ❑ Oct 1959 Cover: 0.10 **NM** value: **16.00**
16 ❑ Dec 1959 Cover: 0.10 **NM** value: **16.00**
17 ❑ Feb 1960 Cover: 0.10 **NM** value: **16.00**
18 ❑ Apr 1960 Cover: 0.10 **NM** value: **16.00**
19 ❑ Jun 1960 Cover: 0.10 **NM** value: **16.00**
20 ❑ Aug 1960 Cover: 0.10 **NM** value: **16.00**
21 ❑ Oct 1960 Cover: 0.10 **NM** value: **12.00**
22 ❑ Dec 1960 Cover: 0.10 **NM** value: **12.00**
23 ❑ Feb 1961 Cover: 0.10 **NM** value: **12.00**
24 ❑ Apr 1961 Cover: 0.10 **NM** value: **12.00**
25 ❑ Jun 1961 Cover: 0.12 **NM** value: **12.00**
26 ❑ Aug 1961 Cover: 0.12 **NM** value: **12.00**
27 ❑ Oct 1961 Cover: 0.12 **NM** value: **12.00**
28 ❑ Dec 1961 Cover: 0.12 **NM** value: **12.00**
29 ❑ Feb 1962 Cover: 0.12 **NM** value: **12.00**
30 ❑ Apr 1962 Cover: 0.12 **NM** value: **12.00**
31 ❑ Jun 1962 Cover: 0.12 **NM** value: **9.00**
32 ❑ Aug 1962 Cover: 0.12 **NM** value: **9.00**
33 ❑ Oct 1962 Cover: 0.12 **NM** value: **9.00**
34 ❑ Dec 1962 Cover: 0.12 **NM** value: **9.00**
35 ❑ Feb 1963 Cover: 0.12 **NM** value: **9.00**
36 ❑ Apr 1963 Cover: 0.12 **NM** value: **9.00**
37 ❑ Jun 1963 Cover: 0.12 **NM** value: **9.00**
38 ❑ Aug 1963 Cover: 0.12 **NM** value: **9.00**
39 ❑ Oct 1963 Cover: 0.12 **NM** value: **9.00**
40 ❑ Dec 1963 Cover: 0.12 **NM** value: **9.00**
41 ❑ Feb 1964 Cover: 0.12 **NM** value: **7.00**
42 ❑ Apr 1964 Cover: 0.12 **NM** value: **7.00**
43 ❑ Jun 1964 Cover: 0.12 **NM** value: **7.00**
44 ❑ Aug 1964 Cover: 0.12 **NM** value: **7.00**
45 ❑ Oct 1964 Cover: 0.12 **NM** value: **7.00**
46 ❑ Dec 1964 Cover: 0.12 **NM** value: **7.00**
47 ❑ Feb 1965 Cover: 0.12 **NM** value: **7.00**
48 ❑ Apr 1965 Cover: 0.12 **NM** value: **7.00**
49 ❑ Jun 1965 Cover: 0.12 **NM** value: **7.00**
50 ❑ Aug 1965 Cover: 0.12 **NM** value: **6.00**
51 ❑ Oct 1965 Cover: 0.12 **NM** value: **6.00**
52 ❑ Dec 1965 Cover: 0.12 **NM** value: **6.00**
53 ❑ Feb 1966 Cover: 0.12 **NM** value: **6.00**
54 ❑ Apr 1966 Cover: 0.12 **NM** value: **6.00**
55 ❑ Jun 1966 Cover: 0.12 **NM** value: **6.00**
56 ❑ Aug 1966 Cover: 0.12 **NM** value: **6.00**
57 ❑ Sep 1966 Cover: 0.12 **NM** value: **6.00**
58 ❑ Oct 1966 Cover: 0.12 **NM** value: **6.00**
59 ❑ Dec 1966 Cover: 0.12 **NM** value: **6.00**
60 ❑ Feb 1967 Cover: 0.12 **NM** value: **6.00**
61 ❑ Apr 1967 Cover: 0.12 **NM** value: **5.00**
62 ❑ Jun 1967 Cover: 0.12 **NM** value: **5.00**
63 ❑ Aug 1967 Cover: 0.12 **NM** value: **5.00**
64 ❑ Oct 1967 Cover: 0.12 **NM** value: **5.00**
65 ❑ Dec 1967 Cover: 0.12 **NM** value: **5.00**
66 ❑ Feb 1968 Cover: 0.12 **NM** value: **5.00**
67 ❑ Apr 1968 Cover: 0.12 **NM** value: **5.00**
68 ❑ Jun 1968 Cover: 0.12 **NM** value: **5.00**
69 ❑ Aug 1968 Cover: 0.12 **NM** value: **5.00**
70 ❑ Oct 1968 Cover: 0.12 **NM** value: **5.00**
71 ❑ Dec 1968 Cover: 0.12 **NM** value: **5.00**
72 ❑ Jan 1969 Cover: 0.12 **NM** value: **5.00**
73 ❑ 1969 Cover: 0.12 **NM** value: **5.00**
74 ❑ May 1969 Cover: 0.12 **NM** value: **5.00**
75 ❑ Jun 1969 Cover: 0.12 **NM** value: **5.00**
• Has 1968 Statement, filed 10/1/68; no circ figures published
76 ❑ Jul 1969 Cover: 0.12 **NM** value: **5.00**
77 ❑ Sep 1969 Cover: 0.15 **NM** value: **5.00**
78 ❑ Oct 1969 Cover: 0.15 **NM** value: **5.00**
79 ❑ Dec 1969 Cover: 0.15 **NM** value: **5.00**
80 ❑ Feb 1970 Cover: 0.15 **NM** value: **5.00**
81 ❑ Apr 1970 Cover: 0.15 **NM** value: **3.00**
82 ❑ Jun 1970 Cover: 0.15 **NM** value: **3.00**
83 ❑ Aug 1970 Cover: 0.15 **NM** value: **3.00**
84 ❑ Oct 1970 Cover: 0.15 **NM** value: **3.00**
85 ❑ Nov 1970 Cover: 0.15 **NM** value: **3.00**
86 ❑ Jan 1971 Cover: 0.15 **NM** value: **3.00**
87 ❑ Feb 1971 Cover: 0.15 **NM** value: **3.00**
88 ❑ Apr 1971 Cover: 0.15 **NM** value: **3.00**
89 ❑ Jun 1971 Cover: 0.15 **NM** value: **3.00**
90 ❑ Aug 1971 Cover: 0.20 **NM** value: **3.00**
91 ❑ Oct 1971 Cover: 0.25 **NM** value: **4.00**
• Giant size. 📖 Big Joke; Close Enough; Fall Guy; The Threat; Usual Day; Good Mistake; Enthusiasm; New Idea; Victim; Dumb; Same Old Bull; Nothing Doing (text); Good Night!; On and On; Bad for Health; Ear Specialist; The Champ; Signs of the Times ★ Appearance of The General, Slob Slobinski.
92 ❑ Dec 1971 Cover: 0.25 **NM** value: **4.00**
• Giant size.
93 ❑ Feb 1972 Cover: 0.25 **NM** value: **4.00**
Circ: Statement: **143,691**
• Giant size.
94 ❑ Apr 1972 Cover: 0.25 **NM** value: **4.00**
Circ: Statement: **143,691**
• Giant size.
95 ❑ Jun 1972 Cover: 0.25 **NM** value: **4.00**
Circ: Statement: **143,691**
• Giant size.
96 ❑ Aug 1972 Cover: 0.25 **NM** value: **4.00**
Circ: Statement: **143,691**
• Giant size.
97 ❑ Oct 1972 Cover: 0.20 **NM** value: **3.00**
Circ: Statement: **143,691**
98 ❑ Dec 1972 Cover: 0.20 **NM** value: **3.00**
Circ: Statement: **143,691**
99 ❑ Feb 1973 Cover: 0.20 **NM** value: **3.00**
Circ: Statement: **157,851**
100 ❑ Apr 1973 Cover: 0.20 **NM** value: **3.00**
Circ: Statement: **157,851**
101 ❑ Jun 1973 Cover: 0.20 **NM** value: **2.00**
Circ: Statement: **157,851**
• Has 1972 Statement, filed 10/1/72; avg print run 290,833; avg sales 143,691; avg subs 0; avg total paid 143,691; samples 345; max existent 144,036; 51% of run returned
102 ❑ Aug 1973 Cover: 0.20 **NM** value: **2.00**
Circ: Statement: **157,851**

CGC-graded: Multiply prices above by **33 for 9.9 M • 16 for 9.8 NM/M • 7 for 9.6 NM+ • 5 for 9.4 NM • 2.5 for 9.2 NM- • 1.5 for 9.0 VF/NM**

103 ❑ Oct 1973 Cover: 0.20 **NM** value: **2.00**
Circ: Statement: **157,851**
104 ❑ Dec 1973 Cover: 0.20 **NM** value: **2.00**
Circ: Statement: **157,851**
105 ❑ Feb 1974 Cover: 0.20 **NM** value: **2.00**
Circ: Statement: **147,946**
106 ❑ Apr 1974 Cover: 0.20 **NM** value: **2.00**
Circ: Statement: **147,946**
• Has 1973 Statement; avg total paid circ 157,851
107 ❑ Jun 1974 Cover: 0.25 **NM** value: **2.00**
Circ: Statement: **147,946**
108 ❑ Aug 1974 Cover: 0.25 **NM** value: **2.00**
Circ: Statement: **147,946**
109 ❑ Oct 1974 Cover: 0.25 **NM** value: **2.00**
Circ: Statement: **147,946**
110 ❑ Dec 1974 Cover: 0.25 **NM** value: **2.00**
Circ: Statement: **147,946**
111 ❑ Feb 1975 Cover: 0.25 **NM** value: **2.00**
Circ: Statement: **123,333**
112 ❑ Apr 1975 Cover: 0.25 **NM** value: **2.00**
Circ: Statement: **123,333**
📖 Laugh, Sarge, Laugh!; The Sarge Version; Keep Em Dry; Wide Awake or Else
113 ❑ Jun 1975 Cover: 0.25 **NM** value: **2.00**
Circ: Statement: **123,333**
• Has 1974 Statement; avg total paid circ 147,946
114 ❑ Aug 1975 Cover: 0.25 **NM** value: **2.00**
Circ: Statement: **123,333**
115 ❑ Oct 1975 Cover: 0.25 **NM** value: **2.00**
Circ: Statement: **123,333**
116 ❑ Dec 1975 Cover: 0.25 **NM** value: **2.00**
Circ: Statement: **123,333**
117 ❑ Feb 1976 Cover: 0.25 **NM** value: **2.00**
118 ❑ Apr 1976 Cover: 0.25 **NM** value: **2.00**
119 ❑ Jun 1976 Cover: 0.25 **NM** value: **2.00**
120 ❑ Aug 1976 Cover: 0.25 **NM** value: **2.00**
121 ❑ Oct 1976 Cover: 0.30 **NM** value: **2.00**
122 ❑ Dec 1976 Cover: 0.30 **NM** value: **2.00**
• Has 1975 Statement; avg total paid circ 123,333
123 ❑ Feb 1977 Cover: 0.30 **NM** value: **2.00**
124 ❑ Apr 1977 Cover: 0.30 **NM** value: **2.00**
125 ❑ Jun 1977 Cover: 0.30 **NM** value: **2.00**
126 ❑ Aug 1977 Cover: 0.30 **NM** value: **2.00**
127 ❑ Oct 1977 Cover: 0.35 **NM** value: **2.00**
128 ❑ Dec 1977 Cover: 0.35 **NM** value: **2.00**
129 ❑ Feb 1978 Cover: 0.35 **NM** value: **2.00**
130 ❑ Apr 1978 Cover: 0.35 **NM** value: **2.00**
131 ❑ Jun 1978 Cover: 0.35 **NM** value: **2.00**
132 ❑ Aug 1978 Cover: 0.35 **NM** value: **2.00**
133 ❑ Oct 1978 Cover: 0.35 **NM** value: **2.00**
134 ❑ Dec 1978 Cover: 0.35 **NM** value: **2.00**
135 ❑ Feb 1979 Cover: 0.35 **NM** value: **2.00**
136 ❑ Apr 1979 Cover: 0.35 **NM** value: **2.00**
137 ❑ Jun 1979 Cover: 0.35 **NM** value: **2.00**
138 ❑ Aug 1979 Cover: 0.35 **NM** value: **2.00**
139 ❑ Oct 1979 Cover: 0.40 **NM** value: **2.00**
140 ❑ Dec 1979 Cover: 0.40 **NM** value: **2.00**
141 ❑ Feb 1980 Cover: 0.40 **NM** value: **2.00**
142 ❑ Apr 1980 Cover: 0.40 **NM** value: **2.00**
143 ❑ Jun 1980 Cover: 0.40 **NM** value: **2.00**
144 ❑ Aug 1980 Cover: 0.40 **NM** value: **2.00**
145 ❑ Oct 1980 Cover: 0.50 **NM** value: **2.00**
146 ❑ Dec 1980 Cover: 0.50 **NM** value: **2.00**
147 ❑ Feb 1981 Cover: 0.50 **NM** value: **2.00**
148 ❑ Apr 1981 Cover: 0.50 **NM** value: **2.00**
149 ❑ Jun 1981 Cover: 0.50 **NM** value: **2.00**
150 ❑ Aug 1981 Cover: 0.50 **NM** value: **2.00**
151 ❑ Oct 1981 Cover: 0.50 **NM** value: **2.00**
152 ❑ Dec 1981 Cover: 0.50 **NM** value: **2.00**
153 ❑ Feb 1982 Cover: 0.60 **NM** value: **2.00**
154 ❑ Apr 1982 Cover: 0.60 **NM** value: **2.00**
155 ❑ Jun 1982 Cover: 0.60 **NM** value: **2.00**

SAD SACK ARMY LIFE PARADE — Harvey

1 ❑ Oct 1963 Cover: 0.25 **NM** value: **35.00**
2 ❑ Feb 1964 Cover: 0.25 **NM** value: **20.00**
3 ❑ May 1964 Cover: 0.25 **NM** value: **15.00**
4 ❑ Aug 1964 Cover: 0.25 **NM** value: **12.00**
5 ❑ Nov 1964 Cover: 0.25 **NM** value: **12.00**
6 ❑ Feb 1965 Cover: 0.25 **NM** value: **10.00**
7 ❑ May 1965 Cover: 0.25 **NM** value: **10.00**
8 ❑ Aug 1965 Cover: 0.25 **NM** value: **10.00**
9 ❑ Nov 1965 Cover: 0.25 **NM** value: **10.00**
10 ❑ Feb 1966 Cover: 0.25 **NM** value: **10.00**
11 ❑ May 1966 Cover: 0.25 **NM** value: **8.00**
12 ❑ Jul 1966 Cover: 0.25 **NM** value: **8.00**
13 ❑ Sep 1966 Cover: 0.25 **NM** value: **8.00**
14 ❑ Oct 1966 Cover: 0.25 **NM** value: **8.00**
15 ❑ Jan 1967 Cover: 0.25 **NM** value: **8.00**
16 ❑ Mar 1967 Cover: 0.25 **NM** value: **8.00**
17 ❑ 1967 Cover: 0.25 **NM** value: **8.00**
18 ❑ Nov 1967 Cover: 0.25 **NM** value: **8.00**
19 ❑ Feb 1968 Cover: 0.25 **NM** value: **8.00**
20 ❑ May 1968 Cover: 0.25 **NM** value: **8.00**
21 ❑ Aug 1968 Cover: 0.25 **NM** value: **6.00**
22 ❑ 1969 Cover: 0.25 **NM** value: **6.00**
23 ❑ Feb 1969 Cover: 0.25 **NM** value: **6.00**
24 ❑ Apr 1969 Cover: 0.25 **NM** value: **6.00**
25 ❑ Aug 1969 Cover: 0.25 **NM** value: **6.00**
26 ❑ Oct 1969 Cover: 0.25 **NM** value: **6.00**
27 ❑ Dec 1969 Cover: 0.25 **NM** value: **6.00**
28 ❑ Feb 1970 Cover: 0.25 **NM** value: **6.00**
29 ❑ Apr 1970 Cover: 0.25 **NM** value: **6.00**
30 ❑ Aug 1970 Cover: 0.25 **NM** value: **6.00**
31 ❑ 1970 Cover: 0.25 **NM** value: **5.00**
32 ❑ 1970 Cover: 0.25 **NM** value: **5.00**
33 ❑ 1971 Cover: 0.25 **NM** value: **5.00**
34 ❑ 1971 Cover: 0.25 **NM** value: **5.00**
35 ❑ Aug 1971 Cover: 0.25 **NM** value: **5.00**
36 ❑ Oct 1971 Cover: 0.25 **NM** value: **5.00**
37 ❑ Dec 1971 Cover: 0.25 **NM** value: **5.00**
38 ❑ Feb 1972 Cover: 0.25 **NM** value: **5.00**
39 ❑ Apr 1972 Cover: 0.25 **NM** value: **5.00**
40 ❑ Jun 1972 Cover: 0.25 **NM** value: **5.00**
41 ❑ Aug 1972 Cover: 0.25 **NM** value: **4.00**
42 ❑ Oct 1972 Cover: 0.25 **NM** value: **4.00**
43 ❑ Dec 1972 Cover: 0.25 **NM** value: **4.00**
44 ❑ Feb 1973 Cover: 0.25 **NM** value: **4.00**
45 ❑ Apr 1973 Cover: 0.25 **NM** value: **4.00**
46 ❑ Jun 1973 Cover: 0.25 **NM** value: **4.00**
47 ❑ Aug 1973 Cover: 0.25 **NM** value: **4.00**
48 ❑ Oct 1973 Cover: 0.25 **NM** value: **4.00**
49 ❑ Dec 1973 Cover: 0.25 **NM** value: **4.00**
50 ❑ Feb 1974 Cover: 0.25 **NM** value: **4.00**
51 ❑ Apr 1974 Cover: 0.25 **NM** value: **2.50**
52 ❑ Jun 1974 Cover: 0.25 **NM** value: **2.50**
53 ❑ Aug 1974 Cover: 0.25 **NM** value: **2.50**
54 ❑ Oct 1974 Cover: 0.25 **NM** value: **2.50**
55 ❑ Dec 1974 Cover: 0.25 **NM** value: **2.50**
56 ❑ Feb 1975 Cover: 0.25 **NM** value: **2.50**
57 ❑ Apr 1975 Cover: 0.25 **NM** value: **2.50**
58 ❑ Jul 1975 Cover: 0.25 **NM** value: **2.50**
59 ❑ 1975 Cover: 0.25 **NM** value: **2.50**
60 ❑ Nov 1975 Cover: 0.25 **NM** value: **2.50**
61 ❑ ca. 1976 Cover: 0.25 **NM** value: **2.50**
final issue.

SAD SACK AT HOME FOR THE HOLIDAYS — Lorne-Harvey

1 ❑ Cover: 2.00 **NM** value: **Cover or less**

SAD SACK IN 3-D — Blackthorne

1 ❑ Cover: 2.50 **NM** value: **Cover or less**

SAD SACK LAUGH SPECIAL — Harvey

1 ❑ Win 1958 Cover: 0.25 **NM** value: **75.00**
2 ❑ Spr 1959 Cover: 0.25 **NM** value: **35.00**
3 ❑ 1959 Cover: 0.25 **NM** value: **35.00**
4 ❑ ca. 1959 Cover: 0.25 **NM** value: **30.00**
5 ❑ ca. 1959 Cover: 0.25 **NM** value: **30.00**
6 ❑ ca. 1960 Cover: 0.25 **NM** value: **30.00**
7 ❑ ca. 1960 Cover: 0.25 **NM** value: **30.00**
8 ❑ ca. 1960 Cover: 0.25 **NM** value: **30.00**
9 ❑ ca. 1961 Cover: 0.25 **NM** value: **30.00**
10 ❑ ca. 1961 Cover: 0.25 **NM** value: **30.00**
11 ❑ ca. 1962 Cover: 0.25 **NM** value: **25.00**
12 ❑ ca. 1962 Cover: 0.25 **NM** value: **25.00**
13 ❑ ca. 1962 Cover: 0.25 **NM** value: **25.00**
14 ❑ ca. 1962 Cover: 0.25 **NM** value: **25.00**
15 ❑ Jan 1963 Cover: 0.25 **NM** value: **25.00**
16 ❑ 1963 Cover: 0.25 **NM** value: **25.00**
17 ❑ 1963 Cover: 0.25 **NM** value: **25.00**
18 ❑ Oct 1963 Cover: 0.25 **NM** value: **25.00**
19 ❑ Cover: 0.25 **NM** value: **25.00**
20 ❑ Apr 1964 Cover: 0.25 **NM** value: **25.00**
21 ❑ Jul 1964 Cover: 0.25 **NM** value: **25.00**
22 ❑ Sep 1964 Cover: 0.25 **NM** value: **25.00**
23 ❑ Dec 1964 Cover: 0.25 **NM** value: **25.00**
24 ❑ Mar 1965 Cover: 0.25 **NM** value: **25.00**
25 ❑ Jun 1965 Cover: 0.25 **NM** value: **25.00**
26 ❑ Sep 1965 Cover: 0.25 **NM** value: **25.00**
27 ❑ Dec 1965 Cover: 0.25 **NM** value: **25.00**
28 ❑ Mar 1966 Cover: 0.25 **NM** value: **25.00**
29 ❑ Jun 1966 Cover: 0.25 **NM** value: **25.00**
• Has 1965 Statement, filed 10/1/65; no circ figures published
30 ❑ Aug 1966 Cover: 0.25 **NM** value: **25.00**
31 ❑ 1966 Cover: 0.25 **NM** value: **20.00**
32 ❑ Oct 1966 Cover: 0.25 **NM** value: **20.00**
33 ❑ Dec 1966 Cover: 0.25 **NM** value: **20.00**
34 ❑ Feb 1967 Cover: 0.25 **NM** value: **20.00**
35 ❑ Apr 1967 Cover: 0.25 **NM** value: **20.00**
36 ❑ Jun 1967 Cover: 0.25 **NM** value: **20.00**
37 ❑ Oct 1967 Cover: 0.25 **NM** value: **20.00**
38 ❑ Nov 1967 Cover: 0.25 **NM** value: **20.00**
39 ❑ 1968 Cover: 0.25 **NM** value: **20.00**
40 ❑ Apr 1968 Cover: 0.25 **NM** value: **20.00**
41 ❑ Jun 1968 Cover: 0.25 **NM** value: **20.00**
• Has 1967 Statement, filed 10/1/67; no circ figures published
42 ❑ Aug 1968 Cover: 0.25 **NM** value: **20.00**
43 ❑ Oct 1968 Cover: 0.25 **NM** value: **20.00**
44 ❑ Dec 1968 Cover: 0.25 **NM** value: **20.00**
45 ❑ Feb 1969 Cover: 0.25 **NM** value: **20.00**
46 ❑ Apr 1969 Cover: 0.25 **NM** value: **20.00**
47 ❑ May 1969 Cover: 0.25 **NM** value: **20.00**
48 ❑ Jul 1969 Cover: 0.25 **NM** value: **20.00**
49 ❑ Sep 1969 Cover: 0.25 **NM** value: **20.00**
50 ❑ Nov 1969 Cover: 0.25 **NM** value: **20.00**
51 ❑ Jan 1970 Cover: 0.25 **NM** value: **20.00**
52 ❑ Mar 1970 Cover: 0.25 **NM** value: **20.00**
53 ❑ May 1970 Cover: 0.25 **NM** value: **20.00**
54 ❑ Jul 1970 Cover: 0.25 **NM** value: **20.00**
55 ❑ Sep 1970 Cover: 0.25 **NM** value: **20.00**
56 ❑ Nov 1970 Cover: 0.25 **NM** value: **20.00**
57 ❑ Jan 1971 Cover: 0.25 **NM** value: **20.00**
58 ❑ Mar 1971 Cover: 0.25 **NM** value: **20.00**
59 ❑ May 1971 Cover: 0.25 **NM** value: **20.00**
60 ❑ Jul 1971 Cover: 0.25 **NM** value: **20.00**
61 ❑ Sep 1971 Cover: 0.25 **NM** value: **15.00**
62 ❑ Nov 1971 Cover: 0.25 **NM** value: **15.00**
63 ❑ Jan 1972 Cover: 0.25 **NM** value: **15.00**
64 ❑ Mar 1972 Cover: 0.25 **NM** value: **15.00**
65 ❑ May 1972 Cover: 0.25 **NM** value: **15.00**
66 ❑ Jul 1972 Cover: 0.25 **NM** value: **15.00**
67 ❑ Sep 1972 Cover: 0.25 **NM** value: **15.00**
68 ❑ Nov 1972 Cover: 0.25 **NM** value: **15.00**
69 ❑ Jan 1973 Cover: 0.25 **NM** value: **15.00**
Circ: Statement: **107,117**
70 ❑ Mar 1973 Cover: 0.25 **NM** value: **15.00**
Circ: Statement: **107,117**
71 ❑ May 1973 Cover: 0.25 **NM** value: **15.00**
Circ: Statement: **107,117**
72 ❑ Jul 1973 Cover: 0.25 **NM** value: **15.00**
Circ: Statement: **107,117**
73 ❑ Sep 1973 Cover: 0.25 **NM** value: **15.00**
Circ: Statement: **107,117**
74 ❑ Nov 1973 Cover: 0.25 **NM** value: **15.00**
Circ: Statement: **107,117**
75 ❑ Jan 1974 Cover: 0.25 **NM** value: **15.00**
Circ: Statement: **117,945**
76 ❑ Mar 1974 Cover: 0.25 **NM** value: **15.00**
Circ: Statement: **117,945**
77 ❑ May 1974 Cover: 0.25 **NM** value: **15.00**
Circ: Statement: **117,945**
• Has 1973 Statement, filed 10/1/73; avg print run 238,780; avg sales 107,102; avg subs 15; avg total paid 107,117; samples 345; max existent 107,462; 55% of run returned
78 ❑ Jul 1974 Cover: 0.25 **NM** value: **15.00**
Circ: Statement: **117,945**
79 ❑ Sep 1974 Cover: 0.25 **NM** value: **15.00**
Circ: Statement: **117,945**
80 ❑ Nov 1974 Cover: 0.25 **NM** value: **15.00**
Circ: Statement: **117,945**
81 ❑ Jan 1975 Cover: 0.25 **NM** value: **10.00**
Circ: Statement: **91,159**
82 ❑ Mar 1975 Cover: 0.25 **NM** value: **10.00**
Circ: Statement: **91,159**
83 ❑ Jun 1975 Cover: 0.25 **NM** value: **10.00**
Circ: Statement: **91,159**
• Has 1974 Statement; avg total paid circ 117,945
84 ❑ Aug 1975 Cover: 0.25 **NM** value: **10.00**
Circ: Statement: **91,159**
85 ❑ Oct 1975 Cover: 0.25 **NM** value: **10.00**
Circ: Statement: **91,159**
86 ❑ Dec 1975 Cover: 0.25 **NM** value: **10.00**
Circ: Statement: **91,159**
87 ❑ Feb 1976 Cover: 0.25 **NM** value: **10.00**
88 ❑ Apr 1976 Cover: 0.25 **NM** value: **10.00**
89 ❑ Jun 1976 Cover: 0.25 **NM** value: **10.00**
90 ❑ Aug 1976 Cover: 0.25 **NM** value: **10.00**
91 ❑ Oct 1976 Cover: 0.25 **NM** value: **10.00**
92 ❑ Dec 1976 Cover: 0.25 **NM** value: **10.00**
93 ❑ Feb 1977 Cover: 0.25 **NM** value: **10.00**

SAD SACK NAVY, GOBS 'N' GALS — Harvey

1 ❑ Aug 1972 Cover: 0.25 **NM** value: **12.00**
2 ❑ Oct 1972 Cover: 0.20 **NM** value: **8.00**
3 ❑ Dec 1972 Cover: 0.20 **NM** value: **6.00**
4 ❑ Feb 1973 Cover: 0.20 **NM** value: **6.00**
5 ❑ Apr 1973 Cover: 0.20 **NM** value: **6.00**
6 ❑ Jun 1973 Cover: 0.20 **NM** value: **4.00**
7 ❑ Aug 1973 Cover: 0.20 **NM** value: **4.00**
8 ❑ Oct 1973 Cover: 0.20 **NM** value: **4.00**
📖 Hot Water; Action at Sea; At Sea; Togetherness; Getting the Message; Spoiled Rotten; **A:** George Baker **W:** George Baker

SAD SACK SACK WORLD — Harvey

1 ❑ Oct 1964 Cover: 0.25 **NM** value: **45.00**
2 ❑ ca. 1965 Cover: 0.25 **NM** value: **25.00**
3 ❑ ca. 1965 Cover: 0.25 **NM** value: **25.00**
4 ❑ ca. 1966 Cover: 0.25 **NM** value: **25.00**
5 ❑ Oct 1966 Cover: 0.25 **NM** value: **25.00**
6 ❑ Dec 1966 Cover: 0.25 **NM** value: **20.00**
7 ❑ Apr 1967 Cover: 0.25 **NM** value: **20.00**
8 ❑ Jun 1967 Cover: 0.25 **NM** value: **20.00**
9 ❑ Aug 1967 Cover: 0.25 **NM** value: **20.00**
10 ❑ 1967 Cover: 0.25 **NM** value: **20.00**
11 ❑ Dec 1967 Cover: 0.25 **NM** value: **15.00**
12 ❑ 1968 Cover: 0.25 **NM** value: **15.00**
13 ❑ 1968 Cover: 0.25 **NM** value: **15.00**
14 ❑ 1968 Cover: 0.25 **NM** value: **15.00**
15 ❑ Nov 1968 Cover: 0.25 **NM** value: **15.00**
16 ❑ Mar 1969 Cover: 0.25 **NM** value: **15.00**
17 ❑ Jun 1969 Cover: 0.25 **NM** value: **15.00**
18 ❑ Sep 1969 Cover: 0.25 **NM** value: **15.00**
19 ❑ Nov 1969 Cover: 0.25 **NM** value: **15.00**
20 ❑ Jan 1970 Cover: 0.25 **NM** value: **15.00**
21 ❑ 1970 Cover: 0.25 **NM** value: **10.00**
22 ❑ 1970 Cover: 0.25 **NM** value: **10.00**
23 ❑ Oct 1970 Cover: 0.25 **NM** value: **10.00**
24 ❑ ca. 1971 Cover: 0.25 **NM** value: **10.00**
25 ❑ ca. 1971 Cover: 0.25 **NM** value: **10.00**
26 ❑ ca. 1971 Cover: 0.25 **NM** value: **10.00**
27 ❑ Sep 1971 Cover: 0.25 **NM** value: **10.00**
28 ❑ ca. 1971 Cover: 0.25 **NM** value: **10.00**
29 ❑ ca. 1972 Cover: 0.25 **NM** value: **10.00**
30 ❑ Mar 1972 Cover: 0.25 **NM** value: **10.00**
31 ❑ ca. 1972 Cover: 0.25 **NM** value: **10.00**
32 ❑ ca. 1972 Cover: 0.25 **NM** value: **10.00**
33 ❑ ca. 1972 Cover: 0.25 **NM** value: **10.00**
34 ❑ ca. 1973 Cover: 0.25 **NM** value: **10.00**
35 ❑ Mar 1973 Cover: 0.25 **NM** value: **10.00**
36 ❑ ca. 1973 Cover: 0.25 **NM** value: **10.00**
37 ❑ ca. 1973 Cover: 0.25 **NM** value: **10.00**
38 ❑ ca. 1973 Cover: 0.25 **NM** value: **10.00**
39 ❑ Oct 1973 Cover: 0.25 **NM** value: **10.00**
40 ❑ Dec 1973 Cover: 0.25 **NM** value: **10.00**
41 ❑ Feb 1973 Cover: 0.20 **NM** value: **7.50**
42 ❑ Apr 1973 Cover: 0.20 **NM** value: **7.50**
43 ❑ Jun 1973 Cover: 0.20 **NM** value: **7.50**
44 ❑ Aug 1973 Cover: 0.20 **NM** value: **7.50**
45 ❑ Oct 1973 Cover: 0.20 **NM** value: **7.50**
46 ❑ Dec 1973 Cover: 0.20 **NM** value: **7.50**

Other grades: Multiply prices above by **1.5 for Mint • 2/3 for Very Fine • 1/3 for Fine • 1/5 for Very Good • 1/8 for Good**

SAD SACK'S FUNNY FRIENDS — Harvey

1 ❑ ca. 1955 Cover: 0.10 **NM** value: **75.00**
• **CGC:** 1 graded, best 8.5
2 ❑ ca. 1956 Cover: 0.10 **NM** value: **50.00**
3 ❑ ca. 1956 Cover: 0.10 **NM** value: **50.00**
4 ❑ ca. 1956 Cover: 0.10 **NM** value: **50.00**
5 ❑ ca. 1957 Cover: 0.10 **NM** value: **50.00**
6 ❑ ca. 1957 Cover: 0.10 **NM** value: **40.00**
7 ❑ ca. 1957 Cover: 0.10 **NM** value: **40.00**
8 ❑ ca. 1957 Cover: 0.10 **NM** value: **40.00**
9 ❑ ca. 1957 Cover: 0.10 **NM** value: **40.00**
10 ❑ ca. 1958 Cover: 0.10 **NM** value: **40.00**
11 ❑ ca. 1958 Cover: 0.10 **NM** value: **25.00**
12 ❑ ca. 1958 Cover: 0.10 **NM** value: **25.00**
13 ❑ ca. 1958 Cover: 0.10 **NM** value: **25.00**
14 ❑ ca. 1959 Cover: 0.10 **NM** value: **25.00**
15 ❑ ca. 1959 Cover: 0.10 **NM** value: **25.00**
16 ❑ ca. 1959 Cover: 0.10 **NM** value: **25.00**
17 ❑ ca. 1959 Cover: 0.10 **NM** value: **25.00**
18 ❑ ca. 1959 Cover: 0.10 **NM** value: **25.00**
19 ❑ ca. 1960 Cover: 0.10 **NM** value: **25.00**
20 ❑ ca. 1960 Cover: 0.10 **NM** value: **25.00**
21 ❑ May 1960 Cover: 0.10 **NM** value: **20.00**
22 ❑ Jul 1960 Cover: 0.10 **NM** value: **20.00**
23 ❑ Sep 1960 Cover: 0.10 **NM** value: **20.00**
24 ❑ Nov 1960 Cover: 0.10 **NM** value: **20.00**
25 ❑ Jan 1961 Cover: 0.10 **NM** value: **20.00**
26 ❑ Mar 1961 Cover: 0.10 **NM** value: **20.00**
• Has 1959 Statement, filed 10/1/59; no circ figures published
27 ❑ May 1961 Cover: 0.10 **NM** value: **20.00**
28 ❑ Jul 1961 Cover: 0.10 **NM** value: **20.00**
29 ❑ Sep 1961 Cover: 0.10 **NM** value: **20.00**
30 ❑ Nov 1961 Cover: 0.10 **NM** value: **20.00**
31 ❑ Jan 1962 Cover: 0.10 **NM** value: **15.00**
32 ❑ Mar 1962 Cover: 0.12 **NM** value: **15.00**
33 ❑ May 1962 Cover: 0.12 **NM** value: **15.00**
34 ❑ Jul 1962 Cover: 0.12 **NM** value: **15.00**
35 ❑ Sep 1962 Cover: 0.12 **NM** value: **15.00**
36 ❑ Nov 1962 Cover: 0.12 **NM** value: **15.00**
37 ❑ Jan 1963 Cover: 0.12 **NM** value: **15.00**
38 ❑ Mar 1963 Cover: 0.12 **NM** value: **15.00**
39 ❑ May 1963 Cover: 0.12 **NM** value: **15.00**
40 ❑ Jul 1963 Cover: 0.12 **NM** value: **15.00**
41 ❑ Sep 1963 Cover: 0.12 **NM** value: **15.00**
42 ❑ Nov 1963 Cover: 0.12 **NM** value: **15.00**
43 ❑ Jan 1964 Cover: 0.12 **NM** value: **15.00**
44 ❑ Mar 1964 Cover: 0.12 **NM** value: **15.00**
45 ❑ May 1964 Cover: 0.12 **NM** value: **15.00**
46 ❑ Jul 1964 Cover: 0.12 **NM** value: **15.00**
47 ❑ Sep 1964 Cover: 0.12 **NM** value: **15.00**
48 ❑ Nov 1964 Cover: 0.12 **NM** value: **15.00**
49 ❑ Jan 1965 Cover: 0.12 **NM** value: **15.00**
50 ❑ Mar 1965 Cover: 0.12 **NM** value: **15.00**
51 ❑ May 1965 Cover: 0.12 **NM** value: **10.00**
52 ❑ Jul 1965 Cover: 0.12 **NM** value: **10.00**
53 ❑ Sep 1965 Cover: 0.12 **NM** value: **10.00**
54 ❑ Nov 1965 Cover: 0.12 **NM** value: **10.00**
55 ❑ Jan 1966 Cover: 0.12 **NM** value: **10.00**
56 ❑ Mar 1966 Cover: 0.12 **NM** value: **10.00**
57 ❑ May 1966 Cover: 0.12 **NM** value: **10.00**
58 ❑ Jul 1966 Cover: 0.12 **NM** value: **10.00**
59 ❑ Sep 1966 Cover: 0.12 **NM** value: **10.00**
60 ❑ Nov 1966 Cover: 0.12 **NM** value: **10.00**
61 ❑ Jan 1967 Cover: 0.12 **NM** value: **10.00**
62 ❑ Mar 1967 Cover: 0.12 **NM** value: **10.00**
63 ❑ May 1967 Cover: 0.12 **NM** value: **10.00**
64 ❑ 1967 Cover: 0.12 **NM** value: **10.00**
65 ❑ Aug 1967 Cover: 0.12 **NM** value: **10.00**
66 ❑ Oct 1967 Cover: 0.12 **NM** value: **10.00**
67 ❑ Jan 1968 Cover: 0.12 **NM** value: **10.00**
68 ❑ Mar 1968 Cover: 0.12 **NM** value: **10.00**
69 ❑ May 1968 Cover: 0.12 **NM** value: **10.00**
• Has 1966 Statement, filed 10/1/66; no circ figures published
70 ❑ 1968 Cover: 0.12 **NM** value: **10.00**
71 ❑ 1968 Cover: 0.12 **NM** value: **10.00**
72 ❑ Jan 1969 Cover: 0.12 **NM** value: **10.00**
73 ❑ Apr 1969 Cover: 0.12 **NM** value: **10.00**
74 ❑ Aug 1969 Cover: 0.15 **NM** value: **10.00**
75 ❑ Oct 1969 Cover: 0.15 **NM** value: **10.00**

SAFEST PLACE IN THE WORLD, THE — Dark Horse

Steve Ditko, the artist famous for creating The Amazing Spider-Man, had a long history creating weird science-fiction and horror comics in the fifties and sixties. Himself was a loner who was virtually never interviewed or photographed, Ditko appropriately developed many characters who didn't "fit in."

This one-shot is Ditko at his alienated best. It's set in a totalitarian regime where the oppressors are involved in complicated schemes for power, with deadly consequences to those around them. The catalyst is a roll of film showing military preparations, taken by agents working against the regime. One by one, the agents are tracked down, until the trail leads to a harmless college professor and his wife. The professor is killed and his wife brutally questioned, but the film is never found by the police. Because it's hidden ... in the safest place in the world.

1 ❑ ca. 1993 Cover: 2.50 **NM** value: **Cover or less**
Circ: CapCity orders: **4,675**
No issue number. Biette Person **A:** Steve Ditko **W:** Steve Ditko

SAFETY-BELT MAN — Sirius

1 ❑ Jun 1994 Cover: 2.50 **NM** value: **Cover or less**
Why Did the Dummy cross the Road?; A Day in the Death of Bill Bardo; Little Goody Two-Hooves **A:** Dark One; Hunter Jackson **W:** Dark One; Hunter Jackson; Robb Horan
2 ❑ Oct 1994 Cover: 2.50 **NM** value: **Cover or less**
3 ❑ Feb 1995 Cover: 2.50 **NM** value: **Cover or less**
4 ❑ Jun 1995 Cover: 2.50 **NM** value: **Cover or less**
The Videon Truth, Part 2; Lady Def • color centerfold **A:** Jozef Szekeres; Joseph Michael Linsner **W:** Joseph Michael Linsner; Robb Horan
5 ❑ Aug 1995 Cover: 2.50 **NM** value: **Cover or less**
6 ❑ Oct 1995 Cover: 2.50 **NM** value: **Cover or less**

SAFETY-BELT MAN: ALL HELL — Sirius

1 ❑ 1996 Cover: 2.95 **NM** value: **Cover or less**
2 ❑ Jun 1996 Cover: 2.95 **NM** value: **Cover or less**
3 ❑ 1996 Cover: 2.95 **NM** value: **Cover or less**
4 ❑ Sep 1996 Cover: 2.95 **NM** value: **Cover or less**
Circ: Diamd. preorders: **3,434**
5 ❑ Jan 1997 Cover: 2.95 **NM** value: **Cover or less**
Circ: Diamd. preorders: **2,982**
6 ❑ Aug 1997 Cover: 2.95 **NM** value: **Cover or less**
Circ: Diamd. preorders: **2,609**

SAFFIRE — Image

1 ❑ Apr 2000 Cover: 2.95 **NM** value: **Cover or less**
Circ: Diamd. preorders: **23,866**
A: Mat Broome **W:** Mat Broome; Mike Woods
2 ❑ Dec 2000 Cover: 2.95 **NM** value: **Cover or less**
Circ: Diamd. preorders: **15,329**
A: Mat Broome **W:** Mat Broome; Mike Woods
3 ❑ Feb 2001 Cover: 2.95 **NM** value: **Cover or less**
Circ: Diamd. preorders: **13,646**
A: Mat Broome **W:** Mat Broome; Mike Woods

SAGA — Odyssey

1 ❑ b&w Cover: 1.95 **NM** value: **Cover or less**
The Apatian Chronicles

SAGA OF CRYSTAR, THE CRYSTAL WARRIOR — Marvel

1 ❑ May 1983 Cover: 2.00 **NM** value: **Cover or less**
The Sundered Throne **A:** Bret Blevins **W:** Mary Jo Duffy ★ Origin of Crystar. ★ 1st Appearance of Crystar.
2 ❑ Jul 1983 Cover: 0.60 **NM** value: **1.00**
Ika **A:** Bret Blevins **W:** Mary Jo Duffy ★ 1st Appearance of Ika.
3 ❑ Sep 1983 Cover: 0.60 **NM** value: **1.00**
In The Sanctum Sanctorum Of Doctor Strange! **A:** Ron Frenz **W:** Mary Jo Duffy ★ Appearance of Doctor Strange.
4 ❑ Nov 1983 Cover: 0.60 **NM** value: **1.00**
5 ❑ Jan 1984 Cover: 0.60 **NM** value: **1.00**
6 ❑ Mar 1984 Cover: 0.60 **NM** value: **1.00**
★ Appearance of Nightcrawler.
7 ❑ May 1984 Cover: 0.60 **NM** value: **1.00**
8 ❑ Jul 1984 Cover: 0.60 **NM** value: **1.00**
9 ❑ Sep 1984 Cover: 0.60 **NM** value: **1.00**
10 ❑ Nov 1984 Cover: 0.60 **NM** value: **1.00**
11 ❑ Feb 1985 Cover: 1.00 **NM** value: **Cover or less**
• Double-size. final issue.★ Appearance of Alpha Flight.

SAGA OF ELF FACE — Exter Entrance

1 ❑ **NM** value: **1.00**
2 ❑ **NM** value: **1.00**

SAGA OF RA'S AL GHUL — DC

1 ❑ Jan 1988 Cover: 2.50 **NM** value: **Cover or less**
Circ: CapCity orders: **14,600**
2 ❑ Feb 1988 Cover: 2.50 **NM** value: **Cover or less**
Circ: CapCity orders: **12,900**
3 ❑ Mar 1988 Cover: 2.50 **NM** value: **Cover or less**
Circ: CapCity orders: **13,900**
4 ❑ Apr 1988 Cover: 2.50 **NM** value: **Cover or less**
Circ: CapCity orders: **13,350**

SAGA OF THE MAN ELF, THE — Trident

1 ❑ Aug 1989 Cover: 2.25 **NM** value: **Cover or less**
Reigns of Power **A:** Steve Whitaker **W:** Guy Lawley
2 ❑ 1989 Cover: 2.25 **NM** value: **Cover or less**
3 ❑ 1989 Cover: 2.25 **NM** value: **Cover or less**
4 ❑ 1990 Cover: 2.25 **NM** value: **Cover or less**
5 ❑ 1990 Cover: 2.25 **NM** value: **Cover or less**

SAGA OF THE ORIGINAL HUMAN TORCH — Marvel

In comics, the word "Saga" in the title tends to tip readers off that they're looking at either a reprint series or a retelling — Marvel Saga, Elektra Saga, etc. True to the pattern, Saga of the Original Human Torch tells the story of, natch, the original Human Torch, an android created by Professor Horton which, due to a design error, burst into flame upon contact with the air. In time this "Human Torch" learned to control his powers and used them to fight criminals (and later, the Nazis). After the war, he resumed his career as a crimefighter until he was buried alive in the 1950s by criminals. Later, his body would be transformed into the Avenger known as Vision.

The Human Torch was Marvel's first super-hero, created by Carl Burgos, who sold the idea to Martin Goodman for his new line of Timely Comics (Marvel's forerunner). He first appeared in a movie theater giveaway, then in Marvel Comics #1. The Torch went on to become one of the most famous super-heroes of the Golden Age, along with Captain America and the Sub-Mariner — who had his own contemporaneous "Saga of the" series from Roy Thomas.

1 ❑ Apr 1990 Cover: 1.50 **NM** value: **Cover or less**
Circ: CapCity orders: **31,500**
The Lighted Torch **A:** Rich Buckler **W:** Roy Thomas ★ Origin of The Human Torch I (android).
2 ❑ May 1990 Cover: 1.50 **NM** value: **Cover or less**
Circ: CapCity orders: **25,000**
A: Rich Buckler **W:** Roy Thomas ★ Origin of Toro.
3 ❑ Jun 1990 Cover: 1.50 **NM** value: **Cover or less**
Circ: CapCity orders: **23,200**
Out Of The Ashes **A:** Rich Buckler **W:** Roy Thomas ★ Death of Hitler.
4 ❑ Jul 1990 Cover: 1.50 **NM** value: **Cover or less**
Circ: CapCity orders: **25,100**
A: Rich Buckler **W:** Roy Thomas

SAGA OF THE REALM — Caliber

1 ❑ b&w Cover: 2.50 **NM** value: **Cover or less**
2 ❑ b&w Cover: 2.50 **NM** value: **Cover or less**
3 ❑ b&w Cover: 2.50 **NM** value: **Cover or less**

SAGA OF THE SUB-MARINER — Marvel

1 ❑ Nov 1988 Cover: 1.25 **NM** value: **1.50**
Circ: CapCity orders: **27,000**
A Legend A-Borning **A:** Rich Buckler **W:** Roy Thomas; Dann Thomas ★ Origin of Sub-Mariner.
2 ❑ Dec 1988 Cover: 1.50 **NM** value: **Cover or less**
Circ: CapCity orders: **20,300**
3 ❑ Jan 1989 Cover: 1.50 **NM** value: **Cover or less**
Circ: CapCity orders: **18,800**
4 ❑ Feb 1989 Cover: 1.50 **NM** value: **Cover or less**
Circ: CapCity orders: **18,000**
★ Appearance of Human Torch.
5 ❑ Mar 1989 Cover: 1.50 **NM** value: **Cover or less**
Circ: CapCity orders: **17,200**
★ Appearance of Human Torch, Captain America, Invaders.
6 ❑ Apr 1989 Cover: 1.50 **NM** value: **Cover or less**
Circ: CapCity orders: **15,300**
★ Appearance of Torch, Human Torch, Captain America, Invaders.
7 ❑ May 1989 Cover: 1.50 **NM** value: **Cover or less**
Circ: CapCity orders: **14,900**
★ Appearance of Fantastic Four.
8 ❑ Jun 1989 Cover: 1.50 **NM** value: **Cover or less**
Circ: CapCity orders: **14,350**
★ Appearance of Fantastic Four, Avengers.
9 ❑ Jul 1989 Cover: 1.50 **NM** value: **Cover or less**
Circ: CapCity orders: **15,100**
★ Appearance of Fantastic Four, Avengers.
10 ❑ Aug 1989 Cover: 1.50 **NM** value: **Cover or less**
Circ: CapCity orders: **13,800**
11 ❑ Sep 1989 Cover: 1.50 **NM** value: **Cover or less**
Circ: CapCity orders: **13,700**
12 ❑ Oct 1989 Cover: 1.50 **NM** value: **Cover or less**
Circ: CapCity orders: **13,800**

SAGA OF THE SWAMP THING, THE — DC

An exception to the rule of thumb about "Saga" series being reprints or retellings, Saga of the Swamp Thing is, instead, a revival — and a successful one at that. Drawn from the mid-seventies monster title, everybody's favorite green monster reemerged in this title in 1982, which eventually changed its name to Swamp Thing with issue #39).

It's the story of Dr. Alec Holland, a biochemist who was immolated by his own chemicals. Trying to save himself, he dove into a swamp, where the burning chemicals interacted with the vegetation in the bog and turned the mild-mannered scientist into the grotesque monster and pitiful hero known as Swamp Thing.

In the years since this title's premiere, it had grown from a monster book into a more mature series, drawing on weird and sometimes beautiful themes of a more adult nature.

1 ❑ May 1982 Cover: 0.60 **NM** value: **3.00**
• **CGC:** 6 graded, best 9.9
What Peace There May Be in Silence **A:** Tom Yeates **W:** Martin Pasko ★ Origin of Swamp Thing.
2 ❑ Jun 1982 Cover: 0.60 **NM** value: **2.00**
3 ❑ Jul 1982 Cover: 0.60 **NM** value: **2.00**
4 ❑ Aug 1982 Cover: 0.60 **NM** value: **2.00**
In the White Room
5 ❑ Sep 1982 Cover: 0.60 **NM** value: **2.00**
6 ❑ Oct 1982 Cover: 0.60 **NM** value: **2.00**
7 ❑ Nov 1982 Cover: 0.60 **NM** value: **2.00**
8 ❑ Dec 1982 Cover: 0.60 **NM** value: **2.00**
9 ❑ Jan 1983 Cover: 0.60 **NM** value: **2.00**
10 ❑ Feb 1983 Cover: 0.60 **NM** value: **2.00**
11 ❑ Mar 1983 Cover: 0.60 **NM** value: **2.00**
12 ❑ Apr 1983 Cover: 0.60 **NM** value: **2.00**
13 ❑ May 1983 Cover: 0.60 **NM** value: **2.00**
14 ❑ Jun 1983 Cover: 0.60 **NM** value: **2.00**
15 ❑ Jul 1983 Cover: 0.60 **NM** value: **2.00**
16 ❑ Aug 1983 Cover: 0.60 **NM** value: **2.00**
17 ❑ Oct 1983 Cover: 0.60 **NM** value: **2.00**
18 ❑ Nov 1983 Cover: 0.60 **NM** value: **2.00**

CGC-graded: Multiply prices above by **33 for 9.9 M • 16 for 9.8 NM/M • 7 for 9.6 NM+ • 5 for 9.4 NM • 2.5 for 9.2 NM- • 1.5 for 9.0 VF/NM**

19 ❑ Dec 1983 Cover: 0.60 **NM** value: **2.00**
20 ❑ Jan 1984 Cover: 0.75 **NM** value: **12.00**
• **CGC:** 13 graded, best 9.6
• Alan Moore scripts begin **W:** Alan Moore
21 ❑ Feb 1984 Cover: 0.75 **NM** value: **10.00**
• **CGC:** 6 graded, best 9.4
W: Alan Moore ★ Origin of Swamp Thing.
22 ❑ Mar 1984 Cover: 0.75 **NM** value: **6.00**
• **CGC:** 3 graded, best 9.6
W: Alan Moore
23 ❑ Apr 1984 Cover: 0.75 **NM** value: **6.00**
• **CGC:** 3 graded, best 9.4
W: Alan Moore
24 ❑ May 1984 Cover: 0.75 **NM** value: **6.00**
• **CGC:** 1 graded, best 9.4
W: Alan Moore ★ Appearance of Justice League.
25 ❑ Jun 1984 Cover: 0.75 **NM** value: **6.00**
W: Alan Moore
26 ❑ Jul 1984 Cover: 0.75 **NM** value: **4.00**
W: Alan Moore
27 ❑ Aug 1984 Cover: 0.75 **NM** value: **4.00**
• **CGC:** 2 graded, best 9.0
W: Alan Moore
28 ❑ Sep 1984 Cover: 0.75 **NM** value: **4.00**
• **CGC:** 3 graded, best 9.4
W: Alan Moore
29 ❑ Oct 1984 Cover: 0.75 **NM** value: **4.00**
• **CGC:** 1 graded, best 8.5
W: Alan Moore
30 ❑ Nov 1984 Cover: 0.75 **NM** value: **4.00**
• **CGC:** 1 graded, best 9.4
W: Alan Moore
31 ❑ Dec 1984 Cover: 0.75 **NM** value: **4.00**
• **CGC:** 2 graded, best 9.6
W: Alan Moore
32 ❑ Jan 1985 Cover: 0.75 **NM** value: **4.00**
• **CGC:** 2 graded, best 9.6
W: Alan Moore
33 ❑ Feb 1985 Cover: 0.75 **NM** value: **3.00**
• **CGC:** 1 graded, best 8.5
34 ❑ Mar 1985 Cover: 0.75 **NM** value: **5.00**
• **CGC:** 3 graded, best 9.8
W: Alan Moore
35 ❑ Apr 1985 Cover: 0.75 **NM** value: **3.00**
• **CGC:** 1 graded, best 9.6
W: Alan Moore
36 ❑ May 1985 Cover: 0.75 **NM** value: **3.00**
Circ: CapCity orders: **10,050** • **CGC:** 1 graded, best 9.4
W: Alan Moore
37 ❑ Jun 1985 Cover: 0.75 **NM** value: **16.00**
Circ: CapCity orders: **9,400** • **CGC:** 23 graded, best 9.9
📖 Growth Patterns **A:** Rick Veitch; John Totleben **W:** Alan Moore ★ 1st Appearance of John Constantine.
38 ❑ Jul 1985 Cover: 0.75 **NM** value: **8.00**
Circ: CapCity orders: **11,350** • **CGC:** 5 graded, best 9.9
📖 Still Waters • Series continues as Swamp Thing **A:** Stan Woch; John Totleben **W:** Alan Moore ★ 2nd Appearance of John Constantine. ★ 2nd Appearance of John Constantine.
39 ❑ Aug 1985 Cover: 0.75 **NM** value: **7.00**
Circ: CapCity orders: **9,700** • **CGC:** 5 graded, best 9.8
📖 Fish Story **A:** Stephen R. Bissette; John Totleben **W:** Alan Moore ★ Appearance of John Constantine.
40 ❑ Sep 1985 Cover: 0.75 **NM** value: **7.00**
Circ: CapCity orders: **9,550** • **CGC:** 2 graded, best 9.4
📖 The Curse **A:** Stephen R. Bissette; John Totleben **W:** Alan Moore ★ Appearance of John Constantine.
41 ❑ Oct 1985 Cover: 0.75 **NM** value: **3.00**
Circ: CapCity orders: **9,050** • **CGC:** 1 graded, best 9.4
W: Alan Moore
42 ❑ Nov 1985 Cover: 0.75 **NM** value: **3.00**
Circ: CapCity orders: **9,850** • **CGC:** 2 graded, best 9.6
W: Alan Moore
43 ❑ Dec 1985 Cover: 0.75 **NM** value: **3.00**
Circ: CapCity orders: **9,950** • **CGC:** 1 graded, best 9.6
W: Alan Moore
44 ❑ Jan 1986 Cover: 0.75 **NM** value: **3.00**
Circ: CapCity orders: **10,450** • **CGC:** 1 graded, best 9.6
W: Alan Moore
45 ❑ Feb 1986 Cover: 0.75 **NM** value: **3.00**
Circ: CapCity orders: **11,050** • **CGC:** 1 graded, best 9.4
• Series continued as "Swamp Thing (2nd Series) #46" **W:** Alan Moore
Anl 1❑ca. 1982 Cover: 1.00 **NM** value: **2.00**
• **CGC:** 2 graded, best 9.6
• 1982 **A:** Mark Texeira; Tony DeZuniga **W:** Bruce Jones; Wes Craven
Anl 2❑ca. 1985 Cover: 1.25 **NM** value: **4.00**
W: Alan Moore ★ Appearance of Demon, Spectre, Deadman, Phantom Stranger.
Anl 3❑ca. 1987 Cover: 2.00 **NM** value: **2.50**
Circ: CapCity orders: **16,700**
📖 Distant Cousins • 1987 **A:** Shawn McManus; Rick Veitch; Stan Woch; Jim Fern **W:** Rick Veitch ★ Appearance of Congorilla.
Bk 1❑ Cover: 10.95 **NM** value: **12.95**
• Trade Paperback. • reprints #21-27
Bk 2❑ Cover: 17.95 **NM** value: **Cover or less**
• Trade Paperback. 📖 Love and Death • Reprints Saga of Swamp Thing #28-34
Bk 3❑ Cover: 19.95 **NM** value: **Cover or less**
• The Curse; Collects Saga of Swamp Thing #35-42 **A:** Stephen R. Bissette; John Totleben **W:** Alan Moore

SAIGON CHRONICLES — Avalon

1 ❑ Cover: 2.95 **NM** value: **Cover or less**
📖 This Crummy War; The Enemy Within; Terror in a Vietcong Tunnel; The Battle for Twombly's Twins

SAILOR MOON COMIC — Mixxzine

The Sailor Moon saga actually began in the mid-1980s with the award-winning story "Love Call" which introduced a teenage girl super-hero named Sailor V. As Sailor V grew in popularity, creator Naoko Takeuchi expanded her story to include other such super-heroes-Sailor Mars, Sailor Jupiter, Sailor Mercury, and Sailor Moon, who eventually replaced Sailor V. The manga saga of these super-powered girls continued to win awards and inspired a very popular anime television series.

In this English-language series, Sailor Moon and the others finally meet Sailor V face-to-face and come to terms with her secret.

This is intriguing, beautifully rendered stuff, in not-always-easy-to-find editions from MixxZine (later TokyoPop).

1 ❑ Oct 1998 Cover: 2.95 **NM** value: **15.00**
• **CGC:** 5 graded, best 9.6
• Continued from MixxZine **A:** Naoko Takeuchi **W:** Naoko Takeuchi
1/A ❑ Oct 1998 Cover: 2.95 **NM** value: **12.00**
• San Diego lmited edition version. **A:** Naoko Takeuchi **W:** Naoko Takeuchi
2 ❑ Nov 1998 Cover: 2.95 **NM** value: **8.00**
Circ: Diamd. preorders: **17,571** • **CGC:** 1 graded, best 9.6
A: Naoko Takeuchi **W:** Naoko Takeuchi
3 ❑ Dec 1998 Cover: 2.95 **NM** value: **8.00**
Circ: Diamd. preorders: **16,874**
• Destruction of the Moon Kingdom (flashback) **A:** Naoko Takeuchi **W:** Naoko Takeuchi ★ Death of Kunzite.
4 ❑ Jan 1999 Cover: 2.95 **NM** value: **8.00**
Circ: Diamd. preorders: **17,085**
A: Naoko Takeuchi **W:** Naoko Takeuchi
5 ❑ Feb 1999 Cover: 2.95 **NM** value: **6.00**
Circ: Diamd. preorders: **18,095**
A: Naoko Takeuchi **W:** Naoko Takeuchi
6 ❑ Mar 1999 Cover: 2.95 **NM** value: **6.00**
Circ: Diamd. preorders: **19,870**
A: Naoko Takeuchi **W:** Naoko Takeuchi
7 ❑ Apr 1999 Cover: 2.95 **NM** value: **6.00**
Circ: Diamd. preorders: **21,298**
A: Naoko Takeuchi **W:** Naoko Takeuchi
8 ❑ May 1999 Cover: 2.95 **NM** value: **5.00**
Circ: Diamd. preorders: **21,364**
A: Naoko Takeuchi **W:** Naoko Takeuchi
9 ❑ Jun 1999 Cover: 2.95 **NM** value: **4.00**
Circ: Diamd. preorders: **21,068**
A: Naoko Takeuchi **W:** Naoko Takeuchi
10 ❑ Jul 1999 Cover: 2.95 **NM** value: **3.00**
Circ: Diamd. preorders: **21,020**
A: Naoko Takeuchi **W:** Naoko Takeuchi
11 ❑ Aug 1999 Cover: 2.95 **NM** value: **3.00**
Circ: Diamd. preorders: **20,466**
A: Naoko Takeuchi **W:** Naoko Takeuchi
12 ❑ Sep 1999 Cover: 2.95 **NM** value: **3.00**
Circ: Diamd. preorders: **20,071**
A: Naoko Takeuchi **W:** Naoko Takeuchi
13 ❑ Oct 1999 Cover: 2.95 **NM** value: **3.00**
Circ: Diamd. preorders: **21,163**
A: Naoko Takeuchi **W:** Naoko Takeuchi
14 ❑ Nov 1999 Cover: 2.95 **NM** value: **3.00**
Circ: Diamd. preorders: **23,772**
A: Naoko Takeuchi **W:** Naoko Takeuchi
15 ❑ Dec 1999 Cover: 2.95 **NM** value: **3.00**
Circ: Diamd. preorders: **20,762**
A: Naoko Takeuchi **W:** Naoko Takeuchi
16 ❑ Jan 2000 Cover: 2.95 **NM** value: **3.00**
Circ: Diamd. preorders: **20,126**
17 ❑ Feb 2000 Cover: 2.95 **NM** value: **3.00**
Circ: Diamd. preorders: **19,047**
18 ❑ Mar 2000 Cover: 2.95 **NM** value: **3.00**
Circ: Diamd. preorders: **19,118**
19 ❑ Apr 2000 Cover: 2.95 **NM** value: **3.00**
Circ: Diamd. preorders: **18,260**
20 ❑ May 2000 Cover: 2.95 **NM** value: **3.00**
Circ: Diamd. preorders: **17,918**
21 ❑ Jun 2000 Cover: 2.95 **NM** value: **3.00**
Circ: Diamd. preorders: **17,764**
22 ❑ Jul 2000 Cover: 2.95 **NM** value: **3.00**
Circ: Diamd. preorders: **17,207**
23 ❑ Aug 2000 Cover: 2.95 **NM** value: **3.00**
Circ: Diamd. preorders: **16,550**
24 ❑ Sep 2000 Cover: 2.95 **NM** value: **3.00**
Circ: Diamd. preorders: **17,141**
25 ❑ Oct 2000 Cover: 2.95 **NM** value: **3.00**
Circ: Diamd. preorders: **17,451**
26 ❑ Nov 2000 Cover: 2.95 **NM** value: **3.00**
Circ: Diamd. preorders: **17,164**
27 ❑ Dec 2000 Cover: 2.95 **NM** value: **3.00**
Circ: Diamd. preorders: **16,693**
28 ❑ Jan 2001 Cover: 2.95 **NM** value: **3.00**
Circ: Diamd. preorders: **15,575**
29 ❑ Feb 2001 Cover: 2.95 **NM** value: **3.00**
Circ: Diamd. preorders: **15,154**
30 ❑ Mar 2001 Cover: 2.95 **NM** value: **3.00**
Circ: Diamd. preorders: **15,175**
31 ❑ Apr 2001 Cover: 2.95 **NM** value: **Cover or less**
Circ: Diamd. preorders: **14,806**
32 ❑ May 2001 Cover: 2.95 **NM** value: **Cover or less**
Circ: Diamd. preorders: **14,721**
33 ❑ Jun 2001 Cover: 2.95 **NM** value: **Cover or less**
Circ: Diamd. preorders: **14,793**
Bk 1❑ Cover: 11.95 **NM** value: **Cover or less**

SAILOR MOON SUPERS — Mixx

1 ❑ Cover: 9.95 **NM** value: **Cover or less**

SAILOR'S STORY, A — Marvel

1 ❑ Cover: 5.95 **NM** value: **Cover or less**
Circ: CapCity orders: **3,850**

SAILOR'S STORY, A: WINDS, DREAMS, AND DRAGONS — Marvel

1 ❑ Cover: 6.95 **NM** value: **Cover or less**
Circ: CapCity orders: **1,600**

SAINT, THE — Avon

1 ❑ Aug 1947 Cover: 0.10 **NM** value: **550.00**
• **CGC:** 4 graded, best 9.2
Bondage cover. **A:** Jack Kamen(cover)
2 ❑ ca. 1947 Cover: 0.10 **NM** value: **300.00**
3 ❑ ca. 1948 Cover: 0.10 **NM** value: **225.00**
• **CGC:** 1 graded, best 9.2
4 ❑ ca. 1948 Cover: 0.10 **NM** value: **225.00**
• **CGC:** 2 graded, best 7.5
5 ❑ ca. 1949 Cover: 0.10 **NM** value: **225.00**
• **CGC:** 1 graded, best 9.4
6 ❑ ca. 1949 Cover: 0.10 **NM** value: **250.00**
• **CGC:** 1 graded, best 9.4
7 ❑ ca. 1950 Cover: 0.10 **NM** value: **165.00**
8 ❑ ca. 1950 Cover: 0.10 **NM** value: **165.00**
9 ❑ ca. 1950 Cover: 0.10 **NM** value: **165.00**
10 ❑ ca. 1951 Cover: 0.10 **NM** value: **125.00**
11 ❑ ca. 1951 Cover: 0.10 **NM** value: **125.00**
• **CGC:** 1 graded, best 9.4
12 ❑ ca. 1952 Cover: 0.10 **NM** value: **125.00**

SAINT ANGEL — Image

0 ❑ Mar 2000 Cover: 2.95 **NM** value: **Cover or less**
Circ: Diamd. preorders: **7,182**
A: Karl Altstaetter **W:** Robert Napton; Karl Altstaetter
1 ❑ Jun 2000 Cover: 3.95 **NM** value: **Cover or less**
Circ: Diamd. preorders: **15,810**
A: Karl Altstaetter **W:** Robert Napton; Karl Altstaetter
2 ❑ Oct 2000 Cover: 3.95 **NM** value: **Cover or less**
Circ: Diamd. preorders: **10,134**
A: Karl Altstaetter **W:** Robert Napton; Karl Altstaetter
3 ❑ Dec 2000 Cover: 3.95 **NM** value: **Cover or less**
Circ: Diamd. preorders: **8,500**
A: Karl Altstaetter **W:** Robert Napton; Karl Altstaetter
4 ❑ Mar 2001 Cover: 3.95 **NM** value: **Cover or less**
Circ: Diamd. preorders: **7,321**
A: Karl Altstaetter **W:** Robert Napton; Karl Altstaetter

SAINT GERMAINE — Caliber

1 ❑ ca. 1997 Cover: 2.95 **NM** value: **Cover or less**

SAINTS, THE — Saturn

0 ❑ Apr 1995, b&w Cover: 2.50 **NM** value: **Cover or less**
1 ❑ Fal 1996, b&w Cover: 2.50 **NM** value: **Cover or less**

SAINT SINNER — Marvel

1 ❑ Oct 1993 Cover: 2.50 **NM** value: **Cover or less**
Circ: CapCity orders: **19,900**
foil cover. 📖 World Without End **A:** Max Douglas **W:** Elaine Lee ★ Origin of Saint Sinner.
2 ❑ Nov 1993 Cover: 1.75 **NM** value: **Cover or less**
Circ: CapCity orders: **11,000**
3 ❑ Dec 1993 Cover: 1.75 **NM** value: **Cover or less**
Circ: CapCity orders: **8,500**
4 ❑ Jan 1994 Cover: 1.75 **NM** value: **Cover or less**
Circ: CapCity orders: **7,500**
5 ❑ Feb 1994 Cover: 1.75 **NM** value: **Cover or less**
Circ: CapCity orders: **6,050**
6 ❑ Mar 1994 Cover: 1.75 **NM** value: **Cover or less**
Circ: CapCity orders: **4,850**
📖 The Child Stealer, Part 1 **A:** Larry Brown **W:** Elaine Lee
7 ❑ Apr 1994 Cover: 1.75 **NM** value: **Cover or less**
Circ: CapCity orders: **4,250**
📖 The Child Stealer, Part 2 **A:** Larry Brown **W:** Elaine Lee
8 ❑ Apr 1994 Cover: 1.75 **NM** value: **Cover or less**

SALAMANDROID — Harris

Ash 1❑ **NM** value: **1.00**
📖 Speculation **A:** Ethan Van Sciver **W:** Ethan Van Sciver

SALIMBA — Blackthorne

1 ❑ b&w Cover: 3.50 **NM** value: **Cover or less**
3D 1❑Aug 1986, b&w Cover: 2.50 **NM** value: **Cover or less**
Circ: CapCity orders: **3,900**
📖 Pirate's Heart! **A:** Paul Chadwick **W:** Steve Perry
3D 2❑Sep 1986 Cover: 2.50 **NM** value: **Cover or less**
Circ: CapCity orders: **3,385**
📖 Well of Night **A:** Paul Chadwick **W:** Steve Perry

SALLY FORTH — Fantagraphics / Eros

1 ❑
1-2 ❑ Jun 1995 Cover: 2.95 **NM** value: **Cover or less**
2 ❑ Oct 1993 Cover: 2.95 **NM** value: **Cover or less**
3 ❑ Feb 1994 Cover: 2.95 **NM** value: **Cover or less**
4 ❑ Apr 1994 Cover: 2.95 **NM** value: **Cover or less**
5 ❑ Jul 1994 Cover: 2.95 **NM** value: **Cover or less**
6 ❑ Sep 1994 Cover: 2.95 **NM** value: **Cover or less**
7 ❑ Nov 1994 Cover: 2.95 **NM** value: **Cover or less**
8 ❑ Jan 1995 Cover: 2.95 **NM** value: **Cover or less**

SAM & MAX, FREELANCE POLICE — Marvel / Epic

1 ❑ Cover: 2.25 **NM** value: **Cover or less**
Circ: CapCity orders: **8,800**
No issue number.

Other grades: Multiply prices above by **1.5 for Mint • 2/3 for Very Fine • 1/3 for Fine • 1/5 for Very Good • 1/8 for Good**

SAM & MAX FREELANCE POLICE SPECIAL — Comico

1 ❑ ca. 1989 Cover: 2.75 **NM** value: **Cover or less**
Circ: CapCity orders: **4,750**
A: Steve Purcell **W:** Steve Purcell

SAM AND MAX, FREELANCE POLICE SPECIAL, THE — Fishwrap

1 ❑ ca. 1987, b&w Cover: 1.75 **NM** value: **Cover or less**

SAM & MAX FREELANCE POLICE SPECIAL COLOR COLLECTION — Marvel / Epic

1 ❑ Cover: 4.95 **NM** value: **Cover or less**
No issue number.

SAM AND TWITCH — Image

Spinning out of the pages of Spawn, Sam and Twitch are retired homicide detectives who are called back into service to investigate a string of unusually gruesome murders.

As a grim calling card, the killer leaves four of the same severed body parts — such as, four thumbs — at the scene of each of the crimes. All Sam and Twitch have to go on is the word of an elderly woman who caught a very brief glimpse of the perp leaving a crime scene. This is grim-and-gritty stuff from writer Brian Michael Bendis and artist Angel Medina (The Incredible Hulk, Kiss: Psycho Circus), but it makes for interesting reading.

1 ❑ Aug 1999 Cover: 2.50 **NM** value: **Cover or less**
Circ: Diamd. preorders: **49,323** • **CGC:** 4 graded, best 9.8
📖 Udaku, Part 1 **A:** Angel Medina **W:** Brian Michael Bendis

2 ❑ Sep 1999 Cover: 2.50 **NM** value: **Cover or less**
Circ: Diamd. preorders: **35,648**
📖 Udaku, Part 2 **A:** Angel Medina **W:** Brian Michael Bendis

3 ❑ Oct 1999 Cover: 2.50 **NM** value: **Cover or less**
Circ: Diamd. preorders: **31,059**
📖 Udaku, Part 3 **A:** Angel Medina **W:** Brian Michael Bendis

4 ❑ Nov 1999 Cover: 2.50 **NM** value: **Cover or less**
Circ: Diamd. preorders: **27,429**
📖 Udaku, Part 4 **A:** Angel Medina **W:** Brian Michael Bendis

5 ❑ Dec 1999 Cover: 2.50 **NM** value: **Cover or less**
Circ: Diamd. preorders: **28,163**
📖 Udaku, Part 5 **A:** Angel Medina **W:** Brian Michael Bendis

6 ❑ Jan 2000 Cover: 2.50 **NM** value: **Cover or less**
Circ: Diamd. preorders: **24,867**
W: Brian Michael Bendis

7 ❑ Feb 2000 Cover: 2.50 **NM** value: **Cover or less**
Circ: Diamd. preorders: **23,067**
W: Brian Michael Bendis

8 ❑ Mar 2000 Cover: 2.50 **NM** value: **Cover or less**
Circ: Diamd. preorders: **23,436**
W: Brian Michael Bendis

9 ❑ Apr 2000 Cover: 2.50 **NM** value: **Cover or less**
Circ: Diamd. preorders: **23,330**
W: Brian Michael Bendis

10 ❑ May 2000 Cover: 2.50 **NM** value: **Cover or less**
Circ: Diamd. preorders: **22,935**
📖 Witchcraft, Part 1 **W:** Brian Michael Bendis

11 ❑ Jun 2000 Cover: 2.50 **NM** value: **Cover or less**
Circ: Diamd. preorders: **22,919**
📖 Witchcraft, Part 2 **W:** Brian Michael Bendis

12 ❑ Jul 2000 Cover: 2.50 **NM** value: **Cover or less**
Circ: Diamd. preorders: **22,373**
📖 Witchcraft, Part 3 **W:** Brian Michael Bendis

13 ❑ Aug 2000 Cover: 2.50 **NM** value: **Cover or less**
Circ: Diamd. preorders: **21,371**
📖 Witchcraft, Part 4 **A:** Alberto Ponticelli **W:** Brian Michael Bendis

14 ❑ Sep 2000 Cover: 2.50 **NM** value: **Cover or less**
Circ: Diamd. preorders: **21,611**
📖 Dumb Laws and Eggs **A:** Clayton Crain **W:** Brian Michael Bendis

15 ❑ Oct 2000 Cover: 2.50 **NM** value: **Cover or less**
Circ: Diamd. preorders: **21,658**
📖 Bounty Hunter Wars, Part 1 **A:** Alex Maleev **W:** Brian Michael Bendis

16 ❑ Nov 2000 Cover: 2.50 **NM** value: **Cover or less**
Circ: Diamd. preorders: **21,718**
📖 Bounty Hunter Wars, Part 2 **A:** Alex Maleev **W:** Brian Michael Bendis

17 ❑ Dec 2000 Cover: 2.50 **NM** value: **Cover or less**
Circ: Diamd. preorders: **21,447**
📖 Bounty Hunter Wars, Part 3 **A:** Alex Maleev **W:** Brian Michael Bendis

18 ❑ Jan 2001 Cover: 2.50 **NM** value: **Cover or less**
Circ: Diamd. preorders: **20,799**
📖 Bounty Hunter Wars, Part 4 **A:** Alex Maleev **W:** Brian Michael Bendis

19 ❑ Feb 2001 Cover: 2.50 **NM** value: **Cover or less**
Circ: Diamd. preorders: **20,251**
📖 Bounty Hunter Wars, Part 5 **A:** Alex Maleev **W:** Brian Michael Bendis

20 ❑ Mar 2001 Cover: 2.50 **NM** value: **Cover or less**
Circ: Diamd. preorders: **19,468**
📖 The John Doe Affair, Part 1 **A:** Alex Maleev **W:** Todd McFarlane

21 ❑ Apr 2001 Cover: 2.50 **NM** value: **Cover or less**
Circ: Diamd. preorders: **18,877**

22 ❑ May 2001 Cover: 2.50 **NM** value: **Cover or less**
Circ: Diamd. preorders: **17,948**

23 ❑ Jun 2001 Cover: 2.50 **NM** value: **Cover or less**
Circ: Diamd. preorders: **19,242**

24 ❑ Jul 2001 Cover: 2.50 **NM** value: **Cover or less**
Circ: Diamd. preorders: **18,110**

Bk 1 ❑ Cover: 21.95 **NM** value: **Cover or less**
📖 Udaku • Udaku; Collects Sam and Twitch# **A:** Alex Maleev **W:** Brian Michael Bendis

SAM BRONX AND THE ROBOTS — Eclipse

1 ❑ Cover: 6.95 **NM** value: **Cover or less**
hardcover.

SAMBU GASSHO (A CHORUS IN THREE PARTS) — Bodo Genki Studios

1 ❑ Aug 1994, b&w **NM** value: **1.00**
No issue number. no cover price.

SAM HILL, PRIVATE EYE — Close-Up

1 ❑ ca. 1950 Cover: 0.10 **NM** value: **65.00**
2 ❑ ca. 1950 Cover: 0.10 **NM** value: **35.00**
3 ❑ ca. 1950 Cover: 0.10 **NM** value: **35.00**
4 ❑ ca. 1950 Cover: 0.10 **NM** value: **30.00**
5 ❑ ca. 1950 Cover: 0.10 **NM** value: **30.00**
6 ❑ ca. 1950 Cover: 0.10 **NM** value: **30.00**
7 ❑ ca. 1950 Cover: 0.10 **NM** value: **30.00**

SAM SLADE, ROBO-HUNTER — Fleetway-Quality

The world of the future has turned heavily to robots to perform virtually every task. Robots of various sorts act as customs agents, cooks, butlers — even policemen. But some robots go bad. That's where Sam Slade comes in.

Sam is a Robo-Hunter: He tracks down and destroys misbehaving robots. He is accompanied in this mission by his faithful robot pals Hoagy and Stogie (a robotic cigar-go figure). Possessing a great deal of chutzpa, Sam sets out for England to ply his chosen trade. There, all humans are on permanent vacation, and the entire business of the country is run by robots. Although penniless, Sam manages to scam his way into a hotel room at the Savoy and writes rubber checks to set up an office on Baker Street. Soon, he begins a new set of offbeat adventures as England's only human Robo-Hunter (and only working human).

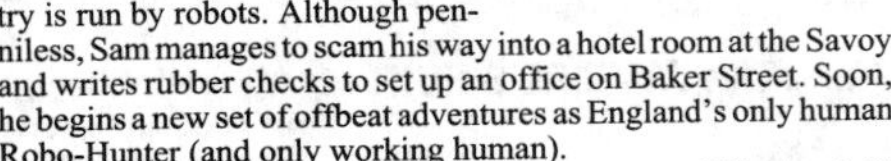

1 ❑ Cover: 0.75 **NM** value: **2.00**
Circ: CapCity orders: **6,725**
📖 Robo-Hunter: The Beast Of Blackheart Manor **A:** Ian Gibson **W:** Pat Mills

2 ❑ Cover: 0.75 **NM** value: **1.50**
Circ: CapCity orders: **5,675**
📖 Robo-Hunter: The Beast Of Blackheart Manor; Ro-Busters: Death on the Orient Express!, Part 2 **A:** Dave Gibbons; Ian Gibson **W:** John Wagner; Pat Mills

3 ❑ Cover: 0.75 **NM** value: **1.50**
Circ: CapCity orders: **4,350**
📖 Robo-Hunter: The Filby Case; Ro-Busters: The Terra-Meks!; Ro-Busters: The Terra-Meks! **A:** Dave Gibbons; Ian Gibson **W:** Alan Grant; Pat Mills

4 ❑ Cover: 0.75 **NM** value: **1.50**
Circ: CapCity orders: **4,300**
📖 Robo-Hunter: The Filby Case; Ro-Busters: The Terra-Meks! **A:** Dave Gibbons; Ian Gibson **W:** Alan Grant; Pat Mills

5 ❑ Cover: 0.75 **NM** value: **1.50**
Circ: CapCity orders: **4,000**
📖 Robo-Hunter: Day of the Droids; Ro-Busters: The Terra-Meks! **A:** Dave Gibbons; Ian Gibson **W:** John Wagner; Pat Mills

6 ❑ Cover: 1.25 **NM** value: **1.50**
Circ: CapCity orders: **3,750**
📖 Ro-Busters: Bax the Burner; ABC Warriors: The Tournament of the Damned; Robo-Hunter **A:** Brett Ewins; Steve Dillon; Ian Gibson **W:** Alan Grant; Alan Moore; Pat Mills

7 ❑ Cover: 1.25 **NM** value: **1.50**
Circ: CapCity orders: **3,900**
📖 Robo-Hunter; ABC Warriors; Steelhorn; Ro-Busters: Old Red Eyes is Back **A:** Mike McMahon; Ian Gibson **W:** Alan Grant; Pat Mills

8 ❑ Cover: 1.25 **NM** value: **1.50**
Circ: CapCity orders: **2,725**
📖 Robo-Hunter; ABC Warriors; Soya Bean Cowboys! **A:** Dave Gibbons; Mike McMahon; Ian Gibson **W:** Alan Grant; Pat Mills

9 ❑ Cover: 1.25 **NM** value: **1.50**
Circ: CapCity orders: **2,350**
📖 Robo-Hunter: Day of the Droids; ABC Warriors; The Red Death! **A:** Mike McMahon; Ian Gibson **W:** Pat Mills; T.B. Grover

10 ❑ Cover: 1.25 **NM** value: **1.50**
Circ: CapCity orders: **1,850**
📖 Robo-Hunter: Day of the Droids; ABC Warriors **A:** Ian Gibson; L.J. Silver **W:** Pat Mills; T.B. Grover

11 ❑ Cover: 1.25 **NM** value: **1.50**
Circ: CapCity orders: **1,875**
📖 Robo-Hunter: Day of the Droids; ABC Warriors • no year of publication **A:** Mike McMahon; Ian Gibson **W:** Pat Mills; T.B. Grover

12 ❑ Cover: 1.25 **NM** value: **1.50**
Circ: CapCity orders: **1,825**
📖 Robo-Hunter: Killing of Kidd; Harlem Heroes **A:** Dave Gibbons; Ian Gibson; Trigo **W:** Alan Grant; Tom Tully

13 ❑ Cover: 1.25 **NM** value: **1.50**
Circ: CapCity orders: **1,750**
📖 Robo-Hunter: Killing of Kidd; Harlem Heroes **A:** Dave Gibbons; Ian Gibson **W:** Alan Grant; Tom Tully

14 ❑ Cover: 1.25 **NM** value: **1.50**
Circ: CapCity orders: **1,650**
📖 Robo-Hunter: Football Crazy; Harlem Heroes **A:** Dave Gibbons; Ian Gibson **W:** Alan Grant; T.B. Grover; Tom Tully

15 ❑ Cover: 1.25 **NM** value: **1.50**
Circ: CapCity orders: **1,425**
📖 Robo-Hunter: Play it Again, Sam; Harlem Heroes **A:** Ian Gibson **W:** Alan Grant; T.B. Grover; Tom Tully

16 ❑ Cover: 1.25 **NM** value: **1.50**
Circ: CapCity orders: **1,350**
📖 Robo-Hunter; Harlem Heroes **A:** Ian Gibson **W:** Alan Grant; T.B. Grover

17 ❑ Cover: 1.25 **NM** value: **1.50**
Circ: CapCity orders: **1,300**
📖 Robo-Hunter: Play it Again, Sam; Harlem Heroes **A:** Dave Gibbons; Ian Gibson **W:** Alan Grant; T.B. Grover; Tom Tully

18 ❑ Cover: 1.25 **NM** value: **1.50**
Circ: CapCity orders: **1,225**
📖 Robo-Hunter: Teeny-Mek Attack; Judge Dredd: The Academy of Law **A:** Dave Gibbons; Ian Gibson **W:** Alan Grant; T.B. Grover

19 ❑ Cover: 1.25 **NM** value: **1.50**
Circ: CapCity orders: **1,250**
📖 Robo-Hunter: The Slaying of Slade; Ace Trucking Co. **A:** Massimo Belardinelli; Ian Gibson **W:** Alan Grant; T.B. Grover

20 ❑ Cover: 1.50 **NM** value: **Cover or less**
Circ: CapCity orders: **1,075**

21 ❑ Cover: 1.50 **NM** value: **Cover or less**
Circ: CapCity orders: **1,100**
• double issue #21/22

22 ❑ Cover: 1.50 **NM** value: **Cover or less**
Circ: CapCity orders: **1,100**

23 ❑ **NM** value: **1.50**
• double issue #23/24

24 ❑ Cover: 1.50 **NM** value: **Cover or less**
Circ: CapCity orders: **1,050**

25 ❑ Cover: 1.50 **NM** value: **Cover or less**
Circ: CapCity orders: **1,025**

26 ❑ **NM** value: **1.50**
📖 Robo-Hunter: Sam Slade's Last Case; The Great Detective Caper: Hemlock Bones-Who He?; Ace Trucking Co. **A:** Massimo Belardinelli; John Higgins; Ian Gibson **W:** Jack Adrian; Alan Grant; T.B. Grover

27 ❑ Cover: 1.50 **NM** value: **Cover or less**
Circ: CapCity orders: **975**
📖 Robo-Hunter: Sam Slade's Last Case; Ulysses Sweet: Fruitcake and Veg!; Ace Trucking Co. **A:** Massimo Belardinelli; Colin MacNeil; Ian Gibson **W:** Grant Morrison; Alan Grant; T.B. Grover

28 ❑ Cover: 1.50 **NM** value: **Cover or less**
Circ: CapCity orders: **975**
📖 Robo-Hunter: Farewell, My Billions; Ace Trucking Co.; Ace Trucking Co.: The Great Mush Race, Part 1; Going Straight **A:** Massimo Belardinelli; Ian Gibson **W:** Alan Grant; T.B. Grover

29 ❑ Cover: 1.50 **NM** value: **Cover or less**
Circ: CapCity orders: **950**
📖 Hap Hazzard; Mirror, Mirror, on the Wall…; Ace Trucking Co.: The Great Mush Rush **A:** Massimo Belardinelli; Ian Gibson **W:** Alan Grant; T.B. Grover

30 ❑ Cover: 1.50 **NM** value: **Cover or less**
Circ: CapCity orders: **925**
📖 Robo-Hunter; Ace Trucking Co.: The Great Mush Rush **A:** Massimo Belardinelli; Ian Gibson **W:** Alan Grant; T.B. Grover

31 ❑ Cover: 1.50 **NM** value: **Cover or less**
Circ: CapCity orders: **900**
📖 Robo-Hunter! Tharg the Mighty: The Shedding **A:** Ian Gibson; Eric Bradbury **W:** Alan Grant; T.B. Grover; T.M.O.

32 ❑ Cover: 1.50 **NM** value: **Cover or less**
Circ: CapCity orders: **825**

33 ❑ Cover: 1.50 **NM** value: **Cover or less**
final issue.

SAMSON — Samson

0.5 ❑ Jan 1995 Cover: 2.50 **NM** value: **Cover or less**
• no indicia

SAMSON (1ST SERIES) — Fox

1 ❑ Fal 1940 Cover: 0.10 **NM** value: **1600.00**
• **CGC:** 2 graded, best 8.0
2 ❑ Dec 1940 Cover: 0.10 **NM** value: **800.00**
3 ❑ Feb 1941 Cover: 0.10 **NM** value: **600.00**
• **CGC:** 1 graded, best 3.5
4 ❑ Apr 1941 Cover: 0.10 **NM** value: **500.00**
5 ❑ Jul 1941 Cover: 0.10 **NM** value: **400.00**
6 ❑ Sep 1941 Cover: 0.10 **NM** value: **400.00**

SAMSON (2ND SERIES) — Ajax

12 ❑ Apr 1955 Cover: 0.10 **NM** value: **200.00**
13 ❑ Jun 1955 Cover: 0.10 **NM** value: **200.00**
14 ❑ Aug 1955 Cover: 0.10 **NM** value: **200.00**

SAMSON: THE KID WHO NEVER GOT A HAIRCUT — Tyndale

1 ❑ Cover: 0.89 **NM** value: **2.00**

SAM STORIES: LEGS — Image / Quality

1 ❑ Dec 1999 Cover: 2.50 **NM** value: **Cover or less**
Circ: Diamd. preorders: **14,215**
A: Sam Kieth **W:** Sam Kieth

There are two different pricing tiers in the modern comic-book hobby. **The prices seen above** are the prices we have seen **loose copies** of these issues reliably fetch in a variety of environments. Condition alters the price by the fractions seen on the bar on the bottom of left-hand pages of this book. **Comics graded by CGC** usually sell for more. Use the guide on the bottom of right-hand pages of this book to estimate what copies have brought on eBay.

CGC-graded: Multiply prices above by **33 for 9.9 M • 16 for 9.8 NM/M • 7 for 9.6 NM+ • 5 for 9.4 NM • 2.5 for 9.2 NM- • 1.5 for 9.0 VF/NM**

SAMURAI — Aircel

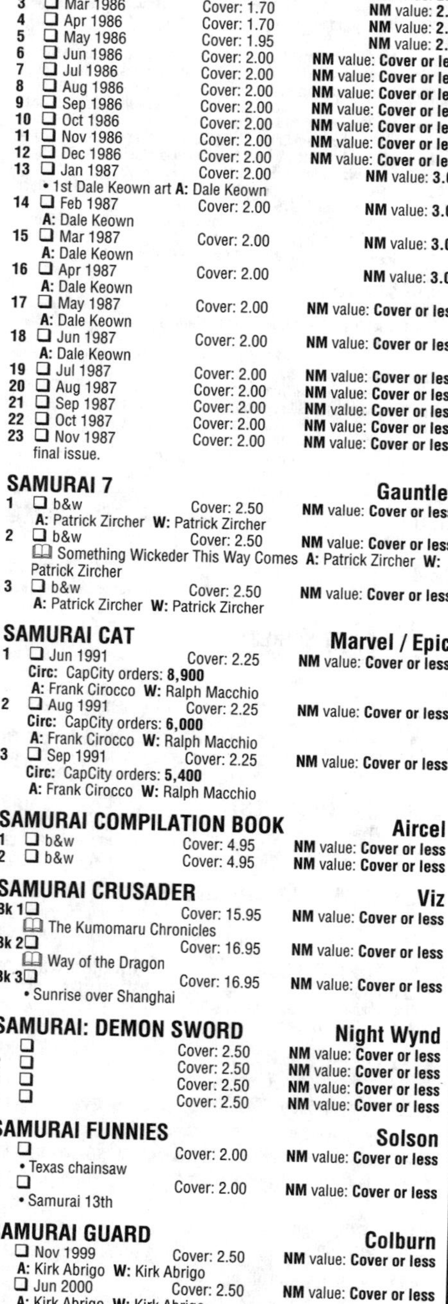

Toronto, Canada, is home to Toshiro Kinura Sahura, a young man with quite a talent with a sword. Toshiro's sword is the subject of this black-and-white series from Aircel Publishing. The Yakuza (Japanese Mafia) is after Toshiro's sword, because a legend states that this very sword was forged to do battle with supernatural beings. Toshiro travels the world in an attempt to evade the Yakuza, as he learns more and more about the sword.

Along the way, he discovers that a second, shorter sword was forged at the same time and for the same purpose. Feeling a moral obligation to keep that sword from the Yakuza, as well, Toshiro travels to Asia, where the sword sits in a religious temple.

Samurai was created, written, and drawn by Barry Blair with help from others. Issue #13 saw the professional debut of artist Dale Keown (Pitt).

1 ❑ Jan 1986 Cover: 1.70 **NM** value: **3.00**
A: Pat McEown; Barry Blair; Bruce Blair **W:** Pat McEown; Barry Blair
1-2 ❑ Cover: 1.70 **NM** value: **2.00**
1-3 ❑ Cover: 1.70 **NM** value: **2.00**
2 ❑ Feb 1986 Cover: 1.70 **NM** value: **2.00**
3 ❑ Mar 1986 Cover: 1.70 **NM** value: **2.00**
4 ❑ Apr 1986 Cover: 1.70 **NM** value: **2.00**
5 ❑ May 1986 Cover: 1.95 **NM** value: **2.00**
6 ❑ Jun 1986 Cover: 2.00 **NM** value: **Cover or less**
7 ❑ Jul 1986 Cover: 2.00 **NM** value: **Cover or less**
8 ❑ Aug 1986 Cover: 2.00 **NM** value: **Cover or less**
9 ❑ Sep 1986 Cover: 2.00 **NM** value: **Cover or less**
10 ❑ Oct 1986 Cover: 2.00 **NM** value: **Cover or less**
11 ❑ Nov 1986 Cover: 2.00 **NM** value: **Cover or less**
12 ❑ Dec 1986 Cover: 2.00 **NM** value: **Cover or less**
13 ❑ Jan 1987 Cover: 2.00 **NM** value: **3.00**
• 1st Dale Keown art **A:** Dale Keown
14 ❑ Feb 1987 Cover: 2.00 **NM** value: **3.00**
A: Dale Keown
15 ❑ Mar 1987 Cover: 2.00 **NM** value: **3.00**
A: Dale Keown
16 ❑ Apr 1987 Cover: 2.00 **NM** value: **3.00**
A: Dale Keown
17 ❑ May 1987 Cover: 2.00 **NM** value: **Cover or less**
A: Dale Keown
18 ❑ Jun 1987 Cover: 2.00 **NM** value: **Cover or less**
A: Dale Keown
19 ❑ Jul 1987 Cover: 2.00 **NM** value: **Cover or less**
20 ❑ Aug 1987 Cover: 2.00 **NM** value: **Cover or less**
21 ❑ Sep 1987 Cover: 2.00 **NM** value: **Cover or less**
22 ❑ Oct 1987 Cover: 2.00 **NM** value: **Cover or less**
23 ❑ Nov 1987 Cover: 2.00 **NM** value: **Cover or less**
final issue.

SAMURAI 7 — Gauntlet

1 ❑ b&w Cover: 2.50 **NM** value: **Cover or less**
A: Patrick Zircher **W:** Patrick Zircher
2 ❑ b&w Cover: 2.50 **NM** value: **Cover or less**
📖 Something Wickeder This Way Comes **A:** Patrick Zircher **W:** Patrick Zircher
3 ❑ b&w Cover: 2.50 **NM** value: **Cover or less**
A: Patrick Zircher **W:** Patrick Zircher

SAMURAI CAT — Marvel / Epic

1 ❑ Jun 1991 Cover: 2.25 **NM** value: **Cover or less**
Circ: CapCity orders: **8,900**
A: Frank Cirocco **W:** Ralph Macchio
2 ❑ Aug 1991 Cover: 2.25 **NM** value: **Cover or less**
Circ: CapCity orders: **6,000**
A: Frank Cirocco **W:** Ralph Macchio
3 ❑ Sep 1991 Cover: 2.25 **NM** value: **Cover or less**
Circ: CapCity orders: **5,400**
A: Frank Cirocco **W:** Ralph Macchio

SAMURAI COMPILATION BOOK — Aircel

1 ❑ b&w Cover: 4.95 **NM** value: **Cover or less**
2 ❑ b&w Cover: 4.95 **NM** value: **Cover or less**

SAMURAI CRUSADER — Viz

Bk 1❑ Cover: 15.95 **NM** value: **Cover or less**
📖 The Kumomaru Chronicles
Bk 2❑ Cover: 16.95 **NM** value: **Cover or less**
📖 Way of the Dragon
Bk 3❑ Cover: 16.95 **NM** value: **Cover or less**
• Sunrise over Shanghai

SAMURAI: DEMON SWORD — Night Wynd

1 ❑ Cover: 2.50 **NM** value: **Cover or less**
2 ❑ Cover: 2.50 **NM** value: **Cover or less**
3 ❑ Cover: 2.50 **NM** value: **Cover or less**
4 ❑ Cover: 2.50 **NM** value: **Cover or less**

SAMURAI FUNNIES — Solson

1 ❑ Cover: 2.00 **NM** value: **Cover or less**
• Texas chainsaw
2 ❑ Cover: 2.00 **NM** value: **Cover or less**
• Samurai 13th

SAMURAI GUARD — Colburn

1 ❑ Nov 1999 Cover: 2.50 **NM** value: **Cover or less**
A: Kirk Abrigo **W:** Kirk Abrigo
2 ❑ Jun 2000 Cover: 2.50 **NM** value: **Cover or less**
A: Kirk Abrigo **W:** Kirk Abrigo
Ash 1❑ **NM** value: **1.00**
A: Kirk Abrigo **W:** Kirk Abrigo

SAMURAI JAM — Slave Labor

1 ❑ Jan 1994 Cover: 2.95 **NM** value: **Cover or less**
2 ❑ Apr 1994 Cover: 2.95 **NM** value: **Cover or less**
3 ❑ Jun 1994 Cover: 2.95 **NM** value: **Cover or less**
📖 Board Walk **A:** Andi Watson **W:** Andi Watson
4 ❑ Sep 1994 Cover: 2.95 **NM** value: **Cover or less**

SAMURAI: MYSTIC CULT — Nightwynd

1 ❑ b&w Cover: 2.50 **NM** value: **Cover or less**
A: Pat McEown **W:** Barry Blair
2 ❑ b&w Cover: 2.50 **NM** value: **Cover or less**
3 ❑ b&w Cover: 2.50 **NM** value: **Cover or less**
4 ❑ b&w Cover: 2.50 **NM** value: **Cover or less**

SAMURAI PENGUIN — Slave Labor

1 ❑ Jun 1986, b&w Cover: 1.50 **NM** value: **Cover or less**
2 ❑ Aug 1986, b&w Cover: 1.50 **NM** value: **Cover or less**
3 ❑ Feb 1987, b&w Cover: 1.50 **NM** value: **Cover or less**
• pink logo version also exist
4 ❑ May 1987, b&w Cover: 1.50 **NM** value: **Cover or less**
5 ❑ Sep 1987, b&w Cover: 1.50 **NM** value: **Cover or less**
6 ❑ Mar 1988 Cover: 1.95 **NM** value: **Cover or less**
★ Death of Samurai Penguin.
7 ❑ Jul 1988 Cover: 1.75 **NM** value: **Cover or less**
8 ❑ May 1989 Cover: 1.75 **NM** value: **Cover or less**

SAMURAI PENGUIN: FOOD CHAIN FOLLIES — Slave Labor

1 ❑ Apr 1991 Cover: 5.95 **NM** value: **Cover or less**
No issue number. One-shot.

SAMURAI SHODOWN — Viz

Bk 1❑ Cover: 15.95 **NM** value: **Cover or less**

SAMURAI SQUIRREL — Spotlight

1 ❑ Cover: 1.75 **NM** value: **Cover or less**
📖 Into The Lair **A:** Kelley Jarvis **W:** Kelley Jarvis
2 ❑ Cover: 1.75 **NM** value: **Cover or less**
A: Kelley Jarvis **W:** Kelley Jarvis

SAMURAI: VAMPIRE'S HUNT — Nightwynd

1 ❑ b&w Cover: 2.50 **NM** value: **Cover or less**
2 ❑ b&w Cover: 2.50 **NM** value: **Cover or less**
3 ❑ b&w Cover: 2.50 **NM** value: **Cover or less**
4 ❑ b&w Cover: 2.50 **NM** value: **Cover or less**

SAMURAI (VOL. 2) — Aircel

1 ❑ Dec 1987 Cover: 2.00 **NM** value: **Cover or less**
2 ❑ Jan 1988 Cover: 2.00 **NM** value: **Cover or less**
3 ❑ Feb 1988 Cover: 2.00 **NM** value: **Cover or less**

SAMURAI (VOL. 3) — Aircel

1 ❑ 1988 Cover: 1.95 **NM** value: **Cover or less**
Circ: CapCity orders: **4,925**
2 ❑ 1988 Cover: 1.95 **NM** value: **Cover or less**
Circ: CapCity orders: **2,950**
3 ❑ 1988 Cover: 1.95 **NM** value: **Cover or less**
Circ: CapCity orders: **2,350**
4 ❑ 1988 Cover: 1.95 **NM** value: **Cover or less**
Circ: CapCity orders: **2,175**
5 ❑ 1988 Cover: 1.95 **NM** value: **Cover or less**
Circ: CapCity orders: **1,925**
6 ❑ Dec 1988 Cover: 1.95 **NM** value: **Cover or less**
7 ❑ Jan 1989 Cover: 1.95 **NM** value: **Cover or less**

SAMURAI (VOL. 4) — Warp

1 ❑ May 1997, b&w Cover: 2.95 **NM** value: **Cover or less**

SAMUREE (1ST SERIES) — Continuity

1 ❑ May 1987 Cover: 2.00 **NM** value: **Cover or less**
Circ: CapCity orders: **7,150**
2 ❑ Aug 1987 Cover: 2.00 **NM** value: **Cover or less**
Circ: CapCity orders: **5,050**
3 ❑ May 1988 Cover: 2.00 **NM** value: **Cover or less**
Circ: CapCity orders: **4,350**
4 ❑ Jan 1989 Cover: 2.00 **NM** value: **Cover or less**
Circ: CapCity orders: **3,975**
5 ❑ Apr 1989 Cover: 2.00 **NM** value: **Cover or less**
Circ: CapCity orders: **3,700**
6 ❑ Aug 1989 Cover: 2.00 **NM** value: **Cover or less**
Circ: CapCity orders: **4,200**
7 ❑ Feb 1990 Cover: 2.00 **NM** value: **Cover or less**
Circ: CapCity orders: **3,650**
8 ❑ Nov 1990 Cover: 2.00 **NM** value: **Cover or less**
Circ: CapCity orders: **3,625**
9 ❑ Jan 1991 Cover: 2.00 **NM** value: **Cover or less**
Circ: CapCity orders: **3,800**

SAMUREE (2ND SERIES) — Continuity

1 ❑ May 1993 Cover: 2.50 **NM** value: **Cover or less**
Circ: CapCity orders: **12,000**
📖 Rise of Magic **A:** Tristan Shane **W:** Neal Adams; Peter Stone
2 ❑ Sep 1993 Cover: 2.50 **NM** value: **Cover or less**
Circ: CapCity orders: **9,475**
📖 Rise of Magic **A:** Tristan Shane **W:** Neal Adams; Peter Stone
3 ❑ Dec 1993 Cover: 2.50 **NM** value: **Cover or less**
Circ: CapCity orders: **8,150**
4 ❑ Jan 1994 Cover: 2.50 **NM** value: **Cover or less**
Circ: CapCity orders: **8,475**

SAMUREE (3RD SERIES) — Acclaim / Windjammer

1 ❑ Oct 1995 Cover: 2.50 **NM** value: **Cover or less**
Circ: CapCity orders: **9,075**
A: Rodolfo DaMaggio **W:** Peter Stone
2 ❑ Nov 1995 Cover: 2.50 **NM** value: **Cover or less**
Circ: CapCity orders: **6,750**
A: Rodolfo DaMaggio **W:** Peter Stone

SANCTUARY PART 1 — Viz

1 ❑ Jun 1993, b&w Cover: 4.95 **NM** value: **6.00**
Circ: CapCity orders: **3,250**
A: Ryoichi Ikegami **W:** Sho Fumimura
2 ❑ Jul 1993, b&w Cover: 4.95 **NM** value: **5.00**
A: Ryoichi Ikegami **W:** Sho Fumimura
3 ❑ Aug 1993 Cover: 4.95 **NM** value: **5.00**
A: Ryoichi Ikegami **W:** Sho Fumimura
4 ❑ Sep 1993 Cover: 4.95 **NM** value: **5.00**
A: Ryoichi Ikegami **W:** Sho Fumimura
5 ❑ Oct 1993 Cover: 4.95 **NM** value: **5.00**
A: Ryoichi Ikegami **W:** Sho Fumimura
6 ❑ Nov 1993 Cover: 4.95 **NM** value: **5.00**
A: Ryoichi Ikegami **W:** Sho Fumimura
7 ❑ Dec 1993 Cover: 4.95 **NM** value: **5.00**
Circ: CapCity orders: **2,400**
A: Ryoichi Ikegami **W:** Sho Fumimura
8 ❑ Jan 1994 Cover: 4.95 **NM** value: **5.00**
Circ: CapCity orders: **2,375**
A: Ryoichi Ikegami **W:** Sho Fumimura
9 ❑ Feb 1994 Cover: 4.95 **NM** value: **5.00**
A: Ryoichi Ikegami **W:** Sho Fumimura
Bk 1❑ Cover: 16.95 **NM** value: **Cover or less**
A: Ryoichi Ikegami **W:** Sho Fumimura
Bk 2❑ Cover: 16.95 **NM** value: **Cover or less**
A: Ryoichi Ikegami **W:** Sho Fumimura

SANCTUARY PART 2 — Viz

1 ❑ Mar 1994 Cover: 4.95 **NM** value: **5.00**
Circ: CapCity orders: **2,700**
A: Ryoichi Ikegami **W:** Sho Fumimura
2 ❑ Apr 1994 Cover: 4.95 **NM** value: **5.00**
A: Ryoichi Ikegami **W:** Sho Fumimura
3 ❑ May 1994 Cover: 4.95 **NM** value: **5.00**
A: Ryoichi Ikegami **W:** Sho Fumimura
4 ❑ Jun 1994 Cover: 4.95 **NM** value: **5.00**
A: Ryoichi Ikegami **W:** Sho Fumimura
5 ❑ Jul 1994 Cover: 4.95 **NM** value: **5.00**
📖 Yakuza **A:** Ryoichi Ikegami **W:** Sho Fumimura
6 ❑ Aug 1994 Cover: 4.95 **NM** value: **5.00**
A: Ryoichi Ikegami **W:** Sho Fumimura
7 ❑ Sep 1994 Cover: 4.95 **NM** value: **5.00**
A: Ryoichi Ikegami **W:** Sho Fumimura
8 ❑ Oct 1994 Cover: 4.95 **NM** value: **5.00**
Circ: CapCity orders: **2,025**
A: Ryoichi Ikegami **W:** Sho Fumimura
9 ❑ Nov 1994 Cover: 4.95 **NM** value: **5.00**
A: Ryoichi Ikegami **W:** Sho Fumimura
Bk 3❑ Jan 1995 Cover: 17.95 **NM** value: **Cover or less**
A: Ryoichi Ikegami **W:** Sho Fumimura
Bk 4❑ Cover: 17.95 **NM** value: **Cover or less**
A: Ryoichi Ikegami **W:** Sho Fumimura

SANCTUARY PART 3 — Viz

1 ❑ Dec 1994, b&w Cover: 3.25 **NM** value: **Cover or less**
Circ: CapCity orders: **2,700**
📖 Oath Of Brotherhood **A:** Ryoichi Ikegami **W:** Sho Fumimura
2 ❑ Jan 1995, b&w Cover: 3.25 **NM** value: **Cover or less**
Circ: CapCity orders: **2,425**
📖 Strategy; Reorganization **A:** Ryoichi Ikegami **W:** Sho Fumimura
3 ❑ Feb 1995, b&w Cover: 3.25 **NM** value: **Cover or less**
Circ: CapCity orders: **2,125**
A: Ryoichi Ikegami **W:** Sho Fumimura
4 ❑ Mar 1995, b&w Cover: 3.25 **NM** value: **Cover or less**
Circ: CapCity orders: **2,075**
A: Ryoichi Ikegami **W:** Sho Fumimura
5 ❑ Apr 1995, b&w Cover: 3.25 **NM** value: **Cover or less**
Circ: CapCity orders: **1,975**
A: Ryoichi Ikegami **W:** Sho Fumimura
6 ❑ May 1995, b&w Cover: 3.25 **NM** value: **Cover or less**
A: Ryoichi Ikegami **W:** Sho Fumimura
7 ❑ Jun 1995, b&w Cover: 3.25 **NM** value: **Cover or less**
A: Ryoichi Ikegami **W:** Sho Fumimura
8 ❑ Jul 1995, b&w Cover: 3.25 **NM** value: **Cover or less**
Circ: CapCity orders: **2,050**
A: Ryoichi Ikegami **W:** Sho Fumimura
Bk 5❑ Cover: 17.95 **NM** value: **Cover or less**
A: Ryoichi Ikegami **W:** Sho Fumimura
Bk 6❑ Cover: 17.95 **NM** value: **Cover or less**
A: Ryoichi Ikegami **W:** Sho Fumimura

SANCTUARY PART 4 — Viz

1 ❑ Aug 1995 Cover: 3.25 **NM** value: **Cover or less**
Circ: CapCity orders: **2,050**
📖 Offense and Defense; Ruthless Pursuit **A:** Ryoichi Ikegami **W:** Sho Fumimura
2 ❑ Sep 1995 Cover: 3.25 **NM** value: **Cover or less**
Circ: CapCity orders: **1,875**
A: Ryoichi Ikegami **W:** Sho Fumimura
3 ❑ Oct 1995 Cover: 3.25 **NM** value: **Cover or less**
A: Ryoichi Ikegami **W:** Sho Fumimura
4 ❑ Nov 1995 Cover: 3.25 **NM** value: **Cover or less**
A: Ryoichi Ikegami **W:** Sho Fumimura
5 ❑ Dec 1995 Cover: 3.25 **NM** value: **Cover or less**
A: Ryoichi Ikegami **W:** Sho Fumimura
6 ❑ Jan 1996 Cover: 3.50 **NM** value: **Cover or less**
A: Ryoichi Ikegami **W:** Sho Fumimura
7 ❑ Feb 1996 Cover: 3.50 **NM** value: **Cover or less**
A: Ryoichi Ikegami **W:** Sho Fumimura
Bk 7❑ Cover: 16.95 **NM** value: **Cover or less**
A: Ryoichi Ikegami **W:** Sho Fumimura

Other grades: Multiply prices above by **1.5 for Mint • 2/3 for Very Fine • 1/3 for Fine • 1/5 for Very Good • 1/8 for Good**

SANCTUARY PART 5 — Viz

1 ❑ Mar 1996 Cover: 3.50 **NM** value: **Cover or less**
A: Ryoichi Ikegami **W:** Sho Fumimura

2 ❑ Apr 1996 Cover: 3.50 **NM** value: **Cover or less**
A: Ryoichi Ikegami **W:** Sho Fumimura

3 ❑ May 1996 Cover: 3.50 **NM** value: **Cover or less**
A: Ryoichi Ikegami **W:** Sho Fumimura

4 ❑ Jun 1996 Cover: 3.50 **NM** value: **Cover or less**
A: Ryoichi Ikegami **W:** Sho Fumimura

5 ❑ Jul 1996 Cover: 3.50 **NM** value: **Cover or less**
A: Ryoichi Ikegami **W:** Sho Fumimura

6 ❑ Aug 1996 Cover: 3.50 **NM** value: **Cover or less**
A: Ryoichi Ikegami **W:** Sho Fumimura

7 ❑ Sep 1996 Cover: 3.50 **NM** value: **Cover or less**
Circ: Diamd. preorders: **4,120**
A: Ryoichi Ikegami **W:** Sho Fumimura

8 ❑ Oct 1996 Cover: 3.50 **NM** value: **Cover or less**
Circ: Diamd. preorders: **3,997**
A: Ryoichi Ikegami **W:** Sho Fumimura

9 ❑ Nov 1996 Cover: 3.50 **NM** value: **Cover or less**
Circ: Diamd. preorders: **3,897**
A: Ryoichi Ikegami **W:** Sho Fumimura

10 ❑ Dec 1996 Cover: 3.50 **NM** value: **Cover or less**
Circ: Diamd. preorders: **3,820**
A: Ryoichi Ikegami **W:** Sho Fumimura

11 ❑ Jan 1997 Cover: 3.50 **NM** value: **Cover or less**
Circ: Diamd. preorders: **3,692**
A: Ryoichi Ikegami **W:** Sho Fumimura

12 ❑ Feb 1997 Cover: 2.95 **NM** value: **3.50**
Circ: Diamd. preorders: **3,370**
A: Ryoichi Ikegami **W:** Sho Fumimura

13 ❑ Mar 1997 Cover: 2.95 **NM** value: **3.50**
Circ: Diamd. preorders: **3,386**
A: Ryoichi Ikegami **W:** Sho Fumimura

Bk 8❑ Cover: 16.95 **NM** value: **Cover or less**
A: Ryoichi Ikegami **W:** Sho Fumimura

Bk 9❑ Cover: 16.95 **NM** value: **Cover or less**
A: Ryoichi Ikegami **W:** Sho Fumimura

SANCTUM — Blackshoe

1/LE❑ Cover: 3.95 **NM** value: **Cover or less**
• Limited edition from 1999 San Diego Comic-Con. **A:** Mike Zittfel **W:** Mike Zittfel

SAN DIEGO COMIC-CON COMICS — Dark Horse

1 ❑ Cover: 2.95 **NM** value: **3.25**
• con giveaway.

2 ❑ Aug 1993 Cover: 2.95 **NM** value: **Cover or less**
• con giveaway. Danger Unlimited; Concrete: Steel Rain; Monkeyman and O'Brien: The Shocking Case of the Brief Journey; Sin City: The Customer is Always Right; Don Martin's Doctor Dork; Mom 'n' Me; Hellboy; Martha Washington Goes to War: State of the Art • 1993 Comic-Con **A:** Matt Wagner; Arthur Adams; Dave Gibbons; Geof Darrow; John Byrne; Rick Geary; Frank Miller; Mike Allred; Paul Chadwick **W:** Arthur Adams; John Byrne; Frank Miller; Paul Chadwick; Don Martin ★ 1st Appearance of Danger Unlimited.

3 ❑ Aug 1994 Cover: 2.50 **NM** value: **Cover or less**
• con giveaway. • 1994 Comic-Con

4 ❑ Aug 1995 Cover: 2.50 **NM** value: **Cover or less**
The Mask in San Diego; Foot Soldiers; Star Wars: Heir to the Empire; Tarzan/John Carter: Warlords of Mars; Cud Comix: Eno and Plum; Motorhead; Tex Avery Comics: Droopy vs. The Red Baron; Fat Man and Little Boy • 1995 Comic-Con **A:** Olivier Vatine; Neil Vokes; Karl Waller; Michael Avon Oeming; Frank Miller; Bret Blevins; Mike Allred; Bill Morrison; Jim Hall; Terry Laban; Fred Blanchard **W:** Frank Miller; Bruce Jones; Terry Laban; Jimmy Janes; Mike Baron; D.G. Chichester; Jim Krueger; Michael Eury; Robert Conte; Timothy Zahn; Vest

SANDMADAM — Spoof

1 ❑ b&w Cover: 2.95 **NM** value: **Cover or less**

SANDMAN — DC

His name is Morpheus, sometimes known by mortals as Sandman. He is lord of the mystical plane known as The Dreaming and he is a member of The Endless, a race which includes Delirium, Delight, Despair — and Dream's sister Death.

But this series is not so much about Morpheus as it is about dreams — dreams, fantasies, and fairy tales. The stories are from contemporary life with a twist of fantasy added or, alternately, old folk tales reworked for a modern audience. Created by noted science-fiction and fantasy writer Neil Gaiman (Miracleman, Death: The High Cost of Living), Sandman is a brilliant, charming, and sometimes profound series.

1 ❑ Jan 1989 Cover: 2.00 **NM** value: **22.00**
Circ: CapCity orders: **20,700** • **CGC:** 87 graded, best 9.8
• Giant-size. **A:** Sam Kieth **W:** Neil Gaiman ★ 1st Appearance of Sandman III (Morpheus).

2 ❑ Feb 1989 Cover: 1.50 **NM** value: **7.00**
Circ: CapCity orders: **16,100** • **CGC:** 4 graded, best 9.4
W: Neil Gaiman ★ Appearance of Abel, Cain.

3 ❑ Mar 1989 Cover: 1.50 **NM** value: **6.00**
Circ: CapCity orders: **15,000** • **CGC:** 2 graded, best 9.6
W: Neil Gaiman ★ Appearance of John Constantine.

4 ❑ Apr 1989 Cover: 1.50 **NM** value: **4.50**
Circ: CapCity orders: **15,050** • **CGC:** 3 graded, best 9.2
W: Neil Gaiman ★ Appearance of Demon.

5 ❑ May 1989 Cover: 1.50 **NM** value: **4.50**
Circ: CapCity orders: **15,900** • **CGC:** 2 graded, best 9.2
W: Neil Gaiman

6 ❑ Jun 1989 Cover: 1.50 **NM** value: **4.00**
Circ: CapCity orders: **15,550** • **CGC:** 1 graded, best 9.2
W: Neil Gaiman

7 ❑ Jul 1989 Cover: 1.50 **NM** value: **4.00**
Circ: CapCity orders: **15,350** • **CGC:** 2 graded, best 9.4
W: Neil Gaiman

8 ❑ Aug 1989 Cover: 1.50 **NM** value: **10.00**
Circ: CapCity orders: **15,900** • **CGC:** 3 graded, best 9.6
• Regular edition, no indicia in inside front cover. The Sound of her Wings **A:** Malcolm Jones III; Mike Dringenberg **W:** Neil Gaiman ★ 1st Appearance of Death (Sandman).

8/LE❑ Aug 1989 Cover: 1.50 **NM** value: **40.00**
• **CGC:** 28 graded, best 9.6
Has indicia in inside front cover, editorial by Karen Berger. • limited edition. The Sound of her Wings • 1000 copies **A:** Malcolm Jones III; Mike Dringenberg **W:** Neil Gaiman ★ 1st Appearance of Death (Sandman).

9 ❑ Sep 1989 Cover: 1.50 **NM** value: **4.00**
Circ: CapCity orders: **16,300** • **CGC:** 2 graded, best 9.4
W: Neil Gaiman

10 ❑ Nov 1989 Cover: 1.50 **NM** value: **4.00**
Circ: CapCity orders: **15,800**
A Doll's House, Part 1 **W:** Neil Gaiman

11 ❑ Dec 1989 Cover: 1.50 **NM** value: **4.00**
Circ: CapCity orders: **15,600**
A Doll's House, Part 2 **W:** Neil Gaiman

12 ❑ Jan 1990 Cover: 1.50 **NM** value: **4.00**
Circ: CapCity orders: **15,550**
A Doll's House, Part 3 **W:** Neil Gaiman

13 ❑ Feb 1990 Cover: 1.50 **NM** value: **4.00**
Circ: CapCity orders: **16,400**
A Doll's House, Part 4 **W:** Neil Gaiman

14 ❑ Mar 1990 Cover: 1.50 **NM** value: **4.00**
Circ: CapCity orders: **16,600**
A Doll's House, Part 5 **W:** Neil Gaiman

15 ❑ Apr 1990 Cover: 1.50 **NM** value: **3.00**
Circ: CapCity orders: **15,600** • **CGC:** 1 graded, best 9.4
A Doll's House, Part 6 **W:** Neil Gaiman

16 ❑ Jun 1990 Cover: 1.50 **NM** value: **3.00**
Circ: CapCity orders: **15,950**
A Doll's House, Part 7 **W:** Neil Gaiman

17 ❑ Jul 1990 Cover: 1.50 **NM** value: **3.00**
Circ: CapCity orders: **16,200**
Dream Country; Calliope **W:** Neil Gaiman

18 ❑ Aug 1990 Cover: 1.50 **NM** value: **3.00**
Circ: CapCity orders: **16,550** • **CGC:** 1 graded, best 9.2
Dream Country; Dream of 1000 Cats **W:** Neil Gaiman

19 ❑ Sep 1990 Cover: 1.50 **NM** value: **3.00**
Circ: CapCity orders: **17,350** • **CGC:** 23 graded, best 9.8
Dream Country • properly printed; Midsummer Night's Dream **A:** Charles Vess **W:** Neil Gaiman

19/A❑ Sep 1990 Cover: 1.50 **NM** value: **3.00**
Circ: CapCity orders: **17,100**
Dream Country • pages out of order; Midsummer Night's Dream **A:** Charles Vess **W:** Neil Gaiman

20 ❑ Oct 1990 Cover: 1.50 **NM** value: **3.00**
Circ: CapCity orders: **17,350**
Dream Country; Facade **W:** Neil Gaiman ★ Death of Element Girl.

21 ❑ Nov 1990 Cover: 1.50 **NM** value: **3.00**
Circ: CapCity orders: **17,800**
Season of Mists prelude **W:** Neil Gaiman

22 ❑ Jan 1991 Cover: 1.50 **NM** value: **4.00**
Circ: CapCity orders: **18,600** • **CGC:** 3 graded, best 9.6
Season of Mists, Part 1 **W:** Neil Gaiman ★ 1st Appearance of Daniel (new Sandman).

23 ❑ Feb 1991 Cover: 1.50 **NM** value: **2.50**
Circ: CapCity orders: **18,700**
Season of Mists, Part 2 **W:** Neil Gaiman

24 ❑ Mar 1991 Cover: 1.50 **NM** value: **2.50**
Circ: CapCity orders: **18,050**
Season of Mists, Part 3 **W:** Neil Gaiman

25 ❑ Apr 1991 Cover: 1.50 **NM** value: **2.50**
Circ: CapCity orders: **18,300**
Season of Mists, Part 4 **W:** Neil Gaiman

26 ❑ May 1991 Cover: 1.50 **NM** value: **2.50**
Circ: CapCity orders: **18,750**
Season of Mists, Part 5 **W:** Neil Gaiman

27 ❑ Jun 1991 Cover: 1.50 **NM** value: **2.50**
Circ: CapCity orders: **19,350**
Season of Mists, Part 6 **W:** Neil Gaiman

28 ❑ Jul 1991 Cover: 1.50 **NM** value: **2.50**
Circ: CapCity orders: **20,100**
Season of Mists, Part 7 **W:** Neil Gaiman

29 ❑ Aug 1991 Cover: 1.50 **NM** value: **2.50**
Circ: CapCity orders: **20,750**
Distant Mirrors **W:** Neil Gaiman

30 ❑ Sep 1991 Cover: 1.50 **NM** value: **2.50**
Circ: CapCity orders: **21,500**
Distant Mirrors **W:** Neil Gaiman

31 ❑ Oct 1991 Cover: 1.50 **NM** value: **2.50**
Circ: CapCity orders: **21,800**
Distant Mirrors **W:** Neil Gaiman

32 ❑ Nov 1991 Cover: 1.50 **NM** value: **2.50**
Circ: CapCity orders: **24,150**
A Game of You, Part 1 **W:** Neil Gaiman

33 ❑ Dec 1991 Cover: 1.50 **NM** value: **2.50**
Circ: CapCity orders: **25,250**
A Game of You, Part 2 **A:** Shawn McManus **W:** Neil Gaiman

34 ❑ Jan 1992 Cover: 1.50 **NM** value: **2.50**
Circ: CapCity orders: **24,050**
A Game of You, Part 3 **W:** Neil Gaiman

35 ❑ Feb 1992 Cover: 1.50 **NM** value: **2.50**
Circ: CapCity orders: **24,000**
A Game of You, Part 4 **A:** Shawn McManus **W:** Neil Gaiman

36 ❑ Apr 1992 Cover: 1.50 **NM** value: **3.00**
Circ: CapCity orders: **24,000**
• Giant-size. A Game of You, Part 5 **A:** Shawn McManus **W:** Neil Gaiman

37 ❑ May 1992 Cover: 1.50 **NM** value: **2.50**
Circ: CapCity orders: **23,900**
A Game of You, Part 6 **W:** Neil Gaiman

38 ❑ Jun 1992 Cover: 1.50 **NM** value: **2.50**
Circ: CapCity orders: **25,350**
Convergence **W:** Neil Gaiman

39 ❑ Jul 1992 Cover: 1.50 **NM** value: **2.50**
Circ: CapCity orders: **25,750**
Convergence **W:** Neil Gaiman

40 ❑ Aug 1992 Cover: 1.50 **NM** value: **2.50**
Circ: CapCity orders: **25,550**
Convergence **W:** Neil Gaiman

41 ❑ Sep 1992 Cover: 1.50 **NM** value: **2.50**
Circ: CapCity orders: **23,950**
Brief Lives, Part 1 **W:** Neil Gaiman

42 ❑ Oct 1992 Cover: 1.50 **NM** value: **2.50**
Circ: CapCity orders: **23,950**
Brief Lives, Part 2 **W:** Neil Gaiman

43 ❑ Nov 1992 Cover: 1.50 **NM** value: **2.50**
Circ: CapCity orders: **24,400**
Brief Lives, Part 3 **W:** Neil Gaiman

44 ❑ Dec 1992 Cover: 1.50 **NM** value: **2.50**
Circ: CapCity orders: **25,000**
Brief Lives, Part 4 **W:** Neil Gaiman

45 ❑ Jan 1993 Cover: 1.75 **NM** value: **2.50**
Circ: CapCity orders: **25,100**
Brief Lives, Part 5 **A:** Jill Thompson **W:** Neil Gaiman

46 ❑ Feb 1993 Cover: 1.75 **NM** value: **2.50**
Circ: CapCity orders: **32,000**
Brief Lives, Part 6 • Brief Lives **A:** Jill Thompson **W:** Neil Gaiman

47 ❑ Mar 1993 Cover: 1.75 **NM** value: **2.50**
Circ: CapCity orders: **40,100**
Brief Lives, Part 7 **A:** Jill Thompson **W:** Neil Gaiman

48 ❑ Apr 1993 Cover: 1.75 **NM** value: **2.50**
Circ: CapCity orders: **34,200**
Brief Lives, Part 8 **A:** Jill Thompson **W:** Neil Gaiman

49 ❑ May 1993 Cover: 1.75 **NM** value: **2.50**
Circ: CapCity orders: **35,200**
Brief Lives, Part 9 **A:** Jill Thompson **W:** Neil Gaiman

50 ❑ Jun 1993 Cover: 2.95 **NM** value: **4.50**
Circ: CapCity orders: **63,950** • **CGC:** 1 graded, best 9.8
• Double-size. Distant Mirrors; Ramadan • Bronze ink **A:** P. Craig Russell; Dave McKean(cover) **W:** Neil Gaiman

50/GO❑ Jun 1993 **NM** value: **20.00**
• **CGC:** 3 graded, best 9.6
• Gold edition. Distant Mirrors; Ramadan **A:** P. Craig Russell **W:** Neil Gaiman

51 ❑ Jul 1993 Cover: 1.95 **NM** value: **2.50**
Circ: CapCity orders: **34,100**
World's End **A:** Bryan Talbot; Dick Giordano; George Pratt; Shawn McManus; Stan Woch; Colleen Doran **W:** Neil Gaiman

52 ❑ Aug 1993 Cover: 1.95 **NM** value: **2.50**
Circ: CapCity orders: **33,850**
World's End **A:** Bryan Talbot; John Watkiss **W:** Neil Gaiman

53 ❑ Sep 1993 Cover: 1.95 **NM** value: **2.50**
Circ: CapCity orders: **33,450**
World's End **A:** Bryan Talbot; Michael Zulli **W:** Neil Gaiman

54 ❑ Oct 1993 Cover: 1.95 **NM** value: **2.50**
Circ: CapCity orders: **31,850**
World's End; The Golden Boy **A:** Bryan Talbot; Mike Allred **W:** Neil Gaiman ★ Origin of Prez Rickard.

55 ❑ Nov 1993 Cover: 1.95 **NM** value: **2.50**
Circ: CapCity orders: **31,350**
World's End **W:** Neil Gaiman

56 ❑ Dec 1993 Cover: 1.95 **NM** value: **2.50**
Circ: CapCity orders: **32,400**
World's End **A:** Bryan Talbot; Gary Amaro **W:** Neil Gaiman

57 ❑ Feb 1994 Cover: 1.95 **NM** value: **2.50**
Circ: CapCity orders: **33,400**
The Kindly Ones, Part 1 **A:** Marc Hempel **W:** Neil Gaiman

58 ❑ Mar 1994 Cover: 1.95 **NM** value: **2.50**
Circ: CapCity orders: **30,050**
The Kindly Ones, Part 2 **A:** Marc Hempel **W:** Neil Gaiman

59 ❑ Apr 1994 Cover: 1.95 **NM** value: **2.50**
Circ: CapCity orders: **29,900**
The Kindly Ones, Part 3 **A:** Marc Hempel **W:** Neil Gaiman

60 ❑ Jun 1994 Cover: 1.95 **NM** value: **2.50**
Circ: CapCity orders: **31,200**
The Kindly Ones, Part 4 **A:** Marc Hempel **W:** Neil Gaiman

61 ❑ Jul 1994 Cover: 1.95 **NM** value: **2.50**
Circ: CapCity orders: **31,150**
The Kindly Ones, Part 5 **A:** Marc Hempel **W:** Neil Gaiman

62 ❑ Aug 1994 Cover: 1.95 **NM** value: **2.50**
Circ: CapCity orders: **31,800**
The Kindly Ones, Part 6 **A:** Dean Ormston; Charles Vess; Glyn Dillon; D'Israeli **W:** Neil Gaiman

63 ❑ Sep 1994 Cover: 1.95 **NM** value: **2.50**
Circ: CapCity orders: **31,300**
The Kindly Ones, Part 7 **A:** Marc Hempel **W:** Neil Gaiman

64 ❑ Nov 1994 Cover: 1.95 **NM** value: **2.50**
Circ: CapCity orders: **30,600**
The Kindly Ones, Part 8 **A:** Teddy Kristiansen **W:** Neil Gaiman

65 ❑ Dec 1994 Cover: 1.95 **NM** value: **2.50**
Circ: CapCity orders: **30,350**
The Kindly Ones, Part 9 **A:** Marc Hempel **W:** Neil Gaiman

66 ❑ Jan 1995 Cover: 1.95 **NM** value: **2.50**
Circ: CapCity orders: **29,050**
The Kindly Ones, Part 10 **A:** Marc Hempel **W:** Neil Gaiman

67 ❑ Mar 1995 Cover: 1.95 **NM** value: **2.50**
Circ: CapCity orders: **28,450**
The Kindly Ones, Part 11 **A:** Marc Hempel **W:** Neil Gaiman

68 ❑ May 1995 Cover: 1.95 **NM** value: **2.50**
Circ: CapCity orders: **27,200**
The Kindly Ones, Part 12 **A:** Marc Hempel **W:** Neil Gaiman

69 ❑ Jul 1995 Cover: 2.50 **NM** value: **3.00**

CGC-graded: Multiply prices above by **33 for 9.9 M • 16 for 9.8 NM/M • 7 for 9.6 NM+ • 5 for 9.4 NM • 2.5 for 9.2 NM- • 1.5 for 9.0 VF/NM**

Circ: CapCity orders: **26,850**
🕮 The Kindly Ones, Part 13 **W:** Neil Gaiman ★ Death of Sandman III (Morpheus).
70 ❑ Aug 1995 Cover: 2.50 **NM** value: **Cover or less**
Circ: CapCity orders: **29,300**
🕮 The Wake, Part 1 **W:** Neil Gaiman
71 ❑ Sep 1995 Cover: 2.50 **NM** value: **Cover or less**
Circ: CapCity orders: **27,175**
🕮 The Wake, Part 2 **W:** Neil Gaiman
72 ❑ Nov 1995 Cover: 2.50 **NM** value: **Cover or less**
🕮 The Wake, Part 3 • burial of Dream **W:** Neil Gaiman
73 ❑ Dec 1995 Cover: 2.50 **NM** value: **Cover or less**
🕮 The Wake, Part 4 **A:** Michael Zulli **W:** Neil Gaiman ★ Appearance of Hob Gadling.
74 ❑ Jan 1996 Cover: 2.50 **NM** value: **Cover or less**
🕮 Exiles **A:** Jon J Muth **W:** Neil Gaiman
75 ❑ Mar 1996 Cover: 3.95 **NM** value: **4.00**
• **CGC:** 1 graded, best 9.6
🕮 The Tempest final issue. • contains timeline **A:** Charles Vess **W:** Neil Gaiman ★ Appearance of William Shakespeare.
Bk 1❑ Cover: 14.95 **NM** value: **Cover or less**
• Trade Paperback. 🕮 Preludes & Nocturnes; Preludes and Nocturnes • collects #1-8 **W:** Neil Gaiman
Bk 2❑ Cover: 12.95 **NM** value: **Cover or less**
• Trade Paperback. 🕮 A Doll's House • collects #8-16 **W:** Neil Gaiman
Bk 2/HC❑ Cover: 29.95 **NM** value: **Cover or less**
hardcover. 🕮 A Doll's House • Collects Sandman #8-16 **W:** Neil Gaiman
Bk 2-2❑ Cover: 12.95 **NM** value: **Cover or less**
Bk 2/HC-2❑ Cover: 29.95 **NM** value: **Cover or less**
Bk 3❑ Cover: 14.95 **NM** value: **Cover or less**
softcover. 🕮 Dream Country • collects #17-20 **W:** Neil Gaiman
Bk 3/HC❑ Cover: 29.95 **NM** value: **Cover or less**
hardcover. 🕮 Dream Country • collects #17-20 **W:** Neil Gaiman
Bk 4❑ Cover: 14.95 **NM** value: **Cover or less**
• Trade Paperback. 🕮 Season of Mists • Collects Sandman #21-28 **W:** Neil Gaiman
Bk 5❑ Cover: 19.95 **NM** value: **Cover or less**
• Trade Paperback. 🕮 A Game of You • Collects Sandman #32-36 **W:** Neil Gaiman
Bk 6❑ Cover: 19.95 **NM** value: **Cover or less**
• Trade Paperback. 🕮 Fables and Reflections; Brief Lives • Collects Sandman #41-48 **W:** Neil Gaiman
Bk 7❑ Cover: 19.95 **NM** value: **Cover or less**
softcover. 🕮 Brief Lives • collects #41-49 **W:** Neil Gaiman
Bk 7/HC❑ Cover: 29.95 **NM** value: **Cover or less**
hardcover. 🕮 Brief Lives • collects #41-49 **W:** Neil Gaiman
Bk 8❑ Cover: 29.95 **NM** value: **Cover or less**
🕮 World's End • collects #51-56 **A:** Marc Hempel; Teddy Kristiansen; Richard Case; Dean Ormston; Charles Vess; Kevin Nowlan; Glyn Dillon; D'Israeli **W:** Neil Gaiman
Bk 8/HC❑ Cover: 34.95 **NM** value: **Cover or less**
• Hardcover edition. 🕮 World's End **A:** Marc Hempel; Teddy Kristiansen; Richard Case; Dean Ormston; Charles Vess; Kevin Nowlan; Glyn Dillon; D'Israeli **W:** Neil Gaiman
Bk 9❑ Cover: 19.95 **NM** value: **Cover or less**
• Trade Paperback. 🕮 The Kindly Ones • collects #57-69 and Vertigo Jam #1 **W:** Neil Gaiman
Bk 9/HC❑ Cover: 34.95 **NM** value: **Cover or less**
Hardcover (3rd printing?). 🕮 The Kindly Ones • collects #57-69 and Vertigo Jam #1 **W:** Neil Gaiman
Bk 10❑ Cover: 19.95 **NM** value: **Cover or less**
🕮 The Wake • collects #70-75 **A:** Jon J. Muth; Michael Zulli; Charles Vess **W:** Neil Gaiman
Bk 10/HC❑ Cover: 29.95 **NM** value: **Cover or less**
hardcover. 🕮 The Wake • collects #70-75 **A:** Jon J. Muth; Michael Zulli; Charles Vess **W:** Neil Gaiman
SE 1❑ ca. 1991 Cover: 3.50 **NM** value: **5.00**
Circ: CapCity orders: **51,250**
Glow-in-the-dark cover. • Orpheus special edition. 🕮 The Song Of The Orpheus **A:** Bryan Talbot **W:** Neil Gaiman

SANDMAN, THE: A GALLERY OF DREAMS — DC / Vertigo

1 ❑ ca. 1994 Cover: 2.95 **NM** value: **Cover or less**
Circ: CapCity orders: **24,850** • **CGC:** 1 graded, best 9.4
No issue number.

SANDMAN COMPANION, THE — DC

1 ❑ Cover: 14.95 **NM** value: **Cover or less**
W: Hy Bender

SANDMAN MIDNIGHT THEATRE — DC / Vertigo

1 ❑ Sep 1995 Cover: 6.95 **NM** value: **Cover or less**
No issue number. • prestige format. • Morpheus meets Wesley Dodds **A:** Teddy Kristiansen **W:** Matt Wagner; Neil Gaiman

SANDMAN MYSTERY THEATRE — DC / Vertigo

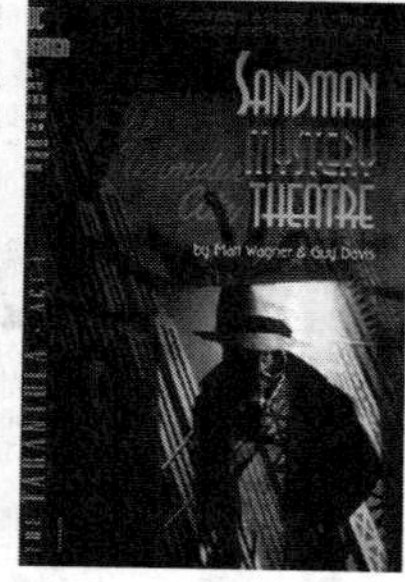

This compelling series is a period piece, set in the midst of the Jazz Age in New York City. To steal a phrase, the city was certainly no safer then, but it was definitely more stylish. The mix of gin joints and socialites, downtown and Chinatown, serves as a perfect backdrop for the central business of murder.

The cast of this mystery theatre presents us with a sea of faces, although an unlikely one seems to keep reappearing: the innocuous, shy countenance of Wesley Dodds. Unknown to others, Dodds wears two faces: his own, and that of the (Golden Age) Sandman. Hidden behind the bulging eyes of a gas mask, and armed with a strange weapon firing gas, Dodds carries out his mysterious plans.

1 ❑ Apr 1993 Cover: 1.95 **NM** value: **4.00**
Circ: CapCity orders: **51,650** • **CGC:** 1 graded, best 9.4
🕮 The Tarantula, Part 1; Tarantula, Part 1 **A:** Guy Davis; Gavin Wilson(cover) **W:** Matt Wagner
2 ❑ May 1993 Cover: 1.95 **NM** value: **3.00**
Circ: CapCity orders: **30,550**
🕮 The Tarantula, Part 2; Tarantula, Part 2 **A:** Guy Davis; Gavin Wilson(cover) **W:** Matt Wagner
3 ❑ Jun 1993 Cover: 1.95 **NM** value: **3.00**
Circ: CapCity orders: **25,550**
🕮 The Tarantula, Part 3; Tarantula, Part 3 **A:** Guy Davis; Gavin Wilson(cover) **W:** Matt Wagner
4 ❑ Jul 1993 Cover: 1.95 **NM** value: **3.00**
Circ: CapCity orders: **24,150**
🕮 The Tarantula, Part 4; Tarantula, Part 4 **W:** Matt Wagner
5 ❑ Aug 1993 Cover: 1.95 **NM** value: **3.00**
Circ: CapCity orders: **21,600**
🕮 The Face, Part 1 **W:** Matt Wagner
6 ❑ Sep 1993 Cover: 1.95 **NM** value: **3.00**
Circ: CapCity orders: **17,900**
🕮 The Face, Part 2 **A:** John Watkiss; Gavin Wilson(cover); Richard Bruning(cover) **W:** Matt Wagner
7 ❑ Oct 1993 Cover: 1.95 **NM** value: **3.00**
Circ: CapCity orders: **16,750**
🕮 The Face, Part 3 **A:** John Watkiss; Gavin Wilson(cover); Richard Bruning(cover) **W:** Matt Wagner
8 ❑ Nov 1993 Cover: 1.95 **NM** value: **3.00**
Circ: CapCity orders: **15,650**
🕮 The Face, Part 4 **A:** John Watkiss; Gavin Wilson(cover); Richard Bruning(cover) **W:** Matt Wagner
9 ❑ Dec 1993 Cover: 1.95 **NM** value: **3.00**
Circ: CapCity orders: **15,000**
🕮 The Brute, Part 1 **A:** R.G. Taylor; Gavin Wilson(cover); Richard Bruning(cover) **W:** Matt Wagner
10 ❑ Jan 1994 Cover: 1.95 **NM** value: **3.00**
Circ: CapCity orders: **13,600**
🕮 The Brute, Part 2 **A:** R.G. Taylor; Gavin Wilson(cover); Richard Bruning(cover) **W:** Matt Wagner
11 ❑ Feb 1994 Cover: 1.95 **NM** value: **2.75**
Circ: CapCity orders: **12,550**
🕮 The Brute, Part 3 **A:** R.G. Taylor; Gavin Wilson(cover); Richard Bruning(cover) **W:** Matt Wagner
12 ❑ Mar 1994 Cover: 1.95 **NM** value: **2.75**
Circ: CapCity orders: **11,800**
🕮 The Brute, Part 4 **A:** R.G. Taylor; Gavin Wilson(cover); Richard Bruning(cover) **W:** Matt Wagner
13 ❑ Apr 1994 Cover: 1.95 **NM** value: **2.75**
Circ: CapCity orders: **11,300**
🕮 The Vamp, Part 1 **W:** Matt Wagner
14 ❑ May 1994 Cover: 1.95 **NM** value: **2.75**
Circ: CapCity orders: **10,900**
🕮 The Vamp, Part 2 **W:** Matt Wagner
15 ❑ Jun 1994 Cover: 1.95 **NM** value: **2.75**
Circ: CapCity orders: **10,700**
🕮 The Vamp, Part 3 **W:** Matt Wagner
16 ❑ Jul 1994 Cover: 1.95 **NM** value: **2.75**
Circ: CapCity orders: **11,000**
🕮 The Vamp, Part 4 **W:** Matt Wagner
17 ❑ Aug 1994 Cover: 1.95 **NM** value: **2.75**
Circ: CapCity orders: **10,700**
🕮 The Scorpion, Part 1 **W:** Matt Wagner
18 ❑ Sep 1994 Cover: 1.95 **NM** value: **2.75**
Circ: CapCity orders: **10,400**
🕮 The Scorpion, Part 2 **W:** Matt Wagner
19 ❑ Oct 1994 Cover: 1.95 **NM** value: **2.75**
Circ: CapCity orders: **10,400**
🕮 The Scorpion, Part 3 **W:** Matt Wagner
20 ❑ Nov 1994 Cover: 1.95 **NM** value: **2.75**
Circ: CapCity orders: **10,200**
🕮 The Scorpion, Part 4 **A:** Guy Davis; Gavin Wilson(cover); Richard Bruning(cover) **W:** Matt Wagner; Steven Seagle
21 ❑ Dec 1994 Cover: 1.95 **NM** value: **2.50**
Circ: CapCity orders: **10,350**
🕮 Dr. Death, Part 1 **A:** Guy Davis **W:** Matt Wagner; Steven Seagle
22 ❑ Jan 1995 Cover: 1.95 **NM** value: **2.50**
Circ: CapCity orders: **9,750**
🕮 Dr. Death, Part 2 **A:** Guy Davis **W:** Matt Wagner; Steven Seagle
23 ❑ Feb 1995 Cover: 1.95 **NM** value: **2.50**
Circ: CapCity orders: **9,375**
🕮 Dr. Death, Part 3 **A:** Guy Davis **W:** Matt Wagner; Steven Seagle
24 ❑ Mar 1995 Cover: 1.95 **NM** value: **2.50**
Circ: CapCity orders: **9,075**
🕮 Dr. Death, Part 4 **A:** Guy Davis **W:** Matt Wagner; Steven Seagle
25 ❑ Apr 1995 Cover: 1.95 **NM** value: **2.50**
Circ: CapCity orders: **8,700**
🕮 Night of the Butcher, Part 1 **W:** Matt Wagner
26 ❑ May 1995 Cover: 2.25 **NM** value: **2.50**
Circ: CapCity orders: **8,700**
🕮 Night of the Butcher, Part 2 **W:** Matt Wagner
27 ❑ Jun 1995 Cover: 2.25 **NM** value: **2.50**
Circ: CapCity orders: **8,350**
🕮 Night of the Butcher, Part 3 **W:** Matt Wagner
28 ❑ Jul 1995 Cover: 2.25 **NM** value: **2.50**
Circ: CapCity orders: **8,575**
🕮 Night of the Butcher, Part 4 **W:** Matt Wagner
29 ❑ Aug 1995 Cover: 2.25 **NM** value: **2.50**
Circ: CapCity orders: **9,075**
🕮 The Hourman, Part 1 **W:** Matt Wagner
30 ❑ Sep 1995 Cover: 2.25 **NM** value: **2.50**
Circ: CapCity orders: **8,725**
🕮 The Hourman, Part 2 **W:** Matt Wagner
31 ❑ Oct 1995 Cover: 2.25 **NM** value: **2.50**
Circ: CapCity orders: **7,650**
🕮 The Hourman, Part 3 **W:** Matt Wagner
32 ❑ Nov 1995 Cover: 2.25 **NM** value: **2.50**
🕮 The Hourman, Part 4 **W:** Matt Wagner
33 ❑ Dec 1995 Cover: 2.25 **NM** value: **2.50**
🕮 The Python, Part 1 **A:** Warren Pleece **W:** Matt Wagner; Steven Seagle
34 ❑ Jan 1996 Cover: 2.25 **NM** value: **2.50**
🕮 The Python, Part 2 **A:** Warren Pleece **W:** Matt Wagner; Steven Seagle
35 ❑ Feb 1996 Cover: 2.25 **NM** value: **2.50**
🕮 The Python, Part 3 **A:** Warren Pleece **W:** Matt Wagner; Steven Seagle
36 ❑ Mar 1996 Cover: 2.25 **NM** value: **2.50**
🕮 The Python, Part 4 **A:** Warren Pleece **W:** Matt Wagner; Steven Seagle
37 ❑ Apr 1996 Cover: 2.25 **NM** value: **2.50**
🕮 The Mist, Part 1 **A:** Guy Davis **W:** Matt Wagner; Steven Seagle
38 ❑ May 1996 Cover: 2.25 **NM** value: **2.50**
🕮 The Mist, Part 2 **A:** Guy Davis **W:** Matt Wagner; Steven Seagle
39 ❑ Jun 1996 Cover: 2.25 **NM** value: **2.50**
🕮 The Mist, Part 3 **A:** Guy Davis **W:** Matt Wagner; Steven Seagle
40 ❑ Jul 1996 Cover: 2.25 **NM** value: **2.50**
🕮 The Mist, Part 4 **A:** Guy Davis **W:** Matt Wagner; Steven Seagle
41 ❑ Aug 1996 Cover: 2.25 **NM** value: **2.50**
🕮 Phantom of the Fair, Part 1; The Phantom of the Fair, Part 1 **A:** Guy Davis **W:** Matt Wagner; Steven Seagle
42 ❑ Sep 1996 Cover: 2.25 **NM** value: **2.50**
🕮 Phantom of the Fair, Part 2; The Phantom of the Fair, Part 2 **A:** Guy Davis **W:** Matt Wagner; Steven Seagle
43 ❑ Oct 1996 Cover: 2.25 **NM** value: **2.50**
🕮 Phantom of the Fair, Part 3; The Phantom of the Fair, Part 3 **A:** Guy Davis **W:** Matt Wagner; Steven Seagle ★ Appearance of Crimson Avenger.
44 ❑ Nov 1996 Cover: 2.50 **NM** value: **Cover or less**
Circ: Diamd. preorders: **20,969**
🕮 Phantom of the Fair, Part 4; The Phantom of the Fair, Part 4 **A:** Guy Davis **W:** Matt Wagner; Steven Seagle
45 ❑ Dec 1996 Cover: 2.50 **NM** value: **Cover or less**
Circ: Diamd. preorders: **21,578**
Photo cover. 🕮 The Blackhawk, Part 1 **A:** Matthew Smith **W:** Matt Wagner; Steven Seagle ★ Appearance of Blackhawk.
46 ❑ Jan 1997 Cover: 2.50 **NM** value: **Cover or less**
Circ: Diamd. preorders: **20,753**
🕮 The Blackhawk, Part 2 **A:** Matthew Smith **W:** Matt Wagner; Steven Seagle
47 ❑ Feb 1997 Cover: 2.50 **NM** value: **Cover or less**
Circ: Diamd. preorders: **20,074**
🕮 The Blackhawk, Part 3 **A:** Matthew Smith **W:** Matt Wagner; Steven Seagle
48 ❑ Mar 1997 Cover: 2.50 **NM** value: **Cover or less**
Circ: Diamd. preorders: **19,655**
Photo cover. 🕮 The Blackhawk, Part 4 **A:** Matthew Smith **W:** Matt Wagner; Steven Seagle
49 ❑ Apr 1997 Cover: 2.50 **NM** value: **Cover or less**
Circ: Diamd. preorders: **19,834**
🕮 Return of the Scarlet Ghost, Part 1 **W:** Matt Wagner
50 ❑ May 1997 Cover: 2.50 **NM** value: **3.50**
Circ: Diamd. preorders: **20,216**
• Giant-size. 🕮 Return of the Scarlet Ghost, Part 2 **W:** Matt Wagner
51 ❑ Jun 1997 Cover: 2.50 **NM** value: **Cover or less**
Circ: Diamd. preorders: **19,735**
🕮 Return of the Scarlet Ghost, Part 3 **W:** Matt Wagner
52 ❑ Jul 1997 Cover: 2.50 **NM** value: **Cover or less**
Circ: Diamd. preorders: **18,470**
🕮 Return of the Scarlet Ghost, Part 4 **W:** Matt Wagner
53 ❑ Aug 1997 Cover: 2.50 **NM** value: **Cover or less**
Circ: Diamd. preorders: **18,352**
🕮 The Crone, Part 1 **A:** Guy Davis **W:** Matt Wagner; Steven Seagle
54 ❑ Sep 1997 Cover: 2.50 **NM** value: **Cover or less**
Circ: Diamd. preorders: **17,691**
🕮 The Crone, Part 2 **A:** Guy Davis **W:** Matt Wagner; Steven Seagle
55 ❑ Oct 1997 Cover: 2.50 **NM** value: **Cover or less**
Circ: Diamd. preorders: **17,589**
🕮 The Crone, Part 3 **A:** Guy Davis **W:** Matt Wagner; Steven Seagle
56 ❑ Nov 1997 Cover: 2.50 **NM** value: **Cover or less**
Circ: Diamd. preorders: **17,305**
🕮 The Crone, Part 4 **A:** Guy Davis **W:** Matt Wagner; Steven Seagle
57 ❑ Dec 1997 Cover: 2.50 **NM** value: **Cover or less**
Circ: Diamd. preorders: **17,163**
🕮 The Cannon, Part 1 **A:** Michael Lark **W:** Matt Wagner; Steven Seagle
58 ❑ Jan 1998 Cover: 2.50 **NM** value: **Cover or less**
Circ: Diamd. preorders: **16,542**
🕮 The Cannon, Part 2 **A:** Michael Lark **W:** Matt Wagner; Steven Seagle
59 ❑ Feb 1998 Cover: 2.50 **NM** value: **Cover or less**
Circ: Diamd. preorders: **16,001**
🕮 The Cannon, Part 3 **A:** Michael Lark **W:** Matt Wagner; Steven Seagle
60 ❑ Mar 1998 Cover: 2.50 **NM** value: **Cover or less**
Circ: Diamd. preorders: **15,717**
🕮 The Cannon, Part 4 **A:** Michael Lark **W:** Matt Wagner; Steven Seagle
61 ❑ Apr 1998 Cover: 2.50 **NM** value: **Cover or less**
Circ: Diamd. preorders: **15,405**
🕮 The City, Part 1
62 ❑ May 1998 Cover: 2.50 **NM** value: **Cover or less**
Circ: Diamd. preorders: **15,080**
🕮 The City, Part 2
63 ❑ Jul 1998 Cover: 2.50 **NM** value: **Cover or less**
Circ: Diamd. preorders: **14,570**
🕮 The City, Part 3
64 ❑ Aug 1998 Cover: 2.50 **NM** value: **Cover or less**
Circ: Diamd. preorders: **13,866**
🕮 The City, Part 4
65 ❑ Sep 1998 Cover: 2.50 **NM** value: **Cover or less**
Circ: Diamd. preorders: **13,663**
🕮 The Goblin, Part 1
66 ❑ Oct 1998 Cover: 2.50 **NM** value: **Cover or less**
Circ: Diamd. preorders: **13,393**
🕮 The Goblin, Part 2

Other grades: Multiply prices above by **1.5 for Mint • 2/3 for Very Fine • 1/3 for Fine • 1/5 for Very Good • 1/8 for Good**

67 ❑ Nov 1998 Cover: 2.50 **NM** value: **Cover or less**
Circ: Diamd. preorders: **13,066**
🕮 The Goblin, Part 3

68 ❑ Dec 1998 Cover: 2.50 **NM** value: **Cover or less**
Circ: Diamd. preorders: **13,012**
🕮 The Goblin, Part 4

69 ❑ Jan 1999 Cover: 2.50 **NM** value: **Cover or less**
Circ: Diamd. preorders: **12,955**
🕮 The Hero; The Hero, Part 1 **A:** Guy Davis **W:** Steven Seagle

70 ❑ Feb 1999 Cover: 2.50 **NM** value: **Cover or less**
Circ: Diamd. preorders: **12,697**
🕮 The Hero; The Hero, Part 2 final issue. **A:** Guy Davis **W:** Steven Seagle

Anl 1❑ Cover: 3.95 **NM** value: **4.00**
Circ: CapCity orders: **10,000**
W: Matt Wagner

Bk 1❑ Cover: 14.95 **NM** value: **Cover or less**
🕮 The Tarantula • collects #1-4

SANDMAN PRESENTS, THE: LOVE STREET — DC / Vertigo

1 ❑ Jul 1999 Cover: 2.95 **NM** value: **Cover or less**
Circ: Diamd. preorders: **25,705**
• John Constantine in the '60s **A:** Michael Zulli **W:** Peter Hogan

2 ❑ Aug 1999 Cover: 2.95 **NM** value: **Cover or less**
Circ: Diamd. preorders: **22,604**
A: Michael Zulli **W:** Peter Hogan

3 ❑ Sep 1999 Cover: 2.95 **NM** value: **Cover or less**
Circ: Diamd. preorders: **21,698**
A: Michael Zulli **W:** Peter Hogan

SANDMAN PRESENTS: LUCIFER — DC / Vertigo

1 ❑ Mar 1999 Cover: 2.95 **NM** value: **Cover or less**
Circ: Diamd. preorders: **28,295**
🕮 The Morningstar Option, Part 1 **A:** Scott Hampton **W:** Mike Carey

2 ❑ Apr 1999 Cover: 2.95 **NM** value: **Cover or less**
Circ: Diamd. preorders: **24,266**
🕮 The Morningstar Option, Part 2 **A:** Scott Hampton **W:** Mike Carey

3 ❑ May 1999 Cover: 2.95 **NM** value: **Cover or less**
Circ: Diamd. preorders: **23,680**
🕮 The Morningstar Option, Part 3 **A:** Scott Hampton **W:** Mike Carey

SANDMAN PRESENTS: PETREFAX — DC / Vertigo

1 ❑ Mar 2000 Cover: 2.95 **NM** value: **Cover or less**
Circ: Diamd. preorders: **18,760**
🕮 Travels in Malegrise, Part 1 **A:** Steve Leialoha **W:** Mike Carey

2 ❑ Apr 2000 Cover: 2.95 **NM** value: **Cover or less**
Circ: Diamd. preorders: **16,201**
🕮 Travels in Malegrise, Part 2 **A:** Steve Leialoha **W:** Mike Carey

3 ❑ May 2000 Cover: 2.95 **NM** value: **Cover or less**
Circ: Diamd. preorders: **13,845**
🕮 Travels in Malegrise, Part 3 **A:** Steve Leialoha **W:** Mike Carey

4 ❑ Jun 2000 Cover: 2.95 **NM** value: **Cover or less**
Circ: Diamd. preorders: **12,755**
🕮 Travels in Malegrise, Part 4 **A:** Steve Leialoha **W:** Mike Carey

SANDMAN, THE — DC

1 ❑ Win 1974 Cover: 0.20 **NM** value: **6.00**
• **CGC:** 21 graded, best 9.8
🕮 The Sandman **A:** Joe Simon; Jack Kirby

2 ❑ May 1975 Cover: 0.25 **NM** value: **4.00**
A: Jack Kirby

3 ❑ Jul 1975 Cover: 0.25 **NM** value: **4.00**
A: Jack Kirby

4 ❑ Sep 1975 Cover: 0.25 **NM** value: **4.00**
🕮 Panic In The Dream Stream **A:** Jack Kirby; Mike Royer **W:** Michael Fleisher ★ Appearance of Demon.

5 ❑ Nov 1975 Cover: 0.25 **NM** value: **4.00**
• **CGC:** 1 graded, best 9.0
🕮 The Invasion of the Frog Men **A:** Jack Kirby

6 ❑ Jan 1976 Cover: 0.25 **NM** value: **4.00**
🕮 The Plot To Destroy Washington, D.C. final issue. **A:** Jack Kirby

SANDMAN, THE: THE DREAM HUNTERS — DC / Vertigo

Sandman creator Neil Gaiman returned to the Dreaming to tell a haunting story of love and sacrifice based on a Japanese fairy tale. Presented as a novel instead of as a traditional comic, the story was beautifully illustrated by Yoshitaka Amano, known for his work in animation and fantasy art, including the cult classic Vampire Hunter D and the Final Fantasy video game.

Dream Hunters is the story of the unlikely love between a modest young monk and an enchantingly beautiful fox. But the monk's fate is entwined with that of the onmyoji, Master of Yin-Yang. For one to live and prosper, the other must die. When the fox overhears demons plotting the monk's demise, she seeks guidance from the King of All Night's Dreaming. Unfortunately, the monk's fate is not so easily escaped, and the fox, who would have gladly died in his place, is left alone, vengeance her only solace.

Bk 1❑ Oct 1999 Cover: 14.95 **NM** value: **Cover or less**
A: Yoshitaka Amano **W:** Neil Gaiman

Bk 1/HC❑ Oct 1999 Cover: 29.95 **NM** value: **Cover or less**
• Hardcover edition. **A:** Yoshitaka Amano **W:** Neil Gaiman

SANDS, THE — Black Eye

1 ❑ b&w Cover: 2.50 **NM** value: **Cover or less**
• smaller than a normal comic book

2 ❑ b&w Cover: 2.50 **NM** value: **Cover or less**
• smaller than a normal comic book

3 ❑ Feb 1997, b&w Cover: 2.50 **NM** value: **Cover or less**
• smaller than a normal comic book

SANDS OF THE SOUTH PACIFIC — Toby

1 ❑ ca. 1953 Cover: 0.10 **NM** value: **150.00**

SAN FRANCISCO COMIC BOOK, THE — San Francisco Comic Book Co.

1 ❑ Cover: 0.50 **NM** value: **5.00**
• **CGC:** 1 graded, best 7.0

2 ❑ Cover: 0.50 **NM** value: **3.00**
🕮 The Adventures o **A:** Larry Welz; Robert Williams; Robert Crumb; Trina Robbins; Rick Griffin; Greg Irons; Jim Osborne; S. Clay Wilson; Spain Rodriguez; Willy Murphy; Dan O'Neill; Kim Dietch; Marvinius **W:** Larry Welz; Robert Williams; Robert Crumb; Trina Robbins; Rick Griffin; Greg Irons; Jim Osborne; S. Clay Wilson; Spain Rodriguez; Willy Murphy; Dan O'Neill; Kim Dietch; Marvinius

3 ❑ Cover: 0.50 **NM** value: **3.00**
🕮 Sacred Goose Thrills; Surreal Comics; Fox; Melody House; Oh-Bow Wow!; Underground Hotline; Take This Woman Comix; The Secret File of Joe Badd Federal Nark; Warped Comics; F*cked Up **A:** Robert Williams; George Metzger; Gilbert Shelton; Robert Crumb; Jerry Beck; Trina Robbins; Jay Lynch; Greg Irons; Kim Deitch; Osborne; Rory Hayes; S. Clay Wilson; Spain Rodriguez; G. Arlington; J. Green; J. Hayes; Mervinius; Simon Dietch; W. Mendes **W:** Robert Williams; George Metzger; Gilbert Shelton; Robert Crumb; Jerry Beck; Trina Robbins; Jay Lynch; Greg Irons; Kim Deitch; Osborne; Rory Hayes; S. Clay Wilson; Spain Rodriguez; G. Arlington; J. Green; J. Hayes; Mervinius; Simon Dietch; W. Mendes

4 ❑ **NM** value: **3.00**
5 ❑ **NM** value: **3.00**
6 ❑ **NM** value: **3.00**
7 ❑ **NM** value: **3.00**

SANTA CLAUS ADVENTURES (WALT KELLY'S...) — Innovation

1 ❑ Cover: 6.95 **NM** value: **Cover or less**
Circ: CapCity orders: **1,125**
No issue number. **A:** Walt Kelly

SANTA CLAUS FUNNIES — Dell

1 ❑ ca. 1942 Cover: 0.10 **NM** value: **400.00**
• **CGC:** 1 graded, best 8.0

2 ❑ ca. 1943 Cover: 0.10 **NM** value: **250.00**

SANTA CLAWS (ETERNITY) — Eternity

1 ❑ b&w Cover: 2.95 **NM** value: **Cover or less**

SANTA CLAWS (THORBY) — Thorby

1 ❑ Cover: 2.95 **NM** value: **Cover or less**

SANTANA — Malibu / Rock-It

1 ❑ May 1994 Cover: 3.95 **NM** value: **5.00**
• magazine. 🕮 The Story of Santana; The Guitars of Santana **A:** Tom Yeates; Timothy Truman **W:** Timothy Truman

SANTA THE BARBARIAN — Maximum

1 ❑ Dec 1996 Cover: 2.99 **NM** value: **Cover or less**
Circ: Diamd. preorders: **14,072**
🕮 The Big Red Slay; The Night Before X-Mas **A:** Dan Fraga; Pop Mhan **W:** Dan Fraga; Pop Mhan

SAPPHIRE — Aircel

All issues are adults only.

1 ❑ Feb 1990 Cover: 2.50 **NM** value: **2.95**
• **CGC:** 1 graded, best 9.6
A: Vince Danks **W:** Vince Danks

2 ❑ Mar 1990 Cover: 2.50 **NM** value: **2.95**
• **CGC:** 1 graded, best 9.2
A: Vince Danks **W:** Vince Danks

3 ❑ Apr 1990 Cover: 2.50 **NM** value: **Cover or less**
• **CGC:** 1 graded, best 9.4

4 ❑ May 1990 Cover: 2.50 **NM** value: **Cover or less**
• **CGC:** 1 graded, best 9.2

5 ❑ Jun 1990 Cover: 2.50 **NM** value: **Cover or less**
6 ❑ Jul 1990 Cover: 2.50 **NM** value: **Cover or less**
7 ❑ Aug 1990 Cover: 2.50 **NM** value: **Cover or less**
8 ❑ Cover: 2.50 **NM** value: **Cover or less**
9 ❑ Sep 1990 Cover: 2.50 **NM** value: **Cover or less**
Bk 1❑ Cover: 9.95 **NM** value: **Cover or less**
• A Wizard's Quest

SAP TUNES — Fantagraphics

1 ❑ b&w Cover: 2.50 **NM** value: **Cover or less**
2 ❑ b&w Cover: 2.50 **NM** value: **Cover or less**

SARAH-JANE HAMILTON PRESENTS SUPERSTARS OF EROTICA — Re-Visionary

1 ❑ Cover: 2.95 **NM** value: **Cover or less**
🕮 Savannah: Piercing the Veil **A:** Chuck Bordell **W:** J. Allen Sanford; Nancy Nemo; Sarah-Jane Hamilton; Savannah

SARGE SNORKEL — Charlton

1 ❑ Oct 1973 **NM** value: **8.00**
2 ❑ Dec 1973 Cover: 0.20 **NM** value: **5.00**
3 ❑ Cover: 0.25 **NM** value: **4.00**
🕮 Lunacy; Sarge & Zero; An Errand for Zero; Good Suggestion; Desperation; Sarge's Lucky Day; Flower Power
4 ❑ Sep 1974 Cover: 0.25 **NM** value: **4.00**
5 ❑ Nov 1974 Cover: 0.25 **NM** value: **4.00**
6 ❑ Jan 1975 Cover: 0.25 **NM** value: **3.00**
7 ❑ Mar 1975 Cover: 0.25 **NM** value: **3.00**
8 ❑ May 1975 Cover: 0.25 **NM** value: **3.00**
9 ❑ Jul 1975 Cover: 0.25 **NM** value: **3.00**
10 ❑ Sep 1975 Cover: 0.25 **NM** value: **3.00**
11 ❑ Nov 1975 Cover: 0.25 **NM** value: **3.00**
12 ❑ Jan 1976 Cover: 0.25 **NM** value: **3.00**
13 ❑ Mar 1976 Cover: 0.25 **NM** value: **3.00**
14 ❑ May 1976 Cover: 0.30 **NM** value: **3.00**
15 ❑ Aug 1976 Cover: 0.30 **NM** value: **3.00**
16 ❑ Oct 1976 Cover: 0.30 **NM** value: **3.00**
17 ❑ Dec 1976 Cover: 0.30 **NM** value: **3.00**

SARGE STEEL — Charlton

1 ❑ Dec 1964 Cover: 0.12 **NM** value: **15.00**
2 ❑ Feb 1965 Cover: 0.12 **NM** value: **10.00**
3 ❑ May 1965 Cover: 0.12 **NM** value: **8.00**
4 ❑ Jul 1965 Cover: 0.12 **NM** value: **8.00**
5 ❑ Sep 1965 Cover: 0.12 **NM** value: **8.00**
6 ❑ Nov 1965 Cover: 0.12 **NM** value: **6.00**
7 ❑ Apr 1966 Cover: 0.12 **NM** value: **6.00**
8 ❑ Oct 1966 Cover: 0.12 **NM** value: **6.00**

SATANIKA — Verotik

0 ❑ ca. 1995 Cover: 2.95 **NM** value: **4.00**
Circ: CapCity orders: **11,095**

1 ❑ Jan 1995 Cover: 2.95 **NM** value: **5.00**
Circ: CapCity orders: **4,470**
W: Glenn Danzig

2 ❑ 1995 Cover: 2.95 **NM** value: **4.00**
Circ: CapCity orders: **4,850**
A: Duke Mighten **W:** Glenn Danzig

3 ❑ 1995 Cover: 2.95 **NM** value: **4.00**
Circ: CapCity orders: **8,525**

4 ❑ 1996 Cover: 2.95 **NM** value: **3.00**

5 ❑ Oct 1996 Cover: 2.95 **NM** value: **3.00**
Circ: Diamd. preorders: **15,004**

6 ❑ Jan 1997 Cover: 2.95 **NM** value: **Cover or less**
Circ: Diamd. preorders: **13,187**

7 ❑ Apr 1997 Cover: 2.95 **NM** value: **Cover or less**
Circ: Diamd. preorders: **11,909**

8 ❑ Sep 1997 Cover: 2.95 **NM** value: **Cover or less**
Circ: Diamd. preorders: **11,570**

9 ❑ Mar 1998 Cover: 2.95 **NM** value: **Cover or less**
Circ: Diamd. preorders: **9,570**

10 ❑ Dec 1998 Cover: 2.95 **NM** value: **Cover or less**
Circ: Diamd. preorders: **5,927**

11 ❑ May 1999 Cover: 3.95 **NM** value: **Cover or less**
Circ: Diamd. preorders: **6,066**

SATANIKA ILLUSTRATIONS, THE — Verotik

All issues are adults only.

1 ❑ Sep 1996 Cover: 3.95 **NM** value: **Cover or less**
Circ: Diamd. preorders: **8,977**
cardstock cover. • pin-ups

SATAN PLACE — Thunderhill

1 ❑ Cover: 3.50 **NM** value: **Cover or less**
🕮 Disposable Love; Say Goodnight, Sophie; Too Much TV; Sally Satan **A:** Jackson Guice; Al Vey; Alfred Ramirez; Jeff Guice **W:** Alfred Ramirez

SATAN'S PLANET (A DAY IN LIFE ON...) — Home-Made Euthanasia

1 ❑ Cover: 1.25 **NM** value: **Cover or less**
2 ❑ Cover: 1.50 **NM** value: **Cover or less**

SATAN'S SIX — Topps

Satan's Six are people (and monsters) trapped in Limbo, qualifying neither for a place in Heaven nor Hell. The pack consists of Brian Bluedragon, an errant knight whose service King Arthur refused; Dezira, a would-be temptress; Hard Luck Harrigan, a gambler; Kuga "the Lion Killer," a seemingly fierce warrior who secretly loves animals; and Frightful, a demon who is sent from Hell to chaperone the others. These six go to Earth in order to qualify for a place in Hades. After all, nothing's worse than sitting around in Limbo for all of Eternity.

Satan's Six is a silly series from the master of adventure, Jack Kirby. Fans of The King won't want to miss the series' backup story, Batton Lash's Wolff & Byrd, Counselors of the Macabre, a hilarious, supernatural take on the problems with lawyers.

1 ❑ Apr 1993 Cover: 2.95 **NM** value: **Cover or less**
Circ: CapCity orders: **57,325**
• trading card; Wolff and Byrd, Counselors of the Macabre backup story **A:** Jack Kirby; Frank Miller **C:** Todd McFarlane; Jack Kirby **W:** Jack Kirby; Tony Isabella ★ Origin of Satan's Six. ★ 1st Appearance of Satan's Six.

2 ❑ May 1993 Cover: 2.95 **NM** value: **Cover or less**
Circ: CapCity orders: **28,875**
🕮 Idol hands • trading cards **A:** John Cleary **W:** Tony Isabella

3 ❑ Jun 1993 Cover: 2.95 **NM** value: **Cover or less**
Circ: CapCity orders: **18,950**
• trading cards

4 ❑ Jul 1993 Cover: 2.95 **NM** value: **Cover or less**
Circ: CapCity orders: **15,475**
• trading cards **W:** Kurt Busiek

SATAN'S SIX: HELLSPAWN — Topps

1 ❑ Jun 1994 Cover: 2.50 **NM** value: **Cover or less**

CGC-graded: Multiply prices above by **33 for 9.9 M • 16 for 9.8 NM/M • 7 for 9.6 NM+ • 5 for 9.4 NM • 2.5 for 9.2 NM- • 1.5 for 9.0 VF/NM**

🕮 A Hell of a Town • Inside index lists it as issue #2 **A:** John Cleary **W:** Len Kaminski; Scott Benson
2 ❑ Jun 1994 Cover: 2.50 **NM** value: **Cover or less**
3 ❑ Jul 1994 Cover: 2.50 **NM** value: **Cover or less**

SATURDAY MORNING: THE COMIC — Marvel
1 ❑ Apr 1996 Cover: 1.95 **NM** value: **Cover or less**
A: Steve Lightle **W:** Mike Lackey; Ralph Sall ★ Appearance of Liz Phair, Matthew Sweet, Ramones, Collective Soul.

SATURDAY MOURNING FLY IN MY EYE — Eclipse
Bk 1❑ b&w Cover: 9.95 **NM** value: **Cover or less**

SATURDAY NITE — Anson Jew
1 ❑ b&w Cover: 2.95 **NM** value: **Cover or less**
🕮 The Samaritan; Youth; Are You Courteous?; Sidewalk **A:** Anson Jew **W:** Anson Jew

SAUCY LITTLE TART — Eros
1 ❑ Dec 1995 Cover: 2.95 **NM** value: **Cover or less**
A: Molly Kiely **W:** Molly Kiely

SAURIANS: UNNATURAL SELECTION — CrossGen
1 ❑ Feb 2002 Cover: 2.95 **NM** value: **Cover or less**
2 ❑ Mar 2002 Cover: 2.95 **NM** value: **Cover or less**

SAVAGE COMBAT TALES — Atlas-Seaboard
1 ❑ Feb 1975 Cover: 0.25 **NM** value: **2.00**
• **CGC:** 1 graded, best 9.4
🕮 Reborn In Battle; Bounty **A:** Jack Sparling; Al Williams **W:** Archie Goodwin ★ Origin of Sgt. Stryker's Death Squad.
2 ❑ Apr 1975 Cover: 0.25 **NM** value: **1.50**
• **CGC:** 1 graded, best 9.4
3 ❑ Jul 1975 Cover: 0.25 **NM** value: **1.50**

SAVAGE DRAGON, THE — Image

Having survived his three-issue limited series, Eric Larsen's Savage Dragon was ready to take off in this, his first regular monthly title.

Two years ago in series time, the amnesiac Dragon was found alive in a burning field. Lt. Frank Darling tricked him into becoming the Chicago Police Department's super-powered ace-in-the-hole in the war on crime. Darling had arranged for super-powered toughs to threaten Darling's brother, Fred, in the hopes that Dragon would see the need to join the side of law and order. The plan succeeded in convincing Dragon, but it also led to the death of Darling's brother. To make matters worse, a villain named Skullface had discovered Darling's scheme, and was now blackmailing Darling with it. The pay-off: Dragon was to be given assignments which didn't interfere with Skullface's real action. But as any fan of this green-finned bad boy knows, reining in the Dragon is easier said than done.

0.5 ❑ ca. 1997 **NM** value: **3.00**
A: Erik Larsen **W:** Erik Larsen
0.5/Pl❑ca. 1997 **NM** value: **4.00**
A: Erik Larsen **W:** Erik Larsen
1 ❑ Jun 1993 Cover: 1.95 **NM** value: **3.00**
• **CGC:** 3 graded, best 9.8
A: Erik Larsen **W:** Erik Larsen
2 ❑ Jul 1993 Cover: 2.95 **NM** value: **3.00**
• Flip book with Vanguard #0 **A:** Erik Larsen **W:** Erik Larsen ★ Appearance of Teenage Mutant Ninja Turtles.
3 ❑ Aug 1993 Cover: 1.95 **NM** value: **2.50**
• Mighty Man back-up feature **A:** Erik Larsen **W:** Erik Larsen
4 ❑ Sep 1993 Cover: 1.95 **NM** value: **2.25**
A: Erik Larsen **W:** Erik Larsen
5 ❑ Oct 1993 Cover: 1.95 **NM** value: **2.25**
A: Erik Larsen **W:** Erik Larsen
6 ❑ Nov 1993 Cover: 1.95 **NM** value: **2.25**
A: Erik Larsen **W:** Erik Larsen
7 ❑ Jan 1994 Cover: 1.95 **NM** value: **2.25**
A: Erik Larsen **W:** Erik Larsen
8 ❑ Mar 1994 Cover: 1.95 **NM** value: **2.00**
A: Erik Larsen **W:** Erik Larsen
9 ❑ Apr 1994 Cover: 1.95 **NM** value: **2.00**
A: Erik Larsen **W:** Erik Larsen
10 ❑ May 1994 Cover: 1.95 **NM** value: **2.00**
alternate cover. • newsstand version **A:** Erik Larsen **W:** Erik Larsen
10/DM❑May 1994 Cover: 1.95 **NM** value: **2.00**
Circ: CapCity orders: **35,100**
A: Erik Larsen **W:** Erik Larsen
11 ❑ Jul 1994 Cover: 1.95 **NM** value: **2.00**
Circ: CapCity orders: **34,600**
A: Erik Larsen **W:** Erik Larsen
12 ❑ Aug 1994 Cover: 1.95 **NM** value: **2.00**
Circ: CapCity orders: **31,675**
• She Dragon **A:** Erik Larsen **W:** Erik Larsen
13 ❑ Jun 1995 Cover: 2.50 **NM** value: **Cover or less**
Circ: CapCity orders: **39,750**
A: Erik Larsen **W:** Erik Larsen ★ 1st Appearance of Condition Red.
13/A❑Jun 1995 Cover: 1.95 **NM** value: **2.50**
Circ: CapCity orders: **17,825**
• Image X month version **A:** Jim Lee; Erik Larsen **W:** Jim Lee
14 ❑ Oct 1994 Cover: 1.95 **NM** value: **Cover or less**
Circ: CapCity orders: **27,650**
A: Erik Larsen **W:** Erik Larsen
15 ❑ Dec 1994 Cover: 2.50 **NM** value: **Cover or less**
Circ: CapCity orders: **25,750**
A: Erik Larsen **W:** Erik Larsen
16 ❑ Jan 1995 Cover: 2.50 **NM** value: **Cover or less**
Circ: CapCity orders: **24,200**
Savage Dragon on cover. **A:** Erik Larsen **W:** Erik Larsen
17/A❑Feb 1995 Cover: 2.50 **NM** value: **Cover or less**
Circ: CapCity orders: **22,350**
A: Erik Larsen **W:** Erik Larsen
18 ❑ Mar 1995 Cover: 2.50 **NM** value: **Cover or less**
Circ: CapCity orders: **20,050**
A: Erik Larsen **W:** Erik Larsen
19 ❑ Apr 1995 Cover: 2.50 **NM** value: **Cover or less**
Circ: CapCity orders: **19,200**
A: Erik Larsen **W:** Erik Larsen
20 ❑ Jul 1995 Cover: 2.50 **NM** value: **Cover or less**
Circ: CapCity orders: **19,675**
A: Erik Larsen **W:** Erik Larsen
21 ❑ Aug 1995 Cover: 2.50 **NM** value: **Cover or less**
Circ: CapCity orders: **19,325**
A: Erik Larsen **W:** Erik Larsen
22 ❑ Sep 1995 Cover: 2.50 **NM** value: **Cover or less**
Circ: CapCity orders: **17,575**
A: Erik Larsen **W:** Erik Larsen ★ Appearance of Teenage Mutant Ninja Turtles.
23 ❑ Oct 1995 Cover: 2.50 **NM** value: **Cover or less**
Circ: CapCity orders: **15,125**
A: Erik Larsen **W:** Erik Larsen
24 ❑ Dec 1995 Cover: 2.50 **NM** value: **Cover or less**
A: Erik Larsen **W:** Erik Larsen
25 ❑ Jan 1996 Cover: 3.95 **NM** value: **Cover or less**
• double-sized. **A:** Erik Larsen **W:** Erik Larsen
25/A❑Jan 1996 Cover: 3.95 **NM** value: **Cover or less**
alternate cover. • double-sized. **A:** Erik Larsen **W:** Erik Larsen
26 ❑ Mar 1996 Cover: 2.50 **NM** value: **Cover or less**
A: Erik Larsen **W:** Erik Larsen
27 ❑ Apr 1996 Cover: 2.50 **NM** value: **Cover or less**
A: Erik Larsen **W:** Erik Larsen
27/A❑Apr 1996 Cover: 2.50 **NM** value: **Cover or less**
alternate cover only available at WonderCon. **A:** Erik Larsen **W:** Erik Larsen
28 ❑ May 1996 Cover: 2.50 **NM** value: **Cover or less**
A: Erik Larsen **W:** Erik Larsen ★ Appearance of Maxx.
29 ❑ Jul 1996 Cover: 2.50 **NM** value: **Cover or less**
A: Erik Larsen **W:** Erik Larsen ★ Appearance of Wildstar.
30 ❑ Aug 1996 Cover: 2.50 **NM** value: **Cover or less**
A: Erik Larsen **W:** Erik Larsen ★ Appearance of Spawn.
31 ❑ Sep 1996 Cover: 2.50 **NM** value: **Cover or less**
censored version says God is good inside Image logo on cover. • God vs. The Devil **A:** Erik Larsen **W:** Erik Larsen
31/A❑Sep 1996 Cover: 2.50 **NM** value: **Cover or less**
• God vs. The Devil; uncensored version **A:** Erik Larsen **W:** Erik Larsen
32 ❑ Oct 1996 Cover: 2.50 **NM** value: **Cover or less**
Circ: Diamd. preorders: **33,955**
A: Erik Larsen **W:** Erik Larsen
33 ❑ Nov 1996 Cover: 2.50 **NM** value: **Cover or less**
Circ: Diamd. preorders: **33,299**
• Birth of Dragon's son **A:** Erik Larsen **W:** Erik Larsen
34 ❑ Dec 1996 Cover: 2.50 **NM** value: **Cover or less**
Circ: Diamd. preorders: **34,427**
A: Mike Mignola; Erik Larsen **W:** Mike Mignola; Erik Larsen ★ Appearance of Hellboy.
35 ❑ Feb 1997 Cover: 2.50 **NM** value: **Cover or less**
Circ: Diamd. preorders: **33,077**
A: Erik Larsen **W:** Erik Larsen ★ Appearance of Hellboy.
36 ❑ Mar 1997 Cover: 2.50 **NM** value: **Cover or less**
Circ: Diamd. preorders: **28,859**
A: Erik Larsen **W:** Erik Larsen ★ 1st Appearance of Zeek.
37 ❑ Apr 1997 Cover: 2.50 **NM** value: **Cover or less**
Circ: Diamd. preorders: **28,149**
A: Erik Larsen **W:** Erik Larsen
38 ❑ May 1997 Cover: 2.50 **NM** value: **Cover or less**
Circ: Diamd. preorders: **28,259**
A: Erik Larsen **W:** Erik Larsen
39 ❑ Jun 1997 Cover: 2.50 **NM** value: **Cover or less**
Circ: Diamd. preorders: **27,693**
A: Erik Larsen **W:** Erik Larsen
40 ❑ Jul 1997 Cover: 2.50 **NM** value: **Cover or less**
Circ: Diamd. preorders: **28,382**
A: Erik Larsen **W:** Erik Larsen
40/A❑Jul 1997 Cover: 2.50 **NM** value: **Cover or less**
Circ: Diamd. preorders: **4,207**
A: Erik Larsen **W:** Erik Larsen
41 ❑ Sep 1997 Cover: 2.50 **NM** value: **Cover or less**
Circ: Diamd. preorders: **24,952**
A: Erik Larsen **W:** Erik Larsen ★ Appearance of Wildstar, Monkeyman, Femforce, E-Man, Zot, Megaton, Madman, Vampirella, Hellboy, DNAgents.
42 ❑ Oct 1997 Cover: 2.50 **NM** value: **Cover or less**
Circ: Diamd. preorders: **25,581**
A: Erik Larsen **W:** Erik Larsen
43 ❑ Nov 1997 Cover: 2.50 **NM** value: **Cover or less**
Circ: Diamd. preorders: **25,304**
A: Erik Larsen **W:** Erik Larsen
44 ❑ Dec 1997 Cover: 2.50 **NM** value: **Cover or less**
Circ: Diamd. preorders: **24,576**
A: Erik Larsen **W:** Erik Larsen
45 ❑ Jan 1998 Cover: 2.50 **NM** value: **Cover or less**
Circ: Diamd. preorders: **24,021**
A: Erik Larsen **W:** Erik Larsen
46 ❑ Feb 1998 Cover: 2.50 **NM** value: **Cover or less**
Circ: Diamd. preorders: **22,954**
A: Erik Larsen **W:** Erik Larsen
47 ❑ Mar 1998 Cover: 2.50 **NM** value: **Cover or less**
Circ: Diamd. preorders: **22,923**
A: Erik Larsen **W:** Erik Larsen
48 ❑ Apr 1998 Cover: 2.50 **NM** value: **Cover or less**
Circ: Diamd. preorders: **23,128**
A: Erik Larsen **W:** Erik Larsen
49 ❑ May 1998 Cover: 2.50 **NM** value: **Cover or less**
Circ: Diamd. preorders: **22,340**
A: Erik Larsen **W:** Erik Larsen
50 ❑ Jun 1998 Cover: 5.95 **NM** value: **Cover or less**
Circ: Diamd. preorders: **24,357**
🕮 Mighty Man: Critter Crime Wave; Mighty Man: Wicked Worm's Circus of Evil; Basic Training; Mighty Man Battles the Conqueror Worm **A:** Vic Bridges; Bill Fugate; Chris Marrinan; Todd McFarlane; Rob Liefeld; Jeff Matsuda; Erik Larsen; Walt Simonson; Dave Johnson; Terry Austin; Larry Marder; Greg Capullo; John Thompson; Jonathan Sibal **W:** Jeph Loeb; Vic Bridges; Erik Larsen; Gary Carlson
51/A❑Jul 1998 Cover: 2.50 **NM** value: **Cover or less**
Circ: Diamd. preorders: **23,170**
• red logo **A:** Erik Larsen **W:** Erik Larsen
51/B❑Jul 1998 Cover: 2.50 **NM** value: **Cover or less**
• yellow logo **A:** Erik Larsen **W:** Erik Larsen
52 ❑ Aug 1998 Cover: 2.50 **NM** value: **Cover or less**
Circ: Diamd. preorders: **22,386**
A: Erik Larsen **W:** Erik Larsen
53 ❑ Sep 1998 Cover: 2.50 **NM** value: **Cover or less**
Circ: Diamd. preorders: **21,947**
A: Erik Larsen **W:** Erik Larsen
54 ❑ Oct 1998 Cover: 2.50 **NM** value: **Cover or less**
Circ: Diamd. preorders: **22,696**
A: Erik Larsen **W:** Erik Larsen
55 ❑ Nov 1998 Cover: 2.50 **NM** value: **Cover or less**
Circ: Diamd. preorders: **22,144**
A: Erik Larsen **W:** Erik Larsen
56 ❑ Dec 1998 Cover: 2.50 **NM** value: **Cover or less**
Circ: Diamd. preorders: **21,308**
A: Erik Larsen **W:** Erik Larsen
57 ❑ Jan 1999 Cover: 2.50 **NM** value: **Cover or less**
Circ: Diamd. preorders: **21,097**
A: Erik Larsen **W:** Erik Larsen
58 ❑ Feb 1999 Cover: 2.50 **NM** value: **Cover or less**
Circ: Diamd. preorders: **20,579**
A: Erik Larsen **W:** Erik Larsen
59 ❑ Mar 1999 Cover: 2.50 **NM** value: **Cover or less**
Circ: Diamd. preorders: **20,647**
A: Erik Larsen **W:** Erik Larsen
60 ❑ Apr 1999 Cover: 2.50 **NM** value: **Cover or less**
Circ: Diamd. preorders: **21,132**
A: Erik Larsen **W:** Erik Larsen
61 ❑ May 1999 Cover: 2.50 **NM** value: **Cover or less**
Circ: Diamd. preorders: **20,876**
A: Erik Larsen **W:** Erik Larsen
62 ❑ Jun 1999 Cover: 2.50 **NM** value: **Cover or less**
Circ: Diamd. preorders: **22,195**
A: Erik Larsen **W:** Erik Larsen
63 ❑ Jun 1999 Cover: 2.50 **NM** value: **Cover or less**
Circ: Diamd. preorders: **21,389**
A: Erik Larsen **W:** Erik Larsen
64 ❑ Jul 1999 Cover: 2.50 **NM** value: **Cover or less**
Circ: Diamd. preorders: **20,858**
A: Erik Larsen **W:** Erik Larsen
65 ❑ Aug 1999 Cover: 2.50 **NM** value: **Cover or less**
Circ: Diamd. preorders: **20,196**
A: Erik Larsen **W:** Erik Larsen
66 ❑ Aug 1999 Cover: 2.50 **NM** value: **Cover or less**
Circ: Diamd. preorders: **20,117**
A: Erik Larsen **W:** Erik Larsen
67 ❑ Sep 1999 Cover: 2.50 **NM** value: **Cover or less**
Circ: Diamd. preorders: **19,600**
A: Erik Larsen **W:** Erik Larsen
68 ❑ Oct 1999 Cover: 2.50 **NM** value: **Cover or less**
Circ: Diamd. preorders: **19,475**
A: Erik Larsen **W:** Erik Larsen
69 ❑ Nov 1999 Cover: 2.50 **NM** value: **Cover or less**
Circ: Diamd. preorders: **18,853**
A: Erik Larsen **W:** Erik Larsen
70 ❑ Dec 1999 Cover: 2.50 **NM** value: **Cover or less**
Circ: Diamd. preorders: **19,585**
A: Erik Larsen **W:** Erik Larsen
71 ❑ Jan 2000 Cover: 2.50 **NM** value: **Cover or less**
Circ: Diamd. preorders: **18,143**
A: Erik Larsen **W:** Erik Larsen
72 ❑ Feb 2000 Cover: 2.50 **NM** value: **Cover or less**
Circ: Diamd. preorders: **17,149**
A: Erik Larsen **W:** Erik Larsen
73 ❑ Mar 2000 Cover: 2.50 **NM** value: **Cover or less**
Circ: Diamd. preorders: **17,735**
A: Erik Larsen **W:** Erik Larsen
74 ❑ Apr 2000 Cover: 2.50 **NM** value: **Cover or less**
Circ: Diamd. preorders: **17,415**
A: Erik Larsen **W:** Erik Larsen
75 ❑ May 2000 Cover: 5.95 **NM** value: **Cover or less**
Circ: Diamd. preorders: **19,092**
• Giant-size. **A:** Erik Larsen **W:** Erik Larsen
76 ❑ Jun 2000 Cover: 2.95 **NM** value: **Cover or less**
Circ: Diamd. preorders: **19,037**
🕮 This Savage World! **A:** Erik Larsen **W:** Erik Larsen
77 ❑ Jul 2000 Cover: 2.95 **NM** value: **Cover or less**
Circ: Diamd. preorders: **19,084**
🕮 Something Wild!! **A:** Erik Larsen **W:** Erik Larsen
78 ❑ Aug 2000 Cover: 2.95 **NM** value: **Cover or less**
Circ: Diamd. preorders: **17,776**
🕮 Mind-Slaves of the Brainchild! **A:** Erik Larsen **W:** Erik Larsen
79 ❑ Sep 2000 Cover: 2.95 **NM** value: **Cover or less**
Circ: Diamd. preorders: **17,888**
🕮 The Attack of the 60-Foot Woman! **A:** Erik Larsen **W:** Erik Larsen
80 ❑ Oct 2000 Cover: 2.95 **NM** value: **Cover or less**
Circ: Diamd. preorders: **17,649**
🕮 The Lurkers Beneath Lake Fear! **A:** Erik Larsen **W:** Erik Larsen
81 ❑ Nov 2000 Cover: 2.95 **NM** value: **Cover or less**
Circ: Diamd. preorders: **17,706**
🕮 The Land Down Under **A:** Erik Larsen **W:** Erik Larsen
82 ❑ Dec 2000 Cover: 2.95 **NM** value: **Cover or less**
Circ: Diamd. preorders: **17,111**
🕮 The Bug Riders! **A:** Erik Larsen **W:** Erik Larsen

Other grades: Multiply prices above by **1.5 for Mint • 2/3 for Very Fine • 1/3 for Fine • 1/5 for Very Good • 1/8 for Good**

83 ❑ Jan 2001 Cover: 2.95 **NM** value: **Cover or less**
Circ: Diamd. preorders: **17,526**
📖 The Arena of Death! **A:** Erik Larsen **W:** Erik Larsen ★ Appearance of Madman.
84 ❑ Feb 2001 Cover: 2.95 **NM** value: **Cover or less**
Circ: Diamd. preorders: **17,081**
📖 Breakout from Command "D" **A:** Erik Larsen **W:** Erik Larsen
85 ❑ Mar 2001 Cover: 2.95 **NM** value: **Cover or less**
Circ: Diamd. preorders: **16,410**
A: Erik Larsen **W:** Erik Larsen
86 ❑ Apr 2001 Cover: 2.95 **NM** value: **Cover or less**
Circ: Diamd. preorders: **15,878**
A: Erik Larsen **W:** Erik Larsen
87 ❑ May 2001 Cover: 2.95 **NM** value: **Cover or less**
Circ: Diamd. preorders: **15,318**
A: Erik Larsen **W:** Erik Larsen
88 ❑ Jun 2001 Cover: 2.95 **NM** value: **Cover or less**
Circ: Diamd. preorders: **15,930**
A: Erik Larsen **W:** Erik Larsen
Bk 1❑ Feb 1996 Cover: 14.95 **NM** value: **Cover or less**
• A Force to Be Reckoned With; collects issues #1-6 of ongoing series **A:** Erik Larsen **W:** Erik Larsen
Bk 1/HC❑ Feb 1996 Cover: 39.95 **NM** value: **Cover or less**
A Force to Be Reckoned With hardcover. • collects issues #1-6 of ongoing series **A:** Erik Larsen **W:** Erik Larsen
Bk 2❑ Nov 1997 Cover: 12.95 **NM** value: **Cover or less**
• The Fallen; collects issues #7-11 **A:** Erik Larsen **W:** Erik Larsen
Bk 3❑ Sep 1998 Cover: 12.95 **NM** value: **13.95**
• Possessed; collects #12-16 and WildC.A.T.S #14 **A:** Erik Larsen **W:** Erik Larsen
Bk 4❑ Cover: 12.95 **NM** value: **13.95**
• Revenge; Collects The Savage Dragon #17-21 **A:** Erik Larsen **W:** Erik Larsen
Bk 5❑ Jun 1997 Cover: 17.95 **NM** value: **Cover or less**
• A Talk with God; collects issues #27-33 **A:** Erik Larsen **W:** Erik Larsen
Bk 5-2❑ Cover: 19.95 **NM** value: **Cover or less**

SAVAGE DRAGON ARCHIVES — Image

1 ❑ Sep 1998 Cover: 2.95 **NM** value: **Cover or less**
A: Erik Larsen **W:** Erik Larsen
2 ❑ Oct 1998 Cover: 2.95 **NM** value: **Cover or less**
📖 Possessed • Reprints Graphic Fantasy #2 **A:** Erik Larsen **W:** Erik Larsen ★ 2nd Appearance of Savage Dragon. ★ 2nd Appearance of Savage Dragon.
3 ❑ Dec 1998 Cover: 2.95 **NM** value: **Cover or less**
📖 Dead Line; To Battle the Dragon **A:** Erik Larsen **W:** Erik Larsen; Gary Carlson
4 ❑ Jan 1999 Cover: 2.95 **NM** value: **Cover or less**
📖 Dungeons & Dragons; The Dragon in Angel Fueled Quake **A:** Erik Larsen **W:** Erik Larsen

SAVAGE DRAGON/DESTROYER DUCK, THE — Image

Eclipse Comics published Destroyer Duck from 1982 until 1984, and proceeds from the sales helped writer Steve Gerber finance his lawsuit to regain ownership of Howard the Duck from Marvel Comics.

Years later, Gerber brought the character from his cause back in this one-shot. Gerber teamed here with Erik Larsen, an outspoken proponent of creators' rights and the Image partner who has best maintained the integrity of his corner of their universe over the years.

Interesting, meaningful stuff from Gerber, Larsen, and penciller Chris Marrinan (Wonder Woman). And just wait 'til you see Leonard the Duck!

1 ❑ Nov 1996 Cover: 3.95 **NM** value: **Cover or less**
Circ: Diamd. preorders: **23,293**
A: Chris Marrinan **W:** Steve Gerber ★ Appearance of Teenage Mutant Ninja Turtles.

SAVAGE DRAGON/MARSHAL LAW, THE — Image

1 ❑ Jul 1997, b&w Cover: 2.95 **NM** value: **Cover or less**
Circ: Diamd. preorders: **18,756**
• indicia says Savage Dragon/Marshall Law **A:** Kevin O'Neill **W:** Pat Mills
2 ❑ Aug 1997, b&w Cover: 2.95 **NM** value: **Cover or less**
Circ: Diamd. preorders: **20,500**
A: Kevin O'Neill **W:** Pat Mills

SAVAGE DRAGON, THE (MINI-SERIES) — Image

1 ❑ Jul 1992 Cover: 1.95 **NM** value: **3.00**
• **CGC:** 1 graded, best 9.6
four cover logo variants (bottom of logo is white, blue, green, or yellow). 📖 Baptism of Fire **A:** Erik Larsen **W:** Erik Larsen ★ 1st Appearance of SuperPatriot, Savage Dragon. ★ Appearance of Spawn.
2 ❑ Oct 1992 Cover: 1.95 **NM** value: **2.50**
• **CGC:** 1 graded, best 9.8
📖 Born Again Patriot • Centerfold Savage Dragon poster **A:** Erik Larsen **W:** Erik Larsen
3 ❑ Dec 1992 Cover: 1.95 **NM** value: **2.50**
• **CGC:** 1 graded, best 9.8
📖 Rock This Town • Centerfold Savage Dragon poster **A:** Erik Larsen **W:** Erik Larsen
Bk 1❑ Cover: 9.95 **NM** value: **Cover or less**
• collects three-issue mini-series
Bk 1/A❑ Cover: 9.95 **NM** value: **Cover or less**
• Diamond Edition. • collects three-issue mini-series
Bk 1/HC❑ Cover: 39.95 **NM** value: **Cover or less**
hardcover. • collects three-issue mini-series **A:** Erik Larsen **W:** Erik Larsen

SAVAGE DRAGON: RED HORIZON — Image

1 ❑ Feb 1997 Cover: 2.50 **NM** value: **Cover or less**
Circ: Diamd. preorders: **22,376**
A: Mike S. Miller **W:** Mike S. Miller
2 ❑ Apr 1997 Cover: 2.50 **NM** value: **Cover or less**
Circ: Diamd. preorders: **20,999**
A: Mike S. Miller **W:** Mike S. Miller
3 ❑ May 1997 Cover: 2.50 **NM** value: **Cover or less**
Circ: Diamd. preorders: **20,252**
A: Mike S. Miller **W:** Mike S. Miller

SAVAGE DRAGON: REVENGE — Image

Bk 1❑ Jul 1999 Cover: 13.95 **NM** value: **Cover or less**

SAVAGE DRAGON: SEX & VIOLENCE — Image

1 ❑ Aug 1997 Cover: 2.50 **NM** value: **Cover or less**
Circ: Diamd. preorders: **24,218**
A: Adam Hughes; Rick Mays; Mark Lipka **W:** Erik Larsen; Mary Bierbaum; Tom Bierbaum
2 ❑ Sep 1997 Cover: 2.50 **NM** value: **Cover or less**
Circ: Diamd. preorders: **21,660**
A: Adam Hughes; Rick Mays; Mark Lipka **W:** Erik Larsen; Mary Bierbaum; Tom Bierbaum

SAVAGE DRAGON: TEAM-UPS — Image

Bk 1❑ Oct 1998 Cover: 19.95 **NM** value: **Cover or less**
No issue number. • Trade Paperback. 📖 Vanguard #3-4; Velocity Vol.1 : #2; Freak Force #10; Savage Dragon #25, 30 • collects Freak Force #10, Savage Dragon #13, 25, 30, Vanguard #3 and 4, and Velocity #2 **A:** Vic Bridges; Rick Leonardi; Jeff Matsuda; Anthony Chun; Erik Larsen; Joe Madureira **W:** Erik Larsen; Kurt Busiek; Gary Carlson

SAVAGE DRAGON/TEENAGE MUTANT NINJA TURTLES CROSSOVER — Mirage

1 ❑ Sep 1993 Cover: 2.75 **NM** value: **Cover or less**
📖 Enter the Savage Dragon! **A:** Michael Dooney **W:** Erik Larsen; Michael Dooney

SAVAGE DRAGON VS. THE SAVAGE MEGATON MAN, THE — Image

1 ❑ Mar 1993 Cover: 1.95 **NM** value: **2.00**
Circ: CapCity orders: **84,000**
📖 Savage Brawl **A:** Donald Simpson; Erik Larsen **W:** Donald Simpson; Erik Larsen
1/GO❑ Mar 1993 Cover: 1.95 **NM** value: **3.00**
Gold foil cover. **A:** Erik Larsen

SAVAGE FISTS OF KUNG FU — Marvel

1 ❑ Cover: 1.50 **NM** value: **8.00**
📖 The Master Plan of Fu Manchu; The Sons of the Tiger!; Shang-Chi: Master of Kung Fu! **A:** Alan Weiss; Al Milgrom; Jim Starlin; John Buscema; Mike Vosburg; Herb Trimpe; Dick Giordano; Dan Adkins **W:** Chris Claremont; Doug Moench; Gerry Conway; Steve Englehart; Tony Isabella ★ Origin of The Sons of the Dragon.

SAVAGE FUNNIES — Vision

1 ❑ Jul 1996 Cover: 1.95 **NM** value: **Cover or less**
2 ❑ Jul 1996 Cover: 1.95 **NM** value: **Cover or less**

SAVAGE HENRY — Vortex

1 ❑ Jan 1987 Cover: 1.75 **NM** value: **2.00**
A: Matt Howarth **W:** Matt Howarth
2 ❑ Feb 1987 Cover: 1.75 **NM** value: **2.00**
📖 Going Interactive **A:** Matt Howarth **W:** Matt Howarth
3 ❑ Apr 1987 Cover: 1.75 **NM** value: **2.00**
A: Matt Howarth **W:** Matt Howarth
4 ❑ 1987 Cover: 1.75 **NM** value: **2.00**
A: Matt Howarth **W:** Matt Howarth
5 ❑ 1987 Cover: 1.75 **NM** value: **2.00**
A: Matt Howarth **W:** Matt Howarth
6 ❑ Mar 1988 Cover: 1.75 **NM** value: **2.00**
A: Matt Howarth **W:** Matt Howarth
7 ❑ Sep 1988, b&w Cover: 1.75 **NM** value: **2.00**
A: Matt Howarth **W:** Matt Howarth
8 ❑ Dec 1988 Cover: 1.75 **NM** value: **2.00**
A: Matt Howarth **W:** Matt Howarth
9 ❑ Feb 1989 Cover: 1.75 **NM** value: **2.00**
A: Matt Howarth **W:** Matt Howarth
10 ❑ Cover: 1.75 **NM** value: **2.00**
A: Matt Howarth **W:** Matt Howarth
11 ❑ 1990 Cover: 2.00 **NM** value: **Cover or less**
A: Matt Howarth **W:** Matt Howarth
12 ❑ 1990 Cover: 2.00 **NM** value: **Cover or less**
A: Matt Howarth **W:** Matt Howarth
13 ❑ 1990 Cover: 2.00 **NM** value: **Cover or less**
• Last Vortex issue **A:** Matt Howarth **W:** Matt Howarth
14 ❑ Mar 1991, b&w Cover: 2.00 **NM** value: **2.50**
• Rip Off begins as publisher **A:** Matt Howarth **W:** Matt Howarth
15 ❑ May 1991, b&w Cover: 2.00 **NM** value: **2.50**
A: Matt Howarth **W:** Matt Howarth
16 ❑ Jul 1991, b&w Cover: 2.50 **NM** value: **Cover or less**
A: Matt Howarth **W:** Matt Howarth
17 ❑ Sep 1991, b&w Cover: 2.50 **NM** value: **Cover or less**
A: Matt Howarth **W:** Matt Howarth
18 ❑ Nov 1991, b&w Cover: 2.50 **NM** value: **Cover or less**
A: Matt Howarth **W:** Matt Howarth
19 ❑ Jan 1992, b&w Cover: 2.50 **NM** value: **Cover or less**
A: Matt Howarth **W:** Matt Howarth
20 ❑ Mar 1992, b&w Cover: 2.50 **NM** value: **Cover or less**
A: Matt Howarth **W:** Matt Howarth
21 ❑ May 1992, b&w Cover: 2.50 **NM** value: **Cover or less**
A: Matt Howarth **W:** Matt Howarth
22 ❑ Jul 1992, b&w Cover: 2.50 **NM** value: **Cover or less**
A: Matt Howarth **W:** Matt Howarth
23 ❑ Sep 1992, b&w Cover: 2.50 **NM** value: **Cover or less**
A: Matt Howarth **W:** Matt Howarth
24 ❑ Nov 1992, b&w Cover: 2.50 **NM** value: **Cover or less**
A: Matt Howarth **W:** Matt Howarth
25 ❑ Jan 1993, b&w Cover: 2.50 **NM** value: **Cover or less**
A: Matt Howarth **W:** Matt Howarth
26 ❑ Mar 1993, b&w Cover: 2.50 **NM** value: **Cover or less**
A: Matt Howarth **W:** Matt Howarth
27 ❑ May 1993 Cover: 2.50 **NM** value: **Cover or less**
A: Matt Howarth **W:** Matt Howarth
28 ❑ Jul 1993, b&w Cover: 2.50 **NM** value: **Cover or less**
A: Matt Howarth **W:** Matt Howarth
29 ❑ Sep 1993, b&w Cover: 2.50 **NM** value: **Cover or less**
A: Matt Howarth **W:** Matt Howarth
30 ❑ Nov 1993, b&w Cover: 2.50 **NM** value: **Cover or less**
final issue. • 1993 **A:** Matt Howarth **W:** Matt Howarth

SAVAGE HENRY: HEADSTRONG — Caliber

1 ❑ b&w Cover: 2.95 **NM** value: **Cover or less**
📖 Headstand **A:** Matt Howarth **W:** Matt Howarth ★ Appearance of Ron Geesin, Fraser Geesin.
2 ❑ b&w Cover: 2.95 **NM** value: **Cover or less**
A: Matt Howarth **W:** Matt Howarth
3 ❑ b&w Cover: 2.95 **NM** value: **Cover or less**
A: Matt Howarth **W:** Matt Howarth

SAVAGE HENRY (ICONOGRAFIX) — Caliber / Iconografix

1 ❑ b&w Cover: 2.95 **NM** value: **Cover or less**
A: Matt Howarth **W:** Matt Howarth
2 ❑ b&w Cover: 2.95 **NM** value: **Cover or less**
A: Matt Howarth **W:** Matt Howarth ★ Appearance of Moby.
3 ❑ b&w Cover: 2.95 **NM** value: **Cover or less**
A: Matt Howarth **W:** Matt Howarth

SAVAGE HULK, THE — Marvel

1 ❑ Jan 1996 Cover: 6.95 **NM** value: **Cover or less**
No issue number. • prestige format. 📖 Courtroom Sequence; Old Friends; The Power of Bullies; The Strongest One There Is; Brief; Vision Quest; Dinner **A:** Tim Sale; Pat McEown; Dave Gibbons; Pascual Ferry; Humberto Ramos; Sam Kieth; Dane McCart **W:** William Messner-Loebs; Tim Sale; Dave Gibbons; Scott Lobdell; B.J. Estes. Matt Wagner; Peter David

SAVAGE LAND, THE — Marvel

Bk 1❑ Cover: 5.95 **NM** value: **Cover or less**
A: Michael Golden; Dave Cockrum

SAVAGE NINJA — Cadillac

1 ❑ Cover: 1.00 **NM** value: **Cover or less**

SAVAGE RETURN OF DRACULA, THE — Marvel

1 ❑ ca. 1992 Cover: 2.00 **NM** value: **Cover or less**
Circ: CapCity orders: **8,200**
📖 Dracula; The Fear Within • Reprints Tomb of Dracula #1, 2 **A:** Gene Colan **W:** Gerry Conway

SAVAGES — Comax

1 ❑ b&w Cover: 2.50 **NM** value: **Cover or less**

SAVAGE SHE-HULK, THE — Marvel

Jennifer Walters was an up-and-coming criminal attorney trying the case of her career against mob boss Nick Trask. In an attack by gunmen hired by Trask, Walters was gravely wounded. Her life was saved only by a last-minute transfusion of blood from her cousin, Bruce Banner.

But Banner's blood carried with it the curse of his alter-ego, The Incredible Hulk. When mob hitmen, disguised as doctors, tried to kill her in the hospital, Walters fought desperately to save her life, and in the struggle found herself changing into the savage She-Hulk.

In this, her first series, Walters learns to deal with her terrible alter-ego. Eventually abandoning her legal practice, she became a full-time super-hero, first as a member of The Avengers, and later as a temporary member of The Fantastic Four.

1 ❑ Feb 1980 Cover: 0.40 **NM** value: **4.00**
• **CGC:** 39 graded, best 9.8
📖 The She-Hulk Lives **A:** John Buscema; Chic Stone **W:** Stan Lee ★ Origin of She-Hulk. ★ 1st Appearance of She-Hulk.
2 ❑ Mar 1980 Cover: 0.40 **NM** value: **3.00**
• **CGC:** 2 graded, best 9.4
📖 Deathrace! **A:** Mike Vosburg **W:** David Anthony Kraft ★ 1st Appearance of Morris Walters, Dan "Zapper" Ridge.
3 ❑ Apr 1980 Cover: 0.40 **NM** value: **2.50**
• **CGC:** 2 graded, best 9.6
4 ❑ May 1980 Cover: 0.40 **NM** value: **2.50**
• **CGC:** 2 graded, best 9.6
5 ❑ Jun 1980 Cover: 0.40 **NM** value: **2.50**
• **CGC:** 1 graded, best 9.4
6 ❑ Jul 1980 Cover: 0.40 **NM** value: **2.00**
★ Appearance of Iron Man.
7 ❑ Aug 1980 Cover: 0.40 **NM** value: **2.00**
8 ❑ Sep 1980 Cover: 0.50 **NM** value: **2.00**
★ Appearance of Man-Thing.

CGC-graded: Multiply prices above by **33 for 9.9 M • 16 for 9.8 NM/M • 7 for 9.6 NM+ • 5 for 9.4 NM • 2.5 for 9.2 NM- • 1.5 for 9.0 VF/NM**

9 ❑ Oct 1980 Cover: 0.50 **NM** value: **2.00**
• **CGC:** 1 graded, best 9.8
10 ❑ Nov 1980 Cover: 0.50 **NM** value: **2.00**
• **CGC:** 1 graded, best 9.6
11 ❑ Dec 1980 Cover: 0.50 **NM** value: **2.00**
12 ❑ Jan 1981 Cover: 0.50 **NM** value: **2.00**
★ Versus Gemini.
13 ❑ Feb 1981 Cover: 0.50 **NM** value: **2.00**
🕮 Through The Crystal! **A:** Mike Vosburg; Frank Springer **W:** David Anthony Kraft ★ Appearance of Man-Wolf.
14 ❑ Mar 1981 Cover: 0.50 **NM** value: **2.00**
🕮 Life In The Bloodstream **A:** Mike Vosburg; Frank Springer **W:** David Anthony Kraft ★ Appearance of Man-Wolf, Hellcat.
15 ❑ Apr 1981 Cover: 0.50 **NM** value: **2.00**
🕮 Delusions **A:** Mike Vosburg; Frank Springer **W:** David Anthony Kraft
16 ❑ May 1981 Cover: 0.50 **NM** value: **2.00**
🕮 The Zapping Of The She-Hulk **A:** Mike Vosburg; Frank Springer **W:** David Anthony Kraft
17 ❑ Jun 1981 Cover: 0.50 **NM** value: **2.00**
★ Versus Man-Elephant.
18 ❑ Jul 1981 Cover: 0.50 **NM** value: **2.00**
★ Versus Grappler.
19 ❑ Aug 1981 Cover: 0.50 **NM** value: **2.00**
20 ❑ Sep 1981 Cover: 0.50 **NM** value: **2.00**
21 ❑ Oct 1981 Cover: 0.50 **NM** value: **2.00**
22 ❑ Nov 1981 Cover: 0.50 **NM** value: **2.00**
★ Versus Radius.
23 ❑ Dec 1981 Cover: 0.50 **NM** value: **2.00**
24 ❑ Jan 1982 Cover: 0.60 **NM** value: **2.00**
25 ❑ Feb 1982 Cover: 1.00 **NM** value: **2.00**
• Giant-size. 🕮 Transmutations final issue. **A:** Mike Vosburg **W:** David Anthony Kraft

SAVAGE SWORD OF CONAN — Marvel

If you're a fan of Conan the Barbarian, there are a few things you should know before you take up Savage Sword of Conan. In Savage Sword, the Conan you know will be a little meaner, the action will be more graphic, and the women will be wearing fewer clothes. If you can deal with this more adult-oriented Conan, then you should love Marvel's rendering of Robert E. Howard's classic character.

In black-and-white, magazine format, Savage Sword of Conan brought several of Howard's most famous Conan adventures to comics form, as well as creating many new Conan epics. From the pits of hell to the cliff nests of monstrous birds, Conan is a savage hero who fears neither man nor monster. Savage Sword of Conan brought readers this legendary character in all his original fury.

1 ❑ Aug 1974, b&w Cover: 1.00 **NM** value: **40.00**
🕮 Curse of the Undead-Man; Red Sonja; Conan's Women Warriors (text); The Birth of Blackmark; An Atlantean in Aquilonia (text); the Frost Giant's Daughter **A:** John Buscema; Neal Adams; Gil Kane; Esteban Maroto; Ross Andru; Roy G. Krenkel; Barry Smith; Boris Vallejo(cover); Hugh Rankin; Severin **W:** Gil Kane; Roy Thomas; Fred Blosser; Glenn Lord; Robert E. Howard ★ Origin of Red Sonja, Blackmark.
2 ❑ Oct 1974 Cover: 1.00 **NM** value: **18.00**
🕮 Black Colossus; Hordes of the Veiled One; Chariot of the Man-Demon; Blackmark; Beast from the Abyss
3 ❑ Dec 1974 Cover: 1.00 **NM** value: **10.00**
🕮 At the Mountain of the Moon-God; The Testing of Blackmark; Kull of Atlantis; Demons of the Summit
4 ❑ Feb 1975 Cover: 1.00 **NM** value: **8.00**
🕮 Iron Shadows in the Moon; What Dreams May Come; The Haunting and the Horror; Blackmark Triumphant; (Conan Art Portfolio) **A:** Boris Vallejo(cover)
5 ❑ Apr 1975 Cover: 1.00 **NM** value: **8.00**
🕮 A Witch Shall BE Born; A People Betrayed; The Tree of Death; A Letter to Nemedia; And Dwell in Darkness; Wolves of the Desert; The Voice in the Crystal; The Shadow from the Temple **A:** Boris Vallejo(cover)
6 ❑ Jun 1975 Cover: 1.00 **NM** value: **8.00**
🕮 The Sleeper Beneath the Sands; People of the Dark
7 ❑ Aug 1975 Cover: 1.00 **NM** value: **8.00**
🕮 The Citadel at the Center of Time; In the Shadow of Fear; Sorcer's Trove; Into Time's Abyss; The Hyborean Age: The Pre-Cataclysmic Age; Lines Written in the Realization That I Must Die (poem with illustrations) **A:** Boris Vallejo(cover)
8 ❑ Oct 1975 Cover: 1.00 **NM** value: **8.00**
🕮 The Forever Phial; Death-Song of Conan the Cimmerian; Sorcer's Summit; The Hyborean Age: The Rise of the Hyboreans; Corsairs Against Stygia
9 ❑ Dec 1975 Cover: 1.00 **NM** value: **8.00**
🕮 The Curse of the Cat-Goddess; When a Tiger Returns to Atlantis **A:** Boris Vallejo(cover)
10 ❑ Feb 1976 Cover: 1.00 **NM** value: **8.00**
A: Boris Vallejo(cover)
11 ❑ Apr 1976 Cover: 1.00 **NM** value: **6.00**
12 ❑ Jun 1976 Cover: 1.00 **NM** value: **6.00**
A: Boris Vallejo(cover)
13 ❑ Aug 1976 Cover: 1.00 **NM** value: **6.00**
14 ❑ Sep 1976 Cover: 1.00 **NM** value: **6.00**
🕮 Shadows of Zamboula
15 ❑ Oct 1976 Cover: 1.00 **NM** value: **6.00**
A: Boris Vallejo(cover)
16 ❑ Dec 1976 Cover: 1.00 **NM** value: **6.00**
17 ❑ Feb 1977 Cover: 1.00 **NM** value: **6.00**
18 ❑ Apr 1977 Cover: 1.00 **NM** value: **6.00**
19 ❑ Jun 1977 Cover: 1.00 **NM** value: **6.00**
20 ❑ Jul 1977 Cover: 1.00 **NM** value: **6.00**
21 ❑ Aug 1977 Cover: 1.00 **NM** value: **5.00**
22 ❑ Sep 1977 Cover: 1.00 **NM** value: **5.00**
23 ❑ Oct 1977 Cover: 1.00 **NM** value: **5.00**
24 ❑ Nov 1977 Cover: 1.00 **NM** value: **5.00**
25 ❑ Dec 1977 Cover: 1.00 **NM** value: **5.00**
26 ❑ Jan 1978 Cover: 1.00 **NM** value: **5.00**
27 ❑ Mar 1978 Cover: 1.00 **NM** value: **5.00**
28 ❑ Apr 1978 Cover: 1.00 **NM** value: **5.00**
29 ❑ May 1978 Cover: 1.00 **NM** value: **5.00**
30 ❑ Jun 1978 Cover: 1.00 **NM** value: **4.00**
31 ❑ Jul 1978 Cover: 1.00 **NM** value: **4.00**
32 ❑ Aug 1978 Cover: 1.00 **NM** value: **4.00**
33 ❑ Sep 1978 Cover: 1.00 **NM** value: **4.00**
34 ❑ Oct 1978 Cover: 1.00 **NM** value: **4.00**
★ 1st Appearance of Garth.
35 ❑ Nov 1978 Cover: 1.00 **NM** value: **4.00**
36 ❑ Dec 1978 Cover: 1.00 **NM** value: **4.00**
37 ❑ Feb 1979 Cover: 1.00 **NM** value: **4.00**
38 ❑ Mar 1979 Cover: 1.00 **NM** value: **4.00**
🕮 The Road of the Eagles; A Gazetteer of the Hyborian Age, Part 6 **A:** John Buscema; Tony DeZuniga **W:** Roy Thomas; L. Sprague de Camp; Lee Falconer; Robert E. Howard
39 ❑ Apr 1979 Cover: 1.00 **NM** value: **4.00**
40 ❑ May 1979 Cover: 1.00 **NM** value: **4.00**
41 ❑ Jun 1979 Cover: 1.00 **NM** value: **4.00**
🕮 Conan the Buccaneer; The Ballad of BTlit; The Return of Sir Richard Grenville **A:** Ernie Chan; David Wenzel; John Buscema; Tony DeZuniga; Steve Gan **W:** Roy Thomas; L. Sprague de Camp; Lin Carter; Robert E. Howard
42 ❑ Jul 1979 Cover: 1.00 **NM** value: **4.00**
🕮 Conan the Buccaneer; A Gazetteer of the Hyborian Age, Part 9; Kings of the Night **A:** John Buscema; Tony DeZuniga **W:** Roy Thomas; L. Sprague de Camp; Lin Carter; Robert E. Howard
43 ❑ Aug 1979 Cover: 1.00 **NM** value: **4.00**
44 ❑ Sep 1979 Cover: 1.00 **NM** value: **4.00**
🕮 The Star of Khorala; Hyborian Heraldry and Cartography; Conan the Conquistador; The Bullpen's Barbarians **A:** Sal Buscema; Tony DeZuniga **W:** Roy Thomas; L. Sprague de Camp; Lin Carter
45 ❑ Oct 1979 Cover: 1.25 **NM** value: **4.00**
46 ❑ Nov 1979 Cover: 1.25 **NM** value: **4.00**
🕮 Moon of Blood; The Savage Swordbooks of Conan; This Sword for Hire **A:** Tony DeZuniga; Ernie Colon **W:** Hal Santiago; Roy Thomas; Don Glut; Fred Blosser; L. Sprague de Camp; Lin Carter
47 ❑ Dec 1979 Cover: 1.25 **NM** value: **4.00**
🕮 The Treasure of Trancios; The Secret of the Black Stranger **A:** John Buscema; Gil Kane; Joe Rubinstein **W:** Roy Thomas; Fred Blosser; L. Sprague de Camp; Robert E. Howard
48 ❑ Jan 1980 Cover: 1.25 **NM** value: **4.00**
Circ: Statement: **100,793**
🕮 Conan the Liberator, Part 1; Chains and Fetters, Part 2; Woman From Khitai **A:** John Buscema; Tony DeZuniga; Gary Brodsky **W:** Roy Thomas; Don Glut; Jim Neal; L. Sprague de Camp; Lin Carter
49 ❑ Feb 1980 Cover: 1.25 **NM** value: **4.00**
Circ: Statement: **100,793**
50 ❑ Mar 1980 Cover: 1.25 **NM** value: **4.00**
Circ: Statement: **100,793**
🕮 Conan the Liberator, part 3; Conan at Fifty **A:** John Buscema; Tony DeZuniga **W:** Roy Thomas; L. Sprague de Camp; Lin Carter
51 ❑ Apr 1980 Cover: 1.25 **NM** value: **3.00**
Circ: Statement: **100,793**
52 ❑ May 1980 Cover: 1.25 **NM** value: **3.00**
Circ: Statement: **100,793**
🕮 Conan the Liberator, Part 5; The Chan Barbarians **A:** Ernie Chan; John Buscema; Tony DeZuniga **W:** Roy Thomas; L. Sprague de Camp; Lin Carter
53 ❑ Jun 1980 Cover: 1.25 **NM** value: **3.00**
Circ: Statement: **100,793**
🕮 Conan and the Sorcerer, Part 1; The Hyborian Reporter; Wings in the Night **A:** David Wenzel; John Buscema; Rudy Nebres **W:** Roy Thomas; Andrew J. Offutt; Don Glut; Robert E. Howard
54 ❑ Jul 1980 Cover: 1.25 **NM** value: **3.00**
Circ: Statement: **100,793**
🕮 Conan and the Sorcerer, Part 2; Satan's Swordbearers; The Chan Barbarians; Wings in the Night **A:** Ricardo Villamonte; Ernie Chan; David Wenzel; John Buscema **W:** Roy Thomas; Andrew J. Offutt; Don Glut; Fred Blosser; Robert E. Howard
55 ❑ Aug 1980 Cover: 1.25 **NM** value: **3.00**
Circ: Statement: **100,793**
🕮 Conan and the Sorcerer, Part 3; Havoc in Hyboria; The New Kids in Town; Warrior and Wizard **A:** Ricardo Villamonte; Will Meugniot; John Buscema; Alfredo Alcala; Joe Jusko; Peter Ledger; Rick Larson; Steve Swenston **W:** Roy Thomas; Andrew J. Offutt; Jim Neal; Lin Carter; Robert E. Howard
56 ❑ Sep 1980 Cover: 1.25 **NM** value: **3.00**
Circ: Statement: **100,793**
🕮 The Sword of Skelos, Part 1; To Kush and Beyond; The DeZuniga Conan **A:** John Buscema; Tony DeZuniga; Gene Day **W:** Roy Thomas; Andrew J. Offutt; Charles R. Saunders
57 ❑ Oct 1980 Cover: 1.25 **NM** value: **3.00**
Circ: Statement: **100,793**
🕮 The Sword of Skelos, Part 2; Surgeons and Scars **A:** John Buscema; Tony DeZuniga **W:** Roy Thomas; Andrew J. Offutt; Jim Neal
58 ❑ Nov 1980 Cover: 1.25 **NM** value: **3.00**
Circ: Statement: **100,793**
🕮 The Sword of Skelos, Part 3; Reh: Bard From the Shadows; Mirror of the Manticore **A:** John Buscema; Tony DeZuniga; Kerry Gammill **W:** Roy Thomas; Fred Blosser; Robert E. Howard
59 ❑ Dec 1980 Cover: 1.25 **NM** value: **3.00**
Circ: Statement: **100,793**
🕮 The City of Skulls; The Kozaks Ride; Wolves Beyond the Border **A:** Ernie Chan; Mike Vosburg; Alfredo Alcala **W:** Roy Thomas; L. Sprague de Camp; Lin Carter; Robert E. Howard
60 ❑ Jan 1981 Cover: 1.25 **NM** value: **3.00**
Circ: Statement: **110,683**
🕮 The Ivory Goddess; Conan of the Storyboards **A:** John Buscema; Dan Bulanadi **W:** Roy Thomas; L. Sprague de Camp; Lin Carter; Mike W. Barr
61 ❑ Feb 1981 Cover: 1.25 **NM** value: **3.00**
Circ: Statement: **110,683**
🕮 The Wizard Fiend of Zingara!; Barbarians by Day **A:** John Buscema **W:** Gene Day; Michael Fleisher
62 ❑ Mar 1981 Cover: 1.25 **NM** value: **3.00**
Circ: Statement: **110,683**
🕮 Temple of the Tiger; The One Black Stain • Has 1980 Statement, filed 10/1/80; avg print run 200,547; avg sales 98,578; avg subs 2,215; avg total paid 100,793; samples 762; office use 835; max existent 102,390; 49% of run returned **A:** Ernie Chan; David Wenzel; John Buscema **W:** Michael Fleisher; Robert E. Howard
63 ❑ Apr 1981 Cover: 1.25 **NM** value: **3.00**
Circ: Statement: **110,683**
🕮 Moat of Blood; Andrax, the Last **A:** Ernie Chan; John Buscema; Gil Kane; Tom Palmer; Bob McLeod **W:** Gil Kane; Michael Fleisher
64 ❑ May 1981 Cover: 1.25 **NM** value: **3.00**
Circ: Statement: **110,683**
🕮 Children of Rhan; The Devil's Bait **A:** Ernie Chan; Alex Toth; John Buscema; Gil Kane **W:** Alex Toth; Gil Kane; Bruce Jones
65 ❑ Jun 1981 Cover: 1.25 **NM** value: **3.00**
Circ: Statement: **110,683**
🕮 Fangs of the Serpent; Bront **A:** John Buscema; Gil Kane **W:** J.M. DeMatteis; Michael Fleisher
66 ❑ Jul 1981 Cover: 1.25 **NM** value: **3.00**
Circ: Statement: **110,683**
🕮 The Sea of No Return; Bront, Part 2 **A:** Ernie Chan; John Buscema; Ernie Colon **W:** Roy Thomas; J.M. DeMatteis
67 ❑ Aug 1981 Cover: 1.25 **NM** value: **3.00**
Circ: Statement: **110,683**
🕮 Plunder of Death Island; In the Desert of Dreams; Deliverance **A:** John Buscema; Gil Kane; Alfredo Alcala; Baron Yoshimoto **W:** Gil Kane; Bruce Jones; Roy Thomas
68 ❑ Sep 1981 Cover: 1.25 **NM** value: **3.00**
Circ: Statement: **110,683**
🕮 Black Cloaks of Ophir; The Lost Race; A Pablos Marcos Portfolio **A:** Ernie Chan; Gene Day; Dan Bulanadi **W:** Roy Thomas; Robert E. Howard
69 ❑ Oct 1981 Cover: 1.25 **NM** value: **3.00**
Circ: Statement: **110,683**
🕮 Eye of the Sorcerer; A Romas Kukalis Portfolio; the Lost Race, Part 2 **A:** Ernie Chan; Gene Day; Dan Bulanadi **W:** Roy Thomas
70 ❑ Nov 1981 Cover: 1.25 **NM** value: **3.00**
Circ: Statement: **110,683**
🕮 Dwellers in the Depths; A Cimmerian in Hollywood; Like Father, Like Daughter **A:** John Buscema; Judith Marcos; Steve Mitchell **W:** Pablo Marcos; Bruce Jones
71 ❑ Dec 1981 Cover: 1.50 **NM** value: **3.00**
Circ: Statement: **110,683**
🕮 Lurker in the Labyrinth; Cimmerian and the Conjeress **A:** Ernie Chan; John Buscema **W:** Michael Fleisher
72 ❑ Jan 1982 Cover: 1.25 **NM** value: **3.00**
Circ: Statement: **125,307**
🕮 The Colossus of Shem **A:** Ernie Chan; John Buscema **W:** Bruce Jones
73 ❑ Feb 1982 Cover: 1.25 **NM** value: **3.00**
Circ: Statement: **125,307**
🕮 The Changeling Quest; Island of Pirates' Doom, Part 1 **A:** John Buscema; Dan Bulanadi **W:** Roy Thomas; Michael Fleisher
74 ❑ Mar 1982 Cover: 1.25 **NM** value: **3.00**
Circ: Statement: **125,307**
🕮 Lady of the Silver Snows; The Black Stone; Conan in Zamora; Island of Pirates' Doom, Part 2 **A:** John Buscema; Val Mayerik; Gene Day; Dan Bulanadi **W:** Roy Thomas; Steven Grant; Chris Claremont; Robert E. Howard
75 ❑ Apr 1982 Cover: 1.25 **NM** value: **3.00**
Circ: Statement: **125,307**
🕮 Temple of the Twelve-Eyed Thing; Conan By Chiodo • Has 1981 Statement, filed 10/1/81; avg print run 199,308; avg sales 107,355; avg subs 3,328; avg total paid 110,683; samples 703; office use 1,022; max existent 112,408; 44% of run returned **A:** Joe Chiodo; Alfredo Alcala **W:** Michael Fleisher
76 ❑ May 1982 Cover: 1.25 **NM** value: **3.00**
Circ: Statement: **125,307**
🕮 Dominion of the Bat; Demons of Ghost Swamp; Easley Does It; Island of the Pirates' Doom, Part 3 **A:** Ricardo Villamonte; Ernie Chan; Joe Chiodo; John Buscema; Alfredo Alcala; Dan Bulanadi **W:** Roy Thomas; Michael Fleisher
77 ❑ Jun 1982 Cover: 1.25 **NM** value: **3.00**
Circ: Statement: **125,307**
🕮 The Cave Dwellers; Islands of Pirates' Doom, Part 4; Through a Glass Darkly **A:** Joe Chiodo; John Buscema; Dan Bulanadi **W:** Bruce Jones; Roy Thomas; Michael Fleisher
78 ❑ Jul 1982 Cover: 1.25 **NM** value: **3.00**
Circ: Statement: **125,307**
🕮 Demons of the Firelight, Part 1; Day of the Sword; Barbarian Spfx; Island of Pirates' Doom, Part 5 **A:** Ernie Chan; John Buscema; Dick Giordano; Terry Austin; Dan Bulanadi **W:** David Anthony Kraft; Roy Thomas; Michael Fleisher
79 ❑ Aug 1982 Cover: 1.25 **NM** value: **3.00**
Circ: Statement: **125,307**
🕮 Demons of the Firelight, Part 2; Bront: In The Halls of Shilme; Island of the Pirates' Doom, Part 6; Chan's Barbarians **A:** Ernie Chan; John Buscema; Dan Bulanadi; David Anthony Kraft **W:** Bruce Jones; David Anthony Kraft; Roy Thomas; Michael Fleisher
80 ❑ Sep 1982 Cover: 1.25 **NM** value: **3.00**
Circ: Statement: **125,307**
🕮 The Colossus of Argos; Bront: The Pact **A:** John Buscema; Alfredo Alcala **W:** Bruce Jones; Michael Fleisher
81 ❑ Oct 1982 Cover: 1.25 **NM** value: **3.00**
Circ: Statement: **125,307**
🕮 The Palace of Pleasure; Bront: The Conclusion **A:** Ernie Chan; John Buscema **W:** Bruce Jones; Michael Fleisher
82 ❑ Nov 1982 Cover: 1.25 **NM** value: **3.00**
Circ: Statement: **125,307**
🕮 Devil in the Dark, Part 1; Song of Red Sonja; Swamp Gas **A:** Ernie Chan; Joe Chiodo; Barry Windsor-Smith; Alfredo Alcala **W:** Bruce Jones; Roy Thomas; Michael Fleisher
83 ❑ Dec 1982 Cover: 1.25 **NM** value: **3.00**
Circ: Statement: **125,307**

Other grades: Multiply prices above by **1.5 for Mint • 2/3 for Very Fine • 1/3 for Fine • 1/5 for Very Good • 1/8 for Good**

Devil in the Dark, Part 2; Hunters and the Hunted; Red Sonja; Red Seas **A:** Ernie Chua; Neal Adams; Alfredo Alcala; Esteban Maroto; Mary Wilshire; Dan Bulanadi **W:** Alan Zelentz; Mary Jo Duffy; Roy Thomas; Michael Fleisher ★ Appearance of Red Sonja.

84 ❑ Jan 1983 Cover: 1.25 **NM** value: **3.00**
Circ: Statement: **133,285**
The Darsome Demon of Rabba Than!; Bonus Pin-Ups **A:** Joe Chiodo; Val Mayerik **W:** Michael Fleisher

85 ❑ Feb 1983 Cover: 1.25 **NM** value: **3.00**
Circ: Statement: **133,285**
Daughter of the God King; The Illuminated Hyborian Age Map **A:** Pablo Marcos; Gil Kane; Jeff Easley **W:** Tim Conrad; Michael Fleisher

86 ❑ Mar 1983 Cover: 1.25 **NM** value: **3.00**
Circ: Statement: **133,285**
Revenge of the Sorcerer; Lion of the Waves • Has 1982 Statement, filed 10/1/82; avg print run 204,278; avg sales 121,009; avg subs 4,298; avg total paid 125,307; samples 627; office use 905; max existent 126,839; 38% of run returned **A:** Gil Kane; Zoran Vanjaka **W:** Alan Zelentz; Michael Fleisher

87 ❑ Apr 1983 Cover: 1.25 **NM** value: **3.00**
Circ: Statement: **133,285**
The Armor of Zulda Thaal!; Escape From the Temple **A:** Ernie Chan; John Buscema **W:** Michael Fleisher

88 ❑ May 1983 Cover: 1.25 **NM** value: **3.00**
Circ: Statement: **133,285**
Isle of the Hunter; The Dark Stranger **A:** John Buscema; Alan Zelentz; Rudy Nebres **W:** Pablo Marcos; Michael Fleisher

89 ❑ Jun 1983 Cover: 1.25 **NM** value: **3.00**
Circ: Statement: **133,285**
Gamesmen of Asgalun; Rite of Blood **A:** Ernie Chan; Nestor Redondo; Armando Gil; Alfredo Alcala; Mary Wilshire; Dan Bulanadi **W:** Gil Kane; Michael Fleisher

90 ❑ Jul 1983 Cover: 1.25 **NM** value: **3.00**
Circ: Statement: **133,285**
Devourer of Souls! **A:** Ernie Chan; Anthony Castrillo; David Wenzel; Nestor Redondo; John Buscema; Gary Kwapisz; Dave Simons **W:** Michael Fleisher

91 ❑ Aug 1983 Cover: 1.25 **NM** value: **3.00**
Circ: Statement: **133,285**
Forest of Fiends!; The Beast; The Chain **A:** John Buscema; Val Mayerik; Pablo Marcos; Gary Kwapisz **W:** James Owsley; Michael Fleisher

92 ❑ Sep 1983 Cover: 1.25 **NM** value: **3.00**
Circ: Statement: **133,285**
The Jeweled Bird **A:** Bob Camp; Ernie Chan; John Buscema **W:** Michael Fleisher

93 ❑ Oct 1983 Cover: 1.25 **NM** value: **3.00**
Circ: Statement: **133,285**
The World Beyond the Mists!; Challenge **A:** Ernie Chan; John Buscema; Pablo Marcos; Rudy Nebres **W:** Michael Fleisher

94 ❑ Nov 1983 Cover: 1.25 **NM** value: **3.00**
Circ: Statement: **133,285**
Death Dwarves of Stygia! **A:** Ernie Chan; Val Mayerik; Vince Colletta **W:** Michael Fleisher

95 ❑ Dec 1983 Cover: 1.25 **NM** value: **3.00**
Circ: Statement: **133,285**
Night of the Rat!; The Hill of Horror **A:** Ernie Chan; John Buscema; Alan Zelentz **W:** Ron Wilson; Michael Fleisher

96 ❑ Jan 1984 Cover: 1.25 **NM** value: **3.00**
Circ: Statement: **133,689**
The Ape-Bat of Marmet Tarn! **A:** John Buscema; Joe Jusko(cover) **W:** Michael Fleisher

97 ❑ Feb 1984 Cover: 1.25 **NM** value: **3.00**
Circ: Statement: **133,689**
The Leopard Men of Darfar! **A:** Pablo Marcos; Gary Kwapisz **W:** Michael Fleisher

98 ❑ Mar 1984 Cover: 1.25 **NM** value: **3.00**
Circ: Statement: **133,689**
The Blood Ruby of Death!; The Lady of the Tower! **A:** John Buscema; Gary Kwapisz **W:** Steve Skeates; Michael Fleisher

99 ❑ Apr 1984 Cover: 1.25 **NM** value: **3.00**
Circ: Statement: **133,689**
The Informer!; One Night At The Maul • Has 1983 Statement, filed 10/06/83; avg print run 220,048; avg sales 128,038; avg subs 5,247; avg total paid 133,285; samples 672; office use 566; max existent 134,523; 39% of run returned **A:** John Buscema; Stan Woch; Ned Sonntag **W:** James Owsley; Michael Fleisher

100 ❑ May 1984 Cover: 1.50 **NM** value: **3.00**
Circ: Statement: **133,689**
When a God Lives!; The Gift **A:** John Buscema; Armando Gil; June Brigman **W:** Larry Yakata; Michael Fleisher

101 ❑ Jun 1984 Cover: 1.50 **NM** value: **2.50**
Circ: Statement: **133,689**
The Siren! **A:** John Buscema **W:** Michael Fleisher

102 ❑ Jul 1984 Cover: 1.50 **NM** value: **2.50**
Circ: Statement: **133,689**
The Iron Lions of the Kharamun! **A:** Ernie Chan; Gary Kwapisz **W:** Michael Fleisher

103 ❑ Aug 1984 Cover: 1.50 **NM** value: **2.50**
Circ: Statement: **133,689**
The White Tiger of Vendhya!; Men of the Shadows!, Part 1 **A:** Pablo Marcos; Gene Day **W:** Roy Thomas; Michael Fleisher

104 ❑ Sep 1984 Cover: 1.50 **NM** value: **2.50**
Circ: Statement: **133,689**
Treachery of the Gray Wolf!; Men of the Shadows!, Part 2 **A:** Ernie Chan; Val Mayerik; Gene Day **W:** Roy Thomas; Michael Fleisher

105 ❑ Oct 1984 Cover: 1.50 **NM** value: **2.50**
Circ: Statement: **133,689**
The Mill; The Crypt **A:** Bob Camp; Geof Isherwood; Gary Kwapisz **W:** William Johnson; Don Krarr

106 ❑ Nov 1984 Cover: 1.50 **NM** value: **2.50**
Circ: Statement: **133,689**
Feud of Blood; Men of the Shadows!, Part 3 **A:** Gene Day; Dave Simons **W:** Roy Thomas; Michael Fleisher

107 ❑ Dec 1984 Cover: 1.50 **NM** value: **2.50**
Circ: Statement: **133,689**
The Eyes of G'Bharr R'Jinn; Deepest Devotion **A:** Tony Salmons; Rudy Nebres **W:** Alan Rowlands; Michael Fleisher

108 ❑ Jan 1985 Cover: 1.50 **NM** value: **2.50**
Circ: Statement: **138,183**
The Claws of the Osprey; Fear of Crom **A:** Michael Docherty; Ernie Chan; Gary Kwapisz **W:** Don Kraar; Michael Fleisher

109 ❑ Feb 1985 Cover: 1.50 **NM** value: **2.50**
Circ: Statement: **138,183**
The Shatterer of Worlds; The Vezek Inn **A:** Michael Docherty; Gary Kwapisz **W:** James Owsley; Michael Fleisher

110 ❑ Mar 1985 Cover: 1.50 **NM** value: **2.50**
Circ: Statement: **138,183**
The Army of the Dead; The Dinner Guest **A:** Ernie Chan; Gary Kwapisz; Tim Burgard **W:** Alan Rowlands; Bill Mantlo

111 ❑ Apr 1985 Cover: 1.50 **NM** value: **2.50**
Circ: Statement: **138,183** CapCity orders: **5,390**
Mud Men of Keshan; In the Eye of the Beholder **A:** Ernie Chan; Gary Kwapisz **W:** Don Kraar; Michael Fleisher

112 ❑ May 1985 Cover: 1.50 **NM** value: **2.50**
Circ: Statement: **138,183** CapCity orders: **5,320**
A Dream of Empire; Mitra Defend Us **A:** William Johnson; Dave Simons; Rey Garcia **W:** Don Kraar; Michael Fleisher

113 ❑ Jun 1985 Cover: 1.50 **NM** value: **2.50**
Circ: Statement: **138,183** CapCity orders: **5,460**
Quest for the Shrine of Luma; A Quiet Place **A:** Ernie Chan; Tony Salmons; William Johnson **W:** Don Kraar; Larry Yakata

114 ❑ Jul 1985 Cover: 1.50 **NM** value: **2.50**
Circ: Statement: **138,183** CapCity orders: **5,250**
The Riddle of the Demuzaar; The Toll **A:** Andy Kubert; Rudy Nebres **W:** Don Kraar; Larry Yakata

115 ❑ Aug 1985 Cover: 1.50 **NM** value: **2.50**
Circ: Statement: **138,183** CapCity orders: **5,250**
Isle of the Faceless Ones; The Warlord of the Castle **A:** Val Mayerik; Rudy Nebres; Henri Bismuth **W:** Craig Anderson; Larry Yakata

116 ❑ Sep 1985 Cover: 1.50 **NM** value: **2.50**
Circ: Statement: **138,183** CapCity orders: **5,320**
Lords of the Falcon; The Boon **A:** Ernie Chan; Sal Buscema; Roy Richardson **W:** Don Kraar; Larry Yakata

117 ❑ Oct 1985 Cover: 1.50 **NM** value: **2.50**
Circ: Statement: **138,183** CapCity orders: **5,250**
The Winds of Aka-Gaar; The Opponents **A:** Gary Kwapisz; Rod Whigham; Roy Richardson **W:** Don Kraar; Larry Yakata

118 ❑ Nov 1985 Cover: 1.50 **NM** value: **2.50**
Circ: Statement: **138,183** CapCity orders: **5,110**
Valley of Howling Shadows; Alchemy **A:** Gary Kwapisz; Tony Salmons **W:** Don Kraar; Larry Yakata

119 ❑ Dec 1985 Cover: 1.50 **NM** value: **2.50**
Circ: Statement: **138,183** CapCity orders: **5,180**
The Homecoming; Kull the Conqueror: From Beyond the Grave! **A:** Ernie Chan; Geof Isherwood **W:** Chuck Dixon; Don Kraar

120 ❑ Jan 1986 Cover: 1.50 **NM** value: **2.50**
Circ: Statement: **135,883** CapCity orders: **5,180**
Star of Thamazhu; Kull the Conqueror; Night of the Monkey **A:** Pablo Marcos; Geof Isherwood **W:** Chuck Dixon; Larry Yakata

121 ❑ Feb 1986 Cover: 1.50 **NM** value: **2.50**
Circ: Statement: **135,883** CapCity orders: **5,180**
The Fountain of Umir; Kull the Conqueror: Pieces of Horror **A:** Geof Isherwood; Rudy Nebres **W:** Chuck Dixon; Larry Yakata

122 ❑ Mar 1986 Cover: 1.50 **NM** value: **2.50**
Circ: Statement: **135,883** CapCity orders: **5,110**
The Blossoms of the Black Lotus; One Against All **A:** Ernie Chan; Val Semeiks **W:** Chuck Dixon; Don Kraar

123 ❑ Apr 1986 Cover: 1.50 **NM** value: **2.50**
Circ: Statement: **135,883** CapCity orders: **4,490**
Secret of the Great Stone; The Debt of the Warrior **A:** Michael Docherty; Ernie Chan; James Baldwin **W:** Larry Yakata

124 ❑ May 1986 Cover: 1.50 **NM** value: **2.50**
Circ: Statement: **135,883** CapCity orders: **5,350**

125 ❑ Jun 1986 Cover: 1.50 **NM** value: **2.50**
Circ: Statement: **135,883** CapCity orders: **5,450**

126 ❑ Jul 1986 Cover: 1.50 **NM** value: **2.50**
Circ: Statement: **135,883** CapCity orders: **5,450**

127 ❑ Aug 1986 Cover: 1.50 **NM** value: **2.50**
Circ: Statement: **135,883** CapCity orders: **5,500**

128 ❑ Sep 1986 Cover: 1.50 **NM** value: **2.50**
Circ: Statement: **135,883** CapCity orders: **5,800**

129 ❑ Oct 1986 Cover: 1.50 **NM** value: **2.50**
Circ: Statement: **135,883** CapCity orders: **5,900**

130 ❑ Nov 1986 Cover: 1.50 **NM** value: **2.50**
Circ: Statement: **135,883** CapCity orders: **5,900**

131 ❑ Dec 1986 Cover: 2.00 **NM** value: **2.50**
Circ: Statement: **135,883** CapCity orders: **5,950**

132 ❑ Jan 1987 Cover: 1.50 **NM** value: **2.50**
Circ: Statement: **132,750** CapCity orders: **5,850**
Master of the Broadsword; The Sea King **A:** Ernie Chan; Gary Kwapisz **W:** Larry Yakata

133 ❑ Feb 1987 Cover: 1.50 **NM** value: **2.50**
Circ: Statement: **132,750** CapCity orders: **6,200**

134 ❑ Mar 1987 Cover: 1.50 **NM** value: **2.50**
Circ: Statement: **132,750** CapCity orders: **6,000**

135 ❑ Apr 1987 Cover: 1.50 **NM** value: **2.50**
Circ: Statement: **132,750** CapCity orders: **6,000**

136 ❑ May 1987 Cover: 1.50 **NM** value: **2.50**
Circ: Statement: **132,750** CapCity orders: **5,900**
The Lost Legion, Part 1; The Brawl **A:** Ernie Chan; Gary Kwapisz; Fraja Bator **W:** Chuck Dixon

137 ❑ Jun 1987 Cover: 1.50 **NM** value: **2.50**
Circ: Statement: **132,750** CapCity orders: **6,100**
The Lost Legion, Part 2; The Brawl **A:** Ernie Chan; Gary Kwapisz; Fraja Bator **W:** Chuck Dixon

138 ❑ Jul 1987 Cover: 1.50 **NM** value: **2.50**
Circ: Statement: **132,750** CapCity orders: **6,300**
Lair of the Lizard; The Mine **A:** Ernie Chan; Gary Kwapisz; Fraja Bator **W:** Chuck Dixon

139 ❑ Aug 1987 Cover: 1.50 **NM** value: **2.50**
Circ: Statement: **132,750** CapCity orders: **6,900**

140 ❑ Sep 1987 Cover: 1.50 **NM** value: **2.50**
Circ: Statement: **132,750** CapCity orders: **7,250**
The Girl of the Haunted Wood; Nightmare **A:** Ernie Chan; Gary Kwapisz; Vincent Waller **W:** Chuck Dixon

141 ❑ Oct 1987 Cover: 1.50 **NM** value: **2.50**
Circ: Statement: **132,750** CapCity orders: **7,400**

142 ❑ Nov 1987 Cover: 1.50 **NM** value: **2.50**
Circ: Statement: **132,750** CapCity orders: **7,050**

143 ❑ Dec 1987 Cover: 1.50 **NM** value: **2.50**
Circ: Statement: **132,750** CapCity orders: **7,400**

144 ❑ Jan 1988 Cover: 1.50 **NM** value: **2.50**
Circ: Statement: **121,310** CapCity orders: **7,400**

145 ❑ Feb 1988 Cover: 1.50 **NM** value: **2.50**
Circ: Statement: **121,310** CapCity orders: **7,450**
Feast of the Stag ★ Appearance of Red Sonja.

146 ❑ Mar 1988 Cover: 1.50 **NM** value: **2.50**
Circ: Statement: **121,310** CapCity orders: **7,500**

147 ❑ Apr 1988 Cover: 1.50 **NM** value: **2.50**
Circ: Statement: **121,310** CapCity orders: **7,300**
Vulture's Shadow; Rites of Passage **A:** Ernie Chan; Gary Kwapisz **W:** William Johnson; Chuck Dixon

148 ❑ May 1988 Cover: 1.50 **NM** value: **2.50**
Circ: Statement: **121,310** CapCity orders: **7,050**

149 ❑ Jun 1988 Cover: 1.50 **NM** value: **2.50**
Circ: Statement: **121,310** CapCity orders: **7,000**

150 ❑ Jul 1988 Cover: 1.50 **NM** value: **2.50**
Circ: Statement: **121,310** CapCity orders: **6,900**
Call to the Slain; Trial by Fear **A:** Ernie Chan; Gary Kwapisz; Mark Pacella **W:** Chuck Dixon; John Arcudi

151 ❑ Aug 1988 Cover: 2.00 **NM** value: **2.50**
Circ: Statement: **121,310** CapCity orders: **6,950**
Fury of the Near-Men; A Bond of Blood **A:** Ernie Chan; Gary Kwapisz; Mark Pacella **W:** Chuck Dixon; John Arcudi

152 ❑ Sep 1988 Cover: 2.00 **NM** value: **2.50**
Circ: Statement: **121,310** CapCity orders: **7,050**
Valley Beyond the Stars; Invictus **A:** Ernie Chan; Dale Eaglesham; Armando Gil; Gary Kwapisz **W:** Chuck Dixon; John Arcudi

153 ❑ Oct 1988 Cover: 2.00 **NM** value: **2.50**
Circ: Statement: **121,310** CapCity orders: **7,350**
Phantasm; Blood on the Sand **A:** Luke McDonnell; Armando Gil; Gary Kwapisz **W:** Chuck Dixon; James Owsley ★ Appearance of Red Sonja.

154 ❑ Nov 1988 Cover: 2.00 **NM** value: **2.50**
Circ: Statement: **121,310** CapCity orders: **7,000**
Return of the Iron Damsels; To Fight Another Day! **A:** Gary Kwapisz; Terry Tidwell; Dave Simons **W:** Chuck Dixon; Don Kraar

155 ❑ Dec 1988 Cover: 2.00 **NM** value: **2.50**
Circ: Statement: **121,310** CapCity orders: **6,700**

156 ❑ Jan 1989 Cover: 2.00 **NM** value: **2.50**
Circ: Statement: **122,965** CapCity orders: **6,500**
Rogue's Honor; Dave Simons Portfolio **A:** Michael Docherty; Dave Simons **W:** Chuck Dixon

157 ❑ Feb 1989 Cover: 2.00 **NM** value: **2.50**
Circ: Statement: **122,965** CapCity orders: **6,650**

158 ❑ Mar 1989 Cover: 2.00 **NM** value: **2.50**
Circ: Statement: **122,965** CapCity orders: **6,800**
Bane of the Dark Brotherhood; Caresses of Mine Enemy **A:** Ernie Chan; Jim Valentino **W:** Chuck Dixon; John Arcudi

159 ❑ Apr 1989 Cover: 2.00 **NM** value: **2.50**
Circ: Statement: **122,965** CapCity orders: **6,950**

160 ❑ May 1989 Cover: 2.00 **NM** value: **2.50**
Circ: Statement: **122,965** CapCity orders: **6,900**

161 ❑ Jun 1989 Cover: 2.00 **NM** value: **2.50**
Circ: Statement: **122,965** CapCity orders: **7,150**

162 ❑ Jul 1989 Cover: 2.00 **NM** value: **2.50**
Circ: Statement: **122,965** CapCity orders: **7,350**

163 ❑ Aug 1989 Cover: 2.00 **NM** value: **2.50**
Circ: Statement: **122,965** CapCity orders: **7,450**

164 ❑ Sep 1989 Cover: 2.25 **NM** value: **2.50**
Circ: Statement: **122,965** CapCity orders: **7,450**

165 ❑ Oct 1989 Cover: 2.25 **NM** value: **2.50**
Circ: Statement: **122,965** CapCity orders: **7,550**
City of Rats; Siege! **A:** Gary Kwapisz; Tony Salmons **W:** Chuck Dixon; John Arcudi

166 ❑ Nov 1989 Cover: 2.25 **NM** value: **2.50**
Circ: Statement: **122,965**

167 ❑ Dec 1989 Cover: 2.25 **NM** value: **2.50**
Circ: Statement: **122,965**

168 ❑ Jan 1990 Cover: 2.25 **NM** value: **2.50**
Circ: Statement: **115,958**

169 ❑ Feb 1990 Cover: 2.25 **NM** value: **2.50**
Circ: Statement: **115,958**

170 ❑ Mar 1990 Cover: 2.25 **NM** value: **2.50**
Circ: Statement: **115,958**

171 ❑ Apr 1990 Cover: 2.25 **NM** value: **2.50**
Circ: Statement: **115,958**

172 ❑ May 1990 Cover: 2.25 **NM** value: **2.50**
Circ: Statement: **115,958**

173 ❑ Jun 1990 Cover: 2.25 **NM** value: **2.50**
Circ: Statement: **115,958**

174 ❑ Jul 1990 Cover: 2.25 **NM** value: **Cover or less**
Circ: Statement: **115,958**
• Series continues as Savage Sworld of Conan the Barbarian

175 ❑ Aug 1990 Cover: 2.25 **NM** value: **Cover or less**
Circ: Statement: **115,958**

176 ❑ Sep 1990 Cover: 2.25 **NM** value: **Cover or less**
Circ: Statement: **115,958**

177 ❑ Oct 1990 Cover: 2.25 **NM** value: **Cover or less**
Circ: Statement: **115,958**

178 ❑ Nov 1990 Cover: 2.25 **NM** value: **Cover or less**
Circ: Statement: **115,958**

179 ❑ Dec 1990 Cover: 2.25 **NM** value: **Cover or less**
Circ: Statement: **115,958**
Fury of the Iron Damsels ★ Appearance of Red Sonja.

180 ❑ Jan 1991 Cover: 2.25 **NM** value: **Cover or less**
181 ❑ Feb 1991 Cover: 2.25 **NM** value: **Cover or less**
182 ❑ Mar 1991 Cover: 2.25 **NM** value: **Cover or less**
183 ❑ Apr 1991 Cover: 2.25 **NM** value: **Cover or less**
184 ❑ May 1991 Cover: 2.25 **NM** value: **Cover or less**
Disciple **A:** Michael Docherty; Alfredo Alcala **W:** Larry Yakata

CGC-graded: Multiply prices above by **33 for 9.9 M • 16 for 9.8 NM/M • 7 for 9.6 NM+ • 5 for 9.4 NM • 2.5 for 9.2 NM- • 1.5 for 9.0 VF/NM**

185 ❑ Jun 1991 Cover: 2.25 **NM** value: **Cover or less**
186 ❑ Jul 1991 Cover: 2.25 **NM** value: **Cover or less**
187 ❑ Aug 1991 Cover: 2.25 **NM** value: **Cover or less**
🕮 Red Sonja Quells the Song of the Siren ★ Appearance of Red Sonja.
188 ❑ Sep 1991 Cover: 2.25 **NM** value: **Cover or less**
189 ❑ Oct 1991 Cover: 2.25 **NM** value: **Cover or less**
190 ❑ Nov 1991 Cover: 2.25 **NM** value: **Cover or less**
191 ❑ Dec 1991 Cover: 2.25 **NM** value: **Cover or less**
192 ❑ Jan 1992 Cover: 2.25 **NM** value: **Cover or less**
193 ❑ Feb 1992 Cover: 2.25 **NM** value: **Cover or less**
Circ: CapCity orders: **7,050**
194 ❑ Mar 1992 Cover: 2.25 **NM** value: **Cover or less**
Circ: CapCity orders: **6,850**
195 ❑ Apr 1992 Cover: 2.25 **NM** value: **Cover or less**
Circ: CapCity orders: **6,700**
196 ❑ May 1992 Cover: 2.25 **NM** value: **Cover or less**
Circ: CapCity orders: **6,500**
197 ❑ Jun 1992 Cover: 2.25 **NM** value: **Cover or less**
Circ: CapCity orders: **6,550**
198 ❑ Jul 1992 Cover: 2.25 **NM** value: **Cover or less**
Circ: CapCity orders: **6,750**
199 ❑ Aug 1992 Cover: 2.25 **NM** value: **Cover or less**
Circ: CapCity orders: **6,650**
200 ❑ Sep 1992 Cover: 2.25 **NM** value: **Cover or less**
Circ: CapCity orders: **9,000**
201 ❑ Oct 1992 Cover: 2.25 **NM** value: **Cover or less**
Circ: CapCity orders: **6,750**
202 ❑ Nov 1992 Cover: 2.25 **NM** value: **Cover or less**
Circ: CapCity orders: **6,500**
203 ❑ Dec 1992 Cover: 2.25 **NM** value: **Cover or less**
Circ: CapCity orders: **6,450**
204 ❑ Jan 1993 Cover: 2.25 **NM** value: **Cover or less**
Circ: CapCity orders: **6,700**
205 ❑ Feb 1993 Cover: 2.25 **NM** value: **Cover or less**
Circ: CapCity orders: **6,250**
206 ❑ Mar 1993 Cover: 2.25 **NM** value: **Cover or less**
Circ: CapCity orders: **6,350**
207 ❑ Apr 1993 Cover: 2.25 **NM** value: **Cover or less**
Circ: CapCity orders: **6,250**
🕮 Conan and the Spider God, Part 1 **A:** John Buscema; E.R. Cruz **W:** Roy Thomas
208 ❑ May 1993 Cover: 2.25 **NM** value: **Cover or less**
Circ: CapCity orders: **6,550**
🕮 Conan and the Spider God, Part 2 **A:** John Buscema; E.R. Cruz
209 ❑ Jun 1993 Cover: 2.25 **NM** value: **Cover or less**
Circ: CapCity orders: **6,600**
🕮 Conan and the Spider God, Part 3 **A:** John Buscema; E.R. Cruz
210 ❑ Jul 1993 Cover: 2.25 **NM** value: **Cover or less**
Circ: CapCity orders: **6,750**
🕮 Conan and the Spider God, Part 4 **A:** John Buscema; E.R. Cruz
211 ❑ Aug 1993 Cover: 2.25 **NM** value: **Cover or less**
Circ: CapCity orders: **6,550**
212 ❑ Sep 1993 Cover: 2.25 **NM** value: **Cover or less**
Circ: CapCity orders: **6,600**
213 ❑ Oct 1993 Cover: 2.25 **NM** value: **Cover or less**
Circ: CapCity orders: **6,300**
214 ❑ Nov 1993 Cover: 2.25 **NM** value: **Cover or less**
Circ: CapCity orders: **6,200**
• Adapted from Robert E. Howard's "Red Nails" **A:** Ernie Chan; E.R. Cruz **W:** Roy Thomas
215 ❑ Dec 1993 Cover: 2.25 **NM** value: **Cover or less**
Circ: CapCity orders: **6,250**
216 ❑ Jan 1994 Cover: 2.25 **NM** value: **Cover or less**
Circ: CapCity orders: **6,250**
217 ❑ Feb 1994 Cover: 2.25 **NM** value: **Cover or less**
Circ: CapCity orders: **6,050**
218 ❑ Mar 1994 Cover: 2.25 **NM** value: **Cover or less**
Circ: CapCity orders: **6,150**
219 ❑ Apr 1994 Cover: 2.25 **NM** value: **Cover or less**
Circ: CapCity orders: **6,050**
220 ❑ May 1994 Cover: 2.25 **NM** value: **Cover or less**
Circ: CapCity orders: **5,750**
221 ❑ May 1994, b&w Cover: 2.25 **NM** value: **Cover or less**
Circ: CapCity orders: **5,800**
222 ❑ Jun 1994, b&w Cover: 2.25 **NM** value: **Cover or less**
Circ: CapCity orders: **5,800**
223 ❑ Jul 1994, b&w Cover: 2.25 **NM** value: **Cover or less**
Circ: CapCity orders: **5,750**
224 ❑ Aug 1994, b&w Cover: 2.25 **NM** value: **Cover or less**
Circ: CapCity orders: **5,800**
225 ❑ Sep 1994, b&w Cover: 2.25 **NM** value: **Cover or less**
Circ: CapCity orders: **5,725**
226 ❑ Oct 1994, b&w Cover: 2.25 **NM** value: **Cover or less**
Circ: CapCity orders: **5,550**
227 ❑ Nov 1994, b&w Cover: 2.25 **NM** value: **Cover or less**
Circ: CapCity orders: **5,250**
228 ❑ Dec 1994, b&w Cover: 2.25 **NM** value: **Cover or less**
Circ: CapCity orders: **5,200**
229 ❑ Jan 1995, b&w Cover: 2.25 **NM** value: **Cover or less**
Circ: CapCity orders: **5,000**
230 ❑ Feb 1995, b&w Cover: 2.25 **NM** value: **Cover or less**
Circ: CapCity orders: **4,750**
231 ❑ Mar 1995, b&w Cover: 2.25 **NM** value: **Cover or less**
Circ: CapCity orders: **4,625**
232 ❑ Apr 1995, b&w Cover: 2.25 **NM** value: **Cover or less**
Circ: CapCity orders: **4,400**
233 ❑ May 1995, b&w Cover: 2.25 **NM** value: **Cover or less**
Circ: CapCity orders: **4,325**
234 ❑ Jun 1995, b&w Cover: 2.25 **NM** value: **Cover or less**
Circ: CapCity orders: **4,300**
235 ❑ Jul 1995, b&w Cover: 2.25 **NM** value: **Cover or less**
Circ: CapCity orders: **4,275**
final issue.
Anl 1 ❑ ca. 1975, b&w Cover: 1.25 **NM** value: **Cover or less**
🕮 Beware the Wrath of Anu; The Forbidden Swamp; The Death-Dance of Thulsa Doom; Web of the Spider-God • reprinted from Conan the Barbarian (1st series) #10 and 13; Kull the Conqueror #3; Monsters on the Prowl #16
SE 1 ❑ ca. 1975 **NM** value: **6.00**

SAVAGE SWORD OF MIKE — Fandom House

1 ❑ b&w Cover: 2.00 **NM** value: **Cover or less**

SAVAGE TALES (1ST SERIES) — Marvel

Following the successful debut of its adaptations of the stories of Robert E. Howard's Conan the Barbarian in its color comics line the year before, Marvel attempted to move to the less-restricted, non-Comics Code arena of the black-and-white magazine format in 1971. Rated "M For The Mature Reader!" the stories presented here contained slightly more daring themes and partial nudity. The lead feature is a Conan story: "The Frost Giant's Daughter" adapted by Roy Thomas and illustrated by Barry Smith. Additional features include the first appearance of The Man-Thing (with art by Gray Morrow) and a more brutal Ka-Zar.

The title was canceled after one issue but revived in 1973, this time with more success. In 1974, Ka-Zar became the lead feature, with Conan headlining a new title, The Savage Sword of Conan. "The Frost Giant's Daughter" was colored to make nude scenes appropriate for the color comic book and saw print in Conan the Barbarian #16.

1 ❑ May 1971 Cover: 0.50 **NM** value: **60.00**
• b&w magazine. 🕮 Conan the Barbarian: The Frost Giant's Daughter; The Fury of the Femizons; Man/Thing; Black Brother; Kazar: The Night of the Looter **A:** Gray Morrow; Gene Colan; John Buscema; Barry Windsor-Smith; John Romita; Barry Smith **W:** Roy Thomas; Stan Lee; Gerry Conway; Sergius O'Shaughnessy ★ Origin of Man-Thing. ★ 1st Appearance of Man-Thing. ★ Appearance of Conan.
2 ❑ Oct 1973 Cover: 0.75 **NM** value: **24.00**
🕮 Conan: Red Nails; Dark Tomorrow; Cimmeria; The Crusader; The Skull of Silence; A Probable Outline of Conan's Career (text with illustrations) • "Crusader" reprinted from The Black Knight #1 **A:** Al Williamson; Gray Morrow; Frank Brunner; Barry Windsor-Smith; Bernie Wrighton
3 ❑ Feb 1974 Cover: 0.75 **NM** value: **15.00**
🕮 The Lurker From the Catacombs; The Crimson Bell; The Fury of the Femizons; He Comes from the Dark • Continues "Red Nails" story from issue #2 **A:** Al Williamson; Frank Brunner; Barry Windsor-Smith; Joe Sinnott
4 ❑ May 1974 Cover: 0.75 **NM** value: **10.00**
A: Neal Adams; Gil Kane
5 ❑ Jul 1974 Cover: 0.75 **NM** value: **10.00**
A: Neal Adams; Gil Kane
6 ❑ Sep 1974 Cover: 0.75 **NM** value: **8.00**
7 ❑ Nov 1974 Cover: 0.75 **NM** value: **8.00**
8 ❑ Jan 1975 Cover: 1.00 **NM** value: **8.00**
9 ❑ Mar 1975 Cover: 1.00 **NM** value: **8.00**
10 ❑ May 1975 Cover: 1.00 **NM** value: **8.00**
11 ❑ Jul 1975 Cover: 1.00 **NM** value: **8.00**
12 ❑ Sum 1975 Cover: 1.25 **NM** value: **6.00**
Anl 1 ❑ ca. 1975, b&w Cover: 1.25 **NM** value: **7.00**
A: Gil Kane ★ Origin of Ka-Zar.

SAVAGE TALES (2ND SERIES) — Marvel

1 ❑ Oct 1985, b&w Cover: 1.50 **NM** value: **4.00**
Circ: CapCity orders: **8,190**
• magazine. • 1st 'Nam story **A:** Michael Golden
2 ❑ Dec 1985 Cover: 1.50 **NM** value: **3.00**
Circ: CapCity orders: **6,370**
• 2nd 'Nam story **A:** John Severin
3 ❑ Feb 1986 Cover: 1.50 **NM** value: **2.50**
Circ: CapCity orders: **4,270**
4 ❑ Apr 1986 Cover: 1.50 **NM** value: **2.50**
Circ: CapCity orders: **3,890**
• 'Nam
5 ❑ Jun 1986 Cover: 1.50 **NM** value: **2.50**
Circ: CapCity orders: **3,600**
A: John Severin
6 ❑ Aug 1986 Cover: 1.50 **NM** value: **2.00**
Circ: CapCity orders: **3,400**
7 ❑ Oct 1986 Cover: 1.50 **NM** value: **2.00**
Circ: CapCity orders: **3,400**
8 ❑ Dec 1986 Cover: 1.50 **NM** value: **2.00**
Circ: CapCity orders: **3,250**
9 ❑ Feb 1987 Cover: 1.50 **NM** value: **2.00**
Circ: CapCity orders: **3,250**
final issue.

SAVANT GARDE — Image

1 ❑ Mar 1997 Cover: 2.50 **NM** value: **Cover or less**
Circ: Diamd. preorders: **37,787**
A: Ryan Odagawa **W:** Barbara Kesel
2 ❑ Apr 1997 Cover: 2.50 **NM** value: **Cover or less**
Circ: Diamd. preorders: **27,353**
★ 1st Appearance of Innuendo.
3 ❑ May 1997 Cover: 2.50 **NM** value: **Cover or less**
Circ: Diamd. preorders: **23,666**
4 ❑ Jun 1997 Cover: 2.50 **NM** value: **Cover or less**
Circ: Diamd. preorders: **20,635**
5 ❑ Jul 1997 Cover: 2.50 **NM** value: **Cover or less**
Circ: Diamd. preorders: **17,394**
6 ❑ Aug 1997 Cover: 2.50 **NM** value: **Cover or less**
Circ: Diamd. preorders: **16,058**
7 ❑ Sep 1997 Cover: 2.50 **NM** value: **Cover or less**
Circ: Diamd. preorders: **14,471**
FAN 1 ❑ Feb 1997 **NM** value: **1.00**
FAN 2 ❑ Mar 1997 **NM** value: **1.00**
A: Christian Uche **W:** Barbara Kesel
FAN 3 ❑ Apr 1997 **NM** value: **1.00**

SAVED BY THE BELL — Harvey

1 ❑ May 1992 Cover: 1.95 **NM** value: **Cover or less**
🕮 A Chillin' Holiday; The Bayside Bugler; High Resolution **A:** Hy Rosen **W:** Angelo De Cesare
2 ❑ Jun 1992 Cover: 1.95 **NM** value: **Cover or less**
3 ❑ Jul 1992 Cover: 1.95 **NM** value: **Cover or less**
4 ❑ Aug 1992 Cover: 1.95 **NM** value: **Cover or less**
5 ❑ Sep 1992 Cover: 1.95 **NM** value: **Cover or less**

SAVIOUR — Trident

All issues are adults only.
1 ❑ 1989b&w Cover: 4.00 **NM** value: **Cover or less**
2 ❑ Feb 1990, b&w Cover: 1.95 **NM** value: **Cover or less**
3 ❑ 1990b&w Cover: 2.50 **NM** value: **Cover or less**
4 ❑ 1990b&w Cover: 2.50 **NM** value: **Cover or less**
5 ❑ 1990b&w Cover: 2.50 **NM** value: **Cover or less**
Bk 1 ❑ Cover: 7.95 **NM** value: **Cover or less**

SAX ROHMER: TWO COMPLETE FU MANCHU ADVENTURES — Eternity

Bk 1 ❑ b&w Cover: 12.95 **NM** value: **Cover or less**

SB NINJA HIGH SCHOOL — Antarctic

1/A ❑ Aug 1992, b&w Cover: 2.95 **NM** value: **Cover or less**
1/B ❑ Aug 1992, b&w Cover: 4.95 **NM** value: **Cover or less**
• trading card
2/A ❑ b&w Cover: 2.95 **NM** value: **Cover or less**
2/B ❑ b&w Cover: 4.95 **NM** value: **Cover or less**
• trading card
3/A ❑ Sep 1994, b&w Cover: 2.75 **NM** value: **Cover or less**
3/B ❑ Sep 1994, b&w Cover: 4.95 **NM** value: **Cover or less**
• trading card
4 ❑ Feb 1995, b&w Cover: 2.75 **NM** value: **Cover or less**
5 ❑ May 1995, b&w Cover: 2.75 **NM** value: **Cover or less**
6 ❑ Aug 1995, b&w Cover: 2.75 **NM** value: **Cover or less**
7 ❑ Nov 1995, b&w Cover: 2.75 **NM** value: **Cover or less**
Bk 1 ❑ Jan 1994 Cover: 6.95 **NM** value: **Cover or less**

SCAB — Fantaco

1 ❑ b&w Cover: 3.50 **NM** value: **Cover or less**
2 ❑ b&w Cover: 3.50 **NM** value: **Cover or less**

SCALES OF THE DRAGON — Sundragon

1 ❑ Mar 1997, b&w Cover: 1.95 **NM** value: **Cover or less**
• Flip-book.

SCAMP (DELL) — Dell

5 ❑ Mar 1958 Cover: 0.10 **NM** value: **40.00**
6 ❑ Jun 1958 Cover: 0.10 **NM** value: **25.00**
7 ❑ Sep 1958 Cover: 0.10 **NM** value: **25.00**
8 ❑ Dec 1958 Cover: 0.10 **NM** value: **25.00**
9 ❑ Mar 1959 Cover: 0.10 **NM** value: **25.00**
10 ❑ Jun 1959 Cover: 0.10 **NM** value: **25.00**
11 ❑ Sep 1959 Cover: 0.10 **NM** value: **25.00**
12 ❑ Dec 1959 Cover: 0.10 **NM** value: **25.00**
• **CGC:** 1 graded, best 9.0
13 ❑ Mar 1960 Cover: 0.10 **NM** value: **25.00**
14 ❑ Jun 1960 Cover: 0.10 **NM** value: **25.00**
15 ❑ Sep 1960 Cover: 0.10 **NM** value: **25.00**
16 ❑ Dec 1960 Cover: 0.10 **NM** value: **25.00**

SCAMP (WALT DISNEY...) — Whitman

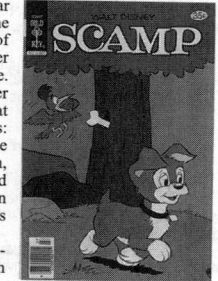

One of Disney's most popular motion pictures was Lady and the Tramp (1955), the lovable story of a heroic mutt and a refined cocker spaniel who meet and fall in love. In the finale of the film (Spoiler Warning), the pair is shown at Christmas, along with their pups: three scampering Ladies and one small Tramp. Not named in the film, Tramp Jr. was quickly dubbed Scamp, and his character design was that of a puppy version of his father.

Scamp starred in this long-running comic-book series, along with a collection of canine friends, including occasional appearances by his mom and dad. In this title, it seemed that Scamp was always either getting into trouble or helping to stop a burglar from climbing in somebody's window. The stories were charming, the Al Hubbard art was top-drawer, and the interplay between Scamp and the supporting characters was delightful. With Scamp, Walt Disney — and Western Publishing — once again proved itself a class act when it comes to family entertainment.

1 ❑ ca. 1968 Cover: 0.12 **NM** value: **10.00**
2 ❑ Mar 1969 Cover: 0.15 **NM** value: **6.00**
3 ❑ ca. 1970 Cover: 0.15 **NM** value: **6.00**
4 ❑ Nov 1970 Cover: 0.15 **NM** value: **6.00**
5 ❑ Feb 1971 Cover: 0.15 **NM** value: **6.00**
6 ❑ Oct 1971 Cover: 0.15 **NM** value: **4.50**
7 ❑ 1972 Cover: 0.15 **NM** value: **4.50**
8 ❑ 1972 Cover: 0.15 **NM** value: **4.50**
9 ❑ Nov 1972 Cover: 0.15 **NM** value: **4.50**
10 ❑ Feb 1973 Cover: 0.20 **NM** value: **4.50**
11 ❑ Jun 1973 Cover: 0.20 **NM** value: **3.50**

12 ❑ Jul 1973 Cover: 0.20 **NM** value: **3.50**
13 ❑ Sep 1973 Cover: 0.20 **NM** value: **3.50**
14 ❑ Nov 1973 Cover: 0.20 **NM** value: **3.50**
15 ❑ Jan 1974 Cover: 0.20 **NM** value: **3.50**
16 ❑ Mar 1974 Cover: 0.20 **NM** value: **3.50**
17 ❑ May 1974 Cover: 0.20 **NM** value: **3.50**
18 ❑ Jul 1974 Cover: 0.20 **NM** value: **3.50**
19 ❑ Sep 1974 Cover: 0.25 **NM** value: **3.50**
20 ❑ Nov 1974 Cover: 0.25 **NM** value: **3.50**
21 ❑ Jan 1975 Cover: 0.25 **NM** value: **2.50**
22 ❑ Mar 1975 Cover: 0.25 **NM** value: **2.50**
23 ❑ May 1975 Cover: 0.25 **NM** value: **2.50**
24 ❑ Jul 1975 Cover: 0.25 **NM** value: **2.50**
25 ❑ Sep 1975 Cover: 0.25 **NM** value: **2.50**
26 ❑ Nov 1975 Cover: 0.25 **NM** value: **2.50**
27 ❑ Jan 1976 Cover: 0.25 **NM** value: **2.50**
28 ❑ Mar 1976 Cover: 0.25 **NM** value: **2.50**
29 ❑ May 1976 Cover: 0.25 **NM** value: **2.50**
30 ❑ Jul 1976 Cover: 0.25 **NM** value: **2.50**
Burglar Baggers; Feats For The Fearless; Hero Hound; The Guest
31 ❑ Sep 1976 Cover: 0.30 **NM** value: **2.50**
32 ❑ Nov 1976 Cover: 0.30 **NM** value: **2.50**
33 ❑ Jan 1977 Cover: 0.30 **NM** value: **2.50**
34 ❑ Mar 1977 Cover: 0.30 **NM** value: **2.50**
35 ❑ May 1977 Cover: 0.30 **NM** value: **2.50**
36 ❑ Jul 1977 Cover: 0.30 **NM** value: **2.50**
37 ❑ Sep 1977 Cover: 0.30 **NM** value: **2.50**
38 ❑ Nov 1977 Cover: 0.30 **NM** value: **2.50**
39 ❑ Jan 1978 Cover: 0.35 **NM** value: **2.50**
40 ❑ Mar 1978 Cover: 0.35 **NM** value: **2.50**
41 ❑ May 1978 Cover: 0.35 **NM** value: **2.00**
42 ❑ Jul 1978 Cover: 0.35 **NM** value: **2.00**
43 ❑ Sep 1978 Cover: 0.35 **NM** value: **2.00**
44 ❑ Nov 1979 Cover: 0.35 **NM** value: **2.00**
45 ❑ Jan 1979 Cover: 0.35 **NM** value: **2.00**
final issue.

SCAN — Iconografix

1 ❑ b&w Cover: 2.95 **NM** value: **Cover or less**
A: Matt Howarth
2 ❑ b&w Cover: 2.95 **NM** value: **Cover or less**
A: Matt Howarth

SCANDALS — Thorby

1 ❑ Cover: 2.95 **NM** value: **Cover or less**

SCANDAL SHEET — Arriba

1 ❑ b&w Cover: 2.50 **NM** value: **Cover or less**

SCARAB — DC / Vertigo

0 ❑ Mar 1994 Cover: 1.95 **NM** value: **Cover or less**
Paradise Defiled **A:** Scot Eaton; Glenn Fabry(cover) **W:** John Smith
1 ❑ Nov 1993 Cover: 1.95 **NM** value: **Cover or less**
Circ: CapCity orders: **18,950**
All Roads Lead to the Minotaur **A:** Scot Eaton; Glenn Fabry(cover) **W:** John Smith
2 ❑ Dec 1993 Cover: 1.95 **NM** value: **Cover or less**
Circ: CapCity orders: **11,600**
Lost and Found **A:** Scot Eaton; Glenn Fabry(cover) **W:** John Smith ★ Appearance of Phantom Stranger.
3 ❑ Jan 1994 Cover: 1.95 **NM** value: **Cover or less**
Circ: CapCity orders: **8,250**
Moveable Feasts **A:** Scot Eaton; Tony Luke(cover) **W:** John Smith
4 ❑ Feb 1994 Cover: 1.95 **NM** value: **Cover or less**
Circ: CapCity orders: **8,950**
A Dawn Chorus **A:** Scot Eaton; Glenn Fabry(cover) **W:** John Smith
5 ❑ Mar 1994 Cover: 1.95 **NM** value: **Cover or less**
Circ: CapCity orders: **8,350**
A: Scot Eaton; Glenn Fabry(cover) **W:** John Smith
6 ❑ Apr 1994 Cover: 1.95 **NM** value: **Cover or less**
Circ: CapCity orders: **7,650**
A: Scot Eaton; Glenn Fabry(cover) **W:** John Smith
7 ❑ May 1994 Cover: 1.95 **NM** value: **Cover or less**
Circ: CapCity orders: **7,300**
The Power and the Glory **A:** Scot Eaton; Glenn Fabry(cover) **W:** John Smith
8 ❑ Jun 1994 Cover: 1.95 **NM** value: **Cover or less**
Circ: CapCity orders: **7,000**
What the Rabbit Saw **A:** Scot Eaton; Glenn Fabry(cover) **W:** John Smith

SCARAMOUCH — Innovation

1 ❑ b&w Cover: 2.25 **NM** value: **Cover or less**
Death Warmed Over **A:** Tom Reyn **W:** Alan Sisson; Dan Tyree
2 ❑ b&w Cover: 2.25 **NM** value: **Cover or less**
A: Tom Reyn **W:** Alan Sisson; Dan Tyree

SCARECROW (VILLAINS) — DC

1 ❑ Feb 1998 Cover: 1.95 **NM** value: **Cover or less**
Mistress of Fear • New Year's Evil **A:** Duncan Fegredo **W:** Peter Milligan

SCARE TACTICS — DC

1 ❑ Dec 1996 Cover: 2.25 **NM** value: **Cover or less**
Circ: Diamd. preorders: **19,373**
Blitzkrieg Bop **A:** Anthony Williams **W:** Len Kaminski ★ Origin of Scare Tactics. ★ 1st Appearance of Screamqueen (Nina Skorzeny), Slither (Jim), Fang (Jake), F, Arnold Burnsteel, Grossout.
2 ❑ Jan 1997 Cover: 2.25 **NM** value: **Cover or less**
Circ: Diamd. preorders: **12,898**
Haunting Season • Road Trip **A:** Anthony Williams **W:** Len Kaminski ★ 1st Appearance of Scaremobile. ★ 2nd Appearance of Slit. ★ 2nd Appearance of Screamqueen (Nina Skorzeny). ★ 2nd Appearance of Slither (Jim). ★ 2nd Appearance of Fang (Jake). ★ 2nd Appearance of Arnold Burnsteel. ★ 2nd Appearance of Grossout.
3 ❑ Feb 1997 Cover: 2.25 **NM** value: **Cover or less**
Circ: Diamd. preorders: **11,365**
A: Anthony Williams **W:** Len Kaminski
4 ❑ Mar 1997 Cover: 2.25 **NM** value: **Cover or less**
Circ: Diamd. preorders: **8,901**
Big for his Age **A:** Anthony Williams **W:** Len Kaminski ★ Origin of Phil.
5 ❑ Apr 1997 Cover: 2.25 **NM** value: **Cover or less**
Circ: Diamd. preorders: **7,432**
Morbid Fascination • Valentine's Day Nightmare **A:** Anthony Williams **W:** Len Kaminski
6 ❑ May 1997 Cover: 2.25 **NM** value: **Cover or less**
Circ: Diamd. preorders: **6,646**
A: Anthony Williams **W:** Len Kaminski
7 ❑ Jun 1997 Cover: 2.25 **NM** value: **Cover or less**
Circ: Diamd. preorders: **6,566**
A: Anthony Williams **W:** Len Kaminski
8 ❑ Jul 1997 Cover: 2.25 **NM** value: **Cover or less**
Circ: Diamd. preorders: **7,166**
Convergenge, Part 4 **A:** Anthony Williams **W:** Len Kaminski
9 ❑ Aug 1997 Cover: 2.25 **NM** value: **Cover or less**
Circ: Diamd. preorders: **5,925**
• series goes on hiatus; story continues in Impulse Plus #1 **A:** Anthony Williams **W:** Len Kaminski ★ Origin of Slither.
10 ❑ Jan 1998 Cover: 2.25 **NM** value: **Cover or less**
Circ: Diamd. preorders: **5,052**
A: Anthony Williams **W:** Len Kaminski ★ Appearance of Batman.
11 ❑ Feb 1998 Cover: 2.25 **NM** value: **Cover or less**
Circ: Diamd. preorders: **5,479**
A: Anthony Williams **W:** Len Kaminski ★ Death of Slither.
12 ❑ Mar 1998 Cover: 2.25 **NM** value: **Cover or less**
Circ: Diamd. preorders: **4,859**
final issue. • Phil transforms **A:** Anthony Williams **W:** Len Kaminski

SCARLET CRUSH — Awesome

1 ❑ Jan 1998 Cover: 2.50 **NM** value: **Cover or less**
Circ: Diamd. preorders: **32,201**
A: John Stinsman **W:** John Stinsman
2 ❑ Feb 1998 Cover: 2.50 **NM** value: **Cover or less**
Circ: Diamd. preorders: **20,591**
A: John Stinsman **W:** John Stinsman

SCARLET IN GASLIGHT — Eternity

Two of literature's most prominent characters meet in this black-and-white tale of horror. Arthur Conan Doyle's famous detective Sherlock Holmes and the ever-present Dr. Watson are drawn into an adventure beyond anything they have ever experienced, when they face the timeless evil of Bram Stoker's Dracula.

Investigating a young woman's mysterious illness, Holmes and Watson find her already under the care of Dr. Van Helsing, whose methods at first seem odd. But when the two detectives find themselves battling her demonic attacker, they barely manage to survive. Unfortunately, the supremely logical mind of Sherlock Holmes is unable to reconcile his concept of reality with the obviously supernatural nature of his vampiric enemy. It appears that Dracula will have free rein to terrorize London, unless Watson and Van Helsing can bring Holmes back from the edge of insanity.

1 ❑ Mar 1988, b&w Cover: 1.95 **NM** value: **Cover or less**
• Sherlock Holmes vs. Dracula **A:** Seppo Makkinen **W:** Martin Powell
2 ❑ Apr 1988 Cover: 1.95 **NM** value: **Cover or less**
A: Seppo Makkinen **W:** Martin Powell
3 ❑ May 1988 Cover: 1.95 **NM** value: **Cover or less**
A: Seppo Makkinen **W:** Martin Powell
4 ❑ Jun 1988 Cover: 1.95 **NM** value: **Cover or less**
A: Seppo Makkinen **W:** Martin Powell
Bk 1 ❑ ca. 1988, b&w Cover: 7.95 **NM** value: **Cover or less**
• Collected #1-4 **A:** Seppo Makkinen **W:** Martin Powell

SCARLET KISS: THE VAMPYRE — All American

1 ❑ b&w Cover: 2.95 **NM** value: **Cover or less**
Dawne Burnes Vampire **A:** Charles Walker **W:** David Gomien

SCARLET SCORPION/DARKSHADE — AC

1 ❑ Jul 1995 Cover: 3.50 **NM** value: **Cover or less**
Ghost **A:** Mark Heike; Darrel Goza; David Jacob Beckett; Eric Coile; Mike Mikolajczyk **W:** Rik Levins; Bill Black
2 ❑ 1995 Cover: 3.50 **NM** value: **Cover or less**

There are two different pricing tiers in the modern comic-book hobby. **The prices seen above** are the prices we have seen **loose copies** of these issues reliably fetch in a variety of environments. Condition alters the price by the fractions seen on the bar on the bottom of left-hand pages of this book. **Comics graded by CGC** usually sell for more. Use the guide on the bottom of right-hand pages of this book to estimate what copies have brought on eBay.

SCARLET SPIDER — Marvel

For a short time in 1995, Marvel's Spider-Man titles went on a brief hiatus, when the infamous "Clone Saga" was in full swing. The Spidey many readers had known and loved since The Amazing Spider-Man #151 was revealed to be a clone, and the clone that had supposedly died in that issue was revealed to be the real McCoy and going by the name Ben Reilly, aka The Scarlet Spider.

Now, the gimmick: For a few months, Marvel replaced its Spider-Man titles with Scarlet Spider titles: The Amazing Spider-Man became The Amazing Scarlet Spider, Web of Spider-Man became Web of Scarlet Spider, The Spectacular Spider-Man became The Spectacular Scarlet Spider, and Spider-Man became Scarlet Spider. Get the picture? This is probably one of the more interesting aspects of the "Clone Saga," since it allowed readers to enjoy an old-fashioned, wisecracking, unmarried "Spider-Man" again.

1 ❑ Nov 1995 Cover: 1.95 **NM** value: **2.00**
Virtual Mortality, Part 3 **A:** Gil Kane **W:** Howard Mackie; Tod DeZago
2 ❑ Dec 1995 Cover: 1.95 **NM** value: **2.00**
Cyberwar, Part 3 • concludes in Spectacular Scarlet Spider #2 **A:** John Romita Jr. **W:** Howard Mackie

SCARLET SPIDER UNLIMITED — Marvel

1 ❑ Nov 1995 Cover: 3.95 **NM** value: **Cover or less**
You Say You Want An Evolution! **A:** Tod Smith **W:** Glenn Herdling

SCARLETT — DC

1 ❑ Jan 1993 Cover: 2.95 **NM** value: **3.00**
Circ: CapCity orders: **16,950**
Blood Of Innocence **A:** Jim Fern **W:** Keith Wilson; Tom Joyner ★ Origin of Scarlett. ★ 1st Appearance of Scarlett.
2 ❑ Feb 1993 Cover: 2.95 **NM** value: **Cover or less**
Circ: CapCity orders: **10,500**
3 ❑ Mar 1993 Cover: 1.75 **NM** value: **2.00**
Circ: CapCity orders: **9,200**
4 ❑ Apr 1993 Cover: 1.75 **NM** value: **Cover or less**
Circ: CapCity orders: **9,900**
5 ❑ May 1993 Cover: 1.75 **NM** value: **Cover or less**
Circ: CapCity orders: **9,300**
6 ❑ Jun 1993 Cover: 1.75 **NM** value: **Cover or less**
Circ: CapCity orders: **8,250**
Blood Of The Damned, Part 1 **A:** Gray Morrow **W:** Keith Wilson; Tom Joyner
7 ❑ Jul 1993 Cover: 1.75 **NM** value: **Cover or less**
Circ: CapCity orders: **7,700**
8 ❑ Aug 1993 Cover: 1.75 **NM** value: **Cover or less**
Circ: CapCity orders: **7,150**
9 ❑ Sep 1993 Cover: 1.75 **NM** value: **Cover or less**
Circ: CapCity orders: **6,100**
10 ❑ Oct 1993 Cover: 1.75 **NM** value: **Cover or less**
Circ: CapCity orders: **5,600**
11 ❑ Nov 1993 Cover: 1.75 **NM** value: **Cover or less**
Circ: CapCity orders: **4,650**
12 ❑ Dec 1993 Cover: 1.75 **NM** value: **Cover or less**
Circ: CapCity orders: **4,450**
13 ❑ Jan 1994 Cover: 1.75 **NM** value: **Cover or less**
Circ: CapCity orders: **3,950**
14 ❑ Feb 1994 Cover: 1.75 **NM** value: **Cover or less**
Circ: CapCity orders: **3,650**
final issue.

SCARLET THUNDER — Slave Labor / Amaze Ink

1 ❑ Nov 1995 Cover: 1.50 **NM** value: **Cover or less**
A: Rick Forgus **W:** Dan Vado ★ Origin of Red Bolt, Blue Streak. ★ 1st Appearance of Red Bolt, Adam Garrison, Jason Pine, Dot.
2 ❑ Feb 1996 Cover: 1.50 **NM** value: **Cover or less**
• 1st apperance Blue Streak **A:** Rick Forgus **W:** Dan Vado ★ 2nd Appearance of Red Bolt. ★ 2nd Appearance of Red Bolt. ★ 2nd Appearance of Adam Garrison. ★ 2nd Appearance of Adam Garrison. ★ 2nd Appearance of Jason Pine. ★ 2nd Appearance of Jason Pine. ★ 2nd Appearance of Dot. ★ 2nd Appearance of Dot.
3 ❑ May 1996 Cover: 2.50 **NM** value: **Cover or less**
A: Rick Forgus **W:** Dan Vado ★ 1st Appearance of Betty Joseph, Oskar (cameo). ★ 2nd Appearance of Blue Streak.
4 ❑ Dec 1996 Cover: 2.50 **NM** value: **Cover or less**
A: Rick Forgus **W:** Dan Vado ★ Origin of Lady Liberty. ★ 1st Appearance of Oskar (full), Lady Liberty. ★ 2nd Appearance of Betty Joseph.

SCARLETT PILGRIM — Last Gasp

1 ❑ Cover: 1.00 **NM** value: **Cover or less**
A: Trina Robbins **W:** Trina Robbins

SCARLET WITCH — Marvel

1 ❑ Jan 1994 Cover: 1.75 **NM** value: **Cover or less**
Circ: CapCity orders: **26,300** • **CGC:** 1 graded, best 9.4
Dark Designs **A:** John Higgins **W:** Andy Lanning; Dan Abnett
2 ❑ Feb 1994 Cover: 1.75 **NM** value: **Cover or less**
Circ: CapCity orders: **16,450**
3 ❑ Mar 1994 Cover: 1.75 **NM** value: **Cover or less**
Circ: CapCity orders: **13,600**
4 ❑ Apr 1994 Cover: 1.75 **NM** value: **Cover or less**
Circ: CapCity orders: **11,350**

SCARLET ZOMBIE, THE — Comax

All issues are adults only.

1 ❑ b&w Cover: 2.95 **NM** value: **Cover or less**

CGC-graded: Multiply prices above by **33 for 9.9 M • 16 for 9.8 NM/M • 7 for 9.6 NM+ • 5 for 9.4 NM • 2.5 for 9.2 NM- • 1.5 for 9.0 VF/NM**

SCARY! — Fantagraphics

Bk 1 ❑ May 1997, b&w — Cover: 12.95 — **NM** value: **Cover or less**

SCARY BOOK, THE — Caliber

1 ❑ b&w — Cover: 2.50 — **NM** value: **Cover or less**
2 ❑ b&w — Cover: 1.75 — **NM** value: **2.50**

SCARY GODMOTHER — Sirius

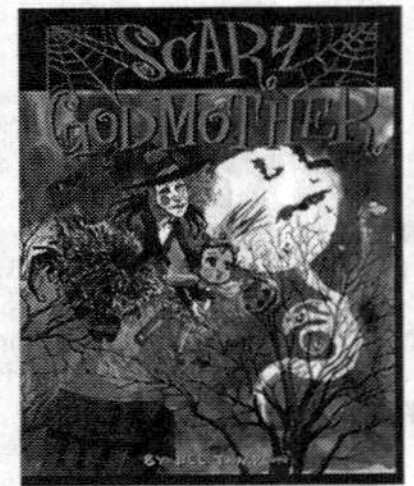

Halloween is a thrilling night for kids, but for Hannah Marie this Halloween is especially exciting. It is the first time she will be going trick-or-treating with the big kids instead of her parents. However, her cousin Jimmy, charged with her care, resents "babysitting" and the hindrance her presence will be to his candy accumulation. He and his friends decide to take Hannah to a large empty house and tell her that she must leave candy as tribute to the hungry monsters. But Jimmy's scheme to scare Hannah into wanting to go home does not take into account Hannah's own special protector, her Scary Godmother.

This is a story that evokes the special naivete of children (even those given to succumbing to selfishness) and the triumph of innocence. Written and illustrated by Jill Thompson (Black Orchid, Sandman), Scary Godmother is a charming fantasy suitable for everyone and especially appropriate for parents to read to their preschoolers.

1 ❑ May 2001 — Cover: 2.95 — **NM** value: **Cover or less**
Circ: Diamd. preorders: **5,628**
🕮 The Search for Mister Boogeylegs **A:** Jill Thompson **W:** Jill Thompson
Bk 1 ❑ Sep 1997 — Cover: 19.95 — **NM** value: **Cover or less**
hardcover. **A:** Jill Thompson **W:** Jill Thompson

SCARY GODMOTHER: BLOODY VALENTINE — Sirius

1 ❑ Feb 1998 — Cover: 3.95 — **NM** value: **Cover or less**
Circ: Diamd. preorders: **5,773**
🕮 The Fright Side **A:** Jill Thompson **W:** Jill Thompson

SCARY GODMOTHER HOLIDAY SPOOKTACULAR — Sirius

1 ❑ Nov 1998, b&w — Cover: 2.95 — **NM** value: **Cover or less**
Circ: Diamd. preorders: **5,888**
wraparound cover. 🕮 The Fright Side; The Search for Mister Boogeylegs; Tricks or Treats **A:** Evan Dorkin; Dan Brereton; Bob Fingerman; Jill Thompson; Terry Laban; Sarah Dyer **W:** Jill Thompson

SCARY GODMOTHER REVENGE OF JIMMY — Sirius

1 ❑ — Cover: 19.95 — **NM** value: **Cover or less**
hardcover. **W:** Jill Thompson

SCARY GODMOTHER: WILD ABOUT HARRY — Sirius

1 ❑ ca. 2000, b&w — Cover: 2.95 — **NM** value: **Cover or less**
Circ: Diamd. preorders: **5,788**
A: Jill Thompson **W:** Jill Thompson
2 ❑ ca. 2000, b&w — Cover: 2.95 — **NM** value: **Cover or less**
Circ: Diamd. preorders: **5,114**
A: Jill Thompson **W:** Jill Thompson
Bk 1 ❑ — Cover: 9.95 — **NM** value: **Cover or less**
• Collects series **A:** Jill Thompson **W:** Jill Thompson

SCARY TALES — Charlton

This Charlton horror title lasted 46 issues in a sporadic run between 1975 and 1984. In a way, it is the archetypical Charlton horror title, featuring the usual cast of monsters, murder, and the walking dead. These stories are generally well-plotted, ironic tales in which evil always got its due. Steve Ditko illustrates many of the stories, using his deceptively simple, slightly quirky artistic style to good effect.

Unfortunately, Scary Tales also epitomizes much of what was wrong with Charlton at the time, including on-and-off publication schedules and some of the worst printing quality in the business. Despite all this, Scary Tales is a worthwhile reading experience for lovers of horror fiction.

1 ❑ Aug 1975 — Cover: 0.35 — **NM** value: **5.00**
★ Origin of Countess Von Bludd. ★ 1st Appearance of Countess Von Bludd.
2 ❑ Oct 1975 — Cover: 0.25 — **NM** value: **3.00**
3 ❑ Dec 1975 — Cover: 0.25 — **NM** value: **3.00**
4 ❑ Feb 1976 — Cover: 0.25 — **NM** value: **3.00**
5 ❑ Apr 1976 — Cover: 0.30 — **NM** value: **3.00**
6 ❑ Jun 1976 — Cover: 0.30 — **NM** value: **2.50**
7 ❑ Sep 1976 — Cover: 0.30 — **NM** value: **2.50**
8 ❑ Nov 1976 — Cover: 0.30 — **NM** value: **2.50**
9 ❑ Jan 1977 — Cover: 0.30 — **NM** value: **2.50**
10 ❑ Sep 1977 — Cover: 0.35 — **NM** value: **2.50**
11 ❑ Jan 1978 — Cover: 0.35 — **NM** value: **2.00**
12 ❑ Mar 1978 — Cover: 0.35 — **NM** value: **2.00**
13 ❑ Apr 1978 — Cover: 0.35 — **NM** value: **2.00**
14 ❑ May 1978 — Cover: 0.35 — **NM** value: **2.00**
🕮 The Heart Of Dibiju; Stop The Clock; Only A Game
15 ❑ Jul 1978 — Cover: 0.35 — **NM** value: **2.00**
16 ❑ Oct 1978 — Cover: 0.35 — **NM** value: **2.00**
17 ❑ Dec 1978 — Cover: 0.35 — **NM** value: **2.00**
18 ❑ Feb 1979 — Cover: 0.35 — **NM** value: **2.00**
19 ❑ Apr 1979 — Cover: 0.40 — **NM** value: **2.00**
20 ❑ Jun 1979 — Cover: 0.40 — **NM** value: **2.00**
21 ❑ Aug 1980 — Cover: 0.40 — **NM** value: **2.00**
22 ❑ Oct 1980 — Cover: 0.50 — **NM** value: **2.00**
23 ❑ Dec 1980 — Cover: 0.50 — **NM** value: **2.00**
24 ❑ Feb 1981 — Cover: 0.50 — **NM** value: **2.00**
25 ❑ Apr 1981 — Cover: 0.50 — **NM** value: **2.00**
26 ❑ Jun 1981 — Cover: 0.50 — **NM** value: **2.00**
27 ❑ Aug 1981 — Cover: 0.50 — **NM** value: **2.00**
28 ❑ Oct 1981 — Cover: 0.50 — **NM** value: **2.00**
29 ❑ Dec 1981 — Cover: 0.50 — **NM** value: **2.00**
30 ❑ Feb 1982 — Cover: 0.60 — **NM** value: **2.00**
31 ❑ Apr 1982 — Cover: 0.60 — **NM** value: **2.00**
32 ❑ Jun 1982 — Cover: 0.60 — **NM** value: **2.00**
33 ❑ Aug 1982 — Cover: 0.60 — **NM** value: **2.00**
34 ❑ Oct 1982 — Cover: 0.60 — **NM** value: **2.00**
35 ❑ Dec 1982 — Cover: 0.60 — **NM** value: **2.00**
36 ❑ Feb 1983 — Cover: 0.60 — **NM** value: **2.00**
37 ❑ Apr 1983 — Cover: 0.60 — **NM** value: **2.00**
38 ❑ Jun 1983 — Cover: 0.60 — **NM** value: **2.00**
39 ❑ Aug 1983 — Cover: 0.60 — **NM** value: **2.00**
40 ❑ Oct 1983 — Cover: 0.60 — **NM** value: **2.00**
41 ❑ Dec 1983 — Cover: 0.60 — **NM** value: **2.00**
42 ❑ Feb 1984 — Cover: 0.60 — **NM** value: **2.00**
43 ❑ Apr 1984 — Cover: 0.60 — **NM** value: **2.00**
44 ❑ Jun 1984 — Cover: 0.60 — **NM** value: **2.00**
45 ❑ Aug 1984 — Cover: 0.75 — **NM** value: **2.00**
46 ❑ Oct 1984 — Cover: 0.75 — **NM** value: **2.00**
final issue.

SCATTERBRAIN — Dark Horse

1 ❑ Jun 1998 — Cover: 2.95 — **NM** value: **Cover or less**
Circ: Diamd. preorders: **9,505**
🕮 Abu Gung and the Beanstalk; Bring on the Robots; Hook, Line, & Sinker; The Cluck of Fear; Tales of Red Erchie; Pop & Norton **A:** Pat McEown; Mike Mignola; Linda Medley; Steve Parkhouse; Dave Cooper; Chris Garbutt; Keith Young **W:** Pat McEown; Mike Mignola; Linda Medley; Steve Parkhouse; Dave Cooper; Chris Garbutt; Gavin McInnes
2 ❑ Jul 1998 — Cover: 2.95 — **NM** value: **Cover or less**
Circ: Diamd. preorders: **5,070**
3 ❑ Aug 1998 — Cover: 2.95 — **NM** value: **Cover or less**
Circ: Diamd. preorders: **4,906**
4 ❑ Sep 1998 — Cover: 2.95 — **NM** value: **Cover or less**
Circ: Diamd. preorders: **5,113**
C: Sergio Aragonés

SCATTERED — Scattered

1 ❑ — Cover: 2.50 — **NM** value: **Cover or less**
2 ❑ — Cover: 2.50 — **NM** value: **Cover or less**
3 ❑ — Cover: 2.50 — **NM** value: **Cover or less**
4 ❑ — Cover: 2.50 — **NM** value: **Cover or less**
5 ❑ — Cover: 2.50 — **NM** value: **Cover or less**
6 ❑ — Cover: 2.50 — **NM** value: **Cover or less**
7 ❑ — Cover: 2.50 — **NM** value: **Cover or less**
8 ❑ — Cover: 2.50 — **NM** value: **Cover or less**
9 ❑ — Cover: 2.50 — **NM** value: **Cover or less**
10 ❑ — Cover: 2.50 — **NM** value: **Cover or less**
11 ❑ — Cover: 2.50 — **NM** value: **Cover or less**
12 ❑ — Cover: 2.50 — **NM** value: **Cover or less**
13 ❑ — Cover: 2.50 — **NM** value: **Cover or less**
14 ❑ — Cover: 2.50 — **NM** value: **Cover or less**
15 ❑ — Cover: 2.50 — **NM** value: **Cover or less**
16 ❑ — Cover: 2.50 — **NM** value: **Cover or less**
17 ❑ — Cover: 2.50 — **NM** value: **Cover or less**
18 ❑ — Cover: 2.50 — **NM** value: **Cover or less**
19 ❑ — Cover: 2.50 — **NM** value: **Cover or less**
20 ❑ — Cover: 2.50 — **NM** value: **Cover or less**
21 ❑ — Cover: 2.50 — **NM** value: **Cover or less**
22 ❑ — Cover: 2.50 — **NM** value: **Cover or less**
23 ❑ — Cover: 2.50 — **NM** value: **Cover or less**
24 ❑ — Cover: 2.50 — **NM** value: **Cover or less**
🕮 Seeker; Comics to Bore and Confuse You • Wendy revealed as Wormwood **A:** Jason Dube; Jesse Hamm **W:** Jason Dube; Jesse Hamm
25 ❑ — Cover: 2.50 — **NM** value: **Cover or less**
🕮 Seeker, Part 2; Comics to Bore and Confuse You; Black • Allen's power revealed **A:** Jason Dube; Jesse Hamm; Mike Banks **W:** Jason Dube; Jesse Hamm; Mike Banks
26 ❑ — Cover: 2.50 — **NM** value: **Cover or less**
🕮 Home Sickness; Comics to Bore and Confuse You **A:** Jason Dube; Jesse Hamm **W:** Jason Dube; Jesse Hamm
27 ❑ — Cover: 2.50 — **NM** value: **Cover or less**
🕮 Suddenly Inevitable; Babies and Carrots **A:** Jason Dube **W:** Jason Dube; Tiffany Jepson
28 ❑ — Cover: 2.50 — **NM** value: **Cover or less**
🕮 Suddenly Inevitable, Part 2; Comics to Bore & Confuse You; The Parting **A:** Jason Dube; Jesse Hamm **W:** Jason Dube; Jesse Hamm; Daniel Sonner
29 ❑ — Cover: 2.50 — **NM** value: **Cover or less**
🕮 Suddenly Inevitable, Part 3 **A:** Jason Dube **W:** Jason Dube
30 ❑ — Cover: 2.50 — **NM** value: **Cover or less**

SCAVENGERS (FLEETWAY/QUALITY) — Fleetway-Quality

1 ❑ Feb 1988 — Cover: 1.25 — **NM** value: **1.50**
Circ: CapCity orders: **2,725**
• Judge Dredd
2 ❑ Mar 1988 — Cover: 1.25 — **NM** value: **1.50**
Circ: CapCity orders: **1,875**
🕮 Flesh; Judge Dredd: Bob & Carol & Ted & Ringo • Judge Dredd **A:** Ron Smith; Ramon Sola **W:** R.E. Wright; T.B. Grover
3 ❑ Apr 1988 — Cover: 1.25 — **NM** value: **1.50**
Circ: CapCity orders: **1,525**
• Judge Dredd
4 ❑ May 1988 — Cover: 1.25 — **NM** value: **1.50**
Circ: CapCity orders: **1,350**
• Judge Dredd
5 ❑ Jun 1988 — Cover: 1.25 — **NM** value: **1.50**
Circ: CapCity orders: **1,325**
6 ❑ Jul 1988 — Cover: 1.50 — **NM** value: **Cover or less**
Circ: CapCity orders: **1,450**
7 ❑ Aug 1988 — Cover: 1.50 — **NM** value: **Cover or less**
Circ: CapCity orders: **1,375**
8 ❑ Sep 1988 — Cover: 1.50 — **NM** value: **Cover or less**
Circ: CapCity orders: **1,275**
9 ❑ Oct 1988 — Cover: 1.50 — **NM** value: **Cover or less**
Circ: CapCity orders: **1,200**
10 ❑ Nov 1988 — Cover: 1.50 — **NM** value: **Cover or less**
Circ: CapCity orders: **1,175**
11 ❑ Dec 1988 — Cover: 1.50 — **NM** value: **Cover or less**
Circ: CapCity orders: **1,125**
12 ❑ Jan 1989 — Cover: 1.50 — **NM** value: **Cover or less**
Circ: CapCity orders: **1,075**
13 ❑ 1989 — Cover: 1.50 — **NM** value: **Cover or less**
Circ: CapCity orders: **1,000**
14 ❑ 1989 — Cover: 1.50 — **NM** value: **Cover or less**
Circ: CapCity orders: **1,025**

SCAVENGERS (TRIUMPHANT) — Triumphant

0 ❑ Mar 1994 — **NM** value: **1.00**
Circ: CapCity orders: **3,235**
• giveaway. **A:** Francheso **W:** John Riley; Eric Shefferman
0/A ❑ Mar 1994 — Cover: 2.50 — **NM** value: **Cover or less**
• 18,000-copy edition. **A:** Francheso **W:** John Riley; Eric Shefferman
0/B ❑ Mar 1994 — Cover: 2.50 — **NM** value: **Cover or less**
• 5000-copy edition. **A:** Francheso **W:** John Riley; Eric Shefferman
1 ❑ Jul 1993 — Cover: 2.50 — **NM** value: **Cover or less**
Circ: CapCity orders: **5,485**
1/Ash ❑ Jul 1993 — Cover: 2.50 — **NM** value: **Cover or less**
• ashcan edition. 🕮 Redemption **A:** Francheso **W:** Jarrod Post
2 ❑ Aug 1993 — Cover: 2.50 — **NM** value: **Cover or less**
3 ❑ Sep 1993 — Cover: 2.50 — **NM** value: **Cover or less**
Circ: CapCity orders: **3,300**
🕮 Counter Strike **A:** David Brewer **W:** John Riley
4 ❑ Oct 1993 — Cover: 2.50 — **NM** value: **Cover or less**
Circ: CapCity orders: **3,350**
5 ❑ Nov 1993 — Cover: 2.50 — **NM** value: **Cover or less**
Circ: CapCity orders: **6,025**
• Unleashed! ★ Death of Jack Hanal.
6 ❑ Dec 1993 — Cover: 2.50 — **NM** value: **Cover or less**
Circ: CapCity orders: **4,830**
• Unleashed!
7 ❑ Jan 1994 — Cover: 2.50 — **NM** value: **Cover or less**
Circ: CapCity orders: **3,910**
8 ❑ Feb 1994 — Cover: 2.50 — **NM** value: **Cover or less**
Circ: CapCity orders: **3,405**
9 ❑ Mar 1994 — Cover: 2.50 — **NM** value: **Cover or less**
Circ: CapCity orders: **2,670**
10 ❑ Apr 1994 — Cover: 2.50 — **NM** value: **Cover or less**
Circ: CapCity orders: **2,237**
🕮 Snowblind **A:** J. Adams Walters **W:** John Riley
11 ❑ May 1994 — Cover: 2.50 — **NM** value: **Cover or less**
Circ: CapCity orders: **1,815**

SCC CONVENTION SPECIAL — Super Crew

1 ❑ — Cover: 2.25 — **NM** value: **Cover or less**
• 1994 Convention Special **A:** Chris Crosby; Bobby Crosby **W:** Chris Crosby; Bobby Crosby

SCENARIO A — Antarctic

1 ❑ Jul 1998, b&w — Cover: 2.95 — **NM** value: **Cover or less**
A: David Hahn **W:** Damon Watson
2 ❑ Sep 1998, b&w — Cover: 2.95 — **NM** value: **Cover or less**
A: David Hahn **W:** Damon Watson

SCENE OF THE CRIME — DC / Vertigo

Jack Herriman is a man with a past. He lost an eye when criminals took revenge on his policeman father for hanging snitches out to dry after a big bust. He's made some mistakes but now he puts his natural ability to get into trouble to good use: He's a private detective.

One night, outside his office, he runs into a person from his past. They are like family, really, but in all the worst ways. He has sent work Jack's way. It seems a beautiful girl has gone missing. Ain't that always the case?

This classic detective story is written by Ed Brubaker (Gangland, Dark Horse Presents), with art provided by Michael Lark (Terminal City). For thoslike a good, hard-boiled detective story, this comic book pulls it off while avoiding plot cliches.

1 ❑ May 1999 — Cover: 2.50 — **NM** value: **Cover or less**
Circ: Diamd. preorders: **14,828**
🕮 A Little Piece of Goodnight, Part 1 **A:** Michael Lark **W:** Ed Brubaker
2 ❑ Jun 1999 — Cover: 2.50 — **NM** value: **Cover or less**
Circ: Diamd. preorders: **12,620**
🕮 A Little Piece of Goodnight, Part 2 **A:** Michael Lark **W:** Ed Brubaker
3 ❑ Jul 1999 — Cover: 2.50 — **NM** value: **Cover or less**

Other grades: Multiply prices above by **1.5 for Mint • 2/3 for Very Fine • 1/3 for Fine • 1/5 for Very Good • 1/8 for Good**

Circ: Diamd. preorders: **11,727**
📖 A Little Piece of Goodnight, Part 3 **A:** Michael Lark **W:** Ed Brubaker
4 ❑ Aug 1999 Cover: 2.50 **NM** value: **Cover or less**
Circ: Diamd. preorders: **11,343**
📖 A Little Piece of Goodnight, Part 4 **A:** Michael Lark **W:** Ed Brubaker
Bk 1 ❑ Jun 2000 Cover: 12.95 **NM** value: **Cover or less**
📖 A Little Piece of Goodnight **A:** Michael Lark **W:** Ed Brubaker

SCHIZO — Antarctic
1 ❑ Dec 1994, b&w Cover: 3.50 **NM** value: **Cover or less**
2 ❑ Jan 1996, b&w Cover: 3.95 **NM** value: **Cover or less**
3 ❑ Mar 1998, b&w Cover: 3.95 **NM** value: **Cover or less**

SCHOOL DAY ROMANCES — Star
1 ❑ Nov 1949 Cover: 0.10 **NM** value: **200.00**
2 ❑ Jan 1950 Cover: 0.10 **NM** value: **150.00**
3 ❑ Mar 1950 Cover: 0.10 **NM** value: **150.00**
4 ❑ May 1950 Cover: 0.10 **NM** value: **150.00**

SCIENCE AFFAIR, A — Antarctic
1 ❑ Mar 1994, b&w Cover: 2.75 **NM** value: **Cover or less**
1/GO ❑ Mar 1994 **NM** value: **3.00**
• Gold edition.
2 ❑ May 1994, b&w Cover: 2.75 **NM** value: **Cover or less**
Bk 1 ❑ Nov 1998, b&w Cover: 4.95 **NM** value: **Cover or less**
• Special Compilation

SCIENCE COMICS (FOX) — Fox
1 ❑ Feb 1940 Cover: 0.10 **NM** value: **3500.00**
• **CGC:** 2 graded, best 5.5
2 ❑ Mar 1940 Cover: 0.10 **NM** value: **1800.00**
• **CGC:** 1 graded, best 5.0
3 ❑ Apr 1940 Cover: 0.10 **NM** value: **1500.00**
• **CGC:** 2 graded, best 7.0
4 ❑ May 1940 Cover: 0.10 **NM** value: **1250.00**
• **CGC:** 1 graded, best 6.0
5 ❑ Jun 1940 Cover: 0.10 **NM** value: **750.00**
• **CGC:** 2 graded, best 7.5
6 ❑ Jul 1940 Cover: 0.10 **NM** value: **750.00**
• **CGC:** 1 graded, best 7.0
7 ❑ Aug 1940 Cover: 0.10 **NM** value: **750.00**
• **CGC:** 2 graded, best 7.5
8 ❑ Sep 1940 Cover: 0.10 **NM** value: **750.00**
• **CGC:** 2 graded, best 9.2

SCIENCE COMICS (HUMOR) — Humor
1 ❑ Jan 1946 Cover: 0.10 **NM** value: **125.00**
• **CGC:** 1 graded, best 9.6
2 ❑ Mar 1946 Cover: 0.10 **NM** value: **75.00**
3 ❑ May 1946 Cover: 0.10 **NM** value: **75.00**
4 ❑ Jul 1946 Cover: 0.10 **NM** value: **75.00**
• **CGC:** 1 graded, best 8.0
5 ❑ Sep 1946 Cover: 0.10 **NM** value: **75.00**

SCIENCE FICTION CLASSICS — Dragon Lady
1 ❑ Cover: 5.95 **NM** value: **Cover or less**
• Twin Earths

SCI-FI — Rough Copy
1 ❑ Cover: 2.95 **NM** value: **Cover or less**
📖 Volcanic Partners; Martian Chronicles; Short 'n' Spacey; Cosmic Cookbook; Pork & Beanz **A:** Eric DeSantis; Mark Nunziati; Marty McCarthy **W:** Eric DeSantis; Mark Nunziati; Marty McCarthy

SCIMIDAR — Eternity
1 ❑ Jun 1988, b&w Cover: 1.95 **NM** value: **2.50**
A: Thomas Derenick **W:** R.A. Jones
2 ❑ 1988b&w Cover: 1.95 **NM** value: **2.50**
📖 Bloody Mary **A:** Thomas Derenick **W:** R.A. Jones
3 ❑ 1988b&w Cover: 1.95 **NM** value: **2.50**
A: Thomas Derenick **W:** R.A. Jones
4/A ❑ Dec 1988 Cover: 1.95 **NM** value: **2.00**
mild cover.
4/B ❑ Dec 1988 Cover: 1.95 **NM** value: **2.00**
hot cover.
Bk 1 ❑ b&w Cover: 5.95 **NM** value: **Cover or less**
• Book I

SCIMIDAR BOOK II — Eternity
All issues are adults only.
1 ❑ b&w **NM** value: **3.00**
1-2 ❑ **NM** value: **3.00**
2 ❑ b&w **NM** value: **3.00**
3 ❑ b&w **NM** value: **3.00**
4 ❑ b&w **NM** value: **3.00**
Bk 1 ❑ b&w **NM** value: **6.00**
• Feast & Famine

SCIMIDAR BOOK III — Eternity
All issues are adults only.
1 ❑ b&w **NM** value: **3.00**
1-2 ❑ **NM** value: **3.00**
2 ❑ b&w **NM** value: **3.00**
3 ❑ b&w **NM** value: **3.00**
4 ❑ b&w **NM** value: **3.00**
Bk 1 ❑ **NM** value: **6.00**
• Twilight Men

SCIMIDAR BOOK IV: "WILD THING" — Eternity
All issues are adults only.
1 ❑ **NM** value: **3.00**
1/Nude ❑ **NM** value: **3.00**
Nude cover.
2 ❑ b&w **NM** value: **3.00**
3 ❑ b&w **NM** value: **3.00**
4 ❑ b&w **NM** value: **3.00**

SCIMIDAR BOOK V: "LIVING COLOR" — Eternity
All issues are adults only.
1 ❑ b&w **NM** value: **3.00**
1/Nude ❑ b&w **NM** value: **3.00**
Nude cover.
2 ❑ b&w **NM** value: **3.00**
3 ❑ b&w **NM** value: **3.00**
4 ❑ b&w **NM** value: **3.00**

SCIMIDAR (CFD) — CFD
1 ❑ b&w Cover: 2.95 **NM** value: **Cover or less**
3 ❑ Cover: 2.75 **NM** value: **Cover or less**

SCIMIDAR PIN-UP BOOK — Eternity
1 ❑ full color Cover: 3.75 **NM** value: **Cover or less**
• unstapled

SCION — CrossGen
In the interwoven worlds of the CrossGen universe, Avalon looks something like Earth's medieval society, but the people residing there have access to electronic and genetic discoveries that make it clear that Avalon's characters populate quite another world.

The rival powers are the kingdoms of East and West, which have opposed each other for centuries. People of the kingdoms of the Heron Dynasty (West) and Raven Dynasty (East)use Lesser Races as slaves, while members of the Underground want to eliminate such discrimination. Prince Ethan (youngest son of the Heron Dynasty) now bears the Sigil, which grants special powers. Unfortunately, the emergence of the Sigil itself plunged East and West into pitched combat, and Ethan finds himself pulled by powerful forces, including his own desire to fight for freedom of the Lesser Races. — Maggie

1 ❑ Jul 2000 Cover: 2.95 **NM** value: **Cover or less**
Circ: Diamd. preorders: **28,445** • **CGC:** 24 graded, best 9.8
A: Jim Cheung **W:** Ron Marz
2 ❑ Aug 2000 Cover: 2.95 **NM** value: **Cover or less**
Circ: Diamd. preorders: **22,208** • **CGC:** 2 graded, best 9.2
A: Jim Cheung **W:** Ron Marz
3 ❑ Sep 2000 Cover: 2.95 **NM** value: **Cover or less**
Circ: Diamd. preorders: **21,042**
A: Jim Cheung **W:** Ron Marz
4 ❑ Oct 2000 Cover: 2.95 **NM** value: **Cover or less**
Circ: Diamd. preorders: **20,988**
A: Jim Cheung **W:** Ron Marz
5 ❑ Nov 2000 Cover: 2.95 **NM** value: **Cover or less**
Circ: Diamd. preorders: **20,886**
6 ❑ Dec 2000 Cover: 2.95 **NM** value: **Cover or less**
Circ: Diamd. preorders: **21,287**
7 ❑ Jan 2001 Cover: 2.95 **NM** value: **Cover or less**
Circ: Diamd. preorders: **20,509**
8 ❑ Feb 2001 Cover: 2.95 **NM** value: **Cover or less**
Circ: Diamd. preorders: **19,983**
9 ❑ Mar 2001 Cover: 2.95 **NM** value: **Cover or less**
Circ: Diamd. preorders: **19,479**
10 ❑ Apr 2001 Cover: 2.95 **NM** value: **Cover or less**
Circ: Diamd. preorders: **19,064**
11 ❑ May 2001 Cover: 2.95 **NM** value: **Cover or less**
Circ: Diamd. preorders: **18,972**
12 ❑ Jun 2001 Cover: 2.95 **NM** value: **Cover or less**
Circ: Diamd. preorders: **18,771**
13 ❑ Jul 2001 Cover: 2.95 **NM** value: **Cover or less**
Circ: Diamd. preorders: **18,821**
14 ❑ Aug 2001 Cover: 2.95 **NM** value: **Cover or less**
Circ: Diamd. preorders: **19,636**
15 ❑ Sep 2001 Cover: 2.95 **NM** value: **Cover or less**
16 ❑ Oct 2001 Cover: 2.95 **NM** value: **Cover or less**
17 ❑ Nov 2001 Cover: 2.95 **NM** value: **Cover or less**
18 ❑ Dec 2001 Cover: 2.95 **NM** value: **Cover or less**
19 ❑ Jan 2002 Cover: 2.95 **NM** value: **Cover or less**
20 ❑ Feb 2002 Cover: 2.95 **NM** value: **Cover or less**
21 ❑ Mar 2002 Cover: 2.95 **NM** value: **Cover or less**

SCI-TECH — DC / Wildstorm
1 ❑ Sep 1999 Cover: 2.50 **NM** value: **Cover or less**
Circ: Diamd. preorders: **24,190**
📖 ...And Then There Was Light **A:** Ed Benés **W:** Brandon Choi; Jonathan Peterson
2 ❑ Oct 1999 Cover: 2.50 **NM** value: **Cover or less**
Circ: Diamd. preorders: **18,319**
📖 The Deep Blue Sea **A:** Ed Benés **W:** Brandon Choi; Jonathan Peterson
3 ❑ Nov 1999 Cover: 2.50 **NM** value: **Cover or less**
Circ: Diamd. preorders: **15,639**
A: Ed Benés **W:** Brandon Choi; Jonathan Peterson
4 ❑ Dec 1999 Cover: 2.50 **NM** value: **Cover or less**
Circ: Diamd. preorders: **13,428**
📖 Reunion **A:** Ed Benés **W:** Brandon Choi; Jonathan Peterson

SCOOBY-DOO (ARCHIE) — Archie
1 ❑ Oct 1995 Cover: 1.50 **NM** value: **Cover or less**
Circ: CapCity orders: **3,425**
2 ❑ Nov 1995 Cover: 1.50 **NM** value: **Cover or less**
Circ: CapCity orders: **2,150**
3 ❑ Dec 1995 Cover: 1.50 **NM** value: **Cover or less**
Circ: CapCity orders: **1,625**
4 ❑ Jan 1996 Cover: 1.50 **NM** value: **Cover or less**
5 ❑ Feb 1996 Cover: 1.50 **NM** value: **Cover or less**
6 ❑ Mar 1996 Cover: 1.50 **NM** value: **Cover or less**
7 ❑ Apr 1996 Cover: 1.50 **NM** value: **Cover or less**
8 ❑ May 1996 Cover: 1.50 **NM** value: **Cover or less**
10 ❑ Jul 1996 Cover: 1.50 **NM** value: **Cover or less**
A: Dan Spiegle **W:** Mark Evanier
11 ❑ Aug 1996 Cover: 1.50 **NM** value: **Cover or less**
12 ❑ Sep 1996 Cover: 1.50 **NM** value: **Cover or less**
14 ❑ Nov 1996 Cover: 1.50 **NM** value: **Cover or less**
15 ❑ Dec 1996 Cover: 1.50 **NM** value: **Cover or less**
Circ: Diamd. preorders: **3,618**
16 ❑ Jan 1997 Cover: 1.50 **NM** value: **Cover or less**
Circ: Diamd. preorders: **3,703**
17 ❑ Feb 1997 Cover: 1.50 **NM** value: **Cover or less**
Circ: Diamd. preorders: **4,005**
18 ❑ Mar 1997 Cover: 1.50 **NM** value: **Cover or less**
Circ: Diamd. preorders: **3,716**
19 ❑ Apr 1997 Cover: 1.50 **NM** value: **Cover or less**
Circ: Diamd. preorders: **3,635**
20 ❑ May 1997 Cover: 1.50 **NM** value: **Cover or less**
Circ: Diamd. preorders: **3,370**
21 ❑ Jun 1997 Cover: 1.50 **NM** value: **Cover or less**
Circ: Diamd. preorders: **3,547**

SCOOBY-DOO BIG BOOK — Harvey
1 ❑ 1992 Cover: 1.95 **NM** value: **Cover or less**
2 ❑ Cover: 1.95 **NM** value: **Cover or less**

SCOOBY-DOO (DC) — DC
As part of its association with the Cartoon Network, DC launched this new Scooby-Doo series in 1997. The form of the series is very much in line with the cartoon: a group of "meddling kids," who seem transported straight out of the 1960s, continually runs across ghosts, goblins, and assorted monsters. Inevitably, the apparition turns out to be the old caretaker of the castle (or some villain who wants to scare people away from his real-estate investments). Scooby-Doo, himself, is the group's dog, an intelligent hound that usually stumbles across the secret to the mystery while searching for Scooby Snacks.

1 ❑ Aug 1997 Cover: 1.75 **NM** value: **2.50**
Circ: Diamd. preorders: **11,095**
2 ❑ Sep 1997 Cover: 1.75 **NM** value: **2.00**
Circ: Diamd. preorders: **7,934**
📖 The Roswell Riddle; Stubble trouble **A:** Tim Harkins; Ernie Colon **W:** Barbara Slate; Chris Duffy; Terrance Griep Jr. Jr.
3 ❑ Oct 1997 Cover: 1.75 **NM** value: **2.00**
Circ: Diamd. preorders: **7,360**
📖 The Truth; Wax Attacks **A:** Joe Staton; Bob Smith **W:** Barbara Slate; Terrance Griep Jr. Jr.
4 ❑ Nov 1997 Cover: 1.75 **NM** value: **2.00**
Circ: Diamd. preorders: **7,076**
📖 The Old Ways; How I Spent my Winter Break **A:** Tim Harkins; Ernie Colon **W:** Terrance Griep Jr.; Sam Henderson
5 ❑ Dec 1997 Cover: 1.95 **NM** value: **2.00**
Circ: Diamd. preorders: **7,157**
📖 Legend of the Silver Scream; The Best Laid Plans... **A:** Tim Harkins; Joe Staton **W:** Chris Duffy; Dan Slott
6 ❑ Jan 1998 Cover: 1.95 **NM** value: **2.00**
Circ: Diamd. preorders: **6,913**
★ Appearance of Stetson Rogers (Shaggy's cousin).
7 ❑ Feb 1998 Cover: 1.95 **NM** value: **2.00**
Circ: Diamd. preorders: **6,558**
8 ❑ Mar 1998 Cover: 1.95 **NM** value: **2.00**
Circ: Diamd. preorders: **6,162**
📖 Kung Fu Month!; Like a Cracked Mirror; Kung-Food Fightin'! **A:** Ernie Colon **W:** Michael Kraiger; Chris Duffy
9 ❑ Apr 1998 Cover: 1.95 **NM** value: **2.00**
Circ: Diamd. preorders: **5,841**
10 ❑ May 1998 Cover: 1.95 **NM** value: **2.00**
Circ: Diamd. preorders: **5,754**
11 ❑ Jun 1998 Cover: 1.95 **NM** value: **2.00**
Circ: Diamd. preorders: **6,021**
12 ❑ Jul 1998 Cover: 1.95 **NM** value: **2.00**
Circ: Diamd. preorders: **5,792**
• mystery at a comic-book convention
13 ❑ Aug 1998 Cover: 1.95 **NM** value: **2.00**
Circ: Diamd. preorders: **6,069**
14 ❑ Sep 1998 Cover: 1.99 **NM** value: **2.00**
Circ: Diamd. preorders: **5,760**
15 ❑ Oct 1998 Cover: 1.99 **NM** value: **2.00**
Circ: Diamd. preorders: **5,381**
16 ❑ Nov 1998 Cover: 1.99 **NM** value: **2.00**
Circ: Diamd. preorders: **5,522**
★ Appearance of Groovy Ghoulie.
17 ❑ Dec 1998 Cover: 1.99 **NM** value: **2.00**
Circ: Diamd. preorders: **5,534**
18 ❑ Jan 1999 Cover: 1.99 **NM** value: **2.00**
Circ: Diamd. preorders: **5,505**
19 ❑ Feb 1999 Cover: 1.99 **NM** value: **2.00**
Circ: Diamd. preorders: **5,432**
📖 The Ghost of Holiday Presents **A:** Joe Staton **W:** John Rozum
20 ❑ Mar 1999 Cover: 1.99 **NM** value: **2.00**
Circ: Diamd. preorders: **5,592**
📖 Revenge of the Mudman; Revenge, Inc. **A:** Joe Staton **W:** Rurik Tyler; Terrance Griep Jr. Jr. ★ Appearance of Mystery, Inc..
21 ❑ Apr 1999 Cover: 1.99 **NM** value: **Cover or less**
Circ: Diamd. preorders: **5,264**
A: Joe Staton **W:** Rurik Tyler; Chris Duffy ★ Appearance of Mystery, Inc..

CGC-graded: Multiply prices above by **33 for 9.9 M • 16 for 9.8 NM/M • 7 for 9.6 NM+ • 5 for 9.4 NM • 2.5 for 9.2 NM- • 1.5 for 9.0 VF/NM**

22 ❑ May 1999 Cover: 1.99 **NM** value: **Cover or less**
Circ: Diamd. preorders: **5,338**

23 ❑ Jun 1999 Cover: 1.99 **NM** value: **Cover or less**
Circ: Diamd. preorders: **5,468**
📖 The Big Lake Fake; The Haunted Halibut **A:** John Delaney; Joe Staton **W:** Rurik Tyler; John Rozum

24 ❑ Jul 1999 Cover: 1.99 **NM** value: **Cover or less**
Circ: Diamd. preorders: **5,541**
📖 Don't Believe What You See!; Surf's Up, Monster's Down **A:** Don Perlin **W:** Paul S. Newman

25 ❑ Aug 1999 Cover: 1.99 **NM** value: **Cover or less**
Circ: Diamd. preorders: **5,783**
📖 The Phantom of the Mosh Pit; Caves of Castle Finn **A:** Don Perlin; Vince Deporter **W:** Terrance Griep Jr.; Joe Edkin

26 ❑ Sep 1999 Cover: 1.99 **NM** value: **Cover or less**
Circ: Diamd. preorders: **5,625**
📖 One Night in Roswell, Part 1 **A:** Joe Staton **W:** Rurik Tyler

27 ❑ Oct 1999 Cover: 1.99 **NM** value: **Cover or less**
Circ: Diamd. preorders: **5,387**
📖 One Night in Roswell, Part 3 **A:** Joe Staton **W:** Rurik Tyler

28 ❑ Nov 1999 Cover: 1.99 **NM** value: **Cover or less**
Circ: Diamd. preorders: **5,280**
📖 Lst of the Mugwumps; High School Ghoul **A:** John Delaney; Joe Staton **W:** Joe Edkin; John Rozum

29 ❑ Dec 1999 Cover: 1.99 **NM** value: **Cover or less**
Circ: Diamd. preorders: **5,604**
📖 Three Shears for Shaggy; The Oceanarium Horror **A:** Joe Staton; Don Perlin **W:** John Rozum

30 ❑ Jan 2000 Cover: 1.99 **NM** value: **Cover or less**
Circ: Diamd. preorders: **5,541**
📖 Spring-Heeled Jack; Dog Gone Ghost **A:** Joe Staton; Vincent DePorter **W:** Terrance Griep Jr.; Chuck Kim

31 ❑ Feb 2000 Cover: 1.99 **NM** value: **Cover or less**
Circ: Diamd. preorders: **5,621**

32 ❑ Mar 2000 Cover: 1.99 **NM** value: **Cover or less**
Circ: Diamd. preorders: **5,291**

33 ❑ Apr 2000 Cover: 1.99 **NM** value: **Cover or less**
Circ: Diamd. preorders: **5,026**

34 ❑ May 2000 Cover: 1.99 **NM** value: **Cover or less**
Circ: Diamd. preorders: **5,129**
📖 The Hound of the Basket Cases; Return of the King **A:** Joe Staton; Chris Jordan **W:** Dan Abnett; Joe Edkin

35 ❑ Jun 2000 Cover: 1.99 **NM** value: **Cover or less**
Circ: Diamd. preorders: **5,039**
📖 Phast Phood Phantom; The Weeping Bride of Lover's Leap! **A:** Joe Staton; Eric Doescher **W:** Bob Fingerman; Joe Edkin

36 ❑ Jul 2000 Cover: 1.99 **NM** value: **Cover or less**
Circ: Diamd. preorders: **5,092**

37 ❑ Aug 2000 Cover: 1.99 **NM** value: **Cover or less**
Circ: Diamd. preorders: **5,360**

38 ❑ Sep 2000 Cover: 1.99 **NM** value: **Cover or less**
Circ: Diamd. preorders: **5,273**

39 ❑ Oct 2000 Cover: 1.99 **NM** value: **Cover or less**
Circ: Diamd. preorders: **5,213**
📖 Two Heads Are Better than None; The Chocalatier Chortled! **A:** Joe Staton; Eric Doescher **W:** Bob Fingerman; John Rozum

40 ❑ Nov 2000 Cover: 1.99 **NM** value: **Cover or less**
Circ: Diamd. preorders: **5,248**
📖 Roc Around the Clock; Ghost Tour **A:** John Delaney; Anthony Williams **W:** Abnett; John Rozum

41 ❑ Dec 2000 Cover: 1.99 **NM** value: **Cover or less**
Circ: Diamd. preorders: **5,226**
📖 Trolley Molly; Down in the Dumps **A:** Joe Staton **W:** Rurik Tyler; John Rozum

42 ❑ Jan 2001 Cover: 1.99 **NM** value: **Cover or less**
Circ: Diamd. preorders: **5,312**
📖 Dig Them Bones; Good Ghost Haunting **A:** Anthony Williams; Joe Staton **W:** Brett Lewis; John Rozum

43 ❑ Feb 2001 Cover: 1.99 **NM** value: **Cover or less**
Circ: Diamd. preorders: **5,245**
📖 Nutcracker Not-So-Sweet; Mascot Madness **A:** Joe Staton **W:** Joe Edkin

44 ❑ Mar 2001 Cover: 1.99 **NM** value: **Cover or less**
Circ: Diamd. preorders: **5,111**
📖 Planet-Terrorium **A:** Joe Staton **W:** Rurik Tyler

45 ❑ Apr 2001 Cover: 1.99 **NM** value: **Cover or less**
Circ: Diamd. preorders: **5,151**
📖 Diamond Dog; Rest in Pizza **A:** Joe Staton; Karen Matchette **W:** Bob Fingerman; John Rozum

46 ❑ May 2001 Cover: 1.99 **NM** value: **Cover or less**
Circ: Diamd. preorders: **5,041**
📖 Ghost Writer; The Ex-Verminators **A:** Joe Staton **W:** Dan Decarlo; Dan Abnett

47 ❑ Jun 2001 Cover: 1.99 **NM** value: **Cover or less**
Circ: Diamd. preorders: **5,385**
📖 Bats What I'm Afraid Of; Tune Goon **A:** Joe Staton; Karen Matchette **W:** Scott Cunningham; Brett Lewis

48 ❑ Jul 2001 Cover: 1.99 **NM** value: **Cover or less**
Circ: Diamd. preorders: **5,420**

49 ❑ Aug 2001 Cover: 1.99 **NM** value: **Cover or less**
Circ: Diamd. preorders: **5,734**

50 ❑ Sep 2001 Cover: 1.99 **NM** value: **Cover or less**
Circ: Diamd. preorders: **6,885**

SE 1❑ Oct 1999 Cover: 3.95 **NM** value: **Cover or less**
📖 Spooky Spectacular; The Comic Book Convention Affair; The Truth; The Old Ways; Hall Dodger • Spooky Spectacular **A:** Joe Staton; Ernie Colon **W:** Mike Kraiger; Terrance Griep Jr. Jr

SE 2❑ Oct 2000 Cover: 3.95 **NM** value: **Cover or less**
Circ: Diamd. preorders: **3,920**
📖 Welcome to Monsterville; The Jersey Devil **A:** Joe Staton **W:** Chris Duffy; Terrence Griep Jr.

SCOOBY-DOO (HARVEY) — Harvey

1 ❑ ca. 1992 Cover: 1.25 **NM** value: **1.50**
Circ: CapCity orders: **3,200**

2 ❑ ca. 1992 Cover: 1.25 **NM** value: **1.50**
📖 Witches' Night Out; The Skeleton Speaks!; Thunder Castle (text) **A:** Jorge Pacheco

3 ❑ ca. 1992 Cover: 1.25 **NM** value: **1.50**

GS 1❑ ca. 1992 Cover: 2.25 **NM** value: **Cover or less**

GS 2❑ ca. 1992 Cover: 2.25 **NM** value: **Cover or less**

SCOOBY-DOO (MARVEL) — Marvel

1 ❑ Oct 1977 Cover: 0.30 **NM** value: **6.00**
• **CGC:** 7 graded, best 9.8
2 ❑ Dec 1977 **NM** value: **4.00**
3 ❑ Feb 1978 **NM** value: **3.00**
4 ❑ Apr 1978 Cover: 0.35 **NM** value: **3.00**
5 ❑ Jun 1978 **NM** value: **3.00**
6 ❑ Aug 1978 **NM** value: **3.00**
7 ❑ Oct 1978 **NM** value: **3.00**
8 ❑ Dec 1978 **NM** value: **3.00**
9 ❑ Feb 1979 **NM** value: **3.00**

SCOOBY DOO, WHERE ARE YOU? (CHARLTON) — Charlton

1 ❑ Apr 1975 **NM** value: **15.00**
• **CGC:** 4 graded, best 9.6
2 ❑ Jun 1975 **NM** value: **10.00**
3 ❑ Aug 1975 **NM** value: **7.00**
4 ❑ Oct 1975 **NM** value: **7.00**
5 ❑ Dec 1975 **NM** value: **7.00**
6 ❑ Feb 1976 **NM** value: **6.00**
7 ❑ Apr 1976 **NM** value: **6.00**
8 ❑ Jun 1976 **NM** value: **6.00**
9 ❑ Aug 1976 **NM** value: **6.00**
10 ❑ Oct 1976 Cover: 0.30 **NM** value: **6.00**
📖 It's Dynamite!; Giant-Size (text story); The Ghost of James Jesse
11 ❑ Dec 1976 Cover: 0.30 **NM** value: **5.00**

SCOOBY DOO, WHERE ARE YOU? (GOLD KEY) — Gold Key

1 ❑ Mar 1970 Cover: 0.15 **NM** value: **50.00**
• **CGC:** 2 graded, best 8.5
2 ❑ Jun 1970 Cover: 0.15 **NM** value: **20.00**
3 ❑ Sep 1970 Cover: 0.15 **NM** value: **20.00**
4 ❑ Dec 1970 Cover: 0.15 **NM** value: **20.00**
5 ❑ Mar 1971 Cover: 0.15 **NM** value: **20.00**
6 ❑ Jun 1971 Cover: 0.15 **NM** value: **20.00**
• **CGC:** 1 graded, best 9.0
7 ❑ Aug 1971 Cover: 0.15 **NM** value: **20.00**
8 ❑ Oct 1971 Cover: 0.15 **NM** value: **20.00**
• **CGC:** 1 graded, best 9.6
9 ❑ Dec 1971 Cover: 0.15 **NM** value: **20.00**
10 ❑ Feb 1972 Cover: 0.15 **NM** value: **20.00**
11 ❑ Apr 1972 Cover: 0.15 **NM** value: **15.00**
12 ❑ Jun 1972 Cover: 0.15 **NM** value: **15.00**
13 ❑ Aug 1972 Cover: 0.15 **NM** value: **15.00**
14 ❑ Oct 1972 Cover: 0.15 **NM** value: **15.00**
15 ❑ Dec 1972 Cover: 0.15 **NM** value: **15.00**
16 ❑ ca. 1973 **NM** value: **10.00**
17 ❑ ca. 1973 **NM** value: **10.00**
18 ❑ ca. 1973 Cover: 0.20 **NM** value: **10.00**
19 ❑ Jul 1973 Cover: 0.20 **NM** value: **10.00**
• **CGC:** 1 graded, best 9.4
20 ❑ Aug 1973 Cover: 0.20 **NM** value: **7.50**
21 ❑ Oct 1973 Cover: 0.20 **NM** value: **7.50**
22 ❑ Dec 1973 Cover: 0.20 **NM** value: **7.50**
23 ❑ Feb 1974 Cover: 0.20 **NM** value: **7.50**
24 ❑ Apr 1974 Cover: 0.20 **NM** value: **7.50**
25 ❑ Jun 1974 Cover: 0.20 **NM** value: **7.50**
26 ❑ ca. 1974 **NM** value: **5.00**
27 ❑ ca. 1974 Cover: 0.25 **NM** value: **5.00**
28 ❑ ca. 1974 Cover: 0.25 **NM** value: **5.00**
29 ❑ Dec 1974 Cover: 0.25 **NM** value: **5.00**
30 ❑ ca. 1975 **NM** value: **5.00**

SCOOP COMICS — Harry A. Chesler

1 ❑ Nov 1941 Cover: 0.10 **NM** value: **1200.00**
2 ❑ Jan 1942 Cover: 0.10 **NM** value: **1000.00**
3 ❑ Mar 1942 Cover: 0.10 **NM** value: **500.00**
8 ❑ ca. 1944 Cover: 0.10 **NM** value: **350.00**
• **CGC:** 1 graded, best 4.0

SCOOTERMAN — Wellzee

1 ❑ Apr 1996, b&w Cover: 2.75 **NM** value: **Cover or less**
2 ❑ Dec 1996, b&w Cover: 2.75 **NM** value: **Cover or less**
• poster
3 ❑ Jul 1997, b&w Cover: 2.75 **NM** value: **Cover or less**

SCORCHED EARTH — Tundra

1 ❑ Apr 1991 Cover: 2.95 **NM** value: **Cover or less**
Circ: CapCity orders: **2,250**
2 ❑ Jun 1991 Cover: 2.95 **NM** value: **Cover or less**
3 ❑ Aug 1991 Cover: 2.95 **NM** value: **Cover or less**

SCORCHY — Forbidden Fruit

All issues are adults only.

1 ❑ b&w Cover: 3.50 **NM** value: **Cover or less**

SCORE, THE — DC / Piranha

All issues are adults only.

The Score is a tale of two cities. The first is New Hollywood, a place of movie stars, beautiful people, and gilded corruption. Next door is the real Hollywood, which the residents call "Hellywood." It's the place where you go, when your dreams have been dashed into the gutter and you have to live like an animal in order to survive.

Phillip Sand was a rock star, one of New Hollywood's exalted residents. Then he fell from grace, his mind and memory blasted away on drugs. Now he wakes up on the mean streets of Hellywood, where he doesn't even know his own name. He would die, were it not for the kindness of a hooker who protects him from the jackals, then introduces him to people who give him a lesson in how the other half lives. Hellywood is a no-man's land where life is cheap and the police belong to the highest bidder. Sand is the key to changing all this, because, although he doesn't know it yet, he knows the Score.

1 ❑ ca. 1989 Cover: 4.95 **NM** value: **Cover or less**
Circ: CapCity orders: **7,900**
A: Mark Badger **W:** Gerard Jones
2 ❑ ca. 1989 Cover: 4.95 **NM** value: **Cover or less**
Circ: CapCity orders: **5,600**
A: Mark Badger **W:** Gerard Jones
3 ❑ ca. 1989 Cover: 4.95 **NM** value: **Cover or less**
Circ: CapCity orders: **5,800**
A: Mark Badger **W:** Gerard Jones
4 ❑ ca. 1989 Cover: 4.95 **NM** value: **Cover or less**
Circ: CapCity orders: **4,450**
A: Mark Badger **W:** Gerard Jones

SCORN: DEADLY REBELLION — SCC Entertainment

0 ❑ Jul 1996, b&w Cover: 2.95 **NM** value: **Cover or less**

SCORN: HEATWAVE — SCC Entertainment

1 ❑ Jan 1997, b&w Cover: 3.95 **NM** value: **Cover or less**
Circ: Diamd. preorders: **3,439**
• follows events in Scorn: Deadly Rebellion

SCORPIA — Miller

1 ❑ Cover: 2.50 **NM** value: **Cover or less**
2 ❑ Cover: 2.50 **NM** value: **Cover or less**

SCORPION — Annruel Studios

1 ❑ b&w Cover: 2.50 **NM** value: **Cover or less**

SCORPION, THE — Atlas-Seaboard

Moro Frost comes from a strange line of adventurers whose number have included a balloonist for the Union during the Civil War and a pilot for the Lafayette Escadrille in World War I. All these men have different names, but the reader wonders whether they are not somehow the same man — known today as The Scorpion.

The Scorpion is a freelance swashbuckler, a sort of "hero for hire" charging outrageous sums for his services but always delivering the goods. He's assisted in his adventures by his secretary, Ruby Bishop, a beautiful woman who can more than fend for herself. Together, they take on all manner of thugs and evildoers.

This series lasted a mere three issues, par for the course for ill-fated Atlas Comics. It was created by Howard Chaykin and bears a striking resemblance to his later characters Dominic Fortune and The Midnight Men.

1 ❑ Feb 1975 Cover: 0.25 **NM** value: **2.00**
• **CGC:** 3 graded, best 9.2
📖 The Death's Gemini Commission **A:** Howard Chaykin **C:** Howard Chaykin **W:** Howard Chaykin ★ 1st Appearance of The Scorpion I (Moro Frost).
2 ❑ Apr 1975 Cover: 0.25 **NM** value: **1.50**
A: Bernie Wrightson; Michael W. Kaluta; Walt Simonson
3 ❑ Jul 1975 Cover: 0.25 **NM** value: **1.50**
final issue. ★ 1st Appearance of The Scorpion II (David Harper).

SCORPION CORPS — Dagger

1 ❑ Nov 1993 Cover: 2.50 **NM** value: **Cover or less**
Circ: CapCity orders: **4,545**
★ 1st Appearance of Streik.
2 ❑ Dec 1993 Cover: 2.50 **NM** value: **Cover or less**
Circ: CapCity orders: **2,520**
A: Jim Royal **W:** Paul Danner
3 ❑ Jan 1994 Cover: 2.50 **NM** value: **Cover or less**
Circ: CapCity orders: **2,200**
4 ❑ Feb 1994 Cover: 2.50 **NM** value: **Cover or less**
5 ❑ Mar 1994 Cover: 2.50 **NM** value: **Cover or less**
6 ❑ Apr 1994 Cover: 2.50 **NM** value: **Cover or less**
📖 Parting Shots **A:** Bill Hobbs **W:** Paul Danner
7 ❑ May 1994 Cover: 2.50 **NM** value: **Cover or less**
8 ❑ Jun 1994 Cover: 2.50 **NM** value: **Cover or less**
9 ❑ Jul 1994 Cover: 2.50 **NM** value: **Cover or less**
10 ❑ Aug 1994 Cover: 2.50 **NM** value: **Cover or less**

SCORPION MOON — Express / Entity

1 ❑ Oct 1994, b&w Cover: 2.95 **NM** value: **Cover or less**
No issue number. cardstock cover. • 4th in a series of Entity illustrated novellas with Zen Intergalactic Ninja **A:** Bill Maus **W:** Don Chin

SCORPIO RISING — Marvel

1 ❑ Oct 1994 Cover: 5.95 **NM** value: **Cover or less**
No issue number. • prestige format one-shot **A:** Shawn McManus **W:** Howard Chaykin

The prices seen above do not represent the highest possible prices seen in online auctions, but rather the prices we have seen these issues reliably fetch in a variety of environments (storefront retail, mail order, auction and convention).

Other grades: Multiply prices above by **1.5 for Mint • 2/3 for Very Fine • 1/3 for Fine • 1/5 for Very Good • 1/8 for Good**

SCORPIO ROSE — Eclipse

Her story began three hundred years ago. In those days, she was simply Rosa, a beautiful gypsy girl. One day, a stranger came to her people's encampment and Rosa danced for him. Afterward, they stole away to a secluded cliff. It was there that Rosa found out the stranger was no human, but harbored a demon from the pit. He violated her body and her soul. He also blessed — or cursed — her with eternal life.

Now Rosa lives in Paris, where she makes her living as a seer. She has learned the ways of magic, but little does she suspect that she will be using them to save her life from the same demon that changed her so many years ago.

Scorpio Rose makes her debut in this two-issue mini-series, originally meant as a story for DC's Madame Xanadu. When DC and creator Steve Englehart disagreed about the script, Englehart turned it into Scorpio Rose's first story.

1 ❑ Jan 1983 Cover: 1.50 **NM** value: **2.00**
A: Marshall Rogers **W:** Steve Englehart ★ Origin of Scorpio Rose. ★ 1st Appearance of Scorpio Rose, Doctor Orient.
2 ❑ Oct 1983 Cover: 1.50 **NM** value: **2.00**

SCOTLAND YARD — Charlton

1 ❑ Jun 1955 Cover: 0.10 **NM** value: **100.00**
2 ❑ Sep 1955 Cover: 0.10 **NM** value: **60.00**
3 ❑ Dec 1955 Cover: 0.10 **NM** value: **60.00**
4 ❑ Mar 1956 Cover: 0.10 **NM** value: **60.00**

SCOUT — Eclipse

SF mercenary Grimjack co-creator (with John Ostrander) Timothy Truman went on to create, write, and draw Scout, in another science-fiction setting: America following a nuclear holocaust. The title character is an Apache warrior fighting corruption and monsters, and Truman worked to provide a comic book that showed drespect for the culture and religion of Native Americans of the Southwest.

Truman won a Haxtur Award for his work on this series and has done other comics work with a focus on Native Americans, including such historical figures as Simon Girty and Tecumseh and such fictional characters as Jonah Hex and The Lone Ranger — and that's not to mention such other creations as Truman's Grateful Dead Comix. — Maggie

1 ❑ Nov 1985 Cover: 1.75 **NM** value: **2.00**
Circ: CapCity orders: **7,550**
A: Tim Truman **W:** Tim Truman
2 ❑ Dec 1985 Cover: 1.75 **NM** value: **2.00**
Circ: CapCity orders: **6,525**
A: Tim Truman **W:** Tim Truman
3 ❑ Jan 1985 Cover: 1.75 **NM** value: **2.00**
Circ: CapCity orders: **6,375**
A: Tim Truman **W:** Tim Truman
4 ❑ Feb 1986 Cover: 1.75 **NM** value: **2.00**
Circ: CapCity orders: **6,075**
A: Tim Truman **W:** Tim Truman
5 ❑ Mar 1986 Cover: 1.75 **NM** value: **2.00**
Circ: CapCity orders: **6,175**
A: Tim Truman **W:** Tim Truman
6 ❑ Apr 1986 Cover: 1.75 **NM** value: **2.00**
Circ: CapCity orders: **6,650**
A: Tim Truman **W:** Tim Truman
7 ❑ May 1986 Cover: 1.75 **NM** value: **2.00**
Circ: CapCity orders: **6,775**
A: Tim Truman **W:** Tim Truman
8 ❑ Jun 1986 Cover: 1.75 **NM** value: **2.00**
Circ: CapCity orders: **6,750**
A: Tim Truman **W:** Tim Truman
9 ❑ Jul 1986 Cover: 1.25 **NM** value: **2.00**
Circ: CapCity orders: **7,525**
• Airboy preview **A:** Tim Truman **W:** Tim Truman
10 ❑ Aug 1986 Cover: 1.25 **NM** value: **2.00**
Circ: CapCity orders: **7,375**
A: Tim Truman **W:** Tim Truman
11 ❑ Sep 1986 Cover: 1.75 **NM** value: **Cover or less**
Circ: CapCity orders: **6,875**
A: Tim Truman **W:** Tim Truman
12 ❑ Oct 1986 Cover: 1.75 **NM** value: **Cover or less**
Circ: CapCity orders: **6,675**
Me and the Devil **A:** Tim Truman **W:** Tim Truman
13 ❑ Nov 1986 Cover: 1.75 **NM** value: **Cover or less**
Circ: CapCity orders: **6,775**
A: Tim Truman **W:** Tim Truman
14 ❑ Dec 1986 Cover: 1.75 **NM** value: **Cover or less**
Circ: CapCity orders: **6,825**
A: Tim Truman **W:** Tim Truman
15 ❑ Jan 1987 Cover: 1.75 **NM** value: **Cover or less**
Circ: CapCity orders: **5,925**
A: Tim Truman **W:** Tim Truman
16 ❑ Feb 1987 Cover: 2.50 **NM** value: **Cover or less**
Circ: CapCity orders: **6,075**
• 3-D. **A:** Tim Truman **W:** Tim Truman
17 ❑ Mar 1987 Cover: 1.75 **NM** value: **Cover or less**
Circ: CapCity orders: **6,075**
A: Tim Truman **W:** Tim Truman
18 ❑ Apr 1987 Cover: 1.75 **NM** value: **Cover or less**
Circ: CapCity orders: **6,675**
A: Tim Truman **W:** Tim Truman
19 ❑ May 1987 Cover: 2.50 **NM** value: **3.00**
Circ: CapCity orders: **6,950**
• flexidisc **A:** Tim Truman **W:** Tim Truman
20 ❑ Jun 1987 Cover: 1.75 **NM** value: **Cover or less**
Circ: CapCity orders: **6,075**
A: Tim Truman **W:** Tim Truman
21 ❑ Jul 1987 Cover: 1.75 **NM** value: **Cover or less**
Circ: CapCity orders: **6,075**
A: Tim Truman **W:** Tim Truman
22 ❑ Aug 1987 Cover: 1.75 **NM** value: **Cover or less**
Circ: CapCity orders: **5,850**
A: Tim Truman **W:** Tim Truman
23 ❑ Sep 1987 Cover: 1.75 **NM** value: **Cover or less**
Circ: CapCity orders: **5,750**
A: Tim Truman **W:** Tim Truman
24 ❑ Oct 1987 Cover: 1.75 **NM** value: **Cover or less**
Circ: CapCity orders: **5,900**
A: Tim Truman **W:** Tim Truman

SCOUT HANDBOOK — Eclipse

1 ❑ Cover: 1.75 **NM** value: **Cover or less**
Circ: CapCity orders: **4,975**
No issue number.

SCOUT: WAR SHAMAN — Eclipse

1 ❑ Mar 1988 Cover: 1.95 **NM** value: **2.00**
Circ: CapCity orders: **7,850**
Down in the Bottom **A:** Tim Truman **W:** Tim Truman
2 ❑ May 1988 Cover: 1.95 **NM** value: **2.00**
Circ: CapCity orders: **6,350**
A: Tim Truman **W:** Tim Truman
3 ❑ Jun 1988 Cover: 1.95 **NM** value: **2.00**
Circ: CapCity orders: **6,175**
A: Tim Truman **W:** Tim Truman
4 ❑ Jul 1988 Cover: 1.95 **NM** value: **2.00**
Circ: CapCity orders: **5,650**
A: Tim Truman **W:** Tim Truman
5 ❑ Aug 1988 Cover: 1.95 **NM** value: **2.00**
Circ: CapCity orders: **5,750**
Wooly Bully•War Movie!!, Part 1 **A:** Tim Truman **W:** Tim Truman
6 ❑ Sep 1988 Cover: 1.95 **NM** value: **2.00**
Circ: CapCity orders: **5,350**
Wooly Bully•War Movie!!, Part 2 **A:** Tim Truman **W:** Tim Truman
7 ❑ Oct 1988 Cover: 1.95 **NM** value: **2.00**
Circ: CapCity orders: **5,100**
A: Tim Truman **W:** Tim Truman
8 ❑ Nov 1988 Cover: 1.95 **NM** value: **2.00**
Circ: CapCity orders: **5,125**
A: Tim Truman **W:** Tim Truman
9 ❑ Dec 1988 Cover: 1.95 **NM** value: **2.00**
Circ: CapCity orders: **5,100**
A: Tim Truman **W:** Tim Truman
10 ❑ Jan 1989 Cover: 1.95 **NM** value: **2.00**
Circ: CapCity orders: **4,900**
A: Tim Truman **W:** Tim Truman
11 ❑ Feb 1989 Cover: 1.95 **NM** value: **2.00**
Circ: CapCity orders: **4,600**
A: Tim Truman **W:** Tim Truman
12 ❑ Mar 1989 Cover: 1.95 **NM** value: **2.00**
Circ: CapCity orders: **4,550**
A: Tim Truman **W:** Tim Truman
13 ❑ Apr 1989 Cover: 1.95 **NM** value: **2.00**
Circ: CapCity orders: **4,450**
A: Tim Truman **W:** Tim Truman
14 ❑ May 1989 Cover: 1.95 **NM** value: **2.00**
Circ: CapCity orders: **4,325**
A: Tim Truman **W:** Tim Truman
15 ❑ Jun 1989 Cover: 1.95 **NM** value: **2.00**
Circ: CapCity orders: **4,375**
A: Tim Truman **W:** Tim Truman
16 ❑ Jul 1989 Cover: 1.95 **NM** value: **2.00**
Circ: CapCity orders: **4,500**
A: Tim Truman **W:** Tim Truman ★ Death of Scout.

SCRAP CITY PACK RATS — Out of the Blue

1 ❑ b&w Cover: 1.50 **NM** value: **Cover or less**
Lightning Strikes
2 ❑ b&w Cover: 1.50 **NM** value: **Cover or less**
3 ❑ b&w Cover: 1.50 **NM** value: **Cover or less**
4 ❑ b&w Cover: 1.75 **NM** value: **Cover or less**
5 ❑ 1986b&w Cover: 1.75 **NM** value: **Cover or less**
Clam on the Lam

SCRATCH — Outside

1 ❑ 1986 Cover: 1.75 **NM** value: **Cover or less**
2 ❑ 1986 Cover: 1.75 **NM** value: **Cover or less**
3 ❑ 1987 Cover: 1.75 **NM** value: **Cover or less**
4 ❑ Apr 1987 Cover: 1.75 **NM** value: **Cover or less**
5 ❑ 1987 Cover: 1.75 **NM** value: **Cover or less**
6 ❑ 1987 Cover: 1.75 **NM** value: **Cover or less**

SCREAM COMICS — Humor

1 ❑ Aut 1944 Cover: 0.10 **NM** value: **75.00**
2 ❑ Jun 1945 Cover: 0.10 **NM** value: **60.00**
3 ❑ Aug 1945 Cover: 0.10 **NM** value: **60.00**
4 ❑ Oct 1945 Cover: 0.10 **NM** value: **60.00**
5 ❑ Dec 1945 Cover: 0.10 **NM** value: **60.00**
6 ❑ Jan 1946 Cover: 0.10 **NM** value: **50.00**
7 ❑ Mar 1946 Cover: 0.10 **NM** value: **50.00**
8 ❑ May 1946 Cover: 0.10 **NM** value: **50.00**
9 ❑ Jul 1946 Cover: 0.10 **NM** value: **50.00**
10 ❑ Sep 1946 Cover: 0.10 **NM** value: **50.00**
11 ❑ Nov 1946 Cover: 0.10 **NM** value: **35.00**
12 ❑ Feb 1947 Cover: 0.10 **NM** value: **35.00**
13 ❑ Apr 1947 Cover: 0.10 **NM** value: **35.00**
14 ❑ Jun 1947 Cover: 0.10 **NM** value: **35.00**
15 ❑ Aug 1947 Cover: 0.10 **NM** value: **35.00**
16 ❑ Oct 1947 Cover: 0.10 **NM** value: **35.00**
17 ❑ Dec 1947 Cover: 0.10 **NM** value: **35.00**
18 ❑ Feb 1948 Cover: 0.10 **NM** value: **35.00**
19 ❑ Apr 1948 Cover: 0.10 **NM** value: **35.00**
• Good Girl art cover

SCREAMERS — Eros

1 ❑ 1995 Cover: 2.95 **NM** value: **Cover or less**
A: Tony Fanning **W:** Tony Fanning
2 ❑ 1995 Cover: 2.95 **NM** value: **Cover or less**
A: Tony Fanning **W:** Tony Fanning
3 ❑ Oct 1995 Cover: 2.95 **NM** value: **Cover or less**
Rock Hard **A:** Tony Fanning **W:** Tony Fanning

SCREEN MONSTERS — Zone

1 ❑ Cover: 2.95 **NM** value: **Cover or less**
A: Chris Taylor; Michael Avon Oeming; Mike Wieringo; Jim Whiting; Dell Barras; Andrew Murphy; Terry Pavlet; Joe Dunn; Bill Cucinotta(cover); Chuck Hyman; Kelly McQuain; Raine Szramski; Rich Rankin; Thomas Bradley **W:** Ron Rockett

SCREENPLAY — Slave Labor

1 ❑ Jun 1989, b&w Cover: 1.75 **NM** value: **Cover or less**

SCREWBALL SQUIRREL — Dark Horse

1 ❑ Jul 1995 Cover: 2.50 **NM** value: **Cover or less**
Circ: CapCity orders: **4,500**
Mauled At The Mall • Wolf & Red back-up **A:** Greg Hyland **W:** Bob Fingerman
2 ❑ Aug 1995 Cover: 2.50 **NM** value: **Cover or less**
Circ: CapCity orders: **3,125**
• Droopy back-up
3 ❑ Sep 1995 Cover: 2.50 **NM** value: **Cover or less**
Circ: CapCity orders: **2,500**
final issue. • Wolf & Red back-up

SCREW COMICS — Fantagraphics / Eros

All issues are adults only.

1 ❑ b&w Cover: 3.50 **NM** value: **Cover or less**
Juden Creature; The Adventures of Truli Godawful, Secretary at **A:** Don Lomax; Kaz; Spain; Charles Pinion; Danny Hellman; Glen Head; Hak; J.T. Quinn III; Ken Pastore; Ken Weiner; Melrose Tweeb; Mr. Six-x; Peter Badge; Sean Taggart; Steve Cerio **W:** Don Lomax; Kaz; Spain; Al Goldstein; Charles Pinion; Danny Hellman; Glen Head; Hak; J.T. Quinn III; Ken Pastore; Ken Weiner; Melrose Tweeb; Mr. Six-x; Peter Badge; Sean Taggart; Steve Cerio

SCREWTAPE LETTERS, THE — Marvel

Bk 1 ❑ Jun 1994 Cover: 9.99 **NM** value: **Cover or less**
• (with Nelson); adapts the C.S. Lewis novel; Neil Gaiman introduction
A: Pat Redding **W:** C. S. Lewis; Charles E. Hall

SCRIBBLY — DC

1 ❑ Aug 1948 Cover: 0.10 **NM** value: **600.00**
2 ❑ Oct 1948 Cover: 0.10 **NM** value: **400.00**
3 ❑ Dec 1948 Cover: 0.10 **NM** value: **400.00**
4 ❑ Feb 1949 Cover: 0.10 **NM** value: **400.00**
5 ❑ Apr 1949 Cover: 0.10 **NM** value: **400.00**
6 ❑ Jun 1949 Cover: 0.10 **NM** value: **300.00**
7 ❑ Aug 1949 Cover: 0.10 **NM** value: **300.00**
8 ❑ Nov 1949 Cover: 0.10 **NM** value: **300.00**
9 ❑ Jan 1950 Cover: 0.10 **NM** value: **300.00**
10 ❑ Mar 1950 Cover: 0.10 **NM** value: **300.00**
11 ❑ May 1950 Cover: 0.10 **NM** value: **250.00**
12 ❑ Jul 1950 Cover: 0.10 **NM** value: **250.00**
13 ❑ Sep 1950 Cover: 0.10 **NM** value: **250.00**
14 ❑ ca. 1951 Cover: 0.10 **NM** value: **250.00**
15 ❑ Dec 1951 Cover: 0.10 **NM** value: **250.00**

SCRUBS IN SCRUBLAND: THE REFLEX — Scrubland Prod.

1 ❑ b&w Cover: 2.50 **NM** value: **Cover or less**

SCUD: TALES FROM THE VENDING MACHINE — Fireman

1 ❑ Jan 1998 Cover: 2.50 **NM** value: **3.00**
Circ: Diamd. preorders: **10,398**
2 ❑ Mar 1998 Cover: 2.50 **NM** value: **Cover or less**
Circ: Diamd. preorders: **8,719**
3 ❑ May 1998 Cover: 2.50 **NM** value: **Cover or less**
Circ: Diamd. preorders: **8,105**
4 ❑ Jul 1998 Cover: 2.50 **NM** value: **Cover or less**
Circ: Diamd. preorders: **8,060**
Rhythmic Metaphor **A:** Jim Mahfood **W:** Jim Mahfood

There are two different pricing tiers in the modern comic-book hobby. **The prices seen above** are the prices we have seen **loose copies** of these issues reliably fetch in a variety of environments. Condition alters the price by the fractions seen on the bar on the bottom of left-hand pages of this book. **Comics graded by CGC** usually sell for more. Use the guide on the bottom of right-hand pages of this book to estimate what copies have brought on eBay.

CGC-graded: Multiply prices above by **33 for 9.9 M • 16 for 9.8 NM/M • 7 for 9.6 NM+ • 5 for 9.4 NM • 2.5 for 9.2 NM- • 1.5 for 9.0 VF/NM**

SCUD: THE DISPOSABLE ASSASSIN

Fireman Press

This series follows Scud, one of many disposable robot assassins which can be purchased at any corner vending machine. For a mere three "franks," a scud can do anything from simply killing its target to murdering everybody in the immediate area, depending on the contempt level to which its owner sets it. After a scud terminates its assigned target, it self-destructs, leaving the customer with no worries.

This is Scud's problem. While carrying out his mission, he notices a sign on his back stating that, once his target dies, so will he. With his target dying on the floor, he quickly calls an ambulance. The target survives but must be kept on life-support. So begins the misadventures of Scud. Now freelancing, he won't self-destruct after completing his missions, but he will need to earn three franks a month to pay for life-support. His assignments lead him on hilarious adventures with high body counts.

1 ❑ Feb 1994, b&w Cover: 2.95 **NM** value: **12.00**
★ 1st Appearance of Scud.
1-2 ❑ Cover: 2.95 **NM** value: **3.00**
1-3 ❑ 1997 Cover: 2.95 **NM** value: **3.00**
2 ❑ May 1994, b&w Cover: 2.95 **NM** value: **6.00**
3 ❑ b&w Cover: 2.95 **NM** value: **5.00**
4 ❑ b&w Cover: 2.95 **NM** value: **5.00**
5 ❑ b&w Cover: 2.95 **NM** value: **5.00**
6 ❑ b&w Cover: 2.95 **NM** value: **4.00**
7 ❑ b&w Cover: 2.95 **NM** value: **4.00**
8 ❑ 1995b&w Cover: 2.95 **NM** value: **4.00**
Circ: CapCity orders: **2,400**
9 ❑ b&w Cover: 2.95 **NM** value: **4.00**
10 ❑ b&w Cover: 2.95 **NM** value: **4.00**
11 ❑ Cover: 2.95 **NM** value: **3.00**
12 ❑ Cover: 2.95 **NM** value: **3.00**
13 ❑ Cover: 2.95 **NM** value: **3.00**
14 ❑ Nov 1996 Cover: 2.95 **NM** value: **3.00**
Circ: Diamd. preorders: **8,892**
15 ❑ Apr 1997 Cover: 2.95 **NM** value: **3.00**
Circ: Diamd. preorders: **9,673**
16 ❑ Jun 1997 Cover: 2.95 **NM** value: **Cover or less**
Circ: Diamd. preorders: **10,242**
17 ❑ Aug 1997 Cover: 2.95 **NM** value: **Cover or less**
Circ: Diamd. preorders: **10,533**
18 ❑ Nov 1997 Cover: 2.95 **NM** value: **Cover or less**
Circ: Diamd. preorders: **10,842**
19 ❑ Dec 1997 Cover: 2.95 **NM** value: **Cover or less**
Circ: Diamd. preorders: **10,706**
20 ❑ Feb 1998 Cover: 2.95 **NM** value: **Cover or less**
Circ: Diamd. preorders: **9,907**
Bk 1❑ Cover: 12.95 **NM** value: **Cover or less**
• Collects Scud: The Disposable Assassin #1-4
Bk 2❑ Cover: 14.95 **NM** value: **Cover or less**
• Collects Scud: The Disposable Assassin #5-9

SCUM OF THE EARTH

Aircel

1 ❑ b&w Cover: 2.50 **NM** value: **Cover or less**
2 ❑ b&w Cover: 2.50 **NM** value: **Cover or less**

SEA DEVILS

DC

The Sea Devils are four adventurers who explore the mysterious world below the waves. The foursome consists of Dane, a master scientist, who's accompanied by Judy, Nicky, and Biff. Operating from their boat, The Sea Witch, these four will strap on scuba gear and dive into waters around the globe. There, they meet everything from sea monsters and alien creatures to more conventional monsters of the human sort.

The team first appeared in a three-issue run in Showcase #27-29. Response was good enough to spin them off into their own series, which ran from 1961-1967. Of note is outstanding art by Russ Heath.

1 ❑ Oct 1961 Cover: 0.10 **NM** value: **325.00**
• **CGC:** 20 graded, best 9.6
2 ❑ Dec 1961 Cover: 0.10 **NM** value: **185.00**
3 ❑ Feb 1962 Cover: 0.12 **NM** value: **125.00**
Circ: Statement: **205,000**
4 ❑ Apr 1962 Cover: 0.12 **NM** value: **90.00**
Circ: Statement: **205,000** • **CGC:** 1 graded, best 8.5
5 ❑ Jun 1962 Cover: 0.12 **NM** value: **90.00**
Circ: Statement: **205,000** • **CGC:** 3 graded, best 9.4
6 ❑ Aug 1962 Cover: 0.12 **NM** value: **60.00**
Circ: Statement: **205,000** • **CGC:** 2 graded, best 9.2
7 ❑ Oct 1962 Cover: 0.12 **NM** value: **60.00**
Circ: Statement: **205,000** • **CGC:** 3 graded, best 9.0
8 ❑ Dec 1962 Cover: 0.12 **NM** value: **60.00**
Circ: Statement: **205,000**
9 ❑ Feb 1963 Cover: 0.12 **NM** value: **60.00**
Circ: Statement: **203,150** • **CGC:** 2 graded, best 9.2
10 ❑ Apr 1963 Cover: 0.12 **NM** value: **60.00**
Circ: Statement: **203,150** • **CGC:** 1 graded, best 8.5
• Has 1962 Statement, filed 10/1/62; avg total paid circ 205,000
11 ❑ Jun 1963 Cover: 0.12 **NM** value: **40.00**
Circ: Statement: **203,150** • **CGC:** 1 graded, best 4.5
12 ❑ Aug 1963 Cover: 0.12 **NM** value: **40.00**
Circ: Statement: **203,150** • **CGC:** 1 graded, best 9.0
13 ❑ Oct 1963 Cover: 0.12 **NM** value: **45.00**
Circ: Statement: **203,150** • **CGC:** 1 graded, best 8.0
A: Gene Colan; Joe Kubert
14 ❑ Dec 1963 Cover: 0.12 **NM** value: **40.00**
Circ: Statement: **203,150** • **CGC:** 1 graded, best 9.2
15 ❑ Feb 1964 Cover: 0.12 **NM** value: **40.00**
Circ: Statement: **198,486** • **CGC:** 2 graded, best 9.2
16 ❑ Apr 1964 Cover: 0.12 **NM** value: **40.00**
Circ: Statement: **198,486**
17 ❑ Jun 1964 Cover: 0.12 **NM** value: **40.00**
Circ: Statement: **198,486**
18 ❑ Aug 1964 Cover: 0.12 **NM** value: **40.00**
Circ: Statement: **198,486** • **CGC:** 2 graded, best 9.2
• Has 1963 Statement, filed 10/1/63; avg print run 336,000; avg sales 203,000; avg subs 150; avg total paid 203,150; samples 370; max existent 203,520; 39% of run returned
19 ❑ Oct 1964 Cover: 0.12 **NM** value: **40.00**
Circ: Statement: **198,486** • **CGC:** 2 graded, best 9.4
20 ❑ Dec 1964 Cover: 0.12 **NM** value: **40.00**
Circ: Statement: **198,486** • **CGC:** 1 graded, best 9.0
📖 The Menace Of the Reptile Men
21 ❑ Feb 1965 Cover: 0.12 **NM** value: **30.00**
Circ: Statement: **182,866** • **CGC:** 1 graded, best 9.2
22 ❑ Apr 1965 Cover: 0.12 **NM** value: **30.00**
Circ: Statement: **182,866** • **CGC:** 1 graded, best 9.2
• Has 1964 Statement, filed 10/1/64; avg print run 317,000; avg sales 198,000; avg subs 486; avg total paid 198,486; samples 387; max existent 198,873; 37% of run returned
23 ❑ Jun 1965 Cover: 0.12 **NM** value: **30.00**
Circ: Statement: **182,866** • **CGC:** 1 graded, best 9.4
24 ❑ Aug 1965 Cover: 0.12 **NM** value: **30.00**
Circ: Statement: **182,866** • **CGC:** 2 graded, best 9.4
25 ❑ Oct 1965 Cover: 0.12 **NM** value: **30.00**
Circ: Statement: **182,866** • **CGC:** 1 graded, best 9.0
26 ❑ Dec 1965 Cover: 0.12 **NM** value: **30.00**
Circ: Statement: **182,866** • **CGC:** 1 graded, best 9.0
27 ❑ Feb 1966 Cover: 0.12 **NM** value: **30.00**
Circ: Statement: **168,731** • **CGC:** 1 graded, best 9.4
28 ❑ Apr 1966 Cover: 0.12 **NM** value: **30.00**
Circ: Statement: **168,731** • **CGC:** 1 graded, best 8.5
• Has 1965 Statement, filed 10/1/65; avg print run 304,000; avg sales 182,000; avg subs 866; avg total paid 182,866; samples 142; max existent 183,008; 40% of run returned
29 ❑ Jun 1966 Cover: 0.12 **NM** value: **30.00**
Circ: Statement: **168,731** • **CGC:** 3 graded, best 9.4
30 ❑ Aug 1966 Cover: 0.12 **NM** value: **30.00**
Circ: Statement: **168,731** • **CGC:** 1 graded, best 9.0
31 ❑ Oct 1966 Cover: 0.12 **NM** value: **30.00**
Circ: Statement: **168,731** • **CGC:** 1 graded, best 9.0
32 ❑ Dec 1966 Cover: 0.12 **NM** value: **30.00**
Circ: Statement: **168,731** • **CGC:** 2 graded, best 8.5
33 ❑ Feb 1967 Cover: 0.12 **NM** value: **30.00**
• **CGC:** 2 graded, best 9.2
34 ❑ Apr 1967 Cover: 0.12 **NM** value: **30.00**
• **CGC:** 3 graded, best 9.2
• Has 1966 Statement, filed 10/1/66; avg print run 309,000; avg sales 168,000; avg subs 731; avg total paid 168,731; samples 265; max existent 168,996; 45% of run returned
35 ❑ Jun 1967 Cover: 0.12 **NM** value: **30.00**
• **CGC:** 4 graded, best 9.2
final issue.

SEADRAGON, THE

Elite

1 ❑ May 1986 Cover: 1.75 **NM** value: **Cover or less**
Circ: CapCity orders: **2,775**
📖 Beward the World of Shadows! **A:** Dennis Yee **W:** Richard Paolinelli
2 ❑ Jun 1986 Cover: 1.75 **NM** value: **Cover or less**
Circ: CapCity orders: **2,125**
3 ❑ Aug 1986 Cover: 1.75 **NM** value: **Cover or less**
Circ: CapCity orders: **2,175**
4 ❑ 1986 Cover: 1.75 **NM** value: **Cover or less**
Circ: CapCity orders: **2,435**
5 ❑ 1986 Cover: 1.75 **NM** value: **Cover or less**
Circ: CapCity orders: **2,750**
6 ❑ 1986 Cover: 1.75 **NM** value: **Cover or less**
Circ: CapCity orders: **2,725**

SEA HOUND

Avon

1 ❑ ca. 1945 Cover: 0.10 **NM** value: **50.00**
• **CGC:** 1 graded, best 9.4
2 ❑ Sep 1945 Cover: 0.10 **NM** value: **50.00**

SEA HUNT

Dell

4 ❑ Mar 1960 Cover: 0.10 **NM** value: **35.00**
• **CGC:** 1 graded, best 9.0
Photo cover. • numbering continues from Dell Four Color
5 ❑ Jun 1960 Cover: 0.10 **NM** value: **35.00**
• **CGC:** 2 graded, best 9.2
Photo cover.
6 ❑ Sep 1960 Cover: 0.10 **NM** value: **35.00**
• **CGC:** 2 graded, best 9.0
Photo cover.
7 ❑ Dec 1960 Cover: 0.10 **NM** value: **30.00**
• **CGC:** 1 graded, best 9.2
Photo cover.
8 ❑ Mar 1961 **NM** value: **30.00**
• **CGC:** 1 graded, best 9.4
no cover price.
9 ❑ Jun 1961 Cover: 0.15 **NM** value: **30.00**
Photo cover. 📖 Underwater Cover-Up; Suspicious Waters
10 ❑ Sep 1961 Cover: 0.15 **NM** value: **25.00**
Photo cover.
11 ❑ Dec 1961 Cover: 0.15 **NM** value: **25.00**
• **CGC:** 1 graded, best 9.6
Photo cover.
12 ❑ Mar 1962 Cover: 0.15 **NM** value: **25.00**
Photo cover.
13 ❑ Jun 1962 Cover: 0.15 **NM** value: **25.00**
Photo cover.

SEALS

Studio Aries

Ash 1❑May 2000, b&w **NM** value: **1.00**
• preview

SEAQUEST

Nemesis

1 ❑ Mar 1994 Cover: 2.25 **NM** value: **2.50**
Circ: CapCity orders: **11,725**
cardstock cover. 📖 Deep Faith • based on TV show **A:** Keith Pollard **W:** D.G. Chichester
2 ❑ 1994 Cover: 2.25 **NM** value: **Cover or less**
Circ: CapCity orders: **6,025**
3 ❑ 1994 Cover: 2.25 **NM** value: **Cover or less**
Circ: CapCity orders: **4,350**

SEARCHERS, THE

Caliber

1 ❑ ca. 1996 Cover: 2.95 **NM** value: **Cover or less**
2 ❑ ca. 1996 Cover: 2.95 **NM** value: **Cover or less**
3 ❑ ca. 1996 Cover: 2.95 **NM** value: **Cover or less**
4 ❑ ca. 1996 Cover: 2.95 **NM** value: **Cover or less**

SEARCHERS, THE: APOSTLE OF MERCY

Caliber

1 ❑ ca. 1997 Cover: 2.95 **NM** value: **Cover or less**
• Giant-size. **A:** Art Wetherell **W:** Chris Dowss; Colin Clayton
2 ❑ ca. 1997 Cover: 3.95 **NM** value: **Cover or less**

SEARCH FOR LOVE

ACG

1 ❑ ca. 1950 Cover: 0.10 **NM** value: **75.00**
2 ❑ ca. 1950 Cover: 0.10 **NM** value: **50.00**

SEBASTIAN O

DC / Vertigo

1 ❑ May 1993 Cover: 1.95 **NM** value: **2.00**
Circ: CapCity orders: **28,850**
📖 The Yellow Book **A:** Steve Yeowell **W:** Grant Morrison ★ 1st Appearance of Sebastian O.
2 ❑ Jun 1993 Cover: 1.95 **NM** value: **2.00**
Circ: CapCity orders: **17,850**
📖 Against Nature **A:** Steve Yeowell **W:** Grant Morrison
3 ❑ Jul 1993 Cover: 1.95 **NM** value: **2.00**
Circ: CapCity orders: **16,050**
📖 The Queen Is Dead **A:** Steve Yeowell **W:** Grant Morrison

SEBASTIAN (WALT DISNEY'S...)

Disney

1 ❑ Cover: 1.50 **NM** value: **2.00**
Circ: CapCity orders: **7,600**
📖 Fiddling Around; Sebastian In Scotland; Out Of Africa And Into The Frying Pan; The Big Finale
2 ❑ Cover: 1.50 **NM** value: **2.00**
Circ: CapCity orders: **6,150**

SECOND CITY

Harrier

1 ❑ Oct 1986 Cover: 1.95 **NM** value: **Cover or less**
A: Phil Elliott **W:** Paul Duncan
2 ❑ Dec 1986 Cover: 1.95 **NM** value: **Cover or less**
A: Phil Elliott **W:** Paul Duncan
3 ❑ Feb 1987 Cover: 1.95 **NM** value: **Cover or less**
A: Phil Elliott **W:** Paul Duncan
4 ❑ Apr 1987 Cover: 1.95 **NM** value: **Cover or less**
A: Phil Elliott **W:** Paul Duncan
Bk 1❑ Apr 1994 Cover: 8.95 **NM** value: **Cover or less**
• collects earlier material

SECOND LIFE OF DOCTOR MIRAGE, THE

Valiant

Doctor Hwen Mirage was a parapsychologist who thought he had stumbled across the find of a lifetime. In many ways he was all too right.

Along with his wife and associate Carmen Ruiz, Hwen was investigating the charred bodies of "Hook" and "Welt," two of Master Darque's operatives. Although the two had died in a propane explosion, the Darque force still inhabited their bodies. When Hwen and Carmen began doing dissections and tissue analyses, the bodies suddenly became animated and attacked them. Hwen and Carmen managed to stop them, and even traced the source of their power to Darque himself. They followed him from New Orleans to Ladakh where Darque had gone to steal the secrets of a dead geomancer. There Hwen confronted Darque, and seemingly lost his life in the process. But Hwen came back from beyond out of love for Carmen, even though he is now an incorporeal ghost!

1 ❑ Nov 1993 Cover: 2.50 **NM** value: **Cover or less**
Circ: CapCity orders: **99,875**
📖 Darque Passage **A:** Bernard Chang **W:** Bob Layton ★ Origin of Doctor Mirage. ★ Appearance of Master Darque. ★ Death of Gwen Mirage.
1/GO❑Nov 1993 **NM** value: **3.00**
• Gold edition.
2 ❑ Dec 1993 Cover: 2.50 **NM** value: **Cover or less**
Circ: CapCity orders: **52,850**
3 ❑ Jan 1994 Cover: 2.50 **NM** value: **Cover or less**
Circ: CapCity orders: **39,900**
4 ❑ Feb 1994 Cover: 2.50 **NM** value: **Cover or less**
Circ: CapCity orders: **32,225**

Other grades: Multiply prices above by **1.5 for Mint • 2/3 for Very Fine • 1/3 for Fine • 1/5 for Very Good • 1/8 for Good**

5 ❑ Mar 1994 Cover: 2.50 **NM** value: **Cover or less**
Circ: CapCity orders: **26,300**
★ Appearance of Shadowman.
6 ❑ Apr 1994 Cover: 2.50 **NM** value: **Cover or less**
Circ: CapCity orders: **21,450**
7 ❑ May 1994 Cover: 2.50 **NM** value: **Cover or less**
Circ: CapCity orders: **25,525**
• trading card ★ Versus Doctor Eclipse.
8 ❑ Jun 1994 Cover: 2.50 **NM** value: **Cover or less**
Circ: CapCity orders: **17,200**
9 ❑ Aug 1994 Cover: 2.50 **NM** value: **Cover or less**
Circ: CapCity orders: **16,075**
10 ❑ Sep 1994 Cover: 2.50 **NM** value: **Cover or less**
Circ: CapCity orders: **15,475**
11 ❑ Oct 1994 Cover: 2.50 **NM** value: **Cover or less**
Circ: CapCity orders: **20,425**
📖 The Chaos Effect: Beta, Part 2 • Chaos Effect
12 ❑ Nov 1994 Cover: 2.50 **NM** value: **Cover or less**
Circ: CapCity orders: **13,375**
13 ❑ Dec 1994 Cover: 2.50 **NM** value: **Cover or less**
Circ: CapCity orders: **12,500**
★ Appearance of Walt Willey.
14 ❑ Jan 1995 Cover: 2.50 **NM** value: **Cover or less**
Circ: CapCity orders: **10,950**
15 ❑ Feb 1995 Cover: 2.50 **NM** value: **Cover or less**
Circ: CapCity orders: **9,950**
16 ❑ Mar 1995 Cover: 2.50 **NM** value: **Cover or less**
Circ: CapCity orders: **8,600**
📖 Building the Perfect Beast, Part 1
17 ❑ Apr 1995 Cover: 2.50 **NM** value: **Cover or less**
Circ: CapCity orders: **7,750**
📖 Building the Perfect Beast, Part 2
18 ❑ May 1995 Cover: 2.50 **NM** value: **Cover or less**
Circ: CapCity orders: **6,775**
📖 Building the Perfect Beast, Part 3 final issue.

SECOND RATE HEROES — Foundation

1 ❑ b&w Cover: 2.50 **NM** value: **Cover or less**
2 ❑ b&w Cover: 2.50 **NM** value: **Cover or less**

SECRET AGENT (CHARLTON) — Charlton

When a grenade blows off his hand in Vietnam, Sarge Steel is given a prosthetic steel hand. He becomes a private detective when he returned to the States but, owing to the popularity of James Bond and the spy motif in the mid-1960s, he undergoes a transformation from private eye to CIA operative.

Mr. Ize, who hypnotizes his subjects to do dirty work, the slinky seductive feline-themed Lynx, and the swastika-wearing Smiling Skull are some of the outrageous villains that Agent Steel goes up against. Although he doesn't utilize his judo expertise as a secret agent, instructional pages left over from his Sarge Steel phase are printed as a backup feature in this title. Secret Agent lasted only two issues after the metamorphosis from Sarge Steel.

9 ❑ Oct 1966 Cover: 0.25 **NM** value: **8.00**
📖 The Warmaker! • Series continued from Sarge Steel #8 **A:** Bill Montes **W:** Joe Gill ★ 1st Appearance of Mr. Ize!.
10 ❑ Oct 1967 Cover: 0.12 **NM** value: **6.00**

SECRET AGENT (GOLD KEY) — Gold Key

1 ❑ Nov 1966 Cover: 0.12 **NM** value: **40.00**
• **CGC:** 4 graded, best 9.4
Photo cover. 📖 The Panic Package
2 ❑ Jan 1968 Cover: 0.12 **NM** value: **25.00**
• **CGC:** 2 graded, best 9.4
Photo cover.

SECRET AGENTS — Personality

1 ❑ b&w Cover: 2.95 **NM** value: **Cover or less**
Circ: CapCity orders: **1,450**
2 ❑ b&w Cover: 2.95 **NM** value: **Cover or less**
3 ❑ b&w Cover: 2.95 **NM** value: **Cover or less**

SECRET CITY SAGA (JACK KIRBY'S...) — Topps

0 ❑ Apr 1993 Cover: 2.95 **NM** value: **Cover or less**
Circ: CapCity orders: **47,804**
📖 Amemoto: Mephistopheles **A:** Walt Simonson; John Cleary **W:** Roy Thomas; Tony Isabella
1 ❑ May 1993 Cover: 2.95 **NM** value: **Cover or less**
Circ: CapCity orders: **35,200**
📖 In Battle Joined • trading cards **A:** Steve Ditko **W:** Steve Ditko
2 ❑ Jun 1993 Cover: 2.95 **NM** value: **Cover or less**
Circ: CapCity orders: **22,900**
• trading cards **A:** Steve Ditko; Bill Sienkiewicz; John Byrne
3 ❑ Jul 1993 Cover: 2.95 **NM** value: **Cover or less**
Circ: CapCity orders: **18,500**
• trading cards **A:** Steve Ditko
4 ❑ Aug 1993 Cover: 2.95 **NM** value: **Cover or less**
Circ: CapCity orders: **12,900**
• trading cards **A:** Steve Ditko

The prices seen above do not represent the highest possible prices seen in online auctions, but rather the prices we have seen these issues reliably fetch in a variety of environments (storefront retail, mail order, auction and convention).

SECRET DEFENDERS — Marvel

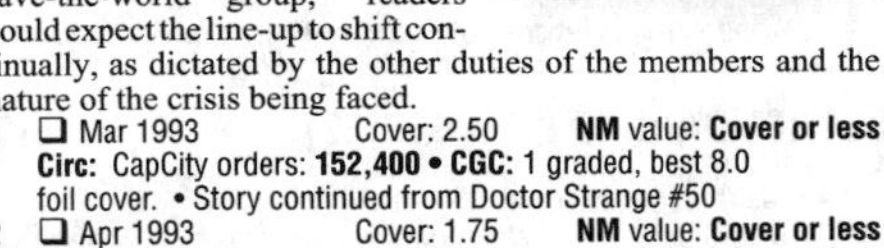

Doctor Strange was once the mightiest of sorcerers, but has since been stripped of his powers as Sorcerer Supreme. Although he is still able to sense the dangers that threaten the world, he often finds himself unable to stop them alone. So, just as he gathered the first team of Defenders, he now gathers others to help fight these greatest of battles.

These "Secret Defenders" (initially comprising Nomad, Darkhawk, Spider-Woman, and Wolverine) are a loose collection of heroes, drawn together to fight the direst of threats. In the case of this "part-time save-the-world group," readers could expect the line-up to shift continually, as dictated by the other duties of the members and the nature of the crisis being faced.

1 ❑ Mar 1993 Cover: 2.50 **NM** value: **Cover or less**
Circ: CapCity orders: **152,400** • **CGC:** 1 graded, best 8.0
foil cover. • Story continued from Doctor Strange #50
2 ❑ Apr 1993 Cover: 1.75 **NM** value: **Cover or less**
Circ: CapCity orders: **66,600**
3 ❑ May 1993 Cover: 1.75 **NM** value: **Cover or less**
Circ: CapCity orders: **50,700**
4 ❑ Jun 1993 Cover: 1.75 **NM** value: **Cover or less**
Circ: CapCity orders: **42,100**
5 ❑ Jul 1993 Cover: 1.75 **NM** value: **Cover or less**
Circ: CapCity orders: **36,400**
6 ❑ Aug 1993 Cover: 1.75 **NM** value: **Cover or less**
Circ: CapCity orders: **29,650**
7 ❑ Sep 1993 Cover: 1.75 **NM** value: **Cover or less**
Circ: CapCity orders: **24,600**
8 ❑ Oct 1993 Cover: 1.75 **NM** value: **Cover or less**
Circ: CapCity orders: **21,500**
A: Andre Coates **W:** Roy Thomas ★ Appearance of Captain America, Spider-Man, Scarlet Witch, Doctor Strange, Xanadu.
9 ❑ Nov 1993 Cover: 1.75 **NM** value: **Cover or less**
Circ: CapCity orders: **19,320**
📖 Revenge, Part 1
10 ❑ Dec 1993 Cover: 1.75 **NM** value: **Cover or less**
Circ: CapCity orders: **17,700**
11 ❑ Jan 1994 Cover: 1.75 **NM** value: **Cover or less**
Circ: CapCity orders: **16,150**
12 ❑ Feb 1994 Cover: 2.50 **NM** value: **Cover or less**
Circ: CapCity orders: **17,700**
foil cover.
13 ❑ Mar 1994 Cover: 1.75 **NM** value: **Cover or less**
Circ: CapCity orders: **13,800**
14 ❑ Apr 1994 Cover: 1.75 **NM** value: **Cover or less**
Circ: CapCity orders: **12,800**
15 ❑ May 1994 Cover: 1.95 **NM** value: **Cover or less**
Circ: CapCity orders: **12,750**
16 ❑ Jun 1994 Cover: 1.95 **NM** value: **Cover or less**
Circ: CapCity orders: **11,900**
17 ❑ Jul 1994 Cover: 1.95 **NM** value: **Cover or less**
Circ: CapCity orders: **11,800**
18 ❑ Aug 1994 Cover: 1.95 **NM** value: **Cover or less**
Circ: CapCity orders: **10,650**
19 ❑ Sep 1994 Cover: 1.95 **NM** value: **Cover or less**
Circ: CapCity orders: **10,100**
20 ❑ Oct 1994 Cover: 1.95 **NM** value: **Cover or less**
Circ: CapCity orders: **9,350**
21 ❑ Nov 1994 Cover: 1.95 **NM** value: **Cover or less**
Circ: CapCity orders: **8,000**
22 ❑ Dec 1994 Cover: 1.95 **NM** value: **Cover or less**
Circ: CapCity orders: **7,650**
23 ❑ Jan 1995 Cover: 1.95 **NM** value: **Cover or less**
Circ: CapCity orders: **6,825**
24 ❑ Feb 1995 Cover: 1.95 **NM** value: **Cover or less**
Circ: CapCity orders: **6,425**
★ Versus original Defenders.
25 ❑ Mar 1995 Cover: 1.95 **NM** value: **2.50**
Circ: CapCity orders: **5,825**
• Giant-size. final issue.

SECRET DIARY OF EERIE ADVENTURES — Avon

1 ❑ ca. 1953 **NM** value: **1500.00**
• **CGC:** 3 graded, best 7.5

SECRET DOORS — Dimension

1 ❑ b&w Cover: 1.50 **NM** value: **Cover or less**

SECRET FANTASIES — Bullseye

1 ❑ b&w and red Cover: 2.25 **NM** value: **Cover or less**
• digest.
2 ❑ b&w Cover: 2.95 **NM** value: **Cover or less**
cardstock cover. • normal-sized.

SECRET FILES — Angel

0 ❑ Jun 1996, b&w Cover: 2.95 **NM** value: **Cover or less**
0/Nude ❑ Jun 1996, b&w Cover: 10.00 **NM** value: **Cover or less**
cardstock cover. • nude cover edition.
1 ❑ Fal 1996, b&w Cover: 2.95 **NM** value: **Cover or less**

SECRET FILES AND ORIGINS GUIDE TO THE DC UNIVERSE 2000 — DC

1 ❑ Mar 2000 Cover: 4.95 **NM** value: **Cover or less**
Circ: Diamd. preorders: **20,534**

SECRET FILES: INVASION DAY — Angel

1 ❑ Cover: 5.00 **NM** value: **Cover or less**
A: Luciano Lima **W:** Mark Valadez; Mort Castle; Robert Gordon Howard
1/Nude ❑ Cover: 5.00 **NM** value: **Cover or less**
A: Luciano Lima **W:** Mark Valadez; Mort Castle; Robert Gordon Howard
2 ❑ Cover: 5.00 **NM** value: **Cover or less**
A: Daniel Horn **W:** Mark Valadez; Mort Castle; Robert Gordon Howard
2/Nude ❑ Cover: 5.00 **NM** value: **Cover or less**
A: Daniel Horn **W:** Mark Valadez; Mort Castle; Robert Gordon Howard

SECRET FILES PRESIDENT LUTHOR — DC

1 ❑ Mar 2001 Cover: 4.95 **NM** value: **Cover or less**
📖 The Why; Most Suitable Person; The Great Debate; Rocket's Red Glare; Power Couple; He's Coming, Mr. Lew-Thor **A:** Yvel Guichet; Paul Pelletier; Stuart Immonen; Jackson Guice; Dale Eaglesham; Mike Wieringo; Louis Small Jr.; Lee Bermejo; Matthew Clark **W:** Jeph Loeb; Karl Kesel; Phil Jimenez; Frank Pittarese; Greg Rucka; Peter David

SECRET FILES: THE STRANGE CASE — Angel

1 ❑ Cover: 2.95 **NM** value: **Cover or less**
📖 Pretty Little Secrets **A:** Al Rio **W:** Lloyd Chasseur

SECRET HEARTS — DC

1 ❑ Sep 1949 Cover: 0.10 **NM** value: **400.00**
• **CGC:** 1 graded, best 9.2
2 ❑ Nov 1949 Cover: 0.10 **NM** value: **250.00**
3 ❑ Feb 1950 Cover: 0.10 **NM** value: **200.00**
4 ❑ Apr 1950 Cover: 0.10 **NM** value: **200.00**
5 ❑ Jun 1950 Cover: 0.10 **NM** value: **200.00**
6 ❑ Aug 1950 Cover: 0.10 **NM** value: **200.00**
7 ❑ Dec 1951 Cover: 0.10 **NM** value: **200.00**
8 ❑ Feb 1952 Cover: 0.10 **NM** value: **150.00**
9 ❑ Apr 1952 Cover: 0.10 **NM** value: **150.00**
10 ❑ Jun 1952 Cover: 0.10 **NM** value: **150.00**
11 ❑ Aug 1952 Cover: 0.10 **NM** value: **100.00**
12 ❑ Oct 1952 Cover: 0.10 **NM** value: **100.00**
13 ❑ Dec 1952 Cover: 0.10 **NM** value: **100.00**
14 ❑ Feb 1953 Cover: 0.10 **NM** value: **100.00**
15 ❑ Apr 1953 Cover: 0.10 **NM** value: **100.00**
16 ❑ Jun 1953 Cover: 0.10 **NM** value: **100.00**
17 ❑ Aug 1953 Cover: 0.10 **NM** value: **100.00**
18 ❑ Oct 1953 Cover: 0.10 **NM** value: **100.00**
19 ❑ Dec 1953 Cover: 0.10 **NM** value: **100.00**
20 ❑ Feb 1954 Cover: 0.10 **NM** value: **100.00**
21 ❑ Apr 1954 Cover: 0.10 **NM** value: **80.00**
22 ❑ Jul 1954 Cover: 0.10 **NM** value: **80.00**
📖 Love Turned Away
23 ❑ Aug 1954 Cover: 0.10 **NM** value: **80.00**
24 ❑ Oct 1954 Cover: 0.10 **NM** value: **80.00**
25 ❑ Dec 1954 Cover: 0.10 **NM** value: **80.00**
26 ❑ Feb 1955 Cover: 0.10 **NM** value: **80.00**
27 ❑ Apr 1955 Cover: 0.10 **NM** value: **80.00**
28 ❑ Jun 1955 Cover: 0.10 **NM** value: **80.00**
29 ❑ Aug 1955 Cover: 0.10 **NM** value: **80.00**
30 ❑ Oct 1955 Cover: 0.10 **NM** value: **80.00**
• **CGC:** 1 graded, best 8.5
31 ❑ Dec 1955 Cover: 0.10 **NM** value: **80.00**
32 ❑ Mar 1956 Cover: 0.10 **NM** value: **80.00**
33 ❑ 1956 Cover: 0.10 **NM** value: **80.00**
34 ❑ 1956 Cover: 0.10 **NM** value: **80.00**
35 ❑ 1956 Cover: 0.10 **NM** value: **80.00**
36 ❑ 1956 Cover: 0.10 **NM** value: **80.00**
37 ❑ 1956 Cover: 0.10 **NM** value: **80.00**
38 ❑ 1956 Cover: 0.10 **NM** value: **80.00**
39 ❑ 1957 Cover: 0.10 **NM** value: **80.00**
40 ❑ 1957 Cover: 0.10 **NM** value: **80.00**
41 ❑ 1957 Cover: 0.10 **NM** value: **45.00**
42 ❑ 1957 Cover: 0.10 **NM** value: **45.00**
43 ❑ 1957 Cover: 0.10 **NM** value: **45.00**
44 ❑ 1957 Cover: 0.10 **NM** value: **45.00**
45 ❑ Feb 1958 Cover: 0.10 **NM** value: **45.00**
46 ❑ Apr 1958 Cover: 0.10 **NM** value: **45.00**
47 ❑ 1958 Cover: 0.10 **NM** value: **45.00**
48 ❑ 1958 Cover: 0.10 **NM** value: **45.00**
49 ❑ 1958 Cover: 0.10 **NM** value: **45.00**
50 ❑ 1958 Cover: 0.10 **NM** value: **45.00**
51 ❑ Nov 1958 Cover: 0.10 **NM** value: **45.00**
52 ❑ 1959 Cover: 0.10 **NM** value: **45.00**
53 ❑ 1959 Cover: 0.10 **NM** value: **45.00**
54 ❑ 1959 Cover: 0.10 **NM** value: **45.00**
55 ❑ 1959 Cover: 0.10 **NM** value: **45.00**
56 ❑ 1959 Cover: 0.10 **NM** value: **45.00**
57 ❑ 1959 Cover: 0.10 **NM** value: **45.00**
58 ❑ 1959 Cover: 0.10 **NM** value: **45.00**
59 ❑ Nov 1959 Cover: 0.10 **NM** value: **45.00**
60 ❑ 1960 Cover: 0.10 **NM** value: **45.00**
61 ❑ 1960 Cover: 0.10 **NM** value: **30.00**
62 ❑ 1960 Cover: 0.10 **NM** value: **30.00**
63 ❑ May 1960 Cover: 0.10 **NM** value: **30.00**
64 ❑ 1960 Cover: 0.10 **NM** value: **30.00**
65 ❑ 1960 Cover: 0.10 **NM** value: **30.00**
66 ❑ 1960 Cover: 0.10 **NM** value: **30.00**
67 ❑ 1960 Cover: 0.10 **NM** value: **30.00**
68 ❑ 1960 Cover: 0.10 **NM** value: **30.00**
69 ❑ 1961 Cover: 0.10 **NM** value: **30.00**
70 ❑ 1961 Cover: 0.10 **NM** value: **30.00**
71 ❑ 1961 Cover: 0.10 **NM** value: **30.00**
72 ❑ 1961 Cover: 0.10 **NM** value: **30.00**
73 ❑ 1961 Cover: 0.10 **NM** value: **30.00**
74 ❑ 1961 Cover: 0.10 **NM** value: **30.00**
75 ❑ 1961 Cover: 0.10 **NM** value: **30.00**
76 ❑ Jan 1962 Cover: 0.10 **NM** value: **30.00**
📖 Too Much to Hope For
77 ❑ 1962 Cover: 0.12 **NM** value: **30.00**
78 ❑ 1962 Cover: 0.12 **NM** value: **30.00**
79 ❑ 1962 Cover: 0.12 **NM** value: **30.00**
80 ❑ 1962 Cover: 0.12 **NM** value: **30.00**
81 ❑ 1962 Cover: 0.12 **NM** value: **25.00**
82 ❑ 1962 Cover: 0.12 **NM** value: **25.00**

CGC-graded: Multiply prices above by **33 for 9.9 M** • **16 for 9.8 NM/M** • **7 for 9.6 NM+** • **5 for 9.4 NM** • **2.5 for 9.2 NM-** • **1.5 for 9.0 VF/NM**

83 ❑ 1962 Cover: 0.12 **NM** value: **25.00**
84 ❑ 1962 Cover: 0.12 **NM** value: **25.00**
85 ❑ 1963 Cover: 0.12 **NM** value: **25.00**
86 ❑ Mar 1963 Cover: 0.12 **NM** value: **25.00**
87 ❑ 1963 Cover: 0.12 **NM** value: **25.00**
88 ❑ 1963 Cover: 0.12 **NM** value: **25.00**
89 ❑ Jul 1963 Cover: 0.12 **NM** value: **25.00**
90 ❑ Sep 1963 Cover: 0.12 **NM** value: **25.00**
91 ❑ Oct 1963 Cover: 0.12 **NM** value: **25.00**
92 ❑ 1963 Cover: 0.12 **NM** value: **25.00**
93 ❑ 1964 Cover: 0.12 **NM** value: **25.00**
94 ❑ 1964 Cover: 0.12 **NM** value: **25.00**
95 ❑ 1964 Cover: 0.12 **NM** value: **25.00**
96 ❑ 1964 Cover: 0.12 **NM** value: **25.00**
97 ❑ 1964 Cover: 0.12 **NM** value: **25.00**
98 ❑ 1964 Cover: 0.12 **NM** value: **25.00**
99 ❑ Oct 1964 Cover: 0.12 **NM** value: **25.00**
100 ❑ 1964 Cover: 0.12 **NM** value: **25.00**
101 ❑ 1964 Cover: 0.12 **NM** value: **20.00**
102 ❑ 1965 Cover: 0.12 **NM** value: **20.00**
103 ❑ 1965 Cover: 0.12 **NM** value: **20.00**
104 ❑ 1965 Cover: 0.12 **NM** value: **20.00**
105 ❑ 1965 Cover: 0.12 **NM** value: **20.00**
106 ❑ Sep 1965 Cover: 0.12 **NM** value: **20.00**
107 ❑ Oct 1965 Cover: 0.12 **NM** value: **20.00**
108 ❑ Dec 1965 Cover: 0.12 **NM** value: **20.00**
109 ❑ Jan 1956 Cover: 0.12 **NM** value: **20.00**
110 ❑ Mar 1966 Cover: 0.12 **NM** value: **20.00**
111 ❑ Apr 1966 Cover: 0.12 **NM** value: **20.00**
📖 Don't Trust Your Boyfriend; Reach For Happiness; In Love With Love
112 ❑ Jun 1966 Cover: 0.12 **NM** value: **20.00**
📖 Don't Tell Me That You Love Me; Reach For Happiness; The Truth About Love
113 ❑ Jul 1966 Cover: 0.12 **NM** value: **20.00**
114 ❑ Sep 1966 Cover: 0.12 **NM** value: **20.00**
115 ❑ Oct 1966 Cover: 0.12 **NM** value: **20.00**
116 ❑ Dec 1966 Cover: 0.12 **NM** value: **20.00**
117 ❑ Jan 1967 Cover: 0.12 **NM** value: **20.00**
Circ: Statement: **149,700**
118 ❑ Mar 1967 Cover: 0.12 **NM** value: **20.00**
Circ: Statement: **149,700**
119 ❑ Apr 1967 Cover: 0.12 **NM** value: **20.00**
Circ: Statement: **149,700**
120 ❑ Jun 1967 Cover: 0.12 **NM** value: **20.00**
Circ: Statement: **149,700**
121 ❑ Jul 1967 Cover: 0.12 **NM** value: **15.00**
Circ: Statement: **149,700**
122 ❑ Sep 1967 Cover: 0.12 **NM** value: **15.00**
Circ: Statement: **149,700**
123 ❑ Oct 1967 Cover: 0.12 **NM** value: **15.00**
Circ: Statement: **149,700**
124 ❑ Dec 1967 Cover: 0.12 **NM** value: **15.00**
Circ: Statement: **149,700**
125 ❑ Jan 1968 Cover: 0.12 **NM** value: **15.00**
126 ❑ Mar 1968 Cover: 0.12 **NM** value: **15.00**
127 ❑ Apr 1968 Cover: 0.12 **NM** value: **15.00**
128 ❑ Jun 1968 Cover: 0.12 **NM** value: **15.00**
129 ❑ Jul 1968 Cover: 0.12 **NM** value: **15.00**
130 ❑ Sep 1968 Cover: 0.12 **NM** value: **15.00**
131 ❑ Oct 1968 Cover: 0.12 **NM** value: **15.00**
132 ❑ Dec 1968 Cover: 0.12 **NM** value: **15.00**
133 ❑ Jan 1969 Cover: 0.12 **NM** value: **15.00**
134 ❑ Mar 1969 Cover: 0.12 **NM** value: **15.00**
135 ❑ Apr 1969 Cover: 0.12 **NM** value: **15.00**
136 ❑ Jun 1969 Cover: 0.12 **NM** value: **15.00**
137 ❑ Jul 1969 **NM** value: **15.00**
138 ❑ Sep 1969 **NM** value: **15.00**
139 ❑ Oct 1969 Cover: 0.15 **NM** value: **15.00**
140 ❑ Dec 1969 Cover: 0.15 **NM** value: **15.00**
141 ❑ Jan 1970 Cover: 0.15 **NM** value: **15.00**
142 ❑ Mar 1970 Cover: 0.15 **NM** value: **15.00**
143 ❑ Apr 1970 Cover: 0.15 **NM** value: **15.00**
144 ❑ Jun 1970 Cover: 0.15 **NM** value: **15.00**
145 ❑ Jul 1970 Cover: 0.15 **NM** value: **15.00**
146 ❑ Sep 1970 Cover: 0.15 **NM** value: **15.00**
147 ❑ Oct 1970 Cover: 0.15 **NM** value: **15.00**
148 ❑ Dec 1970 Cover: 0.15 **NM** value: **15.00**
149 ❑ Jan 1971 Cover: 0.15 **NM** value: **15.00**
150 ❑ Mar 1971 Cover: 0.15 **NM** value: **15.00**
151 ❑ Apr 1971 Cover: 0.15 **NM** value: **15.00**
152 ❑ Jun 1971 **NM** value: **15.00**
153 ❑ Jul 1971 **NM** value: **15.00**

SECRET KILLERS, THE — Bronze Man

1 ❑ Oct 1997, b&w Cover: 2.95 **NM** value: **Cover or less**
📖 Where Dragons Roam, Part 1 **A:** Jerry Williams **W:** Dan Braun
2 ❑ 1997b&w Cover: 2.95 **NM** value: **Cover or less**
📖 Where Dragons Roam, Part 2 **A:** Jerry Williams **W:** Dan Braun
3 ❑ 1998b&w Cover: 2.95 **NM** value: **Cover or less**
4 ❑ 1998b&w Cover: 2.95 **NM** value: **Cover or less**
cover doesn't. • becomes Exit from Shadow; indicia indicates name change

SECRET LOVE (AJAX) — Ajax

1 ❑ ca. 1955 Cover: 0.10 **NM** value: **60.00**
2 ❑ ca. 1956 Cover: 0.10 **NM** value: **40.00**
3 ❑ ca. 1956 Cover: 0.10 **NM** value: **40.00**

SECRET LOVE (FOUR STAR) — Four Star

1 ❑ ca. 1957 Cover: 0.10 **NM** value: **50.00**
2 ❑ ca. 1957 Cover: 0.10 **NM** value: **30.00**
3 ❑ ca. 1957 Cover: 0.10 **NM** value: **30.00**
4 ❑ ca. 1957 Cover: 0.10 **NM** value: **30.00**

SECRET LOVES — Comic Magazines

1 ❑ Nov 1949 Cover: 0.10 **NM** value: **150.00**
2 ❑ Jan 1950 Cover: 0.10 **NM** value: **125.00**
3 ❑ Mar 1950 Cover: 0.10 **NM** value: **100.00**
4 ❑ May 1950 Cover: 0.10 **NM** value: **75.00**
5 ❑ Jul 1950 Cover: 0.10 **NM** value: **75.00**
6 ❑ Sep 1950 Cover: 0.10 **NM** value: **75.00**

SECRET MISSIONS — St. John

1 ❑ Feb 1950 Cover: 0.10 **NM** value: **125.00**
• **CGC:** 1 graded, best 9.0

SECRET MYSTERIES — Ribage

16 ❑ ca. 1954 Cover: 0.10 **NM** value: **175.00**
• **CGC:** 2 graded, best 9.6
17 ❑ ca. 1955 Cover: 0.10 **NM** value: **125.00**
18 ❑ ca. 1955 Cover: 0.10 **NM** value: **125.00**
19 ❑ ca. 1955 Cover: 0.10 **NM** value: **125.00**

SECRET ORIGINS (1ST SERIES) — DC

Anl 1 ❑ Aug 1961 Cover: 0.12 **NM** value: **450.00**
• **CGC:** 10 graded, best 9.0
• second issue published as 80 Page Giant #8. • reprints Silver Age origins **A:** Carmine Infantino; Jack Kirby

SECRET ORIGINS (2ND SERIES) — DC

1 ❑ Mar 1973 Cover: 0.20 **NM** value: **14.00**
• **CGC:** 6 graded, best 9.4
📖 The Ghost; Mystery of the Human Thunderbolt! **A:** Carmine Infantino; Joe Kubert **W:** Robert Kanigher ★ Origin of Superman, Flash, Batman.
2 ❑ May 1973 Cover: 0.20 **NM** value: **8.00**
• **CGC:** 1 graded, best 9.2
3 ❑ Aug 1973 Cover: 0.20 **NM** value: **7.00**
★ Origin of Wonder Woman, Wildcat.
4 ❑ Oct 1973 Cover: 0.20 **NM** value: **7.00**
★ Origin of Kid Eternity, Vigilante.
5 ❑ Dec 1973 Cover: 0.20 **NM** value: **6.00**
• **CGC:** 1 graded, best 9.0
6 ❑ Feb 1974 Cover: 0.20 **NM** value: **6.00**
7 ❑ Oct 1974 Cover: 0.20 **NM** value: **6.00**
★ Origin of Robin I (Dick Grayson), Aquaman.

SECRET ORIGINS (3RD SERIES) — DC

In 1986, just two years shy of its 50th anniversary, DC kicked off a series which chronicled the origins of many of its greatest characters. This second series of Secret Origins told of how everyone from Superman to the Newsboy Legion came into existence. It did this by printing the "secret" origin stories which, in the case of heroes like Wonder Woman, could be quite different than the more widely known origin stories. Published shortly after the events of Crisis on Infinite Earths, the origins were, for the most part, updated and refreshed to reflect the new continuity.

1 ❑ Apr 1986 Cover: 0.75 **NM** value: **3.00**
Circ: CapCity orders: **16,800** • **CGC:** 1 graded, best 9.8
★ Origin of Superman.
2 ❑ May 1986 Cover: 0.75 **NM** value: **2.00**
Circ: CapCity orders: **12,750**
★ Origin of Blue Beetle.
3 ❑ Jun 1986 Cover: 0.75 **NM** value: **2.00**
Circ: CapCity orders: **12,200**
★ Origin of Captain Marvel.
4 ❑ Jul 1986 Cover: 0.75 **NM** value: **2.00**
Circ: CapCity orders: **12,400**
★ Origin of Firestorm.
5 ❑ Aug 1986 Cover: 0.75 **NM** value: **2.00**
Circ: CapCity orders: **14,500**
★ Origin of The Crimson Avenger.
6 ❑ Sep 1986 Cover: 1.25 **NM** value: **2.00**
Circ: CapCity orders: **15,500**
★ Origin of Halo, Batman (Golden Age).
7 ❑ Oct 1986 Cover: 1.25 **NM** value: **2.00**
Circ: CapCity orders: **14,450**
★ Origin of Sandman II (Dr. Garrett Sanford), Green Lantern (Guy Gardner).
8 ❑ Nov 1986 Cover: 1.25 **NM** value: **2.00**
Circ: CapCity orders: **13,900**
★ Origin of Doll Man, Shadow Lass.
9 ❑ Dec 1986 Cover: 1.25 **NM** value: **2.00**
Circ: CapCity orders: **13,150**
★ Origin of Flash I (Jay Garrick), Skyman, Stripsey.
10 ❑ Jan 1987 Cover: 1.25 **NM** value: **2.00**
Circ: CapCity orders: **16,150**
• Legends ★ Origin of Phantom Stranger.
11 ❑ Feb 1987 Cover: 1.25 **NM** value: **2.00**
Circ: CapCity orders: **12,550**
C: Jerry Ordway ★ Origin of Power Girl, Hawkman (Golden Age).
12 ❑ Mar 1987 Cover: 1.25 **NM** value: **2.00**
Circ: CapCity orders: **11,900**
★ Origin of The Fury (Golden Age), Challengers of the Unknown.
13 ❑ Apr 1987 Cover: 1.25 **NM** value: **2.00**
Circ: CapCity orders: **12,950**
★ Origin of Johnny Thunder, Nightwing, Whip.
14 ❑ May 1987 Cover: 1.25 **NM** value: **2.00**
Circ: CapCity orders: **11,850**
• Legends ★ Origin of Suicide Squad.
15 ❑ Jun 1987 Cover: 1.25 **NM** value: **2.00**
Circ: CapCity orders: **12,100**
★ Origin of Spectre, Deadman.
16 ❑ Jul 1987 Cover: 1.25 **NM** value: **2.00**
Circ: CapCity orders: **11,450**
★ Origin of Hourman I (Rex Tyler), Warlord.
17 ❑ Aug 1987 Cover: 1.25 **NM** value: **2.00**
Circ: CapCity orders: **11,550**
★ Origin of Adam Strange, Doctor Occult.
18 ❑ Sep 1987 Cover: 1.25 **NM** value: **2.00**
Circ: CapCity orders: **14,100**
★ Origin of Creeper, Green Lantern I (Alan Scott).
19 ❑ Oct 1987 Cover: 1.25 **NM** value: **2.00**
Circ: CapCity orders: **12,550**
A: Murphy Anderson **C:** Jack Kirby ★ Origin of Uncle Sam, Guardian.
20 ❑ Nov 1987 Cover: 1.25 **NM** value: **2.00**
Circ: CapCity orders: **13,450**
★ Origin of Doctor Mid-Nite (Golden Age), Batgirl.
21 ❑ Dec 1987 Cover: 1.25 **NM** value: **2.00**
Circ: CapCity orders: **12,150**
★ Origin of Black Condor, Jonah Hex.
22 ❑ Jan 1988 Cover: 1.25 **NM** value: **2.00**
Circ: CapCity orders: **18,300**
• Millennium ★ Origin of Manhunters.
23 ❑ Feb 1988 Cover: 1.25 **NM** value: **2.00**
Circ: CapCity orders: **17,550**
• Millennium ★ Origin of Floronic Man, Guardians of the Universe.
24 ❑ Mar 1988 Cover: 1.25 **NM** value: **2.00**
Circ: CapCity orders: **13,400**
★ Origin of Blue Devil, Doctor Fate.
25 ❑ Apr 1988 Cover: 1.25 **NM** value: **2.00**
Circ: CapCity orders: **16,300**
★ Origin of The Atom (Golden Age), the Legion of Super-Heroes.
26 ❑ May 1988 Cover: 1.25 **NM** value: **2.00**
Circ: CapCity orders: **12,750**
★ Origin of Miss America, Black Lightning.
27 ❑ Jun 1988 Cover: 1.50 **NM** value: **2.00**
Circ: CapCity orders: **11,900**
★ Origin of Zatara, Zatanna.
28 ❑ Jul 1988 Cover: 1.50 **NM** value: **2.00**
Circ: CapCity orders: **11,750**
★ Origin of Nightshade, Midnight.
29 ❑ Aug 1988 Cover: 1.50 **NM** value: **2.00**
Circ: CapCity orders: **11,850**
★ Origin of The Atom (Silver Age), Red Tornado (Golden Age), Mr. America.
30 ❑ Sep 1988 Cover: 1.50 **NM** value: **2.00**
Circ: CapCity orders: **11,000**
★ Origin of Plastic Man, Elongated Man.
31 ❑ Oct 1988 Cover: 1.50 **NM** value: **2.00**
Circ: CapCity orders: **11,950**
★ Origin of Justice Society of America.
32 ❑ Nov 1988 Cover: 1.50 **NM** value: **2.00**
Circ: CapCity orders: **15,700**
★ Origin of Justice League of America.
33 ❑ Dec 1988 Cover: 1.50 **NM** value: **2.00**
Circ: CapCity orders: **17,850**
★ Origin of Icemaiden, Green Flame, Mr. Miracle.
34 ❑ Dec 1988 Cover: 1.50 **NM** value: **2.00**
Circ: CapCity orders: **16,700**
★ Origin of Rocket Red, G'Nort, Captain Atom.
35 ❑ Jan 1989 Cover: 1.50 **NM** value: **2.00**
Circ: CapCity orders: **16,850**
★ Origin of Booster Gold, Martian Manhunter, Max Lord.
36 ❑ Jan 1989 Cover: 1.50 **NM** value: **2.00**
Circ: CapCity orders: **12,950**
★ Origin of Green Lantern (Silver Age), Poison Ivy.
37 ❑ Feb 1989 Cover: 1.50 **NM** value: **2.00**
Circ: CapCity orders: **12,600**
★ Origin of Doctor Light, Legion of Substitute Heroes.
38 ❑ Mar 1989 Cover: 1.50 **NM** value: **2.00**
Circ: CapCity orders: **14,900**
★ Origin of Speedy, Green Arrow.
39 ❑ Apr 1989 Cover: 1.50 **NM** value: **2.00**
Circ: CapCity orders: **12,750**
★ Origin of Animal Man, Man-Bat.
40 ❑ May 1989 Cover: 1.50 **NM** value: **2.00**
Circ: CapCity orders: **10,900**
★ Origin of Gorilla Grodd, Congorilla, Detective Chimp.
41 ❑ Jun 1989 Cover: 1.50 **NM** value: **2.00**
Circ: CapCity orders: **11,300**
★ Origin of Flash's Rogue's Gallery.
42 ❑ Jul 1989 Cover: 1.50 **NM** value: **2.00**
Circ: CapCity orders: **11,150**
★ Origin of Grim Ghost, Phantom Girl.
43 ❑ Aug 1989 Cover: 1.50 **NM** value: **2.00**
Circ: CapCity orders: **13,500**
★ Origin of Chris KL-99, Hawk, Dove, Cave Carson.
44 ❑ Sep 1989 Cover: 1.50 **NM** value: **2.00**
★ Origin of Clayface III, Clayface I, Clayface IV, Clayface II.
45 ❑ Oct 1989 Cover: 1.50 **NM** value: **2.00**
Circ: CapCity orders: **10,950**
★ Origin of Blackhawk, El Diablo.
46 ❑ Dec 1989 Cover: 1.75 **NM** value: **2.00**
Circ: CapCity orders: **13,450**
• Blueprints of Teen Titans Headquarters, Legion of Super-Heroes Headquarters
47 ❑ Feb 1990 Cover: 1.75 **NM** value: **2.00**
Circ: CapCity orders: **13,100**
★ Origin of Karate Kid, Chemical King, Ferro Lad.
48 ❑ Apr 1990 Cover: 1.75 **NM** value: **2.00**
★ Origin of Rex the Wonder Dog, Ambush Bug, Trigger Twins, Stanley and His Monster.
49 ❑ Jun 1990 Cover: 1.75 **NM** value: **2.00**
Circ: CapCity orders: **11,300**
★ Origin of Newsboy Legion, Bouncing Boy, Silent Knight.
50 ❑ Aug 1990 Cover: 3.95 **NM** value: **Cover or less**
Circ: CapCity orders: **14,950**
final issue. ★ Origin of Robin I (Dick Grayson), Johnny Thunder (cowboy), Space Museum, Black Canary, Earth-2, Dolphin.
Anl 1 ❑ ca. 1987 Cover: 2.00 **NM** value: **Cover or less**
Circ: CapCity orders: **16,700**
C: John Byrne ★ Origin of The Doom Patrol.

Other grades: Multiply prices above by **1.5 for Mint • 2/3 for Very Fine • 1/3 for Fine • 1/5 for Very Good • 1/8 for Good**

Anl 2❑ca. 1988 Cover: 2.00 NM value: **Cover or less**
Circ: CapCity orders: **15,500**
★ Origin of Flash III (Wally West), Flash II (Barry Allen).
Anl 3❑ca. 1989 Cover: 2.95 NM value: **Cover or less**
★ Origin of Teen Titans. ★ 1st Appearance of Flamebird.
Bk 1❑ Cover: 4.95 NM value: **Cover or less**
Circ: CapCity orders: **14,000**
• Trade Paperback. • new and reprint material ★ Origin of Superman, Flash, Green Lantern, J'onn J'onzz, Batman, The Justice League of America.
GS 1❑Dec 1998 Cover: 4.95 NM value: **Cover or less**
★ Origin of Wonder Girl, Robin III (Tim Drake), Superboy, Impulse, Spoiler, Arrowette, Secret.
SE 1❑Oct 1989 Cover: 2.00 NM value: **Cover or less**
Circ: CapCity orders: **46,500** • **CGC:** 2 graded, best 9.6
★ Origin of Riddler, Two-Face, Penguin.

SECRET ORIGINS FEATURING THE JLA — DC

1 ❑ Cover: 14.95 NM value: **Cover or less**
No issue number. • Trade Paperback. 📖 Star-Seed; Gazing Back; Guy Talk; A Run of Luck; Vulnerability; Left for Dead; Who is…Superman? • collects origins stories from respective Secret Files **A:** Mike S. Miller; Howard Porter; Dick Giordano; Lee Moder; Staz Johnson; Kenny Martinez; Dan Jurgen **W:** Brian Augustyn; Dan Jurgens; Erik Larsen; Grant Morrison; Devin K. Grayson; Joanna Sandsmark; Mark Millar; Mark Waid; Ron Marz

SECRET ORIGINS OF KRANKIN' KOMIX — Krankin' Komix

1 ❑ Nov 1996 Cover: 1.00 NM value: **Cover or less**

SECRET ORIGINS OF SUPER-VILLAINS — DC

GS 1❑Dec 1999 Cover: 4.95 NM value: **Cover or less**
Circ: Diamd. preorders: **21,674**
📖 Random Choice; The Rise of Tartarus; Echoes Past; Dreams in Smoke; Goodness and Mercy; Sorrow Ever More; Original Sin **A:** Cully Hamner; Scott Kolins; Jackson Guice; Rick Burchett; Drew Johnson; Jon Bogdanove; David Goyer **W:** Walt Simonson; Joe Kelly; Devin Grayson; Geoff Johns; Greg Rucka; Ron Marz; Tom Peyer ★ Origin of Amazo, Echo, Johnny Sorrow, Sinestro, Tartarus, Encantadora, Granny Goodness.

SECRET ORIGINS OF THE WORLD'S GREATEST SUPER HEROES — DC

1 ❑ ca. 1989 Cover: 4.95 NM value: **Cover or less**

SECRET ORIGINS REPLICA EDITION — DC

1 ❑ Feb 2000 Cover: 4.95 NM value: **Cover or less**
Circ: Diamd. preorders: **4,602**
cardstock fold-out cover. • reprints Secret Origins #1 (1st series)

SECRET PLOT — Eros

1 ❑ Oct 1997 Cover: 2.95 NM value: **Cover or less**
Circ: Diamd. preorders: **5,762**
📖 Junkie Teacher **A:** New Men **W:** New Men
2 ❑ Nov 1997 Cover: 2.95 NM value: **Cover or less**
Circ: Diamd. preorders: **4,703**

SECRET ROMANCE — Charlton

1 ❑ Oct 1968 Cover: 0.12 NM value: **12.00**
📖 The Wisdom in a Woman's Heart; Just Jeanette (text); Secrets of a Secretary; Love Lies Buried Here **A:** Weston Olivero **W:** Weston Olivero; Jeanette Copeland

#	Date	Cover	NM value
2	❑		**8.00**
3	❑ 1969	0.15	**7.00**
4	❑ 1969	0.15	**7.00**
5	❑ 1969	0.15	**7.00**
6	❑ 1969	0.15	**7.00**
7	❑ 1970	0.15	**7.00**
8	❑ 1970	0.15	**7.00**
9	❑ Oct 1970	0.15	**7.00**
10	❑ Dec 1970	0.15	**7.00**
11	❑ Feb 1971	0.15	**5.00**
12	❑ Apr 1971	0.15	**5.00**
13	❑ Jun 1971	0.15	**5.00**
14	❑ Aug 1971	0.15	**5.00**
15	❑ Oct 1971	0.20	**5.00**
16	❑ Dec 1971	0.20	**5.00**
17	❑ Feb 1972	0.20	**5.00**
18	❑ Apr 1972	0.20	**5.00**
19	❑ Jun 1972	0.20	**5.00**
20	❑ Aug 1972	0.20	**5.00**

📖 Three Loves Have I • David Cassidy on cover

#	Date	Cover	NM value
21	❑ Oct 1972	0.20	**5.00**
22	❑ Dec 1972	0.20	**5.00**
23	❑ Feb 1973	0.20	**5.00**
24	❑ Apr 1973	0.20	**5.00**
25	❑ Jun 1973	0.20	**5.00**
26	❑ Aug 1973	0.20	**5.00**
27	❑ Oct 1973	0.20	**5.00**
28	❑ Dec 1973	0.20	**5.00**
29	❑ 1974	0.20	**5.00**
30	❑ Jan 1975	0.25	**5.00**
31	❑ 1975	0.25	**4.00**
32	❑ 1975	0.25	**4.00**
33	❑ 1975	0.25	**4.00**
34	❑ 1975	0.25	**4.00**
35	❑ 1975	0.25	**4.00**
36	❑ 1976	0.25	**4.00**
37	❑ 1976	0.25	**4.00**
38	❑ 1976	0.25	**4.00**
39	❑ 1976	0.25	**4.00**
40	❑ 1976	0.25	**3.00**
41	❑ Nov 1976	0.25	**3.00**
42	❑ Mar 1979	0.40	**3.00**
43	❑ Jun 1979	0.40	**3.00**
44	❑ Aug 1979	0.40	**3.00**
45	❑ 1979	0.40	**3.00**
46	❑ 1979	0.40	**3.00**
47	❑ 1980	0.40	**3.00**
48	❑ Feb 1980	0.40	**3.00**

SECRET ROMANCES — Superior

#	Date	Cover	NM value
1	❑ Apr 1951	0.10	**45.00**
2	❑ Jun 1951	0.10	**25.00**
3	❑ Aug 1951	0.10	**18.00**
4	❑ Oct 1951	0.10	**18.00**
5	❑ Dec 1951	0.10	**18.00**

📖 I Married a Flirt; Wings of Love; The Kiss Theif; For Sale, Wedding Gown

#	Date	Cover	NM value
6	❑ Feb 1952	0.10	**15.00**
7	❑ Apr 1952	0.10	**15.00**
8	❑ Jun 1952	0.10	**15.00**
9	❑ Aug 1952	0.10	**15.00**
10	❑ Oct 1952	0.10	**15.00**
11	❑ Dec 1952	0.10	**15.00**
12	❑ Feb 1953	0.10	**15.00**
13	❑ Apr 1953	0.10	**15.00**
14	❑ Jun 1953	0.10	**15.00**
15	❑ Aug 1953	0.10	**15.00**
16	❑ Oct 1953	0.10	**15.00**
17	❑ Dec 1953	0.10	**15.00**
18	❑ Feb 1954	0.10	**15.00**
19	❑ Apr 1954	0.10	**15.00**
20	❑ Jun 1954	0.10	**15.00**
21	❑ Aug 1954	0.10	**12.00**
22	❑ Oct 1954	0.10	**12.00**
23	❑ Dec 1954	0.10	**12.00**
24	❑ Feb 1955	0.10	**12.00**
25	❑ Apr 1955	0.10	**12.00**
26	❑ Jun 1955	0.10	**12.00**
27	❑ Aug 1955	0.10	**12.00**

SECRET SIX — DC

Six people — brawny Mike Tempest, physicist Dr. August Durant, escape artist Carlos Di Rienzi, fashionable femme fatale Crimson Dawn, flying ace King Savage, and mistress of disguise Lili DeNeuve — each on the edge of despair and ruin, were saved by a mysterious figure known only as "Mockingbird" and trained to become an international strike force of secret agents.

The espionage and intrigue angle of the Secret Six, reminiscent of the then-popular television series Mission: Impossible, and the dynamic, reality-based artwork of Frank Springer represented something of a departure from the house style of fantasy-driven, super-hero publisher DC.

1 ❑ May 1968 Cover: 0.12 NM value: **30.00**
• **CGC:** 9 graded, best 9.2
splash page is cover. ★ Origin of The Secret Six. ★ 1st Appearance of The Secret Six.
2 ❑ Jul 1968 Cover: 0.12 NM value: **18.00**
• **CGC:** 1 graded, best 9.4
📖 Plunder the Pentagon!
3 ❑ Sep 1968 Cover: 0.12 NM value: **12.00**
• **CGC:** 1 graded, best 7.5
4 ❑ Nov 1968 Cover: 0.12 NM value: **12.00**
• **CGC:** 1 graded, best 9.2
5 ❑ Jan 1969 Cover: 0.12 NM value: **12.00**
• **CGC:** 2 graded, best 9.4
6 ❑ Mar 1969 Cover: 0.12 NM value: **12.00**
7 ❑ May 1969 Cover: 0.12 NM value: **12.00**
final issue.

SECRET SOCIETY OF SUPER-VILLAINS — DC

1 ❑ Jun 1976 Cover: 0.30 NM value: **5.00**
• **CGC:** 18 graded, best 9.6
★ Origin of Secret Society.
2 ❑ Aug 1976 Cover: 0.30 NM value: **3.50**
★ Appearance of Captain Comet.

#	Date	Cover	NM value
3	❑ Oct 1976	0.30	**3.50**
4	❑ Dec 1976	0.30	**3.50**
5	❑ Feb 1977	0.30	**3.50**
6	❑ Apr 1977	0.30	**2.50**
7	❑ Jun 1977	0.30	**2.50**
8	❑ Aug 1977	0.35	**2.50**
9	❑ Sep 1977	0.35	**2.50**
10	❑ Oct 1977	0.35	**2.50**
11	❑ Dec 1977	0.35	**2.50**
12	❑ Jan 1978	0.35	**2.50**
13	❑ Mar 1978	0.35	**2.50**
14	❑ May 1978	0.35	**2.50**
15	❑ Jul 1978	0.35	**2.50**

final issue.

SECRETS OF DRAWING COMICS (RICH BUCKLER'S...) — Showcase

1 ❑ Jan 1994 Cover: 2.50 NM value: **Cover or less**
A: Rich Buckler **W:** Rich Buckler
2 ❑ Cover: 2.50 NM value: **Cover or less**
A: Rich Buckler **W:** Rich Buckler
3 ❑ Cover: 2.50 NM value: **Cover or less**
A: Rich Buckler **W:** Rich Buckler
4 ❑ Cover: 2.50 NM value: **Cover or less**
A: Rich Buckler **W:** Rich Buckler

SECRETS OF HAUNTED HOUSE — DC

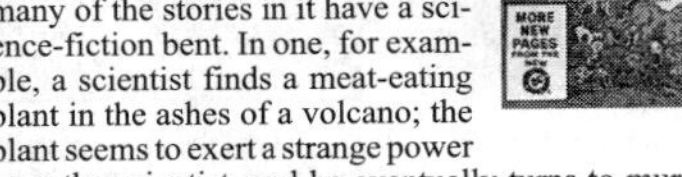

Abel, the timid brother of the horror-tale-spinner Cain, has been appointed caretaker of a haunted house which drove its first inhabitant insane, had its other inhabitants flee in terror from its rooms, and eventually relocated itself near a cemetery directly across from The House of Mystery. Abel hates to be alone but he also likes to to tell frightening stories to his guests, the readers.

Although primarily a horror title, many of the stories in it have a science-fiction bent. In one, for example, a scientist finds a meat-eating plant in the ashes of a volcano; the plant seems to exert a strange power over the scientist, and he eventually turns to murder in order to keep his discovery alive.

Secrets of Haunted House has tales so terrifying that Abel himself gets a little frightened just telling them.

1 ❑ Apr 1975 Cover: 0.25 NM value: **6.00**
• **CGC:** 4 graded, best 9.4
2 ❑ Jun 1975 Cover: 0.25 NM value: **4.00**
• **CGC:** 1 graded, best 6.5
3 ❑ Aug 1975 Cover: 0.25 NM value: **4.00**
• **CGC:** 1 graded, best 7.5
4 ❑ Oct 1975 Cover: 0.25 NM value: **4.00**
5 ❑ Dec 1975 Cover: 0.25 NM value: **4.00**
• **CGC:** 1 graded, best 9.0
6 ❑ Jun 1977 Cover: 0.30 NM value: **3.00**
• **CGC:** 1 graded, best 9.6
7 ❑ Aug 1977 Cover: 0.35 NM value: **3.00**
• **CGC:** 1 graded, best 9.2
8 ❑ Oct 1977 Cover: 0.35 NM value: **3.00**
9 ❑ Dec 1977 Cover: 0.35 NM value: **3.00**
• **CGC:** 1 graded, best 9.2

#	Date	Cover	NM value
10	❑ Feb 1978	0.35	**3.00**
11	❑ Apr 1978	0.35	**3.00**
12	❑ Jun 1978	0.35	**3.00**
13	❑ Aug 1978	0.35	**3.00**
14	❑ Oct 1978	0.50	**3.00**
15	❑ Aug 1979	0.40	**3.00**
16	❑ Sep 1979	0.40	**3.00**
17	❑ Oct 1979	0.40	**3.00**
18	❑ Nov 1979	0.40	**3.00**
19	❑ Dec 1979	0.40	**3.00**
20	❑ Jan 1980	0.40	**3.00**
21	❑ Feb 1980	0.40	**2.00**
22	❑ Mar 1980	0.40	**2.00**
23	❑ Apr 1980	0.40	**2.00**
24	❑ May 1980	0.40	**2.00**
25	❑ Jun 1980	0.40	**2.00**
26	❑ Jul 1980	0.40	**2.00**
27	❑ Aug 1980	0.40	**2.00**
28	❑ Sep 1980	0.40	**2.00**
29	❑ Oct 1980	0.50	**2.00**
30	❑ Nov 1980	0.50	**2.00**
31	❑ Dec 1980	0.50	**3.00**

• **CGC:** 1 graded, best 6.5
★ 1st Appearance of Mister E.

#	Date	Cover	NM value
32	❑ Jan 1981	0.50	**2.00**
33	❑ Feb 1981	0.50	**2.00**
34	❑ Mar 1981	0.50	**2.00**
35	❑ Apr 1981	0.50	**2.00**
36	❑ May 1981	0.50	**2.00**
37	❑ Jun 1981	0.50	**2.00**
38	❑ Jul 1981	0.50	**2.00**
39	❑ Aug 1981	0.50	**2.00**
40	❑ Sep 1981	0.50	**2.00**
41	❑ Oct 1981	0.60	**2.00**
42	❑ Nov 1981	0.60	**2.00**
43	❑ Dec 1981	0.60	**2.00**
44	❑ Jan 1982	0.60	**2.00**
45	❑ Feb 1982	0.60	**2.00**
46	❑ Mar 1982	0.60	**2.00**

final issue.

SECRETS OF SINISTER HOUSE — DC

5 ❑ Jun 1972 Cover: 0.20 NM value: **5.00**
• **CGC:** 2 graded, best 9.2
• Continues from Sinister House of Secret Love #4
6 ❑ Aug 1972 Cover: 0.20 NM value: **4.00**
7 ❑ Nov 1972 Cover: 0.20 NM value: **4.00**
8 ❑ Dec 1972 Cover: 0.20 NM value: **4.00**
9 ❑ Feb 1973 Cover: 0.20 NM value: **4.00**
10 ❑ Mar 1973 Cover: 0.20 NM value: **6.00**
A: Neal Adams
11 ❑ Apr 1973 Cover: 0.20 NM value: **4.00**
• **CGC:** 1 graded, best 9.0
12 ❑ Jun 1973 Cover: 0.20 NM value: **4.00**
• **CGC:** 1 graded, best 8.0
13 ❑ Aug 1973 Cover: 0.20 NM value: **4.00**
• **CGC:** 1 graded, best 5.0
14 ❑ Oct 1973 Cover: 0.20 NM value: **4.00**
15 ❑ Dec 1973 Cover: 0.20 NM value: **4.00**
16 ❑ Feb 1974 Cover: 0.20 NM value: **4.00**
• **CGC:** 1 graded, best 9.6
17 ❑ Apr 1974 Cover: 0.20 NM value: **4.00**
18 ❑ Jun 1974 Cover: 0.20 NM value: **4.00**
📖 The Strange Shop on Demon Street; Mad to Order; One Year to Die…; The House that Death Built; The Half-Lucky charm!; Home, Sweet Homicide (text) final issue. **A:** Gil Kane; Angel B. Luna; Jerry Grandienetti **W:** Leo Dorfman; B. Shotz; D. W. Holtz

CGC-graded: Multiply prices above by **33 for 9.9 M • 16 for 9.8 NM/M • 7 for 9.6 NM+ • 5 for 9.4 NM • 2.5 for 9.2 NM- • 1.5 for 9.0 VF/NM**

SECRETS OF THE LEGION OF SUPER-HEROES DC

The Legion of Super-Heroes is a group of super-powered youngsters who have banded together to preserve peace in the galaxy. This three-issue mini-series gave the inside story of the Legion and many of its chief characters. It began by retelling the story of how Cosmic Boy, Saturn Girl, and Lightning Lad joined together to stop some assassins from murdering R.J. Brande the galaxy's richest man, ultimately leading to the formation of the Legion. This tale was followed in later issues by the origins of Braniac 5, Ultra Boy, Mon-El, and other prominent Legionnaires.

Secrets of the Legion of Super-Heroes is one of the earliest works by writer Paul Kupperberg, who went on to become an editor at DC.

1 ❑ Jan 1981 Cover: 0.50 **NM** value: **2.00**
A: Frank Chiaramonte; Jimmy Janes **W:** E. Nelson Bridwell; Paul Kupperberg ★ Origin of the Legion of Super-Heroes.
2 ❑ Feb 1981 Cover: 0.50 **NM** value: **2.00**
3 ❑ Mar 1981 Cover: 0.50 **NM** value: **2.00**

SECRETS OF THE VALIANT UNIVERSE Valiant

The first issue of this title was released as a special promotional item from Wizard. It served as a useful introduction to new readers of Valiant comics, as well as letting die-hard fans in on new details on their favorite heroes.

The second issue was a regularly available comic, but the title became somewhat misleading. The story it contained was part four of the "beta" phase of Valiant's 1994 mega-crossover, The Chaos Effect. The issue contained a fast-moving story wherein Shadowman regained his sanity; Max St. James (the original Shadowman) battled Master Darque, and Darque launched a nefarious plan to create yet another Shadowman who would do his bidding. Despite all the goings-on, however, no real "secrets of the Valiant universe" were revealed.

1 ❑ May 1994 **NM** value: **2.00**
• Wizard Magazine promo. • no price; bagged with Wizard Special **A:** Rik Levins; Yvel Guichet; Rags Morales; Sean Chen; Don Perlin; Jim Calafiore; Bob Hall; Peter Grau; Mark Moretti; Dave Ross; Bernard Chang; Ted Halsted **W:** Bob Layton; Bob Hall; Mark Moretti; Kevin VanHook; Mike Baron; Antony J.L. Bedard; David Michelinie; Jorge Gonzçlez; Jorge Gonzßlez; Maurice Fontenot
2 ❑ Oct 1994 Cover: 2.25 **NM** value: **Cover or less**
Circ: CapCity orders: **20,525**
🕮 The Chaos Effect: Beta, Part 4 • Chaos Effect **A:** Yvel Guichet **W:** Bob Hall
3 ❑ Oct 1995 Cover: 2.25 **NM** value: **Cover or less**
Circ: CapCity orders: **10,075**
cover says Feb. 🕮 Torn Between Two Mothers • future Rai; indicia says Oct **A:** George Saravia **W:** Bob Layton

SECRET TEACHINGS OF A COMIC BOOK MASTER: THE ART OF ALFREDO ALCALA
Int. Humor Advisory Council

Bk 1❑ Spr 1994, b&w Cover: 11.95 **NM** value: **Cover or less**

SECRETUM SECRETORUM Twilight Twins

0 ❑ Cover: 3.50 **NM** value: **Cover or less**
A: D.C. Nash; Terry Echterling **W:** D.C. Nash; Terry Echterling

SECRET WARS II Marvel

1 ❑ Jul 1985 Cover: 0.75 **NM** value: **2.00**
Circ: CapCity orders: **85,000** • **CGC:** 3 graded, best 9.6
★ Appearance of X-Men, New Mutants.
2 ❑ Aug 1985 Cover: 0.75 **NM** value: **1.50**
Circ: CapCity orders: **65,000**
★ Appearance of Fantastic Four, Spider-Man, Power Man, Iron Fist. ★ Death of Hate-Monger III ("H.M. Unger").
3 ❑ Sep 1985 Cover: 0.75 **NM** value: **1.50**
Circ: CapCity orders: **61,900** • **CGC:** 1 graded, best 9.8
4 ❑ Oct 1985 Cover: 0.75 **NM** value: **1.50**
Circ: CapCity orders: **63,200**
★ Origin of Kurse. ★ 1st Appearance of Kurse. ★ Appearance of Kursei. ★ Versus Avengers.
5 ❑ Nov 1985 Cover: 0.75 **NM** value: **2.50**
Circ: CapCity orders: **59,800**
★ Origin of Boomer (Boom Boom). ★ 1st Appearance of Boomer (Boom Boom). ★ Versus X-Men, Fantastic Four, New Mutants, Avengers.
6 ❑ Dec 1985 Cover: 0.75 **NM** value: **1.50**
Circ: CapCity orders: **54,800**
7 ❑ Jan 1986 Cover: 0.75 **NM** value: **1.50**
Circ: CapCity orders: **49,100**
★ Versus All villains.
8 ❑ Feb 1986 Cover: 0.75 **NM** value: **1.50**
Circ: CapCity orders: **48,600**
★ Origin of Beyonder.
9 ❑ Mar 1986 Cover: 1.25 **NM** value: **1.50**
Circ: CapCity orders: **48,500**
• double-sized. ★ Death of Beyonder.

SECRET WEAPONS Valiant

In May 1992, Solar, Man of the Atom leaves an enemy named Fred Bender to die in the scorching heat of Death Valley. Scarcely a month later, a considerably recuperated Bender appears on the doorstep of Master Darque. He promises Darque that he will do anything, if only Darque will give him the power to destroy Solar.

Darque grants Bender's wish, although it costs Bender his very humanity. Bender becomes the energy creature known as Doctor Eclipse and is able to take out Solar with astonishing ease. Now, he poses a threat to the entire world.

Secret Weapons draws together the Harbinger kids, Shadowman, X-O Manowar, Doctor Mirage, the Eternal Warrior, and Bloodshot, as they join forces to fight Master Darque and the grave new menace he has created.

1 ❑ Sep 1993 Cover: 2.25 **NM** value: **2.50**
Circ: CapCity orders: **141,800**
• Serial number contest ★ Origin of Doctor Eclipse. ★ 1st Appearance of Doctor Eclipse.
1/GO❑ Sep 1993 **NM** value: **3.00**
• Gold edition.
2 ❑ Oct 1993 Cover: 2.25 **NM** value: **Cover or less**
Circ: CapCity orders: **73,300**
3 ❑ Nov 1993 Cover: 2.25 **NM** value: **Cover or less**
Circ: CapCity orders: **53,825**
🕮 Empirical Dynasty, Part 1
4 ❑ Dec 1993 Cover: 2.25 **NM** value: **Cover or less**
Circ: CapCity orders: **42,275**
5 ❑ Jan 1994 Cover: 2.25 **NM** value: **Cover or less**
Circ: CapCity orders: **39,075**
★ Appearance of Ninjak.
6 ❑ Feb 1994 Cover: 2.25 **NM** value: **Cover or less**
Circ: CapCity orders: **30,275**
🕮 The Horror Below, Part 1
7 ❑ Mar 1994 Cover: 2.25 **NM** value: **Cover or less**
Circ: CapCity orders: **23,875**
🕮 The Horror Below, Part 2 ★ Appearance of X-O Manowar, Turok.
8 ❑ Apr 1994 Cover: 2.25 **NM** value: **Cover or less**
Circ: CapCity orders: **20,150**
★ Versus Harbinger.
9 ❑ May 1994 Cover: 2.25 **NM** value: **Cover or less**
Circ: CapCity orders: **24,500**
• trading card ★ Appearance of Bloodshot.
10 ❑ Jun 1994 Cover: 2.25 **NM** value: **Cover or less**
Circ: CapCity orders: **16,075**
11 ❑ Aug 1994 Cover: 2.50 **NM** value: **Cover or less**
Circ: CapCity orders: **20,300**
Enclosed in manila envelope "For Your Eyes Only" cover. • bagged top secret ★ Appearance of Bloodshot.
12 ❑ Sep 1994 Cover: 2.25 **NM** value: **Cover or less**
Circ: CapCity orders: **16,450**
★ Appearance of Bloodshot.
13 ❑ Oct 1994 Cover: 2.25 **NM** value: **Cover or less**
Circ: CapCity orders: **19,975**
🕮 The Chaos Effect: Gamma, Part 2 • Chaos Effect
14 ❑ Nov 1994 Cover: 2.25 **NM** value: **Cover or less**
Circ: CapCity orders: **13,475**
15 ❑ Dec 1994 Cover: 2.25 **NM** value: **Cover or less**
Circ: CapCity orders: **11,600**
16 ❑ Jan 1995 Cover: 2.25 **NM** value: **Cover or less**
Circ: CapCity orders: **10,150**
17 ❑ Feb 1995 Cover: 2.25 **NM** value: **Cover or less**
Circ: CapCity orders: **8,925**
18 ❑ Mar 1995 Cover: 2.25 **NM** value: **Cover or less**
Circ: CapCity orders: **7,450**
★ Appearance of Ninjak.
19 ❑ Apr 1995 Cover: 2.25 **NM** value: **Cover or less**
Circ: CapCity orders: **6,550**
20 ❑ May 1995 Cover: 2.25 **NM** value: **Cover or less**
Circ: CapCity orders: **7,525**
🕮 Rampage, Part 2; Bloodshot Rampage, Part 2 • (see Bloodshot #28)
21 ❑ May 1995 Cover: 2.25 **NM** value: **Cover or less**
Circ: CapCity orders: **7,475**
🕮 Rampage, Part 4; Bloodshot Rampage, Part 4 final issue.

SECTAURS Marvel

The Sectaurs are a strange breed of humanoids with insect-like features (similar to Krkkit from Micronauts). Their world is called Symbion, an appropriate name for a world where organisms like plants are used to form all manner of tools and clothing.

Symbion exists in a state of "enlightened barbarism," where warring factions fight with sword and magic for control. On the side of good is The Shining Realm, led by Prince Dargon. Against them stands General Spiderax and Scorpia of The Dark Domain, who want to conquer the world for themselves. And both sides seek the key to victory: the power of the ancients contained in a legendary Hyve from which all Sectaurs have descended.

Something of a cross between Warriors of Plasm and The Micronauts, Sectaurs is taken from a line of toys from Coleco.

1 ❑ Jun 1985 Cover: 0.75 **NM** value: **1.00**
Circ: CapCity orders: **18,600** • **CGC:** 1 graded, best 8.5
2 ❑ Aug 1985 Cover: 0.75 **NM** value: **1.00**
Circ: CapCity orders: **12,100**
3 ❑ Oct 1985 Cover: 0.75 **NM** value: **1.00**
Circ: CapCity orders: **9,400**
4 ❑ Dec 1985 Cover: 0.75 **NM** value: **1.00**
Circ: CapCity orders: **8,700**
5 ❑ Mar 1986 Cover: 0.75 **NM** value: **1.00**
Circ: CapCity orders: **8,800**
6 ❑ May 1986 Cover: 0.75 **NM** value: **1.00**
Circ: CapCity orders: **8,400**
7 ❑ Jul 1986 Cover: 0.75 **NM** value: **1.00**
Circ: CapCity orders: **7,300**
8 ❑ Sep 1986 Cover: 0.75 **NM** value: **1.00**
Circ: CapCity orders: **6,200**

SECTION 12 Mythic

1 ❑ b&w Cover: 2.95 **NM** value: **Cover or less**
🕮 Awakenings! **A:** Phil Miller **W:** Len Mihalovich

SECTION ZERO Image

1 ❑ Jun 2000 Cover: 2.50 **NM** value: **Cover or less**
Circ: Diamd. preorders: **24,202**
🕮 Ground Zero, Part 1 **A:** Tom Grummett **W:** Karl Kesel
2 ❑ Jul 2000 Cover: 2.50 **NM** value: **Cover or less**
Circ: Diamd. preorders: **15,024**
🕮 Ground Zero, Part 2 **A:** Tom Grummett **W:** Karl Kesel
3 ❑ Sep 2000 Cover: 2.50 **NM** value: **Cover or less**
Circ: Diamd. preorders: **14,209**
🕮 Ground Zero, Part 3 **A:** Tom Grummett **W:** Karl Kesel

SEDUCTION Eternity

1 ❑ b&w Cover: 0.25 **NM** value: **2.50**
🕮 Second Stringer; In Site; Love is not an Alien Thing; Valentinus **A:** Ted Couldron; Sandy Carruthers; John Ross; Scott Dutton **W:** Ted Couldron; Christopher L. Weppler; Roland Mann; Steve Jones

SEDUCTION OF THE INNOCENT Rinehart

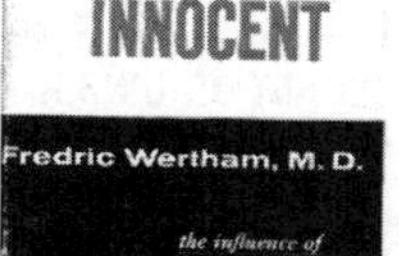

Although not a comic book, Seduction of the Innocent is probably the most influential book in comics history. Written by psychologist Fredric Wertham in 1954, the gist of much of its contents originally ran in a number of different magazine articles, such as one in Ladies' Home Journal, titled "What Parents Don't Know about Comic Books."

While working with juvenile delinquents in the 1940s and 1950s, Wertham became convinced that comics were exerting a corrosive influence on children. Using dubious methodology and a raft of anecdotal "evidence," he accused comics of promoting cruelty in children, carrying (often-hidden) sexual messages, and promoting illiteracy. Batman and Robin were labeled homosexual role models. Wonder Woman was called a lesbian bondage fantasy. Even Superman was portrayed as a fascistic archetype. These charges touched off a firestorm of public outcry (including public comic-book burnings), industry upheaval, and the eventual creation of the Comics Magazine Association of America with its Comics Code for members.

1 ❑ ca. 1953 Cover: 400.00 **NM** value: **Cover or less**
• With bibliography, dust jacket
1-2 ❑ ca. 1954 Cover: 250.00 **NM** value: **Cover or less**

SEDUCTION OF THE INNOCENT (ECLIPSE) Eclipse

1 ❑ Nov 1985 Cover: 1.75 **NM** value: **2.50**
🕮 Adventures into Darkness; Death Dives Deep; Harvest of Death; That Stray Cat; Gift of Murder; Tryst With Terror • Reprints from Adventures into Darkness #6, Out of the Shadows #7, Fantastic Worlds #7, Out of the Shadows #9 **A:** Mort Meskin; Gene Fawcette; Alex Toth; Tom Yeates; George Roussos; Scott **W:** Dave Stevens
2 ❑ Dec 1985 Cover: 1.75 **NM** value: **2.00**
🕮 Was he Death-Proof?; More Deadly Than the Male; Trophies of Doom; Monster in the Maze; The Man Who Was Always on Time **A:** Gene Fawcette; Murphy Anderson; Alex Toth; Matt Baker; Nick Cardy; Mike Peppe; Ruben Moreira; Vic Fodera
3 ❑ Jan 1986 Cover: 1.75 **NM** value: **2.00**
Circ: CapCity orders: **4,600**
🕮 The Crushed Gardenia; The Cup of the Dead; Werewolf; The Phantom Horseman; The Quest of the Chlorophyll Monsters **A:** Alex Toth **W:** Jack Katz; Murphy Anderson; Alex Toth; George Roussos; Mort Mesdin
4 ❑ Feb 1986 Cover: 1.75 **NM** value: **2.00**
Circ: CapCity orders: **3,950**
🕮 Images of Sand; The Beast From the Deep; Rat-Trap; The Man Who Tricked the Devil; Worlds Apart **A:** Alex Toth; John Rosenberger; Nick Cardy; Mel Keefer; Mike Peppe; Tony Mortellaro **W:** Alex Toth; Ray Bradbury
5 ❑ Mar 1986 Cover: 1.75 **NM** value: **2.00**
Circ: CapCity orders: **3,700**
🕮 Phantom Ship; Death Drum; Grip on Life; The Drums of Cajou **A:** Alex Toth; Tom Yeates; Art Saaf **W:** Alex Toth
6 ❑ Apr 1986 Cover: 1.75 **NM** value: **2.00**
Circ: CapCity orders: **3,425**
🕮 The Hands of Don Jose; Your Grave is Ready; The Helmsman; The Mask of Death **A:** Chuck Bekum **W:** Alex Toth; George Tuska; Frank Frazetta; Ross Andru; Jerry Grandienetti
3D 1❑ ca. 1985 Cover: 2.25 **NM** value: **2.50**
Circ: CapCity orders: **6,400**

Other grades: Multiply prices above by **1.5 for Mint • 2/3 for Very Fine • 1/3 for Fine • 1/5 for Very Good • 1/8 for Good**

📖 Adventures into Darkness; Death Dives Deep; Harvest of Death; That Stray Cat; Gift of Murder; Tryst With Terror **A:** Mort Meskin; Gene Fawcette; George Roussos; Scott **C:** Dave Stevens **W:** Dave Stevens

3D 2 ❑ ca. 1986 Cover: 2.25 **NM** value: **2.50**
Circ: CapCity orders: **5,150**
📖 Was He Death-Proof?; More Deadly Than the Male; Trophies of Doom; Monster in the Maze!; The Man Who Was Always on Time! **A:** Gene Fawcette; Alex Toth; Matt Baker; Nick Cardy; Mike Peppe; Vic Fodera **C:** Bernie Wrightson

SEEKER — Caliber

1 ❑ Apr 1994, b&w Cover: 2.95 **NM** value: **Cover or less**
A: Raff Ienco **W:** Joe Martin
2 ❑ 1994b&w Cover: 2.95 **NM** value: **Cover or less**

SEEKERS INTO THE MYSTERY — DC / Vertigo

Lucas Hart is a washed-up writer residing in Los Angeles. He drinks too much, he smokes too much, he takes too many drugs, and, whenever he shut his eyes, he fantasizes that a little man with knives is tearing into him. Though he was once the writer of a cult film masterpiece, it has been ages since he was able to commit anything good to paper. But, as far as his lifestyle goes, he is a true performance artist — doing his best impression of a train wreck in progress.

Then his life takes an abrupt turn, as catastrophe gives way to salvation. Lucas Hart is given a second chance and set upon a new path — to becoming a seeker into life's great mystery.

This series strikes an autobiographical and spiritual chord for creator J.M. DeMatteis (of Moonshadow).

1 ❑ Jan 1996 Cover: 2.50 **NM** value: **Cover or less**
📖 The Pilgrimage of Lucas Hart, Part 1 **A:** Glenn Barr **W:** J.M. DeMatteis
2 ❑ Feb 1996 Cover: 2.50 **NM** value: **Cover or less**
📖 The Pilgrimage of Lucas Hart, Part 2 **A:** Glenn Barr **W:** J.M. DeMatteis
3 ❑ Mar 1996 Cover: 2.50 **NM** value: **Cover or less**
📖 The Pilgrimage of Lucas Hart, Part 3 **A:** Glenn Barr **W:** J.M. DeMatteis
4 ❑ Apr 1996 Cover: 2.50 **NM** value: **Cover or less**
📖 The Pilgrimage of Lucas Hart, Part 4 **A:** Glenn Barr **W:** J.M. DeMatteis
5 ❑ Jun 1996 Cover: 2.50 **NM** value: **Cover or less**
📖 The Pilgrimage of Lucas Hart, Part 5 **A:** Glenn Barr **W:** J.M. DeMatteis
6 ❑ Jul 1996 Cover: 2.50 **NM** value: **Cover or less**
📖 Falling Down to Heaven, Part 1 **A:** Michael Zulli **W:** J.M. DeMatteis
7 ❑ Aug 1996 Cover: 2.50 **NM** value: **Cover or less**
📖 Falling Down to Heaven, Part 2, Gently Stealing **A:** Michael Zulli **W:** J.M. DeMatteis
8 ❑ Sep 1996 Cover: 2.50 **NM** value: **Cover or less**
📖 Falling Down to Heaven, Part 3 **A:** Michael Zulli **W:** J.M. DeMatteis
9 ❑ Oct 1996 Cover: 2.50 **NM** value: **Cover or less**
📖 Falling Down to Heaven, Part 4 **A:** Michael Zulli **W:** J.M. DeMatteis
10 ❑ Nov 1996 Cover: 2.50 **NM** value: **Cover or less**
Circ: Diamd. preorders: **16,922**
📖 Falling Down to Heaven, Part 5 **A:** Jon J. Muth **W:** J.M. DeMatteis
11 ❑ Dec 1996 Cover: 2.50 **NM** value: **Cover or less**
Circ: Diamd. preorders: **16,558**
📖 God's Shadow, Part 1 **A:** Jill Thompson **W:** J.M. DeMatteis
12 ❑ Jan 1997 Cover: 2.50 **NM** value: **Cover or less**
Circ: Diamd. preorders: **15,473**
📖 God's Shadow, Part 2 **A:** Jill Thompson **W:** J.M. DeMatteis
13 ❑ Feb 1997 Cover: 2.50 **NM** value: **Cover or less**
Circ: Diamd. preorders: **14,626**
📖 God's Shadow, Part 3 **A:** Jill Thompson **W:** J.M. DeMatteis
14 ❑ Mar 1997 Cover: 2.50 **NM** value: **Cover or less**
Circ: Diamd. preorders: **14,205**
📖 God's Shadow, Part 4 **A:** Jill Thompson **W:** J.M. DeMatteis
15 ❑ Apr 1997 Cover: 2.50 **NM** value: **2.95**
Circ: Diamd. preorders: **13,417**
📖 The Death of Lucas Hart final issue. **A:** Jon J. Muth **W:** J.M. DeMatteis

SEEKER 3000 — Marvel

1 ❑ Jun 1998 Cover: 2.99 **NM** value: **Cover or less**
Circ: Diamd. preorders: **14,564**
wraparound cover. 📖 A New Beginning… **A:** Andrew Currie **W:** Dan Abnett; Ian Edginton
2 ❑ Jul 1998 Cover: 2.50 **NM** value: **2.99**
Circ: Diamd. preorders: **10,439**
wraparound cover. **A:** Andrew Currie **W:** Dan Abnett; Ian Edginton
3 ❑ Aug 1998 Cover: 2.50 **NM** value: **2.99**
Circ: Diamd. preorders: **8,807**
wraparound cover. **A:** Andrew Currie **W:** Dan Abnett; Ian Edginton
4 ❑ Sep 1998 Cover: 2.50 **NM** value: **2.99**
Circ: Diamd. preorders: **7,836**
wraparound cover. **A:** Andrew Currie **W:** Dan Abnett; Ian Edginton

SEEKER 3000 PREMIERE — Marvel

1 ❑ Jun 1998 Cover: 1.50 **NM** value: **Cover or less**
• reprints Marvel Premiere #41

SEEKER: VENGEANCE — Sky

1 ❑ Nov 1993 Cover: 2.50 **NM** value: **Cover or less**
Circ: CapCity orders: **3,355**
1/GO ❑ Nov 1993 Cover: 2.50 **NM** value: **3.00**
• Gold edition.
2 ❑ 1994 Cover: 2.50 **NM** value: **Cover or less**

SELECT DETECTIVE — D.S.

1 ❑ Aug 1948 Cover: 0.10 **NM** value: **175.00**
2 ❑ Oct 1948 Cover: 0.10 **NM** value: **125.00**
3 ❑ Dec 1948 Cover: 0.10 **NM** value: **100.00**

SELF-LOATHING COMICS — Fantagraphics

1 ❑ 1996 Cover: 3.50 **NM** value: **Cover or less**
Circ: CapCity orders: **3,060**
📖 A Day in the Life; A Day in the Life of Aline Kominsky-Crumb-Crumb; Aline & Bob: ApTritif Tim in the South of France; Aline & Bob: Epismetizin' on the Puppitudes… **A:** R.Crumb **W:** Robert Crumb; Aline Kominsky-Crumb-Crumb
2 ❑ May 1997 Cover: 3.50 **NM** value: **Cover or less**
Circ: Diamd. preorders: **6,102**
A: R.Crumb **W:** Robert Crumb; Aline Kominsky-Crumb-Crumb

SEMPER FI — Marvel

1 ❑ Dec 1988 Cover: 0.75 **NM** value: **1.25**
Circ: CapCity orders: **40,200**
A: John Severin
2 ❑ Jan 1989 Cover: 0.75 **NM** value: **1.25**
Circ: CapCity orders: **26,900**
A: John Severin
3 ❑ Feb 1989 Cover: 0.75 **NM** value: **1.25**
Circ: CapCity orders: **23,600**
A: John Severin
4 ❑ Mar 1989 Cover: 0.75 **NM** value: **1.25**
Circ: CapCity orders: **20,300**
A: John Severin
5 ❑ Apr 1989 Cover: 0.75 **NM** value: **1.25**
Circ: CapCity orders: **17,400**
A: John Severin
6 ❑ May 1989 Cover: 0.75 **NM** value: **1.25**
Circ: CapCity orders: **14,200**
A: John Severin
7 ❑ Jun 1989 Cover: 0.75 **NM** value: **1.25**
Circ: CapCity orders: **12,700**
A: John Severin
8 ❑ Jul 1989 Cover: 0.75 **NM** value: **1.25**
Circ: CapCity orders: **11,800**
A: John Severin
9 ❑ Aug 1989 Cover: 0.75 **NM** value: **1.25**
Circ: CapCity orders: **11,200**
A: John Severin

SENSATIONAL POLICE CASES — Avon

1 ❑ Jan 1954 Cover: 0.10 **NM** value: **300.00**
2 ❑ Mar 1954 Cover: 0.10 **NM** value: **150.00**
3 ❑ May 1954 Cover: 0.10 **NM** value: **150.00**
• **CGC:** 1 graded, best 4.0
4 ❑ Jul 1954 Cover: 0.10 **NM** value: **150.00**

SENSATIONAL SHE-HULK, THE — Marvel

She's big, beautiful, and green...and she's got a license to practice law. So don't ruin her suit, crash into her flying car, or inconveniently appear from another dimension while she's presenting a case to the judge. Because she'll sue you or worse. This is one lady who doesn't need a process server to get even with the bad guys.

This series takes a lighter look at the Incredible Hulk's cousin, Jennifer Walters, Esq., also known as She-Hulk. If you never thought super-heroes — or lawyers — had a sense of humor, check out this title. You'll find it a refreshing change from the usual avenging-vigilante style of super-heroes.

1 ❑ May 1989 Cover: 1.50 **NM** value: **2.50**
Circ: Statement: **234,540** CapCity orders: **59,400**
A: John Byrne **W:** John Byrne
2 ❑ Jun 1989 Cover: 1.50 **NM** value: **2.00**
Circ: Statement: **234,540** CapCity orders: **44,350**
A: John Byrne **W:** John Byrne ★ Versus Toad Men.
3 ❑ Jul 1989 Cover: 1.50 **NM** value: **2.00**
Circ: Statement: **234,540** CapCity orders: **44,700**
A: John Byrne **W:** John Byrne ★ Appearance of Spider-Man.
4 ❑ Aug 1989 Cover: 1.50 **NM** value: **2.00**
Circ: Statement: **234,540** CapCity orders: **42,300**
A: John Byrne **W:** John Byrne ★ Origin of Blonde Phantom. ★ Appearance of Blonde Phantom.
5 ❑ Sep 1989 Cover: 1.50 **NM** value: **2.00**
Circ: Statement: **234,540** CapCity orders: **39,000**
A: John Byrne **W:** John Byrne
6 ❑ Oct 1989 Cover: 1.50 **NM** value: **2.00**
Circ: Statement: **234,540** CapCity orders: **36,300**
A: John Byrne **W:** John Byrne ★ Appearance of Razorback.
7 ❑ Nov 1989 Cover: 1.50 **NM** value: **2.00**
Circ: Statement: **234,540** CapCity orders: **33,600**
A: John Byrne **W:** John Byrne ★ Appearance of Razorback.
8 ❑ Nov 1989 Cover: 1.50 **NM** value: **2.00**
Circ: Statement: **234,540** CapCity orders: **31,900**
A: John Byrne **W:** John Byrne ★ Appearance of Nick St. Christopher.
9 ❑ Dec 1989 Cover: 1.50 **NM** value: **1.75**
Circ: Statement: **234,540** CapCity orders: **26,200**
★ Versus Madcap.
10 ❑ Dec 1989 Cover: 1.50 **NM** value: **1.75**
Circ: Statement: **234,540** CapCity orders: **23,700**
11 ❑ Jan 1990 Cover: 1.50 **NM** value: **1.75**
Circ: Statement: **185,736** CapCity orders: **23,100**
12 ❑ Feb 1990 Cover: 1.50 **NM** value: **1.75**
Circ: Statement: **185,736** CapCity orders: **21,600**
13 ❑ Mar 1990 Cover: 1.50 **NM** value: **1.75**
Circ: Statement: **185,736** CapCity orders: **20,100**
14 ❑ Apr 1990 Cover: 1.50 **NM** value: **1.75**
Circ: Statement: **185,736** CapCity orders: **19,800**
★ Appearance of Howard the Duck.
15 ❑ May 1990 Cover: 1.50 **NM** value: **1.75**
Circ: Statement: **185,736** CapCity orders: **19,000**
★ Appearance of Howard the Duck.
16 ❑ Jun 1990 Cover: 1.50 **NM** value: **1.75**
Circ: Statement: **185,736** CapCity orders: **17,700**
★ Appearance of Howard the Duck.
17 ❑ Jul 1990 Cover: 1.50 **NM** value: **1.75**
Circ: Statement: **185,736** CapCity orders: **17,300**
★ Appearance of Howard the Duck.
18 ❑ Aug 1990 Cover: 1.50 **NM** value: **1.75**
Circ: Statement: **185,736** CapCity orders: **15,900**
📖 The Dentist in the Iron Mask **A:** Tom Artis **W:** Steve Gerber
19 ❑ Sep 1990 Cover: 1.50 **NM** value: **1.75**
Circ: Statement: **185,736** CapCity orders: **15,300**
📖 Year Zero **W:** Bryan Hitch; Jim Sanders; Steve Gerber ★ Appearance of Nosferata the She-Bat.
20 ❑ Oct 1990 Cover: 1.50 **NM** value: **1.75**
Circ: Statement: **185,736** CapCity orders: **15,000**
21 ❑ Nov 1990 Cover: 1.50 **NM** value: **1.75**
Circ: Statement: **185,736** CapCity orders: **13,800**
• Blonde Phantom
22 ❑ Dec 1990 Cover: 1.50 **NM** value: **1.75**
Circ: Statement: **185,736** CapCity orders: **13,500**
• Blonde Phantom
23 ❑ Jan 1991 Cover: 1.50 **NM** value: **1.75**
Circ: Statement: **49,718** CapCity orders: **12,700**
• Blonde Phantom
24 ❑ Feb 1991 Cover: 1.50 **NM** value: **1.75**
Circ: Statement: **49,718** CapCity orders: **12,400**
• Death's Head
25 ❑ Mar 1991 Cover: 1.50 **NM** value: **1.75**
Circ: Statement: **49,718** CapCity orders: **12,200**
• Hercules
26 ❑ Apr 1991 Cover: 1.50 **NM** value: **1.75**
Circ: Statement: **49,718** CapCity orders: **12,200**
27 ❑ May 1991 Cover: 1.50 **NM** value: **1.75**
Circ: Statement: **49,718** CapCity orders: **11,200**
white inside covers.
28 ❑ Jun 1991 Cover: 1.50 **NM** value: **1.75**
Circ: Statement: **49,718** CapCity orders: **11,100**
29 ❑ Jul 1991 Cover: 1.50 **NM** value: **1.75**
Circ: Statement: **49,718** CapCity orders: **34,300**
30 ❑ Aug 1991 Cover: 1.50 **NM** value: **1.75**
Circ: Statement: **49,718** CapCity orders: **17,200**
31 ❑ Sep 1991 Cover: 1.50 **NM** value: **1.75**
Circ: Statement: **49,718** CapCity orders: **23,500**
A: John Byrne **W:** John Byrne
32 ❑ Oct 1991 Cover: 1.50 **NM** value: **1.75**
Circ: Statement: **49,718** CapCity orders: **20,200**
A: John Byrne **W:** John Byrne
33 ❑ Nov 1991 Cover: 1.50 **NM** value: **1.75**
Circ: Statement: **49,718** CapCity orders: **17,800**
A: John Byrne **W:** John Byrne
34 ❑ Dec 1991 Cover: 1.50 **NM** value: **1.75**
Circ: Statement: **49,718** CapCity orders: **17,300**
A: John Byrne **W:** John Byrne
35 ❑ Jan 1992 Cover: 1.50 **NM** value: **1.75**
Circ: Statement: **61,907** CapCity orders: **18,000**
A: John Byrne **W:** John Byrne
36 ❑ Feb 1992 Cover: 1.75 **NM** value: **Cover or less**
Circ: Statement: **61,907** CapCity orders: **16,200**
A: John Byrne **W:** John Byrne ★ Appearance of Wyatt Wingfoot.
37 ❑ Mar 1992 Cover: 1.75 **NM** value: **Cover or less**
Circ: Statement: **61,907** CapCity orders: **15,600**
A: John Byrne **W:** John Byrne
38 ❑ Apr 1992 Cover: 1.75 **NM** value: **Cover or less**
Circ: Statement: **61,907** CapCity orders: **14,800**
A: John Byrne **W:** John Byrne ★ Versus Mahkizmo.
39 ❑ May 1992 Cover: 1.75 **NM** value: **Cover or less**
Circ: Statement: **61,907** CapCity orders: **15,100**
A: John Byrne **W:** John Byrne ★ Appearance of Thing. ★ Versus Mahkizmo.
40 ❑ Jun 1992 Cover: 1.75 **NM** value: **Cover or less**
Circ: Statement: **61,907** CapCity orders: **15,800**
A: John Byrne **W:** John Byrne
41 ❑ Jul 1992 Cover: 1.75 **NM** value: **Cover or less**
Circ: Statement: **61,907** CapCity orders: **15,400**
A: John Byrne **W:** John Byrne
42 ❑ Aug 1992 Cover: 1.75 **NM** value: **Cover or less**
Circ: Statement: **61,907** CapCity orders: **15,600**
A: John Byrne **W:** John Byrne
43 ❑ Sep 1992 Cover: 1.75 **NM** value: **Cover or less**
Circ: Statement: **61,907** CapCity orders: **15,000**
A: John Byrne **W:** John Byrne
44 ❑ Oct 1992 Cover: 1.75 **NM** value: **Cover or less**
Circ: Statement: **61,907** CapCity orders: **14,600**
A: John Byrne **W:** John Byrne
45 ❑ Nov 1992 Cover: 1.75 **NM** value: **Cover or less**
Circ: Statement: **61,907** CapCity orders: **14,300**
A: John Byrne **W:** John Byrne
46 ❑ Dec 1992 Cover: 1.75 **NM** value: **Cover or less**
Circ: Statement: **61,907** CapCity orders: **13,700**
A: John Byrne **W:** John Byrne
47 ❑ Jan 1993 Cover: 1.75 **NM** value: **Cover or less**
Circ: CapCity orders: **13,200**
A: Rik Levins **W:** Simon Furman
48 ❑ Feb 1993 Cover: 1.75 **NM** value: **Cover or less**
Circ: CapCity orders: **13,800**
A: John Byrne **W:** John Byrne
49 ❑ Mar 1993 Cover: 1.75 **NM** value: **Cover or less**
A: John Byrne **W:** John Byrne
50 ❑ Apr 1993 Cover: 2.95 **NM** value: **Cover or less**
Circ: CapCity orders: **50,100**

CGC-graded: Multiply prices above by **33 for 9.9 M • 16 for 9.8 NM/M • 7 for 9.6 NM+ • 5 for 9.4 NM • 2.5 for 9.2 NM- • 1.5 for 9.0 VF/NM**

Green foil cover. • Double-size. **A:** Wendy Pini; John Byrne; Howard Chaykin; Dick Giordano; Frank Miller; Walt Simonson **W:** John Byrne; Frank Miller

51 ❑ May 1993 Cover: 1.75 **NM** value: **Cover or less**
Circ: CapCity orders: **13,300**
• Savage She-Hulk vs. Sensational She-Hulk

52 ❑ Jun 1993 Cover: 1.75 **NM** value: **Cover or less**
Circ: CapCity orders: **17,200**
📖 To Die and Live in L.A., Part 1

53 ❑ Jul 1993 Cover: 1.75 **NM** value: **Cover or less**
Circ: CapCity orders: **13,900**
📖 To Die and Live in L.A., Part 2

54 ❑ Aug 1993 Cover: 1.75 **NM** value: **Cover or less**
Circ: CapCity orders: **12,800**
📖 To Die and Live in L.A., Part 3

55 ❑ Sep 1993 Cover: 1.75 **NM** value: **Cover or less**
Circ: CapCity orders: **11,350**
📖 To Die and Live in L.A., Part 4

56 ❑ Oct 1993 Cover: 1.75 **NM** value: **Cover or less**
Circ: CapCity orders: **11,000**
📖 To Die and Live in L.A., Part 5 **A:** Patrick Olliffe **W:** Michael Eury ★ Appearance of Hulk.

57 ❑ Nov 1993 Cover: 1.75 **NM** value: **Cover or less**
Circ: CapCity orders: **10,050**
📖 To Die and Live in L.A., Part 6 ★ Appearance of Hulk.

58 ❑ Dec 1993 Cover: 1.75 **NM** value: **Cover or less**
Circ: CapCity orders: **9,500**
★ Appearance of Tommy the Gopher. ★ Versus Electro.

59 ❑ Jan 1994 Cover: 1.75 **NM** value: **Cover or less**
Circ: CapCity orders: **8,600**

60 ❑ Feb 1994 Cover: 1.75 **NM** value: **Cover or less**
Circ: CapCity orders: **9,100**
final issue. ★ Appearance of Millie the Model.

SENSATIONAL SHE-HULK IN CEREMONY, THE — Marvel

1 ❑ ca. 1989 Cover: 3.95 **NM** value: **Cover or less**
Circ: CapCity orders: **19,150**
• leg shaving **A:** June Brigman **W:** Dwayne McDuffie

2 ❑ ca. 1989 Cover: 3.95 **NM** value: **Cover or less**
Circ: CapCity orders: **17,750**
A: June Brigman **W:** Dwayne McDuffie; Robin D. Chaplik

SENSATIONAL SPIDER-MAN, THE — Marvel

Sensational Spider-Man was launched in in late 1995 (remember, Marvel post-dates its covers), replacing Web of Spider-Man in the rotation of Spider-titles. That, it should be remembered, replaced Marvel Team-Up.

It was not an auspicious beginning. Sensational Spider-Man started in the middle of the two-year-long "Clone Saga," generally regarded as the single lowest creative period in the history of the series.

Over in the other titles, the clone of Spider-Man, thought killed in Amazing Spider-Man #149, returned and was revealed (only after tortuous and confusing twists) to be the real Peter Parker. Taking the name Ben Reilly, he assumed the mantle of Spider-Man and sent the "other one" off to exile, taking with him only the loyalty of everyone who had read a story about the "fake" Spider-Man over the previous 20 years.

Fans protested and Reilly was eventually killed and replaced by the real thing in #12.

Nothing in this period was going to make anyone regard this series especially fondly, however, and its cancellation brought an end to a Spider-title that had, under four different names and three numbering restarts (counting Web of Scarlet Spider), run continuously since 1972. So passes the glory of this world! — JJM

-1 ❑ Jul 1997 Cover: 1.99 **NM** value: **2.00**
Circ: Diamd. preorders: **63,640**
• Flashback

0 ❑ Jan 1996 Cover: 4.95 **NM** value: **5.00**
• **CGC:** 2 graded, best 9.6
enhanced wraparound cardstock cover with lenticular animation card attached. 📖 Ultimate Commitment • new costume **A:** Dan Jurgens **W:** Dan Jurgens ★ Origin of Spider-Man. ★ 1st Appearance of Armada.

1 ❑ Feb 1996 Cover: 1.95 **NM** value: **2.00**
📖 Media Blizzard, Part 1 • Series picks up subscribers from Web of Spider-Man **A:** Dan Jurgens **W:** Dan Jurgens

2 ❑ Mar 1996 Cover: 1.95 **NM** value: **2.00**
A: Dan Jurgens **W:** Dan Jurgens

2/CS❑ Feb 1996 Cover: 2.95 **NM** value: **Cover or less**
📖 Media Blizzard, Part 1 **A:** Dan Jurgens **W:** Dan Jurgens

3 ❑ Apr 1996 Cover: 1.95 **NM** value: **2.00**
📖 Web of Carnage, Part 1 **A:** Dan Jurgens **W:** Dan Jurgens

4 ❑ May 1996 Cover: 1.95 **NM** value: **2.00**
📖 Blood Brothers, Part 1 • Ben Reilly revealed as Spider-Man

5 ❑ Jun 1996 Cover: 1.95 **NM** value: **2.00**
📖 Blood Brothers, Part 5 ★ Versus Molten Man.

6 ❑ Jul 1996 Cover: 1.95 **NM** value: **2.00**

7 ❑ Aug 1996 Cover: 1.95 **NM** value: **2.00**

8 ❑ Sep 1996 Cover: 1.95 **NM** value: **2.00**
★ Versus Looter.

9 ❑ Oct 1996 Cover: 1.99 **NM** value: **2.00**
★ Appearance of Swarm.

10 ❑ Nov 1996 Cover: 1.99 **NM** value: **2.00**
Circ: Statement: **117,969** Direct Market orders: **74,250**

11 ❑ Dec 1996 Cover: 1.99 **NM** value: **2.00**
Circ: Statement: **117,969** Direct Market orders: **97,750**
📖 Revelations, Part 2

11/CS❑ Dec 1996 **NM** value: **3.00**
📖 Revelations, Part 2

12 ❑ Jan 1997 Cover: 1.99 **NM** value: **2.00**
Circ: Statement: **117,969** Direct Market orders: **72,750**
★ Versus Trapster.

13 ❑ Feb 1997 Cover: 1.99 **NM** value: **2.00**
Circ: Statement: **117,969** Direct Market orders: **72,500**
📖 Deluge, Part 1 **A:** Mike Wieringo **W:** Todd Dezago ★ Appearance of Ka-Zar, Shanna.

14 ❑ Mar 1997 Cover: 1.99 **NM** value: **2.00**
Circ: Statement: **117,969** Direct Market orders: **68,000**
📖 Deluge, Part 2 **A:** Mike Wieringo **W:** Todd Dezago ★ Appearance of Ka-Zar, Shanna, Hulk.

15 ❑ Apr 1997 Cover: 1.99 **NM** value: **2.00**
Circ: Statement: **117,969** Direct Market orders: **66,250**
📖 Deluge, Part 3 **A:** Mike Wieringo **W:** Todd Dezago ★ Appearance of Ka-Zar, Shanna, Hulk.

16 ❑ May 1997 Cover: 1.99 **NM** value: **2.00**
Circ: Statement: **117,969** Diamd. preorders: **65,824**
📖 Paralyzed! **A:** Mike Wieringo **W:** Todd Dezago ★ Versus Prowler.

17 ❑ Jun 1997 Cover: 1.99 **NM** value: **2.00**
Circ: Statement: **117,969** Diamd. preorders: **66,807**
📖 Helpless! **A:** Mike Wieringo **W:** Todd Dezago ★ Versus Vulture.

18 ❑ Aug 1997 Cover: 1.99 **NM** value: **2.00**
Circ: Statement: **117,969** Diamd. preorders: **60,845**
• gatefold summary.

19 ❑ Sep 1997 Cover: 1.99 **NM** value: **2.00**
Circ: Statement: **117,969** Diamd. preorders: **58,608**
• gatefold summary. ★ Versus Living Pharaoh.

20 ❑ Oct 1997 Cover: 1.99 **NM** value: **2.00**
Circ: Statement: **117,969** Diamd. preorders: **57,560**
• gatefold summary.

21 ❑ Nov 1997 Cover: 1.99 **NM** value: **Cover or less**
Circ: Diamd. preorders: **55,506**
• gatefold summary.

22 ❑ Dec 1997 Cover: 1.99 **NM** value: **Cover or less**
Circ: Diamd. preorders: **54,725**
• gatefold summary. ★ Appearance of Doctor Strange.

23 ❑ Jan 1998 Cover: 1.99 **NM** value: **Cover or less**
Circ: Diamd. preorders: **54,208**
• gatefold summary. • Has 1997 Statement, filed 10/1/97; avg print run 211,317; avg sales 114,026; avg subs 3,943; avg total paid 117,969; samples 394; office use 125; max existent 118,488; 44% of run returned

24 ❑ Feb 1998 Cover: 1.99 **NM** value: **Cover or less**
Circ: Diamd. preorders: **52,264**
• gatefold summary. ★ Versus Hydro-Man.

25 ❑ Mar 1998 Cover: 2.99 **NM** value: **Cover or less**
Circ: Diamd. preorders: **60,341** • **CGC:** 1 graded, best 9.4
• double-sized. 📖 Spider-Hunt, Part 1

26 ❑ Apr 1998 Cover: 1.99 **NM** value: **Cover or less**
Circ: Diamd. preorders: **52,042**
• gatefold summary. 📖 Identity Crisis ★ Versus Hydro-Man. ★ Versus Sandman.

27 ❑ May 1998 Cover: 1.99 **NM** value: **Cover or less**
Circ: Diamd. preorders: **61,023**
• gatefold summary. 📖 Identity Crisis

28 ❑ Jun 1998 Cover: 1.99 **NM** value: **Cover or less**
Circ: Diamd. preorders: **60,174**
• gatefold summary. 📖 Identity Crisis ★ Appearance of Hornet.

29 ❑ Jul 1998 Cover: 1.99 **NM** value: **Cover or less**
Circ: Diamd. preorders: **56,595**
• gatefold summary. ★ Appearance of Black Cat.

30 ❑ Aug 1998 Cover: 1.99 **NM** value: **Cover or less**
Circ: Diamd. preorders: **57,135**
• gatefold summary.

31 ❑ Sep 1998 Cover: 1.99 **NM** value: **Cover or less**
Circ: Diamd. preorders: **54,525**
• gatefold summary. ★ Versus Rhino.

32 ❑ Oct 1998 Cover: 1.99 **NM** value: **Cover or less**
Circ: Diamd. preorders: **56,566**
• gatefold summary. 📖 The Gathering of Five, Part 1

33 ❑ Nov 1998 Cover: 1.99 **NM** value: **Cover or less**
Circ: Diamd. preorders: **57,146**
• gatefold summary. 📖 The Gathering of Five, Part 5 final issue. ★ Versus Override.

Anl 1996❑ ca. 1996 Cover: 2.99 **NM** value: **3.00**
Circ: Direct Market orders: **60,250**
📖 Kraven's First Hunt ★ Origin of Kraven the Hunter.

SENSATIONAL SPIDER-MAN IN NOTHING CAN STOP THE JUGGERNAUT, THE — Marvel

1 ❑ Cover: 3.95 **NM** value: **Cover or less**
Circ: CapCity orders: **6,000**
No issue number. 📖 Nothing Can Stop the Juggernaut!; To Fight the Unbeatable Foe! • Reprints Amazing Spider-Man #229-230 **A:** John Romita Jr. **W:** Roger Stern

SENSATION COMICS — DC

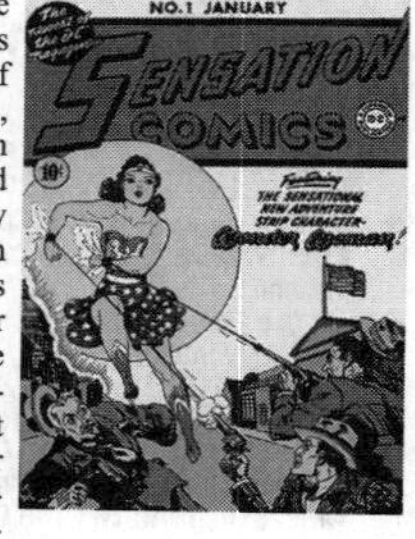

Sensation Comics was one of the cornerstone DC Golden Age titles and the stomping grounds of one of the company's marquee characters, Wonder Woman. Wonder Woman fights Nazis, super-villains, and criminals in adventures written by creator William Moulton Marston (under the pseudonym Charles Moulton) and drawn in a singular style by Harry G. Peter. Memorable backup characters included prize-fighter-turned-crimefighter Wildcat and playboy masked man Mister Terrific. Issue #34 introduced Sargon the Sorcerer, one of DC's longer-lived occult characters.

As the Golden Age wound down in the early 1950s, Wonder Woman departed for the pages of her own title, and adventure-mystery character Johnny Peril moved over from Comic Cavalcade and Danger Trail. The hard-to-find last several issues were entirely mystery-horror, with the title of the series changing to Sensation Mystery from #110 to the final issue, #116.

1 ❑ Jan 1942 Cover: 0.10 **NM** value: **26000.00**
• **CGC:** 9 graded, best 9.4
W: Charles Moulton ★ Origin of Wonder Woman, Wildcat, Mr. Terrific. ★ 1st Appearance of Wildcat, Mr. Terrific.

2 ❑ Feb 1942 Cover: 0.10 **NM** value: **3800.00**
• **CGC:** 3 graded, best 8.5
W: Charles Moulton

3 ❑ Mar 1942 Cover: 0.10 **NM** value: **1900.00**
W: Charles Moulton

4 ❑ Apr 1942 Cover: 0.10 **NM** value: **1250.00**
W: Charles Moulton

5 ❑ May 1942 Cover: 0.10 **NM** value: **950.00**
• **CGC:** 1 graded, best 8.0
W: Charles Moulton

6 ❑ Jun 1942 Cover: 0.10 **NM** value: **900.00**
• **CGC:** 2 graded, best 7.5
W: Charles Moulton

7 ❑ Jul 1942 Cover: 0.10 **NM** value: **775.00**
• **CGC:** 1 graded, best 8.5
W: Charles Moulton

8 ❑ Aug 1942 Cover: 0.10 **NM** value: **775.00**
W: Charles Moulton

9 ❑ Sep 1942 Cover: 0.10 **NM** value: **775.00**
W: Charles Moulton

10 ❑ Oct 1942 Cover: 0.10 **NM** value: **775.00**
W: Charles Moulton

11 ❑ Nov 1942 Cover: 0.10 **NM** value: **650.00**
• **CGC:** 2 graded, best 7.5
W: Charles Moulton

12 ❑ Dec 1942 Cover: 0.10 **NM** value: **650.00**
• **CGC:** 1 graded, best 8.0
W: Charles Moulton

13 ❑ Jan 1943 Cover: 0.10 **NM** value: **650.00**
• **CGC:** 1 graded, best 3.0
W: Charles Moulton

14 ❑ Feb 1943 Cover: 0.10 **NM** value: **650.00**
W: Charles Moulton

15 ❑ Mar 1943 Cover: 0.10 **NM** value: **650.00**
• **CGC:** 3 graded, best 9.0
W: Charles Moulton

16 ❑ Apr 1943 Cover: 0.10 **NM** value: **650.00**
W: Charles Moulton

17 ❑ May 1943 Cover: 0.10 **NM** value: **650.00**
• **CGC:** 1 graded, best 5.5
W: Charles Moulton

18 ❑ Jun 1943 Cover: 0.10 **NM** value: **650.00**
• **CGC:** 1 graded, best 9.2
W: Charles Moulton

19 ❑ Jul 1943 Cover: 0.10 **NM** value: **650.00**
• **CGC:** 2 graded, best 9.2
W: Charles Moulton

20 ❑ Aug 1943 Cover: 0.10 **NM** value: **650.00**
W: Charles Moulton

21 ❑ Sep 1943 Cover: 0.10 **NM** value: **500.00**
W: Charles Moulton

22 ❑ Oct 1943 Cover: 0.10 **NM** value: **500.00**
• **CGC:** 2 graded, best 7.5
W: Charles Moulton

23 ❑ Nov 1943 Cover: 0.10 **NM** value: **500.00**
• **CGC:** 1 graded, best 9.0
W: Charles Moulton

24 ❑ Dec 1943 Cover: 0.10 **NM** value: **500.00**
W: Charles Moulton

25 ❑ Jan 1944 Cover: 0.10 **NM** value: **500.00**
• **CGC:** 1 graded, best 3.0
W: Charles Moulton

26 ❑ Feb 1944 Cover: 0.10 **NM** value: **500.00**
W: Charles Moulton

27 ❑ Mar 1944 Cover: 0.10 **NM** value: **500.00**
W: Charles Moulton

28 ❑ Apr 1944 Cover: 0.10 **NM** value: **500.00**
• **CGC:** 1 graded, best 5.0
W: Charles Moulton

29 ❑ May 1944 Cover: 0.10 **NM** value: **500.00**
W: Charles Moulton

30 ❑ Jun 1944 Cover: 0.10 **NM** value: **500.00**
• **CGC:** 1 graded, best 7.5
W: Charles Moulton

31 ❑ Jul 1944 Cover: 0.10 **NM** value: **400.00**
• **CGC:** 1 graded, best 9.2
W: Charles Moulton

32 ❑ Aug 1944 Cover: 0.10 **NM** value: **400.00**
W: Charles Moulton

33 ❑ Sep 1944 Cover: 0.10 **NM** value: **400.00**
• **CGC:** 2 graded, best 8.5
W: Charles Moulton

34 ❑ Oct 1944 Cover: 0.10 **NM** value: **400.00**
• **CGC:** 1 graded, best 6.0
• Sargon the Sorcerer features begin **W:** Charles Moulton

35 ❑ Nov 1944 Cover: 0.10 **NM** value: **350.00**
• **CGC:** 2 graded, best 9.2
W: Charles Moulton

36 ❑ Dec 1944 Cover: 0.10 **NM** value: **350.00**
• **CGC:** 1 graded, best 5.0
W: Charles Moulton

37 ❑ Jan 1945 Cover: 0.10 **NM** value: **350.00**
• **CGC:** 1 graded, best 9.0
W: Charles Moulton

38 ❑ Feb 1945 Cover: 0.10 **NM** value: **350.00**
• **CGC:** 2 graded, best 7.5
W: Charles Moulton

39 ❑ Mar 1945 Cover: 0.10 **NM** value: **350.00**
• **CGC:** 1 graded, best 8.5
W: Charles Moulton
40 ❑ Apr 1945 Cover: 0.10 **NM** value: **350.00**
W: Charles Moulton
41 ❑ May 1945 Cover: 0.10 **NM** value: **300.00**
• **CGC:** 1 graded, best 7.5
W: Charles Moulton
42 ❑ Jun 1945 Cover: 0.10 **NM** value: **300.00**
W: Charles Moulton
43 ❑ Jul 1945 Cover: 0.10 **NM** value: **300.00**
• **CGC:** 2 graded, best 9.6
W: Charles Moulton
44 ❑ Aug 1945 Cover: 0.10 **NM** value: **300.00**
• **CGC:** 2 graded, best 8.5
W: Charles Moulton
45 ❑ Sep 1945 Cover: 0.10 **NM** value: **300.00**
• **CGC:** 4 graded, best 9.4
W: Charles Moulton
46 ❑ Oct 1945 Cover: 0.10 **NM** value: **300.00**
W: Charles Moulton
47 ❑ Nov 1945 Cover: 0.10 **NM** value: **300.00**
• **CGC:** 1 graded, best 9.2
W: Charles Moulton
48 ❑ Dec 1945 Cover: 0.10 **NM** value: **300.00**
• **CGC:** 1 graded, best 9.2
W: Charles Moulton
49 ❑ Jan 1946 Cover: 0.10 **NM** value: **300.00**
• **CGC:** 1 graded, best 5.5
W: Charles Moulton
50 ❑ Feb 1946 Cover: 0.10 **NM** value: **300.00**
• **CGC:** 1 graded, best 2.0
W: Charles Moulton
51 ❑ Mar 1946 Cover: 0.10 **NM** value: **260.00**
• **CGC:** 1 graded, best 9.0
W: Charles Moulton
52 ❑ Apr 1946 Cover: 0.10 **NM** value: **260.00**
• **CGC:** 2 graded, best 9.4
W: Charles Moulton
53 ❑ May 1946 Cover: 0.10 **NM** value: **260.00**
• **CGC:** 4 graded, best 9.6
W: Charles Moulton
54 ❑ Jun 1946 Cover: 0.10 **NM** value: **260.00**
W: Charles Moulton
55 ❑ Jul 1946 Cover: 0.10 **NM** value: **260.00**
• **CGC:** 3 graded, best 9.4
W: Charles Moulton
56 ❑ Aug 1946 Cover: 0.10 **NM** value: **260.00**
• **CGC:** 2 graded, best 9.0
W: Charles Moulton
57 ❑ Sep 1946 Cover: 0.10 **NM** value: **260.00**
• **CGC:** 3 graded, best 9.4
W: Charles Moulton
58 ❑ Oct 1946 Cover: 0.10 **NM** value: **260.00**
• **CGC:** 1 graded, best 6.5
W: Charles Moulton
59 ❑ Nov 1946 Cover: 0.10 **NM** value: **260.00**
• **CGC:** 6 graded, best 9.6
W: Charles Moulton
60 ❑ Dec 1946 Cover: 0.10 **NM** value: **260.00**
• **CGC:** 2 graded, best 9.4
W: Charles Moulton
61 ❑ Jan 1947 Cover: 0.10 **NM** value: **225.00**
• **CGC:** 2 graded, best 9.0
W: Charles Moulton
62 ❑ Feb 1947 Cover: 0.10 **NM** value: **225.00**
• **CGC:** 2 graded, best 9.0
W: Charles Moulton
63 ❑ Mar 1947 Cover: 0.10 **NM** value: **225.00**
W: Charles Moulton
64 ❑ Apr 1947 Cover: 0.10 **NM** value: **225.00**
W: Charles Moulton
65 ❑ May 1947 Cover: 0.10 **NM** value: **225.00**
• **CGC:** 1 graded, best 9.6
W: Charles Moulton
66 ❑ Jun 1947 Cover: 0.10 **NM** value: **225.00**
• **CGC:** 2 graded, best 9.2
W: Charles Moulton
67 ❑ Jul 1947 Cover: 0.10 **NM** value: **225.00**
• **CGC:** 1 graded, best 7.0
W: Charles Moulton
68 ❑ Aug 1947 Cover: 0.10 **NM** value: **275.00**
W: Charles Moulton ★ Origin of The Huntress I. ★ 1st Appearance of The Huntress I.
69 ❑ Sep 1947 Cover: 0.10 **NM** value: **225.00**
• **CGC:** 1 graded, best 7.0
W: Charles Moulton
70 ❑ Oct 1947 Cover: 0.10 **NM** value: **225.00**
• **CGC:** 2 graded, best 9.0
W: Charles Moulton
71 ❑ Nov 1947 Cover: 0.10 **NM** value: **200.00**
W: Charles Moulton
72 ❑ Dec 1947 Cover: 0.10 **NM** value: **200.00**
W: Charles Moulton
73 ❑ Jan 1948 Cover: 0.10 **NM** value: **200.00**
• **CGC:** 2 graded, best 7.0
W: Charles Moulton
74 ❑ Feb 1948 Cover: 0.10 **NM** value: **200.00**
W: Charles Moulton
75 ❑ Mar 1948 Cover: 0.10 **NM** value: **200.00**
W: Charles Moulton
76 ❑ Apr 1948 Cover: 0.10 **NM** value: **200.00**
• **CGC:** 1 graded, best 5.5
W: Charles Moulton
77 ❑ May 1948 Cover: 0.10 **NM** value: **200.00**
• **CGC:** 1 graded, best 5.0
W: Charles Moulton
78 ❑ Jun 1948 Cover: 0.10 **NM** value: **200.00**
W: Charles Moulton
79 ❑ Jul 1948 Cover: 0.10 **NM** value: **200.00**
W: Charles Moulton
80 ❑ Aug 1948 Cover: 0.10 **NM** value: **200.00**
W: Charles Moulton
81 ❑ Sep 1948 Cover: 0.10 **NM** value: **250.00**
• **CGC:** 2 graded, best 8.0
• Mentioned in Seduction of the Innocent: "So my fellow Americans, it's time to give America back to Americans! Don't let foreigners take your jobs!" **W:** Charles Moulton
82 ❑ Oct 1948 Cover: 0.10 **NM** value: **175.00**
W: Charles Moulton
83 ❑ Nov 1948 Cover: 0.10 **NM** value: **175.00**
• **CGC:** 1 graded, best 5.5
W: Charles Moulton
84 ❑ Dec 1948 Cover: 0.10 **NM** value: **175.00**
W: Charles Moulton
85 ❑ Jan 1949 Cover: 0.10 **NM** value: **175.00**
W: Charles Moulton
86 ❑ Feb 1949 Cover: 0.10 **NM** value: **175.00**
• **CGC:** 1 graded, best 6.0
W: Charles Moulton
87 ❑ Mar 1949 Cover: 0.10 **NM** value: **175.00**
W: Charles Moulton
88 ❑ Apr 1949 Cover: 0.10 **NM** value: **175.00**
W: Charles Moulton
89 ❑ May 1949 Cover: 0.10 **NM** value: **175.00**
W: Charles Moulton
90 ❑ Jun 1949 Cover: 0.10 **NM** value: **175.00**
W: Charles Moulton
91 ❑ Jul 1949 Cover: 0.10 **NM** value: **150.00**
W: Charles Moulton
92 ❑ Aug 1949 Cover: 0.10 **NM** value: **150.00**
• **CGC:** 1 graded, best 5.5
W: Charles Moulton
93 ❑ Sep 1949 Cover: 0.10 **NM** value: **150.00**
• **CGC:** 1 graded, best 7.0
W: Charles Moulton
94 ❑ Nov 1949 Cover: 0.10 **NM** value: **240.00**
W: Charles Moulton
95 ❑ Jan 1950 Cover: 0.10 **NM** value: **150.00**
W: Charles Moulton
96 ❑ Mar 1950 Cover: 0.10 **NM** value: **150.00**
• **CGC:** 1 graded, best 9.6
📖 Kiss Your Sweetheart; Dr. Pat Rx: Report for Romance; Headline Heroines; Beautiful by not Dumb!; Chance Meeting (text story); Romance, Inc.: You Can't Bargain with Love! **A:** Anya Martin; H.G. Peter **W:** Charles Moulton
97 ❑ May 1950 Cover: 0.10 **NM** value: **150.00**
98 ❑ Jul 1950 Cover: 0.10 **NM** value: **150.00**
99 ❑ Sep 1950 Cover: 0.10 **NM** value: **150.00**
100 ❑ Nov 1950 Cover: 0.10 **NM** value: **375.00**
101 ❑ Jan 1951 Cover: 0.10 **NM** value: **375.00**
• **CGC:** 2 graded, best 7.5
102 ❑ Mar 1951 Cover: 0.10 **NM** value: **375.00**
• **CGC:** 1 graded, best 9.0
103 ❑ May 1951 Cover: 0.10 **NM** value: **375.00**
104 ❑ Jul 1951 Cover: 0.10 **NM** value: **375.00**
• **CGC:** 1 graded, best 6.0
105 ❑ Sep 1951 Cover: 0.10 **NM** value: **375.00**
106 ❑ Nov 1951 Cover: 0.10 **NM** value: **375.00**
107 ❑ Jan 1952 Cover: 0.10 **NM** value: **375.00**
• **CGC:** 1 graded, best 5.5
108 ❑ Mar 1952 Cover: 0.10 **NM** value: **375.00**
• **CGC:** 1 graded, best 8.5
109 ❑ May 1952 Cover: 0.10 **NM** value: **375.00**
• **CGC:** 3 graded, best 7.5
• Series continued in Sensation Mystery #110

SENSATION COMICS (2ND SERIES) DC

1 ❑ May 1999 Cover: 1.99 **NM** value: **Cover or less**
📖 Womanly Deeds and Manly Words • Justice Society Returns; Hawkgirl; Speed Saunders **A:** Scott Benefiel **W:** James Robinson; David Goyer ★ Appearance of Wonder Woman, Hawkgirl, Speed Saunders.

SENSATION MYSTERY DC

110 ❑ Jul 1952 Cover: 0.10 **NM** value: **350.00**
• **CGC:** 2 graded, best 9.6
111 ❑ Sep 1952 Cover: 0.10 **NM** value: **350.00**
• **CGC:** 1 graded, best 6.0
112 ❑ Nov 1952 Cover: 0.10 **NM** value: **350.00**
113 ❑ Jan 1953 Cover: 0.10 **NM** value: **350.00**
• **CGC:** 2 graded, best 8.5
114 ❑ Mar 1953 Cover: 0.10 **NM** value: **350.00**
• **CGC:** 1 graded, best 9.0
115 ❑ May 1953 Cover: 0.10 **NM** value: **350.00**
• **CGC:** 1 graded, best 8.0
116 ❑ Jul 1953 Cover: 0.10 **NM** value: **350.00**
• **CGC:** 1 graded, best 5.5

SENSEI First

In the late '80s, First Comics released a series of deluxe-format mini-series that they called First Fiction. The second of these series is Roger Salick and Val Mayerik's Sensei, a four-part story that mixes science-fiction and samurai culture.

Tadashi Natori is one of the people who feel that they were born in the wrong time. Natori was born in the late 20th century, but trained in the ancient art of samurai warfare. For his entire life, he yearned to live in ancient Japan, where he thought he would feel more comfortable. Tadashi gets his chance when his twin brother, Ken, invents a time machine. Tadashi is sent back in time to the California of the Old West. But, while there, he is forced into a deadly confrontation with a crew of murderers. That, coupled with a lab accident back in the future, changes history and throws Natori into a barbaric New California of 2129.

1 ❑ May 1989 Cover: 2.75 **NM** value: **Cover or less**
Circ: CapCity orders: **6,150**
2 ❑ 1989 Cover: 2.75 **NM** value: **Cover or less**
Circ: CapCity orders: **4,825**
3 ❑ 1989 Cover: 2.75 **NM** value: **Cover or less**
Circ: CapCity orders: **4,600**
4 ❑ Dec 1989 Cover: 2.75 **NM** value: **Cover or less**
Circ: CapCity orders: **4,350**

SENTAI Antarctic

1 ❑ Feb 1994, b&w Cover: 2.95 **NM** value: **Cover or less**
• The Journal of Asian SF and Fantasy
2 ❑ Apr 1994, b&w Cover: 2.95 **NM** value: **Cover or less**
• The Journal of Asian SF and Fantasy
3 ❑ Jul 1994, b&w Cover: 2.95 **NM** value: **Cover or less**
• The Journal of Asian SF and Fantasy
4 ❑ Sep 1994, b&w Cover: 2.95 **NM** value: **Cover or less**
• The Journal of Asian SF and Fantasy
5 ❑ Nov 1994 Cover: 3.95 **NM** value: **Cover or less**
• The Journal of Asian SF and Fantasy
6 ❑ Feb 1995, b&w Cover: 2.95 **NM** value: **Cover or less**
• The Journal of Asian SF and Fantasy
7 ❑ Apr 1995, b&w Cover: 2.95 **NM** value: **Cover or less**
• The Journal of Asian SF and Fantasy

SENTINEL Harrier

1 ❑ Dec 1986 Cover: 1.95 **NM** value: **Cover or less**
A: Art Wetherell; Graham Bleathman **W:** Graeme Bassett
2 ❑ Feb 1987 Cover: 1.95 **NM** value: **Cover or less**
A: Art Wetherell; Graham Bleathman **W:** Graeme Bassett
3 ❑ Apr 1987 Cover: 1.95 **NM** value: **Cover or less**
A: Art Wetherell; Graham Bleathman **W:** Graeme Bassett
4 ❑ Jun 1987 Cover: 1.95 **NM** value: **Cover or less**
A: Art Wetherell; Graham Bleathman **W:** Graeme Bassett

SENTINELS OF JUSTICE (2ND SERIES) AC

1 ❑ Cover: 3.95 **NM** value: **Cover or less**
• Avenger **A:** Dick Ayers
2 ❑ Cover: 3.95 **NM** value: **Cover or less**
Circ: CapCity orders: **2,975**
• Jet Girl
3 ❑ Cover: 3.95 **NM** value: **Cover or less**
Circ: CapCity orders: **2,875**
• Yankee Girl

SENTINELS OF JUSTICE COMPACT AC

1 ❑ Cover: 3.95 **NM** value: **Cover or less**
2 ❑ Cover: 3.95 **NM** value: **Cover or less**
3 ❑ Cover: 3.95 **NM** value: **Cover or less**

SENTINELS PRESENTS...CRYSTAL WORLD, THE: PRISONERS OF SPHERIS Academy

1 ❑ Cover: 2.95 **NM** value: **Cover or less**

SENTRY, THE Marvel

Before the Fantastic Four, before the Avengers, there is a hero to rule all heroes, and his name is Sentry. Don't remember this Golden Age icon? Don't worry, neither does the rest of the Marvel Universe. But writer Paul Jenkins and artist Jae Lee looked to change all of that with their five-issue Marvel Knights mini-series.

An interesting occurrence hit the Mighty House of Ideas. Supposedly, fan-favorite writer Jenkins was snooping through the publisher's submission pile one day and just happened to come across a proverbial pot of gold — a "lost file" of work by Stan Lee and Artie Rosen dating back to 1961. It seems the two, upon receiving the mandate to create a new line of super-hero comics, created outlines and character sketches for the Marvel Comics' equivalent to Superman. His name was The Sentry and he had "the power of a million exploding suns." In typical Lee fashion, the character was also an alcoholic, making him that much more accessible to readers. While the concept for the character was later scrapped in favor of The Fantastic Four, Jenkins could not pass on the opportunity of working this truly classic super-hero into mainstream continuity.

The result: Sentry — a five-issue Marvel Knights mini-series that poses the question: Is Sentry a hero that has inexplicably been erased from the Marvel universe? Or is he a madman whose alcoholic delusions of grandeur make him more than he really is?

1 ❑ Sep 2000 Cover: 2.99 **NM** value: **Cover or less**
Circ: Diamd. preorders: **44,412** • **CGC:** 5 graded, best 9.8
📖 The Suit **A:** Jae Lee **W:** Paul Jenkins
2 ❑ Oct 2000 Cover: 2.99 **NM** value: **Cover or less**
Circ: Diamd. preorders: **33,220**
📖 The Unicorn **A:** Jae Lee **W:** Paul Jenkins
3 ❑ Nov 2000 Cover: 2.99 **NM** value: **Cover or less**
Circ: Diamd. preorders: **32,877**
📖 The Photograph **A:** Jae Lee **W:** Paul Jenkins ★ Appearance of Hulk, Spider-Man.
4 ❑ Dec 2000 Cover: 2.99 **NM** value: **Cover or less**
Circ: Diamd. preorders: **33,036**

CGC-graded: Multiply prices above by **33 for 9.9 M • 16 for 9.8 NM/M • 7 for 9.6 NM+ • 5 for 9.4 NM • 2.5 for 9.2 NM- • 1.5 for 9.0 VF/NM**

📖 The Conspiracy **A:** Jae Lee **W:** Paul Jenkins ★ Appearance of Doctor Strange.

5 ❑ Jan 2001 Cover: 2.99 **NM** value: **Cover or less**
Circ: Diamd. preorders: **33,592**
📖 The Betrayal **A:** Jae Lee **W:** Paul Jenkins ★ Appearance of Fantastic Four, Hulk, Spider-Man, Avengers.

SENTRY/FANTASTIC FOUR — Marvel

1 ❑ Feb 2001 Cover: 2.99 **NM** value: **Cover or less**
• **CGC:** 3 graded, best 9.6
📖 The Sentry and Fantastic Four **A:** Phil Winslade **W:** Paul Jenkins

SENTRY/HULK — Marvel

1 ❑ Feb 2001 Cover: 2.99 **NM** value: **Cover or less**
• **CGC:** 2 graded, best 9.6
📖 The Sentry and Hulk **A:** Bill Sienkiewicz **W:** Paul Jenkins

SENTRY SPECIAL — Innovation

1 ❑ Jun 1991 Cover: 2.75 **NM** value: **Cover or less**
Circ: CapCity orders: **2,115**

SENTRY/SPIDER-MAN — Marvel

1 ❑ Feb 2001 Cover: 2.99 **NM** value: **Cover or less**
• **CGC:** 3 graded, best 9.6
📖 The Sentry and Spider-Man **A:** Rick Leonardi **W:** Paul Jenkins

SENTRY/THE VOID — Marvel

1 ❑ Feb 2001 Cover: 2.99 **NM** value: **Cover or less**
Circ: Diamd. preorders: **33,365** • **CGC:** 3 graded, best 9.6
📖 The Sentry and the Truth **A:** Jae Lee **W:** Paul Jenkins

SENTRY/X-MEN — Marvel

1 ❑ Feb 2001 Cover: 2.99 **NM** value: **Cover or less**
• **CGC:** 1 graded, best 9.6
📖 The Sentry and Angel of The X-Men **A:** Mark Texeira **W:** Paul Jenkins

SEPULCHER — Illustration

1 ❑ Mar 2000 Cover: 2.99 **NM** value: **Cover or less**
📖 Hell's Choice **A:** Don Paresi **W:** Don Paresi; Paul Wishinsky
2 ❑ May 2000 Cover: 2.99 **NM** value: **Cover or less**
📖 Eyes of Doom **A:** Don Paresi **W:** Don Paresi; Paul Wishinsky

SEQUENTIAL — I Don't Get It

1 ❑ 2000 Cover: 2.95 **NM** value: **Cover or less**
2 ❑ 2000 Cover: 2.95 **NM** value: **Cover or less**
3 ❑ Jun 1999 Cover: 2.95 **NM** value: **Cover or less**

SERAPHIM — Innovation

1 ❑ May 1990 Cover: 2.50 **NM** value: **Cover or less**
Circ: CapCity orders: **2,800**
A: Doug Talalla **W:** Chris Todd
2 ❑ 1990 Cover: 2.50 **NM** value: **Cover or less**
Circ: CapCity orders: **1,875**
A: Doug Talalla **W:** Chris Todd
3 ❑ 1990 Cover: 2.50 **NM** value: **Cover or less**
A: Doug Talalla **W:** Chris Todd

SERGEANT BARNEY BARKER — Atlas

1 ❑ Aug 1956 Cover: 0.10 **NM** value: **125.00**
2 ❑ Oct 1956 Cover: 0.10 **NM** value: **100.00**
• **CGC:** 1 graded, best 9.0
📖 Untitled stories; Roll Call!; Rocky's Beans (text);
3 ❑ Dec 1956 Cover: 0.10 **NM** value: **100.00**

SGT. BILKO — DC

1 ❑ May 1957 Cover: 0.10 **NM** value: **350.00**
• **CGC:** 2 graded, best 4.5
• based on TV series
2 ❑ Aug 1957 Cover: 0.10 **NM** value: **150.00**
3 ❑ Oct 1957 Cover: 0.10 **NM** value: **100.00**
4 ❑ Dec 1957 Cover: 0.10 **NM** value: **100.00**
5 ❑ Feb 1958 Cover: 0.10 **NM** value: **100.00**
6 ❑ Apr 1958 Cover: 0.10 **NM** value: **75.00**
7 ❑ Jun 1958 Cover: 0.10 **NM** value: **75.00**
8 ❑ Aug 1958 Cover: 0.10 **NM** value: **75.00**
9 ❑ Oct 1958 Cover: 0.10 **NM** value: **75.00**
10 ❑ Dec 1958 Cover: 0.10 **NM** value: **75.00**
11 ❑ Feb 1959 Cover: 0.10 **NM** value: **75.00**
12 ❑ Apr 1959 Cover: 0.10 **NM** value: **75.00**
13 ❑ Jun 1959 Cover: 0.10 **NM** value: **75.00**
14 ❑ Aug 1959 Cover: 0.10 **NM** value: **60.00**
15 ❑ Oct 1959 Cover: 0.10 **NM** value: **60.00**
16 ❑ Dec 1959 Cover: 0.10 **NM** value: **60.00**
17 ❑ Feb 1960 Cover: 0.10 **NM** value: **60.00**
18 ❑ Apr 1960 Cover: 0.10 **NM** value: **60.00**

SGT. BILKO'S PVT. DOBERMAN — DC

1 ❑ Jun 1958 Cover: 0.10 **NM** value: **150.00**
• **CGC:** 4 graded, best 8.5
• spin-off from Sgt. Bilko
2 ❑ Aug 1958 Cover: 0.10 **NM** value: **110.00**
3 ❑ Nov 1958 Cover: 0.10 **NM** value: **90.00**
4 ❑ Jan 1959 Cover: 0.10 **NM** value: **70.00**
5 ❑ Mar 1959 Cover: 0.10 **NM** value: **70.00**
6 ❑ May 1959 Cover: 0.10 **NM** value: **50.00**
7 ❑ Jul 1959 Cover: 0.10 **NM** value: **50.00**
8 ❑ Aug 1959 Cover: 0.10 **NM** value: **50.00**
9 ❑ Sep 1959 Cover: 0.10 **NM** value: **50.00**
10 ❑ Nov 1960 Cover: 0.10 **NM** value: **50.00**
11 ❑ Mar 1960 Cover: 0.10 **NM** value: **50.00**

SGT. FURY — Marvel

Long before he became "Nick Fury, Agent of S.H.I.E.L.D.," Sgt. Fury was the leader of The Howling Commandos, the legendary fighting force of World War II. Comprised of a colorful band of fellow warriors, including future S.H.I.E.L.D. agents Gabriel Jones and Dum-Dum Dugan, The Howlers inflicted untold destruction on the Nazi forces.

During one mission in France, Fury was gravely wounded and came under the emergency care of Professor Berthold. Berthold inoculated him with an experimental "Infinity Formula" which slowed his aging process (which helps to explain how Fury is still going strong in the current day).

1 ❑ Dec 1963 Cover: 0.12 **NM** value: **925.00**
• **CGC:** 24 graded, best 9.4
📖 Sgt. Fury and His Howling Commandos ★ 1st Appearance of General Samuel "Happy Sam" Sawyer, Dum Dum Dugan, Sgt. Nick Fury.
2 ❑ Jan 1964 Cover: 0.12 **NM** value: **325.00**
• **CGC:** 9 graded, best 9.6
📖 Seven Doomed Men
3 ❑ Feb 1964 Cover: 0.12 **NM** value: **175.00**
• **CGC:** 7 graded, best 9.2
📖 Midnight on Massacre Mountain ★ Appearance of Reed Richards.
4 ❑ Mar 1964 Cover: 0.12 **NM** value: **175.00**
• **CGC:** 6 graded, best 9.2
📖 Lord Ha-Ha's Last Laugh ★ Death of Junior Juniper.
5 ❑ Apr 1964 Cover: 0.12 **NM** value: **175.00**
• **CGC:** 6 graded, best 9.2
📖 At the Mercy of Baron Strucker **A:** Jack Kirby **W:** Stan Lee ★ 1st Appearance of Baron Strucker.
6 ❑ May 1964 Cover: 0.12 **NM** value: **115.00**
• **CGC:** 7 graded, best 9.2
📖 The Fangs of the Desert Fox
7 ❑ Jun 1964 Cover: 0.12 **NM** value: **115.00**
• **CGC:** 4 graded, best 9.2
📖 The Court-Martial of Sergeant Fury **A:** Jack Kirby **W:** Stan Lee
8 ❑ Jul 1964 Cover: 0.12 **NM** value: **115.00**
• **CGC:** 6 graded, best 9.4
A: Dick Ayers ★ 1st Appearance of Percival Pinkerton. ★ Versus Doctor Zemo (later Baron Zemo).
9 ❑ Aug 1964 Cover: 0.12 **NM** value: **115.00**
• **CGC:** 4 graded, best 9.4
A: Dick Ayers
10 ❑ Sep 1964 Cover: 0.12 **NM** value: **115.00**
• **CGC:** 6 graded, best 9.2
★ 1st Appearance of Captain Savage.
11 ❑ Oct 1964 Cover: 0.12 **NM** value: **60.00**
• **CGC:** 2 graded, best 9.2
12 ❑ Nov 1964 Cover: 0.12 **NM** value: **60.00**
• **CGC:** 6 graded, best 9.4
13 ❑ Dec 1964 Cover: 0.12 **NM** value: **285.00**
• **CGC:** 43 graded, best 9.4
📖 Fighting Side-By-Side With Captain America and Bucky! **A:** Jack Kirby **W:** Stan Lee ★ Appearance of Captain America.
13-2 ❑ Cover: 0.12 **NM** value: **2.00**
14 ❑ Jan 1965 Cover: 0.12 **NM** value: **60.00**
• **CGC:** 4 graded, best 9.4
★ Appearance of Baron Strucker.
15 ❑ Feb 1965 Cover: 0.12 **NM** value: **60.00**
• **CGC:** 2 graded, best 9.4
A: Dick Ayers ★ 1st Appearance of Hans Rooten.
16 ❑ Mar 1965 Cover: 0.12 **NM** value: **60.00**
• **CGC:** 2 graded, best 9.6
A: Dick Ayers
17 ❑ Apr 1965 Cover: 0.12 **NM** value: **60.00**
• **CGC:** 3 graded, best 9.2
A: Dick Ayers
18 ❑ May 1965 Cover: 0.12 **NM** value: **60.00**
• **CGC:** 6 graded, best 9.6
A: Dick Ayers
19 ❑ Jun 1965 Cover: 0.12 **NM** value: **60.00**
• **CGC:** 6 graded, best 9.6
A: Dick Ayers
20 ❑ Jul 1965 Cover: 0.12 **NM** value: **60.00**
• **CGC:** 3 graded, best 9.2
21 ❑ Aug 1965 Cover: 0.12 **NM** value: **48.00**
• **CGC:** 3 graded, best 9.6
22 ❑ Sep 1965 Cover: 0.12 **NM** value: **48.00**
• **CGC:** 9 graded, best 9.6
23 ❑ Oct 1965 Cover: 0.12 **NM** value: **48.00**
• **CGC:** 5 graded, best 9.6
A: Dick Ayers
24 ❑ Nov 1965 Cover: 0.12 **NM** value: **48.00**
• **CGC:** 9 graded, best 9.6
📖 When the Howlers Hit the Home Front! **A:** Dick Ayers **W:** Stan Lee
25 ❑ Dec 1965 Cover: 0.12 **NM** value: **48.00**
• **CGC:** 5 graded, best 9.6
A: Dick Ayers
26 ❑ Jan 1966 Cover: 0.12 **NM** value: **48.00**
Circ: Statement: **268,499** • **CGC:** 2 graded, best 9.2
A: Dick Ayers
27 ❑ Feb 1966 Cover: 0.12 **NM** value: **48.00**
Circ: Statement: **268,499** • **CGC:** 5 graded, best 9.4
• Explanation of Sgt. Fury's eye patch **A:** Dick Ayers
28 ❑ Mar 1966 Cover: 0.12 **NM** value: **48.00**
Circ: Statement: **268,499** • **CGC:** 4 graded, best 9.4
A: Dick Ayers ★ Versus Baron Strucker.
29 ❑ Apr 1966 Cover: 0.12 **NM** value: **48.00**
Circ: Statement: **268,499** • **CGC:** 3 graded, best 9.4
📖 Armageddon! **A:** Dick Ayers **W:** Roy Thomas ★ Versus Baron Strucker.
30 ❑ May 1966 Cover: 0.12 **NM** value: **48.00**
Circ: Statement: **268,499** • **CGC:** 3 graded, best 9.6
A: Dick Ayers
31 ❑ Jun 1966 Cover: 0.12 **NM** value: **30.00**
Circ: Statement: **268,499** • **CGC:** 1 graded, best 9.4
A: Dick Ayers
32 ❑ Jul 1966 Cover: 0.12 **NM** value: **30.00**
Circ: Statement: **268,499** • **CGC:** 1 graded, best 9.4
A: Dick Ayers
33 ❑ Aug 1966 Cover: 0.12 **NM** value: **30.00**
Circ: Statement: **268,499** • **CGC:** 1 graded, best 9.4
A: Dick Ayers
34 ❑ Sep 1966 Cover: 0.12 **NM** value: **30.00**
Circ: Statement: **268,499**
A: Dick Ayers ★ Origin of Howling Commandos, General Samuel "Happy Sam" Sawyer.
35 ❑ Oct 1966 Cover: 0.12 **NM** value: **30.00**
Circ: Statement: **268,499** • **CGC:** 4 graded, best 9.4
• Eric Koenig joins Howling Commandos **A:** Dick Ayers
36 ❑ Nov 1966 Cover: 0.12 **NM** value: **30.00**
Circ: Statement: **268,499**
A: Dick Ayers
37 ❑ Dec 1966 Cover: 0.12 **NM** value: **30.00**
Circ: Statement: **268,499** • **CGC:** 1 graded, best 9.0
38 ❑ Jan 1967 Cover: 0.12 **NM** value: **30.00**
Circ: Statement: **260,930**
39 ❑ Feb 1967 Cover: 0.12 **NM** value: **30.00**
Circ: Statement: **260,930**
A: Dick Ayers
40 ❑ Mar 1967 Cover: 0.12 **NM** value: **30.00**
Circ: Statement: **260,930** • **CGC:** 6 graded, best 9.6
• Has 1966 Statement, filed 10/1/66; avg print run 430,986; avg sales 267,449; avg subs 1,050; avg total paid 268,499; samples 60; max existent 268,559; 38% of run returned **A:** Dick Ayers
41 ❑ Apr 1967 Cover: 0.12 **NM** value: **24.00**
Circ: Statement: **260,930** • **CGC:** 11 graded, best 9.6
42 ❑ May 1967 Cover: 0.12 **NM** value: **24.00**
Circ: Statement: **260,930** • **CGC:** 1 graded, best 9.6
43 ❑ Jun 1967 Cover: 0.12 **NM** value: **24.00**
Circ: Statement: **260,930** • **CGC:** 1 graded, best 9.6
44 ❑ Jul 1967 Cover: 0.12 **NM** value: **24.00**
Circ: Statement: **260,930**
45 ❑ Aug 1967 Cover: 0.12 **NM** value: **24.00**
Circ: Statement: **260,930**
46 ❑ Sep 1967 Cover: 0.12 **NM** value: **24.00**
Circ: Statement: **260,930**
47 ❑ Oct 1967 Cover: 0.12 **NM** value: **24.00**
Circ: Statement: **260,930**
• Fury on furlough **A:** Dick Ayers
48 ❑ Nov 1967 Cover: 0.12 **NM** value: **24.00**
Circ: Statement: **260,930** • **CGC:** 1 graded, best 9.6
• return of Blitz Squad **A:** John Severin; Dick Ayers
49 ❑ Dec 1967 Cover: 0.12 **NM** value: **24.00**
Circ: Statement: **260,930** • **CGC:** 2 graded, best 9.6
• Howlers in Pacific **A:** John Severin; Dick Ayers
50 ❑ Jan 1968 Cover: 0.12 **NM** value: **24.00**
Circ: Statement: **286,747**
• Howlers in Pacific **A:** John Severin; Dick Ayers
51 ❑ Feb 1968 Cover: 0.12 **NM** value: **18.00**
Circ: Statement: **286,747** • **CGC:** 1 graded, best 9.6
52 ❑ Mar 1968 Cover: 0.12 **NM** value: **18.00**
Circ: Statement: **286,747** • **CGC:** 2 graded, best 9.0
• in Treblinka; Has 1967 Statement, filed 10/1/67; avg print run 445,616; avg sales 259,830; avg subs 1,100; avg total paid 260,930; samples 95; max existent 261,025; 41% of run returned
53 ❑ Apr 1968 Cover: 0.12 **NM** value: **18.00**
Circ: Statement: **286,747**
54 ❑ May 1968 Cover: 0.12 **NM** value: **18.00**
Circ: Statement: **286,747** • **CGC:** 1 graded, best 9.6
55 ❑ Jun 1968 Cover: 0.12 **NM** value: **18.00**
Circ: Statement: **286,747**
56 ❑ Jul 1968 Cover: 0.12 **NM** value: **18.00**
Circ: Statement: **286,747** • **CGC:** 1 graded, best 9.8
📖 Gabriel, Blow Your Horn! **A:** Dick Ayers **W:** Gary Friedrich
57 ❑ Aug 1968 Cover: 0.12 **NM** value: **18.00**
Circ: Statement: **286,747**
📖 The Informer **A:** Tom Sutton; John Severin **W:** Gary Friedrich
58 ❑ Sep 1968 Cover: 0.12 **NM** value: **18.00**
Circ: Statement: **286,747** • **CGC:** 1 graded, best 9.2
A: Dick Ayers
59 ❑ Oct 1968 Cover: 0.12 **NM** value: **18.00**
Circ: Statement: **286,747** • **CGC:** 1 graded, best 9.4
60 ❑ Nov 1968 Cover: 0.12 **NM** value: **18.00**
Circ: Statement: **286,747** • **CGC:** 1 graded, best 9.6
61 ❑ Dec 1968 Cover: 0.12 **NM** value: **18.00**
Circ: Statement: **286,747**
62 ❑ Jan 1969 Cover: 0.12 **NM** value: **18.00**
Circ: Statement: **242,897**
📖 The Name is…Bass…Sergeant Bass! **A:** Dick Ayers **W:** Gary Friedrich ★ Origin of Sgt. Fury.
63 ❑ Feb 1969 Cover: 0.12 **NM** value: **18.00**
Circ: Statement: **242,897**
64 ❑ Mar 1969 Cover: 0.12 **NM** value: **18.00**
Circ: Statement: **242,897**
📖 The Peacemonger! • Story continued from Captain Savage and his Leatherneck Raiders #11; Has 1968 Statement, filed 10/1/68; avg print run 435,250; avg sales 286,117; avg subs 630; avg total paid 286,747; samples 400; max existent 287,147; 34% of run returned **A:** Dick Ayers **W:** Gary Friedrich
65 ❑ Apr 1969 Cover: 0.12 **NM** value: **18.00**
Circ: Statement: **242,897**
📖 Blood is Thicker! **A:** Dick Ayers **W:** Gary Friedrich
66 ❑ May 1969 Cover: 0.12 **NM** value: **18.00**
Circ: Statement: **242,897**
67 ❑ Jun 1969 Cover: 0.12 **NM** value: **18.00**

Other grades: Multiply prices above by **1.5 for Mint • 2/3 for Very Fine • 1/3 for Fine • 1/5 for Very Good • 1/8 for Good**

Circ: Statement: **242,897**
📖 With a Little Help From my Friends **A:** Dick Ayers **C:** John Severin **W:** Gary Friedrich
68 ❑ Jul 1969 Cover: 0.15 **NM** value: **18.00**
Circ: Statement: **242,897**
• Fury goes home on leave **A:** Dick Ayers
69 ❑ Aug 1969 Cover: 0.15 **NM** value: **18.00**
Circ: Statement: **242,897**
A: Dick Ayers ★ 1st Appearance of Jacob Fury (later becomes Scorpio).
70 ❑ Sep 1969 Cover: 0.15 **NM** value: **18.00**
Circ: Statement: **242,897** • **CGC:** 1 graded, best 9.2
A: Dick Ayers ★ 1st Appearance of Missouri Marauders.
71 ❑ Oct 1969 Cover: 0.15 **NM** value: **15.00**
Circ: Statement: **242,897**
72 ❑ Nov 1969 Cover: 0.15 **NM** value: **15.00**
Circ: Statement: **242,897**
A: Dick Ayers
73 ❑ Dec 1969 Cover: 0.15 **NM** value: **15.00**
Circ: Statement: **242,897**
A: Dick Ayers
74 ❑ Jan 1970 Cover: 0.15 **NM** value: **15.00**
75 ❑ Feb 1970 Cover: 0.15 **NM** value: **15.00**
76 ❑ Mar 1970 Cover: 0.15 **NM** value: **15.00**
• Fury's father vs. The Red Baron; Has 1969 Statement; avg print run 423,240; avg sales 242,208; avg subs 689; avg total paid 242,897; max existent 242,897; 43% of run returned **A:** Dick Ayers
77 ❑ Apr 1970 Cover: 0.15 **NM** value: **15.00**
A: Dick Ayers
78 ❑ May 1970 Cover: 0.15 **NM** value: **15.00**
• **CGC:** 1 graded, best 9.4
A: Dick Ayers
79 ❑ Jun 1970 Cover: 0.15 **NM** value: **15.00**
A: Dick Ayers
80 ❑ Sep 1970 Cover: 0.15 **NM** value: **15.00**
81 ❑ Nov 1970 Cover: 0.15 **NM** value: **12.00**
82 ❑ Dec 1970 Cover: 0.15 **NM** value: **12.00**
A: Dick Ayers
83 ❑ Jan 1971 Cover: 0.15 **NM** value: **12.00**
Circ: Statement: **205,326**
• Dum-Dum Dugan vs. Man-Mountain McCoy **A:** Dick Ayers
84 ❑ Feb 1971 Cover: 0.15 **NM** value: **12.00**
Circ: Statement: **205,326** • **CGC:** 1 graded, best 9.6
A: Dick Ayers
85 ❑ Mar 1971 Cover: 0.15 **NM** value: **12.00**
Circ: Statement: **205,326**
A: Dick Ayers
86 ❑ Apr 1971 Cover: 0.15 **NM** value: **12.00**
Circ: Statement: **205,326** • **CGC:** 1 graded, best 9.4
A: Dick Ayers
87 ❑ May 1971 Cover: 0.15 **NM** value: **12.00**
Circ: Statement: **205,326** • **CGC:** 1 graded, best 9.8
A: Dick Ayers
88 ❑ Jun 1971 Cover: 0.15 **NM** value: **12.00**
Circ: Statement: **205,326** • **CGC:** 1 graded, best 9.6
A: Dick Ayers ★ Appearance of Patton.
89 ❑ Jul 1971 Cover: 0.15 **NM** value: **12.00**
Circ: Statement: **205,326**
A: Dick Ayers
90 ❑ Aug 1971 Cover: 0.15 **NM** value: **12.00**
Circ: Statement: **205,326** • **CGC:** 1 graded, best 9.8
📖 ...And One Must Die! **A:** Dick Ayers **W:** Al Kurzrok
91 ❑ Sep 1971 Cover: 0.15 **NM** value: **10.00**
Circ: Statement: **205,326** • **CGC:** 1 graded, best 9.8
A: Dick Ayers
92 ❑ Oct 1971 Cover: 0.25 **NM** value: **10.00**
Circ: Statement: **205,326**
• Giant-size.
93 ❑ Dec 1971 Cover: 0.20 **NM** value: **10.00**
Circ: Statement: **205,326**
📖 A Traitor in Our Midsts! **A:** Dick Ayers **W:** Roy Thomas
94 ❑ Jan 1972 Cover: 0.20 **NM** value: **10.00**
Circ: Statement: **176,011** • **CGC:** 1 graded, best 9.2
📖 Who'll Stop The Rain? **A:** Dick Ayers **W:** Gary Friedrich
95 ❑ Feb 1972 Cover: 0.20 **NM** value: **10.00**
Circ: Statement: **176,011**
📖 Seven Doomed Men • reprints Sgt. Fury #2 **A:** Jack Kirby
96 ❑ Mar 1972 Cover: 0.20 **NM** value: **10.00**
Circ: Statement: **176,011**
📖 This Ravaged Land! **A:** Dick Ayers **W:** Gary Friedrich
97 ❑ Apr 1972 Cover: 0.20 **NM** value: **10.00**
Circ: Statement: **176,011**
A: Dick Ayers
98 ❑ May 1972 Cover: 0.20 **NM** value: **10.00**
Circ: Statement: **176,011** • **CGC:** 1 graded, best 9.6
• Has 1971 Statement, filed 9/23/71; avg print run 350,659; avg sales 204,812; avg subs 514; avg total paid 205,326; samples 110; office use 1,645; max existent 207,081; 41% of run returned **A:** Dick Ayers ★ 1st Appearance of Dugan's Deadly Dozen.
99 ❑ Jun 1972 Cover: 0.20 **NM** value: **10.00**
Circ: Statement: **176,011**
100 ❑ Jul 1972 Cover: 0.20 **NM** value: **10.00**
Circ: Statement: **176,011**
A: Dick Ayers ★ Appearance of Gary Friedrich, Dick Ayers, Martin Goodman, Captain America, Stan Lee.
101 ❑ Sep 1972 Cover: 0.20 **NM** value: **8.00**
Circ: Statement: **176,011**
A: Dick Ayers ★ Origin of the Howling Commandos.
102 ❑ Sep 1972 Cover: 0.20 **NM** value: **7.00**
Circ: Statement: **176,011** • **CGC:** 1 graded, best 9.4
📖 Death for a Dollar! **A:** Dick Ayers **W:** Gary Friedrich
103 ❑ Oct 1972 Cover: 0.20 **NM** value: **7.00**
Circ: Statement: **176,011** • **CGC:** 2 graded, best 9.6
A: Dick Ayers
104 ❑ Nov 1972 Cover: 0.20 **NM** value: **7.00**
Circ: Statement: **176,011**
📖 The Tanks are Coming! **A:** Dick Ayers **W:** Gary Friedrich ★ Appearance of Combat Kelly and Deadly Dozen.
105 ❑ Dec 1972 Cover: 0.20 **NM** value: **7.00**
Circ: Statement: **176,011**
A: Dick Ayers
106 ❑ Jan 1973 Cover: 0.20 **NM** value: **7.00**
Circ: Statement: **184,640**
A: Dick Ayers
107 ❑ Feb 1973 Cover: 0.20 **NM** value: **7.00**
Circ: Statement: **184,640** • **CGC:** 2 graded, best 9.6
A: Dick Ayers
108 ❑ Mar 1973 Cover: 0.20 **NM** value: **7.00**
Circ: Statement: **184,640**
• Has 1972 Statement; avg print run 344,262; avg sales 175,574; avg subs 437; avg total paid 176,011; max existent 176,011; 49% of run returned **A:** Dick Ayers
109 ❑ Apr 1973 Cover: 0.20 **NM** value: **7.00**
Circ: Statement: **184,640**
A: Dick Ayers
110 ❑ May 1973 Cover: 0.20 **NM** value: **7.00**
Circ: Statement: **184,640**
A: Dick Ayers
111 ❑ Jun 1973 Cover: 0.20 **NM** value: **6.00**
Circ: Statement: **184,640**
A: Dick Ayers
112 ❑ Jul 1973 Cover: 0.20 **NM** value: **6.00**
Circ: Statement: **184,640**
A: Dick Ayers ★ Versus Baron Strucker.
113 ❑ Aug 1973 Cover: 0.20 **NM** value: **6.00**
Circ: Statement: **184,640**
A: Dick Ayers
114 ❑ Sep 1973 Cover: 0.20 **NM** value: **6.00**
Circ: Statement: **184,640**
A: Dick Ayers
115 ❑ Oct 1973 Cover: 0.20 **NM** value: **6.00**
Circ: Statement: **184,640**
A: Dick Ayers
116 ❑ Nov 1973 Cover: 0.20 **NM** value: **6.00**
Circ: Statement: **184,640**
A: Dick Ayers
117 ❑ Jan 1974 Cover: 0.20 **NM** value: **6.00**
Circ: Statement: **163,913**
118 ❑ Mar 1974 Cover: 0.20 **NM** value: **6.00**
Circ: Statement: **163,913**
📖 The War Machine **A:** Dick Ayers **W:** Gerry Conway ★ Versus Rommel.
119 ❑ May 1974 Cover: 0.20 **NM** value: **6.00**
Circ: Statement: **163,913**
• Has 1973 Statement; avg total paid circ 184,640 **A:** Dick Ayers
120 ❑ Jul 1974 Cover: 0.20 **NM** value: **6.00**
Circ: Statement: **163,913**
A: Dick Ayers
121 ❑ Sep 1974 Cover: 0.25 **NM** value: **5.00**
Circ: Statement: **163,913**
122 ❑ Oct 1974 Cover: 0.25 **NM** value: **5.00**
Circ: Statement: **163,913**
123 ❑ Nov 1974 Cover: 0.25 **NM** value: **5.00**
Circ: Statement: **163,913**
124 ❑ Jan 1975 Cover: 0.25 **NM** value: **5.00**
Circ: Statement: **162,894**
125 ❑ Mar 1975 Cover: 0.25 **NM** value: **5.00**
Circ: Statement: **162,894**
126 ❑ May 1975 Cover: 0.25 **NM** value: **5.00**
Circ: Statement: **162,894**
127 ❑ Jul 1975 Cover: 0.25 **NM** value: **5.00**
Circ: Statement: **162,894**
• Has 1974 Statement; avg total paid circ 163,913
128 ❑ Sep 1975 Cover: 0.25 **NM** value: **5.00**
Circ: Statement: **162,894**
129 ❑ Oct 1975 Cover: 0.25 **NM** value: **5.00**
Circ: Statement: **162,894**
130 ❑ Nov 1975 Cover: 0.25 **NM** value: **5.00**
Circ: Statement: **162,894**
131 ❑ Jan 1976 Cover: 0.25 **NM** value: **4.00**
Circ: Statement: **120,960**
132 ❑ Mar 1976 Cover: 0.25 **NM** value: **4.00**
Circ: Statement: **120,960** • **CGC:** 1 graded, best 9.4
133 ❑ May 1976 Cover: 0.25 **NM** value: **4.00**
Circ: Statement: **120,960**
134 ❑ Jul 1976 Cover: 0.25 **NM** value: **4.00**
Circ: Statement: **120,960**
135 ❑ Sep 1976 Cover: 0.30 **NM** value: **4.00**
Circ: Statement: **120,960**
136 ❑ Oct 1976 Cover: 0.30 **NM** value: **4.00**
Circ: Statement: **120,960**
137 ❑ Nov 1976 Cover: 0.30 **NM** value: **4.00**
Circ: Statement: **120,960**
138 ❑ Jan 1977 Cover: 0.30 **NM** value: **4.00**
Circ: Statement: **112,882**
139 ❑ Mar 1977 Cover: 0.30 **NM** value: **4.00**
Circ: Statement: **112,882**
140 ❑ May 1977 Cover: 0.30 **NM** value: **4.00**
Circ: Statement: **112,882**
• Has 1976 Statement, filed 9/20/76; avg print run 303,714; avg sales 120,547; avg subs 413; avg total paid 120,960; samples 0; office use 950; max existent 121,910; 60% of run returned
141 ❑ Jul 1977 Cover: 0.30 **NM** value: **4.00**
Circ: Statement: **112,882**
142 ❑ Sep 1977 Cover: 0.30 **NM** value: **4.00**
Circ: Statement: **112,882**
143 ❑ Nov 1977 Cover: 0.30 **NM** value: **4.00**
Circ: Statement: **112,882**
144 ❑ Jan 1978 Cover: 0.30 **NM** value: **4.00**
145 ❑ Mar 1978 Cover: 0.30 **NM** value: **4.00**
146 ❑ May 1978 Cover: 0.30 **NM** value: **4.00**
• Has 1977 Statement; avg total paid circ 112,882
147 ❑ Jul 1978 Cover: 0.30 **NM** value: **4.00**
148 ❑ Sep 1978 Cover: 0.30 **NM** value: **4.00**
149 ❑ Nov 1978 Cover: 0.30 **NM** value: **4.00**
150 ❑ Jan 1979 Cover: 0.30 **NM** value: **4.00**
151 ❑ Mar 1979 Cover: 0.30 **NM** value: **3.00**
152 ❑ Jun 1979 Cover: 0.30 **NM** value: **3.00**
153 ❑ Aug 1979 Cover: 0.30 **NM** value: **3.00**
154 ❑ Oct 1979 Cover: 0.30 **NM** value: **3.00**
155 ❑ Dec 1979 Cover: 0.30 **NM** value: **3.00**
156 ❑ Feb 1980 Cover: 0.30 **NM** value: **3.00**
Circ: Statement: **871,448**
157 ❑ Apr 1980 Cover: 0.30 **NM** value: **3.00**
Circ: Statement: **871,448**
158 ❑ Jun 1980 Cover: 0.30 **NM** value: **3.00**
Circ: Statement: **871,448**
159 ❑ Aug 1980 Cover: 0.30 **NM** value: **3.00**
Circ: Statement: **871,448**
160 ❑ Oct 1980 Cover: 0.30 **NM** value: **3.00**
Circ: Statement: **871,448**
161 ❑ Dec 1980 Cover: 0.30 **NM** value: **3.00**
Circ: Statement: **871,448**
162 ❑ Feb 1981 Cover: 0.30 **NM** value: **3.00**
163 ❑ Apr 1981 Cover: 0.30 **NM** value: **3.00**
• Has 1980 Statement; avg print run 230,675; avg sales 86,821; avg subs 327; avg total paid 87,148; max existent 87,148; 61% of run returned
164 ❑ Jun 1981 Cover: 0.30 **NM** value: **3.00**
165 ❑ Aug 1981 Cover: 0.30 **NM** value: **3.00**
166 ❑ Oct 1981 Cover: 0.30 **NM** value: **3.00**
167 ❑ Dec 1981 Cover: 0.30 **NM** value: **3.00**
• Reprints Sgt. Fury #1
Anl 1 ❑ ca. 1965 Cover: 0.25 **NM** value: **125.00**
• **CGC:** 11 graded, best 9.6
• Korea; reprints from Sgt. Fury #4 and 5
Anl 2 ❑ Aug 1966 Cover: 0.25 **NM** value: **55.00**
• **CGC:** 1 graded, best 9.2
• D-Day ★ Origin of S.H.I.E.L.D..
Anl 3 ❑ Aug 1966 Cover: 0.25 **NM** value: **30.00**
• **CGC:** 2 graded, best 9.4
• Cover reads "King-Size Special". • Vietnam
Anl 4 ❑ Apr 1968 Cover: 0.25 **NM** value: **22.00**
• **CGC:** 1 graded, best 9.6
• Cover reads "King-Size Special". 📖 The Battle of the Bulge; Gary and Dick Up Front! • Battle of the Bulge **A:** Dick Ayers **W:** Gary Friedrich
Anl 5 ❑ Aug 1969 Cover: 0.25 **NM** value: **10.00**
• **CGC:** 1 graded, best 9.6
• Cover reads "King-Size Special". • reprints from Sgt. Fury #6 and 7
Anl 6 ❑ Aug 1970 Cover: 0.25 **NM** value: **9.00**
• **CGC:** 1 graded, best 9.8
• Cover reads "King-Size Special".
Anl 7 ❑ ca. 1971 Cover: 0.25 **NM** value: **9.00**
• Cover reads "King-Size Special".

SGT. PRESTON OF THE YUKON — Dell

5 ❑ Nov 1952 Cover: 0.10 **NM** value: **45.00**
• Earlier issues published as Four Color #344, #373, #397, and #419
6 ❑ Feb 1953 Cover: 0.10 **NM** value: **40.00**
7 ❑ May 1953 Cover: 0.10 **NM** value: **40.00**
8 ❑ Aug 1953 Cover: 0.10 **NM** value: **40.00**
9 ❑ Nov 1953 Cover: 0.10 **NM** value: **40.00**
10 ❑ Feb 1954 Cover: 0.10 **NM** value: **40.00**
11 ❑ May 1954 Cover: 0.10 **NM** value: **40.00**
• **CGC:** 1 graded, best 7.0
12 ❑ Aug 1954 Cover: 0.10 **NM** value: **40.00**
13 ❑ Nov 1954 Cover: 0.10 **NM** value: **50.00**
14 ❑ Feb 1955 Cover: 0.10 **NM** value: **40.00**
15 ❑ May 1955 Cover: 0.10 **NM** value: **40.00**
16 ❑ Aug 1955 Cover: 0.10 **NM** value: **40.00**
17 ❑ Nov 1955 Cover: 0.10 **NM** value: **40.00**
18 ❑ Feb 1956 Cover: 0.10 **NM** value: **45.00**
19 ❑ May 1956 Cover: 0.10 **NM** value: **30.00**
20 ❑ Aug 1956 Cover: 0.10 **NM** value: **30.00**
21 ❑ Nov 1956 Cover: 0.10 **NM** value: **30.00**
22 ❑ Feb 1957 Cover: 0.10 **NM** value: **30.00**
23 ❑ May 1957 Cover: 0.10 **NM** value: **30.00**
24 ❑ Aug 1957 Cover: 0.10 **NM** value: **30.00**
Photo cover. 📖 A Wolf Named Rob; Snow Blind; The Two-Way Trap; Dog Wonder; Gray Wolf: Leader of the Wolf Pack
25 ❑ Nov 1957 Cover: 0.10 **NM** value: **30.00**
26 ❑ Feb 1958 Cover: 0.10 **NM** value: **30.00**
27 ❑ May 1958 Cover: 0.10 **NM** value: **30.00**
28 ❑ Aug 1958 Cover: 0.10 **NM** value: **30.00**
29 ❑ Nov 1958 Cover: 0.10 **NM** value: **30.00**

SGT. ROCK — DC

Formerly known as Our Army at War, Sgt. Rock was the cornerstone of DC's war comics line. First appearing in Our Army at War #81, Sgt. Rock was a battle-hardened veteran who led the men of Easy Company throughout its bloody trudge across Europe in World War II.

By expanding its approach to war comics to include elements of fantasy and science-fiction, Sgt. Rock held its readers long after the war comics genre had fallen from favor. All told, the series lasted more than 30 years, finally ending in 1988 with issue #422.

302 ❑ Mar 1977 Cover: 0.30 **NM** value: **14.00**
Circ: Statement: **137,403**
• Series continued from "Our Army At War"
303 ❑ Apr 1977 Cover: 0.30 **NM** value: **9.00**
Circ: Statement: **137,403**
304 ❑ May 1977 Cover: 0.30 **NM** value: **9.00**
Circ: Statement: **137,403** • **CGC:** 1 graded, best 9.6

CGC-graded: Multiply prices above by **33 for 9.9 M • 16 for 9.8 NM/M • 7 for 9.6 NM+ • 5 for 9.4 NM • 2.5 for 9.2 NM- • 1.5 for 9.0 VF/NM**

305 ❑ Jun 1977 Cover: 0.30 **NM** value: **9.00**
Circ: Statement: **137,403**
306 ❑ Jul 1977 Cover: 0.35 **NM** value: **9.00**
Circ: Statement: **137,403**
307 ❑ Aug 1977 Cover: 0.35 **NM** value: **9.00**
Circ: Statement: **137,403**
308 ❑ Sep 1977 Cover: 0.35 **NM** value: **9.00**
Circ: Statement: **137,403**
309 ❑ Oct 1977 Cover: 0.35 **NM** value: **9.00**
Circ: Statement: **137,403** • **CGC:** 1 graded, best 9.4
310 ❑ Nov 1977 Cover: 0.35 **NM** value: **9.00**
Circ: Statement: **137,403** • **CGC:** 1 graded, best 9.4
311 ❑ Dec 1977 Cover: 0.35 **NM** value: **8.00**
Circ: Statement: **137,403** • **CGC:** 1 graded, best 9.0
312 ❑ Jan 1978 Cover: 0.35 **NM** value: **8.00**
313 ❑ Feb 1978 Cover: 0.35 **NM** value: **8.00**
314 ❑ Mar 1978 Cover: 0.35 **NM** value: **8.00**
315 ❑ Apr 1978 Cover: 0.35 **NM** value: **8.00**
316 ❑ May 1978 Cover: 0.35 **NM** value: **8.00**
• Has 1977 Statement; avg total paid circ 137,403
317 ❑ Jun 1978 Cover: 0.35 **NM** value: **8.00**
318 ❑ Jul 1978 Cover: 0.35 **NM** value: **8.00**
319 ❑ Aug 1978 Cover: 0.35 **NM** value: **8.00**
320 ❑ Sep 1978 Cover: 0.50 **NM** value: **8.00**
• **CGC:** 2 graded, best 9.6
321 ❑ Oct 1978 Cover: 0.50 **NM** value: **6.00**
322 ❑ Nov 1978 Cover: 0.50 **NM** value: **6.00**
323 ❑ Dec 1978 Cover: 0.40 **NM** value: **6.00**
324 ❑ Jan 1979 Cover: 0.40 **NM** value: **6.00**
325 ❑ Feb 1979 Cover: 0.40 **NM** value: **6.00**
326 ❑ Mar 1979 Cover: 0.40 **NM** value: **6.00**
327 ❑ Apr 1979 Cover: 0.40 **NM** value: **6.00**
328 ❑ May 1979 Cover: 0.40 **NM** value: **6.00**
329 ❑ Jun 1979 Cover: 0.40 **NM** value: **6.00**
330 ❑ Jul 1979 Cover: 0.40 **NM** value: **6.00**
331 ❑ Aug 1979 Cover: 0.40 **NM** value: **5.00**
332 ❑ Sep 1979 Cover: 0.40 **NM** value: **5.00**
333 ❑ Oct 1979 Cover: 0.40 **NM** value: **5.00**
334 ❑ Nov 1979 Cover: 0.40 **NM** value: **5.00**
335 ❑ Dec 1979 Cover: 0.40 **NM** value: **5.00**
336 ❑ Jan 1980 Cover: 0.40 **NM** value: **5.00**
337 ❑ Feb 1980 Cover: 0.40 **NM** value: **5.00**
338 ❑ Mar 1980 Cover: 0.40 **NM** value: **5.00**
339 ❑ Apr 1980 Cover: 0.40 **NM** value: **5.00**
340 ❑ May 1980 Cover: 0.40 **NM** value: **5.00**
341 ❑ Jun 1980 Cover: 0.40 **NM** value: **5.00**
342 ❑ Jul 1980 Cover: 0.40 **NM** value: **4.00**
343 ❑ Aug 1980 Cover: 0.40 **NM** value: **4.00**
344 ❑ Sep 1980 Cover: 0.50 **NM** value: **4.00**
345 ❑ Oct 1980 Cover: 0.50 **NM** value: **4.00**
346 ❑ Nov 1980 Cover: 0.50 **NM** value: **4.00**
347 ❑ Dec 1980 Cover: 0.50 **NM** value: **4.00**
348 ❑ Jan 1981 Cover: 0.50 **NM** value: **4.00**
Circ: Statement: **104,000**
349 ❑ Feb 1981 Cover: 0.50 **NM** value: **4.00**
Circ: Statement: **104,000**
350 ❑ Mar 1981 Cover: 0.50 **NM** value: **4.00**
Circ: Statement: **104,000**
351 ❑ Apr 1981 Cover: 0.50 **NM** value: **3.00**
Circ: Statement: **104,000**
352 ❑ May 1981 Cover: 0.50 **NM** value: **3.00**
Circ: Statement: **104,000**
353 ❑ Jun 1981 Cover: 0.50 **NM** value: **3.00**
Circ: Statement: **104,000**
354 ❑ Jul 1981 Cover: 0.50 **NM** value: **3.00**
Circ: Statement: **104,000**
355 ❑ Aug 1981 Cover: 0.50 **NM** value: **3.00**
Circ: Statement: **104,000** • **CGC:** 1 graded, best 9.2
356 ❑ Sep 1981 Cover: 0.50 **NM** value: **3.00**
Circ: Statement: **104,000**
357 ❑ Oct 1981 Cover: 0.60 **NM** value: **3.00**
Circ: Statement: **104,000**
358 ❑ Nov 1981 Cover: 0.60 **NM** value: **3.00**
Circ: Statement: **104,000**
359 ❑ Dec 1981 Cover: 0.60 **NM** value: **3.00**
Circ: Statement: **104,000**
360 ❑ Jan 1982 Cover: 0.60 **NM** value: **3.00**
361 ❑ Feb 1982 Cover: 0.60 **NM** value: **3.00**
📖 Keep Me Alive
362 ❑ Mar 1982 Cover: 0.60 **NM** value: **3.00**
363 ❑ Apr 1982 Cover: 0.60 **NM** value: **3.00**
364 ❑ May 1982 Cover: 0.60 **NM** value: **3.00**
365 ❑ Jun 1982 Cover: 0.60 **NM** value: **3.00**
366 ❑ Jul 1982 Cover: 0.60 **NM** value: **3.00**
367 ❑ Aug 1982 Cover: 0.60 **NM** value: **3.00**
368 ❑ Sep 1982 Cover: 0.60 **NM** value: **3.00**
📖 30 Years Of Dogtags **A:** Joe Kubert **W:** Robert Kanigher
369 ❑ Oct 1982 Cover: 0.60 **NM** value: **3.00**
📖 Too Easy To Die **A:** Frank Redondo **W:** Robert Kanigher
370 ❑ Nov 1982 Cover: 0.60 **NM** value: **3.00**
371 ❑ Dec 1982 Cover: 0.60 **NM** value: **2.50**
372 ❑ Jan 1983 Cover: 0.60 **NM** value: **2.50**
Circ: Statement: **81,514**
373 ❑ Feb 1983 Cover: 0.60 **NM** value: **2.50**
Circ: Statement: **81,514**
📖 Burning Soldier **A:** Trebuk **W:** Robert Kanigher
374 ❑ Mar 1983 Cover: 0.60 **NM** value: **2.50**
Circ: Statement: **81,514**
📖 Trust Me **A:** Frank Redondo **W:** Robert Kanigher
375 ❑ Apr 1983 Cover: 0.60 **NM** value: **2.50**
Circ: Statement: **81,514**
376 ❑ May 1983 Cover: 0.60 **NM** value: **2.50**
Circ: Statement: **81,514**
377 ❑ Jun 1983 Cover: 0.60 **NM** value: **2.50**
Circ: Statement: **81,514**
★ Appearance of Worry Wart.
378 ❑ Jul 1983 Cover: 0.60 **NM** value: **2.50**
Circ: Statement: **81,514**
• Christmas
379 ❑ Aug 1983 Cover: 0.60 **NM** value: **2.50**
Circ: Statement: **81,514**
380 ❑ Sep 1983 Cover: 0.60 **NM** value: **2.50**
Circ: Statement: **81,514**
381 ❑ Oct 1983 Cover: 0.60 **NM** value: **2.50**
Circ: Statement: **81,514**
382 ❑ Nov 1983 Cover: 0.60 **NM** value: **2.50**
Circ: Statement: **81,514**
383 ❑ Dec 1983 Cover: 0.75 **NM** value: **2.50**
Circ: Statement: **81,514**
384 ❑ Jan 1984 Cover: 0.75 **NM** value: **2.50**
Circ: Statement: **69,644**
385 ❑ Feb 1984 Cover: 0.75 **NM** value: **2.50**
Circ: Statement: **69,644**
386 ❑ Mar 1984 Cover: 0.75 **NM** value: **2.50**
Circ: Statement: **69,644**
387 ❑ Apr 1984 Cover: 0.75 **NM** value: **2.50**
Circ: Statement: **69,644**
388 ❑ May 1984 Cover: 0.75 **NM** value: **2.50**
Circ: Statement: **69,644**
389 ❑ Jun 1984 Cover: 0.75 **NM** value: **2.50**
Circ: Statement: **69,644**
390 ❑ Jul 1984 Cover: 0.75 **NM** value: **2.50**
Circ: Statement: **69,644**
391 ❑ Aug 1984 Cover: 0.75 **NM** value: **2.00**
Circ: Statement: **69,644**
392 ❑ Sep 1984 Cover: 0.75 **NM** value: **2.00**
Circ: Statement: **69,644**
393 ❑ Oct 1984 Cover: 0.75 **NM** value: **2.00**
Circ: Statement: **69,644**
394 ❑ Nov 1984 Cover: 0.75 **NM** value: **2.00**
Circ: Statement: **69,644**
395 ❑ Dec 1984 Cover: 0.75 **NM** value: **2.00**
Circ: Statement: **69,644**
396 ❑ Jan 1985 Cover: 0.75 **NM** value: **2.00**
Circ: Statement: **59,632**
397 ❑ Feb 1985 Cover: 0.75 **NM** value: **2.00**
Circ: Statement: **59,632**
398 ❑ Mar 1985 Cover: 0.75 **NM** value: **2.00**
Circ: Statement: **59,632**
399 ❑ Apr 1985 Cover: 0.75 **NM** value: **2.00**
Circ: Statement: **59,632**
400 ❑ May 1985 Cover: 0.75 **NM** value: **2.00**
Circ: Statement: **59,632** CapCity orders: **2,050**
• Has 1984 Statement; avg print run 232,415; avg sales 68,089; avg subs 1,575; avg total paid 69,644; samples 182; office use 2,985; max existent 72,629; 69% of run returned
401 ❑ Jun 1985 Cover: 0.75 **NM** value: **2.00**
Circ: Statement: **59,632** CapCity orders: **1,750**
402 ❑ Jul 1985 Cover: 0.75 **NM** value: **2.00**
Circ: Statement: **59,632** CapCity orders: **1,550**
403 ❑ Aug 1985 Cover: 0.75 **NM** value: **2.00**
Circ: Statement: **59,632** CapCity orders: **1,650**
404 ❑ Sep 1985 Cover: 0.75 **NM** value: **2.00**
Circ: Statement: **59,632** CapCity orders: **2,000**
★ Versus Iron Major.
405 ❑ Oct 1985 Cover: 0.75 **NM** value: **2.00**
Circ: Statement: **59,632** CapCity orders: **1,700**
📖 Angels with Black Wings; Angels With Black Wings, Part 1
406 ❑ Nov 1985 Cover: 0.75 **NM** value: **2.00**
Circ: Statement: **59,632** CapCity orders: **1,600**
📖 Angels with Black Wings; Angels With Black Wings, Part 2
407 ❑ Dec 1985 Cover: 0.75 **NM** value: **2.00**
Circ: Statement: **59,632** CapCity orders: **1,650**
408 ❑ Feb 1986 Cover: 0.75 **NM** value: **2.00**
Circ: Statement: **53,434** CapCity orders: **1,850**
• Shelly Mayer tribute
409 ❑ Apr 1986 Cover: 0.75 **NM** value: **2.00**
Circ: Statement: **53,434** CapCity orders: **1,850**
410 ❑ Jun 1986 Cover: 0.75 **NM** value: **2.00**
Circ: Statement: **53,434** CapCity orders: **2,000**
411 ❑ Aug 1986 Cover: 0.75 **NM** value: **2.00**
Circ: Statement: **53,434** CapCity orders: **2,000**
412 ❑ Oct 1986 Cover: 0.75 **NM** value: **2.00**
Circ: Statement: **53,434** CapCity orders: **2,150**
413 ❑ Dec 1986 Cover: 0.75 **NM** value: **2.00**
Circ: Statement: **53,434** CapCity orders: **2,150**
414 ❑ Feb 1987 Cover: 0.75 **NM** value: **2.00**
Circ: Statement: **41,557** CapCity orders: **2,250**
• Christmas
415 ❑ Apr 1987 Cover: 0.75 **NM** value: **2.00**
Circ: Statement: **41,557** CapCity orders: **2,150**
416 ❑ Jun 1987 Cover: 0.75 **NM** value: **2.00**
Circ: Statement: **41,557** CapCity orders: **1,950**
417 ❑ Aug 1987 Cover: 0.75 **NM** value: **2.00**
Circ: Statement: **41,557** CapCity orders: **2,350**
• looking into future
418 ❑ Oct 1987 Cover: 0.75 **NM** value: **2.00**
Circ: Statement: **41,557**
• looking into future
419 ❑ Dec 1987 Cover: 1.00 **NM** value: **2.00**
Circ: Statement: **41,557**
420 ❑ Feb 1988 Cover: 1.00 **NM** value: **2.00**
Circ: CapCity orders: **2,650**
421 ❑ Apr 1988 Cover: 1.00 **NM** value: **2.00**
Circ: CapCity orders: **2,750**
422 ❑ Jul 1988 Cover: 1.00 **NM** value: **2.00**
Circ: CapCity orders: **2,950**
final issue.
Anl 1 ❑ **NM** value: **4.00**
Anl 2 ❑ Sep 1982 **NM** value: **4.00**
Anl 3 ❑ Aug 1983 **NM** value: **3.00**
Anl 4 ❑ Aug 1984 **NM** value: **3.00**

SGT. ROCK (2ND SERIES) DC

14 ❑ Jul 1991 Cover: 2.00 **NM** value: **Cover or less**
Circ: CapCity orders: **2,800**
• Series continued from Sgt. Rock Special #13
15 ❑ Aug 1991 Cover: 2.00 **NM** value: **Cover or less**
Circ: CapCity orders: **2,750**
16 ❑ Sep 1991 Cover: 2.00 **NM** value: **Cover or less**
Circ: CapCity orders: **2,850**
17 ❑ Oct 1991 Cover: 2.00 **NM** value: **Cover or less**
Circ: CapCity orders: **2,700**
18 ❑ Nov 1991 Cover: 2.00 **NM** value: **Cover or less**
Circ: CapCity orders: **2,600**
📖 Half a Sergeant!; Enemy Ace: Death Whispers-Death Screams! **A:** Michael Golden; Joe Kubert
19 ❑ Dec 1991 Cover: 2.00 **NM** value: **Cover or less**
20 ❑ Jan 1992 Cover: 2.00 **NM** value: **Cover or less**
Circ: CapCity orders: **2,800**
21 ❑ Feb 1992 Cover: 2.00 **NM** value: **Cover or less**
Circ: CapCity orders: **2,600**
SE 1 ❑ Oct 1992 Cover: 2.95 **NM** value: **Cover or less**
Circ: CapCity orders: **5,900**
• 1992 Special **A:** Tim Truman; P. Craig Russell **C:** Walt Simonson
SE 2 ❑ ca. 1994 Cover: 2.95 **NM** value: **Cover or less**
• Commemorates 50th anniversary of the Battle of the Bulge. 📖 The Angel; Hammer and Anvil; The Hunters; Wild Pony • 1994 Special **A:** Howard Chaykin; Graham Nolan; Eduardo Barreto; Russ Heath; Dan Brereton(cover) **W:** Chuck Dixon

SGT. ROCK SPECIAL DC

1 ❑ Sep 1988 Cover: 2.00 **NM** value: **3.00**
Circ: CapCity orders: **3,950**
★ Appearance of Viking Prince.
2 ❑ Dec 1988 Cover: 2.00 **NM** value: **2.50**
Circ: CapCity orders: **4,150**
3 ❑ Mar 1989 Cover: 2.00 **NM** value: **2.50**
Circ: CapCity orders: **3,900**
4 ❑ Jun 1989 Cover: 2.00 **NM** value: **2.50**
Circ: CapCity orders: **3,800**
5 ❑ Sep 1989 Cover: 2.00 **NM** value: **2.50**
Circ: CapCity orders: **4,000**
6 ❑ Dec 1989 Cover: 2.00 **NM** value: **2.50**
Circ: CapCity orders: **4,150**
7 ❑ Mar 1990 Cover: 2.00 **NM** value: **2.50**
Circ: CapCity orders: **3,800** • **CGC:** 1 graded, best 9.6
• reprints Our Fighting Forces #153
8 ❑ Jun 1990 Cover: 2.00 **NM** value: **2.50**
Circ: CapCity orders: **3,450**
9 ❑ Sep 1990 Cover: 2.00 **NM** value: **2.50**
Circ: CapCity orders: **3,250**
10 ❑ Dec 1990 Cover: 2.00 **NM** value: **2.50**
Circ: CapCity orders: **3,250**
11 ❑ Mar 1991 Cover: 2.00 **NM** value: **2.50**
Circ: CapCity orders: **2,950**
12 ❑ May 1991 Cover: 2.00 **NM** value: **2.50**
Circ: CapCity orders: **2,850**
13 ❑ Jun 1991 Cover: 2.00 **NM** value: **2.50**
Circ: CapCity orders: **3,050**

SGT. ROCK'S PRIZE BATTLE TALES REPLICA EDITION DC

1 ❑ ca. 2000 Cover: 5.95 **NM** value: **Cover or less**
Circ: Diamd. preorders: **11,015** • **CGC:** 1 graded, best 9.9
📖 The D.I. And the Sand Fleas!; Silent Fish!; Out in Front!; Island of Armored Giants!; What's the Price of a B-17?; Gun-Jockey!; Calling Easy Co.! **A:** Joe Kubert; Ross Andru; Russ Heath; Irv Novick; Mike Esposito **W:** Robert Kanigher

SERGIO ARAGONÉS DESTROYS DC DC

This fun-filled special finds veteran Mad and Groo the Wanderer artist Sergio Aragones giving his own demented take on the DC universe. The framing story is of Aragones, trying to pick up a job at DC by bringing them the epic of all epics. After gleefully mangling the characters of Superman, Batman, the Legion of Super-Heroes, and other DC stalwarts, Aragones pits them all against that most menacing of all villains...Johnny DC!

It's all fun, frivolity, and fast-paced freneticism courtesy of Aragones and partner-in-crime Mark Evanier.

1 ❑ Jun 1996 Cover: 3.50 **NM** value: **Cover or less**
One-shot. **A:** Sergio Aragonés **W:** Mark Evanier

SERGIO ARAGONÉS MASSACRES MARVEL Marvel

1 ❑ Jun 1996 Cover: 3.50 **NM** value: **Cover or less**
One-shot. wraparound cover.

SERINA Antarctic

1 ❑ Mar 1996, b&w Cover: 2.95 **NM** value: **Cover or less**
📖 Upheaval **A:** Patrick Thornton **W:** Patrick Thornton
2 ❑ May 1996, b&w Cover: 2.95 **NM** value: **Cover or less**
A: David Hahn **W:** David Hahn
3 ❑ Jul 1996 Cover: 2.95 **NM** value: **Cover or less**

SERIUS BOUNTY HUNTER Blackthorne

1 ❑ Nov 1987, b&w Cover: 1.75 **NM** value: **Cover or less**
2 ❑ Jan 1988, b&w Cover: 1.75 **NM** value: **Cover or less**
3 ❑ Mar 1988, b&w Cover: 1.75 **NM** value: **Cover or less**

SERPENTINA Lightning

1/A ❑ Feb 1998, b&w Cover: 2.95 **NM** value: **Cover or less**
Circ: Diamd. preorders: **6,832**
1/B ❑ Feb 1998 Cover: 2.95 **NM** value: **Cover or less**
alternate cover.

Other grades: Multiply prices above by **1.5 for Mint • 2/3 for Very Fine • 1/3 for Fine • 1/5 for Very Good • 1/8 for Good**

SERPENTYNE — Nightwynd

1 ❑ b&w Cover: 2.50 **NM** value: **Cover or less**
2 ❑ b&w Cover: 2.50 **NM** value: **Cover or less**
3 ❑ b&w Cover: 2.50 **NM** value: **Cover or less**

SERRA ANGEL ON THE WORLD OF MAGIC: THE GATHERING — Acclaim / Armada

1 ❑ Aug 1996 Cover: 5.95 **NM** value: **Cover or less**
One-shot. • polybagged with oversized Serra Angel card.

SETH THROB UNDERGROUND ARTIST — Slave Labor

1 ❑ Mar 1994 Cover: 2.95 **NM** value: **Cover or less**
A: Andy Garcia **W:** Andy Garcia
2 ❑ May 1994 Cover: 2.95 **NM** value: **Cover or less**
3 ❑ Aug 1994 Cover: 2.95 **NM** value: **Cover or less**
4 ❑ Dec 1994 Cover: 2.95 **NM** value: **Cover or less**
5 ❑ Mar 1995 Cover: 2.95 **NM** value: **Cover or less**
6 ❑ Jun 1995 Cover: 2.95 **NM** value: **Cover or less**
7 ❑ Sep 1995 Cover: 2.95 **NM** value: **Cover or less**

SETTEI — Antarctic

1 ❑ Feb 1993, b&w Cover: 7.95 **NM** value: **Cover or less**
2 ❑ Apr 1993, b&w Cover: 7.95 **NM** value: **Cover or less**

SETTEI SUPER SPECIAL FEATURING: PROJECT A-KO — Antarctic

1 ❑ Feb 1994, full color Cover: 2.95 **NM** value: **Cover or less**

SEVEN BLOCK — Marvel / Epic

1 ❑ Cover: 4.50 **NM** value: **Cover or less**
Circ: CapCity orders: **5,450**
No issue number. • prestige format. **A:** Jorge Zaffino **W:** Chuck Dixon

SEVEN GUYS OF JUSTICE, THE — False Idol

1 ❑ Apr 2000 Cover: 2.00 **NM** value: **Cover or less**
A: Joshua C. Rowe **W:** Brian Joines
2 ❑ ca. 2000 Cover: 2.00 **NM** value: **Cover or less**
3 ❑ ca. 2000 Cover: 2.00 **NM** value: **Cover or less**
4 ❑ ca. 2000 Cover: 2.00 **NM** value: **Cover or less**
Circ: Diamd. preorders: **1,297**
5 ❑ ca. 2000 Cover: 2.00 **NM** value: **Cover or less**
Circ: Diamd. preorders: **1,225**
6 ❑ ca. 2001 Cover: 2.00 **NM** value: **Cover or less**
Circ: Diamd. preorders: **1,353**
7 ❑ ca. 2001 Cover: 2.00 **NM** value: **Cover or less**
Circ: Diamd. preorders: **1,222**
8 ❑ ca. 2001 Cover: 2.00 **NM** value: **Cover or less**
Circ: Diamd. preorders: **1,144**
9 ❑ ca. 2001 Cover: 2.00 **NM** value: **Cover or less**
Circ: Diamd. preorders: **1,102**
10 ❑ ca. 2001 Cover: 2.00 **NM** value: **Cover or less**

777: WRATH/FAUST FEARBOOK — Rebel

1 ❑ Cover: 14.20 **NM** value: **Cover or less**

SEVEN MILES A SECOND — DC / Vertigo

1 ❑ ca. 1996 Cover: 7.95 **NM** value: **Cover or less**
No issue number. One-shot. • prestige format. **A:** James Romberger **W:** David Wojnarowicz

SEVEN SEAS COMICS — Universal Phoenix

1 ❑ Apr 1946 Cover: 0.10 **NM** value: **750.00**
• **CGC:** 4 graded, best 9.2
2 ❑ Jul 1946 Cover: 0.10 **NM** value: **600.00**
• **CGC:** 3 graded, best 8.5
3 ❑ ca. 1947 Cover: 0.10 **NM** value: **500.00**
• **CGC:** 3 graded, best 9.0
4 ❑ ca. 1947 Cover: 0.10 **NM** value: **500.00**
• **CGC:** 5 graded, best 9.2
5 ❑ ca. 1947 Cover: 0.10 **NM** value: **500.00**
• **CGC:** 4 graded, best 9.2
6 ❑ ca. 1947 Cover: 0.10 **NM** value: **500.00**
• **CGC:** 3 graded, best 7.0

7TH MILLENNIUM — Allied

1 ❑ Cover: 2.50 **NM** value: **Cover or less**
2 ❑ Cover: 2.50 **NM** value: **Cover or less**
3 ❑ Cover: 2.50 **NM** value: **Cover or less**
4 ❑ Cover: 2.50 **NM** value: **Cover or less**

7TH SYSTEM, THE — Sirius

1 ❑ Jan 1998, b&w Cover: 2.95 **NM** value: **Cover or less**
Circ: Diamd. preorders: **8,748**
📖 Kat & Mouse **A:** Roel **W:** Roel; Robb
2 ❑ Feb 1998, b&w Cover: 2.95 **NM** value: **Cover or less**
Circ: Diamd. preorders: **4,599**
3 ❑ Jul 1998, b&w Cover: 2.95 **NM** value: **Cover or less**
Circ: Diamd. preorders: **4,026**
4 ❑ Dec 1998, b&w Cover: 2.95 **NM** value: **Cover or less**
Circ: Diamd. preorders: **2,985**
5 ❑ ca. 1999 Cover: 2.95 **NM** value: **Cover or less**
Circ: Diamd. preorders: **2,563**
6 ❑ Feb 1999, b&w Cover: 2.95 **NM** value: **Cover or less**
Circ: Diamd. preorders: **2,008**

SEWAGE DRAGOON, THE — Parody Press

1 ❑ Cover: 2.50 **NM** value: **Cover or less**
1-2 ❑ Cover: 2.50 **NM** value: **Cover or less**

SEX & DEATH — Acid Rain

1 ❑ b&w Cover: 2.50 **NM** value: **3.95**
📖 Pwdre Ser; The Flea; Terra Em Fogo; Beyond Life; Clouds; Virtual Sexuality **A:** John Bergin; John Bolton; Mike Deodato Jr.; Deodato Filho; H.P. Lovecraft; Jeff Miracola; Scott Rockwell; Terry Pavlet **W:** John Bergin; John Bolton; H.P. Lovecraft; Scott Rockwell; Deodato Borges; T.C. Howards

SEXCAPADES — Eros

1 ❑ Dec 1996 Cover: 2.95 **NM** value: **Cover or less**
Circ: Diamd. preorders: **5,272**
2 ❑ Jan 1997 Cover: 2.95 **NM** value: **Cover or less**
Circ: Diamd. preorders: **4,362**
3 ❑ Feb 1997 Cover: 2.95 **NM** value: **Cover or less**
Circ: Diamd. preorders: **4,368**

SEX DRIVE — M.A.I.N.

1 ❑ Cover: 3.00 **NM** value: **Cover or less**
📖 Demi the Demoness Meets Capt. Fortune Preview; Maid Service; Tattoo Girls Preview; Grave Digger **A:** Ron Fontes; Juan Alcantara; Mike Bradley; Ricky E. Carralero; Warren Elliott **W:** Ron Fontes; Rusty Gilligan; Warren Elliott

SEXECUTIONER — Fantagraphics / Eros

All issues are adults only.
1 ❑ b&w Cover: 2.50 **NM** value: **Cover or less**
2 ❑ b&w Cover: 2.50 **NM** value: **Cover or less**
3 ❑ b&w Cover: 2.50 **NM** value: **Cover or less**

SEXHIBITION — Fantagraphics / Eros

1 ❑ Cover: 2.95 **NM** value: **Cover or less**
2 ❑ Cover: 2.95 **NM** value: **Cover or less**
3 ❑ Cover: 2.95 **NM** value: **Cover or less**
4 ❑ Feb 1996 Cover: 2.95 **NM** value: **Cover or less**

SEX IN THE SINEMA — Comic Zone

All issues are adults only.
1 ❑ b&w Cover: 2.95 **NM** value: **Cover or less**
2 ❑ b&w Cover: 2.95 **NM** value: **Cover or less**
3 ❑ b&w Cover: 2.95 **NM** value: **Cover or less**
4 ❑ b&w Cover: 2.95 **NM** value: **Cover or less**

SEX, LIES AND MUTUAL FUNDS OF THE YUPPIES FROM HELL — Marvel

1 ❑ Cover: 2.95 **NM** value: **Cover or less**
📖 Priorities; Getting Serious; Time To Party; Trash Does Therapy; Love And Marriage **A:** Barbara Slate **W:** Barbara Slate

SEX MACHINE — Fantagraphics / Eros

All issues are adults only.
1 ❑ b&w Cover: 2.50 **NM** value: **Cover or less**
A: Derrick Richardson **W:** Derrick Richardson
2 ❑ b&w Cover: 2.95 **NM** value: **Cover or less**
A: Derrick Richardson **W:** Derrick Richardson
3 ❑ Dec 1997, b&w Cover: 2.95 **NM** value: **Cover or less**
A: Derrick Richardson **W:** Derrick Richardson

SEXPLOITATION CINEMA: A CARTOON HISTORY — Revisionary

All issues are adults only.
1 ❑ Nov 1998, b&w Cover: 3.50 **NM** value: **Cover or less**

SEX TREK: THE NEXT INFILTRATION — Friendly

All issues are adults only.
1 ❑ b&w Cover: 2.95 **NM** value: **Cover or less**

SEX WAD — Eros

1 ❑ Cover: 2.95 **NM** value: **Cover or less**
A: Mike Hersh **W:** Mike Hersh
2 ❑ Cover: 2.95 **NM** value: **Cover or less**
📖 The Rite of Puberty; Modern Lust; I Got an Angel in My Basement; I Wanna be Whipped! **A:** Mike Hersh **W:** Mike Hersh

SEX WARRIOR — Dark Horse

1 ❑ Cover: 2.50 **NM** value: **Cover or less**
Circ: CapCity orders: **8,250**
A: Mike McKone **W:** Pat Mills; Tony Skinner
2 ❑ Cover: 2.50 **NM** value: **Cover or less**
Circ: CapCity orders: **6,625**
A: Mike McKone **W:** Pat Mills; Tony Skinner

SEXX WARS — Immortal

1 ❑ Cover: 2.95 **NM** value: **Cover or less**
📖 Once Upon a Time **A:** Eric C. Smith **W:** Patrick Burnett

SEXY STORIES FROM THE WORLD RELIGIONS — Last Gasp

1 ❑ Cover: 2.50 **NM** value: **Cover or less**
📖 Marozias Secret, The Curse of Saint Dymphna, Divine Anarchy, The Gospel According to Santa and Father Phlem, Fits of Passion, Saint Agnes, Ecclesiasticus 9, 1-9, Santa and New Year's **A:** Joe Sacco; Steve Lafler; Krystine Krittre; M. Fleener; Mike Matthews; Romain Slocombe **W:** Joe Sacco; Steve Lafler; M. Fleener; Romain Slocombe; Lydia Lynch; Mike Furey

SEXY SUPERSPY — Forbidden Fruit

All issues are adults only.
1 ❑ b&w Cover: 2.95 **NM** value: **Cover or less**
2 ❑ b&w Cover: 2.95 **NM** value: **Cover or less**
3 ❑ b&w Cover: 2.95 **NM** value: **Cover or less**
4 ❑ b&w Cover: 2.95 **NM** value: **Cover or less**
5 ❑ b&w Cover: 2.95 **NM** value: **Cover or less**
6 ❑ b&w Cover: 2.95 **NM** value: **Cover or less**
7 ❑ b&w Cover: 2.95 **NM** value: **Cover or less**

SEXY WOMEN — Celebrity

1 ❑ Cover: 2.95 **NM** value: **Cover or less**
2 ❑ Cover: 2.95 **NM** value: **Cover or less**

SFA SPOTLIGHT — Shanda Fantasy Arts

1 ❑ Cover: 2.95 **NM** value: **Cover or less**
2 ❑ Cover: 2.95 **NM** value: **Cover or less**
3 ❑ Cover: 2.95 **NM** value: **Cover or less**
4 ❑ May 1999, b&w Cover: 2.95 **NM** value: **Cover or less**
📖 Tales of the Morphing Period
5 ❑ May 1999, b&w Cover: 4.50 **NM** value: **Cover or less**
• Zebra Comics

SHADE, THE — DC

This mini-series was prompted from The Shade's appearances in DC's Starman series, although he was originally a villain of the Golden Age Flash. The Shade can wield a mysterious, tangible, shadow energy and has lived for hundreds of years, although no explanation for his long life has been offered. His longevity is made even more remarkable given the fact that an entire family — the Ludlows — has taken a vow to kill him in retaliation for his slaughter of their ancestors.

A significant component of this mini-series is the presence of a two-page text piece titled, "From The Shade's Journal" which features the introspective musings and justifications of a man who has lived hundreds of years. The Shade, written by James Robinson (Starman, The Golden Age) features art by such pencillers as Gene Ha and Michael Zulli.

1 ❑ Apr 1997 Cover: 2.25 **NM** value: **2.50**
Circ: Diamd. preorders: **29,508**
📖 A Family Affair **A:** Gene Ha **W:** James Robinson
2 ❑ May 1997 Cover: 2.25 **NM** value: **2.50**
Circ: Diamd. preorders: **23,775**
A: Michael Zulli **W:** James Robinson
3 ❑ Jun 1997 Cover: 2.25 **NM** value: **2.50**
Circ: Diamd. preorders: **25,262**
A: Michael Zulli **W:** James Robinson ★ Appearance of Jay Garrick.
4 ❑ Jul 1997 Cover: 2.25 **NM** value: **2.50**
Circ: Diamd. preorders: **24,894**
📖 Shade: Finale **A:** Michael Zulli **W:** James Robinson

SHADE, THE CHANGING MAN (1ST SERIES) — DC

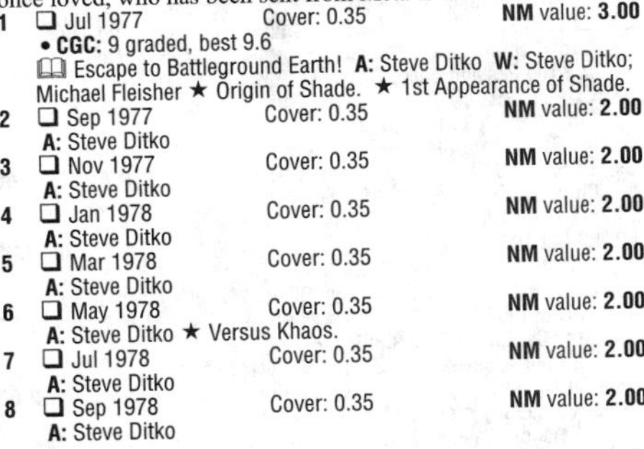

Steve Ditko created Shade, the Changing Man for DC in this 1977 series. Rac Shade is a resident of a dimension known as Meta, separated from Earth by the dreaded Zero Zone. Shade has been wrongly accused of being a traitor to Meta and is sentenced to die. Before the sentence can be carried out, however, a freakish incident casts Shade, along with other criminals, into the Zero Zone. From there, Shade is able to break through to Earth, where he will attempt to prove his innocence.

Shade's power resides in his "M-Vest," which protects him from suffering serious physical harm and acts to reflect people's own fears against them. This makes Shade appear to change constantly, taking on a variety of aspects, as he battles those who framed him as a traitor. Before he can prove his innocence, however, Shade must fight other escapees from his dimension, as well as the woman he once loved, who has been sent from Meta to kill him.

1 ❑ Jul 1977 Cover: 0.35 **NM** value: **3.00**
• **CGC:** 9 graded, best 9.6
📖 Escape to Battleground Earth! **A:** Steve Ditko **W:** Steve Ditko; Michael Fleisher ★ Origin of Shade. ★ 1st Appearance of Shade.
2 ❑ Sep 1977 Cover: 0.35 **NM** value: **2.00**
A: Steve Ditko
3 ❑ Nov 1977 Cover: 0.35 **NM** value: **2.00**
A: Steve Ditko
4 ❑ Jan 1978 Cover: 0.35 **NM** value: **2.00**
A: Steve Ditko
5 ❑ Mar 1978 Cover: 0.35 **NM** value: **2.00**
A: Steve Ditko
6 ❑ May 1978 Cover: 0.35 **NM** value: **2.00**
A: Steve Ditko ★ Versus Khaos.
7 ❑ Jul 1978 Cover: 0.35 **NM** value: **2.00**
A: Steve Ditko
8 ❑ Sep 1978 Cover: 0.35 **NM** value: **2.00**
A: Steve Ditko

SHADE, THE CHANGING MAN (2ND SERIES) — DC

1 ❑ Jul 1990 Cover: 2.50 **NM** value: **3.00**
Circ: CapCity orders: **19,250**
📖 Execution Day **A:** Chris Bachalo **W:** Peter Milligan ★ 1st Appearance of Kathy George, American Scream.
2 ❑ Aug 1990 Cover: 1.50 **NM** value: **2.00**
Circ: CapCity orders: **15,100**
3 ❑ Sep 1990 Cover: 1.50 **NM** value: **2.00**
Circ: CapCity orders: **13,800**
4 ❑ Oct 1990 Cover: 1.50 **NM** value: **2.00**
Circ: CapCity orders: **15,350**
5 ❑ Nov 1990 Cover: 1.50 **NM** value: **2.00**
Circ: CapCity orders: **16,050**
6 ❑ Dec 1990 Cover: 1.50 **NM** value: **2.00**
Circ: CapCity orders: **16,450**
7 ❑ Jan 1991 Cover: 1.50 **NM** value: **2.00**
Circ: CapCity orders: **16,250**

CGC-graded: Multiply prices above by **33 for 9.9 M • 16 for 9.8 NM/M • 7 for 9.6 NM+ • 5 for 9.4 NM • 2.5 for 9.2 NM- • 1.5 for 9.0 VF/NM**

8 ❑ Feb 1991 Cover: 1.50 **NM** value: **2.00**
Circ: CapCity orders: **15,700**
🕮 Love and Haight **A:** Chris Bachalo **W:** Peter Milligan

9 ❑ Mar 1991 Cover: 1.50 **NM** value: **2.00**
Circ: CapCity orders: **13,950**

10 ❑ Apr 1991 Cover: 1.50 **NM** value: **2.00**
Circ: CapCity orders: **12,500**

11 ❑ May 1991 Cover: 1.50 **NM** value: **2.00**
Circ: CapCity orders: **12,050**

12 ❑ Jun 1991 Cover: 1.50 **NM** value: **2.00**
Circ: CapCity orders: **11,250**

13 ❑ Jul 1991 Cover: 1.50 **NM** value: **2.00**
Circ: CapCity orders: **10,700**

14 ❑ Aug 1991 Cover: 1.50 **NM** value: **2.00**
Circ: CapCity orders: **10,400**

15 ❑ Sep 1991 Cover: 1.50 **NM** value: **2.00**
Circ: CapCity orders: **9,950**

16 ❑ Oct 1991 Cover: 1.50 **NM** value: **2.00**
Circ: CapCity orders: **9,800**

17 ❑ Nov 1991 Cover: 1.75 **NM** value: **2.00**
Circ: CapCity orders: **9,100**

18 ❑ Dec 1991 Cover: 1.75 **NM** value: **2.00**
Circ: CapCity orders: **9,000**

19 ❑ Jan 1992 Cover: 1.75 **NM** value: **2.00**
Circ: CapCity orders: **8,800**

20 ❑ Jan 1992 Cover: 1.75 **NM** value: **2.00**
Circ: CapCity orders: **8,350**

21 ❑ Mar 1992 Cover: 1.75 **NM** value: **2.00**
Circ: CapCity orders: **8,200**
🕮 Off the Road, Part 1; Of The Road **A:** Chris Bachalo **W:** Peter Milligan

22 ❑ Apr 1992 Cover: 1.75 **NM** value: **2.00**
Circ: CapCity orders: **7,650**
🕮 Off the Road, Part 2

23 ❑ May 1992 Cover: 1.75 **NM** value: **2.00**
Circ: CapCity orders: **7,750**
🕮 Off the Road, Part 3; The Invisible Loom

24 ❑ Jun 1992 Cover: 1.75 **NM** value: **2.00**
Circ: CapCity orders: **8,150**
🕮 The Road

25 ❑ Jul 1992 Cover: 1.75 **NM** value: **2.00**
Circ: CapCity orders: **7,850**
🕮 The End of the Road

26 ❑ Aug 1992 Cover: 1.75 **NM** value: **2.00**
Circ: CapCity orders: **8,100**

27 ❑ Sep 1992 Cover: 1.75 **NM** value: **2.00**
Circ: CapCity orders: **7,550**

28 ❑ Oct 1992 Cover: 1.75 **NM** value: **2.00**
Circ: CapCity orders: **7,600**

29 ❑ Nov 1992 Cover: 1.75 **NM** value: **2.00**
Circ: CapCity orders: **7,950**

30 ❑ Dec 1992 Cover: 1.75 **NM** value: **2.00**
Circ: CapCity orders: **8,050**

31 ❑ Jan 1993 Cover: 1.75 **NM** value: **2.00**
Circ: CapCity orders: **8,100**
🕮 Ernest And Jim, Part 1

32 ❑ Feb 1993 Cover: 1.75 **NM** value: **2.00**
Circ: CapCity orders: **9,050**
🕮 Ernest And Jim, Part 2 **A:** Colleen Doran **W:** Peter Milligan ★ Death of Talks About Aids insert.

33 ❑ Mar 1993 Cover: 1.75 **NM** value: **2.00**
Circ: CapCity orders: **23,450**
🕮 Birth Pains, Part 1 • Vertigo line starts **A:** Chris Bachalo **W:** Peter Milligan

34 ❑ Apr 1993 Cover: 1.75 **NM** value: **2.00**
Circ: CapCity orders: **11,650**
🕮 Birth Pains, Part 2

35 ❑ May 1993 Cover: 1.75 **NM** value: **2.00**
Circ: CapCity orders: **12,150**

36 ❑ Jun 1993 Cover: 1.95 **NM** value: **2.00**
Circ: CapCity orders: **12,800**
🕮 The Passion Child, Part 1

37 ❑ Jul 1993 Cover: 1.95 **NM** value: **2.00**
Circ: CapCity orders: **12,500**
🕮 The Passion Child, Part 2

38 ❑ Aug 1993 Cover: 1.95 **NM** value: **2.00**
Circ: CapCity orders: **12,200**
🕮 The Great American Novel

39 ❑ Sep 1993 Cover: 1.95 **NM** value: **2.00**
Circ: CapCity orders: **1,100**
🕮 Pond Life

40 ❑ Oct 1993 Cover: 1.95 **NM** value: **2.00**
Circ: CapCity orders: **10,450**
🕮 In Bed With Shade **A:** Glyn Dillon **W:** Peter Milligan

41 ❑ Nov 1993 Cover: 1.95 **NM** value: **2.00**
Circ: CapCity orders: **9,850**
🕮 Angel Dust **A:** Glyn Dillon **W:** Peter Milligan

42 ❑ Dec 1993 Cover: 1.95 **NM** value: **2.00**
Circ: CapCity orders: **10,250**
🕮 History Lesson, Part 1

43 ❑ Jan 1994 Cover: 1.95 **NM** value: **2.00**
Circ: CapCity orders: **9,750**
🕮 History Lesson, Part 2

44 ❑ Feb 1994 Cover: 1.95 **NM** value: **2.00**
Circ: CapCity orders: **9,350**
🕮 History Lesson, Part 3

45 ❑ Mar 1994 Cover: 1.95 **NM** value: **2.00**
Circ: CapCity orders: **8,950**
🕮 A Season in Hell, Part 1

46 ❑ Apr 1994 Cover: 1.95 **NM** value: **2.00**
Circ: CapCity orders: **8,650**
🕮 A Season in Hell, Part 2

47 ❑ May 1994 Cover: 1.95 **NM** value: **2.00**
Circ: CapCity orders: **8,700**
🕮 A Season in Hell, Part 3

48 ❑ Jun 1994 Cover: 1.95 **NM** value: **2.00**
Circ: CapCity orders: **8,500**
🕮 A Season in Hell, Part 4

49 ❑ Jul 1994 Cover: 1.95 **NM** value: **2.00**
Circ: CapCity orders: **8,600**
🕮 A Season in Hell, Part 5

50 ❑ Aug 1994 Cover: 2.95 **NM** value: **3.00**
Circ: CapCity orders: **9,300**
• Giant-size. 🕮 A Season in Hell, Part 6

51 ❑ Sep 1994 Cover: 1.95 **NM** value: **2.00**
Circ: CapCity orders: **8,650**
🕮 The Morning of the Masks, Part 1

52 ❑ Oct 1994 Cover: 1.95 **NM** value: **2.00**
Circ: CapCity orders: **8,550**
🕮 The Morning of the Masks, Part 2

53 ❑ Nov 1994 Cover: 1.95 **NM** value: **2.00**
Circ: CapCity orders: **8,400**
🕮 The Morning of the Masks, Part 3

54 ❑ Dec 1994 Cover: 1.95 **NM** value: **2.00**
Circ: CapCity orders: **8,450**

55 ❑ Jan 1995 Cover: 1.95 **NM** value: **2.00**
Circ: CapCity orders: **7,800**
🕮 Life is Short, Part 1 **A:** Mark Buckingham **W:** Peter Millgan

56 ❑ Feb 1995 Cover: 1.95 **NM** value: **2.00**
Circ: CapCity orders: **7,425**

57 ❑ Mar 1995 Cover: 1.95 **NM** value: **2.00**
Circ: CapCity orders: **7,050**

58 ❑ Apr 1995 Cover: 1.95 **NM** value: **2.00**
Circ: CapCity orders: **6,750**

59 ❑ May 1995 Cover: 2.25 **NM** value: **Cover or less**
Circ: CapCity orders: **6,675**

60 ❑ Jun 1995 Cover: 2.25 **NM** value: **Cover or less**
Circ: CapCity orders: **6,575**

61 ❑ Jul 1995 Cover: 2.25 **NM** value: **Cover or less**
Circ: CapCity orders: **6,475**

62 ❑ Aug 1995 Cover: 2.25 **NM** value: **Cover or less**
Circ: CapCity orders: **6,450**

63 ❑ Sep 1995 Cover: 2.25 **NM** value: **Cover or less**
Circ: CapCity orders: **6,075**

64 ❑ Oct 1995 Cover: 2.25 **NM** value: **Cover or less**
Circ: CapCity orders: **5,300**

65 ❑ Nov 1995 Cover: 2.25 **NM** value: **Cover or less**

66 ❑ Dec 1995 Cover: 2.25 **NM** value: **Cover or less**

67 ❑ Jan 1996 Cover: 2.25 **NM** value: **Cover or less**

68 ❑ Feb 1996 Cover: 2.25 **NM** value: **Cover or less**
🕮 After Kathy, Part 1 **A:** Richard Case **W:** Peter Milligan

69 ❑ Mar 1996 Cover: 2.25 **NM** value: **Cover or less**
🕮 After Kathy, Part 2 **A:** Richard Case **W:** Peter Milligan

70 ❑ Apr 1996 Cover: 2.25 **NM** value: **Cover or less**
final issue.

SHADES AND ANGELS — Candle Light Press

1 ❑ b&w Cover: 2.95 **NM** value: **Cover or less**
🕮 The Shade Pool

SHADES OF BLUE — AMP

1 ❑ Jul 1999, b&w Cover: 2.50 **NM** value: **Cover or less**

SHADES OF GRAY — Lady Luck

1 ❑ ca. 1994 Cover: 2.50 **NM** value: **Cover or less**
2 ❑ Cover: 2.50 **NM** value: **Cover or less**
3 ❑ Cover: 2.50 **NM** value: **Cover or less**
4 ❑ Cover: 2.50 **NM** value: **Cover or less**
5 ❑ Cover: 2.50 **NM** value: **Cover or less**
6 ❑ Cover: 2.50 **NM** value: **Cover or less**
7 ❑ Cover: 2.50 **NM** value: **Cover or less**
8 ❑ Cover: 2.50 **NM** value: **Cover or less**
9 ❑ Cover: 2.50 **NM** value: **Cover or less**
10 ❑ Cover: 2.50 **NM** value: **Cover or less**
11 ❑ Cover: 2.50 **NM** value: **Cover or less**

SHADES OF GRAY COMICS AND STORIES — Tapestry

1 ❑ ca. 1996 Cover: 2.95 **NM** value: **Cover or less**
A: Jimmy Gownley **W:** Jimmy Gownley

2 ❑ Cover: 2.95 **NM** value: **Cover or less**
A: Jimmy Gownley **W:** Jimmy Gownley

3 ❑ Cover: 2.95 **NM** value: **Cover or less**
A: Jimmy Gownley **W:** Jimmy Gownley

4 ❑ Cover: 2.95 **NM** value: **Cover or less**
A: Jimmy Gownley **W:** Jimmy Gownley

SHADE SPECIAL — AC

1 ❑ Oct 1984 Cover: 1.50 **NM** value: **Cover or less**

SHADO: SONG OF THE DRAGON — DC

The tale begins during World War II, when an American G.I. kills a Japanese officer during a fierce fight. As a souvenir, he takes the officer's weapon: a sword. That G.I. is still haunted by the war and the sword 45 years later. To ease his conscience, he decides to return it.

When he brings it to an antique shop for examination, he learns of the sword's origin, an origin rooted with the Yakuza. The antiques store owner (a woman known to Green Arrow fans as Shado) travels with the former G.I. to Japan to try to discover the sword's true owner. What happens is an adventure rich in the mystery and tradition of Japan.

1 ❑ ca. 1992 Cover: 4.95 **NM** value: **Cover or less**
Circ: CapCity orders: **13,550**
🕮 Souvenirs **A:** Michael Lawrence **W:** Mike Grell

2 ❑ ca. 1992 Cover: 4.95 **NM** value: **Cover or less**
Circ: CapCity orders: **10,150**
A: Michael Lawrence **W:** Mike Grell

3 ❑ ca. 1992 Cover: 4.95 **NM** value: **Cover or less**
Circ: CapCity orders: **9,300**
A: Michael Lawrence **W:** Mike Grell

4 ❑ ca. 1992 Cover: 4.95 **NM** value: **Cover or less**
Circ: CapCity orders: **9,400**
🕮 The Black Dragon **A:** Michael Lawrence **W:** Mike Grell

SHADOW, THE (1ST SERIES) — Archie

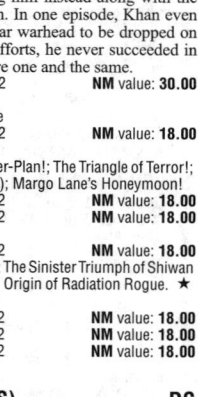

The first Shadow comics title was by far the most lighthearted. Published by Archie's Radio Comics, this rendition of the classic pulp hero stuck mainly to flashy costumes and derring-do.

In this rendition, The Shadow was a member of C.H.I.E.F., the Command Headquarters, International Espionage Forces, a secret agent outfit in the mold of U.N.C.L.E. or S.H.I.E.L.D. His primary enemy was Shiwan Khan, a descendent of Genghis Khan who was determined to conquer the world. Having been defeated so many times in the past by The Shadow, Khan became almost entirely obsessed with crushing him instead-along with the Shadow's "friend," Lamont Cranston. In one episode, Khan even went so far as to arrange for a nuclear warhead to be dropped on Cranston's townhouse. Despite his efforts, he never succeeded in figuring out that his two enemies were one and the same.

1 ❑ Aug 1964 Cover: 0.12 **NM** value: **30.00**
• **CGC:** 1 graded, best 9.6
🕮 The Menace Of Radiation Rogue

2 ❑ Sep 1964 Cover: 0.12 **NM** value: **18.00**
• **CGC:** 1 graded, best 9.4
🕮 Shiwan Khan's Murderous Master-Plan!; The Triangle of Terror!; The Adventures of the Shadow (text); Margo Lane's Honeymoon!

3 ❑ Nov 1964 Cover: 0.12 **NM** value: **18.00**

4 ❑ Jan 1965 Cover: 0.12 **NM** value: **18.00**
• **CGC:** 1 graded, best 9.4

5 ❑ Mar 1965 Cover: 0.12 **NM** value: **18.00**
🕮 The Menace of Radiation Rogue!; The Sinister Triumph of Shiwan Khan!; Doom Stalks the Shadow! ★ Origin of Radiation Rogue. ★ 1st Appearance of Radiation Rogue.

6 ❑ May 1965 Cover: 0.12 **NM** value: **18.00**
7 ❑ Jul 1965 Cover: 0.12 **NM** value: **18.00**
8 ❑ Sep 1965 Cover: 0.12 **NM** value: **18.00**
final issue.

SHADOW, THE (2ND SERIES) — DC

1 ❑ Nov 1973 Cover: 0.20 **NM** value: **20.00**
• **CGC:** 46 graded, best 9.6
🕮 The Doom Puzzle! **A:** Michael W. Kaluta **W:** Denny O'Neil

2 ❑ Jan 1974 Cover: 0.20 **NM** value: **10.00**
• **CGC:** 2 graded, best 9.0
A: Michael W. Kaluta

3 ❑ Mar 1974 Cover: 0.20 **NM** value: **12.00**
• **CGC:** 3 graded, best 9.6
A: Bernie Wrightson; Michael W. Kaluta

4 ❑ May 1974 Cover: 0.20 **NM** value: **9.00**
• **CGC:** 3 graded, best 9.6
A: Michael W. Kaluta

5 ❑ Jul 1974 Cover: 0.20 **NM** value: **6.00**
• **CGC:** 1 graded, best 9.6

6 ❑ Sep 1974 Cover: 0.20 **NM** value: **9.00**
• **CGC:** 2 graded, best 9.6
🕮 Night Of The Ninja **A:** Michael W. Kaluta **W:** Denny O'Neil

7 ❑ Nov 1974 Cover: 0.20 **NM** value: **6.00**
8 ❑ Jan 1975 Cover: 0.20 **NM** value: **6.00**
9 ❑ Mar 1975 Cover: 0.25 **NM** value: **6.00**
10 ❑ May 1975 Cover: 0.25 **NM** value: **6.00**
11 ❑ Jul 1975 Cover: 0.25 **NM** value: **6.00**
★ Appearance of The Avenger.
12 ❑ Sep 1975 Cover: 0.20 **NM** value: **6.00**

SHADOW, THE (3RD SERIES) — DC

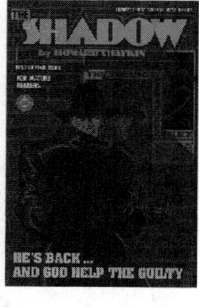

Years had gone by since the Shadow had last appeared to strike terror into the hearts of evildoers. His network of operatives had gone on with their lives, and most were simply growing old.

The Shadow was gone, but he was hardly forgotten. An old enemy named Preston Mayrock had decided it was time to settle old scores. Although wheelchair bound himself, he sent his men on a gruesome murder spree of the Shadow's old agents. But just when all seemed lost, The Shadow returned — and none will escape his vengeance.

Taking a break from his run on American Flagg, Howard Chaykin took on the task of remaking both The Shadow and venerable war hero Blackhawk. In doing so, he managed to add new depth to characters with almost a century of history between them while still maintaining the classic elements which had made them so popular.

1 ❑ May 1986 Cover: 1.50 **NM** value: **3.00**
Circ: CapCity orders: **18,800**
🕮 Blood & Judgment • The Shadow returns **A:** Howard Chaykin **W:** Howard Chaykin

2 ❑ Jun 1986 Cover: 1.50 **NM** value: **2.00**
Circ: CapCity orders: **15,750**
A: Howard Chaykin **W:** Howard Chaykin

Other grades: Multiply prices above by **1.5 for Mint • 2/3 for Very Fine • 1/3 for Fine • 1/5 for Very Good • 1/8 for Good**

3 ❑ Jul 1986 Cover: 1.50 **NM** value: **2.00**
Circ: CapCity orders: **15,850**
A: Howard Chaykin **W:** Howard Chaykin

4 ❑ Aug 1986 Cover: 1.50 **NM** value: **2.00**
Circ: CapCity orders: **20,250**
A: Howard Chaykin **W:** Howard Chaykin

Bk 1❑ Cover: 12.95 **NM** value: **Cover or less**
Circ: CapCity orders: **5,175**
• Reprints The Shadow (3rd Series) #1-4

SHADOW, THE (4TH SERIES) DC

1 ❑ Aug 1987 Cover: 1.50 **NM** value: **2.50**
Circ: CapCity orders: **35,050**
A: Bill Sienkiewicz

2 ❑ Sep 1987 Cover: 1.50 **NM** value: **2.00**
Circ: CapCity orders: **29,450**
A: Bill Sienkiewicz

3 ❑ Oct 1987 Cover: 1.50 **NM** value: **2.00**
Circ: CapCity orders: **29,600**
A: Bill Sienkiewicz

4 ❑ Nov 1987 Cover: 1.50 **NM** value: **2.00**
Circ: CapCity orders: **29,150**
A: Bill Sienkiewicz

5 ❑ Dec 1987 Cover: 1.50 **NM** value: **2.00**
Circ: CapCity orders: **25,500**
A: Bill Sienkiewicz

6 ❑ Jan 1988 Cover: 1.50 **NM** value: **2.00**
Circ: CapCity orders: **23,250**
A: Bill Sienkiewicz

7 ❑ Feb 1988 Cover: 1.75 **NM** value: **2.00**
Circ: CapCity orders: **21,350**

8 ❑ Mar 1988 Cover: 1.75 **NM** value: **2.00**
Circ: CapCity orders: **19,750**
Seven Deadly Finns, Part 1

9 ❑ Apr 1988 Cover: 1.75 **NM** value: **2.00**
Circ: CapCity orders: **18,100**
Seven Deadly Finns, Part 2

10 ❑ May 1988 Cover: 1.75 **NM** value: **2.00**
Circ: CapCity orders: **16,350**
Seven Deadly Finns, Part 3

11 ❑ Jun 1988 Cover: 1.75 **NM** value: **2.00**
Circ: CapCity orders: **15,000**
Seven Deadly Finns, Part 4

12 ❑ Jul 1988 Cover: 1.75 **NM** value: **2.00**
Circ: CapCity orders: **14,200**
Seven Deadly Finns, Part 5

13 ❑ Aug 1988 Cover: 1.75 **NM** value: **2.00**
Circ: CapCity orders: **13,350**
Seven Deadly Finns, Part 6 ★ Death of Shadow.

14 ❑ Sep 1988 Cover: 1.75 **NM** value: **2.00**
Circ: CapCity orders: **13,000**

15 ❑ Oct 1988 Cover: 1.75 **NM** value: **2.00**
Circ: CapCity orders: **12,550**

16 ❑ Nov 1988 Cover: 1.75 **NM** value: **2.00**
Circ: CapCity orders: **11,500**

17 ❑ Dec 1988 Cover: 1.75 **NM** value: **2.00**
Circ: CapCity orders: **11,550**
★ Appearance of Avenger.

18 ❑ Dec 1988 Cover: 1.75 **NM** value: **2.00**
Circ: CapCity orders: **11,200**
★ Appearance of Avenger.

19 ❑ Jan 1989 Cover: 1.75 **NM** value: **2.00**
Circ: CapCity orders: **10,800**
• Shadow alive again

Anl 1❑ca. 1987 Cover: 2.25 **NM** value: **2.50**
Circ: CapCity orders: **23,250**
• EC parody

Anl 2❑ca. 1988 Cover: 2.50 **NM** value: **Cover or less**
Circ: CapCity orders: **11,800**

SHADOW AGENTS Armageddon

1 ❑ May 1991 Cover: 2.50 **NM** value: **Cover or less**
Call to Arms **A:** Christopher Heidt **W:** Kimball Carr

SHADOWALKER Aircel

1 ❑ b&w Cover: 1.50 **NM** value: **Cover or less**

SHADOWALKER CHRONICLES, THE Ground Zero

1 ❑ Cover: 2.25 **NM** value: **Cover or less**
A: Tom Grummettt **W:** Gordon Derry

2 ❑ Cover: 2.25 **NM** value: **Cover or less**
A: Tom Grummettt **W:** Gordon Derry

SHADOW AND DOC SAVAGE, THE Dark Horse

1 ❑ Jul 1995 Cover: 2.95 **NM** value: **Cover or less**
Circ: CapCity orders: **8,450**
The Case of the Shrieking Skeletons, Part 1 **A:** Stan Manoukian; Vince Roucher **W:** Steve Vance

2 ❑ Aug 1995 Cover: 2.95 **NM** value: **Cover or less**
Circ: CapCity orders: **6,175**
The Case of the Shrieking Skeletons, Part 2

SHADOW AND THE MYSTERIOUS 3, THE Dark Horse

1 ❑ Sep 1994 Cover: 2.95 **NM** value: **Cover or less**
No issue number. Fate's Free Fall; Cold Day in Hell; Ceiling Zero
A: Stan Manoukian; Vince Roucher **W:** Michael W. Kaluta; Joel Gross

SHADOWBLADE Hot

1 ❑ Cover: 1.75 **NM** value: **Cover or less**

SHADOW, THE: BLOOD AND JUDGMENT DC

1 ❑ Cover: 12.95 **NM** value: **Cover or less**
A: Howard Chaykin

SHADOW CABINET DC / Milestone

The "Shadow War" was a crossover that brought together Hardware, Icon, Static, Blood Syndicate, and other heroes of Milestone's Dakota universe for the first time. Having run throughout the various Milestone titles, the struggle comes to a head in Shadow Cabinet #0, the first issue of this series.

In that issue, it is revealed that The Big Bang was engineered by a man called Dharma and his Shadow Cabinet, a society of super-powered beings that are out to reshape mankind's destiny. A splinter group called The Star Chamber sought to disperse "de-quantified plasma" over the entire hemisphere, causing a "Big Bang" on a global level. Heroes line up on either side but eventually are forced to unite against The Star Chamber. When it is all over, mankind is saved from immediate danger, although some of the heroes will join The Shadow Cabinet in order to safeguard mankind's future.

0 ❑ Jan 1994 Cover: 2.50 **NM** value: **Cover or less**
Circ: CapCity orders: **16,800**
• Giant-size. Shadow War, Part 6 **A:** John Paul Leon **W:** Robert Washington III ★ Appearance of Xombi, Static, Icon, Hardware, Blood Syndicate.

1 ❑ Jun 1994 Cover: 1.75 **NM** value: **Cover or less**
Circ: CapCity orders: **11,350**
A Handful Of S.A.N.D. **A:** John Paul Leon **W:** Robert Washington III ★ Origin of Iron Butterfly, Sideshow, Corpsicle. ★ 1st Appearance of Corpsicle. ★ Death of Corpsicle.

2 ❑ Jul 1994 Cover: 1.75 **NM** value: **Cover or less**
Circ: CapCity orders: **6,950**

3 ❑ Aug 1994 Cover: 1.75 **NM** value: **Cover or less**
Circ: CapCity orders: **6,050**
★ 1st Appearance of Telesthene.

4 ❑ Sep 1994 Cover: 1.75 **NM** value: **Cover or less**
Circ: CapCity orders: **5,650**

5 ❑ Oct 1994 Cover: 1.75 **NM** value: **Cover or less**
Circ: CapCity orders: **5,300**

6 ❑ Nov 1994 Cover: 1.75 **NM** value: **Cover or less**
Circ: CapCity orders: **4,600**
Red Death, Part 1 **A:** John Paul Leon **W:** Matt Wayne

7 ❑ Dec 1994 Cover: 1.75 **NM** value: **Cover or less**
Circ: CapCity orders: **4,150**
Red Death, Part 2 **A:** John Paul Leon **W:** Matt Wayne

8 ❑ Jan 1995 Cover: 1.75 **NM** value: **Cover or less**
Circ: CapCity orders: **3,600**
Red Death, Part 3 **A:** John Paul Leon **W:** Matt Wayne

9 ❑ Feb 1995 Cover: 1.75 **NM** value: **Cover or less**
Circ: CapCity orders: **3,125**

10 ❑ Mar 1995 Cover: 1.75 **NM** value: **Cover or less**
Circ: CapCity orders: **2,775**

11 ❑ Apr 1995 Cover: 1.75 **NM** value: **Cover or less**
Circ: CapCity orders: **2,525**

12 ❑ May 1995 Cover: 1.75 **NM** value: **Cover or less**
Circ: CapCity orders: **2,475**

13 ❑ Jun 1995 Cover: 2.50 **NM** value: **Cover or less**
Circ: CapCity orders: **2,425**

14 ❑ Jul 1995 Cover: 2.50 **NM** value: **Cover or less**
Circ: CapCity orders: **2,450**

15 ❑ Aug 1995 Cover: 2.50 **NM** value: **Cover or less**
Circ: CapCity orders: **2,425**
Long Hot Summer

16 ❑ Sep 1995 Cover: 2.50 **NM** value: **Cover or less**
Circ: CapCity orders: **2,350**
The Long Hot Summer

17 ❑ Oct 1995 Cover: 2.50 **NM** value: **Cover or less**
Circ: CapCity orders: **1,950**
final issue.

SHADOW COMICS Street & Smith

The Shadow, created by writer Walter Gibson (aka Maxwell Grant) for Street and Smith's pulp The Shadow Magazine in 1933, is one of the most memorable fiction characters of the 20th century. As the first costumed crimefighter, the mysterious Shadow and his agents did battle against underworld menaces throughout the 1930s and 40s in the pulps, radio, movies, and comic books. Though the Shadow was a towering influence on Golden Age super-heroes including Batman, his own comic-book adventures paled in comparison to his super-peers, not to mention Gibson's bi-weekly novels or the radio show which starred a young Orson Welles. The shoddy artwork and dumbed-down pulp stories failed to capture the most important element of the Shadow's mystique — the overbearing atmosphere of dread and mystery. It would be another 30 years before Michael Kaluta and Dennis O'Neil finally got the character right in DC's The Shadow comic.

1 ❑ Mar 1940 Cover: 0.10 **NM** value: **3000.00**
• **CGC:** 3 graded, best 8.0

2 ❑ Apr 1940 Cover: 0.10 **NM** value: **1300.00**
• **CGC:** 1 graded, best 8.5

3 ❑ May 1940 Cover: 0.10 **NM** value: **850.00**
• **CGC:** 1 graded, best 9.0

4 ❑ Jun 1940 Cover: 0.10 **NM** value: **700.00**

5 ❑ Jul 1940 Cover: 0.10 **NM** value: **650.00**
• **CGC:** 2 graded, best 9.0

6 ❑ Aug 1940 Cover: 0.10 **NM** value: **650.00**
• **CGC:** 1 graded, best 9.2

7 ❑ Nov 1940 Cover: 0.10 **NM** value: **550.00**
• **CGC:** 3 graded, best 8.5

8 ❑ Jan 1941 Cover: 0.10 **NM** value: **425.00**
• **CGC:** 2 graded, best 9.0

9 ❑ Mar 1941 Cover: 0.10 **NM** value: **425.00**
• **CGC:** 3 graded, best 9.0

10 ❑ May 1941 Cover: 0.10 **NM** value: **425.00**

11 ❑ Jul 1941 Cover: 0.10 **NM** value: **425.00**
• **CGC:** 2 graded, best 8.5

12 ❑ Sep 1941 Cover: 0.10 **NM** value: **350.00**
• **CGC:** 2 graded, best 9.4
★ Appearance of Dead End Kids.

13 ❑ Oct 1941 Cover: 0.10 **NM** value: **350.00**

14 ❑ Nov 1941 Cover: 0.10 **NM** value: **350.00**
• **CGC:** 4 graded, best 9.4

15 ❑ Mar 1942 Cover: 0.10 **NM** value: **575.00**
• **CGC:** 1 graded, best 9.0
★ 1st Appearance of Supersnipe.

16 ❑ May 1942 Cover: 0.10 **NM** value: **450.00**
• **CGC:** 1 graded, best 7.5

17 ❑ Jul 1942 Cover: 0.10 **NM** value: **450.00**
• **CGC:** 1 graded, best 9.4

18 ❑ Sep 1942 Cover: 0.10 **NM** value: **400.00**

19 ❑ Oct 1942 Cover: 0.10 **NM** value: **400.00**
• **CGC:** 4 graded, best 9.2

20 ❑ Nov 1942 Cover: 0.10 **NM** value: **400.00**
• **CGC:** 2 graded, best 9.4

21 ❑ Dec 1942 Cover: 0.10 **NM** value: **400.00**
• **CGC:** 1 graded, best 9.2

22 ❑ Jan 1943 Cover: 0.10 **NM** value: **400.00**
• **CGC:** 2 graded, best 8.5

23 ❑ Feb 1943 Cover: 0.10 **NM** value: **375.00**

24 ❑ Mar 1943 Cover: 0.10 **NM** value: **375.00**
• **CGC:** 2 graded, best 9.6

25 ❑ Apr 1943 Cover: 0.10 **NM** value: **350.00**
• **CGC:** 1 graded, best 9.6

26 ❑ May 1943 Cover: 0.10 **NM** value: **350.00**
• **CGC:** 1 graded, best 8.0

27 ❑ Jun 1943 Cover: 0.10 **NM** value: **350.00**
• **CGC:** 1 graded, best 9.4

28 ❑ Jul 1943 Cover: 0.10 **NM** value: **350.00**
• **CGC:** 5 graded, best 9.4

29 ❑ Aug 1943 Cover: 0.10 **NM** value: **350.00**
• **CGC:** 1 graded, best 9.4
Monstodamus in Treasure Bay!; At Ghost Manor; The Evil That Lurks in the Hearts of Men; Amazon World; Rain, Rain, Go Away (Text Story); The Mad Hatter!; The Spy Master; **A:** Jack Binder; Al Bare **W:** Bruce Elliot; Ed Gruskin; Maxwell Grant

30 ❑ Sep 1943 Cover: 0.10 **NM** value: **350.00**
• **CGC:** 2 graded, best 9.4

31 ❑ Oct 1943 Cover: 0.10 **NM** value: **350.00**
• **CGC:** 2 graded, best 8.0

32 ❑ Nov 1943 Cover: 0.10 **NM** value: **350.00**
• **CGC:** 2 graded, best 9.6

33 ❑ Dec 1943 Cover: 0.10 **NM** value: **350.00**
• **CGC:** 1 graded, best 9.6

34 ❑ Jan 1944 Cover: 0.10 **NM** value: **350.00**
• **CGC:** 2 graded, best 9.6

35 ❑ Feb 1944 Cover: 0.10 **NM** value: **325.00**
• **CGC:** 2 graded, best 6.5

36 ❑ Mar 1944 Cover: 0.10 **NM** value: **325.00**
• **CGC:** 3 graded, best 9.2

37 ❑ Apr 1944 Cover: 0.10 **NM** value: **325.00**

38 ❑ May 1944 Cover: 0.10 **NM** value: **325.00**

39 ❑ Jun 1944 Cover: 0.10 **NM** value: **325.00**
• **CGC:** 2 graded, best 9.0

40 ❑ Jul 1944 Cover: 0.10 **NM** value: **325.00**
• **CGC:** 1 graded, best 9.2

41 ❑ Aug 1944 Cover: 0.10 **NM** value: **325.00**
• **CGC:** 2 graded, best 9.2

42 ❑ Sep 1944 Cover: 0.10 **NM** value: **325.00**
• **CGC:** 2 graded, best 8.5

43 ❑ Oct 1944 Cover: 0.10 **NM** value: **325.00**
• **CGC:** 4 graded, best 9.0

44 ❑ Nov 1944 Cover: 0.10 **NM** value: **325.00**
• **CGC:** 2 graded, best 9.0

45 ❑ Dec 1944 Cover: 0.10 **NM** value: **325.00**
• **CGC:** 3 graded, best 9.4

46 ❑ Jan 1945 Cover: 0.10 **NM** value: **325.00**
• **CGC:** 2 graded, best 8.5

47 ❑ Feb 1945 Cover: 0.10 **NM** value: **325.00**
• **CGC:** 2 graded, best 9.0

48 ❑ Mar 1945 Cover: 0.10 **NM** value: **325.00**
• **CGC:** 3 graded, best 8.5

49 ❑ Apr 1945 Cover: 0.10 **NM** value: **300.00**
• **CGC:** 2 graded, best 9.2

50 ❑ May 1945 Cover: 0.10 **NM** value: **350.00**

51 ❑ Jun 1945 Cover: 0.10 **NM** value: **325.00**
• **CGC:** 2 graded, best 9.6

52 ❑ Jul 1945 Cover: 0.10 **NM** value: **325.00**
• **CGC:** 3 graded, best 9.4

53 ❑ Aug 1945 Cover: 0.10 **NM** value: **325.00**
• **CGC:** 2 graded, best 9.2

54 ❑ Sep 1945 Cover: 0.10 **NM** value: **325.00**
• **CGC:** 3 graded, best 9.2

55 ❑ Oct 1945 Cover: 0.10 **NM** value: **325.00**
• **CGC:** 2 graded, best 9.4

56 ❑ Nov 1945 Cover: 0.10 **NM** value: **300.00**
• **CGC:** 2 graded, best 7.5

57 ❑ Dec 1945 Cover: 0.10 **NM** value: **300.00**
• **CGC:** 2 graded, best 9.4

58 ❑ Jan 1946 Cover: 0.10 **NM** value: **300.00**

59 ❑ Feb 1946 Cover: 0.10 **NM** value: **300.00**
• **CGC:** 2 graded, best 8.5

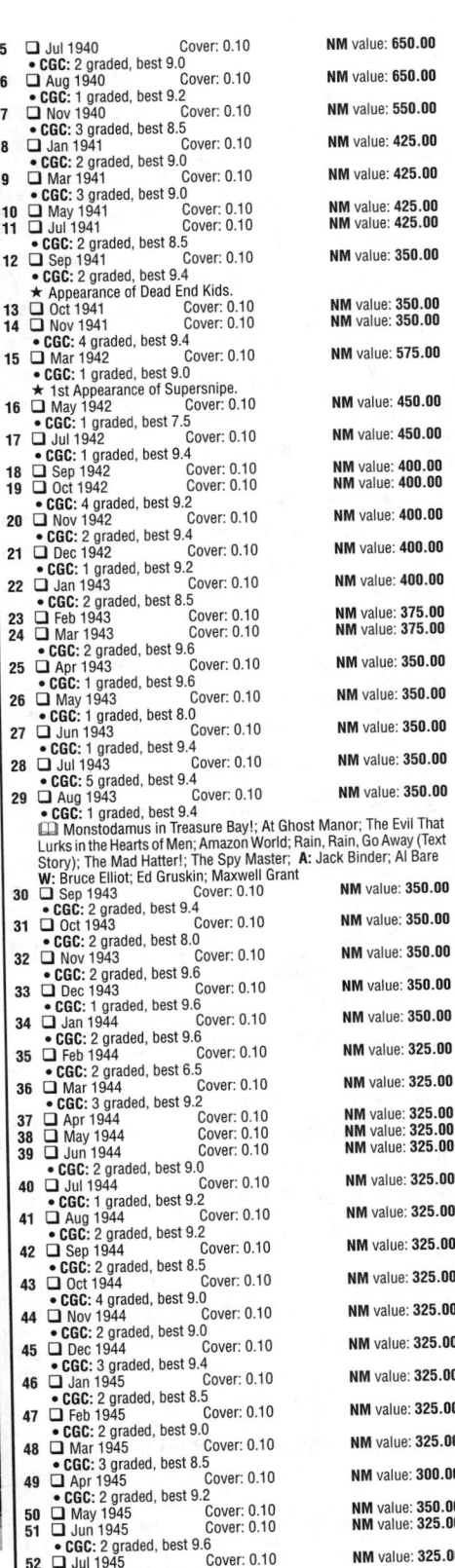

CGC-graded: Multiply prices above by **33 for 9.9 M • 16 for 9.8 NM/M • 7 for 9.6 NM+ • 5 for 9.4 NM • 2.5 for 9.2 NM- • 1.5 for 9.0 VF/NM**

60 ❑ Mar 1946 Cover: 0.10 **NM** value: **300.00**
• **CGC:** 1 graded, best 8.0
61 ❑ Apr 1946 Cover: 0.10 **NM** value: **275.00**
• **CGC:** 1 graded, best 7.0
62 ❑ May 1946 Cover: 0.10 **NM** value: **275.00**
• **CGC:** 1 graded, best 9.4
63 ❑ Jun 1946 Cover: 0.10 **NM** value: **275.00**
64 ❑ Jul 1946 Cover: 0.10 **NM** value: **275.00**
65 ❑ Aug 1946 Cover: 0.10 **NM** value: **275.00**
66 ❑ Sep 1946 Cover: 0.10 **NM** value: **275.00**
• **CGC:** 1 graded, best 8.5
67 ❑ Oct 1946 Cover: 0.10 **NM** value: **275.00**
• **CGC:** 1 graded, best 9.6
68 ❑ Nov 1946 Cover: 0.10 **NM** value: **275.00**
69 ❑ Dec 1946 Cover: 0.10 **NM** value: **275.00**
• **CGC:** 1 graded, best 9.2
70 ❑ Jan 1946 Cover: 0.10 **NM** value: **275.00**
• **CGC:** 1 graded, best 9.4
71 ❑ Feb 1946 Cover: 0.10 **NM** value: **275.00**
72 ❑ Mar 1946 Cover: 0.10 **NM** value: **275.00**
73 ❑ Apr 1946 Cover: 0.10 **NM** value: **275.00**
74 ❑ May 1946 Cover: 0.10 **NM** value: **275.00**
75 ❑ Jun 1946 Cover: 0.10 **NM** value: **275.00**
• **CGC:** 1 graded, best 9.0
76 ❑ Jul 1946 Cover: 0.10 **NM** value: **275.00**
• **CGC:** 1 graded, best 9.0
77 ❑ Aug 1946 Cover: 0.10 **NM** value: **275.00**
78 ❑ Sep 1946 Cover: 0.10 **NM** value: **275.00**
• **CGC:** 1 graded, best 9.0
79 ❑ Oct 1946 Cover: 0.10 **NM** value: **275.00**
• **CGC:** 1 graded, best 8.5
80 ❑ Nov 1946 Cover: 0.10 **NM** value: **275.00**
• **CGC:** 2 graded, best 8.0
81 ❑ Dec 1946 Cover: 0.10 **NM** value: **275.00**
• **CGC:** 1 graded, best 8.5
82 ❑ Jan 1947 Cover: 0.10 **NM** value: **275.00**
• **CGC:** 2 graded, best 7.0
83 ❑ Feb 1947 Cover: 0.10 **NM** value: **275.00**
• **CGC:** 1 graded, best 9.0
84 ❑ Mar 1947 Cover: 0.10 **NM** value: **275.00**
• **CGC:** 1 graded, best 9.2
85 ❑ Apr 1949 Cover: 0.10 **NM** value: **275.00**
• **CGC:** 1 graded, best 9.2
86 ❑ May 1949 Cover: 0.10 **NM** value: **250.00**
• **CGC:** 1 graded, best 9.0
87 ❑ Jun 1949 Cover: 0.10 **NM** value: **250.00**
• **CGC:** 1 graded, best 8.5
88 ❑ Jul 1949 Cover: 0.10 **NM** value: **250.00**
89 ❑ Aug 1949 Cover: 0.10 **NM** value: **250.00**
• **CGC:** 2 graded, best 8.5
90 ❑ Sep 1949 Cover: 0.10 **NM** value: **250.00**
• **CGC:** 2 graded, best 9.0
91 ❑ Oct 1949 Cover: 0.10 **NM** value: **250.00**
92 ❑ Nov 1949 Cover: 0.10 **NM** value: **250.00**
93 ❑ Dec 1949 Cover: 0.10 **NM** value: **250.00**
94 ❑ Jan 1950 Cover: 0.10 **NM** value: **250.00**
95 ❑ Feb 1950 Cover: 0.10 **NM** value: **250.00**
• **CGC:** 1 graded, best 8.0
96 ❑ Mar 1950 Cover: 0.10 **NM** value: **250.00**
• **CGC:** 1 graded, best 8.0
97 ❑ Apr 1950 Cover: 0.10 **NM** value: **200.00**
• **CGC:** 2 graded, best 7.5
98 ❑ May 1950 Cover: 0.10 **NM** value: **200.00**
99 ❑ Jun 1950 Cover: 0.10 **NM** value: **200.00**
• **CGC:** 1 graded, best 9.2
A: Dick Rockwell ★ Appearance of Doc Savage, Nick Carter.
100 ❑ Jul 1950 Cover: 0.10 **NM** value: **200.00**
★ Appearance of Doc Savage.
101 ❑ Aug 1950 Cover: 0.10 **NM** value: **200.00**
• **CGC:** 1 graded, best 8.0

SHADOW COMIX SHOWCASE — Shadow Comix
1 ❑ May 1996 Cover: 2.95 **NM** value: **Cover or less**
Outlander 0.1; Darkblade **A:** Dan Hogan; Jon Larkins **W:** Jon Larkins

SHADOW CROSS — Darkside
1 ❑ Oct 1995 Cover: 2.75 **NM** value: **Cover or less**
A: Les Garner **W:** Les Gerner; Rick Dothager

SHADOWDRAGON — DC
Anl 1 ❑ ca. 1995 Cover: 3.50 **NM** value: **Cover or less**
Circ: CapCity orders: **7,800**
Dawn of the Dragon • Year One **A:** Brett Breeding **W:** Brett Breeding; David Michelinie ★ Origin of Shadowdragon.

SHADOW EMPIRES: FAITH CONQUERS — Dark Horse
1 ❑ Aug 1994 Cover: 2.95 **NM** value: **3.25**
Circ: CapCity orders: **5,775**
A: Christopher Moeller **W:** Christopher Moeller
2 ❑ Sep 1994 Cover: 2.95 **NM** value: **3.00**
Circ: CapCity orders: **4,275**
A: Christopher Moeller **W:** Christopher Moeller
3 ❑ Oct 1994 Cover: 2.95 **NM** value: **3.00**
Circ: CapCity orders: **4,050**
A: Christopher Moeller **W:** Christopher Moeller
4 ❑ Nov 1994 Cover: 2.95 **NM** value: **3.00**
Circ: CapCity orders: **3,950**
A: Christopher Moeller **W:** Christopher Moeller

SHADOWGEAR — Antarctic
1 ❑ Feb 1999 Cover: 2.99 **NM** value: **Cover or less**
Circ: Diamd. preorders: **2,140**
Hardwired, Part 1 **A:** Locke **W:** Locke
2 ❑ Mar 1999 Cover: 2.99 **NM** value: **Cover or less**
Hardwired, Part 2 **A:** Locke **W:** Locke; Dean Morin
3 ❑ Apr 1999 Cover: 2.99 **NM** value: **Cover or less**
Hardwired, Part 3 **A:** Locke **W:** Locke; Dean Morin

SHADOWHAWK GALLERY — Image
1 ❑ Apr 1994 Cover: 1.95 **NM** value: **2.00**
Circ: CapCity orders: **20,200**
A: Jim Valentino **W:** Jim Valentino

SHADOWHAWK: OUT OF THE SHADOWS — Image
Bk 1 ❑ Cover: 19.95 **NM** value: **Cover or less**
Bk 1/HC ❑ Cover: 39.95 **NM** value: **Cover or less**
hardcover.
Bk 1/LE ❑ **NM** value: **20.00**
• limited edition with silver and red logo.

SHADOWHAWKS OF LEGEND — Image
1 ❑ Nov 1995 Cover: 4.95 **NM** value: **Cover or less**
A journey ThroughShadows; The Shadow of Justice; Taka no KagT; L'Ombre AvecLe Faucon; Shadows in the Sand **A:** Kyle Holtz; Jim Valentino; James W. Fry III; Ron Randall; Steve Leialoha **W:** Kurt Busiek; Stan Sakai; Alan Moore; Beau Smith; Len Senecal

SHADOWHAWK-VAMPIRELLA — Image / Harris
2 ❑ Feb 1995 Cover: 4.95 **NM** value: **Cover or less**
Circ: CapCity orders: **27,675**
• crossover; continued from Vampirella – Shadowhawk #1

SHADOWHAWK (VOL. 1) — Image
When the crime rate is skyrocketing out of control, desperate solutions are required. The police have to be accountable to ethics and fair play, when criminals aren't; only a vigilante can set things right.

The mysterious ShadowHawk has stepped out of the shadows to bring swift justice to criminals. He has a nasty habit of breaking the backs — literally — of those he deems worthy of punishment. That way, he figures, they'll never menace innocents again.

Some would say everyone's entitled to a fair and just trial; others think ShadowHawk deserves a medal. Nevertheless, the mystery remains: Who is ShadowHawk?

1 ❑ Aug 1992 Cover: 2.50 **NM** value: **3.00**
Circ: CapCity orders: **119,075** • **CGC:** 5 graded, best 9.8
Embossed cover. A Knightmare Walking **A:** Jim Valentino **W:** Jim Valentino ★ 1st Appearance of Shadowhawk.
1/A ❑ Aug 1992 Cover: 1.95 **NM** value: **2.00**
Embossed cover. • Newsstand edition (no gold stamp). **A:** Jim Valentino **W:** Jim Valentino ★ 1st Appearance of Shadowhawk.
2 ❑ Oct 1992 Cover: 1.95 **NM** value: **2.50**
Circ: CapCity orders: **90,275**
Good Night For Arson **A:** Jim Valentino **W:** Jim Valentino ★ 1st Appearance of Arson. ★ Appearance of Spawn.
3 ❑ Dec 1992 Cover: 1.95 **NM** value: **2.50**
Circ: CapCity orders: **109,250**
Glow-in-the-dark cover. Liquid Fire; Opening Shots **A:** Jim Valentino **W:** Jim Valentino ★ 1st Appearance of The Others, Liquefier.
4 ❑ Mar 1993 Cover: 1.95 **NM** value: **2.00**
Circ: CapCity orders: **97,175**
Enter: The Dragon **A:** Jim Valentino **W:** Jim Valentino ★ Appearance of Savage Dragon.

SHADOWHAWK (VOL. 2) — Image
1 ❑ May 1993 Cover: 3.50 **NM** value: **Cover or less**
Circ: CapCity orders: **178,800**
diecut foil cover. The Shadow Of The Hawk **A:** Jim Valentino **W:** Jim Valentino
1/GO ❑ May 1993 **NM** value: **3.00**
• Gold
2 ❑ Jul 1993 Cover: 1.95 **NM** value: **2.00**
Circ: CapCity orders: **185,750**
Foil-embossed cover. The Secret Revealed • ShadowHawk's identity revealed **A:** Jim Valentino **W:** Jim Valentino ★ 1st Appearance of Hawk's Shadow.
2/GO ❑ Jul 1993 **NM** value: **3.00**
• Gold edition.
3 ❑ Aug 1993 Cover: 2.95 **NM** value: **Cover or less**
Circ: CapCity orders: **103,665**
Cover perforated to allow folding out into poster. Like Lambs To The… **A:** Jim Valentino **W:** Jim Valentino ★ 1st Appearance of The Pact, J.P. Slaughter.
Bk 1 ❑ Cover: 12.95 **NM** value: **Cover or less**
• The Secret Revealed

SHADOWHAWK (VOL. 3) — Image
0 ❑ Oct 1994 Cover: 1.95 **NM** value: **2.50**
Circ: CapCity orders: **35,000**
cover says September. **A:** Rob Liefeld **W:** Jim Valentino; Rob Liefeld; Robert Napton ★ Origin of Shadowhawk. ★ Appearance of Mist, Bloodstrike, Mars Gunther.
1 ❑ Nov 1993 Cover: 1.95 **NM** value: **2.50**
Circ: CapCity orders: **72,125**
Foil-embossed cover. Through The Past, Darkly **A:** Jim Valentino **W:** Jim Valentino ★ 1st Appearance of Valentine.
2 ❑ Dec 1993 Cover: 1.95 **NM** value: **2.00**
Circ: CapCity orders: **49,850**
The Needle And The Damage Done **A:** Jim Valentino **W:** Jim Valentino ★ 1st Appearance of U.S. Male.
3 ❑ Feb 1994 Cover: 1.95 **NM** value: **2.95**
Circ: CapCity orders: **38,225**
Fold-up cover.
4 ❑ Mar 1994 Cover: 1.95 **NM** value: **2.95**
Circ: CapCity orders: **33,775**
12 ❑ Aug 1994 Cover: 1.95 **NM** value: **Cover or less**
Circ: CapCity orders: **26,950**
The Monster Within, Part 1 • (Numbering sequence follows from total of all ShadowHawk books published to this point)
13 ❑ Sep 1994 Cover: 1.95 **NM** value: **Cover or less**
Circ: CapCity orders: **24,700**
The Monster Within, Part 2 ★ Appearance of WildC.A.T.s.
14 ❑ Oct 1994 Cover: 2.50 **NM** value: **Cover or less**
Circ: CapCity orders: **21,750**
Monster Within, Part 3; The Monster Within, Part 3 ★ Appearance of 1963 heroes.
15 ❑ Nov 1994 Cover: 2.50 **NM** value: **Cover or less**
Circ: CapCity orders: **19,075**
Monster Within, Part 4; The Monster Within, Part 4 ★ Appearance of The Others.
16 ❑ Jan 1995 Cover: 2.50 **NM** value: **Cover or less**
Circ: CapCity orders: **15,850**
Monster Within, Part 5; The Monster Within, Part 5 ★ Appearance of Supreme.
17 ❑ Mar 1995 Cover: 2.50 **NM** value: **Cover or less**
Circ: CapCity orders: **17,975**
Monster Within, Part 6 ★ Appearance of Spawn.
18 ❑ May 1995 Cover: 2.50 **NM** value: **Cover or less**
Circ: CapCity orders: **15,175**
final issue. ★ Death of Shadowhawk.
SE 1 ❑ Dec 1994 Cover: 3.50 **NM** value: **Cover or less**
Circ: CapCity orders: **16,225**
• Flip-book. Images of Tomorrow; Images of Yesterday **A:** Jim Valentino; Walter McDaniel **W:** Jim Valentino; Kurt Busiek

SHADOW, THE: HELL'S HEAT WAVE — Dark Horse
1 ❑ Apr 1995 Cover: 2.95 **NM** value: **Cover or less**
Circ: CapCity orders: **6,675**
A: Gary Gianni **W:** Michael W. Kaluta; Joel Goss
2 ❑ May 1995 Cover: 2.95 **NM** value: **Cover or less**
Circ: CapCity orders: **5,525**
A: Gary Gianni **W:** Michael W. Kaluta; Joel Goss
3 ❑ Jun 1995 Cover: 2.95 **NM** value: **Cover or less**
Circ: CapCity orders: **5,200**
A: Gary Gianni **W:** Michael W. Kaluta; Joel Goss

SHADOW, THE: HITLER'S ASTROLOGER — Marvel
1 ❑ Cover: 12.95 **NM** value: **Cover or less**
hardcover.

SHADOW HOUSE — Shadow House Press
1 ❑ Aug 1997, b&w Cover: 2.95 **NM** value: **Cover or less**
Autumn's Arrival, The Revenant, Fetid Matter, Nightmark, Dark Streets **A:** Pat Broderick; Fred Harper; Kirk Van Wormer **W:** James Chambers; Christopher Mills
2 ❑ Oct 1997, b&w Cover: 2.95 **NM** value: **Cover or less**
3 ❑ Dec 1997, b&w Cover: 2.95 **NM** value: **Cover or less**
4 ❑ Feb 1998, b&w Cover: 2.95 **NM** value: **Cover or less**

SHADOWHUNT SPECIAL — Image
1/A ❑ Apr 1996 Cover: 2.50 **NM** value: **Cover or less**
• Part 1 of five-part crossover
1/B ❑ Apr 1996 Cover: 2.50 **NM** value: **Cover or less**
alternate cover. • Part 1 of five-part crossover

SHADOW, THE: IN THE COILS OF LEVIATHAN — Dark Horse
1 ❑ Oct 1993 Cover: 2.95 **NM** value: **Cover or less**
Circ: CapCity orders: **11,025**
A: Gary Gianni **W:** Michael W. Kaluta; Joel Goss
2 ❑ Dec 1993 Cover: 2.95 **NM** value: **Cover or less**
Circ: CapCity orders: **6,625**
3 ❑ Feb 1994 Cover: 2.95 **NM** value: **Cover or less**
Circ: CapCity orders: **6,175**
4 ❑ Apr 1994 Cover: 2.95 **NM** value: **Cover or less**
Circ: CapCity orders: **5,825**

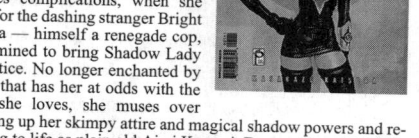

SHADOW LADY (MASAKAZU KATSURA'S...) — Dark Horse / Manga
The Japanese Catwoman? Not exactly, but there are similarities to the DC anti-heroine in this manga mini-series, made available in English by Dark Horse Comics. The sexy Shadow Lady is a playful, mischievous crook who bounces around the city committing crimes and having fun doing it. Rarely inconvenienced by the bumbling cops pursuing her, she nonetheless experiences complications, when she falls for the dashing stranger Bright Honda — himself a renegade cop, determined to bring Shadow Lady to justice. No longer enchanted by a life that has her at odds with the man she loves, she muses over hanging up her skimpy attire and magical shadow powers and returning to life as plain old Aimi Komori. But can she?

Masakazu Katsura's story is lighthearted and funny, and his art dabbles in the kind of sexiness for which this genre is famous. (Men crashing in on women in showers is a recurring theme.) It's all in the name of good, clean fun.

1 ❑ Oct 1998 Cover: 2.50 **NM** value: **3.00**
• **CGC:** 1 graded, best 9.6
Dangeous Love, Part 1; Dangerous Love **A:** Masakazu Katsura **W:** Masakazu Katsura ★ 1st Appearance of Shadow Lady.
2 ❑ Nov 1998 Cover: 2.50 **NM** value: **Cover or less**
Dangeous Love, Part 2; Dangerous Love **A:** Masakazu Katsura **W:** Masakazu Katsura ★ 1st Appearance of Bright Honda. ★ 2nd Appearance of Aimi, Shadow Lady, De-Mo.

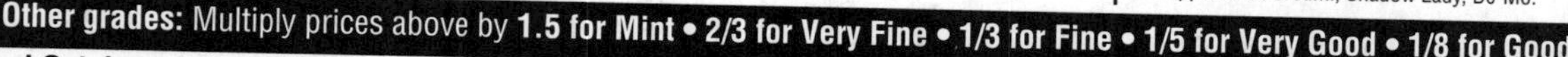

3 ❑ Dec 1998 Cover: 2.50 **NM** value: **Cover or less**
Dangeous Love, Part 3; Dangerous Love **A:** Masakazu Katsura **W:** Masakazu Katsura
4 ❑ Jan 1999 Cover: 2.50 **NM** value: **Cover or less**
Dangeous Love, Part 4; Dangerous Love **A:** Masakazu Katsura **W:** Masakazu Katsura
5 ❑ Feb 1999 Cover: 2.50 **NM** value: **Cover or less**
Dangeous Love, Part 5; Dangerous Love **A:** Masakazu Katsura **W:** Masakazu Katsura
6 ❑ Mar 1999 Cover: 2.50 **NM** value: **Cover or less**
Dangeous Love, Part 6; Dangerous Love **A:** Masakazu Katsura **W:** Masakazu Katsura
7 ❑ Apr 1999 Cover: 2.50 **NM** value: **Cover or less**
The Eyes of a Stranger, Part 1; Dangerous Love; Eyes of a Stranger, Part 1 **A:** Masakazu Katsura **W:** Masakazu Katsura
8 ❑ May 1999 Cover: 2.50 **NM** value: **Cover or less**
The Eyes of a Stranger, Part 2; The Eyes Of A Stranger; Eyes of a Stranger, Part 2 **A:** Masakazu Katsura **W:** Masakazu Katsura
9 ❑ Jun 1999 Cover: 2.50 **NM** value: **Cover or less**
The Eyes Of A Stranger, Part 3; The Eyes Of A Stranger; Eyes of a Stranger, Part 3 **A:** Masakazu Katsura **W:** Masakazu Katsura
10 ❑ Jul 1999 Cover: 2.50 **NM** value: **Cover or less**
The Eyes of a Stranger, Part 4; The Eyes Of A Stranger; Eyes of a Stranger, Part 4 **A:** Masakazu Katsura **W:** Masakazu Katsura
11 ❑ Aug 1999 Cover: 2.50 **NM** value: **Cover or less**
The Eyes Of A Stranger, Part 5; The Eyes Of A Stranger; Eyes of a Stranger, Part 5 **A:** Masakazu Katsura **W:** Masakazu Katsura
12 ❑ Sep 1999 Cover: 2.50 **NM** value: **Cover or less**
The Eyes Of A Stranger, Part 6; The Eyes Of A Stranger
13 ❑ Oct 1999 Cover: 2.50 **NM** value: **Cover or less**
The Awakening
14 ❑ Nov 1999 Cover: 2.50 **NM** value: **Cover or less**
The Awakening
15 ❑ Dec 1999 Cover: 2.50 **NM** value: **Cover or less**
The Awakening
16 ❑ Jan 2000 Cover: 2.50 **NM** value: **Cover or less**
The Awakening
17 ❑ Feb 2000 Cover: 2.50 **NM** value: **Cover or less**
The Awakening
18 ❑ Mar 2000 Cover: 2.50 **NM** value: **Cover or less**
The Awakening
19 ❑ Apr 2000 Cover: 2.50 **NM** value: **Cover or less**
The Awakening
20 ❑ May 2000 Cover: 2.50 **NM** value: **Cover or less**
Sudden Death, Part 1
21 ❑ Jun 2000 Cover: 2.50 **NM** value: **Cover or less**
Sudden Death, Part 2
22 ❑ Jul 2000 Cover: 2.50 **NM** value: **Cover or less**
Sudden Death, Part 3
23 ❑ Aug 2000 Cover: 2.50 **NM** value: **Cover or less**
Sudden Death, Part 4
24 ❑ Sep 2000 Cover: 2.50 **NM** value: **Cover or less**
Sudden Death, Part 5
SE 1❑ Oct 2000 Cover: 3.99 **NM** value: **Cover or less**

SHADOWLAND — Fantagraphics

1 ❑ b&w Cover: 2.25 **NM** value: **Cover or less**
2 ❑ b&w Cover: 2.25 **NM** value: **Cover or less**

SHADOWLINE SPECIAL — Image

1 ❑ **NM** value: **1.00**

SHADOWLORD/TRIUNE — Jet City

1 ❑ Win 1986 Cover: 1.50 **NM** value: **Cover or less**

SHADOWMAN — Valiant

New Orleans is a city rich in music and mystery. Jazz musician Jack Boniface found himself right in the middle of both when he goes home with the wrong woman one night. She attempted to open up his soul to the darkness, though she was forced to flee an unseen assailant before she could finish her task. Nevertheless, Boniface's live has been forever changed.

Now, late at night, Jack dons a simple carnival mask "so the demons don't find him" and carries out a fight against evil. Born of darkness, the night seems to give him strength, even as it turns him into someone else...Shadowman.

0 ❑ Apr 1994 Cover: 2.50 **NM** value: **Cover or less**
Circ: CapCity orders: **43,450**
★ Origin of Shadowman II (Jack Boniface), Shadowman I (Maxim St. James).
0/GO❑ Apr 1994 **NM** value: **4.00**
• Gold edition.
0/SC❑ Apr 1994 Cover: 3.50 **NM** value: **3.95**
chromium cover. ★ Origin of Shadowman II (Jack Boniface), Shadowman I (Maxim St. James).
1 ❑ May 1992 Cover: 2.50 **NM** value: **3.00**
Circ: CapCity orders: **11,500** • **CGC:** 4 graded, best 9.8
A: David Lapham **W:** Jim Shooter; Steve Englehart ★ Origin of Shadowman II (Jack Boniface). ★ 1st Appearance of Shadowman II (Jack Boniface).
2 ❑ Jun 1992 Cover: 2.50 **NM** value: **3.00**
Circ: CapCity orders: **8,100**
3 ❑ Jul 1992 Cover: 2.50 **NM** value: **Cover or less**
Circ: CapCity orders: **9,700**
4 ❑ Aug 1992 Cover: 2.50 **NM** value: **Cover or less**
Circ: CapCity orders: **25,750**
Unity, Part 6 • Unity **A:** Frank Miller(cover) **C:** Frank Miller
5 ❑ Sep 1992 Cover: 2.50 **NM** value: **Cover or less**
Circ: CapCity orders: **30,600**
Unity, Part 14 • Unity **A:** David Lapham **C:** Walt Simonson **W:** Jim Shooter; David Lapham; Bob Layton
6 ❑ Oct 1992 Cover: 2.50 **NM** value: **Cover or less**
Circ: CapCity orders: **17,100**
W: s
7 ❑ Nov 1992 Cover: 2.50 **NM** value: **Cover or less**
Circ: CapCity orders: **17,175**
8 ❑ Dec 1992 Cover: 2.50 **NM** value: **Cover or less**
Circ: CapCity orders: **17,600**
★ 1st Appearance of Master Darque. ★ Versus Master Darque.
9 ❑ Jan 1993 Cover: 2.50 **NM** value: **Cover or less**
Circ: CapCity orders: **17,900**
10 ❑ Feb 1993 Cover: 2.50 **NM** value: **Cover or less**
Circ: CapCity orders: **21,300**
11 ❑ Mar 1993 Cover: 2.50 **NM** value: **Cover or less**
Circ: CapCity orders: **32,300**
12 ❑ Apr 1993 Cover: 2.50 **NM** value: **Cover or less**
Circ: CapCity orders: **39,000**
Dark Rapture **A:** Bob Hall **W:** Bob Hall ★ Versus Master Darque.
13 ❑ May 1993 Cover: 2.50 **NM** value: **Cover or less**
Circ: CapCity orders: **45,900**
14 ❑ Jun 1993 Cover: 2.50 **NM** value: **Cover or less**
Circ: CapCity orders: **57,400**
Crosses **A:** Bob Hall **W:** Bob Hall
15 ❑ Jul 1993 Cover: 2.50 **NM** value: **Cover or less**
Circ: CapCity orders: **71,600**
April Visions **A:** Bob Hall **W:** Bob Hall
16 ❑ Aug 1993 Cover: 2.50 **NM** value: **3.00**
Circ: CapCity orders: **61,000**
★ 1st Appearance of Doctor Mirage.
17 ❑ Sep 1993 Cover: 2.50 **NM** value: **Cover or less**
Circ: CapCity orders: **56,900**
• Serial number contest★ Appearance of Archer & Armstrong.
18 ❑ Oct 1993 Cover: 2.50 **NM** value: **Cover or less**
Circ: CapCity orders: **46,200**
19 ❑ Nov 1993 Cover: 2.50 **NM** value: **Cover or less**
Circ: CapCity orders: **53,425**
• Aerosmith★ Appearance of Aerosmith.
20 ❑ Dec 1993 Cover: 2.50 **NM** value: **Cover or less**
Circ: CapCity orders: **37,400**
21 ❑ Jan 1994 Cover: 2.50 **NM** value: **Cover or less**
Circ: CapCity orders: **33,500**
★ Versus Master Darque.
22 ❑ Feb 1994 Cover: 2.50 **NM** value: **Cover or less**
Circ: CapCity orders: **29,550**
23 ❑ Mar 1994 Cover: 2.50 **NM** value: **Cover or less**
Circ: CapCity orders: **24,350**
★ Appearance of Doctor Mirage.
24 ❑ Apr 1994 Cover: 2.50 **NM** value: **Cover or less**
Circ: CapCity orders: **22,075**
25 ❑ Apr 1994 Cover: 2.50 **NM** value: **Cover or less**
Circ: CapCity orders: **25,925**
• trading card
26 ❑ Jun 1994 Cover: 2.50 **NM** value: **Cover or less**
Circ: CapCity orders: **17,225**
27 ❑ Aug 1994 Cover: 2.50 **NM** value: **Cover or less**
Circ: CapCity orders: **16,475**
28 ❑ Sep 1994 Cover: 2.50 **NM** value: **Cover or less**
Circ: CapCity orders: **15,600**
29 ❑ Oct 1994 Cover: 2.50 **NM** value: **Cover or less**
Circ: CapCity orders: **21,150**
The Chaos Effect: Beta, Part 1 • Chaos Effect
30 ❑ Nov 1994 Cover: 2.50 **NM** value: **Cover or less**
Circ: CapCity orders: **13,775**
31 ❑ Dec 1994 Cover: 2.50 **NM** value: **Cover or less**
Circ: CapCity orders: **12,325**
32 ❑ Jan 1994 Cover: 2.50 **NM** value: **Cover or less**
Circ: CapCity orders: **11,675**
33 ❑ Feb 1994 Cover: 2.50 **NM** value: **Cover or less**
Circ: CapCity orders: **10,550**
34 ❑ Mar 1994 Cover: 2.50 **NM** value: **Cover or less**
Circ: CapCity orders: **9,100**
35 ❑ Apr 1995 Cover: 2.50 **NM** value: **Cover or less**
Circ: CapCity orders: **8,200**
36 ❑ May 1995 Cover: 2.50 **NM** value: **Cover or less**
Circ: CapCity orders: **7,300**
37 ❑ Jun 1995 Cover: 2.50 **NM** value: **Cover or less**
Circ: CapCity orders: **6,550**
A: Bob Hall
38 ❑ Jul 1995 Cover: 2.50 **NM** value: **Cover or less**
Circ: CapCity orders: **6,325**
A: Bob Hall
39 ❑ Aug 1995 Cover: 2.50 **NM** value: **Cover or less**
Circ: CapCity orders: **5,900**
A: Bob Hall
40 ❑ Sep 1995 Cover: 2.50 **NM** value: **Cover or less**
Circ: CapCity orders: **5,825**
A: Bob Hall
41 ❑ Oct 1995 Cover: 2.50 **NM** value: **Cover or less**
Circ: CapCity orders: **5,600**
A: Bob Hall
42 ❑ Nov 1995 Cover: 2.50 **NM** value: **Cover or less**
Circ: CapCity orders: **5,350**
A: Bob Hall
43 ❑ Dec 1995 Cover: 2.50 **NM** value: **Cover or less**
Circ: CapCity orders: **4,625**
A: Bob Hall
Bk 1❑ Cover: 9.95 **NM** value: **Cover or less**
YB 1❑ Dec 1994 Cover: 3.95 **NM** value: **Cover or less**
Circ: CapCity orders: **100,350**
• Yearbook 1.

SHADOWMAN (VOL. 2) — Acclaim

1 ❑ Mar 1997 Cover: 2.50 **NM** value: **Cover or less**
Circ: Diamd. preorders: **37,257**
Deadside, Part 1 **A:** Ashley Wood **W:** Garth Ennis
1/SC❑ Mar 1997 Cover: 2.50 **NM** value: **Cover or less**
Painted cover. Deadside, Part 1 **A:** Ashley Wood **W:** Garth Ennis
2 ❑ Apr 1997 Cover: 2.50 **NM** value: **Cover or less**
Circ: Diamd. preorders: **27,260**
Deadside, Part 2 **A:** Ashley Wood **W:** Garth Ennis
3 ❑ May 1997 Cover: 2.50 **NM** value: **Cover or less**
Circ: Diamd. preorders: **24,257**
Deadside, Part 3 **A:** Ashley Wood **W:** Garth Ennis
4 ❑ Jun 1997 Cover: 2.50 **NM** value: **Cover or less**
Circ: Diamd. preorders: **21,090**
Deadside, Part 4 **A:** Ashley Wood **W:** Garth Ennis
5 ❑ Jul 1997 Cover: 2.50 **NM** value: **Cover or less**
Circ: Diamd. preorders: **18,176**
5/Ash❑ Mar 1997, b&w **NM** value: **1.00**
no cover price. • preview of upcoming issue
6 ❑ Aug 1997 Cover: 2.50 **NM** value: **Cover or less**
Circ: Diamd. preorders: **17,613**
7 ❑ Sep 1997 Cover: 2.50 **NM** value: **Cover or less**
Circ: Diamd. preorders: **15,483**
8 ❑ Oct 1997 Cover: 2.50 **NM** value: **Cover or less**
Circ: Diamd. preorders: **14,018**
9 ❑ Nov 1997 Cover: 2.50 **NM** value: **Cover or less**
Circ: Diamd. preorders: **12,470**
10 ❑ Dec 1997 Cover: 2.50 **NM** value: **Cover or less**
Circ: Diamd. preorders: **11,308**
11 ❑ Jan 1998 Cover: 2.50 **NM** value: **Cover or less**
Circ: Diamd. preorders: **10,145**
12 ❑ Feb 1998 Cover: 2.50 **NM** value: **Cover or less**
Circ: Diamd. preorders: **9,324**
13 ❑ Mar 1998 Cover: 2.50 **NM** value: **Cover or less**
Circ: Diamd. preorders: **8,697**
• Goat Month
14 ❑ Apr 1998 Cover: 2.50 **NM** value: **Cover or less**
Circ: Diamd. preorders: **8,074**
15 ❑ Jan 1998 Cover: 2.50 **NM** value: **Cover or less**
Circ: Diamd. preorders: **7,409**
no cover date. • indicia says Jan
16 ❑ Feb 1998 Cover: 2.50 **NM** value: **Cover or less**
Circ: Diamd. preorders: **8,543**
no cover date. • indicia says Feb
Ash 1❑ Nov 1996, b&w **NM** value: **1.00**
no cover price. • preview of upcoming series
Bk 1❑ Cover: 7.95 **NM** value: **Cover or less**

SHADOWMAN (VOL. 3) — Acclaim

1 ❑ Jul 1999 Cover: 3.95 **NM** value: **Cover or less**
Circ: Diamd. preorders: **5,915**
Mission Unspeakable **A:** Matt Broome; Ryan Benjamin **W:** Andy Lanning; Dan Abnett
2 ❑ Aug 1999 Cover: 3.95 **NM** value: **Cover or less**
Circ: Diamd. preorders: **4,784**
3 ❑ Sep 1999 Cover: 3.95 **NM** value: **Cover or less**
Circ: Diamd. preorders: **4,907**
4 ❑ Oct 1999 Cover: 3.95 **NM** value: **Cover or less**
Circ: Diamd. preorders: **5,467**
Soul Survivor **A:** Ryan Benjamin **W:** Andy Lanning; Dan Abnett

SHADOW MASTER — Psygnosis / Manga

0 ❑ **NM** value: **1.00**
• Preview

SHADOWMASTERS — Marvel

1 ❑ Oct 1989 Cover: 3.95 **NM** value: **4.00**
Circ: CapCity orders: **19,450**
Shadows Of The Past **A:** Dan Lawlis **W:** Carl Potts ★ Origin of Shadowmasters.
2 ❑ Nov 1989 Cover: 3.95 **NM** value: **4.00**
Circ: CapCity orders: **15,450**
A: Dan Lawlis **W:** Carl Potts
3 ❑ Dec 1989 Cover: 3.95 **NM** value: **4.00**
Circ: CapCity orders: **15,250**
A: Dan Lawlis **W:** Carl Potts
4 ❑ Jan 1990 Cover: 3.95 **NM** value: **4.00**
Circ: CapCity orders: **14,550**
Into The Void **A:** Dan Lawlis **W:** Carl Potts

SHADOWMEN — Trident

All issues are adults only.
1 ❑ b&w Cover: 2.25 **NM** value: **Cover or less**
2 ❑ b&w Cover: 2.25 **NM** value: **Cover or less**

SHADOW, THE (MOVIE ADAPTATION) — Dark Horse

1 ❑ Jun 1994 Cover: 2.50 **NM** value: **Cover or less**
Circ: CapCity orders: **14,550**
2 ❑ Jul 1994 Cover: 2.50 **NM** value: **Cover or less**
Circ: CapCity orders: **9,450**

SHADOW OF THE BATMAN — DC

1 ❑ Dec 1985 Cover: 1.75 **NM** value: **3.00**
Circ: CapCity orders: **7,900**
By Death's Eerie Light!; The Master Plan of Dr. Phosphorus **A:** Walt Simonson **W:** Steve Englehart
2 ❑ Jan 1986 Cover: 1.75 **NM** value: **2.00**
Circ: CapCity orders: **6,750**
3 ❑ Feb 1986 Cover: 1.75 **NM** value: **2.00**
Circ: CapCity orders: **7,300**
4 ❑ Mar 1986 Cover: 1.75 **NM** value: **2.00**
Circ: CapCity orders: **7,150**
5 ❑ Apr 1986 Cover: 1.75 **NM** value: **2.00**
Circ: CapCity orders: **6,950**

SHADOW OF THE TORTURER, THE (GENE WOLFE'S...) — Innovation

1 ❑ ca. 1991 Cover: 2.50 **NM** value: **Cover or less**
Circ: CapCity orders: **3,870**
Resurrection and Death **A:** Ted Naifeh **W:** Scott Rockwell
2 ❑ ca. 1991 Cover: 2.50 **NM** value: **Cover or less**
Circ: CapCity orders: **2,940**

CGC-graded: Multiply prices above by **33 for 9.9 M • 16 for 9.8 NM/M • 7 for 9.6 NM+ • 5 for 9.4 NM • 2.5 for 9.2 NM- • 1.5 for 9.0 VF/NM**

3 ❑ ca. 1991 Cover: 2.50 **NM** value: **Cover or less**
Circ: CapCity orders: **2,485**
4 ❑ ca. 1992 Cover: 2.50 **NM** value: **Cover or less**
Circ: CapCity orders: **2,235**
5 ❑ ca. 1992 Cover: 2.50 **NM** value: **Cover or less**
6 ❑ ca. 1992 Cover: 2.50 **NM** value: **Cover or less**

SHADOW PLAY — Whitman

1 ❑ ca. 1982 Cover: 0.60 **NM** value: **3.00**
📖 Monster Clock, the Bracelet, Time for a Change, My Granddaughter will Haunt You!; The Sad Cavalier

SHADOW RAVEN — Poc-It

1 ❑ Jun 1995 Cover: 2.50 **NM** value: **Cover or less**
📖 Fangs Of The Serpent **A:** John Berry **W:** Frank Zanca ★ 1st Appearance of Shadow Raven.

SHADOW REIGNS — Aix C.C.

0 ❑ Dec 1997 Cover: 2.95 **NM** value: **Cover or less**

SHADOW RIDERS — Marvel

1 ❑ Jun 1992 Cover: 2.50 **NM** value: **Cover or less**
Circ: CapCity orders: **55,600**
Embossed cover. 📖 The Screaming Man! **A:** Ross Dearsley **W:** Brian Williamson; John Freeman ★ 1st Appearance of Shadow Riders.
2 ❑ Jul 1992 Cover: 1.75 **NM** value: **Cover or less**
Circ: CapCity orders: **26,700**
3 ❑ Aug 1992 Cover: 1.75 **NM** value: **Cover or less**
Circ: CapCity orders: **17,800**
4 ❑ Sep 1992 Cover: 1.75 **NM** value: **Cover or less**
Circ: CapCity orders: **12,300**

SHADOWS & LIGHT — Marvel

This anthology title boasts such creators as Brian Stelfreeze, Bernie Wrightson, and Steve Ditko telling short stories of Marvel characters, with the artists working only in black-and-white.

While most black-and-white comics are done as such for cost reasons, this is a great example of how, in some cases, it actually can make for more effective storytelling. Stelfreeze mimics the high-contrast approach of Frank Miller's Sin City, giving a dark, clean edge to his Daredevil story "Devils & Angels." Stelfreeze, on the other hand, uses a finished, painted look on his Black Widow story, "Free Fall," giving the flashback story a sort of "old movie" feel which complements it beautifully.

1 ❑ Feb 1998, b&w Cover: 2.99 **NM** value: **Cover or less**
Circ: Diamd. preorders: **33,561**
📖 Free Fall; A Man's Reach; Devils & Angels **A:** Brian Stelfreeze; Steve Ditko; Bernie Wrightson; Gene Ha **W:** Steve Ditko; Bernie Wrightson; Len Wein; Gerard Jones; Ron Marz
2 ❑ Apr 1998, b&w Cover: 2.99 **NM** value: **Cover or less**
Circ: Diamd. preorders: **21,791**
3 ❑ Jul 1998, b&w Cover: 2.99 **NM** value: **Cover or less**
Circ: Diamd. preorders: **16,086**

SHADOW'S EDGE, THE — Lion

1 ❑ Cover: 3.95 **NM** value: **Cover or less**

SHADOWS FALL — DC / Vertigo

1 ❑ Nov 1994 Cover: 2.95 **NM** value: **Cover or less**
Circ: CapCity orders: **13,300**
📖 Absence Makes The Heart **A:** John Van Fleet **W:** John Ney Rieber
2 ❑ Dec 1994 Cover: 2.95 **NM** value: **Cover or less**
Circ: CapCity orders: **9,900**
📖 Toys for the Play of Ghosts **A:** John Van Fleet **W:** John Ney Rieber
3 ❑ Jan 1995 Cover: 2.95 **NM** value: **Cover or less**
Circ: CapCity orders: **8,500**
📖 Windows for the Dark **A:** John Van Fleet **W:** John Ney Rieber
4 ❑ Feb 1995 Cover: 2.95 **NM** value: **Cover or less**
Circ: CapCity orders: **8,125**
📖 Echoes of Who You Are **A:** John Van Fleet **W:** John Ney Rieber
5 ❑ Mar 1995 Cover: 2.95 **NM** value: **Cover or less**
Circ: CapCity orders: **7,400**
📖 Dreamling Alice **A:** John Van Fleet **W:** John Ney Rieber
6 ❑ Apr 1995 Cover: 2.95 **NM** value: **Cover or less**
Circ: CapCity orders: **6,800**
📖 Alone With Mirrors **A:** John Van Fleet **W:** John Ney Rieber

SHADOWS FROM BEYOND — Charlton

50 ❑ Oct 1966 Cover: 0.12 **NM** value: **25.00**
• **CGC:** 1 graded, best 9.2

SHADOWS FROM THE GRAVE — Renegade

1 ❑ b&w Cover: 2.00 **NM** value: **Cover or less**
2 ❑ Mar 1988, b&w Cover: 2.00 **NM** value: **Cover or less**
📖 Blood Will Tell; Creeping Up with the Joneses!; Burial Rites; Epitaph **A:** David Day **W:** Kevin McConnell

SHADOW SLASHER — Pocket Change

1 ❑ Cover: 2.50 **NM** value: **Cover or less**
Circ: CapCity orders: **3,035**
📖 Blood of The City **A:** Scott Shriver **W:** Bob Dixon ★ 1st Appearance of Riplash.

SHADOW SLAYER — Eternity

0 ❑ Cover: 1.95 **NM** value: **Cover or less**

SHADOWSTAR — Shadowstar

1 ❑ Cover: 1.50 **NM** value: **2.00**
A: W.E. Savage **W:** W.E. Savage; Larry Shapiro
2 ❑ Nov 1985 Cover: 1.50 **NM** value: **2.00**
A: W.E. Savage **W:** W.E. Savage; Larry Shapiro
3 ❑ Dec 1985 Cover: 1.50 **NM** value: **2.00**
• first Slave Labor comic book

SHADOW STATE — Broadway

1 ❑ Dec 1995 Cover: 2.50 **NM** value: **Cover or less**
enhanced cardstock cover. 📖 BloodS.C.R.E.A.M.: Scream 'em Down; Till Death Do Us Part: Image Isn't Everything, Part 1; Fatale: Prelude to a Kiss • BloodS.C.R.E.A.M., Fatale **A:** Dave Cockrum; Hoang Nguyen; Stefano Gaudiano **W:** Joe James; Jim Shooter; James S. Jackson-Weiss III; Janet Jackson; Pauline Weiss ★ 1st Appearance of BloodS.C.R.E.A.M..
2 ❑ Jan 1996 Cover: 2.50 **NM** value: **Cover or less**
📖 Till Death Do Us Part: Image Isn't Everything, Part 2 • Till Death Do Us Part; Fatale
3 ❑ Mar 1996 Cover: 2.50 **NM** value: **Cover or less**
• Till Death Do Us Part
4 ❑ Apr 1996 Cover: 2.50 **NM** value: **Cover or less**
• Till Death Do Us Part
5 ❑ May 1996 Cover: 2.50 **NM** value: **Cover or less**
• Till Death Do Us Part
6 ❑ Jun 1996 Cover: 2.95 **NM** value: **Cover or less**
7 ❑ Jul 1996 Cover: 2.95 **NM** value: **Cover or less**
Ash 1❑Sep 1995, b&w **NM** value: **1.00**
• giveaway preview edition. • Till Death Do Us Part, Fatale

SHADOW STRIKES!, THE — DC

1 ❑ Sep 1989 Cover: 1.75 **NM** value: **2.50**
Circ: CapCity orders: **19,550**
📖 Death's Head **A:** Eduardo Barreto **W:** Gerard Jones
2 ❑ Oct 1989 Cover: 1.75 **NM** value: **2.25**
Circ: CapCity orders: **14,650**
3 ❑ Nov 1989 Cover: 1.75 **NM** value: **2.00**
Circ: CapCity orders: **13,050**
4 ❑ Dec 1989 Cover: 1.75 **NM** value: **2.00**
Circ: CapCity orders: **12,950**
5 ❑ Jan 1990 Cover: 1.75 **NM** value: **2.00**
Circ: CapCity orders: **13,800**
★ Appearance of Doc Savage.
6 ❑ Feb 1990 Cover: 1.75 **NM** value: **2.00**
Circ: CapCity orders: **13,050**
★ Appearance of Doc Savage.
7 ❑ Mar 1990 Cover: 1.75 **NM** value: **2.00**
Circ: CapCity orders: **12,200**
8 ❑ Apr 1990 Cover: 1.75 **NM** value: **2.00**
Circ: CapCity orders: **11,400**
★ Versus Shiwan Khan.
9 ❑ May 1990 Cover: 1.75 **NM** value: **2.00**
Circ: CapCity orders: **11,200**
★ Versus Shiwan Khan.
10 ❑ Jun 1990 Cover: 1.75 **NM** value: **2.00**
Circ: CapCity orders: **10,900**
★ Versus Shiwan Khan.
11 ❑ Aug 1990 Cover: 1.75 **NM** value: **2.00**
Circ: CapCity orders: **10,300**
12 ❑ Sep 1990 Cover: 1.75 **NM** value: **2.00**
Circ: CapCity orders: **9,450**
13 ❑ Oct 1990 Cover: 1.75 **NM** value: **2.00**
Circ: CapCity orders: **8,950**
14 ❑ Dec 1990 Cover: 1.75 **NM** value: **2.00**
Circ: CapCity orders: **8,300**
15 ❑ Jan 1991 Cover: 1.75 **NM** value: **2.00**
Circ: CapCity orders: **8,150**
16 ❑ Feb 1991 Cover: 1.75 **NM** value: **2.00**
Circ: CapCity orders: **7,800**
17 ❑ Mar 1991 Cover: 1.75 **NM** value: **2.00**
Circ: CapCity orders: **7,150**
18 ❑ Apr 1991 Cover: 1.75 **NM** value: **2.00**
Circ: CapCity orders: **6,650**
19 ❑ May 1991 Cover: 2.00 **NM** value: **Cover or less**
Circ: CapCity orders: **6,500**
20 ❑ Jun 1991 Cover: 2.00 **NM** value: **Cover or less**
Circ: CapCity orders: **6,450**
21 ❑ Jul 1991 Cover: 2.00 **NM** value: **Cover or less**
Circ: CapCity orders: **6,350**
22 ❑ Aug 1991 Cover: 2.00 **NM** value: **Cover or less**
Circ: CapCity orders: **6,450**
23 ❑ Sep 1991 Cover: 2.00 **NM** value: **Cover or less**
Circ: CapCity orders: **6,150**
24 ❑ Oct 1991 Cover: 2.00 **NM** value: **Cover or less**
Circ: CapCity orders: **6,000**
25 ❑ Nov 1991 Cover: 2.00 **NM** value: **Cover or less**
Circ: CapCity orders: **5,750**
26 ❑ Dec 1991 Cover: 2.00 **NM** value: **Cover or less**
Circ: CapCity orders: **5,700**
27 ❑ Jan 1992 Cover: 2.00 **NM** value: **Cover or less**
Circ: CapCity orders: **5,450**
28 ❑ Feb 1992 Cover: 2.00 **NM** value: **Cover or less**
Circ: CapCity orders: **5,100**
29 ❑ Mar 1992 Cover: 2.00 **NM** value: **Cover or less**
Circ: CapCity orders: **5,000**
30 ❑ Apr 1992 Cover: 2.00 **NM** value: **Cover or less**
Circ: CapCity orders: **5,150**
📖 Disillusions & Illusions
31 ❑ May 1992 Cover: 2.00 **NM** value: **Cover or less**
Circ: CapCity orders: **5,150**
📖 Disillusions & Illusions
Anl 1❑Dec 1989 Cover: 3.50 **NM** value: **Cover or less**
Circ: CapCity orders: **12,300**
A: Dan Spiegle

SHADOWTOWN — Iconografix

1 ❑ Cover: 2.50 **NM** value: **Cover or less**
📖 Break-Out **A:** Terence Anthony **W:** Terence Anthony

SHADOWTOWN: BLACK FIST RISING — Madheart

1 ❑ b&w Cover: 2.50 **NM** value: **Cover or less**

SHADOW WAR OF HAWKMAN, THE — DC

Hawkman was always one of DC's most promising characters, an alien policeman operating with his wife on Earth where they chase down bad guys with a combination of brains, wings, and super-scientific gadgetry.

This 1985 mini-series was an attempt to focus Hawkman's legend and set the groundwork for years to come. Here Hawkman was called upon to prevent the invasion of Earth. This invasion began in the shadows with five Thanagarians appearing out of nowhere to force a petty thief to try to steal Hawkman's anti-gravity device. Hawkman was able to stop that particular theft from occurring, but while he was away, a second squad attacked his wife, Hawkwoman. He returned to help — only to find her image burned into a wall as if by a nuclear explosion!

1 ❑ May 1985 Cover: 0.75 **NM** value: **1.50**
Circ: CapCity orders: **14,000**
📖 The Shadow War of Hawkman **A:** Richard Howell; Alfredo Alcala **W:** Tony Isabella
2 ❑ Jun 1985 Cover: 0.75 **NM** value: **1.25**
Circ: CapCity orders: **11,200**
📖 Fallen Angels **A:** Richard Howell **W:** Tony Isabella
3 ❑ Jul 1985 Cover: 0.75 **NM** value: **1.25**
Circ: CapCity orders: **11,400**
📖 My Worlds Opposed **A:** Richard Howell **W:** Tony Isabella ★ Appearance of Elongated Man. ★ Appearance of Aquaman.
4 ❑ Aug 1985 Cover: 0.75 **NM** value: **1.25**
Circ: CapCity orders: **12,300**
📖 No Sound of Clashing Wars **A:** Richard Howell **W:** Tony Isabella

SHADOW WARRIOR — Gateway

1 ❑ b&w Cover: 1.95 **NM** value: **Cover or less**
A: Bart Ciancone; Terry Krock **W:** Terry Krock

SHAIANA — Express / Entity

1 ❑ Cover: 3.75 **NM** value: **Cover or less**
Circ: CapCity orders: **6,370**
enhanced cover.
2 ❑ Cover: 2.50 **NM** value: **Cover or less**
3 ❑ Cover: 2.50 **NM** value: **Cover or less**
A: Efren Anacleto **W:** Eric Duen

SHALOMAN — Mark 1

1 ❑ b&w Cover: 1.75 **NM** value: **Cover or less**
2 ❑ b&w Cover: 1.75 **NM** value: **Cover or less**
3 ❑ b&w Cover: 1.75 **NM** value: **Cover or less**
4 ❑ b&w Cover: 1.75 **NM** value: **Cover or less**
5 ❑ b&w Cover: 1.75 **NM** value: **Cover or less**
6 ❑ b&w Cover: 1.75 **NM** value: **Cover or less**
7 ❑ b&w Cover: 1.75 **NM** value: **Cover or less**
8 ❑ b&w Cover: 1.75 **NM** value: **Cover or less**
9 ❑ b&w Cover: 1.75 **NM** value: **Cover or less**

SHAMAN — Continuity

0 ❑ **NM** value: **2.00**
Circ: CapCity orders: **3,050**
One-shot.

SHAMAN'S TEARS — Image

Shaman's Tears is Mike Grell's ambitious debut at Image Comics. As the Soviet Union fell apart, a lone cosmonaut was left stranded in space until his new countrymen could find a way to get him down. The cosmonaut had been carrying out advanced genetic experiments, recombining the DNA from many different creatures in order to form new life forms. Under the cover of a brief radio blackout, strangers enter the cosmonaut's ship. They kill him and steal the experiment. Back on Earth, the life forms mature — from half-human, half-monkey space mechanics, to bio-engineered soldiers and warriors. The only question is: Can they be controlled?

Josh Brand, returning home to the Indian reservation he grew up on, will soon have cause to worry about this. He is destined to be an important player in the future of both his tribe — and the world.

0 ❑ Dec 1995 Cover: 1.95 **NM** value: **2.50**
• says 1996 indicia; meant 1995 **A:** Mike Grell; Brian Snoddy **W:** Mike Grell
1 ❑ May 1993 Cover: 2.50 **NM** value: **Cover or less**
foil cover. 📖 Warcry **A:** Mike Grell **W:** Mike Grell
1/PL❑May 1993 Cover: 2.50 **NM** value: **4.00**
• Platinum edition. **A:** Mike Grell
2 ❑ Jul 1993 Cover: 2.50 **NM** value: **Cover or less**
cover says Aug. • indicia says Jul **A:** Mike Grell **W:** Mike Grell
3 ❑ Nov 1994 Cover: 1.95 **NM** value: **Cover or less**
Circ: CapCity orders: **23,525**
A: Mike Grell **W:** Mike Grell
3/Ash❑ **NM** value: **3.00**
• Limited "ashcan" run of Shaman's Tears #3 **A:** Mike Grell **W:** Mike Grell

Other grades: Multiply prices above by **1.5 for Mint • 2/3 for Very Fine • 1/3 for Fine • 1/5 for Very Good • 1/8 for Good**

4 ❑ Dec 1994 Cover: 1.95 **NM** value: **Cover or less**
Circ: CapCity orders: **20,675**
• Title moves back to Image **A:** Mike Grell **W:** Mike Grell

5 ❑ Jan 1995 Cover: 1.95 **NM** value: **Cover or less**
Circ: CapCity orders: **18,775**
A: Mike Grell **W:** Mike Grell

6 ❑ Feb 1995 Cover: 1.95 **NM** value: **Cover or less**
Circ: CapCity orders: **15,500**
A: Mike Grell **W:** Mike Grell

7 ❑ May 1995 Cover: 1.95 **NM** value: **Cover or less**
Circ: CapCity orders: **14,300**
A: Mike Grell **W:** Mike Grell

8 ❑ May 1995 Cover: 1.95 **NM** value: **Cover or less**
Circ: CapCity orders: **13,225**
A: Mike Grell **W:** Mike Grell

9 ❑ Jun 1995 Cover: 1.95 **NM** value: **Cover or less**
Circ: CapCity orders: **12,375**
A: Mike Grell **W:** Mike Grell

10 ❑ Jul 1995 Cover: 1.95 **NM** value: **Cover or less**
Circ: CapCity orders: **12,125**
A: Mike Grell **W:** Mike Grell

11 ❑ Aug 1995 Cover: 2.50 **NM** value: **Cover or less**
Circ: CapCity orders: **11,400**
A: Mike Grell **W:** Mike Grell

12 ❑ Aug 1995 Cover: 2.50 **NM** value: **Cover or less**
A: Mike Grell **W:** Mike Grell

SHAMBALLA — Fleetway-Quality

Bk 1❑ Cover: 8.95 **NM** value: **Cover or less**
• Trade Paperback. • Judge Anderson

SHANDA THE PANDA — Mu

Mike Curtis' Shanda the Panda became one of the longer-running anthropomorphic soap operas. Theater manager Shanda is, of course, a panda, and her co-workers are likewise funny animals.

While early issues are Archie-like with their stories of dating trials and tribulations, Curtis soon brings more adult themes to the storyline. Shanda falls in love with a married raccoon, and their affair is greatly against the wishes of her parents, who insist on an arranged marriage to another panda. Here Curtis actually works animal biology in as a plot point, as Shanda fears falling under the spell of the unwanted suitor's pheromones. Later issues have some nudity and sexual content (if not overly graphic) and follow Shanda's bisexual explorations with her grasshopper best friend Terri.

A bit more cartoony than Omaha the Cat Dancer but in the same soap operatic vein, Shanda built a considerable following in furry comics fandom. And like Omaha, Shanda had been published by several different companies over the years, starting at Mu before moving to Antarctic, Vision, and finally Shanda Fantasy Arts. —JJM

1 ❑ May 1992, b&w Cover: 2.50 **NM** value: **Cover or less**

SHANDA THE PANDA (2ND SERIES) — Antarctic

#	Date	Cover	NM value
1	❑ Jun 1993	Cover: 2.50	**NM** value: **Cover or less**
2	❑ Aug 1993	Cover: 2.50	**NM** value: **Cover or less**
3	❑ Oct 1993	Cover: 2.75	**NM** value: **Cover or less**
4	❑ Dec 1993	Cover: 2.75	**NM** value: **Cover or less**
5	❑ Aug 1994	Cover: 2.75	**NM** value: **Cover or less**
6	❑ Nov 1994	Cover: 2.75	**NM** value: **Cover or less**
7	❑ Jan 1995	Cover: 2.75	**NM** value: **Cover or less**
8	❑ Feb 1995	Cover: 2.75	**NM** value: **Cover or less**
9	❑ May 1995	Cover: 2.75	**NM** value: **Cover or less**
10	❑ Jul 1995	Cover: 2.75	**NM** value: **Cover or less**
11	❑ Sep 1995	Cover: 2.75	**NM** value: **Cover or less**
12	❑ Nov 1995	Cover: 2.75	**NM** value: **Cover or less**
13	❑ Jan 1996	Cover: 2.75	**NM** value: **Cover or less**
14	❑ Mar 1996	Cover: 2.75	**NM** value: **Cover or less**

SHANDA THE PANDA (2ND SERIES) — Vision

15 ❑ May 1996 Cover: 2.75 **NM** value: **Cover or less**
16 ❑ Jul 1996 Cover: 1.95 **NM** value: **Cover or less**
17 ❑ Cover: 1.95 **NM** value: **Cover or less**
18 ❑ Cover: 1.95 **NM** value: **Cover or less**
19 ❑ Cover: 1.95 **NM** value: **Cover or less**
20 ❑ Cover: 1.95 **NM** value: **Cover or less**
21 ❑ Sep 1997 Cover: 2.95 **NM** value: **Cover or less**
Circ: Diamd. preorders: **1,511**
22 ❑ Cover: 2.95 **NM** value: **Cover or less**

SHANDA THE PANDA (2ND SERIES) — Shanda Fantasy Arts

23 ❑ Cover: 2.95 **NM** value: **Cover or less**
24 ❑ Apr 1999 Cover: 2.95 **NM** value: **Cover or less**

SHANGHAI: BIG MACHINE — Brick House Digital

1 ❑ ca. 2000 Cover: 2.95 **NM** value: **Cover or less**
Circ: Diamd. preorders: **4,399**

SHANGHAIED: THE SAGA OF THE BLACK KITE — Eternity

1 ❑ Cover: 1.80 **NM** value: **2.00**
A: Topper Helmers **W:** Tony Hudz
2 ❑ Cover: 1.95 **NM** value: **2.00**
A: Topper Helmers **W:** Tony Hudz
3 ❑ Cover: 1.95 **NM** value: **2.00**
A: Topper Helmers **W:** Tony Hudz

SHANNA THE SHE-DEVIL — Marvel

Shanna was designed as a female counterpart to Marvel's Ka-Zar. Like Ka-Zar, she protects the jungle from all manner of menaces, from game poachers to white slavers. In this, she is accompanied by a pair of leopards, Ina and Biri. Fierce as these animals can be to strangers, Shanna is able to communicate with them through a bond they seem to share.

This same bond didn't seem to exist between Shanna and readers, however, since low sales forced the cancellation of this series after just five issues. Shanna has continued to appear from time to time in jungle adventures starring other Marvel characters.

1 ❑ Dec 1972 Cover: 0.20 **NM** value: **8.00**
• **CGC:** 10 graded, best 9.6
📖 Shanna the She-Devil ★ 1st Appearance of Shanna the She-Devil.

2 ❑ Feb 1973 Cover: 0.20 **NM** value: **5.00**
• **CGC:** 3 graded, best 9.4
📖 The Sahara Connection **A:** Jim Steranko(cover)

3 ❑ Apr 1973 Cover: 0.20 **NM** value: **3.50**
• **CGC:** 2 graded, best 9.4
📖 The Moon of the Fear-Bulls

4 ❑ Jun 1973 Cover: 0.20 **NM** value: **3.50**
• **CGC:** 2 graded, best 9.6
📖 Cry, Mandrill!

5 ❑ Aug 1973 Cover: 0.20 **NM** value: **3.50**
📖 Where Nekra Walks, Death Must Follow

SHAOLIN — Black Tiger

1 ❑ Cover: 2.95 **NM** value: **Cover or less**
A: Rolando Matos **W:** Rolando Matos; Josue Matos ★ Origin of The Tiger. ★ 1st Appearance of The Tiger.
2 ❑ Cover: 2.95 **NM** value: **Cover or less**
A: Rolando Matos **W:** Rolando Matos; Josue Matos
3 ❑ Cover: 2.95 **NM** value: **Cover or less**
A: Rolando Matos **W:** Rolando Matos; Josue Matos
4 ❑ Cover: 2.95 **NM** value: **Cover or less**
A: Rolando Matos **W:** Rolando Matos; Josue Matos
5 ❑ Cover: 2.95 **NM** value: **Cover or less**
A: Rolando Matos **W:** Rolando Matos; Josue Matos

SHAQUILLE O'NEAL VS. MICHAEL JORDAN — Personality

1 ❑ Cover: 2.95 **NM** value: **Cover or less**
Circ: CapCity orders: **5,965**
A: Deborah Max **W:** John Di Meola
2 ❑ Cover: 2.95 **NM** value: **Cover or less**
A: Deborah Max **W:** John Di Meola

SHARDS — Ascension

1 ❑ Feb 1994 Cover: 2.50 **NM** value: **Cover or less**
Circ: Diamd. preorders: **17,199**
A: David W. Miller **W:** Mark A. Clements

SHARKY — Image

Sharky first appeared in the pages of Monster Massacre, an anthology series from Dave Elliott's Atomeka publishing company. Originally meant as the setup for a comics series that never happened, Sharky didn't reappear until this 1998 series.

The focus of this title is the interplay between comic-book hero Sharky, a brawling bruiser of a guy, able to go toe-to-toe with The Mask and catch bullets in mid-air. This tough guy appeals strongly to young Patrick Sharky, who emulates the other Sharky's style of dress but lacks the confidence and power of his comic-book hero. No, Patrick Sharky is just an average awkward teen — at least, he is until the day a rampaging alien and a Norse goddess start a brawl in the middle of the city. Patrick is caught in the inevitable destruction and nearly dies. But, while he lies in a coma, he gets a visit from his hero, who promises him the power to change the world.

1/A ❑ Feb 1998 Cover: 2.50 **NM** value: **Cover or less**
Circ: Diamd. preorders: **4,693**
📖 Lo, He Shall Walk Among Us! **A:** Alex Horley; Alberto Ponticelli **W:** Dave Elliott

1/B ❑ Feb 1998 Cover: 2.50 **NM** value: **Cover or less**
back cover pin-up. 📖 Lo, He Shall Walk Among Us! **A:** Alex Horley; Alberto Ponticelli **W:** Dave Elliott

1/C ❑ Feb 1998 Cover: 2.50 **NM** value: **Cover or less**
• signing tour edition. 📖 Lo, He Shall Walk Among Us! **A:** Alex Horley; Alberto Ponticelli **W:** Dave Elliott

1/D ❑ Feb 1998 Cover: 2.50 **NM** value: **Cover or less**
no cover price. 📖 Lo, He Shall Walk Among Us! • The $1, 000, 000 variant **A:** Alex Horley; Alberto Ponticelli **W:** Dave Elliott

2/A ❑ Apr 1998 Cover: 2.50 **NM** value: **Cover or less**
Circ: Diamd. preorders: **10,303**
📖 Back to School! **A:** Alex Horley; Alberto Ponticelli **W:** Dave Elliott

2/B ❑ Apr 1998 Cover: 2.50 **NM** value: **Cover or less**
alternate wraparound cover (with Savage Dragon). 📖 Back to School! **A:** Alex Horley; Alberto Ponticelli **W:** Dave Elliott

3 ❑ May 1998 Cover: 2.50 **NM** value: **Cover or less**
Circ: Diamd. preorders: **7,854**
📖 Blazin' Glory **A:** Alex Horley; Alberto Ponticelli **W:** Dave Elliott

4 ❑ Jul 1998 Cover: 2.50 **NM** value: **Cover or less**
Circ: Diamd. preorders: **6,255**
Group charging on cover, "The Bad Guy!" inset. 📖 I Get by With a Little Help From my Friends! • gives date of publication as Late **A:** Alex Horley **W:** Dave Elliott

4/A ❑ Jul 1998 Cover: 2.50 **NM** value: **Cover or less**
Circ: Diamd. preorders: **3,560**
variant cover. **A:** Alex Horley **W:** Dave Elliott

SHARP COMICS — Blackerby

1 ❑ Win 1945 Cover: 0.10 **NM** value: **300.00**
2 ❑ Spr 1946 Cover: 0.10 **NM** value: **250.00**

SHATTER (1ST SERIES) — First

Shatter is the first full-length comic book created entirely on computer. Artist Mike Saenz used an early Macintosh to draw, letter, script, and even advertise this series in 1985. Only the coloring was done by hand. It was a startling and appropriate choice of medium for this futuristic crime drama.

Breathtakingly forward-looking in its technology at the time, Shatter now stands as a sign of how far technology has moved in just a few years. By the mid-1990s, computers had become commonplace for comics production work. To many, it seemed that the traditional letterer would be made all but extinct by computerized fontography. Computer coloring and digital effects are now standard on most Marvel titles. Ironically, it is still a comic book's actual drawing — the area Saenz most stressed in Shatter — that is still primarily handled by hand today.

1 ❑ Jun 1985 Cover: 1.75 **NM** value: **2.50**
Circ: CapCity orders: **9,500**
📖 Headhunters • This is the first computer-generated comic book **A:** Mike Saenz **W:** Peter B. Gillis ★ 1st Appearance of Shatter.
1-2 ❑ Cover: 1.75 **NM** value: **2.00**

SHATTER (2ND SERIES) — First

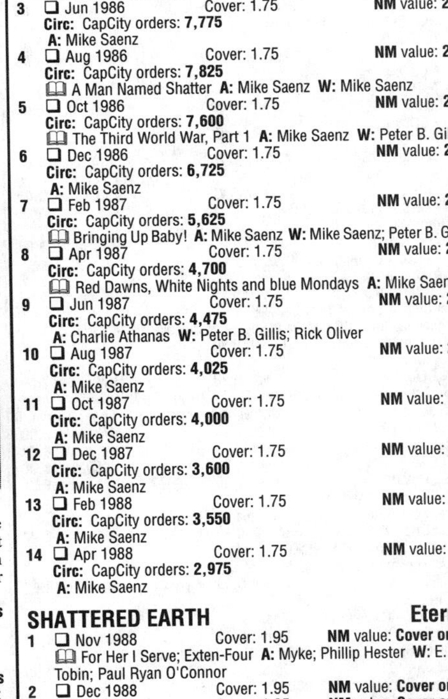

1 ❑ Dec 1985 Cover: 1.75 **NM** value: **2.50**
Circ: CapCity orders: **15,850**
• first computer-drawn comic book; Continued from Shatter one-shot **A:** Mike Saenz

2 ❑ Feb 1986 Cover: 1.75 **NM** value: **2.00**
Circ: CapCity orders: **11,700**
📖 Avenues of Escape **A:** Mike Saenz **W:** Mike Saenz

3 ❑ Jun 1986 Cover: 1.75 **NM** value: **2.00**
Circ: CapCity orders: **7,775**
A: Mike Saenz

4 ❑ Aug 1986 Cover: 1.75 **NM** value: **2.00**
Circ: CapCity orders: **7,825**
📖 A Man Named Shatter **A:** Mike Saenz **W:** Mike Saenz

5 ❑ Oct 1986 Cover: 1.75 **NM** value: **2.00**
Circ: CapCity orders: **7,600**
📖 The Third World War, Part 1 **A:** Mike Saenz **W:** Peter B. Gillis

6 ❑ Dec 1986 Cover: 1.75 **NM** value: **2.00**
Circ: CapCity orders: **6,725**
A: Mike Saenz

7 ❑ Feb 1987 Cover: 1.75 **NM** value: **2.00**
Circ: CapCity orders: **5,625**
📖 Bringing Up Baby! **A:** Mike Saenz **W:** Mike Saenz; Peter B. Gillis

8 ❑ Apr 1987 Cover: 1.75 **NM** value: **2.00**
Circ: CapCity orders: **4,700**
📖 Red Dawns, White Nights and blue Mondays **A:** Mike Saenz

9 ❑ Jun 1987 Cover: 1.75 **NM** value: **2.00**
Circ: CapCity orders: **4,475**
A: Charlie Athanas **W:** Peter B. Gillis; Rick Oliver

10 ❑ Aug 1987 Cover: 1.75 **NM** value: **2.00**
Circ: CapCity orders: **4,025**
A: Mike Saenz

11 ❑ Oct 1987 Cover: 1.75 **NM** value: **2.00**
Circ: CapCity orders: **4,000**
A: Mike Saenz

12 ❑ Dec 1987 Cover: 1.75 **NM** value: **2.00**
Circ: CapCity orders: **3,600**
A: Mike Saenz

13 ❑ Feb 1988 Cover: 1.75 **NM** value: **2.00**
Circ: CapCity orders: **3,550**
A: Mike Saenz

14 ❑ Apr 1988 Cover: 1.75 **NM** value: **2.00**
Circ: CapCity orders: **2,975**
A: Mike Saenz

SHATTERED EARTH — Eternity

1 ❑ Nov 1988 Cover: 1.95 **NM** value: **Cover or less**
📖 For Her I Serve; Exten-Four **A:** Myke; Phillip Hester **W:** E. Paul Tobin; Paul Ryan O'Connor

#	Date	Cover	NM value
2	❑ Dec 1988	Cover: 1.95	**NM** value: **Cover or less**
3	❑ Jan 1989	Cover: 1.95	**NM** value: **Cover or less**
4	❑ Mar 1989	Cover: 1.95	**NM** value: **Cover or less**
5	❑ 1989	Cover: 1.95	**NM** value: **Cover or less**
6	❑ 1989	Cover: 1.95	**NM** value: **Cover or less**
7	❑ 1989	Cover: 1.95	**NM** value: **Cover or less**
8	❑ 1989	Cover: 1.95	**NM** value: **Cover or less**
9	❑ 1989	Cover: 1.95	**NM** value: **Cover or less**

SHATTERED IMAGE — Image

1 ❑ Aug 1996 Cover: 2.50 **NM** value: **Cover or less**
A: Tony Daniel **W:** Kurt Busiek; Barbara Kesel ★ Appearance of Deathblow, Savage Dragon, Gen13, Spawn.

2 ❑ Oct 1996 Cover: 2.50 **NM** value: **Cover or less**
incorrect cover date. **A:** Tony Daniel **W:** Kurt Busiek; Barbara Kesel ★ Appearance of Deathblow, Savage Dragon, Gen13, Spawn.

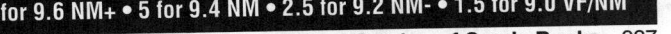

CGC-graded: Multiply prices above by **33 for 9.9 M** • **16 for 9.8 NM/M** • **7 for 9.6 NM+** • **5 for 9.4 NM** • **2.5 for 9.2 NM-** • **1.5 for 9.0 VF/NM**

3 ❑ Nov 1996 Cover: 2.50 **NM** value: **Cover or less**
cover says Oct, indicia says Nov. **A:** Tony Daniel **W:** Kurt Busiek; Barbara Kesel ★ Appearance of Deathblow, Savage Dragon, Gen13, Spawn.

4 ❑ Dec 1996 Cover: 2.50 **NM** value: **Cover or less**
Circ: Diamd. preorders: **55,374**
final issue. **A:** Tony Daniel **W:** Kurt Busiek; Barbara Kesel ★ Appearance of Shadowhawk, Ultiman, Knight Watchman, Savage Dragon, Gen13, Youngblood, Spawn.

SHATTERPOINT — Eternity

1 ❑ b&w Cover: 2.25 **NM** value: **Cover or less**
• Broid

2 ❑ b&w Cover: 2.25 **NM** value: **Cover or less**
• Broid

3 ❑ b&w Cover: 2.25 **NM** value: **Cover or less**
• Broid

4 ❑ b&w Cover: 2.25 **NM** value: **Cover or less**
• Broid

SHAZAM! — DC

The original Captain Marvel was created for Fawcett's Whiz Comics in 1939. Shortly after, DC sued Fawcett, claiming that Captain Marvel, who had superhuman strength, could fly at supersonic speed, and was impervious to bullets, was a copy of Superman. In the early 1950s, tired of publishing and fighting the legal battles, Fawcett retired the hero, but in an act of sheer irony, DC rival Marvel Comics succeeded in locking in a trademark on the name Captain Marvel for one of its super-heroes in the 1960s.

DC brought the original Captain Marvel out of suspended animation in the 1970s for this title which told of how a homeless boy named Billy Batson was given the power to turn into a super-hero by invoking the names of six mighty heroes in the acronym SHAZAM (Solomon, Hercules, Atlas, Zeus, Achilles, and Mercury). Drawn initially by the original artist, C.C. Beck, Shazam! maintained the classic feel of the original Captain Marvel series.

With Marvel's use of the name, DC was forced to title its series after Billy's magic word rather than the character.

1 ❑ Feb 1973 Cover: 0.20 **NM** value: **8.00**
• **CGC:** 25 graded, best 9.8
📖 In The Beginning… **A:** C.C. Beck **W:** Denny O'Neil ★ Origin of Captain Marvel (Golden Age).

2 ❑ Apr 1973 Cover: 0.20 **NM** value: **5.00**
• **CGC:** 1 graded, best 9.2
A: C.C. Beck

3 ❑ Jun 1973 Cover: 0.20 **NM** value: **4.00**
• **CGC:** 1 graded, best 8.5
A: C.C. Beck

4 ❑ Jul 1973 Cover: 0.20 **NM** value: **4.00**
• **CGC:** 1 graded, best 9.0
A: C.C. Beck

5 ❑ Sep 1973 Cover: 0.20 **NM** value: **3.00**
A: C.C. Beck

6 ❑ Oct 1973 Cover: 0.20 **NM** value: **3.00**
• **CGC:** 1 graded, best 9.2
Photo cover. **A:** C.C. Beck

7 ❑ Nov 1973 Cover: 0.20 **NM** value: **3.00**
• **CGC:** 1 graded, best 8.0
A: C.C. Beck

8 ❑ Dec 1973 Cover: 0.50 **NM** value: **10.00**
• **CGC:** 4 graded, best 9.4
• scheduled as DC 100-Page Super-Spectacular #DC-23 **A:** C.C. Beck

9 ❑ Jan 1974 Cover: 0.20 **NM** value: **2.50**
A: C.C. Beck

10 ❑ Feb 1974 Cover: 0.20 **NM** value: **2.50**
📖 Invasion of the Salad Men!; The Thanksgiving Thieves!; The Prize Catch of the Year! • Mary Marvel back-up ★ Versus Aunt Minerva.

11 ❑ Mar 1974 Cover: 0.20 **NM** value: **2.00**
12 ❑ Jun 1974 Cover: 0.60 **NM** value: **8.00**
13 ❑ Aug 1974 Cover: 0.60 **NM** value: **8.00**
14 ❑ Oct 1974 Cover: 0.60 **NM** value: **8.00**
• **CGC:** 2 graded, best 9.6
A: Kurt Schaffenberger ★ Appearance of Monster Society.

15 ❑ Dec 1974 Cover: 0.60 **NM** value: **8.00**
• **CGC:** 1 graded, best 9.0
★ Appearance of Lex Luthor.

16 ❑ Feb 1975 Cover: 0.60 **NM** value: **8.00**
Circ: Statement: **125,000**
★ Versus Seven Deadly Sins.

17 ❑ Apr 1975 Cover: 0.60 **NM** value: **8.00**
Circ: Statement: **125,000** • **CGC:** 4 graded, best 9.6

18 ❑ Jun 1975 Cover: 0.25 **NM** value: **2.00**
Circ: Statement: **125,000**

19 ❑ Aug 1975 Cover: 0.25 **NM** value: **2.00**
Circ: Statement: **125,000**

20 ❑ Oct 1975 Cover: 0.25 **NM** value: **2.00**
Circ: Statement: **125,000**

21 ❑ Dec 1975 Cover: 0.25 **NM** value: **2.00**
Circ: Statement: **125,000**
📖 Captain Marvel **W:** Pete Costanza; C.C. Beck

22 ❑ Feb 1976 Cover: 0.25 **NM** value: **2.00**
• **CGC:** 1 graded, best 9.2
★ Versus King Kull.

23 ❑ Win 1976 Cover: 0.30 **NM** value: **2.00**
24 ❑ Spr 1976 Cover: 0.30 **NM** value: **2.00**
25 ❑ Oct 1976 Cover: 0.30 **NM** value: **3.00**
★ Origin of Isis. ★ 1st Appearance of Isis.

26 ❑ Dec 1976 Cover: 0.30 **NM** value: **2.00**

27 ❑ Feb 1977 Cover: 0.30 **NM** value: **2.00**
Circ: Statement: **100,162**

28 ❑ Apr 1977 Cover: 0.30 **NM** value: **2.00**
Circ: Statement: **100,162**
★ Versus Black Adam.

29 ❑ Jun 1977 Cover: 0.30 **NM** value: **2.00**
Circ: Statement: **100,162**
★ Versus Ibac.

30 ❑ Aug 1977 Cover: 0.35 **NM** value: **2.00**
Circ: Statement: **100,162**

31 ❑ Oct 1977 Cover: 0.35 **NM** value: **2.00**
Circ: Statement: **100,162**
★ Appearance of Minute Man.

32 ❑ Dec 1977 Cover: 0.35 **NM** value: **2.00**
Circ: Statement: **100,162**

33 ❑ Feb 1978 Cover: 0.35 **NM** value: **2.00**
★ Versus Mr. Atom.

34 ❑ Apr 1978 Cover: 0.35 **NM** value: **2.00**
• Captain Marvel Jr. vs. Captain Nazi ★ Origin of Captain Marvel Jr..

35 ❑ Jun 1978 Cover: 0.35 **NM** value: **2.00**
• Has 1977 Statement; avg total paid circ 100,162

SHAZAM! ARCHIVES, THE — DC

1 ❑ Cover: 49.95 **NM** value: **Cover or less**
• Reprints ashcan editions (Flash Comics #1 and Thrill Comics #1) and Captain Marvel stories from Whiz.

2 ❑ Cover: 49.95 **NM** value: **Cover or less**
A: Jack Kirby; C.C. Beck; Charles Sultan **W:** Joe Simon; Bill Parker ★ Appearance of Reprints Shazam!.

SHAZAM! POWER OF HOPE — DC

1 ❑ Cover: 9.95 **NM** value: **Cover or less**
A: Alex Ross **W:** Paul Dini

SHAZAM: THE NEW BEGINNING — DC

1 ❑ Apr 1987 Cover: 0.75 **NM** value: **2.00**
Circ: CapCity orders: **22,650**
A: Tom Mandrake **W:** Roy Thomas; Dann Thomas ★ Origin of Captain Marvel (Golden Age)-new origin.

2 ❑ May 1987 Cover: 0.75 **NM** value: **2.00**
Circ: CapCity orders: **17,850**
📖 "S" is for Wisdom… "H" is for Strength **A:** Tom Mandrake **W:** Roy Thomas; Dann Thomas ★ Versus Black Adam.

3 ❑ Jun 1987 Cover: 0.75 **NM** value: **2.00**
Circ: CapCity orders: **16,300**
A: Tom Mandrake **W:** Roy Thomas; Dann Thomas

4 ❑ Jul 1987 Cover: 0.75 **NM** value: **2.00**
Circ: CapCity orders: **17,850**
A: Tom Mandrake **W:** Roy Thomas; Dann Thomas

SHEBA — Sick Mind

1 ❑ Jul 1996, b&w Cover: 2.95 **NM** value: **Cover or less**
2 ❑ Nov 1996, b&w Cover: 2.95 **NM** value: **Cover or less**
3 ❑ 1997 Cover: 2.50 **NM** value: **Cover or less**
4 ❑ 1997 Cover: 2.50 **NM** value: **Cover or less**

SHEBA (2ND SERIES) — Sirius

1 ❑ Dec 1997, b&w Cover: 2.50 **NM** value: **Cover or less**
2 ❑ Mar 1998, b&w Cover: 2.50 **NM** value: **Cover or less**
3 ❑ Jun 1998, b&w Cover: 2.50 **NM** value: **Cover or less**
4 ❑ Sep 1998, b&w Cover: 2.50 **NM** value: **Cover or less**
5 ❑ 1999b&w Cover: 2.50 **NM** value: **Cover or less**
6 ❑ May 1999, b&w Cover: 2.95 **NM** value: **Cover or less**
📖 Reunions

SHEBA PANTHEON — Sirius

1 ❑ Aug 1998, b&w Cover: 2.50 **NM** value: **Cover or less**
• collects strips and character bios

SHE BUCCANEER — Monster

1 ❑ b&w Cover: 2.25 **NM** value: **Cover or less**
2 ❑ b&w Cover: 2.25 **NM** value: **Cover or less**

SHE-CAT — AC

1 ❑ Jun 1989, b&w Cover: 2.50 **NM** value: **Cover or less**
📖 Stray Cat! **A:** Bill Marimon **W:** Bill Marimon

2 ❑ Apr 1990, b&w Cover: 2.50 **NM** value: **Cover or less**
A: Bill Marimon **W:** Bill Marimon

3 ❑ May 1990, b&w Cover: 2.50 **NM** value: **Cover or less**
A: Bill Marimon **W:** Bill Marimon

4 ❑ Jun 1990, b&w Cover: 2.50 **NM** value: **Cover or less**
A: Bill Marimon **W:** Bill Marimon

SHEEDEVA — Fantagraphics / Eros

All issues are adults only.

1 ❑ Aug 1994, b&w Cover: 2.95 **NM** value: **Cover or less**
A: Sandra Chang **W:** Sandra Chang

2 ❑ Nov 1994, b&w Cover: 2.95 **NM** value: **Cover or less**
A: Sandra Chang **W:** Sandra Chang

SHEENA — Marvel

1 ❑ Dec 1984 Cover: 0.75 **NM** value: **2.00**
A: Gray Morrow

2 ❑ Feb 1985 Cover: 0.75 **NM** value: **2.00**
A: Gray Morrow

SHEENA 3-D SPECIAL — Blackthorne

1 ❑ May 1985 Cover: 2.00 **NM** value: **Cover or less**
A: Morgan Thomas **W:** Morgan Thomas

SHEENA-QUEEN OF THE JUNGLE — London Night

1/A ❑ ca. 1998 Cover: 5.00 **NM** value: **Cover or less**
Alligator cover. **A:** Art Wetherell **W:** Mike Shoemaker

1/B ❑ ca. 1998 Cover: 5.00 **NM** value: **Cover or less**
Leopard cover. **A:** Art Wetherell **W:** Mike Shoemaker

1/C ❑ ca. 1998 Cover: 5.00 **NM** value: **Cover or less**
Zebra cover. **A:** Art Wetherell **W:** Mike Shoemaker

1/D ❑ ca. 1998 Cover: 3.00 **NM** value: **Cover or less**
• Ministry Edition. **A:** Art Wetherell **W:** Mike Shoemaker

1/LE ❑ ca. 1998 Cover: 15.00 **NM** value: **Cover or less**
• White leather edition. **A:** Art Wetherell **W:** Mike Shoemaker

SHEENA, QUEEN OF THE JUNGLE (1ST SERIES) — Fiction House

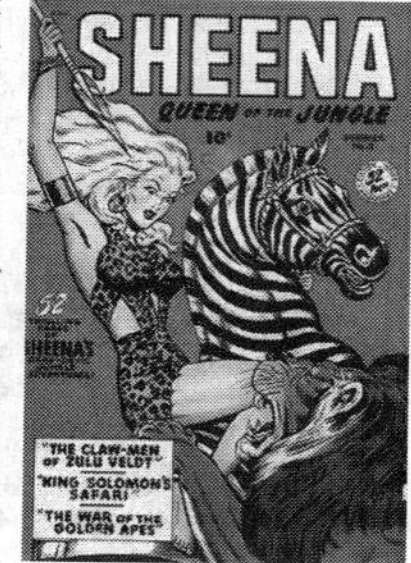

With long blonde hair, a brief leopardskin outfit, a band around both of her upper arms, an ankle bracelet on each ankle, and (ouch!) bare feet, she is in charge of the Congo. "She rules a world of killer beasts and savage men," according to #6, whereas #7 describes her as the "daring, fearless wild beauty of the jungle." The stories are Done in One shorts in which the knife-wielding "golden goddess" and her buddy, Bob Reynolds (who dressed more sensibly but needed rescuing a lot), coped with threats ranging from "Death Trap of the Lion-Men" to "Red Fangs of the Tree-Tribe." She had been introduced in the first issue of the anthology title Jumbo Comics, which was her main stomping ground, and she spun off into a 1955-1956 TV series starring Irish McCalla (1929-2002) and, eventually, into a 1984 film starring Tanya Roberts (1955-). — Maggie

1 ❑ Spr 1942 Cover: 0.10 **NM** value: **2000.00**
• **CGC:** 2 graded, best 7.5

2 ❑ Win 1942 Cover: 0.10 **NM** value: **1000.00**
3 ❑ Spr 1943 Cover: 0.10 **NM** value: **750.00**
4 ❑ Fal 1948 Cover: 0.10 **NM** value: **400.00**
• **CGC:** 6 graded, best 9.0

5 ❑ Sum 1949 Cover: 0.10 **NM** value: **400.00**
• **CGC:** 1 graded, best 9.2

6 ❑ Spr 1950 Cover: 0.10 **NM** value: **350.00**
• **CGC:** 1 graded, best 8.5

7 ❑ ca. 1950 Cover: 0.10 **NM** value: **350.00**
• **CGC:** 1 graded, best 7.5

8 ❑ ca. 1950 Cover: 0.10 **NM** value: **325.00**
• **CGC:** 5 graded, best 8.5

9 ❑ Fal 1950 Cover: 0.10 **NM** value: **325.00**
• **CGC:** 2 graded, best 5.5

10 ❑ Win 1950 Cover: 0.10 **NM** value: **325.00**
• **CGC:** 1 graded, best 8.5

11 ❑ Spr 1951 Cover: 0.10 **NM** value: **300.00**
12 ❑ Sum 1951 Cover: 0.10 **NM** value: **300.00**
• **CGC:** 1 graded, best 8.0

13 ❑ Fal 1951 Cover: 0.10 **NM** value: **300.00**
14 ❑ Win 1951 Cover: 0.10 **NM** value: **300.00**
15 ❑ Spr 1952 Cover: 0.10 **NM** value: **300.00**
16 ❑ Sum 1952 Cover: 0.10 **NM** value: **275.00**
17 ❑ Fal 1952 Cover: 0.10 **NM** value: **275.00**
18 ❑ Win 1952 Cover: 0.10 **NM** value: **275.00**

SHEENA, QUEEN OF THE JUNGLE 3-D — Blackthorne

1 ❑ May 1985 Cover: 2.50 **NM** value: **Cover or less**
A: Dave Stevens

SHEILA TRENT: VAMPIRE HUNTER — Draculina

1 ❑ Cover: 2.50 **NM** value: **Cover or less**
A: Edwin Nieves **W:** Kevin Nagel ★ Origin of Sheila Trent. ★ 1st Appearance of Sheila Trent.

2 ❑ Cover: 2.50 **NM** value: **Cover or less**
A: Edwin Nieves **W:** Kevin Nagel

SHELL SHOCK — Mirage

1 ❑ Cover: 12.95 **NM** value: **Cover or less**

SHERIFF OF TOMBSTONE — Charlton

1 ❑ Nov 1958 Cover: 0.10 **NM** value: **50.00**
2 ❑ Jan 1959 Cover: 0.10 **NM** value: **40.00**
3 ❑ 1959 Cover: 0.10 **NM** value: **30.00**
4 ❑ 1959 Cover: 0.10 **NM** value: **30.00**
5 ❑ Sep 1959 Cover: 0.10 **NM** value: **30.00**
6 ❑ Nov 1959 Cover: 0.10 **NM** value: **25.00**
7 ❑ Jan 1960 Cover: 0.10 **NM** value: **25.00**
8 ❑ Mar 1960 Cover: 0.10 **NM** value: **25.00**
9 ❑ May 1960 Cover: 0.10 **NM** value: **25.00**
10 ❑ Jul 1960 Cover: 0.10 **NM** value: **25.00**
11 ❑ Sep 1960 Cover: 0.10 **NM** value: **20.00**
12 ❑ Nov 1960 Cover: 0.10 **NM** value: **20.00**
13 ❑ Jan 1961 Cover: 0.10 **NM** value: **20.00**
14 ❑ Mar 1961 Cover: 0.10 **NM** value: **20.00**
15 ❑ May 1961 Cover: 0.10 **NM** value: **20.00**
16 ❑ Jul 1961 Cover: 0.10 **NM** value: **20.00**
17 ❑ Sep 1961 Cover: 0.10 **NM** value: **20.00**

SHERLOCK HOLMES: ADVENTURES OF THE OPERA GHOST — Caliber

1 ❑ Cover: 2.95 **NM** value: **Cover or less**
2 ❑ Cover: 2.95 **NM** value: **Cover or less**

SHERLOCK HOLMES: A STUDY IN SCARLET — Thorby

Bk 1 ❑ Cover: 6.95 **NM** value: **Cover or less**

SHERLOCK HOLMES (AVALON) — Avalon

1 ❑ b&w Cover: 2.95 **NM** value: **Cover or less**

Other grades: Multiply prices above by **1.5 for Mint • 2/3 for Very Fine • 1/3 for Fine • 1/5 for Very Good • 1/8 for Good**

SHERLOCK HOLMES CASEBOOK — Eternity

1 ❑ Cover: 2.25 **NM** value: **Cover or less**
📖 The Deadly Inheritance; The Tunnel Scheme • Originally published as New Adventures of Sherlock Holmes

2 ❑ Cover: 2.25 **NM** value: **Cover or less**
📖 The Derelict Ship; The Safe Robber; The Cunning Assassin; Sherlock Holmes' London Haunts • Originally published as New Adventures of Sherlock Holmes

SHERLOCK HOLMES (DC) — DC

1 ❑ Oct 1975 Cover: 0.25 **NM** value: **4.00**
• **CGC:** 5 graded, best 9.6
📖 The Final Problem **A:** E.R. Cruz **W:** Denny O'Neil

SHERLOCK HOLMES: DR. JEKYLL & MR. HOLMES — Caliber / Tome

1 ❑ b&w Cover: 2.95 **NM** value: **Cover or less**
No issue number. One-shot. **A:** Seppo Makkinen **W:** Steve Jones

SHERLOCK HOLMES (ETERNITY) — Eternity

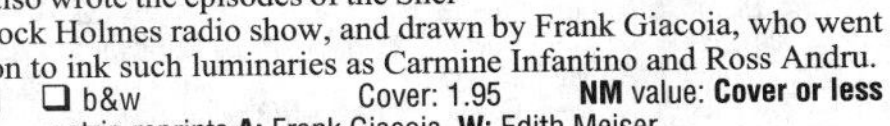

Sir Arthur Conan Doyle's brilliant sleuth and master of condescending repartee comes to the world of comics in this collection of newspaper strips from the 1950s reprinted by Eternity Comics. Since the series was originally published in newspapers, the panel layout is horizontal and necessitates the book be printed in "landscape" orientation.

Accompanied by his faithful, but often befuddled aide, Dr. Watson, Sherlock Holmes retains all of the incredible powers of observation and deduction that he is famous for from books and movies. The strip was written by Edith Meiser, who also wrote the episodes of the Sherlock Holmes radio show, and drawn by Frank Giacoia, who went on to ink such luminaries as Carmine Infantino and Ross Andru.

1 ❑ b&w Cover: 1.95 **NM** value: **Cover or less**
• strip reprints **A:** Frank Giacoia **W:** Edith Meiser

2 ❑ 1988 b&w Cover: 1.95 **NM** value: **Cover or less**
• strip reprints **A:** Frank Giacoia **W:** Edith Meiser

3 ❑ 1988 b&w Cover: 1.95 **NM** value: **Cover or less**
• strip reprints **A:** Frank Giacoia **W:** Edith Meiser

4 ❑ 1988 b&w Cover: 1.95 **NM** value: **Cover or less**
• strip reprints **A:** Frank Giacoia **W:** Edith Meiser

5 ❑ 1988 b&w Cover: 1.95 **NM** value: **Cover or less**
• strip reprints **A:** Frank Giacoia **W:** Edith Meiser

6 ❑ 1988 b&w Cover: 1.95 **NM** value: **Cover or less**
• strip reprints **A:** Frank Giacoia **W:** Edith Meiser

7 ❑ 1988 b&w Cover: 1.95 **NM** value: **Cover or less**
• strip reprints **A:** Frank Giacoia **W:** Edith Meiser

8 ❑ Jan 1989, b&w Cover: 1.95 **NM** value: **Cover or less**
• strip reprints **A:** Frank Giacoia **W:** Edith Meiser

9 ❑ 1989 b&w Cover: 1.95 **NM** value: **Cover or less**
• strip reprints **A:** Frank Giacoia **W:** Edith Meiser

10 ❑ 1989 b&w Cover: 1.95 **NM** value: **Cover or less**
• strip reprints **A:** Frank Giacoia **W:** Edith Meiser

11 ❑ 1989 b&w Cover: 1.95 **NM** value: **Cover or less**
📖 A Case of Blind Fear • strip reprints **A:** Frank Giacoia **W:** Edith Meiser

12 ❑ 1989 b&w Cover: 1.95 **NM** value: **Cover or less**
• strip reprints **A:** Frank Giacoia **W:** Edith Meiser

13 ❑ 1989 b&w Cover: 1.95 **NM** value: **Cover or less**
• strip reprints **A:** Frank Giacoia **W:** Edith Meiser

14 ❑ 1989 b&w Cover: 1.95 **NM** value: **Cover or less**
• strip reprints **A:** Frank Giacoia **W:** Edith Meiser

15 ❑ 1989 b&w Cover: 1.95 **NM** value: **Cover or less**
• strip reprints **A:** Frank Giacoia **W:** Edith Meiser

16 ❑ 1989 Cover: 2.25 **NM** value: **Cover or less**
A: Frank Giacoia **W:** Edith Meiser

17 ❑ 1989 Cover: 2.25 **NM** value: **Cover or less**
A: Frank Giacoia **W:** Edith Meiser

18 ❑ 1990 Cover: 2.25 **NM** value: **Cover or less**
A: Frank Giacoia **W:** Edith Meiser

19 ❑ 1990 Cover: 2.25 **NM** value: **Cover or less**
A: Frank Giacoia **W:** Edith Meiser

20 ❑ 1990 Cover: 2.25 **NM** value: **Cover or less**
A: Frank Giacoia **W:** Edith Meiser

21 ❑ 1990 Cover: 2.50 **NM** value: **Cover or less**
A: Frank Giacoia **W:** Edith Meiser

22 ❑ 1990 Cover: 2.50 **NM** value: **Cover or less**
A: Frank Giacoia **W:** Edith Meiser

23 ❑ 1990 Cover: 2.75 **NM** value: **Cover or less**
final issue. **A:** Frank Giacoia **W:** Edith Meiser

Bk 1 ❑ Cover: 17.95 **NM** value: **Cover or less**
• Trade Paperback. • b&w strip reprints

SHERLOCK HOLMES IN THE CASE OF THE MISSING MARTIAN — Eternity

1 ❑ Jul 1990, b&w Cover: 2.25 **NM** value: **Cover or less**
A: Topper Helmers **W:** Doug Murray

2 ❑ Aug 1990, b&w Cover: 2.25 **NM** value: **Cover or less**
A: Topper Helmers **W:** Doug Murray

3 ❑ Sep 1990, b&w Cover: 2.25 **NM** value: **Cover or less**
A: Topper Helmers **W:** Doug Murray

4 ❑ Oct 1990, b&w Cover: 2.25 **NM** value: **Cover or less**
A: Topper Helmers **W:** Doug Murray

SHERLOCK HOLMES IN THE CURIOUS CASE OF THE VANISHING VILLAIN — Atomeka

1 ❑ Cover: 4.50 **NM** value: **Cover or less**
No issue number.

SHERLOCK HOLMES MYSTERIES — Moonstone

1 ❑ Cover: 2.95 **NM** value: **Cover or less**
📖 The Scorned Mistress; Memories of an Angel **A:** Mike Bianco; Rick Gulick **W:** Joe Gentile

SHERLOCK HOLMES OF THE '30S — Eternity

Sir Arthur Conan Doyle's brilliant, eccentric detective Sherlock Holmes has been adapted numerous times in books, plays, movies, television, newspaper strips, and comic books. One of the first graphic treatments of the character was by illustrator Leo O'Mealia (1884-1960) in 1930. O'Mealia's pulp-illustration, black-and-white, drypoint style was supplemented with blocks of typeset text from actual Sherlock Holmes stories, making the strip more of an illustrated narrative than a comic strip, per se.

Eternity, a division of Malibu Comics, reprinted the stories in a series of seven handsome, 32-page, black-and-white issues, with the participation of the San Francisco Academy of Comic Art. Each features a complete story of Holmes and his faithful friend Dr. Watson solving crimes through observation and deduction.

1 ❑ b&w Cover: 2.95 **NM** value: **Cover or less**
• strip reprints **A:** Leo O'Mealia **W:** Sir Arthur Conan Doyle

2 ❑ b&w Cover: 2.95 **NM** value: **Cover or less**
• strip reprints **A:** Leo O'Mealia **W:** Sir Arthur Conan Doyle

3 ❑ b&w Cover: 2.95 **NM** value: **Cover or less**
• strip reprints **A:** Leo O'Mealia **W:** Sir Arthur Conan Doyle

4 ❑ b&w Cover: 2.95 **NM** value: **Cover or less**
• strip reprints **A:** Leo O'Mealia **W:** Sir Arthur Conan Doyle

5 ❑ b&w Cover: 2.95 **NM** value: **Cover or less**
• strip reprints **A:** Leo O'Mealia **W:** Sir Arthur Conan Doyle

6 ❑ b&w Cover: 2.95 **NM** value: **Cover or less**
• strip reprints **A:** Leo O'Mealia **W:** Sir Arthur Conan Doyle

7 ❑ b&w Cover: 2.95 **NM** value: **Cover or less**
final issue. • strip reprints **A:** Leo O'Mealia **W:** Sir Arthur Conan Doyle

SHERLOCK HOLMES READER — Tome

1 ❑ Sep 1998 Cover: 3.95 **NM** value: **Cover or less**
Circ: Diamd. preorders: **1,995**
📖 The Loch Ness Horror, Part 1 **A:** Seppo Makkinen **W:** Martin Powell

SHERLOCK HOLMES: RETURN OF THE DEVIL — Adventure

1 ❑ Sep 1992, b&w Cover: 2.50 **NM** value: **Cover or less**
2 ❑ 1992b&w Cover: 2.50 **NM** value: **Cover or less**

SHERLOCK JR. — Eternity

1 ❑ b&w Cover: 2.50 **NM** value: **Cover or less**
• strip reprints

2 ❑ b&w Cover: 2.50 **NM** value: **Cover or less**
• strip reprints

3 ❑ b&w Cover: 2.50 **NM** value: **Cover or less**
• strip reprints

SHERMAN'S MARCH THROUGH ATLANTA TO THE SEA — Heritage Collection

1 ❑ Cover: 3.50 **NM** value: **Cover or less**
No issue number. One-shot. wraparound cover. • retells Civil War story

SHERLOCK HOLMES (CHARLTON) — Charlton

1 ❑ ca. 1955 Cover: 0.10 **NM** value: **175.00**
2 ❑ Mar 1956 Cover: 0.10 **NM** value: **150.00**
• **CGC:** 1 graded, best 7.0

SHERRY THE SHOWGIRL — Atlas

1	❑ Aug 1956	Cover: 0.10	**NM** value: **10.00**
2	❑ Oct 1956	Cover: 0.10	**NM** value: **75.00**
3	❑ Dec 1956	Cover: 0.10	**NM** value: **50.00**
4	❑ Feb 1957	Cover: 0.10	**NM** value: **50.00**
5	❑ Apr 1957	Cover: 0.10	**NM** value: **50.00**
6	❑ Jun 1957	Cover: 0.10	**NM** value: **50.00**
7	❑ Aug 1957	Cover: 0.10	**NM** value: **50.00**

SHE'S JOSIE — Archie

1	❑ Feb 1963	Cover: 0.12	**NM** value: **85.00**
2	❑ Aug 1963	Cover: 0.12	**NM** value: **55.00**
3	❑ Oct 1963	Cover: 0.12	**NM** value: **30.00**
4	❑ Nov 1963	Cover: 0.12	**NM** value: **25.00**
5	❑ Feb 1964	Cover: 0.12	**NM** value: **25.00**
6	❑ May 1964	Cover: 0.12	**NM** value: **20.00**
7	❑ Aug 1964	Cover: 0.12	**NM** value: **20.00**
8	❑ Sep 1964	Cover: 0.12	**NM** value: **20.00**
9	❑ Oct 1964	Cover: 0.12	**NM** value: **20.00**
10	❑ Dec 1964	Cover: 0.12	**NM** value: **20.00**
11	❑ Feb 1965	Cover: 0.12	**NM** value: **16.00**
12	❑ Apr 1965	Cover: 0.12	**NM** value: **16.00**
13	❑ Jun 1965	Cover: 0.12	**NM** value: **16.00**
14	❑ Aug 1965	Cover: 0.12	**NM** value: **16.00**
15	❑ Sep 1965	Cover: 0.12	**NM** value: **16.00**
16	❑ Oct 1965	Cover: 0.12	**NM** value: **16.00**

• Series continues as Josie

SHEVA'S WAR — DC / Vertigo

1 ❑ Oct 1998 Cover: 2.95 **NM** value: **Cover or less**
Circ: Diamd. preorders: **11,332**
A: Christopher Moeller **W:** Christopher Moeller

2 ❑ Nov 1998 Cover: 2.95 **NM** value: **Cover or less**
Circ: Diamd. preorders: **8,678**
A: Christopher Moeller **W:** Christopher Moeller

3 ❑ Dec 1998 Cover: 2.95 **NM** value: **Cover or less**
Circ: Diamd. preorders: **7,967**
A: Christopher Moeller **W:** Christopher Moeller

4 ❑ Jan 1999 Cover: 2.95 **NM** value: **Cover or less**
Circ: Diamd. preorders: **7,645**
A: Christopher Moeller **W:** Christopher Moeller

5 ❑ Feb 1999 Cover: 2.95 **NM** value: **Cover or less**
Circ: Diamd. preorders: **7,686**
A: Christopher Moeller **W:** Christopher Moeller

SHI — Crusade

0 ❑ ca. 1996 Cover: 2.99 **NM** value: **Cover or less**
• Flipbook with Wolverine/Shi Night of Justice Preview **A:** Bill Tucci **W:** Bill Tucci

0.5 ❑ ca. 1996 **NM** value: **3.00**
• **CGC:** 2 graded, best 9.8
• Wizard promotional edition with COA. **A:** Jason Orfalas **W:** Tom Sniegoski

SHI: ART OF WAR TOUR BOOK — Crusade

1 ❑ ca. 1998 Cover: 4.95 **NM** value: **Cover or less**
Circ: Diamd. preorders: **6,445**

SHI: BLACK, WHITE, AND RED — Crusade

1 ❑ Mar 1998, b&w and redCover: 2.95 **NM** value: **Cover or less**
Circ: Diamd. preorders: **22,445**

2 ❑ May 1998, b&w and redCover: 2.95 **NM** value: **Cover or less**
Circ: Diamd. preorders: **20,075**

SHI/CYBLADE: THE BATTLE FOR INDEPENDENTS — Crusade

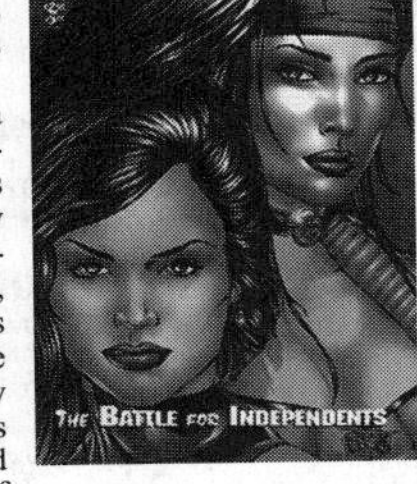

Billy Tucci's Shi and Marc Silvestri's Cyblade team up in this second part of a cross-company story. The story is a special one, as it has a deeper meaning than what is shown on the paper.

Tucci used this crossover as a metaphor for the independent comics' struggle against big companies such as Marvel and DC, which they see as strangling the life out of original comic creations. In this story, Shi and Cyblade find themselves transported to just outside a strange land that is protected by a seemingly impenetrable wall. Dave Sim's Cerebus suddenly appears and helps them over. He warns them of the heroes who have come before them and failed. The two femme fatales are charged with the destruction of a huge machine that keeps killing heroes by nothing more than its sheer size. Along the way, they meet Jeff Smith's Bone, Joe Quesada and Jimmy Palmiotti's Ash, and other independent comics heroes.

1 ❑ Sep 1995 Cover: 2.95 **NM** value: **4.00**
• **CGC:** 2 graded, best 9.8
• crossover; concludes Image's Cyblade/Shi: The Battle for Independents #1; Numerous other independent characters appear **A:** Nelson Asencio; Bill Tucci; Jimmy Palmiotti **W:** Bill Tucci; Gary Cohn ★ 1st Appearance of The Atomik Angels. ★ Appearance of Cerebus, Bone.

1/SC ❑ Sep 1995 Cover: 2.95 **NM** value: **5.00**
• **CGC:** 3 graded, best 9.6
alternate cover. • crossover; concludes Image's Cyblade/Shi: The Battle for Independents #1 **A:** Nelson Asencio; Bill Tucci; Jimmy Palmiotti; Marc Silvestri(cover) **W:** Bill Tucci; Gary Cohn

SHI/DAREDEVIL: HONOR THY MOTHER — Crusade

1 ❑ Jan 1997 Cover: 2.95 **NM** value: **Cover or less**
Circ: Diamd. preorders: **59,754**
• flipbook with TCB Sneak Attack Edition #1. • crossover with Marvel **A:** Bill Tucci **W:** Bill Tucci; Peter Gutierrez; Christopher Golden; Tom Sniegoski

1/LE ❑ Jan 1997 Cover: 10.00 **NM** value: **Cover or less**
• "Banzai" edition.

SHIDIMA — Image

1/A ❑ Jan 2001 Cover: 2.95 **NM** value: **Cover or less**
Circ: Diamd. preorders: **38,712**
Many figures on cover, man center holding rope. 📖 Outlaws Return **A:** Arnakin **W:** Adrian Tsang

1/B ❑ Jan 2001 Cover: 2.95 **NM** value: **Cover or less**
Four figures on cover, man front holding sword. 📖 Outlaws Return **A:** Arnakin **W:** Adrian Tsang

2 ❑ Mar 2001 Cover: 2.95 **NM** value: **Cover or less**
Circ: Diamd. preorders: **31,678**
📖 Reunion **A:** Warui Namekemono **W:** Adrian Tsang

SHI: EAST WIND RAIN — Crusade

1 ❑ Nov 1997 Cover: 3.50 **NM** value: **Cover or less**
Circ: Diamd. preorders: **27,862**
Painted cover. 📖 East Wind Rain **A:** Marc Sasso **W:** Bill Tucci; Gary Cohn

2 ❑ Feb 1998 Cover: 3.50 **NM** value: **Cover or less**
Circ: Diamd. preorders: **24,692**

Ash 1 ❑ Jul 1997 **NM** value: **1.00**
no cover price. • Sneak Teaser Preview

📖 indicates **Story Title** or **Storyline** information.
★ indicates **Character Appearance** information.
W = Writer • A = Artist • C = Cover Artist

CGC-graded: Multiply prices above by **33 for 9.9 M • 16 for 9.8 NM/M • 7 for 9.6 NM+ • 5 for 9.4 NM • 2.5 for 9.2 NM- • 1.5 for 9.0 VF/NM**

SHIELD — Marvel

Sgt. Fury went from the Good War to the Cold War, when he signed up to become director of SHIELD, the Supreme Headquarters International Espionage Law-Enforcement Division. Now a colonel, Fury commands a high-tech group of secret agents, as they try to save the world from the menaces of groups like Hydra, A.I.M., and The Secret Empire.

SHIELD reprints Fury's early adventures from Strange Tales, shortly after he made his debut in SHIELD in Strange Tales #135. These are Fury's glory days, filled with futuristic weaponry, trick spy gadgets, robotic decoys and the SHIELD Helicarrier — their headquarters in the sky. The more outrageous of these devices owed much to the James Bond movies which were popular at the time.

1 ❑ Feb 1973 Cover: 0.20 **NM** value: **8.00**
• **CGC:** 3 graded, best 9.4
🕮 When the Unliving Strike!; The Enemy Within • Nick Fury reprints from Strange Tales **A:** Don Heck; Jack Kirby **W:** Stan Lee

2 ❑ Apr 1973 Cover: 0.20 **NM** value: **5.00**
🕮 Death Before Dishonor; The End of A.I.M. • Nick Fury reprints from Strange Tales

3 ❑ Jun 1973 Cover: 0.20 **NM** value: **5.00**
🕮 Hydra Lives; Overkill • Nick Fury reprints from Strange Tales

4 ❑ Aug 1973 Cover: 0.20 **NM** value: **5.00**
🕮 The Power Of SHIELD!; The Hiding Place • Nick Fury reprints from Strange Tales **A:** Jack Kirby **W:** Stan Lee

5 ❑ Oct 1973 Cover: 0.20 **NM** value: **5.00**
• Nick Fury reprints from Strange Tales

SHIELD (ARCHIE) — Archie / Red Circle

1 ❑ Jun 1983 Cover: 1.00 **NM** value: **Cover or less**
A: Rich Buckler

2 ❑ Aug 1983 Cover: 1.00 **NM** value: **Cover or less**
C: Rich Buckler

3 ❑ Dec 1983 Cover: 1.00 **NM** value: **Cover or less**
• Title changes to Steel Sterling **A:** Eduardo Barreto

SHIELD WIZARD COMICS — M.L.J.

1 ❑ Sum 1940 Cover: 0.10 **NM** value: **3500.00**
• **CGC:** 5 graded, best 9.6

2 ❑ Win 1940 Cover: 0.10 **NM** value: **1500.00**
• **CGC:** 1 graded, best 9.0

3 ❑ Spr 1941 Cover: 0.10 **NM** value: **1000.00**

4 ❑ Sum 1941 Cover: 0.10 **NM** value: **1000.00**
• **CGC:** 1 graded, best 9.6

5 ❑ Fal 1941 Cover: 0.10 **NM** value: **1000.00**
• **CGC:** 2 graded, best 9.4

6 ❑ Win 1941 Cover: 0.10 **NM** value: **800.00**
• **CGC:** 2 graded, best 9.4

7 ❑ Sum 1942 Cover: 0.10 **NM** value: **800.00**
• **CGC:** 3 graded, best 9.4

8 ❑ Fal 1942 Cover: 0.10 **NM** value: **800.00**
• **CGC:** 2 graded, best 9.4

9 ❑ Win 1942 Cover: 0.10 **NM** value: **800.00**
• **CGC:** 2 graded, best 8.5

10 ❑ Spr 1943 Cover: 0.10 **NM** value: **800.00**
• **CGC:** 1 graded, best 8.5

11 ❑ Sum 1943 Cover: 0.10 **NM** value: **700.00**
• **CGC:** 2 graded, best 9.2

12 ❑ Fal 1943 Cover: 0.10 **NM** value: **700.00**

13 ❑ Spr 1944 Cover: 0.10 **NM** value: **700.00**
• **CGC:** 1 graded, best 8.5

SHI: HEAVEN & EARTH — Crusade

1 ❑ Jul 1997 Cover: 2.95 **NM** value: **Cover or less**
Circ: Diamd. preorders: **23,780**

1/A ❑ Jul 1997 Cover: 2.95 **NM** value: **Cover or less**
Circ: Diamd. preorders: **23,808**
alternate cover.

2 ❑ Nov 1997 Cover: 2.95 **NM** value: **Cover or less**
Circ: Diamd. preorders: **31,973**
A: Steve Ellis; Rodney Ramos; Bill Tucci; Juan Pineda **W:** Bill Tucci; Gary Cohn

2/A ❑ Nov 1997 Cover: 2.95 **NM** value: **Cover or less**
logoless cover.

3 ❑ Jan 1998 Cover: 2.95 **NM** value: **Cover or less**
Circ: Diamd. preorders: **27,867**

4/A ❑ Apr 1998 Cover: 2.95 **NM** value: **Cover or less**
Circ: Diamd. preorders: **24,848**
alternate cover (Shi facing right).

Ash 1 ❑ ca. 1997 Cover: 2.95 **NM** value: **Cover or less**
• Special Teaser Preview

SHI: KAIDAN — Crusade

1 ❑ Oct 1996, b&w Cover: 2.95 **NM** value: **Cover or less**
Circ: Diamd. preorders: **45,768**
🕮 The Soul of the Sword!; The Mad Monk; The Master Puppet; The Second • Japanese ghost stories **A:** Michael W. Kaluta; Peter Gutierrez **W:** Peter Gutierrez

1/A ❑ Oct 1996, b&w Cover: 2.95 **NM** value: **3.00**
alternate wraparound cover with no cover copy. 🕮 The Soul of the Sword!; The Mad Monk; The Master Puppet; The Second • Japanese ghost stories **A:** Michael W. Kaluta; Jae Lee(cover); Peter Gutierrez **W:** Peter Gutierrez

SHILOH: THE DEVIL'S OWN DAY — Heritage Collection

1 ❑ Cover: 3.50 **NM** value: **Cover or less**
No issue number. One-shot. wraparound cover. • retells Civil War battle

SHI: MASQUERADE — Crusade

1 ❑ Mar 1998 Cover: 3.50 **NM** value: **Cover or less**
Circ: Diamd. preorders: **22,806**
wraparound painted cover. **A:** Ray Lago **W:** Christopher Golden; Tom Sniegoski

SHIMMER — Avatar

1 ❑ Cover: 3.50 **NM** value: **Cover or less**
A: Rick Lyon3 **W:** Mark Seifert; William Christensen

SHI: NIGHTSTALKERS — Crusade

1 ❑ Sep 1997 Cover: 3.50 **NM** value: **Cover or less**
Circ: Diamd. preorders: **30,508**
🕮 T. C. B. **A:** Val Mayerik **W:** Bill Tucci; Christopher Golden; Gary Cohn

SHION: BLADE OF THE MINSTREL — Viz

1 ❑ Sep 1990, b&w Cover: 9.95 **NM** value: **Cover or less**

SHIP AHOY — Spotlight

1 ❑ ca. 1944 Cover: 0.10 **NM** value: **100.00**

SHIP OF FOOLS (CALIBER) — Caliber

1 ❑ b&w Cover: 2.95 **NM** value: **Cover or less**
A: Michael Avon Oeming; Bryan J.L. Glass **W:** Michael Avon Oeming; Bryan J.L. Glass

2 ❑ Cover: 2.95 **NM** value: **Cover or less**
🕮 Dante's Compass **A:** Michael Avon Oeming; Bryan J.L. Glass **W:** Michael Avon Oeming; Bryan J.L. Glass

3 ❑ b&w Cover: 2.95 **NM** value: **Cover or less**
🕮 Bowling for $$$ **A:** Michael Avon Oeming; Bryan J.L. Glass **W:** Michael Avon Oeming; Bryan J.L. Glass

4 ❑ Cover: 2.95 **NM** value: **Cover or less**
A: Michael Avon Oeming; Bryan J.L. Glass **W:** Michael Avon Oeming; Bryan J.L. Glass

5 ❑ Cover: 2.95 **NM** value: **Cover or less**
A: Michael Avon Oeming; Bryan J.L. Glass **W:** Michael Avon Oeming; Bryan J.L. Glass

6 ❑ Cover: 2.95 **NM** value: **Cover or less**
A: Michael Avon Oeming; Bryan J.L. Glass **W:** Michael Avon Oeming; Bryan J.L. Glass

Bk 1 ❑ Cover: 14.95 **NM** value: **Cover or less**
• Dante's Compass; Collects Ship of Fools (Caliber) #1-6; Compilation published by Image **A:** Michael Avon Oeming; Bryan J.L. Glass **W:** Michael Avon Oeming; Bryan J.L. Glass

SHIP OF FOOLS (IMAGE) — Image

0 ❑ Aug 1997, b&w Cover: 2.95 **NM** value: **Cover or less**
Circ: Diamd. preorders: **5,290**
A: Michael Avon Oeming; Bryan J.L. Glass **W:** Michael Avon Oeming; Bryan J.L. Glass

1 ❑ Oct 1997, b&w Cover: 2.95 **NM** value: **Cover or less**
Circ: Diamd. preorders: **4,901**
🕮 Doesn't Anybody Care, Part 1 **A:** Michael Avon Oeming; Bryan J.L. Glass **W:** Michael Avon Oeming; Bryan J.L. Glass

2 ❑ Dec 1997, b&w Cover: 2.95 **NM** value: **Cover or less**
A: Michael Avon Oeming; Bryan J.L. Glass **W:** Michael Avon Oeming; Bryan J.L. Glass

3 ❑ Feb 1998, b&w Cover: 2.95 **NM** value: **Cover or less**
Circ: Diamd. preorders: **2,447**
🕮 Zombie **A:** Michael Avon Oeming; Bryan J.L. Glass **W:** Michael Avon Oeming; Bryan J.L. Glass

Bk 1 ❑ Cover: 14.95 **NM** value: **Cover or less**
No issue number. • Trade Paperback. • collects mini-series

SHIPWRECKED! — Disney

1 ❑ Cover: 5.95 **NM** value: **Cover or less**
No issue number. **A:** Dan Spiegle **W:** William Rotsler

SHI: REKISHI — Crusade

1 ❑ Jan 1997 Cover: 2.95 **NM** value: **Cover or less**
Circ: Diamd. preorders: **38,001**
• flipbook with Shi: East Wind Rain Sneak Attack Edition #1. **A:** J.G. Jones **W:** Bill Tucci; Christopher Golden

2 ❑ Apr 1997 Cover: 2.95 **NM** value: **Cover or less**
Circ: Diamd. preorders: **29,405**
A: J.G. Jones **W:** Bill Tucci; Christopher Golden

Bk 1 ❑ Aug 1997 Cover: 4.95 **NM** value: **Cover or less**
• Bios and history of characters in Shi: The Way of the Warrior **A:** J.G. Jones **W:** Bill Tucci; Christopher Golden

SHI: SENRYAKU — Crusade

1 ❑ Aug 1995 Cover: 2.95 **NM** value: **3.25**
Circ: CapCity orders: **49,750**

1/SC ❑ Aug 1995 Cover: 2.95 **NM** value: **4.00**
• **CGC:** 1 graded, best 9.6
Variant "virgin" cover with no type. ★ 1st Appearance of 4 cover mix.

2 ❑ Oct 1995 Cover: 2.95 **NM** value: **3.00**
A: Barry Orkin; Amanda Conner; Jae Lee; George Pérez; Dan Jurgens; David Mack; Jim Balent; Marc Silvestri; Caesar; Chris Batista **W:** Gary Cohn

3 ❑ Dec 1995 Cover: 2.95 **NM** value: **3.00**

Bk 1 ❑ Cover: 24.95 **NM** value: **Cover or less**
• Collects Shi: Senryaku #1-3

Bk 1/HC ❑ Cover: 24.95 **NM** value: **Cover or less**
• Hardcover edition. • Collects Shi: Senryaku #1-3

SHI: THE BLOOD OF SAINTS — Crusade

1 ❑ Nov 1996 Cover: 2.95 **NM** value: **Cover or less**

FAN 1 ❑ Nov 1996 **NM** value: **2.00**
• Promotional edition from FAN magazine. **A:** Nelson **W:** Bill Tucci; Peter Gutierrez

SHI: THE SERIES — Crusade

Shi: The Series marks a second phase of the character and its publisher, Crusade Entertainment. Whereas Shi: The Way of the Warrior was a personal, elegantly crafted work by creator Bill Tucci (with contributions by others, as the series went on), Shi: The Series seems a much more conventional comic-book action series.

Ana Ishikawa (Shi) attempted to lay down her sword but was forced to take it up again, when her mother was kidnapped. Now, her friend Tomoe has asked for her aid again — this time to stop an oni (demon) bent on destroying all of Japan. It begins, improbably enough, with Tomoe traveling through time, landing in Hiroshima just before the dropping of the atomic bomb. Tomoe dies trying to escape the city, only to awaken in 1997. There, she seeks Ana's help to stop the oni behind her troubles, and together they travel to Japan, where they discover that the demon has put together a nuclear device that he plans to detonate.

1 ❑ Aug 1997 Cover: 2.95 **NM** value: **3.50**
Circ: Diamd. preorders: **39,630** • **CGC:** 1 graded, best 9.4
A: J.G. Jones **W:** Antony J.L. Bedard

1/A ❑ Aug 1997 Cover: 2.95 **NM** value: **3.50**
• Sneak preview edition with photo cover with Tia Carrera. **A:** J.G. Jones **W:** Antony J.L. Bedard

2 ❑ Sep 1997 Cover: 2.95 **NM** value: **3.00**
Circ: Diamd. preorders: **32,062**

3 ❑ Oct 1997 Cover: 2.95 **NM** value: **3.00**
Circ: Diamd. preorders: **30,938**

4 ❑ Nov 1997 Cover: 2.95 **NM** value: **3.00**
Circ: Diamd. preorders: **28,875**

5 ❑ Dec 1997 Cover: 2.95 **NM** value: **3.00**
Circ: Diamd. preorders: **26,945**

6 ❑ Jan 1998 Cover: 2.95 **NM** value: **Cover or less**
Circ: Diamd. preorders: **25,543**

7 ❑ Feb 1998 Cover: 2.95 **NM** value: **Cover or less**
Circ: Diamd. preorders: **23,610**
manga-style cover.

8 ❑ Mar 1998 Cover: 2.95 **NM** value: **Cover or less**
Circ: Diamd. preorders: **23,003**

9 ❑ Apr 1998 Cover: 2.95 **NM** value: **Cover or less**
Circ: Diamd. preorders: **27,029**

9/A ❑ Apr 1998 Cover: 2.95 **NM** value: **Cover or less**
alternate cover (full moon in background).

9/B ❑ Apr 1998 Cover: 2.95 **NM** value: **Cover or less**
alternate cover (Shi on her back).

9/C ❑ Apr 1998 Cover: 2.95 **NM** value: **Cover or less**
alternate cover (manga-style).

10 ❑ May 1998 Cover: 2.95 **NM** value: **Cover or less**
Circ: Diamd. preorders: **26,941**

10/A ❑ May 1998 Cover: 2.95 **NM** value: **Cover or less**
alternate cover (in water).

10/B ❑ May 1998 Cover: 2.95 **NM** value: **Cover or less**
alternate cover (cherry blossoms).

10/C ❑ May 1998 Cover: 2.95 **NM** value: **Cover or less**
alternate cover (drawing sword).

11 ❑ Jun 1998, b&w Cover: 2.95 **NM** value: **Cover or less**
Circ: Diamd. preorders: **21,060**

12 ❑ Jul 1998 Cover: 2.95 **NM** value: **Cover or less**
Circ: Diamd. preorders: **21,100**

13 ❑ Aug 1998 Cover: 2.95 **NM** value: **Cover or less**
Circ: Diamd. preorders: **20,980**

14 ❑ Aug 1998 Cover: 2.95 **NM** value: **Cover or less**
Circ: Diamd. preorders: **20,916**

15 ❑ Sep 1998 Cover: 2.95 **NM** value: **Cover or less**
Circ: Diamd. preorders: **19,961**

16 ❑ Sep 1998 Cover: 2.95 **NM** value: **Cover or less**
Circ: Diamd. preorders: **20,076**

SHI: THE WAY OF THE WARRIOR — Crusade

Secretly trained in Japanese warrior arts by her grandfather, Ana Ishikawa has come to New York to finally fulfill her vow and avenge the brutal murder of her father and brother. But Ana has an inner struggle she has to face each time she goes into to battle, because, although she grew up and was educated in her father's country, Japan, she was raised by her American expatriate mother, a missionary dedicated to peace. Ana tries to find compromise in using her training to save the innocent from criminal predators, but also regrets that she has to use violence to do so.

Although it's often grouped with "Bad Girl" titles of the 1990s, such as Razor, Lady Death, and Cry for Dawn, Shi: The Way of the Warrior transcends the genre, not only in its characterizations but also in its subtle blending of Western and Eastern art, philosophy, and history.

0.5 ❑ Cover: 5.00 **NM** value: **Cover or less**

0.5/PI ❑ Cover: 20.00 **NM** value: **Cover or less**

1 ❑ Mar 1994 Cover: 2.50 **NM** value: **6.00**
Circ: CapCity orders: **11,255** • **CGC:** 20 graded, best 9.8
A: Bill Tucci **W:** Bill Tucci; Peter Gutierrez

1/A ❑ Mar 1994 Cover: 2.50 **NM** value: **5.00**
A: Bill Tucci **W:** Bill Tucci; Peter Gutierrez

Other grades: Multiply prices above by **1.5 for Mint • 2/3 for Very Fine • 1/3 for Fine • 1/5 for Very Good • 1/8 for Good**

1/B ❑ Mar 1994 Cover: 1.95 **NM value: 8.00**
• **CGC:** 2 graded, best 9.8
• "Fan Appreciation Edition" #1 with no logo on cover. **A:** Bill Tucci **W:** Bill Tucci; Peter Gutierrez

1/C ❑ Mar 1994 **NM value: 8.00**
• **CGC:** 1 graded, best 9.2
Gold logo on cover. • Commemorative edition from the 1994 San Diego Comic Con. **A:** Bill Tucci **W:** Bill Tucci; Peter Gutierrez

2 ❑ Jun 1994 Cover: 2.50 **NM value: 5.00**
Circ: CapCity orders: **20,480** • **CGC:** 3 graded, best 9.6
A: Bill Tucci **W:** Bill Tucci

2/A ❑ Jun 1994 Cover: 2.50 **NM value: 3.00**
• **CGC:** 1 graded, best 5.5
• Fan appreciation edition #2. **A:** Bill Tucci **W:** Bill Tucci

2/Ash❑Jun 1994 **NM value: 5.00**
• Ashcan promotional edition of Shi: The Way of the Warrior #2. **A:** Bill Tucci **W:** Bill Tucci

2/B ❑ Jun 1994 Cover: 2.50 **NM value: 6.00**
• San Diego Comicon edition. **A:** Bill Tucci **W:** Bill Tucci

3 ❑ Oct 1994 Cover: 2.50 **NM value: 4.00**
Circ: CapCity orders: **21,370** • **CGC:** 2 graded, best 9.6
A: Bill Tucci **W:** Bill Tucci

4 ❑ 1995 Cover: 2.50 **NM value: 4.00**
Circ: CapCity orders: **24,185** • **CGC:** 1 graded, best 9.8
A: Bill Tucci **W:** Bill Tucci

5 ❑ Apr 1995 Cover: 2.50 **NM value: 3.00**
Circ: CapCity orders: **26,850** • **CGC:** 1 graded, best 9.6
A: Bill Tucci **W:** Bill Tucci ★ 1st Appearance of Tomoe.

5/SC❑Apr 1995 Cover: 2.50 **NM value: 5.00**
• **CGC:** 3 graded, best 9.8
Silvestri variant cover. **A:** Bill Tucci **W:** Bill Tucci ★ 1st Appearance of Tomoe.

6 ❑ 1995 Cover: 2.95 **NM value: 3.00**
Circ: CapCity orders: **25,900**
A: Bill Tucci **W:** Bill Tucci

6/A ❑ 1995 Cover: 2.95 **NM value: 3.00**
• Fan Appreciation Edition.

6/Ash❑1995 **NM value: 4.00**
• Commemorative edition from 1995 San Diego Comic Con. **A:** Bill Tucci **W:** Bill Tucci

7 ❑ Mar 1996 Cover: 2.50 **NM value: 3.00**
Circ: CapCity orders: **28,025**
• back-up crossover with Lethargic Lad **A:** Bill Tucci **W:** Bill Tucci

7/SC❑Mar 1996 **NM value: 4.00**
no cover price. • chromium edition. • back-up crossover with Lethargic Lad; limited to 5, 000 copies

8 ❑ Jun 1996 Cover: 2.95 **NM value: 3.00**
A: Bill Tucci **W:** Bill Tucci

8/A ❑ Jun 1996 **NM value: 5.00**
• Combo Gold Club version; 5000 publisher; With certificate of Authenticity **A:** Bill Tucci **W:** Bill Tucci

9 ❑ Sep 1996 Cover: 2.95 **NM value: 3.00**
A: Bill Tucci **W:** Bill Tucci

10 ❑ Oct 1996 Cover: 2.95 **NM value: 3.00**
wraparound cover. **A:** Bill Tucci **W:** Bill Tucci

11 ❑ Dec 1996 Cover: 2.95 **NM value: 3.00**
A: Bill Tucci **W:** Bill Tucci

12 ❑ Apr 1997 Cover: 2.95 **NM value: 3.00**
• **CGC:** 1 graded, best 9.2
• contains Angel Fire preview **A:** Bill Tucci **W:** Bill Tucci

Bk 1❑ Cover: 12.95 **NM value: Cover or less**
• Collects Shi: The Way of the Warrior #1-6 **A:** Bill Tucci **W:** Bill Tucci

Bk 1-2❑ Cover: 14.95 **NM value: Cover or less**

Bk 2❑ Cover: 14.95 **NM value: Cover or less**
• Collects issues #5-8

Bk 3❑ Cover: 17.95 **NM value: Cover or less**
• Collects issues #9-12 and Shi vs. Tomoe

FAN 1❑Jan 1995 Cover: 2.95 **NM value: Cover or less**
Circ: CapCity orders: **27,625** Diamd. preorders: **4,716**
• Included with Fan magazine. 📖 The Blood of Saints **A:** Bill Tucci **W:** Bill Tucci

FAN 2❑ **NM value: 1.00**
• Overstreet Fan promotional edition #2.

FAN 3❑ **NM value: 1.00**
• Overstreet Fan promotional edition #3.

SHI/VAMPIRELLA — Crusade

1 ❑ Oct 1997 Cover: 2.95 **NM value: Cover or less**
Circ: Diamd. preorders: **36,673**
📖 In Rashomon • crossover with Harris **A:** Kevin Lau **W:** Warren Ellis

SHI VS. TOMOE — Crusade

1 ❑ Aug 1996 Cover: 3.95 **NM value: Cover or less**
Foil wrap-around cover, color. **A:** Jason Orfalas; Bill Tucci; Poly Wilfredo Feliciano **W:** Bill Tucci; Peter Gutierrez

1/LE❑ Aug 1996 Cover: 5.00 **NM value: Cover or less**
• Preview sold at San Diego Comic Con, black and white **A:** Jason Orfalas; Bill Tucci; Poly Wilfredo Feliciano **W:** Bill Tucci; Peter Gutierrez

SHI: YEAR OF THE DRAGON — Crusade

1 ❑ Sep 2000 Cover: 2.99 **NM value: Cover or less**
Circ: Diamd. preorders: **14,934**
A: Bill Tucci **W:** Gary Kohn

SHMOO COMICS (AL CAPP'S ...) — Toby

1 ❑ ca. 1949 Cover: 0.10 **NM value: 175.00**
2 ❑ ca. 1949 Cover: 0.10 **NM value: 150.00**
3 ❑ ca. 1949 Cover: 0.10 **NM value: 125.00**
4 ❑ ca. 1950 Cover: 0.10 **NM value: 125.00**
5 ❑ ca. 1950 Cover: 0.10 **NM value: 125.00**

SHOCK & SPANK THE MONKEYBOYS SPECIAL — Arrow

1 ❑ b&w Cover: 2.50 **NM value: Cover or less**

SHOCK DETECTIVE CASES — Star

20 ❑ Sep 1952 Cover: 0.10 **NM value: 150.00**
21 ❑ Nov 1952 Cover: 0.10 **NM value: 150.00**
• **CGC:** 1 graded, best 9.0

SHOCKING MYSTERY CASES — Star

50 ❑ Sep 1952 Cover: 0.10 **NM value: 350.00**
51 ❑ Nov 1952 Cover: 0.10 **NM value: 200.00**
• **CGC:** 3 graded, best 8.0
52 ❑ Jan 1953 Cover: 0.10 **NM value: 150.00**
53 ❑ Mar 1953 Cover: 0.10 **NM value: 150.00**
• **CGC:** 1 graded, best 9.6
54 ❑ May 1953 Cover: 0.10 **NM value: 150.00**
• **CGC:** 1 graded, best 1.8
55 ❑ ca. 1953 Cover: 0.10 **NM value: 150.00**
56 ❑ ca. 1953 Cover: 0.10 **NM value: 150.00**
57 ❑ ca. 1954 Cover: 0.10 **NM value: 150.00**
58 ❑ ca. 1954 Cover: 0.10 **NM value: 150.00**
59 ❑ ca. 1954 Cover: 0.10 **NM value: 150.00**
60 ❑ ca. 1954 Cover: 0.10 **NM value: 150.00**
• **CGC:** 1 graded, best 8.0

SHOCKROCKETS — Image

Towards the end of the 21st century, a terrible war wrought by an alien race has ravaged the Earth. To protect the planet from future attacks, an elite squad of space fliers — The Shock Rockets — is formed. These high-tech flyboys (and girls) use ships that are deadly combinations of human and alien technology. But aliens are no longer the problem. The real danger comes from the all-too-human would-be dictator Emilio Korda, who has destroyed the Shock Rockets base as part of his plan to create a global empire subservient only to him. Can Earth's protectors stop him? And when it seems that all has failed, can a young Shock Rocket flyer, dubbed by many as the weak link in the team, save the day? Writer Kurt Busiek's (Marvels, Astro City) six-issue limited series had all the action and flavor of a 1930's movie serial, while Stuart Immonen (Final Night) and Wade von Grawbadger (Starman) provided all the artistic flash and zoom of a turn-of-the-millennium summer blockbuster.

1 ❑ Apr 2000 Cover: 2.50 **NM value: Cover or less**
Circ: Diamd. preorders: **30,570**
A: Stuart Immonen **W:** Kurt Busiek

2 ❑ May 2000 Cover: 2.50 **NM value: Cover or less**
Circ: Diamd. preorders: **22,280**
A: Stuart Immonen **W:** Kurt Busiek

3 ❑ Jun 2000 Cover: 2.50 **NM value: Cover or less**
Circ: Diamd. preorders: **20,059**
📖 The Triangle Trade **A:** Stuart Immonen **W:** Kurt Busiek

4 ❑ Jul 2000 Cover: 2.50 **NM value: Cover or less**
Circ: Diamd. preorders: **18,361**
📖 Rocket Science **A:** Stuart Immonen **W:** Kurt Busiek

5 ❑ Aug 2000 Cover: 2.50 **NM value: Cover or less**
Circ: Diamd. preorders: **16,958**
📖 Base Treachery **A:** Stuart Immonen **W:** Kurt Busiek

6 ❑ Oct 2000 Cover: 2.50 **NM value: Cover or less**
Circ: Diamd. preorders: **16,766**
📖 The Darkest Hour… **A:** Stuart Immonen **W:** Kurt Busiek

SHOCK SUSPENSTORIES (E.C.) — E.C.

From the start, a cover box read, "Jolting tales of tension in the EC tradition!" (a caption that also ran on many issues of Crime SuspenStories). Stories of violence and suspense were illustrated by such E.C. standards as Johnny Craig, Reed Crandall, Jack Davis, George Evans, (Editor) Al Feldstein, Graham Ingels, Jack Kamen, Bernie Krigstein, Joe Orlando, Al Williamson, and Wally Wood. Story sources included Edgar Allan Poe and Ray Bradbury, and the Johnny Craig severed-head cover for #22 was questioned as to its taste in Publisher William Gaines' testimony before Congress. "Carrion Death!" in #9 was Reed Crandall's first story for E.C.

The series came to an end with the Comics Magazine Association of America's implementation of the Comics Code, which forbade much of its type of story in newsstand comics. — Maggie

1 ❑ Feb 1952 Cover: 0.10 **NM value: 625.00**
• **CGC:** 15 graded, best 9.8
Electrocution cover. 📖 The Neat Job; Yellow; Last Will (text piece); Alibi (text piece); Monsters; The Rug • Ray Bradbury adaptation

2 ❑ Apr 1952 Cover: 0.10 **NM value: 350.00**
• **CGC:** 8 graded, best 9.8
📖 Kickback; Gee, Dad…It's a Daisy; The Patriots; Hiding Place (text piece); Halloween

3 ❑ Jun 1952 Cover: 0.10 **NM value: 265.00**
• **CGC:** 3 graded, best 9.8
📖 Just Desserts; The Guilty; Jump-Off (text piece); The Big Stand-Up; Stumped • Brief mention in Seduction of The Innocent

4 ❑ Aug 1952 Cover: 0.10 **NM value: 250.00**
• **CGC:** 5 graded, best 9.6
📖 Split Second; Confession; Doc (text piece); Strictly Business; Uppercut • Brief mention in Seduction of The Innocent

5 ❑ Oct 1952 Cover: 0.10 **NM value: 225.00**
• **CGC:** 9 graded, best 9.8
📖 Well-Traveled; Hate; Justice (text piece); What Fur?; Cold Cuts

6 ❑ Dec 1952 Cover: 0.10 **NM value: 265.00**
• **CGC:** 12 graded, best 9.8
Bondage cover. 📖 Dead Right!; Under Cover!; Not So Tough!; Sugar 'n Spice 'n… **A:** Joe Orlando; Wally Wood; Jack Kamen; Graham Ingels **W:** Joe Orlando; Wally Wood; Jack Kamen; Graham Ingels

7 ❑ Feb 1953 Cover: 0.10 **NM value: 265.00**
• **CGC:** 13 graded, best 9.8
📖 Beauty at the Beach!; The Bribe!; Infiltration; The Small Assassin! • Ray Bradbury adaptation **A:** Joe Orlando; Wally Wood; Jack Kamen; Graham Ingels **W:** Joe Orlando; Wally Wood; Jack Kamen; Graham Ingels; Ray Bradbury

8 ❑ Apr 1953 Cover: 0.10 **NM value: 200.00**
• **CGC:** 7 graded, best 9.8
📖 Piecemeal; The Assault!; The Arrival; Seep No More! **A:** George Evans; Al Williamson; Wally Wood; Jack Kamen **W:** George Evans; Al Williamson; Wally Wood; Jack Kamen

9 ❑ Jun 1953 Cover: 0.10 **NM value: 175.00**
• **CGC:** 4 graded, best 9.8
📖 The October Game; Came the Dawn!; The Meddlers!; Carrion Death! • Ray Bradbury Adaptation **A:** Joe Orlando; Wally Wood; Reed Crandall; Jack Kamen **W:** Joe Orlando; Wally Wood; Reed Crandall; Jack Kamen; Ray Bradbury

10 ❑ Aug 1953 Cover: 0.10 **NM value: 175.00**
• **CGC:** 3 graded, best 9.6
📖 The Sacrifice; …So Shall Ye Reap!; Home Run!; Sweetie-Pie! **A:** Joe Orlando; Wally Wood; Reed Crandall; Jack Kamen **W:** Joe Orlando; Wally Wood; Reed Crandall; Jack Kamen

11 ❑ Oct 1953 Cover: 0.10 **NM value: 175.00**
• **CGC:** 4 graded, best 9.8
📖 The Tryst; In Gratitude…; The Space Suitors; Deadbeat (text story); Three's a Crowd

12 ❑ Dec 1953 Cover: 0.10 **NM value: 190.00**
• **CGC:** 7 graded, best 9.6
📖 Deadline; The Monkey; Last Laugh (text story); The Kidnapper; Fall Guy

13 ❑ Mar 1954 Cover: 0.10 **NM value: 265.00**
• **CGC:** 7 graded, best 9.4
📖 Only Skin-Deep; Blood-Brothers; Upon Reflection; Squeeze Play **A:** Frank Frazetta

14 ❑ May 1954 Cover: 0.10 **NM value: 160.00**
• **CGC:** 3 graded, best 9.6
📖 The Orphan; The Whipping; Slaughter (text story); You, Murderer; As Ye Sow…

15 ❑ Jul 1954 Cover: 0.10 **NM value: 160.00**
• **CGC:** 6 graded, best 9.4
📖 Raw Deal; The Confidant; Proposal (text story); For Cryin' Out Loud!; Well Trained **A:** George Evans; Wally Wood; Reed Crandall; Jack Kamen **W:** George Evans; Wally Wood; Reed Crandall; Jack Kamen

16 ❑ Sep 1954 Cover: 0.10 **NM value: 135.00**
• **CGC:** 4 graded, best 9.6
📖 …My Brother's Keeper; The Hazing; A Kind of Justice; The Pen is Mightier **A:** George Evans; Joe Orlando; Reed Crandall; Jack Kamen **W:** George Evans; Joe Orlando; Reed Crandall; Jack Kamen

17 ❑ Nov 1954 Cover: 0.10 **NM value: 135.00**
• **CGC:** 4 graded, best 9.4
📖 4-Sided Triangle; In Character; The Assassin; The Operation! **A:** George Evans; Joe Orlando; Reed Crandall; Jack Kamen **W:** George Evans; Joe Orlando; Reed Crandall; Jack Kamen

18 ❑ Jan 1955 Cover: 0.10 **NM value: 135.00**
• **CGC:** 4 graded, best 9.4
📖 Cadillac Fever; The Trap; In the Bag; Rundown; Slob! (text story) final issue. **A:** George Evans; Bernie Krigstein; Reed Crandall; Jack Kamen **W:** George Evans; Bernie Krigstein; Reed Crandall; Jack Kamen

SHOCK SUSPENSTORIES (RCP) — Gemstone

1 ❑ Sep 1992 Cover: 1.50 **NM value: 2.00**
Circ: CapCity orders: **4,575**
Electrocution cover. 📖 The Neat Job; Yellow; Last Will (text piece); Alibi (text piece); Monsters; The Rug • Reprints Shock SuspenStories #1; Ray Bradbury adaptation **A:** Joe Orlando; Jack Kamen; Jack Davis; Graham Ingels

2 ❑ Dec 1992 Cover: 1.50 **NM value: 2.00**
Circ: Statement: **22,131** CapCity orders: **4,500**
📖 Kickback; Gee, Dad…It's a Daisy; The Patriots; Hiding Place (text piece); Halloween • Reprints Shock SuspenStories #2

3 ❑ Mar 1993 Cover: 1.50 **NM value: 2.00**
Circ: Statement: **22,131** CapCity orders: **3,700**
📖 Just Desserts; The Guilty; Jump-Off (text piece); The Big Stand-Up; Stumped • Reprints Shock SuspenStories #3

4 ❑ Jun 1993 Cover: 2.00 **NM value: Cover or less**
Circ: Statement: **22,131** CapCity orders: **3,700**
📖 Split Second; Confession; Doc (text piece); Strictly Business; Uppercut • Reprints Shock SuspenStories #4 **A:** Joe Orlando; Wally Wood; Jack Kamen; Jack Davis

5 ❑ Sep 1993 Cover: 2.00 **NM value: Cover or less**
Circ: Statement: **22,131**
📖 Well-Traveled; Hate; Justice (text piece); What Fur?; Cold Cuts • Reprints Shock SuspenStories #5 **A:** Joe Orlando; Wally Wood; Jack Kamen; Jack Davis

6 ❑ Dec 1993 Cover: 2.00 **NM value: Cover or less**
Circ: Statement: **14,828** CapCity orders: **3,250**
📖 Dead Right!; Under Cover!; Not So Tough!; Sugar 'n Spice 'n… • Reprints Shock SuspenStories #6 **A:** Joe Orlando; Wally Wood; Jack Kamen; Graham Ingels **W:** Joe Orlando; Wally Wood; Jack Kamen; Graham Ingels

7 ❑ Mar 1994 Cover: 2.00 **NM value: Cover or less**
Circ: Statement: **14,828** CapCity orders: **2,925**
📖 Beauty at the Beach!; The Bribe!; Infiltration; The Small Assassin! • Reprints Shock SuspenStories #7 **A:** George Evans; Joe Orlando; Jack Kirby; Wally Wood; Jack Kamen; Graham Ingels **C:** Al Feldstein **W:** Joe Orlando; Wally Wood; Jack Kamen; Graham Ingels; Ray Bradbury

CGC-graded: Multiply prices above by **33 for 9.9 M • 16 for 9.8 NM/M • 7 for 9.6 NM+ • 5 for 9.4 NM • 2.5 for 9.2 NM- • 1.5 for 9.0 VF/NM**

8 ❑ Jun 1994 Cover: 2.00 **NM** value: **Cover or less**
Circ: Statement: **14,828** CapCity orders: **2,775**
🕮 Piecemeal; The Assault!; The Arrival; Seep No More! • Reprints Shock SuspenStories #8 **A:** George Evans; Al Williamson; Wally Wood; Jack Kamen **C:** Al Feldstein **W:** George Evans; Al Williamson; Wally Wood; Jack Kamen

9 ❑ Sep 1994 Cover: 2.00 **NM** value: **Cover or less**
Circ: Statement: **14,828**
🕮 The October Game; Came the Dawn!; The Meddlers!; Carrion Death! • Reprints Shock SuspenStories #9 **A:** Joe Orlando; Wally Wood; Reed Crandall; Jack Kamen **W:** Joe Orlando; Wally Wood; Reed Crandall; Jack Kamen; Ray Bradbury

10 ❑ Dec 1994 Cover: 2.00 **NM** value: **Cover or less**
Circ: Statement: **7,281** CapCity orders: **2,750**
🕮 The Sacrifice; ...So Shall Ye Reap!; Home Run!; Sweetie-Pie! • Reprints Shock SuspenStories #10 **A:** Joe Orlando; Wally Wood; Reed Crandall; Jack Kamen **W:** Joe Orlando; Wally Wood; Reed Crandall; Jack Kamen

11 ❑ Mar 1995 Cover: 2.00 **NM** value: **Cover or less**
Circ: Statement: **7,281**
🕮 The Tryst; In Gratitude...; The Space Suitors; Deadbeat (text story); Three's a Crowd • Reprints Shock SuspenStories #11

12 ❑ Jun 1995 Cover: 2.00 **NM** value: **Cover or less**
Circ: Statement: **7,281** CapCity orders: **2,375**
🕮 Deadline; The Monkey; Last Laugh (text story); The Kidnapper; Fall Guy • Reprints Shock SuspenStories #12

13 ❑ Sep 1995 Cover: 2.00 **NM** value: **Cover or less**
Circ: Statement: **7,281** CapCity orders: **2,575**
🕮 Only Skin-Deep; Blood-Brothers; Upon Reflection; Squeeze Play • Reprints Shock SuspenStories #13

14 ❑ Dec 1995 Cover: 2.00 **NM** value: **Cover or less**
Circ: Statement: **6,400**
🕮 The Orphan; The Whipping; Slaughter (text story); You, Murderer; As Ye Sow... • Reprints Shock SuspenStories #14; Has 1995 Statement; avg print run 10,346; avg sales 6,766; avg subs 515; avg total paid 7,281; no newsstand sales during year

15 ❑ Mar 1996 Cover: 2.00 **NM** value: **Cover or less**
Circ: Statement: **6,400**
🕮 Raw Deal; The Confidant; Proposal (text story); For Cryin' Out Loud!; Well Trained • Reprints Shock SuspenStories #15; Cannibalism story **A:** George Evans; Wally Wood; Reed Crandall; Jack Kamen **W:** George Evans; Wally Wood; Reed Crandall; Jack Kamen

16 ❑ Jun 1996 Cover: 2.00 **NM** value: **Cover or less**
Circ: Statement: **6,400**
🕮 ...My Brother's Keeper; The Hazing; A Kind of Justice; The Pen is Mightier • Reprints Shock SuspenStories #16 **A:** George Evans; Joe Orlando; Reed Crandall; Jack Kamen **W:** George Evans; Joe Orlando; Reed Crandall; Jack Kamen

17 ❑ Sep 1996 Cover: 2.50 **NM** value: **Cover or less**
Circ: Statement: **6,400**
🕮 4-Sided Triangle; In Character; The Assassin; The Operation! • Reprints Shock SuspenStories #17 **A:** George Evans; Joe Orlando; Reed Crandall; Jack Kamen **W:** George Evans; Joe Orlando; Reed Crandall; Jack Kamen

18 ❑ Dec 1996 Cover: 2.50 **NM** value: **Cover or less**
Circ: Diamd. preorders: **5,363**
🕮 Cadillac Fever; The Trap; In the Bag; Rundown; Slob! (text story) • Reprints Shock SuspenStories #18; Has 1996 Statement, filed 7/15/96; avg print run 7,832 (not early, series was quarterly); avg sales 5,907; avg subs 493; avg total paid 6,400; office use 1,482; max existent 7,832; no newsstand sales during year **A:** George Evans; Bernie Krigstein; Reed Crandall; Jack Kamen **W:** George Evans; Bernie Krigstein; Reed Crandall; Jack Kamen

Anl 1❑ Cover: 8.95 **NM** value: **Cover or less**
🕮 The Neat Job; Yellow; Last Will (text piece); Alibi (text piece); Monsters; The Rug; Kickback; Gee, Dad...It's a Daisy; The Patri • Reprints Shock SuspenStories #1-5

Anl 2❑ Cover: 9.95 **NM** value: **Cover or less**
🕮 Dead Right!; Under Cover!; Not So Tough!; Sugar 'n Spice 'n... • Reprints Shock SuspenStories #6-10 **A:** Joe Orlando; Wally Wood; Jack Kamen; Graham Ingels **W:** Joe Orlando; Wally Wood; Jack Kamen; Graham Ingels

Anl 3❑ Cover: 8.95 **NM** value: **Cover or less**
🕮 The Tryst; In Gratitude...; The Space Sui • Reprints Shock SuspenStories #11-14

Anl 4❑ Cover: 9.95 **NM** value: **Cover or less**
• Reprints Shock SuspenStories #15-18 **A:** George Evans; Bernie Krigstein; Reed Crandall; Jack Kamen **W:** George Evans; Bernie Krigstein; Reed Crandall; Jack Kamen

SHOCK THE MONKEY — Millennium

1 ❑ Cover: 2.95 **NM** value: **Cover or less**
A: Reuben Rude
2 ❑ b&w Cover: 3.95 **NM** value: **Cover or less**

SHOCK THERAPY — Harrier

1 ❑ Nov 1986 Cover: 1.95 **NM** value: **Cover or less**
🕮 Frog Part 1; Epitaph; Murder Near the Rue Morgue; Fur Exchange; The Inside
2 ❑ Dec 1986 Cover: 1.95 **NM** value: **Cover or less**
3 ❑ Jan 1987 Cover: 1.95 **NM** value: **Cover or less**
🕮 Frog Part 3; Chance of a Ghost; Murder Near the Rue Morgue; Space Race; The Insider **A:** Andy Lanning; Hong; Tom Elmes **W:** Howard Priestley
4 ❑ Feb 1987 Cover: 1.95 **NM** value: **Cover or less**
5 ❑ Mar 1987 Cover: 1.95 **NM** value: **Cover or less**

Do you have changes or corrections for the **Standard Catalog**? Send your original research to us at
allcomics@krause.com

SHOGUN WARRIORS — Marvel

These toy robots from the late 1970s come to life in a title reminiscent of such great Japanese horror films as Godzilla.

The robots — Combatra, Dangard Ace, and Raydeen — are manned respectively by Japanese pilot Genji Odashu, African scientist Ilongo Savage, and American daredevil Richard Carson. They take on Tokyo — destroying Rok-Korr, Maur-Kon, and many more. Both the Shogun Warriors and the monsters are gigantic, and, as could have been expected, they have colossal encounters while dwarfing metropolitan cities.

Relatively long-lived for a series in this genre, Shogun Warriors enjoyed a 20-issue run.

1 ❑ Feb 1979 Cover: 0.35 **NM** value: **2.50**
• **CGC:** 13 graded, best 9.6
🕮 Raydeen! **A:** Herb Trimpe **W:** Doug Moench ★ 1st Appearance of Shogun Warriors.
2 ❑ Mar 1979 Cover: 0.35 **NM** value: **2.00**
3 ❑ Apr 1979 Cover: 0.35 **NM** value: **2.00**
4 ❑ May 1979 Cover: 0.40 **NM** value: **2.00**
5 ❑ Jun 1979 Cover: 0.40 **NM** value: **2.00**
6 ❑ Jul 1979 Cover: 0.40 **NM** value: **2.00**
7 ❑ Aug 1979 Cover: 0.40 **NM** value: **2.00**
8 ❑ Sep 1979 Cover: 0.40 **NM** value: **2.00**
9 ❑ Oct 1979 Cover: 0.40 **NM** value: **2.00**
10 ❑ Nov 1979 Cover: 0.40 **NM** value: **2.00**
11 ❑ Dec 1979 Cover: 0.40 **NM** value: **1.50**
12 ❑ Jan 1980 Cover: 0.40 **NM** value: **1.50**
13 ❑ Feb 1980 Cover: 0.40 **NM** value: **1.50**
14 ❑ Mar 1980 Cover: 0.40 **NM** value: **1.50**
15 ❑ Apr 1980 Cover: 0.40 **NM** value: **1.50**
16 ❑ May 1980 Cover: 0.40 **NM** value: **1.50**
★ Death of Followers.
17 ❑ Jun 1980 Cover: 0.40 **NM** value: **1.50**
18 ❑ Jul 1980 Cover: 0.40 **NM** value: **1.50**
19 ❑ Aug 1980 Cover: 0.40 **NM** value: **1.50**
★ Appearance of Fantastic Four.
20 ❑ Sep 1980 Cover: 0.50 **NM** value: **1.50**
★ Appearance of Fantastic Four.

SHOJO ZEN — Zen

1 ❑ Cover: 2.50 **NM** value: **Cover or less**
🕮 Love and Zen **A:** Lonhee **W:** Lonhee

SHOOTY BEAGLE — Fantagraphics / Eros

All issues are adults only.
1 ❑ b&w Cover: 2.25 **NM** value: **Cover or less**
2 ❑ b&w Cover: 2.25 **NM** value: **Cover or less**
3 ❑ b&w Cover: 2.25 **NM** value: **Cover or less**

SHORT ON PLOT! — Mu

1 ❑ b&w Cover: 2.50 **NM** value: **Cover or less**
No issue number.

SHORT ORDER — Head

1 ❑ **NM** value: **20.00**
A: Art Spiegelman **W:** Art Spiegelman
2 ❑ Jan 1974 Cover: 0.75 **NM** value: **15.00**
🕮 Don't Get Around Much Anymore; The Shlockpeople; A Reason to Live; Tanktown Jollies; Dry Ice; Race Riot; Pillowtalk; Captain **A:** Art Spiegelman; Diane Noomin; Bill Griffith; George Kuchar; Jay Kinney; Joe Schenkman; Michael McMillan; Rory Hayes; Willy Murphy **W:** Art Spiegelman; Diane Noomin; Bill Griffith; George Kuchar; Jay Kinney; Joe Schenkman; Michael McMillan; Rory Hayes; Willy Murphy

SHORTS (PAT KELLEY'S...) — Antarctic

1 ❑ Oct 1997 Cover: 2.95 **NM** value: **Cover or less**
🕮 A B-Movie Primer; As Mr. Ology!: How Does Gravity Work?; Supakik; Tales From the Netherworld; Tales of Grithmonger!; Dr **A:** Pat Kelley **W:** Pat Kelley
2 ❑ Cover: 2.95 **NM** value: **Cover or less**

SHORTSTOP SQUAD — Ultimate Sports Force

1 ❑ ca. 1999 Cover: 3.95 **NM** value: **Cover or less**
• Barry Larkin apperance★ Appearance of Cal Ripken, Jr., Alex Rodriguez, Derek Jeter, Barry Larkin.

SHOTGUN MARY (1ST SERIES) — Antarctic

1 ❑ Sep 1995 Cover: 2.95 **NM** value: **4.00**
Circ: CapCity orders: **13,150**
A: Joseph Wight; Fred Perry(pinup); Pat Kelley(pinup); Shon Howell(pinup) **W:** Herb Mallette
1/CS❑Sep 1995 Cover: 8.95 **NM** value: **9.95**
• CD edition. **A:** Joseph Wight; Fred Perry(pinup); Pat Kelley(pinup); Shon Howell(pinup) **W:** Herb Mallette
1/SC❑Sep 1995 Cover: 2.95 **NM** value: **Cover or less**
alternate cover.
2 ❑ 1995 Cover: 2.95 **NM** value: **3.00**
A: Joseph Wight **W:** Herb Mallette
3 ❑ 1995 Cover: 2.95 **NM** value: **3.00**
• Exists? **A:** Joseph Wight **W:** Herb Mallette
Ash 1❑Sep 1995 Cover: 2.95 **NM** value: **Cover or less**
• ashcan edition.

SHOTGUN MARY (2ND SERIES) — Antarctic

1 ❑ Mar 1998 Cover: 2.95 **NM** value: **Cover or less**
Circ: Diamd. preorders: **9,543**
🕮 Fall **A:** Joseph Wight **W:** Herb Mallette
1/SC❑Mar 1998 Cover: 2.95 **NM** value: **4.00**
• Limited edition cover (purple). 🕮 Fall **A:** Joseph Wight **W:** Herb Mallette
2 ❑ May 1998 Cover: 2.95 **NM** value: **Cover or less**
Circ: Diamd. preorders: **5,726**
🕮 Impact **A:** Kelsey Shannon **W:** Herb Mallette
3 ❑ Jul 1998 Cover: 2.95 **NM** value: **Cover or less**
Circ: Diamd. preorders: **4,746**
🕮 Consciousness final issue. **A:** Kelsey Shannon **W:** Herb Mallette

SHOTGUN MARY: BLOOD LORE — Antarctic

1 ❑ Feb 1997 Cover: 2.95 **NM** value: **Cover or less**
Circ: Diamd. preorders: **9,842**
🕮 Visceral Portent **A:** Neil Googe **W:** Herb Mallette
2 ❑ Apr 1997 Cover: 2.95 **NM** value: **Cover or less**
Circ: Diamd. preorders: **7,897**
🕮 Strange Terrain **A:** Neil Googe **W:** Herb Mallette
3 ❑ Jun 1997 Cover: 2.95 **NM** value: **Cover or less**
Circ: Diamd. preorders: **8,104**
🕮 Surprises **A:** Neil Googe **W:** Herb Mallette
4 ❑ Aug 1997 Cover: 2.95 **NM** value: **Cover or less**
Circ: Diamd. preorders: **7,155**
🕮 Reversals **A:** Neil Googe **W:** Herb Mallette

SHOTGUN MARY: DEVILTOWN — Antarctic

1 ❑ Jul 1996 Cover: 2.95 **NM** value: **Cover or less**
1/LE❑ ca. 1996 Cover: 5.40 **NM** value: **Cover or less**
• Commemorative edition. **A:** Jolyon Yates **W:** Herb Mallette

SHOTGUN MARY SHOOTING GALLERY — Antarctic

1 ❑ Jun 1996 Cover: 2.95 **NM** value: **Cover or less**

SHOTGUN MARY: SON OF THE BEAST — Antarctic

1 ❑ Oct 1997 Cover: 2.95 **NM** value: **Cover or less**
Circ: Diamd. preorders: **9,043**
A: Esad T. Ribic **W:** Miki Horvatic

SHOTTLOOSE — Absolute

1 ❑ Cover: 2.00 **NM** value: **Cover or less**
🕮 A Shot In The Dark **A:** Shane Campos **W:** Bill Henry
2 ❑ Cover: 2.00 **NM** value: **Cover or less**

SHOWCASE — DC

As the name implies, Showcase is an anthology series designed to spotlight various DC creations. Although many such titles make enjoyable reading, they usually have little importance in the larger worlds of the comics universe. Showcase is an exception to that rule. In #4, it introduces readers to Barry Allen, the Silver Age Flash. Four issues later, it gives us the fantastic first appearance of The Challengers of the Unknown.

Later issues keep up the pace, bringing the first appearances of Anthro, Adam Strange, the Silver Age Green Lantern (Hal Jordan), the Silver Age Atom (Ray Palmer), Hawk and Dove, The Creeper, Rip Hunter, the Sea Devils, and many others.

Having run for 14 years between 1956 and 1970, the series came to an end with #93. It was later revived in 1977, running until issue #104.

1 ❑ Apr 1956 Cover: 0.10 **NM** value: **2850.00**
• **CGC:** 2 graded, best 7.0
• Fire Fighters
2 ❑ Jun 1956 Cover: 0.10 **NM** value: **775.00**
• **CGC:** 2 graded, best 8.0
• Kings of Wild **A:** Joe Kubert
3 ❑ Aug 1956 Cover: 0.10 **NM** value: **750.00**
• **CGC:** 4 graded, best 6.5
• Frogmen
4 ❑ Oct 1956 Cover: 0.10 **NM** value: **25000.00**
• **CGC:** 25 graded, best 9.4
🕮 Mystery of the Human Thunderbolt!; The Man Who Broke the Time Barrier • Flash; Begins DC Silver Age revival of heroes **A:** Carmine Infantino; Joe Kubert ★ Origin of Flash II (Barry Allen. ★ 1st Appearance of Flash II (Barry Allen.
5 ❑ Dec 1956 Cover: 0.10 **NM** value: **900.00**
• **CGC:** 2 graded, best 7.5
• Manhunters
6 ❑ Feb 1957 Cover: 0.10 **NM** value: **3500.00**
• **CGC:** 17 graded, best 8.0
🕮 The Secrets of the Sorcerer's Box • 1st appearance/origin Challengers of the Unknown **C:** Jack Kirby ★ Origin of Challengers of the Unknown. ★ 1st Appearance of Challengers of the Unknown.
7 ❑ Apr 1957 Cover: 0.10 **NM** value: **1750.00**
• **CGC:** 6 graded, best 9.2
🕮 Ultivac is Loose • Challengers of the Unknown **C:** Jack Kirby ★ 2nd Appearance of Challengers of the Unknown. ★ 2nd Appearance of Challengers of the Unknown.
8 ❑ Jun 1957 Cover: 0.10 **NM** value: **11000.00**
• **CGC:** 17 graded, best 6.5
🕮 The Coldest Man on Earth; The Secret of the Empty Box • Flash **A:** Carmine Infantino ★ Origin of Captain Cold. ★ 1st Appearance of Captain Cold. ★ 2nd Appearance of Flash II (Barry Allen).
9 ❑ Aug 1957 Cover: 0.10 **NM** value: **6000.00**
• **CGC:** 17 graded, best 9.2
★ Appearance of Lois Lane.
10 ❑ Oct 1957 Cover: 0.10 **NM** value: **2500.00**
• **CGC:** 13 graded, best 9.0
C: Wayne Boring ★ Appearance of Lois Lane.
11 ❑ Dec 1957 Cover: 0.10 **NM** value: **1600.00**
• **CGC:** 7 graded, best 9.0

Other grades: Multiply prices above by **1.5 for Mint • 2/3 for Very Fine • 1/3 for Fine • 1/5 for Very Good • 1/8 for Good**

📖 The Day the Earth Blew Up **C:** Jack Kirby ★ Appearance of Challengers of the Unknown.

12 ❑ Feb 1958 Cover: 0.10 **NM** value: **1600.00**
• **CGC:** 5 graded, best 9.2
📖 The Menace of the Ancient Vials **C:** Jack Kirby ★ Appearance of Challengers of the Unknown.

13 ❑ Apr 1958 Cover: 0.10 **NM** value: **4000.00**
• **CGC:** 10 graded, best 7.5
📖 Around the World in 80 Minutes; Master of the Elements • Flash★ Origin of Mr. Element. ★ 1st Appearance of Mr. Element. ★ Appearance of Flash II (Barry Allen).

14 ❑ Jun 1958 Cover: 0.10 **NM** value: **4200.00**
• **CGC:** 14 graded, best 9.0
📖 Giants of the Time World!; The Man Who Changed the Earth! • Flash★ Origin of Doctor Alchemy. ★ 1st Appearance of Doctor Alchemy. ★ Appearance of Flash II (Barry Allen).

15 ❑ Aug 1958 Cover: 0.10 **NM** value: **1650.00**
• **CGC:** 8 graded, best 8.5
★ 1st Appearance of Space Ranger.

16 ❑ Oct 1958 Cover: 0.10 **NM** value: **900.00**
• **CGC:** 5 graded, best 7.0
• Space Ranger

17 ❑ Dec 1958 Cover: 0.10 **NM** value: **2200.00**
• **CGC:** 10 graded, best 8.5
📖 The Planet and the Pendulum • Adam Strange **C:** Gil Kane ★ Origin of Adam Strange. ★ 1st Appearance of Adam Strange.

18 ❑ Feb 1959 Cover: 0.10 **NM** value: **1100.00**
• **CGC:** 11 graded, best 9.2
• Adam Strange **C:** Gil Kane ★ 1st Appearance of Rann.

19 ❑ Apr 1959 Cover: 0.10 **NM** value: **1100.00**
• **CGC:** 5 graded, best 9.6
• Adam Strange **C:** Gil Kane

20 ❑ Jun 1959 Cover: 0.10 **NM** value: **850.00**
• **CGC:** 6 graded, best 9.4
★ 1st Appearance of Rip Hunter.

21 ❑ Aug 1959 Cover: 0.10 **NM** value: **450.00**
• **CGC:** 4 graded, best 7.5
★ 2nd Appearance of Rip Hunter.

22 ❑ Oct 1959 Cover: 0.10 **NM** value: **4750.00**
• **CGC:** 38 graded, best 9.0
📖 SOS Green Lantern; Secret of the Flaming Spear!; Menace of the Runaway Missile! • Green Lantern **A:** Gil Kane ★ Origin of Green Lantern II (Hal Jordan). ★ 1st Appearance of Green Lantern II (Hal Jordan), Carol Ferris.

23 ❑ Dec 1959 Cover: 0.10 **NM** value: **1550.00**
• **CGC:** 13 graded, best 9.4
📖 Summons from Space!; The Invisible Destroyer! • Green Lantern **A:** Gil Kane ★ 1st Appearance of Invisible Destroyer.

24 ❑ Feb 1960 Cover: 0.10 **NM** value: **1450.00**
Circ: Statement: **213,000** • **CGC:** 23 graded, best 9.0
📖 The Secret of the Black Museum!; The Creature That Couldn't Die! • Green Lantern **A:** Gil Kane

25 ❑ Apr 1960 Cover: 0.10 **NM** value: **275.00**
Circ: Statement: **213,000** • **CGC:** 4 graded, best 7.0
• Rip Hunter **A:** Joe Kubert

26 ❑ Jun 1960 Cover: 0.10 **NM** value: **275.00**
Circ: Statement: **213,000** • **CGC:** 3 graded, best 8.5
• Rip Hunter **A:** Joe Kubert

27 ❑ Aug 1960 Cover: 0.10 **NM** value: **700.00**
Circ: Statement: **213,000** • **CGC:** 14 graded, best 9.2
A: Russ Heath ★ 1st Appearance of Sea Devils.

28 ❑ Oct 1960 Cover: 0.10 **NM** value: **350.00**
Circ: Statement: **213,000** • **CGC:** 6 graded, best 8.0
• Sea Devils **A:** Russ Heath

29 ❑ Dec 1960 Cover: 0.10 **NM** value: **350.00**
Circ: Statement: **213,000** • **CGC:** 9 graded, best 9.0
• Sea Devils **A:** Russ Heath

30 ❑ Feb 1961 Cover: 0.10 **NM** value: **650.00**
Circ: Statement: **240,000** • **CGC:** 24 graded, best 9.0
★ Origin of Aquaman.

31 ❑ Apr 1961 Cover: 0.10 **NM** value: **325.00**
Circ: Statement: **240,000** • **CGC:** 6 graded, best 7.5
• Aquaman; Has 1960 Statement; avg total paid circ 213,000

32 ❑ Jun 1961 Cover: 0.10 **NM** value: **325.00**
Circ: Statement: **240,000** • **CGC:** 4 graded, best 6.5
• Aquaman

33 ❑ Aug 1961 Cover: 0.10 **NM** value: **325.00**
Circ: Statement: **240,000** • **CGC:** 5 graded, best 8.0
• Aquaman

34 ❑ Oct 1961 Cover: 0.10 **NM** value: **1250.00**
Circ: Statement: **240,000** • **CGC:** 44 graded, best 9.4
📖 The Rebirth of the Atom!; Battle of the Tiny Titans!; Inside the Atom, part 1 • Atom **A:** Gil Kane ★ Origin of Atom II (Ray Palmer). ★ 1st Appearance of Atom II (Ray Palmer).

35 ❑ Dec 1961 Cover: 0.10 **NM** value: **700.00**
Circ: Statement: **240,000** • **CGC:** 25 graded, best 9.6
📖 The Dooms from Beyond!; Inside the Atom, part 2 • Atom **A:** Gil Kane ★ 2nd Appearance of Atom II (Ray Palmer). ★ 2nd Appearance of Atom II (Ray Palmer).

36 ❑ Feb 1962 Cover: 0.12 **NM** value: **525.00**
Circ: Statement: **220,000** • **CGC:** 20 graded, best 9.6
📖 Prisoner in a Test Tube!; The "Disappearing Act" Robberies! • Atom **A:** Gil Kane ★ Appearance of Atom II (Ray Palmer).

37 ❑ Apr 1962 Cover: 0.12 **NM** value: **500.00**
Circ: Statement: **220,000** • **CGC:** 18 graded, best 9.2
• Has 1961 Statement; avg total paid circ 240,000★ 1st Appearance of Metal Men.

38 ❑ Jun 1962 Cover: 0.12 **NM** value: **350.00**
Circ: Statement: **220,000** • **CGC:** 14 graded, best 9.8
★ Appearance of Metal Men.

39 ❑ Aug 1962 Cover: 0.12 **NM** value: **300.00**
Circ: Statement: **220,000** • **CGC:** 5 graded, best 8.5
★ 1st Appearance of Chemo. ★ Appearance of Metal Men.

40 ❑ Oct 1962 Cover: 0.12 **NM** value: **300.00**
Circ: Statement: **220,000** • **CGC:** 9 graded, best 9.2
★ Appearance of Metal Men.

41 ❑ Dec 1962 Cover: 0.12 **NM** value: **150.00**
Circ: Statement: **220,000** • **CGC:** 1 graded, best 5.5
• Tommy Tomorrow

42 ❑ Feb 1963 Cover: 0.12 **NM** value: **150.00**
• **CGC:** 1 graded, best 8.5
• Tommy Tomorrow

43 ❑ Apr 1963 Cover: 0.12 **NM** value: **400.00**
• **CGC:** 17 graded, best 9.6
• Doctor No/007; Dr. No/007

44 ❑ Jun 1963 Cover: 0.12 **NM** value: **100.00**
• **CGC:** 2 graded, best 9.4
• Tommy Tomorrow; Has 1962 Statement, filed 10/1/62; avg total paid circ 220,000

45 ❑ Aug 1963 Cover: 0.12 **NM** value: **225.00**
• **CGC:** 5 graded, best 9.2
A: Joe Kubert ★ Origin of Sgt. Rock.

46 ❑ Oct 1963 Cover: 0.12 **NM** value: **95.00**
• **CGC:** 1 graded, best 4.5
• Tommy Tomorrow

47 ❑ Dec 1963 Cover: 0.12 **NM** value: **95.00**
• Tommy Tomorrow

48 ❑ Feb 1964 Cover: 0.12 **NM** value: **65.00**
• **CGC:** 2 graded, best 9.2
• Cave Carson

49 ❑ Apr 1964 Cover: 0.12 **NM** value: **65.00**
• **CGC:** 1 graded, best 9.4
• Cave Carson; Has 1963 Statement, filed 10/1/63; no circ figures published

50 ❑ Jun 1964 Cover: 0.12 **NM** value: **65.00**
• **CGC:** 1 graded, best 9.6
• I Spy **A:** Murphy Anderson; Carmine Infantino

51 ❑ Aug 1964 Cover: 0.12 **NM** value: **65.00**
• I Spy **A:** Murphy Anderson; Carmine Infantino

52 ❑ Oct 1964 Cover: 0.12 **NM** value: **65.00**
• Cave Carson

53 ❑ Dec 1964 Cover: 0.12 **NM** value: **80.00**
• **CGC:** 2 graded, best 9.6
• G.I. Joe **A:** Joe Kubert

54 ❑ Feb 1965 Cover: 0.12 **NM** value: **80.00**
Circ: Statement: **235,091** • **CGC:** 3 graded, best 9.4
• G.I. Joe **A:** Joe Kubert

55 ❑ Apr 1965 Cover: 0.12 **NM** value: **275.00**
Circ: Statement: **235,091** • **CGC:** 24 graded, best 9.8
• Has 1964 Statement, filed 10/1/64; no circ figures published **A:** Murphy Anderson ★ Origin of Doctor Fate.

56 ❑ Jun 1965 Cover: 0.12 **NM** value: **100.00**
Circ: Statement: **235,091** • **CGC:** 10 graded, best 9.6
• Doctor Fate **A:** Murphy Anderson ★ 1st Appearance of Psycho-Pirate II (Roger Hayden).

57 ❑ Aug 1965 Cover: 0.12 **NM** value: **120.00**
Circ: Statement: **235,091** • **CGC:** 2 graded, best 8.0
📖 Killer of the Skies! • Enemy Ace **A:** Joe Kubert

58 ❑ Oct 1965 Cover: 0.12 **NM** value: **120.00**
Circ: Statement: **235,091** • **CGC:** 17 graded, best 9.6
• Enemy Ace **A:** Joe Kubert

59 ❑ Dec 1965 Cover: 0.12 **NM** value: **90.00**
Circ: Statement: **235,091** • **CGC:** 5 graded, best 9.6
★ Appearance of Teen Titans.

60 ❑ Feb 1966 Cover: 0.12 **NM** value: **225.00**
Circ: Statement: **250,512** • **CGC:** 58 graded, best 9.8
A: Murphy Anderson ★ Origin of The Spectre.

61 ❑ Apr 1966 Cover: 0.12 **NM** value: **125.00**
Circ: Statement: **250,512** • **CGC:** 24 graded, best 9.6
• Spectre **A:** Murphy Anderson

62 ❑ Jun 1966 Cover: 0.12 **NM** value: **70.00**
Circ: Statement: **250,512** • **CGC:** 5 graded, best 9.6
A: Joe Orlando ★ Origin of Inferior Five. ★ 1st Appearance of Earth-12, Dumb Bunny, Merryman, Awkwardman, Blimp, White Feather, Inferior Five.

63 ❑ Aug 1966 Cover: 0.12 **NM** value: **35.00**
Circ: Statement: **250,512** • **CGC:** 2 graded, best 9.6
• Inferior Five; Has 1965 Statement, filed 10/1/65; avg print run 388,000; avg sales 234,000; avg subs 1,091; avg total paid 235,091; samples 142; max existent 235,233; 39% of run returned **A:** Joe Orlando

64 ❑ Oct 1966 Cover: 0.12 **NM** value: **125.00**
Circ: Statement: **250,512** • **CGC:** 5 graded, best 9.4
• Spectre **A:** Murphy Anderson

65 ❑ Dec 1966 Cover: 0.12 **NM** value: **35.00**
Circ: Statement: **250,512** • **CGC:** 3 graded, best 9.4
• Inferior Five

66 ❑ Feb 1967 Cover: 0.12 **NM** value: **20.00**
Circ: Statement: **189,500** • **CGC:** 2 graded, best 9.4
★ 1st Appearance of B'wana Beast.

67 ❑ Apr 1967 Cover: 0.12 **NM** value: **20.00**
Circ: Statement: **189,500** • **CGC:** 1 graded, best 9.2
• B'wana Beast; Has 1966 Statement, filed 10/1/66; avg print run 404,000; avg sales 249,000; avg subs 1,512; avg total paid 250,512; samples 265; max existent 250,777; 38% of run returned

68 ❑ Jun 1967 Cover: 0.12 **NM** value: **20.00**
Circ: Statement: **189,500** • **CGC:** 3 graded, best 9.6
• Maniaks

69 ❑ Aug 1967 Cover: 0.12 **NM** value: **20.00**
Circ: Statement: **189,500** • **CGC:** 1 graded, best 9.6
• Maniaks

70 ❑ Oct 1967 Cover: 0.12 **NM** value: **20.00**
Circ: Statement: **189,500** • **CGC:** 2 graded, best 9.4
★ Appearance of Binky.

71 ❑ Dec 1967 Cover: 0.12 **NM** value: **20.00**
Circ: Statement: **189,500** • **CGC:** 1 graded, best 9.2
• Maniaks

72 ❑ Feb 1968 Cover: 0.12 **NM** value: **20.00**
Circ: Statement: **180,400** • **CGC:** 1 graded, best 9.2
• Top Gun **A:** Alex Toth; Joe Kubert

73 ❑ Apr 1968 Cover: 0.12 **NM** value: **110.00**
Circ: Statement: **180,400** • **CGC:** 43 graded, best 9.6
• Has 1967 Statement, filed 10/1/67; avg print run 364,000; avg sales 188,000; avg subs 1,500; avg total paid 189,500; samples 340; max existent 189,840; 48% of run returned **A:** Steve Ditko ★ Origin of Creeper. ★ 1st Appearance of Creeper.

74 ❑ May 1968 Cover: 0.12 **NM** value: **65.00**
Circ: Statement: **180,400** • **CGC:** 11 graded, best 9.4
★ 1st Appearance of Anthro.

75 ❑ Jun 1968 Cover: 0.12 **NM** value: **85.00**
Circ: Statement: **180,400** • **CGC:** 26 graded, best 9.6
📖 The Hawk and the Dove **A:** Steve Ditko **W:** Steve Ditko; Dick Giordano; Steve Skeates ★ Origin of Dove I (Don Hall), Hawk I (Hank Hall). ★ 1st Appearance of Dove I (Don Hall), Hawk I (Hank Hall).

76 ❑ Aug 1968 Cover: 0.12 **NM** value: **40.00**
Circ: Statement: **180,400** • **CGC:** 5 graded, best 9.4
★ 1st Appearance of Bat Lash.

77 ❑ Sep 1968 Cover: 0.12 **NM** value: **45.00**
Circ: Statement: **180,400** • **CGC:** 4 graded, best 9.8
★ 1st Appearance of Angel & Ape.

78 ❑ Nov 1968 Cover: 0.12 **NM** value: **30.00**
Circ: Statement: **180,400** • **CGC:** 3 graded, best 9.6
★ 1st Appearance of Jonny Double.

79 ❑ Dec 1968 Cover: 0.12 **NM** value: **45.00**
Circ: Statement: **180,400** • **CGC:** 4 graded, best 9.6
★ 1st Appearance of Dolphin.

80 ❑ Feb 1969 Cover: 0.12 **NM** value: **35.00**
Circ: Statement: **130,219** • **CGC:** 7 graded, best 9.4
• Phantom Stranger **C:** Neal Adams

81 ❑ Mar 1969 Cover: 0.12 **NM** value: **12.00**
Circ: Statement: **130,219** • **CGC:** 4 graded, best 9.4
• Windy & Willy; Has 1968 Statement, filed 10/1/68; avg print run 342,000; avg sales 180,000; avg subs 400; avg total paid 180,400; samples 386; max existent 180,786; 47% of run returned

82 ❑ May 1969 Cover: 0.12 **NM** value: **45.00**
Circ: Statement: **130,219** • **CGC:** 8 graded, best 9.6
★ 1st Appearance of Nightmaster.

83 ❑ Jun 1969 Cover: 0.12 **NM** value: **40.00**
Circ: Statement: **130,219** • **CGC:** 3 graded, best 9.6
• Nightmaster **A:** Bernie Wrightson; Michael W. Kaluta

84 ❑ Aug 1969 Cover: 0.15 **NM** value: **40.00**
Circ: Statement: **130,219** • **CGC:** 3 graded, best 9.6
• Nightmaster **A:** Bernie Wrightson; Michael W. Kaluta

85 ❑ Sep 1969 Cover: 0.15 **NM** value: **12.00**
Circ: Statement: **130,219**
• Firehair **A:** Joe Kubert

86 ❑ Nov 1969 Cover: 0.15 **NM** value: **12.00**
Circ: Statement: **130,219** • **CGC:** 1 graded, best 9.2
• Firehair **A:** Joe Kubert

87 ❑ Dec 1969 Cover: 0.15 **NM** value: **12.00**
Circ: Statement: **130,219**
• Firehair **A:** Joe Kubert

88 ❑ Feb 1970 Cover: 0.15 **NM** value: **8.00**
• **CGC:** 1 graded, best 9.2
• Jason's Quest

89 ❑ Mar 1970 Cover: 0.15 **NM** value: **8.00**
• Jason's Quest; Has 1969 Statement, filed 10/1/69; avg print run 306,000; avg sales 130,000; avg subs 219; avg total paid 130,219; samples 346; max existent 130,565; 57% of run returned

90 ❑ May 1970 Cover: 0.15 **NM** value: **7.00**
• Manhunter 2070

91 ❑ Jun 1970 Cover: 0.15 **NM** value: **7.00**
• **CGC:** 1 graded, best 7.5
• Manhunter 2070

92 ❑ Aug 1970 Cover: 0.15 **NM** value: **7.00**
• Manhunter 2070

93 ❑ Sep 1970 Cover: 0.15 **NM** value: **7.00**
• Manhunter 2070

94 ❑ Aug 1977 Cover: 0.35 **NM** value: **10.00**
• **CGC:** 5 graded, best 9.6
• Doom Patrol **A:** Joe Staton; Jim Aparo ★ Origin of Doom Patrol II. ★ 1st Appearance of Celsius, Doom Patrol II.

95 ❑ Oct 1977 Cover: 0.35 **NM** value: **8.00**
• Doom Patrol **A:** Joe Staton; Jim Aparo ★ Appearance of The Doom Patrol.

96 ❑ Dec 1977 Cover: 0.35 **NM** value: **8.00**
• Doom Patrol **A:** Joe Staton; Jim Aparo ★ Appearance of The Doom Patrol.

97 ❑ Feb 1978 Cover: 0.35 **NM** value: **5.00**
• **CGC:** 6 graded, best 9.0
• Power Girl

98 ❑ Mar 1978 Cover: 0.35 **NM** value: **5.00**
📖 When The Symbioship Strikes! **A:** Joe Staton **W:** Paul Levitz ★ Origin of Power Girl.

99 ❑ Apr 1978 Cover: 0.35 **NM** value: **5.00**
• Power Girl

100 ❑ May 1978 Cover: 0.60 **NM** value: **5.00**
• **CGC:** 2 graded, best 9.4
• Double-size. • all-star issue

101 ❑ Jun 1978 Cover: 0.35 **NM** value: **5.00**
• **CGC:** 6 graded, best 9.6
📖 Mystery in Space • Hawkman **A:** Al Milgrom; Murphy Anderson **C:** Jack Kirby **W:** Jack Harris

102 ❑ Jul 1978 Cover: 0.35 **NM** value: **5.00**
📖 Strange Adventures • Hawkman **A:** Al Milgrom; Murphy Anderson **C:** Jack Kirby **W:** Jack Harris

103 ❑ Aug 1978 Cover: 0.35 **NM** value: **5.00**
📖 Adventures on Other Worlds • Hawkman **A:** Al Milgrom; Murphy Anderson **C:** Jack Kirby **W:** Jack Harris

104 ❑ Sep 1978 Cover: 0.50 **NM** value: **5.00**
final issue. • OSS Spies

SHOWCASE '93 DC

1 ❑ Jan 1993 Cover: 1.95 **NM** value: **2.25**
Circ: CapCity orders: **28,150**
📖 Catwoman: Sorrow Street; Blue Devil: Speak of the Devil; Cyborg: A Mind is a Terrible Thing…! • Catwoman, Cyborg, Blue Devil **A:** Phil Jimenez; Ed Hannigan; Pete Moriarty **W:** Len Wein; Dan Mishkin; Doug Moench; Gary Cohn

2 ❑ Feb 1993 Cover: 1.95 **NM** value: **2.25**
Circ: CapCity orders: **19,450**
• Catwoman, Cyborg, Blue Devil

3 ❑ Mar 1993 Cover: 1.95 **NM** value: **2.25**
Circ: CapCity orders: **17,600**
• Catwoman, Flash, Blue Devil

4 ❑ Apr 1993 Cover: 1.95 **NM** value: **2.00**
Circ: CapCity orders: **18,100**
• Catwoman, Geo-Force, Blue Devil

CGC-graded: Multiply prices above by **33 for 9.9 M • 16 for 9.8 NM/M • 7 for 9.6 NM+ • 5 for 9.4 NM • 2.5 for 9.2 NM- • 1.5 for 9.0 VF/NM**

5 May 1993 Cover: 1.95 **NM** value: **2.00**
Circ: CapCity orders: **17,900**
• Robin, Peacemaker, Blue Devil

6 Jun 1993 Cover: 1.95 **NM** value: **2.00**
Circ: CapCity orders: **16,700**
• Robin, Peacemaker, Blue Devil

7 Jul 1993 Cover: 1.95 **NM** value: **2.50**
Circ: CapCity orders: **102,600**
Knightfall; Knightfall, Part 13 • Two-Face, Deathstroke, Jade, Obsidian, Peacemaker

8 Aug 1993 Cover: 1.95 **NM** value: **2.50**
Circ: CapCity orders: **102,450**
Knightfall; Knightfall, Part 14 • Two-Face, Batman, Deadshot, Fire and Ice **A:** Klaus Janson **W:** Doug Moench

9 Sep 1993 Cover: 1.95 **NM** value: **2.00**
Circ: CapCity orders: **53,850**
The Huntress: Survival; The Kobra Kronicles, Part 4; Shining Knight • Huntress, Peacemaker, Shining Knight **A:** Bill Willingham; Mike Mayhew; Cary Nord **W:** James Robinson; Mike Baron; Doug Moench

10 Oct 1993 Cover: 1.95 **NM** value: **2.00**
Circ: CapCity orders: **23,600**
• Huntress, Deathstroke, Katana

11 Nov 1993 Cover: 1.95 **NM** value: **2.00**
Circ: CapCity orders: **18,150**
• Nightwing, Robin, Kobra Kronicles

12 Dec 1993 Cover: 1.95 **NM** value: **2.00**
Circ: CapCity orders: **17,400**
• Nightwing, Robin, Green Lantern, Creeper

SHOWCASE '94 — DC

1 Jan 1994 Cover: 1.95 **NM** value: **Cover or less**
Circ: CapCity orders: **28,000**
The Great Pretender • Joker, New Gods, Gunfire **A:** Christian Alamy **W:** James Robinson

2 Feb 1994 Cover: 1.95 **NM** value: **Cover or less**
Circ: CapCity orders: **18,050**
• Joker

3 Mar 1994 Cover: 1.95 **NM** value: **Cover or less**
Circ: CapCity orders: **15,900**
• Arkham Asylum, Blue Beetle, Psyba-Rats

4 Apr 1994 Cover: 1.95 **NM** value: **Cover or less**
Circ: CapCity orders: **14,600**
• Arkham Asylum, Blue Beetle, Psyba-Rats

5 May 1994 Cover: 1.95 **NM** value: **Cover or less**
Circ: CapCity orders: **17,400**
• Huntress, Loose Cannon, Bloodwynd

6 Jun 1994 Cover: 1.95 **NM** value: **Cover or less**
Circ: CapCity orders: **17,700**
• Robin

7 Jul 1994 Cover: 1.95 **NM** value: **Cover or less**
Circ: CapCity orders: **17,400**
• Penguin, Arsenal, Terrorsmith **W:** Kurt Busiek

8 Aug 1994 Cover: 1.95 **NM** value: **Cover or less**
Circ: CapCity orders: **18,750**
• Scarface, Zero Hour Prelude

9 Sep 1994 Cover: 1.95 **NM** value: **Cover or less**
Circ: CapCity orders: **16,650**
• Scarface, Zero Hour Prelude

10 Oct 1994 Cover: 1.95 **NM** value: **Cover or less**
Circ: CapCity orders: **22,050**
• Azrael, Zero Hour, Black Condor

11 Nov 1994 Cover: 1.95 **NM** value: **Cover or less**
• Man-Bat, Starfire, Black Condor

12 Dec 1994 Cover: 1.95 **NM** value: **Cover or less**
Circ: CapCity orders: **15,150**

SHOWCASE '95 — DC

1 Jan 1995 Cover: 2.50 **NM** value: **Cover or less**
Circ: CapCity orders: **19,950**
• Supergirl, Alan Scott, Argus

2 Feb 1995 Cover: 2.50 **NM** value: **Cover or less**
Circ: CapCity orders: **13,275**
• Supergirl, Metal Men, Argus

3 Mar 1995 Cover: 2.50 **NM** value: **Cover or less**
Circ: CapCity orders: **11,725**
Eradicator: No Mercy; Claw: Reunions; The Question: Homecoming • Eradicator, Claw, The Question **A:** Shannon Londin-Gallant; Rick Burchett; Greg LaRocque **W:** Karl Kesel; Denny O'Neil; Steven Seagle

4 Apr 1995 Cover: 2.50 **NM** value: **Cover or less**
Circ: CapCity orders: **12,050**

5 Jun 1995 Cover: 2.50 **NM** value: **Cover or less**
Circ: CapCity orders: **10,725**

6 Jul 1995 Cover: 2.95 **NM** value: **Cover or less**
Circ: CapCity orders: **10,750**
• Bibbo, Lobo, Science Police, Legionnaires

7 Aug 1995 Cover: 2.95 **NM** value: **Cover or less**
Circ: CapCity orders: **10,425**
• Mongul, Arion, New Gods

8 Sep 1995 Cover: 2.95 **NM** value: **Cover or less**
Circ: CapCity orders: **9,275**
• Mongul, Spectre, Arsenal

9 Oct 1995 Cover: 2.95 **NM** value: **Cover or less**
Circ: CapCity orders: **7,750**
• Lois Lane, Lobo, Martian Manhunter

10 Nov 1995 Cover: 2.95 **NM** value: **Cover or less**
• Gangbuster, Ferrin Colos, Hi-Tech

11 Nov 1995 Cover: 2.95 **NM** value: **Cover or less**
• Agent Liberty; Arkham Asylum; Hi-Tech

12 Dec 1995 Cover: 2.95 **NM** value: **Cover or less**
• Supergirl, Maitresse, The Shade

SHOWCASE '96 — DC

1 Jan 1996 Cover: 2.95 **NM** value: **Cover or less**
• Steel and Guy Gardner: Warrior, Aqualad, Metropolis S.C.U.

2 Feb 1996 Cover: 2.95 **NM** value: **Cover or less**
Steel: Good Guy, Bad Buy, and Other Guys; Flesh and Bone • Steel and Guy Gardner: Warrior, Circe, Metallo **A:** Sergio Cariello; J. Alex Morrissey **W:** Beau Smith; Christopher Priest

3 Mar 1996 Cover: 2.95 **NM** value: **Cover or less**
Birds of a Feather; Mercy Killing; Acts of God • Lois Lane and Black Canary, Doctor Fate and The Shade, Lightray **A:** Stan Woch; Jennifer Graves; Alex Morrissey; Wade Von Grawbadger **W:** Jamie Delano; Jordan B. Gorfinkel; Scott Ciencin

4 Apr 1996 Cover: 2.95 **NM** value: **Cover or less**
The Devil's Own; The Shade and Dr. Fate: Day & Night, Night & Bright; The Demon: Street of Darkness • Guardian and Firebrand, Doctor Fate and The Shade, The Demon **A:** Matt Smith; Scot Eaton; Christian Alamy **W:** James Robinson; Brian Augustyn; Jim Higgins

5 Jun 1996 Cover: 2.95 **NM** value: **Cover or less**
• Green Arrow and Thorn, Doctor Fate and The Shade, New Gods

6 Jul 1996 Cover: 2.95 **NM** value: **Cover or less**
• Superboy and The Demon, Firestorm, The Atom

7 Aug 1996 Cover: 2.95 **NM** value: **Cover or less**
• Gangbuster and The Power of Shazam!, Fire, Firestorm

8 Sep 1996 Cover: 2.95 **NM** value: **Cover or less**
• Superboy and Superman, Legionnaires, Supergirl

9 Oct 1996 Cover: 2.95 **NM** value: **Cover or less**
Shadow Dragon: Honor Bound; Illumination • Shadowdragon and Lady Shiva, Doctor Light, Martian Manhunter **A:** Chris Cross; Kevin J. West **W:** Joan Weis; Joseph Illidge

10 Nov 1996 Cover: 2.95 **NM** value: **Cover or less**
Circ: Diamd. preorders: **17,342**
The Bridges of Metropolis County; Captain Comet: The Future; Ultraboy: Straight Time • Bibbo, Ultra Boy, Captain Comet **A:** Denis Rodier; Scot Eaton; Dean Zachary **W:** Paul Castiglia; Ron Boyd; Terrance Griep Jr.

11 Dec 1996 Cover: 2.95 **NM** value: **Cover or less**
Circ: Diamd. preorders: **19,926**
Legion of Super-Heroes: Brain in Vain; Scare Tactics: In the Road; The Scared Path to Justice • Brainiac vs. Legion, Wildcat, Scare Tactics **A:** Anthony Williams; Gary Kwapisz; Derec Aucoin **W:** Len Kaminski; Beau Smith; Daniel Murray; Tom Peyer

12 Win 1996 Cover: 2.95 **NM** value: **Cover or less**
Circ: Diamd. preorders: **17,994**
Roots; Overrun; Rough Air final issue. • Brainiac vs. Legion, Jesse Quick, King Faraday **A:** Brian Augustyn; Stuart Immonen; Derec Aucoin **W:** Stuart Immonen; Mark Waid; Tom Peyer

SHOWGIRLS — Atlas

1 Jun 1957 Cover: 0.10 **NM** value: **75.00**
2 Aug 1957 Cover: 0.10 **NM** value: **50.00**

SHRED — CFW

1 Cover: 2.25 **NM** value: **Cover or less**
2 Cover: 2.25 **NM** value: **Cover or less**
3 Cover: 2.25 **NM** value: **Cover or less**
4 Cover: 2.25 **NM** value: **Cover or less**
5 Cover: 2.25 **NM** value: **Cover or less**
6 Cover: 2.25 **NM** value: **Cover or less**
7 Cover: 2.25 **NM** value: **Cover or less**
8 Cover: 2.25 **NM** value: **Cover or less**

SHRIEK — Fantaco

1 b&w Cover: 4.95 **NM** value: **Cover or less**
2 b&w Cover: 4.95 **NM** value: **Cover or less**
SE 1 b&w Cover: 3.50 **NM** value: **Cover or less**
SE 2 b&w Cover: 3.50 **NM** value: **Cover or less**
• Dangerbrain
SE 3 b&w Cover: 3.50 **NM** value: **Cover or less**

SHRIKE — Victory

1 May 1987, b&w Cover: 1.50 **NM** value: **Cover or less**
Death and a Little Depression **A:** Robert B. Durham **W:** Robert B. Durham

2 Cover: 1.50 **NM** value: **Cover or less**
A: Robert B. Durham **W:** Robert B. Durham

SHROUD, THE — Marvel

The Shroud first appears in Super-Villain Team-Up #5, although he has only made sporadic appearances in the years since. This lack of exposure is especially strange, given the Shroud's interesting origin and modus operandi.

The Shroud's story begins when his parents are killed by criminals. He becomes obsessed with avenging them and dedicates his life to becoming the best law enforcement agent of his generation. But no mere police job can quell his passion for justice. His search for vengeance leads him to the cult of Kali, where he is given occult powers of vengeance — but at a terrible price. His sight is burned away by a branding iron, the mark which emblazons his forehead to this day. In place of his sight, though, he gains the power to sense others around him and to wield darkness itself as a weapon. He then adopts the guise of being a crimelord himself, luring criminals close to him — then striking them down without warning.

1 Mar 1994 Cover: 1.75 **NM** value: **Cover or less**
Circ: CapCity orders: **21,250**
The Deadly Past, Part 1 **A:** M.C. Wyman **W:** Mike W. Barr ★ Origin of The Shroud.

2 Apr 1994 Cover: 1.75 **NM** value: **Cover or less**
Circ: CapCity orders: **13,800**

3 May 1994 Cover: 1.75 **NM** value: **Cover or less**
Circ: CapCity orders: **12,400**

4 Jun 1994 Cover: 1.75 **NM** value: **Cover or less**
Circ: CapCity orders: **12,400**

SHUGGA — Fantagraphics / Eros

All issues are adults only.

1 b&w Cover: 2.50 **NM** value: **Cover or less**
2 b&w Cover: 2.50 **NM** value: **Cover or less**

SHURIKEN (BLACKTHORNE) — Blackthorne

1 Cover: 7.95 **NM** value: **Cover or less**

SHURIKEN: COLD STEEL — Eternity

1 Jul 1989, b&w Cover: 1.50 **NM** value: **Cover or less**
Welcome to Dangertemps, Part 1 • 16 pgs. **A:** Christopher Taylor **W:** S.A. Bennett
2 Aug 1989 Cover: 1.95 **NM** value: **Cover or less**
3 Sep 1989 Cover: 1.95 **NM** value: **Cover or less**
4 Oct 1989 Cover: 1.95 **NM** value: **Cover or less**
5 Nov 1989 Cover: 1.95 **NM** value: **Cover or less**
6 Dec 1989 Cover: 1.95 **NM** value: **Cover or less**

SHURIKEN (ETERNITY) — Eternity

1 Jun 1991, b&w Cover: 2.50 **NM** value: **Cover or less**
A: Wes Abbott **W:** S.A. Bennett
2 ca. 1991, b&w Cover: 2.50 **NM** value: **Cover or less**
3 ca. 1991, b&w Cover: 2.50 **NM** value: **Cover or less**
4 ca. 1991, b&w Cover: 2.50 **NM** value: **Cover or less**
5 ca. 1991, b&w Cover: 2.50 **NM** value: **Cover or less**
6 ca. 1992, b&w Cover: 2.50 **NM** value: **Cover or less**

SHURIKEN TEAM-UP — Eternity

1 ca. 1989, b&w Cover: 1.95 **NM** value: **Cover or less**
• Shuriken, Libra, Kokutai

SHURIKEN (VICTORY) — Victory

1 Win 1985 Cover: 1.50 **NM** value: **Cover or less**
The Enemy • Win-85 **A:** Reggie Byers **W:** Reggie Byers; Neil D. Vokes
2 Fal 1985 Cover: 1.50 **NM** value: **Cover or less**
Scratched! • Fal-85 **A:** Reggie Byers **W:** Reggie Byers; Neil D. Vokes
3 Cover: 1.50 **NM** value: **Cover or less**
4 Nov 1986 Cover: 1.50 **NM** value: **Cover or less**
5 1987 Cover: 1.50 **NM** value: **Cover or less**
6 Feb 1987 Cover: 1.50 **NM** value: **Cover or less**
7 Mar 1987 Cover: 1.50 **NM** value: **Cover or less**
8 Apr 1987 Cover: 1.50 **NM** value: **Cover or less**

SHUT UP AND DIE! — Image

1 Jan 1998 Cover: 2.95 **NM** value: **Cover or less**
Circ: Diamd. preorders: **5,768**
Temptation **A:** Kevin Stokes **W:** James D. Hudnall
2 Mar 1998 Cover: 2.95 **NM** value: **Cover or less**
Circ: Diamd. preorders: **3,480**
A. W. M. (Angry White Man) **A:** Kevin Stokes **W:** James D. Hudnall
3 May 1998 Cover: 2.95 **NM** value: **Cover or less**
Circ: Diamd. preorders: **2,850**
The Bad Week **A:** Kevin Stokes **W:** James D. Hudnall
4 Aug 1998 Cover: 2.95 **NM** value: **Cover or less**
Circ: Diamd. preorders: **2,170**
A: Kevin Stokes **W:** James D. Hudnall
5 ca. 1999 Cover: 2.95 **NM** value: **Cover or less**
A: Kevin Stokes **W:** James D. Hudnall

SICK SMILES — Aiiie!

1 Jun 1994 Cover: 2.50 **NM** value: **Cover or less**
2 Jul 1994 Cover: 2.50 **NM** value: **Cover or less**
3 ca. 1994 Cover: 2.50 **NM** value: **Cover or less**
A: Lee Purvis; Marc Mannheimer; Scott Allie **W:** Lee Purvis; Marc Mannheimer; Scott Allie
4 ca. 1994 Cover: 2.50 **NM** value: **Cover or less**
5 ca. 1994 Cover: 2.50 **NM** value: **Cover or less**
6 ca. 1995 Cover: 2.50 **NM** value: **Cover or less**
7 ca. 1995 Cover: 2.50 **NM** value: **Cover or less**
8 Apr 1995 Cover: 2.95 **NM** value: **Cover or less**

SIDEKICKS — Fanboy

1 Jun 2000 Cover: 2.75 **NM** value: **Cover or less**
Circ: Diamd. preorders: **2,665**
The New Teen Titan, Part 1 **A:** Takeshi Miyazawa **W:** J. Torres

SIDE SHOW — Mature Magic

1 Cover: 1.75 **NM** value: **Cover or less**

SIDESHOW COMICS — Pan Graphics

1 b&w Cover: 2.00 **NM** value: **Cover or less**
2 b&w Cover: 2.00 **NM** value: **Cover or less**
3 Cover: 1.25 **NM** value: **1.75**
4 Cover: 1.25 **NM** value: **1.75**
5 Cover: 1.25 **NM** value: **1.75**
Bad Foot Dealin' **A:** Taylor **W:** Ron Spencer

SIDETRACK CITY AND OTHER TALES — Fantagraphics

Bk 1 Feb 1996 Cover: 9.95 **NM** value: **Cover or less**
No issue number. • oversized squarebound collection of b&w stories.

SIEGE — Image

1 Jan 1997 Cover: 2.50 **NM** value: **Cover or less**
Circ: Diamd. preorders: **26,969**
The Ultimate Conspiracy **A:** Robert Teranishi; Al Vey(inks) **W:** Jonathan Peterson
2 Feb 1997 Cover: 2.50 **NM** value: **Cover or less**
Circ: Diamd. preorders: **20,099**
The Road Less Traveled **A:** Robert Teranishi; Al Vey(inks) **W:** Jonathan Peterson
3 Mar 1997 Cover: 2.50 **NM** value: **Cover or less**
Circ: Diamd. preorders: **19,396**
A: Robert Teranishi; Al Vey(inks) **W:** Jonathan Peterson
4 Apr 1997 Cover: 2.50 **NM** value: **Cover or less**
Circ: Diamd. preorders: **17,899**
A: Robert Teranishi; Al Vey(inks) **W:** Jonathan Peterson

Other grades: Multiply prices above by **1.5 for Mint • 2/3 for Very Fine • 1/3 for Fine • 1/5 for Very Good • 1/8 for Good**

SIEGEL AND SHUSTER: DATELINE 1930S Eclipse
1 ❑ Nov 1984 Cover: 1.50 **NM** value: **1.75**
A: Joe Shuster; Jerry Siegel
2 ❑ Sep 1985 Cover: 1.50 **NM** value: **1.75**
📖 Snoopy and Smiley; Kay; Inko; Bruce Verne G-Man of the Future; The Waif; Gloria Glamour; Horrible Happenings; Cornelius **A:** Joe Shuster; Jerry Siegel

SIEGE OF THE ALAMO Tome Press
1 ❑ Jul 1991, b&w Cover: 2.50 **NM** value: **Cover or less**

SIGHT UNSEEN Fantagraphics
1 ❑ Apr 1997, b&w Cover: 2.95 **NM** value: **Cover or less**
No issue number. wraparound cover. • collects story from The Stranger and The Philadelphia Weekly

SIGIL CrossGen

In the interwoven worlds of the CrossGen universe, this science-fiction title focuses on Samandahl Rey, an old spaceship pilot caring only for himself and his best friend. As a recipient of the powerful Sigil of CrossGen, he finds himself with power — and obligations, as the Planetary Union needs him to combat the Saurian race.

In an early attack, his best friend is killed and her consciousness migrates to his ship's computer system. Later, Rey takes a quick trip around the CrossGen universe, setting the stage for future series. — Maggie

1❑Jul 2000Cover: 2.95NM value: Cover or less
Circ: Diamd. preorders: **28,390** • **CGC:** 13 graded, best 9.9
A: Ben Lai **W:** Barbara Kesel
2 ❑ Aug 2000 Cover: 2.95 **NM** value: **Cover or less**
Circ: Diamd. preorders: **22,150** • **CGC:** 4 graded, best 9.8
A: Ben Lai **W:** Barbara Kesel
3 ❑ Sep 2000 Cover: 2.95 **NM** value: **Cover or less**
Circ: Diamd. preorders: **21,009** • **CGC:** 2 graded, best 9.4
A: Ben Lai **W:** Barbara Kesel
4 ❑ Oct 2000 Cover: 2.95 **NM** value: **Cover or less**
Circ: Diamd. preorders: **20,773**
A: Ben Lai **W:** Barbara Kesel
5 ❑ Nov 2000 Cover: 2.95 **NM** value: **Cover or less**
Circ: Diamd. preorders: **20,424**
6 ❑ Dec 2000 Cover: 2.95 **NM** value: **Cover or less**
Circ: Diamd. preorders: **20,580**
7 ❑ Jan 2001 Cover: 2.95 **NM** value: **Cover or less**
Circ: Diamd. preorders: **19,692**
8 ❑ Feb 2001 Cover: 2.95 **NM** value: **Cover or less**
Circ: Diamd. preorders: **18,997**
9 ❑ Mar 2001 Cover: 2.95 **NM** value: **Cover or less**
Circ: Diamd. preorders: **18,149**
10 ❑ Apr 2001 Cover: 2.95 **NM** value: **Cover or less**
Circ: Diamd. preorders: **17,438**
11 ❑ May 2001 Cover: 2.95 **NM** value: **Cover or less**
Circ: Diamd. preorders: **17,262**
12 ❑ Jun 2001 Cover: 2.95 **NM** value: **Cover or less**
Circ: Diamd. preorders: **17,172**
13 ❑ Jul 2001 Cover: 2.95 **NM** value: **Cover or less**
Circ: Diamd. preorders: **17,533**
14 ❑ Aug 2001 Cover: 2.95 **NM** value: **Cover or less**
Circ: Diamd. preorders: **17,334**
15 ❑ Sep 2001 Cover: 2.95 **NM** value: **Cover or less**
16 ❑ Oct 2001 Cover: 2.95 **NM** value: **Cover or less**
17 ❑ Nov 2001 Cover: 2.95 **NM** value: **Cover or less**
1st printing.
18 ❑ Dec 2001 Cover: 2.95 **NM** value: **Cover or less**
19 ❑ Jan 2002 Cover: 2.95 **NM** value: **Cover or less**
20 ❑ Feb 2002 Cover: 2.95 **NM** value: **Cover or less**
21 ❑ Mar 2002 Cover: 2.95 **NM** value: **Cover or less**

SIGMA Image
1 ❑ Apr 1996 Cover: 2.50 **NM** value: **Cover or less**
📖 Fire From Heaven **A:** Tomm Coker; Ryan Odagawa; Juvaun Kirby **W:** Brandon Choi
2 ❑ May 1996 Cover: 2.50 **NM** value: **Cover or less**
📖 Fire from Heaven, Part 6 **A:** Tomm Coker; Ryan Odagawa; Juvaun Kirby **W:** Brandon Choi
3 ❑ Jun 1996 Cover: 2.50 **NM** value: **Cover or less**
📖 Fire from Heaven, Part 14 **A:** Tomm Coker; Ryan Odagawa; Juvaun Kirby **W:** Brandon Choi

SIGNAL TO NOISE Dark Horse
1 ❑ Cover: 9.99 **NM** value: **15.00**
A: Dave McKean **W:** Neil Gaiman
1-2 ❑ Cover: 14.95 **NM** value: **Cover or less**

SILBUSTER Antarctic
1 ❑ Jan 1994 Cover: 2.95 **NM** value: **Cover or less**
📖 Wandering Siblings **A:** Kazumitsu Sahara **W:** Kazumitsu Sahara
2 ❑ Feb 1994 Cover: 2.95 **NM** value: **Cover or less**
3 ❑ Mar 1994 Cover: 2.95 **NM** value: **Cover or less**
4 ❑ Apr 1994 Cover: 2.95 **NM** value: **Cover or less**
5 ❑ Oct 1994 Cover: 2.95 **NM** value: **Cover or less**
6 ❑ Nov 1994 Cover: 2.95 **NM** value: **Cover or less**
7 ❑ Dec 1994 Cover: 2.95 **NM** value: **Cover or less**
A: Ikkou Sahara **W:** Ikkou Sahara
8 ❑ Jan 1995 Cover: 2.95 **NM** value: **Cover or less**
A: Ikkou Sahara **W:** Ikkou Sahara
9 ❑ Feb 1995 Cover: 2.95 **NM** value: **Cover or less**
A: Ikkou Sahara **W:** Ikkou Sahara
10 ❑ Aug 1995 Cover: 2.95 **NM** value: **Cover or less**
A: Ikkou Sahara **W:** Ikkou Sahara
11 ❑ Oct 1995 Cover: 2.95 **NM** value: **Cover or less**
A: Ikkou Sahara **W:** Ikkou Sahara
12 ❑ Oct 1995 Cover: 2.95 **NM** value: **Cover or less**
A: Ikkou Sahara **W:** Ikkou Sahara
13 ❑ Oct 1995 Cover: 2.95 **NM** value: **Cover or less**
A: Ikkou Sahara **W:** Ikkou Sahara
14 ❑ Oct 1995 Cover: 2.95 **NM** value: **Cover or less**
A: Ikkou Sahara **W:** Ikkou Sahara
15 ❑ May 1996 Cover: 2.95 **NM** value: **Cover or less**
A: Ikkou Sahara **W:** Ikkou Sahara
16 ❑ Jul 1996 Cover: 2.95 **NM** value: **Cover or less**
A: Ikkou Sahara **W:** Ikkou Sahara
17 ❑ Sep 1996 Cover: 2.95 **NM** value: **Cover or less**
A: Ikkou Sahara **W:** Ikkou Sahara
18 ❑ Sep 1996 Cover: 2.95 **NM** value: **Cover or less**
A: Ikkou Sahara **W:** Ikkou Sahara
19 ❑ Jan 1997 Cover: 2.95 **NM** value: **Cover or less**
A: Ikkou Sahara **W:** Ikkou Sahara
Bk 2❑ Nov 1996, b&w Cover: 10.95 **NM** value: **Cover or less**

SILENCERS Caliber
1 ❑ Jul 1991, b&w Cover: 2.50 **NM** value: **Cover or less**
📖 Damage **A:** R.G. Taylor **W:** Mark Askwith
2 ❑ 1991b&w Cover: 2.50 **NM** value: **Cover or less**
📖 Damage Control **A:** R.G. Taylor **W:** Mark Askwith
3 ❑ 1991b&w Cover: 2.50 **NM** value: **Cover or less**
📖 Stories **A:** R.G. Taylor **W:** Mark Askwith
4 ❑ 1991b&w Cover: 2.50 **NM** value: **Cover or less**

SILENT CITY, THE Kitchen Sink
1 ❑ Oct 1995, b&w Cover: 24.95 **NM** value: **Cover or less**
• oversized graphic novel.

SILENT INVASION, THE Renegade
1 ❑ Apr 1986, b&w Cover: 1.70 **NM** value: **2.00**
📖 The Stubbinsville Connection, Part 1 **A:** Michael Cherkas **W:** Larry Hancock
2 ❑ Jun 1986, b&w Cover: 1.70 **NM** value: **2.00**
📖 The Stubbinsville Connection, Part 2 **A:** Michael Cherkas **W:** Larry Hancock
3 ❑ Aug 1986, b&w Cover: 1.70 **NM** value: **2.75**
4 ❑ Oct 1986, b&w Cover: 2.00 **NM** value: **2.75**
📖 A Pink Slip for a Pinko **A:** Michael Cherkas **W:** Larry Hancock
5 ❑ Dec 1986, b&w Cover: 2.00 **NM** value: **2.75**
6 ❑ Feb 1987, b&w Cover: 2.00 **NM** value: **2.75**
7 ❑ May 1987, b&w Cover: 2.00 **NM** value: **2.75**
8 ❑ Jul 1987, b&w Cover: 2.00 **NM** value: **2.75**
9 ❑ Sep 1987, b&w Cover: 2.00 **NM** value: **2.75**
10 ❑ Nov 1987, b&w Cover: 2.00 **NM** value: **2.75**
11 ❑ Jan 1988, b&w Cover: 2.00 **NM** value: **2.75**
12 ❑ Mar 1988, b&w Cover: 2.00 **NM** value: **2.75**

SILENT INVASION, THE: ABDUCTIONS Caliber
1 ❑ May 1998, b&w Cover: 2.95 **NM** value: **Cover or less**

SILENT MÖBIUS: INTO THE LABYRINTH Viz
1 ❑ May 1999 Cover: 2.95 **NM** value: **Cover or less**
Circ: Diamd. preorders: **5,468**
2 ❑ Jun 1999 Cover: 2.95 **NM** value: **Cover or less**
Circ: Diamd. preorders: **4,551**
3 ❑ Jul 1999 Cover: 2.95 **NM** value: **Cover or less**
Circ: Diamd. preorders: **4,263**
4 ❑ Aug 1999 Cover: 2.95 **NM** value: **Cover or less**
Circ: Diamd. preorders: **3,972**
5 ❑ Sep 1999 Cover: 2.95 **NM** value: **Cover or less**
Circ: Diamd. preorders: **3,625**
6 ❑ Oct 1999 Cover: 2.95 **NM** value: **Cover or less**
Circ: Diamd. preorders: **3,690**

SILENT MÖBIUS: KARMA Viz
1 ❑ Nov 1999, b&w Cover: 3.25 **NM** value: **Cover or less**
Circ: Diamd. preorders: **3,992**

SILENT MÖBIUS PART 1 Viz
1 ❑ ca. 1991, full color Cover: 4.95 **NM** value: **Cover or less**
Circ: CapCity orders: **5,550**
📖 Cyber Psychic City, Part 1 **A:** Kia Asamiya **W:** Kia Asamiya
2 ❑ ca. 1991, full color Cover: 4.95 **NM** value: **Cover or less**
📖 Cyber Psychic City, Part 2 **A:** Kia Asamiya **W:** Kia Asamiya
3 ❑ ca. 1991, full color Cover: 4.95 **NM** value: **Cover or less**
Circ: CapCity orders: **3,675**
📖 Cyber Psychic City, Part 3 **A:** Kia Asamiya **W:** Kia Asamiya
4 ❑ ca. 1991, full color Cover: 4.95 **NM** value: **Cover or less**
Circ: CapCity orders: **3,550**
A: Kia Asamiya **W:** Kia Asamiya
5 ❑ ca. 1991, full color Cover: 4.95 **NM** value: **Cover or less**
Circ: CapCity orders: **3,650**
A: Kia Asamiya **W:** Kia Asamiya
6 ❑ ca. 1991, full color Cover: 4.95 **NM** value: **Cover or less**
Circ: CapCity orders: **3,475**
A: Kia Asamiya **W:** Kia Asamiya

SILENT MÖBIUS PART 2 Viz
1 ❑ ca. 1991 Cover: 4.95 **NM** value: **Cover or less**
Circ: CapCity orders: **3,500**
📖 Katsumi Liquer, Part 1 **A:** Kia Asamiya **W:** Kia Asamiya
2 ❑ ca. 1991 Cover: 4.95 **NM** value: **Cover or less**
Circ: CapCity orders: **3,200**
A: Kia Asamiya **W:** Kia Asamiya
3 ❑ ca. 1991 Cover: 4.95 **NM** value: **Cover or less**
Circ: CapCity orders: **3,050**
A: Kia Asamiya **W:** Kia Asamiya
4 ❑ ca. 1991 Cover: 4.95 **NM** value: **Cover or less**
Circ: CapCity orders: **2,950**
A: Kia Asamiya **W:** Kia Asamiya
5 ❑ ca. 1991 Cover: 4.95 **NM** value: **Cover or less**
Circ: CapCity orders: **3,075**
A: Kia Asamiya **W:** Kia Asamiya

SILENT MÖBIUS PART 3 Viz
1 ❑ ca. 1992 Cover: 4.95 **NM** value: **Cover or less**
Circ: CapCity orders: **3,000**
2 ❑ ca. 1992 Cover: 4.95 **NM** value: **Cover or less**
Circ: CapCity orders: **2,725**
3 ❑ ca. 1992 Cover: 2.75 **NM** value: **Cover or less**
Circ: CapCity orders: **2,675**
4 ❑ ca. 1992 Cover: 2.75 **NM** value: **Cover or less**
Circ: CapCity orders: **2,750**
5 ❑ ca. 1992 Cover: 2.75 **NM** value: **Cover or less**
Circ: CapCity orders: **2,950**

SILENT MÖBIUS PART 4 Viz
1 ❑ ca. 1992 Cover: 2.75 **NM** value: **Cover or less**
Circ: CapCity orders: **3,050**
2 ❑ ca. 1992 Cover: 2.75 **NM** value: **Cover or less**
Circ: CapCity orders: **2,725**
3 ❑ ca. 1992 Cover: 2.75 **NM** value: **Cover or less**
4 ❑ ca. 1992 Cover: 2.75 **NM** value: **Cover or less**
5 ❑ ca. 1992 Cover: 2.75 **NM** value: **Cover or less**
Circ: CapCity orders: **2,525**

SILENT RAPTURE Avatar
1 ❑ ca. 1997 Cover: 3.00 **NM** value: **Cover or less**
2 ❑ ca. 1997 Cover: 3.00 **NM** value: **Cover or less**

SILENT SCREAMERS: NOSFERATU Image
1 ❑ Oct 2000 Cover: 4.95 **NM** value: **Cover or less**
Circ: Diamd. preorders: **10,973**
A: Caesar; Gray **W:** Jason Orfalas; Nelson Asencio; Alex Glass; Digger

SILENT WINTER/PINEAPPLEMAN Limelight
1 ❑ Cover: 2.95 **NM** value: **Cover or less**
A: Joy Lampitoc; Laurie Ganaban **W:** Laurie Ganaban

SILKE Dark Horse
1 ❑ Jan 2001 Cover: 2.95 **NM** value: **Cover or less**
Circ: Diamd. preorders: **30,602**
📖 Playing God **A:** Tony Daniel **W:** Tony Daniel
2 ❑ Feb 2001 Cover: 2.99 **NM** value: **Cover or less**
Circ: Diamd. preorders: **19,367**
📖 The Chameleon **A:** Tony Daniel **W:** Tony Daniel

SILLY SYMPHONIES Dell
1 ❑ ca. 1952 Cover: 0.25 **NM** value: **450.00**
• **CGC:** 1 graded, best 9.2
2 ❑ ca. 1953 Cover: 0.25 **NM** value: **400.00**
3 ❑ ca. 1954 Cover: 0.25 **NM** value: **350.00**
4 ❑ ca. 1954 Cover: 0.25 **NM** value: **350.00**
5 ❑ ca. 1955 Cover: 0.25 **NM** value: **300.00**
6 ❑ ca. 1956 Cover: 0.25 **NM** value: **300.00**
7 ❑ ca. 1957 Cover: 0.25 **NM** value: **300.00**
8 ❑ Feb 1958 Cover: 0.25 **NM** value: **300.00**
• **CGC:** 1 graded, best 9.4
9 ❑ ca. 1959 Cover: 0.25 **NM** value: **300.00**

SILLY-CAT Joe Chiappetta
1 ❑ Dec 1997 Cover: 1.00 **NM** value: **Cover or less**
📖 Pickin' an' Grabbin'; Chuck Taylor; Night Walk; Vole Adventures Ten; Silly Batty; Silly Daddy and the Red Shirt Roman; Silly Daddy: Tick Tock; Silly Daddy: Learn Something New Everyday **A:** Joe Chiappetta; John Porcellino **W:** Joe Chiappetta; John Porcellino

SILLY DADDY Joe Chiappetta
Silly Daddy tells Joe Chiapetta's story of fatherhood with a surrealistic flair. Beginning with the three most intense years of his life, when he becomes a father and deals with the comedy and tragedy of family life, each issue presents Chiapetta's odd view of reality.

One issue may serve as a warning to women on the nature of men, while the next may focus on the funny side of parenting. At another juncture in the story, the characters clash with cops at a picnic and later find themselves hiding out in a Big Brother-style future.

And that's all before Daddy meets Psycho Chick, who, at 15, likes her costume skimpy and her enemies beaten to a pulp.

Weird and personal, Joe Chiapetta's Silly Daddy puts a new twist on fatherhood.

1 ❑ Cover: 2.75 **NM** value: **4.00**
A: Joe Chiappetta **W:** Joe Chiappetta
2 ❑ Sep 1995, b&w Cover: 2.75 **NM** value: **3.00**
• flipbook with King Cat back-up **A:** Joe Chiappetta **W:** Joe Chiappetta
3 ❑ Cover: 2.75 **NM** value: **3.00**
A: Joe Chiappetta **W:** Joe Chiappetta
4 ❑ Cover: 2.75 **NM** value: **3.00**
A: Joe Chiappetta **W:** Joe Chiappetta
5 ❑ Cover: 2.75 **NM** value: **3.00**
A: Joe Chiappetta **W:** Joe Chiappetta
6 ❑ Cover: 2.75 **NM** value: **3.00**
A: Joe Chiappetta **W:** Joe Chiappetta
7 ❑ Cover: 2.75 **NM** value: **3.00**
A: Joe Chiappetta **W:** Joe Chiappetta
8 ❑ Cover: 2.75 **NM** value: **3.00**
A: Joe Chiappetta **W:** Joe Chiappetta
9 ❑ Cover: 2.75 **NM** value: **3.00**
A: Joe Chiappetta **W:** Joe Chiappetta

CGC-graded: Multiply prices above by **33 for 9.9 M** • **16 for 9.8 NM/M** • **7 for 9.6 NM+** • **5 for 9.4 NM** • **2.5 for 9.2 NM-** • **1.5 for 9.0 VF/NM**

10 ❑ Mar 1996, b&w Cover: 2.75 **NM** value: **3.00**
A: Joe Chiappetta **W:** Joe Chiappetta

11 ❑ b&w Cover: 2.75 **NM** value: **Cover or less**
📖 A Death in The Family **A:** Joe Chiappetta **W:** Joe Chiappetta

12 ❑ b&w Cover: 2.75 **NM** value: **Cover or less**
A: Joe Chiappetta **W:** Joe Chiappetta

13 ❑ b&w Cover: 2.75 **NM** value: **Cover or less**
A: Joe Chiappetta **W:** Joe Chiappetta

14 ❑ b&w Cover: 2.75 **NM** value: **Cover or less**
no cover price. **A:** Joe Chiappetta **W:** Joe Chiappetta

15 ❑ Cover: 2.75 **NM** value: **Cover or less**
A: Joe Chiappetta **W:** Joe Chiappetta

16 ❑ Cover: 2.75 **NM** value: **Cover or less**
📖 A Death in The Family interlude **A:** Joe Chiappetta **W:** Joe Chiappetta

17 ❑ Cover: 2.75 **NM** value: **Cover or less**
A: Joe Chiappetta **W:** Joe Chiappetta

18 ❑ Cover: 2.75 **NM** value: **Cover or less**
📖 Hit Parade, Baby **A:** Joe Chiappetta **W:** Joe Chiappetta

Bk 1❑ Cover: 8.95 **NM** value: **Cover or less**
• A Death in the Family **A:** Joe Chiappetta **W:** Joe Chiappetta

SILLY TUNES — Timely

1 ❑ Fal 1945 Cover: 0.10 **NM** value: **125.00**
2 ❑ Feb 1946 Cover: 0.10 **NM** value: **75.00**
3 ❑ Apr 1946 Cover: 0.10 **NM** value: **50.00**
4 ❑ Jun 1946 Cover: 0.10 **NM** value: **50.00**
5 ❑ ca. 1946 Cover: 0.10 **NM** value: **50.00**
6 ❑ ca. 1946 Cover: 0.10 **NM** value: **50.00**
7 ❑ Apr 1947 Cover: 0.10 **NM** value: **50.00**

SILVER — Comicolor

1 ❑ Oct 1996 Cover: 2.00 **NM** value: **Cover or less**
Circ: Diamd. preorders: **3,395**

SILVER AGE — DC

Hearkening back to the days of the great big 80-Page Giants of the 1960s, DC released an 80-page special to round out its Silver Age crossover event. In it, the intergalactic villain Agamemno, at one time the ruler of the entire universe, faced off against the mighty Justice League of America, along with many of the great, forgotten heroes of the Silver Age, and a handful of mysterious new heroes. In the final climactic tale, "S.O.S. to Nowhere," writer Mark Waid (Kingdom Come, JLA) and artist Eduardo Barreto (New Teen Titans) delivered a homage to that bygone era. The original Justice League, aided by Robby Reed, the main character from Dial H for Hero, put an end to Agamemno's bid for universal domination. Also included in this issue were two "never before seen" featurettes from DC's vaults, including a Batman story drawn by long-time Superman artist Wayne Boring, and a Jimmy Olsen story. Writer Waid rounded out the book with an "imaginary tale" starring a young Wonder Woman.

1 ❑ Jul 2000 Cover: 2.50 **NM** value: **Cover or less**
Circ: Diamd. preorders: **36,088**
📖 Pawns of the Invincible Immortal! **A:** Terry Dodson **W:** Mark Waid

GS 1❑Jul 2000 Cover: 5.95 **NM** value: **Cover or less**
Circ: Diamd. preorders: **28,139**
📖 S.O.S. to Nowhere; The Mad Hatter's Hat Crimes; The Invaders From Space; Wonder Girl's Mystery Suitor; The Origin of Super-Turtle **A:** Ty Templeton; Pete Costanza; Eduardo Barreto; Wayne Boring **W:** E. Nelson Bridwell; Mark Waid ★ Origin of Super-Turtle.

SILVER AGE: CHALLENGERS OF THE UNKNOWN — DC

1 ❑ Jul 2000 Cover: 2.50 **NM** value: **Cover or less**
Circ: Diamd. preorders: **26,477**
📖 A Small Matter of Time **A:** Drew Johnson **W:** Karl Kesel

SILVER AGE: DIAL H FOR HERO — DC

1 ❑ Jul 2000 Cover: 2.50 **NM** value: **Cover or less**
Circ: Diamd. preorders: **26,235**
📖 The One-Man Justice League **A:** Barry Kitson **W:** Mark Waid

SILVER AGE: DOOM PATROL — DC

1 ❑ Jul 2000 Cover: 2.50 **NM** value: **Cover or less**
Circ: Diamd. preorders: **26,467**
📖 The War of the Super-Weapons **A:** Bachan **W:** Tom Peyer

SILVER AGE: FLASH — DC

1 ❑ Jul 2000 Cover: 2.50 **NM** value: **Cover or less**
Circ: Diamd. preorders: **31,590**
📖 The Flash's Big Day **A:** Ty Templeton **W:** Brian Augustyn

SILVER AGE: GREEN LANTERN — DC

1 ❑ Jul 2000 Cover: 2.50 **NM** value: **Cover or less**
Circ: Diamd. preorders: **33,821**
📖 Alone…Against Injustice! **A:** Brent Anderson **W:** Kurt Busiek

SILVER AGE: JUSTICE LEAGUE OF AMERICA — DC

1 ❑ Jul 2000 Cover: 2.50 **NM** value: **Cover or less**
Circ: Diamd. preorders: **35,670**
📖 The League Without Justice! **A:** Scot Kolins **W:** Mark Millar

SILVER AGE SECRET FILES — DC

1 ❑ Jul 2000 Cover: 4.95 **NM** value: **Cover or less**
Circ: Diamd. preorders: **26,587**
📖 The Silver Age; Justi **A:** Ramona Fradon; Claude St. Aubin; Norm Breyfogle; Kevin Maguire; Ty Templeton; Jim Mooney; Michael Collins; Christopher Jones **W:** Brian Augustyn; D. Curtis Johnson; Jason Hernandez-Rosenblatt; Mark Waid

SILVER AGE: SHOWCASE — DC

1 ❑ Jul 2000 Cover: 2.50 **NM** value: **Cover or less**
Circ: Diamd. preorders: **28,834**
📖 The 7 Soldiers of Victory **A:** Dick Giordano **W:** Geoff Johns

SILVER AGE: TEEN TITANS — DC

1 ❑ Jul 2000 Cover: 2.50 **NM** value: **Cover or less**
Circ: Diamd. preorders: **30,164**
📖 The Tyrannical Terror of Sheriff Law **A:** Pat Oliffe **W:** Marv Wolfman

SILVER AGE: THE BRAVE AND THE BOLD — DC

1 ❑ Jul 2000 Cover: 2.50 **NM** value: **Cover or less**
Circ: Diamd. preorders: **30,673**
📖 The Great Gotham Switcheroo! **A:** Kevin Maguire **W:** Bob Haney

SILVERBACK — Comico

1 ❑ ca. 1990 Cover: 2.50 **NM** value: **Cover or less**
Circ: CapCity orders: **8,300**
📖 The Dreamer **A:** John Peck **W:** William Messner-Loebs; Matt Wagner ★ Origin of Argent.

2 ❑ ca. 1990 Cover: 2.50 **NM** value: **Cover or less**
Circ: CapCity orders: **6,600**
📖 Cold Memories **A:** William Messner-Loebs; John Peck **W:** William Messner-Loebs; Matt Wagner ★ Origin of Argent.

3 ❑ ca. 1990 Cover: 2.50 **NM** value: **Cover or less**
Circ: CapCity orders: **6,150**
★ Origin of Argent.

SILVERBLADE — DC

The English refer to "The California Disease" of wanting to be young forever. For Jonathan Lord, aging actor, that could not be more true. Once a leading man in dozens of movies, he is now a bitter old man, whiling away his final years in his palatial "Shangri-La" estate and rhapsodizing over his early years.

Then he encounters a strange statuette of the Maltese Falcon, which suddenly came to life. It offers to roll back the years for Jonathan, if he will do favors for it, in return. So Jonathan becomes 30 again, while simultaneously being recruited as a "Silverblade," the falcon's paladin against the occult forces of evil. In addition to his restored youth, Jonathan now has the ability to transform into any character he has ever played on film. This could get interesting, since among his roles is Dracula. (And the opposing side manages to find a wooden stake.)

1 ❑ Sep 1987 Cover: 1.25 **NM** value: **Cover or less**
Circ: CapCity orders: **19,300**
📖 The Lord Of Sunset Boulevard **A:** Gene Colan **W:** Cary Bates ★ Origin of Silverblade. ★ 1st Appearance of Silverblade.

2 ❑ Oct 1987 Cover: 1.25 **NM** value: **Cover or less**
Circ: CapCity orders: **16,200**
📖 Son Of Silverblade **A:** Gene Colan **W:** Cary Bates

3 ❑ Nov 1987 Cover: 1.25 **NM** value: **Cover or less**
Circ: CapCity orders: **15,450**
A: Gene Colan

4 ❑ Dec 1987 Cover: 1.25 **NM** value: **Cover or less**
Circ: CapCity orders: **13,050**
A: Gene Colan

5 ❑ Jan 1988 Cover: 1.25 **NM** value: **Cover or less**
Circ: CapCity orders: **11,700**
A: Gene Colan

6 ❑ Feb 1988 Cover: 1.25 **NM** value: **Cover or less**
Circ: CapCity orders: **10,500**
📖 One Through The Heart **A:** Gene Colan **W:** Cary Bates

7 ❑ Mar 1988 Cover: 1.25 **NM** value: **Cover or less**
Circ: CapCity orders: **9,850**
A: Gene Colan

8 ❑ May 1988 Cover: 1.25 **NM** value: **Cover or less**
Circ: CapCity orders: **9,000**
A: Gene Colan

9 ❑ Jun 1988 Cover: 1.25 **NM** value: **Cover or less**
Circ: CapCity orders: **8,050**
A: Gene Colan

10 ❑ Jul 1988 Cover: 1.25 **NM** value: **Cover or less**
Circ: CapCity orders: **6,800**
A: Gene Colan

11 ❑ Aug 1988 Cover: 1.25 **NM** value: **Cover or less**
Circ: CapCity orders: **6,400**
A: Gene Colan

12 ❑ Sep 1988 Cover: 1.25 **NM** value: **Cover or less**
Circ: CapCity orders: **6,150**
A: Gene Colan

SILVER CROSS — Antarctic

1 ❑ Nov 1997 Cover: 2.95 **NM** value: **Cover or less**
Circ: Diamd. preorders: **9,045**
A: Ben Dunn **W:** Ben Dunn

2 ❑ Jan 1998 Cover: 2.95 **NM** value: **Cover or less**
Circ: Diamd. preorders: **5,094**
A: Ben Dunn **W:** Ben Dunn

3 ❑ Mar 1998 Cover: 2.95 **NM** value: **Cover or less**
Circ: Diamd. preorders: **4,091**
A: Ben Dunn **W:** Ben Dunn

SILVERFAWN — Caliber

1 ❑ Cover: 1.95 **NM** value: **Cover or less**
📖 Wings Of Freedom **A:** Mark Winfrey

SILVERHAWKS — Marvel / Star

1 ❑ Aug 1987 Cover: 1.00 **NM** value: **Cover or less**
Circ: CapCity orders: **5,600**
📖 The Origin Story **A:** Mike Witherby **W:** Steve Perry

2 ❑ Oct 1987 Cover: 1.00 **NM** value: **Cover or less**
A: Howard Bender **W:** Steve Perry

3 ❑ Dec 1987 Cover: 1.00 **NM** value: **Cover or less**
A: Howard Bender **W:** Steve Perry

4 ❑ Feb 1988 Cover: 1.00 **NM** value: **Cover or less**
Circ: CapCity orders: **3,100**
A: Howard Bender **W:** Steve Perry

5 ❑ Apr 1988 Cover: 1.00 **NM** value: **Cover or less**
Circ: CapCity orders: **2,600**
A: Howard Bender **W:** Steve Perry

6 ❑ Jun 1988 Cover: 1.00 **NM** value: **Cover or less**
Circ: CapCity orders: **1,950**
📖 A Few Laughs With the Old Crowd final issue. **A:** Howard Bender **W:** Steve Perry

7 ❑ Jul 1988 Cover: 1.00 **NM** value: **Cover or less**
Circ: CapCity orders: **1,600**

SILVERHEELS — Pacific

1 ❑ ca. 1984 Cover: 1.50 **NM** value: **Cover or less**
A: Scott Hampton **W:** Bruce Jones; April Campbell

2 ❑ ca. 1984 Cover: 1.50 **NM** value: **Cover or less**
3 ❑ ca. 1984 Cover: 1.50 **NM** value: **Cover or less**

SILVER KID WESTERN — Key

1 ❑ Oct 1954 Cover: 0.10 **NM** value: **60.00**
2 ❑ Dec 1954 Cover: 0.10 **NM** value: **40.00**
3 ❑ Mar 1955 Cover: 0.10 **NM** value: **30.00**
4 ❑ May 1955 Cover: 0.10 **NM** value: **30.00**
5 ❑ Jul 1955 Cover: 0.10 **NM** value: **30.00**

SILVER SABLE — Marvel

Silver Sable first appears in Amazing Spider-Man #265 as the leader of The Wild Pack. The Wild Pack was formed by Sable's father to hunt down Nazi war criminals. Sable, who was trained by her father as a consummate soldier, takes control of The Wild Pack after her father's death. She then decides to change its direction, concentrating, instead, on renting its services as "guns for hire."

Both Sable and The Wild Pack return in this new title. Marvel decided to make a splash with the first issue and released it with a special, embossed silver cover. Although it looked terrific, Marvel discovered that (ahem!) certain parts of the cover had gained a little too much prominence in the embossing process and it was ultimately slightly de-embossed.

1 ❑ Jun 1992 Cover: 2.00 **NM** value: **Cover or less**
Circ: CapCity orders: **106,800** • **CGC:** 2 graded, best 9.0
Embossed cover. 📖 Personal Stakes **A:** Steven Butler **W:** Greg Wright

2 ❑ Jul 1992 Cover: 1.25 **NM** value: **1.50**
Circ: CapCity orders: **61,200**
📖 Gattling's Big Guns, Part 1 **A:** Steven Butler **W:** Greg Wright

3 ❑ Aug 1992 Cover: 1.25 **NM** value: **1.50**
Circ: CapCity orders: **54,300**
📖 Gattling's Big Guns, Part 2

4 ❑ Sep 1992 Cover: 1.25 **NM** value: **1.50**
Circ: CapCity orders: **50,400**
📖 Infinity War **A:** Steven Butler **W:** Greg Wright

5 ❑ Oct 1992 Cover: 1.25 **NM** value: **Cover or less**
Circ: CapCity orders: **43,800**
📖 Infinity War

6 ❑ Nov 1992 Cover: 1.25 **NM** value: **Cover or less**
Circ: CapCity orders: **32,500**
📖 Museum of Theft **A:** Steve Carr; Deryl Skelton **W:** Greg Wright ★ Appearance of Deathlok.

7 ❑ Dec 1992 Cover: 1.25 **NM** value: **Cover or less**
Circ: CapCity orders: **29,300**
📖 Welcome To My Museum **A:** Steven Butler **W:** Greg Wright ★ Appearance of Deathlok.

8 ❑ Jan 1993 Cover: 1.25 **NM** value: **Cover or less**
Circ: CapCity orders: **26,300**
📖 War Criminal **A:** Steven Butler **W:** Greg Wright

9 ❑ Feb 1993 Cover: 1.25 **NM** value: **Cover or less**
Circ: CapCity orders: **26,200**
📖 Origins **A:** Steven Butler **W:** Greg Wright ★ Origin of Wild Pack.

10 ❑ Mar 1993 Cover: 1.25 **NM** value: **Cover or less**
Circ: CapCity orders: **23,600**
📖 Crossed Purposes **A:** Steven Butler **W:** Greg Wright ★ Appearance of Punisher.

11 ❑ Apr 1993 Cover: 1.25 **NM** value: **Cover or less**
Circ: CapCity orders: **22,600**

12 ❑ May 1993 Cover: 1.25 **NM** value: **Cover or less**
Circ: CapCity orders: **21,500**

13 ❑ Jun 1993 Cover: 1.25 **NM** value: **Cover or less**
Circ: CapCity orders: **20,400**

14 ❑ Jul 1993 Cover: 1.25 **NM** value: **Cover or less**
Circ: CapCity orders: **19,400**

15 ❑ Aug 1993 Cover: 1.25 **NM** value: **Cover or less**
Circ: CapCity orders: **18,200**

16 ❑ Sep 1993 Cover: 1.25 **NM** value: **Cover or less**
Circ: CapCity orders: **18,400**

17 ❑ Oct 1993 Cover: 1.25 **NM** value: **Cover or less**
Circ: CapCity orders: **16,600**
• Infinity Crusade crossover **A:** Steven Butler **W:** Greg Wright ★ Appearance of New Outlaws, Baron Von Strucker, Crippler.

18 ❑ Nov 1993 Cover: 1.25 **NM** value: **Cover or less**
Circ: CapCity orders: **19,050**

19 ❑ Dec 1993 Cover: 1.25 **NM** value: **Cover or less**
Circ: CapCity orders: **18,150**

20 ❑ Jan 1994 Cover: 1.25 **NM** value: **Cover or less**
Circ: Statement: **42,842** CapCity orders: **13,800**

21 ❑ Feb 1994 Cover: 1.25 **NM** value: **Cover or less**
Circ: Statement: **42,842** CapCity orders: **12,800**

22 ❑ Mar 1994 Cover: 1.25 **NM** value: **Cover or less**
Circ: Statement: **42,842** CapCity orders: **11,800**

23 ❑ Apr 1994 Cover: 1.25 **NM** value: **Cover or less**
Circ: Statement: **42,842** CapCity orders: **11,900**
★ Appearance of Daredevil. ★ Versus Deadpool.

24 ❑ May 1994 Cover: 1.50 **NM** value: **Cover or less**
Circ: Statement: **42,842** CapCity orders: **10,750**

25 ❑ Jun 1994 Cover: 2.00 **NM** value: **Cover or less**
Circ: Statement: **42,842** CapCity orders: **12,400**
• Giant-size.

26 ❑ Jul 1994 Cover: 1.50 **NM** value: **Cover or less**
Circ: Statement: **42,842** CapCity orders: **10,600**

27 ❑ Aug 1994 Cover: 1.50 **NM** value: **Cover or less**
Circ: Statement: **42,842** CapCity orders: **9,700**

28 ❑ Sep 1994 Cover: 1.50 **NM** value: **Cover or less**
Circ: Statement: **42,842** CapCity orders: **9,200**

29 ❑ Oct 1994 Cover: 1.50 **NM** value: **Cover or less**
Circ: Statement: **42,842** CapCity orders: **8,650**

30 ❑ Nov 1994 Cover: 1.50 **NM** value: **Cover or less**
Circ: Statement: **42,842**

31 ❑ Dec 1994 Cover: 1.50 **NM** value: **Cover or less**
Circ: Statement: **42,842** CapCity orders: **7,750**

32 ❑ Jan 1995 Cover: 1.50 **NM** value: **Cover or less**
Circ: CapCity orders: **7,075**

33 ❑ Feb 1995 Cover: 1.50 **NM** value: **Cover or less**
Circ: CapCity orders: **6,550**

34 ❑ Mar 1995 Cover: 1.50 **NM** value: **Cover or less**
Circ: CapCity orders: **6,075**
• Has 1994 Statement, filed 10/1/94; avg print run 43,467; avg sales 42,225; avg subs 617; avg total paid 42,842; samples 125; office use 500; max existent 43,467; no newsstand sales during year

35 ❑ Apr 1995 Cover: 1.50 **NM** value: **Cover or less**
Circ: CapCity orders: **5,900**
final issue.

SILVER SCREAM — Recollections

1 ❑ b&w Cover: 2.00 **NM** value: **Cover or less**
2 ❑ b&w Cover: 2.00 **NM** value: **Cover or less**
3 ❑ b&w Cover: 2.00 **NM** value: **Cover or less**

SILVER STAR — Pacific

1 ❑ Feb 1983 Cover: 1.00 **NM** value: **Cover or less**
📖 Silver Star: Homo Geneticus **A:** Jack Kirby **W:** Jack Kirby ★ 1st Appearance of Last of the Viking Heroes.

2 ❑ Apr 1983 Cover: 1.00 **NM** value: **Cover or less**
📖 Darius Drumm **A:** Jack Kirby **W:** Jack Kirby

3 ❑ Jun 1983 Cover: 1.00 **NM** value: **Cover or less**
📖 The Others; Flynn, Part 1 **A:** Jack Kirby; D. Bruce Berry **W:** Jack Kirby; Richard Kyle

4 ❑ Aug 1983 Cover: 1.00 **NM** value: **Cover or less**
📖 The Super-Normals: Are They God's or Satan's Children? **A:** Jack Kirby **W:** Jack Kirby

5 ❑ Nov 1983 Cover: 1.00 **NM** value: **Cover or less**
📖 The World According to Drumm **A:** Jack Kirby **W:** Jack Kirby

6 ❑ Jan 1984 Cover: 1.00 **NM** value: **Cover or less**
📖 Silver Star Battles the Angel of Death **A:** Jack Kirby **W:** Jack Kirby

SILVER STAR (JACK KIRBY'S...) — Topps

1 ❑ Oct 1993 Cover: 2.95 **NM** value: **Cover or less**
Circ: CapCity orders: **14,175**
📖 The Job • trading cards **A:** James W. Fry III **W:** Kurt Busiek

SILVERSTORM (AIRCEL) — Aircel

1 ❑ 1990b&w Cover: 2.25 **NM** value: **Cover or less**
📖 Luck, a Storm-Tossed Coin **A:** Steven Butler **W:** Thomas Fortenberry ★ 1st Appearance of Tempest, Silver Dollar.

2 ❑ 1990b&w Cover: 2.25 **NM** value: **Cover or less**
A: Steven Butler **W:** Thomas Fortenberry

3 ❑ Jul 1990, b&w Cover: 2.25 **NM** value: **Cover or less**
A: Steven Butler **W:** Thomas Fortenberry

4 ❑ 1990b&w Cover: 2.25 **NM** value: **Cover or less**
A: Steven Butler **W:** Thomas Fortenberry

SILVERSTORM (SILVERLINE) — Silverline

1 ❑ Oct 1998 Cover: 2.95 **NM** value: **Cover or less**
A: Jaxon Renick; Keith Mudd **W:** Roland Mann

2 ❑ 1999 Cover: 2.95 **NM** value: **Cover or less**
W: Roland Mann

3 ❑ 1999 Cover: 2.95 **NM** value: **Cover or less**
W: Roland Mann

4 ❑ 1999 Cover: 2.95 **NM** value: **Cover or less**
W: Roland Mann

Capital City orders are the actual sales of comic books by Capital City Distribution, once one of the largest U.S. sellers of comics to comics shops. Capital City's share of comics shop sales, while not known exactly, increases from around 10-20% in the mid-1980s to 30-35% in the mid-1990s. Capital City's share of comic books sold on newsstands (most Marvels and DCs) will be less.

SILVER STREAK COMICS — Lev Gleason

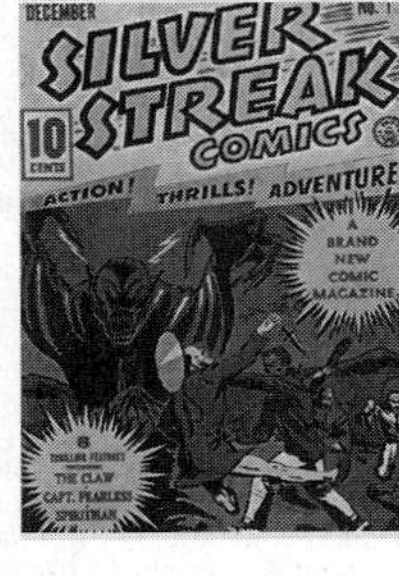

This anthology title is of interest from a number of collecting approaches. Among them: It featured a classic "Yellow Peril" character in "The Claw": a fanged, taloned master criminal (who got ongoing cover play even over his eventual opponent, the Golden Age Daredevil, in many appearances). That was the villain; among costumed characters in the series are the aforementioned Daredevil (in head-to-toe black and blue) and the speedy Silver Streak himself. Another oddity: The cover logo changed and shifted through the run, starting with a slanted silver design and then contorting itself in a number of forms and eventually adding red, white, blue, and stars. Other characters included Sky Wolf, Dickie Dean, Presto Martin, Cloud Curtis, and Captain Battle. Also of interest: The series cover-trumpeted the arrival in #18 of the pulp character The Saint, in stories "written especially for Silver Streak Comics by Leslie Charteris."

Daredevil got his own series and did very well therein, until settling into a luxurious life in a foreign country. But that's another series. — Maggie

1 ❑ Dec 1939 Cover: 0.10 **NM** value: **10000.00**
2 ❑ Jan 1940 Cover: 0.10 **NM** value: **4000.00**
• **CGC:** 1 graded, best 6.5
3 ❑ Mar 1940 Cover: 0.10 **NM** value: **3500.00**
• **CGC:** 1 graded, best 9.2
4 ❑ May 1940 Cover: 0.10 **NM** value: **2000.00**
• **CGC:** 1 graded, best 7.0
5 ❑ Jul 1940 Cover: 0.10 **NM** value: **2000.00**
6 ❑ Sep 1940 Cover: 0.10 **NM** value: **1500.00**
• **CGC:** 2 graded, best 4.5
7 ❑ Jan 1941 Cover: 0.10 **NM** value: **1500.00**
• **CGC:** 3 graded, best 7.5
8 ❑ Mar 1941 Cover: 0.10 **NM** value: **1500.00**
9 ❑ Apr 1941 Cover: 0.10 **NM** value: **1500.00**
10 ❑ May 1941 Cover: 0.10 **NM** value: **1500.00**
11 ❑ Jun 1941 Cover: 0.10 **NM** value: **1000.00**
12 ❑ Jul 1941 Cover: 0.10 **NM** value: **100.00**
13 ❑ Aug 1941 Cover: 0.10 **NM** value: **1000.00**
14 ❑ Sep 1941 Cover: 0.10 **NM** value: **1000.00**
15 ❑ Oct 1941 Cover: 0.10 **NM** value: **1000.00**
• **CGC:** 1 graded, best 6.5
16 ❑ Nov 1941 Cover: 0.10 **NM** value: **750.00**
17 ❑ Dec 1941 Cover: 0.10 **NM** value: **750.00**
18 ❑ Feb 1942 Cover: 0.10 **NM** value: **750.00**
• **CGC:** 2 graded, best 9.2
19 ❑ Mar 1942 Cover: 0.10 **NM** value: **750.00**
20 ❑ Apr 1942 Cover: 0.10 **NM** value: **750.00**
• **CGC:** 1 graded, best 8.0
21 ❑ May 1942 Cover: 0.10 **NM** value: **750.00**
23 ❑ ca. 1946 Cover: 0.10 **NM** value: **750.00**
• **CGC:** 1 graded, best 7.0

SILVER SURFER: DANGEROUS ARTIFACTS — Marvel

1 ❑ Jun 1996 Cover: 3.95 **NM** value: **Cover or less**
One-shot.

SILVER SURFER (FIRESIDE) — Marvel

1 ❑ Cover: 4.95 **NM** value: **Cover or less**
• (Fireside; 1978) **A:** Jack Kirby **W:** Stan Lee

SILVER SURFER: INNER DEMONS — Marvel

1 ❑ Apr 1998 Cover: 3.50 **NM** value: **Cover or less**
One-shot. • collects Silver Surfer #123, 125, 126

SILVER SURFER: JUDGMENT DAY — Marvel

1 ❑ Oct 1988 Cover: 14.95 **NM** value: **Cover or less**
Circ: CapCity orders: **3,400**
hardcover.

SILVER SURFER: LOFTIER THAN MORTALS — Marvel

1 ❑ Oct 1999 Cover: 2.50 **NM** value: **Cover or less**
Circ: Diamd. preorders: **28,806**
A: Sal Velluto **W:** Michael Jan Friedman

2 ❑ Nov 1999 Cover: 2.50 **NM** value: **Cover or less**
Circ: Diamd. preorders: **27,166**
A: Sal Velluto **W:** Michael Jan Friedman

SILVER SURFER: REBIRTH OF THANOS — Marvel

1 ❑ Cover: 12.95 **NM** value: **Cover or less**

SILVER SURFER/SUPERMAN — Marvel

1 ❑ Nov 1996 Cover: 5.95 **NM** value: **Cover or less**
Circ: Direct Market orders: **73,000**
No issue number. • prestige format. 📖 Pop! • crossover with DC **A:** Ron Lim; Terry Austin(inks) **W:** George Pérez

SILVER SURFER: THE ENSLAVERS — Marvel

1 ❑ Mar 1990 Cover: 16.95 **NM** value: **Cover or less**
Circ: CapCity orders: **8,500**
hardcover.

SILVER SURFER VS. DRACULA — Marvel

1 ❑ ca. 1994 Cover: 1.75 **NM** value: **Cover or less**
Circ: CapCity orders: **12,150**
• Reprints Tomb of Dracula #50

SILVER SURFER, THE (VOL. 1) — Marvel

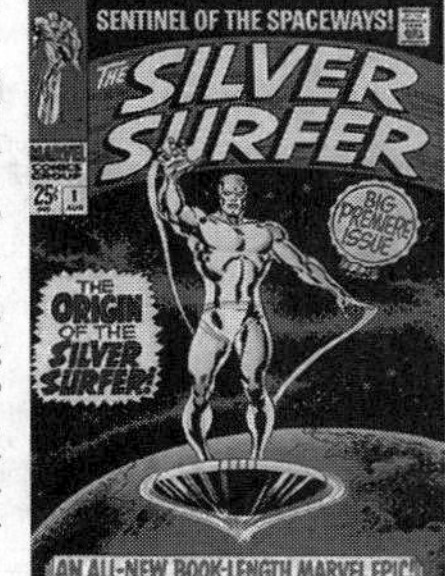

Norrin Radd is an inhabitant of the perfect, boring world of Zenn-La. His only comfort is his love for Shalla Bal. Then tragedy strikes in the form of an alien spaceship bearing Galactus. Zenn-La's best defenses are no match for this devourer of worlds. Galactus would utterly destroy Zenn-La, if Radd did not volunteer to become his herald, helping him find uninhabited worlds to satisfy Galactus' need for energy. Galactus covers Radd with "cosmic glaze" and gives him awesome powers and a sort of interstellar surfboard to travel on.

As The Silver Surfer, Radd serves Galactus for a time, until Galactus insists on destroying Earth, in the story that introduces the characters, starting in Fantastic Four #48 (Mar 66). The Surfer stops him, with the help of The Fantastic Four, but Galactus constructs an energy barrier to trap The Surfer on Earth as punishment for his rebellion. This series chronicles his early adventures on Earth, as he deals with issues of good and evil, scripted by Stan Lee in some of his best work.

1 ❑ Aug 1968 Cover: 0.25 **NM** value: **450.00**
• **CGC:** 211 graded, best 9.6
• Giant-size. 📖 The Origin of the Silver Surfer!; The Wonder of The Watcher! • adaptation from Tales of Suspense #53 **A:** Gene Colan; John Buscema **W:** Stan Lee ★ Origin of Silver Surfer.

2 ❑ Oct 1968 Cover: 0.25 **NM** value: **175.00**
• **CGC:** 112 graded, best 9.8
• Giant-size. 📖 When Lands the Saucer!; The Coming of the Krills! • adaptation from Amazing Adult Fantasy #8 **A:** John Buscema **W:** Stan Lee

3 ❑ Dec 1968 Cover: 0.25 **NM** value: **150.00**
• **CGC:** 53 graded, best 9.6
• Giant-size. 📖 The Power and the Prize!; Duel in the Depths!; Why Won't They Believe Me? • adaptation from Amazing Adult Fantasy #7 **A:** John Buscema **W:** Stan Lee ★ 1st Appearance of Mephisto. ★ Appearance of Thor.

4 ❑ Feb 1969 Cover: 0.25 **NM** value: **375.00**
• **CGC:** 177 graded, best 9.8
• Giant-size. 📖 The Good, the Bad, and the Uncanny; The Terror of Tim Boo Ba! • Scarce; adaptation from Amazing Adult Fantasy #9 **A:** John Buscema **W:** Stan Lee

5 ❑ Apr 1969 Cover: 0.25 **NM** value: **100.00**
• **CGC:** 36 graded, best 9.6
• Giant-size. 📖 And Who Shall Mourn for Him?; Run, Roco, Run! • adaptation from Tales to Astonish #26 **A:** John Buscema **W:** Stan Lee

6 ❑ Jun 1969 Cover: 0.25 **NM** value: **100.00**
• **CGC:** 26 graded, best 9.8
• Giant-size. 📖 Worlds Without End; The Unsuspecting • adaptation from Amazing Adult Fantasy #13 **A:** John Buscema **W:** Stan Lee

7 ❑ Aug 1969 Cover: 0.25 **NM** value: **90.00**
• **CGC:** 24 graded, best 9.6
• Giant-size. 📖 The Heir of Frankenstein!; I, the Gargoyle! • adaptation from Amazing Adult Fantasy #12 **A:** John Buscema **W:** Stan Lee

8 ❑ Sep 1969 Cover: 0.15 **NM** value: **65.00**
• **CGC:** 18 graded, best 9.6
📖 Now Strikes the Ghost! **A:** John Buscema **W:** Stan Lee

9 ❑ Oct 1969 Cover: 0.15 **NM** value: **65.00**
• **CGC:** 25 graded, best 9.6
📖 To Steal The Surfer's Soul! **A:** John Buscema **W:** Stan Lee

10 ❑ Nov 1969 Cover: 0.15 **NM** value: **65.00**
• **CGC:** 22 graded, best 9.6
📖 A World He Never Made **A:** John Buscema **W:** Stan Lee

11 ❑ Dec 1969 Cover: 0.15 **NM** value: **58.00**
• **CGC:** 21 graded, best 9.8
📖 O, Bitter Victory! **A:** John Buscema **W:** Stan Lee

12 ❑ Jan 1970 Cover: 0.15 **NM** value: **58.00**
• **CGC:** 19 graded, best 9.6
📖 Gather, Ye Witches! **A:** John Buscema **W:** Stan Lee

13 ❑ Feb 1970 Cover: 0.15 **NM** value: **58.00**
• **CGC:** 9 graded, best 9.4
📖 The Dawn of the Doomsday Man! **A:** John Buscema **W:** Stan Lee

14 ❑ Mar 1970 Cover: 0.15 **NM** value: **75.00**
• **CGC:** 32 graded, best 9.6
📖 The Surfer and the Spider **A:** John Buscema **W:** Stan Lee ★ Appearance of Spider-Man.

15 ❑ Apr 1970 Cover: 0.15 **NM** value: **45.00**
• **CGC:** 19 graded, best 9.6
📖 The Flame and the Fury **A:** John Buscema **W:** Stan Lee

16 ❑ May 1970 Cover: 0.15 **NM** value: **45.00**
• **CGC:** 15 graded, best 9.6
📖 In the Hands of Mephisto **A:** John Buscema **W:** Stan Lee

17 ❑ Jun 1970 Cover: 0.15 **NM** value: **45.00**
• **CGC:** 18 graded, best 9.4
📖 The Surfer Must Kill! **A:** John Buscema **W:** Stan Lee

18 ❑ Sep 1970 Cover: 0.15 **NM** value: **45.00**
• **CGC:** 24 graded, best 9.8
📖 To Smash the Inhumans final issue. • Inhumans **A:** Jack Kirby **W:** Stan Lee ★ Appearance of Inhumans.

SILVER SURFER, THE (VOL. 2) — Marvel / Epic

1 ❑ Dec 1988 Cover: 1.00 **NM** value: **3.00**
• **CGC:** 34 graded, best 9.8
📖 Parable **A:** Moebius **W:** Stan Lee

2 ❑ Jan 1989 Cover: 1.00 **NM** value: **2.50**
A: Moebius **W:** Stan Lee

Bk 1/HC❑Mar 1989 Cover: 19.95 **NM** value: **Cover or less**
Circ: CapCity orders: **8,550**
hardcover. **A:** Moebius

CGC-graded: Multiply prices above by **33 for 9.9 M • 16 for 9.8 NM/M • 7 for 9.6 NM+ • 5 for 9.4 NM • 2.5 for 9.2 NM- • 1.5 for 9.0 VF/NM**

SILVER SURFER (VOL. 2) Marvel

1 ❑ Jun 1982 Cover: 1.00 **NM** value: **12.00**
📖 Escape-To Terror! **A:** John Byrne **W:** John Byrne; Stan Lee

SILVER SURFER, THE (VOL. 3) Marvel

-1 ❑ Jul 1997 Cover: 1.99 **NM** value: **2.25**
Circ: Diamd. preorders: **39,921**
• Flashback★ Appearance of Stan Lee.
0.5 ❑ ca. 1998 **NM** value: **3.00**
• **CGC:** 7 graded, best 9.8
• Wizard promotional edition (mail-in).
0.5/PI❑ca. 1998 **NM** value: **6.00**
• Wizard promotional edition (mail-in).
1 ❑ Jul 1987 Cover: 1.25 **NM** value: **8.00**
Circ: CapCity orders: **52,900 • CGC:** 11 graded, best 9.8
• Double-size. 📖 Free **A:** Marshall Rogers **W:** Steve Englehart
2 ❑ Aug 1987 Cover: 0.75 **NM** value: **5.00**
Circ: CapCity orders: **43,800**
3 ❑ Sep 1987 Cover: 0.75 **NM** value: **4.00**
Circ: CapCity orders: **45,700**
4 ❑ Oct 1987 Cover: 0.75 **NM** value: **4.00**
Circ: CapCity orders: **46,000 • CGC:** 1 graded, best 9.6
★ Appearance of Mantis.
5 ❑ Nov 1987 Cover: 0.75 **NM** value: **4.00**
Circ: CapCity orders: **44,700 • CGC:** 1 graded, best 9.2
★ Origin of Skrulls. ★ Appearance of Mantis.
6 ❑ Dec 1987 Cover: 0.75 **NM** value: **3.50**
Circ: CapCity orders: **40,600 • CGC:** 1 graded, best 9.6
7 ❑ Jan 1988 Cover: 0.75 **NM** value: **3.50**
Circ: Statement: **221,585** CapCity orders: **38,600 • CGC:** 1 graded, best 9.4
8 ❑ Feb 1988 Cover: 0.75 **NM** value: **3.50**
Circ: Statement: **221,585** CapCity orders: **37,500**
9 ❑ Mar 1988 Cover: 0.75 **NM** value: **3.50**
Circ: Statement: **221,585** CapCity orders: **37,600**
10 ❑ Apr 1988 Cover: 0.75 **NM** value: **3.50**
Circ: Statement: **221,585** CapCity orders: **35,500**
11 ❑ May 1988 Cover: 1.00 **NM** value: **3.00**
Circ: Statement: **221,585** CapCity orders: **32,500**
★ 1st Appearance of Reptyl.
12 ❑ Jun 1988 Cover: 1.00 **NM** value: **3.00**
Circ: Statement: **221,585** CapCity orders: **31,400**
13 ❑ Jul 1988 Cover: 1.00 **NM** value: **3.00**
Circ: Statement: **221,585** CapCity orders: **30,800**
14 ❑ Aug 1988 Cover: 1.00 **NM** value: **3.00**
Circ: Statement: **221,585** CapCity orders: **30,400**
15 ❑ Sep 1988 Cover: 1.00 **NM** value: **4.00**
Circ: Statement: **221,585** CapCity orders: **29,400**
A: Ron Lim
16 ❑ Oct 1988 Cover: 1.00 **NM** value: **3.00**
Circ: Statement: **221,585** CapCity orders: **29,500**
A: Ron Lim ★ Appearance of Fantastic Four.
17 ❑ Nov 1988 Cover: 1.00 **NM** value: **3.00**
Circ: Statement: **221,585** CapCity orders: **29,300**
A: Ron Lim
18 ❑ Dec 1988 Cover: 1.00 **NM** value: **3.00**
Circ: Statement: **221,585** CapCity orders: **30,000**
A: Ron Lim
19 ❑ Jan 1989 Cover: 1.00 **NM** value: **3.00**
Circ: Statement: **165,725** CapCity orders: **29,300**
A: Ron Lim
20 ❑ Feb 1989 Cover: 1.00 **NM** value: **3.00**
Circ: Statement: **165,725** CapCity orders: **28,600**
A: Ron Lim
21 ❑ Mar 1989 Cover: 1.00 **NM** value: **3.00**
Circ: Statement: **165,725** CapCity orders: **29,300**
A: Ron Lim
22 ❑ Apr 1989 Cover: 1.00 **NM** value: **3.00**
Circ: Statement: **165,725** CapCity orders: **30,300**
A: Ron Lim
23 ❑ May 1989 Cover: 1.00 **NM** value: **3.00**
Circ: Statement: **165,725** CapCity orders: **28,500**
A: Ron Lim
24 ❑ Jun 1989 Cover: 1.00 **NM** value: **3.00**
Circ: Statement: **165,725** CapCity orders: **27,600**
A: Ron Lim
25 ❑ Jul 1989 Cover: 1.50 **NM** value: **3.50**
Circ: Statement: **165,725** CapCity orders: **28,700**
• Giant-size. **A:** Ron Lim ★ Versus new Super-Skrull.
26 ❑ Aug 1989 Cover: 1.00 **NM** value: **2.50**
Circ: Statement: **165,725** CapCity orders: **27,800**
A: Ron Lim
27 ❑ Sep 1989 Cover: 1.00 **NM** value: **2.50**
Circ: Statement: **165,725** CapCity orders: **27,000**
A: Ron Lim
28 ❑ Oct 1989 Cover: 1.00 **NM** value: **2.50**
Circ: Statement: **165,725** CapCity orders: **27,400**
A: Ron Lim
29 ❑ Nov 1989 Cover: 1.00 **NM** value: **2.50**
Circ: Statement: **165,725** CapCity orders: **27,500**
A: Ron Lim
30 ❑ Nov 1989 Cover: 1.00 **NM** value: **2.50**
Circ: Statement: **165,725** CapCity orders: **27,600**
A: Ron Lim
31 ❑ Dec 1989 Cover: 1.50 **NM** value: **3.00**
Circ: Statement: **165,725** CapCity orders: **27,200**
• Giant-size. **A:** Ron Lim
32 ❑ Dec 1989 Cover: 1.00 **NM** value: **2.00**
Circ: Statement: **165,725** CapCity orders: **25,400**
33 ❑ Jan 1990 Cover: 1.00 **NM** value: **2.00**
Circ: Statement: **156,024** CapCity orders: **27,000**
34 ❑ Feb 1990 Cover: 1.00 **NM** value: **3.50**
Circ: Statement: **156,024** CapCity orders: **28,700**
★ Appearance of Thanos.
35 ❑ Mar 1990 Cover: 1.00 **NM** value: **3.50**
Circ: Statement: **156,024** CapCity orders: **28,300**
• Drax the Destroyer resurrected★ Appearance of Thanos.
36 ❑ Apr 1990 Cover: 1.00 **NM** value: **3.00**
Circ: Statement: **156,024** CapCity orders: **26,600**
★ Appearance of Thanos.
37 ❑ May 1990 Cover: 1.00 **NM** value: **3.00**
Circ: Statement: **156,024** CapCity orders: **28,900**
• Has 1989 Statement, filed 11/1/89; avg print run 282,185; avg sales 161,685; avg subs 4,040; avg total paid 165,725; samples 125; office use 600; max existent 166,450; 41% of run returned★ Appearance of Thanos.
38 ❑ Jun 1990 Cover: 1.00 **NM** value: **3.00**
Circ: Statement: **156,024** CapCity orders: **29,700**
★ Appearance of Thanos, Silver Surfer vs. Thanos.
39 ❑ Jul 1990 Cover: 1.00 **NM** value: **3.00**
Circ: Statement: **156,024** CapCity orders: **28,200**
★ Appearance of Thanos.
40 ❑ Aug 1990 Cover: 1.00 **NM** value: **2.00**
Circ: Statement: **156,024** CapCity orders: **30,400**
41 ❑ Sep 1990 Cover: 1.00 **NM** value: **2.00**
Circ: Statement: **156,024** CapCity orders: **30,250**
42 ❑ Oct 1990 Cover: 1.00 **NM** value: **2.00**
Circ: Statement: **156,024** CapCity orders: **28,900**
43 ❑ Nov 1990 Cover: 1.00 **NM** value: **2.00**
Circ: Statement: **156,024** CapCity orders: **28,400**
44 ❑ Dec 1990 Cover: 1.00 **NM** value: **2.00**
Circ: Statement: **156,024** CapCity orders: **28,400**
45 ❑ Jan 1991 Cover: 1.00 **NM** value: **2.00**
Circ: Statement: **205,700** CapCity orders: **28,600 • CGC:** 1 graded, best 9.6
46 ❑ Feb 1991 Cover: 1.00 **NM** value: **2.50**
Circ: Statement: **205,700** CapCity orders: **30,900**
• Return of Adam Warlock
47 ❑ Mar 1991 Cover: 1.00 **NM** value: **2.50**
Circ: Statement: **205,700** CapCity orders: **29,700**
• Has 1990 Statement, filed 10/1/90; avg print run 263,249; avg sales 152,308; avg subs 3,716; avg total paid 156,024; samples 100; office use 600; max existent 156,724; 41% of run returned★ Appearance of Warlock.
48 ❑ Apr 1991 Cover: 1.00 **NM** value: **2.00**
Circ: Statement: **205,700** CapCity orders: **33,100 • CGC:** 1 graded, best 9.4
49 ❑ May 1991 Cover: 1.00 **NM** value: **2.00**
Circ: Statement: **205,700** CapCity orders: **44,000**
50 ❑ Jun 1991 Cover: 1.50 **NM** value: **5.00**
Circ: Statement: **205,700 • CGC:** 15 graded, best 9.8
Silver embossed cover. 📖 Deeply Buried Secrets **A:** Ron Lim **W:** Jim Starlin ★ Origin of Silver Surfer.
50-2❑Jun 1991 Cover: 1.50 **NM** value: **2.00**
50-3❑ Cover: 1.50 **NM** value: **2.00**
51 ❑ Jul 1991 Cover: 1.00 **NM** value: **2.00**
Circ: Statement: **205,700** CapCity orders: **57,100**
📖 Infinity Gauntlet • Infinity Gauntlet
52 ❑ Aug 1991 Cover: 1.00 **NM** value: **2.00**
Circ: Statement: **205,700** CapCity orders: **57,500**
📖 Infinity Gauntlet • Infinity Gauntlet★ Appearance of Firelord, Drax.
53 ❑ Aug 1991 Cover: 1.00 **NM** value: **2.00**
Circ: Statement: **205,700** CapCity orders: **55,700**
📖 Infinity Gauntlet • Infinity Gauntlet **A:** Ron Lim **W:** Ron Marz
54 ❑ Sep 1991 Cover: 1.00 **NM** value: **2.00**
Circ: Statement: **205,700** CapCity orders: **62,400**
📖 Infinity Gauntlet • Infinity Gauntlet **A:** Ron Lim **W:** Ron Marz
55 ❑ Sep 1991 Cover: 1.00 **NM** value: **2.00**
Circ: Statement: **205,700** CapCity orders: **64,400**
📖 Infinity Gauntlet • Infinity Gauntlet **W:** Ron Marz
56 ❑ Oct 1991 Cover: 1.00 **NM** value: **2.00**
Circ: Statement: **205,700** CapCity orders: **58,800**
📖 Infinity Gauntlet • Infinity Gauntlet **W:** Ron Marz
57 ❑ Oct 1991 Cover: 1.00 **NM** value: **2.00**
Circ: Statement: **205,700** CapCity orders: **57,800**
📖 Infinity Gauntlet • Infinity Gauntlet **W:** Ron Marz ★ Appearance of Thanos.
58 ❑ Nov 1991 Cover: 1.00 **NM** value: **2.00**
Circ: Statement: **205,700** CapCity orders: **57,500**
📖 Infinity Gauntlet • Infinity Gauntlet **W:** Ron Marz
59 ❑ Nov 1991 Cover: 1.00 **NM** value: **2.00**
Circ: Statement: **205,700** CapCity orders: **57,800**
📖 Infinity Gauntlet • Infinity Gauntlet **A:** Tom Rainey **W:** Ron Marz
60 ❑ Dec 1991 Cover: 1.00 **NM** value: **2.00**
Circ: Statement: **205,700** CapCity orders: **51,800**
W: Ron Marz
61 ❑ Jan 1992 Cover: 1.00 **NM** value: **2.00**
Circ: CapCity orders: **48,300**
📖 Carrier **A:** Ron Lim **W:** Ron Marz
62 ❑ Feb 1992 Cover: 1.25 **NM** value: **2.00**
Circ: CapCity orders: **47,400**
📖 Battlelines **A:** Ron Lim **W:** Ron Marz
63 ❑ Mar 1992 Cover: 1.00 **NM** value: **2.00**
Circ: CapCity orders: **46,200**
W: Ron Marz
64 ❑ Apr 1992 Cover: 1.00 **NM** value: **2.00**
Circ: CapCity orders: **41,700**
📖 Inner Turmoil **A:** Ron Lim **W:** Ron Marz
65 ❑ May 1992 Cover: 1.00 **NM** value: **2.00**
Circ: CapCity orders: **42,300**
📖 Cold Blooded **A:** Ron Lim **W:** Ron Marz
66 ❑ Jun 1992 Cover: 1.00 **NM** value: **2.00**
Circ: CapCity orders: **43,200**
📖 Conflicting Emotions **A:** Steve Carr; Deryl Skelton **W:** Ron Marz ★ 1st Appearance of Avatar.
67 ❑ Jul 1992 Cover: 1.25 **NM** value: **2.00**
Circ: CapCity orders: **60,000**
📖 Infinity war **A:** Kevin West **W:** Ron Marz
68 ❑ Aug 1992 Cover: 1.00 **NM** value: **2.00**
Circ: CapCity orders: **59,400**
📖 Infinity war • Infinity War **A:** Kevin West **W:** Ron Marz
69 ❑ Aug 1992 Cover: 1.00 **NM** value: **2.00**
Circ: CapCity orders: **56,700**
📖 Infinity war **A:** Kevin West **W:** Ron Marz ★ 1st Appearance of Morg.
70 ❑ Sep 1992 Cover: 1.00 **NM** value: **2.00**
Circ: CapCity orders: **48,000**
📖 Herald Ordeal, Part 1 ★ Origin of Morg.
71 ❑ Sep 1992 Cover: 1.00 **NM** value: **2.00**
Circ: CapCity orders: **42,300**
📖 Herald Ordeal, Part 2
72 ❑ Oct 1992 Cover: 1.00 **NM** value: **2.00**
Circ: CapCity orders: **41,200**
📖 Herald Ordeal, Part 3 **A:** M.C. Wyman **W:** Ron Marz
73 ❑ Oct 1992 Cover: 1.00 **NM** value: **2.00**
Circ: CapCity orders: **41,400**
📖 Herald Ordeal, Part 4
74 ❑ Nov 1992 Cover: 1.00 **NM** value: **2.00**
Circ: CapCity orders: **40,600**
📖 Herald Ordeal, Part 5
75 ❑ Nov 1992 Cover: 2.50 **NM** value: **3.50**
Circ: CapCity orders: **118,500 • CGC:** 4 graded, best 9.8
silver foil cover. 📖 Herald Ordeal, Part 6 **A:** Ron Lim **W:** Ron Marz ★ Death of Nova (female).
76 ❑ Dec 1992 Cover: 1.25 **NM** value: **1.50**
Circ: CapCity orders: **39,300**
📖 Prisoners **A:** Ron Lim **W:** Ron Marz
77 ❑ Jan 1993 Cover: 1.25 **NM** value: **1.50**
Circ: Statement: **242,375** CapCity orders: **40,400**
78 ❑ Feb 1993 Cover: 1.25 **NM** value: **1.50**
Circ: Statement: **242,375** CapCity orders: **40,100**
📖 Armored And Dangerous **A:** Ron Lim **W:** Ron Marz
79 ❑ Mar 1993 Cover: 1.25 **NM** value: **1.50**
Circ: Statement: **242,375** CapCity orders: **40,700**
80 ❑ Apr 1993 Cover: 1.25 **NM** value: **1.50**
Circ: Statement: **242,375** CapCity orders: **42,000**
81 ❑ May 1993 Cover: 1.25 **NM** value: **1.50**
Circ: Statement: **242,375** CapCity orders: **39,000**
82 ❑ Jun 1993 Cover: 1.75 **NM** value: **Cover or less**
Circ: Statement: **242,375** CapCity orders: **40,700**
83 ❑ Jul 1993 Cover: 1.75 **NM** value: **Cover or less**
Circ: Statement: **242,375** CapCity orders: **41,500**
84 ❑ Aug 1993 Cover: 1.75 **NM** value: **Cover or less**
Circ: Statement: **242,375** CapCity orders: **39,100**
85 ❑ Sep 1993 Cover: 1.75 **NM** value: **Cover or less**
📖 Compassion • Infinity Crusade **A:** Ernie Stiner **W:** Ron Marz ★ Appearance of Wonder Man, Storm, Goddess.
85/CS❑Sep 1993 Cover: 2.95 **NM** value: **Cover or less**
Circ: Statement: **242,375** CapCity orders: **33,800**
• "Dirtbag special"; Polybagged with Dirt #4; Infinity Crusade crossover **A:** Cully Hammer **W:** Ron Marz ★ Appearance of Wonder Man, Storm, Goddess.
86 ❑ Oct 1993 Cover: 1.75 **NM** value: **Cover or less**
Circ: Statement: **242,375** CapCity orders: **35,950**
87 ❑ Nov 1993 Cover: 1.75 **NM** value: **Cover or less**
Circ: Statement: **242,375** CapCity orders: **34,400**
88 ❑ Jan 1994 Cover: 1.75 **NM** value: **Cover or less**
Circ: Statement: **139,492** CapCity orders: **31,400**
89 ❑ Feb 1994 Cover: 1.25 **NM** value: **1.50**
Circ: Statement: **139,492** CapCity orders: **30,800**
90 ❑ Mar 1994 Cover: 1.95 **NM** value: **Cover or less**
Circ: Statement: **139,492** CapCity orders: **27,300**
• Giant-size.
91 ❑ Apr 1994 Cover: 1.25 **NM** value: **Cover or less**
Circ: Statement: **139,492** CapCity orders: **27,100**
92 ❑ May 1994 Cover: 1.50 **NM** value: **Cover or less**
Circ: Statement: **139,492** CapCity orders: **25,300**
93 ❑ Jun 1994 Cover: 1.50 **NM** value: **Cover or less**
Circ: Statement: **139,492** CapCity orders: **24,950**
94 ❑ Jul 1994 Cover: 1.50 **NM** value: **Cover or less**
Circ: Statement: **139,492** CapCity orders: **24,200**
95 ❑ Aug 1994 Cover: 1.50 **NM** value: **Cover or less**
Circ: Statement: **139,492** CapCity orders: **24,100**
96 ❑ Sep 1994 Cover: 1.50 **NM** value: **Cover or less**
Circ: Statement: **139,492** CapCity orders: **22,600**
97 ❑ Oct 1994 Cover: 1.50 **NM** value: **Cover or less**
Circ: Statement: **139,492** CapCity orders: **21,650**
98 ❑ Nov 1994 Cover: 1.50 **NM** value: **Cover or less**
Circ: Statement: **139,492** CapCity orders: **20,450**
99 ❑ Dec 1994 Cover: 1.50 **NM** value: **Cover or less**
Circ: Statement: **139,492** CapCity orders: **20,900**
100❑ Jan 1995 Cover: 2.25 **NM** value: **2.50**
• Giant-size. **A:** Joe Phillips; Tom Grindberg **W:** Ron Marz
100/SC❑Jan 1995 Cover: 3.95 **NM** value: **Cover or less**
Circ: Statement: **76,280** CapCity orders: **34,350**
enhanced cover. • Giant-size. **A:** Joe Phillips; Tom Grindberg **W:** Ron Marz
101❑ Feb 1995 Cover: 1.50 **NM** value: **Cover or less**
Circ: Statement: **76,280** CapCity orders: **18,825**
102❑ Mar 1995 Cover: 1.50 **NM** value: **Cover or less**
Circ: Statement: **76,280** CapCity orders: **17,550**
• Has 1994 Statement, filed 10/1/94; avg print run 237,942; avg sales 136,017; avg subs 3,475; avg total paid 139,492; samples 125; office use 50; max existent 139,667; 41% of run returned
103❑ Apr 1995 Cover: 1.50 **NM** value: **Cover or less**
Circ: Statement: **76,280** CapCity orders: **17,175**
104❑ May 1995 Cover: 1.50 **NM** value: **Cover or less**
Circ: Statement: **76,280** CapCity orders: **17,050**
105❑ Jun 1995 Cover: 1.50 **NM** value: **Cover or less**
Circ: Statement: **76,280** CapCity orders: **16,775**
★ Versus Super-Skrull.
106❑ Jul 1995 Cover: 1.50 **NM** value: **Cover or less**
Circ: Statement: **76,280** CapCity orders: **15,875**
• Relinquishes Power Cosmic
107❑ Aug 1995 Cover: 1.50 **NM** value: **Cover or less**
Circ: Statement: **76,280**
108❑ Sep 1995 Cover: 1.50 **NM** value: **Cover or less**
Circ: Statement: **76,280**
• regains Power Cosmic
109❑ Oct 1995 Cover: 1.50 **NM** value: **Cover or less**
Circ: Statement: **93,091**

Other grades: Multiply prices above by **1.5 for Mint • 2/3 for Very Fine • 1/3 for Fine • 1/5 for Very Good • 1/8 for Good**

110 ❑ Nov 1995 Cover: 1.50 **NM** value: **Cover or less**
Circ: Statement: **93,091**

111 ❑ Dec 1995 Cover: 1.50 **NM** value: **Cover or less**
Circ: Statement: **93,091**
A: Tom Grindberg **W:** George Pérez

112 ❑ Jan 1996 Cover: 1.95 **NM** value: **Cover or less**
Circ: Statement: **93,091**
• Has 1995 Statement, filed 10/1/95; avg print run 126,250; avg sales 73,780; avg subs 2,500; avg total paid 76,280; samples 750; office use 500; max existent 77,530; 39% of run returned

113 ❑ Feb 1996 Cover: 1.95 **NM** value: **Cover or less**
Circ: Statement: **93,091**

114 ❑ Mar 1996 Cover: 1.95 **NM** value: **Cover or less**
Circ: Statement: **93,091**
Deja Vu? **A:** Tom Grindberg **W:** George Pérez

115 ❑ Apr 1996 Cover: 1.95 **NM** value: **Cover or less**
Circ: Statement: **93,091**

116 ❑ May 1996 Cover: 1.95 **NM** value: **Cover or less**
Circ: Statement: **93,091**

117 ❑ Jun 1996 Cover: 1.95 **NM** value: **Cover or less**
Circ: Statement: **93,091**

118 ❑ Jul 1996 Cover: 1.95 **NM** value: **Cover or less**
Circ: Statement: **93,091**

119 ❑ Aug 1996 Cover: 1.95 **NM** value: **Cover or less**
Circ: Statement: **93,091**

120 ❑ Sep 1996 Cover: 1.50 **NM** value: **1.95**
Circ: Statement: **60,068**

121 ❑ Oct 1996 Cover: 1.50 **NM** value: **1.95**
Circ: Statement: **60,068**

122 ❑ Nov 1996 Cover: 1.50 **NM** value: **1.95**
Circ: Statement: **60,068** Direct Market orders: **37,750**
It's The End Of The World As We Know It! • Has 1996 Statement, filed 10/1/96; avg print run 107,026; avg sales 91,299; avg subs 1,792; avg total paid 93,091; samples 600; office use 125; max existent 93,816; 12% of run returned **A:** Scot Eaton **W:** George Pérez ★ Versus Captain Marvel.

123 ❑ Dec 1996 Cover: 1.50 **NM** value: **1.95**
Circ: Statement: **60,068** Direct Market orders: **40,000**
• Surfer returns to Earth

124 ❑ Jan 1997 Cover: 1.50 **NM** value: **Cover or less**
Circ: Statement: **60,068** Direct Market orders: **38,000**
A Place Called Home **A:** Adriana Melo; Ed Benés **W:** Glenn Greenberg; J.M. DeMatteis ★ Appearance of Kymaera.

125 ❑ Feb 1997 Cover: 2.99 **NM** value: **Cover or less**
Circ: Statement: **60,068** Direct Market orders: **40,250**
wraparound cover. • Giant-size. The Heart of the Beast **A:** Ron Garney **W:** Glenn Greenberg; J.M. DeMatteis ★ Versus Hulk.

126 ❑ Mar 1997 Cover: 1.99 **NM** value: **Cover or less**
Circ: Statement: **60,068** Direct Market orders: **39,000**
The Barrier **A:** Ron Garney **W:** J.M. DeMatteis ★ Appearance of Doctor Strange.

127 ❑ Apr 1997 Cover: 1.99 **NM** value: **Cover or less**
Circ: Statement: **60,068** Direct Market orders: **38,000**
Puppets **A:** Ron Garney **W:** J.M. DeMatteis

128 ❑ May 1997 Cover: 1.99 **NM** value: **Cover or less**
Circ: Statement: **60,068** Diamd. preorders: **38,866**
Beneath the Silver Skin **A:** Ron Garney; Rick Leonardi **W:** J.M. DeMatteis ★ Appearance of Spider-Man, Daredevil.

129 ❑ Jun 1997 Cover: 1.99 **NM** value: **Cover or less**
Circ: Statement: **60,068** Diamd. preorders: **38,899**

130 ❑ Aug 1997 Cover: 1.99 **NM** value: **Cover or less**
Circ: Statement: **60,068** Diamd. preorders: **36,976**
• gatefold summary.

131 ❑ Sep 1997 Cover: 1.99 **NM** value: **Cover or less**
Circ: Diamd. preorders: **35,528**
• gatefold summary.

132 ❑ Oct 1997 Cover: 1.99 **NM** value: **Cover or less**
Circ: Diamd. preorders: **34,586**
• gatefold summary.

133 ❑ Nov 1997 Cover: 1.99 **NM** value: **Cover or less**
Circ: Diamd. preorders: **32,934**
• gatefold summary. ★ Appearance of Puppet Master.

134 ❑ Dec 1997 Cover: 1.99 **NM** value: **Cover or less**
Circ: Diamd. preorders: **32,289**
• gatefold summary. • Has 1997 Statement, filed 10/1/97; avg print run 100,283; avg sales 58,420; avg subs 1,648; avg total paid 60,068; samples 165; office use 125; max existent 60,358; 40% of run returned

135 ❑ Jan 1998 Cover: 1.99 **NM** value: **Cover or less**
Circ: Diamd. preorders: **31,275**
• gatefold summary. ★ Appearance of Agatha Harkness.

136 ❑ Feb 1998 Cover: 1.99 **NM** value: **Cover or less**
Circ: Diamd. preorders: **28,727**
• gatefold summary.

137 ❑ Mar 1998 Cover: 1.99 **NM** value: **Cover or less**
Circ: Diamd. preorders: **31,072**
• gatefold summary. ★ Appearance of Agatha Harkness.

138 ❑ Apr 1998 Cover: 1.99 **NM** value: **Cover or less**
Circ: Diamd. preorders: **29,457**
• gatefold summary. ★ Appearance of Thing.

139 ❑ May 1998 Cover: 1.99 **NM** value: **Cover or less**
Circ: Diamd. preorders: **28,131**
• gatefold summary.

140 ❑ Jun 1998 Cover: 1.99 **NM** value: **Cover or less**
Circ: Diamd. preorders: **30,597**
• gatefold summary.

141 ❑ Jul 1998 Cover: 1.99 **NM** value: **Cover or less**
Circ: Diamd. preorders: **29,406**
• gatefold summary.

142 ❑ Aug 1998 Cover: 1.99 **NM** value: **Cover or less**
Circ: Diamd. preorders: **29,456**
• gatefold summary.

143 ❑ Sep 1998 Cover: 1.99 **NM** value: **Cover or less**
Circ: Diamd. preorders: **27,193**
• gatefold summary. ★ Versus Psycho-Man.

144 ❑ Oct 1998 Cover: 1.99 **NM** value: **Cover or less**
Circ: Diamd. preorders: **26,363**
• gatefold summary.

145 ❑ Oct 1998 Cover: 1.99 **NM** value: **Cover or less**
Circ: Diamd. preorders: **26,126**
• gatefold summary.

146 ❑ Nov 1998 Cover: 1.99 **NM** value: **Cover or less**
Circ: Diamd. preorders: **25,550**
• gatefold summary. final issue.

Anl 1 ❑ ca. 1988 Cover: 1.75 **NM** value: **4.00**
• **CGC:** 1 graded, best 9.4
Evolutionary War, Part 3 **A:** Ron Lim

Anl 2 ❑ ca. 1989 Cover: 2.00 **NM** value: **3.00**
Circ: CapCity orders: **38,900**
Atlantis Attacks, Part 1 • Atlantis Attacks

Anl 3 ❑ ca. 1990 Cover: 2.00 **NM** value: **2.50**
Circ: CapCity orders: **36,900**
Lifeform; Lifeform, Part 4

Anl 4 ❑ ca. 1991 Cover: 2.00 **NM** value: **2.50**
Circ: CapCity orders: **41,200**
Korvac Quest; Korvac Quest, Part 3

Anl 5 ❑ ca. 1992 Cover: 2.25 **NM** value: **2.50**
Circ: CapCity orders: **37,000**
Return of Defenders; Return of the Defenders, Part 3 **A:** Ron Lim; Tom Morgan; Karl Altstaetter **W:** Ron Marz ★ Origin of Nebula.

Anl 6 ❑ ca. 1993 Cover: 2.95 **NM** value: **Cover or less**
Circ: CapCity orders: **29,700**
• trading card; Polybagged **A:** Joe Phillips **W:** Ron Marz ★ 1st Appearance of Legacy. ★ Appearance of Terrax, Jack of Hearts, Ronan the Accuser, Ganymede.

Anl 7 ❑ ca. 1994 Cover: 2.95 **NM** value: **Cover or less**
Circ: CapCity orders: **16,150**

Anl 1997 ❑ ca. 1997 Cover: 2.99 **NM** value: **Cover or less**
Circ: Diamd. preorders: **31,136**
wraparound cover.

Anl 1998 ❑ ca. 1998 Cover: 2.99 **NM** value: **Cover or less**
wraparound cover. • gatefold summary. Millennius! • Silver Surfer/Thor '98 **A:** Ramon Bernado **W:** Tom DeFalco ★ Versus Millennius.

SILVER SURFER/WARLOCK: RESURRECTION — Marvel

1 ❑ Mar 1993 Cover: 2.50 **NM** value: **Cover or less**
Circ: CapCity orders: **94,800**
The Pact **A:** Jim Starlin **W:** Jim Starlin

2 ❑ Apr 1993 Cover: 2.50 **NM** value: **Cover or less**
Circ: CapCity orders: **56,100**

3 ❑ May 1993 Cover: 2.50 **NM** value: **Cover or less**
Circ: CapCity orders: **48,200**
Welcome To Hades! **A:** Jim Starlin **W:** Jim Starlin

4 ❑ Jun 1993 Cover: 2.50 **NM** value: **Cover or less**
Circ: CapCity orders: **40,200**
End Game **A:** Jim Starlin **W:** Jim Starlin

SILVER SURFER/WEAPON ZERO — Marvel

1 ❑ Apr 1997 Cover: 2.95 **NM** value: **Cover or less**
Circ: Direct Market orders: **69,250**
Devil's Reign, Chapter 8; Devil's Reign • crossover with Image **A:** Joe Benitez **W:** Brian Holguin

SILVER SWEETIE, THE — Spoof

1 ❑ b&w Cover: 2.95 **NM** value: **Cover or less**

SILVERWING SPECIAL — Now

1 ❑ Jan 1987 Cover: 0.95 **NM** value: **1.00**

SILVERWOLF COMIC BOOK TRIVIA COMIC BOOK — Silverwolf

1 ❑ b&w Cover: 1.50 **NM** value: **Cover or less**
2 ❑ b&w Cover: 1.50 **NM** value: **Cover or less**

SIMON AND KIRBY CLASSICS — Pure Imagination

1 ❑ Nov 1986 Cover: 2.00 **NM** value: **Cover or less**
Killer in the Big Top; Stuntman Battles the Diamond Curse; Rest Camp for Criminals; Trapped on Wax • new Vagabond Prince and reprints from Stuntman #1, All-New #13 and Green Hornet #39

SIMON CAT IN TAXI — Slab-O-Concrete

1 ❑ **NM** value: **1.50**
• Post card comics **A:** Nigel Auchterlounie **W:** Nigel Auchterlounie

SIMPSONS COMICS — Bongo

TV's favorite dysfunctional cartoon family first appeared in Welsh's 1992 one-shot, Simpsons Comics and Stories. In late 1993, they returned, under the new Bongo Entertainment Group. This title is the flagship of a line that includes Itchy & Scratchy Comics, Radioactive Man, Bartman, Treehouse of Horror, and Bart Simpson Comics.

The Simpsons themselves became something of a national craze in the late Eighties and early Nineties. In particular, the family's exuberant young troublemaker, Bart, was featured on countless T-shirts, lunch boxes, and other merchandise accompanied by personal quotes such as, "Don't have a cow, Man!" Created by cartoonist Matt Groening ("rhymes with 'complaining'"), the Simpsons are a sort of comic antidote to the Brady Bunch. They often drive each other to wits' end, but are ultimately just a lovable family of misfits.

The comics series continues the antics of the TV show.

1 ❑ ca. 1993 Cover: 2.25 **NM** value: **3.00**
Circ: CapCity orders: **57,875** • **CGC:** 7 graded, best 9.8
Fantastic Four #1 homage cover. The Amazing Colossal Homer • Bart Simpsons' Creepy Crawly Tales back-up **A:** Steve Vance **W:** Steve Vance; Cindy Vance

2 ❑ ca. 1994 Cover: 1.95 **NM** value: **2.50**
Circ: CapCity orders: **34,500**
Cool Hand Bart • Patty & Selma's Ill-Fated Romance Comics back-up **A:** Steve Vance **W:** Steve Vance; Cindy Vance ★ Versus Sideshow Bob.

3 ❑ ca. 1994 Cover: 1.95 **NM** value: **2.25**
Circ: CapCity orders: **33,350**
The Perplexing Puzzle of the Springfield Puma; Krusty, Agent of K.L.O.W.N. • Krusty, Agent of K.L.O.W.N. back-up **A:** Steve Vance; Bill Morrison **W:** Steve Vance

4 ❑ ca. 1994 Cover: 2.25 **NM** value: **Cover or less**
Circ: CapCity orders: **31,600**
infinity cover. It's In The Cards; Busman • trading card; Gnarly Adventures of Busman back-up **A:** Steve Vance; Bill Morrison **W:** Steve Vance; Cindy Vance

5 ❑ ca. 1994 Cover: 2.25 **NM** value: **Cover or less**
Circ: CapCity orders: **27,275**
wraparound cover. When Bongos Collide; When Bongos Collide, Part 2 **A:** Steve Vance **W:** Steve Vance; Cindy Vance

6 ❑ ca. 1994 Cover: 2.25 **NM** value: **Cover or less**
Circ: CapCity orders: **21,025**
Be-Bop-A-Lisa • Chief Wiggum's Pre-Code Crime Comics back-up **A:** Bill Morrison **W:** Bill Morrison

7 ❑ ca. 1994 Cover: 2.25 **NM** value: **Cover or less**
Circ: CapCity orders: **17,025**
• McBain Comics back-up

8 ❑ ca. 1995 Cover: 2.25 **NM** value: **Cover or less**
Circ: CapCity orders: **14,975**
I Shrink, Therefore I'm Small • Edna; Queen of the Jungle back-up **A:** Luis Escobar **W:** Gary Glasberg

9 ❑ ca. 1995 Cover: 2.25 **NM** value: **Cover or less**
Circ: CapCity orders: **14,300**
The Purple Prose Of Springfield • Lisa's diary; Barney Gumble back-up **A:** Luis Escobar **W:** Andrew Gottlieb

10 ❑ ca. 1995 Cover: 2.25 **NM** value: **Cover or less**
Circ: CapCity orders: **14,175**
• Apu's Kwik-E Comics back-up

11 ❑ ca. 1995 Cover: 2.25 **NM** value: **Cover or less**
Circ: CapCity orders: **12,150**
• evil Flanders; Homer on the Range back-up

12 ❑ ca. 1995 Cover: 2.25 **NM** value: **Cover or less**
Circ: CapCity orders: **10,925**
• White-Knuckled War Stories back-up

13 ❑ ca. 1995 Cover: 2.25 **NM** value: **Cover or less**
Circ: CapCity orders: **9,200**
• Jimbo Jones' Wedgie Comics back-up

14 ❑ ca. 1995 Cover: 2.25 **NM** value: **Cover or less**
• Cantankerous Coot Classics back-up

15 ❑ ca. 1995 Cover: 2.25 **NM** value: **Cover or less**
• Heinous Funnies back-up

16 ❑ ca. 1996 Cover: 2.25 **NM** value: **Cover or less**
Waitresses In The Sky • Bongo Grab Bag back-up **A:** Phil Ortiz **W:** Jeff Rosenthal; Lona Williams

17 ❑ ca. 1996 Cover: 2.25 **NM** value: **Cover or less**
• Headlight Comics back-up

18 ❑ ca. 1996 Cover: 2.25 **NM** value: **Cover or less**
• Milhouse Comics back-up

19 ❑ ca. 1996 Cover: 2.25 **NM** value: **Cover or less**
• Roswell back-up

20 ❑ ca. 1996 Cover: 2.25 **NM** value: **Cover or less**
Bad homage cover. • Roswell back-up

21 ❑ ca. 1996 Cover: 2.25 **NM** value: **Cover or less**
• Roswell back-up

22 ❑ ca. 1996 Cover: 2.25 **NM** value: **Cover or less**
• Burns and Apu team up; Roswell back-up

23 ❑ ca. 1996 Cover: 2.25 **NM** value: **Cover or less**
• Reverend Lovejoy's Hellfire Comics back-up

24 ❑ ca. 1996 Cover: 2.25 **NM** value: **Cover or less**
Circ: Diamd. preorders: **23,504**
• Li'l Homey back-up

25 ❑ ca. 1996 Cover: 2.25 **NM** value: **Cover or less**
Circ: Diamd. preorders: **24,918**
• Marge gets her own talk show; Itchy & Scratchy back-up

26 ❑ ca. 1996 Cover: 2.25 **NM** value: **Cover or less**
Circ: Diamd. preorders: **21,749**
• Speed parody

27 ❑ ca. 1996 Cover: 2.25 **NM** value: **Cover or less**
Circ: Diamd. preorders: **20,491**
• Homer gets smart

28 ❑ ca. 1997 Cover: 2.25 **NM** value: **Cover or less**
Circ: Diamd. preorders: **22,361**
• Krusty founds his own country

29 ❑ ca. 1997 Cover: 2.25 **NM** value: **Cover or less**
Circ: Diamd. preorders: **22,093**
• Homer becomes a pro wrestler

30 ❑ ca. 1997 Cover: 2.25 **NM** value: **Cover or less**
Circ: Diamd. preorders: **22,289**
• Burns clones Smithers

31 ❑ ca. 1997 Cover: 2.25 **NM** value: **Cover or less**
Circ: Diamd. preorders: **21,113**
• Homer thinks he's Radioactive Man

32 ❑ ca. 1997 Cover: 2.25 **NM** value: **2.95**
Circ: Diamd. preorders: **20,709**
• Krusty's coffee bar

33 ❑ ca. 1997 Cover: 2.25 **NM** value: **Cover or less**
Circ: Diamd. preorders: **21,923**
• Alternate Springfield

34 ❑ ca. 1997 Cover: 2.25 **NM** value: **Cover or less**
Circ: Diamd. preorders: **20,397**
• Burns sponsors Bart as a snowboarder

35 ❑ ca. 1998 Cover: 2.25 **NM** value: **Cover or less**
Circ: Diamd. preorders: **19,967**
• Marge opens a daycare

36 ❑ ca. 1998 Cover: 2.25 **NM** value: **Cover or less**
Circ: Diamd. preorders: **21,591**
• The return of the geeks

CGC-graded: Multiply prices above by **33 for 9.9 M • 16 for 9.8 NM/M • 7 for 9.6 NM+ • 5 for 9.4 NM • 2.5 for 9.2 NM- • 1.5 for 9.0 VF/NM**

37 ❑ ca. 1998 Cover: 2.25 **NM** value: **Cover or less**
Circ: Diamd. preorders: **20,758**
• El Grampo

38 ❑ ca. 1998 Cover: 2.25 **NM** value: **Cover or less**
Circ: Diamd. preorders: **19,303**
• Burns makes addictive donuts

39 ❑ ca. 1998 Cover: 2.25 **NM** value: **Cover or less**
Circ: Diamd. preorders: **20,450**
• Homer and Comic Book Guy on trial

40 ❑ ca. 1998 Cover: 2.50 **NM** value: **Cover or less**
Circ: Diamd. preorders: **19,484**
• Krusty does live show from Simpsons house; Lard Lad back-up

41 ❑ ca. 1999 Cover: 2.50 **NM** value: **Cover or less**
Circ: Diamd. preorders: **18,305**
🕮 Bart Simpson & The Krusty Brand Fun Factory

42 ❑ ca. 1999 Cover: 2.50 **NM** value: **Cover or less**
Circ: Diamd. preorders: **18,883**
• The Homer Show; Slobberwacky back-up

43 ❑ ca. 1999 Cover: 2.50 **NM** value: **Cover or less**
Circ: Diamd. preorders: **18,461**
• story told backwards; Poochie back-up

44 ❑ ca. 1999 Cover: 2.50 **NM** value: **Cover or less**
Circ: Diamd. preorders: **17,248**
• Lisa substitutes; Bartman back-up

45 ❑ ca. 1999 Cover: 2.50 **NM** value: **Cover or less**
Circ: Diamd. preorders: **17,514**
🕮 Hot Dog On A Schtick • Hot Dog On A Schtick

46 ❑ ca. 1999 Cover: 2.50 **NM** value: **Cover or less**
Circ: Diamd. preorders: **16,450**
🕮 Angels with Yellow Faces ★ Appearance of Sideshow Bob.

47 ❑ ca. 2000 Cover: 2.50 **NM** value: **Cover or less**
Circ: Diamd. preorders: **15,266**

48 ❑ ca. 2000 Cover: 2.50 **NM** value: **Cover or less**
Circ: Diamd. preorders: **14,855**

49 ❑ ca. 2000 Cover: 2.50 **NM** value: **Cover or less**
Circ: Diamd. preorders: **15,440**

50 ❑ ca. 2000 Cover: 5.95 **NM** value: **Cover or less**
Circ: Diamd. preorders: **15,215**
• Giant-size. 🕮 Wall or Nothing; The 1001 Costumes of Bartman; Love Gory; Krusty's 11; Planet of the Strange-O's; Li'l Goodfellas; Inside Bongo Comics

51 ❑ ca. 2000 Cover: 2.50 **NM** value: **Cover or less**
Circ: Diamd. preorders: **14,865**
🕮 Bart and Lisa and Marge and Homer and Maggie (to a lesser extent) vs. Thanksgiving!; What Would Possibly Happen If Cletus Went to College • Cletus back-up

52 ❑ ca. 2000 Cover: 2.50 **NM** value: **Cover or less**
Circ: Diamd. preorders: **15,436**
🕮 Worst Christmas Ever!; A Springfield Christmas Carol **A:** Phil Ortiz **W:** Paul Dini

53 ❑ ca. 2000 Cover: 2.50 **NM** value: **Cover or less**
Circ: Diamd. preorders: **15,083**
🕮 The Beer Boys; Around Town with Ned Flanders • Ned Flanders back-up **A:** Phil Ortiz **W:** Doug Tuber; Jesse Leon McCann; Steve Luchsinger; Tim Maile

54 ❑ ca. 2000 Cover: 2.50 **NM** value: **Cover or less**
Circ: Diamd. preorders: **14,801**

55 ❑ ca. 2001 Cover: 2.50 **NM** value: **Cover or less**
Circ: Diamd. preorders: **14,863**

56 ❑ ca. 2001 Cover: 2.50 **NM** value: **Cover or less**
Circ: Diamd. preorders: **15,025**

57 ❑ ca. 2001 Cover: 2.50 **NM** value: **Cover or less**
Circ: Diamd. preorders: **15,405**

58 ❑ ca. 2001 Cover: 2.50 **NM** value: **Cover or less**
Circ: Diamd. preorders: **15,127**

59 ❑ ca. 2001 Cover: 2.50 **NM** value: **Cover or less**
Circ: Diamd. preorders: **15,674**

60 ❑ ca. 2001 Cover: 2.50 **NM** value: **Cover or less**
Circ: Diamd. preorders: **16,163**

Bk 1❑ Cover: 10.00 **NM** value: **Cover or less**
• Extravaganza; collects Simpsons Comics #1-4

Bk 2❑ Cover: 10.00 **NM** value: **Cover or less**
• Spectacular; collects #6-9

Bk 3❑ Cover: 10.00 **NM** value: **Cover or less**
• Bartman: The Best of the Best; Collects Bartman #1-3, Itchy & Scratchy Comics #3, Simpsons Comics #5

Bk 4❑ Cover: 10.95 **NM** value: **Cover or less**
• Simpsons Comics Simpsorama; Collects Simpsons Comics #11-14

Bk 5❑ Cover: 10.95 **NM** value: **Cover or less**
• Simpsons Comics Strike Back; Collects Simpsons Comics #15-18

Bk 6❑ Cover: 11.95 **NM** value: **Cover or less**
• Simpsons Comics Wingding; Collects Simpsons Comics #19-23

Bk 7❑ Cover: 11.95 **NM** value: **Cover or less**
• Simpsons Comics on Parade

Bk 8❑ Cover: 11.95 **NM** value: **Cover or less**
• Big Bonanza; collects #28-31

SIMPSONS COMICS AND STORIES — Welsh

1 ❑ ca. 1993 Cover: 2.50 **NM** value: **4.00**
Circ: CapCity orders: **36,550** • **CGC:** 2 graded, best 9.2
🕮 Lo, There Shall Come…A Bartman • with poster **A:** Steve Vance **W:** Steve Vance; Cindy Vance ★ Origin of Bartman, Bartman. ★ 1st Appearance of The Simpsons.

SIMPSONS COMICS (MAGAZINE) — Bongo

1 ❑ Mar 1997 Cover: 2.00 **NM** value: **4.00**
2 ❑ Apr 1997 Cover: 2.00 **NM** value: **3.25**
3 ❑ May 1997 Cover: 2.00 **NM** value: **3.25**
🕮 The Perplexing Puzzle of the Springfield Puma; Krusty, Agent of K.L.O.W.N. **A:** Steve Vance; Bill Morrison **W:** Steve Vance
4 ❑ Jun 1997 Cover: 2.00 **NM** value: **3.25**
5 ❑ Jul 1997 Cover: 2.00 **NM** value: **3.25**
6 ❑ Aug 1997 Cover: 2.00 **NM** value: **3.25**
7 ❑ Sep 1997 Cover: 2.00 **NM** value: **3.25**
8 ❑ Oct 1997 Cover: 2.00 **NM** value: **3.25**
9 ❑ Nov 1997 Cover: 2.00 **NM** value: **3.25**
10 ❑ Dec 1997 Cover: 2.00 **NM** value: **3.25**
11 ❑ Jan 1998 Cover: 2.00 **NM** value: **3.25**
12 ❑ Feb 1998 Cover: 2.00 **NM** value: **3.25**
13 ❑ Mar 1998 Cover: 2.00 **NM** value: **3.25**
🕮 Give Me Merchandising or Give Me Death!; Cabin Fervor; Rebel Without a Clutch **A:** Phil Ortiz; Shaun Cashman **W:** Barry Dutter; Gary Glasberg
14 ❑ Apr 1998 Cover: 2.00 **NM** value: **3.25**
15 ❑ May 1998 Cover: 2.00 **NM** value: **3.25**
16 ❑ Jun 1998 Cover: 2.00 **NM** value: **3.25**
17 ❑ Jul 1998 Cover: 2.00 **NM** value: **3.25**
18 ❑ Aug 1998 Cover: 2.00 **NM** value: **3.25**
19 ❑ Sep 1998 Cover: 2.00 **NM** value: **3.25**
20 ❑ Oct 1998 Cover: 2.00 **NM** value: **3.25**
21 ❑ Nov 1998 Cover: 2.00 **NM** value: **3.25**
22 ❑ Dec 1998 Cover: 2.00 **NM** value: **3.25**
23 ❑ Jan 1999 Cover: 2.00 **NM** value: **3.25**
24 ❑ Feb 1999 Cover: 2.00 **NM** value: **3.25**
25 ❑ Mar 1999 Cover: 2.00 **NM** value: **3.25**
🕮 Get off the Bus!; The Comic Cover Caper! • Reprints Bartman #1 **A:** Phil Ortiz **W:** Steve Vance; Rob Hammersley; Todd J. Greenwald

SIMPSONS COMICS PRESENTS BART SIMPSON — Bongo

1 ❑ Cover: 2.50 **NM** value: **Cover or less**
🕮 Big Fat Trouble in Little Springfield; Grrrl-Whirl; Close Encounters of the Nerd Kind **A:** John Costanza; Phil Ortiz; Caroline Kelly **W:** Chris Yambar; George Gladir; James Bates

2 ❑ Cover: 2.50 **NM** value: **Cover or less**
🕮 Bart's Day at the Zoo; Talent Hunt; Maximum Bart!; Futility Belt **A:** Dan Decarlo; Phil Ortiz; Francis Dinglasan; Igor Baranko; Mike Rote **W:** Gail Simone; George Gladir; James W. Bates ★ Appearance of Bartman.

SIN — Tragedy Strikes

1 ❑ b&w Cover: 2.95 **NM** value: **Cover or less**
2 ❑ b&w Cover: 2.95 **NM** value: **Cover or less**
3 ❑ b&w Cover: 2.95 **NM** value: **Cover or less**

SINBAD — Adventure

Sinbad, the sailor from the Arabian Nights adventures, is one of the oldest heroes in literature. He's a daring rogue who lives by his wits and his sword, taking what treasure he can while breaking the hearts of damsels along the way.

Writer R.A. Jones and artists M. C. Wyman, Bruce McCorkindale, and Bobby Blair did justice to the scope and grandeur of the Sinbad legend. In 1989, they introduced this atmospheric and well-illustrated series for Malibu's Adventure Comics line. Rendered in black-and-white, with lush wash tones applied by Blair, their Sinbad adaptation followed the format of the Arabian Nights original right down to the framing story of the princess Shaharazad (sic).

1 ❑ Nov 1989, b&w Cover: 2.25 **NM** value: **Cover or less**
cardstock cover. 🕮 The Four Trials of Sinbad **A:** M.C. Wyman **W:** R.A. Jones

2 ❑ Dec 1989, b&w Cover: 2.25 **NM** value: **Cover or less**
cardstock cover. **A:** M.C. Wyman **W:** R.A. Jones

3 ❑ Jan 1990, b&w Cover: 2.25 **NM** value: **Cover or less**
cardstock cover. **A:** M.C. Wyman **W:** R.A. Jones

4 ❑ Mar 1990, b&w Cover: 2.25 **NM** value: **Cover or less**
A: M.C. Wyman **W:** R.A. Jones

SINBAD BOOK II — Adventure

1 ❑ Mar 1991, b&w Cover: 2.50 **NM** value: **Cover or less**
🕮 House of God; In the House of God **A:** M.C. Wyman **W:** R.A. Jones

2 ❑ Apr 1991, b&w Cover: 2.50 **NM** value: **Cover or less**
🕮 House of God **A:** M.C. Wyman **W:** R.A. Jones

3 ❑ May 1991, b&w Cover: 2.50 **NM** value: **Cover or less**
🕮 House of God **A:** M.C. Wyman **W:** R.A. Jones

4 ❑ Jun 1991, b&w Cover: 2.50 **NM** value: **Cover or less**
🕮 House of God **A:** M.C. Wyman **W:** R.A. Jones

SIN CITY: A DAME TO KILL FOR — Dark Horse

1 ❑ Nov 1993, b&w Cover: 2.95 **NM** value: **3.50**
Circ: CapCity orders: **30,825** • **CGC:** 1 graded, best 9.8
A: Frank Miller **W:** Frank Miller

2 ❑ b&w Cover: 2.95 **NM** value: **3.25**
Circ: CapCity orders: **22,825**
A: Frank Miller **W:** Frank Miller

3 ❑ 1994b&w Cover: 2.95 **NM** value: **3.00**
Circ: CapCity orders: **21,400**
A: Frank Miller **W:** Frank Miller

4 ❑ Mar 1994, b&w Cover: 2.95 **NM** value: **3.00**
Circ: CapCity orders: **21,500**
A: Frank Miller **W:** Frank Miller

5 ❑ Apr 1994, b&w Cover: 2.95 **NM** value: **3.00**
Circ: CapCity orders: **22,275**
A: Frank Miller **W:** Frank Miller

6 ❑ May 1994, b&w Cover: 2.95 **NM** value: **3.00**
Circ: CapCity orders: **32,150**
A: Frank Miller **W:** Frank Miller

Bk 1❑ Cover: 15.00 **NM** value: **Cover or less**
• Trade Paperback. • Collects Sin City: A Dame to Kill For #1-6 **A:** Frank Miller **W:** Frank Miller

Bk 1/HC❑ Cover: 25.00 **NM** value: **Cover or less**
• hardcover (1st edition misprinted). • Collects Sin City: A Dame to Kill For #1-6 **A:** Frank Miller **W:** Frank Miller

Bk 1/LE❑ Cover: 100.00 **NM** value: **Cover or less**
• Limited edition hardcover. • Collects Sin City: A Dame to Kill for #1-6 **A:** Frank Miller **W:** Frank Miller

Bk 1-2❑ Cover: 15.00 **NM** value: **Cover or less**

SIN CITY: BOOZE, BROADS, & BULLETS — Dark Horse

Bk 1❑ Dec 1998 Cover: 15.00 **NM** value: **Cover or less**
No issue number. • Trade Paperback. • collects Babe Wore Red And Other Stories, Silent Night, A Decade of Dark Horse, Lost; Lonely & Lethal, Sex & Violence, and Just Another Saturday Night **A:** Frabj Miller **W:** Frabj Miller

SIN CITY (COZMIC) — Cozmic

1 ❑ Cover: 0.75 **NM** value: **1.50**
🕮 2001 A Haze Odyssey; Sin City Suicide; No Hiding Place; Tough Shit; Underground; Mrs. Higgins-Char **A:** Angus McKie; Bill Sanderson; Edward B.; J. T. B.; Paul Simmons; Wyndham Raine **W:** Angus McKie; Bill Sanderson; J. T. B.; Paul Simmons; Wyndham Raine; Dick Pountain; Felix; Ian Penman; the Cozmic Crew

SIN CITY (DARK HORSE) — Dark Horse

Using stark, high contrast black-and-white imagery and a newfound penchant for noir storytelling, Frank Miller once again revitalized the comics form with his landmark Sin City series. The original story, collected here from the Dark Horse Presents serial, is that of a scarred hulk of a man named Marv as he searches for justice — and a reason to live — in a dark world where life is cheap. Marv's tale began when a woman he had no right to expect would ever give him the time of day instead gave him a night to remember. The next morning, she was dead — killed beside him while he slept off the previous night's booze. Marv was haunted by her memory and determined to find the killer. Even while he was hunted as the girl's supposed killer, Marv had to uncover the grisly truth behind the woman's death. And in doing so, he would lay bare the true face of power in Sin City.

1 ❑ Jan 1993 Cover: 15.00 **NM** value: **Cover or less**
A: Frank Miller **W:** Frank Miller
1/HC❑ Dec 1994 Cover: 30.00 **NM** value: **Cover or less**
A: Frank Miller **W:** Frank Miller
1/LE❑ Cover: 100.00 **NM** value: **Cover or less**
A: Frank Miller **W:** Frank Miller
1-2 ❑ Cover: 15.00 **NM** value: **Cover or less**
1-3 ❑ Cover: 15.00 **NM** value: **Cover or less**
1-4 ❑ Cover: 15.00 **NM** value: **Cover or less**
1-5 ❑ Cover: 15.00 **NM** value: **Cover or less**
1-6 ❑ Cover: 15.00 **NM** value: **Cover or less**
Dlx 1❑ Cover: 30.00 **NM** value: **Cover or less**
• 1st edition in slipcase. **A:** Frank Miller **W:** Frank Miller

SIN CITY: FAMILY VALUES — Dark Horse

1 ❑ Oct 1997, b&w Cover: 10.00 **NM** value: **15.00**
No issue number. One-shot. **A:** Frank Miller **W:** Frank Miller
1/A ❑ Oct 1997 **NM** value: **15.00**
Cover has Roller-skating girl. **A:** Frank Miller **W:** Frank Miller
1/LE❑ Oct 1997 Cover: 75.00 **NM** value: **Cover or less**
• Limited edition hardcover. **A:** Frank Miller **W:** Frank Miller

SIN CITY: HELL AND BACK — Dark Horse / Maverick

1 ❑ Jul 1999, b&w Cover: 2.95 **NM** value: **Cover or less**
Circ: Diamd. preorders: **49,425**
cardstock cover. **A:** Frank Miller **W:** Frank Miller

2 ❑ Aug 1999, b&w Cover: 2.95 **NM** value: **Cover or less**
Circ: Diamd. preorders: **44,207**
cardstock cover. **A:** Frank Miller **W:** Frank Miller

3 ❑ Sep 1999, b&w Cover: 2.95 **NM** value: **Cover or less**
Circ: Diamd. preorders: **42,077**
cardstock cover. **A:** Frank Miller **W:** Frank Miller

4 ❑ Oct 1999, b&w Cover: 2.95 **NM** value: **Cover or less**
Circ: Diamd. preorders: **41,319**
cardstock cover. **A:** Frank Miller **W:** Frank Miller

5 ❑ Nov 1999, b&w Cover: 2.95 **NM** value: **Cover or less**
Circ: Diamd. preorders: **38,988**
cardstock cover. **A:** Frank Miller **W:** Frank Miller

6 ❑ Dec 1999, b&w Cover: 2.95 **NM** value: **Cover or less**
Circ: Diamd. preorders: **42,619**
cardstock cover. **A:** Frank Miller **W:** Frank Miller

7 ❑ Jan 2000, b&w Cover: 2.95 **NM** value: **Cover or less**
Circ: Diamd. preorders: **37,489**
cardstock cover. **A:** Frank Miller **W:** Frank Miller

8 ❑ b&w Cover: 2.95 **NM** value: **Cover or less**
Circ: Diamd. preorders: **35,310**
cardstock cover. **A:** Frank Miller **W:** Frank Miller

9 ❑ b&w Cover: 2.95 **NM** value: **Cover or less**
Circ: Diamd. preorders: **35,352**
cardstock cover. **A:** Frank Miller **W:** Frank Miller

SIN CITY: JUST ANOTHER SATURDAY NIGHT — Dark Horse

0.5 ❑ Aug 1997 Cover: 2.50 **NM** value: **3.00**
Circ: Diamd. preorders: **36,492** • **CGC:** 3 graded, best 9.6
• Wizard promotional edition. **A:** Frank Miller **W:** Frank Miller

1 ❑ Oct 1998, b&w Cover: 2.50 **NM** value: **Cover or less**
No issue number. One-shot. **A:** Frank Miller **W:** Frank Miller

SIN CITY: LOST, LONELY, & LETHAL — Dark Horse / Legend

1 ❑ Dec 1996 Cover: 2.95 **NM** value: **Cover or less**
Circ: Diamd. preorders: **56,265**

Other grades: Multiply prices above by **1.5 for Mint • 2/3 for Very Fine • 1/3 for Fine • 1/5 for Very Good • 1/8 for Good**

No issue number. One-shot. cardstock cover. • b&w and blue **A:** Frank Miller **W:** Frank Miller

SIN CITY: SEX & VIOLENCE — Dark Horse

1 ❑ Mar 1997, b&w Cover: 2.95 **NM** value: **Cover or less**
Circ: Diamd. preorders: **56,334**
No issue number. One-shot. cardstock cover. 📖 Wrong Turn; Wrong Track **A:** Frank Miller **W:** Frank Miller

SIN CITY: SILENT NIGHT — Dark Horse / Legend

1 ❑ Nov 1995, b&w Cover: 2.95 **NM** value: **Cover or less**
No issue number. One-shot. cardstock cover. **A:** Frank Miller **W:** Frank Miller

SIN CITY: THAT YELLOW BASTARD — Dark Horse / Legend

1 ❑ Feb 1996 Cover: 2.95 **NM** value: **Cover or less**
A: Frank Miller **W:** Frank Miller
2 ❑ Feb 1996 Cover: 2.95 **NM** value: **Cover or less**
A: Frank Miller **W:** Frank Miller
3 ❑ Apr 1996 Cover: 2.95 **NM** value: **Cover or less**
A: Frank Miller **W:** Frank Miller
4 ❑ May 1996 Cover: 2.95 **NM** value: **Cover or less**
A: Frank Miller **W:** Frank Miller
5 ❑ Jun 1996 Cover: 2.95 **NM** value: **Cover or less**
A: Frank Miller **W:** Frank Miller
6 ❑ Jul 1996 Cover: 2.95 **NM** value: **Cover or less**
A: Frank Miller **W:** Frank Miller
Bk 1❑ Jul 1997 Cover: 15.00 **NM** value: **Cover or less**
A: Frank Miller **W:** Frank Miller
Bk 1/HC❑Sep 1997 Cover: 25.00 **NM** value: **Cover or less**
hardcover. **A:** Frank Miller **W:** Frank Miller

SIN CITY: THE BABE WORE RED AND OTHER STORIES — Dark Horse

1 ❑ Nov 1994, b&w and redCover: 2.95 **NM** value: **Cover or less**
Circ: CapCity orders: **23,700** Diamd. preorders: **5,005**
No issue number. **A:** Frank Miller **W:** Frank Miller

SIN CITY: THE BIG FAT KILL — Dark Horse

1 ❑ Nov 1994, b&w Cover: 2.95 **NM** value: **Cover or less**
Circ: CapCity orders: **24,525**
A: Frank Miller **W:** Frank Miller
2 ❑ Dec 1994, b&w Cover: 2.95 **NM** value: **Cover or less**
Circ: CapCity orders: **22,125**
cardstock cover. **A:** Frank Miller **W:** Frank Miller
3 ❑ Jan 1995, b&w Cover: 2.95 **NM** value: **Cover or less**
Circ: CapCity orders: **20,250**
cardstock cover. **A:** Frank Miller **W:** Frank Miller
4 ❑ Feb 1995, b&w Cover: 2.95 **NM** value: **Cover or less**
Circ: CapCity orders: **20,050**
cardstock cover. **A:** Frank Miller **W:** Frank Miller
5 ❑ Mar 1995, b&w Cover: 2.95 **NM** value: **Cover or less**
Circ: CapCity orders: **20,200**
cardstock cover. **A:** Frank Miller **W:** Frank Miller

SINDY — Forbidden Fruit

All issues are adults only.
1 ❑ b&w Cover: 2.95 **NM** value: **Cover or less**
2 ❑ b&w Cover: 2.95 **NM** value: **Cover or less**
3 ❑ b&w Cover: 2.95 **NM** value: **Cover or less**
4 ❑ b&w Cover: 2.95 **NM** value: **Cover or less**
5 ❑ b&w Cover: 2.95 **NM** value: **Cover or less**

SINERGY — Caliber

1 ❑ ca. 1994, b&w Cover: 2.95 **NM** value: **Cover or less**
1/LE❑ ca. 1994 Cover: 5.95 **NM** value: **Cover or less**
• limited edition.
2 ❑ ca. 1994, b&w Cover: 2.95 **NM** value: **Cover or less**
2/LE❑ ca. 1994 Cover: 5.95 **NM** value: **Cover or less**
• limited edition.
3 ❑ ca. 1994, b&w Cover: 2.95 **NM** value: **Cover or less**
3/LE❑ ca. 1994 Cover: 5.95 **NM** value: **Cover or less**
• limited edition.
4 ❑ ca. 1994, b&w Cover: 2.95 **NM** value: **Cover or less**
4/LE❑ ca. 1994 Cover: 5.95 **NM** value: **Cover or less**
• limited edition.
5 ❑ ca. 1994, b&w Cover: 2.95 **NM** value: **Cover or less**
5/LE❑ ca. 1994 Cover: 5.95 **NM** value: **Cover or less**
• limited edition.
Bk 1❑ ca. 1994, b&w Cover: 14.95 **NM** value: **Cover or less**
• A Journey Through Hell

SINGLE SERIES — United Feature

1 ❑ Dec 1939 Cover: 0.10 **NM** value: **750.00**
• **CGC:** 1 graded, best 3.5
2 ❑ Cover: 0.10 **NM** value: **400.00**
3 ❑ Cover: 0.10 **NM** value: **300.00**
4 ❑ Cover: 0.10 **NM** value: **500.00**
5 ❑ Cover: 0.10 **NM** value: **300.00**
• **CGC:** 1 graded, best 5.0
6 ❑ Cover: 0.10 **NM** value: **300.00**
7 ❑ Cover: 0.10 **NM** value: **300.00**
8 ❑ Cover: 0.10 **NM** value: **300.00**
9 ❑ Cover: 0.10 **NM** value: **300.00**
10 ❑ Cover: 0.10 **NM** value: **300.00**
11 ❑ Cover: 0.10 **NM** value: **250.00**
12 ❑ Cover: 0.10 **NM** value: **250.00**
13 ❑ Cover: 0.10 **NM** value: **250.00**
14 ❑ Cover: 0.10 **NM** value: **250.00**
15 ❑ Cover: 0.10 **NM** value: **250.00**
16 ❑ ca. 1940 Cover: 0.10 **NM** value: **250.00**
17 ❑ ca. 1940 Cover: 0.10 **NM** value: **250.00**
18 ❑ ca. 1940 Cover: 0.10 **NM** value: **400.00**
19 ❑ ca. 1940 Cover: 0.10 **NM** value: **350.00**
20 ❑ ca. 1940 Cover: 0.10 **NM** value: **250.00**
• **CGC:** 2 graded, best 8.5
21 ❑ ca. 1940 Cover: 0.10 **NM** value: **250.00**
22 ❑ ca. 1940 Cover: 0.10 **NM** value: **250.00**
23 ❑ ca. 1940 Cover: 0.10 **NM** value: **250.00**
24 ❑ ca. 1940 Cover: 0.10 **NM** value: **250.00**
25 ❑ Cover: 0.10 **NM** value: **250.00**
26 ❑ Cover: 0.10 **NM** value: **250.00**
27 ❑ Cover: 0.10 **NM** value: **250.00**
28 ❑ Cover: 0.10 **NM** value: **250.00**

SINISTER HOUSE OF SECRET LOVE, THE — DC

1 ❑ Oct 1971 Cover: 0.25 **NM** value: **12.00**
• **CGC:** 11 graded, best 9.6
2 ❑ Dec 1971 Cover: 0.25 **NM** value: **8.00**
• **CGC:** 2 graded, best 9.4
📖 To Wed the Devil; Shattered Dreams; Interrupted Journey; Time for Revelation; Marriage of Fear; Epilogue (text) **A:** Tony DeZuniga **W:** Joe Orlando; Len Wein
3 ❑ Feb 1972 Cover: 0.25 **NM** value: **8.00**
• **CGC:** 1 graded, best 9.0
4 ❑ Apr 1972 Cover: 0.25 **NM** value: **8.00**
📖 Kiss Of The Serpent • Series continued in Secrets of Sinister House #5 **A:** Tony DeZuniga **W:** Mary DeZuniga; Michael Fleisher

SINISTER ROMANCE — Harrier

1 ❑ b&w Cover: 1.95 **NM** value: **2.00**
📖 The Isis Syndrome!; You Put a Spell on Me!; Know What I Mean? **A:** Glenn Dakin; Warren Pleece; Trevs Phoenix **W:** Glenn Dakin; Warren Pleece; Trevs Phoenix
2 ❑ b&w Cover: 1.95 **NM** value: **2.00**
3 ❑ b&w Cover: 1.95 **NM** value: **Cover or less**
4 ❑ b&w Cover: 1.95 **NM** value: **Cover or less**

SINJA: DEADLY SINS — Lightning

In 13th century Japan, Junan, the Sinja Master of the Daka-Rya clan, casts a spell to give life to the elements — and he succeeds. Chi (Earth), Ka (Fire), Sui (Water), Moku (Wood), and Kin (Metal) come forth, destroy Junan and his clan, and overrun Japan. Among the dead of the clan is Haratsu Taganaga, but his spirit is rescued by Seishin, the spirit of life. She offers him the opportunity to return to the world of the living and to be reunited with his wife and child — if he will be her warrior against the elemental demons. Of course, he agrees, and his battle commences.

This is a reasonably interesting piece of work, but the sketchy, faux-Jim Lee art distracts from the quality of the story.

1 ❑ Cover: 3.00 **NM** value: **Cover or less**
A: John Cleary **W:** John Cleary; Joseph A. Zyskowski; Tim Cleary
1/A ❑ Cover: 5.95 **NM** value: **Cover or less**
• Commemorative edition. **A:** John Cleary **W:** John Cleary; Joseph A. Zyskowski; Tim Cleary
1/B ❑ Cover: 9.95 **NM** value: **Cover or less**
• Nude edition. **A:** John Cleary **W:** John Cleary; Joseph A. Zyskowski; Tim Cleary

SINJA: RESURRECTION — Lightning

1 ❑ Aug 1996 Cover: 3.00 **NM** value: **Cover or less**
cover says Kunoichi. • flipbook with Kunoichi #1; indicia says Sinja: Resurrection

SINNAMON (VOL. 1) — Catfish

1 ❑ Dec 1995 Cover: 2.50 **NM** value: **Cover or less**
📖 Girls Will be Girls **A:** M. Gerald Delaney **W:** Angelo Furlan ★ 1st Appearance of Sinnamon.

SINNAMON (VOL. 2) — Catfish

1 ❑ 1996 Cover: 2.75 **NM** value: **Cover or less**
A: M. Gerald Delaney **W:** Angelo Furlan
2 ❑ 1996 Cover: 2.75 **NM** value: **Cover or less**
A: M. Gerald Delaney **W:** Angelo Furlan
3 ❑ 1996 Cover: 2.75 **NM** value: **Cover or less**
A: M. Gerald Delaney **W:** Angelo Furlan
4 ❑ 1996 Cover: 2.75 **NM** value: **Cover or less**
A: M. Gerald Delaney **W:** Angelo Furlan
4/SC❑1996 **NM** value: **5.00**
• Variant cover edition (500 printed). **A:** M. Gerald Delaney **W:** Angelo Furlan
5 ❑ 1996 Cover: 2.75 **NM** value: **Cover or less**
A: M. Gerald Delaney **W:** Angelo Furlan
5/SC❑1996 **NM** value: **4.00**
• Variant cover edition (500 printed). **A:** M. Gerald Delaney; Dave Roman(cover); Nick Poliwko(cover) **W:** Angelo Furlan
6 ❑ 1996 Cover: 2.75 **NM** value: **Cover or less**
A: M. Gerald Delaney **W:** Angelo Furlan
7 ❑ 1996 Cover: 2.75 **NM** value: **Cover or less**
📖 The Pyre-Anna Saga, Part 1 **A:** M. Gerald Delaney **W:** Angelo Furlan
8 ❑ 1996 Cover: 2.75 **NM** value: **Cover or less**
• Sinnamon vs. Aerobica **A:** M. Gerald Delaney **W:** Angelo Furlan

SINNER — Fantagraphics

1 ❑ Cover: 2.95 **NM** value: **Cover or less**
2 ❑ Cover: 2.95 **NM** value: **Cover or less**
3 ❑ Cover: 2.95 **NM** value: **Cover or less**
4 ❑ Cover: 2.95 **NM** value: **Cover or less**
5 ❑ Cover: 2.95 **NM** value: **Cover or less**

SINNERS, THE — DC / Piranha

1 ❑ Cover: 9.95 **NM** value: **Cover or less**
Circ: CapCity orders: **2,000**

SINNIN! — Fantagraphics / Eros

All issues are adults only.
1 ❑ b&w Cover: 2.25 **NM** value: **Cover or less**
2 ❑ b&w Cover: 2.25 **NM** value: **Cover or less**

SIN OF THE MUMMY — Fantagraphics / Eros

All issues are adults only.
1 ❑ b&w Cover: 2.50 **NM** value: **Cover or less**
A: P.W. Williams **W:** P.W. Williams

SINS OF YOUTH: AQUABOY/LAGOON MAN — DC

1 ❑ May 2000 Cover: 2.50 **NM** value: **Cover or less**
Circ: Diamd. preorders: **23,302**
📖 Turning Back the Tides of Time **A:** Sunny Lee **W:** Ben Raab

SINS OF YOUTH: BATBOY AND ROBIN — DC

1 ❑ May 2000 Cover: 2.50 **NM** value: **Cover or less**
Circ: Diamd. preorders: **30,590**
📖 Big Magic **A:** Cary Nord **W:** Chuck Dixon

SINS OF YOUTH: JLA, JR. — DC

1 ❑ May 2000 Cover: 2.50 **NM** value: **Cover or less**
Circ: Diamd. preorders: **32,281**
📖 You Gotta Be Kidding! **A:** Carlo Barberi **W:** Danny Curtis Johnson

SINS OF YOUTH: KID FLASH/IMPULSE — DC

1 ❑ May 2000 Cover: 2.50 **NM** value: **Cover or less**
Circ: Diamd. preorders: **27,003**
📖 Media Blitz **A:** Angel Unzueta **W:** Dwayne McDuffie

SINS OF YOUTH SECRET FILES — DC

1 ❑ May 2000 Cover: 4.95 **NM** value: **Cover or less**
📖 Disaffected Youth; CD-TV ad; Crisis on Infantile Earths; Wisdom, Like Age; Klarion and Kitty Cat **A:** Cully Hamner; Mike Miller; Pascual Ferry; Carlo Barberi; Sunny Lee **W:** Jim Alexander; Scott Beatty; Larry Stucker; Ben Raab; Geoff Johns; Jay Faerber

SINS OF YOUTH: STARWOMAN AND THE JSA (JUNIOR SOCIETY) — DC

1 ❑ May 2000 Cover: 2.50 **NM** value: **Cover or less**
Circ: Diamd. preorders: **26,690**
📖 Stars and Tykes **A:** Drew Johnson **W:** Geoff Johns

SINS OF YOUTH: SUPERMAN, JR./SUPERBOY, SR. — DC

1 ❑ May 2000 Cover: 2.50 **NM** value: **Cover or less**
Circ: Diamd. preorders: **28,461**
📖 The Adventures of Superboy when he wa a Man! **A:** Rob Haynes **W:** Karl Kesel

SINS OF YOUTH: THE SECRET/DEADBOY — DC

1 ❑ May 2000 Cover: 2.50 **NM** value: **Cover or less**
Circ: Diamd. preorders: **23,635**
📖 Looking for Trouble **A:** Michael Avon Oeming **W:** Todd Dezago

SINS OF YOUTH: WONDER GIRLS — DC

1 ❑ May 2000 Cover: 2.50 **NM** value: **Cover or less**
Circ: Diamd. preorders: **25,431**
📖 Coming of Age **A:** Scott Kolins **W:** Brian K. Vaughan

SINTHIA — Lightning

1/A ❑ Oct 1997 Cover: 2.95 **NM** value: **Cover or less**
Circ: Diamd. preorders: **6,181**
A: Rod Perry **W:** Joseph Adams
1/B ❑ Oct 1997 Cover: 2.95 **NM** value: **Cover or less**
Circ: Diamd. preorders: **5,372**
alternate cover. **A:** Rod Perry **W:** Joseph Adams
1/PL❑ Oct 1997 Cover: 9.95 **NM** value: **Cover or less**
• Platinum edition.
2/A ❑ Jan 1998 Cover: 3.00 **NM** value: **Cover or less**
Circ: Diamd. preorders: **6,101**
2/B ❑ Jan 1998 Cover: 3.00 **NM** value: **Cover or less**

SIR CHARLES BARKLEY AND THE REFEREE MURDERS — Hamilton

1 ❑ ca. 1993 Cover: 9.95 **NM** value: **Cover or less**
A: Jim Starlin

SIREN (MALIBU) — Malibu / Ultraverse

0 ❑ Sep 1995 Cover: 1.50 **NM** value: **Cover or less**
• Black September; #Infinity **A:** Kevin West **W:** Hank Kanalz
0/A ❑ Sep 1995 Cover: 1.50 **NM** value: **Cover or less**
alternate cover.
1 ❑ Oct 1995 Cover: 1.50 **NM** value: **Cover or less**
A: Kevin West **W:** Hank Kanalz ★ Versus War Machine.
2 ❑ Nov 1995 Cover: 1.50 **NM** value: **Cover or less**
A: Kevin West **W:** Hank Kanalz ★ Versus War Machine.
3 ❑ Dec 1995 Cover: 1.50 **NM** value: **Cover or less**
📖 Choosing Sides final issue. • continues in Siren Special #1 **A:** Kevin West **W:** Hank Kanalz
SE 1❑ Feb 1996 Cover: 1.95 **NM** value: **Cover or less**
★ Origin of Siren.

SIREN: SHAPES — Image

1 ❑ May 1998 Cover: 2.95 **NM** value: **Cover or less**
Circ: Diamd. preorders: **4,823**
📖 Shapes, Part 1 **A:** Tim Levins **W:** J. Torres
2 ❑ Sep 1998 Cover: 2.95 **NM** value: **Cover or less**
Circ: Diamd. preorders: **2,965**
📖 Shapes, Part 2 **A:** Tim Levins **W:** J. Torres
3 ❑ Nov 1998 Cover: 2.95 **NM** value: **Cover or less**
Circ: Diamd. preorders: **2,806**
📖 Shapes, Part 3 **A:** Tim Levins **W:** J. Torres
Bk 1❑ Cover: 9.95 **NM** value: **Cover or less**

CGC-graded: Multiply prices above by **33 for 9.9 M • 16 for 9.8 NM/M • 7 for 9.6 NM+ • 5 for 9.4 NM • 2.5 for 9.2 NM- • 1.5 for 9.0 VF/NM**

SIRENS OF THE LOST WORLD
Comax

All issues are adults only.

1 ❑ b&w Cover: 2.95 **NM** value: **Cover or less**

SIRIUS GALLERY 1999
Sirius

1 ❑ Apr 1999 **NM** value: **2.00**
Circ: Diamd. preorders: **7,867**
cardstock cover. • pin-ups

SISTER ARMAGEDDON
Draculina

1 ❑ Cover: 2.75 **NM** value: **Cover or less**
★ 1st Appearance of Sister Armageddon.
2 ❑ b&w Cover: 2.50 **NM** value: **2.75**
3 ❑ b&w Cover: 2.95 **NM** value: **3.00**
4 ❑ Cover: 3.00 **NM** value: **Cover or less**

SISTERHOOD OF STEEL
Marvel / Epic

This series tells the tale of a group of women warriors known as "the Sisterhood." Living in the age of the longsword and the crossbow, these women exist apart from men, honing their skills as warriors in a separate society. Although the women are allowed to use men for their own pleasure, they are forbidden to fall in love or marry, and any attempt to leave the Sisterhood carries a penalty of death.

This story centers on Boronwd, a woman who is coming of age and facing the final tests of membership into the Sisterhood. When her best friend decides to leave the Sisterhood to run off with a man she loves, Boronwd has to choose between loyalty to her friend and duty to the Sisterhood.

1 ❑ Dec 1984 Cover: 1.50 **NM** value: **2.00**
A: Mike Vosburg **W:** Christy Marx
2 ❑ Feb 1985 Cover: 1.50 **NM** value: **2.00**
A: Mike Vosburg **W:** Christy Marx
3 ❑ Apr 1985 Cover: 1.50 **NM** value: **2.00**
Circ: CapCity orders: **8,100**
A: Mike Vosburg **W:** Christy Marx
4 ❑ Jun 1985 Cover: 1.50 **NM** value: **2.00**
Circ: CapCity orders: **7,450**
A: Mike Vosburg **W:** Christy Marx
5 ❑ Aug 1985 Cover: 1.50 **NM** value: **2.00**
Circ: CapCity orders: **7,350**
📖 Passion, Pain, And Politics **A:** Mike Vosburg **W:** Christy Marx
6 ❑ Oct 1985 Cover: 1.50 **NM** value: **2.00**
Circ: CapCity orders: **6,850**
📖 Loyalties **A:** Mike Vosburg **W:** Christy Marx
7 ❑ Dec 1985 Cover: 1.50 **NM** value: **2.00**
Circ: CapCity orders: **6,100**
📖 Vows And Vengeances **A:** Mike Vosburg **W:** Christy Marx
8 ❑ Feb 1986 Cover: 1.50 **NM** value: **2.00**
Circ: CapCity orders: **5,800**
📖 Judgement And Justice **A:** Mike Vosburg **W:** Christy Marx
Bk 1❑ Cover: 9.95 **NM** value: **Cover or less**
• Trade Paperback. **A:** Mike Vosburg **W:** Christy Marx
Bk 1/HC❑ Cover: 15.95 **NM** value: **Cover or less**
hardcover. **A:** Mike Vosburg **W:** Christy Marx

SISTERS OF DARKNESS
Illustration

1/A ❑ 1997 Cover: 3.25 **NM** value: **Cover or less**
Adult cover. **A:** Don Paresi; Steve Woron
1/B ❑ 1997 Cover: 3.25 **NM** value: **Cover or less**
tame cover. **A:** Don Paresi; Steve Woron
2/A ❑ 1997 Cover: 3.25 **NM** value: **Cover or less**
Adult cover. **A:** Don Paresi; Steve Woron
2/B ❑ 1997 Cover: 3.25 **NM** value: **Cover or less**
tame cover. **A:** Don Paresi; Steve Woron
3 ❑ Aug 1997 Cover: 3.25 **NM** value: **Cover or less**
A: Don Paresi; Steve Woron

SISTERS OF MERCY
Maximum

1 ❑ Dec 1995 Cover: 2.50 **NM** value: **Cover or less**
★ 1st Appearance of Sisters of Mercy (super-heroes), Doctor Vincent Casey.
1/A ❑ Dec 1995 Cover: 2.50 **NM** value: **Cover or less**
alternate cover.
2 ❑ 1996 Cover: 2.50 **NM** value: **Cover or less**
3 ❑ 1996 Cover: 2.50 **NM** value: **Cover or less**
4 ❑ 1996 Cover: 2.50 **NM** value: **Cover or less**
5 ❑ 1996 Cover: 2.50 **NM** value: **Cover or less**

SISTERS OF MERCY (VOL. 2)
London Night

0 ❑ Mar 1997 Cover: 1.50 **NM** value: **Cover or less**
Circ: Diamd. preorders: **7,532**
A: Mark Williams **W:** Rikki Rockett

SISTERS OF MERCY: WHEN RAZORS CRY CRIMSON TEARS
No Mercy

1 ❑ Oct 1996 Cover: 2.50 **NM** value: **Cover or less**
Circ: Diamd. preorders: **4,171**

SISTER VAMPIRE
Angel

1 ❑ Cover: 2.95 **NM** value: **Cover or less**
📖 A World of Gray **A:** R. Adolfson **W:** Sally Meer

6, THE
Virtual

1 ❑ Oct 1996 Cover: 2.50 **NM** value: **Cover or less**
Circ: Diamd. preorders: **6,224**
📖 Lethal Origins, Part 1 **A:** Greg Luzniak **W:** Fabian Nicieza; Louise Simonson
2 ❑ Nov 1996 Cover: 2.50 **NM** value: **Cover or less**
Circ: Diamd. preorders: **4,053**
📖 Lethal Origins, Part 2 **A:** Greg Luzniak **W:** Fabian Nicieza; Louise Simonson
3 ❑ Dec 1996 Cover: 2.50 **NM** value: **Cover or less**
Circ: Diamd. preorders: **3,814**
📖 Lethal Origins, Part 3 **A:** Greg Luzniak **W:** Fabian Nicieza; Louise Simonson

SIX DEGREES
Heretic Press

1 ❑ b&w Cover: 2.95 **NM** value: **3.50**
A: Marc Laming **W:** Martin Shipp
1/Aut❑ Cover: 2.95 **NM** value: **6.00**
A: Marc Laming **W:** Martin Shipp
2 ❑ b&w Cover: 2.95 **NM** value: **Cover or less**
A: Marc Laming **W:** Martin Shipp
3 ❑ b&w Cover: 2.95 **NM** value: **Cover or less**
A: Marc Laming; Sean Phillips(cover) **W:** Martin Shipp
4 ❑ b&w Cover: 2.95 **NM** value: **Cover or less**
A: Marc Laming **W:** Martin Shipp
5 ❑ b&w Cover: 2.95 **NM** value: **Cover or less**
A: Marc Laming; Jay Dyke(cover) **W:** Martin Shipp

SIX FROM SIRIUS
Marvel / Epic

The galaxy teeters on the brink of catastrophe, as two worlds prepare to go to war. In a desperate bid for peace, the worlds agree to hold talks — but a key ambassador, a telepath known as Phaedra, has been kidnapped by forces wanting to sabotage the peace process. To avert Armageddon, the galactic federation known as Sirius Swarm sends a team of crack troubleshooters to rescue her. But what begins as a straightforward mission quickly turns ugly, as a strange collection of foes tries to stop the six from rescuing Phaedra.

Created by Doug Moench and Paul Gulacy, Six from Sirius is a brilliant tale of interstellar adventure and intrigue.

1 ❑ Jul 1984 Cover: 1.50 **NM** value: **2.00**
📖 Phaedrea **A:** Paul Gulacy **W:** Doug Moench
2 ❑ Aug 1984 Cover: 1.50 **NM** value: **2.00**
📖 Masterfax **A:** Paul Gulacy **W:** Doug Moench
3 ❑ Sep 1984 Cover: 1.50 **NM** value: **2.00**
📖 Heavenstone **A:** Paul Gulacy **W:** Doug Moench
4 ❑ Oct 1984 Cover: 1.50 **NM** value: **2.00**
📖 Mind-Prime **A:** Paul Gulacy **W:** Doug Moench
Bk 1❑ Cover: 8.95 **NM** value: **Cover or less**
Circ: CapCity orders: **1,400**
• Collects Six From Sirius #1-4 **A:** Paul Gulacy **W:** Doug Moench

SIX FROM SIRIUS 2
Marvel / Epic

1 ❑ Feb 1986 Cover: 1.75 **NM** value: **2.00**
Circ: CapCity orders: **9,000**
A: Paul Gulacy **W:** Doug Moench
2 ❑ Mar 1986 Cover: 1.75 **NM** value: **2.00**
Circ: CapCity orders: **7,850**
A: Paul Gulacy **W:** Doug Moench
3 ❑ Apr 1986 Cover: 1.75 **NM** value: **2.00**
Circ: CapCity orders: **7,750**
A: Paul Gulacy **W:** Doug Moench
4 ❑ May 1986 Cover: 1.75 **NM** value: **2.00**
Circ: CapCity orders: **7,700**
A: Paul Gulacy **W:** Doug Moench

SIX-GUN HEROES (FAWCETT)
Fawcett

1 ❑ Mar 1950 Cover: 0.10 **NM** value: **350.00**
2 ❑ May 1950 Cover: 0.10 **NM** value: **200.00**
3 ❑ Jul 1950 Cover: 0.10 **NM** value: **150.00**
4 ❑ Sep 1950 Cover: 0.10 **NM** value: **150.00**
5 ❑ Nov 1950 Cover: 0.10 **NM** value: **150.00**
6 ❑ Jan 1951 Cover: 0.10 **NM** value: **125.00**
7 ❑ Mar 1951 Cover: 0.10 **NM** value: **125.00**
8 ❑ May 1951 Cover: 0.10 **NM** value: **125.00**
9 ❑ Jul 1951 Cover: 0.10 **NM** value: **125.00**
10 ❑ Sep 1951 Cover: 0.10 **NM** value: **125.00**
11 ❑ Nov 1951 Cover: 0.10 **NM** value: **100.00**
12 ❑ Jan 1952 Cover: 0.10 **NM** value: **100.00**
13 ❑ Mar 1952 Cover: 0.10 **NM** value: **100.00**
14 ❑ May 1952 Cover: 0.10 **NM** value: **100.00**
15 ❑ Jul 1952 Cover: 0.10 **NM** value: **100.00**
16 ❑ Sep 1952 Cover: 0.10 **NM** value: **75.00**
17 ❑ Nov 1952 Cover: 0.10 **NM** value: **75.00**
18 ❑ Jan 1953 Cover: 0.10 **NM** value: **75.00**
• Hopalong Cassidy, Monte Hale, Rocky Lane, Lash Larue photo cover
📖 The Marks of Innocence
19 ❑ Mar 1953 Cover: 0.10 **NM** value: **75.00**
20 ❑ May 1953 Cover: 0.10 **NM** value: **75.00**
21 ❑ Jul 1953 Cover: 0.10 **NM** value: **75.00**
22 ❑ Sep 1953 Cover: 0.10 **NM** value: **75.00**
23 ❑ Nov 1953 Cover: 0.10 **NM** value: **75.00**

SIX-GUN HEROES (CHARLTON)
Charlton

24 ❑ ca. 1954 Cover: 0.10 **NM** value: **150.00**
25 ❑ ca. 1954 Cover: 0.10 **NM** value: **75.00**
26 ❑ ca. 1954 Cover: 0.10 **NM** value: **50.00**
27 ❑ ca. 1954 Cover: 0.10 **NM** value: **50.00**
28 ❑ ca. 1954 Cover: 0.10 **NM** value: **50.00**
29 ❑ ca. 1954 Cover: 0.10 **NM** value: **50.00**
30 ❑ ca. 1955 Cover: 0.10 **NM** value: **50.00**
31 ❑ ca. 1955 Cover: 0.10 **NM** value: **50.00**
32 ❑ ca. 1955 Cover: 0.10 **NM** value: **50.00**
33 ❑ ca. 1955 Cover: 0.10 **NM** value: **50.00**
34 ❑ ca. 1955 Cover: 0.10 **NM** value: **50.00**
35 ❑ ca. 1955 Cover: 0.10 **NM** value: **50.00**
36 ❑ ca. 1956 Cover: 0.10 **NM** value: **50.00**
37 ❑ ca. 1956 Cover: 0.10 **NM** value: **50.00**
38 ❑ ca. 1956 Cover: 0.10 **NM** value: **50.00**
39 ❑ ca. 1956 Cover: 0.10 **NM** value: **50.00**
40 ❑ ca. 1956 Cover: 0.10 **NM** value: **50.00**
41 ❑ ca. 1956 Cover: 0.10 **NM** value: **50.00**
42 ❑ ca. 1957 Cover: 0.10 **NM** value: **50.00**
43 ❑ ca. 1957 Cover: 0.10 **NM** value: **50.00**
44 ❑ ca. 1957 Cover: 0.10 **NM** value: **50.00**
45 ❑ ca. 1957 Cover: 0.10 **NM** value: **50.00**
46 ❑ ca. 1957 Cover: 0.10 **NM** value: **50.00**
47 ❑ ca. 1957 Cover: 0.10 **NM** value: **50.00**
• **CGC:** 1 graded, best 5.5
48 ❑ ca. 1958 Cover: 0.10 **NM** value: **50.00**
49 ❑ ca. 1958 Cover: 0.10 **NM** value: **50.00**
50 ❑ ca. 1958 Cover: 0.10 **NM** value: **50.00**
51 ❑ ca. 1958 Cover: 0.10 **NM** value: **40.00**
52 ❑ ca. 1958 Cover: 0.10 **NM** value: **40.00**
53 ❑ ca. 1958 Cover: 0.10 **NM** value: **40.00**
54 ❑ ca. 1959 Cover: 0.10 **NM** value: **40.00**
55 ❑ ca. 1959 Cover: 0.10 **NM** value: **40.00**
56 ❑ ca. 1959 Cover: 0.10 **NM** value: **40.00**
57 ❑ ca. 1959 Cover: 0.10 **NM** value: **40.00**
58 ❑ ca. 1959 Cover: 0.10 **NM** value: **40.00**
59 ❑ ca. 1959 Cover: 0.10 **NM** value: **40.00**
60 ❑ ca. 1960 Cover: 0.10 **NM** value: **40.00**
61 ❑ ca. 1960 Cover: 0.10 **NM** value: **40.00**
62 ❑ ca. 1960 Cover: 0.10 **NM** value: **40.00**
63 ❑ ca. 1960 Cover: 0.10 **NM** value: **40.00**
64 ❑ ca. 1960 Cover: 0.10 **NM** value: **40.00**
65 ❑ ca. 1961 Cover: 0.10 **NM** value: **40.00**
66 ❑ ca. 1961 Cover: 0.10 **NM** value: **40.00**
67 ❑ ca. 1961 Cover: 0.10 **NM** value: **40.00**
68 ❑ ca. 1961 Cover: 0.12 **NM** value: **40.00**
69 ❑ Jul 1962 Cover: 0.12 **NM** value: **40.00**
• Gunmaster, Wyatt Earp, Annie Oakley
70 ❑ ca. 1962 Cover: 0.12 **NM** value: **40.00**
71 ❑ ca. 1962 Cover: 0.12 **NM** value: **25.00**
72 ❑ ca. 1962 Cover: 0.12 **NM** value: **25.00**
73 ❑ ca. 1962 Cover: 0.12 **NM** value: **25.00**
74 ❑ ca. 1962 Cover: 0.12 **NM** value: **25.00**
75 ❑ ca. 1963 Cover: 0.12 **NM** value: **25.00**
76 ❑ ca. 1963 Cover: 0.12 **NM** value: **25.00**
77 ❑ ca. 1963 Cover: 0.12 **NM** value: **25.00**
• Gunmaster, Wyatt Earp, Annie Oakley
78 ❑ ca. 1963 Cover: 0.12 **NM** value: **25.00**
79 ❑ ca. 1964 Cover: 0.12 **NM** value: **25.00**
80 ❑ ca. 1964 Cover: 0.12 **NM** value: **25.00**
81 ❑ ca. 1964 Cover: 0.12 **NM** value: **25.00**
82 ❑ ca. 1964 Cover: 0.12 **NM** value: **25.00**
83 ❑ ca. 1964 Cover: 0.12 **NM** value: **25.00**

SIX-GUN WESTERN
Atlas

1 ❑ Jan 1957 Cover: 0.10 **NM** value: **150.00**
2 ❑ Mar 1957 Cover: 0.10 **NM** value: **125.00**
3 ❑ May 1957 Cover: 0.10 **NM** value: **125.00**
4 ❑ Jul 1957 Cover: 0.10 **NM** value: **100.00**

SIX-GUN WESTERN (TROJAN)
Trojan

1 ❑ Cover: 0.25 **NM** value: **50.00**
📖 Six-Gun Rampage (text story) • Pulp **A:** Fred Yates; Oren Waggener; R. Hayden; Robert Mccarty; W. M. Allison; William Meilink **W:** Arthur S. Paacker; Calvin L. Boswell; Cliff Walters; E. Hoffman Price; Gerald James; John Kane; Ralph Fritz; Ralph Sedgwick

6, THE: LETHAL ORIGINS
Virtual

1 ❑ May 1996 Cover: 3.99 **NM** value: **Cover or less**
No issue number. • digest.

SIX MILLION DOLLAR MAN, THE
Charlton

Steve Austin is an astronaut and test pilot who suffers a critical accident on reentry. His body shattered by the crash, he is rushed into emergency, experimental surgery. Both legs and an arm are replaced with bionic implants, making them several time stronger than his original limbs. In addition, one eye is replaced with a bionic camera, which acts like a high-powered telephoto lens. It costs the government $6 million to rebuild Steve, providing a name for the series. In his new life, Steve works as an agent in OSI (Office of Scientific Information), reporting to Oscar Goldman.

The Six Million Dollar Man was an incredibly successful TV show running from 1974 to 1978 and spinning off the series The Bionic Woman, which was also adapted to comic-book format. Steve Austin's saga was based on Martin Caidin's novel Cyborg.

1 ❑ Jun 1976 Cover: 0.30 **NM** value: **5.00**
• **CGC:** 17 graded, best 9.8
📖 The Beginning of The Six Million Dollar Man **A:** Joe Staton **W:** Joe Gill ★ Origin of The Six Million Dollar Man. ★ 1st Appearance of The Six Million Dollar Man (in comics).
2 ❑ Aug 1976 Cover: 0.30 **NM** value: **3.50**
📖 The Effigy; Win a few (text) • Nicola Cuti, Joe Staton credits; Action figure tie-in **A:** Joe Staton **W:** Nicola Cutii
3 ❑ Oct 1976 Cover: 0.30 **NM** value: **3.00**
📖 Second Chance; Forbidden Reef (text) • Nicola Cuti, Joe Staton credits

Other grades: Multiply prices above by **1.5 for Mint • 2/3 for Very Fine • 1/3 for Fine • 1/5 for Very Good • 1/8 for Good**

4 ❑ Dec 1977 Cover: 0.30 **NM** value: **3.00**
5 ❑ Oct 1977 Cover: 0.35 **NM** value: **3.00**
📖 The Man Who Isn't There; Counter Punch (text)
6 ❑ Feb 1978 Cover: 0.35 **NM** value: **2.00**
7 ❑ Mar 1978 Cover: 0.35 **NM** value: **2.00**
📖 Hostage!; The Deadly Image; The Escape (text) • Boyette and Himes credits
8 ❑ May 1978 Cover: 0.35 **NM** value: **2.00**
9 ❑ Jun 1978 Cover: 0.35 **NM** value: **2.00**

SIX MILLION DOLLAR MAN, THE (MAGAZINE) Charlton
1 ❑ **NM** value: **6.00**
2 ❑ **NM** value: **5.00**
3 ❑ **NM** value: **4.00**
4 ❑ **NM** value: **4.00**
5 ❑ **NM** value: **4.00**
6 ❑ **NM** value: **4.00**
7 ❑ **NM** value: **4.00**

666: THE MARK OF THE BEAST Fleetway-Quality
1 ❑ ca. 1986 Cover: 1.95 **NM** value: **2.50**
Circ: CapCity orders: **4,800**
2 ❑ ca. 1986 Cover: 1.95 **NM** value: **2.00**
3 ❑ ca. 1986 Cover: 1.95 **NM** value: **2.00**
4 ❑ ca. 1986 Cover: 1.95 **NM** value: **2.00**
5 ❑ ca. 1986 Cover: 1.95 **NM** value: **2.00**
📖 The Dead **A:** Massimo Belardinelli **W:** Peter Milligan
6 ❑ ca. 1986 Cover: 1.95 **NM** value: **2.00**
7 ❑ ca. 1986 Cover: 1.95 **NM** value: **2.00**
8 ❑ ca. 1986 Cover: 1.95 **NM** value: **2.00**
9 ❑ ca. 1986 Cover: 1.95 **NM** value: **2.00**
10 ❑ ca. 1987 Cover: 1.95 **NM** value: **2.00**
📖 The Drowning Pond
11 ❑ ca. 1987 Cover: 1.95 **NM** value: **2.00**
12 ❑ ca. 1987 Cover: 1.95 **NM** value: **2.00**
• Alan Moore special **W:** Alan Moore
13 ❑ ca. 1987 Cover: 1.95 **NM** value: **2.00**
14 ❑ ca. 1987 Cover: 1.95 **NM** value: **2.00**
15 ❑ ca. 1987 Cover: 1.95 **NM** value: **2.00**
16 ❑ ca. 1987 Cover: 1.95 **NM** value: **2.00**
17 ❑ ca. 1987 Cover: 1.95 **NM** value: **2.00**
18 ❑ ca. 1987 Cover: 1.95 **NM** value: **2.00**
final issue.

SIX STRING SAMURAI Awesome
1 ❑ Sep 1998 Cover: 2.95 **NM** value: **Cover or less**
Circ: Diamd. preorders: **8,476**
A: Dan Fraga; John Stinsman **W:** Rob Liefeld; Matt Hawkins

SIXTY NINE Eros
1 ❑ Cover: 2.75 **NM** value: **Cover or less**
A: Patrick N. Cosgrove **W:** Patrick N. Cosgrove
2 ❑ Cover: 2.75 **NM** value: **Cover or less**
A: Patrick N. Cosgrove **W:** Patrick N. Cosgrove
3 ❑ Cover: 2.75 **NM** value: **Cover or less**
A: Patrick N. Cosgrove **W:** Patrick N. Cosgrove
4 ❑ Jul 1994 Cover: 2.75 **NM** value: **Cover or less**
📖 Primed & Cut **A:** Patrick N. Cosgrove **W:** Patrick N. Cosgrove

67 SECONDS Marvel / Epic
1 ❑ Cover: 15.95 **NM** value: **Cover or less**

SIXX Zygotic Studios
1 ❑ Cover: 2.50 **NM** value: **Cover or less**
A: Thomas F. Strating **W:** Thomas F. Strating
2 ❑ Cover: 2.50 **NM** value: **Cover or less**
A: Thomas F. Strating **W:** Thomas F. Strating
3 ❑ Cover: 2.50 **NM** value: **Cover or less**
A: Thomas F. Strating **W:** Thomas F. Strating
4 ❑ Cover: 2.50 **NM** value: **Cover or less**
A: Thomas F. Strating **W:** Thomas F. Strating

SIZZLE THEATRE Slave Labor
All issues are adults only.
1 ❑ Aug 1991, b&w Cover: 2.50 **NM** value: **Cover or less**

SIZZLIN' SISTERS Eros
1 ❑ 1997 Cover: 2.95 **NM** value: **Cover or less**
A: Art Wetherell **W:** Art Wetherell
2 ❑ Aug 1997 Cover: 2.95 **NM** value: **Cover or less**
A: Art Wetherell **W:** Art Wetherell

SKATEMAN Pacific
1 ❑ Nov 1983 Cover: 1.50 **NM** value: **Cover or less**
📖 Skateman; Futureworld; Rock Warrior **A:** Neal Adams; Paul S. Power **W:** Neal Adams; Paul S. Power ★ Origin of Skateman. ★ 1st Appearance of Skateman.

SKELETON GIRL Slave Labor
1 ❑ Dec 1995 Cover: 2.95 **NM** value: **Cover or less**
📖 Today I; Stacy pinup; What Do You Want to Do?; Stacy's Guide to Life; Toilet Trouble!; Stacy's School of Eloquent Communication; Attention Men!!!; Introducing the New Stacy Action Figure Doll; The Story of Cousin Frank; Dana, Meg, and Stacy…X; Stacy Sez **A:** Cris Dornaus **W:** Cris Dornaus; Rich "Luber" Withrow ★ 1st Appearance of J.J., Skeleton Boy, Skeleton Girl, Stacy the Maniacal, Angst-Filled Hate Girl.
2 ❑ Apr 1996 Cover: 2.95 **NM** value: **Cover or less**
📖 The Stitch; Utterly, Ridiculously Inane and Frustrating Couple Fight #1; Space! **A:** Cris Dornaus **W:** Cris Dornaus ★ 2nd Appearance of J.J., Skeleton Boy, Skeleton Girl.
3 ❑ Sep 1996 Cover: 2.95 **NM** value: **Cover or less**
📖 Confessions of and X-Phile!!; Space! The Conclusion!!! **A:** Cris Dornaus **W:** Cris Dornaus

SKELETON HAND Avalon
1 ❑ Cover: 2.99 **NM** value: **Cover or less**
📖 Deathless Mortal; Sea of Retribution; Death for Hire; Monster of the Deep; The Ghost of Company C (text story)

SKELETON HAND (1ST SERIES) ACG
1 ❑ Sep 1952 Cover: 0.10 **NM** value: **300.00**
• **CGC:** 1 graded, best 7.0
2 ❑ Nov 1952 Cover: 0.10 **NM** value: **200.00**
3 ❑ Jan 1953 Cover: 0.10 **NM** value: **150.00**
• **CGC:** 2 graded, best 9.2
4 ❑ Mar 1953 Cover: 0.10 **NM** value: **150.00**
5 ❑ May 1953 Cover: 0.10 **NM** value: **150.00**
6 ❑ Jul 1953 Cover: 0.10 **NM** value: **150.00**

SKELETON KEY Slave Labor / Amaze Ink
1 ❑ Jul 1995 Cover: 1.50 **NM** value: **2.00**
2 ❑ Aug 1995 Cover: 1.50 **NM** value: **2.00**
3 ❑ Sep 1995 Cover: 1.50 **NM** value: **2.00**
4 ❑ Oct 1995 Cover: 1.50 **NM** value: **2.00**
5 ❑ Nov 1995 Cover: 1.50 **NM** value: **2.00**
6 ❑ Dec 1995 Cover: 1.50 **NM** value: **2.00**
7 ❑ Jan 1996 Cover: 1.50 **NM** value: **2.00**
8 ❑ Feb 1996 Cover: 1.50 **NM** value: **2.00**
9 ❑ Mar 1996 Cover: 1.50 **NM** value: **2.00**
10 ❑ Apr 1996 Cover: 1.75 **NM** value: **2.00**
11 ❑ May 1996 Cover: 1.75 **NM** value: **Cover or less**
12 ❑ Jun 1996 Cover: 1.75 **NM** value: **Cover or less**
13 ❑ Jul 1996 Cover: 1.75 **NM** value: **Cover or less**
14 ❑ Aug 1996 Cover: 1.75 **NM** value: **Cover or less**
15 ❑ Sep 1996 Cover: 1.75 **NM** value: **Cover or less**
cover says Aug, indicia says Sep.
16 ❑ Oct 1996 Cover: 1.75 **NM** value: **Cover or less**
17 ❑ Nov 1996 Cover: 1.75 **NM** value: **Cover or less**
18 ❑ Dec 1996 Cover: 1.75 **NM** value: **Cover or less**
19 ❑ Jan 1997 Cover: 1.75 **NM** value: **Cover or less**
20 ❑ Feb 1997 Cover: 1.75 **NM** value: **Cover or less**
21 ❑ Mar 1997 Cover: 1.75 **NM** value: **Cover or less**
22 ❑ Apr 1997 Cover: 1.75 **NM** value: **Cover or less**
23 ❑ May 1997 Cover: 1.75 **NM** value: **Cover or less**
24 ❑ Jun 1997 Cover: 1.75 **NM** value: **Cover or less**
25 ❑ Jul 1997 Cover: 1.75 **NM** value: **Cover or less**
26 ❑ Aug 1997 Cover: 1.75 **NM** value: **Cover or less**
27 ❑ Sep 1997 Cover: 1.75 **NM** value: **Cover or less**
28 ❑ Oct 1997 Cover: 1.75 **NM** value: **Cover or less**
29 ❑ Nov 1997 Cover: 1.75 **NM** value: **Cover or less**
30 ❑ Dec 1997 Cover: 1.75 **NM** value: **Cover or less**
Bk 1❑ Jun 1996 Cover: 11.95 **NM** value: **Cover or less**
• Beyond the Threshold; collects issues #1-6
Bk 2❑ Jun 1996 Cover: 11.95 **NM** value: **Cover or less**
• The Celestial Calendar; collects issues #7-18

SKELETON WARRIORS Marvel
1 ❑ Apr 1995 Cover: 1.50 **NM** value: **Cover or less**
Circ: CapCity orders: **8,525**
📖 Dark Dawn **A:** Greg Pro **W:** Adam Bezark; Gary Goodman ★ Origin of The Skeleton Warriors. ★ 1st Appearance of Prince Lightstar, Doctor Cyborn, Grimskull, Talyn, Baron Dark.
2 ❑ May 1995 Cover: 1.50 **NM** value: **Cover or less**
Circ: CapCity orders: **5,350**
3 ❑ Jun 1995 Cover: 1.50 **NM** value: **Cover or less**
Circ: CapCity orders: **4,600**
4 ❑ Jul 1995 Cover: 1.50 **NM** value: **Cover or less**
Circ: CapCity orders: **3,200**
final issue.

SKETCHBOOK SERIES, THE Tundra
1 ❑ Cover: 3.95 **NM** value: **Cover or less**
Circ: CapCity orders: **2,300**
• Melting Pot **A:** Kevin Eastman
2 ❑ Cover: 3.95 **NM** value: **Cover or less**
Circ: CapCity orders: **1,700**
• Totleben
3 ❑ Cover: 3.95 **NM** value: **Cover or less**
Circ: CapCity orders: **1,650**
• Zulli
4 ❑ Cover: 3.95 **NM** value: **Cover or less**
5 ❑ Cover: 3.95 **NM** value: **Cover or less**
A: Charles Vess
6 ❑ Cover: 3.95 **NM** value: **Cover or less**
• Screaming Masks **A:** Rick McCollum; Bill Anderson
7 ❑ Cover: 3.95 **NM** value: **Cover or less**
8 ❑ Cover: 3.95 **NM** value: **Cover or less**
• Forg
9 ❑ Cover: 3.95 **NM** value: **Cover or less**
10 ❑ Cover: 4.95 **NM** value: **Cover or less**
A: Paul Mavrides

SKIDMARKS Tundra
1 ❑ b&w Cover: 2.95 **NM** value: **Cover or less**
2 ❑ b&w Cover: 2.95 **NM** value: **Cover or less**
3 ❑ b&w Cover: 2.95 **NM** value: **Cover or less**

SKIM LIZARD Puppy Toss
1 ❑ Cover: 2.95 **NM** value: **Cover or less**
📖 Fil **A:** Eric Jones; Dylan Williams; Aldyth Beltrane; Boby Madness; Chris Hatfield; Fawn Gehweiler; Gabrielle Gamboa; K. Capelli; Lisa Onomoro; Scott Hsu-Storaker **W:** Dylan Williams; Aldyth Beltrane; Boby Madness; Chris Hatfield; Fawn Gehweiler; Gabrielle Gamboa; K. Capelli; Landry Q. Walker; Lisa Onomoro; Scott Hsu-Storaker

SKIN Tundra
1 ❑ Cover: 8.95 **NM** value: **Cover or less**

SKIN GRAFT Iconografix
1 ❑ b&w Cover: 3.50 **NM** value: **Cover or less**

SKIN GRAFT: THE ADVENTURES OF A TATTOOED MAN DC / Vertigo
1 ❑ Jul 1993 Cover: 2.50 **NM** value: **Cover or less**
Circ: CapCity orders: **21,450**
📖 Blood And Ink **A:** Warren Pleece **W:** Jerry Prosser
2 ❑ Aug 1993 Cover: 2.50 **NM** value: **Cover or less**
Circ: CapCity orders: **13,050**
📖 Skin And Bone **A:** Warren Pleece **W:** Jerry Prosser
3 ❑ Sep 1993 Cover: 2.50 **NM** value: **Cover or less**
Circ: CapCity orders: **10,350**
📖 Body and Soul **A:** Warren Pleece **W:** Jerry Prosser
4 ❑ Oct 1993 Cover: 2.50 **NM** value: **Cover or less**
Circ: CapCity orders: **10,050**
📖 Dissolve And Combine **A:** Warren Pleece **W:** Jerry Prosser

SKINHEADS IN LOVE Fantagraphics / Eros
All issues are adults only.
1 ❑ b&w Cover: 2.25 **NM** value: **Cover or less**

SKIN13 Express / Parody
0.5/A❑ Oct 1995, b&w Cover: 2.50 **NM** value: **Cover or less**
• Amazing SKIN Thir-Teen; reprints Skin13 #1 **A:** Bill Maus **W:** Bill Maus
0.5/B❑ Oct 1995, b&w Cover: 2.50 **NM** value: **Cover or less**
• Barbari-SKIN; reprints Skin13 #1 **A:** Bill Maus **W:** Bill Maus
0.5/C❑ Oct 1995, b&w Cover: 2.50 **NM** value: **Cover or less**
• SKIN-et Jackson; reprints Skin13 #1 **A:** Bill Maus **W:** Bill Maus
0.5/A-2❑ Cover: 2.50 **NM** value: **Cover or less**
0.5/B-2❑ Cover: 2.50 **NM** value: **Cover or less**
0.5/C-2❑ Cover: 2.50 **NM** value: **Cover or less**
1/A ❑ b&w Cover: 2.50 **NM** value: **Cover or less**
Circ: CapCity orders: **3,690**
A: Bill Maus **W:** Bill Maus
1/B ❑ b&w Cover: 2.50 **NM** value: **Cover or less**
Heavy Metal-style cover. **A:** Bill Maus **W:** Bill Maus
1/C ❑ b&w Cover: 2.50 **NM** value: **Cover or less**
Spider-Man #1-style cover. **A:** Bill Maus **W:** Bill Maus

SKIZZ Fleetway-Quality
1 ❑ Cover: 1.95 **NM** value: **Cover or less**
A: Jim Baikie **W:** Alan Moore
2 ❑ Cover: 1.95 **NM** value: **Cover or less**
3 ❑ Cover: 1.95 **NM** value: **Cover or less**

SKREEMER DC
1 ❑ May 1989 Cover: 2.00 **NM** value: **Cover or less**
Circ: CapCity orders: **16,250**
2 ❑ Jun 1989 Cover: 2.00 **NM** value: **Cover or less**
Circ: CapCity orders: **12,250**
3 ❑ Jul 1989 Cover: 2.00 **NM** value: **Cover or less**
Circ: CapCity orders: **11,050**
4 ❑ Aug 1989 Cover: 2.00 **NM** value: **Cover or less**
Circ: CapCity orders: **10,550**
📖 His Corpse To Wake **A:** Brett Ewins; Steve Dillon **W:** Peter Milligan
5 ❑ Sep 1989 Cover: 2.00 **NM** value: **Cover or less**
Circ: CapCity orders: **9,600**
6 ❑ Oct 1989 Cover: 2.00 **NM** value: **Cover or less**
Circ: CapCity orders: **8,750**
📖 Finnegan's Wake **A:** Brett Ewins; Steve Dillon **W:** Peter Milligan

SKROG Comico
1 ❑ b&w Cover: 3.50 **NM** value: **Cover or less**
A: Bill Cucinotta **W:** Bill Cucinotta

SKROG (YIP, YIP, YAY) SPECIAL Crystal
1 ❑ b&w Cover: 2.50 **NM** value: **Cover or less**

SKRULL KILL KREW Marvel
1 ❑ Sep 1995 Cover: 2.95 **NM** value: **Cover or less**
cardstock cover. 📖 Skrull Meat **A:** Steve Yeowell **W:** Grant Morrison; Mark Millar
2 ❑ Oct 1995 Cover: 2.95 **NM** value: **Cover or less**
cardstock cover. 📖 Goin' Krazy! **A:** Steve Yeowell **W:** Grant Morrison; Mark Millar ★ Appearance of Captain America.
3 ❑ Nov 1995 Cover: 2.95 **NM** value: **Cover or less**
cardstock cover. **A:** Steve Yeowell **W:** Grant Morrison; Mark Millar ★ Appearance of Captain America.
4 ❑ Dec 1995 Cover: 2.95 **NM** value: **Cover or less**
cardstock cover. **A:** Steve Yeowell **W:** Grant Morrison; Mark Millar ★ Appearance of Fantastic Four.
5 ❑ Jan 1996 Cover: 2.95 **NM** value: **Cover or less**
cardstock cover. final issue. **A:** Steve Yeowell **W:** Grant Morrison; Mark Millar

SKULKER, THE Thorby
1 ❑ Cover: 2.95 **NM** value: **Cover or less**

SKULL & BONES DC
1 ❑ ca. 1992 Cover: 4.95 **NM** value: **Cover or less**
Circ: CapCity orders: **11,100**
📖 Revolution Day **A:** Ed Hannigan **W:** Ed Hannigan
2 ❑ ca. 1992 Cover: 4.95 **NM** value: **Cover or less**
Circ: CapCity orders: **7,200**
📖 Evil Empire **A:** Ed Hannigan **W:** Ed Hannigan
3 ❑ ca. 1992 Cover: 4.95 **NM** value: **Cover or less**
Circ: CapCity orders: **6,000**
📖 Iron Curtain **A:** Ed Hannigan **W:** Ed Hannigan

SKULL COMICS Last Gasp
1 ❑ **NM** value: **10.00**
2 ❑ Jan 1970 Cover: 0.50 **NM** value: **6.00**
📖 Lame Lem's Love; Tall Tail; Pussy Whipped! **A:** Richard Corben; Gilbert Shelton; Jaxon; Dave Sheridan; R. Gore **W:** Richard Corben; Gilbert Shelton; Jaxon; Dave Sheridan; R. Gore
3 ❑ Cover: 0.50 **NM** value: **4.00**
4 ❑ Cover: 0.50 **NM** value: **4.00**

CGC-graded: Multiply prices above by **33 for 9.9 M • 16 for 9.8 NM/M • 7 for 9.6 NM+ • 5 for 9.4 NM • 2.5 for 9.2 NM- • 1.5 for 9.0 VF/NM**

5 ❑ Jan 1972 Cover: 0.50 **NM** value: **4.00**
📖 The Rats in the Walls; Wilfred Kreel and the Hand of KaS; To a Dreamer; The Shadow from the Abyss; **A:** Jaxon; Dave Sheridan; Dallas; Deitch; H.P. Lovecraft; R. Gore; Spain; Todd **W:** Jaxon; Dave Sheridan; Dallas; Deitch; H.P. Lovecraft; R. Gore; Spain; Todd
6 ❑ Jun 1972 Cover: 0.50 **NM** value: **4.00**
📖 A Gothic Tale **A:** Richard Corben; Greg Irons **W:** Tom Veitch

SKULL THE SLAYER — Marvel

On a bright, clear day in 1975, Sgt. Jim Scully was being taken from Bermuda to Miami to stand trial for the murder of his brother. Although the death was accidental, Scully flees and has only recently been tracked down. As the plane travels through the fabled Bermuda Triangle, it passes through some sort of strange turbulence that begins to tear it apart. When it emerges, it is over land — strange, tropical land. The plane breaks apart in midair and crashes to the ground in two pieces. Only Scully and three other passengers survive.

These survivors discover that they have moved back in time, to an epoch when dinosaurs and cavemen roamed the Earth. Separated from the others, Scully uses his military training to survive and conquer. Eventually, "Jim Scully" becomes Skull the Slayer.

1 ❑ Aug 1975 Cover: 0.25 **NM** value: **2.50**
• **CGC:** 7 graded, best 9.8
📖 The Coming Of Skull The Slayer! **A:** Gil Kane(cover); Steve Gan **W:** Marv Wolfman ★ Origin of Skull the Slayer.
2 ❑ Nov 1975 Cover: 0.25 **NM** value: **1.50**
3 ❑ Jan 1976 Cover: 0.25 **NM** value: **1.50**
4 ❑ Mar 1976 Cover: 0.25 **NM** value: **1.50**
5 ❑ May 1976 Cover: 0.25 **NM** value: **1.50**
• **CGC:** 1 graded, best 9.4
6 ❑ Jul 1976 Cover: 0.25 **NM** value: **1.50**
• **CGC:** 1 graded, best 9.6
7 ❑ Sep 1976 Cover: 0.30 **NM** value: **1.50**
• **CGC:** 1 graded, best 4.5
8 ❑ Nov 1976 Cover: 0.30 **NM** value: **1.50**

SKUNK — Mu Press

All issues are adults only.

1 ❑ Dec 1993, b&w Cover: 2.50 **NM** value: **Cover or less**
No issue number.

SKUNK, THE — Express / Entity

3 ❑ Jul 1996, b&w Cover: 2.75 **NM** value: **Cover or less**
cover says #tree.
4 ❑ Sep 1996, b&w Cover: 2.75 **NM** value: **Cover or less**
5 ❑ Sep 1996, b&w Cover: 2.75 **NM** value: **Cover or less**
cover says Cinco de Mayo.
6 ❑ Oct 1996, b&w Cover: 2.75 **NM** value: **Cover or less**
cover says #sick.

SKY APE (LES ADVENTURES) — Slave Labor

1 ❑ Jun 1997, b&w Cover: 2.95 **NM** value: **Cover or less**
2 ❑ Sep 1997, b&w Cover: 2.95 **NM** value: **Cover or less**
3 ❑ Jan 1998, b&w Cover: 2.95 **NM** value: **Cover or less**
Bk 1❑ Cover: 12.95 **NM** value: **Cover or less**

SKY COMICS PRESENTS MONTHLY — Sky Comics

1 ❑ b&w Cover: 2.50 **NM** value: **Cover or less**

SKYE BLUE — Mu Press

1 ❑ b&w Cover: 2.50 **NM** value: **Cover or less**
A: Dwight Decker **W:** The Superhero Option
2 ❑ b&w Cover: 2.50 **NM** value: **Cover or less**
3 ❑ Cover: 2.50 **NM** value: **Cover or less**

SKY GAL — AC

1 ❑ Cover: 3.95 **NM** value: **Cover or less**
📖 Ginger And The Gremlins!; Blood On The Typewriter!; Indian Nut In The Air; The Sheik Of Air-O-Bee!; High Flyin' Ginger! • some reprint; Reprints Sky Gal stories from Jumbo Comics #68, others plus new story **A:** Matt Baker; Brad Gorby; Alex Blum **W:** Matt Baker; Brad Gorby; Alex Blum ★ 1st Appearance of Sky Gal.
2 ❑ Cover: 3.95 **NM** value: **Cover or less**
• some color; some reprint; Reprints Sky Gal stories from Jumbo Comics plus new story **A:** Matt Baker
3 ❑ Cover: 3.95 **NM** value: **Cover or less**
• some color; some reprint; Reprints Sky Gal stories from Jumbo Comics plus new story **A:** Matt Baker

SKY MASTERS — Pure Imagination

1 ❑ ca. 1991, b&w Cover: 7.95 **NM** value: **Cover or less**
• strip reprints **A:** Jack Kirby; Wally Wood

SKYNN & BONES — Brainstorm

1 ❑ Cover: 2.95 **NM** value: **Cover or less**
📖 Red Zone; Assault **A:** Bill Ruth; Juan Pineda; Mishimbo Kuumba **W:** Andrew Lynch; Brian Hodge; Elizabeth Massie; Paul Anthony

SKY PILOT — Ziff-Davis

10 ❑ ca. 1951 Cover: 0.10 **NM** value: **100.00**
11 ❑ Apr 1951 Cover: 0.10 **NM** value: **100.00**

SKYWOLF — Eclipse

1 ❑ Mar 1988 Cover: 1.75 **NM** value: **2.00**
Circ: CapCity orders: **6,175**
📖 The War Garden **A:** Tom Lyle **W:** Chuck Dixon
2 ❑ May 1988 Cover: 1.75 **NM** value: **2.00**
Circ: CapCity orders: **4,375**
📖 Bamboo Gauntlet **A:** Tom Lyle **W:** Chuck Dixon
3 ❑ Oct 1988 Cover: 1.95 **NM** value: **2.00**
Circ: CapCity orders: **4,025**
📖 Breakout **A:** Tom Lyle **W:** Chuck Dixon

SLACKER COMICS — Slave Labor

Doug Slack has put together a living tribute to high-school life in general and to the outcasts with alternative lifestyles who don't give a fig what other people think of them. An adult black-and-white due to language, this series has lasted so long because the reader actually starts to care about the characters and is shown that they are people just like us, with dreams and the problems of everyday life. Wak, Patricia, Mitch, Dana, and the ever-graphic Randy survive the rigors of high-school life and puberty in these middle-length to short stories intertwined with various spots, featuring not only Schmenkie but Doug Slack himself.

1 ❑ Aug 1994 Cover: 2.95 **NM** value: **3.00**
A: Doug Slack **W:** Doug Slack
1-2 ❑ Apr 1995 Cover: 2.95 **NM** value: **Cover or less**
2 ❑ Nov 1994 Cover: 2.95 **NM** value: **Cover or less**
A: Doug Slack **W:** Doug Slack
3 ❑ Feb 1995 Cover: 2.95 **NM** value: **Cover or less**
A: Doug Slack **W:** Doug Slack
4 ❑ May 1995 Cover: 2.95 **NM** value: **Cover or less**
A: Doug Slack **W:** Doug Slack
5 ❑ Sep 1995 Cover: 2.95 **NM** value: **Cover or less**
A: Doug Slack **W:** Doug Slack
6 ❑ Dec 1995 Cover: 2.95 **NM** value: **Cover or less**
📖 What's Wrong with Wak?!?; Today Is the Worst Day of the Rest of Your Life; Con Job, Part II; Schmenkie Gets a Job; And Now, a Personal Apology from Doug Slack **A:** Doug Slack **W:** Doug Slack
7 ❑ Feb 1996 Cover: 2.95 **NM** value: **Cover or less**
📖 Randy, the Heartbreaker; Randy, the Angry Little Grunge Puppy **A:** Doug Slack **W:** Doug Slack
8 ❑ May 1996 Cover: 2.95 **NM** value: **Cover or less**
A: Doug Slack **W:** Doug Slack
9 ❑ Aug 1996 Cover: 2.95 **NM** value: **Cover or less**
📖 A List of Things that Jus **A:** Doug Slack **W:** Doug Slack
10 ❑ 1996 Cover: 2.95 **NM** value: **Cover or less**
📖 Randy's Pals 'n' Gals; If You Will Be so Kind as to Indulge Me for a Minute...; Bizarre Wrestling Women, Part III; Mitch...Beeper Blunder; Male Bonding; The Slacker Comics Fun Page!!!; Lil' Frank, Jr. Detective...Young Cthul! **A:** Doug Slack **W:** Doug Slack
11 ❑ Jan 1997 Cover: 2.95 **NM** value: **Cover or less**
📖 Hang the D.J.; Lil' Frank, Jr. Detective **A:** Doug Slack **W:** Doug Slack; Bryan Slugger
12 ❑ 1997 Cover: 2.95 **NM** value: **Cover or less**
📖 Randy; The Slacker Fun Page; The Wak Master Takes It Off; For Motion Discomfort; Randy's Gal Patricia **A:** Doug Slack **W:** Doug Slack
13 ❑ Apr 1997 Cover: 2.95 **NM** value: **Cover or less**
📖 Popular Alternative Mu **A:** Doug Slack **W:** Doug Slack
14 ❑ May 1997 Cover: 2.95 **NM** value: **Cover or less**
📖 Wotta' Rip!; I Was a Teenage Singing Banana; Boy! • Slacker Annual; Also titled "Annual #1" **A:** Doug Slack **W:** Doug Slack
15 ❑ 1997 Cover: 2.95 **NM** value: **Cover or less**
📖 Patricia, the Happy Little Goth Chick; Epilogue...; David Hasselhoff Must Die; Chasing Amy the Monkey • no indicia **A:** Doug Slack **W:** Doug Slack
16 ❑ Apr 1998 Cover: 2.95 **NM** value: **Cover or less**
📖 Retaility Bites; A Gag Reflex Cartoon **A:** Doug Slack **W:** Doug Slack
17 ❑ Jul 1998 Cover: 2.95 **NM** value: **Cover or less**
📖 Slacker's Soapbox; Baptism of Fire; Randy, the Surly Little Failure; Editorial; Sioban; True Tales of a Popcorn Monkey; Patricia; Mitch...Bootycall; Slacker Asks the Hard Questions...; Randy **A:** Doug Slack **W:** Doug Slack
18 ❑ Oct 1998 Cover: 2.95 **NM** value: **Cover or less**
📖 Slacker Asks More of the Hard Questions; The Wake, Pt. I; Binky! The Clown; Bonus! Popcorn Monkey Movie Tip #38; The Wake, Pt. II; The Wak Master Lives!; Tickle Me, Elmer! Kill! Kill!; The Wake, Pt. III **A:** Doug Slack **W:** Doug Slack
Bk 1❑ May 1996 Cover: 11.95 **NM** value: **Cover or less**
📖 Meet Randy • Randy $ells Out; collects Slacker Comics #1-4 **A:** Doug Slack **W:** Doug Slack

SLÁINE THE BERSERKER — Fleetway-Quality

1 ❑ Jul 1987 Cover: 1.25 **NM** value: **1.50**
Circ: CapCity orders: **3,300**
2 ❑ Aug 1987 Cover: 1.25 **NM** value: **1.50**
3 ❑ Sep 1987 Cover: 1.25 **NM** value: **1.50**
Circ: CapCity orders: **2,075**
4 ❑ Oct 1987 Cover: 1.25 **NM** value: **1.50**
Circ: CapCity orders: **1,775**
5 ❑ Nov 1987 Cover: 1.25 **NM** value: **1.50**
Circ: CapCity orders: **1,700**
6 ❑ Dec 1987 Cover: 1.25 **NM** value: **1.50**
Circ: CapCity orders: **1,600**
7 ❑ Jan 1988 Cover: 1.25 **NM** value: **1.50**
Circ: CapCity orders: **1,375**
8 ❑ Feb 1988 Cover: 1.25 **NM** value: **1.50**
Circ: CapCity orders: **1,300**
9 ❑ Mar 1988 Cover: 1.25 **NM** value: **1.50**
Circ: CapCity orders: **1,250**
10 ❑ Apr 1988 Cover: 1.25 **NM** value: **1.50**
Circ: CapCity orders: **1,125**
11 ❑ May 1988 Cover: 1.25 **NM** value: **1.50**
Circ: CapCity orders: **1,100**
12 ❑ Jun 1988 Cover: 1.25 **NM** value: **1.50**
Circ: CapCity orders: **1,075**
13 ❑ Jul 1988 Cover: 1.50 **NM** value: **Cover or less**
Circ: CapCity orders: **1,375**
14 ❑ Aug 1988 Cover: 1.50 **NM** value: **Cover or less**
Circ: CapCity orders: **1,025**
• double issue #14/15
16 ❑ Sep 1988 Cover: 1.50 **NM** value: **Cover or less**
Circ: CapCity orders: **1,000**
• double issue #16/17
18 ❑ Oct 1988 Cover: 1.50 **NM** value: **Cover or less**
Circ: CapCity orders: **1,025**
19 ❑ Nov 1988 Cover: 1.50 **NM** value: **Cover or less**
Circ: CapCity orders: **1,000**
20 ❑ Dec 1988 Cover: 1.50 **NM** value: **Cover or less**
Circ: CapCity orders: **975**

SLÁINE THE HORNED GOD — Fleetway-Quality

1 ❑ ca. 1990 Cover: 2.95 **NM** value: **3.50**
Circ: CapCity orders: **1,300** • **CGC:** 1 graded, best 9.2
2 ❑ Cover: 2.95 **NM** value: **3.00**
Circ: CapCity orders: **4,725**
3 ❑ Cover: 2.95 **NM** value: **3.00**
Circ: CapCity orders: **3,950**
4 ❑ Cover: 2.95 **NM** value: **3.00**
Circ: CapCity orders: **3,625**
5 ❑ Cover: 2.95 **NM** value: **3.00**
Circ: CapCity orders: **3,975**
6 ❑ Cover: 2.95 **NM** value: **3.00**
Circ: CapCity orders: **3,925**

SLÁINE THE KING — Fleetway-Quality

21 ❑ Jan 1989 Cover: 1.50 **NM** value: **Cover or less**
Circ: CapCity orders: **925**
22 ❑ Feb 1989 Cover: 1.50 **NM** value: **Cover or less**
Circ: CapCity orders: **925**
23 ❑ 1989 Cover: 1.50 **NM** value: **Cover or less**
Circ: CapCity orders: **900**
24 ❑ 1989 Cover: 1.50 **NM** value: **Cover or less**
Circ: CapCity orders: **925**
25 ❑ 1989 Cover: 1.50 **NM** value: **Cover or less**
Circ: CapCity orders: **875**
26 ❑ 1989 Cover: 1.50 **NM** value: **Cover or less**
Circ: CapCity orders: **850**
27 ❑ 1989 Cover: 1.50 **NM** value: **Cover or less**
Circ: CapCity orders: **850**
28 ❑ 1989 Cover: 1.50 **NM** value: **Cover or less**
Circ: CapCity orders: **925**

SLAM BANG COMICS — Fawcett

1 ❑ Mar 1940 Cover: 0.10 **NM** value: **1500.00**
• **CGC:** 4 graded, best 5.0
2 ❑ Apr 1940 Cover: 0.10 **NM** value: **750.00**
3 ❑ May 1940 Cover: 0.10 **NM** value: **750.00**
4 ❑ Jun 1940 Cover: 0.10 **NM** value: **600.00**
5 ❑ Jul 1940 Cover: 0.10 **NM** value: **600.00**
• **CGC:** 1 graded, best 5.0
6 ❑ Aug 1940 Cover: 0.10 **NM** value: **600.00**
7 ❑ Sep 1940 Cover: 0.10 **NM** value: **600.00**
• **CGC:** 1 graded, best 9.4

SLAM DUNK KINGS — Personality

1 ❑ Mar 1992, b&w Cover: 2.95 **NM** value: **Cover or less**
• Michael Jordan **A:** Wayne Reid **W:** Paul A. Schleicher
2 ❑ 1992b&w Cover: 2.95 **NM** value: **Cover or less**
3 ❑ 1992b&w Cover: 2.95 **NM** value: **Cover or less**
4 ❑ 1992b&w Cover: 2.95 **NM** value: **Cover or less**

SLAPSTICK — Marvel

1 ❑ Nov 1992 Cover: 1.25 **NM** value: **Cover or less**
Circ: CapCity orders: **22,800**
📖 The Totally Awesome Origin Of Slapstick! **A:** James W. Fry III **W:** Len Kaminski ★ Origin of Slapstick. ★ 1st Appearance of Slapstick.
2 ❑ Dec 1992 Cover: 1.25 **NM** value: **Cover or less**
Circ: CapCity orders: **15,200**
A: James W. Fry III **W:** Len Kaminski
3 ❑ Jan 1993 Cover: 1.25 **NM** value: **Cover or less**
Circ: CapCity orders: **10,700**
A: James W. Fry III **W:** Len Kaminski
4 ❑ Feb 1993 Cover: 1.25 **NM** value: **Cover or less**
Circ: CapCity orders: **9,900**
A: James W. Fry III **W:** Len Kaminski ★ Appearance of Ghost Rider.

SLASH — Northstar

All issues are adults only.

1 ❑ Aug 1993, b&w Cover: 2.95 **NM** value: **Cover or less**
📖 Blood Rape of the Lust Ghouls; Night City: Music on the Bridge; Werewolf **A:** Mark A. Nelson; Tommy Pons; James O'Barr **W:** Tommy Pons; David J. Schow; Mort Castle
1/SE❑ Aug 1993 Cover: 4.95 **NM** value: **Cover or less**
📖 Blood Rape of the Lust Ghouls; Night City: Music on the Bridge; Werewolf **A:** Mark A. Nelson; Tommy Pons; James O'Barr **W:** Tommy Pons; David J. Schow; Mort Castle
2 ❑ 1993b&w Cover: 2.95 **NM** value: **Cover or less**
3 ❑ 1993b&w Cover: 2.95 **NM** value: **Cover or less**
4 ❑ 1993b&w Cover: 2.95 **NM** value: **Cover or less**
5 ❑ Oct 1993 Cover: 2.95 **NM** value: **Cover or less**
📖 Burn; A Mission From God; ...So Goes The Empire **A:** Kyle Holtz; Adam McDaniel; Steve Carter **W:** Frank Gomez; Steve Carter; David de Vries

For up-to-the-week CGC ratios, consult the current issue of **Comics Buyer's Guide**.

Other grades: Multiply prices above by **1.5 for Mint • 2/3 for Very Fine • 1/3 for Fine • 1/5 for Very Good • 1/8 for Good**

SLASH MARAUD — DC

Earth of the near future finds itself overrun by a group of aliens known as Shapers. In their own state, the Shapers resemble large fuzzy-headed humanoids. However, no future-dweller would ever confuse them with teddy bears: They're as likely to blow away human beings as to cuddle up to them. The Shapers are nearly indestructible and can assume any form — even that of humans. They have fled their own dying world to come to Earth and have since unleashed a bio-plague which is slowly transforming Earth into a copy of their old planet. There's only one small problem: By then, Earth will be uninhabitable by humans.

Slash Maraud is one of the few who have dared to stand against the Shapers, but he has made a habit of looking after himself before anyone else. Then an old flame approaches him with important news: The chief Shaper bio-engineer has defected. With his — and Slash's — help, they might be able to take back their world.

1 ❑ Nov 1987 Cover: 1.75 **NM** value: **2.25**
Circ: CapCity orders: **24,000**
📖 Beautiful Blues! **A:** Paul Gulacy **W:** Doug Moench

2 ❑ Dec 1987 Cover: 1.75 **NM** value: **2.00**
Circ: CapCity orders: **17,750**
A: Paul Gulacy **W:** Doug Moench

3 ❑ Jan 1988 Cover: 1.75 **NM** value: **2.00**
Circ: CapCity orders: **16,400**
A: Paul Gulacy **W:** Doug Moench

4 ❑ Feb 1988 Cover: 1.75 **NM** value: **2.00**
Circ: CapCity orders: **15,900**
📖 Halfway To Hyde On The Mulloid Express **A:** Paul Gulacy **W:** Doug Moench

5 ❑ Mar 1988 Cover: 1.75 **NM** value: **2.00**
Circ: CapCity orders: **15,250**
A: Paul Gulacy **W:** Doug Moench

6 ❑ Apr 1988 Cover: 1.75 **NM** value: **2.00**
Circ: CapCity orders: **14,450**
A: Paul Gulacy **W:** Doug Moench

SLAUGHTERMAN — Comico

1 ❑ b&w Cover: 3.50 **NM** value: **Cover or less**
2 ❑ b&w Cover: 3.50 **NM** value: **Cover or less**

SLAVE GIRL — Eternity

1 ❑ Mar 1989, b&w Cover: 2.25 **NM** value: **Cover or less**

SLAVE GIRL COMICS — Avon

1 ❑ Feb 1949 Cover: 0.10 **NM** value: **800.00**
• **CGC:** 8 graded, best 9.2

2 ❑ Apr 1949 Cover: 0.10 **NM** value: **600.00**
• **CGC:** 3 graded, best 9.6

SLAVE LABOR STORIES — Slave Labor

1 ❑ Feb 1992, b&w Cover: 2.95 **NM** value: **Cover or less**
📖 Stretching; Do Scientists Dream of Electric Sheep?; My Mommy Lied!; Father Tim; Rex Mallard: How to Deal With a Fanboy • Doctor Radium; Dr. Radium **A:** Gino Attanasio; Scott Saavedra; Gordon Purcell; Bob Simpkins **W:** Dan Vado; Scott Saavedra; Bob Simpkins

2 ❑ Apr 1992, b&w Cover: 2.95 **NM** value: **Cover or less**
📖 Milk and Cheese: Con Job!; Eating Elvis; Last Night; The Peasants: A Leo Tolstoy Adventure • Milk & Cheese **A:** Ted Couldron; Evan Dorkin; Aldin Baroza; Bob Simpkins **W:** Ted Couldron; Evan Dorkin; Aldin Baroza; Bob Simpkins; Jill Miller

3 ❑ Jul 1992, b&w Cover: 2.95 **NM** value: **Cover or less**
📖 Biill the Clown; Frozen Embryo; Jake Gunther vs. the NFL; Tales of the Odd Folk; Hero; The Nature Fixer Uppers • Bill the Clown **A:** Ted Couldron; Norman Felchle; Troy Nixey; Andy Garcia; Bob Simpkins **W:** Dan Vado; Ted Couldron; Andy Garcia; Bob Simpkins; Bill McDougall

4 ❑ Nov 1992, b&w Cover: 2.95 **NM** value: **Cover or less**
📖 Why We Hate the French; A Letter; Fat People • Samurai Penguin **A:** Ted Couldron; Bob Simpkins **W:** Ted Couldron; Bob Simpkins

SLAVE PIT FUNNIES — Slave Pit

1 ❑ Cover: 4.95 **NM** value: **Cover or less**
📖 Salve Escape; Tales of the Toolbox; Mid Galactic Championship Wrestling; Welcome to... Stalingrad 1942; When Heroes Roamed the Earth; Gwar Interview with Techno Destructo; Slymenstrs Hymen 1680 B.C. **A:** Bob Gorman; Danyell; Dave Brockie; Hunter Jackson; Matt Maguire; Mike Bishop **W:** Bob Gorman; Dave Brockie; Hunter Jackson; Matt Maguire; Chuck Varga

SLAYERS — CPM Manga

1 ❑ Oct 1998 Cover: 2.95 **NM** value: **Cover or less**
Circ: Diamd. preorders: **8,338**
A: Rui Araizumi **W:** Hajime Kanzaka

2 ❑ Nov 1998 Cover: 2.95 **NM** value: **Cover or less**
Circ: Diamd. preorders: **6,235**
📖 The Black Fox **A:** Rui Araizumi **W:** Hajime Kanzaka

3 ❑ Dec 1998 Cover: 2.95 **NM** value: **Cover or less**
Circ: Diamd. preorders: **5,658**
A: Rui Araizumi **W:** Hajime Kanzaka

4 ❑ Jan 1999 Cover: 2.95 **NM** value: **Cover or less**
Circ: Diamd. preorders: **6,318**
A: Rui Araizumi **W:** Hajime Kanzaka

5 ❑ Feb 1999 Cover: 2.95 **NM** value: **Cover or less**
Circ: Diamd. preorders: **6,097**
A: Rui Araizumi **W:** Hajime Kanzaka

SLEAZY SCANDALS OF THE SILVER SCREEN — Kitchen Sink

1 ❑ Cover: 2.50 **NM** value: **Cover or less**
📖 Fatty's Fatal Fling; The Suicide of Lupe Velez; Clara Bow Takes on the Thundering Herd; Tallulah Bankhead; Piano Lessons Paid Off for Liberace; The Mysterious Death of William Desmond Taylor **A:** Art Spiegelman; Bill Griffith; Jim Osborne; Kim Deitch; Spain Rodriguez **W:** Art Spiegelman; Bill Griffith; Jim Osborne; Kim Deitch; Spain Rodriguez

SLEDGE HAMMER — Marvel

1 ❑ Feb 1988 Cover: 1.00 **NM** value: **Cover or less**
Circ: CapCity orders: **9,850**
📖 Creephouse! • TV tie-in **A:** Alex Saviuk **W:** Jim Salicrup ★ 1st Appearance of Sledge Hammer. ★ Appearance of Satana.

2 ❑ Mar 1988 Cover: 1.00 **NM** value: **Cover or less**
• TV tie-in **A:** Alex Saviuk **W:** Jim Salicrup ★ Appearance of Spider-Man.

SLEEPWALKER — Marvel

1 ❑ Jun 1991 Cover: 1.00 **NM** value: **1.50**
Circ: Statement: **356,925** CapCity orders: **59,300**
📖 To Sleep Perchance To Scream! **A:** Bret Blevins **W:** Bob Budiansky ★ 1st Appearance of Sleepwalker.

2 ❑ Jul 1991 Cover: 1.00 **NM** value: **Cover or less**
Circ: Statement: **356,925** CapCity orders: **37,800**
★ 1st Appearance of 8-Ball.

3 ❑ Aug 1991 Cover: 1.00 **NM** value: **Cover or less**
Circ: Statement: **356,925** CapCity orders: **51,000**

4 ❑ Sep 1991 Cover: 1.00 **NM** value: **Cover or less**
Circ: Statement: **356,925** CapCity orders: **31,000**

5 ❑ Oct 1991 Cover: 1.00 **NM** value: **Cover or less**
Circ: Statement: **356,925** CapCity orders: **40,800**
★ Appearance of Spider-Man.

6 ❑ Nov 1991 Cover: 1.00 **NM** value: **Cover or less**
Circ: Statement: **356,925** CapCity orders: **38,600**
★ Appearance of Spider-Man.

7 ❑ Dec 1991 Cover: 1.00 **NM** value: **Cover or less**
Circ: Statement: **356,925** CapCity orders: **36,100**
• Infinity Gauntlet

8 ❑ Jan 1992 Cover: 1.25 **NM** value: **Cover or less**
Circ: Statement: **158,275** CapCity orders: **38,400**
★ Appearance of Deathlok.

9 ❑ Feb 1992 Cover: 1.25 **NM** value: **Cover or less**
Circ: Statement: **158,275** CapCity orders: **28,100**

10 ❑ Mar 1992 Cover: 1.25 **NM** value: **Cover or less**
Circ: Statement: **158,275** CapCity orders: **25,600**

11 ❑ Apr 1992 Cover: 1.25 **NM** value: **Cover or less**
Circ: Statement: **158,275** CapCity orders: **29,700**

12 ❑ May 1992 Cover: 1.25 **NM** value: **Cover or less**
Circ: Statement: **158,275** CapCity orders: **23,700**

13 ❑ Jun 1992 Cover: 1.25 **NM** value: **Cover or less**
Circ: Statement: **158,275** CapCity orders: **23,300**
📖 Color Blindness, Part 1 ★ 1st Appearance of Spectra.

14 ❑ Jul 1992 Cover: 1.25 **NM** value: **Cover or less**
Circ: Statement: **158,275** CapCity orders: **22,800**
📖 Color Blindness, Part 2

15 ❑ Aug 1992 Cover: 1.25 **NM** value: **Cover or less**
Circ: Statement: **158,275** CapCity orders: **21,700**
📖 Color Blindness, Part 3 **A:** Bret Blevins **W:** Bob Budiansky

16 ❑ Sep 1992 Cover: 1.25 **NM** value: **Cover or less**
Circ: Statement: **158,275** CapCity orders: **18,300**
📖 Color Blindness, Part 4

17 ❑ Oct 1992 Cover: 1.25 **NM** value: **Cover or less**
Circ: Statement: **158,275** CapCity orders: **21,100**

18 ❑ Nov 1992 Cover: 1.25 **NM** value: **Cover or less**
Circ: Statement: **158,275** CapCity orders: **25,400**

19 ❑ Dec 1992 Cover: 2.00 **NM** value: **Cover or less**
Circ: Statement: **158,275**
Die-cut cover. 📖 Mindfield, Part 1

20 ❑ Jan 1993 Cover: 1.25 **NM** value: **Cover or less**
Circ: CapCity orders: **16,600**
📖 Mindfield, Part 2

21 ❑ Feb 1993 Cover: 1.25 **NM** value: **Cover or less**
Circ: CapCity orders: **15,800**
📖 Mindfield, Part 3

22 ❑ Mar 1993 Cover: 1.25 **NM** value: **Cover or less**
Circ: CapCity orders: **14,700**
📖 Mindfield, Part 4

23 ❑ Apr 1993 Cover: 1.25 **NM** value: **Cover or less**
Circ: CapCity orders: **14,300**
📖 Mindfield, Part 5

24 ❑ May 1993 Cover: 1.25 **NM** value: **Cover or less**
Circ: CapCity orders: **13,900**
📖 Mindfield, Part 6 **A:** Kelly Krantz **W:** Bob Budiansky

25 ❑ Jun 1993 Cover: 2.95 **NM** value: **Cover or less**
Circ: CapCity orders: **26,800**
Holo-grafix cover.

26 ❑ Jul 1993 Cover: 1.25 **NM** value: **Cover or less**
Circ: CapCity orders: **12,600**

27 ❑ Aug 1993 Cover: 1.25 **NM** value: **Cover or less**
Circ: CapCity orders: **12,350**

28 ❑ Sep 1993 Cover: 1.25 **NM** value: **Cover or less**
Circ: CapCity orders: **11,100**

29 ❑ Oct 1993 Cover: 1.25 **NM** value: **Cover or less**
Circ: CapCity orders: **9,500**
A: Kelly Krantz **W:** Bob Budiansky ★ Appearance of Spectra.

30 ❑ Nov 1993 Cover: 1.25 **NM** value: **Cover or less**
Circ: CapCity orders: **9,050**

31 ❑ Dec 1993 Cover: 1.25 **NM** value: **Cover or less**
Circ: CapCity orders: **8,450**

32 ❑ Jan 1994 Cover: 1.25 **NM** value: **Cover or less**
Circ: CapCity orders: **7,350**

33 ❑ Feb 1994 Cover: 1.25 **NM** value: **Cover or less**
Circ: CapCity orders: **7,100**
final issue.

HS 1❑ Cover: 2.00 **NM** value: **Cover or less**
Circ: CapCity orders: **13,000**

SLEEPWALKING — Hall of Heroes

1 ❑ Jan 1996, b&w Cover: 2.50 **NM** value: **Cover or less**
1/SC❑ Jan 1996, b&w Cover: 9.95 **NM** value: **Cover or less**
alternate logoless cover. • Black Magic edition.
2 ❑ Jun 1997, b&w Cover: 2.50 **NM** value: **Cover or less**
2/SC❑ Jun 1997, b&w Cover: 2.50 **NM** value: **Cover or less**
alternate logoless cover.

SLEEPY HOLLOW — DC / Vertigo

1 ❑ Jan 2000 Cover: 7.95 **NM** value: **Cover or less**
Circ: Diamd. preorders: **10,167**
A: Kelley Jones **W:** Steven Seagle

SLEEZE BROTHERS — Marvel / Epic

1 ❑ Aug 1989 Cover: 1.75 **NM** value: **Cover or less**
Circ: CapCity orders: **8,900**
📖 Nice 'N' Sleazy **A:** Andy Lanning **W:** John Carnell

2 ❑ Sep 1989 Cover: 1.75 **NM** value: **Cover or less**
Circ: CapCity orders: **5,800**

3 ❑ Oct 1989 Cover: 1.75 **NM** value: **Cover or less**
Circ: CapCity orders: **4,700**

4 ❑ Nov 1989 Cover: 1.75 **NM** value: **Cover or less**
Circ: CapCity orders: **3,850**

5 ❑ Dec 1989 Cover: 1.75 **NM** value: **Cover or less**
Circ: CapCity orders: **3,750**

6 ❑ Jan 1990 Cover: 1.75 **NM** value: **Cover or less**
Circ: CapCity orders: **3,450**

SLEEZE BROTHERS, THE (2ND SERIES) — Marvel / Epic

1 ❑ ca. 1991 Cover: 3.95 **NM** value: **Cover or less**
Circ: CapCity orders: **2,500**
No issue number.

SLICE — Express / Entity

1 ❑ Oct 1996, b&w Cover: 2.75 **NM** value: **Cover or less**

SLICK CHICK — Leader

1 ❑ ca. 1946 Cover: 0.10 **NM** value: **75.00**
2 ❑ ca. 1946 Cover: 0.10 **NM** value: **50.00**
3 ❑ ca. 1946 Cover: 0.10 **NM** value: **50.00**

SLIDERS — Acclaim / Armada

1 ❑ Jun 1996 Cover: 2.50 **NM** value: **3.00**
• based on TV series

2 ❑ Jul 1996 Cover: 2.50 **NM** value: **Cover or less**
• based on TV series

3 ❑ Sep 1996 Cover: 2.50 **NM** value: **Cover or less**
📖 Ultimatum, Part 1

4 ❑ Sep 1996 Cover: 2.50 **NM** value: **Cover or less**
📖 Ultimatum, Part 2 **A:** Bernard Chang **W:** D.G. Chichester

5 ❑ Oct 1996 Cover: 2.50 **NM** value: **Cover or less**
📖 Darkest Hour, Part 1 **W:** D.G. Chichester

6 ❑ Nov 1996 Cover: 2.50 **NM** value: **Cover or less**
📖 Darkest Hour, Part 2 **W:** D.G. Chichester

7 ❑ Dec 1996 Cover: 2.50 **NM** value: **Cover or less**
📖 Darkest Hour, Part 3 **A:** Val Mayerik; Kevin Kobasic; Dennis Calero **W:** D.G. Chichester

SE 1❑ Nov 1996 Cover: 3.95 **NM** value: **Cover or less**
Circ: Diamd. preorders: **11,512**
📖 Narcotica • Narcotica **W:** Jerry O'Connell

SE 2❑ Jan 1997 Cover: 3.95 **NM** value: **Cover or less**
Circ: Diamd. preorders: **10,857**
📖 Blood & Splendor **A:** Rags Morales **W:** Jeff Somers; Jeof Vita; Tracy Tormé

SE 3❑ Mar 1997 Cover: 3.95 **NM** value: **Cover or less**
• Deadly Secrets

SLIGHTLY BENT COMICS — Slightly Bent

1 ❑ Fal 1998, b&w Cover: 3.00 **NM** value: **Cover or less**
📖 Dude-Guy, Earth's Best Pal; Those Dang Gnats!; Mel Cool: Mall Cop: The Mystery of the Missing Morons!; Smirk Du Jour; Danger Dad; Attorney in Space **A:** Don Secrease; Paul Daly; Craig Skaggs; Jim Riley; Tony Patti **W:** Walt Jaschek

2 ❑ Win 1999, b&w Cover: 3.00 **NM** value: **Cover or less**

SLIMER! — Now

1 ❑ May 1989 Cover: 1.75 **NM** value: **2.00**
Circ: CapCity orders: **4,225**
📖 A Kindly Ghost; Ghostly Plumbing **A:** Dave Schwartz; Gary Fields **W:** Hilarie Staton

2 ❑ Jun 1989 Cover: 1.75 **NM** value: **2.00**
Circ: CapCity orders: **2,675**

3 ❑ Jul 1989 Cover: 1.75 **NM** value: **2.00**
Circ: CapCity orders: **2,650**

4 ❑ Aug 1989 Cover: 1.75 **NM** value: **Cover or less**
Circ: CapCity orders: **2,300**

5 ❑ Sep 1989 Cover: 1.75 **NM** value: **Cover or less**
Circ: CapCity orders: **2,200**

6 ❑ Oct 1989 Cover: 1.75 **NM** value: **Cover or less**

7 ❑ Nov 1989 Cover: 1.75 **NM** value: **Cover or less**
Circ: CapCity orders: **2,075**

8 ❑ Dec 1989 Cover: 1.75 **NM** value: **Cover or less**
Circ: CapCity orders: **2,150**

9 ❑ Jan 1990 Cover: 1.75 **NM** value: **Cover or less**
Circ: CapCity orders: **2,025**

10 ❑ Feb 1990 Cover: 1.75 **NM** value: **Cover or less**
Circ: CapCity orders: **1,925**
📖 Thanksgiving Nightmares; Sleepless Nights **A:** Mark Braun; Howard Bender **W:** Hilarie Staton

11 ❑ Mar 1990 Cover: 1.75 **NM** value: **Cover or less**
Circ: CapCity orders: **1,850**

12 ❑ Apr 1990 Cover: 1.75 **NM** value: **Cover or less**
Circ: CapCity orders: **1,725**

CGC-graded: Multiply prices above by **33 for 9.9 M • 16 for 9.8 NM/M • 7 for 9.6 NM+ • 5 for 9.4 NM • 2.5 for 9.2 NM- • 1.5 for 9.0 VF/NM**

🕮 Supernatural Bowl; Fooled for Love **A:** Mark Braun; Steve Parkhouse; Dave Harwood; Tim Perkins; Brian Williamson **W:** Dennys McCoy; Jane Fabian; John Carnell; Pamela Hickey

13 ❑ May 1990 Cover: 1.75 **NM** value: **Cover or less**
Circ: CapCity orders: **1,600**
🕮 Stupid Cupid; Car-Wash Spook; The Ghost House **A:** Anthony Williams; Mark Braun; Dave Harwood; Tony O'Donnell **W:** Dennys McCoy; Graham Watson; Jane Fabian; Larry Parr; Pamela Hickey

14 ❑ Jun 1990 Cover: 1.75 **NM** value: **Cover or less**
Circ: CapCity orders: **1,500**
🕮 Art For Slimer's Sake; Trans-Mutant Terror; Haunted Melodies **A:** Phil Elliott; Anthony Williams; Andrew Wildman; Kev Hopgood; Dave Elliott; Dave Harwood; Dave Hine; Gordon Morrison **W:** Dennys McCoy; John Carnell; Pamela Hickey; Sue Flaxman

15 ❑ Jul 1990 Cover: 1.75 **NM** value: **Cover or less**
Circ: CapCity orders: **1,525**
🕮 Genie With the Light Green Slime; Monster Movie; Highway Haunt **A:** Anthony Williams; Mark Braun; Paul Marshall; Tim Perkins; Tony O'Donnell **W:** Andrew Brenner; John Carnell; Larry Parr

16 ❑ Aug 1990 Cover: 1.75 **NM** value: **Cover or less**
Circ: CapCity orders: **1,425**
🕮 The Ghostly Egg; Ray's From the Grave; An Inspectre Calls **A:** Phil Elliott; Anthony Williams; Dave Elliott; Dave Harwood; Gordon Morrison **W:** Dan Abnett; Diane Piron; John Carnell

17 ❑ Sep 1990 Cover: 1.75 **NM** value: **Cover or less**
Circ: CapCity orders: **1,350**

18 ❑ Oct 1990 Cover: 1.75 **NM** value: **Cover or less**
Circ: CapCity orders: **1,350**
🕮 A Bird in the Slime; Surgical Spirit; Too Many Ghost Busters; Ghost Boaster! **A:** Mark Braun; Anthony Larcombe; Tim Perkins; Brian Williamson **W:** John Carnell; Larry Parr; Nancy Hazel

19 ❑ Nov 1990 Cover: 1.75 **NM** value: **Cover or less**
Circ: CapCity orders: **1,250**
🕮 Rind Around the Slime; Doomsday Mask! **A:** Mark Braun; Andy Lanning; Dave Hine **W:** John Carnell; Larry Parr

Bk 1❑ Cover: 5.95 **NM** value: **Cover or less**
• Slimer Compendium

SLINGERS — Marvel

Four teen-agers have been chosen to become part of a most unusual team. A mysterious figure has given each of them a super-heroic persona once used by Spider-Man.

Ricochet, the rowdiest of the group, utilizes bouncing disks and has the personality to match. Hornet is most at home in his winged exoskeleton, perhaps because it allows him to escape the handicaps he faces in the real world. Prodigy, grim and driven, will let nothing, whether bullets or other people, stand in his way. And Dusk, shy and confused, is not even certain she wants to be part of The Slingers.

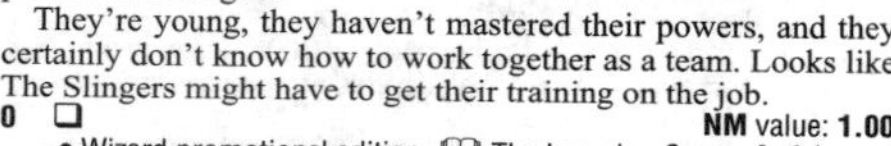

They're young, they haven't mastered their powers, and they certainly don't know how to work together as a team. Looks like The Slingers might have to get their training on the job.

0 ❑ **NM** value: **1.00**
• Wizard promotional edition. 🕮 The Learning Curve **A:** Adam Pollina **W:** Joseph Harris

1/A ❑ Dec 1998 Cover: 2.99 **NM** value: **Cover or less**
Circ: Diamd. preorders: **104,655**
variant cover with caption "Prodigy: Prepare for Justice!". • gatefold summary. 🕮 So Whose Idea Was this Anyway? **A:** Chris Cross **W:** Joseph Harris ★ Appearance of Ricochet, Dusk, Hornet, Prodigy, and Black Marvel.

1/B ❑ Dec 1998 Cover: 2.99 **NM** value: **Cover or less**
Caption "Dusk Falls Over Manhattan" on cover.

1/C ❑ Dec 1998 Cover: 2.99 **NM** value: **Cover or less**
variant cover with caption "Hornet: Feel the Sting!".

1/D ❑ Dec 1998 Cover: 2.99 **NM** value: **Cover or less**
variant cover with caption "Ricochet Springs into Action!".

2 ❑ Jan 1999 Cover: 1.99 **NM** value: **2.00**
Circ: Diamd. preorders: **45,315**
Cover A. • gatefold summary.

2/SC❑Jan 1999 Cover: 1.99 **NM** value: **2.00**
Cover B.

3 ❑ Feb 1999 Cover: 1.99 **NM** value: **Cover or less**
Circ: Diamd. preorders: **34,917**
A: Chriscross **W:** Mike Harris ★ Appearance of Spider-Man, Prodigy.

4 ❑ Mar 1999 Cover: 1.99 **NM** value: **Cover or less**
Circ: Diamd. preorders: **32,095**
A: Chriscross **W:** Mike Harris ★ Appearance of Prodigy.

5 ❑ Apr 1999 Cover: 1.99 **NM** value: **Cover or less**
Circ: Diamd. preorders: **28,062**
A: Chriscross **W:** Mike Harris ★ Appearance of Black Marvel.

6 ❑ May 1999 Cover: 1.99 **NM** value: **Cover or less**
Circ: Diamd. preorders: **25,852**

7 ❑ Jun 1999 Cover: 1.99 **NM** value: **Cover or less**
Circ: Diamd. preorders: **24,362**
★ Versus Griz.

8 ❑ Jul 1999 Cover: 1.99 **NM** value: **Cover or less**
Circ: Diamd. preorders: **22,685**

9 ❑ Aug 1999 Cover: 1.99 **NM** value: **Cover or less**
Circ: Diamd. preorders: **22,133**
• Ricochet vs. Nanny and Orphanmaker

10 ❑ Sep 1999 Cover: 1.99 **NM** value: **Cover or less**
Circ: Diamd. preorders: **21,413**

12 ❑ Nov 1999 Cover: 1.99 **NM** value: **Cover or less**
Circ: Diamd. preorders: **18,592**

SLOTH PARK — Blatant

1 ❑ Jun 1998 Cover: 2.95 **NM** value: **Cover or less**
Circ: Diamd. preorders: **5,005**

SLOW BURN — Eros

1 ❑ Cover: 2.95 **NM** value: **Cover or less**
A: Bené **W:** Bené

SLOW DEATH — Last Gasp

1 ❑ **NM** value: **10.00**

2 ❑ Jan 1970 **NM** value: **6.00**
🕮 The Sex Evolsors of Tecnicus **A:** Jaxon; Dave Sheridan; Osborne; R. Gore **W:** Jaxon; Dave Sheridan; Osborne; R. Gore

3 ❑ **NM** value: **5.00**

4 ❑ Jan 1972 Cover: 0.50 **NM** value: **5.00**
🕮 Eyes of the Beholder; Ecotopia 2001; The Awakening; Mangle, Robot Mangler; Homesick **A:** George Metzger; Jaxon; Dave Sheridan; Greg Irons; William Corben **W:** George Metzger; Jaxon; Dave Sheridan; Greg Irons; William Corben

5 ❑ Jan 1973 Cover: 0.75 **NM** value: **5.00**
🕮 Last Gasp; Recycled; Museum Piece; Melton's Big Game **A:** Jaxon; Charles Dallas; Dave Sheridan; Greg Irons; Tom Veitch **W:** Jaxon; Charles Dallas; Dave Sheridan; Greg Irons; Tom Veitch

6 ❑ **NM** value: **3.00**

7 ❑ Dec 1976 **NM** value: **3.00**
🕮 Nits Make Lice; Armistace: 1918; Bonus Army **A:** William Wray; Jaxon; Greg Irons; William Stout **W:** William Wray; Jaxon; Greg Irons; William Stout

8 ❑ Jul 1977 Cover: 1.00 **NM** value: **3.00**
🕮 The Honour & Glory of Whaling; The Bengal Blues; Rites of Spring; Animals Your Children Will Never See!; Ozean-Oinken; Balance; Condor's End; The Last Dinosaur; The Ol' Salt's Tale; Perfect Evening; The Stink Goes On • Greenpeace issue **A:** William Wray; Tim Boxell; Michael T. Gilbert; Doug Hansen; Greg Irons; Roger Brand; William Stout; Brenda Bernu; Dennis Ellefson; Michael Jerry Becker; Sam Wray; Shelby Sampson **W:** William Wray; Tim Boxell; Michael T. Gilbert; Doug Hansen; Greg Irons; Roger Brand; William Stout; Brenda Bernu; Dennis Ellefson; Michael Jerry Becker; Sam Wray; Shelby Sampson

9 ❑ **NM** value: **3.00**
10 ❑ **NM** value: **3.00**
11 ❑ **NM** value: **3.00**

SLOWPOKE COMIX — Alternative

1 ❑ Nov 1998, b&w Cover: 2.95 **NM** value: **Cover or less**
🕮 The Umbrella; The Giraffe Quandary; Problem People; Miracle Umbrella; Midi Minni; Gus's Blues; Still Blue; Drool Julie; Great Escapists; Mystery of Mr. P #37B; Highly Symbolic Comix; Minnie's Box **A:** Jennifer Sorensen **W:** Jennifer Sorensen

SLUDGE — Malibu / Ultraverse

1 ❑ Oct 1993 Cover: 2.50 **NM** value: **Cover or less**
Circ: CapCity orders: **40,525**
🕮 Rune, Part A • Rune **A:** Aaron Lopresti; Barry Windsor-Smith **W:** Steve Gerber ★ Origin of Sludge. ★ 1st Appearance of Sludge.

1/LE❑ Oct 1993 Cover: 5.00 **NM** value: **Cover or less**
🕮 Rune, Part A • Ultra Ltd.

2 ❑ Nov 1993 Cover: 1.95 **NM** value: **2.00**
Circ: CapCity orders: **22,575**
A: Aaron Lopresti **W:** Steve Gerber ★ 1st Appearance of Bloodstorm.

3 ❑ Dec 1993 Cover: 1.95 **NM** value: **2.00**
Circ: CapCity orders: **21,275**
🕮 Break-Thru • Break-Thru **A:** Aaron Lopresti **W:** Steve Gerber ★ 1st Appearance of Lord Pumpkin.

4 ❑ Jan 1994 Cover: 1.95 **NM** value: **2.00**
Circ: CapCity orders: **17,875**
🕮 Cold Blood **A:** Aaron Lopresti **W:** Steve Gerber ★ Origin of Mantra.

5 ❑ Feb 1994 Cover: 1.95 **NM** value: **2.00**
Circ: CapCity orders: **15,350**
🕮 Creatures Of The Night **A:** Aaron Lopresti **W:** Aaron Lopresti

6 ❑ Mar 1994 Cover: 1.95 **NM** value: **Cover or less**
Circ: CapCity orders: **13,450**
W: Steve Gerber ★ Versus Lord Pumpkin.

7 ❑ Jun 1994 Cover: 1.95 **NM** value: **Cover or less**
Circ: CapCity orders: **12,625**
W: Steve Gerber

8 ❑ Jul 1994 Cover: 1.95 **NM** value: **Cover or less**
Circ: CapCity orders: **11,800**
W: Steve Gerber ★ Versus Bloodstorm.

9 ❑ Sep 1994 Cover: 1.95 **NM** value: **Cover or less**
Circ: CapCity orders: **11,075**
🕮 Zuke 'em Till They Glow! **A:** Robb Phipps; Aaron Lopresti(cover) **W:** Steve Gerber ★ Versus Lord Pumpkin.

10 ❑ Oct 1994 Cover: 1.95 **NM** value: **Cover or less**
Circ: CapCity orders: **10,000**
🕮 Form Follows Unction **A:** Robb Phipps; Aaron Lopresti(cover) **W:** Steve Gerber ★ 1st Appearance of Bash Brothers, Organism 0.9B, and Vinaigrette.

11 ❑ Nov 1994 Cover: 1.95 **NM** value: **Cover or less**
Circ: CapCity orders: **7,700**
🕮 Intellectual Exercise! **A:** Robb Phipps; Aaron Lopresti(cover) **W:** Steve Gerber ★ Versus Bash Brothers.

12 ❑ Dec 1994 Cover: 3.50 **NM** value: **Cover or less**
Circ: CapCity orders: **7,250**
🕮 Neverland Blues, Part 2; Grenade and Electrocute: Soldiers of Fortune; Wrath: In the Belly of the Beast, Part 1 • flipbook with Ultraverse Premiere #8 **A:** Aaron Lopresti; Steve Scott; Keith Conroy; Brian Kong **W:** Aaron Lopresti; James D. Hudnall; Mike W. Barr; R.A. Jones ★ 1st Appearance of Witch, and Mr. Mischief. ★ Appearance of Prime.

13 ❑ Jan 1995 Cover: 1.95 **NM** value: **Cover or less**
Circ: CapCity orders: **6,275**
final issue. **W:** Steve Gerber

SLUGGER — Lev Gleason

1 ❑ Apr 1956 Cover: 0.10 **NM** value: **35.00**

SLUG 'N' GINGER — Fantagraphics / Eros

All issues are adults only.

1 ❑ b&w Cover: 2.25 **NM** value: **Cover or less**

SLUTBURGER STORIES — Rip Off

All issues are adults only.

1 ❑ Jul 1990, b&w Cover: 2.50 **NM** value: **Cover or less**
2 ❑ Jul 1991, b&w Cover: 2.50 **NM** value: **Cover or less**

SMALL KILLING, A — VG

1 ❑ Cover: 15.00 **NM** value: **Cover or less**
A: Oscar Zarate **W:** Alan Moore

1-2 ❑ Cover: 11.95 **NM** value: **Cover or less**
• American 2nd printing **A:** Oscar Zarate **W:** Alan Moore

SMALL PRESS EXPO — Insight

1995❑ca. 1995 Cover: 2.95 **NM** value: **Cover or less**
🕮 Swimsuit Pin-ups • Benefit Comic for American Cancer Society

1996❑ca. 1996 Cover: 2.95 **NM** value: **Cover or less**

1997❑ca. 1997 Cover: 2.95 **NM** value: **Cover or less**
Circ: Diamd. preorders: **5,226**
🕮 The Staros Report...SPX; Silly Daddy: Actual Thoughts; Jane's High School Reunion; True Artist Tales; The Same Day; A Wrong Number Down at the Deli; The Stup • Benefit comic for Comic Legal Defense Fund **A:** Alex Robinson; Brian Biggs; Ed Brubaker; Joe Chiappetta; John Porcellino; Pete Mullins; Scott Gilbert; Chris Staros; Dave Lasky; Edgar Keret; Josue Menjivar; Matt Madden; Rutu Modan; Tony Consiglio; Yvonne Mojica; Tom Har **W:** Alex Robinson; Brian Biggs; Ed Brubaker; Joe Chiappetta; John Porcellino; Pete Mullins; Scott Gilbert; Chris Staros; Dave Lasky; Edgar Keret; Josue Menjivar; Matt Madden; Rutu Modan; Tom Ha; Tony Consiglio; Yvonne Mojica

SMALL PRESS SWIMSUIT SPECTACULAR — Allied

1 ❑ Jun 1995, b&w Cover: 2.95 **NM** value: **Cover or less**
• pin-ups; benefit comic for American Cancer Society

SMASH COMICS — Quality

Smash Comics is one of the flagship titles of the Quality line, a first-rank publisher of the Golden Age. Early issues struggle to find a star amid a lineup of perennial backups like Espionage and Hooded Justice. Issue #14 introduces The Ray, a hero who can turn himself into a beam of light. Lavishly illustrated by Lou Fine, one of the great Golden Age artists, The Ray gains enough popularity to be revived many years later by DC in The Freedom Fighters and Justice League of America. Four issues later, he is joined by Midnight, one of many imitators of Will Eisner's Spirit. However, writer-artist Jack Cole (creator of Plastic Man, among others) is one of the few creators who can approach Eisner's skill and wit, and Midnight soon develops its own distinct personality. Midnight kept Smash going until Quality folded.

1 ❑ Aug 1939 Cover: 0.10 **NM** value: **1650.00**
• **CGC:** 1 graded, best 6.5
2 ❑ Sep 1939 Cover: 0.10 **NM** value: **650.00**
3 ❑ Oct 1939 Cover: 0.10 **NM** value: **475.00**
4 ❑ Nov 1939 Cover: 0.10 **NM** value: **425.00**
5 ❑ Dec 1939 Cover: 0.10 **NM** value: **425.00**
6 ❑ Jan 1940 Cover: 0.10 **NM** value: **350.00**
7 ❑ Feb 1940 Cover: 0.10 **NM** value: **350.00**
8 ❑ Mar 1940 Cover: 0.10 **NM** value: **350.00**
• **CGC:** 1 graded, best 9.6
9 ❑ Apr 1940 Cover: 0.10 **NM** value: **350.00**
10 ❑ May 1940 Cover: 0.10 **NM** value: **350.00**
• **CGC:** 1 graded, best .5
11 ❑ Jun 1940 Cover: 0.10 **NM** value: **325.00**
12 ❑ Jul 1940 Cover: 0.10 **NM** value: **325.00**
13 ❑ Aug 1940 Cover: 0.10 **NM** value: **350.00**
14 ❑ Sep 1940 Cover: 0.10 **NM** value: **1500.00**
• **CGC:** 1 graded, best 5.5
★ 1st Appearance of The Ray I.
15 ❑ Oct 1940 Cover: 0.10 **NM** value: **725.00**
16 ❑ Nov 1940 Cover: 0.10 **NM** value: **700.00**
17 ❑ Dec 1940 Cover: 0.10 **NM** value: **800.00**
• **CGC:** 1 graded, best 8.0
• Plastic Man prototype?
18 ❑ Jan 1941 Cover: 0.10 **NM** value: **1000.00**
A: Jack Cole ★ 1st Appearance of Midnight.
19 ❑ Feb 1941 Cover: 0.10 **NM** value: **550.00**
20 ❑ Mar 1941 Cover: 0.10 **NM** value: **550.00**
21 ❑ Apr 1941 Cover: 0.10 **NM** value: **500.00**
• **CGC:** 1 graded, best 6.5
22 ❑ May 1941 Cover: 0.10 **NM** value: **500.00**
23 ❑ Jun 1941 Cover: 0.10 **NM** value: **500.00**
24 ❑ Jul 1941 Cover: 0.10 **NM** value: **500.00**
• **CGC:** 1 graded, best 7.0
25 ❑ Aug 1941 Cover: 0.10 **NM** value: **550.00**
26 ❑ Sep 1941 Cover: 0.10 **NM** value: **500.00**
27 ❑ Oct 1941 Cover: 0.10 **NM** value: **500.00**
28 ❑ Nov 1941 Cover: 0.10 **NM** value: **500.00**
29 ❑ Dec 1941 Cover: 0.10 **NM** value: **500.00**
30 ❑ Jan 1942 Cover: 0.10 **NM** value: **500.00**
31 ❑ Feb 1942 Cover: 0.10 **NM** value: **385.00**
32 ❑ Mar 1942 Cover: 0.10 **NM** value: **385.00**
33 ❑ May 1942 Cover: 0.10 **NM** value: **385.00**
• **CGC:** 2 graded, best 3.5
34 ❑ Jul 1942 Cover: 0.10 **NM** value: **385.00**
35 ❑ Sep 1942 Cover: 0.10 **NM** value: **385.00**
• **CGC:** 1 graded, best 2.5
36 ❑ Oct 1942 Cover: 0.10 **NM** value: **385.00**
• **CGC:** 1 graded, best 3.5
37 ❑ Nov 1942 Cover: 0.10 **NM** value: **385.00**
• **CGC:** 1 graded, best 9.4
38 ❑ Dec 1942 Cover: 0.10 **NM** value: **385.00**
• **CGC:** 1 graded, best 9.2

Other grades: Multiply prices above by **1.5 for Mint • 2/3 for Very Fine • 1/3 for Fine • 1/5 for Very Good • 1/8 for Good**

39 ❑ Jan 1943 Cover: 0.10 **NM** value: **385.00**
• **CGC:** 1 graded, best 9.0
40 ❑ Feb 1943 Cover: 0.10 **NM** value: **385.00**
41 ❑ Mar 1943 Cover: 0.10 **NM** value: **275.00**
42 ❑ Apr 1943 Cover: 0.10 **NM** value: **275.00**
• **CGC:** 1 graded, best 9.4
43 ❑ Jun 1943 Cover: 0.10 **NM** value: **275.00**
• **CGC:** 1 graded, best 9.0
44 ❑ Jul 1943 Cover: 0.10 **NM** value: **275.00**
45 ❑ Aug 1943 Cover: 0.10 **NM** value: **275.00**
• **CGC:** 1 graded, best 9.0
46 ❑ Sep 1943 Cover: 0.10 **NM** value: **275.00**
47 ❑ Oct 1943 Cover: 0.10 **NM** value: **275.00**
48 ❑ Nov 1943 Cover: 0.10 **NM** value: **275.00**
49 ❑ Jan 1944 Cover: 0.10 **NM** value: **275.00**
50 ❑ Feb 1944 Cover: 0.10 **NM** value: **275.00**
51 ❑ Mar 1944 Cover: 0.10 **NM** value: **185.00**
52 ❑ Apr 1944 Cover: 0.10 **NM** value: **185.00**
53 ❑ May 1944 Cover: 0.10 **NM** value: **185.00**
• **CGC:** 1 graded, best 7.5
54 ❑ Aug 1944 Cover: 0.10 **NM** value: **185.00**
55 ❑ Oct 1944 Cover: 0.10 **NM** value: **185.00**
56 ❑ Dec 1944 Cover: 0.10 **NM** value: **185.00**
57 ❑ Feb 1945 Cover: 0.10 **NM** value: **185.00**
• **CGC:** 1 graded, best 9.2
58 ❑ Apr 1945 Cover: 0.10 **NM** value: **185.00**
59 ❑ Jun 1945 Cover: 0.10 **NM** value: **185.00**
60 ❑ Aug 1945 Cover: 0.10 **NM** value: **185.00**
61 ❑ Oct 1945 Cover: 0.10 **NM** value: **135.00**
62 ❑ Dec 1945 Cover: 0.10 **NM** value: **135.00**
📖 Midnight; Daffy; Rookie Rankin; Spunky; Dead Man's Mountain (Text Story); Let Peace return to Earth!; The Jester!; **A:** Klaus Nordling; Ginger; Sid Lazarus **W:** Klaus Nordling; Ginger; Sid Lazarus
63 ❑ Feb 1946 Cover: 0.10 **NM** value: **135.00**
• **CGC:** 1 graded, best 3.0
64 ❑ Apr 1946 Cover: 0.10 **NM** value: **135.00**
65 ❑ Jun 1946 Cover: 0.10 **NM** value: **135.00**
66 ❑ Aug 1946 Cover: 0.10 **NM** value: **135.00**
67 ❑ Oct 1946 Cover: 0.10 **NM** value: **135.00**
68 ❑ Dec 1946 Cover: 0.10 **NM** value: **135.00**
• **CGC:** 1 graded, best 9.0
69 ❑ Feb 1947 Cover: 0.10 **NM** value: **135.00**
• **CGC:** 1 graded, best 7.5
70 ❑ Apr 1947 Cover: 0.10 **NM** value: **135.00**
• **CGC:** 1 graded, best 7.0
71 ❑ Jun 1947 Cover: 0.10 **NM** value: **100.00**
• **CGC:** 1 graded, best 7.0
72 ❑ Aug 1947 Cover: 0.10 **NM** value: **100.00**
• **CGC:** 1 graded, best 8.5
73 ❑ Oct 1947 Cover: 0.10 **NM** value: **100.00**
• **CGC:** 2 graded, best 9.2
74 ❑ Dec 1947 Cover: 0.10 **NM** value: **100.00**
75 ❑ Feb 1948 Cover: 0.10 **NM** value: **100.00**
• **CGC:** 1 graded, best 6.5
76 ❑ Apr 1948 Cover: 0.10 **NM** value: **100.00**
• **CGC:** 1 graded, best 8.0
77 ❑ Jun 1948 Cover: 0.10 **NM** value: **100.00**
78 ❑ Aug 1948 Cover: 0.10 **NM** value: **100.00**
79 ❑ Oct 1948 Cover: 0.10 **NM** value: **100.00**
80 ❑ Dec 1948 Cover: 0.10 **NM** value: **100.00**
81 ❑ Feb 1949 Cover: 0.10 **NM** value: **100.00**
• **CGC:** 1 graded, best 8.0
82 ❑ Apr 1949 Cover: 0.10 **NM** value: **100.00**
83 ❑ Jun 1949 Cover: 0.10 **NM** value: **100.00**
84 ❑ Aug 1949 Cover: 0.10 **NM** value: **100.00**
85 ❑ Oct 1949 Cover: 0.10 **NM** value: **100.00**

SMASH COMICS (2ND SERIES) — DC
1 ❑ May 1999 Cover: 1.99 **NM** value: **Cover or less**
Circ: Diamd. preorders: **42,239**
📖 Name Your Poison • Justice Society Returns **A:** Stephen Sadowski **W:** Tom Peyer ★ Appearance of Doctor Mid-Nite, Hourman.

SMILE (KITCHEN SINK) — Kitchen Sink
1 ❑ Cover: 0.50 **NM** value: **3.00**
📖 Fang; Humble There a Rocky Start!; The Making of a Hipster; Wouldn't it be Nice if Everyone Were Children AgainSmile **A:** Jim Mitchell **W:** Jim Mitchell

SMILE (MIXX) — Mixx
1 ❑ Dec 1998 Cover: 3.99 **NM** value: **Cover or less**
• Sailor Moon
2 ❑ 1999 Cover: 3.99 **NM** value: **Cover or less**
3 ❑ 1999 Cover: 3.99 **NM** value: **Cover or less**
4 ❑ 1999 Cover: 3.99 **NM** value: **Cover or less**
5 ❑ 1999 Cover: 3.99 **NM** value: **Cover or less**
6 ❑ 1999 Cover: 3.99 **NM** value: **Cover or less**
7 ❑ Dec 1999 Cover: 3.99 **NM** value: **Cover or less**
8 ❑ Cover: 3.99 **NM** value: **Cover or less**

SMILEY — Chaos
1 ❑ Jun 1998 Cover: 2.95 **NM** value: **Cover or less**
Circ: Diamd. preorders: **21,604**
W: Brian Pulido

SMILEY ANTI-HOLIDAY SPECIAL — Chaos!
1 ❑ Jan 1999 Cover: 2.95 **NM** value: **Cover or less**
Circ: Diamd. preorders: **14,286**

SMILEY BURNETT WESTERN — Fawcett
1 ❑ Mar 1950 Cover: 0.10 **NM** value: **350.00**
2 ❑ 1950 Cover: 0.10 **NM** value: **200.00**
3 ❑ 1950 Cover: 0.10 **NM** value: **200.00**
4 ❑ Oct 1950 Cover: 0.10 **NM** value: **200.00**

SMILEY'S SPRING BREAK — Chaos!
1 ❑ Apr 1999 Cover: 2.95 **NM** value: **Cover or less**

SMILEY WRESTLING SPECIAL — Chaos!
1 ❑ May 1999 Cover: 2.95 **NM** value: **Cover or less**
Circ: Diamd. preorders: **11,778**
No issue number. One-shot.

SMILIN' ED — Fantaco
1 ❑ 1982, b&w Cover: 1.25 **NM** value: **Cover or less**
A: Fred Hembeck; Raoul Vezina **W:** Raoul Vezina
2 ❑ 1982, b&w Cover: 1.25 **NM** value: **Cover or less**
A: Fred Hembeck; Raoul Vezina **W:** Raoul Vezina
3 ❑ 1982, b&w Cover: 1.25 **NM** value: **Cover or less**
A: Fred Hembeck; Raoul Vezina **W:** Raoul Vezina
4 ❑ 1982, b&w Cover: 1.25 **NM** value: **Cover or less**
A: Fred Hembeck; Raoul Vezina **W:** Raoul Vezina

SMILIN' JACK — Dell
1 ❑ Jan 1948 Cover: 0.10 **NM** value: **100.00**
2 ❑ Apr 1948 Cover: 0.10 **NM** value: **50.00**
3 ❑ Jul 1948 Cover: 0.10 **NM** value: **35.00**
4 ❑ Oct 1948 Cover: 0.10 **NM** value: **35.00**
5 ❑ Jan 1949 Cover: 0.10 **NM** value: **35.00**
• **CGC:** 1 graded, best 5.0
6 ❑ Apr 1949 Cover: 0.10 **NM** value: **35.00**
7 ❑ Jul 1949 Cover: 0.10 **NM** value: **35.00**
8 ❑ Oct 1949 Cover: 0.10 **NM** value: **35.00**

SMITH BROWN JONES — Kiwi Studios
Smith Brown Jones is a goofy send-up of 1990s X-Files culture courtesy of independent creator Jon "Bean" Hastings. Smith Brown Jones is a bumbling Everyman alien, accompanied by a disembodied floating troublemaker named Pops. They are pursued by the vaguely sinister Mel and Chuck, agents of a goofy, alien mastermind named Mr. Phtang. And that's way more than anyone needs to know about the plot, since most of the enjoyment of Smith Brown Jones comes from the Marx Brothers school of non-sequitur humor combined with an offbeat art style that, at its best, mixes equal parts Mad's Don Martin and Cerebus' Dave Sim.

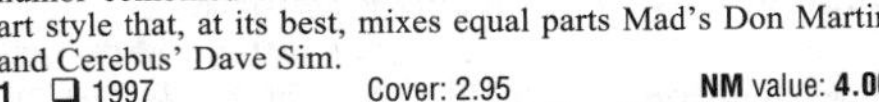

1 ❑ 1997 Cover: 2.95 **NM** value: **4.00**
A: Jon "Bean" Hastings(Bean) **W:** Jon "Bean" Hastings(Bean)
2 ❑ 1997 Cover: 2.95 **NM** value: **Cover or less**
📖 All Mirth & No Matter **A:** Jon "Bean" Hastings(Bean) **W:** Jon "Bean" Hastings(Bean)
3 ❑ 1997 Cover: 2.95 **NM** value: **Cover or less**
A: Jon "Bean" Hastings(Bean) **W:** Jon "Bean" Hastings(Bean)
4 ❑ 1998 Cover: 2.95 **NM** value: **Cover or less**
📖 We Have Met the Enemy and He is You! **A:** Jon "Bean" Hastings(Bean) **W:** Jon "Bean" Hastings(Bean)
5 ❑ 1998 Cover: 2.95 **NM** value: **Cover or less**

SMITH BROWN JONES: ALIEN ACCOUNTANT — Slave Labor
1 ❑ May 1998 Cover: 2.95 **NM** value: **Cover or less**
📖 The Hero & The Sidekick **A:** Jon "Bean" Hastings(Bean) **W:** Jon "Bean" Hastings(Bean)
2 ❑ Aug 1998 Cover: 2.95 **NM** value: **Cover or less**
📖 The Troll **A:** Jon "Bean" Hastings(Bean) **W:** Jon "Bean" Hastings(Bean)
3 ❑ Nov 1998 Cover: 2.95 **NM** value: **Cover or less**
📖 The Vampire Unicorn **A:** Jon "Bean" Hastings(Bean) **W:** Jon "Bean" Hastings(Bean)
4 ❑ Feb 1999 Cover: 2.95 **NM** value: **Cover or less**
📖 The Brother **A:** Jon "Bean" Hastings(Bean) **W:** Jon "Bean" Hastings(Bean)

SMITH BROWN JONES: HALLOWEEN SPECIAL — Slave Labor
1 ❑ Oct 1998, b&w Cover: 2.95 **NM** value: **Cover or less**

SMITTY — Dell
1 ❑ Feb 1948 Cover: 0.10 **NM** value: **55.00**
A: Walter Berndt **W:** Walter Berndt ★ Appearance of Series continued from.
2 ❑ Feb 1948 Cover: 0.10 **NM** value: **35.00**
A: Walter Berndt **W:** Walter Berndt
3 ❑ May 1948 Cover: 0.10 **NM** value: **25.00**
A: Walter Berndt **W:** Walter Berndt
4 ❑ Aug 1948 Cover: 0.10 **NM** value: **25.00**
A: Walter Berndt **W:** Walter Berndt
5 ❑ Nov 1948 Cover: 0.10 **NM** value: **25.00**
A: Walter Berndt **W:** Walter Berndt
6 ❑ Feb 1949 Cover: 0.10 **NM** value: **20.00**
A: Walter Berndt **W:** Walter Berndt
7 ❑ May 1949 Cover: 0.10 **NM** value: **20.00**
A: Walter Berndt **W:** Walter Berndt

SMOKEHOUSE FIVE — Platinum
Bk 1❑ Cover: 9.95 **NM** value: **Cover or less**
A: Sergio Aragonés

SMOOT — Skip Williamson
1 ❑ Cover: 2.95 **NM** value: **Cover or less**
📖 Snappy Sammy Smoot; Citizen Smoot; Sammy Gets Fat **A:** Skip Williamson **W:** Skip Williamson

SMURFS — Marvel
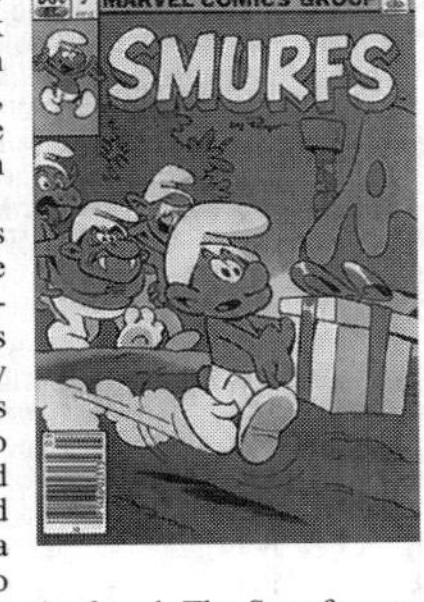

The small blue crew known as the Smurfs were a national craze back in the early 1980s. Stars of their own Saturday morning television show, they quickly began appearing in the toy stores, and on everything from lunch boxes to adhesive bandages.

For their own part, the Smurfs were an almost nauseatingly cute group of munchkins that lived peacefully in a tiny village. Each one was a bit of a character, such as Handy Smurf who would devise ingenious and overcomplicated solutions to any problem; Lazy Smurf who liked nothing better than to sit around and eat Smurfberries; wise old Papa Smurf; and Smurfette, a blonde, who mysteriously was the only female to be found. The Smurfs were constantly set upon by a mean human named Gargamel, along with his cat Azrael. Gargamel despised the Smurfs' cuteness, but all his schemes to put an end to them were inevitably foiled.

1 ❑ Dec 1982 Cover: 0.60 **NM** value: **2.00**
• **CGC:** 1 graded, best 8.5
2 ❑ Jan 1983 Cover: 0.60 **NM** value: **2.00**
• **CGC:** 1 graded, best 9.0
3 ❑ Feb 1983 Cover: 0.60 **NM** value: **2.00**
• **CGC:** 1 graded, best 9.0
Bk 1❑ Cover: 2.50 **NM** value: **4.00**
• Treasury edition. • Collects Smurfs #1-3

SMUT THE ALTERNATIVE COMIC — Wiltshire
1 ❑ Cover: 0.80 **NM** value: **3.00**

SNACK BAR — Big Town
1 ❑ Cover: 2.95 **NM** value: **Cover or less**

SNAGGLEPUSS — Gold Key
1 ❑ Oct 1962 Cover: 0.15 **NM** value: **50.00**
• **CGC:** 1 graded, best 9.0
2 ❑ Dec 1962 Cover: 0.12 **NM** value: **35.00**
3 ❑ Mar 1963 Cover: 0.12 **NM** value: **35.00**
4 ❑ Jun 1963 Cover: 0.12 **NM** value: **35.00**

SNAKE, THE — Special Studio
1 ❑ Dec 1989, b&w Cover: 3.50 **NM** value: **Cover or less**
📖 The Den of Madame Joy **A:** Ron Hobbs **W:** Dave Darrigo

SNAKE EYES — Fantagraphics
1 ❑ b&w Cover: 7.95 **NM** value: **Cover or less**
2 ❑ b&w Cover: 7.95 **NM** value: **Cover or less**
3 ❑ b&w Cover: 7.95 **NM** value: **Cover or less**

SNAK POSSE — HCOM
1 ❑ Jun 1994 Cover: 1.95 **NM** value: **Cover or less**
• 1st ap **A:** Denny Fincke **W:** David Pettigrew ★ 1st Appearance of Silky Stalker, Snak Posse, Flash, Blush, Kernel, Banana Bolt, Carrot Ship.
2 ❑ Jul 1994 Cover: 1.95 **NM** value: **Cover or less**

SNAP — Harry A. Chesler
9 ❑ ca. 1944 **NM** value: **100.00**

SNAP THE PUNK TURTLE — Super Crew
0.5 ❑ Cover: 2.25 **NM** value: **Cover or less**
A: Chris Crosby **W:** Chris Crosby

SNARF — Kitchen Sink
All issues are adults only.

Snarf is a collection of short black-and-white comic stories by some of the most offbeat talent in the field. The topics range from "The Adventures of Jesus" (as we see him puttering around the house trying to meet the utility bills) to "Raising Nancies," a takeoff on the old "Sea Monkeys" ads in comics—except that this time the cute little critter being raised is a comic-book character. Popular independent newspaper cartoonist P.S. Mueller has also contributed work to this series and a Spirit story appears in the first issue.

1 ❑ Feb 1972 Cover: 0.50**NM** value: **5.00**
2 ❑ Aug 1972 Cover: 0.50 **NM** value: **4.00**
3 ❑ Nov 1972 Cover: 0.50 **NM** value: **4.00**
A: Will Eisner(cover) **C:** Will Eisner
4 ❑ Mar 1973 Cover: 0.50 **NM** value: **4.00**
5 ❑ Mar 1974 Cover: 0.65 **NM** value: **3.00**
C: Harvey Kurtzman
6 ❑ Feb 1976 Cover: 0.75 **NM** value: **3.00**
📖 Life in the Ice and Salt Works; Crutch or Cure?; Computer Date; How The Mona Lisa Got Her Smile; Don't Rain on My Parade; Food Trip **A:** Denis Kitchen; L.B. Armstrong **C:** Richard Corben **W:** Dave Schreiner; Harvey Pekar
7 ❑ Feb 1977 Cover: 1.00 **NM** value: **3.00**
C: Art Spiegelman
8 ❑ Oct 1978 Cover: 1.00 **NM** value: **3.00**
9 ❑ Feb 1981 Cover: 1.50 **NM** value: **3.00**
10 ❑ Feb 1987 Cover: 2.00 **NM** value: **3.00**
C: Will Elder ★ Appearance of Omaha the Cat Dancer.

CGC-graded: Multiply prices above by **33 for 9.9 M • 16 for 9.8 NM/M • 7 for 9.6 NM+ • 5 for 9.4 NM • 2.5 for 9.2 NM- • 1.5 for 9.0 VF/NM**

11 ❑ Feb 1989 Cover: 2.00 **NM** value: **Cover or less**
🕮 Latex Love; Mr. Ned the Talking Gila Monster; California; The Town Where Time Went Bad; Head Case
12 ❑ Cover: 2.00 **NM** value: **Cover or less**
🕮 Raising Nancies; Uncle Mud; At Home With Jesus; The Man With The Autonomous Tongue; Waiting For Gummo; What Superman Means To Me **A:** Howard Cruse **W:** Howard Cruse
13 ❑ Cover: 2.00 **NM** value: **Cover or less**
14 ❑ Cover: 2.00 **NM** value: **Cover or less**
15 ❑ Cover: 2.50 **NM** value: **Cover or less**

SNARL — Caliber

1 ❑ b&w Cover: 2.50 **NM** value: **Cover or less**
🕮 Eaters; The Dog **A:** Kevin Atkinson **W:** Kevin Atkinson
2 ❑ b&w Cover: 2.50 **NM** value: **Cover or less**
3 ❑ b&w Cover: 2.50 **NM** value: **Cover or less**

SNIFFY THE PUP — Standard

5 ❑ ca. 1949 Cover: 0.10 **NM** value: **75.00**
6 ❑ ca. 1949 Cover: 0.10 **NM** value: **35.00**
7 ❑ ca. 1950 Cover: 0.10 **NM** value: **35.00**
8 ❑ ca. 1950 Cover: 0.10 **NM** value: **35.00**
9 ❑ ca. 1950 Cover: 0.10 **NM** value: **35.00**
10 ❑ ca. 1951 Cover: 0.10 **NM** value: **35.00**
11 ❑ ca. 1951 Cover: 0.10 **NM** value: **30.00**
12 ❑ ca. 1951 Cover: 0.10 **NM** value: **30.00**
13 ❑ ca. 1952 Cover: 0.10 **NM** value: **30.00**
14 ❑ ca. 1952 Cover: 0.10 **NM** value: **30.00**
15 ❑ ca. 1952 Cover: 0.10 **NM** value: **30.00**
16 ❑ ca. 1953 Cover: 0.10 **NM** value: **25.00**
17 ❑ ca. 1953 Cover: 0.10 **NM** value: **25.00**
18 ❑ ca. 1953 Cover: 0.10 **NM** value: **25.00**

SNOID COMICS — Kitchen Sink

Robert Crumb strikes again with this Adults Only comic dedicated to one of his most popular characters, Snoid. Brimming with hostility and hatred toward his fellow man, Snoid unleashes his unique brand of comedy on the stereotypical woman- the female who is inexplicably attracted to the man who treats her with the utmost disrespect.

Yet, the artist's attention to illustrative detail coupled with his thought-provoking social commentary manages to find its way onto pages in between. Using 12 panels and no captions/dialogue, "A Short History of America" manages to tell a centuries old tale of destruction and pollution thanks to uncontrolled urbanization. "Those Dharma Bhums" captures the plight of a modern day bohemian- one struggling to find answers, while never losing sight of the beautiful love by his side. Perhaps this Crumb isn't as perverse as some would like to think.

1 ❑ Dec 1979 Cover: 2.00 **NM** value: **Cover or less**
• **CGC:** 2 graded, best 9.2
🕮 This Cartooning is Tricky Busuness; The Snoid Goes Bohemian; Bearzy Wearzy; A Short History of America; Those Dharma Bhums; One Foot to Heaven; Among his Fellow Humans **A:** Robert Crumb **W:** Robert Crumb

SNOOPER AND BLABBER DETECTIVES — Gold Key

1 ❑ Nov 1962 Cover: 0.12 **NM** value: **75.00**
• **CGC:** 1 graded, best 7.5
2 ❑ Feb 1963 Cover: 0.12 **NM** value: **50.00**
3 ❑ May 1963 Cover: 0.12 **NM** value: **50.00**

S'NOT FOR KIDS — Vortex

1 ❑ b&w Cover: 6.95 **NM** value: **Cover or less**

SNOWMAN — Express / Entity

1 ❑ Nov 1996 Cover: 2.50 **NM** value: **5.00**
Circ: Diamd. preorders: **3,375**
🕮 Terror Eyes **A:** Matthew Martin **W:** Matthew Martin ★ 1st Appearance of Snowman.
1/A ❑ 1996 Cover: 2.50 **NM** value: **6.00**
variant cover. 🕮 Terror Eyes **A:** Matthew Martin; Ethan Van Sciver(cover) **W:** Matthew Martin ★ 1st Appearance of Snowman.
1-2 ❑ 1996b&w Cover: 2.50 **NM** value: **Cover or less**
2 ❑ 1996 Cover: 2.50 **NM** value: **4.00**
2/A ❑ 1996 Cover: 2.50 **NM** value: **5.00**
variant cover.
2-2 ❑ 1996 Cover: 2.50 **NM** value: **Cover or less**
3 ❑ 1996 Cover: 2.50 **NM** value: **3.00**
3/A ❑ 1996 Cover: 2.50 **NM** value: **3.00**
variant cover.

SNOW WHITE — Marvel

1 ❑ Jan 1995 Cover: 1.95 **NM** value: **2.00**
Circ: CapCity orders: **12,175**
No issue number. • lead story is reprint of Dell Four Color #49

SNOW WHITE AND THE SEVEN DWARFS (WALT DISNEY'S...) — Gladstone

1 ❑ Cover: 2.95 **NM** value: **3.50**
Circ: CapCity orders: **4,550**
🕮 The Many Faces f Snow White; Three Faces of Snow White and Tenggren's Evil Witch; The Tenggren Gallery; Whatever Happened to Prince Bucketheead?; Snow White and the Seven Dwarfs-The Sunday Pages **A:** Ron Dias

SNUFF — Boneyard

All issues are adults only.
1 ❑ May 1997, b&w Cover: 2.95 **NM** value: **Cover or less**

SOB: SPECIAL OPERATIONS BRANCH — Promethean

1 ❑ May 1994, b&w Cover: 2.25 **NM** value: **Cover or less**
★ 1st Appearance of SOB, Polymorph, Ferret (Prometheus), Orion (Major James T. Greene), Bandwidth. ★ Death of Bandwidth.

SOCKETEER, THE — Kardia

1 ❑ b&w Cover: 2.25 **NM** value: **Cover or less**
• parody

SOCK MONKEY — Dark Horse

Remember those sock monkeys? Homemade stuffed animals from your youth? Well, Tony Millionaire brought a bit of that youth into the 1990s with an animated and jovial sock-monkey adventurer. Sock Monkey (dubbed Uncle Gabby) and his restless companion, the Crow, live in a world in which toys sing and play while people are away. It's a thoroughly odd and puzzling mini-series, since Uncle Gabby and Crow speak with intelligence but display none of that intelligence in their actions. The art has a minimalist tone and the plots could benefit from more character definition, but readers who enjoy bizarre and offbeat humor will be singing its virtues to the masses and nominating it for awards. The scripting is reminiscent of that by Winsor McCay, and those who dislike whimsical comics probably won't enjoy Millionaire's fantasy world.

1 ❑ Sep 1998, b&w Cover: 2.95 **NM** value: **Cover or less**
Circ: Diamd. preorders: **4,006**
2 ❑ Oct 1998, b&w Cover: 2.95 **NM** value: **Cover or less**
Circ: Diamd. preorders: **3,066**

SOCK MONKEY (TONY MILLIONAIRE'S...) — Dark Horse / Maverick

1 ❑ Jul 1999, b&w Cover: 2.95 **NM** value: **Cover or less**
Circ: Diamd. preorders: **6,190**
A: Tony Millionaire **W:** Tony Millionaire
2 ❑ Aug 1999, b&w Cover: 2.95 **NM** value: **Cover or less**
Circ: Diamd. preorders: **5,499**
A: Tony Millionaire **W:** Tony Millionaire

SOCK MONKEY (VOL. 3) (TONY MILLIONAIRE'S...) — Dark Horse / Maverick

1 ❑ Nov 2000 Cover: 2.99 **NM** value: **Cover or less**
Circ: Diamd. preorders: **6,272**
A: Tony Millionaire **W:** Tony Millionaire
2 ❑ Dec 2000 Cover: 2.99 **NM** value: **Cover or less**
Circ: Diamd. preorders: **5,580**
A: Tony Millionaire **W:** Tony Millionaire

SO DARK THE ROSE — CFD

1 ❑ Oct 1995 Cover: 2.95 **NM** value: **Cover or less**
• **CGC:** 1 graded, best 9.4
No issue number.

SOFA JET CITY CRISIS — Visual Assault

1 ❑ b&w Cover: 6.95 **NM** value: **Cover or less**
No issue number.

S.O.F.T. CORPS — Spoof

1 ❑ Cover: 2.95 **NM** value: **Cover or less**
A: Allan Jacobsen **W:** Mike Halbleib

SOJOURN — Dreamer

1 ❑ May 1998 Cover: 2.95 **NM** value: **Cover or less**
Circ: Diamd. preorders: **25,846**
2 ❑ Cover: 2.10 **NM** value: **Cover or less**
3 ❑ Cover: 2.10 **NM** value: **Cover or less**
4 ❑ Cover: 2.10 **NM** value: **Cover or less**
5 ❑ Cover: 2.10 **NM** value: **Cover or less**
6 ❑ Cover: 3.15 **NM** value: **Cover or less**
7 ❑ Cover: 3.15 **NM** value: **Cover or less**
8 ❑ Cover: 3.15 **NM** value: **Cover or less**
9 ❑ Cover: 3.15 **NM** value: **Cover or less**
10 ❑ Cover: 3.15 **NM** value: **Cover or less**

SOJOURN (CROSSGEN) — CrossGen

1 ❑ Aug 2001 Cover: 2.95 **NM** value: **Cover or less**
• **CGC:** 11 graded, best 9.8
2 ❑ Sep 2001 Cover: 2.95 **NM** value: **Cover or less**
• **CGC:** 1 graded, best 9.6
3 ❑ Oct 2001 Cover: 2.95 **NM** value: **Cover or less**
• **CGC:** 1 graded, best 9.6
4 ❑ Nov 2001 Cover: 2.95 **NM** value: **Cover or less**
5 ❑ Dec 2001 Cover: 2.95 **NM** value: **Cover or less**
6 ❑ Jan 2002 Cover: 2.95 **NM** value: **Cover or less**
7 ❑ Feb 2002 Cover: 2.95 **NM** value: **Cover or less**
8 ❑ Mar 2002 Cover: 2.95 **NM** value: **Cover or less**
SE 1 ❑ Sep 2001 Cover: 3.95 **NM** value: **Cover or less**
• Collects Prequel and #1

SOLAR LORD — Image

1 ❑ Mar 1999 Cover: 2.50 **NM** value: **Cover or less**
Circ: Diamd. preorders: **14,026**
A: Khoo Fuk Lung **W:** Khoo Fuk Lung; James D. Hudnall
2 ❑ Apr 1999 Cover: 2.50 **NM** value: **Cover or less**
Circ: Diamd. preorders: **9,483**
A: Khoo Fuk Lung **W:** Khoo Fuk Lung; James D. Hudnall
3 ❑ May 1999 Cover: 2.50 **NM** value: **Cover or less**
Circ: Diamd. preorders: **8,998**
A: Khoo Fuk Lung **W:** Khoo Fuk Lung; James D. Hudnall
4 ❑ Jun 1999 Cover: 2.50 **NM** value: **Cover or less**
Circ: Diamd. preorders: **10,014**
A: Khoo Fuk Lung **W:** Khoo Fuk Lung; James D. Hudnall
5 ❑ Jul 1999 Cover: 2.50 **NM** value: **Cover or less**
Circ: Diamd. preorders: **8,720**
A: Khoo Fuk Lung **W:** Khoo Fuk Lung; James D. Hudnall
6 ❑ Aug 1999 Cover: 2.50 **NM** value: **Cover or less**
Circ: Diamd. preorders: **7,860**
A: Khoo Fuk Lung **W:** Khoo Fuk Lung; James D. Hudnall
7 ❑ Sep 1999 Cover: 2.50 **NM** value: **Cover or less**
Circ: Diamd. preorders: **7,085**
A: Khoo Fuk Lung **W:** Khoo Fuk Lung; James D. Hudnall

SOLARMAN — Marvel

1 ❑ Jan 1989 Cover: 1.00 **NM** value: **Cover or less**
Circ: CapCity orders: **11,000**
🕮 Star Burst! **A:** Jim Mooney **W:** Stan Lee ★ Origin of Solarman.
2 ❑ May 1990 Cover: 1.00 **NM** value: **Cover or less**
Circ: CapCity orders: **14,200**
🕮 This Silent Death, This Hostage Earth **A:** Mike Zeck **W:** Stan Lee

SOLAR, MAN OF THE ATOM — Valiant

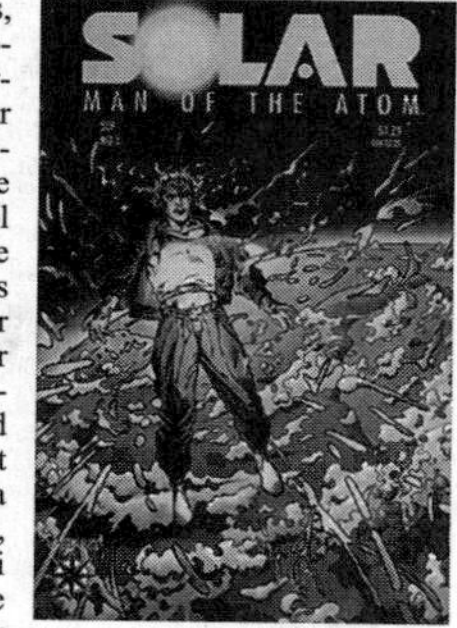

With the success of its Magnus, Robot Fighter series, Valiant updated the first Gold Key superhero with this series. Doctor Solar is Dr. Phil Saleski, an atomic scientist chosen by fate to receive the awesome power to control matter on the atomic level. The same accident that gave him his powers also gave Erica Pierce her powers — which she would later use to destroy Solar in Unity. Solar's strange story is complicated by the fact that Phil Saleski first appeared from the future in a black hole of his own creation, later merging into the Phil Saleski from the current day. The future Saleski had inadvertently brought about terrible tragedy in his day and could only hope that he can avoid making the same mistakes in this, his second chance.

Saleski now lives in Cupertino, California, with his girlfriend, Gayle. He has had to leave those quiet surroundings frequently, however, to do battle with everyone from the Harbinger corporation to a race of spider-aliens, determined to feed on all of mankind.

1 ❑ Sep 1991 Cover: 1.75 **NM** value: **3.00**
Circ: CapCity orders: **14,800** • **CGC:** 10 graded, best 9.6
🕮 Second Death, Part 1 **A:** Barry Windsor-Smith ★ Origin of Solar.
2 ❑ Oct 1991 Cover: 1.75 **NM** value: **2.00**
Circ: CapCity orders: **11,200**
🕮 Second Death, Part 2 **A:** Barry Windsor-Smith ★ Origin of Solar.
3 ❑ Nov 1991 Cover: 1.75 **NM** value: **2.00**
Circ: CapCity orders: **12,700** • **CGC:** 2 graded, best 9.4
🕮 Second Death, Part 3 **A:** Barry Windsor-Smith ★ Origin of Solar. ★ 1st Appearance of Toyo Harada, Harbinger Foundation.
4 ❑ Dec 1991 Cover: 1.75 **NM** value: **2.00**
Circ: CapCity orders: **13,000**
🕮 Second Death, Part 4 **A:** Barry Windsor-Smith ★ Origin of Solar.
5 ❑ Jan 1992 Cover: 1.95 **NM** value: **2.00**
Circ: CapCity orders: **14,000**
A: Barry Windsor-Smith
6 ❑ Feb 1992 Cover: 1.95 **NM** value: **2.00**
Circ: CapCity orders: **13,100**
A: Barry Windsor-Smith ★ Versus Spider-Aliens.
7 ❑ Mar 1992 Cover: 1.95 **NM** value: **2.00**
Circ: CapCity orders: **11,500**
A: Barry Windsor-Smith ★ Versus X-O armor.
8 ❑ Apr 1992 Cover: 2.25 **NM** value: **Cover or less**
Circ: CapCity orders: **11,400**
A: Barry Windsor-Smith
9 ❑ May 1992 Cover: 2.25 **NM** value: **Cover or less**
Circ: CapCity orders: **10,300**
A: Barry Windsor-Smith
10 ❑ Jun 1992 Cover: 3.95 **NM** value: **4.00**
Circ: CapCity orders: **11,300** • **CGC:** 3 graded, best 9.4
All-black embossed cover. **A:** Barry Windsor-Smith **C:** Barry Windsor-Smith ★ 1st Appearance of Eternal Warrior (cameo).
10-2 ❑ Cover: 3.95 **NM** value: **Cover or less**
11 ❑ Jul 1992 Cover: 2.25 **NM** value: **2.50**
Circ: CapCity orders: **12,100**
★ 1st Appearance of Eternal Warrior (full appearance).
12 ❑ Aug 1992 Cover: 2.25 **NM** value: **2.50**
Circ: CapCity orders: **26,950**
🕮 Unity, Part 9 • Unity **A:** Frank Miller(cover) **C:** Frank Miller
13 ❑ Sep 1992 Cover: 2.25 **NM** value: **2.50**
Circ: CapCity orders: **31,300**
🕮 Unity, Part 17 • Unity **C:** Walt Simonson
14 ❑ Oct 1992 Cover: 2.25 **NM** value: **Cover or less**
Circ: CapCity orders: **19,200**
★ 1st Appearance of Fred Bender.
15 ❑ Nov 1992 Cover: 2.25 **NM** value: **Cover or less**
Circ: CapCity orders: **18,800**
16 ❑ Dec 1992 Cover: 2.25 **NM** value: **Cover or less**
Circ: CapCity orders: **18,400**
★ Death of Lyja (Valiant).
17 ❑ Jan 1993 Cover: 2.25 **NM** value: **Cover or less**
Circ: CapCity orders: **21,700**
🕮 Seed of Destruction, Part 3 ★ Appearance of X-O Manowar.

Other grades: Multiply prices above by **1.5 for Mint • 2/3 for Very Fine • 1/3 for Fine • 1/5 for Very Good • 1/8 for Good**

18 ❑ Feb 1993 Cover: 2.25 **NM** value: **Cover or less**
Circ: CapCity orders: **24,425**

19 ❑ Mar 1993 Cover: 2.25 **NM** value: **Cover or less**
Circ: CapCity orders: **30,900**
Virtually Real **A:** Peter Grau **W:** Kevin VanHook

20 ❑ Apr 1993 Cover: 2.25 **NM** value: **Cover or less**
Circ: CapCity orders: **40,200**

21 ❑ May 1993 Cover: 2.25 **NM** value: **Cover or less**
Circ: CapCity orders: **51,300**
Afraid of the Darque, Part 1 ★ Versus Master Darque.

22 ❑ Jun 1993 Cover: 2.25 **NM** value: **Cover or less**
Circ: CapCity orders: **64,500**
Afraid of the Darque, Part 2; Where Do Gods Go to Pray? **A:** Peter Grau **W:** Kevin VanHook ★ Versus Master Darque.

23 ❑ Jul 1993 Cover: 2.25 **NM** value: **Cover or less**
Circ: CapCity orders: **80,500**
Afraid of the Darque, Part 3; Split Decision **A:** Peter Grau **W:** Kevin VanHook ★ 1st Appearance of Solar the Destroyer.

24 ❑ Aug 1993 Cover: 2.25 **NM** value: **Cover or less**
Circ: CapCity orders: **65,300**
Half a Man **A:** Peter Grau **C:** Mike Mignola **W:** Kevin VanHook

25 ❑ Sep 1993 Cover: 2.25 **NM** value: **Cover or less**
Circ: CapCity orders: **74,600**
Solar Eclipse • Secret Weapons x-over **A:** Peter Grau **W:** Kevin VanHook ★ Versus Doctor Eclipse.

26 ❑ Oct 1993 Cover: 2.25 **NM** value: **Cover or less**
Circ: CapCity orders: **47,600**

27 ❑ Nov 1993 Cover: 2.25 **NM** value: **Cover or less**
Circ: CapCity orders: **42,325**
Awake in the Dreamtime **A:** Peter Grau **W:** Kevin VanHook

28 ❑ Dec 1993 Cover: 2.25 **NM** value: **Cover or less**
Circ: CapCity orders: **39,175**
• Solar the Destroyer vs. spiders

29 ❑ Jan 1994 Cover: 2.25 **NM** value: **Cover or less**
Circ: CapCity orders: **49,200**
• Valiant Vision

30 ❑ Feb 1994 Cover: 2.25 **NM** value: **Cover or less**
Circ: CapCity orders: **31,850**

31 ❑ Mar 1994 Cover: 2.25 **NM** value: **Cover or less**
Circ: CapCity orders: **26,000**

32 ❑ Apr 1994 Cover: 2.25 **NM** value: **Cover or less**
Circ: CapCity orders: **22,125**

33 ❑ May 1994 Cover: 2.25 **NM** value: **Cover or less**
Circ: CapCity orders: **29,500**
• Valiant Vision; trading card

34 ❑ Jun 1994 Cover: 2.25 **NM** value: **Cover or less**
Circ: CapCity orders: **20,925**
• Valiant Vision

35 ❑ Aug 1994 Cover: 2.25 **NM** value: **Cover or less**
Circ: CapCity orders: **21,300**
• Valiant Vision

36 ❑ Sep 1994 Cover: 2.25 **NM** value: **Cover or less**
Circ: CapCity orders: **17,450**
Revenge Times Two, Part 1 ★ Versus Ravenus. ★ Versus Doctor Eclipse.

37 ❑ Oct 1994 Cover: 2.25 **NM** value: **Cover or less**
Circ: CapCity orders: **16,350**
Revenge Times Two, Part 2 ★ Versus Ravenus. ★ Versus Doctor Eclipse.

38 ❑ Nov 1994 Cover: 2.25 **NM** value: **Cover or less**
Circ: CapCity orders: **21,700**
The Chaos Effect: Epsilon, Part 1 • Chaos Effect

39 ❑ Dec 1994 Cover: 2.25 **NM** value: **Cover or less**
Circ: CapCity orders: **13,525**

40 ❑ Jan 1995 Cover: 2.25 **NM** value: **Cover or less**
Circ: CapCity orders: **12,050**

41 ❑ Feb 1995 Cover: 2.25 **NM** value: **Cover or less**
Circ: CapCity orders: **11,050**

42 ❑ Mar 1995 Cover: 2.25 **NM** value: **Cover or less**
Circ: CapCity orders: **9,650**
Elements of Evil, Part 1

43 ❑ Apr 1995 Cover: 2.25 **NM** value: **Cover or less**
Circ: CapCity orders: **8,700**
Elements of Evil, Part 2

44 ❑ May 1995 Cover: 2.25 **NM** value: **Cover or less**
Circ: CapCity orders: **7,700**

45 ❑ Jun 1995 Cover: 2.25 **NM** value: **Cover or less**
Circ: CapCity orders: **6,800**

46 ❑ Jul 1995 Cover: 2.50 **NM** value: **Cover or less**
Circ: CapCity orders: **8,750**
A: Dick Giordano; Dan Jurgens

47 ❑ Aug 1995 Cover: 2.50 **NM** value: **Cover or less**
Circ: CapCity orders: **7,700**
A: Dick Giordano; Dan Jurgens

48 ❑ Sep 1995 Cover: 2.50 **NM** value: **Cover or less**
Circ: CapCity orders: **7,950**
A: Dick Giordano; Dan Jurgens

49 ❑ Sep 1995 Cover: 2.50 **NM** value: **Cover or less**
A: Dick Giordano; Dan Jurgens

50 ❑ Oct 1995 Cover: 2.50 **NM** value: **Cover or less**
Circ: CapCity orders: **9,400**
A: Dick Giordano; Dan Jurgens

51 ❑ Nov 1995 Cover: 2.50 **NM** value: **Cover or less**
Circ: CapCity orders: **7,850**
A: Dick Giordano; Dan Jurgens

52 ❑ Nov 1995 Cover: 2.50 **NM** value: **Cover or less**
Circ: CapCity orders: **7,800**
A: Dick Giordano; Dan Jurgens

53 ❑ Dec 1995 Cover: 2.50 **NM** value: **Cover or less**
Circ: CapCity orders: **6,775**
A: Dick Giordano; Dan Jurgens

54 ❑ Dec 1995 Cover: 2.50 **NM** value: **Cover or less**
Circ: CapCity orders: **6,750**
A: Dick Giordano; Dan Jurgens

55 ❑ Jan 1996 Cover: 2.50 **NM** value: **Cover or less**
Circ: CapCity orders: **5,425**

56 ❑ Jan 1996 Cover: 2.50 **NM** value: **Cover or less**
Circ: CapCity orders: **5,425**

57 ❑ Feb 1996 Cover: 2.50 **NM** value: **Cover or less**

58 ❑ Feb 1996 Cover: 2.50 **NM** value: **Cover or less**

59 ❑ Mar 1996 Cover: 2.50 **NM** value: **Cover or less**
• Texas destroyed

60 ❑ Apr 1996 Cover: 2.50 **NM** value: **Cover or less**

36801❑ Cover: 3.95 **NM** value: **Cover or less**

Bk 1❑ Cover: 9.95 **NM** value: **Cover or less**
Alpha and Omega • "Second Death" trade paperback; Reprints Solar, Man of the Atom #1-4

SOLAR, MAN OF THE ATOM-HELL ON EARTH — Acclaim

1 ❑ Jan 1998 Cover: 2.50 **NM** value: **Cover or less**
Circ: Diamd. preorders: **14,091**
Domino **A:** Patrick Zircher **W:** Christopher Priest

2 ❑ Feb 1998 Cover: 2.50 **NM** value: **Cover or less**
Circ: Diamd. preorders: **11,896**
A: Patrick Zircher **W:** Christopher Priest

3 ❑ Mar 1998 Cover: 2.50 **NM** value: **Cover or less**
Circ: Diamd. preorders: **11,020**
A: Patrick Zircher **W:** Christopher Priest

4 ❑ Apr 1998 Cover: 2.50 **NM** value: **Cover or less**
Circ: Diamd. preorders: **10,696**
A: Patrick Zircher **W:** Christopher Priest

SOLAR, MAN OF THE ATOM-REVELATIONS — Acclaim

1 ❑ Nov 1997 Cover: 3.95 **NM** value: **Cover or less**
One-shot.

SOLAR, MAN OF THE ATOM (VOL. 2) — Acclaim / Valiant

1 ❑ May 1997 Cover: 3.95 **NM** value: **Cover or less**
No issue number. One-shot. • lays groundwork for second Valiant universe **A:** Darick Robertson **W:** Warren Ellis

SOLAR STELLA — Sirius

1 ❑ Aug 2000, b&w Cover: 2.95 **NM** value: **Cover or less**
Circ: Diamd. preorders: **2,099**
One-shot. Solar Stella meets the Dark Master **A:** J. Bone **W:** J. Bone

SOLDIER & MARINE COMICS — Charlton

9 ❑ ca. 1955 Cover: 0.10 **NM** value: **50.00**
11 ❑ Dec 1954 Cover: 0.10 **NM** value: **30.00**
12 ❑ Feb 1955 Cover: 0.10 **NM** value: **30.00**
13 ❑ Apr 1955 Cover: 0.10 **NM** value: **25.00**
14 ❑ Jun 1955 Cover: 0.10 **NM** value: **25.00**
15 ❑ Aug 1955 Cover: 0.10 **NM** value: **25.00**

SOLDIER COMICS — Fawcett

1 ❑ Jan 1952 Cover: 0.10 **NM** value: **55.00**
2 ❑ Mar 1952 Cover: 0.10 **NM** value: **30.00**
3 ❑ May 1952 Cover: 0.10 **NM** value: **30.00**
This is How It Is; Whippersnappers...Camp Life!; Most and Least; I'll Take You Home, Kathleen; Pvt. Salter; Spy Jinks (text); That Makes Us Even! **W:** John Martin
4 ❑ Jul 1952 Cover: 0.10 **NM** value: **25.00**
• **CGC:** 1 graded, best 8.5
5 ❑ Sep 1952 Cover: 0.10 **NM** value: **25.00**
6 ❑ Nov 1952 Cover: 0.10 **NM** value: **16.00**
7 ❑ Jan 1953 Cover: 0.10 **NM** value: **16.00**
8 ❑ Mar 1953 Cover: 0.10 **NM** value: **16.00**
9 ❑ May 1953 Cover: 0.10 **NM** value: **16.00**
10 ❑ Jul 1953 Cover: 0.10 **NM** value: **16.00**
11 ❑ Sep 1953 Cover: 0.10 **NM** value: **16.00**
final issue.

SOLDIERS OF FORTUNE — ACG

1 ❑ Mar 1952 Cover: 0.10 **NM** value: **150.00**
2 ❑ May 1952 Cover: 0.10 **NM** value: **75.00**
• Captain Crossbones; Lance Larson; Ace Carter
3 ❑ Jul 1952 Cover: 0.10 **NM** value: **60.00**
4 ❑ Sep 1952 Cover: 0.10 **NM** value: **60.00**
5 ❑ Nov 1952 Cover: 0.10 **NM** value: **60.00**
6 ❑ Feb 1953 Cover: 0.10 **NM** value: **50.00**
7 ❑ Apr 1953 Cover: 0.10 **NM** value: **50.00**
8 ❑ Jun 1953 Cover: 0.10 **NM** value: **50.00**
9 ❑ Aug 1953 Cover: 0.10 **NM** value: **50.00**
10 ❑ Oct 1953 Cover: 0.10 **NM** value: **50.00**
11 ❑ Dec 1953 Cover: 0.10 **NM** value: **35.00**
12 ❑ Feb 1954 Cover: 0.10 **NM** value: **35.00**
13 ❑ Apr 1954 Cover: 0.10 **NM** value: **35.00**

SOLDIERS OF FREEDOM — AC

1 ❑ Jul 1987 Cover: 1.75 **NM** value: **Cover or less**
Circ: CapCity orders: **3,325**
2 ❑ Aug 1987 Cover: 1.95 **NM** value: **Cover or less**

SOLD OUT — Fantaco

1 ❑ Cover: 1.50 **NM** value: **Cover or less**
A: John M. Hebert **W:** Augustus Mattick III; Roger Green; Tom Skulan
2 ❑ Cover: 1.50 **NM** value: **Cover or less**

SOLITAIRE — Malibu / Ultraverse

1 ❑ Nov 1993 Cover: 1.95 **NM** value: **2.00**
Circ: CapCity orders: **35,275**
The Pleasure Principle • Comes polybagged with one of 4 "ace" trading cards **A:** Jeff Johnson **W:** Gerard Jones ★ 1st Appearance of Solitaire.

1/CS❑ Nov 1993 **NM** value: **2.50**
Circ: CapCity orders: **4,150**
• trading card

2 ❑ Dec 1993 Cover: 1.95 **NM** value: **2.00**
Circ: CapCity orders: **21,350**
Break-Thru • Break-Thru **A:** Jeff Johnson **W:** Gerard Jones

3 ❑ Feb 1994 Cover: 1.95 **NM** value: **2.00**
Circ: CapCity orders: **17,350**
Curse of the Monkey Woman **A:** Patrick Rolo **W:** Gerard Jones ★ Origin of Night Man.

4 ❑ Mar 1994 Cover: 1.95 **NM** value: **2.00**
Circ: CapCity orders: **13,775**
Bad Monkey **A:** Jeff Johnson **W:** Gerard Jones ★ Origin of Solitaire.

5 ❑ Apr 1994 Cover: 1.95 **NM** value: **2.00**
Circ: CapCity orders: **13,000**
Even In Death **A:** Jeff Johnson **W:** Gerard Jones

6 ❑ May 1994 Cover: 1.95 **NM** value: **Cover or less**
Circ: CapCity orders: **12,025**
W: Gerard Jones

7 ❑ Sep 1994 Cover: 1.95 **NM** value: **Cover or less**
Circ: CapCity orders: **11,150**
On the Edge **A:** Jeff Parker; J.B. Jones; Sam Liu(cover) **W:** Gerard Jones; Julie Huffman ★ 1st Appearance of Double Edge.

8 ❑ Sep 1994 Cover: 1.95 **NM** value: **Cover or less**
Circ: CapCity orders: **9,925**
Criss-Cross **A:** Jeff Parker; Mike Wieringo(cover) **W:** Gerard Jones ★ 1st Appearance of The Degenerate.

9 ❑ Sep 1994 Cover: 1.95 **NM** value: **Cover or less**
Circ: CapCity orders: **8,850**
Talkin' 'Bout My Degeneration **A:** Jeff Parker **W:** Gerard Jones ★ Death of The Degenerate.

10 ❑ Oct 1994 Cover: 1.95 **NM** value: **Cover or less**
Circ: CapCity orders: **7,975**
Hostile Takeover; Hostile Takeover, Part 2 **A:** Jeff Parker; Ernie Stiner; Scott Kolins(cover) **W:** Gerard Jones

11 ❑ Nov 1994 Cover: 1.95 **NM** value: **Cover or less**
Circ: CapCity orders: **7,200**
Whose Life is It? **A:** Jeff Parker; Scott Kolins(cover) **W:** Gerard Jones

12 ❑ Dec 1994 Cover: 1.95 **NM** value: **Cover or less**
Circ: CapCity orders: **3,675**
Womb of Fire final issue. **A:** Jeff Parker; Scott Kolins(cover) **W:** Gerard Jones ★ Death of Jinn. ★ Death of Anton Lone.

SOLO AVENGERS — Marvel

1 ❑ Dec 1987 Cover: 0.75 **NM** value: **1.00**
Circ: CapCity orders: **38,200**
Here Comes Hawkeye • I.D. card; 1st solo Mockingbird story **A:** Mark D. Bright **W:** Tom DeFalco

2 ❑ Jan 1988 Cover: 0.75 **NM** value: **1.00**
Circ: CapCity orders: **32,100**
• Captain Marvel

3 ❑ Feb 1988 Cover: 0.75 **NM** value: **1.00**
Circ: CapCity orders: **31,200**
• Moon Knight vs. Shroud ★ Versus Batroc.

4 ❑ Mar 1988 Cover: 0.75 **NM** value: **1.00**
Circ: CapCity orders: **29,800**
• Black Knight

5 ❑ Apr 1988 Cover: 0.75 **NM** value: **1.00**
Circ: CapCity orders: **27,000**
• Scarlet Witch

6 ❑ May 1988 Cover: 0.75 **NM** value: **1.00**
Circ: CapCity orders: **24,600**
• Falcon

7 ❑ Jun 1988 Cover: 0.75 **NM** value: **1.00**
Circ: CapCity orders: **23,000**
• Black Widow

8 ❑ Jul 1988 Cover: 0.75 **NM** value: **1.00**
Circ: CapCity orders: **22,900**
• Hank Pym

9 ❑ Aug 1988 Cover: 0.75 **NM** value: **1.00**
Circ: CapCity orders: **22,200**
• Hellcat

10 ❑ Sep 1988 Cover: 0.75 **NM** value: **1.00**
Circ: CapCity orders: **22,100**
• Doctor Druid

11 ❑ Oct 1988 Cover: 0.75 **NM** value: **1.00**
Circ: CapCity orders: **21,500**
• Hercules

12 ❑ Nov 1988 Cover: 0.75 **NM** value: **1.00**
Circ: CapCity orders: **20,500**

13 ❑ Dec 1988 Cover: 0.75 **NM** value: **1.00**
Circ: CapCity orders: **20,200**
• Wonder Man

14 ❑ Jan 1989 Cover: 0.75 **NM** value: **1.00**
Circ: CapCity orders: **19,600**
• Black Widow

15 ❑ Feb 1989 Cover: 0.75 **NM** value: **1.00**
Circ: CapCity orders: **18,000**

16 ❑ Mar 1989 Cover: 0.75 **NM** value: **1.00**
Circ: CapCity orders: **17,750**
• Moondragon

17 ❑ Apr 1989 Cover: 0.75 **NM** value: **1.00**
• Sub-Mariner

18 ❑ May 1989 Cover: 0.75 **NM** value: **1.00**
• Moondragon

19 ❑ Jun 1989 Cover: 0.75 **NM** value: **1.00**
• Black Panther

20 ❑ Jul 1989 Cover: 0.75 **NM** value: **1.00**
• Moondragon; series continues as Avengers Spotlight

SOLO (DARK HORSE) — Dark Horse

1 ❑ Jul 1996 Cover: 2.50 **NM** value: **Cover or less**
A: Shannon-Gallant **W:** Rick Geary
2 ❑ Aug 1996 Cover: 2.50 **NM** value: **Cover or less**
final issue. **A:** Shannon-Gallant **W:** Rick Geary

SOLO EX-MUTANTS — Eternity

1 ❑ 1987 Cover: 1.95 **NM** value: **2.00**
2 ❑ Feb 1988 Cover: 1.95 **NM** value: **2.00**
3 ❑ Apr 1988 Cover: 1.95 **NM** value: **2.00**
4 ❑ 1988 Cover: 1.95 **NM** value: **2.00**

CGC-graded: Multiply prices above by **33 for 9.9 M • 16 for 9.8 NM/M • 7 for 9.6 NM+ • 5 for 9.4 NM • 2.5 for 9.2 NM- • 1.5 for 9.0 VF/NM**

5 ❑ 1988 Cover: 1.95 **NM** value: **2.00**
6 ❑ Jan 1989 Cover: 1.95 **NM** value: **2.00**

SOLO (MARVEL) — Marvel

1 ❑ Sep 1994 Cover: 1.75 **NM** value: **Cover or less**
Circ: CapCity orders: **18,600**
📖 Blood Of The Hunted, Part 1 **A:** Ron Randall **W:** Eric Fein ★ Origin of Solo.
2 ❑ Oct 1994 Cover: 1.75 **NM** value: **Cover or less**
Circ: CapCity orders: **12,000**
📖 Blood Of The Hunted, Part 2 **A:** Ron Randall **W:** Eric Fein
3 ❑ Nov 1994 Cover: 1.75 **NM** value: **Cover or less**
Circ: CapCity orders: **9,400**
📖 Blood Of The Hunted, Part 3 **A:** Ron Randall **W:** Eric Fein
4 ❑ Dec 1994 Cover: 1.75 **NM** value: **Cover or less**
Circ: CapCity orders: **8,200**
📖 Blood Of The Hunted, Part 4 final issue. **A:** Ron Randall **W:** Eric Fein

SOLOMON KANE — Marvel

1 ❑ Sep 1985 Cover: 1.25 **NM** value: **1.50**
Circ: CapCity orders: **12,600**
• Double-size. 📖 Red Shadows **A:** Steve Carr; Bret Blevins **W:** Ralph Macchio
2 ❑ Nov 1985 Cover: 0.65 **NM** value: **1.25**
Circ: CapCity orders: **11,200**
📖 And Faith, Undying… **A:** Bret Blevins **W:** Ralph Macchio
3 ❑ Jan 1986 Cover: 0.65 **NM** value: **1.25**
Circ: CapCity orders: **9,100**
📖 Blades Of The Brotherhood **A:** Bret Blevins **W:** Ralph Macchio
4 ❑ Mar 1986 Cover: 0.75 **NM** value: **1.25**
Circ: CapCity orders: **8,500**
📖 The Prophet **A:** Mike Mignola **W:** Ralph Macchio
5 ❑ May 1986 Cover: 0.75 **NM** value: **1.25**
Circ: CapCity orders: **8,200**
📖 Hills Of The Dead **A:** Jon Bogdanove **W:** Ralph Macchio
6 ❑ Jul 1986 Cover: 0.75 **NM** value: **1.25**
Circ: CapCity orders: **8,200**
A: Al Williamson **W:** Ralph Macchio

SOLOMON KANE IN 3-D — Blackthorne

1 ❑ Cover: 2.50 **NM** value: **Cover or less**
Circ: CapCity orders: **950**

SOLSON CHRISTMAS SPECIAL — Solson

1 ❑ ca. 1986 **NM** value: **3.00**
• **CGC:** 1 graded, best 9.4
• Samurai Santa; 1st Jim Lee art **A:** Jim Lee

SOLSON'S COMIC TALENT STARSEARCH — Solson

1 ❑ Cover: 1.50 **NM** value: **Cover or less**
A: John Holiwski **W:** John Holiwski
2 ❑ Cover: 1.50 **NM** value: **Cover or less**

SOLUTION, THE — Malibu / Ultraverse

If you've got a problem, this team is the solution. The Solution is a quartet of ultra-powered heroes for hire. Their roster consists of martial artist Dropkick; alien sorceress Shadowmage; Outrage, a shape-changing member of the Darkulon race; and team leader Lela Cho, a.k.a. Tech, a capable fighter who also possesses the ability to control machines through "wetware" implanted in her skull. Lela has been using the Solution to wage war against the Dragon Fang, a gang of criminals who stole her previous company.

In addition to pursuing Cho's vendetta, the Solution specializes in tackling cases that are too rough-or too weird-for conventional handling. The series begins as the Solution tries to stop a group of ultras from stealing nuclear warheads from bases around the world.

0 ❑ Jan 1994 **NM** value: **2.50**
no cover price. • Promotional (coupon redemption) edition. **A:** Darick Robertson **W:** James D. Hudnall
1 ❑ Sep 1993 Cover: 1.95 **NM** value: **2.00**
Circ: CapCity orders: **29,450**
📖 The Problem •; **A:** Darick Robertson **W:** James D. Hudnall ★ 1st Appearance of Quattro, The Solution, Outrage, Dropkick, Tech, Shadowmage.
1/LE❑ Sep 1993 Cover: 1.95 **NM** value: **3.00**
• Ultra-Limited foil edition. 📖 The Problem •; **A:** Darick Robertson **W:** James D. Hudnall ★ 1st Appearance of Quattro, The Solution, Outrage, Dropkick, Tech, Shadowmage.
2 ❑ Oct 1993 Cover: 2.50 **NM** value: **Cover or less**
Circ: CapCity orders: **28,350**
📖 Rune, Part K • Rune **A:** Barry Windsor-Smith; Darick Robertson **W:** James D. Hudnall
3 ❑ Nov 1993 Cover: 1.95 **NM** value: **2.00**
Circ: CapCity orders: **20,100**
📖 The Hunted **A:** Darick Robertson **W:** James D. Hudnall
4 ❑ Dec 1993 Cover: 1.95 **NM** value: **2.00**
Circ: CapCity orders: **20,075**
📖 Break-Thru • Break-Thru **W:** James D. Hudnall
5 ❑ Jan 1994 Cover: 1.95 **NM** value: **Cover or less**
Circ: CapCity orders: **16,775**
📖 It's A Hard World • Dropkick solo story **A:** Alan Jackson **W:** James D. Hudnall ★ Origin of The Strangers.
6 ❑ Feb 1994 Cover: 1.95 **NM** value: **Cover or less**
Circ: CapCity orders: **14,600**
W: James D. Hudnall ★ Origin of The Solution, Tech.
7 ❑ Mar 1994 Cover: 1.95 **NM** value: **Cover or less**
Circ: CapCity orders: **12,825**
W: James D. Hudnall ★ Origin of The Solution.
8 ❑ Apr 1994 Cover: 1.95 **NM** value: **Cover or less**
Circ: CapCity orders: **12,150**
W: James D. Hudnall ★ Origin of The Solution.
9 ❑ Jun 1994 Cover: 1.95 **NM** value: **Cover or less**
Circ: CapCity orders: **11,275**
W: James D. Hudnall
10 ❑ Jul 1994 Cover: 1.95 **NM** value: **Cover or less**
Circ: CapCity orders: **10,425**
📖 Backtrack, Part 1 **A:** John Statema; Dan Brereton(cover) **W:** James D. Hudnall
11 ❑ Aug 1994 Cover: 1.95 **NM** value: **Cover or less**
Circ: CapCity orders: **9,450**
📖 Backtrack, Part 2 **A:** John Statema; Dan Brereton(cover) **W:** James D. Hudnall
12 ❑ Oct 1994 Cover: 1.95 **NM** value: **Cover or less**
Circ: CapCity orders: **8,850**
📖 Backtrack, Part 3 **A:** John Statema **W:** James D. Hudnall
13 ❑ Oct 1994 Cover: 1.95 **NM** value: **Cover or less**
Circ: CapCity orders: **7,725**
📖 Hostile Takeover; Hostile Takeover, Part 3 **A:** Scott Benefiel; Frank Gomez(cover) **W:** James D. Hudnall
14 ❑ Dec 1994 Cover: 1.95 **NM** value: **Cover or less**
Circ: CapCity orders: **6,900**
📖 Killing Spree **A:** Hoang Nguyen; John Statema(cover) **W:** James D. Hudnall
15 ❑ Jan 1995 Cover: 1.95 **NM** value: **Cover or less**
Circ: CapCity orders: **6,125**
📖 The Trap, Part 1 **A:** George Dove; John Statema(cover) **W:** James D. Hudnall
16 ❑ Jan 1995 Cover: 3.50 **NM** value: **Cover or less**
Circ: CapCity orders: **5,950**
📖 The Trap, Part 2; Manic Monday; Bad Citizen; Catharsis, Part 1; A New Game of Death, Part 2 • flipbook with Ultraverse Premiere #10 **A:** Steve Scott; Greg Horn; Steve Ellis; Mike Zeck; Daerick Gröss Jr.; Chris Gardner; John Statema(cover) **W:** Buzz Dixon; Hank Kanalz; James D. Hudnall; Len Strazewski; Roland Mann
17 ❑ Feb 1995 Cover: 2.50 **NM** value: **Cover or less**
Circ: CapCity orders: **4,975**
📖 The Trap, Part 3 **A:** John Statema **W:** James D. Hudnall

SOMEPLACE STRANGE — Marvel / Epic

1 ❑ Cover: 6.95 **NM** value: **Cover or less**
Circ: CapCity orders: **5,400**

SOMERSET HOLMES — Pacific

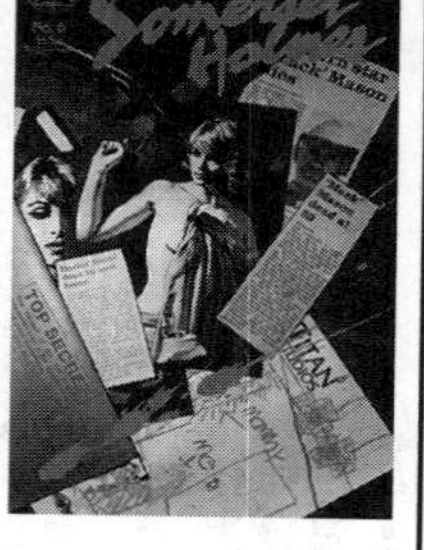

She was an actress once, she knows that now. She had also been a mother, but her daughter is dead. She may have killed someone herself. But all that was before the coma.

Awakening at a state facility for the criminally insane, a woman who calls herself "Somerset Holmes" makes a desperate escape. She doesn't remember much about herself, but she knows that someone wants to kill her.

Somerset Holmes is a stylish mystery thriller by Bruce Jones and Brent Anderson. Its issues included a special backup feature called "Cliffhanger"- a comic book version of an action/adventure cliffhanger series.

1 ❑ Sep 1983 Cover: 1.50 **NM** value: **2.50**
• **CGC:** 1 graded, best 9.4
A: Brent Anderson **W:** Bruce Jones
2 ❑ Nov 1983 Cover: 1.50 **NM** value: **2.00**
A: Brent Anderson
3 ❑ Feb 1984 Cover: 1.50 **NM** value: **2.00**
A: Brent Anderson **W:** Bruce Jones
4 ❑ Apr 1984 Cover: 1.50 **NM** value: **2.00**
A: Brent Anderson
5 ❑ Nov 1984 Cover: 1.50 **NM** value: **2.00**
A: Brent Anderson
6 ❑ Dec 1984 Cover: 1.50 **NM** value: **2.00**
A: Brent Anderson
Bk 1❑ ca. 1985 Cover: 15.95 **NM** value: **Cover or less**
Circ: CapCity orders: **974**
• Trade Paperback. • Collects Somerset Holmes #1-6 **A:** Brent Anderson
Bk 1/HC❑ ca. 1985 Cover: 25.95 **NM** value: **Cover or less**
Circ: CapCity orders: **122**
• Cloth bound edition. • Collects Somerset Holmes #1-6 **A:** Brent Anderson
Bk 1/LE❑ ca. 1985 Cover: 36.00 **NM** value: **Cover or less**
Circ: CapCity orders: **266**
• Collects Somerset Holmes #1-6 **A:** Brent Anderson

SOME TALES FROM GIMBLEY — Harrier

1 ❑ Jun 1987 Cover: 1.95 **NM** value: **Cover or less**
📖 A Tale from Gimbley **A:** Phil Elliott **W:** Phil Elliott

SOMETHING — Strictly Underground

1 ❑ Cover: 2.95 **NM** value: **Cover or less**
📖 The Eighth Seal **W:** Derrell Spicy; Joe Robinson Currie; John Rogers

SOMETHING AT THE WINDOW IS SCRATCHING — Slave Labor

1 ❑ Cover: 9.95 **NM** value: **Cover or less**
A: Roman Dirge **W:** Roman Dirge

SOMETHING DIFFERENT — Wooga Central

All issues are adults only.

1 ❑ b&w Cover: 2.00 **NM** value: **Cover or less**
2 ❑ Spr 1992 Cover: 2.00 **NM** value: **Cover or less**
📖 Mark Twain's 1601 • flexidisc

SOMNAMBULO: SLEEP OF THE JUST — 9th Circle Studios

1 ❑ Aug 1996, b&w Cover: 2.95 **NM** value: **Cover or less**

SONGBOOK (ALAN MOORE'S…) — Caliber

1 ❑ Cover: 5.95 **NM** value: **Cover or less**
📖 Rose Madder; Me and Dorothy Parker; The Murders on the Rue Morgue; London; Positively Bridge Street; Leopard-Man at C & A's; The Hair of the Snake that Bit Me; Litvinov's Book; Trampling Tokyo; Madame October; 14.2.99; Chiaroscuro; Fires I Wish I'd Seen • Collected from issues of Negative Burn **A:** Michael Gaydos; Arthur Adams; Dave Gibbons; Richard Case; Richard Pace; Jordan Raskin; Dave Johnson; James Owen; Terry Moore; Ande Parks; Colleen Doran; Phil Hester; Neil Gaiman **W:** Alan Moore

SONG OF THE CID — Tome Press

1 ❑ b&w Cover: 2.95 **NM** value: **Cover or less**
2 ❑ b&w Cover: 2.95 **NM** value: **Cover or less**

SONG OF THE SIRENS — Millennium

1 ❑ b&w Cover: 2.95 **NM** value: **Cover or less**
2 ❑ b&w Cover: 2.95 **NM** value: **Cover or less**

SONGS OF BASTARDS — Conquest

1 ❑ b&w Cover: 2.95 **NM** value: **Cover or less**

SONIC & KNUCKLES: MECHA MADNESS SPECIAL — Archie

1 ❑ Cover: 2.00 **NM** value: **Cover or less**

SONIC & KNUCKLES SPECIAL — Archie

1 ❑ Aug 1995 Cover: 2.00 **NM** value: **Cover or less**

SONIC BLAST SPECIAL — Archie

1 ❑ Oct 1996 Cover: 2.00 **NM** value: **Cover or less**
Circ: Diamd. preorders: **6,231**

SONIC DISRUPTORS — DC

The U.S. had been taken over by a military coup. For years, the military had sat by while gays, communists, and other minorities achieved prominence in the national agenda. Then came the final straw: a female president. The military could stand no more and decided it was time to act.

Today, armed militia patrol the streets and more and more citizens are counted among the "vanished." The only remaining thorn in the government's side is The Sonic Disruptors, a group of disc jockeys and revolutionaries who broadcast from an orbital space station. Led by Myron Speece, aka Sheik Rattle Enroll, they beam banned music and revolutionary politics to the world below. What's more, the government can't shoot them down as the ship also carries tons of nuclear waste.

Sonic Disruptors was originally scheduled as a 12-issue maxi-series, but was abruptly cancelled with #7 due to low sales.

1 ❑ Dec 1987 Cover: 1.75 **NM** value: **Cover or less**
Circ: CapCity orders: **19,450**
📖 Are You Ready To Rock? **A:** Barry Crain **W:** Mike Baron
2 ❑ Jan 1988 Cover: 1.75 **NM** value: **Cover or less**
Circ: CapCity orders: **15,500**
W: Mike Baron
3 ❑ Feb 1988 Cover: 1.75 **NM** value: **Cover or less**
Circ: CapCity orders: **14,150**
W: Mike Baron
4 ❑ Mar 1988 Cover: 1.75 **NM** value: **Cover or less**
Circ: CapCity orders: **12,200**
W: Mike Baron
5 ❑ May 1988 Cover: 1.75 **NM** value: **Cover or less**
Circ: CapCity orders: **10,650**
W: Mike Baron
6 ❑ Jun 1988 Cover: 1.75 **NM** value: **Cover or less**
Circ: CapCity orders: **8,550**
W: Mike Baron
7 ❑ Jul 1988 Cover: 1.75 **NM** value: **Cover or less**
Circ: CapCity orders: **7,550**
final issue. • series goes on hiatus with unresolved storyline; Series cancelled **W:** Mike Baron

SONIC LIVE SPECIAL — Archie

1 ❑ Cover: 2.00 **NM** value: **Cover or less**
One-shot. • Knuckles back-up continues in Sonic the Hedgehog #45

SONIC QUEST – THE DEATH EGG SAGA — Archie

2 ❑ Jan 1997 Cover: 1.50 **NM** value: **Cover or less**
Circ: Diamd. preorders: **5,299**

SONIC'S FRIENDLY NEMESIS KNUCKLES — Archie

1 ❑ Jul 1996 Cover: 1.50 **NM** value: **3.00**
2 ❑ Aug 1996 Cover: 1.50 **NM** value: **2.00**
3 ❑ Sep 1996 Cover: 1.50 **NM** value: **2.00**

Other grades: Multiply prices above by **1.5 for Mint • 2/3 for Very Fine • 1/3 for Fine • 1/5 for Very Good • 1/8 for Good**

SONIC THE HEDGEHOG **Archie**

When game machine-maker Sega launched their challenge to market leader Nintendo, they needed a game which showed off the fast graphics of their new Genesis system. The answer was a furiously fun game called Sonic the Hedgehog. The game proved so popular that several follow-ons were created, and eventually it even became a comic book.

The heroic hedgehog is a bundle of energy with supersonic sneakers that let him run incredibly fast. He needs all his skill and speed to stop the evil Doctor Robotnik, who plans to turn all the furry creatures of Mobius into robots. However, with the help of friends Princess Sally, Tails, and Knuckles, he's ready to take on any nasty plan that Robotnik can cook up.

0 ❑ Feb 1993 Cover: 1.25 **NM** value: **4.00**
• **CGC:** 2 graded, best 9.8
📖 Meet Me at the Corner of Hedgehog & Vine!; You Bet My Life!; I'd Like to Thank...; Fast Food!; Keep Looking Up! **A:** Dave Manak **W:** Michael Gallagher

1 ❑ Jul 1993 Cover: 1.25 **NM** value: **10.00**
• **CGC:** 6 graded, best 9.8
📖 Meet Me at the Corner of Hedgehog & Vine!; You Bet My Life!; I'd Like to Thank...; Fast Food!; Keep Looking Up! **A:** Dave Manak **W:** Michael Gallagher

2 ❑ Sep 1993 Cover: 1.25 **NM** value: **6.00**
• **CGC:** 2 graded, best 9.4

3 ❑ Oct 1993 Cover: 1.25 **NM** value: **5.00**
• **CGC:** 1 graded, best 9.2

4 ❑ Nov 1993 Cover: 1.25 **NM** value: **5.00**
• **CGC:** 1 graded, best 9.6

5 ❑ Dec 1993 Cover: 1.25 **NM** value: **5.00**

6 ❑ Jan 1994 Cover: 1.25 **NM** value: **4.00**

7 ❑ Feb 1994 Cover: 1.25 **NM** value: **4.00**
• **CGC:** 1 graded, best 9.2

8 ❑ Mar 1994 Cover: 1.25 **NM** value: **4.00**

9 ❑ Apr 1994 Cover: 1.25 **NM** value: **4.00**

10 ❑ May 1994 Cover: 1.25 **NM** value: **4.00**

11 ❑ Jun 1994 Cover: 1.25 **NM** value: **3.00**
• **CGC:** 1 graded, best 9.2

12 ❑ Jul 1994 Cover: 1.25 **NM** value: **3.00**

13 ❑ Aug 1994 Cover: 1.50 **NM** value: **3.00**

14 ❑ Sep 1994 Cover: 1.50 **NM** value: **3.00**

15 ❑ Oct 1994 Cover: 1.50 **NM** value: **3.00**

16 ❑ Nov 1994 Cover: 1.50 **NM** value: **3.00**

17 ❑ Dec 1994 Cover: 1.50 **NM** value: **3.00**

18 ❑ Jan 1995 Cover: 1.50 **NM** value: **3.00**

19 ❑ Feb 1995 Cover: 1.50 **NM** value: **3.00**

20 ❑ Mar 1995 Cover: 1.50 **NM** value: **3.00**

21 ❑ Apr 1995 Cover: 1.50 **NM** value: **2.00**

22 ❑ May 1995 Cover: 1.50 **NM** value: **2.00**

23 ❑ Jun 1995 Cover: 1.50 **NM** value: **2.00**
📖 Ivo Robotnik, Freedom Fighter; Sonic's Pal, Antoine: The Vol-Ant-Teer! **A:** Dave Manak **W:** Angelo Decesare

24 ❑ Jul 1995 Cover: 1.50 **NM** value: **2.00**

25 ❑ Aug 1995 Cover: 1.50 **NM** value: **2.00**

26 ❑ Sep 1995 Cover: 1.50 **NM** value: **2.00**

27 ❑ Oct 1995 Cover: 1.50 **NM** value: **2.00**

28 ❑ Nov 1995 Cover: 1.50 **NM** value: **2.00**

29 ❑ Dec 1995 Cover: 1.50 **NM** value: **2.00**

30 ❑ Jan 1996 Cover: 1.50 **NM** value: **2.00**
Circ: Statement: **67,610**

31 ❑ Feb 1996 Cover: 1.50 **NM** value: **2.00**
Circ: Statement: **67,610**

32 ❑ Mar 1996 Cover: 1.50 **NM** value: **2.00**
Circ: Statement: **67,610**

33 ❑ Apr 1996 Cover: 1.50 **NM** value: **2.00**
Circ: Statement: **67,610**

34 ❑ May 1996 Cover: 1.50 **NM** value: **2.00**
Circ: Statement: **67,610**

35 ❑ Jun 1996 Cover: 1.50 **NM** value: **2.00**
Circ: Statement: **67,610**

36 ❑ Jul 1996 Cover: 1.50 **NM** value: **2.00**
Circ: Statement: **67,610**

37 ❑ Aug 1996 Cover: 1.50 **NM** value: **2.00**
Circ: Statement: **67,610**
• Bunnie Rabbot back-up story

38 ❑ Sep 1996 Cover: 1.50 **NM** value: **2.00**
Circ: Statement: **67,610**
• Tails solo story

39 ❑ Oct 1996 Cover: 1.50 **NM** value: **2.00**
Circ: Statement: **67,610**
📖 Mecha Madness

40 ❑ Nov 1996 Cover: 1.50 **NM** value: **2.00**
Circ: Statement: **67,610**

41 ❑ Dec 1996 Cover: 1.50 **NM** value: **2.00**
Circ: Statement: **67,610** Diamd. preorders: **5,579**

42 ❑ Jan 1997 Cover: 1.50 **NM** value: **2.00**
Circ: Statement: **70,574** Diamd. preorders: **6,238**

43 ❑ Feb 1997 Cover: 1.50 **NM** value: **2.00**
Circ: Statement: **70,574** Diamd. preorders: **6,784**

44 ❑ Mar 1997 Cover: 1.50 **NM** value: **2.00**
Circ: Statement: **70,574** Diamd. preorders: **6,535**

45 ❑ Apr 1997 Cover: 1.50 **NM** value: **2.00**
Circ: Statement: **70,574** Diamd. preorders: **6,499**
• Has 1996 Statement, filed 9/27/96; avg print run 194,766; avg sales 62,129; avg subs 5,481; avg total paid 67,610; samples 554; office use 14,651; max existent 82,815; 50% of run returned

46 ❑ May 1997 Cover: 1.50 **NM** value: **2.00**
Circ: Statement: **70,574** Diamd. preorders: **5,906**

47 ❑ Jun 1997 Cover: 1.50 **NM** value: **2.00**
Circ: Statement: **70,574** Diamd. preorders: **6,359**
📖 End Game, Part 1

48 ❑ Jul 1997 Cover: 1.50 **NM** value: **2.00**
Circ: Statement: **70,574** Diamd. preorders: **6,833**
📖 End Game, Part 2

49 ❑ Aug 1997 Cover: 1.50 **NM** value: **2.00**
Circ: Statement: **70,574** Diamd. preorders: **7,019**
📖 End Game, Part 3

50 ❑ Sep 1997 Cover: 1.50 **NM** value: **2.00**
Circ: Statement: **70,574** Diamd. preorders: **8,738**
📖 End Game, Part 4

51 ❑ Oct 1997 Cover: 1.50 **NM** value: **Cover or less**
Circ: Statement: **70,574** Diamd. preorders: **7,945**

52 ❑ Nov 1997 Cover: 1.50 **NM** value: **Cover or less**
Circ: Statement: **70,574** Diamd. preorders: **8,580**
• noir issue

53 ❑ Dec 1997 Cover: 1.50 **NM** value: **Cover or less**
Circ: Statement: **70,574** Diamd. preorders: **8,887**

54 ❑ Jan 1998 Cover: 1.75 **NM** value: **Cover or less**
Circ: Diamd. preorders: **9,296**

55 ❑ Feb 1998 Cover: 1.75 **NM** value: **Cover or less**
Circ: Diamd. preorders: **9,454**

56 ❑ Mar 1998 Cover: 1.75 **NM** value: **Cover or less**
Circ: Diamd. preorders: **9,122**

57 ❑ Apr 1998 Cover: 1.75 **NM** value: **Cover or less**
Circ: Diamd. preorders: **8,201**
• Has 1997 Statement, filed 11/1/97; avg print run 182,024; avg sales 64,389; avg subs 6,185; avg total paid 70,574; samples 535; office use 9,027; max existent 80,136; 56% of run returned

58 ❑ May 1998 Cover: 1.75 **NM** value: **Cover or less**
Circ: Diamd. preorders: **8,056**

59 ❑ Jun 1998 Cover: 1.75 **NM** value: **Cover or less**
Circ: Diamd. preorders: **8,273**

60 ❑ Jul 1998 Cover: 1.75 **NM** value: **Cover or less**
Circ: Diamd. preorders: **8,459**

61 ❑ Aug 1998 Cover: 1.75 **NM** value: **Cover or less**
Circ: Diamd. preorders: **8,130**

62 ❑ Sep 1998 Cover: 1.75 **NM** value: **Cover or less**
Circ: Diamd. preorders: **8,218**

63 ❑ Oct 1998 Cover: 1.75 **NM** value: **Cover or less**
Circ: Diamd. preorders: **7,883**

64 ❑ Nov 1998 Cover: 1.75 **NM** value: **Cover or less**
Circ: Diamd. preorders: **7,570**
📖 The Naugus Trilogy, Part 1; On His Majesty's Secret Service **A:** Steven Butler; Art Mawhinney; Pam Eklund **W:** Ken Penders; Karl Bollers

65 ❑ Dec 1998 Cover: 1.75 **NM** value: **Cover or less**
Circ: Diamd. preorders: **7,751**
📖 The Naugus Trilogy, Part 2

66 ❑ Jan 1999 Cover: 1.75 **NM** value: **Cover or less**
Circ: Diamd. preorders: **7,758**
📖 The Naugus Trilogy, Part 3

67 ❑ Feb 1999 Cover: 1.75 **NM** value: **Cover or less**
Circ: Diamd. preorders: **7,894**

68 ❑ Mar 1999 Cover: 1.75 **NM** value: **Cover or less**
Circ: Diamd. preorders: **7,547**

69 ❑ Apr 1999 Cover: 1.79 **NM** value: **Cover or less**
Circ: Diamd. preorders: **7,130**

70 ❑ May 1999 Cover: 1.79 **NM** value: **Cover or less**
Circ: Diamd. preorders: **6,861**

71 ❑ Jun 1999 Cover: 1.79 **NM** value: **Cover or less**
Circ: Diamd. preorders: **6,763**

72 ❑ Jul 1999 Cover: 1.79 **NM** value: **Cover or less**
Circ: Diamd. preorders: **6,689**

73 ❑ Aug 1999 Cover: 1.79 **NM** value: **Cover or less**
Circ: Diamd. preorders: **6,513**

74 ❑ Sep 1999 Cover: 1.79 **NM** value: **Cover or less**
Circ: Diamd. preorders: **6,305**

75 ❑ Oct 1999 Cover: 1.79 **NM** value: **Cover or less**
Circ: Diamd. preorders: **6,680**

76 ❑ Nov 1999 Cover: 1.79 **NM** value: **Cover or less**
Circ: Diamd. preorders: **6,136**

77 ❑ Dec 1999 Cover: 1.79 **NM** value: **Cover or less**
Circ: Diamd. preorders: **5,807**

78 ❑ Jan 2000 Cover: 1.79 **NM** value: **Cover or less**
Circ: Diamd. preorders: **6,279**

79 ❑ Feb 2000 Cover: 1.79 **NM** value: **Cover or less**
Circ: Diamd. preorders: **5,991**

80 ❑ Mar 2000 Cover: 1.79 **NM** value: **Cover or less**
Circ: Diamd. preorders: **5,867**

81 ❑ Apr 2000 Cover: 1.79 **NM** value: **Cover or less**
Circ: Diamd. preorders: **5,500**

82 ❑ May 2000 Cover: 1.79 **NM** value: **Cover or less**
Circ: Diamd. preorders: **5,199**

83 ❑ Jun 2000 Cover: 1.99 **NM** value: **Cover or less**
Circ: Diamd. preorders: **5,208**

84 ❑ Jul 2000 Cover: 1.99 **NM** value: **Cover or less**
Circ: Diamd. preorders: **5,176**

85 ❑ Aug 2000 Cover: 1.99 **NM** value: **Cover or less**
Circ: Diamd. preorders: **5,254**

86 ❑ Sep 2000 Cover: 1.99 **NM** value: **Cover or less**
Circ: Diamd. preorders: **5,480**

87 ❑ Oct 2000 Cover: 1.99 **NM** value: **Cover or less**
Circ: Diamd. preorders: **5,389**

88 ❑ Nov 2000 Cover: 1.99 **NM** value: **Cover or less**
Circ: Diamd. preorders: **4,998**

89 ❑ Dec 2000 Cover: 1.99 **NM** value: **Cover or less**
Circ: Diamd. preorders: **5,106**

90 ❑ Jan 2001 Cover: 1.99 **NM** value: **Cover or less**
Circ: Statement: **30,665** Diamd. preorders: **5,051**

91 ❑ Feb 2001 Cover: 1.99 **NM** value: **Cover or less**
Circ: Statement: **30,665** Diamd. preorders: **4,961**

92 ❑ Mar 2001 Cover: 1.99 **NM** value: **Cover or less**
Circ: Statement: **30,665** Diamd. preorders: **4,790**

93 ❑ Apr 2001 Cover: 1.99 **NM** value: **Cover or less**
Circ: Statement: **30,665** Diamd. preorders: **4,602**

94 ❑ May 2001 Cover: 1.99 **NM** value: **Cover or less**
Circ: Statement: **30,665** Diamd. preorders: **4,529**

95 ❑ Jun 2001 Cover: 1.99 **NM** value: **Cover or less**
Circ: Statement: **30,665** Diamd. preorders: **4,400**

96 ❑ Jul 2001 Cover: 1.99 **NM** value: **Cover or less**
Circ: Statement: **30,665** Diamd. preorders: **4,582**

97 ❑ Aug 2001 Cover: 1.99 **NM** value: **Cover or less**
Circ: Statement: **30,665** Diamd. preorders: **4,493**

98 ❑ Sep 2001 Cover: 1.99 **NM** value: **Cover or less**
Circ: Statement: **30,665** Diamd. preorders: **4,359**

99 ❑ Oct 2001 Cover: 1.99 **NM** value: **Cover or less**
Circ: Statement: **30,665** Diamd. preorders: **4,723**

100 ❑ Nov 2001 Cover: 1.99 **NM** value: **Cover or less**
Circ: Statement: **30,665** Diamd. preorders: **6,147**

SS 1 ❑ Nov 1997 Cover: 2.00 **NM** value: **Cover or less**
Circ: Diamd. preorders: **8,222**

SS 2 ❑ ca. 1997 Cover: 2.00 **NM** value: **Cover or less**
• Brave New World

SS 3 ❑ Jan 1997 Cover: 2.00 **NM** value: **2.25**
Circ: Diamd. preorders: **6,910**
• Firsts

SS 4 ❑ Mar 1998 Cover: 2.25 **NM** value: **Cover or less**
Circ: Diamd. preorders: **7,306**
📖 Return of the King

SS 5 ❑ Jun 1998 Cover: 2.25 **NM** value: **Cover or less**
Circ: Diamd. preorders: **6,690**
• Sonic Kids

SS 6 ❑ Sep 1998 Cover: 2.25 **NM** value: **Cover or less**
Circ: Diamd. preorders: **6,856**
• Director's Cut; expanded version of Sonic #50

SS 7 ❑ Dec 1998 Cover: 2.25 **NM** value: **Cover or less**
Circ: Diamd. preorders: **9,141**
• crossover with Image

SS 8 ❑ Mar 1999 Cover: 2.25 **NM** value: **Cover or less**
Circ: Diamd. preorders: **6,830**

SS 9 ❑ Jun 1999 Cover: 2.29 **NM** value: **Cover or less**
Circ: Diamd. preorders: **5,947**

SS 10 ❑ Sep 1999 Cover: 2.29 **NM** value: **Cover or less**
Circ: Diamd. preorders: **6,134**
★ Appearance of Sabrina.

SS 11 ❑ Dec 1999 Cover: 2.29 **NM** value: **Cover or less**
Circ: Diamd. preorders: **5,306**

SS 12 ❑ Apr 2000 Cover: 2.29 **NM** value: **Cover or less**
Circ: Diamd. preorders: **4,985**

SS 13 ❑ Jun 2000 Cover: 2.29 **NM** value: **Cover or less**
Circ: Diamd. preorders: **4,755**

SS 14 ❑ Sep 2000 Cover: 2.29 **NM** value: **Cover or less**
Circ: Diamd. preorders: **4,874**

SS 15 ❑ Feb 2001 Cover: 2.49 **NM** value: **Cover or less**
Circ: Diamd. preorders: **4,428**

SONIC THE HEDGEHOG IN YOUR FACE SPECIAL **Archie**

1 ❑ Cover: 2.00 **NM** value: **Cover or less**

SONIC THE HEDGEHOG (MINI-SERIES) **Archie**

1 ❑ ca. 1993 Cover: 1.25 **NM** value: **20.00**
Circ: CapCity orders: **2,550**

2 ❑ ca. 1993 Cover: 1.25 **NM** value: **10.00**

3 ❑ ca. 1993 Cover: 1.25 **NM** value: **10.00**

SONIC THE HEDGEHOG TRIPLE TROUBLE SPECIAL **Archie**

1 ❑ Oct 1995 Cover: 2.00 **NM** value: **Cover or less**

SONIC VS. KNUCKLES BATTLE ROYAL SPECIAL **Archie**

1 ❑ ca. 1997 Cover: 2.00 **NM** value: **Cover or less**
Circ: Diamd. preorders: **6,396**

SON OF AMBUSH BUG **DC**

Son of Ambush Bug follows on the heels of the Ambush Bug Stocking Stuffer. In it, we once again find AB down on his luck, out of work, and talking obsessively to his toy doll, Cheeks. The six issues of this mini-series feature Ambush Bug in a variety of goofy vignettes. These include a Japanese monster movie remake of Ambush Bug ("Gauguin, Friend of Rodin"), Jack Kirby parody "Amber Butane," and a series of bizarre encounters with letters column character Jonni DC. Cheeks also gets his turn in the spotlight, starring in tales such as "Combat Cheeks, Frontline Medic."

1 ❑ Jul 1986 Cover: 0.75 **NM** value: **1.50**
Circ: CapCity orders: **12,150**
📖 How Come You Do Me Like You Do Do Do? **A:** Keith Giffen **W:** Robert Loren Flemming

2 ❑ Aug 1986 Cover: 0.75 **NM** value: **1.50**
Circ: CapCity orders: **10,300**
A: Keith Giffen

3 ❑ Sep 1986 Cover: 0.75 **NM** value: **1.50**
Circ: CapCity orders: **10,200**
A: Keith Giffen

4 ❑ Oct 1986 Cover: 0.75 **NM** value: **1.50**
Circ: CapCity orders: **9,750**
A: Keith Giffen

5 ❑ Nov 1986 Cover: 0.75 **NM** value: **1.50**
Circ: CapCity orders: **8,950**
A: Keith Giffen

6 ❑ Dec 1986 Cover: 0.75 **NM** value: **1.50**
Circ: CapCity orders: **8,900**
A: Keith Giffen

CGC-graded: Multiply prices above by **33 for 9.9 M • 16 for 9.8 NM/M • 7 for 9.6 NM+ • 5 for 9.4 NM • 2.5 for 9.2 NM- • 1.5 for 9.0 VF/NM**

SON OF CELLULOID — Eclipse

Bk 1❑ Cover: 6.95 **NM** value: **Cover or less**
W: Clive Barker

SON OF MUTANT WORLD — Fantagor

1 ❑ full color Cover: 2.00 **NM** value: **3.00**
Circ: CapCity orders: **4,700**
📖 Targets; The Small World of Lewis Stillman **A:** Richard Corben; Bruce Jones **W:** Richard Corben; Bruce Jones; William F. Nolan

2 ❑ full color Cover: 2.00 **NM** value: **2.50**
Circ: CapCity orders: **3,975**
📖 Watching You; Inna Pit; Fireworks **A:** Richard Corben; Bruce Jones; Jan Strnad; Rich Margopoulos **W:** Richard Corben; Bruce Jones; Jan Strnad; Rich Margopoulos

3 ❑ b&w Cover: 1.75 **NM** value: **2.00**
Circ: CapCity orders: **4,200**
📖 Dead Run; Twilight of the Dogs • Black and white issues begin **A:** Richard Corben; Bruce Jones; Jan Strnad **W:** Richard Corben; Bruce Jones; Jan Strnad

4 ❑ b&w Cover: 1.75 **NM** value: **2.00**
📖 Afterthought; Different; The Inducement **A:** Richard Corben; Bruce Jones; Rich Margopoulos **W:** Richard Corben; Bruce Jones; Rich Margopoulos

5 ❑ b&w Cover: 1.75 **NM** value: **2.00**
📖 Flypaper; Silver, Emeralds and Rubies; Da Dork Planet: Da Official Adaptation **A:** Richard Corben; Bruce Jones; Brian Buniak; Jan Strnad; Rich Margopoulous **W:** Richard Corben; Bruce Jones; Brian Buniak; Jan Strnad; Rich Margopoulous

SON OF ORIGINS OF MARVEL COMICS — Marvel

Bk 1❑ Cover: 6.95 **NM** value: **Cover or less**
• (Fireside)

SON OF SATAN — Marvel

1 ❑ Dec 1975 Cover: 0.25 **NM** value: **10.00**
• **CGC:** 12 graded, best 9.4
2 ❑ Feb 1976 Cover: 0.25 **NM** value: **8.00**
• **CGC:** 2 graded, best 9.2
📖 The Possession! **A:** Sonny Trinidad **W:** John Warner
3 ❑ Apr 1976 Cover: 0.25 **NM** value: **6.00**
4 ❑ Jun 1976 Cover: 0.25 **NM** value: **6.00**
📖 Cloud of Witness! **A:** P. Craig Russell; Sonny Trinidad **W:** John Warner
5 ❑ Aug 1976 Cover: 0.25 **NM** value: **6.00**
6 ❑ Oct 1976 Cover: 0.30 **NM** value: **5.00**
7 ❑ Dec 1976 Cover: 0.30 **NM** value: **5.00**
8 ❑ Feb 1977 Cover: 0.30 **NM** value: **5.00**

SON OF SINBAD — St. John

1 ❑ Feb 1950 Cover: 0.10 **NM** value: **300.00**
• **CGC:** 2 graded, best 9.0

SON OF SUPERMAN — DC

1 ❑ Cover: 14.95 **NM** value: **Cover or less**
A: J.H. Williams **W:** Howard Chaykin; David Tischman

SON OF YUPPIES FROM HELL — Marvel

1 ❑ Cover: 3.50 **NM** value: **Cover or less**
A: Barbara Slate **W:** Barbara Slate

SONS OF KATIE ELDER — Dell

1 ❑ Sep 1965 Cover: 0.12 **NM** value: **50.00**
• **CGC:** 1 graded, best 2.0

SOPHISTIKATS KATCH-UP KOLLECTION, THE — Silk Purrs Press

1 ❑ Jul 1995, b&w Cover: 5.95 **NM** value: **Cover or less**
No issue number.

SORCERER'S CHILDREN, THE — Sillwill Press

1 ❑ Dec 1998 Cover: 2.95 **NM** value: **Cover or less**
2 ❑ Feb 1999 Cover: 2.95 **NM** value: **Cover or less**
3 ❑ Apr 1999 Cover: 2.95 **NM** value: **Cover or less**
4 ❑ Jul 1999 Cover: 2.95 **NM** value: **Cover or less**

SORORITY SECRETS — Toby

1 ❑ ca. 1954 Cover: 0.10 **NM** value: **50.00**

S.O.S. — Fantagraphics

All issues are adults only.

1 ❑ b&w Cover: 2.75 **NM** value: **Cover or less**
No issue number.

SOUL — Flashpoint

1 ❑ Mar 1994 Cover: 2.50 **NM** value: **Cover or less**
📖 The Wakening **A:** Lance Sells **W:** Peter Caravette; Thomas Grozan
1/GO❑ Mar 1994 Cover: 2.50 **NM** value: **3.00**
• Gold edition. 📖 The Wakening **A:** Lance Sells **W:** Peter Caravette; Thomas Grozan

SOULQUEST — Innovation

1 ❑ Apr 1989 Cover: 3.95 **NM** value: **Cover or less**
Circ: CapCity orders: **2,236**
📖 Unfinished Portraits **A:** Glen Johnson **W:** Peter Quinones

SOUL SAGA — Top Cow

1 ❑ Feb 2000 Cover: 5.95 **NM** value: **Cover or less**
Circ: Diamd. preorders: **66,272** • **CGC:** 6 graded, best 9.9
A: Stephen Platt **W:** Stephen Platt; Christian Lichtner
2 ❑ Apr 2000 Cover: 2.50 **NM** value: **Cover or less**
Circ: Diamd. preorders: **41,942** • **CGC:** 2 graded, best 9.9
A: Stephen Platt **W:** Stephen Platt; Christian Lichtner
3 ❑ Aug 2000 Cover: 2.50 **NM** value: **Cover or less**
Circ: Diamd. preorders: **46,773**
A: Stephen Platt **W:** Stephen Platt; Christian Lichtner
4 ❑ Oct 2000 Cover: 2.95 **NM** value: **Cover or less**
Circ: Diamd. preorders: **45,358** • **CGC:** 1 graded, best 9.9
A: Stephen Platt **W:** Stephen Platt; Christian Lichtner
5 ❑ Apr 2001 Cover: 2.95 **NM** value: **Cover or less**
Circ: Diamd. preorders: **43,039**
A: Stephen Platt **W:** Stephen Platt; Christian Lichtner
Bk 1❑ Apr 2000 Cover: 5.95 **NM** value: **Cover or less**
• **CGC:** 1 graded, best 9.8
A: Stephen Platt **W:** Stephen Platt; Christian Lichtner

SOULSEARCHERS AND COMPANY — Claypool

Peter David is known for his long run on Marvel's Hulk, for his scripts for the recent form of DC's Supergirl, for his Star Trek prose novels, for co-creating the TV series Space Cases, for his ongoing column in Comics Buyer's Guide — What he's not as widely known for is his long-time scripting of Claypool's Soulsearchers and Company, devoted to a strange group of paranormal researchers. While they're working on getting rid of "otherworldly weirdness" from Mystic Grove, they're pretty weird themselves. The group comprises Arnold (a talking prairie dog), Baraka (a fire-demon from an Arabic Hell), Bridget (a former Olympic athlete), Janocz (a changeling), Kelly (an apprentice witch), and Peterson (an accountant with a magic bag). Their success as a group has had its ups and downs, but it's usually safe to say that even good days have unsettling aspects.

Thanks to the involvement of David and Editor Richard Howell, the series is loaded with slapstick, parody, and puns. That's fair warning. — Maggie

1 ❑ 1993 Cover: 2.50 **NM** value: **4.00**
• **CGC:** 1 graded, best 9.2
📖 Puppet Dictatorship **A:** Amanda Conner **W:** Richard Howell; Peter David
2 ❑ 1993 Cover: 2.50 **NM** value: **3.00**
W: Peter David
3 ❑ Aug 1993 Cover: 2.50 **NM** value: **3.00**
• Sandman parody **W:** Peter David
4 ❑ Sep 1993 Cover: 2.50 **NM** value: **3.00**
W: Peter David
5 ❑ Oct 1993 Cover: 2.50 **NM** value: **3.00**
W: Peter David
6 ❑ Feb 1994 Cover: 2.50 **NM** value: **Cover or less**
W: Peter David
7 ❑ May 1994 Cover: 2.50 **NM** value: **Cover or less**
W: Peter David
8 ❑ Jul 1994 Cover: 2.50 **NM** value: **Cover or less**
W: Peter David
9 ❑ 1995 Cover: 2.50 **NM** value: **Cover or less**
W: Peter David
10 ❑ Jan 1995 Cover: 2.50 **NM** value: **Cover or less**
W: Peter David
11 ❑ Feb 1995 Cover: 2.50 **NM** value: **Cover or less**
📖 Liquid Assets **A:** Richard Howell **W:** Peter David
12 ❑ May 1995 Cover: 2.50 **NM** value: **Cover or less**
W: Peter David
13 ❑ Jul 1995 Cover: 2.50 **NM** value: **Cover or less**
W: Peter David
14 ❑ Oct 1995 Cover: 2.50 **NM** value: **Cover or less**
W: Peter David
15 ❑ Dec 1995 Cover: 2.50 **NM** value: **Cover or less**
W: Peter David
16 ❑ Feb 1996 Cover: 2.50 **NM** value: **Cover or less**
W: Peter David
17 ❑ Apr 1996 Cover: 2.50 **NM** value: **Cover or less**
W: Peter David
18 ❑ Jun 1996 Cover: 2.50 **NM** value: **Cover or less**
W: Peter David
19 ❑ Aug 1996 Cover: 2.50 **NM** value: **Cover or less**
W: Peter David
20 ❑ Oct 1996 Cover: 2.50 **NM** value: **Cover or less**
W: Peter David
21 ❑ Dec 1996 Cover: 2.50 **NM** value: **Cover or less**
W: Peter David
22 ❑ Feb 1997 Cover: 2.50 **NM** value: **Cover or less**
W: Peter David
23 ❑ Apr 1997 Cover: 2.50 **NM** value: **Cover or less**
W: Peter David
24 ❑ Jun 1997 Cover: 2.50 **NM** value: **Cover or less**
W: Peter David
25 ❑ Aug 1997 Cover: 2.50 **NM** value: **Cover or less**
W: Peter David
26 ❑ Oct 1997 Cover: 2.50 **NM** value: **Cover or less**
W: Peter David
27 ❑ Dec 1997 Cover: 2.50 **NM** value: **Cover or less**
W: Peter David
28 ❑ Feb 1998 Cover: 2.50 **NM** value: **Cover or less**
W: Peter David
29 ❑ Apr 1998 Cover: 2.50 **NM** value: **Cover or less**
📖 Animal Crackers! **A:** Dave Cockrum; Jim Mooney; Brent Carpenter **W:** Peter David
30 ❑ Jun 1998 Cover: 2.50 **NM** value: **Cover or less**
W: Peter David
31 ❑ Aug 1998 Cover: 2.50 **NM** value: **Cover or less**
• Li'l Soulsearchers **W:** Peter David
32 ❑ Sep 1998 Cover: 2.50 **NM** value: **Cover or less**
W: Peter David
33 ❑ Nov 1998 Cover: 2.50 **NM** value: **Cover or less**
W: Peter David
34 ❑ Jan 1999 Cover: 2.50 **NM** value: **Cover or less**
W: Peter David
35 ❑ Mar 1999 Cover: 2.50 **NM** value: **Cover or less**
W: Peter David
36 ❑ May 1999 Cover: 2.50 **NM** value: **Cover or less**
W: Peter David
37 ❑ Jul 1999 Cover: 2.50 **NM** value: **Cover or less**
W: Peter David
38 ❑ Sep 1999 Cover: 2.50 **NM** value: **Cover or less**
W: Peter David
39 ❑ Nov 1999 Cover: 2.50 **NM** value: **Cover or less**
📖 Festival of Lights **A:** Neil Vokes **W:** Peter David
40 ❑ Jan 2000 Cover: 2.50 **NM** value: **Cover or less**
W: Peter David
41 ❑ Mar 2000 Cover: 2.50 **NM** value: **Cover or less**
W: Peter David
42 ❑ May 2000 Cover: 2.50 **NM** value: **Cover or less**
📖 Kelly the Demon Slayer **W:** Peter David
43 ❑ Jul 2000 Cover: 2.50 **NM** value: **Cover or less**
📖 It's in the Bag **A:** Dave Cockrum **W:** Peter David
44 ❑ Sep 2000 Cover: 2.50 **NM** value: **Cover or less**
• **CGC:** 1 graded, best 9.4
📖 Town 4 Sale! **A:** Chris Marrinan; Dave Cockrum; John Heebink **W:** Peter David
45 ❑ Nov 2000 Cover: 2.50 **NM** value: **Cover or less**
46 ❑ Jan 2001 Cover: 2.50 **NM** value: **Cover or less**
Circ: Diamd. preorders: **674**
47 ❑ Mar 2001 Cover: 2.50 **NM** value: **Cover or less**
48 ❑ May 2001 Cover: 2.50 **NM** value: **Cover or less**
• **CGC:** 1 graded, best 9.0
49 ❑ Jul 2001 Cover: 2.50 **NM** value: **Cover or less**
Bk 1❑ b&w Cover: 12.95 **NM** value: **Cover or less**
• collects issues #1-6; On the Case! trade paperback **W:** Peter David
Bk 2❑ b&w Cover: 12.95 **NM** value: **Cover or less**
• Trade Paperback. 📖 Frothy Fun! • collects issues #7-12 **A:** Neil Vokes; Amanda Conner **W:** Peter David

SOUL TREK — Spoof

1 ❑ b&w Cover: 2.95 **NM** value: **Cover or less**
• parody
2 ❑ b&w Cover: 2.95 **NM** value: **Cover or less**
• parody

SOULWIND — Image

1 ❑ Mar 1997, b&w Cover: 2.95 **NM** value: **Cover or less**
Circ: Diamd. preorders: **12,115**
A: C. Scott Morse **W:** C. Scott Morse
2 ❑ Apr 1997, b&w Cover: 2.95 **NM** value: **Cover or less**
Circ: Diamd. preorders: **7,606**
A: C. Scott Morse **W:** C. Scott Morse
3 ❑ May 1997, b&w Cover: 2.95 **NM** value: **Cover or less**
Circ: Diamd. preorders: **7,060**
A: C. Scott Morse **W:** C. Scott Morse
4 ❑ Jun 1997, b&w Cover: 2.95 **NM** value: **Cover or less**
Circ: Diamd. preorders: **6,663**
A: C. Scott Morse **W:** C. Scott Morse
5 ❑ Oct 1997, b&w Cover: 2.95 **NM** value: **Cover or less**
Circ: Diamd. preorders: **5,019**
📖 The Day I Tried to Live, Part 1 **A:** C. Scott Morse **W:** C. Scott Morse
6 ❑ Dec 1997, b&w Cover: 2.95 **NM** value: **Cover or less**
Circ: Diamd. preorders: **4,195**
📖 The Day I Tried to Live, Part 2 **A:** C. Scott Morse **W:** C. Scott Morse
7 ❑ Feb 1998, b&w Cover: 2.95 **NM** value: **Cover or less**
Circ: Diamd. preorders: **3,557**
📖 The Day I Tried to Live, Part 3 **A:** C. Scott Morse **W:** C. Scott Morse
8 ❑ Apr 1998, b&w Cover: 2.95 **NM** value: **Cover or less**
Circ: Diamd. preorders: **3,385**
📖 The Day I Tried to Live, Part 4 **A:** C. Scott Morse **W:** C. Scott Morse
Bk 1❑ b&w Cover: 9.95 **NM** value: **Cover or less**
• The Boy from Planet Earth; collects issues #1-4

SOUTHERN BLOOD — Jm Comics

1 ❑ b&w Cover: 2.50 **NM** value: **Cover or less**
2 ❑ b&w Cover: 2.50 **NM** value: **Cover or less**

SOUTHERN COMFORT — Ceros

All issues are adults only.

1 ❑ Cover: 2.95 **NM** value: **Cover or less**

SOUTHERN-FRIED HOMICIDE — Cremo / Shel-Tone

1 ❑ b&w Cover: 7.95 **NM** value: **Cover or less**
No issue number. cardstock cover.

SOUTHERN KNIGHTS — Guild

A regional super-hero group (billed as "the super-team of the South") that had more than a decade's run, The Southern Knights were one of Comics Interview's few comics series. Combining fantasy elements with super-hero themes, the stories featured both dragons and crimefighting.

In addition to their own adventures, The Knights also helped get the Aristocratic Xtra-terrestrial Time-Traveling Thieves' ongoing series underway by helping Fred and Bianca steal the Coca-Cola formula in an early issue of that series. — Brent

2 ❑ Apr 1983 **NM** value: **2.00**
• Title changes to Southern Knights
3 ❑ Jul 1983 Cover: 1.50 **NM** value: **2.00**
4 ❑ 1983 **NM** value: **2.00**
5 ❑ 1984 **NM** value: **2.00**
6 ❑ Jun 1984 **NM** value: **2.00**

Other grades: Multiply prices above by **1.5 for Mint • 2/3 for Very Fine • 1/3 for Fine • 1/5 for Very Good • 1/8 for Good**

7 ❑ Sep 1984 NM value: **2.00**
8 ❑ Apr 1985 NM value: **2.00**
9 ❑ Jun 1985 NM value: **2.00**
10 ❑ Aug 1985 NM value: **2.00**
11 ❑ Oct 1985 NM value: **2.00**
12 ❑ Dec 1985 NM value: **2.00**
13 ❑ Feb 1986 NM value: **2.00**
14 ❑ Apr 1986 NM value: **2.00**
15 ❑ Jun 1986 NM value: **2.00**
16 ❑ Aug 1986 Cover: 1.75 NM value: **2.00**
17 ❑ Oct 1986 Cover: 1.75 NM value: **2.00**
18 ❑ Dec 1986 Cover: 1.75 NM value: **2.00**
19 ❑ Feb 1987 Cover: 1.75 NM value: **2.00**
20 ❑ Apr 1987 Cover: 1.75 NM value: **2.00**
21 ❑ Jun 1987 Cover: 1.75 NM value: **2.00**
22 ❑ Aug 1987 Cover: 1.75 NM value: **2.00**
23 ❑ Dec 1987 Cover: 1.75 NM value: **2.00**
24 ❑ Dec 1987 Cover: 1.75 NM value: **2.00**
25 ❑ Feb 1988 Cover: 1.75 NM value: **2.00**
26 ❑ Apr 1988 Cover: 1.75 NM value: **2.00**
27 ❑ Jun 1988 Cover: 1.75 NM value: **2.00**
28 ❑ Aug 1988 Cover: 1.95 NM value: **2.00**
29 ❑ Aug 1988 Cover: 1.95 NM value: **2.00**
30 ❑ Sep 1988 Cover: 1.95 NM value: **2.00**
31 ❑ Oct 1988 Cover: 1.95 NM value: **2.00**
32 ❑ Jan 1989 Cover: 1.95 NM value: **2.00**
33 ❑ Sep 1989 Cover: 1.95 NM value: **2.00**
34 ❑ Cover: 2.25 NM value: **Cover or less**
35 ❑ b&w Cover: 3.50 NM value: **Cover or less**
36 ❑ b&w Cover: 3.50 NM value: **Cover or less**
HS 1❑Oct 1988 Cover: 2.25 NM value: **Cover or less**
• Wizard promotional edition. • Dread Halloween Special; b&w Reprint
SE 1❑Apr 1989, b&w Cover: 2.25 NM value: **Cover or less**

SOUTHERN KNIGHTS PRIMER — Comics Interview
1 ❑ b&w Cover: 2.25 NM value: **Cover or less**

SOUTHERN SQUADRON (2ND SERIES) — Eternity
1 ❑ 1991 Cover: 2.50 NM value: **Cover or less**
2 ❑ 1991 Cover: 2.50 NM value: **Cover or less**
3 ❑ 1991 Cover: 2.50 NM value: **Cover or less**
4 ❑ 1991 Cover: 2.50 NM value: **Cover or less**

SOUTHERN SQUADRON, THE (AIRCEL) — Aircel
1 ❑ Aug 1990 Cover: 2.25 NM value: **Cover or less**
📖 Moving Home **A:** Gary Chaloner **C:** Mike Grell **W:** Dave DeVries ★ 1st Appearance of Nightlifter, Southern Squadron, The Dingo.
2 ❑ Sep 1990 Cover: 2.25 NM value: **Cover or less**
3 ❑ Sep 1990 Cover: 2.25 NM value: **Cover or less**
4 ❑ Nov 1990 Cover: 2.25 NM value: **Cover or less**
C: Paul Gulacy

SOUTHERN SQUADRON: THE FREEDOM OF INFORMATION ACT — Eternity
1 ❑ Jan 1992 Cover: 2.50 NM value: **Cover or less**
Fantastic Four #1 homage cover.
2 ❑ Feb 1992 Cover: 2.50 NM value: **Cover or less**
3 ❑ Mar 1992 Cover: 2.50 NM value: **Cover or less**

SOVEREIGN SEVEN — DC

Seven beings from another dimension find themselves in a town called Crossroads. In Crossroads, they try to assimilate into human society. The team is super-powered and all of the members possess high moral virtues. The team is comprised of Rampart, Reflex, Conal, Cascade, Network, Indigo, and their leader, Cruiser. Cruiser's mother is an evil being who has the power to either rule or destroy the world. This power causes Darkseid, one of DC's most powerful villains, to fear her, adding a powerful enemy to the growing list of people who want the team dead.

With this series, writer Chris Claremont returned to the DC Comics stable. Known mostly for his work on Marvel's Uncanny X-Men, Claremont was the creative force behind the introduction of Sovereign Seven in 1995.

1 ❑ Jul 1995 Cover: 1.95 NM value: **2.50**
Circ: CapCity orders: **61,175**
📖 It Was a Dark and Stormy Night... **A:** Dwayne Turner **W:** Chris Claremont ★ 1st Appearance of Conal, Sovereign Seven, Cruiser, Network, Reflex, Indigo, Rampart, Cascade.
1/SC❑Jul 1995 Cover: 10.00 NM value: **Cover or less**
no cover price. • foil edition. **A:** Dwayne Turner **W:** Chris Claremont
2 ❑ Aug 1995 Cover: 1.95 NM value: **2.00**
Circ: CapCity orders: **46,775**
A: Dwayne Turner **W:** Chris Claremont
3 ❑ Sep 1995 Cover: 1.95 NM value: **2.00**
Circ: CapCity orders: **40,725**
📖 Costume Drama **A:** Dwayne Turner **W:** Chris Claremont
4 ❑ Oct 1995 Cover: 1.95 NM value: **2.00**
Circ: CapCity orders: **25,550**
A: Dwayne Turner **W:** Chris Claremont
5 ❑ Nov 1995 Cover: 1.95 NM value: **2.00**
A: Dwayne Turner **W:** Chris Claremont
6 ❑ Dec 1995 Cover: 1.95 NM value: **2.00**
A: Dwayne Turner **W:** Chris Claremont
7 ❑ Jan 1996 Cover: 1.95 NM value: **2.00**
A: Dwayne Turner **W:** Chris Claremont
8 ❑ Feb 1996 Cover: 1.95 NM value: **2.00**
📖 The Wild Hunt **A:** Dwayne Turner **W:** Chris Claremont
9 ❑ Mar 1996 Cover: 1.95 NM value: **2.00**
📖 12th Night **A:** Dwayne Turner **W:** Chris Claremont
10 ❑ Apr 1996 Cover: 1.95 NM value: **2.00**
📖 Road Trip, Part 1 **A:** Dwayne Turner **W:** Chris Claremont
11 ❑ Jun 1996 Cover: 1.95 NM value: **Cover or less**
📖 Road Trip, Part 2 **A:** Dwayne Turner **W:** Chris Claremont
12 ❑ Jul 1996 Cover: 1.95 NM value: **Cover or less**
📖 Road Trip, Part 3 **A:** Dwayne Turner **W:** Chris Claremont
13 ❑ Aug 1996 Cover: 1.95 NM value: **Cover or less**
📖 Lost Souls, Part 1 **A:** Ron Lim **W:** Chris Claremont
14 ❑ Sep 1996 Cover: 1.95 NM value: **Cover or less**
📖 Lost Souls, Part 2 **A:** Dwayne Turner **W:** Chris Claremont
15 ❑ Oct 1996 Cover: 1.95 NM value: **Cover or less**
📖 Prom Night **A:** Dwayne Turner **W:** Chris Claremont
16 ❑ Nov 1996 Cover: 1.95 NM value: **Cover or less**
Circ: Diamd. preorders: **29,504**
• Final Night **A:** Dwayne Turner **W:** Chris Claremont
17 ❑ Dec 1996 Cover: 1.95 NM value: **Cover or less**
Circ: Diamd. preorders: **23,174**
📖 Hot Pursuit **A:** Dwayne Turner **W:** Chris Claremont
18 ❑ Jan 1997 Cover: 1.95 NM value: **Cover or less**
Circ: Diamd. preorders: **22,420**
📖 Meridian: Force Twenty • Cascade quits **A:** Ron Lim **W:** Chris Claremont
19 ❑ Feb 1997 Cover: 1.95 NM value: **Cover or less**
Circ: Diamd. preorders: **21,024**
📖 Bolo **A:** Ron Lim **W:** Chris Claremont ★ Appearance of Clark Kent.
20 ❑ Mar 1997 Cover: 1.95 NM value: **Cover or less**
Circ: Diamd. preorders: **20,192**
📖 Q&A **A:** Vince Giarrano **W:** Chris Claremont
21 ❑ Apr 1997 Cover: 1.95 NM value: **Cover or less**
Circ: Diamd. preorders: **18,909**
📖 Casey the Spy! **A:** Ron Lim **W:** Chris Claremont
22 ❑ May 1997 Cover: 1.95 NM value: **Cover or less**
Circ: Diamd. preorders: **18,343**
W: Chris Claremont
23 ❑ Jun 1997 Cover: 1.95 NM value: **Cover or less**
Circ: Diamd. preorders: **18,045**
W: Chris Claremont
24 ❑ Jul 1997 Cover: 1.95 NM value: **Cover or less**
Circ: Diamd. preorders: **17,564**
W: Chris Claremont ★ Appearance of Superman.
25 ❑ Aug 1997 Cover: 1.95 NM value: **Cover or less**
Circ: Diamd. preorders: **17,972**
W: Chris Claremont ★ Appearance of Power Girl.
26 ❑ Sep 1997 Cover: 2.25 NM value: **Cover or less**
Circ: Diamd. preorders: **17,416**
W: Chris Claremont ★ Appearance of Hitman.
27 ❑ Oct 1997 Cover: 2.25 NM value: **Cover or less**
Circ: Diamd. preorders: **19,237**
• Genesis **W:** Chris Claremont
28 ❑ Nov 1997 Cover: 2.25 NM value: **Cover or less**
Circ: Diamd. preorders: **16,780**
📖 Whatever Happened to Power Girl? **A:** Ron Lim **W:** Chris Claremont ★ Appearance of Impulse.
29 ❑ Dec 1997 Cover: 2.25 NM value: **Cover or less**
Circ: Diamd. preorders: **16,623**
Face cover. 📖 Busted! **A:** Ron Lim **W:** Chris Claremont
30 ❑ Jan 1998 Cover: 2.25 NM value: **Cover or less**
Circ: Diamd. preorders: **15,981**
W: Chris Claremont
31 ❑ Feb 1998 Cover: 2.25 NM value: **Cover or less**
Circ: Diamd. preorders: **15,312**
W: Chris Claremont
32 ❑ Mar 1998 Cover: 2.25 NM value: **Cover or less**
Circ: Diamd. preorders: **14,430**
📖 Night of the Hunters **A:** Ron Lim **W:** Chris Claremont
33 ❑ Apr 1998 Cover: 2.25 NM value: **Cover or less**
Circ: Diamd. preorders: **13,465**
W: Chris Claremont
34 ❑ May 1998 Cover: 2.25 NM value: **Cover or less**
Circ: Diamd. preorders: **13,040**
W: Chris Claremont
35 ❑ Jun 1998 Cover: 2.25 NM value: **Cover or less**
Circ: Diamd. preorders: **12,949**
W: Chris Claremont
36 ❑ Jul 1998 Cover: 2.25 NM value: **Cover or less**
Circ: Diamd. preorders: **12,653**
final issue. **W:** Chris Claremont
Anl 1❑ca. 1995 Cover: 3.95 NM value: **Cover or less**
• Year One; Big Barda **W:** Chris Claremont ★ Appearance of Lobo.
Anl 2❑ca. 1996 Cover: 2.95 NM value: **Cover or less**
Circ: Diamd. preorders: **20,514**
📖 Memento Mori • Legends of the Dead Earth; 1996 Annual **A:** Rick Leonardi **W:** Chris Claremont
Bk 1❑ Cover: 12.95 NM value: **Cover or less**
• collects issues #1-5, Annual #1, and story from Showcase '95 #12 **A:** Alan Davis; Dwayne Turner; Jeff Johnson **W:** Chris Claremont

SOVEREIGN SEVEN PLUS — DC
1 ❑ Feb 1997 Cover: 2.95 NM value: **Cover or less**
Circ: Diamd. preorders: **21,011**
★ Appearance of Legion.

SOVIET SUPER SOLDIERS — Marvel
1 ❑ Nov 1992 Cover: 2.00 NM value: **Cover or less**
Circ: CapCity orders: **25,300**
📖 The Red Triangle Agenda **A:** Angel Medina; Javier Saltares **W:** Fabian Nicieza

SPACE ACTION — Ace
1 ❑ Jun 1952 Cover: 0.10 NM value: **600.00**
• **CGC:** 6 graded, best 9.0
2 ❑ Aug 1952 Cover: 0.10 NM value: **400.00**
• **CGC:** 3 graded, best 9.0
3 ❑ Oct 1952 Cover: 0.10 NM value: **400.00**
• **CGC:** 5 graded, best 9.2

SPACE SQUADRON — Atlas
1 ❑ Jun 1951 Cover: 0.10 NM value: **500.00**
2 ❑ Aug 1951 Cover: 0.10 NM value: **450.00**
3 ❑ Oct 1951 Cover: 0.10 NM value: **350.00**
• **CGC:** 1 graded, best 5.0
4 ❑ Dec 1951 Cover: 0.10 NM value: **350.00**
• **CGC:** 1 graded, best 5.0
5 ❑ Feb 1952 Cover: 0.10 NM value: **350.00**
• **CGC:** 1 graded, best 7.0

SPACE: 1999 — Charlton
1 ❑ Nov 1975 Cover: 0.25 NM value: **5.00**
📖 Moonless Night **A:** Joe Staton **W:** Nicola Cutii ★ Origin of Moonbase Alpha.
2 ❑ Jan 1976 Cover: 0.25 NM value: **3.00**
• **CGC:** 1 graded, best 9.4
3 ❑ Mar 1976 Cover: 0.25 NM value: **4.00**
A: John Byrne
4 ❑ May 1976 Cover: 0.30 NM value: **4.00**
A: John Byrne
5 ❑ Jul 1976 Cover: 0.30 NM value: **4.00**
A: John Byrne
6 ❑ Sep 1976 Cover: 0.30 NM value: **4.00**
A: John Byrne
7 ❑ Nov 1976 Cover: 0.30 NM value: **2.50**

SPACE: 34-24-34 — MN Design
1 ❑ b&w Cover: 4.50 NM value: **Cover or less**
• photos

SPACE: ABOVE AND BEYOND — Topps
1 ❑ Jan 1996 Cover: 2.95 NM value: **Cover or less**
📖 Out of the Silent Space **A:** Yanick Paquette **W:** Roy Thomas
2 ❑ Feb 1996 Cover: 2.95 NM value: **Cover or less**
📖 Mars Ain't the Kind of Place to Raise Your Kids... **A:** Yanick Paquette **W:** Roy Thomas
3 ❑ Mar 1996 Cover: 2.95 NM value: **Cover or less**
A: Yanick Paquette **W:** Roy Thomas

SPACE: ABOVE AND BEYOND-THE GAUNTLET — Topps
1 ❑ May 1996 Cover: 2.95 NM value: **Cover or less**
📖 Running the Gauntlet **A:** Yanick Paquette **W:** Roy Thomas
2 ❑ Jun 1996 Cover: 2.95 NM value: **Cover or less**
📖 A Gauntlet Hurled **A:** Yanick Paquette **W:** Roy Thomas

SPACE ACE — Magazine Enterprises
5 ❑ ca. 1952 Cover: 0.10 NM value: **400.00**
• **CGC:** 7 graded, best 9.4

SPACE ADVENTURES — Charlton

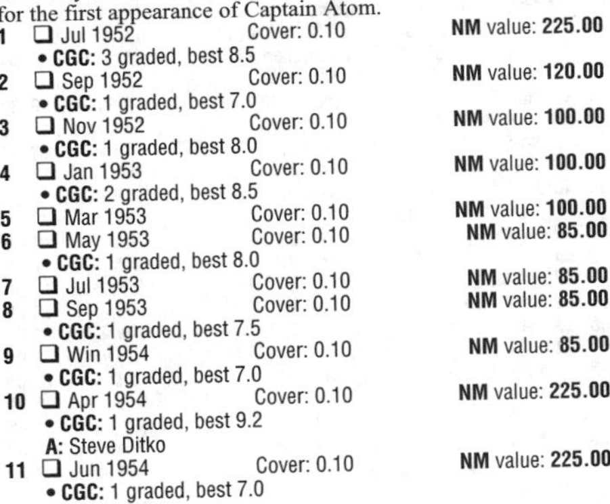

Supersophisticated androids that can pass for human? Robots that turn on their creators to take control of their world? Strange alien armies secretly infiltrating the earth? Men rocketing through the galaxy as easily as taking an average Sunday drive in the country? Come on, that stuff is just a bunch of science fiction, right?

You bet it is! Published every two months, Charlton Comics presented a new collection of short stories about mankind's long-dreamed-of exploration of the rest of the solar system...and beyond!

This series is notable for its many stories by Steve Ditko (creator of The Amazing Spider-Man), and for the first appearance of Captain Atom.

1 ❑ Jul 1952 Cover: 0.10 NM value: **225.00**
• **CGC:** 3 graded, best 8.5
2 ❑ Sep 1952 Cover: 0.10 NM value: **120.00**
• **CGC:** 1 graded, best 7.0
3 ❑ Nov 1952 Cover: 0.10 NM value: **100.00**
• **CGC:** 1 graded, best 8.0
4 ❑ Jan 1953 Cover: 0.10 NM value: **100.00**
• **CGC:** 2 graded, best 8.5
5 ❑ Mar 1953 Cover: 0.10 NM value: **100.00**
6 ❑ May 1953 Cover: 0.10 NM value: **85.00**
• **CGC:** 1 graded, best 8.0
7 ❑ Jul 1953 Cover: 0.10 NM value: **85.00**
8 ❑ Sep 1953 Cover: 0.10 NM value: **85.00**
• **CGC:** 1 graded, best 7.5
9 ❑ Win 1954 Cover: 0.10 NM value: **85.00**
• **CGC:** 1 graded, best 7.0
10 ❑ Apr 1954 Cover: 0.10 NM value: **225.00**
• **CGC:** 1 graded, best 9.2
A: Steve Ditko
11 ❑ Jun 1954 Cover: 0.10 NM value: **225.00**
• **CGC:** 1 graded, best 7.0
A: Steve Ditko
12 ❑ Aug 1954 Cover: 0.10 NM value: **225.00**
• **CGC:** 2 graded, best 8.0
📖 The Boy and the Stars; Captain Atom: An Ageless Weapon; Captain Atom: Test-Pilot's Nightmare; Captain Atom: Silver Lady From Venus; A Strange Kiss • Steve Ditko credits **A:** Steve Ditko
13 ❑ Oct 1954 Cover: 0.10 NM value: **85.00**
• **CGC:** 12 graded, best 9.6
14 ❑ Dec 1954 Cover: 0.10 NM value: **85.00**
• **CGC:** 1 graded, best 9.4
15 ❑ Mar 1955 Cover: 0.10 NM value: **85.00**
16 ❑ May 1955 Cover: 0.10 NM value: **85.00**
17 ❑ Jul 1955 Cover: 0.10 NM value: **85.00**
• **CGC:** 1 graded, best 9.4

CGC-graded: Multiply prices above by **33 for 9.9 M • 16 for 9.8 NM/M • 7 for 9.6 NM+ • 5 for 9.4 NM • 2.5 for 9.2 NM- • 1.5 for 9.0 VF/NM**

18 ❑ Sep 1955 Cover: 0.10 **NM** value: **85.00**
• **CGC:** 1 graded, best 9.4
19 ❑ Nov 1955 Cover: 0.10 **NM** value: **85.00**
20 ❑ Jan 1956 Cover: 0.10 **NM** value: **100.00**
• **CGC:** 1 graded, best 8.0
21 ❑ Mar 1956 Cover: 0.10 **NM** value: **70.00**
• Series continued in War at Sea #22
23 ❑ May 1958 Cover: 0.10 **NM** value: **100.00**
• Series continued from Nyoka, the Jungle Girl #22
24 ❑ Jul 1958 Cover: 0.10 **NM** value: **70.00**
• **CGC:** 1 graded, best 8.5
25 ❑ Sep 1958 Cover: 0.10 **NM** value: **70.00**
• **CGC:** 1 graded, best 9.4
26 ❑ Nov 1958 Cover: 0.10 **NM** value: **70.00**
27 ❑ Feb 1959 Cover: 0.10 **NM** value: **70.00**
• **CGC:** 1 graded, best 9.2
28 ❑ 1959 Cover: 0.10 **NM** value: **70.00**
29 ❑ Jul 1959 Cover: 0.10 **NM** value: **70.00**
30 ❑ Sep 1959 Cover: 0.10 **NM** value: **70.00**
31 ❑ Dec 1959 Cover: 0.10 **NM** value: **70.00**
32 ❑ Jan 1960 Cover: 0.10 **NM** value: **70.00**
Circ: Statement: **110,166** • **CGC:** 2 graded, best 9.2
33 ❑ Mar 1960 Cover: 0.10 **NM** value: **325.00**
Circ: Statement: **110,166**
A: Steve Ditko ★ Origin of Captain Atom. ★ 1st Appearance of Captain Atom.
34 ❑ Jun 1960 Cover: 0.10 **NM** value: **150.00**
Circ: Statement: **110,166** • **CGC:** 1 graded, best 8.5
A: Steve Ditko ★ 2nd Appearance of Captain Atom.
35 ❑ Aug 1960 Cover: 0.10 **NM** value: **125.00**
Circ: Statement: **110,166** • **CGC:** 1 graded, best 7.0
A: Steve Ditko ★ Appearance of Captain Atom.
36 ❑ Oct 1960 Cover: 0.10 **NM** value: **125.00**
Circ: Statement: **110,166**
A: Steve Ditko ★ Appearance of Captain Atom.
37 ❑ Dec 1960 Cover: 0.10 **NM** value: **125.00**
Circ: Statement: **110,166**
A: Steve Ditko ★ Appearance of Captain Atom.
38 ❑ Feb 1961 Cover: 0.10 **NM** value: **125.00**
A: Steve Ditko ★ Appearance of Captain Atom.
39 ❑ Apr 1961 Cover: 0.10 **NM** value: **125.00**
• Has 1960 Statement; avg total paid circ 110,166 **A:** Steve Ditko ★ Appearance of Captain Atom.
40 ❑ Jun 1961 Cover: 0.10 **NM** value: **125.00**
A: Steve Ditko ★ Appearance of Captain Atom.
41 ❑ Aug 1961 Cover: 0.10 **NM** value: **25.00**
42 ❑ Oct 1961 Cover: 0.10 **NM** value: **75.00**
• **CGC:** 1 graded, best 9.2
A: Steve Ditko ★ Appearance of Captain Atom.
43 ❑ Dec 1961 **NM** value: **25.00**
44 ❑ Feb 1962 **NM** value: **25.00**
• **CGC:** 5 graded, best 9.6
45 ❑ May 1962 Cover: 0.12 **NM** value: **25.00**
46 ❑ Jul 1962 Cover: 0.12 **NM** value: **25.00**
47 ❑ Sep 1962 Cover: 0.12 **NM** value: **25.00**
48 ❑ Nov 1962 Cover: 0.12 **NM** value: **25.00**
📖 A True Friend; The Ambassador From Earth; Silent World; Space Speech (text story); The Lively Forest
49 ❑ Jan 1963 Cover: 0.12 **NM** value: **25.00**
Circ: Statement: **117,623**
50 ❑ Mar 1963 Cover: 0.12 **NM** value: **25.00**
Circ: Statement: **117,623**
51 ❑ May 1963 Cover: 0.12 **NM** value: **18.00**
Circ: Statement: **117,623**
52 ❑ Jul 1963 Cover: 0.12 **NM** value: **18.00**
Circ: Statement: **117,623**
53 ❑ Sep 1963 Cover: 0.12 **NM** value: **18.00**
Circ: Statement: **117,623**
54 ❑ Nov 1963 Cover: 0.12 **NM** value: **18.00**
Circ: Statement: **117,623**
55 ❑ Mar 1964 Cover: 0.12 **NM** value: **18.00**
56 ❑ May 1964 Cover: 0.12 **NM** value: **18.00**
• Has 1963 Statement, filed 9/30/63; avg print run 190,781; avg sales 117,604; avg subs 19; avg total paid 117,623; samples 25; max existent 117,648; 38% of run returned
57 ❑ Jul 1964 Cover: 0.12 **NM** value: **18.00**
58 ❑ Sep 1964 Cover: 0.12 **NM** value: **18.00**
59 ❑ Nov 1964 Cover: 0.12 **NM** value: **18.00**
60 ❑ Oct 1967 Cover: 0.12 **NM** value: **18.00**
61 ❑ Jul 1968 Cover: 0.12 **NM** value: **12.00**
• **CGC:** 2 graded, best 8.0
62 ❑ Sep 1968 Cover: 0.12 **NM** value: **12.00**
63 ❑ Nov 1968 Cover: 0.12 **NM** value: **12.00**
64 ❑ Jan 1969 Cover: 0.12 **NM** value: **12.00**
65 ❑ Mar 1969 Cover: 0.12 **NM** value: **12.00**
66 ❑ May 1969 Cover: 0.12 **NM** value: **12.00**
67 ❑ Jul 1969 Cover: 0.15 **NM** value: **12.00**
68 ❑ May 1978 Cover: 0.35 **NM** value: **12.00**
69 ❑ 1978 Cover: 0.35 **NM** value: **12.00**
70 ❑ 1978 Cover: 0.35 **NM** value: **12.00**
71 ❑ Jan 1979 Cover: 0.35 **NM** value: **12.00**
72 ❑ Mar 1979 Cover: 0.35 **NM** value: **12.00**
• **CGC:** 1 graded, best 9.6

SPACE ARK — AC

1 ❑ Cover: 1.75 **NM** value: **Cover or less**
Circ: CapCity orders: **2,700**
📖 No Time for Space Ark! **A:** Ken Mitchroney **W:** Ken Mitchroney; Mark Cantrell
2 ❑ Cover: 1.75 **NM** value: **Cover or less**
Circ: CapCity orders: **1,775**
📖 Cattycornered **A:** Ken Mitchroney **W:** Ken Mitchroney; Mark Cantrell
3 ❑ b&w Cover: 1.75 **NM** value: **Cover or less**
A: Ken Mitchroney **W:** Ken Mitchroney; Mark Cantrell
4 ❑ b&w Cover: 1.75 **NM** value: **Cover or less**
A: Ken Mitchroney **W:** Ken Mitchroney; Mark Cantrell
5 ❑ b&w Cover: 1.75 **NM** value: **Cover or less**
A: Ken Mitchroney **W:** Ken Mitchroney; Mark Cantrell

SPACE BANANAS — Karl Art

0 ❑ Cover: 1.95 **NM** value: **Cover or less**
📖 The Shrinking Gas Strikes! **A:** Chris Allan; Joe Dator **W:** Joe Dator; Barry Kraus

SPACE BEAVER — Ten-Buck

1 ❑ Oct 1986 Cover: 1.50 **NM** value: **Cover or less**
A: Darick Robertson **W:** Darick Robertson
2 ❑ Cover: 1.50 **NM** value: **Cover or less**
A: Darick Robertson **W:** Darick Robertson
3 ❑ Feb 1987 Cover: 1.50 **NM** value: **Cover or less**
A: Darick Robertson **W:** Darick Robertson
4 ❑ 1987 Cover: 1.50 **NM** value: **Cover or less**
5 ❑ 1987 Cover: 1.50 **NM** value: **Cover or less**
6 ❑ Sep 1987 Cover: 1.50 **NM** value: **Cover or less**
7 ❑ Oct 1987 Cover: 1.50 **NM** value: **Cover or less**
8 ❑ Nov 1987 Cover: 1.50 **NM** value: **Cover or less**
9 ❑ Dec 1987 Cover: 1.50 **NM** value: **Cover or less**
10 ❑ Jan 1988 Cover: 1.50 **NM** value: **Cover or less**
11 ❑ Feb 1988 Cover: 1.50 **NM** value: **Cover or less**

SPACE BUSTERS — Ziff-Davis

1 ❑ Spr 1952 Cover: 0.10 **NM** value: **700.00**
2 ❑ Fal 1952 Cover: 0.10 **NM** value: **500.00**

SPACE CIRCUS — Dark Horse

1 ❑ Jul 2000 Cover: 2.95 **NM** value: **Cover or less**
Circ: Diamd. preorders: **10,900**
A: Sergio Aragonés **W:** Mark Evanier
2 ❑ Aug 2000 Cover: 2.95 **NM** value: **Cover or less**
Circ: Diamd. preorders: **9,087**
A: Sergio Aragonés **W:** Mark Evanier
3 ❑ Sep 2000 Cover: 2.95 **NM** value: **Cover or less**
Circ: Diamd. preorders: **8,843**
A: Sergio Aragonés **W:** Mark Evanier
4 ❑ Oct 2000 Cover: 2.95 **NM** value: **Cover or less**
Circ: Diamd. preorders: **8,593**
A: Sergio Aragonés **W:** Mark Evanier

SPACE COMICS — Avon

4 ❑ Mar 1954 Cover: 0.10 **NM** value: **25.00**
5 ❑ May 1954 Cover: 0.10 **NM** value: **25.00**

SPACED — Unbridled Ambition

1 ❑ Cover: 1.60 **NM** value: **2.00**
2 ❑ Cover: 1.60 **NM** value: **2.00**
3 ❑ Cover: 1.60 **NM** value: **2.00**
4 ❑ Cover: 1.60 **NM** value: **2.00**
5 ❑ Cover: 1.60 **NM** value: **2.00**
6 ❑ Cover: 1.60 **NM** value: **2.00**
7 ❑ Cover: 1.60 **NM** value: **2.00**
8 ❑ Cover: 1.60 **NM** value: **2.00**
📖 Beer, Wine & Set-Ups **W:** John Williams; Tom Stazer
9 ❑ Cover: 1.60 **NM** value: **2.00**
10 ❑ b&w Cover: 1.50 **NM** value: **2.00**
• Eclipse publisher
11 ❑ b&w Cover: 1.50 **NM** value: **2.00**
12 ❑ b&w Cover: 1.50 **NM** value: **2.00**
13 ❑ b&w Cover: 1.50 **NM** value: **2.00**

SPACED (COMICS AND COMIX) — Comics and Comix

1 ❑ Cover: 1.00 **NM** value: **4.00**

SPACE DETECTIVE — Avon

1 ❑ Jul 1951 Cover: 0.10 **NM** value: **800.00**
• **CGC:** 2 graded, best 9.2
2 ❑ Nov 1951 Cover: 0.10 **NM** value: **450.00**
• **CGC:** 3 graded, best 7.0
3 ❑ Feb 1952 Cover: 0.10 **NM** value: **300.00**
• **CGC:** 3 graded, best 8.0
4 ❑ Apr 1952 Cover: 0.10 **NM** value: **300.00**
• **CGC:** 3 graded, best 9.4

SPACED OUT (FORBIDDEN FRUIT) — Forbidden Fruit

1 ❑ Jul 1992 Cover: 2.95 **NM** value: **Cover or less**
📖 Cyborg 28-H; Downed; The Buy **A:** Don Lomax **W:** Don Lomax

SPACED OUT (PRINT MINT) — Print Mint

1 ❑ Cover: 0.50 **NM** value: **3.00**
📖 Run!; Perish the Thought; Space Bum; Of Good and Evil **A:** Jim Pinkoski; Ron Roach **W:** Jim Pinkoski; Ron Roach

SPACE FAMILY ROBINSON — Gold Key

Space Family Robinson was the inspiration for the hit 1960s TV show "Lost In Space." In this original comics version, the family consisted of Craig and June Robinson and their children Tim and Tam. (The TV series' Robot joined the devious Doctor Smith and the stalwart Major West for the TV version.)

In the comics version, the Robinson family was cast adrift in space due to an accident, while the TV Robinsons were the victims of sabotage on the part of Smith. Their goal was to eventually find their way back to Earth, but a series of mishaps and alien encounters always seems to send them spinning off into space just as they were beginning to get back on course.

This series began in 1962, some years before the television show. When the show became a hit, the comic changed its name to "Space Family Robinson Lost in Space" (later even adding "On Space Station One").

1 ❑ Dec 1962 Cover: 0.12 **NM** value: **150.00**
• **CGC:** 4 graded, best 8.5
• Low circulation
2 ❑ Mar 1963 Cover: 0.12 **NM** value: **75.00**
• Robinson's become lost in space
3 ❑ Jun 1963 Cover: 0.12 **NM** value: **50.00**
4 ❑ Sep 1963 Cover: 0.12 **NM** value: **50.00**
5 ❑ Dec 1963 Cover: 0.12 **NM** value: **50.00**
6 ❑ Feb 1964 Cover: 0.12 **NM** value: **40.00**
Circ: Statement: **231,629** • **CGC:** 1 graded, best 9.2
7 ❑ Apr 1964 Cover: 0.12 **NM** value: **40.00**
Circ: Statement: **231,629** • **CGC:** 1 graded, best 9.6
8 ❑ Jun 1964 Cover: 0.12 **NM** value: **40.00**
Circ: Statement: **231,629**
9 ❑ Aug 1964 Cover: 0.12 **NM** value: **40.00**
Circ: Statement: **231,629**
10 ❑ Oct 1964 Cover: 0.12 **NM** value: **40.00**
Circ: Statement: **231,629** • **CGC:** 1 graded, best 9.6
11 ❑ Dec 1964 Cover: 0.12 **NM** value: **25.00**
Circ: Statement: **231,629**
12 ❑ Apr 1965 Cover: 0.12 **NM** value: **25.00**
Circ: Statement: **216,775**
📖 The Iron Dwarfs
13 ❑ Jul 1965 Cover: 0.12 **NM** value: **25.00**
Circ: Statement: **216,775** • **CGC:** 1 graded, best 9.8
14 ❑ Oct 1965 Cover: 0.12 **NM** value: **25.00**
Circ: Statement: **216,775**
15 ❑ Jan 1966 Cover: 0.12 **NM** value: **25.00**
Circ: Statement: **253,025** • **CGC:** 1 graded, best 9.6
• Title changes to "Space Family Robinson Lost in Space"
16 ❑ Apr 1966 Cover: 0.12 **NM** value: **20.00**
Circ: Statement: **253,025** • **CGC:** 1 graded, best 9.4
17 ❑ Jul 1966 Cover: 0.12 **NM** value: **20.00**
Circ: Statement: **253,025**
18 ❑ Oct 1966 Cover: 0.12 **NM** value: **20.00**
Circ: Statement: **253,025**
19 ❑ Dec 1966 Cover: 0.12 **NM** value: **20.00**
Circ: Statement: **253,025**
20 ❑ Feb 1967 Cover: 0.12 **NM** value: **20.00**
Circ: Statement: **264,667**
21 ❑ Apr 1967 Cover: 0.12 **NM** value: **18.00**
Circ: Statement: **264,667**
📖 Operation Survival!
22 ❑ Jun 1967 Cover: 0.12 **NM** value: **18.00**
Circ: Statement: **264,667** • **CGC:** 1 graded, best 9.6
23 ❑ Aug 1967 Cover: 0.12 **NM** value: **18.00**
Circ: Statement: **264,667**
24 ❑ Oct 1967 Cover: 0.12 **NM** value: **18.00**
Circ: Statement: **264,667**
📖 The Savage Earth; captain Venture: The Big Wave
25 ❑ Dec 1967 Cover: 0.12 **NM** value: **18.00**
Circ: Statement: **264,667** • **CGC:** 1 graded, best 9.0
26 ❑ Feb 1968 Cover: 0.12 **NM** value: **18.00**
27 ❑ Apr 1968 Cover: 0.12 **NM** value: **18.00**
• **CGC:** 1 graded, best 9.0
28 ❑ Jun 1968 Cover: 0.12 **NM** value: **18.00**
• **CGC:** 1 graded, best 9.0
📖 When Suns Collide
29 ❑ Aug 1968, four-color Cover: 0.15 **NM** value: **18.00**
📖 The Formless Foe; Captain Venture in the Cavern of Ages
30 ❑ Oct 1968 Cover: 0.15 **NM** value: **18.00**
31 ❑ Dec 1968 Cover: 0.15 **NM** value: **18.00**
• **CGC:** 2 graded, best 9.4
32 ❑ Feb 1969 Cover: 0.15 **NM** value: **18.00**
33 ❑ Apr 1969 Cover: 0.15 **NM** value: **18.00**
34 ❑ Jun 1969 Cover: 0.15 **NM** value: **18.00**
35 ❑ Aug 1969 Cover: 0.15 **NM** value: **18.00**
36 ❑ Oct 1969 **NM** value: **18.00**
• Final issue of original run
37 ❑ Oct 1973 Cover: 0.20 **NM** value: **18.00**
• Series begins again
38 ❑ Jan 1974 Cover: 0.20 **NM** value: **18.00**
• Title changes to "Space Family Robinson, Lost in Space on Space Station One"
39 ❑ Apr 1974 Cover: 0.20 **NM** value: **18.00**
40 ❑ Jul 1974 Cover: 0.20 **NM** value: **18.00**
41 ❑ Oct 1974 Cover: 0.25 **NM** value: **18.00**
42 ❑ Cover: 0.25 **NM** value: **18.00**
43 ❑ Apr 1975 Cover: 0.25 **NM** value: **18.00**
44 ❑ Aug 1975 Cover: 0.25 **NM** value: **18.00**
45 ❑ Oct 1975 Cover: 0.25 **NM** value: **8.00**
46 ❑ Cover: 0.25 **NM** value: **8.00**
47 ❑ Apr 1976 Cover: 0.25 **NM** value: **8.00**
48 ❑ Aug 1976 Cover: 0.25 **NM** value: **8.00**
49 ❑ **NM** value: **8.00**
50 ❑ **NM** value: **8.00**
51 ❑ **NM** value: **8.00**
52 ❑ **NM** value: **8.00**
53 ❑ **NM** value: **8.00**
54 ❑ Nov 1978 **NM** value: **8.00**
55 ❑ 1982 **NM** value: **5.00**
• Series begins again
56 ❑ **NM** value: **5.00**
57 ❑ **NM** value: **5.00**
58 ❑ Feb 1982 **NM** value: **5.00**
59 ❑ **NM** value: **5.00**
final issue.

SPACE FUNNIES — Archival

1 ❑ Cover: 5.95 **NM** value: **Cover or less**
A: Basil Wolverton

Other grades: Multiply prices above by **1.5 for Mint • 2/3 for Very Fine • 1/3 for Fine • 1/5 for Very Good • 1/8 for Good**

SPACEGAL COMICS — Thorby
1 ❑ Cover: 2.95 **NM** value: **Cover or less**
A: Mike Kadin **W:** Mike Kadin
2 ❑ Cover: 2.95 **NM** value: **Cover or less**
• Flip-Book with Johnny Cosmic #1★ Origin of Spacegal.

SPACE GHOST (COMICO) — Comico
1 ❑ Dec 1987 Cover: 3.50 **NM** value: **Cover or less**
Circ: CapCity orders: **1,925** • **CGC:** 2 graded, best 9.8
The Sinister Spectre **A:** Steve Rude **W:** Steve Rude; Mark Evanier

SPACE GHOST (GOLD KEY) — Gold Key
1 ❑ Mar 1967 Cover: 0.12 **NM** value: **150.00**
• **CGC:** 6 graded, best 9.4

SPACE GIANTS, THE — Boneyard
1 ❑ Cover: 2.75 **NM** value: **Cover or less**
A: Mark Texeira **W:** Pat Gabriele

SPACEGIRL COMICS — Bill Jones Graphics
1 ❑ Nov 1995, b&w Cover: 2.50 **NM** value: **Cover or less**
2 ❑ Nov 1995, b&w Cover: 2.50 **NM** value: **Cover or less**

SPACEHAWK — Dark Horse
1 ❑ ca. 1989 Cover: 2.00 **NM** value: **Cover or less**
Spacehawk vs. The Brain Bats of Venus **A:** Basil Wolverton **W:** Basil Wolverton
2 ❑ ca. 1989 Cover: 2.00 **NM** value: **Cover or less**
Vulture Men from the Void; The Superhuman Enemy of Crime **A:** Basil Wolverton **W:** Basil Wolverton
3 ❑ ca. 1989 Cover: 2.00 **NM** value: **2.25**
Visit to the Planet of Terror **A:** Basil Wolverton **W:** Basil Wolverton
4 ❑ ca. 1989 Cover: 2.25 **NM** value: **Cover or less**
Spacehawk: Superhuman Enemy of Crime; Spacehawk: Lone Wolf of the Void **A:** Basil Wolverton **W:** Basil Wolverton
5 ❑ Jan 1993 Cover: 2.50 **NM** value: **Cover or less**
A: Basil Wolverton **W:** Basil Wolverton

SPACE HUSTLERS — Slave Labor
1 ❑ Mar 1997, b&w Cover: 2.95 **NM** value: **Cover or less**
Sewercide **A:** Steve Owen **W:** Steve Owen

SPACE JAM — DC
1 ❑ Oct 1996 Cover: 2.50 **NM** value: **5.95**
Circ: Diamd. preorders: **17,048**
No issue number. • prestige format. **A:** Alberto Saichann; Horacio Ottolini; Leo Batic **W:** David Cody Weiss

SPACEKNIGHTS — Marvel
1 ❑ Oct 2000 Cover: 2.99 **NM** value: **Cover or less**
Circ: Diamd. preorders: **21,334**
Ebon Tidings **A:** Chris Batista **W:** Jim Starlin; Chris Batista
2 ❑ Nov 2000 Cover: 2.99 **NM** value: **Cover or less**
Circ: Diamd. preorders: **17,320**
Dishonor! **A:** Chris Batista **W:** Jim Starlin; Chris Batista
3 ❑ Dec 2000 Cover: 2.99 **NM** value: **Cover or less**
Circ: Diamd. preorders: **16,459**
Redemption! **A:** Chris Batista **W:** Jim Starlin; Chris Batista
4 ❑ Jan 2001 Cover: 2.99 **NM** value: **Cover or less**
Circ: Diamd. preorders: **14,885**
... Retreat and Regroup! **A:** Chris Batista **W:** Jim Starlin; Chris Batista
5 ❑ Feb 2001 Cover: 2.99 **NM** value: **Cover or less**
Circ: Diamd. preorders: **14,005**
War! **A:** Chris Batista **W:** Jim Starlin; Chris Batista

SPACEMAN — Dell
2 ❑ Jun 1962 Cover: 0.12 **NM** value: **35.00**
★ Appearance of Series continued from.
3 ❑ Sep 1962 Cover: 0.12 **NM** value: **28.00**
4 ❑ 1963 Cover: 0.12 **NM** value: **22.00**
Our Solar System: Venus; Space Man; Flight from Way Out (text); The Space Hogs
5 ❑ Jun 1963 Cover: 0.12 **NM** value: **22.00**
Our Solar System: Jupiter; Space Man; Old Faithful (text); The Space Hogs; Solar System Oddballs
6 ❑ Sep 1963 Cover: 0.12 **NM** value: **22.00**
7 ❑ Dec 1964 Cover: 0.12 **NM** value: **20.00**
Space Man: Space Battle; The Time Niche (text); Space Hogs: Bewitched; Stardust
8 ❑ Mar 1964 Cover: 0.12 **NM** value: **20.00**
The Moon; Space Man: The Soulless One; Surprise! (text); The Space Hogs; The Solar System
9 ❑ ca. 1972 Cover: 0.20 **NM** value: **5.00**
• Reprints Space Man #1
10 ❑ ca. 1972 Cover: 0.20 **NM** value: **5.00**
• Reprints Space Man #2

SPACEMAN (ATLAS) — Atlas
1 ❑ Sep 1953 Cover: 0.10 **NM** value: **600.00**
• **CGC:** 2 graded, best 7.5
2 ❑ Nov 1953 Cover: 0.10 **NM** value: **300.00**
3 ❑ Jan 1954 Cover: 0.10 **NM** value: **250.00**
4 ❑ Mar 1954 Cover: 0.10 **NM** value: **250.00**
5 ❑ May 1954 Cover: 0.10 **NM** value: **250.00**
6 ❑ Jul 1954 Cover: 0.10 **NM** value: **250.00**

SPACE MOUSE — Avon
1 ❑ Spr 1953 Cover: 0.10 **NM** value: **60.00**
2 ❑ Sum 1953 Cover: 0.10 **NM** value: **40.00**
3 ❑ Fal 1953 Cover: 0.10 **NM** value: **30.00**
4 ❑ Win 1953 Cover: 0.10 **NM** value: **30.00**
5 ❑ Spr 1954 Cover: 0.10 **NM** value: **30.00**

SPACE PATROL (ADVENTURE) — Adventure
1 ❑ Cover: 2.50 **NM** value: **Cover or less**
A: Doug Wheatley **W:** Christopher Weppler
2 ❑ b&w Cover: 2.50 **NM** value: **Cover or less**
A: Doug Wheatley **W:** Christopher Weppler
3 ❑ Cover: 2.50 **NM** value: **Cover or less**
A: Doug Wheatley **W:** Christopher Weppler

SPACE PATROL (ZIFF-DAVIS) — Ziff-Davis
1 ❑ Sum 1952 Cover: 0.10 **NM** value: **750.00**
• **CGC:** 3 graded, best 9.0
2 ❑ Oct 1952 Cover: 0.10 **NM** value: **500.00**
• **CGC:** 1 graded, best 8.5

SPACE SLUTZ — Comic Zone
All issues are adults only.
1 ❑ b&w Cover: 3.95 **NM** value: **Cover or less**

SPACE THRILLERS — Avon
1 ❑ ca. 1954 Cover: 0.25 **NM** value: **1000.00**

SPACE TIME SHUFFLE A TRILOGY — Alpha Productions
1 ❑ b&w Cover: 1.95 **NM** value: **Cover or less**
2 ❑ b&w Cover: 1.95 **NM** value: **Cover or less**

SPACE TRIP TO THE MOON — Avalon
1 ❑ ca. 1999, b&w Cover: 2.95 **NM** value: **Cover or less**
• adapts Destination: Moon

SPACE USAGI — Mirage
1 ❑ Jun 1992, b&w Cover: 2.00 **NM** value: **3.00**
Circ: CapCity orders: **5,625**
2 ❑ Jul 1992, b&w Cover: 2.00 **NM** value: **3.00**
Circ: CapCity orders: **4,250**
3 ❑ Aug 1992, b&w Cover: 2.00 **NM** value: **3.00**
Circ: CapCity orders: **3,975**

SPACE USAGI (VOL. 2) — Mirage
1 ❑ Nov 1993 Cover: 2.75 **NM** value: **3.00**
Circ: CapCity orders: **4,825**
White Star Rising, Part 1 **A:** Stan Sakai **W:** Stan Sakai
2 ❑ Jan 1994 Cover: 2.75 **NM** value: **3.00**
Circ: CapCity orders: **3,600**
White Star Rising, Part 2 **A:** Stan Sakai **W:** Stan Sakai
3 ❑ Mar 1994 Cover: 2.75 **NM** value: **3.00**
Circ: CapCity orders: **3,300**
White Star Rising, Part 3 **A:** Stan Sakai **W:** Stan Sakai

SPACE USAGI (VOL. 3) — Dark Horse
1 ❑ Jan 1996, b&w Cover: 2.95 **NM** value: **Cover or less**
Warrior, Part 1 **A:** Stan Sakai **W:** Stan Sakai
2 ❑ Feb 1996, b&w Cover: 2.95 **NM** value: **Cover or less**
Warrior, Part 2 **A:** Stan Sakai **W:** Stan Sakai
3 ❑ Mar 1996, b&w Cover: 2.95 **NM** value: **Cover or less**
Warrior, Part 3 **A:** Stan Sakai **W:** Stan Sakai
Bk 1 ❑ Dec 1998 Cover: 16.95 **NM** value: **Cover or less**
• collects all mini-series and other material

SPACE WAR — Charlton
1 ❑ Oct 1959 Cover: 0.10 **NM** value: **85.00**
• **CGC:** 1 graded, best 9.6
2 ❑ Dec 1959 Cover: 0.10 **NM** value: **50.00**
• **CGC:** 1 graded, best 7.5
3 ❑ Feb 1960 Cover: 0.10 **NM** value: **50.00**
• **CGC:** 1 graded, best 8.5
4 ❑ Apr 1960 Cover: 0.10 **NM** value: **90.00**
• **CGC:** 1 graded, best 9.4
A: Steve Ditko
5 ❑ Jun 1960 Cover: 0.10 **NM** value: **90.00**
• **CGC:** 1 graded, best 9.2
A: Steve Ditko
6 ❑ Aug 1960 Cover: 0.10 **NM** value: **90.00**
• **CGC:** 1 graded, best 8.5
A: Steve Ditko
7 ❑ Oct 1960 Cover: 0.10 **NM** value: **28.00**
8 ❑ Dec 1960 Cover: 0.10 **NM** value: **90.00**
A: Steve Ditko
9 ❑ Feb 1961 Cover: 0.10 **NM** value: **28.00**
10 ❑ Apr 1961 Cover: 0.10 **NM** value: **90.00**
A: Steve Ditko
11 ❑ Jun 1961 Cover: 0.10 **NM** value: **28.00**
12 ❑ Aug 1961 Cover: 0.12 **NM** value: **28.00**
13 ❑ Oct 1961 Cover: 0.12 **NM** value: **28.00**
The Snail From Uranus; Earth's Deadly Weapon; Day of Destiny
14 ❑ Dec 1961 Cover: 0.12 **NM** value: **28.00**
• **CGC:** 4 graded, best 9.6
15 ❑ 1962 Cover: 0.12 **NM** value: **28.00**
16 ❑ 1962 Cover: 0.12 **NM** value: **15.00**
Rescue in Space; The Greatest Adventure; The Friendly Creatures; The Space Serpent
17 ❑ 1962 Cover: 0.12 **NM** value: **15.00**
18 ❑ 1962 Cover: 0.12 **NM** value: **15.00**
The Great Powers of Space; The Peacemakers; No Surrender; A Look At A Backward Planet
19 ❑ 1962 Cover: 0.12 **NM** value: **15.00**
The Long Orbit!; The Imitators
20 ❑ Jan 1963 Cover: 0.12 **NM** value: **15.00**
Circ: Statement: **121,581**
Underworld; The Beginning; The Brain Master
21 ❑ Mar 1963 Cover: 0.12 **NM** value: **15.00**
Circ: Statement: **121,581** • **CGC:** 1 graded, best 9.4
An Ugly World; Easy Victory; Double Danger; The Odd One
22 ❑ May 1963 Cover: 0.12 **NM** value: **15.00**
Circ: Statement: **121,581**
The Raiders; The Mercenaries; The Terrible Foe; The End of the Long Long War; Strange World; Terms of Surrender
23 ❑ Jul 1963 Cover: 0.12 **NM** value: **15.00**
Circ: Statement: **121,581**
The War Mongers; The End of Time; Ten Enemies; Space Flotsam; Century Without War; The Aggressors
24 ❑ Sep 1963 Cover: 0.12 **NM** value: **15.00**
Circ: Statement: **121,581**
The Emerald Moon; Assault Force; Gift of the Mojii; The Hive Planet; The Ultimate Weapon
25 ❑ Nov 1963 Cover: 0.12 **NM** value: **15.00**
Circ: Statement: **121,581**
Action At Station 4!; Darken The Sun; This Better World; Princess Of Chaos
26 ❑ Jan 1964 Cover: 0.12 **NM** value: **15.00**
27 ❑ Mar 1964 Cover: 0.12 **NM** value: **15.00**
• Series continued in Fightin' 5 #28; Has 1963 Statement, filed 9/30/63; avg print run 196,293; avg sales 121,574; avg subs 7; avg total paid 121,581; samples 25; max existent 121,606
28 ❑ Mar 1978 Cover: 0.35 **NM** value: **3.50**
• Series begins again (1978)
29 ❑ May 1978 Cover: 0.35 **NM** value: **3.50**
• **CGC:** 1 graded, best 9.4
30 ❑ Jun 1978 Cover: 0.35 **NM** value: **3.50**
• **CGC:** 1 graded, best 9.4
Lifelong Companion; The Anywhere Machine; The King Of Planetoid X
31 ❑ Oct 1978 Cover: 0.35 **NM** value: **3.50**
• **CGC:** 1 graded, best 9.6
32 ❑ ca. 1979 Cover: 0.35 **NM** value: **3.50**
Circ: Statement: **130,490**

SPACE WAR CLASSICS — Avalon
1 ❑ b&w Cover: 2.95 **NM** value: **Cover or less**

SPACE WESTERN COMICS — Charlton
40 ❑ Oct 1952 Cover: 0.10 **NM** value: **500.00**
41 ❑ Dec 1952 Cover: 0.10 **NM** value: **350.00**
42 ❑ Feb 1953 Cover: 0.10 **NM** value: **350.00**
43 ❑ Apr 1953 Cover: 0.10 **NM** value: **300.00**
• **CGC:** 1 graded, best 9.2
44 ❑ Jun 1953 Cover: 0.10 **NM** value: **300.00**
45 ❑ Aug 1953 Cover: 0.10 **NM** value: **300.00**

SPACE WOLF — Antarctic
1 ❑ b&w Cover: 2.50 **NM** value: **Cover or less**
2 ❑ b&w Cover: 2.50 **NM** value: **Cover or less**

SPACE WORLDS — Atlas
6 ❑ **NM** value: **300.00**

SPAM — Alpha Productions
1 ❑ b&w Cover: 1.50 **NM** value: **Cover or less**
2 ❑ b&w Cover: 1.50 **NM** value: **Cover or less**

SPANDEX TIGHTS — Lost Cause
1 ❑ Sep 1994, b&w Cover: 1.95 **NM** value: **2.50**
Couched Terms **A:** Sky Owens **W:** Bryan J.L. Glass
2 ❑ Nov 1994, b&w Cover: 2.25 **NM** value: **Cover or less**
W: Bryan J.L. Glass
3 ❑ b&w Cover: 2.25 **NM** value: **Cover or less**
W: Bryan J.L. Glass
4 ❑ Mar 1995, b&w Cover: 2.25 **NM** value: **Cover or less**
W: Bryan J.L. Glass
5 ❑ May 1995, b&w Cover: 2.25 **NM** value: **Cover or less**
W: Bryan J.L. Glass
6 ❑ Jul 1995, b&w Cover: 2.50 **NM** value: **Cover or less**
false cover for Mighty Awful Sour Rangers #1. **W:** Bryan J.L. Glass
★ Versus Mighty Awful Sour Rangers.

SPANDEX TIGHTS (VOL. 2) — Lost Cause
1 ❑ Jan 1997, b&w Cover: 2.95 **NM** value: **Cover or less**
W: Bryan J.L. Glass
2 ❑ Mar 1997, b&w Cover: 2.95 **NM** value: **Cover or less**
The Strange Secret of Huggy Love **A:** Bob Dix **W:** Bryan J.L. Glass
3 ❑ May 1997, b&w Cover: 2.95 **NM** value: **Cover or less**
Space Opera, Part 1 **A:** Bob Dix **W:** Bryan J.L. Glass

SPANISH FLY — Eros
1 ❑ Cover: 2.95 **NM** value: **Cover or less**
A: Tobalina **W:** Tobalina
2 ❑ Cover: 2.95 **NM** value: **Cover or less**
A: Tobalina **W:** Tobalina
3 ❑ Cover: 2.95 **NM** value: **Cover or less**
A: Tobalina **W:** Tobalina
4 ❑ Cover: 2.95 **NM** value: **Cover or less**
A: Tobalina **W:** Tobalina
5 ❑ May 1996 Cover: 2.95 **NM** value: **Cover or less**
Ursula **A:** Tobalina **W:** Tobalina

SPANK — Fantagraphics / Eros
All issues are adults only.
2 ❑ b&w Cover: 2.25 **NM** value: **Cover or less**
3 ❑ b&w Cover: 2.25 **NM** value: **Cover or less**
4 ❑ b&w Cover: 2.25 **NM** value: **Cover or less**

SPANK THE MONKEY — Arrow
1 ❑ Jul 1999, b&w Cover: 2.95 **NM** value: **Cover or less**

SPANNER'S GALAXY — DC
1 ❑ Dec 1984 Cover: 2.00 **NM** value: **Cover or less**
Castling • mini-series **A:** Tom Mandrake **W:** Nicola Cutii
2 ❑ Jan 1985 Cover: 1.00 **NM** value: **Cover or less**
A: Tom Mandrake **W:** Nicola Cutii
3 ❑ Feb 1985 Cover: 1.00 **NM** value: **Cover or less**
A: Tom Mandrake **W:** Nicola Cutii
4 ❑ Mar 1985 Cover: 1.00 **NM** value: **Cover or less**
A: Tom Mandrake **W:** Nicola Cutii
5 ❑ Apr 1985 Cover: 1.00 **NM** value: **Cover or less**
A: Tom Mandrake **W:** Nicola Cutii

CGC-graded: Multiply prices above by **33 for 9.9 M • 16 for 9.8 NM/M • 7 for 9.6 NM+ • 5 for 9.4 NM • 2.5 for 9.2 NM- • 1.5 for 9.0 VF/NM**

6 ❑ May 1985 Cover: 1.00 **NM** value: **Cover or less**
Circ: CapCity orders: **7,050**
A: Tom Mandrake **W:** Nicola Cutii

SPARKLE COMICS — United Feature

1 ❑ Oct 1948 Cover: 0.10 **NM** value: **100.00**
2 ❑ Dec 1948 Cover: 0.10 **NM** value: **50.00**
3 ❑ Feb 1949 Cover: 0.10 **NM** value: **40.00**
4 ❑ Apr 1949 Cover: 0.10 **NM** value: **40.00**
5 ❑ Jun 1949 Cover: 0.10 **NM** value: **40.00**
6 ❑ Aug 1949 Cover: 0.10 **NM** value: **40.00**
7 ❑ Oct 1949 Cover: 0.10 **NM** value: **40.00**
8 ❑ Dec 1949 Cover: 0.10 **NM** value: **40.00**
9 ❑ Feb 1950 Cover: 0.10 **NM** value: **40.00**
10 ❑ Apr 1950 Cover: 0.10 **NM** value: **40.00**
11 ❑ Jun 1950 Cover: 0.10 **NM** value: **35.00**
12 ❑ Aug 1950 Cover: 0.10 **NM** value: **35.00**
13 ❑ Oct 1950 Cover: 0.10 **NM** value: **35.00**
• **CGC:** 1 graded, best 8.0
14 ❑ Dec 1950 Cover: 0.10 **NM** value: **35.00**
• **CGC:** 1 graded, best 9.0
15 ❑ Feb 1951 Cover: 0.10 **NM** value: **35.00**
16 ❑ Apr 1951 Cover: 0.10 **NM** value: **35.00**
17 ❑ Jun 1951 Cover: 0.10 **NM** value: **35.00**
18 ❑ Aug 1951 Cover: 0.10 **NM** value: **35.00**
19 ❑ Oct 1951 Cover: 0.10 **NM** value: **35.00**
20 ❑ Dec 1951 Cover: 0.10 **NM** value: **35.00**
21 ❑ ca. 1952 Cover: 0.10 **NM** value: **30.00**
22 ❑ ca. 1952 Cover: 0.10 **NM** value: **30.00**
23 ❑ ca. 1952 Cover: 0.10 **NM** value: **30.00**
24 ❑ ca. 1952 Cover: 0.10 **NM** value: **30.00**
25 ❑ ca. 1952 Cover: 0.10 **NM** value: **30.00**
• **CGC:** 1 graded, best 9.4
26 ❑ ca. 1952 Cover: 0.10 **NM** value: **30.00**
27 ❑ ca. 1953 Cover: 0.10 **NM** value: **30.00**
28 ❑ ca. 1953 Cover: 0.10 **NM** value: **30.00**
29 ❑ ca. 1953 Cover: 0.10 **NM** value: **30.00**
30 ❑ ca. 1953 Cover: 0.10 **NM** value: **30.00**
31 ❑ ca. 1953 Cover: 0.10 **NM** value: **25.00**
32 ❑ ca. 1953 Cover: 0.10 **NM** value: **25.00**
33 ❑ Dec 1953 Cover: 0.10 **NM** value: **25.00**

SPARKLER COMICS (1ST SERIES) — United Feature

Two issues of Sparkler Comics (1st series) were published by United Features Syndicate in 1940, but the one that most people remember is the second series, which ran from 1941 until 1955.

As one might expect, the stars of this long-running series were primarily United Features comic strip characters: Tarzan (by the legendary Burne Hogarth); Nancy (by Ernie Bushmiller); The Captain and the Kids; Li'l Abner; and Abbie & Slats.

The title also introduced the super-hero Spark Man who went through two or three costume changes over the course of the series, but was only cover-featured 11 times.

1st Series
1❑ Jul 1940Cover: 0.10 **NM** value: **300.00**
• **CGC:** 2 graded, best 4.5
2 ❑ Aug 1940 Cover: 0.10 **NM** value: **300.00**

2nd Series
1 ❑ Jul 1941 Cover: 0.10 **NM** value: **1350.00**
★ Origin of Sparkman. ★ 1st Appearance of Sparkman.
2 ❑ Aug 1941 Cover: 0.10 **NM** value: **550.00**
3 ❑ Sep 1941 Cover: 0.10 **NM** value: **375.00**
4 ❑ Oct 1941 Cover: 0.10 **NM** value: **375.00**
5 ❑ Dec 1941 Cover: 0.10 **NM** value: **330.00**
• **CGC:** 1 graded, best 9.0
6 ❑ Jan 1942 Cover: 0.10 **NM** value: **330.00**
7 ❑ Feb 1942 Cover: 0.10 **NM** value: **330.00**
8 ❑ Mar 1942 Cover: 0.10 **NM** value: **330.00**
9 ❑ Apr 1942 Cover: 0.10 **NM** value: **330.00**
10 ❑ May 1942 Cover: 0.10 **NM** value: **330.00**
11 ❑ Jun 1942 Cover: 0.10 **NM** value: **265.00**
12 ❑ Jul 1942 Cover: 0.10 **NM** value: **265.00**
13 ❑ Aug 1952 Cover: 0.10 **NM** value: **265.00**
14 ❑ Sep 1942 Cover: 0.10 **NM** value: **265.00**
15 ❑ Oct 1942 Cover: 0.10 **NM** value: **265.00**
16 ❑ Nov 1942 Cover: 0.10 **NM** value: **265.00**
17 ❑ Dec 1942 Cover: 0.10 **NM** value: **265.00**
18 ❑ Jan 1943 Cover: 0.10 **NM** value: **265.00**
19 ❑ Feb 1943 Cover: 0.10 **NM** value: **265.00**
20 ❑ Mar 1943 Cover: 0.10 **NM** value: **265.00**
21 ❑ Apr 1943 Cover: 0.10 **NM** value: **200.00**
22 ❑ Jun 1943 Cover: 0.10 **NM** value: **200.00**
23 ❑ Jul 1943 Cover: 0.10 **NM** value: **200.00**
24 ❑ Aug 1943 Cover: 0.10 **NM** value: **200.00**
25 ❑ Sep 1943 Cover: 0.10 **NM** value: **200.00**
26 ❑ Oct 1943 Cover: 0.10 **NM** value: **200.00**
27 ❑ Nov 1943 Cover: 0.10 **NM** value: **200.00**
28 ❑ Dec 1943 Cover: 0.10 **NM** value: **200.00**
29 ❑ Jan 1944 Cover: 0.10 **NM** value: **200.00**
30 ❑ Feb 1944 Cover: 0.10 **NM** value: **140.00**
31 ❑ Mar 1944 Cover: 0.10 **NM** value: **140.00**
32 ❑ Apr 1944 Cover: 0.10 **NM** value: **140.00**
33 ❑ Jun 1944 Cover: 0.10 **NM** value: **140.00**
34 ❑ Jul 1944 Cover: 0.10 **NM** value: **140.00**
35 ❑ Aug 1944 Cover: 0.10 **NM** value: **140.00**
36 ❑ Sep 1944 Cover: 0.10 **NM** value: **140.00**
37 ❑ Oct 1944 Cover: 0.10 **NM** value: **140.00**
38 ❑ Nov 1944 Cover: 0.10 **NM** value: **140.00**
39 ❑ Dec 1944 Cover: 0.10 **NM** value: **140.00**
40 ❑ Jan 1945 Cover: 0.10 **NM** value: **140.00**
41 ❑ Feb 1945 Cover: 0.10 **NM** value: **125.00**
42 ❑ Mar 1945 Cover: 0.10 **NM** value: **125.00**
43 ❑ Apr 1945 Cover: 0.10 **NM** value: **125.00**
44 ❑ Jun 1945 Cover: 0.10 **NM** value: **125.00**
45 ❑ Jul 1945 Cover: 0.10 **NM** value: **125.00**
• Katzenjammer kids cover
46 ❑ Aug 1945 Cover: 0.10 **NM** value: **125.00**
47 ❑ Sep 1945 Cover: 0.10 **NM** value: **125.00**
48 ❑ Oct 1945 Cover: 0.10 **NM** value: **125.00**
49 ❑ Nov 1945 Cover: 0.10 **NM** value: **125.00**
50 ❑ Dec 1945 Cover: 0.10 **NM** value: **125.00**
51 ❑ Jan 1946 Cover: 0.10 **NM** value: **85.00**
52 ❑ Feb 1946 Cover: 0.10 **NM** value: **85.00**
53 ❑ Mar 1946 Cover: 0.10 **NM** value: **85.00**
54 ❑ Apr 1946 Cover: 0.10 **NM** value: **85.00**
55 ❑ May 1946 Cover: 0.10 **NM** value: **85.00**
56 ❑ Jun 1946 Cover: 0.10 **NM** value: **85.00**
57 ❑ Jul 1946 Cover: 0.10 **NM** value: **85.00**
58 ❑ Aug 1946 Cover: 0.10 **NM** value: **85.00**
59 ❑ Sep 1946 Cover: 0.10 **NM** value: **85.00**
60 ❑ Oct 1946 Cover: 0.10 **NM** value: **85.00**
61 ❑ Nov 1946 Cover: 0.10 **NM** value: **58.00**
62 ❑ Dec 1946 Cover: 0.10 **NM** value: **58.00**
63 ❑ Jan 1947 Cover: 0.10 **NM** value: **58.00**
64 ❑ Feb 1947 Cover: 0.10 **NM** value: **58.00**
65 ❑ Mar 1947 Cover: 0.10 **NM** value: **58.00**
66 ❑ Apr 1947 Cover: 0.10 **NM** value: **58.00**
67 ❑ May 1947 Cover: 0.10 **NM** value: **58.00**
68 ❑ Jun 1947 Cover: 0.10 **NM** value: **58.00**
69 ❑ Jul 1947 Cover: 0.10 **NM** value: **58.00**
70 ❑ Aug 1947 Cover: 0.10 **NM** value: **58.00**
71 ❑ Sep 1947 Cover: 0.10 **NM** value: **45.00**
72 ❑ Oct 1947 Cover: 0.10 **NM** value: **45.00**
📖 Nancy; Tarzan; Li'L Abner; The Captain and The Kids; Dink O'Day; Abbie an' Slats; **A:** Ernie Bushmiller; Edgar Rice Burrough; R. Dirks; Rae Van Buren **W:** Ernie Bushmiller; Edgar Rice Burrough; R. Dirks; Rae Van Buren
73 ❑ Nov 1947 Cover: 0.10 **NM** value: **45.00**
74 ❑ Dec 1947 Cover: 0.10 **NM** value: **45.00**
75 ❑ Jan 1948 Cover: 0.10 **NM** value: **45.00**
76 ❑ Feb 1948 Cover: 0.10 **NM** value: **45.00**
77 ❑ Mar 1948 Cover: 0.10 **NM** value: **45.00**
78 ❑ Apr 1948 Cover: 0.10 **NM** value: **45.00**
79 ❑ May 1948 Cover: 0.10 **NM** value: **45.00**
80 ❑ Jun 1948 Cover: 0.10 **NM** value: **45.00**
81 ❑ Jul 1948 Cover: 0.10 **NM** value: **45.00**
82 ❑ Aug 1948 Cover: 0.10 **NM** value: **45.00**
83 ❑ Sep 1948 Cover: 0.10 **NM** value: **45.00**
84 ❑ Nov 1948 Cover: 0.10 **NM** value: **45.00**
85 ❑ Jan 1949 Cover: 0.10 **NM** value: **45.00**
86 ❑ Mar 1949 Cover: 0.10 **NM** value: **45.00**
87 ❑ May 1949 Cover: 0.10 **NM** value: **45.00**
88 ❑ Jul 1949 Cover: 0.10 **NM** value: **45.00**
89 ❑ Sep 1949 Cover: 0.10 **NM** value: **45.00**
90 ❑ Nov 1949 Cover: 0.10 **NM** value: **45.00**
91 ❑ Jan 1950 Cover: 0.10 **NM** value: **35.00**
92 ❑ Mar 1950 Cover: 0.10 **NM** value: **35.00**
93 ❑ May 1950 Cover: 0.10 **NM** value: **35.00**
94 ❑ Jul 1950 Cover: 0.10 **NM** value: **35.00**
95 ❑ Sep 1950 Cover: 0.10 **NM** value: **35.00**
96 ❑ Nov 1950 Cover: 0.10 **NM** value: **35.00**
97 ❑ Jan 1951 Cover: 0.10 **NM** value: **35.00**
98 ❑ Mar 1951 Cover: 0.10 **NM** value: **35.00**
99 ❑ May 1951 Cover: 0.10 **NM** value: **35.00**
100❑ Jul 1951 Cover: 0.10 **NM** value: **35.00**
101❑ Sep 1951 Cover: 0.10 **NM** value: **24.00**
102❑ Nov 1951 Cover: 0.10 **NM** value: **24.00**
103❑ Jan 1952 Cover: 0.10 **NM** value: **24.00**
104❑ Mar 1952 Cover: 0.10 **NM** value: **24.00**
105❑ May 1952 Cover: 0.10 **NM** value: **24.00**
106❑ Jul 1952 Cover: 0.10 **NM** value: **24.00**
107❑ Sep 1952 Cover: 0.10 **NM** value: **24.00**
108❑ Nov 1952 Cover: 0.10 **NM** value: **24.00**
109❑ Jan 1953 Cover: 0.10 **NM** value: **24.00**
110❑ Mar 1953 Cover: 0.10 **NM** value: **24.00**
111❑ May 1953 Cover: 0.10 **NM** value: **24.00**
112❑ Jul 1953 Cover: 0.10 **NM** value: **24.00**
113❑ Sep 1953 Cover: 0.10 **NM** value: **24.00**
114❑ Nov 1953 Cover: 0.10 **NM** value: **24.00**
115❑ Jan 1954 Cover: 0.10 **NM** value: **24.00**
116❑ Mar 1954 Cover: 0.10 **NM** value: **24.00**
117❑ Apr 1954 Cover: 0.10 **NM** value: **24.00**
118❑ Jun 1954 Cover: 0.10 **NM** value: **24.00**
119❑ Aug 1954 Cover: 0.10 **NM** value: **24.00**
120❑ Oct 1954 Cover: 0.10 **NM** value: **24.00**

SPARKLING STARS — Holyoke

1 ❑ Jun 1944 Cover: 0.10 **NM** value: **80.00**
2 ❑ Jul 1944 Cover: 0.10 **NM** value: **50.00**
3 ❑ Aug 1944 Cover: 0.10 **NM** value: **38.00**
4 ❑ Sep 1944 Cover: 0.10 **NM** value: **30.00**
5 ❑ Oct 1944 Cover: 0.10 **NM** value: **30.00**
6 ❑ Nov 1944 Cover: 0.10 **NM** value: **30.00**
7 ❑ Dec 1944 Cover: 0.10 **NM** value: **30.00**
8 ❑ Jan 1945 Cover: 0.10 **NM** value: **30.00**
9 ❑ Feb 1945 Cover: 0.10 **NM** value: **30.00**
10 ❑ Feb 1946 Cover: 0.10 **NM** value: **30.00**
11 ❑ Mar 1946 Cover: 0.10 **NM** value: **24.00**
12 ❑ Apr 1946 Cover: 0.10 **NM** value: **24.00**
13 ❑ May 1946 Cover: 0.10 **NM** value: **24.00**
★ Origin of Jungo, the Man-Beast. ★ 1st Appearance of Jungo, the Man-Beast.
14 ❑ Jun 1946 Cover: 0.10 **NM** value: **24.00**
15 ❑ Jul 1946 Cover: 0.10 **NM** value: **24.00**
16 ❑ Aug 1946 Cover: 0.10 **NM** value: **24.00**
17 ❑ Sep 1946 Cover: 0.10 **NM** value: **24.00**
18 ❑ Oct 1946 Cover: 0.10 **NM** value: **24.00**
19 ❑ Nov 1946 Cover: 0.10 **NM** value: **24.00**
20 ❑ Dec 1946 Cover: 0.10 **NM** value: **24.00**
★ 1st Appearance of Fangs the Wolfboy.
21 ❑ Jan 1947 Cover: 0.10 **NM** value: **24.00**
22 ❑ Apr 1947 Cover: 0.10 **NM** value: **24.00**
23 ❑ May 1947 Cover: 0.10 **NM** value: **24.00**
24 ❑ Jun 1947 Cover: 0.10 **NM** value: **24.00**
25 ❑ Jul 1947 Cover: 0.10 **NM** value: **24.00**
26 ❑ Aug 1947 Cover: 0.10 **NM** value: **24.00**
27 ❑ Sep 1947 Cover: 0.10 **NM** value: **24.00**
28 ❑ Oct 1947 Cover: 0.10 **NM** value: **24.00**
29 ❑ Nov 1947 Cover: 0.10 **NM** value: **24.00**
Bondage cover.
30 ❑ Dec 1947 Cover: 0.10 **NM** value: **24.00**
31 ❑ Jan 1948 Cover: 0.10 **NM** value: **24.00**
32 ❑ Feb 1948 Cover: 0.10 **NM** value: **24.00**
33 ❑ Mar 1948 Cover: 0.10 **NM** value: **24.00**
final issue.

SPARKPLUG — Heroic

1 ❑ b&w Cover: 2.95 **NM** value: **Cover or less**
📖 Once Upon A Time In Deutschland **A:** Scott Clark **W:** Lou Mougin
2 ❑ b&w Cover: 3.95 **NM** value: **Cover or less**
• trading card
3 ❑ Cover: 2.95 **NM** value: **Cover or less**

SPARKY & TIM — Aaron Warner

1 ❑ Feb 1999 Cover: 5.95 **NM** value: **Cover or less**
A: Aaron Warner; Denver Brubaker **W:** Aaron Warner; Denver Brubaker

SPARKY WATTS — Publication Enterprises

Sparky Watts was a lighthearted adventure strip of the 1940s, written and drawn by Boody Rogers. Sparky, along with his pal Doc (the world's greatest inventor) and Slap Happy (a big-footed, slow-witted oaf) travel the world in all manner of madcap plots. In their travels, they encounter spies, international crooks, supernatural creatures like mummies and werewolves, and the other staples of 1940s adventure fiction. Strongly inspired by humor/adventure strips like Alley Oop and Brick Bradford, Sparky Watts provided plenty of entertainment and fun, goofy stories, living up to the Columbia Comics motto, "clean comics for everyone."

1 ❑ ca. 1942 Cover: 0.10 **NM** value: **225.00**
2 ❑ ca. 1943 Cover: 0.10 **NM** value: **125.00**
3 ❑ ca. 1944 Cover: 0.10 **NM** value: **85.00**
4 ❑ ca. 1944 Cover: 0.10 **NM** value: **70.00**
5 ❑ ca. 1947 Cover: 0.10 **NM** value: **45.00**
6 ❑ ca. 1947 Cover: 0.10 **NM** value: **45.00**
7 ❑ ca. 1948 Cover: 0.10 **NM** value: **35.00**
8 ❑ ca. 1948 Cover: 0.10 **NM** value: **30.00**
9 ❑ ca. 1949 Cover: 0.10 **NM** value: **30.00**
10 ❑ ca. 1949 Cover: 0.10 **NM** value: **30.00**
📖 Cranberry Boggs; Sparky Watts **A:** Boody Rogers; Don Dean **W:** Boody Rogers; Don Dean

SPARROW (DC/PIRANHA) — DC / Piranha

Bk 1❑ b&w Cover: 9.95 **NM** value: **Cover or less**
• paperback

SPARROW (MILLENNIUM) — Millennium

1 ❑ 1995b&w Cover: 2.95 **NM** value: **Cover or less**
📖 Where Demons Dwell **A:** Mitchell Reichgut; Tom Tonkin **W:** Mitchell Reichgut
2 ❑ Apr 1995, b&w Cover: 2.95 **NM** value: **Cover or less**
3 ❑ May 1995, b&w Cover: 2.95 **NM** value: **Cover or less**
4 ❑ Jul 1995, b&w Cover: 2.95 **NM** value: **Cover or less**

SPARTAN: WARRIOR SPIRIT — Image

1 ❑ Jul 1995 Cover: 2.50 **NM** value: **Cover or less**
Circ: CapCity orders: **25,225**
A: Mike McKone **W:** Kurt Busiek
2 ❑ Sep 1995 Cover: 2.50 **NM** value: **Cover or less**
Circ: CapCity orders: **16,875**
A: Mike McKone **W:** Kurt Busiek
3 ❑ Oct 1995 Cover: 2.50 **NM** value: **Cover or less**
Circ: CapCity orders: **13,875**
W: Kurt Busiek
4 ❑ Nov 1995 Cover: 2.50 **NM** value: **Cover or less**
Circ: CapCity orders: **7,675**
W: Kurt Busiek

SPARTAN X: HELL-BENT-HERO-FOR-HIRE (JACKIE CHAN'S...) — Image

1 ❑ Mar 1998 Cover: 2.95 **NM** value: **Cover or less**
📖 The Armor of Heaven, Part 1 **A:** Michael Golden **W:** Michael Golden; Ric Meyers
2 ❑ Apr 1998 Cover: 2.95 **NM** value: **Cover or less**
📖 The Armor of Heaven, Part 2 **A:** Michael Golden **W:** Michael Golden; Ric Meyers
3 ❑ May 1998 Cover: 2.95 **NM** value: **Cover or less**
cover says Jun, indicia says May. 📖 The Armor of Heaven, Part 3 **A:** Michael Golden **W:** Michael Golden; Ric Meyers
4 ❑ Jul 1998 Cover: 2.95 **NM** value: **Cover or less**
cover says Aug, indicia says Jul. 📖 The Armor of Heaven, Part 4 **A:** Michael Golden **W:** Michael Golden; Ric Meyers

SPARTAN X: THE ARMOUR OF HEAVEN (JACKIE CHAN'S...) — Topps

1 ❑ May 1997 Cover: 2.95 **NM** value: **Cover or less**

SPASM (PARODY PRESS) — Parody Press

1 ❑ Cover: 9.95 **NM** value: **Cover or less**

SPASM (ROUGH COPY) — Rough Copy

1 ❑ Cover: 2.95 **NM** value: **Cover or less**
2 ❑ Cover: 2.95 **NM** value: **Cover or less**
3 ❑ Cover: 2.95 **NM** value: **Cover or less**
4 ❑ Cover: 2.95 **NM** value: **Cover or less**
5 ❑ Cover: 2.95 **NM** value: **Cover or less**
📖 Meet Oomori: Full Time Student/Part Time Assassin; Ode to a Grecian Formula; Sparky; **A:** Alan Lau **W:** Alan Lau

SPAWN — Image

After a stint at DC on such titles as Infinity, Inc. and All-Star Squadron, the multi-talented Todd McFarlane moved to Marvel, bringing his dynamic writing and artistry to a number of titles, most notably the Amazing Spider-Man. Having proved himself, Marvel awarded him his own title, Spider-Man, whose premiere issue was the best-selling comic book of 1991. Eventually, McFarlane set his sights even higher, leaving Marvel to help found Image.

Spawn was McFarlane's first title at Image. Its title character is a former mercenary, dead for five years, who is brought back to life as a cloaked Hellspawn, or "'Spawn." In life, he was Al Simmons, but more than that he remembers only in flashes: a wife, the shadowy organization he worked for, and murders...including his own.

1 ❑ May 1992 Cover: 1.95 **NM** value: **9.00**
Circ: CapCity orders: **204,760** • **CGC:** 1016 graded, best 10.0
📖 Questions **A:** Todd McFarlane **W:** Todd McFarlane ★ 1st Appearance of Spawn. ★ 1st Appearance of Spawn.

1/A ❑ Sep 1997, b&w Cover: 1.95 **NM** value: **Cover or less**
• **CGC:** 36 graded, best 9.8
• promo with Spawn #65 **A:** Todd McFarlane

2 ❑ Jul 1992 Cover: 1.95 **NM** value: **6.00**
Circ: CapCity orders: **137,025** • **CGC:** 102 graded, best 9.9
cover says Jun, indicia says Jul. **A:** Todd McFarlane **W:** Todd McFarlane ★ 1st Appearance of Violator.

3 ❑ Aug 1992 Cover: 1.95 **NM** value: **5.00**
Circ: CapCity orders: **136,600** • **CGC:** 83 graded, best 10.0
A: Todd McFarlane **W:** Todd McFarlane

4 ❑ Sep 1992 Cover: 1.95 **NM** value: **5.00**
Circ: CapCity orders: **135,875** • **CGC:** 159 graded, best 9.9
• with coupon **A:** Todd McFarlane **W:** Todd McFarlane

5 ❑ Oct 1992 Cover: 1.95 **NM** value: **4.00**
Circ: CapCity orders: **124,675** • **CGC:** 34 graded, best 9.8
A: Todd McFarlane **W:** Todd McFarlane

6 ❑ Nov 1992 Cover: 1.95 **NM** value: **3.00**
Circ: CapCity orders: **132,975** • **CGC:** 11 graded, best 9.8
📖 Payback, Part 1 **A:** Todd McFarlane **W:** Todd McFarlane ★ 1st Appearance of Overt-Kill. ★ 1st Appearance of Overt-Kill.

7 ❑ Jan 1993 Cover: 1.95 **NM** value: **3.00**
Circ: CapCity orders: **143,225** • **CGC:** 14 graded, best 9.8
📖 Payback, Part 2 **A:** Todd McFarlane **W:** Todd McFarlane

8 ❑ Mar 1993 Cover: 1.95 **NM** value: **3.00**
Circ: CapCity orders: **225,675** • **CGC:** 34 graded, best 9.8
cover says Feb, indicia says Mar. 📖 In Heaven **A:** Todd McFarlane **W:** Alan Moore

9 ❑ Mar 1993 Cover: 1.95 **NM** value: **4.00**
Circ: CapCity orders: **204,600** • **CGC:** 43 graded, best 9.8
📖 Angela **A:** Todd McFarlane **W:** Neil Gaiman ★ 1st Appearance of Angela.

10 ❑ May 1993 Cover: 1.95 **NM** value: **3.25**
Circ: CapCity orders: **210,500** • **CGC:** 16 graded, best 9.9
📖 Crossing Over **A:** Todd McFarlane **W:** Dave Sim ★ Appearance of Cerebus.

11 ❑ Jun 1993 Cover: 1.95 **NM** value: **3.00**
Circ: CapCity orders: **234,150** • **CGC:** 17 graded, best 9.8
📖 Home **A:** Todd McFarlane **W:** Frank Miller

12 ❑ Jul 1993 Cover: 1.95 **NM** value: **3.00**
Circ: CapCity orders: **225,150** • **CGC:** 14 graded, best 9.8
📖 Flashback **A:** Todd McFarlane **W:** Todd McFarlane

13 ❑ Aug 1993 Cover: 1.95 **NM** value: **3.00**
Circ: CapCity orders: **207,400** • **CGC:** 12 graded, best 9.8
• Spawn vs. Chapel **A:** Todd McFarlane **W:** Todd McFarlane

14 ❑ Sep 1993 Cover: 1.95 **NM** value: **3.00**
Circ: CapCity orders: **198,575** • **CGC:** 1 graded, best 9.6
📖 Myths, Part 1 **A:** Todd McFarlane **W:** Todd McFarlane ★ Appearance of Violator.

15 ❑ Nov 1993 Cover: 1.95 **NM** value: **3.00**
Circ: CapCity orders: **166,675** • **CGC:** 3 graded, best 9.6
A: Todd McFarlane **W:** Todd McFarlane

16 ❑ Dec 1993 Cover: 1.95 **NM** value: **3.00**
Circ: CapCity orders: **140,500** • **CGC:** 1 graded, best 9.2
📖 Reflections, Part 1 **A:** Todd McFarlane; Greg Capullo **W:** Grant Morrison ★ 1st Appearance of Anti-Spawn.

17 ❑ Jan 1994 Cover: 1.95 **NM** value: **2.50**
Circ: CapCity orders: **130,950** • **CGC:** 5 graded, best 9.6
📖 Reflections, Part 2 • Spawn vs. Anti-Spawn **A:** Todd McFarlane; Greg Capullo **W:** Grant Morrison ★ 1st Appearance of Anti-Spawn.

18 ❑ Feb 1994 Cover: 1.95 **NM** value: **2.50**
Circ: CapCity orders: **119,400** • **CGC:** 23 graded, best 9.8
📖 Reflections, Part 3 **A:** Todd McFarlane; Greg Capullo **W:** Grant Morrison

19 ❑ Oct 1994 Cover: 1.95 **NM** value: **2.00**
Circ: CapCity orders: **93,700** • **CGC:** 5 graded, best 9.8
• Published out of sequence with fill-in art **A:** Todd McFarlane

20 ❑ Nov 1994 Cover: 1.95 **NM** value: **2.00**
Circ: CapCity orders: **93,400** • **CGC:** 2 graded, best 9.8
• Published out of sequence with fill-in art **A:** Todd McFarlane

21 ❑ May 1994 Cover: 1.95 **NM** value: **2.50**
Circ: CapCity orders: **103,900** • **CGC:** 26 graded, best 9.9
A: Todd McFarlane

22 ❑ Jun 1994 Cover: 1.95 **NM** value: **2.25**
Circ: CapCity orders: **110,550** • **CGC:** 3 graded, best 9.8
A: Todd McFarlane

23 ❑ Aug 1994 Cover: 1.95 **NM** value: **2.25**
Circ: CapCity orders: **106,225** • **CGC:** 4 graded, best 9.8
A: Todd McFarlane

24 ❑ Sep 1994 Cover: 1.95 **NM** value: **2.25**
Circ: CapCity orders: **102,175** • **CGC:** 3 graded, best 9.8
A: Todd McFarlane

25 ❑ Oct 1994 Cover: 1.95 **NM** value: **2.25**
Circ: CapCity orders: **94,600** • **CGC:** 2 graded, best 9.6
A: Todd McFarlane

26 ❑ Dec 1994 Cover: 1.95 **NM** value: **2.25**
Circ: CapCity orders: **87,125**
A: Todd McFarlane

27 ❑ Jan 1995 Cover: 1.95 **NM** value: **2.25**
Circ: CapCity orders: **85,200**
A: Todd McFarlane; Greg Capullo

28 ❑ Feb 1995 Cover: 1.95 **NM** value: **2.25**
Circ: CapCity orders: **79,500**
A: Todd McFarlane; Greg Capullo

29 ❑ Mar 1995 Cover: 1.95 **NM** value: **2.25**
Circ: CapCity orders: **77,850**
A: Todd McFarlane

30 ❑ Apr 1995 Cover: 1.95 **NM** value: **2.25**
Circ: CapCity orders: **78,400**
A: Todd McFarlane

31 ❑ May 1995 Cover: 1.95 **NM** value: **2.25**
Circ: CapCity orders: **77,900**
📖 The Homecoming **A:** Todd McFarlane; Greg Capullo **W:** Todd McFarlane

32 ❑ Jun 1995 Cover: 1.95 **NM** value: **2.25**
Circ: CapCity orders: **94,625**
📖 Appearances **A:** Todd McFarlane; Greg Capullo **W:** Todd McFarlane

33 ❑ Jul 1995 Cover: 1.95 **NM** value: **2.25**
Circ: CapCity orders: **85,975**
📖 Shadows, Part 1 **A:** Todd McFarlane; Greg Capullo **W:** Todd McFarlane

34 ❑ Aug 1995 Cover: 1.95 **NM** value: **2.25**
Circ: CapCity orders: **89,750**
📖 Shadows, Part 2 **A:** Todd McFarlane; Greg Capullo **W:** Todd McFarlane

35 ❑ Sep 1995 Cover: 1.95 **NM** value: **2.25**
Circ: CapCity orders: **80,125**
A: Todd McFarlane **W:** Todd McFarlane

36 ❑ Oct 1995 Cover: 1.95 **NM** value: **2.25**
Circ: CapCity orders: **70,275**
A: Todd McFarlane **W:** Todd McFarlane

37 ❑ Nov 1995 Cover: 1.95 **NM** value: **2.25**
Circ: CapCity orders: **50,150**
A: Todd McFarlane **W:** Todd McFarlane

38 ❑ Dec 1995 Cover: 1.95 **NM** value: **2.25**
cover says Aug, indicia says Dec. **A:** Todd McFarlane **W:** Todd McFarlane ★ 1st Appearance of Cy-Gor.

39 ❑ Dec 1995 Cover: 1.95 **NM** value: **2.25**
• **CGC:** 1 graded, best 7.0
📖 Noel • Christmas story **A:** Todd McFarlane **W:** Todd McFarlane

40 ❑ Jan 1996 Cover: 1.95 **NM** value: **2.25**
📖 Fugitives, Part 1 **W:** Todd McFarlane

41 ❑ Jan 1996 Cover: 1.95 **NM** value: **2.00**
📖 Fugitives, Part 2 **W:** Todd McFarlane

42 ❑ Feb 1996 Cover: 1.95 **NM** value: **2.00**
📖 Fanboy **W:** Todd McFarlane

43 ❑ Feb 1996 Cover: 1.95 **NM** value: **2.00**
W: Todd McFarlane

44 ❑ Mar 1996 Cover: 1.95 **NM** value: **2.00**
W: Todd McFarlane

45 ❑ Mar 1996 Cover: 1.95 **NM** value: **2.00**
W: Todd McFarlane

46 ❑ Apr 1996 Cover: 1.95 **NM** value: **2.00**
W: Todd McFarlane

47 ❑ Apr 1996 Cover: 1.95 **NM** value: **2.00**
W: Todd McFarlane

48 ❑ May 1996 Cover: 1.95 **NM** value: **2.00**
W: Todd McFarlane

49 ❑ May 1996 Cover: 1.95 **NM** value: **2.00**
W: Todd McFarlane

50 ❑ Jun 1996 Cover: 3.95 **NM** value: **Cover or less**
• **CGC:** 7 graded, best 9.8
W: Todd McFarlane

51 ❑ Aug 1996 Cover: 1.95 **NM** value: **Cover or less**
cover says Jul, indicia says Aug. **W:** Todd McFarlane

52 ❑ Aug 1996 Cover: 1.95 **NM** value: **Cover or less**
W: Todd McFarlane

53 ❑ Sep 1996 Cover: 1.95 **NM** value: **Cover or less**
W: Todd McFarlane

54 ❑ Oct 1996 Cover: 1.95 **NM** value: **Cover or less**
Circ: Diamd. preorders: **161,450**
W: Todd McFarlane

55 ❑ Nov 1996 Cover: 1.95 **NM** value: **Cover or less**
Circ: Diamd. preorders: **162,895**
📖 Sabotage **A:** Greg Capullo **W:** Todd McFarlane

56 ❑ Dec 1996 Cover: 1.95 **NM** value: **Cover or less**
Circ: Diamd. preorders: **163,273**
📖 Kahn **A:** Greg Capullo **W:** Todd McFarlane

57 ❑ Jan 1997 Cover: 1.95 **NM** value: **Cover or less**
Circ: Diamd. preorders: **158,221**
📖 The Beast **A:** Greg Capullo **W:** Todd McFarlane

58 ❑ Feb 1997 Cover: 1.95 **NM** value: **Cover or less**
Circ: Diamd. preorders: **153,594**
W: Todd McFarlane

59 ❑ Mar 1997 Cover: 1.95 **NM** value: **Cover or less**
Circ: Diamd. preorders: **145,623**
W: Todd McFarlane

60 ❑ Apr 1997 Cover: 1.95 **NM** value: **Cover or less**
Circ: Diamd. preorders: **140,759**
W: Todd McFarlane

61 ❑ May 1997 Cover: 1.95 **NM** value: **Cover or less**
Circ: Diamd. preorders: **141,122**
W: Todd McFarlane

62 ❑ Jun 1997 Cover: 1.95 **NM** value: **Cover or less**
Circ: Diamd. preorders: **167,373**
W: Todd McFarlane ★ Appearance of Angela.

63 ❑ Jul 1997 Cover: 1.95 **NM** value: **Cover or less**
Circ: Diamd. preorders: **134,822**
W: Todd McFarlane

64 ❑ Aug 1997 Cover: 1.95 **NM** value: **Cover or less**
Circ: Diamd. preorders: **134,161**
• polybagged with McFarlane Toys catalog **W:** Todd McFarlane

65 ❑ Sep 1997 Cover: 1.95 **NM** value: **Cover or less**
Circ: Diamd. preorders: **165,233**
Photo cover. 📖 The Past **A:** Greg Capullo **W:** Todd McFarlane

66 ❑ Oct 1997 Cover: 1.95 **NM** value: **Cover or less**
Circ: Diamd. preorders: **147,350**
📖 Demons **A:** Greg Capullo **W:** Todd McFarlane

67 ❑ Nov 1997 Cover: 1.95 **NM** value: **Cover or less**
Circ: Diamd. preorders: **156,354**
📖 Homeland **A:** Greg Capullo **W:** Todd McFarlane

68 ❑ Jan 1998 Cover: 1.95 **NM** value: **Cover or less**
Circ: Diamd. preorders: **156,454**
📖 Intersection **A:** Greg Capullo **W:** Todd McFarlane

69 ❑ Jan 1998 Cover: 1.95 **NM** value: **Cover or less**
Circ: Diamd. preorders: **147,249**
📖 Freaky **A:** Greg Capullo **W:** Todd McFarlane

70 ❑ Feb 1998 Cover: 1.95 **NM** value: **Cover or less**
Circ: Diamd. preorders: **138,051**
📖 Darkness **A:** Greg Capullo **W:** Todd McFarlane

71 ❑ Apr 1998 Cover: 1.95 **NM** value: **Cover or less**
Circ: Diamd. preorders: **128,561**
📖 Apparitions **A:** Greg Capullo **W:** Todd McFarlane; Brian Holguin

72 ❑ May 1998 Cover: 1.95 **NM** value: **Cover or less**
Circ: Diamd. preorders: **131,782**
📖 Bloodless **A:** Greg Capullo **W:** Todd McFarlane; Brian Holguin

73 ❑ Jun 1998 Cover: 1.95 **NM** value: **Cover or less**
Circ: Diamd. preorders: **130,809**
📖 The Heap **A:** Greg Capullo **W:** Todd McFarlane; Brian Holguin

74 ❑ Jul 1998 Cover: 1.95 **NM** value: **Cover or less**
Circ: Diamd. preorders: **130,506**
📖 The Void **A:** Greg Capullo **W:** Todd McFarlane; Brian Holguin

75 ❑ Aug 1998 Cover: 1.95 **NM** value: **Cover or less**
Circ: Diamd. preorders: **125,256**
📖 Sacred Ground **A:** Greg Capullo; Todd McFarlane(cover) **W:** Todd McFarlane; Brian Holguin

76 ❑ Sep 1998 Cover: 1.95 **NM** value: **Cover or less**
Circ: Diamd. preorders: **116,010**
📖 Farewell Dance **A:** Dwayne Turner **W:** Todd McFarlane; Brian Holguin

77 ❑ Oct 1998 Cover: 1.95 **NM** value: **Cover or less**
Circ: Diamd. preorders: **116,721**
📖 Relics **A:** Dwayne Turner **W:** Todd McFarlane; Brian Holguin

78 ❑ Nov 1998 Cover: 1.95 **NM** value: **Cover or less**
Circ: Diamd. preorders: **110,227**

79 ❑ Jan 1999 Cover: 1.95 **NM** value: **Cover or less**
Circ: Diamd. preorders: **111,391**
A: Greg Capullo **W:** Todd McFarlane; Brian Holguin

80 ❑ Feb 1999 Cover: 1.95 **NM** value: **Cover or less**
Circ: Diamd. preorders: **107,473**
A: Brian Holguin **W:** Todd McFarlane; Brian Holguin

81 ❑ Mar 1999 Cover: 1.95 **NM** value: **Cover or less**
Circ: Diamd. preorders: **103,367**
📖 Devil Inside, Part 1 **A:** Brian Holguin **W:** Todd McFarlane; Brian Holguin

82 ❑ Apr 1999 Cover: 1.95 **NM** value: **Cover or less**
Circ: Diamd. preorders: **101,528**
📖 Devil Inside, Part 2 **A:** Greg Capullo **W:** Todd McFarlane; Brian Holguin

83 ❑ May 1999 Cover: 1.95 **NM** value: **Cover or less**
Circ: Diamd. preorders: **99,008**
📖 The Conqueror **A:** Greg Capullo **W:** Todd McFarlane; Brian Holguin

84 ❑ Jun 1999 Cover: 1.95 **NM** value: **Cover or less**
Circ: Diamd. preorders: **97,144**
📖 The Waiting **A:** Greg Capullo **W:** Todd McFarlane; Brian Holguin

85 ❑ Jul 1999 Cover: 1.95 **NM** value: **Cover or less**
Circ: Diamd. preorders: **98,058**
📖 EndGame **A:** Greg Capullo **W:** Todd McFarlane; Brian Holguin

86 ❑ Aug 1999 Cover: 1.95 **NM** value: **Cover or less**
Circ: Diamd. preorders: **94,215**
📖 Abdication **A:** Greg Capullo **W:** Todd McFarlane; Brian Holguin

87 ❑ Sep 1999 Cover: 1.95 **NM** value: **Cover or less**
Circ: Diamd. preorders: **91,799**
📖 Folklore **A:** Greg Capullo **W:** Todd McFarlane; Brian Holguin

88 ❑ Oct 1999 Cover: 1.95 **NM** value: **Cover or less**
Circ: Diamd. preorders: **90,087**
📖 Seasons of Change **A:** Greg Capullo **W:** Todd McFarlane; Brian Holguin

89 ❑ Nov 1999 Cover: 1.95 **NM** value: **Cover or less**
Circ: Diamd. preorders: **86,616**
📖 The Devil You Know **A:** Greg Capullo **W:** Todd McFarlane; Brian Holguin

90 ❑ Dec 1999 Cover: 1.95 **NM** value: **Cover or less**
Circ: Diamd. preorders: **82,737**
📖 Three Uses of the Knife **A:** Greg Capullo **W:** Todd McFarlane; Brian Holguin

91 ❑ Jan 2000 Cover: 1.95 **NM** value: **Cover or less**
Circ: Diamd. preorders: **83,271**

92 ❑ Feb 2000 Cover: 1.95 **NM** value: **Cover or less**
Circ: Diamd. preorders: **79,634**

93 ❑ Mar 2000 Cover: 1.95 **NM** value: **Cover or less**
Circ: Diamd. preorders: **80,010**

The Devil's Banquet **A:** Greg Capullo **W:** Todd McFarlane; Brian Holguin

94 ❑ Apr 2000 Cover: 1.95 **NM** value: **Cover or less**
Circ: Diamd. preorders: **73,516**
The Children's Hour **A:** Greg Capullo **W:** Todd McFarlane; Brian Holguin

95 ❑ May 2000 Cover: 1.95 **NM** value: **Cover or less**
Circ: Diamd. preorders: **68,776**

96 ❑ Jun 2000 Cover: 1.95 **NM** value: **Cover or less**
Circ: Diamd. preorders: **68,966**

97 ❑ Jul 2000 Cover: 1.95 **NM** value: **Cover or less**
Circ: Diamd. preorders: **70,102**
Heaven's Folly **A:** Greg Capullo **W:** Todd McFarlane; Brian Holguin

98 ❑ Aug 2000 Cover: 2.50 **NM** value: **Cover or less**
Circ: Diamd. preorders: **67,865**
The Trouble With Angels **A:** Greg Capullo **W:** Todd McFarlane; Brian Holguin

99 ❑ Sep 2000 Cover: 2.50 **NM** value: **Cover or less**
Circ: Diamd. preorders: **68,073**
The Edge of Darkness **A:** Greg Capullo **W:** Todd McFarlane; Brian Holguin

100/A❑Nov 2000 Cover: 4.95 **NM** value: **Cover or less**
Circ: Diamd. preorders: **143,493** • **CGC:** 13 graded, best 9.8
Todd McFarlane cover. • Giant-size. Milestone **A:** Greg Capullo **W:** Todd McFarlane; Brian Holguin

100/B❑Nov 2000 Cover: 4.95 **NM** value: **Cover or less**
• **CGC:** 4 graded, best 9.8
Ashley Wood cover. • Giant-size. Milestone **A:** Greg Capullo **W:** Todd McFarlane; Brian Holguin

100/C❑Nov 2000 Cover: 4.95 **NM** value: **Cover or less**
• **CGC:** 2 graded, best 9.8
Frank Miller cover. • Giant-size. Milestone **A:** Greg Capullo **W:** Todd McFarlane; Brian Holguin

100/D❑Nov 2000 Cover: 4.95 **NM** value: **Cover or less**
Mike Mignola Cover. • Giant-size. Milestone **A:** Greg Capullo **W:** Todd McFarlane; Brian Holguin

100/E❑Nov 2000 Cover: 4.95 **NM** value: **Cover or less**
• **CGC:** 53 graded, best 9.9
Alex Ross cover. • Giant-size. Milestone **A:** Greg Capullo **W:** Todd McFarlane; Brian Holguin

100/F❑Nov 2000 Cover: 4.95 **NM** value: **Cover or less**
Greg Capullo cover. • Giant-size. Milestone **A:** Greg Capullo **W:** Todd McFarlane; Brian Holguin

101 ❑ Dec 2000 Cover: 2.50 **NM** value: **Cover or less**
Circ: Diamd. preorders: **64,022**
Aftermath **A:** Angel Medina **W:** Todd McFarlane

102 ❑ Jan 2001 Cover: 2.50 **NM** value: **Cover or less**
Circ: Diamd. preorders: **64,051**
Cautionary Tales, Part 1 **A:** Angel Medina **W:** Todd McFarlane

103 ❑ Feb 2001 Cover: 2.50 **NM** value: **Cover or less**
Circ: Diamd. preorders: **63,688** • **CGC:** 1 graded, best 9.6
Cautionary Tales, Part 2 **A:** Angel Medina **W:** Todd McFarlane

104 ❑ Feb 2001 Cover: 2.50 **NM** value: **Cover or less**
Circ: Diamd. preorders: **63,741**
Cautionary Tales, Part 3 **A:** Angel Medina **W:** Todd McFarlane; Brian Holguin

105 ❑ Feb 2001 Cover: 2.50 **NM** value: **Cover or less**
Circ: Diamd. preorders: **63,544**
Retribution Overdrive, Part 1 **A:** Angel Medina **W:** Todd McFarlane; Steve Niles

106 ❑ Mar 2001 Cover: 2.50 **NM** value: **Cover or less**
Circ: Diamd. preorders: **62,685**
Retribution Overdrive, Part 2 **A:** Angel Medina **W:** Todd McFarlane; Steve Niles

107 ❑ Apr 2001 Cover: 2.50 **NM** value: **Cover or less**
Circ: Diamd. preorders: **61,689**
The Kingdom, Part 1 **A:** Angel Medina **W:** Todd McFarlane; Brian Holguin

108 ❑ May 2001 Cover: 2.50 **NM** value: **Cover or less**
Circ: Diamd. preorders: **59,201**

109 ❑ Jun 2001 Cover: 2.50 **NM** value: **Cover or less**
Circ: Diamd. preorders: **57,512**

110 ❑ Jul 2001 Cover: 2.50 **NM** value: **Cover or less**
Circ: Diamd. preorders: **55,911**

111 ❑ Aug 2001 Cover: 2.50 **NM** value: **Cover or less**
Circ: Diamd. preorders: **55,443**

112 ❑ Sep 2001 Cover: 2.50 **NM** value: **Cover or less**
Circ: Diamd. preorders: **57,189**

Anl 1❑May 1999 Cover: 4.95 **NM** value: **Cover or less**
Circ: Diamd. preorders: **72,333**
Blood and Shadows • squarebound **A:** Ashley Wood **W:** Paul Jenkin

Bk 1❑ Cover: 9.95 **NM** value: **Cover or less**
Circ: CapCity orders: **7,400**
• collects Spawn #1-6 **A:** Todd McFarlane **W:** Todd McFarlane

Bk 1/A❑ **NM** value: **9.95**
• Capital City Collection; collects first six issues

Bk 2❑ Cover: 9.95 **NM** value: **Cover or less**
• collects Spawn #7-11 **A:** Todd McFarlane **W:** Todd McFarlane

Bk 3❑ Cover: 9.95 **NM** value: **Cover or less**
• collects Spawn #12-15 **A:** Todd McFarlane **W:** Todd McFarlane

Bk 4❑ Cover: 9.95 **NM** value: **Cover or less**
• collects Spawn #16-20 **A:** Todd McFarlane **W:** Todd McFarlane

Bk 5❑ Cover: 9.95 **NM** value: **Cover or less**
• collects Spawn #21-25 **A:** Todd McFarlane; Greg Capullo **W:** Todd McFarlane

Bk 6❑ Cover: 9.95 **NM** value: **Cover or less**
Book of the Droid • collects Spawn #26-30 **A:** Greg Capullo **W:** Todd McFarlane

Bk 7❑ Cover: 9.95 **NM** value: **Cover or less**
Deadman's Touch • collects Spawn #31-34 **A:** Todd McFarlane; Greg Capullo **W:** Todd McFarlane

Bk 8❑ Cover: 9.95 **NM** value: **Cover or less**
Betrayal of Blood • Collects issues #35-38 **A:** Todd McFarlane; Greg Capullo; Tony Daniel; Kevin Conrad **W:** Todd McFarlane; Alan Moore

Bk 9❑ Oct 1999 Cover: 9.95 **NM** value: **Cover or less**
• Collects issues #39-42 **A:** Todd McFarlane; Greg Capullo; Tony Daniel; Kevin Conrad **W:** Todd McFarlane

Bk 10❑ **NM** value: **9.95**

Bk 11❑ Cover: 10.95 **NM** value: **Cover or less**
Crossroads • Collects Spawn #48-50 **A:** Todd McFarlane; Greg Capullo; Tony Daniel; Danny Miki; Kevin Conrad **W:** Todd McFarlane

Bk 12❑ Cover: 10.95 **NM** value: **Cover or less**
Immortality • Collects Spawn #51-54 **A:** Todd McFarlane; Greg Capullo; Danny Miki **W:** Todd McFarlane

FAN 1❑ **NM** value: **1.00**
• Promotional edition included in Overstreet Fan.

FAN 2❑ **NM** value: **1.00**
• Promotional edition included in Overstreet Fan.

FAN 3❑Oct 1996 **NM** value: **1.00**
• Promotional edition included in Overstreet Fan. **A:** Brad Gorby **W:** Beau Smith

SPAWN: ANGELA'S HUNT — Image

Bk 1❑ Cover: 9.95 **NM** value: **Cover or less**
A: Greg Capullo; Mark Pennington **W:** Neil Gaiman

Bk 1-2❑ Cover: 7.95 **NM** value: **Cover or less**

SPAWN-BATMAN — Image

1 ❑ ca. 1994 Cover: 3.95 **NM** value: **4.00**
Circ: CapCity orders: **141,550** • **CGC:** 20 graded, best 9.8
No issue number. **A:** Todd McFarlane **W:** Frank Miller

SPA.WN BIBLE — Image

1 ❑ Aug 1996 Cover: 1.95 **NM** value: **Cover or less**
• background on series **A:** Greg Capullo **W:** Todd McFarlane; Andrew Grossberg; Beau Smith; Tom Orzechowski

SPAWN BLOOD AND SALVATION — Image

1 ❑ Nov 1999 Cover: 4.95 **NM** value: **Cover or less**
Circ: Diamd. preorders: **29,577**
A: Ashley Wood **W:** Alan McElroy

SPAWN BLOOD FEUD — Image

1 ❑ Jun 1995 Cover: 2.25 **NM** value: **Cover or less**
Circ: CapCity orders: **80,175** • **CGC:** 5 graded, best 9.6
Part 1 **A:** Tony Daniel; Kevin Conrad **W:** Alan Moore

2 ❑ Jul 1995 Cover: 2.25 **NM** value: **Cover or less**
Circ: CapCity orders: **71,900**
Part 2 **A:** Tony Daniel; Kevin Conrad **W:** Alan Moore

3 ❑ Aug 1995 Cover: 2.25 **NM** value: **Cover or less**
Circ: CapCity orders: **62,050**
Part 3 **A:** Tony Daniel; Kevin Conrad **W:** Alan Moore

4 ❑ Sep 1995 Cover: 2.25 **NM** value: **Cover or less**
Circ: CapCity orders: **51,600**
W: Alan Moore

SPAWN MOVIE ADAPTATION — Image

1 ❑ Dec 1997 Cover: 4.95 **NM** value: **Cover or less**
Circ: Diamd. preorders: **41,873** • **CGC:** 5 graded, best 9.9
No issue number. • prestige format. **A:** Carlos D'Anda **W:** Alan McElroy; Mark Dippe; Ted Adams

SPAWN: THE DARK AGES — Image

The Dark Ages opens a new chapter in Todd McFarlane's popular Spawn series, this time set in medieval times.

In a graveyard, a half-human devil appears, filled with pain and hunger. Haunted by faint memories of a beautiful woman and the blood of legions upon his sword, he is drawn to a deserted castle. He is now Spawn, Hell's own Black Knight, but in the past he was just a man named Lord Iain Covenant.

Visions of the Hell that Spawn escaped flood his mind, but what were the sins of his past that had condemned him there? And why has he been returned to Earth to wreak vengeance on the unholy?

Like the modern Spawn, this series is about one man's search for redemption in a world of violence. But, in the Dark Ages, that world is filled with battlefields, kings, and villainous knights.

1 ❑ Mar 1999 Cover: 2.50 **NM** value: **3.00**
Circ: Diamd. preorders: **113,645** • **CGC:** 9 graded, best 9.8
Devil's Knight **A:** Liam McCormack-Sharp; Glenn Fabry(cover) **W:** Brian Holguin

1/SC❑Mar 1999 Cover: 2.50 **NM** value: **Cover or less**
• **CGC:** 4 graded, best 9.6
Variant cover by McFarlane. Devil's Knight **A:** Liam McCormack-Sharp; Todd McFarlane(cover) **W:** Brian Holguin

2 ❑ Apr 1999 Cover: 2.50 **NM** value: **Cover or less**
Circ: Diamd. preorders: **81,979**
Forsaken **A:** Liam McCormack-Sharp; Todd McFarlane(cover) **W:** Brian Holguin

3 ❑ May 1999 Cover: 2.50 **NM** value: **Cover or less**
Circ: Diamd. preorders: **72,442**
Unward **A:** Liam McCormack-Sharp **W:** Brian Holguin

4 ❑ Jun 1999 Cover: 2.50 **NM** value: **Cover or less**
Circ: Diamd. preorders: **64,829**
Death and Glory **A:** Liam McCormack-Sharp **W:** Brian Holguin

5 ❑ Jul 1999 Cover: 2.50 **NM** value: **Cover or less**
Circ: Diamd. preorders: **57,887**
Crimson Shadow **A:** Liam McCormack-Sharp **W:** Brian Holguin

6 ❑ Aug 1999 Cover: 2.50 **NM** value: **Cover or less**
Circ: Diamd. preorders: **52,006**
Benediction **A:** Liam McCormack-Sharp **W:** Brian Holguin

7 ❑ Sep 1999 Cover: 2.50 **NM** value: **Cover or less**
Circ: Diamd. preorders: **46,188**
Providence **A:** Liam McCormack-Sharp **W:** Brian Holguin

8 ❑ Oct 1999 Cover: 2.50 **NM** value: **Cover or less**
Circ: Diamd. preorders: **42,584**
Acts of Contrition **A:** Liam McCormack-Sharp **W:** Brian Holguin

9 ❑ Nov 1999 Cover: 2.50 **NM** value: **Cover or less**
Circ: Diamd. preorders: **38,381**
A Merry Round of Cheer **A:** Liam McCormack-Sharp **W:** Brian Holguin

10 ❑ Dec 1999 Cover: 2.50 **NM** value: **Cover or less**
Circ: Diamd. preorders: **37,233**
A Child's Crusade, Part 1 **A:** Liam McCormack-Sharp **W:** Brian Holguin

11 ❑ Jan 2000 Cover: 2.50 **NM** value: **Cover or less**
Circ: Diamd. preorders: **33,105**

12 ❑ Feb 2000 Cover: 2.50 **NM** value: **Cover or less**
Circ: Diamd. preorders: **29,800**

13 ❑ Mar 2000 Cover: 2.50 **NM** value: **Cover or less**
Circ: Diamd. preorders: **28,963**

14 ❑ Apr 2000 Cover: 2.50 **NM** value: **Cover or less**
Circ: Diamd. preorders: **27,671**

15 ❑ May 2000 Cover: 2.50 **NM** value: **Cover or less**
Circ: Diamd. preorders: **26,139**

16 ❑ Jun 2000 Cover: 2.50 **NM** value: **Cover or less**
Circ: Diamd. preorders: **26,191**
Heart of the Hellspawn **A:** Nat Jones **W:** Steve Niles

17 ❑ Jul 2000 Cover: 2.50 **NM** value: **Cover or less**
Circ: Diamd. preorders: **24,930**
The Circle and the Worm **A:** Nat Jones **W:** Steve Niles

18 ❑ Aug 2000 Cover: 2.50 **NM** value: **Cover or less**
Circ: Diamd. preorders: **23,511**
Crucified **A:** Nat Jones **W:** Steve Niles

19 ❑ Sep 2000 Cover: 2.50 **NM** value: **Cover or less**
Circ: Diamd. preorders: **22,912**
Like Any Other Man **A:** Nat Jones **W:** Steve Niles

20 ❑ Oct 2000 Cover: 2.50 **NM** value: **Cover or less**
Circ: Diamd. preorders: **23,073**
Voices in the Dark **A:** Nat Jones **W:** Steve Niles

21 ❑ Nov 2000 Cover: 2.50 **NM** value: **Cover or less**
Circ: Diamd. preorders: **22,295**
Sins of the Hellspawn **A:** Nat Jones **W:** Steve Niles

22 ❑ Jan 2001 Cover: 2.50 **NM** value: **Cover or less**
Circ: Diamd. preorders: **21,480**
The Seeding **A:** Nat Jones **W:** Steve Niles

23 ❑ Feb 2001 Cover: 2.50 **NM** value: **Cover or less**
Circ: Diamd. preorders: **20,016**
The Beast **A:** Nat Jones **W:** Steve Niles

24 ❑ Mar 2001 Cover: 2.50 **NM** value: **Cover or less**
Circ: Diamd. preorders: **19,813**
Bleed, Pagan Bleed **A:** Nat Jones **W:** Steve Niles

SPAWN THE IMPALER — Image

1 ❑ Oct 1996 Cover: 2.95 **NM** value: **Cover or less**
Circ: Diamd. preorders: **172,837** • **CGC:** 1 graded, best 9.4
A: Mike Grell; Rob Prior **W:** Mike Grell

2 ❑ Nov 1996 Cover: 2.95 **NM** value: **Cover or less**
Circ: Diamd. preorders: **135,548**
A: Mike Grell; Rob Prior **W:** Mike Grell

3 ❑ Dec 1996 Cover: 2.95 **NM** value: **Cover or less**
Circ: Diamd. preorders: **125,198**
A: Mike Grell; Rob Prior **W:** Mike Grell

SPAWN THE UNDEAD — Image

1 ❑ Jun 1999 Cover: 1.95 **NM** value: **2.00**
Circ: Diamd. preorders: **93,780** • **CGC:** 6 graded, best 9.8
A face in the Crowd **A:** Dwayne Turner **W:** Paul Jenkins

2 ❑ Jul 1999 Cover: 1.95 **NM** value: **Cover or less**
Circ: Diamd. preorders: **68,174**
The Door to Nowhere **A:** Dwayne Turner **W:** Paul Jenkins

3 ❑ Aug 1999 Cover: 1.95 **NM** value: **Cover or less**
Circ: Diamd. preorders: **57,460**
My Soul to Keep **A:** Dwayne Turner **W:** Paul Jenkins

4 ❑ Sep 1999 Cover: 1.95 **NM** value: **Cover or less**
Circ: Diamd. preorders: **49,715**
Song Sung Bloo **A:** Dwayne Turner **W:** Paul Jenkins

5 ❑ Oct 1999 Cover: 1.95 **NM** value: **Cover or less**
Circ: Diamd. preorders: **44,988**
The Wind that Shakes the Barley, Part 1 **A:** Dwayne Turner **W:** Paul Jenkins

6 ❑ Nov 1999 Cover: 1.95 **NM** value: **Cover or less**
Circ: Diamd. preorders: **40,239**
The Wind that Shakes the Barley, Part 2 **A:** Dwayne Turner **W:** Paul Jenkins

7 ❑ Dec 1999 Cover: 1.95 **NM** value: **Cover or less**
Circ: Diamd. preorders: **38,777**
Up the Down Stairs **A:** Dwayne Turner **W:** Paul Jenkins

SPAWN/WILDC.A.T.S — Image

1 ❑ Jan 1996 Cover: 2.50 **NM** value: **3.00**
Devilday, Part 1 **A:** Scott Clark **W:** Alan Moore

2 ❑ Feb 1996 Cover: 2.50 **NM** value: **Cover or less**
Devilday, Part 2 **A:** Scott Clark **W:** Alan Moore

3 ❑ Mar 1996 Cover: 2.50 **NM** value: **Cover or less**
Devilday, Part 3 **A:** Scott Clark **W:** Alan Moore

4 ❑ Apr 1996 Cover: 2.50 **NM** value: **Cover or less**
Devilday, Part 4 **A:** Scott Clark **W:** Alan Moore

SPECIAL AGENT — Parents' Magazine Institute

1 ❑ Dec 1947 Cover: 0.10 **NM** value: **75.00**
2 ❑ Mar 1948 Cover: 0.10 **NM** value: **45.00**
3 ❑ Jun 1948 Cover: 0.10 **NM** value: **35.00**
4 ❑ Sep 1948 Cover: 0.10 **NM** value: **35.00**
5 ❑ Dec 1948 Cover: 0.10 **NM** value: **35.00**
6 ❑ Mar 1949 Cover: 0.10 **NM** value: **35.00**
7 ❑ Jun 1949 Cover: 0.10 **NM** value: **35.00**
8 ❑ Sep 1949 Cover: 0.10 **NM** value: **35.00**

SPECIAL COMICS — M.L.J.

1 ❑ Win 1941 Cover: 0.10 **NM** value: **2000.00**
• **CGC:** 2 graded, best 6.0

Other grades: Multiply prices above by **1.5 for Mint • 2/3 for Very Fine • 1/3 for Fine • 1/5 for Very Good • 1/8 for Good**

SPECIAL EDITION COMICS — Fawcett

1 ❑ Aug 1940 Cover: 0.10 **NM** value: **10000.00**
• **CGC:** 8 graded, best 9.8

SPECIAL HUGGING AND OTHER CHILDHOOD TALES — Slave Labor

1 ❑ Apr 1989, b&w Cover: 1.95 **NM** value: **Cover or less**

SPECIAL MARVEL EDITION — Marvel

Beginning in 1971, Special Marvel Edition spent most of its three-year run as home to a nondescript sereis, first of Thor reprints, then of Sgt. Fury reprints.

Its last two issues were a different story. With #15, Special Marvel Edition introduced Shang-Chi, the Master of Kung Fu. Shang-Chi was a hit, drawing on the kung fu craze of the day. Beginning with #17, Special Marvel Edition was renamed after its new hero, becoming Master of Kung Fu.

By the way, while Shang-Chi is the better-known character today, his introduction actually involved a well-known existing fictional villain, Sax Rohmer's Dr. Fu Manchu. Rohmer (1883-1959) introduced the character in 1912, and Fu Manchu's schemes for world domination were fought (in a number of books over the years) by Sir Denis Nayland Smith and his friends. Smith and Manchu appeared in Shang-Chi stories until Marvel eased them out of continuity.

1 ❑ Jan 1971 Cover: 0.25 **NM** value: **6.00**
• **CGC:** 4 graded, best 9.6
📖 Into the Blaze of Battle!; To Kill a Thunder God!; Tales of Asgard: The Golden Apples!; The Day of the Destroyer! • reprints Thor stories from Journey into Mystery #117-119; Thor reprints begin **A:** Jack Kirby **W:** Stan Lee

2 ❑ 1971 Cover: 0.25 **NM** value: **4.00**
📖 With My Hammer in Hand; The Power, The Passion, The Pride; The Secret of Sigurd; Where Mortals Fear to Tread • reprints Thor stories from Journey into Mystery #120-122

3 ❑ Sep 1971 Cover: 0.25 **NM** value: **4.00**
📖 While a Universe Trembles; The Grandeur and the Glory; When Meet the Immortals; The Coming of Loki • reprints Thor stories from Journey into Mystery #123-125

4 ❑ Feb 1972 Cover: 0.25 **NM** value: **4.00**
📖 Whom the Gods Would Destroy; A Viper in Our Midst; The Hammer and the Holocaust • reprints Thor #126 and #127; Thor reprints end

5 ❑ Jul 1972 Cover: 0.20 **NM** value: **3.00**
• Sgt. Fury reprints begin

6 ❑ Sep 1972 Cover: 0.20 **NM** value: **3.00**

7 ❑ Nov 1972 Cover: 0.20 **NM** value: **3.00**
• Sgt. Fury

8 ❑ Jan 1973 Cover: 0.20 **NM** value: **3.00**

9 ❑ Mar 1973 Cover: 0.20 **NM** value: **3.00**

10 ❑ May 1973 Cover: 0.20 **NM** value: **3.00**

11 ❑ Jul 1973 Cover: 0.20 **NM** value: **3.00**
★ Appearance of Captain America.

12 ❑ Sep 1973 Cover: 0.20 **NM** value: **3.00**

13 ❑ Oct 1973 Cover: 0.20 **NM** value: **3.00**
📖 Too Small to Fight, Too Young to Die! **A:** Steve Ditko **W:** Dick Ayers

14 ❑ Nov 1973 Cover: 0.20 **NM** value: **3.00**
• Sgt. Fury reprints end

15 ❑ Dec 1973 Cover: 0.20 **NM** value: **20.00**
• **CGC:** 41 graded, best 9.6
📖 Fu Manchu • Master of Kung Fu **A:** Jim Starlin ★ 1st Appearance of Shang-Chi, Master of Kung Fu, Nayland Smith.

16 ❑ Feb 1974 Cover: 0.20 **NM** value: **10.00**
• **CGC:** 9 graded, best 9.6
📖 Midnight Brings Dark Death! • series continues as Master of Kung Fu **A:** Jim Starlin ★ Origin of Midnight. ★ 1st Appearance of Midnight. ★ 2nd Appearance of Shang-Chi, Master of Kung Fu.

SPECIAL WAR SERIES — Charlton

1 ❑ Aug 1965 Cover: 0.12 **NM** value: **10.00**

2 ❑ Sep 1965 Cover: 0.12 **NM** value: **8.00**

3 ❑ Oct 1965 Cover: 0.12 **NM** value: **8.00**
📖 Terror in the Caves; Special Service 3X (text story); Hero the Hard Way; Learning the Trade; Crisis in Korea • War and Attack **A:** Nicholas Alascia

4 ❑ Nov 1965 Cover: 0.12 **NM** value: **16.00**
★ Origin of Judomaster. ★ 1st Appearance of Judomaster.

SPECIES — Dark Horse

1 ❑ Jun 1995 Cover: 2.50 **NM** value: **Cover or less**
Circ: CapCity orders: **15,150**
📖 Species **A:** Jon Foster **W:** Dennis Feldman

2 ❑ Jul 1995 Cover: 2.50 **NM** value: **Cover or less**
Circ: CapCity orders: **10,750**
A: Jon Foster **W:** Dennis Feldman

3 ❑ Aug 1995 Cover: 2.50 **NM** value: **Cover or less**
Circ: CapCity orders: **9,325**
A: Jon Foster **W:** Dennis Feldman

4 ❑ Sep 1995 Cover: 2.50 **NM** value: **Cover or less**
Circ: CapCity orders: **7,850**
A: Jon Foster **W:** Dennis Feldman

SPECIES: HUMAN RACE — Dark Horse

1 ❑ Nov 1996 Cover: 2.95 **NM** value: **Cover or less**
Circ: Diamd. preorders: **17,500**
A: Phil Hester **W:** Gordon Rennie

2 ❑ Dec 1996 Cover: 2.95 **NM** value: **Cover or less**
Circ: Diamd. preorders: **13,395**
A: Phil Hester **W:** Ed Gorman

3 ❑ Jan 1997 Cover: 2.95 **NM** value: **Cover or less**
Circ: Diamd. preorders: **11,784**
A: Denys Cowan **W:** Stephen Blue

4 ❑ Feb 1997 Cover: 2.95 **NM** value: **Cover or less**
Circ: Diamd. preorders: **9,517**
A: Mark A. Nelson **W:** Stephen R. Bissette

Bk 1 ❑ Jul 1997 Cover: 11.95 **NM** value: **Cover or less**

SPECTACLES — Alternative Press

1 ❑ Feb 1997, b&w Cover: 2.95 **NM** value: **Cover or less**
Circ: Diamd. preorders: **2,241**
📖 The Frost Chances; Land of The Early Bird; Eye of Potential Harm
A: Jon Lewis **W:** Jon Lewis

2 ❑ May 1997, b&w Cover: 2.95 **NM** value: **Cover or less**
A: Jon Lewis **W:** Jon Lewis

3 ❑ Sep 1997, b&w Cover: 2.95 **NM** value: **Cover or less**
📖 Deeper than your Strangest Dreams; Shell Men **A:** Jon Lewis **W:** Jon Lewis

4 ❑ Jan 1998, b&w Cover: 2.95 **NM** value: **Cover or less**
A: Jon Lewis **W:** Jon Lewis

SPECTACULAR FEATURES MAGAZINE — Fox

11 ❑ Apr 1950 Cover: 0.10 **NM** value: **200.00**
• **CGC:** 1 graded, best 7.5

12 ❑ Jun 1950 Cover: 0.10 **NM** value: **200.00**

3 ❑ Aug 1950 Cover: 0.10 **NM** value: **200.00**

SPECTACULAR SCARLET SPIDER — Marvel

1 ❑ Nov 1995 Cover: 1.95 **NM** value: **Cover or less**
📖 Virtual Mortality, Part 4

2 ❑ Dec 1995 Cover: 1.95 **NM** value: **Cover or less**
📖 Cyberwar, Part 4 **A:** Sal Buscema; Bill Sienkiewicz(inker) **W:** Todd Dezago

SPECTACULAR SPIDER-MAN, THE — Marvel

Marvel launched its second ongoing title for Spider-Man in 1976, labeling it Peter Parker, The Spectacular Spider-Man. However, as years went by, many retailers racked it under "Spectacular" — probably to be closer to other Spider-Man related material — and the name officially changed, even though many still referred to it as "Peter Parker."

Whatever the title, the beginning of the series was inauspicious, with such lame characters as Razorback making the scene. A Frank Miller team-up starring Daredevil is the sole high-point of the run's early years. But in the 1980s, Bill Mantlo energized the title with the introduction of Cloak & Dagger in #64 and a romance between Spider-Man and the Black Cat. Later, Peter David provided a distinguished run, beginning with "Who Killed Jean DeWolff?"

Eventually, the series would become more wrapped up in Amazing Spider-Man's continuity, serving as basically one part of a weekly serial — and it had lost much of its individual personality when it ended in 1998. Despite its name, the replacement companion for Amazing Spider-Man, called Peter Parker, Spider-Man, is actually the continuation of the "adjectiveless" Spider-Man series, not this one (at least, according to the postal license). — JJM

-1 ❑ Jul 1997 Cover: 1.99 **NM** value: **2.00**
Circ: Diamd. preorders: **64,874**
• Flashback

1 ❑ Dec 1976 Cover: 0.30 **NM** value: **16.00**
• **CGC:** 460 graded, best 9.8
📖 Lo, This Monster; In the Beginning • Tarantula **A:** Sal Buscema; John Romita; Larry Lieber **W:** John Romita; Stan Lee

2 ❑ Jan 1977 Cover: 0.30 **NM** value: **6.00**
• **CGC:** 18 graded, best 9.6
📖 The Goblin Lives • Kraven **A:** Sal Buscema; John Romita; Jim Mooney **W:** John Romita; Stan Lee

3 ❑ Feb 1977 Cover: 0.30 **NM** value: **4.00**
• **CGC:** 19 graded, best 9.8
A: Sal Buscema ★ Origin of Lightmaster. ★ 1st Appearance of Lightmaster.

4 ❑ Mar 1977 Cover: 0.30 **NM** value: **4.00**
• **CGC:** 16 graded, best 9.9
A: Sal Buscema ★ Versus Vulture.

5 ❑ Apr 1977 Cover: 0.30 **NM** value: **4.00**
• **CGC:** 10 graded, best 9.8
A: Sal Buscema ★ Versus Vulture.

6 ❑ May 1977 Cover: 0.30 **NM** value: **3.50**
• **CGC:** 16 graded, best 9.9
★ Appearance of Morbius. ★ Versus Morbius.

7 ❑ Jun 1977 Cover: 0.30 **NM** value: **3.50**
• **CGC:** 10 graded, best 9.8
★ Appearance of Morbius. ★ Versus Morbius.

8 ❑ Jul 1977 Cover: 0.30 **NM** value: **3.50**
• **CGC:** 8 graded, best 9.8
★ Appearance of Morbius. ★ Versus Morbius.

9 ❑ Aug 1977 Cover: 0.30 **NM** value: **3.00**
• **CGC:** 10 graded, best 9.8
★ Appearance of White Tiger.

10 ❑ Sep 1977 Cover: 0.30 **NM** value: **3.00**
• **CGC:** 2 graded, best 9.8
★ Appearance of White Tiger.

11 ❑ Oct 1977 Cover: 0.35 **NM** value: **3.00**
• **CGC:** 1 graded, best 9.4
A: Sal Buscema

12 ❑ Nov 1977 Cover: 0.35 **NM** value: **3.00**
A: Sal Buscema ★ 1st Appearance of Razorback (partial). ★ 1st Appearance of Razorback (partial). ★ Appearance of Brother Power.

13 ❑ Dec 1977 Cover: 0.35 **NM** value: **3.00**
• **CGC:** 1 graded, best 9.6
A: Sal Buscema ★ Origin of Razorback. ★ 1st Appearance of Razorback (full).

14 ❑ Jan 1978 Cover: 0.35 **NM** value: **3.00**
A: Sal Buscema ★ Versus Hatemonger.

15 ❑ Feb 1978 Cover: 0.35 **NM** value: **3.00**
A: Sal Buscema ★ Appearance of Razorback.

16 ❑ Mar 1978 Cover: 0.35 **NM** value: **3.00**
• **CGC:** 1 graded, best 9.4
A: Sal Buscema ★ Versus Beetle.

17 ❑ Apr 1978 Cover: 0.35 **NM** value: **3.00**
★ Appearance of Iceman, Angel.

18 ❑ May 1978 Cover: 0.35 **NM** value: **3.00**
★ Appearance of Iceman, Angel.

19 ❑ Jun 1978 Cover: 0.35 **NM** value: **3.00**
★ Versus Enforcers.

20 ❑ Jul 1978 Cover: 0.35 **NM** value: **3.00**
• **CGC:** 1 graded, best 9.4
★ Versus Light Master.

21 ❑ Aug 1978 Cover: 0.35 **NM** value: **2.50**
★ Appearance of Moon Knight.

22 ❑ Sep 1978 Cover: 0.35 **NM** value: **2.50**
★ Appearance of Moon Knight.

23 ❑ Oct 1978 Cover: 0.35 **NM** value: **2.50**
• **CGC:** 2 graded, best 9.6
★ Appearance of Moon Knight.

24 ❑ Nov 1978 Cover: 0.35 **NM** value: **2.50**

25 ❑ Dec 1978 Cover: 0.35 **NM** value: **2.50**
★ 1st Appearance of Carrion I.

26 ❑ Jan 1979 Cover: 0.35 **NM** value: **2.50**
Circ: Statement: **219,169**
★ Appearance of Daredevil.

27 ❑ Feb 1979 Cover: 0.35 **NM** value: **5.00**
Circ: Statement: **219,169** • **CGC:** 37 graded, best 9.9
• Frank Miller's first Daredevil art **A:** Frank Miller; Dave Cockrum ★ Appearance of Daredevil.

28 ❑ Mar 1979 Cover: 0.35 **NM** value: **4.00**
Circ: Statement: **219,169** • **CGC:** 12 graded, best 9.8
A: Frank Miller ★ Appearance of Daredevil.

29 ❑ Apr 1979 Cover: 0.35 **NM** value: **2.50**
Circ: Statement: **219,169**
★ Versus Carrion.

30 ❑ May 1979 Cover: 0.40 **NM** value: **2.50**
Circ: Statement: **219,169** • **CGC:** 1 graded, best 9.6
★ Versus Carrion.

31 ❑ Jun 1979 Cover: 0.40 **NM** value: **2.50**
Circ: Statement: **219,169**
★ Origin of Carrion I. ★ Death of Carrion I.

32 ❑ Jul 1979 Cover: 0.40 **NM** value: **2.50**
Circ: Statement: **219,169**

33 ❑ Aug 1979 Cover: 0.40 **NM** value: **2.50**
Circ: Statement: **219,169**
★ Origin of Iguana.

34 ❑ Sep 1979 Cover: 0.40 **NM** value: **2.50**
Circ: Statement: **219,169** • **CGC:** 1 graded, best 9.8
★ Versus Lizard.

35 ❑ Oct 1979 Cover: 0.40 **NM** value: **2.50**
Circ: Statement: **219,169**

36 ❑ Nov 1979 Cover: 0.40 **NM** value: **2.50**
Circ: Statement: **219,169** • **CGC:** 1 graded, best 9.8
★ Versus Swarm.

37 ❑ Dec 1979 Cover: 0.40 **NM** value: **2.50**
Circ: Statement: **219,169**
★ Versus Swarm.

38 ❑ Jan 1980 Cover: 0.40 **NM** value: **2.50**
Circ: Statement: **211,327**
★ Appearance of Morbius. ★ Versus Morbius.

39 ❑ Feb 1980 Cover: 0.40 **NM** value: **2.50**
Circ: Statement: **211,327**
★ Versus Schizoid Man.

40 ❑ Mar 1980 Cover: 0.40 **NM** value: **2.50**
Circ: Statement: **211,327** • **CGC:** 1 graded, best 9.6
• Has 1979 Statement, filed 10/1/79; avg print run 424,891; avg sales 214,483; avg subs 4,686; avg total paid 219,169; samples 590; office use 1,115; max existent 220,874; 48% of run returned ★ Versus Lizard.

41 ❑ Apr 1980 Cover: 0.40 **NM** value: **2.50**
Circ: Statement: **211,327**
★ Versus Meteor Man.

42 ❑ May 1980 Cover: 0.40 **NM** value: **2.50**
Circ: Statement: **211,327**
★ Appearance of Human Torch.

43 ❑ Jun 1980 Cover: 0.40 **NM** value: **2.50**
Circ: Statement: **211,327** • **CGC:** 1 graded, best 9.4
★ 1st Appearance of Belladonna.

44 ❑ Jul 1980 Cover: 0.40 **NM** value: **2.50**
Circ: Statement: **211,327**

45 ❑ Aug 1980 Cover: 0.40 **NM** value: **2.50**
Circ: Statement: **211,327**
• Vulture

46 ❑ Sep 1980 Cover: 0.50 **NM** value: **2.50**
Circ: Statement: **211,327**
• Cobra **A:** Frank Miller(cover) **C:** Frank Miller

47 ❑ Oct 1980 Cover: 0.50 **NM** value: **2.50**
Circ: Statement: **211,327**

48 ❑ Nov 1980 Cover: 0.50 **NM** value: **2.50**
Circ: Statement: **211,327**
📖 Double Defeat! **A:** Marie Severin; Frank Miller(cover) **W:** Roger Stern

49 ❑ Dec 1980 Cover: 0.50 **NM** value: **2.50**
Circ: Statement: **211,327**

CGC-graded: Multiply prices above by **33 for 9.9 M • 16 for 9.8 NM/M • 7 for 9.6 NM+ • 5 for 9.4 NM • 2.5 for 9.2 NM- • 1.5 for 9.0 VF/NM**

• Title changes to Peter Parker, The Spectacular Spider-Man **A:** Frank Miller(cover) ★ Appearance of Prowler.

50 ❑ Jan 1981 Cover: 0.50 **NM** value: **2.50**
Circ: Statement: **171,839** • **CGC:** 1 graded, best 9.4
• Smuggler **A:** John Romita Jr.; Jim Mooney; Frank Miller(cover)

51 ❑ Feb 1981 Cover: 0.50 **NM** value: **2.50**
Circ: Statement: **171,839**
A: Frank Miller(cover) **C:** Frank Miller ★ Versus Mysterio.

52 ❑ Mar 1981 Cover: 0.50 **NM** value: **2.50**
Circ: Statement: **171,839**
A: Frank Miller(cover) **C:** Frank Miller ★ Appearance of White Tiger.

53 ❑ Apr 1981 Cover: 0.50 **NM** value: **2.50**
Circ: Statement: **171,839**
• Has 1980 Statement, filed 10/1/80; avg print run 434,466; avg sales 205,391; avg subs 5,936; avg total paid 211,327; samples 596; office use 3,168; max existent 215,091; 51% of run returned **A:** Jim Mooney; Frank Springer ★ Versus Tinkerer.

54 ❑ May 1981 Cover: 0.50 **NM** value: **2.50**
Circ: Statement: **171,839**
A: Frank Miller(cover) **C:** Frank Miller

55 ❑ Jun 1981 Cover: 0.50 **NM** value: **2.50**
Circ: Statement: **171,839**
A: Frank Miller(cover) ★ Versus Nitro.

56 ❑ Jul 1981 Cover: 0.50 **NM** value: **4.00**
Circ: Statement: **171,839** • **CGC:** 2 graded, best 9.6
A: Frank Miller(cover) **C:** Frank Miller ★ 2nd Appearance of Jack O'Lantern II. ★ 2nd Appearance of Jack O'Lantern II. ★ Versus Jack O'Lantern II.

57 ❑ Aug 1981 Cover: 0.50 **NM** value: **2.50**
Circ: Statement: **171,839**
A: Frank Miller(cover)

58 ❑ Sep 1981 Cover: 0.50 **NM** value: **2.50**
Circ: Statement: **171,839** • **CGC:** 1 graded, best 9.6
Ring Out The Old, Ring In The New **A:** John Byrne **W:** Roger Stern ★ Versus Ringer.

59 ❑ Oct 1981 Cover: 0.50 **NM** value: **2.50**
Circ: Statement: **171,839**
A: Jim Mooney

60 ❑ Nov 1981 Cover: 0.75 **NM** value: **2.50**
Circ: Statement: **171,839**
• Giant-size. **A:** Frank Miller(cover) **C:** Frank Miller; Jim Mooney ★ Origin of Spider-Man. ★ Versus Beetle.

61 ❑ Dec 1981 Cover: 0.50 **NM** value: **2.50**
Circ: Statement: **171,839**
By The Light Of The Silvery Moonstone...! **A:** Ed Hannigan; Jim Mooney **W:** Roger Stern; Bill Mantlo ★ Appearance of Moonstone.

62 ❑ Jan 1982 Cover: 0.60 **NM** value: **2.50**
Circ: Statement: **172,262**
A: Frank Miller(cover) ★ Versus Gold Bug.

63 ❑ Feb 1982 Cover: 0.60 **NM** value: **2.50**
Circ: Statement: **172,262**
★ Versus Molten Man.

64 ❑ Mar 1982 Cover: 0.60 **NM** value: **4.50**
Circ: Statement: **172,262** • **CGC:** 4 graded, best 9.8
★ 1st Appearance of Cloak & Dagger.

65 ❑ Apr 1982 Cover: 0.60 **NM** value: **2.00**
Circ: Statement: **172,262**
• Has 1981 Statement, filed 10/1/81; avg print run 414,166; avg sales 164,833; avg subs 6,956; avg total paid 171,839; samples 601; office use 2,670; max existent 175,060; 58% of run returned ★ Versus Kraven.

66 ❑ May 1982 Cover: 0.60 **NM** value: **2.00**
Circ: Statement: **172,262**
★ Versus Electro.

67 ❑ Jun 1982 Cover: 0.60 **NM** value: **2.00**
Circ: Statement: **172,262**
★ Versus Kingpin.

68 ❑ Jul 1982 Cover: 0.60 **NM** value: **2.00**
Circ: Statement: **172,262**
★ Versus Robot Master.

69 ❑ Aug 1982 Cover: 0.60 **NM** value: **2.00**
Circ: Statement: **172,262**
★ Appearance of Cloak & Dagger.

70 ❑ Sep 1982 Cover: 0.60 **NM** value: **2.00**
Circ: Statement: **172,262**
★ Appearance of Cloak & Dagger.

71 ❑ Oct 1982 Cover: 0.60 **NM** value: **2.00**
Circ: Statement: **172,262**
• Gun control story

72 ❑ Nov 1982 Cover: 0.60 **NM** value: **2.00**
Circ: Statement: **172,262**
★ Versus Doctor Octopus.

73 ❑ Dec 1982 Cover: 0.60 **NM** value: **2.00**
Circ: Statement: **172,262**
★ Versus Owl.

74 ❑ Jan 1983 Cover: 0.60 **NM** value: **2.00**
Circ: Statement: **172,290**
Fantasia! **A:** Bob Hall **W:** Bill Mantlo ★ Appearance of Black Cat.

75 ❑ Feb 1983 Cover: 1.00 **NM** value: **2.50**
Circ: Statement: **172,290**
• Giant-size. ★ Appearance of Black Cat.

76 ❑ Mar 1983 Cover: 0.60 **NM** value: **2.00**
Circ: Statement: **172,290**
★ Appearance of Black Cat.

77 ❑ Apr 1983 Cover: 0.60 **NM** value: **2.00**
Circ: Statement: **172,290**
★ Appearance of Gladiator.

78 ❑ May 1983 Cover: 0.60 **NM** value: **2.00**
Circ: Statement: **172,290**
• Has 1982 Statement, filed 10/11/82; avg print run 377,302; avg sales 164,590; avg subs 7,672; avg total paid 172,262; samples 700; office use 1,233; max existent 174,195; 54% of run returned ★ Versus Doctor Octopus.

79 ❑ Jun 1983 Cover: 0.60 **NM** value: **2.00**
Circ: Statement: **172,290**
★ Versus Doctor Octopus.

80 ❑ Jul 1983 Cover: 0.60 **NM** value: **2.00**
Circ: Statement: **172,290**
• J. Jonah Jameson solo story

81 ❑ Aug 1983 Cover: 0.60 **NM** value: **2.00**
Circ: Statement: **172,290** • **CGC:** 2 graded, best 9.8
Stalkers In The Shadows **A:** Al Milgrom; Jim Mooney **W:** Bill Mantlo ★ Appearance of Punisher, Cloak & Dagger.

82 ❑ Sep 1983 Cover: 0.60 **NM** value: **2.50**
Circ: Statement: **172,290** • **CGC:** 1 graded, best 9.6
★ Appearance of Punisher, Cloak & Dagger.

83 ❑ Oct 1983 Cover: 0.60 **NM** value: **3.00**
Circ: Statement: **172,290** • **CGC:** 2 graded, best 9.8
★ Appearance of Punisher.

84 ❑ Nov 1983 Cover: 0.60 **NM** value: **2.00**
Circ: Statement: **172,290**

85 ❑ Dec 1983 Cover: 0.60 **NM** value: **4.00**
Circ: Statement: **172,290** • **CGC:** 7 graded, best 9.9
★ Appearance of Hobgoblin (Ned Leeds). ★ Versus Hobgoblin.

86 ❑ Jan 1984 Cover: 0.60 **NM** value: **2.00**
Circ: Statement: **180,498** • **CGC:** 1 graded, best 9.6
• Asst. Editor Month ★ Appearance of Fred Hembeck.

87 ❑ Feb 1984 Cover: 0.60 **NM** value: **2.00**
Circ: Statement: **180,498**
Mistaken Identities • reveals identity **A:** Al Milgrom **W:** Bill Mantlo

88 ❑ Mar 1984 Cover: 0.60 **NM** value: **2.00**
Circ: Statement: **180,498** • **CGC:** 1 graded, best 9.6
★ Appearance of Black Cat. ★ Versus Mr. Hyde. ★ Versus Cobra.

89 ❑ Apr 1984 Cover: 0.60 **NM** value: **2.00**
Circ: Statement: **180,498** • **CGC:** 1 graded, best 9.6
• Fantastic Four apperance ★ Appearance of Fantastic Four, Kingpin.

90 ❑ May 1984 Cover: 0.60 **NM** value: **2.00**
Circ: Statement: **180,498** • **CGC:** 1 graded, best 9.6
• new costume; Black Cat's new powers; Has 1983 Statement, filed 10/3/83; avg print run 351,448; avg sales 163,595; avg subs 8,695; avg total paid 172,290; samples 760; office use 6,080; max existent 179,130; 49% of run returned **A:** Al Milgrom

91 ❑ Jun 1984 Cover: 0.60 **NM** value: **2.00**
Circ: Statement: **180,498**
★ Versus Blob.

92 ❑ Jul 1984 Cover: 0.60 **NM** value: **2.00**
Circ: Statement: **180,498**
★ 1st Appearance of The Answer. ★ Versus Answer.

93 ❑ Aug 1984 Cover: 0.60 **NM** value: **2.00**
Circ: Statement: **180,498**
★ Versus Answer.

94 ❑ Sep 1984 Cover: 0.60 **NM** value: **2.00**
Circ: Statement: **180,498**
★ Appearance of Cloak & Dagger. ★ Versus Silvermane.

95 ❑ Oct 1984 Cover: 0.60 **NM** value: **2.00**
Circ: Statement: **180,498**
★ Appearance of Cloak & Dagger. ★ Versus Silvermane.

96 ❑ Nov 1984 Cover: 0.60 **NM** value: **2.00**
Circ: Statement: **180,498**
★ Appearance of Cloak & Dagger. ★ Versus Silvermane.

97 ❑ Dec 1984 Cover: 0.60 **NM** value: **2.00**
Circ: Statement: **180,498**
★ Versus Hermit.

98 ❑ Jan 1985 Cover: 0.60 **NM** value: **2.00**
Circ: Statement: **247,916**
★ 1st Appearance of Spot. ★ Versus Kingpin.

99 ❑ Feb 1985 Cover: 0.60 **NM** value: **2.00**
Circ: Statement: **247,916**
★ Versus Spot.

100 ❑ Mar 1985 Cover: 1.00 **NM** value: **4.00**
Circ: Statement: **247,916** • **CGC:** 2 graded, best 9.6
• Giant-size. ★ Versus Spot.

101 ❑ Apr 1985 Cover: 0.65 **NM** value: **2.00**
Circ: Statement: **247,916** • **CGC:** 2 graded, best 9.6
• Has 1984 Statement, filed 9/28/84; avg print run 337,108; avg sales 171,814; avg subs 8,684; avg total paid 180,498; samples 140; office use 3,652; max existent 184,290; 45% of run returned ★ Versus Blacklash.

102 ❑ May 1985 Cover: 0.65 **NM** value: **2.00**
Circ: Statement: **247,916** CapCity orders: **19,100**
★ Versus Killer Shrike.

103 ❑ Jun 1985 Cover: 0.65 **NM** value: **2.00**
Circ: Statement: **247,916** CapCity orders: **18,200**

104 ❑ Jul 1985 Cover: 0.65 **NM** value: **2.00**
Circ: Statement: **247,916** CapCity orders: **19,300**
★ Origin of Rocket Racer. ★ Versus Rocket Racer.

105 ❑ Aug 1985 Cover: 0.65 **NM** value: **2.00**
Circ: Statement: **247,916** CapCity orders: **18,300**
★ Appearance of Wasp.

106 ❑ Sep 1985 Cover: 0.65 **NM** value: **2.00**
Circ: Statement: **247,916** CapCity orders: **18,900**
★ Appearance of Wasp.

107 ❑ Oct 1985 Cover: 0.65 **NM** value: **2.00**
Circ: Statement: **247,916** CapCity orders: **18,700**
★ Death of Jean DeWolff.

108 ❑ Nov 1985 Cover: 0.65 **NM** value: **2.00**
Circ: Statement: **247,916** CapCity orders: **19,000**

109 ❑ Dec 1985 Cover: 0.65 **NM** value: **2.00**
Circ: Statement: **247,916** CapCity orders: **18,700**

110 ❑ Jan 1986 Cover: 0.65 **NM** value: **2.00**
Circ: Statement: **214,047** CapCity orders: **18,400**
★ Appearance of Daredevil.

111 ❑ Feb 1986 Cover: 0.75 **NM** value: **2.00**
Circ: Statement: **214,047** CapCity orders: **26,100**
Secret Wars II • Secret Wars II

112 ❑ Mar 1986 Cover: 0.75 **NM** value: **2.00**
Circ: Statement: **214,047** CapCity orders: **20,400**
• Christmas story

113 ❑ Apr 1986 Cover: 0.75 **NM** value: **2.00**
Circ: Statement: **214,047** CapCity orders: **21,000**

114 ❑ May 1986 Cover: 0.75 **NM** value: **2.00**
Circ: Statement: **214,047** CapCity orders: **22,200**

115 ❑ Jun 1986 Cover: 0.75 **NM** value: **2.00**
Circ: Statement: **214,047** CapCity orders: **21,400**
★ Appearance of Doctor Strange.

116 ❑ Jul 1986 Cover: 0.75 **NM** value: **3.00**
Circ: Statement: **214,047** CapCity orders: **22,300** • **CGC:** 2 graded, best 9.6
★ Appearance of Sabretooth.

117 ❑ Aug 1986 Cover: 0.75 **NM** value: **2.00**
Circ: Statement: **214,047** CapCity orders: **22,500**
★ Appearance of Doctor Strange.

118 ❑ Sep 1986 Cover: 0.75 **NM** value: **2.00**
Circ: Statement: **214,047** CapCity orders: **22,700**

119 ❑ Oct 1986 Cover: 0.75 **NM** value: **3.00**
Circ: Statement: **214,047** CapCity orders: **22,000** • **CGC:** 4 graded, best 9.6
★ Appearance of Sabretooth.

120 ❑ Nov 1986 Cover: 0.75 **NM** value: **2.00**
Circ: Statement: **214,047** CapCity orders: **23,100**

121 ❑ Dec 1986 Cover: 0.75 **NM** value: **2.00**
Circ: Statement: **214,047** CapCity orders: **22,800**

122 ❑ Jan 1987 Cover: 0.75 **NM** value: **2.00**
Circ: Statement: **213,758** CapCity orders: **22,700**

123 ❑ Feb 1987 Cover: 0.75 **NM** value: **2.00**
Circ: Statement: **213,758** CapCity orders: **23,200** • **CGC:** 1 graded, best 9.4
With Friends Like These **A:** Dwayne Turner **W:** Peter David ★ Versus Blaze.

124 ❑ Mar 1987 Cover: 0.75 **NM** value: **2.00**
Circ: Statement: **213,758** CapCity orders: **23,100**
★ Versus Doctor Octopus.

125 ❑ Apr 1987 Cover: 0.75 **NM** value: **2.00**
Circ: Statement: **213,758** CapCity orders: **23,100**
★ Appearance of Spider Woman.

126 ❑ May 1987 Cover: 0.75 **NM** value: **2.00**
Circ: Statement: **213,758** CapCity orders: **21,400**
★ Appearance of Spider Woman.

127 ❑ Jun 1987 Cover: 0.75 **NM** value: **2.00**
Circ: Statement: **213,758** CapCity orders: **22,300**
Among Us Lurks...A Lizard! **A:** Alan Kupperberg **W:** Len Kaminski ★ Versus Lizard.

128 ❑ Jul 1987 Cover: 0.75 **NM** value: **2.00**
Circ: Statement: **213,758** CapCity orders: **22,000**
★ Appearance of Silver Sable.

129 ❑ Aug 1987 Cover: 0.75 **NM** value: **2.00**
Circ: Statement: **213,758** CapCity orders: **22,800**
★ Versus Foreigner.

130 ❑ Sep 1987 Cover: 0.75 **NM** value: **3.00**
Circ: Statement: **213,758** CapCity orders: **24,000**
★ Appearance of Hobgoblin. ★ Versus Hobgoblin.

131 ❑ Oct 1987 Cover: 0.75 **NM** value: **5.00**
Circ: Statement: **213,758** CapCity orders: **27,900**
Kraven's Last Hunt, Part 3 • Kraven **A:** Mike Zeck **W:** J.M. DeMatteis

132 ❑ Nov 1987 Cover: 0.75 **NM** value: **4.00**
Circ: Statement: **213,758** CapCity orders: **29,500**
Kraven's Last Hunt, Part 6 • Kraven

133 ❑ Dec 1987 Cover: 0.75 **NM** value: **3.00**
Circ: Statement: **213,758** CapCity orders: **27,700**
A: Bill Sienkiewicz

134 ❑ Jan 1988 Cover: 0.75 **NM** value: **2.00**
Circ: Statement: **228,340** CapCity orders: **27,900**
★ Versus Sin Eater.

135 ❑ Feb 1988 Cover: 0.75 **NM** value: **2.00**
Circ: Statement: **228,340** CapCity orders: **29,600**
• Title returns to The Spectacular Spider-Man ★ Versus Sin Eater. ★ Versus Electro.

136 ❑ Mar 1988 Cover: 0.75 **NM** value: **2.00**
Circ: Statement: **228,340** CapCity orders: **30,200**
★ Versus Sin Eater.

137 ❑ Apr 1988 Cover: 0.75 **NM** value: **2.00**
Circ: Statement: **228,340** CapCity orders: **31,600**
★ Versus Tarantula.

138 ❑ May 1988 Cover: 1.00 **NM** value: **2.00**
Circ: Statement: **228,340** CapCity orders: **30,100**
★ Appearance of Captain America. ★ Versus Tarantula.

139 ❑ Jun 1988 Cover: 1.00 **NM** value: **3.00**
Circ: Statement: **228,340** CapCity orders: **28,100**
★ Origin of Tombstone.

140 ❑ Jul 1988 Cover: 1.00 **NM** value: **2.00**
Circ: Statement: **228,340** CapCity orders: **32,600**
★ Appearance of Punisher.

141 ❑ Aug 1988 Cover: 1.00 **NM** value: **2.00**
Circ: Statement: **228,340** CapCity orders: **32,000** • **CGC:** 1 graded, best 9.4
★ Appearance of Punisher.

142 ❑ Sep 1988 Cover: 1.00 **NM** value: **2.00**
Circ: Statement: **228,340** CapCity orders: **31,700**
★ Appearance of Punisher.

143 ❑ Oct 1988 Cover: 1.00 **NM** value: **2.00**
Circ: Statement: **228,340** CapCity orders: **32,600**
★ Appearance of Punisher.

144 ❑ Nov 1988 Cover: 1.00 **NM** value: **2.00**
Circ: Statement: **228,340** CapCity orders: **29,300**
• in San Diego ★ Versus Boomerang.

145 ❑ Dec 1988 Cover: 1.00 **NM** value: **2.00**
Circ: Statement: **228,340** CapCity orders: **29,400**

146 ❑ Jan 1989 Cover: 1.00 **NM** value: **2.00**
Circ: Statement: **205,425** CapCity orders: **33,800**
Inferno • Inferno **A:** Sal Buscema **W:** Gerry Conway

147 ❑ Feb 1989 Cover: 1.00 **NM** value: **10.00**
Circ: Statement: **205,425** CapCity orders: **33,700** • **CGC:** 7 graded, best 9.8
• Inferno ★ 1st Appearance of Hobgoblin III.

148 ❑ Mar 1989 Cover: 1.00 **NM** value: **2.00**
Circ: Statement: **205,425** CapCity orders: **33,800**
• Inferno

149 ❑ Apr 1989 Cover: 1.00 **NM** value: **3.00**
Circ: Statement: **205,425** CapCity orders: **29,100**
★ Origin of Carrion II (Malcolm McBride). ★ 1st Appearance of Carrion II (Malcolm McBride).

150 ❑ May 1989 Cover: 1.00 **NM** value: **2.00**
Circ: Statement: **205,425** CapCity orders: **30,000**
★ Versus Tombstone.

151 ❑ Jun 1989 Cover: 1.00 **NM** value: **2.00**
Circ: Statement: **205,425** CapCity orders: **28,000**
★ Versus Tombstone.

Other grades: Multiply prices above by **1.5 for Mint • 2/3 for Very Fine • 1/3 for Fine • 1/5 for Very Good • 1/8 for Good**

152 ❑ Jul 1989 Cover: 1.00 **NM** value: **2.00**
Circ: Statement: **205,425** CapCity orders: **28,600**
🕮 A Wolf's Tale... **A:** Sal Buscema **W:** Gerry Conway ★ Versus Lobo Brothers.

153 ❑ Aug 1989 Cover: 1.00 **NM** value: **2.00**
Circ: Statement: **205,425** CapCity orders: **28,400**
★ Versus Tombstone.

154 ❑ Sep 1989 Cover: 1.00 **NM** value: **2.00**
Circ: Statement: **205,425** CapCity orders: **28,000**
★ Versus Puma.

155 ❑ Oct 1989 Cover: 1.00 **NM** value: **2.00**
Circ: Statement: **205,425** CapCity orders: **28,800**
★ Versus Tombstone.

156 ❑ Nov 1989 Cover: 1.00 **NM** value: **2.00**
Circ: Statement: **205,425** CapCity orders: **29,300**
★ Versus Banjo.

157 ❑ Nov 1989 Cover: 1.00 **NM** value: **2.00**
Circ: Statement: **205,425** CapCity orders: **29,900**
★ Versus Electro.

158 ❑ Dec 1989 Cover: 1.00 **NM** value: **5.00**
Circ: Statement: **205,425** CapCity orders: **35,300** • **CGC:** 3 graded, best 9.6
🕮 Acts of Vengeance • Acts of Vengeance; Spider-Man gets cosmic powers ★ Versus Trapster.

159 ❑ Dec 1989 Cover: 1.00 **NM** value: **4.00**
Circ: Statement: **205,425** CapCity orders: **33,800**
🕮 Acts of Vengeance • Acts of Vengeance; Cosmic-powered Spider-Man ★ Versus Brothers Grimm.

160 ❑ Jan 1990 Cover: 1.00 **NM** value: **1.50**
Circ: Statement: **215,441** CapCity orders: **36,000**
🕮 Acts of Vengeance • Acts of Vengeance; Cosmic-powered Spider-Man ★ Versus Doctor Doom.

161 ❑ Feb 1990 Cover: 1.00 **NM** value: **1.50**
Circ: Statement: **215,441** CapCity orders: **33,500**
★ Appearance of Hobgoblin III. ★ Versus Hobgoblin III.

162 ❑ Mar 1990 Cover: 1.00 **NM** value: **1.50**
Circ: Statement: **215,441** CapCity orders: **33,600**
★ Appearance of Hobgoblin III. ★ Versus Carrion.

163 ❑ Apr 1990 Cover: 1.00 **NM** value: **1.50**
Circ: Statement: **215,441** CapCity orders: **35,100**
★ Appearance of Hobgoblin III. ★ Versus Hobgoblin III. ★ Versus Carrion.

164 ❑ May 1990 Cover: 1.00 **NM** value: **1.50**
Circ: Statement: **215,441** CapCity orders: **34,200**
★ Versus Beetle.

165 ❑ Jun 1990 Cover: 1.00 **NM** value: **1.50**
Circ: Statement: **215,441** CapCity orders: **34,500**
★ Death of Arranger.

166 ❑ Jul 1990 Cover: 1.00 **NM** value: **1.50**
Circ: Statement: **215,441** CapCity orders: **35,100**
🕮 The Deadly Lads From Liverpool **A:** Sal Buscema **W:** Gerry Conway

167 ❑ Aug 1990 Cover: 1.00 **NM** value: **1.50**
Circ: Statement: **215,441** CapCity orders: **34,500**
🕮 A Misty Kind Of Memory **A:** Sal Buscema **W:** Gerry Conway

168 ❑ Sep 1990 Cover: 1.00 **NM** value: **1.50**
Circ: Statement: **215,441** CapCity orders: **35,100**
• Avengers

169 ❑ Oct 1990 Cover: 1.00 **NM** value: **1.50**
Circ: Statement: **215,441** CapCity orders: **33,600**
• Avengers

170 ❑ Nov 1990 Cover: 1.00 **NM** value: **1.50**
Circ: Statement: **215,441** CapCity orders: **33,300**
• Avengers

171 ❑ Dec 1990 Cover: 1.00 **NM** value: **1.50**
Circ: Statement: **215,441** CapCity orders: **34,200**
🕮 Ordeal, Part 1 **A:** Sal Buscema **W:** Gerry Conway ★ Versus Puma.

172 ❑ Jan 1991 Cover: 1.00 **NM** value: **1.50**
Circ: CapCity orders: **33,900**
★ Versus Puma.

173 ❑ Feb 1991 Cover: 1.00 **NM** value: **1.50**
Circ: CapCity orders: **33,900**
🕮 Creatures Stirring • Doctor Octopus **A:** Sal Buscema **W:** David Michelinie; Gerry Conway

174 ❑ Mar 1991 Cover: 1.00 **NM** value: **1.50**
Circ: CapCity orders: **33,600**
🕮 Dedication (Or Jonah Goes TO Pieces! • Doctor Octopus **A:** Sal Buscema **W:** Terry Kavanagh; David Michelinie; Gerry Conway

175 ❑ Apr 1991 Cover: 1.00 **NM** value: **1.50**
Circ: CapCity orders: **33,000**
🕮 Spouse Trap • Doctor Octopus **A:** Sal Buscema **W:** David Michelinie

176 ❑ May 1991 Cover: 1.00 **NM** value: **1.50**
Circ: CapCity orders: **33,300**
🕮 The Love Of Power **A:** Sal Buscema **W:** Kurt Busiek ★ Origin of Corona. ★ 1st Appearance of Corona.

177 ❑ Jun 1991 Cover: 1.00 **NM** value: **1.50**
Circ: CapCity orders: **32,400**
🕮 Fever Pitch **A:** Sal Buscema **W:** Kurt Busiek

178 ❑ Jul 1991 Cover: 1.00 **NM** value: **1.50**
Circ: CapCity orders: **33,600**
🕮 The Child Within, Part 1 **A:** Sal Buscema **W:** J.M. DeMatteis ★ Versus Vermin.

179 ❑ Aug 1991 Cover: 1.00 **NM** value: **1.50**
Circ: CapCity orders: **35,400**
🕮 The Child Within, Part 2 **A:** Sal Buscema **W:** J.M. DeMatteis ★ Versus Vermin.

180 ❑ Sep 1991 Cover: 1.00 **NM** value: **1.50**
Circ: CapCity orders: **34,800**
🕮 The Child Within, Part 3 **A:** Sal Buscema **W:** J.M. DeMatteis ★ Appearance of Green Goblin. ★ Versus Green Goblin.

181 ❑ Oct 1991 Cover: 1.00 **NM** value: **1.50**
Circ: CapCity orders: **35,700**
🕮 The Child Within, Part 4 **A:** Sal Buscema **W:** J.M. DeMatteis ★ Appearance of Green Goblin. ★ Versus Green Goblin.

182 ❑ Nov 1991 Cover: 1.00 **NM** value: **1.50**
Circ: CapCity orders: **35,100**
🕮 The Child Within, Part 5 **A:** Sal Buscema **W:** J.M. DeMatteis ★ Origin of Vermin, Green Goblin. ★ Versus Green Goblin.

183 ❑ Dec 1991 Cover: 1.00 **NM** value: **1.50**
Circ: CapCity orders: **36,300**
🕮 The Child Within, Part 6 **A:** Sal Buscema **W:** J.M. DeMatteis ★ Appearance of Green Goblin. ★ Versus Green Goblin.

184 ❑ Jan 1992 Cover: 1.00 **NM** value: **1.50**
Circ: Statement: **261,308** CapCity orders: **35,400**
A: Sal Buscema **W:** J.M. DeMatteis ★ Appearance of Green Goblin.

185 ❑ Feb 1992 Cover: 1.25 **NM** value: **1.50**
Circ: Statement: **261,308** CapCity orders: **32,400**
A: Sal Buscema **W:** J.M. DeMatteis ★ Appearance of Frogman.

186 ❑ Mar 1992 Cover: 1.25 **NM** value: **1.50**
Circ: Statement: **261,308** CapCity orders: **33,200**
🕮 Funeral Arrangements, Part 1 **A:** Sal Buscema **W:** J.M. DeMatteis ★ Versus Vulture.

187 ❑ Apr 1992 Cover: 1.25 **NM** value: **1.50**
Circ: Statement: **261,308** CapCity orders: **31,200**
🕮 Funeral Arrangements, Part 2 **A:** Sal Buscema **W:** J.M. DeMatteis ★ Versus Vulture.

188 ❑ May 1992 Cover: 1.25 **NM** value: **1.50**
Circ: Statement: **261,308** CapCity orders: **32,400**
🕮 Funeral Arrangements, Part 3 **A:** Sal Buscema **W:** J.M. DeMatteis ★ Versus Vulture.

189 ❑ Jun 1992 Cover: 2.95 **NM** value: **4.00**
Circ: Statement: **261,308** CapCity orders: **85,100** • **CGC:** 4 graded, best 9.8
• 30th Anniversary Issue. 🕮 The Osborn Legacy • Gatefold painted poster **A:** Sal Buscema **W:** J.M. DeMatteis

189-2 ❑ Jun 1992 Cover: 2.95 **NM** value: **3.00**
Circ: CapCity orders: **50,100**

190 ❑ Jul 1992 Cover: 1.25 **NM** value: **1.50**
Circ: Statement: **261,308** CapCity orders: **37,500**
🕮 The Horns Of A Dilemma **A:** Sal Buscema **W:** J.M. DeMatteis

191 ❑ Aug 1992 Cover: 1.25 **NM** value: **1.50**
Circ: Statement: **261,308** CapCity orders: **37,100**
🕮 Eye of the Puma, Part 1 **A:** Sal Buscema **W:** J.M. DeMatteis

192 ❑ Sep 1992 Cover: 1.25 **NM** value: **1.50**
Circ: Statement: **261,308** CapCity orders: **34,800**
🕮 Eye of the Puma, Part 2 **A:** Sal Buscema **W:** J.M. DeMatteis

193 ❑ Oct 1992 Cover: 1.25 **NM** value: **1.50**
Circ: Statement: **261,308** CapCity orders: **35,300**
🕮 Eye of the Puma, Part 3 **A:** Sal Buscema **W:** J.M. DeMatteis ★ Versus Puma.

194 ❑ Nov 1992 Cover: 1.25 **NM** value: **1.50**
Circ: Statement: **261,308** CapCity orders: **36,200**
🕮 Death of Vermin, Part 1 **A:** Sal Buscema **W:** J.M. DeMatteis ★ Versus Vermin.

195 ❑ Dec 1992 Cover: 1.25 **NM** value: **1.50**
🕮 Death of Vermin, Part 2 **A:** Sal Buscema **W:** J.M. DeMatteis ★ Versus Vermin.

195/CS ❑ Dec 1992 Cover: 2.50 **NM** value: **Cover or less**
Circ: Statement: **261,308** CapCity orders: **29,300**
• Polybagged with Dirt Magazine #2, cassette sampler tape. 🕮 Death of Vermin, Part 2 • "Dirtbag Special" **A:** Sal Buscema **W:** J.M. DeMatteis

196 ❑ Jan 1993 Cover: 1.25 **NM** value: **1.50**
Circ: Statement: **295,925** CapCity orders: **35,100**
🕮 Death of Vermin, Part 3 **A:** Sal Buscema **W:** J.M. DeMatteis ★ Death of Vermin.

197 ❑ Feb 1993 Cover: 1.25 **NM** value: **1.50**
Circ: Statement: **295,925** CapCity orders: **44,100**
🕮 Power Play! **A:** Sal Buscema **W:** J.M. DeMatteis

198 ❑ Mar 1993 Cover: 1.25 **NM** value: **1.50**
Circ: Statement: **295,925** CapCity orders: **41,400**
A: Sal Buscema **W:** J.M. DeMatteis ★ Appearance of X-Men.

199 ❑ Apr 1993 Cover: 1.25 **NM** value: **1.50**
Circ: Statement: **295,925** CapCity orders: **43,900**
🕮 Falling! **A:** Sal Buscema **W:** J.M. DeMatteis ★ Appearance of X-Men.

200 ❑ May 1993 Cover: 2.95 **NM** value: **3.00**
Circ: Statement: **295,925** CapCity orders: **149,600** • **CGC:** 15 graded, best 9.9
foil cover. 🕮 Best Of Enemies **A:** Sal Buscema **W:** J.M. DeMatteis ★ Appearance of Green Goblin. ★ Death of Green Goblin.

201 ❑ Jun 1993 Cover: 1.25 **NM** value: **1.50**
Circ: Statement: **295,925** CapCity orders: **122,400**
🕮 Maximum Carnage, Part 5 **A:** Sal Buscema **W:** J.M. DeMatteis ★ Appearance of Carnage, Venom.

202 ❑ Jul 1993 Cover: 1.25 **NM** value: **1.50**
Circ: Statement: **295,925** CapCity orders: **106,200**
🕮 Maximum Carnage, Part 9 **A:** Sal Buscema **W:** J.M. DeMatteis ★ Appearance of Carnage, Venom.

203 ❑ Aug 1993 Cover: 1.25 **NM** value: **1.50**
Circ: Statement: **295,925** CapCity orders: **107,700**
🕮 Maximum Carnage, Part 13 **A:** Sal Buscema **W:** J.M. DeMatteis ★ Appearance of Carnage, Venom.

204 ❑ Sep 1993 Cover: 1.25 **NM** value: **1.50**
Circ: Statement: **295,925** CapCity orders: **50,000**
🕮 Death by Tombstone, Part 1 **A:** Sal Buscema ★ Appearance of Tombstone. ★ Versus Tombstone.

205 ❑ Oct 1993 Cover: 1.25 **NM** value: **1.50**
Circ: Statement: **295,925** CapCity orders: **44,500**
🕮 Death by Tombstone, Part 2 **A:** Sal Buscema **W:** Steven Grant ★ Appearance of Tombstone. ★ Versus Tombstone.

206 ❑ Nov 1993 Cover: 1.25 **NM** value: **1.50**
Circ: Statement: **295,925** CapCity orders: **45,500**
★ Versus Tombstone.

207 ❑ Dec 1993 Cover: 1.25 **NM** value: **1.50**
Circ: Statement: **295,925** CapCity orders: **42,800**
★ Versus Shroud.

208 ❑ Jan 1994 Cover: 1.25 **NM** value: **1.50**
Circ: Statement: **236,723** CapCity orders: **37,500**
A: Sal Buscema ★ Versus Shroud.

209 ❑ Feb 1994 Cover: 1.25 **NM** value: **1.50**
Circ: Statement: **236,723** CapCity orders: **36,100**
A: Sal Buscema ★ Versus Foreigner.

210 ❑ Mar 1994 Cover: 1.25 **NM** value: **1.50**
Circ: Statement: **236,723** CapCity orders: **32,600**
A: Sal Buscema ★ Versus Foreigner.

211 ❑ Apr 1994 Cover: 1.25 **NM** value: **1.50**
Circ: Statement: **236,723** CapCity orders: **39,100**
🕮 Pursuit, Part 2

212 ❑ May 1994 Cover: 1.25 **NM** value: **1.50**
Circ: Statement: **236,723** CapCity orders: **29,750**

213 ❑ Jun 1994 Cover: 1.50 **NM** value: **Cover or less**
🕮 Hail Mary, Part 1 ★ Versus Typhoid Mary.

213/CS ❑ Jun 1994 Cover: 2.95 **NM** value: **Cover or less**
Circ: Statement: **236,723** CapCity orders: **46,650**
🕮 Hail Mary, Part 1 • TV preview; print ★ Versus Typhoid Mary.

214 ❑ Jul 1994 Cover: 1.50 **NM** value: **Cover or less**
Circ: Statement: **236,723** CapCity orders: **31,200**
★ Versus Bloody Mary.

215 ❑ Aug 1994 Cover: 1.50 **NM** value: **Cover or less**
Circ: Statement: **236,723** CapCity orders: **29,350**

216 ❑ Sep 1994 Cover: 1.50 **NM** value: **Cover or less**
Circ: Statement: **236,723** CapCity orders: **29,000**
★ Versus Scorpion.

217 ❑ Oct 1994 Cover: 2.95 **NM** value: **Cover or less**
🕮 Power & Responsibility; Power and Responsibility, Part 4 **A:** Liam Sharp **W:** J.M. DeMatteis ★ Appearance of Ben Reilly.

217/SC ❑ Oct 1994 Cover: 2.95 **NM** value: **Cover or less**
Circ: Statement: **236,723** CapCity orders: **39,000**
enhanced cover. • Giant-size. 🕮 Power and Responsibility, Part 4; The Double, Part 4 • flip-book with back-up story **A:** Liam Sharp **W:** J.M. DeMatteis ★ Origin of Ben Reilly. ★ Appearance of Ben Reilly.

218 ❑ Nov 1994 Cover: 1.50 **NM** value: **Cover or less**
Circ: Statement: **236,723** CapCity orders: **38,300**
🕮 Back from the Edge, Part 2 ★ Versus Puma.

219 ❑ Dec 1994 Cover: 1.50 **NM** value: **Cover or less**
Circ: Statement: **236,723** CapCity orders: **33,750**
🕮 Back from the Edge, Part 4

220 ❑ Jan 1995 Cover: 2.25 **NM** value: **2.50**
Circ: Statement: **184,508** CapCity orders: **34,350**
• Giant-size. • flip book with illustrated story from The Ultimate Spider-Man back-up

221 ❑ Feb 1995 Cover: 1.50 **NM** value: **3.00**
Circ: Statement: **184,508** CapCity orders: **37,650**
🕮 Web of Death, Part 4 ★ Death of Doctor Octopus.

222 ❑ Mar 1995 Cover: 1.50 **NM** value: **Cover or less**
Circ: Statement: **184,508** CapCity orders: **32,850**
🕮 Players & Pawns, Part 1 **A:** Bill Sienkiewicz; Sal Buscema **W:** Tom DeFalco

223 ❑ Apr 1995 Cover: 2.50 **NM** value: **Cover or less**
• Giant-size.

223/SC ❑ Apr 1995 Cover: 2.95 **NM** value: **Cover or less**
Circ: Statement: **184,508** CapCity orders: **38,950**
enhanced cover. • Giant-size.

224 ❑ May 1995 Cover: 1.50 **NM** value: **Cover or less**
Circ: Statement: **184,508** CapCity orders: **34,450**

225 ❑ Jun 1995 Cover: 2.95 **NM** value: **3.95**
• Giant-size. 🕮 Return of the Green Goblin; He was Such a Nice Boy **A:** Sal Buscema **W:** Tom DeFalco ★ 1st Appearance of Green Goblin IV.

225/SC ❑ Jun 1995 Cover: 3.95 **NM** value: **Cover or less**
Circ: Statement: **184,508** CapCity orders: **35,300** • **CGC:** 1 graded, best 9.6
Hologram on cover.

226 ❑ Jul 1995 Cover: 1.50 **NM** value: **Cover or less**
Circ: Statement: **184,508** CapCity orders: **38,025**
🕮 The Trial of Peter Parker, Part 4 • identity of clone revealed

227 ❑ Aug 1995 Cover: 1.50 **NM** value: **Cover or less**
Circ: Statement: **184,508**

228 ❑ Sep 1995 Cover: 1.50 **NM** value: **Cover or less**
Circ: Statement: **184,508**
🕮 Time Bomb, Part 1 • continues in Web of Spider-Man #129

229 ❑ Oct 1995 Cover: 2.50 **NM** value: **Cover or less**
• **CGC:** 1 graded, best 9.8
wraparound cover. • Giant-size. 🕮 The Greatest Responsibility, Part 3 • the clone retires **A:** Bill Sienkiewicz; Sal Buscema **W:** Tom DeFalco

229/SC ❑ Oct 1995 Cover: 3.95 **NM** value: **Cover or less**
Circ: Statement: **135,110**
enhanced acetate outer cover. 🕮 The Greatest Responsibility, Part 3 • the clone retires

230 ❑ Jan 1996 Cover: 1.50 **NM** value: **3.95**
Circ: Statement: **135,110**
Special cover. • Giant-size. 🕮 Vengeance Is Mine-Sayeth The Sword • Has 1995 Statement, filed 10/1/95; avg print run 324,277; avg sales 181,142; avg subs 3,366; avg total paid 184,508; samples 750; office use 500; max existent 185,758; 43% of run returned ★ Versus D.K..

231 ❑ Feb 1996 Cover: 1.50 **NM** value: **Cover or less**
Circ: Statement: **135,110**
🕮 The Return of Kaine, Part 1 **A:** Sal Buscema **W:** Todd Dezago

232 ❑ Mar 1996 Cover: 1.50 **NM** value: **Cover or less**
Circ: Statement: **135,110**
🕮 A Show of Force • New Doctor Octopus returns **A:** Sal Buscema **W:** Todd Dezago

233 ❑ Apr 1996 Cover: 1.50 **NM** value: **Cover or less**
Circ: Statement: **135,110**
🕮 Web of Carnage, Part 4 **A:** Sal Buscema; Art Thibert; John Stanisci **W:** Todd Dezago

234 ❑ May 1996 Cover: 1.50 **NM** value: **Cover or less**
Circ: Statement: **135,110**
🕮 Blood Brothers, Part 4

235 ❑ Jun 1996 Cover: 1.50 **NM** value: **Cover or less**
Circ: Statement: **135,110**
• return of Will o' the Wisp

236 ❑ Jul 1996 Cover: 1.50 **NM** value: **Cover or less**
Circ: Statement: **135,110**
★ Versus Dragon-Man.

237 ❑ Aug 1996 Cover: 1.50 **NM** value: **Cover or less**
Circ: Statement: **135,110**
★ Versus Lizard.

238 ❑ Sep 1996 Cover: 1.50 **NM** value: **Cover or less**
Circ: Statement: **135,110**
★ Origin of second Lizard.

239 ❑ Oct 1996 Cover: 1.50 **NM** value: **Cover or less**
Circ: Statement: **128,297**
★ Versus Lizard.

CGC-graded: Multiply prices above by **33 for 9.9 M • 16 for 9.8 NM/M • 7 for 9.6 NM+ • 5 for 9.4 NM • 2.5 for 9.2 NM- • 1.5 for 9.0 VF/NM**

240 ❑ Nov 1996 Cover: 1.50 **NM value: Cover or less**
Circ: Statement: **128,297** Direct Market orders: **165,500**
📖 Revelations, Part 1 **A:** Luke Ross **W:** Todd Dezago
241 ❑ Dec 1996 Cover: 1.50 **NM value: Cover or less**
Circ: Statement: **128,297** Direct Market orders: **99,750**
📖 A New Day Dawning **A:** Luke Ross **W:** J.M. DeMatteis
242 ❑ Jan 1997 Cover: 1.50 **NM value: Cover or less**
Circ: Statement: **128,297** Direct Market orders: **76,750**
📖 Facedancing **A:** Luke Ross **W:** J.M. DeMatteis ★ Versus Chameleon.
243 ❑ Feb 1997 Cover: 1.50 **NM value: Cover or less**
Circ: Statement: **128,297** Direct Market orders: **75,500**
📖 Who Am I? **A:** Luke Ross **W:** J.M. DeMatteis ★ Versus Chameleon.
244 ❑ Mar 1997 Cover: 1.99 **NM value: Cover or less**
Circ: Statement: **128,297** Direct Market orders: **71,500**
📖 Backlash **A:** Luke Ross **W:** J.M. DeMatteis ★ 1st Appearance of Kangaroo II. ★ Versus Kraven.
245 ❑ Apr 1997 Cover: 1.99 **NM value: Cover or less**
Circ: Statement: **128,297** Direct Market orders: **70,250**
📖 Kravinov's Revenge **A:** Luke Ross **W:** J.M. DeMatteis ★ Versus Chameleon.
246 ❑ May 1997 Cover: 1.99 **NM value: Cover or less**
Circ: Statement: **128,297** Diamd. preorders: **69,097**
📖 The Legion of Losers! **A:** Luke Ross **W:** Glenn Greenberg; J.M. DeMatteis ★ Versus Legion of Losers (Gibbon, Spot, Kangaroo, Grizzly).
247 ❑ Jun 1997 Cover: 1.99 **NM value: Cover or less**
Circ: Statement: **128,297** Diamd. preorders: **69,482**
248 ❑ Aug 1997 Cover: 1.99 **NM value: Cover or less**
Circ: Statement: **128,297** Diamd. preorders: **63,330**
• gatefold summary.
249 ❑ Sep 1997 Cover: 1.99 **NM value: Cover or less**
Circ: Statement: **128,297** Diamd. preorders: **61,103**
• gatefold summary. • Norman Osborn buys Daily Bugle
250 ❑ Oct 1997 Cover: 3.25 **NM value: Cover or less**
Circ: Diamd. preorders: **70,212**
wraparound cover. • Giant-size.
251 ❑ Nov 1997 Cover: 1.99 **NM value: Cover or less**
Circ: Diamd. preorders: **59,888**
• gatefold summary. ★ Versus Kraven.
252 ❑ Dec 1997 Cover: 1.99 **NM value: Cover or less**
Circ: Diamd. preorders: **59,159**
• gatefold summary. • Has 1997 Statement; avg total paid circ 128,297★ Versus Kraven.
253 ❑ Jan 1998 Cover: 1.99 **NM value: Cover or less**
Circ: Diamd. preorders: **59,072**
• gatefold summary. ★ Versus Kraven. ★ Versus Calypso.
254 ❑ Feb 1998 Cover: 1.99 **NM value: Cover or less**
Circ: Diamd. preorders: **56,727**
• gatefold summary.
255 ❑ Mar 1998 Cover: 2.99 **NM value: Cover or less**
Circ: Diamd. preorders: **60,883**
• gatefold summary. 📖 Spider-Hunt, Part 4
256 ❑ Apr 1998 Cover: 1.99 **NM value: Cover or less**
Circ: Diamd. preorders: **55,520**
• gatefold summary. ★ Versus White Rabbit.
257 ❑ May 1998 Cover: 1.99 **NM value: Cover or less**
Circ: Diamd. preorders: **62,761**
has second cover with The Spectacular Prodigy #1. • gatefold summary. • Identity Crisis
258 ❑ Jun 1998 Cover: 1.99 **NM value: Cover or less**
Circ: Diamd. preorders: **62,591**
• gatefold summary. 📖 Identity Crisis
259 ❑ Jul 1998 Cover: 1.99 **NM value: Cover or less**
Circ: Diamd. preorders: **58,587**
• gatefold summary. 📖 Goblins at the Gate, Part 1
260 ❑ Aug 1998 Cover: 1.99 **NM value: Cover or less**
Circ: Diamd. preorders: **60,150**
• gatefold summary. 📖 Goblins at the Gate, Part 2
261 ❑ Sep 1998 Cover: 1.99 **NM value: Cover or less**
Circ: Diamd. preorders: **57,267**
• gatefold summary. 📖 Goblins at the Gate, Part 3
262 ❑ Oct 1998 Cover: 1.99 **NM value: Cover or less**
Circ: Diamd. preorders: **58,445**
• gatefold summary. 📖 The Gathering of Five, Part 4
263 ❑ Nov 1998 Cover: 1.99 **NM value: Cover or less**
Circ: Diamd. preorders: **63,650** • **CGC:** 1 graded, best 9.6
• gatefold summary. 📖 The Final Chapter, Part 3 final issue. **C:** John Byrne
Anl 1 ❑ Dec 1979 Cover: 0.75 **NM value: 5.00**
• **CGC:** 8 graded, best 9.8
• Doctor Octopus **A:** Rich Buckler; Jim Mooney
Anl 2 ❑ Sep 1980 Cover: 0.75 **NM value: 4.00**
📖 Vengeance Is Mine-Sayeth The Sword **A:** Jim Mooney **W:** Ralph Macchio ★ Origin of Rapier. ★ 1st Appearance of Rapier.
Anl 3 ❑ Nov 1981 Cover: 0.75 **NM value: 3.00**
📖 Dark Side Of The Moon **A:** Alan Weiss; James Sherman **W:** David Anthony Kraft
Anl 4 ❑ Nov 1984 Cover: 1.00 **NM value: 3.00**
• Title changes to Peter Parker, The Spectacular Spider-Man Annual★ Origin of Ben Parker ("Uncle Ben").
Anl 5 ❑ Oct 1985 Cover: 1.25 **NM value: 3.00**
Circ: CapCity orders: **17,200**
Anl 6 ❑ Oct 1986 Cover: 1.25 **NM value: 3.00**
Circ: CapCity orders: **19,700** • **CGC:** 1 graded, best 9.2
• series continues as Spectacular Spider-Man Annual
Anl 7 ❑ ca. 1987 Cover: 1.25 **NM value: 3.00**
Circ: CapCity orders: **32,200**
• Title returns to Spectacular Spider-Man Annual★ Versus Puma.
Anl 8 ❑ ca. 1988 Cover: 1.75 **NM value: 4.00**
Circ: CapCity orders: **36,400**
📖 Evolutionary War, Part 10
Anl 9 ❑ ca. 1989 Cover: 2.00 **NM value: 2.50**
Circ: CapCity orders: **38,900** • **CGC:** 1 graded, best 9.4
📖 Atlantis attacks, Part 6 • Atlantis Attacks
Anl 10 ❑ ca. 1990 Cover: 2.00 **NM value: 2.50**
Circ: CapCity orders: **44,700** • **CGC:** 1 graded, best 9.0
📖 Spidey's Totally Tiny Adventure, Part 2 • tiny Spider-Man **A:** Alan Kupperberg; Rich Buckler; Todd McFarlane; Ross Andru **W:** Stan Lee; Gerry Conway; Glenn Herdling; Tony Isabella
Anl 11 ❑ ca. 1991 Cover: 2.00 **NM value: 2.50**
Circ: CapCity orders: **44,100**
📖 Vibranium Vendetta; The Vibranium Vendetta **A:** Alan Kupperberg; Fred Hembeck; Marie Severin; Terry Kavanagh **W:** Fred Hembeck; David Michelinie; Gerry Conway
Anl 12 ❑ ca. 1992 Cover: 2.25 **NM value: 2.50**
Circ: CapCity orders: **49,500**
📖 Hero Killers; Hero Killers, Part 2 • Venom back-up story **A:** Vince Evans; Aaron Lopresti; Scott McDaniel; Tod Smith **W:** David Michelinie; Eric Fein; Glenn Herdling; Mike Kanterovich; Tom Brevoort ★ Appearance of New Warriors.
Anl 13 ❑ ca. 1993 Cover: 2.95 **NM value: Cover or less**
Circ: CapCity orders: **41,200**
• trading card
Anl 14 ❑ ca. 1994 Cover: 2.95 **NM value: Cover or less**
★ Versus Green Goblin.
Anl 1997 ❑ ca. 1997 Cover: 2.99 **NM value: Cover or less**
📖 Dead Men Walking • Peter Parker Spider-Man '97 **A:** Shawn McManus **W:** Glenn Herdling
SE 1 ❑ ca. 1995 Cover: 3.95 **NM value: Cover or less**
• **CGC:** 1 graded, best 9.6
• Flip-book. 📖 Planet of the Symbiotes, Part 4, Invasion!; Growing Pains, Part 4, Party Monster • Super special **A:** Jean-Claude St. Aubin; Darick Robertson **W:** Terry Kavanagh; David Michelinie ★ Appearance of Scarlet Spider, The Lizard, Carnage, Venom.

SPECTACULAR SPIDER-MAN (MAGAZINE) — Marvel

1 ❑ Jul 1968, b&w Cover: 0.35 **NM value: 35.00**
• magazine. **A:** John Romita ★ 1st Appearance of Richard Raleigh, Man Monster.
2 ❑ Nov 1968 Cover: 0.40 **NM value: 50.00**
• color magazine. **A:** John Romita ★ Versus Green Goblin.

SPECTACULAR SPIDER-MAN SUPER SPECIAL, THE — Marvel

1 ❑ Sep 1995 Cover: 3.95 **NM value: Cover or less**
Circ: CapCity orders: **19,750** • **CGC:** 1 graded, best 9.6
• Flip-book. 📖 Planet of the Symbiotes, Part 4 • two of the stories conclude in Web of Spider-Man Super Special #1 **A:** Darick Robertson **W:** David Michelinie

SPECTACULAR STORIES MAGAZINE — Fox

3 ❑ 1950 Cover: 0.12 **NM value: 300.00**
4 ❑ Jul 1950 Cover: 0.12 **NM value: 200.00**
• **CGC:** 1 graded, best 9.0

SPECTRE, THE (1ST SERIES) — DC

The Spectre first appeared in 1940's More Fun Comics #52. One of the longest-"lived" comics super-heroes, he was actually the ghost of a dead man.

The Spectre's story began when detective Jim Corrigan was captured by mobsters, sealed in a barrel of cement, and dumped into the river. Dying, he heard a voice which commanded him to return to the land of the living and continue his fight against evil. As The Spectre, he wielded incredible supernatural powers which he used to bring criminals to justice. Later he would fight super-powered menaces as a member of the Justice Society of America.

This first Spectre series presented The Spectre at his best. His powers were literally cosmic in scope, and the stories featured early artwork by comics greats Neal Adams and Bernie Wrightson.

1 ❑ Dec 1967 Cover: 0.12 **NM value: 90.00**
• **CGC:** 25 graded, best 9.4
A: Murphy Anderson; Gene Colan
2 ❑ Feb 1968 Cover: 0.12 **NM value: 60.00**
• **CGC:** 20 graded, best 9.8
A: Neal Adams
3 ❑ Apr 1968 Cover: 0.12 **NM value: 60.00**
• **CGC:** 19 graded, best 9.6
A: Neal Adams
4 ❑ Jun 1968 Cover: 0.12 **NM value: 60.00**
• **CGC:** 11 graded, best 9.6
A: Neal Adams
5 ❑ Aug 1968 Cover: 0.12 **NM value: 60.00**
• **CGC:** 8 graded, best 9.4
A: Neal Adams
6 ❑ Oct 1968 Cover: 0.12 **NM value: 35.00**
• **CGC:** 4 graded, best 9.2
A: Murphy Anderson
7 ❑ Dec 1968 Cover: 0.12 **NM value: 35.00**
• **CGC:** 6 graded, best 9.8
A: Murphy Anderson
8 ❑ Feb 1969 Cover: 0.12 **NM value: 35.00**
• **CGC:** 5 graded, best 9.4
A: Murphy Anderson
9 ❑ Apr 1969 Cover: 0.12 **NM value: 35.00**
• **CGC:** 4 graded, best 9.4
A: Bernie Wrightson
10 ❑ Jun 1969 Cover: 0.12 **NM value: 35.00**
• **CGC:** 2 graded, best 9.2

📖 indicates **Story Title** or **Storyline** information.
★ indicates **Character Appearance** information.

SPECTRE, THE (2ND SERIES) — DC

The Spectre was one of the most intriguing characters of the Golden Age of comics. He first appeared in More Fun Comics #52 in 1940, later materializing in All Star Comics where he became a member of the Justice Society. He seemed to vanish with the end of the Golden Age, reappearing in 1965's Showcase #60 and later starring in his own title, The Spectre (1st Series), a title which introduced the remarkable comic artist Neal Adams in issue #2. Nevertheless, that series lasted only 10 issues, after which the Spectre virtually vanished.

In 1987, he returned in this, his second self-titled series. His spirit had been languishing in the vortex as punishment for his failure to live up to the responsibilities that his godlike powers entailed. Then, the universe decided on another fate for him. In greatly diminished form, he was sent back to Earth — landing in the parlor of Madame Xanadu — and tasked with meting out punishment to evildoers.

He was also tied to the resurrected body of Jim Corrigan and separation for more than 24 hours would doom them both.

1 ❑ Apr 1987 Cover: 1.00 **NM value: 3.00**
Circ: CapCity orders: **20,350**
📖 Vessels **A:** Gene Colan; Steve Mitchell **W:** Doug Moench
2 ❑ May 1987 Cover: 1.00 **NM value: 2.50**
Circ: CapCity orders: **15,650**
3 ❑ Jun 1987 Cover: 1.00 **NM value: 2.50**
Circ: CapCity orders: **14,900**
4 ❑ Jul 1987 Cover: 1.00 **NM value: 2.50**
Circ: CapCity orders: **15,150**
5 ❑ Aug 1987 Cover: 1.00 **NM value: 2.50**
Circ: CapCity orders: **15,650**
6 ❑ Sep 1987 Cover: 1.00 **NM value: 2.25**
Circ: CapCity orders: **15,850**
📖 Murder Of My Mystery **A:** Gene Colan; Steve Mitchell **W:** Doug Moench
7 ❑ Oct 1987 Cover: 1.00 **NM value: 2.25**
Circ: CapCity orders: **15,700**
★ Appearance of Zatanna.
8 ❑ Nov 1987 Cover: 1.00 **NM value: 2.25**
Circ: CapCity orders: **15,550**
9 ❑ Dec 1987 Cover: 1.25 **NM value: 2.25**
Circ: CapCity orders: **13,750**
10 ❑ Jan 1988 Cover: 1.25 **NM value: 2.25**
Circ: CapCity orders: **18,050**
• Millennium
11 ❑ Feb 1988 Cover: 1.25 **NM value: 2.00**
Circ: CapCity orders: **17,500**
• Millennium
12 ❑ Mar 1988 Cover: 1.25 **NM value: 2.00**
Circ: CapCity orders: **12,700**
13 ❑ Apr 1988 Cover: 1.25 **NM value: 2.00**
Circ: CapCity orders: **13,600**
14 ❑ May 1988 Cover: 1.25 **NM value: 2.00**
Circ: CapCity orders: **12,150**
15 ❑ Jun 1988 Cover: 1.25 **NM value: 2.00**
Circ: CapCity orders: **11,100**
16 ❑ Jul 1988 Cover: 1.25 **NM value: 2.00**
Circ: CapCity orders: **10,800**
📖 Secret Weapon **A:** Chris Wozniak; Mark Farmer **W:** Doug Moench
17 ❑ Aug 1988 Cover: 1.25 **NM value: 1.75**
Circ: CapCity orders: **10,150**
18 ❑ Sep 1988 Cover: 1.25 **NM value: 1.75**
Circ: CapCity orders: **10,000**
19 ❑ Oct 1988 Cover: 1.25 **NM value: 1.75**
Circ: CapCity orders: **10,000**
20 ❑ Nov 1988 Cover: 1.25 **NM value: 1.75**
Circ: CapCity orders: **9,200**
21 ❑ Dec 1988 Cover: 1.25 **NM value: 1.50**
Circ: CapCity orders: **9,050**
22 ❑ Dec 1988 Cover: 1.25 **NM value: 1.50**
Circ: CapCity orders: **8,700**
23 ❑ Jan 1989 Cover: 1.25 **NM value: 1.50**
Circ: CapCity orders: **10,650**
• Invasion!
24 ❑ Feb 1989 Cover: 1.25 **NM value: 1.50**
Circ: CapCity orders: **9,000**
📖 Ghosts in the Machine, Part 1 **A:** Ralph Cabrera; Tom Artis **W:** Doug Moench
25 ❑ Apr 1989 Cover: 1.50 **NM value: Cover or less**
Circ: CapCity orders: **8,450**
📖 Ghosts in the Machine, Part 2 **W:** Doug Moench
26 ❑ May 1989 Cover: 1.50 **NM value: Cover or less**
Circ: CapCity orders: **8,100**
📖 Ghosts in the Machine, Part 3 **A:** Tom Artis **W:** Doug Moench
27 ❑ Jun 1989 Cover: 1.50 **NM value: Cover or less**
Circ: CapCity orders: **8,450**
📖 Ghosts in the Machine, Part 4
28 ❑ Aug 1989 Cover: 1.50 **NM value: Cover or less**
Circ: CapCity orders: **8,150**
📖 Ghosts in the Machine, Part 5
29 ❑ Sep 1989 Cover: 1.50 **NM value: Cover or less**
Circ: CapCity orders: **8,050**
📖 Ghosts in the Machine, Part 6
30 ❑ Oct 1989 Cover: 1.50 **NM value: Cover or less**
Circ: CapCity orders: **7,800**
31 ❑ Nov 1989 Cover: 1.50 **NM value: Cover or less**
Circ: CapCity orders: **7,250**
Anl 1 ❑ ca. 1988 Cover: 2.00 **NM value: 2.50**
Circ: CapCity orders: **11,550**
📖 Ghost, Dead Man, Devil-Child ... ★ Appearance of Deadman.

Other grades: Multiply prices above by **1.5 for Mint • 2/3 for Very Fine • 1/3 for Fine • 1/5 for Very Good • 1/8 for Good**

SPECTRE, THE (3RD SERIES) DC

0 ❑ Oct 1994 Cover: 1.95 **NM** value: **2.50**
Circ: CapCity orders: **19,850**
🕮 The Temptation Of The Spectre **A:** Tom Mandrake **W:** John Ostrander ★ Origin of The Spectre.

1 ❑ Dec 1992 Cover: 1.75 **NM** value: **6.00**
Circ: CapCity orders: **37,900** • **CGC:** 3 graded, best 9.6
Glow-in-the-dark cover. 🕮 Crimes Of Violence **A:** Tom Mandrake **W:** John Ostrander ★ Origin of The Spectre.

2 ❑ Jan 1993 Cover: 1.75 **NM** value: **5.00**
Circ: CapCity orders: **18,150**
A: Tom Mandrake **W:** John Ostrander

3 ❑ Feb 1993 Cover: 1.75 **NM** value: **4.00**
Circ: CapCity orders: **16,000**
A: Tom Mandrake **W:** John Ostrander

4 ❑ Mar 1993 Cover: 1.75 **NM** value: **3.00**
Circ: CapCity orders: **17,950**
🕮 Crime And Judgement **A:** Tom Mandrake **W:** John Ostrander

5 ❑ Apr 1993 Cover: 1.75 **NM** value: **3.00**
Circ: CapCity orders: **20,450**
A: Tom Mandrake **C:** Charles Vess **W:** John Ostrander

6 ❑ May 1993 Cover: 1.75 **NM** value: **3.00**
Circ: CapCity orders: **18,650**
🕮 The Bleeding Gun **A:** Tom Mandrake **W:** John Ostrander

7 ❑ Jun 1993 Cover: 1.75 **NM** value: **3.00**
Circ: CapCity orders: **16,950**
A: Tom Mandrake **W:** John Ostrander

8 ❑ Jul 1993 Cover: 2.50 **NM** value: **3.50**
Glow-in-the-dark cover. **A:** Tom Mandrake **W:** John Ostrander

9 ❑ Aug 1993 Cover: 1.75 **NM** value: **3.00**
Circ: CapCity orders: **16,450**
🕮 No Good Deed Goes Unpunished **A:** Tom Mandrake **W:** John Ostrander

10 ❑ Sep 1993 Cover: 1.75 **NM** value: **3.00**
Circ: CapCity orders: **15,700**
A: Tom Mandrake **C:** Michael W. Kaluta **W:** John Ostrander

11 ❑ Oct 1993 Cover: 1.75 **NM** value: **3.00**
Circ: CapCity orders: **14,750**
🕮 The Deepest Cut **A:** Tom Mandrake **W:** John Ostrander

12 ❑ Nov 1993 Cover: 1.75 **NM** value: **3.00**
Circ: CapCity orders: **13,100**
A: Tom Mandrake **W:** John Ostrander

13 ❑ Dec 1993 Cover: 1.75 **NM** value: **3.00**
Circ: CapCity orders: **17,650**
Glow-in-the-dark cover. 🕮 Righteousness **A:** Tom Mandrake **W:** John Ostrander

14 ❑ Jan 1994 Cover: 1.75 **NM** value: **2.50**
Circ: CapCity orders: **12,950**

15 ❑ Feb 1994 Cover: 1.75 **NM** value: **2.50**
Circ: CapCity orders: **12,700**

16 ❑ Mar 1994 Cover: 1.75 **NM** value: **2.50**
Circ: CapCity orders: **12,150** • **CGC:** 1 graded, best 9.4
🕮 Call for Blood **A:** Jim Aparo **W:** John Ostrander

17 ❑ Apr 1994 Cover: 1.75 **NM** value: **2.50**
Circ: CapCity orders: **11,750**

18 ❑ May 1994 Cover: 1.75 **NM** value: **2.50**
Circ: CapCity orders: **11,900**

19 ❑ Jun 1994 Cover: 1.75 **NM** value: **2.50**
Circ: CapCity orders: **11,650**

20 ❑ Jul 1994 Cover: 1.75 **NM** value: **2.50**
Circ: CapCity orders: **12,200**

21 ❑ Aug 1994 Cover: 1.95 **NM** value: **2.00**
Circ: CapCity orders: **12,450**

22 ❑ Sep 1994 Cover: 1.95 **NM** value: **2.00**
Circ: CapCity orders: **14,000**
★ Appearance of Spear of Destiny. ★ Versus Superman.

23 ❑ Nov 1994 Cover: 1.95 **NM** value: **2.00**
Circ: CapCity orders: **12,550**

24 ❑ Dec 1994 Cover: 1.95 **NM** value: **2.00**
Circ: CapCity orders: **13,050**

25 ❑ Jan 1995 Cover: 1.95 **NM** value: **2.00**
Circ: CapCity orders: **13,250**
🕮 Malicious **A:** Tom Mandrake **W:** John Ostrander

26 ❑ Feb 1995 Cover: 1.95 **NM** value: **2.00**
Circ: CapCity orders: **12,400**

27 ❑ Mar 1995 Cover: 1.95 **NM** value: **2.00**
Circ: CapCity orders: **11,800**

28 ❑ Apr 1995 Cover: 1.95 **NM** value: **2.00**
Circ: CapCity orders: **11,300**

29 ❑ May 1995 Cover: 1.95 **NM** value: **2.00**
Circ: CapCity orders: **10,675**

30 ❑ Jun 1995 Cover: 2.25 **NM** value: **Cover or less**
Circ: CapCity orders: **10,450**

31 ❑ Jul 1995 Cover: 2.25 **NM** value: **Cover or less**
Circ: CapCity orders: **10,475**

32 ❑ Aug 1995 Cover: 2.25 **NM** value: **Cover or less**
Circ: CapCity orders: **10,625**

33 ❑ Sep 1995 Cover: 2.25 **NM** value: **Cover or less**
Circ: CapCity orders: **9,975**

34 ❑ Oct 1995 Cover: 2.25 **NM** value: **Cover or less**
Circ: CapCity orders: **8,425**

35 ❑ Nov 1995 Cover: 2.25 **NM** value: **Cover or less**
• Underworld Unleashed

36 ❑ Dec 1995 Cover: 2.25 **NM** value: **Cover or less**
• Underworld Unleashed

37 ❑ Jan 1996 Cover: 2.25 **NM** value: **2.50**
🕮 The Haunting of America, Part 1 **A:** Tom Mandrake **W:** John Ostrander

38 ❑ Feb 1996 Cover: 2.25 **NM** value: **2.50**
🕮 The Haunting of America, Part 2 **A:** Tom Mandrake **W:** John Ostrander ★ Origin of Uncle Sam.

39 ❑ Mar 1996 Cover: 2.25 **NM** value: **2.50**
🕮 The Haunting of America, Part 3 **A:** Tom Mandrake **W:** John Ostrander ★ Origin of Shadrach.

40 ❑ Apr 1996 Cover: 2.25 **NM** value: **2.50**
🕮 The Haunting of America, Part 4 **A:** Tom Mandrake **W:** John Ostrander ★ Origin of Captain Fear.

41 ❑ May 1996 Cover: 2.25 **NM** value: **2.50**
🕮 The Haunting of America, Part 5 **A:** Tom Mandrake **W:** John Ostrander

42 ❑ Jun 1996 Cover: 2.25 **NM** value: **2.50**
🕮 The Haunting of America, Part 6 **A:** Tom Mandrake **W:** John Ostrander

43 ❑ Jul 1996 Cover: 2.25 **NM** value: **2.50**
🕮 The Haunting of America, Part 7 **A:** Tom Mandrake **W:** John Ostrander

44 ❑ Aug 1996 Cover: 2.25 **NM** value: **2.50**
🕮 The Haunting of America, Part 8 **A:** Tom Mandrake **W:** John Ostrander

45 ❑ Sep 1996 Cover: 2.25 **NM** value: **2.50**
🕮 The Haunting of America, Part 9 • homosexuality issues **A:** Tom Mandrake **W:** John Ostrander

46 ❑ Oct 1996 Cover: 2.25 **NM** value: **2.50**
🕮 The Haunting of America, Part 10 • National Interest acquires Spear of Destiny **A:** Tom Mandrake **W:** John Ostrander

47 ❑ Nov 1996 Cover: 2.25 **NM** value: **2.50**
Circ: Diamd. preorders: **27,315**
🕮 The Haunting of America, Part 11 • Final Night **A:** Tom Mandrake **W:** John Ostrander

48 ❑ Dec 1996 Cover: 2.25 **NM** value: **2.50**
Circ: Diamd. preorders: **21,543**
🕮 The Haunting of America, Part 12 **A:** Tom Mandrake **W:** John Ostrander

49 ❑ Jan 1997 Cover: 2.50 **NM** value: **Cover or less**
Circ: Diamd. preorders: **20,726**
🕮 The Haunting of America, Part 13 **A:** Tom Mandrake **W:** John Ostrander

50 ❑ Feb 1997 Cover: 2.50 **NM** value: **Cover or less**
Circ: Diamd. preorders: **21,623**
🕮 The Haunting of America, Part 14 (Conclusion); The Haunting of America, Part 14 **A:** John Bolton(cover) **W:** John Ostrander

51 ❑ Mar 1997 Cover: 2.50 **NM** value: **Cover or less**
Circ: Diamd. preorders: **26,046**
🕮 The Haunting of Jim Corrigan; A Savage Innocence **A:** Tom Mandrake **W:** John Ostrander

52 ❑ Apr 1997 Cover: 2.50 **NM** value: **Cover or less**
Circ: Diamd. preorders: **20,297**
🕮 The Haunting of Jim Corrigan

53 ❑ May 1997 Cover: 2.50 **NM** value: **Cover or less**
Circ: Diamd. preorders: **19,677**
🕮 The Haunting of Jim Corrigan

54 ❑ Jun 1997 Cover: 2.50 **NM** value: **Cover or less**
Circ: Diamd. preorders: **21,328**
🕮 The Haunting of Jim Corrigan

55 ❑ Jul 1997 Cover: 2.50 **NM** value: **Cover or less**
Circ: Diamd. preorders: **20,036**
🕮 The Haunting of Jim Corrigan

56 ❑ Aug 1997 Cover: 2.50 **NM** value: **Cover or less**
Circ: Diamd. preorders: **19,252**
🕮 The Haunting of Jim Corrigan

57 ❑ Sep 1997 Cover: 2.50 **NM** value: **Cover or less**
Circ: Diamd. preorders: **18,622**

58 ❑ Oct 1997 Cover: 2.50 **NM** value: **Cover or less**
Circ: Diamd. preorders: **21,073**

59 ❑ Nov 1997 Cover: 2.50 **NM** value: **Cover or less**
Circ: Diamd. preorders: **18,502**
🕮 True Believers **A:** Tom Mandrake **W:** John Ostrander

60 ❑ Dec 1997 Cover: 2.50 **NM** value: **Cover or less**
Circ: Diamd. preorders: **18,924**
Face cover. 🕮 Within **A:** Tom Mandrake **W:** John Ostrander

61 ❑ Jan 1998 Cover: 2.50 **NM** value: **Cover or less**
Circ: Diamd. preorders: **18,621**

62 ❑ Feb 1998 Cover: 2.50 **NM** value: **Cover or less**
Circ: Diamd. preorders: **19,660** • **CGC:** 1 graded, best 9.6
final issue. • funeral of Jim Corrigan

Anl 1 ❑ ca. 1995 Cover: 3.95 **NM** value: **Cover or less**
• Year One ★ Appearance of Doctor Fate.

SPECTRE, THE (4TH SERIES) DC

1 ❑ Mar 2001 Cover: 2.50 **NM** value: **Cover or less**
Circ: Diamd. preorders: **39,023** • **CGC:** 21 graded, best 9.8
A: Ryan Sook **W:** J.M. DeMatteis

2 ❑ Apr 2001 Cover: 2.50 **NM** value: **Cover or less**
Circ: Diamd. preorders: **32,678**
🕮 Redeeming the Demon, Part 1 **A:** Ryan Sook **W:** J.M. DeMatteis

3 ❑ May 2001 Cover: 2.50 **NM** value: **Cover or less**
Circ: Diamd. preorders: **31,366**
🕮 Redeeming the Demon, Part 2 **A:** Ryan Sook **W:** J.M. DeMatteis

4 ❑ Jun 2001 Cover: 2.50 **NM** value: **Cover or less**
Circ: Diamd. preorders: **31,388**
🕮 Redeeming the Demon, Part 3 **A:** Ryan Sook **W:** J.M. DeMatteis

5 ❑ Jul 2001 Cover: 2.50 **NM** value: **Cover or less**
Circ: Diamd. preorders: **30,389**

6 ❑ Aug 2001 Cover: 2.50 **NM** value: **Cover or less**
Circ: Diamd. preorders: **30,110**

7 ❑ Sep 2001 Cover: 2.50 **NM** value: **Cover or less**
Circ: Diamd. preorders: **29,644**

SPECTRESCOPE Spectre

1 ❑ Mar 1994 **NM** value: **1.00**
no cover price. • giveaway.

SPECTRUM New Horizons

1 ❑ Jul 1987, b&w Cover: 1.50 **NM** value: **Cover or less**

SPECTRUM COMICS PREVIEWS Spectrum

1 ❑ Feb 1983 Cover: 3.00 **NM** value: **Cover or less**
🕮 In the Beginning… **A:** Steve Woron **W:** Steve Woron ★ 1st Appearance of Survivors.

SPEEDBALL Marvel

Robbie Benson was a teenager, not quite old enough to have his learner's permit to drive. His father, a district attorney, wanted him to study the law in college. His mother, a former star of the stage, wanted him to get involved in the arts. For now, Robbie just worked after school sweeping up at the laboratory of Doctor Hammond. One day, Robbie decided to secretly observe an experiment that the doctor was conducting- an experiment that inadvertently released a strange energy from the warp. This energy struck Robbie, who later discovered that whenever he hit anything hard, the kinetic energy rebounded with increasing force, turning him into the human jumping bean super-hero known as Speedball.

Although he first appeared in Amazing Spider-Man Annual #22, this title served as the first real introduction to the bouncing boy super-hero. Afterward, Speedball would become famous as a member of the New Warriors.

1 ❑ Sep 1988 Cover: 0.75 **NM** value: **1.00**
Circ: CapCity orders: **23,400**
A: Steve Ditko **W:** Steve Ditko; Roger Stern ★ Origin of Speedball.

2 ❑ Oct 1988 Cover: 0.75 **NM** value: **1.00**
Circ: CapCity orders: **15,300**
🕮 Stuck on You! **A:** Steve Ditko **W:** Steve Ditko; Roger Stern

3 ❑ Nov 1988 Cover: 0.75 **NM** value: **1.00**
Circ: CapCity orders: **13,500**
A: Steve Ditko

4 ❑ Dec 1988 Cover: 0.75 **NM** value: **1.00**
Circ: CapCity orders: **11,800**
A: Steve Ditko

5 ❑ Jan 1989 Cover: 0.75 **NM** value: **1.00**
Circ: CapCity orders: **12,600**
A: Steve Ditko

6 ❑ Feb 1989 Cover: 0.75 **NM** value: **1.00**
Circ: CapCity orders: **9,900**
A: Steve Ditko

7 ❑ Mar 1989 Cover: 0.75 **NM** value: **1.00**
Circ: CapCity orders: **9,100**
A: Steve Ditko

8 ❑ Apr 1989 Cover: 0.75 **NM** value: **1.00**
Circ: CapCity orders: **8,600**
A: Steve Ditko

9 ❑ May 1989 Cover: 0.75 **NM** value: **1.00**
Circ: CapCity orders: **7,500**
A: Steve Ditko

10 ❑ Jun 1989 Cover: 0.75 **NM** value: **1.00**
Circ: CapCity orders: **7,000**
A: Steve Ditko

SPEED BUGGY Charlton

1 ❑ May 1975 Cover: 0.25 **NM** value: **12.00**
• **CGC:** 8 graded, best 9.8

2 ❑ Sep 1975 Cover: 0.25 **NM** value: **8.00**

3 ❑ Nov 1975 Cover: 0.25 **NM** value: **8.00**

4 ❑ Jan 1976 Cover: 0.25 **NM** value: **8.00**

5 ❑ Mar 1976 Cover: 0.25 **NM** value: **8.00**
🕮 Safari Nice Place to Visit But…; Old Timers Day; Don't Be Fuelish (text); Get a Blindfold

6 ❑ May 1976 Cover: 0.25 **NM** value: **8.00**

7 ❑ Jul 1976 Cover: 0.25 **NM** value: **8.00**

8 ❑ Sep 1976 Cover: 0.25 **NM** value: **8.00**

9 ❑ Nov 1976 Cover: 0.25 **NM** value: **8.00**
🕮 Magnetic Menace; Speed and the Black Baron

SPEED COMICS Harvey

Speed Comics (which experienced a slight title hiccup with #24, when it was New Speed Comics for one issue)is probably best known as the home of the often cover-featured Shock Gibson ("the human dynamo"), though The Black Cat (complete with a repeat of her origin) joined the anthology title with #17, and Captain Freedom (who could easily have been mistaken for Captain America, complete with similar headpiece and occasional stars-and-stripes short design — oh, and even some of Schomburg's cluttered covers) was introduced in #13.

The focus was on World War II action, with an assortment of heroic characters clouting an assortment of Axis foes. — Maggie

1 ❑ Oct 1939 Cover: 0.10 **NM** value: **3000.00**
• **CGC:** 3 graded, best 8.5

2 ❑ Nov 1939 Cover: 0.10 **NM** value: **1500.00**
• **CGC:** 1 graded, best 4.5

3 ❑ Dec 1939 Cover: 0.10 **NM** value: **750.00**

4 ❑ Jan 1940 Cover: 0.10 **NM** value: **500.00**

5 ❑ Feb 1940 Cover: 0.10 **NM** value: **500.00**

6 ❑ Mar 1940 Cover: 0.10 **NM** value: **400.00**

7 ❑ Apr 1940 Cover: 0.10 **NM** value: **400.00**

8 ❑ May 1940 Cover: 0.10 **NM** value: **400.00**

9 ❑ Jun 1940 Cover: 0.10 **NM** value: **400.00**

10 ❑ Jul 1940 Cover: 0.10 **NM** value: **400.00**

11 ❑ Aug 1940 Cover: 0.10 **NM** value: **350.00**

12 ❑ Mar 1941 Cover: 0.10 **NM** value: **350.00**

13 ❑ May 1941 Cover: 0.10 **NM** value: **350.00**

CGC-graded: Multiply prices above by **33 for 9.9 M • 16 for 9.8 NM/M • 7 for 9.6 NM+ • 5 for 9.4 NM • 2.5 for 9.2 NM- • 1.5 for 9.0 VF/NM**

14 ❑ Sep 1941 Cover: 0.10 NM value: **350.00**
15 ❑ Nov 1941 Cover: 0.10 NM value: **350.00**
• **CGC:** 1 graded, best .5
16 ❑ Jan 1942 Cover: 0.10 NM value: **350.00**
17 ❑ Apr 1942 Cover: 0.10 NM value: **350.00**
• **CGC:** 1 graded, best 9.6
18 ❑ May 1942 Cover: 0.10 NM value: **350.00**
19 ❑ Jun 1942 Cover: 0.10 NM value: **350.00**
20 ❑ Jul 1942 Cover: 0.10 NM value: **350.00**
21 ❑ Aug 1942 Cover: 0.10 NM value: **300.00**
22 ❑ Sep 1942 Cover: 0.10 NM value: **300.00**
23 ❑ Oct 1942 Cover: 0.10 NM value: **300.00**
24 ❑ Dec 1942 Cover: 0.10 NM value: **300.00**
25 ❑ Feb 1943 Cover: 0.10 NM value: **300.00**
26 ❑ Apr 1943 Cover: 0.10 NM value: **300.00**
27 ❑ Jul 1943 Cover: 0.10 NM value: **300.00**
28 ❑ Sep 1943 Cover: 0.10 NM value: **300.00**
29 ❑ Nov 1943 Cover: 0.10 NM value: **300.00**
• **CGC:** 1 graded, best 9.4
30 ❑ Jan 1944 Cover: 0.10 NM value: **300.00**
31 ❑ Mar 1944 Cover: 0.10 NM value: **250.00**
32 ❑ May 1944 Cover: 0.10 NM value: **250.00**
33 ❑ Jul 1944 Cover: 0.10 NM value: **250.00**
34 ❑ Sep 1944 Cover: 0.10 NM value: **250.00**
35 ❑ Nov 1944 Cover: 0.10 NM value: **250.00**
36 ❑ Mar 1945 Cover: 0.10 NM value: **250.00**
• **CGC:** 1 graded, best 9.6
37 ❑ May 1945 Cover: 0.10 NM value: **250.00**
38 ❑ Jul 1945 Cover: 0.10 NM value: **250.00**
• **CGC:** 3 graded, best 9.6
39 ❑ Sep 1945 Cover: 0.10 NM value: **250.00**
• **CGC:** 2 graded, best 9.4
40 ❑ Nov 1945 Cover: 0.10 NM value: **250.00**
• **CGC:** 3 graded, best 9.2
41 ❑ Jan 1946 Cover: 0.10 NM value: **250.00**
• **CGC:** 1 graded, best 9.2
42 ❑ Mar 1946 Cover: 0.10 NM value: **250.00**
• **CGC:** 1 graded, best 9.4
43 ❑ May 1946 Cover: 0.10 NM value: **250.00**
• **CGC:** 4 graded, best 9.0
44 ❑ Jan 1947 Cover: 0.10 NM value: **250.00**
• **CGC:** 2 graded, best 9.4

SPEED DEMON — Marvel / Amalgam

1 ❑ Apr 1996 Cover: 1.95 NM value: **2.00**
Demon's Night **A:** Al Milgrom; Salvador Larroca **W:** Howard Mackie; James Felder

SPEED FORCE — DC

1 ❑ Nov 1997 Cover: 3.95 NM value: **Cover or less**
Circ: Diamd. preorders: **40,095**
Burning Secrets; Like Straws in a Hurricane; Child's Play; A Stranger With My Face • anthology series with stories of the various Flashes **A:** John Byrne; Dusty Abell; Kenny Martinez; Jim Aparo; Drew Geraci **W:** William Messner-Loebs; Brian Augustyn; John Byrne; Mark Waid

SPEED RACER (1ST SERIES) — Now

Beloved as kitchy fun by some and loathed as irritating dreck by others, Speed Racer was one of the first Japanese animation series to really strike it big in America. The show starred a fearless boy race car driver who outwitted bad guys using his wits and driving skill. Of course, it doesn't hurt that he drives the best car on the road: the "fabulous Mach 5."

The title character was always referred to simply as "Speed," but this Now Comics adaptation reveals that his real name is Greg (thus the "G" on his shirts). It also tells the story of how his father, Rex Racer, was killed by Alpha racing team and sent flying over a cliff. Speed was then adopted and taught to follow in his departed father's footsteps. Only with Speed, it's always the bad guys who get their comeuppance. Rex, meanwhile, would reappear as the mysterious Racer X, popping up periodically just in time to save Speed from danger.

1 ❑ Aug 1987 Cover: 1.50 NM value: **2.50**
Circ: CapCity orders: **5,050** • **CGC:** 1 graded, best 9.4
Death of a Racer **A:** Gary Thomas Washington **W:** Len Strazewski
★ Origin of Speed Racer.
1-2 ❑ Cover: 1.50 NM value: **Cover or less**
2 ❑ Sep 1987 Cover: 1.50 NM value: **2.00**
Circ: CapCity orders: **4,475**
3 ❑ Oct 1987 Cover: 1.50 NM value: **2.00**
Circ: CapCity orders: **4,175**
4 ❑ Nov 1987 Cover: 1.75 NM value: **Cover or less**
Circ: CapCity orders: **6,075**
5 ❑ Dec 1987 Cover: 1.75 NM value: **Cover or less**
Circ: CapCity orders: **6,775**
Dead Heat **A:** Jill Thompson **W:** Brian Thomas
6 ❑ Jan 1988 Cover: 1.75 NM value: **Cover or less**
Circ: CapCity orders: **7,100**
7 ❑ Mar 1988 Cover: 1.75 NM value: **Cover or less**
Circ: CapCity orders: **6,775**
8 ❑ Apr 1988 Cover: 1.75 NM value: **Cover or less**
Circ: CapCity orders: **5,725**
9 ❑ May 1988 Cover: 1.75 NM value: **Cover or less**
Circ: CapCity orders: **4,950**
10 ❑ Jun 1988 Cover: 1.75 NM value: **Cover or less**
Circ: CapCity orders: **4,925**
11 ❑ Jul 1988 Cover: 1.75 NM value: **Cover or less**
Circ: CapCity orders: **4,325**
12 ❑ Aug 1988 Cover: 1.75 NM value: **Cover or less**
Circ: CapCity orders: **4,325**
13 ❑ Sep 1988 Cover: 1.75 NM value: **Cover or less**
Circ: CapCity orders: **4,150**
14 ❑ Oct 1988 Cover: 1.75 NM value: **Cover or less**
Circ: CapCity orders: **3,750**
15 ❑ Nov 1988 Cover: 1.75 NM value: **Cover or less**
Circ: CapCity orders: **3,700**
16 ❑ Dec 1988 Cover: 1.75 NM value: **Cover or less**
Circ: CapCity orders: **3,275**
17 ❑ Jan 1989 Cover: 1.75 NM value: **Cover or less**
Circ: CapCity orders: **3,350**
18 ❑ Mar 1989 Cover: 1.75 NM value: **Cover or less**
Circ: CapCity orders: **3,325**
19 ❑ Apr 1989 Cover: 1.75 NM value: **Cover or less**
Circ: CapCity orders: **3,075**
20 ❑ May 1989 Cover: 1.75 NM value: **Cover or less**
Circ: CapCity orders: **2,925**
21 ❑ Jun 1989 Cover: 1.75 NM value: **Cover or less**
Circ: CapCity orders: **2,650**
22 ❑ Jul 1989 Cover: 1.75 NM value: **Cover or less**
Circ: CapCity orders: **2,600**
23 ❑ Aug 1989 Cover: 1.75 NM value: **Cover or less**
Circ: CapCity orders: **2,475**
A: Norm Dwyer **W:** Lamar Waldron
24 ❑ Sep 1989 Cover: 1.75 NM value: **Cover or less**
Circ: CapCity orders: **2,425**
25 ❑ Oct 1989 Cover: 1.75 NM value: **Cover or less**
26 ❑ Nov 1989 Cover: 1.75 NM value: **Cover or less**
Circ: CapCity orders: **2,300**
27 ❑ Dec 1989 Cover: 1.75 NM value: **Cover or less**
Circ: CapCity orders: **2,325**
28 ❑ Jan 1990 Cover: 1.75 NM value: **Cover or less**
Circ: CapCity orders: **2,200**
29 ❑ Feb 1990 Cover: 1.75 NM value: **Cover or less**
Circ: CapCity orders: **2,100**
30 ❑ Mar 1990 Cover: 1.75 NM value: **Cover or less**
Circ: CapCity orders: **2,125**
31 ❑ Apr 1990 Cover: 1.75 NM value: **Cover or less**
Circ: CapCity orders: **2,000**
32 ❑ May 1990 Cover: 1.75 NM value: **Cover or less**
Circ: CapCity orders: **1,950**
33 ❑ Jun 1990 Cover: 1.75 NM value: **Cover or less**
Circ: CapCity orders: **1,800**
34 ❑ Jul 1990 Cover: 1.75 NM value: **Cover or less**
Circ: CapCity orders: **1,850**
35 ❑ Aug 1990 Cover: 1.75 NM value: **Cover or less**
Circ: CapCity orders: **1,750**
36 ❑ Sep 1990 Cover: 1.75 NM value: **Cover or less**
37 ❑ Oct 1990 Cover: 1.75 NM value: **Cover or less**
Circ: CapCity orders: **1,600**
38 ❑ Nov 1990 Cover: 1.75 NM value: **Cover or less**
Circ: CapCity orders: **1,650**
final issue.
SE 1 ❑ Mar 1988 Cover: 2.00 NM value: **2.50**
Circ: CapCity orders: **8,700**
★ Origin of the Mach 5 (Speed Racer's Car).
SE 1-2 ❑ Sep 1988 Cover: 1.75 NM value: **Cover or less**
Circ: CapCity orders: **5,300**

SPEED RACER (2ND SERIES) — DC / Wildstorm

1 ❑ Oct 1999 Cover: 2.50 NM value: **Cover or less**
Circ: Diamd. preorders: **23,858** • **CGC:** 1 graded, best 9.0
Born to Race **A:** Tommy Yune **W:** Tommy Yune
2 ❑ Nov 1999 Cover: 2.50 NM value: **Cover or less**
Circ: Diamd. preorders: **17,987**
A: Tommy Yune **W:** Tommy Yune
3 ❑ Dec 1999 Cover: 2.50 NM value: **Cover or less**
Circ: Diamd. preorders: **19,038**
Enter the Mach 5 **A:** Tommy Yune **W:** Tommy Yune
Bk 1 ❑ Cover: 9.95 NM value: **Cover or less**
Born to Race • Born to Race; Collects series **A:** Tommy Yune **W:** Tommy Yune

SPEED RACER 3-D SPECIAL — Now

1 ❑ Jan 1993 Cover: 2.95 NM value: **Cover or less**

SPEED RACER CLASSICS — Now

1 ❑ Oct 1988, b&w Cover: 3.75 NM value: **Cover or less**
Circ: CapCity orders: **2,025**
2 ❑ Feb 1989, b&w Cover: 3.95 NM value: **Cover or less**
Circ: CapCity orders: **1,525**

SPEED RACER FEATURING NINJA HIGH SCHOOL — Now / Eternity

1 ❑ Aug 1993 Cover: 2.50 NM value: **Cover or less**
Quandary In Quagmire • trading card **A:** George Broderick Jr. **W:** Mark Levine; Dan Danko; Ian Ward
2 ❑ Sep 1993 Cover: 2.50 NM value: **Cover or less**
• two trading cards **A:** George Broderick Jr. **W:** Mark Levine; Dan Danko; Ian Ward

SPEED RACER (MINI-SERIES) — Now

1 ❑ NM value: **2.50**
Best Laid Plans… **A:** Joe Koziarski; Mark Stegbauer(coveR) **W:** Tony Caputo
1/DM ❑ Cover: 2.50 NM value: **Cover or less**
cardstock cover. • Direct Market edition. Best Laid Plans… **A:** Joe Koziarski; Max Siebel(cover) **W:** Tony Caputo
2 ❑ NM value: **2.50**
A: Joe Koziarski **W:** Tony Caputo
3 ❑ NM value: **2.50**
A: Joe Koziarski **W:** Tony Caputo

SPEED RACER: RETURN OF THE GRX — Now

1 ❑ Mar 1994 Cover: 1.95 NM value: **Cover or less**
Circ: CapCity orders: **2,200**
The Haunted Engine **A:** George Booker **W:** Lamar Waldron
2 ❑ Apr 1994 Cover: 1.95 NM value: **Cover or less**
A: George Booker **W:** Lamar Waldron

SPEED SMITH, THE HOT ROD KING — Ziff-Davis

1 ❑ ca. 1952 Cover: 0.10 NM value: **100.00**

SPEED TRIBES — Nemicron

1 ❑ Aug 1998 Cover: 2.95 NM value: **Cover or less**
Circ: Diamd. preorders: **1,853**
The Beginning… **A:** Anthony Vu **W:** Mark Alamares; Russell Scott

SPELLBINDERS — Fleetway-Quality

1 ❑ Dec 1986 Cover: 1.25 NM value: **1.50**
Circ: CapCity orders: **5,825**
Sláine: The Beast in the Broch; Nemesis: The Gothic Empire; Amadeus Wolf: Kalak the Evil; Sláine: The Beast in the Broch **A:** Massimo Belardinelli; Eric Bradbury; Kevin O'Neill **W:** Ken Mennell; Pat Mills
2 ❑ Jan 1986 Cover: 1.25 NM value: **1.50**
Circ: CapCity orders: **4,725**
3 ❑ Feb 1986 Cover: 1.25 NM value: **1.50**
Circ: CapCity orders: **3,925**
4 ❑ Mar 1986 Cover: 1.25 NM value: **1.50**
Circ: CapCity orders: **3,700**
5 ❑ Apr 1986 Cover: 1.25 NM value: **1.50**
Circ: CapCity orders: **3,475**
6 ❑ May 1986 Cover: 1.25 NM value: **1.50**
Circ: CapCity orders: **2,650**
7 ❑ Jun 1986 Cover: 1.25 NM value: **1.50**
Circ: CapCity orders: **2,125**
8 ❑ Jul 1986 Cover: 1.25 NM value: **1.50**
Circ: CapCity orders: **1,775**
9 ❑ Aug 1986 Cover: 1.25 NM value: **1.50**
Circ: CapCity orders: **1,725**
10 ❑ Sep 1986 Cover: 1.25 NM value: **1.50**
Circ: CapCity orders: **1,700**
11 ❑ Oct 1986 Cover: 1.25 NM value: **1.50**
Circ: CapCity orders: **1,650**
12 ❑ Nov 1986 Cover: 1.25 NM value: **1.50**
Circ: CapCity orders: **1,350**

SPELLBOUND (ATLAS) — Atlas

1 ❑ Mar 1952 Cover: 0.10 NM value: **500.00**
• **CGC:** 4 graded, best 6.5
2 ❑ Apr 1952 Cover: 0.10 NM value: **250.00**
• **CGC:** 3 graded, best 8.0
3 ❑ May 1952 Cover: 0.10 NM value: **250.00**
4 ❑ Jun 1952 Cover: 0.10 NM value: **250.00**
• **CGC:** 2 graded, best 9.2
5 ❑ Jul 1952 Cover: 0.10 NM value: **250.00**
6 ❑ Aug 1952 Cover: 0.10 NM value: **200.00**
• **CGC:** 1 graded, best 9.4
7 ❑ Sep 1952 Cover: 0.10 NM value: **200.00**
8 ❑ Oct 1952 Cover: 0.10 NM value: **200.00**
• **CGC:** 2 graded, best 5.5
9 ❑ Nov 1952 Cover: 0.10 NM value: **200.00**
• **CGC:** 1 graded, best 8.0
10 ❑ Dec 1952 Cover: 0.10 NM value: **200.00**
• **CGC:** 1 graded, best 9.2
11 ❑ Jan 1953 Cover: 0.10 NM value: **175.00**
12 ❑ Feb 1953 Cover: 0.10 NM value: **175.00**
13 ❑ Mar 1953 Cover: 0.10 NM value: **175.00**
• **CGC:** 1 graded, best 8.0
14 ❑ Apr 1953 Cover: 0.10 NM value: **175.00**
15 ❑ Jun 1953 Cover: 0.10 NM value: **175.00**
16 ❑ Aug 1953 Cover: 0.10 NM value: **150.00**
17 ❑ Sep 1953 Cover: 0.10 NM value: **150.00**
18 ❑ Dec 1953 Cover: 0.10 NM value: **150.00**
19 ❑ Feb 1954 Cover: 0.10 NM value: **150.00**
20 ❑ Mar 1954 Cover: 0.10 NM value: **150.00**
• **CGC:** 1 graded, best 7.5
21 ❑ Apr 1954 Cover: 0.10 NM value: **125.00**
22 ❑ May 1954 Cover: 0.10 NM value: **125.00**
23 ❑ Jun 1954 Cover: 0.10 NM value: **125.00**
• **CGC:** 1 graded, best 8.5
24 ❑ 1954 Cover: 0.10 NM value: **125.00**
25 ❑ Dec 1954 Cover: 0.10 NM value: **125.00**
26 ❑ Feb 1955 Cover: 0.10 NM value: **125.00**
27 ❑ Apr 1955 Cover: 0.10 NM value: **125.00**
28 ❑ Jun 1955 Cover: 0.10 NM value: **125.00**
29 ❑ Aug 1955 Cover: 0.10 NM value: **125.00**
30 ❑ Oct 1952 Cover: 0.10 NM value: **125.00**
31 ❑ Dec 1956 Cover: 0.10 NM value: **100.00**
32 ❑ Feb 1957 Cover: 0.10 NM value: **100.00**
• **CGC:** 2 graded, best 7.5
33 ❑ Apr 1957 Cover: 0.10 NM value: **100.00**
• **CGC:** 1 graded, best 9.0

SPELLBOUND — Marvel

1 ❑ Jan 1988 Cover: 1.50 NM value: **Cover or less**
Circ: CapCity orders: **20,600**
Power! **A:** Terry Shoemaker **W:** Louise Simonson
2 ❑ Feb 1988 Cover: 1.50 NM value: **Cover or less**
Circ: CapCity orders: **16,800**
3 ❑ Feb 1988 Cover: 1.50 NM value: **Cover or less**
Circ: CapCity orders: **16,350**
4 ❑ Mar 1988 Cover: 1.50 NM value: **Cover or less**
Circ: CapCity orders: **17,800**
5 ❑ Apr 1988 Cover: 1.50 NM value: **Cover or less**
Circ: CapCity orders: **16,100**
6 ❑ Apr 1988 Cover: 2.25 NM value: **Cover or less**
Circ: CapCity orders: **14,500**
• Double Size.

SPELLCASTER — Medusa

1 ❑ Cover: 2.95 NM value: **Cover or less**
The Past **A:** Eric Wolfe Hanson **W:** Aaron Michael Hĕbrich; Aaron Michael Hĕbrich

Other grades: Multiply prices above by **1.5 for Mint • 2/3 for Very Fine • 1/3 for Fine • 1/5 for Very Good • 1/8 for Good**

2 ❑ Cover: 2.95 NM value: **Cover or less**
3 ❑ Cover: 2.95 NM value: **Cover or less**

SPELLJAMMER — DC

1 ❑ Sep 1990 Cover: 1.75 NM value: **Cover or less**
Circ: CapCity orders: **17,300**
📖 Journey's Song, Kirstig's Tale **A:** Mike Collins **W:** Barbara Kesel
2 ❑ Oct 1990 Cover: 1.75 NM value: **Cover or less**
Circ: CapCity orders: **12,950**
3 ❑ Nov 1990 Cover: 1.75 NM value: **Cover or less**
Circ: CapCity orders: **11,500**
4 ❑ Dec 1990 Cover: 1.75 NM value: **Cover or less**
Circ: CapCity orders: **10,900**
5 ❑ Jan 1991 Cover: 1.75 NM value: **Cover or less**
Circ: CapCity orders: **10,250**
6 ❑ Feb 1991 Cover: 1.75 NM value: **Cover or less**
Circ: CapCity orders: **9,900**
📖 Circle Of Fear **A:** Mike Collins **W:** Barbara Kesel
7 ❑ Mar 1991 Cover: 1.75 NM value: **Cover or less**
Circ: CapCity orders: **8,600**
8 ❑ Apr 1991 Cover: 1.75 NM value: **Cover or less**
Circ: CapCity orders: **7,850**
9 ❑ May 1991 Cover: 1.75 NM value: **Cover or less**
Circ: CapCity orders: **7,850**
10 ❑ Jun 1991 Cover: 1.75 NM value: **Cover or less**
Circ: CapCity orders: **7,950**
11 ❑ Jul 1991 Cover: 1.75 NM value: **Cover or less**
Circ: CapCity orders: **7,800**
12 ❑ Aug 1991 Cover: 1.75 NM value: **Cover or less**
Circ: CapCity orders: **7,950**
13 ❑ Sep 1991 Cover: 1.75 NM value: **Cover or less**
Circ: CapCity orders: **7,600**
14 ❑ Oct 1991 Cover: 1.75 NM value: **Cover or less**
Circ: CapCity orders: **7,300**
📖 Nimone **A:** Kevin West **W:** Don Kraar
15 ❑ Nov 1991 Cover: 1.75 NM value: **Cover or less**
Circ: CapCity orders: **7,350**
16 ❑ Dec 1991 Cover: 1.75 NM value: **Cover or less**
Circ: CapCity orders: **6,950**
17 ❑ Jan 1992 Cover: 1.75 NM value: **Cover or less**
Circ: CapCity orders: **6,650**
18 ❑ Feb 1992 Cover: 1.75 NM value: **Cover or less**
Circ: CapCity orders: **6,100**

SPEX-7 — Shadow Shock

1 ❑ Sum 1994, b&w Cover: 1.50 NM value: **Cover or less**

SPHINX — Print Mint

1 ❑ Cover: 0.50 NM value: **3.00**
2 ❑ Cover: 0.50 NM value: **3.00**
3 ❑ Cover: 0.50 NM value: **3.00**
📖 Agents of Dread **A:** Susan Morris **W:** Susan Morris

SPICECAPADES — Fantagraphics

1 ❑ Spr 1999 Cover: 4.95 NM value: **Cover or less**
Circ: Diamd. preorders: **3,495**
No issue number. wraparound cover. • magazine-sized. 📖 Why I'm Ga-Ga Over Baby Spice; The Spice Girls Forget the Words; Sporty Spice: An Appreciation; Rejected Spice Girls; Monkey Spice and Mashed Potatoes; • Spice Girls parody **A:** Gilbert Hernandez; Tony Millionaire; Ariel Bordeaux; Eric Reynolds; Kaz; Shawn Belschwe **W:** Gilbert Hernandez; Kaz; Arielle Greenberg; Michael McPadden; Peter Landau; Quee

SPICY ADULT STORIES — Aircel

1 ❑ Mar 1991 Cover: 2.50 NM value: **Cover or less**
• pulp reprints
2 ❑ Apr 1991 Cover: 2.50 NM value: **Cover or less**
• pulp reprints
3 ❑ May 1991 Cover: 2.50 NM value: **Cover or less**
• pulp reprints
4 ❑ Cover: 2.50 NM value: **Cover or less**
• pulp reprints

SPICY DETECTIVE STORIES — Eternity

Bk 1❑ Cover: 6.95 NM value: **Cover or less**
• magazine reprints.

SPICY HORROR STORIES — Eternity

Bk 1❑ Cover: 9.95 NM value: **Cover or less**
• magazine reprints.

SPICY MYSTERY STORIES — Eternity

Bk 1❑ Dec 1988 Cover: 6.95 NM value: **Cover or less**
• magazine reprints.

SPICY TALES — Eternity

1 ❑ Apr 1988, b&w Cover: 1.95 NM value: **Cover or less**
2 ❑ Jun 1988, b&w Cover: 1.95 NM value: **Cover or less**
3 ❑ Aug 1988, b&w Cover: 1.95 NM value: **Cover or less**
4 ❑ Oct 1988, b&w Cover: 1.95 NM value: **Cover or less**
5 ❑ Dec 1988, b&w Cover: 1.95 NM value: **Cover or less**
6 ❑ Feb 1989, b&w Cover: 1.95 NM value: **Cover or less**
7 ❑ b&w Cover: 1.95 NM value: **Cover or less**
8 ❑ b&w Cover: 1.95 NM value: **Cover or less**
9 ❑ b&w Cover: 1.95 NM value: **Cover or less**
10 ❑ Cover: 2.25 NM value: **Cover or less**
11 ❑ Cover: 2.25 NM value: **Cover or less**
12 ❑ Cover: 2.25 NM value: **Cover or less**
13 ❑ Cover: 2.25 NM value: **Cover or less**
14 ❑ Cover: 2.25 NM value: **Cover or less**
15 ❑ Cover: 2.25 NM value: **Cover or less**
16 ❑ Cover: 2.50 NM value: **Cover or less**
17 ❑ Cover: 2.50 NM value: **Cover or less**
📖 The Hidden Murder; News Ace; Death Trumps The Joker; Diana Daw; The Torso Murders **W:** Pierre Charpentier
18 ❑ Cover: 2.95 NM value: **Cover or less**
19 ❑ Cover: 2.95 NM value: **Cover or less**
20 ❑ Cover: 2.95 NM value: **Cover or less**
Bk 1❑ b&w Cover: 9.95 NM value: **Cover or less**
SE 1❑ Feb 1989, b&w Cover: 2.25 NM value: **Cover or less**
SE 2❑ b&w Cover: 2.25 NM value: **Cover or less**

SPICY WESTERN STORIES — Eternity

Bk 1❑ Cover: 9.95 NM value: **Cover or less**
• magazine reprints.

SPIDER, THE — Eclipse

1 ❑ Jun 1991 Cover: 4.95 NM value: **Cover or less**
Circ: CapCity orders: **10,300**
📖 Blood Dance **A:** Tim Truman **W:** Tim Truman
2 ❑ Aug 1991 Cover: 4.95 NM value: **Cover or less**
Circ: CapCity orders: **7,300**
3 ❑ Oct 1991 Cover: 4.95 NM value: **Cover or less**
Circ: CapCity orders: **4,425**

SPIDERBABY COMIX (S.R. BISSETTE'S...) — Spiderbaby

1 ❑ Nov 1996 Cover: 3.95 NM value: **Cover or less**
Circ: Diamd. preorders: **3,931**
📖 Cell Food; Cries from the Vegetable Kingdom; The Tell-Tale Fart; Scraps; Earth Invasion; Sans; Tobias Impressions; Dark Time **A:** Rick Veitch; Stephen R. Bissette; Spider **W:** Rick Veitch; Stephen R. Bissette; Spider; Lawrence Shell

SPIDER-BOY — Marvel / Amalgam

1 ❑ Apr 1996 Cover: 1.95 NM value: **2.50**
• **CGC:** 1 graded, best 8.0
📖 Big Trouble! **A:** Mike Wieringo **W:** Karl Kesel

SPIDER-BOY TEAM-UP — Marvel / Amalgam

1 ❑ Jun 1997 Cover: 1.95 NM value: **Cover or less**
Circ: Diamd. preorders: **131,096**
📖 Too Many Heroes…Too Little Time! **A:** J.O. Ladronn **W:** R.K. Sternsel

SPIDER-FEMME — Spoof

1 ❑ Cover: 2.50 NM value: **Cover or less**
• parody

SPIDER-GIRL — Marvel

0 ❑ Oct 1998 Cover: 2.99 NM value: **3.00**
Circ: Diamd. preorders: **53,123** • **CGC:** 2 graded, best 9.8
• reprints What If? #105 **A:** Patrick Olliffe **W:** Tom DeFalco ★ Origin of Spider-Girl.
0.5 ❑ NM value: **3.00**
• **CGC:** 8 graded, best 9.6
• Wizard promotional edition.
1 ❑ Oct 1998 Cover: 1.99 NM value: **3.00**
Circ: Statement: **81,637** Diamd. preorders: **62,804** • **CGC:** 12 graded, best 9.8
White cover with Spider-Girl facing forward. 📖 Choices **A:** Patrick Olliffe **W:** Tom DeFalco
1/A ❑ Oct 1998 Cover: 1.99 NM value: **3.00**
variant cover. 📖 Choices **A:** Patrick Olliffe **W:** Tom DeFalco
2 ❑ Nov 1998 Cover: 1.99 NM value: **2.00**
Circ: Statement: **81,637** • **CGC:** 3 graded, best 9.6
• gatefold summary. **A:** Patrick Olliffe **W:** Tom DeFalco ★ Appearance of Darkdevil.
3 ❑ Dec 1998 Cover: 1.99 NM value: **2.00**
Circ: Statement: **81,637** Diamd. preorders: **56,100**
• gatefold summary. **A:** Patrick Olliffe **W:** Tom DeFalco ★ Appearance of Fantastic Five.
4 ❑ Jan 1999 Cover: 1.99 NM value: **2.00**
Circ: Statement: **81,637** Diamd. preorders: **55,891**
A: Patrick Olliffe **W:** Tom DeFalco ★ Versus Dragon King.
5 ❑ Feb 1999 Cover: 1.99 NM value: **2.00**
Circ: Statement: **81,637** Diamd. preorders: **54,449**
📖 Ghosts of the Past **A:** Patrick Olliffe **W:** Tom DeFalco ★ 1st Appearance of Spider-Venom. ★ Appearance of Venom.
6 ❑ Mar 1999 Cover: 1.99 NM value: **Cover or less**
Circ: Statement: **81,637** Diamd. preorders: **49,796**
📖 Majority Rules! **A:** Patrick Olliffe **W:** Tom DeFalco ★ Appearance of Ladyhawk, Green Goblin.
7 ❑ Apr 1999 Cover: 1.99 NM value: **Cover or less**
Circ: Statement: **81,637** Diamd. preorders: **46,615**
📖 The Last Days of Spider-Man **A:** Patrick Olliffe **W:** Tom DeFalco ★ Appearance of Nova, Mary Jane Parker.
8 ❑ May 1999 Cover: 1.99 NM value: **Cover or less**
Circ: Statement: **81,637** Diamd. preorders: **45,203**
A: Patrick Olliffe **W:** Tom DeFalco ★ Appearance of Kingpin. ★ Versus Mr. Nobody. ★ Versus Crazy Eight.
9 ❑ Jun 1999 Cover: 1.99 NM value: **Cover or less**
Circ: Statement: **81,637** Diamd. preorders: **44,716**
A: Patrick Olliffe **W:** Tom DeFalco ★ Versus Killer Watt.
10 ❑ Jul 1999 Cover: 1.99 NM value: **Cover or less**
Circ: Statement: **81,637** Diamd. preorders: **44,387**
A: Patrick Olliffe **W:** Tom DeFalco ★ Appearance of Spider-Man.
11 ❑ Aug 1999 Cover: 1.99 NM value: **Cover or less**
Circ: Statement: **81,637** Diamd. preorders: **42,597**
A: Patrick Olliffe **W:** Tom DeFalco ★ Appearance of Human Torch, Spider-Man. ★ Versus Spider-Slayer.
12 ❑ Sep 1999 Cover: 1.99 NM value: **Cover or less**
Circ: Statement: **81,637** Diamd. preorders: **42,131**
A: Patrick Olliffe **W:** Tom DeFalco
13 ❑ Oct 1999 Cover: 1.99 NM value: **Cover or less**
Circ: Diamd. preorders: **40,747**
A: Patrick Olliffe **W:** Tom DeFalco
14 ❑ Nov 1999 Cover: 1.99 NM value: **Cover or less**
Circ: Diamd. preorders: **38,917**
A: Patrick Olliffe **W:** Tom DeFalco
15 ❑ Dec 1999 Cover: 1.99 NM value: **Cover or less**
Circ: Diamd. preorders: **39,231**
📖 Swingin 'n' Slammin' With Speedball **A:** Patrick Olliffe **W:** Tom DeFalco
16 ❑ Jan 2000 Cover: 2.25 NM value: **Cover or less**
Circ: Diamd. preorders: **37,439**
17 ❑ Feb 2000 Cover: 2.25 NM value: **Cover or less**
Circ: Diamd. preorders: **36,569**
18 ❑ Mar 2000 Cover: 2.25 NM value: **Cover or less**
Circ: Diamd. preorders: **34,844**
19 ❑ Apr 2000 Cover: 2.25 NM value: **Cover or less**
Circ: Diamd. preorders: **32,842**
20 ❑ May 2000 Cover: 2.25 NM value: **Cover or less**
Circ: Diamd. preorders: **32,704**
21 ❑ Jun 2000 Cover: 2.25 NM value: **Cover or less**
Circ: Diamd. preorders: **31,441**
22 ❑ Jul 2000 Cover: 2.25 NM value: **Cover or less**
Circ: Diamd. preorders: **31,272**
23 ❑ Aug 2000 Cover: 2.25 NM value: **Cover or less**
Circ: Diamd. preorders: **30,845**
24 ❑ Sep 2000 Cover: 2.25 NM value: **Cover or less**
Circ: Diamd. preorders: **30,281**
25 ❑ Oct 2000 Cover: 2.99 NM value: **Cover or less**
Circ: Diamd. preorders: **28,496**
26 ❑ Nov 2000 Cover: 2.25 NM value: **Cover or less**
Circ: Diamd. preorders: **27,858**
📖 Passages! **A:** Patrick Olliffe **W:** Tom DeFalco
27 ❑ Dec 2000 Cover: 2.25 NM value: **Cover or less**
Circ: Diamd. preorders: **27,423**
📖 End Game **A:** Patrick Olliffe **W:** Tom DeFalco
28 ❑ Jan 2001 Cover: 2.25 NM value: **Cover or less**
Circ: Diamd. preorders: **26,737**
📖 Unfinished Business! **A:** Patrick Olliffe **W:** Tom DeFalco
29 ❑ Feb 2001 Cover: 2.25 NM value: **Cover or less**
Circ: Diamd. preorders: **26,442**
📖 Strange Allies! **A:** Patrick Olliffe **W:** Tom DeFalco
30 ❑ Mar 2001 Cover: 2.25 NM value: **Cover or less**
Circ: Diamd. preorders: **25,915**
📖 The Winds of War! **A:** Patrick Olliffe **W:** Tom DeFalco
31 ❑ Apr 2001 Cover: 2.25 NM value: **Cover or less**
Circ: Diamd. preorders: **25,428**
📖 With Friends Like These **A:** Patrick Olliffe **W:** Tom DeFalco
32 ❑ May 2001 Cover: 2.25 NM value: **Cover or less**
Circ: Diamd. preorders: **25,494**
33 ❑ Jun 2001 Cover: 2.25 NM value: **Cover or less**
Circ: Diamd. preorders: **25,985**
34 ❑ Jul 2001 Cover: 2.25 NM value: **Cover or less**
Circ: Diamd. preorders: **25,596**
35 ❑ Aug 2001 Cover: 2.25 NM value: **Cover or less**
Circ: Diamd. preorders: **26,098**
36 ❑ Sep 2001 Cover: 2.25 NM value: **Cover or less**
Circ: Diamd. preorders: **27,333**
37 ❑ Oct 2001 Cover: 2.25 NM value: **Cover or less**
Circ: Diamd. preorders: **27,490**
Anl 1999❑ ca. 1999 Cover: 3.99 NM value: **Cover or less**
Circ: Diamd. preorders: **34,638**
A: Patrick Olliffe **W:** Tom DeFalco
Bk 1❑ Jan 1999 Cover: 5.99 NM value: **9.95**
• A Fresh Start; collects #1 and #2 **A:** Patrick Olliffe **W:** Tom DeFalco
38 ❑ Nov 2001 Cover: 2.25 NM value: **Cover or less**
Circ: Diamd. preorders: **25,858**
39 ❑ Dec 2001 Cover: 2.25 NM value: **Cover or less**
Circ: Diamd. preorders: **25,229**
40 ❑ Jan 2002 Cover: 2.25 NM value: **Cover or less**
Circ: Diamd. preorders: **25,647**
41 ❑ Feb 2002 Cover: 2.25 NM value: **Cover or less**
Circ: Diamd. preorders: **25,335**
42 ❑ Mar 2002 Cover: 2.25 NM value: **Cover or less**
Circ: Diamd. preorders: **24,713**
43 ❑ Mar 2002 Cover: 2.25 NM value: **Cover or less**
Circ: Diamd. preorders: **24,769**
44 ❑ Apr 2002 Cover: 2.25 NM value: **Cover or less**
Circ: Diamd. preorders: **25,226**

SPIDER-GIRL BATTLEBOOK — Marvel

1 ❑ Cover: 3.99 NM value: **Cover or less**

SPIDER-MAN — Marvel

Believe it or not, the first comic-book series called simply Spider-Man didn't appear until 1990. It made a serious splash. Todd McFarlane, who had become a comics superstar for his very spidery-looking renditions of the title character of Amazing Spider-Man, was given the chance to start a Spidey title that would be all his own: "adjective-less," as it would commonly be called.

Retailers wopuld call it a license to print money, as sales on the first issue went far beyond the wildest expectations. The issue came with special "bagged" editions — the logic being that if you opened the bag, you destroyed the resale value of the comic book. That particular bit of lunacy didn't survive the end of the 1990s speculator glut, but it had a good deal to do with getting it going in the first place. (It should be noted, in fact, that there is no such thing as a CGC-graded copy of the "bagged edition." CGC has to unbag comics to grade them, making them just like all the others that people — horrors! — opened and read.)

McFarlane eventually left the series to form Image, and the title became more closely related to the other Spider-series. It was cancelled in 1998 and restarted as Peter Parker, Spider-Man. — JJM

-1 ❑ Jul 1997 Cover: 1.95 NM value: **2.00**
Circ: Diamd. preorders: **69,070**
• Flashback

CGC-graded: Multiply prices above by **33 for 9.9 M • 16 for 9.8 NM/M • 7 for 9.6 NM+ • 5 for 9.4 NM • 2.5 for 9.2 NM- • 1.5 for 9.0 VF/NM**

0.5 ❑ ca. 1999 NM value: **4.00**
• **CGC:** 26 graded, best 10.0
0.5/PI❑ca. 1999 NM value: **6.00**
• Platinum edition.
1 ❑ Aug 1990 Cover: 1.75 NM value: **3.00**
Circ: CapCity orders: **426,200** • **CGC:** 298 graded, best 10.0
Green cover (newsstand). 📖 Torment, Part 1 **A:** Todd McFarlane **W:** Todd McFarlane
1/CG❑Aug 1990 Cover: 1.75 NM value: **4.00**
• **CGC:** 16 graded, best 9.6
📖 Torment, Part 1 • bagged newsstand (green)
1/CS❑Aug 1990 Cover: 2.00 NM value: **6.00**
• **CGC:** 51 graded, best 9.6
bagged silver cover.
1/PL❑Aug 1990 Cover: 1.75 NM value: **60.00**
• **CGC:** 106 graded, best 9.6 • giveaway.
1/SI❑ Aug 1990 Cover: 1.75 NM value: **3.00**
• **CGC:** 391 graded, best 10.0
silver cover.
1/DM-2❑ Cover: 1.75 NM value: **125.00**
1-2 ❑ Aug 1990 Cover: 1.75 NM value: **2.50**
• **CGC:** 128 graded, best 9.9 • Gold w. upc box
2 ❑ Sep 1990 Cover: 1.75 NM value: **3.00**
Circ: CapCity orders: **168,600** • **CGC:** 29 graded, best 9.8
📖 Torment, Part 2 • Lizard **A:** Todd McFarlane **W:** Todd McFarlane
3 ❑ Oct 1990 Cover: 1.75 NM value: **3.00**
Circ: CapCity orders: **151,900** • **CGC:** 17 graded, best 9.9
📖 Torment, Part 3 • Lizard **A:** Todd McFarlane **W:** Todd McFarlane
4 ❑ Nov 1990 Cover: 1.75 NM value: **3.00**
Circ: CapCity orders: **141,000** • **CGC:** 5 graded, best 9.6
📖 Torment, Part 4 • Lizard **A:** Todd McFarlane **W:** Todd McFarlane
5 ❑ Dec 1990 Cover: 1.75 NM value: **3.00**
Circ: CapCity orders: **143,400** • **CGC:** 7 graded, best 9.8
📖 Torment, Part 5 • Lizard **A:** Todd McFarlane **W:** Todd McFarlane
6 ❑ Jan 1991 Cover: 1.75 NM value: **3.00**
Circ: CapCity orders: **202,500** • **CGC:** 8 graded, best 9.6
📖 Masques, Part 1 **A:** Todd McFarlane **W:** Todd McFarlane ★ Appearance of Hobgoblin, Ghost Rider. ★ Versus Hobgoblin.
7 ❑ Feb 1991 Cover: 1.75 NM value: **3.00**
Circ: CapCity orders: **180,500** • **CGC:** 4 graded, best 9.6
📖 Masques, Part 2 **A:** Todd McFarlane **W:** Todd McFarlane ★ Appearance of Hobgoblin, Ghost Rider. ★ Versus Hobgoblin.
8 ❑ Mar 1991 Cover: 1.75 NM value: **2.50**
Circ: CapCity orders: **190,500** • **CGC:** 4 graded, best 9.8
📖 Perceptions, Part 1 **A:** Todd McFarlane **W:** Todd McFarlane ★ Appearance of Wolverine. ★ Versus Wendigo.
9 ❑ Apr 1991 Cover: 1.75 NM value: **2.50**
Circ: CapCity orders: **162,600** • **CGC:** 21 graded, best 9.9
📖 Perceptions, Part 2 **A:** Todd McFarlane **W:** Todd McFarlane ★ Appearance of Wolverine. ★ Versus Wendigo.
10 ❑ May 1991 Cover: 1.75 NM value: **2.50**
Circ: CapCity orders: **150,600** • **CGC:** 27 graded, best 9.9
📖 Perceptions, Part 3 **A:** Todd McFarlane **W:** Todd McFarlane ★ Appearance of Wolverine. ★ Versus Wendigo.
11 ❑ Jun 1991 Cover: 1.75 NM value: **2.50**
Circ: CapCity orders: **140,100** • **CGC:** 15 graded, best 9.9
📖 Perceptions, Part 4 **A:** Todd McFarlane **W:** Todd McFarlane ★ Appearance of Wolverine. ★ Versus Wendigo.
12 ❑ Jul 1991 Cover: 1.75 NM value: **2.50**
Circ: CapCity orders: **143,400** • **CGC:** 24 graded, best 9.9
📖 Perceptions, Part 5 **A:** Todd McFarlane **W:** Todd McFarlane ★ Appearance of Wolverine. ★ Versus Wendigo.
13 ❑ Aug 1991 Cover: 1.75 NM value: **2.50**
Circ: CapCity orders: **138,000** • **CGC:** 3 graded, best 9.8
📖 Sub City, Part 1 • Spider-Man wears black costume **A:** Todd McFarlane **W:** Todd McFarlane
14 ❑ Sep 1991 Cover: 1.75 NM value: **2.50**
Circ: CapCity orders: **132,300** • **CGC:** 1 graded, best 9.6
📖 Sub City, Part 2 **A:** Todd McFarlane **W:** Todd McFarlane
15 ❑ Oct 1991 Cover: 1.75 NM value: **2.00**
Circ: CapCity orders: **130,500**
📖 The Mutant Factor **A:** Erik Larsen **W:** Erik Larsen ★ Appearance of Beast.
16 ❑ Nov 1991 Cover: 1.75 NM value: **2.00**
Circ: CapCity orders: **228,900** • **CGC:** 1 graded, best 9.6
📖 Sabotage, Part 1 • X-Force; Sideways printing **A:** Todd McFarlane **W:** Todd McFarlane
17 ❑ Dec 1991 Cover: 1.75 NM value: **2.00**
Circ: CapCity orders: **111,300**
📖 No One Gets Outta Here Alive! **A:** Al Williamson **W:** Ann Nocenti ★ Appearance of Thanos. ★ Versus Thanos.
18 ❑ Jan 1992 Cover: 1.75 NM value: **2.00**
Circ: Statement: **574,825** CapCity orders: **105,600**
📖 Revenge of the Sinister Six, Part 1; Revenge of Sinister Six, Part 1 • Ghost Rider **A:** Erik Larsen **W:** Erik Larsen
19 ❑ Feb 1992 Cover: 1.75 NM value: **2.00**
Circ: Statement: **574,825** CapCity orders: **100,500**
📖 Revenge of the Sinister Six, Part 2; Revenge of Sinister Six, Part 2 **A:** Erik Larsen **W:** Erik Larsen ★ Appearance of Hulk.
20 ❑ Mar 1992 Cover: 1.75 NM value: **2.00**
Circ: Statement: **574,825** CapCity orders: **92,700**
📖 Revenge of the Sinister Six, Part 3; Revenge of Sinister Six, Part 3 **A:** Erik Larsen **W:** Erik Larsen ★ Appearance of Nova, Hulk, Solo, Deathlok.
21 ❑ Apr 1992 Cover: 1.75 NM value: **2.00**
Circ: Statement: **574,825** CapCity orders: **90,600**
📖 Revenge of the Sinister Six, Part 4; Revenge of Sinister Six, Part 4; Dealing Rams • Deathlok appearnace **A:** Erik Larsen **W:** Erik Larsen ★ Appearance of Solo, Deathlok.
22 ❑ May 1992 Cover: 1.75 NM value: **2.00**
Circ: Statement: **574,825**
📖 Revenge of the Sinister Six, Part 5; Revenge of Sinister Six, Part 5 **A:** Erik Larsen **W:** Erik Larsen ★ Appearance of Sleepwalker, Hulk, Ghost Rider, Deathlok.
23 ❑ Jun 1992 Cover: 1.75 NM value: **2.00**
Circ: Statement: **574,825** CapCity orders: **103,500**
📖 Revenge of the Sinister Six, Part 6; Revenge of Sinister Six, Part 6 **A:** Erik Larsen **W:** Erik Larsen ★ Appearance of Fantastic Four, Hulk, Ghost Rider, Deathlok.
24 ❑ Jul 1992 Cover: 1.75 NM value: **2.00**
Circ: Statement: **574,825** CapCity orders: **104,700**
📖 Infinity War • Infinity War **A:** Larry Alexander **W:** Howard Mackie
25 ❑ Aug 1992 Cover: 1.75 NM value: **2.00**
Circ: Statement: **574,825** CapCity orders: **105,500**
📖 Why Me? **A:** Chris Marrinan **W:** Terry Kavanagh ★ Appearance of Phoenix.
26 ❑ Sep 1992 Cover: 3.50 NM value: **4.00**
Circ: Statement: **574,825** CapCity orders: **250,600** • **CGC:** 6 graded, best 9.8
Hologram cover. • 30th Anniversary Edition. 📖 With Great Responsibility-! • Gatefold poster **A:** Ron Frenz **W:** Mark Bagley; Tom DeFalco ★ Origin of Spider-Man.
27 ❑ Oct 1992 Cover: 1.75 NM value: **2.00**
Circ: Statement: **574,825** CapCity orders: **87,100**
📖 There's Something About a Gun, Part 1 **A:** Marshall Rogers **W:** Don McGregor
28 ❑ Nov 1992 Cover: 1.75 NM value: **2.00**
Circ: Statement: **574,825** CapCity orders: **81,300**
📖 There's Something About a Gun, Part 2
29 ❑ Dec 1992 Cover: 1.75 NM value: **2.00**
Circ: Statement: **574,825** CapCity orders: **75,100**
📖 Return to the Mad Dog Ward, Part 1
30 ❑ Jan 1993 Cover: 1.75 NM value: **2.00**
Circ: CapCity orders: **67,500** • **CGC:** 1 graded, best 9.6
📖 Return to the Mad Dog Ward, Part 2 **A:** Chris Marrinan **W:** Ann Nocenti
31 ❑ Feb 1993 Cover: 1.75 NM value: **2.00**
Circ: CapCity orders: **62,700** • **CGC:** 1 graded, best 9.8
📖 Return to the Mad Dog Ward, Part 3 **A:** Chris Marrinan **W:** Ann Nocenti
32 ❑ Mar 1993 Cover: 1.75 NM value: **2.00**
Circ: CapCity orders: **60,900** • **CGC:** 1 graded, best 9.8
📖 Vengeance, Part 1 **A:** Bob McLeod **W:** Steven Grant
33 ❑ Apr 1993 Cover: 1.75 NM value: **2.00**
Circ: CapCity orders: **58,400** • **CGC:** 2 graded, best 9.8
📖 Vengeance, Part 2 • Has 1992 Statement, filed 10/1/92; avg print run 778,067; avg sales 567,250; avg subs 7,575; avg total paid 574,825; samples 250; office use 500; max existent 575,575; 26% of run returned **A:** Bob McLeod **W:** Steven Grant ★ Appearance of Punisher.
34 ❑ May 1993 Cover: 1.75 NM value: **2.00**
Circ: CapCity orders: **56,200** • **CGC:** 2 graded, best 9.6
📖 Vengeance, Part 3 **A:** Bob McLeod; Lee Weeks **W:** Steven Grant ★ Appearance of Punisher.
35 ❑ Jun 1993 Cover: 1.75 NM value: **2.00**
Circ: CapCity orders: **128,500**
📖 Maximum Carnage, Part 4 **A:** Tom Lyle **W:** David Michelinie ★ Appearance of Carnage, Venom.
36 ❑ Jul 1993 Cover: 1.75 NM value: **2.00**
Circ: CapCity orders: **112,700**
📖 Maximum Carnage, Part 8 ★ Appearance of Carnage, Venom.
37 ❑ Aug 1993 Cover: 1.75 NM value: **2.00**
Circ: CapCity orders: **111,000**
📖 Maximum Carnage, Part 12 ★ Appearance of Carnage, Venom.
38 ❑ Sep 1993 Cover: 1.75 NM value: **2.00**
Circ: CapCity orders: **59,200**
📖 Light the Night, Part 1 **A:** Klaus Janson **W:** J.M. DeMatteis
39 ❑ Oct 1993 Cover: 1.75 NM value: **2.00**
Circ: CapCity orders: **57,400**
📖 Light the Night, Part 2 **A:** Klaus Janson **W:** J.M. DeMatteis ★ Appearance of Electro.
40 ❑ Nov 1993 Cover: 1.75 NM value: **2.00**
Circ: CapCity orders: **56,500** • **CGC:** 1 graded, best 9.8
📖 Light the Night, Part 3 **A:** Klaus Janson **W:** J.M. DeMatteis ★ Versus Electro.
41 ❑ Dec 1993 Cover: 1.75 NM value: **2.00**
Circ: CapCity orders: **62,300**
📖 Storm Warnings, Part 1
42 ❑ Jan 1994 Cover: 1.75 NM value: **2.00**
Circ: Statement: **256,883** CapCity orders: **55,500**
📖 Storm Warnings, Part 2 **A:** Jae Lee **W:** Terry Kavanagh
43 ❑ Feb 1994 Cover: 1.75 NM value: **2.00**
Circ: Statement: **256,883** CapCity orders: **48,800** • **CGC:** 1 graded, best 9.6
44 ❑ Mar 1994 Cover: 1.75 NM value: **2.00**
Circ: Statement: **256,883** CapCity orders: **41,750** • **CGC:** 1 graded, best 9.6
45 ❑ Apr 1994 Cover: 1.75 NM value: **2.00**
Circ: Statement: **256,883** CapCity orders: **45,650** • **CGC:** 1 graded, best 9.8
📖 Pursuit, Part 1
46 ❑ May 1994 Cover: 1.95 NM value: **2.00**
Circ: Statement: **256,883** CapCity orders: **37,600** • **CGC:** 1 graded, best 9.6
📖 Beware the Rage of a Desperate Man, Part 1 **A:** Tom Lyle **W:** Howard Mackie
46/CS❑May 1994 Cover: 2.75 NM value: **3.00**
Circ: Statement: **256,883** CapCity orders: **52,550**
📖 Beware the Rage of a Desperate Man, Part 1 • with print **A:** Tom Lyle **W:** Howard Mackie
47 ❑ Jun 1994 Cover: 1.95 NM value: **2.00**
Circ: Statement: **256,883** CapCity orders: **37,900**
📖 Beware the Rage of a Desperate Man, Part 2 **A:** Tom Lyle **W:** Howard Mackie ★ Versus Hobgoblin.
48 ❑ Jul 1994 Cover: 1.95 NM value: **2.00**
Circ: Statement: **256,883** CapCity orders: **38,950**
★ Versus Hobgoblin.
49 ❑ Aug 1994 Cover: 1.95 NM value: **2.00**
Circ: Statement: **256,883** CapCity orders: **38,350** • **CGC:** 1 graded, best 9.8
50 ❑ Sep 1994 Cover: 2.50 NM value: **Cover or less**
50/SC❑Sep 1994 Cover: 3.95 NM value: **Cover or less**
Circ: Statement: **256,883** CapCity orders: **57,350**
Holo-grafix cover.
51 ❑ Oct 1994 Cover: 1.95 NM value: **2.50**
📖 Power and Responsibility, Part 3 **A:** Tom Lyle **W:** Howard Mackie ★ Appearance of Ben Reilly.
51/SC❑Oct 1994 Cover: 2.95 NM value: **Cover or less**
Circ: Statement: **256,883** CapCity orders: **43,400** • **CGC:** 1 graded, best 9.6
enhanced cover. • Giant-size. 📖 Power and Responsibility, Part 3; The Double, Part 3 • flip-book with back-up **A:** Tom Lyle; Ron Liam **W:** Howard Mackie; J.M. DeMatteis ★ Origin of Ben Reilly. ★ Appearance of Ben Reilly.
52 ❑ Nov 1994 Cover: 1.95 NM value: **2.00**
Circ: Statement: **256,883** CapCity orders: **45,150**
• The clone vs. Venom
53 ❑ Dec 1994 Cover: 1.95 NM value: **2.00**
Circ: Statement: **256,883** CapCity orders: **41,450**
• The clone defeats Venom
54 ❑ Jan 1995 Cover: 2.75 NM value: **Cover or less**
Circ: Statement: **199,974** CapCity orders: **39,175**
📖 Web of Life, Part 2 • flip book with illustrated story from The Ultimate Spider-Man back-up
55 ❑ Feb 1995 Cover: 1.95 NM value: **2.00**
Circ: Statement: **199,974** CapCity orders: **38,925**
📖 Web of Life, Part 4
56 ❑ Mar 1995 Cover: 1.95 NM value: **2.00**
Circ: Statement: **199,974** CapCity orders: **37,050**
57 ❑ Apr 1995 Cover: 2.50 NM value: **Cover or less**
Circ: Statement: **199,974**
• Giant-size. 📖 Aftershocks, Part 1; The Parker Legacy, Part 2 **A:** John Romita Jr. **W:** Howard Mackie; J.M. DeMatteis
57/SC❑Apr 1995 Cover: 2.95 NM value: **Cover or less**
Circ: Statement: **199,974** CapCity orders: **42,475** • **CGC:** 2 graded, best 9.8
enhanced cardstock cover. • Giant-size. 📖 Aftershocks, Part 1; The Parker Legacy, Part 2
58 ❑ May 1995 Cover: 1.95 NM value: **2.00**
Circ: Statement: **199,974** CapCity orders: **37,600** • **CGC:** 1 graded, best 9.6
59 ❑ Jun 1995 Cover: 1.95 NM value: **2.00**
Circ: Statement: **199,974** CapCity orders: **35,850**
60 ❑ Jul 1995 Cover: 1.95 NM value: **2.00**
Circ: Statement: **199,974** CapCity orders: **36,475**
📖 The Trial of Peter Parker, Part 3 • Kaine's identity revealed
61 ❑ Aug 1995 Cover: 1.95 NM value: **2.00**
Circ: Statement: **199,974** CapCity orders: **39,300**
📖 Maximum Clonage, Part 4
62 ❑ Sep 1995 Cover: 1.95 NM value: **2.00**
Circ: Statement: **199,974**
📖 Exiled, Part 3
63 ❑ Oct 1995 Cover: 1.95 NM value: **2.00**
Circ: Statement: **199,974**
📖 The Greatest Responsibility, Part 2 • OverPower game cards bound-in
64 ❑ Jan 1996 Cover: 1.95 NM value: **2.00**
Circ: Statement: **165,342**
• Has 1995 Statement, filed 10/1/95; avg print run 342,896; avg sales 196,974; avg subs 3,000; avg total paid 199,974; samples 750; office use 500; max existent 201,224; 41% of run returned ★ Versus Poison.
65 ❑ Feb 1996 Cover: 1.95 NM value: **2.00**
Circ: Statement: **165,342**
📖 Media Blizzard, Part 3
66 ❑ Mar 1996 Cover: 1.95 NM value: **2.00**
Circ: Statement: **165,342** • **CGC:** 1 graded, best 9.6
📖 The Return of Kaine, Part 4 **A:** John Romita Jr. **W:** Howard Mackie
67 ❑ Apr 1996 Cover: 1.95 NM value: **2.00**
Circ: Statement: **165,342**
📖 Web of Carnage, Part 3 **A:** John Romita Jr.; Al Milgrom(inks); Al Williamson(inks) **W:** John Romita Jr.; Howard Mackie
68 ❑ May 1996 Cover: 1.95 NM value: **2.00**
Circ: Statement: **165,342**
📖 Blood Brothers, Part 3
69 ❑ Jun 1996 Cover: 1.95 NM value: **2.00**
Circ: Statement: **165,342**
70 ❑ Jul 1996 Cover: 1.95 NM value: **2.00**
Circ: Statement: **165,342**
★ Appearance of Hammerhead.
71 ❑ Aug 1996 Cover: 1.95 NM value: **2.00**
Circ: Statement: **165,342**
A: John Romita Jr. ★ Versus Hammerhead.
72 ❑ Sep 1996 Cover: 1.95 NM value: **2.00**
Circ: Statement: **165,342**
📖 Onslaught: Impact 2 **A:** John Romita Jr. ★ Versus Sentinels.
73 ❑ Oct 1996 Cover: 1.99 NM value: **2.00**
Circ: Statement: **165,342**
A: John Romita Jr.
74 ❑ Nov 1996 Cover: 1.99 NM value: **2.00**
Circ: Statement: **140,059** Direct Market orders: **82,750**
A: John Romita Jr. ★ Appearance of Daredevil.
75 ❑ Dec 1996 Cover: 2.99 NM value: **3.50**
Circ: Statement: **140,059** Direct Market orders: **124,750**
wraparound cover. • Giant-size. 📖 Revelations, Part 4 • return of original Green Goblin **A:** John Romita Jr. **W:** Howard Mackie ★ Death of Ben Reilly.
76 ❑ Jan 1997 Cover: 1.99 NM value: **2.00**
Circ: Statement: **140,059** Direct Market orders: **83,000**
📖 SHOC **A:** John Romita Jr. **W:** Howard Mackie ★ Appearance of S.H.O.C.. ★ Versus S.H.O.C..
77 ❑ Feb 1997 Cover: 1.95 NM value: **2.00**
Circ: Statement: **140,059** Direct Market orders: **81,250**
★ Versus Morbius.
78 ❑ Mar 1997 Cover: 1.99 NM value: **2.00**
Circ: Statement: **140,059** Direct Market orders: **75,250**
📖 The Love of a Woman **A:** John Romita Jr. **W:** Howard Mackie ★ Versus Morbius.
79 ❑ Apr 1997 Cover: 1.99 NM value: **2.00**
Circ: Statement: **140,059** Direct Market orders: **74,250**
📖 After the Fall **A:** John Romita Jr. **W:** Howard Mackie ★ Appearance of Morbius. ★ Versus S.H.O.C..

Other grades: Multiply prices above by **1.5 for Mint • 2/3 for Very Fine • 1/3 for Fine • 1/5 for Very Good • 1/8 for Good**

80 ❑ May 1997 Cover: 1.99 **NM** value: **2.00**
Circ: Statement: **140,059** Diamd. preorders: **74,207**
📖 Blood Simple **A:** John Romita Jr. **W:** Howard Mackie ★ Appearance of Morbius. ★ Versus Hammerhead.

81 ❑ Jun 1997 Cover: 1.99 **NM** value: **2.00**
Circ: Statement: **140,059** Diamd. preorders: **74,066**
📖 Shadow of the Cat **A:** John Romita Jr. **W:** Howard Mackie

82 ❑ Aug 1997 Cover: 1.99 **NM** value: **2.00**
Circ: Statement: **140,059** Diamd. preorders: **67,266**
• gatefold summary.

83 ❑ Sep 1997 Cover: 1.99 **NM** value: **2.00**
Circ: Statement: **140,059** Diamd. preorders: **64,804**
• gatefold summary.

84 ❑ Oct 1997 Cover: 1.99 **NM** value: **2.00**
Circ: Diamd. preorders: **64,387** • **CGC:** 1 graded, best 8.5
• gatefold summary. ★ Versus Juggernaut.

85 ❑ Nov 1997 Cover: 1.99 **NM** value: **2.00**
Circ: Diamd. preorders: **62,314**
• gatefold summary. ★ Versus Shocker.

86 ❑ Dec 1997 Cover: 1.99 **NM** value: **2.00**
Circ: Diamd. preorders: **61,230**
• gatefold summary. • Has 1997 Statement, filed 10/1/97; avg print run 256,717; avg sales 136,895; avg subs 3,164; avg total paid 140,059; samples 316; office use 125; max existent 140,500; 45% of run returned★ Appearance of Trapster. ★ Versus Shocker.

87 ❑ Jan 1998 Cover: 1.99 **NM** value: **2.00**
Circ: Diamd. preorders: **60,482**
• gatefold summary. ★ Versus Shocker.

88 ❑ Feb 1998 Cover: 1.99 **NM** value: **2.00**
• gatefold summary.

89 ❑ Mar 1998 Cover: 1.99 **NM** value: **2.00**
Circ: Diamd. preorders: **61,997**
• gatefold summary. 📖 Spider-Hunt, Part 3 ★ Versus Punisher. ★ Versus Shotgun.

90 ❑ Apr 1998 Cover: 1.99 **NM** value: **2.00**
• gatefold summary. 📖 Identity Crisis ★ 1st Appearance of Spidey as Dusk. ★ Versus Blastaar.

91 ❑ May 1998 Cover: 1.99 **NM** value: **2.00**
• gatefold summary. 📖 Identity Crisis, Part 3 • Identity Crisis

92 ❑ Jun 1998 Cover: 1.99 **NM** value: **2.00**
• gatefold summary. • Identity Crisis

93 ❑ Jul 1998 Cover: 1.99 **NM** value: **2.00**
• gatefold summary. ★ Appearance of Ghost Rider.

94 ❑ Aug 1998 Cover: 1.99 **NM** value: **2.00**
• gatefold summary.

95 ❑ Sep 1998 Cover: 1.99 **NM** value: **2.00**
Circ: Diamd. preorders: **59,733**
• gatefold summary. ★ Versus Nitro.

96 ❑ Oct 1998 Cover: 1.99 **NM** value: **2.00**
Circ: Diamd. preorders: **60,278**
• gatefold summary. 📖 The Gathering of Five, Part 3 ★ Appearance of Madame Web.

97 ❑ Nov 1998 Cover: 1.99 **NM** value: **2.00**
• gatefold summary. 📖 The Final Chapter, Part 2 **C:** John Byrne

98/A❑ Nov 1998 Cover: 1.99 **NM** value: **2.00**
• **CGC:** 1 graded, best 9.8
• gatefold summary. 📖 The Final Chapter, Part 4 final issue.

98/B❑ Nov 1998 Cover: 1.99 **NM** value: **2.00**
• **CGC:** 1 graded, best 9.6
alternate cover. • gatefold summary. 📖 The Final Chapter, Part 4 final issue. • series begins again as Peter Parker: Spider-Man **C:** John Byrne

Anl 1997❑ ca. 1997 Cover: 2.99 **NM** value: **Cover or less**
Circ: Diamd. preorders: **55,100**
• 1997 Annual

Anl 1998❑ ca. 1998 Cover: 2.99 **NM** value: **Cover or less**
wraparound cover. • gatefold summary. ★ Appearance of Devil Dinosaur, Moon Boy.

GS 1❑ Dec 1998 Cover: 3.99 **NM** value: **Cover or less**
Circ: Diamd. preorders: **20,200**
• Giant-Sized Spider-Man.

HS 1995❑ Hol 1995 Cover: 2.95 **NM** value: **Cover or less**
No issue number. One-shot. • Trade Paperback. • 1995 Holiday Special★ Appearance of Human Torch, Venom.

SPIDER-MAN ADVENTURES — Marvel

1 ❑ Dec 1994 Cover: 1.50 **NM** value: **Cover or less**
📖 Night of the Lizard • adapts animated series **A:** Alex Saviuk **W:** Nel Yomtov

1/SC❑ Dec 1994 Cover: 2.95 **NM** value: **Cover or less**
Circ: CapCity orders: **33,800**
enhanced cover. 📖 Night of the Lizard • Adapts animated series **A:** Alex Saviuk **W:** Nel Yomtov

2 ❑ Jan 1995 Cover: 1.50 **NM** value: **Cover or less**
Circ: CapCity orders: **16,825**
• adapts animated series **A:** Alex Saviuk **W:** Nel Yomtov

3 ❑ Feb 1995 Cover: 1.50 **NM** value: **Cover or less**
Circ: CapCity orders: **11,250**
• adapts animated series **A:** Alex Saviuk **W:** Nel Yomtov ★ Versus Spider-Slayer.

4 ❑ Mar 1995 Cover: 1.50 **NM** value: **Cover or less**
Circ: CapCity orders: **9,250**
• adapts animated series **A:** Alex Saviuk **W:** Nel Yomtov

5 ❑ Apr 1995 Cover: 1.50 **NM** value: **Cover or less**
Circ: CapCity orders: **8,200**
• adapts animated series **A:** Alex Saviuk **W:** Nel Yomtov ★ Versus Mysterio.

6 ❑ May 1995 Cover: 1.50 **NM** value: **Cover or less**
Circ: CapCity orders: **6,650**
• adapts animated series **A:** Alex Saviuk **W:** Nel Yomtov

7 ❑ Jun 1995 Cover: 1.50 **NM** value: **Cover or less**
Circ: CapCity orders: **6,075**
• adapts animated series **A:** Alex Saviuk **W:** Nel Yomtov

8 ❑ Jul 1995 Cover: 1.50 **NM** value: **Cover or less**
Circ: CapCity orders: **6,275**
• Adapts animated series **A:** Alex Saviuk **W:** Nel Yomtov

9 ❑ Aug 1995 Cover: 1.50 **NM** value: **Cover or less**
• Adapts animated series **A:** Alex Saviuk **W:** Nel Yomtov ★ Versus Shocker.

10 ❑ Sep 1995 Cover: 1.50 **NM** value: **Cover or less**
• Adapts animated series **A:** Alex Saviuk **W:** Nel Yomtov ★ Versus Venom.

11 ❑ Oct 1995 Cover: 1.50 **NM** value: **Cover or less**
• Adapts animated series **A:** Alex Saviuk **W:** Nel Yomtov ★ Versus Hobgoblin.

12 ❑ Nov 1995 Cover: 1.50 **NM** value: **Cover or less**
• Adapts animated series **A:** Alex Saviuk **W:** Nel Yomtov ★ Versus Hobgoblin.

13 ❑ Dec 1995 Cover: 1.50 **NM** value: **Cover or less**
• Adapts animated series **A:** Alex Saviuk **W:** Nel Yomtov ★ Appearance of S.H.I.E.L.D., Chameleon, Nick Fury. ★ Versus Chameleon.

14 ❑ Jan 1996 Cover: 1.50 **NM** value: **Cover or less**
• Adapts animated series★ Versus Doctor Octopus.

15 ❑ Feb 1996 Cover: 1.50 **NM** value: **Cover or less**
final issue. • Adapts animated series; Continues in Adventures of Spider-Man #1★ Versus Lizard.

SPIDER-MAN AND BATMAN — Marvel

1 ❑ Sep 1995 Cover: 5.95 **NM** value: **Cover or less**
• **CGC:** 3 graded, best 9.8
No issue number. • prestige format.

SPIDER-MAN AND DAREDEVIL SPECIAL EDITION — Marvel

1 ❑ Mar 1984 Cover: 2.00 **NM** value: **Cover or less**
• **CGC:** 3 graded, best 9.4

SPIDER-MAN AND HIS AMAZING FRIENDS — Marvel

1 ❑ Dec 1981 Cover: 0.50 **NM** value: **2.50**
• **CGC:** 7 graded, best 9.4
📖 The Triumph of the Green Goblin • Adapted from television show **A:** Dan Spiegle **W:** Dennis Marks ★ 1st Appearance of Firestar. ★ Appearance of Iceman, Green Goblin.

SPIDER-MAN AND MYSTERIO — Marvel

1 ❑ Jan 2001 Cover: 2.99 **NM** value: **Cover or less**
says Spider-Man: The Mysterio Manifesto on the cover. 📖 Jack's Back **A:** Lee Weeks **W:** Tom DeFalco ★ Appearance of Daredevil.

2 ❑ Feb 2001 Cover: 2.99 **NM** value: **Cover or less**
says Spider-Man: The Mysterio Manifesto on the cover. 📖 Even the Dead Can Lie! **A:** Lee Weeks **W:** Tom DeFalco ★ Appearance of Daredevil.

3 ❑ Mar 2001 Cover: 2.99 **NM** value: **Cover or less**
says Spider-Man: The Mysterio Manifesto on the cover. 📖 False Truths! **A:** Lee Weeks **W:** Tom DeFalco ★ Appearance of Daredevil.

SPIDER-MAN AND THE DALLAS COWBOYS — Marvel

1 ❑ Sep 1983 **NM** value: **10.00**
• **CGC:** 2 graded, best 9.6
No issue number. • Danger in Dallas giveaway.

SPIDER-MAN AND THE INCREDIBLE HULK — Marvel

1 ❑ Sep 1981 **NM** value: **10.00**
• **CGC:** 3 graded, best 9.6
No issue number. • Chaos in Kansas City giveaway.

SPIDER-MAN & THE NEW MUTANTS — Marvel

1 ❑ **NM** value: **3.00**
No issue number. • giveaway. • child abuse

SPIDER-MAN AND X-FACTOR: SHADOWGAMES — Marvel

1 ❑ May 1994 Cover: 1.95 **NM** value: **2.25**
Circ: CapCity orders: **46,650**
📖 Shadow-Games, Part 1 **A:** Pat Broderick **W:** Kurt Busiek ★ Origin of Shadow Force. ★ 1st Appearance of Shadow Force.

2 ❑ Jun 1994 Cover: 1.95 **NM** value: **2.25**
Circ: CapCity orders: **37,350**
📖 Shadow-Games, Part 2 **A:** Pat Broderick **W:** Kurt Busiek

3 ❑ Jul 1994 Cover: 1.95 **NM** value: **2.25**
Circ: CapCity orders: **33,950**
📖 Shadow-Games, Part 3 **A:** Pat Broderick **W:** Kurt Busiek

SPIDER-MAN ANNUAL — Marvel / Grandreams

1 ❑ Cover: 3.95 **NM** value: **Cover or less**
hardcover.

SPIDER-MAN/BADROCK — Maximum

1/A ❑ Mar 1997 Cover: 2.99 **NM** value: **Cover or less**
Circ: Diamd. preorders: **42,083**
• first part of story

1/B ❑ Mar 1997 Cover: 2.99 **NM** value: **Cover or less**
• second part of story

SPIDER-MAN BATTLEBOOK — Marvel

1 ❑ Cover: 3.99 **NM** value: **Cover or less**

SPIDER-MAN: CARNAGE — Marvel

1 ❑ **NM** value: **8.95**

> The CGC numbers printed in individual listings above represent the **number of copies examined** and given a **Universal** grade by CGC and the **best such copy** graded at press time. For current populations, watch for special ***Comics Buyer's Guide*** issues or check **www.cgccomics.com.**

SPIDER-MAN: CHAPTER ONE — Marvel

After allowing their flagship hero to flounder through clone sagas and alien symbiote storylines, Marvel brought in writer and artist John Byrne to take Spider-Man back to his roots. This limited series retold the webslinger's earliest adventures — including classic run-ins with the likes of Doctors Octopus and Doom, The Sandman, and The Vulture — tweaking the longstanding Spider-continuity here and there in an attempt to bring Spidey into the 1990s. While it was obvious that Byrne was having fun with the work, many fans did not agree with the changes and the series was canceled after 13 issues.

0 ❑ May 1999 Cover: 2.50 **NM** value: **Cover or less**
Circ: Diamd. preorders: **56,286**
📖 Where Walks the Lizard **A:** John Byrne **W:** John Byrne ★ Origin of Lizard, Vulture, Sandman.

1 ❑ Dec 1998 Cover: 2.50 **NM** value: **Cover or less**
Circ: Diamd. preorders: **100,162**
📖 Bitter Lesson **A:** John Byrne **W:** John Byrne ★ Origin of Doctor Octopus, Spider-Man.

1/A ❑ Dec 1998 Cover: 6.95 **NM** value: **Cover or less**
DFE alternate cover. 📖 Bitter Lesson **A:** John Byrne **W:** John Byrne ★ Origin of Doctor Octopus, Spider-Man.

1/B ❑ Dec 1998 Cover: 19.63 **NM** value: **Cover or less**
📖 Bitter Lesson **A:** John Byrne **W:** John Byrne ★ Origin of Doctor Octopus, Spider-Man.

1/C ❑ Dec 1998 Cover: 19.63 **NM** value: **Cover or less**
📖 Bitter Lesson **A:** John Byrne **W:** John Byrne ★ Origin of Doctor Octopus, Spider-Man.

2/A ❑ Dec 1998 Cover: 2.50 **NM** value: **Cover or less**
Circ: Diamd. preorders: **100,651**
Cover A. **A:** John Byrne **W:** John Byrne

2/B ❑ Dec 1998 Cover: 2.50 **NM** value: **Cover or less**
Cover B. **A:** John Byrne **W:** John Byrne

2/C ❑ Dec 1998 Cover: 6.95 **NM** value: **Cover or less**
Cover forms diptych with issue #1 DFE cover. **A:** John Byrne **W:** John Byrne

3 ❑ Jan 1999 Cover: 2.50 **NM** value: **Cover or less**
Circ: Diamd. preorders: **79,574**
A: John Byrne **W:** John Byrne ★ Origin of Vulture. ★ Appearance of Mad Thinker.

4 ❑ Feb 1999 Cover: 2.50 **NM** value: **Cover or less**
Circ: Diamd. preorders: **71,919**
A: John Byrne **W:** John Byrne ★ Appearance of Doctor Octopus, Doctor Doom. ★ Versus Doctor Octopus. ★ Versus Doctor Doom.

5 ❑ Mar 1999 Cover: 2.50 **NM** value: **Cover or less**
Circ: Diamd. preorders: **64,916**
A: John Byrne **W:** John Byrne ★ Appearance of Lizard, Doctor Doom. ★ Versus Lizard.

6 ❑ Apr 1999 Cover: 2.50 **NM** value: **Cover or less**
Circ: Diamd. preorders: **59,254**
A: John Byrne **W:** John Byrne ★ Appearance of Human Torch, Electro. ★ Versus Electro.

7 ❑ May 1999 Cover: 2.50 **NM** value: **Cover or less**
Circ: Diamd. preorders: **55,479**
A: John Byrne **W:** John Byrne ★ Versus Mysterio.

8 ❑ Jun 1999 Cover: 2.50 **NM** value: **Cover or less**
Circ: Diamd. preorders: **54,142**
A: John Byrne **W:** John Byrne ★ Appearance of Hulk. ★ Versus Green Goblin.

9 ❑ Jul 1999 Cover: 2.50 **NM** value: **Cover or less**
Circ: Diamd. preorders: **50,875**
A: John Byrne **W:** John Byrne ★ Appearance of Daredevil. ★ Versus Kraven.

10 ❑ Aug 1999 Cover: 2.50 **NM** value: **Cover or less**
Circ: Diamd. preorders: **47,754**
A: John Byrne **W:** John Byrne ★ Versus Green Goblin.

11 ❑ Sep 1999 Cover: 2.50 **NM** value: **Cover or less**
Circ: Diamd. preorders: **45,097**
A: John Byrne **W:** John Byrne ★ Appearance of Giant-Man.

12 ❑ Oct 1999 Cover: 3.50 **NM** value: **Cover or less**
Circ: Diamd. preorders: **42,916**
final issue. **A:** John Byrne **W:** John Byrne ★ Versus Sandman.

Dlx 1❑ Cover: 29.95 **NM** value: **Cover or less**
A: John Byrne **W:** John Byrne

Dlx 1/LE❑ Cover: 29.95 **NM** value: **Cover or less**
A: John Byrne **W:** John Byrne

SPIDER-MAN: CHRISTMAS IN DALLAS — Marvel

1 ❑ Dec 1983 **NM** value: **10.00**
No issue number. • giveaway.

SPIDER-MAN CLASSICS — Marvel

1 ❑ Apr 1993 Cover: 1.25 **NM** value: **2.00**
Circ: CapCity orders: **26,400**
📖 The Origin Of Doctor Strange • Reprints Amazing Fantasy #15 & Strange Tales #115 **A:** Steve Ditko **W:** Stan Lee ★ Origin of Spider-Man, Doctor Strange. ★ 1st Appearance of Spider-Man.

2 ❑ May 1993 Cover: 1.25 **NM** value: **1.50**
Circ: CapCity orders: **17,900**
📖 Spider-Man; Spider-Man vs. the Chameleon • Reprints Amazing Spider-Man #1 **A:** Steve Ditko **W:** Steve Ditko; Stan Lee ★ Origin of Spider-Man. ★ 1st Appearance of J. Jonah Jameson, Chameleon. ★ Appearance of Fantastic Four.

3 ❑ Jun 1993 Cover: 1.25 **NM** value: **1.50**
Circ: CapCity orders: **19,100**
📖 Duel to the Death with the Vulture; The Uncanny Threat of the Terrible Tinkerer • Reprints Amazing Spider-Man #2 **A:** Steve Ditko

CGC-graded: Multiply prices above by **33 for 9.9 M • 16 for 9.8 NM/M • 7 for 9.6 NM+ • 5 for 9.4 NM • 2.5 for 9.2 NM- • 1.5 for 9.0 VF/NM**

W: Steve Ditko; Stan Lee ★ 1st Appearance of Mysterio (as "alien"), Tinkerer, Vulture.

4 ❑ Jul 1993 Cover: 1.25 **NM** value: **1.50**
Circ: CapCity orders: **14,500**
📖 Spider-Man Versus Doctor Octopus • Reprints Amazing Spider-Man #3 **A:** Steve Ditko **W:** Steve Ditko; Stan Lee ★ Origin of Doctor Octopus. ★ 1st Appearance of Doctor Octopus.

5 ❑ Aug 1993 Cover: 1.25 **NM** value: **1.50**
Circ: CapCity orders: **13,500**
📖 Nothing Can Stop the Sandman • Reprints Amazing Spider-Man #4 **A:** Steve Ditko **W:** Steve Ditko; Stan Lee ★ Origin of Sandman (Marvel). ★ 1st Appearance of Betty Brant, Sandman (Marvel).

6 ❑ Sep 1993 Cover: 1.25 **NM** value: **1.50**
Circ: CapCity orders: **12,200**
📖 Marked for Destruction by Dr. Doom • Reprints Amazing Spider-Man #5 **A:** Steve Ditko **W:** Steve Ditko; Stan Lee ★ Appearance of Doctor Doom.

7 ❑ Oct 1993 Cover: 1.25 **NM** value: **1.50**
Circ: CapCity orders: **11,000**
📖 Face-to-Face with the Lizard • Reprints Amazing Spider-Man #6 **A:** Steve Ditko **W:** Steve Ditko; Stan Lee ★ Origin of The Lizard. ★ 1st Appearance of The Lizard.

8 ❑ Nov 1993 Cover: 1.25 **NM** value: **1.50**
Circ: CapCity orders: **10,800**
📖 Return of the Vulture • Reprints Amazing Spider-Man #7 **A:** Steve Ditko **W:** Steve Ditko; Stan Lee ★ 2nd Appearance of The Vulture.

9 ❑ Dec 1993 Cover: 1.25 **NM** value: **1.50**
Circ: CapCity orders: **10,300**
📖 The Terrible Threat of the Living Brain • Reprints Amazing Spider-Man #8 **A:** Steve Ditko **W:** Steve Ditko; Stan Lee ★ 1st Appearance of The Living Brain. ★ Appearance of Human Torch.

10 ❑ Jan 1994 Cover: 1.25 **NM** value: **1.50**
Circ: CapCity orders: **8,800**
📖 The Man Called Electro • Reprints Amazing Spider-Man #9 **A:** Steve Ditko **W:** Steve Ditko; Stan Lee ★ Origin of Electro. ★ 1st Appearance of Electro.

11 ❑ Feb 1994 Cover: 1.25 **NM** value: **1.50**
Circ: CapCity orders: **9,100**
📖 The Enforcers • Reprints Amazing Spider-Man #10 **A:** Steve Ditko **W:** Steve Ditko; Stan Lee ★ 1st Appearance of Big Man, Enforcers.

12 ❑ Mar 1994 Cover: 1.25 **NM** value: **1.50**
Circ: CapCity orders: **7,800**
📖 Turning Point • Reprints Amazing Spider-Man #11 **A:** Steve Ditko **W:** Steve Ditko; Stan Lee ★ 2nd Appearance of Doctor Octopus.

13 ❑ Apr 1994 Cover: 1.25 **NM** value: **Cover or less**
Circ: CapCity orders: **7,350**

14 ❑ May 1994 Cover: 1.25 **NM** value: **Cover or less**
Circ: CapCity orders: **7,000**

15 ❑ Jun 1994 Cover: 1.25 **NM** value: **Cover or less**
★ 1st Appearance of Green Goblin I (Norman Osborn).

15/CS❑ Jun 1994 Cover: 2.95 **NM** value: **Cover or less**
Circ: CapCity orders: **17,200**
• polybagged with animation print ★ 1st Appearance of Green Goblin I (Norman Osborn).

16 ❑ Jul 1994 Cover: 1.25 **NM** value: **Cover or less**
Circ: CapCity orders: **7,150**

SPIDER-MAN COLLECTORS' PREVIEW — Marvel

1 ❑ Dec 1994 Cover: 1.50 **NM** value: **Cover or less**
Circ: CapCity orders: **10,300**

SPIDER-MAN COMICS MAGAZINE — Marvel

1 ❑ Jan 1987 Cover: 1.50 **NM** value: **Cover or less**
• digest-sized.

2 ❑ Mar 1987 Cover: 1.50 **NM** value: **Cover or less**
• digest-sized.

3 ❑ May 1987 Cover: 1.50 **NM** value: **Cover or less**
• digest-sized.

4 ❑ Jul 1987 Cover: 1.50 **NM** value: **Cover or less**
• digest-sized.

5 ❑ Sep 1987 Cover: 1.50 **NM** value: **Cover or less**
• digest-sized.

6 ❑ Nov 1987 Cover: 1.50 **NM** value: **Cover or less**
• digest-sized.

7 ❑ Jan 1988 Cover: 1.50 **NM** value: **Cover or less**
• digest-sized.

8 ❑ Mar 1988 Cover: 1.50 **NM** value: **Cover or less**
• digest-sized.

9 ❑ May 1988 Cover: 1.50 **NM** value: **Cover or less**
• digest-sized.

10 ❑ Jul 1988 Cover: 1.50 **NM** value: **Cover or less**
• digest-sized.

11 ❑ Sep 1988 Cover: 1.50 **NM** value: **Cover or less**
• digest-sized.

12 ❑ Nov 1988 Cover: 1.50 **NM** value: **Cover or less**
• digest-sized. **A:** John Romita; Jim Mooney **W:** Stan Lee

13 ❑ Jan 1989 Cover: 1.50 **NM** value: **Cover or less**
• digest-sized.

SPIDER-MAN: DEAD MAN'S HAND — Marvel

1 ❑ Apr 1997 Cover: 2.99 **NM** value: **Cover or less**
Circ: Direct Market orders: **52,500**
wraparound cover. **A:** Darick Robertson; Dan Lawlis **W:** Roger Stern; Joe Edkin

SPIDER-MAN: DEATH AND DESTINY — Marvel

1 ❑ Aug 2000 Cover: 2.99 **NM** value: **Cover or less**
Circ: Diamd. preorders: **30,970**
📖 Focus **A:** Lee Weeks **W:** Lee Weeks

2 ❑ Sep 2000 Cover: 2.99 **NM** value: **Cover or less**
Circ: Diamd. preorders: **27,642**
📖 The Camera Doesn't Lie **A:** Lee Weeks **W:** Lee Weeks

3 ❑ Oct 2000 Cover: 2.99 **NM** value: **Cover or less**
Circ: Diamd. preorders: **23,607**
📖 D...ja Vu All Over Again **A:** Lee Weeks **W:** Lee Weeks

SPIDER-MAN/DR. STRANGE: THE WAY TO DUSTY DEATH — Marvel

1 ❑ Cover: 6.95 **NM** value: **Cover or less**
• graphic novel **A:** Michael Bair **W:** Roy Thomas; Gerry Conway

SPIDER-MAN: FEARFUL SYMMETRY — Marvel

Bk 1❑ Cover: 15.95 **NM** value: **Cover or less**
Bk 1/HC❑ Cover: 19.95 **NM** value: **Cover or less**
hardcover.

SPIDER-MAN: FEAR ITSELF — Marvel

1 ❑ Feb 1992 Cover: 12.95 **NM** value: **Cover or less**
Circ: CapCity orders: **8,350**
A: Ross Andru **W:** Stan Lee; Gerry Conway

SPIDER-MAN, FIRE-STAR AND ICEMAN — Marvel

1 ❑ **NM** value: **10.00**
No issue number. • Danger in Denver giveaway.

SPIDER-MAN: FRIENDS & ENEMIES — Marvel

1 ❑ Jan 1995 Cover: 1.95 **NM** value: **Cover or less**
Circ: CapCity orders: **17,825**
A: Ron Lim **W:** Danny Fingeroth ★ Origin of The Metahumes. ★ 1st Appearance of The Metahumes.

2 ❑ Feb 1995 Cover: 1.95 **NM** value: **Cover or less**
Circ: CapCity orders: **12,625**
A: Ron Lim **W:** Danny Fingeroth

3 ❑ Mar 1995 Cover: 1.95 **NM** value: **Cover or less**
Circ: CapCity orders: **11,325**
A: Ron Lim **W:** Danny Fingeroth

4 ❑ Apr 1995 Cover: 1.95 **NM** value: **Cover or less**
Circ: CapCity orders: **10,525**
📖 Fire Of Freedom **A:** Ron Lim **W:** Danny Fingeroth

SPIDER-MAN: FUNERAL FOR AN OCTOPUS — Marvel

1 ❑ Mar 1995 Cover: 1.50 **NM** value: **Cover or less**
Circ: CapCity orders: **16,625**
📖 Eight Arms Beyond the Grave **A:** Stewart Johnson; Al Milgrom **W:** Mike Kanterovich; Tom Brevoort

2 ❑ Apr 1995 Cover: 1.50 **NM** value: **Cover or less**
Circ: CapCity orders: **13,475**
A: Stewart Johnson; Al Milgrom **W:** Mike Kanterovich; Tom Brevoort

3 ❑ May 1995 Cover: 1.50 **NM** value: **Cover or less**
Circ: CapCity orders: **14,525**
A: Stewart Johnson; Al Milgrom **W:** Mike Kanterovich; Tom Brevoort

4 ❑ Jun 1995 Cover: 1.50 **NM** value: **Cover or less**
A: Stewart Johnson; Al Milgrom **W:** Mike Kanterovich; Tom Brevoort

SPIDER-MAN/GEN13 — Marvel

1 ❑ Nov 1996 Cover: 4.95 **NM** value: **Cover or less**
Circ: Direct Market orders: **106,500** • **CGC:** 1 graded, best 9.8
No issue number. • prestige format. 📖 Crossed Generations **A:** Stuart Immonen **W:** Peter David

SPIDER-MAN: HIS GREATEST TEAM-UP BATTLES — Marvel

Bk 1❑ Cover: 2.50 **NM** value: **Cover or less**

SPIDER-MAN: HOBGOBLIN LIVES — Marvel

1 ❑ Jan 1997 Cover: 2.50 **NM** value: **Cover or less**
Circ: Direct Market orders: **63,750**
wraparound cover. 📖 Victims **A:** Scott Hanna; Jerome Moore; Ron Frenz **W:** Roger Stern ★ Death of Jason Macendale.

2 ❑ Feb 1997 Cover: 2.50 **NM** value: **Cover or less**
Circ: Direct Market orders: **56,500**
wraparound cover. 📖 Back In Business **A:** Scott Hanna; Jerome Moore; Ron Frenz **W:** Roger Stern

3 ❑ Apr 1997 Cover: 2.50 **NM** value: **Cover or less**
Circ: Direct Market orders: **52,500**
wraparound cover. 📖 Secrets final issue. • identity of Hobgoblin revealed; True identity of Hobgoblin I revealed **A:** Scott Hanna; Jerome Moore; Ron Frenz **W:** Roger Stern

SPIDER-MAN/KINGPIN: TO THE DEATH — Marvel

1 ❑ Cover: 5.95 **NM** value: **Cover or less**
No issue number. • prestige format. ★ Appearance of Daredevil.

SPIDER-MAN: LEGACY OF EVIL — Marvel

1 ❑ Jun 1996 Cover: 3.95 **NM** value: **Cover or less**
• **CGC:** 1 graded, best 9.4
One-shot. • retells history of Green Goblin **A:** Mark Texeira **W:** Kurt Busiek

SPIDER-MAN: LIFELINE — Marvel

1 ❑ Apr 2001 Cover: 2.99 **NM** value: **Cover or less**
Circ: Diamd. preorders: **35,050** • **CGC:** 3 graded, best 9.9
📖 Pieces of Fate **A:** Steve Rude **W:** Fabian Nicieza ★ Appearance of Doctor Strange.

2 ❑ May 2001 Cover: 2.99 **NM** value: **Cover or less**
Circ: Diamd. preorders: **33,124**
📖 Snakes in the Grass **A:** Steve Rude **W:** Fabian Nicieza ★ Appearance of Lizard, Doctor Strange.

3 ❑ Jun 2001 Cover: 2.99 **NM** value: **Cover or less**
Circ: Diamd. preorders: **31,202**
📖 A Taste of Infinity **A:** Steve Rude **W:** Fabian Nicieza ★ Appearance of Lizard, Doctor Strange.

SPIDER-MAN: MADE MEN — Marvel

1 ❑ Aug 1999 Cover: 5.99 **NM** value: **Cover or less**
A: Norman Felchle **W:** Howard Mackie

SPIDER-MAN MAGAZINE — Marvel

1 ❑ Win 1994 Cover: 1.95 **NM** value: **2.00**
Circ: Statement: **52,740** CapCity orders: **11,150**
No issue number.

2 ❑ Jun 1994 Cover: 1.95 **NM** value: **2.00**
Circ: Statement: **52,740** CapCity orders: **5,400**

3 ❑ Jul 1994 Cover: 1.95 **NM** value: **2.00**
Circ: Statement: **52,740**

4 ❑ Aug 1994 Cover: 1.95 **NM** value: **2.00**
Circ: Statement: **52,740**
• X-Men

5 ❑ Sep 1994 Cover: 1.95 **NM** value: **2.00**
Circ: Statement: **52,740**

6 ❑ Oct 1994 Cover: 1.95 **NM** value: **2.00**
Circ: Statement: **52,740**
• X-Men

7 ❑ Nov 1994 Cover: 1.95 **NM** value: **2.00**
Circ: Statement: **52,740**

8 ❑ Dec 1994 Cover: 1.95 **NM** value: **2.00**
Circ: Statement: **52,740**

9 ❑ Jan 1995 Cover: 1.95 **NM** value: **2.00**
• flip book with Iron Man back-up

10 ❑ Feb 1995 Cover: 1.95 **NM** value: **2.00**
• flip book with X-Men back-up

SPIDER-MAN MAGAZINE (2ND SERIES) — Marvel

1 ❑ Spr 1995 Cover: 2.50 **NM** value: **Cover or less**
No issue number.

SPIDER-MAN: MAXIMUM CARNAGE — Marvel

Bk 1❑ Aug 1994 Cover: 24.95 **NM** value: **Cover or less**
• collects Amazing Spider-Man #378-80, Spectacular Spider-Man #201-3, Spider-Man #35-7, Spider-Man Unlimited #1-2, Web of Spider-Man #101-103

SPIDER-MAN: MAXIMUM CLONAGE ALPHA — Marvel

1 ❑ Aug 1995 Cover: 4.95 **NM** value: **5.00**
Circ: CapCity orders: **42,775** • **CGC:** 10 graded, best 10.0
Acetate wraparound cover overlay. 📖 and the Jackal Cries, "Death" **A:** Ron Lim **W:** Tom DeFalco; Todd Dezago

SPIDER-MAN: MAXIMUM CLONAGE OMEGA — Marvel

1 ❑ Aug 1995 Cover: 4.95 **NM** value: **5.00**
• **CGC:** 8 graded, best 10.0
enhanced wraparound cover. ★ Death of The Jackal.

SPIDER-MAN MEGAZINE — Marvel

This 100-page (including covers) reprint title hit the stands in late 1994 and reprinted Spider-Man stories from various eras of his publishing history: classic Steve Ditko-illustrated stories from the 1960s; Spidey/Human Torch from the early 1970s and the early issues of Marvel Team-Up; and Spidey's early encounters with the beauteous Black Cat from the 1980s.

An excellent package of nostalgia, Spider-Man Megazine offered up important moments from the web-slinger's past for the enjoyment of fans, both new and old, for only $2.95 an issue. Unfortunately, low sales forced the cancellation of this and Marvel's other "megazines" after only six issues. Too bad, especially since inexpensive reprints of classic stories are hard to come by these days.

1 ❑ Oct 1994 Cover: 2.50 **NM** value: **Cover or less**
Circ: CapCity orders: **5,200**

2 ❑ Nov 1994 Cover: 2.95 **NM** value: **Cover or less**
Circ: CapCity orders: **3,250**
📖 But the Cat Came Back...; Goin' Straight!; And Spidey Makes Four!; The Return of the Green Goblin! **A:** Steve Ditko; John Romita Jr.; Ross Andru; Jim Mooney **W:** Roger Stern; Stan Lee; Gerry Conway

3 ❑ Dec 1994 Cover: 2.95 **NM** value: **Cover or less**
Circ: CapCity orders: **3,600**

4 ❑ Jan 1995 Cover: 2.95 **NM** value: **Cover or less**
Circ: CapCity orders: **3,000**

5 ❑ Feb 1995 Cover: 2.95 **NM** value: **Cover or less**
Circ: CapCity orders: **2,725**

6 ❑ Mar 1995 Cover: 2.95 **NM** value: **Cover or less**
Circ: CapCity orders: **2,400**
final issue.

SPIDER-MAN MYSTERIES — Marvel

1 ❑ Aug 1998 **NM** value: **1.00**
No issue number. no cover price. • prototype for children's comic

SPIDER-MAN: POWER OF TERROR — Marvel

1 ❑ Jan 1995 Cover: 1.95 **NM** value: **Cover or less**
Circ: CapCity orders: **17,375**
📖 Beneficial Alliances **A:** Darick Robertson **W:** Greg Wright

2 ❑ Feb 1995 Cover: 1.95 **NM** value: **Cover or less**
Circ: CapCity orders: **12,550**

3 ❑ Mar 1995 Cover: 1.95 **NM** value: **Cover or less**
Circ: CapCity orders: **11,625**

4 ❑ Apr 1995 Cover: 1.95 **NM** value: **Cover or less**
Circ: CapCity orders: **10,300**

SPIDER-MAN, POWER PACK — Marvel

1 ❑ Aug 1984 **NM** value: **1.00**
Circ: CapCity orders: **31,500**
no cover price. • Giveaway from the National Committee for Prevention of Child Abuse. 📖 Secrets • sexual abuse **A:** Jim Mooney **W:** Jim Salicrup

Other grades: Multiply prices above by **1.5 for Mint • 2/3 for Very Fine • 1/3 for Fine • 1/5 for Very Good • 1/8 for Good**

SPIDER-MAN/PUNISHER: FAMILY PLOT Marvel

1 ❑ Feb 1996 Cover: 2.95 **NM** value: **Cover or less**
📖 The Fall **A:** Dick Giordano; Shawn McManus; Mike Manley; Harris **W:** Tom Lyle

2 ❑ Feb 1996 Cover: 2.95 **NM** value: **Cover or less**
📖 Redemption **A:** Joe Bennett **W:** Tom Lyle

SPIDER-MAN, PUNISHER, SABRETOOTH: DESIGNER GENES Marvel

1 ❑ Cover: 8.95 **NM** value: **Cover or less**
• **CGC:** 1 graded, best 9.8
No issue number.

SPIDER-MAN: REDEMPTION Marvel

1 ❑ Sep 1996 Cover: 1.50 **NM** value: **Cover or less**
• no ads **A:** Mike Zeck **W:** J.M. DeMatteis

2 ❑ Oct 1996 Cover: 1.50 **NM** value: **Cover or less**
A: Mike Zeck **W:** J.M. DeMatteis

3 ❑ Nov 1996 Cover: 1.50 **NM** value: **Cover or less**
Circ: Direct Market orders: **55,500**
A: Mike Zeck **W:** J.M. DeMatteis

4 ❑ Dec 1996 Cover: 1.50 **NM** value: **Cover or less**
Circ: Direct Market orders: **53,500**
📖 Burning Bright **A:** Mike Zeck **W:** J.M. DeMatteis

SPIDER-MAN: REVENGE OF THE GREEN GOBLIN Marvel

1 ❑ Oct 2000 Cover: 2.99 **NM** value: **Cover or less**
Circ: Diamd. preorders: **32,576**
📖 Madness Takes Its Toll **A:** Ron Frenz **W:** Roger Stern

2 ❑ Nov 2000 Cover: 2.99 **NM** value: **Cover or less**
Circ: Diamd. preorders: **29,126**
📖 Lives in the Balance! **A:** Ron Frenz **W:** Roger Stern

3 ❑ Dec 2000 Cover: 2.99 **NM** value: **Cover or less**
Circ: Diamd. preorders: **28,950**
📖 Surrender to the Dark! • events lead in to Amazing Spider-Man #25 and Peter Parker, Spider-Man #25 **A:** Ron Frenz **W:** Roger Stern

SPIDER-MAN SAGA Marvel

1 ❑ Nov 1991 Cover: 2.95 **NM** value: **Cover or less**
Circ: CapCity orders: **32,400**
A: Steve Lightle(cover) **W:** Glenn Herdling

2 ❑ Dec 1991 Cover: 2.95 **NM** value: **Cover or less**
Circ: CapCity orders: **26,800**
W: Glenn Herdling

3 ❑ Jan 1992 Cover: 2.95 **NM** value: **Cover or less**
Circ: CapCity orders: **24,900**
A: Al Milgrom(cover) **W:** Glenn Herdling

4 ❑ Feb 1992 Cover: 2.95 **NM** value: **Cover or less**
Circ: CapCity orders: **23,900**
W: Glenn Herdling

SPIDER-MAN SPECIAL EDITION Marvel

1 ❑ Nov 1992 Cover: 1.25 **NM** value: **3.00**
• **CGC:** 18 graded, best 9.8
Embossed cover. • "The Trial of Venom" special edition to benefit Unicef. 📖 The Trial Of Venom **A:** Jim Craig **W:** Peter David ★ Appearance of Venom.

SPIDER-MAN: SPIRITS OF THE EARTH Marvel

1 ❑ Cover: 18.95 **NM** value: **Cover or less**
Circ: CapCity orders: **12,650**
hardcover.

SPIDER-MAN, STORM AND POWER MAN Marvel

1 ❑ Apr 1982 **NM** value: **2.00**
• **CGC:** 1 graded, best 8.0
No issue number. • Smokescreen giveaway.

SPIDER-MAN SUPER SPECIAL Marvel

1 ❑ Jul 1995 Cover: 3.95 **NM** value: **Cover or less**
• Flip-book. • two of the stories continue in Venom Super Special #1

SPIDER-MAN TEAM-UP Marvel

1 ❑ Dec 1995 Cover: 2.95 **NM** value: **3.00**
A: Ken Lashley **W:** Mark Waid ★ Appearance of X-Men, Cyclops, Archangel, Hellfire Club, Beast, Phoenix, Psylocke.

2 ❑ Mar 1996 Cover: 2.95 **NM** value: **3.00**
📖 Ambush **A:** Tom Grindberg **W:** George Pérez; Roger Stern ★ Appearance of Silver Surfer.

3 ❑ Jun 1996 Cover: 2.95 **NM** value: **3.00**
★ Appearance of Fantastic Four.

4 ❑ Sep 1996 Cover: 2.95 **NM** value: **3.00**
★ Appearance of Avengers.

5 ❑ Dec 1996 Cover: 2.99 **NM** value: **3.00**
Circ: Direct Market orders: **47,750**
★ Appearance of Howard the Duck, Gambit.

6 ❑ Mar 1997 Cover: 2.99 **NM** value: **3.00**
Circ: Direct Market orders: **38,500**
📖 Breaking And Entering; Lost Souls **A:** Tom Palmer; Bob McLeod; Dietrich Smith **W:** Larry Hama; J.M. DeMatteis; Marv Wolfman ★ Appearance of Dracula, Aquarian, Hulk, Doctor Strange.

7 ❑ Jun 1997 Cover: 2.99 **NM** value: **3.00**
Circ: Diamd. preorders: **39,228**
📖 Old Scores **A:** Sal Buscema; Dick Giordano **W:** Kurt Busiek ★ Appearance of Thunderbolts.

SPIDER-MAN: THE ARACHNIS PROJECT Marvel

1 ❑ Aug 1994 Cover: 1.75 **NM** value: **2.00**
Circ: CapCity orders: **26,400**

2 ❑ Sep 1994 Cover: 1.75 **NM** value: **2.00**
Circ: CapCity orders: **19,850**

3 ❑ Oct 1994 Cover: 1.75 **NM** value: **2.00**
Circ: CapCity orders: **17,500**

4 ❑ Nov 1994 Cover: 1.75 **NM** value: **2.00**
Circ: CapCity orders: **15,000**

5 ❑ Dec 1994 Cover: 1.75 **NM** value: **2.00**
Circ: CapCity orders: **13,850**

6 ❑ Jan 1995 Cover: 1.75 **NM** value: **2.00**
Circ: CapCity orders: **12,550**

SPIDER-MAN: THE CLONE JOURNAL Marvel

1 ❑ Mar 1995 Cover: 2.95 **NM** value: **3.00**
Circ: CapCity orders: **11,850**
One-shot. 📖 Puppet **A:** Mark Bagley; Sal Buscema; Steven Butler; Mike Manley; Phil Gosier; Tom Lyle **W:** Howard Mackie; Terry Kavanagh; Tom DeFalco; J.M. DeMatteis; Todd Dezago ★ Origin of Ben Reilly.

SPIDER-MAN: THE COSMIC ADVENTURES Marvel

Bk 1❑ Cover: 19.95 **NM** value: **Cover or less**

SPIDER-MAN: THE DEATH OF CAPTAIN STACY Marvel

1 ❑ Aug 2000 Cover: 3.50 **NM** value: **Cover or less**
Circ: Diamd. preorders: **9,954**
📖 The Arms of Doctor Octopus!; Doc Ock Lives!; And Death Shall Come!; And Death Sall Come! • Reprints Amazing Spider-Man #88-90 **A:** Gil Kane; John Romita **W:** Stan Lee ★ Death of Captain Stacy.

SPIDER-MAN: THE FINAL ADVENTURE Marvel

1 ❑ Dec 1995 Cover: 2.95 **NM** value: **3.00**
enhanced cardstock cover. 📖 Destiny's Web • clone returns to action one last time **A:** Darick Robertson **W:** Fabian Nicieza

2 ❑ Jan 1996 Cover: 2.95 **NM** value: **3.00**
enhanced cardstock cover. **A:** Darick Robertson **W:** Fabian Nicieza

3 ❑ Feb 1996 Cover: 2.95 **NM** value: **3.00**
enhanced cardstock cover. 📖 Skin Deep **A:** Darick Robertson **W:** Fabian Nicieza

4 ❑ Mar 1996 Cover: 2.95 **NM** value: **3.00**
enhanced cardstock cover. 📖 To End The Begin • Peter loses his powers **A:** Darick Robertson **W:** Fabian Nicieza

SPIDER-MAN: THE JACKAL FILES Marvel

The Spider-Man clone storyline of the mid-1990s was one of the most polarizing and controversial plot devices in the web slinger's long history. It occurred to the editors of the Spider-Man group that a Who's Who of key characters was in order, since it was nealy impossible to keep it all straight. Thus was born The Jackal Files. This one-shot offers numerous one-page biographies of the cast of Spidey characters up to that point, including Scarlet Spider, Kaine, Gwen Stacy, Mary Jane Watson, and most of the popular villains, including Venom and Carnage. The information is relayed as data being downloaded into the brain of yet another Peter Parker clone produced by the evil scientist Jackal.

If nothing else, the book features some nifty art by the likes of George Perez (New Teen Titans, Avengers), Mark Buckingham (Miracleman), and Michael Bair (Vampirella).

1 ❑ Aug 1995 Cover: 1.95 **NM** value: **Cover or less**
Circ: CapCity orders: **22,525**
One-shot. • files on main Spider-Man characters and equipment **A:** Roger Robinson; Guy Dorian; Michael Bair; Pat Olliffe; Liam Sharp; Mark Buckingham; George Pérez; Patrick Zircher; Jordan Raskin; Dan Lawlis; Joe St. Pierre **W:** Todd Dezago

SPIDER-MAN: THE LOST YEARS Marvel

0 ❑ Jan 1996 Cover: 3.95 **NM** value: **Cover or less**
📖 The Double; The Parker Legacy • collects clone origin back-up stories; Collects prologue chapters to series **A:** Liam Sharp; John Romita Jr. **W:** J.M. DeMatteis

1 ❑ Aug 1995 Cover: 2.95 **NM** value: **3.00**
Circ: CapCity orders: **28,950**
enhanced cardstock cover. **A:** John Romita Jr. **W:** J.M. DeMatteis

2 ❑ Sep 1995 Cover: 2.95 **NM** value: **3.00**
enhanced cardstock cover. 📖 Intimacies **A:** John Romita Jr. **W:** J.M. DeMatteis

3 ❑ Oct 1995 Cover: 2.95 **NM** value: **3.00**
enhanced cardstock cover. **A:** John Romita Jr. **W:** J.M. DeMatteis

SPIDER-MAN: THE MANGA Marvel

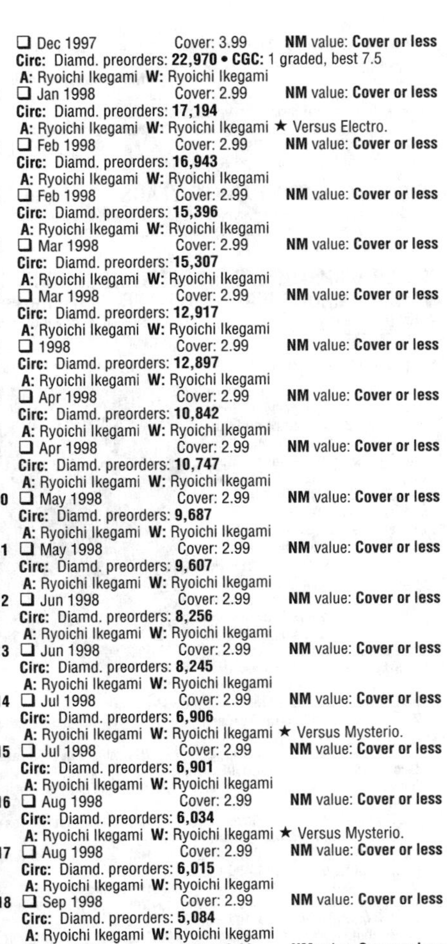

In order to appeal to the Japanese market, Marvel commissioned manga favorite Ryoichi Ikegami to adapt Spider-Man to Japanese tastes. The result was a black-and-white series in traditional manga style where Peter Parker and the rest of the gang look like Japanese schoolkids, and Aunt May looks as if she could be running the local Japanese restaurant. The setting has been moved from America to Tokyo. 5All in all, it was a credible attempt by Marvel to capitalize on the popularity of its characters while moving them into the most comics-literate culture on Earth.

The strange part came in 1997 when Marvel imported the Japanese version into America as Spider-Man: The Manga. While an interesting idea, this, and Marvel's X-Men manga import, turned out to be two of its worst-selling titles in the States ever.

1 ❑ Dec 1997 Cover: 3.99 **NM** value: **Cover or less**
Circ: Diamd. preorders: **22,970** • **CGC:** 1 graded, best 7.5
A: Ryoichi Ikegami **W:** Ryoichi Ikegami

2 ❑ Jan 1998 Cover: 2.99 **NM** value: **Cover or less**
Circ: Diamd. preorders: **17,194**
A: Ryoichi Ikegami **W:** Ryoichi Ikegami ★ Versus Electro.

3 ❑ Feb 1998 Cover: 2.99 **NM** value: **Cover or less**
Circ: Diamd. preorders: **16,943**
A: Ryoichi Ikegami **W:** Ryoichi Ikegami

4 ❑ Feb 1998 Cover: 2.99 **NM** value: **Cover or less**
Circ: Diamd. preorders: **15,396**
A: Ryoichi Ikegami **W:** Ryoichi Ikegami

5 ❑ Mar 1998 Cover: 2.99 **NM** value: **Cover or less**
Circ: Diamd. preorders: **15,307**
A: Ryoichi Ikegami **W:** Ryoichi Ikegami

6 ❑ Mar 1998 Cover: 2.99 **NM** value: **Cover or less**
Circ: Diamd. preorders: **12,917**
A: Ryoichi Ikegami **W:** Ryoichi Ikegami

7 ❑ 1998 Cover: 2.99 **NM** value: **Cover or less**
Circ: Diamd. preorders: **12,897**
A: Ryoichi Ikegami **W:** Ryoichi Ikegami

8 ❑ Apr 1998 Cover: 2.99 **NM** value: **Cover or less**
Circ: Diamd. preorders: **10,842**
A: Ryoichi Ikegami **W:** Ryoichi Ikegami

9 ❑ Apr 1998 Cover: 2.99 **NM** value: **Cover or less**
Circ: Diamd. preorders: **10,747**
A: Ryoichi Ikegami **W:** Ryoichi Ikegami

10 ❑ May 1998 Cover: 2.99 **NM** value: **Cover or less**
Circ: Diamd. preorders: **9,687**
A: Ryoichi Ikegami **W:** Ryoichi Ikegami

11 ❑ May 1998 Cover: 2.99 **NM** value: **Cover or less**
Circ: Diamd. preorders: **9,607**
A: Ryoichi Ikegami **W:** Ryoichi Ikegami

12 ❑ Jun 1998 Cover: 2.99 **NM** value: **Cover or less**
Circ: Diamd. preorders: **8,256**
A: Ryoichi Ikegami **W:** Ryoichi Ikegami

13 ❑ Jun 1998 Cover: 2.99 **NM** value: **Cover or less**
Circ: Diamd. preorders: **8,245**
A: Ryoichi Ikegami **W:** Ryoichi Ikegami

14 ❑ Jul 1998 Cover: 2.99 **NM** value: **Cover or less**
Circ: Diamd. preorders: **6,906**
A: Ryoichi Ikegami **W:** Ryoichi Ikegami ★ Versus Mysterio.

15 ❑ Jul 1998 Cover: 2.99 **NM** value: **Cover or less**
Circ: Diamd. preorders: **6,901**
A: Ryoichi Ikegami **W:** Ryoichi Ikegami

16 ❑ Aug 1998 Cover: 2.99 **NM** value: **Cover or less**
Circ: Diamd. preorders: **6,034**
A: Ryoichi Ikegami **W:** Ryoichi Ikegami ★ Versus Mysterio.

17 ❑ Aug 1998 Cover: 2.99 **NM** value: **Cover or less**
Circ: Diamd. preorders: **6,015**
A: Ryoichi Ikegami **W:** Ryoichi Ikegami

18 ❑ Sep 1998 Cover: 2.99 **NM** value: **Cover or less**
Circ: Diamd. preorders: **5,084**
A: Ryoichi Ikegami **W:** Ryoichi Ikegami

19 ❑ Sep 1998 Cover: 2.99 **NM** value: **Cover or less**
Circ: Diamd. preorders: **5,155**
A: Ryoichi Ikegami **W:** Ryoichi Ikegami

20 ❑ Oct 1998 Cover: 2.99 **NM** value: **Cover or less**
Circ: Diamd. preorders: **4,368**
A: Ryoichi Ikegami **W:** Ryoichi Ikegami

21 ❑ Oct 1998 Cover: 2.99 **NM** value: **Cover or less**
Circ: Diamd. preorders: **4,345**
A: Ryoichi Ikegami **W:** Ryoichi Ikegami

22 ❑ ca. 1998 Cover: 2.99 **NM** value: **Cover or less**
Circ: Diamd. preorders: **3,822**
A: Ryoichi Ikegami **W:** Ryoichi Ikegami

23 ❑ ca. 1998 Cover: 2.99 **NM** value: **Cover or less**
Circ: Diamd. preorders: **3,818**
A: Ryoichi Ikegami **W:** Ryoichi Ikegami

24 ❑ ca. 1998 Cover: 2.99 **NM** value: **Cover or less**
Circ: Diamd. preorders: **3,744**
A: Ryoichi Ikegami **W:** Ryoichi Ikegami

25 ❑ ca. 1998 Cover: 2.99 **NM** value: **Cover or less**
Circ: Diamd. preorders: **3,598**
A: Ryoichi Ikegami **W:** Ryoichi Ikegami

26 ❑ ca. 1999 Cover: 2.99 **NM** value: **Cover or less**
Circ: Diamd. preorders: **3,330**
A: Ryoichi Ikegami **W:** Ryoichi Ikegami ★ Appearance of Mitsuo Kitano.

27 ❑ ca. 1999 Cover: 2.99 **NM** value: **Cover or less**
Circ: Diamd. preorders: **3,417**
A: Ryoichi Ikegami **W:** Ryoichi Ikegami ★ Appearance of Mitsuo Kitano.

28 ❑ ca. 1999 Cover: 2.99 **NM** value: **Cover or less**
Circ: Diamd. preorders: **3,521**
A: Ryoichi Ikegami **W:** Ryoichi Ikegami ★ Appearance of Mitsuo Kitano.

29 ❑ ca. 1999 Cover: 2.99 **NM** value: **Cover or less**
Circ: Diamd. preorders: **3,483**
A: Ryoichi Ikegami **W:** Ryoichi Ikegami ★ Appearance of Mitsuo Kitano.

30 ❑ ca. 1999 Cover: 2.99 **NM** value: **Cover or less**
Circ: Diamd. preorders: **2,895**
A: Ryoichi Ikegami **W:** Ryoichi Ikegami ★ Appearance of Mitsuo Kitano.

31 ❑ ca. 1999 Cover: 2.99 **NM** value: **Cover or less**
Circ: Diamd. preorders: **2,776**
A: Ryoichi Ikegami **W:** Ryoichi Ikegami

SPIDER-MAN: THE MUTANT AGENDA Marvel

0 ❑ Mar 1994 Cover: 1.25 **NM** value: **Cover or less**
Circ: CapCity orders: **35,900**
cover says Feb, indicia says Mar. • strip reprints; Spaces to paste in newspaper strip ★ Origin of Spider-Man. ★ Appearance of Beast. ★ Versus Hobgoblin.

1 ❑ Mar 1994 Cover: 1.75 **NM** value: **Cover or less**
Circ: CapCity orders: **32,350**

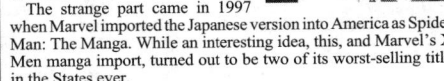

CGC-graded: Multiply prices above by **33 for 9.9 M** • **16 for 9.8 NM/M** • **7 for 9.6 NM+** • **5 for 9.4 NM** • **2.5 for 9.2 NM-** • **1.5 for 9.0 VF/NM**

• Ties in with daily Spider-Man newspaper strip ★ Appearance of Beast. ★ Versus Hobgoblin.

2 ❑ Apr 1994 Cover: 1.75 **NM** value: **Cover or less**
Circ: CapCity orders: **19,700**
★ Appearance of Beast. ★ Versus Hobgoblin.

3 ❑ May 1994 Cover: 1.75 **NM** value: **Cover or less**
Circ: CapCity orders: **17,150**
★ Appearance of Beast. ★ Versus Hobgoblin.

SPIDER-MAN: THE PARKER YEARS Marvel

1 ❑ Nov 1995 Cover: 2.50 **NM** value: **Cover or less**
One-shot. • retells events in the clone's life from Amazing Spider-Man #150 to the present

SPIDER-MAN: THE SECRET STORY OF MARVEL'S WORLD-FAMOUS WALL-CRAWLER Marvel

Bk 1❑ Dec 1981 Cover: 2.95 **NM** value: **Cover or less**
• (Ideals)

SPIDER-MAN 2099 Marvel

Marvel introduced its vision of the future with Spider-Man 2099. Ravage 2099, Doom 2099, and Punisher 2099 soon followed, needlessly adding one more offshoot line of comics to a Marvel already stretched creatively thin during the glut of the early 1990s.

In the 2099 future, the population is controlled by drug abuse and police-state tactics, with the strings being pulled by powerful corporations. One of those corporations, Alchemax, employs Miguel O'Hara to create a sort of super-human "corporate raider," modelled after the 20th century's Spider-Man. O'Hara rebelled, however, and in doing so, was transformed into a spider-like creature, Spider-Man 2099.

Written by Peter David, Spider-Man 2099 was the best of the line — but still not really necessary.

1 ❑ Nov 1992 Cover: 1.75 **NM** value: **Cover or less**
Circ: CapCity orders: **300,000**
foil cover. **A:** Rick Leonardi **W:** Peter David ★ Origin of Spider-Man 2099. ★ 1st Appearance of Tyler Stone.

1/Aut❑Nov 1992 Cover: 1.75 **NM** value: **Cover or less**
foil cover. • with certificate of authenticity

2 ❑ Dec 1992 Cover: 1.25 **NM** value: **Cover or less**
Circ: CapCity orders: **134,400**
A: Rick Leonardi **W:** Peter David ★ Origin of Spider-Man 2099.

3 ❑ Jan 1993 Cover: 1.25 **NM** value: **Cover or less**
Circ: CapCity orders: **119,100**
📖 Nothing Gained **A:** Rick Leonardi **W:** Peter David ★ Origin of Spider-Man 2099.

4 ❑ Feb 1993 Cover: 1.25 **NM** value: **Cover or less**
Circ: CapCity orders: **108,300**
📖 The Specialist **A:** Rick Leonardi **W:** Peter David ★ 1st Appearance of The Specialist.

5 ❑ Mar 1993 Cover: 1.25 **NM** value: **Cover or less**
Circ: CapCity orders: **93,900**
A: Rick Leonardi **W:** Peter David

6 ❑ Apr 1993 Cover: 1.25 **NM** value: **Cover or less**
Circ: CapCity orders: **91,500**
A: Rick Leonardi **W:** Peter David ★ 1st Appearance of Vulture 2099.

7 ❑ May 1993 Cover: 1.25 **NM** value: **Cover or less**
Circ: CapCity orders: **86,600**
📖 Wing And A Prayer **A:** Rick Leonardi **W:** Peter David

8 ❑ Jun 1993 Cover: 1.25 **NM** value: **Cover or less**
Circ: CapCity orders: **84,200**
A: Rick Leonardi **W:** Peter David

9 ❑ Jul 1993 Cover: 1.25 **NM** value: **Cover or less**
Circ: CapCity orders: **78,600**
A: Rick Leonardi **W:** Peter David

10 ❑ Aug 1993 Cover: 1.25 **NM** value: **Cover or less**
Circ: CapCity orders: **73,400**
A: Rick Leonardi **W:** Peter David

11 ❑ Sep 1993 Cover: 1.25 **NM** value: **Cover or less**
Circ: CapCity orders: **64,700**
A: Rick Leonardi **W:** Peter David

12 ❑ Oct 1993 Cover: 1.25 **NM** value: **Cover or less**
Circ: CapCity orders: **59,000**
A: Rick Leonardi **W:** Peter David

13 ❑ Nov 1993 Cover: 1.25 **NM** value: **Cover or less**
Circ: CapCity orders: **57,800**
W: Peter David

14 ❑ Dec 1993 Cover: 1.25 **NM** value: **Cover or less**
Circ: CapCity orders: **53,000**
W: Peter David

15 ❑ Jan 1994 Cover: 1.25 **NM** value: **Cover or less**
Circ: Statement: **221,317** CapCity orders: **48,200**
W: Peter David

16 ❑ Feb 1994 Cover: 1.25 **NM** value: **Cover or less**
Circ: Statement: **221,317** CapCity orders: **56,100**
📖 Fall of the Hammer, Part 1 **W:** Peter David

17 ❑ Mar 1994 Cover: 1.25 **NM** value: **Cover or less**
Circ: Statement: **221,317** CapCity orders: **42,250**
W: Peter David

18 ❑ Apr 1994 Cover: 1.25 **NM** value: **Cover or less**
Circ: Statement: **221,317** CapCity orders: **39,750**
W: Peter David

19 ❑ May 1994 Cover: 1.50 **NM** value: **Cover or less**
Circ: Statement: **221,317** CapCity orders: **38,850**
W: Peter David

20 ❑ Jun 1994 Cover: 1.50 **NM** value: **Cover or less**
Circ: Statement: **221,317** CapCity orders: **37,450**
W: Peter David

21 ❑ Jul 1994 Cover: 1.50 **NM** value: **Cover or less**
Circ: Statement: **221,317** CapCity orders: **35,900**
W: Peter David

22 ❑ Aug 1994 Cover: 1.50 **NM** value: **Cover or less**
Circ: Statement: **221,317** CapCity orders: **33,200**
W: Peter David

23 ❑ Sep 1994 Cover: 1.50 **NM** value: **Cover or less**
Circ: Statement: **221,317** CapCity orders: **31,450**
W: Peter David

24 ❑ Oct 1994 Cover: 1.50 **NM** value: **Cover or less**
Circ: Statement: **221,317** CapCity orders: **29,400**
W: Peter David

25 ❑ Nov 1994 Cover: 2.25 **NM** value: **Cover or less**
• Giant-size. **W:** Peter David

25/SC❑Nov 1994 Cover: 2.95 **NM** value: **Cover or less**
Circ: Statement: **221,317** CapCity orders: **27,500**
enhanced cover. • Giant-size. **W:** Peter David

26 ❑ Dec 1994 Cover: 1.50 **NM** value: **Cover or less**
Circ: Statement: **221,317** CapCity orders: **26,950**
W: Peter David

27 ❑ Jan 1995 Cover: 1.50 **NM** value: **Cover or less**
Circ: Statement: **97,998** CapCity orders: **25,150**
W: Peter David

28 ❑ Feb 1995 Cover: 1.50 **NM** value: **Cover or less**
Circ: Statement: **97,998** CapCity orders: **23,850**
W: Peter David

29 ❑ Mar 1995 Cover: 1.50 **NM** value: **Cover or less**
Circ: Statement: **97,998** CapCity orders: **21,675**
• Has 1994 Statement, filed 10/1/94; avg print run 381,067; avg sales 214,692; avg subs 6,625; avg total paid 221,317; samples 125; office use 500; max existent 221,942; 42% of run returned **W:** Peter David

30 ❑ Apr 1995 Cover: 1.50 **NM** value: **Cover or less**
Circ: Statement: **97,998** CapCity orders: **20,450**
W: Peter David

31 ❑ May 1995 Cover: 1.50 **NM** value: **Cover or less**
Circ: Statement: **97,998** CapCity orders: **20,575**
W: Peter David

32 ❑ Jun 1995 Cover: 1.50 **NM** value: **1.95**
Circ: Statement: **97,998** CapCity orders: **20,025**
W: Peter David

33 ❑ Jul 1995 Cover: 1.95 **NM** value: **Cover or less**
Circ: Statement: **97,998** CapCity orders: **19,275**
W: Peter David ★ Appearance of Strange 2099.

34 ❑ Aug 1995 Cover: 1.95 **NM** value: **Cover or less**
Circ: Statement: **97,998** CapCity orders: **18,400**
W: Peter David

35 ❑ Sep 1995 Cover: 1.95 **NM** value: **Cover or less**
W: Peter David

35/SC❑Sep 1995 Cover: 1.95 **NM** value: **Cover or less**
Circ: Statement: **97,998**
alternate cover. **W:** Peter David

36 ❑ Oct 1995 Cover: 1.95 **NM** value: **Cover or less**
Spiderman 2099 on cover. **W:** Peter David

36/SC❑Oct 1995 Cover: 1.95 **NM** value: **Cover or less**
alternate cover. • says Venom 2099; forms diptych **W:** Peter David

37 ❑ Nov 1995 Cover: 1.95 **NM** value: **Cover or less**
W: Peter David

37/SC❑Nov 1995 Cover: 1.95 **NM** value: **Cover or less**
alternate cover. • says Venom 2099

38 ❑ Dec 1995 Cover: 1.95 **NM** value: **Cover or less**
Spiderman 2099 on cover. **A:** Andrew Wildman **W:** Peter David

38/SC❑Dec 1995 Cover: 1.95 **NM** value: **Cover or less**
alternate cover. • says Venom 2099; forms diptych **A:** Andrew Wildman **W:** Peter David

39 ❑ Jan 1996 Cover: 1.95 **NM** value: **Cover or less**
• Has 1995 Statement, filed 10/1/95; avg print run 175,740; avg sales 95,923; avg subs 275; avg total paid 97,998; samples 750; office use 500; max existent 97,448; 44% of run returned **W:** Peter David

40 ❑ Feb 1996 Cover: 1.95 **NM** value: **Cover or less**
W: Peter David ★ Versus Goblin 2099.

41 ❑ Mar 1996 Cover: 1.95 **NM** value: **Cover or less**
W: Peter David

42 ❑ Apr 1996 Cover: 1.95 **NM** value: **Cover or less**
📖 Earth **A:** Andrew Wildman; Bill Sienkiewicz(inks) **W:** Peter David

43 ❑ May 1996 Cover: 1.95 **NM** value: **Cover or less**
📖 Water **A:** Andrew Wildman; Ron Lim **W:** Peter David

44 ❑ Jun 1996 Cover: 1.95 **NM** value: **Cover or less**

45 ❑ Jul 1996 Cover: 1.95 **NM** value: **Cover or less**
★ Versus Goblin 2099.

46 ❑ Aug 1996 Cover: 1.95 **NM** value: **Cover or less**
final issue. • story continues in Fantastic Four 2099 #8 ★ Versus Vulture 2099.

Anl 1❑ca. 1994 Cover: 2.95 **NM** value: **Cover or less**
Circ: CapCity orders: **23,500**
• 1994 Annual

SE 1❑Nov 1995 Cover: 3.95 **NM** value: **Cover or less**

SPIDER-MAN 2099 MEETS SPIDER-MAN Marvel

1 ❑ Nov 1995 Cover: 5.95 **NM** value: **Cover or less**
No issue number. **A:** Rick Leonardi **W:** Peter David

SPIDER-MAN UNIVERSE Marvel

1 ❑ Mar 2000 Cover: 4.99 **NM** value: **Cover or less**
Circ: Diamd. preorders: **4,427**
📖 Living in Oblivion; The Time Before; War & Pieces • Reprints Peter Parker: Spider-Man #13, Webspinners #13, Spider-Woman (2nd Series) #8 **A:** Graham Nolan; Lee Weeks **W:** John Byrne; Howard Mackie ★ Death of Mary Jane (revealed).

SPIDER-MAN UNLIMITED Marvel

1 ❑ May 1993 Cover: 3.95 **NM** value: **5.00**
Circ: CapCity orders: **186,900** • **CGC:** 9 graded, best 9.9
📖 Maximum Carnage, Part 1 **A:** Ron Lim **W:** Tom DeFalco ★ Appearance of Carnage, Venom.

2 ❑ Aug 1993 Cover: 3.95 **NM** value: **4.50**
Circ: CapCity orders: **118,300**
📖 Maximum Carnage; Maximum Carnage, Part 14 **W:** Kurt Busiek ★ Appearance of Carnage, Venom.

3 ❑ Nov 1993 Cover: 3.95 **NM** value: **4.50**
Circ: CapCity orders: **52,500**
• Doctor Octopus **W:** Kurt Busiek

4 ❑ Feb 1994 Cover: 3.95 **NM** value: **4.50**
Circ: CapCity orders: **48,350**
📖 The Man Who Would be Spider-Man!; Still Living in Fear • Mysterio **A:** Kevin West; Ron Lim **W:** Kurt Busiek; Tom DeFalco

5 ❑ May 1994 Cover: 3.95 **NM** value: **4.50**
Circ: CapCity orders: **26,950**
• Human Torch **W:** Kurt Busiek

6 ❑ Aug 1994 Cover: 3.95 **NM** value: **4.00**
Circ: CapCity orders: **23,450**

7 ❑ Nov 1994 Cover: 3.95 **NM** value: **4.00**
Circ: CapCity orders: **20,800**
• Spider-Man and clone

8 ❑ Feb 1995 Cover: 3.95 **NM** value: **4.00**
Circ: CapCity orders: **18,350**
• Spider-Man and clone

9 ❑ May 1995 Cover: 3.95 **NM** value: **4.00**
Circ: CapCity orders: **22,600**
📖 Mark of Kaine, Part 5

10 ❑ Sep 1995 Cover: 3.95 **NM** value: **4.00**
📖 Exiled, Part 4 ★ Versus Vulture.

11 ❑ Jan 1996 Cover: 3.95 **NM** value: **4.00**
📖 The Skull Jackets; Night Work **A:** Sal Buscema; Dave Hoover **W:** Fabian Nicieza; Adam Santangelo ★ 1st Appearance of Skull Jacket. ★ Appearance of Black Cat.

12 ❑ May 1996 Cover: 3.95 **NM** value: **4.00**
★ Versus Shocker. ★ Versus Boomerang. ★ Versus Jack O'Lantern. ★ Versus Beetle. ★ Versus Scorpia.

13 ❑ Aug 1996 Cover: 3.95 **NM** value: **Cover or less**
★ Appearance of Luke Cage, Iron Fist. ★ Versus Scorpion.

14 ❑ Dec 1996 Cover: 2.99 **NM** value: **Cover or less**
Circ: Direct Market orders: **53,500**
📖 Game's End **A:** Joe Bennett **W:** Glenn Herdling ★ Death of Polestar. ★ Death of Nightwatch.

15 ❑ Feb 1997 Cover: 2.99 **NM** value: **Cover or less**
Circ: Direct Market orders: **49,500**
📖 Facing the Void **A:** Joe Bennett **W:** Tom DeFalco ★ Versus Puma.

16 ❑ May 1997 Cover: 2.99 **NM** value: **Cover or less**
Circ: Diamd. preorders: **47,299**
📖 The Wages of Conquest **A:** Joe Bennett **W:** Mark Bernardo ★ Appearance of Silver Sable.

17 ❑ Aug 1997 Cover: 2.99 **NM** value: **Cover or less**
Circ: Diamd. preorders: **43,478**
• gatefold summary. ★ Versus Robot Master.

18 ❑ Nov 1997 Cover: 2.99 **NM** value: **Cover or less**
Circ: Diamd. preorders: **39,882**
• gatefold summary. ★ Origin of Doctor Octopus.

19 ❑ Feb 1998 Cover: 2.99 **NM** value: **Cover or less**
Circ: Diamd. preorders: **37,704**
• gatefold summary. ★ Versus Lizard.

20 ❑ May 1998 Cover: 2.99 **NM** value: **Cover or less**
Circ: Diamd. preorders: **36,213**
• gatefold summary. ★ Appearance of Hannibal King.

21 ❑ Aug 1998 Cover: 2.99 **NM** value: **Cover or less**
Circ: Diamd. preorders: **35,001**
• gatefold summary. ★ Appearance of Frankenstein's Monster.

22 ❑ Nov 1998 Cover: 2.99 **NM** value: **Cover or less**
Circ: Diamd. preorders: **32,283**
• gatefold summary. final issue. ★ Versus Scorpion.

SPIDER-MAN UNLIMITED (2ND SERIES) Marvel

1 ❑ Dec 1999 Cover: 2.99 **NM** value: **Cover or less**
Circ: Diamd. preorders: **26,906**
📖 Worlds Apart • based on animated television show **A:** Andy Kuhn **W:** Eric Stephenson

SPIDER-MAN UNMASKED Marvel

1 ❑ Nov 1996 Cover: 5.95 **NM** value: **Cover or less**
Circ: Direct Market orders: **25,750**
No issue number.

SPIDER-MAN: VENOM AGENDA Marvel

1 ❑ Jan 1998 Cover: 2.99 **NM** value: **Cover or less**
Circ: Diamd. preorders: **39,269**
One-shot. • gatefold summary.

SPIDER-MAN: VENOM RETURNS Marvel

Bk 1❑ Cover: 12.95 **NM** value: **Cover or less**

SPIDER-MAN VS. DRACULA Marvel

1 ❑ Cover: 1.75 **NM** value: **2.00**
Circ: CapCity orders: **17,450** • **CGC:** 1 graded, best 9.4
📖 Ship Of Fiends! **A:** Ross Andru **W:** Len Wein

SPIDER-MAN VS. PUNISHER Marvel

1 ❑ Jul 2000 Cover: 2.99 **NM** value: **Cover or less**
Circ: Diamd. preorders: **24,618**
📖 No One Here Gets Out Alive **A:** Michael Lopez **W:** Joseph Harris

SPIDER-MAN VS. THE HULK Marvel

1 ❑ ca. 1979 **NM** value: **1.00**
No issue number. • giveaway.

SPIDER-MAN VS. WOLVERINE Marvel

1 ❑ Feb 1987 Cover: 2.50 **NM** value: **Cover or less**
Circ: CapCity orders: **41,600** • **CGC:** 77 graded, best 9.9
★ Death of Ned Leeds.

1-2 ❑ Aug 1990 Cover: 4.95 **NM** value: **Cover or less**
Circ: CapCity orders: **5,750**
cardstock cover. ★ Death of Ned Leeds.

SPIDER-MAN: WEB OF DOOM Marvel

1 ❑ Aug 1994 Cover: 1.75 **NM** value: **2.00**

Other grades: Multiply prices above by **1.5 for Mint • 2/3 for Very Fine • 1/3 for Fine • 1/5 for Very Good • 1/8 for Good**

Circ: CapCity orders: **27,800**
A: Scott Kolins W: Jack Harris

2 ❑ Sep 1994 Cover: 1.75 **NM** value: **2.00**
Circ: CapCity orders: **20,950**

3 ❑ Oct 1994 Cover: 1.75 **NM** value: **2.00**
Circ: CapCity orders: **18,550**

SPIDER, THE: REIGN OF THE VAMPIRE KING — Eclipse

1 ❑ ca. 1992 Cover: 4.95 **NM** value: **Cover or less**
Circ: CapCity orders: **6,200**
A: Enrique Alcatena W: Tim Truman

2 ❑ ca. 1992 Cover: 5.95 **NM** value: **Cover or less**
Circ: CapCity orders: **4,750**
A: Enrique Alcatena W: Tim Truman

3 ❑ ca. 1992 Cover: 5.95 **NM** value: **Cover or less**
Circ: CapCity orders: **4,425**
A: Enrique Alcatena W: Tim Truman

SPIDER'S WEB, THE — Blazing

1 ❑ Cover: 1.50 **NM** value: **Cover or less**
• Flip-book. 📖 Web-Man in The Web of Time; G-8 and His Battle Aces A: Sam Glanzman W: Chuck Dixon

SPIDER-WOMAN — Marvel

Jessica Drew's father was a visionary scientist who dreamed of someday combining the adaptive abilities of the spider with human genes. His theory was put to the test when he placed his daughter, who was dying of radiation poisoning, n his Genetic Accelerator.

Years later, Jessica found she had incredible strength, could stick to walls, and was able to generate "venom bolts" from her own bio-system. These powers caused others to fear her, and she escaped their wrath only when she was recruited into Hydra. She soon learned the true nature of Hydra, however, and turned against them — becoming a super-hero.

Spider-Woman's creation was perceived by many as an attempt by Marvel to protect its trademark options, and her frequently dark series never really caught on. A plot device in the series' final issue made it so everyone in the Marvel universe would forget she had ever existed — whic, sadly, wasn't that hard.

1 ❑ Apr 1978 Cover: 0.35 **NM** value: **4.00**
• **CGC:** 77 graded, best 9.8
📖 ...A Future Uncertain! A: Carmine Infantino W: Marv Wolfman ★ Origin of Spider-Woman I (Jessica Drew).

2 ❑ May 1978 Cover: 0.35 **NM** value: **3.00**
• **CGC:** 1 graded, best 9.6
★ 1st Appearance of Morgan LeFay.

3 ❑ Jun 1978 Cover: 0.35 **NM** value: **2.50**
• **CGC:** 2 graded, best 9.4
★ 1st Appearance of Brothers Grimm.

4 ❑ Jul 1978 Cover: 0.35 **NM** value: **2.00**
• **CGC:** 1 graded, best 9.6

5 ❑ Aug 1978 Cover: 0.35 **NM** value: **2.00**
• **CGC:** 1 graded, best 9.6

6 ❑ Sep 1978 Cover: 0.35 **NM** value: **1.75**
• **CGC:** 1 graded, best 9.6

7 ❑ Oct 1978 Cover: 0.35 **NM** value: **1.75**

8 ❑ Nov 1978 Cover: 0.35 **NM** value: **1.75**

9 ❑ Dec 1978 Cover: 0.35 **NM** value: **1.75**
★ Origin of Needle. ★ 1st Appearance of Needle.

10 ❑ Jan 1979 Cover: 0.35 **NM** value: **1.75**
Circ: Statement: **126,875** • **CGC:** 1 graded, best 9.8

11 ❑ Feb 1979 Cover: 0.35 **NM** value: **1.50**
Circ: Statement: **126,875**

12 ❑ Mar 1979 Cover: 0.35 **NM** value: **1.50**
Circ: Statement: **126,875**
★ Death of Brothers Grimm.

13 ❑ Apr 1979 Cover: 0.35 **NM** value: **1.50**
Circ: Statement: **126,875**

14 ❑ May 1979 Cover: 0.40 **NM** value: **1.50**
Circ: Statement: **126,875**

15 ❑ Jun 1979 Cover: 0.40 **NM** value: **1.50**
Circ: Statement: **126,875**

16 ❑ Jul 1979 Cover: 0.40 **NM** value: **1.50**
Circ: Statement: **126,875**

17 ❑ Aug 1979 Cover: 0.40 **NM** value: **1.50**
Circ: Statement: **126,875**

18 ❑ Sep 1979 Cover: 0.40 **NM** value: **1.50**
Circ: Statement: **126,875**

19 ❑ Oct 1979 Cover: 0.40 **NM** value: **1.50**
Circ: Statement: **126,875**
★ Versus Werewolf.

20 ❑ Nov 1979 Cover: 0.40 **NM** value: **1.50**
Circ: Statement: **126,875** • **CGC:** 1 graded, best 9.4
★ Appearance of Spider-Man.

21 ❑ Dec 1979 Cover: 0.40 **NM** value: **1.50**
Circ: Statement: **126,875**

22 ❑ Jan 1980 Cover: 0.40 **NM** value: **1.50**
Circ: Statement: **128,006**

23 ❑ Feb 1980 Cover: 0.40 **NM** value: **1.50**
Circ: Statement: **128,006**

24 ❑ Mar 1980 Cover: 0.40 **NM** value: **1.50**
Circ: Statement: **128,006**
📖 Trapped-In The Doomsday Room! • Has 1979 Statement, filed 10/1/79; avg print run 331,645; avg sales 126,438; avg subs 437; avg total paid 126,875; samples 590; office use 1,619; max existent 129,084; 61% of run returned A: Trevor Von Eeden; Mike Esposito W: Michael Fleisher

25 ❑ Apr 1980 Cover: 0.40 **NM** value: **1.50**
Circ: Statement: **128,006**
📖 To Free A Felon! A: Steve Leialoha W: Michael Fleisher

26 ❑ May 1980 Cover: 0.40 **NM** value: **1.50**
Circ: Statement: **128,006**
C: John Byrne

27 ❑ Jun 1980 Cover: 0.40 **NM** value: **1.50**
Circ: Statement: **128,006**

28 ❑ Jul 1980 Cover: 0.40 **NM** value: **1.50**
Circ: Statement: **128,006**
★ Appearance of Spider-Man.

29 ❑ Aug 1980 Cover: 0.40 **NM** value: **1.50**
Circ: Statement: **128,006**
★ Appearance of Spider-Man.

30 ❑ Sep 1980 Cover: 0.50 **NM** value: **1.50**
Circ: Statement: **128,006**
★ 1st Appearance of Doctor Karl Malus.

31 ❑ Oct 1980 Cover: 0.50 **NM** value: **1.50**
Circ: Statement: **128,006**
A: Frank Miller(cover)

32 ❑ Nov 1980 Cover: 0.50 **NM** value: **1.50**
Circ: Statement: **128,006**
A: Frank Miller(cover)

33 ❑ Dec 1980 Cover: 0.50 **NM** value: **1.50**
Circ: Statement: **128,006**
★ Origin of Turner D. Century. ★ 1st Appearance of Turner D. Century.

34 ❑ Jan 1981 Cover: 0.50 **NM** value: **1.50**
Circ: Statement: **102,474**

35 ❑ Feb 1981 Cover: 0.50 **NM** value: **1.50**
Circ: Statement: **102,474**

36 ❑ Mar 1981 Cover: 0.50 **NM** value: **1.50**
Circ: Statement: **102,474**
📖 The Wanderer! A: Steve Leialoha; Bruce Patterson W: Chris Claremont

37 ❑ Apr 1981 Cover: 0.50 **NM** value: **4.00**
Circ: Statement: **102,474** • **CGC:** 1 graded, best 9.6
• Has 1980 Statement, filed 10/1/80; avg print run 283,001; avg sales 127,036; avg subs 970; avg total paid 128,006; samples 636; office use 2,160; max existent 130,802; 54% of run returned A: Terry Austin ★ 1st Appearance of Siryn. ★ Appearance of X-Men.

38 ❑ Jun 1981 Cover: 0.50 **NM** value: **3.00**
Circ: Statement: **102,474** • **CGC:** 3 graded, best 9.8
★ Appearance of X-Men.

39 ❑ Aug 1981 Cover: 0.50 **NM** value: **1.25**
Circ: Statement: **102,474**

40 ❑ Oct 1981 Cover: 0.50 **NM** value: **1.25**
Circ: Statement: **102,474**

41 ❑ Dec 1981 Cover: 0.50 **NM** value: **1.25**
Circ: Statement: **102,474**

42 ❑ Feb 1982 Cover: 0.60 **NM** value: **1.25**

43 ❑ Apr 1982 Cover: 0.60 **NM** value: **1.25**
• Has 1981 Statement, filed 10/1/1981; avg print run 252,763; avg sales 99,112; avg subs 3,362; avg total paid 102,474; samples 591; office use 767; max existent 103,832; 59% of run returned

44 ❑ Jun 1982 Cover: 0.60 **NM** value: **1.25**

45 ❑ Aug 1982 Cover: 0.60 **NM** value: **1.25**

46 ❑ Oct 1982 Cover: 0.60 **NM** value: **1.25**

47 ❑ Dec 1982 Cover: 0.60 **NM** value: **1.25**

48 ❑ Feb 1983 Cover: 0.60 **NM** value: **1.25**

49 ❑ Apr 1983 Cover: 0.60 **NM** value: **1.25**

50 ❑ Jun 1983 Cover: 1.00 **NM** value: **4.00**
Photo cover. • Giant-size. final issue.★ Death of Spider-Woman I (Jessica Drew).

SPIDER-WOMAN (2ND SERIES) — Marvel

1 ❑ Nov 1993 Cover: 1.75 **NM** value: **Cover or less**
Circ: CapCity orders: **49,900**

2 ❑ Dec 1993 Cover: 1.75 **NM** value: **Cover or less**
Circ: CapCity orders: **27,500**

3 ❑ Jan 1994 Cover: 1.75 **NM** value: **Cover or less**
Circ: CapCity orders: **21,800**

4 ❑ Feb 1994 Cover: 1.75 **NM** value: **Cover or less**
Circ: CapCity orders: **18,150**

SPIDER-WOMAN (3RD SERIES) — Marvel

1 ❑ Jul 1999 Cover: 2.99 **NM** value: **Cover or less**
Circ: Statement: **74,561** Diamd. preorders: **66,854**
📖 Spider Spider A: Bart Sears W: John Byrne

2 ❑ Aug 1999 Cover: 1.99 **NM** value: **2.99**
Circ: Statement: **74,561** Diamd. preorders: **58,596**

3 ❑ Sep 1999 Cover: 1.99 **NM** value: **Cover or less**
Circ: Statement: **74,561** Diamd. preorders: **46,432**

4 ❑ Oct 1999 Cover: 1.99 **NM** value: **Cover or less**
Circ: Statement: **74,561** Diamd. preorders: **42,054**

5 ❑ Nov 1999 Cover: 1.99 **NM** value: **Cover or less**
Circ: Statement: **74,561** Diamd. preorders: **37,272**

6 ❑ Dec 1999 Cover: 1.99 **NM** value: **Cover or less**
Circ: Statement: **74,561** Diamd. preorders: **35,888**

7 ❑ Jan 2000 Cover: 1.99 **NM** value: **Cover or less**
Circ: Diamd. preorders: **32,128**

8 ❑ Feb 2000 Cover: 1.99 **NM** value: **Cover or less**
Circ: Diamd. preorders: **30,565**

9 ❑ Mar 2000 Cover: 1.99 **NM** value: **Cover or less**
Circ: Diamd. preorders: **28,456**

10 ❑ Apr 2000 Cover: 2.25 **NM** value: **Cover or less**
Circ: Diamd. preorders: **25,789**

11 ❑ May 2000 Cover: 2.25 **NM** value: **Cover or less**
Circ: Diamd. preorders: **25,267**

12 ❑ Jun 2000 Cover: 2.25 **NM** value: **Cover or less**
Circ: Diamd. preorders: **24,104**

13 ❑ Jul 2000 Cover: 2.25 **NM** value: **Cover or less**
Circ: Diamd. preorders: **23,232**

14 ❑ Aug 2000 Cover: 2.25 **NM** value: **Cover or less**
Circ: Diamd. preorders: **22,909**

15 ❑ Sep 2000 Cover: 2.25 **NM** value: **Cover or less**
Circ: Diamd. preorders: **22,174**

16 ❑ Oct 2000 Cover: 2.25 **NM** value: **Cover or less**
Circ: Diamd. preorders: **19,903**

17 ❑ Nov 2000 Cover: 2.25 **NM** value: **Cover or less**
Circ: Diamd. preorders: **19,573**

18 ❑ Dec 2000 Cover: 2.25 **NM** value: **Cover or less**
Circ: Diamd. preorders: **18,753**
📖 Dry Bones final issue. A: Bart Sears W: John Byrne

SPIDER-WOMAN (BOOK) — Marvel

Bk 1❑ Cover: 2.50 **NM** value: **4.00**
• (Pocket newsstand pb)

SPIDERY-MON: MAXIMUM CARCASS — Parody Press

1/A ❑ Cover: 3.25 **NM** value: **Cover or less**
Covers of the three variants join together to form a mural. • Variant edition A. A: Bob Hanon W: Bill Maus

1/B ❑ Cover: 3.25 **NM** value: **Cover or less**
Covers of the three variants join together to form a mural. • Variant edition B. A: Bob Hanon W: Bill Maus

1/C ❑ Cover: 3.25 **NM** value: **Cover or less**
Covers of the three variants join together to form a mural. • Variant edition C. A: Bob Hanon W: Bill Maus

SPIDEY SUPER STORIES — Marvel

On PBS stations in the 1970s, The Electric Company was Children's Television Workshop's hip follow-up to Sesame Street, teaching kids phonemes and spelling rules through sketch comedy from a troupe of players including Morgan Freeman, Rita Moreno, and Bill Cosby. Later in the series' run, Children's Television Workshop entered into an agreement with Marvel and presented live-action skits featuring a mute Spider-Man (actually, Freeman in a suit).

For Marvel's part, it published an original series of easy-to-read comics starring Spider-Man and introducing readers not just to reading, but to a roster of Marvel guest-stars including the X-Men's Storm and Shanna the She-Devil.

A wonderful effort, and one long overlooked by collectors.

— JJM

1 ❑ Oct 1974 Cover: 0.35 **NM** value: **6.00**
• **CGC:** 16 graded, best 9.6
📖 Spider-Man is Born!; Spidey Signs Up!; Spidey Meets the Spoiler; Help! I'm Spider-Man! ★ Origin of Spider-Man.

2 ❑ Nov 1974 Cover: 0.35 **NM** value: **4.00**
📖 In the Hands of the Hunter; Spidey vs. Mister Measles; The Long Arms of the Law-Breaker

3 ❑ Dec 1974 Cover: 0.35 **NM** value: **3.00**
📖 The Big-Top Bust; The Evil Dr. Fly; Mysterio, Master of Masks and Mystery ★ Versus Circus of Crime.

4 ❑ Jan 1975 Cover: 0.35 **NM** value: **3.00**
• **CGC:** 1 graded, best 9.4
📖 Spidey: Beware of the Hair; The Beastly Banana; Beat the Beetle

5 ❑ Feb 1975 Cover: 0.35 **NM** value: **3.00**
📖 The Wings and the Web-Slinger; Spidey Fights Dr. Fright; The Shocker

6 ❑ Mar 1975 Cover: 0.35 **NM** value: **2.50**
📖 Webbing in a Winter Wonderland; The Book-Worm Bully; The Rage of the Rhino

7 ❑ Apr 1975 Cover: 0.35 **NM** value: **2.50**
📖 The Vanisher Shows Up; Spidey Jumps the Thumper; Lizard on the Loose

8 ❑ May 1975 Cover: 0.35 **NM** value: **2.50**
📖 Power to the People; Spidey Up Against the Wall; 20,000 Feet Underground

9 ❑ Jun 1975 Cover: 0.35 **NM** value: **2.50**
📖 The Day of Doom; Spidey Fights the Funny Bunny; Guess What's Coming to Dinner? • Hulk★ Versus Dr. Doom. ★ Versus Doctor Doom.

10 ❑ Jul 1975 Cover: 0.35 **NM** value: **2.50**
📖 Green Grows the Goblin; There's No Fool Like an April Fool; A TV Rock Group in King Arthur's Court

11 ❑ Aug 1975 Cover: 0.35 **NM** value: **2.50**
📖 Spider-Woman?; The Show-Stopper Strikes; The Return of Doctor Octopus

12 ❑ Sep 1975 Cover: 0.35 **NM** value: **2.50**
📖 The Law of the Claw; Trick the Tickler; The Purple Pirates

13 ❑ Oct 1975 Cover: 0.35 **NM** value: **2.50**
📖 Spidey and the Sandman; The Sitter; Win With the Wing

14 ❑ Dec 1975 Cover: 0.35 **NM** value: **2.50**
📖 Haunting Season; The Birthday Bandit; The Trapper ★ Appearance of Shanna.

15 ❑ Feb 1976 Cover: 0.35 **NM** value: **2.50**
★ Appearance of Storm.

16 ❑ Apr 1976 Cover: 0.35 **NM** value: **2.50**

17 ❑ Jun 1976 Cover: 0.35 **NM** value: **2.50**

18 ❑ Aug 1976 Cover: 0.35 **NM** value: **2.50**

19 ❑ Oct 1976 Cover: 0.35 **NM** value: **2.50**

20 ❑ Dec 1976 Cover: 0.35 **NM** value: **2.50**

21 ❑ Feb 1977 Cover: 0.35 **NM** value: **2.50**

22 ❑ Apr 1977 Cover: 0.35 **NM** value: **2.50**

23 ❑ Jun 1977 Cover: 0.35 **NM** value: **2.50**
📖 The Amazing Shrinking Spidey A: Kolfax Mingo W: Kolfax Mingo

24 ❑ Jul 1977 Cover: 0.35 **NM** value: **2.50**
★ Appearance of Thundra.

25 ❑ Aug 1977 Cover: 0.35 **NM** value: **2.50**

26 ❑ Sep 1977 Cover: 0.35 **NM** value: **2.50**

CGC-graded: Multiply prices above by **33 for 9.9 M • 16 for 9.8 NM/M • 7 for 9.6 NM+ • 5 for 9.4 NM • 2.5 for 9.2 NM- • 1.5 for 9.0 VF/NM**

27 ❑ Oct 1977 Cover: 0.35 **NM** value: **2.50**
28 ❑ Nov 1977 Cover: 0.35 **NM** value: **2.50**
29 ❑ Dec 1977 Cover: 0.35 **NM** value: **2.50**
★ Versus Kingpin.
30 ❑ Jan 1978 Cover: 0.35 **NM** value: **2.50**
★ Versus Kang the Conqueror.
31 ❑ Feb 1978 Cover: 0.35 **NM** value: **2.50**
• **CGC:** 1 graded, best 9.2
32 ❑ Mar 1978 Cover: 0.35 **NM** value: **2.50**
33 ❑ Apr 1978 Cover: 0.35 **NM** value: **2.50**
★ Appearance of Hulk.
34 ❑ May 1978 Cover: 0.35 **NM** value: **2.50**
35 ❑ Jul 1978 Cover: 0.35 **NM** value: **2.50**
★ Appearance of Shanna.
36 ❑ Sep 1978 Cover: 0.35 **NM** value: **2.50**
37 ❑ Nov 1978 Cover: 0.35 **NM** value: **2.50**
38 ❑ Jan 1979 Cover: 0.35 **NM** value: **2.50**
39 ❑ Mar 1979 Cover: 0.35 **NM** value: **2.50**
• **CGC:** 1 graded, best 9.0
★ Appearance of Thanos, Hellcat.
40 ❑ May 1979 Cover: 0.40 **NM** value: **2.50**
41 ❑ Jul 1979 Cover: 0.40 **NM** value: **2.50**
42 ❑ Sep 1979 Cover: 0.40 **NM** value: **2.50**
43 ❑ Nov 1979 Cover: 0.40 **NM** value: **2.50**
44 ❑ Jan 1980 Cover: 0.40 **NM** value: **2.50**
45 ❑ Mar 1980 Cover: 0.40 **NM** value: **2.50**
★ Appearance of Doctor Doom, Silver Surfer.
46 ❑ May 1980 Cover: 0.50 **NM** value: **2.50**
47 ❑ Jul 1980 Cover: 0.50 **NM** value: **2.50**
48 ❑ Sep 1980 Cover: 0.50 **NM** value: **2.50**
• **CGC:** 1 graded, best 8.5
49 ❑ Nov 1980 Cover: 0.50 **NM** value: **2.50**
50 ❑ Jan 1981 Cover: 0.50 **NM** value: **2.50**
51 ❑ Mar 1981 Cover: 0.50 **NM** value: **2.50**
52 ❑ May 1981 Cover: 0.50 **NM** value: **2.50**
53 ❑ Jul 1981 Cover: 0.50 **NM** value: **2.50**
54 ❑ Sep 1981 Cover: 0.50 **NM** value: **2.50**
55 ❑ Nov 1981 Cover: 0.50 **NM** value: **2.50**
★ Versus Kingpin.
56 ❑ Jan 1982 Cover: 0.60 **NM** value: **2.50**
• **CGC:** 1 graded, best 9.2
57 ❑ Mar 1982 Cover: 0.60 **NM** value: **2.50**
• **CGC:** 1 graded, best 9.4
final issue.

SPIKE AND TYKE (M.G.M.'S...) — Dell

4 ❑ Dec 1955 Cover: 0.10 **NM** value: **14.00**
★ Appearance of Series numbering continued from.
5 ❑ Mar 1956 Cover: 0.10 **NM** value: **12.00**
6 ❑ Jun 1956 Cover: 0.10 **NM** value: **10.00**
7 ❑ Sep 1956 Cover: 0.10 **NM** value: **10.00**
8 ❑ Dec 1956 Cover: 0.10 **NM** value: **10.00**
9 ❑ Mar 1957 Cover: 0.10 **NM** value: **10.00**
10 ❑ Jun 1957 Cover: 0.10 **NM** value: **10.00**
11 ❑ Sep 1957 Cover: 0.10 **NM** value: **8.00**
12 ❑ Dec 1957 Cover: 0.10 **NM** value: **8.00**
13 ❑ Mar 1958 Cover: 0.10 **NM** value: **8.00**
14 ❑ Jun 1958 Cover: 0.10 **NM** value: **8.00**
15 ❑ Sep 1958 Cover: 0.10 **NM** value: **8.00**
16 ❑ Dec 1958 Cover: 0.10 **NM** value: **8.00**
17 ❑ Mar 1959 Cover: 0.10 **NM** value: **8.00**
18 ❑ Jun 1959 Cover: 0.10 **NM** value: **8.00**
19 ❑ Sep 1959 Cover: 0.10 **NM** value: **8.00**
20 ❑ Dec 1959 Cover: 0.10 **NM** value: **8.00**
21 ❑ Mar 1960 Cover: 0.10 **NM** value: **8.00**
📖 Growing-Up Games; Pampered Pooches; Hound in the Pound; Tom and Jerry: The Lost Gold Mine; Coyote Chorus (text story); Bird Watchers
22 ❑ Jun 1960 Cover: 0.10 **NM** value: **8.00**
23 ❑ Sep 1960 Cover: 0.10 **NM** value: **8.00**
24 ❑ Dec 1960 Cover: 0.10 **NM** value: **8.00**
final issue.

SPINELESS-MAN $2099 — Parody Press

1 ❑ Cover: 2.50 **NM** value: **Cover or less**

SPINE-TINGLING TALES (DR. SPEKTOR PRESENTS...) — Gold Key

1 ❑ May 1975 Cover: 0.25 **NM** value: **3.00**
• **CGC:** 1 graded, best 9.4
2 ❑ Aug 1975 Cover: 0.25 **NM** value: **2.00**
3 ❑ Nov 1975 Cover: 0.25 **NM** value: **2.00**
4 ❑ Feb 1976 Cover: 0.25 **NM** value: **2.00**

SPINWORLD — Slave Labor / Amaze Ink

1 ❑ Jul 1997, b&w Cover: 2.95 **NM** value: **Cover or less**
📖 The Snake and the Staff **A:** Brent Anderson; Chuck Anderson **W:** Eric Vinicoff
2 ❑ Aug 1997, b&w Cover: 2.95 **NM** value: **Cover or less**
📖 Spacing Dutchman **A:** Brent Anderson; Chuck Anderson **W:** Eric Vinicoff
3 ❑ Oct 1997, b&w Cover: 2.95 **NM** value: **Cover or less**
📖 Spacing Dutchman **A:** Brent Anderson; Chuck Anderson **W:** Eric Vinicoff
4 ❑ Jan 1998, b&w Cover: 3.95 **NM** value: **Cover or less**
📖 Politics of Plenty **A:** Brent Anderson; Chuck Anderson **W:** Eric Vinicoff

SPIRAL PATH, THE — Eclipse

1 ❑ ca. 1986 Cover: 1.50 **NM** value: **1.75**
A: Geoff Senior **W:** Steve Parkhouse
2 ❑ ca. 1986 Cover: 1.50 **NM** value: **1.75**
A: Geoff Senior **W:** Steve Parkhouse

SPIRAL ZONE — DC

1 ❑ Feb 1988 Cover: 1.00 **NM** value: **Cover or less**
📖 Colossus Of Doom **A:** Carmine Infantino; Dick Giordano **W:** Michael Fleisher
2 ❑ Mar 1988 Cover: 1.00 **NM** value: **Cover or less**
A: Carmine Infantino; Dick Giordano
3 ❑ Apr 1988 Cover: 1.00 **NM** value: **Cover or less**
Circ: CapCity orders: **5,850**
A: Carmine Infantino; Dick Giordano
4 ❑ May 1988 Cover: 1.00 **NM** value: **Cover or less**
Circ: CapCity orders: **4,500**
A: Carmine Infantino; Dick Giordano

SPIRIT, THE (1st SERIES) See page 973

SPIRIT, THE (2ND SERIES) — Quality

1 ❑ ca. 1944 Cover: 0.10 **NM** value: **600.00**
• **CGC:** 1 graded, best 7.0
📖 Wanted Dead or Alive! • Quality publishes **A:** Will Eisner **W:** Will Eisner
2 ❑ ca. 1944 Cover: 0.10 **NM** value: **350.00**
• **CGC:** 3 graded, best 9.4
📖 Crime Doesn't Pay! **A:** Will Eisner **W:** Will Eisner
3 ❑ Win 1945 Cover: 0.10 **NM** value: **250.00**
• **CGC:** 1 graded, best 8.0
📖 Murder Runs Wild! **A:** Will Eisner **W:** Will Eisner
4 ❑ Spr 1946 Cover: 0.10 **NM** value: **185.00**
• **CGC:** 1 graded, best 9.0
A: Will Eisner **W:** Will Eisner
5 ❑ Sum 1946 Cover: 0.10 **NM** value: **185.00**
A: Will Eisner **W:** Will Eisner
6 ❑ Fal 1946 Cover: 0.10 **NM** value: **150.00**
• **CGC:** 2 graded, best 9.4
A: Will Eisner **W:** Will Eisner
7 ❑ Win 1946 Cover: 0.10 **NM** value: **150.00**
• **CGC:** 1 graded, best 7.0
A: Will Eisner **W:** Will Eisner
8 ❑ Spr 1947 Cover: 0.10 **NM** value: **150.00**
A: Will Eisner **W:** Will Eisner
9 ❑ Sum 1947 Cover: 0.10 **NM** value: **150.00**
• **CGC:** 2 graded, best 8.5
A: Will Eisner **W:** Will Eisner
10 ❑ Fal 1947 Cover: 0.10 **NM** value: **150.00**
• **CGC:** 1 graded, best 8.0
A: Will Eisner **W:** Will Eisner
11 ❑ Spr 1948 Cover: 0.10 **NM** value: **125.00**
• **CGC:** 1 graded, best 9.0
A: Will Eisner **W:** Will Eisner
12 ❑ Sum 1948 Cover: 0.10 **NM** value: **200.00**
Eisner cover. **A:** Will Eisner **W:** Will Eisner
13 ❑ Fal 1948 Cover: 0.10 **NM** value: **200.00**
• **CGC:** 1 graded, best 7.5
Eisner cover. **A:** Will Eisner **W:** Will Eisner
14 ❑ Win 1948 Cover: 0.10 **NM** value: **200.00**
• **CGC:** 1 graded, best 8.5
Eisner cover. **A:** Will Eisner **W:** Will Eisner
15 ❑ Spr 1949 Cover: 0.10 **NM** value: **200.00**
Eisner cover. **A:** Will Eisner **W:** Will Eisner
16 ❑ Jul 1949 Cover: 0.10 **NM** value: **200.00**
• **CGC:** 1 graded, best 8.0
Eisner cover. **A:** Will Eisner **W:** Will Eisner
17 ❑ Sep 1949 Cover: 0.10 **NM** value: **200.00**
Eisner cover. **A:** Will Eisner **W:** Will Eisner
18 ❑ Nov 1949 Cover: 0.10 **NM** value: **250.00**
• **CGC:** 1 graded, best 6.5
Eisner cover. **A:** Will Eisner **W:** Will Eisner
19 ❑ Jan 1950 Cover: 0.10 **NM** value: **250.00**
Eisner cover. **A:** Will Eisner **W:** Will Eisner
20 ❑ Apr 1950 Cover: 0.10 **NM** value: **250.00**
Eisner cover. **A:** Will Eisner **W:** Will Eisner
21 ❑ Jun 1950 Cover: 0.10 **NM** value: **250.00**
• **CGC:** 1 graded, best 8.5
Eisner cover. **A:** Will Eisner **W:** Will Eisner
22 ❑ Aug 1950 Cover: 0.10 **NM** value: **350.00**
• **CGC:** 5 graded, best 8.0
Classic Eisner cover. **A:** Will Eisner **W:** Will Eisner

SPIRIT, THE (3RD SERIES) — Fiction House

1 ❑ Mar 1952 Cover: 0.10 **NM** value: **250.00**
📖 The Case of the Counterfeit Killer; The Curse of Claymore Castle; The Plot of the Perfect Crime; Panic on Pier 8 • Fiction House publishes
2 ❑ ca. 1952 Cover: 0.10 **NM** value: **200.00**
• **CGC:** 2 graded, best 8.0
A: Will Eisner **W:** Will Eisner
3 ❑ ca. 1953 Cover: 0.10 **NM** value: **175.00**
A: Will Eisner **W:** Will Eisner
4 ❑ ca. 1953 Cover: 0.10 **NM** value: **175.00**
A: Will Eisner **W:** Will Eisner
5 ❑ ca. 1954 Cover: 1.10 **NM** value: **175.00**

SPIRIT, THE (4TH SERIES) — Super

Super is known for its rereleases of earlier titles with its own imprint, as if it were the originating publisher. The cover did not convey the quality of the contents. — Maggie

11 ❑ Cover: 0.12 **NM** value: **15.00**
• I.W./Super; Reprints Spirit (2nd Series), #19 **A:** Will Eisner **W:** Will Eisner
12 ❑ Cover: 0.12 **NM** value: **15.00**
• Reprints Spirit (2nd Series), #17 **A:** Will Eisner **W:** Will Eisner

SPIRIT, THE (5TH SERIES) — Harvey

1 ❑ ca. 1967 Cover: 0.25 **NM** value: **50.00**
• **CGC:** 3 graded, best 9.4
• Harvey **A:** Will Eisner **W:** Will Eisner ★ Origin of The Spirit.
2 ❑ ca. 1967 Cover: 0.25 **NM** value: **42.00**
• **CGC:** 4 graded, best 9.6
A: Will Eisner **W:** Will Eisner

SPIRIT, THE (6TH SERIES) — Kitchen Sink

All issues are adults only.

1 ❑ Jan 1973, b&w Cover: 0.50 **NM** value: **14.00**
• **CGC:** 4 graded, best 9.6
• Krupp/Kitchen Sink publishes
2 ❑ 1973 Cover: 0.50 **NM** value: **14.00**
• **CGC:** 3 graded, best 9.8

SPIRIT, THE (7TH SERIES) — Ken Pierce

1 ❑ Cover: 3.95 **NM** value: **18.00**
2 ❑ Cover: 5.95 **NM** value: **18.00**
3 ❑ Cover: 5.95 **NM** value: **18.00**
4 ❑ Cover: 6.95 **NM** value: **18.00**

SPIRIT, THE (8TH SERIES) — Kitchen Sink

1 ❑ Oct 1983, full color Cover: 1.75 **NM** value: **5.00**
📖 The Christmas Spirit; The Return of the Villains of '42; Hilde and the Kid Gang; Dolan's Origin of the Spirit • Kitchen Sink publishes; #291, 292, 293, 294 **A:** Will Eisner **W:** Will Eisner ★ Origin of The Spirit.
2 ❑ Dec 1983, full color Cover: 1.75 **NM** value: **4.00**
📖 Hildie and Satin; The Siberian Dagger; The Atomic Bomb; As Ever Orange • #295, 296, 297, 298 **A:** Will Eisner **W:** Will Eisner
3 ❑ Feb 1984, full color Cover: 1.75 **NM** value: **4.00**
📖 Introducing Blubber; Rockhead Stone; The Feud; The Fly • #299, 300, 301, 302 **A:** Will Eisner **W:** Will Eisner
4 ❑ Mar 1984, full color Cover: 2.00 **NM** value: **3.50**
📖 Nylon Rose; The Last Trolley; Yafodder's Mustache; The Lipstick Print Case • #303, 304; Reprints Police Comics #98 Spirit Story **A:** Will Eisner **W:** Will Eisner
5 ❑ Jun 1984 Cover: 2.00 **NM** value: **3.50**
A: Will Eisner **W:** Will Eisner
6 ❑ Aug 1984 Cover: 2.00 **NM** value: **3.50**
📖 Welcome Home, Ebony!; Carrion's Rock; Magnifying Glasses; Tidal Wave **A:** Will Eisner **W:** Will Eisner
7 ❑ Oct 1984 Cover: 2.95 **NM** value: **3.50**
Circ: Statement: **13,644**
A: Will Eisner **W:** Will Eisner
8 ❑ Feb 1985 Cover: 2.95 **NM** value: **3.50**
Circ: Statement: **13,644**
A: Will Eisner **W:** Will Eisner
9 ❑ Apr 1985 Cover: 2.95 **NM** value: **3.50**
Circ: Statement: **13,644** CapCity orders: **3,325**
A: Will Eisner **W:** Will Eisner
10 ❑ Jun 1985 Cover: 2.95 **NM** value: **Cover or less**
Circ: Statement: **13,644** CapCity orders: **3,175**
A: Will Eisner **W:** Will Eisner
11 ❑ Aug 1985 Cover: 2.95 **NM** value: **Cover or less**
Circ: Statement: **13,644** CapCity orders: **2,925**
A: Will Eisner **W:** Will Eisner
12 ❑ Oct 1985 Cover: 1.95 **NM** value: **2.00**
Circ: Statement: **11,722** CapCity orders: **2,625**
• Has 1985 Statement, filed 9/6/85; avg print run 15,352; avg sales 13,391; avg subs 229; avg total paid 13,644; samples 75; office use 1,633; max existent 15,328; no newsstand sales this year **A:** Will Eisner **W:** Will Eisner
13 ❑ Nov 1985 Cover: 1.95 **NM** value: **2.00**
Circ: Statement: **11,722**
A: Will Eisner **W:** Will Eisner
14 ❑ Dec 1985 Cover: 1.95 **NM** value: **2.00**
Circ: Statement: **11,722**
A: Will Eisner **W:** Will Eisner
15 ❑ Jan 1986 Cover: 1.95 **NM** value: **2.00**
Circ: Statement: **11,722**
📖 Hoagy the Yogi; April Fool; The Pinhead; Escape • #356, 357, 358, 359 **A:** Will Eisner **W:** Will Eisner
16 ❑ Feb 1986 Cover: 1.95 **NM** value: **2.00**
Circ: Statement: **11,722**
A: Will Eisner **W:** Will Eisner
17 ❑ Mar 1986 Cover: 1.95 **NM** value: **2.00**
Circ: Statement: **11,722**
A: Will Eisner **W:** Will Eisner
18 ❑ Apr 1986 Cover: 1.95 **NM** value: **2.00**
Circ: Statement: **11,722**
A: Will Eisner **W:** Will Eisner
19 ❑ May 1986 Cover: 1.95 **NM** value: **2.00**
Circ: Statement: **11,722**
📖 Black Gold; Hangly Hollyer Mansion; Whiffenpoof; Wanted **A:** Will Eisner **W:** Will Eisner
20 ❑ Jun 1986 Cover: 1.95 **NM** value: **2.00**
Circ: Statement: **11,722**
📖 Hanzel and Gretel; Li'l Adam; The Lamp; Competition **A:** Will Eisner **W:** Will Eisner
21 ❑ Jul 1986 Cover: 1.95 **NM** value: **2.00**
Circ: Statement: **11,722**
A: Will Eisner **W:** Will Eisner
22 ❑ Aug 1986 Cover: 1.95 **NM** value: **2.00**
Circ: Statement: **11,722**
📖 A Killer At Large; Into the Light; End of the S.S. Raven; UFO **A:** Will Eisner **W:** Will Eisner
23 ❑ Sep 1986 Cover: 1.95 **NM** value: **2.00**
Circ: Statement: **10,767**
📖 Cinderella; Mr. McDool; Doppelganger; The Burning of P.S. 43 **A:** Will Eisner **W:** Will Eisner
24 ❑ Oct 1986 Cover: 1.95 **NM** value: **2.00**
Circ: Statement: **10,767**
A: Will Eisner **W:** Will Eisner
25 ❑ Nov 1986 Cover: 1.95 **NM** value: **2.00**
Circ: Statement: **10,767**
• Has 1986 Statement, filed 10/1/86; avg print run 12,309; avg sales 11,552; avg subs 170; avg total paid 11,722; samples 75; office use 512; max existent 12.309; no newsstand sales this year **A:** Will Eisner **W:** Will Eisner
26 ❑ Dec 1986 Cover: 1.95 **NM** value: **2.00**
Circ: Statement: **10,767**
A: Will Eisner **W:** Will Eisner
27 ❑ Jan 1987 Cover: 2.00 **NM** value: **Cover or less**
Circ: Statement: **10,767**

Other grades: Multiply prices above by **1.5 for Mint • 2/3 for Very Fine • 1/3 for Fine • 1/5 for Very Good • 1/8 for Good**

SPIRIT, THE (1ST SERIES)

Will Eisner's work on The Spirit, created as a comic-book-sized weekly newspaper insert, has become internationally accepted as a classic work of art. Denny Colt, in the first installment, is declared dead and literally goes underground (with his hideout in a cemetery) to fight the forces of evil. The premise may be stereotypical, but the feature was anything but: It was a wildly entertaining, pioneering use of the art form. And the stories featured the work of such creators as Andre LeBlanc, Jules Feiffer, and Wally Wood.

Because the sections ran with different papers, there are variant formats: newspaper-page size as well as comic-book size; Spirit story only as well as anthology length with such features as Lady Luck and Mr. Mystic. The 645 issues are identified by the date of the newspaper, printed on the first page; the Near Mint values appear next to them. — Maggie

Issue	NM price
6/2/40	700.00
6/9/40	325.00
6/16/40	175.00
6/23/40	125.00
6/30/40	125.00
7/7/40	100.00
7/14/40	100.00
7/21/40	100.00
7/28/40	100.00
8/4/40	100.00
8/11/40	75.00
8/18/40	75.00
8/25/40	75.00
9/1/40	75.00
9/8/40	75.00
9/15/40	75.00
9/22/40	75.00
9/29/40	75.00
10/6/40	75.00
10/13/40	75.00
10/20/40	55.00
10/27/40	55.00
11/3/40	55.00
11/10/40	55.00
11/17/40	55.00
11/24/40	55.00
12/1/40	55.00
12/8/40	55.00
12/15/40	55.00
12/22/40	55.00
12/29/40	55.00
1/5/41	55.00
1/12/41	55.00
1/19/41	55.00
1/26/41	55.00
2/2/41	55.00
2/9/41	55.00
2/16/41	55.00
2/23/41	55.00
3/2/41	55.00
3/9/41	55.00
3/16/41	55.00
3/23/41	55.00
3/30/41	55.00
4/6/41	55.00
4/13/41	55.00
4/20/41	55.00
4/27/41	55.00
5/4/41	55.00
5/11/41	55.00
5/18/41	55.00
5/25/41	55.00
6/1/41	45.00
6/8/41	45.00
6/15/41	45.00
6/22/41	45.00
6/29/41	45.00
7/6/41	45.00
7/13/41	45.00
7/20/41	45.00
7/27/41	45.00
8/3/41	45.00
8/10/41	45.00
8/17/41	45.00
8/24/41	45.00
8/31/41	45.00
9/7/41	45.00
9/14/41	45.00
9/21/41	45.00
9/28/41	45.00
10/5/41	45.00
10/12/41	45.00

Issue	NM price
10/19/41	45.00
10/26/41	45.00
11/2/41	45.00
11/9/41	45.00
11/16/41	45.00
11/23/41	45.00
11/30/41	45.00
12/7/41	45.00
12/14/41	45.00
12/21/41	45.00
12/28/41	45.00
1/4/42	35.00
1/11/42	35.00
1/18/42	35.00
1/25/42	35.00
2/1/42	35.00
2/8/42	35.00
2/15/42	35.00
2/22/42	35.00
3/1/42	35.00
3/8/42	35.00
3/15/42	35.00
3/22/42	35.00
3/29/42	35.00
4/5/42	35.00
4/12/42	35.00
4/19/42	35.00
4/26/42	35.00
5/3/42	35.00
5/10/42	35.00
5/17/42	35.00
5/24/42	35.00
5/31/42	35.00
6/7/42	35.00
6/14/42	35.00
6/21/42	35.00
6/28/42	35.00
7/5/42	35.00
7/12/42	35.00
7/19/42	35.00
7/26/42	35.00
8/2/42	35.00
8/9/42	35.00
8/16/42	35.00
8/23/42	35.00
8/30/42	35.00
9/6/42	35.00
9/13/42	35.00
9/20/42	35.00
9/27/42	35.00
10/4/42	35.00
10/11/42	35.00
10/18/42	35.00
10/25/42	35.00
11/1/42	35.00
11/8/42	35.00
11/15/42	35.00
11/22/42	35.00
11/29/42	35.00
12/6/42	35.00
12/13/42	35.00
12/20/42	35.00
12/27/42	35.00
1/3/43	28.00
1/10/43	28.00
1/17/43	28.00
1/24/43	28.00
1/31/43	28.00
2/7/43	28.00
2/14/43	28.00
2/21/43	28.00
2/28/43	28.00

Issue	NM price
3/7/43	28.00
3/14/43	28.00
3/21/43	28.00
3/28/43	28.00
4/4/43	28.00
4/11/43	28.00
4/18/43	28.00
4/25/43	28.00
5/2/43	28.00
5/9/43	28.00
5/16/43	28.00
5/23/43	28.00
5/30/43	28.00
6/6/43	28.00
6/13/43	28.00
6/20/43	28.00
6/27/43	28.00
7/4/43	28.00
7/11/43	28.00
7/18/43	28.00
7/25/43	28.00
8/1/43	28.00
8/8/43	28.00
8/15/43	28.00
8/22/43	28.00
8/29/43	28.00
9/5/43	28.00
9/12/43	28.00
9/19/43	28.00
9/26/43	28.00
10/3/43	28.00
10/10/43	28.00
10/17/43	28.00
10/24/43	28.00
10/31/43	28.00
11/7/43	28.00
11/14/43	28.00
11/21/43	28.00
11/28/43	28.00
12/5/43	28.00
12/12/43	28.00
12/19/43	28.00
12/26/43	28.00
1/2/44	20.00
1/9/44	20.00
1/16/44	20.00
1/23/44	20.00
1/30/44	20.00
2/6/44	20.00
2/13/44	20.00
2/20/44	20.00
2/27/44	20.00
3/5/44	20.00
3/12/44	20.00
3/19/44	20.00
3/26/44	20.00
4/2/44	20.00
4/9/44	20.00
4/16/44	20.00
4/23/44	20.00
4/30/44	20.00
5/7/44	20.00
5/14/44	20.00
5/21/44	20.00
5/28/44	20.00
6/4/44	20.00
6/11/44	20.00
6/18/44	20.00
6/25/44	20.00
7/2/44	20.00
7/9/44	20.00
7/16/44	20.00

Issue	NM price
7/23/44	20.00
7/30/44	20.00
8/6/44	20.00
8/13/44	20.00
8/20/44	20.00
8/27/44	20.00
9/3/44	20.00
9/10/44	20.00
9/17/44	20.00
9/24/44	20.00
10/1/44	20.00
10/8/44	20.00
10/15/44	20.00
10/22/44	20.00
10/29/44	20.00
11/5/44	20.00
11/12/44	20.00
11/19/44	20.00
11/26/44	20.00
12/3/44	20.00
12/10/44	20.00
12/17/44	20.00
12/24/44	20.00
12/31/44	20.00
1/7/45	16.00
1/14/45	16.00
1/21/45	16.00
1/28/45	16.00
2/4/45	16.00
2/11/45	16.00
2/18/45	16.00
2/25/45	16.00
3/4/45	16.00
3/11/45	16.00
3/18/45	16.00
3/25/45	16.00
4/1/45	16.00
4/8/45	16.00
4/15/45	16.00
4/22/45	16.00
4/29/45	16.00
5/6/45	16.00
5/13/45	16.00
5/20/45	16.00
5/27/45	16.00
6/3/45	16.00
6/10/45	16.00
6/17/45	16.00
6/24/45	16.00
7/1/45	16.00
7/8/45	16.00
7/15/45	16.00
7/22/45	16.00
7/29/45	16.00
8/5/45	16.00
8/12/45	16.00
8/19/45	16.00
8/26/45	16.00
9/2/45	16.00
9/9/45	16.00
9/16/45	16.00
9/23/45	16.00
9/30/45	16.00
10/7/45	16.00
10/14/45	16.00
10/21/45	16.00
10/28/45	16.00
11/4/45	16.00
11/11/45	16.00
11/18/45	16.00
11/25/45	16.00
12/2/45	16.00

Issue	NM price
12/9/45	16.00
12/16/45	16.00
12/23/45	35.00
12/30/45	35.00
1/6/46	35.00
1/13/46	35.00
1/20/46	35.00
1/27/46	35.00
2/3/46	35.00
2/10/46	35.00
2/17/46	35.00
2/24/46	35.00
3/3/46	35.00
3/10/46	35.00
3/17/46	35.00
3/24/46	35.00
3/31/46	35.00
4/7/46	35.00
4/14/46	35.00
4/21/46	35.00
4/28/46	35.00
5/5/46	35.00
5/12/46	35.00
5/19/46	35.00
5/26/46	35.00
6/2/46	35.00
6/9/46	35.00
6/16/46	35.00
6/23/46	35.00
6/30/46	35.00
7/7/46	35.00
7/14/46	35.00
7/21/46	35.00
7/28/46	35.00
8/4/46	35.00
8/11/46	35.00
8/18/46	35.00
8/25/46	35.00
9/1/46	35.00
9/8/46	35.00
9/15/46	35.00
9/22/46	35.00
9/29/46	35.00
10/6/46	35.00
10/13/46	35.00
10/20/46	35.00
10/27/46	35.00
11/3/46	35.00
11/10/46	35.00
11/17/46	35.00
11/24/46	35.00
12/1/46	35.00
12/8/46	35.00
12/15/46	35.00
12/22/46	35.00
12/29/46	35.00
1/5/47	35.00
1/12/47	35.00
1/19/47	35.00
1/26/47	35.00
2/2/47	35.00
2/9/47	35.00
2/16/47	35.00
2/23/47	35.00
3/2/47	35.00
3/9/47	35.00
3/16/47	35.00
3/23/47	35.00
3/30/47	35.00
4/6/47	35.00
4/13/47	35.00
4/20/47	35.00
4/27/47	35.00
5/4/47	35.00
5/11/47	35.00
5/18/47	35.00
5/25/47	35.00
6/1/47	35.00
6/8/47	35.00
6/15/47	35.00
6/22/47	35.00
6/29/47	35.00
7/6/47	35.00
7/13/47	35.00
7/20/47	35.00
7/27/47	35.00
8/3/47	35.00
8/10/47	35.00
8/17/47	35.00
8/24/47	35.00

Issue	NM price
8/31/47	35.00
9/7/47	35.00
9/14/47	35.00
9/21/47	35.00
9/28/47	35.00
10/5/47	35.00
10/12/47	35.00
10/19/47	35.00
10/26/47	35.00
11/2/47	35.00
11/9/47	35.00
11/16/47	35.00
11/23/47	35.00
11/30/47	35.00
12/7/47	35.00
12/14/47	35.00
12/21/47	35.00
12/28/47	35.00
1/4/48	30.00
1/11/48	30.00
1/18/48	30.00
1/25/48	30.00
2/1/48	30.00
2/8/48	30.00
2/15/48	30.00
2/22/48	30.00
2/29/48	30.00
3/7/48	30.00
3/14/48	30.00
3/21/48	30.00
3/28/48	30.00
4/4/48	30.00
4/11/48	30.00
4/18/48	30.00
4/25/48	30.00
5/2/48	30.00
5/9/48	30.00
5/16/48	30.00
5/23/48	30.00
5/30/48	30.00
6/6/48	30.00
6/13/48	30.00
6/20/48	30.00
6/27/48	30.00
7/4/48	30.00
7/11/48	30.00
7/18/48	30.00
7/25/48	30.00
8/1/48	30.00
8/8/48	30.00
8/15/48	30.00
8/22/48	30.00
8/29/48	30.00
9/5/48	30.00
9/12/48	30.00
9/19/48	30.00
9/26/48	30.00
10/3/48	30.00
10/10/48	30.00
10/17/48	30.00
10/24/48	30.00
10/31/48	30.00
11/7/48	30.00
11/14/48	30.00
11/21/48	30.00
11/28/48	30.00
12/5/48	30.00
12/12/48	30.00
12/19/48	30.00
12/26/48	30.00
1/2/49	30.00
1/9/49	30.00
1/16/49	30.00
1/23/49	30.00
1/30/49	30.00
2/6/49	30.00
2/13/49	30.00
2/20/49	30.00
2/27/49	30.00
3/6/49	30.00
3/13/49	30.00
3/20/49	30.00
3/27/49	30.00
4/3/49	30.00
4/10/49	30.00
4/17/49	30.00
4/24/49	30.00
5/1/49	30.00
5/8/49	30.00
5/15/49	30.00

Issue	NM price
5/22/49	30.00
5/29/49	30.00
6/5/49	30.00
6/12/49	30.00
6/19/49	30.00
6/26/49	30.00
7/3/49	30.00
7/10/49	30.00
7/17/49	30.00
7/24/49	30.00
7/31/49	30.00
8/7/49	30.00
8/14/49	30.00
8/21/49	30.00
8/28/49	30.00
9/4/49	30.00
9/11/49	30.00
9/18/49	30.00
9/25/49	30.00
10/2/49	30.00
10/9/49	30.00
10/16/49	30.00
10/23/49	30.00
10/30/49	30.00
11/6/49	30.00
11/13/49	30.00
11/20/49	30.00
11/27/49	30.00
12/4/49	30.00
12/11/49	30.00
12/18/49	30.00
12/25/49	30.00
1/1/50	30.00
1/8/50	30.00
1/15/50	30.00
1/22/50	30.00
1/29/50	30.00
2/5/50	30.00
2/12/50	30.00
2/19/50	30.00
2/26/50	30.00
3/5/50	30.00
3/12/50	30.00
3/19/50	30.00
3/26/50	30.00
4/2/50	30.00
4/9/50	30.00
4/16/50	30.00
4/23/50	30.00
4/30/50	30.00
5/7/50	30.00
5/14/50	30.00
5/21/50	30.00
5/28/50	30.00
6/4/50	30.00
6/11/50	30.00
6/18/50	30.00
6/25/50	30.00
7/2/50	30.00
7/9/50	30.00
7/16/50	30.00
7/23/50	30.00
7/30/50	30.00
8/6/50	30.00
8/13/50	30.00
8/20/50	30.00
8/27/50	30.00
9/3/50	30.00
9/10/50	30.00
9/17/50	30.00
9/24/50	30.00
10/1/50	30.00
10/8/50	30.00
10/15/50	30.00
10/22/50	30.00
10/29/50	30.00
11/5/50	30.00
11/12/50	30.00
11/19/50	30.00
11/26/50	30.00
12/3/50	30.00
12/10/50	30.00
12/17/50	30.00
12/24/50	30.00
12/31/50	30.00
1/7/51	30.00
1/14/51	30.00
1/21/51	30.00
1/28/51	30.00
2/4/51	30.00

Issue	NM price
2/11/51	30.00
2/18/51	30.00
2/25/51	30.00
3/4/51	30.00
3/11/51	30.00
3/18/51	30.00
3/25/51	30.00
4/1/51	30.00
4/8/51	30.00
4/15/51	30.00
4/22/51	30.00
4/29/51	30.00
5/6/51	30.00
5/13/51	30.00
5/20/51	30.00
5/27/51	30.00
6/3/51	30.00
6/10/51	30.00
6/17/51	30.00
6/24/51	30.00
7/1/51	30.00
7/8/51	30.00
7/15/51	30.00
7/22/51	30.00
7/29/51	30.00
8/5/51	30.00
8/12/51	30.00
8/19/51	15.00
8/26/51	15.00
9/2/51	15.00
9/9/51	15.00
9/16/51	15.00
9/23/51	15.00
9/30/51	15.00
10/7/51	15.00
10/14/51	15.00
10/21/51	15.00
10/28/51	15.00
11/4/51	15.00
11/11/51	15.00
11/18/51	15.00
11/25/51	15.00
12/2/51	15.00
12/9/51	15.00
12/16/51	15.00
12/23/51	15.00
12/30/51	15.00
1/6/52	15.00
1/13/52	15.00
1/20/52	15.00
1/27/52	15.00
2/3/52	15.00
2/10/52	15.00
2/17/52	15.00
2/24/52	15.00
3/2/52	15.00
3/9/52	15.00
3/16/52	15.00
3/23/52	15.00
3/30/52	15.00
4/6/52	15.00
4/13/52	15.00
4/20/52	15.00
4/27/52	15.00
5/4/52	15.00
5/11/52	15.00
5/18/52	15.00
5/25/52	15.00
6/1/52	15.00
6/8/52	15.00
6/15/52	15.00
6/22/52	15.00
6/29/52	15.00
7/6/52	15.00
7/13/52	15.00
7/20/52	15.00
7/27/52	125.00
A: Wally Wood begins	
8/3/52	125.00
8/10/52	125.00
8/17/52	125.00
8/24/52	125.00
8/31/52	125.00
9/7/52	125.00
9/14/52	75.00
9/21/52	125.00
9/28/52	125.00
10/5/52	75.00

CGC-graded: Multiply prices above by **33 for 9.9 M • 16 for 9.8 NM/M • 7 for 9.6 NM+ • 5 for 9.4 NM • 2.5 for 9.2 NM- • 1.5 for 9.0 VF/NM**

Montabaldo; Blackmail; The Tragedy of Merry Andrew **A:** Will Eisner **W:** Will Eisner

28 ❑ Feb 1987 Cover: 2.00 **NM** value: **Cover or less**
Circ: Statement: **10,767**
A: Will Eisner **W:** Will Eisner

29 ❑ Mar 1987 Cover: 2.00 **NM** value: **Cover or less**
Circ: Statement: **10,767**
A: Will Eisner **W:** Will Eisner

30 ❑ Apr 1987 Cover: 2.00 **NM** value: **Cover or less**
Circ: Statement: **10,767**
A: Will Eisner **W:** Will Eisner

31 ❑ May 1987 Cover: 2.00 **NM** value: **Cover or less**
Circ: Statement: **10,767**
A: Will Eisner **W:** Will Eisner

32 ❑ Jun 1987 Cover: 2.00 **NM** value: **Cover or less**
Circ: Statement: **10,767**
Cheap is Cheap; Murder,...Bloodless Type; The Spirit Takes a Vacation; Cromlech Was a Nature Boy! **A:** Will Eisner **W:** Will Eisner

33 ❑ Jul 1987 Cover: 2.00 **NM** value: **Cover or less**
Circ: Statement: **10,767**
A: Will Eisner **W:** Will Eisner

34 ❑ Aug 1987 Cover: 2.00 **NM** value: **Cover or less**
Circ: Statement: **9,383**
A: Will Eisner **W:** Will Eisner

35 ❑ Sep 1987 Cover: 2.00 **NM** value: **Cover or less**
Circ: Statement: **9,383**
A: Will Eisner **W:** Will Eisner

36 ❑ Oct 1987 Cover: 2.00 **NM** value: **Cover or less**
Circ: Statement: **9,383**
• Has 1987 Statement, filed 9/16/87; avg print run 11,409; avg sales 10,614; avg subs 153; avg total paid 10,614; samples 75; office use 75; max existent 11,409; no newsstand sales this year **A:** Will Eisner **W:** Will Eisner

37 ❑ Nov 1987 Cover: 2.00 **NM** value: **Cover or less**
Circ: Statement: **9,383**
A: Will Eisner **W:** Will Eisner

38 ❑ Dec 1988 Cover: 2.00 **NM** value: **Cover or less**
Circ: Statement: **9,383**
A: Will Eisner **W:** Will Eisner

39 ❑ Jan 1988 Cover: 2.00 **NM** value: **Cover or less**
Circ: Statement: **9,383**
Almanac of the Year 1948; Ice; A Prisoner of Love; The Explorer **A:** Will Eisner **W:** Will Eisner

40 ❑ Feb 1988 Cover: 2.00 **NM** value: **Cover or less**
Circ: Statement: **9,383**
A: Will Eisner **W:** Will Eisner

41 ❑ Mar 1988 Cover: 2.00 **NM** value: **Cover or less**
Circ: Statement: **9,383**
• Wertham parody **A:** Will Eisner **W:** Will Eisner

42 ❑ Apr 1988 Cover: 2.00 **NM** value: **Cover or less**
Circ: Statement: **9,383**
A: Will Eisner **W:** Will Eisner

43 ❑ May 1988 Cover: 2.00 **NM** value: **Cover or less**
Circ: Statement: **9,383**
A: Will Eisner **W:** Will Eisner

44 ❑ Jun 1988 Cover: 2.00 **NM** value: **Cover or less**
Circ: Statement: **9,383**
A: Will Eisner **W:** Will Eisner

45 ❑ Jul 1988 Cover: 2.00 **NM** value: **Cover or less**
Circ: Statement: **9,383**
A: Will Eisner **W:** Will Eisner

46 ❑ Aug 1988 Cover: 2.00 **NM** value: **Cover or less**
Circ: Statement: **8,785**
A: Will Eisner **W:** Will Eisner

47 ❑ Sep 1988 Cover: 2.00 **NM** value: **Cover or less**
Circ: Statement: **8,785**
Matua; The Return; The Candidate; White Cloud **A:** Will Eisner **W:** Will Eisner

48 ❑ Oct 1988 Cover: 2.00 **NM** value: **Cover or less**
Circ: Statement: **8,785**
Rat-Tat The Toy Machine Gun; Ten Minutes; Lurid Love; The Return of Vino Red **A:** Will Eisner **W:** Will Eisner

49 ❑ Nov 1988 Cover: 2.00 **NM** value: **Cover or less**
Circ: Statement: **8,785**
Crime; Death of Autumn Mews; The Curse; Fox At Bay • Has 1988 Statement, filed 9/30/88; avg print run 10,127; avg sales 9,216; avg subs 167; avg total paid 9,383; samples 75; office use 669; max existent 10,127; no newsstand sales this year **A:** Will Eisner **W:** Will Eisner

50 ❑ Dec 1988 Cover: 2.00 **NM** value: **Cover or less**
Circ: Statement: **8,785**
Elect Miss Rhinemaiden; The Inner Voice; Surgery; The Thanksgiving **A:** Will Eisner **W:** Will Eisner

51 ❑ Jan 1989 Cover: 2.00 **NM** value: **Cover or less**
Circ: Statement: **8,785**
The Embezzler; Winter Haven; Flaxen Weaver; Lonesome Cool **A:** Will Eisner **W:** Will Eisner

52 ❑ Feb 1989 Cover: 2.00 **NM** value: **Cover or less**
Circ: Statement: **8,785**
The Christmas Spirit; Fan Mail; Sand Saref **A:** Will Eisner **W:** Will Eisner

53 ❑ Mar 1989 Cover: 2.00 **NM** value: **Cover or less**
Circ: Statement: **8,785**
The Predictions of Druid Peer; Nickless Nerser; Roller Derby **A:** Will Eisner **W:** Will Eisner

54 ❑ Apr 1989 Cover: 2.00 **NM** value: **Cover or less**
Circ: Statement: **8,785**
A: Will Eisner **W:** Will Eisner

55 ❑ May 1989 Cover: 2.00 **NM** value: **Cover or less**
Circ: Statement: **8,785**
Carrion; The Island; Water; Rescue **A:** Will Eisner **W:** Will Eisner

56 ❑ Jun 1989 Cover: 2.00 **NM** value: **Cover or less**
Circ: Statement: **8,785**
Taxes; A Day At the Zoo; Wanted: Dangerous Job; Pito **A:** Will Eisner **W:** Will Eisner

57 ❑ Jul 1989 Cover: 2.00 **NM** value: **Cover or less**
Circ: Statement: **8,785**
A: Will Eisner **W:** Will Eisner

58 ❑ Aug 1989 Cover: 2.00 **NM** value: **Cover or less**
Circ: Statement: **8,398**
Sammy the Explorer; Willum and the Baron; Census '50; The Moment of Glory **A:** Will Eisner **W:** Will Eisner

59 ❑ Sep 1989 Cover: 2.00 **NM** value: **Cover or less**
Circ: Statement: **8,398**
The Ship vs. darling O'Shea; The Desert; Dick Whittler; The Chase **A:** Will Eisner **W:** Will Eisner

60 ❑ Oct 1989 Cover: 2.00 **NM** value: **Cover or less**
Circ: Statement: **8,398**
Investigation; The Wreck of Old 78; The First Man; Camp Wachoobee • Reprints #532, 533, 534, 535; Has 1989 Statement, filed 9/28/89; avg print run 9,340; avg sales 8,644; avg subs 141; avg total paid 8,785; samples 75; office use 480; max existent 9,340; no newsstand sales this year **A:** Will Eisner **W:** Will Eisner

61 ❑ Nov 1989 Cover: 2.00 **NM** value: **Cover or less**
Circ: Statement: **8,398**
Cape Cod Vacation; Teacher's Pet!; The Story of Sam; Sound • Reprints #536, 537, 538, 539 **A:** Will Eisner **W:** Will Eisner

62 ❑ Dec 1989 Cover: 2.00 **NM** value: **Cover or less**
Circ: Statement: **8,398**
The Big Win; O'Shea's Uncle; Lizzy's Boys; The Haircut **A:** Will Eisner **W:** Will Eisner

63 ❑ Jan 1990 Cover: 2.00 **NM** value: **Cover or less**
Circ: Statement: **8,398**
Halloween; Vietnam '50; Ellen Dolan for Mayor; La Cucaracha **A:** Will Eisner **W:** Will Eisner

64 ❑ Feb 1990 Cover: 2.00 **NM** value: **Cover or less**
Circ: Statement: **8,398**
Little Willum; The Winnah; Snowbound; Sammy and Willum Take Over **A:** Will Eisner **W:** Will Eisner

65 ❑ Mar 1990 Cover: 2.00 **NM** value: **Cover or less**
Circ: Statement: **8,398**
The Christmas Spirit; Happy New Year; Rife **A:** Will Eisner **W:** Will Eisner

66 ❑ Apr 1990 Cover: 2.00 **NM** value: **Cover or less**
Circ: Statement: **8,398**
Future Death; The Meanest Man in the World; Showdown; The Octopus is Back **A:** Will Eisner **W:** Will Eisner

67 ❑ May 1990 Cover: 2.00 **NM** value: **Cover or less**
Circ: Statement: **8,398**
To the Spirit With Love; Portier Fortune; Death is My Destiny; The Case of the Double Jones **A:** Will Eisner **W:** Will Eisner

68 ❑ Jun 1990 Cover: 2.00 **NM** value: **Cover or less**
Circ: Statement: **8,398**
A: Will Eisner **W:** Will Eisner

69 ❑ Jul 1990 Cover: 2.00 **NM** value: **Cover or less**
Circ: Statement: **8,398**
Time Bomb; Hobart; Help Wanted; The Facts **A:** Will Eisner **W:** Will Eisner

70 ❑ Aug 1990 Cover: 2.00 **NM** value: **Cover or less**
The Hero; The 7th Husband; King Wang; The Thing in the Jungle Eisner **W:** Will Eisner

71 ❑ Sep 1990 Cover: 2.00 **NM** value: **Cover or less**
Wanchu; Khyber Bill; School is Out; A Ticket Home **A:** Will Eisner **W:** Will Eisner

72 ❑ Oct 1990 Cover: 2.00 **NM** value: **Cover or less**
The Loot of Robinson Crusoe; Heat; Quiet!; Veta Barra • Has 1990 Statement, filed 9/17/90; avg print run 9,340; avg sales 8,254; avg subs 144; avg total paid 8,398; samples 100; office use 842; max existent 9,340; no newsstand sales this year **A:** Will Eisner **W:** Will Eisner

73 ❑ Nov 1990 Cover: 2.00 **NM** value: **Cover or less**
The Return of the Narcissus; The Foxtrot Poll; Night on the Waterfront; Deacon Mantis

74 ❑ Dec 1990 Cover: 2.00 **NM** value: **Cover or less**
Dance of the Bullfighter; Dr. Schyzoid; The Counterfeit Kitter; Stony Keefer

75 ❑ Jan 1991 Cover: 2.00 **NM** value: **Cover or less**
Roamin Umpire; The Suicide Town; Tiny Buttrix; A Guide to Clean Living;

76 ❑ Feb 1991 Cover: 2.00 **NM** value: **Cover or less**
A Perfect Crime Plot; Claymore Castle's Curse; Vote For Scallion; Baleful Buddha

77 ❑ Mar 1991 Cover: 2.00 **NM** value: **Cover or less**
The League of Liars; The Man From Mars; The Balloons; The Spirit Gets Older

78 ❑ Apr 1991 Cover: 2.00 **NM** value: **Cover or less**
Joe Fix; Joshua Blows His Horn; Fabian Skimp; Design for Doomsday

79 ❑ May 1991 Cover: 2.00 **NM** value: **Cover or less**
A Witness to Murder; The First Man on Mars; A Man Named Nero; The Snow Fort Massacre • #608, 609, 610, 611

80 ❑ Jun 1991 Cover: 2.00 **NM** value: **Cover or less**
Leap Year; It Kills by Dark; The Miami Beach Rumble; A Walking Corpse • #612, 613, 614, 615

81 ❑ Jul 1991 Cover: 2.00 **NM** value: **Cover or less**
Dolan Walks a Beat; Staple Springs; Water; Links Robbery • #616, 617, 618, 619

82 ❑ Aug 1991 Cover: 2.00 **NM** value: **Cover or less**
Ellen Dolan for Mayor!; The Great Galactic Mystery; A Different Face; L'Spirit • #620, 621, 622, 623

83 ❑ Sep 1991 Cover: 2.00 **NM** value: **Cover or less**
The Incident of the Sitting Duck; Assassins Incorporated; Sammy Falls in Love • #625, 626, 627, 628

84 ❑ Oct 1991 Cover: 2.00 **NM** value: **Cover or less**
What Are You Really Like?; 500 Papers; The Golden Lily; Rube Potter

85 ❑ Nov 1991 Cover: 2.00 **NM** value: **Cover or less**
The Ballad of Greenly Sleeve; Matt Slugg; Marry the Spirit; Outer Space • #632, 633, 634, 635

86 ❑ Dec 1991 Cover: 2.00 **NM** value: **Cover or less**

87 ❑ Jan 1992 Cover: 2.00 **NM** value: **Cover or less**
final issue.

SPIRIT ARCHIVES, THE (WILL EISNER'S...) DC

1 ❑ Cover: 49.95 **NM** value: **Cover or less**
• Reprints strips #1-31 **A:** Will Eisner **W:** Will Eisner

2 ❑ Cover: 49.95 **NM** value: **Cover or less**
• Reprints strips #32-57 **A:** Will Eisner **W:** Will Eisner

3 ❑ Cover: 49.95 **NM** value: **Cover or less**
• Reprints strips #58-83 **A:** Will Eisner **W:** Will Eisner

SPIRIT CASEBOOK, THE Kitchen Sink

1 ❑ Cover: 12.95 **NM** value: **Cover or less**

SPIRIT COLLECTOR'S EDITION REPRINTS Will Eisner

1 ❑ Oct 1972 **NM** value: **2.00**
A: Will Eisner **W:** Will Eisner

2 ❑ Oct 1972 **NM** value: **2.00**
A: Will Eisner **W:** Will Eisner

3 ❑ Oct 1972 **NM** value: **2.00**
A: Will Eisner **W:** Will Eisner

4 ❑ Oct 1972 **NM** value: **2.00**
A: Will Eisner **W:** Will Eisner

5 ❑ Oct 1972 **NM** value: **2.00**
A: Will Eisner **W:** Will Eisner

6 ❑ Oct 1972 **NM** value: **2.00**
A: Will Eisner **W:** Will Eisner

7 ❑ Oct 1972 **NM** value: **2.00**
A: Will Eisner **W:** Will Eisner

8 ❑ Oct 1972 **NM** value: **2.00**
A: Will Eisner **W:** Will Eisner

9 ❑ Oct 1972 **NM** value: **2.00**
A: Will Eisner **W:** Will Eisner

10 ❑ Oct 1972 **NM** value: **2.00**
A: Will Eisner **W:** Will Eisner

11 ❑ Dec 1972 **NM** value: **2.00**
A: Will Eisner **W:** Will Eisner

12 ❑ Dec 1972 **NM** value: **2.00**
A: Will Eisner **W:** Will Eisner

13 ❑ Dec 1972 **NM** value: **2.00**
A: Will Eisner **W:** Will Eisner

14 ❑ Dec 1972 **NM** value: **2.00**
A: Will Eisner **W:** Will Eisner

15 ❑ Dec 1972 **NM** value: **2.00**
A: Will Eisner **W:** Will Eisner

16 ❑ Dec 1972 **NM** value: **2.00**
A: Will Eisner **W:** Will Eisner

17 ❑ Dec 1972 **NM** value: **2.00**
A: Will Eisner **W:** Will Eisner

18 ❑ Dec 1972 **NM** value: **2.00**
A: Will Eisner **W:** Will Eisner

19 ❑ Dec 1972 **NM** value: **2.00**
A: Will Eisner **W:** Will Eisner

20 ❑ Dec 1972 **NM** value: **2.00**
A: Will Eisner **W:** Will Eisner

21 ❑ Dec 1972 **NM** value: **2.00**
A: Will Eisner **W:** Will Eisner

22 ❑ Dec 1972 **NM** value: **2.00**
A: Will Eisner **W:** Will Eisner

23 ❑ Dec 1972 **NM** value: **2.00**
A: Will Eisner **W:** Will Eisner

24 ❑ Dec 1972 **NM** value: **2.00**
A: Will Eisner **W:** Will Eisner

25 ❑ Dec 1972 **NM** value: **2.00**
A: Will Eisner **W:** Will Eisner

26 ❑ Dec 1972 **NM** value: **2.00**
A: Will Eisner **W:** Will Eisner

27 ❑ Dec 1972 **NM** value: **2.00**
A: Will Eisner **W:** Will Eisner

28 ❑ Dec 1972 **NM** value: **2.00**
A: Will Eisner **W:** Will Eisner

29 ❑ Dec 1972 **NM** value: **2.00**
A: Will Eisner **W:** Will Eisner

30 ❑ Dec 1972 **NM** value: **2.00**
A: Will Eisner **W:** Will Eisner

31 ❑ Jan 1973 **NM** value: **2.00**
A: Will Eisner **W:** Will Eisner

32 ❑ Jan 1973 **NM** value: **2.00**
A: Will Eisner **W:** Will Eisner

33 ❑ Jan 1973 **NM** value: **2.00**
A: Will Eisner **W:** Will Eisner

34 ❑ Jan 1973 **NM** value: **2.00**
A: Will Eisner **W:** Will Eisner

35 ❑ Jan 1973 **NM** value: **2.00**
A: Will Eisner **W:** Will Eisner

36 ❑ Jan 1973 **NM** value: **2.00**
A: Will Eisner **W:** Will Eisner

37 ❑ Jan 1973 **NM** value: **2.00**
A: Will Eisner **W:** Will Eisner

38 ❑ Jan 1973 **NM** value: **2.00**
A: Will Eisner **W:** Will Eisner

39 ❑ Jan 1973 **NM** value: **2.00**
A: Will Eisner **W:** Will Eisner

40 ❑ Jan 1973 **NM** value: **2.00**
A: Will Eisner **W:** Will Eisner

Dlx 1 ❑ Jan 1973 **NM** value: **20.00**
• Issues #1-10 (sold as (lot); Each includes back-page commentary by Eisner **A:** Will Eisner **W:** Will Eisner

Dlx 2 ❑ Dec 1972 **NM** value: **20.00**
• Issues #11-20 (sold as lot); Each includes back-page commentary by Eisner **A:** Will Eisner **W:** Will Eisner

Dlx 3 ❑ Dec 1972 **NM** value: **20.00**
• Issues #21-30 (sold as lot); Commentary continues **A:** Will Eisner **W:** Will Eisner

Dlx 4 ❑ Jan 1973 **NM** value: **20.00**
• #31-40 (sold as lot) **A:** Will Eisner **W:** Will Eisner

SPIRIT JAM Kitchen Sink

1 ❑ Cover: 5.95 **NM** value: **Cover or less**

Other grades: Multiply prices above by **1.5 for Mint • 2/3 for Very Fine • 1/3 for Fine • 1/5 for Very Good • 1/8 for Good**

SPIRIT, THE (MAGAZINE) — Warren

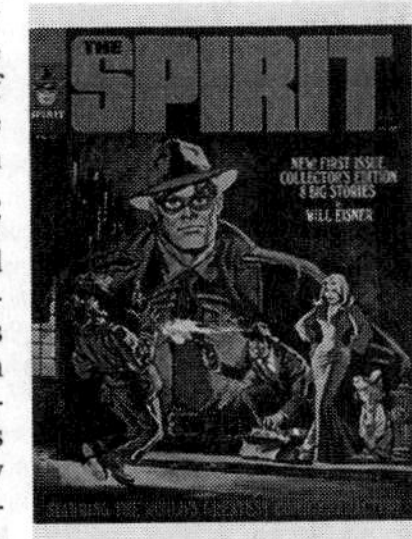

The first 16 issues of this mostly black-and-white reprint magazine were published by Warren — of Creepy, Eerie, and Vampirella fame — from 1974 until 1976. Kitchen Sink picked up the reins after that, producing #17-41 between 1977 and 1983. Here, readers will find classic stories starring comic-book-industry legend Will Eisner's masked vigilante; the originals ran as supplements to newspapers between 1940 and 1952. The Spirit's adventures are equal parts mystery and pure whimsy and showcase Eisner's incredible talent for comic-book storytelling — heck, they're practically how-to guides!

One of the highlights of this magazine's run was #30, a jam issue that featured a new Spirit story by Eisner himself, as well work by as creators like Chris Claremont, John Byrne, Brian Bolland, and Frank Miller.

1 ❑ Apr 1974 Cover: 1.00 **NM** value: **15.00**
📖 The Last Trolley; Escape; Li'l Adam; The Criminal; El Spirito; The Killer; Granule of Time; The Partner **A:** Will Eisner; Basil Gogos(cover) **W:** Will Eisner

2 ❑ Jun 1974 Cover: 1.00 **NM** value: **8.00**
A: Will Eisner **W:** Will Eisner

3 ❑ Aug 1974 Cover: 1.00 **NM** value: **7.00**
A: Will Eisner **W:** Will Eisner

4 ❑ Oct 1974 Cover: 1.00 **NM** value: **5.00**
A: Will Eisner **W:** Will Eisner

5 ❑ Dec 1974 Cover: 1.00 **NM** value: **5.00**
A: Will Eisner **W:** Will Eisner

6 ❑ Feb 1975 Cover: 1.25 **NM** value: **5.00**
A: Will Eisner **W:** Will Eisner

7 ❑ Apr 1975 Cover: 1.25 **NM** value: **5.00**
A: Will Eisner **W:** Will Eisner

8 ❑ Jun 1975 Cover: 1.25 **NM** value: **5.00**
A: Will Eisner **W:** Will Eisner

9 ❑ Aug 1975 Cover: 1.25 **NM** value: **5.00**
A: Will Eisner **W:** Will Eisner

10 ❑ Oct 1975 Cover: 1.25 **NM** value: **5.00**
A: Will Eisner **W:** Will Eisner

11 ❑ Dec 1975 Cover: 1.25 **NM** value: **3.00**
A: Will Eisner **W:** Will Eisner

12 ❑ Feb 1976 Cover: 1.25 **NM** value: **3.00**
A: Will Eisner **W:** Will Eisner

13 ❑ Apr 1976 Cover: 1.25 **NM** value: **3.00**
A: Will Eisner **W:** Will Eisner

14 ❑ Jun 1976 Cover: 1.25 **NM** value: **3.00**
A: Will Eisner **W:** Will Eisner

15 ❑ Aug 1976 Cover: 1.25 **NM** value: **3.00**
A: Will Eisner **W:** Will Eisner

16 ❑ Oct 1976 Cover: 1.25 **NM** value: **3.00**
A: Will Eisner **W:** Will Eisner

17 ❑ Nov 1977 Cover: 1.50 **NM** value: **3.00**
A: Will Eisner **W:** Will Eisner

18 ❑ May 1978 Cover: 1.50 **NM** value: **3.00**
A: Will Eisner **W:** Will Eisner

19 ❑ Oct 1978 Cover: 1.50 **NM** value: **3.00**
A: Will Eisner **W:** Will Eisner

20 ❑ Mar 1979 Cover: 1.50 **NM** value: **3.00**
A: Will Eisner **W:** Will Eisner

21 ❑ Jul 1979 Cover: 1.75 **NM** value: **3.00**
A: Will Eisner **W:** Will Eisner

22 ❑ Dec 1979 Cover: 1.75 **NM** value: **3.00**
A: Will Eisner **W:** Will Eisner

23 ❑ Feb 1980 Cover: 1.75 **NM** value: **3.00**
A: Will Eisner **W:** Will Eisner

24 ❑ May 1980 Cover: 1.75 **NM** value: **3.00**
A: Will Eisner **W:** Will Eisner

25 ❑ Aug 1980 Cover: 1.75 **NM** value: **3.00**
A: Will Eisner **W:** Will Eisner

26 ❑ Dec 1980 Cover: 2.00 **NM** value: **3.00**
📖 The Public Interest; The Confessions of Monks Mallon; Nylon Rose; The Kissing Caper; Umbrellas!; The Last Chapter; The Man in the Moon **A:** Will Eisner; Wally Wood **W:** Will Eisner; Wally Wood

27 ❑ Feb 1981 Cover: 2.00 **NM** value: **3.00**
A: Will Eisner **W:** Will Eisner

28 ❑ Apr 1981 Cover: 2.00 **NM** value: **3.00**
A: Will Eisner **W:** Will Eisner

29 ❑ Jun 1981 Cover: 2.00 **NM** value: **3.00**
A: Will Eisner **W:** Will Eisner

30 ❑ Jul 1981 Cover: 2.00 **NM** value: **3.00**
A: Will Eisner **W:** Will Eisner

31 ❑ Oct 1981 Cover: 2.00 **NM** value: **3.00**
A: Will Eisner **W:** Will Eisner

32 ❑ Dec 1981 Cover: 2.50 **NM** value: **3.00**
A: Will Eisner **W:** Will Eisner

33 ❑ Feb 1982 Cover: 2.50 **NM** value: **3.00**
A: Will Eisner **W:** Will Eisner

34 ❑ Apr 1982 Cover: 2.50 **NM** value: **3.00**
A: Will Eisner **W:** Will Eisner

35 ❑ Jun 1982 Cover: 2.50 **NM** value: **3.00**
A: Will Eisner **W:** Will Eisner

36 ❑ Aug 1982 Cover: 2.95 **NM** value: **3.00**
A: Will Eisner **W:** Will Eisner

37 ❑ Oct 1982 Cover: 2.95 **NM** value: **3.00**
A: Will Eisner **W:** Will Eisner

38 ❑ Dec 1982 Cover: 2.95 **NM** value: **3.00**
A: Will Eisner **W:** Will Eisner

39 ❑ Feb 1983 Cover: 2.95 **NM** value: **3.00**
A: Will Eisner **W:** Will Eisner

40 ❑ Apr 1983 Cover: 2.95 **NM** value: **3.00**
A: Will Eisner **W:** Will Eisner

41 ❑ Jun 1983 Cover: 2.95 **NM** value: **3.00**
A: Will Eisner **W:** Will Eisner

SPIRIT OF THE TAO, THE — Image

Written by D-Tron (aka Duy Truong) and featuring pencils by Billy Tan, The Spirit of the Tao owes much of its style to D-Tron's popular Witchblade series. The basic story is of an ages-old evil that threatens humanity and the few modern descendants of an elder race that stand against it.

The good guys are called the Jaikaps — only a handful of whom survive today. Two Jaikaps, Jasmine and Lance, are schooled by their master Lang to fulfill their destiny. On their 18th birthday, they are confronted by a group called the Tao Hunters, who seek to test their mettle before allying themselves with them to begin the fight anew against the great evil.

As the series develops, so, too, do the themes of universal balance and the unity of opposites into a whole (as in yin and yang).

1 ❑ Jun 1998 Cover: 2.50 **NM** value: **4.00**
Circ: Diamd. preorders: **74,844** • **CGC:** 1 graded, best 9.8
A: Billy Tan **W:** Billy Tan; D-Tron

2 ❑ Jul 1998 Cover: 2.50 **NM** value: **3.00**
Circ: Diamd. preorders: **58,858**
📖 Ta Chuan (The Great Commentary), Part1 **A:** Billy Tan **W:** Billy Tan; D-Tron

3 ❑ Aug 1998 Cover: 2.50 **NM** value: **3.00**
Circ: Diamd. preorders: **53,901**
A: Billy Tan **W:** Malachy Coney; D-Tron

4 ❑ Sep 1998 Cover: 2.50 **NM** value: **Cover or less**
Circ: Diamd. preorders: **48,731**
A: Billy Tan **W:** Malachy Coney; Billy Tan; D-Tron

5 ❑ Nov 1998 Cover: 2.50 **NM** value: **Cover or less**
Circ: Diamd. preorders: **42,544**
A: Billy Tan **W:** Malachy Coney; Billy Tan; D-Tron

6 ❑ Dec 1998 Cover: 2.50 **NM** value: **Cover or less**
Circ: Diamd. preorders: **35,907**
A: Billy Tan **W:** Malachy Coney; Billy Tan; D-Tron

7 ❑ Feb 1999 Cover: 2.50 **NM** value: **Cover or less**
Circ: Diamd. preorders: **34,065**
A: Billy Tan **W:** Malachy Coney; Billy Tan; D-Tron

8 ❑ Apr 1999 Cover: 2.50 **NM** value: **Cover or less**
Circ: Diamd. preorders: **30,921**
A: Billy Tan **W:** Malachy Coney; Billy Tan; D-Tron

9 ❑ May 1999 Cover: 2.50 **NM** value: **Cover or less**
Circ: Diamd. preorders: **29,140**
A: Billy Tan **W:** Malachy Coney; Billy Tan; D-Tron

10 ❑ Jun 1999 Cover: 2.50 **NM** value: **Cover or less**
Circ: Diamd. preorders: **27,722**
A: Billy Tan **W:** D-Tron

11 ❑ Aug 1999 Cover: 2.50 **NM** value: **Cover or less**
Circ: Diamd. preorders: **26,872**
A: Billy Tan **W:** D-Tron

12 ❑ Oct 1999 Cover: 2.50 **NM** value: **Cover or less**
Circ: Diamd. preorders: **24,777**
A: Billy Tan **W:** D-Tron

13 ❑ Nov 1999 Cover: 2.50 **NM** value: **Cover or less**
Circ: Diamd. preorders: **23,391**
A: Billy Tan **W:** Billy Tan; D-Tron

Ash 1❑ **NM** value: **8.00**
A: Billy Tan **W:** Billy Tan; D-Tron ★ 1st Appearance of Jasmine, Lance.

SPIRIT OF THE WIND — Chocolate Mouse

1 ❑ b&w Cover: 2.00 **NM** value: **Cover or less**

SPIRIT OF WONDER — Dark Horse / Manga

1 ❑ Apr 1996, b&w Cover: 2.95 **NM** value: **Cover or less**
A: Kenji Tsuruta **W:** Kenji Tsuruta

2 ❑ May 1996, b&w Cover: 2.95 **NM** value: **Cover or less**
A: Kenji Tsuruta **W:** Kenji Tsuruta

3 ❑ Jun 1996, b&w Cover: 2.95 **NM** value: **Cover or less**
A: Kenji Tsuruta **W:** Kenji Tsuruta

4 ❑ Jul 1996, b&w Cover: 2.95 **NM** value: **Cover or less**
📖 China Strikes Back, Part 1 **A:** Kenji Tsuruta **W:** Kenji Tsuruta

5 ❑ Aug 1996, b&w Cover: 2.95 **NM** value: **Cover or less**
📖 China Strikes Back, Part 2 final issue. **A:** Kenji Tsuruta **W:** Kenji Tsuruta

Bk 1❑ Jun 1998, b&w Cover: 12.95 **NM** value: **Cover or less**
• Collects Spirit of Wonder #1-5 **A:** Kenji Tsuruta **W:** Kenji Tsuruta

SPIRITS — Mind Walker

3 ❑ Sep 1995, b&w Cover: 2.95 **NM** value: **Cover or less**

SPIRITS OF VENOM — Marvel

1 ❑ Cover: 9.95 **NM** value: **Cover or less**
📖 Storm Shadows; Chasing Shadows; Enemies: Ahate Story; Last Rites **A:** Adam Kubert; Alex Saviuk **W:** Howard Mackie

> **Capital City** orders are the actual sales of comic books by Capital City Distribution, once one of the largest U.S. sellers of comics to comics shops. Capital City's share of comics shop sales, while not known exactly, increases from around 10-20% in the mid-1980s to 30-35% in the mid-1990s. Capital City's share of comic books sold on newsstands (most Marvels and DCs) will be less.

SPIRIT, THE: THE NEW ADVENTURES — Kitchen Sink

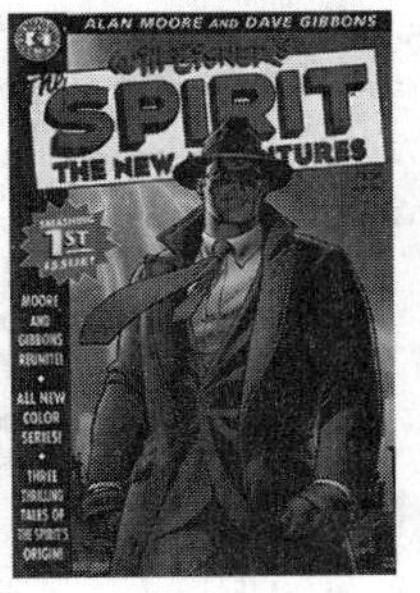

The Spirit is widely recognized as one of the high points of comic-book art. Created by Will Eisner, The Spirit started as a popular newspaper feature before making his way into newsstand comic books in Police Comics #11. It was in comics that Eisner's storytelling gained its trademark fluidity and inventiveness. Eisner proved himself to be a master of the medium, using different types of lighting, points of view, and other cinematic techniques to enhance the story. He then went further to pioneer new techniques, such as using overlapping panels to relate two characters' points of view of similar events, or putting comics themselves in the story by having the characters read about their own actions. Moreover, he was a pioneer of creative studios, and much of the newspaper material was produced by a top-notch team of writers and artists, including Jules Feiffer, Wally Wood, and Andre LeBlanc.

With its 1997 debut, this series continued in Eisner's tradition while using such more modern creators as Alan Moore, Dave Gibbons, and Neil Gaiman. Although the master himself contributes only occasionally, this series serves as an impressive testament to how much he has brought to comics.

1 ❑ Mar 1998 Cover: 3.50 **NM** value: **Cover or less**
Circ: Diamd. preorders: **22,434**
📖 The Most Important Meal; Force of Arms; Gossip and Gertrude French **A:** Dave Gibbons **W:** Alan Moore

2 ❑ Apr 1998 Cover: 3.50 **NM** value: **Cover or less**
Circ: Diamd. preorders: **18,070**
📖 The Return of Mink Stole; Sunday in the Park with St. George; Spinx the Jinx in The Game of Life **A:** Eddie Campbell; Carlos Ezquerra; Dan Burr **W:** James Vance; John Wagner; Neil Gaiman

3 ❑ May 1998 Cover: 3.50 **NM** value: **Cover or less**
Circ: Diamd. preorders: **17,120**
📖 Last Night I Dreamed of Dr. Cobra; Ellen's Stalker **A:** Bo Hampton; Daniel Torres **W:** Alan Moore; Mark Kneece

4 ❑ Jun 1998 Cover: 3.50 **NM** value: **Cover or less**
Circ: Diamd. preorders: **18,114**
📖 The Samovar of Shooshnipoor; The Weapon; Dr. Broca von Bitelbaum **A:** David Lloyd; Brent Anderson; Mike Allred; Matt Brundage; Michael Avon-Oeming **W:** Mike Allred; Kurt Busiek; Mark Schultz

5 ❑ Jul 1998 Cover: 3.50 **NM** value: **Cover or less**
Circ: Diamd. preorders: **16,243**
📖 Cursed Beauty **A:** Paul Chadwick **W:** Paul Chadwick

6 ❑ Sep 1998 Cover: 3.50 **NM** value: **Cover or less**
Circ: Diamd. preorders: **13,726**
📖 Swami Vashtibubu; Baby Eichberg **A:** Tom Mandrake; Scott Hampton **W:** Scott Hampton; John Ostrander; Mark Kneece

7 ❑ Oct 1998 Cover: 3.50 **NM** value: **Cover or less**
Circ: Diamd. preorders: **13,710**
📖 Golf Anyone?; The Pacifist; The Ghost of Tiger Traps **A:** Eddie Campbell; Paul Pope; Gene Fama; Pete Mullins **W:** Eddie Campbell; Jay Stephens; Dennis P. Eichhorn; Marcus Moore

8 ❑ Nov 1998 Cover: 3.50 **NM** value: **Cover or less**
Circ: Diamd. preorders: **12,804**
📖 Sweetheart **A:** John Lucas **W:** Joe R. Lansdale

SPIRIT: THE ORIGIN YEARS — Kitchen Sink

1 ❑ May 1992 Cover: 2.95 **NM** value: **Cover or less**
📖 The Origin of the Spirit; The Return of Dr. Cobra; The Black Queen; Voodoo in Manhattan **A:** Will Eisner **W:** Will Eisner ★ Origin of The Spirit.

2 ❑ Jul 1992 Cover: 2.95 **NM** value: **Cover or less**
A: Will Eisner **W:** Will Eisner

3 ❑ Sep 1992 Cover: 2.95 **NM** value: **Cover or less**
A: Will Eisner **W:** Will Eisner

4 ❑ Nov 1992 Cover: 2.95 **NM** value: **Cover or less**
A: Will Eisner **W:** Will Eisner

5 ❑ Jan 1993 Cover: 2.95 **NM** value: **Cover or less**
A: Will Eisner **W:** Will Eisner

6 ❑ Mar 1993 Cover: 2.95 **NM** value: **Cover or less**
A: Will Eisner **W:** Will Eisner

7 ❑ May 1993 Cover: 2.95 **NM** value: **Cover or less**
A: Will Eisner **W:** Will Eisner

8 ❑ Jul 1993 Cover: 2.95 **NM** value: **Cover or less**
A: Will Eisner **W:** Will Eisner

9 ❑ Sep 1993 Cover: 2.95 **NM** value: **Cover or less**
A: Will Eisner **W:** Will Eisner

10 ❑ Dec 1993 Cover: 2.95 **NM** value: **Cover or less**
A: Will Eisner **W:** Will Eisner

SPIRIT WORLD — DC

1 ❑ Jul 1971 Cover: 0.25 **NM** value: **35.00**
📖 The President Must Die; House of Horror; Children of the Flaming Wheel (text); The Screaming Woman; Amazing Predictions **A:** Jack Kirby **W:** Jack Kirby

SPIROU & FANTASIO: Z IS FOR ZORGLUB — Fantasy Flight

1 ❑ Cover: 8.95 **NM** value: **Cover or less**
• graphic novel

SPITFIRE AND THE TROUBLESHOOTERS — Marvel

1 ❑ Oct 1986 Cover: 0.75 **NM** value: **1.00**
Circ: CapCity orders: **36,300**
📖 Beginnings **A:** Herb Trimpe **W:** Eliot Brown; Gerry Conway; John Morelli

2 ❑ Nov 1986 Cover: 0.75 **NM** value: **1.00**
Circ: CapCity orders: **25,700**

CGC-graded: Multiply prices above by **33 for 9.9 M • 16 for 9.8 NM/M • 7 for 9.6 NM+ • 5 for 9.4 NM • 2.5 for 9.2 NM- • 1.5 for 9.0 VF/NM**

3 ❑ Dec 1986 Cover: 0.75 **NM** value: **1.00**
Circ: CapCity orders: **20,500**
4 ❑ Jan 1987 Cover: 0.75 **NM** value: **1.00**
Circ: CapCity orders: **17,200**
A: Todd McFarlane
5 ❑ Feb 1987 Cover: 0.75 **NM** value: **1.00**
Circ: CapCity orders: **16,600**
6 ❑ Mar 1987 Cover: 0.75 **NM** value: **1.00**
Circ: CapCity orders: **15,000**
7 ❑ Apr 1987 Cover: 0.75 **NM** value: **1.00**
Circ: CapCity orders: **13,600**
8 ❑ May 1987 Cover: 0.75 **NM** value: **1.00**
Circ: CapCity orders: **11,800**
📖 Down And Dirty **A:** Alan Kupperberg **W:** Cary Bates
9 ❑ Jun 1987 Cover: 0.75 **NM** value: **1.00**
Circ: CapCity orders: **10,700**
• Series continued in "Code Name: Spitfire"

SPITFIRE COMICS — Harvey

1 ❑ Aug 1941 Cover: 0.10 **NM** value: **350.00**
2 ❑ Oct 1941 Cover: 0.10 **NM** value: **300.00**

SPITTIN' IMAGE — Eclipse

1 ❑ Cover: 2.50 **NM** value: **Cover or less**
Circ: CapCity orders: **4,025**
No issue number. 📖 Fred Schiller • b&w parody **W:** Terry Dodson; David Ammerman; Ben Herrera; Tom Simonton; David Williams

SPIT WAD COMICS — Spit Wad Press

1 ❑ Jun 1983, b&w Cover: 2.50 **NM** value: **Cover or less**

SPLAT! — Mad Dog

1 ❑ b&w Cover: 2.50 **NM** value: **Cover or less**
2 ❑ Mar 1987 Cover: 2.50 **NM** value: **Cover or less**
📖 Cartoon Man's Best Friend; Steroids; The Amazons; Dead-End Job; Characters From Everyday Life; Help for the Dyslexic; Maxwell the Magic Cat; Deadlines; Danger Dan; Growing up Weird; Donald Dogfly **A:** Eddie Campbell; J.R. Williams; Marc Hempel; Peter Bagge; Phil Elliott; Robin Ator; Dennis Fujitake; Hunt Emerson; Alan Moore; Dave McDonnell; George Kochell; J. Thackray; P.S. Mueller **W:** Eddie Campbell; J.R. Williams; Marc Hempel; Peter Bagge; Phil Elliott; Robin Ator; Dennis Fujitake; Hunt Emerson; Alan Moore; Dave McDonnell; George Kochell; J. Thackray; P.S. Mueller
3 ❑ Cover: 2.50 **NM** value: **Cover or less**
A: B.Kliban

SPLATTER (ARPAD) — Arpad

1 ❑ b&w Cover: 2.50 **NM** value: **Cover or less**

SPLATTER (NORTHSTAR) — Northstar

All issues are adults only.
1 ❑ b&w Cover: 2.75 **NM** value: **4.95**
2 ❑ b&w Cover: 2.75 **NM** value: **Cover or less**
W: Tim Vigil
3 ❑ b&w Cover: 2.75 **NM** value: **Cover or less**
4 ❑ b&w Cover: 2.75 **NM** value: **Cover or less**
W: Tim Vigil
5 ❑ b&w Cover: 2.75 **NM** value: **Cover or less**
6 ❑ b&w Cover: 2.75 **NM** value: **Cover or less**
7 ❑ b&w Cover: 2.75 **NM** value: **Cover or less**
📖 Klownshock: Through the Looking Glass; Conversation O'er a Corpse; Vicious Circle **A:** Jeremie Johnson; Rich Longmore **W:** Eric Dinehart; Rafael Nieves
8 ❑ Cover: 2.75 **NM** value: **Cover or less**
Anl 1 ❑ Cover: 4.95 **NM** value: **Cover or less**

SPLITTING IMAGE — Image

1 ❑ Mar 1993 Cover: 1.95 **NM** value: **Cover or less**
Circ: CapCity orders: **51,550**
📖 Based On A True Story! • parody **A:** Donald Simpson **W:** Donald Simpson
2 ❑ Apr 1993 Cover: 1.95 **NM** value: **Cover or less**
Circ: CapCity orders: **47,100**
• parody

SPOOF — Marvel

1 ❑ ca. 1970 Cover: 0.15 **NM** value: **6.00**
📖 Darn Shadows!; Marooned; Clod Squad; The Spoof Report On Crime **A:** Marie Severin; Stu Schwartzberg **W:** Len Wein; Roy Thomas; Stu Schwartzberg
2 ❑ Nov 1972 Cover: 0.20 **NM** value: **4.00**
3 ❑ Jan 1973 Cover: 0.20 **NM** value: **4.00**
• **CGC:** 1 graded, best 9.0
4 ❑ Mar 1973 Cover: 0.20 **NM** value: **4.00**
5 ❑ May 1973 Cover: 0.20 **NM** value: **4.00**
• **CGC:** 1 graded, best 9.4
📖 Nut Gallery; 177 Sick final issue. **A:** Win Mortimer; Marie Severin **W:** Stu Schwartzberg; Marv Wolfman

SPOOF COMICS — Spoof

0 ❑ 1992, b&w Cover: 2.50 **NM** value: **Cover or less**
• Imp-Unity
1 ❑ 1992, b&w Cover: 2.50 **NM** value: **Cover or less**
• Spider-Femme
1-2 ❑ 1992, full color Cover: 2.50 **NM** value: **Cover or less**
2 ❑ 1992b&w Cover: 2.50 **NM** value: **Cover or less**
• Batbabe
2-2 ❑ 1992full color Cover: 2.50 **NM** value: **Cover or less**
• Batbabe
3 ❑ Aug 1992, b&w Cover: 2.95 **NM** value: **Cover or less**
• Wolverbroad
4 ❑ Sep 1992, b&w Cover: 2.95 **NM** value: **Cover or less**
• Superbabe
5 ❑ Oct 1992, b&w Cover: 2.95 **NM** value: **Cover or less**
• Daredame
6 ❑ 1992b&w Cover: 2.95 **NM** value: **Cover or less**
• X-Babes
7 ❑ 1993b&w Cover: 2.95 **NM** value: **Cover or less**
• Justice Broads
8 ❑ 1993b&w Cover: 2.95 **NM** value: **Cover or less**
• Fantastic Femmes
9 ❑ 1993b&w Cover: 2.95 **NM** value: **Cover or less**
• Hobo
10 ❑ 1993b&w Cover: 2.95 **NM** value: **Cover or less**
11 ❑ 1993b&w Cover: 2.95 **NM** value: **Cover or less**
12 ❑ Mar 1993, b&w Cover: 2.95 **NM** value: **Cover or less**
• Deathlocks

SPOOK (1ST SERIES) — Star

1 ❑ ca. 1946 Cover: 0.10 **NM** value: **200.00**
• **CGC:** 1 graded, best 9.0

SPOOK (2ND SERIES) — Star

22 ❑ Jan 1953 Cover: 0.10 **NM** value: **300.00**
23 ❑ Mar 1953 Cover: 0.10 **NM** value: **200.00**
• **CGC:** 1 graded, best 9.2
24 ❑ May 1953 Cover: 0.10 **NM** value: **200.00**
• **CGC:** 3 graded, best 9.4
25 ❑ Jul 1953 Cover: 0.10 **NM** value: **200.00**
• **CGC:** 1 graded, best 9.0
26 ❑ Aug 1953 Cover: 0.10 **NM** value: **175.00**
27 ❑ 1953 Cover: 0.10 **NM** value: **175.00**
28 ❑ 1954 Cover: 0.10 **NM** value: **175.00**
29 ❑ 1954 Cover: 0.10 **NM** value: **175.00**
30 ❑ 1954 Cover: 0.10 **NM** value: **175.00**
• **CGC:** 3 graded, best 9.2

SPOOK CITY — Mythic

1 ❑ Nov 1997, b&w Cover: 2.95 **NM** value: **Cover or less**

SPOOKGIRL — Slave Labor

1 ❑ ca. 2000 Cover: 2.95 **NM** value: **Cover or less**
Circ: Diamd. preorders: **3,323**

SPOOKY DIGEST — Harvey

1 ❑ Cover: 1.75 **NM** value: **2.00**
2 ❑ Cover: 1.75 **NM** value: **2.00**

SPOOKY MYSTERIES — Your Guide

1 ❑ ca. 1947 Cover: 0.10 **NM** value: **58.00**
📖 Mr. Spooky; Ludge Hunt; Super Snooper Hound for Clues; Barney Bungle (text story); Pinky Girl Detective; Crazy Crimes; Barney Bungle **A:** JCA **W:** JCA; Kate Phillips

SPOOKY SPOOKTOWN — Harvey

Like many of Casper's friends, Spooky proved popular enough to gain his own title. Sporting a mobster-like accent and a "doiby" hat, Spooky spends much of his time protecting his reputation as a "tuff little ghost." Part of his rep is the skill and power of his scaring ability, and Spooky prides himself on being able to out-Boo pretty much any other ghost around.

But the truth is that his tough demeanor is pretty much an act, as Spooky often goes to great effort to help those in need. Of course, all the time he's out doing good deeds, he's fussing and complaining about it. And though his patented Boo comes in handy when defeating the bad guys, Spooky also puts a lot of energy into not scaring. Why would a self-styled tough guy try not to be tough? Well, mostly to impress his best girlfriend, a sweet ghost called "Poil."

Many Harvey characters got a second series with a geographical-sounding name, such as Little Lotta FoodLand or Little Dot Dotland. Even for the 1960s, the unfortunate name chosen for Spooky's spinoff should have raised eyebrows.

1 ❑ Sep 1961 Cover: 0.25 **NM** value: **85.00**
2 ❑ Sep 1962 Cover: 0.25 **NM** value: **45.00**
3 ❑ ca. 1962 Cover: 0.25 **NM** value: **30.00**
4 ❑ ca. 1963 Cover: 0.25 **NM** value: **30.00**
5 ❑ ca. 1963 Cover: 0.25 **NM** value: **30.00**
6 ❑ ca. 1963 Cover: 0.25 **NM** value: **22.00**
7 ❑ ca. 1963 Cover: 0.25 **NM** value: **22.00**
8 ❑ ca. 1964 Cover: 0.25 **NM** value: **22.00**
9 ❑ ca. 1964 Cover: 0.25 **NM** value: **22.00**
10 ❑ ca. 1964 Cover: 0.25 **NM** value: **22.00**
11 ❑ ca. 1964 Cover: 0.25 **NM** value: **15.00**
12 ❑ ca. 1964 Cover: 0.25 **NM** value: **15.00**
13 ❑ ca. 1965 Cover: 0.25 **NM** value: **15.00**
14 ❑ ca. 1965 Cover: 0.25 **NM** value: **15.00**
15 ❑ Sep 1965 Cover: 0.25 **NM** value: **15.00**
16 ❑ Mar 1966 Cover: 0.25 **NM** value: **15.00**
17 ❑ Sep 1966 Cover: 0.25 **NM** value: **15.00**
18 ❑ ca. 1967 Cover: 0.25 **NM** value: **15.00**
19 ❑ ca. 1967 Cover: 0.25 **NM** value: **15.00**
20 ❑ May 1967 Cover: 0.25 **NM** value: **15.00**
21 ❑ Sep 1967 Cover: 0.25 **NM** value: **8.00**
22 ❑ Nov 1967 Cover: 0.25 **NM** value: **8.00**
23 ❑ ca. 1968 Cover: 0.25 **NM** value: **8.00**
24 ❑ ca. 1968 Cover: 0.25 **NM** value: **8.00**
25 ❑ Jul 1968 Cover: 0.25 **NM** value: **8.00**
26 ❑ ca. 1968 Cover: 0.25 **NM** value: **8.00**
27 ❑ Dec 1968 Cover: 0.25 **NM** value: **8.00**
28 ❑ ca. 1969 Cover: 0.25 **NM** value: **8.00**
29 ❑ ca. 1969 Cover: 0.25 **NM** value: **8.00**
30 ❑ ca. 1969 Cover: 0.25 **NM** value: **5.00**
31 ❑ Oct 1969 Cover: 0.25 **NM** value: **5.00**
32 ❑ ca. 1970 Cover: 0.25 **NM** value: **5.00**
33 ❑ ca. 1970 Cover: 0.25 **NM** value: **5.00**
34 ❑ ca. 1970 Cover: 0.25 **NM** value: **5.00**
35 ❑ ca. 1970 Cover: 0.25 **NM** value: **5.00**
36 ❑ Oct 1970 Cover: 0.25 **NM** value: **5.00**
37 ❑ ca. 1971 Cover: 0.25 **NM** value: **5.00**
38 ❑ ca. 1971 Cover: 0.25 **NM** value: **5.00**
39 ❑ ca. 1971 Cover: 0.25 **NM** value: **5.00**
40 ❑ ca. 1971 Cover: 0.25 **NM** value: **5.00**
41 ❑ ca. 1971 Cover: 0.25 **NM** value: **3.00**
42 ❑ Dec 1971 Cover: 0.25 **NM** value: **3.00**
43 ❑ Mar 1972 Cover: 0.25 **NM** value: **3.00**
44 ❑ Jun 1972 Cover: 0.25 **NM** value: **3.00**
45 ❑ Sep 1972 Cover: 0.25 **NM** value: **3.00**
46 ❑ Dec 1972 Cover: 0.20 **NM** value: **3.00**
• **CGC:** 1 graded, best 3.0
47 ❑ Feb 1973 Cover: 0.20 **NM** value: **3.00**
📖 Spooky: No Boos are Good Boos; Spooky and the Jeannie; Casper: Ghost Wanted; Wendy and the Lazy Witch;
48 ❑ Apr 1973 Cover: 0.20 **NM** value: **3.00**
49 ❑ Jun 1973 Cover: 0.20 **NM** value: **3.00**
50 ❑ Aug 1973 Cover: 0.20 **NM** value: **3.00**
51 ❑ Oct 1973 Cover: 0.20 **NM** value: **3.00**
52 ❑ Dec 1973 Cover: 0.20 **NM** value: **3.00**
53 ❑ Oct 1974 Cover: 0.25 **NM** value: **3.00**
54 ❑ Dec 1974 Cover: 0.25 **NM** value: **3.00**
55 ❑ Feb 1975 Cover: 0.25 **NM** value: **3.00**
56 ❑ Apr 1975 Cover: 0.25 **NM** value: **3.00**
57 ❑ Jun 1975 Cover: 0.25 **NM** value: **3.00**
58 ❑ Aug 1975 Cover: 0.25 **NM** value: **3.00**
59 ❑ Oct 1975 Cover: 0.25 **NM** value: **3.00**
60 ❑ Dec 1975 Cover: 0.25 **NM** value: **3.00**
61 ❑ Feb 1976 Cover: 0.25 **NM** value: **3.00**
62 ❑ Apr 1976 Cover: 0.25 **NM** value: **3.00**
📖 A Monstrous Tale; The Ghostly Trio; A Prince of a Baron; Nightmare…The Ghostly Octopus; Casper…The Abominable Slowman ★ Appearance of Casper, Nightmare.
63 ❑ Jun 1976 Cover: 0.25 **NM** value: **3.00**
64 ❑ Aug 1976 Cover: 0.25 **NM** value: **3.00**
65 ❑ Oct 1976 Cover: 0.25 **NM** value: **3.00**
66 ❑ Dec 1976 Cover: 0.25 **NM** value: **3.00**

SPOOKY THE DOG CATCHER — Paw Prints

1 ❑ Oct 1994, b&w Cover: 2.50 **NM** value: **Cover or less**

SPOOKY (VOL. 1) — Harvey

1 ❑ Nov 1955 Cover: 0.10 **NM** value: **200.00**
• **CGC:** 1 graded, best 7.5
2 ❑ Jan 1956 Cover: 0.10 **NM** value: **110.00**
3 ❑ Mar 1956 Cover: 0.10 **NM** value: **65.00**
4 ❑ May 1956 Cover: 0.10 **NM** value: **50.00**
5 ❑ Jul 1956 Cover: 0.10 **NM** value: **50.00**
6 ❑ Sep 1956 Cover: 0.10 **NM** value: **35.00**
7 ❑ Nov 1956 Cover: 0.10 **NM** value: **35.00**
8 ❑ Jan 1957 Cover: 0.10 **NM** value: **35.00**
9 ❑ Mar 1957 Cover: 0.10 **NM** value: **35.00**
10 ❑ May 1957 Cover: 0.10 **NM** value: **35.00**
11 ❑ Jul 1957 Cover: 0.10 **NM** value: **24.00**
12 ❑ Sep 1957 Cover: 0.10 **NM** value: **24.00**
13 ❑ Nov 1957 Cover: 0.10 **NM** value: **24.00**
14 ❑ Dec 1957 Cover: 0.10 **NM** value: **24.00**
15 ❑ Jan 1958 Cover: 0.10 **NM** value: **24.00**
16 ❑ Feb 1958 Cover: 0.10 **NM** value: **24.00**
17 ❑ Mar 1958 Cover: 0.10 **NM** value: **24.00**
18 ❑ Apr 1958 Cover: 0.10 **NM** value: **24.00**
19 ❑ May 1958 Cover: 0.10 **NM** value: **24.00**
20 ❑ Jun 1958 Cover: 0.10 **NM** value: **24.00**
21 ❑ Jul 1958 Cover: 0.10 **NM** value: **20.00**
22 ❑ Aug 1958 Cover: 0.10 **NM** value: **20.00**
23 ❑ Sep 1958 Cover: 0.10 **NM** value: **20.00**
24 ❑ Oct 1958 Cover: 0.10 **NM** value: **20.00**
25 ❑ Nov 1958 Cover: 0.10 **NM** value: **20.00**
26 ❑ Dec 1958 Cover: 0.10 **NM** value: **20.00**
27 ❑ Jan 1959 Cover: 0.10 **NM** value: **20.00**
28 ❑ Feb 1959 Cover: 0.10 **NM** value: **20.00**
29 ❑ Mar 1959 Cover: 0.10 **NM** value: **20.00**
30 ❑ Apr 1959 Cover: 0.10 **NM** value: **18.00**
31 ❑ May 1959 Cover: 0.10 **NM** value: **18.00**
32 ❑ Jun 1959 Cover: 0.10 **NM** value: **18.00**
33 ❑ Jul 1959 Cover: 0.10 **NM** value: **18.00**
34 ❑ Sep 1959 Cover: 0.10 **NM** value: **18.00**
35 ❑ Aug 1959 Cover: 0.10 **NM** value: **18.00**
36 ❑ Oct 1959 Cover: 0.10 **NM** value: **18.00**
37 ❑ Nov 1959 Cover: 0.10 **NM** value: **18.00**
38 ❑ Dec 1959 Cover: 0.10 **NM** value: **18.00**
39 ❑ Jan 1960 Cover: 0.10 **NM** value: **18.00**
40 ❑ Feb 1960 Cover: 0.10 **NM** value: **15.00**
41 ❑ Mar 1960 Cover: 0.10 **NM** value: **15.00**
42 ❑ Apr 1960 Cover: 0.10 **NM** value: **15.00**
43 ❑ May 1960 Cover: 0.10 **NM** value: **15.00**
44 ❑ Jun 1960 Cover: 0.10 **NM** value: **15.00**
45 ❑ Jul 1960 Cover: 0.10 **NM** value: **15.00**
46 ❑ Aug 1960 Cover: 0.10 **NM** value: **15.00**
• **CGC:** 1 graded, best 8.5
47 ❑ Sep 1960 Cover: 0.10 **NM** value: **15.00**
48 ❑ Oct 1960 Cover: 0.10 **NM** value: **15.00**
49 ❑ Nov 1960 Cover: 0.10 **NM** value: **15.00**
50 ❑ Dec 1960 Cover: 0.10 **NM** value: **15.00**
51 ❑ Jan 1961 Cover: 0.10 **NM** value: **12.00**
52 ❑ Feb 1961 Cover: 0.10 **NM** value: **12.00**
53 ❑ Mar 1961 Cover: 0.10 **NM** value: **12.00**
54 ❑ Apr 1961 Cover: 0.12 **NM** value: **12.00**
55 ❑ May 1961 Cover: 0.12 **NM** value: **12.00**
56 ❑ Jun 1961 Cover: 0.12 **NM** value: **12.00**
57 ❑ Jul 1961 Cover: 0.12 **NM** value: **12.00**
58 ❑ Aug 1961 Cover: 0.12 **NM** value: **12.00**
59 ❑ Sep 1961 Cover: 0.12 **NM** value: **12.00**
60 ❑ Oct 1961 Cover: 0.12 **NM** value: **12.00**
61 ❑ Nov 1961 Cover: 0.12 **NM** value: **12.00**

62 ❑ Dec 1961 Cover: 0.12 **NM** value: **12.00**
63 ❑ Jan 1962 Cover: 0.12 **NM** value: **12.00**
64 ❑ Feb 1962 Cover: 0.12 **NM** value: **12.00**
65 ❑ Mar 1962 Cover: 0.12 **NM** value: **12.00**
66 ❑ Apr 1962 Cover: 0.12 **NM** value: **12.00**
67 ❑ May 1962 Cover: 0.12 **NM** value: **12.00**
68 ❑ Jun 1962 Cover: 0.12 **NM** value: **12.00**
69 ❑ Aug 1962 Cover: 0.12 **NM** value: **12.00**
70 ❑ Oct 1962 Cover: 0.12 **NM** value: **12.00**
71 ❑ Dec 1962 Cover: 0.12 **NM** value: **8.00**
72 ❑ Feb 1963 Cover: 0.12 **NM** value: **8.00**
73 ❑ Apr 1963 Cover: 0.12 **NM** value: **8.00**
74 ❑ Jun 1963 Cover: 0.12 **NM** value: **8.00**
75 ❑ Aug 1963 Cover: 0.12 **NM** value: **8.00**
76 ❑ Oct 1963 Cover: 0.12 **NM** value: **8.00**
77 ❑ Dec 1963 Cover: 0.12 **NM** value: **8.00**
78 ❑ Feb 1964 Cover: 0.12 **NM** value: **8.00**
79 ❑ Apr 1964 Cover: 0.12 **NM** value: **8.00**
80 ❑ Jun 1964 Cover: 0.12 **NM** value: **8.00**
81 ❑ Aug 1964 Cover: 0.12 **NM** value: **8.00**
82 ❑ Oct 1964 Cover: 0.12 **NM** value: **8.00**
83 ❑ Dec 1964 Cover: 0.12 **NM** value: **8.00**
84 ❑ Feb 1965 Cover: 0.12 **NM** value: **8.00**
85 ❑ Apr 1965 Cover: 0.12 **NM** value: **8.00**
86 ❑ Jun 1965 Cover: 0.12 **NM** value: **8.00**
87 ❑ Aug 1965 Cover: 0.12 **NM** value: **8.00**
88 ❑ Oct 1965 Cover: 0.12 **NM** value: **8.00**
89 ❑ Dec 1965 Cover: 0.12 **NM** value: **8.00**
90 ❑ Feb 1966 Cover: 0.12 **NM** value: **8.00**
91 ❑ Apr 1966 Cover: 0.12 **NM** value: **6.00**
92 ❑ Jun 1966 Cover: 0.12 **NM** value: **6.00**
93 ❑ Aug 1966 Cover: 0.12 **NM** value: **6.00**
94 ❑ Oct 1966 Cover: 0.12 **NM** value: **6.00**
95 ❑ Dec 1966 Cover: 0.12 **NM** value: **6.00**
96 ❑ Feb 1967 Cover: 0.12 **NM** value: **6.00**
Circ: Statement: **177,303**
97 ❑ Apr 1967 Cover: 0.12 **NM** value: **6.00**
Circ: Statement: **177,303**
98 ❑ Jun 1967 Cover: 0.12 **NM** value: **6.00**
Circ: Statement: **177,303**
99 ❑ Aug 1967 Cover: 0.12 **NM** value: **6.00**
Circ: Statement: **177,303**
100 ❑ Oct 1967 Cover: 0.12 **NM** value: **6.00**
Circ: Statement: **177,303**
101 ❑ Dec 1967 Cover: 0.12 **NM** value: **6.00**
Circ: Statement: **177,303**
102 ❑ Feb 1968 Cover: 0.12 **NM** value: **6.00**
103 ❑ Apr 1968 Cover: 0.12 **NM** value: **6.00**
104 ❑ Jun 1968 Cover: 0.12 **NM** value: **6.00**
• Has 1967 Statement, filed 10/1/67; avg print run 351,568; avg sales 177,263; avg subs 40; avg total paid 177,303; samples 345; max existent 177,648; 50% of run returned
105 ❑ Aug 1968 Cover: 0.12 **NM** value: **6.00**
106 ❑ Oct 1968 Cover: 0.12 **NM** value: **6.00**
107 ❑ Dec 1968 Cover: 0.12 **NM** value: **6.00**
108 ❑ Feb 1969 Cover: 0.12 **NM** value: **6.00**
109 ❑ 1969 Cover: 0.12 **NM** value: **6.00**
110 ❑ May 1969 Cover: 0.12 **NM** value: **6.00**
111 ❑ 1969 Cover: 0.15 **NM** value: **5.00**
112 ❑ 1969 Cover: 0.15 **NM** value: **5.00**
113 ❑ Oct 1969 Cover: 0.15 **NM** value: **5.00**
114 ❑ 1969 Cover: 0.15 **NM** value: **5.00**
115 ❑ Jan 1970 Cover: 0.15 **NM** value: **5.00**
116 ❑ Mar 1970 Cover: 0.15 **NM** value: **5.00**
117 ❑ May 1970 Cover: 0.15 **NM** value: **5.00**
118 ❑ Jul 1970 Cover: 0.15 **NM** value: **5.00**
119 ❑ Sep 1970 Cover: 0.15 **NM** value: **5.00**
120 ❑ Nov 1970 Cover: 0.15 **NM** value: **5.00**
121 ❑ Dec 1970 Cover: 0.15 **NM** value: **5.00**
122 ❑ Feb 1971 Cover: 0.15 **NM** value: **5.00**
123 ❑ 1971 Cover: 0.15 **NM** value: **5.00**
124 ❑ Jun 1971 Cover: 0.15 **NM** value: **5.00**
125 ❑ 1971 Cover: 0.15 **NM** value: **5.00**
126 ❑ Sep 1971 Cover: 0.15 **NM** value: **5.00**
127 ❑ Oct 1971 Cover: 0.25 **NM** value: **5.00**
128 ❑ Dec 1971 Cover: 0.25 **NM** value: **5.00**
129 ❑ Cover: 0.25 **NM** value: **5.00**
130 ❑ May 1972 Cover: 0.25 **NM** value: **5.00**
📖 Having a Wonderful Time; The Gallopin' Ghost; The Silent Ghost; Is Booing Necessary?; Healthy Haunt; The Phony Ghost!; Wendy: The Wand Tester
131 ❑ Jul 1972 Cover: 0.25 **NM** value: **4.00**
132 ❑ Sep 1972 Cover: 0.25 **NM** value: **4.00**
133 ❑ Nov 1972 Cover: 0.20 **NM** value: **4.00**
134 ❑ Jan 1973 Cover: 0.20 **NM** value: **4.00**
Circ: Statement: **126,488**
135 ❑ Mar 1973 Cover: 0.20 **NM** value: **4.00**
Circ: Statement: **126,488**
136 ❑ May 1973 Cover: 0.20 **NM** value: **4.00**
Circ: Statement: **126,488**
137 ❑ Jul 1973 Cover: 0.20 **NM** value: **4.00**
Circ: Statement: **126,488**
138 ❑ Sep 1973 Cover: 0.20 **NM** value: **4.00**
Circ: Statement: **126,488**
139 ❑ Nov 1973 Cover: 0.20 **NM** value: **4.00**
Circ: Statement: **126,488**
140 ❑ Jul 1974 Cover: 0.25 **NM** value: **4.00**
Circ: Statement: **137,137**
• Has 1973 Statement; avg total paid circ 126,488
141 ❑ Sep 1974 Cover: 0.25 **NM** value: **4.00**
Circ: Statement: **137,137**
142 ❑ Nov 1974 Cover: 0.25 **NM** value: **4.00**
Circ: Statement: **137,137**
143 ❑ Jan 1975 Cover: 0.25 **NM** value: **4.00**
Circ: Statement: **120,020**
144 ❑ Mar 1975 Cover: 0.25 **NM** value: **4.00**
Circ: Statement: **120,020**
• Has 1974 Statement; avg total paid circ 137,137
145 ❑ May 1975 Cover: 0.25 **NM** value: **4.00**
Circ: Statement: **120,020**
146 ❑ Jul 1975 Cover: 0.25 **NM** value: **4.00**
Circ: Statement: **120,020**
147 ❑ Sep 1975 Cover: 0.25 **NM** value: **4.00**
Circ: Statement: **120,020**
148 ❑ Nov 1975 Cover: 0.25 **NM** value: **4.00**
Circ: Statement: **120,020**
149 ❑ Jan 1976 Cover: 0.25 **NM** value: **4.00**
150 ❑ Mar 1976 Cover: 0.25 **NM** value: **4.00**
151 ❑ May 1976 Cover: 0.25 **NM** value: **4.00**
152 ❑ Jul 1976 Cover: 0.25 **NM** value: **4.00**
153 ❑ Sep 1976 Cover: 0.25 **NM** value: **4.00**
154 ❑ Nov 1976 Cover: 0.30 **NM** value: **4.00**
155 ❑ Jan 1977 Cover: 0.30 **NM** value: **4.00**
156 ❑ Dec 1977 Cover: 0.30 **NM** value: **4.00**
157 ❑ Feb 1978 Cover: 0.30 **NM** value: **4.00**
158 ❑ Apr 1978 Cover: 0.30 **NM** value: **4.00**
159 ❑ Sep 1978 Cover: 0.35 **NM** value: **4.00**
160 ❑ Oct 1979 Cover: 0.40 **NM** value: **4.00**
161 ❑ Sep 1980 Cover: 0.50 **NM** value: **4.00**

SPOOKY (VOL. 2) — Harvey

1 ❑ ca. 1991 Cover: 1.25 **NM** value: **Cover or less**
2 ❑ ca. 1991 Cover: 1.25 **NM** value: **Cover or less**
3 ❑ ca. 1991 Cover: 1.25 **NM** value: **Cover or less**
4 ❑ ca. 1991 Cover: 1.25 **NM** value: **Cover or less**
📖 No Boos are Good Boos; Nightmare The Galloping Ghost; Spooky and the Jeannie; Casper: Ghost Wanted; Wendy the Good Little Witch and the Lazy Witch

SPORT COMICS — Street & Smith

1 ❑ Oct 1940 Cover: 0.10 **NM** value: **350.00**
• **CGC:** 2 graded, best 6.5
2 ❑ 1941 Cover: 0.10 **NM** value: **200.00**
3 ❑ 1941 Cover: 0.10 **NM** value: **200.00**
4 ❑ 1941 Cover: 0.10 **NM** value: **200.00**

SPORTS ACTION — Atlas

2 ❑ Feb 1950 Cover: 0.10 **NM** value: **250.00**
• **CGC:** 1 graded, best 9.4
3 ❑ Jun 1950 Cover: 0.10 **NM** value: **150.00**
4 ❑ Oct 1950 Cover: 0.10 **NM** value: **150.00**
5 ❑ Jan 1951 Cover: 0.10 **NM** value: **150.00**
6 ❑ Mar 1951 Cover: 0.10 **NM** value: **125.00**
7 ❑ May 1951 Cover: 0.10 **NM** value: **125.00**
8 ❑ Aug 1951 Cover: 0.10 **NM** value: **125.00**
9 ❑ Oct 1951 Cover: 0.10 **NM** value: **125.00**
10 ❑ Jan 1952 Cover: 0.10 **NM** value: **125.00**
11 ❑ Mar 1952 Cover: 0.10 **NM** value: **100.00**
12 ❑ May 1952 Cover: 0.10 **NM** value: **100.00**
13 ❑ Jul 1952 Cover: 0.10 **NM** value: **100.00**
14 ❑ Sep 1952 Cover: 0.10 **NM** value: **100.00**

SPORTS CLASSICS — Personality

1 ❑ Cover: 2.95 **NM** value: **Cover or less**
1/LE ❑ Cover: 5.95 **NM** value: **Cover or less**
• limited edition.
2 ❑ Cover: 2.95 **NM** value: **Cover or less**
3 ❑ Cover: 2.95 **NM** value: **Cover or less**
4 ❑ Cover: 2.95 **NM** value: **Cover or less**
5 ❑ Cover: 2.95 **NM** value: **Cover or less**

SPORTS COMICS — Personality

1 ❑ Cover: 2.50 **NM** value: **Cover or less**
2 ❑ Cover: 2.50 **NM** value: **Cover or less**
3 ❑ Cover: 2.50 **NM** value: **Cover or less**
4 ❑ Cover: 2.50 **NM** value: **Cover or less**

SPORTS HALL OF SHAME IN 3-D — Blackthorne

1 ❑ Cover: 2.50 **NM** value: **Cover or less**
• baseball

SPORTS LEGENDS — Revolutionary

1 ❑ Sep 1992, b&w Cover: 2.50 **NM** value: **Cover or less**
• Joe Namath
2 ❑ Oct 1992, b&w Cover: 2.50 **NM** value: **Cover or less**
• Gordie Howe
3 ❑ Nov 1992, b&w Cover: 2.50 **NM** value: **Cover or less**
• Arthur Ashe
4 ❑ Dec 1992, full color Cover: 2.50 **NM** value: **Cover or less**
• Muhammad Ali
5 ❑ Jan 1993, full color Cover: 2.50 **NM** value: **Cover or less**
• O.J. Simpson
6 ❑ Feb 1993, full color Cover: 2.50 **NM** value: **Cover or less**
• K.A. Jabbar
7 ❑ Mar 1993, b&w Cover: 2.95 **NM** value: **Cover or less**
• Walter Payton
8 ❑ Apr 1993, b&w Cover: 2.95 **NM** value: **Cover or less**
• Wilt Chamberlain
9 ❑ May 1993, b&w Cover: 2.95 **NM** value: **Cover or less**
• Joe Louis

SPORTS LEGENDS SPECIAL – BREAKING THE COLOR BARRIER — Revolutionary

1 ❑ Oct 1993, b&w Cover: 2.95 **NM** value: **Cover or less**

SPORTS PERSONALITIES — Personality

1 ❑ Cover: 2.95 **NM** value: **Cover or less**
• Bo Jackson
2 ❑ Cover: 2.95 **NM** value: **Cover or less**
• Nolan Ryan
3 ❑ Cover: 2.95 **NM** value: **Cover or less**
• Rickey Henderson
4 ❑ Cover: 2.95 **NM** value: **Cover or less**
• Magic Johnson
5 ❑ Cover: 2.95 **NM** value: **Cover or less**
6 ❑ Cover: 2.95 **NM** value: **Cover or less**
7 ❑ Cover: 2.95 **NM** value: **Cover or less**
8 ❑ Cover: 2.95 **NM** value: **Cover or less**
9 ❑ Cover: 2.95 **NM** value: **Cover or less**
10 ❑ Cover: 2.95 **NM** value: **Cover or less**
11 ❑ Cover: 2.95 **NM** value: **Cover or less**
12 ❑ Cover: 2.95 **NM** value: **Cover or less**
13 ❑ Cover: 2.95 **NM** value: **Cover or less**

SPORT STARS (1ST SERIES) — Parents' Magazine Institute

1 ❑ Feb 1946 Cover: 0.10 **NM** value: **300.00**
2 ❑ Apr 1946 Cover: 0.10 **NM** value: **200.00**
3 ❑ Jun 1946 Cover: 1.10 **NM** value: **150.00**
4 ❑ Sep 1946 Cover: 0.10 **NM** value: **150.00**

SPORT STARS (2ND SERIES) — Atlas

1 ❑ Nov 1949 Cover: 0.10 **NM** value: **300.00**

SPORTS SUPERSTARS — Revolutionary

1 ❑ Apr 1992, b&w Cover: 2.50 **NM** value: **Cover or less**
• Michael Jordan
2 ❑ May 1992, b&w Cover: 2.50 **NM** value: **Cover or less**
• Wayne Gretzsky
3 ❑ Jun 1992, b&w Cover: 2.50 **NM** value: **Cover or less**
• Magic Johnson **A:** Ken Landgraf **W:** John Harrington
4 ❑ Jul 1992, b&w Cover: 2.50 **NM** value: **Cover or less**
• Joe Montana
5 ❑ Aug 1992, b&w Cover: 2.50 **NM** value: **Cover or less**
• Mike Tyson
6 ❑ Sep 1992, b&w Cover: 2.50 **NM** value: **Cover or less**
• Larry Bird
7 ❑ Oct 1992, b&w Cover: 2.50 **NM** value: **Cover or less**
• John Elway
8 ❑ Nov 1992, b&w Cover: 2.50 **NM** value: **Cover or less**
• Julius Erving
9 ❑ Dec 1992, full color Cover: 2.75 **NM** value: **Cover or less**
• Barry Sanders
10 ❑ Jan 1993, full color Cover: 2.75 **NM** value: **Cover or less**
• Isiah Thomas
11 ❑ Feb 1992, full color Cover: 2.95 **NM** value: **Cover or less**
• **CGC:** 1 graded, best 8.5
• Mario Lemieux
12 ❑ Mar 1993, b&w Cover: 2.95 **NM** value: **Cover or less**
• Dan Marino
13 ❑ Apr 1993, b&w Cover: 2.95 **NM** value: **Cover or less**
• Deion Sanders
14 ❑ May 1993, b&w Cover: 2.95 **NM** value: **Cover or less**
• Patrick Ewing
15 ❑ Jun 1993, b&w Cover: 2.95 **NM** value: **Cover or less**
• Charles Barkley
16 ❑ Aug 1993, b&w Cover: 2.95 **NM** value: **Cover or less**
• Shaquille O'neal, Christian Laettner
Anl 1 ❑ Feb 1993, full color Cover: 2.75 **NM** value: **Cover or less**
• Michael Jordan II

SPOTLIGHT — Marvel

1 ❑ Sep 1978 Cover: 0.35 **NM** value: **8.00**
• Huckleberry Hound
2 ❑ Nov 1978 Cover: 0.35 **NM** value: **6.00**
3 ❑ Jan 1979 Cover: 0.35 **NM** value: **6.00**
4 ❑ Mar 1979 Cover: 0.35 **NM** value: **6.00**

SPOTLIGHT COMICS — Harry A. Chesler

1 ❑ Nov 1944 Cover: 0.10 **NM** value: **500.00**
• **CGC:** 1 graded, best 8.5
2 ❑ Jan 1945 Cover: 0.10 **NM** value: **350.00**
3 ❑ Mar 1945 Cover: 0.10 **NM** value: **350.00**
• **CGC:** 1 graded, best 8.5

SPOTLIGHT ON THE GENIUS THAT IS JOE SACCO — Fantagraphics

1 ❑ b&w Cover: 4.95 **NM** value: **Cover or less**
No issue number.

SPOTTY THE PUP — Avon

1 ❑ 1953 Cover: 0.10 **NM** value: **25.00**
2 ❑ 1953 Cover: 0.10 **NM** value: **25.00**
3 ❑ 1953 Cover: 0.10 **NM** value: **25.00**

SPRING BREAK COMICS — AC

1 ❑ Mar 1987, b&w Cover: 1.00 **NM** value: **1.50**
Circ: CapCity orders: **900**

SPRING-HEEL JACK — Rebel

1 ❑ b&w Cover: 2.25 **NM** value: **Cover or less**
2 ❑ b&w Cover: 2.25 **NM** value: **Cover or less**

SPRINGTIME TALES (WALT KELLY'S...) — Eclipse

1 ❑ Cover: 2.50 **NM** value: **Cover or less**
• Peter Wheat **A:** Walt Kelly

SPUD — Spud Press

1 ❑ Sum 1996, b&w Cover: 3.50 **NM** value: **Cover or less**

SPUNGIFEEL PRIMER, THE — Spungifeel Comix

Bk 1 ❑ b&w Cover: 11.95 **NM** value: **Cover or less**

SPUNKY — Standard

1 ❑ ca. 1949 Cover: 0.10 **NM** value: **50.00**
2 ❑ ca. 1949 Cover: 0.10 **NM** value: **40.00**
3 ❑ ca. 1949 Cover: 0.10 **NM** value: **25.00**
4 ❑ ca. 1950 Cover: 0.10 **NM** value: **25.00**
5 ❑ ca. 1950 Cover: 0.10 **NM** value: **25.00**

CGC-graded: Multiply prices above by **33 for 9.9 M • 16 for 9.8 NM/M • 7 for 9.6 NM+ • 5 for 9.4 NM • 2.5 for 9.2 NM- • 1.5 for 9.0 VF/NM**

6 ❑ ca. 1950 Cover: 0.10 **NM** value: **25.00**
7 ❑ ca. 1950 Cover: 0.10 **NM** value: **25.00**

SPUNKY KNIGHT — Fantagraphics / Eros

1 ❑ May 1996 Cover: 2.95 **NM** value: **Cover or less**
2 ❑ Jun 1996 Cover: 2.95 **NM** value: **Cover or less**
3 ❑ Jul 1996 Cover: 2.95 **NM** value: **Cover or less**

SPUNKY THE SMILING SPOOK — Ajax

1 ❑ Aug 1957 Cover: 0.10 **NM** value: **50.00**
2 ❑ Oct 1957 Cover: 0.10 **NM** value: **35.00**
3 ❑ Jan 1958 Cover: 0.10 **NM** value: **35.00**
4 ❑ Apr 1958 Cover: 0.10 **NM** value: **35.00**

SPUNKY TODD: THE PSYCHIC BOY — Caliber

1 ❑ b&w Cover: 2.95 **NM** value: **Cover or less**

SPY AND COUNTERSPY — ACG

1 ❑ Aug 1949 Cover: 0.10 **NM** value: **175.00**
2 ❑ Oct 1949 Cover: 0.10 **NM** value: **100.00**

SPYBOY — Dark Horse

Alex gets bullied in high school, tries to avoid the girl claimed by the local schoolyard tough, and wishes he had the skills of his favorite martial arts and spy movie heroes at his disposal. He doesn't realize that his father and grandfather hold secrets or that the mysterious blonde outside his window will play a big role in his future.

But when a secret code is spoken to him after a particularly rough couple of days at school, Alex finds himself transformed: in command of a nifty arsenal, a set of killer kung fu moves, and at the center of attention of some really bald, really bad, guys in black. And then the fun begins.

Writer Peter David's career includes runs on such titles as The Incredible Hulk and Soulsearchers and Company. He teams with artist Pop Mhan, who brings an anime look to the series.

1 ❑ Oct 1999 Cover: 2.50 **NM** value: **4.00**
Circ: Diamd. preorders: **19,149**
A: Pop Mhan **W:** Peter David

2 ❑ Nov 1999 Cover: 2.50 **NM** value: **3.00**
Circ: Diamd. preorders: **14,264**
📖 Live and Let Fry **A:** Pop Mhan **W:** Peter David

3 ❑ Dec 1999 Cover: 2.50 **NM** value: **3.00**
Circ: Diamd. preorders: **15,638**
📖 From Russia With Fries and a Coke **A:** Pop Mhan **W:** Peter David

4 ❑ Jan 2000 Cover: 2.50 **NM** value: **3.00**
Circ: Diamd. preorders: **13,223**
W: Peter David

5 ❑ Feb 2000 Cover: 2.50 **NM** value: **3.00**
Circ: Diamd. preorders: **12,568**
W: Peter David

6 ❑ Mar 2000 Cover: 2.50 **NM** value: **Cover or less**
Circ: Diamd. preorders: **12,651**
W: Peter David

7 ❑ Apr 2000 Cover: 2.50 **NM** value: **Cover or less**
Circ: Diamd. preorders: **12,457**
W: Peter David

8 ❑ May 2000 Cover: 2.50 **NM** value: **Cover or less**
Circ: Diamd. preorders: **12,377**
A: Carlos Meglia **W:** Peter David

9 ❑ Jun 2000 Cover: 2.50 **NM** value: **Cover or less**
Circ: Diamd. preorders: **12,324**
📖 Boldfinger **A:** Pop Mhan **W:** Peter David

10 ❑ Jul 2000 Cover: 2.50 **NM** value: **Cover or less**
Circ: Diamd. preorders: **12,283**
W: Peter David

11 ❑ Aug 2000 Cover: 2.50 **NM** value: **Cover or less**
Circ: Diamd. preorders: **11,602**
W: Peter David

12 ❑ Sep 2000 Cover: 2.95 **NM** value: **Cover or less**
Circ: Diamd. preorders: **11,778**
📖 Spygirl! **A:** Pop Mhan **W:** Peter David

13 ❑ Oct 2000 Cover: 2.95 **NM** value: **Cover or less**
A: Pop Mhan **W:** Peter David

14 ❑ Nov 2000 Cover: 2.99 **NM** value: **Cover or less**
Circ: Diamd. preorders: **11,740**
📖 The Beer and the Dragon **A:** Pop Mhan **W:** Peter David

15 ❑ Jan 2001 Cover: 2.99 **NM** value: **Cover or less**
Circ: Diamd. preorders: **12,839**
📖 The Deadly Gourmet Affair **A:** Pop Mhan **W:** Peter David

16 ❑ Mar 2001 Cover: 2.99 **NM** value: **Cover or less**
Circ: Diamd. preorders: **11,007**
📖 Fatal Election! **A:** Pop Mhan **W:** Peter David

SPY CASES — Atlas

26 ❑ Sep 1950 Cover: 0.10 **NM** value: **150.00**
• **CGC:** 1 graded, best 4.5
27 ❑ Nov 1950 Cover: 0.10 **NM** value: **100.00**
28 ❑ Feb 1951 Cover: 0.10 **NM** value: **100.00**
4 ❑ Apr 1951 Cover: 0.10 **NM** value: **75.00**
📖 Discs of Death; Secret Invasion; The Secret of Hakin's Harem
5 ❑ Jun 1951 Cover: 0.10 **NM** value: **75.00**
6 ❑ Aug 1951 Cover: 0.10 **NM** value: **75.00**
7 ❑ Oct 1951 Cover: 0.10 **NM** value: **75.00**
8 ❑ Dec 1951 Cover: 0.10 **NM** value: **75.00**
9 ❑ Feb 1952 Cover: 0.10 **NM** value: **75.00**
10 ❑ Apr 1952 Cover: 0.10 **NM** value: **75.00**
11 ❑ Jun 1952 Cover: 0.10 **NM** value: **50.00**
12 ❑ Aug 1952 Cover: 0.10 **NM** value: **50.00**
13 ❑ Oct 1952 Cover: 0.10 **NM** value: **50.00**
14 ❑ Dec 1952 Cover: 0.10 **NM** value: **50.00**
15 ❑ Feb 1953 Cover: 0.10 **NM** value: **50.00**
16 ❑ Apr 1953 Cover: 0.10 **NM** value: **50.00**
17 ❑ Jun 1953 Cover: 0.10 **NM** value: **50.00**
18 ❑ Aug 1953 Cover: 0.10 **NM** value: **50.00**
19 ❑ Oct 1953 Cover: 0.10 **NM** value: **50.00**

SPY FIGHTERS — Atlas

1 ❑ Mar 1951 Cover: 0.10 **NM** value: **150.00**
2 ❑ May 1951 Cover: 0.10 **NM** value: **100.00**
3 ❑ Jul 1951 Cover: 0.10 **NM** value: **75.00**
4 ❑ Sep 1951 Cover: 0.10 **NM** value: **75.00**
5 ❑ Nov 1951 Cover: 0.10 **NM** value: **75.00**
6 ❑ Jan 1952 Cover: 0.10 **NM** value: **75.00**
7 ❑ Mar 1952 Cover: 0.10 **NM** value: **75.00**
8 ❑ May 1952 Cover: 0.10 **NM** value: **75.00**
9 ❑ Jul 1952 Cover: 0.10 **NM** value: **75.00**
10 ❑ Sep 1952 Cover: 0.10 **NM** value: **75.00**
11 ❑ Nov 1952 Cover: 0.10 **NM** value: **75.00**
12 ❑ Jan 1953 Cover: 0.10 **NM** value: **75.00**
13 ❑ Mar 1953 Cover: 0.10 **NM** value: **75.00**
14 ❑ May 1953 Cover: 0.10 **NM** value: **75.00**
15 ❑ Jul 1953 Cover: 0.10 **NM** value: **75.00**

SPY HUNTERS — ACG

3 ❑ Dec 1949 Cover: 0.10 **NM** value: **175.00**
• **CGC:** 1 graded, best 8.5
4 ❑ Feb 1950 Cover: 0.10 **NM** value: **100.00**
• Commie sub cover ★ Appearance of Adolf Hitler.
5 ❑ Apr 1950 Cover: 0.10 **NM** value: **100.00**
6 ❑ Jun 1950 Cover: 0.10 **NM** value: **100.00**
7 ❑ Aug 1950 Cover: 0.10 **NM** value: **100.00**
8 ❑ Oct 1950 Cover: 0.10 **NM** value: **100.00**
• **CGC:** 1 graded, best 9.2
9 ❑ Dec 1950 Cover: 0.10 **NM** value: **100.00**
10 ❑ Feb 1951 Cover: 0.10 **NM** value: **100.00**
11 ❑ Apr 1951 Cover: 0.10 **NM** value: **75.00**
12 ❑ Jun 1951 Cover: 0.10 **NM** value: **75.00**
13 ❑ Aug 1951 Cover: 0.10 **NM** value: **75.00**
14 ❑ Oct 1951 Cover: 0.10 **NM** value: **75.00**
• Red China cover
15 ❑ Dec 1951 Cover: 0.10 **NM** value: **75.00**
16 ❑ Feb 1952 Cover: 0.10 **NM** value: **75.00**
17 ❑ May 1952 Cover: 0.10 **NM** value: **75.00**
18 ❑ Jul 1952 Cover: 0.10 **NM** value: **75.00**
19 ❑ Sep 1952 Cover: 0.10 **NM** value: **75.00**
20 ❑ Nov 1952 Cover: 0.10 **NM** value: **75.00**
21 ❑ Jan 1953 Cover: 0.10 **NM** value: **60.00**
22 ❑ Mar 1953 Cover: 0.10 **NM** value: **60.00**
23 ❑ May 1953 Cover: 0.10 **NM** value: **60.00**
• **CGC:** 1 graded, best 7.0
24 ❑ Jul 1953 Cover: 0.10 **NM** value: **60.00**

SPYKE — Marvel / Epic

1 ❑ Jul 1993 Cover: 2.50 **NM** value: **Cover or less**
Circ: CapCity orders: **18,000**
Embossed cover. **A:** Bill Reinhold **W:** Mike Baron ★ 1st Appearance of Spyke Jones.

2 ❑ Aug 1993 Cover: 1.95 **NM** value: **Cover or less**
Circ: CapCity orders: **8,200**
A: Bill Reinhold **W:** Mike Baron

3 ❑ Sep 1993 Cover: 1.95 **NM** value: **Cover or less**
Circ: CapCity orders: **6,100**
A: Bill Reinhold **W:** Mike Baron

4 ❑ Oct 1993 Cover: 1.95 **NM** value: **Cover or less**
Circ: CapCity orders: **4,800**
A: Bill Reinhold **W:** Mike Baron ★ Appearance of Muffy, Sonia.

SPY SMASHER — Fawcett

Though his own title designates him "hero of Whiz Comics," Spy Smasher gets his own title as well, for a time, as he "battles the sharks of steel," "whacks the Japs," and "batters the Axis." With the 10th issue asking on the cover, "Did Spy Smasher kill Hitler?" (long before Hitler's death), it's clear that the character, introduced in Whiz Comics in February 1940 (before America joined the fight in World War II), quickly became enmeshed in combat. In fact, he didn't survive long after the conflict ended, even in Whiz.

Of interest is the Republic 12-chapter movie serial, complicating the premise with twins wearing the goggles and red cape, as they defended democracy. — Maggie

1 ❑ Fal 1941 Cover: 0.10 **NM** value: **3000.00**
• **CGC:** 3 graded, best 5.5
2 ❑ Win 1941 Cover: 0.10 **NM** value: **1500.00**
• **CGC:** 3 graded, best 9.0
3 ❑ Feb 1942 Cover: 0.10 **NM** value: **1000.00**
• **CGC:** 1 graded, best 7.0
4 ❑ Apr 1942 Cover: 0.10 **NM** value: **1000.00**
• **CGC:** 1 graded, best 8.0
5 ❑ Jun 1942 Cover: 0.10 **NM** value: **1000.00**
• **CGC:** 1 graded, best 3.5
6 ❑ Aug 1942 Cover: 0.10 **NM** value: **750.00**
• **CGC:** 1 graded, best 4.5
7 ❑ Oct 1942 Cover: 0.10 **NM** value: **750.00**
• **CGC:** 2 graded, best 9.2
8 ❑ Nov 1942 Cover: 0.10 **NM** value: **750.00**
• **CGC:** 1 graded, best 9.6
9 ❑ Dec 1942 Cover: 0.10 **NM** value: **750.00**
10 ❑ Jan 1943 Cover: 0.10 **NM** value: **750.00**
• **CGC:** 2 graded, best 7.5
11 ❑ Feb 1943 Cover: 0.10 **NM** value: **750.00**
• **CGC:** 1 graded, best 3.5

SPY THRILLERS — Atlas

1 ❑ Nov 1954 Cover: 0.10 **NM** value: **150.00**
2 ❑ Jan 1955 Cover: 0.10 **NM** value: **90.00**
3 ❑ Mar 1955 Cover: 0.10 **NM** value: **75.00**
4 ❑ May 1955 Cover: 0.10 **NM** value: **75.00**

SQUADRON SUPREME — Marvel

Squadron Supreme is a 12-issue mini-series which paints a dark vision of super-heroes determining the fate of the world. Although it uses Marvel characters, it should be thought of as an "alternate reality" story.

It begins when Kyle Richmond (Nighthawk) quits the Defenders, deciding he can help the world more by becoming a congressman. He succeeds and eventually becomes president of the United States. Then, a being called the Overmind strikes, controlling Richmond's mind, the minds of his top advisors, and those of the Squadron Supreme (the government's top super-heroes). Under the Overmind's influence, America wages war against the entire world, eventually conquering it. By the time the Squadron Supreme throws off the Overmind's control, the world is in shambles. They decide to embark on a bold new plan: to use their powers to turn the world into a utopia. The catch: They will become its absolute rulers.

1 ❑ Sep 1985 Cover: 1.25 **NM** value: **1.50**
Circ: CapCity orders: **24,400**
📖 The Utopia Principle **A:** Bob Hall **W:** Mark Gruenwald

2 ❑ Oct 1985 Cover: 0.75 **NM** value: **1.00**
Circ: CapCity orders: **19,600**
W: Mark Gruenwald ★ Versus Scarlet Centurion.

3 ❑ Nov 1985 Cover: 0.75 **NM** value: **1.00**
Circ: CapCity orders: **20,400**
W: Mark Gruenwald

4 ❑ Dec 1985 Cover: 0.75 **NM** value: **1.00**
Circ: CapCity orders: **19,300**
W: Mark Gruenwald

5 ❑ Jan 1986 Cover: 0.75 **NM** value: **1.00**
Circ: CapCity orders: **19,100**
W: Mark Gruenwald ★ Versus Institute of Evil.

6 ❑ Feb 1986 Cover: 0.75 **NM** value: **1.00**
Circ: CapCity orders: **19,300**
W: Mark Gruenwald

7 ❑ Mar 1986 Cover: 0.75 **NM** value: **1.00**
Circ: CapCity orders: **18,600**
W: Mark Gruenwald

8 ❑ Apr 1986 Cover: 0.75 **NM** value: **1.00**
Circ: CapCity orders: **18,100**
W: Mark Gruenwald

9 ❑ May 1986 Cover: 0.75 **NM** value: **1.00**
Circ: CapCity orders: **17,100**
W: Mark Gruenwald ★ Death of Tom Thumb.

10 ❑ Jun 1986 Cover: 0.75 **NM** value: **1.00**
Circ: CapCity orders: **16,500**
W: Mark Gruenwald

11 ❑ Jul 1986 Cover: 0.75 **NM** value: **1.00**
Circ: CapCity orders: **16,100**
W: Mark Gruenwald

12 ❑ Aug 1986 Cover: 1.25 **NM** value: **Cover or less**
Circ: CapCity orders: **16,800**
W: Mark Gruenwald

Bk 1 ❑ Dec 1989 Cover: 9.95 **NM** value: **24.99**
Circ: CapCity orders: **4,650**
• Collects Squadron Supreme #1-12; Printed after Mark Gruenwald's death-includes part of his remains mixed in ink. **W:** Mark Gruenwald ★ Death of a Universe.

SQUALOR — First

1 ❑ Dec 1989 Cover: 2.75 **NM** value: **Cover or less**
Circ: CapCity orders: **7,425**
📖 Quiet Island • 1st comics work by Stefan Petrucha **A:** Tom Sutton **W:** Stefan Petrucha

2 ❑ Jun 1990 Cover: 2.75 **NM** value: **Cover or less**
Circ: CapCity orders: **4,525**
A: Tom Sutton **W:** Stefan Petrucha

3 ❑ Jul 1990 Cover: 2.75 **NM** value: **Cover or less**
Circ: CapCity orders: **3,950**
A: Tom Sutton **W:** Stefan Petrucha

4 ❑ Aug 1990 Cover: 2.75 **NM** value: **Cover or less**
Circ: CapCity orders: **4,000**
A: Tom Sutton **W:** Stefan Petrucha

There are two different pricing tiers in the modern comic-book hobby. **The prices seen above** are the prices we have seen **loose copies** of these issues reliably fetch in a variety of environments. Condition alters the price by the fractions seen on the bar on the bottom of left-hand pages of this book. **Comics graded by CGC** usually sell for more. Use the guide on the bottom of right-hand pages of this book to estimate what copies have brought on eBay.

Other grades: Multiply prices above by **1.5 for Mint • 2/3 for Very Fine • 1/3 for Fine • 1/5 for Very Good • 1/8 for Good**

SQUEE! — Slave Labor

Jhonen Vasquez, creator of Squee! and Johnny the Homicidal Maniac is the Tim Burton of comics. Using deliciously nightmarish imagery, he specializes in drawing the reader into the terrifying moments of childhood — like when you really get to know what that thing in your closet is, or when the thing under the bed starts talking back to you.

Some might say that Squee (the little-boy hero of the series) just has an overactive imagination, but he knows the real truth. He knows that lurking horrors inhabit the closed stalls in convenience-store bathrooms and that future versions of himself occasionally appear to warn him of some grave disaster — then forget what they were meant to say. Worse yet, he knows all about his next-door neighbor Johnny.

1 ❑ Apr 1997 Cover: 2.95 **NM** value: **7.00**
Circ: Diamd. preorders: **11,302**
📖 A Walk to School; Tickle Me Hellmo!; Fun with Filler **A:** Jhonen Vasquez **W:** Jhonen Vasquez

1-2 ❑ 1997 Cover: 2.95 **NM** value: **Cover or less**
Circ: Diamd. preorders: **721**

2 ❑ Jul 1997 Cover: 2.95 **NM** value: **5.00**
Circ: Diamd. preorders: **12,145**
A: Jhonen Vasquez **W:** Jhonen Vasquez

3 ❑ Nov 1997 Cover: 2.95 **NM** value: **3.50**
Circ: Diamd. preorders: **13,134**
📖 Just Before Bedtime; The Space Monkey; A Little Visitor; True Tales of Human Drama!; A Brief Friend; Meanwhile; Dinner With Satan **A:** Jhonen Vasquez **W:** Jhonen Vasquez

4 ❑ Feb 1998 Cover: 2.95 **NM** value: **3.50**
Circ: Diamd. preorders: **13,428**
A: Jhonen Vasquez **W:** Jhonen Vasquez

Bk 1 ❑ Cover: 15.95 **NM** value: **Cover or less**
A: Jhonen Vasquez **W:** Jhonen Vasquez

SQUEEKS — Lev Gleason

1 ❑ Oct 1953 Cover: 0.10 **NM** value: **50.00**
2 ❑ Dec 1953 Cover: 0.10 **NM** value: **25.00**
3 ❑ Feb 1954 Cover: 0.10 **NM** value: **25.00**
4 ❑ Apr 1954 Cover: 0.10 **NM** value: **25.00**
5 ❑ Jun 1954 Cover: 0.10 **NM** value: **25.00**

SRI KRISHNA — Chakra

1 ❑ Cover: 3.50 **NM** value: **Cover or less**
📖 The Advent

STACIA STORIES — Kitchen Sink Press

1 ❑ Jun 1995, b&w Cover: 2.95 **NM** value: **Cover or less**

STAIN — Fathom

1 ❑ **NM** value: **2.95**

STAINLESS STEEL ARMADILLO — Antarctic

1 ❑ Feb 1995, b&w Cover: 2.95 **NM** value: **Cover or less**
Circ: CapCity orders: **4,245**
A: Ryukihei **W:** Ryukihei

2 ❑ Apr 1995, b&w Cover: 2.95 **NM** value: **Cover or less**
Circ: CapCity orders: **2,935**
A: Ryukihei **W:** Ryukihei

3 ❑ Jun 1995, b&w Cover: 2.95 **NM** value: **Cover or less**
Circ: CapCity orders: **2,740**
A: Ryukihei **W:** Ryukihei

4 ❑ Aug 1995, b&w Cover: 2.95 **NM** value: **Cover or less**
A: Ryukihei **W:** Ryukihei

5 ❑ Oct 1995, b&w Cover: 2.95 **NM** value: **Cover or less**
A: Ryukihei **W:** Ryukihei

STAINLESS STEEL RAT — Eagle

1 ❑ Oct 1985 Cover: 2.25 **NM** value: **2.50**
• Reprinted from 2000 A.D. #140-145 **A:** Carlos Ezquerra **W:** Kelvin Gosnell

2 ❑ Nov 1985 Cover: 1.50 **NM** value: **2.50**
Circ: CapCity orders: **5,700**
• Reprinted from 2000 A.D. #146-151

3 ❑ Dec 1985 Cover: 1.50 **NM** value: **2.50**
Circ: CapCity orders: **5,325**

4 ❑ Jan 1986 Cover: 1.75 **NM** value: **2.50**
Circ: CapCity orders: **4,775**

5 ❑ Feb 1986 Cover: 1.75 **NM** value: **2.50**
Circ: CapCity orders: **4,950**

6 ❑ Mar 1986 Cover: 1.75 **NM** value: **2.50**
Circ: CapCity orders: **4,575**

STALKER — DC

1 ❑ Jul 1975 Cover: 0.25 **NM** value: **1.50**
• **CGC:** 2 graded, best 9.4
A: Steve Ditko; Wally Wood **W:** Paul Levitz ★ Origin of Stalker. ★ 1st Appearance of Stalker.

2 ❑ Sep 1975 Cover: 0.25 **NM** value: **1.50**
• **CGC:** 1 graded, best 9.2

3 ❑ Nov 1975 Cover: 0.25 **NM** value: **1.50**
4 ❑ Jan 1976 Cover: 0.25 **NM** value: **1.50**

STALKERS — Marvel / Epic

1 ❑ Apr 1990 Cover: 1.50 **NM** value: **Cover or less**
Circ: CapCity orders: **17,650**
📖 Motown Madness **A:** Mark Texeira **W:** Mark Verheiden; Jan Strnad

2 ❑ May 1990 Cover: 1.50 **NM** value: **Cover or less**
Circ: CapCity orders: **11,700**

3 ❑ Jun 1990 Cover: 1.50 **NM** value: **Cover or less**
Circ: CapCity orders: **10,700**

4 ❑ Jul 1990 Cover: 1.50 **NM** value: **Cover or less**
Circ: CapCity orders: **10,800**

5 ❑ Aug 1990 Cover: 1.50 **NM** value: **Cover or less**
Circ: CapCity orders: **9,800**

6 ❑ Sep 1990 Cover: 1.50 **NM** value: **Cover or less**
Circ: CapCity orders: **9,350**

7 ❑ Oct 1990 Cover: 1.50 **NM** value: **Cover or less**
Circ: CapCity orders: **8,400**

8 ❑ Nov 1990 Cover: 1.50 **NM** value: **Cover or less**
Circ: CapCity orders: **7,550**

9 ❑ Dec 1990 Cover: 1.50 **NM** value: **Cover or less**
Circ: CapCity orders: **6,500**
📖 Inside Out **A:** Mark Verheiden **W:** Jan Strnad

10 ❑ Jan 1991 Cover: 1.50 **NM** value: **Cover or less**
Circ: CapCity orders: **5,750**

11 ❑ Feb 1991 Cover: 1.50 **NM** value: **Cover or less**
Circ: CapCity orders: **5,400**

12 ❑ Mar 1991 Cover: 1.50 **NM** value: **Cover or less**
Circ: CapCity orders: **4,800**

STALKING RALPH — Aeon

1 ❑ Oct 1995 Cover: 4.95 **NM** value: **Cover or less**
No issue number. One-shot. cardstock cover.

STAMPS COMICS — Youthful

1 ❑ Oct 1951 Cover: 0.15 **NM** value: **200.00**
• **CGC:** 1 graded, best 6.0
2 ❑ Dec 1951 Cover: 0.10 **NM** value: **125.00**
3 ❑ Feb 1952 Cover: 0.10 **NM** value: **100.00**
4 ❑ Apr 1952 Cover: 0.10 **NM** value: **100.00**
5 ❑ Jun 1952 Cover: 0.10 **NM** value: **100.00**
6 ❑ Aug 1952 Cover: 0.10 **NM** value: **100.00**
• **CGC:** 1 graded, best 7.0
7 ❑ Oct 1952 Cover: 0.10 **NM** value: **100.00**

STAND UP COMIX (BOB RUMBA'S...) — Grey

1 ❑ b&w Cover: 2.50 **NM** value: **Cover or less**

STANLEY AND HIS MONSTER — DC

Phil Foglio took the storyline about a bright boy and his seven-foot-tall purple monster (which ran in Fox and the Crow in the mid-1960s, ultimately taking over the title and its numbering) and updated it for the '90s in this hilarious new series.

The monster, who in the first series was merely wandering the world looking for a safe place to hide from humanity, was now cast as an escapee from Hell. The monster, however, was still the best friend a kid could have, since he could carry off piles of lumber (for a tree house) and he told the scariest stories (demon stories, of course.)

It's a pity it only ran as a four-part mini-series because this '90s version of a boy and his demon was loaded with charm.

Foglio gave a similar treatment to Angel and the Ape with a tie-in to The Inferior Five.

1 ❑ Feb 1993 Cover: 1.50 **NM** value: **2.50**
Circ: CapCity orders: **9,000**
📖 How To Build A Tree Fort **A:** Phil Foglio **W:** Phil Foglio

2 ❑ Mar 1993 Cover: 1.50 **NM** value: **2.00**
Circ: CapCity orders: **6,150**
📖 Old Friends **A:** Phil Foglio **W:** Phil Foglio

3 ❑ Apr 1993 Cover: 1.50 **NM** value: **2.00**
Circ: CapCity orders: **5,800**
📖 Parental Discretion **A:** Phil Foglio **W:** Phil Foglio

4 ❑ May 1993 Cover: 1.50 **NM** value: **2.00**
Circ: CapCity orders: **5,100**
📖 Going Down **A:** Phil Foglio **W:** Phil Foglio

STANLEY THE SNAKE WITH THE OVERACTIVE IMAGINATION — Emerald

1 ❑ b&w Cover: 1.50 **NM** value: **Cover or less**
2 ❑ b&w Cover: 1.50 **NM** value: **Cover or less**

STAR — Image

Star is an altruistic man with a mysterious past. He patrols the streets of Chicago, constantly searching out evil. Since he's considered to be a lawless vigilante, his main nemesis is the police officer extraordinary, the Savage Dragon. Star's weapon of choice is the throwing shuriken, also known as a throwing star (which gives him his nickname).

Erik Larsen's Star first appeared in three panels of the very first issue of The Savage Dragon mini-series, which Larsen also created. Star was popular with the fans, and letters numbering in the hundreds found their way to Larsen's studios. In June 1995, nearly three years after his introduction, Star's first issue was released in comics stores across the country.

1 ❑ Jun 1995 Cover: 2.50 **NM** value: **Cover or less**
Circ: CapCity orders: **16,325**
A: Ben Herrera **W:** Mary Bierbaum; Tom Bierbaum

2 ❑ Jul 1995 Cover: 2.50 **NM** value: **Cover or less**
Circ: CapCity orders: **12,375**
A: Ben Herrera **W:** Mary Bierbaum; Tom Bierbaum

3 ❑ Aug 1995 Cover: 2.50 **NM** value: **Cover or less**
Circ: CapCity orders: **9,275**
A: Ben Herrera **W:** Mary Bierbaum; Tom Bierbaum

4 ❑ Oct 1995 Cover: 2.50 **NM** value: **Cover or less**
Circ: CapCity orders: **7,025**
cover says Aug, indicia says Oct. **A:** Ben Herrera **W:** Mary Bierbaum; Tom Bierbaum

STARBIKERS — Renegade

1 ❑ b&w Cover: 2.00 **NM** value: **Cover or less**

STARBLAST — Marvel

1 ❑ Jan 1994 Cover: 2.00 **NM** value: **Cover or less**
Circ: CapCity orders: **30,700**
📖 Once in a Blue Moon **A:** Herb Trimpe **W:** Mark Gruenwald

2 ❑ Feb 1994 Cover: 1.75 **NM** value: **Cover or less**
Circ: CapCity orders: **17,250**

3 ❑ Mar 1994 Cover: 1.75 **NM** value: **Cover or less**
Circ: CapCity orders: **15,150**

4 ❑ Apr 1994 Cover: 1.75 **NM** value: **Cover or less**
Circ: CapCity orders: **12,850**

STAR BLAZERS — Comico

1 ❑ Apr 1987 Cover: 1.75 **NM** value: **2.00**
Circ: CapCity orders: **13,125**

2 ❑ ca. 1987 Cover: 1.75 **NM** value: **2.00**
Circ: CapCity orders: **10,550**

3 ❑ ca. 1987 Cover: 1.75 **NM** value: **2.00**
Circ: CapCity orders: **9,650**

4 ❑ ca. 1987 Cover: 1.75 **NM** value: **2.00**
Circ: CapCity orders: **9,125**

STAR BLAZERS: THE MAGAZINE OF SPACE BATTLESHIP YAMATO — Argo

0 ❑ 1995 Cover: 2.95 **NM** value: **Cover or less**
Circ: CapCity orders: **4,255**
📖 Scarlet Scarf **A:** Tim Eldred **W:** Tim Eldred

1 ❑ Mar 1995 Cover: 2.95 **NM** value: **Cover or less**
Circ: CapCity orders: **3,710**
📖 The Gift

STAR BLAZERS (VOL. 2) — Comico

1 ❑ ca. 1989 Cover: 1.95 **NM** value: **2.00**
Circ: CapCity orders: **8,100**
📖 The Jackals Come To Feed! **A:** Harrison Fong; Bill Anderson **W:** Mark Alan Joplin

2 ❑ 1989 Cover: 1.95 **NM** value: **2.00**
Circ: CapCity orders: **6,400**

3 ❑ 1989 Cover: 2.50 **NM** value: **Cover or less**
Circ: CapCity orders: **6,550**

4 ❑ 1989 Cover: 2.50 **NM** value: **Cover or less**
Circ: CapCity orders: **5,650**

5 ❑ 1989 Cover: 2.50 **NM** value: **Cover or less**
Circ: CapCity orders: **5,000**

STAR BLECCH: DEEP SPACE DINER — Parody Press

1/A ❑ Cover: 2.50 **NM** value: **Cover or less**
Star Blecch: Deep Space Diner cover. **A:** H.J. Cho; Bill Maus **W:** Ross Turner; Don Chin; Laura Davis Chin

1/B ❑ Cover: 2.50 **NM** value: **Cover or less**
Star Blecch: The Degeneration cover.

STAR BRAND, THE — Marvel

For those willing to read between the lines, Jim Shooter's New Universe, a setting separate from the Marvel universe, was more than simply a marketing successor to his Secret Wars series; since the Beyonder "dies" in those series by turning into a universe, some have interpreted that this is the one. Either way, it's a world without superheroes — until it's transformed by the "White Event."

In the flagship title of the New Universe, the Star Brand is a marking of power carried by an ancient man — who releases the uncontrollable energies and causes the White Event. Retaining some power, he gave it to Pittsburgh native Kenneth Connell, who then is faced with using the power for good.

It's a not-particularly-original flagship for a lackluster line, which foundered within a few years. Several other companies have since used their own "White Events" to jump-start their own superhero universes. — JJM

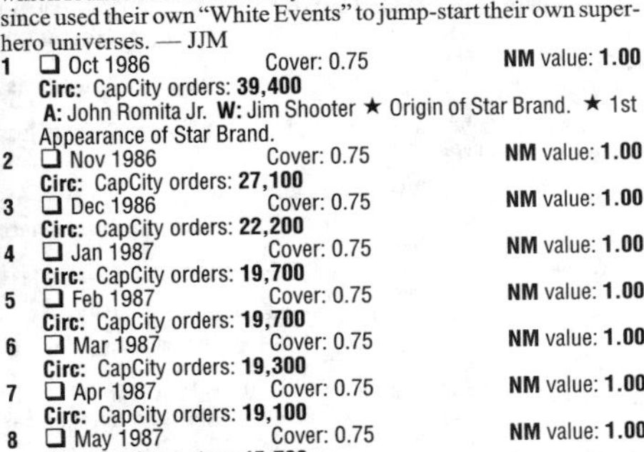

1 ❑ Oct 1986 Cover: 0.75 **NM** value: **1.00**
Circ: CapCity orders: **39,400**
A: John Romita Jr. **W:** Jim Shooter ★ Origin of Star Brand. ★ 1st Appearance of Star Brand.

2 ❑ Nov 1986 Cover: 0.75 **NM** value: **1.00**
Circ: CapCity orders: **27,100**

3 ❑ Dec 1986 Cover: 0.75 **NM** value: **1.00**
Circ: CapCity orders: **22,200**

4 ❑ Jan 1987 Cover: 0.75 **NM** value: **1.00**
Circ: CapCity orders: **19,700**

5 ❑ Feb 1987 Cover: 0.75 **NM** value: **1.00**
Circ: CapCity orders: **19,700**

6 ❑ Mar 1987 Cover: 0.75 **NM** value: **1.00**
Circ: CapCity orders: **19,300**

7 ❑ Apr 1987 Cover: 0.75 **NM** value: **1.00**
Circ: CapCity orders: **19,100**

8 ❑ May 1987 Cover: 0.75 **NM** value: **1.00**
Circ: CapCity orders: **15,700**

CGC-graded: Multiply prices above by **33 for 9.9 M • 16 for 9.8 NM/M • 7 for 9.6 NM+ • 5 for 9.4 NM • 2.5 for 9.2 NM- • 1.5 for 9.0 VF/NM**

9 ❑ Jun 1987 Cover: 0.75 **NM** value: **1.00**
Circ: CapCity orders: **15,800**
10 ❑ Jul 1987 Cover: 0.75 **NM** value: **1.00**
11 ❑ Jan 1988 Cover: 0.75 **NM** value: **1.00**
Circ: CapCity orders: **24,800**
• Title changes to The Star Brand **A:** John Byrne
12 ❑ Mar 1988 Cover: 0.75 **NM** value: **1.00**
Circ: CapCity orders: **25,800**
• Prelude to The Pitt **A:** John Byrne ★ Origin of Star Brand, New Universe (explains "White Event").
13 ❑ May 1988 Cover: 1.25 **NM** value: **Cover or less**
Circ: CapCity orders: **20,700**
A: John Byrne
14 ❑ Jul 1988 Cover: 1.25 **NM** value: **Cover or less**
Circ: CapCity orders: **19,400**
A: John Byrne
15 ❑ Sep 1988 Cover: 1.25 **NM** value: **Cover or less**
Circ: CapCity orders: **17,900**
A: John Byrne
16 ❑ Nov 1988 Cover: 1.25 **NM** value: **Cover or less**
Circ: CapCity orders: **13,250**
A: John Byrne
17 ❑ Jan 1989 Cover: 1.50 **NM** value: **Cover or less**
Circ: CapCity orders: **15,300**
A: John Byrne
18 ❑ Mar 1989 Cover: 1.50 **NM** value: **Cover or less**
Circ: CapCity orders: **13,600**
A: John Byrne
19 ❑ May 1989 Cover: 1.50 **NM** value: **Cover or less**
Circ: CapCity orders: **13,100**
final issue. **A:** John Byrne
Anl 1❑ca. 1987 Cover: 1.25 **NM** value: **Cover or less**
Circ: CapCity orders: **14,900**

STARCHILD — Taliesen Press

0 ❑ Apr 1993, b&w Cover: 2.50 **NM** value: **4.00**
A: James Owen **W:** James Owen
1 ❑ b&w Cover: 2.25 **NM** value: **4.00**
wraparound cover. 📖 Awakenings, Part 1 **A:** James Owen **W:** James Owen
1-2 ❑ **NM** value: **2.25**
2 ❑ 1993b&w Cover: 2.25 **NM** value: **4.00**
wraparound cover. 📖 Awakenings, Part 2; Children Of The Storm **A:** James Owen **W:** James Owen
2-2 ❑ Feb 1994, b&w Cover: 2.50 **NM** value: **Cover or less**
2-3 ❑ Feb 1994, b&w Cover: 2.50 **NM** value: **Cover or less**
3 ❑ 1993b&w Cover: 2.50 **NM** value: **3.00**
wraparound cover. 📖 Awakenings, Part 3 **A:** James Owen **W:** James Owen
4 ❑ 1993b&w Cover: 2.50 **NM** value: **3.00**
wraparound cover. 📖 Awakenings, Part 4 **A:** James Owen **W:** James Owen
5 ❑ Jan 1994, b&w Cover: 2.50 **NM** value: **3.00**
wraparound cover. 📖 Awakenings, Part 5 **A:** James Owen **W:** James Owen
6 ❑ Feb 1994, b&w Cover: 2.50 **NM** value: **3.00**
wraparound cover. 📖 Awakenings, Part 6 **A:** James Owen **W:** James Owen
7 ❑ Mar 1994, b&w Cover: 2.50 **NM** value: **Cover or less**
wraparound cover. 📖 Awakenings, Part 7 **A:** James Owen **W:** James Owen
8 ❑ Apr 1994, b&w Cover: 2.50 **NM** value: **Cover or less**
wraparound cover. 📖 Awakenings, Part 8 **A:** James Owen **W:** James Owen
9 ❑ May 1994, b&w Cover: 2.50 **NM** value: **Cover or less**
wraparound cover. 📖 Awakenings, Part 9 **A:** James Owen **W:** James Owen
10 ❑ b&w Cover: 2.50 **NM** value: **Cover or less**
wraparound cover. 📖 Awakenings, Part 10 **A:** James Owen **W:** James Owen
11 ❑ b&w Cover: 2.50 **NM** value: **Cover or less**
wraparound cover. 📖 Awakenings, Part 11 **A:** James Owen **W:** James Owen
12 ❑ Jun 1995, b&w Cover: 2.50 **NM** value: **Cover or less**
wraparound cover. 📖 Awakenings, Part 12 **A:** James Owen **W:** James Owen
13 ❑ Cover: 2.50 **NM** value: **Cover or less**
A: James Owen **W:** James Owen
14 ❑ Cover: 2.50 **NM** value: **Cover or less**
final issue. **A:** James Owen **W:** James Owen
Bk 1❑ Jun 1995 Cover: 20.00 **NM** value: **Cover or less**
• Awakenings **A:** James Owen **W:** James Owen
Bk 1/HC❑Jun 1995 Cover: 35.00 **NM** value: **Cover or less**
Awakenings hardcover. **A:** James Owen **W:** James Owen
Bk 1/LE❑Jun 1995 Cover: 100.00 **NM** value: **Cover or less**
• Awakenings limited edition hardcover with slipcase.
Bk 1-2❑Sep 1995 Cover: 20.00 **NM** value: **Cover or less**
• Awakenings 2nd Printing

STARCHILD: CROSSROADS — Coppervale

1 ❑ Nov 1995, b&w Cover: 2.95 **NM** value: **Cover or less**
📖 The Weaver's Tale
2 ❑ Jan 1996, b&w Cover: 2.95 **NM** value: **Cover or less**
📖 The Innkeeper's Tale
3 ❑ Mar 1996, b&w Cover: 2.95 **NM** value: **Cover or less**
📖 The Wanderer's Tale

STARCHILD: MYTHOPOLIS — Image

0 ❑ Jul 1997, b&w Cover: 2.95 **NM** value: **Cover or less**
Circ: Diamd. preorders: **7,407**
1 ❑ Sep 1997, b&w Cover: 2.95 **NM** value: **Cover or less**
Circ: Diamd. preorders: **7,193**
📖 Pinehead, Part 1 **A:** James Owen **W:** James Owen
2 ❑ Nov 1997, b&w Cover: 2.95 **NM** value: **Cover or less**
Circ: Diamd. preorders: **5,144**
📖 Pinehead, Part 2 **A:** James Owen **W:** James Owen
3 ❑ Jan 1998, b&w Cover: 2.95 **NM** value: **Cover or less**
Circ: Diamd. preorders: **4,425**
📖 Pinehead, Part 3 **A:** James Owen **W:** James Owen
4 ❑ Apr 1998, b&w Cover: 2.95 **NM** value: **Cover or less**
Circ: Diamd. preorders: **3,778**
📖 The Fisher King, Part 1 **A:** James Owen **W:** James Owen
5 ❑ Cover: 2.95 **NM** value: **Cover or less**
📖 The Fisher King, Part 2 **A:** James Owen **W:** James Owen
6 ❑ Cover: 2.95 **NM** value: **Cover or less**
A: James Owen **W:** James Owen

STARCHY — Excel

1 ❑ Cover: 1.95 **NM** value: **Cover or less**
A: Mark McElligott **W:** Mark McElligott

STAR COMICS MAGAZINE — Marvel / Star

1 ❑ Dec 1986 Cover: 1.50 **NM** value: **3.00**
Circ: CapCity orders: **1,200**
• digest-sized.
2 ❑ Feb 1987 Cover: 1.50 **NM** value: **2.00**
• digest-sized.
3 ❑ Apr 1987 Cover: 1.50 **NM** value: **2.00**
Circ: CapCity orders: **825**
• digest-sized.
4 ❑ Jun 1987 Cover: 1.50 **NM** value: **2.00**
Circ: CapCity orders: **400**
• digest-sized.
5 ❑ Aug 1987 Cover: 1.50 **NM** value: **2.00**
• digest-sized.
6 ❑ Oct 1987 Cover: 1.50 **NM** value: **2.00**
• digest-sized.
7 ❑ Dec 1987 Cover: 1.50 **NM** value: **2.00**
• digest-sized.
8 ❑ Feb 1988 Cover: 1.50 **NM** value: **2.00**
• digest-sized.
9 ❑ Apr 1988 Cover: 1.50 **NM** value: **2.00**
• digest-sized.
10 ❑ Jun 1988 Cover: 1.50 **NM** value: **2.00**
Circ: CapCity orders: **250**
• digest-sized.
11 ❑ Aug 1988 Cover: 1.50 **NM** value: **2.00**
• digest-sized.
12 ❑ Oct 1988 Cover: 1.50 **NM** value: **2.00**
• digest-sized.
13 ❑ Dec 1988 Cover: 1.50 **NM** value: **2.00**
• digest-sized.

S.T.A.R. CORPS — DC

1 ❑ Nov 1993 Cover: 1.50 **NM** value: **Cover or less**
Circ: CapCity orders: **22,350**
A: Norman Felchle **W:** Dan Vado
2 ❑ Dec 1993 Cover: 1.50 **NM** value: **Cover or less**
Circ: CapCity orders: **11,500**
A: Norman Felchle **W:** Dan Vado
3 ❑ Jan 1994 Cover: 1.50 **NM** value: **Cover or less**
Circ: CapCity orders: **9,750**
📖 Star Pupil **A:** Norman Felchle **W:** Dan Vado
4 ❑ Feb 1994 Cover: 1.50 **NM** value: **Cover or less**
Circ: CapCity orders: **8,350**
A: Norman Felchle **W:** Dan Vado
5 ❑ Mar 1994 Cover: 1.50 **NM** value: **Cover or less**
Circ: CapCity orders: **7,350**
📖 Trauma **A:** Norman Felchle **W:** Dan Vado
6 ❑ Apr 1994 Cover: 1.50 **NM** value: **Cover or less**
Circ: CapCity orders: **6,200**
A: Norman Felchle **W:** Dan Vado

STAR CROSSED — DC / Helix

1 ❑ Jun 1997 Cover: 2.50 **NM** value: **Cover or less**
Circ: Diamd. preorders: **11,400**
📖 The Black Holes of Logic **A:** Matt Howarth **W:** Matt Howarth
2 ❑ Jul 1997 Cover: 2.50 **NM** value: **Cover or less**
Circ: Diamd. preorders: **8,072**
A: Matt Howarth **W:** Matt Howarth
3 ❑ Aug 1997 Cover: 2.50 **NM** value: **Cover or less**
Circ: Diamd. preorders: **7,527**
A: Matt Howarth **W:** Matt Howarth

STARDUSTERS — Nightwynd

1 ❑ b&w Cover: 2.50 **NM** value: **Cover or less**
A: Angel de Mioche **W:** Angel de Mioche
2 ❑ b&w Cover: 2.50 **NM** value: **Cover or less**
A: Angel de Mioche **W:** Angel de Mioche
3 ❑ b&w Cover: 2.50 **NM** value: **Cover or less**
A: Angel de Mioche **W:** Angel de Mioche
4 ❑ b&w Cover: 2.50 **NM** value: **Cover or less**
A: Angel de Mioche **W:** Angel de Mioche

STARDUST (NEIL GAIMAN AND CHARLES VESS'...) — DC / Vertigo

The vision of writer Neil Gaiman, architect of the Sandman saga and Books of Magic, is complemented by the art of Charles Vess. Gaiman tells this fantasy of quests and magic in text, punctuated by full-page paintings by Vess.

Stardust follows the adventures of young Tristan Thorn, living on the edge of the land of faerie, who has sworn an oath to fetch a fallen star for the most beautiful girl in his village. From this gentle premise, Gaiman crafts a tale in the great tradition of 19th and early 20th century children's stories that are equally charming to readers of any age.

1 ❑ Cover: 5.95 **NM** value: **6.50**
• prestige format. 📖 Being a Romance Within the Realms of Faerie **A:** Charles Vess **W:** Neil Gaiman
2 ❑ Cover: 5.95 **NM** value: **6.00**
• prestige format. **A:** Charles Vess **W:** Neil Gaiman
3 ❑ Cover: 5.95 **NM** value: **6.00**
• prestige format. **A:** Charles Vess **W:** Neil Gaiman
4 ❑ Cover: 6.95 **NM** value: **Cover or less**
• prestige format. **A:** Charles Vess **W:** Neil Gaiman
Bk 1❑ Cover: 19.95 **NM** value: **Cover or less**
A: Charles Vess **W:** Neil Gaiman

STARFIRE — DC

1 ❑ Sep 1976 Cover: 0.30 **NM** value: **1.50**
• **CGC:** 9 graded, best 9.6
📖 A World Made Of War **A:** Mike Vosburg; Robert Smith **W:** David Michelinie ★ Origin of Starfire I. ★ 1st Appearance of Starfire I.
2 ❑ Nov 1976 Cover: 0.30 **NM** value: **1.00**
3 ❑ Jan 1977 Cover: 0.30 **NM** value: **1.00**
4 ❑ Mar 1977 Cover: 0.30 **NM** value: **1.00**
5 ❑ May 1977 Cover: 0.30 **NM** value: **1.00**
6 ❑ Jul 1977 Cover: 0.30 **NM** value: **1.00**
7 ❑ Sep 1977 Cover: 0.30 **NM** value: **1.00**
8 ❑ Nov 1977 Cover: 0.30 **NM** value: **1.00**

STAR FORCES — The Other Faculty / Helix

1 ❑ Cover: 0.50 **NM** value: **3.00**
📖 The First Encounter **A:** Pat Wilson; Roger Brand **W:** Sherry Venit; Susan Knapp

STARFORCE SIX SPECIAL — AC

1 ❑ Nov 1984 Cover: 1.50 **NM** value: **Cover or less**

STARGATE — Express / Entity

1 ❑ Jul 1996 Cover: 2.95 **NM** value: **Cover or less**
1/SC❑Jul 1996 Cover: 3.50 **NM** value: **Cover or less**
Photo cover.
2 ❑ Aug 1996 Cover: 2.95 **NM** value: **Cover or less**
• photo section back-up
2/SC❑Aug 1996 Cover: 3.50 **NM** value: **Cover or less**
Photo cover. • photo section back-up
3 ❑ Sep 1996 Cover: 2.95 **NM** value: **Cover or less**
• photo section back-up
3/SC❑Sep 1996 Cover: 3.50 **NM** value: **Cover or less**
Photo cover. • photo section back-up
4 ❑ Oct 1996 Cover: 2.95 **NM** value: **Cover or less**
final issue. • photo section back-up
4/SC❑Oct 1996 Cover: 3.50 **NM** value: **Cover or less**
Photo cover. final issue. • photo section back-up

STARGATE DOOMSDAY WORLD — Entity

1 ❑ Nov 1996 Cover: 2.95 **NM** value: **Cover or less**
Circ: Diamd. preorders: **3,232**
A: Raff Ienco **W:** Raff Ienco; John Migliore
2 ❑ Dec 1996 Cover: 2.95 **NM** value: **Cover or less**
Circ: Diamd. preorders: **2,636**
3 ❑ Jan 1997 Cover: 2.95 **NM** value: **Cover or less**
Circ: Diamd. preorders: **2,231**

STARGATE: THE NEW ADVENTURES COLLECTION — Entity

1 ❑ ca. 1997 Cover: 5.95 **NM** value: **Cover or less**
• Collects Stargate: One Nation Under Ra; Stargate: Underworld **A:** Bill Maus **W:** John Migliore

STARGATE UNDERWORLD — Entity

1 ❑ ca. 1997 Cover: 2.95 **NM** value: **Cover or less**

STARGODS — Antarctic

1 ❑ Jul 1998 Cover: 2.95 **NM** value: **Cover or less**
Circ: Diamd. preorders: **13,415**
📖 Anachron **A:** Dean Zachary; Scott Clark **W:** Dean Zachary; Scott Clark
1/CS❑Jul 1998 Cover: 5.95 **NM** value: **Cover or less**
alternate cover. 📖 Anachron • poster **A:** Dean Zachary; Scott Clark **W:** Dean Zachary; Scott Clark
2 ❑ Sep 1998 Cover: 2.95 **NM** value: **Cover or less**
Circ: Diamd. preorders: **9,338**
📖 The Golden Bow **A:** Dean Zachary; Scott Clark **W:** Dean Zachary; Scott Clark
2/CS❑Sep 1998 Cover: 5.95 **NM** value: **Cover or less**
alternate cover. 📖 The Golden Bow • poster **A:** Dean Zachary; Scott Clark **W:** Dean Zachary; Scott Clark

STARGODS: VISIONS — Antarctic

1 ❑ Dec 1998 Cover: 2.95 **NM** value: **Cover or less**
• pin-ups **A:** Dean Zachary; Scott Clark; David Beaty **W:** Dean Zachary; Scott Clark; David Beaty

CGC price ratios appearing on the bottom of right-hand pages are for pre-1990 comic books "slabbed" by Comics Guaranty Corp.

They represent the median price offered on eBay above our printed prices for comics in each grade. These are only a guide; individual prices vary by interest in the issue and the number of CGC-graded copies on the market.

For up-to-the-week CGC ratios, consult the current issue of **Comics Buyer's Guide**.

Other grades: Multiply prices above by **1.5 for Mint • 2/3 for Very Fine • 1/3 for Fine • 1/5 for Very Good • 1/8 for Good**

STAR HAWKS — Avalon

Gil Kane is of course best known for his substantial body of work at Marvel and DC, on some of their greatest heroes. But along the way he also brought his unique artistic stylings to the Sunday newspapers, teaming with well-known science fiction writer Ron Goulart on a weekly adventure strip. This late 1970s science fiction drama is collected, reprinted, and resurrected by ACG Comics in this series.

Action focuses on a pair of "star hawks"-interstellar cops-named Rex and Chavez (one is reluctant to get involved, the other as gung-ho as a law officer could be), and their myriad adventures which often involve saving damsels in distress. Published in black-and-white...regrettably.

1 ❑ Cover: 2.95 **NM** value: **Cover or less**
A: Gil Kane **W:** Ron Goulart
2 ❑ Cover: 2.95 **NM** value: **Cover or less**
A: Gil Kane **W:** Ron Goulart

STARHEAD PRESENTS — Starhead

1 ❑ Cover: 0.95 **NM** value: **1.00**
2 ❑ Cover: 0.95 **NM** value: **1.00**
🕮 Curse Of The Baby Monster **A:** R.K. Sloane **W:** R.K. Sloane
3 ❑ Cover: 0.95 **NM** value: **1.00**
• Bad Teens

STAR HUNTERS — DC

1 ❑ Nov 1977 Cover: 0.35 **NM** value: **1.00**
• **CGC:** 4 graded, best 9.6
2 ❑ Jan 1978 Cover: 0.35 **NM** value: **1.00**
🕮 The Annihilist Factor **A:** Bob Layton; Larry Hama **W:** David Michelinie
3 ❑ Mar 1978 Cover: 0.35 **NM** value: **1.00**
🕮 The Sowers Of Holocaust **A:** Mike Nasser; Bob Layton **W:** David Michelinie
4 ❑ May 1978 Cover: 0.35 **NM** value: **1.00**
5 ❑ Jul 1978 Cover: 0.35 **NM** value: **1.00**
6 ❑ Sep 1978 Cover: 0.35 **NM** value: **1.00**
7 ❑ Nov 1978 Cover: 0.35 **NM** value: **1.00**
final issue.

STAR JACKS — Antarctic

1 ❑ Jun 1994, b&w Cover: 2.75 **NM** value: **Cover or less**

STAR JAM COMICS — Revolutionary

1 ❑ Apr 1992, b&w Cover: 2.50 **NM** value: **Cover or less**
• M.C. Hammer story
2 ❑ Jun 1992, b&w Cover: 2.50 **NM** value: **Cover or less**
• Janet Jackson story
3 ❑ Aug 1992, b&w Cover: 2.50 **NM** value: **Cover or less**
🕮 Genesis and Revelation • Beverly Hills 90210 story **A:** Joe Paradise **W:** Jay Allen Sanford
4 ❑ Sep 1992, b&w Cover: 2.50 **NM** value: **Cover or less**
• Beverly Hills 90210 story
5 ❑ Oct 1992, b&w Cover: 2.50 **NM** value: **Cover or less**
• Beverly Hills 90210 story
6 ❑ Nov 1992, b&w Cover: 2.50 **NM** value: **Cover or less**
• Kriss Kross story
7 ❑ Dec 1992, b&w Cover: 2.50 **NM** value: **Cover or less**
• Marky Mark story
8 ❑ Jan 1993, b&w Cover: 2.50 **NM** value: **Cover or less**
• Madonna story
9 ❑ Feb 1993, b&w Cover: 2.50 **NM** value: **Cover or less**
• Jennie Garth story
10 ❑ Mar 1993, b&w Cover: 2.50 **NM** value: **Cover or less**
• Melrose Place story

STARJAMMERS — Marvel

1 ❑ Oct 1995 Cover: 2.95 **NM** value: **Cover or less**
enhanced cardstock cover. 🕮 Cepheid Variable • OverPower cards bound-in **A:** Carlos Pacheco **W:** Warren Ellis
2 ❑ Nov 1995 Cover: 2.95 **NM** value: **Cover or less**
enhanced cardstock cover. **A:** Carlos Pacheco **W:** Warren Ellis
3 ❑ Dec 1995 Cover: 2.95 **NM** value: **Cover or less**
enhanced cardstock cover. **A:** Carlos Pacheco **W:** Warren Ellis
4 ❑ Jan 1996 Cover: 2.95 **NM** value: **Cover or less**
enhanced cardstock cover. final issue. **A:** Carlos Pacheco **W:** Warren Ellis

STARJONGLEUR, THE — Trylvertel

1 ❑ Aug 1986, b&w Cover: 2.00 **NM** value: **Cover or less**
🕮 Plots Primeval **A:** Gary Davis **W:** Gary Davis
2 ❑ Win 1987, b&w Cover: 2.00 **NM** value: **Cover or less**

STARK: FUTURE — Aircel

1 ❑ Aug 1986, b&w Cover: 2.00 **NM** value: **Cover or less**
A: David Day; Tim McEown **W:** Gordon Derry
2 ❑ Sep 1986 Cover: 1.70 **NM** value: **2.00**
A: Tim McEown **W:** Gordon Derry
3 ❑ Oct 1986 Cover: 1.70 **NM** value: **2.00**
4 ❑ Nov 1986 Cover: 1.70 **NM** value: **2.00**
5 ❑ Dec 1986 Cover: 1.70 **NM** value: **2.00**
6 ❑ Jan 1987 Cover: 1.70 **NM** value: **2.00**
🕮 What are Dreams Made Of? **A:** Jim Somerville **W:** Gordon Derry
7 ❑ Feb 1987 Cover: 1.70 **NM** value: **2.00**
8 ❑ Mar 1987 Cover: 1.70 **NM** value: **2.00**
9 ❑ Apr 1987 Cover: 1.70 **NM** value: **2.00**
10 ❑ May 1987 Cover: 1.70 **NM** value: **2.00**
11 ❑ Jun 1987 Cover: 1.70 **NM** value: **2.00**
12 ❑ Jul 1987 Cover: 1.70 **NM** value: **2.00**
13 ❑ Aug 1987 Cover: 1.70 **NM** value: **2.00**
14 ❑ Sep 1987 Cover: 1.70 **NM** value: **2.00**
15 ❑ Oct 1987 Cover: 1.70 **NM** value: **2.00**
16 ❑ Nov 1987 Cover: 1.70 **NM** value: **2.00**
17 ❑ Dec 1987 Cover: 1.70 **NM** value: **2.00**

STARKID — Dark Horse

1 ❑ Jan 1998 Cover: 2.95 **NM** value: **Cover or less**
No issue number. 🕮 Brood Storm • prequel to movie **A:** John Stokes **W:** Manny Coto

STARK RAVEN — Endless Horizons

1 ❑ Sep 2000 Cover: 2.95 **NM** value: **Cover or less**
Circ: Diamd. preorders: **3,393**
🕮 The Screaming Rain, Part 1 **A:** Walter McDaniel **W:** Ken Smith

STARLET O'HARA IN HOLLYWOOD — Standard

1 ❑ Win 1948 Cover: 0.10 **NM** value: **100.00**
2 ❑ Spr 1949 Cover: 0.10 **NM** value: **75.00**
3 ❑ Sum 1949 Cover: 0.10 **NM** value: **50.00**
4 ❑ Fal 1949 Cover: 0.10 **NM** value: **50.00**

STARLIGHT — Eternity

1 ❑ Oct 1987 Cover: 1.95 **NM** value: **Cover or less**
🕮 The Outer Space Babes **A:** Uriel Antonio **W:** C.J. Henderson ★ Appearance of Outer Space Babes.

STARLIGHT AGENCY, THE — Antarctic

1 ❑ Jun 1991, b&w Cover: 1.95 **NM** value: **2.50**
2 ❑ Aug 1991, b&w Cover: 1.95 **NM** value: **2.50**
3 ❑ Sep 1991, b&w Cover: 1.95 **NM** value: **2.50**

STARLION: A PAWN'S GAME — Storm

1 ❑ Feb 1993 Cover: 2.25 **NM** value: **Cover or less**
🕮 Puppet Strings and Captain's Chairs **A:** David Jorgenson **W:** Anthony Bruno

STARLORD — Marvel

1 ❑ Dec 1996 Cover: 2.50 **NM** value: **Cover or less**
Circ: Direct Market orders: **28,750**
A: Dan Lawlis **W:** Timothy Zahn
2 ❑ Jan 1997 Cover: 2.50 **NM** value: **Cover or less**
Circ: Direct Market orders: **21,000**
🕮 Time Quake; Strontium Dog; Planet of the Damned; Ro-Busters **A:** Dan Lawlis; Carlos Pino; Leopoldo Pena **W:** Pat Mills; R.E. Wright; Timothy Zahn
3 ❑ Feb 1997 Cover: 2.50 **NM** value: **Cover or less**
Circ: Direct Market orders: **16,000**
final issue. **A:** Dan Lawlis **W:** Timothy Zahn

STARLORD MEGAZINE — Marvel

1 ❑ Nov 1996 Cover: 2.95 **NM** value: **Cover or less**
Circ: Direct Market orders: **9,250**
back cover pin-up. • Reprints Star-Lord, The Special Edition #1. **A:** Michael Golden; John Byrne **W:** Chris Claremont

STAR-LORD, THE SPECIAL EDITION — Marvel

1 ❑ Feb 1982 Cover: 1.50 **NM** value: **2.00**
A: Michael Golden; John Byrne **W:** Chris Claremont

STARLOVE — Forbidden Fruit

All issues are adults only.
1 ❑ b&w Cover: 2.95 **NM** value: **Cover or less**
2 ❑ b&w Cover: 3.50 **NM** value: **Cover or less**

STARMAN (1ST SERIES) — DC

This new Starman is actually the fourth person to bear the name. His story begins in a secret laboratory in Western Utah where scientists had been conducting experiments to create new super-heroes. After years of research, they had gathered the subjects with the unique body chemistry required. Then, they put a special satellite in orbit, the Stellartron-5, which would convert the sun's energy into a beam and use it to transform the subjects into super-heroes. As the beam was energized, however, the satellite was hit by space junk. Instead of striking the intended subjects, it hit a camper named William Peyton, knocking him unconscious for a month.

When he awoke, he found his entire body had changed. He suddenly had superhuman strength and speed, could emit bursts of light, and even fly. Although he had no intention of becoming "one of those egotistical super-heroes," he soon found the call of duty too strong to resist.

1 ❑ Oct 1988 Cover: 1.00 **NM** value: **2.00**
Circ: CapCity orders: **20,600**
🕮 Grassroots Hero **A:** Tom Lyle **W:** Roger Stern ★ Origin of Starman IV (William Payton). ★ 1st Appearance of Starman IV (William Payton).
2 ❑ Nov 1988 Cover: 1.00 **NM** value: **1.50**
Circ: CapCity orders: **14,850**
3 ❑ Dec 1988 Cover: 1.00 **NM** value: **1.50**
Circ: CapCity orders: **13,250**
★ Versus Bolt.
4 ❑ Win 1988 Cover: 1.00 **NM** value: **1.50**
Circ: CapCity orders: **12,550**
★ Versus Power Elite.
5 ❑ Hol 1989 Cover: 1.00 **NM** value: **1.50**
Circ: CapCity orders: **14,400**
• Invasion!
6 ❑ Jan 1989 Cover: 1.00 **NM** value: **1.50**
Circ: CapCity orders: **13,350**
• Invasion!
7 ❑ Feb 1989 Cover: 1.00 **NM** value: **1.50**
Circ: CapCity orders: **12,200**
8 ❑ Mar 1989 Cover: 1.00 **NM** value: **1.50**
Circ: CapCity orders: **11,850**
★ Appearance of Lady Quark.
9 ❑ Apr 1989 Cover: 1.00 **NM** value: **1.50**
Circ: CapCity orders: **13,600**
★ Origin of Blockbuster. ★ Appearance of Batman.
10 ❑ May 1989 Cover: 1.00 **NM** value: **1.50**
Circ: CapCity orders: **14,900**
★ Origin of Blockbuster. ★ Appearance of Batman.
11 ❑ Jun 1989 Cover: 1.00 **NM** value: **1.25**
Circ: CapCity orders: **12,950**
12 ❑ Jul 1989 Cover: 1.00 **NM** value: **1.25**
Circ: CapCity orders: **13,000**
13 ❑ Aug 1989 Cover: 1.00 **NM** value: **1.25**
Circ: CapCity orders: **12,800**
14 ❑ Sep 1989 Cover: 1.00 **NM** value: **1.25**
Circ: CapCity orders: **13,400**
• Superman
15 ❑ Oct 1989 Cover: 1.00 **NM** value: **1.25**
Circ: CapCity orders: **12,550**
★ 1st Appearance of Deadline.
16 ❑ Nov 1989 Cover: 1.00 **NM** value: **1.25**
Circ: CapCity orders: **11,850**
17 ❑ Dec 1989 Cover: 1.00 **NM** value: **1.25**
Circ: CapCity orders: **17,950**
• Power Girl
18 ❑ Jan 1990 Cover: 1.00 **NM** value: **1.25**
Circ: CapCity orders: **12,200**
19 ❑ Feb 1990 Cover: 1.00 **NM** value: **1.25**
Circ: CapCity orders: **11,800**
20 ❑ Mar 1990 Cover: 1.00 **NM** value: **1.25**
Circ: CapCity orders: **11,600**
21 ❑ Apr 1990 Cover: 1.00 **NM** value: **1.25**
Circ: CapCity orders: **11,400**
22 ❑ May 1990 Cover: 1.00 **NM** value: **1.25**
★ Versus Deadline.
23 ❑ Jun 1990 Cover: 1.00 **NM** value: **1.25**
Circ: CapCity orders: **11,050**
24 ❑ Jul 1990 Cover: 1.00 **NM** value: **1.25**
Circ: CapCity orders: **11,000**
25 ❑ Aug 1990 Cover: 1.00 **NM** value: **1.25**
Circ: CapCity orders: **10,800**
26 ❑ Sep 1990 Cover: 1.00 **NM** value: **2.00**
Circ: CapCity orders: **10,700**
★ 1st Appearance of David Knight.
27 ❑ Oct 1990 Cover: 1.00 **NM** value: **1.25**
Circ: CapCity orders: **10,250**
🕮 Riders On The Storm **A:** Dave Hoover **W:** Roger Stern ★ Origin of Starman III (David Knight).
28 ❑ Nov 1990 Cover: 1.00 **NM** value: **1.25**
Circ: CapCity orders: **11,200**
• Superman
29 ❑ Dec 1990 Cover: 1.00 **NM** value: **1.25**
Circ: CapCity orders: **10,600**
30 ❑ Jan 1991 Cover: 1.00 **NM** value: **1.25**
Circ: CapCity orders: **10,800**
31 ❑ Feb 1991 Cover: 1.00 **NM** value: **1.25**
Circ: CapCity orders: **11,200**
32 ❑ Mar 1991 Cover: 1.00 **NM** value: **1.25**
Circ: CapCity orders: **10,700**
33 ❑ Apr 1991 Cover: 1.00 **NM** value: **1.25**
Circ: CapCity orders: **10,400**
34 ❑ May 1991 Cover: 1.00 **NM** value: **1.25**
Circ: CapCity orders: **11,900**
35 ❑ Jun 1991 Cover: 1.00 **NM** value: **1.25**
Circ: CapCity orders: **10,000**
36 ❑ Jul 1991 Cover: 1.00 **NM** value: **1.25**
Circ: CapCity orders: **10,050**
🕮 Intruder Alert! **A:** Dave Hoover **W:** Len Strazewski
37 ❑ Aug 1991 Cover: 1.00 **NM** value: **1.25**
Circ: CapCity orders: **10,200**
38 ❑ Sep 1991 Cover: 1.00 **NM** value: **1.25**
Circ: CapCity orders: **11,500**
🕮 War of the Gods, Part 6 • War of the Gods
39 ❑ Oct 1991 Cover: 1.00 **NM** value: **1.25**
Circ: CapCity orders: **10,700**
40 ❑ Nov 1991 Cover: 1.00 **NM** value: **1.25**
Circ: CapCity orders: **10,550**
41 ❑ Dec 1991 Cover: 1.00 **NM** value: **1.25**
Circ: CapCity orders: **10,200**
42 ❑ Jan 1992 Cover: 1.00 **NM** value: **1.25**
Circ: CapCity orders: **10,400**
43 ❑ Feb 1992 Cover: 1.00 **NM** value: **1.25**
Circ: CapCity orders: **11,350**
44 ❑ Mar 1992 Cover: 1.25 **NM** value: **Cover or less**
Circ: CapCity orders: **10,400**
• Lobo
45 ❑ Apr 1992 Cover: 1.25 **NM** value: **Cover or less**
Circ: CapCity orders: **8,500**
• Lobo

Capital City orders are the actual sales of comic books by Capital City Distribution, once one of the largest U.S. sellers of comics to comics shops. Capital City's share of comics shop sales, while not known exactly, increases from around 10-20% in the mid-1980s to 30-35% in the mid-1990s. Capital City's share of comic books sold on newsstands (most Marvels and DCs) will be less.

CGC-graded: Multiply prices above by **33 for 9.9 M** • **16 for 9.8 NM/M** • **7 for 9.6 NM+** • **5 for 9.4 NM** • **2.5 for 9.2 NM-** • **1.5 for 9.0 VF/NM**

STARMAN (2ND SERIES) DC

The original Starman was Ted Knight, an amateur astronomer who became a super-hero and member of both the Justice Society of America and the All-Star Squadron. His adventures began in Adventure Comics #61, making Starman a key hero of DC's Golden Age. For years, Ted Knight's presence made his home town of Opal City one of the big cities in the country.

But now The Mist, an enemy from Starman's past, returned for revenge. The Mist hospitalized Ted, killed his son David, and began a reign of terror in Opal City. Only Ted's other son, Jack, remained to fight against him. Unfortunately, Jack was a callow youth who never wanted to wear the "silly costume" that his father made famous. Moreover, Jack managed to lose the Cosmic Belt that gave Starman most of his power, letting it fall into the hands of the Mist. Unless Jack could become a hero using his father's old Gravity Rod from the 1940s, everything he holds dear will be lost. And Opal City would burn down around him.

After surviving his first adventure, Jack eventually grew into the role of his city's protector. Writer James Robinson delved into Golden Age lore and delivered new insights into what makes a hero throughout the series' run.

0 ❑ Oct 1994 Cover: 1.95 **NM** value: **5.00**
Circ: CapCity orders: **23,500** • **CGC:** 2 graded, best 9.8
📖 Sins of the Father, Part 1 **W:** James Robinson

1 ❑ Nov 1994 Cover: 1.95 **NM** value: **5.00**
Circ: CapCity orders: **23,800** • **CGC:** 2 graded, best 9.4
📖 Sins of the Father, Part 2 **A:** Tony Harris **W:** James Robinson

2 ❑ Dec 1994 Cover: 1.95 **NM** value: **4.00**
Circ: CapCity orders: **17,000** • **CGC:** 1 graded, best 9.6
📖 Sins of the Father, Part 3 **A:** Tony Harris **W:** James Robinson

3 ❑ Jan 1995 Cover: 1.95 **NM** value: **4.00**
Circ: CapCity orders: **15,450**
📖 Night Flight **A:** Tony Harris **W:** James Robinson

4 ❑ Feb 1995 Cover: 1.95 **NM** value: **3.00**
Circ: CapCity orders: **13,900**
A: Tony Harris **W:** James Robinson

5 ❑ Mar 1995 Cover: 1.95 **NM** value: **3.00**
Circ: CapCity orders: **12,975**
A: Tony Harris **W:** James Robinson

6 ❑ Apr 1995 Cover: 1.95 **NM** value: **3.00**
Circ: CapCity orders: **12,300**
A: Tony Harris **W:** James Robinson

7 ❑ May 1995 Cover: 1.95 **NM** value: **3.00**
Circ: CapCity orders: **11,975**
📖 A Knight at the Circus, Part 1 **A:** Tony Harris **W:** James Robinson

8 ❑ Jun 1995 Cover: 2.25 **NM** value: **3.00**
Circ: CapCity orders: **12,275**
📖 A Knight at the Circus, Part 2 **A:** Tony Harris **W:** James Robinson

9 ❑ Jul 1995 Cover: 2.25 **NM** value: **3.00**
Circ: CapCity orders: **12,200**
📖 Shards **A:** Tony Harris **W:** James Robinson

10 ❑ Aug 1995 Cover: 2.25 **NM** value: **3.00**
Circ: CapCity orders: **12,400**
📖 The Day Before the Day to Come **A:** Tony Harris **W:** James Robinson ★ Versus Solomon Grundy.

11 ❑ Sep 1995 Cover: 2.25 **NM** value: **2.50**
Circ: CapCity orders: **11,625**
A: Tony Harris **W:** James Robinson

12 ❑ Oct 1995 Cover: 2.25 **NM** value: **2.50**
Circ: CapCity orders: **10,150**
📖 Sins of the Child, Part 1 **A:** Tony Harris **W:** James Robinson

13 ❑ Nov 1995 Cover: 2.25 **NM** value: **2.50**
📖 Sins of the Child, Part 2 • Underworld Unleashed **A:** Tony Harris **W:** James Robinson

14 ❑ Dec 1995 Cover: 2.25 **NM** value: **2.50**
📖 Sins of the Child, Part 3 **A:** Tony Harris **W:** James Robinson

15 ❑ Jan 1996 Cover: 2.25 **NM** value: **2.50**
📖 Sins of the Child, Part 4 **A:** Tony Harris **W:** James Robinson

16 ❑ Feb 1996 Cover: 2.25 **NM** value: **2.50**
📖 Sins of the Child, Part 5 **A:** Tony Harris **W:** James Robinson

17 ❑ Mar 1996 Cover: 2.25 **NM** value: **2.50**
📖 Beyond Sins **A:** Tony Harris **W:** James Robinson

18 ❑ Apr 1996 Cover: 2.25 **NM** value: **2.50**
📖 First Joust • Original Starman versus The Mist **A:** John Watkiss **W:** James Robinson

19 ❑ Jun 1996 Cover: 2.25 **NM** value: **2.50**
📖 Talking with David '96 • Times Past **A:** Tony Harris **W:** James Robinson

20 ❑ Jul 1996 Cover: 2.25 **NM** value: **2.50**
📖 Sand and Stars, Part 1; Sand of the Stars, Part 1 **A:** Tony Harris **W:** James Robinson ★ Appearance of Wesley Dodds, Wesley Dodds, Dian Belmont.

21 ❑ Aug 1996 Cover: 2.25 **NM** value: **2.50**
📖 Sand and Stars, Part 2; Sand of the Stars, Part 2 **A:** Tony Harris **W:** James Robinson

22 ❑ Sep 1996 Cover: 2.25 **NM** value: **2.50**
📖 Sand and Stars, Part 3; Sand of the Stars, Part 3 **A:** Tony Harris **W:** James Robinson

23 ❑ Oct 1996 Cover: 2.25 **NM** value: **2.50**
📖 Sand and Stars, Part 4; Sand of the Stars, Part 4 **A:** Tony Harris **W:** James Robinson

24 ❑ Nov 1996 Cover: 2.25 **NM** value: **2.50**
Circ: Diamd. preorders: **31,405**
📖 Demon Quest, Part 1; Hell & Back, Part 1 **A:** Tony Harris **W:** James Robinson

25 ❑ Dec 1996 Cover: 2.25 **NM** value: **2.50**
Circ: Diamd. preorders: **31,303**
📖 Demon Quest, Part 2; Hell & Back, Part 2 **A:** Tony Harris **W:** James Robinson

26 ❑ Jan 1997 Cover: 2.25 **NM** value: **2.50**
Circ: Diamd. preorders: **30,147**
📖 Demon Quest, Part 3; Hell & Back, Part 3 **A:** Tony Harris **W:** James Robinson

27 ❑ Feb 1997 Cover: 2.25 **NM** value: **2.50**
Circ: Diamd. preorders: **29,324**
📖 Christmas Knight **A:** Steve Yeowell **W:** James Robinson

28 ❑ Mar 1997 Cover: 2.25 **NM** value: **2.50**
Circ: Diamd. preorders: **28,265**
📖 Superfreaks & Backstabbers **A:** Craig Hamilton **W:** James Robinson

29 ❑ Apr 1997 Cover: 2.25 **NM** value: **2.50**
Circ: Diamd. preorders: **32,056**
W: James Robinson

30 ❑ May 1997 Cover: 2.25 **NM** value: **2.50**
Circ: Diamd. preorders: **29,453**
📖 Infernal Devices, Part 1 **W:** James Robinson

31 ❑ Jun 1997 Cover: 2.25 **NM** value: **2.50**
Circ: Diamd. preorders: **30,643**
📖 Infernal Devices, Part 2 **W:** James Robinson

32 ❑ Jul 1997 Cover: 2.25 **NM** value: **2.50**
Circ: Diamd. preorders: **30,183**
📖 Infernal Devices, Part 3 **W:** James Robinson

33 ❑ Aug 1997 Cover: 2.25 **NM** value: **2.50**
Circ: Diamd. preorders: **32,457**
📖 Dark Knights **W:** James Robinson ★ Appearance of Solomon Grundy, Sentinel, Batman.

34 ❑ Sep 1997 Cover: 2.25 **NM** value: **2.50**
Circ: Diamd. preorders: **31,597**
W: James Robinson ★ Appearance of Ted Knight, Solomon Grundy, Sentinel, Batman, Jason Woodrue.

35 ❑ Oct 1997 Cover: 2.25 **NM** value: **2.50**
Circ: Diamd. preorders: **33,994**
• Genesis **W:** James Robinson

36 ❑ Nov 1997 Cover: 2.25 **NM** value: **2.50**
Circ: Diamd. preorders: **31,794**
W: James Robinson ★ Appearance of Will Payton.

37 ❑ Dec 1997 Cover: 2.25 **NM** value: **2.50**
Circ: Diamd. preorders: **31,934**
Face cover. 📖 Talking with David '97 **A:** Tony Harris **W:** James Robinson

38 ❑ Jan 1998 Cover: 2.25 **NM** value: **2.50**
Circ: Diamd. preorders: **31,474**
📖 ...La Fraternite De Justice Et Liberte! • Mist vs. Justice League Europe **A:** Dusty Abell **W:** James Robinson ★ 1st Appearance of Baby Starman.

39 ❑ Feb 1998 Cover: 2.25 **NM** value: **2.50**
Circ: Diamd. preorders: **32,630**
cover forms diptych with Starman #40. 📖 Lightning and Stars, Part 1 • continues in Power of Shazam! #35 **W:** James Robinson

40 ❑ Mar 1998 Cover: 2.25 **NM** value: **2.50**
Circ: Diamd. preorders: **31,982**
cover forms diptych with Starman #39. 📖 Lightning and Stars, Part 3 **W:** James Robinson

41 ❑ Apr 1998 Cover: 2.25 **NM** value: **Cover or less**
Circ: Diamd. preorders: **29,779**
📖 Villain's Redemption **A:** Gary Erskine **W:** James Robinson ★ Versus Doctor Phosphorus.

42 ❑ May 1998 Cover: 2.25 **NM** value: **Cover or less**
Circ: Diamd. preorders: **30,108**
📖 Science and Sorcery 1944 **W:** James Robinson ★ Appearance of Demon.

43 ❑ Jun 1998 Cover: 2.25 **NM** value: **Cover or less**
Circ: Diamd. preorders: **31,452**
W: James Robinson ★ Appearance of Justice League of America.

44 ❑ Jul 1998 Cover: 2.25 **NM** value: **Cover or less**
Circ: Diamd. preorders: **29,462**
📖 Things That Go Bump in the Night 1944 **W:** James Robinson ★ Appearance of Phantom Lady.

45 ❑ Aug 1998 Cover: 2.25 **NM** value: **Cover or less**
Circ: Diamd. preorders: **29,565**
📖 Journey to the Stars **W:** James Robinson

46 ❑ Sep 1998 Cover: 2.25 **NM** value: **Cover or less**
Circ: Diamd. preorders: **28,788**
📖 Times Past: Good Men and Bad 1954 **W:** James Robinson

47 ❑ Oct 1998 Cover: 2.50 **NM** value: **Cover or less**
Circ: Diamd. preorders: **28,128**
📖 City Without Light, Part 1 **W:** James Robinson

48 ❑ Dec 1998 Cover: 2.50 **NM** value: **Cover or less**
Circ: Diamd. preorders: **28,041**
📖 Stars My Destination: A Blue World **W:** James Robinson ★ Appearance of Solomon Grundy.

49 ❑ Jan 1999 Cover: 2.50 **NM** value: **Cover or less**
Circ: Diamd. preorders: **28,250**
📖 Stars My Destination: Talking with David '99 **W:** James Robinson

50 ❑ Feb 1999 Cover: 3.95 **NM** value: **Cover or less**
Circ: Diamd. preorders: **30,622**
📖 Stars My Destination **A:** Peter Snejbjerg **W:** James Robinson ★ Appearance of Legion.

51 ❑ Mar 1999 Cover: 2.50 **NM** value: **Cover or less**
Circ: Diamd. preorders: **28,122**
📖 Stars My Destination • on Krypton **A:** Peter Snejbjerg **W:** James Robinson ★ Appearance of Jor-El.

52 ❑ Apr 1999 Cover: 2.50 **NM** value: **Cover or less**
Circ: Diamd. preorders: **27,006**
📖 Stars My Destination • on Rann **A:** Peter Snejbjerg **W:** James Robinson ★ Appearance of Turran Kha, Adam Strange.

53 ❑ May 1999 Cover: 2.50 **NM** value: **Cover or less**
Circ: Diamd. preorders: **27,188**
📖 Stars My Destination • on Rann **W:** James Robinson ★ Appearance of Adam Strange.

54 ❑ Jun 1999 Cover: 2.50 **NM** value: **Cover or less**
Circ: Diamd. preorders: **27,551**
📖 Times Past; 1899: A Rich Man's Family; A Rich Man's Folly • Times Past **A:** Craig Hamilton **W:** James Robinson

55 ❑ Jul 1999 Cover: 2.50 **NM** value: **Cover or less**
Circ: Diamd. preorders: **26,672**
📖 Stars My Destination; Taxicab Confessions **A:** Peter Snejbjerg; Keith Champagne; McCrea; Weston **W:** James Robinson ★ Appearance of Space Cabbie.

56 ❑ Aug 1999 Cover: 2.50 **NM** value: **Cover or less**
Circ: Diamd. preorders: **26,323**
📖 City Without Light, Part 2 **A:** Stephen Sadowski **W:** James Robinson; David Goyer

57 ❑ Sep 1999 Cover: 2.50 **NM** value: **Cover or less**
Circ: Diamd. preorders: **27,549**
📖 Stars My Destination; The Welcome Wagon • on Throneworld **A:** Peter Snejbjerg **W:** James Robinson; David Goyer ★ Appearance of Fastbak, Tigorr.

58 ❑ Oct 1999 Cover: 2.50 **NM** value: **Cover or less**
Circ: Diamd. preorders: **26,456**
📖 Stars My Destination; Familiar Faces, Some Forgotten **A:** Peter Snejbjerg **W:** James Robinson; David Goyer ★ Appearance of Will Payton.

59 ❑ Nov 1999 Cover: 2.50 **NM** value: **Cover or less**
Circ: Diamd. preorders: **26,158**
📖 Stars My Destination; The Secret of Will Payton **A:** Peter Snejbjerg **W:** James Robinson; David Goyer

60 ❑ Dec 1999 Cover: 2.50 **NM** value: **Cover or less**
Circ: Diamd. preorders: **26,625**
📖 Stars My Destination • Jack returns to Earth

61 ❑ Jan 2000 Cover: 2.50 **NM** value: **Cover or less**
Circ: Diamd. preorders: **25,807**
📖 In Tranquility and Fire **A:** Peter Snejbjerg **W:** James Robinson

62 ❑ Feb 2000 Cover: 2.50 **NM** value: **Cover or less**
Circ: Diamd. preorders: **25,630**
📖 Grand Guignol, Part 1 **A:** Peter Snejbjerg **W:** James Robinson

63 ❑ Mar 2000 Cover: 2.50 **NM** value: **Cover or less**
Circ: Diamd. preorders: **24,785**
📖 Grand Guignol, Part 2 **A:** Peter Snejbjerg **W:** James Robinson

64 ❑ Apr 2000 Cover: 2.50 **NM** value: **Cover or less**
Circ: Diamd. preorders: **23,728**
📖 Grand Guignol, Part 3 **A:** Peter Snejbjerg **W:** James Robinson

65 ❑ May 2000 Cover: 2.50 **NM** value: **Cover or less**
Circ: Diamd. preorders: **24,182**
📖 Grand Guignol, Part 4 **A:** Peter Snejbjerg **W:** James Robinson

66 ❑ Jun 2000 Cover: 2.50 **NM** value: **Cover or less**
Circ: Diamd. preorders: **24,033**
📖 Grand Guignol, Part 5 **A:** Peter Snejbjerg **W:** James Robinson

67 ❑ Jul 2000 Cover: 2.50 **NM** value: **Cover or less**
Circ: Diamd. preorders: **24,038**
📖 Grand Guignol, Part 6 **A:** Peter Snejbjerg **W:** James Robinson

68 ❑ Aug 2000 Cover: 2.50 **NM** value: **Cover or less**
Circ: Diamd. preorders: **24,282**
📖 Grand Guignol, Part 7 **A:** Peter Snejbjerg **W:** James Robinson

69 ❑ Sep 2000 Cover: 2.50 **NM** value: **Cover or less**
Circ: Diamd. preorders: **24,978**
📖 Grand Guignol, Part 8 **A:** Peter Snejbjerg **W:** James Robinson

70 ❑ Oct 2000 Cover: 2.50 **NM** value: **Cover or less**
Circ: Diamd. preorders: **23,205**
📖 Grand Guignol, Part 9 **A:** Peter Snejbjerg **W:** James Robinson

71 ❑ Nov 2000 Cover: 2.50 **NM** value: **Cover or less**
Circ: Diamd. preorders: **23,713**
📖 Grand Guignol, Part 10 **A:** Peter Snejbjerg **W:** James Robinson

72 ❑ Dec 2000 Cover: 2.50 **NM** value: **Cover or less**
Circ: Diamd. preorders: **23,472**
📖 Grand Guignol, Part 11 **A:** Peter Snejbjerg **W:** James Robinson

73 ❑ Jan 2001 Cover: 2.50 **NM** value: **Cover or less**
Circ: Diamd. preorders: **23,561**
📖 Grand Guignol, Part 12 **A:** Peter Snejbjerg **W:** James Robinson

74 ❑ Feb 2001 Cover: 2.50 **NM** value: **Cover or less**
Circ: Diamd. preorders: **23,369**
📖 His Death and the Dying of It • Times Past **A:** Russ Heath **W:** James Robinson

75 ❑ Mar 2001 Cover: 2.50 **NM** value: **Cover or less**
Circ: Diamd. preorders: **23,336**
📖 Sons and Fathers **A:** Peter Snejbjerg **W:** James Robinson

76 ❑ Apr 2001 Cover: 2.50 **NM** value: **Cover or less**
Circ: Diamd. preorders: **22,867**
📖 Talking with David (and Ted) **A:** Peter Snejbjerg **W:** James Robinson

77 ❑ May 2001 Cover: 2.50 **NM** value: **Cover or less**
Circ: Diamd. preorders: **23,060**
📖 1951, Part 1 **A:** Peter Snejbjerg **W:** James Robinson; David Goyer

78 ❑ Jun 2001 Cover: 2.50 **NM** value: **Cover or less**
Circ: Diamd. preorders: **23,290**
📖 1951, Part 2 **A:** Peter Snejbjerg **W:** James Robinson; David Goyer

1000000 ❑ Nov 1998 Cover: 2.50 **NM** value: **Cover or less**
Circ: Diamd. preorders: **37,173**
📖 All the Starlight Shining **A:** Peter Snejbjerg **W:** James Robinson

Anl 1 ❑ ca. 1996 Cover: 3.50 **NM** value: **Cover or less**
Circ: Diamd. preorders: **28,280**
• Legends of the Dead Earth; Shade tells stories of Ted Knight and Gavyn; 1996 Annual **A:** Bret Blevins; J.H. Williams III; Craig Hamilton **W:** James Robinson

Anl 2 ❑ ca. 1997 Cover: 3.95 **NM** value: **Cover or less**
Circ: Diamd. preorders: **27,020**
📖 Stars in my Eyes! • Pulp Heroes; 1997 annual **A:** Mitch Byrd **W:** James Robinson

Bk 1 ❑ Cover: 12.95 **NM** value: **Cover or less**
📖 Sins of the Father • Sins of the Father; Collects issues #0-5 **A:** Tony Harris **W:** James Robinson

Bk 2 ❑ Cover: 14.95 **NM** value: **Cover or less**
📖 Night and Day • Night and Day; collects #7-10 and #12-16 **W:** James Robinson

Bk 3 ❑ Cover: 17.95 **NM** value: **Cover or less**
📖 Times Past • A Wicked Inclination; collects #17; 19-27 **W:** James Robinson

Bk 4 ❑ Aug 1999 Cover: 17.95 **NM** value: **Cover or less**
📖 Talking With Ted.../Talking With Jack...; An Entry From the Shade's Journal; 1882, Back Stage, Back Then; 13 Years Ago: Five Friends; First Joust; 1971, Super Freaks and Backstabbers; Legends of the Dead Earth • Times Past; Collects stories from Starman Secret Files #1, Starman (2nd Series) #6, 11, 18, 28, Anl 1 **A:** Matt Smith; Teddy Kristiansen; Phil Jimenez; Bret Blevins; John Watkiss; J.H. Williams III; Craig Hamilton; Lee Weeks; Mick Gray; Ray Snyder; Robert Campanella; Tony Harris(cover) **W:** James Robinson

Other grades: Multiply prices above by **1.5 for Mint • 2/3 for Very Fine • 1/3 for Fine • 1/5 for Very Good • 1/8 for Good**

Bk 5❑ Cover: 17.95 **NM** value: **Cover or less**
• Infernal Devices; Collects Starman (2nd Series) #29-35, 37-38 **A:** Tony Harris; Mark Buckingham; Steve Yeowell; Dusty Abell **W:** James Robinson

GS 1❑Jan 1999 Cover: 4.95 **NM** value: **Cover or less**
W: James Robinson

STARMAN: SECRET FILES — DC

1 ❑ Apr 1998 Cover: 4.95 **NM** value: **Cover or less**
Circ: Diamd. preorders: **25,370**
• background on series

STARMAN: THE MIST — DC

1 ❑ Jun 1998 Cover: 1.95 **NM** value: **Cover or less**
Circ: Diamd. preorders: **33,823**
One-shot. 📖 Good Girls and Bad • Girlfrenzy **A:** John Lucas; Richard Case **W:** James Robinson

STARMASTERS (AC) — AC

1 ❑ Cover: 1.50 **NM** value: **Cover or less**
📖 The Women of W.O.S.P.; Breed **A:** Paul Ryan; Tom Lyle **W:** Paul Ryan; Tom Lyle

STAR MASTERS (MARVEL) — Marvel

1 ❑ Dec 1995 Cover: 1.95 **NM** value: **Cover or less**
📖 The Stars, My Desperation **A:** Scot Eaton **W:** Mark Gruenwald ★ Appearance of Quasar, The Silver Surfer, Beta Ray Bill, Silver Surfer.

2 ❑ Jan 1996 Cover: 1.95 **NM** value: **Cover or less**
📖 The Cauldron of Conversion **A:** Scot Eaton **W:** Mark Gruenwald ★ Appearance of Quasar, Beta Ray Thor, Silver Surfer.

3 ❑ Feb 1996 Cover: 1.95 **NM** value: **Cover or less**
final issue. • continues in Cosmic Powers Unlimited #4 **A:** Scot Eaton **W:** Mark Gruenwald ★ Appearance of Quasar, Beta Ray Thor, Silver Surfer.

STAR RANGER — Centaur

#	Date	Cover	NM value
1	❑ Feb 1937	Cover: 0.10	**NM** value: **800.00**
2	❑ Apr 1937	Cover: 0.10	**NM** value: **400.00**
3	❑ May 1937	Cover: 0.10	**NM** value: **400.00**
4	❑ Jun 1937	Cover: 0.10	**NM** value: **400.00**
5	❑ Jul 1937	Cover: 0.10	**NM** value: **350.00**
6	❑ Sep 1937	Cover: 0.10	**NM** value: **350.00**
7	❑ Oct 1937	Cover: 0.10	**NM** value: **350.00**
8	❑ Dec 1937	Cover: 0.10	**NM** value: **350.00**
9	❑ Jan 1938	Cover: 0.10	**NM** value: **350.00**
10	❑ Mar 1938	Cover: 0.10	**NM** value: **300.00**
11	❑ Apr 1938	Cover: 0.10	**NM** value: **300.00**
12	❑ May 1938	Cover: 0.10	**NM** value: **300.00**

STAR RANGER FUNNIES — Centaur

15 ❑ Oct 1939 Cover: 0.10 **NM** value: **250.00**
1 ❑ Jan 1939 Cover: 0.10 **NM** value: **450.00**
• **CGC:** 1 graded, best 9.4
2 ❑ Apr 1939 Cover: 0.10 **NM** value: **300.00**
3 ❑ Jun 1939 Cover: 0.10 **NM** value: **300.00**
4 ❑ Aug 1939 Cover: 0.10 **NM** value: **300.00**
5 ❑ Oct 1939 Cover: 0.10 **NM** value: **300.00**

STAR RANGERS — Adventure

1 ❑ Oct 1987 Cover: 1.95 **NM** value: **Cover or less**
📖 Community of Victims **A:** Jim Mooney **W:** Mark Ellis
2 ❑ Nov 1987 Cover: 1.95 **NM** value: **Cover or less**
3 ❑ Dec 1987 Cover: 1.95 **NM** value: **Cover or less**
📖 Pilots of the Purple Twilight, Part 2

STAR*REACH — Star*Reach

1 ❑ ca. 1974 Cover: 0.75 **NM** value: **2.00**
📖 ...The Birth of Death!; Fish Myths; Suburban Fish; A Tale of Sword & Sorcery; Cody Starbuck; The Origin of God **A:** Jim Starlin; Howard Chaykin; Walt Simonson; Steve Skeates **W:** Jim Starlin; Howard Chaykin; Steve Skeates; Ed Wicks
2 ❑ ca. 1975 Cover: 1.25 **NM** value: **2.00**
📖 "In the Light of Future Days..." **A:** Dick Giordano **W:** Mike Friedrich
3 ❑ ca. 1975 Cover: 1.00 **NM** value: **2.00**
4 ❑ ca. 1976 Cover: 1.00 **NM** value: **2.00**
5 ❑ ca. 1976 Cover: 1.25 **NM** value: **1.50**
6 ❑ Oct 1976 Cover: 1.25 **NM** value: **1.50**
📖 Elric: The Prisoner of Pan-Pang; Childsong; Why Viking Lander I Mars?; Gods of Mount Olympus; Out of Space•Out of Time **A:** Joe Staton; Gene Day; Alex Nino; Gary Lyda; Bob Gould; Alex Ni±o **W:** Gary Lyda; Ray Bradbury; Eric Kimball; Gary Petras; Johnny Achziger
7 ❑ ca. 1977 Cover: 1.25 **NM** value: **1.50**
8 ❑ ca. 1977 Cover: 1.25 **NM** value: **1.50**
9 ❑ ca. 1977 Cover: 1.25 **NM** value: **1.50**
10 ❑ ca. 1977 Cover: 1.25 **NM** value: **1.50**
11 ❑ ca. 1977 Cover: 1.25 **NM** value: **1.50**
12 ❑ ca. 1978 Cover: 1.50 **NM** value: **Cover or less**
13 ❑ ca. 1978 Cover: 1.50 **NM** value: **Cover or less**
14 ❑ ca. 1978 Cover: 1.50 **NM** value: **Cover or less**
15 ❑ ca. 1978 Cover: 1.75 **NM** value: **Cover or less**
16 ❑ ca. 1979 Cover: 1.75 **NM** value: **Cover or less**
17 ❑ ca. 1979 Cover: 1.75 **NM** value: **Cover or less**
18 ❑ ca. 1979 Cover: 1.75 **NM** value: **Cover or less**
Bk 1❑ Cover: 6.95 **NM** value: **Cover or less**
• Greatest Hits

STAR*REACH CLASSICS — Eclipse

1 ❑ Mar 1984 Cover: 1.75 **NM** value: **2.00**
A: Dick Giordano
2 ❑ Apr 1984 Cover: 1.75 **NM** value: **2.00**
3 ❑ May 1984 Cover: 1.75 **NM** value: **2.00**
4 ❑ Jun 1984 Cover: 1.75 **NM** value: **2.00**
5 ❑ Jul 1984 Cover: 1.75 **NM** value: **2.00**
A: Howard Chaykin
6 ❑ Aug 1984 Cover: 1.75 **NM** value: **2.00**
A: P. Craig Russell

STARRIORS — Marvel

1 ❑ Nov 1984 Cover: 0.75 **NM** value: **1.00**
📖 Discovery **A:** Michael Chen **W:** Louise Simonson
2 ❑ Dec 1984 Cover: 0.75 **NM** value: **1.00**
📖 Under Fire! **A:** Michael Chen **W:** Louise Simonson
3 ❑ Jan 1985 Cover: 0.75 **NM** value: **1.00**
📖 Assault! **A:** Michael Chen **W:** Louise Simonson
4 ❑ Feb 1985 Cover: 0.75 **NM** value: **1.00**
📖 Quest's End! **A:** Michael Chen **W:** Louise Simonson

STAR ROVERS — Comax

All issues are adults only.

1 ❑ b&w Cover: 2.95 **NM** value: **Cover or less**

STARS AND S.T.R.I.P.E. — DC

Courtney Whitmore is the new Star-Spangled Kid, a brash and impulsive brat. She's environmentally conscious and an animal rights activist at heart. Meanwhile, the Kid's overly protective sidekick, S.T.R.I.P.E., is actually Courtney's stepfather, Pat Dugan formerly known as Stripesy. Beneath the self-confident exterior, Courtney is hiding the fact that she's scared of making a mistake. Intuitively, she knows a mistake at this level could cost someone his or her life. Pat's S.T.R.I.P.E. armor is an excellent metaphor for masking his concern for her own well-being. There are plenty of conflicts in this book: generation gap, stepfather-stepdaughter, old school vs. hip-hop, et al. All of this and fighting super-powered criminals, too.

0 ❑ Jul 1999 Cover: 2.95 **NM** value: **Cover or less**
Circ: Diamd. preorders: **30,238**
📖 A Chilly Day in Opal **A:** Lee Moder; Chris Weston **W:** James Robinson; Geoff Johns ★ Appearance of Starman.
1 ❑ Aug 1999 Cover: 2.50 **NM** value: **2.95**
Circ: Diamd. preorders: **29,851**
📖 New Kid on the Block **A:** Lee Moder **W:** Lee Moder; Geoff Johns
2 ❑ Sep 1999 Cover: 2.50 **NM** value: **2.95**
Circ: Diamd. preorders: **22,548**
📖 True Colors **A:** Lee Moder **W:** Lee Moder; Geoff Johns
3 ❑ Oct 1999 Cover: 2.50 **NM** value: **2.95**
Circ: Diamd. preorders: **19,260**
📖 Bloodrush **A:** Lee Moder **W:** Geoff Johns ★ 1st Appearance of Skeeter.
4 ❑ Nov 1999 Cover: 2.50 **NM** value: **2.95**
Circ: Diamd. preorders: **19,802**
📖 Waking the Dead! • Day of Judgment **A:** Lee Moder **W:** Lee Moder; Geoff Johns ★ Appearance of Captain Marvel.
5 ❑ Dec 1999 Cover: 2.95 **NM** value: **Cover or less**
Circ: Diamd. preorders: **15,932**
📖 The Subs, Part 1 **A:** Lee Moder **W:** Lee Moder; Geoff Johns ★ Appearance of Young Justice.
6 ❑ Jan 2000 Cover: 2.95 **NM** value: **Cover or less**
Circ: Diamd. preorders: **14,672**
📖 The Subs, Part 2 **A:** Lee Moder **W:** Lee Moder; Geoff Johns
7 ❑ Feb 2000 Cover: 2.95 **NM** value: **Cover or less**
Circ: Diamd. preorders: **13,461**
📖 You Kids Today! **A:** Lee Moder **W:** Lee Moder; Geoff Johns
8 ❑ Mar 2000 Cover: 2.95 **NM** value: **Cover or less**
Circ: Diamd. preorders: **12,668**
📖 Crisis in Blue Valley
9 ❑ Apr 2000 Cover: 2.95 **NM** value: **Cover or less**
Circ: Diamd. preorders: **11,624**
📖 The Final Hour for the 7 Soldiers of Victory!
10 ❑ May 2000 Cover: 2.50 **NM** value: **Cover or less**
Circ: Diamd. preorders: **11,317**
📖 Shortcuts **A:** Scott Kolins **W:** Geoff Johns
11 ❑ Jun 2000 Cover: 2.50 **NM** value: **Cover or less**
Circ: Diamd. preorders: **11,015**
📖 Knight Time **A:** Scott Kolins **W:** Geoff Johns

STARS AND STRIPES COMICS — Centaur

2 ❑ May 1941 Cover: 0.10 **NM** value: **1500.00**
3 ❑ Jul 1941 Cover: 0.10 **NM** value: **1000.00**
4 ❑ Sep 1941 Cover: 0.10 **NM** value: **1000.00**
5 ❑ Nov 1941 Cover: 0.10 **NM** value: **800.00**
6 ❑ Dec 1941 Cover: 0.10 **NM** value: **800.00**

STAR SEED — Broadway

7 ❑ Jul 1996 Cover: 2.95 **NM** value: **Cover or less**
• Series continued from Powers That Be #6
8 ❑ Aug 1996 Cover: 2.95 **NM** value: **Cover or less**
9 ❑ Sep 1996 Cover: 2.95 **NM** value: **Cover or less**
📖 It's the End of the World as we Know It, Part 5 final issue.

STARSHIP TROOPERS — Dark Horse

1 ❑ Oct 1997 Cover: 2.95 **NM** value: **Cover or less**
Circ: Diamd. preorders: **16,724**
A: Mitch Byrd **W:** Bruce Jones; Robert Heinlein
2 ❑ Nov 1997 Cover: 2.95 **NM** value: **Cover or less**
Circ: Diamd. preorders: **14,809**
A: Mitch Byrd **W:** Bruce Jones; Robert Heinlein

STARSHIP TROOPERS: BRUTE CREATIONS — Dark Horse

1 ❑ Sep 1997 Cover: 2.95 **NM** value: **Cover or less**
Circ: Diamd. preorders: **12,370**
No issue number. One-shot. **A:** Tommy Lee Edwards **W:** Jan Strnad

STARSHIP TROOPERS: DOMINANT SPECIES — Dark Horse

1 ❑ Aug 1998 Cover: 2.95 **NM** value: **Cover or less**
Circ: Diamd. preorders: **10,953**
2 ❑ Sep 1998 Cover: 2.95 **NM** value: **Cover or less**
Circ: Diamd. preorders: **9,801**
A: David Fabrii **W:** Jan Strnad
3 ❑ Oct 1998 Cover: 2.95 **NM** value: **Cover or less**
Circ: Diamd. preorders: **9,058**
A: David Fabrii **W:** Jan Strnad
4 ❑ Nov 1998 Cover: 2.95 **NM** value: **Cover or less**
Circ: Diamd. preorders: **8,614**

STARSHIP TROOPERS: INSECT TOUCH — Dark Horse

1 ❑ May 1997 Cover: 2.95 **NM** value: **Cover or less**
Circ: Diamd. preorders: **18,797**
cardstock cover. **A:** Paolo Parente; David Fabrii **W:** Warren Ellis
2 ❑ Jun 1997 Cover: 2.95 **NM** value: **Cover or less**
Circ: Diamd. preorders: **13,620**
cardstock cover. **A:** Paolo Parente; David Fabrii **W:** Warren Ellis; Gordon Rennie
3 ❑ Jul 1997 Cover: 2.95 **NM** value: **Cover or less**
Circ: Diamd. preorders: **12,913**
cardstock cover. **A:** Paolo Parente; David Fabrii **W:** Warren Ellis; Gordon Rennie

STAR SLAMMERS (MALIBU) — Malibu / Bravura

In a world of big guns and big wars, the Star Slammers are a race of men that can kill, fight, and shoot better than anyone in the galaxy. The Slammers are mercenaries, paid vast sums and considered unstoppable.

But one day the unthinkable happened. While running a strike-and-sweep operation against a "backwater galactic empire," a Slammer named Rojas got cut off and was captured. He was the first Star Slammer ever taken alive, a real feather in the empire's cap. As this series begins, they've immobilized Rojas and are carrying him back to homeworld aboard a starship filled with soldiers. In other words, Rojas' odds are just about even.

Star Slammers first appeared in a Marvel Graphic Novel several years before this 1994 series for Bravura. Its creator, Walter Simonson, is a comics veteran famous for his work on titles ranging from Thor to Cyberforce.

1 ❑ May 1994 Cover: 2.50 **NM** value: **Cover or less**
Circ: CapCity orders: **25,850**
📖 The Minoan Agendas, Part 1 **A:** Walt Simonson **W:** Walt Simonson
2 ❑ Jun 1994 Cover: 2.50 **NM** value: **Cover or less**
Circ: CapCity orders: **18,175**
📖 The Minoan Agendas, Part 2 **A:** Walt Simonson **W:** Walt Simonson
3 ❑ Aug 1994 Cover: 2.50 **NM** value: **Cover or less**
Circ: CapCity orders: **15,750**
📖 The Minoan Agendas, Part 3 **A:** Walt Simonson **W:** Walt Simonson
4 ❑ Feb 1995 Cover: 2.50 **NM** value: **Cover or less**
Circ: CapCity orders: **11,900**
📖 The Minoan Agendas, Part 4 **A:** Walt Simonson **W:** Walt Simonson

STAR SLAMMERS SPECIAL — Dark Horse / Legend

1 ❑ Jun 1996 Cover: 2.95 **NM** value: **Cover or less**
No issue number. One-shot. **A:** Walt Simonson **W:** Walt Simonson

STARSLAYER — Pacific

Starslayer is Torin Mac Quillon, a Celt, who began the first part of his life in ancient Britain. When the Romans began their invasion of that island country in 43 A.D., Torin took up arms against them. Although the Roman army was ultimately unstoppable, Torin fought bravely. The gods must have smiled upon him, for just as he faced his end, a bolt of energy stole him out of time and placed him in the distant future. There this barbarian began a different kind of battle.

Starslayers was one of the earliest titles from Pacific Comics during the independent publisher boom of the early 1980s. Created by Mike Grell, it was in many ways the counterpoint to Warlord, Grell's first comic book creation. In addition to the adventures of Starslayer, the title became notable for hosting the first comic appearance of the Rocketeer, as well as giving birth to Grimjack with issue #10.

1 ❑ Feb 1982 Cover: 1.00 **NM** value: **2.00**
• **CGC:** 1 graded, best 9.6
A: Mike Grell **W:** Mike Grell ★ Origin of Starslayer. ★ 1st Appearance of Rocketeer (cameo).
2 ❑ Apr 1982 Cover: 1.00 **NM** value: **5.00**
• **CGC:** 13 graded, best 9.8

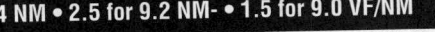

CGC-graded: Multiply prices above by **33 for 9.9 M • 16 for 9.8 NM/M • 7 for 9.6 NM+ • 5 for 9.4 NM • 2.5 for 9.2 NM- • 1.5 for 9.0 VF/NM**

• Rocketeer backup story **A:** Sergio Aragonés; Mike Grell; Dave Stevens **W:** Mike Grell ★ Origin of Rocketeer. ★ 1st Appearance of Rocketeer (full appearance).

3 ❑ Jun 1982 Cover: 1.00 **NM** value: **3.00**
• **CGC:** 3 graded, best 9.8
• Rocketeer backup story **A:** Mike Grell; Dave Stevens **W:** Mike Grell ★ Appearance of Rocketeer.

4 ❑ Aug 1982 Cover: 1.00 **NM** value: **1.50**
A: Mike Grell **W:** Mike Grell

5 ❑ Nov 1982 Cover: 1.00 **NM** value: **3.00**
• **CGC:** 2 graded, best 9.8
A: Sergio Aragonés; Mike Grell **W:** Mike Grell; Mark Evanier ★ Appearance of Groo.

6 ❑ Apr 1983 Cover: 1.00 **NM** value: **1.50**
A: Mike Grell **W:** Mike Grell

7 ❑ Aug 1983 Cover: 1.00 **NM** value: **1.50**
• First Comics begins publishing

8 ❑ Sep 1983 Cover: 1.00 **NM** value: **1.50**

9 ❑ Oct 1983 Cover: 1.00 **NM** value: **1.50**

10 ❑ Nov 1983 Cover: 1.00 **NM** value: **2.00**
★ 1st Appearance of Grimjack.

11 ❑ Dec 1983 Cover: 1.00 **NM** value: **1.50**
★ Appearance of Grimjack.

12 ❑ Jan 1984 Cover: 1.00 **NM** value: **1.50**
★ Appearance of Grimjack.

13 ❑ Feb 1984 Cover: 1.00 **NM** value: **1.50**
★ Appearance of Grimjack.

14 ❑ Mar 1984 Cover: 1.00 **NM** value: **1.50**
★ Appearance of Grimjack.

15 ❑ Apr 1984 Cover: 1.00 **NM** value: **1.50**
★ Appearance of Grimjack.

16 ❑ May 1984 Cover: 1.00 **NM** value: **1.50**
★ Appearance of Grimjack.

17 ❑ Jun 1984 Cover: 1.00 **NM** value: **1.50**
★ Appearance of Grimjack.

18 ❑ Jul 1984 Cover: 1.00 **NM** value: **1.50**
★ Appearance of Grimjack.

19 ❑ Aug 1984 Cover: 1.00 **NM** value: **1.50**

20 ❑ Sep 1984 Cover: 1.00 **NM** value: **1.50**

21 ❑ Oct 1984 Cover: 1.00 **NM** value: **1.25**

22 ❑ Nov 1984 Cover: 1.25 **NM** value: **Cover or less**

23 ❑ Dec 1984 Cover: 1.25 **NM** value: **Cover or less**

24 ❑ Jan 1985 Cover: 1.25 **NM** value: **Cover or less**

25 ❑ Feb 1985 Cover: 1.25 **NM** value: **Cover or less**
• The Black Flame back-up story

26 ❑ Mar 1985 Cover: 1.25 **NM** value: **Cover or less**

27 ❑ Apr 1985 Cover: 1.25 **NM** value: **Cover or less**

28 ❑ May 1985 Cover: 1.25 **NM** value: **Cover or less**
Circ: CapCity orders: **5,775**

29 ❑ Jun 1985 Cover: 1.25 **NM** value: **Cover or less**
Circ: CapCity orders: **5,275**

30 ❑ Jul 1985 Cover: 1.25 **NM** value: **Cover or less**
Circ: CapCity orders: **5,025**

31 ❑ Aug 1985 Cover: 1.25 **NM** value: **Cover or less**
Circ: CapCity orders: **5,050**

32 ❑ Sep 1985 Cover: 1.25 **NM** value: **Cover or less**
Circ: CapCity orders: **5,450**

33 ❑ Oct 1985 Cover: 1.25 **NM** value: **Cover or less**
Circ: CapCity orders: **4,800**

34 ❑ Nov 1985 Cover: 1.25 **NM** value: **Cover or less**
Circ: CapCity orders: **4,550**
final issue.

STARSLAYER: THE DIRECTOR'S CUT — Acclaim / Windjammer

1 ❑ Jun 1995 Cover: 2.50 **NM** value: **Cover or less**
Circ: CapCity orders: **7,950**
• New story and artwork **A:** Mike Grell; S. Clarke Hawbaker **W:** Mike Grell

2 ❑ Jun 1995 Cover: 2.50 **NM** value: **Cover or less**
Circ: CapCity orders: **7,500**
• Reprints Starslayer #1 **A:** Mike Grell **W:** Mike Grell

3 ❑ Jul 1995 Cover: 2.50 **NM** value: **Cover or less**
Circ: CapCity orders: **5,650**
• Reprints Starslayer #2 **A:** Mike Grell **W:** Mike Grell

4 ❑ Jul 1995 Cover: 2.50 **NM** value: **Cover or less**
Circ: CapCity orders: **5,600**
• Reprints Starslayer #3 **A:** Mike Grell **W:** Mike Grell

5 ❑ Aug 1995 Cover: 2.50 **NM** value: **Cover or less**
Circ: CapCity orders: **4,950**
• Reprints Starslayer #4 **A:** Mike Grell **W:** Mike Grell

6 ❑ Sep 1995 Cover: 2.50 **NM** value: **Cover or less**
Circ: CapCity orders: **4,875**
cover says Aug, indicia says Sep. • Reprints Starslayer #5 **A:** Mike Grell **W:** Mike Grell

7 ❑ Sep 1995 Cover: 2.50 **NM** value: **Cover or less**
Circ: CapCity orders: **4,375**
• Reprints Starslayer #6 **A:** Mike Grell **W:** Mike Grell

8 ❑ Dec 1995 Cover: 2.50 **NM** value: **Cover or less**
Circ: CapCity orders: **4,375**
• New story and artwork **A:** Mike Grell **W:** Mike Grell

Diamond preorders are the estimated number of comics sold, prior to their release, to comics shops in North America by Diamond Comic Distributors, the largest distributor. These figures underreport the actual number of circulating copies by the amount of reorders Diamond took (usually 5-10% again of the preorders) and sales by publishers to newsstand and bookstore distributors. For many independent publishers, Diamond's preorders may be quite close to the actual number of copies in circulation.

STAR SPANGLED COMICS — DC

Beginning, appropriately enough, with the adventures of The Star-Spangled Kid and Stripesy, this DC anthology series eventually became home to Joe Simon and Jack Kirby's Guardian and The Newsboy Legion, as well as Robotman, The Tarantula, and a series of solo Robin stories.

In 1949, while still featuring Robin stories, the series' focus shifted to the Revolutionary War adventures of Tomahawk and concluded its run with the adventures of Ghost Breaker, a supernatural investigator.

The series became Star Spangled War Stories following #130.
— Brent

1 ❑ Oct 1941 Cover: 0.10 **NM** value: **3500.00**
• **CGC:** 7 graded, best 9.4
★ 1st Appearance of Tarantula.

2 ❑ Nov 1941 Cover: 0.10 **NM** value: **1250.00**
• **CGC:** 3 graded, best 9.0

3 ❑ Dec 1941 Cover: 0.10 **NM** value: **800.00**
• **CGC:** 1 graded, best 4.0

4 ❑ Jan 1942 Cover: 0.10 **NM** value: **750.00**
• **CGC:** 2 graded, best 9.0

5 ❑ Feb 1942 Cover: 0.10 **NM** value: **750.00**
• **CGC:** 1 graded, best 4.5

6 ❑ Mar 1942 Cover: 0.10 **NM** value: **6000.00**
• **CGC:** 1 graded, best 8.0
A: Jack Kirby **W:** Joe Simon ★ 1st Appearance of The Newsboy Legion, Robotman.

7 ❑ Apr 1942 Cover: 0.10 **NM** value: **1850.00**
• **CGC:** 4 graded, best 9.4
Newsboy Legion • 1st appearance Newsboy Legion

8 ❑ May 1942 Cover: 0.10 **NM** value: **1400.00**
• **CGC:** 2 graded, best 9.0
Last Mile Alley • Newsboy Legion

9 ❑ Jun 1942 Cover: 0.10 **NM** value: **1400.00**
• **CGC:** 1 graded, best 8.0
The Rookie Takes the Rap • Newsboy Legion

10 ❑ Jul 1942 Cover: 0.10 **NM** value: **1400.00**
• **CGC:** 1 graded, best 9.2
Kings for A Day • Newsboy Legion

11 ❑ Aug 1942 Cover: 0.10 **NM** value: **1000.00**
• **CGC:** 2 graded, best 8.5
Paradise Prison • Newsboy Legion

12 ❑ Sep 1942 Cover: 0.10 **NM** value: **1000.00**
• **CGC:** 1 graded, best 4.5
Prevue of Peril • Newsboy Legion

13 ❑ Oct 1942 Cover: 0.10 **NM** value: **1000.00**
• **CGC:** 4 graded, best 9.2
The Scoop of Suicide Slum • Newsboy Legion

14 ❑ Nov 1942 Cover: 0.10 **NM** value: **1000.00**
• **CGC:** 4 graded, best 9.4
The Meanest Man on Earth • Newsboy Legion

15 ❑ Dec 1942 Cover: 0.10 **NM** value: **1000.00**
• **CGC:** 1 graded, best 8.5
Playmates of Peril • Newsboy Legion

16 ❑ Jan 1943 Cover: 0.10 **NM** value: **1000.00**
• **CGC:** 2 graded, best 7.5
• Newsboy Legion

17 ❑ Feb 1943 Cover: 0.10 **NM** value: **1275.00**
• **CGC:** 4 graded, best 9.8
The Rafferty Mob • Newsboy Legion★ Origin of The Star Spangled Kid.

18 ❑ Mar 1943 Cover: 0.10 **NM** value: **850.00**
• **CGC:** 2 graded, best 4.0
The Education of Iron Man Gukin • Newsboy Legion

19 ❑ Apr 1943 Cover: 0.10 **NM** value: **850.00**
• **CGC:** 2 graded, best 8.0
The Furher of Suicide Slum • Newsboy Legion

20 ❑ May 1943 Cover: 0.10 **NM** value: **700.00**
• **CGC:** 3 graded, best 9.4
• Newsboy Legion

21 ❑ Jun 1943 Cover: 0.10 **NM** value: **700.00**
• **CGC:** 2 graded, best 8.0
• Newsboy Legion

22 ❑ Jul 1943 Cover: 0.10 **NM** value: **700.00**
• **CGC:** 1 graded, best 5.5
Brains for Sale • Newsboy Legion

23 ❑ Aug 1943 Cover: 0.10 **NM** value: **700.00**
• **CGC:** 4 graded, best 9.2
Art for the Scrapper Sale • Newsboy Legion

24 ❑ Sep 1943 Cover: 0.10 **NM** value: **700.00**
• **CGC:** 5 graded, best 9.2
Death Strikes a Bargain • Newsboy Legion

25 ❑ Oct 1943 Cover: 0.10 **NM** value: **700.00**
• **CGC:** 4 graded, best 9.4
Victuals for Victory • Newsboy Legion

26 ❑ Nov 1943 Cover: 0.10 **NM** value: **700.00**
• **CGC:** 1 graded, best 7.5
Louie the Lug Goes Literary • Newsboy Legion

27 ❑ Dec 1943 Cover: 0.10 **NM** value: **700.00**
• **CGC:** 6 graded, best 9.4
Turn on the Heat • Newsboy Legion

28 ❑ Jan 1944 Cover: 0.10 **NM** value: **700.00**
• **CGC:** 4 graded, best 9.0
• Newsboy Legion

29 ❑ Feb 1944 Cover: 0.10 **NM** value: **700.00**
• **CGC:** 1 graded, best 9.0
Cabbages and Comics • Newsboy Legion

30 ❑ Mar 1944 Cover: 0.10 **NM** value: **700.00**
• **CGC:** 2 graded, best 9.4

31 ❑ Apr 1944 Cover: 0.10 **NM** value: **440.00**

32 ❑ May 1944 Cover: 0.10 **NM** value: **440.00**
• **CGC:** 3 graded, best 9.2

33 ❑ Jun 1944 Cover: 0.10 **NM** value: **440.00**
• **CGC:** 5 graded, best 9.6

34 ❑ Jul 1944 Cover: 0.10 **NM** value: **440.00**
• **CGC:** 2 graded, best 8.5

35 ❑ Aug 1944 Cover: 0.10 **NM** value: **440.00**
• **CGC:** 2 graded, best 9.4

36 ❑ Sep 1944 Cover: 0.10 **NM** value: **440.00**
• **CGC:** 3 graded, best 9.6

37 ❑ Oct 1944 Cover: 0.10 **NM** value: **440.00**
• **CGC:** 1 graded, best 7.0

38 ❑ Nov 1944 Cover: 0.10 **NM** value: **440.00**
• **CGC:** 1 graded, best 9.2

39 ❑ Dec 1944 Cover: 0.10 **NM** value: **440.00**
• **CGC:** 3 graded, best 9.2

40 ❑ Jan 1945 Cover: 0.10 **NM** value: **440.00**
• **CGC:** 3 graded, best 9.6

41 ❑ Feb 1945 Cover: 0.10 **NM** value: **365.00**
• **CGC:** 1 graded, best 8.0

42 ❑ Mar 1945 Cover: 0.10 **NM** value: **365.00**
• **CGC:** 1 graded, best 8.0

43 ❑ Apr 1945 Cover: 0.10 **NM** value: **365.00**
• **CGC:** 2 graded, best 9.0

44 ❑ May 1945 Cover: 0.10 **NM** value: **365.00**
• **CGC:** 3 graded, best 9.2

45 ❑ Jun 1945 Cover: 0.10 **NM** value: **365.00**
• **CGC:** 2 graded, best 9.0

46 ❑ Jul 1945 Cover: 0.10 **NM** value: **365.00**
• **CGC:** 2 graded, best 9.4

47 ❑ Aug 1945 Cover: 0.10 **NM** value: **365.00**
• **CGC:** 2 graded, best 8.5

48 ❑ Sep 1945 Cover: 0.10 **NM** value: **365.00**
• **CGC:** 2 graded, best 9.6

49 ❑ Oct 1945 Cover: 0.10 **NM** value: **365.00**
• **CGC:** 1 graded, best 9.4

50 ❑ Nov 1945 Cover: 0.10 **NM** value: **365.00**
• **CGC:** 2 graded, best 9.4

51 ❑ Dec 1945 Cover: 0.10 **NM** value: **325.00**
• **CGC:** 2 graded, best 9.4

52 ❑ Jan 1946 Cover: 0.10 **NM** value: **325.00**
• **CGC:** 2 graded, best 7.5

53 ❑ Feb 1946 Cover: 0.10 **NM** value: **325.00**
• **CGC:** 1 graded, best 7.0
• Newsboy Legion

54 ❑ Mar 1946 Cover: 0.10 **NM** value: **325.00**
• **CGC:** 3 graded, best 9.6
• Newsboy Legion

55 ❑ Apr 1946 Cover: 0.10 **NM** value: **325.00**
• **CGC:** 5 graded, best 9.8
• Newsboy Legion

56 ❑ May 1946 Cover: 0.10 **NM** value: **325.00**
• **CGC:** 1 graded, best 8.5
• Newsboy Legion

57 ❑ Jun 1946 Cover: 0.10 **NM** value: **325.00**
• **CGC:** 2 graded, best 9.6
• Newsboy Legion

58 ❑ Jul 1946 Cover: 0.10 **NM** value: **325.00**
• **CGC:** 1 graded, best 9.4
• Newsboy Legion

59 ❑ Aug 1946 Cover: 0.10 **NM** value: **325.00**
• **CGC:** 2 graded, best 8.5
• Newsboy Legion

60 ❑ Sep 1946 Cover: 0.10 **NM** value: **325.00**
• **CGC:** 1 graded, best 3.0

61 ❑ Oct 1946 Cover: 0.10 **NM** value: **300.00**
• **CGC:** 3 graded, best 9.2

62 ❑ Nov 1946 Cover: 0.10 **NM** value: **300.00**
• **CGC:** 2 graded, best 9.2

63 ❑ Dec 1946 Cover: 0.10 **NM** value: **300.00**

64 ❑ Jan 1947 Cover: 0.10 **NM** value: **300.00**
• **CGC:** 1 graded, best 8.0

65 ❑ Feb 1947 Cover: 0.10 **NM** value: **850.00**
• **CGC:** 2 graded, best 7.0
• Robin stories begin

66 ❑ Mar 1947 Cover: 0.10 **NM** value: **540.00**
• **CGC:** 4 graded, best 9.6

67 ❑ Apr 1947 Cover: 0.10 **NM** value: **540.00**
• **CGC:** 1 graded, best 9.4

68 ❑ May 1947 Cover: 0.10 **NM** value: **540.00**
• **CGC:** 2 graded, best 9.2

69 ❑ Jun 1947 Cover: 0.10 **NM** value: **650.00**
• **CGC:** 4 graded, best 9.2
★ 1st Appearance of Tomahawk.

70 ❑ Jul 1947 Cover: 0.10 **NM** value: **540.00**
• **CGC:** 1 graded, best 7.5

71 ❑ Aug 1947 Cover: 0.10 **NM** value: **475.00**
• **CGC:** 2 graded, best 9.0

72 ❑ Sep 1947 Cover: 0.10 **NM** value: **475.00**
• **CGC:** 1 graded, best 8.0

73 ❑ Oct 1947 Cover: 0.10 **NM** value: **475.00**
• **CGC:** 3 graded, best 9.4

74 ❑ Nov 1947 Cover: 0.10 **NM** value: **475.00**
• **CGC:** 1 graded, best 8.0

75 ❑ Dec 1947 Cover: 0.10 **NM** value: **475.00**
• **CGC:** 1 graded, best 9.0

76 ❑ Jan 1948 Cover: 0.10 **NM** value: **475.00**
• **CGC:** 2 graded, best 8.5

77 ❑ Feb 1948 Cover: 0.10 **NM** value: **475.00**
• **CGC:** 1 graded, best 7.5

78 ❑ Mar 1948 Cover: 0.10 **NM** value: **475.00**
• **CGC:** 1 graded, best 9.2

79 ❑ Apr 1948 Cover: 0.10 **NM** value: **475.00**
• **CGC:** 2 graded, best 9.2

80 ❑ May 1948 Cover: 0.10 **NM** value: **475.00**
• **CGC:** 2 graded, best 9.6

81 ❑ Jun 1948 Cover: 0.10 **NM** value: **390.00**
• **CGC:** 1 graded, best 7.0

Other grades: Multiply prices above by **1.5 for Mint • 2/3 for Very Fine • 1/3 for Fine • 1/5 for Very Good • 1/8 for Good**

82 ❑ Jul 1948 Cover: 0.10 **NM** value: **390.00**
• **CGC:** 4 graded, best 9.0
83 ❑ Aug 1948 Cover: 0.10 **NM** value: **390.00**
• **CGC:** 2 graded, best 8.0
84 ❑ Sep 1948 Cover: 0.10 **NM** value: **525.00**
• **CGC:** 3 graded, best 8.5
85 ❑ Oct 1948 Cover: 0.10 **NM** value: **390.00**
• **CGC:** 1 graded, best 5.5
86 ❑ Nov 1948 Cover: 0.10 **NM** value: **390.00**
• **CGC:** 1 graded, best 6.5
87 ❑ Dec 1948 Cover: 0.10 **NM** value: **525.00**
• **CGC:** 1 graded, best 9.2
88 ❑ Jan 1949 Cover: 0.10 **NM** value: **400.00**
• **CGC:** 1 graded, best 6.5
★ Appearance of Batman.
89 ❑ Feb 1949 Cover: 0.10 **NM** value: **400.00**
• **CGC:** 2 graded, best 5.5
★ Appearance of Batman.
90 ❑ Mar 1949 Cover: 0.10 **NM** value: **400.00**
• **CGC:** 2 graded, best 8.5
★ Appearance of Batman.
91 ❑ Apr 1949 Cover: 0.10 **NM** value: **400.00**
• **CGC:** 3 graded, best 8.0
★ Appearance of Batman.
92 ❑ May 1949 Cover: 0.10 **NM** value: **400.00**
• **CGC:** 2 graded, best 7.5
★ Appearance of Batman.
93 ❑ Jun 1949 Cover: 0.10 **NM** value: **400.00**
• **CGC:** 2 graded, best 8.0
★ Appearance of Batman.
94 ❑ Jul 1949 Cover: 0.10 **NM** value: **400.00**
★ Appearance of Batman.
95 ❑ Aug 1949 Cover: 0.10 **NM** value: **225.00**
• **CGC:** 1 graded, best 4.0
96 ❑ Sep 1949 Cover: 0.10 **NM** value: **225.00**
• **CGC:** 2 graded, best 8.5
97 ❑ Oct 1949 Cover: 0.10 **NM** value: **225.00**
98 ❑ Nov 1949 Cover: 0.10 **NM** value: **225.00**
99 ❑ Dec 1949 Cover: 0.10 **NM** value: **225.00**
• **CGC:** 2 graded, best 9.0
100 ❑ Jan 1950 Cover: 0.10 **NM** value: **250.00**
101 ❑ Feb 1950 Cover: 0.10 **NM** value: **185.00**
102 ❑ Mar 1950 Cover: 0.10 **NM** value: **185.00**
103 ❑ Apr 1950 Cover: 0.10 **NM** value: **185.00**
104 ❑ May 1950 Cover: 0.10 **NM** value: **185.00**
• **CGC:** 2 graded, best 8.5
105 ❑ Jun 1950 Cover: 0.10 **NM** value: **185.00**
• **CGC:** 3 graded, best 8.5
106 ❑ Jul 1950 Cover: 0.10 **NM** value: **185.00**
• **CGC:** 3 graded, best 8.0
107 ❑ Aug 1950 Cover: 0.10 **NM** value: **185.00**
• **CGC:** 3 graded, best 7.5
108 ❑ Sep 1950 Cover: 0.10 **NM** value: **185.00**
• **CGC:** 1 graded, best 8.0
109 ❑ Oct 1950 Cover: 0.10 **NM** value: **185.00**
• **CGC:** 1 graded, best 8.0
110 ❑ Nov 1950 Cover: 0.10 **NM** value: **185.00**
111 ❑ Dec 1950 Cover: 0.10 **NM** value: **160.00**
112 ❑ Jan 1951 Cover: 0.10 **NM** value: **160.00**
• **CGC:** 1 graded, best 8.5
113 ❑ Feb 1951 Cover: 0.10 **NM** value: **300.00**
• **CGC:** 3 graded, best 9.4
A: Frank Frazetta
114 ❑ Mar 1951 Cover: 0.10 **NM** value: **275.00**
• **CGC:** 1 graded, best 7.5
★ Origin of Robin.
115 ❑ Apr 1951 Cover: 0.10 **NM** value: **160.00**
116 ❑ May 1951 Cover: 0.10 **NM** value: **160.00**
117 ❑ Jun 1951 Cover: 0.10 **NM** value: **160.00**
118 ❑ Jul 1951 Cover: 0.10 **NM** value: **160.00**
• **CGC:** 1 graded, best 7.5
119 ❑ Aug 1951 Cover: 0.10 **NM** value: **160.00**
• **CGC:** 3 graded, best 9.4
120 ❑ Sep 1951 Cover: 0.10 **NM** value: **160.00**
• **CGC:** 2 graded, best 9.0
• Has 1964 Statement, filed 10/1/64; no circ figures published
121 ❑ Oct 1951 Cover: 0.10 **NM** value: **160.00**
• **CGC:** 1 graded, best 8.5
122 ❑ Nov 1951 Cover: 0.10 **NM** value: **160.00**
• **CGC:** 1 graded, best 8.0
123 ❑ Dec 1951 Cover: 0.10 **NM** value: **160.00**
• **CGC:** 1 graded, best 7.5
124 ❑ Jan 1952 Cover: 0.10 **NM** value: **160.00**
• **CGC:** 1 graded, best 5.0
125 ❑ Feb 1952 Cover: 0.10 **NM** value: **160.00**
126 ❑ Mar 1952 Cover: 0.10 **NM** value: **160.00**
127 ❑ Apr 1952 Cover: 0.10 **NM** value: **160.00**
128 ❑ May 1952 Cover: 0.10 **NM** value: **160.00**
• **CGC:** 1 graded, best 9.0
129 ❑ Jun 1952 Cover: 0.10 **NM** value: **160.00**
130 ❑ Jul 1952 Cover: 0.10 **NM** value: **160.00**
131 ❑ Aug 1952 Cover: 0.10 **NM** value: **500.00**
final issue. • Becomes Star Spangled War Stories; Has 1966 Statement; avg print run 387,000; avg sales 214,000; avg subs 1,495; avg total paid 215,495; samples 265; max existent 215,760; 44% of run returned

STAR SPANGLED COMICS (2ND SERIES) DC

1 ❑ May 1999 Cover: 1.99 **NM** value: **2.00**
Circ: Diamd. preorders: **42,080**
📖 ...A Terrifying Hour! • Justice Society Returns **A:** Chris Weston **W:** Geoff Johns ★ Appearance of Star Spangled Kid, Sandman.

STAR SPANGLED WAR STORIES DC

From 1952 until 1977, Star Spangled War Stories was one of DC's line of war comics. In the course of those 20 years, it brought readers tales of Enemy Ace, Viking Prince, and many other notables. Although these features were popular with readers, it was not until issue #151, with the introduction of The Unknown Soldier that Star Spangled War Stories found its star.

Star Spangled War Stories grew out of an earlier title, Star Spangled Comics. After issue #130 of that title, it switched names to Star Spangled War Stories, although it continued its numbering sequence through issue #133. At that point, it retroactively decided that issue #131 was really a first issue and began numbering its next issues #4, 5, etc. All this was cleared up somewhat when Star Spangled War Stories changed names again (to Unknown Soldier) following issue #205.

1 ❑ Sep 1952 Cover: 0.10 **NM** value: **750.00**
Cover reads #131 (series' #s continued from Star Spangled Comics).
2 ❑ Oct 1952 Cover: 0.10 **NM** value: **550.00**
Cover reads #132 (#s from Star Spangled Comics).
3 ❑ Nov 1952 Cover: 0.10 **NM** value: **475.00**
Cover reads #133 (#s from Star Spangled Comics).
4 ❑ Dec 1952 Cover: 0.10 **NM** value: **285.00**
• **CGC:** 1 graded, best 7.5
5 ❑ Jan 1953 Cover: 0.10 **NM** value: **285.00**
6 ❑ Feb 1953 Cover: 0.10 **NM** value: **285.00**
7 ❑ Mar 1953 Cover: 0.10 **NM** value: **220.00**
8 ❑ Apr 1953 Cover: 0.10 **NM** value: **220.00**
9 ❑ May 1953 Cover: 0.10 **NM** value: **220.00**
• **CGC:** 1 graded, best 8.5
10 ❑ Jun 1953 Cover: 0.10 **NM** value: **220.00**
• **CGC:** 1 graded, best 8.5
11 ❑ Jul 1953 Cover: 0.10 **NM** value: **185.00**
12 ❑ Aug 1953 Cover: 0.10 **NM** value: **185.00**
13 ❑ Sep 1953 Cover: 0.10 **NM** value: **185.00**
14 ❑ Oct 1953 Cover: 0.10 **NM** value: **185.00**
15 ❑ Nov 1953 Cover: 0.10 **NM** value: **185.00**
16 ❑ Dec 1953 Cover: 0.10 **NM** value: **185.00**
17 ❑ Jan 1954 Cover: 0.10 **NM** value: **185.00**
18 ❑ Feb 1954 Cover: 0.10 **NM** value: **185.00**
• **CGC:** 1 graded, best 6.5
19 ❑ Mar 1954 Cover: 0.10 **NM** value: **185.00**
• **CGC:** 1 graded, best 7.0
20 ❑ Apr 1954 Cover: 0.10 **NM** value: **185.00**
• **CGC:** 1 graded, best 9.0
21 ❑ May 1954 Cover: 0.10 **NM** value: **130.00**
• **CGC:** 1 graded, best 7.5
22 ❑ Jun 1954 Cover: 0.10 **NM** value: **130.00**
23 ❑ Jul 1954 Cover: 0.10 **NM** value: **130.00**
24 ❑ Aug 1954 Cover: 0.10 **NM** value: **130.00**
• **CGC:** 1 graded, best 8.5
25 ❑ Sep 1954 Cover: 0.10 **NM** value: **130.00**
26 ❑ Oct 1954 Cover: 0.10 **NM** value: **130.00**
• **CGC:** 2 graded, best 8.0
27 ❑ Nov 1954 Cover: 0.10 **NM** value: **130.00**
28 ❑ Dec 1954 Cover: 0.10 **NM** value: **130.00**
29 ❑ Jan 1955 Cover: 0.10 **NM** value: **130.00**
• **CGC:** 1 graded, best 7.5
30 ❑ Feb 1955 Cover: 0.10 **NM** value: **130.00**
31 ❑ Mar 1955 Cover: 0.10 **NM** value: **90.00**
32 ❑ Apr 1955 Cover: 0.10 **NM** value: **90.00**
• **CGC:** 1 graded, best 9.2
33 ❑ May 1955 Cover: 0.10 **NM** value: **90.00**
34 ❑ Jun 1955 Cover: 0.10 **NM** value: **90.00**
35 ❑ Jul 1955 Cover: 0.10 **NM** value: **90.00**
36 ❑ Aug 1955 Cover: 0.10 **NM** value: **90.00**
37 ❑ Sep 1955 Cover: 0.10 **NM** value: **90.00**
38 ❑ Oct 1955 Cover: 0.10 **NM** value: **90.00**
39 ❑ Nov 1955 Cover: 0.10 **NM** value: **90.00**
40 ❑ Dec 1955 Cover: 0.10 **NM** value: **90.00**
• **CGC:** 1 graded, best 7.0
41 ❑ Jan 1956 Cover: 0.10 **NM** value: **70.00**
42 ❑ Feb 1956 Cover: 0.10 **NM** value: **70.00**
43 ❑ Mar 1956 Cover: 0.10 **NM** value: **70.00**
44 ❑ Apr 1956 Cover: 0.10 **NM** value: **70.00**
45 ❑ May 1956 Cover: 0.10 **NM** value: **70.00**
46 ❑ Jun 1956 Cover: 0.10 **NM** value: **70.00**
47 ❑ Jul 1956 Cover: 0.10 **NM** value: **70.00**
📖 Sidekick!; The Ghost Raider!; Bull's-Eye Letter!; Private Pete; Battle Parade; Fighting Engineers (text)
48 ❑ Aug 1956 Cover: 0.10 **NM** value: **70.00**
📖 Battle Hills!; The Real War!; Bazooka Battle Roll!; Private Pete; Underground Soldier!; The Invisible Crew (text)
49 ❑ Sep 1956 Cover: 0.10 **NM** value: **70.00**
50 ❑ Oct 1956 Cover: 0.10 **NM** value: **70.00**
51 ❑ Nov 1956 Cover: 0.10 **NM** value: **60.00**
52 ❑ Dec 1956 Cover: 0.10 **NM** value: **60.00**
53 ❑ Jan 1957 Cover: 0.10 **NM** value: **60.00**
54 ❑ Feb 1957 Cover: 0.10 **NM** value: **60.00**
55 ❑ Mar 1957 Cover: 0.10 **NM** value: **60.00**
56 ❑ Apr 1957 Cover: 0.10 **NM** value: **60.00**
57 ❑ May 1957 Cover: 0.10 **NM** value: **60.00**
58 ❑ Jun 1957 Cover: 0.10 **NM** value: **60.00**
59 ❑ Jul 1957 Cover: 0.10 **NM** value: **60.00**
60 ❑ Aug 1957 Cover: 0.10 **NM** value: **60.00**
61 ❑ Sep 1957 Cover: 0.10 **NM** value: **60.00**
62 ❑ Oct 1957 Cover: 0.10 **NM** value: **60.00**
63 ❑ Nov 1957 Cover: 0.10 **NM** value: **60.00**
64 ❑ Dec 1957 Cover: 0.10 **NM** value: **60.00**
65 ❑ Jan 1958 Cover: 0.10 **NM** value: **60.00**
66 ❑ Feb 1958 Cover: 0.10 **NM** value: **60.00**
67 ❑ Mar 1958 Cover: 0.10 **NM** value: **60.00**
68 ❑ Apr 1958 Cover: 0.10 **NM** value: **60.00**
69 ❑ May 1958 Cover: 0.10 **NM** value: **60.00**
70 ❑ Jun 1958 Cover: 0.10 **NM** value: **60.00**
• **CGC:** 1 graded, best 8.5
71 ❑ Jul 1958 Cover: 0.10 **NM** value: **55.00**
72 ❑ Aug 1958 Cover: 0.10 **NM** value: **55.00**
73 ❑ Sep 1958 Cover: 0.10 **NM** value: **55.00**
74 ❑ Oct 1958 Cover: 0.10 **NM** value: **55.00**
75 ❑ Nov 1958 Cover: 0.10 **NM** value: **55.00**
76 ❑ Dec 1958 Cover: 0.10 **NM** value: **55.00**
77 ❑ Jan 1959 Cover: 0.10 **NM** value: **55.00**
78 ❑ Feb 1959 Cover: 0.10 **NM** value: **55.00**
79 ❑ Mar 1959 Cover: 0.10 **NM** value: **55.00**
80 ❑ Apr 1959 Cover: 0.10 **NM** value: **55.00**
81 ❑ May 1959 Cover: 0.10 **NM** value: **55.00**
82 ❑ Jun 1959 Cover: 0.10 **NM** value: **55.00**
83 ❑ Jul 1959 Cover: 0.10 **NM** value: **55.00**
84 ❑ Aug 1959 Cover: 0.10 **NM** value: **125.00**
• **CGC:** 1 graded, best 5.0
★ Origin of Mademoiselle Marie. ★ 1st Appearance of Mademoiselle Marie.
85 ❑ Sep 1959 Cover: 0.10 **NM** value: **80.00**
★ Appearance of Mademoiselle Marie.
86 ❑ Oct 1959 Cover: 0.10 **NM** value: **80.00**
★ Appearance of Mademoiselle Marie.
87 ❑ Nov 1959 Cover: 0.10 **NM** value: **80.00**
★ Appearance of Mademoiselle Marie.
88 ❑ Jan 1960 Cover: 0.10 **NM** value: **65.00**
Circ: Statement: **169,000**
89 ❑ Mar 1960 Cover: 0.10 **NM** value: **65.00**
Circ: Statement: **169,000**
90 ❑ May 1960 Cover: 0.10 **NM** value: **325.00**
Circ: Statement: **169,000** • **CGC:** 1 graded, best 4.5
• Island of Armored Giants (dinosaur) story ★ 1st Appearance of Dinosaur Island.
91 ❑ Jul 1960 Cover: 0.10 **NM** value: **45.00**
Circ: Statement: **169,000**
92 ❑ Sep 1960 Cover: 0.10 **NM** value: **110.00**
Circ: Statement: **169,000**
• Dinosaurs
93 ❑ Nov 1960 Cover: 0.10 **NM** value: **45.00**
Circ: Statement: **169,000**
94 ❑ Jan 1961 Cover: 0.10 **NM** value: **110.00**
Circ: Statement: **205,000**
• Dinosaurs
95 ❑ Mar 1961 Cover: 0.10 **NM** value: **110.00**
Circ: Statement: **205,000**
• Dinosaurs
96 ❑ May 1961 Cover: 0.10 **NM** value: **110.00**
Circ: Statement: **205,000**
• Dinosaurs
97 ❑ Jul 1961 Cover: 0.10 **NM** value: **110.00**
Circ: Statement: **205,000**
• Dinosaurs
98 ❑ Sep 1961 Cover: 0.10 **NM** value: **110.00**
Circ: Statement: **205,000** • **CGC:** 1 graded, best 7.0
• Dinosaurs
99 ❑ Nov 1961 Cover: 0.10 **NM** value: **110.00**
Circ: Statement: **205,000**
• Dinosaurs
100 ❑ Jan 1962 Cover: 0.12 **NM** value: **145.00**
• Dinosaurs
101 ❑ Mar 1962 Cover: 0.12 **NM** value: **75.00**
• Dinosaurs
102 ❑ May 1962 Cover: 0.12 **NM** value: **75.00**
• Dinosaurs
103 ❑ Jul 1962 Cover: 0.12 **NM** value: **75.00**
• Dinosaurs
104 ❑ Sep 1962 Cover: 0.12 **NM** value: **75.00**
• Dinosaurs
105 ❑ Nov 1962 Cover: 0.12 **NM** value: **75.00**
• **CGC:** 1 graded, best 9.2
• Dinosaurs
106 ❑ Jan 1963 Cover: 0.12 **NM** value: **75.00**
• Dinosaurs
107 ❑ Mar 1963 Cover: 0.12 **NM** value: **75.00**
• Dinosaurs
108 ❑ May 1963 Cover: 0.12 **NM** value: **75.00**
• Dinosaurs
109 ❑ Jul 1963 Cover: 0.12 **NM** value: **75.00**
• Dinosaurs
110 ❑ Sep 1963 Cover: 0.12 **NM** value: **75.00**
• Dinosaurs
111 ❑ Nov 1963 Cover: 0.12 **NM** value: **75.00**
📖 War That Time Forgot • Dinosaurs
112 ❑ Jan 1964 Cover: 0.12 **NM** value: **75.00**
• Dinosaurs
113 ❑ Mar 1964 Cover: 0.12 **NM** value: **75.00**
• Dinosaurs
114 ❑ May 1964 Cover: 0.12 **NM** value: **75.00**
• Dinosaurs
115 ❑ Jul 1964 Cover: 0.12 **NM** value: **75.00**
• Dinosaurs
116 ❑ Sep 1964 Cover: 0.12 **NM** value: **75.00**
📖 War That Time Forgot: Dead Man's Curve!; Baker's Dozen • Dinosaurs
117 ❑ Nov 1964 Cover: 0.12 **NM** value: **75.00**
• Dinosaurs
118 ❑ Jan 1965 Cover: 0.12 **NM** value: **75.00**
Circ: Statement: **243,700**
• Dinosaurs
119 ❑ Mar 1965 Cover: 0.12 **NM** value: **75.00**
Circ: Statement: **243,700**
• Dinosaurs

CGC-graded: Multiply prices above by **33 for 9.9 M** • **16 for 9.8 NM/M** • **7 for 9.6 NM+** • **5 for 9.4 NM** • **2.5 for 9.2 NM-** • **1.5 for 9.0 VF/NM**

120 ❑ Apr 1965 Cover: 0.12 **NM** value: **75.00**
Circ: Statement: **243,700**
• Dinosaurs
121 ❑ Jun 1965 Cover: 0.12 **NM** value: **75.00**
Circ: Statement: **243,700**
• Dinosaurs
122 ❑ Aug 1965 Cover: 0.12 **NM** value: **75.00**
Circ: Statement: **243,700 • CGC:** 1 graded, best 9.2
• Dinosaurs
123 ❑ Oct 1965 Cover: 0.12 **NM** value: **75.00**
Circ: Statement: **243,700 • CGC:** 2 graded, best 9.0
• Dinosaurs
124 ❑ Dec 1965 Cover: 0.12 **NM** value: **75.00**
Circ: Statement: **243,700 • CGC:** 3 graded, best 9.4
• Dinosaurs
125 ❑ Feb 1966 Cover: 0.12 **NM** value: **75.00**
Circ: Statement: **215,495 • CGC:** 1 graded, best 8.5
War That Time Forgot: Tidbit for a Tyrannosaurus!; A Navy Named Smith • Dinosaurs
126 ❑ Apr 1966 Cover: 0.12 **NM** value: **75.00**
Circ: Statement: **215,495**
★ 1st Appearance of Sgt. Gorilla.
127 ❑ Jun 1966 Cover: 0.12 **NM** value: **75.00**
Circ: Statement: **215,495**
• Dinosaurs
128 ❑ Aug 1966 Cover: 0.12 **NM** value: **75.00**
Circ: Statement: **215,495 • CGC:** 1 graded, best 9.0
• Dinosaurs
129 ❑ Oct 1966 Cover: 0.12 **NM** value: **75.00**
Circ: Statement: **215,495**
• Dinosaurs
130 ❑ Dec 1966 Cover: 0.12 **NM** value: **75.00**
Circ: Statement: **215,495**
War That Time Forgot: Secrets Die on Monster Island; Stakeout on Red Beach! • Dinosaurs
131 ❑ Mar 1967 Cover: 0.12 **NM** value: **75.00**
Circ: Statement: **160,000 • CGC:** 1 graded, best 9.0
• Dinosaurs
132 ❑ May 1967 Cover: 0.12 **NM** value: **75.00**
Circ: Statement: **160,000 • CGC:** 1 graded, best 9.0
• Dinosaurs
133 ❑ Jul 1967 Cover: 0.12 **NM** value: **75.00**
Circ: Statement: **160,000 • CGC:** 3 graded, best 9.6
• Dinosaurs
134 ❑ Sep 1967 Cover: 0.12 **NM** value: **80.00**
Circ: Statement: **160,000 • CGC:** 1 graded, best 9.0
War That Time Forgot: The Killing Ground!; Ace of the Death Cloud! • Dinosaurs **A:** Neal Adams
135 ❑ Nov 1967 Cover: 0.12 **NM** value: **75.00**
Circ: Statement: **160,000 • CGC:** 1 graded, best 9.6
War That Time Forgot • Dinosaurs
136 ❑ Jan 1968 Cover: 0.12 **NM** value: **75.00**
Circ: Statement: **170,310 • CGC:** 2 graded, best 9.4
• Dinosaurs
137 ❑ Mar 1968 Cover: 0.12 **NM** value: **75.00**
Circ: Statement: **170,310 • CGC:** 2 graded, best 9.2
War That Time Forgot: Fight to the Last!; Mud Soldier!; Human Booby Trap! • Dinosaurs
138 ❑ May 1968 Cover: 0.12 **NM** value: **75.00**
Circ: Statement: **170,310 • CGC:** 2 graded, best 9.4
• Enemy Ace stories begin; Has 1967 Statement, filed 10/1/67; avg print run 359,000; avg sales 159,000; avg subs 1,000; avg total paid 160,000; samples 340; max existent 160,340; 55% of run returned
139 ❑ Jul 1968 Cover: 0.12 **NM** value: **60.00**
Circ: Statement: **170,310 • CGC:** 4 graded, best 9.0
★ Origin of Enemy Ace.
140 ❑ Sep 1968 Cover: 0.12 **NM** value: **35.00**
Circ: Statement: **170,310**
• Enemy Ace
141 ❑ Nov 1968 Cover: 0.12 **NM** value: **35.00**
Circ: Statement: **170,310 • CGC:** 2 graded, best 9.4
Enemy Ace Meets the Bull • Enemy Ace
142 ❑ Jan 1969 Cover: 0.12 **NM** value: **35.00**
Circ: Statement: **149,170 • CGC:** 2 graded, best 9.2
• Enemy Ace
143 ❑ Mar 1969 Cover: 0.12 **NM** value: **35.00**
Circ: Statement: **149,170 • CGC:** 4 graded, best 9.4
• Enemy Ace; Has 1968 Statement, filed 10/1/68; avg print run 335,000; avg sales 170,000; avg subs 310; avg total paid 170,310; samples 386; max existent 170,696; 49% of run returned
144 ❑ May 1969 Cover: 0.12 **NM** value: **40.00**
Circ: Statement: **149,170 • CGC:** 4 graded, best 9.4
Death Takes No Holiday! • Enemy Ace **A:** Joe Kubert; Neal Adams
145 ❑ Jul 1969 Cover: 0.12 **NM** value: **35.00**
Circ: Statement: **149,170 • CGC:** 1 graded, best 7.5
• Enemy Ace
146 ❑ Sep 1969 Cover: 0.15 **NM** value: **24.00**
Circ: Statement: **149,170 • CGC:** 3 graded, best 9.4
Enemy Ace; Brother Enemy • Enemy Ace
147 ❑ Nov 1969 Cover: 0.15 **NM** value: **24.00**
Circ: Statement: **149,170 • CGC:** 1 graded, best 8.5
A Grave in the Sky! • Enemy Ace **A:** Joe Kubert
148 ❑ Jan 1970 Cover: 0.15 **NM** value: **24.00**
Circ: Statement: **136,204 • CGC:** 5 graded, best 9.4
• Enemy Ace
149 ❑ Mar 1970 Cover: 0.15 **NM** value: **24.00**
Circ: Statement: **136,204 • CGC:** 1 graded, best 7.5
150 ❑ May 1970 Cover: 0.15 **NM** value: **24.00**
Circ: Statement: **136,204 • CGC:** 2 graded, best 9.4
3 Graves to Home!; Monster of the Viking Sea!; The Great Battles of History: The Marne • Enemy Ace, Viking Prince; Has 1969 Statement, filed 10/1/69; avg print run 317,000; avg sales 149,000; avg subs 170; avg total paid 149,170; samples 346; max existent 149,516; 53% of run returned **A:** Joe Kubert
151 ❑ Jul 1970 Cover: 0.15 **NM** value: **100.00**
Circ: Statement: **136,204 • CGC:** 11 graded, best 9.6
A: Joe Kubert ★ 1st Appearance of Unknown Soldier.
152 ❑ Sep 1970 Cover: 0.15 **NM** value: **25.00**
Circ: Statement: **136,204**
Instant Glory!; Battle Album: Lafayette Escadrille; Enemy Ace: Rain Above...Mud Below! ★ 2nd Appearance of The Unknown Soldier.
153 ❑ Nov 1970 Cover: 0.15 **NM** value: **25.00**
Circ: Statement: **136,204**
Everybody Dies; Enemy Ace: Fokker Fury; U.S.S. Stevens: Double Rescue!; The Jet and the Prop! **A:** Joe Kubert
154 ❑ Jan 1971 Cover: 0.15 **NM** value: **70.00**
Circ: Statement: **156,713 • CGC:** 10 graded, best 9.4
I'll Never Die!; Killer of the Skies! • Unknown Soldier; Enemy Ace **A:** Joe Kubert ★ Origin of Unknown Soldier.
155 ❑ Mar 1971 Cover: 0.15 **NM** value: **16.00**
Circ: Statement: **156,713**
• reprints Enemy Ace story
156 ❑ May 1971 Cover: 0.15 **NM** value: **14.00**
Circ: Statement: **156,713**
Assassination!; Battle Album: Fokker-D-VII; A Dream Came True! • Unknown Soldier; Enemy Ace back-up; Has 1970 Statement, filed 10/1/70; avg print run 288,160; avg sales 136,098; avg subs 106; avg total paid 136,204; samples 122; max existent 136,326; 53% of run returned
157 ❑ Jul 1971 Cover: 0.15 **NM** value: **14.00**
Circ: Statement: **156,713**
Unknown Soldier (Untitled); Battle Album: Royalty Over Viet Nam; Fokker Fury! • Unknown Soldier meets Easy Co.; Enemy Ace back-up
158 ❑ Sep 1971 Cover: 0.25 **NM** value: **14.00**
Circ: Statement: **156,713**
159 ❑ Nov 1971 Cover: 0.25 **NM** value: **14.00**
Circ: Statement: **156,713**
160 ❑ Jan 1972 Cover: 0.25 **NM** value: **14.00**
Circ: Statement: **145,869**
161 ❑ Mar 1972 Cover: 0.25 **NM** value: **14.00**
Circ: Statement: **145,869**
• Regular Enemy Ace stories end
162 ❑ May 1972 Cover: 0.25 **NM** value: **6.00**
Circ: Statement: **145,869**
• Has 1971 Statement, filed 10/1/71; avg print run 288,333; avg sales 156,713; avg subs 0; avg total paid 156,713; samples 0; office use 334; max existent 157,047; 46% of run returned
163 ❑ Jul 1972 Cover: 0.25 **NM** value: **6.00**
Circ: Statement: **145,869 • CGC:** 2 graded, best 9.4
Kill the General!; The Ace who Died Twice!; Sgt. Storm Cloud; Misnomers of Wa! **A:** Carmine Infantino; Joe Kubert; Dan Spiegel **W:** Bob Kanigher
164 ❑ Sep 1972 Cover: 0.20 **NM** value: **6.00**
Circ: Statement: **145,869 • CGC:** 1 graded, best 9.2
Remittance Man!; Battle Album: Hannibal; Bob Kanigher's Galler of War: White Devil, Yellow Devil **A:** Alex Toth; Dan Spiegel **W:** Bob Haney; Bob Kanigher
165 ❑ Nov 1972 Cover: 0.20 **NM** value: **6.00**
Circ: Statement: **145,869**
Witness For A Coward; Shot'n'Shell; Medal Of Honor; The Vengeance Of Horus
166 ❑ Jan 1973 Cover: 0.20 **NM** value: **6.00**
Circ: Statement: **144,292**
167 ❑ Feb 1973 Cover: 0.20 **NM** value: **6.00**
Circ: Statement: **144,292 • CGC:** 1 graded, best 9.4
168 ❑ Mar 1973 Cover: 0.20 **NM** value: **6.00**
Circ: Statement: **144,292 • CGC:** 2 graded, best 9.0
The Glory Hound!; The Last Raid • Has 1972 Statement, filed 10/1/72; avg print run 288,000; avg sales 145,761; avg subs 108; avg total paid 145,869; samples 523; office use 297; max existent 146,689; 49% of run returned **A:** Jack Sparling; Tom Sutfon **W:** Tom Sutton; Archie Goodwin
169 ❑ Apr 1973 Cover: 0.20 **NM** value: **6.00**
Circ: Statement: **144,292**
Destroy the Devil's Broomstick!; Battle Album: The Little Big Horn!; Mine Eyes Have Seen... **A:** Jack Sparling; Joe Kubert(cover); Ken Barr **W:** Archie Goodwin; J. David Warner
170 ❑ Jun 1973 Cover: 0.20 **NM** value: **6.00**
Circ: Statement: **144,292**
171 ❑ Jul 1973 Cover: 0.20 **NM** value: **6.00**
Circ: Statement: **144,292**
Appointment in Prague!; Who to Believe!; First! **A:** Sam Glanzman; Jack Sparling; Joe Kubert(cover) **W:** Sam Glanzman; Archie Goodwin ★ Origin of The Unknown Soldier.
172 ❑ Aug 1973 Cover: 0.20 **NM** value: **6.00**
Circ: Statement: **144,292**
173 ❑ Sep 1973 Cover: 0.20 **NM** value: **6.00**
Circ: Statement: **144,292**
174 ❑ Oct 1973 Cover: 0.20 **NM** value: **6.00**
Circ: Statement: **144,292**
Operation Snafu!; King of the Hill; Battle Album: Tirpitz! **A:** Sam Glanzman; Jack Sparling; Jack Kubert(cover) **W:** Frank Robbins; Sam Glanzman
175 ❑ Nov 1973 Cover: 0.20 **NM** value: **6.00**
Circ: Statement: **144,292**
176 ❑ Dec 1973 Cover: 0.20 **NM** value: **6.00**
Circ: Statement: **144,292**
Target: The Unknown Soldier; Charge!; Warrior! **A:** Frank Thorne; Jack Sparling **W:** Frank Robbins; Sam Glanzman; Archie Goodwin
177 ❑ Jan 1974 Cover: 0.20 **NM** value: **6.00**
Circ: Statement: **144,765**
178 ❑ Feb 1974 Cover: 0.20 **NM** value: **6.00**
Circ: Statement: **144,765**
179 ❑ Mar 1974 Cover: 0.20 **NM** value: **6.00**
Circ: Statement: **144,765**
A Town Called Hate!; Warrior!
180 ❑ Jun 1974 Cover: 0.20 **NM** value: **6.00**
Circ: Statement: **144,765**
• Has 1973 Statement; avg total paid circ 144,292
181 ❑ Aug 1974 Cover: 0.20 **NM** value: **5.00**
Circ: Statement: **144,765**
One Guy in the Right Place...; The Balloon Buster: Hell's Angels **A:** Frank Thorne; Jack Sparling **W:** Frank Robbins; Robert Kanigher
182 ❑ Oct 1974 Cover: 0.20 **NM** value: **5.00**
Circ: Statement: **144,765**
A Thirst for Death! **A:** Jack Sparling **W:** Frank Robbins
183 ❑ Dec 1974 Cover: 0.25 **NM** value: **5.00**
Circ: Statement: **144,765**
184 ❑ Feb 1975 Cover: 0.25 **NM** value: **5.00**
Circ: Statement: **145,000**
A Sense of Obligation; War Games; Death on the Russian Front **A:** Ramona Fradon; Sergio Aragonés; Gerry Talaoc **W:** Sergio Aragonés; Steve Skeates; David Michelinie
185 ❑ Mar 1975 Cover: 0.25 **NM** value: **5.00**
Circ: Statement: **145,000**
186 ❑ Apr 1975 Cover: 0.25 **NM** value: **5.00**
Circ: Statement: **145,000**
Man of God...Man of War; The Last Kill **W:** Gerry Talaoc; David Miichelinie
187 ❑ May 1975 Cover: 0.25 **NM** value: **5.00**
Circ: Statement: **145,000**
A Death in the Chapel; Waiting for a Legend • Has 1974 Statement, filed 10/1/74; avg print run 307,217; avg sales 144,200; avg subs 565; avg total paid 144,765; samples 100; office use 2,652; max existent 147,517; 52% of run returned **A:** Gerry Talaoc; Quico Redondo **W:** Gerry Talaoc; David Miichelinie; Don Kaar
188 ❑ Jun 1975 Cover: 0.25 **NM** value: **5.00**
Circ: Statement: **145,000**
Encounter **A:** Gerry Talaoc **W:** David Michelinie
189 ❑ Jul 1975 Cover: 0.25 **NM** value: **5.00**
Circ: Statement: **145,000**
The Cadaver Gap Massacres; Midway!; **A:** Gerry Talaoc; Fred Carillo; Joe Kubert(cover) **W:** Archie Goodwin; David Michelinie
190 ❑ Aug 1975 Cover: 0.25 **NM** value: **5.00**
Circ: Statement: **145,000**
Project: Omega **A:** Gerry Talaoc; Joe Kubert(cover) **W:** David Michelinie
191 ❑ Sep 1975 Cover: 0.25 **NM** value: **5.00**
Circ: Statement: **145,000**
192 ❑ Oct 1975 Cover: 0.25 **NM** value: **5.00**
Circ: Statement: **145,000**
Vendetta **A:** Gerry Talaoc; Joe Kubert(cover) **W:** David Michelinie
193 ❑ Nov 1975 Cover: 0.25 **NM** value: **5.00**
Circ: Statement: **145,000**
Save the Children!; There Are No Guns on a Showboat **A:** Gerry Talaoc; Quico Redondo **W:** Arnold Drake; Gerry Conway
194 ❑ Dec 1975 Cover: 0.25 **NM** value: **5.00**
Circ: Statement: **145,000**
195 ❑ Jan 1976 Cover: 0.25 **NM** value: **5.00**
Circ: Statement: **124,000**
The Deathmasters; Duel in the Desert; War Games: Last Request **A:** Bill Draut; Dave Manak; Gerry Talaoc **W:** D. Edwing; David Michelinie; Jack Oleck
196 ❑ Feb 1976 Cover: 0.25 **NM** value: **5.00**
Circ: Statement: **124,000**
Target Red; Just One More **A:** Gerry Talaoc; Tenny Henson **W:** Steve Skeates; David Michelinie
197 ❑ Mar 1976 Cover: 0.25 **NM** value: **5.00**
Circ: Statement: **124,000**
198 ❑ Apr 1976 Cover: 0.30 **NM** value: **5.00**
Circ: Statement: **124,000**
The Unknown Soldier: Traitor!; The Last Battle **A:** Frank Redondo; Gerry Talaoc **W:** Arnold Drake; David Michelinie
199 ❑ May 1976 Cover: 0.30 **NM** value: **5.00**
Circ: Statement: **124,000**
The Crime Of Sgt. Schepke; Killing Machine **A:** Gerry Talaoc; Tenny Henson **W:** Steve Skeates; David Michelinie
200 ❑ Jul 1976 Cover: 0.30 **NM** value: **5.00**
Circ: Statement: **124,000**
Deathride; Enemy Ace: Shooting Star **A:** Joe Kubert; Gerry Talaoc **W:** David Michelinie ★ Appearance of Mademoiselle Marie.
201 ❑ Sep 1976 Cover: 0.30 **NM** value: **5.00**
Circ: Statement: **124,000**
The Back-Alley War **A:** Gerry Talaoc; Joe Kubert(cover) **W:** David Michelinie
202 ❑ Nov 1976 Cover: 0.30 **NM** value: **5.00**
Circ: Statement: **124,000**
The Cure **A:** Gerry Talaoc **W:** David Michelinie
203 ❑ Jan 1977 Cover: 0.30 **NM** value: **5.00**
Circ: Statement: **126,071**
Curtain Call **A:** Gerry Talaoc; Joe Kubert(cover) **W:** David Michelinie
204 ❑ Mar 1977 Cover: 0.30 **NM** value: **5.00**
Circ: Statement: **126,071**
The Unknown Soldier Must Die!; A Walk Up a Hill • Series continues as Unknown Soldier **A:** Dick Ayers; Bob McLeod; Gerry Talaoc **W:** Bob Haney; Bob Kanigher

STARSTONE — Aircel

1 ❑ b&w Cover: 1.70 **NM** value: **Cover or less**
A: Adrian Kleinbergen **W:** Gordon Derry
2 ❑ b&w Cover: 1.70 **NM** value: **Cover or less**
A: Adrian Kleinbergen **W:** Gordon Derry
3 ❑ b&w Cover: 1.70 **NM** value: **Cover or less**
A: Adrian Kleinbergen **W:** Gordon Derry

STARSTREAM — Gold Key / Whitman

1 ❑ ca. 1976 Cover: 0.79 **NM** value: **3.00**
2 ❑ 1976 Cover: 0.79 **NM** value: **3.00**
Night of the Storm; The Brain Traveler; Flight of the Horse; Collecting Team; The Utopia Tree; Phoenix Planet • Stories by Science-Fiction writers
3 ❑ 1976 Cover: 0.79 **NM** value: **3.00**
4 ❑ 1976 Cover: 0.79 **NM** value: **3.00**
Call Me Joe; Ben Franklin, Martian; Does A Bee Care?; The City; Report To The Plenary Council; And The Blood Ran Green **A:** Adolfo Buylla; Jack Abel; Nevio Zeccara; Pamela Eckard **W:** Pamela Eckard; Roger Elwood; A. Moniz; Arnold Drake; Isaac Asimov; Poul Anderson; Robert Bloch; Stephan Goldin

STARSTRUCK (DARK HORSE) — Dark Horse

1 ❑ Aug 1990, b&w Cover: 2.95 **NM** value: **Cover or less**
Silver Bells and Cockle Shells **A:** Michael W. Kaluta **W:** Elaine Lee

Other grades: Multiply prices above by **1.5 for Mint • 2/3 for Very Fine • 1/3 for Fine • 1/5 for Very Good • 1/8 for Good**

2 ❑ 1990b&w Cover: 2.95 **NM** value: **Cover or less**
A: Michael W. Kaluta **W:** Elaine Lee
3 ❑ Jan 1991, b&w Cover: 2.95 **NM** value: **Cover or less**
📖 The Right Bait **A:** Michael W. Kaluta **W:** Elaine Lee
4 ❑ Mar 1991 Cover: 2.95 **NM** value: **Cover or less**
📖 Mother's Little Helpers • trading cards **A:** Michael W. Kaluta **W:** Elaine Lee

STARSTRUCK (EPIC) — Marvel / Epic

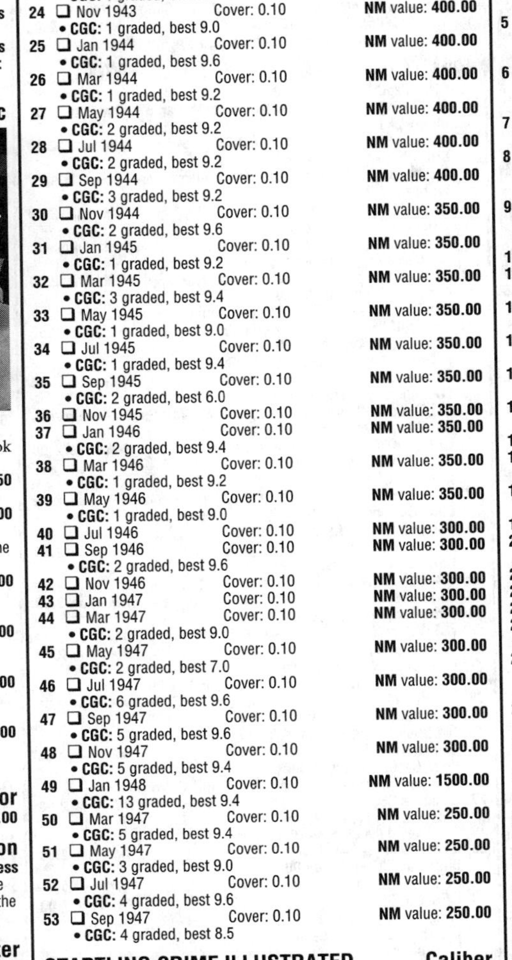

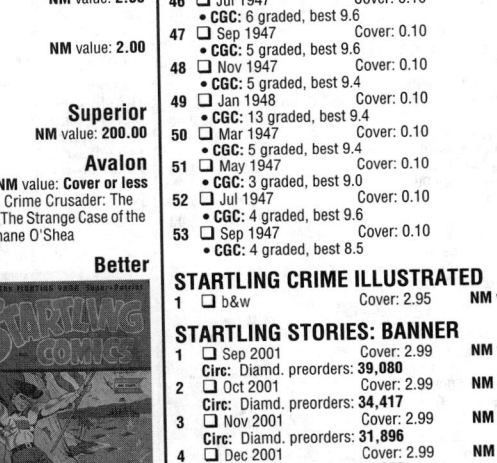

Elaine Lee (Vamps) and Michael Kaluta brought us this ambitious tale of mystery, love, and cybernetics. It followed bartender and ex-rebel Harry Palmer as he searched the underworld of the future for a certain lost property: a pleasure droid named Erotica Ann. Ann was more than machinery: she was Palmer's companion, and a link to his past. She was missing, and Palmer would follow any lead-human or robotic-to find her.

Epic Comics released the first issue of Starstruck in February of 1985. However, this was not the first time that Starstruck was introduced to the public. Over the years, it went from a stage play, to a graphic novel, to this comic book series.

1 ❑ Feb 1985 Cover: 1.50 **NM** value: **2.50**
📖 Liar's Poker **A:** Michael W. Kaluta **W:** Elaine Lee
2 ❑ Apr 1985 Cover: 1.50 **NM** value: **2.00**
Circ: CapCity orders: **7,800**
📖 Conspicuous By Their Absence **A:** Michael W. Kaluta **W:** Elaine Lee
3 ❑ Jun 1985 Cover: 1.50 **NM** value: **2.00**
Circ: CapCity orders: **6,300**
A: Michael W. Kaluta **W:** Elaine Lee
4 ❑ Aug 1985 Cover: 1.50 **NM** value: **2.00**
Circ: CapCity orders: **6,250**
A: Michael W. Kaluta **W:** Elaine Lee
5 ❑ Oct 1985 Cover: 1.50 **NM** value: **2.00**
Circ: CapCity orders: **4,750**
A: Michael W. Kaluta **W:** Elaine Lee
6 ❑ Feb 1986 Cover: 1.50 **NM** value: **2.00**
Circ: CapCity orders: **4,600**
A: Michael W. Kaluta **W:** Elaine Lee

STAR STUDDED — Superior

1 ❑ ca. 1945 Cover: 0.25 **NM** value: **200.00**

STARTLING COMICS — Avalon

1 ❑ Cover: 2.95 **NM** value: **Cover or less**
📖 Nemesis: Hitler, Wanted Dead or Alive!; Crime Crusader: The Case of the Careful Guardian; The Crash Kid: The Strange Case of the Black Dragon Gods **A:** Stone-Hickey **W:** Shane O'Shea

STARTLING COMICS (BETTER) — Better

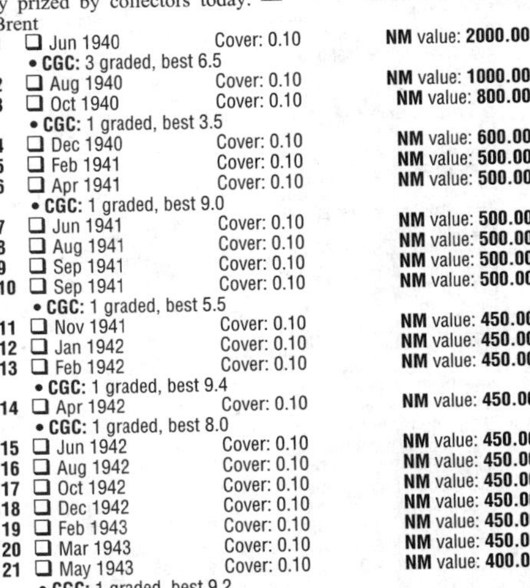

Better's Startling Comics began as a standard super-hero series featuring the adventures of Captain Future — Man of Tomorrow, The Fighting Yank, The Scarab, and Pyroman. Early artists on the stories included Max Plaisted, Jack Binder, and Bill Everett.

Alex Schomburg contributed covers to the series in the midst of its run.

Later in the 1940s with super-heroes on the wane, the series shifted focus to science-fiction themes with Schomburg returning for several memorable covers, which are highly prized by collectors today. — Brent

1 ❑ Jun 1940 Cover: 0.10 **NM** value: **2000.00**
• **CGC:** 3 graded, best 6.5
2 ❑ Aug 1940 Cover: 0.10 **NM** value: **1000.00**
3 ❑ Oct 1940 Cover: 0.10 **NM** value: **800.00**
• **CGC:** 1 graded, best 3.5
4 ❑ Dec 1940 Cover: 0.10 **NM** value: **600.00**
5 ❑ Feb 1941 Cover: 0.10 **NM** value: **500.00**
6 ❑ Apr 1941 Cover: 0.10 **NM** value: **500.00**
• **CGC:** 1 graded, best 9.0
7 ❑ Jun 1941 Cover: 0.10 **NM** value: **500.00**
8 ❑ Aug 1941 Cover: 0.10 **NM** value: **500.00**
9 ❑ Sep 1941 Cover: 0.10 **NM** value: **500.00**
10 ❑ Sep 1941 Cover: 0.10 **NM** value: **500.00**
• **CGC:** 1 graded, best 5.5
11 ❑ Nov 1941 Cover: 0.10 **NM** value: **450.00**
12 ❑ Jan 1942 Cover: 0.10 **NM** value: **450.00**
13 ❑ Feb 1942 Cover: 0.10 **NM** value: **450.00**
• **CGC:** 1 graded, best 9.4
14 ❑ Apr 1942 Cover: 0.10 **NM** value: **450.00**
• **CGC:** 1 graded, best 8.0
15 ❑ Jun 1942 Cover: 0.10 **NM** value: **450.00**
16 ❑ Aug 1942 Cover: 0.10 **NM** value: **450.00**
17 ❑ Oct 1942 Cover: 0.10 **NM** value: **450.00**
18 ❑ Dec 1942 Cover: 0.10 **NM** value: **450.00**
19 ❑ Feb 1943 Cover: 0.10 **NM** value: **450.00**
20 ❑ Mar 1943 Cover: 0.10 **NM** value: **450.00**
21 ❑ May 1943 Cover: 0.10 **NM** value: **400.00**
• **CGC:** 1 graded, best 9.2
22 ❑ Jul 1943 Cover: 0.10 **NM** value: **400.00**
• **CGC:** 1 graded, best 9.2
23 ❑ Sep 1943 Cover: 0.10 **NM** value: **400.00**
• **CGC:** 1 graded, best 9.0
24 ❑ Nov 1943 Cover: 0.10 **NM** value: **400.00**
• **CGC:** 1 graded, best 9.0
25 ❑ Jan 1944 Cover: 0.10 **NM** value: **400.00**
• **CGC:** 1 graded, best 9.6
26 ❑ Mar 1944 Cover: 0.10 **NM** value: **400.00**
• **CGC:** 1 graded, best 9.2
27 ❑ May 1944 Cover: 0.10 **NM** value: **400.00**
• **CGC:** 2 graded, best 9.2
28 ❑ Jul 1944 Cover: 0.10 **NM** value: **400.00**
• **CGC:** 2 graded, best 9.2
29 ❑ Sep 1944 Cover: 0.10 **NM** value: **400.00**
• **CGC:** 3 graded, best 9.2
30 ❑ Nov 1944 Cover: 0.10 **NM** value: **350.00**
• **CGC:** 2 graded, best 9.6
31 ❑ Jan 1945 Cover: 0.10 **NM** value: **350.00**
• **CGC:** 1 graded, best 9.2
32 ❑ Mar 1945 Cover: 0.10 **NM** value: **350.00**
• **CGC:** 3 graded, best 9.4
33 ❑ May 1945 Cover: 0.10 **NM** value: **350.00**
• **CGC:** 1 graded, best 9.0
34 ❑ Jul 1945 Cover: 0.10 **NM** value: **350.00**
• **CGC:** 1 graded, best 9.4
35 ❑ Sep 1945 Cover: 0.10 **NM** value: **350.00**
• **CGC:** 2 graded, best 6.0
36 ❑ Nov 1945 Cover: 0.10 **NM** value: **350.00**
37 ❑ Jan 1946 Cover: 0.10 **NM** value: **350.00**
• **CGC:** 2 graded, best 9.4
38 ❑ Mar 1946 Cover: 0.10 **NM** value: **350.00**
• **CGC:** 1 graded, best 9.2
39 ❑ May 1946 Cover: 0.10 **NM** value: **350.00**
• **CGC:** 1 graded, best 9.0
40 ❑ Jul 1946 Cover: 0.10 **NM** value: **300.00**
41 ❑ Sep 1946 Cover: 0.10 **NM** value: **300.00**
• **CGC:** 2 graded, best 9.6
42 ❑ Nov 1946 Cover: 0.10 **NM** value: **300.00**
43 ❑ Jan 1947 Cover: 0.10 **NM** value: **300.00**
44 ❑ Mar 1947 Cover: 0.10 **NM** value: **300.00**
• **CGC:** 2 graded, best 9.0
45 ❑ May 1947 Cover: 0.10 **NM** value: **300.00**
• **CGC:** 2 graded, best 7.0
46 ❑ Jul 1947 Cover: 0.10 **NM** value: **300.00**
• **CGC:** 6 graded, best 9.6
47 ❑ Sep 1947 Cover: 0.10 **NM** value: **300.00**
• **CGC:** 5 graded, best 9.6
48 ❑ Nov 1947 Cover: 0.10 **NM** value: **300.00**
• **CGC:** 5 graded, best 9.4
49 ❑ Jan 1948 Cover: 0.10 **NM** value: **1500.00**
• **CGC:** 13 graded, best 9.4
50 ❑ Mar 1947 Cover: 0.10 **NM** value: **250.00**
• **CGC:** 5 graded, best 9.4
51 ❑ May 1947 Cover: 0.10 **NM** value: **250.00**
• **CGC:** 3 graded, best 9.0
52 ❑ Jul 1947 Cover: 0.10 **NM** value: **250.00**
• **CGC:** 4 graded, best 9.6
53 ❑ Sep 1947 Cover: 0.10 **NM** value: **250.00**
• **CGC:** 4 graded, best 8.5

STARTLING CRIME ILLUSTRATED — Caliber

1 ❑ b&w Cover: 2.95 **NM** value: **Cover or less**

STARTLING STORIES: BANNER — Marvel

1 ❑ Sep 2001 Cover: 2.99 **NM** value: **Cover or less**
Circ: Diamd. preorders: **39,080**
2 ❑ Oct 2001 Cover: 2.99 **NM** value: **Cover or less**
Circ: Diamd. preorders: **34,417**
3 ❑ Nov 2001 Cover: 2.99 **NM** value: **Cover or less**
Circ: Diamd. preorders: **31,896**
4 ❑ Dec 2001 Cover: 2.99 **NM** value: **Cover or less**
Circ: Diamd. preorders: **31,092**

STARTLING TERROR TALES (1ST SERIES) — Star

10 ❑ May 1952 Cover: 0.10 **NM** value: **600.00**
• **CGC:** 4 graded, best 9.0
11 ❑ Jul 1952 Cover: 0.10 **NM** value: **750.00**
• **CGC:** 9 graded, best 9.2
12 ❑ Sep 1952 Cover: 0.10 **NM** value: **250.00**
13 ❑ Dec 1952 Cover: 0.10 **NM** value: **250.00**
• **CGC:** 3 graded, best 9.0
14 ❑ Feb 1953 Cover: 0.10 **NM** value: **250.00**
• **CGC:** 1 graded, best 8.0

STARTLING TERROR TALES (2ND SERIES) — Star

4 ❑ 1953 Cover: 0.10 **NM** value: **200.00**
5 ❑ Apr 1953 Cover: 0.10 **NM** value: **200.00**
• **CGC:** 1 graded, best 5.5
6 ❑ 1953 Cover: 0.10 **NM** value: **200.00**
7 ❑ Nov 1953 Cover: 0.10 **NM** value: **200.00**
• **CGC:** 1 graded, best 8.0
8 ❑ 1954 Cover: 0.10 **NM** value: **200.00**
9 ❑ 1954 Cover: 0.10 **NM** value: **200.00**
10 ❑ Aug 1954 Cover: 0.10 **NM** value: **175.00**
• **CGC:** 4 graded, best 9.0
11 ❑ Nov 1954 Cover: 0.10 **NM** value: **175.00**
• **CGC:** 2 graded, best 6.0

STAR TREK (1ST SERIES) — Gold Key

1 ❑ Oct 1967 Cover: 0.12 **NM** value: **285.00**
• **CGC:** 15 graded, best 9.4
wraparound photo cover.
2 ❑ Jun 1968 Cover: 0.12 **NM** value: **185.00**
• **CGC:** 7 graded, best 9.4
Photo cover.
3 ❑ Dec 1968 Cover: 0.15 **NM** value: **140.00**
• **CGC:** 6 graded, best 9.4
Photo cover.
4 ❑ Jun 1969 Cover: 0.15 **NM** value: **140.00**
• **CGC:** 14 graded, best 9.4
Photo cover.
5 ❑ Sep 1969 Cover: 0.15 **NM** value: **140.00**
• **CGC:** 4 graded, best 9.2
Photo cover.
6 ❑ Dec 1969 Cover: 0.15 **NM** value: **115.00**
• **CGC:** 6 graded, best 9.4
Photo cover.
7 ❑ Mar 1970 Cover: 0.15 **NM** value: **115.00**
Photo cover.
8 ❑ Sep 1970 Cover: 0.15 **NM** value: **115.00**
• **CGC:** 3 graded, best 8.5
Photo cover.
9 ❑ Feb 1971 Cover: 0.15 **NM** value: **115.00**
• **CGC:** 2 graded, best 9.0
last photo cover.
10 ❑ May 1971 Cover: 0.15 **NM** value: **60.00**
11 ❑ Aug 1971 Cover: 0.15 **NM** value: **60.00**
• **CGC:** 13 graded, best 9.6
12 ❑ Nov 1971 Cover: 0.15 **NM** value: **60.00**
• **CGC:** 20 graded, best 9.6
13 ❑ Feb 1972 Cover: 0.15 **NM** value: **60.00**
• **CGC:** 1 graded, best 3.0
14 ❑ May 1972 Cover: 0.15 **NM** value: **60.00**
• **CGC:** 2 graded, best 9.4
15 ❑ Aug 1972 Cover: 0.15 **NM** value: **60.00**
• **CGC:** 18 graded, best 9.6
16 ❑ Nov 1972 Cover: 0.15 **NM** value: **60.00**
17 ❑ Feb 1973 Cover: 0.15 **NM** value: **60.00**
• **CGC:** 1 graded, best 9.4
18 ❑ May 1973 Cover: 0.15 **NM** value: **60.00**
• **CGC:** 2 graded, best 9.4
19 ❑ Jul 1973 Cover: 0.15 **NM** value: **60.00**
20 ❑ Sep 1973 Cover: 0.20 **NM** value: **60.00**
• **CGC:** 3 graded, best 9.4
21 ❑ Nov 1973 Cover: 0.20 **NM** value: **45.00**
22 ❑ Jan 1974 Cover: 0.20 **NM** value: **45.00**
23 ❑ Mar 1974 Cover: 0.20 **NM** value: **45.00**
24 ❑ May 1974 Cover: 0.20 **NM** value: **45.00**
• **CGC:** 2 graded, best 9.2
25 ❑ Jul 1974 Cover: 0.25 **NM** value: **45.00**
• **CGC:** 2 graded, best 9.4
📖 Dwarf Planet
26 ❑ Sep 1974 Cover: 0.25 **NM** value: **45.00**
📖 The Perfect Dream
27 ❑ Nov 1974 Cover: 0.25 **NM** value: **45.00**
• **CGC:** 1 graded, best 9.4
28 ❑ Jan 1975 Cover: 0.25 **NM** value: **45.00**
• **CGC:** 1 graded, best 9.2
29 ❑ Mar 1975 Cover: 0.25 **NM** value: **45.00**
30 ❑ May 1975 Cover: 0.25 **NM** value: **45.00**
• **CGC:** 2 graded, best 9.2
31 ❑ Jul 1975 Cover: 0.25 **NM** value: **35.00**
32 ❑ Aug 1975 **NM** value: **35.00**
33 ❑ Sep 1975 **NM** value: **35.00**
• **CGC:** 2 graded, best 9.4
34 ❑ Oct 1975 **NM** value: **35.00**
35 ❑ Nov 1975 **NM** value: **35.00**
36 ❑ Mar 1976 **NM** value: **35.00**
• **CGC:** 2 graded, best 9.2
37 ❑ May 1976 **NM** value: **35.00**
• **CGC:** 2 graded, best 9.4
38 ❑ Jul 1976 **NM** value: **35.00**
39 ❑ Aug 1976 **NM** value: **35.00**
• **CGC:** 1 graded, best 9.0
40 ❑ Sep 1976 **NM** value: **35.00**
• **CGC:** 2 graded, best 9.6
41 ❑ Nov 1976 **NM** value: **24.00**
42 ❑ Jan 1977 **NM** value: **24.00**
43 ❑ Feb 1977 **NM** value: **24.00**
44 ❑ May 1977 **NM** value: **24.00**
45 ❑ Jul 1977 **NM** value: **24.00**
46 ❑ Aug 1977 **NM** value: **24.00**
47 ❑ Sep 1977 **NM** value: **24.00**
48 ❑ Oct 1977 **NM** value: **24.00**
49 ❑ Nov 1977 **NM** value: **24.00**
50 ❑ Jan 1978 **NM** value: **24.00**
• **CGC:** 1 graded, best 4.0
51 ❑ Mar 1978 Cover: 0.35 **NM** value: **24.00**
📖 Destination Annihilation! ★ Appearance of Professor Whipple.
52 ❑ May 1978 **NM** value: **24.00**
• **CGC:** 1 graded, best 9.6
53 ❑ Jul 1978 **NM** value: **24.00**
• **CGC:** 1 graded, best 6.0
54 ❑ Aug 1978 **NM** value: **24.00**
55 ❑ Sep 1978 **NM** value: **24.00**
• **CGC:** 1 graded, best 9.0
56 ❑ Oct 1978 **NM** value: **24.00**
• **CGC:** 1 graded, best 8.5
57 ❑ Nov 1978 **NM** value: **24.00**
• **CGC:** 2 graded, best 8.5
58 ❑ Dec 1978 **NM** value: **24.00**
• **CGC:** 1 graded, best 7.0
59 ❑ Jan 1979 **NM** value: **24.00**
• **CGC:** 1 graded, best 8.0
60 ❑ Feb 1979 **NM** value: **20.00**
61 ❑ Mar 1979 **NM** value: **20.00**
• **CGC:** 1 graded, best 8.5
final issue.
Bk 1 ❑ Aug 1976 Cover: 1.95 **NM** value: **25.00**
• Enterprise Logs
Bk 2 ❑ Feb 1977 Cover: 1.95 **NM** value: **25.00**
• Enterprise Logs
Bk 3 ❑ Aug 1977 Cover: 1.95 **NM** value: **25.00**
• Enterprise Logs
Bk 4 ❑ Oct 1977 Cover: 1.95 **NM** value: **25.00**
• Enterprise Logs

CGC-graded: Multiply prices above by **33 for 9.9 M • 16 for 9.8 NM/M • 7 for 9.6 NM+ • 5 for 9.4 NM • 2.5 for 9.2 NM- • 1.5 for 9.0 VF/NM**

STAR TREK (2ND SERIES) — Marvel

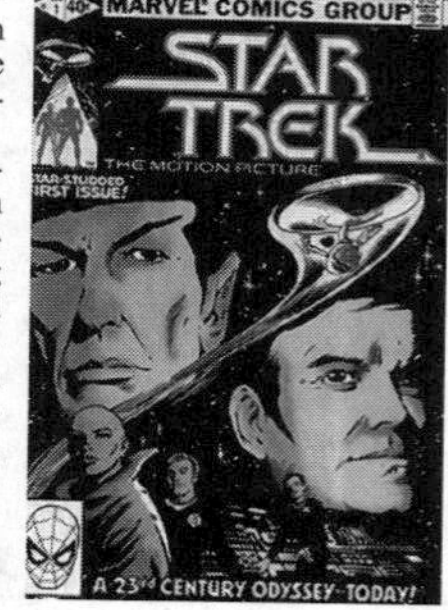

This series began with an adaptation of Star Trek: The Motion Picture which helped revive the franchise after years of syndicated reruns.

After the Starship U.S.S. Enterprise, commanded by Captain James T. Kirk, completed its historic five-year mission exploring the galaxy, the ship received a full systems and structural overhaul. Most of her crew stayed on with notable exceptions. McCoy retired and returned home to be an "old country doctor." Spock returned to Vulcan and began the Ritual of Kohlinar that would eventually purge his remaining human emotions. Kirk was promoted to admiral and foolishly accepted a desk-bound assignment. Two-and-a-half years later, an immensely powerful alien probe traveling towards Earth and cleaving a wide path of destruction reunited the entire crew of the Enterprise. As a movie adaptation, the first three issues didn't deviate from the screenplay-which was widely panned as lacking the best qualities of the show.

Later issues of the 18-issue run attempted to carry on with new missions, but were hampered by not being able to expand much, if at all, from the events of the movie.

1 ❑ Apr 1980 Cover: 0.40 **NM** value: **4.00**
• **CGC:** 20 graded, best 9.8
📖 Star Trek: The Motion Picture • adapts Star Trek: The Motion Picture **A:** Dave Cockrum; Klaus Janson **W:** Alan Dean Foster; Gene Roddenberry; Harold Livingston; Marv Wolfman

2 ❑ May 1980 Cover: 0.40 **NM** value: **3.00**
• **CGC:** 1 graded, best 9.6
📖 V'Ger • adapts Star Trek: The Motion Picture **A:** Dave Cockrum; Klaus Janson **W:** Alan Dean Foster; Gene Roddenberry; Harold Livingston; Marv Wolfman

3 ❑ Jun 1980 Cover: 0.40 **NM** value: **2.00**
• **CGC:** 2 graded, best 9.6
📖 Evolutions • adapts Star Trek: The Motion Picture **A:** Dave Cockrum; Klaus Janson **W:** Alan Dean Foster; Gene Roddenberry; Harold Livingston; Marv Wolfman

4 ❑ Jul 1980 Cover: 0.40 **NM** value: **2.00**
📖 The Haunting of Thallus!

5 ❑ Aug 1980 Cover: 0.40 **NM** value: **2.00**
📖 The Haunting of the Enterprise!

6 ❑ Sep 1980 Cover: 0.50 **NM** value: **2.00**
📖 The Enterprise Murder Case!

7 ❑ Oct 1980 Cover: 0.50 **NM** value: **2.00**
📖 Tomorrow or Yesterday

8 ❑ Nov 1980 Cover: 0.50 **NM** value: **2.00**
📖 The Expansionist Syndrome

9 ❑ Dec 1980 Cover: 0.50 **NM** value: **2.00**
📖 Experiment in Vengeance!

10 ❑ Jan 1981 Cover: 0.50 **NM** value: **2.00**
📖 Domain of the Dragon God! • Starfleet files

11 ❑ Feb 1981 Cover: 0.50 **NM** value: **2.00**
📖 Like a Woman Scorned!

12 ❑ Mar 1981 Cover: 0.50 **NM** value: **2.00**
📖 Eclipse of Reason

13 ❑ Apr 1981 Cover: 0.50 **NM** value: **2.00**
📖 All the Infinite Ways ★ Appearance of McCoy's daughter.

14 ❑ Jun 1981 Cover: 0.50 **NM** value: **2.00**
📖 We Are Dying, Egypt, Dying!

15 ❑ Aug 1981 Cover: 0.50 **NM** value: **2.00**
📖 The Quality of Mercy

16 ❑ Oct 1981 Cover: 0.50 **NM** value: **2.00**
📖 There's No Space Like Gnomes!

17 ❑ Dec 1981 Cover: 0.50 **NM** value: **2.00**
📖 The Long Night's Dawn!

18 ❑ Feb 1982 Cover: 0.60 **NM** value: **2.00**
📖 A Thousand Deaths final issue.

STAR TREK (3RD SERIES) — DC

1 ❑ Feb 1984 Cover: 0.75 **NM** value: **4.00**
• **CGC:** 12 graded, best 9.8
📖 The Wormhole Connection • Part 1 **A:** Tom Sutton; Ricardo Villagran **W:** Mike W. Barr ★ 1st Appearance of Bearclaw.

2 ❑ Mar 1984 Cover: 0.75 **NM** value: **3.00**
• **CGC:** 1 graded, best 9.6
📖 The Only Good Klingon • Part 2 **A:** Tom Sutton **W:** Mike W. Barr

3 ❑ Apr 1984 Cover: 0.75 **NM** value: **3.00**
• **CGC:** 1 graded, best 9.8
📖 Errand of War! • Part 3 **A:** Tom Sutton **W:** Mike W. Barr

4 ❑ May 1984 Cover: 0.75 **NM** value: **3.00**
• **CGC:** 1 graded, best 9.6
📖 Deadly Allies! • Part 4 **A:** Tom Sutton **W:** Mike W. Barr

5 ❑ Jun 1984 Cover: 0.75 **NM** value: **3.00**
• **CGC:** 1 graded, best 9.8
📖 Mortal Gods **A:** Tom Sutton **W:** Mike W. Barr

6 ❑ Jul 1984 Cover: 0.75 **NM** value: **2.50**
📖 Who Is Enigma? **A:** Tom Sutton **W:** Mike W. Barr

7 ❑ Aug 1984 Cover: 0.75 **NM** value: **2.50**
📖 Pon Far! **A:** Tom Sutton **W:** Mike W. Barr ★ Origin of Saavik.

8 ❑ Nov 1984 Cover: 0.75 **NM** value: **2.50**
📖 Blood Fever **A:** Tom Sutton **W:** Mike W. Barr ★ Versus Romulans.

9 ❑ Dec 1984 Cover: 0.75 **NM** value: **2.50**
📖 Promises to Keep • New Frontiers, Part 1; Return of Mirror Universe **A:** Tom Sutton **W:** Mike W. Barr

10 ❑ Jan 1985 Cover: 0.75 **NM** value: **2.50**
📖 Double Image • New Frontiers, Part 2 **A:** Tom Sutton **W:** Mike W. Barr

11 ❑ Feb 1985 Cover: 0.75 **NM** value: **2.00**
📖 Deadly Perfection • New Frontiers, Part 3; The two Spocks mind-meld **A:** Tom Sutton **W:** Mike W. Barr

12 ❑ Mar 1985 Cover: 0.75 **NM** value: **2.00**
📖 The Tantalus Trap! • New Frontiers, Part 4; Mirror Universe Enterprise's engineering hull destroyed **A:** Tom Sutton **W:** Mike W. Barr

13 ❑ Apr 1985 Cover: 0.75 **NM** value: **2.00**
📖 Masquerade! • New Frontiers, Part 5 **A:** Tom Sutton **W:** Mike W. Barr

14 ❑ May 1985 Cover: 0.75 **NM** value: **2.00**
Circ: CapCity orders: **9,150**
📖 Behind Enemy Lines! • New Frontiers, Part 6 **A:** Tom Sutton **W:** Mike W. Barr

15 ❑ Jun 1985 Cover: 0.75 **NM** value: **2.00**
Circ: CapCity orders: **8,950**
📖 The Beginning of the End • New Frontiers, Part 7 **A:** Tom Sutton **W:** Mike W. Barr

16 ❑ Jul 1985 Cover: 0.75 **NM** value: **2.00**
Circ: CapCity orders: **8,800**
📖 Homecoming • New Frontiers, Part 8; Kirk receives command of Excelsior **A:** Tom Sutton **W:** Mike W. Barr

17 ❑ Aug 1985 Cover: 0.75 **NM** value: **2.00**
Circ: CapCity orders: **8,800**
📖 The D'Artagnan Three **A:** Tom Sutton

18 ❑ Sep 1985 Cover: 0.75 **NM** value: **2.00**
Circ: CapCity orders: **9,000**
📖 Rest and Recreation! **A:** Tom Sutton

19 ❑ Oct 1985 Cover: 0.75 **NM** value: **2.00**
Circ: CapCity orders: **9,350**
📖 Chekov's Choice • Written by Koenig **A:** Tom Sutton; Dan Spiegle **W:** Walter Koenig; Walter Koenig(Chekov)

20 ❑ Nov 1985 Cover: 0.75 **NM** value: **2.00**
Circ: CapCity orders: **8,750**
📖 Giri **A:** Tom Sutton

21 ❑ Dec 1985 Cover: 0.75 **NM** value: **2.00**
Circ: CapCity orders: **8,550**
📖 Dreamworld **A:** Tom Sutton

22 ❑ Jan 1986 Cover: 0.75 **NM** value: **2.00**
Circ: CapCity orders: **8,600**
📖 Wolf on the Prowl • return of Redjac **A:** Tom Sutton

23 ❑ Feb 1986 Cover: 0.75 **NM** value: **2.00**
Circ: CapCity orders: **8,550**
📖 Wolf at the Door • return of Redjac **A:** Tom Sutton

24 ❑ Mar 1986 Cover: 0.75 **NM** value: **2.00**
Circ: CapCity orders: **8,900**
📖 Double Blind • Part 1 **A:** Tom Sutton

25 ❑ Apr 1986 Cover: 0.75 **NM** value: **2.00**
Circ: CapCity orders: **8,100**
📖 Double Blind • Part 2 **A:** Tom Sutton

26 ❑ May 1986 Cover: 0.75 **NM** value: **2.00**
Circ: CapCity orders: **8,000**
📖 The Trouble With Transporters **A:** Tom Sutton

27 ❑ Jun 1986 Cover: 0.75 **NM** value: **2.00**
Circ: CapCity orders: **7,900**
📖 Around the Clock **A:** Tom Sutton

28 ❑ Jul 1986 Cover: 0.75 **NM** value: **2.00**
Circ: CapCity orders: **8,000**
📖 The Last Word **A:** Tom Sutton; Gray Morrow

29 ❑ Aug 1986 Cover: 0.75 **NM** value: **2.00**
Circ: CapCity orders: **8,000**
📖 The Trouble with Bearclaw **A:** Tom Sutton

30 ❑ Sep 1986 Cover: 0.75 **NM** value: **2.00**
Circ: CapCity orders: **7,900**
📖 Uhura's Story **A:** Tom Sutton

31 ❑ Oct 1986 Cover: 0.75 **NM** value: **2.00**
Circ: CapCity orders: **8,150**
📖 Maggie's World! **A:** Tom Sutton

32 ❑ Nov 1986 Cover: 0.75 **NM** value: **2.00**
Circ: CapCity orders: **8,150**
📖 Judgment Day! **A:** Tom Sutton

33 ❑ Dec 1986 Cover: 1.25 **NM** value: **2.00**
Circ: CapCity orders: **8,850**
• 20th Anniversary of Star Trek issue. 📖 Vicious Circle! • original Enterprise meets Excelsior

34 ❑ Jan 1987 Cover: 0.75 **NM** value: **2.00**
Circ: CapCity orders: **8,200**
📖 Death Ship! • The Doomsday Bug, part 1

35 ❑ Feb 1987 Cover: 0.75 **NM** value: **2.00**
Circ: CapCity orders: **8,800**
📖 Stand-Off! • The Doomsday Bug, part 2 **A:** Gray Morrow

36 ❑ Mar 1987 Cover: 0.75 **NM** value: **2.00**
Circ: CapCity orders: **11,250**
📖 The Apocalypse Scenario! • The Doomsday Bug, part 3; returns to Vulcan

37 ❑ Apr 1987 Cover: 0.75 **NM** value: **2.00**
Circ: CapCity orders: **10,700**
📖 Choices! • follows events of Star Trek IV **A:** Curt Swan

38 ❑ May 1987 Cover: 0.75 **NM** value: **2.00**
Circ: CapCity orders: **9,980**
📖 The Argon Affair!

39 ❑ Jun 1987 Cover: 0.75 **NM** value: **2.00**
Circ: CapCity orders: **10,350**
📖 When You Wish Upon a Star • return of Harry Mudd **W:** Len Wein

40 ❑ Jul 1987 Cover: 0.75 **NM** value: **2.00**
Circ: CapCity orders: **11,000**
📖 Mudd's Magic! ★ Appearance of Harry Mudd.

41 ❑ Aug 1987 Cover: 0.75 **NM** value: **2.00**
Circ: CapCity orders: **11,850**
📖 What Goes Around **W:** Mike Carlin ★ Versus Orion pirates.

42 ❑ Sep 1987 Cover: 0.75 **NM** value: **2.00**
Circ: CapCity orders: **12,300**
📖 The Corbomite Effect! **W:** Mike Carlin

43 ❑ Oct 1987 Cover: 0.75 **NM** value: **2.00**
Circ: CapCity orders: **12,250**
📖 Paradise Lost! • The Return of the Serpent, part 1 **W:** Mike Carlin

44 ❑ Nov 1987 Cover: 0.75 **NM** value: **2.00**
Circ: CapCity orders: **12,300**
📖 Past Perfect • The Return of the Serpent, part 2 **W:** Mike Carlin

45 ❑ Dec 1987 Cover: 0.75 **NM** value: **2.00**
Circ: CapCity orders: **11,800**
📖 Devil Down Below! • The Return of the Serpent, part 3 **W:** Mike Carlin

46 ❑ Jan 1988 Cover: 0.75 **NM** value: **2.00**
Circ: CapCity orders: **11,600**
📖 Getaway **W:** Mike Carlin

47 ❑ Feb 1988 Cover: 0.75 **NM** value: **2.00**
Circ: CapCity orders: **11,450**
📖 Idol Threats **W:** Mike Carlin

48 ❑ Mar 1988 Cover: 0.75 **NM** value: **2.00**
Circ: CapCity orders: **11,550**
📖 The Stars in Secret Influence • first Peter David script **W:** Peter David ★ 1st Appearance of Moron.

49 ❑ Apr 1988 Cover: 1.00 **NM** value: **2.00**
Circ: CapCity orders: **11,850**
📖 Aspiring to be Angels **W:** Peter David

50 ❑ May 1988 Cover: 1.50 **NM** value: **2.00**
Circ: CapCity orders: **12,900**
• Giant-size. 📖 Marriage of Inconvenience **W:** Peter David

51 ❑ Jun 1988 Cover: 1.00 **NM** value: **2.00**
Circ: CapCity orders: **11,300**
📖 Haunted Honeymoon **W:** Peter David

52 ❑ Jul 1988 Cover: 1.00 **NM** value: **2.00**
Circ: CapCity orders: **11,750**
📖 Hell in a Handbasket • Dante's Inferno **W:** Peter David

53 ❑ Aug 1988 Cover: 1.00 **NM** value: **2.00**
Circ: CapCity orders: **12,050**
📖 You're Dead, Jim **W:** Peter David

54 ❑ Sep 1988 Cover: 1.00 **NM** value: **2.00**
Circ: CapCity orders: **11,850**
📖 Old Loyalties • Return of Finnegan **W:** Peter David

55 ❑ Oct 1988 Cover: 1.00 **NM** value: **2.00**
Circ: CapCity orders: **11,650**
📖 Finnegan's Wake! **W:** Peter David

56 ❑ Nov 1988 Cover: 1.00 **NM** value: **2.00**
Circ: CapCity orders: **11,150**
📖 A Small Matter of Faith final issue. • set during first five-year mission **W:** Peter David

Anl 1❑ca. 1985 Cover: 1.25 **NM** value: **2.00**
Circ: CapCity orders: **10,200**
📖 All Those Years Ago... • Kirk's first mission on The Enterprise

Anl 2❑ca. 1986 Cover: 1.25 **NM** value: **2.00**
Circ: CapCity orders: **8,650**
📖 The Final Voyage • The final mission of the first five-year mission **A:** Dan Jurgens ★ Appearance of Captain Pike.

Anl 3❑ca. 1988 Cover: 1.25 **NM** value: **2.00**
📖 Retrospect • Scotty's romances **A:** Curt Swan

STAR TREK (4TH SERIES) — DC

Following hot on the heels of DC's first Star Trek series, this second DC series didn't tie itself as tightly to movie continuity as the first series did, a move that didn't force story changes in mid-stream.

Initially written by Peter David, the series was set in a nebulous time following the events of Star Trek IV and V. David delved more deeply into the continuity of the original TV episodes, including putting Captain Kirk on trial for all the times he had "bent" the Prime Directive or Starfleet regulations during those original missions.

Another memorable storyline, co-written with Bill Mumy (Lost in Space's Will Robinson), was a sort of crossover between Star Trek and that competing CBS show. These comics adventures were a real treat for fans of the original TV show, with special guests popping out at every turn.

— Brent

1 ❑ Oct 1989 Cover: 1.50 **NM** value: **5.00**
Circ: CapCity orders: **30,900** • **CGC:** 2 graded, best 9.8
📖 The Return! **A:** James W. Fry **W:** Peter David

2 ❑ Nov 1989 Cover: 1.50 **NM** value: **4.00**
Circ: CapCity orders: **21,650**
📖 The Sentence

3 ❑ Dec 1989 Cover: 1.50 **NM** value: **3.00**
Circ: CapCity orders: **19,600**
📖 Death Before Dishonor

4 ❑ Jan 1990 Cover: 1.50 **NM** value: **3.00**
• **CGC:** 1 graded, best 9.6
📖 Repercussions ★ 1st Appearance of R.J. Blaise.

5 ❑ Feb 1990 Cover: 1.50 **NM** value: **2.50**
Circ: CapCity orders: **20,150**
📖 Fast Friends

6 ❑ Mar 1990 Cover: 1.50 **NM** value: **2.50**
Circ: CapCity orders: **20,500**
📖 Cure All

7 ❑ Apr 1990 Cover: 1.50 **NM** value: **2.50**
Circ: CapCity orders: **19,700**
📖 Not Sweeney!

8 ❑ May 1990 Cover: 1.50 **NM** value: **2.50**
Circ: CapCity orders: **19,850**
📖 Going, Going... ★ Versus Sweeney.

9 ❑ Jun 1990 Cover: 1.50 **NM** value: **2.50**
Circ: CapCity orders: **19,300**
📖 ...Gone! ★ Versus Sweeney.

10 ❑ Jul 1990 Cover: 1.50 **NM** value: **2.50**
Circ: CapCity orders: **19,000**
📖 The First Thing We Do... • The Trial of James T. Kirk ★ Appearance of Areel Shaw, Samuel Cogsley.

11 ❑ Aug 1990 Cover: 1.50 **NM** value: **2.00**
Circ: CapCity orders: **18,050**
📖 ...Let's Kill All the Lawyers! • The Trial of James T. Kirk ★ Appearance of Bella Oxmyx, Leonard James Akaar.

12 ❑ Sep 1990 Cover: 1.50 **NM** value: **2.00**
Circ: CapCity orders: **17,750**
📖 Trial and Error • The Trial of James T. Kirk

Other grades: Multiply prices above by **1.5 for Mint • 2/3 for Very Fine • 1/3 for Fine • 1/5 for Very Good • 1/8 for Good**

13 ❑ Oct 1990 Cover: 1.50 **NM** value: **2.00**
Circ: CapCity orders: **17,300**
📖 A Rude Awakening! • The Return of the Worthy

14 ❑ Dec 1990 Cover: 1.50 **NM** value: **2.00**
Circ: CapCity orders: **17,300**
📖 Great Expectations! • The Return of the Worthy

15 ❑ Jan 1991 Cover: 1.50 **NM** value: **2.00**
Circ: CapCity orders: **17,050**
📖 Tomorrow Never Knows! • The Return of the Worthy; final Peter David issue **W:** Peter David

16 ❑ Feb 1991 Cover: 1.50 **NM** value: **2.00**
Circ: CapCity orders: **17,550**
📖 Worldsinger • Written by Straczynski **W:** J. Michael Straczynski

17 ❑ Mar 1991 Cover: 1.50 **NM** value: **2.00**
Circ: CapCity orders: **16,750**
📖 Partners? • Part 1

18 ❑ Apr 1991 Cover: 1.50 **NM** value: **2.00**
Circ: CapCity orders: **15,950**
📖 Partners? • Part 2

19 ❑ May 1991 Cover: 1.50 **NM** value: **2.00**
Circ: CapCity orders: **15,850**
📖 Once a Hero! • Peter David

20 ❑ Jun 1991 Cover: 1.50 **NM** value: **2.00**
Circ: CapCity orders: **15,750**
📖 Gods' Gauntlet • Gods' Gauntlet, part 1

21 ❑ Jul 1991 Cover: 1.75 **NM** value: **2.00**
Circ: CapCity orders: **16,400**
📖 The Last Stand! • Gods' Gauntlet, part 2

22 ❑ Aug 1991 Cover: 1.75 **NM** value: **2.00**
Circ: CapCity orders: **17,100**
📖 Mission: Muddled • Return of Harry Mudd, Part 1

23 ❑ Sep 1991 Cover: 1.75 **NM** value: **2.00**
Circ: CapCity orders: **17,100**
📖 The Sky Above... The Mudd Below • Return of Harry Mudd, Part 2★ Appearance of Harry Mudd.

24 ❑ Oct 1991 Cover: 2.95 **NM** value: **3.00**
Circ: CapCity orders: **17,100**
• 25th anniversary of Star Trek. 📖 Target = Mudd!; Moments To Remember (text); Fitzgerald Never Saw Star Trek (text); It's TV Guide's Fault (text); 25 Years... (text); Pin-Up gallery • Return of Harry Mudd, Part 3; 25th Anniversary issue; Text pieces by Chris Claremont, Michael Jan Friedman, Peter David and Howard Weinstein★ Appearance of Harry Mudd.

25 ❑ Nov 1991 Cover: 1.75 **NM** value: **2.00**
Circ: CapCity orders: **16,350**
📖 Class Reunion ★ Appearance of Saavik, Captain Styles.

26 ❑ Dec 1991 Cover: 1.75 **NM** value: **2.00**
Circ: CapCity orders: **17,000**
📖 Where There's a Will

27 ❑ Jan 1992 Cover: 1.75 **NM** value: **2.00**
Circ: CapCity orders: **17,150**
📖 Secrets

28 ❑ Feb 1992 Cover: 1.75 **NM** value: **2.00**
Circ: CapCity orders: **17,250**
📖 Truth or Treachery

29 ❑ Mar 1992 Cover: 1.75 **NM** value: **2.00**
Circ: CapCity orders: **17,050**
📖 The Price of Admission!

30 ❑ Apr 1992 Cover: 1.75 **NM** value: **2.00**
Circ: CapCity orders: **16,350**
📖 Veritas • Veritas, part 1

31 ❑ May 1992 Cover: 1.75 **NM** value: **2.00**
Circ: CapCity orders: **16,600**
📖 Sacrifices and Survivors • Veritas, part 2

32 ❑ Jun 1992 Cover: 1.75 **NM** value: **2.00**
Circ: CapCity orders: **16,550**
📖 Danger on Ice! • Veritas, part 3

33 ❑ Jul 1992 Cover: 1.75 **NM** value: **2.00**
Circ: CapCity orders: **16,550**
📖 Cold Comfort! • Veritas, part 4

34 ❑ Aug 1992 Cover: 1.75 **NM** value: **2.00**
Circ: CapCity orders: **16,450**
📖 The Tree of Life, the Branches of Heaven

35 ❑ Sep 1992 Cover: 1.75 **NM** value: **2.00**
Circ: CapCity orders: **14,700**
📖 Divide and Conquer • The Tabukan Syndrome, Part 1

36 ❑ Sep 1992 Cover: 1.75 **NM** value: **2.00**
Circ: CapCity orders: **14,700**
📖 Battle Stations! • The Tabukan Syndrome, Part 2

37 ❑ Oct 1992 Cover: 1.75 **NM** value: **2.00**
Circ: CapCity orders: **15,250**
📖 Prisoners of War? • The Tabukan Syndrome, Part 3

38 ❑ Oct 1992 Cover: 1.75 **NM** value: **2.00**
Circ: CapCity orders: **15,150**
📖 Consequences! • The Tabukan Syndrome, Part 4

39 ❑ Nov 1992 Cover: 1.75 **NM** value: **2.00**
Circ: CapCity orders: **14,900**
📖 Collision Course • The Tabukan Syndrome, Part 5

40 ❑ Nov 1992 Cover: 1.75 **NM** value: **2.00**
Circ: CapCity orders: **14,900**
📖 Showdown! • The Tabukan Syndrome, Part 6

41 ❑ Dec 1992 Cover: 1.75 **NM** value: **2.00**
Circ: CapCity orders: **14,700**
📖 Runaway

42 ❑ Jan 1993 Cover: 1.75 **NM** value: **2.00**
Circ: CapCity orders: **14,450**
📖 A Little Adventure... • Part 1

43 ❑ Feb 1993 Cover: 1.75 **NM** value: **2.00**
Circ: CapCity orders: **15,200**
📖 (A Little Adventure) Goes a Long Way • Part 2

44 ❑ Mar 1993 Cover: 1.75 **NM** value: **2.00**
Circ: CapCity orders: **14,900**
📖 Acceptable Risk

45 ❑ Apr 1993 Cover: 1.75 **NM** value: **2.00**
Circ: CapCity orders: **15,250**
📖 A Little Man-To-Man Talk • Return of Trelane

46 ❑ May 1993 Cover: 1.75 **NM** value: **2.00**
Circ: CapCity orders: **15,350**
📖 Coup D'etat • Deceptions, part 1

47 ❑ May 1993 Cover: 1.75 **NM** value: **2.00**
Circ: CapCity orders: **15,500**
📖 Deceptions! • Deceptions, part 2

48 ❑ Jun 1993 Cover: 1.75 **NM** value: **2.00**
Circ: CapCity orders: **15,400**
📖 Deceptions! • Deceptions, part 3

49 ❑ Jun 1993 Cover: 1.75 **NM** value: **2.00**
Circ: CapCity orders: **15,550**
📖 The Peacekeeper • Part 1

50 ❑ Jul 1993 Cover: 3.50 **NM** value: **Cover or less**
Circ: CapCity orders: **20,650**
• Giant-size anniversary special. 📖 The Peacekeeper • Part 2; Double-sized issue★ Appearance of Gary Seven.

51 ❑ Aug 1993 Cover: 1.75 **NM** value: **2.00**
Circ: CapCity orders: **15,650**
📖 Renegade

52 ❑ Sep 1993 Cover: 1.75 **NM** value: **2.00**
Circ: CapCity orders: **15,150**
📖 Epic Proportions

53 ❑ Oct 1993 Cover: 1.75 **NM** value: **2.00**
Circ: CapCity orders: **14,750**
📖 Time Crime • Time Crime, Part 1

54 ❑ Nov 1993 Cover: 1.75 **NM** value: **2.00**
Circ: CapCity orders: **14,750**
📖 Nightmares • Time Crime, Part 2 **A:** Rod Whigham **W:** Howard Weinstein

55 ❑ Dec 1993 Cover: 1.75 **NM** value: **2.00**
Circ: CapCity orders: **15,000**
📖 Time to Time • Time Crime, Part 3

56 ❑ Jan 1994 Cover: 1.75 **NM** value: **2.00**
Circ: CapCity orders: **15,250**
📖 Call Back Yesterday • Time Crime, Part 4

57 ❑ Feb 1994 Cover: 1.75 **NM** value: **2.00**
Circ: CapCity orders: **15,000**
📖 Seems Like Old Times • Time Crime, Part 5

58 ❑ Mar 1994 Cover: 1.75 **NM** value: **2.00**
Circ: CapCity orders: **14,700**
cover forms triptych with issues #59 and 60. 📖 No Compromise • Part 1; Chekov's first days on the Enterprise

59 ❑ Apr 1994 Cover: 1.75 **NM** value: **2.00**
Circ: CapCity orders: **13,800**
cover forms triptych with issues #58 and 60. 📖 No Compromise • Part 2; Chekov's first days on the Enterprise

60 ❑ Jun 1994 Cover: 1.75 **NM** value: **2.00**
Circ: CapCity orders: **13,700**
cover forms triptych with issues #57 and 58. 📖 No Compromise • Part 3; Chekov's first days on the Enterprise

61 ❑ Jul 1994 Cover: 1.95 **NM** value: **2.00**
Circ: CapCity orders: **13,600**
📖 Door in the Cage • return to Talos IV

62 ❑ Aug 1994 Cover: 1.95 **NM** value: **2.00**
Circ: CapCity orders: **13,500**
📖 The Lone Alone • Part 1 **A:** Rod Whigham **W:** Kevin J. Ryan

63 ❑ Sep 1994 Cover: 1.95 **NM** value: **2.00**
Circ: CapCity orders: **13,100**
📖 The Lone Alone • Part 2

64 ❑ Oct 1994 Cover: 1.95 **NM** value: **2.00**
Circ: CapCity orders: **13,000**
📖 Gary • follows events of Where No Man Has Gone Before

65 ❑ Nov 1994 Cover: 1.95 **NM** value: **2.00**
Circ: CapCity orders: **12,350**
📖 Bait and Switch

66 ❑ Dec 1994 Cover: 1.95 **NM** value: **2.00**
Circ: CapCity orders: **12,600**
📖 Rivals • Part 1

67 ❑ Jan 1995 Cover: 1.95 **NM** value: **2.00**
Circ: CapCity orders: **12,000**
📖 Rivals • Part 2

68 ❑ Feb 1995 Cover: 1.95 **NM** value: **2.00**
Circ: CapCity orders: **11,550**
📖 Rivals • Part 3

69 ❑ Mar 1995 Cover: 1.95 **NM** value: **2.00**
Circ: CapCity orders: **11,200**
📖 Wolf in Cheap Clothing • Part 1

70 ❑ Apr 1995 Cover: 1.95 **NM** value: **2.00**
Circ: CapCity orders: **11,050**
📖 Wolf in Cheap Clothing • Part 2

71 ❑ May 1995 Cover: 2.50 **NM** value: **Cover or less**
Circ: CapCity orders: **11,075**

72 ❑ Jun 1995 Cover: 2.50 **NM** value: **Cover or less**
Circ: CapCity orders: **10,650**

73 ❑ Jul 1995 Cover: 2.50 **NM** value: **Cover or less**
Circ: CapCity orders: **10,400**
📖 Star-Crossed • Part 1 **A:** Rachel Ketchum **W:** Howard Weinstein

74 ❑ Aug 1995 Cover: 2.50 **NM** value: **Cover or less**
Circ: CapCity orders: **10,575**
📖 Star-Crossed • Part 2 **A:** Rachel Ketchum **W:** Howard Weinstein

75 ❑ Sep 1995 Cover: 3.95 **NM** value: **Cover or less**
Circ: CapCity orders: **11,050**

76 ❑ Oct 1995 Cover: 2.50 **NM** value: **Cover or less**
Circ: CapCity orders: **8,600**
📖 Prisoners

77 ❑ Nov 1995 Cover: 2.50 **NM** value: **Cover or less**
📖 Deadlock

78 ❑ Dec 1995 Cover: 2.50 **NM** value: **Cover or less**
📖 The Hunted • The Chosen, Part 1 **A:** Rachel Forbes-Sense **W:** Kevin J. Ryan

79 ❑ Jan 1996 Cover: 2.50 **NM** value: **Cover or less**
📖 Blood Enemies • The Chosen, Part 2 **A:** Rachel Forbes-Sense **W:** Kevin J. Ryan

80 ❑ Feb 1996 Cover: 2.50 **NM** value: **Cover or less**
final issue. • The Chosen, Part 3 **A:** Rachel Forbes-Sense **W:** Kevin J. Ryan

Anl 1❑ca. 1990 Cover: 2.95 **NM** value: **3.50**
📖 So Near the Touch • Story by George Takei **W:** George Takei(Sulu); Peter David

Anl 2❑ca. 1991 Cover: 2.95 **NM** value: **3.25**
Circ: CapCity orders: **15,600**
📖 Starfleet Academy! • Kirk at Starfleet Academy

Anl 3❑ca. 1992 Cover: 3.50 **NM** value: **Cover or less**
Circ: CapCity orders: **12,350**
📖 Homeworld **A:** Norm Dwyer **W:** Howard Weinstein

Anl 4❑ca. 1993 Cover: 3.50 **NM** value: **Cover or less**
Circ: CapCity orders: **14,900**
📖 To Walk the Night • Spock on Enterprise with Captain Pike

Anl 5❑ca. 1994 Cover: 3.95 **NM** value: **Cover or less**
Circ: CapCity orders: **11,550**
📖 The Dream Walkers • 1994 Annual

Anl 6❑ca. 1995 Cover: 3.95 **NM** value: **Cover or less**
📖 Split Infinities • Convergence, Part 1; continues in Star Trek: TNG Annual #6; 1995 Annual★ Death of Gary Seven.

Bk 1❑ Cover: 19.95 **NM** value: **Cover or less**
• Revisitations; collects #22-24; 49-50★ Origin of Gary Seven. ★ Appearance of Harry Mudd.

Bk 2❑ Cover: 17.95 **NM** value: **Cover or less**
• Tests of Courage; collects #35-40

Bk 3❑ Cover: 14.95 **NM** value: **Cover or less**
• Debt of Honor

Bk 3/HC❑ Cover: 25.00 **NM** value: **Cover or less**
Debt of Honor hardcover.

Bk 4❑ Cover: 14.95 **NM** value: **Cover or less**
• The Ashes of Eden; adapts William Shatner novel of same name

SE 1❑Spr 1994 Cover: 3.50 **NM** value: **Cover or less**
Circ: CapCity orders: **16,750**
📖 Blaise of Glory

SE 2❑Win 1994 Cover: 3.95 **NM** value: **Cover or less**
📖 Raise the Defiant

SE 3❑Win 1995 Cover: 3.95 **NM** value: **Cover or less**
Circ: CapCity orders: **11,800**
📖 The Unforgiven; Echoes of Yesterday

STAR TREK: DEEP SPACE NINE, THE CELEBRITY SERIES: BLOOD AND HONOR Malibu

1 ❑ May 1995 Cover: 2.95 **NM** value: **Cover or less**
📖 Blood & Honor • Written by Mark Lenard **W:** Mark Lenard(Sarek)

STAR TREK: DEEP SPACE NINE HEARTS AND MINDS Malibu

1 ❑ Jun 1994 Cover: 2.50 **NM** value: **Cover or less**
Circ: CapCity orders: **18,250 • CGC:** 1 graded, best 9.8
📖 For the Glory of the Empire • an original Deep Space Nine mini series **A:** Rob Davis **W:** Mark A. Altman

2 ❑ Jul 1994 Cover: 2.50 **NM** value: **Cover or less**
Circ: CapCity orders: **13,950**
📖 On the Edge of Armageddon

3 ❑ Aug 1994 Cover: 2.50 **NM** value: **Cover or less**
Circ: CapCity orders: **13,050**
📖 Into the Abyss

4 ❑ Sep 1994 Cover: 2.50 **NM** value: **Cover or less**
Circ: CapCity orders: **12,325**
📖 Masters of War

STAR TREK: DEEP SPACE NINE: LIGHTSTORM Malibu

1 ❑ Dec 1994 Cover: 3.50 **NM** value: **Cover or less**
Circ: CapCity orders: **12,900**
A: Rob Davis **W:** Mark Altman

STAR TREK: DEEP SPACE NINE (MALIBU) Malibu

This adaptation of the popular television series chronicles the adventures of the later additions to the Star Trek family.

After 50 years, the citizens of Bajor had freed themselves from the cruel Cardassian occupation. Lacking sufficient resources to guarantee their hard-won freedom, they welcomed the assistance of the Federation. But what was meant to be a token presence soon becomes one of the most pivotal of Starfleet assignments. The discovery of a stable wormhole in an unexplored area of the galaxy turns Bajor, a remote frontier planet, into an interstellar hub of activity. The new crew of the former Cardassian space station (Terok Nor) must maintain the fragile peace between Bajor and Cardassia, as well as the Dominion, a new threat from beyond the wormhole.

In addition to being based on the syndicated series, the title featured writing by some of the actors.

0 ❑ Jan 1995 Cover: 28.00 **NM** value: **Cover or less**
• premium limited edition. • QVC offer

1/A ❑ Aug 1993 Cover: 2.50 **NM** value: **3.00**
Circ: CapCity orders: **42,600 • CGC:** 4 graded, best 9.6
photo cover (newsstand). 📖 Stowaway • Part 1 **A:** Gordon Purcell **W:** Mike W. Barr

1/B ❑ Aug 1993 Cover: 2.50 **NM** value: **3.00**
line-drawing cover. 📖 Stowaway • Part 1 **A:** Gordon Purcell **W:** Mike W. Barr

1/C ❑ Aug 1993 Cover: 19.95 **NM** value: **Cover or less**
• deluxe edition (black/foil). 📖 Stowaway • Part 1 **A:** Gordon Purcell **W:** Mike W. Barr

2 ❑ Sep 1993 Cover: 2.50 **NM** value: **Cover or less**
Circ: CapCity orders: **24,200**
📖 Stowaway • Part 2; trading card

3 ❑ Oct 1993 Cover: 2.50 **NM** value: **Cover or less**
Circ: CapCity orders: **21,325**
📖 Old Wounds

4 ❑ Nov 1993 Cover: 2.50 **NM** value: **Cover or less**
Circ: CapCity orders: **19,850**
📖 Emancipation • Part 1

CGC-graded: Multiply prices above by **33 for 9.9 M • 16 for 9.8 NM/M • 7 for 9.6 NM+ • 5 for 9.4 NM • 2.5 for 9.2 NM- • 1.5 for 9.0 VF/NM**

5 ❑ Dec 1993 Cover: 2.50 **NM** value: **Cover or less**
Circ: CapCity orders: **17,950**
🕮 Emancipation • Part 2

6 ❑ Jan 1994 Cover: 2.50 **NM** value: **Cover or less**
Circ: CapCity orders: **17,200**
🕮 Field Trip

7 ❑ Feb 1994 Cover: 2.50 **NM** value: **Cover or less**
Circ: CapCity orders: **16,125**
🕮 Working Vacation

8 ❑ May 1994 Cover: 2.50 **NM** value: **Cover or less**
Circ: CapCity orders: **15,625**
🕮 Requiem • Part 1 **A:** Gordon Purcell

9 ❑ Jun 1994 Cover: 2.50 **NM** value: **Cover or less**
Circ: CapCity orders: **14,800**
🕮 Requiem • Part 2

10 ❑ Jun 1994 Cover: 2.50 **NM** value: **Cover or less**
Circ: CapCity orders: **14,550**
🕮 Decendants

11 ❑ Jul 1994 Cover: 2.50 **NM** value: **Cover or less**
Circ: CapCity orders: **14,925**
🕮 A Short Fuse

12 ❑ Jul 1994 Cover: 2.50 **NM** value: **Cover or less**
Circ: CapCity orders: **14,100**
🕮 Baby on Board

13 ❑ Aug 1994 Cover: 2.50 **NM** value: **Cover or less**
Circ: CapCity orders: **13,350**
🕮 Lapse

14 ❑ Sep 1994 Cover: 2.50 **NM** value: **Cover or less**
Circ: CapCity orders: **12,725**
🕮 Dax's Comet • Part 1

15 ❑ Sep 1994 Cover: 2.50 **NM** value: **Cover or less**
Circ: CapCity orders: **12,700**
🕮 Dax's Comet • Part 2

16 ❑ Nov 1994 Cover: 2.50 **NM** value: **Cover or less**
Circ: CapCity orders: **11,700**
🕮 Shanghaied

17 ❑ Dec 1994 Cover: 2.50 **NM** value: **Cover or less**
Circ: CapCity orders: **11,725**

18 ❑ Jan 1995 Cover: 2.50 **NM** value: **Cover or less**
Circ: CapCity orders: **11,550**
🕮 Hearts of Old

19 ❑ Feb 1995 Cover: 2.50 **NM** value: **Cover or less**
Circ: CapCity orders: **11,375**

20 ❑ Mar 1995 Cover: 2.50 **NM** value: **Cover or less**
Circ: CapCity orders: **10,950**

21 ❑ Apr 1995 Cover: 2.50 **NM** value: **Cover or less**
Circ: CapCity orders: **13,250**
🕮 Fadeout!

22 ❑ May 1995 Cover: 2.50 **NM** value: **Cover or less**
Circ: CapCity orders: **10,150**
🕮 Deep Space Mine!

23 ❑ May 1995 Cover: 2.50 **NM** value: **Cover or less**
Circ: CapCity orders: **10,125**
🕮 The Search • The Secret of the Lost Orb, Part 1

24 ❑ Jun 1995 Cover: 2.50 **NM** value: **Cover or less**
Circ: CapCity orders: **10,000**
• The Secret of the Lost Orb, Part 2

25 ❑ Jul 1995 Cover: 3.50 **NM** value: **Cover or less**
🕮 Gods of War • The Secret of the Lost Orb, Part 3; Double-sized issue

26 ❑ Jul 1995 Cover: 2.50 **NM** value: **Cover or less**
🕮 Genesis Denied • Part 1

27 ❑ Aug 1995 Cover: 2.50 **NM** value: **Cover or less**
🕮 Genesis Denied • Part 2

28 ❑ Sep 1995 Cover: 2.50 **NM** value: **Cover or less**

29 ❑ Oct 1995 Cover: 2.50 **NM** value: **Cover or less**
🕮 Sole Asylum; Enemies & Allies • Part 1; Part 1; Commander Riker; Mirror Tuvok **A:** Rod Whigham **W:** Mark Paniccia; Tim Russ ★ Appearance of Mirror Universe Tuvok, Thomas Riker, Captain Sisko, Will Riker, Bashir.

30 ❑ Nov 1995 Cover: 2.50 **NM** value: **Cover or less**

31 ❑ Dec 1995 Cover: 2.50 **NM** value: **3.95**

32 ❑ Jan 1996 Cover: 2.50 **NM** value: **3.50**
final issue.

Anl 1❑ca. 1995 Cover: 3.95 **NM** value: **Cover or less**
Circ: CapCity orders: **11,075**

Ash 1❑ **NM** value: **5.00**
• limited edition ashcan.

SE 1❑ca. 1995 Cover: 3.50 **NM** value: **Cover or less**
Circ: CapCity orders: **9,550**

STAR TREK: DEEP SPACE NINE, THE MAQUIS
Malibu

1 ❑ Feb 1995 Cover: 2.50 **NM** value: **Cover or less**
Circ: CapCity orders: **15,300**
🕮 Vacation's Over • Soldier of Peace, Part 1 **A:** Rob Davis **W:** Mark Altman

2 ❑ Mar 1995 Cover: 2.50 **NM** value: **Cover or less**
Circ: CapCity orders: **10,525**
🕮 Rats in a Maze • Soldier of Peace, Part 2 **A:** Rob Davis **W:** Mark Altman

3 ❑ Apr 1995 Cover: 2.50 **NM** value: **Cover or less**
Circ: CapCity orders: **10,350**
🕮 Victims of Deceit • Soldier of Peace, Part 3 **A:** Rob Davis **W:** Mark Altman

STAR TREK: DEEP SPACE NINE (MARVEL)
Marvel / Paramount

1 ❑ Nov 1996 Cover: 1.99 **NM** value: **2.00**
Circ: Statement: **57,266** Direct Market orders: **66,750**
🕮 Judgment Day • Part 1; DS9 is drawn into the wormhole **A:** Tom Grindberg **W:** Howard Weinstein

2 ❑ Dec 1996 Cover: 1.99 **NM** value: **2.00**
Circ: Statement: **57,266** Direct Market orders: **37,750**
🕮 Judgment Day • Part 2

3 ❑ Jan 1997 Cover: 1.99 **NM** value: **2.00**
Circ: Statement: **57,266** Direct Market orders: **35,500**
🕮 The Cancer Within • Part 1 **A:** Tom Grindberg **W:** Mariano

4 ❑ Feb 1997 Cover: 1.99 **NM** value: **2.00**
Circ: Statement: **57,266** Direct Market orders: **35,500**
🕮 The Cancer Within • Part 1 **A:** Tom Grindberg **W:** Mariano

5 ❑ Mar 1997 Cover: 1.99 **NM** value: **2.00**
Circ: Statement: **57,266** Direct Market orders: **30,250**
🕮 The Shadow Group **A:** Tom Grindberg **W:** Mariano

6 ❑ Apr 1997 Cover: 1.99 **NM** value: **2.00**
Circ: Statement: **57,266** Direct Market orders: **24,000**
🕮 Risk **A:** Tom Grindberg **W:** Howard Weinstein

7 ❑ May 1997 Cover: 1.99 **NM** value: **2.00**
Circ: Statement: **57,266** Diamd. preorders: **26,712**

8 ❑ Aug 1997 Cover: 1.99 **NM** value: **2.00**
Circ: Statement: **57,266** Diamd. preorders: **26,095**

9 ❑ Sep 1997 Cover: 1.99 **NM** value: **2.00**
Circ: Statement: **57,266** Diamd. preorders: **22,491**

10 ❑ Oct 1997 Cover: 1.99 **NM** value: **2.00**
Circ: Diamd. preorders: **22,209**

11 ❑ Nov 1997 Cover: 1.99 **NM** value: **2.00**
Circ: Diamd. preorders: **20,252**
• gatefold summary. • Telepathy War, Part 1; Crossover with ST: Starfleet Academy, ST: Telepathy War one-shot, ST Unlimited and ST: Voyager;

12 ❑ Dec 1997 Cover: 1.99 **NM** value: **2.00**
Circ: Diamd. preorders: **20,480**
• gatefold summary. 🕮 Command Decisions • Telepathy War, Part 2; Crossover with ST: Starfleet Academy, ST: Telepathy War one-shot, ST Unlimited and ST: Voyager; Has 1997 Statement; avg total paid circ 57,266

13 ❑ Jan 1998 Cover: 1.99 **NM** value: **2.00**
Circ: Diamd. preorders: **19,110**
• gatefold summary.

14 ❑ Feb 1998 Cover: 1.99 **NM** value: **2.00**
Circ: Diamd. preorders: **18,683**
• gatefold summary. ★ Appearance of Tribbles.

15 ❑ Mar 1998 Cover: 1.99 **NM** value: **2.00**
Circ: Diamd. preorders: **18,291**
• gatefold summary. 🕮 Requiem in Obsidian final issue.

STAR TREK: DEEP SPACE NINE-N-VECTOR
DC / Wildstorm

1 ❑ Aug 2000 Cover: 2.50 **NM** value: **Cover or less**
Circ: Diamd. preorders: **14,313**
🕮 N-Vector **A:** Toby Cypress **W:** K.W. Jeter

2 ❑ Sep 2000 Cover: 2.50 **NM** value: **Cover or less**
Circ: Diamd. preorders: **13,398**
A: Toby Cypress **W:** K.W. Jeter

3 ❑ Oct 2000 Cover: 2.50 **NM** value: **Cover or less**
Circ: Diamd. preorders: **11,790**
A: Toby Cypress **W:** K.W. Jeter

4 ❑ Nov 2000 Cover: 2.50 **NM** value: **Cover or less**
Circ: Diamd. preorders: **11,142**
A: Toby Cypress **W:** K.W. Jeter

STAR TREK: DEEP SPACE NINE: RULES OF DIPLOMACY
Malibu

1 ❑ Aug 1995 Cover: 2.95 **NM** value: **Cover or less**
🕮 Rules Of Diplomacy • Co-Author Aron Eisenberg plays "Nog" in series **A:** Leonard Kirk **W:** Mark Paniccia; Aron Eisenberg; Aron Eisenberg(Nog)

STAR TREK: DEEP SPACE NINE/STAR TREK: THE NEXT GENERATION
Malibu

1 ❑ Oct 1994 Cover: 2.50 **NM** value: **Cover or less**
Circ: CapCity orders: **19,700**
🕮 The Wormhole Trap! • part two of a four-part crossover with DC; Deep Space Nine/The Next Generation crossover, Part 2; Continued from Star Trek: The Next Generation/Star Trek: Deep Space Nine #1; Continues in Star Trek: The Next Generation/Star Trek: Deep Space Nine #2 **A:** Gordon Purcell **W:** Michael Jan Friedman; Mike W. Barr

2 ❑ Nov 1994 Cover: 2.50 **NM** value: **Cover or less**
🕮 The Othersiders! • part three of a four-part crossover with DC; Deep Space Nine/The Next Generation crossover, Part 4; Continued from Star Trek: The Next Generation/Star Trek: Deep Space Nine #2 **A:** Gordon Purcell **W:** Michael Jan Friedman; Mike W. Barr

Ash 1❑ **NM** value: **1.00**
no cover price. • Ashcan preview; flip-book with DC's Star Trek: The Next Generation/Star Trek: Deep Space Nine Ashcan

STAR TREK: DEEP SPACE NINE: TEROK NOR
Malibu

0 ❑ Jan 1995 Cover: 2.95 **NM** value: **Cover or less**
Circ: CapCity orders: **12,325**
🕮 Terok Nor **A:** Trevor Goring **W:** Mark Altman ★ Origin of Deep Space Nine.

STAR TREK: DEEP SPACE NINE, ULTIMATE ANNUAL
Malibu

1 ❑ ca. 1995 Cover: 5.95 **NM** value: **Cover or less**
🕮 No Time Like The Present **A:** Leonard Kirk **W:** Laurie Sutton

STAR TREK: DEEP SPACE NINE, WORF SPECIAL
Malibu

0 ❑ Dec 1995 Cover: 3.95 **NM** value: **Cover or less**
🕮 Bonds of Honor **A:** Steve Erwin **W:** Dan Mishkin

Statement of Ownership figures are the average number of copies originally sold, as cited by the publisher to the U.S. Postal Service. These estimate **all** sales, in comics shops and on newsstands.

STAR TREK: EARLY VOYAGES
Marvel / Paramount

Before the galaxy-spanning adventures of Jean-Luc Picard, and before the five-year mission of James T. Kirk, the starship Enterprise had another captain. Christopher Pike was first introduced in the original Star Trek episode, The Cage, the pilot for the series. The show eventually aired with several changes, the most notable being the replacement of Pike with Kirk.

The pilot episode was later incorporated into The Menagerie, a two-part flashback episode, firmly placing Pike as Kirk's predecessor in the show's continuity.

With its second round with the Star Trek license Marvel told Pike's adventures from the very beginning, starting with the selection of his crew. The Enterprise is the best ship the Federation has to offer, and her crew needs to meet the same standards. They include Mr. Spock as a cadet-in-training, and the intelligent but enigmatic female First Officer known as Number One. Like the crews in the television shows, the rest of Pike's team is a mix of aliens and humans.

In a time-traveling story arc, the crew has a run-in with Kirk and Scotty from an alternate history.

1 ❑ Feb 1997 Cover: 2.99 **NM** value: **Cover or less**
Circ: Statement: **44,273** Direct Market orders: **35,250**
🕮 Flesh of My Flesh • Christopher Pike as Enterprise captain **A:** Patrick Zircher **W:** Dan Abnett; Ian Edginton

2 ❑ Mar 1997 Cover: 1.99 **NM** value: **Cover or less**
Circ: Statement: **44,273** Direct Market orders: **29,750**
🕮 The Fires of Pharos • Battle with the Klingons **A:** Patrick Zircher **W:** Dan Abnett; Ian Edginton ★ Versus Klingons.

3 ❑ Apr 1997 Cover: 1.99 **NM** value: **Cover or less**
Circ: Statement: **44,273** Direct Market orders: **28,000**
🕮 Our Dearest Blood • prequel to The Cage **A:** Patrick Zircher **W:** Dan Abnett; Ian Edginton

4 ❑ May 1997 Cover: 1.99 **NM** value: **Cover or less**
Circ: Statement: **44,273** Diamd. preorders: **26,975**
🕮 Nor Iron Bars a Cage • Yeoman Colt's POV on The Cage **A:** Patrick Zircher **W:** Dan Abnett; Ian Edginton

5 ❑ Jun 1997 Cover: 1.99 **NM** value: **Cover or less**
Circ: Statement: **44,273** Diamd. preorders: **25,590**
🕮 Cloak and Dagger • Part 1

6 ❑ Jul 1997 Cover: 1.99 **NM** value: **Cover or less**
Circ: Statement: **44,273** Diamd. preorders: **22,193**
🕮 Cloak and Dagger • Part 2

7 ❑ Aug 1997 Cover: 1.99 **NM** value: **Cover or less**
Circ: Statement: **44,273** Diamd. preorders: **21,834**
• gatefold summary. 🕮 The Flat, Gold Forever • Pike vs. Kaaj

8 ❑ Sep 1997 Cover: 1.99 **NM** value: **Cover or less**
Circ: Statement: **44,273** Diamd. preorders: **20,646**
• gatefold summary. 🕮 Immortal Wounds

9 ❑ Oct 1997 Cover: 1.99 **NM** value: **Cover or less**
Circ: Diamd. preorders: **20,111**
• gatefold summary. 🕮 One of a Kind

10 ❑ Nov 1997 Cover: 1.99 **NM** value: **Cover or less**
Circ: Diamd. preorders: **19,530**
• gatefold summary. 🕮 The Fallen • Part 1 ★ Versus Chakuun.

11 ❑ Dec 1997 Cover: 1.99 **NM** value: **Cover or less**
Circ: Diamd. preorders: **18,654**
• gatefold summary. 🕮 The Fallen • Part 2; Has 1997 Statement, filed 10/1/1997; avg print run 81,313; avg sales 44,072; avg subs 201; avg total paid 44,273; samples 20; office use 125; max existent 44,418; 45% of run returned

12 ❑ Jan 1998 Cover: 1.99 **NM** value: **Cover or less**
Circ: Diamd. preorders: **18,182**
• gatefold summary. 🕮 Futures • Part 1 ★ Appearance of Robert April.

13 ❑ Feb 1998 Cover: 1.99 **NM** value: **Cover or less**
Circ: Diamd. preorders: **71,823**
• gatefold summary. 🕮 Future Tense • Part 2 ★ Appearance of Kirk, Scotty.

14 ❑ Mar 1998 Cover: 1.99 **NM** value: **Cover or less**
Circ: Diamd. preorders: **17,455**
• gatefold summary. 🕮 Futures • Pike vs. Kirk ★ Appearance of Kirk, Scotty.

15 ❑ Apr 1998 Cover: 1.99 **NM** value: **Cover or less**
Circ: Diamd. preorders: **16,769**
• gatefold summary. 🕮 Now and Then ★ Appearance of Kirk, Scotty.

16 ❑ May 1998 Cover: 1.99 **NM** value: **Cover or less**
Circ: Diamd. preorders: **16,456**
Pike goes undercover. • gatefold summary. 🕮 Thanatos

17 ❑ Jun 1998 Cover: 1.99 **NM** value: **Cover or less**
Circ: Diamd. preorders: **16,986**
• gatefold summary. 🕮 Nemesis final issue.

STAR TREK: ENTER THE WOLVES
WildStorm / Paramount

1 ❑ ca. 2001 Cover: 5.99 **NM** value: **Cover or less**
Circ: Diamd. preorders: **10,222**
A: Howard Weinstein **W:** R.C Crispin

STAR TREK: FIRST CONTACT
Marvel / Paramount

1 ❑ Nov 1996 Cover: 5.99 **NM** value: **Cover or less**
Circ: Direct Market orders: **29,000**
cardstock cover. • prestige format. • Movie adaptation **A:** Rod Whigham; Terry Pallot **W:** Brannon Braga; John Vornhort; Rick Berman; Roland D. Moore

STAR TREK GENERATIONS — DC

1 ❑ Cover: 3.95 **NM** value: **Cover or less**
Circ: CapCity orders: **14,550**
One-shot. • Movie adaptation; Newstand edition **A:** Gordon Purcell **W:** Michael Jan Friedman; Brannon Braga; Rick Berman; Ronald D. Moore

1/PR❑ Cover: 5.95 **NM** value: **Cover or less**
• Movie adaptation; Prestige format one-shot **A:** Gordon Purcell **W:** Michael Jan Friedman; Brannon Braga; Rick Berman; Ronald D. Moore

STAR TREKKER — Antarctic

1 ❑ Dec 1992, b&w Cover: 2.95 **NM** value: **Cover or less**
Circ: CapCity orders: **2,625**
• parody (never distributed)

Bk 1❑ Dec 1991 Cover: 9.95 **NM** value: **Cover or less**

STAR TREK: MIRROR MIRROR — Marvel / Paramount

1 ❑ Feb 1997 Cover: 3.99 **NM** value: **Cover or less**
Circ: Direct Market orders: **30,750**
📖 Fragile Glass • one-shot sequel to original series episode **A:** Mark Bagley **W:** Tom DeFalco

STAR TREK MOVIE SPECIAL — DC

3 ❑ ca. 1984 Cover: 1.50 **NM** value: **2.00**
📖 Star Trek III: The Search for Spock • Movie adaptation

4 ❑ ca. 1987 Cover: 2.00 **NM** value: **Cover or less**
Circ: CapCity orders: **12,250**
📖 Star Trek IV: The Voyage Home • Movie adaptation

5 ❑ ca. 1989 Cover: 2.00 **NM** value: **Cover or less**
Circ: CapCity orders: **17,350**
📖 Star Trek V: The Final Frontier • Movie adaptation

STAR TREK: NEW FRONTIER-DOUBLE TIME — DC / Wildstorm

1 ❑ Nov 2000 Cover: 5.95 **NM** value: **Cover or less**
• Captain Calhoun on the USS Excalibur **A:** Michael Collins **W:** Peter David

STAR TREK: OPERATION ASSIMILATION — Marvel / Paramount

1 ❑ Apr 1997 Cover: 2.99 **NM** value: **Cover or less**
Circ: Direct Market orders: **34,000**
One-shot. • Romulans as Borg **A:** Steve Erwin; Terry Pallot **W:** Paul Jenkins

STAR TREK: OTHER REALITIES — WildStorm / Paramount

2001❑2001 Cover: 14.95 **NM** value: **Cover or less**
📖 Star Trek: All of Me; Star Trek: Deep Space Nine: N-Vector; Star Trek: New Frontier: Double Time **A:** Aaron Lopresti; Toby Cypress; Michael Collins **W:** Bob Ingersoll; K. W. Jetter; Peter David; Tony Isabella

STAR TREK SPECIAL — WildStorm

1 ❑ Feb 2001 Cover: 6.95 **NM** value: **Cover or less**
Circ: Diamd. preorders: **12,032**
📖 Bloodline; A Rolling Stone Gathers No Nanoprobes; When the Stars Come A-Calling; Exercises in Futility; The Legacy of Elenor Dain; The Wake • Prestige format; stories for Star Trek, Next Generation, Deep Space Nine and Voyager **A:** Steve Lieber; Paul Neary; John Lucas; Gordon Purcell; Carlos Mota; Tommy Lee Edwards **W:** Jeffrey Lang; Andy Mangels; Ben Raab; Christopher Hinz; Ian Edginton; Stuart Moore

STAR TREK: STARFLEET ACADEMY — Marvel / Paramount

1 ❑ Dec 1996 Cover: 1.99 **NM** value: **2.00**
Circ: Statement: **50,703** Direct Market orders: **42,750**
📖 Prime Directives **A:** Chris Renaud **W:** Chris Cooper ★ Appearance of Nog.

2 ❑ Jan 1997 Cover: 1.99 **NM** value: **2.00**
Circ: Statement: **50,703** Direct Market orders: **35,250**
📖 Liberty **A:** Chris Renaud **W:** Chris Cooper

3 ❑ Feb 1997 Cover: 1.99 **NM** value: **2.00**
Circ: Statement: **50,703** Direct Market orders: **31,250**
📖 Loyalty Test **A:** John Royle **W:** Chris Cooper

4 ❑ Mar 1997 Cover: 1.99 **NM** value: **2.00**
Circ: Statement: **50,703** Direct Market orders: **29,000**
📖 War and Peace • Part 1 **A:** Chris Renaud **W:** Chris Cooper

5 ❑ Apr 1997 Cover: 1.99 **NM** value: **2.00**
Circ: Statement: **50,703** Direct Market orders: **27,500**
📖 Love and Death **A:** Chris Renaud **W:** Chris Cooper ★ Death of Kamilah.

6 ❑ May 1997 Cover: 1.99 **NM** value: **2.00**
Circ: Statement: **50,703** Diamd. preorders: **26,172**
📖 Passages **A:** Chris Renaud **W:** Chris Cooper

7 ❑ Jun 1997 Cover: 1.99 **NM** value: **2.00**
Circ: Statement: **50,703** Diamd. preorders: **24,830**
📖 Hide & Seek

8 ❑ Jul 1997 Cover: 1.99 **NM** value: **2.00**
Circ: Statement: **50,703** Diamd. preorders: **21,807**
• return of Charlie X

9 ❑ Aug 1997 Cover: 1.99 **NM** value: **2.00**
Circ: Statement: **50,703** Diamd. preorders: **20,354**
• gatefold summary. • on Talos IV★ Appearance of Pike.

10 ❑ Sep 1997 Cover: 1.99 **NM** value: **2.00**
Circ: Statement: **50,703** Diamd. preorders: **21,430**
• gatefold summary.

11 ❑ Oct 1997 Cover: 1.99 **NM** value: **2.00**
Circ: Diamd. preorders: **19,924**
• gatefold summary. • cadets on trial for going to Talos IV

12 ❑ Nov 1997 Cover: 1.99 **NM** value: **2.00**
Circ: Diamd. preorders: **20,083**
• gatefold summary. 📖 Telepathy War • Part 1; Crossover with ST: Deep Space Nine, ST: Telepathy War one-shot; ST Unlimited and ST: Voyager

13 ❑ Dec 1997 Cover: 1.99 **NM** value: **2.00**
Circ: Diamd. preorders: **18,705**
• gatefold summary. • Has 1997 Statement; avg total paid circ 50,703

14 ❑ Jan 1998 Cover: 1.99 **NM** value: **2.00**
Circ: Diamd. preorders: **18,291**
• gatefold summary. 📖 T'Priell Revealed • Part 1

15 ❑ Feb 1998 Cover: 1.99 **NM** value: **2.00**
Circ: Diamd. preorders: **17,912**
• gatefold summary. 📖 T'Priell Revealed • Part 2

16 ❑ Mar 1998 Cover: 1.99 **NM** value: **2.00**
Circ: Diamd. preorders: **17,449**
• gatefold summary. 📖 T'Priell Revealed • Part 3

17 ❑ Apr 1998 Cover: 1.99 **NM** value: **2.00**
Circ: Diamd. preorders: **16,557**
• gatefold summary.

18/A❑ May 1998 Cover: 1.99 **NM** value: **2.00**
Circ: Diamd. preorders: **15,495**
• English language edition. 📖 Cadet Challenge • English language edition

18/B❑ May 1998 Cover: 1.99 **NM** value: **2.00**
Circ: Diamd. preorders: **13,805**
• Klingon language edition. 📖 Cadet Challenge • Klingon language edition

19 ❑ Jun 1998 Cover: 1.99 **NM** value: **2.00**
• gatefold summary. 📖 Between Love and Hate final issue.

STAR TREK: TELEPATHY WAR — Marvel / Paramount

1 ❑ Nov 1997 Cover: 2.99 **NM** value: **Cover or less**
Circ: Diamd. preorders: **22,129**
One-shot. • concludes crossover between ST: Deep Space Nine, ST: Starfleet Academy; ST Unlimited and ST: Voyager

STAR TREK: THE MIRROR UNIVERSE SAGA — DC

Bk 1❑ Cover: 19.95 **NM** value: **Cover or less**
Circ: CapCity orders: **2,550**

STAR TREK-THE MODALA IMPERATIVE — DC

1 ❑ Jul 1991 Cover: 1.75 **NM** value: **2.50**
Circ: CapCity orders: **25,250**
📖 A Little Seasoning **A:** Pablo Marcos **W:** Michael Jan Friedman

2 ❑ Aug 1991 Cover: 1.75 **NM** value: **2.00**
Circ: CapCity orders: **20,600**
📖 Tools of Tyranny **A:** Pablo Marcos **W:** Michael Jan Friedman

3 ❑ Aug 1991 Cover: 1.75 **NM** value: **2.00**
Circ: CapCity orders: **20,450**
📖 The Price of Freedom **A:** Pablo Marcos **W:** Michael Jan Friedman

4 ❑ Sep 1991 Cover: 1.75 **NM** value: **2.00**
Circ: CapCity orders: **19,800**
📖 For Whom the Bell Tolls **A:** Pablo Marcos **W:** Michael Jan Friedman

Bk 1❑ Cover: 19.95 **NM** value: **Cover or less**
• Collects series, as well as Star Trek: The Next Generation-The Modala Imperative **A:** Pablo Marcos **W:** Michael Jan Friedman; Peter David

STAR TREK: THE NEXT GENERATION — DC

Inspired by the second Star Trek TV series, this series sent the characters on further adventures through time and space in the 23rd century. The stories hold true to the themes and lessons in the show, and the special effects, if anything, are bigger and better (since pen and ink costs considerably less than soundstages and sets). This was definitely a must-read both for Star Trek fans and for anyone who loves great fiction.

Paramount's licensing, while still strict, did allow writers and artists to build on the foundation established by the TV series.

1 ❑ Oct 1989 Cover: 1.50 **NM** value: **5.00**
Circ: CapCity orders: **32,050** • **CGC:** 3 graded, best 9.6
📖 Return to Raimon **A:** Pablo Marcos; Gordon Purcell **W:** John DeLancie

2 ❑ Nov 1989 Cover: 1.50 **NM** value: **4.00**
Circ: CapCity orders: **21,956**
📖 Murder, Most Foul

3 ❑ Dec 1989 Cover: 1.50 **NM** value: **3.00**
Circ: CapCity orders: **19,900**
📖 The Derelict

4 ❑ Jan 1990 Cover: 1.50 **NM** value: **3.00**
Circ: CapCity orders: **19,900**
📖 The Hero Factor

5 ❑ Feb 1990 Cover: 1.50 **NM** value: **3.00**
Circ: CapCity orders: **20,650**
📖 Serafin's Survivors

6 ❑ Mar 1990 Cover: 1.50 **NM** value: **2.50**
Circ: CapCity orders: **19,950**
📖 Shadows in the Garden

7 ❑ Apr 1990 Cover: 1.50 **NM** value: **2.50**
Circ: CapCity orders: **19,350**
📖 The Pilot

8 ❑ May 1990 Cover: 1.50 **NM** value: **2.50**
Circ: CapCity orders: **19,650**
📖 The Battle Within

9 ❑ Jun 1990 Cover: 1.50 **NM** value: **2.50**
Circ: CapCity orders: **19,000**
📖 The Pay Off!

10 ❑ Jul 1990 Cover: 1.50 **NM** value: **2.50**
Circ: CapCity orders: **18,850**
📖 The Noise of Justice

11 ❑ Aug 1990 Cover: 1.50 **NM** value: **2.50**
Circ: CapCity orders: **17,800**
📖 The Impostor

12 ❑ Sep 1990 Cover: 1.50 **NM** value: **2.50**
Circ: CapCity orders: **17,050**
📖 Whoever Fights Monsters

13 ❑ Oct 1990 Cover: 1.50 **NM** value: **2.50**
Circ: CapCity orders: **16,450**
📖 The Hand of the Assassin

14 ❑ Dec 1990 Cover: 1.50 **NM** value: **2.50**
Circ: CapCity orders: **16,650**
📖 Holiday on Ice **A:** Pablo Marcos **W:** Michael Jan Friedman

15 ❑ Jan 1991 Cover: 1.50 **NM** value: **2.50**
Circ: CapCity orders: **16,750**
📖 Prisoners of the Ferengi ★ Versus Ferengi.

16 ❑ Feb 1991 Cover: 1.50 **NM** value: **2.50**
Circ: CapCity orders: **16,700**

17 ❑ Mar 1991 Cover: 1.50 **NM** value: **2.50**
Circ: CapCity orders: **16,400**

18 ❑ Apr 1991 Cover: 1.50 **NM** value: **2.50**
Circ: CapCity orders: **15,800**
📖 Forbidden Fruit

19 ❑ May 1991 Cover: 1.50 **NM** value: **2.50**
Circ: CapCity orders: **16,000**
📖 The Lesson

20 ❑ Jun 1991 Cover: 1.50 **NM** value: **2.50**
Circ: CapCity orders: **15,800**
📖 The Flight of the Albert Einstein

21 ❑ Jul 1991 Cover: 1.75 **NM** value: **2.00**
Circ: CapCity orders: **16,350**
📖 Mourning Star

22 ❑ Aug 1991 Cover: 1.75 **NM** value: **2.00**
Circ: CapCity orders: **16,600**
📖 Trapped

23 ❑ Sep 1991 Cover: 1.75 **NM** value: **2.00**
Circ: CapCity orders: **16,900**
📖 The Barrier

24 ❑ Oct 1991 Cover: 2.50 **NM** value: **Cover or less**
Circ: CapCity orders: **17,000**
• double-sized. 📖 Homecoming • Double-sized 25th Anniversary issue

25 ❑ Nov 1991 Cover: 1.50 **NM** value: **2.00**
Circ: CapCity orders: **17,050**
• Giant-size. 📖 Wayward Son

26 ❑ Dec 1991 Cover: 1.50 **NM** value: **2.00**
Circ: CapCity orders: **17,700**
📖 Strangers in Strange Lands

27 ❑ Jan 1992 Cover: 1.50 **NM** value: **2.00**
Circ: CapCity orders: **17,900**
📖 City Life

28 ❑ Feb 1992 Cover: 1.50 **NM** value: **2.00**
Circ: CapCity orders: **17,950**
📖 The Remembered One • Return of K'ehleyr

29 ❑ Mar 1992 Cover: 1.50 **NM** value: **2.00**
Circ: CapCity orders: **17,950**
📖 Honorbound!

30 ❑ Apr 1992 Cover: 1.50 **NM** value: **2.00**
Circ: CapCity orders: **17,550**
📖 The Rift!

31 ❑ May 1992 Cover: 1.75 **NM** value: **2.00**
Circ: CapCity orders: **17,550**
📖 Kingdom of the Damned

32 ❑ Jun 1992 Cover: 1.75 **NM** value: **2.00**
Circ: CapCity orders: **17,950**
📖 Wet Behind the Ears

33 ❑ Jul 1992 Cover: 1.75 **NM** value: **2.00**
Circ: CapCity orders: **17,800**
📖 The Way of the Warrior • Q turns the crew into Klingons

34 ❑ Jul 1992 Cover: 1.75 **NM** value: **2.00**
Circ: CapCity orders: **17,800**
📖 Devil's Brew!

35 ❑ Aug 1992 Cover: 1.75 **NM** value: **2.00**
Circ: CapCity orders: **16,000**
📖 The Dogs of War

36 ❑ Aug 1992 Cover: 1.75 **NM** value: **2.00**
Circ: CapCity orders: **15,900**
📖 Shoreleave in Shanzibar! • Part 1

37 ❑ Sep 1992 Cover: 1.75 **NM** value: **2.00**
Circ: CapCity orders: **15,650**
📖 Consorting with the Devil! • Part 2

38 ❑ Sep 1992 Cover: 1.75 **NM** value: **2.00**
Circ: CapCity orders: **15,700**
📖 Dirty Work • Part 3

39 ❑ Oct 1992 Cover: 1.75 **NM** value: **2.00**
Circ: CapCity orders: **16,200**
📖 Bridges

40 ❑ Nov 1992 Cover: 1.75 **NM** value: **2.00**
Circ: CapCity orders: **16,000**
📖 Bone of Contention • Part 1

41 ❑ Dec 1992 Cover: 1.75 **NM** value: **2.00**
Circ: CapCity orders: **15,650**
📖 Separation Anxiety! • Part 2

42 ❑ Jan 1993 Cover: 1.75 **NM** value: **2.00**
Circ: CapCity orders: **15,600**
📖 Second Chances! • Part 3

43 ❑ Feb 1993 Cover: 1.75 **NM** value: **2.00**
Circ: CapCity orders: **16,350**
📖 Strange Bedfellows • Part 4

44 ❑ Mar 1993 Cover: 1.75 **NM** value: **2.00**
Circ: CapCity orders: **16,050**
📖 Restoration • Part 5

45 ❑ Apr 1993 Cover: 1.75 **NM** value: **2.00**
Circ: CapCity orders: **16,800**
📖 Childish Things

46 ❑ May 1993 Cover: 1.75 **NM** value: **2.00**
Circ: CapCity orders: **16,950**
📖 The Maze

47 ❑ Jun 1993 Cover: 1.75 **NM** value: **2.00**
Circ: CapCity orders: **17,400**
📖 The Bludgeonings of Chance! • Worst of Both Worlds, Part 1

CGC-graded: Multiply prices above by **33 for 9.9 M • 16 for 9.8 NM/M • 7 for 9.6 NM+ • 5 for 9.4 NM • 2.5 for 9.2 NM- • 1.5 for 9.0 VF/NM**

48 ❑ Jul 1993 Cover: 1.75 **NM** value: **2.00**
Circ: CapCity orders: **17,200**
📖 The Belly of the Beast! • Worst of Both Worlds, Part 2

49 ❑ Aug 1993 Cover: 1.75 **NM** value: **2.00**
Circ: CapCity orders: **17,400**
📖 The Armies of the Night • Worst of Both Worlds, Part 3

50 ❑ Sep 1993 Cover: 3.50 **NM** value: **Cover or less**
Circ: CapCity orders: **20,150**
• Giant-size. 📖 And Death Shall Have No Dominion • Worst of Both Worlds, Part 4; Double-sized issue

51 ❑ Oct 1993 Cover: 1.75 **NM** value: **2.00**
Circ: CapCity orders: **15,050**
📖 Life Signs

52 ❑ Oct 1993 Cover: 1.75 **NM** value: **2.00**
Circ: CapCity orders: **16,150**
📖 The Rich and the Dead! • Part 1; Dixon Hill story **A:** Pablo Marcos **W:** Michael Jan Friedman

53 ❑ Nov 1993 Cover: 1.75 **NM** value: **2.00**
Circ: CapCity orders: **16,350**
📖 Reductions and Deductions • Part 2

54 ❑ Nov 1993 Cover: 1.75 **NM** value: **2.00**
Circ: CapCity orders: **15,950**
📖 Hidden Agendas! • Part 3

55 ❑ Dec 1993 Cover: 1.75 **NM** value: **2.00**
Circ: CapCity orders: **16,750**
📖 The Good of the Many!

56 ❑ Jan 1994 Cover: 1.75 **NM** value: **2.00**
Circ: CapCity orders: **16,900**
📖 Companionship **A:** Deryl Skelton **W:** Michael Jan Friedman

57 ❑ Mar 1994 Cover: 1.75 **NM** value: **2.00**
Circ: CapCity orders: **16,350**
📖 Of Two Minds

58 ❑ Apr 1994 Cover: 1.75 **NM** value: **2.00**
Circ: CapCity orders: **15,800**
📖 Bodies of Evidence

59 ❑ May 1994 Cover: 1.75 **NM** value: **2.00**
Circ: CapCity orders: **15,250**
📖 Children of Chaos

60 ❑ Jun 1994 Cover: 1.75 **NM** value: **2.00**
Circ: CapCity orders: **15,150**
📖 Mother of Madness

61 ❑ Jul 1994 Cover: 1.95 **NM** value: **2.00**
Circ: CapCity orders: **15,250**
📖 Brothers in Darkness **A:** Deryl Skelton **W:** Michael Jan Friedman

62 ❑ Aug 1994 Cover: 1.95 **NM** value: **2.00**
Circ: CapCity orders: **15,150**
📖 The Victim

63 ❑ Sep 1994 Cover: 1.95 **NM** value: **2.00**
Circ: CapCity orders: **14,800**
📖 A Matter of Conscience

64 ❑ Oct 1994 Cover: 1.95 **NM** value: **2.00**
Circ: CapCity orders: **14,200**
📖 The Deceivers

65 ❑ Nov 1994 Cover: 1.95 **NM** value: **2.00**
Circ: CapCity orders: **13,700**
📖 The Truth Elusive

66 ❑ Dec 1994 Cover: 1.95 **NM** value: **2.00**
Circ: CapCity orders: **14,050**
📖 Just Desserts!

67 ❑ Jan 1995 Cover: 1.95 **NM** value: **2.00**
Circ: CapCity orders: **13,200**
📖 Friends and Other Strangers • Part 1 **A:** Deryl Skelton **W:** Michael Jan Friedman

68 ❑ Feb 1995 Cover: 1.95 **NM** value: **2.00**
Circ: CapCity orders: **17,900**
📖 The Bajoran and the Beast • Part 2

69 ❑ Mar 1995 Cover: 1.95 **NM** value: **2.00**
Circ: CapCity orders: **12,625**
📖 Dreams Die • Part 3

70 ❑ Apr 1995 Cover: 1.95 **NM** value: **2.00**
Circ: CapCity orders: **12,350**
• Part 4

71 ❑ May 1995 Cover: 1.95 **NM** value: **2.00**
Circ: CapCity orders: **12,250**

72 ❑ Jun 1995 Cover: 2.50 **NM** value: **Cover or less**
Circ: CapCity orders: **11,925**
• War and Madness, Part 1 **A:** Gordon Purcell **W:** Michael Jan Friedman

73 ❑ Jul 1995 Cover: 2.50 **NM** value: **Cover or less**
Circ: CapCity orders: **11,650**
• War and Madness, Part 2 **A:** Gordon Purcell **W:** Michael Jan Friedman

74 ❑ Aug 1995 Cover: 2.50 **NM** value: **Cover or less**
Circ: CapCity orders: **11,900**
📖 Ceremony of Innocence • War and Madness, Part 3 **A:** Gordon Purcell **W:** Michael Jan Friedman

75 ❑ Sep 1995 Cover: 3.95 **NM** value: **Cover or less**
Circ: CapCity orders: **12,400**
• Giant-size. 📖 Cry Havoc! • War and Madness, Part 4; Double-sized issue ★ Versus Borg.

76 ❑ Oct 1995 Cover: 2.50 **NM** value: **Cover or less**
Circ: CapCity orders: **9,600**

77 ❑ Nov 1995 Cover: 2.50 **NM** value: **Cover or less**
📖 Gateway

78 ❑ Dec 1995 Cover: 2.50 **NM** value: **Cover or less**
📖 The Unconquered

79 ❑ Jan 1996 Cover: 2.50 **NM** value: **Cover or less**
📖 Artificiality • Q transforms the crew into androids **A:** Gordon Purcell **W:** Michael Jan Friedman

80 ❑ Feb 1996 Cover: 2.50 **NM** value: **Cover or less**
📖 The Abandoned final issue. **A:** Gordon Purcell **W:** Michael Jan Friedman

Anl 1❑ca. 1990 Cover: 2.95 **NM** value: **3.50**
📖 The Gift • Q story written by deLancie; Stardate back-up feature (puts comics & books in conjunction with TV series); 1990 Annual **W:** John deLancie(Q)

Anl 2❑ca. 1991 Cover: 3.50 **NM** value: **Cover or less**
Circ: CapCity orders: **17,450**
📖 Thin Ice • 1991 Annual

Anl 3❑ca. 1992 Cover: 3.50 **NM** value: **Cover or less**
Circ: CapCity orders: **14,900**
📖 The Broken Moon! • 1992 Annual

Anl 4❑ca. 1993 Cover: 3.50 **NM** value: **Cover or less**
Circ: CapCity orders: **14,800**
📖 A House Divided • 1993 Annual

Anl 5❑ca. 1994 Cover: 3.95 **NM** value: **Cover or less**
Circ: CapCity orders: **12,150**
📖 Brother's Keeper • 1994 Annual **A:** Rachel Ketchum **W:** Howard Weinstein

Anl 6❑ca. 1995 Cover: 3.95 **NM** value: **Cover or less**
📖 Convergence • Part 2; continued from Star Trek Annual #6; 1995 Annual **A:** Ken Save **W:** Michael Jan Friedman

Bk 1❑ Cover: 14.95 **NM** value: **Cover or less**
• The Star Lost

Bk 2❑ Cover: 19.95 **NM** value: **Cover or less**
• Best of Star Trek: The Next Generation

SE 1❑ca. 1993 Cover: 3.50 **NM** value: **Cover or less**
Circ: CapCity orders: **17,500**
📖 Good Listener!; A True Son of Kahless; Spot's Day • 1993 Special

SE 2❑Sum 1994 Cover: 3.95 **NM** value: **Cover or less**
Circ: CapCity orders: **13,950**
📖 The Choice; Cry Vengeance; Out of Time • Captain Bateson of the Bozeman; 1994 Special

SE 3❑Win 1995 Cover: 3.95 **NM** value: **Cover or less**
Circ: CapCity orders: **8,925**
📖 Pandora's Prodigy; Old Debts • 1995 Special

STAR TREK: THE NEXT GENERATION/DEEP SPACE NINE — DC

1 ❑ Dec 1994 Cover: 2.50 **NM** value: **Cover or less**
Circ: CapCity orders: **23,150**
📖 Prophets and Losses • crossover with Malibu; Deep Space Nine/The Next Generation crossover, Part 1; Continues in Star Trek: Deep Space Nine/The Next Generation #1 **A:** Gordon Purcell **W:** Michael Jan Friedman; Mike W. Barr

2 ❑ Jan 1995 Cover: 2.50 **NM** value: **Cover or less**
Circ: CapCity orders: **16,600**
📖 The Enemy Unseen • crossover with Malibu; Deep Space Nine/The Next Generation crossover, Part 4; Continued from Star Trek: Deep Space Nine/The Next Generation #1; Continues in Star Trek: Deep Space Nine/The Next Generation #2 **A:** Gordon Purcell **W:** Michael Jan Friedman; Mike W. Barr

Ash 1❑ **NM** value: **1.00**
no cover price. • flip-book with Malibu's Deep Space Nine/Star Trek: The Next Generation Ashcan

STAR TREK: THE NEXT GENERATION-ILL WIND — DC

1 ❑ Nov 1995 Cover: 2.50 **NM** value: **Cover or less**
A: Deryl Skelton **W:** Diane Duane

2 ❑ Dec 1995 Cover: 2.50 **NM** value: **Cover or less**
A: Deryl Skelton **W:** Diane Duane

3 ❑ Jan 1996 Cover: 2.50 **NM** value: **Cover or less**
A: Deryl Skelton **W:** Diane Duane

4 ❑ Feb 1996 Cover: 2.50 **NM** value: **Cover or less**
A: Deryl Skelton **W:** Diane Duane

STAR TREK: THE NEXT GENERATION (MINI-SERIES) — DC

1 ❑ Feb 1988 Cover: 1.50 **NM** value: **3.00**
Circ: CapCity orders: **24,000** • **CGC:** 1 graded, best 9.6
📖 Where No One Has Gone Before **A:** Pablo Marcos **W:** Mike Carlin

2 ❑ Mar 1988 Cover: 1.00 **NM** value: **2.00**
Circ: CapCity orders: **19,850**
📖 Spirit in the Sky! **A:** Pablo Marcos **W:** Mike Carlin

3 ❑ Apr 1988 Cover: 1.00 **NM** value: **2.00**
Circ: CapCity orders: **18,350**
📖 Q Factor **A:** Pablo Marcos **W:** Mike Carlin

4 ❑ May 1988 Cover: 1.00 **NM** value: **2.00**
Circ: CapCity orders: **18,550**
📖 Q's Day **A:** Pablo Marcos **W:** Mike Carlin

5 ❑ Jun 1988 Cover: 1.00 **NM** value: **2.00**
Circ: CapCity orders: **16,850**
📖 Q Affects! **A:** Pablo Marcos **W:** Mike Carlin ★ Death of Geordi.

6 ❑ Jul 1988 Cover: 1.00 **NM** value: **2.00**
Circ: CapCity orders: **16,600**
📖 Here Today **A:** Pablo Marcos **W:** Mike Carlin

Bk 1❑ Cover: 19.95 **NM** value: **Cover or less**
• Beginnings

STAR TREK: THE NEXT GENERATION-PERCHANCE TO DREAM — DC / Wildstorm

1 ❑ Feb 2000 Cover: 2.50 **NM** value: **Cover or less**
Circ: Diamd. preorders: **20,030**
📖 To Take Arms Against a Sea of Troubles **A:** Peter Pachoumis **W:** Keith R.A. DeCandido

2 ❑ Mar 2000 Cover: 2.50 **NM** value: **Cover or less**
Circ: Diamd. preorders: **18,051**
📖 By a Sleep to Say We End **A:** Peter Pachoumis **W:** Keith R.A. DeCandido

3 ❑ Apr 2000 Cover: 2.50 **NM** value: **Cover or less**
Circ: Diamd. preorders: **15,774**
📖 In the Sleep of Death, What Dreams May Come **A:** Peter Pachoumis **W:** Keith R.A. DeCandido

4 ❑ May 2000 Cover: 2.50 **NM** value: **Cover or less**
Circ: Diamd. preorders: **15,093**
📖 Enterprises of Great Pitch and Moment **A:** Peter Pachoumis **W:** Keith R.A. DeCandido

STAR TREK: THE NEXT GENERATION: RIKER — Marvel / Paramount

1 ❑ Jul 1998 Cover: 3.50 **NM** value: **Cover or less**
One-shot. 📖 The Enemy of My Enemy

STAR TREK:THE NEXT GENERATION-SHADOWHEART — DC

1 ❑ Dec 1994 Cover: 1.95 **NM** value: **Cover or less**
Circ: CapCity orders: **18,950**
📖 The Lion and the Lamb **A:** Steve Erwin **W:** Michael Jan Friedman

2 ❑ Jan 1995 Cover: 1.95 **NM** value: **Cover or less**
Circ: CapCity orders: **13,650**
📖 Dealers in Darkness **A:** Steve Erwin **W:** Michael Jan Friedman

3 ❑ Feb 1995 Cover: 1.95 **NM** value: **Cover or less**
Circ: CapCity orders: **12,950**
📖 My Brother's Keeper **A:** Steve Erwin **W:** Michael Jan Friedman

4 ❑ Mar 1995 Cover: 1.95 **NM** value: **Cover or less**
Circ: CapCity orders: **12,325**
📖 The Prince of Madness **A:** Steve Erwin **W:** Michael Jan Friedman

STAR TREK: THE NEXT GENERATION-THE GORN CRISIS — DC / Wildstorm

1/HC❑ Cover: 29.95 **NM** value: **Cover or less**
A: Igor Kordey **W:** Kevin J. Anderson; Rebecca Moesta

STAR TREK: THE NEXT GENERATION-THE KILLING SHADOWS — DC / Wildstorm

1 ❑ Nov 2000 Cover: 2.50 **NM** value: **Cover or less**
Circ: Diamd. preorders: **13,001**
📖 The Trap **A:** Andrew Currie **W:** Scott Ciencin

2 ❑ Dec 2000 Cover: 2.50 **NM** value: **Cover or less**
Circ: Diamd. preorders: **11,996**
📖 The Hunted **A:** Andrew Currie **W:** Scott Ciencin

3 ❑ Jan 2001 Cover: 2.50 **NM** value: **Cover or less**
Circ: Diamd. preorders: **11,434**
📖 The Trap **A:** Andrew Currie **W:** Scott Ciencin

4 ❑ Feb 2001 Cover: 2.50 **NM** value: **Cover or less**
Circ: Diamd. preorders: **11,559**
📖 The Secret **A:** Andrew Currie **W:** Scott Ciencin

STAR TREK: THE NEXT GENERATION-THE SERIES FINALE — DC

1 ❑ ca. 1994 Cover: 3.95 **NM** value: **Cover or less**
Circ: CapCity orders: **18,950**
No issue number. • adapts final TV episode

STAR TREK: THE NEXT GENERATION/ X-MEN — Marvel

1 ❑ ca. 1998 Cover: 4.95 **NM** value: **Cover or less**
Circ: Diamd. preorders: **57,277**
A: Cary Nord **W:** Dan Abnett; Ian Edginton

1/SC❑ca. 1998 **NM** value: **8.00**
Cover has Wolverine, Data, Riker, Sentinel in background. **A:** Cary Nord **W:** Dan Abnett; Ian Edginton

STAR TREK UNLIMITED — Marvel / Paramount

1 ❑ Nov 1996 Cover: 2.99 **NM** value: **3.00**
Circ: Direct Market orders: **67,500**
📖 Directives; Dying of the Light • Original crew story; Next Generation story **A:** Jerome Moore; Carlos Garzon; Mark Buckingham; Ron Randall **W:** Dan Abnett; Ian Edginton

2 ❑ Jan 1997 Cover: 2.99 **NM** value: **3.00**
Circ: Direct Market orders: **53,500**
📖 Action of the Tiger; The Unkindest Cut • Original crew story; Next Generation story **A:** Mark Buckingham; Ron Randall **W:** Dan Abnett; Ian Edginton

3 ❑ Apr 1997 Cover: 2.99 **NM** value: **3.00**
Circ: Direct Market orders: **30,000**
• Original crew story; Next Generation story

4 ❑ May 1997 Cover: 2.99 **NM** value: **3.00**
Circ: Diamd. preorders: **27,269**
• Original crew story; Next Generation story; Original series and Next Generation stories crossover

5 ❑ Sep 1997 Cover: 2.99 **NM** value: **3.00**
Circ: Diamd. preorders: **21,162**
• Original series and Next Generation stories crossover; Original crew story; Next Generation story

6 ❑ Nov 1997 Cover: 2.99 **NM** value: **3.00**
Circ: Diamd. preorders: **20,737**
📖 Telepathy War • Part 4; Crossover with ST: Deep Space Nine, ST: Starfleet Academy, ST: Telepathy War one-shot and ST: Voyager;

7 ❑ Jan 1998 Cover: 2.99 **NM** value: **3.00**
Circ: Diamd. preorders: **19,623**

8 ❑ Mar 1998 Cover: 2.99 **NM** value: **3.00**
Circ: Diamd. preorders: **18,625**
• Kang vs. Sulu

9 ❑ May 1998 Cover: 2.99 **NM** value: **3.00**
Circ: Diamd. preorders: **17,641**
• Chekov wins a Klingon cruiser

10 ❑ Jul 1998 Cover: 2.99 **NM** value: **3.00**
Circ: Diamd. preorders: **17,722**
📖 A Piece of Reaction

STAR TREK: UNTOLD VOYAGES — Marvel / Paramount

1 ❑ Mar 1998 Cover: 2.50 **NM** value: **Cover or less**
Circ: Diamd. preorders: **20,204**
📖 Renewal **A:** Mike Collins **W:** Glenn Greenberg

2 ❑ Apr 1998 Cover: 2.50 **NM** value: **Cover or less**
Circ: Diamd. preorders: **17,467**
★ Appearance of Saavik.

3 ❑ May 1998 Cover: 2.50 **NM** value: **Cover or less**
Circ: Diamd. preorders: **17,041**
★ Appearance of Onlies.

4 ❑ Jun 1998 Cover: 2.50 **NM** value: **Cover or less**
Circ: Diamd. preorders: **17,403**
• Sulu takes command

5 ❑ Jul 1998 Cover: 3.50 **NM** value: **Cover or less**
Circ: Diamd. preorders: **16,648**
final issue.

STAR TREK VI: THE UNDISCOVERED COUNTRY
DC

1 ❑ ca. 1992 Cover: 2.95 **NM** value: **Cover or less**
The Undiscovered Country. • Movie adaptation; Newsstand edition
1/DM❑ca. 1992 Cover: 5.95 **NM** value: **Cover or less**
The Undiscovered Country. • prestige format. • Movie adaptation

STAR TREK: VOYAGER **Marvel / Paramount**
1 ❑ Nov 1996 Cover: 1.95 **NM** value: **2.00**
Circ: Statement: **56,869** Direct Market orders: **69,000**
A: Jesus Redondo **W:** Laurie Sutton
2 ❑ Dec 1996 Cover: 1.95 **NM** value: **2.00**
Circ: Statement: **56,869** Direct Market orders: **38,250**
📖 Under Ion Skies **A:** Jesus Redondo **W:** Laurie Sutton
3 ❑ Jan 1997 Cover: 1.99 **NM** value: **2.00**
Circ: Statement: **56,869** Direct Market orders: **36,500**
📖 Repercussions **A:** Jesus Redondo **W:** Laurie Sutton
4 ❑ Feb 1997 Cover: 1.99 **NM** value: **2.00**
Circ: Statement: **56,869** Direct Market orders: **33,750**
📖 Homeostasis • Part 1 **A:** Jesus Redondo **W:** Howard Weinstein
5 ❑ Mar 1997 Cover: 1.99 **NM** value: **2.00**
Circ: Statement: **56,869** Direct Market orders: **31,000**
📖 Homeostasis • Part 2 **A:** Jesus Redondo **W:** Howard Weinstein
6 ❑ Apr 1997 Cover: 1.99 **NM** value: **2.00**
Circ: Statement: **56,869** Direct Market orders: **29,000**
📖 RelicQuest • Part 1 **A:** Jesus Redondo **W:** Ben Raab
7 ❑ May 1997 Cover: 1.99 **NM** value: **2.00**
Circ: Statement: **56,869** Diamd. preorders: **27,837**
📖 RelicQuest • Part 2 **A:** Jesus Redondo **W:** Ben Raab
8 ❑ Jun 1997 Cover: 1.99 **NM** value: **2.00**
Circ: Statement: **56,869** Diamd. preorders: **26,709**
9 ❑ Sep 1997 Cover: 1.99 **NM** value: **2.00**
Circ: Statement: **56,869** Diamd. preorders: **20,808**
• gatefold summary.
10 ❑ Oct 1997 Cover: 1.99 **NM** value: **2.00**
Circ: Statement: **56,869** Diamd. preorders: **20,663**
• gatefold summary. • replays events at Wolf 359
11 ❑ Nov 1997 Cover: 1.99 **NM** value: **2.00**
Circ: Diamd. preorders: **19,921**
• gatefold summary. ★ Versus Leviathan.
12 ❑ Dec 1997 Cover: 1.99 **NM** value: **2.00**
Circ: Diamd. preorders: **19,177**
• gatefold summary.
13 ❑ Jan 1998 Cover: 1.99 **NM** value: **2.00**
Circ: Diamd. preorders: **19,032**
• gatefold summary. 📖 Telepathy War • Part 5; Crossover with ST: Deep Space Nine, ST: Starfleet Academy, ST: Telepathy War one-shot and ST Unlimited; Has 1997 Statement; avg total paid circ 56,869
14 ❑ Feb 1998 Cover: 1.99 **NM** value: **2.00**
Circ: Diamd. preorders: **18,639**
• gatefold summary. ★ 1st Appearance of Seven of Nine.
15 ❑ Mar 1998 Cover: 1.99 **NM** value: **2.00**
Circ: Diamd. preorders: **18,307**
• gatefold summary. final issue.

STAR TREK: VOYAGER-FALSE COLORS
DC / Wildstorm

1 ❑ Jan 2000 Cover: 5.95 **NM** value: **Cover or less**
A: Jeffrey Moy **W:** Nathan Archer

STAR TREK: VOYAGER: SPLASHDOWN
Marvel / Paramount

1 ❑ Apr 1998 Cover: 2.50 **NM** value: **Cover or less**
Circ: Diamd. preorders: **19,636**
• gatefold summary. **A:** Terry Pallot **W:** Laurie Sutton
2 ❑ May 1998 Cover: 2.50 **NM** value: **Cover or less**
Circ: Diamd. preorders: **17,520**
• gatefold summary. **A:** Terry Pallot **W:** Laurie Sutton
3 ❑ Jun 1998 Cover: 2.50 **NM** value: **Cover or less**
Circ: Diamd. preorders: **17,078**
• gatefold summary. **A:** Terry Pallot **W:** Laurie Sutton
4 ❑ Jul 1998 Cover: 2.50 **NM** value: **Cover or less**
Circ: Diamd. preorders: **17,205**
• gatefold summary. • final Marvel Star Trek comic book **A:** Terry Pallot **W:** Laurie Sutton

STAR TREK: VOYAGER-THE PLANET KILLER
DC / Wildstorm

1 ❑ Mar 2001 Cover: 2.95 **NM** value: **Cover or less**
Circ: Diamd. preorders: **11,689**
📖 Ultimate Weapon **A:** Robert Teranishi **W:** Dean Wesley Smith; Kristine Katherine Busch
2 ❑ Apr 2001 Cover: 2.95 **NM** value: **Cover or less**
Circ: Diamd. preorders: **11,007**
📖 Old Tricks **A:** Robert Teranishi **W:** Dean Wesley Smith; Kristine Katherine Busch
3 ❑ May 2001 Cover: 2.95 **NM** value: **Cover or less**
Circ: Diamd. preorders: **10,818**
📖 Death **A:** Robert Teranishi **W:** Dean Wesley Smith; Kristine Katherine Busch

STAR TREK/X-MEN **Marvel / Paramount**
1 ❑ Dec 1996 Cover: 4.95 **NM** value: **5.00**
• **CGC:** 1 graded, best 9.6
One-shot. 📖 Star Trex • X-Men meet original Enterprise crew **A:** David Finch; Brian Ching; Billy Tan; Marc Silvestri; Anthony Winn **W:** Scott Lobdell

STAR TREK/X-MEN: SECOND CONTACT
Marvel / Paramount

1 ❑ May 1998 Cover: 4.99 **NM** value: **5.00**
One-shot. 📖 Second Contact • X-Men meet Next Generation crew; Sentinels; continues in Star Trek: The Next Generation/X-Men: Planet X novel ★ Appearance of Kang.

STAR WARS **Marvel**
The long connection between Star Wars and comics began in the mid-1970s, when Marvel Editor Roy Thomas made the acquaintance of director George Lucas, a fan of Carl Barks' Uncle Scrooge comics. Lucas later conveyed his interest in Thomas producing an adaptation of his new film, yet an unknown quantity, for Marvel. An unprecedented six-issue presentation was planned.

The rest is history. Issues of #1-6 were reprinted heavily in bagged editions, and a test-marketed 35-cent edition of #1 became one of the holy grails of 1970s comics. Marvel continued with its own stories, including distinguished runs by writers Archie Goodwin and David Michelinie. Marvel's Empire Strikes Back adaptation took place in #39-44.

Readers lost interest after Return of the Jedi was released, and Marvel let the license go. Unlike Marvel's series, that of Dark Horse would be regarded as "canonical" by Lucasfilm, giving them an added cachet. But many consider the Marvel series to include some of the best comics stories featuring Star Wars characters. For a time, they were, after all, the only place to read more about them. — JJM

1 ❑ Jul 1977 Cover: 0.30 **NM** value: **25.00**
• **CGC:** 413 graded, best 9.8
📖 Star Wars, Part 1 **A:** Howard Chaykin **W:** Roy Thomas
1/A ❑ Jul 1977 Cover: 0.35 **NM** value: **250.00**
• **CGC:** 11 graded, best 8.5
📖 Star Wars, Part 1 • 35 cent variation; Rare variation; Price is in a square area, and UPC code appears with a line drawn through it **A:** Howard Chaykin **W:** Roy Thomas
1-2 ❑ Cover: 0.30 **NM** value: **4.00**
• **CGC:** 1 graded, best 8.0
2 ❑ Aug 1977 Cover: 0.30 **NM** value: **15.00**
• **CGC:** 23 graded, best 9.8
📖 Star Wars, Part 2: Six Against the Galaxy **A:** Howard Chaykin **W:** Roy Thomas
2-2 ❑ Cover: 0.35 **NM** value: **3.50**
3 ❑ Sep 1977 Cover: 0.30 **NM** value: **15.00**
• **CGC:** 15 graded, best 9.6
📖 Star Wars, Part 3: Death Star! **A:** Howard Chaykin **W:** Roy Thomas
3-2 ❑ Cover: 0.35 **NM** value: **3.50**
4 ❑ Oct 1977 Cover: 0.30 **NM** value: **15.00**
• **CGC:** 17 graded, best 9.6
📖 Star Wars, Part 4: In Battle with Darth Vader • low distribution **A:** Howard Chaykin **W:** Roy Thomas
4-2 ❑ Cover: 0.35 **NM** value: **3.50**
5 ❑ Nov 1977 Cover: 0.35 **NM** value: **15.00**
• **CGC:** 6 graded, best 9.8
📖 Star Wars, Part 5: Lo, the Moons of Yavin! **A:** Howard Chaykin; Steve Leialoha **W:** Roy Thomas
5-2 ❑ Cover: 0.35 **NM** value: **3.50**
6 ❑ Dec 1977 Cover: 0.35 **NM** value: **15.00**
• **CGC:** 6 graded, best 9.4
📖 Star Wars, Part 6: The Final Chapter? **A:** Howard Chaykin **W:** Roy Thomas
6-2 ❑ Cover: 0.35 **NM** value: **3.50**
7 ❑ Jan 1978 Cover: 0.35 **NM** value: **12.00**
• **CGC:** 6 graded, best 9.6
📖 New Planets, New Perils! **A:** Howard Chaykin **W:** Roy Thomas
7-2 ❑ Cover: 0.35 **NM** value: **3.00**
8 ❑ Feb 1978 Cover: 0.35 **NM** value: **12.00**
• **CGC:** 7 graded, best 9.6
📖 Eight For Aduba-3 **A:** Howard Chaykin **W:** Roy Thomas
8-2 ❑ Cover: 0.35 **NM** value: **3.00**
9 ❑ Mar 1978 Cover: 0.35 **NM** value: **12.00**
• **CGC:** 4 graded, best 9.4
📖 Showdown On A Wasteland World! **A:** Howard Chaykin **W:** Roy Thomas
9-2 ❑ Cover: 0.35 **NM** value: **3.00**
10 ❑ Apr 1978 Cover: 0.35 **NM** value: **8.00**
• **CGC:** 3 graded, best 9.4
📖 Behemoth From The World Below **A:** Alan Kupperberg; Howard Chaykin **W:** Don Glut
11 ❑ May 1978 Cover: 0.35 **NM** value: **7.00**
📖 Star Search!
12 ❑ Jun 1978 Cover: 0.35 **NM** value: **7.00**
• **CGC:** 1 graded, best 9.6
📖 Doomworld!
13 ❑ Jul 1978 Cover: 0.35 **NM** value: **7.00**
• **CGC:** 5 graded, best 9.6
📖 Day of the Dragon Lords! **A:** Carmine Infantino
14 ❑ Aug 1978 Cover: 0.35 **NM** value: **7.00**
• **CGC:** 5 graded, best 9.4
📖 The Sound Of Armageddon! **A:** Carmine Infantino; Terry Austin **W:** Archie Goodwin
15 ❑ Sep 1978 Cover: 0.35 **NM** value: **7.00**
• **CGC:** 3 graded, best 9.6
📖 Star Duel! **A:** Carmine Infantino; Terry Austin **W:** Archie Goodwin ★ Death of Crimson Jack.
16 ❑ Oct 1978 Cover: 0.35 **NM** value: **7.00**
• **CGC:** 3 graded, best 9.4
📖 The Hunter ★ 1st Appearance of Valance the bounty hunter.
17 ❑ Nov 1978 Cover: 0.35 **NM** value: **7.00**
• **CGC:** 1 graded, best 9.4
📖 Crucible! • low distribution; Tatooine adventure set before first movie **A:** Al Milgrom; Herb Trimpe **W:** Archie Goodwin; Chris Claremont
18 ❑ Dec 1978 Cover: 0.35 **NM** value: **7.00**
• **CGC:** 4 graded, best 9.6
📖 The Empire Strikes • low distribution
19 ❑ Jan 1979 Cover: 0.35 **NM** value: **7.00**
Circ: Statement: **278,759** • **CGC:** 1 graded, best 9.0
📖 The Ultimate Gamble! • low distribution **A:** Carmine Infantino; Bob Wiacek **W:** Archie Goodwin
20 ❑ Feb 1979 Cover: 0.35 **NM** value: **7.00**
Circ: Statement: **278,759** • **CGC:** 2 graded, best 9.6
📖 Deathgame **A:** Carmine Infantino; Bob Wiacek **W:** Archie Goodwin
21 ❑ Mar 1979 Cover: 0.35 **NM** value: **5.00**
Circ: Statement: **278,759** • **CGC:** 1 graded, best 9.6
📖 Shadow of a Dark Lord
22 ❑ Apr 1979 Cover: 0.35 **NM** value: **5.00**
Circ: Statement: **278,759**
📖 To the Last Gladiator!
23 ❑ May 1979 Cover: 0.40 **NM** value: **5.00**
Circ: Statement: **278,759** • **CGC:** 5 graded, best 9.6
📖 Flight Into Fury! **A:** Carmine Infantino; Bob Wiacek **W:** Archie Goodwin
24 ❑ Jun 1979 Cover: 0.40 **NM** value: **5.00**
Circ: Statement: **278,759** • **CGC:** 8 graded, best 9.6
📖 Silent Drifting • flashback to before first movie **A:** Carmine Infantino; Bob Wiacek **W:** Mary Jo Duffy
25 ❑ Jul 1979 Cover: 0.40 **NM** value: **5.00**
Circ: Statement: **278,759** • **CGC:** 1 graded, best 9.6
📖 Seige at Yavin!
26 ❑ Aug 1979 Cover: 0.40 **NM** value: **5.00**
Circ: Statement: **278,759** • **CGC:** 1 graded, best 9.8
📖 Doom Mission!
27 ❑ Sep 1979 Cover: 0.40 **NM** value: **5.00**
Circ: Statement: **278,759** • **CGC:** 1 graded, best 9.6
📖 Return Of The Hunter **A:** Carmine Infantino; Bob Wiacek **W:** Archie Goodwin
28 ❑ Oct 1979 Cover: 0.40 **NM** value: **5.00**
Circ: Statement: **278,759** • **CGC:** 12 graded, best 9.6
📖 What Ever Happened To Jabba The Hut **A:** Carmine Infantino; Bob Wiacek **W:** Archie Goodwin ★ Appearance of Jabba the Hutt (not movie version).
29 ❑ Nov 1979 Cover: 0.40 **NM** value: **5.00**
Circ: Statement: **278,759** • **CGC:** 2 graded, best 9.8
📖 Dark Encounter **A:** Carmine Infantino; Bob Wiacek **W:** Archie Goodwin ★ Appearance of Darth Vader.
30 ❑ Dec 1979 Cover: 0.40 **NM** value: **5.00**
Circ: Statement: **278,759**
📖 A Princess Alone! **A:** Carmine Infantino; Gene Day **W:** Archie Goodwin
31 ❑ Jan 1980 Cover: 0.40 **NM** value: **4.00**
Circ: Statement: **255,985**
📖 Return To Tatooine! • return to Tatooine **A:** Carmine Infantino; Bob Wiacek **W:** Archie Goodwin
32 ❑ Feb 1980 Cover: 0.40 **NM** value: **4.00**
Circ: Statement: **255,985**
📖 The Jawa Express **A:** Carmine Infantino; Bob Wiacek **W:** Archie Goodwin
33 ❑ Mar 1980 Cover: 0.40 **NM** value: **4.00**
Circ: Statement: **255,985**
📖 Saber Clash! • Has 1979 Statement, filed 10/1/79; avg print run 497,018; avg sales 255,590; avg subs 23,169; avg total paid 278,759; samples 615; office use 2,095; max existent 281,469; 43% of run returned **A:** Carmine Infantino; Gene Day **W:** Archie Goodwin
34 ❑ Apr 1980 Cover: 0.40 **NM** value: **4.00**
Circ: Statement: **255,985**
📖 Thunder in the Stars ★ Death of Baron Tagge.
35 ❑ May 1980 Cover: 0.40 **NM** value: **4.00**
Circ: Statement: **255,985**
📖 Dark Lord's Gambit ★ Appearance of Darth Vader, Luke Skywalker.
36 ❑ Jun 1980 Cover: 0.40 **NM** value: **4.00**
Circ: Statement: **255,985** • **CGC:** 1 graded, best 9.6
📖 Red Queen Rising!
37 ❑ Jul 1980 Cover: 0.40 **NM** value: **4.00**
Circ: Statement: **255,985**
📖 In Mortal Combat! • 1st Vader/Luke duel **A:** Carmine Infantino; Gene Day **W:** Archie Goodwin
38 ❑ Aug 1980 Cover: 0.40 **NM** value: **4.00**
Circ: Statement: **255,985**
📖 Rider in the Void! • living spaceship **A:** Michael Golden; Terry Austin
39 ❑ Sep 1980 Cover: 0.50 **NM** value: **4.00**
Circ: Statement: **255,985** • **CGC:** 7 graded, best 9.8
📖 Empire Strikes Back; The Empire Strikes Back, Part 1 • movie adaptation **A:** Al Williamson
40 ❑ Oct 1980 Cover: 0.50 **NM** value: **4.00**
Circ: Statement: **255,985** • **CGC:** 5 graded, best 9.6
📖 Empire Strikes Back; The Empire Strikes Back, Part 2: Battleground Hoth • movie adaptation **A:** Al Williamson
41 ❑ Nov 1980 Cover: 0.50 **NM** value: **4.00**
Circ: Statement: **255,985** • **CGC:** 5 graded, best 9.6
📖 Empire Strikes Back; The Empire Strikes Back, Part 3: Imperial Persuit • movie adaptation **A:** Al Williamson
42 ❑ Dec 1980 Cover: 0.50 **NM** value: **4.00**
Circ: Statement: **255,985** • **CGC:** 13 graded, best 9.8
📖 Empire Strikes Back; The Empire Strikes Back, Part 4: To Be a Jedi! • movie adaptation **A:** Al Williamson
43 ❑ Jan 1981 Cover: 0.50 **NM** value: **4.00**
Circ: Statement: **229,901** • **CGC:** 1 graded, best 9.6
📖 Empire Strikes Back; The Empire Strikes Back, Part 5: Betrayal at Bespin • movie adaptation **A:** Al Williamson
44 ❑ Feb 1981 Cover: 0.50 **NM** value: **4.00**
Circ: Statement: **229,901** • **CGC:** 4 graded, best 9.8
📖 Empire Strikes Back; The Empire Strikes Back, Part 6: Duel a Dark Lord • movie adaptation **A:** Al Williamson
45 ❑ Mar 1981 Cover: 0.50 **NM** value: **3.00**
Circ: Statement: **229,901**
📖 Death Probe • first post-Empire Strikes Back story
46 ❑ Apr 1981 Cover: 0.50 **NM** value: **3.00**
Circ: Statement: **229,901**

CGC-graded: Multiply prices above by **33 for 9.9 M • 16 for 9.8 NM/M • 7 for 9.6 NM+ • 5 for 9.4 NM • 2.5 for 9.2 NM- • 1.5 for 9.0 VF/NM**

📖 The Dreams of Cody Sunn-Childe! • Has 1980 Statement, filed 10/1/80; avg print run 484,446; avg sales 230,308; avg subs 25,677; avg total paid 255,985; samples 620; office use 7,267; max existent 263,872; 46% of run returned

47 ❑ May 1981 Cover: 0.50 **NM** value: **3.00**
Circ: Statement: **229,901**
📖 Droid World! **A:** Frank Miller(cover)

48 ❑ Jun 1981 Cover: 0.50 **NM** value: **3.00**
Circ: Statement: **229,901**
📖 The Third Law

49 ❑ Jul 1981 Cover: 0.50 **NM** value: **3.00**
Circ: Statement: **229,901**
📖 The Last Jedi! • low distribution

50 ❑ Aug 1981 Cover: 0.75 **NM** value: **3.00**
Circ: Statement: **229,901** • **CGC:** 6 graded, best 9.6
• double-sized. 📖 The Crimson Forever! **A:** Al Williamson; Tom Palmer; Walt Simonson

51 ❑ Sep 1981 Cover: 0.50 **NM** value: **3.00**
Circ: Statement: **229,901**
📖 Resurrection of Evil ★ Appearance of Tarkin, Star II appearance, Star II appearance.

52 ❑ Oct 1981 Cover: 0.50 **NM** value: **3.00**
Circ: Statement: **229,901**
📖 To Take the Tarkin ★ Appearance of Tarkin, Star II appearance, Star II appearance.

53 ❑ Nov 1981 Cover: 0.50 **NM** value: **3.00**
Circ: Statement: **229,901**
📖 The Last Gift from Alderaan

54 ❑ Dec 1981 Cover: 0.50 **NM** value: **3.00**
Circ: Statement: **229,901**
📖 Starfire Rising!

55 ❑ Jan 1982 Cover: 0.60 **NM** value: **3.00**
Circ: Statement: **205,179**
📖 Plif!

56 ❑ Feb 1982 Cover: 0.60 **NM** value: **3.00**
Circ: Statement: **205,179**
📖 Coffin in the Clouds

57 ❑ Mar 1982 Cover: 0.60 **NM** value: **3.00**
Circ: Statement: **205,179** • **CGC:** 2 graded, best 9.2
📖 Hello, Bespin, Good-Bye!

58 ❑ Apr 1982 Cover: 0.60 **NM** value: **3.00**
Circ: Statement: **205,179**
📖 Sundown • Return to Cloud City; Has 1981 Statement, filed 10/1/81; avg print run 455,651; avg sales 209,023; avg subs 20,876; avg total paid 229,901; samples 627; office use 4,353; max existent 234,879; 49% of run returned

59 ❑ May 1982 Cover: 0.60 **NM** value: **3.00**
Circ: Statement: **205,179**
📖 Bazarre

60 ❑ Jun 1982 Cover: 0.60 **NM** value: **3.00**
Circ: Statement: **205,179**
📖 Shira's Story

61 ❑ Jul 1982 Cover: 0.60 **NM** value: **3.00**
Circ: Statement: **205,179**
📖 Screams in the Void

62 ❑ Aug 1982 Cover: 0.60 **NM** value: **3.00**
Circ: Statement: **205,179**
📖 Pariah! • Luke kicked out of Alliance

63 ❑ Sep 1982 Cover: 0.60 **NM** value: **3.00**
Circ: Statement: **205,179** • **CGC:** 2 graded, best 9.4
📖 The Mind Spider!

64 ❑ Oct 1982 Cover: 0.60 **NM** value: **3.00**
Circ: Statement: **205,179**
📖 Serphidian Eyes **A:** Brent Anderson(cover)

65 ❑ Nov 1982 Cover: 0.60 **NM** value: **3.00**
Circ: Statement: **205,179**
📖 Golrath Never Forgets!

66 ❑ Dec 1982 Cover: 0.60 **NM** value: **3.00**
Circ: Statement: **205,179**
📖 The Water Bandits!

67 ❑ Jan 1983 Cover: 0.60 **NM** value: **3.00**
Circ: Statement: **180,213**
📖 The Darker

68 ❑ Feb 1983 Cover: 0.60 **NM** value: **3.00**
Circ: Statement: **180,213** • **CGC:** 8 graded, best 9.4
📖 The Search Begins

69 ❑ Mar 1983 Cover: 0.60 **NM** value: **3.00**
Circ: Statement: **180,213**
📖 Death in the City of Bone

70 ❑ Apr 1983 Cover: 0.60 **NM** value: **3.00**
Circ: Statement: **180,213**
📖 The Stenax Shuffle • Has 1982 Statement, filed 10/11/82; avg print run 447,075; avg sales 173,285; avg subs 31,894; avg total paid 205,179; samples 719; office use 5,211; max existent 211,109; 53% of run returned

71 ❑ May 1983 Cover: 0.60 **NM** value: **3.00**
Circ: Statement: **180,213**
📖 Return to Stenos

72 ❑ Jun 1983 Cover: 0.60 **NM** value: **3.00**
Circ: Statement: **180,213**
📖 Fool's Bounty

73 ❑ Jul 1983 Cover: 0.60 **NM** value: **3.00**
Circ: Statement: **180,213**
📖 Lahsbane

74 ❑ Aug 1983 Cover: 0.60 **NM** value: **3.00**
Circ: Statement: **180,213**
📖 The Iskalon Effect

75 ❑ Sep 1983 Cover: 0.60 **NM** value: **3.00**
Circ: Statement: **180,213**
📖 Tidal

76 ❑ Oct 1983 Cover: 0.60 **NM** value: **3.00**
Circ: Statement: **180,213**
📖 Artoo-Detoo to the Rescue

77 ❑ Nov 1983 Cover: 0.60 **NM** value: **3.00**
Circ: Statement: **180,213**
📖 Chanteuse of the Stars

78 ❑ Dec 1983 Cover: 0.60 **NM** value: **3.00**
Circ: Statement: **180,213** • **CGC:** 1 graded, best 9.4
📖 Hoth Stuff!

79 ❑ Jan 1984 Cover: 0.60 **NM** value: **3.00**
Circ: Statement: **179,917**
📖 The Big Con

80 ❑ Feb 1984 Cover: 0.60 **NM** value: **3.00**
Circ: Statement: **179,917**
📖 Ellie

81 ❑ Mar 1984 Cover: 0.60 **NM** value: **3.00**
Circ: Statement: **179,917** • **CGC:** 1 graded, best 9.4
Photo cover. 📖 Jawas of Doom • first post-Return of the Jedi story

82 ❑ Apr 1984 Cover: 0.60 **NM** value: **3.00**
Circ: Statement: **179,917**
📖 Diplomacy • Has 1983 Statement, filed 10/6/83; avg print run 389,772; avg sales 142,681; avg subs 37,532; avg total paid 180,213; samples 784; office use 6,855; max existent 187,852; 52% of run returned

83 ❑ May 1984 Cover: 0.60 **NM** value: **3.00**
Circ: Statement: **179,917**
📖 Sweetheart Contract

84 ❑ Jun 1984 Cover: 0.60 **NM** value: **3.00**
Circ: Statement: **179,917**
📖 Seoul Searching

85 ❑ Jul 1984 Cover: 0.60 **NM** value: **3.00**
Circ: Statement: **179,917**
📖 The Hero

86 ❑ Aug 1984 Cover: 0.60 **NM** value: **3.00**
Circ: Statement: **179,917**
📖 The Alderaan Factor

87 ❑ Sep 1984 Cover: 0.60 **NM** value: **3.00**
Circ: Statement: **179,917**
📖 Still Active after All These Years

88 ❑ Oct 1984 Cover: 0.60 **NM** value: **3.00**
Circ: Statement: **179,917**
📖 Figurehead

89 ❑ Nov 1984 Cover: 0.60 **NM** value: **3.00**
Circ: Statement: **179,917**
📖 I'll See You in the Throne Room

90 ❑ Dec 1984 Cover: 0.60 **NM** value: **3.00**
Circ: Statement: **179,917**
📖 The Choice

91 ❑ Jan 1985 Cover: 0.60 **NM** value: **3.00**
Circ: Statement: **141,489** • **CGC:** 1 graded, best 9.2
📖 Wookiee World

92 ❑ Feb 1985 Cover: 1.00 **NM** value: **3.00**
Circ: Statement: **141,489** • **CGC:** 1 graded, best 8.5
• Giant-size. 📖 The Dream

93 ❑ Mar 1985 Cover: 0.60 **NM** value: **3.00**
Circ: Statement: **141,489** • **CGC:** 1 graded, best 9.0
📖 Catspaw

94 ❑ Apr 1985 Cover: 0.65 **NM** value: **3.00**
Circ: Statement: **141,489**
📖 Small Wars • Has 1984 Statement, filed 9/28/84; avg print run 343,390; avg sales 144,451; avg subs 35,466; avg total paid 179,917; samples 859; office use 4,177; max existent 184,953; 46% of run returned

95 ❑ May 1985 Cover: 0.65 **NM** value: **3.00**
Circ: Statement: **141,489** CapCity orders: **7,700**
📖 No Zeltrons

96 ❑ Jun 1985 Cover: 0.65 **NM** value: **3.00**
Circ: Statement: **141,489** CapCity orders: **7,800**
📖 Duel with a Dark Lady

97 ❑ Jul 1985 Cover: 0.65 **NM** value: **3.00**
Circ: Statement: **141,489** CapCity orders: **8,600** • **CGC:** 1 graded, best 9.4
📖 Escape

98 ❑ Aug 1985 Cover: 0.65 **NM** value: **3.00**
Circ: Statement: **141,489** CapCity orders: **8,600** • **CGC:** 1 graded, best 9.4
📖 Supply and Demand

99 ❑ Sep 1985 Cover: 0.65 **NM** value: **3.00**
Circ: Statement: **141,489** CapCity orders: **7,900** • **CGC:** 2 graded, best 9.4
📖 Touch of the Goddess

100 ❑ Oct 1985 Cover: 1.25 **NM** value: **3.00**
Circ: Statement: **141,489** CapCity orders: **9,800** • **CGC:** 4 graded, best 9.4
• Giant-size. 📖 First Strike

101 ❑ Nov 1985 Cover: 0.65 **NM** value: **3.00**
Circ: Statement: **141,489** CapCity orders: **7,900**
📖 Far, Far Away

102 ❑ Dec 1985 Cover: 0.65 **NM** value: **3.00**
Circ: Statement: **141,489** CapCity orders: **7,600** • **CGC:** 1 graded, best 9.4
📖 School Spirit

103 ❑ Jan 1986 Cover: 0.65 **NM** value: **3.00**
Circ: CapCity orders: **7,500** • **CGC:** 3 graded, best 9.6
📖 Tai

104 ❑ Mar 1986 Cover: 0.75 **NM** value: **3.00**
Circ: CapCity orders: **7,200** • **CGC:** 1 graded, best 9.0
📖 Nagais and Dolls

105 ❑ May 1986 Cover: 0.75 **NM** value: **3.00**
Circ: CapCity orders: **7,300**
📖 The Party's Over • Has 1985 Statement, filed 10/1/85; avg print run 303,029; avg sales 117,881; avg subs 23,208; avg total paid 141,489; samples 877; office use 813; max existent 142,779; 53% of run returned

106 ❑ Jul 1986 Cover: 0.75 **NM** value: **3.00**
Circ: CapCity orders: **7,200** • **CGC:** 3 graded, best 9.4
📖 My Hiromi

107 ❑ Sep 1986 Cover: 0.75 **NM** value: **25.00**
Circ: CapCity orders: **7,000** • **CGC:** 62 graded, best 9.6
📖 All Together Now final issue. **W:** Whilce Portacio

Anl 1 ❑ Dec 1979 Cover: 0.75 **NM** value: **8.00**
• **CGC:** 5 graded, best 9.9
📖 The Long Hunt **W:** Chris Claremont

Anl 2 ❑ ca. 1982 Cover: 1.00 **NM** value: **5.00**
📖 Shadeshine!

Anl 3 ❑ ca. 1983 Cover: 1.00 **NM** value: **5.00**
📖 The Apprentice

Bk 1 ❑ Cover: 2.50 **NM** value: **4.00**
• mass-market paperback

Bk 2 ❑ Cover: 1.75 **NM** value: **4.00**
• mass-market paperback

STAR WARS: A NEW HOPE MANGA — Dark Horse

1 ❑ Jul 1998 Cover: 9.95 **NM** value: **Cover or less**

2 ❑ Jul 1998 Cover: 9.95 **NM** value: **Cover or less**

3 ❑ Sep 1998 Cover: 9.95 **NM** value: **Cover or less**

4 ❑ Oct 1998 Cover: 9.95 **NM** value: **Cover or less**

STAR WARS: A NEW HOPE-THE SPECIAL EDITION — Dark Horse

1 ❑ Jan 1997 Cover: 2.95 **NM** value: **Cover or less**
Circ: Diamd. preorders: **50,538**
A: Eduardo Barreto; Al Williamson(inks) **W:** Bruce Jones

2 ❑ Feb 1997 Cover: 2.95 **NM** value: **Cover or less**
Circ: Diamd. preorders: **41,844**
A: Eduardo Barreto; Al Williamson(inks) **W:** Bruce Jones

3 ❑ Mar 1997 Cover: 2.95 **NM** value: **Cover or less**
Circ: Diamd. preorders: **37,506**
A: Eduardo Barreto; Al Williamson(inks) **W:** Bruce Jones

4 ❑ Apr 1997 Cover: 2.95 **NM** value: **Cover or less**
Circ: Diamd. preorders: **38,480**
A: Eduardo Barreto; Al Williamson(inks); Dave Dorman(cover) **W:** Bruce Jones

Bk 1 ❑ Cover: 9.95 **NM** value: **Cover or less**

STAR WARS: BOBA FETT — Dark Horse

0.5 ❑ Dec 1997 Cover: 5.00 **NM** value: **Cover or less**
• **CGC:** 5 graded, best 9.8
• Wizard mail-in edition.

0.5/GO ❑ Dec 1997 Cover: 10.00 **NM** value: **Cover or less**
• Gold edition.

1 ❑ Dec 1995 Cover: 3.95 **NM** value: **Cover or less**
cardstock cover. 📖 Bounty on Bar-Kooda **A:** Cam Kennedy **W:** John Wagner

2 ❑ Sep 1996 Cover: 3.95 **NM** value: **Cover or less**
Circ: Diamd. preorders: **61,757**
cardstock cover. 📖 When the Fat Lady Sings **A:** Cam Kennedy **W:** John Wagner

3 ❑ Aug 1997 Cover: 3.95 **NM** value: **Cover or less**
Circ: Diamd. preorders: **41,308**
cardstock cover. 📖 Murder Most Foul **A:** Cam Kennedy **W:** John Wagner

STAR WARS: BOBA FETT-AGENT OF DOOM — Dark Horse

1 ❑ Nov 2000 Cover: 2.99 **NM** value: **Cover or less**
Circ: Diamd. preorders: **29,842**
A: Cam Kennedy **W:** John Ostrander

STAR WARS: BOBA FETT: ENEMY OF THE EMPIRE — Dark Horse

1 ❑ Jan 1999 Cover: 2.95 **NM** value: **Cover or less**
Circ: Diamd. preorders: **42,430**
A: Ian Gibson **W:** John Wagner

2 ❑ Feb 1999 Cover: 2.95 **NM** value: **Cover or less**
Circ: Diamd. preorders: **36,259**
A: Ian Gibson **W:** John Wagner

3 ❑ Mar 1999 Cover: 2.95 **NM** value: **Cover or less**
Circ: Diamd. preorders: **35,737**
A: Ian Gibson **W:** John Wagner

4 ❑ Apr 1999 Cover: 2.95 **NM** value: **Cover or less**
Circ: Diamd. preorders: **37,356**
A: Ian Gibson **W:** John Wagner

STAR WARS: BOBA FETT-TWIN ENGINES OF DESTRUCTION — Dark Horse

1 ❑ Jan 1997 Cover: 2.95 **NM** value: **Cover or less**
Circ: Diamd. preorders: **53,990**
No issue number. **A:** John Nadeau **W:** Andy Mangels

STAR WARS: CHEWBACCA — Dark Horse

1 ❑ Jan 2000 Cover: 2.95 **NM** value: **Cover or less**
Circ: Diamd. preorders: **30,154** • **CGC:** 1 graded, best 9.6
A: Brent Anderson; Igor Kordey **W:** Darko Macan

2 ❑ Feb 2000 Cover: 2.95 **NM** value: **Cover or less**
Circ: Diamd. preorders: **26,393**
A: Brent Anderson; Igor Kordey **W:** Darko Macan

3 ❑ Mar 2000 Cover: 2.95 **NM** value: **Cover or less**
Circ: Diamd. preorders: **26,680**
A: Brent Anderson; Igor Kordey **W:** Darko Macan

4 ❑ Apr 2000 Cover: 2.95 **NM** value: **Cover or less**
Circ: Diamd. preorders: **27,201**
A: Brent Anderson; Igor Kordey **W:** Darko Macan

STAR WARS: CRIMSON EMPIRE — Dark Horse

1 ❑ Dec 1997 Cover: 2.95 **NM** value: **6.00**
• **CGC:** 1 graded, best 9.6
A: Paul Gulacy **W:** Mike Richardson; Randy Stradley

2 ❑ Jan 1998 Cover: 2.95 **NM** value: **5.00**
Circ: Diamd. preorders: **38,486**
A: Paul Gulacy **W:** Mike Richardson; Randy Stradley

3 ❑ Feb 1998 Cover: 2.95 **NM** value: **5.00**
Circ: Diamd. preorders: **36,568**
A: Paul Gulacy **W:** Mike Richardson; Randy Stradley

4 ❑ Mar 1998 Cover: 2.95 **NM** value: **5.00**
Circ: Diamd. preorders: **38,158**
A: Paul Gulacy **W:** Mike Richardson; Randy Stradley

5 ❑ Apr 1998 Cover: 2.95 **NM** value: **5.00**
Circ: Diamd. preorders: **41,203**
📖 Crimson Empire, Part 5 **A:** Paul Gulacy **W:** Mike Richardson; Randy Stradley

6 ❑ May 1998 Cover: 2.95 **NM** value: **5.00**
Circ: Diamd. preorders: **40,599**

Other grades: Multiply prices above by **1.5 for Mint • 2/3 for Very Fine • 1/3 for Fine • 1/5 for Very Good • 1/8 for Good**

📖 Council of blood **A:** Paul Gulacy **W:** Mike Richardson; Randy Stradley
Bk 1❑ Dec 1998 Cover: 17.95 **NM** value: **Cover or less**

STAR WARS: CRIMSON EMPIRE II: COUNCIL OF BLOOD — Dark Horse

1 ❑ Nov 1998 Cover: 2.95 **NM** value: **4.00**
Circ: Diamd. preorders: **40,383**
A: Paul Gulacy **W:** Mike Richardson; Randy Stradley
2 ❑ Dec 1998 Cover: 2.95 **NM** value: **Cover or less**
Circ: Diamd. preorders: **36,459**
A: Paul Gulacy **W:** Mike Richardson; Randy Stradley
3 ❑ Jan 1999 Cover: 2.95 **NM** value: **Cover or less**
Circ: Diamd. preorders: **35,622**
A: Paul Gulacy **W:** Mike Richardson; Randy Stradley
4 ❑ Feb 1999 Cover: 2.95 **NM** value: **Cover or less**
Circ: Diamd. preorders: **33,542**
A: Paul Gulacy **W:** Mike Richardson; Randy Stradley
5 ❑ Mar 1999 Cover: 2.95 **NM** value: **Cover or less**
Circ: Diamd. preorders: **33,100**
A: Paul Gulacy **W:** Mike Richardson; Randy Stradley
6 ❑ Apr 1999 Cover: 2.95 **NM** value: **Cover or less**
Circ: Diamd. preorders: **33,991**
A: Paul Gulacy **W:** Mike Richardson; Randy Stradley

STAR WARS: DARK EMPIRE — Dark Horse

1 ❑ Dec 1991 Cover: 2.95 **NM** value: **6.00**
Circ: CapCity orders: **46,550** • **CGC:** 25 graded, best 9.8
cardstock cover. **A:** Cam Kennedy **W:** Tom Veitch
1-2 ❑ Aug 1992 Cover: 2.95 **NM** value: **3.00**
2 ❑ Feb 1992 Cover: 2.95 **NM** value: **4.00**
Circ: CapCity orders: **30,725** • **CGC:** 2 graded, best 9.6
cardstock cover. **A:** Cam Kennedy **W:** Tom Veitch
2-2 ❑ Aug 1992 Cover: 2.95 **NM** value: **3.00**
3 ❑ Apr 1992 Cover: 2.95 **NM** value: **4.00**
Circ: CapCity orders: **36,650** • **CGC:** 1 graded, best 9.6
cardstock cover. 📖 The Battle for Calamari **A:** Cam Kennedy **W:** Tom Veitch
3-2 ❑ Cover: 2.95 **NM** value: **3.00**
4 ❑ Apr 1992 Cover: 2.95 **NM** value: **4.00**
Circ: CapCity orders: **41,700** • **CGC:** 1 graded, best 9.6
cardstock cover. **A:** Cam Kennedy **W:** Tom Veitch
5 ❑ Aug 1992 Cover: 2.95 **NM** value: **3.00**
Circ: CapCity orders: **38,775** • **CGC:** 4 graded, best 9.8
cardstock cover. **A:** Cam Kennedy **W:** Tom Veitch
6 ❑ Oct 1992 Cover: 2.95 **NM** value: **3.00**
Circ: CapCity orders: **37,900** • **CGC:** 2 graded, best 9.8
cardstock cover. final issue. **A:** Cam Kennedy **W:** Tom Veitch
Ash 1❑Mar 1996 Cover: 0.99 **NM** value: **1.00**
No issue number. wraparound cover. • newsprint preview of trade paperback collection of mini-series **A:** Cam Kennedy **W:** Tom Veitch
Bk 1❑ Cover: 16.95 **NM** value: **Cover or less**
A: Cam Kennedy **W:** Tom Veitch
Bk 1/HC❑ Cover: 99.95 **NM** value: **Cover or less**
A: Cam Kennedy **W:** Tom Veitch

STAR WARS: DARK EMPIRE II — Dark Horse

1 ❑ Dec 1994 Cover: 2.95 **NM** value: **Cover or less**
Circ: CapCity orders: **47,175**
cardstock cover. **A:** Cam Kennedy **W:** Tom Veitch
2 ❑ Jan 1995 Cover: 2.95 **NM** value: **Cover or less**
Circ: CapCity orders: **39,125**
cardstock cover. 📖 Uel on Nar Shaddaa **A:** Cam Kennedy **W:** Tom Veitch
3 ❑ Feb 1995 Cover: 2.95 **NM** value: **Cover or less**
Circ: CapCity orders: **37,500**
cardstock cover. **A:** Cam Kennedy **W:** Tom Veitch
4 ❑ Mar 1995 Cover: 2.95 **NM** value: **Cover or less**
Circ: CapCity orders: **38,250**
cardstock cover. **A:** Cam Kennedy **W:** Tom Veitch
5 ❑ Apr 1995 Cover: 2.95 **NM** value: **Cover or less**
Circ: CapCity orders: **38,550**
cardstock cover. **A:** Cam Kennedy **W:** Tom Veitch
6 ❑ May 1995 Cover: 2.95 **NM** value: **Cover or less**
Circ: CapCity orders: **39,075**
cardstock cover. **A:** Cam Kennedy **W:** Tom Veitch
Bk 1/A❑Aug 1995 Cover: 17.95 **NM** value: **Cover or less**
Circ: CapCity orders: **2,475**
A: Cam Kennedy **W:** Tom Veitch
Bk 1/B❑Aug 1995 Cover: 17.95 **NM** value: **Cover or less**
alternate cover. • embossed foil logo **A:** Cam Kennedy **W:** Tom Veitch
Bk 1/HC❑Aug 1995 Cover: 79.95 **NM** value: **Cover or less**
• Limited edition hardcover. **A:** Cam Kennedy **W:** Tom Veitch

STAR WARS: DARK FORCE RISING — Dark Horse

1 ❑ May 1997 Cover: 2.95 **NM** value: **Cover or less**
Circ: Diamd. preorders: **60,145**
cardstock cover. • adapts Timothy Zahn novel **A:** Terry Dodson **W:** Mike Baron; Timothy Zahn
2 ❑ Jun 1997 Cover: 2.95 **NM** value: **Cover or less**
Circ: Diamd. preorders: **50,285**
cardstock cover. • adapts Timothy Zahn novel **A:** Terry Dodson **W:** Mike Baron; Timothy Zahn
3 ❑ Jul 1997 Cover: 2.95 **NM** value: **Cover or less**
Circ: Diamd. preorders: **46,793**
cardstock cover. • adapts Timothy Zahn novel **A:** Terry Dodson **W:** Mike Baron; Timothy Zahn
4 ❑ Aug 1997 Cover: 2.95 **NM** value: **Cover or less**
Circ: Diamd. preorders: **43,249**
cardstock cover. • adapts Timothy Zahn novel **A:** Terry Dodson **W:** Mike Baron; Timothy Zahn
5 ❑ Sep 1997 Cover: 2.95 **NM** value: **Cover or less**
Circ: Diamd. preorders: **40,536**
cardstock cover. • adapts Timothy Zahn novel **A:** Terry Dodson **W:** Mike Baron; Timothy Zahn
6 ❑ Oct 1997 Cover: 2.95 **NM** value: **Cover or less**
Circ: Diamd. preorders: **39,852**
cardstock cover. • adapts Timothy Zahn novel **A:** Terry Dodson **W:** Mike Baron; Timothy Zahn
Bk 1❑ Feb 1998 Cover: 17.95 **NM** value: **Cover or less**

STAR WARS: DARK FORCES-REBEL AGENT — Dark Horse

Bk 1❑ Apr 1999 Cover: 14.95 **NM** value: **Cover or less**
• prose story with illustrations
Bk 1/HC❑Apr 1998 Cover: 24.95 **NM** value: **Cover or less**
• prose story with illustrations

STAR WARS: DARK FORCES-SOLDIER FOR THE EMPIRE — Dark Horse

Bk 1/HC❑Apr 1998 Cover: 24.95 **NM** value: **Cover or less**
hardcover. • prose story with illustrations based on Dark Forces computer game

STAR WARS (DARK HORSE) — Dark Horse

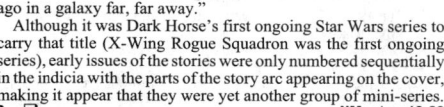

In this series from writer Jan Strnad and artist Anthony Winn, Jedi Knight Ki-Adi-Mundi's story is told both in the past and in the present. He is accused of a murder he did not commit, stunned by the loss of a dear friend, and uncertain of how to deal with a rebellious teen-age daughter; however, glimpses of his Jedi training years before by the master Yoda reveal that Ki has always struggled with the concept of a bad day, and that he must search for the good that seems to remain hidden from him. More layers are added to George Lucas' increasingly sprawling saga of worlds that existed "a long time ago in a galaxy far, far away."

Although it was Dark Horse's first ongoing Star Wars series to carry that title (X-Wing Rogue Squadron was the first ongoing series), early issues of the stories were only numbered sequentially in the indicia with the parts of the story arc appearing on the cover, making it appear that they were yet another group of mini-series.

0 ❑ **NM** value: **10.00**
• **CGC:** 5 graded, best 9.8
• American Entertainment exclusive **A:** Howard Chaykin
1 ❑ Dec 1998 Cover: 2.50 **NM** value: **4.00**
Circ: Diamd. preorders: **49,321**
📖 Prelude to Rebellion, Part 1 **A:** Anthony Winn **W:** Jan Strnad
2 ❑ Jan 1999 Cover: 2.50 **NM** value: **3.00**
Circ: Diamd. preorders: **39,691**
📖 Prelude to Rebellion, Part 2 **A:** Anthony Winn **W:** Jan Strnad
3 ❑ Feb 1999 Cover: 2.50 **NM** value: **3.00**
Circ: Diamd. preorders: **37,051**
📖 Prelude to Rebellion, Part 3 **A:** Anthony Winn **W:** Jan Strnad
4 ❑ Mar 1999 Cover: 2.50 **NM** value: **3.00**
Circ: Diamd. preorders: **34,946**
📖 Prelude to Rebellion, Part 4 **A:** Anthony Winn **W:** Jan Strnad
5 ❑ Apr 1999 Cover: 2.50 **NM** value: **3.00**
Circ: Diamd. preorders: **35,336**
📖 Prelude to Rebellion, Part 5 **A:** Anthony Winn **W:** Jan Strnad
6 ❑ May 1999 Cover: 2.50 **NM** value: **3.00**
Circ: Diamd. preorders: **35,238**
📖 Prelude to Rebellion, Part 6 **A:** Anthony Winn **W:** Jan Strnad
7 ❑ Jun 1999 Cover: 2.50 **NM** value: **Cover or less**
Circ: Diamd. preorders: **35,619**
📖 Outlander, Part 1 **A:** Tom Raney; Rob Pereira **W:** Tim Truman
8 ❑ Jul 1999 Cover: 2.50 **NM** value: **Cover or less**
Circ: Diamd. preorders: **33,863**
📖 Outlander, Part 2 **A:** Rick Leonardi **W:** Tim Truman
9 ❑ Aug 1999 Cover: 2.50 **NM** value: **Cover or less**
Circ: Diamd. preorders: **31,128**
📖 Outlander, Part 3 **A:** Rod Pereira **W:** Tim Truman
10 ❑ Sep 1999 Cover: 2.50 **NM** value: **Cover or less**
Circ: Diamd. preorders: **31,795**
📖 Outlander, Part 4 **A:** Rick Leonardi **W:** Tim Truman
11 ❑ Oct 1999 Cover: 2.50 **NM** value: **Cover or less**
Circ: Diamd. preorders: **32,008**
📖 Outlander, Part 5 **A:** Al Rio **W:** Tim Truman
12 ❑ Nov 1999 Cover: 2.50 **NM** value: **Cover or less**
Circ: Diamd. preorders: **30,490**
📖 Outlander, Part 6 **A:** Al Rio **W:** Tim Truman
13 ❑ Dec 1999 Cover: 2.50 **NM** value: **Cover or less**
Circ: Diamd. preorders: **29,336**
📖 Emissaries to Malastare, Part 1 **A:** Tom Lyle **W:** Tim Truman
14 ❑ Jan 2000 Cover: 2.50 **NM** value: **Cover or less**
Circ: Diamd. preorders: **28,711**
📖 Emissaries to Malastare, Part 2 **A:** Tom Lyle **W:** Tim Truman
15 ❑ Feb 2000 Cover: 2.50 **NM** value: **Cover or less**
Circ: Diamd. preorders: **27,155**
📖 Emissaries to Malastare, Part 3 **W:** Tim Truman
16 ❑ Mar 2000 Cover: 2.50 **NM** value: **Cover or less**
Circ: Diamd. preorders: **27,396**
📖 Emissaries to Malastare, Part 4 **W:** Tim Truman
17 ❑ Apr 2000 Cover: 2.50 **NM** value: **Cover or less**
Circ: Diamd. preorders: **27,535**
📖 Emissaries to Malastare, Part 5 **W:** Tim Truman
18 ❑ May 2000 Cover: 2.50 **NM** value: **Cover or less**
Circ: Diamd. preorders: **25,751**
📖 Emissaries to Malastare, Part 6 **A:** John Nadeau **W:** Tim Truman
19 ❑ Jun 2000 Cover: 2.50 **NM** value: **Cover or less**
Circ: Diamd. preorders: **27,193**
📖 Twilight, Part 1 **A:** Jan Duursema **W:** John Ostrander
20 ❑ Jul 2000 Cover: 2.50 **NM** value: **Cover or less**
Circ: Diamd. preorders: **26,589**
📖 Twilight, Part 2 **A:** Jan Duursema **W:** John Ostrander
21 ❑ Aug 2000 Cover: 2.50 **NM** value: **Cover or less**
Circ: Diamd. preorders: **25,057**
📖 Twilight, Part 3 **A:** Jan Duursema **W:** John Ostrander
22 ❑ Sep 2000 Cover: 2.50 **NM** value: **Cover or less**
Circ: Diamd. preorders: **25,307**
📖 Twilight, Part 4 **A:** Jan Duursema **W:** John Ostrander
23 ❑ Oct 2000 Cover: 2.50 **NM** value: **Cover or less**
Circ: Diamd. preorders: **24,963**
📖 Infinity's End, Part 1 **A:** Ramon F. Bachs **W:** Pat Mills
24 ❑ Nov 2000 Cover: 2.50 **NM** value: **Cover or less**
Circ: Diamd. preorders: **24,774**
📖 Infinity's End, Part 2 **A:** Ramon F. Bachs **W:** Pat Mills
25 ❑ Dec 2000 Cover: 2.50 **NM** value: **Cover or less**
Circ: Diamd. preorders: **24,339**
📖 Infinity's End, Part 3 **A:** Ramon F. Bachs **W:** Pat Mills
26 ❑ Jan 2001 Cover: 2.50 **NM** value: **Cover or less**
Circ: Diamd. preorders: **23,670**
📖 Infinity's End, Part 4 **A:** Ramon F. Bachs **W:** Pat Mills
27 ❑ Feb 2001 Cover: 2.99 **NM** value: **Cover or less**
Circ: Diamd. preorders: **23,481**
📖 Starcrash **A:** Randy Green **W:** Doug Petrie
28 ❑ Mar 2001 Cover: 2.99 **NM** value: **Cover or less**
Circ: Diamd. preorders: **24,324**
📖 The Hunt for Aurra Sing, Part 1 **A:** Davidé Fabbri **W:** Tim Truman
29 ❑ Apr 2001 Cover: 2.99 **NM** value: **Cover or less**
Circ: Diamd. preorders: **23,637**
📖 The Hunt for Aurra Sing, Part 2 **A:** Davidé Fabbri **W:** Tim Truman
30 ❑ May 2001 Cover: 2.99 **NM** value: **Cover or less**
Circ: Diamd. preorders: **23,668**
31 ❑ Jun 2001 Cover: 2.99 **NM** value: **Cover or less**
Circ: Diamd. preorders: **23,848**
32 ❑ Jul 2001 Cover: 2.99 **NM** value: **Cover or less**
Circ: Diamd. preorders: **25,151**

STAR WARS: DARTH MAUL — Dark Horse

1 ❑ Sep 2000 Cover: 2.95 **NM** value: **Cover or less**
Circ: Diamd. preorders: **35,391** • **CGC:** 1 graded, best 9.8
A: Jan Duursema **W:** Ron Marz
1/SC❑Sep 2000 Cover: 2.95 **NM** value: **Cover or less**
Photo cover. **A:** Jan Duursema **W:** Ron Marz
2 ❑ Oct 2000 Cover: 2.99 **NM** value: **Cover or less**
Circ: Diamd. preorders: **35,846**
A: Jan Duursema **W:** Ron Marz
2/SC❑Oct 2000 Cover: 2.99 **NM** value: **Cover or less**
Photo cover. **A:** Jan Duursema **W:** Ron Marz
3 ❑ Nov 2000 Cover: 2.99 **NM** value: **Cover or less**
Circ: Diamd. preorders: **37,905**
A: Jan Duursema **W:** Ron Marz
3/SC❑Nov 2000 Cover: 2.99 **NM** value: **Cover or less**
Photo cover. **A:** Jan Duursema **W:** Ron Marz
4 ❑ Dec 2000 Cover: 2.99 **NM** value: **Cover or less**
Circ: Diamd. preorders: **38,127**
A: Jan Duursema **W:** Ron Marz
4/SC❑Dec 2000 Cover: 2.99 **NM** value: **Cover or less**
Photo cover. **A:** Jan Duursema **W:** Ron Marz

STAR WARS: DROIDS (VOL. 1) — Dark Horse

1 ❑ Apr 1994 Cover: 2.95 **NM** value: **3.00**
Circ: CapCity orders: **34,250**
enhanced cover. **A:** Bill Hughes **W:** Dan Thorsland
2 ❑ May 1994 Cover: 2.50 **NM** value: **2.75**
Circ: CapCity orders: **28,275**
A: Bill Hughes **W:** Dan Thorsland
3 ❑ Jun 1994 Cover: 2.50 **NM** value: **2.75**
Circ: CapCity orders: **27,175**
📖 The Scarlet Pirate; End of the Game **A:** Bill Hughes **W:** Dan Thorsland
4 ❑ Jul 1994 Cover: 2.50 **NM** value: **Cover or less**
Circ: CapCity orders: **24,525**
A: Bill Hughes **W:** Dan Thorsland
5 ❑ Aug 1994 Cover: 2.50 **NM** value: **Cover or less**
Circ: CapCity orders: **21,175**
A: Bill Hughes **W:** Dan Thorsland
6 ❑ Sep 1994 Cover: 2.50 **NM** value: **Cover or less**
Circ: CapCity orders: **19,250**
A: Bill Hughes **W:** Dan Thorsland
Bk 1❑ Jun 1995 Cover: 17.95 **NM** value: **Cover or less**
• Trade Paperback. 📖 The Kalarba Adventures • Collects Star Wars Droids Special, issues #1-6, and an eight-page story from Star Wars Galaxy **A:** Bill Hughes **W:** Dan Thorsland
Bk 1/LE❑Jun 1995 Cover: 99.95 **NM** value: **Cover or less**
• Limited edition hardcover. 📖 The Kalarba Adventures • Collects Star Wars Droids Special, issues #1-6, and an eight-page story from Star Wars Galaxy **A:** Bill Hughes **W:** Dan Thorsland
SE 1❑ Jan 1995 Cover: 2.50 **NM** value: **Cover or less**
Circ: CapCity orders: **13,650**
• Special edition. • Reprints serial from Dark Horse Comics **A:** Bill Hughes **W:** Dan Thorsland

STAR WARS: DROIDS (VOL. 2) — Dark Horse

1 ❑ Apr 1995 Cover: 2.50 **NM** value: **Cover or less**
Circ: CapCity orders: **18,775**
📖 Rebellion, Part 1 **A:** Ian Gibson **W:** Ryder Windham
2 ❑ May 1995 Cover: 2.50 **NM** value: **Cover or less**
Circ: CapCity orders: **16,775**
📖 Rebellion, Part 2 **A:** Ian Gibson **W:** Ryder Windham
3 ❑ Jun 1995 Cover: 2.50 **NM** value: **Cover or less**
Circ: CapCity orders: **15,500**
📖 Rebellion, Part 3 **A:** Ian Gibson **W:** Ryder Windham
4 ❑ Jul 1995 Cover: 2.50 **NM** value: **Cover or less**
Circ: CapCity orders: **15,000**
📖 Rebellion, Part 4 **A:** Ian Gibson **W:** Ryder Windham
5 ❑ Sep 1995 Cover: 2.50 **NM** value: **Cover or less**
Circ: CapCity orders: **11,100**
6 ❑ Oct 1995 Cover: 2.50 **NM** value: **Cover or less**
Circ: CapCity orders: **7,675**
7 ❑ Nov 1995 Cover: 2.50 **NM** value: **Cover or less**
8 ❑ Dec 1995 Cover: 2.50 **NM** value: **Cover or less**
Bk 1❑ Jan 1997 Cover: 14.95 **NM** value: **Cover or less**
• Rebellion

CGC-graded: Multiply prices above by **33 for 9.9 M • 16 for 9.8 NM/M • 7 for 9.6 NM+ • 5 for 9.4 NM • 2.5 for 9.2 NM- • 1.5 for 9.0 VF/NM**

STAR WARS: EMPIRE'S END — Dark Horse

1 ❑ Oct 1995 Cover: 2.95 **NM** value: **Cover or less**
Circ: CapCity orders: **20,075**
cardstock cover. **A:** Jim Baikie; Dave Dorman(cover) **W:** Tom Veitch
2 ❑ Nov 1995 Cover: 2.95 **NM** value: **Cover or less**
cardstock cover. **A:** Jim Baikie; Dave Dorman(cover) **W:** Tom Veitch
Bk 1❑ Sep 1997 Cover: 5.95 **NM** value: **Cover or less**
Circ: Diamd. preorders: **4,795**
A: Jim Baikie; Dave Dorman(cover) **W:** Tom Veitch

STAR WARS: EPISODE I ANAKIN SKYWALKER — Dark Horse

1 ❑ May 1999 Cover: 2.95 **NM** value: **Cover or less**
Circ: Diamd. preorders: **69,359**
cardstock cover. **A:** Steve Crespo **W:** Tim Truman
1/SC❑May 1999 Cover: 2.95 **NM** value: **Cover or less**
Photo cover. **A:** Steve Crespo **W:** Tim Truman

STAR WARS: EPISODE I OBI-WAN KENOBI — Dark Horse

1 ❑ May 1999 Cover: 2.95 **NM** value: **Cover or less**
Circ: Diamd. preorders: **69,266**
cardstock cover. **A:** Martin Egeland **W:** Henry Gilroy
1/SC❑May 1999 Cover: 2.95 **NM** value: **Cover or less**
Photo cover. **A:** Martin Egeland **W:** Henry Gilroy

STAR WARS: EPISODE I QUEEN AMIDALA — Dark Horse

1 ❑ Jun 1999 Cover: 2.95 **NM** value: **Cover or less**
Circ: Diamd. preorders: **60,944**
cardstock cover. **A:** Galen Showman **W:** Mark Schultz
1/SC❑Jun 1999 Cover: 2.95 **NM** value: **Cover or less**
Photo cover. **A:** Galen Showman **W:** Mark Schultz

STAR WARS: EPISODE I QUI-GON JINN — Dark Horse

1 ❑ Jun 1999 Cover: 2.95 **NM** value: **Cover or less**
Circ: Diamd. preorders: **60,810**
cardstock cover. **A:** Robert Teranishi **W:** Ryder Windham
1/SC❑Jun 1999 Cover: 2.95 **NM** value: **Cover or less**
Photo cover. **A:** Robert Teranishi **W:** Ryder Windham

STAR WARS: EPISODE I THE PHANTOM MENACE — Dark Horse

Two Jedi Knights are sent to intervene in a Trade Federation blockade of the small planet Naboo, but they soon discover that a Sith Lord, master of the evil Dark Side of the Force, is behind the federation's actions.

Forced to flee with Naboo's queen, the Jedi find themselves seeking aid and repairs on the desert planet Tattooine. There, they discover a young boy named Anakin Skywalker, whose potential for controlling the Force is overwhelming. The two knights risk all by assuming responsibility for the boy, but they sense he is critical to their victory. Their mission seems simple enough: defeat the robot hordes that hold Naboo imprisoned, unite the planet's two races, restore the queen's throne, and defeat Darth Maul, the Sith Lord's apprentice.

Phantom Menace is a prequel to the hit 1970s movie, Star Wars, which detailed the adventures of Luke Skywalker against Darth Vader and the evil empire.

The best part of this adaptation is not having to listen to the annoying strains of Jar Jar Binks.

1 ❑ May 1999 Cover: 2.95 **NM** value: **Cover or less**
Circ: Diamd. preorders: **88,437** • **CGC:** 10 graded, best 9.9
cardstock cover. **A:** Rodolfo DaMaggio **W:** George Lucas; Henry Gilroy
1/SC❑May 1999 Cover: 2.95 **NM** value: **Cover or less**
• **CGC:** 2 graded, best 9.8
Photo cover. **A:** Rodolfo DaMaggio **W:** George Lucas; Henry Gilroy
2 ❑ May 1999 Cover: 2.95 **NM** value: **Cover or less**
Circ: Diamd. preorders: **83,639**
cardstock cover. **A:** Rodolfo DaMaggio **W:** George Lucas; Henry Gilroy
2/SC❑May 1999 Cover: 2.95 **NM** value: **Cover or less**
Photo cover. **A:** Rodolfo DaMaggio **W:** George Lucas; Henry Gilroy
3 ❑ May 1999 Cover: 2.95 **NM** value: **Cover or less**
Circ: Diamd. preorders: **82,345**
cardstock cover. **A:** Rodolfo DaMaggio **W:** George Lucas; Henry Gilroy
3/SC❑May 1999 Cover: 2.95 **NM** value: **Cover or less**
Photo cover. **A:** Rodolfo DaMaggio **W:** George Lucas; Henry Gilroy
4 ❑ May 1999 Cover: 2.95 **NM** value: **Cover or less**
Circ: Diamd. preorders: **81,965**
cardstock cover. **A:** Rodolfo DaMaggio **W:** George Lucas; Henry Gilroy
4/SC❑May 1999 Cover: 2.95 **NM** value: **Cover or less**
Photo cover. **A:** Rodolfo DaMaggio **W:** George Lucas; Henry Gilroy

STAR WARS HANDBOOK — Dark Horse

1 ❑ Jul 1998 Cover: 2.95 **NM** value: **Cover or less**
Circ: Diamd. preorders: **22,480**
• X-Wing Rogue Squadron profiles
2 ❑ Jul 1999 Cover: 2.95 **NM** value: **Cover or less**
Circ: Diamd. preorders: **24,874**
• Crimson Empire profiles **A:** Alex Maleev; Robert Teranishi; Paul Gulacy; Steve Crespo; Dave Ross; Martin Egeland; John Nadeau; Tom Raney; Jordi Ensign **W:** Michael D. Hansen

STAR WARS: HEIR TO THE EMPIRE — Dark Horse

1 ❑ Oct 1995 Cover: 2.95 **NM** value: **Cover or less**
Circ: CapCity orders: **20,350** • **CGC:** 1 graded, best 9.8
A: Olivier Vatine; Fred Blanchard **W:** Mike Baron
2 ❑ Nov 1995 Cover: 2.95 **NM** value: **Cover or less**
A: Olivier Vatine; Fred Blanchard **W:** Mike Baron
3 ❑ Dec 1995 Cover: 2.95 **NM** value: **Cover or less**
A: Olivier Vatine; Fred Blanchard **W:** Mike Baron
4 ❑ Jan 1996 Cover: 2.95 **NM** value: **Cover or less**
A: Olivier Vatine; Fred Blanchard **W:** Mike Baron
5 ❑ Mar 1996 Cover: 2.95 **NM** value: **Cover or less**
A: Olivier Vatine; Fred Blanchard **W:** Mike Baron
6 ❑ Apr 1996 Cover: 2.95 **NM** value: **Cover or less**
A: Olivier Vatine; Fred Blanchard **W:** Mike Baron
Bk 1❑ Sep 1996 Cover: 19.95 **NM** value: **Cover or less**
A: Olivier Vatine; Fred Blanchard **W:** Mike Baron
Bk 1/HC❑Sep 1996 Cover: 79.95 **NM** value: **Cover or less**
• Limited edition hardcover. • 1000 copies printed **A:** Olivier Vatine; Fred Blanchard **W:** Mike Baron

STAR WARS IN 3-D — Blackthorne

1 ❑ Dec 1987 Cover: 2.50 **NM** value: **Cover or less**
Circ: CapCity orders: **5,400**
• a.k.a. Blackthorne in 3-D #30

STAR WARS: JABBA THE HUTT — Dark Horse

1 ❑ Apr 1995 Cover: 2.50 **NM** value: **Cover or less**
Circ: CapCity orders: **26,300**
📖 The Gaar Suppoon Hit **A:** Art Wetherell **W:** Jim Woodring
2 ❑ Jun 1995 Cover: 2.50 **NM** value: **Cover or less**
Circ: CapCity orders: **20,750**
📖 The Hunger of Princess Nampi
3 ❑ Aug 1995 Cover: 2.50 **NM** value: **Cover or less**
📖 The Dynasty Trap
4 ❑ Feb 1996 Cover: 2.50 **NM** value: **Cover or less**
📖 The Betrayal
Bk 1❑ Jun 1998 Cover: 9.95 **NM** value: **Cover or less**
📖 The Art of the Deal • collects one-shots; Collects Jabba the Hutt one-shots

STAR WARS: JEDI ACADEMY-LEVIATHAN — Dark Horse

1 ❑ Oct 1998 Cover: 2.95 **NM** value: **Cover or less**
Circ: Diamd. preorders: **30,111**
A: Dario Carrasco Jr. **W:** Kevin J. Anderson
2 ❑ Nov 1998 Cover: 2.95 **NM** value: **Cover or less**
Circ: Diamd. preorders: **27,418**
A: Dario Carrasco Jr. **W:** Kevin J. Anderson
3 ❑ Dec 1998 Cover: 2.95 **NM** value: **Cover or less**
Circ: Diamd. preorders: **26,918**
A: Dario Carrasco Jr. **W:** Kevin J. Anderson
4 ❑ Jan 1999 Cover: 2.95 **NM** value: **Cover or less**
Circ: Diamd. preorders: **26,901**
A: Dario Carrasco Jr. **W:** Kevin J. Anderson

STAR WARS: JEDI COUNCIL: ACTS OF WAR — Dark Horse

1 ❑ Jun 2000 Cover: 2.95 **NM** value: **Cover or less**
Circ: Diamd. preorders: **28,275**
A: Davidé Fabbri **W:** Randy Stradley
2 ❑ Jul 2000 Cover: 2.95 **NM** value: **Cover or less**
Circ: Diamd. preorders: **26,293**
A: Davidé Fabbri **W:** Randy Stradley
3 ❑ Aug 2000 Cover: 2.95 **NM** value: **Cover or less**
Circ: Diamd. preorders: **24,490**
A: Davidé Fabbri **W:** Randy Stradley
4 ❑ Sep 2000 Cover: 2.95 **NM** value: **Cover or less**
Circ: Diamd. preorders: **24,624**
A: Davidé Fabbri **W:** Randy Stradley

STAR WARS: JEDI VS. SITH — Dark Horse

1 ❑ Apr 2001 Cover: 2.99 **NM** value: **Cover or less**
Circ: Diamd. preorders: **28,680**
A: Ramon F. Bachs **W:** Darko Macan
2 ❑ May 2001 Cover: 2.99 **NM** value: **Cover or less**
Circ: Diamd. preorders: **25,384**
A: Ramon F. Bachs **W:** Darko Macan
3 ❑ Jun 2001 Cover: 2.99 **NM** value: **Cover or less**
Circ: Diamd. preorders: **25,100**
A: Ramon F. Bachs **W:** Darko Macan
4 ❑ Jul 2001 Cover: 2.99 **NM** value: **Cover or less**
Circ: Diamd. preorders: **26,535**
A: Ramon F. Bachs **W:** Darko Macan
5 ❑ Aug 2001 Cover: 2.99 **NM** value: **Cover or less**
Circ: Diamd. preorders: **26,861**
A: Ramon F. Bachs **W:** Darko Macan
6 ❑ Sep 2001 Cover: 2.99 **NM** value: **Cover or less**
Circ: Diamd. preorders: **25,139**
A: Ramon F. Bachs **W:** Darko Macan

STAR WARS (MAGAZINE) — Dark Horse

1 ❑ Oct 1992 Cover: 2.50 **NM** value: **5.00**
📖 Star Wars: Dark Empire; Indiana Jones and the Fate of Atlantis **A:** Dan Barry; Cam Kennedy **W:** William Messner-Loebs; Noah Falstein; Tom Veitchm Hal Harwood
2 ❑ Cover: 2.50 **NM** value: **4.00**
3 ❑ Cover: 2.50 **NM** value: **3.00**
4 ❑ Cover: 2.50 **NM** value: **3.00**
5 ❑ Cover: 2.50 **NM** value: **3.00**
6 ❑ Cover: 2.50 **NM** value: **3.00**
7 ❑ Cover: 2.50 **NM** value: **3.00**
8 ❑ Cover: 2.50 **NM** value: **3.00**
9 ❑ Cover: 2.50 **NM** value: **3.00**
10 ❑ Cover: 2.50 **NM** value: **3.00**

STAR WARS: MARA JADE — Dark Horse

1 ❑ Aug 1998 Cover: 2.95 **NM** value: **3.00**
Circ: Diamd. preorders: **31,689**
📖 By the Emperor's Hand, Part 1 **A:** Carlos Ezquerra **W:** Michael A. Stackpole; Timothy Zahn
2 ❑ Sep 1998 Cover: 2.95 **NM** value: **Cover or less**
Circ: Diamd. preorders: **29,170**
📖 By the Emperor's Hand, Part 2 **A:** Carlos Ezquerra **W:** Michael A. Stackpole; Timothy Zahn ★ 2nd Appearance of Mara Jade. ★ 2nd Appearance of Mara Jade.
3 ❑ Oct 1998 Cover: 2.95 **NM** value: **Cover or less**
Circ: Diamd. preorders: **29,522**
📖 By the Emperor's Hand, Part 3 **A:** Carlos Ezquerra **W:** Michael A. Stackpole; Timothy Zahn
4 ❑ Nov 1998 Cover: 2.95 **NM** value: **Cover or less**
Circ: Diamd. preorders: **30,567**
📖 By the Emperor's Hand, Part 4 • Darth Vader cameo; Luke Skywalker cameo; Emperor cameo **A:** Carlos Ezquerra **W:** Michael A. Stackpole; Timothy Zahn
5 ❑ Dec 1998 Cover: 2.95 **NM** value: **Cover or less**
Circ: Diamd. preorders: **30,097**
📖 By the Emperor's Hand, Part 5 **A:** Carlos Ezquerra **W:** Michael A. Stackpole; Timothy Zahn
6 ❑ Jan 1999 Cover: 2.95 **NM** value: **Cover or less**
Circ: Diamd. preorders: **30,279**
📖 By the Emperor's Hand, Part 6 **A:** Carlos Ezquerra **W:** Michael A. Stackpole; Timothy Zahn
Bk 1❑ Cover: 15.95 **NM** value: **Cover or less**
📖 By The Emperor's Hand • collects issues #1-6

STAR WARS (NEWSPAPER STRIP) — Marvel

Bk 1❑ Cover: 1.50 **NM** value: **4.00**
• Del Rey mass-market paperback

STAR WARS: QUI-GON & OBI-WAN-LAST STAND ON ORD MANTELL — Dark Horse

1/A ❑ Dec 2000 Cover: 2.99 **NM** value: **Cover or less**
Obi-Wan leaping on cover, Qui-Gon standing. **A:** Ramon F. Bachs **W:** Ryder Windham
1/B ❑ Dec 2000 Cover: 2.99 **NM** value: **Cover or less**
Qui-gon and Obi-Wan standing on cover, Obi-Wan has light sabre out. **A:** Ramon F. Bachs **W:** Ryder Windham
1/C ❑ Dec 2000 Cover: 2.99 **NM** value: **Cover or less**
Photo cover. **A:** Ramon F. Bachs **W:** Ryder Windham
2/A ❑ Feb 2001 Cover: 2.99 **NM** value: **Cover or less**
Drawn cover. **A:** Ramon F. Bachs **W:** Ryder Windham
2/B ❑ Feb 2001 Cover: 2.99 **NM** value: **Cover or less**
Photo cover. **A:** Ramon F. Bachs **W:** Ryder Windham
3/A ❑ Mar 2001 Cover: 2.99 **NM** value: **Cover or less**
Drawn cover. **A:** Ramon F. Bachs **W:** Ryder Windham
3/B ❑ Mar 2001 Cover: 2.99 **NM** value: **Cover or less**
Photo cover. **A:** Ramon F. Bachs **W:** Ryder Windham

STAR WARS: RETURN OF THE JEDI — Marvel

1 ❑ Oct 1983 Cover: 0.60 **NM** value: **4.00**
• **CGC:** 3 graded, best 9.6
📖 At The Hands Of Jabba The Hut • Reprints Marvel Super Special #27 **A:** Al Williamson; Carlos Garzon **W:** Archie Goodwin
2 ❑ Nov 1983 Cover: 0.60 **NM** value: **4.00**
• Reprints Marvel Super Special #27 **A:** Al Williamson; Carlos Garzon **W:** Archie Goodwin
3 ❑ Dec 1983 Cover: 0.60 **NM** value: **4.00**
• **CGC:** 1 graded, best 9.6
📖 Mission To Endor • Reprints Marvel Super Special #27 **A:** Al Williamson; Carlos Garzon **W:** Archie Goodwin
4 ❑ Jan 1984 Cover: 0.60 **NM** value: **4.00**
• Reprints Marvel Super Special #27 **A:** Al Williamson; Carlos Garzon **W:** Archie Goodwin
Bk 1❑ Cover: 2.50 **NM** value: **Cover or less**
• mass-market paperback
Bk 1-2❑Feb 1997 Cover: 9.95 **NM** value: **Cover or less**
• collects Marvel's Star Wars: Return of the Jedi #1-4

STAR WARS: RETURN OF THE JEDI – MANGA Dark Horse

Bk 1❑ Jul 1999 Cover: 9.95 **NM** value: **Cover or less**
Bk 2❑ Aug 1999 Cover: 9.95 **NM** value: **Cover or less**
Bk 3❑ Sep 1999 Cover: 9.95 **NM** value: **Cover or less**
Bk 4❑ Oct 1999 Cover: 9.95 **NM** value: **Cover or less**

STAR WARS: RIVER OF CHAOS — Dark Horse

1 ❑ Jun 1995 Cover: 2.50 **NM** value: **Cover or less**
Circ: CapCity orders: **29,300**
A: June Brigman **W:** Louise Simonson
2 ❑ Jul 1995 Cover: 2.50 **NM** value: **Cover or less**
Circ: CapCity orders: **25,025**
A: June Brigman **W:** Louise Simonson
3 ❑ Sep 1995 Cover: 2.50 **NM** value: **Cover or less**
Circ: CapCity orders: **24,550**
A: June Brigman **W:** Louise Simonson
4 ❑ Nov 1995 Cover: 2.50 **NM** value: **Cover or less**
Circ: CapCity orders: **16,175**
A: June Brigman **W:** Louise Simonson

STAR WARS: SHADOWS OF EMPIRE-EVOLUTION — Dark Horse

1 ❑ Feb 1998 Cover: 2.95 **NM** value: **Cover or less**
Circ: Diamd. preorders: **34,828** • **CGC:** 4 graded, best 9.8
A: Ron Randall **W:** Steve Perry
2 ❑ Mar 1998 Cover: 2.95 **NM** value: **Cover or less**
Circ: Diamd. preorders: **32,515**
📖 The Journey of a Thousand Light-Years **A:** Ron Randall **W:** Steve Perry

Other grades: Multiply prices above by **1.5 for Mint • 2/3 for Very Fine • 1/3 for Fine • 1/5 for Very Good • 1/8 for Good**

3 ❑ Apr 1998 Cover: 2.95 **NM** value: **Cover or less**
Circ: Diamd. preorders: **33,452**
A: Ron Randall **W:** Steve Perry

4 ❑ May 1998 Cover: 2.95 **NM** value: **Cover or less**
Circ: Diamd. preorders: **32,272**
A: Ron Randall **W:** Steve Perry

5 ❑ Jun 1998 Cover: 2.95 **NM** value: **Cover or less**
Circ: Diamd. preorders: **32,114**
A: Ron Randall **W:** Steve Perry

STAR WARS: SHADOWS OF THE EMPIRE — Dark Horse

1 ❑ May 1996 Cover: 2.95 **NM** value: **Cover or less**
A: Kilian Plunkett **W:** John Wagner

2 ❑ Jun 1996 Cover: 2.95 **NM** value: **Cover or less**
A: Kilian Plunkett **W:** John Wagner

3 ❑ Jul 1996 Cover: 2.95 **NM** value: **Cover or less**
A: Kilian Plunkett **W:** John Wagner

4 ❑ Aug 1996 Cover: 2.95 **NM** value: **Cover or less**
A: Kilian Plunkett **W:** John Wagner

5 ❑ Sep 1996 Cover: 2.95 **NM** value: **Cover or less**
Circ: Diamd. preorders: **70,572**
A: Kilian Plunkett **W:** John Wagner

6 ❑ Oct 1996 Cover: 2.95 **NM** value: **Cover or less**
Circ: Diamd. preorders: **70,987**
A: Kilian Plunkett; John Nadeau **W:** John Wagner

Bk 1❑ Apr 1997 Cover: 17.95 **NM** value: **Cover or less**
A: Kilian Plunkett; John Nadeau **W:** John Wagner

Bk 1/HC❑ Apr 1997 Cover: 79.95 **NM** value: **Cover or less**
• Limited edition hardcover. **A:** Kilian Plunkett; John Nadeau **W:** John Wagner

STAR WARS: SHADOW STALKER — Dark Horse

1 ❑ Sep 1997 Cover: 2.95 **NM** value: **Cover or less**
Circ: Diamd. preorders: **33,118**
No issue number. One-shot.

STAR WARS: SPLINTER OF THE MIND'S EYE — Dark Horse

1 ❑ Dec 1995 Cover: 2.50 **NM** value: **Cover or less**
📖 After the Fall **A:** Chris Sprouse **W:** Terry Austin; Alan Dean Foster

2 ❑ Feb 1996 Cover: 2.50 **NM** value: **Cover or less**
A: Chris Sprouse **W:** Terry Austin; Alan Dean Foster

3 ❑ Apr 1996 Cover: 2.95 **NM** value: **Cover or less**
A: Chris Sprouse **W:** Terry Austin; Alan Dean Foster

4 ❑ Jun 1996 Cover: 2.95 **NM** value: **Cover or less**
final issue. **A:** Chris Sprouse **W:** Terry Austin; Alan Dean Foster

Bk 1❑ Dec 1996 Cover: 14.95 **NM** value: **Cover or less**
• Collects series **A:** Chris Sprouse **W:** Terry Austin; Alan Dean Foster

STAR WARS TALES — Dark Horse

One of the biggest problems early on with Dark Horse's comics based on Star Wars was the infrequent use made of the "original cast," which in Star Trek parlance (if that can be legally used here) means those heroes from the original three films, not counting the umpteen less-than-memorable Jedi and Sith created to populate the novels, video games, and comics. Dark Horse got greater leeway to use those characters in the late 1990s, and this anthology is one result. Creators who don't normally work on Star Wars titles had the chance to do their own short stories, some of which are "non-canonical" but most of which are entertaining. Favorites include Peter David's "Skippy: The Jedi Droid."
— JJM

1 ❑ Sep 1999 Cover: 4.95 **NM** value: **Cover or less**
Circ: Diamd. preorders: **29,908**
📖 Life, Death, and the Living Force; Mara Jade: A Night On the Town; Extinction; Skippy the Jedi Droid **A:** Robert Teranishi; Martin Egeland; Igor Kordey; Claudia Castellini **W:** Jim Woodring; Peter David; Ron Marz; Timothy Zahn

2 ❑ Dec 1999 Cover: 4.95 **NM** value: **Cover or less**
Circ: Diamd. preorders: **26,342**
📖 Routine; Darth Vader: Extinction, Part 2; Stop that Jawa!; Incident at Horn Station **A:** Sean Phillips; Claudio Castellini; Dave Cooper; John Nadeau **W:** Dave Cooper; Dan Jolley; Ron Marz; Tony Isabella

3 ❑ Mar 2000 Cover: 4.95 **NM** value: **Cover or less**
Circ: Diamd. preorders: **23,695**

4 ❑ Jun 2000 Cover: 4.95 **NM** value: **Cover or less**
Circ: Diamd. preorders: **23,170**

5 ❑ Sep 2000 Cover: 4.95 **NM** value: **Cover or less**
Circ: Diamd. preorders: **21,474**
📖 Yaddle's Tale: The One Below; What They Called Me; A Summer's Dream; Hoth; Lando's Commandos: On Eagle's Wings **A:** Cliff Richards; Jesus Saiz; Tony Millionaire; Carlos Meglia; Craig Thompson **W:** Dean Motter; Tony Millionaire; Terry Moore; Craig Thompson; Ian Edginton

STAR WARS: TALES FROM MOS EISLEY — Dark Horse

1 ❑ Mar 1996 Cover: 2.95 **NM** value: **Cover or less**
No issue number. 📖 Light Duty **A:** Bret Blevins **W:** Bruce Jones

STAR WARS: TALES OF THE JEDI — Dark Horse

1 ❑ Oct 1993 Cover: 2.50 **NM** value: **4.00**
Circ: CapCity orders: **59,200**
📖 Ulic Qel-Droma And The Beast Wars Of Onderon **A:** Chris Gossett **W:** Tom Veitch

2 ❑ Nov 1993 Cover: 2.50 **NM** value: **3.50**
Circ: CapCity orders: **42,850**
A: Chris Gossett **W:** Tom Veitch

3 ❑ Dec 1993 Cover: 2.50 **NM** value: **3.25**
Circ: CapCity orders: **39,100**
A: Chris Gossett **W:** Tom Veitch

4 ❑ Jan 1994 Cover: 2.50 **NM** value: **Cover or less**
Circ: CapCity orders: **35,025**
A: Chris Gossett **W:** Tom Veitch

5 ❑ Feb 1994 Cover: 2.50 **NM** value: **Cover or less**
Circ: CapCity orders: **33,350**
A: Chris Gossett **W:** Tom Veitch

Bk 1❑ Cover: 14.95 **NM** value: **Cover or less**
• Trade Paperback. • Collects Star Wars: Tales of the Jedi #1-5 **A:** Chris Gossett **W:** Tom Veitch

STAR WARS: TALES OF THE JEDI-DARK LORDS OF THE SITH — Dark Horse

1 ❑ Oct 1994 Cover: 2.50 **NM** value: **3.00**
Circ: CapCity orders: **39,325**
A: Art Wetherell; Chris Gossett **W:** Tom Veitch; Kevin J. Anderson

2 ❑ Nov 1994 Cover: 2.50 **NM** value: **3.00**
Circ: CapCity orders: **32,225**
A: Art Wetherell; Chris Gossett **W:** Tom Veitch; Kevin J. Anderson

3 ❑ Dec 1994 Cover: 2.50 **NM** value: **3.00**
Circ: CapCity orders: **31,650**
A: Art Wetherell; Chris Gossett **W:** Tom Veitch; Kevin J. Anderson

4 ❑ Jan 1995 Cover: 2.50 **NM** value: **3.00**
Circ: CapCity orders: **29,575**
A: Art Wetherell; Chris Gossett **W:** Tom Veitch; Kevin J. Anderson

5 ❑ Feb 1995 Cover: 2.50 **NM** value: **3.00**
Circ: CapCity orders: **28,950**
A: Art Wetherell; Chris Gossett **W:** Tom Veitch; Kevin J. Anderson

6 ❑ Mar 1995 Cover: 2.50 **NM** value: **3.00**
Circ: CapCity orders: **30,575**
A: Art Wetherell; Chris Gossett **W:** Tom Veitch; Kevin J. Anderson

Bk 1❑ Feb 1996 Cover: 17.95 **NM** value: **Cover or less**
A: Art Wetherell; Chris Gossett **W:** Tom Veitch; Kevin J. Anderson

STAR WARS: TALES OF THE JEDI-FALL OF THE SITH EMPIRE — Dark Horse

1 ❑ Jun 1997 Cover: 2.95 **NM** value: **Cover or less**
Man with marionettes on cover. **A:** Dario Carrasco Jr.; Duncan Fegredo(cover) **W:** Kevin J. Anderson

1/A ❑ Jun 1997 Cover: 2.95 **NM** value: **Cover or less**
Variant cover, flame in background. **A:** Dario Carrasco Jr. **W:** Kevin J. Anderson

2 ❑ Jul 1997 Cover: 2.95 **NM** value: **Cover or less**
A: Dario Carrasco Jr. **W:** Kevin J. Anderson

3 ❑ Aug 1997 Cover: 2.95 **NM** value: **Cover or less**
A: Dario Carrasco Jr. **W:** Kevin J. Anderson

4 ❑ Sep 1997 Cover: 2.95 **NM** value: **Cover or less**
A: Dario Carrasco Jr. **W:** Kevin J. Anderson

5 ❑ Oct 1997 Cover: 2.95 **NM** value: **Cover or less**
A: Dario Carrasco Jr. **W:** Kevin J. Anderson

Bk 1❑ May 1998 Cover: 15.95 **NM** value: **Cover or less**
Die-cut cover.

STAR WARS: TALES OF THE JEDI-REDEMPTION — Dark Horse

1 ❑ Jul 1998 Cover: 2.95 **NM** value: **Cover or less**
Circ: Diamd. preorders: **29,788**
📖 A Gathering of Jedi **A:** Chris Gossett **W:** Kevin J. Anderson

2 ❑ Aug 1998 Cover: 2.95 **NM** value: **Cover or less**
Circ: Diamd. preorders: **28,201**
A: Chris Gossett **W:** Kevin J. Anderson

3 ❑ Sep 1998 Cover: 2.95 **NM** value: **Cover or less**
Circ: Diamd. preorders: **27,311**
📖 Homecoming **A:** Chris Gossett **W:** Kevin J. Anderson

4 ❑ Oct 1998 Cover: 2.95 **NM** value: **Cover or less**
Circ: Diamd. preorders: **27,470**
📖 The Trials of a Jedi **A:** Chris Gossett **W:** Kevin J. Anderson

5 ❑ Nov 1998 Cover: 2.95 **NM** value: **Cover or less**
Circ: Diamd. preorders: **27,387**
A: Chris Gossett **W:** Kevin J. Anderson

STAR WARS: TALES OF THE JEDI-THE FREEDON NADD UPRISING — Dark Horse

1 ❑ Aug 1994 Cover: 2.50 **NM** value: **Cover or less**
Circ: CapCity orders: **36,525**
A: Denis Rodier; Tony Atkins **W:** Tom Veitch

2 ❑ Sep 1994 Cover: 2.50 **NM** value: **Cover or less**
Circ: CapCity orders: **31,100**
final issue. **A:** Denis Rodier; Tony Atkins **W:** Tom Veitch

Bk 1❑ Dec 1997 Cover: 5.95 **NM** value: **Cover or less**
A: Denis Rodier; Tony Atkins **W:** Tom Veitch

STAR WARS: TALES OF THE JEDI-THE GOLDEN AGE OF THE SITH — Dark Horse

0 ❑ ca. 1996 Cover: 0.99 **NM** value: **Cover or less**
📖 Conquest And Unification **A:** Chris Gossett **W:** Kevin J. Anderson

1 ❑ Oct 1996 Cover: 2.95 **NM** value: **Cover or less**
📖 Into The Unknown **A:** Dario Carrasco Jr. **W:** Kevin J. Anderson

2 ❑ Nov 1996 Cover: 2.95 **NM** value: **Cover or less**
📖 Funeral for a Dark Lord **A:** Dario Carrasco Jr. **W:** Kevin J. Anderson

3 ❑ Dec 1996 Cover: 2.95 **NM** value: **Cover or less**
📖 The Fabric of an Empire **A:** Dario Carrasco Jr. **W:** Kevin J. Anderson

4 ❑ Jan 1997 Cover: 2.95 **NM** value: **Cover or less**
📖 Pawns of the Sith Lord **A:** Dario Carrasco Jr. **W:** Kevin J. Anderson

5 ❑ Feb 1997 Cover: 2.95 **NM** value: **Cover or less**
📖 The Flight of Starbreaker 12 **A:** Dario Carrasco Jr. **W:** Kevin J. Anderson

Bk 1❑ Aug 1997 Cover: 16.95 **NM** value: **Cover or less**

STAR WARS: TALES OF THE JEDI-THE SITH WAR — Dark Horse

1 ❑ Aug 1995 Cover: 2.50 **NM** value: **Cover or less**
Circ: CapCity orders: **28,350**
A: Dario Carrasco Jr. **W:** Kevin J. Anderson

2 ❑ Sep 1995 Cover: 2.50 **NM** value: **Cover or less**
Circ: CapCity orders: **21,450**
A: Dario Carrasco Jr. **W:** Kevin J. Anderson

3 ❑ Oct 1995 Cover: 2.50 **NM** value: **Cover or less**
Circ: CapCity orders: **15,225**
A: Dario Carrasco Jr. **W:** Kevin J. Anderson

4 ❑ Nov 1995 Cover: 2.50 **NM** value: **Cover or less**
A: Dario Carrasco Jr. **W:** Kevin J. Anderson

5 ❑ Dec 1995 Cover: 2.50 **NM** value: **Cover or less**
A: Dario Carrasco Jr. **W:** Kevin J. Anderson

6 ❑ Jan 1996 Cover: 2.50 **NM** value: **Cover or less**
A: Dario Carrasco Jr. **W:** Kevin J. Anderson

Bk 1❑ Jul 1996 Cover: 17.95 **NM** value: **Cover or less**
A: Dario Carrasco Jr. **W:** Kevin J. Anderson

STAR WARS: THE BOUNTY HUNTERS-AURRA SING — Dark Horse

1 ❑ Jul 1999 Cover: 2.95 **NM** value: **Cover or less**
No issue number. One-shot. **A:** Tim Truman **W:** Tim Truman

STAR WARS: THE BOUNTY HUNTERS-KENIX KIL — Dark Horse

1 ❑ Oct 1999 Cover: 2.95 **NM** value: **Cover or less**
• one shot **A:** Javier Saltares **W:** Randy Stradley

STAR WARS: THE BOUNTY HUNTERS-SCOUNDREL'S WAGES — Dark Horse

1 ❑ Aug 1999 Cover: 2.95 **NM** value: **Cover or less**
Circ: Diamd. preorders: **28,924**
No issue number. One-shot. **A:** Mel Rubi **W:** Mark Schultz

STAR WARS: THE EMPIRE STRIKES BACK — Marvel

Bk 1❑ Cover: 2.50 **NM** value: **Cover or less**
• mass-market paperback

Bk 1-2❑ Feb 1997 Cover: 9.95 **NM** value: **Cover or less**
• reprints Marvel's Star Wars #39-44

STAR WARS: THE EMPIRE STRIKES BACK-MANGA — Dark Horse

1 ❑ Jan 1999 Cover: 9.95 **NM** value: **Cover or less**
2 ❑ Feb 1999 Cover: 9.95 **NM** value: **Cover or less**
3 ❑ Mar 1999 Cover: 9.95 **NM** value: **Cover or less**
4 ❑ Apr 1999 Cover: 9.95 **NM** value: **Cover or less**

STAR WARS: THE JABBA TAPE — Dark Horse

1 ❑ Dec 1998 Cover: 2.95 **NM** value: **Cover or less**
Circ: Diamd. preorders: **24,343**
No issue number. **A:** Kilian Plunkett **W:** John Wagner

STAR WARS: THE LAST COMMAND — Dark Horse

1 ❑ Nov 1997 Cover: 2.95 **NM** value: **3.50**
Circ: Diamd. preorders: **41,741**
A: Edvin Biukovic **W:** Mike Baron; Timothy Zahn

2 ❑ Dec 1997 Cover: 2.95 **NM** value: **3.00**
Circ: Diamd. preorders: **36,320**
A: Edvin Biukovic **W:** Mike Baron; Timothy Zahn

3 ❑ Feb 1998 Cover: 2.95 **NM** value: **3.00**
Circ: Diamd. preorders: **32,967**
A: Edvin Biukovic **W:** Mike Baron; Timothy Zahn

4 ❑ Mar 1998 Cover: 2.95 **NM** value: **3.00**
Circ: Diamd. preorders: **32,669**
A: Edvin Biukovic **W:** Mike Baron; Timothy Zahn

5 ❑ Apr 1998 Cover: 2.95 **NM** value: **3.00**
Circ: Diamd. preorders: **33,848**
A: Edvin Biukovic **W:** Mike Baron; Timothy Zahn

6 ❑ Jul 1998 Cover: 2.95 **NM** value: **Cover or less**
Circ: Diamd. preorders: **30,297**
A: Edvin Biukovic **W:** Mike Baron; Timothy Zahn

Bk 1❑ Jun 1999 Cover: 17.95 **NM** value: **Cover or less**
• Trade Paperback. • collects mini-series

STAR WARS: THE PROTOCOL OFFENSIVE — Dark Horse

1 ❑ Sep 1997 Cover: 4.95 **NM** value: **Cover or less**
Circ: Diamd. preorders: **26,696**
No issue number. One-shot. • prestige format. • Co-written by actor who played C-3PO **A:** Igor Kordey **W:** Anthony Daniels; Anthony Daniels(C-3PO); Brian Daley; Ryder Windham

STAR WARS: UNDERWORLD-THE YAVIN VASSILIKA — Dark Horse

1/A ❑ Dec 2000 Cover: 2.99 **NM** value: **Cover or less**
Circ: Diamd. preorders: **32,515**
Drawn cover with Hand Solo, Lando Calrisian, and Boba Fett. **A:** Carlos Meglia **W:** Mike Kennedy

1/B ❑ Dec 2000 Cover: 2.99 **NM** value: **Cover or less**
Painted cover with Jabba the Hutt. **A:** Carlos Meglia **W:** Mike Kennedy

2/A ❑ Jan 2001 Cover: 2.99 **NM** value: **Cover or less**
Circ: Diamd. preorders: **28,041**
A: Carlos Meglia **W:** Mike Kennedy

2/B ❑ Jan 2001 Cover: 2.99 **NM** value: **Cover or less**
Photo cover. **A:** Carlos Meglia **W:** Mike Kennedy

3/A ❑ Feb 2001 Cover: 2.99 **NM** value: **Cover or less**
Circ: Diamd. preorders: **15,026**
Drawn cover with Hand Solo, Lando Calrisian, and Boba Fett. **A:** Carlos Meglia **W:** Mike Kennedy

3/B ❑ Feb 2001 Cover: 2.99 **NM** value: **Cover or less**
Circ: Diamd. preorders: **11,963**

CGC-graded: Multiply prices above by **33 for 9.9 M • 16 for 9.8 NM/M • 7 for 9.6 NM+ • 5 for 9.4 NM • 2.5 for 9.2 NM- • 1.5 for 9.0 VF/NM**

Photo cover featuring Harrison Ford. **A:** Carlos Meglia **W:** Mike Kennedy

4/A ❑ Mar 2001 Cover: 2.99 **NM** value: **Cover or less**
Circ: Diamd. preorders: **26,002**
A: Carlos Meglia **W:** Mike Kennedy

4/B ❑ Mar 2001 Cover: 2.99 **NM** value: **Cover or less**
Photo cover with bounty hunters. **A:** Carlos Meglia **W:** Mike Kennedy

5/A ❑ Apr 2001 Cover: 2.99 **NM** value: **Cover or less**
Circ: Diamd. preorders: **26,193**
A: Carlos Meglia **W:** Mike Kennedy

5/B ❑ Apr 2001 Cover: 2.99 **NM** value: **Cover or less**
A: Carlos Meglia **W:** Mike Kennedy

STAR WARS: UNION — Dark Horse

1 ❑ Nov 1999 Cover: 2.95 **NM** value: **14.00**
Circ: Diamd. preorders: **35,885**
A: Robert Teranshi **W:** Michael A. Stackpole

2 ❑ Dec 1999 Cover: 2.95 **NM** value: **10.00**
Circ: Diamd. preorders: **30,597**
A: Robert Teranshi **W:** Michael A. Stackpole

3 ❑ Jan 2000 Cover: 2.95 **NM** value: **7.00**
Circ: Diamd. preorders: **30,133**
A: Robert Teranshi **W:** Michael A. Stackpole

4 ❑ Feb 2000 Cover: 2.95 **NM** value: **5.00**
Circ: Diamd. preorders: **29,067**
• Wedding of Luke Skywalker & Mara Jade **A:** Robert Teranshi **W:** Michael A. Stackpole

Bk 1❑ 2000 Cover: 14.95 **NM** value: **Cover or less**
• Collects series **A:** Robert Teranshi **W:** Michael A. Stackpole

STAR WARS: VADER'S QUEST — Dark Horse

1 ❑ Feb 1999 Cover: 2.95 **NM** value: **Cover or less**
Circ: Diamd. preorders: **40,820**
A: Dave Gibbons **W:** Darko Macan

2 ❑ Mar 1999 Cover: 2.95 **NM** value: **Cover or less**
Circ: Diamd. preorders: **36,039**
A: Dave Gibbons **W:** Darko Macan

3 ❑ Apr 1999 Cover: 2.95 **NM** value: **Cover or less**
Circ: Diamd. preorders: **36,494**
A: Dave Gibbons **W:** Darko Macan

4 ❑ May 1999 Cover: 2.95 **NM** value: **Cover or less**
Circ: Diamd. preorders: **36,096**
A: Dave Gibbons **W:** Darko Macan

STAR WARS: X-WING ROGUE SQUADRON — Dark Horse

Who is the only pilot to be in both assaults on the Death Stars? Most Star Wars fans answer Luke Skywalker. The right answer, however is Wedge Antilles, Luke's childhood friend who left to join the Rebellion. This series, written by Michael Stackpole and based characters from his novels, chronicles Wedge's adventures after the Alliance's victory.

In the opening story arc, "The Rebel Opposition," Wedge and three others are ordered to escort a cargo ship from the planet Cilpar. Before they even clear Cilpar, they find a dozen Imperial tie fighters waiting for them. The only explanation for the ambush is that someone is leaking information about their activities. As the story unfolds, the only thing that's clear is that the situation on Cilpar is far more complicated than Wedge had expected. Rumors abounded that the Alliance had made a deal with the Empire to quash a local rebellion. Although it had come seeking refuge, the Rogue Squadron found itself caught in a three-way war.

Later stories in the series, although numbered as if they were separate mini-series on the cover, were actually part of an ongoing numbering that is recorded in each issue's indicia.

0.5 ❑ Feb 1997 **NM** value: **3.00**
• **CGC:** 6 graded, best 9.8
• Wizard mail-in edition.

0.5/Pl❑Feb 1997 Cover: 10.00 **NM** value: **Cover or less**
• Platinum edition.

1 ❑ Jul 1995 Cover: 2.95 **NM** value: **4.00**
Circ: CapCity orders: **34,400**
Rebel Opposition, Part 1; The Rebel Opposition, Part 1 **A:** Allen Nunis; Dave Dorman(cover) **W:** Mike Baron; Michael A. Stackpole

2 ❑ Aug 1995 Cover: 2.95 **NM** value: **3.50**
Circ: CapCity orders: **26,400**
Rebel Opposition, Part 2; The Rebel Opposition, Part 2 **A:** Allen Nunis; Dave Dorman(cover) **W:** Mike Baron; Michael A. Stackpole

3 ❑ Sep 1995 Cover: 2.95 **NM** value: **3.50**
Circ: CapCity orders: **20,800**
Rebel Opposition, Part 3; The Rebel Opposition, Part 3 **A:** Allen Nunis; Dave Dorman(cover) **W:** Mike Baron; Michael A. Stackpole

4 ❑ Oct 1995 Cover: 2.95 **NM** value: **3.50**
Circ: CapCity orders: **14,300**
Rebel Opposition, Part 4; The Rebel Opposition, Part 4 **A:** Allen Nunis; Dave Dorman(cover) **W:** Mike Baron; Michael A. Stackpole

5 ❑ Feb 1996 Cover: 2.95 **NM** value: **3.00**
The Phantom Affair, Part 1 **A:** Edvin Biukovic **W:** Darko Macan; Michael A. Stackpole

6 ❑ Mar 1996 Cover: 2.95 **NM** value: **3.00**
The Phantom Affair, Part 2 **A:** Edvin Biukovic **W:** Darko Macan; Michael A. Stackpole

7 ❑ Apr 1996 Cover: 2.95 **NM** value: **3.00**
The Phantom Affair, Part 3 **A:** Edvin Biukovic **W:** Darko Macan; Michael A. Stackpole

8 ❑ Jun 1996 Cover: 2.95 **NM** value: **3.00**
The Phantom Affair, Part 4 **A:** Edvin Biukovic **W:** Darko Macan; Michael A. Stackpole

9 ❑ Jul 1996 Cover: 2.95 **NM** value: **3.00**
Battleground: Tatooine, Part 1 **A:** John Nadeau; Mark Harrison(cover) **W:** Jan Strnad; Michael A. Stackpole

10 ❑ Jul 1996 Cover: 2.95 **NM** value: **3.00**
Battleground: Tatooine, Part 2 **A:** John Nadeau; Mark Harrison(cover) **W:** Jan Strnad; Michael A. Stackpole

11 ❑ Aug 1996 Cover: 2.95 **NM** value: **3.00**
Battleground: Tatooine, Part 3 **A:** John Nadeau; Mark Harrison(cover) **W:** Jan Strnad; Michael A. Stackpole

12 ❑ Sep 1996 Cover: 2.95 **NM** value: **3.00**
Circ: Diamd. preorders: **45,306**
Battleground: Tatooine, Part 4 **A:** John Nadeau; Mark Harrison(cover) **W:** Jan Strnad; Michael A. Stackpole

13 ❑ Oct 1996 Cover: 2.95 **NM** value: **3.00**
Circ: Diamd. preorders: **46,332**
The Warrior Princess, Part 1 **A:** John Nadeau; Mark Harrison(cover) **W:** Scott Tolson; Michael A. Stackpole

14 ❑ Dec 1996 Cover: 2.95 **NM** value: **3.00**
Circ: Diamd. preorders: **42,817**
The Warrior Princess, Part 2 **A:** John Nadeau; Mark Harrison(cover) **W:** Scott Tolson; Michael A. Stackpole

15 ❑ Jan 1997 Cover: 2.95 **NM** value: **3.00**
Circ: Diamd. preorders: **40,644**
The Warrior Princess, Part 3 **A:** John Nadeau; Mark Harrison(cover) **W:** Scott Tolson; Michael A. Stackpole

16 ❑ Feb 1997 Cover: 2.95 **NM** value: **3.00**
Circ: Diamd. preorders: **37,962**
The Warrior Princess, Part 4 **A:** John Nadeau; Mark Harrison(cover) **W:** Scott Tolson; Michael A. Stackpole

17 ❑ Mar 1997 Cover: 2.95 **NM** value: **3.00**
Circ: Diamd. preorders: **38,115**
Requiem for a Rogue, Part 1 **A:** Gary Erskine **W:** Jan Strnad; Michael A. Stackpole

18 ❑ Apr 1997 Cover: 2.95 **NM** value: **3.00**
Circ: Diamd. preorders: **35,888**
Requiem for a Rogue, Part 2 **A:** Gary Erskine **W:** Jan Strnad; Michael A. Stackpole

19 ❑ May 1997 Cover: 2.95 **NM** value: **3.00**
Circ: Diamd. preorders: **33,068**
Requiem for a Rogue, Part 3 **A:** Gary Erskine **W:** Jan Strnad; Michael A. Stackpole

20 ❑ Jun 1997 Cover: 2.95 **NM** value: **3.00**
Circ: Diamd. preorders: **32,292**
Requiem for a Rogue, Part 4 **A:** Gary Erskine **W:** Jan Strnad; Michael A. Stackpole

21 ❑ Aug 1997 Cover: 2.95 **NM** value: **3.00**
Circ: Diamd. preorders: **33,771**
In the Empire's Service, Part 1 **A:** John Nadeau **W:** Jan Strnad; Michael A. Stackpole

22 ❑ Sep 1997 Cover: 2.95 **NM** value: **3.00**
Circ: Diamd. preorders: **31,022**
In the Empire's Service, Part 2 **A:** John Nadeau **W:** Jan Strnad; Michael A. Stackpole

23 ❑ Oct 1997 Cover: 2.95 **NM** value: **3.00**
Circ: Diamd. preorders: **30,922**
In the Empire's Service, Part 3 **A:** John Nadeau **W:** Jan Strnad; Michael A. Stackpole

24 ❑ Nov 1997 Cover: 2.95 **NM** value: **3.00**
Circ: Diamd. preorders: **29,598**
In the Empire's Service, Part 4 **A:** John Nadeau **W:** Jan Strnad; Michael A. Stackpole

25 ❑ Dec 1997 Cover: 3.95 **NM** value: **4.00**
Circ: Diamd. preorders: **29,014**
• Giant-size. The Making of Baron Fel **A:** Steve Crespo **W:** Michael A. Stackpole ★ Origin of Baron Fel.

26 ❑ Jan 1998 Cover: 2.95 **NM** value: **Cover or less**
Circ: Diamd. preorders: **28,803**
Family Ties, Part 1 **A:** Jim Hall **W:** Michael A. Stackpole

27 ❑ Feb 1998 Cover: 2.95 **NM** value: **Cover or less**
Circ: Diamd. preorders: **27,062**
Family Ties, Part 2 **A:** Jim Hall **W:** Michael A. Stackpole

28 ❑ Mar 1998 Cover: 2.95 **NM** value: **Cover or less**
Circ: Diamd. preorders: **27,987**
Masquerade, Part 1 **A:** Drew Johnson **W:** Michael A. Stackpole

29 ❑ Apr 1998 Cover: 2.95 **NM** value: **Cover or less**
Circ: Diamd. preorders: **28,066**
Masquerade, Part 2 **A:** Drew Johnson **W:** Michael A. Stackpole

30 ❑ May 1998 Cover: 2.95 **NM** value: **Cover or less**
Circ: Diamd. preorders: **26,817**
Masquerade, Part 3 **A:** Drew Johnson; Jim Hall **W:** Michael A. Stackpole

31 ❑ Jun 1998 Cover: 2.95 **NM** value: **Cover or less**
Circ: Diamd. preorders: **26,906**
Masquerade, Part 4 **A:** Drew Johnson **W:** Michael A. Stackpole

32 ❑ Jul 1998 Cover: 2.95 **NM** value: **Cover or less**
Circ: Diamd. preorders: **25,665**
Mandatory Retirement, Part 1 **A:** Steve Crespo **W:** Michael A. Stackpole

33 ❑ Aug 1998 Cover: 2.95 **NM** value: **Cover or less**
Circ: Diamd. preorders: **24,388**
Mandatory Retirement, Part 2 **A:** Steve Crespo **W:** Michael A. Stackpole

34 ❑ Sep 1998 Cover: 2.95 **NM** value: **Cover or less**
Circ: Diamd. preorders: **23,882**
Mandatory Retirement, Part 3 **A:** Steve Crespo **W:** Michael A. Stackpole

35 ❑ Nov 1998 Cover: 2.95 **NM** value: **Cover or less**
Circ: Diamd. preorders: **23,856**
Mandatory Retirement, Part 4 **A:** Steve Crespo **W:** Michael A. Stackpole

Bk 1❑ Cover: 12.95 **NM** value: **Cover or less**
The Phantom Affair **A:** Edvin Biukovic **W:** Michael A. Stackpole

Bk 2❑ Nov 1997 Cover: 12.95 **NM** value: **Cover or less**
The Phantom Affair; Battleground: Tatooine • collects story-arc from issues #5-8 **A:** John Nadeau; Mark Harrison(cover) **W:** Michael A. Stackpole

Bk 3❑ Apr 1998 Cover: 12.95 **NM** value: **Cover or less**
• collects issues #9-12 plus Apple Jacks giveaway. Battleground Tatooine; The Warrior Princess **A:** John Nadeau; Mark Harrison(cover) **W:** Michael A. Stackpole

Bk 4❑ Nov 1998 Cover: 12.95 **NM** value: **Cover or less**
The Warrior Princess; Requiem for a Rogue • collects #13-16 **A:** Gary Erskine **W:** Michael A. Stackpole

Bk 5❑ Feb 1999 Cover: 12.95 **NM** value: **Cover or less**
Requiem For A Rogue; In the Empire's Service • collects story from #17-20 **A:** John Nadeau **W:** Michael A. Stackpole

Bk 6❑ May 1999 Cover: 12.95 **NM** value: **Cover or less**
In The Empire's Service; Blood & Honor • collects #21-24 **W:** Michael A. Stackpole

Bk 7❑ May 1999 Cover: 12.95 **NM** value: **Cover or less**
• Blood And Honor; collects #25-27

SE 1❑ Aug 1995 **NM** value: **1.00**
• **CGC:** 2 graded, best 9.6
No issue number. • promotional giveaway with Kellogg's Apple Jacks.

STAR WEEVILS — Rip Off

1 ❑ Cover: 1.00 **NM** value: **Cover or less**
A: J. Michael Leonard **W:** J. Michael Leonard

STAR WESTERN — Avalon

Wild Bill Hickok in "Last Stage to Cheyenne." Lash LaRue and "The Killers in the Hills." Tex Ritter in "Wanted: Dead or Alive!" The legendary Wyatt Earp in "Gun-Crazy Marshal." And, just to prove there's not a gender bias when it comes to gunplay, Annie Oakley in "Queen of Alkali Flats." These and other short comics stories of heroes, villains, and legends of the Old West, originally presented decades earlier, are collected and reprinted in black and white by Avalon.

But that's not all. In addition to these rippin' yarns of action and danger, back-up features provide added value to each issue. Ever wanted to understand Indian sign language? Curious as to the origins of the phrase "dead man's hand"? The answers are here. Moreover, each issue features a photo cover of an old Western movie star — including John Wayne and Jimmy Stewart — and biographical overviews of the actor and his relevant work. Finally, even though all tales are unfortunately uncredited, readers with an eye for art might spot early efforts from creators (for example, John Romita) who went on to greater fame.

1 ❑ Cover: 5.95 **NM** value: **Cover or less**

2 ❑ Cover: 5.95 **NM** value: **Cover or less**
Tom Mix: Blackmail!; Wyatt Earp: Gun-Crazy Marshal; Annie Oakley: Queen of Alkali Flats; Jingles and Wild Bill Hickok: Carniv • John Wayne feature

3 ❑ Cover: 5.95 **NM** value: **Cover or less**
Lash Larue: King of the Camp; Black Jack; Annie Oakley: Whena Dude Ain't a Dude; Denve • Clint Eastwood feature

4 ❑ Cover: 5.95 **NM** value: **Cover or less**

5 ❑ Cover: 5.95 **NM** value: **Cover or less**

S.T.A.T. — Majestic

1 ❑ Dec 1993 Cover: 2.25 **NM** value: **Cover or less**
Circ: CapCity orders: **8,700**
A: Phil Hester **W:** Fred Schiller

1/SC❑Dec 1993 Cover: 2.25 **NM** value: **Cover or less**
foil cover.

STATIC — DC / Milestone

In every high school there's the kid who doesn't fit in- the brainy little guy who tries hard to be cool, but instead just gets beat up a lot by the local bullies. In Ernest Hemingway High School, that person goes by the name of Virgil Ovid Hawkins. Virgil, to put it bluntly, is a geek.

But ever since he was caught up in the "Big Bang," when he inhaled the strange gas being used by police, Virgil has also been something else: a super-hero. Called Static because he controls electrostatic energy, using it to do everything from "flying" atop a garbage can lid to throwing taser-like punches against his enemies, his real secret weapon is the same inspired intellect that makes him a social outcast at school.

1 ❑ Jun 1993 Cover: 1.50 **NM** value: **2.00**
Circ: CapCity orders: **30,200** • **CGC:** 1 graded, best 9.2
Trail By Fire **A:** John Paul Leon **W:** Robert Washington III; Dwayne McDuffie ★ 1st Appearance of Hotstreak, Frieda Goren, Static.

1/CS❑Jun 1993 Cover: 2.95 **NM** value: **3.00**
• **CGC:** 1 graded, best 9.4
Trail By Fire • poster; trading card; Collector's Set **A:** John Paul Leon **W:** Robert Washington III; Dwayne McDuffie ★ 1st Appearance of Hotstreak, Frieda Goren, Static.

1/SI❑ Jun 1993 **NM** value: **3.00**
• Silver (limited promotional) edition. Trail By Fire **A:** John Paul Leon **W:** Robert Washington III; Dwayne McDuffie ★ 1st Appearance of Hotstreak, Frieda Goren, Static.

2 ❑ Jul 1993 Cover: 1.50 **NM** value: **Cover or less**
Circ: CapCity orders: **16,800**

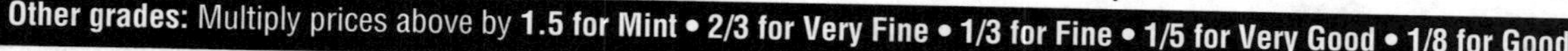
Other grades: Multiply prices above by **1.5 for Mint • 2/3 for Very Fine • 1/3 for Fine • 1/5 for Very Good • 1/8 for Good**

📖 Everything But The Girl **A:** John Paul Leon **W:** Robert Washington III; Dwayne McDuffie ★ Origin of Static. ★ 1st Appearance of Tarmack.

3 ❑ Aug 1993 Cover: 1.50 **NM** value: **Cover or less**
Circ: CapCity orders: **13,350**
📖 Pounding The Pavement **A:** John Paul Leon **W:** Robert Washington III; Dwayne McDuffie

4 ❑ Sep 1993 Cover: 1.50 **NM** value: **Cover or less**
Circ: CapCity orders: **11,000**
★ 1st Appearance of Don Giacomo Cornelius.

5 ❑ Oct 1993 Cover: 1.50 **NM** value: **Cover or less**
Circ: CapCity orders: **8,800**
📖 Megablast **A:** John Paul Leon **W:** Robert Washington III ★ 1st Appearance of Commando X.

6 ❑ Nov 1993 Cover: 1.50 **NM** value: **Cover or less**
Circ: CapCity orders: **8,750**

7 ❑ Dec 1993 Cover: 1.50 **NM** value: **Cover or less**
Circ: CapCity orders: **8,550**

8 ❑ Jan 1994 Cover: 1.50 **NM** value: **Cover or less**
Circ: CapCity orders: **11,650**
📖 Shadow War, Part 5 • Shadow War

9 ❑ Feb 1994 Cover: 1.50 **NM** value: **Cover or less**
Circ: CapCity orders: **7,450**
📖 Static Needs A New Pair Of Shoes **A:** John Paul Leon **W:** Robert Washington III ★ 1st Appearance of Virus.

10 ❑ Mar 1994 Cover: 1.50 **NM** value: **Cover or less**
Circ: CapCity orders: **6,750**
★ 1st Appearance of Puff, Coil.

11 ❑ Apr 1994 Cover: 1.50 **NM** value: **Cover or less**
Circ: CapCity orders: **6,200**

12 ❑ May 1994 Cover: 1.50 **NM** value: **Cover or less**
Circ: CapCity orders: **5,950**
📖 Full Yellow Jacket **A:** Humberto Ramos **W:** Adam Blaustein; Yves Fezzani ★ 1st Appearance of Snakefinger.

13 ❑ Jun 1994 Cover: 1.50 **NM** value: **Cover or less**
Circ: CapCity orders: **5,950**

14 ❑ Aug 1994 Cover: 2.50 **NM** value: **Cover or less**
Circ: CapCity orders: **19,050**
• Giant-size. 📖 Worlds Collide; Worlds Collide, Part 14

15 ❑ Sep 1994 Cover: 1.75 **NM** value: **Cover or less**
Circ: CapCity orders: **5,900**

16 ❑ Oct 1994 Cover: 1.75 **NM** value: **Cover or less**
Circ: CapCity orders: **5,800**
📖 What are Little Boys Made Of? ★ 1st Appearance of Joyride.

17 ❑ Nov 1994 Cover: 1.75 **NM** value: **Cover or less**
Circ: CapCity orders: **5,400**
📖 What are Little Boys Made Of?

18 ❑ Dec 1994 Cover: 1.75 **NM** value: **Cover or less**
Circ: CapCity orders: **5,100**
📖 What are Little Boys Made Of? **A:** Wilfred **W:** Robert Washington III

19 ❑ Jan 1995 Cover: 1.75 **NM** value: **Cover or less**
Circ: CapCity orders: **4,550**
📖 What are Little Boys Made Of?

20 ❑ Feb 1995 Cover: 1.75 **NM** value: **Cover or less**
Circ: CapCity orders: **4,050**
📖 What are Little Boys Made Of?

21 ❑ Mar 1995 Cover: 1.75 **NM** value: **Cover or less**
Circ: CapCity orders: **3,650**
★ Appearance of Blood Syndicate.

22 ❑ Apr 1995 Cover: 1.75 **NM** value: **Cover or less**
Circ: CapCity orders: **3,350**

23 ❑ Jun 1995 Cover: 1.75 **NM** value: **Cover or less**
Circ: CapCity orders: **3,200**

24 ❑ Jul 1995 Cover: 1.75 **NM** value: **Cover or less**
Circ: CapCity orders: **3,300**

25 ❑ Jul 1995 Cover: 3.95 **NM** value: **Cover or less**
Circ: CapCity orders: **3,550**
• Double-size. 📖 Long Hot Summer

26 ❑ Aug 1995 Cover: 2.50 **NM** value: **Cover or less**
Circ: CapCity orders: **3,275**
📖 Long Hot Summer

27 ❑ Sep 1995 Cover: 0.99 **NM** value: **2.50**
Circ: CapCity orders: **3,575**
📖 Long Hot Summer

28 ❑ Oct 1995 Cover: 2.50 **NM** value: **Cover or less**
Circ: CapCity orders: **2,625**

29 ❑ Nov 1995 Cover: 2.50 **NM** value: **Cover or less**
📖 The Long Hot Summer

30 ❑ Dec 1995 Cover: 2.50 **NM** value: **Cover or less**
★ Death of Larry.

31 ❑ Jan 1996 Cover: 0.99 **NM** value: **Cover or less**
📖 Cape Fear **A:** Gil Kane **W:** Adam Blaustein; Yves Fezzani

32 ❑ Feb 1996 Cover: 2.50 **NM** value: **Cover or less**
33 ❑ Mar 1996 Cover: 2.50 **NM** value: **Cover or less**
📖 Bee, My Love **A:** Jeff Moore **W:** Adam Blaustein; Yves Fezzani

34 ❑ Apr 1996 Cover: 2.50 **NM** value: **Cover or less**
📖 Blame it on Picasso **A:** Jeff Moore **W:** Adam Blaustein; Yves Fezzani

35 ❑ May 1996 Cover: 2.50 **NM** value: **Cover or less**
36 ❑ Jun 1996 Cover: 2.50 **NM** value: **Cover or less**
37 ❑ Jul 1996 Cover: 2.50 **NM** value: **Cover or less**
38 ❑ Aug 1996 Cover: 2.50 **NM** value: **Cover or less**
39 ❑ Sep 1996 Cover: 2.50 **NM** value: **Cover or less**
40 ❑ Oct 1996 Cover: 2.50 **NM** value: **Cover or less**
📖 Boyz Night Out **A:** Keith Pollard **W:** Brian McDonald

41 ❑ Nov 1996 Cover: 2.50 **NM** value: **Cover or less**
Circ: Diamd. preorders: **5,476**
📖 Love Bites, Part 1; Love ites, Part 1 **A:** Jeff Moore **W:** Jaqueline Ching

42 ❑ Dec 1996 Cover: 2.50 **NM** value: **Cover or less**
Circ: Diamd. preorders: **5,279**
📖 Love Bites, Part 2; Love ites, Part 2 **A:** Jeff Moore **W:** Jaqueline Ching

43 ❑ Jan 1997 Cover: 2.50 **NM** value: **Cover or less**
Circ: Diamd. preorders: **5,110**
📖 Power Struggle; Power Strugge **A:** Wilfred **W:** Joseph Illidge

44 ❑ Feb 1997 Cover: 2.50 **NM** value: **Cover or less**
Circ: Diamd. preorders: **4,901**

45 ❑ Mar 1997 Cover: 2.50 **NM** value: **Cover or less**
Circ: Diamd. preorders: **4,766**

46 ❑ Apr 1997 Cover: 2.50 **NM** value: **Cover or less**
Circ: Diamd. preorders: **4,572**

47 ❑ May 1997 Cover: 2.50 **NM** value: **Cover or less**
Circ: Diamd. preorders: **4,816**
final issue.

Bk 1 ❑ Cover: 9.95 **NM** value: **Cover or less**
📖 Trial by Fire • Static Shock: Trial by Fire; Collects Static #1-4 **A:** Robert Washington III **W:** Dwayne McDuffie

STATIC SHOCK!: REBIRTH OF THE COOL — DC / Milestone

1 ❑ Jan 2001 Cover: 2.50 **NM** value: **Cover or less**
Circ: Diamd. preorders: **7,716**
📖 As I Was Saying Before I Was Interrupted... **A:** John Paul Leon **W:** Dwayne McDuffie

2 ❑ Feb 2001 Cover: 2.50 **NM** value: **Cover or less**
Circ: Diamd. preorders: **6,206**
📖 Standing on the Verge of Getting it On **A:** John Paul Leon **W:** Dwayne McDuffie

3 ❑ Mar 2001 Cover: 2.50 **NM** value: **Cover or less**
Circ: Diamd. preorders: **5,366**
📖 The Story So Far... **A:** John Paul Leon **W:** Dwayne McDuffie

4 ❑ Apr 2001 Cover: 2.50 **NM** value: **Cover or less**
Circ: Diamd. preorders: **5,100**

STEALTH FORCE — Malibu

1 ❑ Jul 1987 Cover: 1.95 **NM** value: **Cover or less**
A: Patrick Olliffe **W:** Mike Valerio

2 ❑ Aug 1987 Cover: 1.95 **NM** value: **Cover or less**
A: Patrick Olliffe **W:** Mike Valerio

3 ❑ Sep 1987 Cover: 1.95 **NM** value: **Cover or less**
A: Patrick Olliffe **W:** Mike Valerio

4 ❑ Oct 1987 Cover: 1.95 **NM** value: **Cover or less**
A: Patrick Olliffe **W:** Mike Valerio

5 ❑ Nov 1987 Cover: 1.95 **NM** value: **Cover or less**
A: Patrick Olliffe **W:** Mike Valerio

6 ❑ Dec 1987 Cover: 1.95 **NM** value: **Cover or less**
A: Patrick Olliffe **W:** Mike Valerio

7 ❑ Jan 1988 Cover: 1.95 **NM** value: **Cover or less**
A: Patrick Olliffe **W:** Mike Valerio

8 ❑ Feb 1988 Cover: 1.95 **NM** value: **Cover or less**
• Eternity begins as publisher **A:** Patrick Olliffe **W:** Mike Valerio

STEALTH SQUAD — Petra

0 ❑ Cover: 2.50 **NM** value: **Cover or less**
Circ: CapCity orders: **3,235**
★ Origin of Stealth Squad.

1 ❑ Cover: 2.50 **NM** value: **Cover or less**
📖 All Fall Down! **A:** Philip Lane **W:** Michael Willis ★ 1st Appearance of Fire Flare, Swoop, Kid Mammoth, Solar Blade, Stealth One, Strikeforce Champion, Stealth Squad.

2 ❑ Cover: 2.50 **NM** value: **Cover or less**
3 ❑ Cover: 2.50 **NM** value: **Cover or less**
4 ❑ Cover: 2.50 **NM** value: **Cover or less**

STEAM DETECTIVES — Viz

Bk 1 ❑ Aug 1998, b&w Cover: 15.95 **NM** value: **Cover or less**

STEAMPUNK — WildStorm

1 ❑ Apr 2000 Cover: 2.50 **NM** value: **Cover or less**
Circ: Diamd. preorders: **46,892** • **CGC:** 2 graded, best 9.6
📖 Birth Pangs **A:** Joe Kelly **W:** Joe Kelly; Chris Bachalo

2 ❑ May 2000 Cover: 2.50 **NM** value: **Cover or less**
Circ: Diamd. preorders: **38,530**
📖 100 Dragons **A:** Joe Kelly **W:** Joe Kelly; Chris Bachalo

3 ❑ Jun 2000 Cover: 2.50 **NM** value: **Cover or less**
Circ: Diamd. preorders: **36,667**
A: Joe Kelly **W:** Joe Kelly; Chris Bachalo

4 ❑ Jul 2000 Cover: 2.50 **NM** value: **Cover or less**
Circ: Diamd. preorders: **39,675**
A: Joe Kelly **W:** Joe Kelly; Chris Bachalo

5 ❑ Oct 2000 Cover: 2.50 **NM** value: **Cover or less**
Circ: Diamd. preorders: **34,197**
📖 Contrition **A:** Joe Kelly **W:** Joe Kelly; Chris Bachalo

6 ❑ Jan 2001 Cover: 2.50 **NM** value: **Cover or less**
Circ: Diamd. preorders: **30,725**
📖 Mechanica Sundown, Part 1 **A:** Joe Kelly **W:** Joe Kelly; Chris Bachalo

7 ❑ Apr 2001 Cover: 2.50 **NM** value: **Cover or less**
Circ: Diamd. preorders: **23,777**
📖 Mechanica Sundown, Part 2 **A:** Joe Kelly **W:** Joe Kelly; Chris Bachalo

8 ❑ Jun 2001 Cover: 2.50 **NM** value: **Cover or less**
Circ: Diamd. preorders: **22,366**

9 ❑ Sep 2001 Cover: 2.50 **NM** value: **Cover or less**
Circ: Diamd. preorders: **21,895**

STEAMPUNK: CATECHISM — WildStorm

1 ❑ Jan 2000 Cover: 2.50 **NM** value: **Cover or less**
Circ: Diamd. preorders: **38,261**
A: Joe Kelly **W:** Joe Kelly; Chris Bachalo

STECH — Silverwolf

1 ❑ Dec 1986, b&w Cover: 1.50 **NM** value: **Cover or less**
📖 Triad, Part 1 **A:** Lorenzo Lizana **W:** Kris Silver; SP Cook

STEED AND MRS. PEEL — Eclipse

1 ❑ Dec 1990 Cover: 4.95 **NM** value: **5.00**
Circ: CapCity orders: **3,975**
📖 Crown And Anchor **A:** Ian Gibson **W:** Grant Morrison

2 ❑ May 1991 Cover: 4.95 **NM** value: **5.00**
Circ: CapCity orders: **6,200**
A: Ian Gibson **W:** Grant Morrison

3 ❑ Cover: 4.95 **NM** value: **5.00**
Circ: CapCity orders: **5,600**
A: Ian Gibson **W:** Grant Morrison

STEEL — DC

John Henry Irons was working as a steelworker when the monster Doomsday dropped a building on him. Superman saved Irons that day, and Irons vowed his gratitude. So when Doomsday later killed Superman, Irons used his engineering skills to forge a suit of high-powered armor and become the new "Man of Steel."

When Superman came back from the dead, Irons decided to go back and clean up his old neighborhood, Washington D.C. Irons onced worked as a weapons designer for a firm named AmerTek where he created the awesomely powerful BG-80 "Toastmaster" gun. Now street gangs were using these guns to chop each other up, killing innocents in the crossfire. Someone had to put a stop to it, and that someone was John Henry Irons, a.k.a. Steel.

0 ❑ Oct 1994 Cover: 1.50 **NM** value: **2.00**
Circ: CapCity orders: **31,550**
📖 In The Beginning! **A:** Chris Batista **W:** Louise Simonson

1 ❑ Feb 1994 Cover: 1.50 **NM** value: **2.00**
Circ: CapCity orders: **80,400**
📖 Wrought Iron **A:** Chris Batista **W:** Jon Bogdanove; Louise Simonson

2 ❑ Mar 1994 Cover: 1.50 **NM** value: **Cover or less**
Circ: CapCity orders: **40,900**
📖 Turf War! **A:** Chris Batista **W:** Jon Bogdanove; Louise Simonson

3 ❑ Apr 1994 Cover: 1.50 **NM** value: **Cover or less**
Circ: CapCity orders: **33,750**

4 ❑ May 1994 Cover: 1.50 **NM** value: **Cover or less**
Circ: CapCity orders: **32,200**

5 ❑ Jun 1994 Cover: 1.50 **NM** value: **Cover or less**
Circ: CapCity orders: **29,150**
📖 Retaliation **A:** Chris Batista **W:** Louise Simonson

6 ❑ Jul 1994 Cover: 1.50 **NM** value: **Cover or less**
Circ: CapCity orders: **35,600**
📖 Worlds Collide, Part 5 ★ Appearance of Hardware.

7 ❑ Aug 1994 Cover: 1.50 **NM** value: **Cover or less**
Circ: CapCity orders: **31,550**
📖 Worlds Collide, Part 12 ★ Appearance of Icon, Hardware.

8 ❑ Sep 1994 Cover: 1.50 **NM** value: **Cover or less**
Circ: CapCity orders: **26,100**

9 ❑ Nov 1994 Cover: 1.50 **NM** value: **Cover or less**
Circ: CapCity orders: **22,600**

10 ❑ Dec 1994 Cover: 1.50 **NM** value: **Cover or less**
Circ: CapCity orders: **21,000**

11 ❑ Jan 1995 Cover: 1.50 **NM** value: **Cover or less**
Circ: CapCity orders: **19,000**
📖 Maximum Orbit, Part 1 **A:** Chris Batista **W:** Louise Simonson

12 ❑ Feb 1995 Cover: 1.50 **NM** value: **Cover or less**
Circ: CapCity orders: **16,825**
📖 Maximum Orbit, Part 2

13 ❑ Mar 1995 Cover: 1.50 **NM** value: **Cover or less**
Circ: CapCity orders: **14,750**
📖 Maximum Orbit, Part 3

14 ❑ Apr 1995 Cover: 1.50 **NM** value: **Cover or less**
Circ: CapCity orders: **14,500**

15 ❑ May 1995 Cover: 1.50 **NM** value: **Cover or less**
Circ: CapCity orders: **12,950**

16 ❑ Jun 1995 Cover: 1.95 **NM** value: **Cover or less**
Circ: CapCity orders: **12,225**

17 ❑ Jul 1995 Cover: 1.95 **NM** value: **Cover or less**
Circ: CapCity orders: **12,220**

18 ❑ Aug 1995 Cover: 1.95 **NM** value: **Cover or less**
Circ: CapCity orders: **12,000**

19 ❑ Sep 1995 Cover: 1.95 **NM** value: **Cover or less**
Circ: CapCity orders: **10,825**

20 ❑ Oct 1995 Cover: 1.95 **NM** value: **Cover or less**
Circ: CapCity orders: **8,875**

21 ❑ Nov 1995 Cover: 1.95 **NM** value: **Cover or less**
• Underworld Unleashed

22 ❑ Dec 1995 Cover: 1.95 **NM** value: **Cover or less**
★ Appearance of Supergirl, Eradicator.

23 ❑ Jan 1996 Cover: 1.95 **NM** value: **Cover or less**
📖 Wired! **A:** Phil Gosier **W:** Louise Simonson

24 ❑ Feb 1996 Cover: 1.95 **NM** value: **Cover or less**
📖 Countdown to Destiny **A:** Lee Sullivan **W:** Louise Simonson

25 ❑ Mar 1996 Cover: 1.95 **NM** value: **Cover or less**
📖 Family Feud, Part 1 **A:** Phil Gosier **W:** Louise Simonson

26 ❑ May 1996 Cover: 1.95 **NM** value: **Cover or less**
27 ❑ Jun 1996 Cover: 1.95 **NM** value: **Cover or less**
28 ❑ Jul 1996 Cover: 1.95 **NM** value: **Cover or less**
★ Versus Plasmus.

29 ❑ Aug 1996 Cover: 1.95 **NM** value: **Cover or less**
30 ❑ Sep 1996 Cover: 1.95 **NM** value: **Cover or less**
31 ❑ Oct 1996 Cover: 1.95 **NM** value: **Cover or less**
📖 Possession **A:** Phil Gosier **W:** Louise Simonson

32 ❑ Nov 1996 Cover: 1.95 **NM** value: **Cover or less**
Circ: Diamd. preorders: **19,295**
📖 Herculean Labors **A:** Roger Robinson **W:** Darren Vincenzo ★ Versus Blockbuster.

33 ❑ Dec 1996 Cover: 1.95 **NM** value: **Cover or less**
Circ: Diamd. preorders: **19,078**
📖 Withdrawal Symptoms **A:** Peter J. Tomasi **W:** Peter J. Tomasi

34 ❑ Jan 1997 Cover: 1.95 **NM** value: **Cover or less**
Circ: Diamd. preorders: **21,153**
📖 Bang • new armor **A:** Denys Cowan; Tom Palmer **W:** Christopher Priest ★ Appearance of Margot.

35 ❑ Feb 1997 Cover: 1.95 **NM** value: **Cover or less**
Circ: Diamd. preorders: **18,700**

CGC-graded: Multiply prices above by **33 for 9.9 M • 16 for 9.8 NM/M • 7 for 9.6 NM+ • 5 for 9.4 NM • 2.5 for 9.2 NM- • 1.5 for 9.0 VF/NM**

36 ❑ Mar 1997 Cover: 1.95 **NM** value: **Cover or less**
Circ: Diamd. preorders: **17,948**
Home **A:** De\ **W:** Christopher Priest

37 ❑ Apr 1997 Cover: 1.95 **NM** value: **Cover or less**
Circ: Diamd. preorders: **17,106**

38 ❑ May 1997 Cover: 1.95 **NM** value: **Cover or less**
Circ: Diamd. preorders: **16,811**

39 ❑ Jun 1997 Cover: 1.95 **NM** value: **Cover or less**
Circ: Diamd. preorders: **16,677**

40 ❑ Jul 1997 Cover: 1.95 **NM** value: **2.25**
Circ: Diamd. preorders: **16,220**
The Never Ending Story **A:** Vince Giarrano **W:** Christopher Priest ★ 1st Appearance of new hammer.

41 ❑ Aug 1997 Cover: 1.95 **NM** value: **Cover or less**
Circ: Diamd. preorders: **15,735**

42 ❑ Sep 1997 Cover: 1.95 **NM** value: **Cover or less**
Circ: Diamd. preorders: **16,076**

43 ❑ Oct 1997 Cover: 1.95 **NM** value: **Cover or less**
Circ: Diamd. preorders: **18,299**
• Genesis ★ Appearance of Superman.

44 ❑ Nov 1997 Cover: 1.95 **NM** value: **Cover or less**
Circ: Diamd. preorders: **15,114**

45 ❑ Dec 1997 Cover: 1.95 **NM** value: **Cover or less**
Circ: Diamd. preorders: **15,351**
Face cover. Fire **A:** Denys Cowan; Tom Palmer **W:** Christopher Priest

46 ❑ Jan 1998 Cover: 1.95 **NM** value: **Cover or less**
Circ: Diamd. preorders: **14,651**
Bori **A:** Denys Cowan; Tom Palmer **W:** Christopher Priest ★ Appearance of Superboy.

47 ❑ Feb 1998 Cover: 1.95 **NM** value: **2.50**
Circ: Diamd. preorders: **13,380**

48 ❑ Mar 1998 Cover: 2.50 **NM** value: **Cover or less**
Circ: Diamd. preorders: **12,815**

49 ❑ Apr 1998 Cover: 2.50 **NM** value: **Cover or less**
Circ: Diamd. preorders: **12,212**
Heart **A:** Denys Cowan; Tom Palmer **W:** Christopher Priest

50 ❑ May 1998 Cover: 2.50 **NM** value: **Cover or less**
Circ: Diamd. preorders: **18,561**
• Millennium Giants ★ Appearance of Superman.

51 ❑ Jun 1998 Cover: 2.50 **NM** value: **Cover or less**
Circ: Diamd. preorders: **12,454**

52 ❑ Jul 1998 Cover: 2.50 **NM** value: **Cover or less**
Circ: Diamd. preorders: **13,235**
final issue.

Anl 1❑ca. 1994 Cover: 2.95 **NM** value: **Cover or less**
Circ: CapCity orders: **20,050**
• Elseworlds

Anl 2❑ca. 1995 Cover: 3.95 **NM** value: **Cover or less**
Circ: CapCity orders: **9,250**
• Year One

Bk 1❑ Cover: 19.95 **NM** value: **Cover or less**
The Forging of a Hero **A:** Kevin West; Jon Bogdanove; Chris Batista **W:** Jon Bogdanove; Louise Simonson ★ Appearance of Collects early Steel.

STEEL ANGEL — Gauntlet

1 ❑ Cover: 2.50 **NM** value: **Cover or less**
A: Fredd Gorham **W:** Scott Friedermeyer

STEEL CLAW, THE — Fleetway-Quality

1 ❑ Dec 1986 Cover: 0.75 **NM** value: **1.50**
Circ: CapCity orders: **6,675**
A: Gary Leach; Jesus Blasco **W:** H. Ken Bulmer

2 ❑ Jan 1987 Cover: 0.75 **NM** value: **1.50**
Circ: CapCity orders: **5,500**

3 ❑ Feb 1987 Cover: 0.75 **NM** value: **1.50**
Circ: CapCity orders: **8,410**

4 ❑ Mar 1987 Cover: 1.25 **NM** value: **1.50**
Circ: CapCity orders: **3,750**

5 ❑ Apr 1987 Cover: 1.25 **NM** value: **1.50**

STEELDRAGON STORIES — Steeldragon

1 ❑ Cover: 1.50 **NM** value: **Cover or less**

STEELE DESTINIES — Nightscapes

1 ❑ Apr 1995, b&w Cover: 2.95 **NM** value: **Cover or less**
2 ❑ Jun 1995, b&w Cover: 2.95 **NM** value: **Cover or less**
3 ❑ Sep 1995, b&w Cover: 2.95 **NM** value: **Cover or less**

STEELGRIP STARKEY — Marvel / Epic

1 ❑ Jun 1986 Cover: 1.50 **NM** value: **1.75**
Circ: CapCity orders: **10,700**
Working Man's Myth! **A:** Alan Weiss **W:** Alan Weiss

2 ❑ Aug 1986 Cover: 1.50 **NM** value: **1.75**
Circ: CapCity orders: **8,700**

3 ❑ Nov 1986 Cover: 1.50 **NM** value: **1.75**
Circ: CapCity orders: **7,700**

4 ❑ Dec 1986 Cover: 1.50 **NM** value: **1.75**
Circ: CapCity orders: **7,400**

5 ❑ Jan 1987 Cover: 1.50 **NM** value: **1.75**
Circ: CapCity orders: **6,000**

6 ❑ May 1987 Cover: 1.75 **NM** value: **Cover or less**
Circ: CapCity orders: **5,750**

STEEL, THE INDESTRUCTIBLE MAN — DC

1 ❑ Mar 1978 Cover: 0.35 **NM** value: **3.00**
• **CGC:** 2 graded, best 9.4
From Hell Is Forged…A Hero! **A:** Don Heck **W:** Gerry Conway ★ Origin of Steel. ★ 1st Appearance of Steel.

2 ❑ Apr 1978 Cover: 0.35 **NM** value: **2.00**
3 ❑ Jun 1978 Cover: 0.35 **NM** value: **2.00**
4 ❑ Sep 1978 Cover: 0.35 **NM** value: **2.00**
5 ❑ Nov 1978 Cover: 0.50 **NM** value: **2.00**

STEEL PULSE — True Fiction

1 ❑ Mar 1986, b&w Cover: 2.00 **NM** value: **Cover or less**
This Belt is Mine!; Arthur "Sherlock" Jones Wrestling Detective: Death Grip **A:** Richard W. Florence **W:** Dennis J. Pimple

2 ❑ b&w Cover: 2.00 **NM** value: **Cover or less**
3 ❑ b&w Cover: 2.00 **NM** value: **Cover or less**
4 ❑ Cover: 3.50 **NM** value: **Cover or less**

STEEL STERLING — Archie / Red Circle

4 ❑ Jan 1984 Cover: 1.00 **NM** value: **Cover or less**
A License to Kill • Red Circle publishes **A:** Eduardo Barreto **W:** Robert Kanigher

5 ❑ Mar 1984 Cover: 1.00 **NM** value: **Cover or less**
The Young Steelers: Too Easy to Kill • Archie publishes **A:** McLaughlin **W:** Robert Kanigher

6 ❑ May 1984 Cover: 1.00 **NM** value: **Cover or less**
7 ❑ Jul 1984 Cover: 1.00 **NM** value: **Cover or less**

STEEL: THE FORGING OF A HERO — DC

Bk 1❑ Cover: 19.95 **NM** value: **Cover or less**
• collects Adventures of Superman #500, Superman: The Man of Steel #22, and Steel #1-6, 8, 0

STEEL: THE OFFICIAL COMIC ADAPTATION OF THE WARNER BROS. MOTION PICTURE — DC

1 ❑ Sep 1997 Cover: 4.95 **NM** value: **Cover or less**
Circ: Diamd. preorders: **9,908**
No issue number. • prestige format.

STEELTOWN ROCKERS — Marvel

1 ❑ Apr 1990 Cover: 1.00 **NM** value: **Cover or less**
Circ: CapCity orders: **13,400**
Held For Ransom **A:** Steve Leialoha **W:** Elaine Lee

2 ❑ May 1990 Cover: 1.00 **NM** value: **Cover or less**
Circ: CapCity orders: **9,800**
A: Steve Leialoha **W:** Elaine Lee

3 ❑ Jun 1990 Cover: 1.00 **NM** value: **Cover or less**
Circ: CapCity orders: **6,200**
A: Steve Leialoha **W:** Elaine Lee

4 ❑ Jul 1990 Cover: 1.00 **NM** value: **Cover or less**
Circ: CapCity orders: **4,900**
A: Steve Leialoha **W:** Elaine Lee

5 ❑ Aug 1990 Cover: 1.00 **NM** value: **Cover or less**
Circ: CapCity orders: **4,100**
A: Steve Leialoha **W:** Elaine Lee

6 ❑ Sep 1990 Cover: 1.00 **NM** value: **Cover or less**
Circ: CapCity orders: **3,600**
A: Steve Leialoha **W:** Elaine Lee

STELLAR COMICS — Stellar

1 ❑ Cover: 2.50 **NM** value: **Cover or less**
Noble: The Jungle; Hello, Goodbye, Part 1; Idestep: Prologue **A:** Dave Johnson **W:** Dave Johnson; H.F. Richardson III

STELLAR LOSERS — Antarctic

1 ❑ Feb 1993, b&w Cover: 2.50 **NM** value: **Cover or less**
2 ❑ Apr 1993, b&w Cover: 2.50 **NM** value: **Cover or less**
3 ❑ Jun 1993, b&w Cover: 2.50 **NM** value: **Cover or less**

STEPHEN DARKLORD — Rak

1 ❑ b&w Cover: 1.75 **NM** value: **Cover or less**
2 ❑ b&w Cover: 1.75 **NM** value: **Cover or less**
3 ❑ b&w Cover: 1.75 **NM** value: **Cover or less**

STEPS TO A DRUG FREE LIFE — David G. Brown Studios

1 ❑ Feb 1998 **NM** value: **1.00**
No issue number. • promotional comic done for the Alcohol and Drug Council of Greater L.A. and Share Inc.

STERN WHEELER — Spotlight

1 ❑ Cover: 1.75 **NM** value: **Cover or less**

STEVE CANYON COMICS — Harvey

Steve Canyon was designed to be the ultimate adventurer: he's a ruggedly handsome and charming ladies' man, as well as a skilled fighter and pilot. Along with a crew of other ex-Air Force members, he's formed an international air service called Horizon's Unlimited. For them, no danger is too great, no job is too small.

Of course, when they find themselves working for the beautiful but calculating Copper Calhoun, known on Wall Street as the Copperhead, they just might change their minds.

Writer/Artist Milton Caniff was well-known for his newspaper strips, as well as other artistic endeavors. His most memorable work was a strip called Terry and the Pirates, but he gave that up in 1947 for more personal control over his work. Steve Canyon ran as a newspaper strip for 41 years, ending with Caniff's death in 1988.

1 ❑ Feb 1948 Cover: 0.10 **NM** value: **110.00**
• **CGC:** 1 graded, best 7.0
Special Assignment; Take-Off for Adventure; Dangerous Flight (text); Kid Brother; Plane Talk; Cartoons & Jokes; Flossie; Puzzle Fun (activity); Call to Action (text) • Reprints comic strips, Bio of Milton Caniff **A:** Milton Caniff; Frank Engli **W:** Milton Caniff; Frank Engli

2 ❑ Apr 1948 Cover: 0.10 **NM** value: **75.00**
• **CGC:** 1 graded, best 9.0
• Reprints comic strips **A:** Milton Caniff **W:** Milton Caniff

3 ❑ Jun 1948 Cover: 0.10 **NM** value: **55.00**
• Reprints comic strips **A:** Milton Caniff **W:** Milton Caniff

4 ❑ Aug 1948 Cover: 0.10 **NM** value: **55.00**
• **CGC:** 1 graded, best 9.4
• Reprints comic strips **A:** Milton Caniff **W:** Milton Caniff

5 ❑ Oct 1948 Cover: 0.10 **NM** value: **55.00**
• Reprints comic strips **A:** Milton Caniff **W:** Milton Caniff

6 ❑ Dec 1948 Cover: 0.10 **NM** value: **55.00**
• Reprints comic strips **A:** Milton Caniff **W:** Milton Caniff

STEVE CANYON COMICS (KITCHEN SINK) — Kitchen Sink

Bk 1❑ Jan 1983 Cover: 5.00 **NM** value: **Cover or less**
Bk 2❑ May 1983 Cover: 5.00 **NM** value: **Cover or less**
Bk 3❑ Aug 1983 Cover: 5.00 **NM** value: **Cover or less**
Bk 4❑ Dec 1983 Cover: 5.00 **NM** value: **Cover or less**
Bk 5❑ Mar 1984 Cover: 5.00 **NM** value: **Cover or less**
Bk 6❑ Jun 1984 Cover: 5.00 **NM** value: **Cover or less**
Bk 7❑ Sep 1984 Cover: 5.00 **NM** value: **Cover or less**
Bk 8❑ Dec 1984 Cover: 5.00 **NM** value: **Cover or less**
Bk 9❑ Feb 1985 Cover: 5.00 **NM** value: **Cover or less**
Bk 10❑May 1985 Cover: 5.00 **NM** value: **Cover or less**
Bk 11❑Jul 1985 Cover: 5.00 **NM** value: **Cover or less**
Bk 12❑Sep 1985 Cover: 5.00 **NM** value: **Cover or less**
Bk 13❑Nov 1985 Cover: 5.00 **NM** value: **Cover or less**
Bk 14❑Feb 1986 Cover: 5.00 **NM** value: **Cover or less**
Bk 15❑Apr 1986 Cover: 5.00 **NM** value: **Cover or less**
Bk 16❑Jun 1986 Cover: 5.00 **NM** value: **Cover or less**
Bk 17❑Aug 1986 Cover: 6.95 **NM** value: **Cover or less**
Bk 18❑Sep 1987 Cover: 6.95 **NM** value: **Cover or less**
Bk 19❑Dec 1987 Cover: 7.95 **NM** value: **Cover or less**
• 40th anniv.

Bk 19/HC❑ Cover: 19.95 **NM** value: **Cover or less**
40th anniv. hardcover.

Bk 20❑Mar 1988 Cover: 5.95 **NM** value: **Cover or less**
Bk 21❑Dec 1988 Cover: 6.95 **NM** value: **Cover or less**
Bk 22❑ Cover: 11.95 **NM** value: **Cover or less**
• book format

Bk 23❑ Cover: 11.95 **NM** value: **Cover or less**
• book format

Bk 24❑ Cover: 13.95 **NM** value: **Cover or less**
• book format

STEVE CANYON MAGAZINE (MILTON CANIFF'S…) — Kitchen Sink

1 ❑ Jan 1983 Cover: 2.95 **NM** value: **Cover or less**
A: Milton Caniff **W:** Milton Caniff

2 ❑ May 1983 Cover: 2.95 **NM** value: **Cover or less**
A: Milton Caniff **W:** Milton Caniff

3 ❑ Aug 1983 Cover: 2.95 **NM** value: **Cover or less**
Male Call, Part 1 **A:** Milton Caniff **W:** Milton Caniff

4 ❑ Dec 1983 Cover: 2.95 **NM** value: **Cover or less**
A: Milton Caniff **W:** Milton Caniff

5 ❑ Mar 1984 Cover: 2.95 **NM** value: **3.50**
Circ: Statement: **6,421**
Male Call, Part 2 **A:** Milton Caniff **W:** Milton Caniff

6 ❑ Jun 1984 Cover: 3.50 **NM** value: **Cover or less**
Circ: Statement: **6,421**
A: Milton Caniff **W:** Milton Caniff

7 ❑ Sep 1984 Cover: 3.50 **NM** value: **Cover or less**
Circ: Statement: **6,421**
A: Milton Caniff **W:** Milton Caniff

8 ❑ Dec 1984 Cover: 4.95 **NM** value: **Cover or less**
Circ: Statement: **6,421**
A: Milton Caniff **W:** Milton Caniff

9 ❑ Mar 1985 Cover: 4.95 **NM** value: **Cover or less**
Circ: Statement: **4,976**
A: Milton Caniff **W:** Milton Caniff

10 ❑ Jun 1985 Cover: 4.95 **NM** value: **Cover or less**
Circ: Statement: **4,976**
A: Milton Caniff **W:** Milton Caniff

11 ❑ Sep 1985 Cover: 4.95 **NM** value: **Cover or less**
Circ: Statement: **4,976**
A: Milton Caniff **W:** Milton Caniff

12 ❑ Dec 1985 Cover: 4.95 **NM** value: **Cover or less**
Circ: Statement: **4,976**
A: Milton Caniff **W:** Milton Caniff

13 ❑ 1986 Cover: 5.95 **NM** value: **Cover or less**
Circ: Statement: **4,368**
• Giant-size. **A:** Milton Caniff **W:** Milton Caniff

14 ❑ 1986 Cover: 4.95 **NM** value: **Cover or less**
Circ: Statement: **4,368**
A: Milton Caniff **W:** Milton Caniff

3D 1❑Jun 1986 Cover: 2.25 **NM** value: **Cover or less**
Circ: CapCity orders: **3,925**
• prestige format. • 3-D Special #1 **A:** Milton Caniff **W:** Milton Caniff

STEVEN — Kitchen Sink

Doug Allen first began drawing the truculent little cuss known as Steven back in 1976. As he puts it, "I had a lot of anger and Steven was an outlet for it. Twelve years later, I still have a lot of anger, but I think Steven has kept me from killing somebody. I let him do it for me."

And anger is certainly one of the key traits of this diminutive character. He has assaulted Santa Claus, murdered fellow cartoon characters, and generally has gotten nastiness down to an art. But he's also very funny, a fact that has made him a long-running favorite in Newspaper, a Providence, Rhode Island weekly. This title collects those weekly strips into comic book form.

1 ❑ b&w Cover: 2.95 **NM** value: **3.00**
A: Doug Allen **W:** Doug Allen

2 ❑ b&w Cover: 2.95 **NM** value: **3.00**
A: Doug Allen **W:** Doug Allen

Other grades: Multiply prices above by **1.5 for Mint • 2/3 for Very Fine • 1/3 for Fine • 1/5 for Very Good • 1/8 for Good**

3 ❑ May 1999, b&w Cover: 2.95 **NM** value: **3.00**
Circ: Diamd. preorders: **2,048**
A: Doug Allen **W:** Doug Allen
4 ❑ b&w Cover: 2.95 **NM** value: **3.00**
A: Doug Allen **W:** Doug Allen
5 ❑ Cover: 3.50 **NM** value: **Cover or less**
A: Doug Allen **W:** Doug Allen
6 ❑ b&w Cover: 3.50 **NM** value: **Cover or less**
A: Doug Allen **W:** Doug Allen
7 ❑ Cover: 3.50 **NM** value: **Cover or less**
A: Doug Allen **W:** Doug Allen
8 ❑ Dec 1996, b&w Cover: 3.50 **NM** value: **Cover or less**
cardstock cover. • over-sized. **A:** Doug Allen **W:** Doug Allen

STEVEN PRESENTS DUMPY — Fantagraphics
1 ❑ May 1999, b&w Cover: 2.95 **NM** value: **Cover or less**

STEVEN'S COMICS — DK Press / Yell Comics
3 ❑ b&w Cover: 3.00 **NM** value: **Cover or less**

STEVE ROPER — Famous Funnies
1 ❑ Apr 1948 Cover: 0.10 **NM** value: **75.00**
2 ❑ Jun 1948 Cover: 0.10 **NM** value: **50.00**
3 ❑ Aug 1948 Cover: 0.10 **NM** value: **35.00**
4 ❑ Oct 1948 Cover: 0.10 **NM** value: **35.00**
5 ❑ Dec 1948 Cover: 0.10 **NM** value: **35.00**

STEVE ZODIAK AND THE FIREBALL XL-5 — Gold Key
1 ❑ Jan 1964 **NM** value: **75.00**
• **CGC:** 2 graded, best 9.2

STEVIE — Magazine Publications
1 ❑ ca. 1952 Cover: 0.10 **NM** value: **35.00**
• **CGC:** 1 graded, best 6.5
2 ❑ ca. 1953 Cover: 0.10 **NM** value: **25.00**
3 ❑ ca. 1953 Cover: 0.10 **NM** value: **25.00**
4 ❑ ca. 1953 Cover: 0.10 **NM** value: **25.00**
5 ❑ ca. 1953 Cover: 0.10 **NM** value: **25.00**
6 ❑ ca. 1954 Cover: 0.10 **NM** value: **25.00**

ST. GEORGE — Marvel / Epic
1 ❑ Jun 1988 Cover: 1.25 **NM** value: **1.50**
Circ: CapCity orders: **24,300**
📖 When Mercy Seasons Justice **A:** Klaus Janson; Bill Sienkiewicz(cover) **W:** D.G. Chichester; Margaret Clark
2 ❑ Aug 1988 Cover: 1.25 **NM** value: **1.50**
Circ: CapCity orders: **15,100**
3 ❑ Oct 1988 Cover: 1.50 **NM** value: **Cover or less**
Circ: CapCity orders: **11,900**
4 ❑ Dec 1988 Cover: 1.50 **NM** value: **Cover or less**
Circ: CapCity orders: **10,000**
5 ❑ Feb 1989 Cover: 1.50 **NM** value: **Cover or less**
Circ: CapCity orders: **8,900**
6 ❑ Apr 1989 Cover: 1.50 **NM** value: **Cover or less**
Circ: CapCity orders: **7,600**
7 ❑ Jun 1989 Cover: 1.50 **NM** value: **Cover or less**
Circ: CapCity orders: **6,850**
8 ❑ Aug 1989 Cover: 1.50 **NM** value: **Cover or less**
Circ: CapCity orders: **6,200**

STICKBOY (FANTAGRAPHICS) — Fantagraphics
1 ❑ b&w Cover: 2.50 **NM** value: **Cover or less**
1-2 ❑ Cover: 2.75 **NM** value: **Cover or less**
2 ❑ b&w Cover: 2.50 **NM** value: **Cover or less**
3 ❑ b&w Cover: 2.50 **NM** value: **Cover or less**
4 ❑ Nov 1990, b&w Cover: 2.95 **NM** value: **Cover or less**
5 ❑ Feb 1992, b&w Cover: 2.50 **NM** value: **Cover or less**

STICKBOY (STARHEAD) — Starhead
1 ❑ b&w Cover: 2.50 **NM** value: **Cover or less**
2 ❑ b&w Cover: 2.50 **NM** value: **Cover or less**
3 ❑ b&w Cover: 2.50 **NM** value: **Cover or less**
4 ❑ b&w Cover: 2.50 **NM** value: **Cover or less**
5 ❑ b&w Cover: 2.50 **NM** value: **Cover or less**
6 ❑ b&w Cover: 2.50 **NM** value: **Cover or less**

STIG'S INFERNO — Vortex
1 ❑ ca. 1989 Cover: 1.95 **NM** value: **2.00**
2 ❑ 1989 Cover: 1.95 **NM** value: **2.00**
3 ❑ 1989 Cover: 3.50 **NM** value: **Cover or less**
4 ❑ 1989 Cover: 3.50 **NM** value: **Cover or less**
5 ❑ 1989 Cover: 1.75 **NM** value: **Cover or less**
6 ❑ 1989b&w Cover: 1.50 **NM** value: **Cover or less**
7 ❑ 1989b&w Cover: 1.50 **NM** value: **Cover or less**
Bk 1❑ b&w Cover: 6.95 **NM** value: **Cover or less**

STIMULATOR — Fantagraphics / Eros
All issues are adults only.
1 ❑ b&w Cover: 2.50 **NM** value: **Cover or less**

STING — Artline Studios
1 ❑ Cover: 2.50 **NM** value: **Cover or less**
• flip book with Killer Synthetic Toads

STING OF THE GREEN HORNET — Now
1 ❑ Jun 1992 Cover: 2.50 **NM** value: **Cover or less**
Circ: CapCity orders: **4,825**
📖 Out of the Shadows • bagged with poster **A:** Jeff Butler **W:** Jeff Butler; Ron Fortier ★ Appearance of Adolf Hitler.
1/CS❑Jun 1992 Cover: 2.75 **NM** value: **Cover or less**
Circ: CapCity orders: **6,550**
📖 Out of the Shadows **A:** Jeff Butler **W:** Jeff Butler; Ron Fortier ★ Appearance of Adolf Hitler.
2 ❑ Jul 1992 Cover: 2.50 **NM** value: **Cover or less**
Circ: CapCity orders: **3,625**
A: Jeff Butler **W:** Jeff Butler; Ron Fortier
2/CS❑Jul 1992 Cover: 2.75 **NM** value: **Cover or less**
• bagged with poster **A:** Jeff Butler **W:** Jeff Butler; Ron Fortier
3 ❑ Aug 1992 Cover: 2.50 **NM** value: **Cover or less**
Circ: CapCity orders: **5,600**
📖 The Terror Express **A:** Jeff Butler **W:** Jeff Butler; Ron Fortier
3/CS❑Aug 1992 Cover: 2.75 **NM** value: **Cover or less**
📖 The Terror Express • bagged with poster **A:** Jeff Butler **W:** Jeff Butler; Ron Fortier
4 ❑ Sep 1992 Cover: 2.50 **NM** value: **Cover or less**
A: Jeff Butler **W:** Jeff Butler; Ron Fortier
4/CS❑Sep 1992 Cover: 2.75 **NM** value: **Cover or less**
• stitched with poster **A:** Jeff Butler **W:** Jeff Butler; Ron Fortier

STINZ (1ST SERIES) — Fantagraphics

Donna Barr's work is like nothing else in comics, featuring (in this case) a structured world of gutsy, macho farmer centaurs who interact with humans and fantastic characters. Her series over the years have featured four worlds, those of: Bosom Enemies, The Desert Peach, Hader and the Colonel — and Stinz.

Centaur Stinz Lowhard is the mayor of the Geiselthal Valley, in which the centaurs and humans ("two-leggers") live and work together. Barr herself notes of Stinz, "He is nothing like the classical half-man, half-horse creatures of Greek myth. He is his own man and his own horse, in a world tht in everything except the form of him and his people is just as everyday as our own." Barr's stories have a beginning, a middle, and an end — and a point. Her projects are outstanding and rewarding drawn books. — Maggie

1 ❑ Aug 1989, b&w Cover: 2.00 **NM** value: **4.00**
📖 Draft Horse **A:** Donna Barr **W:** Donna Barr
2 ❑ Oct 1989, b&w Cover: 2.00 **NM** value: **3.00**
📖 Breaking to Harness **A:** Donna Barr **W:** Donna Barr
3 ❑ ca. 1989, b&w Cover: 2.00 **NM** value: **3.00**
📖 Breaking In **A:** Donna Barr **W:** Donna Barr
4 ❑ Feb 1990, b&w Cover: 2.00 **NM** value: **2.50**
📖 Sorting That Out • Moves to Brave New Words **A:** Donna Barr **W:** Donna Barr
5 ❑ ca. 1990 Cover: 2.50 **NM** value: **Cover or less**
📖 Wedding Hell • Published by Brave New Words **A:** Donna Barr **W:** Donna Barr

STINZ (2ND SERIES) — Brave New Words
1 ❑ ca. 1990, b&w Cover: 2.50 **NM** value: **Cover or less**
📖 On a Pale Horse **A:** Donna Barr **W:** Donna Barr
2 ❑ ca. 1991, b&w Cover: 2.50 **NM** value: **Cover or less**
📖 Freed Elections **A:** Donna Barr **W:** Donna Barr
3 ❑ ca. 1991 Cover: 2.95 **NM** value: **Cover or less**
📖 Pipe Dream **A:** Donna Barr **W:** Donna Barr
Bk 1❑ ca. 1992 Cover: 12.95 **NM** value: **Cover or less**
• Wartime And Wedding Bells

STINZ (3RD SERIES) — Mu
1 ❑ Oct 1994 Cover: 2.50 **NM** value: **Cover or less**
📖 Family Values **A:** Donna Barr **W:** Donna Barr
2 ❑ Oct 1994 Cover: 2.50 **NM** value: **Cover or less**
📖 Old Man Out **A:** Donna Barr **W:** Donna Barr
3 ❑ Feb 1995 Cover: 2.50 **NM** value: **Cover or less**
📖 The BobWar **A:** Donna Barr **W:** Donna Barr
4 ❑ Oct 1995 Cover: 2.50 **NM** value: **Cover or less**
📖 Bum Steer **A:** Donna Barr **W:** Donna Barr
5 ❑ Jan 1997 Cover: 4.95 **NM** value: **Cover or less**
📖 A Stranger to Our Kind • Last Mu issue; moves to A Fine Line **A:** Donna Barr **W:** Donna Barr
6 ❑ Jun 1998 Cover: 5.50 **NM** value: **Cover or less**
📖 A Marvelous Resistance • First A Fine Line Press issue **A:** Donna Barr **W:** Donna Barr
7 ❑ Aug 1998 Cover: 4.95 **NM** value: **Cover or less**
📖 A Dog's Life **A:** Donna Barr **W:** Donna Barr
Bk 1❑ Cover: 12.95 **NM** value: **Cover or less**
📖 Horsebrush and Other Tales • Stinz stories from Dreamery comics **A:** Donna Barr **W:** Donna Barr

STINZ: WARHORSE — Mu
Bk 1❑ Mar 1993 Cover: 9.95 **NM** value: **Cover or less**

STONE — Image
1 ❑ Aug 1998 Cover: 2.50 **NM** value: **Cover or less**
Circ: Diamd. preorders: **47,368**
📖 The Awakening, part 1 **A:** Whilce Portacio **W:** Brian Haberlin
1/A ❑ Aug 1998 Cover: 2.50 **NM** value: **Cover or less**
Variant cover with white background. 📖 The Awakening, part 1 **A:** Whilce Portacio **W:** Brian Haberlin
1/B ❑ Aug 1998 Cover: 2.50 **NM** value: **Cover or less**
Variant cover with side view of Stone, jewel showing in armband. 📖 The Awakening, part 1 **A:** Whilce Portacio **W:** Brian Haberlin
2 ❑ Sep 1998 Cover: 2.50 **NM** value: **Cover or less**
Circ: Diamd. preorders: **36,829**
📖 The Awakening, part 2 **A:** Whilce Portacio **W:** Brian Haberlin
2/A ❑ Sep 1998 Cover: 2.50 **NM** value: **6.00**
DFE chrome cover. 📖 The Awakening, part 2 • reprints indicia from #1 **A:** Whilce Portacio **W:** Brian Haberlin
2/B ❑ Sep 1998 Cover: 2.50 **NM** value: **4.00**
alternate cover (white border). 📖 The Awakening, part 2 **A:** Whilce Portacio **W:** Brian Haberlin
3 ❑ Nov 1998 Cover: 2.50 **NM** value: **Cover or less**
Circ: Diamd. preorders: **34,214**
📖 The Awakening, part 3 **A:** Whilce Portacio **W:** Brian Haberlin
4 ❑ Apr 1999 Cover: 2.50 **NM** value: **Cover or less**
Circ: Diamd. preorders: **29,833**
📖 The Awakening, part 4 **A:** Whilce Portacio **W:** Brian Haberlin

STONE COLD STEVE AUSTIN — Chaos
1 ❑ Oct 1999 Cover: 2.95 **NM** value: **Cover or less**
Circ: Diamd. preorders: **38,830**
cover says Nov, indicia says Oct. 📖 Tougher than the Rest **A:** James Fry **W:** Steven Grant
2 ❑ Nov 1999 Cover: 2.95 **NM** value: **Cover or less**
Circ: Diamd. preorders: **27,890**
A: James Fry **W:** Steven Grant
3 ❑ Dec 1999 Cover: 2.95 **NM** value: **Cover or less**
Circ: Diamd. preorders: **22,992**
A: James Fry **W:** Steven Grant
4 ❑ Jan 2000 Cover: 2.95 **NM** value: **Cover or less**
Circ: Diamd. preorders: **19,591**
A: James Fry **W:** Steven Grant

STONE PROTECTORS — Harvey
1 ❑ May 1994 Cover: 1.50 **NM** value: **Cover or less**
📖 The Legend of the Stone Protectors **A:** Bill Vallely **W:** Michael Kirschenbaum ★ Origin of the Stone Protectors. ★ 1st Appearance of the Stone Protectors.
2 ❑ Cover: 1.50 **NM** value: **Cover or less**
A: Bill Vallely **W:** Michael Kirschenbaum
3 ❑ Sep 1994 Cover: 1.50 **NM** value: **Cover or less**
📖 The Mystic of Mythrandir **A:** Bill Vallely **W:** Michael Kirschenbaum

STONE (VOL. 2) — Image
1 ❑ Aug 1999 Cover: 2.50 **NM** value: **Cover or less**
Circ: Diamd. preorders: **28,241**
A: Whilce Portacio **W:** Brian Haberlin
1/SC❑Aug 1999 Cover: 6.95 **NM** value: **Cover or less**
Chrome cover. **A:** Whilce Portacio **W:** Brian Haberlin
2 ❑ Sep 1999 Cover: 2.50 **NM** value: **Cover or less**
Circ: Diamd. preorders: **23,388**
A: Whilce Portacio **W:** Brian Haberlin
3 ❑ Dec 1999 Cover: 2.50 **NM** value: **Cover or less**
Circ: Diamd. preorders: **21,729**
A: Whilce Portacio **W:** Brian Haberlin

STONEWALL IN THE SHENANDOAH — Heritage Collection
1 ❑ Cover: 3.50 **NM** value: **Cover or less**
No issue number. wraparound cover.

STORIES FROM BOSNIA — Drawn and Quarterly
1 ❑ b&w Cover: 3.95 **NM** value: **Cover or less**
cardstock cover. • Oversized.

STORIES OF ROMANCE — Atlas
5 ❑ Mar 1956 Cover: 0.10 **NM** value: **60.00**
6 ❑ May 1956 Cover: 0.10 **NM** value: **40.00**
7 ❑ Jul 1956 Cover: 0.10 **NM** value: **40.00**
8 ❑ Sep 1956 Cover: 0.10 **NM** value: **40.00**
9 ❑ Nov 1956 Cover: 0.10 **NM** value: **40.00**
11 ❑ Mar 1957 Cover: 0.10 **NM** value: **35.00**
12 ❑ May 1957 Cover: 0.10 **NM** value: **35.00**
13 ❑ Jul 1957 Cover: 0.10 **NM** value: **35.00**
10 ❑ Jan 1957 Cover: 0.10 **NM** value: **40.00**

STORIES OF THE FANTASTIC — NBM
1 ❑ **NM** value: **9.95**
A: Francois Schuiten **W:** Benoit Peeters
2 ❑ Cover: 9.95 **NM** value: **Cover or less**
📖 The Great Walls of Samaris **A:** Francois Schuiten **W:** Benoit Peeters
3 ❑ Cover: 12.95 **NM** value: **Cover or less**
📖 Feber in Urbicand **A:** Francois Schuiten **W:** Benoit Peeters

STORM — Marvel

Storm made her first appearance along with the rest of the new X-Men in Giant Sized X-Men (1st Series) #1. She has the mutant ability to control the weather and can conjure rain, snow, wind, tornadoes, and lightning at will. For many years, she had been the X-Men's leader, but in this four-issue limited series, Storm begins to question her ability to make the tough decisions. In a previous adventure she had been forced to kill a little girl who had been transformed into a Morlock terrorist, in order to save the lives of others. The series deals with her struggle as she searches for inner strength and the conviction required to continue as the X-Men's leader. In pursuing these goals she would find herself drawn into another, even greater challenge.

This series was written by Warren Ellis and drawn by Terry Dodson.

1 ❑ Feb 1996 Cover: 2.95 **NM** value: **Cover or less**
• **CGC:** 1 graded, best 9.6
enhanced cardstock cover. 📖 Sunburst And Snowblind **A:** Terry Dodson; Karl Story **W:** Warren Ellis
2 ❑ Mar 1996 Cover: 2.95 **NM** value: **Cover or less**
enhanced cardstock cover. 📖 The Ghost Has No Home **A:** Terry Dodson; Karl Story **W:** Warren Ellis
3 ❑ Apr 1996 Cover: 2.95 **NM** value: **Cover or less**
enhanced cardstock cover. 📖 The Tinderbox Of A Heart **A:** Terry Dodson; Karl Story **W:** Warren Ellis
4 ❑ May 1996 Cover: 2.95 **NM** value: **Cover or less**
enhanced cardstock cover. final issue. **A:** Terry Dodson; Karl Story **W:** Warren Ellis

CGC-graded: Multiply prices above by **33 for 9.9 M • 16 for 9.8 NM/M • 7 for 9.6 NM+ • 5 for 9.4 NM • 2.5 for 9.2 NM- • 1.5 for 9.0 VF/NM**

STORM BATTLEBOOK — Marvel

1 ❑ Cover: 3.99 **NM** value: **Cover or less**

STORMQUEST — Caliber / Sky

1 ❑ Nov 1994 Cover: 1.95 **NM** value: **Cover or less**
2 ❑ Dec 1994 Cover: 1.95 **NM** value: **Cover or less**
3 ❑ 1995 Cover: 1.95 **NM** value: **Cover or less**
4 ❑ 1995 Cover: 1.95 **NM** value: **Cover or less**
5 ❑ 1995 Cover: 1.95 **NM** value: **Cover or less**
6 ❑ 1955 Cover: 1.95 **NM** value: **Cover or less**

STORMWATCH — Image

Think of StormWatch as a super-powered United Nations task force. Far above the earth, the U.N.'s Skywatch orbital platform monitors the goings-on across the Earth. There, a solemn man fitted with cyborg appendages analyzes world crisis points. When things get too hot in places such as Kuwait or Sarajevo, this man- Weatherman One- orders in the StormWatch team.

StormWatch One consists of Fuji, a hulking Japanese powerhouse; Diva, a beautiful mutant with a sonic scream; Winter, a Russian with cold powers, Hellstrike, a flyer capable of firing withering energy blasts, and their leader, Battalion, a psionic who (with the help of his Cyber-Tran suit) possesses the awesome firepower of his namesake. Like the U.N., these heroes come from different nations, but they have all pledged their lives to defend the global community.

0 ❑ Aug 1993 Cover: 2.50 **NM** value: **Cover or less**
Circ: CapCity orders: **192,900**
• Polybagged **A:** Brett Booth; Jeffrey Scott **W:** Jim Lee; Brandon Choi ★ 1st Appearance of Backlash, Flashpoint, Nautica, Warguard.
1 ❑ Mar 1993 Cover: 1.95 **NM** value: **2.50**
Circ: CapCity orders: **220,575**
★ 1st Appearance of Hellstrike, Battalion, Diva, Winter, Strafe, StormWatch, Synergy, Deathtrap, Fuji.
1/GO❑ Mar 1993 Cover: 1.95 **NM** value: **4.00**
Gold foil cover.
2 ❑ May 1993 Cover: 1.95 **NM** value: **2.00**
Circ: CapCity orders: **173,800**
★ 1st Appearance of Regent, Cannon, Fahrenheit, Ion & Lance.
3 ❑ Jul 1993 Cover: 1.95 **NM** value: **2.00**
Circ: CapCity orders: **172,175**
★ 1st Appearance of LaSalle. ★ Appearance of Backlash.
4 ❑ Aug 1993 Cover: 1.95 **NM** value: **Cover or less**
Circ: CapCity orders: **93,850**
cover says Oct. ★ Versus Warguard.
5 ❑ Nov 1993 Cover: 1.95 **NM** value: **Cover or less**
Circ: CapCity orders: **72,950**
6 ❑ Dec 1993 Cover: 1.95 **NM** value: **Cover or less**
Circ: CapCity orders: **64,000**
7 ❑ 1994 Cover: 1.95 **NM** value: **Cover or less**
Circ: CapCity orders: **57,625**
★ 1st Appearance of Sunburst.
8 ❑ 1994 Cover: 1.95 **NM** value: **Cover or less**
Circ: CapCity orders: **42,900**
★ 1st Appearance of Rainmaker.
9 ❑ Apr 1994 Cover: 2.50 **NM** value: **Cover or less**
Circ: CapCity orders: **37,100**
10 ❑ Jun 1994 Cover: 1.95 **NM** value: **Cover or less**
Circ: CapCity orders: **40,950**
10/A❑ Jun 1994 Cover: 1.95 **NM** value: **5.00**
• Variant edition cover.
10/B❑ Jun 1994 Cover: 1.95 **NM** value: **5.00**
variant cover.
11 ❑ Aug 1994 Cover: 1.95 **NM** value: **Cover or less**
Circ: CapCity orders: **36,425**
12 ❑ Aug 1994 Cover: 1.95 **NM** value: **Cover or less**
Circ: CapCity orders: **36,600**
13 ❑ Sep 1994 Cover: 1.95 **NM** value: **Cover or less**
Circ: CapCity orders: **35,850**
14 ❑ Sep 1994 Cover: 1.95 **NM** value: **Cover or less**
Circ: CapCity orders: **35,850**
15 ❑ Oct 1994 Cover: 1.95 **NM** value: **Cover or less**
Circ: CapCity orders: **33,750**
16 ❑ Nov 1994 Cover: 1.95 **NM** value: **Cover or less**
Circ: CapCity orders: **32,800**
17 ❑ Dec 1994 Cover: 2.50 **NM** value: **Cover or less**
Circ: CapCity orders: **30,025**
18 ❑ Jan 1995 Cover: 2.50 **NM** value: **Cover or less**
Circ: CapCity orders: **27,325**
19 ❑ Feb 1995 Cover: 2.50 **NM** value: **Cover or less**
Circ: CapCity orders: **22,925**
20 ❑ Mar 1995 Cover: 2.50 **NM** value: **Cover or less**
Circ: CapCity orders: **22,325**
21 ❑ Apr 1995 Cover: 2.50 **NM** value: **Cover or less**
Circ: CapCity orders: **21,475**
cover says #1. ★ 1st Appearance of Tao.
22 ❑ May 1995 Cover: 2.50 **NM** value: **Cover or less**
Circ: CapCity orders: **30,325**
WildStorm Rising Chapter 9; Wildstorm Rising, Part 9 • bound-in trading cards
23 ❑ Jun 1995 Cover: 2.50 **NM** value: **Cover or less**
Circ: CapCity orders: **22,100**
24 ❑ Jul 1995 Cover: 2.50 **NM** value: **Cover or less**
Circ: CapCity orders: **21,000**
25 ❑ May 1994 Cover: 2.50 **NM** value: **Cover or less**
Circ: CapCity orders: **17,175**
cover says Jun 95. • Images of Tomorrow; Shipped out of sequence as preview to future events (after #9)
25-2❑ Aug 1995 Cover: 2.50 **NM** value: **Cover or less**
26 ❑ Aug 1995 Cover: 2.50 **NM** value: **Cover or less**
Circ: CapCity orders: **21,950**
27 ❑ Aug 1995 Cover: 2.50 **NM** value: **Cover or less**
Circ: CapCity orders: **19,975**
28 ❑ Sep 1995 Cover: 2.50 **NM** value: **Cover or less**
Circ: CapCity orders: **17,275**
cover forms right half of diptych with issue #29. ★ 1st Appearance of Swift, Storm Force, Flint.
29 ❑ Oct 1995 Cover: 2.50 **NM** value: **Cover or less**
cover says Nov. • indicia says Oct
30 ❑ Nov 1995 Cover: 2.50 **NM** value: **Cover or less**
31 ❑ Dec 1995 Cover: 2.50 **NM** value: **Cover or less**
32 ❑ Jan 1996 Cover: 2.50 **NM** value: **Cover or less**
33 ❑ Feb 1996 Cover: 2.50 **NM** value: **Cover or less**
34 ❑ Mar 1996 Cover: 2.50 **NM** value: **Cover or less**
35 ❑ Apr 1996 Cover: 2.50 **NM** value: **Cover or less**
Fire from Heaven, Part 5
36 ❑ Jun 1996 Cover: 2.50 **NM** value: **Cover or less**
Fire from Heaven, Part 12
37 ❑ Jul 1996 Cover: 3.50 **NM** value: **Cover or less**
• **CGC:** 2 graded, best 9.6
• Giant-size. ★ 1st Appearance of Hawksmoor, Jenny Sparks.
38 ❑ Aug 1996 Cover: 2.50 **NM** value: **Cover or less**
39 ❑ Aug 1996 Cover: 2.50 **NM** value: **Cover or less**
40 ❑ Oct 1996 Cover: 2.50 **NM** value: **Cover or less**
Circ: Diamd. preorders: **31,265**
41 ❑ Oct 1996 Cover: 2.50 **NM** value: **Cover or less**
Circ: Diamd. preorders: **30,232**
42 ❑ Nov 1996 Cover: 2.50 **NM** value: **Cover or less**
Circ: Diamd. preorders: **28,344**
43 ❑ Dec 1996 Cover: 2.50 **NM** value: **Cover or less**
Circ: Diamd. preorders: **27,032**
A: Tom Raney **W:** Warren Ellis
44/A❑ Jan 1997 Cover: 2.50 **NM** value: **Cover or less**
Circ: Diamd. preorders: **28,139**
Torrid Tales cover. • homages to various comics eras **A:** Tom Raney **W:** Warren Ellis ★ Origin of Jenny Sparks.
44/B❑ Jan 1997 Cover: 2.50 **NM** value: **Cover or less**
Pop Art Masterpiece cover. **A:** Tom Raney **C:** Gil Kane **W:** Warren Ellis ★ Origin of Jenny Sparks.
44/C❑ Jan 1997 Cover: 2.50 **NM** value: **Cover or less**
Who Watches The Weathermen cover. **A:** Tom Raney **W:** Warren Ellis ★ Origin of Jenny Sparks.
45 ❑ Feb 1997 Cover: 2.50 **NM** value: **Cover or less**
Circ: Diamd. preorders: **24,966**
46 ❑ Mar 1997 Cover: 2.50 **NM** value: **Cover or less**
Circ: Diamd. preorders: **25,726**
47 ❑ Apr 1997 Cover: 2.50 **NM** value: **Cover or less**
Circ: Diamd. preorders: **31,202**
48 ❑ May 1997 Cover: 2.50 **NM** value: **Cover or less**
Circ: Diamd. preorders: **25,250**
A: Tom Raney **W:** Warren Ellis
49 ❑ Jun 1997 Cover: 2.50 **NM** value: **Cover or less**
Circ: Diamd. preorders: **24,820**
A: Tom Raney **W:** Warren Ellis
50 ❑ Jul 1997 Cover: 4.50 **NM** value: **Cover or less**
Circ: Diamd. preorders: **25,171**
• Giant-size. final issue. **A:** Tom Raney **W:** Warren Ellis
Bk 1❑ Cover: 14.95 **NM** value: **Cover or less**
No issue number. • Trade Paperback. Change or Die; Terminal Zone; Strange Weather • Change Or Die **A:** Michael Ryan; Oscar Jimenez; Tom Raney **W:** Warren Ellis
Bk 2❑ Cover: 14.95 **NM** value: **Cover or less**
Lightning Strikes • Collects StormWatch #43-47 **A:** Jim Lee; Tom Raney **W:** Warren Ellis
SE 1❑ Jan 1994 Cover: 3.50 **NM** value: **Cover or less**
★ 1st Appearance of Argos.
SE 2❑ May 1995 Cover: 3.50 **NM** value: **Cover or less**
Circ: CapCity orders: **16,175**

STORMWATCH (2ND SERIES) — Image

1 ❑ Oct 1997 Cover: 2.50 **NM** value: **Cover or less**
Circ: Diamd. preorders: **29,993**
Strange Weather, Part 1 **A:** Oscar Jimenez **W:** Warren Ellis
1/A ❑ Oct 1997 Cover: 2.50 **NM** value: **Cover or less**
alternate cover (white background).
1/B ❑ Oct 1997 Cover: 2.50 **NM** value: **Cover or less**
• Voyager pack
2 ❑ Nov 1997 Cover: 2.50 **NM** value: **Cover or less**
Circ: Diamd. preorders: **27,723** • **CGC:** 1 graded, best 9.6
Strange Weather, Part 2 **A:** Oscar Jimenez **W:** Warren Ellis
3 ❑ Dec 1997 Cover: 2.50 **NM** value: **Cover or less**
Circ: Diamd. preorders: **26,755**
Strange Weather, Part 3 **A:** Oscar Jimenez **W:** Warren Ellis
4 ❑ Feb 1998 Cover: 2.50 **NM** value: **Cover or less**
Circ: Diamd. preorders: **23,324** • **CGC:** 3 graded, best 9.6
A Finer World, Part 1 **A:** Paul Neary; Bryan Hitch **W:** Warren Ellis
5 ❑ Mar 1998 Cover: 2.50 **NM** value: **Cover or less**
Circ: Diamd. preorders: **22,801**
A Finer World, Part 2 **A:** Paul Neary; Bryan Hitch **W:** Warren Ellis
5/A ❑ Mar 1998 Cover: 2.50 **NM** value: **Cover or less**
alternate cover. • group flying
6 ❑ Apr 1998 Cover: 2.50 **NM** value: **Cover or less**
Circ: Diamd. preorders: **23,445**
A Finer World, Part 3 **A:** Paul Neary; Bryan Hitch **W:** Warren Ellis
7 ❑ May 1998 Cover: 2.50 **NM** value: **Cover or less**
Circ: Diamd. preorders: **22,114**
Bleed, Part 1 **A:** Paul Neary; Bryan Hitch **W:** Warren Ellis
8 ❑ Jun 1998 Cover: 2.50 **NM** value: **Cover or less**
Circ: Diamd. preorders: **22,485**
Bleed, Part 2 **A:** Paul Neary; Bryan Hitch **W:** Warren Ellis
9 ❑ Jul 1998 Cover: 2.50 **NM** value: **Cover or less**
Circ: Diamd. preorders: **21,599**
Bleed, Part 3 **A:** Paul Neary; Bryan Hitch **W:** Warren Ellis
10 ❑ Aug 1998 Cover: 2.50 **NM** value: **Cover or less**
Circ: Diamd. preorders: **21,305** • **CGC:** 1 graded, best 9.6
Bleed, Part 2; No Reason **A:** Paul Neary; Bryan Hitch **W:** Warren Ellis
11 ❑ Sep 1998 Cover: 2.50 **NM** value: **Cover or less**
Circ: Diamd. preorders: **20,922** • **CGC:** 1 graded, best 9.4
No Direction Home **A:** Paul Neary; Bryan Hitch **W:** Warren Ellis
Bk 1❑ Cover: 14.95 **NM** value: **Cover or less**
A Finer World • Collects StormWatch (2nd Series) #4-9 **A:** Paul Neary; Bryan Hitch **W:** Warren Ellis

STORMWATCHER — Eclipse

1 ❑ Apr 1989, b&w Cover: 2.00 **NM** value: **Cover or less**
Back in Business **A:** Andrew Currie **W:** Alan Cowshill; Ian Abbinnett
2 ❑ May 1989, b&w Cover: 2.00 **NM** value: **Cover or less**
3 ❑ b&w Cover: 2.00 **NM** value: **Cover or less**
4 ❑ b&w Cover: 2.00 **NM** value: **Cover or less**

STORMWATCH SOURCEBOOK — Image

1 ❑ Jan 1994 Cover: 2.50 **NM** value: **Cover or less**
Circ: CapCity orders: **30,675**

STORY OF MARTHA WAYNE, THE — Argo

1 ❑ **NM** value: **25.00**

STRAIGHT ARROW — Magazine Enterprises

By day, ranch hand Steve Adams helps out around the farms and grazing lands of the old West. But when problems require solutions outside the reach of the law, he dons the Indian garb of Straight Arrow to take on the rustlers, robbers, and outlaws that plague the frontier. Trusted by the Indians and feared by white men, Straight Arrow often strayed beyond the boundaries of the Old West to explore ancient civilizations, tangle with prehistoric creatures, and tackle the issue of drugs — powerful stuff in the 1950s.

Straight Arrow was drawn by Fred Meagher, with covers occasionally supplied by future fantasy art superstar Frank Frazetta. Readers could count on three or four full-length Straight Arrow stories each issue.

1 ❑ Feb 1950 Cover: 0.10 **NM** value: **175.00**
• **CGC:** 1 graded, best 6.0
2 ❑ Apr 1950 Cover: 0.10 **NM** value: **110.00**
3 ❑ Jun 1950 Cover: 0.10 **NM** value: **125.00**
A: Frank Frazetta(cover)
4 ❑ Aug 1950 Cover: 0.10 **NM** value: **55.00**
5 ❑ Sep 1950 Cover: 0.10 **NM** value: **55.00**
6 ❑ Oct 1950 Cover: 0.10 **NM** value: **50.00**
7 ❑ Nov 1950 Cover: 0.10 **NM** value: **50.00**
• **CGC:** 1 graded, best 9.0
8 ❑ Dec 1950 Cover: 0.10 **NM** value: **50.00**
• **CGC:** 1 graded, best 9.0
9 ❑ Jan 1951 Cover: 0.10 **NM** value: **50.00**
10 ❑ Feb 1951 Cover: 0.10 **NM** value: **50.00**
11 ❑ Mar 1951 Cover: 0.10 **NM** value: **45.00**
12 ❑ Apr 1951 Cover: 0.10 **NM** value: **45.00**
13 ❑ May 1951 Cover: 0.10 **NM** value: **45.00**
14 ❑ Jun 1951 Cover: 0.10 **NM** value: **45.00**
15 ❑ Jul 1951 Cover: 0.10 **NM** value: **45.00**
The Disappearing Lake; Gunsmoke Trail; The Coup-Stick Of Crying Calf; The Young Chief; 4
16 ❑ Aug 1951 Cover: 0.10 **NM** value: **45.00**
17 ❑ Sep 1951 Cover: 0.10 **NM** value: **45.00**
18 ❑ Oct 1951 Cover: 0.10 **NM** value: **45.00**
19 ❑ Nov 1951 Cover: 0.10 **NM** value: **45.00**
20 ❑ Dec 1951 Cover: 0.10 **NM** value: **45.00**
21 ❑ Jan 1952 Cover: 0.10 **NM** value: **40.00**
22 ❑ Feb 1952 Cover: 0.10 **NM** value: **75.00**
• **CGC:** 1 graded, best 9.0
A: Frank Frazetta(cover)
23 ❑ Mar 1952 Cover: 0.10 **NM** value: **35.00**
24 ❑ Apr 1952 Cover: 0.10 **NM** value: **35.00**
25 ❑ Jun 1952 Cover: 0.10 **NM** value: **35.00**
26 ❑ Aug 1952 Cover: 0.10 **NM** value: **35.00**
27 ❑ Oct 1952 Cover: 0.10 **NM** value: **35.00**
28 ❑ Dec 1952 Cover: 0.10 **NM** value: **35.00**
29 ❑ Feb 1953 Cover: 0.10 **NM** value: **35.00**
30 ❑ Apr 1953 Cover: 0.10 **NM** value: **35.00**
31 ❑ Jun 1953 Cover: 0.10 **NM** value: **28.00**
32 ❑ Aug 1953 Cover: 0.10 **NM** value: **28.00**
33 ❑ Oct 1953 Cover: 0.10 **NM** value: **28.00**
34 ❑ Dec 1953 Cover: 0.10 **NM** value: **28.00**
35 ❑ Feb 1954 Cover: 0.10 **NM** value: **28.00**
36 ❑ Apr 1954 Cover: 0.10 **NM** value: **28.00**
★ 1st Appearance of Hazard.
37 ❑ Jun 1954 Cover: 0.10 **NM** value: **28.00**
38 ❑ Aug 1954 Cover: 0.10 **NM** value: **28.00**
39 ❑ Oct 1954 Cover: 0.10 **NM** value: **28.00**
40 ❑ Dec 1954 Cover: 0.10 **NM** value: **28.00**
41 ❑ Jan 1955 Cover: 0.10 **NM** value: **20.00**
42 ❑ Feb 1955 Cover: 0.10 **NM** value: **20.00**
43 ❑ Mar 1955 Cover: 0.10 **NM** value: **20.00**
44 ❑ Apr 1955 Cover: 0.10 **NM** value: **20.00**
45 ❑ May 1955 Cover: 0.10 **NM** value: **20.00**
46 ❑ Jun 1955 Cover: 0.10 **NM** value: **20.00**
47 ❑ Jul 1955 Cover: 0.10 **NM** value: **20.00**
48 ❑ Aug 1955 Cover: 0.10 **NM** value: **20.00**
49 ❑ Sep 1955 Cover: 0.10 **NM** value: **20.00**
50 ❑ Oct 1955 Cover: 0.10 **NM** value: **20.00**
51 ❑ Nov 1955 Cover: 0.10 **NM** value: **16.00**
52 ❑ Dec 1955 Cover: 0.10 **NM** value: **16.00**

Other grades: Multiply prices above by **1.5 for Mint • 2/3 for Very Fine • 1/3 for Fine • 1/5 for Very Good • 1/8 for Good**

53 ❑ Jan 1956 Cover: 0.10 **NM** value: **16.00**
54 ❑ Feb 1956 Cover: 0.10 **NM** value: **16.00**
55 ❑ Mar 1956 Cover: 0.10 **NM** value: **16.00**
final issue.

STRAIGHT UP TO SEE THE SKY — Eclipse

Bk 1❑ Cover: 14.95 **NM** value: **Cover or less**
• text with illustrations **A:** Tim Truman

STRAND — Trident

1 ❑ Nov 1990, b&w Cover: 2.50 **NM** value: **Cover or less**
Strand Episode 1; Where Angels Fear to Tread; Under The Bed; Tulpa Episode 1 **A:** Gary Caldwell; Simon Fraser; Daniel Vallely; Richard Elson **W:** Daniel Vallely; Richard Elson; Eleanor Hughes; John Kaiine
2 ❑ b&w Cover: 2.50 **NM** value: **Cover or less**

STRANDED ON PLANET X — Radio

1 ❑ Jun 1999 Cover: 2.95 **NM** value: **Cover or less**

STRANGE ADVENTURES — DC

For most of its 244-issue run, Strange Adventures was host to a rather unremarkable collection of science-fiction and monster stories. Several of the characters that got their start here, however, were remade into some of DC's most inventive and original heroes.

First came the Atomic Knights in issue #117. These long-running characters were a sort of post-apocalyptic Knights of the Round Table. Later, their origin was revised, a la Miracleman, to state that the adventures had all been computer-inspired delusions of the lead character. Issue #180 saw the introduction of Animal Man, a rather plain hero who took on the powers of animals around him. Writer Grant Morrison gave him a surreal bent, and used him to represent man's struggle with nature. Finally came the eerie Deadman in issue #205, a great character from the start. Deadman was the spirit of a murdered aerialist who inhabits the bodies the living in order to fight evil.

1 ❑ Aug 1950 Cover: 0.10 **NM** value: **2000.00**
• **CGC:** 23 graded, best 9.0
★ 1st Appearance of Chris KL-99.
2 ❑ Oct 1950 Cover: 0.10 **NM** value: **900.00**
• **CGC:** 7 graded, best 9.0
3 ❑ Dec 1950 Cover: 0.10 **NM** value: **660.00**
• **CGC:** 5 graded, best 9.6
4 ❑ Jan 1951 Cover: 0.10 **NM** value: **625.00**
• **CGC:** 2 graded, best 9.2
5 ❑ Feb 1951 Cover: 0.10 **NM** value: **500.00**
• **CGC:** 6 graded, best 9.4
6 ❑ Mar 1951 Cover: 0.10 **NM** value: **500.00**
• **CGC:** 1 graded, best 7.5
7 ❑ Apr 1951 Cover: 0.10 **NM** value: **500.00**
• **CGC:** 1 graded, best 9.0
8 ❑ May 1951 Cover: 0.10 **NM** value: **500.00**
• **CGC:** 5 graded, best 9.4
9 ❑ Jun 1951 Cover: 0.10 **NM** value: **1150.00**
• **CGC:** 9 graded, best 9.6
★ Origin of Captain Comet. ★ 1st Appearance of Captain Comet.
10 ❑ Jul 1951 Cover: 0.10 **NM** value: **500.00**
• **CGC:** 5 graded, best 9.8
11 ❑ Aug 1951 Cover: 0.10 **NM** value: **400.00**
• **CGC:** 3 graded, best 9.2
12 ❑ Sep 1951 Cover: 0.10 **NM** value: **400.00**
• **CGC:** 5 graded, best 9.2
13 ❑ Oct 1951 Cover: 0.10 **NM** value: **400.00**
• **CGC:** 5 graded, best 9.6
14 ❑ Nov 1951 Cover: 0.10 **NM** value: **400.00**
• **CGC:** 5 graded, best 9.2
15 ❑ Dec 1951 Cover: 0.10 **NM** value: **400.00**
• **CGC:** 3 graded, best 9.4
16 ❑ Jan 1952 Cover: 0.10 **NM** value: **365.00**
• **CGC:** 4 graded, best 9.4
17 ❑ Feb 1952 Cover: 0.10 **NM** value: **365.00**
• **CGC:** 4 graded, best 9.6
18 ❑ Mar 1952 Cover: 0.10 **NM** value: **365.00**
• **CGC:** 2 graded, best 9.0
19 ❑ Apr 1952 Cover: 0.10 **NM** value: **365.00**
• **CGC:** 2 graded, best 9.0
20 ❑ May 1952 Cover: 0.10 **NM** value: **365.00**
21 ❑ Jun 1952 Cover: 0.10 **NM** value: **285.00**
• **CGC:** 1 graded, best 9.4
22 ❑ Jul 1952 Cover: 0.10 **NM** value: **285.00**
• **CGC:** 1 graded, best 7.5
23 ❑ Aug 1952 Cover: 0.10 **NM** value: **285.00**
24 ❑ Sep 1952 Cover: 0.10 **NM** value: **285.00**
• **CGC:** 1 graded, best 8.5
25 ❑ Oct 1952 Cover: 0.10 **NM** value: **285.00**
26 ❑ Nov 1952 Cover: 0.10 **NM** value: **250.00**
• **CGC:** 1 graded, best 7.0
27 ❑ Dec 1952 Cover: 0.10 **NM** value: **250.00**
• **CGC:** 1 graded, best 5.0
28 ❑ Jan 1953 Cover: 0.10 **NM** value: **250.00**
• **CGC:** 1 graded, best 5.0
29 ❑ Feb 1953 Cover: 0.10 **NM** value: **250.00**
• **CGC:** 1 graded, best 4.5
30 ❑ Mar 1953 Cover: 0.10 **NM** value: **250.00**
31 ❑ Apr 1953 Cover: 0.10 **NM** value: **225.00**
• **CGC:** 1 graded, best 5.0
32 ❑ May 1953 Cover: 0.10 **NM** value: **225.00**
33 ❑ Jun 1953 Cover: 0.10 **NM** value: **225.00**
• **CGC:** 1 graded, best 4.0
34 ❑ Jul 1953 Cover: 0.10 **NM** value: **225.00**
• **CGC:** 1 graded, best 2.0
35 ❑ Aug 1953 Cover: 0.10 **NM** value: **225.00**
• **CGC:** 1 graded, best 8.5
36 ❑ Sep 1953 Cover: 0.10 **NM** value: **225.00**
• **CGC:** 1 graded, best 3.5
37 ❑ Oct 1953 Cover: 0.10 **NM** value: **225.00**
• **CGC:** 2 graded, best 5.0
38 ❑ Nov 1953 Cover: 0.10 **NM** value: **225.00**
39 ❑ Dec 1953 Cover: 0.10 **NM** value: **325.00**
• **CGC:** 1 graded, best 7.0
• Mentioned in Seduction of the Innocent
40 ❑ Jan 1954 Cover: 0.10 **NM** value: **200.00**
41 ❑ Feb 1954 Cover: 0.10 **NM** value: **200.00**
• **CGC:** 1 graded, best 3.0
42 ❑ Mar 1954 Cover: 0.10 **NM** value: **200.00**
• **CGC:** 1 graded, best 4.5
43 ❑ Apr 1954 Cover: 0.10 **NM** value: **200.00**
• **CGC:** 1 graded, best 2.5
44 ❑ May 1954 Cover: 0.10 **NM** value: **200.00**
45 ❑ Jun 1954 Cover: 0.10 **NM** value: **200.00**
• **CGC:** 1 graded, best 5.5
46 ❑ Jul 1954 Cover: 0.10 **NM** value: **200.00**
47 ❑ Aug 1954 Cover: 0.10 **NM** value: **200.00**
• **CGC:** 1 graded, best 3.0
48 ❑ Sep 1954 Cover: 0.10 **NM** value: **200.00**
• **CGC:** 1 graded, best 3.0
49 ❑ Oct 1954 Cover: 0.10 **NM** value: **200.00**
50 ❑ Nov 1954 Cover: 0.10 **NM** value: **200.00**
• **CGC:** 1 graded, best 3.0
51 ❑ Dec 1954 Cover: 0.10 **NM** value: **165.00**
• **CGC:** 1 graded, best 2.5
52 ❑ Jan 1955 Cover: 0.10 **NM** value: **165.00**
• **CGC:** 1 graded, best 4.5
53 ❑ Feb 1955 Cover: 0.10 **NM** value: **165.00**
• **CGC:** 1 graded, best 4.0
54 ❑ Mar 1955 Cover: 0.10 **NM** value: **100.00**
• **CGC:** 1 graded, best 1.8
• Code-approved issues begin
55 ❑ Apr 1955 Cover: 0.10 **NM** value: **100.00**
56 ❑ May 1955 Cover: 0.10 **NM** value: **100.00**
57 ❑ Jun 1955 Cover: 0.10 **NM** value: **100.00**
• **CGC:** 1 graded, best 5.0
58 ❑ Jul 1955 Cover: 0.10 **NM** value: **100.00**
59 ❑ Aug 1955 Cover: 0.10 **NM** value: **100.00**
• **CGC:** 1 graded, best 3.0
60 ❑ Sep 1955 Cover: 0.10 **NM** value: **100.00**
61 ❑ Oct 1955 Cover: 0.10 **NM** value: **90.00**
62 ❑ Nov 1955 Cover: 0.10 **NM** value: **90.00**
63 ❑ Dec 1955 Cover: 0.10 **NM** value: **90.00**
64 ❑ Jan 1956 Cover: 0.10 **NM** value: **90.00**
65 ❑ Feb 1956 Cover: 0.10 **NM** value: **90.00**
66 ❑ Mar 1956 Cover: 0.10 **NM** value: **90.00**
• **CGC:** 2 graded, best 9.0
67 ❑ Apr 1956 Cover: 0.10 **NM** value: **90.00**
• **CGC:** 1 graded, best 6.0
68 ❑ May 1956 Cover: 0.10 **NM** value: **90.00**
69 ❑ Jun 1956 Cover: 0.10 **NM** value: **90.00**
70 ❑ Jul 1956 Cover: 0.10 **NM** value: **90.00**
• **CGC:** 2 graded, best 8.0
71 ❑ Aug 1956 Cover: 0.10 **NM** value: **80.00**
• **CGC:** 1 graded, best 6.0
72 ❑ Sep 1956 Cover: 0.10 **NM** value: **80.00**
• **CGC:** 1 graded, best 5.0
73 ❑ Oct 1956 Cover: 0.10 **NM** value: **80.00**
• **CGC:** 1 graded, best 5.5
74 ❑ Nov 1956 Cover: 0.10 **NM** value: **80.00**
• **CGC:** 1 graded, best 7.0
75 ❑ Dec 1956 Cover: 0.10 **NM** value: **80.00**
76 ❑ Jan 1957 Cover: 0.10 **NM** value: **80.00**
77 ❑ Feb 1957 Cover: 0.10 **NM** value: **80.00**
78 ❑ Mar 1957 Cover: 0.10 **NM** value: **80.00**
79 ❑ Apr 1957 Cover: 0.10 **NM** value: **80.00**
• **CGC:** 1 graded, best 7.5
80 ❑ May 1957 Cover: 0.10 **NM** value: **80.00**
81 ❑ Jun 1957 Cover: 0.10 **NM** value: **70.00**
82 ❑ Jul 1957 Cover: 0.10 **NM** value: **70.00**
83 ❑ Aug 1957 Cover: 0.10 **NM** value: **70.00**
84 ❑ Sep 1957 Cover: 0.10 **NM** value: **70.00**
• **CGC:** 1 graded, best 6.5
85 ❑ Oct 1957 Cover: 0.10 **NM** value: **70.00**
• **CGC:** 1 graded, best 1.5
86 ❑ Nov 1957 Cover: 0.10 **NM** value: **70.00**
87 ❑ Dec 1957 Cover: 0.10 **NM** value: **70.00**
88 ❑ Jan 1958 Cover: 0.10 **NM** value: **70.00**
89 ❑ Feb 1958 Cover: 0.10 **NM** value: **70.00**
• **CGC:** 1 graded, best 9.0
90 ❑ Mar 1958 Cover: 0.10 **NM** value: **70.00**
91 ❑ Apr 1958 Cover: 0.10 **NM** value: **65.00**
92 ❑ May 1958 Cover: 0.10 **NM** value: **65.00**
93 ❑ Jun 1958 Cover: 0.10 **NM** value: **65.00**
94 ❑ Jul 1958 Cover: 0.10 **NM** value: **65.00**
95 ❑ Aug 1958 Cover: 0.10 **NM** value: **65.00**
96 ❑ Sep 1958 Cover: 0.10 **NM** value: **65.00**
97 ❑ Oct 1958 Cover: 0.10 **NM** value: **65.00**
98 ❑ Nov 1958 Cover: 0.10 **NM** value: **65.00**
99 ❑ Dec 1958 Cover: 0.10 **NM** value: **65.00**
100 ❑ Jan 1959 Cover: 0.10 **NM** value: **90.00**
• 100th anniversary issue.
101 ❑ Feb 1959 Cover: 0.10 **NM** value: **50.00**
• **CGC:** 1 graded, best 7.0
102 ❑ Mar 1959 Cover: 0.10 **NM** value: **50.00**
103 ❑ Apr 1959 Cover: 0.10 **NM** value: **50.00**
104 ❑ May 1959 Cover: 0.10 **NM** value: **50.00**
★ 1st Appearance of Space Museum.
105 ❑ Jun 1959 Cover: 0.10 **NM** value: **50.00**
106 ❑ Jul 1959 Cover: 0.10 **NM** value: **50.00**
107 ❑ Aug 1959 Cover: 0.10 **NM** value: **50.00**
108 ❑ Sep 1959 Cover: 0.10 **NM** value: **50.00**
109 ❑ Oct 1959 Cover: 0.10 **NM** value: **50.00**
110 ❑ Nov 1959 Cover: 0.10 **NM** value: **50.00**
111 ❑ Dec 1959 Cover: 0.10 **NM** value: **45.00**
112 ❑ Jan 1960 Cover: 0.10 **NM** value: **45.00**
Circ: Statement: **207,000**
113 ❑ Feb 1960 Cover: 0.10 **NM** value: **45.00**
Circ: Statement: **207,000**
114 ❑ Mar 1960 Cover: 0.10 **NM** value: **45.00**
Circ: Statement: **207,000**
★ 1st Appearance of Star Hawkins.
115 ❑ Apr 1960 Cover: 0.10 **NM** value: **45.00**
Circ: Statement: **207,000**
116 ❑ May 1960 Cover: 0.10 **NM** value: **45.00**
Circ: Statement: **207,000**
117 ❑ Jun 1960 Cover: 0.10 **NM** value: **450.00**
Circ: Statement: **207,000** • **CGC:** 6 graded, best 9.2
★ 1st Appearance of The Atomic Knights.
118 ❑ Jul 1960 Cover: 0.10 **NM** value: **60.00**
Circ: Statement: **207,000**
119 ❑ Aug 1960 Cover: 0.10 **NM** value: **60.00**
Circ: Statement: **207,000**
120 ❑ Sep 1960 Cover: 0.10 **NM** value: **200.00**
Circ: Statement: **207,000** • **CGC:** 6 graded, best 9.0
★ 2nd Appearance of The Atomic Knights.
121 ❑ Oct 1960 Cover: 0.10 **NM** value: **55.00**
Circ: Statement: **207,000**
122 ❑ Nov 1960 Cover: 0.10 **NM** value: **55.00**
Circ: Statement: **207,000**
123 ❑ Dec 1960 Cover: 0.10 **NM** value: **55.00**
Circ: Statement: **207,000**
124 ❑ Jan 1961 Cover: 0.10 **NM** value: **55.00**
Circ: Statement: **210,000** • **CGC:** 1 graded, best 6.5
125 ❑ Feb 1961 Cover: 0.10 **NM** value: **55.00**
Circ: Statement: **210,000**
• Has 1960 Statement, filed 10/1/60; avg total paid circ 207,000
126 ❑ Mar 1961 Cover: 0.10 **NM** value: **55.00**
Circ: Statement: **210,000**
127 ❑ Apr 1961 Cover: 0.10 **NM** value: **55.00**
Circ: Statement: **210,000**
128 ❑ May 1961 Cover: 0.10 **NM** value: **55.00**
Circ: Statement: **210,000**
129 ❑ Jun 1961 Cover: 0.10 **NM** value: **55.00**
Circ: Statement: **210,000** • **CGC:** 1 graded, best 9.0
130 ❑ Jul 1961 Cover: 0.10 **NM** value: **55.00**
Circ: Statement: **210,000**
131 ❑ Aug 1961 Cover: 0.10 **NM** value: **48.00**
Circ: Statement: **210,000**
132 ❑ Sep 1961 Cover: 0.10 **NM** value: **48.00**
Circ: Statement: **210,000**
133 ❑ Oct 1961 Cover: 0.10 **NM** value: **48.00**
Circ: Statement: **210,000**
134 ❑ Nov 1961 Cover: 0.10 **NM** value: **48.00**
Circ: Statement: **210,000**
135 ❑ Dec 1961 Cover: 0.10 **NM** value: **35.00**
Circ: Statement: **210,000** • **CGC:** 1 graded, best 9.0
136 ❑ Jan 1962 Cover: 0.12 **NM** value: **35.00**
Circ: Statement: **180,000**
137 ❑ Feb 1962 Cover: 0.12 **NM** value: **35.00**
Circ: Statement: **180,000**
• Has 1961 Statement, filed 10/1/61; avg total paid circ 210,000
138 ❑ Mar 1962 Cover: 0.12 **NM** value: **35.00**
Circ: Statement: **180,000**
★ Appearance of The Atomic Knights.
139 ❑ Apr 1962 Cover: 0.12 **NM** value: **35.00**
Circ: Statement: **180,000**
140 ❑ May 1962 Cover: 0.12 **NM** value: **35.00**
Circ: Statement: **180,000**
141 ❑ Jun 1962 Cover: 0.12 **NM** value: **35.00**
Circ: Statement: **180,000**
142 ❑ Jul 1962 Cover: 0.12 **NM** value: **35.00**
Circ: Statement: **180,000** • **CGC:** 1 graded, best 7.0
143 ❑ Aug 1962 Cover: 0.12 **NM** value: **35.00**
Circ: Statement: **180,000**
144 ❑ Sep 1962 Cover: 0.12 **NM** value: **35.00**
Circ: Statement: **180,000** • **CGC:** 2 graded, best 8.5
★ Appearance of The Atomic Knights.
145 ❑ Oct 1962 Cover: 0.12 **NM** value: **35.00**
Circ: Statement: **180,000** • **CGC:** 1 graded, best 9.2
146 ❑ Nov 1962 Cover: 0.12 **NM** value: **35.00**
Circ: Statement: **180,000** • **CGC:** 3 graded, best 9.4
147 ❑ Dec 1962 Cover: 0.12 **NM** value: **35.00**
Circ: Statement: **180,000** • **CGC:** 3 graded, best 9.0
★ Appearance of The Atomic Knights.
148 ❑ Jan 1963 Cover: 0.12 **NM** value: **35.00**
• **CGC:** 1 graded, best 9.4
149 ❑ Feb 1963 Cover: 0.12 **NM** value: **35.00**
• **CGC:** 1 graded, best 9.6
• Has 1962 Statement, filed 10/1/62; avg total paid circ 180,000
150 ❑ Mar 1963 Cover: 0.12 **NM** value: **35.00**
• **CGC:** 2 graded, best 9.6
★ Appearance of The Atomic Knights.
151 ❑ Apr 1963 Cover: 0.12 **NM** value: **30.00**
• **CGC:** 2 graded, best 9.6
152 ❑ May 1963 Cover: 0.12 **NM** value: **30.00**
• **CGC:** 1 graded, best 9.4
153 ❑ Jun 1963 Cover: 0.12 **NM** value: **30.00**
• **CGC:** 2 graded, best 9.8
★ Appearance of The Atomic Knights.
154 ❑ Jul 1963 Cover: 0.12 **NM** value: **30.00**
• **CGC:** 1 graded, best 9.6
155 ❑ Aug 1963 Cover: 0.12 **NM** value: **30.00**
• **CGC:** 2 graded, best 9.4
156 ❑ Sep 1963 Cover: 0.12 **NM** value: **30.00**
• **CGC:** 1 graded, best 9.4
★ Appearance of The Atomic Knights.

CGC-graded: Multiply prices above by **33 for 9.9 M • 16 for 9.8 NM/M • 7 for 9.6 NM+ • 5 for 9.4 NM • 2.5 for 9.2 NM- • 1.5 for 9.0 VF/NM**

157 ❑ Oct 1963 Cover: 0.12 **NM** value: **30.00**
• **CGC:** 2 graded, best 9.8
158 ❑ Nov 1963 Cover: 0.12 **NM** value: **30.00**
• **CGC:** 2 graded, best 8.0
159 ❑ Dec 1963 Cover: 0.12 **NM** value: **30.00**
• **CGC:** 1 graded, best 9.6
160 ❑ Jan 1964 Cover: 0.12 **NM** value: **30.00**
• **CGC:** 1 graded, best 9.4
★ Appearance of The Atomic Knights.
161 ❑ Feb 1964 Cover: 0.12 **NM** value: **18.00**
• **CGC:** 1 graded, best 9.8
• Has 1963 Statement, filed 10/1/63; no circ figures published
162 ❑ Mar 1964 Cover: 0.12 **NM** value: **18.00**
• **CGC:** 1 graded, best 9.2
163 ❑ Apr 1964 Cover: 0.12 **NM** value: **18.00**
• **CGC:** 1 graded, best 9.6
164 ❑ May 1964 Cover: 0.12 **NM** value: **18.00**
• **CGC:** 1 graded, best 9.6
165 ❑ Jun 1964 Cover: 0.12 **NM** value: **18.00**
• **CGC:** 2 graded, best 9.6
166 ❑ Jul 1964 Cover: 0.12 **NM** value: **18.00**
• **CGC:** 2 graded, best 9.6
167 ❑ Aug 1964 Cover: 0.12 **NM** value: **18.00**
• **CGC:** 1 graded, best 9.4
168 ❑ Sep 1964 Cover: 0.12 **NM** value: **18.00**
• **CGC:** 2 graded, best 9.6
169 ❑ Oct 1964 Cover: 0.12 **NM** value: **18.00**
• **CGC:** 1 graded, best 9.8
170 ❑ Nov 1964 Cover: 0.12 **NM** value: **18.00**
• **CGC:** 1 graded, best 9.6
171 ❑ Dec 1964 Cover: 0.12 **NM** value: **18.00**
• **CGC:** 1 graded, best 9.4
172 ❑ Jan 1965 Cover: 0.12 **NM** value: **18.00**
173 ❑ Feb 1965 Cover: 0.12 **NM** value: **18.00**
• **CGC:** 1 graded, best 4.0
174 ❑ Mar 1965 Cover: 0.12 **NM** value: **18.00**
• Has 1964 Statement, filed 10/1/64; no circ figures published
175 ❑ Apr 1965 Cover: 0.12 **NM** value: **18.00**
• **CGC:** 2 graded, best 9.4
176 ❑ May 1965 Cover: 0.12 **NM** value: **18.00**
177 ❑ Jun 1965 Cover: 0.12 **NM** value: **18.00**
★ Origin of Immortal Man. ★ 1st Appearance of Immortal Man.
178 ❑ Jul 1965 Cover: 0.12 **NM** value: **18.00**
• **CGC:** 1 graded, best 3.5
179 ❑ Aug 1965 Cover: 0.12 **NM** value: **18.00**
• **CGC:** 1 graded, best 7.0
180 ❑ Sep 1965 Cover: 0.12 **NM** value: **100.00**
• **CGC:** 7 graded, best 9.8
★ Origin of Animal Man (no costume). ★ 1st Appearance of Animal Man (no costume).
181 ❑ Oct 1965 Cover: 0.12 **NM** value: **13.00**
182 ❑ Nov 1965 Cover: 0.12 **NM** value: **13.00**
183 ❑ Dec 1965 Cover: 0.12 **NM** value: **13.00**
184 ❑ Jan 1966 Cover: 0.12 **NM** value: **70.00**
Circ: Statement: **174,922** • **CGC:** 7 graded, best 9.4
★ Appearance of Animal Man.
185 ❑ Feb 1966 Cover: 0.12 **NM** value: **13.00**
Circ: Statement: **174,922** • **CGC:** 1 graded, best 9.2
★ Appearance of Immortal Man, Star Hawkins.
186 ❑ Mar 1966 Cover: 0.12 **NM** value: **13.00**
Circ: Statement: **174,922** • **CGC:** 1 graded, best 9.0
• Has 1965 Statement, filed 10/1/65; no circ figures published
187 ❑ Apr 1966 Cover: 0.12 **NM** value: **13.00**
Circ: Statement: **174,922**
★ Origin of The Enchantress. ★ 1st Appearance of The Enchantress.
188 ❑ May 1966 Cover: 0.12 **NM** value: **13.00**
Circ: Statement: **174,922**
189 ❑ Jun 1966 Cover: 0.12 **NM** value: **13.00**
Circ: Statement: **174,922** • **CGC:** 1 graded, best 9.2
190 ❑ Jul 1966 Cover: 0.12 **NM** value: **75.00**
Circ: Statement: **174,922** • **CGC:** 10 graded, best 9.6
★ 1st Appearance of Animal Man (in costume).
191 ❑ Aug 1966 Cover: 0.12 **NM** value: **10.00**
Circ: Statement: **174,922**
192 ❑ Sep 1966 Cover: 0.12 **NM** value: **10.00**
Circ: Statement: **174,922**
193 ❑ Oct 1966 Cover: 0.12 **NM** value: **10.00**
Circ: Statement: **174,922**
194 ❑ Nov 1966 Cover: 0.12 **NM** value: **10.00**
Circ: Statement: **174,922** • **CGC:** 1 graded, best 9.2
195 ❑ Dec 1966 Cover: 0.12 **NM** value: **45.00**
Circ: Statement: **174,922** • **CGC:** 7 graded, best 9.8
★ Appearance of Animal Man.
196 ❑ Jan 1967 Cover: 0.12 **NM** value: **10.00**
Circ: Statement: **146,600** • **CGC:** 1 graded, best 9.2
197 ❑ Feb 1967 Cover: 0.12 **NM** value: **10.00**
Circ: Statement: **146,600** • **CGC:** 2 graded, best 9.6
• Has 1966 Statement, filed 10/1/66; avg print run 310,000; avg sales 174,000; avg subs 922; avg total paid 174,922; samples 265; max existent 175,187; 44% of run returned
198 ❑ Mar 1967 Cover: 0.12 **NM** value: **10.00**
Circ: Statement: **146,600**
199 ❑ Apr 1967 Cover: 0.12 **NM** value: **10.00**
Circ: Statement: **146,600**
200 ❑ May 1967 Cover: 0.12 **NM** value: **10.00**
Circ: Statement: **146,600** • **CGC:** 3 graded, best 9.6
201 ❑ Jun 1967 Cover: 0.12 **NM** value: **30.00**
Circ: Statement: **146,600**
★ Appearance of Animal Man.
202 ❑ Jul 1967 Cover: 0.12 **NM** value: **9.00**
Circ: Statement: **146,600**
203 ❑ Aug 1967 Cover: 0.12 **NM** value: **9.00**
Circ: Statement: **146,600**
🕮 The Winged Beasts Of Nightmare Swamp!; The Split Man!
204 ❑ Sep 1967 Cover: 0.12 **NM** value: **9.00**
Circ: Statement: **146,600**
205 ❑ Oct 1967 Cover: 0.12 **NM** value: **70.00**
Circ: Statement: **146,600** • **CGC:** 13 graded, best 9.4
★ Origin of Deadman. ★ 1st Appearance of Deadman.
206 ❑ Nov 1967 Cover: 0.12 **NM** value: **45.00**
Circ: Statement: **146,600** • **CGC:** 2 graded, best 9.6
★ 2nd Appearance of Deadman.
207 ❑ Dec 1967 Cover: 0.12 **NM** value: **32.00**
Circ: Statement: **146,600** • **CGC:** 4 graded, best 9.8
• Deadman
208 ❑ Jan 1968 Cover: 0.12 **NM** value: **32.00**
Circ: Statement: **165,190** • **CGC:** 1 graded, best 9.4
• Deadman
209 ❑ Feb 1968 Cover: 0.12 **NM** value: **32.00**
Circ: Statement: **165,190** • **CGC:** 3 graded, best 9.4
• Deadman; Has 1967 Statement, filed 10/1/67; avg print run 299,000; avg sales 146,000; avg subs 600; avg total paid 146,600; samples 340; max existent 146,940; 51% of run returned
210 ❑ Mar 1968 Cover: 0.12 **NM** value: **32.00**
Circ: Statement: **165,190** • **CGC:** 1 graded, best 9.4
• Deadman
211 ❑ Apr 1968 Cover: 0.12 **NM** value: **28.00**
Circ: Statement: **165,190** • **CGC:** 1 graded, best 9.4
• Deadman
212 ❑ Jun 1968 Cover: 0.12 **NM** value: **28.00**
Circ: Statement: **165,190** • **CGC:** 1 graded, best 9.4
• Deadman
213 ❑ Aug 1968 Cover: 0.12 **NM** value: **28.00**
Circ: Statement: **165,190** • **CGC:** 3 graded, best 9.6
• Deadman
214 ❑ Oct 1968 Cover: 0.12 **NM** value: **28.00**
Circ: Statement: **165,190** • **CGC:** 2 graded, best 9.4
• Deadman
215 ❑ Dec 1968 Cover: 0.12 **NM** value: **28.00**
Circ: Statement: **165,190** • **CGC:** 3 graded, best 9.4
• Deadman ★ 1st Appearance of League of Assassins, Sensei.
216 ❑ Feb 1969 Cover: 0.12 **NM** value: **28.00**
Circ: Statement: **141,179** • **CGC:** 4 graded, best 9.4
• Deadman
217 ❑ Apr 1969 Cover: 0.12 **NM** value: **7.00**
Circ: Statement: **141,179** • **CGC:** 1 graded, best 9.0
• Has 1968 Statement, filed 10/1/68; avg print run 312,000; avg sales 165,000; avg subs 190; avg total paid 165,190; samples 386; max existent 165,576; 47% of run returned
218 ❑ Jun 1969 Cover: 0.12 **NM** value: **7.00**
Circ: Statement: **141,179** • **CGC:** 2 graded, best 9.4
219 ❑ Aug 1969 Cover: 0.15 **NM** value: **7.00**
Circ: Statement: **141,179**
220 ❑ Oct 1969 Cover: 0.15 **NM** value: **7.00**
Circ: Statement: **141,179**
221 ❑ Dec 1969 Cover: 0.15 **NM** value: **7.00**
Circ: Statement: **141,179**
222 ❑ Feb 1970 Cover: 0.15 **NM** value: **10.00**
Circ: Statement: **136,047**
• New Adam Strange story **A:** Neal Adams
223 ❑ Apr 1970 Cover: 0.15 **NM** value: **7.00**
Circ: Statement: **136,047** • **CGC:** 2 graded, best 9.6
• Has 1969 Statement, filed 10/1/69; avg print run 293,000; avg sales 141,000; avg subs 179; avg total paid 141,179; samples 346; max existent 141,525; 52% of run returned
224 ❑ Jun 1970 Cover: 0.15 **NM** value: **7.00**
Circ: Statement: **136,047** • **CGC:** 2 graded, best 9.4
225 ❑ Aug 1970 Cover: 0.15 **NM** value: **7.00**
Circ: Statement: **136,047**
226 ❑ Oct 1970 Cover: 0.25 **NM** value: **7.00**
Circ: Statement: **136,047**
• giant series begins
227 ❑ Dec 1970 Cover: 0.25 **NM** value: **7.00**
Circ: Statement: **136,047**
C: Joe Kubert
228 ❑ Feb 1971 Cover: 0.25 **NM** value: **7.00**
Circ: Statement: **135,265**
229 ❑ Apr 1971 Cover: 0.25 **NM** value: **7.00**
Circ: Statement: **135,265**
• Has 1970 Statement, filed 10/1/70; avg print run 280,328; avg sales 135,866; avg subs 181; avg total paid 136,047; samples 122; max existent 136,169; 52% of run returned
230 ❑ Jun 1971 Cover: 0.25 **NM** value: **7.00**
Circ: Statement: **135,265**
231 ❑ Aug 1971 Cover: 0.25 **NM** value: **4.00**
Circ: Statement: **135,265**
232 ❑ Oct 1971 Cover: 0.25 **NM** value: **4.00**
Circ: Statement: **135,265**
233 ❑ Dec 1971 Cover: 0.25 **NM** value: **4.00**
Circ: Statement: **135,265**
234 ❑ Feb 1972 Cover: 0.25 **NM** value: **4.00**
Circ: Statement: **135,706** • **CGC:** 1 graded, best 9.2
235 ❑ Apr 1972 Cover: 0.25 **NM** value: **4.00**
Circ: Statement: **135,706** • **CGC:** 1 graded, best 9.4
• Has 1971 Statement, filed 10/1/71; avg print run 276,666; avg sales 135,265; avg subs 0; avg total paid 135,265; samples 0; office use 666; max existent 135,931; 51% of run returned
236 ❑ Jun 1972 Cover: 0.25 **NM** value: **4.00**
Circ: Statement: **135,706**
237 ❑ Jun 1972 Cover: 0.20 **NM** value: **4.00**
Circ: Statement: **135,706** • **CGC:** 1 graded, best 9.6
🕮 The Skyscraper That Came To Life!; Ray-Gun In The Sky!; The Case Of The Counterfeit Humans
238 ❑ Oct 1972 Cover: 0.20 **NM** value: **4.00**
Circ: Statement: **135,706**
🕮 The Secret of the Tomb Thumb Spacemen!; The Man Who Killed Himself!; Adam Strange: Shadow People of the Eclipse! **A:** Murphy Anderson; Carmine Infantino; Bernard Sachs; John Giunta; Sid Greene **W:** Gardner Fox; John Broome
239 ❑ Dec 1972 Cover: 0.20 **NM** value: **4.00**
Circ: Statement: **135,706**
240 ❑ Feb 1973 Cover: 0.20 **NM** value: **4.00**
241 ❑ Apr 1973 Cover: 0.20 **NM** value: **4.00**
• Has 1972 Statement, filed 10/1/72; avg print run 275,000; avg sales 135,676; avg subs 30; avg total paid 135,706; samples 523; office use 208; max existent 136,437; 50% of run returned
242 ❑ Jul 1973 Cover: 0.20 **NM** value: **4.00**
243 ❑ Sep 1973 Cover: 0.20 **NM** value: **4.00**
244 ❑ Nov 1973 Cover: 0.20 **NM** value: **4.00**
final issue.

STRANGE ADVENTURES (HARVEY KURTZMAN'S...) Marvel / Epic

Bk 1/HC ❑ Oct 1990 Cover: 19.95 **NM** value: **Cover or less**
hardcover.

STRANGE ADVENTURES (MINI-SERIES) DC / Vertigo

1 ❑ Nov 1999 Cover: 2.50 **NM** value: **Cover or less**
Circ: Diamd. preorders: **17,801**
2 ❑ Dec 1999 Cover: 2.50 **NM** value: **Cover or less**
Circ: Diamd. preorders: **14,214**
🕮 Third Toe, Left Boot; Ice Cream Comes to Wharftown; Expiration Date **A:** Edvin Biukovic; Klaus Janson; James Romberger **W:** Bruce Jones; Klaus Janson; Colin Raff
3 ❑ Jan 2000 Cover: 2.50 **NM** value: **Cover or less**
Circ: Diamd. preorders: **13,264**
🕮 The Split; Driving Miss 134; Metal Fatigue **A:** Pat McEown; Richard Corben; John Toteben **W:** Mark Schultz; Doselle Young; Joe R. Lansdale
4 ❑ Feb 2000 Cover: 2.50 **NM** value: **Cover or less**
Circ: Diamd. preorders: **13,906**

STRANGE ATTRACTORS Retrografix

Sophie, the introverted curator of the Museum of Lost Things, finds a mysterious amulet, and her life is suddenly changed forever. First she is caught up in a romance with the mysterious stranger, Meson, who later abandons her when he falls under the influence of the magical amulet. Her life spins even more out of control when Sophie discovers Meson plans to marry her childhood friend, Widow, heiress to the largest fortune in the solar system.

But when Meson assassinates Widow's father, Sophie sets out on a desperate attempt to help Widow. She is joined by her faithful robot, Roshi, and the legendary adventurer, Pirate Peg. They soon discover that there is more to the strange happenings than just murder, as they are all swept up in a timeless struggle between the forces of science and sorcery.

1 ❑ May 1993 Cover: 2.50 **NM** value: **4.00**
🕮 The Sorrows of Young Sophie **A:** Mark Sherman; Michael Cohen **W:** Mark Sherman; Michael Cohen
1-2 ❑ Jul 1994 Cover: 2.50 **NM** value: **2.75**
2 ❑ Aug 1993 Cover: 2.50 **NM** value: **3.50**
🕮 I Went to See the Gypsy **A:** Mark Sherman; Michael Cohen **W:** Mark Sherman; Michael Cohen
2-2 ❑ Jul 1993 Cover: 2.50 **NM** value: **2.75**
3 ❑ Nov 1993 Cover: 2.50 **NM** value: **3.50**
🕮 Dear Diary **A:** Mark Sherman; Michael Cohen **W:** Mark Sherman; Michael Cohen
3-2 ❑ Jun 1993 Cover: 2.50 **NM** value: **2.75**
4 ❑ Feb 1994 Cover: 2.50 **NM** value: **3.00**
🕮 Heart Of Stone **A:** Mark Sherman; Michael Cohen **W:** Mark Sherman; Michael Cohen
4-2 ❑ Jun 1994 Cover: 2.50 **NM** value: **2.75**
5 ❑ May 1994 Cover: 2.50 **NM** value: **3.00**
A: Mark Sherman; Michael Cohen **W:** Mark Sherman; Michael Cohen
6 ❑ Aug 1994 Cover: 2.50 **NM** value: **Cover or less**
A: Mark Sherman; Michael Cohen **W:** Mark Sherman; Michael Cohen
7 ❑ Nov 1994 Cover: 2.50 **NM** value: **Cover or less**
A: Mark Sherman; Michael Cohen **W:** Mark Sherman; Michael Cohen
8 ❑ Jan 1995 Cover: 2.50 **NM** value: **Cover or less**
A: Mark Sherman; Michael Cohen **W:** Mark Sherman; Michael Cohen
9 ❑ Apr 1995 Cover: 2.50 **NM** value: **Cover or less**
A: Mark Sherman; Michael Cohen **W:** Mark Sherman; Michael Cohen
10 ❑ Jun 1995 Cover: 2.50 **NM** value: **Cover or less**
A: Mark Sherman; Michael Cohen **W:** Mark Sherman; Michael Cohen
11 ❑ Sep 1995 Cover: 2.50 **NM** value: **Cover or less**
A: Mark Sherman; Michael Cohen **W:** Mark Sherman; Michael Cohen
12 ❑ Nov 1995 Cover: 2.50 **NM** value: **Cover or less**
A: Mark Sherman; Michael Cohen **W:** Mark Sherman; Michael Cohen
13 ❑ Feb 1996 Cover: 2.95 **NM** value: **Cover or less**
A: Mark Sherman; Michael Cohen **W:** Mark Sherman; Michael Cohen
14 ❑ Jul 1996 Cover: 2.95 **NM** value: **Cover or less**
A: Mark Sherman; Michael Cohen **W:** Mark Sherman; Michael Cohen
15 ❑ Feb 1997 Cover: 2.95 **NM** value: **Cover or less**
A: Mark Sherman; Michael Cohen **W:** Mark Sherman; Michael Cohen
Bk 1 ❑ May 1996, b&w Cover: 14.95 **NM** value: **Cover or less**
• Chaos Jitterbug; collects issues #1-7 **A:** Mark Sherman; Michael Cohen **W:** Mark Sherman; Michael Cohen
Bk 2 ❑ **NM** value: **18.95**
• Collects Strange Attractors #8-15 **A:** Mark Sherman; Michael Cohen **W:** Mark Sherman; Michael Cohen

STRANGE ATTRACTORS: MOON FEVER Caliber

1 ❑ Feb 1997, b&w Cover: 2.95 **NM** value: **Cover or less**
Circ: Diamd. preorders: **1,910**
A: Mark Sherman; Michael Cohen **W:** Mark Sherman
2 ❑ 1997 Cover: 2.95 **NM** value: **Cover or less**
A: Mark Sherman; Michael Cohen **W:** Mark Sherman
3 ❑ 1997 Cover: 2.95 **NM** value: **Cover or less**
A: Mark Sherman; Michael Cohen **W:** Mark Sherman

STRANGE AVENGING TALES (STEVE DITKO'S...) Fantagraphics

1 ❑ Feb 1997 Cover: 2.95 **NM** value: **Cover or less**
Circ: Diamd. preorders: **5,558**

Other grades: Multiply prices above by **1.5 for Mint • 2/3 for Very Fine • 1/3 for Fine • 1/5 for Very Good • 1/8 for Good**

The Baffler in All Mine; The Spoiler Files; Clyde and Claude; Speak for Yourself and not for Reality **A:** Steve Ditko **W:** Steve Ditko

STRANGE BREW — Aardvark-Vanaheim

1 ❑ **NM** value: **3.00**

STRANGE COMBAT TALES — Marvel / Epic

1 ❑ Oct 1993 Cover: 2.50 **NM** value: **Cover or less**
Circ: CapCity orders: **5,000**
March Of The Dead **A:** Dave Matthews **W:** Aubrey Singer; Rob Stofega ★ Appearance of Julian Drake.
2 ❑ Nov 1993 Cover: 2.50 **NM** value: **Cover or less**
Circ: CapCity orders: **2,100**
A: Dave Matthews **W:** Aubrey Singer; Rob Stofega
3 ❑ Dec 1993 Cover: 2.50 **NM** value: **Cover or less**
A: Dave Matthews **W:** Aubrey Singer; Rob Stofega
4 ❑ Jan 1984 Cover: 2.50 **NM** value: **Cover or less**
Midnight Crusade **A:** Dave Matthews **W:** Aubrey Singer; Rob Stofega

STRANGE DAYS — Eclipse

1 ❑ Cover: 1.50 **NM** value: **Cover or less**
Freakwave; Tales from the 4th Dimesion; Johnny Nemo; Krazy Foam; Paradax **A:** Brett Ewins; McCarthy; Milligan **W:** Brett Ewins; McCarthy; Milligan
2 ❑ Cover: 1.50 **NM** value: **Cover or less**
Circ: CapCity orders: **4,225**
3 ❑ Cover: 1.50 **NM** value: **Cover or less**
Circ: CapCity orders: **4,050**

STRANGE EMBRACE — Atomeka

1 ❑ b&w Cover: 3.95 **NM** value: **Cover or less**
2 ❑ b&w Cover: 3.95 **NM** value: **Cover or less**
3 ❑ b&w Cover: 3.95 **NM** value: **Cover or less**

STRANGE FANTASY — Farrell

Like its sister publication Voodoo (Farrell), Strange Fantasy seemed to be somehow weirder than most other horror anthologies of its day. Published in the years prior to the inception of the Comics Code, it featured plenty of vampires, zombies, and other monsters. Its oddest pieces, however, were about the human reactions to circumstances they had set up with no supernatural help. These include the mortician who flees from his lover in Paris, kills her when she shows up to ruin his happy marriage in America (dismembering the body to prevent identification), then kills himself when the body is found floating behind his own house.

1 ❑ Aug 1952 Cover: 0.10 **NM** value: **200.00**
• **CGC:** 1 graded, best 9.2
#2 on cover.
2 ❑ Oct 1952 Cover: 0.10 **NM** value: **175.00**
3 ❑ Dec 1952 Cover: 0.10 **NM** value: **150.00**
• **CGC:** 1 graded, best 3.0
4 ❑ Feb 1953 Cover: 0.10 **NM** value: **100.00**
5 ❑ Apr 1953 Cover: 0.10 **NM** value: **100.00**
• **CGC:** 1 graded, best 9.2
6 ❑ Jun 1953 Cover: 0.10 **NM** value: **100.00**
• **CGC:** 2 graded, best 9.4
7 ❑ Aug 1953 Cover: 0.10 **NM** value: **125.00**
• Madam Satan
8 ❑ Oct 1953 Cover: 0.10 **NM** value: **100.00**
• **CGC:** 1 graded, best 9.4
9 ❑ Dec 1953 Cover: 0.10 **NM** value: **125.00**
A: Steve Ditko
10 ❑ Feb 1954 Cover: 0.10 **NM** value: **100.00**
11 ❑ Apr 1954 Cover: 0.10 **NM** value: **90.00**
In a Lonely Place; Death Packs a Suitcase; Frozen in Stone!; Mice and Old Rice (text story); Doom Deferred
12 ❑ Jun 1954 Cover: 0.10 **NM** value: **90.00**
13 ❑ Aug 1954 Cover: 0.10 **NM** value: **90.00**
14 ❑ Oct 1954 Cover: 0.10 **NM** value: **90.00**
final issue.

STRANGEHAVEN — Abiogenesis Press

1 ❑ Jun 1995 Cover: 2.95 **NM** value: **5.00**
A: Gary Spencer Millidge **W:** Gary Spencer Millidge
2 ❑ Cover: 2.95 **NM** value: **4.00**
A: Gary Spencer Millidge **W:** Gary Spencer Millidge
3 ❑ Dec 1995 Cover: 2.95 **NM** value: **4.00**
Call No Man Happy; My Alien Retina; Too Many Questions **A:** Gary Spencer Millidge **W:** Gary Spencer Millidge
4 ❑ Jun 1996 Cover: 2.95 **NM** value: **Cover or less**
A: Gary Spencer Millidge **W:** Gary Spencer Millidge
5 ❑ Nov 1996 Cover: 2.95 **NM** value: **Cover or less**
A: Gary Spencer Millidge **W:** Gary Spencer Millidge
6 ❑ May 1997 Cover: 2.95 **NM** value: **Cover or less**
Circ: Diamd. preorders: **2,301**
A: Gary Spencer Millidge **W:** Gary Spencer Millidge
7 ❑ Cover: 2.95 **NM** value: **Cover or less**
A: Gary Spencer Millidge **W:** Gary Spencer Millidge
8 ❑ 1997 Cover: 2.95 **NM** value: **Cover or less**
A: Gary Spencer Millidge **W:** Gary Spencer Millidge
9 ❑ Jun 1998 Cover: 2.95 **NM** value: **Cover or less**
A: Gary Spencer Millidge **W:** Gary Spencer Millidge
10 ❑ Nov 1998 Cover: 2.95 **NM** value: **Cover or less**
Circ: Diamd. preorders: **1,888**
A: Gary Spencer Millidge **W:** Gary Spencer Millidge
11 ❑ Apr 1999 Cover: 2.95 **NM** value: **Cover or less**
Circ: Diamd. preorders: **1,835**
A: Gary Spencer Millidge **W:** Gary Spencer Millidge
12 ❑ Oct 1999 Cover: 2.95 **NM** value: **Cover or less**
Circ: Diamd. preorders: **1,820**
A: Gary Spencer Millidge **W:** Gary Spencer Millidge

STRANGE HEROES — Lone Star

1 ❑ Jun 2000 Cover: 2.95 **NM** value: **Cover or less**
Spellbinder; Otherland **A:** Bobby Diaz; Kelsey Shannon **W:** Bill Willingham

STRANGE JOURNEY — America's Best

1 ❑ Sep 1957 Cover: 0.10 **NM** value: **125.00**
2 ❑ Nov 1957 Cover: 0.10 **NM** value: **75.00**
3 ❑ Feb 1958 Cover: 0.10 **NM** value: **75.00**
4 ❑ ca. 1958 Cover: 0.10 **NM** value: **75.00**

STRANGELOVE — Express / Entity

1 ❑ b&w Cover: 2.50 **NM** value: **Cover or less**
Circ: CapCity orders: **2,460**
2 ❑ b&w Cover: 2.50 **NM** value: **Cover or less**

STRANGE MYSTERIES — Superior

1 ❑ Sep 1951 Cover: 0.10 **NM** value: **500.00**
• **CGC:** 9 graded, best 9.2
2 ❑ Nov 1951 Cover: 0.10 **NM** value: **250.00**
• **CGC:** 2 graded, best 9.0
3 ❑ Jan 1952 Cover: 0.10 **NM** value: **200.00**
• **CGC:** 2 graded, best 9.2
4 ❑ Mar 1952 Cover: 0.10 **NM** value: **200.00**
• **CGC:** 1 graded, best 6.0
5 ❑ May 1952 Cover: 0.10 **NM** value: **200.00**
Eyes of Evil; Dead Men Never Die; Bury us Not; Blood of the Zombies
6❑ Jul 1952Cover: 0.10 **NM** value: **200.00**
• **CGC:** 1 graded, best 9.4
7 ❑ Sep 1952 Cover: 0.10 **NM** value: **200.00**
8 ❑ Nov 1952 Cover: 0.10 **NM** value: **200.00**
• **CGC:** 1 graded, best 5.5
9 ❑ Jan 1953 Cover: 0.10 **NM** value: **200.00**
10 ❑ Mar 1953 Cover: 0.10 **NM** value: **200.00**
• **CGC:** 2 graded, best 7.5
11 ❑ May 1953 Cover: 0.10 **NM** value: **175.00**
If the Coffin Fits; Dial C for Coward; Date with the Devil; Recipe for Horror
12 ❑ Jul 1953 Cover: 0.10 **NM** value: **175.00**
13 ❑ Sep 1953 Cover: 0.10 **NM** value: **175.00**
14 ❑ Nov 1953 Cover: 0.10 **NM** value: **175.00**
15 ❑ Jan 1954 Cover: 0.10 **NM** value: **175.00**
16 ❑ Mar 1954 Cover: 0.10 **NM** value: **150.00**
• **CGC:** 1 graded, best 7.5
17 ❑ May 1954 Cover: 0.10 **NM** value: **150.00**
18 ❑ Jul 1954 Cover: 0.10 **NM** value: **150.00**
19 ❑ Sep 1954 Cover: 0.10 **NM** value: **150.00**
20 ❑ Nov 1954 Cover: 0.10 **NM** value: **150.00**
21 ❑ Jan 1955 Cover: 0.10 **NM** value: **150.00**

STRANGER IN A STRANGE LAND — Rip Off

All issues are adults only.

1 ❑ Jun 1989, b&w Cover: 2.00 **NM** value: **Cover or less**
Stranger in a Strange Land; What Wine Goes with Face…?; Pit Stop; Of Romance and Vegetable; First Meeting; Battle of the Sexes; Mall Walker **A:** Bruce Bolinger **W:** Bruce Bolinger
2 ❑ May 1990, b&w Cover: 2.00 **NM** value: **Cover or less**
Inside Every Fat Man There's a Thin Man Dying; Brilliant Finish; Just a couple Iceholes; Lunch Break in Hell; Wally Upizarse at Work; Robo-Crotch **A:** Bruce Bolinger **W:** Bruce Bolinger
3 ❑ Sep 1991, b&w Cover: 2.50 **NM** value: **Cover or less**
A: Bruce Bolinger **W:** Bruce Bolinger

STRANGERS, THE — Malibu / Ultraverse

Over fifty complete strangers were on the Powell Street cable car when it was hit by what looked like lightning. The cable car crashed into a sports car, apparently killing its driver (but actually, creating the Night Man). Miraculously, nobody on the cable car seemed seriously hurt. Still, in an all-too-real way the cable car's passengers found that the accident had changed them.

Within hours, this cross section of humanity found itself blessed (or cursed) with super-human abilities. These range from a pair of art students, with the powers to explode and transmute matter, to a young street kid with incredible speed. Strangest of all is Candy, a robotic experiment of magnate J.D. Hunt, who somehow gains both powers and sentience in the freak "lightning" known around the world as "the Jumpstart."

1 ❑ Jun 1993 Cover: 1.95 **NM** value: **2.00**
Circ: CapCity orders: **55,825**
Jumpstart! **A:** Rick Hoberg **W:** Steve Englehart ★ Origin of The Strangers. ★ 1st Appearance of The Strangers, The Night Man (out of costume).
1/Hol❑Jun 1993 **NM** value: **5.00**
• hologram edition. **W:** Steve Englehart
1/LE❑ Jun 1993 Cover: 1.95 **NM** value: **4.00**
• Ultra-limited edition. **W:** Steve Englehart
2 ❑ Jul 1993 Cover: 1.95 **NM** value: **2.00**
Circ: CapCity orders: **20,475**
• card **W:** Steve Englehart
3 ❑ Aug 1993 Cover: 1.95 **NM** value: **2.00**
Circ: CapCity orders: **17,600**
A: Rick Hoberg **W:** Steve Englehart ★ 1st Appearance of TNTNT.
4 ❑ Sep 1993 Cover: 1.95 **NM** value: **2.00**
Circ: CapCity orders: **29,250**
W: Steve Englehart ★ Appearance of Hardcase.
5 ❑ Oct 1993 Cover: 2.50 **NM** value: **Cover or less**
Dynamic Tension!; Rune, Part G • Rune **A:** Rick Hoberg; Barry Windsor-Smith **W:** Barry Windsor-Smith; Chris Ulm; Steve Englehart
6 ❑ Nov 1993 Cover: 1.95 **NM** value: **Cover or less**
Circ: CapCity orders: **21,900**
W: Steve Englehart
7 ❑ Dec 1993 Cover: 1.95 **NM** value: **Cover or less**
Circ: CapCity orders: **22,650**
Break-Thru • Break-Thru **W:** Steve Englehart
8 ❑ Jan 1994 Cover: 1.95 **NM** value: **Cover or less**
Circ: CapCity orders: **18,525**
Taken By The Sky! **A:** Rick Hoberg; Steve Skroce **W:** Steve Englehart ★ Origin of The Solution.
9 ❑ Feb 1994 Cover: 1.95 **NM** value: **Cover or less**
Circ: CapCity orders: **15,800**
W: Steve Englehart
10 ❑ Mar 1994 Cover: 1.95 **NM** value: **Cover or less**
Circ: CapCity orders: **14,125**
W: Steve Englehart
11 ❑ Apr 1994 Cover: 1.95 **NM** value: **Cover or less**
Circ: CapCity orders: **13,525**
W: Steve Englehart
12 ❑ May 1994 Cover: 1.95 **NM** value: **Cover or less**
Circ: CapCity orders: **12,750**
W: Steve Englehart
13 ❑ Jun 1994 Cover: 3.50 **NM** value: **Cover or less**
Circ: CapCity orders: **15,125**
This Space Still Available; Anatomy of a Hero, Part 2; Market Realities • contains Ultraverse Premiere #4 **A:** Mike Gustovich; Frank Gomez; Frank Gomez(cover); Kris Renkewitz; Rick Hoberg(cover) **W:** Kurt Busiek; Len Strazewski; Steve Englehart ★ 1st Appearance of Pilgrim.
14 ❑ Jul 1994 Cover: 1.95 **NM** value: **Cover or less**
Circ: CapCity orders: **11,200**
the Man of Power **A:** Rick Hoberg **W:** Steve Englehart ★ 1st Appearance of Byter.
15 ❑ Aug 1994 Cover: 1.95 **NM** value: **Cover or less**
Circ: CapCity orders: **9,800**
Homeboy **A:** Rick Hoberg **W:** Steve Englehart ★ 1st Appearance of Lightshow, Generator X, Rodent.
16 ❑ Sep 1994 Cover: 1.95 **NM** value: **Cover or less**
Circ: CapCity orders: **8,775**
Party Time **A:** Rick Hoberg **W:** Steve Englehart
17 ❑ Oct 1994 Cover: 1.95 **NM** value: **Cover or less**
Circ: CapCity orders: **8,325**
Blood of an Ultra **A:** Rick Hoberg **W:** Steve Englehart ★ Appearance of Rafferty.
18 ❑ Nov 1994 Cover: 1.95 **NM** value: **Cover or less**
Circ: CapCity orders: **7,200**
The Pitch **A:** Rick Hoberg **W:** Steve Englehart
19 ❑ Dec 1994 Cover: 1.95 **NM** value: **Cover or less**
Circ: CapCity orders: **6,700**
The Teknight Before Christmas **A:** Steve Ellis; Rick Hoberg(cover) **W:** Steve Englehart
20 ❑ Jan 1995 Cover: 1.95 **NM** value: **Cover or less**
Circ: CapCity orders: **3,025**
The Name of the Game is Fear **A:** Rick Hoberg(cover); Sam Payne **W:** Steve Englehart ★ 1st Appearance of Beater, M.C. Zed.
21 ❑ Feb 1995 Cover: 2.50 **NM** value: **Cover or less**
Circ: CapCity orders: **5,650**
Life in Wartime! **A:** Paul Abrams; Rick Hoberg(cover) **W:** Steve Englehart
22 ❑ Mar 1995 Cover: 2.50 **NM** value: **Cover or less**
Circ: CapCity orders: **5,425**
Machines in Wartime! **A:** Paul Abrams; Rick Hoberg(cover) **W:** Steve Englehart
23 ❑ Apr 1995 Cover: 2.50 **NM** value: **Cover or less**
Circ: CapCity orders: **5,025**
The Subject is…Taboo! **A:** Rick Hoberg **W:** Steve Englehart
24 ❑ May 1995 Cover: 2.50 **NM** value: **Cover or less**
Circ: CapCity orders: **4,675**
The Subject is…TNTNT II! final issue. **A:** Rick Hoberg **W:** Steve Englehart
Anl 1❑ca. 1994 Cover: 3.95 **NM** value: **Cover or less**
Circ: CapCity orders: **5,875**
The Pilgrim Conundrum, Part 2 **A:** Rick Hoberg; Barb Kaalberg **W:** Steve Englehart

STRANGERS IN PARADISE — Antarctic

Terry Moore has been the hand at the helm, both writing and drawing, Strangers in Paradise since its inception. It could be termed a romance series, since it's definitely focused on attraction, repulsion, relationships, elation, affection, and hate. It might be an adventure series, since it's featured pulse-quickening cliffhangers. It could be called a mystery series, because several characters have secrets they haven't divulged: secrets that affect their lives. It's not a super-hero strip, but there are delicious panels of "Good Girl Art."

Friends accounting clerk Francine Peters, artist Katina "Katchoo" Choovanski, and art student David Qin are the focal characters, with Katchoo perhaps the most outrageous of the three. The early issues have been collected in trade paperbacks, so it's simple enough to get into the storyline from the beginning. Its circle of admirers continues to grow. — Maggie

0 ❑ b&w **NM** value: **70.00**
1 ❑ Nov 1993, b&w Cover: 2.75 **NM** value: **60.00**
• **CGC:** 3 graded, best 9.2
1-2 ❑ Mar 1994, b&w Cover: 2.75 **NM** value: **5.00**
1-3 ❑ Apr 1994, b&w Cover: 2.75 **NM** value: **3.00**

CGC-graded: Multiply prices above by **33 for 9.9 M • 16 for 9.8 NM/M • 7 for 9.6 NM+ • 5 for 9.4 NM • 2.5 for 9.2 NM- • 1.5 for 9.0 VF/NM**

2 ☐ Dec 1993, b&w Cover: 2.75 **NM** value: **15.00**
• **CGC:** 2 graded, best 8.5

3 ☐ Feb 1994, b&w Cover: 2.75 **NM** value: **15.00**

Bk 1☐ Cover: 14.95 **NM** value: **Cover or less**
• Immortal Enemies

Bk 2☐ Cover: 8.95 **NM** value: **Cover or less**
• The Collected Strangers In Paradise

STRANGERS IN PARADISE (2ND SERIES)
Abstract

1 ☐ Sep 1994, b&w Cover: 2.75 **NM** value: **25.00**
• **CGC:** 4 graded, best 9.6
A: Terry Moore **W:** Terry Moore

1/SC☐ Cover: 2.75 **NM** value: **4.00**
• Gold logo edition. **A:** Terry Moore **W:** Terry Moore

1-2 ☐ Apr 1995, b&w Cover: 2.75 **NM** value: **Cover or less**

2 ☐ Nov 1994, b&w Cover: 2.75 **NM** value: **12.00**
• **CGC:** 3 graded, best 9.9
A: Terry Moore **W:** Terry Moore

2/SC☐ Cover: 2.75 **NM** value: **3.00**
• Gold logo edition. **A:** Terry Moore **W:** Terry Moore

3 ☐ Jan 1995, b&w Cover: 2.75 **NM** value: **10.00**
• **CGC:** 1 graded, best 9.4
A: Terry Moore **W:** Terry Moore

3/SC☐ Cover: 2.75 **NM** value: **3.00**
• Gold logo edition. **A:** Terry Moore **W:** Terry Moore

4 ☐ Mar 1995, b&w Cover: 2.75 **NM** value: **8.00**
Circ: CapCity orders: **3,800**
A: Terry Moore **W:** Terry Moore

4/SC☐ Cover: 2.75 **NM** value: **Cover or less**
• Gold logo edition. **A:** Terry Moore **W:** Terry Moore

5 ☐ Jun 1995, b&w Cover: 2.75 **NM** value: **8.00**
Circ: CapCity orders: **4,280** • **CGC:** 1 graded, best 9.2
A: Terry Moore **W:** Terry Moore

5/SC☐ Cover: 2.75 **NM** value: **Cover or less**
• Gold logo edition. **A:** Terry Moore **W:** Terry Moore

6 ☐ Jul 1995, b&w Cover: 2.75 **NM** value: **6.00**
Circ: CapCity orders: **4,345** • **CGC:** 1 graded, best 9.6
A: Terry Moore **W:** Terry Moore

6/SC☐ Cover: 2.75 **NM** value: **Cover or less**
• Gold logo edition. **A:** Terry Moore **W:** Terry Moore

7 ☐ Sep 1995, b&w Cover: 2.75 **NM** value: **6.00**
Circ: CapCity orders: **4,115**
A: Terry Moore **W:** Terry Moore

7/SC☐ Cover: 2.75 **NM** value: **Cover or less**
• Gold logo edition. **A:** Terry Moore **W:** Terry Moore

8 ☐ Nov 1995, b&w Cover: 2.75 **NM** value: **6.00**
A: Terry Moore **W:** Terry Moore

8/SC☐ Cover: 2.75 **NM** value: **Cover or less**
• Gold logo edition. **A:** Terry Moore **W:** Terry Moore

9 ☐ Jan 1996, b&w Cover: 2.75 **NM** value: **6.00**
A: Terry Moore **W:** Terry Moore

9/SC☐ Cover: 2.75 **NM** value: **Cover or less**
• Gold logo edition. **A:** Terry Moore **W:** Terry Moore

10 ☐ Feb 1996, b&w Cover: 2.75 **NM** value: **6.00**
A: Terry Moore **W:** Terry Moore

10/SC☐ Cover: 2.75 **NM** value: **Cover or less**
• Gold logo edition. **A:** Terry Moore **W:** Terry Moore

11 ☐ b&w Cover: 2.75 **NM** value: **4.00**
A: Terry Moore **W:** Terry Moore

11/SC☐ Cover: 2.75 **NM** value: **Cover or less**
• Gold logo edition. **A:** Terry Moore **W:** Terry Moore

12 ☐ May 1996, b&w Cover: 2.75 **NM** value: **4.00**
A: Terry Moore **W:** Terry Moore

12/SC☐ Cover: 2.75 **NM** value: **Cover or less**
• Gold logo edition. **A:** Terry Moore **W:** Terry Moore

13 ☐ Jun 1996, b&w Cover: 2.75 **NM** value: **3.00**
A: Terry Moore **W:** Terry Moore

14 ☐ Jul 1996 Cover: 2.75 **NM** value: **Cover or less**
📖 Molly & Poo • continues in 3rd series (Image); Titled: Terry Moore's Strangers in Paradise **A:** Terry Moore **W:** Terry Moore

Bk 1☐ Aug 1994 Cover: 6.95 **NM** value: **16.95**
• collects stories from Strangers in Paradise #1-3 and Negative Burn #13 along with new material; I Dream of You trade paperback **A:** Terry Moore **W:** Terry Moore

Bk 2☐ Cover: 8.95 **NM** value: **Cover or less**
• Trade Paperback. • It's A Good Life **A:** Terry Moore **W:** Terry Moore

SE 1☐ Cover: 2.75 **NM** value: **3.00**
• Molly & Poo Special **A:** Terry Moore **W:** Terry Moore

STRANGERS IN PARADISE (3RD SERIES)
Homage

1 ☐ Oct 1996, b&w Cover: 2.75 **NM** value: **4.00**
• **CGC:** 3 graded, best 9.8
A: Terry Moore **W:** Terry Moore

2 ☐ Dec 1996, b&w Cover: 2.75 **NM** value: **3.00**
Circ: Diamd. preorders: **25,352** • **CGC:** 1 graded, best 9.6
A: Terry Moore **W:** Terry Moore

3 ☐ Jan 1997, b&w Cover: 2.75 **NM** value: **3.00**
Circ: Diamd. preorders: **25,904**
A: Terry Moore **W:** Terry Moore

4 ☐ Feb 1997, b&w Cover: 2.75 **NM** value: **3.00**
Circ: Diamd. preorders: **26,660**
A: Terry Moore **W:** Terry Moore

5 ☐ Apr 1997, b&w Cover: 2.75 **NM** value: **3.00**
Circ: Diamd. preorders: **27,084**
cover says Mar, indicia says Apr. **A:** Terry Moore **W:** Terry Moore

6 ☐ May 1997, b&w Cover: 2.75 **NM** value: **3.00**
Circ: Diamd. preorders: **27,144**
A: Terry Moore **W:** Terry Moore

7 ☐ Jul 1997, b&w Cover: 2.75 **NM** value: **3.00**
Circ: Diamd. preorders: **26,618**
A: Terry Moore **W:** Terry Moore

8 ☐ Aug 1997, b&w Cover: 2.75 **NM** value: **3.00**
Circ: Diamd. preorders: **25,929**
• returns to Abstract **A:** Terry Moore **W:** Terry Moore

9 ☐ Sep 1997 Cover: 2.75 **NM** value: **3.00**
Circ: Diamd. preorders: **23,018**
A: Terry Moore **W:** Terry Moore

10 ☐ Oct 1997 Cover: 2.75 **NM** value: **3.00**
Circ: Diamd. preorders: **22,509**
A: Terry Moore **W:** Terry Moore

11 ☐ Dec 1997 Cover: 2.75 **NM** value: **3.00**
Circ: Diamd. preorders: **21,539**
A: Terry Moore **W:** Terry Moore

12 ☐ Jan 1997 Cover: 2.75 **NM** value: **3.00**
Circ: Diamd. preorders: **20,761**
A: Terry Moore **W:** Terry Moore

13 ☐ Mar 1998 Cover: 2.75 **NM** value: **3.00**
Circ: Diamd. preorders: **20,511**
A: Terry Moore **W:** Terry Moore

14 ☐ Apr 1998 Cover: 2.75 **NM** value: **3.00**
Circ: Diamd. preorders: **20,747** • **CGC:** 1 graded, best 9.6
A: Terry Moore **W:** Terry Moore

15 ☐ May 1998 Cover: 2.75 **NM** value: **3.00**
Circ: Diamd. preorders: **19,960**
A: Terry Moore **W:** Terry Moore

16 ☐ Jul 1998 Cover: 2.75 **NM** value: **3.00**
• **CGC:** 2 graded, best 9.4

17 ☐ Aug 1998 Cover: 2.75 **NM** value: **3.00**
Circ: Diamd. preorders: **19,144**

18 ☐ Oct 1998 Cover: 2.75 **NM** value: **3.00**
Circ: Diamd. preorders: **18,910**

19 ☐ Nov 1998 Cover: 2.75 **NM** value: **3.00**
Circ: Diamd. preorders: **19,061**

20 ☐ Dec 1998 Cover: 2.75 **NM** value: **3.00**
Circ: Diamd. preorders: **18,755**

21 ☐ Jan 1999 Cover: 2.75 **NM** value: **3.00**
Circ: Diamd. preorders: **18,935**

22 ☐ Feb 1999 Cover: 2.75 **NM** value: **3.00**
Circ: Diamd. preorders: **17,777**

23 ☐ Apr 1999 Cover: 2.75 **NM** value: **3.00**
Circ: Diamd. preorders: **18,265**

24 ☐ Jun 1999 Cover: 2.75 **NM** value: **3.00**
Circ: Diamd. preorders: **17,628**

25 ☐ Jul 1999 Cover: 2.75 **NM** value: **3.00**
Circ: Diamd. preorders: **18,011**

26 ☐ Aug 1999 Cover: 2.75 **NM** value: **3.00**
Circ: Diamd. preorders: **17,829**

27 ☐ Sep 1999 Cover: 2.75 **NM** value: **3.00**
Circ: Diamd. preorders: **17,480**

28 ☐ Nov 1999 Cover: 2.75 **NM** value: **3.00**
Circ: Diamd. preorders: **17,492**

29 ☐ Dec 1999 Cover: 2.75 **NM** value: **3.00**
Circ: Diamd. preorders: **17,507**

30 ☐ Feb 2000 Cover: 2.75 **NM** value: **3.00**
Circ: Diamd. preorders: **16,210**

31 ☐ Mar 2000 Cover: 2.75 **NM** value: **2.95**
Circ: Diamd. preorders: **16,934**

32 ☐ May 2000 Cover: 2.75 **NM** value: **2.95**
Circ: Diamd. preorders: **16,467**

33 ☐ Jun 2000 Cover: 2.75 **NM** value: **2.95**
Circ: Diamd. preorders: **17,108**

34 ☐ Aug 2000 Cover: 2.75 **NM** value: **2.95**
Circ: Diamd. preorders: **15,828**

35 ☐ Sep 2000 Cover: 2.75 **NM** value: **2.95**
Circ: Diamd. preorders: **16,170**

36 ☐ Nov 2000 Cover: 2.75 **NM** value: **2.95**
Circ: Diamd. preorders: **15,876**

37 ☐ Dec 2000 Cover: 2.75 **NM** value: **2.95**
Circ: Diamd. preorders: **15,431**

38 ☐ Jan 2001 Cover: 2.95 **NM** value: **Cover or less**
Circ: Diamd. preorders: **15,183**

39 ☐ Jun 2001 Cover: 2.95 **NM** value: **Cover or less**
Circ: Diamd. preorders: **14,831**

40 ☐ Jul 2001 Cover: 2.95 **NM** value: **Cover or less**
Circ: Diamd. preorders: **15,071**

41 ☐ Aug 2001 Cover: 2.95 **NM** value: **Cover or less**
Circ: Diamd. preorders: **14,765**

42 ☐ Oct 2001 Cover: 2.95 **NM** value: **Cover or less**
Circ: Diamd. preorders: **15,824**

Bk 1☐ Cover: 12.95 **NM** value: **Cover or less**
• Love Me Tender; Reprints Strangers in Paradise (3rd Series) #1-5
A: Terry Moore **W:** Terry Moore

SE 1☐ Feb 1999 Cover: 2.75 **NM** value: **3.00**
• Lyrics and Poems **A:** Terry Moore **W:** Terry Moore

STRANGER'S TALE, A
Vineyard

1 ☐ b&w Cover: 2.00 **NM** value: **Cover or less**
cardstock cover. 📖 Temple; Spork; G.U.N.S. **A:** Jr.; Sanford Green; Thomas Washington; Joey Robinson **W:** Duane Schilz; Philip Looney; Trip Brown

STRANGER THAN FICTION
Impact Studios

1 ☐ 1998b&w Cover: 1.99 **NM** value: **Cover or less**
A: Lee Ferguson **W:** Josh Roberts

2 ☐ Jul 1998, b&w Cover: 1.99 **NM** value: **Cover or less**
A: Lee Ferguson **W:** Josh Roberts

3 ☐ 1998 Cover: 1.99 **NM** value: **Cover or less**
A: Lee Ferguson **W:** Josh Roberts

4 ☐ 1998 Cover: 1.99 **NM** value: **Cover or less**
A: Lee Ferguson **W:** Josh Roberts

There are two different pricing tiers in the modern comic-book hobby. **The prices seen above** are the prices we have seen **loose copies** of these issues reliably fetch in a variety of environments. Condition alters the price by the fractions seen on the bar on the bottom of left-hand pages of this book. **Comics graded by CGC** usually sell for more. Use the guide on the bottom of right-hand pages of this book to estimate what copies have brought on eBay.

STRANGE SPORTS STORIES
DC

After a double-tryout in The Brave and the Bold, Strange Sports Stories became a feature in its own right in this series of the early 1970s. At a time when the comics market was glutted with mystery and horror comics, this title was a breath of fresh air. Its stories combined sports and the bizarre in a mix that avoided most of the cliches found in competing offerings.

The inspiration behind many of the stories here seemed to be early colonial fiction. "To Beat the Devil" told of how a baseball team used the letter of the rule book to outsmart Satan, in a move reminiscent of The Devil and Daniel Webster. Similarly, "A Tall Tale of Tenpins" drew on the Rip Van Winkle legend to tell how Rip's latter-day ancestor learned to bowl perfect games, courtesy of the same "wee people" who ensorceled Rip Van Winkle.

1 ☐ Oct 1973 Cover: 0.20 **NM** value: **10.00**
• **CGC:** 4 graded, best 9.8
📖 To Beat The Devil; A Tall Tale Of Tenpins **A:** Bob Oksner; Dick Giordano; Curt Swan **W:** Frank Robbins

2 ☐ Dec 1973 Cover: 0.20 **NM** value: **7.00**
📖 Karate on the Moon!; Volley of Death; Tall in the Saddle! **A:** Murphy Anderson; Dick Giordano; Curt Swan; Irv Novick **W:** Frank Robbins; Denny O'Neil

3 ☐ Feb 1974 Cover: 0.20 **NM** value: **5.00**
📖 Gridiron Knightmare!; Man Who Leaped Over the Earth! **A:** Dick Giordano; Curt Swan **W:** Frank Robbins; Elliott S! Maggin

4 ☐ Apr 1974 Cover: 0.20 **NM** value: **5.00**
📖 The Challenge of the Faceless Five; Man with the Golden Gloves! **A:** Dick Giordano; John Rosenberger; Irv Novick **W:** Cary Bates; Denny O'Neil

5 ☐ Jun 1974 Cover: 0.20 **NM** value: **5.00**

6 ☐ Aug 1974 Cover: 0.20 **NM** value: **5.00**

STRANGE SPORTS STORIES (ADVENTURE)
Adventure

1 ☐ Cover: 2.50 **NM** value: **Cover or less**

STRANGE STORIES
Avalon

1 ☐ b&w Cover: 2.95 **NM** value: **Cover or less**
• reprints John Force and Magic Man stories

STRANGE STORIES FROM ANOTHER WORLD
Fawcett

2 ☐ Aug 1952 Cover: 0.10 **NM** value: **400.00**
• **CGC:** 1 graded, best 6.0

3 ☐ Oct 1952 Cover: 0.10 **NM** value: **300.00**

4 ☐ Dec 1953 Cover: 0.10 **NM** value: **300.00**

5 ☐ Feb 1953 Cover: 0.10 **NM** value: **300.00**
• **CGC:** 1 graded, best 7.0

STRANGE STORIES OF SUSPENSE
Atlas

5 ☐ Oct 1955 Cover: 0.10 **NM** value: **300.00**
• **CGC:** 1 graded, best 7.5

6 ☐ Dec 1955 Cover: 0.10 **NM** value: **175.00**
• **CGC:** 1 graded, best 8.5

7 ☐ Feb 1956 Cover: 0.10 **NM** value: **175.00**
• **CGC:** 1 graded, best 5.5

8 ☐ Apr 1956 Cover: 0.10 **NM** value: **175.00**
• **CGC:** 2 graded, best 7.5

9 ☐ Jun 1956 Cover: 0.10 **NM** value: **175.00**
• **CGC:** 2 graded, best 8.5

10 ☐ Aug 1956 Cover: 0.10 **NM** value: **175.00**

11 ☐ Oct 1956 Cover: 0.10 **NM** value: **150.00**
• **CGC:** 2 graded, best 7.5

12 ☐ Dec 1956 Cover: 0.10 **NM** value: **150.00**

13 ☐ Feb 1957 Cover: 0.10 **NM** value: **150.00**
• **CGC:** 1 graded, best 8.0

14 ☐ Apr 1957 Cover: 0.10 **NM** value: **150.00**
• **CGC:** 2 graded, best 9.2

15 ☐ Jun 1957 Cover: 0.10 **NM** value: **150.00**

16 ☐ Aug 1957 Cover: 0.10 **NM** value: **150.00**
• **CGC:** 1 graded, best 8.5

STRANGE SUSPENSE STORIES
Charlton / ACG

The perennial also-ran publisher Charlton experienced a flash of brilliance in 1967, when artist and art director Dick Giordano was promoted to editor and brought a wave of talented young writers and artists into the fold. Strange Suspense Stories is a revival of one of Charlton's most successful titles of the 1950s: a blend of horror, science fiction, and mystery in the mold of E.C.'s Shock SuspenStories. The 1960s revival issues feature some of the earliest professional work of Dennis O'Neill (at that time using the alias Sergius O'Shaughnessy), who went on to become the longtime editor of Batman, and Jim Aparo, who did memorable work at DC in the 1970s and 1980s. Strange Suspense Stories during Giordano's editorship provided solid storytelling and art, with tales that anticipated DC's efforts in House of Mystery several years later.

1 ☐ Jun 1952 Cover: 0.10 **NM** value: **450.00**
• **CGC:** 6 graded, best 9.2
• Fawcett publishes

Other grades: Multiply prices above by **1.5 for Mint • 2/3 for Very Fine • 1/3 for Fine • 1/5 for Very Good • 1/8 for Good**

2 ❑ Aug 1952 Cover: 0.10 NM value: 325.00
3 ❑ Oct 1952 Cover: 0.10 NM value: 275.00
4 ❑ Dec 1952 Cover: 0.10 NM value: 275.00
5 ❑ Mar 1953 Cover: 0.10 NM value: 275.00
• CGC: 1 graded, best 8.5
• Series continued with issue #16
16 ❑ Jan 1954 Cover: 0.12 NM value: 150.00
17 ❑ Mar 1954 Cover: 0.12 NM value: 110.00
• CGC: 1 graded, best 7.5
18 ❑ May 1954 Cover: 0.12 NM value: 160.00
• CGC: 1 graded, best 8.5
A: Steve Ditko
19 ❑ Jul 1954 Cover: 0.12 NM value: 200.00
• CGC: 4 graded, best 9.0
A: Steve Ditko
20 ❑ Sep 1954 Cover: 0.12 NM value: 160.00
• CGC: 2 graded, best 9.4
A: Steve Ditko
21 ❑ Oct 1954 Cover: 0.12 NM value: 110.00
• CGC: 2 graded, best 9.6
22 ❑ Nov 1954 Cover: 0.12 NM value: 135.00
• CGC: 1 graded, best 9.2
• Series continued in This is Suspense #23 A: Steve Ditko(cover)
27 ❑ Oct 1955 Cover: 0.12 NM value: 60.00
• CGC: 1 graded, best 8.0
• Code-approved issues begin; Series continued from This is Suspense #26
28 ❑ Cover: 0.12 NM value: 50.00
29 ❑ Cover: 0.12 NM value: 50.00
30 ❑ 1957 Cover: 0.12 NM value: 50.00
31 ❑ 1957 Cover: 0.12 NM value: 100.00
A: Steve Ditko
32 ❑ 1957 Cover: 0.12 NM value: 100.00
A: Steve Ditko
33 ❑ 1957 Cover: 0.12 NM value: 100.00
A: Steve Ditko
34 ❑ Nov 1957 Cover: 0.12 NM value: 200.00
• CGC: 2 graded, best 7.5
• Gaines A: Steve Ditko
35 ❑ Cover: 0.12 NM value: 100.00
A: Steve Ditko
36 ❑ 1958 Cover: 0.15 NM value: 145.00
• Giant-size. A: Steve Ditko
37 ❑ 1958 Cover: 0.12 NM value: 100.00
A: Steve Ditko
38 ❑ 1958 Cover: 0.12 NM value: 45.00
39 ❑ Nov 1958 Cover: 0.12 NM value: 80.00
• CGC: 1 graded, best 9.0
A: Steve Ditko
40 ❑ 1959 Cover: 0.12 NM value: 80.00
A: Steve Ditko
41 ❑ 1959 Cover: 0.12 NM value: 80.00
A: Steve Ditko
42 ❑ Jun 1959 Cover: 0.12 NM value: 20.00
• CGC: 1 graded, best 8.5
43 ❑ 1959 Cover: 0.12 NM value: 20.00
44 ❑ 1959 Cover: 0.12 NM value: 20.00
45 ❑ Jan 1960 Cover: 0.12 NM value: 80.00
A: Steve Ditko
46 ❑ Mar 1960 Cover: 0.12 NM value: 20.00
47 ❑ May 1960 Cover: 0.12 NM value: 80.00
A: Steve Ditko
48 ❑ Jul 1960 Cover: 0.12 NM value: 80.00
A: Steve Ditko
49 ❑ Sep 1960 Cover: 0.12 NM value: 20.00
Up into the Unknown; Mad Dog; Honeymoon; Indian Taboo! (text story); The Old Well
50 ❑ Nov 1960 Cover: 0.12 NM value: 75.00
A: Steve Ditko
51 ❑ Jan 1961 Cover: 0.12 NM value: 75.00
A: Steve Ditko
52 ❑ Mar 1961 Cover: 0.12 NM value: 50.00
A: Steve Ditko
53 ❑ 1961 Cover: 0.12 NM value: 50.00
A: Steve Ditko
54 ❑ 1961 Cover: 0.12 NM value: 50.00
A: Steve Ditko
55 ❑ 1961 Cover: 0.12 NM value: 20.00
56 ❑ 1961 Cover: 0.12 NM value: 20.00
57 ❑ 1961 Cover: 0.12 NM value: 20.00
58 ❑ 1962 Cover: 0.12 NM value: 20.00
Circ: Statement: 127,740
59 ❑ 1962 Cover: 0.12 NM value: 20.00
Circ: Statement: 127,740
60 ❑ 1962 Cover: 0.12 NM value: 20.00
Circ: Statement: 127,740
61 ❑ 1962 Cover: 0.12 NM value: 14.00
Circ: Statement: 127,740
62 ❑ 1962 Cover: 0.12 NM value: 14.00
Circ: Statement: 127,740
63 ❑ 1963 Cover: 0.12 NM value: 14.00
64 ❑ 1963 Cover: 0.12 NM value: 14.00
65 ❑ Jun 1963 Cover: 0.12 NM value: 14.00
66 ❑ Aug 1963 Cover: 0.12 NM value: 14.00
67 ❑ Oct 1963 Cover: 0.12 NM value: 14.00
68 ❑ Dec 1963 Cover: 0.12 NM value: 14.00
The Disenchanter; The Too Late, Late Show!; From Beyond (text story); The Exotic Beauty; Monsters Forever; The Protector
69 ❑ Feb 1964 Cover: 0.12 NM value: 14.00
70 ❑ 1964 Cover: 0.12 NM value: 14.00
71 ❑ 1964 Cover: 0.12 NM value: 14.00
72 ❑ 1964 Cover: 0.12 NM value: 14.00
73 ❑ Jan 1965 Cover: 0.12 NM value: 14.00
Circ: Statement: 131,350
74 ❑ 1965 Cover: 0.12 NM value: 14.00
Circ: Statement: 131,350
75 ❑ Jun 1965 Cover: 0.12 NM value: 90.00
Circ: Statement: 131,350 • CGC: 7 graded, best 9.8
A: Steve Ditko W: Steve Ditko ★ 1st Appearance of Captain Atom.
76 ❑ Aug 1965 Cover: 0.12 NM value: 20.00
Circ: Statement: 131,350 • CGC: 3 graded, best 9.6
A: Steve Ditko W: Steve Ditko
77 ❑ Oct 1965 Cover: 0.12 NM value: 20.00
Circ: Statement: 131,350 • CGC: 4 graded, best 9.8
final issue. A: Steve Ditko W: Steve Ditko

STRANGE SUSPENSE STORIES (VOL. 3) Charlton

1 ❑ Oct 1967 Cover: 0.12 NM value: 20.00
• CGC: 1 graded, best 9.2
2 ❑ 1968 Cover: 0.12 NM value: 12.00
3 ❑ Sep 1968 Cover: 0.12 NM value: 12.00
• CGC: 1 graded, best 8.0
4 ❑ Nov 1968 Cover: 0.12 NM value: 12.00
5 ❑ Jan 1969 Cover: 0.12 NM value: 12.00
6 ❑ Mar 1969 Cover: 0.12 NM value: 12.00
7 ❑ May 1969 Cover: 0.12 NM value: 12.00
Rendezvous!; Strange Homecoming; Another Time; Enemy Agent (text); The Old Lady's Curse A: Nicholas Alascia; Ram W: Nicholas Alascia; Ram
8 ❑ Jul 1969 Cover: 0.12 NM value: 12.00
9 ❑ Sep 1969 Cover: 0.12 NM value: 12.00

STRANGE TALES (1ST SERIES) Marvel

Strange Tales began as a straightforward horror comic book, gradually switching to include super-hero appearances by the likes of The Human Torch. In issue #110, it made a breakthrough, introducing readers to Stephen Strange, better known as "Doctor Strange, Master of the Mystic Arts."

Strange Tales featured a pair of stories each month. Initially, Dr. Strange battled cosmic foes in one story and The Torch, often teamed with The Thing, starred in the other. The Torch stories were replaced, in #135, when Strange Tales introduced Nick Fury, Agent of S.H.I.E.L.D.

With issue #169, Doctor Strange took over the entire issue and its numbering.

In the mid-1970s, the series returned picking up its numbering with #169 and featuring single stories each month featuring first Brother Voodoo, then Warlock. These new characters failed to catch on, though, and the series concluded with issue #188.

1 ❑ Jun 1951 Cover: 0.10 NM value: 2250.00
• CGC: 3 graded, best 8.5
2 ❑ Aug 1951 Cover: 0.10 NM value: 775.00
• CGC: 2 graded, best 8.5
3 ❑ Oct 1951 Cover: 0.10 NM value: 600.00
• CGC: 1 graded, best 5.5
4 ❑ Dec 1951 Cover: 0.10 NM value: 600.00
• CGC: 1 graded, best .5
5 ❑ Feb 1952 Cover: 0.10 NM value: 600.00
6 ❑ Apr 1952 Cover: 0.10 NM value: 425.00
• CGC: 1 graded, best 5.0
7 ❑ Jun 1952 Cover: 0.10 NM value: 425.00
• CGC: 1 graded, best 9.0
8 ❑ Jul 1952 Cover: 0.10 NM value: 425.00
9 ❑ Aug 1952 Cover: 0.10 NM value: 425.00
• CGC: 1 graded, best 8.5
10 ❑ Sep 1952 Cover: 0.10 NM value: 425.00
• CGC: 1 graded, best 4.5
11 ❑ Oct 1952 Cover: 0.10 NM value: 290.00
12 ❑ Nov 1952 Cover: 0.10 NM value: 290.00
• CGC: 2 graded, best 8.5
13 ❑ Dec 1952 Cover: 0.10 NM value: 290.00
14 ❑ Jan 1953 Cover: 0.10 NM value: 290.00
• CGC: 1 graded, best 9.0
15 ❑ Feb 1953 Cover: 0.10 NM value: 290.00
• CGC: 1 graded, best 6.0
16 ❑ Mar 1953 Cover: 0.10 NM value: 290.00
• CGC: 1 graded, best 9.0
17 ❑ Apr 1953 Cover: 0.10 NM value: 290.00
18 ❑ May 1953 Cover: 0.10 NM value: 290.00
19 ❑ Jun 1953 Cover: 0.10 NM value: 290.00
20 ❑ Jul 1953 Cover: 0.10 NM value: 290.00
21 ❑ Aug 1953 Cover: 0.10 NM value: 225.00
22 ❑ Sep 1953 Cover: 0.10 NM value: 225.00
23 ❑ Oct 1953 Cover: 0.10 NM value: 225.00
• CGC: 1 graded, best 9.0
24 ❑ Dec 1953 Cover: 0.10 NM value: 225.00
25 ❑ Feb 1954 Cover: 0.10 NM value: 225.00
26 ❑ Mar 1954 Cover: 0.10 NM value: 225.00
27 ❑ Apr 1954 Cover: 0.10 NM value: 225.00
• CGC: 2 graded, best 6.0
28 ❑ May 1954 Cover: 0.10 NM value: 225.00
29 ❑ Jun 1954 Cover: 0.10 NM value: 225.00
30 ❑ Jul 1954 Cover: 0.10 NM value: 225.00
• CGC: 3 graded, best 9.0
31 ❑ Aug 1954 Cover: 0.10 NM value: 200.00
• CGC: 2 graded, best 7.5
32 ❑ Oct 1954 Cover: 0.10 NM value: 200.00
• CGC: 2 graded, best 8.0
33 ❑ Dec 1954 Cover: 0.10 NM value: 200.00
• CGC: 2 graded, best 8.0
34 ❑ Feb 1955 Cover: 0.10 NM value: 200.00
• CGC: 2 graded, best 3.5
35 ❑ Apr 1955 Cover: 0.10 NM value: 200.00
36 ❑ Jun 1955 Cover: 0.10 NM value: 200.00
37 ❑ Aug 1955 Cover: 0.10 NM value: 200.00
38 ❑ Sep 1955 Cover: 0.10 NM value: 200.00
39 ❑ Oct 1955 Cover: 0.10 NM value: 200.00
40 ❑ Nov 1955 Cover: 0.10 NM value: 200.00
• CGC: 1 graded, best 5.5
41 ❑ Dec 1955 Cover: 0.10 NM value: 200.00
42 ❑ Jan 1956 Cover: 0.10 NM value: 200.00
43 ❑ Feb 1956 Cover: 0.10 NM value: 200.00
44 ❑ Mar 1956 Cover: 0.10 NM value: 200.00
45 ❑ Apr 1956 Cover: 0.10 NM value: 155.00
46 ❑ May 1956 Cover: 0.10 NM value: 155.00
47 ❑ Jun 1956 Cover: 0.10 NM value: 155.00
48 ❑ Jul 1956 Cover: 0.10 NM value: 155.00
49 ❑ Aug 1956 Cover: 0.10 NM value: 155.00
• CGC: 1 graded, best 7.0
50 ❑ Sep 1956 Cover: 0.10 NM value: 155.00
• CGC: 1 graded, best 4.5
51 ❑ Oct 1956 Cover: 0.10 NM value: 155.00
• CGC: 1 graded, best 8.5
52 ❑ Nov 1956 Cover: 0.10 NM value: 155.00
• CGC: 1 graded, best 2.5
53 ❑ Dec 1956 Cover: 0.10 NM value: 155.00
• CGC: 2 graded, best 8.0
54 ❑ Jan 1957 Cover: 0.10 NM value: 155.00
55 ❑ Feb 1957 Cover: 0.10 NM value: 155.00
• CGC: 2 graded, best 8.0
56 ❑ Mar 1957 Cover: 0.10 NM value: 155.00
• CGC: 1 graded, best 7.0
57 ❑ Apr 1957 Cover: 0.10 NM value: 155.00
• CGC: 1 graded, best 6.0
58 ❑ 1957 Cover: 0.10 NM value: 165.00
A: Al Williamson
59 ❑ Jul 1957 Cover: 0.10 NM value: 185.00
A: Bernie Krigstein
60 ❑ Aug 1957 Cover: 0.10 NM value: 155.00
61 ❑ Cover: 0.10 NM value: 185.00
A: Bernie Krigstein
62 ❑ 1958 Cover: 0.10 NM value: 135.00
63 ❑ 1958 Cover: 0.10 NM value: 135.00
64 ❑ 1958 Cover: 0.10 NM value: 165.00
A: Al Williamson
65 ❑ 1958 Cover: 0.10 NM value: 130.00
66 ❑ 1958 Cover: 0.10 NM value: 130.00
67 ❑ Feb 1959 Cover: 0.10 NM value: 175.00
• Quicksilver prototype?
68 ❑ Apr 1959 Cover: 0.10 NM value: 130.00
69 ❑ Jun 1959 Cover: 0.10 NM value: 160.00
• CGC: 1 graded, best 5.0
• Professor X prototype?
70 ❑ Aug 1959 Cover: 0.10 NM value: 125.00
• CGC: 1 graded, best 6.0
71 ❑ Oct 1959 Cover: 0.10 NM value: 125.00
• CGC: 1 graded, best 7.5
72 ❑ Dec 1959 Cover: 0.10 NM value: 125.00
• CGC: 1 graded, best 7.0
73 ❑ Feb 1960 Cover: 0.10 NM value: 125.00
74 ❑ Apr 1960 Cover: 0.10 NM value: 125.00
75 ❑ Jun 1960 Cover: 0.10 NM value: 125.00
76 ❑ Aug 1960 Cover: 0.10 NM value: 125.00
77 ❑ Oct 1960 Cover: 0.10 NM value: 125.00
• CGC: 1 graded, best 9.0
78 ❑ Nov 1960 Cover: 0.10 NM value: 125.00
• CGC: 2 graded, best 9.0
79 ❑ Dec 1960 Cover: 0.10 NM value: 215.00
• CGC: 2 graded, best 9.0
• Doctor Strange try-out character
80 ❑ Jan 1961 Cover: 0.10 NM value: 125.00
• CGC: 1 graded, best 6.0
81 ❑ Feb 1961 Cover: 0.10 NM value: 115.00
• CGC: 4 graded, best 9.2
82 ❑ Mar 1961 Cover: 0.10 NM value: 115.00
• CGC: 2 graded, best 8.0
The Thing Called It
83 ❑ Apr 1961 Cover: 0.10 NM value: 105.00
From Out of the Black Pit Came Grogg
84 ❑ May 1961 Cover: 0.10 NM value: 190.00
• CGC: 2 graded, best 8.0
Magneto • Magneto prototype character (?)
85 ❑ Jun 1961 Cover: 0.10 NM value: 115.00
The Return of Gargantus
86 ❑ Jul 1961 Cover: 0.10 NM value: 115.00
• CGC: 1 graded, best 4.0
I Created Mechano
87 ❑ Aug 1961 Cover: 0.10 NM value: 115.00
The Return of Grogg
88 ❑ Sep 1961 Cover: 0.10 NM value: 115.00
Zzutak, the Thing That Shouldn't Exist
89 ❑ Oct 1961 Cover: 0.10 NM value: 250.00
• CGC: 6 graded, best 9.0
Fin Fang Foom A: Jack Kirby ★ Origin of Fin Fang Foom. ★ 1st Appearance of Fin Fang Foom.
90 ❑ Nov 1961 Cover: 0.10 NM value: 115.00
• CGC: 1 graded, best 8.0
91 ❑ Dec 1961 Cover: 0.10 NM value: 115.00
• CGC: 3 graded, best 8.5
92 ❑ Jan 1962 Cover: 0.10 NM value: 115.00
Circ: Statement: 136,637 • CGC: 1 graded, best 5.0
93 ❑ Feb 1962 Cover: 0.10 NM value: 105.00
Circ: Statement: 136,637 • CGC: 2 graded, best 7.5
94 ❑ Mar 1962 Cover: 0.10 NM value: 105.00
Circ: Statement: 136,637
95 ❑ Apr 1962 Cover: 0.10 NM value: 105.00
Circ: Statement: 136,637 • CGC: 1 graded, best 8.5
96 ❑ May 1962 Cover: 0.10 NM value: 105.00
Circ: Statement: 136,637 • CGC: 2 graded, best 7.5
97 ❑ Jun 1962 Cover: 0.10 NM value: 325.00
Circ: Statement: 136,637 • CGC: 11 graded, best 8.0
• Aunt May & Uncle Ben prototype characters (?)
98 ❑ Jul 1962 Cover: 0.10 NM value: 105.00
Circ: Statement: 136,637

CGC-graded: Multiply prices above by **33 for 9.9 M • 16 for 9.8 NM/M • 7 for 9.6 NM+ • 5 for 9.4 NM • 2.5 for 9.2 NM- • 1.5 for 9.0 VF/NM**

99 ❑ Aug 1962 Cover: 0.10 **NM** value: **105.00**
Circ: Statement: **136,637** • **CGC:** 1 graded, best 7.5

100 ❑ Sep 1962 Cover: 0.12 **NM** value: **105.00**
Circ: Statement: **136,637** • **CGC:** 2 graded, best 8.5

101 ❑ Oct 1962 Cover: 0.12 **NM** value: **825.00**
Circ: Statement: **136,637** • **CGC:** 28 graded, best 9.4
The Human Torch; The Flaming Fury Strikes Back; The Impossible Spaceship; What Is X-35?; Sdrawkcab (text) • Human Torch features begin **A:** Steve Ditko; Jack Kirby

102 ❑ Nov 1962 Cover: 0.12 **NM** value: **300.00**
Circ: Statement: **136,637** • **CGC:** 18 graded, best 9.6
Prisoner of the Wizard; Wizard's Wiles; The Secret of the Hidden Planet; Who Needs You?; The Treasure (text) • Human Torch **A:** Steve Ditko; Jack Kirby ★ Appearance of Human Torch.

103 ❑ Dec 1962 Cover: 0.12 **NM** value: **240.00**
Circ: Statement: **136,637** • **CGC:** 9 graded, best 9.4
Prisoner of the 5th Dimension; Trapped in Another World; The End of Zemu; The Little People; Jasper's Jalopy; Lady Luck (text) • Human Torch **A:** Steve Ditko; Jack Kirby ★ Appearance of Human Torch.

104 ❑ Jan 1963 Cover: 0.12 **NM** value: **240.00**
Circ: Statement: **189,305** • **CGC:** 15 graded, best 9.4
The Human Torch Meets Paste-Pot Pete; Markham's Magic Crayon; The Frog-Man; Venus (text) • Human Torch **A:** Steve Ditko; Jack Kirby ★ Origin of Paste-Pot Pete. ★ 1st Appearance of Paste-Pot Pete. ★ Appearance of Human Torch.

105 ❑ Feb 1963 Cover: 0.12 **NM** value: **240.00**
Circ: Statement: **189,305** • **CGC:** 14 graded, best 9.4
The Return of the Wizard; Man Alone; The Supernatural; Discovery (text) • Human Torch **A:** Steve Ditko; Jack Kirby ★ Appearance of Human Torch.

106 ❑ Mar 1963 Cover: 0.12 **NM** value: **175.00**
Circ: Statement: **189,305** • **CGC:** 13 graded, best 9.6
The Threat of the Torrid Twosome; Man on the Scaffold; The Mystery of the Purple Planet; The Recipie (text) • Human Torch **A:** Steve Ditko ★ Appearance of Fantastic Four. ★ Appearance of Human Torch.

107 ❑ Apr 1963 Cover: 0.12 **NM** value: **190.00**
Circ: Statement: **189,305** • **CGC:** 19 graded, best 9.6
The Master of Flame vs. the Monarch of the Sea; The Secret Weapon; The Treasure of Planetoid 12; The Universal Gadget (text) • Human Torch vs. Sub-Mariner **A:** Steve Ditko

108 ❑ May 1963 Cover: 0.12 **NM** value: **175.00**
Circ: Statement: **189,305** • **CGC:** 12 graded, best 9.6
The Painter of a Thousand Perils; The Silent Giant; The Iron Warrior; The Heat's On (text) • Human Torch **A:** Steve Ditko; Jack Kirby ★ Appearance of Human Torch.

109 ❑ Jun 1963 Cover: 0.12 **NM** value: **175.00**
Circ: Statement: **189,305** • **CGC:** 18 graded, best 9.6
The Sorcerer and Pandora's Box; Earth Is Off-Limits; Time Was; The Comic (text) • Human Torch **A:** Steve Ditko; Jack Kirby ★ 1st Appearance of Circe (later becomes Sersi). ★ Appearance of Human Torch.

110 ❑ Jul 1963 Cover: 0.12 **NM** value: **1000.00**
Circ: Statement: **189,305** • **CGC:** 61 graded, best 9.6
The Human Torch vs. the Wizard and Paste-Pot Pete; We Search the Stars; Dr. Strange, Master of Black Magic; Silent Stranger (text) • Human Torch, Dr. Strange **A:** Steve Ditko ★ 1st Appearance of The Ancient One, Doctor Strange, Wong (Doctor Strange's manservant). ★ Appearance of Human Torch.

111 ❑ Aug 1963 Cover: 0.12 **NM** value: **300.00**
Circ: Statement: **189,305** • **CGC:** 17 graded, best 9.6
Fighting to the Death with the Asbestos Man; Beware the Machine; Face-To-Face with the Magic of Baron Mordo; Masquerade (text) • Human Torch, Dr. Strange **A:** Steve Ditko ★ 1st Appearance of Asbestos, Baron Mordo, Eel I (Leopold Stryke). ★ 2nd Appearance of Doctor Strange. ★ Appearance of Human Torch.

112 ❑ Sep 1963 Cover: 0.12 **NM** value: **110.00**
Circ: Statement: **189,305** • **CGC:** 8 graded, best 9.6
The Living Bomb; The Man Who Dared; I Saw the Impossible World **A:** Steve Ditko ★ Appearance of Human Torch.

113 ❑ Oct 1963 Cover: 0.12 **NM** value: **110.00**
Circ: Statement: **189,305** • **CGC:** 3 graded, best 9.6
The Coming of the Plantman; The Search for Shanng; The Shoemaker's Strange Assistants; New Glasses (text) **A:** Steve Ditko ★ 1st Appearance of Plantman. ★ Appearance of Human Torch.

114 ❑ Nov 1963 Cover: 0.12 **NM** value: **250.00**
Circ: Statement: **189,305** • **CGC:** 37 graded, best 9.6
The Human Torch Meets Captain America; The Return of the Omnipotent Baron Mordo; The Bridge (text) • Villain (The Acrobat) appears, dressed as Captain America; Dr. Strange **A:** Steve Ditko; Jack Kirby ★ Appearance of Human Torch.

115 ❑ Dec 1963 Cover: 0.12 **NM** value: **375.00**
Circ: Statement: **189,305** • **CGC:** 48 graded, best 9.6
The Sandman Strikes; The Origin of Dr. Strange; Zero of Time (text) • Human Torch, Dr. Strange **A:** Steve Ditko ★ Origin of Doctor Strange. ★ Appearance of Human Torch.

116 ❑ Jan 1964 Cover: 0.12 **NM** value: **85.00**
Circ: Statement: **215,090** • **CGC:** 11 graded, best 9.6
In the Clutches of the Puppet Master; Return to the Nightmare World; The Radio (text) • Human Torch vs. Thing; Dr. Strange

117 ❑ Feb 1964 Cover: 0.12 **NM** value: **70.00**
Circ: Statement: **215,090** • **CGC:** 5 graded, best 9.6
The Return of the Eel; The Many Traps of Baron Mordo; From Outer Space (text) • Human Torch, Dr. Strange ★ Appearance of Human Torch.

118 ❑ Mar 1964 Cover: 0.12 **NM** value: **70.00**
Circ: Statement: **215,090** • **CGC:** 7 graded, best 9.4
The Man Who Became the Torch; The Possessed; The Weatherman (text) • Human Torch, Dr. Strange ★ Appearance of Human Torch.

119 ❑ Apr 1964 Cover: 0.12 **NM** value: **90.00**
Circ: Statement: **215,090** • **CGC:** 6 graded, best 9.6
The Torch Goes Wild; Beyond the Purple Veil • Human Torch, Dr. Strange ★ Appearance of Human Torch, Spider-Man.

120 ❑ May 1964 Cover: 0.12 **NM** value: **85.00**
Circ: Statement: **215,090** • **CGC:** 7 graded, best 9.8
The Torch Meets Iceman; The House of Shadows; The Salesman (text, part 1) • Human Torch, Iceman; Dr. Strange ★ Appearance of Human Torch, Iceman.

121 ❑ Jun 1964 Cover: 0.12 **NM** value: **48.00**
Circ: Statement: **215,090** • **CGC:** 6 graded, best 9.4
Prisoner of the Plantman; Witchcraft in the Wax Museum; The Salesman (text, part 2) • Has 1963 Statement, filed 10/1/63; avg print run 321,212; avg sales 189,160; avg subs 145; avg total paid 189,305; samples 175; max existent 189,480; 41% of run returned ★ Appearance of Human Torch.

122 ❑ Jul 1964 Cover: 0.12 **NM** value: **48.00**
Circ: Statement: **215,090** • **CGC:** 9 graded, best 9.6
Three Against the Torch; The World Beyond; Strange Mission (text, part 1) ★ Appearance of Human Torch.

123 ❑ Aug 1964 Cover: 0.12 **NM** value: **48.00**
Circ: Statement: **215,090** • **CGC:** 8 graded, best 9.6
The Birth of the Beetle; The Challenge of Loki; Strange Mission (text, part 2) ★ Origin of The Beetle. ★ 1st Appearance of The Beetle. ★ Appearance of Thing, Human Torch, Thor.

124 ❑ Sep 1964 Cover: 0.12 **NM** value: **48.00**
Circ: Statement: **215,090** • **CGC:** 4 graded, best 9.4
Paste-Pot Pete; The Lady From Nowhere ★ Appearance of Thing, Human Torch.

125 ❑ Oct 1964 Cover: 0.12 **NM** value: **48.00**
Circ: Statement: **215,090** • **CGC:** 5 graded, best 9.6
The Sub-Mariner Must Be Stopped; Mordo Must Not Catch Me; The Message (text, part 1) ★ Appearance of Human Torch.

126 ❑ Nov 1964 Cover: 0.12 **NM** value: **55.00**
Circ: Statement: **215,090** • **CGC:** 10 graded, best 9.8
Pawns of the Deadly Duo; The Domain of the Dread Dormammu ★ 1st Appearance of Dormammu, Clea. ★ Appearance of Human Torch.

127 ❑ Dec 1964 Cover: 0.12 **NM** value: **42.00**
Circ: Statement: **215,090** • **CGC:** 5 graded, best 9.6
The Mystery Villain; Duel With the Dread Dormammu ★ Appearance of Human Torch.

128 ❑ Jan 1965 Cover: 0.12 **NM** value: **42.00**
Circ: Statement: **230,285** • **CGC:** 4 graded, best 9.6
Quicksilver and the Scarlet Witch; The Demon's Desciple ★ Appearance of Human Torch.

129 ❑ Feb 1965 Cover: 0.12 **NM** value: **42.00**
Circ: Statement: **230,285** • **CGC:** 10 graded, best 9.6
The Terrible Trio; Beware Tiboro, the Tyrant of the Sixth Dimension ★ Appearance of Human Torch.

130 ❑ Mar 1965 Cover: 0.12 **NM** value: **48.00**
Circ: Statement: **230,285** • **CGC:** 7 graded, best 9.4
Meet the Beatles; The Defeat of Dr. Strange **A:** Steve Ditko ★ Appearance of Human Torch, Beatles.

131 ❑ Apr 1965 Cover: 0.12 **NM** value: **42.00**
Circ: Statement: **230,285** • **CGC:** 7 graded, best 9.8
The Bouncing Ball of Doom; The Hunter and the Hunted • Has 1964 Statement, filed 10/1/64; avg print run 315,500; avg sales 214,800; avg subs 290; avg total paid 215,090; samples 125; max existent 215,215; 32% of run returned **A:** Steve Ditko ★ Appearance of Thing, Human Torch.

132 ❑ May 1965 Cover: 0.12 **NM** value: **42.00**
Circ: Statement: **230,285** • **CGC:** 6 graded, best 9.4
The Sinister Space Trap; Face-To-Face at Last with Baron Mordo **A:** Steve Ditko ★ Appearance of Thing, Human Torch.

133 ❑ Jun 1965 Cover: 0.12 **NM** value: **42.00**
Circ: Statement: **230,285** • **CGC:** 12 graded, best 9.6
The Terrible Toys; A Nameless Land, a Timeless Time **A:** Steve Ditko ★ Appearance of Thing, Human Torch.

134 ❑ Jul 1965 Cover: 0.12 **NM** value: **42.00**
Circ: Statement: **230,285** • **CGC:** 7 graded, best 9.6
The Challenge of the Watcher; Earth Be My Battleground • Last Human Torch issue **A:** Steve Ditko ★ Appearance of Torch, Human Torch, Watcher.

135 ❑ Aug 1965 Cover: 0.12 **NM** value: **85.00**
Circ: Statement: **230,285** • **CGC:** 27 graded, best 9.6
Nick Fury, Agent of S.H.I.E.L.D.: The Man for the Job!; Eternity Beckons! • Origin of Nick Fury, Doctor Strange **A:** Steve Ditko; Jack Kirby; Dick Ayers(inks) **W:** Stan Lee ★ Origin of Nick Fury, Agent of SHIELD. ★ 1st Appearance of S.H.I.E.L.D., Nick Fury, Agent of SHIELD, Hydra.

136 ❑ Sep 1965 Cover: 0.12 **NM** value: **28.00**
Circ: Statement: **230,285** • **CGC:** 4 graded, best 9.6
Find Fury or Die; What Lurks Beneath the Mask? • Doctor Strange, Nick Fury **A:** Steve Ditko; Jack Kirby

137 ❑ Oct 1965 Cover: 0.12 **NM** value: **28.00**
Circ: Statement: **230,285** • **CGC:** 6 graded, best 9.6
The Prize is Earth; When Meet the Mystic Minds • Doctor Strange, Nick Fury

138 ❑ Nov 1965 Cover: 0.12 **NM** value: **28.00**
Circ: Statement: **230,285** • **CGC:** 16 graded, best 9.6
Sometimes the Good Guys Loose; If Eternity Should Fail • Doctor Strange, Nick Fury ★ 1st Appearance of Eternity.

139 ❑ Dec 1965 Cover: 0.12 **NM** value: **28.00**
Circ: Statement: **230,285** • **CGC:** 7 graded, best 9.6
The Brave Die Hard; Beware, Dormammu is Watching • Doctor Strange, Nick Fury

140 ❑ Jan 1966 Cover: 0.12 **NM** value: **28.00**
Circ: Statement: **261,069** • **CGC:** 5 graded, best 9.8
The End of Hydra; The Pincers of Power • Doctor Strange, Nick Fury

141 ❑ Feb 1966 Cover: 0.12 **NM** value: **28.00**
Circ: Statement: **261,069** • **CGC:** 5 graded, best 9.8
Operation: Brain Blast; Let There Be Victory • Doctor Strange, Nick Fury ★ 1st Appearance of The Fixer, Mentallo.

142 ❑ Mar 1966 Cover: 0.12 **NM** value: **28.00**
Circ: Statement: **261,069** • **CGC:** 5 graded, best 9.6
Who Strikes at S.H.I.E.L.D.?; Those Who Would Destroy Me • Doctor Strange, Nick Fury

143 ❑ Apr 1966 Cover: 0.12 **NM** value: **28.00**
Circ: Statement: **261,069** • **CGC:** 10 graded, best 9.6
To Free a Brain Slave; With None Beside Me • Doctor Strange, Nick Fury; Has 1965 Statement, filed 10/1/65; avg print run 380,992; avg sales 229,760; avg subs 525; avg total paid 230,285; samples 60; max existent 230,345; 40% of run returned

144 ❑ May 1966 Cover: 0.12 **NM** value: **28.00**
Circ: Statement: **261,069** • **CGC:** 9 graded, best 9.6
The Day of the Druid; Where Man Hath Never Trod • Doctor Strange, Nick Fury ★ 1st Appearance of The Druid, Jasper Sitwell (SHIELD agent).

145 ❑ Jun 1966 Cover: 0.12 **NM** value: **28.00**
Circ: Statement: **261,069** • **CGC:** 10 graded, best 9.6
Lo, the Eggs Shall Hatch; To Catch a Magician • Doctor Strange, Nick Fury

146 ❑ Jul 1966 Cover: 0.12 **NM** value: **30.00**
Circ: Statement: **261,069** • **CGC:** 7 graded, best 9.6
The End At Last!; When the Unliving Strike! • Doctor Strange, Nick Fury ★ 1st Appearance of Advanced Idea Mechanics (A.I.M.).

147 ❑ Aug 1966 Cover: 0.12 **NM** value: **28.00**
Circ: Statement: **261,069** • **CGC:** 25 graded, best 9.8
The Enemy Within; From the Nameless Nowhere Comes Kaluu • Doctor Strange, Nick Fury ★ Origin of Kaluu. ★ 1st Appearance of Kaluu.

148 ❑ Sep 1966 Cover: 0.12 **NM** value: **50.00**
Circ: Statement: **261,069** • **CGC:** 9 graded, best 9.4
Death Before Dishonor; The Origin of the Ancient One • Doctor Strange, Nick Fury **A:** Bill Everett; Jack Kirby ★ Origin of The Ancient One.

149 ❑ Oct 1966 Cover: 0.12 **NM** value: **28.00**
Circ: Statement: **261,069** • **CGC:** 8 graded, best 9.8
The End of A.I.M.; If Kaluu Should Triumph • Doctor Strange, Nick Fury **A:** Bill Everett; Jack Kirby

150 ❑ Nov 1966 Cover: 0.12 **NM** value: **32.00**
Circ: Statement: **261,069** • **CGC:** 7 graded, best 9.6
HYDRA Lives; The Conquest of Kaluu • 1st John Buscema art at Marvel **A:** John Buscema; Bill Everett; Jack Kirby ★ 1st Appearance of Umar.

151 ❑ Dec 1966 Cover: 0.12 **NM** value: **42.00**
Circ: Statement: **261,069** • **CGC:** 8 graded, best 9.6
Overkill; Umar Strikes • 1st Jim Steranko art at Marvel **A:** Bill Everett; Jack Kirby; Jim Steranko

152 ❑ Jan 1967 Cover: 0.12 **NM** value: **25.00**
Circ: Statement: **241,561** • **CGC:** 5 graded, best 9.6
The Power of S.H.I.E.L.D.; Into the Dimension of Death • Doctor Strange, Nick Fury

153 ❑ Feb 1967 Cover: 0.12 **NM** value: **25.00**
Circ: Statement: **241,561** • **CGC:** 4 graded, best 9.6
The Hiding Place; Alone Against the Mindless Ones • Doctor Strange, Nick Fury

154 ❑ Mar 1967 Cover: 0.12 **NM** value: **25.00**
Circ: Statement: **241,561** • **CGC:** 7 graded, best 9.6
Beware the Deadly Dreadnaught; Clea Must Die • Doctor Strange, Nick Fury ★ 1st Appearance of Dreadnought (original).

155 ❑ Apr 1967 Cover: 0.12 **NM** value: **25.00**
Circ: Statement: **241,561** • **CGC:** 5 graded, best 9.6
Death Trap; The Fearful Finish • Doctor Strange, Nick Fury; Has 1966 Statement, filed 10/1/66; avg print run 420,036; avg sales 259,844; avg subs 1,225; avg total paid 261,069; samples 60; max existent 261,129; 38% of run returned

156 ❑ May 1967 Cover: 0.12 **NM** value: **25.00**
Circ: Statement: **241,561** • **CGC:** 4 graded, best 9.6
The Tribunal; Umar Walks the Earth • Doctor Strange, Nick Fury ★ Appearance of Daredevil.

157 ❑ Jun 1967 Cover: 0.12 **NM** value: **25.00**
Circ: Statement: **241,561** • **CGC:** 3 graded, best 9.6
Crisis; The End of the Ancient One • Doctor Strange, Nick Fury ★ 1st Appearance of Living Tribunal.

158 ❑ Jul 1967 Cover: 0.12 **NM** value: **25.00**
Circ: Statement: **241,561** • **CGC:** 9 graded, best 9.6
Final Encounter; The Sands of Death • Doctor Strange, Nick Fury ★ Death of Baron Strucker.

159 ❑ Aug 1967 Cover: 0.12 **NM** value: **32.00**
Circ: Statement: **241,561** • **CGC:** 8 graded, best 9.6
Spy School; The Evil That Men Do • Doctor Strange, Nick Fury **A:** Jim Steranko ★ Origin of Nick Fury, Agent of SHIELD, Fury. ★ 1st Appearance of Val Fontaine. ★ Appearance of Captain America.

160 ❑ Sep 1967 Cover: 0.12 **NM** value: **25.00**
Circ: Statement: **241,561** • **CGC:** 5 graded, best 9.4
Project: Blackout (part 1); If This Planet You Would Save • Doctor Strange, Nick Fury ★ Appearance of Captain America.

161 ❑ Oct 1967 Cover: 0.12 **NM** value: **25.00**
Circ: Statement: **241,561** • **CGC:** 3 graded, best 9.6
The Second Doom (part 2); And A Scourge Shall Come Upon You • Doctor Strange, Nick Fury ★ Appearance of Captain America.

162 ❑ Nov 1967 Cover: 0.12 **NM** value: **25.00**
Circ: Statement: **241,561** • **CGC:** 3 graded, best 9.2
So Evil, The Night; From the Never-World Comes Nebulos • Doctor Strange, Nick Fury ★ Appearance of Captain America.

163 ❑ Dec 1967 Cover: 0.12 **NM** value: **25.00**
Circ: Statement: **241,561** • **CGC:** 5 graded, best 9.4
And the Dragon Cried Death; Three Faces of Doom • Doctor Strange, Nick Fury

164 ❑ Jan 1968 Cover: 0.12 **NM** value: **25.00**
Circ: Statement: **266,422** • **CGC:** 4 graded, best 9.4
Nightmare; When Comes Black Noon • Doctor Strange, Nick Fury ★ 1st Appearance of Yandroth.

165 ❑ Feb 1968 Cover: 0.12 **NM** value: **25.00**
Circ: Statement: **266,422** • **CGC:** 6 graded, best 9.6
Behold the Savage Sky; The Mystic and the Machine • Doctor Strange, Nick Fury

166 ❑ Mar 1968 Cover: 0.12 **NM** value: **25.00**
Circ: Statement: **266,422** • **CGC:** 2 graded, best 9.4
Nothing Can Halt Voltorg; If Death Be My Destiny • Doctor Strange, Nick Fury

167 ❑ Apr 1968 Cover: 0.12 **NM** value: **25.00**
Circ: Statement: **266,422** • **CGC:** 8 graded, best 9.6

Other grades: Multiply prices above by **1.5 for Mint** • **2/3 for Very Fine** • **1/3 for Fine** • **1/5 for Very Good** • **1/8 for Good**

📖 Armageddon; This Dream, This Doom • Doctor Strange, Nick Fury; Has 1967 Statement, filed 10/1/67; avg print run 428,603; avg sales 240,336; avg subs 1,225; avg total paid 241,561; samples 95; max existent 241,656; 44% of run returned **A:** Jim Steranko; Dan Adkins

168 ❑ May 1968 Cover: 0.12 **NM** value: **25.00**
Circ: Statement: **266,422** • **CGC:** 3 graded, best 9.0
📖 Exile; Today Earth Died • original series continues as Doctor Strange; Nick Fury, Agent of SHIELD series ends **A:** Jim Steranko; Dan Adkins ★ Origin of Brother Voodoo.

169 ❑ Jun 1973 Cover: 0.20 **NM** value: **3.50**
• **CGC:** 2 graded, best 9.4
📖 Brother Voodoo • second series begins; Brother Voodoo

170 ❑ Aug 1973 Cover: 0.20 **NM** value: **3.50**
📖 Baptism of Fire and Blood! • Brother Voodoo

171 ❑ Oct 1973 Cover: 0.20 **NM** value: **3.50**
📖 March of the Dead! • Brother Voodoo ★ 1st Appearance of Baron Samedi.

172 ❑ Dec 1973 Cover: 0.20 **NM** value: **3.50**
📖 Fiend in the Fog! • Brother Voodoo

173 ❑ Feb 1974 Cover: 0.20 **NM** value: **3.50**
📖 Sacrifice Play! • Brother Voodoo **A:** Gene Colan **W:** Len Wein ★ 1st Appearance of Black Talon I (Desmond Drew).

174 ❑ Jun 1974 Cover: 0.25 **NM** value: **3.50**
📖 There Walks The Golem! • Golem **A:** John Buscema; Jim Mooney **W:** Len Wein ★ Origin of Golem.

175 ❑ Aug 1974 Cover: 0.25 **NM** value: **3.50**
📖 Torr; Midnight in the Wax Museum • Rep-Torr; reprints Amazing Adventures #1 **A:** Steve Ditko

176 ❑ Oct 1974 Cover: 0.25 **NM** value: **3.50**
📖 Black Crossing • Golem

177 ❑ Dec 1974 Cover: 0.25 **NM** value: **3.50**
📖 There Comes Now Raging Fire! • Golem **A:** Tony DeZuniga **W:** Mike Friedrich

178 ❑ Feb 1975 Cover: 0.25 **NM** value: **15.00**
• **CGC:** 13 graded, best 9.6
📖 Who is Adam Warlock? • Warlock **A:** Jim Starlin ★ Origin of Warlock. ★ 1st Appearance of Magus.

179 ❑ Apr 1975 Cover: 0.25 **NM** value: **10.00**
• **CGC:** 1 graded, best 9.2
📖 Death Ship! • Warlock **A:** Jim Starlin ★ 1st Appearance of Pip. ★ Appearance of Warlock.

180 ❑ Jun 1975 Cover: 0.25 **NM** value: **10.00**
• **CGC:** 1 graded, best 9.6
📖 The Judgement • Warlock **A:** Jim Starlin ★ 1st Appearance of Gamora. ★ Appearance of Warlock.

181 ❑ Aug 1975 Cover: 0.25 **NM** value: **10.00**
• **CGC:** 1 graded, best 9.4
📖 1000 Clowns • Warlock **A:** Jim Starlin ★ Appearance of Warlock.

182 ❑ Oct 1975 Cover: 0.25 **NM** value: **3.00**
📖 The Challenge of Loki; The Lady from Nowhere • reprinted from Strange Tales #123 and 124

183 ❑ Dec 1975 Cover: 0.25 **NM** value: **3.00**
📖 The Defeat of Dr. Strange; The Hunter and the Hunted • reprinted from Strange Tales #130 and 131

184 ❑ Feb 1976 Cover: 0.25 **NM** value: **3.00**
📖 Face-To-Face at Last With Baron Mordo; A Nameless Land, a Nameless Time • reprinted from Strange Tales #132 and 133

185 ❑ Apr 1976 Cover: 0.25 **NM** value: **3.00**
📖 Earth Be My Battleground • reprinted from Strange Tales #134 and 135

186 ❑ Jun 1976 Cover: 0.25 **NM** value: **3.00**
📖 What Lurks Beneath the Mask? • reprinted from Strange Tales #136 and 137

187 ❑ Aug 1976 Cover: 0.30 **NM** value: **3.00**
📖 If Eternity Should Fail • reprinted from Strange Tales #138 and 139

188 ❑ Oct 1976 Cover: 0.30 **NM** value: **3.00**
📖 The Pincers of Power • reprinted from Strange Tales #140 and 141

Anl 1 ❑ ca. 1962 Cover: 0.25 **NM** value: **325.00**
• **CGC:** 13 graded, best 9.2
📖 I Unleashed Shagg Upon the World; I Come From the Shadow World; He Waits for Us in the Glacier; I Became a Human Bomb; Grottu, King of the Insects; I Know the Secret of the Poltergeist; I Saw the Serpent That Saved the World; The Stranger in Space; I Saw Diablo, the Demon from the Fifth Dimension; I Found the Giant in the Sky; Beware! The Ghosts Surround Me; I Saw the Invasion of the Stone Men; A Martian Walks Among Us • reprinted from Journey Into Mystery #53, 55 and 59; Strange Tales #73, 76 and 78; Tales of Suspense #7 and 9; Tales to Astonish #1,6 and 7

Anl 2 ❑ ca. 1963 Cover: 0.25 **NM** value: **350.00**
• **CGC:** 27 graded, best 9.6
📖 On the Trail of the Amazing Spider-Man; I Was the Invisible Man; I Was a Prisoner on the Planet of Plunder; I am Robot; Worlds Within Worlds; I Was the Man Who Lived Twice; I Fly to the Stars; Prison 2000 A.D.; I am the Scourge of Atlantis; Nightmare Planet; I Captured the Abominable Snowman • Spider-Man new, all others reprinted from Strange Tales #67; Strange Worlds #1,2 and 3; World of Fantasy #16 ★ Appearance of Human Torch, Spider-Man.

STRANGE TALES (2ND SERIES) — Marvel

1 ❑ Apr 1987 Cover: 0.75 **NM** value: **1.50**
Circ: CapCity orders: **25,100**
📖 Cloak & Dagger; And Have Not Charity • Doctor Strange, Cloak & Dagger **A:** Bret Blevins; Chris Warner **W:** Bill Mantlo; Peter B. Gillis

2 ❑ May 1987 Cover: 0.75 **NM** value: **1.25**
Circ: CapCity orders: **18,000**
📖 All In The Family; The World Well Lost For Love-! **A:** Bret Blevins; Chris Warner **W:** Bill Mantlo; Peter B. Gillis

3 ❑ Jun 1987 Cover: 0.75 **NM** value: **1.25**
Circ: CapCity orders: **17,100**

4 ❑ Jul 1987 Cover: 0.75 **NM** value: **1.25**
Circ: CapCity orders: **17,500**

5 ❑ Aug 1987 Cover: 0.75 **NM** value: **1.25**
Circ: CapCity orders: **17,500**

6 ❑ Sep 1987 Cover: 0.75 **NM** value: **1.25**
Circ: CapCity orders: **18,000**

7 ❑ Oct 1987 Cover: 0.75 **NM** value: **1.25**
Circ: CapCity orders: **17,700**
• Defenders

8 ❑ Nov 1987 Cover: 0.75 **NM** value: **1.25**
Circ: CapCity orders: **17,300**

9 ❑ Dec 1987 Cover: 0.75 **NM** value: **1.25**
Circ: CapCity orders: **16,400**

10 ❑ Jan 1988 Cover: 0.75 **NM** value: **1.25**
Circ: CapCity orders: **16,350**

11 ❑ Feb 1988 Cover: 0.75 **NM** value: **1.25**
Circ: CapCity orders: **16,100**

12 ❑ Mar 1988 Cover: 0.75 **NM** value: **1.25**
Circ: CapCity orders: **18,300**
• Black Cat

13 ❑ Apr 1988 Cover: 0.75 **NM** value: **1.75**
Circ: CapCity orders: **19,100**
★ Appearance of Punisher.

14 ❑ May 1988 Cover: 0.75 **NM** value: **1.75**
Circ: CapCity orders: **17,600**
★ Appearance of Punisher.

15 ❑ Jun 1988 Cover: 0.75 **NM** value: **1.25**
Circ: CapCity orders: **15,000**

16 ❑ Jul 1988 Cover: 0.75 **NM** value: **1.25**
Circ: CapCity orders: **14,700**

17 ❑ Aug 1988 Cover: 0.75 **NM** value: **1.50**
Circ: CapCity orders: **14,700**

18 ❑ Sep 1988 Cover: 0.75 **NM** value: **1.25**
Circ: CapCity orders: **14,700**
• X-Factor ★ Appearance of X-Factor.

19 ❑ Oct 1988 Cover: 0.75 **NM** value: **1.25**
Circ: CapCity orders: **13,900**
final issue.

STRANGE TALES (3RD SERIES) — Marvel

1 ❑ Nov 1994 Cover: 6.95 **NM** value: **Cover or less**
Circ: CapCity orders: **24,750** • **CGC:** 2 graded, best 9.9
acetate overlay cover. • prestige format. **A:** Ricardo Villagran **W:** Kurt Busiek ★ 1st Appearance of Orrgo the Unconquerable, Golden Gator, Khlog.

STRANGE TALES (4TH SERIES) — Marvel

Following a one-shot prestige format issue featuring the characters that starred in the first series, Marvel released a new rendition of one of its most famous titles in 1998. The new version of Strange Tales started off with a giant-sized anthology starring Werewolf by Night and Marvel's muck monster, Man-Thing. The title is anchored by solo stories of the two headliners, with a third (generally horror) story filling out each issue.

The Werewolf and Man-Thing stories were continued from each of their respective titles, presenting something of a problem for new readers of this series who might have expected to come in at the beginning of the story.

1 ❑ Sep 1998 Cover: 4.99 **NM** value: **Cover or less**
Circ: Diamd. preorders: **15,139**
• gatefold summary. 📖 Man-Thing: Destroyer of Worlds; Werewolf: Love is Colder Than Death, Part 2; A Tomb for Two **A:** Liam Sharp; Mark Pajarillo; Leonardo Manco **W:** Glenn Herdling; J.M. DeMatteis; Paul Jenkins ★ Appearance of Werewolf, Man-Thing.

2 ❑ Oct 1998 Cover: 4.99 **NM** value: **Cover or less**
Circ: Diamd. preorders: **14,994**
• gatefold summary. ★ Appearance of Werewolf, Man-Thing.

3 ❑ Nov 1998 Cover: 4.99 **NM** value: **Cover or less**
Circ: Diamd. preorders: **11,300**

4 ❑ Dec 1998 Cover: 4.99 **NM** value: **Cover or less**
Circ: Diamd. preorders: **10,363**

STRANGE TALES: DARK CORNERS — Marvel

1 ❑ May 1998 Cover: 3.99 **NM** value: **Cover or less**
Circ: Diamd. preorders: **16,510**
• gatefold summary. 📖 Cloak & Dagger: Expressway to Hell; Morbius the Living Vampire: Desiring Martine; Gargoyle: In Stone **A:** Alex Maleev; Mark Badger; Mike Dringenberg **W:** Mike Baron; Don McGregor; J.M. DeMatteis

STRANGE TALES OF THE UNUSUAL — Atlas

1 ❑ Dec 1955 Cover: 0.10 **NM** value: **350.00**
• **CGC:** 4 graded, best 9.0

2 ❑ Feb 1956 Cover: 0.10 **NM** value: **200.00**
• **CGC:** 1 graded, best 9.0

3 ❑ Apr 1956 Cover: 0.10 **NM** value: **200.00**
• **CGC:** 2 graded, best 8.5

4 ❑ Jun 1956 Cover: 0.10 **NM** value: **200.00**
• **CGC:** 1 graded, best 9.2
📖 The Long Wait!; The Life Saver!; Flames of Fury!; The Warning Voice; The Talking Horse!; Mission to Jupiter; The Money Miracle (text)

5 ❑ Aug 1956 Cover: 0.10 **NM** value: **200.00**
• **CGC:** 1 graded, best 7.5

6 ❑ Oct 1956 Cover: 0.10 **NM** value: **150.00**

7 ❑ Dec 1956 Cover: 0.10 **NM** value: **150.00**
• **CGC:** 1 graded, best 9.2

8 ❑ Feb 1957 Cover: 0.10 **NM** value: **150.00**
• **CGC:** 1 graded, best 8.5

9 ❑ Apr 1957 Cover: 0.10 **NM** value: **150.00**
• **CGC:** 3 graded, best 9.0

10 ❑ Jun 1957 Cover: 0.10 **NM** value: **150.00**
• **CGC:** 2 graded, best 8.5

11 ❑ Aug 1957 Cover: 0.10 **NM** value: **150.00**
• **CGC:** 1 graded, best 8.5

STRANGE TERRORS — St. John

1 ❑ Jun 1952 Cover: 0.10 **NM** value: **400.00**
• **CGC:** 3 graded, best 9.2

2 ❑ Aug 1952 Cover: 0.10 **NM** value: **200.00**
• **CGC:** 2 graded, best 7.0

3 ❑ Sep 1952 Cover: 0.10 **NM** value: **200.00**
• **CGC:** 1 graded, best 9.2

4 ❑ Nov 1952 Cover: 0.10 **NM** value: **200.00**
• **CGC:** 4 graded, best 9.4

5 ❑ Dec 1952 Cover: 0.10 **NM** value: **200.00**
• **CGC:** 1 graded, best 9.2

6 ❑ Jan 1953 Cover: 0.10 **NM** value: **150.00**

7 ❑ Mar 1953 Cover: 0.10 **NM** value: **150.00**
• **CGC:** 2 graded, best 8.0

STRANGE WEATHER LATELY — Metaphrog

1 ❑ 1997 Cover: 3.50 **NM** value: **Cover or less**
2 ❑ Dec 1997 Cover: 3.50 **NM** value: **Cover or less**
3 ❑ Feb 1998 Cover: 3.50 **NM** value: **Cover or less**
4 ❑ 1998 Cover: 3.50 **NM** value: **Cover or less**
5 ❑ Jun 1998 Cover: 3.50 **NM** value: **Cover or less**
6 ❑ Aug 1998 Cover: 3.50 **NM** value: **Cover or less**
7 ❑ Oct 1998 Cover: 3.00 **NM** value: **Cover or less**
8 ❑ 1999 Cover: 3.00 **NM** value: **Cover or less**
9 ❑ 1999 Cover: 3.00 **NM** value: **Cover or less**
10 ❑ May 1999 Cover: 3.50 **NM** value: **Cover or less**
Bk 1 ❑ Cover: 9.95 **NM** value: **Cover or less**
• Trade Paperback. • collects #1-5
Bk 2 ❑ Cover: 9.95 **NM** value: **Cover or less**

STRANGE WINK (JOHN BOLTON'S...) — Dark Horse

1 ❑ Mar 1998, b&w Cover: 2.95 **NM** value: **Cover or less**
A: John Bolton **W:** John Bolton; Christina Rossetti; Goethe; Graham Marks

2 ❑ Apr 1998, b&w Cover: 2.95 **NM** value: **Cover or less**
A: John Bolton **W:** John Bolton; Graham Marks; Nicholas Vince

3 ❑ May 1998, b&w Cover: 2.95 **NM** value: **Cover or less**
A: John Bolton **W:** John Bolton; Ann Nocenti; Graham Marks

STRANGE WORLD OF YOUR DREAMS — Prize

1 ❑ Aug 1952 Cover: 0.10 **NM** value: **500.00**
• **CGC:** 1 graded, best 9.6

2 ❑ Sep 1952 Cover: 0.10 **NM** value: **400.00**
• **CGC:** 1 graded, best 8.5

3 ❑ Nov 1952 Cover: 0.10 **NM** value: **400.00**
• **CGC:** 1 graded, best 9.0

4 ❑ Jan 1953 Cover: 0.10 **NM** value: **300.00**

STRANGE WORLDS (ATLAS) — Atlas

1 ❑ Dec 1958 Cover: 0.10 **NM** value: **700.00**
• **CGC:** 3 graded, best 6.0
2 ❑ Feb 1959 Cover: 0.10 **NM** value: **400.00**
3 ❑ Apr 1959 Cover: 0.10 **NM** value: **300.00**
4 ❑ Jun 1959 Cover: 0.10 **NM** value: **300.00**
5 ❑ Aug 1959 Cover: 0.10 **NM** value: **250.00**

STRANGE WORLDS (AVON) — Avon

18 ❑ Dec 1954 Cover: 0.10 **NM** value: **200.00**
📖 Attack on Planet Mars **A:** Joe Kubert
19 ❑ Feb 1955 Cover: 0.10 **NM** value: **200.00**
20 ❑ Apr 1955 Cover: 0.10 **NM** value: **100.00**
21 ❑ Jun 1955 Cover: 0.10 **NM** value: **100.00**
22 ❑ Sep 1955 Cover: 0.10 **NM** value: **100.00**

STRANGE WORLDS (ETERNITY) — Eternity

1 ❑ b&w Cover: 3.95 **NM** value: **Cover or less**

STRANGE WORLDS (NORTH COAST) — North Coast Studios

1 ❑ b&w Cover: 4.00 **NM** value: **Cover or less**
cardstock cover. • magazine.

STRANGLING DESDEMONA — Ningen Manga

1 ❑ b&w Cover: 2.95 **NM** value: **Cover or less**

STRAPPED (DERRECK WAYNE JACKSON'S...) — Gothic Images

1 ❑ Cover: 2.00 **NM** value: **Cover or less**
📖 The Confrontation Factor, Part 1 **A:** Derreck Wayne Jackson **W:** Derreck Wayne Jackson

2 ❑ Cover: 2.00 **NM** value: **Cover or less**
📖 The Confrontation Factor, Part 2 **A:** Derreck Wayne Jackson **W:** Derreck Wayne Jackson

3 ❑ Cover: 2.00 **NM** value: **Cover or less**
📖 The Confrontation Factor, Part 3 **A:** Derreck Wayne Jackson **W:** Derreck Wayne Jackson

4 ❑ Cover: 2.00 **NM** value: **Cover or less**
📖 The Confrontation Factor, Part 4 **A:** Derreck Wayne Jackson **W:** Derreck Wayne Jackson

STRATA — Renegade

1 ❑ Jan 1986, b&w Cover: 2.00 **NM** value: **Cover or less**
2 ❑ 1986b&w Cover: 1.70 **NM** value: **2.00**
3 ❑ 1986 Cover: 2.00 **NM** value: **Cover or less**
4 ❑ 1986 Cover: 2.00 **NM** value: **Cover or less**
5 ❑ Cover: 2.00 **NM** value: **Cover or less**

STRATONAUT — Nightwynd

1 ❑ b&w Cover: 2.50 **NM** value: **Cover or less**
2 ❑ b&w Cover: 2.50 **NM** value: **Cover or less**
3 ❑ b&w Cover: 2.50 **NM** value: **Cover or less**
4 ❑ b&w Cover: 2.50 **NM** value: **Cover or less**

STRATOSFEAR — Caliber

1 ❑ Cover: 2.95 **NM** value: **Cover or less**
A: Gary Crutchley; Shane Oakley **W:** Paul Birch

CGC-graded: Multiply prices above by **33 for 9.9 M** • **16 for 9.8 NM/M** • **7 for 9.6 NM+** • **5 for 9.4 NM** • **2.5 for 9.2 NM-** • **1.5 for 9.0 VF/NM**

STRAWBERRY SHORTCAKE **Marvel / Star**

Strawberry Shortcake, the cute little heroine of this children's series, lives in the wondrous Strawberryland, where she and her friends play and never grow up. It's a charming place, if a little, er, baking-oriented. Strawberry's friends include Blueberry Muffin, Raspberry, Huckleberry, Raisin Cane, and a cat called Custard. Even the villains seem to hail from the kitchen: Sour Grapes and the Peculiar Purple Pieman of Porcupine Peak.

Inspired by the popular toy line and Saturday morning children's TV show, Strawberry Shortcake became the focus of a 2001 debate over back-issue sales when a prominent dealer explained he could get $10 apiece for issues — simply because he's the only retailer in the country who bothers to stock it. There's good logic there, but we've still found that these issues are plentiful and cheap if you care enough to dig a little.

1 ❑ Apr 1985 Cover: 0.65 **NM** value: **1.00**
• **CGC:** 2 graded, best 9.4
📖 The Great Pie Baking Contest; Secret Land **A:** Howie Post **W:** Stan Kay

2 ❑ Jun 1985 Cover: 0.65 **NM** value: **1.00**
Circ: CapCity orders: **2,500**
📖 Goblin' Goblin; Bigger and Bigger **A:** Howie Post **W:** Stan Kay

3 ❑ Aug 1985 Cover: 0.65 **NM** value: **1.00**
Circ: CapCity orders: **2,800**
A: Howie Post **W:** Stan Kay

4 ❑ Oct 1985 Cover: 0.65 **NM** value: **1.00**
Circ: CapCity orders: **2,300**
A: Howie Post **W:** Stan Kay

5 ❑ Dec 1985 Cover: 0.65 **NM** value: **1.00**
Circ: CapCity orders: **1,800**
📖 Who's Your Really, Really Best Friend? **A:** Howie Post **W:** Stan Kay

6 ❑ Feb 1986 Cover: 0.65 **NM** value: **1.00**
Circ: CapCity orders: **1,700**
A: Howie Post **W:** Stan Kay

7 ❑ Apr 1986 Cover: 0.65 **NM** value: **1.00**
Circ: CapCity orders: **1,500**
A: Howie Post **W:** Stan Kay

STRAW MEN **All American**

1 ❑ 1989b&w Cover: 1.95 **NM** value: **Cover or less**
2 ❑ 1989b&w Cover: 1.95 **NM** value: **Cover or less**
Circ: CapCity orders: **1,500**
3 ❑ 1989b&w Cover: 1.95 **NM** value: **Cover or less**
4 ❑ Jan 1990, b&w Cover: 1.95 **NM** value: **Cover or less**
📖 The New Geneticists **A:** Rob Davis **W:** Michale Vance; R.A. Jones
5 ❑ 1990b&w Cover: 1.95 **NM** value: **Cover or less**
6 ❑ 1990b&w Cover: 1.95 **NM** value: **Cover or less**
7 ❑ 1990b&w Cover: 1.95 **NM** value: **Cover or less**
8 ❑ 1990b&w Cover: 1.95 **NM** value: **Cover or less**

STRAY **Homage / Star**

1 ❑ Mar 2001 Cover: 5.95 **NM** value: **Cover or less**
Circ: Diamd. preorders: **8,052**
A: Adam Pollina **W:** Scott Lobdell; Jimmy Palmiotti

STRAY BULLETS **El Capitan**

Stray Bullets kicks off at two o'clock in the morning, sometime in the summer of 1997. Two mob henchmen were driving to the woods to dump a body when their car blew a tire. The younger mook, a low IQ-type named Joey, was sent into the woods with the body while the older one, Frank, began changing the tire. Then the cop drove up.

Frank had almost talked his way out of the situation when the cop saw the bloodstains. Before the cop could act, Joey appeared and shot him. That's when the evening began to get truly out of hand. Before sunrise, the car would be stuffed with bodies, the pair would blow up a diner, and Joey would declare his undying love for a corpse.

David Lapham hails from Valiant (where he helped create Rai, Harbinger and Shadowman) and Defiant (where he co-created Warriors of Plasm). In Stray Bullets, he brings readers a memorable crime saga in classic pulp style.

1 ❑ 1995 Cover: 2.95 **NM** value: **5.00**
• **CGC:** 3 graded, best 9.4
📖 The Look Of Love **A:** David Lapham **W:** David Lapham
1-2 ❑ Cover: 2.95 **NM** value: **3.00**
1-3 ❑ Cover: 2.95 **NM** value: **3.00**
1-4 ❑ Cover: 2.95 **NM** value: **3.00**
2 ❑ Apr 1995 Cover: 2.95 **NM** value: **4.00**
📖 Victimology **A:** David Lapham **W:** David Lapham
2-2 ❑ Cover: 2.95 **NM** value: **3.00**
2-3 ❑ Cover: 2.95 **NM** value: **3.00**
2-4 ❑ Cover: 2.95 **NM** value: **3.00**
3 ❑ May 1995 Cover: 2.95 **NM** value: **3.00**
📖 The Party **A:** David Lapham **W:** David Lapham
3-2 ❑ Cover: 2.95 **NM** value: **3.00**

4 ❑ 1995 Cover: 2.95 **NM** value: **3.00**
Circ: CapCity orders: **2,330**
• indicia contains information for issue #3 **A:** David Lapham **W:** David Lapham

5 ❑ 1995 Cover: 2.95 **NM** value: **3.00**
Circ: CapCity orders: **3,325**
• indicia contains information for issue #4 **A:** David Lapham **W:** David Lapham

6 ❑ Sep 1995 Cover: 2.95 **NM** value: **3.00**
Circ: CapCity orders: **3,645**
📖 How I Spent My Summer Vacation or The Rocket Ship Of Life Is Goin My Way or Three Cheers For God-He's Certainly A Swell Guy or Home Is Where Mom Lives or I Don't Care, As Long As I Gots Me Space Munchies **A:** David Lapham **W:** David Lapham

7 ❑ Nov 1995 Cover: 2.95 **NM** value: **3.00**
A: David Lapham **W:** David Lapham
8 ❑ Feb 1996 Cover: 2.95 **NM** value: **3.00**
A: David Lapham **W:** David Lapham
9 ❑ May 1996 Cover: 2.95 **NM** value: **3.00**
A: David Lapham **W:** David Lapham
10 ❑ Aug 1996 Cover: 2.95 **NM** value: **3.00**
A: David Lapham **W:** David Lapham
11 ❑ Oct 1996 Cover: 2.95 **NM** value: **Cover or less**
Circ: Diamd. preorders: **18,154**
A: David Lapham **W:** David Lapham
12 ❑ Jan 1997 Cover: 2.95 **NM** value: **Cover or less**
Circ: Diamd. preorders: **17,119**
A: David Lapham **W:** David Lapham
13 ❑ Apr 1997 Cover: 2.95 **NM** value: **Cover or less**
Circ: Diamd. preorders: **16,458**
A: David Lapham **W:** David Lapham
14 ❑ Jun 1997 Cover: 2.95 **NM** value: **Cover or less**
Circ: Diamd. preorders: **15,354**
A: David Lapham **W:** David Lapham
15 ❑ Jul 1998 Cover: 2.95 **NM** value: **Cover or less**
Circ: Diamd. preorders: **12,134**
📖 Sex and Violence, part 1 **A:** David Lapham **W:** David Lapham
16 ❑ Aug 1998 Cover: 2.95 **NM** value: **Cover or less**
Circ: Diamd. preorders: **11,692**
📖 Two-Week Vacation **A:** David Lapham **W:** David Lapham
17 ❑ Nov 1998 Cover: 2.95 **NM** value: **Cover or less**
Circ: Diamd. preorders: **11,096**
📖 While Ricky Fish Was Sleeping… **A:** David Lapham **W:** David Lapham
18 ❑ Feb 1999 Cover: 2.95 **NM** value: **Cover or less**
Circ: Diamd. preorders: **11,251**
A: David Lapham **W:** David Lapham
19 ❑ Apr 1999 Cover: 2.95 **NM** value: **Cover or less**
Circ: Diamd. preorders: **10,740**
A: David Lapham **W:** David Lapham
20 ❑ Jul 1999 Cover: 2.95 **NM** value: **Cover or less**
Circ: Diamd. preorders: **10,314**
A: David Lapham **W:** David Lapham
Bk 1/HC❑ Cover: 24.50 **NM** value: **24.95**
Innocence of Nihilism hardcover. • Reprints Stray Bullets #1-7 **A:** David Lapham **W:** David Lapham
Bk 1/HC-2❑ Cover: 29.95 **NM** value: **Cover or less**

STRAY CATS **Twilight Twins**

1 ❑ Jan 1999, b&w Cover: 2.50 **NM** value: **Cover or less**
Circ: Diamd. preorders: **2,272**
A: Lillian Mousli **W:** Lillian Mousli

STRAY TOASTERS **Marvel / Epic**

A demon prepares to take a vacation on Earth and his children implore him to bring back a present-something really slimy and awful. The demon has the perfect idea: he'll bring them a lawyer...

A demented child will eat only jam, nothing but jam. When his parents die horribly, he realizes that the toaster will deliver no more jam sandwiches...

An alcoholic doctor, dangerously insane, lives in a world where he is torn at by robotic birds who inject him with hallucinogens from their talons...

This is the mad, brilliant world of Bill Sienkiewicz. This is the world of the stray toasters.

1 ❑ Cover: 3.50 **NM** value: **4.50**
Circ: CapCity orders: **14,700**
A: Bill Sienkiewicz **W:** Bill Sienkiewicz
2 ❑ Cover: 3.50 **NM** value: **4.50**
Circ: CapCity orders: **12,650**
A: Bill Sienkiewicz **W:** Bill Sienkiewicz
3 ❑ Cover: 3.50 **NM** value: **4.50**
Circ: CapCity orders: **11,900**
📖 Sicker Here…Than Over There **A:** Bill Sienkiewicz **W:** Bill Sienkiewicz
4 ❑ Cover: 3.50 **NM** value: **4.50**
Circ: CapCity orders: **12,450**
A: Bill Sienkiewicz **W:** Bill Sienkiewicz
Bk 1❑ **NM** value: **12.95**
Circ: CapCity orders: **1,700**
• Collects series **A:** Bill Sienkiewicz **W:** Bill Sienkiewicz

STREAK OF CHALK **NBM**

1 ❑ Cover: 15.95 **NM** value: **Cover or less**

STREET FIGHTER II: THE ANIMATED MOVIE **Viz**

1 ❑ Cover: 2.95 **NM** value: **Cover or less**
A: Takayuki Sakai **W:** Takayuki Sakai
2 ❑ Cover: 2.95 **NM** value: **Cover or less**
A: Takayuki Sakai **W:** Takayuki Sakai
3 ❑ Cover: 2.95 **NM** value: **Cover or less**
A: Takayuki Sakai **W:** Takayuki Sakai
4 ❑ Cover: 2.95 **NM** value: **Cover or less**
A: Takayuki Sakai **W:** Takayuki Sakai
5 ❑ Cover: 2.95 **NM** value: **Cover or less**
A: Takayuki Sakai **W:** Takayuki Sakai

STREET FIGHTER II (TOKUMA SHOTEN) **Tokuma Shoten**

1 ❑ Apr 1994 Cover: 2.95 **NM** value: **Cover or less**

STREET FIGHTER II (VIZ) **Viz**

1 ❑ Apr 1994 Cover: 2.95 **NM** value: **Cover or less**
Circ: CapCity orders: **16,075**
A: Masaomi Kanzaki **W:** Masaomi Kanzaki
2 ❑ May 1994 Cover: 2.95 **NM** value: **Cover or less**
Circ: CapCity orders: **11,025**
A: Masaomi Kanzaki **W:** Masaomi Kanzaki
3 ❑ Jun 1994 Cover: 2.95 **NM** value: **Cover or less**
Circ: CapCity orders: **11,075**
A: Masaomi Kanzaki **W:** Masaomi Kanzaki
4 ❑ Jul 1994 Cover: 2.95 **NM** value: **Cover or less**
Circ: CapCity orders: **9,900**
A: Masaomi Kanzaki **W:** Masaomi Kanzaki
5 ❑ Aug 1994 Cover: 2.95 **NM** value: **Cover or less**
Circ: CapCity orders: **9,175**
A: Masaomi Kanzaki **W:** Masaomi Kanzaki
6 ❑ Sep 1994 Cover: 2.95 **NM** value: **Cover or less**
Circ: CapCity orders: **8,975**
A: Masaomi Kanzaki **W:** Masaomi Kanzaki
7 ❑ Oct 1994 Cover: 2.95 **NM** value: **Cover or less**
Circ: CapCity orders: **8,875**
A: Masaomi Kanzaki **W:** Masaomi Kanzaki
8 ❑ Nov 1994 Cover: 2.95 **NM** value: **Cover or less**
Circ: CapCity orders: **8,250**
A: Masaomi Kanzaki **W:** Masaomi Kanzaki

STREET FIGHTER (MALIBU) **Malibu**

1 ❑ Sep 1993 Cover: 2.95 **NM** value: **Cover or less**
Circ: CapCity orders: **23,200**
📖 Battle Scars **A:** Don Hillsman **W:** Len Strazewski
1/GO❑Sep 1993 Cover: 15.00 **NM** value: **Cover or less**
• gold foil edition. 📖 Battle Scars **A:** Don Hillsman **W:** Len Strazewski
2 ❑ Oct 1993 Cover: 2.95 **NM** value: **Cover or less**
Circ: CapCity orders: **11,700**
A: Don Hillsman **W:** Len Strazewski
2/GO❑Oct 1993 Cover: 15.00 **NM** value: **Cover or less**
• gold foil edition. **A:** Don Hillsman **W:** Len Strazewski
3 ❑ Nov 1993 Cover: 2.95 **NM** value: **Cover or less**
Circ: CapCity orders: **10,800**
A: Don Hillsman **W:** Len Strazewski
3/GO❑Nov 1993 Cover: 15.00 **NM** value: **Cover or less**
• gold foil edition. **A:** Don Hillsman **W:** Len Strazewski

STREETFIGHTER (OCEAN) **Ocean**

1 ❑ Aug 1986 Cover: 1.75 **NM** value: **2.00**
Circ: CapCity orders: **4,800**
📖 Flame in the Night **A:** Gary Kato **W:** Ron Fortier ★ 1st Appearance of Streetfighter.
2 ❑ Nov 1986 Cover: 1.75 **NM** value: **2.00**
Circ: CapCity orders: **3,825**
📖 The Sacrifice **A:** Gary Kato **W:** Ron Fortier ★ 2nd Appearance of Streetfighter. ★ 2nd Appearance of Streetfighter.
3 ❑ Feb 1987 Cover: 1.75 **NM** value: **2.00**
Circ: CapCity orders: **1,650**
A: Gary Kato **W:** Ron Fortier
4 ❑ May 1987 Cover: 1.75 **NM** value: **2.00**
A: Gary Kato **W:** Ron Fortier

STREET FIGHTER: THE BATTLE FOR SHADALOO **DC**

1 ❑ Cover: 3.95 **NM** value: **Cover or less**
No issue number. • polybagged with trading card and temporary tattoos

STREET HEROES 2005 **Eternity**

1 ❑ Jan 1989, b&w Cover: 1.95 **NM** value: **Cover or less**
📖 Night Shift **A:** Chris Jones **W:** Steve Jones
2 ❑ Feb 1989, b&w Cover: 1.95 **NM** value: **Cover or less**
3 ❑ Mar 1989, b&w Cover: 1.95 **NM** value: **Cover or less**

STREET MUSIC **Fantagraphics**

1 ❑ b&w Cover: 2.95 **NM** value: **Cover or less**
2 ❑ b&w Cover: 2.95 **NM** value: **Cover or less**
3 ❑ b&w Cover: 2.95 **NM** value: **Cover or less**
4 ❑ b&w Cover: 2.95 **NM** value: **Cover or less**
5 ❑ b&w Cover: 2.95 **NM** value: **Cover or less**
6 ❑ b&w Cover: 2.95 **NM** value: **Cover or less**

STREET POET RAY (BLACKTHORNE) **Blackthorne**

1 ❑ Apr 1989, b&w Cover: 2.00 **NM** value: **Cover or less**
W: Michael Redmond
2 ❑ b&w Cover: 2.00 **NM** value: **Cover or less**

The prices seen above do not represent the highest possible prices seen in online auctions, but rather the prices we have seen these issues reliably fetch in a variety of environments (storefront retail, mail order, auction and convention).

Other grades: Multiply prices above by **1.5 for Mint • 2/3 for Very Fine • 1/3 for Fine • 1/5 for Very Good • 1/8 for Good**

STREET POET RAY (MARVEL) — Marvel

Michael Redmond has a friend, a street poet named Ray, who makes his living telling short poems about life. Ray's concerns range from supporting the Red Cross to the plight of working mothers to people who burn flags. He tells it like he sees it, and each day, he has a new poem about it.

Redmond worked with Ray to bring his poetic works to comic form. The result is this obscure but enjoyable four-issue set of graphic novels. The truly devoted are also given a 900 number in the back where they can call to hear the "rap of the day" — direct from Ray.

Why is this series obscure? Not for anything good: this was reputed to have been Marvel's single lowest circulation comic book in its history, with a print run on the last issue of around 3,500.

Bk 1❑ ca. 1990, b&w Cover: 2.95 **NM** value: **Cover or less**
cardstock cover. 📖 Street Players **A:** Junko Hosizawa **W:** Michael Redmond
Bk 2❑ ca. 1990, b&w Cover: 2.95 **NM** value: **Cover or less**
cardstock cover. **W:** Michael Redmond
Bk 3❑ ca. 1990, b&w Cover: 2.95 **NM** value: **Cover or less**
cardstock cover. **W:** Michael Redmond
Bk 4❑ ca. 1990, b&w Cover: 2.95 **NM** value: **Cover or less**
cardstock cover. **W:** Michael Redmond

STREETS — DC

1 ❑ ca. 1993 Cover: 4.95 **NM** value: **Cover or less**
Circ: CapCity orders: **4,750**
📖 Tenderloin **A:** John Estes **W:** James D. Hudnall
2 ❑ ca. 1993 Cover: 4.95 **NM** value: **Cover or less**
Circ: CapCity orders: **3,700**
W: James D. Hudnall
3 ❑ ca. 1993 Cover: 4.95 **NM** value: **Cover or less**
Circ: CapCity orders: **3,550**
W: James D. Hudnall

STREET SHARKS — Archie

1 ❑ May 1996 Cover: 1.50 **NM** value: **Cover or less**
3 ❑ Aug 1996 Cover: 1.50 **NM** value: **Cover or less**

STREET SHARKS (MINI-SERIES) — Archie

1 ❑ Jan 1996 Cover: 1.50 **NM** value: **Cover or less**
• based on toy line and animated series ★ 1st Appearance of The Street Sharks, Doctor Pirahnoid.
2 ❑ Feb 1996 Cover: 1.50 **NM** value: **Cover or less**
3 ❑ Mar 1996 Cover: 1.50 **NM** value: **Cover or less**
📖 Sharkstorm **A:** Nelson Ortega **W:** Martha Moran

STREET WOLF — Blackthorne

1 ❑ Jul 1986, b&w Cover: 2.00 **NM** value: **Cover or less**
📖 When Angels Cry **A:** Dennis Francis **W:** Mark Wayne Harris
2 ❑ Sep 1986, b&w Cover: 2.00 **NM** value: **Cover or less**
📖 Black Rain **A:** Dennis Francis **W:** Mark Wayne Harris
3 ❑ b&w Cover: 2.00 **NM** value: **Cover or less**
A: Dennis Francis **W:** Mark Wayne Harris

STRICTLY INDEPENDENT! — One Shot Press

1 ❑ Jan 1996, b&w Cover: 2.50 **NM** value: **Cover or less**
2 ❑ b&w Cover: 2.50 **NM** value: **Cover or less**
• Flip-book. • Flip Book, Elvira, Killer Clowns

STRICTLY PRIVATE — Eastern Color

1 ❑ ca. 1942 Cover: 0.10 **NM** value: **150.00**
2 ❑ ca. 1942 Cover: 0.10 **NM** value: **150.00**

STRIKE! — Eclipse

1 ❑ Aug 1987 Cover: 1.75 **NM** value: **Cover or less**
Circ: CapCity orders: **6,425**
📖 The Inheritance **A:** Tom Lyle **W:** Chuck Dixon ★ Origin of Sgt. Strike, Strike. ★ 1st Appearance of Strike.
2 ❑ Sep 1987 Cover: 1.75 **NM** value: **Cover or less**
Circ: CapCity orders: **4,550**
★ Origin of Sgt. Strike.
3 ❑ Oct 1987 Cover: 1.75 **NM** value: **Cover or less**
Circ: CapCity orders: **4,075**
★ Origin of Sgt. Strike.
4 ❑ Nov 1987 Cover: 1.75 **NM** value: **Cover or less**
Circ: CapCity orders: **3,925**
★ Origin of Sgt. Strike.
5 ❑ Dec 1987 Cover: 1.75 **NM** value: **Cover or less**
Circ: CapCity orders: **3,575**
★ Origin of Sgt. Strike.
6 ❑ Feb 1988 Cover: 1.75 **NM** value: **Cover or less**
Circ: CapCity orders: **3,200**
final issue. ★ Origin of Sgt. Strike.

STRIKEBACK! (IMAGE) — Image

1 ❑ Jan 1996 Cover: 2.50 **NM** value: **Cover or less**
Reprints Strikeback (Malibu) #1 with new cover. **A:** Kevin Maguire **W:** Jonathan Peterson
2 ❑ Feb 1996 Cover: 2.50 **NM** value: **Cover or less**
Reprints Strikeback (Malibu) #2 with new cover. **A:** Kevin Maguire **W:** Jonathan Peterson
3 ❑ Mar 1996 Cover: 2.50 **NM** value: **Cover or less**
Reprints Strikeback (Malibu) #3 with new cover. **A:** Kevin Maguire **W:** Jonathan Peterson
4 ❑ Apr 1996 Cover: 2.50 **NM** value: **Cover or less**
A: Kevin Maguire **W:** Jonathan Peterson
5 ❑ Jun 1996 Cover: 2.50 **NM** value: **Cover or less**
final issue. **A:** Kevin Maguire **W:** Jonathan Peterson
6 ❑ 1996 Cover: 2.50 **NM** value: **Cover or less**
A: Kevin Maguire **W:** Jonathan Peterson

STRIKEBACK! (MALIBU) — Malibu / Bravura

1 ❑ Oct 1994 Cover: 2.95 **NM** value: **Cover or less**
Circ: CapCity orders: **12,125**
A: Kevin Maguire **W:** Jonathan Peterson
2 ❑ Nov 1994 Cover: 2.95 **NM** value: **Cover or less**
Circ: CapCity orders: **8,025**
A: Kevin Maguire **W:** Jonathan Peterson
3 ❑ Dec 1994 Cover: 2.95 **NM** value: **Cover or less**
Circ: CapCity orders: **6,450**
• Final issue; series announced as six issues, but title cancelled after Marvel's purchase of Malibu **A:** Kevin Maguire **W:** Jonathan Peterson

STRIKE FORCE AMERICA — Comico

1 ❑ Aug 1992 Cover: 2.50 **NM** value: **Cover or less**
Circ: CapCity orders: **8,600**
📖 Black Dog **A:** Scott Clark **W:** David de Vries

STRIKE FORCE LEGACY — Comico

1 ❑ Cover: 3.95 **NM** value: **Cover or less**
A: Mike Leeke **W:** Jack Herman; Bill Willingham

STRIKEFORCE: MORITURI — Marvel

Earth had been invaded by the malevolent alien Horde. Entire cities had been destroyed, and countless people had been enslaved by these vicious raiders. Even the most advanced armaments Earth had to offer were no match for alien technology.

Then a scientist, Dr. Kimmo Tuolema, discovered the Morituri process. This process replaced a subject's metabolism with an entirely new one. As a result the subject gained superhuman abilities, making them powerful soldiers in Earth's war for freedom. The only problem was that the new metabolism was inherently incompatible with a human body, killing the subjects within a year. The Morituri process made life worth living for many who would receive it, but it was also a death sentence.

This imaginative series featured the first work by artist Whilce Portacio.

1 ❑ Dec 1986 Cover: 0.75 **NM** value: **2.00**
Circ: CapCity orders: **33,700** • **CGC:** 1 graded, best 9.6
📖 We Who Are About To Die • Whilce Portacio's 1st pro work **A:** Whilce Portacio; Brent Anderson **W:** Peter B. Gillis ★ 1st Appearance of Strikeforce: Morituri.
2 ❑ Jan 1987 Cover: 0.75 **NM** value: **1.50**
Circ: CapCity orders: **22,900**
A: Brent Anderson
3 ❑ Feb 1987 Cover: 0.75 **NM** value: **1.50**
Circ: CapCity orders: **20,200**
A: Brent Anderson
4 ❑ Mar 1987 Cover: 0.75 **NM** value: **1.75**
Circ: CapCity orders: **18,500**
A: Whilce Portacio; Brent Anderson
5 ❑ Apr 1987 Cover: 0.75 **NM** value: **1.25**
Circ: CapCity orders: **18,200**
A: Brent Anderson
6 ❑ May 1987 Cover: 0.75 **NM** value: **1.25**
Circ: CapCity orders: **16,100**
A: Brent Anderson
7 ❑ Jun 1987 Cover: 0.75 **NM** value: **1.25**
Circ: CapCity orders: **15,100**
A: Brent Anderson
8 ❑ Jul 1987 Cover: 0.75 **NM** value: **1.25**
Circ: CapCity orders: **14,200**
A: Brent Anderson
9 ❑ Aug 1987 Cover: 0.75 **NM** value: **1.25**
Circ: CapCity orders: **15,300**
A: Brent Anderson
10 ❑ Sep 1987 Cover: 0.75 **NM** value: **1.25**
Circ: CapCity orders: **15,000**
• 1st full story by Whilce Portacio **A:** Whilce Portacio
11 ❑ Oct 1987 Cover: 0.75 **NM** value: **1.25**
Circ: CapCity orders: **14,500**
A: Brent Anderson
12 ❑ Nov 1987 Cover: 0.75 **NM** value: **1.25**
Circ: CapCity orders: **15,100**
A: Brent Anderson
13 ❑ Dec 1987 Cover: 1.25 **NM** value: **1.50**
Circ: CapCity orders: **14,600**
• Giant-size. **A:** Brent Anderson
14 ❑ Jan 1988 Cover: 0.75 **NM** value: **1.25**
Circ: CapCity orders: **14,000**
A: Brent Anderson
15 ❑ Feb 1988 Cover: 1.00 **NM** value: **1.25**
Circ: CapCity orders: **14,100**
A: Brent Anderson
16 ❑ Mar 1988 Cover: 1.00 **NM** value: **1.25**
Circ: CapCity orders: **14,250**
A: Whilce Portacio
17 ❑ Apr 1988 Cover: 1.00 **NM** value: **1.25**
Circ: CapCity orders: **13,950**
A: Whilce Portacio
18 ❑ May 1988 Cover: 1.00 **NM** value: **1.25**
Circ: CapCity orders: **13,600**
A: Brent Anderson
19 ❑ Jun 1988 Cover: 1.00 **NM** value: **1.25**
Circ: CapCity orders: **12,500**
A: Brent Anderson
20 ❑ Jul 1988 Cover: 1.00 **NM** value: **1.25**
Circ: CapCity orders: **12,000**
A: Brent Anderson
21 ❑ Sep 1988 Cover: 1.25 **NM** value: **Cover or less**
Circ: CapCity orders: **11,300**
22 ❑ Oct 1988 Cover: 1.25 **NM** value: **Cover or less**
Circ: CapCity orders: **11,000**
23 ❑ Nov 1988 Cover: 1.25 **NM** value: **Cover or less**
Circ: CapCity orders: **10,200**
24 ❑ Dec 1988 Cover: 1.50 **NM** value: **Cover or less**
Circ: CapCity orders: **9,800**
25 ❑ Jan 1989 Cover: 1.25 **NM** value: **1.50**
Circ: CapCity orders: **9,000**
26 ❑ Feb 1989 Cover: 1.50 **NM** value: **Cover or less**
Circ: CapCity orders: **8,500**
27 ❑ Mar 1989 Cover: 1.50 **NM** value: **Cover or less**
Circ: CapCity orders: **8,200**
28 ❑ Apr 1989 Cover: 1.50 **NM** value: **Cover or less**
Circ: CapCity orders: **8,200**
29 ❑ May 1989 Cover: 1.50 **NM** value: **Cover or less**
Circ: CapCity orders: **7,900**
30 ❑ Jun 1989 Cover: 1.50 **NM** value: **Cover or less**
Circ: CapCity orders: **7,700**
31 ❑ Jul 1989 Cover: 1.50 **NM** value: **Cover or less**
Circ: CapCity orders: **7,900**
final issue.

STRIKEFORCE: MORITURI: ELECTRIC UNDERTOW — Marvel

1 ❑ Dec 1989 Cover: 3.95 **NM** value: **Cover or less**
Circ: CapCity orders: **11,900**
📖 Street Moves • Strikeforce: Morituri **A:** Mark Bagley **W:** James D. Hudnall
2 ❑ Dec 1989 Cover: 3.95 **NM** value: **Cover or less**
Circ: CapCity orders: **8,850**
• Strikeforce: Morituri **A:** Mark Bagley **W:** James D. Hudnall
3 ❑ Jan 1990 Cover: 3.95 **NM** value: **Cover or less**
Circ: CapCity orders: **8,350**
• Strikeforce: Morituri **A:** Mark Bagley **W:** James D. Hudnall
4 ❑ Feb 1990 Cover: 3.95 **NM** value: **Cover or less**
Circ: CapCity orders: **7,200**
• Strikeforce: Morituri **A:** Mark Bagley **W:** James D. Hudnall
5 ❑ Mar 1990 Cover: 3.95 **NM** value: **Cover or less**
Circ: CapCity orders: **6,850**
📖 The Battle • Strikeforce: Morituri **A:** Mark Bagley **W:** James D. Hudnall

STRIKER — Viz

1 ❑ b&w Cover: 2.75 **NM** value: **Cover or less**
Circ: CapCity orders: **4,625**
📖 Overture **A:** Ryoji Minagawa **W:** Hiroshi Takashige
2 ❑ b&w Cover: 2.75 **NM** value: **Cover or less**
A: Ryoji Minagawa **W:** Hiroshi Takashige
3 ❑ b&w Cover: 2.75 **NM** value: **Cover or less**
Circ: CapCity orders: **2,900**
A: Ryoji Minagawa **W:** Hiroshi Takashige
4 ❑ b&w Cover: 2.75 **NM** value: **Cover or less**
A: Ryoji Minagawa **W:** Hiroshi Takashige
Bk 1❑ Apr 1998 Cover: 16.95 **NM** value: **Cover or less**
• The Armored Warrior; Collects Striker mini-series **A:** Ryoji Minagawa **W:** Hiroshi Takashige
Bk 1-2❑ Cover: 16.95 **NM** value: **Cover or less**

STRIKER: SECRET OF THE BERSERKER — Viz

1 ❑ b&w Cover: 2.75 **NM** value: **Cover or less**
Circ: CapCity orders: **3,025**
A: Ryoji Minagawa **W:** Hiroshi Takashige
2 ❑ b&w Cover: 2.75 **NM** value: **Cover or less**
Circ: CapCity orders: **2,450**
3 ❑ b&w Cover: 2.75 **NM** value: **Cover or less**
Circ: CapCity orders: **2,350**
4 ❑ b&w Cover: 2.75 **NM** value: **Cover or less**
Circ: CapCity orders: **2,375**

STRIKER: THE FOREST OF NO RETURN — Viz

Bk 1❑ Jun 1998 Cover: 15.95 **NM** value: **Cover or less**

STRIKER VS. THE THIRD REICH — Viz

Bk 1❑ Feb 1999 Cover: 15.95 **NM** value: **Cover or less**

STRIKE! VERSUS SGT. STRIKE SPECIAL — Eclipse

1 ❑ May 1988 Cover: 1.95 **NM** value: **Cover or less**
Circ: CapCity orders: **3,925**
📖 The Man **A:** Tom Lyle **W:** Chuck Dixon

STRIPPED — Fantagraphics

Bk 1❑ May 1995, b&w Cover: 9.95 **NM** value: **Cover or less**
No issue number. • unauthorized autobiography of Peter Kuper

STRIPPERS AND SEX QUEENS OF THE EXOTIC WORLD — Fantagraphics

All issues are adults only.

1 ❑ Cover: 3.95 **NM** value: **Cover or less**
2 ❑ Cover: 3.95 **NM** value: **Cover or less**
3 ❑ Jun 1994, b&w Cover: 3.95 **NM** value: **Cover or less**
cardstock cover.
4 ❑ Oct 1994, b&w Cover: 3.95 **NM** value: **Cover or less**
final issue.

STRIPS — Rip Off

All issues are adults only.

1 ❑ Dec 1989, b&w Cover: 2.50 **NM** value: **Cover or less**
2 ❑ Feb 1990, b&w Cover: 2.50 **NM** value: **Cover or less**
3 ❑ Apr 1990, b&w Cover: 2.50 **NM** value: **Cover or less**
4 ❑ Jun 1990, b&w Cover: 2.50 **NM** value: **Cover or less**
5 ❑ Nov 1990, b&w Cover: 2.50 **NM** value: **Cover or less**

6 ❑ Dec 1990, b&w Cover: 2.50 **NM** value: **Cover or less**
7 ❑ Feb 1991, b&w Cover: 2.50 **NM** value: **Cover or less**
8 ❑ Mar 1991, b&w Cover: 2.50 **NM** value: **Cover or less**
9 ❑ Jun 1991, b&w Cover: 2.50 **NM** value: **Cover or less**
• series goes on hiatus
10 ❑ b&w Cover: 2.95 **NM** value: **Cover or less**
wraparound cover. • series returns (1997)
11 ❑ b&w Cover: 2.95 **NM** value: **Cover or less**
wraparound cover.
12 ❑ b&w Cover: 2.95 **NM** value: **Cover or less**
SE 1❑ Cover: 2.95 **NM** value: **Cover or less**
• reprints Rip Off issues with additional material
SE 2❑ Cover: 2.95 **NM** value: **Cover or less**
• reprints Rip Off issues with additional material

STRONG GUY REBORN — Marvel

1 ❑ Sep 1997 Cover: 2.99 **NM** value: **Cover or less**
Circ: Diamd. preorders: **35,595**
One-shot. • gatefold summary. 🕮 The Heart of the Matter **A:** Andy Smith **W:** Todd Dezago

STRONTIUM BITCH — Fleetway-Quality

1 ❑ Cover: 2.95 **NM** value: **Cover or less**
🕮 Island of the Damned Part 1-6 **A:** Carlos Ezquerra **W:** Alan Moore
2 ❑ Cover: 2.95 **NM** value: **Cover or less**
🕮 Island of the Damned Part 7-12 **A:** Carlos Ezquerra **W:** Alan Moore

STRONTIUM DOG — Fleetway-Quality

They are called Strontium Dogs: a whole race of people who have been mutated since birth by exposure to strontium-90. They face terrible discrimination throughout the galaxy, and, as a result, are allowed to work at only the very worst jobs. In their case, that meant becoming bounty hunters.

Johnny Alpha is the star of this series and a bounty hunter beyond compare. His particular mutation serves him well in his career, as his glowing eyes are able to see through solid objects. This ability comes in handy for planning and avoiding ambushes. He's accompanied on his missions by his steadfast friend, Wulf Sternhammer, a latter-day Viking and able warrior. Together, they lead a life of danger and adventure-even if the rest of the world thinks of their kind only as Strontium Dogs.

These stories are reprinted from 2000 A.D. in this North American edition.

1 ❑ 1997 Cover: 1.25 **NM** value: **1.50**
Circ: CapCity orders: **2,950**
🕮 Only The Best Survive **A:** Carlos Ezquerra **W:** John Wagner
2 ❑ 1997 Cover: 1.25 **NM** value: **Cover or less**
3 ❑ 1997 Cover: 1.25 **NM** value: **Cover or less**
Circ: CapCity orders: **2,200**
4 ❑ 1997 Cover: 1.25 **NM** value: **Cover or less**
Circ: CapCity orders: **1,925**
🕮 The Moses Incident, Part 1 **A:** Carlos Ezquerra **W:** Alan Grant
5 ❑ 1997 Cover: 1.25 **NM** value: **Cover or less**
Circ: CapCity orders: **1,825**
6 ❑ 1997 Cover: 1.25 **NM** value: **Cover or less**
Circ: CapCity orders: **1,700**
🕮 The Killing **A:** Carlos Ezquerra **W:** Alan Grant
7 ❑ 1988 Cover: 1.25 **NM** value: **Cover or less**
Circ: CapCity orders: **1,550**
🕮 Strontium Dog: The Killing; Strontium Dog: The Two-Faced Terror; Tharg's Future Shocks: Long Division
8 ❑ Feb 1988 Cover: 1.25 **NM** value: **Cover or less**
Circ: CapCity orders: **1,450**
9 ❑ Mar 1988 Cover: 1.25 **NM** value: **Cover or less**
Circ: CapCity orders: **1,375**
🕮 Strontium Dog: Outlaw; Tharg's Future Shocks: With a Bang **A:** Carlos Ezquerra **W:** Alan Grant
10 ❑ Apr 1988 Cover: 1.25 **NM** value: **Cover or less**
Circ: CapCity orders: **1,275**
🕮 Strontium Dog: Outlaw **A:** Carlos Ezquerra **W:** Alan Grant
11 ❑ 1988 Cover: 1.25 **NM** value: **Cover or less**
Circ: CapCity orders: **1,225**
🕮 Strontium Dog; Strontium Dog: The Slavers of Drule; Tharg's Future Shocks: The War with the Slobb!! **A:** Barry Kitson; Carlos Ezquerra **W:** Peter Milligan; Alan Grant
12 ❑ 1988 Cover: 1.25 **NM** value: **Cover or less**
Circ: CapCity orders: **1,225**
13 ❑ 1988 Cover: 1.50 **NM** value: **Cover or less**
Circ: CapCity orders: **1,150**
14 ❑ 1988 Cover: 1.50 **NM** value: **Cover or less**
Circ: CapCity orders: **1,150**
• double issue #14/15
15 ❑ 1988 Cover: 1.50 **NM** value: **Cover or less**
Circ: CapCity orders: **1,150**
16 ❑ 1988 Cover: 1.50 **NM** value: **Cover or less**
Circ: CapCity orders: **1,100**
• double issue #16/17
17 ❑ 1988 Cover: 1.50 **NM** value: **Cover or less**
Circ: CapCity orders: **1,075**
18 ❑ 1988 Cover: 1.50 **NM** value: **Cover or less**
Circ: CapCity orders: **1,075**
19 ❑ **NM** value: **1.50**
20 ❑ Dec 1988 Cover: 1.50 **NM** value: **Cover or less**
Circ: CapCity orders: **1,050**
21 ❑ Jan 1989 Cover: 1.50 **NM** value: **Cover or less**
Circ: CapCity orders: **1,075**
22 ❑ Feb 1989 Cover: 1.50 **NM** value: **Cover or less**
Circ: CapCity orders: **1,025**
23 ❑ Cover: 1.50 **NM** value: **Cover or less**
Circ: CapCity orders: **1,050**
24 ❑ Cover: 1.50 **NM** value: **Cover or less**
Circ: CapCity orders: **1,075**
25 ❑ Cover: 1.50 **NM** value: **Cover or less**
Circ: CapCity orders: **1,000**
26 ❑ Cover: 1.50 **NM** value: **Cover or less**
Circ: CapCity orders: **950**
27 ❑ Cover: 1.50 **NM** value: **Cover or less**
Circ: CapCity orders: **950**
28 ❑ Cover: 1.50 **NM** value: **Cover or less**
Circ: CapCity orders: **975**
29 ❑ Cover: 1.50 **NM** value: **Cover or less**
Circ: CapCity orders: **1,000**
SE 1❑ Cover: 1.50 **NM** value: **Cover or less**
Circ: CapCity orders: **4,150**
• Special Edition #1. 🕮 Strontium Dog: The Wolrogs; Grawks Bearing Gifts • Reprints from 2000 A.D. #87-94 **A:** Ian Gibson; Carlos Ezquerra **W:** Alan Moore; John Wagner

STRONTIUM DOG (MINI-SERIES) — Eagle

1 ❑ 1985 Cover: 1.25 **NM** value: **1.50**
Circ: CapCity orders: **6,025**
🕮 Strontium Dog: Portrait of a Mutant **A:** Carlos Ezquerra **W:** Alan Grant ★ Origin of Johnny Alpha.
2 ❑ 1985 Cover: 1.25 **NM** value: **1.50**
Circ: CapCity orders: **4,925**
🕮 Strontium Dog: Portrait of a Mutant **A:** Carlos Ezquerra **W:** Alan Grant
3 ❑ 1985 Cover: 1.25 **NM** value: **1.50**
Circ: CapCity orders: **4,450**
🕮 Strontium Dog: Portrait of a Mutant **A:** Carlos Ezquerra **W:** Alan Grant
4 ❑ 1985 Cover: 1.25 **NM** value: **1.50**
Circ: CapCity orders: **4,050**

STRÜDEL WAR — Rough Copy

1 ❑ Cover: 2.95 **NM** value: **Cover or less**
• Flip-book. 🕮 I Am a Chimpazee; Frida and Friends: The Metallic Necklace; Close Encounters with Northern Exposure; The Mission; Picasso Soda; Meet Omori (Flip book) **A:** Alan Lau; Manny Bello **W:** Alan Lau; Manny Bello

STRYFE'S STRIKE FILE — Marvel

1 ❑ Jan 1993 Cover: 1.75 **NM** value: **Cover or less**
Circ: CapCity orders: **77,700**
• Follows X-Cutioner's Song x-over series **A:** Whilce Portacio; Andy Kubert; Jim Lee; Brandon Peterson; Marc Silvestri; Larry Stroman; Greg Capullo **W:** Scott Lobdell; Fabian Nicieza
1-2 ❑ Jan 1993 Cover: 1.75 **NM** value: **Cover or less**

STRYKE — London Night

0 ❑ Cover: 2.95 **NM** value: **3.00**
Circ: CapCity orders: **10,135**
🕮 Ice… **A:** Richard Pollard **W:** Everette Hartsoe; Kevin Hill
0/A ❑ Cover: 2.95 **NM** value: **4.00**
alternate cover. 🕮 Ice… **A:** Richard Pollard **W:** Everette Hartsoe; Kevin Hill
1 ❑ Cover: 2.95 **NM** value: **3.00**

ST. SWITHIN'S DAY — Trident

1 ❑ ca. 1990, b&w Cover: 2.50 **NM** value: **3.00**
Circ: CapCity orders: **3,175**
One-shot. **A:** Paul Grist **W:** Grant Morrison
1-2 ❑ b&w Cover: 2.95 **NM** value: **Cover or less**

ST. SWITHIN'S DAY (ONI) — Oni

1 ❑ Mar 1998 Cover: 2.95 **NM** value: **Cover or less**
Circ: Diamd. preorders: **5,478**
A: Paul Grist **W:** Grant Morrison

ST. TAIL COMIC — Mixx

1 ❑ Oct 2000 Cover: 2.95 **NM** value: **Cover or less**
Circ: Diamd. preorders: **4,157**
A: Megumi Tachikawa **W:** Megumi Tachikawa
2 ❑ Nov 2000 Cover: 2.95 **NM** value: **Cover or less**
Circ: Diamd. preorders: **3,109**
3 ❑ Dec 2000 Cover: 2.95 **NM** value: **Cover or less**
Circ: Diamd. preorders: **2,683**
4 ❑ Feb 2001 Cover: 2.95 **NM** value: **Cover or less**
Circ: Diamd. preorders: **2,402**
5 ❑ Mar 2001 Cover: 2.95 **NM** value: **Cover or less**
Circ: Diamd. preorders: **2,309**
6 ❑ Apr 2001 Cover: 2.95 **NM** value: **Cover or less**
Circ: Diamd. preorders: **2,347**
7 ❑ May 2001 Cover: 2.95 **NM** value: **Cover or less**
Circ: Diamd. preorders: **2,170**
8 ❑ Jun 2001 Cover: 2.95 **NM** value: **Cover or less**
Circ: Diamd. preorders: **2,241**
9 ❑ Jul 2001 Cover: 2.95 **NM** value: **Cover or less**
Circ: Diamd. preorders: **2,288**

STUCK RUBBER BABY — DC / Paradox

1 ❑ b&w Cover: 14.00 **NM** value: **Cover or less**
1/HC❑ b&w Cover: 24.95 **NM** value: **Cover or less**
hardcover.

STUDIO COMICS PRESENTS — Studio

1 ❑ May 1995 Cover: 2.50 **NM** value: **Cover or less**
🕮 Lion's Mayne • Battle Bunnies **A:** Jeff Welborn **W:** Jeff Welborn

STUMBO TINYTOWN — Harvey

1 ❑ Aug 1963 Cover: 0.25 **NM** value: **65.00**
• **CGC:** 1 graded, best 9.2
2 ❑ Oct 1963 Cover: 0.25 **NM** value: **40.00**
3 ❑ Jan 1964 Cover: 0.25 **NM** value: **30.00**
🕮 Stumbo the Giant: In the Big Sport; The Big Bank Robbery; The Big Lazy Bones; Cloudy Skies; The Big Show Off
4 ❑ Apr 1964 Cover: 0.25 **NM** value: **20.00**
5 ❑ Oct 1964 Cover: 0.25 **NM** value: **20.00**
6 ❑ 1965 Cover: 0.25 **NM** value: **15.00**
7 ❑ 1965 Cover: 0.25 **NM** value: **15.00**
8 ❑ 1965 Cover: 0.25 **NM** value: **15.00**
9 ❑ 1965 Cover: 0.25 **NM** value: **15.00**
10 ❑ 1966 Cover: 0.25 **NM** value: **15.00**
11 ❑ 1966 Cover: 0.25 **NM** value: **15.00**
12 ❑ 1966 Cover: 0.25 **NM** value: **15.00**
13 ❑ 1966 Cover: 0.25 **NM** value: **15.00**

STUNT DAWGS — Harvey

1 ❑ Mar 1993 Cover: 1.25 **NM** value: **Cover or less**
🕮 Rom Russia with Like! **A:** Nelson Dewey **W:** Michael Gallagher

STUNTMAN COMICS — Harvey

1 ❑ Apr 1946 Cover: 0.10 **NM** value: **750.00**
• **CGC:** 5 graded, best 8.5
🕮 Killer in the Bigtop; The Crime on Cauliflower Row; The House of Madness; The Boy Explorers Meet Commodore Sinbad
2 ❑ Jun 1946 Cover: 0.10 **NM** value: **600.00**
• **CGC:** 2 graded, best 9.2
🕮 Curtain Call for Death; The Rescu of Robin Hood; His Highness, the Duke of Broadway; Triumph for the Boy Explorers
3 ❑ Aug 1946 Cover: 0.10 **NM** value: **500.00**

STUPID — Image

1 ❑ May 1993 Cover: 1.95 **NM** value: **Cover or less**
Circ: CapCity orders: **62,800**
🕮 Spewn • parody **A:** Hilary Barta **W:** Hilary Barta

STUPID COMICS — Oni

1 ❑ Jul 2000, b&w Cover: 2.95 **NM** value: **Cover or less**
Circ: Diamd. preorders: **4,113**
No issue number. • collects Mahfood's strips from Java Magazine. **A:** Jim Mahfood **W:** Jim Mahfood

STUPID HEROES — Mirage / Next

1 ❑ Aug 1994 Cover: 2.75 **NM** value: **Cover or less**
Circ: CapCity orders: **5,625**
🕮 Super Crooks **A:** Peter Laird **W:** Peter Laird ★ 1st Appearance of Muscle Master, Rock Boy, Scott Poundstone, Cinder.
2 ❑ Oct 1994 Cover: 2.75 **NM** value: **Cover or less**
🕮 Wall Crawling Weirdos! **A:** Peter Laird **W:** Peter Laird ★ 1st Appearance of MISTer.
3 ❑ Dec 1994 Cover: 2.75 **NM** value: **Cover or less**
🕮 Betrayal! **A:** Peter Laird **W:** Peter Laird

STUPIDMAN — Parody

1 ❑ Cover: 2.50 **NM** value: **Cover or less**

STUPIDMAN: BURIAL FOR A BUDDY — Parody

1/A ❑ b&w Cover: 2.50 **NM** value: **Cover or less**
🕮 Gloomsday **A:** Mac Meyers **W:** Mac Meyers
1/B ❑ b&w Cover: 2.50 **NM** value: **Cover or less**

STUPIDMAN: RAIN ON THE STUPIDMEN — Parody

1/A ❑ b&w Cover: 2.95 **NM** value: **Cover or less**
🕮 I Am…Stupidman **A:** Roy Burdine **W:** Mac Meyers
1/B ❑ b&w Cover: 2.95 **NM** value: **Cover or less**

STUPID, STUPID RAT TAILS — Cartoon Books

1 ❑ Dec 1999 Cover: 2.95 **NM** value: **Cover or less**
Circ: Diamd. preorders: **18,199**
A: Jeff Smith **W:** Tom Sniegoski
2 ❑ 2000 Cover: 2.95 **NM** value: **Cover or less**
Circ: Diamd. preorders: **16,476**
A: Jeff Smith **W:** Tom Sniegoski
3 ❑ 2000 Cover: 2.95 **NM** value: **Cover or less**
Circ: Diamd. preorders: **15,713**
A: Jeff Smith **W:** Tom Sniegoski
Bk 1❑ b&w Cover: 9.95 **NM** value: **Cover or less**
• Trade Paperback. • collects mini-series **A:** Jeff Smith **W:** Tom Sniegoski

STYGMATA — Express / Entity

0 ❑ Cover: 2.95 **NM** value: **Cover or less**
Circ: CapCity orders: **4,720**
A: Raff Ienco **W:** John Migliore ★ Origin of Stygmata.
1 ❑ Jul 1994, b&w Cover: 2.95 **NM** value: **Cover or less**
enhanced cover.
2 ❑ Cover: 2.95 **NM** value: **Cover or less**
Foil-stamped cover. 🕮 Paradise Remembered **A:** Raff Ienco **W:** John Migliore ★ Origin of Stygmata. ★ 1st Appearance of The Sieger, Savanna.
3 ❑ Oct 1994, b&w Cover: 2.95 **NM** value: **Cover or less**

SUBHUMAN — Dark Horse

1 ❑ Nov 1998 Cover: 2.95 **NM** value: **Cover or less**
Circ: Diamd. preorders: **9,957**
A: Roger Petersen **W:** Michael Ryan; Mark Schultz
2 ❑ Dec 1998 Cover: 2.95 **NM** value: **Cover or less**
Circ: Diamd. preorders: **7,573**
A: Roger Petersen **W:** Michael Ryan; Mark Schultz
3 ❑ Jan 1999 Cover: 2.95 **NM** value: **Cover or less**
Circ: Diamd. preorders: **7,461**
A: Roger Petersen **W:** Michael Ryan; Mark Schultz
4 ❑ Feb 1999 Cover: 2.95 **NM** value: **Cover or less**
Circ: Diamd. preorders: **6,843**
A: Roger Petersen **W:** Michael Ryan; Mark Schultz

Other grades: Multiply prices above by **1.5 for Mint • 2/3 for Very Fine • 1/3 for Fine • 1/5 for Very Good • 1/8 for Good**

SUB-MARINER COMICS — Timely

When Prince Namor, The Sub-Mariner, was introduced in the Golden Age, he was not a nice guy. Enraged at what the surface world had been doing, The Sub-Mariner would rampage through the streets of Manhatten, punch holes in ships, and otherwise bedevil humans. Written and drawn by Bill Everett, his initial big splash (as opposed to the little-circulated Motion Picture Funnies Weekly) was in Marvel Comics #1 (Oct-Nov 39). The character was the result of a romance between a human explorer and a sea-dwelling member of the royal family, so he was a super-powered prince of the sea who could live in either world. When America entered World War II, Namor joined Timely's super-powered heroes and turned his hostility on the Axis powers.

In the Golden Age, he popped up in such titles as Marvel Mystery Comics, The Human Torch Comics, All Winners Comics, Daring Comics, Namora, and Young Men. — Maggie

1 ❑ Spr 1941 Cover: 0.10 **NM** value: **25000.00**
• **CGC:** 12 graded, best 9.0
2 ❑ Sum 1941 Cover: 0.10 **NM** value: **7500.00**
• **CGC:** 2 graded, best 6.5
3 ❑ Fal 1941 Cover: 0.10 **NM** value: **4000.00**
• **CGC:** 3 graded, best 9.0
4 ❑ Win 1941 Cover: 0.10 **NM** value: **3000.00**
• **CGC:** 1 graded, best 3.5
5 ❑ Spr 1942 Cover: 0.10 **NM** value: **3000.00**
• **CGC:** 2 graded, best 6.5
6 ❑ Sum 1942 Cover: 0.10 **NM** value: **2500.00**
7 ❑ Fal 1942 Cover: 0.10 **NM** value: **2500.00**
• **CGC:** 1 graded, best 3.5
8 ❑ Win 1942 Cover: 0.10 **NM** value: **2500.00**
• **CGC:** 2 graded, best 8.0
9 ❑ Spr 1943 Cover: 0.10 **NM** value: **2500.00**
• **CGC:** 1 graded, best 9.4
10 ❑ Sum 1943 Cover: 0.10 **NM** value: **2500.00**
• **CGC:** 3 graded, best 9.0
11 ❑ Fal 1943 Cover: 0.10 **NM** value: **1500.00**
• **CGC:** 2 graded, best 7.5
12 ❑ Win 1943 Cover: 0.10 **NM** value: **1500.00**
• **CGC:** 1 graded, best 3.5
13 ❑ Spr 1944 Cover: 0.10 **NM** value: **1500.00**
• **CGC:** 1 graded, best 8.5
14 ❑ Win 1944 Cover: 0.10 **NM** value: **1500.00**
• **CGC:** 3 graded, best 8.0
15 ❑ Win 1944 Cover: 0.10 **NM** value: **1500.00**
• **CGC:** 3 graded, best 7.5
16 ❑ Spr 1945 Cover: 0.10 **NM** value: **1000.00**
• **CGC:** 1 graded, best 5.0
17 ❑ Fal 1945 Cover: 0.10 **NM** value: **1000.00**
• **CGC:** 6 graded, best 8.5
18 ❑ Win 1945 Cover: 0.10 **NM** value: **1000.00**
• **CGC:** 6 graded, best 9.2
19 ❑ Spr 1946 Cover: 0.10 **NM** value: **1000.00**
• **CGC:** 3 graded, best 9.0
20 ❑ Sum 1946 Cover: 0.10 **NM** value: **1000.00**
• **CGC:** 5 graded, best 8.5
21 ❑ Win 1946 Cover: 0.10 **NM** value: **1000.00**
• **CGC:** 3 graded, best 7.5
22 ❑ Spr 1947 Cover: 0.10 **NM** value: **1000.00**
• **CGC:** 3 graded, best 9.2
23 ❑ Sum 1947 Cover: 0.10 **NM** value: **1000.00**
• **CGC:** 3 graded, best 8.0
24 ❑ Win 1947 Cover: 0.10 **NM** value: **1000.00**
25 ❑ Apr 1948 Cover: 0.10 **NM** value: **1000.00**
26 ❑ Jun 1948 Cover: 0.10 **NM** value: **1000.00**
• **CGC:** 4 graded, best 9.0
27 ❑ Aug 1948 Cover: 0.10 **NM** value: **1000.00**
• **CGC:** 1 graded, best 8.5
28 ❑ Oct 1948 Cover: 0.10 **NM** value: **1000.00**
29 ❑ Dec 1948 Cover: 0.10 **NM** value: **1000.00**
30 ❑ Feb 1949 Cover: 0.10 **NM** value: **1000.00**
31 ❑ Apr 1949 Cover: 0.10 **NM** value: **850.00**
• **CGC:** 1 graded, best 7.0
32 ❑ Jun 1949 Cover: 0.10 **NM** value: **850.00**
• **CGC:** 3 graded, best 7.0
33 ❑ Apr 1954 Cover: 0.10 **NM** value: **850.00**
• **CGC:** 1 graded, best 4.5
34 ❑ Jun 1954 Cover: 0.10 **NM** value: **850.00**
• **CGC:** 7 graded, best 8.5
35 ❑ Aug 1954 Cover: 0.10 **NM** value: **850.00**
36 ❑ Nov 1954 Cover: 0.10 **NM** value: **850.00**
• **CGC:** 1 graded, best 7.0
37 ❑ Dec 1954 Cover: 0.10 **NM** value: **850.00**
• **CGC:** 1 graded, best 6.5
38 ❑ Feb 1955 Cover: 0.10 **NM** value: **850.00**
39 ❑ Apr 1955 Cover: 0.10 **NM** value: **850.00**
• **CGC:** 1 graded, best 6.0
40 ❑ Jun 1955 Cover: 0.10 **NM** value: **850.00**
41 ❑ Aug 1955 Cover: 0.10 **NM** value: **850.00**
• **CGC:** 1 graded, best 7.0
42 ❑ Oct 1955 Cover: 0.10 **NM** value: **850.00**
• **CGC:** 2 graded, best 8.0

Statement of Ownership figures are the average number of copies originally sold, as cited by the publisher to the U.S. Postal Service. These estimate **all** sales, in comics shops and on newsstands.

SUB-MARINER, THE (VOL. 2) — Marvel

Following Iron Man & Sub-Mariner #1 — the bridge issue for Sub-Mariner fans who had been following him in Tales to Astonish — this series continued the adventures of the Prince of Atlantis.

Prince Namor remains a prince of Atlantis, born of a mermaid and an American seaman. He possesses incredible strength and the ability to fly. He's shown at his fiercest in this series, even taking on the entire U.S. Navy in one issue.

But while lasting longer than either of the titles split off from Strange Tales, this showcase for Subby was nowhere near as successful as its former conjoined twin in Tales to Astonish, The Incredible Hulk. Even a revival a couple of decades later couldn't get herds of Marvel fans to really warm up to this cold fish... — JJM

1 ❑ May 1968 Cover: 0.12 **NM** value: **90.00**
• **CGC:** 205 graded, best 9.8
📖 Years of Glory, Day of Doom **A:** John Buscema ★ Origin of Sub-Mariner.
36740❑ Cover: 0.12 **NM** value: **1.50**
2 ❑ Jun 1968 Cover: 0.12 **NM** value: **40.00**
• **CGC:** 45 graded, best 9.8
📖 Cry Triton! **A:** John Buscema ★ Appearance of Triton.
3 ❑ Jul 1968 Cover: 0.12 **NM** value: **22.00**
• **CGC:** 10 graded, best 9.6
📖 On a Clear Day You Can See the Leviathan! **A:** John Buscema ★ Appearance of Triton.
4 ❑ Aug 1968 Cover: 0.12 **NM** value: **22.00**
• **CGC:** 5 graded, best 9.4
📖 Who Strikes for Atlantis? **A:** John Buscema
5 ❑ Sep 1968 Cover: 0.12 **NM** value: **24.00**
• **CGC:** 10 graded, best 9.6
📖 Watch Out for Tiger Shark! **A:** John Buscema ★ Origin of Tiger Shark. ★ 1st Appearance of Tiger Shark.
6 ❑ Oct 1968 Cover: 0.12 **NM** value: **22.00**
• **CGC:** 34 graded, best 9.6
📖 And To the Vanquished, Death! **A:** John Buscema
7 ❑ Nov 1968 Cover: 0.12 **NM** value: **22.00**
• **CGC:** 20 graded, best 9.8
photo background cover. 📖 For President – The Man Called Destiny! **A:** John Buscema **W:** Roy Thomas ★ 1st Appearance of Ikthon.
8 ❑ Dec 1968 Cover: 0.12 **NM** value: **22.00**
• **CGC:** 20 graded, best 9.6
📖 In the Rage of Battle! **A:** John Buscema **W:** Roy Thomas ★ Versus Thing.
8-2 ❑ Cover: 0.12 **NM** value: **1.50**
9 ❑ Jan 1969 Cover: 0.12 **NM** value: **22.00**
• **CGC:** 12 graded, best 9.4
📖 The Spell of the Serpent! **A:** Marie Severin **W:** Roy Thomas ★ 1st Appearance of Lemuria, Naga.
10 ❑ Feb 1969 Cover: 0.12 **NM** value: **22.00**
• **CGC:** 8 graded, best 9.6
📖 Never Bother a Barracuda ★ Origin of Naga.
11 ❑ Mar 1969 Cover: 0.12 **NM** value: **16.00**
• **CGC:** 3 graded, best 9.4
📖 The Choice and the Challenge!
12 ❑ Apr 1969 Cover: 0.12 **NM** value: **16.00**
• **CGC:** 4 graded, best 9.2
📖 A World Against Me!
13 ❑ May 1969 Cover: 0.12 **NM** value: **16.00**
• **CGC:** 4 graded, best 9.2
📖 Death, Thou Shalt Die!
14 ❑ Jun 1969 Cover: 0.12 **NM** value: **30.00**
• **CGC:** 4 graded, best 9.4
📖 Burn, Namor, Burn! ★ Appearance of Human Torch. ★ Death of Toro.
15 ❑ Jul 1969 Cover: 0.12 **NM** value: **12.00**
• **CGC:** 2 graded, best 9.4
📖 The Day of the Dragon!
16 ❑ Aug 1969 Cover: 0.15 **NM** value: **10.00**
• **CGC:** 2 graded, best 9.6
📖 The Sea That Time Forgot! ★ 1st Appearance of Thakos.
17 ❑ Sep 1969 Cover: 0.15 **NM** value: **10.00**
• **CGC:** 1 graded, best 9.6
📖 From the Stars... The Stalker! ★ 1st Appearance of Kormok.
18 ❑ Oct 1969 Cover: 0.15 **NM** value: **10.00**
• **CGC:** 1 graded, best 9.4
📖 Side By Side with Triton!
19 ❑ Nov 1969 Cover: 0.15 **NM** value: **10.00**
• **CGC:** 1 graded, best 9.2
📖 Support Your Local Sting-Ray ★ Origin of Stingray. ★ 1st Appearance of Stingray.
20 ❑ Dec 1969 Cover: 0.15 **NM** value: **10.00**
📖 In the Darkness Dwells... Doom!
21 ❑ Jan 1970 Cover: 0.15 **NM** value: **7.00**
• **CGC:** 2 graded, best 9.6
📖 Invasion from the Ocean Floor!
22 ❑ Feb 1970 Cover: 0.15 **NM** value: **7.00**
📖 The Monarch and the Mystic ★ Appearance of Doctor Strange.
23 ❑ Mar 1970 Cover: 0.15 **NM** value: **7.00**
📖 The Coming of... Orka! ★ Origin of Orka. ★ 1st Appearance of Orka.
24 ❑ Apr 1970 Cover: 0.15 **NM** value: **7.00**
• **CGC:** 1 graded, best 9.4
📖 The Lady and the Tiger Shark!
25 ❑ May 1970 Cover: 0.15 **NM** value: **7.00**
• **CGC:** 1 graded, best 9.4
📖 A World My Enemy! ★ Origin of Atlantis.
26 ❑ Jun 1970 Cover: 0.15 **NM** value: **7.00**
📖 "Kill," Cried the Raven! ★ Appearance of Red Raven. ★ Death of Red Raven.
27 ❑ Jul 1970 Cover: 0.15 **NM** value: **7.00**
📖 When Walks the Kraken! **A:** Sal Buscema ★ 1st Appearance of Commander Kraken.
28 ❑ Aug 1970 Cover: 0.15 **NM** value: **7.00**
📖 Youthquake!
29 ❑ Sep 1970 Cover: 0.15 **NM** value: **7.00**
📖 Fear Is the Hunter **A:** Sal Buscema ★ Versus Hercules.
30 ❑ Oct 1970 Cover: 0.15 **NM** value: **7.00**
• **CGC:** 2 graded, best 9.4
📖 Calling Captain Marvel! **A:** Sal Buscema ★ Appearance of Captain Marvel.
31 ❑ Nov 1970 Cover: 0.15 **NM** value: **7.00**
• **CGC:** 3 graded, best 9.6
📖 Attuma Triumphant!
32 ❑ Dec 1970 Cover: 0.15 **NM** value: **7.00**
📖 Call Her Llyra, Call Her Legend! ★ Origin of Llyra. ★ 1st Appearance of Llyra.
33 ❑ Jan 1971 Cover: 0.15 **NM** value: **7.00**
• **CGC:** 1 graded, best 9.6
📖 Come the Cataclysm! **A:** Sal Buscema; Jim Mooney ★ 1st Appearance of Namora.
34 ❑ Feb 1971 Cover: 0.15 **NM** value: **15.00**
• **CGC:** 7 graded, best 9.4
📖 Titans Three! • Leads into Defenders #1 **A:** Sal Buscema; Jim Mooney ★ Appearance of Hulk, Silver Surfer.
35 ❑ Mar 1971 Cover: 0.15 **NM** value: **15.00**
• **CGC:** 6 graded, best 9.4
📖 Confrontation! **A:** Sal Buscema; Jim Mooney ★ Appearance of Hulk, Silver Surfer.
36 ❑ Apr 1971 Cover: 0.15 **NM** value: **7.00**
📖 What the Gods Have Joined Together! • Wedding of Lady Dorma **A:** Bernie Wrightson; Sal Buscema ★ 1st Appearance of The Octo-Meks.
37 ❑ May 1971 Cover: 0.15 **NM** value: **7.00**
• **CGC:** 2 graded, best 9.2
📖 The Way to Dusty Death! **A:** Ross Andru **W:** Roy Thomas ★ Death of Lady Dorma.
38 ❑ Jun 1971 Cover: 0.15 **NM** value: **7.00**
• **CGC:** 2 graded, best 9.6
📖 Namor Agonistes! **A:** John Severin; Ross Andru **W:** Roy Thomas ★ Origin of Sub-Mariner.
39 ❑ Jul 1971 Cover: 0.15 **NM** value: **7.00**
📖 ...And Here I'll Stand **A:** Ross Andru; Jim Mooney **W:** Roy Thomas
40 ❑ Aug 1971 Cover: 0.15 **NM** value: **7.00**
📖 Under the Name of Ritual ★ Appearance of Spider-Man.
41 ❑ Sep 1971 Cover: 0.15 **NM** value: **4.00**
• **CGC:** 1 graded, best 5.5
📖 Whom the Sky Would Destroy! **A:** George Tuska
42 ❑ Oct 1971 Cover: 0.15 **NM** value: **4.00**
📖 And a House Whose Name ... is Death! **A:** George Tuska **W:** Gerry Conway
43 ❑ Nov 1971 Cover: 0.25 **NM** value: **4.00**
• Giant-size. 📖 Mind-Quake!; And tehPower of His Mind; The Changeling War
44 ❑ Dec 1971 Cover: 0.20 **NM** value: **4.00**
• **CGC:** 1 graded, best 9.4
📖 Namor – Betrayed! ★ Appearance of Human Torch.
45 ❑ Jan 1972 Cover: 0.20 **NM** value: **4.00**
• **CGC:** 1 graded, best 9.0
📖 And Fire Stalks the Skies!
46 ❑ Feb 1972 Cover: 0.20 **NM** value: **4.00**
📖 Even the Noble Die **A:** Gene Colan
47 ❑ Mar 1972 Cover: 0.20 **NM** value: **4.00**
📖 Doomsmasque! **A:** Gene Colan
48 ❑ Apr 1972 Cover: 0.20 **NM** value: **4.00**
• **CGC:** 1 graded, best 9.2
📖 Twilight of the Hunted! **A:** Gene Colan
49 ❑ May 1972 Cover: 0.20 **NM** value: **4.00**
📖 The Dreamstone **A:** Gene Colan
50 ❑ Jun 1972 Cover: 0.20 **NM** value: **7.00**
📖 Who Am I? **A:** Bill Everett ★ 1st Appearance of Namorita.
51 ❑ Jul 1972 Cover: 0.20 **NM** value: **4.00**
📖 Armageddon... At Fifty Fathoms Full! **A:** Bill Everett
52 ❑ Aug 1972 Cover: 0.20 **NM** value: **4.00**
📖 Atomic Samurai! **A:** Bill Everett
53 ❑ Sep 1972 Cover: 0.20 **NM** value: **4.00**
📖 And the Rising Sun Shall Fall!; The Return of the Nautilus • Reprinted from Sub-Mariner (Vol. 1) #41 **A:** Bill Everett
54 ❑ Oct 1972 Cover: 0.20 **NM** value: **4.00**
📖 Comes Now the Decision; The Mer-Mutants; A Lesson in Humility from Namora • Reprinted from Sub-Mariner (Vol. 1) #39 **A:** Bill Everett ★ 1st Appearance of Lorvex.
55 ❑ Nov 1972 Cover: 0.20 **NM** value: **4.00**
📖 The Abominable Snow-King! **A:** Bill Everett
56 ❑ Dec 1972 Cover: 0.20 **NM** value: **4.00**
📖 Atlantis Mon Amour ★ 1st Appearance of Tamara Rahn.
57 ❑ Jan 1973 Cover: 0.20 **NM** value: **4.00**
📖 In the Lap of the Gods!
58 ❑ Feb 1973 Cover: 0.20 **NM** value: **4.00**
📖 Hands Across the Water, Hands Across the Skies **A:** Bill Everett
59 ❑ Mar 1973 Cover: 0.20 **NM** value: **4.00**
📖 Thunder Over the Seas! **A:** Bill Everett
60 ❑ Apr 1973 Cover: 0.20 **NM** value: **4.00**
📖 The Invasion of New York! **A:** Bill Everett
61 ❑ May 1973 Cover: 0.20 **NM** value: **4.00**
📖 The Prince and the Pirate
62 ❑ Jun 1973 Cover: 0.20 **NM** value: **4.00**
📖 A Realm Besieged; Tales of Atlantis • Tales of Atlantis
63 ❑ Jul 1973 Cover: 0.20 **NM** value: **4.00**
📖 And the Seas Shall Explode!; Cataclysm! • Tales of Atlantis ★ 1st Appearance of Arkus, Volpan.
64 ❑ Aug 1973 Cover: 0.20 **NM** value: **4.00**
📖 Voyage Into Chaos; In the Wake of the Warriors • Tales of Atlantis ★ 1st Appearance of Madoxx.
65 ❑ Sep 1973 Cover: 0.20 **NM** value: **4.00**
📖 The Cry of the She-Beast!; The Lurker in the Ruins! • Tales of Atlantis
66 ❑ Oct 1973 Cover: 0.20 **NM** value: **4.00**

CGC-graded: Multiply prices above by **33 for 9.9 M • 16 for 9.8 NM/M • 7 for 9.6 NM+ • 5 for 9.4 NM • 2.5 for 9.2 NM- • 1.5 for 9.0 VF/NM**

• **CGC:** 1 graded, best 9.6
📖 Rise, Thou Killer Whale!; The Sword in the Throne • Tales of Atlantis ★ 1st Appearance of Raman.
67 ❑ Nov 1973 Cover: 0.20 **NM** value: **4.00**
📖 Seawinds of Change
68 ❑ Jan 1974 Cover: 0.20 **NM** value: **4.00**
📖 On the Brink of Madness!
69 ❑ Mar 1974 Cover: 0.20 **NM** value: **4.00**
• **CGC:** 1 graded, best 9.6
📖 Two Worlds and Dark Destiny
70 ❑ May 1974 Cover: 0.25 **NM** value: **4.00**
📖 Namor Unchained!
71 ❑ Jul 1974 Cover: 0.25 **NM** value: **4.00**
📖 Comes the Pirahna!
72 ❑ Sep 1974 Cover: 0.25 **NM** value: **4.00**
📖 From the Void it Came… final issue. **A:** Dan Adkins **W:** Steve Skeates
SE 1❑ ca. 1971 Cover: 0.25 **NM** value: **6.00**
• **CGC:** 5 graded, best 9.4
• Sub-Mariner Special Edition #1. 📖 The Start of the Quest; Escape to Nowhere; A Prince There Was; By Force of Arms • Reprinted from Tales to Astonish #70-73 **A:** Sal Buscema
SE 2❑ ca. 1972 Cover: 0.25 **NM** value: **6.00**
• Sub-Mariner Special Edition #2. 📖 When Fails the Quest; The End of the Quest; Uneasy Hangs the Head • Reprinted from Tales to Astonish #74-76 **A:** Bill Everett

SUBMISSIVE SUZANNE — Fantagraphics / Eros

All issues are adults only.
1 ❑ b&w Cover: 2.50 **NM** value: **Cover or less**
A: Gnnther Von Wegen **W:** Gnnther Von Wegen; Conny Hahn
2 ❑ b&w Cover: 2.50 **NM** value: **Cover or less**
A: Gnnther Von Wegen **W:** Gnnther Von Wegen; Conny Hahn
3 ❑ b&w **NM** value: **2.95**
A: Gnnther Von Wegen **W:** Gnnther Von Wegen; Conny Hahn
4 ❑ b&w **NM** value: **2.95**
A: Gnnther Von Wegen **W:** Gnnther Von Wegen; Conny Hahn
5 ❑ b&w **NM** value: **2.95**
A: Gnnther Von Wegen **W:** Gnnther Von Wegen; Conny Hahn
6 ❑ Aug 1998, b&w Cover: 2.95 **NM** value: **Cover or less**
A: Gnnther Von Wegen **W:** Gnnther Von Wegen; Conny Hahn

SUBSPECIES — Eternity

1 ❑ May 1991 Cover: 2.50 **NM** value: **Cover or less**
Circ: CapCity orders: **2,210**
📖 Blood Feud **A:** M.C. Wyman; Adam Adamowicz(cover) **W:** Lowell Cunningham
2 ❑ 1991 Cover: 2.50 **NM** value: **Cover or less**
A: M.C. Wyman; Adam Adamowicz(cover) **W:** Lowell Cunningham
3 ❑ 1991 Cover: 2.50 **NM** value: **Cover or less**
A: M.C. Wyman; Adam Adamowicz(cover) **W:** Lowell Cunningham
4 ❑ 1991 Cover: 2.50 **NM** value: **Cover or less**
A: M.C. Wyman; Adam Adamowicz(cover) **W:** Lowell Cunningham

SUBSTANCE AFFECT — Crazyfish

1 ❑ Cover: 2.95 **NM** value: **Cover or less**
📖 Dare You Resist The Magic Pickle; Grrrl Scout; Chab; Valentine Shmalentine; Junk Culture; Mega-Stuf; One Track Mind **A:** John Green; C. Scott Morse; Jim Mahfood; Dave Roman; Jason Faust; Lawrence Marvit **W:** John Green; C. Scott Morse; Jim Mahfood; Dave Roman; Jason Faust; Lawrence Marvit

SUBSTANCE QUARTERLY — Substance

1 ❑ Spr 1994, b&w Cover: 3.00 **NM** value: **Cover or less**
★ Origin of Misfits. ★ 1st Appearance of Misfits.
2 ❑ Sum 1994, b&w Cover: 3.00 **NM** value: **Cover or less**
★ 1st Appearance of Faerie King.
3 ❑ Fal 1994, b&w Cover: 3.00 **NM** value: **Cover or less**
📖 The Faerie King; Misfits **A:** Josh McClenahan **W:** Chris Yambar
★ Origin of Faerie King. ★ 1st Appearance of Nash, Platt.

SUBTERRA — Forbidden Fruit

Bk 1❑ b&w Cover: 8.98 **NM** value: **Cover or less**

SUBTLE VIOLENTS — Cry for Dawn

1 ❑ ca. 1991 Cover: 2.50 **NM** value: **15.00**
• **CGC:** 1 graded, best 9.4
📖 Rhyder; Ahryssia; The New Order; Odd Man Out **A:** Kevin J. Taylor; Joseph Michael Linsner; Tim Conrad; Thomas Derenick **W:** Kevin J. Taylor; Joseph Michael Linsner; Tim Conrad; Joseph A. Monks
1/A ❑ ca. 1991 Cover: 2.50 **NM** value: **160.00**
• **CGC:** 1 graded, best 9.2
• San Diego Comic-Con edition. 📖 Rhyder; Ahryssia; The New Order; Odd Man Out **A:** Kevin J. Taylor; Joseph Michael Linsner; Tim Conrad; Thomas Derenick **W:** Kevin J. Taylor; Joseph Michael Linsner; Tim Conrad; Joseph A. Monks

SUBURBAN HIGH LIFE — Slave Labor

1 ❑ Jun 1987 Cover: 1.75 **NM** value: **Cover or less**
📖 Amazing 2-D Glasses; Scientific Novelty Company; Suburban Romance; The Moderne Family; Weird Wild Par **A:** Scott Saavedra; Rick Geary; Trina Robbins; Frank Cirocco; Basilio Amaro; Norman Dog; Ron Winnick **W:** Scott Saavedra; Rick Geary; Trina Robbins; Frank Cirocco; Basilio Amaro; Norman Dog; Ron Winnick
1-2 ❑ Feb 1988 Cover: 1.75 **NM** value: **Cover or less**
2 ❑ Aug 1987 Cover: 1.75 **NM** value: **Cover or less**
📖 Audience Participation; House of Floyd; Geek Patrol; Suburban Romance; Philosophy for Idiots; Normans of Hollywood; Suburban Adventure; Hey; The big Mean Weenie; More Philosophy for Idiots; Late Watch Theater **A:** Scott Saavedra; Rick Geary; Frank Cirocco; Basilio Amaro; Norman Dog **W:** Scott Saavedra; Rick Geary; Frank Cirocco; Basilio Amaro; Norman Dog
3 ❑ Oct 1987 Cover: 1.75 **NM** value: **Cover or less**
📖 The Happy Homemaker; Javatown; The Possession of Beaver; Papoose; How we do It; Everybody Loves Meat; Blow-Up!; White Collar Incursion **W:** Joe Sacco; Mark Martin; Scott Saavedra; Rick Geary; Frank Cirocco; Norman Dog; Tom Tomorrow

SUBURBAN HIGH LIFE (VOL. 2) — Slave Labor

1 ❑ May 1988 Cover: 5.95 **NM** value: **Cover or less**
• Oversized.

SUBURBAN NIGHTMARES — Renegade

1 ❑ Jul 1988, b&w Cover: 2.00 **NM** value: **Cover or less**
📖 Dark Secrets of Green Valley, Part 1 **A:** Michael Cherkas; John Van Bruggen **W:** Michael Cherkas; John Van Bruggen; Larry Hancock
2 ❑ Jul 1988, b&w Cover: 2.00 **NM** value: **Cover or less**
📖 Dark Secrets of Green Valley, Part 2 **A:** Michael Cherkas; John Van Bruggen **W:** Michael Cherkas; John Van Bruggen; Larry Hancock
3 ❑ Aug 1988, b&w Cover: 2.00 **NM** value: **Cover or less**
📖 Dark Secrets of Green Valley, Part 3; Just Another Joe **A:** Michael Cherkas; John Van Bruggen **W:** Michael Cherkas; John Van Bruggen; Larry Hancock
4 ❑ Aug 1988, b&w Cover: 2.00 **NM** value: **Cover or less**
Bk 1❑ Oct 1996 Cover: 11.95 **NM** value: **Cover or less**
• Childhood Secrets; collects stories from Renegade series

SUBURBAN SHE-DEVILS — Marvel

1 ❑ Cover: 1.50 **NM** value: **Cover or less**
Circ: CapCity orders: **6,050**
Cover reads Suburban Jersey Ninja She-Devils. 📖 Jagged Image **A:** Amanda Conner **W:** Steve Gerber

SUBURBAN VOODOO — Fantagraphics

1 ❑ b&w Cover: 2.50 **NM** value: **Cover or less**

SUCCUBUS — Fantagraphics / Eros

All issues are adults only.
1 ❑ b&w Cover: 2.50 **NM** value: **Cover or less**

SUCKER THE COMIC — Troma

1 ❑ Cover: 2.50 **NM** value: **Cover or less**

SUCKLE — Fantagraphics

All issues are adults only.
1 ❑ Jan 1996, b&w Cover: 14.95 **NM** value: **Cover or less**
No issue number. • digest.

SUGAR & SPIKE — DC

At a time when most comics were derivative and formulaic, Sheldon Mayer's wildly fun, charming, and hilarious Sugar and Spike stood out as a beacon of creative inspiration for over 15 years. Sugar Plumm and Cecil "Spike" Wilson are two tiny toddlers, not yet able to speak recognizable English, but fluent in the universal language of baby talk. Their efforts to puzzle out the world of grown-ups and their matter-of-fact delight in kiddie play are an inexhaustible source of gut-splitting laughs and magical moments for readers of all ages.

Issues of Sugar and Spike were packed with features ranging from 16-pagers to three-panel gag strips, plus activities, pages printed in black-and-white for kids to color or write their own dialogue, cut-out dolls, and the letters page, "We Got Letters!" ("They sound better than they taste," remarked Spike). Meyer's delightful series later became a cult classic among collectors.

1 ❑ May 1956 Cover: 0.10 **NM** value: **1150.00**
A: Sheldon Mayer **W:** Sheldon Mayer
2 ❑ Jul 1956 Cover: 0.10 **NM** value: **500.00**
• **CGC:** 1 graded, best 7.5
A: Sheldon Mayer **W:** Sheldon Mayer
3 ❑ Sep 1956 Cover: 0.10 **NM** value: **410.00**
A: Sheldon Mayer **W:** Sheldon Mayer
4 ❑ Nov 1956 Cover: 0.10 **NM** value: **410.00**
A: Sheldon Mayer **W:** Sheldon Mayer
5 ❑ Jan 1957 Cover: 0.10 **NM** value: **410.00**
A: Sheldon Mayer **W:** Sheldon Mayer
6 ❑ Mar 1957 Cover: 0.10 **NM** value: **265.00**
A: Sheldon Mayer **W:** Sheldon Mayer
7 ❑ May 1957 Cover: 0.10 **NM** value: **265.00**
A: Sheldon Mayer **W:** Sheldon Mayer
8 ❑ Jun 1957 Cover: 0.10 **NM** value: **265.00**
A: Sheldon Mayer **W:** Sheldon Mayer
9 ❑ Aug 1957 Cover: 0.10 **NM** value: **265.00**
A: Sheldon Mayer **W:** Sheldon Mayer
10 ❑ Sep 1957 Cover: 0.10 **NM** value: **265.00**
A: Sheldon Mayer **W:** Sheldon Mayer
11 ❑ Oct 1957 Cover: 0.10 **NM** value: **210.00**
A: Sheldon Mayer **W:** Sheldon Mayer
12 ❑ Dec 1957 Cover: 0.10 **NM** value: **210.00**
A: Sheldon Mayer **W:** Sheldon Mayer
13 ❑ Feb 1958 Cover: 0.10 **NM** value: **210.00**
• Has 1957 Statement, filed 10/1/57; no circ figures published **A:** Sheldon Mayer **W:** Sheldon Mayer
14 ❑ Mar 1958 Cover: 0.10 **NM** value: **210.00**
A: Sheldon Mayer **W:** Sheldon Mayer
15 ❑ Apr 1958 Cover: 0.10 **NM** value: **210.00**
• left-handedness **A:** Sheldon Mayer **W:** Sheldon Mayer
16 ❑ Jun 1958 Cover: 0.10 **NM** value: **210.00**
A: Sheldon Mayer **W:** Sheldon Mayer
17 ❑ Aug 1958 Cover: 0.10 **NM** value: **210.00**
A: Sheldon Mayer **W:** Sheldon Mayer
18 ❑ Sep 1958 Cover: 0.10 **NM** value: **210.00**
A: Sheldon Mayer **W:** Sheldon Mayer
19 ❑ Oct 1958 Cover: 0.10 **NM** value: **210.00**
A: Sheldon Mayer **W:** Sheldon Mayer
20 ❑ Dec 1958 Cover: 0.10 **NM** value: **210.00**
• **CGC:** 1 graded, best 4.5
A: Sheldon Mayer **W:** Sheldon Mayer
21 ❑ Mar 1959 Cover: 0.10 **NM** value: **135.00**
• **CGC:** 1 graded, best 8.5
• Has 1958 Statement, filed 10/1/58; no circ figures published **A:** Sheldon Mayer **W:** Sheldon Mayer
22 ❑ May 1959 Cover: 0.10 **NM** value: **135.00**
A: Sheldon Mayer **W:** Sheldon Mayer
23 ❑ Jul 1959 Cover: 0.10 **NM** value: **135.00**
• **CGC:** 1 graded, best 7.0
A: Sheldon Mayer **W:** Sheldon Mayer
24 ❑ Sep 1959 Cover: 0.10 **NM** value: **135.00**
A: Sheldon Mayer **W:** Sheldon Mayer
25 ❑ Nov 1959 Cover: 0.10 **NM** value: **135.00**
• Halloween issue **A:** Sheldon Mayer **W:** Sheldon Mayer
26 ❑ Jan 1960 Cover: 0.10 **NM** value: **135.00**
Circ: Statement: **209,000**
• Christmas issue **A:** Sheldon Mayer **W:** Sheldon Mayer
27 ❑ Mar 1960 Cover: 0.10 **NM** value: **135.00**
Circ: Statement: **209,000**
• Valentine's issue; Has 1959 Statement, filed 10/1/59; no circ figures published **A:** Sheldon Mayer **W:** Sheldon Mayer
28 ❑ May 1960 Cover: 0.10 **NM** value: **135.00**
Circ: Statement: **209,000**
A: Sheldon Mayer **W:** Sheldon Mayer
29 ❑ Jul 1960 Cover: 0.10 **NM** value: **135.00**
Circ: Statement: **209,000**
A: Sheldon Mayer **W:** Sheldon Mayer
30 ❑ Sep 1960 Cover: 0.10 **NM** value: **135.00**
Circ: Statement: **209,000**
A: Sheldon Mayer **W:** Sheldon Mayer
31 ❑ Nov 1960 Cover: 0.10 **NM** value: **100.00**
Circ: Statement: **209,000**
• Halloween issue **A:** Sheldon Mayer **W:** Sheldon Mayer
32 ❑ Jan 1961 Cover: 0.10 **NM** value: **100.00**
Circ: Statement: **195,000**
• Christmas issue **A:** Sheldon Mayer **W:** Sheldon Mayer
33 ❑ Mar 1961 Cover: 0.10 **NM** value: **100.00**
Circ: Statement: **195,000**
A: Sheldon Mayer **W:** Sheldon Mayer
34 ❑ May 1961 Cover: 0.10 **NM** value: **100.00**
Circ: Statement: **195,000**
A: Sheldon Mayer **W:** Sheldon Mayer
35 ❑ Jul 1961 Cover: 0.10 **NM** value: **100.00**
Circ: Statement: **195,000**
A: Sheldon Mayer **W:** Sheldon Mayer ★ Appearance of Grampa Plumm.
36 ❑ Sep 1961 Cover: 0.10 **NM** value: **100.00**
Circ: Statement: **195,000**
📖 The Big Yacht Race; Small War; Spike's Tough Day; The Big Giant Mystery! **A:** Sheldon Mayer **W:** Sheldon Mayer
37 ❑ Nov 1961 Cover: 0.10 **NM** value: **100.00**
Circ: Statement: **195,000**
📖 The Day the Trees Got Sloppy; Mystery Toy; The Rise of Sugar & Spike • Halloween issue **A:** Sheldon Mayer **W:** Sheldon Mayer
38 ❑ Jan 1962 Cover: 0.12 **NM** value: **100.00**
Circ: Statement: **160,000**
• Christmas issue with Christmas cards **A:** Sheldon Mayer **W:** Sheldon Mayer
39 ❑ Mar 1962 Cover: 0.12 **NM** value: **100.00**
Circ: Statement: **160,000**
• Valentine's issue with valentines; Has 1961 Statement, filed 10/1/61; avg total paid circ 195,000 **A:** Sheldon Mayer **W:** Sheldon Mayer
40 ❑ May 1962 Cover: 0.12 **NM** value: **100.00**
Circ: Statement: **160,000**
📖 Space Sprout; Who's Who **A:** Sheldon Mayer **W:** Sheldon Mayer
★ 1st Appearance of Space Sprout.
41 ❑ Jul 1962 Cover: 0.12 **NM** value: **70.00**
Circ: Statement: **160,000**
📖 The Adventure of the Wet Stuff… The Shiny Thing… and the Sweet Mush; The New Hat **A:** Sheldon Mayer **W:** Sheldon Mayer
42 ❑ Sep 1962 Cover: 0.12 **NM** value: **70.00**
Circ: Statement: **160,000**
• Vacation issue **A:** Sheldon Mayer **W:** Sheldon Mayer
43 ❑ Nov 1962 Cover: 0.12 **NM** value: **70.00**
Circ: Statement: **160,000**
📖 Uncle Charlie's Talking Pumpkin; Sugar and Spike Get Up in the World; Space Sprout Returns • Halloween issue **A:** Sheldon Mayer **W:** Sheldon Mayer
44 ❑ Jan 1963 Cover: 0.12 **NM** value: **70.00**
• Christmas issue with Christmas cards **A:** Sheldon Mayer **W:** Sheldon Mayer
45 ❑ Mar 1963 Cover: 0.12 **NM** value: **70.00**
• Valentine's issue with valentines; Has 1962 Statement, filed 10/1/62; avg total paid circ 160,000 **A:** Sheldon Mayer **W:** Sheldon Mayer
46 ❑ May 1963 Cover: 0.12 **NM** value: **70.00**
Wedding cover. 📖 Adventure with the Wooden Pussy-Cat; Sugar's Greatest Discovery **A:** Sheldon Mayer **W:** Sheldon Mayer
47 ❑ Jul 1963 Cover: 0.12 **NM** value: **70.00**
📖 Who Stole Our Ocean?; Growing Pains **A:** Sheldon Mayer **W:** Sheldon Mayer
48 ❑ Sep 1963 Cover: 0.12 **NM** value: **70.00**
📖 The 4,000-Year Old Baby; Sugar Becomes an Indian Chief **A:** Sheldon Mayer **W:** Sheldon Mayer
49 ❑ Nov 1963 Cover: 0.12 **NM** value: **70.00**
• Halloween issue **A:** Sheldon Mayer **W:** Sheldon Mayer
50 ❑ Jan 1964 Cover: 0.12 **NM** value: **70.00**
• Christmas issue with Christmas cards **A:** Sheldon Mayer **W:** Sheldon Mayer
51 ❑ Mar 1964 Cover: 0.12 **NM** value: **55.00**
• Valentine's issue with valentines; Has 1963 Statement, filed 10/1/63; no circ figures published **A:** Sheldon Mayer **W:** Sheldon Mayer
52 ❑ May 1964 Cover: 0.12 **NM** value: **55.00**
A: Sheldon Mayer **W:** Sheldon Mayer
53 ❑ Jul 1964 Cover: 0.12 **NM** value: **55.00**
A: Sheldon Mayer **W:** Sheldon Mayer
54 ❑ Sep 1964 Cover: 0.12 **NM** value: **55.00**
A: Sheldon Mayer **W:** Sheldon Mayer
55 ❑ Nov 1964 Cover: 0.12 **NM** value: **55.00**
📖 Halloween Goblin • Halloween issue **A:** Sheldon Mayer **W:** Sheldon Mayer

Other grades: Multiply prices above by **1.5 for Mint • 2/3 for Very Fine • 1/3 for Fine • 1/5 for Very Good • 1/8 for Good**

56 ❑ Jan 1965 Cover: 0.12 **NM** value: **55.00**
Circ: Statement: **175,089**
• Christmas issue with Christmas cards **A:** Sheldon Mayer **W:** Sheldon Mayer

57 ❑ Mar 1965 Cover: 0.12 **NM** value: **55.00**
Circ: Statement: **175,089**
• Valentine's issue with valentines **A:** Sheldon Mayer **W:** Sheldon Mayer

58 ❑ May 1965 Cover: 0.12 **NM** value: **55.00**
Circ: Statement: **175,089**
• Has 1964 Statement, filed 10/1/64; no circ figures published **A:** Sheldon Mayer **W:** Sheldon Mayer

59 ❑ Jul 1965 Cover: 0.12 **NM** value: **55.00**
Circ: Statement: **175,089**
A: Sheldon Mayer **W:** Sheldon Mayer

60 ❑ Sep 1965 Cover: 0.12 **NM** value: **55.00**
Circ: Statement: **175,089**
A: Sheldon Mayer **W:** Sheldon Mayer

61 ❑ Nov 1965 Cover: 0.12 **NM** value: **45.00**
Circ: Statement: **175,089**
📖 Halloween Cats • Halloween issue **A:** Sheldon Mayer **W:** Sheldon Mayer ★ Appearance of Uncle Charley.

62 ❑ Jan 1966 Cover: 0.12 **NM** value: **45.00**
Circ: Statement: **190,515**
• Christmas issue with Christmas cards **A:** Sheldon Mayer **W:** Sheldon Mayer

63 ❑ Mar 1966 Cover: 0.12 **NM** value: **45.00**
Circ: Statement: **190,515**
• Valentine's issue with valentines **A:** Sheldon Mayer **W:** Sheldon Mayer

64 ❑ May 1966 Cover: 0.12 **NM** value: **45.00**
Circ: Statement: **190,515**
A: Sheldon Mayer **W:** Sheldon Mayer

65 ❑ Jul 1966 Cover: 0.12 **NM** value: **45.00**
Circ: Statement: **190,515**
📖 Impossible Adventure • Summer issue **A:** Sheldon Mayer **W:** Sheldon Mayer

66 ❑ Sep 1966 Cover: 0.12 **NM** value: **45.00**
Circ: Statement: **190,515**
• Has 1965 Statement, filed 10/1/65 (Second statement published, this time with figures); avg print run 317,000; avg sales 174,000; avg subs 1,089; avg total paid 175,089; samples 142; max existent 175,231; 45% of run returned **A:** Sheldon Mayer **W:** Sheldon Mayer

67 ❑ Nov 1966 Cover: 0.12 **NM** value: **45.00**
Circ: Statement: **190,515**
📖 Halloween Magic • Halloween issue **A:** Sheldon Mayer **W:** Sheldon Mayer

68 ❑ Jan 1967 Cover: 0.12 **NM** value: **45.00**
Circ: Statement: **150,200**
• Christmas issue **A:** Sheldon Mayer **W:** Sheldon Mayer

69 ❑ Mar 1967 Cover: 0.12 **NM** value: **45.00**
Circ: Statement: **150,200**
• Has 1966 Statement, filed 10/1/66; avg print run 365,000; avg sales 189,000; avg subs 1,515; avg total paid 190,515; samples 265; max existent 190,780; 48% of run returned **A:** Sheldon Mayer **W:** Sheldon Mayer ★ 1st Appearance of Tornado Tot.

70 ❑ May 1967 Cover: 0.12 **NM** value: **45.00**
Circ: Statement: **150,200**
• Sugar & Spike become giants **A:** Sheldon Mayer **W:** Sheldon Mayer

71 ❑ Jul 1967 Cover: 0.12 **NM** value: **45.00**
Circ: Statement: **150,200**
A: Sheldon Mayer **W:** Sheldon Mayer

72 ❑ Sep 1967 Cover: 0.12 **NM** value: **45.00**
Circ: Statement: **150,200** • **CGC:** 1 graded, best 7.5
📖 Bernie the Brain! **A:** Sheldon Mayer **W:** Sheldon Mayer ★ 1st Appearance of Bernie the Brain.

73 ❑ Nov 1967 Cover: 0.12 **NM** value: **45.00**
Circ: Statement: **150,200**
A: Sheldon Mayer **W:** Sheldon Mayer

74 ❑ Jan 1968 Cover: 0.12 **NM** value: **45.00**
Circ: Statement: **174,410**
A: Sheldon Mayer **W:** Sheldon Mayer

75 ❑ Mar 1968 Cover: 0.12 **NM** value: **45.00**
Circ: Statement: **174,410** • **CGC:** 1 graded, best 9.2
📖 The Mystery of the Mischevious Marble! **A:** Sheldon Mayer **W:** Sheldon Mayer ★ 1st Appearance of M.C.P. pellet.

76 ❑ May 1968 Cover: 0.12 **NM** value: **45.00**
Circ: Statement: **174,410**
• Has 1967 Statement, filed 10/1/67; avg print run 304,000; avg sales 149,000; avg subs 1,200; avg total paid 150,200; samples 340; max existent 150,540; 51% of run returned **A:** Sheldon Mayer **W:** Sheldon Mayer

77 ❑ Jul 1968 Cover: 0.12 **NM** value: **45.00**
Circ: Statement: **174,410**
A: Sheldon Mayer **W:** Sheldon Mayer ★ Appearance of Bernie the Brain.

78 ❑ Sep 1968 Cover: 0.12 **NM** value: **45.00**
Circ: Statement: **174,410**
A: Sheldon Mayer **W:** Sheldon Mayer

79 ❑ Nov 1968 Cover: 0.12 **NM** value: **45.00**
Circ: Statement: **174,410**
A: Sheldon Mayer **W:** Sheldon Mayer

80 ❑ Jan 1969 Cover: 0.12 **NM** value: **45.00**
Circ: Statement: **171,227**
A: Sheldon Mayer **W:** Sheldon Mayer ★ Appearance of Bernie the Brain.

81 ❑ Mar 1969 Cover: 0.12 **NM** value: **32.00**
Circ: Statement: **171,227**
A: Sheldon Mayer **W:** Sheldon Mayer

82 ❑ May 1969 Cover: 0.12 **NM** value: **32.00**
Circ: Statement: **171,227**
• Sugar & Spike as grown-ups; Has 1968 Statement, filed 10/1/69; avg print run 310,000; avg sales 174,000; avg subs 410; avg total paid 174,410; samples 174,410; office use 386; max existent 174,796; 44% of run returned **A:** Sheldon Mayer **W:** Sheldon Mayer

83 ❑ Jul 1969 Cover: 0.12 **NM** value: **32.00**
Circ: Statement: **171,227**
• super-powers **A:** Sheldon Mayer **W:** Sheldon Mayer

84 ❑ Sep 1969 Cover: 0.15 **NM** value: **32.00**
Circ: Statement: **171,227**
📖 Bernie the Brain's Biggest Blunder!; Mayhem by Machine; Rambunctious Robots **A:** Sheldon Mayer **W:** Sheldon Mayer

85 ❑ Oct 1969 Cover: 0.25 **NM** value: **32.00**
Circ: Statement: **171,227** • **CGC:** 1 graded, best 9.2
A: Sheldon Mayer **W:** Sheldon Mayer

86 ❑ Nov 1969 Cover: 0.15 **NM** value: **32.00**
Circ: Statement: **171,227**
A: Sheldon Mayer **W:** Sheldon Mayer

87 ❑ Jan 1970 Cover: 0.15 **NM** value: **32.00**
Circ: Statement: **135,093**
A: Sheldon Mayer **W:** Sheldon Mayer ★ 1st Appearance of Marvin the Midget.

88 ❑ Mar 1970 Cover: 0.15 **NM** value: **32.00**
Circ: Statement: **135,093**
A: Sheldon Mayer **W:** Sheldon Mayer

89 ❑ May 1970 Cover: 0.15 **NM** value: **32.00**
Circ: Statement: **135,093**
• Has 1969 Statement, filed 10/1/69; avg print run 355,000; avg sales 171,000; avg subs 227; avg total paid 171,227; samples 346; max existent 171,573; 52% of run returned **A:** Sheldon Mayer **W:** Sheldon Mayer

90 ❑ Jul 1970 Cover: 0.15 **NM** value: **32.00**
Circ: Statement: **135,093** • **CGC:** 1 graded, best 9.0
A: Sheldon Mayer **W:** Sheldon Mayer ★ 1st Appearance of Flumsh.

91 ❑ Sep 1970 Cover: 0.15 **NM** value: **32.00**
Circ: Statement: **135,093**
A: Sheldon Mayer **W:** Sheldon Mayer

92 ❑ Nov 1970 Cover: 0.15 **NM** value: **32.00**
Circ: Statement: **135,093**
A: Sheldon Mayer **W:** Sheldon Mayer

93 ❑ Jan 1971 Cover: 0.15 **NM** value: **32.00**
A: Sheldon Mayer **W:** Sheldon Mayer

94 ❑ Mar 1971 Cover: 0.15 **NM** value: **32.00**
A: Sheldon Mayer **W:** Sheldon Mayer ★ 1st Appearance of Raymond.

95 ❑ May 1971 Cover: 0.15 **NM** value: **32.00**
• **CGC:** 1 graded, best 9.4
• Has 1970 Statement, filed 10/1/70; avg print run 307,824; avg sales 134,913; avg subs 180; avg total paid 135,093; samples 122; max existent 135,215; 56% of run returned **A:** Sheldon Mayer **W:** Sheldon Mayer

96 ❑ Jul 1971 Cover: 0.25 **NM** value: **32.00**
📖 The Shiny Round Roller **A:** Sheldon Mayer **W:** Sheldon Mayer

97 ❑ Sep 1971 Cover: 0.25 **NM** value: **32.00**
• **CGC:** 1 graded, best 8.5
A: Sheldon Mayer **W:** Sheldon Mayer

98 ❑ Nov 1971 Cover: 0.25 **NM** value: **32.00**
final issue. **A:** Sheldon Mayer **W:** Sheldon Mayer

SUGAR BOWL COMICS — Famous Funnies

1 ❑ May 1948 Cover: 0.10 **NM** value: **100.00**
• **CGC:** 1 graded, best 8.5
2 ❑ Jul 1948 Cover: 0.10 **NM** value: **75.00**
3 ❑ Sep 1948 Cover: 0.10 **NM** value: **50.00**
4 ❑ Nov 1948 Cover: 0.10 **NM** value: **50.00**
5 ❑ Jan 1949 Cover: 0.10 **NM** value: **50.00**

SUGAR BUZZ — Slave Labor

1 ❑ Jan 1998, b&w Cover: 2.95 **NM** value: **Cover or less**
📖 Valenteen in Bad Hair Day!; Mr. Extra the Super Evolved Man; Urbane Gorilla; Upchuck Duck; Darren Danger Galactic Enforcer; Tattle Tails **A:** Woodrow Phoenix **W:** Ian Carney
2 ❑ 1998 Cover: 2.95 **NM** value: **Cover or less**
3 ❑ 1998 Cover: 2.95 **NM** value: **Cover or less**
4 ❑ 1998 Cover: 2.95 **NM** value: **Cover or less**

SUGAR RAY FINHEAD — Wolf Press

1 ❑ Cover: 2.50 **NM** value: **Cover or less**
2 ❑ Cover: 2.95 **NM** value: **Cover or less**
3 ❑ Cover: 2.95 **NM** value: **Cover or less**
4 ❑ Cover: 2.95 **NM** value: **Cover or less**
5 ❑ Cover: 2.95 **NM** value: **Cover or less**
6 ❑ Jul 1994 Cover: 2.95 **NM** value: **Cover or less**
7 ❑ Cover: 2.95 **NM** value: **Cover or less**
8 ❑ Cover: 2.95 **NM** value: **Cover or less**
9 ❑ Cover: 2.95 **NM** value: **Cover or less**
10 ❑ Sep 1997 Cover: 2.95 **NM** value: **Cover or less**
11 ❑ Oct 1998 Cover: 2.95 **NM** value: **Cover or less**

SUGARVIRUS — Atomeka

1 ❑ b&w Cover: 3.95 **NM** value: **Cover or less**
No issue number.

SUICIDE SQUAD — DC

In the 1960s, The Suicide Squad was a military group who were sent on missions that there was little chance of returning from, but they always did.

In the mid-1980s Legends series, the group was resurrected, this time as a gathering of villains who were promised reduced sentences for their cooperation.

Lead by the enigmatic Amanda Waller (who had deep secrets of her own), the group often had its own agendas that ran counter to the super-heroes of the world, bringing the group into conflict with the Justice League. Later in the series, the super-secret group clashed with the super-secret government agency Checkmate. — Brent

1 ❑ May 1987 Cover: 0.75 **NM** value: **1.50**
Circ: CapCity orders: **24,450** • **CGC:** 1 graded, best 9.6
📖 Trial By Blood **C:** Howard Chaykin

2 ❑ Jun 1987 Cover: 0.75 **NM** value: **1.25**
Circ: CapCity orders: **17,100**

3 ❑ Jul 1987 Cover: 0.75 **NM** value: **1.25**
Circ: CapCity orders: **16,850**
★ Death of Mindboggler. ★ Versus Female Furies.

4 ❑ Aug 1987 Cover: 0.75 **NM** value: **1.25**
Circ: CapCity orders: **18,500**

5 ❑ Sep 1987 Cover: 0.75 **NM** value: **1.25**
Circ: CapCity orders: **19,450**

6 ❑ Oct 1987 Cover: 0.75 **NM** value: **1.25**
Circ: CapCity orders: **19,250**

7 ❑ Nov 1987 Cover: 0.75 **NM** value: **1.25**
Circ: CapCity orders: **18,650**

8 ❑ Dec 1987 Cover: 0.75 **NM** value: **1.25**
Circ: CapCity orders: **17,400**

9 ❑ Jan 1988 Cover: 0.75 **NM** value: **1.25**
Circ: CapCity orders: **21,000**
• Millennium Week 4 ★ 1st Appearance of Duchess.

10 ❑ Feb 1988 Cover: 0.75 **NM** value: **1.25**
Circ: CapCity orders: **20,750**
★ Appearance of Batman.

11 ❑ Mar 1988 Cover: 0.75 **NM** value: **1.25**
Circ: CapCity orders: **16,450**
★ Appearance of Speedy, Vixen.

12 ❑ Apr 1988 Cover: 0.75 **NM** value: **1.25**
Circ: CapCity orders: **15,850**

13 ❑ May 1988 Cover: 0.75 **NM** value: **1.25**
Circ: CapCity orders: **22,700**
• continued from Justice League International #13; Suicide Squad view of Justice League ★ Appearance of Justice League International.

14 ❑ Jun 1988 Cover: 0.75 **NM** value: **1.25**
Circ: CapCity orders: **16,450**
📖 Nightshade Odyssey, Part 1

15 ❑ Jul 1988 Cover: 0.75 **NM** value: **1.25**
Circ: CapCity orders: **15,200**
📖 Nightshade Odyssey, Part 2

16 ❑ Aug 1988 Cover: 1.00 **NM** value: **Cover or less**
Circ: CapCity orders: **15,500**
📖 Nightshade Odyssey, Part 3 ★ Appearance of Shade, the Changing Man.

17 ❑ Sep 1988 Cover: 1.00 **NM** value: **Cover or less**
Circ: CapCity orders: **14,800**
★ Versus Jihad.

18 ❑ Oct 1988 Cover: 1.00 **NM** value: **Cover or less**
Circ: CapCity orders: **14,250**
• Ravan vs. Bronze Tiger

19 ❑ Nov 1988 Cover: 1.00 **NM** value: **Cover or less**
Circ: CapCity orders: **13,350**

20 ❑ Dec 1988 Cover: 1.00 **NM** value: **Cover or less**
Circ: CapCity orders: **13,050**

21 ❑ Dec 1988 Cover: 1.00 **NM** value: **Cover or less**
Circ: CapCity orders: **12,250**

22 ❑ Jan 1989 Cover: 1.00 **NM** value: **Cover or less**
Circ: CapCity orders: **11,700**

23 ❑ Jan 1989 Cover: 1.00 **NM** value: **Cover or less**
Circ: CapCity orders: **11,550**

24 ❑ Feb 1989 Cover: 1.00 **NM** value: **Cover or less**
Circ: CapCity orders: **11,800**

25 ❑ Mar 1989 Cover: 1.00 **NM** value: **Cover or less**
Circ: CapCity orders: **11,250**

26 ❑ Apr 1989 Cover: 1.00 **NM** value: **Cover or less**
Circ: CapCity orders: **11,300**

27 ❑ May 1989 Cover: 1.00 **NM** value: **Cover or less**
Circ: CapCity orders: **12,800**
📖 Janus Directive

28 ❑ May 1989 Cover: 1.00 **NM** value: **Cover or less**
Circ: CapCity orders: **12,600**
📖 Janus Directive ★ Versus Force of July.

29 ❑ Jun 1989 Cover: 1.00 **NM** value: **Cover or less**
Circ: CapCity orders: **12,750**
📖 Janus Directive

30 ❑ Jun 1989 Cover: 1.00 **NM** value: **Cover or less**
Circ: CapCity orders: **12,700**
📖 Janus Directive

31 ❑ Jul 1989 Cover: 1.00 **NM** value: **Cover or less**
Circ: CapCity orders: **11,900**

32 ❑ Aug 1989 Cover: 1.00 **NM** value: **Cover or less**
Circ: CapCity orders: **12,250**

33 ❑ Sep 1989 Cover: 1.00 **NM** value: **Cover or less**
Circ: CapCity orders: **12,400**

34 ❑ Oct 1989 Cover: 1.00 **NM** value: **Cover or less**
Circ: CapCity orders: **12,550**

35 ❑ Nov 1989 Cover: 1.00 **NM** value: **Cover or less**
Circ: CapCity orders: **11,500**

36 ❑ Dec 1989 Cover: 1.00 **NM** value: **Cover or less**
Circ: CapCity orders: **11,300**

37 ❑ Jan 1990 Cover: 1.00 **NM** value: **Cover or less**
Circ: CapCity orders: **11,200**

38 ❑ Feb 1990 Cover: 1.00 **NM** value: **Cover or less**
Circ: CapCity orders: **11,000**

39 ❑ Mar 1990 Cover: 1.00 **NM** value: **Cover or less**
Circ: CapCity orders: **10,950**

40 ❑ Apr 1990 Cover: 1.00 **NM** value: **Cover or less**
Circ: CapCity orders: **27,650**
📖 Phoenix Gambit

41 ❑ May 1990 Cover: 1.00 **NM** value: **Cover or less**
Circ: CapCity orders: **22,500**
📖 Phoenix Gambit

42 ❑ Jun 1990 Cover: 1.00 **NM** value: **Cover or less**
Circ: CapCity orders: **20,350**
📖 Phoenix Gambit

43 ❑ Jul 1990 Cover: 1.00 **NM** value: **Cover or less**
Circ: CapCity orders: **22,000**
📖 Phoenix Gambit

44 ❑ Aug 1990 Cover: 1.00 **NM** value: **Cover or less**
Circ: CapCity orders: **12,650**
• Flash

45 ❑ Sep 1990 Cover: 1.00 **NM** value: **Cover or less**
Circ: CapCity orders: **12,300**

CGC-graded: Multiply prices above by **33 for 9.9 M • 16 for 9.8 NM/M • 7 for 9.6 NM+ • 5 for 9.4 NM • 2.5 for 9.2 NM- • 1.5 for 9.0 VF/NM**

46 ❑ Oct 1990 Cover: 1.00 NM value: **Cover or less**
Circ: CapCity orders: **12,050**
47 ❑ Nov 1990 Cover: 1.00 NM value: **Cover or less**
Circ: CapCity orders: **11,600**
📖 choice Of Dooms **A:** Geof Isherwood **W:** Kim Yale; John Ostrander
48 ❑ Dec 1990 Cover: 1.00 NM value: **Cover or less**
Circ: CapCity orders: **11,550**
• Joker
49 ❑ Jan 1991 Cover: 1.00 NM value: **Cover or less**
Circ: CapCity orders: **11,050**
50 ❑ Feb 1991 Cover: 2.00 NM value: **Cover or less**
Circ: CapCity orders: **11,500**
51 ❑ Mar 1991 Cover: 1.00 NM value: **Cover or less**
Circ: CapCity orders: **10,450**
52 ❑ Apr 1991 Cover: 1.00 NM value: **Cover or less**
Circ: CapCity orders: **10,550**
53 ❑ May 1991 Cover: 1.00 NM value: **Cover or less**
Circ: CapCity orders: **10,850**
54 ❑ Jun 1991 Cover: 1.00 NM value: **Cover or less**
Circ: CapCity orders: **10,350**
55 ❑ Jul 1991 Cover: 1.00 NM value: **Cover or less**
Circ: CapCity orders: **10,050**
56 ❑ Aug 1991 Cover: 1.00 NM value: **Cover or less**
Circ: CapCity orders: **10,100**
57 ❑ Sep 1991 Cover: 1.00 NM value: **Cover or less**
Circ: CapCity orders: **9,950**
58 ❑ Oct 1991 Cover: 1.00 NM value: **Cover or less**
Circ: CapCity orders: **15,050**
📖 War of the Gods; War of the Gods, Part 16 ★ Appearance of Black Adam.
59 ❑ Nov 1991 Cover: 1.25 NM value: **Cover or less**
Circ: CapCity orders: **11,250**
60 ❑ Dec 1991 Cover: 1.25 NM value: **Cover or less**
Circ: CapCity orders: **12,650**
61 ❑ Jan 1992 Cover: 1.25 NM value: **Cover or less**
Circ: CapCity orders: **13,000**
62 ❑ Feb 1992 Cover: 1.25 NM value: **Cover or less**
Circ: CapCity orders: **12,450**
63 ❑ Mar 1992 Cover: 1.25 NM value: **Cover or less**
Circ: CapCity orders: **9,900**
64 ❑ Apr 1992 Cover: 1.25 NM value: **Cover or less**
Circ: CapCity orders: **9,650**
📖 Nasty As They Want To Be! **A:** Geof Isherwood **W:** Kim Yale; John Ostrander
65 ❑ May 1992 Cover: 1.25 NM value: **Cover or less**
Circ: CapCity orders: **9,300**
66 ❑ Jun 1992 Cover: 1.25 NM value: **Cover or less**
Circ: CapCity orders: **9,900**
final issue.
Anl 1❑ Cover: 1.50 NM value: **Cover or less**
Circ: CapCity orders: **14,100**
• secret of Argent revealed ★ Appearance of Manhunter.

SUIT, THE — Virtual

1 ❑ May 1996 Cover: 3.99 NM value: **Cover or less**
Circ: Diamd. preorders: **5,440**
📖 Invasion, Part 1
2 ❑ Jun 1997 Cover: 3.99 NM value: **Cover or less**
Circ: Diamd. preorders: **3,653**
📖 Invasion, Part 2

SULTRY TEENAGE SUPER FOXES — Solson

1 ❑ b&w Cover: 2.00 NM value: **Cover or less**
2 ❑ b&w Cover: 2.00 NM value: **Cover or less**

SUMMER LOVE — Charlton

46 ❑ ca. 1965 Cover: 0.12 NM value: **80.00**
47 ❑ Oct 1966 Cover: 0.12 NM value: **100.00**
📖 The Beatles Saved My Romance! • **CGC:** 7 graded, best 9.0
Notes: Beatles cover drawings in ad for Help! and Hard Days Night
48 ❑ ca. 1967 Cover: 0.12 NM value: **50.00**

SUNBURN — Alternative

1 ❑ Aug 2000, b&w Cover: 2.95 NM value: **Cover or less**
No issue number. • smaller than normal comic book **A:** James Kochalka **W:** James Kochalka

SUN DEVILS — DC

1 ❑ Jul 1984 Cover: 1.25 NM value: **1.50**
📖 Planet Kill **A:** Dan Jurgens **W:** Dan Jurgens; Gerry Conway
2 ❑ Aug 1984 Cover: 1.50 NM value: **Cover or less**
3 ❑ Sep 1984 Cover: 1.50 NM value: **Cover or less**
4 ❑ Oct 1984 Cover: 1.50 NM value: **Cover or less**
5 ❑ Nov 1984 Cover: 1.50 NM value: **Cover or less**
6 ❑ Dec 1984 Cover: 1.50 NM value: **Cover or less**
7 ❑ Jan 1985 Cover: 1.50 NM value: **Cover or less**
8 ❑ Feb 1985 Cover: 1.50 NM value: **Cover or less**
9 ❑ Mar 1985 Cover: 1.50 NM value: **Cover or less**
10 ❑ Apr 1985 Cover: 1.50 NM value: **Cover or less**
11 ❑ May 1985 Cover: 1.50 NM value: **Cover or less**
Circ: CapCity orders: **6,000**
12 ❑ Jun 1985 Cover: 1.50 NM value: **Cover or less**
Circ: CapCity orders: **6,050**

SUNFIRE & BIG HERO SIX — Marvel

1 ❑ Sep 1998 Cover: 2.50 NM value: **Cover or less**
Circ: Diamd. preorders: **29,216**
📖 Land of the Rising Sun, Part 1 **A:** Gus Vazquez **W:** Scott Lobdell ★ Appearance of Honey Lemon, Gogo Tomago, Baymax, Hiro, Silver Samurai.
2 ❑ Oct 1998 Cover: 2.50 NM value: **Cover or less**
Circ: Diamd. preorders: **23,627**
📖 Land of the Rising Sun, Part 2 **A:** Gus Vazquez **W:** Scott Lobdell ★ Appearance of Honey Lemon, Gogo Tomago, Baymax, Hiro, Silver Samurai.
3 ❑ Nov 1998 Cover: 2.50 NM value: **Cover or less**
Circ: Diamd. preorders: **22,683**
📖 Land of the Rising Sun, Part 3 **A:** Gus Vazquez **W:** Scott Lobdell ★ Appearance of Honey Lemon, Gogo Tomago, Baymax, Hiro, Silver Samurai.

SUN FUN KOMIKS — Sun

1 ❑ ca. 1939 Cover: 0.15 NM value: **200.00**

SUN GIRL — Marvel

1 ❑ Aug 1948 Cover: 0.10 NM value: **700.00**
2 ❑ Oct 1948 Cover: 0.10 NM value: **500.00**
• **CGC:** 1 graded, best 6.0
3 ❑ Dec 1948 Cover: 0.10 NM value: **500.00**

SUNGLASSES AFTER DARK — Verotik

1 ❑ Cover: 5.00 NM value: **Cover or less**
2 ❑ Cover: 3.50 NM value: **Cover or less**
3 ❑ Cover: 2.95 NM value: **Cover or less**

SUNNY, AMERICA'S SWEETHEART — Fox

11 ❑ Dec 1947 Cover: 0.10 NM value: **650.00**
• **CGC:** 1 graded, best 8.0
12 ❑ Feb 1948 Cover: 0.10 NM value: **500.00**
13 ❑ Apr 1948 Cover: 0.10 NM value: **500.00**
14 ❑ Jun 1948 Cover: 0.10 NM value: **500.00**

SUNRISE — Harrier

1 ❑ Dec 1986 Cover: 1.95 NM value: **Cover or less**
2 ❑ May 1987 Cover: 1.95 NM value: **Cover or less**

SUN-RUNNERS — Pacific

Sun-Runners takes place in a future where the distribution of energy requires a network that spans thousands of worlds. On a huge power station called Daybreak, a group led by Mark Dancer acts as troubleshooters, patching up problems both mechanical and humanoid. Dancer's crew includes Delphi, the ship's captain and a powerful psychic; Doctor Gibraltar, an elephant-like powerhouse who is also a near-genius; and Scooter, their sentient engineering robot.

Sun-Runners was one of the raft of creator-owned comics produced by independent Pacific Comics in the mid-1980s. It featured art by Pat Broderick as well as early color work by Steve Oliff (who would later become famous for his Olyoptics computer coloring for Image Comics).

1 ❑ Feb 1984 Cover: 1.50 NM value: **Cover or less**
A: Pat Broderick **W:** Roger McKenzie
2 ❑ Mar 1984 Cover: 1.50 NM value: **Cover or less**
A: Pat Broderick **W:** Roger McKenzie
3 ❑ May 1984 Cover: 1.50 NM value: **Cover or less**
A: Pat Broderick
4 ❑ 1984 Cover: 1.75 NM value: **Cover or less**
5 ❑ 1984 Cover: 1.75 NM value: **Cover or less**
Circ: CapCity orders: **4,725**
6 ❑ 1984 Cover: 1.75 NM value: **Cover or less**
7 ❑ 1984 Cover: 1.75 NM value: **Cover or less**
final issue.
HS 1❑ Cover: 1.95 NM value: **Cover or less**
• Double-size.
SE 1❑ Cover: 1.95 NM value: **Cover or less**
• Special edition.

SUNSET CARSON — Charlton

1 ❑ Feb 1951 Cover: 0.10 NM value: **700.00**
2 ❑ Apr 1951 Cover: 0.10 NM value: **500.00**
3 ❑ Jun 1951 Cover: 0.10 NM value: **400.00**
4 ❑ Aug 1951 Cover: 0.10 NM value: **400.00**

SUPERBOY (1ST SERIES) — DC

Encouraged by the long-lasting popularity of Superman, DC decided to launch several follow-up titles. Titles such as Superman's Girl Friend Lois Lane, and Superman's Pal Jimmy Olsen concentrated on supporting cast, and Superboy went back into his own past, telling of Clark Kent's adventures as a teenager.

The stories here were light-hearted and often gimmicky. A Bizarro-Superboy, Super-Baby, Super-Dog, and even a Super-Monkey were concocted for this series. Superboy's main problems, however, were balancing the need to save the world, protecting his secret identity, and fending off the romantic advances of Lana Lang and others.

With issue #231, the title became known as Superboy and the Legion of Super-Heroes. With issue #259, Superboy faded from view, and the title's name changed officially to The Legion of Super-Heroes.

1 ❑ Mar 1949 Cover: 0.10 NM value: **5200.00**
• **CGC:** 25 graded, best 9.2
Superman on cover. 📖 The Man Who Could See Tomorrow!; Rocket Plane; Shorty; The Boy Vandals; Daffy & Doodle; The Language of the Sea; Sagebrush Sam; Superboy Meets Mighty Boy!; Homer **A:** Henry Boltinoff; Win Mortimer; Ed Dobrotka; John Sikela; Lit-Win **W:** Henry Boltinoff; Lit-Win; Cliff Rhodes; Edmond Hamilton
2 ❑ May 1949 Cover: 0.10 NM value: **1450.00**
• **CGC:** 5 graded, best 8.0
• Cited in Seduction of The Innocent (p35-36, 226), "Superboy rewrites American history, too. In one story he helps George Washington's campaign and saves his life by hitting a Hessian with a snowball..."
3 ❑ Jul 1949 Cover: 0.10 NM value: **1050.00**
• **CGC:** 1 graded, best 7.0
4 ❑ Sep 1949 Cover: 0.10 NM value: **800.00**
• **CGC:** 1 graded, best 4.5
5 ❑ Nov 1949 Cover: 0.10 NM value: **700.00**
• **CGC:** 2 graded, best 7.0
★ Appearance of Supergirl.
6 ❑ Jan 1950 Cover: 0.10 NM value: **625.00**
• **CGC:** 1 graded, best 9.4
7 ❑ Mar 1950 Cover: 0.10 NM value: **625.00**
• **CGC:** 3 graded, best 4.0
8 ❑ May 1950 Cover: 0.10 NM value: **625.00**
• **CGC:** 1 graded, best 8.5
★ 1st Appearance of Superbaby.
9 ❑ Jul 1950 Cover: 0.10 NM value: **625.00**
• **CGC:** 2 graded, best 9.0
10 ❑ Sep 1950 Cover: 0.10 NM value: **625.00**
• **CGC:** 4 graded, best 9.0
★ 1st Appearance of Lana Lang.
11 ❑ Nov 1950 Cover: 0.10 NM value: **475.00**
• **CGC:** 1 graded, best 9.0
12 ❑ Jan 1951 Cover: 0.10 NM value: **475.00**
• **CGC:** 3 graded, best 8.0
13 ❑ Mar 1951 Cover: 0.10 NM value: **475.00**
• **CGC:** 1 graded, best 7.0
14 ❑ May 1951 Cover: 0.10 NM value: **475.00**
• **CGC:** 2 graded, best 7.0
15 ❑ Jul 1951 Cover: 0.10 NM value: **475.00**
• **CGC:** 3 graded, best 9.2
16 ❑ Sep 1951 Cover: 0.10 NM value: **350.00**
• **CGC:** 2 graded, best 8.0
17 ❑ Nov 1951 Cover: 0.10 NM value: **350.00**
• **CGC:** 2 graded, best 9.2
18 ❑ Feb 1952 Cover: 0.10 NM value: **350.00**
• **CGC:** 2 graded, best 9.6
19 ❑ Apr 1952 Cover: 0.10 NM value: **350.00**
• **CGC:** 1 graded, best 9.0
20 ❑ Jun 1952 Cover: 0.10 NM value: **350.00**
• **CGC:** 2 graded, best 9.0
21 ❑ Aug 1952 Cover: 0.10 NM value: **275.00**
• **CGC:** 1 graded, best 5.0
22 ❑ Oct 1952 Cover: 0.10 NM value: **275.00**
• **CGC:** 3 graded, best 9.2
23 ❑ Dec 1952 Cover: 0.10 NM value: **275.00**
24 ❑ Feb 1953 Cover: 0.10 NM value: **275.00**
25 ❑ Apr 1953 Cover: 0.10 NM value: **275.00**
• **CGC:** 1 graded, best 4.5
26 ❑ Jun 1953 Cover: 0.10 NM value: **275.00**
27 ❑ Aug 1953 Cover: 0.10 NM value: **275.00**
• Scarcer
28 ❑ Oct 1953 Cover: 0.10 NM value: **275.00**
29 ❑ Dec 1953 Cover: 0.10 NM value: **275.00**
30 ❑ Jan 1954 Cover: 0.10 NM value: **275.00**
• **CGC:** 1 graded, best 5.0
31 ❑ Mar 1954 Cover: 0.10 NM value: **200.00**
32 ❑ Apr 1954 Cover: 0.10 NM value: **200.00**
• **CGC:** 1 graded, best 5.0
33 ❑ Jun 1954 Cover: 0.10 NM value: **200.00**
34 ❑ Jul 1954 Cover: 0.10 NM value: **200.00**
• **CGC:** 2 graded, best 6.5
35 ❑ Sep 1954 Cover: 0.10 NM value: **200.00**
• **CGC:** 2 graded, best 4.5
36 ❑ Oct 1954 Cover: 0.10 NM value: **200.00**
37 ❑ Dec 1954 Cover: 0.10 NM value: **200.00**
38 ❑ Jan 1955 Cover: 0.10 NM value: **200.00**
• **CGC:** 1 graded, best 3.5
39 ❑ Mar 1955 Cover: 0.10 NM value: **140.00**
• **CGC:** 1 graded, best 1.0
• First Comics Code-approved issue
40 ❑ Apr 1955 Cover: 0.10 NM value: **140.00**
• **CGC:** 1 graded, best 3.5
41 ❑ Jun 1955 Cover: 0.10 NM value: **140.00**
42 ❑ Jul 1955 Cover: 0.10 NM value: **140.00**
• **CGC:** 2 graded, best 5.0
43 ❑ Sep 1955 Cover: 0.10 NM value: **140.00**
• **CGC:** 1 graded, best 4.0
44 ❑ Oct 1955 Cover: 0.10 NM value: **140.00**
45 ❑ Dec 1955 Cover: 0.10 NM value: **140.00**
46 ❑ Jan 1956 Cover: 0.10 NM value: **140.00**
47 ❑ Mar 1956 Cover: 0.10 NM value: **140.00**
• **CGC:** 1 graded, best 7.5
48 ❑ Apr 1956 Cover: 0.10 NM value: **140.00**
49 ❑ May 1956 Cover: 0.10 NM value: **185.00**
★ 1st Appearance of Metallo.
50 ❑ Jul 1956 Cover: 0.10 NM value: **140.00**
• **CGC:** 1 graded, best 7.0
51 ❑ Sep 1956 Cover: 0.10 NM value: **110.00**
52 ❑ Oct 1956 Cover: 0.10 NM value: **110.00**
53 ❑ Dec 1956 Cover: 0.10 NM value: **110.00**
• **CGC:** 1 graded, best 7.0
54 ❑ Jan 1957 Cover: 0.10 NM value: **110.00**
• **CGC:** 3 graded, best 8.0
55 ❑ Mar 1957 Cover: 0.10 NM value: **110.00**
• **CGC:** 1 graded, best 7.0
56 ❑ Apr 1957 Cover: 0.10 NM value: **110.00**
57 ❑ Jun 1957 Cover: 0.10 NM value: **110.00**
• **CGC:** 2 graded, best 7.0
58 ❑ Jul 1957 Cover: 0.10 NM value: **110.00**
• **CGC:** 1 graded, best 8.0

59 ❑ Sep 1957 Cover: 0.10 **NM** value: **110.00**
• **CGC:** 3 graded, best 8.5

60 ❑ Oct 1957 Cover: 0.10 **NM** value: **110.00**
• **CGC:** 1 graded, best 6.0

61 ❑ Dec 1957 Cover: 0.10 **NM** value: **90.00**
• **CGC:** 1 graded, best 8.0

62 ❑ Jan 1958 Cover: 0.10 **NM** value: **90.00**
• **CGC:** 2 graded, best 6.5

63 ❑ Mar 1958 Cover: 0.10 **NM** value: **90.00**

64 ❑ Apr 1958 Cover: 0.10 **NM** value: **90.00**
• **CGC:** 1 graded, best 6.5

65 ❑ Jun 1958 Cover: 0.10 **NM** value: **90.00**
• **CGC:** 2 graded, best 5.5

66 ❑ Jul 1958 Cover: 0.10 **NM** value: **90.00**

67 ❑ Sep 1958 Cover: 0.10 **NM** value: **90.00**
• **CGC:** 2 graded, best 6.0
• Origin of Klax-Ar. ★ 1st Appearance of Klax-Ar.

68 ❑ Oct 1958 Cover: 0.10 **NM** value: **475.00**
• **CGC:** 5 graded, best 6.5
• Origin of Bizarro. ★ 1st Appearance of Bizarro.

69 ❑ Dec 1958 Cover: 0.10 **NM** value: **70.00**
• **CGC:** 3 graded, best 7.5

70 ❑ Jan 1959 Cover: 0.10 **NM** value: **70.00**
• **CGC:** 1 graded, best 4.5
★ Origin of Mr. Mxyzptlk.

71 ❑ Mar 1959 Cover: 0.10 **NM** value: **70.00**
• **CGC:** 2 graded, best 6.5

72 ❑ Apr 1959 Cover: 0.10 **NM** value: **70.00**
• **CGC:** 1 graded, best 7.5

73 ❑ Jun 1959 Cover: 0.10 **NM** value: **70.00**
• **CGC:** 1 graded, best 3.5

74 ❑ Jul 1959 Cover: 0.10 **NM** value: **70.00**

75 ❑ Sep 1959 Cover: 0.10 **NM** value: **70.00**
• **CGC:** 1 graded, best 5.0

76 ❑ Oct 1959 Cover: 0.10 **NM** value: **70.00**
• **CGC:** 3 graded, best 7.5
★ 1st Appearance of Supermonkey.

77 ❑ Dec 1959 Cover: 0.10 **NM** value: **70.00**
• **CGC:** 2 graded, best 9.0

78 ❑ Jan 1960 Cover: 0.10 **NM** value: **135.00**
Circ: Statement: **635,000** • **CGC:** 1 graded, best 6.0
★ Origin of Mr. Mxyzptlk.

79 ❑ Mar 1960 Cover: 0.10 **NM** value: **70.00**
Circ: Statement: **635,000**

80 ❑ Apr 1960 Cover: 0.10 **NM** value: **110.00**
Circ: Statement: **635,000**
• Superboy meets Supergirl

81 ❑ Jun 1960 Cover: 0.10 **NM** value: **52.00**
Circ: Statement: **635,000** • **CGC:** 3 graded, best 9.4

82 ❑ Jul 1960 Cover: 0.10 **NM** value: **52.00**
Circ: Statement: **635,000** • **CGC:** 1 graded, best 8.5
★ Appearance of Bizarro Krypto.

83 ❑ Sep 1960 Cover: 0.10 **NM** value: **52.00**
Circ: Statement: **635,000** • **CGC:** 1 graded, best 9.4
★ Origin of Kryptonite Kid. ★ 1st Appearance of Kryptonite Kid.

84 ❑ Oct 1960 Cover: 0.10 **NM** value: **52.00**
Circ: Statement: **635,000** • **CGC:** 1 graded, best 4.5
★ Versus Rainbow Raider.

85 ❑ Dec 1960 Cover: 0.10 **NM** value: **52.00**
Circ: Statement: **635,000** • **CGC:** 2 graded, best 9.2

86 ❑ Jan 1961 Cover: 0.10 **NM** value: **125.00**
Circ: Statement: **655,000** • **CGC:** 2 graded, best 8.0
📖 The Army of Living Kryptonite Men ★ 1st Appearance of Pete Ross. ★ Appearance of Legion of Super-Heroes.

87 ❑ Mar 1961 Cover: 0.10 **NM** value: **52.00**
Circ: Statement: **655,000** • **CGC:** 1 graded, best 9.2

88 ❑ Apr 1961 Cover: 0.10 **NM** value: **52.00**
Circ: Statement: **655,000**

89 ❑ Jun 1961 Cover: 0.10 **NM** value: **220.00**
Circ: Statement: **655,000** • **CGC:** 3 graded, best 8.5
📖 Superboy's Big Brother ★ Origin of Mon-El. ★ 1st Appearance of Mon-El.

90 ❑ Jul 1961 Cover: 0.10 **NM** value: **48.00**
Circ: Statement: **655,000** • **CGC:** 2 graded, best 9.2

91 ❑ Sep 1961 Cover: 0.10 **NM** value: **48.00**
Circ: Statement: **655,000** • **CGC:** 1 graded, best 9.4

92 ❑ Oct 1961 Cover: 0.10 **NM** value: **48.00**
Circ: Statement: **655,000**

93 ❑ Dec 1961 Cover: 0.12 **NM** value: **48.00**
Circ: Statement: **655,000** • **CGC:** 3 graded, best 9.0
★ Appearance of Legion of Super-Heroes.

94 ❑ Jan 1962 Cover: 0.12 **NM** value: **35.00**
Circ: Statement: **605,000** • **CGC:** 3 graded, best 9.2

95 ❑ Mar 1962 Cover: 0.12 **NM** value: **35.00**
Circ: Statement: **605,000** • **CGC:** 2 graded, best 9.4
• Has 1961 Statement; avg total paid circ 655,000

96 ❑ Apr 1962 Cover: 0.12 **NM** value: **35.00**
Circ: Statement: **605,000** • **CGC:** 3 graded, best 9.0

97 ❑ Jun 1962 Cover: 0.12 **NM** value: **35.00**
Circ: Statement: **605,000** • **CGC:** 1 graded, best 9.4

98 ❑ Jul 1962 Cover: 0.12 **NM** value: **45.00**
Circ: Statement: **605,000** • **CGC:** 4 graded, best 9.4
📖 The Boy With Ultra-Powers ★ Origin of Ultra Boy. ★ 1st Appearance of Ultra Boy. ★ Appearance of Legion of Super-Heroes.

99 ❑ Sep 1962 Cover: 0.12 **NM** value: **35.00**
Circ: Statement: **605,000** • **CGC:** 2 graded, best 8.5

100 ❑ Oct 1962 Cover: 0.12 **NM** value: **175.00**
Circ: Statement: **605,000** • **CGC:** 10 graded, best 9.2
• 100th anniversary issue. ★ 1st Appearance of Phantom Zone villains. ★ Appearance of Legion of Super-Heroes.

101 ❑ Dec 1962 Cover: 0.12 **NM** value: **16.00**
Circ: Statement: **605,000**

102 ❑ Jan 1963 Cover: 0.12 **NM** value: **16.00**
• **CGC:** 1 graded, best 9.2
• Superbaby back-up

103 ❑ Mar 1963 Cover: 0.12 **NM** value: **16.00**
• Red K story; Has 1962 Statement, filed 10/1/62; avg total paid circ 605,000

104 ❑ Apr 1963 Cover: 0.12 **NM** value: **16.00**
★ Origin of Phantom Zone.

105 ❑ Jun 1963 Cover: 0.12 **NM** value: **16.00**

106 ❑ Jul 1963 Cover: 0.12 **NM** value: **16.00**
• **CGC:** 1 graded, best 7.0

107 ❑ Sep 1963 Cover: 0.12 **NM** value: **16.00**
• **CGC:** 3 graded, best 9.2

108 ❑ Oct 1963 Cover: 0.12 **NM** value: **16.00**

109 ❑ Dec 1963 Cover: 0.12 **NM** value: **16.00**

110 ❑ Jan 1964 Cover: 0.12 **NM** value: **16.00**
• **CGC:** 1 graded, best 6.5

111 ❑ Mar 1964 Cover: 0.12 **NM** value: **15.00**
• Has 1963 Statement, filed 10/1/63; no circ figures published

112 ❑ Apr 1964 Cover: 0.12 **NM** value: **15.00**
• **CGC:** 1 graded, best 6.5

113 ❑ Jun 1964 Cover: 0.12 **NM** value: **15.00**
• **CGC:** 3 graded, best 9.2

114 ❑ Jul 1964 Cover: 0.12 **NM** value: **15.00**

115 ❑ Sep 1964 Cover: 0.12 **NM** value: **15.00**
• Atomic Superboy

116 ❑ Oct 1964 Cover: 0.12 **NM** value: **15.00**
• **CGC:** 1 graded, best 7.5
📖 Superboy, King of the Wolf-Pack!; The False Superboy of Smallville!; The Ordeal of Chief Parker

117 ❑ Dec 1964 Cover: 0.12 **NM** value: **15.00**
• **CGC:** 1 graded, best 9.2
📖 Superboy and the Five Legion Traitors ★ Appearance of Legion.

118 ❑ Jan 1965 Cover: 0.12 **NM** value: **15.00**
Circ: Statement: **672,681** • **CGC:** 2 graded, best 9.2

119 ❑ Mar 1965 Cover: 0.12 **NM** value: **15.00**
Circ: Statement: **672,681** • **CGC:** 1 graded, best 9.2

120 ❑ Apr 1965 Cover: 0.12 **NM** value: **15.00**
Circ: Statement: **672,681**
• Has 1964 Statement, filed 10/1/64; no circ figures published

121 ❑ Jun 1965 Cover: 0.12 **NM** value: **10.00**
Circ: Statement: **672,681** • **CGC:** 2 graded, best 9.0
• Clark loses his super-powers; Jor-El back-up

122 ❑ Jul 1965 Cover: 0.12 **NM** value: **10.00**
Circ: Statement: **672,681** • **CGC:** 1 graded, best 8.5

123 ❑ Sep 1965 Cover: 0.12 **NM** value: **10.00**
Circ: Statement: **672,681** • **CGC:** 2 graded, best 9.0

124 ❑ Oct 1965 Cover: 0.12 **NM** value: **10.00**
Circ: Statement: **672,681** • **CGC:** 1 graded, best 8.5
📖 The Insect Queen of Smallville ★ 1st Appearance of Insect Queen.

125 ❑ Dec 1965 Cover: 0.12 **NM** value: **10.00**
Circ: Statement: **672,681** • **CGC:** 3 graded, best 9.6
📖 The Sacrifice of Kid Psycho ★ Origin of Kid Psycho. ★ 1st Appearance of Kid Psycho.

126 ❑ Jan 1966 Cover: 0.12 **NM** value: **10.00**
Circ: Statement: **608,386** • **CGC:** 1 graded, best 9.4
★ Origin of Krypto.

127 ❑ Mar 1966 Cover: 0.12 **NM** value: **10.00**
Circ: Statement: **608,386** • **CGC:** 1 graded, best 7.0

128 ❑ Apr 1966 Cover: 0.12 **NM** value: **10.00**
Circ: Statement: **608,386**
• Imaginary Story ★ Appearance of Dev-Em, Kryptonite Kid.

129 ❑ May 1966 Cover: 0.25 **NM** value: **13.00**
Circ: Statement: **608,386** • **CGC:** 2 graded, best 9.0
• Giant-size.

130 ❑ Jun 1966 Cover: 0.12 **NM** value: **8.00**
Circ: Statement: **608,386**
• Superbaby

131 ❑ Jul 1966 Cover: 0.12 **NM** value: **8.00**
Circ: Statement: **608,386** • **CGC:** 1 graded, best 6.0

132 ❑ Sep 1966 Cover: 0.12 **NM** value: **8.00**
Circ: Statement: **608,386** • **CGC:** 1 graded, best 7.0
• Has 1965 Statement, filed 10/1/65; avg total paid circ 672,681

133 ❑ Oct 1966 Cover: 0.12 **NM** value: **8.00**
Circ: Statement: **608,386** • **CGC:** 1 graded, best 6.0
★ Appearance of Robin.

134 ❑ Dec 1966 Cover: 0.12 **NM** value: **8.00**
Circ: Statement: **608,386** • **CGC:** 1 graded, best 9.2
• Krypto back-up

135 ❑ Jan 1967 Cover: 0.12 **NM** value: **8.00**
Circ: Statement: **547,100** • **CGC:** 2 graded, best 9.2

136 ❑ Mar 1967 Cover: 0.12 **NM** value: **8.00**
Circ: Statement: **547,100** • **CGC:** 3 graded, best 9.4
• Has 1966 Statement; avg print run 952,000; avg sales 601,000; avg subs 7,386; avg total paid 608,386; samples 330; max existent 608,716; 36% of run returned

137 ❑ Apr 1967 Cover: 0.12 **NM** value: **8.00**
Circ: Statement: **547,100** • **CGC:** 2 graded, best 8.5

138 ❑ Jun 1967 Cover: 0.25 **NM** value: **13.00**
Circ: Statement: **547,100** • **CGC:** 2 graded, best 9.0
• Giant-size.

139 ❑ Jun 1967 Cover: 0.12 **NM** value: **7.00**
Circ: Statement: **547,100** • **CGC:** 1 graded, best 9.6

140 ❑ Jul 1967 Cover: 0.12 **NM** value: **7.00**
Circ: Statement: **547,100**

141 ❑ Sep 1967 Cover: 0.12 **NM** value: **6.00**
Circ: Statement: **547,100**

142 ❑ Oct 1967 Cover: 0.12 **NM** value: **6.00**
Circ: Statement: **547,100** • **CGC:** 1 graded, best 9.2
★ Appearance of Beppo.

143 ❑ Dec 1967 Cover: 0.12 **NM** value: **6.00**
Circ: Statement: **547,100** • **CGC:** 4 graded, best 9.4
C: Neal Adams

144 ❑ Jan 1968 Cover: 0.12 **NM** value: **6.00**
Circ: Statement: **532,135** • **CGC:** 2 graded, best 9.4
C: Curt Swan

145 ❑ Mar 1968 Cover: 0.12 **NM** value: **6.00**
Circ: Statement: **532,135** • **CGC:** 3 graded, best 9.4
• Has 1967 Statement; avg total paid circ 547,100 **C:** Neal Adams

146 ❑ Apr 1968 Cover: 0.12 **NM** value: **6.00**
Circ: Statement: **532,135** • **CGC:** 2 graded, best 9.4
C: Neal Adams

147 ❑ Jun 1968 Cover: 0.25 **NM** value: **10.00**
Circ: Statement: **532,135** • **CGC:** 1 graded, best 9.2
• Giant-size. 📖 The Origin of the Legion ★ Origin of Saturn Girl, Cosmic Boy.

148 ❑ Jun 1968 Cover: 0.12 **NM** value: **6.00**
Circ: Statement: **532,135** • **CGC:** 3 graded, best 9.4
C: Neal Adams

149 ❑ Jul 1968 Cover: 0.12 **NM** value: **6.00**
Circ: Statement: **532,135**
C: Neal Adams

150 ❑ Sep 1968 Cover: 0.12 **NM** value: **6.00**
Circ: Statement: **532,135** • **CGC:** 1 graded, best 8.0
C: Neal Adams ★ Versus Mr. Cipher.

151 ❑ Oct 1968 Cover: 0.12 **NM** value: **6.00**
Circ: Statement: **532,135** • **CGC:** 1 graded, best 9.4
C: Neal Adams

152 ❑ Dec 1968 Cover: 0.12 **NM** value: **6.00**
Circ: Statement: **532,135** • **CGC:** 2 graded, best 9.4
A: Wally Wood **C:** Neal Adams

153 ❑ Jan 1969 Cover: 0.12 **NM** value: **6.00**
Circ: Statement: **465,462** • **CGC:** 3 graded, best 9.4
📖 Challenge of the Cosmic Invaders! **A:** Wally Wood; Bob Brown **C:** Neal Adams **W:** Frank Robbins

154 ❑ Mar 1969 Cover: 0.12 **NM** value: **6.00**
Circ: Statement: **465,462** • **CGC:** 2 graded, best 9.4
• Has 1968 Statement, filed 10/1/68; avg print run 892,000; avg sales 531,000; avg subs 1,135; avg total paid 532,135; samples 386; max existent 532,521; 40% of run returned **A:** Wally Wood **C:** Neal Adams

155 ❑ Apr 1969 Cover: 0.12 **NM** value: **6.00**
Circ: Statement: **465,462** • **CGC:** 1 graded, best 8.5
A: Wally Wood **C:** Neal Adams

156 ❑ Jun 1969 Cover: 0.25 **NM** value: **9.00**
Circ: Statement: **465,462** • **CGC:** 2 graded, best 9.2
• Giant-size.

157 ❑ Jun 1969 Cover: 0.12 **NM** value: **6.00**
Circ: Statement: **465,462** • **CGC:** 2 graded, best 9.4
A: Wally Wood

158 ❑ Jul 1969 Cover: 0.15 **NM** value: **6.00**
Circ: Statement: **465,462**
A: Wally Wood

159 ❑ Sep 1969 Cover: 0.15 **NM** value: **6.00**
Circ: Statement: **465,462**
A: Wally Wood

160 ❑ Oct 1969 Cover: 0.15 **NM** value: **6.00**
Circ: Statement: **465,462** • **CGC:** 3 graded, best 9.4
A: Wally Wood

161 ❑ Dec 1969 Cover: 0.15 **NM** value: **6.00**
Circ: Statement: **465,462** • **CGC:** 2 graded, best 9.2
📖 The Strange Death Of Superboy! **A:** Wally Wood; Bob Brown **W:** Frank Robbins

162 ❑ Jan 1970 Cover: 0.15 **NM** value: **6.00**
Circ: Statement: **377,525** • **CGC:** 1 graded, best 9.2

163 ❑ Mar 1970 Cover: 0.15 **NM** value: **6.00**
Circ: Statement: **377,525**
• Has 1969 Statement; avg print run 856,000; avg sales 465,000; avg subs 462; avg total paid 465,462; max existent 465,462; 46% of run returned **C:** Neal Adams

164 ❑ Apr 1970 Cover: 0.15 **NM** value: **6.00**
Circ: Statement: **377,525** • **CGC:** 3 graded, best 9.4
C: Neal Adams

165 ❑ Jun 1970 Cover: 0.25 **NM** value: **9.00**
Circ: Statement: **377,525** • **CGC:** 1 graded, best 9.0
• Giant-size.

166 ❑ Jun 1970 Cover: 0.15 **NM** value: **6.00**
Circ: Statement: **377,525**
C: Neal Adams

167 ❑ Jul 1970 Cover: 0.15 **NM** value: **6.00**
Circ: Statement: **377,525** • **CGC:** 1 graded, best 9.0
C: Neal Adams

168 ❑ Sep 1970 Cover: 0.15 **NM** value: **6.00**
Circ: Statement: **377,525**
C: Neal Adams

169 ❑ Oct 1970 Cover: 0.15 **NM** value: **6.00**
Circ: Statement: **377,525**

170 ❑ Dec 1970 Cover: 0.15 **NM** value: **6.00**
Circ: Statement: **377,525**

171 ❑ Jan 1971 Cover: 0.15 **NM** value: **4.00**
Circ: Statement: **353,642**

172 ❑ Mar 1971 Cover: 0.15 **NM** value: **5.00**
Circ: Statement: **353,642**
📖 Brotherly Hate! • Has 1970 Statement; avg print run 737,080; avg sales 377,251; avg subs 274; avg total paid 377,525; max existent 377,525; 49% of run returned ★ Appearance of Legion of Super-Heroes.

173 ❑ Apr 1971 Cover: 0.15 **NM** value: **4.00**
Circ: Statement: **353,642**
📖 Trust Me or Kill Me! **A:** George Tuska; Dick Giordano **C:** Neal Adams ★ Origin of Cosmic Boy.

174 ❑ Jun 1971 Cover: 0.25 **NM** value: **7.00**
Circ: Statement: **353,642** • **CGC:** 2 graded, best 9.4
• Giant-size. • reprints Adventure #219, #225, and #262, Superboy #53 and #105

175 ❑ Jun 1971 Cover: 0.15 **NM** value: **4.00**
Circ: Statement: **353,642**
A: Murphy Anderson **C:** Neal Adams

176 ❑ Jul 1971 Cover: 0.15 **NM** value: **4.00**
Circ: Statement: **353,642** • **CGC:** 1 graded, best 9.2
📖 Invisible Invader! **A:** Murphy Anderson; George Tuska; Wally Wood **C:** Neal Adams ★ Appearance of Legion of Super-Heroes.

177 ❑ Sep 1971 Cover: 0.25 **NM** value: **4.00**
Circ: Statement: **353,642** • **CGC:** 1 graded, best 9.2
• Giant-size. **A:** Murphy Anderson

178 ❑ Oct 1971 Cover: 0.25 **NM** value: **4.00**
Circ: Statement: **353,642**
• Giant-size. **A:** Murphy Anderson **C:** Neal Adams

179 ❑ Nov 1971 Cover: 0.25 **NM** value: **4.00**
Circ: Statement: **353,642** • **CGC:** 2 graded, best 9.2
• Giant-size.

180 ❑ Dec 1971 Cover: 0.25 **NM** value: **4.00**
Circ: Statement: **353,642** • **CGC:** 1 graded, best 9.2
• Giant-size.

181 ❑ Jan 1972 Cover: 0.25 **NM** value: **4.00**
Circ: Statement: **265,877** • **CGC:** 2 graded, best 9.6

CGC-graded: Multiply prices above by **33 for 9.9 M** • **16 for 9.8 NM/M** • **7 for 9.6 NM+** • **5 for 9.4 NM** • **2.5 for 9.2 NM-** • **1.5 for 9.0 VF/NM**

• Giant-size. • reprints Adventure #355
182 ❑ Feb 1972 Cover: 0.25 **NM** value: **4.00**
Circ: Statement: **265,877 • CGC:** 2 graded, best 9.2
• Giant-size.
183 ❑ Mar 1972 Cover: 0.25 **NM** value: **4.00**
Circ: Statement: **265,877 • CGC:** 1 graded, best 9.6
• Giant-size. War of the Wraith-Mates! • Has 1971 Statement; avg print run 656,250; avg sales 353,570; avg subs 72; avg total paid 353,642; samples 0; office use 428; max existent 354,070; 46% of run returned
184 ❑ Apr 1972 Cover: 0.25 **NM** value: **4.00**
Circ: Statement: **265,877 • CGC:** 2 graded, best 9.6
• Giant-size. One Leagionnaire Must Go! ★ Origin of Dial "H" For Hero.
185 ❑ May 1972 Cover: 0.50 **NM** value: **4.00**
Circ: Statement: **265,877 • CGC:** 1 graded, best 9.2
wraparound cover. • a.k.a. DC 100-Page Super Spectacular #185 ★ Appearance of Legion of Super-Heroes.
186 ❑ May 1972 Cover: 0.25 **NM** value: **4.00**
Circ: Statement: **265,877 • CGC:** 2 graded, best 9.2
187 ❑ Jun 1972 Cover: 0.25 **NM** value: **4.00**
Circ: Statement: **265,877**
188 ❑ Jul 1972 Cover: 0.20 **NM** value: **4.00**
Circ: Statement: **265,877**
Curse of the Blood Crystals! ★ Origin of Karkan.
189 ❑ Aug 1972 Cover: 0.20 **NM** value: **4.00**
Circ: Statement: **265,877**
190 ❑ Sep 1972 Cover: 0.20 **NM** value: **4.00**
Circ: Statement: **265,877 • CGC:** 3 graded, best 9.4
Murder the Leader!
191 ❑ Oct 1972 Cover: 0.20 **NM** value: **4.00**
Circ: Statement: **265,877 • CGC:** 1 graded, best 9.4
Attack of the Sun-Scavenger! ★ Origin of Sunboy.
192 ❑ Dec 1972 Cover: 0.20 **NM** value: **4.00**
Circ: Statement: **265,877 • CGC:** 4 graded, best 9.4
• Superbaby
193 ❑ Feb 1973 Cover: 0.20 **NM** value: **4.00**
Circ: Statement: **238,992**
War Between the Nights and Days!
194 ❑ Apr 1973 Cover: 0.20 **NM** value: **4.00**
Circ: Statement: **238,992 • CGC:** 1 graded, best 9.4
• Has 1972 Statement; avg print run 556,000; avg sales 265,172; avg subs 705; avg total paid 265,877; max existent 265,877; 52% of run returned
195 ❑ Jun 1973 Cover: 0.20 **NM** value: **4.00**
Circ: Statement: **238,992**
One-Shot Hero • Wildfire joins team ★ 1st Appearance of Wildfire. ★ 1st Appearance of Wildfire. ★ Appearance of Legion of Super-Heroes.
196 ❑ Jul 1973 Cover: 0.20 **NM** value: **4.00**
Circ: Statement: **238,992**
• last Superboy solo story
197 ❑ Sep 1973 Cover: 0.20 **NM** value: **6.00**
Circ: Statement: **238,992 • CGC:** 3 graded, best 9.2
Timber Wolf: Dead Hero, Live Executioner! • Legion of Super-Heroes stories begin **A:** Murphy Anderson
198 ❑ Oct 1973 Cover: 0.20 **NM** value: **4.00**
Circ: Statement: **238,992**
The Fatal Five Who Twisted Time! ★ Versus Fatal Five.
199 ❑ Nov 1973 Cover: 0.20 **NM** value: **4.00**
Circ: Statement: **238,992 • CGC:** 3 graded, best 9.4
The Gun That Mastered Men!
200 ❑ Feb 1974 Cover: 0.20 **NM** value: **6.00**
Circ: Statement: **225,427 • CGC:** 3 graded, best 9.4
The Legionnaire Bride of Starfinger • Wedding of Bouncing Boy and Duo Damsel
201 ❑ Apr 1974 Cover: 0.20 **NM** value: **3.00**
Circ: Statement: **225,427 • CGC:** 3 graded, best 9.4
The Betrayer From Beyond; The Silent Death
202 ❑ Jun 1974 Cover: 0.60 **NM** value: **3.00**
Circ: Statement: **225,427 • CGC:** 4 graded, best 9.6
Lost: a Million Miles From Home!; The Legionnaire Who Killed!; The Super-Stalag of Space!; The Execution of Matter-Eater Lad!; The Lore of the Legion!; The Wrath of Devilfish!; The Superboy of Bigville! • Has 1973 Statement; avg print run 533,600; avg sales 237,991; avg subs 1,101; avg total paid 238,992; max existent 239,092; 55% of run returned
203 ❑ Aug 1974 Cover: 0.20 **NM** value: **3.00**
Circ: Statement: **225,427 • CGC:** 6 graded, best 9.4
Massacre By Remote Control ★ Death of Invisible Kid I (Lyle Norg). ★ Versus Validus.
204 ❑ Oct 1974 Cover: 0.20 **NM** value: **3.00**
Circ: Statement: **225,427 • CGC:** 3 graded, best 9.6
The Legionnaire Nobody Remembered; Braniac 5's Secret Weakness! ★ 1st Appearance of Anti Lad.
205 ❑ Dec 1974 Cover: 0.60 **NM** value: **3.00**
Circ: Statement: **225,427 • CGC:** 4 graded, best 9.4
The Legion of Super-Executioners; The One-Man Team!; The Outcast Super-Heroes!; Lore of the Legion; The Forgotten Legion!; Meet "Iron Mike" Grell (text) • reprints Superboy #88, Adventure #350 and #351
206 ❑ Jan 1975 Cover: 0.25 **NM** value: **3.00**
Circ: Statement: **222,000 • CGC:** 4 graded, best 9.8
The Legionnaires Who Haunted Superboy; Welcome Home, Daughter… Now Die!
207 ❑ Feb 1975 Cover: 0.25 **NM** value: **3.00**
Circ: Statement: **222,000**
The Rookie Who Betrayed the Legion; Lightning Lad's Day of Dread
208 ❑ Apr 1975 Cover: 0.50 **NM** value: **3.00**
Circ: Statement: **222,000 • CGC:** 1 graded, best 6.5
Vengeance of the Super-Villains; The Legion of Substitute Heroes
209 ❑ Jun 1975 Cover: 0.25 **NM** value: **3.00**
Circ: Statement: **222,000 • CGC:** 3 graded, best 9.2
Who Can Save the Princess?; Hero For a Day • Has 1974 Statement; avg print run 487,060; avg sales 222,750; avg subs 2,677; avg total paid 225,427; max existent 225,427; 52% of run returned
210 ❑ Aug 1975 Cover: 0.25 **NM** value: **3.00**
Circ: Statement: **222,000**
Soljer's Private War; The Lair of the Black Dragon ★ Origin of Karate Kid.
211 ❑ Sep 1975 Cover: 0.25 **NM** value: **3.00**
Circ: Statement: **222,000 • CGC:** 2 graded, best 9.2
The Ultimate Revenge; The Legion's Lost Home ★ Appearance of Legion Subs.
212 ❑ Oct 1975 Cover: 0.25 **NM** value: **3.00**
Circ: Statement: **222,000**
Last Fight For a Legionnaire; A Death Stroke at Dawn • Matter-Eater Lad leaves team
213 ❑ Dec 1975 Cover: 0.25 **NM** value: **3.00**
Circ: Statement: **222,000**
The Jaws of Fear; Trapped to Live, Free to Die! ★ Appearance of Miracle Machine.
214 ❑ Jan 1976 Cover: 0.25 **NM** value: **3.00**
Circ: Statement: **218,000**
No Price Too High; Stay Small or Die!
215 ❑ Mar 1976 Cover: 0.25 **NM** value: **3.00**
Circ: Statement: **218,000**
The Final Eclipse of Sun Boy; The Hero Who Wouldn't Fight
216 ❑ Apr 1976 Cover: 0.30 **NM** value: **3.00**
Circ: Statement: **218,000**
The Hero Who Hated the Legion; 1+1=3 ★ 1st Appearance of Tyroc.
217 ❑ Jun 1976 Cover: 0.30 **NM** value: **3.00**
Circ: Statement: **218,000 • CGC:** 1 graded, best 9.6
The Charge of the Doomed Legionnaires; Future Shock for Superboy • Has 1975 Statement; avg print run 445,000; avg sales 219,000; avg subs 3,000; avg total paid 222,000; max existent 222,000; 49% of run returned ★ 1st Appearance of Laurel Kent.
218 ❑ Jul 1976 Cover: 0.30 **NM** value: **3.00**
Circ: Statement: **218,000**
The Secret Villain the World Never Knew • Tyroc joins team; Bicentennial #22
219 ❑ Sep 1976 Cover: 0.30 **NM** value: **3.00**
Circ: Statement: **218,000**
The Plunder Ploy of the Fatal Five ★ Versus Fatal Five.
220 ❑ Oct 1976 Cover: 0.30 **NM** value: **3.00**
Circ: Statement: **218,000**
The Super Soldiers of the Slave-Maker; Dream Girl's Living Nightmare
221 ❑ Nov 1976 Cover: 0.30 **NM** value: **2.00**
Circ: Statement: **218,000 • CGC:** 1 graded, best 9.4
The Trillion-Dollar Trophies ★ Origin of Charma, Grimbor. ★ 1st Appearance of Charma, Grimbor.
222 ❑ Dec 1976 Cover: 0.30 **NM** value: **2.00**
Circ: Statement: **218,000**
This Legionnaire Is Condemned!; Death of a Legend
223 ❑ Jan 1977 Cover: 0.30 **NM** value: **2.00**
Circ: Statement: **184,528**
We Can't Escape the Trap in Time! ★ 1st Appearance of Pulsar Stargrave. ★ Versus Time Trapper.
224 ❑ Feb 1977 Cover: 0.30 **NM** value: **2.00**
Circ: Statement: **184,528**
When Stargrave Strikes! ★ Versus Stargrave.
225 ❑ Mar 1977 Cover: 0.30 **NM** value: **2.00**
Circ: Statement: **184,528**
And Who Shall Lead Them?; A Matter of Priorities ★ 1st Appearance of Dawnstar.
226 ❑ Apr 1977 Cover: 0.30 **NM** value: **2.00**
Circ: Statement: **184,528**
The Dazzling Debut of Dawnstar!; Five Against One • Dawnstar joins team; Stargrave's identity revealed
227 ❑ May 1977 Cover: 0.30 **NM** value: **2.00**
Circ: Statement: **184,528**
War at World's End! • Has 1976 Statement; avg print run 478,000; avg sales 214,000; avg subs 4,000; avg total paid 218,000; max existent 218,000; 54% of run returned
228 ❑ Jun 1977 Cover: 0.35 **NM** value: **2.00**
Circ: Statement: **184,528**
That a World Might Live, a Legionnaire Must Die! ★ Death of Chemical King.
229 ❑ Jul 1977 Cover: 0.35 **NM** value: **2.00**
Circ: Statement: **184,528**
Hunt for a Hero-Killer
230 ❑ Aug 1977 Cover: 0.35 **NM** value: **2.00**
Circ: Statement: **184,528**
The Creature Who Conned the Legion; The Bouncing Boy Bounced Back • Bouncing Boy's powers restored; series continues as Superboy and the Legion of Super-Heroes
Anl 1 ❑ Sum 1964 Cover: 0.25 **NM** value: **135.00**
• **CGC:** 9 graded, best 9.6
The Return of Joe-El and Lara; The Voyage to New Krypton; The Orphan of Steel; Superbaby in Scotland Yard; The Blind Boy of Steel; How Superboy Learned to Fly; The Day Clark Kent Got a Haircut; The Power-Boy from Earth; The Space Adventures of Krypto; Ways Red Kryptonite Has Affected Superboy (text); Superboy's Kryptonian Ancestors (text); The Phantom Zone Criminals (text)
SP 1 ❑ ca. 1980 Cover: 1.00 **NM** value: **3.00**
Circ: CapCity orders: **7,450**
pin-up back cover. • Superboy Spectacular; giant

There are two different pricing tiers in the modern comic-book hobby. **The prices seen above** are the prices we have seen **loose copies** of these issues reliably fetch in a variety of environments. Condition alters the price by the fractions seen on the bar on the bottom of left-hand pages of this book. **Comics graded by CGC** usually sell for more. Use the guide on the bottom of right-hand pages of this book to estimate what copies have brought on eBay.

SUPERBOY (2ND SERIES) DC

This second Superboy series kicked off in conjunction with 1990's Superboy television show. Although the TV show was for the most part a weak attempt to give the Man of Steel youthful appeal, the corresponding comic was an unexpected delight. It was set in the same "world" as the show, but it managed to combine humor and action in just the right proportion.

One of the masterstrokes of both series was the creation of Nicknack, the Master of Toys. Nicknack was played on television by comedian Gilbert Gottfried, whose routine consisted almost solely of a hyper-active whining. The fictional world played this to the hilt, with characters constantly torturing Nicknack by saying how much he looked like "that comedian."

For its last few issues, this series was known as "The Adventures of Superboy."

1 ❑ Jan 1990 Cover: 1.00 **NM** value: **2.00**
Circ: CapCity orders: **28,650**
Photo cover from TV show. The Superboy **A:** Jim Mooney **W:** John Moore
2 ❑ Feb 1990 Cover: 1.00 **NM** value: **1.50**
Circ: CapCity orders: **19,400**
Jokes My Father Never Told Me
3 ❑ Mar 1990 Cover: 1.00 **NM** value: **1.50**
Circ: CapCity orders: **16,300**
Forever Is a Lot Longer Than You Think!
4 ❑ Apr 1990 Cover: 1.00 **NM** value: **1.50**
Circ: CapCity orders: **13,900**
Big Man on Campus
5 ❑ May 1990 Cover: 1.00 **NM** value: **1.50**
Circ: CapCity orders: **12,050**
With Friends Like These
6 ❑ Jun 1990 Cover: 1.00 **NM** value: **1.50**
Circ: CapCity orders: **10,700**
Kryptonite Reigns!
7 ❑ Jul 1990 Cover: 1.00 **NM** value: **1.50**
Circ: CapCity orders: **9,550**
Murmurs of the Heart!
8 ❑ Aug 1990 Cover: 1.00 **NM** value: **1.50**
Circ: CapCity orders: **9,550**
But, Am It Art? • Bizarro
9 ❑ Sep 1990 Cover: 1.00 **NM** value: **1.50**
Circ: CapCity orders: **8,650**
The Phantom Zone **A:** Curt Swan
10 ❑ Oct 1990 Cover: 1.00 **NM** value: **1.50**
Circ: CapCity orders: **8,000**
Superboy's Pal, Lex Luthor? **A:** Curt Swan
11 ❑ Nov 1990 Cover: 1.00 **NM** value: **1.50**
Circ: CapCity orders: **7,650**
Rock & Roll Refugee **A:** Curt Swan
12 ❑ Dec 1990 Cover: 1.00 **NM** value: **1.50**
Circ: CapCity orders: **7,400**
Holidazed & Confused **A:** Curt Swan
13 ❑ Jan 1991 Cover: 1.00 **NM** value: **1.50**
Circ: CapCity orders: **7,100**
Untold Stories • Mxyzptlk
14 ❑ Feb 1991 Cover: 1.00 **NM** value: **1.50**
Circ: CapCity orders: **6,700**
The Chaos Child! ★ Versus Brimstone.
15 ❑ Mar 1991 Cover: 1.00 **NM** value: **1.50**
Circ: CapCity orders: **6,450**
It's the End of the World As We Know It (And I Steal Time)!
16 ❑ Apr 1991 Cover: 1.25 **NM** value: **1.50**
Circ: CapCity orders: **6,250**
★ Appearance of Superman.
17 ❑ May 1991 Cover: 1.25 **NM** value: **1.50**
Circ: CapCity orders: **6,000**
The Superboy File
18 ❑ Jun 1991 Cover: 1.25 **NM** value: **1.50**
Soon to Be a Major Motion Picture • Series continued in Adventures of Superboy #19
19 ❑ Aug 1991 Cover: 1.25 **NM** value: **Cover or less**
All in Vein • Title changes to The Adventures of Superboy

SUPERBOY (3RD SERIES) DC

This isn't the Superboy of old. That is, it's not Clark Kent when he was a boy, or even Clark Kent from some alternate timeline or from a parallel Earth-2 (etc. etc. etc.).

This Superboy is actually a clone of Superman developed at Project Cadmus. The new Superboy first appeared during the "Reign of the Supermen" as one of the four newcomers vying for the role of Superman after his death at the hands of Doomsday. In those days, this Superboy rebelled against being called "SuperBOY," preferring the title "SuperMAN" (or even "the Metropolis Kid").

Of course, Superman eventually "got better," and this newcomer resigned himself to being known as "Superboy." This shouldn't concern him too much, however, as he's usually busy

Other grades: Multiply prices above by **1.5 for Mint • 2/3 for Very Fine • 1/3 for Fine • 1/5 for Very Good • 1/8 for Good**

showing a boyish flair for self-promotion, flirting with women, and humiliating would-be super-villains.

0 ❑ Oct 1994 Cover: 1.50 **NM** value: **2.00**
Circ: CapCity orders: **40,700**
Sidearm- One! Superboy- Zero! • Comes between issues #8 and 9 **A:** Tom Grummettt **W:** Karl Kesel ★ Origin of Superboy (clone).

1 ❑ Feb 1994 Cover: 1.50 **NM** value: **2.50**
Circ: CapCity orders: **87,650**
Trouble In Paradise! **A:** Tom Grummettt **W:** Karl Kesel

2 ❑ Mar 1994 Cover: 1.50 **NM** value: **2.00**
Circ: CapCity orders: **47,200**
Knockout! ★ 1st Appearance of Scavenger, Knockout.

3 ❑ Apr 1994 Cover: 1.50 **NM** value: **2.00**
Circ: CapCity orders: **39,450**
Remains of the Dead! ★ Versus Scavenger.

4 ❑ May 1994 Cover: 1.50 **NM** value: **2.00**
Circ: CapCity orders: **37,700**
Superboy, the Animated Series

5 ❑ Jun 1994 Cover: 1.50 **NM** value: **2.00**
Circ: CapCity orders: **36,050**
Live By the Sword, Die By the Sword!

6 ❑ Jul 1994 Cover: 1.50 **NM** value: **2.00**
Circ: CapCity orders: **41,100**
Changing Realities! • Worlds Collide, Part 3; crossover with Milestone Media

7 ❑ Aug 1994 Cover: 1.50 **NM** value: **2.00**
Circ: CapCity orders: **37,450**
Menace 2 Societies! • Worlds Collide, Part 8; crossover with Milestone Media **A:** Tom Grummettt **W:** Karl Kesel

8 ❑ Sep 1994 Cover: 1.50 **NM** value: **2.00**
Circ: CapCity orders: **34,650**
Big Trouble in Smallville! • Zero Hour; meets original Superboy

9 ❑ Nov 1994 Cover: 1.50 **NM** value: **2.00**
Circ: CapCity orders: **31,000**
King Shark!

10 ❑ Dec 1994 Cover: 1.50 **NM** value: **2.00**
Circ: CapCity orders: **31,700**
Hilo Monsters!

11 ❑ Jan 1995 Cover: 1.50 **NM** value: **2.00**
Circ: CapCity orders: **27,650**
Reality Bites! **A:** Tom Grummettt **W:** Eddie Berganza

12 ❑ Feb 1995 Cover: 1.50 **NM** value: **2.00**
Circ: CapCity orders: **25,225**
Compound Troubles!

13 ❑ Mar 1995 Cover: 1.50 **NM** value: **2.00**
Circ: CapCity orders: **22,975**
Suicidal Tendencies • Watery Grave, Part 1

14 ❑ Apr 1995 Cover: 1.50 **NM** value: **2.00**
Circ: CapCity orders: **21,150**
Kill Them All! • Watery Grave, Part 2

15 ❑ May 1995 Cover: 1.50 **NM** value: **2.00**
Circ: CapCity orders: **20,600**
Honor Among Thieves • Watery Grave, Part 3

16 ❑ Jun 1995 Cover: 1.95 **NM** value: **2.00**
Circ: CapCity orders: **20,250**
School and Hard Knocks ★ Versus Loose Cannon.

17 ❑ Jul 1995 Cover: 1.95 **NM** value: **2.00**
Circ: CapCity orders: **19,575**
Neon!

18 ❑ Aug 1995 Cover: 1.95 **NM** value: **2.00**
Circ: CapCity orders: **19,850**
Battle of the Century! ★ Versus Valor.

19 ❑ Sep 1995 Cover: 1.95 **NM** value: **2.00**
Circ: CapCity orders: **18,375**
T-K-O! • Valor enters Phantom Zone

20 ❑ Oct 1995 Cover: 1.95 **NM** value: **2.00**
Circ: CapCity orders: **15,425**
The Hunt! ★ Appearance of Green Lantern.

21 ❑ Nov 1995 Cover: 1.95 **NM** value: **2.00**
Making History! • Future Tense, Part 1; continues in Legion of Super-Heroes #74

22 ❑ Dec 1995 Cover: 1.95 **NM** value: **2.00**
Fire and Ice • Underworld Unleashed ★ Appearance of Killer Frost.

23 ❑ Jan 1996 Cover: 1.95 **NM** value: **2.00**
The Limits of Power

24 ❑ Feb 1996 Cover: 1.95 **NM** value: **2.00**
Like Damocles' Sword • Knockout's past revealed **A:** Tom Grummettt **W:** Karl Kesel ★ Versus Silver Sword.

25 ❑ Mar 1996 Cover: 2.95 **NM** value: **3.00**
• Giant-size. Whom the Gods Would Destroy! • Losin' It, Part 1; pin-up pages **A:** Steve Mattsson **W:** Karl Kesel

26 ❑ Apr 1996 Cover: 1.95 **NM** value: **2.00**
Strange Bedfellows • Losin' It, Part 2 **A:** Steve Mattsson **W:** Karl Kesel

27 ❑ May 1996 Cover: 1.95 **NM** value: **2.00**
Ensnared! • Losin' It, Part 3 **A:** Steve Mattsson **W:** Karl Kesel

28 ❑ Jun 1996 Cover: 1.95 **NM** value: **2.00**
Tough Love • Losin' It, Part 4 **A:** Steve Mattsson **W:** Karl Kesel ★ Appearance of Supergirl.

29 ❑ Jul 1996 Cover: 1.95 **NM** value: **2.00**
Imminent Eruption! • Losin' It, Part 5 **A:** Steve Mattsson **W:** Karl Kesel

30 ❑ Aug 1996 Cover: 1.95 **NM** value: **2.00**
Lost & Found • Losin' It, Part 6; Knockout captured **A:** Steve Mattsson **W:** Karl Kesel

31 ❑ Sep 1996 Cover: 1.95 **NM** value: **2.00**
Wipeout!

32 ❑ Oct 1996 Cover: 1.95 **NM** value: **2.00**
So, Tell Me About Superboy **A:** Ramon Bernado **W:** Ron Marz ★ Origin of Superboy.

33 ❑ Nov 1996 Cover: 1.95 **NM** value: **2.00**
Circ: Diamd. preorders: **43,102**
Running Hot and Cold • Final Night **A:** Ramon Bernado **W:** Ron Marz

34 ❑ Dec 1996 Cover: 1.95 **NM** value: **2.00**
Circ: Diamd. preorders: **37,471**
Going Mental • Dubbilex regains powers **A:** Ramon Bernado **W:** Ron Marz

35 ❑ Jan 1997 Cover: 1.95 **NM** value: **2.00**
Circ: Diamd. preorders: **36,389**
Kidnapped! **A:** Ramon Bernado **W:** Ron Marz ★ 1st Appearance of The Agenda.

36 ❑ Feb 1997 Cover: 1.95 **NM** value: **2.00**
Circ: Diamd. preorders: **34,355**
Grudge Match **A:** Ramon Bernado **W:** Ron Marz ★ Versus Match.

37 ❑ Mar 1997 Cover: 1.95 **NM** value: **2.00**
Circ: Diamd. preorders: **32,685**
Sledge-Hammered! **A:** Sal Buscema **W:** Ron Marz

38 ❑ Apr 1997 Cover: 1.95 **NM** value: **2.00**
Circ: Diamd. preorders: **31,113**
Meltdown, Part 1: Breakout! **A:** Ramon Bernado **W:** Ron Marz

39 ❑ May 1997 Cover: 1.95 **NM** value: **2.00**
Circ: Diamd. preorders: **30,458**
Meltdown, Part 2: Freak Show! **A:** Ramon Bernado **W:** Ron Marz

40 ❑ Jun 1997 Cover: 1.95 **NM** value: **2.00**
Circ: Diamd. preorders: **30,539**
Meltdown, Part 3: Life Support • continues in Superboy & the Ravers #10 **A:** Ramon Bernado **W:** Ron Marz

41 ❑ Jul 1997 Cover: 1.95 **NM** value: **2.00**
Circ: Diamd. preorders: **29,429**
Meltdown, Part 5: The Cure

42 ❑ Aug 1997 Cover: 1.95 **NM** value: **2.00**
Circ: Diamd. preorders: **28,612**
Ashes to Ashes

43 ❑ Sep 1997 Cover: 1.95 **NM** value: **2.00**
Circ: Diamd. preorders: **28,160**
Caught!

44 ❑ Oct 1997 Cover: 1.95 **NM** value: **2.00**
Circ: Diamd. preorders: **27,736**
Going Nowhere • Superboy goes to timeless island

45 ❑ Nov 1997 Cover: 1.95 **NM** value: **2.00**
Circ: Diamd. preorders: **27,333**
Invaders from the Future! **A:** Georges Jeanty **W:** Ron Marz ★ Appearance of Legion of Super-Heroes. ★ Versus Silver Sword.

46 ❑ Dec 1997 Cover: 1.95 **NM** value: **2.00**
Circ: Diamd. preorders: **26,358**
Face cover. Sword Play **A:** Georges Jeanty **W:** Ron Marz

47 ❑ Jan 1998 Cover: 1.95 **NM** value: **2.00**
Circ: Diamd. preorders: **28,958**
Idol Worship, Part 2 • Continued from Green Lantern #94 ★ Appearance of Green Lantern.

48 ❑ Feb 1998 Cover: 1.95 **NM** value: **2.00**
Circ: Diamd. preorders: **25,092**
Superboy, the Event

49 ❑ Mar 1998 Cover: 1.95 **NM** value: **2.00**
Circ: Diamd. preorders: **24,664**
Searching…

50 ❑ Apr 1998 Cover: 1.95 **NM** value: **2.00**
Circ: Diamd. preorders: **27,559**
Survival of the Fittest! • Last Boy on Earth, Part 1

51 ❑ May 1998 Cover: 1.95 **NM** value: **Cover or less**
Circ: Diamd. preorders: **24,512**
The Test! • Last Boy on Earth, Part 2

52 ❑ Jun 1998 Cover: 1.95 **NM** value: **Cover or less**
Circ: Diamd. preorders: **25,086**
Destination: Unknown! • Last Boy on Earth, Part 3; Superboy returns to Hawaii

53 ❑ Jul 1998 Cover: 1.95 **NM** value: **Cover or less**
Circ: Diamd. preorders: **25,175**
Pearl Harbor 2! • Last Boy on Earth, Part 4

54 ❑ Aug 1998 Cover: 1.95 **NM** value: **Cover or less**
Circ: Diamd. preorders: **25,060**
Darkness & Light ★ Appearance of Guardian.

55 ❑ Sep 1998 Cover: 1.99 **NM** value: **Cover or less**
Circ: Diamd. preorders: **24,165**
Hexed! ★ 1st Appearance of new Hex. ★ Versus Grokk.

56 ❑ Oct 1998 Cover: 1.99 **NM** value: **Cover or less**
Circ: Diamd. preorders: **23,554**
Here There Be Monsters! • Mechanic takes over Cadmus

57 ❑ Dec 1998 Cover: 1.99 **NM** value: **Cover or less**
Circ: Diamd. preorders: **22,519**
Dangerous Curves • Demolition Run, Part 1

58 ❑ Jan 1999 Cover: 1.99 **NM** value: **Cover or less**
Circ: Diamd. preorders: **22,353**
Crash & Burn! • Demolition Run, Part 2

59 ❑ Feb 1999 Cover: 1.99 **NM** value: **Cover or less**
Circ: Diamd. preorders: **23,948**
Mission to Krypton • on Krypton **A:** Dusty Abell **W:** Karl Kesel ★ Appearance of Superman, Project: Cadmus.

60 ❑ Mar 1999 Cover: 1.99 **NM** value: **Cover or less**
Circ: Diamd. preorders: **26,281**
Hyper-Tension, Part 1: Big Bang Theory! **A:** Tom Grummettt **W:** Karl Kesel

61 ❑ Apr 1999 Cover: 1.99 **NM** value: **Cover or less**
Circ: Diamd. preorders: **23,740**
Hyper-Tension, Part 2: Superboy of Infinite Worlds • learns Superman's identity **A:** Tom Grummettt **W:** Karl Kesel

62 ❑ May 1999 Cover: 1.99 **NM** value: **Cover or less**
Circ: Diamd. preorders: **24,372**
Hyper-Tension, Part 3: Divided By Zero **A:** Tom Grummettt **W:** Karl Kesel ★ Origin of Black Zero.

63 ❑ Jun 1999 Cover: 1.99 **NM** value: **Cover or less**
Circ: Diamd. preorders: **26,954**
Hyper-Tension, Part 4: For Every World A Doomsday! **A:** Tom Grummettt **W:** Karl Kesel ★ Versus Doomsdays.

64 ❑ Jul 1999 Cover: 1.99 **NM** value: **Cover or less**
Circ: Diamd. preorders: **27,560**
Hyper-Tension, Part 5: Zero Tolerance **A:** Tom Grummettt **W:** Karl Kesel

65 ❑ Aug 1999 Cover: 1.99 **NM** value: **Cover or less**
Circ: Diamd. preorders: **27,906**
Hyper-Tension, Part 6: Out of Hyper-Time! **A:** Tom Grummettt **W:** Karl Kesel ★ Appearance of Metal Men, Steel, Inferno, Green Lantern, Impulse, Creeper, Robin, Hero Hotline, Damage.

66 ❑ Sep 1999 Cover: 1.99 **NM** value: **Cover or less**
Circ: Diamd. preorders: **25,514**
Wild Hunt! • back to Wild Lands **A:** Aaron Lopresti **W:** Karl Kesel

67 ❑ Oct 1999 Cover: 1.99 **NM** value: **Cover or less**
Circ: Diamd. preorders: **24,754**
Tooth & Claw **A:** Aaron Lopresti **W:** Karl Kesel ★ Versus King Shark.

68 ❑ Nov 1999 Cover: 1.99 **NM** value: **Cover or less**
Circ: Diamd. preorders: **26,810**
Demons! • Day of Judgment

69 ❑ Dec 1999 Cover: 1.99 **NM** value: **Cover or less**
Circ: Diamd. preorders: **22,971**
Hawaii-Hana Hou! **A:** Tom Grummettt **W:** Karl Kesel

70 ❑ Jan 2000 Cover: 1.99 **NM** value: **Cover or less**
Circ: Diamd. preorders: **22,207**
The Evil Factory, Part 1: Evil Factory! **A:** Tom Grummettt **W:** Karl Kesel

71 ❑ Feb 2000 Cover: 1.99 **NM** value: **Cover or less**
Circ: Diamd. preorders: **22,123**
The Evil Factory, Part 2: Prisoners of the Project! **W:** Karl Kesel

72 ❑ Mar 2000 Cover: 1.99 **NM** value: **Cover or less**
Circ: Diamd. preorders: **20,340**
The Evil Factory, Part 3: The Hex Files **W:** Karl Kesel

73 ❑ Apr 2000 Cover: 1.99 **NM** value: **Cover or less**
Circ: Diamd. preorders: **19,248**
The Evil Factory, Part 4: Point of No Return! **A:** Adam DeKraker **W:** Karl Kesel

74 ❑ May 2000 Cover: 1.99 **NM** value: **Cover or less**
Circ: Diamd. preorders: **23,809**
The Evil Factory, Part 5: Game, Set & Match! • Sins of Youth **A:** Tom Grummettt **W:** Karl Kesel

75 ❑ Jun 2000 Cover: 1.99 **NM** value: **Cover or less**
Circ: Diamd. preorders: **20,137**
My Greatest Adventure! **A:** Tom Grummettt **W:** Karl Kesel

76 ❑ Jul 2000 Cover: 1.99 **NM** value: **Cover or less**
Circ: Diamd. preorders: **19,595**
The New Superboy **A:** Tom Grummettt **W:** Karl Kesel

77 ❑ Aug 2000 Cover: 1.99 **NM** value: **Cover or less**
Circ: Diamd. preorders: **20,384**
Into the Fire! **A:** Tom Grummettt **W:** Karl Kesel

78 ❑ Sep 2000 Cover: 2.25 **NM** value: **Cover or less**
Circ: Diamd. preorders: **20,292**
Give Me Liberty…! **A:** Tom Grummettt **W:** Karl Kesel

79 ❑ Oct 2000 Cover: 2.25 **NM** value: **Cover or less**
Circ: Diamd. preorders: **19,304**
The Power & The Prize! **A:** Tom Grummettt **W:** Karl Kesel

80 ❑ Nov 2000 Cover: 2.25 **NM** value: **Cover or less**
Circ: Diamd. preorders: **18,955**
Boiling Point **A:** Ben Herrera **W:** Jay Faerber

81 ❑ Dec 2000 Cover: 2.25 **NM** value: **Cover or less**
Circ: Diamd. preorders: **18,879**
Fever Pitch **A:** Ben Herrera **W:** Jay Faerber

82 ❑ Jan 2001 Cover: 2.25 **NM** value: **Cover or less**
Circ: Diamd. preorders: **18,133**
Power Lunch **A:** Sunny Lee **W:** Jay Faerber

83 ❑ Feb 2001 Cover: 2.25 **NM** value: **Cover or less**
Circ: Diamd. preorders: **19,172**
How Kon-El Got His Groove Back **A:** Pascual Ferry **W:** Joe Kelly

84 ❑ Mar 2001 Cover: 2.25 **NM** value: **Cover or less**
Circ: Diamd. preorders: **18,054**
Smells Like Rage **A:** Pascual Ferry **W:** Joe Kelly

85 ❑ Apr 2001 Cover: 2.25 **NM** value: **Cover or less**
Circ: Diamd. preorders: **18,930**
Silent, But Deadly **A:** Pascual Ferry **W:** Joe Kelly

86 ❑ May 2001 Cover: 2.25 **NM** value: **Cover or less**
Circ: Diamd. preorders: **17,808**
Southern Cookin' **A:** Paco Medina **W:** Joe Kelly

87 ❑ Jun 2001 Cover: 2.25 **NM** value: **Cover or less**
Circ: Diamd. preorders: **18,243**

88 ❑ Jul 2001 Cover: 2.25 **NM** value: **Cover or less**
Circ: Diamd. preorders: **18,442**

89 ❑ Aug 2001 Cover: 2.25 **NM** value: **Cover or less**
Circ: Diamd. preorders: **22,723**

90 ❑ Sep 2001 Cover: 2.25 **NM** value: **Cover or less**
Circ: Diamd. preorders: **24,570**

1000000 ❑ Nov 1998 Cover: 1.99 **NM** value: **2.00**
Circ: Diamd. preorders: **30,854**
Omac: One Million and Counting • Comes between issues #56 and 57 **A:** Tom Grummettt **W:** Karl Kesel

Anl 1 ❑ ca. 1994 Cover: 2.95 **NM** value: **3.00**
Circ: CapCity orders: **27,900**
The Super Seven: Men of Steel! • Elseworlds; concludes story from Adventures of Superman Annual #6

Anl 2 ❑ ca. 1995 Cover: 3.95 **NM** value: **4.00**
The Lost Boys • Year One; Identity of being who Superboy was cloned from is revealed

Anl 3 ❑ ca. 1996 Cover: 2.95 **NM** value: **Cover or less**
Fathers and Suns • Legends of the Dead Earth

Anl 4 ❑ ca. 1997 Cover: 3.95 **NM** value: **Cover or less**
Circ: Diamd. preorders: **26,215**
Savageboy: The Adventures of Superboy When He Was in the Jungle • Pulp Heroes

SUPERBOY AND THE LEGION OF SUPER-HEROES
DC

231 ❑ Sep 1977 Cover: 0.60 **NM** value: **2.00**
Circ: Statement: **184,528** • **CGC:** 5 graded, best 9.8
A Day in the Death of a World! • Giant-Size ★ Versus Fatal Five.

232 ❑ Oct 1977 Cover: 0.60 **NM** value: **2.00**
Circ: Statement: **184,528**

233 ❑ Nov 1977 Cover: 0.60 **NM** value: **2.00**
Circ: Statement: **184,528**
The Infinite Man Who Conquered the Legion!; The Final Illusion ★ Origin of Infinite Man. ★ 1st Appearance of Infinite Man.

CGC-graded: Multiply prices above by **33 for 9.9 M • 16 for 9.8 NM/M • 7 for 9.6 NM+ • 5 for 9.4 NM • 2.5 for 9.2 NM- • 1.5 for 9.0 VF/NM**

234 ❑ Dec 1977 Cover: 0.60 **NM** value: **2.00**
Circ: Statement: **184,528**

235 ❑ Jan 1978 Cover: 0.60 **NM** value: **2.00**
Circ: Statement: **141,277**

236 ❑ Feb 1978 Cover: 0.60 **NM** value: **2.00**
Circ: Statement: **141,277**
📖 A World Born Anew!; Mon-El's One-Man War!; Words Never Spoken!

237 ❑ Mar 1978 Cover: 0.60 **NM** value: **2.00**
Circ: Statement: **141,277**
📖 No Price Too High • Saturn Girl leaves team; Lightning Lad leaves team **A:** Walt Simonson

238 ❑ Apr 1978 Cover: 0.60 **NM** value: **2.00**
Circ: Statement: **141,277**
wraparound cover. 📖 The Outlawed Legionnaires!; The Legion Chain Gang! • reprints Adventure Comics #359 and 360

239 ❑ May 1978 Cover: 0.60 **NM** value: **2.00**
Circ: Statement: **141,277** • **CGC:** 1 graded, best 9.6
📖 Murder Most Foul • Has 1977 Statement; avg print run 441,198; avg sales 181,050; avg subs 3,478; avg total paid 184,528; max existent 184,528; 57% of run returned

240 ❑ Jun 1978 Cover: 0.60 **NM** value: **2.00**
Circ: Statement: **141,277**
📖 The Man Who Manacled the Legion; Dawnstar Rising ★ Origin of Dawnstar. ★ Versus Grimbor.

241 ❑ Jul 1978 Cover: 0.60 **NM** value: **2.00**
Circ: Statement: **141,277**

242 ❑ Aug 1978 Cover: 0.60 **NM** value: **2.00**
Circ: Statement: **141,277** • **CGC:** 1 graded, best 8.0
📖 Startarget: Earth; Girls' Night Out

243 ❑ Sep 1978 Cover: 0.50 **NM** value: **2.00**
Circ: Statement: **141,277** • **CGC:** 1 graded, best 9.4
📖 Earth's Last Stand ★ Appearance of Legion Subs.

244 ❑ Oct 1978 Cover: 0.50 **NM** value: **2.00**
Circ: Statement: **141,277**
📖 The Dark Circle That Crushed Earth • Mordru returns

245 ❑ Nov 1978 Cover: 0.50 **NM** value: **2.00**
Circ: Statement: **141,277**
📖 Mordru, Master of Earth! • Lightning Lad and Saturn Girl rejoin

246 ❑ Dec 1978 Cover: 0.40 **NM** value: **2.00**
Circ: Statement: **141,277**

247 ❑ Jan 1979 Cover: 0.40 **NM** value: **2.00**
Circ: Statement: **162,265**

248 ❑ Feb 1979 Cover: 0.40 **NM** value: **2.00**
Circ: Statement: **162,265**
📖 Beneath the Streets Lurks Death!

249 ❑ Mar 1979 Cover: 0.40 **NM** value: **2.00**
Circ: Statement: **162,265**
📖 Capital Crimes of the Chemical Conquerer!; The Arctoraan Jewel Case

250 ❑ Apr 1979 Cover: 0.40 **NM** value: **2.00**
Circ: Statement: **162,265**
• Has 1978 Statement; avg print run 384,845; avg sales 138,740; avg subs 2,537; avg total paid 141,277; max existent 141,277; 62% of run returned

251 ❑ May 1979 Cover: 0.40 **NM** value: **1.50**
Circ: Statement: **162,265**

252 ❑ Jun 1979 Cover: 0.40 **NM** value: **1.50**
Circ: Statement: **162,265**
📖 Postscript to Holocaust

253 ❑ Jul 1979 Cover: 0.40 **NM** value: **1.50**
Circ: Statement: **162,265**
📖 Night of the Super-Assassins! ★ 1st Appearance of Blok. ★ Versus League of Super-Assassins.

254 ❑ Aug 1979 Cover: 0.40 **NM** value: **1.50**
Circ: Statement: **162,265**
📖 A Madman Shall Leave Them

255 ❑ Sep 1979 Cover: 0.40 **NM** value: **1.50**
Circ: Statement: **162,265**
📖 The Super-Spectacles Swipe! • Legion visits Krypton before it's destroyed

256 ❑ Oct 1979 Cover: 0.40 **NM** value: **1.50**
Circ: Statement: **162,265**
📖 This Is Your Life and Death, Braniac 5! ★ Origin of Brainiac 5.

257 ❑ Nov 1979 Cover: 0.40 **NM** value: **1.50**
Circ: Statement: **162,265**
📖 Who Stole the Legion?; Once a Legionnaire! • Return of Bouncing Boy; Return of Duo Damsel **A:** Steve Ditko

258 ❑ Dec 1979 Cover: 0.40 **NM** value: **1.50**
Circ: Statement: **162,265**
📖 The Mind-Attack of the Psycho-Warrior! • series continues as Legion of Super-Heroes ★ Versus Psycho Warrior.

SUPERBOY & THE RAVERS — DC

1 ❑ Sep 1996 Cover: 1.95 **NM** value: **2.50**
📖 House Rules, Part 1: The Never-Ending Party **A:** Paul Pelletier **W:** Karl Kesel; Steve Mattsson

2 ❑ Oct 1996 Cover: 1.95 **NM** value: **2.00**
📖 House Rules, Part 2: This Ain't No Party! **A:** Paul Pelletier **W:** Karl Kesel; Steve Mattsson

3 ❑ Nov 1996 Cover: 1.95 **NM** value: **2.00**
Circ: Diamd. preorders: **32,378**
📖 House Rules, Part 3: Illegal Aliens **A:** Paul Pelletier **W:** Karl Kesel; Steve Mattsson ★ 1st Appearance of Half-Life.

4 ❑ Dec 1996 Cover: 1.95 **NM** value: **2.00**
Circ: Diamd. preorders: **31,716**
📖 House Rules, Part 4: Political Party **A:** Paul Pelletier **W:** Karl Kesel; Steve Mattsson

5 ❑ Jan 1997 Cover: 1.95 **NM** value: **2.00**
Circ: Diamd. preorders: **29,185**
📖 Dial "X" for X-Mas **A:** Paul Pelletier **W:** Karl Kesel; Steve Mattsson ★ Versus Scavenger.

6 ❑ Feb 1997 Cover: 1.95 **NM** value: **2.00**
Circ: Diamd. preorders: **26,427**
📖 Truth or Dare **A:** Paul Pelletier **W:** Karl Kesel; Steve Mattsson

7 ❑ Mar 1997 Cover: 1.95 **NM** value: **2.00**
Circ: Diamd. preorders: **24,681**
📖 Road Trip: First Stop – Speed Kills **A:** Paul Pelletier **W:** Karl Kesel; Steve Mattsson ★ Appearance of Impulse.

8 ❑ Apr 1997 Cover: 1.95 **NM** value: **2.00**
Circ: Diamd. preorders: **22,748**
📖 Road Trip: Second Stop – The Romance of the Road ★ Appearance of Warrior.

9 ❑ May 1997 Cover: 1.95 **NM** value: **2.00**
Circ: Diamd. preorders: **21,394**
📖 Road Trip: Part 3 – The Road Not Taken ★ Appearance of Superman.

10 ❑ Jun 1997 Cover: 1.95 **NM** value: **2.00**
Circ: Diamd. preorders: **21,833**
📖 Meltdown, Part 4: Flatline • continued from Superboy #40, continues in Superboy #41

11 ❑ Jul 1997 Cover: 1.95 **NM** value: **2.00**
Circ: Diamd. preorders: **20,434**
📖 Kindred, Part 1: Funeral for a Friend

12 ❑ Aug 1997 Cover: 1.95 **NM** value: **2.00**
Circ: Diamd. preorders: **19,851**
📖 Kindred, Part 2: Reunion

13 ❑ Sep 1997 Cover: 1.95 **NM** value: **2.00**
Circ: Diamd. preorders: **19,608**
📖 My Precious…

14 ❑ Oct 1997 Cover: 1.95 **NM** value: **2.00**
Circ: Diamd. preorders: **21,190**
• Genesis ★ Versus Female Furies.

15 ❑ Nov 1997 Cover: 1.95 **NM** value: **2.00**
Circ: Diamd. preorders: **18,267**
📖 Edge of the Event Horizon **A:** Josh Hood **W:** Karl Kesel; Steve Mattsson

16 ❑ Dec 1997 Cover: 1.95 **NM** value: **2.00**
Circ: Diamd. preorders: **18,012**
📖 Half-Life of the Party! **A:** Josh Hood **W:** Karl Kesel; Steve Mattsson

17 ❑ Jan 1998 Cover: 1.95 **NM** value: **2.00**
Circ: Diamd. preorders: **17,537**
📖 Love Is All That Anti-Matters: Part 1 – No Weddings and a Funeral

18 ❑ Feb 1998 Cover: 1.95 **NM** value: **2.00**
Circ: Diamd. preorders: **16,586**
📖 Love Is All That Anti-Matters: Part 2 – The Deadliest of the Species

19 ❑ Mar 1998 Cover: 1.95 **NM** value: **2.00**
Circ: Diamd. preorders: **15,743**
📖 Love Is All That Anti-Matters: Part 3 – Last Dance final issue.

SUPERBOY PLUS — DC

1 ❑ Jan 1997 Cover: 2.95 **NM** value: **Cover or less**
Circ: Diamd. preorders: **35,949**
📖 Junior Partners **A:** Andy Smith **W:** Ron Marz ★ Appearance of Captain Marvel Jr..

2 ❑ Fal 1997 Cover: 2.95 **NM** value: **Cover or less**
Circ: Diamd. preorders: **21,055**
📖 The Serpent and the Rainbow • continues in Catwoman Plus #1 ★ Appearance of Slither.

SUPERBOY/RISK DOUBLE-SHOT — DC

1 ❑ Feb 1998 Cover: 1.95 **NM** value: **Cover or less**
Circ: Diamd. preorders: **24,881**
📖 Bad Times at Montridge High

SUPERBOY/ROBIN: WORLD'S FINEST THREE — DC

1 ❑ ca. 1996 Cover: 4.95 **NM** value: **Cover or less**
• prestige format. **A:** Tom Grummett **W:** Karl Kesel; Chuck Dixon ★ Versus Metallo. ★ Versus Poison Ivy.

2 ❑ ca. 1996 Cover: 4.95 **NM** value: **Cover or less**
• prestige format. **A:** Tom Grummett **W:** Karl Kesel; Chuck Dixon ★ Versus Metallo. ★ Versus Poison Ivy.

SUPERBOY'S LEGION — DC

1 ❑ Apr 2001 Cover: 5.95 **NM** value: **Cover or less**
Circ: Diamd. preorders: **22,975** • **CGC:** 5 graded, best 10.0
A: Alan Davis **W:** Mark Farmer

2 ❑ May 2001 Cover: 5.95 **NM** value: **Cover or less**
Circ: Diamd. preorders: **21,584**
A: Alan Davis **W:** Mark Farmer

SUPER BRAT — Toby

1	❑ ca. 1954	Cover: 0.10	**NM** value: **35.00**
2	❑ ca. 1954	Cover: 0.10	**NM** value: **25.00**
3	❑ ca. 1954	Cover: 0.10	**NM** value: **25.00**
4	❑ ca. 1954	Cover: 0.10	**NM** value: **25.00**

SUPER CAT (AJAX) — Ajax

1	❑ Aug 1957	Cover: 0.10	**NM** value: **50.00**
2	❑ Nov 1957	Cover: 0.10	**NM** value: **35.00**
3	❑ Feb 1958	Cover: 0.10	**NM** value: **35.00**
4	❑ May 1958	Cover: 0.10	**NM** value: **35.00**

SUPER CAT (STAR) — Star

56	❑ Nov 1953	Cover: 0.10	**NM** value: **150.00**
57	❑ Feb 1954	Cover: 0.10	**NM** value: **150.00**
58	❑ May 1954	Cover: 0.10	**NM** value: **150.00**

SUPER CIRCUS — Cross

1 ❑ Jan 1951 Cover: 0.10 **NM** value: **80.00**
• Cliffy the Clown, Claude Kirchner photo cover

2	❑ Mar 1951	Cover: 0.10	**NM** value: **50.00**
3	❑ May 1951	Cover: 0.10	**NM** value: **30.00**
4	❑ Jul 1951	Cover: 0.10	**NM** value: **30.00**
5	❑ Sep 1951	Cover: 0.10	**NM** value: **30.00**

Do you have changes or corrections for the **Standard Catalog**? Send your original research to us at
allcomics@krause.com

SUPER COMICS — Dell

Super Comics was primarily an anthology of comic-strip reprints, a popular format in the early days of comic books. Early features included Terry and the Pirates, Dick Tracy, Little Orphan Annie, Tiny Tim, Winnie Winkle, and Smitty. Many of these strips eventually moved on to their own titles, establishing continuity that ran far beyond these funnies and helping cement the comic book's standing as a medium of its own.

Though a few of the covers featured the comedy characters of Smitty, the primary focus was on action, with Dick Tracy and his pals often featured.

1 ❑ May 1938 Cover: 0.10 **NM** value: **1700.00**
• **CGC:** 1 graded, best 3.0
2 ❑ Jun 1938 Cover: 0.10 **NM** value: **700.00**
3 ❑ Jul 1938 Cover: 0.10 **NM** value: **550.00**
4 ❑ Aug 1938 Cover: 0.10 **NM** value: **415.00**
• **CGC:** 1 graded, best 4.0
5 ❑ Sep 1938 Cover: 0.10 **NM** value: **415.00**
6 ❑ Oct 1938 Cover: 0.10 **NM** value: **325.00**
• **CGC:** 1 graded, best 7.5
7 ❑ Nov 1938 Cover: 0.10 **NM** value: **325.00**
8 ❑ Dec 1938 Cover: 0.10 **NM** value: **325.00**
9 ❑ Jan 1939 Cover: 0.10 **NM** value: **325.00**
10 ❑ Mar 1939 Cover: 0.10 **NM** value: **325.00**
11 ❑ Apr 1939 Cover: 0.10 **NM** value: **265.00**
12 ❑ May 1939 Cover: 0.10 **NM** value: **265.00**
13 ❑ Jun 1939 Cover: 0.10 **NM** value: **265.00**
14 ❑ Jul 1939 Cover: 0.10 **NM** value: **265.00**
15 ❑ Aug 1939 Cover: 0.10 **NM** value: **265.00**
16 ❑ Sep 1939 Cover: 0.10 **NM** value: **265.00**
17 ❑ Oct 1939 Cover: 0.10 **NM** value: **265.00**
18 ❑ Nov 1939 Cover: 0.10 **NM** value: **265.00**
19 ❑ Dec 1939 Cover: 0.10 **NM** value: **265.00**
20 ❑ Jan 1940 Cover: 0.10 **NM** value: **265.00**
21 ❑ Feb 1940 Cover: 0.10 **NM** value: **265.00**
22 ❑ Mar 1940 Cover: 0.10 **NM** value: **265.00**
23 ❑ Apr 1940 Cover: 0.10 **NM** value: **265.00**
24 ❑ May 1940 Cover: 0.10 **NM** value: **265.00**
25 ❑ Jun 1940 Cover: 0.10 **NM** value: **265.00**
26 ❑ Jul 1940 Cover: 0.10 **NM** value: **185.00**
27 ❑ Aug 1940 Cover: 0.10 **NM** value: **185.00**
28 ❑ Sep 1940 Cover: 0.10 **NM** value: **185.00**
29 ❑ Oct 1940 Cover: 0.10 **NM** value: **185.00**
• **CGC:** 1 graded, best 4.0
30 ❑ Nov 1940 Cover: 0.10 **NM** value: **275.00**
📖 The Sea Hawk
31 ❑ Dec 1940 Cover: 0.10 **NM** value: **140.00**
32 ❑ Jan 1941 Cover: 0.10 **NM** value: **140.00**
33 ❑ Feb 1941 Cover: 0.10 **NM** value: **140.00**
• **CGC:** 1 graded, best 4.5
34 ❑ Mar 1941 Cover: 0.10 **NM** value: **140.00**
• Magic Morro, Dick Tracy, Smilin' Jack, Jim Ellis **C:** Ken Ernst
35 ❑ Apr 1941 Cover: 0.10 **NM** value: **140.00**
• Dick Tracy, Smilin' Jack, Terry and the Pirates, Magic Morro, Jim Ellis
36 ❑ May 1941 Cover: 0.10 **NM** value: **140.00**
• **CGC:** 1 graded, best 5.0
37 ❑ Jun 1941 Cover: 0.10 **NM** value: **140.00**
• Dick Tracy, Harold Teen, Little Orphan Annie, Terry and the Pirates, Moon Mullins, Smitty
38 ❑ Jul 1941 Cover: 0.10 **NM** value: **140.00**
39 ❑ Aug 1941 Cover: 0.10 **NM** value: **140.00**
• **CGC:** 1 graded, best 8.0
40 ❑ Sep 1941 Cover: 0.10 **NM** value: **140.00**
41 ❑ Oct 1941 Cover: 0.10 **NM** value: **125.00**
42 ❑ Nov 1941 Cover: 0.10 **NM** value: **125.00**
43 ❑ Dec 1941 Cover: 0.10 **NM** value: **125.00**
44 ❑ Jan 1942 Cover: 0.10 **NM** value: **125.00**
45 ❑ Feb 1942 Cover: 0.10 **NM** value: **125.00**
46 ❑ Mar 1942 Cover: 0.10 **NM** value: **125.00**
47 ❑ Apr 1942 Cover: 0.10 **NM** value: **125.00**
48 ❑ May 1942 Cover: 0.10 **NM** value: **125.00**
49 ❑ Jun 1942 Cover: 0.10 **NM** value: **125.00**
50 ❑ Jul 1942 Cover: 0.10 **NM** value: **125.00**
• **CGC:** 1 graded, best 7.0
51 ❑ Aug 1942 Cover: 0.10 **NM** value: **80.00**
52 ❑ Sep 1942 Cover: 0.10 **NM** value: **80.00**
• **CGC:** 1 graded, best 9.2
53 ❑ Oct 1942 Cover: 0.10 **NM** value: **80.00**
54 ❑ Nov 1942 Cover: 0.10 **NM** value: **80.00**
55 ❑ Dec 1942 Cover: 0.10 **NM** value: **80.00**
56 ❑ Jan 1943 Cover: 0.10 **NM** value: **80.00**
57 ❑ Feb 1943 Cover: 0.10 **NM** value: **80.00**
58 ❑ Mar 1943 Cover: 0.10 **NM** value: **80.00**
59 ❑ Apr 1943 Cover: 0.10 **NM** value: **80.00**
60 ❑ May 1943 Cover: 0.10 **NM** value: **80.00**
61 ❑ Jun 1943 Cover: 0.10 **NM** value: **80.00**
62 ❑ Jul 1943 Cover: 0.10 **NM** value: **80.00**
• **CGC:** 1 graded, best 9.0
63 ❑ Aug 1943 Cover: 0.10 **NM** value: **80.00**
64 ❑ Sep 1943 Cover: 0.10 **NM** value: **80.00**
65 ❑ Oct 1943 Cover: 0.10 **NM** value: **80.00**
66 ❑ Nov 1943 Cover: 0.10 **NM** value: **80.00**
67 ❑ Dec 1943 Cover: 0.10 **NM** value: **80.00**
68 ❑ Jan 1944 Cover: 0.10 **NM** value: **80.00**
69 ❑ Feb 1944 Cover: 0.10 **NM** value: **80.00**
70 ❑ Mar 1944 Cover: 0.10 **NM** value: **80.00**
71 ❑ Apr 1944 Cover: 0.10 **NM** value: **60.00**
72 ❑ May 1944 Cover: 0.10 **NM** value: **60.00**
• **CGC:** 1 graded, best 9.4

Other grades: Multiply prices above by **1.5 for Mint • 2/3 for Very Fine • 1/3 for Fine • 1/5 for Very Good • 1/8 for Good**

73 ❑ Jun 1944 Cover: 0.10 **NM** value: **60.00**
74 ❑ Jul 1944 Cover: 0.10 **NM** value: **60.00**
• **CGC:** 1 graded, best 9.2
75 ❑ Aug 1944 Cover: 0.10 **NM** value: **60.00**
76 ❑ Sep 1944 Cover: 0.10 **NM** value: **60.00**
77 ❑ Oct 1944 Cover: 0.10 **NM** value: **60.00**
78 ❑ Nov 1944 Cover: 0.10 **NM** value: **60.00**
79 ❑ Dec 1944 Cover: 0.10 **NM** value: **60.00**
80 ❑ Jan 1945 Cover: 0.10 **NM** value: **60.00**
81 ❑ Feb 1945 Cover: 0.10 **NM** value: **60.00**
82 ❑ Mar 1945 Cover: 0.10 **NM** value: **60.00**
83 ❑ Apr 1945 Cover: 0.10 **NM** value: **60.00**
84 ❑ May 1945 Cover: 0.10 **NM** value: **60.00**
• **CGC:** 1 graded, best 9.4
85 ❑ Jun 1945 Cover: 0.10 **NM** value: **60.00**
86 ❑ Jul 1945 Cover: 0.10 **NM** value: **60.00**
87 ❑ Aug 1945 Cover: 0.10 **NM** value: **60.00**
88 ❑ Sep 1945 Cover: 0.10 **NM** value: **60.00**
89 ❑ Oct 1945 Cover: 0.10 **NM** value: **60.00**
• **CGC:** 1 graded, best 9.2
90 ❑ Nov 1945 Cover: 0.10 **NM** value: **60.00**
91 ❑ Dec 1945 Cover: 0.10 **NM** value: **50.00**
• **CGC:** 1 graded, best 9.2
92 ❑ Jan 1946 Cover: 0.10 **NM** value: **50.00**
• **CGC:** 1 graded, best 9.6
93 ❑ Feb 1946 Cover: 0.10 **NM** value: **50.00**
• **CGC:** 1 graded, best 6.5
94 ❑ Mar 1946 Cover: 0.10 **NM** value: **50.00**
95 ❑ Apr 1946 Cover: 0.10 **NM** value: **50.00**
96 ❑ May 1946 Cover: 0.10 **NM** value: **50.00**
97 ❑ Jun 1946 Cover: 0.10 **NM** value: **50.00**
• **CGC:** 1 graded, best 9.4
98 ❑ Jul 1946 Cover: 0.10 **NM** value: **50.00**
99 ❑ Aug 1946 Cover: 0.10 **NM** value: **50.00**
100 ❑ Sep 1946 Cover: 0.10 **NM** value: **50.00**
101 ❑ Oct 1946 Cover: 0.10 **NM** value: **35.00**
102 ❑ Nov 1946 Cover: 0.10 **NM** value: **35.00**
103 ❑ Dec 1946 Cover: 0.10 **NM** value: **35.00**
104 ❑ Jan 1947 Cover: 0.10 **NM** value: **35.00**
📖 Dick Tracy; Sweeney & Son; Smith; Little Joe; Winnie Winkle, the Breadwinner; Moon Mullins; Harold Teen; Clyde Beaty; Tiny Tim **W:** Chester Gould; Walter Berndt; Martin Branner; Carl Ed; Frank Willard; Posenz; Stanley Link ★ Appearance of Dick Tracy.
105 ❑ Feb 1947 Cover: 0.10 **NM** value: **35.00**
106 ❑ Mar 1947 Cover: 0.10 **NM** value: **35.00**
107 ❑ Apr 1947 Cover: 0.10 **NM** value: **35.00**
108 ❑ May 1947 Cover: 0.10 **NM** value: **35.00**
109 ❑ Jun 1947 Cover: 0.10 **NM** value: **35.00**
110 ❑ Jul 1947 Cover: 0.10 **NM** value: **35.00**
111 ❑ Aug 1947 Cover: 0.10 **NM** value: **26.00**
112 ❑ Sep 1947 Cover: 0.10 **NM** value: **26.00**
113 ❑ Oct 1947 Cover: 0.10 **NM** value: **26.00**
114 ❑ Nov 1947 Cover: 0.10 **NM** value: **26.00**
115 ❑ Dec 1947 Cover: 0.10 **NM** value: **26.00**
116 ❑ ca. 1948 Cover: 0.10 **NM** value: **26.00**
117 ❑ ca. 1948 Cover: 0.10 **NM** value: **26.00**
118 ❑ ca. 1948 Cover: 0.10 **NM** value: **26.00**
119 ❑ ca. 1948 Cover: 0.10 **NM** value: **26.00**
120 ❑ ca. 1948 Cover: 0.10 **NM** value: **26.00**
121 ❑ ca. 1949 Cover: 0.10 **NM** value: **26.00**
final issue.

SUPERCOPS — Now

1 ❑ Sep 1990 Cover: 2.75 **NM** value: **Cover or less**
Circ: CapCity orders: **4,250**
• double-sized.
2 ❑ Oct 1990 Cover: 1.75 **NM** value: **Cover or less**
Circ: CapCity orders: **3,025**
📖 2nd Generation **A:** Peter Grau **W:** Chuck Dixon
3 ❑ Nov 1990 Cover: 1.75 **NM** value: **Cover or less**
Circ: CapCity orders: **2,325**
4 ❑ Feb 1991 Cover: 1.75 **NM** value: **Cover or less**
Circ: CapCity orders: **3,050**

SUPER COPS, THE — Red Circle

1 ❑ ca. 1974 Cover: 0.25 **NM** value: **2.00**
📖 Crime Is Out Of Fashion **A:** Gray Morrow **W:** Marv Channing

SUPER DC GIANT — DC

13 ❑ Sep 1970 **NM** value: **75.00**
• **CGC:** 1 graded, best 8.5
• really S-13; Binky
14 ❑ Sep 1970 Cover: 0.25 **NM** value: **30.00**
• **CGC:** 2 graded, best 9.2
• really S-14; Westerns
15 ❑ Sep 1970 Cover: 0.25 **NM** value: **30.00**
• really S-15; Westerns
16 ❑ Sep 1970 Cover: 0.25 **NM** value: **30.00**
• **CGC:** 2 graded, best 9.6
• really S-16; Brave & the Bold
17 ❑ Sep 1970 **NM** value: **100.00**
• **CGC:** 7 graded, best 9.2
• really S-17; Romance
18 ❑ Oct 1970 **NM** value: **50.00**
• **CGC:** 3 graded, best 9.2
• really S-18; Three Mouseketeers
19 ❑ Oct 1970 **NM** value: **50.00**
• **CGC:** 2 graded, best 9.4
• really S-19; Jerry Lewis
20 ❑ Oct 1970 **NM** value: **40.00**
• really S-20; House of Mystery
21 ❑ Jan 1971 **NM** value: **150.00**
• **CGC:** 8 graded, best 9.4
• really S-21; Romance
22 ❑ Mar 1971 Cover: 0.25 **NM** value: **25.00**
• **CGC:** 1 graded, best 9.4
• really S-22; Westerns
23 ❑ Mar 1971 **NM** value: **30.00**
• **CGC:** 1 graded, best 9.2
• really S-23; Unexpected
24 ❑ May 1971 Cover: 0.25 **NM** value: **30.00**
• **CGC:** 4 graded, best 9.4
📖 The Girl With the X-Ray Mind; The Girl Who Was Supergirl's Double; The Forbidden Weapons of Krypton; The Super-Powers of Lex Luthor; Fashions From Fans • really S-24; Supergirl
25 ❑ Aug 1971 Cover: 0.25 **NM** value: **25.00**
📖 The Man Who Stole the Future; Captives of the Space Circus; The Wizard of Time • really S-25; Challengers of the Unknown
26 ❑ Aug 1971 Cover: 0.25 **NM** value: **25.00**
• really S-26; Aquaman
27 ❑ Sum 1976 **NM** value: **15.00**
• **CGC:** 1 graded, best 7.0
• Flying Saucers

SUPER DUCK COMICS — Archie

1 ❑ Fal 1944 Cover: 0.10 **NM** value: **325.00**
★ Origin of Super Duck.
2 ❑ Win 1944 Cover: 0.10 **NM** value: **150.00**
3 ❑ Spr 1945 Cover: 0.10 **NM** value: **100.00**
4 ❑ Sum 1945 Cover: 0.10 **NM** value: **80.00**
5 ❑ Fal 1945 Cover: 0.10 **NM** value: **80.00**
6 ❑ Feb 1946 Cover: 0.10 **NM** value: **65.00**
7 ❑ Apr 1946 Cover: 0.10 **NM** value: **65.00**
8 ❑ Jun 1946 Cover: 0.10 **NM** value: **65.00**
9 ❑ Aug 1946 Cover: 0.10 **NM** value: **65.00**
10 ❑ Oct 1946 Cover: 0.10 **NM** value: **65.00**
11 ❑ Dec 1946 Cover: 0.10 **NM** value: **55.00**
• Atom Bomb cover reference
12 ❑ Feb 1947 Cover: 0.10 **NM** value: **55.00**
13 ❑ Apr 1947 Cover: 0.10 **NM** value: **55.00**
14 ❑ Jun 1947 Cover: 0.10 **NM** value: **55.00**
15 ❑ Aug 1947 Cover: 0.10 **NM** value: **55.00**
16 ❑ Oct 1947 Cover: 0.10 **NM** value: **55.00**
17 ❑ Dec 1947 Cover: 0.10 **NM** value: **55.00**
18 ❑ Feb 1948 Cover: 0.10 **NM** value: **55.00**
19 ❑ Apr 1948 Cover: 0.10 **NM** value: **55.00**
20 ❑ Jun 1948 Cover: 0.10 **NM** value: **55.00**
21 ❑ Aug 1948 Cover: 0.10 **NM** value: **42.00**
22 ❑ Oct 1948 Cover: 0.10 **NM** value: **42.00**
23 ❑ Dec 1948 Cover: 0.10 **NM** value: **42.00**
24 ❑ Feb 1949 Cover: 0.10 **NM** value: **42.00**
25 ❑ Apr 1949 Cover: 0.10 **NM** value: **42.00**
26 ❑ Jun 1949 Cover: 0.10 **NM** value: **42.00**
27 ❑ Aug 1949 Cover: 0.10 **NM** value: **42.00**
28 ❑ Oct 1949 Cover: 0.10 **NM** value: **42.00**
29 ❑ Dec 1949 Cover: 0.10 **NM** value: **42.00**
30 ❑ Feb 1950 Cover: 0.10 **NM** value: **42.00**
📖 The Invisible Duck; Forget Me Nots; The Gift of Politeness; A Sweeping Climax; Cubby the Bear in It's for the Birds; Groaning Home; Movie News; It Shouldn't Happen to a Dog; A Sad Tail; A Current Event; Picnic a la Cart **A:** "Red" Holmdale; Al Fagaly **W:** "Red" Holmdale; Al Fagaly ★ Appearance of Cubby the Bear, Uwanna, Fauntleroy, Hamburger.
31 ❑ Apr 1950 Cover: 0.10 **NM** value: **30.00**
32 ❑ Jun 1950 Cover: 0.10 **NM** value: **30.00**
33 ❑ Aug 1950 Cover: 0.10 **NM** value: **30.00**
34 ❑ Oct 1950 Cover: 0.10 **NM** value: **30.00**
35 ❑ Dec 1950 Cover: 0.10 **NM** value: **30.00**
36 ❑ Feb 1951 Cover: 0.10 **NM** value: **30.00**
37 ❑ Apr 1951 Cover: 0.10 **NM** value: **30.00**
38 ❑ Jun 1951 Cover: 0.10 **NM** value: **30.00**
39 ❑ Aug 1951 Cover: 0.10 **NM** value: **30.00**
40 ❑ Oct 1951 Cover: 0.10 **NM** value: **30.00**
• **CGC:** 1 graded, best 9.2
41 ❑ Dec 1951 Cover: 0.10 **NM** value: **30.00**
42 ❑ Feb 1952 Cover: 0.10 **NM** value: **30.00**
43 ❑ Apr 1952 Cover: 0.10 **NM** value: **30.00**
44 ❑ Jun 1952 Cover: 0.10 **NM** value: **30.00**
45 ❑ Aug 1952 Cover: 0.10 **NM** value: **30.00**
46 ❑ Oct 1952 Cover: 0.10 **NM** value: **30.00**
47 ❑ Dec 1952 Cover: 0.10 **NM** value: **30.00**
48 ❑ Feb 1953 Cover: 0.10 **NM** value: **30.00**
49 ❑ Apr 1953 Cover: 0.10 **NM** value: **30.00**
50 ❑ Jun 1953 Cover: 0.10 **NM** value: **30.00**
51 ❑ Aug 1953 Cover: 0.10 **NM** value: **24.00**
52 ❑ Oct 1953 Cover: 0.10 **NM** value: **24.00**
53 ❑ Dec 1953 Cover: 0.10 **NM** value: **24.00**
54 ❑ Feb 1954 Cover: 0.10 **NM** value: **24.00**
55 ❑ Apr 1954 Cover: 0.10 **NM** value: **24.00**
56 ❑ Jun 1954 Cover: 0.10 **NM** value: **24.00**
57 ❑ Aug 1954 Cover: 0.10 **NM** value: **24.00**
58 ❑ Oct 1954 Cover: 0.10 **NM** value: **24.00**
59 ❑ Dec 1954 Cover: 0.10 **NM** value: **24.00**
60 ❑ Feb 1955 Cover: 0.10 **NM** value: **24.00**
61 ❑ Apr 1955 Cover: 0.10 **NM** value: **24.00**
62 ❑ Jun 1955 Cover: 0.10 **NM** value: **24.00**
63 ❑ Aug 1955 Cover: 0.10 **NM** value: **24.00**
64 ❑ Oct 1955 Cover: 0.10 **NM** value: **24.00**
65 ❑ Dec 1955 Cover: 0.10 **NM** value: **24.00**
66 ❑ Feb 1956 Cover: 0.10 **NM** value: **24.00**
67 ❑ Apr 1956 Cover: 0.10 **NM** value: **24.00**
68 ❑ Jun 1956 Cover: 0.10 **NM** value: **24.00**
📖 Protective Pest!; Wig Wag!; Fauntleroy…The Old Pelter; Deuces Wild!; On the ★ Appearance of Mushnoggin, Uwanna, Fauntleroy, Hamburger, Squintly.
69 ❑ Aug 1956 Cover: 0.10 **NM** value: **24.00**
70 ❑ Oct 1956 Cover: 0.10 **NM** value: **24.00**
71 ❑ Dec 1956 Cover: 0.10 **NM** value: **20.00**
72 ❑ Feb 1957 Cover: 0.10 **NM** value: **20.00**
73 ❑ Apr 1957 Cover: 0.10 **NM** value: **20.00**
74 ❑ Jun 1957 Cover: 0.10 **NM** value: **20.00**
75 ❑ Aug 1957 Cover: 0.10 **NM** value: **20.00**
76 ❑ Oct 1957 Cover: 0.10 **NM** value: **20.00**
77 ❑ Dec 1957 Cover: 0.10 **NM** value: **20.00**
78 ❑ Feb 1958 Cover: 0.10 **NM** value: **20.00**
79 ❑ Apr 1958 Cover: 0.10 **NM** value: **20.00**
80 ❑ Jun 1958 Cover: 0.10 **NM** value: **20.00**
81 ❑ Aug 1958 Cover: 0.10 **NM** value: **20.00**
82 ❑ 1958 Cover: 0.10 **NM** value: **20.00**
83 ❑ 1958 Cover: 0.10 **NM** value: **20.00**
84 ❑ 1959 Cover: 0.10 **NM** value: **20.00**
85 ❑ 1959 Cover: 0.10 **NM** value: **20.00**
86 ❑ 1959 Cover: 0.10 **NM** value: **20.00**
87 ❑ Sep 1959 Cover: 0.10 **NM** value: **20.00**
88 ❑ 1959 Cover: 0.10 **NM** value: **20.00**
89 ❑ 1960 Cover: 0.10 **NM** value: **20.00**
90 ❑ Apr 1960 Cover: 0.10 **NM** value: **20.00**
91 ❑ Jun 1960 Cover: 0.10 **NM** value: **20.00**
92 ❑ Aug 1960 Cover: 0.10 **NM** value: **20.00**
93 ❑ Oct 1960 Cover: 0.10 **NM** value: **20.00**
94 ❑ Dec 1960 Cover: 0.10 **NM** value: **20.00**
• Final; issue

SUPERFAN — Mark 1

1 ❑ b&w Cover: 1.95 **NM** value: **Cover or less**

SUPERFIST AYUMI — Eros

1 ❑ Oct 1996 Cover: 2.95 **NM** value: **Cover or less**
Circ: Diamd. preorders: **4,830**
2 ❑ Nov 1996 Cover: 2.95 **NM** value: **Cover or less**
Circ: Diamd. preorders: **4,236**

SUPER FRIENDS — DC

All the DC favorites — Superman, Batman, Wonder Woman, Aquaman, and Robin — team up in this series based on the ABC-TV Saturday morning cartoon of the same name.

During the adventures, some new heroes and villains appear. Extraterrestrial super-children, the Wonder Twins (who can "charge" each other up and then take on other forms), appeared in this series and hung around for most of it, as did the Ice Maiden, Dr. Mist, Fire, and Green Fury. Other friends, such as the Atom, Plastic Man, and Black Orchid also showed up to share the team's adventures.

As kitschy as the TV show, it's a little hard to read these issues without imagining Ted Knight's narration.

1 ❑ Nov 1976 Cover: 0.30 **NM** value: **5.00**
• **CGC:** 19 graded, best 9.6
2 ❑ Dec 1976 Cover: 0.30 **NM** value: **2.00**
3 ❑ Feb 1977 Cover: 0.30 **NM** value: **2.00**
• **CGC:** 2 graded, best 9.6
4 ❑ Apr 1977 Cover: 0.30 **NM** value: **2.00**
• **CGC:** 1 graded, best 9.6
5 ❑ Jun 1977 Cover: 0.35 **NM** value: **2.00**
6 ❑ Aug 1977 Cover: 0.35 **NM** value: **2.00**
7 ❑ Oct 1977 Cover: 0.35 **NM** value: **2.00**
★ 1st Appearance of Wonder Twins, Tasmanian Devil.
8 ❑ Nov 1977 Cover: 0.35 **NM** value: **2.00**
9 ❑ Dec 1977 Cover: 0.35 **NM** value: **2.00**
• **CGC:** 1 graded, best 9.2
★ 1st Appearance of Iron Maiden.
10 ❑ Mar 1978 Cover: 0.35 **NM** value: **2.00**
11 ❑ May 1978 Cover: 0.35 **NM** value: **1.50**
12 ❑ Jul 1978 Cover: 0.35 **NM** value: **1.50**
• **CGC:** 1 graded, best 9.0
★ 1st Appearance of Doctor Mist.
13 ❑ Sep 1978 Cover: 0.35 **NM** value: **1.50**
14 ❑ Nov 1978 Cover: 0.50 **NM** value: **1.50**
15 ❑ Dec 1978 Cover: 0.40 **NM** value: **1.50**
16 ❑ Jan 1979 Cover: 0.40 **NM** value: **1.50**
17 ❑ Feb 1979 Cover: 0.40 **NM** value: **1.50**
18 ❑ Mar 1979 Cover: 0.40 **NM** value: **1.50**
19 ❑ Apr 1979 Cover: 0.40 **NM** value: **1.50**
20 ❑ May 1979 Cover: 0.40 **NM** value: **1.50**
21 ❑ Jun 1979 Cover: 0.40 **NM** value: **1.50**
22 ❑ Jul 1979 Cover: 0.40 **NM** value: **1.50**
23 ❑ Aug 1979 Cover: 0.40 **NM** value: **1.50**
24 ❑ Sep 1979 Cover: 0.40 **NM** value: **1.50**
25 ❑ Oct 1979 Cover: 0.40 **NM** value: **1.50**
★ 1st Appearance of Fire.
26 ❑ Nov 1979 Cover: 0.40 **NM** value: **1.50**
27 ❑ Dec 1979 Cover: 0.40 **NM** value: **1.50**
• **CGC:** 1 graded, best 9.4
28 ❑ Jan 1980 Cover: 0.40 **NM** value: **1.50**
29 ❑ Feb 1980 Cover: 0.40 **NM** value: **1.50**
30 ❑ Mar 1980 Cover: 0.40 **NM** value: **1.50**
31 ❑ Apr 1980 Cover: 0.40 **NM** value: **1.50**
★ Appearance of Black Orchid.
32 ❑ May 1980 Cover: 0.40 **NM** value: **1.50**
• **CGC:** 1 graded, best 9.6
33 ❑ Jun 1980 Cover: 0.40 **NM** value: **1.50**
34 ❑ Jul 1980 Cover: 0.40 **NM** value: **1.50**
35 ❑ Aug 1980 Cover: 0.40 **NM** value: **1.50**
36 ❑ Sep 1980 Cover: 0.50 **NM** value: **1.50**
37 ❑ Oct 1980 Cover: 0.50 **NM** value: **1.50**
38 ❑ Nov 1980 Cover: 0.50 **NM** value: **1.50**
39 ❑ Dec 1980 Cover: 0.50 **NM** value: **1.50**
40 ❑ Jan 1981 Cover: 0.50 **NM** value: **1.50**
41 ❑ Feb 1981 Cover: 0.50 **NM** value: **1.50**
42 ❑ Mar 1981 Cover: 0.50 **NM** value: **1.50**
★ 1st Appearance of Green Flame.
43 ❑ Apr 1981 Cover: 0.50 **NM** value: **1.50**
44 ❑ May 1981 Cover: 0.50 **NM** value: **1.50**

CGC-graded: Multiply prices above by **33 for 9.9 M • 16 for 9.8 NM/M • 7 for 9.6 NM+ • 5 for 9.4 NM • 2.5 for 9.2 NM- • 1.5 for 9.0 VF/NM**

45 ☐ Jun 1981 Cover: 0.50 **NM** value: **1.50**
46 ☐ Jul 1981 Cover: 0.50 **NM** value: **1.50**
47 ☐ Aug 1981 Cover: 0.50 **NM** value: **1.50**
final issue.
SE 1☐ ca. 1981 **NM** value: **2.00**
says A TV Comic on cover. • giveaway.

SUPER FUNNIES — Superior

1 ☐ Dec 1953 Cover: 0.10 **NM** value: **250.00**
• **CGC:** 1 graded, best 7.0
2 ☐ Mar 1954 Cover: 0.10 **NM** value: **100.00**
3 ☐ Jun 1954 Cover: 0.10 **NM** value: **50.00**
4 ☐ Sep 1954 Cover: 0.10 **NM** value: **50.00**

SUPERGIRL (1ST SERIES) — DC

Although a longtime member of the Legion of Super-Heroes, this 1972 title was Supergirl's first solo series. At the time, her costume consisted of a V-neck suit with a choker cape. The Maid of Steel lived a double-life as brunette girl's school student "Linda Lee" and as the blonde hero Supergirl. In her latter identity, she had powers similar to her cousin Superman's, including strength, invulnerability, heat vision, and the ability to fly. She used these powers to come to the rescue of any number of people, often fellow classmates, saving them from falling buildings, alien invaders, and other dangers.

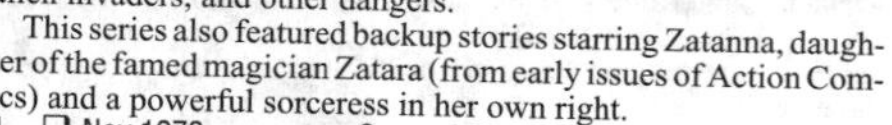

This series also featured backup stories starring Zatanna, daughter of the famed magician Zatara (from early issues of Action Comics) and a powerful sorceress in her own right.

1 ☐ Nov 1972 Cover: 0.20 **NM** value: **15.00**
• **CGC:** 9 graded, best 9.6
2 ☐ Cover: 0.20 **NM** value: **10.00**
3 ☐ Feb 1973 Cover: 0.20 **NM** value: **8.00**
📖 The Garden of Death **A:** Art Saaf; Vince Colletta **W:** Cary Bates
4 ☐ Apr 1973 Cover: 0.20 **NM** value: **8.00**
• **CGC:** 2 graded, best 9.2
5 ☐ Jun 1973 Cover: 0.20 **NM** value: **8.00**
• **CGC:** 4 graded, best 9.6
📖 The Devil's Brother; The Girl Who Split in Two! • origin of Zatana **A:** John Rosenberger; Vince Colletta **W:** Arnold Drake
6 ☐ Aug 1973 Cover: 0.20 **NM** value: **8.00**
7 ☐ Oct 1973 Cover: 0.20 **NM** value: **8.00**
• **CGC:** 1 graded, best 9.2
8 ☐ Nov 1973 Cover: 0.20 **NM** value: **8.00**
• **CGC:** 1 graded, best 9.4
9 ☐ Jan 1974 Cover: 0.20 **NM** value: **8.00**
• **CGC:** 8 graded, best 9.4
10 ☐ Sep 1974 Cover: 0.20 **NM** value: **8.00**
• **CGC:** 6 graded, best 9.8
📖 Death of a Prez!; Her Brother's Keeper! final issue. ★ Appearance of Prez.

SUPERGIRL (2ND SERIES) — DC

This title is a continuation of the Daring New Adventures of Supergirl. Its title character, Kara Zor-El (Supergirl) first showed up in Action Comics #252, back in 1959. Kara was the cousin of fellow Kryptonian Ka-El, better known as Superman. Their home planet, Krypton, had exploded years before her appearance, and Superman was believed to be the only survivor. As the years went by, however, Kryptonians kept showing up, including the criminals who had been imprisoned in the Phantom Zone and the people of the bottled city of Kandor.

Supergirl herself was born in the domed city of Argo which had been sent flying off into space by the explosion that destroyed Krypton. For a time, the city's dome protected it, but the dome's integrity was eventually breached. In desperation, her parents sent the teen-aged Kara on a rocket to Earth. There she eventually met up with Kal-El, who taught her how to use her powers.

14 ☐ Dec 1983 Cover: 0.75 **NM** value: **3.00**
• Title changes to Supergirl; Series continued from "Daring New Adventures of Supergirl"
15 ☐ Jan 1984 Cover: 0.75 **NM** value: **3.00**
16 ☐ Feb 1984 Cover: 0.75 **NM** value: **3.00**
📖 Bug-Out! **A:** Carmine Infantino **W:** Paul Kupperberg ★ Appearance of Ambush Bug.
17 ☐ Mar 1984 Cover: 0.75 **NM** value: **3.00**
📖 Publish and Perish!
18 ☐ Apr 1984 Cover: 0.75 **NM** value: **3.00**
📖 Call Me Kraken!
19 ☐ May 1984 Cover: 0.75 **NM** value: **3.00**
📖 Who Stole Supergirl's Life?
20 ☐ Jun 1984 Cover: 0.75 **NM** value: **3.00**
★ Appearance of Teen Titans, Justice League of America.
21 ☐ Jul 1984 Cover: 0.75 **NM** value: **3.00**
A: Carmine Infantino
22 ☐ Aug 1984 Cover: 0.75 **NM** value: **3.00**
A: Carmine Infantino
23 ☐ Sep 1984 Cover: 0.75 **NM** value: **3.00**
final issue. **A:** Carmine Infantino
DOT 1☐ ca. 1984 **NM** value: **3.00**
• Department of Transportation giveaway. **A:** Angelo Torres **W:** Joe Orlando; Andy Helfer; Barry Marx; Robert Loren Flemming

SUPERGIRL (3RD SERIES) — DC

Originally Kara Zor-El, another survivor of Krypton, the Silver Age Supergirl came to Earth years after her famous cousin had established his super-heroic career.

In the 1986 revamp of the Superman titles, The Man of Steel was his planet's sole survivor, leaving fans to wonder if or when Supergirl would reappear. The answer came just a couple of years later when Superman visited a "pocket universe" created by The Time Trapper that contained Superboy and most of the Silver Age continuity. Here though, Lex Luthor was a hero who had created a new Supergirl out of a protoplasmic matrix.

Eventually, the new Supergirl made her way to Superman's home dimension where she began her own super-heroic career. In this series, written by Peter David with art by Gary Frank, Supergirl bonds with Linda Danvers, the victim of a demon. Utilizing more humor than previous incarnations, this series pits Supergirl against all types of supernatural horrors. — Brent

1 ☐ Sep 1996 Cover: 1.95 **NM** value: **6.00**
• **CGC:** 9 graded, best 9.6
📖 Body & Soul • Matrix merges with Linda Danvers **A:** Gary Frank **W:** Peter David
1-2 ☐ Sep 1996 Cover: 1.95 **NM** value: **3.00**
2 ☐ Oct 1996 Cover: 1.95 **NM** value: **4.00**
📖 Cat's Paw • Matrix learns more of Linda Danvers' past **A:** Gary Frank **W:** Peter David
3 ☐ Nov 1996 Cover: 1.95 **NM** value: **3.50**
Circ: Diamd. preorders: **67,425**
📖 And No Dawn to Follow the Darkness • Final Night **A:** Gary Frank **W:** Peter David ★ Versus Gorilla Grodd.
4 ☐ Dec 1996 Cover: 1.95 **NM** value: **3.00**
Circ: Diamd. preorders: **67,311**
📖 Belly of the Beast **A:** Gary Frank **W:** Peter David ★ Versus Gorilla Grodd.
5 ☐ Jan 1997 Cover: 1.95 **NM** value: **3.00**
Circ: Diamd. preorders: **62,443**
📖 Chemical Imbalance **A:** Gary Frank **W:** Peter David ★ Versus Chemo.
6 ☐ Feb 1997 Cover: 1.95 **NM** value: **2.50**
Circ: Diamd. preorders: **59,871**
📖 Trust Fund **A:** Gary Frank **W:** Peter David ★ Appearance of Superman. ★ Versus Rampage.
7 ☐ Mar 1997 Cover: 1.95 **NM** value: **2.50**
Circ: Diamd. preorders: **57,100**
📖 Art History **A:** Gary Frank **W:** Gary Frank; Peter David
8 ☐ Apr 1997 Cover: 1.95 **NM** value: **2.00**
Circ: Diamd. preorders: **53,519**
📖 My Dinner With Buzz **W:** Peter David
9 ☐ May 1997 Cover: 1.95 **NM** value: **2.00**
Circ: Diamd. preorders: **53,325**
📖 Tempus Fugit **W:** Peter David ★ Versus Tempus.
10 ☐ Jun 1997 Cover: 1.95 **NM** value: **2.00**
Circ: Diamd. preorders: **52,081**
📖 Hidden Things **W:** Peter David
11 ☐ Jul 1997 Cover: 1.95 **NM** value: **2.00**
Circ: Diamd. preorders: **50,892**
📖 Sound and Fury **W:** Peter David ★ Versus Silver Banshee.
12 ☐ Aug 1997 Cover: 1.95 **NM** value: **2.00**
Circ: Diamd. preorders: **49,173**
📖 Cries in the Darkness **W:** Peter David
13 ☐ Sep 1997 Cover: 1.95 **NM** value: **2.00**
Circ: Diamd. preorders: **46,305**
📖 Incubus **W:** Peter David
14 ☐ Oct 1997 Cover: 1.95 **NM** value: **2.00**
Circ: Diamd. preorders: **47,601**
• Genesis **W:** Peter David
15 ☐ Nov 1997 Cover: 1.95 **NM** value: **2.00**
Circ: Diamd. preorders: **43,387**
📖 Gods of the Twilight **A:** Leonard Kirk **W:** Peter David ★ Versus Extremists.
16 ☐ Dec 1997 Cover: 1.95 **NM** value: **2.00**
Circ: Diamd. preorders: **43,285**
Face cover. 📖 Blonde Justice **A:** Leonard Kirk **W:** Peter David ★ Versus Extremists.
17 ☐ Jan 1998 Cover: 1.95 **NM** value: **2.00**
Circ: Diamd. preorders: **41,792**
W: Peter David ★ Versus Despero.
18 ☐ Feb 1998 Cover: 1.95 **NM** value: **2.00**
Circ: Diamd. preorders: **40,263**
W: Peter David ★ Versus Despero.
19 ☐ Mar 1998 Cover: 1.95 **NM** value: **2.00**
Circ: Diamd. preorders: **38,737**
📖 Middle-Aged Crisis **A:** Leonard Kirk **W:** Peter David ★ Versus Blastoff.
20 ☐ Apr 1998 Cover: 1.95 **NM** value: **2.00**
Circ: Diamd. preorders: **40,422**
• Millennium Giants **W:** Peter David
21 ☐ May 1998 Cover: 1.95 **NM** value: **2.00**
Circ: Diamd. preorders: **37,287**
W: Peter David
22 ☐ Jun 1998 Cover: 1.95 **NM** value: **2.00**
Circ: Diamd. preorders: **37,692**
W: Peter David
23 ☐ Jul 1998 Cover: 1.95 **NM** value: **2.00**
Circ: Diamd. preorders: **36,624**
W: Peter David ★ Appearance of Steel.
24 ☐ Aug 1998 Cover: 1.95 **NM** value: **2.00**
Circ: Diamd. preorders: **37,476**
W: Peter David ★ Appearance of Resurrection Man.
25 ☐ Sep 1998 Cover: 1.99 **NM** value: **2.00**
Circ: Diamd. preorders: **34,953**
W: Peter David
26 ☐ Oct 1998 Cover: 1.99 **NM** value: **2.00**
Circ: Diamd. preorders: **33,842**
W: Peter David ★ Origin of Comet.
27 ☐ Dec 1998 Cover: 1.99 **NM** value: **2.00**
Circ: Diamd. preorders: **33,150**
A: Gary Frank **W:** Peter David ★ Versus Female Furies.
28 ☐ Jan 1999 Cover: 1.99 **NM** value: **2.00**
Circ: Diamd. preorders: **32,804**
W: Peter David ★ Versus Female Furies.
29 ☐ Feb 1999 Cover: 1.99 **NM** value: **2.00**
Circ: Diamd. preorders: **31,708**
W: Peter David ★ Appearance of Twilight, Female Furies, Granny Goodness.
30 ☐ Mar 1999 Cover: 1.99 **NM** value: **2.00**
Circ: Diamd. preorders: **30,937**
W: Peter David ★ Appearance of Matrix. ★ Versus Matrix.
31 ☐ Apr 1999 Cover: 1.99 **NM** value: **Cover or less**
Circ: Diamd. preorders: **29,732**
W: Peter David ★ Versus Matrix.
32 ☐ May 1999 Cover: 1.99 **NM** value: **Cover or less**
Circ: Diamd. preorders: **29,236**
📖 The Quality of Mercy **A:** Sean Phillips **W:** Peter David
33 ☐ Jun 1999 Cover: 1.99 **NM** value: **Cover or less**
Circ: Diamd. preorders: **29,691**
📖 Above a Murmur **A:** Jason Orfalas **W:** Peter David
34 ☐ Jul 1999 Cover: 1.99 **NM** value: **Cover or less**
Circ: Diamd. preorders: **29,146**
📖 We'll Always Have Parasite **A:** Leonard Kirk **W:** Peter David ★ Versus Parasite.
35 ☐ Aug 1999 Cover: 1.99 **NM** value: **Cover or less**
Circ: Diamd. preorders: **28,548**
📖 For Those Who Came Late… **A:** Leonard Kirk **W:** Peter David ★ Versus Parasite.
36 ☐ Sep 1999 Cover: 1.99 **NM** value: **Cover or less**
Circ: Diamd. preorders: **31,328**
📖 Justice Delayed **A:** Leonard Kirk **W:** Peter David ★ Appearance of Young Justice.
37 ☐ Oct 1999 Cover: 1.99 **NM** value: **Cover or less**
Circ: Diamd. preorders: **29,556**
📖 Heck's Angels, Part 4 **A:** Leonard Kirk **W:** Peter David ★ Appearance of Young Justice.
38 ☐ Nov 1999 Cover: 1.99 **NM** value: **Cover or less**
Circ: Diamd. preorders: **29,918**
• Day of Judgment **A:** Leonard Kirk **W:** Peter David ★ Appearance of Zauriel.
39 ☐ Dec 1999 Cover: 1.99 **NM** value: **Cover or less**
Circ: Diamd. preorders: **27,806**
📖 On Ice **A:** Leonard Kirk **W:** Peter David
40 ☐ Jan 2000 Cover: 1.99 **NM** value: **Cover or less**
Circ: Diamd. preorders: **27,283**
📖 Fading Ember **A:** Leonard Kirk **W:** Peter David
41 ☐ Feb 2000 Cover: 1.99 **NM** value: **Cover or less**
Circ: Diamd. preorders: **28,603**
W: Peter David
42 ☐ Mar 2000 Cover: 1.99 **NM** value: **Cover or less**
Circ: Diamd. preorders: **25,616**
W: Peter David
43 ☐ Apr 2000 Cover: 1.99 **NM** value: **Cover or less**
Circ: Diamd. preorders: **24,447**
📖 Damned if you do… **A:** Leonard Kirk **W:** Peter David
44 ☐ May 2000 Cover: 1.99 **NM** value: **Cover or less**
Circ: Diamd. preorders: **24,197**
📖 Shadows of Doubt **A:** Leonard Kirk **W:** Peter David
45 ☐ Jun 2000 Cover: 1.99 **NM** value: **Cover or less**
Circ: Diamd. preorders: **23,806**
A: Leonard Kirk **W:** Peter David
46 ☐ Jul 2000 Cover: 1.99 **NM** value: **Cover or less**
Circ: Diamd. preorders: **23,565**
A: Leonard Kirk **W:** Peter David
47 ☐ Aug 2000 Cover: 1.99 **NM** value: **Cover or less**
Circ: Diamd. preorders: **23,651**
A: Leonard Kirk **W:** Peter David
48 ☐ Sep 2000 Cover: 2.25 **NM** value: **Cover or less**
Circ: Diamd. preorders: **23,605**
📖 Fallen Angel **A:** Leonard Kirk **W:** Peter David
49 ☐ Oct 2000 Cover: 2.25 **NM** value: **Cover or less**
Circ: Diamd. preorders: **22,510**
📖 Through a Mirror Darkly **A:** Leonard Kirk; Derec Aucoin; Robin Riggs **W:** Peter David
50 ☐ Nov 2000 Cover: 3.95 **NM** value: **Cover or less**
Circ: Diamd. preorders: **24,102**
• Giant-size. 📖 Wally's Angels **A:** Leonard Kirk **W:** Peter David
51 ☐ Dec 2000 Cover: 2.25 **NM** value: **Cover or less**
Circ: Diamd. preorders: **22,857**
📖 Making a Splash **A:** Leonard Kirk **W:** Peter David
52 ☐ Jan 2001 Cover: 2.25 **NM** value: **Cover or less**
Circ: Diamd. preorders: **22,468** • **CGC:** 1 graded, best 9.6
📖 Supergirl, Interrupted **A:** Leonard Kirk; Robin Riggs **W:** Peter David
53 ☐ Feb 2001 Cover: 2.25 **NM** value: **Cover or less**
Circ: Diamd. preorders: **22,311**
📖 Art for Art's Sake **A:** Leonard Kirk; Robin Riggs **W:** Peter David
54 ☐ Mar 2001 Cover: 2.25 **NM** value: **Cover or less**
Circ: Diamd. preorders: **22,355**
📖 Statue of Limitations **A:** Leonard Kirk **W:** Peter David
55 ☐ Apr 2001 Cover: 2.25 **NM** value: **Cover or less**
Circ: Diamd. preorders: **22,065**
📖 Dale of the Mule **A:** Derec Aucoin **W:** Peter David
56 ☐ May 2001 Cover: 2.25 **NM** value: **Cover or less**
Circ: Diamd. preorders: **21,593**
📖 Demon Rum **A:** Leonard Kirk **W:** Peter David
57 ☐ Jun 2001 Cover: 2.25 **NM** value: **Cover or less**
Circ: Diamd. preorders: **21,906**
58 ☐ Jul 2001 Cover: 2.25 **NM** value: **Cover or less**
Circ: Diamd. preorders: **21,796**

Other grades: Multiply prices above by **1.5 for Mint • 2/3 for Very Fine • 1/3 for Fine • 1/5 for Very Good • 1/8 for Good**

59 ❑ Aug 2001 Cover: 2.25 **NM** value: **Cover or less**
Circ: Diamd. preorders: **26,269**
60 ❑ Sep 2001 Cover: 2.25 **NM** value: **Cover or less**
Circ: Diamd. preorders: **27,963**
1000000❑Nov 1998 Cover: 1.99 **NM** value: **Cover or less**
Circ: Diamd. preorders: **40,912**
📖 When She Was Good… **A:** Dusty Abell **W:** Peter David ★ Appearance of R'E'L.
Anl 1❑ca. 1996 Cover: 2.95 **NM** value: **Cover or less**
• Legends of the Dead Earth
Anl 2❑ca. 1997 Cover: 3.95 **NM** value: **Cover or less**
Circ: Diamd. preorders: **36,745**
• Pulp Heroes
Bk 1❑ Cover: 14.95 **NM** value: **Cover or less**
• collects issues #1-9 and Showcase '96 #12

SUPERGIRL/LEX LUTHOR SPECIAL — DC

1 ❑ ca. 1993 Cover: 2.50 **NM** value: **Cover or less**
Circ: CapCity orders: **47,800**
One-shot. cover says Supergirl and Team Luthor. 📖 The Future of Metropolis!; Shelter • includes pin-up gallery

SUPERGIRL (MINI-SERIES) — DC

1 ❑ Feb 1994 Cover: 1.50 **NM** value: **3.00**
Circ: CapCity orders: **73,700**
📖 Trial Run **A:** June Brigman **W:** Roger Stern
2 ❑ Mar 1994 Cover: 1.50 **NM** value: **2.50**
Circ: CapCity orders: **43,050**
📖 Demands **A:** June Brigman **W:** Roger Stern
3 ❑ Apr 1994 Cover: 1.50 **NM** value: **2.50**
Circ: CapCity orders: **36,000**
📖 End of Innocence
4 ❑ May 1994 Cover: 1.50 **NM** value: **2.50**
Circ: CapCity orders: **34,850**
📖 The Big Hurt

SUPERGIRL MOVIE SPECIAL — DC

1 ❑ Cover: 1.25 **NM** value: **Cover or less**
📖 Supergirl • Movie adaptation **A:** Gray Morrow

SUPERGIRL PLUS — DC

1 ❑ Feb 1997 Cover: 2.95 **NM** value: **Cover or less**
Circ: Diamd. preorders: **49,880**
★ Appearance of Mary Marvel.

SUPERGIRL/PRYSM DOUBLE SHOT — DC

1 ❑ Feb 1998 Cover: 1.95 **NM** value: **Cover or less**
Circ: Diamd. preorders: **31,424**
One-shot.

SUPER GOOF (WALT DISNEY…) — Gold Key

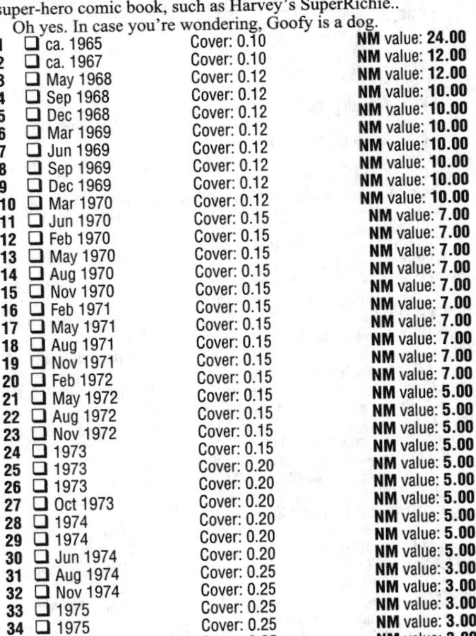

Disney's Goofy gained super-powers by eating super-peanuts (called "Super Goobers"). Still goofy as ever, he now has powers that rival Superman's. As Super Goof, Goofy has the ability to fly, X-ray vision, super-breath, invulnerability, and other powers. Joined by a wide assortment of friends, including gadget-master Gyro Gearloose and brainy nephew Gilbert, he battles evildoers, including the Phantom Blot, wherever they may be.

Super Goof's lighthearted style made it a fine companion to other Disney titles, and it fares better than some other attempt to create a kids' super-hero comic book, such as Harvey's SuperRichie..

Oh yes. In case you're wondering, Goofy is a dog.

1 ❑ ca. 1965 Cover: 0.10 **NM** value: **24.00**
2 ❑ ca. 1967 Cover: 0.10 **NM** value: **12.00**
3 ❑ May 1968 Cover: 0.12 **NM** value: **12.00**
4 ❑ Sep 1968 Cover: 0.12 **NM** value: **10.00**
5 ❑ Dec 1968 Cover: 0.12 **NM** value: **10.00**
6 ❑ Mar 1969 Cover: 0.12 **NM** value: **10.00**
7 ❑ Jun 1969 Cover: 0.12 **NM** value: **10.00**
8 ❑ Sep 1969 Cover: 0.12 **NM** value: **10.00**
9 ❑ Dec 1969 Cover: 0.12 **NM** value: **10.00**
10 ❑ Mar 1970 Cover: 0.12 **NM** value: **10.00**
11 ❑ Jun 1970 Cover: 0.15 **NM** value: **7.00**
12 ❑ Feb 1970 Cover: 0.15 **NM** value: **7.00**
13 ❑ May 1970 Cover: 0.15 **NM** value: **7.00**
14 ❑ Aug 1970 Cover: 0.15 **NM** value: **7.00**
15 ❑ Nov 1970 Cover: 0.15 **NM** value: **7.00**
16 ❑ Feb 1971 Cover: 0.15 **NM** value: **7.00**
17 ❑ May 1971 Cover: 0.15 **NM** value: **7.00**
18 ❑ Aug 1971 Cover: 0.15 **NM** value: **7.00**
19 ❑ Nov 1971 Cover: 0.15 **NM** value: **7.00**
20 ❑ Feb 1972 Cover: 0.15 **NM** value: **7.00**
21 ❑ May 1972 Cover: 0.15 **NM** value: **5.00**
22 ❑ Aug 1972 Cover: 0.15 **NM** value: **5.00**
23 ❑ Nov 1972 Cover: 0.15 **NM** value: **5.00**
24 ❑ 1973 Cover: 0.15 **NM** value: **5.00**
25 ❑ 1973 Cover: 0.20 **NM** value: **5.00**
26 ❑ 1973 Cover: 0.20 **NM** value: **5.00**
27 ❑ Oct 1973 Cover: 0.20 **NM** value: **5.00**
28 ❑ 1974 Cover: 0.20 **NM** value: **5.00**
29 ❑ 1974 Cover: 0.20 **NM** value: **5.00**
30 ❑ Jun 1974 Cover: 0.20 **NM** value: **5.00**
31 ❑ Aug 1974 Cover: 0.25 **NM** value: **3.00**
32 ❑ Nov 1974 Cover: 0.25 **NM** value: **3.00**
33 ❑ 1975 Cover: 0.25 **NM** value: **3.00**
34 ❑ 1975 Cover: 0.25 **NM** value: **3.00**
35 ❑ Sep 1975 Cover: 0.25 **NM** value: **3.00**
36 ❑ Dec 1975 Cover: 0.25 **NM** value: **3.00**
37 ❑ Feb 1976 Cover: 0.25 **NM** value: **3.00**
38 ❑ Jun 1976 Cover: 0.25 **NM** value: **3.00**
39 ❑ Sep 1976 Cover: 0.30 **NM** value: **3.00**
40 ❑ Nov 1976 Cover: 0.30 **NM** value: **3.00**
📖 The Crystal Egg Affair; The Worlds Strongest Weakling; Seeing Double
41 ❑ Feb 1977 Cover: 0.30 **NM** value: **3.00**
42 ❑ Jun 1977 Cover: 0.30 **NM** value: **3.00**
43 ❑ Sep 1977 Cover: 0.30 **NM** value: **3.00**
44 ❑ Nov 1977 Cover: 0.30 **NM** value: **3.00**
45 ❑ Feb 1978 Cover: 0.35 **NM** value: **3.00**
46 ❑ Apr 1978 Cover: 0.35 **NM** value: **3.00**
47 ❑ Jun 1978 Cover: 0.35 **NM** value: **3.00**
48 ❑ Aug 1978 Cover: 0.35 **NM** value: **3.00**
49 ❑ Oct 1978 Cover: 0.35 **NM** value: **3.00**
50 ❑ Dec 1978 Cover: 0.35 **NM** value: **3.00**
51 ❑ Feb 1979 Cover: 0.35 **NM** value: **2.50**
52 ❑ Apr 1979 Cover: 0.35 **NM** value: **2.50**
53 ❑ Jun 1979 Cover: 0.40 **NM** value: **2.50**
54 ❑ Aug 1979 Cover: 0.40 **NM** value: **2.50**
55 ❑ Oct 1979 Cover: 0.40 **NM** value: **2.50**
56 ❑ Dec 1979 Cover: 0.40 **NM** value: **2.50**
57 ❑ Jan 1980 Cover: 0.40 **NM** value: **2.50**
58 ❑ Mar 1980 Cover: 0.40 **NM** value: **2.50**
59 ❑ May 1980 Cover: 0.40 **NM** value: **2.50**
60 ❑ Jul 1980 Cover: 0.40 **NM** value: **2.50**
61 ❑ Oct 1980 Cover: 0.40 **NM** value: **2.50**
62 ❑ Dec 1980 Cover: 0.40 **NM** value: **2.50**
63 ❑ Jan 1981 Cover: 0.50 **NM** value: **2.50**
64 ❑ 1981 Cover: 0.50 **NM** value: **2.50**
65 ❑ 1981 Cover: 0.50 **NM** value: **2.50**
66 ❑ Dec 1981 Cover: 0.50 **NM** value: **2.50**
67 ❑ Feb 1982 Cover: 0.60 **NM** value: **2.50**
📖 Mini But Mighty; The Runaway Planet; The Mysterious Mystery; The Mighty Knight: The Gimmick Knight
68 ❑ 1982 Cover: 0.60 **NM** value: **2.50**
69 ❑ 1982 Cover: 0.60 **NM** value: **2.50**
70 ❑ 1982 Cover: 0.60 **NM** value: **2.50**
71 ❑ 1982 Cover: 0.60 **NM** value: **2.50**
72 ❑ 1983 Cover: 0.60 **NM** value: **2.50**
73 ❑ Jul 1983 Cover: 0.60 **NM** value: **2.50**
74 ❑ 1983 Cover: 0.60 **NM** value: **2.50**
final issue.

SUPER GREEN BERET — Milson

Captain Wilson had bravely risked his life to save a group of Vietnamese monks from the Viet Cong guerillas. In gratitude, the had abbot bestowed jungle magic upon Wilson's beret with the qualification that only one who is young and noble by nature will have the sorcery at his command. The captain didn't believe that there was anything to the old monk's words, but when his nephew, Tod, placed the beret on his head, he was transformed into a full-grown adult who has amazing magical powers.

As Super Green Beret, Tod hears telepathic messages and transports himself to combat zones to aid soldiers in dangerous situations. He later discovers that the magic Green Beret can even transport him back in time to aid soldiers in World War II.

A strange cross between the standard war comic book and the magic boy-to-adult motif of Captain Marvel, Super Green Beret seemed even then to be a stilted attempt to capitalize on the public knowledge of the Green Berets. Today, it seems even more a product of its time. There's no question of the nobility of war in Vietnam in this series, and the Vietcong are faceless villains, depicted much like the Japanese were in comics two decades earlier.

1 ❑ Apr 1967 Cover: 0.25 **NM** value: **30.00**
📖 Super Green Beret; True Combat Action; Rebel Rat-Hole; White Magic in the Black Forest!; Give me a Little Man Anytime; Sorcery Against Saboteurs!
2 ❑ Cover: 0.25 **NM** value: **24.00**

SUPERHEROES — Dell

1 ❑ ca. 1967 Cover: 0.12 **NM** value: **20.00**
📖 The Origin Of The Fab Four **A:** Sal Trapani ★ Origin of The Fab Four. ★ 1st Appearance of The Fab Four, Endo-Man.
2 ❑ ca. 1967 Cover: 0.12 **NM** value: **12.00**
3 ❑ ca. 1967 Cover: 0.12 **NM** value: **12.00**
4 ❑ ca. 1967 Cover: 0.12 **NM** value: **12.00**
final issue.

SUPER HEROES BATTLE SUPER GORILLAS — DC

1 ❑ Win 1976 Cover: 0.50 **NM** value: **7.00**
• **CGC:** 1 graded, best 9.2

SUPER HEROES PUZZLES AND GAMES — Marvel

1 ❑ Apr 1980 **NM** value: **2.00**
No issue number. • giveaway. ★ Origin of Captain America, Spider-Man, The Hulk, Spider-Woman.

SUPER HEROES STAMP ALBUM — USPS / DC

1 ❑ Cover: 2.95 **NM** value: **Cover or less**
• 1900-1909 **A:** Paul Ryan; Doug Hazlewood **W:** Doug Moench
2 ❑ Cover: 2.95 **NM** value: **Cover or less**
• 1910-1919
3 ❑ Cover: 2.95 **NM** value: **Cover or less**
• 1920-1929
4 ❑ Cover: 2.95 **NM** value: **Cover or less**
no Snow White coverage. • 1930-1939
5 ❑ Cover: 2.95 **NM** value: **Cover or less**
• 1940-1949
6 ❑ Cover: 2.95 **NM** value: **Cover or less**
• 1950-1959; 3-D stamp **W:** Bronwyn Carlton
7 ❑ Cover: 2.95 **NM** value: **Cover or less**
• 1960-1969
8 ❑ Cover: 2.95 **NM** value: **Cover or less**
• 1970-1979
9 ❑ Cover: 2.95 **NM** value: **Cover or less**
• 1980-1989 **W:** Bob Rozakis
10 ❑ Cover: 2.95 **NM** value: **Cover or less**
• 1990-1999

SUPER HEROES VERSUS SUPER VILLAINS — Archie

1 ❑ ca. 1966 **NM** value: **50.00**
• **CGC:** 3 graded, best 9.4

SUPERHERO WOMEN, THE — Marvel

Bk 1❑ Cover: 6.95 **NM** value: **15.00**
📖 Make Way For…Medusa!; Eyes of the Gorg • (Fireside) **A:** John Buscema; Frank Thorne; Jack Kirby; John Romita; Wally Wood; Ross Andru; Jim Mooney; Marie Severin **W:** Jack Kirby; Bruce Jones; Stan Lee; Carole Seuling; Gerry Conway; Linda Fite

SUPERICHIE — Harvey

1 ❑ Sep 1975 Cover: 0.35 **NM** value: **5.00**
• **CGC:** 1 graded, best 8.0
2 ❑ Nov 1975 Cover: 0.35 **NM** value: **3.00**
3 ❑ Jan 1976 Cover: 0.35 **NM** value: **3.00**
• **CGC:** 1 graded, best 9.2
4 ❑ Mar 1976 Cover: 0.35 **NM** value: **3.00**
5 ❑ 1976 Cover: 0.40 **NM** value: **3.00**
6 ❑ Nov 1976 Cover: 0.40 **NM** value: **2.00**
📖 Badman Strikes!; The Personality Changer; Space Emergency Landing!; Little Dot: Game Kids!; Treasured Chest; Clothes Make the Play
7 ❑ ca. 1977 Cover: 0.40 **NM** value: **2.00**
8 ❑ ca. 1977 Cover: 0.40 **NM** value: **2.00**
9 ❑ ca. 1977 Cover: 0.40 **NM** value: **2.00**
10 ❑ ca. 1977 Cover: 0.40 **NM** value: **2.00**
11 ❑ ca. 1977 Cover: 0.40 **NM** value: **2.00**
12 ❑ ca. 1977 Cover: 0.50 **NM** value: **2.00**
13 ❑ ca. 1978 Cover: 0.50 **NM** value: **2.00**
14 ❑ ca. 1978 Cover: 0.50 **NM** value: **2.00**
15 ❑ ca. 1978 Cover: 0.50 **NM** value: **2.00**
16 ❑ ca. 1978 Cover: 0.50 **NM** value: **2.00**
17 ❑ Oct 1978 Cover: 0.50 **NM** value: **2.00**
18 ❑ Jan 1979 Cover: 0.50 **NM** value: **2.00**

SUPER INFORMATION HIJINKS: REALITY CHECK — Tavicat

1 ❑ Oct 1995, b&w Cover: 2.95 **NM** value: **Cover or less**
📖 Insomniacs! **A:** Tavisha Wolfgarth; Rosearik Rikki **W:** Rosearik Rikki
2 ❑ Dec 1995, b&w Cover: 2.95 **NM** value: **Cover or less**
A: Tavisha Wolfgarth; Rosearik Rikki **W:** Rosearik Rikki
3 ❑ 1996 Cover: 2.95 **NM** value: **Cover or less**
A: Tavisha Wolfgarth; Rosearik Rikki **W:** Rosearik Rikki
4 ❑ 1996 Cover: 2.95 **NM** value: **Cover or less**
A: Tavisha Wolfgarth; Rosearik Rikki **W:** Rosearik Rikki
5 ❑ 1996 Cover: 2.95 **NM** value: **Cover or less**
A: Tavisha Wolfgarth; Rosearik Rikki **W:** Rosearik Rikki

SUPER INFORMATION HIJINKS: REALITY CHECK! (2ND SERIES) — Sirius

1 ❑ Sep 1996 Cover: 2.95 **NM** value: **Cover or less**
Circ: Diamd. preorders: **5,690**
2 ❑ Oct 1996 Cover: 2.95 **NM** value: **Cover or less**
Circ: Diamd. preorders: **4,298**
3 ❑ Nov 1996 Cover: 2.95 **NM** value: **Cover or less**
Circ: Diamd. preorders: **3,815**
4 ❑ Dec 1996 Cover: 2.95 **NM** value: **Cover or less**
Circ: Diamd. preorders: **3,957**
5 ❑ Jan 1997 Cover: 2.95 **NM** value: **Cover or less**
Circ: Diamd. preorders: **4,077**
6 ❑ Feb 1997 Cover: 2.95 **NM** value: **Cover or less**
Circ: Diamd. preorders: **3,695**
7 ❑ Mar 1997 Cover: 2.95 **NM** value: **Cover or less**
Circ: Diamd. preorders: **3,930**
8 ❑ Jan 1998 Cover: 2.95 **NM** value: **Cover or less**
Circ: Diamd. preorders: **3,530**
📖 When Kittens Collide! **A:** Tavisha Wolfgarth; Rosearik Rikki Simons **W:** Rosearik Rikki Simons
9 ❑ Mar 1998 Cover: 2.95 **NM** value: **Cover or less**
Circ: Diamd. preorders: **3,453**
10 ❑ May 1998 Cover: 2.95 **NM** value: **Cover or less**
Circ: Diamd. preorders: **3,237**
11 ❑ Jul 1998 Cover: 2.95 **NM** value: **Cover or less**
Circ: Diamd. preorders: **3,208**
12 ❑ Oct 1998 Cover: 2.95 **NM** value: **Cover or less**
Circ: Diamd. preorders: **3,102**
Bk 1❑ Dec 1997 Cover: 2.95 **NM** value: **Cover or less**
• Trade Paperback. • collects #1-6

SUPERIOR SEVEN — Imagine This Productions

1 ❑ Cover: 2.95 **NM** value: **Cover or less**
📖 The Starcore Saga, Part 1 **A:** Deon Nuchols **W:** Chris Henry; Rodney Fyke
2 ❑ Cover: 2.95 **NM** value: **Cover or less**
📖 The Starcore Saga, Part 2 **A:** Deon Nuchols **W:** Chris Henry; Rodney Fyke
3 ❑ Cover: 2.95 **NM** value: **Cover or less**
📖 The Starcore Saga, Part 3 **A:** Deon Nuchols **W:** Chris Henry; Rodney Fyke
4 ❑ Cover: 1.95 **NM** value: **2.00**
📖 Somebodies Gonna Get a Punchn' Da Head **A:** Deon Nuchols **W:** Chris Henry; Rodney Fyke

CGC-graded: Multiply prices above by **33 for 9.9 M • 16 for 9.8 NM/M • 7 for 9.6 NM+ • 5 for 9.4 NM • 2.5 for 9.2 NM- • 1.5 for 9.0 VF/NM**

5 ❑ Cover: 1.95 NM value: 2.00
A: Deon Nuchols W: Chris Henry; Rodney Fyke

SUPER MAGIC — Street & Smith

1 ❑ May 1941 Cover: 0.10 NM value: 1000.00
• CGC: 2 graded, best 4.5
• Continues as Super Magician

SUPER MAGICIAN — Street & Smith

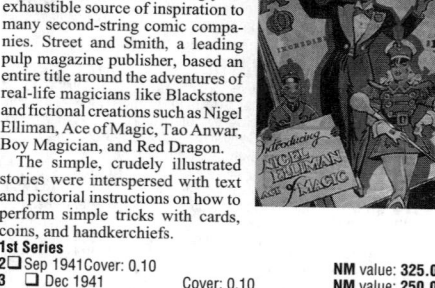

In the early days of comics, the notion that stage magicians could use tricks like hypnotism and sleight of hand as "super powers" to fight crime was a seemingly inexhaustible source of inspiration to many second-string comic companies. Street and Smith, a leading pulp magazine publisher, based an entire title around the adventures of real-life magicians like Blackstone and fictional creations such as Nigel Elliman, Ace of Magic, Tao Anwar, Boy Magician, and Red Dragon.

The simple, crudely illustrated stories were interspersed with text and pictorial instructions on how to perform simple tricks with cards, coins, and handkerchiefs.

1st Series

2 ❑ Sep 1941 Cover: 0.10 NM value: 325.00
3 ❑ Dec 1941 Cover: 0.10 NM value: 250.00
4 ❑ Mar 1942 Cover: 0.10 NM value: 225.00
5 ❑ May 1942 Cover: 0.10 NM value: 225.00
6 ❑ Jul 1942 Cover: 0.10 NM value: 200.00
7 ❑ Sep 1942 Cover: 0.10 NM value: 200.00
8 ❑ Nov 1942 Cover: 0.10 NM value: 225.00
9 ❑ Jan 1943 Cover: 0.10 NM value: 200.00
• CGC: 1 graded, best 6.0
10 ❑ Feb 1943 Cover: 0.10 NM value: 200.00
11 ❑ Mar 1943 Cover: 0.10 NM value: 175.00
12 ❑ Apr 1943 Cover: 0.10 NM value: 175.00
• CGC: 1 graded, best 8.0

2nd Series

1 ❑ May 1943 Cover: 0.10 NM value: 225.00
2 ❑ Jun 1943 Cover: 0.10 NM value: 110.00
• CGC: 1 graded, best 9.0
3 ❑ Jul 1943 Cover: 0.10 NM value: 110.00
• CGC: 1 graded, best 9.2
4 ❑ Aug 1943 Cover: 0.10 NM value: 110.00
5 ❑ Sep 1943 Cover: 0.10 NM value: 110.00
6 ❑ Oct 1943 Cover: 0.10 NM value: 110.00
• CGC: 1 graded, best 9.0
7 ❑ Nov 1943 Cover: 0.10 NM value: 110.00
• CGC: 1 graded, best 7.0
8 ❑ Dec 1943 Cover: 0.10 NM value: 110.00
9 ❑ Jan 1944 Cover: 0.10 NM value: 110.00
10 ❑ Feb 1944 Cover: 0.10 NM value: 110.00
• CGC: 1 graded, best 7.5
11 ❑ Mar 1944 Cover: 0.10 NM value: 110.00
• CGC: 1 graded, best 9.2
12 ❑ Apr 1944 Cover: 0.10 NM value: 110.00

3rd Series

1 ❑ May 1944 Cover: 0.10 NM value: 100.00
2 ❑ Jun 1944 Cover: 0.10 NM value: 100.00
• CGC: 1 graded, best 7.5
3 ❑ Jul 1944 Cover: 0.10 NM value: 100.00
4 ❑ Aug 1944 Cover: 0.10 NM value: 100.00
5 ❑ Sep 1944 Cover: 0.10 NM value: 100.00
6 ❑ Oct 1944 Cover: 0.10 NM value: 100.00
7 ❑ Nov 1944 Cover: 0.10 NM value: 100.00
• CGC: 1 graded, best 9.2
8 ❑ Dec 1944 Cover: 0.10 NM value: 100.00
9 ❑ Jan 1945 Cover: 0.10 NM value: 100.00
10 ❑ Feb 1945 Cover: 0.10 NM value: 100.00
11 ❑ Mar 1945 Cover: 0.10 NM value: 100.00
12 ❑ Apr 1945 Cover: 0.10 NM value: 100.00

4th Series

1 ❑ May 1945 Cover: 0.10 NM value: 90.00
2 ❑ Jun 1945 Cover: 0.10 NM value: 90.00
3 ❑ Jul 1945 Cover: 0.10 NM value: 90.00
4 ❑ Aug 1945 Cover: 0.10 NM value: 90.00
5 ❑ Sep 1945 Cover: 0.10 NM value: 90.00
6 ❑ Oct 1945 Cover: 0.10 NM value: 90.00
7 ❑ Nov 1945 Cover: 0.10 NM value: 90.00
8 ❑ Dec 1945 Cover: 0.10 NM value: 90.00
9 ❑ Jan 1946 Cover: 0.10 NM value: 90.00
• CGC: 2 graded, best 9.0
10 ❑ Feb 1946 Cover: 0.10 NM value: 90.00
11 ❑ Mar 1946 Cover: 0.10 NM value: 90.00
12 ❑ Apr 1946 Cover: 0.10 NM value: 90.00

5th Series

1 ❑ May 1946 Cover: 0.10 NM value: 75.00
2 ❑ Jun 1946 Cover: 0.10 NM value: 75.00
3 ❑ Jul 1946 Cover: 0.10 NM value: 75.00
4 ❑ Aug 1946 Cover: 0.10 NM value: 75.00
• CGC: 1 graded, best 8.5
5 ❑ Sep 1946 Cover: 0.10 NM value: 75.00
6 ❑ Oct 1946 Cover: 0.10 NM value: 75.00
7 ❑ Dec 1946 Cover: 0.10 NM value: 75.00
8 ❑ Feb 1947 Cover: 0.10 NM value: 75.00

SUPERMAN (1ST SERIES) — DC

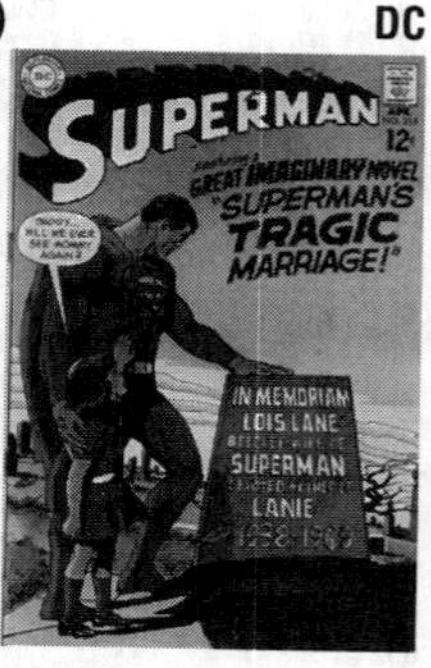

When Jor-El, the top scientist of the planet Krypton, realized that his world was doomed, he sent his baby son, Kal-El, off into space in a rocket ship. The ship traveled far from the red sun of the exploding planet Krypton, eventually landing on Earth. There, the baby was found by a kindly old couple, the Kents, who dubbed him Clark and raised him as their own son. Our world's yellow sun gave Clark incredible powers, eventually turning him into the legendary hero Superman.

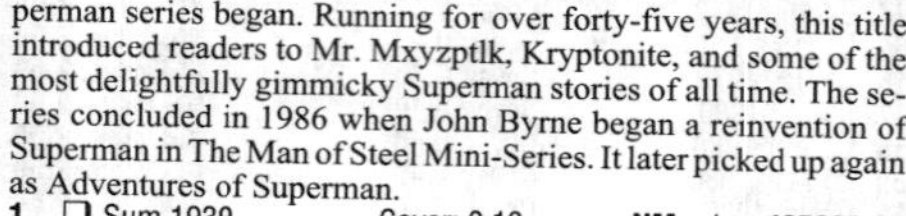

Siegel and Shuster's creation was already the headliner in Action Comics when this solo Superman series began. Running for over forty-five years, this title introduced readers to Mr. Mxyzptlk, Kryptonite, and some of the most delightfully gimmicky Superman stories of all time. The series concluded in 1986 when John Byrne began a reinvention of Superman in The Man of Steel Mini-Series. It later picked up again as Adventures of Superman.

1 ❑ Sum 1939 Cover: 0.10 NM value: 135000.00
• CGC: 6 graded, best 8.0
📖 Superman-Champion of the Oppressed!; Scientific Explanation of Superman's Amazing Strength!; Cave-In at the Blakely Mine!; Superman-Football Hero!; Superman • Reprints and expands early Superman stories from Action Comics #1-4 A: Joe Shuster W: Jerry Siegel ★ Origin of Superman.
2 ❑ Fal 1939 Cover: 0.10 NM value: 10500.00
• CGC: 12 graded, best 8.5
3 ❑ Win 1939 Cover: 0.10 NM value: 7000.00
• CGC: 12 graded, best 8.0
• Reprints Superman stories from Action Comics #5, 6
4 ❑ Spr 1940 Cover: 0.10 NM value: 5000.00
• CGC: 16 graded, best 8.0
★ 2nd Appearance of Lex Luthor (with hair). ★ 2nd Appearance of Lex Luthor (with hair).
5 ❑ Sum 1940 Cover: 0.10 NM value: 3525.00
• CGC: 11 graded, best 8.5
6 ❑ Sep 1940 Cover: 0.10 NM value: 2575.00
• CGC: 9 graded, best 7.5
7 ❑ Nov 1940 Cover: 0.10 NM value: 2575.00
• CGC: 9 graded, best 9.0
★ 1st Appearance of Perry White.
8 ❑ Jan 1941 Cover: 0.10 NM value: 2175.00
• CGC: 13 graded, best 9.4
9 ❑ Mar 1941 Cover: 0.10 NM value: 2175.00
• CGC: 11 graded, best 8.5
10 ❑ May 1941 Cover: 0.10 NM value: 2175.00
• CGC: 14 graded, best 9.4
★ 1st Appearance of Lex Luthor (bald).
11 ❑ Jul 1941 Cover: 0.10 NM value: 1650.00
• CGC: 17 graded, best 9.0
12 ❑ Sep 1941 Cover: 0.10 NM value: 1650.00
• CGC: 8 graded, best 7.0
13 ❑ Nov 1941 Cover: 0.10 NM value: 1650.00
• CGC: 9 graded, best 8.5
Anti-Axis cover. ★ Appearance of Lex Luthor.
14 ❑ Jan 1942 Cover: 0.10 NM value: 2550.00
• CGC: 9 graded, best 9.0
Classic flag cover.
15 ❑ Mar 1942 Cover: 0.10 NM value: 1575.00
• CGC: 4 graded, best 7.0
16 ❑ May 1942 Cover: 0.10 NM value: 1350.00
• CGC: 8 graded, best 9.0
17 ❑ Jul 1942 Cover: 0.10 NM value: 1350.00
• CGC: 5 graded, best 7.5
Hitler/Mussolini cover.
18 ❑ Sep 1942 Cover: 0.10 NM value: 1359.00
• CGC: 7 graded, best 7.5
19 ❑ Nov 1942 Cover: 0.10 NM value: 1350.00
• CGC: 9 graded, best 6.5
20 ❑ Jan 1943 Cover: 0.10 NM value: 1350.00
• CGC: 9 graded, best 9.0
21 ❑ Mar 1943 Cover: 0.10 NM value: 1100.00
• CGC: 3 graded, best 8.0
22 ❑ May 1943 Cover: 0.10 NM value: 950.00
• CGC: 9 graded, best 8.0
23 ❑ Jul 1943 Cover: 0.10 NM value: 950.00
• CGC: 11 graded, best 9.2
Anti-Axis cover.
24 ❑ Sep 1943 Cover: 0.10 NM value: 1100.00
• CGC: 11 graded, best 8.5
Flag cover.
25 ❑ Nov 1943 Cover: 0.10 NM value: 925.00
• CGC: 6 graded, best 9.2
26 ❑ Jan 1944 Cover: 0.10 NM value: 825.00
• CGC: 8 graded, best 8.0
Anti-Axis cover.
27 ❑ Mar 1944 Cover: 0.10 NM value: 825.00
• CGC: 7 graded, best 9.0
28 ❑ May 1944 Cover: 0.10 NM value: 825.00
• CGC: 6 graded, best 9.0
29 ❑ Jul 1944 Cover: 0.10 NM value: 825.00
• CGC: 12 graded, best 9.4
30 ❑ Sep 1944 Cover: 0.10 NM value: 1450.00
• CGC: 11 graded, best 9.4
• Spelling originally "Mxyztplk"★ Origin of Mr. Mxyzptlk. ★ 1st Appearance of Mr. Mxyzptlk.
31 ❑ Nov 1944 Cover: 0.10 NM value: 725.00
• CGC: 14 graded, best 8.5
32 ❑ Jan 1945 Cover: 0.10 NM value: 725.00
• CGC: 8 graded, best 8.0
33 ❑ Mar 1945 Cover: 0.10 NM value: 725.00
• CGC: 10 graded, best 8.0
★ Appearance of Mr. Mxyzptlk.
34 ❑ May 1945 Cover: 0.10 NM value: 725.00
• CGC: 11 graded, best 9.0
35 ❑ Jul 1945 Cover: 0.10 NM value: 725.00
• CGC: 5 graded, best 9.0
36 ❑ Sep 1945 Cover: 0.10 NM value: 725.00
• CGC: 8 graded, best 9.0
37 ❑ Nov 1945 Cover: 0.10 NM value: 725.00
• CGC: 8 graded, best 6.5
38 ❑ Jan 1946 Cover: 0.10 NM value: 750.00
• CGC: 16 graded, best 9.4
Atom bomb cover.
39 ❑ Mar 1946 Cover: 0.10 NM value: 725.00
• CGC: 10 graded, best 9.0
40 ❑ May 1946 Cover: 0.10 NM value: 725.00
• CGC: 8 graded, best 9.4
41 ❑ Jul 1946 Cover: 0.10 NM value: 575.00
• CGC: 4 graded, best 8.5
42 ❑ Sep 1946 Cover: 0.10 NM value: 575.00
• CGC: 9 graded, best 9.0
43 ❑ Nov 1946 Cover: 0.10 NM value: 575.00
• CGC: 6 graded, best 8.0
44 ❑ Jan 1947 Cover: 0.10 NM value: 575.00
• CGC: 5 graded, best 7.0
45 ❑ Mar 1947 Cover: 0.10 NM value: 575.00
• CGC: 7 graded, best 9.0
46 ❑ May 1947 Cover: 0.10 NM value: 575.00
• CGC: 7 graded, best 8.5
47 ❑ Jul 1947 Cover: 0.10 NM value: 575.00
• CGC: 5 graded, best 8.5
48 ❑ Sep 1947 Cover: 0.10 NM value: 575.00
• CGC: 8 graded, best 9.4
49 ❑ Nov 1947 Cover: 0.10 NM value: 575.00
• CGC: 6 graded, best 7.5
50 ❑ Jan 1948 Cover: 0.10 NM value: 575.00
• CGC: 2 graded, best 3.5
51 ❑ Mar 1948 Cover: 0.10 NM value: 475.00
• CGC: 1 graded, best 1.8
52 ❑ May 1948 Cover: 0.10 NM value: 475.00
• CGC: 5 graded, best 9.2
53 ❑ Jul 1948 Cover: 0.10 NM value: 2000.00
• CGC: 25 graded, best 9.4
• 10th anniversary issue. ★ Origin of Superman.
54 ❑ Sep 1948 Cover: 0.10 NM value: 475.00
• CGC: 5 graded, best 7.0
55 ❑ Nov 1948 Cover: 0.10 NM value: 475.00
• CGC: 2 graded, best 6.0
56 ❑ Jan 1949 Cover: 0.10 NM value: 475.00
• CGC: 2 graded, best 7.5
57 ❑ Mar 1949 Cover: 0.10 NM value: 475.00
• CGC: 3 graded, best 9.0
58 ❑ May 1949 Cover: 0.10 NM value: 475.00
• CGC: 8 graded, best 7.0
59 ❑ Jul 1949 Cover: 0.10 NM value: 475.00
• CGC: 9 graded, best 8.0
60 ❑ Sep 1949 Cover: 0.10 NM value: 475.00
• CGC: 3 graded, best 5.0
61 ❑ Nov 1949 Cover: 0.10 NM value: 925.00
• CGC: 3 graded, best 7.0
★ Origin of Green Kryptonite, Superman. ★ 1st Appearance of Kryptonite, Green Kryptonite.
62 ❑ Jan 1950 Cover: 0.10 NM value: 450.00
• CGC: 7 graded, best 9.2
★ Appearance of Orson Welles.
63 ❑ Mar 1950 Cover: 0.10 NM value: 450.00
• CGC: 2 graded, best 7.0
• Has 1949 Statement, filed 10/1/1949; no circ figures published
64 ❑ May 1950 Cover: 0.10 NM value: 450.00
• CGC: 1 graded, best 6.0
65 ❑ Jul 1950 Cover: 0.10 NM value: 450.00
• CGC: 3 graded, best 8.5
★ 1st Appearance of Mala.
66 ❑ Sep 1950 Cover: 0.10 NM value: 450.00
• CGC: 5 graded, best 8.0
67 ❑ Nov 1950 Cover: 0.10 NM value: 450.00
• CGC: 4 graded, best 8.0
68 ❑ Jan 1951 Cover: 0.10 NM value: 450.00
• CGC: 2 graded, best 3.0
69 ❑ Mar 1951 Cover: 0.10 NM value: 450.00
• CGC: 4 graded, best 5.5
★ 2nd Appearance of Superbaby. ★ 2nd Appearance of Superbaby.
70 ❑ May 1951 Cover: 0.10 NM value: 450.00
• CGC: 3 graded, best 8.0
71 ❑ Jul 1951 Cover: 0.10 NM value: 425.00
• CGC: 2 graded, best 6.5
72 ❑ Sep 1951 Cover: 0.10 NM value: 425.00
• CGC: 7 graded, best 9.2
73 ❑ Nov 1951 Cover: 0.10 NM value: 425.00
• CGC: 4 graded, best 7.5
74 ❑ Jan 1952 Cover: 0.10 NM value: 425.00
• CGC: 13 graded, best 9.0
75 ❑ Mar 1952 Cover: 0.10 NM value: 425.00
• CGC: 7 graded, best 9.4
76 ❑ May 1952 Cover: 0.10 NM value: 1300.00
• CGC: 17 graded, best 9.0
📖 The Mightiest Team in the World • Superman and Batman learn each other's secret identities★ Appearance of Batman.
77 ❑ Jul 1952 Cover: 0.10 NM value: 375.00
• CGC: 3 graded, best 9.2
78 ❑ Sep 1952 Cover: 0.10 NM value: 375.00
• CGC: 3 graded, best 6.5
79 ❑ Nov 1952 Cover: 0.10 NM value: 375.00
• CGC: 3 graded, best 7.5
80 ❑ Jan 1953 Cover: 0.10 NM value: 375.00
• CGC: 4 graded, best 5.0
81 ❑ Mar 1953 Cover: 0.10 NM value: 350.00
• CGC: 1 graded, best 7.5

82 ❑ May 1953 Cover: 0.10 **NM** value: **350.00**
• **CGC:** 2 graded, best 4.5
83 ❑ Jul 1953 Cover: 0.10 **NM** value: **350.00**
• **CGC:** 2 graded, best 5.0
84 ❑ Sep 1953 Cover: 0.10 **NM** value: **350.00**
• **CGC:** 5 graded, best 8.0
85 ❑ Nov 1953 Cover: 0.10 **NM** value: **350.00**
• **CGC:** 4 graded, best 8.0
86 ❑ Jan 1954 Cover: 0.10 **NM** value: **350.00**
• **CGC:** 2 graded, best 2.5
87 ❑ Feb 1954 Cover: 0.10 **NM** value: **350.00**
• **CGC:** 3 graded, best 7.5
88 ❑ Mar 1954 Cover: 0.10 **NM** value: **350.00**
• **CGC:** 2 graded, best 8.0
• Prankster/Toy Man super-villain team-up
89 ❑ May 1954 Cover: 0.10 **NM** value: **350.00**
• **CGC:** 4 graded, best 7.0
90 ❑ Jul 1954 Cover: 0.10 **NM** value: **350.00**
• **CGC:** 2 graded, best 4.5
91 ❑ Aug 1954 Cover: 0.10 **NM** value: **335.00**
• **CGC:** 4 graded, best 9.0
92 ❑ Sep 1954 Cover: 0.10 **NM** value: **335.00**
• **CGC:** 4 graded, best 7.0
93 ❑ Nov 1954 Cover: 0.10 **NM** value: **335.00**
• **CGC:** 6 graded, best 8.5
94 ❑ Jan 1955 Cover: 0.10 **NM** value: **335.00**
• **CGC:** 5 graded, best 7.0
95 ❑ Feb 1955 Cover: 0.10 **NM** value: **335.00**
• **CGC:** 5 graded, best 6.0
96 ❑ Mar 1955 Cover: 0.10 **NM** value: **300.00**
• **CGC:** 2 graded, best 7.0
97 ❑ May 1955 Cover: 0.10 **NM** value: **300.00**
• **CGC:** 3 graded, best 9.2
98 ❑ Jul 1955 Cover: 0.10 **NM** value: **300.00**
• **CGC:** 5 graded, best 7.5
99 ❑ Aug 1955 Cover: 0.10 **NM** value: **300.00**
• **CGC:** 7 graded, best 7.5
100 ❑ Sep 1955 Cover: 0.10 **NM** value: **1600.00**
• **CGC:** 21 graded, best 8.0
• 100th anniversary issue.
101 ❑ Nov 1955 Cover: 0.10 **NM** value: **260.00**
• **CGC:** 3 graded, best 7.0
102 ❑ Jan 1956 Cover: 0.10 **NM** value: **260.00**
• **CGC:** 4 graded, best 8.0
103 ❑ Feb 1956 Cover: 0.10 **NM** value: **260.00**
• **CGC:** 3 graded, best 7.5
104 ❑ Mar 1956 Cover: 0.10 **NM** value: **260.00**
• **CGC:** 5 graded, best 9.0
105 ❑ May 1956 Cover: 0.10 **NM** value: **260.00**
• **CGC:** 4 graded, best 9.0
106 ❑ Jul 1956 Cover: 0.10 **NM** value: **260.00**
• **CGC:** 2 graded, best 6.0
107 ❑ Aug 1956 Cover: 0.10 **NM** value: **260.00**
• **CGC:** 2 graded, best 8.5
108 ❑ Sep 1956 Cover: 0.10 **NM** value: **260.00**
• **CGC:** 3 graded, best 5.5
109 ❑ Nov 1956 Cover: 0.10 **NM** value: **260.00**
• **CGC:** 4 graded, best 9.0
110 ❑ Jan 1957 Cover: 0.10 **NM** value: **260.00**
• **CGC:** 1 graded, best 8.0
111 ❑ Feb 1957 Cover: 0.10 **NM** value: **225.00**
• **CGC:** 3 graded, best 6.5
112 ❑ Mar 1957 Cover: 0.10 **NM** value: **225.00**
• **CGC:** 1 graded, best 8.5
113 ❑ May 1957 Cover: 0.10 **NM** value: **225.00**
• **CGC:** 2 graded, best 8.5
114 ❑ Jul 1957 Cover: 0.10 **NM** value: **225.00**
• **CGC:** 1 graded, best 4.5
115 ❑ Aug 1957 Cover: 0.10 **NM** value: **225.00**
• **CGC:** 2 graded, best 7.0
116 ❑ Sep 1957 Cover: 0.10 **NM** value: **225.00**
• **CGC:** 1 graded, best 7.0
117 ❑ Nov 1957 Cover: 0.10 **NM** value: **225.00**
• **CGC:** 1 graded, best 8.0
118 ❑ 1958 Cover: 0.10 **NM** value: **225.00**
119 ❑ Feb 1958 Cover: 0.10 **NM** value: **225.00**
• **CGC:** 1 graded, best 8.0
120 ❑ Mar 1958 Cover: 0.10 **NM** value: **225.00**
• **CGC:** 1 graded, best 7.5
121 ❑ May 1958 Cover: 0.10 **NM** value: **185.00**
• **CGC:** 1 graded, best 9.0
122 ❑ Jul 1958 Cover: 0.10 **NM** value: **185.00**
• **CGC:** 1 graded, best 8.0
123 ❑ Aug 1958 Cover: 0.10 **NM** value: **200.00**
📖 The Three Magic Wishes: The Girl of Steel; The Lost Super-Powers; Superman's Return to Krypton • Supergirl prototype
124 ❑ Sep 1958 Cover: 0.10 **NM** value: **185.00**
• **CGC:** 1 graded, best 5.0
125 ❑ Nov 1958 Cover: 0.10 **NM** value: **185.00**
• **CGC:** 1 graded, best 6.5
126 ❑ Jan 1959 Cover: 0.10 **NM** value: **185.00**
• **CGC:** 1 graded, best 4.0
127 ❑ Feb 1959 Cover: 0.10 **NM** value: **185.00**
• **CGC:** 1 graded, best 4.0
★ Origin of Titano. ★ 1st Appearance of Titano.
128 ❑ Apr 1959 Cover: 0.10 **NM** value: **185.00**
• **CGC:** 1 graded, best 6.5
129 ❑ May 1959 Cover: 0.10 **NM** value: **185.00**
• **CGC:** 3 graded, best 8.0
★ Origin of Lori Lemaris. ★ 1st Appearance of Lori Lemaris.
130 ❑ Jul 1959 Cover: 0.10 **NM** value: **185.00**
• **CGC:** 4 graded, best 8.5
131 ❑ Aug 1959 Cover: 0.10 **NM** value: **145.00**
• **CGC:** 2 graded, best 9.2
132 ❑ Oct 1959 Cover: 0.10 **NM** value: **145.00**
• **CGC:** 1 graded, best 4.0
133 ❑ Nov 1959 Cover: 0.10 **NM** value: **145.00**
• **CGC:** 2 graded, best 8.5
134 ❑ Jan 1960 Cover: 0.10 **NM** value: **145.00**
Circ: Statement: **810,000**
135 ❑ Feb 1960 Cover: 0.10 **NM** value: **145.00**
Circ: Statement: **810,000**
136 ❑ Apr 1960 Cover: 0.10 **NM** value: **145.00**
Circ: Statement: **810,000**
137 ❑ May 1960 Cover: 0.10 **NM** value: **145.00**
Circ: Statement: **810,000** • **CGC:** 1 graded, best 4.0
138 ❑ Jul 1960 Cover: 0.10 **NM** value: **145.00**
Circ: Statement: **810,000** • **CGC:** 2 graded, best 7.0
139 ❑ Aug 1960 Cover: 0.10 **NM** value: **145.00**
Circ: Statement: **810,000** • **CGC:** 2 graded, best 5.0
140 ❑ Oct 1960 Cover: 0.10 **NM** value: **170.00**
Circ: Statement: **810,000** • **CGC:** 3 graded, best 8.5
★ 1st Appearance of Bizarro Jr., Blue Kryptonite, Bizarro Supergirl.
★ Appearance of Lex Luthor.
141 ❑ Nov 1960 Cover: 0.10 **NM** value: **110.00**
Circ: Statement: **810,000** • **CGC:** 4 graded, best 9.4
142 ❑ Jan 1961 Cover: 0.10 **NM** value: **110.00**
Circ: Statement: **820,000** • **CGC:** 3 graded, best 9.4
143 ❑ Feb 1961 Cover: 0.10 **NM** value: **110.00**
Circ: Statement: **820,000** • **CGC:** 2 graded, best 5.5
144 ❑ Apr 1961 Cover: 0.10 **NM** value: **110.00**
Circ: Statement: **820,000** • **CGC:** 4 graded, best 6.5
★ Appearance of Lex Luthor.
145 ❑ May 1961 Cover: 0.10 **NM** value: **110.00**
Circ: Statement: **820,000** • **CGC:** 3 graded, best 9.4
146 ❑ Jul 1961 Cover: 0.10 **NM** value: **150.00**
Circ: Statement: **820,000** • **CGC:** 7 graded, best 9.2
• Superman's life ★ Origin of Superman.
147 ❑ Aug 1961 Cover: 0.10 **NM** value: **135.00**
Circ: Statement: **820,000** • **CGC:** 8 graded, best 9.4
📖 The Legion of Super-Villains **A:** Curt Swan ★ 1st Appearance of Legion of Super-Heroes (adult), Legion of Super-Villains.
148 ❑ Oct 1961 Cover: 0.10 **NM** value: **110.00**
Circ: Statement: **820,000** • **CGC:** 4 graded, best 8.5
A: Curt Swan ★ Versus Mxyzptlk.
149 ❑ Nov 1961 Cover: 0.10 **NM** value: **125.00**
Circ: Statement: **820,000** • **CGC:** 3 graded, best 8.5
A: Curt Swan ★ Appearance of Legion of Super-Heroes.
150 ❑ Jan 1962 Cover: 0.12 **NM** value: **65.00**
Circ: Statement: **740,000** • **CGC:** 2 graded, best 9.4
📖 The One Minute of Doom
151 ❑ Feb 1962 Cover: 0.12 **NM** value: **65.00**
Circ: Statement: **740,000** • **CGC:** 2 graded, best 9.2
• Has 1961 Statement; avg total paid circ 820,000
152 ❑ Apr 1962 Cover: 0.12 **NM** value: **65.00**
Circ: Statement: **740,000** • **CGC:** 1 graded, best 9.2
★ Appearance of Legion of Super-Heroes.
153 ❑ May 1962 Cover: 0.12 **NM** value: **65.00**
Circ: Statement: **740,000** • **CGC:** 5 graded, best 9.0
154 ❑ Jul 1962 Cover: 0.12 **NM** value: **65.00**
Circ: Statement: **740,000** • **CGC:** 2 graded, best 9.0
A: Curt Swan
155 ❑ Aug 1962 Cover: 0.12 **NM** value: **65.00**
Circ: Statement: **740,000** • **CGC:** 3 graded, best 9.0
156 ❑ Oct 1962 Cover: 0.12 **NM** value: **65.00**
Circ: Statement: **740,000** • **CGC:** 1 graded, best 9.2
157 ❑ Nov 1962 Cover: 0.12 **NM** value: **65.00**
Circ: Statement: **740,000** • **CGC:** 1 graded, best 9.0
★ 1st Appearance of Gold Kryptonite.
158 ❑ Jan 1963 Cover: 0.12 **NM** value: **65.00**
• **CGC:** 1 graded, best 4.0
A: Curt Swan ★ 1st Appearance of Nightwing, Flamebird.
159 ❑ Feb 1963 Cover: 0.12 **NM** value: **65.00**
• Has 1962 Statement, filed 10/1/62; avg total paid circ 740,000
160 ❑ Apr 1963 Cover: 0.12 **NM** value: **65.00**
• **CGC:** 2 graded, best 8.0
161 ❑ May 1963 Cover: 0.12 **NM** value: **65.00**
• **CGC:** 4 graded, best 8.5
★ Death of Ma & Pa Kent.
162 ❑ Jul 1963 Cover: 0.12 **NM** value: **50.00**
• **CGC:** 1 graded, best 6.0
A: Curt Swan
163 ❑ Aug 1963 Cover: 0.12 **NM** value: **50.00**
• **CGC:** 1 graded, best 4.0
164 ❑ Oct 1963 Cover: 0.12 **NM** value: **50.00**
• **CGC:** 2 graded, best 9.0
A: Curt Swan
165 ❑ Nov 1963 Cover: 0.12 **NM** value: **50.00**
• **CGC:** 1 graded, best 3.5
166 ❑ Jan 1964 Cover: 0.12 **NM** value: **50.00**
• **CGC:** 1 graded, best 6.5
167 ❑ Feb 1964 Cover: 0.12 **NM** value: **50.00**
• **CGC:** 4 graded, best 9.2
• Has 1963 Statement, filed 10/1/63; no circ figures published **A:** Curt Swan ★ Origin of Brainiac (new origin), Braniac 5 (new origin).
168 ❑ Apr 1964 Cover: 0.12 **NM** value: **50.00**
• **CGC:** 2 graded, best 9.0
169 ❑ May 1964 Cover: 0.12 **NM** value: **50.00**
• **CGC:** 3 graded, best 9.0
170 ❑ Jul 1964 Cover: 0.12 **NM** value: **50.00**
• **CGC:** 1 graded, best 7.5
★ Appearance of John F. Kennedy.
171 ❑ Aug 1964 Cover: 0.12 **NM** value: **50.00**
• **CGC:** 5 graded, best 9.0
A: Curt Swan
172 ❑ Oct 1964 Cover: 0.12 **NM** value: **50.00**
• **CGC:** 3 graded, best 8.0
173 ❑ Nov 1964 Cover: 0.12 **NM** value: **50.00**
• **CGC:** 2 graded, best 7.5
174 ❑ Jan 1965 Cover: 0.12 **NM** value: **50.00**
Circ: Statement: **823,829** • **CGC:** 2 graded, best 9.2
175 ❑ Feb 1965 Cover: 0.12 **NM** value: **50.00**
Circ: Statement: **823,829**
• Imaginary Story
176 ❑ Apr 1965 Cover: 0.12 **NM** value: **50.00**
Circ: Statement: **823,829**
• Has 1964 Statement, filed 10/1/64; no circ figures published **A:** Curt Swan
177 ❑ May 1965 Cover: 0.12 **NM** value: **50.00**
Circ: Statement: **823,829**
📖 The Menace Called "It"
178 ❑ Jul 1965 Cover: 0.12 **NM** value: **50.00**
Circ: Statement: **823,829** • **CGC:** 1 graded, best 9.2
179 ❑ Aug 1965 Cover: 0.12 **NM** value: **50.00**
Circ: Statement: **823,829** • **CGC:** 2 graded, best 9.2
📖 Tales of Kryptonite, Part 4
180 ❑ Oct 1965 Cover: 0.12 **NM** value: **50.00**
Circ: Statement: **823,829** • **CGC:** 4 graded, best 9.4
181 ❑ Nov 1965 Cover: 0.12 **NM** value: **35.00**
Circ: Statement: **823,829** • **CGC:** 5 graded, best 9.6
A: Curt Swan
182 ❑ Jan 1966 Cover: 0.12 **NM** value: **35.00**
Circ: Statement: **719,976** • **CGC:** 2 graded, best 9.2
★ Versus Toyman.
183 ❑ Jan 1966 Cover: 0.25 **NM** value: **45.00**
Circ: Statement: **719,976** • **CGC:** 4 graded, best 9.6
• Giant-size. • Golden Age reprints
184 ❑ Feb 1966 Cover: 0.12 **NM** value: **35.00**
Circ: Statement: **719,976** • **CGC:** 6 graded, best 9.4
185 ❑ Apr 1966 Cover: 0.12 **NM** value: **35.00**
Circ: Statement: **719,976** • **CGC:** 1 graded, best 9.0
186 ❑ May 1966 Cover: 0.12 **NM** value: **35.00**
Circ: Statement: **719,976**
A: Curt Swan
187 ❑ Jun 1966 Cover: 0.25 **NM** value: **45.00**
Circ: Statement: **719,976** • **CGC:** 8 graded, best 9.6
• Giant-size. • Fortress stories
188 ❑ Jul 1966 Cover: 0.12 **NM** value: **35.00**
Circ: Statement: **719,976** • **CGC:** 2 graded, best 7.5
• Has 1965 Statement, filed 10/1/65 (second one printed, this one with figures); avg print run 1,179,000; avg sales 805,000; avg subs 18,829; avg total paid 823,829; samples 142; max existent 823,971; 30% of run returned **A:** Curt Swan
189 ❑ Aug 1966 Cover: 0.12 **NM** value: **35.00**
Circ: Statement: **719,976** • **CGC:** 2 graded, best 9.0
190 ❑ Oct 1966 Cover: 0.12 **NM** value: **35.00**
Circ: Statement: **719,976** • **CGC:** 2 graded, best 9.0
191 ❑ Nov 1966 Cover: 0.12 **NM** value: **30.00**
Circ: Statement: **719,976** • **CGC:** 3 graded, best 9.4
★ Versus D.E.M.O.N..
192 ❑ Jan 1967 Cover: 0.12 **NM** value: **30.00**
Circ: Statement: **649,300** • **CGC:** 7 graded, best 9.4
• Imaginary Story **A:** Curt Swan
193 ❑ Feb 1967 Cover: 0.25 **NM** value: **40.00**
Circ: Statement: **649,300** • **CGC:** 8 graded, best 9.8
• Giant-size. • reprints Action #223 and Superman #149
194 ❑ Feb 1967 Cover: 0.12 **NM** value: **30.00**
Circ: Statement: **649,300** • **CGC:** 4 graded, best 9.2
• Has 1966 Statement, filed 10/1/66; avg print run 1,091,000; avg sales 707,000; avg subs 12,976; avg total paid 719,976; samples 330; max existent 720,306; 34% of run returned **A:** Curt Swan
195 ❑ Apr 1967 Cover: 0.12 **NM** value: **30.00**
Circ: Statement: **649,300** • **CGC:** 3 graded, best 9.4
A: Curt Swan
196 ❑ May 1967 Cover: 0.12 **NM** value: **30.00**
Circ: Statement: **649,300** • **CGC:** 3 graded, best 9.4
197 ❑ Jul 1967 Cover: 0.25 **NM** value: **40.00**
Circ: Statement: **649,300** • **CGC:** 5 graded, best 9.6
• Giant-size. • All Clark Kent issue
198 ❑ Jul 1967 Cover: 0.12 **NM** value: **30.00**
Circ: Statement: **649,300** • **CGC:** 2 graded, best 9.2
A: Curt Swan
199 ❑ Aug 1967 Cover: 0.12 **NM** value: **200.00**
Circ: Statement: **649,300** • **CGC:** 22 graded, best 9.4
• 1st Flash/Superman race; 1st Superman/Flash race
200 ❑ Oct 1967 Cover: 0.12 **NM** value: **30.00**
Circ: Statement: **649,300** • **CGC:** 10 graded, best 9.8
201 ❑ Nov 1967 Cover: 0.12 **NM** value: **20.00**
Circ: Statement: **649,300** • **CGC:** 1 graded, best 9.2
A: Curt Swan
202 ❑ Dec 1967 Cover: 0.25 **NM** value: **30.00**
Circ: Statement: **649,300** • **CGC:** 7 graded, best 9.8
• Giant-size. • Bizarro issue
203 ❑ Jan 1968 Cover: 0.12 **NM** value: **20.00**
Circ: Statement: **636,400** • **CGC:** 4 graded, best 9.2
C: Curt Swan
204 ❑ Feb 1968 Cover: 0.12 **NM** value: **20.00**
Circ: Statement: **636,400** • **CGC:** 1 graded, best 7.5
C: Neal Adams ★ 1st Appearance of Q-energy.
205 ❑ Apr 1968 Cover: 0.12 **NM** value: **20.00**
Circ: Statement: **636,400** • **CGC:** 4 graded, best 9.2
• Has 1967 Statement, filed 10/1/67; avg print run 1,140,000; avg sales 640,000; avg subs 9,300; avg total paid 649,300; samples 340; max existent 649,640; 43% of run returned
206 ❑ May 1968 Cover: 0.12 **NM** value: **20.00**
Circ: Statement: **636,400** • **CGC:** 3 graded, best 9.4
207 ❑ Jul 1968 Cover: 0.25 **NM** value: **30.00**
Circ: Statement: **636,400** • **CGC:** 3 graded, best 9.4
• Giant-size.
208 ❑ Jul 1968 Cover: 0.12 **NM** value: **20.00**
Circ: Statement: **636,400** • **CGC:** 5 graded, best 9.4
209 ❑ Aug 1968 Cover: 0.12 **NM** value: **20.00**
Circ: Statement: **636,400** • **CGC:** 3 graded, best 9.8
210 ❑ Oct 1968 Cover: 0.12 **NM** value: **20.00**
Circ: Statement: **636,400** • **CGC:** 2 graded, best 9.2
211 ❑ Nov 1968 Cover: 0.12 **NM** value: **20.00**
Circ: Statement: **636,400** • **CGC:** 5 graded, best 9.4
212 ❑ Jan 1969 Cover: 0.25 **NM** value: **30.00**
Circ: Statement: **511,984** • **CGC:** 4 graded, best 9.6
• Giant-size. • Superbabies
213 ❑ Jan 1969 Cover: 0.12 **NM** value: **20.00**
Circ: Statement: **511,984** • **CGC:** 4 graded, best 9.6
📖 The Most Dangerous Door in the World!; The Orphans of Space!
★ Appearance of Lex Luthor.

CGC-graded: Multiply prices above by **33 for 9.9 M** • **16 for 9.8 NM/M** • **7 for 9.6 NM+** • **5 for 9.4 NM** • **2.5 for 9.2 NM-** • **1.5 for 9.0 VF/NM**

214 ☐ Feb 1969 Cover: 0.12 **NM** value: **20.00**
Circ: Statement: **511,984 • CGC:** 1 graded, best 9.2

215 ☐ Apr 1969 Cover: 0.12 **NM** value: **20.00**
Circ: Statement: **511,984 • CGC:** 5 graded, best 9.4
📖 Lois Lane ... Dead ... Yet Alive; Superman's First Exploit • Imaginary Story; Superman as widower; Has 1968 Statement, filed 10/1/68; avg print run 1,076,000; avg sales 634,000; avg subs 2,400; avg total paid 636,400; samples 386;max existent 636,786; 41% of run returned

216 ☐ May 1969 Cover: 0.12 **NM** value: **20.00**
Circ: Statement: **511,984 • CGC:** 6 graded, best 9.6
• in Vietnam

217 ☐ Jul 1969 Cover: 0.25 **NM** value: **30.00**
Circ: Statement: **511,984 • CGC:** 2 graded, best 9.2
• Giant-size. **C:** Curt Swan

218 ☐ Jul 1969 Cover: 0.15 **NM** value: **20.00**
Circ: Statement: **511,984 • CGC:** 2 graded, best 9.4

219 ☐ Aug 1969 Cover: 0.15 **NM** value: **20.00**
Circ: Statement: **511,984 • CGC:** 2 graded, best 9.2

220 ☐ Oct 1969 Cover: 0.15 **NM** value: **20.00**
Circ: Statement: **511,984 • CGC:** 2 graded, best 9.4

221 ☐ Nov 1969 Cover: 0.15 **NM** value: **20.00**
Circ: Statement: **511,984 • CGC:** 2 graded, best 9.4

222 ☐ Jan 1970 Cover: 0.25 **NM** value: **30.00**
Circ: Statement: **446,678 • CGC:** 5 graded, best 9.4
• Giant-size.

223 ☐ Jan 1970 Cover: 0.15 **NM** value: **20.00**
Circ: Statement: **446,678 • CGC:** 3 graded, best 9.6

224 ☐ Feb 1970 Cover: 0.15 **NM** value: **20.00**
Circ: Statement: **446,678 • CGC:** 3 graded, best 9.6
• Imaginary Story

225 ☐ Apr 1970 Cover: 0.15 **NM** value: **20.00**
Circ: Statement: **446,678 • CGC:** 1 graded, best 9.2
• Has 1969 Statement, filed 10/1/69; avg print run 959,000; avg sales 511,000; avg subs 984; avg total paid 511,984; samples 346; max existent 512,330; 47% of run returned

226 ☐ May 1970 Cover: 0.15 **NM** value: **20.00**
Circ: Statement: **446,678 • CGC:** 2 graded, best 9.6

227 ☐ Jul 1970 Cover: 0.25 **NM** value: **30.00**
Circ: Statement: **446,678 • CGC:** 2 graded, best 9.6
• Giant-size.

228 ☐ Jul 1970 Cover: 0.15 **NM** value: **20.00**
Circ: Statement: **446,678**
A: Curt Swan; Dan Adkins

229 ☐ Aug 1970 Cover: 0.15 **NM** value: **20.00**
Circ: Statement: **446,678 • CGC:** 3 graded, best 9.2
📖 The Ex-Superman; Clark Kent, Assassin! **A:** Curt Swan; Dan Adkins; Wayne Boring

230 ☐ Oct 1970 Cover: 0.15 **NM** value: **20.00**
Circ: Statement: **446,678 • CGC:** 1 graded, best 9.4
• Imaginary Story **A:** Curt Swan; Dan Adkins

231 ☐ Nov 1970 Cover: 0.15 **NM** value: **20.00**
Circ: Statement: **446,678 • CGC:** 2 graded, best 9.2
• Imaginary Story **A:** Neal Adams; Curt Swan

232 ☐ Jan 1971 Cover: 0.25 **NM** value: **30.00**
Circ: Statement: **421,948 • CGC:** 3 graded, best 9.6
• Giant-size.

233 ☐ Jan 1971 Cover: 0.15 **NM** value: **20.00**
Circ: Statement: **421,948 • CGC:** 18 graded, best 9.4
📖 Kryptonite No More

234 ☐ Feb 1971 Cover: 0.15 **NM** value: **20.00**
Circ: Statement: **421,948 • CGC:** 5 graded, best 9.6
★ Appearance of Sand Superman.

235 ☐ Mar 1971 Cover: 0.15 **NM** value: **20.00**
Circ: Statement: **421,948 • CGC:** 4 graded, best 9.2
• Has 1970 Statement, filed 10/1/70; avg print run 859,811; avg sales 446,019; avg subs 659; avg total paid 446,678; samples 127; max existent 446,805; 48% of run returned

236 ☐ Apr 1971 Cover: 0.15 **NM** value: **20.00**
Circ: Statement: **421,948 • CGC:** 2 graded, best 9.6
• World of Krypton back-up

237 ☐ May 1971 Cover: 0.15 **NM** value: **20.00**
Circ: Statement: **421,948 • CGC:** 2 graded, best 9.4

238 ☐ Jun 1971 Cover: 0.15 **NM** value: **20.00**
Circ: Statement: **421,948 • CGC:** 7 graded, best 9.6
★ Appearance of Sand Superman.

239 ☐ Jul 1971 Cover: 0.25 **NM** value: **30.00**
Circ: Statement: **421,948 • CGC:** 2 graded, best 9.4
• Giant-size. • reprints Action #267 and #268, Superman #127 and #164 **A:** Murphy Anderson; Gray Morrow; Curt Swan

240 ☐ Jul 1971 Cover: 0.15 **NM** value: **8.00**
Circ: Statement: **421,948 • CGC:** 2 graded, best 9.4
★ Appearance of I-Ching.

241 ☐ Aug 1971 Cover: 0.25 **NM** value: **7.00**
Circ: Statement: **421,948 • CGC:** 3 graded, best 9.4
• giant ★ Appearance of I-Ching, Sand Superman.

242 ☐ Sep 1971 Cover: 0.25 **NM** value: **7.00**
Circ: Statement: **421,948**
★ Appearance of final.

243 ☐ Oct 1971 Cover: 0.25 **NM** value: **7.00**
Circ: Statement: **421,948 • CGC:** 2 graded, best 9.2

244 ☐ Nov 1971 Cover: 0.25 **NM** value: **7.00**
Circ: Statement: **421,948 • CGC:** 2 graded, best 9.0

245 ☐ Jan 1972 Cover: 0.50 **NM** value: **12.00**
Circ: Statement: **317,990 • CGC:** 5 graded, best 9.0
back cover pin-up. • a.k.a. DC 100-Page Super-Spectacular #DC-7; reprints from All-Star Western #117, The Atom #3, Detective #66, Kid Eternity #3, Mystery in Space #89, and Superman #87, and #167 **A:** Curt Swan; Marshall Rogers

246 ☐ Dec 1971 Cover: 0.25 **NM** value: **6.00**
Circ: Statement: **317,990 • CGC:** 1 graded, best 9.2
📖 Danger – Monster at Work

247 ☐ Jan 1972 Cover: 0.25 **NM** value: **6.00**
Circ: Statement: **317,990**
📖 Must There Be a Superman? • 1st Private Life of Clark Kent; Superman of Tomorrow back-up ★ Appearance of Guardians of the Universe.

248 ☐ Feb 1972 Cover: 0.25 **NM** value: **6.00**
Circ: Statement: **317,990**

249 ☐ Mar 1972 Cover: 0.25 **NM** value: **10.00**
Circ: Statement: **317,990 • CGC:** 5 graded, best 9.6
• Has 1971 Statement, filed 10/1/71; avg print run 793,000; avg sales 421,790; avg subs 158; avg total paid 421,948; office use 617; max existent 422,565; 47% of run returned **A:** Neal Adams; Curt Swan ★ Origin of Terra-Man. ★ 1st Appearance of Terra-Man.

250 ☐ Apr 1972 Cover: 0.25 **NM** value: **6.00**
Circ: Statement: **317,990 • CGC:** 3 graded, best 9.4

251 ☐ May 1972 Cover: 0.25 **NM** value: **6.00**
Circ: Statement: **317,990 • CGC:** 1 graded, best 9.2
A: Murphy Anderson; Curt Swan

252 ☐ Jun 1972 Cover: 0.50 **NM** value: **12.00**
Circ: Statement: **317,990 • CGC:** 11 graded, best 9.6
wraparound cover. • a.k.a. DC 100-Page Super Spectacular #DC-13
A: Murphy Anderson; Curt Swan

253 ☐ Jun 1972 Cover: 0.25 **NM** value: **6.00**
Circ: Statement: **317,990 • CGC:** 4 graded, best 9.4
A: Murphy Anderson; Curt Swan

254 ☐ Jul 1972 Cover: 0.20 **NM** value: **12.00**
Circ: Statement: **317,990 • CGC:** 1 graded, best 9.6
A: Neal Adams; Curt Swan

255 ☐ Aug 1972 Cover: 0.20 **NM** value: **3.00**
Circ: Statement: **317,990 • CGC:** 1 graded, best 9.4

256 ☐ Sep 1972 Cover: 0.20 **NM** value: **3.00**
Circ: Statement: **317,990**

257 ☐ Oct 1972 Cover: 0.20 **NM** value: **3.00**
Circ: Statement: **317,990 • CGC:** 4 graded, best 9.4

258 ☐ Nov 1972 Cover: 0.20 **NM** value: **3.00**
Circ: Statement: **317,990**
📖 The Fury of the Energy Eater

259 ☐ Dec 1972 Cover: 0.20 **NM** value: **3.00**
Circ: Statement: **317,990 • CGC:** 3 graded, best 9.6

260 ☐ Jan 1973 Cover: 0.20 **NM** value: **3.00**
Circ: Statement: **309,318**

261 ☐ Feb 1973 Cover: 0.20 **NM** value: **3.00**
Circ: Statement: **309,318 • CGC:** 3 graded, best 9.6

262 ☐ Mar 1973 Cover: 0.20 **NM** value: **3.00**
Circ: Statement: **309,318**
📖 The Skyscraper That Screamed for It's Life • Has 1972 Statement, filed 10/1/72; avg print run 704,000; avg sales 316,617; avg subs 1,373; avg total paid 317,990; samples 518; office use 689; max existent 319,197; 55% of run returned

263 ☐ Apr 1973 Cover: 0.20 **NM** value: **3.00**
Circ: Statement: **309,318 • CGC:** 1 graded, best 9.6

264 ☐ Jun 1973 Cover: 0.20 **NM** value: **4.00**
Circ: Statement: **309,318 • CGC:** 1 graded, best 9.6
★ 1st Appearance of Steve Lombard.

265 ☐ Jul 1973 Cover: 0.20 **NM** value: **3.00**
Circ: Statement: **309,318 • CGC:** 2 graded, best 9.6

266 ☐ Aug 1973 Cover: 0.20 **NM** value: **3.00**
Circ: Statement: **309,318**

267 ☐ Sep 1973 Cover: 0.20 **NM** value: **3.00**
Circ: Statement: **309,318 • CGC:** 1 graded, best 9.4

268 ☐ Oct 1973 Cover: 0.20 **NM** value: **3.00**
Circ: Statement: **309,318 • CGC:** 1 graded, best 9.6

269 ☐ Nov 1973 Cover: 0.20 **NM** value: **3.00**
Circ: Statement: **309,318**

270 ☐ Dec 1973 Cover: 0.20 **NM** value: **3.00**
Circ: Statement: **309,318 • CGC:** 1 graded, best 9.0

271 ☐ Jan 1974 Cover: 0.20 **NM** value: **3.00**
Circ: Statement: **285,634**

272 ☐ Feb 1974 Cover: 0.50 **NM** value: **7.00**
Circ: Statement: **285,634 • CGC:** 2 graded, best 9.4
A: Bob Oksner; Curt Swan

273 ☐ Mar 1974 Cover: 0.20 **NM** value: **3.00**
Circ: Statement: **285,634 • CGC:** 8 graded, best 9.6
A: Bob Oksner; Curt Swan

274 ☐ Apr 1974 Cover: 0.20 **NM** value: **3.00**
Circ: Statement: **285,634 • CGC:** 2 graded, best 9.6
• Has 1973 Statement, filed 10/1/73; avg print run 670,667; avg sales 307,425; avg subs 1,893; avg total paid 309,318; samples 100; office use 4,061; max existent 313,479; 53% of run returned **A:** Bob Oksner; Curt Swan

275 ☐ May 1974 Cover: 0.20 **NM** value: **3.00**
Circ: Statement: **285,634 • CGC:** 1 graded, best 9.2
A: Bob Oksner; Curt Swan

276 ☐ Jun 1974 Cover: 0.20 **NM** value: **3.00**
Circ: Statement: **285,634 • CGC:** 1 graded, best 7.0
A: Bob Oksner; Curt Swan ★ 1st Appearance of Captain Thunder.

277 ☐ Jul 1974 Cover: 0.20 **NM** value: **3.00**
Circ: Statement: **285,634**
A: Bob Oksner; Curt Swan

278 ☐ Aug 1974 Cover: 0.60 **NM** value: **6.00**
Circ: Statement: **285,634 • CGC:** 4 graded, best 9.2
A: Bob Oksner; Curt Swan

279 ☐ Sep 1974 Cover: 0.20 **NM** value: **3.00**
Circ: Statement: **285,634**
★ Appearance of Batgirl.

280 ☐ Oct 1974 Cover: 0.20 **NM** value: **3.00**
Circ: Statement: **285,634 • CGC:** 10 graded, best 9.6

281 ☐ Nov 1974 Cover: 0.20 **NM** value: **3.00**
Circ: Statement: **285,634**

282 ☐ Dec 1974 Cover: 0.20 **NM** value: **3.00**
Circ: Statement: **285,634 • CGC:** 2 graded, best 9.4

283 ☐ Jan 1975 Cover: 0.20 **NM** value: **3.00**
Circ: Statement: **296,000**

284 ☐ Feb 1975 Cover: 0.60 **NM** value: **6.00**
Circ: Statement: **296,000 • CGC:** 5 graded, best 9.4
A: Bob Oksner; Curt Swan

285 ☐ Mar 1975 Cover: 0.25 **NM** value: **2.50**
Circ: Statement: **296,000**
★ Appearance of Roy Raymond.

286 ☐ Apr 1975 Cover: 0.25 **NM** value: **2.50**
Circ: Statement: **296,000**
★ Versus Luthor. ★ Versus Parasite.

287 ☐ May 1975 Cover: 0.25 **NM** value: **2.50**
Circ: Statement: **296,000 • CGC:** 1 graded, best 9.2
• Return of Krypto; Has 1974 Statement; avg total paid circ 285,634

288 ☐ Jun 1975 Cover: 0.25 **NM** value: **2.50**
Circ: Statement: **296,000 • CGC:** 1 graded, best 8.5

289 ☐ Jul 1975 Cover: 0.25 **NM** value: **2.50**
Circ: Statement: **296,000**

290 ☐ Aug 1975 Cover: 0.25 **NM** value: **2.50**
Circ: Statement: **296,000 • CGC:** 1 graded, best 9.2

291 ☐ Sep 1975 Cover: 0.25 **NM** value: **2.50**
Circ: Statement: **296,000 • CGC:** 2 graded, best 9.4

292 ☐ Oct 1975 Cover: 0.25 **NM** value: **4.00**
Circ: Statement: **296,000 • CGC:** 2 graded, best 9.4
A: Bob Oksner; Curt Swan ★ Origin of Lex Luthor.

293 ☐ Nov 1975 Cover: 0.25 **NM** value: **2.50**
Circ: Statement: **296,000**

294 ☐ Dec 1975 Cover: 0.25 **NM** value: **2.50**
Circ: Statement: **296,000**

295 ☐ Jan 1976 Cover: 0.25 **NM** value: **2.50**
Circ: Statement: **273,000 • CGC:** 1 graded, best 9.4

296 ☐ Feb 1976 Cover: 0.25 **NM** value: **2.50**
Circ: Statement: **273,000**
• Superman loses powers when not in costume

297 ☐ Mar 1976 Cover: 0.25 **NM** value: **2.50**
Circ: Statement: **273,000**

298 ☐ Apr 1976 Cover: 0.30 **NM** value: **2.50**
Circ: Statement: **273,000 • CGC:** 3 graded, best 9.2

299 ☐ May 1976 Cover: 0.30 **NM** value: **2.50**
Circ: Statement: **273,000**
• Has 1975 Statement, filed 10/1/75; avg print run 644,000; avg sales 293,000; avg subs 3,000; avg total paid 296,000; samples 1,000; office use 5,000; max existent 302,000; 53% of run returned

300 ☐ Jun 1976 Cover: 0.30 **NM** value: **6.00**
Circ: Statement: **273,000 • CGC:** 8 graded, best 9.6
• 300th anniversary issue. **A:** Bob Oksner; Curt Swan ★ Origin of Superman of 2001.

301 ☐ Jul 1976 Cover: 0.30 **NM** value: **2.50**
Circ: Statement: **273,000 • CGC:** 1 graded, best 9.4

302 ☐ Aug 1976 Cover: 0.30 **NM** value: **2.50**
Circ: Statement: **273,000**

303 ☐ Sep 1976 Cover: 0.30 **NM** value: **2.50**
Circ: Statement: **273,000 • CGC:** 1 graded, best 9.2

304 ☐ Oct 1976 Cover: 0.30 **NM** value: **2.50**
Circ: Statement: **273,000**

305 ☐ Nov 1976 Cover: 0.30 **NM** value: **2.50**
Circ: Statement: **273,000 • CGC:** 1 graded, best 9.4

306 ☐ Dec 1976 Cover: 0.30 **NM** value: **2.50**
Circ: Statement: **273,000 • CGC:** 1 graded, best 9.0
★ Versus Bizarro.

307 ☐ Jan 1977 Cover: 0.30 **NM** value: **2.50**
Circ: Statement: **235,430**
A: Frank Springer; José Luis Garcia-Lopez **C:** Neal Adams

308 ☐ Feb 1977 Cover: 0.30 **NM** value: **2.50**
Circ: Statement: **235,430**
A: Frank Springer; José Luis Garcia-Lopez **C:** Neal Adams

309 ☐ Mar 1977 Cover: 0.30 **NM** value: **2.50**
Circ: Statement: **235,430**

310 ☐ Apr 1977 Cover: 0.30 **NM** value: **2.50**
Circ: Statement: **235,430 • CGC:** 1 graded, best 9.2

311 ☐ May 1977 Cover: 0.30 **NM** value: **2.50**
Circ: Statement: **235,430**

312 ☐ Jun 1977 Cover: 0.35 **NM** value: **2.50**
Circ: Statement: **235,430**

313 ☐ Jul 1977 Cover: 0.35 **NM** value: **2.50**
Circ: Statement: **235,430**
A: Curt Swan; Dan Adkins **C:** Neal Adams

314 ☐ Aug 1977 Cover: 0.35 **NM** value: **2.50**
Circ: Statement: **235,430**

315 ☐ Sep 1977 Cover: 0.35 **NM** value: **2.50**
Circ: Statement: **235,430**

316 ☐ Oct 1977 Cover: 0.35 **NM** value: **2.50**
Circ: Statement: **235,430 • CGC:** 1 graded, best 9.2

317 ☐ Nov 1977 Cover: 0.35 **NM** value: **2.50**
Circ: Statement: **235,430**
• Return of Lana Lang **C:** Neal Adams

318 ☐ Dec 1977 Cover: 0.35 **NM** value: **2.50**
Circ: Statement: **235,430**
A: Curt Swan

319 ☐ Jan 1978 Cover: 0.35 **NM** value: **2.50**
Circ: Statement: **223,222**
A: Curt Swan

320 ☐ Feb 1978 Cover: 0.35 **NM** value: **2.50**
Circ: Statement: **223,222 • CGC:** 1 graded, best 9.6
A: Curt Swan

321 ☐ Mar 1978 Cover: 0.35 **NM** value: **2.50**
Circ: Statement: **223,222**

322 ☐ Apr 1978 Cover: 0.35 **NM** value: **2.50**
Circ: Statement: **223,222**
★ Versus Parasite.

323 ☐ May 1978 Cover: 0.35 **NM** value: **2.50**
Circ: Statement: **223,222**
• Has 1977 Statement; avg total paid circ 235,430 ★ 1st Appearance of Atomic Skull. ★ Versus Atomic Skull.

324 ☐ Jun 1978 Cover: 0.35 **NM** value: **2.50**
Circ: Statement: **223,222**
★ Versus Titano.

325 ☐ Jul 1978 Cover: 0.35 **NM** value: **2.50**
Circ: Statement: **223,222**

326 ☐ Aug 1978 Cover: 0.35 **NM** value: **2.50**
Circ: Statement: **223,222**

327 ☐ Sep 1978 Cover: 0.50 **NM** value: **2.50**
Circ: Statement: **223,222**

328 ☐ Oct 1978 Cover: 0.50 **NM** value: **2.50**
Circ: Statement: **223,222**

329 ☐ Nov 1978 Cover: 0.50 **NM** value: **2.50**
Circ: Statement: **223,222**

330 ☐ Dec 1978 Cover: 0.40 **NM** value: **2.50**
Circ: Statement: **223,222**

331 ☐ Jan 1979 Cover: 0.40 **NM** value: **2.50**

332 ☐ Feb 1979 Cover: 0.40 **NM** value: **2.50**

333 ☐ Mar 1979 Cover: 0.40 **NM** value: **2.50**

Other grades: Multiply prices above by **1.5 for Mint • 2/3 for Very Fine • 1/3 for Fine • 1/5 for Very Good • 1/8 for Good**

334 ❑ Apr 1979 Cover: 0.40 **NM** value: **2.50**
335 ❑ May 1979 Cover: 0.40 **NM** value: **2.50**
★ Versus Mxyzptlk.
336 ❑ Jun 1979 Cover: 0.40 **NM** value: **2.50**
337 ❑ Jul 1979 Cover: 0.40 **NM** value: **2.50**
338 ❑ Aug 1979 Cover: 0.40 **NM** value: **2.50**
📖 Let My People Grow • Kandor enlarged
339 ❑ Sep 1979 Cover: 0.40 **NM** value: **2.50**
340 ❑ Oct 1979 Cover: 0.40 **NM** value: **2.50**
341 ❑ Nov 1979 Cover: 0.40 **NM** value: **2.50**
★ Appearance of J. Wilbur Wolfingham.
342 ❑ Dec 1979 Cover: 0.40 **NM** value: **2.50**
343 ❑ Jan 1980 Cover: 0.40 **NM** value: **2.50**
344 ❑ Feb 1980 Cover: 0.40 **NM** value: **2.50**
📖 The Electronic Ghost of Metropolis
345 ❑ Mar 1980 Cover: 0.40 **NM** value: **2.50**
346 ❑ Apr 1980 Cover: 0.40 **NM** value: **2.50**
347 ❑ May 1980 Cover: 0.40 **NM** value: **2.50**
348 ❑ Jun 1980 Cover: 0.40 **NM** value: **2.50**
349 ❑ Jul 1980 Cover: 0.40 **NM** value: **2.50**
• **CGC:** 1 graded, best 9.4
350 ❑ Aug 1980 Cover: 0.40 **NM** value: **2.50**
351 ❑ Sep 1980 Cover: 0.40 **NM** value: **2.00**
📖 The Island That Invaded the Earth
352 ❑ Oct 1980 Cover: 0.50 **NM** value: **2.00**
353 ❑ Nov 1980 Cover: 0.50 **NM** value: **2.00**
354 ❑ Dec 1980 Cover: 0.50 **NM** value: **2.00**
355 ❑ Jan 1981 Cover: 0.50 **NM** value: **2.00**
Circ: Statement: **148,637**
A: Jim Starlin
356 ❑ Feb 1981 Cover: 0.50 **NM** value: **2.00**
Circ: Statement: **148,637**
357 ❑ Mar 1981 Cover: 0.50 **NM** value: **2.00**
Circ: Statement: **148,637**
358 ❑ Apr 1981 Cover: 0.50 **NM** value: **2.00**
Circ: Statement: **148,637**
359 ❑ May 1981 Cover: 0.50 **NM** value: **2.00**
Circ: Statement: **148,637**
360 ❑ Jun 1981 Cover: 0.50 **NM** value: **2.00**
Circ: Statement: **148,637**
361 ❑ Jul 1981 Cover: 0.50 **NM** value: **2.00**
Circ: Statement: **148,637**
362 ❑ Aug 1981 Cover: 0.50 **NM** value: **2.00**
Circ: Statement: **148,637**
• Lana and Lois contract deadly virus that killed Kents
363 ❑ Sep 1981 Cover: 0.50 **NM** value: **2.00**
Circ: Statement: **148,637**
★ Appearance of Lex Luthor.
364 ❑ Oct 1981 Cover: 0.50 **NM** value: **2.00**
Circ: Statement: **148,637**
365 ❑ Nov 1981 Cover: 0.50 **NM** value: **2.00**
Circ: Statement: **148,637**
• Superboy back-up ★ Appearance of Supergirl.
366 ❑ Dec 1981 Cover: 0.50 **NM** value: **2.00**
Circ: Statement: **148,637**
367 ❑ Jan 1982 Cover: 0.60 **NM** value: **2.00**
368 ❑ Feb 1982 Cover: 0.60 **NM** value: **2.00**
369 ❑ Mar 1982 Cover: 0.60 **NM** value: **2.00**
★ Versus Parasite.
370 ❑ Apr 1982 Cover: 0.60 **NM** value: **2.00**
371 ❑ May 1982 Cover: 0.60 **NM** value: **2.00**
372 ❑ Jun 1982 Cover: 0.60 **NM** value: **2.00**
373 ❑ Jul 1982 Cover: 0.60 **NM** value: **2.00**
374 ❑ Aug 1982 Cover: 0.60 **NM** value: **2.00**
375 ❑ Sep 1982 Cover: 0.60 **NM** value: **2.00**
376 ❑ Oct 1982 Cover: 0.60 **NM** value: **2.00**
377 ❑ Nov 1982 Cover: 0.60 **NM** value: **2.00**
378 ❑ Dec 1982 Cover: 0.60 **NM** value: **2.00**
379 ❑ Jan 1983 Cover: 0.60 **NM** value: **2.00**
Circ: Statement: **126,279** • **CGC:** 1 graded, best 9.0
★ Appearance of Bizarro.
380 ❑ Feb 1983 Cover: 0.60 **NM** value: **2.00**
Circ: Statement: **126,279**
381 ❑ Mar 1983 Cover: 0.60 **NM** value: **2.00**
Circ: Statement: **126,279**
382 ❑ Apr 1983 Cover: 0.60 **NM** value: **2.00**
Circ: Statement: **126,279**
383 ❑ May 1983 Cover: 0.60 **NM** value: **2.00**
Circ: Statement: **126,279**
384 ❑ Jun 1983 Cover: 0.60 **NM** value: **2.00**
Circ: Statement: **126,279**
385 ❑ Jul 1983 Cover: 0.60 **NM** value: **2.00**
Circ: Statement: **126,279**
386 ❑ Aug 1983 Cover: 0.60 **NM** value: **2.00**
Circ: Statement: **126,279**
387 ❑ Sep 1983 Cover: 0.60 **NM** value: **2.00**
Circ: Statement: **126,279**
388 ❑ Oct 1983 Cover: 0.60 **NM** value: **2.00**
Circ: Statement: **126,279**
📖 The Kid Who Played Superman
389 ❑ Nov 1983 Cover: 0.60 **NM** value: **2.00**
Circ: Statement: **126,279**
390 ❑ Dec 1983 Cover: 0.75 **NM** value: **2.00**
Circ: Statement: **126,279**
391 ❑ Jan 1984 Cover: 0.75 **NM** value: **2.00**
Circ: Statement: **111,073**
392 ❑ Feb 1984 Cover: 0.75 **NM** value: **2.00**
Circ: Statement: **111,073**
393 ❑ Mar 1984 Cover: 0.75 **NM** value: **2.00**
Circ: Statement: **111,073**
394 ❑ Apr 1984 Cover: 0.75 **NM** value: **2.00**
Circ: Statement: **111,073**
395 ❑ May 1984 Cover: 0.75 **NM** value: **2.00**
Circ: Statement: **111,073**
396 ❑ Jun 1984 Cover: 0.75 **NM** value: **2.00**
Circ: Statement: **111,073**
397 ❑ Jul 1984 Cover: 0.75 **NM** value: **2.00**
Circ: Statement: **111,073**
398 ❑ Aug 1984 Cover: 0.75 **NM** value: **2.00**
Circ: Statement: **111,073**
399 ❑ Sep 1984 Cover: 0.75 **NM** value: **2.00**
Circ: Statement: **111,073**
400 ❑ Oct 1984 Cover: 1.50 **NM** value: **5.00**
Circ: Statement: **111,073** • **CGC:** 2 graded, best 9.4
• Giant-size. **A:** Jayson Disbrow; Al Williamson; Steve Ditko; Jerry Ordway; Will Eisner; Mike Grell; Jack Kirby; Frank Miller; Walt Simonson; Frank Miller(back cover)
401 ❑ Nov 1984 Cover: 0.75 **NM** value: **2.00**
Circ: Statement: **111,073**
402 ❑ Dec 1984 Cover: 0.75 **NM** value: **2.00**
Circ: Statement: **111,073**
403 ❑ Jan 1985 Cover: 0.75 **NM** value: **2.00**
Circ: Statement: **98,767**
404 ❑ Feb 1985 Cover: 0.75 **NM** value: **2.00**
Circ: Statement: **98,767**
405 ❑ Mar 1985 Cover: 0.75 **NM** value: **2.00**
Circ: Statement: **98,767**
406 ❑ Apr 1985 Cover: 0.75 **NM** value: **2.00**
Circ: Statement: **98,767**
407 ❑ May 1985 Cover: 0.75 **NM** value: **2.00**
Circ: Statement: **98,767** CapCity orders: **4,600**
• powers passed along
408 ❑ Jun 1985 Cover: 0.75 **NM** value: **2.00**
Circ: Statement: **98,767** CapCity orders: **4,750**
• nuclear nightmare
409 ❑ Jul 1985 Cover: 0.75 **NM** value: **2.00**
Circ: Statement: **98,767** CapCity orders: **4,600**
410 ❑ Aug 1985 Cover: 0.75 **NM** value: **2.00**
Circ: Statement: **98,767** CapCity orders: **4,650**
411 ❑ Sep 1985 Cover: 0.75 **NM** value: **2.00**
Circ: Statement: **98,767** CapCity orders: **4,750**
• Julius Schwartz' birthday
412 ❑ Oct 1985 Cover: 0.75 **NM** value: **2.00**
Circ: Statement: **98,767** CapCity orders: **7,550**
413 ❑ Nov 1985 Cover: 0.75 **NM** value: **2.00**
Circ: Statement: **98,767** CapCity orders: **9,000**
414 ❑ Dec 1985 Cover: 0.75 **NM** value: **2.00**
Circ: Statement: **98,767** CapCity orders: **5,800**
📖 Crisis on Infinite Earths • Crisis
415 ❑ Jan 1986 Cover: 0.75 **NM** value: **2.00**
Circ: Statement: **98,443** CapCity orders: **7,700**
📖 Crisis on Infinite Earths • Crisis
416 ❑ Feb 1986 Cover: 0.75 **NM** value: **2.00**
Circ: Statement: **98,443** CapCity orders: **5,250**
• Superman learns Luthor's connection to Einstein
417 ❑ Mar 1986 Cover: 0.75 **NM** value: **2.00**
Circ: Statement: **98,443** CapCity orders: **5,550**
📖 What if Kal-El's rocket landed on Mars?
418 ❑ Apr 1986 Cover: 0.75 **NM** value: **2.00**
Circ: Statement: **98,443** CapCity orders: **5,900**
419 ❑ May 1986 Cover: 0.75 **NM** value: **2.00**
Circ: Statement: **98,443** CapCity orders: **5,650**
420 ❑ Jun 1986 Cover: 0.75 **NM** value: **2.00**
Circ: Statement: **98,443** CapCity orders: **5,500**
421 ❑ Jul 1986 Cover: 0.75 **NM** value: **2.00**
Circ: Statement: **98,443** CapCity orders: **5,750**
422 ❑ Aug 1986 Cover: 0.75 **NM** value: **2.00**
Circ: Statement: **98,443** CapCity orders: **5,750**
423 ❑ Sep 1986 Cover: 0.75 **NM** value: **8.00**
Circ: Statement: **98,443** CapCity orders: **16,400** • **CGC:** 19 graded, best 9.8
final issue. • series continues as Adventures of Superman **W:** Alan Moore
Anl 1 ❑ Oct 1960 Cover: 0.25 **NM** value: **550.00**
• **CGC:** 9 graded, best 9.0
• Reprints Action Comics #252 ★ Origin of Supergirl. ★ 1st Appearance of Supergirl, Supergirl reprinted.
Anl 2 ❑ ca. 1960 Cover: 0.25 **NM** value: **300.00**
• **CGC:** 11 graded, best 9.2
★ Origin of Titano.
Anl 3 ❑ Sum 1961 Cover: 0.25 **NM** value: **200.00**
• **CGC:** 3 graded, best 9.0
• Strange Lives of Superman
Anl 4 ❑ Win 1961 Cover: 0.25 **NM** value: **175.00**
• **CGC:** 4 graded, best 9.4
📖 The Origin & Powers of the Legion of Super-Heroes ★ Origin of Legion of Super-Heroes. ★ Appearance of Legion of Super-Heroes.
Anl 5 ❑ Sum 1962 Cover: 0.25 **NM** value: **100.00**
• **CGC:** 6 graded, best 9.4
📖 The Second Coming of Superman • Krypton
Anl 6 ❑ Win 1962 Cover: 0.25 **NM** value: **85.00**
• **CGC:** 5 graded, best 9.6
• Reprints Adventure Comics #247 ★ 1st Appearance of Legion of Super-Heroes.
Anl 7 ❑ Jun 1963 Cover: 0.25 **NM** value: **60.00**
• **CGC:** 7 graded, best 9.6
• 25th anniversary. ★ Origin of Superman-Batman team.
Anl 8 ❑ Sum 1963 Cover: 0.25 **NM** value: **45.00**
• **CGC:** 6 graded, best 9.8
• Untold Stories and Secret Origins
Anl 9 ❑ ca. 1983 Cover: 1.00 **NM** value: **5.00**
Anl 10 ❑ ca. 1984 Cover: 1.25 **NM** value: **5.00**
📖 Sword of Superman **A:** Curt Swan
Anl 11 ❑ ca. 1985 Cover: 1.25 **NM** value: **4.00**
Circ: CapCity orders: **8,700**
A: Dave Gibbons **W:** Alan Moore ★ Appearance of Wonder Woman, Robin, Batman. ★ Versus Mongul.
Anl 12 ❑ ca. 1986 Cover: 1.25 **NM** value: **3.00**
Circ: CapCity orders: **7,000**
★ Versus Luthor's Warsuit.
SE 1 ❑ ca. 1983 Cover: 1.00 **NM** value: **4.00**
A: Gil Kane
SE 2 ❑ Apr 1984 Cover: 1.25 **NM** value: **4.00**
SE 3 ❑ Apr 1985 Cover: 1.25 **NM** value: **4.00**
★ Versus Amazo.
Anl 1-2 ❑ Oct 1998 Cover: 4.95 **NM** value: **5.00**
Circ: Diamd. preorders: **27,434**
cardstock cover. • Replica Edition; reprints Giant Superman Annual #1

SUPERMAN (2ND SERIES) DC

One of the temptations for a character like Superman is to make him seem more and more powerful, with each new feat outdoing the last. Over the years since his first appearance in Action Comics #1, this has certainly been the case, going even so far at one point as to show Superman moving Earth back into its orbit. However, such a daunting character has a hard time finding an adequate challenge, and in time can get a little boring. DC comics realized this and decided to reinvent the Superman character, altering his origin somewhat and scaling back his powers to a more comprehensible level.

With this second volume, we see a far more interesting Superman than ever before. He has to try a little harder, and alter-ego Clark Kent is a more interesting character. Killed in an event that made national news, this new, modern Superman even settled down with Lois Lane, a feat she'd been trying to accomplish for more than 50 years.

0 ❑ Oct 1994 Cover: 1.50 **NM** value: **3.00**
Circ: CapCity orders: **62,850**
📖 Peer Pressure, Part 2 • ▲1994-38 **A:** Dan Jurgens **W:** Dan Jurgens
1 ❑ Jan 1987 Cover: 0.75 **NM** value: **5.00**
Circ: Statement: **161,859** CapCity orders: **91,650** • **CGC:** 38 graded, best 9.9
📖 Heart Of Stone **A:** John Byrne; Terry Austin **W:** John Byrne ★ 1st Appearance of Metallo (new).
2 ❑ Feb 1987 Cover: 0.75 **NM** value: **3.50**
Circ: Statement: **161,859** CapCity orders: **59,100** • **CGC:** 2 graded, best 9.8
A: John Byrne; Terry Austin
3 ❑ Mar 1987 Cover: 0.75 **NM** value: **3.00**
Circ: Statement: **161,859** CapCity orders: **50,650**
📖 Legends **A:** John Byrne; Terry Austin ★ 1st Appearance of Amazing Grace.
4 ❑ Apr 1987 Cover: 0.75 **NM** value: **2.50**
Circ: Statement: **161,859** CapCity orders: **40,050** • **CGC:** 1 graded, best 9.8
A: John Byrne ★ 1st Appearance of Bloodsport.
5 ❑ May 1987 Cover: 0.75 **NM** value: **2.50**
Circ: Statement: **161,859** CapCity orders: **34,750**
A: John Byrne
6 ❑ Jun 1987 Cover: 0.75 **NM** value: **2.00**
Circ: Statement: **161,859** CapCity orders: **25,950**
A: John Byrne
7 ❑ Jul 1987 Cover: 0.75 **NM** value: **2.00**
Circ: Statement: **161,859** CapCity orders: **30,350**
A: John Byrne ★ Origin of Rampage (DC). ★ 1st Appearance of Rampage (DC).
8 ❑ Aug 1987 Cover: 0.75 **NM** value: **2.00**
Circ: Statement: **161,859** CapCity orders: **31,900**
A: John Byrne ★ Appearance of Superboy, Legion of Super-Heroes.
9 ❑ Sep 1987 Cover: 0.75 **NM** value: **3.50**
Circ: Statement: **161,859** CapCity orders: **31,650**
A: John Byrne ★ Appearance of Joker. ★ Versus Joker. ★ Versus Luthor.
10 ❑ Oct 1987 Cover: 0.75 **NM** value: **2.00**
Circ: Statement: **161,859** CapCity orders: **31,050**
A: John Byrne
11 ❑ Nov 1987 Cover: 0.75 **NM** value: **2.00**
Circ: Statement: **161,859** CapCity orders: **32,550**
A: John Byrne ★ Origin of Mr. Mxyzptlk.
12 ❑ Dec 1987 Cover: 0.75 **NM** value: **2.00**
Circ: Statement: **161,859** CapCity orders: **30,750**
A: John Byrne ★ Origin of Lori Lemaris.
13 ❑ Jan 1988 Cover: 0.75 **NM** value: **2.00**
Circ: CapCity orders: **35,050**
• Millennium **A:** John Byrne
14 ❑ Feb 1988 Cover: 0.75 **NM** value: **2.00**
Circ: CapCity orders: **35,550**
• Millennium **A:** John Byrne ★ Appearance of Green Lantern.
15 ❑ Mar 1988 Cover: 0.75 **NM** value: **2.00**
Circ: CapCity orders: **31,100**
A: John Byrne
16 ❑ Apr 1988 Cover: 0.75 **NM** value: **2.00**
Circ: CapCity orders: **31,150**
A: John Byrne ★ Versus Prankster.
17 ❑ May 1988 Cover: 0.75 **NM** value: **2.00**
Circ: CapCity orders: **31,950**
A: John Byrne ★ Versus Silver Banshee.
18 ❑ Jun 1988 Cover: 0.75 **NM** value: **2.00**
Circ: CapCity orders: **28,250**
• return to Krypton **A:** John Byrne
19 ❑ Jul 1988 Cover: 0.75 **NM** value: **2.00**
Circ: CapCity orders: **27,750**
A: John Byrne ★ 1st Appearance of Dreadnaught, Psi-Phon.
20 ❑ Aug 1988 Cover: 0.75 **NM** value: **2.00**
Circ: CapCity orders: **27,300**
A: John Byrne ★ Appearance of Doom Patrol.
21 ❑ Sep 1988 Cover: 0.75 **NM** value: **2.00**
Circ: CapCity orders: **31,050**
• Supergirl **A:** John Byrne
22 ❑ Oct 1988 Cover: 0.75 **NM** value: **2.00**
Circ: CapCity orders: **28,100**
• Supergirl **A:** John Byrne
23 ❑ Nov 1988 Cover: 0.75 **NM** value: **2.00**
Circ: CapCity orders: **24,350**
★ Appearance of Batman.

CGC-graded: Multiply prices above by **33 for 9.9 M • 16 for 9.8 NM/M • 7 for 9.6 NM+ • 5 for 9.4 NM • 2.5 for 9.2 NM- • 1.5 for 9.0 VF/NM**

24 ❑ Dec 1988 Cover: 0.75 **NM** value: **2.00**
Circ: CapCity orders: **23,400**
25 ❑ Dec 1988 Cover: 0.75 **NM** value: **2.00**
Circ: CapCity orders: **22,550**
26 ❑ Jan 1989 Cover: 0.75 **NM** value: **2.00**
Circ: CapCity orders: **24,125**
• Invasion!
27 ❑ Jan 1989 Cover: 0.75 **NM** value: **2.00**
Circ: CapCity orders: **22,550**
• Invasion!
28 ❑ Feb 1989 Cover: 0.75 **NM** value: **2.00**
Circ: CapCity orders: **20,850**
• in space
29 ❑ Mar 1989 Cover: 0.75 **NM** value: **2.00**
Circ: CapCity orders: **20,800**
• in space
30 ❑ Apr 1989 Cover: 0.75 **NM** value: **2.00**
Circ: CapCity orders: **20,800**
• in space
31 ❑ May 1989 Cover: 0.75 **NM** value: **2.00**
Circ: CapCity orders: **21,700**
• Mxyzptlk vs. Luthor
32 ❑ Jun 1989 Cover: 0.75 **NM** value: **2.00**
Circ: CapCity orders: **23,350**
★ Versus Mongul.
33 ❑ Jul 1989 Cover: 0.75 **NM** value: **2.00**
Circ: CapCity orders: **23,200**
34 ❑ Aug 1989 Cover: 0.75 **NM** value: **2.00**
Circ: CapCity orders: **23,500**
★ Versus Skyhook.
35 ❑ Sep 1989 Cover: 0.75 **NM** value: **2.00**
Circ: CapCity orders: **23,750**
★ Appearance of Black Racer.
36 ❑ Oct 1989 Cover: 0.75 **NM** value: **2.00**
Circ: CapCity orders: **24,900**
★ Versus Prankster.
37 ❑ Nov 1989 Cover: 0.75 **NM** value: **2.00**
Circ: CapCity orders: **24,250**
★ Appearance of Newsboys.
38 ❑ Dec 1989 Cover: 0.75 **NM** value: **2.00**
Circ: CapCity orders: **23,100**
39 ❑ Jan 1990 Cover: 0.75 **NM** value: **2.00**
Circ: CapCity orders: **22,600**
40 ❑ Feb 1990 Cover: 0.75 **NM** value: **2.00**
Circ: CapCity orders: **21,950**
41 ❑ Mar 1990 Cover: 0.75 **NM** value: **2.00**
Circ: CapCity orders: **21,550**
📖 Day of the Krypton Man, Part 1 ★ Appearance of Lobo.
42 ❑ Apr 1990 Cover: 0.75 **NM** value: **2.00**
Circ: CapCity orders: **20,450**
📖 Day of the Krypton Man, Part 4
43 ❑ May 1990 Cover: 0.75 **NM** value: **2.00**
Circ: CapCity orders: **20,750**
★ Versus Kryptonite Man.
44 ❑ Jun 1990 Cover: 0.75 **NM** value: **2.00**
Circ: CapCity orders: **34,000**
📖 Dark Knight over Metropolis ★ Appearance of Batman.
45 ❑ Jul 1990 Cover: 0.75 **NM** value: **2.00**
Circ: CapCity orders: **22,650**
46 ❑ Aug 1990 Cover: 0.75 **NM** value: **2.00**
Circ: CapCity orders: **21,700**
★ Appearance of Jade, Obsidian. ★ Versus Terraman.
47 ❑ Sep 1990 Cover: 0.75 **NM** value: **2.00**
Circ: CapCity orders: **23,300**
★ Versus Blaze.
48 ❑ Oct 1990 Cover: 0.75 **NM** value: **2.00**
Circ: CapCity orders: **22,450**
★ Appearance of Sinbad.
49 ❑ Nov 1990 Cover: 0.75 **NM** value: **2.00**
Circ: CapCity orders: **21,700**
📖 Krisis of the Krimson Kryptonite, Part 1
50 ❑ Dec 1990 Cover: 1.50 **NM** value: **5.00**
Circ: CapCity orders: **22,250** • **CGC:** 3 graded, best 9.4
📖 Krisis of the Krimson Kryptonite, Part 4; The Human Factor • Clark Kent proposes to Lois Lane **A:** Brett Breeding; Jerry Ordway; John Byrne; Dan Jurgens; Curt Swan; Kerry Gammill; Dennis Janke **W:** Jerry Ordway
50-2❑ Dec 1990 Cover: 1.50 **NM** value: **1.75**
51 ❑ Jan 1991 Cover: 1.00 **NM** value: **2.00**
Circ: CapCity orders: **19,750**
📖 Mister Z! • ▲1991-1 **A:** Jerry Ordway **W:** Jerry Ordway ★ 1st Appearance of Mister Z. ★ Versus Mr. Z.
52 ❑ Feb 1991 Cover: 1.00 **NM** value: **2.00**
Circ: CapCity orders: **19,900**
★ Versus Terraman.
52-2❑ Feb 1991 Cover: 1.00 **NM** value: **1.50**
53 ❑ Mar 1991 Cover: 1.00 **NM** value: **2.50**
Circ: CapCity orders: **35,200**
📖 Truth, Justice, And The American Way • Lois reacts to Superman disclosing identity **A:** Dennis Janke **W:** Jerry Ordway
53-2❑ Mar 1991 Cover: 1.00 **NM** value: **1.50**
54 ❑ Apr 1991 Cover: 1.00 **NM** value: **1.75**
Circ: CapCity orders: **24,050**
📖 Time & Time Again, Part 3 • in 40s
55 ❑ May 1991 Cover: 1.00 **NM** value: **1.75**
Circ: CapCity orders: **24,350**
📖 Time & Time Again, Part 6 • in Middle Ages ★ Appearance of Demon.
56 ❑ Jun 1991 Cover: 1.00 **NM** value: **1.75**
Circ: CapCity orders: **25,550**
📖 Red Glass
57 ❑ Jul 1991 Cover: 1.75 **NM** value: **2.00**
Circ: CapCity orders: **36,800**
• Double-size. 📖 Return Of The Krypton Man • Krypton Man **A:** Dan Jurgens; Bob McLeod; Tom Grummettt; Jon Bogdanove; Art Thibert **W:** Dan Jurgens
58 ❑ Aug 1991 Cover: 1.00 **NM** value: **1.50**
Circ: CapCity orders: **28,050**
★ Versus Bloodhounds.
59 ❑ Sep 1991 Cover: 1.00 **NM** value: **1.50**
Circ: CapCity orders: **28,200**
📖 Blackout, Part 1
60 ❑ Oct 1991 Cover: 1.00 **NM** value: **2.00**
Circ: CapCity orders: **29,350**
📖 Blackout, Part 2 ★ 1st Appearance of Agent Liberty. ★ Versus Intergang.
61 ❑ Nov 1991 Cover: 1.00 **NM** value: **1.50**
Circ: CapCity orders: **27,200**
📖 Blackout, Part 3 ★ Appearance of Linear Men, Waverider.
62 ❑ Dec 1991 Cover: 1.00 **NM** value: **1.50**
Circ: CapCity orders: **24,950** • **CGC:** 1 graded, best 9.6
📖 Blackout, Part 4 **A:** Dan Jurgens **W:** Dan Jurgens
63 ❑ Jan 1992 Cover: 1.00 **NM** value: **1.50**
Circ: CapCity orders: **23,900**
★ Appearance of Aquaman.
64 ❑ Feb 1992 Cover: 1.00 **NM** value: **1.50**
Circ: CapCity orders: **22,000**
• Christmas issue
65 ❑ Mar 1992 Cover: 1.00 **NM** value: **1.50**
Circ: CapCity orders: **24,850**
📖 Panic in the Sky Second Strike ★ Appearance of Guy Gardner, Deathstroke, Captain Marvel, Batman, Aquaman.
66 ❑ Apr 1992 Cover: 1.00 **NM** value: **1.50**
Circ: CapCity orders: **22,300**
📖 Panic in the Sky Final Strike ★ Appearance of Guy Gardner, Deathstroke, Captain Marvel, Batman, Aquaman.
67 ❑ May 1992 Cover: 1.00 **NM** value: **1.50**
Circ: CapCity orders: **19,600**
68 ❑ Jun 1992 Cover: 1.25 **NM** value: **1.50**
Circ: CapCity orders: **23,050**
• Deathstroke
69 ❑ Jul 1992 Cover: 1.25 **NM** value: **1.50**
Circ: CapCity orders: **22,300**
70 ❑ Aug 1992 Cover: 1.25 **NM** value: **1.50**
Circ: CapCity orders: **26,300**
• Robin
71 ❑ Sep 1992 Cover: 1.25 **NM** value: **1.50**
Circ: CapCity orders: **20,350**
72 ❑ Oct 1992 Cover: 1.25 **NM** value: **1.50**
Circ: CapCity orders: **19,900**
73 ❑ Nov 1992 Cover: 1.25 **NM** value: **3.00**
Circ: CapCity orders: **19,250**
📖 Doomsday ★ Appearance of Doomsday, Waverider.
73-2❑ Cover: 1.25 **NM** value: **1.75**
74 ❑ Dec 1992 Cover: 1.25 **NM** value: **4.00**
Circ: CapCity orders: **25,900** • **CGC:** 7 graded, best 9.8
📖 Countdown to Doomsday! • Doomsday; ▲1992-74 **A:** Dan Jurgens **W:** Dan Jurgens
74-2❑ Dec 1992 Cover: 1.25 **NM** value: **1.50**
📖 Countdown to Doomsday! • ▲1992-74 **A:** Dan Jurgens **W:** Dan Jurgens
75 ❑ Jan 1993 Cover: 1.25 **NM** value: **4.00**
• **CGC:** 33 graded, best 9.8
📖 Doomsday! • newsstand; unbagged **A:** Dan Jurgens **W:** Dan Jurgens ★ Death of Superman.
75/CS❑ Jan 1993 Cover: 2.50 **NM** value: **10.00**
Circ: CapCity orders: **281,400** • **CGC:** 32 graded, best 9.6
📖 Doomsday! **A:** Dan Jurgens **W:** Dan Jurgens ★ Death of Superman.
75/PL❑ Jan 1993 Cover: 1.25 **NM** value: **35.00**
• **CGC:** 21 graded, best 9.6
• Platinum edition. 📖 Doomsday! **A:** Dan Jurgens **W:** Dan Jurgens ★ Death of Superman.
75-2❑ Jan 1993 Cover: 1.25 **NM** value: **2.00**
75-3❑ Jan 1993 Cover: 1.25 **NM** value: **1.50**
75-4❑ Jan 1993 Cover: 1.25 **NM** value: **1.50**
76 ❑ Feb 1993 Cover: 1.25 **NM** value: **2.50**
Circ: CapCity orders: **84,950**
📖 Funeral for a Friend, Part 4 **A:** Brett Breeding **W:** Dan Jurgens
77 ❑ Mar 1993 Cover: 1.25 **NM** value: **2.50**
Circ: CapCity orders: **145,300**
📖 Funeral for a Friend, Part 8 **A:** Brett Breeding **W:** Dan Jurgens
78 ❑ Jun 1993 Cover: 1.50 **NM** value: **2.00**
Circ: CapCity orders: **110,100** • **CGC:** 2 graded, best 9.8
📖 Reign of the Supermen **A:** Brett Breeding **W:** Dan Jurgens ★ 1st Appearance of Cyborg Superman.
78/CS❑ Jun 1993 Cover: 1.95 **NM** value: **2.50**
Circ: CapCity orders: **401,850**
Die-cut cover. **A:** Brett Breeding **W:** Dan Jurgens ★ 1st Appearance of Cyborg Superman.
79 ❑ Jul 1993 Cover: 1.50 **NM** value: **2.00**
Circ: CapCity orders: **122,700**
📖 Reign of the Supermen
80 ❑ Aug 1993 Cover: 1.50 **NM** value: **2.00**
Circ: CapCity orders: **110,100**
📖 Reign of the Supermen • Coast City destroyed; Cyborg Superman revealed as evil ★ Versus Mongul.
81 ❑ Sep 1993 Cover: 1.50 **NM** value: **2.00**
Circ: CapCity orders: **89,950**
📖 Reign of the Supermen; Resurrections **A:** Dan Jurgens **W:** Dan Jurgens
82 ❑ Oct 1993 Cover: 1.50 **NM** value: **2.00**
📖 Reign of the Supermen • return of Superman; Reign of the Superman ends; True Superman revealed **A:** Brett Breeding **W:** Dan Jurgens
82/SC❑ Oct 1993 Cover: 2.00 **NM** value: **3.50**
Circ: CapCity orders: **224,700** • **CGC:** 3 graded, best 9.6
chromium cover. • with poster; Reign of the Superman ends; True Superman revealed **A:** Brett Breeding **W:** Dan Jurgens
83 ❑ Nov 1993 Cover: 1.50 **NM** value: **2.00**
Circ: CapCity orders: **79,300**
📖 Funeral for a Friend Epilogue
84 ❑ Dec 1993 Cover: 1.50 **NM** value: **2.00**
Circ: CapCity orders: **82,100**
★ Death of Adam Grant. ★ Versus Toyman.
85 ❑ Jan 1994 Cover: 1.50 **NM** value: **2.00**
Circ: CapCity orders: **79,200**
86 ❑ Feb 1994 Cover: 1.50 **NM** value: **2.00**
Circ: CapCity orders: **81,650**
87 ❑ Mar 1994 Cover: 1.50 **NM** value: **2.00**
Circ: CapCity orders: **66,500**
📖 Bizarro's World, Part 1 • Bizarro **A:** Stuart Immonen **W:** Dan Jurgens
88 ❑ Apr 1994 Cover: 1.50 **NM** value: **2.00**
Circ: CapCity orders: **58,950**
• Bizarro
89 ❑ May 1994 Cover: 1.50 **NM** value: **2.00**
Circ: CapCity orders: **54,950**
90 ❑ Jun 1994 Cover: 1.50 **NM** value: **2.00**
Circ: CapCity orders: **56,350**
A: Brent Anderson
91 ❑ Jul 1994 Cover: 1.50 **NM** value: **2.00**
Circ: CapCity orders: **56,200**
A: Brent Anderson
92 ❑ Aug 1994 Cover: 1.50 **NM** value: **2.00**
Circ: CapCity orders: **51,900**
📖 Massacre in Metropolis, Part 1
93 ❑ Sep 1994 Cover: 1.50 **NM** value: **2.00**
Circ: CapCity orders: **53,850**
📖 Zero Hour • Zero Hour **A:** Dan Jurgens **W:** Dan Jurgens
94 ❑ Nov 1994 Cover: 1.50 **NM** value: **2.00**
Circ: CapCity orders: **46,350**
📖 Dead Again
95 ❑ Dec 1994 Cover: 1.50 **NM** value: **2.00**
Circ: CapCity orders: **45,250**
📖 Dead Again ★ Appearance of Atom.
96 ❑ Jan 1995 Cover: 1.50 **NM** value: **2.00**
Circ: CapCity orders: **42,800**
📖 Dead Again • ▲1995-2 **A:** Dan Jurgens **W:** Dan Jurgens
97 ❑ Feb 1995 Cover: 1.50 **NM** value: **2.00**
Circ: CapCity orders: **40,850**
★ 1st Appearance of Shadowdragon.
98 ❑ Mar 1995 Cover: 1.50 **NM** value: **2.00**
Circ: CapCity orders: **38,200**
99 ❑ Apr 1995 Cover: 1.50 **NM** value: **2.00**
Circ: CapCity orders: **36,300**
★ Appearance of Agent Liberty.
100❑ May 1995 Cover: 2.95 **NM** value: **3.00**
• 100th anniversary edition. 📖 Death of Clark Kent, Part 1; The Death Of Clark Kent • ▲1995-18 **A:** Dan Jurgens **W:** Dan Jurgens
100/SC❑ May 1995 Cover: 3.95 **NM** value: **4.00**
Circ: CapCity orders: **70,900**
enhanced cover. • 100th anniversary edition. 📖 The Death Of Clark Kent • ▲1995-18 **A:** Dan Jurgens **W:** Dan Jurgens
101❑ Jun 1995 Cover: 1.95 **NM** value: **2.00**
Circ: CapCity orders: **41,350**
📖 Grief • ▲1995-22
102❑ Jul 1995 Cover: 1.95 **NM** value: **2.00**
Circ: CapCity orders: **34,775**
★ Versus Captain Marvel.
103❑ Aug 1995 Cover: 1.95 **NM** value: **2.00**
Circ: CapCity orders: **34,250**
★ Versus Arclight.
104❑ Sep 1995 Cover: 1.95 **NM** value: **2.00**
Circ: CapCity orders: **32,900**
• Cyborg is released by Darkseid
105❑ Oct 1995 Cover: 1.95 **NM** value: **2.00**
Circ: CapCity orders: **27,700**
★ Appearance of Green Lantern.
106❑ Nov 1995 Cover: 1.95 **NM** value: **2.00**
📖 Trial of Superman
107❑ Dec 1995 Cover: 1.95 **NM** value: **2.00**
📖 Trial of Superman
108❑ Jan 1996 Cover: 1.95 **NM** value: **2.00**
📖 Trial of Superman ★ Death of Mope.
109❑ Feb 1996 Cover: 1.95 **NM** value: **2.00**
📖 The Kill Fee! • Christmas story; return of Lori Lemaris; ▲1996-7 **A:** Ron Frenz; Joe Rubinstein **W:** Dan Jurgens
110❑ Mar 1996 Cover: 1.95 **NM** value: **2.00**
📖 The Treasure Hunt Caper • ▲1996-11 **A:** Ron Frenz; Joe Rubinstein **W:** Dan Jurgens; Jerry Conway ★ Appearance of Plastic Man.
111❑ Apr 1996 Cover: 1.95 **NM** value: **2.00**
📖 Divisions • ▲1996-16 **A:** Denis Rodier; Brett Breeding; Ron Frenz **W:** Dan Jurgens
112❑ Jun 1996 Cover: 1.95 **NM** value: **2.00**
113❑ Jul 1996 Cover: 1.95 **NM** value: **2.00**
114❑ Aug 1996 Cover: 1.95 **NM** value: **2.00**
115❑ Sep 1996 Cover: 1.95 **NM** value: **2.00**
• Lois becomes foreign correspondent
116❑ Oct 1996 Cover: 1.95 **NM** value: **2.00**
📖 The Bottle City, Part 3 • Teen Titans preview
117❑ Nov 1996 Cover: 1.95 **NM** value: **2.00**
Circ: Diamd. preorders: **64,985**
📖 Sanctuary • Final Night; ▲1996-42 **A:** Ron Frenz; Joe Rubinstein **W:** Dan Jurgens
118❑ Dec 1996 Cover: 1.95 **NM** value: **2.00**
Circ: Diamd. preorders: **62,704**
📖 From the Heart • Lois decides to return to Metropolis; ▲1996-46 **A:** Ron Frenz; Joe Rubinstein **W:** Dan Jurgens ★ Appearance of Wonder Woman.
119❑ Jan 1997 Cover: 1.95 **NM** value: **2.00**
Circ: Diamd. preorders: **64,361**
📖 Power Struggle; Subburned! • ▲1997-1 **A:** Ron Frenz; Joe Rubinstein **W:** Dan Jurgens ★ Appearance of Legion.
120❑ Feb 1997 Cover: 1.95 **NM** value: **2.00**
Circ: Diamd. preorders: **58,127**
📖 To Be a Superman
121❑ Mar 1997 Cover: 1.95 **NM** value: **2.00**
Circ: Diamd. preorders: **56,462**
📖 They Call It Suicide Slum • ▲1997-10 **A:** Dan Jurgens; Joe Rubinstein **W:** Dan Jurgens
122❑ Apr 1997 Cover: 1.95 **NM** value: **2.00**
Circ: Diamd. preorders: **54,510**
• energy powers begin to manifest
123❑ May 1997 Cover: 1.95 **NM** value: **3.00**
Circ: Diamd. preorders: **49,963** • **CGC:** 2 graded, best 9.6
📖 Superman…Reborn! • New costume

Other grades: Multiply prices above by **1.5 for Mint • 2/3 for Very Fine • 1/3 for Fine • 1/5 for Very Good • 1/8 for Good**

123/SC❑May 1997 Cover: 1.95 **NM** value: **5.00**
Circ: Diamd. preorders: **213,481** • **CGC:** 15 graded, best 9.8
glow-in-the-dark cardstock cover. Superman…Reborn! • New costume

124 ❑ Jun 1997 Cover: 1.95 **NM** value: **2.00**
Circ: Diamd. preorders: **77,045**
★ Appearance of Booster Gold.

125 ❑ Jul 1997 Cover: 1.95 **NM** value: **2.00**
Circ: Diamd. preorders: **73,694**
• in Kandor★ Appearance of Atom.

126 ❑ Aug 1997 Cover: 1.95 **NM** value: **2.00**
Circ: Diamd. preorders: **71,532**
★ Appearance of Batman.

127 ❑ Sep 1997 Cover: 1.95 **NM** value: **2.00**
Circ: Diamd. preorders: **67,630**
• Superman Revenge Squad leader's identity revealed

128 ❑ Oct 1997 Cover: 1.95 **NM** value: **2.00**
Circ: Diamd. preorders: **67,754**
• Genesis★ Versus Cyborg Superman.

129 ❑ Nov 1997 Cover: 1.95 **NM** value: **2.00**
Circ: Diamd. preorders: **62,213**
Within Human Reach • ▲1997-44 **A:** Paul Ryan **W:** Dan Jurgens
★ Appearance of Scorn.

130 ❑ Dec 1997 Cover: 1.95 **NM** value: **2.00**
Circ: Diamd. preorders: **60,493**
Face cover. the Longest Halloween **A:** Norm Breyfogle **W:** Dan Jurgens

131 ❑ Jan 1998 Cover: 1.95 **NM** value: **2.00**
Circ: Diamd. preorders: **57,875**
• birth of Lena Luthor★ Death of Mayor Berkowitz.

132 ❑ Feb 1998 Cover: 1.95 **NM** value: **2.00**
Circ: Diamd. preorders: **65,628**

133 ❑ Mar 1998 Cover: 1.95 **NM** value: **2.00**
Circ: Diamd. preorders: **54,700**

134 ❑ Apr 1998 Cover: 1.95 **NM** value: **2.00**
Circ: Diamd. preorders: **53,363**
• Millennium Giants

135 ❑ May 1998 Cover: 1.95 **NM** value: **2.00**
Circ: Diamd. preorders: **55,210**
• leads into Superman Forever #1; End of Superman Red/Blue

136 ❑ Jul 1998 Cover: 1.95 **NM** value: **2.00**
Circ: Diamd. preorders: **54,597**
Superman 2999

137 ❑ Aug 1998 Cover: 1.95 **NM** value: **2.00**
Circ: Diamd. preorders: **54,927**
Superman 2999 ★ Versus Muto.

138 ❑ Sep 1998 Cover: 1.99 **NM** value: **2.00**
Circ: Diamd. preorders: **51,454**
★ Appearance of Kismet. ★ Versus Dominus.

139 ❑ Oct 1998 Cover: 1.99 **NM** value: **Cover or less**
Circ: Diamd. preorders: **49,374**
★ Versus Dominus.

140 ❑ Dec 1998 Cover: 1.99 **NM** value: **Cover or less**
Circ: Diamd. preorders: **47,617**
• in Kandor; Inventor's identity revealed

141 ❑ Jan 1999 Cover: 1.99 **NM** value: **Cover or less**
Circ: Diamd. preorders: **46,373**
★ 1st Appearance of Outburst.

142 ❑ Feb 1999 Cover: 1.99 **NM** value: **Cover or less**
Circ: Diamd. preorders: **47,406**
A: Georges Jeanty **W:** Dan Jurgens ★ Appearance of Outburst.

143 ❑ Mar 1999 Cover: 1.99 **NM** value: **Cover or less**
Circ: Diamd. preorders: **40,824**
A: Steve Epting **W:** Dan Jurgens ★ Appearance of Supermen of America, Superman Robots.

144 ❑ Apr 1999 Cover: 1.99 **NM** value: **Cover or less**
Circ: Diamd. preorders: **40,052**
• Fortress destroyed **A:** Steve Epting **W:** Dan Jurgens

145 ❑ Jun 1999 Cover: 1.99 **NM** value: **Cover or less**
Circ: Diamd. preorders: **41,433**
Public Hearing • ♦1999-23 **A:** Steve Epting **W:** Dan Jurgens

146 ❑ Jul 1999 Cover: 1.99 **NM** value: **Cover or less**
Circ: Diamd. preorders: **41,045**
Rough Day at the Office **A:** Dan Jurgens; Joe Rubinstein **W:** Dan Jurgens ★ Appearance of Toyman.

147 ❑ Aug 1999 Cover: 1.99 **NM** value: **Cover or less**
Circ: Diamd. preorders: **43,533**
One-Man JLA; Secret Origin Part 1: The Knight • Superman as Green Lantern **A:** Tom Grindberg **W:** Ron Marz

148 ❑ Sep 1999 Cover: 1.99 **NM** value: **Cover or less**
Circ: Diamd. preorders: **40,716**
Champions **A:** Steve Epting **W:** Dan Jurgens

149 ❑ Oct 1999 Cover: 1.99 **NM** value: **Cover or less**
Circ: Diamd. preorders: **41,710**
Who is Strange Visitor?, Part 1 • ♦1999-40 **A:** Sal Buscema; Ron Frenz; Rand Frenz **W:** Ron Frenz; Ran Frenz

150 ❑ Nov 1999 Cover: 1.99 **NM** value: **Cover or less**
Circ: Diamd. preorders: **15,116**

150/SC❑Nov 1999 Cover: 3.95 **NM** value: **Cover or less**
Circ: Diamd. preorders: **40,458**
Special cover.

151 ❑ Dec 1999 Cover: 1.99 **NM** value: **Cover or less**
Circ: Diamd. preorders: **41,509**
• Daily Planet reopens

152 ❑ Jan 2000 Cover: 1.99 **NM** value: **Cover or less**
Circ: Diamd. preorders: **38,905**
Deadline U.S.A. • ▲2000-1 **A:** Mike McKone **W:** Jeph Loeb

153 ❑ Feb 2000 Cover: 1.99 **NM** value: **Cover or less**
Circ: Diamd. preorders: **39,008**
Say Goodbye • ▲2000-5 **A:** Mike McKone **W:** Jeph Loeb

154 ❑ Mar 2000 Cover: 1.99 **NM** value: **Cover or less**
Circ: Diamd. preorders: **40,258**

155 ❑ Apr 2000 Cover: 1.99 **NM** value: **Cover or less**
Circ: Diamd. preorders: **38,990**

156 ❑ May 2000 Cover: 1.99 **NM** value: **Cover or less**
Circ: Diamd. preorders: **41,191**
The Tender Trap • ▲2000-18 **A:** Ed McGuinness **W:** Jeph Loeb

157 ❑ Jun 2000 Cover: 1.99 **NM** value: **Cover or less**
Circ: Diamd. preorders: **41,869**
Superman's Enemy Lois Lane • ▲2000-22 **A:** Ed McGuinness **W:** Jeph Loeb

158 ❑ Jul 2000 Cover: 1.99 **NM** value: **Cover or less**
Circ: Diamd. preorders: **41,861**

159 ❑ Aug 2000 Cover: 1.99 **NM** value: **Cover or less**
Circ: Diamd. preorders: **43,896**

160 ❑ Sep 2000 Cover: 1.99 **NM** value: **Cover or less**
Circ: Diamd. preorders: **47,274**

161 ❑ Oct 2000 Cover: 2.25 **NM** value: **Cover or less**
Circ: Diamd. preorders: **42,788**
The Reign of Emperor Joker, Part 2 • ▲2000-39 **A:** Ed McGuinness **W:** Jeph Loeb

162 ❑ Nov 2000 Cover: 2.25 **NM** value: **Cover or less**
Circ: Diamd. preorders: **42,375**
American Dream • ▲2000-43 **A:** Ed McGuinness **W:** Jeph Loeb

163 ❑ Dec 2000 Cover: 2.25 **NM** value: **Cover or less**
Circ: Diamd. preorders: **42,392**
Where Monsters Lurk! • ▲2000-47 **A:** Ed McGuinness **W:** Jeph Loeb

164 ❑ Jan 2001 Cover: 2.25 **NM** value: **Cover or less**
Circ: Diamd. preorders: **42,152**
Tales From the Bizarro World • ▲2001-1 **A:** Carlo Barbieri; Ed McGuinness **W:** Jeph Loeb

165 ❑ Feb 2001 Cover: 2.25 **NM** value: **Cover or less**
Circ: Diamd. preorders: **41,470**
Help! • ▲2001-6 **A:** Cam Smith; Ed McGuinness **W:** Jeph Loeb

166 ❑ Mar 2001 Cover: 2.25 **NM** value: **Cover or less**
Circ: Diamd. preorders: **51,297** • **CGC:** 34 graded, best 10.0
Fathers… • ▲2001-10 **A:** Ed McGuinness **W:** Jeph Loeb

167 ❑ Apr 2001 Cover: 2.25 **NM** value: **Cover or less**
Circ: Diamd. preorders: **41,896**
Return to Krypton, Part 1 • ▲2001-14 **A:** Ed McGuinness **W:** Jeph Loeb

168 ❑ May 2001 Cover: 2.25 **NM** value: **Cover or less**
Circ: Diamd. preorders: **47,703** • **CGC:** 3 graded, best 9.8
With This Ring… • ▲2001-18 **A:** Ed McGuinness **W:** Jeph Loeb

169 ❑ Jun 2001 Cover: 2.25 **NM** value: **Cover or less**
Circ: Diamd. preorders: **41,929**
Infestation, Part 1 • ▲2001-22 **A:** Paco Medina **W:** Marv Wolfman

170 ❑ Jul 2001 Cover: 2.25 **NM** value: **Cover or less**
Circ: Diamd. preorders: **44,181**

171 ❑ Aug 2001 Cover: 2.25 **NM** value: **Cover or less**
Circ: Diamd. preorders: **51,673** • **CGC:** 4 graded, best 9.9

172 ❑ Sep 2001 Cover: 2.25 **NM** value: **Cover or less**
Circ: Diamd. preorders: **52,681**
A: Ed McGuinness **W:** Jeph Loeb

1000000❑Nov 1998 Cover: 1.99 **NM** value: **Cover or less**
Circ: Diamd. preorders: **57,893**
Down to Earth **A:** Andy Lanning **W:** Dan Abnett

1000000/LE❑ Cover: 14.99 **NM** value: **Cover or less**
Down to Earth **A:** Andy Lanning **W:** Dan Abnett

3D 1❑ Cover: 3.95 **NM** value: **Cover or less**

Anl 1❑ca. 1987 Cover: 1.25 **NM** value: **4.00**
Circ: CapCity orders: **28,650**
★ Origin of Titano.

Anl 2❑ca. 1988 Cover: 1.50 **NM** value: **3.00**
Circ: CapCity orders: **24,600**
• Private Lives

Anl 3❑ca. 1991 Cover: 2.00 **NM** value: **2.50**
Circ: CapCity orders: **36,700**
Armageddon 2001, Part 2 • Armageddon 2001

Anl 3-2❑ Cover: 2.00 **NM** value: **Cover or less**

Anl 3-3❑ Cover: 2.00 **NM** value: **Cover or less**

Anl 4❑ca. 1992 Cover: 2.50 **NM** value: **Cover or less**
Circ: CapCity orders: **27,000**
Eclipso: The Darkness Within, Part 5 • Eclipso: The Darkness Within **A:** Scott Benefiel **W:** Dan Vado

Anl 5❑ca. 1993 Cover: 2.50 **NM** value: **Cover or less**
Circ: CapCity orders: **57,700**
Bloodlines • Bloodlines★ 1st Appearance of Myriad.

Anl 6❑ca. 1994 Cover: 2.95 **NM** value: **Cover or less**
Circ: CapCity orders: **33,550**
• Elseworlds **C:** Mike Mignola

Anl 7❑ca. 1995 Cover: 3.95 **NM** value: **Cover or less**
Circ: CapCity orders: **24,875**
• Year One★ Appearance of Dr. Occult, Doctor Occult.

Anl 8❑ca. 1996 Cover: 2.95 **NM** value: **Cover or less**
• Legends of the Dead Earth; The League of Supermen

Anl 9❑Jul 1997 Cover: 3.95 **NM** value: **Cover or less**
Circ: Diamd. preorders: **54,283**
• Pulp Heroes★ Appearance of Doc Savage.

Anl 10❑Oct 1998 Cover: 2.95 **NM** value: **Cover or less**
Circ: Diamd. preorders: **37,431**
• Ghosts★ Appearance of Phantom Zone villains.

Anl 11❑Oct 1999 Cover: 2.95 **NM** value: **Cover or less**
Circ: Diamd. preorders: **33,297**
The Apes of Wrath • JLApe **A:** Joe Phillips **W:** Andy Lanning; Dan Abnett

GS 1❑Feb 1999 Cover: 4.95 **NM** value: **Cover or less**
Circ: Diamd. preorders: **31,704**

GS 2❑Jun 1999 Cover: 4.95 **NM** value: **Cover or less**
Circ: Diamd. preorders: **27,707**
Under Control; If I Had a Hammer; Redemption; Who Do You Trust?; Sibs; Frustration Eternal; From Krypton With Love **A:** Peter Doherty; Mike Collins; Sean Phillips; Michael Avon Oeming; Gordon Purcell; Scott Beatty; Brian Denham **W:** Joe Casey; Michael Jan Friedman; Dan Jurgens; Chuck Dixon; Doselle Young; Eric Luke; Mark Millar

GS 3❑Nov 2000 Cover: 4.95 **NM** value: **Cover or less**
Circ: Diamd. preorders: **22,339**
I, Witness **A:** Yvel Guichet; Mark Bagley; Ron Lim; Paul Ryan; Justiniano; Carlo Barberi; Sunny Lee **W:** Jay Faerber

SE 1❑ca. 1992 Cover: 3.50 **NM** value: **4.00**
Circ: CapCity orders: **31,650**
The Sand Man • 1992 Special **A:** Walt Simonson **W:** Walt Simonson

SUPERMAN 3-D — DC

1 ❑ Dec 1998 Cover: 3.95 **NM** value: **4.00**
Circ: Diamd. preorders: **30,120** • **CGC:** 1 graded, best 7.5
Bad Trip to Nowhere **A:** Neil Vokes **W:** Louise Simonson

SUPERMAN ACTION ARCHIVES — DC

1 ❑ Cover: 49.95 **NM** value: **Cover or less**
• Collects Superman stories from Action Comics #1, 7-20 **A:** Joe Shuster; Jerry Siegel **W:** Joe Shuster; Jerry Siegel ★ Origin of Superman. ★ 1st Appearance of Superman.

2 ❑ Cover: 49.95 **NM** value: **Cover or less**
• Collects Superman stories from Action Comics #21-36 **A:** Joe Shuster; Jerry Siegel **W:** Joe Shuster; Jerry Siegel

SUPERMAN ADVENTURES — DC

1 ❑ Nov 1996 Cover: 1.75 **NM** value: **3.00**
Circ: Diamd. preorders: **47,893**
Men of Steel • based on animated series; follow-up to pilot episode **A:** Rick Burchett **W:** Scott McCloud

2 ❑ Dec 1996 Cover: 1.75 **NM** value: **2.50**
Circ: Diamd. preorders: **34,391**
Be Careful What You Wish For **A:** Rick Burchett **W:** Scott McCloud ★ Versus Metallo.

3 ❑ Jan 1997 Cover: 1.75 **NM** value: **2.50**
Circ: Diamd. preorders: **32,350**
Distant Thunder **A:** Rick Burchett **W:** Scott McCloud ★ Versus Brainiac.

4 ❑ Feb 1997 Cover: 1.75 **NM** value: **2.00**
Circ: Diamd. preorders: **28,855**
Eye to Eye **A:** Rick Burchett **W:** Scott McCloud

5 ❑ Mar 1997 Cover: 1.75 **NM** value: **2.00**
Circ: Diamd. preorders: **26,287**
Balance of Power **A:** Bret Blevins **W:** Scott McCloud ★ Versus Livewire.

6 ❑ Apr 1997 Cover: 1.75 **NM** value: **2.00**
Circ: Diamd. preorders: **24,311**

7 ❑ May 1997 Cover: 1.75 **NM** value: **2.00**
Circ: Diamd. preorders: **23,793**
All Creatures Great and Small, Part 1 **A:** Rick Burchett **W:** Scott McCloud ★ Versus Mala. ★ Versus Jax-ur. ★ Versus Jax-ur, Mala.

8 ❑ Jun 1997 Cover: 1.75 **NM** value: **2.00**
Circ: Diamd. preorders: **23,845**
All Creatures Great and Small, Part 2 **A:** Rick Burchett **W:** Scott McCloud ★ Versus Mala. ★ Versus Jax-ur. ★ Versus Jax-ur, Mala.

9 ❑ Jul 1997 Cover: 1.75 **NM** value: **2.00**
Circ: Diamd. preorders: **22,409**
Return of the Hero **A:** Mike Manley **W:** Scott McCloud

10 ❑ Aug 1997 Cover: 1.75 **NM** value: **2.00**
Circ: Diamd. preorders: **21,690**
★ Versus Toyman.

11 ❑ Sep 1997 Cover: 1.75 **NM** value: **2.00**
Circ: Diamd. preorders: **20,663**

12 ❑ Oct 1997 Cover: 1.75 **NM** value: **2.00**
Circ: Diamd. preorders: **19,877**
The War Within, Part 2 **A:** Rick Burchett **W:** Scott McCloud

13 ❑ Nov 1997 Cover: 1.75 **NM** value: **2.00**
Circ: Diamd. preorders: **19,033**

14 ❑ Dec 1997 Cover: 1.75 **NM** value: **2.00**
Circ: Diamd. preorders: **18,615**
Face cover. Stop the Presses! **A:** Neil Vokes **W:** Mark Evanier

15 ❑ Jan 1998 Cover: 1.95 **NM** value: **2.00**
Circ: Diamd. preorders: **18,008**
Maximum Effort! **A:** Rick Burchett **W:** Mark Evanier ★ Appearance of Bibbo.

16 ❑ Feb 1998 Cover: 1.95 **NM** value: **2.00**
Circ: Diamd. preorders: **17,813**
Clark Kent, You're a Nobody! **A:** Aluir Amancio **W:** Mark Millar

17 ❑ Mar 1998 Cover: 1.95 **NM** value: **2.00**
Circ: Diamd. preorders: **16,719**

18 ❑ Apr 1998 Cover: 1.95 **NM** value: **2.00**
Circ: Diamd. preorders: **15,976**
It's a Super Life **A:** Aluir Amancio **W:** Devin K. Grayson

19 ❑ May 1998 Cover: 1.95 **NM** value: **2.00**
Circ: Diamd. preorders: **15,681**
The Bodyguard of Steel **A:** Aluir Amancio **W:** Mark Millar

20 ❑ Jun 1998 Cover: 1.95 **NM** value: **2.00**
Circ: Diamd. preorders: **16,455**

21 ❑ Jul 1998 Cover: 3.95 **NM** value: **Cover or less**
Circ: Diamd. preorders: **19,745** • **CGC:** 1 graded, best 9.4
• double-sized. • adapts Supergirl episode

22 ❑ Aug 1998 Cover: 1.95 **NM** value: **2.00**
Circ: Diamd. preorders: **15,347**

23 ❑ Sep 1998 Cover: 1.99 **NM** value: **2.00**
Circ: Diamd. preorders: **15,110**
★ Appearance of Livewire. ★ Versus Brainiac.

24 ❑ Oct 1998 Cover: 1.99 **NM** value: **2.00**
Circ: Diamd. preorders: **15,327**
★ Versus Parasite.

25 ❑ Nov 1998 Cover: 1.99 **NM** value: **2.00**
Circ: Diamd. preorders: **16,054**
★ Appearance of Batgirl.

26 ❑ Dec 1998 Cover: 1.99 **NM** value: **2.00**
Circ: Diamd. preorders: **14,299**
★ Versus Mxyzptlk.

27 ❑ Jan 1999 Cover: 1.99 **NM** value: **2.00**
Circ: Diamd. preorders: **14,627**
★ 1st Appearance of Superior-Man.

28 ❑ Feb 1999 Cover: 1.99 **NM** value: **2.00**
Circ: Diamd. preorders: **14,013**
• Jimmy and Superman switch bodies **A:** Mike Manley **W:** Mark Millar ★ Appearance of Jimmy Olsen.

29 ❑ Mar 1999 Cover: 1.99 **NM** value: **2.00**
Circ: Diamd. preorders: **13,943**
• Lobo apperance **A:** Aluir Amancio **W:** Mark Millar ★ Appearance of Bizarro, Lobo.

30 ❑ Apr 1999 Cover: 1.99 **NM** value: **2.00**
Circ: Diamd. preorders: **13,292**
A: Aluir Amancio **W:** Mark Millar

CGC-graded: Multiply prices above by **33 for 9.9 M • 16 for 9.8 NM/M • 7 for 9.6 NM+ • 5 for 9.4 NM • 2.5 for 9.2 NM- • 1.5 for 9.0 VF/NM**

31 ❑ May 1999 Cover: 1.99 **NM** value: **2.00**
Circ: Diamd. preorders: **13,205**

32 ❑ Jun 1999 Cover: 1.99 **NM** value: **2.00**
Circ: Diamd. preorders: **13,923**
Sullivan's Girl Friend, Lois Lane **A:** Neil Vokes **W:** David Michelinie

33 ❑ Jul 1999 Cover: 1.99 **NM** value: **2.00**
Circ: Diamd. preorders: **13,770**
Clark Kent is Superman and I Can Prove It! **A:** Neil Vokes **W:** Mark Millar

34 ❑ Aug 1999 Cover: 1.99 **NM** value: **2.00**
Circ: Diamd. preorders: **13,573**
Sanctuary **A:** Mike Manley **W:** Mark Millar ★ Appearance of Doctor Fate.

35 ❑ Sep 1999 Cover: 1.99 **NM** value: **2.00**
Circ: Diamd. preorders: **13,188**
Never Play with the Toyman's Toys! **A:** Aluir Amancio **W:** Mark Millar ★ Versus Toyman.

36 ❑ Oct 1999 Cover: 1.99 **NM** value: **2.00**
Circ: Diamd. preorders: **12,746**
This is a Job for Superman **A:** Aluir Amancio **W:** Mark Millar

37 ❑ Nov 1999 Cover: 1.99 **NM** value: **2.00**
Circ: Diamd. preorders: **12,505**
Clark Kent: Public Enemy **A:** Aluir Amancio **W:** Mark Millar ★ Versus Multi-Face.

38 ❑ Dec 1999 Cover: 1.99 **NM** value: **2.00**
Circ: Diamd. preorders: **12,405**
If I Ruled the World! **A:** Aluir Amancio **W:** Mark Millar

39 ❑ Jan 2000 Cover: 1.99 **NM** value: **2.00**
Circ: Diamd. preorders: **12,108**
Reunion **A:** Bret Blevins **W:** Evan Dorkin; Sarah Dyer

40 ❑ Feb 2000 Cover: 1.99 **NM** value: **2.00**
Circ: Diamd. preorders: **11,477**
Old Wounds **A:** Neil Vokes **W:** Ty Templeton; Dan Slott

41 ❑ Mar 2000 Cover: 1.99 **NM** value: **Cover or less**
Circ: Diamd. preorders: **11,526**

42 ❑ Apr 2000 Cover: 1.99 **NM** value: **Cover or less**
Circ: Diamd. preorders: **11,145**

43 ❑ May 2000 Cover: 1.99 **NM** value: **Cover or less**
Circ: Diamd. preorders: **10,899**
Are You My Mother Box? **A:** Min S. Ku **W:** Jordan B. Gorfinkel

44 ❑ Jun 2000 Cover: 1.99 **NM** value: **Cover or less**
Circ: Diamd. preorders: **11,111**
Law and Orders **A:** Aluir Amancio **W:** David Michelinie

45 ❑ Jul 2000 Cover: 1.99 **NM** value: **Cover or less**
Circ: Diamd. preorders: **10,770**

46 ❑ Aug 2000 Cover: 1.99 **NM** value: **Cover or less**
Circ: Diamd. preorders: **11,116**

47 ❑ Sep 2000 Cover: 1.99 **NM** value: **Cover or less**
Circ: Diamd. preorders: **10,832**

48 ❑ Oct 2000 Cover: 1.99 **NM** value: **Cover or less**
Circ: Diamd. preorders: **10,262**
The Believer **A:** Neil Vokes **W:** Jay Faerber

49 ❑ Nov 2000 Cover: 1.99 **NM** value: **Cover or less**
Circ: Diamd. preorders: **10,066**
The Challenge **A:** Aluir Amancio **W:** Michael Reeves

50 ❑ Dec 2000 Cover: 1.99 **NM** value: **Cover or less**
Circ: Diamd. preorders: **10,214**
A: Min S. Ku **W:** Jordan B. Gorfinkel

51 ❑ Jan 2001 Cover: 1.99 **NM** value: **Cover or less**
Circ: Diamd. preorders: **9,750**
How Many Miles to Nowhere Atoll...? **A:** Neil Vokes **W:** Dean Motter

52 ❑ Feb 2001 Cover: 1.99 **NM** value: **Cover or less**
Circ: Diamd. preorders: **9,939**
A Death in the Family **A:** Aluir Amancio **W:** Mark Millar

53 ❑ Mar 2001 Cover: 1.99 **NM** value: **Cover or less**
Circ: Diamd. preorders: **9,378**
The Greatest Escape! **A:** Neil Vokes **W:** Mark Evanier

54 ❑ Apr 2001 Cover: 1.99 **NM** value: **Cover or less**
Circ: Diamd. preorders: **9,428**
Kryptonite No More!, Part 1 **A:** Aluir Amancio **W:** Dean Motter

55 ❑ May 2001 Cover: 1.99 **NM** value: **Cover or less**
Circ: Diamd. preorders: **9,394**
Kryptonite No More!, Part 2 **A:** Aluir Amancio **W:** Dean Motter

56 ❑ Jun 2001 Cover: 1.99 **NM** value: **Cover or less**
Circ: Diamd. preorders: **9,477**

57 ❑ Jul 2001 Cover: 1.99 **NM** value: **Cover or less**
Circ: Diamd. preorders: **9,268**

58 ❑ Aug 2001 Cover: 1.99 **NM** value: **Cover or less**
Circ: Diamd. preorders: **11,948**

59 ❑ Sep 2001 Cover: 1.99 **NM** value: **Cover or less**
Circ: Diamd. preorders: **9,936**

Anl 1 ❑ ca. 1997 Cover: 3.95 **NM** value: **Cover or less**
Circ: Diamd. preorders: **19,290**
Dark Planes Drifter • ties in with Adventures in the DC Universe Annual #1 and Batman and Robin Adventures Annual #2 **A:** Joe Staton **W:** Hilary J. Bader

Bk 1 ❑ Cover: 7.95 **NM** value: **Cover or less**
• Adventures of the Man of Steel; collects Superman Adventures #1-6

SE 1 ❑ Feb 1998 Cover: 2.95 **NM** value: **Cover or less**
Circ: Diamd. preorders: **20,370**
★ Versus Lobo.

SUPERMAN: A NATION DIVIDED — DC

1 ❑ Cover: 4.95 **NM** value: **Cover or less**
Circ: Diamd. preorders: **27,657**
No issue number. • prestige format. • Elseworlds; Superman in Civil War **A:** Eduardo Barreto **W:** Roger Stern

SUPERMAN & BATMAN: GENERATIONS — DC

1 ❑ Jan 1999 Cover: 4.95 **NM** value: **Cover or less**
Circ: Diamd. preorders: **43,998**
1939, The Vigilantes • Elseworlds story **A:** John Byrne **W:** John Byrne ★ Versus Ultra-Humanite. ★ Versus Lex Luthor. ★ Versus Joker.

2 ❑ Feb 1999 Cover: 4.95 **NM** value: **Cover or less**
Circ: Diamd. preorders: **38,547**
• Elseworlds story **A:** John Byrne **W:** John Byrne ★ Versus Bat-Mite. ★ Versus Joker Junior. ★ Versus Mxyzptlk.

3 ❑ Mar 1999 Cover: 4.95 **NM** value: **Cover or less**
Circ: Diamd. preorders: **38,380**
• Elseworlds story **A:** John Byrne **W:** John Byrne ★ Appearance of Ra's Al Ghul. ★ Death of Luthor.

4 ❑ Apr 1999 Cover: 4.95 **NM** value: **Cover or less**
Circ: Diamd. preorders: **37,160**
• Elseworlds story **A:** John Byrne **W:** John Byrne ★ Appearance of Lana Lang.

Bk 1 ❑ ca. 1999 Cover: 14.95 **NM** value: **Cover or less**
A: John Byrne **W:** John Byrne

SUPERMAN & BATMAN MAGAZINE — Welsh

1 ❑ Sum 1993 Cover: 2.95 **NM** value: **3.00**
Circ: CapCity orders: **6,800**
• bagged with poster

2 ❑ Fal 1993 Cover: 1.95 **NM** value: **2.00**
Circ: CapCity orders: **4,410**

3 ❑ Win 1993 Cover: 2.95 **NM** value: **3.00**
Circ: CapCity orders: **4,160**
• trading cards

4 ❑ Spr 1994 Cover: 1.95 **NM** value: **2.00**

5 ❑ Sum 1994 Cover: 1.95 **NM** value: **2.00**
• magazine.

7 ❑ Win 1995 Cover: 1.95 **NM** value: **2.00**
• magazine.

8 ❑ Spr 1995 Cover: 1.95 **NM** value: **2.00**
• magazine.

SUPERMAN AND BATMAN: WORLD'S FUNNEST — DC

Bat-Mite and Mr. Mxyzptlk, magical imps from the 5th Dimension, have always been more annoying than dangerous. But if they really cut loose, could even the World's Finest heroes stop them?

In this "Elseworlds" story their childish rivalry escalates when they accidentally kill Batman. Grief-stricken at the loss of his idol, Bat-Mite lashes out, killing Superman, too. Soon, the feuding maniacs have slaughtered all of DC's heroes and destroyed the entire universe. An inter-dimensional blood bath ensues, showcasing the many interpretations of the DC Universe, from the Golden Age worlds of the Justice Society and Shazam, to the grim futures of the Dark Knight and Kingdom Come. Eventually, every possible alternate universe, parallel world, and divergent timeline, including our "real" world, is obliterated.

This story was written by Evan Dorkin, of Milk & Cheese fame, and illustrated by over twenty artists, including Mike Allred, Frank Miller, and Alex Ross.

1 ❑ ca. 2000 Cover: 6.95 **NM** value: **Cover or less**
Circ: Diamd. preorders: **25,804** • **CGC:** 1 graded, best 9.9
Last Imp Standing **A:** Brian Bolland; Frank Miller; Frank Cho; Mike Allred; Step **W:** Evan Dorkin

SUPERMAN & BUGS BUNNY — DC

1 ❑ Jul 2000 Cover: 2.50 **NM** value: **Cover or less**
Circ: Diamd. preorders: **21,656**
A: Joe Staton; Tom Palmer; Mike DeCarlo **W:** Mark Evanier

2 ❑ Aug 2000 Cover: 2.50 **NM** value: **Cover or less**
Circ: Diamd. preorders: **19,362**
A: Joe Staton; Tom Palmer; Mike DeCarlo **W:** Mark Evanier

3 ❑ Sep 2000 Cover: 2.50 **NM** value: **Cover or less**
Circ: Diamd. preorders: **18,919**
The Duck Knight Returns! **A:** Joe Staton; Tom Palmer; Mike DeCarlo **W:** Mark Evanier

4 ❑ Oct 2000 Cover: 2.50 **NM** value: **Cover or less**
Circ: Diamd. preorders: **17,854**
Cwisis on Infinite Earths **A:** Joe Staton; Tom Palmer; Mike DeCarlo **W:** Mark Evanier

SUPERMAN AND SPIDER-MAN — Marvel

Bk 1 ❑ Cover: 2.50 **NM** value: **3.00**
• Warner mass-market paperback

SUPERMAN ARCHIVES — DC

1 ❑ Dec 1989 Cover: 39.95 **NM** value: **Cover or less**
Circ: CapCity orders: **4,200**
• reprint #1-4; 1939-1940

2 ❑ Dec 1990 Cover: 39.95 **NM** value: **Cover or less**
• reprint #5-8; 1940

3 ❑ Dec 1991 Cover: 39.95 **NM** value: **Cover or less**
• reprint #9-12; 1941

4 ❑ Cover: 49.95 **NM** value: **Cover or less**
• reprint #13-16; 1941-42

5 ❑ Cover: 49.95 **NM** value: **Cover or less**
• reprint #17-20

SUPERMAN: BIZARRO'S WORLD — DC

1 ❑ Cover: 9.95 **NM** value: **Cover or less**
• Collects story from Superman 87-88, Adventures of Superman #510, Action Comics #697, and Superman: the Man of Steel #32 **A:** Stuart Immonen; Jackson Guice; Barry Kitson; Jon Bogdanove **W:** Karl Kesel; Dan Jurgens; Louise Simonson; Roger Stern

SUPERMAN: DISTANT FIRES — DC

1 ❑ Feb 1998 Cover: 5.95 **NM** value: **Cover or less**
Circ: Diamd. preorders: **31,319**
No issue number. • prestige format. • Elseworlds

SUPERMAN/DOOMSDAY: HUNTER/PREY — DC

1 ❑ ca. 1994 Cover: 4.95 **NM** value: **6.00**
Circ: CapCity orders: **84,350** • **CGC:** 1 graded, best 9.8
• prestige format. **A:** Dan Jurgens **W:** Dan Jurgens

2 ❑ ca. 1994 Cover: 4.95 **NM** value: **6.00**
Circ: CapCity orders: **79,050** • **CGC:** 3 graded, best 9.8
• prestige format. ★ Origin of Doomsday.

3 ❑ ca. 1994 Cover: 4.95 **NM** value: **6.00**
Circ: CapCity orders: **73,500** • **CGC:** 1 graded, best 9.6
• prestige format. ★ Death of Doomsday.

Bk 1 ❑ Cover: 14.95 **NM** value: **Cover or less**

SUPERMAN: EMPEROR JOKER — DC

1 ❑ Oct 2000 Cover: 3.50 **NM** value: **Cover or less**
Circ: Diamd. preorders: **36,778**
It's a Joker World, Baby, We Just Live in It! **A:** Duncan Rouleau; Scott McDaniel; Carlo Barberi; Todd Nauck **W:** Jeph Loeb; Joe Kelly

SUPERMAN: ENDGAME — DC

1 ❑ Cover: 14.95 **NM** value: **Cover or less**
• Collects story from Superman Y2K #1, Superman (2nd Series) #154, Adventures of Superman #576, Superman: The Man of Steel #98, Action Comics #763

SUPERMAN: END OF THE CENTURY — DC

1 ❑ **NM** value: **5.95**

SUPERMAN: EXILE — DC

Bk 1 ❑ Cover: 14.95 **NM** value: **Cover or less**
• collects Action #643, Action Annual #2, Adventures of Superman #451-456, and Superman #28-30, 32, 33

SUPERMAN FAMILY, THE — DC

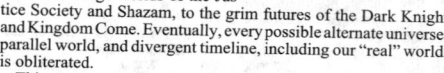

Why should Superman get all the publicity when everyone around him is just as brave and adventurous as the Man of Steel? This series treated readers to stories featuring Supergirl, Lois Lane, Lana Lang, Jimmy Olsen, and many others. The stories were great, showing that the characters could hold their own, though it didn't hurt that they could call on the old Supester when they got into trouble over their heads.

Originally this series was entitled "Superman's Pal Jimmy Olsen," but no doubt Lois Lane and friends wanted to get into the action as well. This series had some unique plots, including a marriage between Batman and Catwoman on Earth-2.

164 ❑ May 1974 Cover: 0.60 **NM** value: **15.00**
Circ: Statement: **178,478** • **CGC:** 8 graded, best 9.4
• Series continued from "Superman's Pal Jimmy Olsen"; Has 1973 Statement; avg print run 432,900; avg sales 194,398; avg subs 759; avg total paid 195,157; max existent 195,157; 55% of run returned

165 ❑ Jul 1974 Cover: 0.60 **NM** value: **12.00**
Circ: Statement: **178,478** • **CGC:** 5 graded, best 9.8
• reprints from Action #296, Jimmy Olsen #59, Lois Lane #47, Superboy #111, #133, and Superman #186

166 ❑ Sep 1974 Cover: 0.60 **NM** value: **12.00**
Circ: Statement: **178,478** • **CGC:** 2 graded, best 9.0

167 ❑ Nov 1974 Cover: 0.60 **NM** value: **12.00**
Circ: Statement: **178,478** • **CGC:** 3 graded, best 9.6

168 ❑ Jan 1975 Cover: 0.60 **NM** value: **12.00**
Circ: Statement: **169,000** • **CGC:** 1 graded, best 2.5

169 ❑ Mar 1975 Cover: 0.60 **NM** value: **12.00**
Circ: Statement: **169,000** • **CGC:** 1 graded, best 8.5

170 ❑ May 1975 Cover: 0.50 **NM** value: **12.00**
Circ: Statement: **169,000**

171 ❑ Jul 1975 Cover: 0.50 **NM** value: **10.00**
Circ: Statement: **169,000**
• Has 1974 Statement; avg print run 400,413; avg sales 176,286; avg subs 2,192; avg total paid 178,478; max existent 178,478; 55% of run returned

172 ❑ Sep 1975 Cover: 0.50 **NM** value: **10.00**
Circ: Statement: **169,000** • **CGC:** 1 graded, best 9.4

173 ❑ Nov 1975 Cover: 0.50 **NM** value: **10.00**
Circ: Statement: **169,000**

174 ❑ Jan 1976 Cover: 0.50 **NM** value: **10.00**
Circ: Statement: **163,000**

175 ❑ Mar 1976 Cover: 0.50 **NM** value: **10.00**
Circ: Statement: **163,000**

176 ❑ May 1976 Cover: 0.50 **NM** value: **10.00**
Circ: Statement: **163,000** • **CGC:** 1 graded, best 9.6

177 ❑ Jul 1976 Cover: 0.50 **NM** value: **10.00**
Circ: Statement: **163,000**
• reprints from Jimmy Olsen #74 and Lois Lane #53; Has 1975 Statement; avg print run 361,000; avg sales 167,000; avg subs 2,000; avg total paid 169,000; max existent 169,000; 52% of run returned

178 ❑ Sep 1976 Cover: 0.50 **NM** value: **5.00**
Circ: Statement: **163,000**

179 ❑ Oct 1976 Cover: 0.50 **NM** value: **5.00**
Circ: Statement: **163,000**

180 ❑ Nov 1976 Cover: 0.50 **NM** value: **5.00**
Circ: Statement: **163,000**

181 ❑ Jan 1977 Cover: 0.50 **NM** value: **3.50**
Circ: Statement: **141,557**

182 ❑ Apr 1977 Cover: 1.00 **NM** value: **3.50**
Circ: Statement: **141,557**

183 ❑ Jun 1977 Cover: 1.00 **NM** value: **3.50**
Circ: Statement: **141,557**
• Has 1976 Statement; avg print run 360,000; avg sales 159,000; avg subs 4,000; avg total paid 163,000; max existent 163,000; 54% of run returned

184 ❑ Aug 1977 Cover: 1.00 **NM** value: **3.50**
Circ: Statement: **141,557**
★ Versus Prankster.

Other grades: Multiply prices above by **1.5 for Mint • 2/3 for Very Fine • 1/3 for Fine • 1/5 for Very Good • 1/8 for Good**

185 ☐ Oct 1977 Cover: 1.00 **NM** value: **3.50**
Circ: Statement: **141,557**

186 ☐ Dec 1977 Cover: 1.00 **NM** value: **3.50**
Circ: Statement: **141,557**
★ Appearance of Earth-2 Superman.

187 ☐ Feb 1978 Cover: 1.00 **NM** value: **3.50**
Circ: Statement: **117,594**
★ Appearance of Earth-2 Superman.

188 ☐ Apr 1978 Cover: 1.00 **NM** value: **3.50**
Circ: Statement: **117,594**

189 ☐ Jun 1978 Cover: 1.00 **NM** value: **3.50**
Circ: Statement: **117,594**
• Has 1977 Statement; avg print run 361,349; avg sales 138,829; avg subs 2,728; avg total paid 141,557; samples 400; office use 131; max existent 141,688; 61% of run returned

190 ☐ Aug 1978 Cover: 1.00 **NM** value: **3.50**
Circ: Statement: **117,594**

191 ☐ Oct 1978 Cover: 1.00 **NM** value: **3.50**
Circ: Statement: **117,594**

192 ☐ Dec 1978 Cover: 1.00 **NM** value: **3.50**
Circ: Statement: **117,594**

193 ☐ Feb 1979 Cover: 1.00 **NM** value: **3.50**
Circ: Statement: **76,693**

194 ☐ Apr 1979 Cover: 1.00 **NM** value: **3.50**
Circ: Statement: **76,693**
A: Marshall Rogers ★ Versus Jimmy clones.

195 ☐ Jun 1979 Cover: 1.00 **NM** value: **3.50**
Circ: Statement: **76,693**
• Has 1978 Statement; avg print run 304,142; avg sales 115,527; avg subs 2,067; avg total paid 117,594; samples 105; office use 2,380; max existent 119,974; 61% of run returned

196 ☐ Aug 1979 Cover: 1.00 **NM** value: **3.50**
Circ: Statement: **76,693**

197 ☐ Oct 1979 Cover: 1.00 **NM** value: **3.50**
Circ: Statement: **76,693**

198 ☐ Dec 1979 Cover: 1.00 **NM** value: **3.50**
Circ: Statement: **76,693**

199 ☐ Feb 1980 Cover: 1.00 **NM** value: **3.50**
Circ: Statement: **82,076**

200 ☐ Apr 1980 Cover: 1.00 **NM** value: **3.50**
Circ: Statement: **82,076**
• Imaginary Story

201 ☐ Jun 1980 Cover: 1.00 **NM** value: **3.00**
Circ: Statement: **82,076**
• Has 1979 Statement; avg print run 220,383; avg sales 75,519; avg subs 1,174; avg total paid 76,693; samples 0; office use 127; max existent 76,820; 65% of run returned

202 ☐ Aug 1980 Cover: 1.00 **NM** value: **3.00**
Circ: Statement: **82,076**

203 ☐ Oct 1980 Cover: 1.00 **NM** value: **3.00**
Circ: Statement: **82,076**
★ 1st Appearance of Lana Lang.

204 ☐ Dec 1980 Cover: 1.00 **NM** value: **3.00**
Circ: Statement: **82,076**
★ Versus Enchantress.

205 ☐ Feb 1981 Cover: 1.00 **NM** value: **3.00**
Circ: Statement: **68,561**
★ 1st Appearance of H.I.V.E.. ★ Versus Enchantress.

206 ☐ Apr 1981 Cover: 1.00 **NM** value: **3.00**
Circ: Statement: **68,561**
★ Appearance of Lesla-Lar.

207 ☐ Jun 1981 Cover: 1.00 **NM** value: **3.00**
Circ: Statement: **68,561**
• Has 1980 Statement; avg print run 236,369; avg sales 80,899; avg subs 1,177; avg total paid 82,076; max existent 82,076; 64% of run returned ★ Appearance of Legion. ★ Versus Universo.

208 ☐ Jul 1981 Cover: 1.00 **NM** value: **3.00**
Circ: Statement: **68,561**
• Supergirl relocates to New York

209 ☐ Aug 1981 Cover: 1.00 **NM** value: **3.00**
Circ: Statement: **68,561**

210 ☐ Sep 1981 Cover: 1.00 **NM** value: **3.00**
Circ: Statement: **68,561**

211 ☐ Oct 1981 Cover: 1.00 **NM** value: **3.00**
Circ: Statement: **68,561**

212 ☐ Nov 1981 Cover: 1.00 **NM** value: **3.00**
Circ: Statement: **68,561**

213 ☐ Dec 1981 Cover: 1.00 **NM** value: **3.00**
Circ: Statement: **68,561**
★ 1st Appearance of Insect Queen (Lana Lang).

214 ☐ Jan 1982 Cover: 1.00 **NM** value: **3.00**

215 ☐ Feb 1982 Cover: 1.00 **NM** value: **3.00**

216 ☐ Mar 1982 Cover: 1.00 **NM** value: **3.00**

217 ☐ Apr 1982 Cover: 1.00 **NM** value: **3.00**

218 ☐ May 1982 Cover: 1.00 **NM** value: **3.00**
• Has 1981 Statement; avg print run 226,140; avg sales 66,991; avg subs 1,570; avg total paid 68,561; samples 17; office use 260; max existent 68,821; 69% of run returned

219 ☐ Jun 1982 Cover: 1.00 **NM** value: **3.00**
★ Versus Master Jailer.

220 ☐ Jul 1982 Cover: 1.00 **NM** value: **3.00**
• **CGC:** 1 graded, best 9.4
★ Versus Master Jailer.

221 ☐ Aug 1982 Cover: 1.00 **NM** value: **3.00**
★ Versus Master Jailer.

222 ☐ Sep 1982 Cover: 1.00 **NM** value: **3.00**
final issue.

SUPERMAN/FANTASTIC FOUR — DC

1 ☐ Cover: 9.95 **NM** value: **Cover or less**
A: Dan Jurgens **W:** Dan Jurgens

SUPERMAN FOR ALL SEASONS — DC

1 ☐ Sep 1998 Cover: 4.95 **NM** value: **Cover or less**
Circ: Diamd. preorders: **47,336** • **CGC:** 4 graded, best 9.8
• prestige format. 📖 Spring • Spring **A:** Tim Sale **W:** Jeph Loeb

2 ☐ Oct 1998 Cover: 4.95 **NM** value: **Cover or less**
Circ: Diamd. preorders: **41,722**
• prestige format. 📖 Summer • Summer **A:** Tim Sale **W:** Jeph Loeb

3 ☐ Nov 1998 Cover: 4.95 **NM** value: **Cover or less**
Circ: Diamd. preorders: **42,613**
• prestige format. 📖 Fall • Fall **A:** Tim Sale **W:** Jeph Loeb

4 ☐ Dec 1998 Cover: 4.95 **NM** value: **Cover or less**
Circ: Diamd. preorders: **43,354**
• prestige format. 📖 Winter • Winter **A:** Tim Sale **W:** Jeph Loeb

SUPERMAN FOR EARTH — DC

1 ☐ Apr 1991 Cover: 4.95 **NM** value: **Cover or less**
Circ: CapCity orders: **16,000**
No issue number. **C:** Joe Orlando

SUPERMAN FOREVER — DC

1 ☐ Jun 1998 Cover: 4.95 **NM** value: **5.50**
Circ: Diamd. preorders: **27,826** • **CGC:** 1 graded, best 9.9
• newsstand edition. • Superman returns to normal powers **A:** Norm Breyfogle; Scot Eaton; Kieron Dwyer; Anthony Williams; Stuart Immonen; Steve Yeowell; John Byrne; Paul Ryan; Val Semeiks; Dick Giordano; Dan Jurgens; Tom Grummettt; Jon Bogdanove **W:** Karl Kesel; Stuart Immonen; Dan Jurgens; Jon Bogdanove; Louise Simonson

1/Aut ☐ Jun 1998 Cover: 4.95 **NM** value: **30.00**
A: Norm Breyfogle; Scot Eaton; Kieron Dwyer; Anthony Williams; Stuart Immonen; Steve Yeowell; John Byrne; Paul Ryan; Val Semeiks; Dick Giordano; Dan Jurgens; Tom Grummettt; Jon Bogdanove **W:** Karl Kesel; Stuart Immonen; Dan Jurgens; Jon Bogdanove; Louise Simonson

1/SC ☐ Jun 1998 Cover: 5.95 **NM** value: **7.00**
Circ: Diamd. preorders: **113,791** • **CGC:** 9 graded, best 9.8
lenticular animation cover. • prestige format. • Superman returns to normal powers

SUPER MANGA BLAST! — Dark Horse

Dark Horse Comics has a long history of importing such great Japanese comics as Akira and Lone Wolf and Cub. In Super Manga Blast, it continued to bring Japanese manga to a larger audience in this anthology series which showcases a variety of popular stories.

In a format similar to Pulp from Viz, Dark Horse presents here some of Japan's most popular titles are translated into English for the first time and presented in a thick, traditional Japanese format, weighing in at over 120 pages per issue.

Highlights include early Oh My Goddess! stories not included in the original series from Dark Horse; hilarious What's Michael? shorts, and such science fiction epics as Shadow Star and Seraphic Feather.

1 ☐ Mar 2000 Cover: 4.95 **NM** value: **Cover or less**
Circ: Diamd. preorders: **11,929**

2 ☐ Apr 2000 Cover: 4.95 **NM** value: **Cover or less**
Circ: Diamd. preorders: **9,578**

3 ☐ May 2000 Cover: 4.95 **NM** value: **Cover or less**
Circ: Diamd. preorders: **8,926**

4 ☐ Jun 2000 Cover: 4.95 **NM** value: **Cover or less**
Circ: Diamd. preorders: **9,047**
📖 3x3 Eyes; What's Michael; Shadow Star; Seraphic Feather; Oh My Goddess! **A:** Yuzo Takada; Kosuke Fujishima; Hiroyuki Uttane; Makoto Kobayashi; Mohiro Kitoh; Yo Morimoto **W:** Yuzo Takada; Kosuke Fujishima; Hiroyuki Uttane; Makoto Kobayashi; Mohiro Kitoh; Yo Morimoto

5 ☐ Jul 2000 Cover: 4.95 **NM** value: **Cover or less**
Circ: Diamd. preorders: **8,346**

6 ☐ Aug 2000 Cover: 4.95 **NM** value: **Cover or less**
Circ: Diamd. preorders: **8,618**

7 ☐ Sep 2000 Cover: 4.95 **NM** value: **Cover or less**
Circ: Diamd. preorders: **8,227**

8 ☐ Nov 2000 Cover: 4.95 **NM** value: **Cover or less**
Circ: Diamd. preorders: **9,145**

9 ☐ Jan 2001 Cover: 4.95 **NM** value: **Cover or less**
Circ: Diamd. preorders: **7,794**

10 ☐ Feb 2001 Cover: 4.99 **NM** value: **Cover or less**
Circ: Diamd. preorders: **7,725**
📖 Seraphic Feather; Oh My Goddess!; 3x3 Eyes; What's Michael?; Shadow Star **A:** Yuzo Takada; Kosuke Fujishima; Hiroyuki Utatane; Makoto Kobayashi; Mohiro Kitoh; Yo Morimoto **W:** Yuzo Takada; Kosuke Fujishima; Hiroyuki Utatane; Makoto Kobayashi; Mohiro Kitoh; Yo Morimoto

11 ☐ Mar 2001 Cover: 4.99 **NM** value: **Cover or less**
Circ: Diamd. preorders: **7,596**

12 ☐ May 2001 Cover: 4.99 **NM** value: **Cover or less**
Circ: Diamd. preorders: **7,668**
📖 Club 9; 3x3 Eyes; What's Michael?; Shadowstar; Seraphic Feather; Oh My Goddess! **A:** Yuzo Takada; Kosuke Fujishima; Hiroyuki Utatane; Makoto Kobayashi; Mihiro Kitoh; Yo Morimoto **W:** Yuzo Takada; Kosuke Fujishima; Hiroyuki Utatane; Makoto Kobayashi; Mihiro Kitoh; Yo Morimoto

13 ☐ Jun 2001 Cover: 4.99 **NM** value: **Cover or less**
Circ: Diamd. preorders: **7,615**

14 ☐ Jul 2001 Cover: 4.99 **NM** value: **Cover or less**
Circ: Diamd. preorders: **7,850**

SUPERMAN GALLERY, THE — DC

1 ☐ ca. 1993 Cover: 2.95 **NM** value: **Cover or less**
Circ: CapCity orders: **36,550**

SUPERMAN/GEN13 — WildStorm

1 ☐ Jun 2000 Cover: 2.50 **NM** value: **Cover or less**
Circ: Diamd. preorders: **38,211**
📖 The Never-Ending Prattle **A:** Lee Bermejo **W:** Adam Hughes

1/A ☐ Jun 2000 Cover: 2.50 **NM** value: **Cover or less**
Fairchild opening shirt to show Supergirl costume on cover. 📖 The Never-Ending Prattle **A:** Lee Bermejo **W:** Adam Hughes

2 ☐ Jul 2000 Cover: 2.50 **NM** value: **Cover or less**
Circ: Diamd. preorders: **31,998**
Supergirl/Fairchild cover. **A:** Lee Bermejo **W:** Adam Hughes

2/A ☐ Jul 2000 Cover: 2.50 **NM** value: **Cover or less**
Large figures looking down on cover. **A:** Lee Bermejo **W:** Adam Hughes

3 ☐ Aug 2000 Cover: 2.50 **NM** value: **Cover or less**
Circ: Diamd. preorders: **31,952**
A: Lee Bermejo **W:** Adam Hughes

SUPERMAN (GIVEAWAYS) — DC

1 ☐ **NM** value: **1.00**
• game giveaway.

2 ☐ **NM** value: **1.00**
• Pizza Hut

3 ☐ Jul 1980 **NM** value: **1.00**
• Radio Shack

4 ☐ **NM** value: **1.00**
• Radio Shack

5 ☐ **NM** value: **1.00**
• Radio Shack

SUPERMAN, INC. — DC

1 ☐ Jan 2000 Cover: 6.95 **NM** value: **Cover or less**
Circ: Diamd. preorders: **20,056**
A: Jose Luis Garcia-Lopez **W:** Steve Vance

SUPERMAN IN EUROPA — DC

Bk 1 ☐ Cover: 9.95 **NM** value: **Cover or less**

SUPERMAN IN THE SEVENTIES — DC

Bk 1 ☐ Cover: 19.95 **NM** value: **Cover or less**
📖 Make Way for Captain Thunder!; Judge, Jury…And No Justice!; The Man Who Murdered the Earth!; The Man Who Murdered Metropolis!; The Cha • Collects 1970s Superman adventures **A:** Bob Oksner; Murphy Anderson; Carmine Infantino; Dick Giordano; Jack Kirby; Curt Swan; Ross Andru; Jose Luis Garcia-Lopez; Werner Roth; Elliot S! Maggin **W:** Bob Oksner; Jack Kirby; Len Wein; Cary Bates; Elliot S! Maggin; Robert Kanigher

SUPERMAN IN THE SIXTIES — DC

Bk 1 ☐ Cover: 19.95 **NM** value: **Cover or less**
No issue number. • Trade Paperback. • collects 1960s Superman adventures

SUPERMAN IV MOVIE SPECIAL — DC

1 ☐ Oct 1987 Cover: 2.00 **NM** value: **Cover or less**
Circ: CapCity orders: **12,500**

SUPERMAN: KAL — DC

1 ☐ Cover: 5.95 **NM** value: **Cover or less**
Circ: CapCity orders: **18,975**
No issue number. • prestige format one-shot

SUPERMAN: KING OF THE WORLD — DC

1 ☐ Jun 1999 Cover: 3.95 **NM** value: **Cover or less**
📖 King of the World • ▲1999-22 **A:** Dougie Braithwaite **W:** Karl Kesel

1/GO ☐ Jun 1999 Cover: 4.95 **NM** value: **Cover or less**
enhanced cardstock cover. 📖 King of the World • ▲1999-22 **A:** Dougie Braithwaite **W:** Karl Kesel

SUPERMAN: KRISIS OF THE KRIMSON KRYPTONITE — DC

1 ☐ Cover: 12.95 **NM** value: **Cover or less**
• Reprints story from Advemtures of Superman #472-473, Action Comics #659-660, Starman #28, Superman (2nd Series) #49-50 **A:** Jerry Ordway; Dave Hoover; John Byrne; Dan Jurgens; Curt Swan; Kerry Gammill; Bob McLeod **W:** Jerry Ordway; Dan Jurgens; Roger Stern

SUPERMAN: LAST SON OF EARTH — DC

1 ☐ Sep 2000 Cover: 5.95 **NM** value: **Cover or less**
Circ: Diamd. preorders: **23,892**
A: Doug Wheatley **W:** Steve Gerber

2 ☐ Oct 2000 Cover: 5.95 **NM** value: **Cover or less**
Circ: Diamd. preorders: **20,740**
A: Doug Wheatley **W:** Steve Gerber

SUPERMAN: LEX 2000 — DC

Savior of Metropolis, rebuilder of Gotham, genius, industrialist- just about everyone likes Lex Luthor. So who better to run this great nation of ours than someone who promises to get rid of fossil fuel burning autos and put a flying car in every garage? Who better to become President of these United States?

Some people know him better. These are people who have fought Luthor at every turn and know what he is capable of. And to see one of the most devious, self-centered uncaught criminals of our time in the seat of the highest office in the land is a terrifying prospect. Batman fears the worst and attempts to combat his greatest concern while Superman is torn between his job to impartially report the news and his knowledge that America will be in for some hard times if Luthor takes office.

Superman: Lex 2000 gives us some behind-the-scene looks at one of the most unusual elections in recorded history- candidate Lex Luthor's road to the White House.

CGC-graded: Multiply prices above by **33 for 9.9 M • 16 for 9.8 NM/M • 7 for 9.6 NM+ • 5 for 9.4 NM • 2.5 for 9.2 NM- • 1.5 for 9.0 VF/NM**

1 ❑ Jan 2001 Cover: 3.50 **NM** value: **Cover or less**
Circ: Diamd. preorders: **35,409**
📖 Triumph over Tragedy; One or the Other; Where Were You?; He Knows; Lana's Story; Word Around Metropolis **A:** Doug Mahnke; Tony Harris; Dwayne Turner; Ed McGuinness; Todd Nauck **W:** Jeph Loeb; Greg Rucka

SUPERMAN: LOIS LANE — DC

1 ❑ Jun 1998 Cover: 1.95 **NM** value: **Cover or less**
Circ: Diamd. preorders: **41,317**
One-shot. • Girlfrenzy **A:** Amanda Conner **W:** Barbara Kesel

SUPERMAN/MADMAN HULLABALOO, THE — Dark Horse / DC

1 ❑ Jun 1997 Cover: 2.95 **NM** value: **Cover or less**
Circ: Diamd. preorders: **46,487**
📖 Man and Super-Madman! • crossover with DC **A:** Mike Allred **W:** Mike Allred

2 ❑ Jul 1997 Cover: 2.95 **NM** value: **Cover or less**
Circ: Diamd. preorders: **39,610**
📖 Hot Dang! Yin Yang! • crossover with DC **A:** Mike Allred **W:** Mike Allred

3 ❑ Aug 1997 Cover: 2.95 **NM** value: **Cover or less**
Circ: Diamd. preorders: **36,815**
• crossover with DC **A:** Mike Allred **W:** Mike Allred

Bk 1❑ Cover: 8.95 **NM** value: **Cover or less**
• Collects Superman/Madman Hullabaloo #1-3 **A:** Mike Allred **W:** Mike Allred

SUPERMAN MEETS THE QUIK BUNNY — DC

1 ❑ **NM** value: **1.00**
No issue number. • promotional giveaway from Nestle. 📖 Quik Thinking **A:** Carmine Infantino; Dick Giordano **W:** Mike Carlin

SUPERMAN METROPOLIS SECRET FILES — DC

1 ❑ Jul 2000 Cover: 4.95 **NM** value: **Cover or less**
📖 Metropolica; Fortress of Solitude; Municipal Bonds; The City of Tomorrow; Unbearable Brightness of Being; 5th Dimension Fun **A:** German Garcia; Cully Hamner; Pascual Ferry; Doug Mahnke; Chuck Wojtkiewicz; Stuart Immonen; Howard Porter; Mike McKone; Duncan Rouleau; Coy Turnbull; Jeff Matsuda; Pablo Raimondi; Ed McGuinness; Louis Small Jr.; Kano **W:** Jeph Loeb; Joe Kelly; Mark Schultz

SUPERMAN MOVIE SPECIAL — DC

1 ❑ ca. 1983 Cover: 1.00 **NM** value: **2.00**

SUPERMAN MOVIE SPECIAL, THE — DC

1 ❑ Sep 1983 Cover: 1.00 **NM** value: **2.00**
Photo cover. • adapts Superman III **A:** Gray Morrow; Curt Swan

SUPERMAN: NO LIMITS! — DC

1 ❑ Cover: 14.95 **NM** value: **Cover or less**
• Reprints from Action Comics #760-761, Adventures of Superman #574, Superman #151-153, Superman: The Man of Steel #95-97 **A:** Mike McKone **W:** Jeph Loeb

SUPERMAN: PEACE ON EARTH — DC

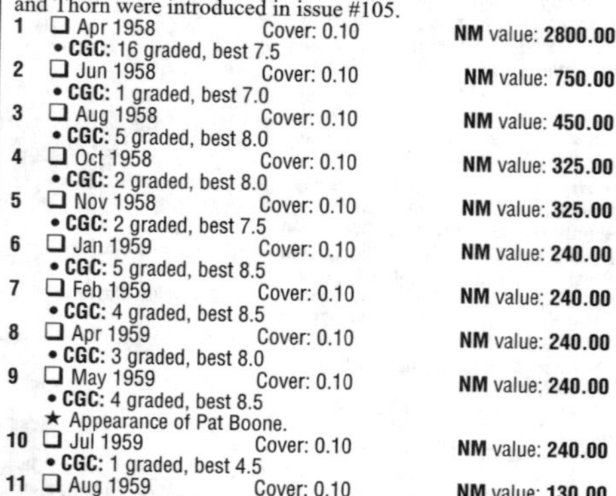

This book is a winner in every way. Alex Ross's gorgeous painted artwork is coupled with a thoughtful script by Paul Dini, making this a perfect holiday tale.

As Superman prepared to celebrate Christmas, his attention turned to the hungry people both in Metropolis and around the world. He faced the age-old dilemma: in the midst of such riches and power, why couldn't the hungry be fed? He knew from the start that he alone couldn't solve the problem, but he hoped that by launching an all-out effort to transport unneeded grain to the needy around the world, he might kick start a worldwide effort that could at last solve the problem. In the course of his one-man war on hunger, he learned two powerful lessons. Most hunger is not due purely to a lack of food, but to the human elements which prevent it from getting to those in need. He also learned that a man who is given food eats that day. When he learns to grow it, he eats for a lifetime.

1 ❑ Jan 1999 Cover: 9.95 **NM** value: **Cover or less**
• Oversized. 📖 Peace on Earth **A:** Alex Ross **W:** Paul Dini

1/Aut❑ Cover: 22.95 **NM** value: **Cover or less**
• Oversized. 📖 Peace on Earth **A:** Alex Ross **W:** Paul Dini

SUPERMAN PLUS — DC

1 ❑ Feb 1997 Cover: 2.95 **NM** value: **Cover or less**
Circ: Diamd. preorders: **49,834**
📖 Yesterday, Today, and Tomorrow **A:** Bernard Chang **W:** Tom Peyer ★ Appearance of Legion.

SUPERMAN RED/SUPERMAN BLUE — DC

1 ❑ Feb 1998 Cover: 3.95 **NM** value: **Cover or less**
Circ: Diamd. preorders: **25,855**
📖 Superman Red/Superman Blue **A:** Stuart Immonen; Paul Ryan; Ron Frenz; Tom Grummettt; Jon Bogdanove **W:** Dan Jurgens ★ 1st Appearance of Superman Red.

Dlx 1❑ Feb 1998 Cover: 4.95 **NM** value: **Cover or less**
Circ: Diamd. preorders: **79,720** • **CGC:** 1 graded, best 9.4
No issue number. one-shot with 3-D cover. • Superman splits into two beings

SUPERMAN: SAVE THE PLANET — DC

1 ❑ Oct 1998 Cover: 2.95 **NM** value: **Cover or less**
Circ: Diamd. preorders: **13,904**
• Daily Planet sold to Lex Luthor

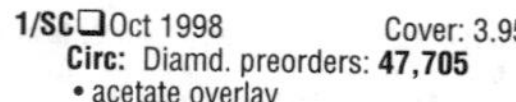

1/SC❑ Oct 1998 Cover: 3.95 **NM** value: **Cover or less**
Circ: Diamd. preorders: **47,705**
• acetate overlay

SUPERMAN: SECRET FILES — DC

1 ❑ Jan 1998 Cover: 4.95 **NM** value: **Cover or less**
Circ: Diamd. preorders: **42,549**
📖 Secret Origin; Jimmy Olsen's Past Lives; Daily Planet; Whitty Banter's "Super 8"; National Whisper; Superman's Fortress; Who watched Metropolis during Superman's Honeymoon?; What Happened During Lois & Clark's Honeymoon? • background material **A:** Scot Eaton; Steve Lieber; Kieron Dwyer; Stuart Immonen; Jerry Ordway; Dan Jurgens; Peter Krause; Tom Grummettt; Jon Bogdanove; Georgés Jeanty **W:** Karl Kesel; Stuart Immonen; Dan Jurgens; Scott Beatty; Kevin Dooley; Whitty Banter ★ Origin of Superman.

2 ❑ May 1999 Cover: 4.95 **NM** value: **Cover or less**
Circ: Diamd. preorders: **24,224**
• background material

SUPERMAN'S GIRL FRIEND LOIS LANE — DC

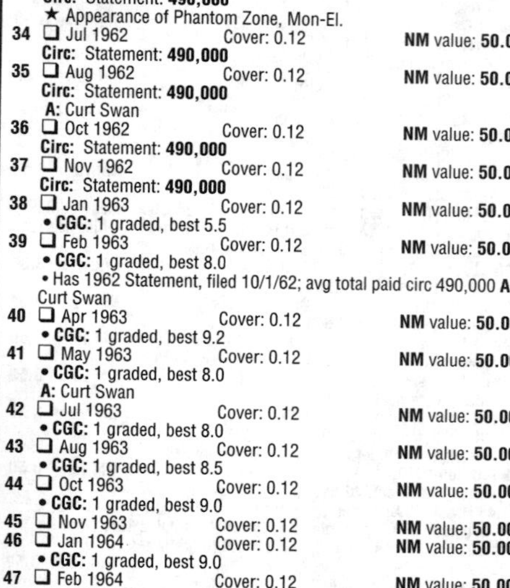

Lois Lane got her first taste of the spotlight in Showcase #9-10 before going on to star in this long-running title. Lois may have been a star reporter for the Daily Planet, but in this long-running series, her real career was Superman. Her entire life seemed to be centered around finding out his secret identity and in luring him into proposing marriage. She tried no end of schemes to accomplish these ends, including trying to gain super-powers so that she could truly become Mrs. Superman.

It seemed that anytime another woman made an appearance in this series, it would inevitably end in a catfight. Naturally, DC took every opportunity to exploit this, regularly featuring Catwoman, Wonder Woman, Lori Lemaris, and other vexing vixens. Things got even worse for Lois when Rose and Thorn were introduced in issue #105.

1 ❑ Apr 1958 Cover: 0.10 **NM** value: **2800.00**
• **CGC:** 16 graded, best 7.5

2 ❑ Jun 1958 Cover: 0.10 **NM** value: **750.00**
• **CGC:** 1 graded, best 7.0

3 ❑ Aug 1958 Cover: 0.10 **NM** value: **450.00**
• **CGC:** 5 graded, best 8.0

4 ❑ Oct 1958 Cover: 0.10 **NM** value: **325.00**
• **CGC:** 2 graded, best 8.0

5 ❑ Nov 1958 Cover: 0.10 **NM** value: **325.00**
• **CGC:** 2 graded, best 7.5

6 ❑ Jan 1959 Cover: 0.10 **NM** value: **240.00**
• **CGC:** 5 graded, best 8.5

7 ❑ Feb 1959 Cover: 0.10 **NM** value: **240.00**
• **CGC:** 4 graded, best 8.5

8 ❑ Apr 1959 Cover: 0.10 **NM** value: **240.00**
• **CGC:** 3 graded, best 8.0

9 ❑ May 1959 Cover: 0.10 **NM** value: **240.00**
• **CGC:** 4 graded, best 8.5
★ Appearance of Pat Boone.

10 ❑ Jul 1959 Cover: 0.10 **NM** value: **240.00**
• **CGC:** 1 graded, best 4.5

11 ❑ Aug 1959 Cover: 0.10 **NM** value: **130.00**
• **CGC:** 4 graded, best 8.5

12 ❑ Oct 1959 Cover: 0.10 **NM** value: **130.00**
• **CGC:** 1 graded, best 6.0

13 ❑ Nov 1959 Cover: 0.10 **NM** value: **130.00**
• **CGC:** 1 graded, best 4.0

14 ❑ Jan 1960 Cover: 0.10 **NM** value: **130.00**
Circ: Statement: **458,000** • **CGC:** 1 graded, best 4.5

15 ❑ Feb 1960 Cover: 0.10 **NM** value: **130.00**
Circ: Statement: **458,000** • **CGC:** 1 graded, best 5.0

16 ❑ Apr 1960 Cover: 0.10 **NM** value: **130.00**
Circ: Statement: **458,000** • **CGC:** 2 graded, best 9.0

17 ❑ May 1960 Cover: 0.10 **NM** value: **130.00**
Circ: Statement: **458,000** • **CGC:** 2 graded, best 7.0

18 ❑ Jul 1960 Cover: 0.10 **NM** value: **130.00**
Circ: Statement: **458,000** • **CGC:** 1 graded, best 5.0

19 ❑ Aug 1960 Cover: 0.10 **NM** value: **130.00**
Circ: Statement: **458,000** • **CGC:** 2 graded, best 9.0

20 ❑ Oct 1960 Cover: 0.10 **NM** value: **130.00**
Circ: Statement: **458,000** • **CGC:** 3 graded, best 8.5

21 ❑ Nov 1960 Cover: 0.10 **NM** value: **90.00**
Circ: Statement: **458,000** • **CGC:** 1 graded, best 3.5

22 ❑ Jan 1961 Cover: 0.10 **NM** value: **90.00**
Circ: Statement: **515,000** • **CGC:** 2 graded, best 7.5

23 ❑ Feb 1961 Cover: 0.10 **NM** value: **90.00**
Circ: Statement: **515,000** • **CGC:** 2 graded, best 9.0
• Has 1960 Statement; avg total paid circ 458,000

24 ❑ Apr 1961 Cover: 0.10 **NM** value: **90.00**
Circ: Statement: **515,000** • **CGC:** 2 graded, best 7.0

25 ❑ May 1961 Cover: 0.10 **NM** value: **90.00**
Circ: Statement: **515,000** • **CGC:** 3 graded, best 7.0

26 ❑ Jul 1961 Cover: 0.10 **NM** value: **90.00**
Circ: Statement: **515,000**

27 ❑ Aug 1961 Cover: 0.10 **NM** value: **90.00**
Circ: Statement: **515,000** • **CGC:** 1 graded, best 5.0

28 ❑ Oct 1961 Cover: 0.10 **NM** value: **90.00**
Circ: Statement: **515,000** • **CGC:** 2 graded, best 8.0

29 ❑ Nov 1961 Cover: 0.10 **NM** value: **90.00**
Circ: Statement: **515,000** • **CGC:** 2 graded, best 9.4

30 ❑ Jan 1962 Cover: 0.10 **NM** value: **50.00**
Circ: Statement: **490,000** • **CGC:** 1 graded, best 6.5

31 ❑ Feb 1962 Cover: 0.12 **NM** value: **50.00**
Circ: Statement: **490,000** • **CGC:** 1 graded, best 5.5
• Has 1961 Statement; avg total paid circ 515,000

32 ❑ Apr 1962 Cover: 0.12 **NM** value: **50.00**
Circ: Statement: **490,000**

33 ❑ May 1962 Cover: 0.12 **NM** value: **50.00**
Circ: Statement: **490,000**
★ Appearance of Phantom Zone, Mon-El.

34 ❑ Jul 1962 Cover: 0.12 **NM** value: **50.00**
Circ: Statement: **490,000**

35 ❑ Aug 1962 Cover: 0.12 **NM** value: **50.00**
Circ: Statement: **490,000**
A: Curt Swan

36 ❑ Oct 1962 Cover: 0.12 **NM** value: **50.00**
Circ: Statement: **490,000**

37 ❑ Nov 1962 Cover: 0.12 **NM** value: **50.00**
Circ: Statement: **490,000**

38 ❑ Jan 1963 Cover: 0.12 **NM** value: **50.00**
• **CGC:** 1 graded, best 5.5

39 ❑ Feb 1963 Cover: 0.12 **NM** value: **50.00**
• **CGC:** 1 graded, best 8.0
• Has 1962 Statement, filed 10/1/62; avg total paid circ 490,000 **A:** Curt Swan

40 ❑ Apr 1963 Cover: 0.12 **NM** value: **50.00**
• **CGC:** 1 graded, best 9.2

41 ❑ May 1963 Cover: 0.12 **NM** value: **50.00**
• **CGC:** 1 graded, best 8.0
A: Curt Swan

42 ❑ Jul 1963 Cover: 0.12 **NM** value: **50.00**
• **CGC:** 1 graded, best 8.0

43 ❑ Aug 1963 Cover: 0.12 **NM** value: **50.00**
• **CGC:** 1 graded, best 8.5

44 ❑ Oct 1963 Cover: 0.12 **NM** value: **50.00**
• **CGC:** 1 graded, best 9.0

45 ❑ Nov 1963 Cover: 0.12 **NM** value: **50.00**

46 ❑ Jan 1964 Cover: 0.12 **NM** value: **50.00**
• **CGC:** 1 graded, best 9.0

47 ❑ Feb 1964 Cover: 0.12 **NM** value: **50.00**
• Has 1963 Statement, filed 10/1/63; no circ figures published

48 ❑ Apr 1964 Cover: 0.12 **NM** value: **50.00**
• **CGC:** 1 graded, best 8.5

49 ❑ May 1964 Cover: 0.12 **NM** value: **50.00**

50 ❑ Jul 1964 Cover: 0.12 **NM** value: **50.00**
• **CGC:** 2 graded, best 9.2
📖 Lois Lane's Luckiest Day

51 ❑ Aug 1964 Cover: 0.12 **NM** value: **35.00**
• **CGC:** 2 graded, best 8.0

52 ❑ Oct 1964 Cover: 0.12 **NM** value: **35.00**
• **CGC:** 1 graded, best 9.0

53 ❑ Nov 1964 Cover: 0.12 **NM** value: **35.00**
• **CGC:** 2 graded, best 9.2
📖 How Lois Lane Fell in Love with Superman!; Superman's Hometown Sweetheart; When Lois and Lana Were Brides! • How Lois fell in love with Superman **A:** Kurt Schaffenberger

54 ❑ Jan 1965 Cover: 0.12 **NM** value: **35.00**
Circ: Statement: **556,091** • **CGC:** 2 graded, best 9.4

55 ❑ Feb 1965 Cover: 0.12 **NM** value: **35.00**
Circ: Statement: **556,091**
• Has 1964 Statement; no circ figures published

56 ❑ Apr 1965 Cover: 0.12 **NM** value: **35.00**
Circ: Statement: **556,091** • **CGC:** 2 graded, best 9.4

57 ❑ May 1965 Cover: 0.12 **NM** value: **35.00**
Circ: Statement: **556,091**

58 ❑ Jul 1965 Cover: 0.12 **NM** value: **35.00**
Circ: Statement: **556,091**

59 ❑ Aug 1965 Cover: 0.12 **NM** value: **35.00**
Circ: Statement: **556,091** • **CGC:** 1 graded, best 6.0

60 ❑ Oct 1965 Cover: 0.12 **NM** value: **35.00**
Circ: Statement: **556,091** • **CGC:** 3 graded, best 9.4

61 ❑ Nov 1965 Cover: 0.12 **NM** value: **35.00**
Circ: Statement: **556,091** • **CGC:** 2 graded, best 9.4

62 ❑ Jan 1966 Cover: 0.12 **NM** value: **35.00**
Circ: Statement: **530,808**

63 ❑ Feb 1966 Cover: 0.12 **NM** value: **35.00**
Circ: Statement: **530,808** • **CGC:** 2 graded, best 9.2
• Noel Neill interview ★ Versus S.K.U.L..

64 ❑ Apr 1966 Cover: 0.12 **NM** value: **35.00**
Circ: Statement: **530,808** • **CGC:** 1 graded, best 9.2

65 ❑ May 1966 Cover: 0.12 **NM** value: **35.00**
Circ: Statement: **530,808** • **CGC:** 2 graded, best 9.4

66 ❑ Jul 1966 Cover: 0.12 **NM** value: **35.00**
Circ: Statement: **530,808** • **CGC:** 2 graded, best 8.5

67 ❑ Aug 1966 Cover: 0.12 **NM** value: **35.00**
Circ: Statement: **530,808** • **CGC:** 2 graded, best 9.2
• Has 1965 Statement, filed 10/1/65; avg print run 821,000; avg sales 552,000; avg subs 4,091; avg total paid 556,091; samples 142; max existent 556,233; 32% of run returned

68 ❑ Sep 1966 Cover: 0.12 **NM** value: **45.00**
Circ: Statement: **530,808** • **CGC:** 8 graded, best 9.8
• Giant-size.

69 ❑ Oct 1966 Cover: 0.12 **NM** value: **35.00**
Circ: Statement: **530,808** • **CGC:** 1 graded, best 9.4

70 ❑ Nov 1966 Cover: 0.12 **NM** value: **225.00**
Circ: Statement: **530,808** • **CGC:** 10 graded, best 9.4
• 1st Catwoman in Silver Age ★ Appearance of Catwoman.

71 ❑ Jan 1967 Cover: 0.12 **NM** value: **130.00**
Circ: Statement: **448,400** • **CGC:** 6 graded, best 9.2
★ Appearance of Catwoman.

72 ❑ Feb 1967 Cover: 0.12 **NM** value: **16.00**
Circ: Statement: **448,400** • **CGC:** 1 graded, best 9.4
• Has 1966 Statement; avg print run 801,000; avg sales 572,000; avg subs 3,808; avg total paid 530,808; max existent 575,808; 28% of run returned

73 ❑ Apr 1967 Cover: 0.12 **NM** value: **16.00**
Circ: Statement: **448,400** • **CGC:** 1 graded, best 9.2

74 ❑ May 1967 Cover: 0.12 **NM** value: **35.00**
Circ: Statement: **448,400** • **CGC:** 2 graded, best 9.2
★ 1st Appearance of Bizarro Flash.

75 ❑ Jul 1967 Cover: 0.12 **NM** value: **16.00**
Circ: Statement: **448,400** • **CGC:** 1 graded, best 9.4

76 ❑ Aug 1967 Cover: 0.12 **NM** value: **16.00**
Circ: Statement: **448,400**

77 ❑ Sep 1967 Cover: 0.12 **NM** value: **25.00**
Circ: Statement: **448,400** • **CGC:** 3 graded, best 9.4
• Giant-size.

Other grades: Multiply prices above by **1.5 for Mint • 2/3 for Very Fine • 1/3 for Fine • 1/5 for Very Good • 1/8 for Good**

78 ❑ Oct 1967 Cover: 0.12 **NM** value: **16.00**
Circ: Statement: **448,400** • **CGC:** 1 graded, best 9.4
79 ❑ Nov 1967 Cover: 0.12 **NM** value: **10.00**
Circ: Statement: **448,400**
80 ❑ Jan 1968 Cover: 0.12 **NM** value: **10.00**
Circ: Statement: **461,725** • **CGC:** 3 graded, best 9.6
81 ❑ Feb 1968 Cover: 0.12 **NM** value: **10.00**
Circ: Statement: **461,725** • **CGC:** 1 graded, best 9.2
82 ❑ Apr 1968 Cover: 0.12 **NM** value: **10.00**
Circ: Statement: **461,725** • **CGC:** 1 graded, best 4.5
• Has 1967 Statement; avg print run 777,000; avg sales 446,000; avg subs 2,400; avg total paid 448,400; samples 340; max existent 448,740; 42% of run returned
83 ❑ May 1968 Cover: 0.12 **NM** value: **10.00**
Circ: Statement: **461,725** • **CGC:** 2 graded, best 9.4
84 ❑ Jul 1968 Cover: 0.12 **NM** value: **10.00**
Circ: Statement: **461,725** • **CGC:** 1 graded, best 8.0
85 ❑ Aug 1968 Cover: 0.12 **NM** value: **10.00**
Circ: Statement: **461,725** • **CGC:** 1 graded, best 9.0
86 ❑ Sep 1968 Cover: 0.25 **NM** value: **18.00**
Circ: Statement: **461,725** • **CGC:** 3 graded, best 9.6
• Giant-size. **A:** Neal Adams
87 ❑ Oct 1968 Cover: 0.12 **NM** value: **10.00**
Circ: Statement: **461,725** • **CGC:** 1 graded, best 9.2
88 ❑ Nov 1968 Cover: 0.12 **NM** value: **10.00**
Circ: Statement: **461,725** • **CGC:** 3 graded, best 9.4
89 ❑ Jan 1969 Cover: 0.12 **NM** value: **10.00**
Circ: Statement: **397,346** • **CGC:** 2 graded, best 9.2
• Imaginary Story; Lois marries Batman
90 ❑ Feb 1969 Cover: 0.12 **NM** value: **10.00**
Circ: Statement: **397,346** • **CGC:** 3 graded, best 9.6
• Has 1968 Statement; avg print run 742,000; avg sales 461,000; avg subs 725; avg total paid 461,725; samples 386; max existent 462,111; 38% of run returned
91 ❑ Apr 1969 Cover: 0.12 **NM** value: **10.00**
Circ: Statement: **397,346**
92 ❑ May 1969 Cover: 0.12 **NM** value: **10.00**
Circ: Statement: **397,346**
93 ❑ Jul 1969 Cover: 0.15 **NM** value: **10.00**
Circ: Statement: **397,346** • **CGC:** 3 graded, best 9.4
★ Appearance of Wonder Woman.
94 ❑ Aug 1969 Cover: 0.15 **NM** value: **10.00**
Circ: Statement: **397,346** • **CGC:** 1 graded, best 9.0
95 ❑ Sep 1969 Cover: 0.15 **NM** value: **18.00**
Circ: Statement: **397,346** • **CGC:** 2 graded, best 9.0
• Giant-size.
96 ❑ Oct 1969 Cover: 0.15 **NM** value: **8.00**
Circ: Statement: **397,346** • **CGC:** 1 graded, best 9.4
97 ❑ Nov 1969 Cover: 0.15 **NM** value: **8.00**
Circ: Statement: **397,346** • **CGC:** 1 graded, best 6.0
98 ❑ Jan 1970 Cover: 0.15 **NM** value: **8.00**
Circ: Statement: **355,561** • **CGC:** 1 graded, best 9.4
99 ❑ Feb 1970 Cover: 0.15 **NM** value: **8.00**
Circ: Statement: **355,561** • **CGC:** 1 graded, best 9.2
100 ❑ Apr 1970 Cover: 0.15 **NM** value: **8.00**
Circ: Statement: **355,561** • **CGC:** 2 graded, best 9.2
• Has 1969 Statement, filed 10/1/69; avg print run 727,000; avg sales 397,000; avg subs 346; avg total paid 397,346; samples 346; max existent 397,692; 45% of run returned
101 ❑ May 1970 Cover: 0.15 **NM** value: **8.00**
Circ: Statement: **355,561** • **CGC:** 2 graded, best 9.2
102 ❑ Jul 1970 Cover: 0.15 **NM** value: **8.00**
Circ: Statement: **355,561** • **CGC:** 2 graded, best 9.4
103 ❑ Aug 1970 Cover: 0.15 **NM** value: **8.00**
Circ: Statement: **355,561**
104 ❑ Sep 1970 Cover: 0.15 **NM** value: **18.00**
Circ: Statement: **355,561** • **CGC:** 3 graded, best 9.2
• Giant-size.
105 ❑ Oct 1970 Cover: 0.15 **NM** value: **15.00**
Circ: Statement: **355,561** • **CGC:** 5 graded, best 9.4
★ Origin of Rose & Thorn II (Rose Forrest). ★ 1st Appearance of Rose & Thorn II (Rose Forrest), The 1,000.
106 ❑ Nov 1970 Cover: 0.15 **NM** value: **6.00**
Circ: Statement: **355,561** • **CGC:** 2 graded, best 9.2
107 ❑ Dec 1970 Cover: 0.15 **NM** value: **6.00**
Circ: Statement: **355,561**
108 ❑ Feb 1971 Cover: 0.15 **NM** value: **6.00**
Circ: Statement: **331,145** • **CGC:** 1 graded, best 9.4
109 ❑ Apr 1971 Cover: 0.15 **NM** value: **6.00**
Circ: Statement: **331,145** • **CGC:** 1 graded, best 9.4
• Has 1970 Statement, filed 10/1/70; avg print run 659,881; avg sales 355,253; avg subs 308; avg total paid 355,561; samples 122; max existent 355,683; 46% of run returned
110 ❑ May 1971 Cover: 0.15 **NM** value: **6.00**
Circ: Statement: **331,145** • **CGC:** 2 graded, best 9.2
111 ❑ Jul 1971 Cover: 0.15 **NM** value: **6.00**
Circ: Statement: **331,145** • **CGC:** 3 graded, best 9.4
112 ❑ Aug 1971 Cover: 0.15 **NM** value: **6.00**
Circ: Statement: **331,145** • **CGC:** 2 graded, best 9.4
113 ❑ Sep 1971 Cover: 0.15 **NM** value: **15.00**
Circ: Statement: **331,145** • **CGC:** 4 graded, best 9.4
• Giant-size.
114 ❑ Sep 1971 Cover: 0.15 **NM** value: **6.00**
Circ: Statement: **331,145** • **CGC:** 1 graded, best 9.4
115 ❑ Oct 1971 Cover: 0.20 **NM** value: **6.00**
Circ: Statement: **331,145** • **CGC:** 1 graded, best 9.6
116 ❑ Nov 1971 Cover: 0.20 **NM** value: **6.00**
Circ: Statement: **331,145**
117 ❑ Dec 1971 Cover: 0.20 **NM** value: **6.00**
Circ: Statement: **331,145** • **CGC:** 2 graded, best 9.4
118 ❑ Jan 1972 Cover: 0.20 **NM** value: **6.00**
Circ: Statement: **232,067** • **CGC:** 1 graded, best 9.6
119 ❑ Feb 1972 Cover: 0.20 **NM** value: **6.00**
• **CGC:** 1 graded, best 7.5
120 ❑ Mar 1972 Cover: 0.20 **NM** value: **6.00**
• **CGC:** 2 graded, best 9.6
• Has 1971 Statement; avg print run 604,375; avg sales 331,145; avg subs 0; avg total paid 331,145; max existent 331,145; 45% of run returned
121 ❑ Apr 1972 Cover: 0.20 **NM** value: **5.00**
• **CGC:** 3 graded, best 9.4
122 ❑ May 1972 Cover: 0.20 **NM** value: **5.00**
• **CGC:** 2 graded, best 9.6
123 ❑ Jun 1972 Cover: 0.20 **NM** value: **5.00**
• **CGC:** 1 graded, best 9.4
124 ❑ Jul 1972 Cover: 0.20 **NM** value: **5.00**
• **CGC:** 1 graded, best 9.4
125 ❑ Aug 1972 Cover: 0.20 **NM** value: **5.00**
• **CGC:** 2 graded, best 9.2
126 ❑ Sep 1972 Cover: 0.20 **NM** value: **5.00**
• **CGC:** 7 graded, best 9.6
127 ❑ Oct 1972 Cover: 0.20 **NM** value: **5.00**
128 ❑ Dec 1972 Cover: 0.20 **NM** value: **5.00**
129 ❑ Feb 1973 Cover: 0.20 **NM** value: **5.00**
• **CGC:** 1 graded, best 8.5
📖 Serpent in Paradise; Rose and the Thorn: The Million Dollar Night! **A:** John Rosenberger **W:** Maxine Fabe
130 ❑ Apr 1973 Cover: 0.20 **NM** value: **5.00**
• Has 1972 Statement; avg print run 517,000; avg sales 231,813; avg subs 254; avg total paid 232,067; max existent 232,067; 55% of run returned
131 ❑ Jun 1973 Cover: 0.20 **NM** value: **5.00**
132 ❑ Jul 1973 Cover: 0.20 **NM** value: **5.00**
133 ❑ Sep 1973 Cover: 0.20 **NM** value: **5.00**
134 ❑ Oct 1973 Cover: 0.20 **NM** value: **5.00**
135 ❑ Nov 1973 Cover: 0.20 **NM** value: **5.00**
136 ❑ Jan 1974 Cover: 0.20 **NM** value: **5.00**
• **CGC:** 1 graded, best 9.6
★ Appearance of Wonder Woman.
137 ❑ ca. 1974 Cover: 0.20 **NM** value: **5.00**
Anl 1 ❑ Sum 1962 Cover: 0.25 **NM** value: **100.00**
Anl 2 ❑ Sum 1963 **NM** value: **60.00**
• **CGC:** 1 graded, best 7.0

SUPERMAN: SILVER BANSHEE DC

1 ❑ Dec 1998 Cover: 2.25 **NM** value: **Cover or less**
Circ: Diamd. preorders: **30,722**
📖 Superman: Silver Banshee **A:** Joyce Chin **W:** Dan Brereton
2 ❑ Jan 1999 Cover: 2.25 **NM** value: **Cover or less**
Circ: Diamd. preorders: **27,681**

SUPERMAN'S METROPOLIS DC

1 ❑ Jan 1997 Cover: 5.95 **NM** value: **Cover or less**
No issue number. • prestige format. • Elseworlds **A:** Ted McKeever **W:** R.J.M. Lofficier; Roy Thomas

SUPERMAN'S NEMESIS: LEX LUTHOR DC

1 ❑ Mar 1999 Cover: 2.50 **NM** value: **Cover or less**
Circ: Diamd. preorders: **29,116**
📖 Dark Victory, Part 1 **A:** Val Semeiks **W:** David Michelinie
2 ❑ Apr 1999 Cover: 2.50 **NM** value: **Cover or less**
Circ: Diamd. preorders: **24,897**
📖 Dark Victory, Part 2 **A:** Val Semeiks **W:** David Michelinie ★ Appearance of Demolitia. ★ Versus Demolitia.
3 ❑ May 1999 Cover: 2.50 **NM** value: **Cover or less**
Circ: Diamd. preorders: **23,739**
📖 Dark Victory, Part 3 **A:** Val Semeiks **W:** David Michelinie
4 ❑ Jun 1999 Cover: 2.50 **NM** value: **Cover or less**
Circ: Diamd. preorders: **22,046**
📖 Dark Victory, Part 4 **A:** Val Semeiks **W:** David Michelinie

SUPERMAN'S PAL JIMMY OLSEN DC

In 1954, Daily Planet cub reporter Jimmy Olsen got a title of his own. Always on the lookout for a story, Jimmy embarked on a long series of humorous adventures taking him from undersea cities to encounters with aliens. If the action got too hot, Jimmy could use his signal watch to call Superman for a rescue. Indeed, it seemed like not an issue went by that Superman wasn't saving Jimmy from one menace or another.

Jimmy had several chances to become a super-hero during the course of this series. At different times, he became Elastic Lad, Flamebird, and even giant ape Congorilla. In the end, however, he always decided that super-heroing was not for him. Possibly, this was because he was so busy chasing after Lucy Lane, Lois Lane's sister.

1 ❑ Oct 1954 Cover: 0.10 **NM** value: **4000.00**
• **CGC:** 13 graded, best 7.0
📖 The Boy of 100 Faces!; Case of the Lumberjack Jinx!; Peg; Cruelist Critter in the Sea (text story); The Man of Steel's Substitute!; Varsity Vic **A:** Curt Swan **W:** Otto Binder
2 ❑ Dec 1954 Cover: 0.10 **NM** value: **1250.00**
• **CGC:** 1 graded, best 1.8
📖 The Flying Jimmy Olsen!; Jimmy Olsen, Superman's Ex-Pal
3 ❑ Feb 1955 Cover: 0.10 **NM** value: **675.00**
• **CGC:** 2 graded, best 5.5
4 ❑ Apr 1955 Cover: 0.10 **NM** value: **475.00**
• **CGC:** 1 graded, best 1.5
5 ❑ Jun 1955 Cover: 0.10 **NM** value: **475.00**
• **CGC:** 2 graded, best 9.0
6 ❑ Aug 1955 Cover: 0.10 **NM** value: **335.00**
7 ❑ Sep 1955 Cover: 0.10 **NM** value: **335.00**
• **CGC:** 1 graded, best 5.0
8 ❑ Nov 1955 Cover: 0.10 **NM** value: **335.00**
9 ❑ Dec 1955 Cover: 0.10 **NM** value: **335.00**
• **CGC:** 1 graded, best 7.5
10 ❑ Feb 1956 Cover: 0.10 **NM** value: **335.00**
• **CGC:** 1 graded, best 3.0
11 ❑ Mar 1956 Cover: 0.10 **NM** value: **235.00**
• **CGC:** 1 graded, best 7.5
12 ❑ Apr 1956 Cover: 0.10 **NM** value: **235.00**
• **CGC:** 2 graded, best 6.0
13 ❑ Jun 1956 Cover: 0.10 **NM** value: **235.00**
• **CGC:** 1 graded, best 7.5
14 ❑ Aug 1956 Cover: 0.10 **NM** value: **235.00**
15 ❑ Sep 1956 Cover: 0.10 **NM** value: **235.00**
• **CGC:** 2 graded, best 7.5
16 ❑ Oct 1956 Cover: 0.10 **NM** value: **235.00**
• **CGC:** 1 graded, best 9.2
17 ❑ Dec 1956 Cover: 0.10 **NM** value: **235.00**
• **CGC:** 2 graded, best 6.5
18 ❑ Feb 1957 Cover: 0.10 **NM** value: **235.00**
19 ❑ Mar 1957 Cover: 0.10 **NM** value: **235.00**
• **CGC:** 3 graded, best 8.5
20 ❑ Apr 1957 Cover: 0.10 **NM** value: **235.00**
21 ❑ Jun 1957 Cover: 0.10 **NM** value: **150.00**
• **CGC:** 1 graded, best 7.0
22 ❑ Aug 1957 Cover: 0.10 **NM** value: **150.00**
• **CGC:** 1 graded, best 4.0
23 ❑ Sep 1957 Cover: 0.10 **NM** value: **150.00**
• **CGC:** 1 graded, best 9.0
24 ❑ Oct 1957 Cover: 0.10 **NM** value: **150.00**
25 ❑ Dec 1957 Cover: 0.10 **NM** value: **150.00**
• **CGC:** 2 graded, best 9.2
26 ❑ Feb 1958 Cover: 0.10 **NM** value: **150.00**
• **CGC:** 1 graded, best 7.0
27 ❑ Mar 1958 Cover: 0.10 **NM** value: **150.00**
28 ❑ Apr 1958 Cover: 0.10 **NM** value: **150.00**
29 ❑ Jun 1958 Cover: 0.10 **NM** value: **150.00**
• **CGC:** 1 graded, best 9.0
30 ❑ Aug 1958 Cover: 0.10 **NM** value: **150.00**
31 ❑ Sep 1958 Cover: 0.10 **NM** value: **100.00**
★ 1st Appearance of Elastic Lad (Jimmy Olsen).
32 ❑ Oct 1958 Cover: 0.10 **NM** value: **100.00**
33 ❑ Dec 1958 Cover: 0.10 **NM** value: **100.00**
• **CGC:** 2 graded, best 8.0
34 ❑ Jan 1959 Cover: 0.10 **NM** value: **100.00**
35 ❑ Mar 1959 Cover: 0.10 **NM** value: **100.00**
• **CGC:** 2 graded, best 7.5
36 ❑ Apr 1959 Cover: 0.10 **NM** value: **100.00**
★ 1st Appearance of Lucy Lane.
37 ❑ Jun 1959 Cover: 0.10 **NM** value: **100.00**
📖 The Elastic Lad of Metropolis
38 ❑ Jul 1959 Cover: 0.10 **NM** value: **100.00**
• **CGC:** 1 graded, best 7.0
39 ❑ Sep 1959 Cover: 0.10 **NM** value: **100.00**
📖 The Superlad of Space
40 ❑ Oct 1959 Cover: 0.10 **NM** value: **100.00**
• **CGC:** 1 graded, best 4.5
41 ❑ Dec 1959 Cover: 0.10 **NM** value: **75.00**
• **CGC:** 1 graded, best 3.0
42 ❑ Jan 1960 Cover: 0.10 **NM** value: **75.00**
Circ: Statement: **498,000**
43 ❑ Mar 1960 Cover: 0.10 **NM** value: **75.00**
Circ: Statement: **498,000** • **CGC:** 1 graded, best 6.5
44 ❑ Apr 1960 Cover: 0.10 **NM** value: **75.00**
Circ: Statement: **498,000** • **CGC:** 1 graded, best 4.0
45 ❑ Jun 1960 Cover: 0.10 **NM** value: **75.00**
Circ: Statement: **498,000**
46 ❑ Jul 1960 Cover: 0.10 **NM** value: **75.00**
Circ: Statement: **498,000**
47 ❑ Sep 1960 Cover: 0.10 **NM** value: **75.00**
Circ: Statement: **498,000** • **CGC:** 1 graded, best 7.0
48 ❑ Oct 1960 Cover: 0.10 **NM** value: **75.00**
Circ: Statement: **498,000** • **CGC:** 1 graded, best 9.0
★ 1st Appearance of Superman Emergency Squad.
49 ❑ Dec 1960 Cover: 0.10 **NM** value: **75.00**
Circ: Statement: **498,000** • **CGC:** 1 graded, best 9.4
• Jimmy Olsen becomes Congorilla
50 ❑ Jan 1961 Cover: 0.10 **NM** value: **75.00**
Circ: Statement: **520,000**
51 ❑ Mar 1961 Cover: 0.10 **NM** value: **50.00**
Circ: Statement: **520,000**
52 ❑ Apr 1961 Cover: 0.12 **NM** value: **50.00**
Circ: Statement: **520,000** • **CGC:** 1 graded, best 9.2
53 ❑ Jun 1961 Cover: 0.12 **NM** value: **50.00**
Circ: Statement: **520,000** • **CGC:** 3 graded, best 9.4
54 ❑ Jul 1961 Cover: 0.12 **NM** value: **50.00**
Circ: Statement: **520,000** • **CGC:** 2 graded, best 9.6
55 ❑ Sep 1961 Cover: 0.12 **NM** value: **50.00**
Circ: Statement: **520,000** • **CGC:** 3 graded, best 9.6
56 ❑ Oct 1961 Cover: 0.12 **NM** value: **50.00**
Circ: Statement: **520,000** • **CGC:** 2 graded, best 9.6
57 ❑ Dec 1961 Cover: 0.12 **NM** value: **30.00**
Circ: Statement: **520,000** • **CGC:** 3 graded, best 9.4
A: Curt Swan ★ Appearance of Supergirl.
58 ❑ Jan 1962 Cover: 0.12 **NM** value: **30.00**
Circ: Statement: **470,000** • **CGC:** 2 graded, best 9.4
59 ❑ Mar 1962 Cover: 0.12 **NM** value: **30.00**
Circ: Statement: **470,000** • **CGC:** 2 graded, best 8.0
• Has 1961 Statement, filed 10/1/61; avg total paid circ 520,000 **A:** Curt Swan
60 ❑ Apr 1962 Cover: 0.12 **NM** value: **30.00**
Circ: Statement: **470,000** • **CGC:** 1 graded, best 4.5
61 ❑ Jun 1962 Cover: 0.12 **NM** value: **30.00**
Circ: Statement: **470,000**
62 ❑ Jul 1962 Cover: 0.12 **NM** value: **30.00**
Circ: Statement: **470,000** • **CGC:** 1 graded, best 9.2
• Elastic Lad in Phantom Zone
63 ❑ Sep 1962 Cover: 0.12 **NM** value: **30.00**
Circ: Statement: **470,000**
64 ❑ Oct 1962 Cover: 0.12 **NM** value: **30.00**
Circ: Statement: **470,000**

CGC-graded: Multiply prices above by **33 for 9.9 M • 16 for 9.8 NM/M • 7 for 9.6 NM+ • 5 for 9.4 NM • 2.5 for 9.2 NM- • 1.5 for 9.0 VF/NM**

65 ❑ Dec 1962 Cover: 0.12 **NM** value: **30.00**
Circ: Statement: **470,000**
66 ❑ Jan 1963 Cover: 0.12 **NM** value: **30.00**
67 ❑ Mar 1963 Cover: 0.12 **NM** value: **30.00**
• Has 1962 Statement, filed 10/1/62; avg total paid circ 470,000
68 ❑ Apr 1963 Cover: 0.12 **NM** value: **30.00**
69 ❑ Jun 1963 Cover: 0.12 **NM** value: **30.00**
A: Curt Swan
70 ❑ Jul 1963 Cover: 0.12 **NM** value: **30.00**
• Silver Kryptonite
71 ❑ Sep 1963 Cover: 0.12 **NM** value: **25.00**
72 ❑ Oct 1963 Cover: 0.12 **NM** value: **30.00**
• **CGC:** 1 graded, best 5.5
📖 The World of Doomed Olsens **A:** Curt Swan ★ Appearance of Legion of Super-Heroes.
73 ❑ Dec 1963 Cover: 0.12 **NM** value: **30.00**
74 ❑ Jan 1964 Cover: 0.12 **NM** value: **25.00**
A: Curt Swan ★ Appearance of Lex Luthor.
75 ❑ Mar 1964 Cover: 0.12 **NM** value: **25.00**
• **CGC:** 1 graded, best 4.0
• Has 1963 Statement, filed 10/1/63; no circ figures published ★ Appearance of Supergirl.
76 ❑ Apr 1964 Cover: 0.12 **NM** value: **30.00**
• **CGC:** 1 graded, best 5.5
📖 Elastic Lad Jimmy and His Legion Romances ★ Appearance of Lightning Lad, Saturn Girl, Lightning Lass, Triplicate Girl, Triplicate Girl, Saturn Girl.
77 ❑ Jun 1964 Cover: 0.12 **NM** value: **25.00**
• **CGC:** 1 graded, best 6.5
78 ❑ Jul 1964 Cover: 0.12 **NM** value: **25.00**
• **CGC:** 1 graded, best 4.0
79 ❑ Sep 1964 Cover: 0.12 **NM** value: **25.00**
• **CGC:** 1 graded, best 4.5
• Jimmy as Beatle
80 ❑ Oct 1964 Cover: 0.12 **NM** value: **25.00**
• **CGC:** 2 graded, best 8.5
★ 1st Appearance of Bizarro-Jimmy Olsen.
81 ❑ Dec 1964 Cover: 0.12 **NM** value: **25.00**
• **CGC:** 3 graded, best 9.2
82 ❑ Jan 1965 Cover: 0.12 **NM** value: **25.00**
Circ: Statement: **554,931** • **CGC:** 2 graded, best 9.4
83 ❑ Mar 1965 Cover: 0.12 **NM** value: **25.00**
Circ: Statement: **554,931** • **CGC:** 2 graded, best 9.4
• Has 1964 Statement, filed 10/1/64; no circ figures published
84 ❑ Apr 1965 Cover: 0.12 **NM** value: **25.00**
Circ: Statement: **554,931**
A: Curt Swan
85 ❑ Jun 1965 Cover: 0.12 **NM** value: **25.00**
Circ: Statement: **554,931**
A: Curt Swan
86 ❑ Jul 1965 Cover: 0.12 **NM** value: **25.00**
Circ: Statement: **554,931** • **CGC:** 2 graded, best 7.0
87 ❑ Sep 1965 Cover: 0.12 **NM** value: **25.00**
Circ: Statement: **554,931** • **CGC:** 2 graded, best 7.5
★ Appearance of Legion of Super-Villains, Bizarro Jimmy.
88 ❑ Oct 1965 Cover: 0.12 **NM** value: **20.00**
Circ: Statement: **554,931**
89 ❑ Dec 1965 Cover: 0.12 **NM** value: **20.00**
Circ: Statement: **554,931** • **CGC:** 2 graded, best 9.4
90 ❑ Jan 1966 Cover: 0.12 **NM** value: **20.00**
Circ: Statement: **523,455** • **CGC:** 2 graded, best 9.4
91 ❑ Mar 1966 Cover: 0.12 **NM** value: **16.00**
Circ: Statement: **523,455** • **CGC:** 2 graded, best 9.4
92 ❑ Apr 1966 Cover: 0.12 **NM** value: **16.00**
Circ: Statement: **523,455** • **CGC:** 2 graded, best 9.2
★ Appearance of Batman.
93 ❑ Jun 1966 Cover: 0.12 **NM** value: **16.00**
Circ: Statement: **523,455** • **CGC:** 1 graded, best 9.0
94 ❑ Jul 1966 Cover: 0.12 **NM** value: **16.00**
Circ: Statement: **523,455** • **CGC:** 3 graded, best 9.4
95 ❑ Aug 1966 Cover: 0.12 **NM** value: **25.00**
Circ: Statement: **523,455** • **CGC:** 5 graded, best 9.4
• Giant-size.
96 ❑ Sep 1966 Cover: 0.12 **NM** value: **16.00**
Circ: Statement: **523,455** • **CGC:** 2 graded, best 9.4
97 ❑ Oct 1966 Cover: 0.12 **NM** value: **16.00**
Circ: Statement: **523,455** • **CGC:** 1 graded, best 9.2
98 ❑ Dec 1966 Cover: 0.12 **NM** value: **16.00**
Circ: Statement: **523,455** • **CGC:** 2 graded, best 9.4
99 ❑ Jan 1967 Cover: 0.12 **NM** value: **16.00**
Circ: Statement: **450,700** • **CGC:** 3 graded, best 9.4
• Jimmy as one-man Legion
100 ❑ Mar 1967 Cover: 0.12 **NM** value: **25.00**
Circ: Statement: **450,700** • **CGC:** 2 graded, best 9.6
• Wedding of Jimmy and Lucy Lane; Has 1966 Statement, filed 10/1/66; avg print run 786,000; avg sales 520,000; avg subs 3,455; avg total paid 523,455; samples 330; office use 0; max existent 523,785; 33% of run returned
101 ❑ Apr 1967 **NM** value: **12.00**
Circ: Statement: **450,700** • **CGC:** 2 graded, best 9.2
📖 Olsen's Time-Trip to Save Krypton
102 ❑ Jun 1967 **NM** value: **12.00**
Circ: Statement: **450,700** • **CGC:** 1 graded, best 9.4
103 ❑ Jul 1967 **NM** value: **12.00**
Circ: Statement: **450,700** • **CGC:** 2 graded, best 9.2
104 ❑ Aug 1967 Cover: 0.25 **NM** value: **25.00**
Circ: Statement: **450,700** • **CGC:** 2 graded, best 9.4
• Giant-size. • giant; Weird Adventures
105 ❑ Sep 1967 Cover: 0.12 **NM** value: **12.00**
Circ: Statement: **450,700**
📖 World of 1,000 Olsens
106 ❑ Oct 1967 **NM** value: **12.00**
Circ: Statement: **450,700** • **CGC:** 2 graded, best 9.4
📖 The Lone Wolf Legionnaire Reporter!
107 ❑ Dec 1967 **NM** value: **12.00**
Circ: Statement: **450,700** • **CGC:** 1 graded, best 9.4
A: Curt Swan
108 ❑ Jan 1968 **NM** value: **12.00**
Circ: Statement: **460,560**
A: Curt Swan
109 ❑ Mar 1968 Cover: 0.12 **NM** value: **12.00**
Circ: Statement: **460,560** • **CGC:** 1 graded, best 9.0
• Has 1967 Statement, filed 10/1/67; avg print run 791,000; avg sales 448,000 avg subs 2,700; avg total paid 450,700; samples 340; max existent 451,040; 43% of run returned ★ Appearance of Luthor.
110 ❑ Apr 1968 **NM** value: **12.00**
Circ: Statement: **460,560** • **CGC:** 2 graded, best 9.0
A: Curt Swan
111 ❑ Jun 1968 **NM** value: **12.00**
Circ: Statement: **460,560** • **CGC:** 4 graded, best 9.6
112 ❑ Jul 1968 **NM** value: **12.00**
Circ: Statement: **460,560** • **CGC:** 3 graded, best 9.4
113 ❑ Aug 1968 Cover: 0.25 **NM** value: **25.00**
Circ: Statement: **460,560** • **CGC:** 3 graded, best 9.2
• Anti-Superman issue
114 ❑ Sep 1968 **NM** value: **12.00**
Circ: Statement: **460,560** • **CGC:** 1 graded, best 9.0
115 ❑ Oct 1968 Cover: 0.12 **NM** value: **12.00**
Circ: Statement: **460,560** • **CGC:** 3 graded, best 9.6
★ Appearance of Aquaman.
116 ❑ Dec 1968 Cover: 0.12 **NM** value: **12.00**
Circ: Statement: **460,560** • **CGC:** 2 graded, best 9.2
117 ❑ Jan 1969 **NM** value: **12.00**
118 ❑ Mar 1969 **NM** value: **12.00**
• **CGC:** 3 graded, best 9.2
• Has 1968 Statement, filed 10/1/68; avg print run 748,000; avg sales 460,000; avg subs 560; avg total paid 460,560; samples 386; max existent 460,946; 38% of run returned
119 ❑ Apr 1969 **NM** value: **12.00**
• **CGC:** 2 graded, best 9.6
120 ❑ Jun 1969 **NM** value: **10.00**
• **CGC:** 1 graded, best 9.2
121 ❑ Jul 1969 **NM** value: **10.00**
• **CGC:** 2 graded, best 9.4
122 ❑ Aug 1969 **NM** value: **10.00**
• **CGC:** 3 graded, best 9.4
123 ❑ Sep 1969 Cover: 0.15 **NM** value: **10.00**
• **CGC:** 1 graded, best 9.4
124 ❑ Oct 1969 Cover: 0.15 **NM** value: **10.00**
• **CGC:** 2 graded, best 9.6
125 ❑ Dec 1969 Cover: 0.15 **NM** value: **10.00**
• **CGC:** 2 graded, best 9.4
📖 Superman's Saddest Day!; The Spendthrift and the Miser
126 ❑ Jan 1970 Cover: 0.15 **NM** value: **10.00**
Circ: Statement: **333,539** • **CGC:** 2 graded, best 9.6
★ Appearance of Kryptonite Plus.
127 ❑ Mar 1970 Cover: 0.15 **NM** value: **10.00**
Circ: Statement: **333,539** • **CGC:** 1 graded, best 9.0
128 ❑ Apr 1970 Cover: 0.15 **NM** value: **10.00**
Circ: Statement: **333,539** • **CGC:** 1 graded, best 9.2
129 ❑ Jun 1970 Cover: 0.15 **NM** value: **10.00**
Circ: Statement: **333,539**
130 ❑ Jul 1970 Cover: 0.15 **NM** value: **10.00**
Circ: Statement: **333,539** • **CGC:** 1 graded, best 9.6
131 ❑ Aug 1970 Cover: 0.15 **NM** value: **8.00**
Circ: Statement: **333,539** • **CGC:** 2 graded, best 9.4
132 ❑ Sep 1970 Cover: 0.15 **NM** value: **8.00**
Circ: Statement: **333,539** • **CGC:** 1 graded, best 9.6
📖 Winner's Prize... The Loser's Grave
133 ❑ Oct 1970 Cover: 0.15 **NM** value: **10.00**
Circ: Statement: **333,539** • **CGC:** 4 graded, best 9.2
📖 The Newsboy Legion • Newsboy Legion **A:** Jack Kirby ★ 1st Appearance of Newsboy Legion, Habitat. ★ Appearance of Newsboy Legion.
134 ❑ Dec 1970 Cover: 0.15 **NM** value: **25.00**
Circ: Statement: **333,539** • **CGC:** 11 graded, best 9.2
📖 The Mountain of Judgment • 1st appearance Darkseid ★ 1st Appearance of Darkseid.
135 ❑ Jan 1971 Cover: 0.15 **NM** value: **12.00**
Circ: Statement: **299,882** • **CGC:** 6 graded, best 9.4
📖 Evil Factory ★ 1st Appearance of Project Cadmus.
136 ❑ Mar 1971 Cover: 0.15 **NM** value: **12.00**
Circ: Statement: **299,882** • **CGC:** 2 graded, best 9.4
📖 The Saga of the D.N.Aliens • Has 1970 Statement, filed 10/1/70; avg print run 627,102; avg sales 333,361; avg subs 178; avg total paid 333,539; samples 122; max existent 333,661; 47% of run returned ★ Origin of Guardian (new).
137 ❑ Apr 1971 Cover: 0.15 **NM** value: **12.00**
Circ: Statement: **299,882** • **CGC:** 3 graded, best 9.6
📖 The Four-Armed Terror
138 ❑ Jun 1971 Cover: 0.15 **NM** value: **12.00**
Circ: Statement: **299,882** • **CGC:** 4 graded, best 9.6
📖 The Big Room
139 ❑ Jul 1971 Cover: 0.15 **NM** value: **12.00**
Circ: Statement: **299,882** • **CGC:** 2 graded, best 9.2
📖 The Guardian Fights Again ★ Appearance of Don Rickles.
140 ❑ Aug 1971 Cover: 0.35 **NM** value: **12.00**
Circ: Statement: **299,882** • **CGC:** 2 graded, best 9.4
• reprints Jimmy Olsen #69, #72, and Superman #158
141 ❑ Sep 1971 Cover: 0.25 **NM** value: **10.00**
Circ: Statement: **299,882**
📖 Will the Real Don Rickles Panic?
142 ❑ Oct 1971 Cover: 0.25 **NM** value: **10.00**
Circ: Statement: **299,882** • **CGC:** 3 graded, best 9.6
📖 The Man from Transilvane
143 ❑ Nov 1971 Cover: 0.25 **NM** value: **10.00**
Circ: Statement: **299,882** • **CGC:** 1 graded, best 9.6
📖 Genocide Spray **A:** Jack Kirby
144 ❑ Dec 1971 Cover: 0.25 **NM** value: **10.00**
Circ: Statement: **299,882** • **CGC:** 4 graded, best 9.6
📖 A Big Thing in a Deep Scottish Lake **A:** Jack Kirby
145 ❑ Jan 1972 Cover: 0.25 **NM** value: **10.00**
Circ: Statement: **203,492** • **CGC:** 6 graded, best 9.8
146 ❑ Feb 1972 Cover: 0.25 **NM** value: **10.00**
Circ: Statement: **203,492** • **CGC:** 1 graded, best 9.6
147 ❑ Mar 1972 Cover: 0.25 **NM** value: **10.00**
Circ: Statement: **203,492** • **CGC:** 3 graded, best 9.6
📖 A Superman in Supertown • Has 1971 Statement; avg print run 555,000; avg sales 229,810; avg subs 72; avg total paid 299,882; office use 803; max existent 3000,685; 46% of run returned
148 ❑ Apr 1972 Cover: 0.25 **NM** value: **10.00**
Circ: Statement: **203,492** • **CGC:** 3 graded, best 9.6
149 ❑ May 1972 Cover: 0.25 **NM** value: **10.00**
Circ: Statement: **203,492** • **CGC:** 1 graded, best 9.2
150 ❑ Jun 1972 Cover: 0.25 **NM** value: **10.00**
Circ: Statement: **203,492** • **CGC:** 1 graded, best 9.0
151 ❑ Jul 1972 Cover: 0.20 **NM** value: **8.00**
Circ: Statement: **203,492**
152 ❑ Sep 1972 Cover: 0.20 **NM** value: **7.00**
Circ: Statement: **203,492** • **CGC:** 4 graded, best 9.4
153 ❑ Oct 1972 Cover: 0.20 **NM** value: **7.00**
Circ: Statement: **203,492** • **CGC:** 3 graded, best 9.6
154 ❑ Nov 1972 Cover: 0.20 **NM** value: **7.00**
Circ: Statement: **203,492** • **CGC:** 1 graded, best 9.6
155 ❑ Jan 1973 Cover: 0.20 **NM** value: **7.00**
Circ: Statement: **195,157**
156 ❑ Feb 1973 Cover: 0.20 **NM** value: **7.00**
Circ: Statement: **195,157**
157 ❑ Mar 1973 Cover: 0.20 **NM** value: **7.00**
Circ: Statement: **195,157**
📖 The Strange Second Life of Jimmy Olsen
158 ❑ 1973 Cover: 0.20 **NM** value: **7.00**
Circ: Statement: **195,157**
159 ❑ Aug 1973 Cover: 0.20 **NM** value: **7.00**
Circ: Statement: **195,157** • **CGC:** 1 graded, best 9.0
160 ❑ 1973 Cover: 0.20 **NM** value: **7.00**
Circ: Statement: **195,157**
161 ❑ Nov 1973 Cover: 0.20 **NM** value: **7.00**
Circ: Statement: **195,157**
162 ❑ Dec 1973 Cover: 0.20 **NM** value: **7.00**
Circ: Statement: **195,157**
163 ❑ Feb 1974 Cover: 0.20 **NM** value: **7.00**
Circ: Statement: **178,478**
final issue. • Series continues as The Superman Family

SUPERMAN SPECTACULAR — DC

1 ❑ Cover: 1.00 **NM** value: **3.00**
Circ: CapCity orders: **25,300**
No issue number. ★ Versus Luthor. ★ Versus Brainiac.

SUPERMAN: SPEEDING BULLETS — DC

1 ❑ ca. 1993 Cover: 4.95 **NM** value: **Cover or less**
Circ: CapCity orders: **38,400**
No issue number. • prestige format. • Elseworlds **A:** Eduardo Barreto **W:** J.M. DeMatteis

SUPERMAN: THE DAILIES — DC

This superb collection released by D.C. Comics and Kitchen Sink Press includes all the daily newspaper strips featuring The Man of Steel, which ran from 1939 to 1942. Originally released as a single volume hardcover and later as three separate trade paperbacks, these comics showcase the burgeoning talents of Superman's creators Jerry Siegal and Joe Shuster.

Highlights include one of Superman's longest stories which ran for an astounding eight months and pitted Superman against numerous villains from the underworld determined to collect a million dollar reward for Superman's death. Probably one of the funniest moments from the series shows Superman spanking his enemy and admirer the Blonde Tigress.

Also, featured are informative introductions, which add insight to the comics and discuss such topics as Superman's early Hollywood career. This collection is not only an entertaining read, but also an important piece of history preserving the legacy of one of America's greatest icons.

1 ❑ ca. 2000 Cover: 14.95 **NM** value: **Cover or less**
📖 Superman Comes to Earth; War Against Crime; The Comeback of Larry Trent; Jewel Smugglers; Skyscraper of Death; The Most Deadly Weapon; Superman and the Runaway; Royal Deathplot; Underworld Politics; Unnatural Disasters • 1939-1940 **A:** Paul Cassidy **W:** Joe Shuster; Jerry Siegel; James Vance
2 ❑ ca. 2001 Cover: 14.95 **NM** value: **Cover or less**
📖 Clark Kent-Spy; Superman Goes to War; Trouble in the Tenements; The Big Boss; "The Unknown" Strikes; King of the Kidnapping Ring; The Hooded Saboteur; Pawns of the Master; The Meekest Man in the World • 1940-1941 **A:** Paul Cassidy **W:** Joe Shuster; Jerry Siegel; James Vance
3 ❑ ca. 2001 Cover: 14.95 **NM** value: **Cover or less**
📖 Superman Goes Hollywood; The League to Destroy Superman; The Scientists of Sudden Death; The Death Ray; The Pseudo-Superman; The Deadly Dwarf; Explosion; The Electric Rod; The Blond Tigress Regrets; Superman's Hollywood Debut • 1941-1942 **A:** Paul Cassidy **W:** Joe Shuster; Jerry Siegel; James Vance

SUPERMAN: THE DARK SIDE — DC

1 ❑ Oct 1998 Cover: 4.95 **NM** value: **Cover or less**
Circ: Diamd. preorders: **34,945**
A: Hilary Barta **W:** John Francis Moore
2 ❑ Nov 1998 Cover: 4.95 **NM** value: **Cover or less**
Circ: Diamd. preorders: **31,383**
A: Hilary Barta **W:** John Francis Moore
3 ❑ Dec 1998 Cover: 4.95 **NM** value: **Cover or less**
Circ: Diamd. preorders: **32,661**
A: Hilary Barta **W:** John Francis Moore
Bk 1 ❑ Cover: 12.95 **NM** value: **Cover or less**
No issue number. • Trade Paperback. • collects mini-series **A:** Hilary Barta **W:** John Francis Moore

SUPERMAN: THE DEATH OF CLARK KENT DC

Bk 1❑ Cover: 19.95 **NM value: Cover or less**
• Reprints story from Adventures of Superman #523-525, Action Comics #706-711, Superman (2nd Series) #99-102, Superman: The Man of Steel #43-46, Superman: The Man of Tomorrow #1 **A:** Stuart Immonen; Jackson Guice; Gil Kane; Dan Jurgens; Tom Grummett; Jon Bogdanove **W:** Karl Kesel; Dan Jurgens; Louise Simonson; Roger Stern; David Michelinie

SUPERMAN: THE DOOMSDAY WARS DC

1 ❑ ca. 1999 Cover: 4.95 **NM value: Cover or less**
Circ: Diamd. preorders: **42,531**
📖 Birth **A:** Dan Jurgens **W:** Dan Jurgens ★ Appearance of Justice League of America, Pete Ross, Lana Lang.

1/LE❑ Cover: 24.95 **NM value: Cover or less**
A: Dan Jurgens **W:** Dan Jurgens

2 ❑ ca. 1999 Cover: 4.95 **NM value: Cover or less**
Circ: Diamd. preorders: **37,734** • **CGC:** 1 graded, best 9.8
A: Dan Jurgens **W:** Dan Jurgens

3 ❑ ca. 1999 Cover: 4.95 **NM value: Cover or less**
Circ: Diamd. preorders: **37,367** • **CGC:** 1 graded, best 9.8
A: Dan Jurgens **W:** Dan Jurgens

Bk 1❑ Feb 2000 Cover: 12.95 **NM value: Cover or less**
• Collects Series **A:** Dan Jurgens **W:** Dan Jurgens

SUPERMAN: THE EARTH STEALERS DC

1 ❑ May 1988 Cover: 2.95 **NM value: Cover or less**
No issue number. One-shot. **A:** Jerry Ordway; Curt Swan **W:** John Byrne

SUPERMAN: THE LAST GOD OF KRYPTON DC

1 ❑ Aug 1999 Cover: 4.95 **NM value: Cover or less**
Circ: Diamd. preorders: **30,601**
No issue number. • prestige format. **A:** Greg Hildebrandt; Tim Hildebrandt **W:** Walt Simonson

SUPERMAN: THE LEGACY OF SUPERMAN DC

1 ❑ Mar 1993 Cover: 2.50 **NM value: Cover or less**
📖 The Guardians Of Metropolis; Gangbuster Of Suicidal Slum; Funeral Pyres; • Follows up after Superman's demise **A:** Curt Swan; Walt Simonson; Dennis Janke **W:** William Messner-Loebs; Karl Kesel; Jerry Ordway

SUPERMAN: THE MAN OF STEEL DC

He was born as Kal-El, on the planet Krypton where his father, Jor-El, was that world's greatest scientist. When Jor-El, realized that their world was doomed, he placed his son in a lone spaceship and sent it to Earth. There, the boy was found by a kind elderly couple, the Kents, who named him Clark, and raised him as if he were their own son. As the boy grew, he developed extraordinary powers: super-strength, X-ray vision, the ability to fly, and more. When he sheds his identity of Clark Kent, he becomes Superman: The Man of Steel.

The most recent Superman series, this title continues to bring readers the adventures of the world's best-known super-hero, intertwining its stories with the stories contained in Superman (2nd Series), Action Comics, and Adventures of Superman. To keep things straight, each issue features a triangle-number on the cover showing the sequence of the stories.

0 ❑ Oct 1994 Cover: 1.50 **NM value: 2.50**
Circ: CapCity orders: **60,150**
📖 Peer Pressure, Part 1 • ▲1994-37 **A:** Jon Bogdanove **W:** Louise Simonson

1 ❑ Jul 1991 Cover: 1.75 **NM value: 3.50**
Circ: CapCity orders: **86,400** • **CGC:** 2 graded, best 9.4
📖 Man of Steel/Man of Fire! • ▲1991-19 **A:** Jon Bogdanove **W:** Louise Simonson ★ 1st Appearance of Cerberus.

2 ❑ Aug 1991 Cover: 1.00 **NM value: 2.50**
Circ: CapCity orders: **51,000**
★ Versus Sgt. Belcher. ★ Versus Rorc.

3 ❑ Sep 1991 Cover: 1.00 **NM value: 2.50**
Circ: CapCity orders: **48,700**
📖 War of the Gods, Part 2 • War of the Gods

4 ❑ Oct 1991 Cover: 1.00 **NM value: 2.00**
Circ: CapCity orders: **38,000**
★ Versus Angstrom.

5 ❑ Nov 1991 Cover: 1.00 **NM value: 2.00**
Circ: CapCity orders: **33,000**
★ Versus Atomic Skull.

6 ❑ Dec 1991 Cover: 1.00 **NM value: 2.00**
Circ: CapCity orders: **29,450**
📖 Blackout, Part 3

7 ❑ Jan 1992 Cover: 1.00 **NM value: 2.00**
Circ: CapCity orders: **25,050**
★ Versus Blockhouse. ★ Versus Jolt.

8 ❑ Feb 1992 Cover: 1.00 **NM value: 2.00**
Circ: CapCity orders: **22,350**
★ Versus Blockhouse. ★ Versus Jolt.

9 ❑ Mar 1992 Cover: 1.00 **NM value: 2.00**
Circ: CapCity orders: **24,150**
📖 Panic in the Sky First Strike

10 ❑ Apr 1992 Cover: 1.00 **NM value: 2.00**
Circ: CapCity orders: **22,450**
📖 Panic in the Sky Fifth Strike

11 ❑ May 1992 Cover: 1.25 **NM value: 1.50**
Circ: CapCity orders: **19,750**

12 ❑ Jun 1992 Cover: 1.25 **NM value: 1.50**
Circ: CapCity orders: **21,500**

13 ❑ Jul 1992 Cover: 1.25 **NM value: 1.50**
Circ: CapCity orders: **21,150**

14 ❑ Aug 1992 Cover: 1.25 **NM value: 1.50**
Circ: CapCity orders: **25,700**
★ Appearance of Robin.

15 ❑ Sep 1992 Cover: 1.25 **NM value: 1.50**
Circ: CapCity orders: **19,350**
★ Appearance of Satanus, Blaze.

16 ❑ Oct 1992 Cover: 1.25 **NM value: 1.50**
Circ: CapCity orders: **19,500**

17 ❑ Nov 1992 Cover: 1.25 **NM value: 3.00**
Circ: CapCity orders: **18,700** • **CGC:** 2 graded, best 9.4
📖 Doomsday! ★ 1st Appearance of Doomsday (cameo).

18 ❑ Dec 1992 Cover: 1.25 **NM value: 4.00**
Circ: CapCity orders: **26,350** • **CGC:** 17 graded, best 9.8
📖 Doomsday! • ▲1992-18 **A:** Jon Bogdanove **W:** Louise Simonson ★ 1st Appearance of Doomsday (full appearance).

18-2❑ Dec 1992 Cover: 1.25 **NM value: 2.00**

18-3❑ Dec 1992 Cover: 1.25 **NM value: 1.50**

19 ❑ Jan 1993 Cover: 1.25 **NM value: 3.00**
Circ: CapCity orders: **96,700** • **CGC:** 6 graded, best 9.8
📖 Doomsday is Here! • ▲1993-1 **A:** Jon Bogdanove **W:** Louise Simonson ★ Versus Doomsday.

20 ❑ Feb 1993 Cover: 1.25 **NM value: 2.50**
Circ: CapCity orders: **84,250**
📖 Funeral for a Friend, Part 3 **A:** Jon Bogdanove **W:** Louise Simonson

21 ❑ Mar 1993 Cover: 1.25 **NM value: 2.50**
Circ: CapCity orders: **138,050**
📖 Funeral for a Friend, Part 7 • Pa Kent has heart attack **A:** Jon Bogdanove **W:** Louise Simonson

22 ❑ Jun 1993 Cover: 1.50 **NM value: 2.00**
Circ: CapCity orders: **109,350**
📖 Reign of the Supermen; Steel **A:** Jon Bogdanove **W:** Louise Simonson ★ 1st Appearance of Steel (John Henry Irons).

22/SC❑ Jun 1993 Cover: 1.95 **NM value: 2.50**
Circ: CapCity orders: **400,450**
Die-cut cover. 📖 Steel **A:** Jon Bogdanove **W:** Louise Simonson

23 ❑ Jul 1993 Cover: 1.50 **NM value: 2.00**
Circ: CapCity orders: **122,250**
📖 Reign of the Supermen • Steel vs. Superboy

24 ❑ Aug 1993 Cover: 1.50 **NM value: 2.00**
Circ: CapCity orders: **108,900**
📖 Reign of the Supermen; Impact! • Steel vs. Last Son of Krypton **A:** Jon Bogdanove **W:** Louise Simonson

25 ❑ Sep 1993 Cover: 1.50 **NM value: 2.00**
Circ: CapCity orders: **91,700**
📖 Reign of the Supermen

26 ❑ Oct 1993 Cover: 1.50 **NM value: 2.00**
Circ: CapCity orders: **104,850**
📖 Reign of the Supermen; Blast Off! **A:** Jon Bogdanove **W:** Louise Simonson

27 ❑ Nov 1993 Cover: 1.50 **NM value: 2.00**
Circ: CapCity orders: **77,700**

28 ❑ Dec 1993 Cover: 1.50 **NM value: 2.00**
Circ: CapCity orders: **81,450**

29 ❑ Jan 1994 Cover: 1.50 **NM value: 2.00**
Circ: CapCity orders: **78,350**
📖 Spilled Blood

30 ❑ Feb 1994 Cover: 1.50 **NM value: 2.00**
• Lobo

30/SC❑ Feb 1994 Cover: 2.50 **NM value: 3.00**
Circ: CapCity orders: **97,000** • **CGC:** 3 graded, best 9.8
vinyl clings cover.

31 ❑ Mar 1994 Cover: 1.50 **NM value: 2.00**
Circ: CapCity orders: **64,650**
📖 Obsessions! **A:** M.D. Bright **W:** Louise Simonson

32 ❑ Apr 1994 Cover: 1.50 **NM value: 2.00**
Circ: CapCity orders: **57,900**
• Bizarro

33 ❑ May 1994 Cover: 1.50 **NM value: 2.00**
Circ: CapCity orders: **54,450**

34 ❑ Jun 1994 Cover: 1.50 **NM value: 2.00**
Circ: CapCity orders: **55,250**
📖 Battle for Metropolis

35 ❑ Jul 1994 Cover: 1.50 **NM value: 2.00**
Circ: CapCity orders: **58,150**
📖 Worlds Collide, Part 1 • crossover with Milestone Media

36 ❑ Aug 1994 Cover: 1.50 **NM value: 2.00**
Circ: CapCity orders: **51,800**
📖 Worlds Collide, Part 10 • ▲1994-29 **A:** Jon Bogdanove **W:** Louise Simonson ★ Appearance of Static, Icon, Hardware.

37 ❑ Sep 1994 Cover: 1.50 **NM value: 2.00**
Circ: CapCity orders: **53,200** • **CGC:** 1 graded, best 9.8
• Zero Hour

38 ❑ Nov 1994 Cover: 1.50 **NM value: 2.00**
Circ: CapCity orders: **45,850**
📖 Dead Again

39 ❑ Dec 1994 Cover: 1.50 **NM value: 2.00**
Circ: CapCity orders: **44,600**
📖 Dead Again

40 ❑ Jan 1995 Cover: 1.50 **NM value: 2.00**
Circ: CapCity orders: **42,250**
📖 Dead Again • ▲1995-1 **A:** Jon Bogdanove **W:** Louise Simonson

41 ❑ Feb 1995 Cover: 1.50 **NM value: 2.00**
Circ: CapCity orders: **40,225**

42 ❑ Mar 1995 Cover: 1.50 **NM value: 2.00**
Circ: CapCity orders: **37,300**

43 ❑ Apr 1995 Cover: 1.50 **NM value: 2.00**
Circ: CapCity orders: **35,300**
★ Appearance of Mr. Miracle.

44 ❑ May 1995 Cover: 1.50 **NM value: 2.00**
Circ: CapCity orders: **44,625**

45 ❑ Jun 1995 Cover: 1.95 **NM value: 2.00**
Circ: CapCity orders: **40,450**

46 ❑ Jul 1995 Cover: 1.95 **NM value: 2.00**
Circ: CapCity orders: **33,425**

47 ❑ Aug 1995 Cover: 1.95 **NM value: 2.00**
Circ: CapCity orders: **33,225**

48 ❑ Sep 1995 Cover: 1.95 **NM value: 2.00**
Circ: CapCity orders: **31,850**
★ Appearance of Aquaman.

49 ❑ Oct 1995 Cover: 1.95 **NM value: 2.00**
Circ: CapCity orders: **26,575**

50 ❑ Nov 1995 Cover: 2.95 **NM value: 3.00**
• Giant-size. 📖 Trial of Superman

51 ❑ Dec 1995 Cover: 1.95 **NM value: 2.00**
📖 Trial of Superman ★ Versus Freelance.

52 ❑ Jan 1996 Cover: 1.95 **NM value: 2.00**
📖 Trial of Superman ★ Versus Cyborg.

53 ❑ Feb 1996 Cover: 1.95 **NM value: 2.00**
📖 The Game **A:** Jon Bogdanove **W:** Louise Simonson ★ Versus Brawl.

54 ❑ Mar 1996 Cover: 1.95 **NM value: 2.00**
📖 Ghosts • ▲1996-10 **A:** Denys Cowan **W:** Louise Simonson ★ Appearance of Spectre.

55 ❑ Apr 1996 Cover: 1.95 **NM value: 2.00**
📖 Something Fishy • ▲1996-15 **A:** Jon Bogdanove **W:** Louise Simonson ★ Death of Jeb Friedman.

56 ❑ May 1996 Cover: 1.95 **NM value: 2.00**
★ Versus Mxyzptlk.

57 ❑ Jun 1996 Cover: 1.95 **NM value: 2.00**
★ Appearance of Golden Age Flash.

58 ❑ Jul 1996 Cover: 1.95 **NM value: 2.00**

59 ❑ Aug 1996 Cover: 1.95 **NM value: 2.00**
★ Versus Parasite.

60 ❑ Sep 1996 Cover: 1.95 **NM value: 2.00**
📖 The Bottle City, Part 2

61 ❑ Oct 1996 Cover: 1.95 **NM value: 2.00**
📖 Losin' It • polybagged with On the Edge; ▲1996-41 **A:** Jon Bogdanove **W:** Louise Simonson

62 ❑ Oct 1996 Cover: 1.95 **NM value: 2.00**
Circ: Diamd. preorders: **62,398**
📖 To Build a Fire • Final Night; ▲1996-45 **A:** Jon Bogdanove **W:** Louise Simonson ★ Origin of Superman.

63 ❑ Dec 1996 Cover: 1.95 **NM value: 2.00**
Circ: Diamd. preorders: **89,466**
📖 Hawaiian Honeymoon; Fireworks • Lois rescues Clark from terrorists; ▲1996-50 **A:** Jon Bogdanove **W:** Louise Simonson

64 ❑ Jan 1997 Cover: 1.95 **NM value: 2.00**
Circ: Diamd. preorders: **59,712**
📖 Power Struggle; Into the Fire! • ▲1997-4 **A:** Ron Lim **W:** Louise Simonson

65 ❑ Mar 1997 Cover: 1.95 **NM value: 2.00**
Circ: Diamd. preorders: **54,255**
📖 Losers • ▲1997-9 **A:** Sal Buscema **W:** Louise Simonson ★ Versus Superman Revenge Squad.

66 ❑ Apr 1997 Cover: 1.95 **NM value: 2.00**
Circ: Diamd. preorders: **52,059**

67 ❑ May 1997 Cover: 1.95 **NM value: 2.00**
Circ: Diamd. preorders: **88,415**
• destruction of old costume★ Appearance of Scorn.

68 ❑ Jun 1997 Cover: 1.95 **NM value: 2.00**
Circ: Diamd. preorders: **72,272**
★ Versus Metallo.

69 ❑ Jul 1997 Cover: 1.95 **NM value: 2.00**
Circ: Diamd. preorders: **69,503**
• in Kandor★ Appearance of Atom.

70 ❑ Aug 1997 Cover: 1.95 **NM value: 2.00**
Circ: Diamd. preorders: **67,728**
★ Appearance of Scorn. ★ Versus Saviour.

71 ❑ Sep 1997 Cover: 1.95 **NM value: 2.00**
Circ: Diamd. preorders: **65,039**
★ 1st Appearance of Baud.

72 ❑ Oct 1997 Cover: 1.95 **NM value: 2.00**
Circ: Diamd. preorders: **64,974**
• Genesis★ Versus Mainframe.

73 ❑ Nov 1997 Cover: 1.95 **NM value: 2.00**
Circ: Diamd. preorders: **59,681**
★ Versus Parademons.

74 ❑ Dec 1997 Cover: 1.95 **NM value: 2.00**
Circ: Diamd. preorders: **58,276**
Face cover. 📖 Subterranean Terror • ▲1997-47 **A:** Scot Eaton **W:** Louise Simonson ★ Appearance of Sam Lane. ★ Versus Rajiv.

75 ❑ Jan 1998 Cover: 1.95 **NM value: 2.00**
Circ: Diamd. preorders: **60,341**
📖 The Death of Mr. Mxyptlk • ▲1998-1 **A:** Jon Bogdanove **W:** Jon Bogdanove; Louise Simonson ★ Appearance of Mike Carlin. ★ Death of Mr. Mxyzptlk.

76 ❑ Feb 1998 Cover: 1.95 **NM value: 2.00**
Circ: Diamd. preorders: **53,632**
★ Appearance of Simyan, Morgan Edge, Mokkari.

77 ❑ Mar 1998 Cover: 1.95 **NM value: 2.00**
Circ: Diamd. preorders: **51,874**
cover forms diptych with Action Comics #742. 📖 Triangles **A:** Paul Ryan **W:** Louise Simonson

78 ❑ Apr 1998 Cover: 1.95 **NM value: 2.00**
Circ: Diamd. preorders: **51,027**
• Millennium Giants

79 ❑ May 1998 Cover: 1.95 **NM value: 2.00**
Circ: Diamd. preorders: **52,256**
• Millennium Giants aftermath

80 ❑ Jun 1998 Cover: 1.95 **NM value: 2.00**
Circ: Diamd. preorders: **58,382**
• set in late '30s

81 ❑ Jul 1998 Cover: 1.95 **NM value: 2.00**
Circ: Diamd. preorders: **52,790**
• set in late '30s

82 ❑ Aug 1998 Cover: 1.95 **NM value: 2.00**
Circ: Diamd. preorders: **52,056**
★ Appearance of Kismet. ★ Versus Dominus.

83 ❑ Sep 1998 Cover: 1.99 **NM value: 2.00**
Circ: Diamd. preorders: **49,321**
★ Appearance of Waverider.

84 ❑ Dec 1998 Cover: 1.99 **NM value: 2.00**
Circ: Diamd. preorders: **46,357**
• in Kandor★ 1st Appearance of Inventor.

CGC-graded: Multiply prices above by **33 for 9.9 M • 16 for 9.8 NM/M • 7 for 9.6 NM+ • 5 for 9.4 NM • 2.5 for 9.2 NM- • 1.5 for 9.0 VF/NM**

85 ❑ Jan 1999 Cover: 1.99 **NM** value: **2.00**
Circ: Diamd. preorders: **44,683**
★ Versus Simyan. ★ Versus Mokkari.

86 ❑ Feb 1999 Cover: 1.99 **NM** value: **2.00**
Circ: Diamd. preorders: **42,621**
A: Scot Eaton **W:** Louise Simonson

87 ❑ Mar 1999 Cover: 1.99 **NM** value: **2.00**
Circ: Diamd. preorders: **41,138**
A: Doug Mahnke **W:** Mark Schultz ★ Appearance of Steel, Superboy, Supergirl.

88 ❑ May 1999 Cover: 1.99 **NM** value: **2.00**
Circ: Diamd. preorders: **38,988**
A: Doug Mahnke **W:** Mark Schultz ★ Versus Robots.

89 ❑ Jun 1999 Cover: 1.99 **NM** value: **2.00**
Circ: Diamd. preorders: **40,390**
Prelude to a Coronation • ▲1999-21 **A:** Doug Mahnke **W:** Mark Schultz ★ Versus Dominus.

90 ❑ Jul 1999 Cover: 1.99 **NM** value: **2.00**
Circ: Diamd. preorders: **40,099**
A Girl and her Robot • ▲1999-26 **A:** Mike Collins **W:** Mark Schultz

91 ❑ Aug 1999 Cover: 1.99 **NM** value: **Cover or less**
Circ: Diamd. preorders: **39,726**
Nemesis • ▲1999-31 **A:** Charles Adlard **W:** John Rozum

92 ❑ Sep 1999 Cover: 1.99 **NM** value: **Cover or less**
Circ: Diamd. preorders: **39,871**
One-Man JLA; Secret Origins, Part 4 • Superman as Martian Manhunter; ▲1999-35 **A:** Tom Grindberg **W:** Tom Peyer

93 ❑ Oct 1999 Cover: 1.99 **NM** value: **Cover or less**
Circ: Diamd. preorders: **37,580**
The Sea Beast of Metropolis! • ▲1999-39 **A:** Doug Mahnke **W:** Mrk Schultz

94 ❑ Nov 1999 Cover: 1.99 **NM** value: **Cover or less**
Circ: Diamd. preorders: **36,998**
W: Mrk Schultz ★ Appearance of Strange Visitor. ★ Versus Parasite.

95 ❑ Dec 1999 Cover: 1.99 **NM** value: **Cover or less**
Circ: Diamd. preorders: **39,489**
Krypton Lives • ▲1999-48 **A:** Doug Mahnke **W:** Mrk Schultz

96 ❑ Jan 2000 Cover: 1.99 **NM** value: **Cover or less**
Circ: Diamd. preorders: **37,057**
Home • ?2000-3 **A:** Doug Mahnke **W:** Mrk Schultz

97 ❑ Feb 2000 Cover: 1.99 **NM** value: **Cover or less**
Circ: Diamd. preorders: **38,689**
W: Mrk Schultz

98 ❑ Mar 2000 Cover: 1.99 **NM** value: **Cover or less**
Circ: Diamd. preorders: **37,255**
W: Mrk Schultz

99 ❑ Apr 2000 Cover: 1.99 **NM** value: **Cover or less**
Circ: Diamd. preorders: **35,943**
All that Dwell in Dark Waters • ?2000-16 **A:** Pablo Raimondi **W:** Mark Schultz

100 ❑ May 2000 Cover: 2.99 **NM** value: **Cover or less**
Circ: Diamd. preorders: **12,432**
• Giant-size. Creation Story • ?2000-20 **A:** Doug Mahnke **W:** Mark Schultz

100/SC ❑ May 2000 Cover: 3.99 **NM** value: **Cover or less**
Circ: Diamd. preorders: **39,256** • **CGC:** 1 graded, best 9.6
Special fold-out cover. • Giant-size. Creation Story • ?2000-20 **A:** Doug Mahnke **W:** Mark Schultz

101 ❑ Jun 2000 Cover: 1.99 **NM** value: **Cover or less**
Circ: Diamd. preorders: **38,018**
A: Doug Mahnke **W:** Mark Schultz

102 ❑ Jul 2000 Cover: 1.99 **NM** value: **Cover or less**
Circ: Diamd. preorders: **37,922**
A: Doug Mahnke **W:** Mark Schultz

103 ❑ Aug 2000 Cover: 1.99 **NM** value: **Cover or less**
Circ: Diamd. preorders: **38,720**
A: Doug Mahnke **W:** Mark Schultz

104 ❑ Sep 2000 Cover: 2.25 **NM** value: **Cover or less**
Circ: Diamd. preorders: **43,161**
No Axioms • ?2000-36 **A:** Doug Mahnke **W:** Mark Schultz

105 ❑ Oct 2000 Cover: 2.25 **NM** value: **Cover or less**
Circ: Diamd. preorders: **39,532**
Emperor Joker, Part 3 • (c)2000-41 **A:** Doug Mahnke **W:** Mark Schultz

106 ❑ Nov 2000 Cover: 2.25 **NM** value: **Cover or less**
Circ: Diamd. preorders: **37,800**
Under the Waterfront • ?2000-45 **A:** Carlo Barberi **W:** Mark Schultz

107 ❑ Dec 2000 Cover: 2.25 **NM** value: **Cover or less**
Circ: Diamd. preorders: **37,979**
In the Zone • ?2000-49 **A:** Doug Mahnke **W:** Mark Schultz

108 ❑ Jan 2001 Cover: 2.25 **NM** value: **Cover or less**
Circ: Diamd. preorders: **37,563**
Metropolis is Burning • ?2001-4 **A:** Doug Mahnke; Paco Medina **W:** Mark Schultz

109 ❑ Feb 2001 Cover: 2.25 **NM** value: **Cover or less**
Circ: Diamd. preorders: **35,625**
World Without Superman • ?2001-8 **A:** Duncan Rouleau **W:** Mark Schultz

110 ❑ Mar 2001 Cover: 2.25 **NM** value: **Cover or less**
Circ: Diamd. preorders: **34,893**
Saints • ?2001-12 **A:** Doug Mahnke **W:** Mark Schultz ★ Appearance of Stars and S.T.R.I.P.E..

111 ❑ Apr 2001 Cover: 2.25 **NM** value: **Cover or less**
Circ: Diamd. preorders: **36,937**
The Most Dangerous Kryptonian Game • ?2001-16 **A:** Doug Mahnke **W:** Mark Schultz

112 ❑ May 2001 Cover: 2.25 **NM** value: **Cover or less**
Circ: Diamd. preorders: **34,243**
The Adventures of...Krypto! • ?2001-20 **A:** Yanick Paquette; Olivier Cuipel **W:** Mark Schultz

113 ❑ Jun 2001 Cover: 2.25 **NM** value: **Cover or less**
Circ: Diamd. preorders: **36,500**

114 ❑ Jul 2001 Cover: 2.25 **NM** value: **Cover or less**
Circ: Diamd. preorders: **36,017**

115 ❑ Aug 2001 Cover: 2.25 **NM** value: **Cover or less**
Circ: Diamd. preorders: **44,831**

116 ❑ Sep 2001 Cover: 2.25 **NM** value: **Cover or less**
Circ: Diamd. preorders: **47,020**

1000000 ❑ Nov 1998 Cover: 1.99 **NM** value: **Cover or less**
Circ: Diamd. preorders: **56,176**
Fear & Loathing **A:** Jerry Ordway **W:** Karl Kesel

Anl 1 ❑ ca. 1992 Cover: 2.50 **NM** value: **3.00**
Circ: CapCity orders: **29,200**
Eclipso: The Darkness Within, Part 2 ★ Appearance of Eclipso.

Anl 2 ❑ ca. 1993 Cover: 2.50 **NM** value: **3.00**
Circ: CapCity orders: **58,700**
Bloodlines • Bloodlines ★ 1st Appearance of Edge.

Anl 3 ❑ ca. 1994 Cover: 2.95 **NM** value: **3.00**
Circ: CapCity orders: **39,050**
• Elseworlds **C:** Mike Mignola

Anl 4 ❑ ca. 1995 Cover: 2.95 **NM** value: **3.00**
Circ: CapCity orders: **27,250**
Superman: Year One • Year One **A:** John Paul Leon **W:** Louise Simonson ★ Appearance of Justice League.

Anl 5 ❑ Nov 1996 Cover: 2.95 **NM** value: **3.00**
Circ: Diamd. preorders: **46,596**
The Never-Ending Battle • Legends of the Dead Earth **A:** Paul Ryan; Joe Rubinstein **W:** Kurt Busiek ★ 1st Appearance of Kaleb.

Anl 6 ❑ Aug 1997 Cover: 3.95 **NM** value: **Cover or less**
Circ: Diamd. preorders: **47,196**
• Pulp Heroes

SUPERMAN: THE MAN OF STEEL GALLERY — DC

1 ❑ Dec 1995 Cover: 3.50 **NM** value: **Cover or less**
• pin-ups

SUPERMAN: THE MAN OF TOMORROW — DC

Beginning with issues dated January 1991, the three regular Superman titles, Superman, The Adventures of Superman, and Action Comics, began a tight, integrated continuity. Stories were continued, not from one month's issue to the same title the next month, but to the issue that would be appearing the next week regardless of its title. When Superman: The Man of Steel appeared in July of 1991, it tied into the other three Superman titles, virtually guaranteeing a Superman story every week. Virtually, but not literally, since some months contain five weeks. Hence came Superman: The Man of Tomorrow in 1995 to cover that vexing fifth week. Usually published every thirteen weeks, this title bears a season in its indicia rather than a month and assures Superman fans that they will receive a steady chronicle of the adventures of the first and foremost super-hero.

1 ❑ Sum 1995 Cover: 1.95 **NM** value: **2.00**
Circ: CapCity orders: **41,200**

2 ❑ Fal 1995 Cover: 1.95 **NM** value: **2.00**
Circ: CapCity orders: **25,175**
★ Appearance of Alpha Centurion.

3 ❑ Win 1995 Cover: 1.95 **NM** value: **2.00**
Trial of Superman • Underworld Unleashed ★ Appearance of how Luthor regained strength and.

4 ❑ Spr 1996 Cover: 1.95 **NM** value: **2.00**
...The World's Mightiest Mortals! • ▲1996-13 **A:** Brett Breeding; Tom Grummett **W:** Roger Stern ★ Appearance of Captain Marvel.

5 ❑ Sum 1996 Cover: 1.95 **NM** value: **2.00**
• Wedding of Lex Luthor and Contessa

6 ❑ Fal 1996 Cover: 1.95 **NM** value: **2.00**
Going to Extremes • ▲1996-38 **A:** Paul Ryan **W:** Roger Stern ★ Versus Jackal.

7 ❑ Win 1997 Cover: 1.95 **NM** value: **2.00**
Circ: Diamd. preorders: **50,823**
★ Versus Maxima.

8 ❑ Sum 1997 Cover: 1.95 **NM** value: **2.00**
Circ: Diamd. preorders: **49,172**
★ Versus Rock.

9 ❑ Fal 1997 Cover: 1.95 **NM** value: **2.00**
Circ: Diamd. preorders: **56,056**
• Ma and Pa Kent remember Superman's career

10 ❑ Win 1998 Cover: 1.95 **NM** value: **2.00**
Circ: Diamd. preorders: **47,899**
• Obsession vs. Maxima

11 ❑ Fal 1998 Cover: 1.99 **NM** value: **2.00**
Circ: Diamd. preorders: **43,163**
Timewar

12 ❑ Win 1998 Cover: 1.99 **NM** value: **2.00**
Circ: Diamd. preorders: **40,489**

13 ❑ Spr 1998 Cover: 1.99 **NM** value: **2.00**
Circ: Diamd. preorders: **38,135**

14 ❑ Sum 1998 Cover: 1.99 **NM** value: **2.00**
Circ: Diamd. preorders: **37,305**
★ Versus Riot.

15 ❑ Fal 1998 Cover: 2.95 **NM** value: **3.00**
Circ: Diamd. preorders: **36,398**
• Day of Judgment ★ Versus Neron.

1000000 ❑ Nov 1998 Cover: 1.99 **NM** value: **2.00**
Circ: Diamd. preorders: **53,156**

SUPERMAN: THE ODYSSEY — DC

1 ❑ Jul 1999 Cover: 4.95 **NM** value: **Cover or less**
Circ: Diamd. preorders: **26,854**
No issue number. One-shot. • prestige format. **A:** Graham Nolan **W:** Graham Nolan; Chuck Dixon

SUPERMAN: THE SECRET YEARS — DC

1 ❑ Feb 1985 Cover: 0.75 **NM** value: **1.50**
A: Curt Swan; Frank Miller(cover) **W:** Bob Rozakis

2 ❑ Mar 1985 Cover: 0.75 **NM** value: **1.50**
• Clark reveals his secret to Billy Cramer **A:** Curt Swan; Frank Miller(cover) **W:** Bob Rozakis ★ Appearance of Lori Lemaris.

3 ❑ Apr 1985 Cover: 0.75 **NM** value: **1.50**
Terminus **A:** Curt Swan; Frank Miller(cover) **W:** Bob Rozakis ★ Death of Billy Cramer.

4 ❑ May 1985 Cover: 0.75 **NM** value: **1.50**
Circ: CapCity orders: **10,350**
• Superboy becomes Superman; Clark Kent meets Perry White **A:** Curt Swan; Frank Miller(cover) **W:** Bob Rozakis

SUPERMAN: THE TRIAL OF SUPERMAN — DC

1 ❑ Cover: 14.95 **NM** value: **Cover or less**
• Collects story from Action Comics #716-717, Adventures of Superman #529-531, Superman #106-108, Superman: the Man of Steel #50-52, Superman: The Man of Tomorrow #3 **A:** Kieron Dwyer; Stuart Immonen; Ron Frenz; Tom Grummett; Jon Bogdanove **W:** Karl Kesel; Stuart Immonen; Dan Jurgens; Roger Stern; David Michelinie; Louise Simons

SUPERMAN: THE WEDDING ALBUM — DC

1 ❑ Dec 1996 Cover: 4.95 **NM** value: **Cover or less**
Circ: Diamd. preorders: **291,056** • **CGC:** 5 graded, best 9.8
• newsstand edition with gatefold back cover. • Wedding of Clark Kent and Lois Lane; ▲1996-47 **A:** Kieron Dwyer; Brett Breeding; Stuart Immonen; Jerry Ordway; George Pérez; John Byrne; Jackson Guice; Paul Ryan; Gil Kane; Dan Jurgens; Curt Swan; Ron Frenz; Kerry Gammill; Jim Mooney; Bob McLeod; Jon Bogdanove; Terry Austin; Dennis Janke **W:** Karl Kesel; Dan Jurgens; Louise Simonson; Roger Stern; David Michelinie

1/DM ❑ Dec 1996 Cover: 4.95 **NM** value: **Cover or less**
Circ: Diamd. preorders: **55,082** • **CGC:** 17 graded, best 9.8
white cardstock wraparound cover with gatefold back cover. • Wedding of Clark Kent and Lois Lane

SUPERMAN: THE WEDDING & BEYOND — DC

Bk 1 ❑ Cover: 14.95 **NM** value: **Cover or less**
• collects Superman: The Wedding Album, Superman #118, Action Comics #728, Adventures of Superman #541, and Superman: The Man of Steel #63

SUPERMAN: THEY SAVED LUTHOR'S BRAIN — DC

1 ❑ **NM** value: **4.95**

SUPERMAN/TOYMAN — DC

1 ❑ Cover: 1.95 **NM** value: **Cover or less**
One-shot. • promo for toy line

SUPERMAN TRANSFORMED! — DC

Bk 1 ❑ Cover: 12.95 **NM** value: **Cover or less**
• collects Action Comics #729 and #732, Adventures of Superman #542 and #545, Superman #119, #122, and #123, Superman: The Man of Steel #64 and #67

SUPERMAN: UNDER A YELLOW SUN — DC

1 ❑ ca. 1994 Cover: 5.95 **NM** value: **Cover or less**
Circ: CapCity orders: **23,500**
No issue number. • prestige format one-shot **A:** Eduardo Barreto; Kerry Gammill **W:** John Francis Moore

SUPERMAN VS. ALIENS — DC / Dark Horse

1 ❑ Jul 1995 Cover: 4.95 **NM** value: **Cover or less**
Circ: CapCity orders: **46,025** • **CGC:** 2 graded, best 9.8
• prestige format. • crossover with Dark Horse **A:** Dan Jurgens; Kevin Nowlan **W:** Dan Jurgens

2 ❑ Aug 1995 Cover: 4.95 **NM** value: **Cover or less**
Circ: CapCity orders: **40,425**
• prestige format. • crossover with Dark Horse **A:** Dan Jurgens; Kevin Nowlan **W:** Dan Jurgens

3 ❑ Sep 1995 Cover: 4.95 **NM** value: **Cover or less**
Circ: CapCity orders: **37,850**
• prestige format. • crossover with Dark Horse **A:** Dan Jurgens; Kevin Nowlan **W:** Dan Jurgens

Bk 1 ❑ Jun 1996 Cover: 14.95 **NM** value: **Cover or less**

SUPERMAN VS. PREDATOR — DC / Dark Horse

1 ❑ Jul 2000 Cover: 4.95 **NM** value: **Cover or less**
Circ: Diamd. preorders: **27,746**
A: Alex Maleev **W:** David Michelinie

2 ❑ Aug 2000 Cover: 4.95 **NM** value: **Cover or less**
Circ: Diamd. preorders: **27,002**
A: Alex Maleev **W:** David Michelinie

3 ❑ Sep 2000 Cover: 4.95 **NM** value: **Cover or less**
Circ: Diamd. preorders: **25,551**
A: Alex Maleev **W:** David Michelinie

SUPERMAN VS. THE AMAZING SPIDER-MAN — DC / Marvel

1 ❑ Cover: 2.00 **NM** value: **20.00**
• treasury-sized. • first DC/Marvel crossover **A:** Dick Giordano; Ross Andru ★ Versus Lex Luthor. ★ Versus Doctor Octopus. ★ Versus Lex Luthor, Doc Ock.

SUPERMAN VS. THE REVENGE SQUAD — DC

1 ❑ Cover: 12.95 **NM** value: **Cover or less**
• Collects story from Adventures of Superman #539, 542, 543, Action Comics #726, 730, Superman: The Man of Steel #61, 65, Superman: The Man of Tomorrow #7 **A:** Denis Rodier; Brett Breeding; Stuart Immonen; Ron Lim; Paul Ryan; Tom Morgan; Tom Grummettt; Jon Bogdanove **W:** Karl Kesel; Jerry Ordway; Louise Simonson; Roger Stern; David Michelinie

SUPERMAN VS. THE TERMINATOR: DEATH TO THE FUTURE — Dark Horse

1 ❑ Dec 1999 Cover: 2.95 **NM** value: **Cover or less**
Circ: Diamd. preorders: **33,052**
A: Steve Pugh **W:** Alan Grant

Other grades: Multiply prices above by **1.5 for Mint • 2/3 for Very Fine • 1/3 for Fine • 1/5 for Very Good • 1/8 for Good**

2 ❑ Jan 2000 Cover: 2.95 **NM** value: **Cover or less**
Circ: Diamd. preorders: **27,074**
A: Steve Pugh **W:** Alan Grant
3 ❑ Feb 2000 Cover: 2.95 **NM** value: **Cover or less**
Circ: Diamd. preorders: **25,425**
A: Steve Pugh **W:** Alan Grant
4 ❑ Mar 2000 Cover: 2.95 **NM** value: **Cover or less**
Circ: Diamd. preorders: **25,834**
A: Steve Pugh **W:** Alan Grant

SUPERMAN VILLAINS SECRET FILES DC

1 ❑ Jun 1998 Cover: 4.95 **NM** value: **Cover or less**
Circ: Diamd. preorders: **32,478**
• biographical info on Superman's Rogues Gallery **W:** Stuart Immonen

SUPERMAN: WAR OF THE WORLDS DC

1 ❑ Dec 1998 Cover: 5.95 **NM** value: **Cover or less**
Circ: Diamd. preorders: **31,171**
No issue number. • prestige format one-shot; Elseworlds
1/LE❑ ca. 1999 Cover: 18.95 **NM** value: **Cover or less**

SUPERMAN: "WHATEVER HAPPENED TO THE MAN OF TOMORROW?" DC

1 ❑ Feb 1997 Cover: 5.95 **NM** value: **Cover or less**
Circ: Diamd. preorders: **20,406**
No issue number. • prestige format collection of Action Comics #583 and Superman #423 **W:** Alan Moore

SUPERMAN/WONDER WOMAN: WHOM GODS DESTROY DC

1 ❑ Dec 1996 Cover: 4.95 **NM** value: **Cover or less**
Circ: Diamd. preorders: **53,372**
• prestige format. 📖 TheDream • Elseworlds **A:** Dusty Abell **W:** Chris Claremont
2 ❑ Jan 1997 Cover: 4.95 **NM** value: **Cover or less**
Circ: Diamd. preorders: **47,539**
• prestige format. 📖 The Hunt • Elseworlds **A:** Dusty Abell **W:** Chris Claremont
3 ❑ Feb 1997 Cover: 4.95 **NM** value: **Cover or less**
Circ: Diamd. preorders: **41,164**
• prestige format. • Elseworlds **A:** Dusty Abell **W:** Chris Claremont
4 ❑ Mar 1997 Cover: 4.95 **NM** value: **Cover or less**
Circ: Diamd. preorders: **38,792**
• prestige format. 📖 The Price final issue. • Elseworlds **A:** Dusty Abell **W:** Chris Claremont

SUPERMAN Y2K DC

1 ❑ Feb 2000 Cover: 2.95 **NM** value: **Cover or less**
Circ: Diamd. preorders: **29,131**

SUPER MARIO BROS. (1ST SERIES) Valiant

By 1993, Valiant was the darling of the comics industry, having revitalized old properties like Solar, Man of the Atom and Magnus, Robot Fighter, merging them with new heroes into a unique, highly connected super-hero universe. Valiant was hotter than hot...and it all seemed to come out of nowhere.

But while speculators were busy bidding up the price of Harbinger #1, few realized that Valiant had an earlier history publishing kids comics based on video games from Nintendo.

Super Mario Bros. was one of those early comics, serving up harmless, lighthearted adventures based on the star characters of so many Nintendo video games.

Ironically, Valiant would be bought by Acclaim, a video-game company — which would find it next-to-impossible to play on the synergies of comics and video games in the post-glut market of the mid-1990s.

1 ❑ ca. 1991 Cover: 1.95 **NM** value: **Cover or less**
Circ: CapCity orders: **6,400** • **CGC:** 1 graded, best 8.5
2 ❑ ca. 1991 Cover: 1.95 **NM** value: **Cover or less**
Circ: CapCity orders: **4,600**
3 ❑ ca. 1991 Cover: 1.95 **NM** value: **Cover or less**
Circ: CapCity orders: **2,600**
4 ❑ ca. 1991 Cover: 1.95 **NM** value: **Cover or less**
Circ: CapCity orders: **2,300**
5 ❑ ca. 1991 Cover: 1.95 **NM** value: **Cover or less**
Circ: CapCity orders: **1,800**
📖 Dug Stoopid Bomb! **A:** George Wildman; Bill Vallely; Carol Smith; Ken Shooter; Mark McClellan; P. Zorito; Rod Ollerenshaw **W:** George Wildman; Bill Vallely; Carol Smith; Ken Shooter; Mark McClellan; P. Zorito; Rod Ollerenshaw
6 ❑ ca. 1991 Cover: 1.95 **NM** value: **Cover or less**
Circ: CapCity orders: **1,600**
📖 The Buddy System; Weight Up; Kitchen Kraziness; It's Always Fair Weather **A:** George Wildman; Heather Eastman; Jade; Kathryn Bolinger; P. Zorito; Sikorski; Slinchak **W:** Mark McClellan; Bill Valley; John Walker
SE 1❑ ca. 1990 Cover: 1.95 **NM** value: **Cover or less**
Circ: CapCity orders: **6,300** • **CGC:** 1 graded, best 9.2
📖 The Legend; Mutiny on the Fungi; Koopa's Health and Beauty Tips; Dear Princess Toadstool; A Mouser in the Houser **A:** Art Nichols **W:** George Caragonne

SUPER MARIO BROS. (2ND SERIES) Valiant

1 ❑ ca. 1991 Cover: 1.50 **NM** value: **Cover or less**
2 ❑ ca. 1991 Cover: 1.50 **NM** value: **Cover or less**
3 ❑ ca. 1991 Cover: 1.50 **NM** value: **Cover or less**
4 ❑ ca. 1991 Cover: 1.50 **NM** value: **Cover or less**
5 ❑ ca. 1991 Cover: 1.50 **NM** value: **Cover or less**

SUPERMEN OF AMERICA DC

1 ❑ Mar 1999 Cover: 3.95 **NM** value: **Cover or less**
Circ: Diamd. preorders: **9,734**
📖 Fire From Heaven **A:** Norm Breyfogle **W:** Stuart Immonen ★ Origin of Supermen of America.
1/CS❑ Mar 1999 Cover: 4.95 **NM** value: **Cover or less**
Circ: Diamd. preorders: **32,532**
Gatefold cardstock cover. • Collector's edition. 📖 Fire From Heaven **A:** Norm Breyfogle **W:** Stuart Immonen ★ Origin of Supermen of America.
2 ❑ Apr 1999 Cover: 2.50 **NM** value: **Cover or less**
Circ: Diamd. preorders: **18,999**
3 ❑ May 1999 Cover: 2.50 **NM** value: **Cover or less**
Circ: Diamd. preorders: **16,063**
📖 A Piece of the Action **A:** Doug Braithwaite **W:** Fabian Nicieza
4 ❑ Jun 1999 Cover: 2.50 **NM** value: **Cover or less**
Circ: Diamd. preorders: **13,985**
📖 Up, Up, and Away... **A:** Doug Braithwaite **W:** Fabian Nicieza

SUPERMODELS IN THE RAINFOREST Sirius

1 ❑ Dec 1998, b&w Cover: 2.95 **NM** value: **Cover or less**
Circ: Diamd. preorders: **6,341**
📖 Welcome to the Amazon; The Lost World **A:** Kevin J. Taylor; Dark One **W:** Kevin J. Taylor; Mark Bellis; Robb Horan
2 ❑ Feb 1999, b&w Cover: 2.95 **NM** value: **Cover or less**
Circ: Diamd. preorders: **3,582**
3 ❑ Apr 1999 Cover: 2.95 **NM** value: **Cover or less**
Circ: Diamd. preorders: **2,355**

SUPERMOUSE, THE BIG CHEESE Pines

With a few bites of supercheese, Supermouse, the hero of Animalville, U.I.A., is able to bend steel bars in his mighty hands and change the course of mighty rivers as he flies through the skies in his red-and-blue outfit with the yellow "S" emblazoned across his chest. His main opponent is Terrible Tom, a wily feline who escapes with alarming frequency only to be tossed back in by the mouse of might. His girl friend Mabel actually does help in many adventures, slipping him a chuck of supercheese before Terrible Tom's latest plan destroys the big cheese for good.

Supermouse is a more obvious compilation of Superman and Mighty Mouse, and may even predate Underdog in his use of a strength enhancing substance to gain superpowers. Some of the stories may seem a politically incorrect today, but were pro forma for the 1950's.

1 ❑ ca. 1949 Cover: 0.10 **NM** value: **150.00**
• Frank Frazetta text illustrations
2 ❑ Feb 1950 Cover: 0.10 **NM** value: **90.00**
• Frank Frazetta text illustrations
3 ❑ May 1950 Cover: 0.10 **NM** value: **70.00**
• Frank Frazetta text illustrations
4 ❑ Aug 1950 Cover: 0.10 **NM** value: **55.00**
• Frank Frazetta text illustrations
5 ❑ Nov 1950 Cover: 0.10 **NM** value: **55.00**
• Frank Frazetta text illustrations
6 ❑ Feb 1951 Cover: 0.10 **NM** value: **55.00**
• Frank Frazetta text illustrations
7 ❑ 1951 Cover: 0.10 **NM** value: **28.00**
8 ❑ 1951 Cover: 0.10 **NM** value: **28.00**
9 ❑ 1951 Cover: 0.10 **NM** value: **28.00**
10 ❑ 1951 Cover: 0.10 **NM** value: **28.00**
11 ❑ 1951 Cover: 0.10 **NM** value: **20.00**
12 ❑ 1951 Cover: 0.10 **NM** value: **20.00**
13 ❑ 1951 Cover: 0.10 **NM** value: **20.00**
14 ❑ Cover: 0.10 **NM** value: **20.00**
15 ❑ Cover: 0.10 **NM** value: **20.00**
16 ❑ 1952 Cover: 0.10 **NM** value: **20.00**
17 ❑ 1952 Cover: 0.10 **NM** value: **20.00**
18 ❑ 1952 Cover: 0.10 **NM** value: **20.00**
19 ❑ 1952 Cover: 0.10 **NM** value: **20.00**
20 ❑ 1952 Cover: 0.10 **NM** value: **20.00**
21 ❑ 1952 Cover: 0.10 **NM** value: **15.00**
22 ❑ 1952 Cover: 0.10 **NM** value: **15.00**
23 ❑ 1952 Cover: 0.10 **NM** value: **15.00**
24 ❑ 1952 Cover: 0.10 **NM** value: **15.00**
25 ❑ Cover: 0.10 **NM** value: **15.00**
26 ❑ Cover: 0.10 **NM** value: **15.00**
27 ❑ Cover: 0.10 **NM** value: **15.00**
28 ❑ Dec 1954 Cover: 0.10 **NM** value: **15.00**
29 ❑ ca. 1955 Cover: 0.10 **NM** value: **15.00**
30 ❑ ca. 1955 Cover: 0.10 **NM** value: **15.00**
31 ❑ ca. 1955 Cover: 0.10 **NM** value: **15.00**
32 ❑ ca. 1955 Cover: 0.10 **NM** value: **15.00**
33 ❑ ca. 1955 Cover: 0.10 **NM** value: **15.00**
34 ❑ ca. 1955 Cover: 0.10 **NM** value: **15.00**
35 ❑ ca. 1956 Cover: 0.10 **NM** value: **15.00**
36 ❑ ca. 1956 Cover: 0.10 **NM** value: **15.00**
37 ❑ ca. 1956 Cover: 0.10 **NM** value: **15.00**
38 ❑ ca. 1956 Cover: 0.10 **NM** value: **15.00**
39 ❑ ca. 1957 Cover: 0.10 **NM** value: **15.00**
40 ❑ ca. 1957 Cover: 0.10 **NM** value: **15.00**
41 ❑ ca. 1957 Cover: 0.10 **NM** value: **12.00**
42 ❑ ca. 1957 Cover: 0.10 **NM** value: **12.00**
43 ❑ ca. 1958 Cover: 0.10 **NM** value: **12.00**
44 ❑ ca. 1958 Cover: 0.10 **NM** value: **12.00**
45 ❑ ca. 1958 Cover: 0.10 **NM** value: **12.00**
GS 1❑ ca. 1957 Cover: 0.25 **NM** value: **50.00**
📖 Tommy Turtle...Sharps and Flat Work; Monsters on the Loose; Lucky Duck...Safe but not Sane; A Whale of a Story; Rocky Rabbit...Doctor's Orders; Lucky Duck...Mountain Madness; Sniffy th • Tommy Turtle app
GS 2❑ ca. 1958 Cover: 0.25 **NM** value: **45.00**

SUPER-MYSTERY COMICS Ace

1st Series
1 ❑ Jul 1940 Cover: 0.10 **NM** value: **1500.00**
• **CGC:** 3 graded, best 9.4
2 ❑ Aug 1940 Cover: 0.10 **NM** value: **750.00**
• **CGC:** 1 graded, best 2.5
3 ❑ Oct 1940 Cover: 0.10 **NM** value: **600.00**
• **CGC:** 1 graded, best 9.6
4 ❑ Nov 1940 Cover: 0.10 **NM** value: **450.00**
• **CGC:** 1 graded, best 9.2
5 ❑ Dec 1940 Cover: 0.10 **NM** value: **450.00**
6 ❑ Feb 1941 Cover: 0.10 **NM** value: **450.00**
2nd Series
1 ❑ Apr 1941 Cover: 0.10 **NM** value: **400.00**
• **CGC:** 1 graded, best 9.4
2 ❑ Jun 1941 Cover: 0.10 **NM** value: **350.00**
• **CGC:** 1 graded, best 9.6
3 ❑ Aug 1941 Cover: 0.10 **NM** value: **350.00**
• **CGC:** 1 graded, best 3.0
4 ❑ Oct 1941 Cover: 0.10 **NM** value: **350.00**
• **CGC:** 1 graded, best 6.0
5 ❑ Dec 1941 Cover: 0.10 **NM** value: **350.00**
• **CGC:** 2 graded, best 9.6
6 ❑ Feb 1942 Cover: 0.10 **NM** value: **350.00**
• **CGC:** 1 graded, best 4.0
3rd Series
1 ❑ Apr 1942 Cover: 0.10 **NM** value: **300.00**
• **CGC:** 1 graded, best 6.5
2 ❑ Jul 1942 Cover: 0.10 **NM** value: **300.00**
3 ❑ Jan 1943 Cover: 0.10 **NM** value: **300.00**
4 ❑ Apr 1943 Cover: 0.10 **NM** value: **300.00**
• **CGC:** 2 graded, best 8.5
5 ❑ Jul 1943 Cover: 0.10 **NM** value: **300.00**
6 ❑ Oct 1943 Cover: 0.10 **NM** value: **300.00**
4th Series
1 ❑ Jan 1944 Cover: 0.10 **NM** value: **200.00**
2 ❑ Apr 1944 Cover: 0.10 **NM** value: **200.00**
3 ❑ Jul 1944 Cover: 0.10 **NM** value: **200.00**
• **CGC:** 1 graded, best 7.5
4 ❑ Oct 1944 Cover: 0.10 **NM** value: **200.00**
5 ❑ Jan 1945 Cover: 0.10 **NM** value: **200.00**
6 ❑ Apr 1945 Cover: 0.10 **NM** value: **200.00**
5th Series
1 ❑ Jul 1945 Cover: 0.10 **NM** value: **175.00**
2 ❑ Oct 1945 Cover: 0.10 **NM** value: **175.00**
3 ❑ Dec 1945 Cover: 0.10 **NM** value: **175.00**
• **CGC:** 1 graded, best 9.2
4 ❑ Feb 1946 Cover: 0.10 **NM** value: **175.00**
• **CGC:** 1 graded, best 7.0
5 ❑ Apr 1946 Cover: 0.10 **NM** value: **175.00**
6 ❑ Jun 1946 Cover: 0.10 **NM** value: **175.00**
6th Series
1 ❑ Aug 1946 Cover: 0.10 **NM** value: **150.00**
• **CGC:** 1 graded, best 9.0
2 ❑ Oct 1946 Cover: 0.10 **NM** value: **150.00**
• **CGC:** 1 graded, best 3.5
3 ❑ Dec 1946 Cover: 0.10 **NM** value: **150.00**
• **CGC:** 4 graded, best 9.2
4 ❑ Feb 1947 Cover: 0.10 **NM** value: **150.00**
• **CGC:** 1 graded, best 8.5
5 ❑ Apr 1947 Cover: 0.10 **NM** value: **150.00**
6 ❑ Jul 1947 Cover: 0.10 **NM** value: **150.00**
7th Series
1 ❑ Sep 1947 Cover: 0.10 **NM** value: **150.00**
• Mister Risk; Uno, the United Nations Superhero
2 ❑ Nov 1947 Cover: 0.10 **NM** value: **150.00**
3 ❑ Jan 1948 Cover: 0.10 **NM** value: **150.00**
• **CGC:** 1 graded, best 9.2
4 ❑ Mar 1948 Cover: 0.10 **NM** value: **150.00**
5 ❑ May 1948 Cover: 0.10 **NM** value: **150.00**
6 ❑ Jul 1948 Cover: 0.10 **NM** value: **150.00**
8th Series
1 ❑ Sep 1948 Cover: 0.10 **NM** value: **125.00**
2 ❑ Nov 1948 Cover: 0.10 **NM** value: **125.00**
• **CGC:** 1 graded, best 8.5
3 ❑ Jan 1949 Cover: 0.10 **NM** value: **125.00**
4 ❑ Mar 1949 Cover: 0.10 **NM** value: **125.00**
5 ❑ May 1949 Cover: 0.10 **NM** value: **125.00**
• **CGC:** 1 graded, best 7.5
6 ❑ Jul 1949 Cover: 0.10 **NM** value: **125.00**

SUPERNATURAL LAW Exhibit A Press

24 ❑ Oct 1999 Cover: 2.50 **NM** value: **Cover or less**
📖 You'll Never Suck Blood in This Town Again • was Wolff & Byrd, Counselors of the Macabre **A:** Batton Lash **W:** Batton Lash
25 ❑ Cover: 2.50 **NM** value: **Cover or less**
A: Batton Lash **W:** Batton Lash
26 ❑ May 2000 Cover: 2.50 **NM** value: **Cover or less**
📖 Black Market Souls! **A:** Batton Lash **W:** Batton Lash
27 ❑ Jul 2000 Cover: 2.50 **NM** value: **Cover or less**
📖 Bright Lights, Big Feet; Jury Duty **A:** Batton Lash **W:** Batton Lash
28 ❑ Oct 2000 Cover: 2.50 **NM** value: **Cover or less**
📖 Is Everyone Courting Disaster? **A:** Batton Lash **W:** Batton Lash
29 ❑ Jul 2000 Cover: 2.50 **NM** value: **Cover or less**
📖 The Inevitable Hank **A:** Batton Lash **W:** Batton Lash
30 ❑ Mar 2001 Cover: 2.50 **NM** value: **Cover or less**
Circ: Diamd. preorders: **1,088**
A: Batton Lash **W:** Batton Lash
31 ❑ Cover: 2.50 **NM** value: **Cover or less**
A: Batton Lash **W:** Batton Lash

CGC-graded: Multiply prices above by **33 for 9.9 M • 16 for 9.8 NM/M • 7 for 9.6 NM+ • 5 for 9.4 NM • 2.5 for 9.2 NM- • 1.5 for 9.0 VF/NM**

SUPERNATURALS, THE — Marvel

1/A ❑ Dec 1998 Cover: 3.99 **NM** value: **Cover or less**
Circ: Diamd. preorders: **29,680**
📖 Design Demons **A:** Ivan Reis **W:** Brian Pulido; Mark Andreyko
1/B ❑ Dec 1998 Cover: 3.99 **NM** value: **Cover or less**
📖 Design Demons **A:** Ivan Reis **W:** Brian Pulido; Mark Andreyko
1/C ❑ Dec 1998 Cover: 3.99 **NM** value: **Cover or less**
📖 Design Demons **A:** Ivan Reis **W:** Brian Pulido; Mark Andreyko
1/D ❑ Dec 1998 Cover: 3.99 **NM** value: **Cover or less**
📖 Design Demons **A:** Ivan Reis **W:** Brian Pulido; Mark Andreyko
1/E ❑ Dec 1998 Cover: 3.99 **NM** value: **4.50**
📖 Design Demons **A:** Ivan Reis **W:** Brian Pulido; Mark Andreyko
1/LE ❑ Dec 1998 Cover: 14.95 **NM** value: **29.99**
📖 Design Demons **A:** Ivan Reis **W:** Brian Pulido; Mark Andreyko
2 ❑ Dec 1998 Cover: 3.99 **NM** value: **Cover or less**
Circ: Diamd. preorders: **27,601**
A: Ivan Reis **W:** Brian Pulido; Mark Andreyko
3 ❑ Dec 1998 Cover: 3.99 **NM** value: **Cover or less**
Circ: Diamd. preorders: **27,257**
A: Ivan Reis **W:** Brian Pulido; Mark Andreyko
4 ❑ Dec 1998 Cover: 3.99 **NM** value: **Cover or less**
Circ: Diamd. preorders: **27,112**
A: Ivan Reis **W:** Brian Pulido; Mark Andreyko
Ash 1 ❑ Cover: 2.99 **NM** value: **Cover or less**
• Character bios, sketches, creator bios **A:** Ivan Reis **W:** Brian Pulido; Mark Andreyko

SUPERNATURALS TOUR BOOK, THE — Marvel

1 ❑ Oct 1998 Cover: 2.99 **NM** value: **Cover or less**
No issue number. cardstock cover. • preview of series

SUPERNATURAL THRILLERS — Marvel

1 ❑ Dec 1972 Cover: 0.20 **NM** value: **8.00**
• **CGC:** 3 graded, best 9.6
• It! (Theodore Sturgeon adaptation) **A:** Marie Severin; Frank Giacoia **W:** Roy Thomas
2 ❑ Feb 1973 Cover: 0.20 **NM** value: **5.00**
• **CGC:** 1 graded, best 9.2
• Invisible Man
3 ❑ Apr 1973 Cover: 0.20 **NM** value: **4.00**
• **CGC:** 1 graded, best 9.6
📖 The Valley of the Worm • The Valley of the Worm **A:** Gil Kane **W:** Roy Thomas; Gerry Conway; Robert E. Howard
4 ❑ Jun 1973 Cover: 0.20 **NM** value: **4.00**
• Dr. Jekyll and Mr. Hyde
5 ❑ Aug 1973 Cover: 0.20 **NM** value: **4.00**
• **CGC:** 20 graded, best 9.6
★ Origin of Living Mummy. ★ 1st Appearance of Living Mummy.
6 ❑ 1974 Cover: 0.20 **NM** value: **3.50**
• The Headless Horseman
7 ❑ 1974 Cover: 0.25 **NM** value: **3.50**
★ Appearance of Living Mummy.
8 ❑ 1974 Cover: 0.25 **NM** value: **3.50**
★ Appearance of Living Mummy.
9 ❑ 1974 Cover: 0.25 **NM** value: **3.50**
★ Appearance of Living Mummy.
10 ❑ 1974 Cover: 0.25 **NM** value: **3.50**
★ Appearance of Living Mummy.
11 ❑ Feb 1975 Cover: 0.25 **NM** value: **3.50**
• **CGC:** 1 graded, best 9.0
★ Appearance of Living Mummy.
12 ❑ Apr 1975 Cover: 0.25 **NM** value: **3.50**
★ Appearance of Living Mummy.
13 ❑ Jun 1975 Cover: 0.25 **NM** value: **3.50**
• **CGC:** 2 graded, best 9.4
★ Appearance of Living Mummy.
14 ❑ Aug 1975 Cover: 0.25 **NM** value: **3.50**
★ Appearance of Living Mummy.
15 ❑ Oct 1975 Cover: 0.25 **NM** value: **3.50**
• **CGC:** 1 graded, best 9.4
📖 Armageddon At The Aleph! **A:** Tom Sutton **W:** John Warner ★ Appearance of Living Mummy.

SUPERPATRIOT — Image

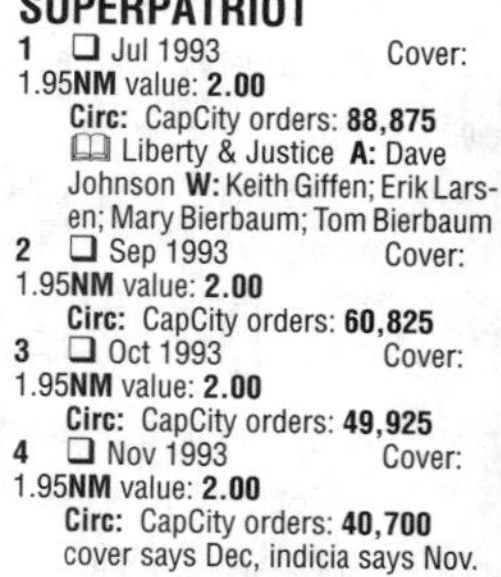

1 ❑ Jul 1993 Cover: 1.95 **NM** value: **2.00**
Circ: CapCity orders: **88,875**
📖 Liberty & Justice **A:** Dave Johnson **W:** Keith Giffen; Erik Larsen; Mary Bierbaum; Tom Bierbaum
2 ❑ Sep 1993 Cover: 1.95 **NM** value: **2.00**
Circ: CapCity orders: **60,825**
3 ❑ Oct 1993 Cover: 1.95 **NM** value: **2.00**
Circ: CapCity orders: **49,925**
4 ❑ Nov 1993 Cover: 1.95 **NM** value: **2.00**
Circ: CapCity orders: **40,700**
cover says Dec, indicia says Nov.

SUPERPATRIOT: LIBERTY & JUSTICE — Image

1 ❑ Jun 1995 Cover: 2.50 **NM** value: **Cover or less**
Circ: CapCity orders: **14,300**
2 ❑ Aug 1995 Cover: 2.50 **NM** value: **Cover or less**
Circ: CapCity orders: **10,775**
3 ❑ Sep 1995 Cover: 2.50 **NM** value: **Cover or less**
Circ: CapCity orders: **9,125**
4 ❑ Oct 1995 Cover: 2.50 **NM** value: **Cover or less**
Circ: CapCity orders: **7,675**

SUPER POWERS (1ST SERIES) — DC

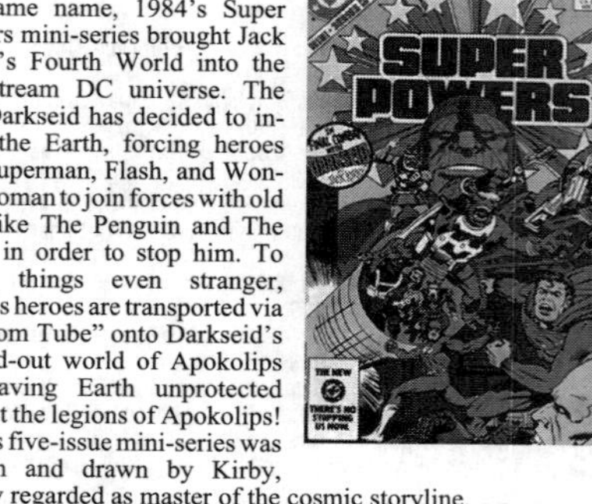

Based on a Kenner toy line of the same name, 1984's Super Powers mini-series brought Jack Kirby's Fourth World into the mainstream DC universe. The evil Darkseid has decided to invade the Earth, forcing heroes like Superman, Flash, and Wonder Woman to join forces with old foes like The Penguin and The Joker in order to stop him. To make things even stranger, Earth's heroes are transported via a "Boom Tube" onto Darkseid's blasted-out world of Apokolips — leaving Earth unprotected against the legions of Apokolips!

This five-issue mini-series was written and drawn by Kirby, widely regarded as master of the cosmic storyline.

1 ❑ Jul 1984 Cover: 0.75 **NM** value: **1.00**
📖 Power Beyond Price **C:** Jack Kirby
2 ❑ Aug 1984 Cover: 0.75 **NM** value: **1.00**
📖 Clash Against Chaos **C:** Jack Kirby
3 ❑ Sep 1984 Cover: 0.75 **NM** value: **1.00**
📖 Amazons At War **C:** Jack Kirby
4 ❑ Oct 1984 Cover: 0.75 **NM** value: **1.00**
📖 Earth's Last Stand **C:** Jack Kirby
5 ❑ Nov 1984 Cover: 0.75 **NM** value: **1.00**
📖 Spaceship Earth, We're All on It **A:** Jack Kirby **C:** Jack Kirby **W:** Jack Kirby

SUPER POWERS (2ND SERIES) — DC

1 ❑ Sep 1985 Cover: 0.75 **NM** value: **1.00**
Circ: CapCity orders: **13,900**
📖 Seeds Of Doom! **A:** Jack Kirby **W:** Paul Kupperberg
2 ❑ Oct 1985 Cover: 0.75 **NM** value: **1.00**
Circ: CapCity orders: **11,150**
📖 When Past and Present Meet **A:** Jack Kirby
3 ❑ Nov 1985 Cover: 0.75 **NM** value: **1.00**
Circ: CapCity orders: **10,000**
📖 Time Upon Time Upon Time **A:** Jack Kirby
4 ❑ Dec 1985 Cover: 0.75 **NM** value: **1.00**
Circ: CapCity orders: **9,050**
📖 There's No Place Like Rome **A:** Jack Kirby
5 ❑ Jan 1986 Cover: 0.75 **NM** value: **1.00**
Circ: CapCity orders: **8,200**
📖 Once Upon Tomorrow **A:** Jack Kirby
6 ❑ Feb 1986 Cover: 0.75 **NM** value: **1.00**
Circ: CapCity orders: **8,050**
📖 Darkseid Of The Moon **A:** Jack Kirby

SUPER POWERS (3RD SERIES) — DC

1 ❑ Sep 1986 Cover: 0.75 **NM** value: **1.00**
Circ: CapCity orders: **10,900**
📖 Threshold **A:** Carmine Infantino **W:** Paul Kupperberg
2 ❑ Oct 1986 Cover: 0.75 **NM** value: **1.00**
Circ: CapCity orders: **8,650**
A: Carmine Infantino
3 ❑ Nov 1986 Cover: 0.75 **NM** value: **1.00**
Circ: CapCity orders: **8,450**
A: Carmine Infantino
4 ❑ Dec 1986 Cover: 0.75 **NM** value: **1.00**
Circ: CapCity orders: **7,700**
A: Carmine Infantino

SUPER PUP — Avon

4 ❑ ca. 1940 Cover: 0.10 **NM** value: **25.00**
5 ❑ ca. 1940 Cover: 0.10 **NM** value: **25.00**

SUPER RABBIT — Timely

1 ❑ Fal 1943 Cover: 0.10 **NM** value: **350.00**
2 ❑ Win 1943 Cover: 0.10 **NM** value: **175.00**
3 ❑ Spr 1944 Cover: 0.10 **NM** value: **125.00**
4 ❑ Sum 1944 Cover: 0.10 **NM** value: **125.00**
5 ❑ Fal 1944 Cover: 0.10 **NM** value: **125.00**
6 ❑ Win 1944 Cover: 0.10 **NM** value: **100.00**
7 ❑ Spr 1945 Cover: 0.10 **NM** value: **100.00**
8 ❑ Sum 1945 Cover: 0.10 **NM** value: **100.00**
9 ❑ Jan 1948 Cover: 0.10 **NM** value: **100.00**
10 ❑ Mar 1948 Cover: 0.10 **NM** value: **100.00**
11 ❑ May 1948 Cover: 0.10 **NM** value: **75.00**
12 ❑ Jul 1948 Cover: 0.10 **NM** value: **75.00**
13 ❑ Sep 1948 Cover: 0.10 **NM** value: **75.00**
14 ❑ Nov 1948 Cover: 0.10 **NM** value: **75.00**

SUPER SEXXX — Fantagraphics / Eros

All issues are adults only.
1 ❑ b&w Cover: 3.25 **NM** value: **Cover or less**

SUPER SHARK HUMANOIDS — Fish Tales

1 ❑ Apr 1992 Cover: 2.75 **NM** value: **Cover or less**
A: Michael Leighton **W:** Michael Peters

The CGC numbers printed in individual listings above represent the **number of copies examined** and given a **Universal** grade by CGC and the **best such copy** graded at press time. For current populations, watch for special ***Comics Buyer's Guide*** issues or check **www.cgccomics.com.**

SUPERSNIPE COMICS — Street & Smith

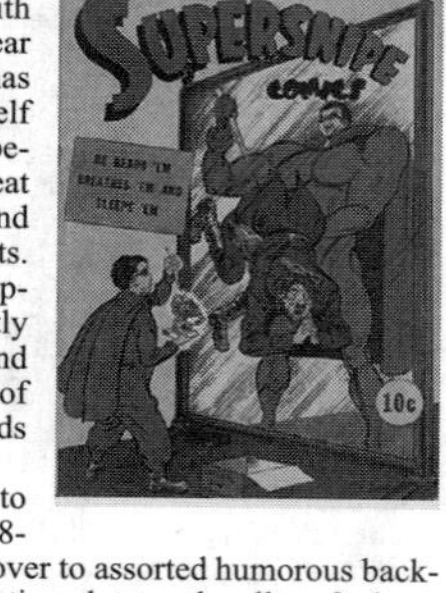

Koppy McFad is the kid with the most comic books in America. With these treasures to feed his 10-year old imagination, plus red pajamas and a mask, Koppy pictures himself as the masked avenger Supersnipe-solver of crimes, doer of great deeds, allowed to stay up late and have as much ice cream as he wants. Supersnipe had such immediate appeal that the character promptly took over the former Army and Navy Comics in the middle of World War II, and entertained kids throughout the 1940s.

Supersnipe's adventures ran to epic length, often 32 pages of a 48-page issue (the remainder given over to assorted humorous backups). With quick pacing, imaginative plots, and well-crafted artwork to rival the best kid strips of the era (including Disney's), Supersnipe gained a cult following of fans and anchored the otherwise-average Street and Smith comics line.

Volume 1
6 ❑ Oct 1942 Cover: 0.10 **NM** value: **575.00**
• Series continued from Army & Navy #5
7 ❑ Jan 1943 Cover: 0.10 **NM** value: **375.00**
8 ❑ Apr 1943 Cover: 0.10 **NM** value: **400.00**
• **CGC:** 1 graded, best 5.0
9 ❑ Jun 1943 Cover: 0.10 **NM** value: **425.00**
10 ❑ Aug 1943 Cover: 0.10 **NM** value: **350.00**
11 ❑ Oct 1943 Cover: 0.10 **NM** value: **325.00**
• **CGC:** 1 graded, best 7.0
📖 Snowbound; Butterfinger!; The Ice Has it!; Crisis in The Comics! (Text Story); A Better Mouse Trap
12 ❑ Dec 1943 Cover: 0.10 **NM** value: **325.00**
• **CGC:** 2 graded, best 8.5

Volume 2
1 ❑ Feb 1944 Cover: 0.10 **NM** value: **240.00**
• **CGC:** 3 graded, best 9.4
2 ❑ Apr 1944 Cover: 0.10 **NM** value: **210.00**
• Huck Finn
3 ❑ Jun 1944 Cover: 0.10 **NM** value: **210.00**
• Huck Finn
4 ❑ Aug 1944 Cover: 0.10 **NM** value: **200.00**
• Huck Finn
5 ❑ Oct 1944 Cover: 0.10 **NM** value: **200.00**
• **CGC:** 1 graded, best 9.0
• Huck Finn
6 ❑ Dec 1944 Cover: 0.10 **NM** value: **200.00**
• Huck Finn
7 ❑ Feb 1945 Cover: 0.10 **NM** value: **200.00**
• **CGC:** 1 graded, best 9.6
• Wing WooWoo
8 ❑ Apr 1945 Cover: 0.10 **NM** value: **200.00**
• Huck Finn
9 ❑ Jun 1945 Cover: 0.10 **NM** value: **200.00**
• Dotty
10 ❑ Aug 1945 Cover: 0.10 **NM** value: **200.00**
• Huck Finn
11 ❑ Oct 1945 Cover: 0.10 **NM** value: **200.00**
• **CGC:** 1 graded, best 9.0
• Dotty
12 ❑ Nov 1945 Cover: 0.10 **NM** value: **200.00**
• **CGC:** 2 graded, best 8.5
• Dotty

Volume 3
1 ❑ Jan 1946 Cover: 0.10 **NM** value: **185.00**
• Huck Finn
2 ❑ Mar 1946 Cover: 0.10 **NM** value: **160.00**
• **CGC:** 1 graded, best 9.4
3 ❑ May 1946 Cover: 0.10 **NM** value: **160.00**
• **CGC:** 1 graded, best 9.2
• Dotty
4 ❑ Jul 1946 Cover: 0.10 **NM** value: **160.00**
• **CGC:** 1 graded, best 8.0
• Wacky
5 ❑ Sep 1946 Cover: 0.10 **NM** value: **160.00**
6 ❑ Nov 1946 Cover: 0.10 **NM** value: **160.00**
7 ❑ Dec 1946 Cover: 0.10 **NM** value: **160.00**
8 ❑ Jan 1947 Cover: 0.10 **NM** value: **160.00**
9 ❑ Feb 1947 Cover: 0.10 **NM** value: **160.00**
• Christmas issue
10 ❑ Mar 1947 Cover: 0.10 **NM** value: **160.00**
11 ❑ Apr 1947 Cover: 0.10 **NM** value: **160.00**
• **CGC:** 1 graded, best 7.5
12 ❑ Jun 1947 Cover: 0.10 **NM** value: **160.00**

Volume 4
1 ❑ Aug 1947 Cover: 0.10 **NM** value: **125.00**
2 ❑ Oct 1947 Cover: 0.10 **NM** value: **125.00**
3 ❑ Dec 1947 Cover: 0.10 **NM** value: **125.00**
• Wacky's Think Machine
4 ❑ Feb 1948 Cover: 0.10 **NM** value: **125.00**
5 ❑ Apr 1948 Cover: 0.10 **NM** value: **125.00**
6 ❑ Jun 1948 Cover: 0.10 **NM** value: **125.00**
7 ❑ Aug 1948 Cover: 0.10 **NM** value: **125.00**
8 ❑ Oct 1948 Cover: 0.10 **NM** value: **125.00**
9 ❑ Dec 1948 Cover: 0.10 **NM** value: **125.00**
10 ❑ Feb 1949 Cover: 0.10 **NM** value: **125.00**
11 ❑ Apr 1949 Cover: 0.10 **NM** value: **125.00**
12 ❑ Jun 1949 Cover: 0.10 **NM** value: **125.00**

Volume 5
1 ❑ Aug 1949 Cover: 0.10 **NM** value: **100.00**

SUPER SOLDIER — DC / Amalgam

1 ❑ Apr 1996 Cover: 1.95 **NM** value: **Cover or less**
📖 Secret Of The K-Bombs **A:** Dave Gibbons **W:** Mark Waid ★ Origin of Super Soldier.

SUPER SOLDIER: MAN OF WAR — DC / Amalgam
1 ❑ Jun 1997 Cover: 1.95 **NM** value: **Cover or less**
Circ: Diamd. preorders: **127,807**
🕮 Deadly Cargo **A:** Dave Gibbons **W:** Dave Gibbons; Mark Waid

SUPER SOLDIERS — Marvel
1 ❑ Apr 1993 Cover: 2.50 **NM** value: **Cover or less**
Circ: CapCity orders: **52,700** • **CGC:** 1 graded, best 9.2
foil cover. 🕮 Memories, Part 1 **A:** Andrew Currie **W:** Lee Stevens; Michael Bennett
2 ❑ May 1993 Cover: 1.75 **NM** value: **Cover or less**
Circ: CapCity orders: **21,600**
🕮 Memories, Part 2 **A:** Andrew Currie **W:** Lee Stevens; Michael Bennett
3 ❑ Jun 1993 Cover: 1.75 **NM** value: **Cover or less**
Circ: CapCity orders: **17,500**
4 ❑ Jul 1993 Cover: 1.75 **NM** value: **Cover or less**
Circ: CapCity orders: **16,800**
5 ❑ Aug 1993 Cover: 1.75 **NM** value: **Cover or less**
Circ: CapCity orders: **12,200**
6 ❑ Sep 1993 Cover: 1.75 **NM** value: **Cover or less**
Circ: CapCity orders: **10,300**
7 ❑ Oct 1993 Cover: 1.75 **NM** value: **Cover or less**
Circ: CapCity orders: **7,500**
• X-Men cameo **A:** Andrew Currie **W:** Lee Stevens ★ Appearance of Nick Fury.
8 ❑ Nov 1993 Cover: 1.75 **NM** value: **Cover or less**
Circ: CapCity orders: **6,450**

SUPERSONIC SOUL PUDDIN COMICS & STORIES — Four Cats Funny Books
1 ❑ Jun 1995 Cover: 3.50 **NM** value: **Cover or less**

SUPER SONIC VS. HYPER KNUCKLES — Archie
1 ❑ Cover: 2.00 **NM** value: **Cover or less**
One-shot.

SUPER SPY — Centaur
1 ❑ Oct 1940 **NM** value: **1000.00**
• **CGC:** 1 graded, best 9.6
2 ❑ Nov 1940 **NM** value: **600.00**
• **CGC:** 1 graded, best 9.2

SUPER STREET FIGHTER II: CAMMY — Viz
Bk 1❑ Cover: 15.95 **NM** value: **Cover or less**

SUPERSWINE — Caliber
1 ❑ b&w Cover: 2.50 **NM** value: **Cover or less**
2 ❑ b&w Cover: 2.50 **NM** value: **Cover or less**

SUPER TABOO — Fantagraphics / Eros
1 ❑ Dec 1995 Cover: 2.95 **NM** value: **Cover or less**
A: Wolf Ogami **W:** Wolf Ogami
2 ❑ Jan 1996 Cover: 2.95 **NM** value: **Cover or less**
A: Wolf Ogami **W:** Wolf Ogami

SUPER-TEAM FAMILY — DC
Super-Team Family was a giant-sized showcase for some of DC's longest-running characters. Its run mixed reprints and new stories, as well as text pieces which gave origin and other information on the characters. Of the 15 issues in this 1975-1978 series, the best came in the middle when DC brought out new stories featuring the Challengers of the Unknown along with classic reprints of the Doom Patrol. Other heroes featured in Super-Team Family included Superman, Batman, Green Arrow (with kid sidekick Speedy), Wonder Woman, Supergirl, and The Creeper.

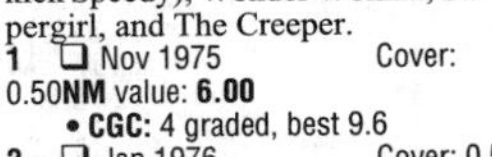

1 ❑ Nov 1975 Cover: 0.50 **NM** value: **6.00**
• **CGC:** 4 graded, best 9.6
2 ❑ Jan 1976 Cover: 0.50 **NM** value: **4.00**
🕮 Showdown in San Lorenzo!; The Track of the Hook!; The Case of the Vanishing Arrows ★ Appearance of Speedy, Wildcat, Deadman, Superman, Green Arrow, Creeper, Batman.
3 ❑ Mar 1976 Cover: 0.50 **NM** value: **4.00**
4 ❑ May 1976 Cover: 0.50 **NM** value: **4.00**
🕮 The Revenge of Solomon Grundy!; The Menace of the Moonman! ★ Appearance of Justice Society of America, Superman, Solomon Grundy, Robin, Batman.
5 ❑ Jul 1976 Cover: 0.50 **NM** value: **3.00**
6 ❑ Sep 1976 Cover: 0.50 **NM** value: **3.00**
7 ❑ Nov 1976 Cover: 0.50 **NM** value: **3.00**
• Teen Titans
8 ❑ Jan 1977 Cover: 0.50 **NM** value: **4.00**
• **CGC:** 1 graded, best 9.2
• New stories begin ★ Appearance of Challengers of the Unknown.
9 ❑ Mar 1977 Cover: 0.50 **NM** value: **4.00**
★ Appearance of Challengers of the Unknown.
10 ❑ May 1977 Cover: 0.50 **NM** value: **4.00**
★ Appearance of Challengers of the Unknown.
11 ❑ Jul 1977 Cover: 0.60 **NM** value: **3.00**
• **CGC:** 1 graded, best 8.0
• Flash, Atom, Supergirl
12 ❑ Sep 1977 Cover: 0.60 **NM** value: **3.00**
• **CGC:** 1 graded, best 9.0
13 ❑ Nov 1977 Cover: 0.60 **NM** value: **3.00**
• Atom, Aquaman, Captain Comet
14 ❑ Jan 1978 Cover: 0.60 **NM** value: **3.00**
15 ❑ Apr 1978 Cover: 0.60 **NM** value: **3.00**

SUPER-VILLAIN CLASSICS — Marvel
1 ❑ May 1983 Cover: 0.60 **NM** value: **3.00**
• **CGC:** 5 graded, best 9.6
★ Origin of Galactus.

SUPER-VILLAIN TEAM-UP — Marvel
1 ❑ Aug 1975 Cover: 0.25 **NM** value: **7.00**
• **CGC:** 19 graded, best 9.8
🕮 Slayers from the Sea! An Alliance Asunder?; Frenzy on the Loating Fortress! **A:** George Evans; Bill Everett; George Tuska **W:** Tony Isabella ★ Appearance of Doctor Doom, Sub-Mariner.
2 ❑ Oct 1975 Cover: 0.25 **NM** value: **5.00**
🕮 In the Midst of Life...!; The Way to Dusty Death! **A:** Sal Buscema **W:** Tony Isabella ★ Appearance of Doctor Doom, Sub-Mariner.
3 ❑ Dec 1975 Cover: 0.25 **NM** value: **4.00**
🕮 In Vengeance Fails! ★ Appearance of Doctor Doom, Sub-Mariner.
4 ❑ Feb 1976 Cover: 0.25 **NM** value: **4.00**
• **CGC:** 1 graded, best 9.4
🕮 A Duel of Titans! ★ Appearance of Doctor Doom, Sub-Mariner.
5 ❑ Apr 1976 Cover: 0.25 **NM** value: **4.00**
• **CGC:** 1 graded, best 9.4
🕮 And Be a Villain ★ 1st Appearance of Shroud. ★ 1st Appearance of Shroud. ★ Appearance of Doctor Doom, Sub-Mariner.
6 ❑ Jun 1976 Cover: 0.25 **NM** value: **3.00**
🕮 Prisoner! ★ Appearance of Doctor Doom, Sub-Mariner.
7 ❑ Aug 1976 Cover: 0.25 **NM** value: **3.00**
🕮 Who Is the Shroud? ★ Origin of Shroud. ★ Appearance of Doctor Doom, Sub-Mariner.
8 ❑ Oct 1976 Cover: 0.30 **NM** value: **3.00**
★ 1st Appearance of Rajah. ★ 1st Appearance of Rajah. ★ Appearance of Doctor Doom, Sub-Mariner.
9 ❑ Dec 1976 Cover: 0.30 **NM** value: **3.00**
🕮 Pawns of Attuma! ★ Appearance of Doctor Doom, Sub-Mariner.
10 ❑ Feb 1977 Cover: 0.30 **NM** value: **3.00**
🕮 The Sign of the Skull; While Atlantis Sleeps ★ Appearance of Doctor Doom, Sub-Mariner.
11 ❑ Apr 1977 Cover: 0.30 **NM** value: **3.00**
🕮 MyAlly, My Enemy
12 ❑ Jun 1977 Cover: 0.30 **NM** value: **3.00**
🕮 Death-Duel
13 ❑ Aug 1977 Cover: 0.30 **NM** value: **3.00**
14 ❑ Oct 1977 Cover: 0.30 **NM** value: **3.00**
• **CGC:** 1 graded, best 9.6
15 ❑ Nov 1977 Cover: 0.30 **NM** value: **3.00**
★ Appearance of Red Skull, Doctor Doom.
16 ❑ May 1979 Cover: 0.40 **NM** value: **3.00**
★ Appearance of Red Skull, Doctor Doom.
17 ❑ Jun 1980 Cover: 0.40 **NM** value: **3.00**
★ Appearance of Red Skull, Doctor Doom.
GS 1❑Mar 1975 Cover: 0.50 **NM** value: **5.00**
🕮 Encounter at Land's End; Sub-Mariner Rising; Into the Darkness Dwells Doom; This Man, This Demon • Reprinted from Sub-Mariner #20 and Marvel Super-Heroes #20
GS 2❑Jun 1975 Cover: 0.50 **NM** value: **5.00**
🕮 To Bestride the World; The Slaying of a Titan; When Monarchs Meet; The Armies of Andro; The Living Brain • Reprints story from Amazing Spider-Man #8

SUPERWORLD COMICS — Hugo Gernsback
1 ❑ Apr 1940 Cover: 0.10 **NM** value: **6000.00**
• **CGC:** 2 graded, best 5.5
2 ❑ May 1940 Cover: 0.10 **NM** value: **3000.00**
3 ❑ Aug 1940 Cover: 0.10 **NM** value: **2000.00**
• **CGC:** 1 graded, best 6.0

SUPPRESSED! — Tome Press
1 ❑ b&w Cover: 2.95 **NM** value: **Cover or less**
🕮 Columbus; Pilgrims; Doctor Riots; Gangs; Cop vs. Cop; The Invisible Empire; Draft Riots; Stinkin' Lincoln; Catholics; WWI Propaganda; 100% Americanism; The Jews; Trading Cards; Cuba; Philippines; Hemp; Zoot Suit Riots; Christmas **A:** Al Frank; James Burchett **W:** Starlen Baxter

SUPREME — Image
Appearing for the first time in this series — inexplicably labelled "Volume 2" in parts — series, Supreme is the brainchild of Rob Liefeld, creator of Youngblood for Image. Supreme is the closest thing to a supreme being as the Image universe has, measuring a "Level 10" on the powers scale. Supreme has a history dating back 50 years on Earth, and in this series is just returning to see what's happened in his absence.

Something else that was inexplicable for many was the decision of Alan Moore to write later issues of this series, given that that celebrated writer had eschewed more commercial super-hero work for some time. But his work here, a thinly veiled homage to Superman, perhaps opened the door for his development of the Amercia's Best Comics line for Wildstorm (which would be bought out by DC).

0 ❑ Aug 1995 Cover: 2.50 **NM** value: **Cover or less**
Circ: CapCity orders: **12,625**
🕮 The Weight **A:** Todd Nauck; Rob Liefeld(cover); Stephen Platt(cover) **W:** Eric Stephenson
1 ❑ Nov 1992 Cover: 1.95 **NM** value: **2.50**
Circ: CapCity orders: **130,325** • **CGC:** 1 graded, best 9.8
silver foil-embossed cover. 🕮 Second Coming **A:** Brian Murray **W:** Rob Liefeld; Brian Murray
1/GO❑Nov 1992 **NM** value: **2.50**
• **CGC:** 1 graded, best 9.8
Embossed cover. • Gold promotional edition. 🕮 Second Coming
2 ❑ Feb 1993 Cover: 1.95 **NM** value: **2.00**
Circ: CapCity orders: **88,900**
covers says May, indicia says Feb. ★ 1st Appearance of Grizlock.
3 ❑ Jun 1993 Cover: 1.95 **NM** value: **2.00**
Circ: CapCity orders: **84,950**
★ 1st Appearance of Khrome.
4 ❑ Jul 1993 Cover: 1.95 **NM** value: **2.00**
Circ: CapCity orders: **71,275**
5 ❑ Aug 1993 Cover: 1.95 **NM** value: **2.00**
Circ: CapCity orders: **63,225**
★ 1st Appearance of Thor (Image).
6 ❑ Oct 1993 Cover: 1.95 **NM** value: **2.00**
Circ: CapCity orders: **56,500**
★ 1st Appearance of the Starguard.
7 ❑ Nov 1993 Cover: 1.95 **NM** value: **2.00**
Circ: CapCity orders: **55,500**
8 ❑ Dec 1993 Cover: 1.95 **NM** value: **2.00**
Circ: CapCity orders: **47,625**
9 ❑ Jan 1994 Cover: 1.95 **NM** value: **2.00**
Circ: CapCity orders: **38,425**
10 ❑ Feb 1994 Cover: 1.95 **NM** value: **2.00**
Circ: CapCity orders: **29,475**
11 ❑ Mar 1994 Cover: 1.95 **NM** value: **2.00**
Circ: CapCity orders: **28,900**
🕮 Extreme Prejudice, Part 4
12 ❑ Apr 1994 Cover: 1.95 **NM** value: **2.00**
Circ: CapCity orders: **25,875**
13 ❑ Jun 1994 Cover: 2.50 **NM** value: **Cover or less**
Circ: CapCity orders: **31,350**
🕮 Supreme Madness, Part 1
14 ❑ Jun 1994 Cover: 2.50 **NM** value: **Cover or less**
Circ: CapCity orders: **30,175**
🕮 Supreme Madness, Part 2
15 ❑ Jul 1994 Cover: 2.50 **NM** value: **Cover or less**
Circ: CapCity orders: **30,050**
🕮 Supreme Madness, Part 3
16 ❑ Jul 1994 Cover: 2.50 **NM** value: **Cover or less**
Circ: CapCity orders: **27,125**
🕮 Supreme Madness, Part 4
17 ❑ Aug 1994 Cover: 2.50 **NM** value: **Cover or less**
Circ: CapCity orders: **27,275**
🕮 Supreme Madness, Part 5 ★ Versus Pitt.
18 ❑ Aug 1994 Cover: 2.50 **NM** value: **Cover or less**
Circ: CapCity orders: **27,200**
🕮 Supreme Madness, Part 6
19 ❑ Sep 1994 Cover: 2.50 **NM** value: **Cover or less**
Circ: CapCity orders: **23,550**
20 ❑ Oct 1994 Cover: 2.50 **NM** value: **Cover or less**
Circ: CapCity orders: **21,800**
★ Appearance of Kid Supreme.
21 ❑ Nov 1994 Cover: 2.50 **NM** value: **Cover or less**
Circ: CapCity orders: **19,375**
🕮 God War, Part 1
22 ❑ Dec 1994 Cover: 2.50 **NM** value: **Cover or less**
Circ: CapCity orders: **17,825**
🕮 God War, Part 2
23 ❑ Jan 1995 Cover: 2.50 **NM** value: **Cover or less**
Circ: CapCity orders: **20,325**
🕮 Extreme Sacrifice, Part 2; Extreme Sacrifice, Part 1 • polybagged with trading card
24 ❑ Feb 1995 Cover: 2.50 **NM** value: **Cover or less**
Circ: CapCity orders: **13,875**
🕮 Extreme Sacrifice Aftermath
25 ❑ May 1994 Cover: 1.95 **NM** value: **2.50**
• Images of Tomorrow; Shipped out of sequence after #12 to give preview of future **A:** Stephen Platt(cover)
26 ❑ Mar 1995 Cover: 2.50 **NM** value: **Cover or less**
Circ: CapCity orders: **12,950**
★ Versus Kid Supreme.
27 ❑ Apr 1995 Cover: 2.50 **NM** value: **Cover or less**
Circ: CapCity orders: **12,100**
28/A❑May 1995 Cover: 2.50 **NM** value: **Cover or less**
Circ: CapCity orders: **12,175**
★ Appearance of Glory.
28/B❑May 1995 Cover: 2.50 **NM** value: **Cover or less**
★ Appearance of Glory.
29 ❑ Jun 1995 Cover: 2.50 **NM** value: **Cover or less**
Circ: CapCity orders: **13,550**
🕮 Supreme Apocalypse, Part 1 • polybagged with Power Cardz
30 ❑ Jul 1995 Cover: 2.50 **NM** value: **Cover or less**
Circ: CapCity orders: **14,500**
🕮 Supreme Apocalypse, Part 5 • polybagged with Power Cardz
31 ❑ Aug 1995 Cover: 2.50 **NM** value: **Cover or less**
Circ: CapCity orders: **9,275**
32 ❑ Oct 1995 Cover: 2.50 **NM** value: **Cover or less**
Circ: CapCity orders: **6,050**
33 ❑ Nov 1995 Cover: 2.50 **NM** value: **Cover or less**
• Babewatch
34 ❑ Dec 1995 Cover: 2.50 **NM** value: **Cover or less**
35 ❑ Jan 1996 Cover: 2.50 **NM** value: **Cover or less**
🕮 Extreme Destroyer, Part 7 • polybagged with Lady Supreme card
36 ❑ Feb 1996 Cover: 2.50 **NM** value: **Cover or less**
37 ❑ Mar 1996 Cover: 2.50 **NM** value: **Cover or less**
37/A❑Mar 1996 Cover: 2.50 **NM** value: **Cover or less**
alternate cover.
37/B❑Mar 1996 Cover: 2.50 **NM** value: **Cover or less**
alternate cover.
38 ❑ Apr 1996 Cover: 2.50 **NM** value: **Cover or less**
39 ❑ May 1996 Cover: 2.50 **NM** value: **Cover or less**
★ Versus Loki.
40 ❑ Jul 1996 Cover: 2.50 **NM** value: **Cover or less**
41 ❑ Aug 1996 Cover: 2.50 **NM** value: **3.50**
• Newmen Special Preview Edition back-up. **W:** Alan Moore
41/A❑Aug 1996 Cover: 2.50 **NM** value: **3.50**
alternate cover (Superman homage). • Newmen Special Preview Edition back-up. **W:** Alan Moore

CGC-graded: Multiply prices above by **33 for 9.9 M • 16 for 9.8 NM/M • 7 for 9.6 NM+ • 5 for 9.4 NM • 2.5 for 9.2 NM- • 1.5 for 9.0 VF/NM**

41/B ❑ Aug 1996 Cover: 2.50 **NM** value: **15.00**
alternate cover (Superman homage). • limited edition.
41/C ❑ Aug 1996 Cover: 2.50 **NM** value: **9.00**
alternate cover (American Entertainment exclusive).
41-2 ❑ Cover: 2.50 **NM** value: **Cover or less**
42 ❑ Sep 1996 Cover: 2.50 **NM** value: **3.00**
Circ: Diamd. preorders: **20,003**
• Superman homage; moves to Maximum Press **W:** Alan Moore
43 ❑ Oct 1996 Cover: 2.50 **NM** value: **3.00**
Circ: Diamd. preorders: **20,171**
• Superman homage **W:** Alan Moore
44 ❑ Jan 1997 Cover: 2.50 **NM** value: **3.00**
Circ: Diamd. preorders: **17,960**
W: Alan Moore
45 ❑ Jan 1997 Cover: 2.50 **NM** value: **Cover or less**
Circ: Diamd. preorders: **18,055**
W: Alan Moore
46 ❑ Feb 1997 Cover: 2.50 **NM** value: **Cover or less**
Circ: Diamd. preorders: **17,779**
W: Alan Moore ★ 1st Appearance of Suprema.
47 ❑ Mar 1997 Cover: 2.50 **NM** value: **Cover or less**
Circ: Diamd. preorders: **17,535**
W: Alan Moore ★ 1st Appearance of Twilight.
48 ❑ Apr 1997 Cover: 2.50 **NM** value: **Cover or less**
Circ: Diamd. preorders: **18,787**
W: Alan Moore
49 ❑ May 1997 Cover: 2.50 **NM** value: **Cover or less**
Circ: Diamd. preorders: **17,131**
cover says Jun, indicia says May. **W:** Alan Moore
50 ❑ Jun 1997 Cover: 2.50 **NM** value: **Cover or less**
Circ: Diamd. preorders: **20,646**
• Giant-size. **W:** Alan Moore
51 ❑ Jul 1997 Cover: 2.50 **NM** value: **Cover or less**
Circ: Diamd. preorders: **17,433**
W: Alan Moore
52/A ❑ Sep 1997 Cover: 2.50 **NM** value: **3.50**
Circ: Diamd. preorders: **14,891**
W: Alan Moore
52/B ❑ Sep 1997 Cover: 2.50 **NM** value: **Cover or less**
Circ: Diamd. preorders: **14,164**
W: Alan Moore
53 ❑ Sep 1997 Cover: 2.50 **NM** value: **Cover or less**
Circ: Diamd. preorders: **17,428**
W: Alan Moore
54 ❑ Nov 1997 Cover: 2.50 **NM** value: **Cover or less**
Circ: Diamd. preorders: **17,455**
W: Alan Moore
55 ❑ Nov 1997 Cover: 2.50 **NM** value: **Cover or less**
Circ: Diamd. preorders: **17,319**
cover says Dec, indicia says Nov. 📖 Silence at Gettysburg **A:** Chris Sprouse; Gil Kane **W:** Alan Moore
56 ❑ Feb 1998 Cover: 2.50 **NM** value: **Cover or less**
Circ: Diamd. preorders: **16,396**
Anl 1 ❑ May 1995 Cover: 2.95 **NM** value: **Cover or less**
★ Appearance of The Allies.

SUPREME: GLORY DAYS — Image
1 ❑ Oct 1994 Cover: 2.95 **NM** value: **3.00**
Circ: CapCity orders: **22,800**
A: David Williams **W:** Rob Liefeld; Kurt Hathaway
2 ❑ Dec 1994 Cover: 2.50 **NM** value: **Cover or less**
Circ: CapCity orders: **15,025**
final issue. **A:** David Williams **W:** Rob Liefeld; Kurt Hathaway

SUPREME: THE RETURN — Awesome
1 ❑ May 1999 Cover: 2.99 **NM** value: **Cover or less**
Circ: Diamd. preorders: **29,026**
• continues story from Supreme #56
2 ❑ Jun 1999 Cover: 2.99 **NM** value: **Cover or less**
Circ: Diamd. preorders: **24,332**
• infinite Darius Daxes
3 ❑ Cover: 2.99 **NM** value: **Cover or less**
4 ❑ Mar 2000 Cover: 2.99 **NM** value: **Cover or less**
Circ: Diamd. preorders: **11,626**
5 ❑ May 2000 Cover: 2.99 **NM** value: **Cover or less**
Circ: Diamd. preorders: **11,556**
📖 Suddenly ... The Supremium Man! **A:** Ian Churchill; Rick Veitch **W:** Alan Moore ★ Appearance of Supremium Man, Master Meteor.
6 ❑ Jun 2000 Cover: 2.99 **NM** value: **Cover or less**
Circ: Diamd. preorders: **11,486**
📖 New Jack City! **A:** Rob Liefeld; Rick Veitch **W:** Alan Moore

SUPREMIE — Parody
1 ❑ b&w Cover: 2.50 **NM** value: **Cover or less**
📖 The Babe of Steel **A:** Rus Sever **W:** Don Chin

SURE-FIRE COMICS — Ace
1 ❑ Jun 1940 Cover: 0.10 **NM** value: **1500.00**
2 ❑ Aug 1940 Cover: 0.10 **NM** value: **750.00**
• **CGC:** 1 graded, best 2.0
3 ❑ Sep 1940 Cover: 0.10 **NM** value: **500.00**

SURFCRAZED COMICS — Pacifica
1 ❑ Cover: 2.50 **NM** value: **Cover or less**
3 ❑ Cover: 3.95 **NM** value: **Cover or less**
• 3-D.
4 ❑ Cover: 2.50 **NM** value: **Cover or less**

SURF SUMO — Star Tiger
1 ❑ Cover: 2.95 **NM** value: **Cover or less**
📖 Clone Wars **A:** Mitch Scheele **W:** Mitch Scheele
1-2 ❑ Cover: 2.95 **NM** value: **Cover or less**
📖 Clone Wars • 2nd printing with insert noting rights had reverted to Mighty Graphics; June 1997 **A:** Mitch Scheele **W:** Mitch Scheele

SURGE — Eclipse
1 ❑ Jul 1984 Cover: 1.50 **NM** value: **1.75**
📖 Human Hunt **A:** Rick Hoberg **W:** Mark Evanier
2 ❑ Aug 1984 Cover: 1.50 **NM** value: **1.75**
A: Rick Hoberg **W:** Mark Evanier
3 ❑ Oct 1984 Cover: 1.50 **NM** value: **1.75**
A: Rick Hoberg **W:** Mark Evanier
4 ❑ Jan 1985 Cover: 1.50 **NM** value: **1.75**
A: Rick Hoberg **W:** Mark Evanier

SURREAL SCHOOL STORIES — Gratuitous Bunny
1 ❑ Cover: 1.30 **NM** value: **2.00**
Price on cover: 1/2 pence. 📖 Strange Doings as Tycho **A:** Terry Wiley **W:** Terry Wiley
2 ❑ Cover: 1.30 **NM** value: **2.00**
📖 Late Seventies Masonettes **A:** Terry Wiley **W:** Terry Wiley
3 ❑ Cover: 1.30 **NM** value: **2.00**
📖 A Week in Politics **A:** Terry Wiley **W:** Terry Wiley
4 ❑ Cover: 1.30 **NM** value: **2.00**
📖 Lost in France **A:** Terry Wiley **W:** Terry Wiley
5 ❑ Cover: 1.30 **NM** value: **2.00**
📖 Ascension **A:** Terry Wiley **W:** Terry Wiley

SURROGATE SAVIOUR — Hot Brazen Comics
1 ❑ Sep 1995, b&w Cover: 2.50 **NM** value: **Cover or less**
2 ❑ Nov 1995, b&w Cover: 2.75 **NM** value: **Cover or less**
3 ❑ Jun 1996, b&w Cover: 2.95 **NM** value: **Cover or less**

SURVIVE! — Apple
1 ❑ b&w Cover: 2.75 **NM** value: **Cover or less**

SURVIVORS, THE (BURNSIDE) — Burnside
1 ❑ Cover: 1.95 **NM** value: **Cover or less**

SURVIVORS (FANTAGRAPHICS) — Fantagraphics
1 ❑ Cover: 2.50 **NM** value: **Cover or less**
2 ❑ Cover: 2.50 **NM** value: **Cover or less**

SURVIVORS, THE (PRELUDE) — Prelude
1 ❑ Oct 1986 Cover: 1.95 **NM** value: **Cover or less**
📖 Destinies **A:** Steve Woron **W:** Steve Woron
2 ❑ Cover: 1.95 **NM** value: **Cover or less**

SURVIVORS (SPECTRUM) — Spectrum
1 ❑ Cover: 2.00 **NM** value: **Cover or less**
2 ❑ Cover: 2.00 **NM** value: **Cover or less**
3 ❑ Cover: 2.00 **NM** value: **Cover or less**
4 ❑ Cover: 2.00 **NM** value: **Cover or less**

SUSHI — Shunga
All issues are adults only.
1 ❑ b&w Cover: 2.50 **NM** value: **3.00**
A: Tokyo Jones **W:** Tokyo Jones
1-2 ❑ Cover: 2.50 **NM** value: **Cover or less**
2 ❑ b&w Cover: 2.50 **NM** value: **3.00**
3 ❑ b&w Cover: 2.50 **NM** value: **3.00**
4 ❑ b&w Cover: 2.50 **NM** value: **3.00**
5 ❑ b&w Cover: 2.50 **NM** value: **3.00**
6 ❑ b&w Cover: 2.50 **NM** value: **3.00**
7 ❑ Cover: 2.50 **NM** value: **Cover or less**
8 ❑ Cover: 2.50 **NM** value: **Cover or less**

SUSPENSE — Atlas
1 ❑ Dec 1949 Cover: 0.10 **NM** value: **500.00**
2 ❑ Feb 1950 Cover: 0.10 **NM** value: **250.00**
3 ❑ May 1950 Cover: 0.10 **NM** value: **250.00**
4 ❑ Aug 1950 Cover: 0.10 **NM** value: **200.00**
5 ❑ Nov 1950 Cover: 0.10 **NM** value: **200.00**
6 ❑ Jan 1951 Cover: 0.10 **NM** value: **200.00**
• **CGC:** 1 graded, best 8.0
7 ❑ Mar 1951 Cover: 0.10 **NM** value: **200.00**
8 ❑ May 1951 Cover: 0.10 **NM** value: **200.00**
9 ❑ Jul 1951 Cover: 0.10 **NM** value: **200.00**
• **CGC:** 1 graded, best 7.0
10 ❑ Sep 1951 Cover: 0.10 **NM** value: **200.00**
• **CGC:** 2 graded, best 9.0
11 ❑ Nov 1951 Cover: 0.10 **NM** value: **175.00**
• **CGC:** 1 graded, best 9.0
12 ❑ Dec 1951 Cover: 0.10 **NM** value: **175.00**
• **CGC:** 2 graded, best 9.2
13 ❑ Jan 1952 Cover: 0.10 **NM** value: **175.00**
C: Joe Maneely **A:** Joe Maneely
14 ❑ Feb 1952 Cover: 0.10 **NM** value: **175.00**
• **CGC:** 1 graded, best 7.0
15 ❑ Mar 1952 Cover: 0.10 **NM** value: **175.00**
• **CGC:** 2 graded, best 7.0
16 ❑ Apr 1952 Cover: 0.10 **NM** value: **150.00**
17 ❑ Apr 1952 Cover: 0.10 **NM** value: **150.00**
• **CGC:** 1 graded, best 6.0
18 ❑ May 1952 Cover: 0.10 **NM** value: **150.00**
• **CGC:** 2 graded, best 8.0
📖 The Cozy Coffin
19 ❑ Jun 1952 Cover: 0.10 **NM** value: **150.00**
20 ❑ Jul 1952 Cover: 0.10 **NM** value: **150.00**
21 ❑ Aug 1952 Cover: 0.10 **NM** value: **125.00**
22 ❑ Sep 1952 Cover: 0.10 **NM** value: **125.00**
23 ❑ Oct 1952 Cover: 0.10 **NM** value: **125.00**
24 ❑ Nov 1952 Cover: 0.10 **NM** value: **125.00**
• **CGC:** 3 graded, best 8.5
25 ❑ Dec 1952 Cover: 0.10 **NM** value: **125.00**
26 ❑ Jan 1953 Cover: 0.10 **NM** value: **100.00**
• **CGC:** 1 graded, best 9.2
27 ❑ Feb 1953 Cover: 0.10 **NM** value: **100.00**
28 ❑ Mar 1953 Cover: 0.10 **NM** value: **100.00**
• **CGC:** 1 graded, best 8.0
29 ❑ Apr 1953 Cover: 0.10 **NM** value: **100.00**

SUSPENSE COMICS — Continental
1 ❑ Dec 1943 Cover: 0.10 **NM** value: **4000.00**
• **CGC:** 2 graded, best 8.5
2 ❑ Feb 1944 Cover: 0.10 **NM** value: **2000.00**
• **CGC:** 2 graded, best 6.0
3 ❑ Apr 1944 Cover: 0.10 **NM** value: **10000.00**
• **CGC:** 4 graded, best 7.0
4 ❑ Jun 1944 Cover: 0.10 **NM** value: **2000.00**
• **CGC:** 1 graded, best 5.5
5 ❑ Aug 1944 Cover: 0.10 **NM** value: **2000.00**
• **CGC:** 4 graded, best 9.2
6 ❑ Oct 1944 Cover: 0.10 **NM** value: **2000.00**
• **CGC:** 3 graded, best 8.0
7 ❑ Dec 1944 Cover: 0.10 **NM** value: **1500.00**
• **CGC:** 5 graded, best 9.2
8 ❑ Jun 1945 Cover: 0.10 **NM** value: **1500.00**
• **CGC:** 5 graded, best 7.0
9 ❑ Win 1945 Cover: 0.10 **NM** value: **1500.00**
• **CGC:** 4 graded, best 8.5
10 ❑ Jun 1946 Cover: 0.10 **NM** value: **1500.00**
• **CGC:** 7 graded, best 9.2
11 ❑ 1946 Cover: 0.10 **NM** value: **1500.00**
• **CGC:** 6 graded, best 9.4
12 ❑ Sep 1946 Cover: 0.10 **NM** value: **1500.00**
• **CGC:** 4 graded, best 9.0

SUSPENSE DETECTIVE — Fawcett
1 ❑ Jun 1952 Cover: 0.10 **NM** value: **350.00**
• **CGC:** 1 graded, best 7.0
2 ❑ Aug 1952 Cover: 0.10 **NM** value: **200.00**
3 ❑ Oct 1952 Cover: 0.10 **NM** value: **150.00**
4 ❑ Dec 1952 Cover: 0.10 **NM** value: **150.00**
5 ❑ Feb 1953 Cover: 0.10 **NM** value: **150.00**

SUSPIRA: THE GREAT WORKING — Chaos
1 ❑ Mar 1997 Cover: 2.95 **NM** value: **Cover or less**
Circ: Diamd. preorders: **32,558**
A: Michael Okamoto **W:** Brian Pulido; Phil Nutman
2 ❑ Apr 1997 Cover: 2.95 **NM** value: **Cover or less**
Circ: Diamd. preorders: **24,885**
A: Michael Okamoto **W:** Brian Pulido; Phil Nutman
3 ❑ May 1997 Cover: 2.95 **NM** value: **Cover or less**
Circ: Diamd. preorders: **20,106**
A: Michael Okamoto **W:** Brian Pulido; Phil Nutman
4 ❑ Jun 1997 Cover: 2.95 **NM** value: **Cover or less**
Circ: Diamd. preorders: **19,586**
A: Michael Okamoto **W:** Brian Pulido; Phil Nutman

SUSSEX VAMPIRE, THE — Caliber
1 ❑ Cover: 2.95 **NM** value: **Cover or less**
A: Craig Gilmore **W:** Warren Ellis

SUSTAH-GIRL: QUEEN OF THE BLACK AGE — Onli Studios
1 ❑ b&w Cover: 2.00 **NM** value: **Cover or less**

SUZIE COMICS — M.L.J. / Archie
49 ❑ Spr 1945 Cover: 0.10 **NM** value: **150.00**
50 ❑ Sum 1945 Cover: 0.10 **NM** value: **100.00**
51 ❑ Fal 1945 Cover: 0.10 **NM** value: **100.00**
52 ❑ Win 1945 Cover: 0.10 **NM** value: **100.00**
C: Al Fagaly
53 ❑ Spr 1946 Cover: 0.10 **NM** value: **100.00**
54 ❑ Sum 1946 Cover: 0.10 **NM** value: **100.00**
55 ❑ Win 1946 Cover: 0.10 **NM** value: **100.00**
56 ❑ Apr 1947 Cover: 0.10 **NM** value: **100.00**
57 ❑ Jun 1947 Cover: 0.10 **NM** value: **100.00**
58 ❑ Aug 1947 Cover: 0.10 **NM** value: **100.00**
59 ❑ Oct 1947 Cover: 0.10 **NM** value: **100.00**
60 ❑ Dec 1947 Cover: 0.10 **NM** value: **100.00**
• **CGC:** 1 graded, best 9.2
61 ❑ Feb 1948 Cover: 0.10 **NM** value: **75.00**
62 ❑ Apr 1948 Cover: 0.10 **NM** value: **75.00**
63 ❑ Jun 1948 Cover: 0.10 **NM** value: **75.00**
64 ❑ Aug 1948 Cover: 0.10 **NM** value: **75.00**
C: Al Fagaly
65 ❑ Oct 1948 Cover: 0.10 **NM** value: **75.00**
66 ❑ Dec 1948 Cover: 0.10 **NM** value: **75.00**
67 ❑ Feb 1949 Cover: 0.10 **NM** value: **75.00**
68 ❑ Apr 1949 Cover: 0.10 **NM** value: **75.00**
69 ❑ Jun 1949 Cover: 0.10 **NM** value: **75.00**
70 ❑ Aug 1949 Cover: 0.10 **NM** value: **75.00**
71 ❑ Oct 1949 Cover: 0.10 **NM** value: **75.00**
72 ❑ Dec 1949 Cover: 0.10 **NM** value: **75.00**
73 ❑ Feb 1950 Cover: 0.10 **NM** value: **75.00**
74 ❑ Apr 1950 Cover: 0.10 **NM** value: **75.00**
75 ❑ Jun 1950 Cover: 0.10 **NM** value: **75.00**
76 ❑ Aug 1950 Cover: 0.10 **NM** value: **75.00**
77 ❑ Oct 1950 Cover: 0.10 **NM** value: **75.00**
78 ❑ Dec 1950 Cover: 0.10 **NM** value: **75.00**
79 ❑ Feb 1951 Cover: 0.10 **NM** value: **75.00**
80 ❑ Apr 1951 Cover: 0.10 **NM** value: **75.00**
81 ❑ Jun 1951 Cover: 0.10 **NM** value: **50.00**
82 ❑ Aug 1951 Cover: 0.10 **NM** value: **50.00**
83 ❑ Oct 1951 Cover: 0.10 **NM** value: **50.00**
84 ❑ Dec 1951 Cover: 0.10 **NM** value: **50.00**
• **CGC:** 1 graded, best 8.5
85 ❑ Feb 1952 Cover: 0.10 **NM** value: **50.00**
86 ❑ Apr 1952 Cover: 0.10 **NM** value: **50.00**
87 ❑ Jun 1952 Cover: 0.10 **NM** value: **50.00**
88 ❑ Aug 1952 Cover: 0.10 **NM** value: **50.00**
89 ❑ Oct 1952 Cover: 0.10 **NM** value: **50.00**
90 ❑ Dec 1952 Cover: 0.10 **NM** value: **50.00**
91 ❑ Feb 1953 Cover: 0.10 **NM** value: **50.00**
92 ❑ Apr 1953 Cover: 0.10 **NM** value: **50.00**
93 ❑ Jun 1953 Cover: 0.10 **NM** value: **50.00**
94 ❑ Aug 1953 Cover: 0.10 **NM** value: **50.00**
95 ❑ Oct 1953 Cover: 0.10 **NM** value: **50.00**
96 ❑ Dec 1953 Cover: 0.10 **NM** value: **50.00**
97 ❑ Feb 1954 Cover: 0.10 **NM** value: **50.00**

Other grades: Multiply prices above by **1.5 for Mint • 2/3 for Very Fine • 1/3 for Fine • 1/5 for Very Good • 1/8 for Good**

98 ❑ Apr 1954 Cover: 0.10 **NM** value: **50.00**
99 ❑ Jun 1954 Cover: 0.10 **NM** value: **50.00**
100 ❑ Aug 1954 Cover: 0.10 **NM** value: **50.00**

SWAMP FEVER — Big Muddy

1 ❑ Cover: 0.50 **NM** value: **3.00**
📖 Split! Splat!; The Real Dope on Drugs **A:** Dany Frolich; Sol Wright **W:** Dany Frolich; Sol Wright

SWAMP THING (1ST SERIES) — DC

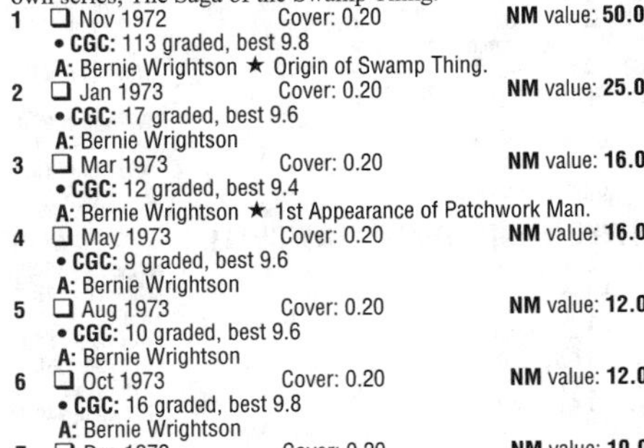

Swamp Thing, who first appeared in House of Secrets #92, was once Dr. Alec Holland, a brilliant biochemist who was working on research in the far recesses of the bayou. When he refused to sell out his research to a gang of thugs, they bombed his laboratory. Holland was covered in the flaming chemicals, which interacted with the swampy vegetation to transform him into this hideous man/monster.

This first Swamp Thing title began in 1972, and featured art by the great Bernie Wrightson, who penciled the first 10 issues. It continued to run until issue #24 in 1976. Afterward, Swampie continued to make guest appearances in various titles for the next few years. In 1982, he once again starred in his own series, The Saga of the Swamp Thing.

1 ❑ Nov 1972 Cover: 0.20 **NM** value: **50.00**
• **CGC:** 113 graded, best 9.8
A: Bernie Wrightson ★ Origin of Swamp Thing.
2 ❑ Jan 1973 Cover: 0.20 **NM** value: **25.00**
• **CGC:** 17 graded, best 9.6
A: Bernie Wrightson
3 ❑ Mar 1973 Cover: 0.20 **NM** value: **16.00**
• **CGC:** 12 graded, best 9.4
A: Bernie Wrightson ★ 1st Appearance of Patchwork Man.
4 ❑ May 1973 Cover: 0.20 **NM** value: **16.00**
• **CGC:** 9 graded, best 9.6
A: Bernie Wrightson
5 ❑ Aug 1973 Cover: 0.20 **NM** value: **12.00**
• **CGC:** 10 graded, best 9.6
A: Bernie Wrightson
6 ❑ Oct 1973 Cover: 0.20 **NM** value: **12.00**
• **CGC:** 16 graded, best 9.8
A: Bernie Wrightson
7 ❑ Dec 1973 Cover: 0.20 **NM** value: **10.00**
• **CGC:** 19 graded, best 9.6
• Batman **A:** Bernie Wrightson ★ Appearance of Batman.
8 ❑ Feb 1974 Cover: 0.20 **NM** value: **8.00**
• **CGC:** 11 graded, best 9.6
A: Bernie Wrightson
9 ❑ Apr 1974 Cover: 0.20 **NM** value: **8.00**
• **CGC:** 15 graded, best 9.6
A: Bernie Wrightson
10 ❑ Jun 1974 Cover: 0.20 **NM** value: **8.00**
• **CGC:** 9 graded, best 9.6
A: Bernie Wrightson
11 ❑ Aug 1974 Cover: 0.20 **NM** value: **4.50**
• **CGC:** 1 graded, best 9.0
📖 The Conqueror Worms! **A:** Nestor Redondo **W:** Len Wein
12 ❑ Oct 1974 Cover: 0.20 **NM** value: **4.50**
• **CGC:** 1 graded, best 9.0
A: Nestor Redondo
13 ❑ Dec 1974 Cover: 0.20 **NM** value: **4.50**
• **CGC:** 2 graded, best 9.4
A: Nestor Redondo
14 ❑ Feb 1975 Cover: 0.25 **NM** value: **4.50**
Circ: Statement: **176,000**
A: Nestor Redondo
15 ❑ Apr 1975 Cover: 0.25 **NM** value: **4.50**
Circ: Statement: **176,000**
A: Nestor Redondo
16 ❑ May 1975 Cover: 0.25 **NM** value: **4.50**
Circ: Statement: **176,000** • **CGC:** 2 graded, best 9.4
A: Nestor Redondo
17 ❑ Jul 1975 Cover: 0.25 **NM** value: **4.50**
Circ: Statement: **176,000**
A: Nestor Redondo
18 ❑ Sep 1975 Cover: 0.25 **NM** value: **4.50**
Circ: Statement: **176,000**
A: Nestor Redondo
19 ❑ Oct 1975 Cover: 0.25 **NM** value: **4.50**
Circ: Statement: **176,000**
A: Nestor Redondo
20 ❑ Jan 1976 Cover: 0.25 **NM** value: **4.50**
A: Nestor Redondo
21 ❑ Mar 1976 Cover: 0.25 **NM** value: **4.50**
A: Nestor Redondo
22 ❑ May 1976 Cover: 0.30 **NM** value: **4.50**
A: Nestor Redondo
23 ❑ Jul 1976 Cover: 0.30 **NM** value: **4.50**
A: Nestor Redondo
24 ❑ Sep 1976 Cover: 0.30 **NM** value: **4.50**
final issue. **A:** Nestor Redondo

The prices seen above do not represent the highest possible prices seen in online auctions, but rather the prices we have seen these issues reliably fetch in a variety of environments (storefront retail, mail order, auction and convention).

SWAMP THING (2ND SERIES) — DC

This second Swamp Thing title, called The Saga of the Swamp Thing at its start, continued to develop the man/monster as a character for readers with mature tastes. By the latter part of the series, in fact, the series was moved under the Vertigo label, becoming the second pillar of that DC mature-readers line (following Neil Gaiman's Sandman).

Controversy surrounded this series in 1989 when writer Rick Veitch resigned from the series, after DC rejected his plans for #88. His time-travel story was to hyave involved the series' characters in the life of Christ. As a result, Neil Gaiman and Chirs Bachalo also stepped back from plans to work on the title.

A third series, following the Swamp Thing's daughter, followed years later. — JJM

46 ❑ Mar 1986 Cover: 0.75 **NM** value: **4.00**
Circ: CapCity orders: **13,850** • **CGC:** 1 graded, best 9.6
• Crisis; Series continued from "Saga of the Swamp Thing" **W:** Alan Moore ★ Appearance of John Constantine.
47 ❑ Apr 1986 Cover: 0.75 **NM** value: **3.00**
Circ: CapCity orders: **11,500** • **CGC:** 1 graded, best 9.4
W: Alan Moore ★ 1st Appearance of Parliament of Trees.
48 ❑ May 1986 Cover: 0.75 **NM** value: **3.00**
Circ: CapCity orders: **11,550**
W: Alan Moore
49 ❑ Jun 1986 Cover: 0.75 **NM** value: **3.00**
Circ: CapCity orders: **11,800** • **CGC:** 1 graded, best 9.4
W: Alan Moore
50 ❑ Jul 1986 Cover: 1.25 **NM** value: **4.00**
Circ: CapCity orders: **14,000** • **CGC:** 1 graded, best 9.6
• Giant-size. **W:** Alan Moore ★ Death of Sargon.
51 ❑ Aug 1986 Cover: 0.75 **NM** value: **3.00**
Circ: CapCity orders: **13,000** • **CGC:** 1 graded, best 9.4
W: Alan Moore
52 ❑ Sep 1986 Cover: 0.75 **NM** value: **4.00**
Circ: CapCity orders: **12,000** • **CGC:** 1 graded, best 9.2
• Joker **W:** Alan Moore ★ Appearance of Arkham Asylum, Joke.
53 ❑ Oct 1986 Cover: 0.75 **NM** value: **4.50**
Circ: CapCity orders: **15,500** • **CGC:** 1 graded, best 9.4
• Arkham Asylum story **W:** Alan Moore ★ Appearance of Batman.
54 ❑ Nov 1986 Cover: 0.75 **NM** value: **3.00**
Circ: CapCity orders: **13,000** • **CGC:** 1 graded, best 9.0
W: Alan Moore
55 ❑ Dec 1986 Cover: 0.75 **NM** value: **3.00**
Circ: CapCity orders: **12,600**
W: Alan Moore
56 ❑ Jan 1987 Cover: 0.75 **NM** value: **3.00**
Circ: CapCity orders: **12,950**
📖 My Blue Heaven **A:** Alfredo Alcala; Rick Veitch **W:** Alan Moore
57 ❑ Feb 1987 Cover: 0.75 **NM** value: **3.00**
Circ: CapCity orders: **13,550**
W: Alan Moore
58 ❑ Mar 1987 Cover: 0.75 **NM** value: **3.00**
Circ: CapCity orders: **12,850** • **CGC:** 1 graded, best 9.4
• Spectre preview **W:** Alan Moore
59 ❑ Apr 1987 Cover: 0.75 **NM** value: **3.00**
Circ: CapCity orders: **13,400**
W: Alan Moore
60 ❑ May 1987 Cover: 0.75 **NM** value: **3.00**
Circ: CapCity orders: **13,100**
• new format **W:** Alan Moore
61 ❑ Jun 1987 Cover: 1.00 **NM** value: **3.00**
Circ: CapCity orders: **13,550**
W: Alan Moore
62 ❑ Jul 1987 Cover: 1.00 **NM** value: **3.00**
Circ: CapCity orders: **12,550**
W: Alan Moore
63 ❑ Aug 1987 Cover: 1.00 **NM** value: **3.00**
Circ: CapCity orders: **15,650**
W: Alan Moore
64 ❑ Sep 1987 Cover: 1.00 **NM** value: **3.00**
Circ: CapCity orders: **17,750**
• last with Moore **W:** Alan Moore
65 ❑ Oct 1987 Cover: 1.00 **NM** value: **3.00**
Circ: CapCity orders: **15,000**
• Arkham Asylum ★ 1st Appearance of Sprout.
66 ❑ Nov 1987 Cover: 1.00 **NM** value: **2.50**
Circ: CapCity orders: **15,100**
• Arkham Asylum
67 ❑ Dec 1987 Cover: 1.25 **NM** value: **2.50**
Circ: CapCity orders: **14,050**
★ 1st Appearance of Hellblazer.
68 ❑ Jan 1988 Cover: 1.25 **NM** value: **2.50**
Circ: CapCity orders: **13,850**
69 ❑ Feb 1988 Cover: 1.25 **NM** value: **2.50**
Circ: CapCity orders: **13,650**
70 ❑ Mar 1988 Cover: 1.25 **NM** value: **2.50**
Circ: CapCity orders: **13,650**
71 ❑ Apr 1988 Cover: 1.25 **NM** value: **2.50**
Circ: CapCity orders: **13,150**
72 ❑ May 1988 Cover: 1.25 **NM** value: **2.50**
Circ: CapCity orders: **12,800**
73 ❑ Jun 1988 Cover: 1.25 **NM** value: **2.50**
Circ: CapCity orders: **12,050**
74 ❑ Jul 1988 Cover: 1.25 **NM** value: **2.50**
Circ: CapCity orders: **11,900**
75 ❑ Aug 1988 Cover: 1.25 **NM** value: **2.50**
Circ: CapCity orders: **11,700**
76 ❑ Sep 1988 Cover: 1.25 **NM** value: **2.50**
Circ: CapCity orders: **12,100**
77 ❑ Oct 1988 Cover: 1.25 **NM** value: **2.50**
Circ: CapCity orders: **12,000**
📖 Infernal Triangles **A:** Tom Mandrake; Alfredo Alcala(inks) **W:** Jamie Delano
78 ❑ Nov 1988 Cover: 1.25 **NM** value: **2.50**
Circ: CapCity orders: **11,250**
📖 To Sow One's Seed in the Wind **A:** Tom Mandrake; Alfredo Alcala **W:** Stephen R. Bissette
79 ❑ Dec 1988 Cover: 1.25 **NM** value: **2.50**
Circ: CapCity orders: **12,500**
★ Appearance of Superman.
80 ❑ Win 1988 Cover: 1.25 **NM** value: **2.50**
Circ: CapCity orders: **11,850**
81 ❑ Hol 1989 Cover: 1.25 **NM** value: **2.50**
Circ: CapCity orders: **13,900**
📖 Invasion!; Widows Weed • Invasion!
82 ❑ Jan 1989 Cover: 1.25 **NM** value: **2.25**
Circ: CapCity orders: **12,350**
• Sgt. Rock
83 ❑ Feb 1989 Cover: 1.25 **NM** value: **2.25**
Circ: CapCity orders: **12,350**
• Enemy Ace
84 ❑ Mar 1989 Cover: 1.25 **NM** value: **5.00**
Circ: CapCity orders: **12,000** • **CGC:** 1 graded, best 9.6
★ Appearance of Sandman.
85 ❑ Apr 1989 Cover: 1.25 **NM** value: **2.25**
Circ: CapCity orders: **12,100**
• Jonah Hex, Bat Lash
86 ❑ May 1989 Cover: 1.50 **NM** value: **2.25**
Circ: CapCity orders: **11,850**
• Tomahawk, Rip Hunter, Demon
87 ❑ Jun 1989 Cover: 1.50 **NM** value: **2.25**
Circ: CapCity orders: **12,000**
• Shining Knight, Demon
88 ❑ Sep 1989 Cover: 1.50 **NM** value: **2.25**
Circ: CapCity orders: **11,900**
📖 Survival of the Fittest
89 ❑ Oct 1989 Cover: 1.50 **NM** value: **2.25**
Circ: CapCity orders: **12,150**
📖 Founding Fathers
90 ❑ Dec 1989 Cover: 1.50 **NM** value: **2.50**
Circ: CapCity orders: **12,050**
📖 Journeys • Formerly known as Sprout ★ 1st Appearance of Tefé Holland.
91 ❑ Jan 1990 Cover: 1.50 **NM** value: **2.25**
Circ: CapCity orders: **11,700**
★ Appearance of Woodgod.
92 ❑ Feb 1990 Cover: 1.50 **NM** value: **2.25**
Circ: CapCity orders: **11,500**
93 ❑ Mar 1990 Cover: 1.50 **NM** value: **2.25**
Circ: CapCity orders: **11,350**
94 ❑ Apr 1990 Cover: 1.50 **NM** value: **2.25**
Circ: CapCity orders: **10,800**
95 ❑ May 1990 Cover: 1.50 **NM** value: **2.25**
Circ: CapCity orders: **10,900**
96 ❑ Jun 1990 Cover: 1.50 **NM** value: **2.25**
Circ: CapCity orders: **10,550**
97 ❑ Jul 1990 Cover: 1.50 **NM** value: **2.25**
Circ: CapCity orders: **10,550**
98 ❑ Aug 1990 Cover: 1.50 **NM** value: **2.25**
Circ: CapCity orders: **10,200**
99 ❑ Sep 1990 Cover: 1.50 **NM** value: **2.25**
Circ: CapCity orders: **10,300**
100 ❑ Oct 1990 Cover: 2.50 **NM** value: **3.00**
Circ: CapCity orders: **11,550**
• Giant-size.
101 ❑ Nov 1990 Cover: 1.50 **NM** value: **2.25**
Circ: CapCity orders: **10,250**
102 ❑ Dec 1990 Cover: 1.50 **NM** value: **2.25**
Circ: CapCity orders: **10,800**
103 ❑ Jan 1991 Cover: 1.50 **NM** value: **2.25**
Circ: CapCity orders: **10,850**
104 ❑ Feb 1991 Cover: 1.50 **NM** value: **2.25**
Circ: CapCity orders: **11,050**
105 ❑ Mar 1991 Cover: 1.50 **NM** value: **2.25**
Circ: CapCity orders: **10,450**
106 ❑ Apr 1991 Cover: 1.50 **NM** value: **2.25**
Circ: CapCity orders: **9,700**
107 ❑ May 1991 Cover: 1.50 **NM** value: **2.25**
Circ: CapCity orders: **9,650**
108 ❑ Jun 1991 Cover: 1.50 **NM** value: **2.25**
Circ: CapCity orders: **9,450**
109 ❑ Jul 1991 Cover: 1.50 **NM** value: **2.25**
Circ: CapCity orders: **9,550**
110 ❑ Aug 1991 Cover: 1.75 **NM** value: **2.25**
Circ: CapCity orders: **9,800**
111 ❑ Sep 1991 Cover: 1.75 **NM** value: **2.25**
Circ: CapCity orders: **9,500**
112 ❑ Oct 1991 Cover: 1.75 **NM** value: **2.25**
Circ: CapCity orders: **10,100**
113 ❑ Nov 1991 Cover: 1.75 **NM** value: **2.25**
Circ: CapCity orders: **9,350**
114 ❑ Dec 1991 Cover: 1.75 **NM** value: **2.25**
Circ: CapCity orders: **10,000**
115 ❑ Jan 1992 Cover: 1.75 **NM** value: **2.25**
Circ: CapCity orders: **9,550**
116 ❑ Feb 1992 Cover: 1.75 **NM** value: **2.25**
Circ: CapCity orders: **9,050**
117 ❑ Mar 1992 Cover: 1.75 **NM** value: **2.25**
Circ: CapCity orders: **8,800**
118 ❑ Apr 1992 Cover: 1.75 **NM** value: **2.25**
Circ: CapCity orders: **8,650**
119 ❑ May 1992 Cover: 1.75 **NM** value: **2.25**
Circ: CapCity orders: **8,300**
★ 1st Appearance of Lady Jane.
120 ❑ Jun 1992 Cover: 1.75 **NM** value: **2.25**
Circ: CapCity orders: **9,100**

CGC-graded: Multiply prices above by **33 for 9.9 M • 16 for 9.8 NM/M • 7 for 9.6 NM+ • 5 for 9.4 NM • 2.5 for 9.2 NM- • 1.5 for 9.0 VF/NM**

121 ❑ Jul 1992 Cover: 1.75 **NM** value: **2.00**
Circ: CapCity orders: **8,800**
122 ❑ Aug 1992 Cover: 1.75 **NM** value: **2.00**
Circ: CapCity orders: **8,950**
📖 The Eye Of The Needleman **A:** Scot Eaton; Kim Demulder **W:** Nancy Collins
123 ❑ Sep 1992 Cover: 1.75 **NM** value: **2.00**
Circ: CapCity orders: **8,050**
📖 Punctures **A:** Scot Eaton **W:** Nancy Collins
124 ❑ Oct 1992 Cover: 1.75 **NM** value: **2.00**
Circ: CapCity orders: **8,250**
125 ❑ Nov 1992 Cover: 2.95 **NM** value: **3.25**
Circ: CapCity orders: **9,700**
• 20th Anniversary Issue. 📖 Family Reunion • Arcane **A:** Scot Eaton; Kim Demulder **W:** Nancy Collins
126 ❑ Dec 1992 Cover: 1.75 **NM** value: **2.00**
Circ: CapCity orders: **8,450**
📖 The Big Picture **A:** Scot Eaton **W:** Dick Foreman
127 ❑ Jan 1993 Cover: 1.75 **NM** value: **2.00**
Circ: CapCity orders: **8,750**
📖 Project Proteus, Part 1
128 ❑ Feb 1993 Cover: 1.75 **NM** value: **2.00**
Circ: CapCity orders: **9,350**
📖 Project Proteus, Part 2 • Vertigo line begins **A:** Scot Eaton; Kim Demulder **W:** Nancy Collins
129 ❑ Mar 1993 Cover: 1.75 **NM** value: **2.00**
Circ: CapCity orders: **23,800**
📖 Swamp Fever **A:** Scot Eaton; Kim Demulder **W:** Nancy Collins
130 ❑ Apr 1993 Cover: 1.75 **NM** value: **2.00**
Circ: CapCity orders: **12,050**
131 ❑ May 1993 Cover: 1.75 **NM** value: **2.00**
Circ: CapCity orders: **12,350**
📖 Folk Remedy **A:** Scot Eaton; Kim Demulder **W:** Nancy Collins
132 ❑ Jun 1993 Cover: 1.95 **NM** value: **2.00**
Circ: CapCity orders: **12,450**
133 ❑ Jul 1993 Cover: 1.95 **NM** value: **2.00**
Circ: CapCity orders: **11,750**
134 ❑ Aug 1993 Cover: 1.95 **NM** value: **2.00**
Circ: CapCity orders: **12,100**
135 ❑ Sep 1993 Cover: 1.95 **NM** value: **2.00**
Circ: CapCity orders: **11,000**
136 ❑ Oct 1993 Cover: 1.95 **NM** value: **2.00**
Circ: CapCity orders: **10,500**
137 ❑ Nov 1993 Cover: 1.95 **NM** value: **2.00**
Circ: CapCity orders: **10,000**
138 ❑ Dec 1993 Cover: 1.95 **NM** value: **2.00**
Circ: CapCity orders: **10,000**
📖 And in the End… **A:** Scot Eaton; Kim Demulder **W:** Nancy Collins
139 ❑ Jan 1994 Cover: 1.95 **NM** value: **2.00**
Circ: CapCity orders: **10,050**
📖 The Mind Fields, Part 2 **A:** Rebecca Guay **W:** Dick Foreman
140 ❑ Mar 1994 Cover: 1.95 **NM** value: **2.00**
Circ: CapCity orders: **18,000**
📖 Bad Gumbo, Part 1
140/PL ❑ Mar 1994 **NM** value: **6.00**
• **CGC:** 1 graded, best 9.4
• platinum
141 ❑ Apr 1994 Cover: 1.95 **NM** value: **2.00**
Circ: CapCity orders: **13,350**
142 ❑ May 1994 Cover: 1.95 **NM** value: **2.00**
Circ: CapCity orders: **11,100**
143 ❑ Jun 1994 Cover: 1.95 **NM** value: **2.00**
Circ: CapCity orders: **11,300**
📖 Desert Hearts **A:** Kim Demulder **W:** Mark Millar
144 ❑ Jul 1994 Cover: 1.95 **NM** value: **2.00**
Circ: CapCity orders: **11,000**
145 ❑ Aug 1994 Cover: 1.95 **NM** value: **2.00**
Circ: CapCity orders: **10,750**
146 ❑ Sep 1994 Cover: 1.95 **NM** value: **2.00**
Circ: CapCity orders: **10,450**
147 ❑ Oct 1994 Cover: 1.95 **NM** value: **2.00**
Circ: CapCity orders: **9,650**
148 ❑ Nov 1994 Cover: 1.95 **NM** value: **2.00**
Circ: CapCity orders: **9,150**
149 ❑ Dec 1994 Cover: 1.95 **NM** value: **2.00**
Circ: CapCity orders: **8,900**
150 ❑ Jan 1995 Cover: 2.95 **NM** value: **3.00**
Circ: CapCity orders: **8,600**
• Giant-size. 📖 Illumination, The **A:** Kim Demulder **W:** Mark Millar
151 ❑ Feb 1995 Cover: 2.95 **NM** value: **Cover or less**
Circ: CapCity orders: **7,825**
152 ❑ Mar 1995 Cover: 2.95 **NM** value: **Cover or less**
Circ: CapCity orders: **7,425**
📖 River Run, Part 1
153 ❑ Apr 1995 Cover: 1.95 **NM** value: **2.00**
Circ: CapCity orders: **7,250**
154 ❑ May 1995 Cover: 2.25 **NM** value: **Cover or less**
Circ: CapCity orders: **7,000**
155 ❑ Jun 1995 Cover: 2.25 **NM** value: **Cover or less**
Circ: CapCity orders: **6,900**
156 ❑ Jul 1995 Cover: 2.25 **NM** value: **Cover or less**
Circ: CapCity orders: **7,075**
157 ❑ Aug 1995 Cover: 2.25 **NM** value: **Cover or less**
Circ: CapCity orders: **7,025**
158 ❑ Sep 1995 Cover: 2.25 **NM** value: **Cover or less**
Circ: CapCity orders: **6,575**
159 ❑ Oct 1995 Cover: 2.25 **NM** value: **2.50**
Circ: CapCity orders: **5,800**
Photo cover.
160 ❑ Nov 1995 Cover: 2.25 **NM** value: **2.50**
161 ❑ Dec 1995 Cover: 2.25 **NM** value: **2.50**
162 ❑ Jan 1996 Cover: 2.25 **NM** value: **2.50**
163 ❑ Feb 1996 Cover: 2.25 **NM** value: **2.50**
📖 Trees of Knowledge **A:** Kim Demulder; Phil Hester **W:** Mark Millar
164 ❑ Mar 1996 Cover: 2.25 **NM** value: **2.50**
📖 The Parliament of Vapors **A:** Kim Demulder; Phil Hester **W:** Mark Millar
165 ❑ Apr 1996 Cover: 2.25 **NM** value: **2.50**
📖 Chester Williams: American Cop **A:** Curt Swan **W:** Mark Millar
166 ❑ May 1996 Cover: 2.25 **NM** value: **2.50**
167 ❑ Jun 1996 Cover: 2.25 **NM** value: **2.50**
168 ❑ Jul 1996 Cover: 2.25 **NM** value: **2.50**
169 ❑ Aug 1996 Cover: 2.25 **NM** value: **2.50**
170 ❑ Sep 1996 Cover: 2.25 **NM** value: **2.50**
171 ❑ Oct 1996 Cover: 2.25 **NM** value: **2.50**
📖 Trial by Fire final issue. **A:** Phil Hester **W:** Mark Millar
Anl 4 ❑ Cover: 2.00 **NM** value: **3.50**
Circ: CapCity orders: **13,550**
★ Appearance of Batman.
Anl 5 ❑ Cover: 2.95 **NM** value: **3.50**
Circ: CapCity orders: **13,100**
★ Appearance of Brother Power.
Anl 6 ❑ Cover: 2.95 **NM** value: **Cover or less**
Circ: CapCity orders: **9,700**
Anl 7 ❑ Cover: 3.95 **NM** value: **Cover or less**
Circ: CapCity orders: **13,100**
📖 The Children's Crusade, Part 4 • Children's Crusade
Bk 1 ❑ Dec 1990 Cover: 17.95 **NM** value: **Cover or less**
Circ: CapCity orders: **2,900**
• Love And Death

SWAMP THING (3RD SERIES) — DC / Vertigo

1 ❑ May 2000 Cover: 2.50 **NM** value: **3.00**
Circ: Diamd. preorders: **25,063**
📖 In Lieu of Flowers **A:** Roger Peterson **W:** Brian K. Vaughan
2 ❑ Jun 2000 Cover: 2.50 **NM** value: **Cover or less**
Circ: Diamd. preorders: **20,400**
📖 A Tree Falls in the Forest **A:** Roger Peterson **W:** Brian K. Vaughan
3 ❑ Jul 2000 Cover: 2.50 **NM** value: **Cover or less**
Circ: Diamd. preorders: **18,744**
A: Roger Peterson **W:** Brian K. Vaughan
4 ❑ Aug 2000 Cover: 2.50 **NM** value: **Cover or less**
Circ: Diamd. preorders: **18,511**
📖 Killing Time, Part 1 **A:** Roger Peterson **W:** Brian K. Vaughan
5 ❑ Sep 2000 Cover: 2.50 **NM** value: **Cover or less**
Circ: Diamd. preorders: **17,464**
📖 Killing Time, Part 2 **A:** Roger Peterson **W:** Brian K. Vaughan
6 ❑ Oct 2000 Cover: 2.50 **NM** value: **Cover or less**
Circ: Diamd. preorders: **15,787**
📖 Killing Time, Part 3 **A:** Roger Peterson **W:** Brian K. Vaughan
7 ❑ Nov 2000 Cover: 2.50 **NM** value: **Cover or less**
Circ: Diamd. preorders: **15,236**
📖 Concrete Jungle, Part 1 **A:** Roger Peterson **W:** Brian K. Vaughan
8 ❑ Dec 2000 Cover: 2.50 **NM** value: **Cover or less**
Circ: Diamd. preorders: **14,529**
📖 Concrete Jungle, Part 2 **A:** Roger Peterson **W:** Brian K. Vaughan
9 ❑ Jan 2001 Cover: 2.50 **NM** value: **Cover or less**
Circ: Diamd. preorders: **13,957**
📖 Concrete Jungle, Part 3 **A:** Steve Lieber; Paul Pope; Guy Davis; Roger Peterson; Rick Magyar **W:** Brian K. Vaughan
10 ❑ Feb 2001 Cover: 2.50 **NM** value: **Cover or less**
Circ: Diamd. preorders: **13,583**
📖 Silk Cut **A:** Roger Peterson; Glenn Fabry(cover) **W:** Brian K. Vaughan
11 ❑ Mar 2001 Cover: 2.50 **NM** value: **Cover or less**
Circ: Diamd. preorders: **12,736**
📖 Red Harvest, Part 1 **A:** Roger Peterson; Glenn Fabry(cover) **W:** Brian K. Vaughan
12 ❑ Apr 2001 Cover: 2.50 **NM** value: **Cover or less**
Circ: Diamd. preorders: **12,615**
📖 Red Harvest, Part 2 **A:** Giuseppe Camuncoli **W:** Brian K. Vaughan
13 ❑ May 2001 Cover: 2.50 **NM** value: **Cover or less**
Circ: Diamd. preorders: **12,452**
📖 Red Harvest, Part 3 **A:** Giuseppe Camuncoli **W:** Brian K. Vaughan
14 ❑ Jun 2001 Cover: 2.50 **NM** value: **Cover or less**
Circ: Diamd. preorders: **12,393**
📖 Red Harvest, Part 4 **A:** Giuseppe Camuncoli **W:** Brian K. Vaughan
15 ❑ Jul 2001 Cover: 2.50 **NM** value: **Cover or less**
Circ: Diamd. preorders: **11,838**
16 ❑ Aug 2001 Cover: 2.50 **NM** value: **Cover or less**
Circ: Diamd. preorders: **11,803**
17 ❑ Sep 2001 Cover: 2.50 **NM** value: **Cover or less**
Circ: Diamd. preorders: **12,123**

SWAMP THING: DARK GENESIS — DC

Bk 1 ❑ Cover: 19.95 **NM** value: **Cover or less**
A: Bernie Wrightson

SWAMP THING: ROOTS — DC / Vertigo

1 ❑ Cover: 7.95 **NM** value: **Cover or less**
No issue number. • prestige format one-shot **A:** Jon J. Muth **W:** Jon J. Muth

SWAN — Little Idylls

1 ❑ Jun 1995, b&w Cover: 2.95 **NM** value: **Cover or less**
2 ❑ Jun 1995, b&w Cover: 2.95 **NM** value: **Cover or less**

SWARM — Mushroom

1 ❑ Cover: 2.50 **NM** value: **Cover or less**

SWEENEY — Standard

4 ❑ ca. 1949 Cover: 0.10 **NM** value: **50.00**
5 ❑ ca. 1949 Cover: 0.10 **NM** value: **50.00**

SWEET — Adept

1 ❑ Cover: 3.95 **NM** value: **Cover or less**

SWEETCHILDE — New Moon

All issues are adults only.
1 ❑ b&w Cover: 2.95 **NM** value: **Cover or less**

SWEET CHILDE: LOST CONFESSIONS — Anarchy Bridgeworks

1 ❑ Cover: 2.95 **NM** value: **Cover or less**
A: Marcus Shockley **W:** Vinson Watson

SWEETHEART DIARY (CHARLTON) — Charlton

32 ❑ Oct 1955 Cover: 0.10 **NM** value: **40.00**
33 ❑ Apr 1956 Cover: 0.10 **NM** value: **25.00**
34 ❑ ca. 1956 Cover: 0.10 **NM** value: **25.00**
35 ❑ ca. 1956 Cover: 0.10 **NM** value: **25.00**
36 ❑ ca. 1956 Cover: 0.10 **NM** value: **25.00**
37 ❑ ca. 1956 Cover: 0.10 **NM** value: **25.00**
38 ❑ ca. 1956 Cover: 0.10 **NM** value: **25.00**
39 ❑ ca. 1957 Cover: 0.10 **NM** value: **25.00**
40 ❑ ca. 1957 Cover: 0.10 **NM** value: **25.00**
41 ❑ ca. 1957 Cover: 0.10 **NM** value: **20.00**
42 ❑ ca. 1957 Cover: 0.10 **NM** value: **20.00**
43 ❑ ca. 1957 Cover: 0.10 **NM** value: **20.00**
44 ❑ ca. 1957 Cover: 0.10 **NM** value: **20.00**
45 ❑ Feb 1958 Cover: 0.10 **NM** value: **20.00**
46 ❑ Apr 1958 Cover: 0.10 **NM** value: **20.00**
47 ❑ ca. 1958 Cover: 0.10 **NM** value: **20.00**
48 ❑ ca. 1958 Cover: 0.10 **NM** value: **20.00**
49 ❑ ca. 1958 Cover: 0.10 **NM** value: **20.00**
50 ❑ Oct 1958 Cover: 0.10 **NM** value: **20.00**
51 ❑ ca. 1959 Cover: 0.10 **NM** value: **20.00**
52 ❑ ca. 1959 Cover: 0.10 **NM** value: **20.00**
53 ❑ Jul 1959 Cover: 0.10 **NM** value: **20.00**
54 ❑ Jun 1960 Cover: 0.10 **NM** value: **20.00**
55 ❑ ca. 1960 Cover: 0.10 **NM** value: **20.00**
56 ❑ ca. 1960 Cover: 0.10 **NM** value: **20.00**
57 ❑ ca. 1961 Cover: 0.10 **NM** value: **20.00**
58 ❑ ca. 1961 Cover: 0.10 **NM** value: **20.00**
59 ❑ Jul 1961 Cover: 0.10 **NM** value: **20.00**
60 ❑ Sep 1961 Cover: 0.10 **NM** value: **20.00**
61 ❑ Nov 1961 Cover: 0.10 **NM** value: **15.00**
62 ❑ Jan 1962 Cover: 0.10 **NM** value: **15.00**
Circ: Statement: **118,845**
63 ❑ ca. 1962 Cover: 0.12 **NM** value: **15.00**
Circ: Statement: **118,845**
64 ❑ ca. 1962 Cover: 0.12 **NM** value: **15.00**
Circ: Statement: **118,845**
65 ❑ Aug 1962 Cover: 0.12 **NM** value: **15.00**
Circ: Statement: **118,845**

SWEETHEART DIARY (FAWCETT) — Fawcett

1 ❑ Win 1949 Cover: 0.10 **NM** value: **100.00**
2 ❑ Spr 1950 Cover: 0.10 **NM** value: **75.00**
3 ❑ Jun 1950 Cover: 0.10 **NM** value: **50.00**
4 ❑ Aug 1950 Cover: 0.10 **NM** value: **50.00**
5 ❑ Oct 1950 Cover: 0.10 **NM** value: **50.00**
6 ❑ ca. 1951 Cover: 0.10 **NM** value: **40.00**
7 ❑ Sep 1951 Cover: 0.10 **NM** value: **40.00**
📖 Stolen Happiness; Fatman Blackmail
8 ❑ Dec 1951 Cover: 0.10 **NM** value: **40.00**
9 ❑ ca. 1952 Cover: 0.10 **NM** value: **40.00**
10 ❑ May 1952 Cover: 0.10 **NM** value: **40.00**
11 ❑ Jul 1952 Cover: 0.10 **NM** value: **35.00**
12 ❑ Sep 1952 Cover: 0.10 **NM** value: **35.00**
13 ❑ Nov 1952 Cover: 0.10 **NM** value: **35.00**
14 ❑ Jan 1953 Cover: 0.10 **NM** value: **35.00**

SWEETHEARTS (VOL. 1) — Fawcett

Early issues of Sweethearts (a title which, inexplicably, had once been Captain Midnight) featured the usual combination of lovelorn melodrama, cheesecake, and photo covers that had made romance comics popular.

In 1955, Fawcett passed the series to Charlton, which also started its numbering well past #1. Strangely enough, the less-than-inspired workmanship that Charlton brought to the table in Vol. 2 meshed well with the cliche-ridden genre that romance comics had become by the mid-50s. Always a reflection of the stultifying insecurity and sexual frustration of American middle class suburbia, such love comics as Sweethearts epitomized kitsch culture and became icons of pop art in 1960s. By that time, however, Sweethearts and other romance comics had embraced "hip" 1960s fashions and slang, as well as an embarrassingly shallow take on "radical" social values, providing lots of unintended laughs for modern readers.

68 ❑ Oct 1948 Cover: 0.10 **NM** value: **100.00**
69 ❑ Nov 1948 Cover: 0.10 **NM** value: **40.00**
• Glenn Ford back cover photo
70 ❑ Dec 1948 Cover: 0.10 **NM** value: **40.00**
71 ❑ Jan 1949 Cover: 0.10 **NM** value: **40.00**
72 ❑ Feb 1949 Cover: 0.10 **NM** value: **40.00**
73 ❑ Mar 1949 Cover: 0.10 **NM** value: **40.00**
74 ❑ Apr 1949 Cover: 0.10 **NM** value: **40.00**
75 ❑ May 1949 Cover: 0.10 **NM** value: **40.00**
76 ❑ Jun 1949 Cover: 0.10 **NM** value: **40.00**
77 ❑ Jul 1949 Cover: 0.10 **NM** value: **40.00**
78 ❑ Aug 1949 Cover: 0.10 **NM** value: **40.00**
79 ❑ Sep 1949 Cover: 0.10 **NM** value: **40.00**
80 ❑ Oct 1949 Cover: 0.10 **NM** value: **40.00**
81 ❑ Nov 1949 Cover: 0.10 **NM** value: **30.00**
82 ❑ Dec 1949 Cover: 0.10 **NM** value: **30.00**
83 ❑ Jan 1950 Cover: 0.10 **NM** value: **30.00**
84 ❑ Feb 1950 Cover: 0.10 **NM** value: **30.00**
85 ❑ Mar 1950 Cover: 0.10 **NM** value: **30.00**
86 ❑ Apr 1950 Cover: 0.10 **NM** value: **30.00**
87 ❑ May 1950 Cover: 0.10 **NM** value: **30.00**
88 ❑ Jun 1950 Cover: 0.10 **NM** value: **30.00**
89 ❑ Jul 1950 Cover: 0.10 **NM** value: **30.00**
90 ❑ Aug 1950 Cover: 0.10 **NM** value: **30.00**
91 ❑ Sep 1950 Cover: 0.10 **NM** value: **30.00**

Other grades: Multiply prices above by **1.5 for Mint • 2/3 for Very Fine • 1/3 for Fine • 1/5 for Very Good • 1/8 for Good**

92 ❑ Oct 1950 Cover: 0.10 **NM** value: **30.00**
93 ❑ Nov 1950 Cover: 0.10 **NM** value: **30.00**
94 ❑ Dec 1950 Cover: 0.10 **NM** value: **30.00**
95 ❑ Jan 1951 Cover: 0.10 **NM** value: **30.00**
96 ❑ Feb 1951 Cover: 0.10 **NM** value: **30.00**
97 ❑ Mar 1951 Cover: 0.10 **NM** value: **30.00**
98 ❑ Apr 1951 Cover: 0.10 **NM** value: **30.00**
99 ❑ May 1951 Cover: 0.10 **NM** value: **30.00**
100 ❑ Jun 1951 Cover: 0.10 **NM** value: **30.00**
101 ❑ Jul 1951 Cover: 0.10 **NM** value: **25.00**
102 ❑ Aug 1951 Cover: 0.10 **NM** value: **25.00**
103 ❑ Sep 1951 Cover: 0.10 **NM** value: **25.00**
104 ❑ Oct 1951 Cover: 0.10 **NM** value: **25.00**
105 ❑ Nov 1951 Cover: 0.10 **NM** value: **25.00**
106 ❑ Dec 1951 Cover: 0.10 **NM** value: **25.00**
107 ❑ Jan 1952 Cover: 0.10 **NM** value: **25.00**
108 ❑ Feb 1952 Cover: 0.10 **NM** value: **25.00**
109 ❑ Mar 1952 Cover: 0.10 **NM** value: **25.00**
110 ❑ Apr 1952 Cover: 0.10 **NM** value: **25.00**
111 ❑ May 1952 Cover: 0.10 **NM** value: **20.00**
112 ❑ Jun 1952 Cover: 0.10 **NM** value: **20.00**
113 ❑ Jul 1952 Cover: 0.10 **NM** value: **20.00**
114 ❑ Aug 1952 Cover: 0.10 **NM** value: **20.00**
115 ❑ Sep 1952 Cover: 0.10 **NM** value: **20.00**
116 ❑ Oct 1952 Cover: 0.10 **NM** value: **20.00**
117 ❑ Nov 1952 Cover: 0.10 **NM** value: **20.00**
118 ❑ Dec 1952 Cover: 0.10 **NM** value: **20.00**
119 ❑ Jan 1953 Cover: 0.10 **NM** value: **20.00**
120 ❑ Mar 1953 Cover: 0.10 **NM** value: **20.00**
121 ❑ May 1953 Cover: 0.10 **NM** value: **20.00**
122 ❑ ca. 1954 Cover: 0.10 **NM** value: **20.00**

SWEETHEARTS (VOL. 2) — Charlton

23 ❑ ca. 1954 Cover: 0.10 **NM** value: **12.00**
24 ❑ ca. 1954 Cover: 0.10 **NM** value: **12.00**
25 ❑ ca. 1954 Cover: 0.10 **NM** value: **12.00**
26 ❑ ca. 1954 Cover: 0.10 **NM** value: **12.00**
27 ❑ ca. 1954 Cover: 0.10 **NM** value: **12.00**
28 ❑ ca. 1955 Cover: 0.10 **NM** value: **12.00**
29 ❑ ca. 1955 Cover: 0.10 **NM** value: **12.00**
30 ❑ ca. 1955 Cover: 0.10 **NM** value: **12.00**
31 ❑ ca. 1955 Cover: 0.10 **NM** value: **10.00**
32 ❑ ca. 1955 Cover: 0.10 **NM** value: **10.00**
33 ❑ ca. 1955 Cover: 0.10 **NM** value: **10.00**
34 ❑ Cover: 0.10 **NM** value: **10.00**
35 ❑ Cover: 0.10 **NM** value: **10.00**
36 ❑ Cover: 0.10 **NM** value: **10.00**
37 ❑ Cover: 0.10 **NM** value: **10.00**
38 ❑ Cover: 0.10 **NM** value: **10.00**
39 ❑ Cover: 0.10 **NM** value: **10.00**
40 ❑ Cover: 0.10 **NM** value: **16.00**
Photo cover.
41 ❑ Cover: 0.10 **NM** value: **9.00**
42 ❑ Cover: 0.10 **NM** value: **35.00**
Ricky Nelson photo cover.
43 ❑ Cover: 0.10 **NM** value: **9.00**
44 ❑ Cover: 0.10 **NM** value: **9.00**
45 ❑ Cover: 0.10 **NM** value: **9.00**
46 ❑ Cover: 0.10 **NM** value: **15.00**
Photo cover.
47 ❑ Cover: 0.10 **NM** value: **9.00**
48 ❑ Cover: 0.10 **NM** value: **9.00**
49 ❑ Cover: 0.10 **NM** value: **9.00**
50 ❑ Cover: 0.10 **NM** value: **9.00**
51 ❑ Cover: 0.10 **NM** value: **7.00**
52 ❑ Cover: 0.10 **NM** value: **7.00**
53 ❑ Cover: 0.10 **NM** value: **7.00**
54 ❑ Cover: 0.10 **NM** value: **7.00**
55 ❑ Cover: 0.10 **NM** value: **7.00**
56 ❑ Cover: 0.10 **NM** value: **7.00**
57 ❑ Cover: 0.10 **NM** value: **7.00**
58 ❑ Cover: 0.10 **NM** value: **7.00**
59 ❑ Cover: 0.10 **NM** value: **7.00**
60 ❑ Cover: 0.10 **NM** value: **7.00**
61 ❑ Cover: 0.10 **NM** value: **6.00**
62 ❑ Cover: 0.10 **NM** value: **6.00**
63 ❑ Cover: 0.10 **NM** value: **6.00**
64 ❑ **NM** value: **6.00**
65 ❑ **NM** value: **6.00**
66 ❑ **NM** value: **6.00**
67 ❑ **NM** value: **6.00**
68 ❑ ca. 1961 **NM** value: **6.00**
69 ❑ Jan 1962 Cover: 0.12 **NM** value: **6.00**
70 ❑ Cover: 0.12 **NM** value: **6.00**
71 ❑ Cover: 0.12 **NM** value: **4.00**
72 ❑ Cover: 0.12 **NM** value: **4.00**
73 ❑ Cover: 0.12 **NM** value: **4.00**
74 ❑ Cover: 0.12 **NM** value: **4.00**
75 ❑ Cover: 0.12 **NM** value: **4.00**
76 ❑ Cover: 0.12 **NM** value: **4.00**
77 ❑ Cover: 0.12 **NM** value: **4.00**
78 ❑ Cover: 0.12 **NM** value: **4.00**
📖 Stormy Love
79 ❑ 1964 Cover: 0.12 **NM** value: **4.00**
80 ❑ Jan 1965 Cover: 0.12 **NM** value: **4.00**
Circ: Statement: **142,208**
81 ❑ 1965 Cover: 0.12 **NM** value: **4.00**
Circ: Statement: **142,208**
82 ❑ 1965 Cover: 0.12 **NM** value: **4.00**
Circ: Statement: **142,208**
83 ❑ Aug 1965 Cover: 0.12 **NM** value: **4.00**
Circ: Statement: **142,208**
84 ❑ Cover: 0.12 **NM** value: **4.00**
Circ: Statement: **142,208**
📖 A Fool for Love
85 ❑ 1966 Cover: 0.12 **NM** value: **4.00**
86 ❑ 1966 Cover: 0.12 **NM** value: **4.00**
87 ❑ 1966 Cover: 0.12 **NM** value: **4.00**
88 ❑ 1966 Cover: 0.12 **NM** value: **4.00**
89 ❑ 1966 Cover: 0.12 **NM** value: **4.00**
90 ❑ Cover: 0.12 **NM** value: **4.00**
91 ❑ Feb 1967 Cover: 0.12 **NM** value: **4.00**
Circ: Statement: **120,713**
92 ❑ Apr 1967 Cover: 0.12 **NM** value: **4.00**
Circ: Statement: **120,713**
93 ❑ Jun 1967 Cover: 0.12 **NM** value: **4.00**
Circ: Statement: **120,713**
94 ❑ Aug 1967 Cover: 0.12 **NM** value: **4.00**
Circ: Statement: **120,713**
95 ❑ Oct 1967 Cover: 0.12 **NM** value: **4.00**
Circ: Statement: **120,713**
96 ❑ Dec 1967 Cover: 0.12 **NM** value: **4.00**
Circ: Statement: **120,713**
97 ❑ 1968 Cover: 0.12 **NM** value: **4.00**
98 ❑ Cover: 0.12 **NM** value: **4.00**
99 ❑ Cover: 0.12 **NM** value: **4.00**
100 ❑ Cover: 0.12 **NM** value: **4.00**
101 ❑ Cover: 0.12 **NM** value: **3.00**
102 ❑ Cover: 0.12 **NM** value: **3.00**
103 ❑ 1969 **NM** value: **3.00**
104 ❑ 1969 **NM** value: **3.00**
105 ❑ 1969 **NM** value: **3.00**
106 ❑ **NM** value: **3.00**
107 ❑ **NM** value: **3.00**
📖 Weekend in Kicksville; Unlovable Me!; Plan Your Kisses **A:** Nicholas Alascia; Nicholas Ferme
108 ❑ **NM** value: **3.00**
109 ❑ Mar 1970 Cover: 0.15 **NM** value: **3.00**
110 ❑ May 1970 Cover: 0.15 **NM** value: **3.00**
111 ❑ Jul 1970 Cover: 0.15 **NM** value: **3.00**
112 ❑ Sep 1970 Cover: 0.15 **NM** value: **3.00**
113 ❑ Nov 1970 Cover: 0.15 **NM** value: **3.00**
114 ❑ Jan 1971 Cover: 0.15 **NM** value: **3.00**
115 ❑ Mar 1971 Cover: 0.15 **NM** value: **3.00**
116 ❑ May 1971 Cover: 0.15 **NM** value: **3.00**
117 ❑ Jul 1971 Cover: 0.15 **NM** value: **3.00**
118 ❑ Sep 1971 Cover: 0.15 **NM** value: **3.00**
119 ❑ Oct 1971 Cover: 0.20 **NM** value: **3.00**
120 ❑ Nov 1971 Cover: 0.20 **NM** value: **3.00**
121 ❑ Cover: 0.20 **NM** value: **3.00**
122 ❑ ca. 1972 Cover: 0.20 **NM** value: **3.00**
123 ❑ ca. 1972 Cover: 0.20 **NM** value: **3.00**
124 ❑ ca. 1972 Cover: 0.20 **NM** value: **3.00**
125 ❑ ca. 1972 Cover: 0.20 **NM** value: **3.00**
126 ❑ Jul 1972 Cover: 0.20 **NM** value: **3.00**
127 ❑ Aug 1972 Cover: 0.20 **NM** value: **3.00**
📖 A Homey Type
128 ❑ Cover: 0.20 **NM** value: **3.00**
129 ❑ Cover: 0.20 **NM** value: **3.00**
130 ❑ ca. 1973 Cover: 0.20 **NM** value: **3.00**
131 ❑ ca. 1973 Cover: 0.20 **NM** value: **3.00**
132 ❑ ca. 1973 Cover: 0.20 **NM** value: **3.00**
133 ❑ ca. 1973 Cover: 0.20 **NM** value: **3.00**
134 ❑ ca. 1973 Cover: 0.20 **NM** value: **3.00**
135 ❑ ca. 1973 Cover: 0.20 **NM** value: **3.00**
136 ❑ ca. 1973 Cover: 0.20 **NM** value: **3.00**
137 ❑ ca. 1973 Cover: 0.20 **NM** value: **3.00**
final issue.

SWEETIE PIE — Ajax

1 ❑ ca. 1956 Cover: 0.10 **NM** value: **40.00**
2 ❑ ca. 1956 Cover: 0.10 **NM** value: **25.00**
3 ❑ ca. 1956 Cover: 0.10 **NM** value: **25.00**
4 ❑ ca. 1956 Cover: 0.10 **NM** value: **25.00**
5 ❑ ca. 1956 Cover: 0.10 **NM** value: **25.00**
6 ❑ ca. 1956 Cover: 0.10 **NM** value: **20.00**
7 ❑ ca. 1956 Cover: 0.10 **NM** value: **20.00**
8 ❑ ca. 1956 Cover: 0.10 **NM** value: **20.00**
9 ❑ ca. 1956 Cover: 0.10 **NM** value: **20.00**
10 ❑ ca. 1956 Cover: 0.10 **NM** value: **20.00**
11 ❑ ca. 1956 Cover: 0.10 **NM** value: **20.00**
12 ❑ ca. 1956 Cover: 0.10 **NM** value: **20.00**
13 ❑ ca. 1956 Cover: 0.10 **NM** value: **20.00**
14 ❑ ca. 1956 Cover: 0.10 **NM** value: **20.00**
15 ❑ ca. 1956 Cover: 0.10 **NM** value: **20.00**

SWEET LOVE — Harvey

1 ❑ Sep 1949 Cover: 0.10 **NM** value: **50.00**
2 ❑ Nov 1949 Cover: 0.10 **NM** value: **35.00**
• **CGC:** 1 graded, best 7.5
3 ❑ Jan 1950 Cover: 0.10 **NM** value: **30.00**
• **CGC:** 1 graded, best 8.5
4 ❑ Mar 1950 Cover: 0.10 **NM** value: **30.00**
5 ❑ May 1950 Cover: 0.10 **NM** value: **30.00**

SWEET LUCY — Brainstorm

1 ❑ Jun 1993, b&w Cover: 2.95 **NM** value: **Cover or less**
2 ❑ b&w Cover: 2.95 **NM** value: **Cover or less**

SWEET LUCY: BLONDE STEELE — Brainstorm

1 ❑ Cover: 2.95 **NM** value: **Cover or less**
📖 Blonde Steel; Technophelia **A:** Scott Harrison **W:** Scott Harrison

SWEET LUCY COMMEMORATIVE EDITION — Brainstorm

1 ❑ Cover: 3.95 **NM** value: **Cover or less**
A: Scott Harrison **W:** Scott Harrison

SWEETMEATS — Atomeka

1 ❑ Cover: 3.95 **NM** value: **Cover or less**
No issue number. • b&w one-shot

SWEET SIXTEEN — Parents' Magazine Institute

1 ❑ Aug 1946 Cover: 0.10 **NM** value: **125.00**
2 ❑ Nov 1946 Cover: 0.10 **NM** value: **100.00**
3 ❑ Jan 1947 Cover: 0.10 **NM** value: **100.00**
4 ❑ Mar 1947 Cover: 0.10 **NM** value: **100.00**
5 ❑ May 1947 Cover: 0.10 **NM** value: **100.00**
6 ❑ Jun 1947 Cover: 0.10 **NM** value: **75.00**
7 ❑ Jul 1947 Cover: 0.10 **NM** value: **75.00**
8 ❑ Aug 1947 Cover: 0.10 **NM** value: **75.00**
9 ❑ Sep 1947 Cover: 0.10 **NM** value: **75.00**
10 ❑ Oct 1947 Cover: 0.10 **NM** value: **75.00**
11 ❑ Nov 1947 Cover: 0.10 **NM** value: **60.00**
12 ❑ Dec 1947 Cover: 0.10 **NM** value: **60.00**
13 ❑ Jan 1948 Cover: 0.10 **NM** value: **60.00**

SWEET XVI — Marvel

This title examines the trials and tribulations of teenagers during Roman times, when life was much simpler. Princess Cornelia and Aria are two best friends who do the usual teen-age things together — go to the mall, hang out at Jupiter's diner and dream about boys, especially their friends, Anthony and Seneca. Add to this a few more friends, Diana and Virgil and Aria's little sister, budding scientist Alexandria, and you have the makings for fun and wholesome entertainment for young and old alike.

Written and drawn by Barb Slate, the series also included fashion tips.

1 ❑ May 1991 Cover: 1.00 **NM** value: **Cover or less**
Circ: CapCity orders: **5,750**
📖 The Invitation; How to Make a Roman Braid; Event of the Century; I Didn't Get an Invitation!; How Could a Plebe be so Lucky? **A:** Barbara Slate **W:** Barbara Slate
2 ❑ Jun 1991 Cover: 1.00 **NM** value: **Cover or less**
Circ: CapCity orders: **3,550**
A: Barbara Slate **W:** Barbara Slate
3 ❑ Jul 1991 Cover: 1.00 **NM** value: **Cover or less**
Circ: CapCity orders: **2,750**
A: Barbara Slate **W:** Barbara Slate
4 ❑ Aug 1991 Cover: 1.00 **NM** value: **Cover or less**
Circ: CapCity orders: **2,150**
A: Barbara Slate **W:** Barbara Slate
5 ❑ Sep 1991 Cover: 1.00 **NM** value: **Cover or less**
Circ: CapCity orders: **1,700**
A: Barbara Slate **W:** Barbara Slate
6 ❑ Oct 1991 Cover: 1.00 **NM** value: **Cover or less**
Circ: CapCity orders: **1,450**
A: Barbara Slate **W:** Barbara Slate
SE 1 ❑ Cover: 2.25 **NM** value: **Cover or less**
• Back to School Special **A:** Barbara Slate **W:** Barbara Slate

SWERVE — Slave Labor / Amaze Ink

1 ❑ Dec 1995 Cover: 1.50 **NM** value: **Cover or less**
📖 False Start **A:** Kyle Hunter **W:** Kyle Hunter
2 ❑ Mar 1996 Cover: 1.50 **NM** value: **Cover or less**
A: Kyle Hunter **W:** Kyle Hunter

SWIFT ARROW (1ST SERIES) — Ajax

1 ❑ Feb 1954 Cover: 0.10 **NM** value: **75.00**
2 ❑ Apr 1954 Cover: 0.10 **NM** value: **50.00**
3 ❑ Jun 1954 Cover: 0.10 **NM** value: **40.00**
4 ❑ Aug 1954 Cover: 0.10 **NM** value: **40.00**
5 ❑ Oct 1954 Cover: 0.10 **NM** value: **40.00**

SWIFT ARROW (2ND SERIES) — Ajax

1 ❑ Apr 1957 Cover: 0.10 **NM** value: **40.00**
2 ❑ Jun 1957 Cover: 0.10 **NM** value: **40.00**
3 ❑ Aug 1957 Cover: 0.10 **NM** value: **40.00**

SWIFT ARROW'S GUNFIGHTERS — Ajax

4 ❑ Oct 1957 Cover: 0.10 **NM** value: **35.00**

SWIFTSURE — Harrier

1 ❑ May 1985 Cover: 1.75 **NM** value: **2.00**
📖 Arrival; A Fall From Grace; The Assassin; Brazen Invasion Part 1; Codename: Andromeda Chapter 1 **A:** Dave Harwood; R.F. O'Roake; Stephen Baskerville **W:** Stephen Baskerville; Bill W. Ryan; Lew Stringer; Martin Lock
2 ❑ Cover: 1.75 **NM** value: **2.00**
3 ❑ Aug 1985 Cover: 1.75 **NM** value: **2.00**
4 ❑ Cover: 1.75 **NM** value: **2.00**
5 ❑ Nov 1985 Cover: 1.75 **NM** value: **2.00**
6 ❑ Jan 1986 Cover: 1.75 **NM** value: **2.00**
7 ❑ Mar 1986 Cover: 1.75 **NM** value: **2.00**
8 ❑ May 1986 Cover: 1.75 **NM** value: **2.00**
9 ❑ Jul 1986 Cover: 1.75 **NM** value: **2.00**
• Redfox
10 ❑ Sep 1986 Cover: 1.50 **NM** value: **2.00**
11 ❑ Nov 1986 Cover: 1.50 **NM** value: **2.00**
12 ❑ Jan 1987 Cover: 1.50 **NM** value: **2.00**
13 ❑ Mar 1987 Cover: 1.95 **NM** value: **2.00**
14 ❑ May 1987 Cover: 1.95 **NM** value: **2.00**
15 ❑ Jul 1987 Cover: 1.95 **NM** value: **2.00**
16 ❑ Sep 1987 Cover: 1.95 **NM** value: **2.00**
17 ❑ Nov 1987 Cover: 1.95 **NM** value: **2.00**
18 ❑ Jan 1988 Cover: 1.95 **NM** value: **2.00**

SWIFTSURE & CONQUEROR — Harrier

1 ❑ Cover: 1.75 **NM** value: **2.00**
2 ❑ Cover: 1.75 **NM** value: **Cover or less**

CGC-graded: Multiply prices above by **33 for 9.9 M • 16 for 9.8 NM/M • 7 for 9.6 NM+ • 5 for 9.4 NM • 2.5 for 9.2 NM- • 1.5 for 9.0 VF/NM**

3 ❑ Cover: 1.75 NM value: **Cover or less**
4 ❑ Cover: 1.75 NM value: **Cover or less**
5 ❑ Cover: 1.75 NM value: **Cover or less**
6 ❑ Cover: 1.75 NM value: **Cover or less**
7 ❑ Cover: 1.75 NM value: **Cover or less**
8 ❑ Cover: 1.75 NM value: **Cover or less**
9 ❑ Cover: 1.75 NM value: **2.50**
★ Appearance of Redfox.
10 ❑ Cover: 1.50 NM value: **Cover or less**
11 ❑ Cover: 1.50 NM value: **Cover or less**
12 ❑ Cover: 1.50 NM value: **Cover or less**
13 ❑ Cover: 1.95 NM value: **Cover or less**
📖 Tales of the Rugged Reptile: One Too Many; Lieutenant Ff'ff: Nowhere to Run; Forest: Phase Two; Codename: Andromeda: Team-Up **A:** Steve Yeowell; Ashley Watkins; Dave Harwood; Glenn Fleming; Tem Latham **W:** Bill W. Ryan; Dave Coleman; Doris Telford; Martin Lock
14 ❑ Cover: 1.95 NM value: **Cover or less**
15 ❑ Cover: 1.95 NM value: **Cover or less**
16 ❑ Cover: 1.95 NM value: **Cover or less**
17 ❑ Cover: 1.95 NM value: **Cover or less**
18 ❑ Cover: 1.95 NM value: **Cover or less**

SWIMSUITS & MERMAIDS — Image Guild
1 ❑ Cover: 3.50 NM value: **Cover or less**
A: Steve Woron
1-2 ❑ Cover: 3.50 NM value: **Cover or less**

SWING WITH SCOOTER — DC
1 ❑ Jul 1966 Cover: 0.12 NM value: **30.00**
2 ❑ Sep 1966 Cover: 0.12 NM value: **18.00**
3 ❑ Nov 1966 Cover: 0.12 NM value: **15.00**
📖 Action at the Auction **A:** Joe Orlando **W:** B. F.; J. M.
4 ❑ Jan 1967 Cover: 0.12 NM value: **12.00**
5 ❑ Mar 1967 Cover: 0.12 NM value: **12.00**
6 ❑ May 1967 Cover: 0.12 NM value: **10.00**
7 ❑ Jul 1967 Cover: 0.12 NM value: **10.00**
8 ❑ Sep 1967 Cover: 0.12 NM value: **10.00**
9 ❑ Nov 1967 Cover: 0.12 NM value: **10.00**
10 ❑ Jan 1968 Cover: 0.12 NM value: **10.00**
11 ❑ Mar 1968 Cover: 0.12 NM value: **8.00**
12 ❑ May 1968 Cover: 0.12 NM value: **8.00**
• **CGC:** 1 graded, best 9.6
13 ❑ Jul 1968 Cover: 0.12 NM value: **8.00**
14 ❑ Sep 1968 Cover: 0.12 NM value: **8.00**
15 ❑ Nov 1968 Cover: 0.12 NM value: **8.00**
16 ❑ Jan 1969 Cover: 0.12 NM value: **8.00**
17 ❑ Mar 1969 Cover: 0.12 NM value: **8.00**
18 ❑ May 1969 Cover: 0.12 NM value: **8.00**
19 ❑ Jul 1969 Cover: 0.12 NM value: **8.00**
20 ❑ Aug 1969 Cover: 0.12 NM value: **8.00**
21 ❑ Sep 1969 Cover: 0.12 NM value: **6.00**
22 ❑ Oct 1969 Cover: 0.12 NM value: **6.00**
• **CGC:** 1 graded, best 9.0
23 ❑ 1969 Cover: 0.12 NM value: **6.00**
24 ❑ 1970 Cover: 0.12 NM value: **6.00**
25 ❑ Feb 1970 Cover: 0.12 NM value: **6.00**
26 ❑ 1970 Cover: 0.12 NM value: **6.00**
27 ❑ 1970 Cover: 0.12 NM value: **6.00**
28 ❑ 1970 Cover: 0.12 NM value: **6.00**
29 ❑ 1970 Cover: 0.12 NM value: **6.00**
30 ❑ Oct 1970 Cover: 0.12 NM value: **6.00**
31 ❑ Nov 1970 Cover: 0.12 NM value: **5.00**
32 ❑ Mar 1971 Cover: 0.25 NM value: **5.00**
33 ❑ 1971 Cover: 0.25 NM value: **5.00**
34 ❑ 1971 Cover: 0.25 NM value: **5.00**
35 ❑ 1971 Cover: 0.25 NM value: **10.00**
36 ❑ Aug 1971 Cover: 0.12 NM value: **5.00**
final issue.

SWITCHBLADE — Silverline
1 ❑ Dec 1997 Cover: 2.95 NM value: **Cover or less**

SWORD IN THE STONE — Gold Key
1 ❑ Feb 1964 NM value: **60.00**
• **CGC:** 1 graded, best 8.0

SWORD OF DAMOCLES — Image
1 ❑ Mar 1996 Cover: 2.50 NM value: **Cover or less**
📖 Fire from Heaven Prelude 1 **A:** Randy Green **W:** Warren Ellis ★ 1st Appearance of Sword of Damocles, Fire From Heaven.
2 ❑ Jul 1996 Cover: 2.50 NM value: **Cover or less**
📖 Fire from Heaven Finale 1; Fire From Heaven Finale, Part 1 **A:** Randy Green **W:** Warren Ellis

SWORD OF SORCERY — DC
1 ❑ Mar 1973 Cover: 0.20 NM value: **3.00**
• **CGC:** 14 graded, best 9.6
• Fafhrd and The Gray Mouser **A:** Howard Chaykin; Neal Adams **W:** Denny O'Neil
2 ❑ May 1973 Cover: 0.20 NM value: **2.00**
• **CGC:** 3 graded, best 9.4
• Fafhrd and The Gray Mouser **A:** Howard Chaykin
3 ❑ Aug 1973 Cover: 0.20 NM value: **2.00**
• **CGC:** 3 graded, best 9.6
• Fafhrd and The Gray Mouser **A:** Howard Chaykin
4 ❑ Oct 1973 Cover: 0.20 NM value: **2.00**
• **CGC:** 1 graded, best 8.5
• Fafhrd and The Gray Mouser **A:** Howard Chaykin; Walt Simonson
5 ❑ Dec 1973 Cover: 0.20 NM value: **2.00**
final issue. • Fafhrd and The Gray Mouser **A:** John Severin; Walt Simonson

SWORD OF THE ATOM — DC

Ray Palmer's life had been strange ever since he used the remnants of a white dwarf star to build the device that let him become The Atom. But things got even stranger for the diminutive hero in this four-issue mini-series.

The pressures of Palmer's unique lifestyle had taken a toll on his marriage to Jean Loring. One night, Ray found his wife in the arms of another man. He decided to escape his problems by going "on vacation" for six weeks to find another white dwarf star remnant in South America. Unfortunately, the pilots of the plane he was using were running a drug operation, and when Ray's search got too close, they decided to kill him. Ray used his size-changing powers to overwhelm his attackers — but then lightning struck the plane, shorting out Ray's size controls and causing the plane to crash into the dense rain forest. Stuck at six inches, Ray then discovered the strangest thing of all: a miniature civilization in the midst of the jungle!

1 ❑ Sep 1983 Cover: 0.60 NM value: **1.50**
📖 Stormy Passage **A:** Gil Kane **W:** Jan Strnad
2 ❑ Oct 1983 Cover: 0.60 NM value: **1.50**
A: Gil Kane
3 ❑ Nov 1983 Cover: 0.60 NM value: **1.50**
A: Gil Kane
4 ❑ Dec 1983 Cover: 0.60 NM value: **1.50**
A: Gil Kane
SE 1 ❑ ca. 1984 Cover: 1.25 NM value: **1.50**
A: Gil Kane
SE 2 ❑ ca. 1985 Cover: 1.25 NM value: **1.50**
Circ: CapCity orders: **9,600**
A: Gil Kane
SE 3 ❑ ca. 1988 Cover: 1.25 NM value: **1.50**
A: Pat Broderick

SWORD OF THE SAMURAI — Avalon
1 ❑ b&w Cover: 2.50 NM value: **Cover or less**

SWORD OF VALOR — A+
1 ❑ Cover: 2.50 NM value: **Cover or less**
📖 Kuno: Son of Steel; The Tower Maiden; Thane of Bagarth, Part 1; Sir Lancelot and the Haunted Tower; Through the Time Warp; Cursed Sword; The Black Flight **A:** John Buscema; Dick Giordano; Gene Day; Jim Aparo; Edd Ashe; Frank Frazetta(cover); Nicola Cutii; Tom Hickey **W:** Tom Sutton; Dick Giordano; Gene Day; Steve Skeates; Charles Lacoste; Kurato Osaki
2 ❑ Cover: 2.50 NM value: **Cover or less**
📖 Thane of Bagarth, Part 2
3 ❑ Cover: 2.50 NM value: **Cover or less**
📖 The Promise; Thane of Bagarth, Part 3; The Eagle of Genghis Khan; The Temple of the Spider; Pirates for the King **A:** Sam Glanzman; Sanho Kim; Walt Simonson; Jim Aparo **W:** Sam Glanzman; Sanho Kim; Walt Simonson; Jim Aparo
4 ❑ Cover: 2.50 NM value: **Cover or less**

SWORDSMEN AND SAURIANS — Eclipse
1 ❑ b&w Cover: 19.95 NM value: **Cover or less**
A: Roy G. Krenkel

SWORDS OF CEREBUS — Aardvark-Vanaheim
1 ❑ Cover: 5.00 NM value: **Cover or less**
1-2 ❑ Cover: 5.00 NM value: **Cover or less**
1-3 ❑ Cover: 5.00 NM value: **Cover or less**
2 ❑ Cover: 5.00 NM value: **Cover or less**
2-2 ❑ Cover: 5.00 NM value: **Cover or less**
3 ❑ Cover: 6.00 NM value: **Cover or less**
3-2 ❑ Cover: 6.00 NM value: **Cover or less**
3-3 ❑ Cover: 6.00 NM value: **Cover or less**
4 ❑ Cover: 6.00 NM value: **Cover or less**
4-2 ❑ Cover: 6.00 NM value: **Cover or less**
5 ❑ Cover: 5.00 NM value: **Cover or less**
6 ❑ Cover: 5.00 NM value: **Cover or less**
• first printing omitted issue #25

SWORDS OF CEREBUS SUPPLEMENT — Aardvark-Vanaheim
1 ❑ NM value: **1.00**
• giveaway to buyers of Swords of Cerebus #6 first printing. • reprinted issue #25

SWORDS OF SHAR-PEI — Caliber
1 ❑ b&w Cover: 2.50 NM value: **Cover or less**
📖 Path of Freedom **A:** Mark Masztal **W:** Thomas e. Sniegoski
2 ❑ b&w Cover: 2.50 NM value: **Cover or less**

SWORDS OF TEXAS — Eclipse
1 ❑ Oct 1987 Cover: 1.75 NM value: **Cover or less**
Circ: CapCity orders: **6,075**
📖 Lost Highway **A:** Ben Dunn **W:** Chuck Dixon
2 ❑ Cover: 1.75 NM value: **Cover or less**
Circ: CapCity orders: **5,175**
3 ❑ Jan 1988 Cover: 1.75 NM value: **Cover or less**
Circ: CapCity orders: **5,175**
4 ❑ Mar 1988 Cover: 1.75 NM value: **Cover or less**
Circ: CapCity orders: **4,975**

For up-to-the-week CGC ratios, consult the current issue of **Comics Buyer's Guide**.

SWORDS OF THE SWASHBUCKLERS — Marvel / Epic

Swords of the Swashbucklers first appeared in Marvel Graphic Novel #14, and Epic, a division of Marvel, began publishing it as an ongoing title in 1985. Created by Bill Mantlo and Jackson Guice, it could best be described as Treasure Island meets Star Wars.

It's set in an alternate dimension to Earth in which the inhabitants resemble Earth's pirates of old. A powerful, evil race of aliens known as the Colonizers controls the dimension while rebel "Swashbucklers" rob and pillage their oppressors so that they might survive. In one battle, The Admiral of the Colonizers' armada, J'Rel discovers Earth and kidnaps two of the Swashbuckler's leader's descendants. The couple's daughter, Domino, finds the Swashbucklers and agrees to use her unique powers to fight the Colonizers if the Swashbucklers help her rescue her parents. The series chronicles the war between the two races.

1 ❑ May 1985 Cover: 1.50 NM value: **2.00**
Circ: CapCity orders: **11,500**
📖 Shockwaves **A:** Jackson Guice **W:** Bill Mantlo
2 ❑ Jul 1985 Cover: 1.50 NM value: **1.75**
Circ: CapCity orders: **8,550**
A: Jackson Guice **W:** Bill Mantlo
3 ❑ Sep 1985 Cover: 1.50 NM value: **1.75**
Circ: CapCity orders: **6,950**
A: Jackson Guice **W:** Bill Mantlo
4 ❑ Nov 1985 Cover: 1.50 NM value: **Cover or less**
Circ: CapCity orders: **6,500**
📖 The Wierdling **A:** Jackson Guice **W:** Bill Mantlo
5 ❑ Jan 1986 Cover: 1.50 NM value: **Cover or less**
Circ: CapCity orders: **5,800**
A: Jackson Guice **W:** Bill Mantlo
6 ❑ Mar 1986 Cover: 1.50 NM value: **Cover or less**
Circ: CapCity orders: **5,550**
A: Jackson Guice **W:** Bill Mantlo
7 ❑ May 1986 Cover: 1.50 NM value: **Cover or less**
Circ: CapCity orders: **5,200**
A: Jackson Guice **W:** Bill Mantlo
8 ❑ Jul 1986 Cover: 1.50 NM value: **Cover or less**
Circ: CapCity orders: **5,150**
A: Jackson Guice **W:** Bill Mantlo
9 ❑ Sep 1986 Cover: 1.50 NM value: **Cover or less**
Circ: CapCity orders: **4,950**
A: Jackson Guice **W:** Bill Mantlo
10 ❑ Nov 1986 Cover: 1.50 NM value: **Cover or less**
Circ: CapCity orders: **4,650**
A: Jackson Guice **W:** Bill Mantlo
11 ❑ Jan 1987 Cover: 1.50 NM value: **Cover or less**
Circ: CapCity orders: **4,250**
A: Jackson Guice **W:** Bill Mantlo
12 ❑ Mar 1987 Cover: 1.75 NM value: **Cover or less**
Circ: CapCity orders: **4,000**
A: Jackson Guice **W:** Bill Mantlo

SWORDS OF VALOR — A-Plus
1 ❑ b&w Cover: 2.50 NM value: **Cover or less**
2 ❑ b&w Cover: 2.50 NM value: **Cover or less**
3 ❑ b&w Cover: 2.50 NM value: **Cover or less**
4 ❑ b&w Cover: 2.50 NM value: **Cover or less**

SYMBOLS OF JUSTICE — High Impact
1 ❑ Jun 1995 Cover: 2.95 NM value: **Cover or less**
A: Rick Lyon **W:** Ricky Carralero

SYNN, THE GIRL FROM LSD — AC
1 ❑ Aug 1990, b&w Cover: 3.95 NM value: **Cover or less**

SYNTHETIC ASSASSIN, THE — Night Realm
1 ❑ Cover: 1.50 NM value: **Cover or less**
A: Fred Diana **W:** Fred Diana

SYPHONS — Now
1 ❑ Jul 1986 Cover: 1.50 NM value: **2.00**
Circ: CapCity orders: **4,325**
📖 Night Moves **A:** Allen Curtis **W:** Allen Curtis ★ Origin of Syphons. ★ 1st Appearance of Syphons.
2 ❑ Sep 1986 Cover: 1.50 NM value: **Cover or less**
Circ: CapCity orders: **3,100**
3 ❑ Nov 1986 Cover: 1.50 NM value: **Cover or less**
Circ: CapCity orders: **3,725**
4 ❑ Jan 1987 Cover: 1.50 NM value: **Cover or less**
Circ: CapCity orders: **3,075**
5 ❑ Mar 1987 Cover: 1.50 NM value: **Cover or less**
Circ: CapCity orders: **2,450**
6 ❑ Jul 1987 Cover: 1.50 NM value: **Cover or less**
Circ: CapCity orders: **2,075**
7 ❑ Aug 1987 Cover: 1.50 NM value: **Cover or less**

SYPHONS: THE SYGATE STRATAGEM — Now
1 ❑ ca. 1994 Cover: 2.95 NM value: **Cover or less**
Circ: CapCity orders: **3,525**
A: Jr.; Naser Subashi; Rich Buchler; Rich Bucker; Sr. **W:** Allen Curtis
2 ❑ ca. 1994 Cover: 2.95 NM value: **Cover or less**
3 ❑ ca. 1994 Cover: 2.95 NM value: **Cover or less**

SYPHONS (VOL. 2) — Now
0 ❑ Dec 1993 NM value: **1.00**
• Preview edition. 📖 Load and Run, Part 1 **A:** Mark Beachum; Patrick Williams **W:** Allen Curtis

Other grades: Multiply prices above by **1.5 for Mint • 2/3 for Very Fine • 1/3 for Fine • 1/5 for Very Good • 1/8 for Good**

1 ❑ May 1994 Cover: 2.95 **NM** value: **Cover or less**
Circ: CapCity orders: **5,090**
Load and Run, Part 1 **A:** Mark Beachum; Patrick Williams **W:** Allen Curtis
2 ❑ Jun 1994 Cover: 2.50 **NM** value: **Cover or less**
Circ: CapCity orders: **3,530**
Drag and Drop **A:** Mark Beachum; Patrick Williams **W:** Allen Curtis
3 ❑ Jul 1994 Cover: 2.50 **NM** value: **Cover or less**
Circ: CapCity orders: **3,550**

SYSTEM, THE — DC / Vertigo
1 ❑ May 1996 Cover: 2.95 **NM** value: **Cover or less**
A: Peter Kuper **W:** Peter Kuper
2 ❑ Jun 1996 Cover: 2.95 **NM** value: **Cover or less**
A: Peter Kuper **W:** Peter Kuper
3 ❑ Jul 1996 Cover: 2.95 **NM** value: **Cover or less**
A: Peter Kuper **W:** Peter Kuper
Bk 1❑ Cover: 12.95 **NM** value: **Cover or less**

SYSTEM SEVEN — Arrow
1 ❑ Dec 1987 Cover: 1.50 **NM** value: **Cover or less**
T.E.S.T. Results **A:** Mark Winfrey **W:** Mark Winfrey; Ralph Griffith
2 ❑ Cover: 1.50 **NM** value: **Cover or less**
3 ❑ Cover: 1.50 **NM** value: **Cover or less**

T2: CYBERNETIC DAWN — Malibu
0 ❑ Apr 1996 Cover: 2.95 **NM** value: **3.00**
• Flip-Book with T2 Nuclear Twilight #0
1 ❑ Nov 1995 Cover: 2.50 **NM** value: **Cover or less**
Lost & Found • immediately follows events of T2 Judgment Day **A:** Rod Whigham **W:** Dan Abnett
2 ❑ Dec 1995 Cover: 2.50 **NM** value: **Cover or less**
Search Mode **A:** Gordon Purcell; Rod Whigham **W:** Dan Abnett
3 ❑ Jan 1996 Cover: 2.50 **NM** value: **Cover or less**
Judgement Impaired **A:** Rod Whigham **W:** Dan Abnett
4 ❑ Feb 1996 Cover: 2.50 **NM** value: **Cover or less**

T2: NUCLEAR TWILIGHT — Malibu
0 ❑ Apr 1996 Cover: 2.95 **NM** value: **3.00**
The Programming Of Fate • Flip-book with T2 Cybernetic Dawn #0 **A:** Gary Erskine **W:** Mark Paniccia
1 ❑ Nov 1995 Cover: 2.50 **NM** value: **Cover or less**
• prequel to first Terminator movie
2 ❑ Dec 1995 Cover: 2.50 **NM** value: **Cover or less**
Suicide Mission **A:** Gary Erskine **W:** Mark Paniccia
3 ❑ Jan 1996 Cover: 2.50 **NM** value: **Cover or less**
Dead Men Walking **A:** Gary Erskine **W:** Mark Paniccia
4 ❑ Feb 1996 Cover: 2.50 **NM** value: **Cover or less**
Father's Day **A:** Gary Erskine **W:** Mark Paniccia

TABOO — Spiderbaby / Tundra
1 ❑ b&w Cover: 9.95 **NM** value: **Cover or less**
2 ❑ b&w Cover: 9.95 **NM** value: **Cover or less**
3 ❑ b&w Cover: 9.95 **NM** value: **Cover or less**
4 ❑ b&w Cover: 14.95 **NM** value: **Cover or less**
5 ❑ Cover: 14.95 **NM** value: **Cover or less**
Circ: CapCity orders: **2,175**
6 ❑ Cover: 14.95 **NM** value: **Cover or less**
• with booklet
7 ❑ Cover: 14.95 **NM** value: **Cover or less**
• with booklet
8 ❑ Jun 1995, b&w Cover: 14.95 **NM** value: **Cover or less**
A: David Lloyd; Jeff Jones; P. Craig Russell; Moebius; Stephen R. Bissette; Jeff Nicholson; Greg Capullo; Al Columbia; Rick Grimes **W:** David Lloyd; P. Craig Russell; Stephen R. Bissette; Jeff Nicholson; Greg Capullo; Al Columbia; Rick Grimes
9 ❑ Cover: 14.95 **NM** value: **Cover or less**
In the Garden; Worms; After Life **A:** Mike Hoffman; Tim Truman; Tony Salmons; Stephen Blue; Aidan Potts; Alec Stevens; David Thorpe; Rick Grimes **W:** Mike Hoffman; Tim Truman; Tony Salmons; Stephen Blue; Aidan Potts; Alec Stevens; David Thorpe; Rick Grimes

TABOUX — Antarctic
1 ❑ Aug 1996 Cover: 3.95 **NM** value: **Cover or less**
The Evil Legacy **A:** Reuben Njaa **W:** Vivian Lushliner
2 ❑ Aug 1996 Cover: 3.95 **NM** value: **Cover or less**
Just Deserts **A:** Reuben Njaa **W:** Vivian Lushliner

TAFFY COMICS — Rural Home
1 ❑ Mar 1945 Cover: 0.10 **NM** value: **450.00**
• **CGC:** 1 graded, best 9.0
2 ❑ May 1945 Cover: 0.10 **NM** value: **200.00**
3 ❑ Cover: 0.10 **NM** value: **150.00**
4 ❑ Sep 1946 Cover: 0.10 **NM** value: **150.00**
5 ❑ Nov 1946 Cover: 0.10 **NM** value: **150.00**
6 ❑ Feb 1947 Cover: 0.10 **NM** value: **125.00**
7 ❑ Apr 1947 Cover: 0.10 **NM** value: **125.00**
8 ❑ Jun 1947 Cover: 0.10 **NM** value: **125.00**
9 ❑ Aug 1947 Cover: 0.10 **NM** value: **125.00**
10 ❑ Oct 1947 Cover: 0.10 **NM** value: **125.00**
11 ❑ Dec 1947 Cover: 0.10 **NM** value: **125.00**
12 ❑ Feb 1948 Cover: 0.10 **NM** value: **125.00**

TAILGUNNER JO — DC
1 ❑ Sep 1988 Cover: 1.25 **NM** value: **Cover or less**
Circ: CapCity orders: **13,400**
The Curve Of Binding Energy **A:** Tom Artis **W:** Peter B. Gillis
2 ❑ Oct 1988 Cover: 1.25 **NM** value: **Cover or less**
Circ: CapCity orders: **10,550**
3 ❑ Nov 1988 Cover: 1.25 **NM** value: **Cover or less**
Circ: CapCity orders: **9,700**
4 ❑ Dec 1988 Cover: 1.25 **NM** value: **Cover or less**
Circ: CapCity orders: **8,450**
5 ❑ Win 1988 Cover: 1.25 **NM** value: **Cover or less**
Circ: CapCity orders: **7,700**
6 ❑ Jan 1989 Cover: 1.25 **NM** value: **Cover or less**
Circ: CapCity orders: **7,150**

TAILS — Archie
1 ❑ Dec 1995 Cover: 1.50 **NM** value: **Cover or less**
2 ❑ Jan 1996 Cover: 1.50 **NM** value: **Cover or less**
3 ❑ Feb 1996 Cover: 1.50 **NM** value: **Cover or less**

TAINTED — DC / Vertigo
1 ❑ Feb 1995 Cover: 4.95 **NM** value: **Cover or less**

TAINTED BLOOD — Weirdling / Vertigo
1 ❑ Apr 1996 Cover: 2.95 **NM** value: **Cover or less**
Bury My Lovely **A:** Darrel Kindle **W:** Brian Babyok

TAKEN UNDER COMPENDIUM — Caliber
1 ❑ b&w Cover: 2.95 **NM** value: **Cover or less**
No issue number. A Faint Smell of Violet; Only Say the Word; The Devil's Teeth; Of All That is Seen & Unseen **A:** Michael Lark **W:** D.M. Rodia

TAKION — DC
1 ❑ Jun 1996 Cover: 1.75 **NM** value: **Cover or less**
Birth Pains **A:** Aaron Lopresti **W:** Paul Kupperberg
2 ❑ Jul 1996 Cover: 1.75 **NM** value: **Cover or less**
A: Aaron Lopresti **W:** Paul Kupperberg ★ Versus Flash. ★ Versus Green Lantern. ★ Versus Captain Atom.
3 ❑ Aug 1996 Cover: 1.75 **NM** value: **Cover or less**
A: Aaron Lopresti **W:** Paul Kupperberg
4 ❑ Sep 1996 Cover: 1.75 **NM** value: **Cover or less**
Blind Faith **A:** Aaron Lopresti **W:** Paul Kupperberg
5 ❑ Oct 1996 Cover: 1.75 **NM** value: **Cover or less**
Homecoming **A:** Aaron Lopresti **W:** Paul Kupperberg
6 ❑ Nov 1996 Cover: 1.75 **NM** value: **Cover or less**
Circ: Diamd. preorders: **16,590**
Dark Dawn **A:** Aaron Lopresti **W:** Paul Kupperberg
7 ❑ Dec 1996 Cover: 1.75 **NM** value: **Cover or less**
Circ: Diamd. preorders: **9,984**
Moonlight final issue. • Lightray returns **A:** Aaron Lopresti **W:** Paul Kupperberg

TALE OF HALIMA, THE — Fantagraphics / Eros
All issues are adults only.
1 ❑ b&w Cover: 2.75 **NM** value: **Cover or less**
2 ❑ b&w Cover: 2.75 **NM** value: **Cover or less**

TALE OF MYA ROM, THE — Aircel
1 ❑ b&w Cover: 1.70 **NM** value: **Cover or less**
A: Sam Dixon **W:** Sam Dixon

TALE OF ONE BAD RAT, THE — Dark Horse
Helen had not lived a happy life. Her home situation, never exactly ideal, got worse when her parents began to have marital problems. And it became much, much worse when her father began sneaking into her bedroom in the dark of night.

She flees, at the all-too-young age of 13, to London, where she and her pet rat try to survive on the mean streets. Homeless, hungry, and alone, she fantasizes about throwing herself beneath oncoming subway trains and jumping off bridges. For her, the world is a horrific fairy tale, a bit like the Beatrix Potter "Tale of Two Bad Mice," she had read as a younger child.

Bryan Talbot's award-winning mini-series is a moving and powerful tale of child abuse, and the will to survive. As the introduction from Neil Gaiman says, "the work — and fine work it is, and I do not flatter — speaks for itself."

1 ❑ Oct 1994 Cover: 2.95 **NM** value: **4.00**
Circ: CapCity orders: **3,925**
Town • Introduction by Neil Gaiman **A:** Bryan Talbot **W:** Bryan Talbot; Neil Gaiman
2 ❑ Nov 1994 Cover: 2.95 **NM** value: **3.00**
Circ: CapCity orders: **3,125**
A: Bryan Talbot **W:** Bryan Talbot
3 ❑ Dec 1994 Cover: 2.95 **NM** value: **3.00**
Circ: CapCity orders: **2,900**
A: Bryan Talbot **W:** Bryan Talbot
4 ❑ Jan 1995 Cover: 2.95 **NM** value: **3.00**
Circ: CapCity orders: **3,475**
A: Bryan Talbot **W:** Bryan Talbot
Bk 1❑ Oct 1995 Cover: 14.95 **NM** value: **Cover or less**
• Trade Paperback. • Collects The Tale of One Bad Rat #1-4 **A:** Bryan Talbot **W:** Bryan Talbot
Bk 1/HC❑ Cover: 69.95 **NM** value: **Cover or less**
• Hardcover edition. • Collects The Tale of One Bad Rat #1-4 **A:** Bryan Talbot **W:** Bryan Talbot

TALE OF THE BODY THIEF, THE (ANNE RICE'S...) — Sicilian Dragon
1 ❑ 1999 Cover: 2.95 **NM** value: **Cover or less**
A: Travis Moore **W:** Anne Rice; Faye Perozich
2 ❑ Oct 1999 Cover: 2.95 **NM** value: **Cover or less**
A: Travis Moore **W:** Anne Rice; Faye Perozich
3 ❑ 1999 Cover: 2.95 **NM** value: **Cover or less**
A: Travis Moore **W:** Anne Rice; Faye Perozich
4 ❑ 2000 Cover: 2.95 **NM** value: **Cover or less**
A: Travis Moore **W:** Anne Rice; Faye Perozich
5 ❑ 2000 Cover: 2.95 **NM** value: **Cover or less**
A: Travis Moore **W:** Anne Rice; Faye Perozich
6 ❑ 2000 Cover: 2.95 **NM** value: **Cover or less**
A: Travis Moore **W:** Anne Rice; Faye Perozich
7 ❑ 2000 Cover: 2.95 **NM** value: **Cover or less**
A: Travis Moore **W:** Anne Rice; Faye Perozich
8 ❑ 2000 Cover: 2.95 **NM** value: **Cover or less**
A: Travis Moore **W:** Anne Rice; Faye Perozich
9 ❑ 2000 Cover: 2.95 **NM** value: **Cover or less**
A: Travis Moore **W:** Anne Rice; Faye Perozich
10 ❑ 2000 Cover: 2.95 **NM** value: **Cover or less**
A: Travis Moore **W:** Anne Rice; Faye Perozich
11 ❑ 2000 Cover: 2.95 **NM** value: **Cover or less**
A: Travis Moore **W:** Anne Rice; Faye Perozich
12 ❑ 2000 Cover: 2.95 **NM** value: **Cover or less**
A: Travis Moore **W:** Anne Rice; Faye Perozich

TALES CALCULATED TO DRIVE YOU BATS — Archie
1 ❑ Nov 1961 Cover: 0.10 **NM** value: **75.00**
2 ❑ Jan 1962 Cover: 0.12 **NM** value: **50.00**
Count Congo; Witchcraft Then & Now; Igor & Freddie in Memories; Monster News; Transylvanian Word Game; Monster Crisis; Jake the Spider Spins a Tale; Igor & Freddie: Memories **A:** Orlando Busino **W:** George Gladir
3 ❑ Mar 1962 Cover: 0.12 **NM** value: **30.00**
4 ❑ May 1962 Cover: 0.12 **NM** value: **30.00**
5 ❑ Jul 1962 Cover: 0.12 **NM** value: **30.00**
6 ❑ Sep 1962 Cover: 0.12 **NM** value: **30.00**
7 ❑ Nov 1962 Cover: 0.12 **NM** value: **30.00**

TALES CALCULATED TO DRIVE YOU MAD — E.C.
Mad magazine has been around since the 1950s, but most of its readership hasn't. Not to worry, the classic strips from decades past live on and continue to find a new audience, in this series that reprints a collection of those time-lost tales. Typical buffoonery includes spoofs of cartoons and comics like "Superman" and "Gasoline Alley"; "Ripley's Believe It Or Not!" parodies; and goofy adaptations of popular films. Art includes classic work from well-known creators like Wally Wood and Bill Elder.

Published quarterly in magazine format, and in full-color too, by E.C. Publications. The series also features a narrative history of the magazine that brought smiles to generations.

1 ❑ ca. 1997 Cover: 3.99 **NM** value: **Cover or less**
2 ❑ ca. 1997 Cover: 3.99 **NM** value: **Cover or less**
3 ❑ ca. 1997 Cover: 3.99 **NM** value: **Cover or less**
4 ❑ ca. 1998 Cover: 3.99 **NM** value: **Cover or less**
5 ❑ ca. 1998 Cover: 3.99 **NM** value: **Cover or less**
6 ❑ Mar 1999 Cover: 3.99 **NM** value: **Cover or less**
Circ: Diamd. preorders: **5,126**
• Reprints Mad #16-18
7 ❑ Nov 1999 Cover: 4.99 **NM** value: **Cover or less**
Circ: Diamd. preorders: **4,913**
8 ❑ Jan 2000 Cover: 4.99 **NM** value: **Cover or less**
Circ: Diamd. preorders: **4,965**
• Reprints Mad #22, 23

TALES FROM GROUND ZERO — Excel
1 ❑ b&w Cover: 4.95 **NM** value: **Cover or less**

TALES FROM NECROPOLIS — Brainstorm
1 ❑ b&w Cover: 2.95 **NM** value: **Cover or less**
Wood Werk; Ghost in the Machine; Warebeast **A:** Jeff Wright; Juan Pineda; Ken Becker **W:** Jeff Wright; Ken Becker; Amy Wasp-Wimberger

TALES FROM SLEAZE CASTLE — Gratuitous Bunny
1 ❑ **NM** value: **2.50**
2 ❑ **NM** value: **2.50**
3 ❑ **NM** value: **2.50**
Rest and Recuperation **A:** Terry Wiley; Dave Mckinnon **W:** Terry Wiley; Dave Mckinnon

TALES FROM THE AGE OF APOCALYPSE: SINISTER BLOODLINES — Marvel
1 ❑ Dec 1996 Cover: 5.95 **NM** value: **Cover or less**
No issue number.

TALES FROM THE ANIVERSE (ARROW) — Arrow
A black and white collection of short stories revolving around high-tech, intelligent animals that populate the Aniverse, the title calls forth memories of such sci-fi classics as Star Wars and Star Trek and adds a bit of the Looney Tunes in for good measure.

Characters include Falterous, a Darth Vader-like bull who terrorizes the Aniverse with his group of space pirates, and Retro Ram, the heroic champion of the Avian Conflict who emerges from retirement to defend the Aniverse from evil. Also included is Ms. Chevious, the feline bounty hunter whose allegiance is sold to the highest bidder.

1 ❑ Cover: 1.50 **NM** value: **2.00**
2 ❑ Cover: 1.50 **NM** value: **Cover or less**
3 ❑ Cover: 1.50 **NM** value: **Cover or less**
The Politics of Piracy; Retro Ram and his Rocket Rangers **A:** Randy Zimmerman **W:** Randy Zimmerman; Susan Van Camp
4 ❑ Cover: 1.50 **NM** value: **Cover or less**
Ms. Chevious and Ganda: A Matter of Style; J.B. Space: Much to Stew About Nothing **A:** Guy Davis; Randy Zimmerman **W:** Randy Zimmerman; Susan Van Camp

CGC-graded: Multiply prices above by **33 for 9.9 M • 16 for 9.8 NM/M • 7 for 9.6 NM+ • 5 for 9.4 NM • 2.5 for 9.2 NM- • 1.5 for 9.0 VF/NM**

5 ❑ Cover: 1.50 **NM** value: **Cover or less**
6 ❑ Cover: 1.50 **NM** value: **Cover or less**

TALES FROM THE ANIVERSE (MASSIVE) Massive

1 ❑ Jan 1992, b&w Cover: 2.25 **NM** value: **Cover or less**
2 ❑ 1992 Cover: 2.75 **NM** value: **Cover or less**
3 ❑ 1992 Cover: 2.25 **NM** value: **Cover or less**
• **CGC:** 1 graded, best 9.2

TALES FROM THE BOG Aberration

1 ❑ Nov 1995, b&w Cover: 2.95 **NM** value: **Cover or less**
2 ❑ Feb 1996, b&w Cover: 2.95 **NM** value: **Cover or less**
3 ❑ Jun 1996, b&w Cover: 2.95 **NM** value: **Cover or less**
4 ❑ Sep 1996, b&w Cover: 2.95 **NM** value: **Cover or less**
5 ❑ Apr 1997, b&w Cover: 2.95 **NM** value: **Cover or less**
Circ: Diamd. preorders: **2,201**
6 ❑ Jun 1997, b&w Cover: 2.95 **NM** value: **Cover or less**
7 ❑ Nov 1997, b&w Cover: 3.95 **NM** value: **Cover or less**
Bk 1❑ Cover: 6.95 **NM** value: **Cover or less**
• collects first four issues

TALES FROM THE BOG (DIRECTOR'S CUT) Aberration

1 ❑ b&w Cover: 2.95 **NM** value: **Cover or less**

TALES FROM THE CLONEZONE Dark Horse

1 ❑ Cover: 1.75 **NM** value: **Cover or less**

TALES FROM THE CRYPT (COCHRAN) Cochran

1 ❑ Cover: 2.00 **NM** value: **Cover or less**
A: Al Williamson; Johnny Craig; Jack Kamen; Jack Davis; Graham Ingels
2 ❑ Oct 1991 Cover: 2.00 **NM** value: **Cover or less**
A: Al Williamson; Johnny Craig; Jack Kamen; Jack Davis; Graham Ingels
3 ❑ Dec 1991 Cover: 2.00 **NM** value: **Cover or less**
A: Al Williamson; Johnny Craig; Jack Kamen; Jack Davis; Graham Ingels
4 ❑ Feb 1992 Cover: 2.00 **NM** value: **Cover or less**
A: Al Williamson; Johnny Craig; Jack Kamen; Jack Davis; Graham Ingels
5 ❑ Mar 1992 Cover: 2.00 **NM** value: **Cover or less**
A: Al Williamson; Johnny Craig; Jack Kamen; Jack Davis; Graham Ingels
6 ❑ May 1992 Cover: 2.00 **NM** value: **Cover or less**
A: Al Williamson; Johnny Craig; Jack Kamen; Jack Davis; Graham Ingels
7 ❑ Jul 1992 Cover: 2.00 **NM** value: **Cover or less**
A: Al Williamson; Johnny Craig; Jack Kamen; Jack Davis; Graham Ingels

TALES FROM THE CRYPT (COCHRAN ONE-SHOT) Cochran

1 ❑ Jul 1991 Cover: 3.95 **NM** value: **Cover or less**
• over-sized reprint of Tales #31 and Crime SuspenStories #12.

TALES FROM THE CRYPT (E.C.) E.C.

This was the final evolution of the title that had begun as International Comics, continued as International Crime Patrol, which continued as Crime Patrol, which evolved as The Crypt of Terror and wound up as Tales from the Crypt, eventually labeled as part of E.C.' "New Trend" line of titles.

The title carried work of those thought of as the core artists that made E.C. the focus of fan attention: Johnny Craig, Harvey Kurtzman, Al Feldstein, Graham Ingels, Jack Davis, Jack Kamen, Reed Crandall, George Evans, Bernie Krigstein, Al Williamson (whose first E.C. work appeared in this title), Joe Orlando, and Wally Wood. Some of the stories were adaptations of stories by the likes of Bennett Cerf, Edgar Allan Poe, and Ray Bradbury. In #31, there was a comics-oriented story featuring E.C. staffers, "Kamen's Kalamity!" The series came to an end with the Comics Magazine Association of America's implementation of the Comics Code, which forbade "all scenes of horror" in newsstand comics. — Maggie

20 ❑ Oct 1951 Cover: 0.10 **NM** value: **650.00**
• **CGC:** 8 graded, best 9.8
🕮 The Thing From the Sea!; End of the Search (text story); A Fatal Caper!; Rx...Death!; Impending Doom! • Series continued from Crypt of Terror #19
21 ❑ Dec 1950 Cover: 0.10 **NM** value: **750.00**
• **CGC:** 9 graded, best 9.8
🕮 A Shocking Way to Die!; Terror Ride!; House of Horror; Death Suited Him!
22 ❑ Feb 1951 Cover: 0.10 **NM** value: **600.00**
• **CGC:** 13 graded, best 9.6
23 ❑ Apr 1951 Cover: 0.10 **NM** value: **450.00**
• **CGC:** 9 graded, best 9.6
24 ❑ Jun 1951 Cover: 0.10 **NM** value: **450.00**
• **CGC:** 5 graded, best 9.8
25 ❑ Aug 1951 Cover: 0.10 **NM** value: **450.00**
• **CGC:** 11 graded, best 9.8
26 ❑ Oct 1951 Cover: 0.10 **NM** value: **350.00**
• **CGC:** 5 graded, best 9.6
27 ❑ Dec 1951 Cover: 0.10 **NM** value: **350.00**
• **CGC:** 10 graded, best 9.6
🕮 Well-Cooked Hams!; Madame Bluebeard; Return!; Horror! Head...It Off! **A:** Joe Orlando; Jack Kamen; Jack Davis; Graham Ingels **W:** Joe Orlando; Jack Kamen; Jack Davis; Graham Ingels
28 ❑ Feb 1952 Cover: 0.10 **NM** value: **350.00**
• **CGC:** 14 graded, best 9.6
🕮 Bargain in Death!; Ants in Her Trance!; A Corny Story; The Ventriloquist's Dummy! **A:** Joe Orlando; Jack Kamen; Jack Davis; Graham Ingels **W:** Joe Orlando; Jack Kamen; Jack Davis; Graham Ingels
29 ❑ Apr 1952 Cover: 0.10 **NM** value: **350.00**
• **CGC:** 7 graded, best 9.6
🕮 Grounds...For Horror! **A:** Joe Orlando; Jack Kamen; Jack Davis; Graham Ingels **W:** Joe Orlando; Jack Kamen; Jack Davis; Graham Ingels
30 ❑ Jun 1952 Cover: 0.10 **NM** value: **350.00**
• **CGC:** 9 graded, best 9.8
🕮 Gas-tly Prospects!; A Hollywood Ending!; Auntie, It's Coal Inside!; Mournin', Ambrose...! **A:** Joe Orlando; Jack Kamen; Jack Davis; Graham Ingels **W:** Joe Orlando; Jack Kamen; Jack Davis; Graham Ingels
31 ❑ Aug 1952 Cover: 0.10 **NM** value: **400.00**
• **CGC:** 11 graded, best 9.8
🕮 Survival...Or Death!; The Thing in the 'Glades!; Kamen's Kalamity!; Buried Treasure! • 1st Al Williamson art at EC **A:** Al Williamson; Jack Kamen; Jack Davis; Graham Ingels **W:** Al Williamson; Jack Kamen; Jack Davis; Graham Ingels
32 ❑ Oct 1952 Cover: 0.10 **NM** value: **280.00**
• **CGC:** 10 graded, best 9.6
🕮 T Ain't the Meat...It's the Humanity!; Roped In!; Cutting Cards!; Squash...Anyone? **A:** George Evans; Jack Davis; Fred Peters; Graham Ingels **W:** George Evans; Jack Davis; Fred Peters; Graham Ingels
33 ❑ Dec 1952 Cover: 0.10 **NM** value: **525.00**
• **CGC:** 13 graded, best 9.6
🕮 Lower Berth!; This Trick'll Kill You!; The Funeral; None but the Lonely Heart! **A:** George Evans; Jack Kamen; Jack Davis; Graham Ingels **W:** George Evans; Jack Kamen; Jack Davis; Graham Ingels ★ Origin of The Crypt Keeper.
34 ❑ Feb 1953 Cover: 0.10 **NM** value: **275.00**
• **CGC:** 7 graded, best 9.6
🕮 Mirror, Mirror, on the Wall!; Oil's Well that Ends Well!; Attacks of Horror!; There was an Old Woman! • Contains Ray Bradbury adaptation **A:** George Evans; Jack Kamen; Jack Davis; Graham Ingels; Ray Bradbury **W:** George Evans; Jack Kamen; Jack Davis; Graham Ingels
35 ❑ Apr 1953 Cover: 0.10 **NM** value: **275.00**
• **CGC:** 7 graded, best 9.6
🕮 By the Fright of the Silvery Moon!; Midnight Mess!; Busted Marriage; This Wraps it Up! **A:** Joe Orlando; Jack Kamen; Jack Davis; Graham Ingels **W:** Joe Orlando; Jack Kamen; Jack Davis; Graham Ingels
36 ❑ Jun 1953 Cover: 0.10 **NM** value: **275.00**
• **CGC:** 8 graded, best 9.8
🕮 Fare Tonight, Followed by Increasing Clottiness...; Curiousity Killed...; How Green was My Alley; The Handler • Contains Ray Bradbury adaptation **A:** George Evans; Jack Kamen; Jack Davis; Graham Ingels; Ray Bradbury **W:** George Evans; Jack Kamen; Jack Davis; Graham Ingels
37 ❑ Aug 1953 Cover: 0.10 **NM** value: **275.00**
• **CGC:** 3 graded, best 9.4
🕮 Dead Right!; Pleasant Screams; Strop! You're Killing Me!; The Rover Boys! **A:** Joe Orlando; Bill Elder; Jack Davis; Graham Ingels **W:** Joe Orlando; Bill Elder; Jack Davis; Graham Ingels
38 ❑ Oct 1953 Cover: 0.10 **NM** value: **275.00**
• **CGC:** 4 graded, best 9.4
🕮 Tight Grip!; ...Only Skin Deep!; Last Laugh; Mournin' Mess **A:** Bill Elder; Reed Crandall; Jack Davis; Graham Ingels **W:** Bill Elder; Reed Crandall; Jack Davis; Graham Ingels
39 ❑ Dec 1953 Cover: 0.10 **NM** value: **275.00**
• **CGC:** 6 graded, best 9.6
🕮 Undertaking Palor; The Craving Grave; The Sleeping Beauty; Shadow of Death **A:** Joe Orlando; Jack Kamen; Jack Davis; Graham Ingels **W:** Joe Orlando; Jack Kamen; Jack Davis; Graham Ingels
40 ❑ Feb 1954 Cover: 0.10 **NM** value: **275.00**
• **CGC:** 7 graded, best 9.4
🕮 Food for Though; Pearly to Dead; Prairie Schooner; Half-Baked **A:** George Evans; Bernie Krigstein; Jack Davis; Graham Ingels **W:** George Evans; Bernie Krigstein; Jack Davis; Graham Ingels
41 ❑ Apr 1954 Cover: 0.10 **NM** value: **275.00**
• **CGC:** 7 graded, best 9.4
🕮 Operation Friendship; Come Back, Little Linda!; Current Attraction; Mess Call **A:** George Evans; Jack Kamen; Jack Davis; Graham Ingels **W:** George Evans; Jack Kamen; Jack Davis; Graham Ingels
42 ❑ Jun 1954 Cover: 0.10 **NM** value: **275.00**
• **CGC:** 4 graded, best 9.4
43 ❑ Aug 1954 Cover: 0.10 **NM** value: **275.00**
• **CGC:** 4 graded, best 9.4
44 ❑ Oct 1954 Cover: 0.10 **NM** value: **275.00**
• **CGC:** 6 graded, best 9.6
45 ❑ Dec 1954 Cover: 0.10 **NM** value: **275.00**
• **CGC:** 4 graded, best 9.2
46 ❑ Feb 1955 Cover: 0.10 **NM** value: **275.00**
• **CGC:** 8 graded, best 9.4
final issue.

TALES FROM THE CRYPT (GLADSTONE) Gladstone

1 ❑ Jul 1990 Cover: 1.95 **NM** value: **3.00**
Circ: CapCity orders: **15,600**
🕮 Lower Birth!; This Trick'll Kill You; Grim Fairy Tale!; The Witch's Cauldron; Touch And Go!; One For The Money; Fired!; Two For The Show! • Reprints Tales From the Crypt #33, Crime SuspenStories #17 **A:** George Evans; Al Williamson; Johnny Craig; Frank Frazetta; Bill Elder; Jack Kamen; Jack Davis; Graham Ingels; Will Elder **W:** George Evans; Al Williamson; Frank Frazetta; Bill Elder; Jack Davis; Graham Ingels; Ray Bradbury ★ Origin of Crypt-Keeper.
2 ❑ Sep 1990 Cover: 1.95 **NM** value: **2.50**
Circ: CapCity orders: **12,900**
🕮 By the Fright of the Silvery Moon!; Midnight Mess; Busted Marriage; This Wra[s it Up; Out of the Frying Pan...; A Trace of Murder; The Escaped Maniac; Partnership Dissolved • Reprints Tales From the Crypt #35, Crime SuspenStories #18 **A:** Joe Orlando; Johnny Craig; Jack Kamen; Jack Davis; George Roussos; Graham Ingels **W:** Joe Orlando; Johnny Craig; Jack Kamen; Jack Davis; George Roussos; Graham Ingels
3 ❑ Nov 1990 Cover: 1.95 **NM** value: **2.50**
Circ: CapCity orders: **12,600**
🕮 Undertaking Pallor; The Craving Grave; The Sleeping Beauty; Shadow of Death; Murder May Boomerang; Death's Double-Cross; A Snapshot of Death; High Tide! • Reprints Tales From the Crypt #39, Crime SuspenStories #1 **A:** Harvey Kurtzman; Joe Orlando; Johnny Craig; Wally Wood; Jack Kamen; Jack Davis; Graham Ingels **W:** Harvey Kurtzman; Joe Orlando; Wally Wood; Jack Kamen; Jack Davis; Graham Ingels
4 ❑ Jan 1991 Cover: 2.00 **NM** value: **2.50**
Circ: CapCity orders: **12,650**
• Reprints Tales From the Crypt #18, Crime SuspenStories #16 **A:** Al Feldstein; Al Williamson; Harvey Kurtzman; Joe Orlando; Johnny Craig; Jack Kamen
5 ❑ Mar 1991 Cover: 2.00 **NM** value: **2.50**
Circ: CapCity orders: **10,850**
• Reprints Tales From the Crypt #45, Crime SuspenStories #5 **A:** Johnny Craig; Bernie Krigstein; Jack Kamen; Jack Davis; Graham Ingels
6 ❑ May 1991 Cover: 2.00 **NM** value: **2.50**
Circ: CapCity orders: **9,000**
• Reprints Tales From the Crypt #42, Crime SuspenStories #27 **A:** Johnny Craig; Bernie Krigstein; Jack Kamen; Jack Davis; Graham Ingels

TALES FROM THE CRYPT (RCP) Gemstone

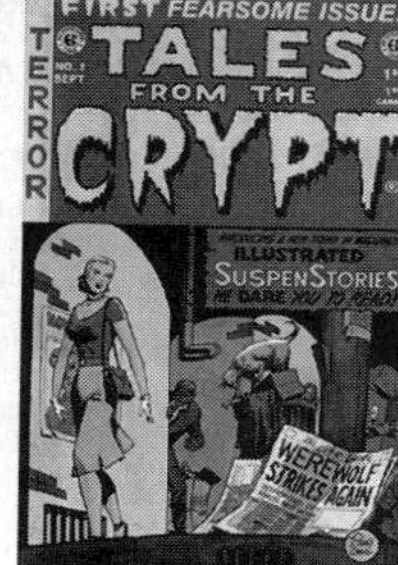

In 1993, Russ Cochran Presents began reprinting Tales From the Crypt, perhaps the most famous horror series of all time. RCP's version was extremely faithful to the original, reprinting the series in the order it first appeared, and bringing back all the ghoulish tales which frightened readers 40 years earlier. With original Crypt issues fetching hundreds of dollars apiece, the $1.50 cover price (later $2.00) of this reprint series was a true bargain.

In addition, these much less valuable reprints allowed those who just want to read the stories an inexpensive chance to do so.

1 ❑ Sep 1992 Cover: 1.50 **NM** value: **2.00**
Circ: CapCity orders: **5,975**
🕮 Death Must Come; The Man Who Was Death; Alibi...On Ice (text story); Tell-Tale Marks (text story); The Corpse Nobody Knew; Curse of the Full Moon • Reprints Crypt of Terror (EC) #17 **A:** Al Feldstein; Johnny Craig
2 ❑ Dec 1992 Cover: 1.50 **NM** value: **2.00**
Circ: Statement: **25,587** CapCity orders: **4,800**
🕮 The Maestro's Hand; The Living Corpse; Portrait of Life...And Death (text story); Madness at Manderville; Mute Witness to Murder • Reprints Crypt of Terror (EC) #18
3 ❑ Mar 1993 Cover: 1.50 **NM** value: **2.00**
Circ: Statement: **25,587** CapCity orders: **4,800**
🕮 Ghost Ship; The Hungry Grave; Cave Man; Zombie • Reprints Crypt of Terror (EC) #19
4 ❑ Jun 1993 Cover: 2.00 **NM** value: **Cover or less**
Circ: Statement: **25,587** CapCity orders: **4,600**
🕮 The Thing From the Sea!; End of the Search (text story); A Fatal Caper!; Rx...Death!; Impending Doom! • Reprints Tales From the Crypt (EC) #20 **A:** Al Feldstein; Johnny Craig; Jack Kamen; Graham Ingels
5 ❑ Sep 1993 Cover: 2.00 **NM** value: **Cover or less**
Circ: Statement: **25,587** CapCity orders: **4,270**
🕮 A Shocking Way to Die!; Terror Ride!; House of Horror; Death Suited Him! • Reprints Tales From the Crypt (EC) #21 **A:** Al Feldstein; Harvey Kurtzman; Wally Wood; Graham Ingels
6 ❑ Dec 1993 Cover: 2.00 **NM** value: **Cover or less**
Circ: Statement: **20,746** CapCity orders: **4,125**
🕮 The Thing From The Grave!; Blood Type 'V'!; Death's Run; The Curse Of The Arnold Clan!; • Reprints Tales From the Crypt (EC) #22 **A:** Al Feldstein; Johnny Craig; Graham Ingels
7 ❑ Mar 1994 Cover: 2.00 **NM** value: **Cover or less**
Circ: Statement: **20,746** CapCity orders: **3,750**
• Reprints Tales From the Crypt (EC) #23 **A:** Al Feldstein; Johnny Craig; Jack Davis; Graham Ingels
8 ❑ Jun 1994 Cover: 2.00 **NM** value: **Cover or less**
Circ: Statement: **20,746** CapCity orders: **3,475**
• Reprints Tales From the Crypt (EC) #24 **A:** Johnny Craig; Wally Wood; Jack Davis; Graham Ingels **C:** Al Feldstein
9 ❑ Sep 1994 Cover: 2.00 **NM** value: **Cover or less**
Circ: Statement: **20,746** CapCity orders: **3,525**
• Reprints Tales From the Crypt (EC) #25
10 ❑ Dec 1994 Cover: 2.00 **NM** value: **Cover or less**
Circ: Statement: **14,390** CapCity orders: **3,625**
• Reprints Tales From the Crypt (EC) #26
11 ❑ Mar 1995 Cover: 2.00 **NM** value: **Cover or less**
Circ: Statement: **14,390** CapCity orders: **3,250**
🕮 Well-Cooked Hams!; Madame Bluebeard; Return!; Horror! Head...It Off! • Reprints Tales From the Crypt (EC) #27 **A:** Joe Orlando; Jack Kamen; Jack Davis; Graham Ingels **W:** Joe Orlando; Jack Kamen; Jack Davis; Graham Ingels
12 ❑ Jun 1995 Cover: 2.00 **NM** value: **Cover or less**
Circ: Statement: **14,390** CapCity orders: **3,175**
🕮 Bargain in Death!; Ants in Her Trance!; A Corny Story; The Ventriloquist's Dummy! • Reprints Tales From the Crypt (EC) #28 **A:** Joe Orlando; Jack Kamen; Jack Davis; Graham Ingels **W:** Joe Orlando; Jack Kamen; Jack Davis; Graham Ingels

Other grades: Multiply prices above by **1.5 for Mint • 2/3 for Very Fine • 1/3 for Fine • 1/5 for Very Good • 1/8 for Good**

13 ❑ Sep 1995 Cover: 2.00 **NM** value: **Cover or less**
Circ: Statement: **14,390** CapCity orders: **3,425**
📖 Grounds…For Horror! • Reprints Tales From the Crypt (EC) #29 **A:** Joe Orlando; Jack Kamen; Jack Davis; Graham Ingels **W:** Joe Orlando; Jack Kamen; Jack Davis; Graham Ingels

14 ❑ Dec 1995 Cover: 2.00 **NM** value: **Cover or less**
Circ: Statement: **12,317**
📖 Gas-tly Prospects!; A Hollywood Ending!; Auntie, It's Coal Inside!; Mournin', Ambrose…! • Reprints Tales From the Crypt (EC) #30; Has 1995 Statement; avg print run 18,256; avg sales 13,350; avg subs 1,040; avg total paid 14,390 **A:** Joe Orlando; Jack Kamen; Jack Davis; Graham Ingels **W:** Joe Orlando; Jack Kamen; Jack Davis; Graham Ingels

15 ❑ Mar 1996 Cover: 2.00 **NM** value: **Cover or less**
Circ: Statement: **12,317**
📖 Survival…Or Death!; The Thing in the 'Glades!; Kamen's Kalamity!; Buried Treasure! • Reprints Tales From the Crypt (EC) #31 **A:** Al Williamson; Jack Kamen; Jack Davis; Graham Ingels **W:** Al Williamson; Jack Kamen; Jack Davis; Graham Ingels

16 ❑ Jun 1996 Cover: 2.00 **NM** value: **2.50**
Circ: Statement: **12,317**
📖 T Ain't the Meat…It's the Humanity!; Roped In!; Cutting Cards!; Squash…Anyone? • Reprints Tales From the Crypt (EC) #32 **A:** George Evans; Jack Davis; Fred Peters; Graham Ingels **W:** George Evans; Jack Davis; Fred Peters; Graham Ingels

17 ❑ Sep 1996 Cover: 2.50 **NM** value: **Cover or less**
Circ: Statement: **12,317**
📖 Lower Berth!; This Trick'll Kill You!; The Funeral; None but the Lonely Heart! • Reprints Tales From the Crypt (EC) #33 **A:** George Evans; Jack Kamen; Jack Davis; Graham Ingels **W:** George Evans; Jack Kamen; Jack Davis; Graham Ingels ★ Origin of the The Crypt Keeper.

18 ❑ Dec 1996 Cover: 2.50 **NM** value: **Cover or less**
Circ: Statement: **10,049** Diamd. preorders: **6,959**
📖 Mirror, Mirror, on the Wall!; Oil's Well that Ends Well!; Attacks of Horror!; There was an Old Woman! • Reprints Tales From the Crypt (EC) #34; Has 1996 Statement, filed 7/15/96 (not early, title was quarterly); avg print run 13,936; avg sales 11,439; avg subs 878; avg total paid 12,317; office use 1,619; max existent 13,936; no newsstand sales this year **A:** George Evans; Jack Kamen; Jack Davis; Graham Ingels; Ray Bradbury **W:** George Evans; Jack Kamen; Jack Davis; Graham Ingels

19 ❑ Mar 1997 Cover: 2.50 **NM** value: **Cover or less**
Circ: Statement: **10,049** Diamd. preorders: **6,612**
📖 By the Fright of the Silvery Moon!; Midnight Mess!; Busted Marriage; This Wraps it Up! • Reprints Tales From the Crypt (EC) #35 **A:** Joe Orlando; Jack Kamen; Jack Davis; Graham Ingels **W:** Joe Orlando; Jack Kamen; Jack Davis; Graham Ingels

20 ❑ Jun 1997 Cover: 2.50 **NM** value: **Cover or less**
Circ: Statement: **10,049** Diamd. preorders: **6,688**
📖 Fare Tonight, Followed by Increasing Clottiness…; Curiousity Killed…; How Green was My Alley; The Handler • Reprints Tales From the Crypt (EC) #36 **A:** George Evans; Jack Kamen; Jack Davis; Graham Ingels **W:** George Evans; Jack Kamen; Jack Davis; Graham Ingels

21 ❑ Sep 1997 Cover: 2.50 **NM** value: **Cover or less**
Circ: Statement: **10,049** Diamd. preorders: **6,269**
📖 Dead Right!; Pleasant Screams; Strop! You're Killing Me!; The Rover Boys! • Reprints Tales From the Crypt (EC) #37 **A:** Joe Orlando; Bill Elder; Jack Davis; Graham Ingels **W:** Joe Orlando; Bill Elder; Jack Davis; Graham Ingels

22 ❑ Dec 1997 Cover: 2.50 **NM** value: **Cover or less**
Circ: Diamd. preorders: **6,308**
📖 Tight Grip!; …Only Skin Deep!; Last Laugh; Mournin' Mess • Reprints Tales From the Crypt (EC) #38; Has 1997 Statement; avg total paid circ 10,049 **A:** Bill Elder; Reed Crandall; Jack Davis; Graham Ingels **W:** Bill Elder; Reed Crandall; Jack Davis; Graham Ingels

23 ❑ Mar 1998 Cover: 2.50 **NM** value: **Cover or less**
Circ: Diamd. preorders: **5,753**
📖 Undertaking Palor; The Craving Grave; The Sleeping Beauty; Shadow of Death • Reprints Tales From the Crypt (EC) #39 **A:** Joe Orlando; Jack Kamen; Jack Davis; Graham Ingels **W:** Joe Orlando; Jack Kamen; Jack Davis; Graham Ingels

24 ❑ Jun 1998 Cover: 2.50 **NM** value: **Cover or less**
Circ: Diamd. preorders: **5,724**
📖 Food for Though; Pearly to Dead; Prairie Schooner; Half-Baked • Reprints Tales From the Crypt (EC) #40 **A:** George Evans; Bernie Krigstein; Jack Davis; Graham Ingels **W:** George Evans; Bernie Krigstein; Jack Davis; Graham Ingels

25 ❑ Sep 1998 Cover: 2.50 **NM** value: **Cover or less**
Circ: Diamd. preorders: **5,208**
📖 Operation Friendship; Come Back, Little Linda!; Current Attraction; Mess Call • Reprints Tales From the Crypt (EC) #41 **A:** George Evans; Jack Kamen; Jack Davis; Graham Ingels **W:** George Evans; Jack Kamen; Jack Davis; Graham Ingels

26 ❑ Dec 1998 Cover: 2.50 **NM** value: **Cover or less**
Circ: Diamd. preorders: **5,226**
• Reprints Tales From the Crypt (EC) #42

27 ❑ Mar 1999 Cover: 2.50 **NM** value: **Cover or less**
Circ: Diamd. preorders: **4,723**
• Reprints Tales From the Crypt (EC) #43

28 ❑ Jun 1999 Cover: 2.50 **NM** value: **Cover or less**
Circ: Diamd. preorders: **4,819**
• Reprints Tales From the Crypt (EC) #44

29 ❑ Sep 1999 Cover: 2.50 **NM** value: **Cover or less**
Circ: Diamd. preorders: **4,478**
• Reprints Tales From the Crypt (EC) #45

30 ❑ Dec 1999 Cover: 2.50 **NM** value: **Cover or less**
Circ: Diamd. preorders: **4,655**
📖 Upon Reflection; Blind Alleys; Success Story; Tatter Up! • Reprints Tales From the Crypt (EC) #46; material originally prepared for Crypt of Terror #1

Anl 1❑ Cover: 8.95 **NM** value: **Cover or less**
• Collects Tales From the Crypt #1-5

Anl 2❑ Cover: 9.95 **NM** value: **Cover or less**
Anl 3❑ Cover: 10.95 **NM** value: **Cover or less**
Anl 4❑ Cover: 12.95 **NM** value: **Cover or less**
Anl 5❑ Cover: 13.50 **NM** value: **Cover or less**
• Collects Tales From the Crypt #37-41

TALES FROM THE EDGE! — Vanguard

1 ❑ Jun 1993, b&w Cover: 2.95 **NM** value: **3.50**
2 ❑ Sep 1993, b&w Cover: 2.95 **NM** value: **10.00**
3 ❑ Dec 1993, b&w Cover: 2.95 **NM** value: **3.00**
4 ❑ Jul 1994, b&w Cover: 2.95 **NM** value: **3.00**
5 ❑ 1994 Cover: 2.95 **NM** value: **3.00**
6 ❑ 1995 Cover: 2.95 **NM** value: **3.00**
7 ❑ Jul 1995, b&w Cover: 2.95 **NM** value: **3.00**
8 ❑ b&w Cover: 2.95 **NM** value: **6.00**
9 ❑ b&w Cover: 2.95 **NM** value: **10.00**
10 ❑ b&w Cover: 2.95 **NM** value: **6.00**
11 ❑ **NM** value: **5.00**
12 ❑ Cover: 4.00 **NM** value: **Cover or less**
📖 Sacred Monkey Man **A:** Marshall Arisman **W:** Marshall Arisman
13 ❑ **NM** value: **3.00**
14 ❑ **NM** value: **5.00**
15 ❑ Cover: 5.55 **NM** value: **Cover or less**
Circ: Diamd. preorders: **2,552**
• Bill Sienkiewicz Special **A:** Bill Sienkiewicz **W:** J. David Spurlock
Smr 1❑Aug 1994, b&w Cover: 3.50 **NM** value: **Cover or less**
cardstock cover.

TALES FROM THE FRIDGE — Kitchen Sink

1 ❑ Jun 1973, b&w Cover: 0.75 **NM** value: **3.00**

TALES FROM THE GREAT BOOK — Famous Funnies

1 ❑ Feb 1955 Cover: 0.10 **NM** value: **30.00**
📖 Joseph and his Brothers (text story); Young Daniel's Faith; The Saga of Samson **A:** John Lehti **W:** John Lehti
2 ❑ May 1955 Cover: 0.10 **NM** value: **24.00**
• **CGC:** 1 graded, best 8.0
3 ❑ Sep 1955 Cover: 0.10 **NM** value: **24.00**
4 ❑ Jan 1956 Cover: 0.10 **NM** value: **24.00**

TALES FROM THE HEART — Entropy

Autobiographical comics have been around for a while, but few have tackled the subject matter that this ongoing series did. Subtitled "The African experiences of a young Peace Corps volunteer," each issue features stories of a young woman and her struggles in dealing with an often cruel and frustrating world around her. One day it's the lack of water; the next it's healthcare struggles; and on another, it's quality entertainment in a land where something as simple as kicking a soccer ball can bring happiness to scores of African children. There are even moments of beauty and joy, which must be appreciated since they are few and far between.

Published by Entropy and Slave Labor Graphics, the series offers a glimpse into a world that most readers will never confront, but can now comprehend from the printed page. Written by Cindy Goff and Rafael Nieves, and drawn by Aldin Baroza, it's not a pretty world, but it is real.

1 ❑ 1988 Cover: 1.50 **NM** value: **4.00**
no cover date. **A:** Aldin Baroza **W:** Cindy Goff; Rafael Nieves
2 ❑ 1988 Cover: 1.50 **NM** value: **3.25**
A: Aldin Baroza **W:** Cindy Goff; Rafael Nieves
3 ❑ Dec 1988, b&w Cover: 1.75 **NM** value: **3.00**
A: Aldin Baroza **W:** Cindy Goff; Rafael Nieves
4 ❑ Jan 1989, b&w Cover: 1.75 **NM** value: **3.00**
A: Aldin Baroza **W:** Cindy Goff; Rafael Nieves
5 ❑ May 1989, b&w Cover: 1.75 **NM** value: **2.95**
A: Aldin Baroza **W:** Cindy Goff; Rafael Nieves
6 ❑ Oct 1989, b&w Cover: 1.75 **NM** value: **2.95**
A: Aldin Baroza **W:** Cindy Goff; Rafael Nieves
7 ❑ Nov 1990 Cover: 2.95 **NM** value: **Cover or less**
A: Aldin Baroza **W:** Cindy Goff; Rafael Nieves
8 ❑ Apr 1991 Cover: 2.50 **NM** value: **2.95**
📖 Monkey Business **A:** Aldin Baroza **W:** Cindy Goff; Rafael Nieves
9 ❑ Aug 1992 Cover: 2.50 **NM** value: **2.95**
📖 A Day in the Life **A:** Aldin Baroza **W:** Cindy Goff; Rafael Nieves
10 ❑ Mar 1993, b&w Cover: 2.95 **NM** value: **Cover or less**
📖 Mawa **A:** Aldin Baroza **W:** Cindy Goff; Rafael Nieves
11 ❑ May 1994, b&w Cover: 2.95 **NM** value: **Cover or less**
📖 Taking It **A:** Aldin Baroza **W:** Cindy Goff; Rafael Nieves
Bk 1❑ Jun 1994 Cover: 10.95 **NM** value: **14.95**
• Hearts of Africa; collects Tales from the Heart #1-3 **A:** Aldin Baroza **W:** Cindy Goff; Rafael Nieves
Bk 2❑ Cover: 14.95 **NM** value: **Cover or less**
📖 Hearts of Africa, Vol. 2, Trials • Collects issues #4-6 **A:** Aldin Baroza **W:** Cindy Goff; Rafael Nieves

TALES FROM THE HEART OF AFRICA: THE TEMPORARY NATIVES — Marvel / Epic

1 ❑ Aug 1990 Cover: 3.95 **NM** value: **Cover or less**
Circ: CapCity orders: **3,150**
No issue number. One-shot. **A:** Seitu Hayden **W:** Cindy Goff; Rafael Nieves

TALES FROM THE KIDS — David G. Brown Studios

1 ❑ Apr 1996, b&w **NM** value: **2.00**
no cover price. • anthology by children; produced for L.A. Cultural Affairs Dept.

TALES FROM THE LEATHER NUN — Last Gasp

1 ❑ Cover: 0.50 **NM** value: **14.00**
📖 Tales of the Leather Nun; The Adventures of Robert Crumb Himself; The Leather Nun Gets Hers; Tales of the Leather Nun's Grandmother; Father Justin Thyme: Confessions of a Teenage Confessor; Br'er Dragon's Dream! or The Meat Will Please Come to Order! **A:** Robert Crumb; Jaxon; Dave Sheridan; Pat Ryan; Roger Brand; Spain Rodriguez **W:** Robert Crumb; Jaxon; Dave Sheridan; Pat Ryan; Roger Brand; Spain Rodriguez

TALES FROM THE MAHABHARATA — Amar Chitra Katha

16 ❑ Cover: 3.50 **NM** value: **Cover or less**
📖 The Golden Mongoose; The Pigeon's Sacrifice; Aruni; Uttanka; Friends and Foes **A:** Madhu Powle(cover); Pradeep Sathe; Pratap Mulick; Ram Waeerkar **W:** Kamala Chandrakant; Luis M. Fernandes; Toni Patel

TALES FROM THE OUTER BOROUGHS — Fantagraphics

1 ❑ b&w Cover: 2.25 **NM** value: **Cover or less**
2 ❑ b&w Cover: 2.25 **NM** value: **Cover or less**
3 ❑ b&w Cover: 2.25 **NM** value: **Cover or less**
4 ❑ b&w Cover: 2.50 **NM** value: **Cover or less**
5 ❑ b&w Cover: 2.50 **NM** value: **Cover or less**

TALES FROM THE PLAGUE — Eclipse

1 ❑ Cover: 3.95 **NM** value: **Cover or less**

TALES FROM THE RAVAGED LANDS — Magi Studios

0 ❑ Cover: 2.00 **NM** value: **Cover or less**
No issue number. • no indicia; b&w introduction to series
1 ❑ b&w Cover: 2.50 **NM** value: **Cover or less**
no indicia or cover date.
2 ❑ b&w Cover: 2.50 **NM** value: **Cover or less**
no indicia or cover date.
3 ❑ Jan 1996, b&w Cover: 2.50 **NM** value: **Cover or less**
4 ❑ b&w Cover: 2.50 **NM** value: **Cover or less**
no indicia or cover date.

TALES FROM THE STONE TROLL CAFÉ — Planet X

1 ❑ Cover: 1.75 **NM** value: **Cover or less**
A: Tony Basilicato **W:** Tony Basilicato

TALES FROM THE TOMB — Dell

1 ❑ Oct 1962 Cover: 0.12 **NM** value: **150.00**
• **CGC:** 1 graded, best 8.5

TALES FROM THE TUBE — Print Mint

1 ❑ Cover: 0.50 **NM** value: **3.00**
📖 The Tides that Bind!; Maui No Ka Oe; The Bushongo Brothers Match Wits with Morambo the Mighty; Mexico; Cosmic Shangrila; Murphy and His Pal Hit it!; Salty Dog Sam Goes Surfin'! **A:** Rick Griffin **W:** Rick Griffin

TALES OF A CHECKERED MAN — D.W. Brubaker Productions

1 ❑ b&w **NM** value: **2.00**
no cover price.

TALES OF ASGARD (VOL. 1) — Marvel

1 ❑ Oct 1968 Cover: 0.25 **NM** value: **30.00**
• **CGC:** 18 graded, best 9.6
📖 Odin Battles Ymir, King of the Ice Giants; Surtur the Fire Demon!; The Storm Giants; The Invasion of Asgard!; Death Comes to Thor!; Thor's Mission to Mirmir!; Heimdall: Guardian of he Mystic Rainbow Bridge; When Heimdall Failed!; Balder the Brave • reprints "Tales of Asgard" stories from Journey Into Mystery #98-106 **A:** Jack Kirby **W:** Stan Lee

TALES OF ASGARD (VOL. 2) — Marvel

1 ❑ Feb 1984 Cover: 1.25 **NM** value: **1.50**
📖 The Hordes of Harokin!; The Fateful Change!; The Warlock's Eye!; The Dark Horse Of Death!; Valhalla!; When Speaks The Dragon!; The Fiery Breath Of Fafnir!; There Shall Come A Miracle! • reprints "Tales of Asgard" stories from Journey Into Mystery #129-136 **A:** Jack Kirby; Walt Simonson(cover) **W:** Stan Lee

TALES OF BEATRIX FARMER — Mu

1 ❑ Feb 1996, b&w Cover: 2.95 **NM** value: **Cover or less**
No issue number.

TALES OF BLUE & GREY — Avalon

1 ❑ b&w Cover: 2.95 **NM** value: **Cover or less**

TALES OF EVIL — Atlas-Seaboard

1 ❑ Feb 1975 Cover: 0.25 **NM** value: **2.00**
• **CGC:** 5 graded, best 9.4
📖 Spawn Of The Devil!; A Matter Of Breeding, Stake Out **A:** Mike Sekowsky; Jerry Grandienetti **W:** Russ Jones; Jack Younger
2 ❑ Apr 1975 Cover: 0.25 **NM** value: **1.50**
📖 The Fifty Dollar Body!; The Last Train; Requiem For A Werewolf! **A:** Tom Sutton; Jack Sparling; Jerry Grandienetti **W:** John Albano; Russ Jones; Marv Channing
3 ❑ Jul 1975 Cover: 0.25 **NM** value: **1.50**
📖 Man-Monster!; **A:** Rich Buckler **W:** Rich Buckler; Gary Friedrich; Tony Isabella

TALES OF GHOST CASTLE — DC

1 ❑ May 1975 Cover: 0.25 **NM** value: **2.00**
• **CGC:** 10 graded, best 9.6
📖 A Child's Garden Of Graves; A Soul A Day Keeps The Devil Away; Ghost Cackles; The Mushroom Man **A:** Nestor Redondo; Martin Pasko; Quico Redondo; Ruben Yandoc **W:** Paul Levitz; David Michelinie
2 ❑ Jul 1975 Cover: 0.25 **NM** value: **2.00**
📖 Snake-Eyes; The Inheritors, The Fate Of The Fortune Hunter **A:** E.R. Cruz; Ruben Yandoc; Alex Ni±o **W:** Jack Oleck; Mal Warwick; Robert Kanigher
3 ❑ Sep 1975 Cover: 0.25 **NM** value: **2.00**

CGC-graded: Multiply prices above by **33 for 9.9 M • 16 for 9.8 NM/M • 7 for 9.6 NM+ • 5 for 9.4 NM • 2.5 for 9.2 NM- • 1.5 for 9.0 VF/NM**

TALES OF G.I. JOE — Marvel

1 ❑ Jan 1988 Cover: 2.25 **NM** value: **Cover or less**
Circ: CapCity orders: **17,450**
📖 Operation: Last Doomsday; Hot Potato! • Reprints G.I. Joe, A Real America Hero #1 **A:** Herb Trimpe; Don Perlin **W:** Larry Hama

2 ❑ Feb 1988 Cover: 1.50 **NM** value: **Cover or less**
Circ: CapCity orders: **12,250**
• Reprints G.I. Joe, A Real America Hero #2

3 ❑ Mar 1988 Cover: 1.50 **NM** value: **Cover or less**
Circ: CapCity orders: **10,600**
• Reprints G.I. Joe, A Real America Hero #3

4 ❑ Apr 1988 Cover: 1.50 **NM** value: **Cover or less**
Circ: CapCity orders: **9,400**
• Reprints G.I. Joe, A Real America Hero #4

5 ❑ May 1988 Cover: 1.50 **NM** value: **Cover or less**
Circ: CapCity orders: **7,800**
• Reprints G.I. Joe, A Real America Hero #5

6 ❑ Jun 1988 Cover: 1.50 **NM** value: **Cover or less**
Circ: CapCity orders: **6,800**
• Reprints G.I. Joe, A Real America Hero #6

7 ❑ Jul 1988 Cover: 1.50 **NM** value: **Cover or less**
Circ: CapCity orders: **6,295**
• Reprints G.I. Joe, A Real America Hero #7

8 ❑ Aug 1988 Cover: 1.50 **NM** value: **Cover or less**
Circ: CapCity orders: **5,800**
• Reprints G.I. Joe, A Real America Hero #8

9 ❑ Sep 1988 Cover: 1.50 **NM** value: **Cover or less**
Circ: CapCity orders: **5,400**
• Reprints G.I. Joe, A Real America Hero #9

10 ❑ Oct 1988 Cover: 1.50 **NM** value: **Cover or less**
Circ: CapCity orders: **5,100**
• Reprints G.I. Joe, A Real America Hero #10

11 ❑ Nov 1988 Cover: 1.50 **NM** value: **Cover or less**
Circ: CapCity orders: **4,800**
• Reprints G.I. Joe, A Real America Hero #11

12 ❑ Dec 1988 Cover: 1.50 **NM** value: **Cover or less**
Circ: CapCity orders: **4,400**
• Reprints G.I. Joe, A Real America Hero #12

13 ❑ Jan 1989 Cover: 1.50 **NM** value: **Cover or less**
Circ: CapCity orders: **4,000**
• Reprints G.I. Joe, A Real America Hero #13

14 ❑ Feb 1989 Cover: 1.50 **NM** value: **Cover or less**
Circ: CapCity orders: **3,900**
• Reprints G.I. Joe, A Real America Hero #14

15 ❑ Mar 1989 Cover: 1.50 **NM** value: **Cover or less**
Circ: CapCity orders: **3,900**
• Reprints G.I. Joe, A Real America Hero #15

TALES OF HORROR — Toby

1 ❑ Jun 1952 Cover: 0.10 **NM** value: **300.00**
• **CGC:** 2 graded, best 9.2
2 ❑ Aug 1952 Cover: 0.10 **NM** value: **250.00**
3 ❑ Oct 1952 Cover: 0.10 **NM** value: **150.00**
4 ❑ Dec 1952 Cover: 0.10 **NM** value: **150.00**
5 ❑ Feb 1953 Cover: 0.10 **NM** value: **150.00**
📖 Hand of Fate; The Man Who Lost His Shadow
6 ❑ Apr 1953 Cover: 0.10 **NM** value: **150.00**
7 ❑ Jun 1953 Cover: 0.10 **NM** value: **150.00**
8 ❑ Aug 1953 Cover: 0.10 **NM** value: **150.00**
9 ❑ Oct 1953 Cover: 0.10 **NM** value: **150.00**
10 ❑ Jan 1954 Cover: 0.10 **NM** value: **150.00**
11 ❑ Apr 1954 Cover: 0.10 **NM** value: **150.00**
12 ❑ Jul 1954 Cover: 0.10 **NM** value: **150.00**
13 ❑ Oct 1954 Cover: 0.10 **NM** value: **150.00**
• **CGC:** 2 graded, best 6.5

TALES OF JERRY — Hacienda

1 ❑ b&w Cover: 2.50 **NM** value: **Cover or less**
2 ❑ Cover: 2.50 **NM** value: **Cover or less**
3 ❑ Cover: 2.50 **NM** value: **Cover or less**
4 ❑ Cover: 2.50 **NM** value: **Cover or less**
5 ❑ Cover: 2.50 **NM** value: **Cover or less**
6 ❑ Cover: 2.50 **NM** value: **Cover or less**
7 ❑ Cover: 2.50 **NM** value: **Cover or less**
8 ❑ Cover: 2.50 **NM** value: **Cover or less**
9 ❑ Cover: 2.50 **NM** value: **Cover or less**
10 ❑ Cover: 2.50 **NM** value: **Cover or less**

TALES OF LETHARGY — Alpha

1 ❑ b&w Cover: 2.50 **NM** value: **Cover or less**
📖 Guy With A Gun; The Evil Thumb **A:** Steve Reman **W:** Greg Hyland

2 ❑ b&w Cover: 2.50 **NM** value: **Cover or less**
📖 Guy With A Gun; Dream Date; Green And Dirty **A:** Greg Hyland **W:** Greg Hyland; John Migliore

3 ❑ b&w Cover: 2.50 **NM** value: **Cover or less**
📖 Guy With A Gun; Spider-San; The Trial; Walrus-Boy; Brian Lemay **A:** Greg Hyland; Steve Reman **W:** Greg Hyland; Steve Reman

TALES OF ORDINARY MADNESS — Dark Horse

1 ❑ b&w Cover: 2.50 **NM** value: **Cover or less**
2 ❑ b&w Cover: 2.50 **NM** value: **Cover or less**
3 ❑ b&w Cover: 2.50 **NM** value: **Cover or less**
4 ❑ b&w Cover: 2.50 **NM** value: **Cover or less**

TALES OF SCREAMING HORROR — Fantaco

1 ❑ b&w Cover: 3.50 **NM** value: **Cover or less**

TALES OF SEX AND DEATH — Print Mint

1 ❑ Apr 1971 Cover: 0.50 **NM** value: **3.00**
📖 Soupygoy; God Takes Him From Me; The Big Sewer; One Too Many; Country Capers **A:** Justin Green; Simon Deitch; Kim Deitch; Paul Rogers; Roger Brand; Rory Hayes; S. Clay Wilson; Bill Griffth **W:** Justin Green; Simon Deitch; Kim Deitch; Paul Rogers; Roger Brand; Rory Hayes; S. Clay Wilson; Bill Griffth

2 ❑ Cover: 0.75 **NM** value: **3.00**
📖 The Greening of America; If Brains Were Muscles; Nite-Lifer; Nocturnal Rendesvous; Pills in M' Pussy; The Head, The Brain, and The Body **W:** Justin Green; Charles Dallas; Dave Geiser; Kim Deitch; Roger Brand; Rory Hayes; Spain

TALES OF SHAUNDRA — Rip Off

1 ❑ Cover: 12.95 **NM** value: **Cover or less**
A: Philo **W:** Philo

TALES OF SUSPENSE — Marvel

Like many early Marvel titles, Tales of Suspense began as a collection of horror/science-fiction stories and eventually evolved into a super-hero title. Tales of Suspense made the big change in issue #39, when Stan Lee introduced Tony Stark, the billionaire inventor who would become Iron Man. An immediate hit, Iron Man soon joined the Avengers, becoming a key character in the Marvel Universe.

Beginning with issue #59, Tales of Suspense went to a double-feature format, co-starring Captain America in his first solo stories of the Silver Age. The issues that followed would be remembered as Marvel classics.

Following issue #99, Marvel decided to "graduate" these two characters to their own titles. Iron Man started over with issue #1 (after the bridging Iron Man and Sub-Mariner #1), and Captain America inherited Tales of Suspense's numbering sequence, starting with issue #100.

1 ❑ Jan 1959 Cover: 0.10 **NM** value: **1400.00**
• **CGC:** 7 graded, best 7.5
📖 I Dared to Explore the Unknown Emptiness

2 ❑ Mar 1959 Cover: 0.10 **NM** value: **540.00**
• **CGC:** 2 graded, best 8.0
📖 Robot in Hiding

3 ❑ May 1959 Cover: 0.10 **NM** value: **475.00**
• **CGC:** 2 graded, best 8.5
📖 The Aliens Who Captured Earth

4 ❑ Jul 1959 Cover: 0.10 **NM** value: **450.00**
• **CGC:** 1 graded, best 4.0
📖 One of Us is A Martian **A:** Al Williamson

5 ❑ Sep 1959 Cover: 0.10 **NM** value: **325.00**
• **CGC:** 1 graded, best 4.0
📖 Tunnel to Nowhere; I Became a Human Robot

6 ❑ Nov 1959 Cover: 0.10 **NM** value: **325.00**
• **CGC:** 4 graded, best 8.5
📖 I Heard It Howl in the Swamp

7 ❑ Jan 1960 Cover: 0.10 **NM** value: **325.00**
• **CGC:** 1 graded, best 5.5
📖 I Fought the Molten Man-Thing ★ 1st Appearance of Neptune.

8 ❑ Mar 1960 Cover: 0.10 **NM** value: **325.00**
• **CGC:** 1 graded, best 3.5
📖 Monstro

9 ❑ May 1960 Cover: 0.10 **NM** value: **325.00**
• **CGC:** 7 graded, best 9.2
📖 Diablo ★ 1st Appearance of Chondu the Mystic.

10 ❑ Jul 1960 Cover: 0.10 **NM** value: **325.00**
• **CGC:** 3 graded, best 7.0
📖 The Shadow **A:** Al Hartley

11 ❑ Sep 1960 Cover: 0.10 **NM** value: **240.00**
• **CGC:** 1 graded, best 4.5
📖 I Created Sporr, the Thing that Could not Die

12 ❑ Nov 1960 Cover: 0.10 **NM** value: **240.00**
• **CGC:** 3 graded, best 9.0
📖 Gor-Kill The Living Demon

13 ❑ Jan 1961 Cover: 0.10 **NM** value: **240.00**
Circ: Statement: **184,635** • **CGC:** 2 graded, best 6.5
📖 Elektro

14 ❑ Feb 1961 Cover: 0.10 **NM** value: **240.00**
Circ: Statement: **184,635** • **CGC:** 2 graded, best 7.0
📖 I Created the Colossus ★ 1st Appearance of It, the Living Colossus.

15 ❑ Mar 1961 Cover: 0.10 **NM** value: **240.00**
Circ: Statement: **184,635** • **CGC:** 4 graded, best 7.0
📖 Behold Goom! The Thing From Planet X!

16 ❑ Apr 1961 Cover: 0.10 **NM** value: **240.00**
Circ: Statement: **184,635** • **CGC:** 3 graded, best 8.0
📖 The Thing Called Metallo • Iron Man prototype

17 ❑ May 1961 Cover: 0.10 **NM** value: **240.00**
Circ: Statement: **184,635** • **CGC:** 2 graded, best 8.0
📖 Googam, Son of Goom

18 ❑ Jun 1961 Cover: 0.10 **NM** value: **240.00**
Circ: Statement: **184,635** • **CGC:** 3 graded, best 6.5
📖 Kraa the Unhuman

19 ❑ Jul 1961 Cover: 0.10 **NM** value: **240.00**
Circ: Statement: **184,635** • **CGC:** 1 graded, best 5.5
📖 The Green Thing

20 ❑ Aug 1961 Cover: 0.10 **NM** value: **240.00**
Circ: Statement: **184,635** • **CGC:** 2 graded, best 7.5
📖 Colossus Lives Again

21 ❑ Sep 1961 Cover: 0.10 **NM** value: **150.00**
Circ: Statement: **184,635** • **CGC:** 3 graded, best 8.0

22 ❑ Oct 1961 Cover: 0.10 **NM** value: **150.00**
Circ: Statement: **184,635** • **CGC:** 3 graded, best 7.5

23 ❑ Nov 1961 Cover: 0.10 **NM** value: **150.00**
Circ: Statement: **184,635** • **CGC:** 3 graded, best 9.0

24 ❑ Dec 1961 Cover: 0.10 **NM** value: **150.00**
Circ: Statement: **184,635** • **CGC:** 2 graded, best 7.0

25 ❑ Jan 1962 Cover: 0.10 **NM** value: **150.00**
Circ: Statement: **126,140** • **CGC:** 3 graded, best 9.4

26 ❑ Feb 1962 Cover: 0.12 **NM** value: **150.00**
Circ: Statement: **126,140** • **CGC:** 1 graded, best 7.0

27 ❑ Mar 1962 Cover: 0.12 **NM** value: **150.00**
Circ: Statement: **126,140**

28 ❑ Apr 1962 Cover: 0.12 **NM** value: **150.00**
Circ: Statement: **126,140** • **CGC:** 5 graded, best 8.5

29 ❑ May 1962 Cover: 0.12 **NM** value: **150.00**
Circ: Statement: **126,140** • **CGC:** 3 graded, best 9.6
• Has 1961 Statement; avg total paid circ 184,635

30 ❑ Jun 1962 Cover: 0.12 **NM** value: **150.00**
Circ: Statement: **126,140** • **CGC:** 1 graded, best 6.5

31 ❑ Jul 1962 Cover: 0.12 **NM** value: **150.00**
Circ: Statement: **126,140** • **CGC:** 3 graded, best 9.0
★ 1st Appearance of Doctor Doom-prototype ("The Monster in the Iron Mask").

32 ❑ Aug 1962 Cover: 0.12 **NM** value: **150.00**
Circ: Statement: **126,140**
📖 Sazzik, The Sorcerer • prototype Doctor Strange ★ 1st Appearance of Doctor Strange-prototype ("Sazik the Sorcerer").

33 ❑ Sep 1962 Cover: 0.12 **NM** value: **135.00**
Circ: Statement: **126,140** • **CGC:** 2 graded, best 4.5

34 ❑ Oct 1962 Cover: 0.12 **NM** value: **135.00**
Circ: Statement: **126,140** • **CGC:** 2 graded, best 6.5

35 ❑ Nov 1962 Cover: 0.12 **NM** value: **135.00**
Circ: Statement: **126,140** • **CGC:** 5 graded, best 9.0

36 ❑ Dec 1962 Cover: 0.12 **NM** value: **135.00**
Circ: Statement: **126,140** • **CGC:** 4 graded, best 9.2

37 ❑ Jan 1963 Cover: 0.12 **NM** value: **135.00**
Circ: Statement: **188,110** • **CGC:** 5 graded, best 9.4

38 ❑ Feb 1963 Cover: 0.12 **NM** value: **135.00**
Circ: Statement: **188,110** • **CGC:** 5 graded, best 9.6
📖 The Teenager Who Ruled the World!

39 ❑ Mar 1963 Cover: 0.12 **NM** value: **3600.00**
Circ: Statement: **188,110** • **CGC:** 114 graded, best 9.6
📖 Iron Man Is Born; The Last Rocket; Gundar; The Treasure (text) • Grey armor; Iron Man stories begin **A:** Jack Kirby ★ Origin of Iron Man. ★ 1st Appearance of Iron Man.

40 ❑ Apr 1963 Cover: 0.12 **NM** value: **1350.00**
Circ: Statement: **188,110** • **CGC:** 42 graded, best 9.4
📖 Iron Man Versus Gargantus; Work of Art; Prophet of Doom; Wrong Number (text) • Iron Man **A:** Jack Kirby ★ 1st Appearance of Iron Man gold armor. ★ 2nd Appearance of Iron Man.

41 ❑ May 1963 Cover: 0.12 **NM** value: **650.00**
Circ: Statement: **188,110** • **CGC:** 21 graded, best 9.4
📖 The Stronghold of Doctor Strange; The Sorcerer's Spell; The End of the Universe; Music Master (text) • Iron Man **A:** Jack Kirby

42 ❑ Jun 1963 Cover: 0.12 **NM** value: **300.00**
Circ: Statement: **188,110** • **CGC:** 16 graded, best 9.4
📖 Trapped by the Red Barbarian; I Speak of the Haunted House; Escape into Space; Discovery (text) • Iron Man **A:** Steve Ditko; Don Heck ★ 1st Appearance of Mad Pharoah.

43 ❑ Jul 1963 Cover: 0.12 **NM** value: **300.00**
Circ: Statement: **188,110** • **CGC:** 11 graded, best 9.4
📖 Iron Man Versus Kala, Queen of the Netherworld; You Can't Change the Past; Victim of Venus; The Journey (text) • Iron Man ★ Origin of Kala. ★ 1st Appearance of Kala.

44 ❑ Aug 1963 Cover: 0.12 **NM** value: **300.00**
Circ: Statement: **188,110** • **CGC:** 9 graded, best 9.4
📖 The Mad Pharoah; One of Us Must Die; I Come from the Sky; The Tree (text) • Iron Man

45 ❑ Sep 1963 Cover: 0.12 **NM** value: **300.00**
Circ: Statement: **188,110** • **CGC:** 16 graded, best 9.4
📖 The Icy Fingers of Jack Frost; I Come From Far Centaurus • Iron Man ★ 1st Appearance of Pepper Potts, Happy Hogan, Jack Frost II (Gregor Shapanka), Jack Frost II (Gregor Shapanka). ★ Versus Jack Frost II (Gregor Shapanka).

46 ❑ Oct 1963 Cover: 0.12 **NM** value: **185.00**
Circ: Statement: **188,110** • **CGC:** 15 graded, best 9.6
📖 Iron Man Faces the Crimson Dynamo; Mr. Flubb's Flashlight; The Gargoyles; The Utopia (text) • Iron Man ★ 1st Appearance of Crimson Dynamo.

47 ❑ Nov 1963 Cover: 0.12 **NM** value: **185.00**
Circ: Statement: **188,110** • **CGC:** 18 graded, best 9.2
📖 The Mysterious Melter; Shock; The Green Man (text) • Iron Man ★ Origin of Melter. ★ 1st Appearance of Melter.

48 ❑ Dec 1963 Cover: 0.12 **NM** value: **215.00**
Circ: Statement: **188,110** • **CGC:** 28 graded, best 9.4
📖 The Mysterious Mister Doll; Kraddak; The Pact (text) • New armor for Iron Man (red and gold) **A:** Steve Ditko

49 ❑ Jan 1964 Cover: 0.12 **NM** value: **165.00**
Circ: Statement: **207,065** • **CGC:** 18 graded, best 9.4
📖 The New Iron Man Meets the Angel; The Saga of the Sneepers; Strange Encounter (text) • Watcher back-up **A:** Steve Ditko ★ Appearance of Angel II.

50 ❑ Feb 1964 Cover: 0.12 **NM** value: **115.00**
Circ: Statement: **207,065** • **CGC:** 8 graded, best 9.4
📖 The Hands of the Mandarin; Journey's End; Them • Watcher back-up **A:** Don Heck ★ 1st Appearance of The Mandarin.

51 ❑ Mar 1964 Cover: 0.12 **NM** value: **90.00**
Circ: Statement: **207,065** • **CGC:** 8 graded, best 9.6
📖 The Sinister Scarecrow; The Primitive; The Green Thing; The Recipe (text) • Watcher back-up **A:** Don Heck ★ Origin of Scarecrow (Marvel). ★ 1st Appearance of Scarecrow (Marvel).

52 ❑ Apr 1964 Cover: 0.12 **NM** value: **135.00**
Circ: Statement: **207,065** • **CGC:** 13 graded, best 9.4
📖 The Crimson Dynamo Strikes Again; The Failure; The Séance; The Magician (text) • Watcher back-up; Has 1963 Statement, filed 10/1/63; avg print run 318,932; avg sales 188,005; avg subs 105; avg total paid 188,110; samples 175; max existent 188,285; 41% of run returned **A:** Don Heck ★ 1st Appearance of Black Widow.

53 ❑ May 1964 Cover: 0.12 **NM** value: **115.00**
Circ: Statement: **207,065** • **CGC:** 17 graded, best 9.6
📖 The Black Widow Strikes Again; The Way It Began • Watcher back-up **A:** Don Heck ★ Origin of The Watcher.

54 ❑ Jun 1964 Cover: 0.12 **NM** value: **60.00**
Circ: Statement: **207,065** • **CGC:** 15 graded, best 9.6
📖 The Mandarin's Revenge; Hands Off! • Watcher back-up **A:** Don Heck ★ 1st Appearance of Black Knight II (Nathan Garrett).

55 ❑ Jul 1964 Cover: 0.12 **NM** value: **60.00**
Circ: Statement: **207,065** • **CGC:** 11 graded, best 9.4
📖 No One Escapes the Mandarin; The Sun Stealer; various pin-ups • Watcher back-up

56 ❑ Aug 1964 Cover: 0.12 **NM** value: **60.00**
Circ: Statement: **207,065** • **CGC:** 10 graded, best 9.6

Other grades: Multiply prices above by **1.5 for Mint • 2/3 for Very Fine • 1/3 for Fine • 1/5 for Very Good • 1/8 for Good**

🕮 The Uncanny Unicorn; The Watcher's Sacrifice • Watcher back-up **A:** Don Heck ★ 1st Appearance of Unicorn I (Milos Masaryk).

57 ❑ Sep 1964 Cover: 0.12 **NM** value: **160.00**
Circ: Statement: **207,065 • CGC:** 25 graded, best 9.4
🕮 Hawkeye, The Marksman; The Watcher's Power • Watcher back-up **A:** Don Heck ★ 1st Appearance of Hawkeye. ★ Appearance of Black Widow.

58 ❑ Oct 1964 Cover: 0.12 **NM** value: **265.00**
Circ: Statement: **207,065 • CGC:** 28 graded, best 9.4
🕮 In Mortal Combat with Captain America; The Watcher Must Die • Watcher back-up **A:** Don Heck ★ Appearance of Captain America.

59 ❑ Nov 1964 Cover: 0.12 **NM** value: **265.00**
Circ: Statement: **207,065 • CGC:** 54 graded, best 9.6
🕮 The Black Knight; Captain America • Captain America second feature begins **A:** Don Heck; Jack Kirby ★ 1st Appearance of Jarvis. ★ Versus Black Knight.

60 ❑ Dec 1964 Cover: 0.12 **NM** value: **115.00**
Circ: Statement: **207,065 • CGC:** 15 graded, best 9.6
🕮 Suspected of Murder; The Army of Assassins Strikes **A:** Jack Kirby; Dan Jurgens

61 ❑ Jan 1965 Cover: 0.12 **NM** value: **65.00**
Circ: Statement: **222,060 • CGC:** 10 graded, best 9.4
🕮 The Death of Tony Stark; The Strength of the Sumo **A:** Don Heck; Jack Kirby

62 ❑ Feb 1965 Cover: 0.12 **NM** value: **65.00**
Circ: Statement: **222,060 • CGC:** 7 graded, best 9.4
🕮 The Origin of the Mandarin; Break-Out in Cell Block 10 • redesign of Iron Man's helmet **A:** Don Heck; Jack Kirby ★ Origin of Mandarin.

63 ❑ Mar 1965 Cover: 0.12 **NM** value: **175.00**
Circ: Statement: **222,060 • CGC:** 31 graded, best 9.6
🕮 Somewhere Lurks the Phantom; The Origin of Captain America ★ Origin of Bucky, Captain America. ★ Appearance of Doctor Erskine, Dr. Erskine, General Phillips, Sgt. Duffy.

64 ❑ Apr 1965 Cover: 0.12 **NM** value: **70.00**
Circ: Statement: **222,060 • CGC:** 19 graded, best 9.6
🕮 Hawkeye and the New Black Widow Strike Again; Among Us, Wreckers Dwell • Has 1964 Statement, filed 10/1/64; avg print run 312,400; avg sales 206,800; avg subs 265; avg total paid 207,065; samples 125; max existent 207,190; 34% of run returned ★ 1st Appearance of Agent 13 (Peggy Carter).

65 ❑ May 1965 Cover: 0.12 **NM** value: **120.00**
Circ: Statement: **222,060 • CGC:** 15 graded, best 9.6
🕮 When Titans Clash; The Red Skull Strikes ★ Appearance of Red Skull.

66 ❑ Jun 1965 Cover: 0.12 **NM** value: **120.00**
Circ: Statement: **222,060 • CGC:** 28 graded, best 9.6
🕮 If I Fail, a World is Lost; The Fantastic Origin of the Red Skull • Red Skull returns ★ Origin of Red Skull.

67 ❑ Jul 1965 Cover: 0.12 **NM** value: **50.00**
Circ: Statement: **222,060 • CGC:** 10 graded, best 9.4
🕮 Where Walk the Villains; Lest Tyranny Triumph

68 ❑ Aug 1965 Cover: 0.12 **NM** value: **50.00**
Circ: Statement: **222,060 • CGC:** 9 graded, best 9.6
🕮 If a Man Be Mad; The Sentinel and the Spy

69 ❑ Sep 1965 Cover: 0.12 **NM** value: **50.00**
Circ: Statement: **222,060 • CGC:** 5 graded, best 9.6
🕮 If I Must Die, Let it Be With Honor; Midnight in Greymoor Castle ★ 1st Appearance of Titanium Man I (Boris Bullski).

70 ❑ Oct 1965 Cover: 0.12 **NM** value: **50.00**
Circ: Statement: **222,060 • CGC:** 12 graded, best 9.8
🕮 Fight On, For A World is Watching; If This Be Treason

71 ❑ Nov 1965 Cover: 0.12 **NM** value: **45.00**
Circ: Statement: **222,060 • CGC:** 12 graded, best 9.6
🕮 What Price, Victory?; When You Lie Down With Dogs

72 ❑ Dec 1965 Cover: 0.12 **NM** value: **45.00**
Circ: Statement: **222,060 • CGC:** 11 graded, best 9.6
🕮 Hoorah For the Conquering Hero; The Sleeper Shall Awake

73 ❑ Jan 1966 Cover: 0.12 **NM** value: **45.00**
Circ: Statement: **252,239 • CGC:** 13 graded, best 9.8
🕮 My Life for Yours; Where Walks the Sleeper ★ Death of Black Knight II (Nathan Garrett).

74 ❑ Feb 1966 Cover: 0.12 **NM** value: **45.00**
Circ: Statement: **252,239 • CGC:** 44 graded, best 9.8
🕮 If This Guilt Be Mine; The Final Sleep

75 ❑ Mar 1966 Cover: 0.12 **NM** value: **45.00**
Circ: Statement: **252,239 • CGC:** 12 graded, best 9.6
🕮 The Fury of the Freak; 30 Minutes to Live ★ 1st Appearance of Second Agent 13 (Sharon Carter), Batroc.

76 ❑ Apr 1966 Cover: 0.12 **NM** value: **45.00**
Circ: Statement: **252,239 • CGC:** 8 graded, best 9.6
🕮 Here Lies the Unspeakable Ultimo; The Gladiator, the Girl, and the Glory • Has 1965 Statement, filed 10/1/65; avg print run 367,728; avg sales 221,535; avg subs 525; avg total paid 222,060; samples 60; max existent 222,120; 40% of run returned ★ 1st Appearance of Ultimo (cameo).

77 ❑ May 1966 Cover: 0.12 **NM** value: **45.00**
Circ: Statement: **252,239 • CGC:** 10 graded, best 9.6
🕮 Ultimo Lives; If a Hostage Should Die ★ Origin of Ultimo. ★ 1st Appearance of Ultimo (full appearance), Peggy Carter.

78 ❑ Jun 1966 Cover: 0.12 **NM** value: **45.00**
Circ: Statement: **252,239 • CGC:** 7 graded, best 9.6
🕮 Crescendo; Them ★ Appearance of Nick Fury.

79 ❑ Jul 1966 Cover: 0.12 **NM** value: **45.00**
Circ: Statement: **252,239 • CGC:** 8 graded, best 9.8
🕮 Disaster; The Red Skull Lives ★ 1st Appearance of Cosmic Cube (Kubik).

80 ❑ Aug 1966 Cover: 0.12 **NM** value: **45.00**
Circ: Statement: **252,239 • CGC:** 37 graded, best 9.8
🕮 When Fall the Mighty; He Who Holds the Cosmic Cume • Cosmic Cube; Sub-Mariner vs. Iron Man

81 ❑ Sep 1966 Cover: 0.12 **NM** value: **40.00**
Circ: Statement: **252,239 • CGC:** 8 graded, best 9.6
🕮 The Return of the Titanium Man; The Red Skull Supreme

82 ❑ Oct 1966 Cover: 0.12 **NM** value: **40.00**
Circ: Statement: **252,239 • CGC:** 17 graded, best 9.6
🕮 By Force of Arms; The Maddening Mystery of the Inconceivable Adaptoid ★ 1st Appearance of Adaptoid.

83 ❑ Nov 1966 Cover: 0.12 **NM** value: **40.00**
Circ: Statement: **252,239 • CGC:** 30 graded, best 9.6
🕮 Victory; Enter the Tumbler

84 ❑ Dec 1966 Cover: 0.12 **NM** value: **40.00**
Circ: Statement: **252,239 • CGC:** 10 graded, best 9.6
🕮 The Other Iron Man; The Super-Adaptoid ★ 1st Appearance of Super-Adaptoid.

85 ❑ Jan 1967 Cover: 0.12 **NM** value: **40.00**
Circ: Statement: **257,342 • CGC:** 19 graded, best 9.4
🕮 Into the Jaws of Death; The Blitzkreig of Batroc • Happy substitutes as Iron Man **A:** Gene Colan; Gil Kane ★ Versus Mandarin.

86 ❑ Feb 1967 Cover: 0.12 **NM** value: **40.00**
Circ: Statement: **257,342 • CGC:** 20 graded, best 9.8
🕮 Death Duel For The Life Of Happy Hogan; The Secret! **A:** Gene Colan; Jack Kirby **W:** Stan Lee

87 ❑ Mar 1967 Cover: 0.12 **NM** value: **40.00**
Circ: Statement: **257,342 • CGC:** 15 graded, best 9.6
🕮 Crisis at the Earth's Core; Wanted: Captain America

88 ❑ Apr 1967 Cover: 0.12 **NM** value: **40.00**
Circ: Statement: **257,342 • CGC:** 29 graded, best 9.6
🕮 Beyond All Rescue; If Bucky Lives • Has 1966 Statement, filed 10/1/66; avg print run 405,137; avg sales 251,239; avg subs 1,000; avg total paid 252,239; samples 60; max existent 252,299; 38% of run returned **A:** Gene Colan; Gil Kane

89 ❑ May 1967 Cover: 0.12 **NM** value: **40.00**
Circ: Statement: **257,342 • CGC:** 32 graded, best 9.8
🕮 The Monstrous Menace of the Mysterious Melter; Back from the Dead **A:** Gene Colan; Gil Kane

90 ❑ Jun 1967 Cover: 0.12 **NM** value: **40.00**
Circ: Statement: **257,342 • CGC:** 11 graded, best 9.6
🕮 The Golden Ghost; And Men Shall Call Him Traitor **A:** Gene Colan; Gil Kane ★ Origin of Byrrah.

91 ❑ Jul 1967 Cover: 0.12 **NM** value: **40.00**
Circ: Statement: **257,342 • CGC:** 11 graded, best 9.6
🕮 The Uncanny Challenge of the Crusher; The Last Defeat **A:** Gene Colan; Gil Kane

92 ❑ Aug 1967 Cover: 0.12 **NM** value: **40.00**
Circ: Statement: **257,342 • CGC:** 13 graded, best 9.6
🕮 Within the Vastness of Viet Nam; Before My Eyes, Nick Fury Dead **A:** Gene Colan; Gil Kane

93 ❑ Sep 1967 Cover: 0.12 **NM** value: **40.00**
Circ: Statement: **257,342 • CGC:** 11 graded, best 9.6
🕮 The Golden Gladiator and the Giant; Into the Jaws of A.I.M. **A:** Gene Colan; Gil Kane

94 ❑ Oct 1967 Cover: 0.12 **NM** value: **40.00**
Circ: Statement: **257,342 • CGC:** 13 graded, best 9.8
🕮 The Tragedy and theTriumph; If This Be MODOK ★ 1st Appearance of M.O.D.O.K..

95 ❑ Nov 1967 Cover: 0.12 **NM** value: **40.00**
Circ: Statement: **257,342 • CGC:** 7 graded, best 9.6
🕮 If Man Be Stone; A Time to Die, A Time to Live • Captain America's identity revealed **A:** Gene Colan; Gil Kane ★ 1st Appearance of Walter Newell (later becomes Stingray).

96 ❑ Dec 1967 Cover: 0.12 **NM** value: **40.00**
Circ: Statement: **257,342 • CGC:** 13 graded, best 9.8
🕮 The Deadly Victory; To Be Reborn **A:** Gene Colan; Gil Kane

97 ❑ Jan 1968 Cover: 0.12 **NM** value: **40.00**
Circ: Statement: **273,476 • CGC:** 17 graded, best 9.4
🕮 The Coming of Whiplash!; And So It Begins ... **A:** Gene Colan; Jack Kirby; Gil Kane **W:** Stan Lee ★ 1st Appearance of Whiplash. ★ Appearance of Black Panther.

98 ❑ Feb 1968 Cover: 0.12 **NM** value: **40.00**
Circ: Statement: **273,476 • CGC:** 23 graded, best 9.8
🕮 The Claw of the Panther; The Warrior and the Whip **A:** Gene Colan; Gil Kane ★ Origin of Whitney Frost. ★ 1st Appearance of Whitney Frost.

99 ❑ Mar 1968 Cover: 0.12 **NM** value: **40.00**
Circ: Statement: **273,476 • CGC:** 15 graded, best 9.6
🕮 At the Mercy of the Maggia; The Man Who Lived Twice • series continues as Captain America; Series continued in Captain America #100, Iron Man #1 **A:** Gene Colan; Gil Kane ★ Versus Red Skull.

TALES OF SUSPENSE (VOL. 2) — Marvel

1 ❑ Jan 1995 Cover: 6.95 **NM** value: **Cover or less**
Circ: CapCity orders: **29,300 • CGC:** 4 graded, best 10.0
acetate outer cover. 🕮 Men And Machines • prestige format one-shot **A:** Colin MacNeil **W:** James Robinson

TALES OF TERROR — Eclipse

1 ❑ Jul 1985 Cover: 1.75 **NM** value: **2.00**
Circ: CapCity orders: **6,200 • CGC:** 1 graded, best 9.2

2 ❑ Sep 1985 Cover: 1.75 **NM** value: **2.00**
Circ: CapCity orders: **5,050**

3 ❑ Nov 1985 Cover: 1.75 **NM** value: **2.00**
Circ: CapCity orders: **4,575**

4 ❑ Jan 1986 Cover: 1.75 **NM** value: **2.00**
Circ: CapCity orders: **4,600**

5 ❑ Mar 1986 Cover: 1.75 **NM** value: **2.00**
Circ: CapCity orders: **4,225**

6 ❑ May 1986 Cover: 1.75 **NM** value: **2.00**
Circ: CapCity orders: **4,175**
🕮 Change of Scene; Good Neighbors; The Painting of Kwajim Kaji **A:** Larry Elmore; Nicholas Koenig; Eric Dinehart **W:** Bruce Jones; Chuck Dixon; Eric Dinehart

7 ❑ Jul 1986 Cover: 1.75 **NM** value: **2.00**
Circ: CapCity orders: **4,650**

8 ❑ Sep 1986 Cover: 1.75 **NM** value: **2.00**
Circ: CapCity orders: **4,425**

9 ❑ Nov 1986 Cover: 1.75 **NM** value: **2.00**
Circ: CapCity orders: **4,450**
🕮 The Dark Man; The Cubicle; Queen of the Worms; Free **A:** John Bolton; John Ridgway; Rick Geary; Jim Seed **W:** Rick Geary; Bruce Jones; Chuck Dixon

10 ❑ Jan 1987 Cover: 2.00 **NM** value: **Cover or less**
Circ: CapCity orders: **3,875**

11 ❑ Mar 1987 Cover: 2.00 **NM** value: **Cover or less**
Circ: CapCity orders: **3,925**

12 ❑ May 1987 Cover: 2.00 **NM** value: **Cover or less**
Circ: CapCity orders: **4,200**

13 ❑ Jul 1987 Cover: 2.00 **NM** value: **Cover or less**
Circ: CapCity orders: **3,950**

TALES OF TERROR ANNUAL — E.C.

1 ❑ ca. 1951 Cover: 0.25 **NM** value: **2500.00**
• **CGC:** 2 graded, best 9.0

2 ❑ ca. 1952 Cover: 0.25 **NM** value: **2000.00**
• **CGC:** 4 graded, best 9.2

3 ❑ ca. 1953 Cover: 0.25 **NM** value: **1500.00**
• **CGC:** 6 graded, best 9.2

TALES OF THE ARMORKINS — Co. & Sons

1 ❑ Cover: 0.50 **NM** value: **3.00**
🕮 Prisoners of Love; the Amazing Liver **A:** Larry S. Todd **W:** Larry S. Todd

TALES OF THE BEANWORLD — Eclipse

Beanworld and the zones beneath make up a weird fantasy dimension which operates under its own rules. It has a hero, Mr. Spook; the artist-dreamer Beanish; the intellectual Professor Garbanzo; a rock 'n' roll band; a mythical protector, Gran'ma'pa; and the faceless masses of the Beanworld army. Still, it's not really about destruction or violence. Instead, the stories are about relationships between the different inhabitants and forces of nature in and around the Beanworld. Every action has its reaction, sometimes with ramifications far beyond expectations.

It's a remarkably innovative and engaging series from Larry Marder, who would go on to herd cats as the executive director of Image Comics in the 1990s.

1 ❑ 1985 Cover: 1.50 **NM** value: **4.00**
A: Larry Marder **W:** Larry Marder

2 ❑ 1985 Cover: 1.50 **NM** value: **3.00**
A: Larry Marder **W:** Larry Marder

3 ❑ 1986 Cover: 1.50 **NM** value: **3.00**
A: Larry Marder **W:** Larry Marder

4 ❑ 1986 Cover: 1.50 **NM** value: **3.00**
A: Larry Marder **W:** Larry Marder

5 ❑ 1986 Cover: 1.50 **NM** value: **3.00**
A: Larry Marder **W:** Larry Marder

6 ❑ Apr 1987 Cover: 2.00 **NM** value: **3.00**
A: Larry Marder **W:** Larry Marder

7 ❑ 1987 Cover: 2.00 **NM** value: **3.00**
A: Larry Marder **W:** Larry Marder

8 ❑ 1987 Cover: 2.00 **NM** value: **3.00**
A: Larry Marder **W:** Larry Marder

9 ❑ 1988 Cover: 2.00 **NM** value: **3.00**
A: Larry Marder **W:** Larry Marder

10 ❑ 1988 Cover: 2.00 **NM** value: **3.00**
A: Larry Marder **W:** Larry Marder

11 ❑ 1988 Cover: 2.00 **NM** value: **Cover or less**
A: Larry Marder **W:** Larry Marder

12 ❑ Feb 1989 Cover: 2.00 **NM** value: **Cover or less**
A: Larry Marder **W:** Larry Marder

13 ❑ 1989 Cover: 2.00 **NM** value: **Cover or less**
A: Larry Marder **W:** Larry Marder

14 ❑ 1989 Cover: 2.00 **NM** value: **Cover or less**
A: Larry Marder **W:** Larry Marder

15 ❑ 1990 Cover: 2.00 **NM** value: **Cover or less**
A: Larry Marder **W:** Larry Marder

16 ❑ 1990 Cover: 2.00 **NM** value: **Cover or less**
A: Larry Marder **W:** Larry Marder

17 ❑ 1990 Cover: 2.00 **NM** value: **Cover or less**
🕮 The Mystery Pods Must Go! **A:** Larry Marder **W:** Larry Marder

18 ❑ 1991 Cover: 2.00 **NM** value: **Cover or less**
🕮 Tale Of The Goofy Jerks **A:** Larry Marder **W:** Larry Marder

19 ❑ 1991 Cover: 2.00 **NM** value: **Cover or less**
A: Larry Marder **W:** Larry Marder

20 ❑ 1993 Cover: 2.50 **NM** value: **Cover or less**
A: Larry Marder **W:** Larry Marder

21 ❑ 1993 Cover: 2.95 **NM** value: **Cover or less**
🕮 The First Time Professor Garbanzo Discovered The Four Realities
A: Larry Marder **W:** Larry Marder

Bk 1 ❑ 1993 Cover: 9.95 **NM** value: **10.95**
• Trade Paperback. • Larry Marder's Beanworld **A:** Larry Marder **W:** Larry Marder

Bk 1/LE ❑ Cover: 30.95 **NM** value: **Cover or less**
• Limited hardcover edition. **A:** Larry Marder **W:** Larry Marder

TALES OF THE CLOSET — Hetricmartin

1 ❑ b&w Cover: 2.50 **NM** value: **Cover or less**
2 ❑ b&w Cover: 2.50 **NM** value: **Cover or less**
3 ❑ b&w Cover: 2.50 **NM** value: **Cover or less**
4 ❑ b&w Cover: 2.50 **NM** value: **Cover or less**
5 ❑ b&w Cover: 2.50 **NM** value: **Cover or less**
6 ❑ b&w Cover: 2.50 **NM** value: **Cover or less**

TALES OF THE CYBORG GERBILS — Harrier

1 ❑ Nov 1987 Cover: 1.95 **NM** value: **Cover or less**
🕮 The Prof; Shopping; The Dealers; The Conversation **A:** John Jackson **W:** John Jackson

TALES OF THE DARKNESS — Image

0.5 ❑ Apr 1998 Cover: 2.95 **NM** value: **Cover or less**
• **CGC:** 3 graded, best 9.8
A: Clarence Lansang; Bill Sienkiewicz; Dan Fraga; Cedric Nocon; Joe Benitez; Steve Firchow; Marc Silvestri; Dean White; Jason Gorder; Joe Weems V; Liquid!; Matt Nelson; Peter Steigerwald **W:** Malachy Coney; Garth Ennis

1 ❑ Apr 1998 Cover: 2.95 **NM** value: **Cover or less**
Circ: Diamd. preorders: **93,698 • CGC:** 3 graded, best 9.6
A: Whilce Portacio **W:** Malachy Coney; Brian Haberlin

CGC-graded: Multiply prices above by **33 for 9.9 M • 16 for 9.8 NM/M • 7 for 9.6 NM+ • 5 for 9.4 NM • 2.5 for 9.2 NM- • 1.5 for 9.0 VF/NM**

2 ❑ Jun 1998 Cover: 2.95 **NM** value: **Cover or less**
Circ: Diamd. preorders: **64,199**
A: Whilce Portacio **W:** Malachy Coney; Brian Haberlin
3 ❑ Aug 1998 Cover: 2.95 **NM** value: **Cover or less**
Circ: Diamd. preorders: **55,829**
A: Clarence Lansang; Cedric Nocon **W:** Malachy Coney
4 ❑ Dec 1998 Cover: 2.95 **NM** value: **Cover or less**
Circ: Diamd. preorders: **43,167**
W: Malachy Coney

TALES OF THE FEHNNIK (ANTARCTIC) Antarctic
1 ❑ Aug 1995, b&w Cover: 2.95 **NM** value: **Cover or less**

TALES OF THE FEHNNIK (RADIO) Radio
1 ❑ Jun 1998, b&w Cover: 2.95 **NM** value: **Cover or less**

TALES OF THE GREAT UNSPOKEN Top Shelf
1 ❑ b&w **NM** value: **1.00**
No issue number. no cover price.

TALES OF THE GREEN BERET Dell
1 ❑ Jan 1967 Cover: 0.12 **NM** value: **30.00**
2 ❑ Mar 1967 Cover: 0.12 **NM** value: **20.00**
• **CGC:** 1 graded, best 9.0
3 ❑ Jun 1967 Cover: 0.12 **NM** value: **20.00**
🕮 The Charlie Trap; Don't Call me Chicken; My Enemy-My Brother
4 ❑ Sep 1967 Cover: 0.12 **NM** value: **20.00**
5 ❑ ca. 1968 Cover: 0.12 **NM** value: **20.00**

TALES OF THE GREEN BERETS Avalon
1 ❑ Cover: 2.95 **NM** value: **Cover or less**
• "The Green Berets" in the indicia **A:** Joe Kubert **W:** Robin Moore
2 ❑ Cover: 2.95 **NM** value: **Cover or less**
• "The Green Berets" in the indicia **A:** Joe Kubert **W:** Robin Moore
3 ❑ Cover: 2.95 **NM** value: **Cover or less**
• "The Green Berets" in the indicia **A:** Joe Kubert **W:** Robin Moore
4 ❑ Cover: 2.95 **NM** value: **Cover or less**
A: Joe Kubert **W:** Robin Moore
5 ❑ Cover: 2.95 **NM** value: **Cover or less**
A: Joe Kubert **W:** Robin Moore
6 ❑ Cover: 2.95 **NM** value: **Cover or less**
A: Joe Kubert **W:** Robin Moore
7 ❑ Cover: 2.95 **NM** value: **Cover or less**
• "Green Berets" in the indicia **A:** Joe Kubert **W:** Robin Moore

TALES OF THE GREEN HORNET (1ST SERIES) Now
1 ❑ Sep 1990 Cover: 1.75 **NM** value: **2.00**
W: Van Williams
2 ❑ Oct 1990 Cover: 1.75 **NM** value: **2.00**

TALES OF THE GREEN HORNET (2ND SERIES) Now
1 ❑ Jan 1992 Cover: 1.95 **NM** value: **Cover or less**
Circ: CapCity orders: **11,075**
🕮 Destiny, Part 1
2 ❑ Feb 1992 Cover: 1.95 **NM** value: **Cover or less**
Circ: CapCity orders: **8,275**
🕮 Destiny, Part 2 **A:** Dell Barras **W:** James Van Hise ★ Origin of The Green Hornet.
3 ❑ Mar 1992 Cover: 1.95 **NM** value: **Cover or less**
Circ: CapCity orders: **6,975**
4 ❑ Apr 1992 Cover: 1.95 **NM** value: **Cover or less**
Circ: CapCity orders: **6,250**

TALES OF THE GREEN HORNET (3RD SERIES) Now
1 ❑ Sep 1992 Cover: 2.75 **NM** value: **Cover or less**
Circ: CapCity orders: **8,425**
• bagged with hologram card
2 ❑ Oct 1992 Cover: 2.50 **NM** value: **Cover or less**
Circ: CapCity orders: **5,025**
3 ❑ Nov 1992 Cover: 2.50 **NM** value: **Cover or less**
Circ: CapCity orders: **4,875**

TALES OF THE GREEN LANTERN CORPS DC
1 ❑ May 1981 Cover: 0.50 **NM** value: **1.50**
🕮 Challenge **A:** Frank McLaughlin; John Severin; John Costanza **W:** Len Wein; Mike W. Barr ★ Origin of Green Lantern.
2 ❑ Jun 1981 Cover: 0.50 **NM** value: **1.25**
A: Frank McLaughlin; John Severin
3 ❑ Jul 1981 Cover: 0.50 **NM** value: **1.25**
🕮 Triumph! **A:** Frank McLaughlin; Joe Staton; John Severin **W:** Len Wein; Mike W. Barr
Anl 1❑ Cover: 1.25 **NM** value: **Cover or less**

TALES OF THE JACKALOPE Blackthorne
1 ❑ 1986 Cover: 2.00 **NM** value: **Cover or less**
2 ❑ 1986 Cover: 2.00 **NM** value: **Cover or less**
3 ❑ 1986 Cover: 2.00 **NM** value: **Cover or less**
4 ❑ 1986 Cover: 2.00 **NM** value: **Cover or less**
5 ❑ 1986 Cover: 2.00 **NM** value: **Cover or less**
6 ❑ 1986 Cover: 2.00 **NM** value: **Cover or less**
🕮 Throwing Continuity To The Wind; The One That Got Away
7 ❑ Feb 1987 Cover: 2.00 **NM** value: **Cover or less**

TALES OF THE KUNG FU WARRIORS CFW
1 ❑ Cover: 1.95 **NM** value: **2.00**
★ 1st Appearance of Ethereal Black. ★ 1st Appearance of Squamous.
2 ❑ Cover: 2.00 **NM** value: **Cover or less**
3 ❑ Cover: 2.00 **NM** value: **Cover or less**
4 ❑ Cover: 2.00 **NM** value: **Cover or less**
5 ❑ Cover: 2.00 **NM** value: **Cover or less**
6 ❑ Cover: 2.00 **NM** value: **Cover or less**
7 ❑ Cover: 2.00 **NM** value: **Cover or less**
8 ❑ Cover: 2.00 **NM** value: **Cover or less**
9 ❑ Cover: 2.00 **NM** value: **Cover or less**
10 ❑ Cover: 2.25 **NM** value: **Cover or less**
11 ❑ Cover: 2.25 **NM** value: **Cover or less**
12 ❑ Cover: 2.25 **NM** value: **Cover or less**
13 ❑ Cover: 2.25 **NM** value: **Cover or less**
14 ❑ Cover: 2.25 **NM** value: **Cover or less**
★ 1st Appearance of Sumo.

TALES OF THE LEGION DC
314❑ Aug 1984 Cover: 0.75 **NM** value: **1.50**
Circ: Statement: **140,018**
★ Origin of White Witch.
315❑ Sep 1984 Cover: 0.75 **NM** value: **1.50**
Circ: Statement: **140,018**
🕮 Judgement! **A:** Karl Kesel; Keith Giffen; Terry Shoemaker **W:** Keith Giffen; Paul Levitz ★ Versus Dark Circle.
316❑ Oct 1984 Cover: 0.75 **NM** value: **1.50**
Circ: Statement: **140,018**
★ Origin of White Witch.
317❑ Nov 1984 Cover: 0.75 **NM** value: **1.50**
Circ: Statement: **140,018**
318❑ Dec 1984 Cover: 0.75 **NM** value: **1.50**
Circ: Statement: **140,018**
★ Versus Persuader.
319❑ Jan 1985 Cover: 0.75 **NM** value: **1.50**
Circ: Statement: **109,126**
320❑ Feb 1985 Cover: 0.75 **NM** value: **1.50**
Circ: Statement: **109,126**
321❑ Mar 1985 Cover: 0.75 **NM** value: **1.50**
Circ: Statement: **109,126**
322❑ Apr 1985 Cover: 0.75 **NM** value: **1.50**
Circ: Statement: **109,126**
323❑ May 1985 Cover: 0.75 **NM** value: **1.50**
Circ: Statement: **109,126** CapCity orders: **11,150**
• Has 1984 Statement; avg print run 304,901; avg sales 137,692; avg subs 2,326; avg total paid 140,018; max existent 140,018; 53% of run returned
324❑ Jun 1985 Cover: 0.75 **NM** value: **1.50**
Circ: Statement: **109,126** CapCity orders: **10,950**
★ Versus Dark Circle.
325❑ Jul 1985 Cover: 0.75 **NM** value: **1.50**
Circ: Statement: **109,126** CapCity orders: **10,850**
🕮 5 to the Infinite Power **A:** Dan Jurgens **W:** Paul Levitz; Mindy Newell
326❑ Aug 1985 Cover: 0.75 **NM** value: **1.25**
Circ: Statement: **109,126** CapCity orders: **8,550**
• begins reprints of Legion of Super-Heroes (3rd series); Reprints begin ★ Versus Legion of Super-Villains.
327❑ Sep 1985 Cover: 0.75 **NM** value: **1.25**
Circ: Statement: **109,126** CapCity orders: **8,050**
★ Versus Legion of Super-Villains.
328❑ Oct 1985 Cover: 0.75 **NM** value: **1.25**
Circ: Statement: **109,126** CapCity orders: **7,450**
★ Versus Legion of Super-Villains.
329❑ Nov 1985 Cover: 0.75 **NM** value: **1.25**
Circ: Statement: **109,126** CapCity orders: **6,450**
★ Death of Karate Kid. ★ Versus Legion of Super-Villains.
330❑ Dec 1985 Cover: 0.75 **NM** value: **1.25**
Circ: Statement: **109,126** CapCity orders: **5,900**
★ Versus Legion of Super-Villains.
331❑ Jan 1986 Cover: 0.75 **NM** value: **1.25**
Circ: Statement: **71,507** CapCity orders: **5,550**
★ Origin of Lightning Lord, Lightning Lass, Lightning Lad.
332❑ Feb 1986 Cover: 0.75 **NM** value: **1.25**
Circ: Statement: **71,507** CapCity orders: **5,500**
333❑ Mar 1986 Cover: 0.75 **NM** value: **1.25**
Circ: Statement: **71,507** CapCity orders: **5,300**
334❑ Apr 1986 Cover: 0.75 **NM** value: **1.25**
Circ: Statement: **71,507** CapCity orders: **5,200**
335❑ May 1986 Cover: 0.75 **NM** value: **1.25**
Circ: Statement: **71,507** CapCity orders: **4,850**
336❑ Jun 1986 Cover: 0.75 **NM** value: **1.25**
Circ: Statement: **71,507** CapCity orders: **4,850**
337❑ Jul 1986 Cover: 0.75 **NM** value: **1.25**
Circ: Statement: **71,507** CapCity orders: **4,900**
338❑ Aug 1986 Cover: 0.75 **NM** value: **1.25**
Circ: Statement: **71,507** CapCity orders: **4,750**
339❑ Sep 1986 Cover: 0.75 **NM** value: **1.25**
Circ: Statement: **71,507** CapCity orders: **4,600**
• Magnetic Kid joins team; Tellus joins team; Polar Boy joins team; Quislet joins team; Sensor Girl joins team
340❑ Oct 1986 Cover: 0.75 **NM** value: **1.25**
Circ: Statement: **71,507** CapCity orders: **4,650**
★ Versus Doctor Regulus.
341❑ Nov 1986 Cover: 0.75 **NM** value: **1.25**
Circ: Statement: **71,507** CapCity orders: **4,600**
342❑ Dec 1986 Cover: 0.75 **NM** value: **1.25**
Circ: Statement: **71,507** CapCity orders: **4,700**
343❑ Jan 1987 Cover: 0.75 **NM** value: **1.25**
Circ: CapCity orders: **4,750**
★ Origin of Wildfire.
344❑ Feb 1987 Cover: 0.75 **NM** value: **1.25**
Circ: CapCity orders: **4,700**
345❑ Mar 1987 Cover: 0.75 **NM** value: **1.25**
Circ: CapCity orders: **4,750**
346❑ Apr 1987 Cover: 0.75 **NM** value: **1.25**
Circ: CapCity orders: **5,500**
347❑ May 1987 Cover: 0.75 **NM** value: **1.25**
Circ: CapCity orders: **4,350**
★ Versus Universo.
348❑ Jun 1987 Cover: 0.75 **NM** value: **1.25**
Circ: CapCity orders: **4,100**
• in Phantom Zone
349❑ Jul 1987 Cover: 0.75 **NM** value: **1.25**
Circ: CapCity orders: **4,050**
350❑ Aug 1987 Cover: 0.75 **NM** value: **1.25**
Circ: CapCity orders: **4,400**
• Sensor Girl's identity revealed
351❑ Sep 1987 Cover: 0.75 **NM** value: **1.25**
Circ: CapCity orders: **4,550**
★ Versus Fatal Five.
352❑ Oct 1987 Cover: 0.75 **NM** value: **1.25**
Circ: CapCity orders: **4,500**
353❑ Nov 1987 Cover: 1.00 **NM** value: **1.25**
Circ: CapCity orders: **4,500**
354❑ Dec 1987 Cover: 1.00 **NM** value: **1.25**
Circ: CapCity orders: **4,510**
final issue.
Anl 4❑ Cover: 1.25 **NM** value: **1.50**
Circ: CapCity orders: **5,000**
Anl 5❑ Cover: 1.25 **NM** value: **1.50**
Circ: CapCity orders: **5,150**
★ Origin of Validus.

TALES OF THE MANS Skit
Ash 1❑ **NM** value: **1.00**
A: Denny Riccelli **W:** Denny Riccelli

TALES OF THE MARVELS: BLOCKBUSTER Marvel
1 ❑ Apr 1995 Cover: 5.95 **NM** value: **Cover or less**
Circ: CapCity orders: **16,350** • **CGC:** 1 graded, best 9.8
One-shot. acetate overlay outer cover. • prestige format. **A:** Shawn Martinbrough **W:** Mike Baron

TALES OF THE MARVELS: INNER DEMONS Marvel
1 ❑ Cover: 5.95 **NM** value: **Cover or less**
No issue number. One-shot. acetate overlay outer cover.

TALES OF THE MARVELS: WONDER YEARS Marvel
1 ❑ Aug 1995 Cover: 4.95 **NM** value: **Cover or less**
• **CGC:** 1 graded, best 9.8
wraparound acetate outer cover. **A:** Igor Kordey **W:** Andy Lanning; Dan Abnett
2 ❑ Sep 1995 Cover: 4.95 **NM** value: **Cover or less**
• **CGC:** 1 graded, best 9.8
wraparound acetate outer cover. **A:** Igor Kordey **W:** Andy Lanning; Dan Abnett

TALES OF THE MARVEL UNIVERSE Marvel
1 ❑ Feb 1997 Cover: 2.99 **NM** value: **Cover or less**
wraparound cover. 🕮 Onslaught epilogue • Ka-Zar appearace; Doctor Strange apperance **A:** Aaron Lopresti; Mark Bagley; Rick Leonardi; Andy Kubert; Pat Chau; Klaus Janson **W:** Kurt Busiek; Howard Mackie; Tom DeFalco; J.M. DeMatteis; Mark Bernardo; Mark Waid ★ Appearance of Ka-Zar, Doctor Strange, Kristoff, Thunderbolts.

TALES OF THE MYSTERIOUS TRAVELER (CHARLTON) Charlton
He wears a trench coat and fedora and speaks in cryptic mysteries as he moves, omniscient and distant, through the shadows of this Charlton title, narrating odd tales with a twist. In a typical issue of this series (inspired by the Mysterious Traveler radio dramas), the traveler watches a man who hears voices struggle with his ability to levitate; a scientist's attempts to create the ultimate microscope; a truck driver deals with an alien invasion. Then the traveler tells what really happened to that dog sent up into space by the Russians.

The title ran from 1956 to 1959 and returned briefly from DC Comics in 1985.

1 ❑ Aug 1956 Cover: 0.10 **NM** value: **240.00**
2 ❑ Nov 1956 Cover: 0.10 **NM** value: **185.00**
3 ❑ May 1957 Cover: 0.10 **NM** value: **145.00**
• **CGC:** 2 graded, best 9.2
4 ❑ 1957 Cover: 0.10 **NM** value: **125.00**
5 ❑ 1957 Cover: 0.10 **NM** value: **125.00**
6 ❑ 1958 Cover: 0.10 **NM** value: **100.00**
7 ❑ Mar 1958 Cover: 0.10 **NM** value: **100.00**
8 ❑ Jul 1958 Cover: 0.10 **NM** value: **100.00**
9 ❑ Sep 1958 Cover: 0.10 **NM** value: **100.00**
10 ❑ Nov 1958 Cover: 0.10 **NM** value: **100.00**
11 ❑ Feb 1959 Cover: 0.10 **NM** value: **85.00**
12 ❑ Apr 1959 Cover: 0.10 **NM** value: **85.00**
• **CGC:** 1 graded, best 8.0
🕮 A Man Alone!; A Day of "Fun with Pop"; Ad Infinitum; I Was There!; Satisfied Customers
13 ❑ Jun 1959 Cover: 0.10 **NM** value: **85.00**
🕮 Final issue of original run
14 ❑ Oct 1985 Cover: 0.75 **NM** value: **3.00**
15 ❑ Dec 1985 Cover: 0.75 **NM** value: **3.00**

TALES OF THE MYSTERIOUS TRAVELER (ECLIPSE) Eclipse
1 ❑ **NM** value: **3.00**

Statement of Ownership figures are the average number of copies originally sold, as cited by the publisher to the U.S. Postal Service. These estimate **all** sales, in comics shops and on newsstands.

Other grades: Multiply prices above by **1.5 for Mint • 2/3 for Very Fine • 1/3 for Fine • 1/5 for Very Good • 1/8 for Good**

TALES OF THE NEW TEEN TITANS — DC

The New Teen Titans first appeared in DC Comics Presents #26. In 1982, DC featured the new group in this four-issue mini-series which related the full origins of the new characters on the team.

First up was Victor Stone (Cyborg), son of a pair of researchers who raised him as their own experiment in increasing human intelligence. Thanks to their efforts young Victor achieved genius level IQ. Still, he missed having a normal childhood and eventually rebelled against his parents. Fate intervened, however, when he was attacked by the same extradimensional being that killed his mother at S.T.A.R. Labs. To save his life, his father had to graft a new body of metal onto the remains of Victor's old body, turning him into a cyborg.

Later issues in this series related the origins of Raven, Starfire II (the alien Koriand'r), and Changeling.

1 ❑ Jun 1982 Cover: 0.60 **NM** value: **1.50**
• **CGC:** 1 graded, best 9.8
📖 Cyborg **A:** George Pérez **W:** Marv Wolfman ★ Origin of Cyborg.

2 ❑ Jul 1982 Cover: 0.60 **NM** value: **1.00**
📖 Raven **A:** George Pérez **W:** Marv Wolfman ★ Origin of Raven.

3 ❑ Aug 1982 Cover: 0.60 **NM** value: **1.00**
📖 The Changeling **A:** George Pérez; Gene Day **W:** Marv Wolfman ★ Origin of Changeling.

4 ❑ Sep 1982 Cover: 0.60 **NM** value: **1.00**
📖 Starfire **A:** George Pérez; Ernie Colon **W:** Marv Wolfman ★ Origin of Starfire II (Koriand'r). ★ 1st Appearance of Ryand'r.

TALES OF THE NINJA WARRIORS — CFW

1 ❑ b&w Cover: 2.25 **NM** value: **Cover or less**
2 ❑ b&w Cover: 2.25 **NM** value: **Cover or less**
3 ❑ b&w Cover: 2.25 **NM** value: **Cover or less**
4 ❑ b&w Cover: 2.25 **NM** value: **Cover or less**
5 ❑ b&w Cover: 2.25 **NM** value: **Cover or less**
6 ❑ b&w Cover: 2.25 **NM** value: **Cover or less**
7 ❑ b&w Cover: 2.25 **NM** value: **Cover or less**
8 ❑ b&w Cover: 2.25 **NM** value: **Cover or less**
9 ❑ b&w Cover: 2.25 **NM** value: **Cover or less**
10 ❑ b&w Cover: 2.25 **NM** value: **Cover or less**
11 ❑ b&w Cover: 2.25 **NM** value: **Cover or less**
12 ❑ b&w Cover: 2.25 **NM** value: **Cover or less**
13 ❑ b&w Cover: 2.25 **NM** value: **Cover or less**
14 ❑ b&w Cover: 2.25 **NM** value: **Cover or less**
15 ❑ b&w Cover: 2.25 **NM** value: **Cover or less**
📖 Parallax: The Third Wave; Kabuki Kid, Part 2; Blackangel; Flint, Part 5 **A:** Chris Gossett; Dell Barras; Doran Fish; S. David Lee **W:** Chris Gossett; Doran Fish; Nijel Pompeii
16 ❑ b&w Cover: 2.25 **NM** value: **Cover or less**

TALES OF THE SUN RUNNERS — Sirius

1 ❑ Jul 1986 Cover: 1.50 **NM** value: **Cover or less**
Circ: CapCity orders: **4,250**
📖 Dancing in the Dark **A:** Glen Johnson **W:** Roger McKenzie
2 ❑ 1986 Cover: 1.95 **NM** value: **Cover or less**
Circ: CapCity orders: **3,575**
3 ❑ 1986 Cover: 1.95 **NM** value: **Cover or less**
Circ: CapCity orders: **3,675**

TALES OF THE TEENAGE MUTANT NINJA TURTLES — Mirage

1 ❑ May 1987 Cover: 1.50 **NM** value: **3.00**
A: Jim Lawson **W:** Kevin Eastman; Peter Laird
2 ❑ Jul 1987 Cover: 1.50 **NM** value: **2.00**
3 ❑ Oct 1987 Cover: 1.50 **NM** value: **2.00**
4 ❑ Feb 1988 Cover: 1.50 **NM** value: **2.00**
cover says Jan, indicia says Feb.
5 ❑ May 1988 Cover: 1.50 **NM** value: **2.00**
6 ❑ Aug 1988 Cover: 1.50 **NM** value: **2.00**
7 ❑ Aug 1989 Cover: 1.50 **NM** value: **2.00**
cover says Apr, indicia says Aug. final issue.

TALES OF THE TEEN TITANS — DC

41 ❑ Apr 1984 Cover: 0.75 **NM** value: **2.00**
Circ: CapCity orders: **3,500**
📖 Baptism of Blood • Series continued from New Teen Titans (1st Series) #40 **A:** George Pérez **W:** Marv Wolfman ★ Appearance of Brother Blood.

42 ❑ May 1984 Cover: 0.75 **NM** value: **2.00**
📖 Judas Contract, Part 1; The Judas Contract, Part 1, The Eyes of Tara Markov **A:** George Pérez **W:** Marv Wolfman ★ Versus Deathstroke.

43 ❑ Jun 1984 Cover: 0.75 **NM** value: **2.00**
• **CGC:** 1 graded, best 9.6
📖 Judas Contract, Part 2; The Judas Contract, Part 2, Betrayal **A:** George Pérez **W:** Marv Wolfman ★ Versus Deathstroke. ★ Versus H.I.V.E..

44 ❑ Jul 1984 Cover: 0.75 **NM** value: **6.00**
• **CGC:** 59 graded, best 9.8
📖 Judas Contract, Part 3; The Judas Contract **A:** George Pérez **W:** Marv Wolfman ★ Origin of Jericho. ★ 1st Appearance of Nightwing.

45 ❑ Aug 1984 Cover: 0.75 **NM** value: **1.50**
• **CGC:** 1 graded, best 9.8
A: George Pérez **W:** Marv Wolfman ★ Appearance of Aquagirl, Aqualad.

46 ❑ Sep 1984 Cover: 0.75 **NM** value: **1.50**
• **CGC:** 1 graded, best 9.4
📖 Showdown! **A:** George Pérez **W:** Marv Wolfman ★ Versus H.I.V.E..

47 ❑ Oct 1984 Cover: 0.75 **NM** value: **1.50**
• **CGC:** 1 graded, best 9.8
📖 Final Conflict! **A:** George Pérez **W:** Marv Wolfman ★ Versus H.I.V.E..

48 ❑ Nov 1984 Cover: 0.75 **NM** value: **1.50**
📖 The Recombatants **A:** George Pérez; Steve Rude **W:** Marv Wolfman ★ Versus Recombatants.

49 ❑ Dec 1984 Cover: 0.75 **NM** value: **1.50**
📖 The Light That Failed **A:** Carmine Infantino; George Pérez **W:** Marv Wolfman ★ Versus Doctor Light. ★ Versus Dr. Light.

50 ❑ Feb 1985 Cover: 1.25 **NM** value: **2.00**
Circ: Statement: **182,189**
• Giant-size. 📖 We Are Gathered Here Today… • Wedding of Wonder Girl **A:** George Pérez **W:** Marv Wolfman

51 ❑ Mar 1985 Cover: 0.75 **NM** value: **1.50**
Circ: Statement: **182,189**
★ 1st Appearance of Azrael (not Batman character). ★ Versus Cheshire.

52 ❑ Apr 1985 Cover: 0.75 **NM** value: **1.50**
Circ: Statement: **182,189** • **CGC:** 1 graded, best 9.8
★ Versus Cheshire.

53 ❑ May 1985 Cover: 0.75 **NM** value: **1.50**
Circ: Statement: **182,189** CapCity orders: **23,950**
★ Appearance of Deathstroke.

54 ❑ Jun 1985 Cover: 0.75 **NM** value: **1.50**
Circ: Statement: **182,189** CapCity orders: **22,200**
📖 Blind Justice! • Trial of Deathstroke **A:** Rich Buckler; Dick Giordano; Mike DeCarlo **W:** Marv Wolfman ★ Appearance of Deathstroke.

55 ❑ Jul 1985 Cover: 0.75 **NM** value: **1.50**
Circ: Statement: **182,189** CapCity orders: **21,550**
• Changeling vs. Deathstroke

56 ❑ Aug 1985 Cover: 0.75 **NM** value: **1.50**
Circ: Statement: **182,189** CapCity orders: **20,600**
★ Versus Fearsome Five.

57 ❑ Sep 1985 Cover: 0.75 **NM** value: **1.50**
Circ: Statement: **182,189** CapCity orders: **20,950**
• Cyborg transformed★ Versus Fearsome Five.

58 ❑ Oct 1985 Cover: 0.75 **NM** value: **1.50**
Circ: Statement: **182,189** CapCity orders: **20,200**
★ Appearance of Monitor, Harbinger. ★ Versus Fearsome Five.

59 ❑ Nov 1985 Cover: 0.75 **NM** value: **1.50**
Circ: Statement: **182,189** CapCity orders: **16,000**
• reprints DC Comics Presents #26

60 ❑ Dec 1985 Cover: 0.75 **NM** value: **1.00**
Circ: Statement: **182,189** CapCity orders: **13,250**
• series begins reprinting New Teen Titans (second series)★ Versus Trigon.

61 ❑ Jan 1986 Cover: 0.75 **NM** value: **1.00**
Circ: Statement: **106,853** CapCity orders: **9,800**
★ Versus Trigon.

62 ❑ Feb 1986 Cover: 0.75 **NM** value: **1.00**
Circ: Statement: **106,853** CapCity orders: **9,500**
★ Versus Trigon.

63 ❑ Mar 1986 Cover: 0.75 **NM** value: **1.00**
Circ: Statement: **106,853** CapCity orders: **9,000**
★ Versus Trigon.

64 ❑ Apr 1986 Cover: 0.75 **NM** value: **1.00**
Circ: Statement: **106,853** CapCity orders: **8,650**
• Has 1985 Statement, filed 10/1/85; avg print run 366,796; avg sales 178,629; avg subs 3,560; avg total paid 182,189; samples 108; max existent 182,297; 49% of run returned★ Versus Trigon.

65 ❑ May 1986 Cover: 0.75 **NM** value: **1.00**
Circ: Statement: **106,853** CapCity orders: **8,250**

66 ❑ Jun 1986 Cover: 0.75 **NM** value: **1.00**
Circ: Statement: **106,853** CapCity orders: **7,700**
★ Origin of Lilith.

67 ❑ Jul 1986 Cover: 0.75 **NM** value: **1.00**
Circ: Statement: **106,853** CapCity orders: **7,800**

68 ❑ Aug 1986 Cover: 0.75 **NM** value: **1.00**
Circ: Statement: **106,853** CapCity orders: **7,200**
★ Appearance of Kole.

69 ❑ Sep 1986 Cover: 0.75 **NM** value: **1.00**
Circ: Statement: **106,853** CapCity orders: **6,850**

70 ❑ Oct 1986 Cover: 0.75 **NM** value: **1.00**
Circ: Statement: **106,853** CapCity orders: **7,050**
★ Origin of Kole.

71 ❑ Nov 1986 Cover: 0.75 **NM** value: **1.00**
Circ: Statement: **106,853** CapCity orders: **7,000**

72 ❑ Dec 1986 Cover: 0.75 **NM** value: **1.00**
Circ: Statement: **106,853** CapCity orders: **6,750**
★ Appearance of Outsiders.

73 ❑ Jan 1987 Cover: 0.75 **NM** value: **1.00**
Circ: Statement: **70,507** CapCity orders: **6,150**

74 ❑ Feb 1987 Cover: 0.75 **NM** value: **1.00**
Circ: Statement: **70,507** CapCity orders: **6,150**

75 ❑ Mar 1987 Cover: 0.75 **NM** value: **1.00**
Circ: Statement: **70,507** CapCity orders: **6,150**
★ Appearance of Omega Men.

76 ❑ Apr 1987 Cover: 0.75 **NM** value: **1.00**
Circ: Statement: **70,507** CapCity orders: **6,150**
• Wedding of Starfire; Has 1986 Statement, filed 10/1/86; avg print run 286,516; avg sales 104,223; avg subs 2,630; avg total paid 106,853; samples 162; office use 2,796; max existent 109,811; 62% of run returned

77 ❑ May 1987 Cover: 0.75 **NM** value: **1.00**
Circ: Statement: **70,507** CapCity orders: **5,400**

78 ❑ Jun 1987 Cover: 0.75 **NM** value: **1.00**
Circ: Statement: **70,507** CapCity orders: **5,250**
• new team

79 ❑ Jul 1987 Cover: 0.75 **NM** value: **1.00**
Circ: Statement: **70,507** CapCity orders: **5,250**

80 ❑ Aug 1987 Cover: 0.75 **NM** value: **1.00**
Circ: Statement: **70,507** CapCity orders: **5,600**
★ Appearance of Cheshire, Lian.

81 ❑ Sep 1987 Cover: 0.75 **NM** value: **1.00**
Circ: Statement: **70,507** CapCity orders: **5,900**

82 ❑ Oct 1987 Cover: 0.75 **NM** value: **1.00**
Circ: Statement: **70,507** CapCity orders: **5,850**

83 ❑ Nov 1987 Cover: 0.75 **NM** value: **1.00**
Circ: Statement: **70,507** CapCity orders: **5,700**

84 ❑ Dec 1987 Cover: 0.75 **NM** value: **1.00**
Circ: Statement: **70,507** CapCity orders: **5,550**

85 ❑ Jan 1988 Cover: 0.75 **NM** value: **1.00**
Circ: CapCity orders: **5,550**

86 ❑ Feb 1988 Cover: 0.75 **NM** value: **1.00**
Circ: CapCity orders: **5,600**
★ Versus Twister.

87 ❑ Mar 1988 Cover: 0.75 **NM** value: **1.00**
Circ: CapCity orders: **5,450**
★ Versus Brotherhood of Evil.

88 ❑ Apr 1988 Cover: 0.75 **NM** value: **1.00**
Circ: CapCity orders: **5,400**
• Has 1987 Statement, filed 10/5/87; avg print run 203,000; avg sales 69,327; avg subs 1,180; avg total paid 70,507; samples 980; office use 5,572; max existent 77,059; 62% of run returned★ Versus Brother Blood.

89 ❑ May 1988 Cover: 1.35 **NM** value: **Cover or less**
Circ: CapCity orders: **5,200**
★ Versus Brother Blood.

90 ❑ Jun 1988 Cover: 0.75 **NM** value: **1.00**
Circ: CapCity orders: **5,000**

91 ❑ Jul 1988 Cover: 0.75 **NM** value: **1.00**
Circ: CapCity orders: **4,750**
final issue.

Anl 4❑ Cover: 1.25 **NM** value: **Cover or less**
Circ: CapCity orders: **7,350**
• reprints New Teen Titans Annual #1★ Appearance of Superman. ★ Versus Vanguard.

Anl 5❑ **NM** value: **1.25**
Circ: CapCity orders: **5,950**

Bk 1❑ Dec 1988 Cover: 14.95 **NM** value: **Cover or less**
• The Judas Contract **A:** George Pérez

TALES OF THE UNEXPECTED — DC

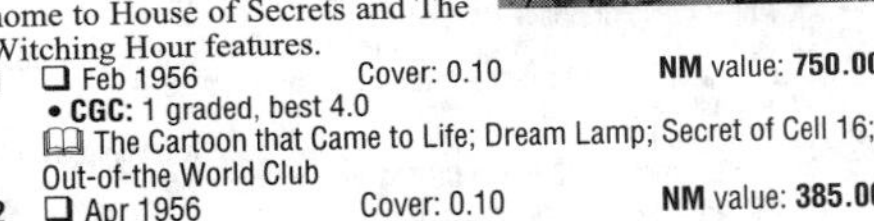

From silly science-fiction tales to poignant fantasy stories, Tales of the Unexpected sought to serve up something for everyone. In the best DC fantasy tradition, this series showcased stories and art that inspired a generation of fiction writers.

The series became simply The Unexpected with #105, featuring artwork by horror master Bernie Wrightson, among others.

As the market for non-super-hero titles continued to dry up in the late 1970s, The Unexpected became home to House of Secrets and The Witching Hour features.

1 ❑ Feb 1956 Cover: 0.10 **NM** value: **750.00**
• **CGC:** 1 graded, best 4.0
📖 The Cartoon that Came to Life; Dream Lamp; Secret of Cell 16; Out-of-the World Club

2 ❑ Apr 1956 Cover: 0.10 **NM** value: **385.00**
📖 The Gorilla Who Saved the World

3 ❑ Jul 1956 Cover: 0.10 **NM** value: **275.00**
• **CGC:** 1 graded, best 6.0
📖 The Master of 100 Wigs; Highway to Tomorrow; Man Nobody Could See; I Lost My Past

4 ❑ Aug 1956 Cover: 0.10 **NM** value: **225.00**
📖 The House Where Dreams Come True

5 ❑ Sep 1956 Cover: 0.10 **NM** value: **225.00**
• **CGC:** 1 graded, best 8.0
📖 The Second Life of Geoffrey Hawkes

6 ❑ Oct 1956 Cover: 0.10 **NM** value: **165.00**
• **CGC:** 1 graded, best 9.2
📖 The Girl in the Bottle; Telecast from the Future; Dial M for Magic; Forbidden Flowers

7 ❑ Nov 1956 Cover: 0.10 **NM** value: **165.00**
• **CGC:** 1 graded, best 7.5
📖 The Face in the Clock; Beware, I Can Read Your Mind; Forbidden Wish; The Pen That Lied

8 ❑ Dec 1956 Cover: 0.10 **NM** value: **165.00**
• **CGC:** 1 graded, best 7.5
📖 The 3-D Camera That Could Rob; Secret of the Elephant's Tusk; The Man Who Stole a Genie; Four Seeds of Destiny

9 ❑ Jan 1957 Cover: 0.10 **NM** value: **165.00**
• **CGC:** 2 graded, best 7.5
📖 The Man Who Ate Fire

10 ❑ Feb 1957 Cover: 0.10 **NM** value: **165.00**
• **CGC:** 1 graded, best 5.0
📖 Slave to the Wizard's Lamp; The Duplicate Man; Strangest Circus on Earth; The Phantom Mariner

11 ❑ Mar 1957 Cover: 0.10 **NM** value: **125.00**
• **CGC:** 1 graded, best 8.5
📖 The Man Who Hated Green

12 ❑ Apr 1957 Cover: 0.10 **NM** value: **125.00**
• **CGC:** 1 graded, best 4.0
📖 The Indestructible Man

13 ❑ May 1957 Cover: 0.10 **NM** value: **125.00**
📖 The Face Behind the Mask

14 ❑ Jun 1957 Cover: 0.10 **NM** value: **125.00**
📖 The Green Gorilla

15 ❑ Jul 1957 Cover: 0.10 **NM** value: **125.00**
• **CGC:** 1 graded, best 6.5
📖 City of Three Dooms

16 ❑ Aug 1957 Cover: 0.10 **NM** value: **125.00**
• **CGC:** 1 graded, best 5.0

17 ❑ Sep 1957 Cover: 0.10 **NM** value: **125.00**
• **CGC:** 1 graded, best 7.5
📖 The Impossible Voyage

18 ❑ Oct 1957 Cover: 0.10 **NM** value: **125.00**
• **CGC:** 2 graded, best 9.0

19 ❑ Nov 1957 Cover: 0.10 **NM** value: **125.00**
📖 The Menace of the Fireball

CGC-graded: Multiply prices above by **33 for 9.9 M • 16 for 9.8 NM/M • 7 for 9.6 NM+ • 5 for 9.4 NM • 2.5 for 9.2 NM- • 1.5 for 9.0 VF/NM**

20 ❑ Dec 1957 Cover: 0.10 **NM** value: **125.00**
• **CGC:** 1 graded, best 8.0
21 ❑ Jan 1958 Cover: 0.10 **NM** value: **100.00**
22 ❑ Feb 1958 Cover: 0.10 **NM** value: **100.00**
23 ❑ Mar 1958 Cover: 0.10 **NM** value: **100.00**
• **CGC:** 1 graded, best 8.0
24 ❑ Apr 1958 Cover: 0.10 **NM** value: **100.00**
25 ❑ May 1958 Cover: 0.10 **NM** value: **100.00**
26 ❑ Jun 1958 Cover: 0.10 **NM** value: **100.00**
• **CGC:** 1 graded, best 9.0
27 ❑ Jul 1958 Cover: 0.10 **NM** value: **100.00**
28 ❑ Aug 1958 Cover: 0.10 **NM** value: **100.00**
• **CGC:** 1 graded, best 8.5
29 ❑ Sep 1958 Cover: 0.10 **NM** value: **100.00**
30 ❑ Oct 1958 Cover: 0.10 **NM** value: **100.00**
• **CGC:** 2 graded, best 8.0
31 ❑ Nov 1958 Cover: 0.10 **NM** value: **85.00**
• **CGC:** 1 graded, best 9.4
32 ❑ Dec 1958 Cover: 0.10 **NM** value: **85.00**
33 ❑ Jan 1959 Cover: 0.10 **NM** value: **85.00**
34 ❑ Feb 1959 Cover: 0.10 **NM** value: **85.00**
35 ❑ Mar 1959 Cover: 0.10 **NM** value: **85.00**
• **CGC:** 1 graded, best 9.0
36 ❑ Apr 1959 Cover: 0.10 **NM** value: **85.00**
• **CGC:** 1 graded, best 8.5
37 ❑ May 1959 Cover: 0.10 **NM** value: **85.00**
38 ❑ Jun 1959 Cover: 0.10 **NM** value: **85.00**
• **CGC:** 1 graded, best 9.4
39 ❑ Jul 1959 Cover: 0.10 **NM** value: **85.00**
40 ❑ Aug 1959 Cover: 0.10 **NM** value: **650.00**
• **CGC:** 6 graded, best 9.0
📖 Battle of the Colossal Creatures • Space Ranger stories begin
41 ❑ Sep 1959 Cover: 0.10 **NM** value: **275.00**
• **CGC:** 6 graded, best 9.4
★ Appearance of Space Ranger.
42 ❑ Oct 1959 Cover: 0.10 **NM** value: **275.00**
• **CGC:** 3 graded, best 9.2
★ Appearance of Space Ranger.
43 ❑ Nov 1959 Cover: 0.10 **NM** value: **450.00**
• **CGC:** 2 graded, best 8.5
Space Ranger cover. ★ Appearance of Space Ranger.
44 ❑ Dec 1959 Cover: 0.10 **NM** value: **200.00**
★ Appearance of Space Ranger.
45 ❑ Jan 1960 Cover: 0.10 **NM** value: **200.00**
Circ: Statement: **192,000**
★ Appearance of Space Ranger.
46 ❑ Feb 1960 Cover: 0.10 **NM** value: **150.00**
Circ: Statement: **192,000** • **CGC:** 1 graded, best 9.2
★ Appearance of Space Ranger.
47 ❑ Mar 1960 Cover: 0.10 **NM** value: **150.00**
Circ: Statement: **192,000** • **CGC:** 1 graded, best 9.2
★ Appearance of Space Ranger.
48 ❑ Apr 1960 Cover: 0.10 **NM** value: **150.00**
Circ: Statement: **192,000** • **CGC:** 1 graded, best 7.5
★ Appearance of Space Ranger.
49 ❑ May 1960 Cover: 0.10 **NM** value: **150.00**
Circ: Statement: **192,000** • **CGC:** 1 graded, best 8.5
★ Appearance of Space Ranger.
50 ❑ Jun 1960 Cover: 0.10 **NM** value: **150.00**
Circ: Statement: **192,000** • **CGC:** 1 graded, best 9.2
★ Appearance of Space Ranger.
51 ❑ Jul 1960 Cover: 0.10 **NM** value: **125.00**
Circ: Statement: **192,000**
★ Appearance of Space Ranger.
52 ❑ Aug 1960 Cover: 0.10 **NM** value: **125.00**
Circ: Statement: **192,000** • **CGC:** 2 graded, best 9.4
★ Appearance of Space Ranger.
53 ❑ Sep 1960 Cover: 0.10 **NM** value: **125.00**
Circ: Statement: **192,000** • **CGC:** 1 graded, best 9.0
★ Appearance of Space Ranger.
54 ❑ Oct 1960 Cover: 0.10 **NM** value: **125.00**
Circ: Statement: **192,000** • **CGC:** 1 graded, best 8.5
★ Appearance of Space Ranger.
55 ❑ Nov 1960 Cover: 0.10 **NM** value: **125.00**
Circ: Statement: **192,000**
★ Appearance of Space Ranger.
56 ❑ Dec 1960 Cover: 0.10 **NM** value: **100.00**
Circ: Statement: **192,000**
★ Appearance of Space Ranger.
57 ❑ Jan 1961 Cover: 0.10 **NM** value: **100.00**
Circ: Statement: **195,000** • **CGC:** 2 graded, best 9.0
★ Appearance of Space Ranger.
58 ❑ Feb 1961 Cover: 0.10 **NM** value: **100.00**
Circ: Statement: **195,000**
• Has 1960 Statement; avg total paid circ 192,000★ Appearance of Space Ranger.
59 ❑ Mar 1961 Cover: 0.10 **NM** value: **100.00**
Circ: Statement: **195,000**
★ Appearance of Space Ranger.
60 ❑ Apr 1961 Cover: 0.10 **NM** value: **100.00**
Circ: Statement: **195,000**
★ Appearance of Space Ranger.
61 ❑ May 1961 Cover: 0.10 **NM** value: **85.00**
Circ: Statement: **195,000**
★ Appearance of Space Ranger.
62 ❑ Jun 1961 Cover: 0.10 **NM** value: **85.00**
Circ: Statement: **195,000**
★ Appearance of Space Ranger.
63 ❑ Jul 1961 Cover: 0.10 **NM** value: **85.00**
Circ: Statement: **195,000**
★ Appearance of Space Ranger.
64 ❑ Aug 1961 Cover: 0.10 **NM** value: **85.00**
Circ: Statement: **195,000**
★ Appearance of Space Ranger.
65 ❑ Sep 1961 Cover: 0.10 **NM** value: **85.00**
Circ: Statement: **195,000** • **CGC:** 2 graded, best 8.5
★ Appearance of Space Ranger.
66 ❑ Oct 1961 Cover: 0.10 **NM** value: **85.00**
Circ: Statement: **195,000**
★ Appearance of Space Ranger.
67 ❑ Nov 1961 Cover: 0.10 **NM** value: **85.00**
Circ: Statement: **195,000** • **CGC:** 1 graded, best 8.0
★ Appearance of Space Ranger.
68 ❑ Dec 1961 Cover: 0.12 **NM** value: **85.00**
Circ: Statement: **195,000** • **CGC:** 1 graded, best 7.0
★ Appearance of Space Ranger.
69 ❑ Feb 1962 Cover: 0.12 **NM** value: **85.00**
Circ: Statement: **180,000**
• Has 1961 Statement, filed 10/1/61; avg total paid circ 195,000★ Appearance of Space Ranger.
70 ❑ Apr 1962 Cover: 0.12 **NM** value: **85.00**
Circ: Statement: **180,000** • **CGC:** 1 graded, best 8.0
★ Appearance of Space Ranger.
71 ❑ Jun 1962 Cover: 0.12 **NM** value: **60.00**
Circ: Statement: **180,000** • **CGC:** 1 graded, best 8.0
★ Appearance of Space Ranger.
72 ❑ Aug 1962 Cover: 0.12 **NM** value: **60.00**
Circ: Statement: **180,000**
★ Appearance of Space Ranger.
73 ❑ Oct 1962 Cover: 0.12 **NM** value: **60.00**
Circ: Statement: **180,000** • **CGC:** 2 graded, best 9.4
★ Appearance of Space Ranger.
74 ❑ Jan 1963 Cover: 0.12 **NM** value: **60.00**
• **CGC:** 2 graded, best 9.6
★ Appearance of Space Ranger.
75 ❑ Feb 1963 Cover: 0.12 **NM** value: **50.00**
• **CGC:** 1 graded, best 9.2
• Has 1962 Statement, filed 10/1/62; avg total paid circ 180,000★ Appearance of Space Ranger.
76 ❑ Apr 1963 Cover: 0.12 **NM** value: **50.00**
• **CGC:** 1 graded, best 9.4
★ Appearance of Space Ranger.
77 ❑ Jun 1963 Cover: 0.12 **NM** value: **50.00**
• **CGC:** 1 graded, best 9.4
★ Appearance of Space Ranger.
78 ❑ Aug 1963 Cover: 0.12 **NM** value: **50.00**
• **CGC:** 1 graded, best 9.8
★ Appearance of Space Ranger.
79 ❑ Oct 1963 Cover: 0.12 **NM** value: **50.00**
• **CGC:** 1 graded, best 9.4
★ Appearance of Space Ranger.
80 ❑ Dec 1963 Cover: 0.12 **NM** value: **50.00**
• **CGC:** 1 graded, best 9.6
★ Appearance of Space Ranger.
81 ❑ Feb 1964 Cover: 0.12 **NM** value: **50.00**
• **CGC:** 1 graded, best 9.6
• Has 1963 Statement, filed 10/1/63; no circ figures published★ Appearance of Space Ranger.
82 ❑ Apr 1964 Cover: 0.12 **NM** value: **50.00**
• **CGC:** 3 graded, best 9.6
★ Appearance of Space Ranger.
83 ❑ Jun 1964 Cover: 0.12 **NM** value: **30.00**
• **CGC:** 1 graded, best 9.6
84 ❑ Aug 1964 Cover: 0.12 **NM** value: **30.00**
85 ❑ Oct 1964 Cover: 0.12 **NM** value: **30.00**
86 ❑ Dec 1964 Cover: 0.12 **NM** value: **30.00**
87 ❑ Feb 1965 Cover: 0.12 **NM** value: **30.00**
88 ❑ Apr 1965 Cover: 0.12 **NM** value: **30.00**
• Has 1964 Statement, filed 10/1/64; no circ figures published
89 ❑ Jun 1965 Cover: 0.12 **NM** value: **30.00**
90 ❑ Aug 1965 Cover: 0.12 **NM** value: **30.00**
91 ❑ Oct 1965 Cover: 0.12 **NM** value: **22.00**
92 ❑ Dec 1965 Cover: 0.12 **NM** value: **22.00**
93 ❑ Feb 1966 Cover: 0.12 **NM** value: **22.00**
Circ: Statement: **185,650**
94 ❑ Apr 1966 Cover: 0.12 **NM** value: **22.00**
Circ: Statement: **185,650** • **CGC:** 1 graded, best 4.5
• Has 1965 Statement, filed 10/1/65; no circ figures published
95 ❑ Jun 1966 Cover: 0.12 **NM** value: **22.00**
Circ: Statement: **185,650** • **CGC:** 1 graded, best 9.2
96 ❑ Aug 1966 Cover: 0.12 **NM** value: **22.00**
Circ: Statement: **185,650**
97 ❑ Oct 1966 Cover: 0.12 **NM** value: **22.00**
Circ: Statement: **185,650** • **CGC:** 1 graded, best 7.5
📖 One Month to Die!; The Human Stallion; Automan vs. Mutant-Man! ★ Appearance of Automan.
98 ❑ Dec 1966 Cover: 0.12 **NM** value: **22.00**
Circ: Statement: **185,650**
99 ❑ Feb 1967 Cover: 0.12 **NM** value: **22.00**
Circ: Statement: **162,600** • **CGC:** 1 graded, best 9.0
• Has 1966 Statement, filed 10/1/66; avg print run 312,000; avg sales 185,000; avg subs 650; avg total paid 185,650; samples 265; max existent 185,915; 40% of run returned
100 ❑ Apr 1967 Cover: 0.12 **NM** value: **22.00**
Circ: Statement: **162,600**
101 ❑ Jun 1967 Cover: 0.12 **NM** value: **20.00**
Circ: Statement: **162,600** • **CGC:** 1 graded, best 9.0
102 ❑ Aug 1967 Cover: 0.12 **NM** value: **20.00**
Circ: Statement: **162,600**
103 ❑ Oct 1967 Cover: 0.12 **NM** value: **20.00**
Circ: Statement: **162,600**
104 ❑ Dec 1967 Cover: 0.12 **NM** value: **20.00**
Circ: Statement: **162,600**
• Series continues as The Unexpected

TALES OF THE WITCHBLADE — Image

0.5 ❑ Jun 1997 Cover: 2.95 **NM** value: **5.00**
• **CGC:** 4 graded, best 9.4
• Wizard promotional item
0.5/A❑Jun 1997 **NM** value: **10.00**
• Wizard "Certified Authentic" exclusive
0.5/GO❑Jun 1997 Cover: 2.95 **NM** value: **5.00**
• Wizard promotional item; gold logo
1 ❑ Nov 1996 Cover: 2.95 **NM** value: **4.00**
Circ: Diamd. preorders: **87,245** • **CGC:** 3 graded, best 9.8
📖 Anne Bonny **A:** Tony Daniel **W:** Christina Z.
1/A ❑ Nov 1996 Cover: 2.95 **NM** value: **5.00**
alternate cover. 📖 Anne Bonny • Green background with Witchblade front, arms behind back **A:** Tony Daniel; Michael Turner(cover) **W:** Christina Z.
1/B ❑ Nov 1996 Cover: 2.95 **NM** value: **Cover or less**
alternate cover (blue background with black panther).
1/GO❑Nov 1996 Cover: 2.95 **NM** value: **5.00**
• Gold edition.
1/PL❑Nov 1996 Cover: 2.95 **NM** value: **8.00**
• **CGC:** 3 graded, best 9.6
• Platinum edition.
2 ❑ Jun 1997 Cover: 2.95 **NM** value: **3.00**
Circ: Diamd. preorders: **76,827**
📖 Annabella Altavista **A:** David Finch; Billy Tan **W:** David Finch; Christina Z.; David Wohl
3 ❑ Oct 1997 Cover: 2.95 **NM** value: **3.00**
Circ: Diamd. preorders: **74,293**
4 ❑ Jan 1998 Cover: 2.95 **NM** value: **Cover or less**
Circ: Diamd. preorders: **66,292**
📖 Selena **A:** Billy Tan **W:** Warren Ellis
5 ❑ May 1998 Cover: 2.95 **NM** value: **Cover or less**
Circ: Diamd. preorders: **61,195**
📖 Maitea **A:** Richard Bennett **W:** Christina Z.; David Wohl
6 ❑ Sep 1998 Cover: 2.95 **NM** value: **Cover or less**
Circ: Diamd. preorders: **51,960**
📖 Samantha **A:** Clarence Lansang; Dan Fraga; Cedric Nocon; Randy Green; Billy Tan **W:** David Finch
7/A ❑ Jun 1999 Cover: 2.95 **NM** value: **Cover or less**
Circ: Diamd. preorders: **45,464**
Woman turning around, eyes in background on cover. 📖 Raquel **A:** Clarence Lansang; Christian Zanier; Keu Cha **W:** Michael Turner; Bill O'Neil
7/B ❑ Jun 1999 Cover: 2.95 **NM** value: **Cover or less**
Alternate cover (woman standing before pyramid). 📖 Raquel **A:** Clarence Lansang; Christian Zanier; Keu Cha **W:** Michael Turner; Bill O'Neil
8 ❑ Oct 1999 Cover: 2.95 **NM** value: **Cover or less**
Circ: Diamd. preorders: **34,397**
A: Christian Zanier **W:** Michael Turner; Bill O'Neil
9 ❑ Jan 2001 Cover: 2.95 **NM** value: **Cover or less**
Circ: Diamd. preorders: **25,379**
📖 Raquel **A:** David Boller; Brian Denham **W:** Bill O'Neill
Bk 1❑ May 1998 Cover: 4.95 **NM** value: **Cover or less**
Circ: Diamd. preorders: **10,741**
• prestige format. 📖 Anne Bonney, Annabella Altavista • collects issues #1 and 2 **A:** Clarence Lansang; Dan Fraga; Cedric Nocon; Randy Green; Billy Tan **W:** David Finch; Christina Z.; David Wohl
Bk 2❑ Nov 1999 Cover: 5.95 **NM** value: **Cover or less**
Circ: Diamd. preorders: **5,288**
📖 Selena, Maitea **A:** Billy Tan; Richard Bennett **W:** Warren Ellis; Christina Z; David Wohl

TALES OF THE ZOMBIE — Marvel

1 ❑ Aug 1973, b&w Cover: 0.75 **NM** value: **8.00**
• magazine. ★ Origin of Zombie.
2 ❑ Oct 1973 Cover: 0.75 **NM** value: **5.00**
3 ❑ Jan 1974 Cover: 0.75 **NM** value: **4.00**
4 ❑ Mar 1974 Cover: 0.75 **NM** value: **4.00**
5 ❑ May 1974 Cover: 0.75 **NM** value: **4.00**
6 ❑ Jul 1974 Cover: 0.75 **NM** value: **4.00**
7 ❑ Sep 1974 Cover: 0.75 **NM** value: **4.00**
8 ❑ Nov 1974 Cover: 0.75 **NM** value: **4.00**
9 ❑ Jan 1975 Cover: 0.75 **NM** value: **4.00**
10 ❑ Mar 1975 Cover: 0.75 **NM** value: **4.00**
Anl 1❑ Cover: 1.25 **NM** value: **4.00**

TALE SPIN — Disney

1 ❑ Jun 1991 Cover: 1.50 **NM** value: **Cover or less**
Circ: CapCity orders: **5,800**
2 ❑ Jul 1991 Cover: 1.50 **NM** value: **Cover or less**
Circ: CapCity orders: **4,900**
3 ❑ Aug 1991 Cover: 1.50 **NM** value: **Cover or less**
Circ: CapCity orders: **4,750**
4 ❑ Sep 1991 Cover: 1.50 **NM** value: **Cover or less**
Circ: CapCity orders: **4,500**
5 ❑ Oct 1991 Cover: 1.50 **NM** value: **Cover or less**
6 ❑ Nov 1991 Cover: 1.50 **NM** value: **Cover or less**
Circ: CapCity orders: **4,500**
7 ❑ Jan 1991 Cover: 1.50 **NM** value: **Cover or less**
Circ: CapCity orders: **4,000**

TALE SPIN LIMITED SERIES — Disney

1 ❑ Jan 1991 Cover: 1.50 **NM** value: **Cover or less**
Circ: CapCity orders: **6,250**
📖 Take Off, Part 1 **A:** Bat; Sal Quartieri; Valenti **W:** Bobbi J.G. Weiss
2 ❑ Feb 1991 Cover: 1.50 **NM** value: **Cover or less**
Circ: CapCity orders: **4,850**
📖 Take Off, Part 2 **A:** Bat; Sal Quartieri; Valenti **W:** Bobbi J.G. Weiss
3 ❑ Mar 1991 Cover: 1.50 **NM** value: **Cover or less**
Circ: CapCity orders: **4,650**
📖 Take Off, Part 3 **A:** Bat; Sal Quartieri; Valenti **W:** Bobbi J.G. Weiss
4 ❑ Apr 1991 Cover: 1.50 **NM** value: **Cover or less**
Circ: CapCity orders: **4,600**
📖 Take Off, Part 4 **A:** Bat; Sal Quartieri; Valenti **W:** Bobbi J.G. Weiss

TALESPIN (ONE-SHOT) — Disney

1 ❑ Cover: 3.50 **NM** value: **Cover or less**
No issue number. • Sky-Raker

There are two different pricing tiers in the modern comic-book hobby. **The prices seen above** are the prices we have seen **loose copies** of these issues reliably fetch in a variety of environments. Condition alters the price by the fractions seen on the bar on the bottom of left-hand pages of this book. **Comics graded by CGC** usually sell for more. Use the guide on the bottom of right-hand pages of this book to estimate what copies have brought on eBay.

Other grades: Multiply prices above by **1.5 for Mint • 2/3 for Very Fine • 1/3 for Fine • 1/5 for Very Good • 1/8 for Good**

TALES TO ASTONISH (VOL. 1) — Marvel

Like Strange Tales and Tales of Suspense, this title was one of the great breeding grounds for today's Marvel super-heroes. Formerly a horror/science-fiction title, it introduced Hank Pym, a.k.a. Antman, in issue #27. Antman, who could shrink to ant size at will and control his insect contemporaries through a special helmet, would later become a member of the Avengers. He would be joined in issue #44 by his future wife, Janet Van Dyne, the Wasp.

Beginning in issue #60, these new super-heroes would be displaced by Marvel's new sensation, a green goliath known as the Incredible Hulk. Ten issues later, the title would switch to a Hulk/Sub-Mariner double-feature. This would last until Hulk took over the series; it became Incredible Hulk with #102. Subby's storyline moved to Iron Man and Sub-Mariner and then to Sub-Mariner Vol. 2, which itself was reprinted much later in Tales to Astonish Vol. 2., after which these two characters would both move to their own titles.

1 ❑ Jan 1959 Cover: 0.10 **NM** value: **1500.00**
• **CGC:** 7 graded, best 5.5

2 ❑ Mar 1959 Cover: 0.10 **NM** value: **565.00**
• **CGC:** 2 graded, best 9.2

3 ❑ May 1959 Cover: 0.10 **NM** value: **390.00**
• **CGC:** 2 graded, best 7.0

4 ❑ Jul 1959 Cover: 0.10 **NM** value: **390.00**
• **CGC:** 2 graded, best 7.0

5 ❑ Sep 1959 Cover: 0.10 **NM** value: **390.00**
• **CGC:** 2 graded, best 7.0

6 ❑ Nov 1959 Cover: 0.10 **NM** value: **315.00**
• **CGC:** 1 graded, best 7.0

7 ❑ Jan 1960 Cover: 0.10 **NM** value: **315.00**
Circ: Statement: **163,156** • **CGC:** 2 graded, best 4.5

8 ❑ Mar 1960 Cover: 0.10 **NM** value: **315.00**
Circ: Statement: **163,156** • **CGC:** 4 graded, best 6.0

9 ❑ May 1960 Cover: 0.10 **NM** value: **315.00**
Circ: Statement: **163,156** • **CGC:** 3 graded, best 8.0

10 ❑ Jul 1960 Cover: 0.10 **NM** value: **315.00**
Circ: Statement: **163,156** • **CGC:** 1 graded, best 5.5

11 ❑ Sep 1960 Cover: 0.10 **NM** value: **235.00**
Circ: Statement: **163,156** • **CGC:** 2 graded, best 5.0

12 ❑ Oct 1960 Cover: 0.10 **NM** value: **235.00**
Circ: Statement: **163,156** • **CGC:** 4 graded, best 8.5

13 ❑ Nov 1960 Cover: 0.10 **NM** value: **235.00**
Circ: Statement: **163,156** • **CGC:** 2 graded, best 9.2

14 ❑ Dec 1960 Cover: 0.10 **NM** value: **235.00**
Circ: Statement: **163,156** • **CGC:** 5 graded, best 9.2

15 ❑ Jan 1961 Cover: 0.10 **NM** value: **235.00**
Circ: Statement: **184,895** • **CGC:** 4 graded, best 8.0

16 ❑ Feb 1961 Cover: 0.10 **NM** value: **235.00**
Circ: Statement: **184,895** • **CGC:** 6 graded, best 9.2

17 ❑ Mar 1961 Cover: 0.10 **NM** value: **235.00**
Circ: Statement: **184,895** • **CGC:** 4 graded, best 7.5

18 ❑ Apr 1961 Cover: 0.10 **NM** value: **235.00**
Circ: Statement: **184,895** • **CGC:** 3 graded, best 7.0

19 ❑ May 1961 Cover: 0.10 **NM** value: **235.00**
Circ: Statement: **184,895** • **CGC:** 1 graded, best 5.0

20 ❑ Jun 1961 Cover: 0.10 **NM** value: **235.00**
Circ: Statement: **184,895** • **CGC:** 1 graded, best 7.5

21 ❑ Jul 1961 Cover: 0.10 **NM** value: **175.00**
Circ: Statement: **184,895** • **CGC:** 1 graded, best 8.5
A: Jack Kirby

22 ❑ Aug 1961 Cover: 0.10 **NM** value: **175.00**
Circ: Statement: **184,895** • **CGC:** 2 graded, best 5.0

23 ❑ Sep 1961 Cover: 0.10 **NM** value: **175.00**
Circ: Statement: **184,895** • **CGC:** 3 graded, best 7.0

24 ❑ Oct 1961 Cover: 0.10 **NM** value: **175.00**
Circ: Statement: **184,895** • **CGC:** 2 graded, best 7.5

25 ❑ Nov 1961 Cover: 0.10 **NM** value: **175.00**
Circ: Statement: **184,895** • **CGC:** 2 graded, best 5.5

26 ❑ Dec 1961 Cover: 0.10 **NM** value: **175.00**
Circ: Statement: **184,895** • **CGC:** 2 graded, best 6.5

27 ❑ Jan 1962 Cover: 0.10 **NM** value: **3000.00**
Circ: Statement: **139,167** • **CGC:** 40 graded, best 9.2
A: Steve Ditko; Jack Kirby ★ 1st Appearance of Ant-Man (out of costume), Hijacker.

28 ❑ Feb 1962 Cover: 0.12 **NM** value: **150.00**
Circ: Statement: **139,167** • **CGC:** 2 graded, best 9.2
A: Steve Ditko; Jack Kirby

29 ❑ Mar 1962 Cover: 0.12 **NM** value: **150.00**
Circ: Statement: **139,167** • **CGC:** 1 graded, best 4.0
A: Steve Ditko; Jack Kirby

30 ❑ Apr 1962 Cover: 0.12 **NM** value: **150.00**
Circ: Statement: **139,167** • **CGC:** 4 graded, best 8.0
A: Steve Ditko; Jack Kirby

31 ❑ May 1962 Cover: 0.12 **NM** value: **150.00**
Circ: Statement: **139,167** • **CGC:** 3 graded, best 9.0
A: Steve Ditko; Jack Kirby

32 ❑ Jun 1962 Cover: 0.12 **NM** value: **150.00**
Circ: Statement: **139,167**
A: Steve Ditko; Jack Kirby

33 ❑ Jul 1962 Cover: 0.12 **NM** value: **150.00**
Circ: Statement: **139,167** • **CGC:** 3 graded, best 8.0
A: Steve Ditko; Jack Kirby

34 ❑ Aug 1962 Cover: 0.12 **NM** value: **150.00**
Circ: Statement: **139,167** • **CGC:** 5 graded, best 8.5
A: Steve Ditko; Jack Kirby

35 ❑ Sep 1962 Cover: 0.12 **NM** value: **1450.00**
Circ: Statement: **139,167** • **CGC:** 36 graded, best 9.6
📖 Return of the Ant-Man; The Doorway to Nowhere; The Thing from Outer Space; Strange Encounter (text) **A:** Steve Ditko; Jack Kirby ★ 1st Appearance of Ant-Man (in costume). ★ 2nd Appearance of Ant-Man.

36 ❑ Oct 1962 Cover: 0.12 **NM** value: **550.00**
Circ: Statement: **139,167** • **CGC:** 17 graded, best 9.6
📖 The Challenge of Comrade X; The Hands of Time; The Search for Pan; From Outer Space (text) **A:** Steve Ditko; Jack Kirby

37 ❑ Nov 1962 Cover: 0.12 **NM** value: **310.00**
Circ: Statement: **139,167** • **CGC:** 21 graded, best 9.6
📖 Trapped by the Protector; Afraid to Dream; The Star Raiders; The Magician (text) **A:** Steve Ditko; Jack Kirby

38 ❑ Dec 1962 Cover: 0.12 **NM** value: **310.00**
Circ: Statement: **139,167** • **CGC:** 16 graded, best 9.6
📖 Betrayed by the Ants; I Found the Impossible World; Secret of the Statues; Strange Mission (text) ★ 1st Appearance of Egghead.

39 ❑ Jan 1963 Cover: 0.12 **NM** value: **310.00**
Circ: Statement: **189,390** • **CGC:** 16 graded, best 9.6
📖 The Vengeance of the Scarlet Beetle; Ozamm the Terrible; The Toy Soldiers; The Remedy Oil (text)

40 ❑ Feb 1963 Cover: 0.12 **NM** value: **310.00**
Circ: Statement: **189,390** • **CGC:** 11 graded, best 9.6
📖 The Day that Ant-Man Failed; I Was Trapped in the Mad Universe; The Worst Man on Earth; Bird Talk (text)

41 ❑ Mar 1963 Cover: 0.12 **NM** value: **200.00**
Circ: Statement: **189,390** • **CGC:** 12 graded, best 9.4
📖 Prisoner of the Slave World; When the Beast Walks; The Curse; Tricky Travel (text) **A:** Steve Ditko; Don Heck

42 ❑ Apr 1963 Cover: 0.12 **NM** value: **200.00**
Circ: Statement: **189,390** • **CGC:** 10 graded, best 9.6
📖 The Voice of Doom; The Eye of the Mummy; I Am Not Human; Secret Mission (text) **A:** Steve Ditko; Don Heck ★ Origin of The Voice. ★ 1st Appearance of The Voice.

43 ❑ May 1963 Cover: 0.12 **NM** value: **200.00**
Circ: Statement: **189,390** • **CGC:** 5 graded, best 9.4
📖 The Mad Master of Time; Frankie's Fast Ball; My Fatal Mistake; Lady Luck (text) **A:** Steve Ditko; Don Heck

44 ❑ Jun 1963 Cover: 0.12 **NM** value: **250.00**
Circ: Statement: **189,390** • **CGC:** 21 graded, best 9.4
📖 The Creature from Kosmos; Hunted; Blueprint for Victory (text) **A:** Steve Ditko; Jack Kirby ★ Origin of Wasp. ★ 1st Appearance of Wasp.

45 ❑ Jul 1963 Cover: 0.12 **NM** value: **125.00**
Circ: Statement: **189,390** • **CGC:** 9 graded, best 9.6
📖 The Terrible Traps of Egghead; Bronson's Brain; It Walks Like a Man; The Future (text) **A:** Steve Ditko; Don Heck

46 ❑ Aug 1963 Cover: 0.12 **NM** value: **125.00**
Circ: Statement: **189,390** • **CGC:** 7 graded, best 9.4
📖 When Cyclops Walks the Earth; The Secret of the Swamp; The Most Dangerous Weapon; Ride to the Future (text) **A:** Steve Ditko; Don Heck

47 ❑ Sep 1963 Cover: 0.12 **NM** value: **125.00**
Circ: Statement: **189,390** • **CGC:** 14 graded, best 9.6
📖 Music to Scream By; The Smiling Gods; Target: Earth; The Disappearance (text) **A:** Steve Ditko; Don Heck

48 ❑ Oct 1963 Cover: 0.12 **NM** value: **125.00**
Circ: Statement: **189,390** • **CGC:** 11 graded, best 9.6
📖 Ant-Man and the Wasp Defy the Porcupine; Grayson's Gorilla; The Little Green Man; The Inventor (text) **A:** Steve Ditko; Don Heck ★ Origin of Porcupine. ★ 1st Appearance of Porcupine.

49 ❑ Nov 1963 Cover: 0.12 **NM** value: **175.00**
Circ: Statement: **189,390** • **CGC:** 16 graded, best 9.6
📖 The Birth of Giant-Man; The End of a World; Odd Skulls (text) • Ant-Man becomes Giant Man **A:** Don Heck; Jack Kirby ★ 1st Appearance of Giant Man.

50 ❑ Dec 1963 Cover: 0.12 **NM** value: **85.00**
Circ: Statement: **189,390** • **CGC:** 8 graded, best 9.4
📖 The Human Top; The Secret of Sagittus; No Ending; Mystery Trip (text) **A:** Steve Ditko; Jack Kirby ★ Origin of Human Top (later becomes Whirlwind). ★ 1st Appearance of Human Top (later becomes Whirlwind).

51 ❑ Jan 1964 Cover: 0.12 **NM** value: **85.00**
Circ: Statement: **207,365** • **CGC:** 9 graded, best 9.4
📖 Showdown with the Human Top; No Place to Turn; Somewhere Waits a Wobbow; The Sorcerer (text) **A:** Jack Kirby

52 ❑ Feb 1964 Cover: 0.12 **NM** value: **85.00**
Circ: Statement: **207,365** • **CGC:** 12 graded, best 9.4
📖 The Black Knight Strikes; Not What They Seem ★ Origin of Black Knight II (Nathan Garrett).

53 ❑ Mar 1964 Cover: 0.12 **NM** value: **85.00**
Circ: Statement: **207,365** • **CGC:** 10 graded, best 9.6
📖 Trapped by the Porcupine; When Wakes the Colossus; The Clock (text)

54 ❑ Apr 1964 Cover: 0.12 **NM** value: **85.00**
Circ: Statement: **207,365** • **CGC:** 6 graded, best 9.6
📖 No Place to Hide; There Were Five Frightened Men; The Treasure, Part 1 (text) • Has 1963 Statement, filed 10/1/63; avg print run 321,646; avg sales 189,270; avg subs 120; avg total paid 189,390; samples 175; max existent 189,465; 41% of run returned

55 ❑ May 1964 Cover: 0.12 **NM** value: **85.00**
Circ: Statement: **207,365** • **CGC:** 12 graded, best 9.6
📖 On the Trail of the Human Top; The Gypsy's Secret; The Treasure, Part 2 (text)

56 ❑ Jun 1964 Cover: 0.12 **NM** value: **85.00**
Circ: Statement: **207,365** • **CGC:** 8 graded, best 9.6
📖 The Coming of the Magician; Beware the Bog Beast ★ Versus Magician.

57 ❑ Jul 1964 Cover: 0.12 **NM** value: **110.00**
Circ: Statement: **207,365** • **CGC:** 28 graded, best 9.6
📖 On the Trail of the Amazing Spider-Man; A Voice in the Dark ★ Appearance of Spider-Man.

58 ❑ Aug 1964 Cover: 0.12 **NM** value: **85.00**
Circ: Statement: **207,365** • **CGC:** 3 graded, best 9.4
📖 The Coming of Colossus; The Magician and the Maiden

59 ❑ Sep 1964 Cover: 0.12 **NM** value: **125.00**
Circ: Statement: **207,365** • **CGC:** 26 graded, best 9.4
📖 Enter: The Hulk; Let's Learn About Hank and Jan • Giant-Man vs. Hulk

60 ❑ Oct 1964 Cover: 0.12 **NM** value: **150.00**
Circ: Statement: **207,365** • **CGC:** 25 graded, best 9.6
📖 The Beasts of Berlin; The Incredible Hulk • Giant Man/Hulk double feature begins

61 ❑ Nov 1964 Cover: 0.12 **NM** value: **56.00**
Circ: Statement: **207,365** • **CGC:** 5 graded, best 9.6
📖 Now Walks the Android; Captured at Last

62 ❑ Dec 1964 Cover: 0.12 **NM** value: **56.00**
Circ: Statement: **207,365** • **CGC:** 10 graded, best 9.4
📖 Giant-Man versus the Wonderful Wasp; Enter the Chameleon ★ 1st Appearance of The Leader.

63 ❑ Jan 1965 Cover: 0.12 **NM** value: **56.00**
Circ: Statement: **224,346** • **CGC:** 12 graded, best 9.6
📖 The Gangsters and the Giant; A Titan Rides the Train ★ Origin of The Leader. ★ 1st Appearance of The Wrecker II.

64 ❑ Feb 1965 Cover: 0.12 **NM** value: **56.00**
Circ: Statement: **224,346** • **CGC:** 6 graded, best 9.6
📖 When Attuma Strikes; The Horde of Humanoids

65 ❑ Mar 1965 Cover: 0.12 **NM** value: **56.00**
Circ: Statement: **224,346** • **CGC:** 19 graded, best 9.4
📖 The New Giant-Man; On the Rampage Against the Reds • Giant-Man's new costume

66 ❑ Apr 1965 Cover: 0.12 **NM** value: **56.00**
Circ: Statement: **224,346** • **CGC:** 8 graded, best 9.4
📖 The Menace of Madam Macabre; The Power of Doctor Banner • Has 1964 Statement, filed 10/1/64; avg print run 312,900; avg sales 207,100; avg subs 265; avg total paid 207,365; samples 125; max existent 207,490; 34% of run returned

67 ❑ May 1965 Cover: 0.12 **NM** value: **56.00**
Circ: Statement: **224,346** • **CGC:** 9 graded, best 9.4
📖 The Hidden Man and His Rays of Doom; Where Strides the Behemoth

68 ❑ Jun 1965 Cover: 0.12 **NM** value: **56.00**
Circ: Statement: **224,346** • **CGC:** 12 graded, best 9.4
📖 Peril from the Long-Dead Past; Back from the Dead ★ Versus Leader.

69 ❑ Jul 1965 Cover: 0.12 **NM** value: **56.00**
Circ: Statement: **224,346** • **CGC:** 6 graded, best 9.6
📖 Oh, Wasp, Where is Thy Sting; Trapped in the Lair of the Leader • Giant Man feature ends

70 ❑ Aug 1965 Cover: 0.12 **NM** value: **85.00**
Circ: Statement: **224,346** • **CGC:** 14 graded, best 9.6
📖 The Start of the Quest; To Live Again • Sub-Mariner begins

71 ❑ Sep 1965 Cover: 0.12 **NM** value: **44.00**
Circ: Statement: **224,346** • **CGC:** 4 graded, best 9.6
📖 Escape to Nowhere; Like a Beast at Bay ★ 1st Appearance of Vashti.

72 ❑ Oct 1965 Cover: 0.12 **NM** value: **44.00**
Circ: Statement: **224,346** • **CGC:** 3 graded, best 9.6
📖 A Prince There Was; Within the Monster Dwells a Man

73 ❑ Nov 1965 Cover: 0.12 **NM** value: **44.00**
Circ: Statement: **224,346** • **CGC:** 5 graded, best 9.4
📖 By Force of Arms; Another World, Another Foe

74 ❑ Dec 1965 Cover: 0.12 **NM** value: **44.00**
Circ: Statement: **224,346** • **CGC:** 10 graded, best 9.6
📖 When Fails the Quest!; The Wisdom of the Watcher

75 ❑ Jan 1966 Cover: 0.12 **NM** value: **44.00**
Circ: Statement: **256,145** • **CGC:** 10 graded, best 9.6
📖 The End of the Quest; Not All My Power Can Save Me ★ 1st Appearance of Behemoth.

76 ❑ Feb 1966 Cover: 0.12 **NM** value: **44.00**
Circ: Statement: **256,145** • **CGC:** 7 graded, best 9.9
📖 Uneasy Hangs the Head; I, Against a World

77 ❑ Mar 1966 Cover: 0.12 **NM** value: **44.00**
Circ: Statement: **256,145** • **CGC:** 7 graded, best 9.8
📖 To Walk Amongst Men; Bruce Banner is the Hulk • Banner revealed as Hulk

78 ❑ Apr 1966 Cover: 0.12 **NM** value: **44.00**
Circ: Statement: **256,145** • **CGC:** 7 graded, best 9.4
📖 The Prince and the Puppet; The Hulk Must Die • Has 1965 Statement, filed 10/1/65; avg print run 368,525; avg sales 223,866; avg subs 480; avg total paid 224,346; samples 60; max existent 224,406; 39% of run returned

79 ❑ May 1966 Cover: 0.12 **NM** value: **44.00**
Circ: Statement: **256,145** • **CGC:** 15 graded, best 9.8
📖 When Rises the Behemoth; The Titan and the Torment

80 ❑ Jun 1966 Cover: 0.12 **NM** value: **44.00**
Circ: Statement: **256,145** • **CGC:** 5 graded, best 9.4
📖 To the Death; They Dwell in the Depths **A:** Gene Colan; Jack Kirby

81 ❑ Jul 1966 Cover: 0.12 **NM** value: **44.00**
Circ: Statement: **256,145** • **CGC:** 10 graded, best 9.4
📖 When a Monarch Goes Mad; The Stage is Set **A:** Gene Colan; Jack Kirby ★ 1st Appearance of Boomerang.

82 ❑ Aug 1966 Cover: 0.12 **NM** value: **65.00**
Circ: Statement: **256,145** • **CGC:** 13 graded, best 9.6
📖 The Power of Iron Man!; The Battle-Cry of the Boomerang! • Iron Man vs. Sub-Mariner; Hulk **A:** Gene Colan; Jack Kirby

83 ❑ Sep 1966 Cover: 0.12 **NM** value: **44.00**
Circ: Statement: **256,145** • **CGC:** 17 graded, best 9.4
📖 The Sub-Mariner Strikes!; Less Than Monster, More Than Man • Sub-Mariner, Hulk

84 ❑ Oct 1966 Cover: 0.12 **NM** value: **44.00**
Circ: Statement: **256,145** • **CGC:** 17 graded, best 9.8
📖 Like a Beast at Bay; Rampage in the City

85 ❑ Nov 1966 Cover: 0.12 **NM** value: **44.00**
Circ: Statement: **256,145** • **CGC:** 16 graded, best 9.6
📖 And One Shall Die; The Missile and the Monster

86 ❑ Dec 1966 Cover: 0.12 **NM** value: **44.00**
Circ: Statement: **256,145** • **CGC:** 18 graded, best 9.8
📖 The Wrath of Warlord Krang; The Birth of the Hulk-Killer

87 ❑ Jan 1967 Cover: 0.12 **NM** value: **44.00**
Circ: Statement: **269,132** • **CGC:** 15 graded, best 9.6
📖 Moment of Truth; The Humanoid and the Hero

88 ❑ Feb 1967 Cover: 0.12 **NM** value: **44.00**
Circ: Statement: **269,132** • **CGC:** 8 graded, best 9.6
📖 A Stranger Strikes from Space; Boomerang and the Brute

89 ❑ Mar 1967 Cover: 0.12 **NM** value: **44.00**
Circ: Statement: **269,132** • **CGC:** 13 graded, best 9.6
📖 The Prince of Power; Then, There Shall Come a Stranger

CGC-graded: Multiply prices above by **33 for 9.9 M** • **16 for 9.8 NM/M** • **7 for 9.6 NM+** • **5 for 9.4 NM** • **2.5 for 9.2 NM-** • **1.5 for 9.0 VF/NM**

90 ❑ Apr 1967 Cover: 0.12 **NM** value: **44.00**
Circ: Statement: **269,132 • CGC:** 9 graded, best 9.6
📖 To Be Beaten By Byrrah; The Abomination • Has 1966 Statement, filed 10/1/66; avg print run 404,314; avg sales 255,045; avg subs 100; avg total paid 256,145; samples 60; max existent 255,205; 37% of run returned ★ 1st Appearance of The Abomination, Byrrah.

91 ❑ May 1967 Cover: 0.12 **NM** value: **42.00**
Circ: Statement: **269,132 • CGC:** 19 graded, best 9.6
📖 Outside the Gates Waits Death; Whosoever Harms the Hulk • Sub-Mariner story continues in Avengers #40

92 ❑ Jun 1967 Cover: 0.12 **NM** value: **55.00**
Circ: Statement: **269,132 • CGC:** 10 graded, best 9.8
📖 It Walks Like a Man; Turning Point • Sub-Mariner story continued from Avengers #40 ★ Appearance of Silver Surfer.

93 ❑ Jul 1967 Cover: 0.12 **NM** value: **55.00**
Circ: Statement: **269,132 • CGC:** 23 graded, best 9.6
📖 The Monarch and the Monster; He Who Strikes the Silver Surfer ★ Appearance of Silver Surfer.

94 ❑ Aug 1967 Cover: 0.12 **NM** value: **42.00**
Circ: Statement: **269,132 • CGC:** 11 graded, best 9.8
📖 Hepless at the Hands of Dragorr; To the Beckoning Stars • Hulk story continues from Thor #135

95 ❑ Sep 1967 Cover: 0.12 **NM** value: **42.00**
Circ: Statement: **269,132 • CGC:** 12 graded, best 9.6
📖 The Power of the Plunderer; A World He Never Made • Sub-Mariner story continues from Daredevil #24

96 ❑ Oct 1967 Cover: 0.12 **NM** value: **42.00**
Circ: Statement: **269,132 • CGC:** 11 graded, best 9.6
📖 Somewhere Stands Skull Island; What Have I Created?

97 ❑ Nov 1967 Cover: 0.12 **NM** value: **42.00**
Circ: Statement: **269,132 • CGC:** 10 graded, best 9.6
📖 The Sovereign and the Savages; The Legions of the Living Lightning

98 ❑ Dec 1967 Cover: 0.12 **NM** value: **42.00**
Circ: Statement: **269,132 • CGC:** 12 graded, best 9.8
📖 To Destroy the Realm Eternal; The Puppet and the Power ★ 1st Appearance of Seth (Namor's advisor).

99 ❑ Jan 1968 Cover: 0.12 **NM** value: **42.00**
Circ: Statement: **277,857 • CGC:** 12 graded, best 9.6
📖 When the Monster Wakes; When Falls the Holocaust

100 ❑ Feb 1968 Cover: 0.12 **NM** value: **58.00**
Circ: Statement: **277,857 • CGC:** 27 graded, best 9.8
📖 Let there Be Battle • Hulk vs. Sub-Mariner

101 ❑ Mar 1968 Cover: 0.12 **NM** value: **75.00**
Circ: Statement: **277,857 • CGC:** 24 graded, best 9.6
📖 Where Walk the Immortals; And Evil Shall Beckon • Hulk feature continued in Incredible Hulk #102; Sub-Mariner feature continued in Iron Man & Sub-Mariner #1

TALES TO ASTONISH (VOL. 2) — Marvel

1 ❑ Dec 1979 Cover: 0.40 **NM** value: **2.00**
• **CGC:** 1 graded, best 9.6
A: John Buscema

2 ❑ Jan 1980 Cover: 0.40 **NM** value: **1.50**
• **CGC:** 1 graded, best 5.0
A: John Buscema

3 ❑ Feb 1980 Cover: 0.40 **NM** value: **1.50**
A: John Buscema

4 ❑ Mar 1980 Cover: 0.40 **NM** value: **1.50**
A: John Buscema

5 ❑ Apr 1980 Cover: 0.40 **NM** value: **1.50**
A: John Buscema

6 ❑ May 1980 Cover: 0.40 **NM** value: **1.50**
A: John Buscema

7 ❑ Jun 1980 Cover: 0.40 **NM** value: **1.50**
A: John Buscema

8 ❑ Jul 1980 Cover: 0.40 **NM** value: **1.50**
A: John Buscema

9 ❑ Aug 1980 Cover: 0.40 **NM** value: **1.50**
A: John Buscema

10 ❑ Sep 1980 Cover: 0.40 **NM** value: **1.50**
A: John Buscema

11 ❑ Oct 1980 Cover: 0.40 **NM** value: **1.50**
A: John Buscema

12 ❑ Nov 1980 Cover: 0.40 **NM** value: **1.50**
A: John Buscema

13 ❑ Dec 1980 Cover: 0.50 **NM** value: **1.50**
A: John Buscema

14 ❑ Jan 1981 Cover: 0.50 **NM** value: **1.50**
A: John Buscema

TALES TO ASTONISH (VOL. 3) — Marvel

1 ❑ Dec 1994 Cover: 6.95 **NM** value: **Cover or less**
Circ: CapCity orders: **33,850 • CGC:** 5 graded, best 9.9
acetate outer cover. 📖 Loki's Dream • prestige format one-shot **A:** John Estes **W:** Peter David

TALES TO OFFEND — Dark Horse

1 ❑ Jul 1997 Cover: 2.95 **NM** value: **Cover or less**
Circ: Diamd. preorders: **29,932**
📖 Lance Blastoff; Daddy's Little Girl; America's Favorite Hero! • Lance Blastoff **A:** Frank Miller **W:** Frank Miller

TALES TOO TERRIBLE TO TELL — NEC

1 ❑ b&w Cover: 2.95 **NM** value: **Cover or less**
📖 Vampire; Clumsy; Insane; The House in the Sky (text Story); Wall of Coahuila; Terrology; Purple Claw; Fit to Die; Hunger; Henpecked; The Tick: I Had a Bad Day; That Terrible, Terrible Sound • Reprints from Mister Mystery #13, Weird Chills #1, Weird Chills #3, Mister Mystery #16, Purple Claw #1, Strange Mysteries #7, Mister Mystery #17 **A:** Ben Edlund **C:** Stephen R. Bissette **W:** Ben Edlund; E. Hughes; Gerald Altman; Iger Studios

1-2 ❑ May 1993 Cover: 3.50 **NM** value: **Cover or less**
2nd printing with new cover. 📖 Horror of Mixed Torsos! • Reprints from Mister Mystery #13, Weird Chills #1, Weird Chills #3, Mister Mystery #16, Purple Claw #1, Strange Mysteries #7, Mister Mystery #17 **A:** Ben Edlund **W:** Ben Edlund; Gerald Altman

2 ❑ Mar 1991, b&w Cover: 3.50 **NM** value: **Cover or less**
📖 Head of Horror; The Door; No Rest for the Dead; Colorama; The Sunken Grave; The Curse of the Zamboori!; The Man Who Came to Dinner; • Reprints from Strange Mysteries #6, Weird Mysteries #11, Unseen #14, Black Cat Mystery #45, Journey into Fear #5, Ghoul Tales #3, Dark Mysteries #13

3 ❑ Jun 1991, b&w Cover: 3.50 **NM** value: **Cover or less**
📖 Voice of Doom; The Disguise; The Hatchet Man; Eternal Death; Hallucinations!; Monster in a Maze; Night People; Death Kiss • Reprints from Weird Chills #3, Weird Mysteries #10, Weird Chills #1, Adventures into Darkness #13, Horrific #5

4 ❑ Dec 1991, b&w Cover: 3.50 **NM** value: **Cover or less**
📖 The Gossips!; Fiends From the Crypt; Monsters of the Deep; No Rest for the Dead; Hollow Horror; The Devil is a Dame!; Black Death; Rack of Terror! • Reprints from Mister Mystery #13, Fantastic Fears #8, Unseen #14, Journey into Fear #12, Fantastic Fears #6, Purple Claw #1, Fantastic Fears #4, Dark Mysteries #19 **A:** Steve Ditko(cover)

5 ❑ 1992b&w Cover: 3.50 **NM** value: **Cover or less**
6 ❑ 1992b&w Cover: 3.50 **NM** value: **Cover or less**
7 ❑ 1992b&w Cover: 3.50 **NM** value: **Cover or less**

TALISMEN: SCSI VOODOO — Blink

1 ❑ Cover: 2.75 **NM** value: **Cover or less**
2 ❑ Cover: 2.75 **NM** value: **Cover or less**
3 ❑ Cover: 2.75 **NM** value: **Cover or less**

TALK DIRTY — Fantagraphics / Eros

All issues are adults only.

1 ❑ b&w Cover: 2.50 **NM** value: **Cover or less**
2 ❑ b&w Cover: 2.50 **NM** value: **Cover or less**
3 ❑ b&w Cover: 2.95 **NM** value: **Cover or less**

TALKING ORANGUTANS IN BORNEO — GT-Labs

1 ❑ ca. 1999, b&w Cover: 3.50 **NM** value: **Cover or less**
No issue number. • efforts to educate orangutans to communicate via sign language

TALL TAILS — Golden Realm

1 ❑ b&w Cover: 1.50 **NM** value: **2.00**
2 ❑ Cover: 1.50 **NM** value: **2.00**
📖 Firequest **A:** Daphne Lage **W:** Jose Calderon
3 ❑ Cover: 2.95 **NM** value: **Cover or less**
4 ❑ Cover: 2.95 **NM** value: **Cover or less**
5 ❑ Cover: 2.95 **NM** value: **Cover or less**
6 ❑ Cover: 2.95 **NM** value: **Cover or less**
7 ❑ Cover: 2.95 **NM** value: **Cover or less**
Bk 1 ❑ Cover: 8.95 **NM** value: **Cover or less**

TALLY-HO COMICS — Bailey

1 ❑ Dec 1944 Cover: 0.10 **NM** value: **300.00**
• **CGC:** 2 graded, best 9.0

TALONZ — Stop Dragon

1 ❑ Jan 1987, b&w Cover: 1.50 **NM** value: **Cover or less**
A: Rudy Holmes **W:** Jeff Dunkerson

TALOS OF THE WILDERNESS SEA — DC

1 ❑ ca. 1985 Cover: 2.00 **NM** value: **Cover or less**
Circ: CapCity orders: **12,750**
📖 To the Wilderness Sea **A:** Gil Kane **W:** Gil Kane; Jan Strnad

TAMMAS — Pandemonium

1 ❑ Dec 1986 Cover: 1.50 **NM** value: **Cover or less**
📖 Hail and Farewell **A:** Fred Rugar **W:** Fred Rugar; Pan

TANGENT COMICS/DOOM PATROL — DC

1 ❑ Dec 1997 Cover: 2.95 **NM** value: **Cover or less**
Circ: Diamd. preorders: **47,702**
One-shot. 📖 Saving Time • alternate universe **A:** Sean Chen **W:** Dan Jurgens

TANGENT COMICS/GREEN LANTERN — DC

"The Only Thing You Know is the Names" was the tag line that promoted the Tangent imprint from DC in the summer of 1997.

This title is the most unusual of the Tangent line. Rather than a super-hero, the Green Lantern of the Tangent Universe is a mysterious woman who uses her lantern to return the dead to life so they can perform one final mission and rest in peace. The title character serves as host and narrator in a framing sequence before and after each story, much like Cain or Abel of DC's mystery titles, House of Mystery and House of Secrets, although her style of narration is much more colloquial. The stories feature characters that support events in other Tangent titles, such as the escalation of the Cuban Missile Crisis and the United State's subsequent war in Czechoslovakia.

1 ❑ Dec 1997 Cover: 2.95 **NM** value: **Cover or less**
Circ: Diamd. preorders: **54,376**
One-shot. 📖 From Beyond the Unknown • alternate universe **A:** J.H. Williams **W:** James Robinson

TANGENT COMICS/JLA — DC

1 ❑ Sep 1998 Cover: 1.95 **NM** value: **Cover or less**
Circ: Diamd. preorders: **47,146**
One-shot. • alternate universe

TANGENT COMICS/METAL MEN — DC

1 ❑ Dec 1997 Cover: 2.95 **NM** value: **Cover or less**
Circ: Diamd. preorders: **47,657**
One-shot. 📖 Secrets & Lies • alternate universe **A:** Mike McKone **W:** Ron Marz

TANGENT COMICS/NIGHTWING — DC

1 ❑ Dec 1997 Cover: 2.95 **NM** value: **Cover or less**
Circ: Diamd. preorders: **51,079**
One-shot. 📖 The Most Dangerous Man in the World • alternate universe **A:** Jan Duursema **W:** John Ostrander

TANGENT COMICS/NIGHTWING: NIGHT FORCE — DC

1 ❑ Sep 1998 Cover: 1.95 **NM** value: **Cover or less**
Circ: Diamd. preorders: **37,243**
One-shot. • alternate universe

TANGENT COMICS/POWERGIRL — DC

1 ❑ Sep 1998 Cover: 1.95 **NM** value: **Cover or less**
Circ: Diamd. preorders: **33,730**
One-shot. • alternate universe

TANGENT COMICS/SEA DEVILS — DC

1 ❑ Dec 1997 Cover: 2.95 **NM** value: **Cover or less**
Circ: Diamd. preorders: **48,389**
One-shot. 📖 Devils and the Deep • alternate universe **A:** Vince Giarrano **W:** Kurt Busiek

TANGENT COMICS/SECRET SIX — DC

1 ❑ Dec 1997 Cover: 2.95 **NM** value: **Cover or less**
Circ: Diamd. preorders: **48,591**
One-shot. 📖 Bad Moon • alternate universe **A:** Tom Grummettt **W:** Chuck Dixon

TANGENT COMICS/TALES OF THE GREEN LANTERN — DC

1 ❑ Sep 1998 Cover: 1.95 **NM** value: **Cover or less**
Circ: Diamd. preorders: **40,323**
One-shot. • alternate universe

TANGENT COMICS/THE ATOM — DC

1 ❑ Dec 1997 Cover: 2.95 **NM** value: **Cover or less**
Circ: Diamd. preorders: **49,030**
One-shot. 📖 Truth • alternate universe **A:** Paul Ryan **W:** Dan Jurgens

TANGENT COMICS/THE BATMAN — DC

1 ❑ Sep 1998 Cover: 1.95 **NM** value: **Cover or less**
Circ: Diamd. preorders: **42,251**
One-shot. • alternate universe

TANGENT COMICS/THE FLASH — DC

1 ❑ Dec 1997 Cover: 2.95 **NM** value: **Cover or less**
Circ: Diamd. preorders: **52,480**
One-shot. 📖 Premiere • alternate universe **A:** Gary Frank **W:** Todd Dezago

TANGENT COMICS/THE JOKER — DC

1 ❑ Dec 1997 Cover: 2.95 **NM** value: **Cover or less**
Circ: Diamd. preorders: **54,359**
One-shot. 📖 Laugh 'Till it Hurts • alternate universe **A:** Matt Haley **W:** Karl Kesel

TANGENT COMICS/THE JOKER'S WILD — DC

1 ❑ Sep 1998 Cover: 1.95 **NM** value: **Cover or less**
Circ: Diamd. preorders: **38,281**
One-shot. • alternate universe

TANGENT COMICS/THE SUPERMAN — DC

1 ❑ Sep 1998 Cover: 1.95 **NM** value: **Cover or less**
Circ: Diamd. preorders: **41,437**
One-shot. • alternate universe

TANGENT COMICS/THE TRIALS OF THE FLASH — DC

1 ❑ Sep 1998 Cover: 1.95 **NM** value: **Cover or less**
Circ: Diamd. preorders: **36,938**
One-shot. • alternate universe

TANGENT COMICS/WONDER WOMAN — DC

1 ❑ Sep 1998 Cover: 1.95 **NM** value: **Cover or less**
Circ: Diamd. preorders: **36,924**
One-shot. • alternate universe

TANGENTS — NBM

All issues are adults only.

1 ❑ Cover: 16.95 **NM** value: **Cover or less**
hardcover.

TANGLED WEB — Marvel

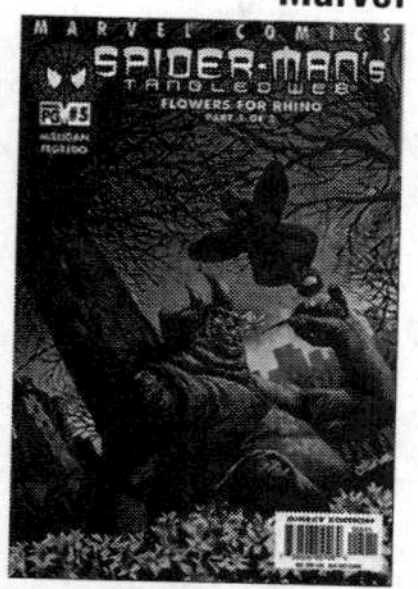

Much like DC's Batman: Legends of the Dark Knight, Marvel's Tangled Web series offers creators an opportunity to focus on specific Spider-Man villains as well as aspects of the hero himself that have only been hinted at in the ongoing series.

Stories in the series include "Flowers for Rhino," in which the super-villain acquires super-intelligence but learns it comes with a price; "Severance Package," in which a Kingpin henchman faces the consequences of his mistakes; and "Open All Night," a Valen-

Other grades: Multiply prices above by **1.5 for Mint • 2/3 for Very Fine • 1/3 for Fine • 1/5 for Very Good • 1/8 for Good**

tine's tale in which Peter Parker has made dates with two different women on the same night. — Brent

1 ❑ Jun 2001 Cover: 2.99 **NM** value: **Cover or less**
Circ: Diamd. preorders: **53,233** • **CGC:** 15 graded, best 9.8
2 ❑ Jul 2001 Cover: 2.99 **NM** value: **Cover or less**
Circ: Diamd. preorders: **46,803**
3 ❑ Aug 2001 Cover: 2.99 **NM** value: **Cover or less**
Circ: Diamd. preorders: **46,628**
4 ❑ Sep 2001 Cover: 2.99 **NM** value: **Cover or less**
Circ: Diamd. preorders: **41,310**
5 ❑ Oct 2001 Cover: 2.99 **NM** value: **Cover or less**
Circ: Diamd. preorders: **40,178**
6 ❑ Nov 2001 Cover: 2.99 **NM** value: **Cover or less**
Circ: Diamd. preorders: **36,202**
7 ❑ Dec 2001 Cover: 2.99 **NM** value: **Cover or less**
Circ: Diamd. preorders: **32,940**
8 ❑ Jan 2002 Cover: 2.99 **NM** value: **Cover or less**
Circ: Diamd. preorders: **32,899**
9 ❑ Feb 2002 Cover: 2.99 **NM** value: **Cover or less**
Circ: Diamd. preorders: **32,173**
10 ❑ Mar 2002 Cover: 2.99 **NM** value: **Cover or less**
Circ: Diamd. preorders: **31,184**

TANK GIRL — Dark Horse

"What's bald and smelly, snogs kangaroos, wears shoes that don't fit and a bra that's too tight, (and knickers that need a good wash), smokes, drinks, and fights too much for her own good, and at this very moment in time has a mega hangover?" Who else could it be, except the one and only Tank Girl!

Jamie Hewlett and Alan Martin's rambunctious creation first appeared in Britain's Deadline magazine. She soon became the star attraction there, and eventually found her way into numerous comic spinoffs, and even a feature movie. This 1991 Dark Horse mini-series reprints her earliest adventures, giving American fans a rare look at this fun-loving catastrophe in a 40,000 pound tank.

1 ❑ May 1991, b&w Cover: 2.25 **NM** value: **3.50**
• trading cards; British **A:** Jamie Hewlett **W:** Alan Martin ★ 1st Appearance of Tank Girl (in American comics).
2 ❑ Jun 1991, b&w Cover: 2.25 **NM** value: **3.00**
• British **A:** Jamie Hewlett **W:** Alan Martin
3 ❑ Jul 1991, b&w Cover: 2.25 **NM** value: **3.00**
• British **A:** Jamie Hewlett **W:** Alan Martin
4 ❑ Aug 1991, b&w Cover: 2.25 **NM** value: **3.00**
• British **A:** Jamie Hewlett **W:** Alan Martin

TANK GIRL 2 — Dark Horse

1 ❑ Jun 1993, b&w and colorCover: 2.50 **NM** value: **3.00**
Circ: CapCity orders: **6,175**
📖 I've Got Friends At Bells End… • British **A:** Jamie Hewlett **W:** Alan Martin
2 ❑ Jul 1993, b&w and colorCover: 2.50 **NM** value: **3.00**
Circ: CapCity orders: **4,700**
• British **A:** Jamie Hewlett **W:** Alan Martin
3 ❑ Aug 1993, b&w and colorCover: 2.50 **NM** value: **3.00**
Circ: CapCity orders: **4,175**
• British **A:** Jamie Hewlett **W:** Alan Martin
4 ❑ Sep 1993, b&w and colorCover: 2.50 **NM** value: **3.00**
Circ: CapCity orders: **3,900**
• British **A:** Jamie Hewlett **W:** Alan Martin
Bk 1❑ Cover: 17.95 **NM** value: **Cover or less**
• Trade Paperback. • Collects Tank Girl 2 #1-4 **A:** Jamie Hewlett **W:** Alan Martin
Bk 1-2❑ Cover: 17.95 **NM** value: **Cover or less**

TANK GIRL: APOCALYPSE — DC / Vertigo

1 ❑ Nov 1995 Cover: 2.25 **NM** value: **Cover or less**
• Tank Girl becomes pregnant **A:** Andy Pritchett **W:** Alan Grant
2 ❑ Dec 1995 Cover: 2.25 **NM** value: **Cover or less**
A: Andy Pritchett **W:** Alan Grant
3 ❑ Jan 1996 Cover: 2.25 **NM** value: **Cover or less**
A: Andy Pritchett **W:** Alan Grant
4 ❑ Feb 1996 Cover: 2.25 **NM** value: **Cover or less**
📖 So Long, It's Been Good To Know Ya • Tank Girl gives birth **A:** Andy Pritchett **W:** Alan Grant

TANK GIRL MOVIE ADAPTATION — DC / Vertigo

1 ❑ Cover: 5.95 **NM** value: **Cover or less**
Circ: CapCity orders: **4,750**
No issue number. • prestige format one-shot **A:** Andy Pritchett; John Bolton(cover) **W:** Peter Milligan

TANK GIRL: THE ODYSSEY — DC / Vertigo

1 ❑ Jun 1995 Cover: 2.25 **NM** value: **Cover or less**
Circ: CapCity orders: **11,850**
A: Jamie Hewlett **W:** Peter Milligan
2 ❑ Jul 1995 Cover: 2.25 **NM** value: **Cover or less**
Circ: CapCity orders: **9,950**
A: Jamie Hewlett **W:** Peter Milligan
3 ❑ Aug 1995 Cover: 2.25 **NM** value: **Cover or less**
Circ: CapCity orders: **9,050**
A: Jamie Hewlett **W:** Peter Milligan
4 ❑ Oct 1995 Cover: 2.25 **NM** value: **Cover or less**
Circ: CapCity orders: **8,325**
A: Jamie Hewlett **W:** Peter Milligan

TANK VIXENS — Antarctic

1 ❑ Jan 1994 Cover: 2.95 **NM** value: **Cover or less**
A: Mike Sagara; Paul Kidd **W:** Mike Sagara; Paul Kidd
2 ❑ Mar 1994 Cover: 2.95 **NM** value: **Cover or less**
A: Mike Sagara; Paul Kidd **W:** Mike Sagara; Paul Kidd
3 ❑ ca. 1995 Cover: 2.95 **NM** value: **Cover or less**
4 ❑ Mar 1996 Cover: 2.95 **NM** value: **Cover or less**

TANTALIZING STORIES — Tundra

1 ❑ Oct 1992 Cover: 2.25 **NM** value: **Cover or less**
2 ❑ Dec 1992 Cover: 2.25 **NM** value: **Cover or less**
3 ❑ Feb 1993 Cover: 2.25 **NM** value: **Cover or less**
4 ❑ Apr 1993 Cover: 2.25 **NM** value: **Cover or less**
6 ❑ Jun 1993 Cover: 2.50 **NM** value: **Cover or less**

TAOLAND — Sumitek

1 ❑ Nov 1994, b&w Cover: 1.50 **NM** value: **2.00**
cardstock cover. 📖 Yingpeng's Friends **A:** Jeff Amano **W:** Jeff Amano
2 ❑ Aug 1995, b&w Cover: 2.95 **NM** value: **5.95**
cardstock cover. **A:** Jeff Amano **W:** Jeff Amano
3 ❑ Sep 1995, b&w Cover: 3.25 **NM** value: **5.95**
cardstock cover. **A:** Jeff Amano **W:** Jeff Amano
4 ❑ Feb 1996, b&w Cover: 3.25 **NM** value: **5.95**
A: Jeff Amano **W:** Jeff Amano
5 ❑ Dec 1996 Cover: 5.95 **NM** value: **Cover or less**
• prestige format. 📖 Night & Day **A:** Jeff Amano **W:** Jeff Amano

TAOLAND ADVENTURES — Antarctic

1 ❑ Mar 1999 Cover: 2.99 **NM** value: **3.50**
Circ: Diamd. preorders: **1,845**
A: Jeff Amano **W:** Jeff Amano
2 ❑ May 1999 Cover: 3.50 **NM** value: **Cover or less**
Circ: Diamd. preorders: **1,356**
A: Jeff Amano **W:** Jeff Amano

TAP — Promethean

1 ❑ Sep 1994 Cover: 2.95 **NM** value: **Cover or less**
A: Marvin P. Mann; C.P. Smith **W:** Phil Adams
2 ❑ Jan 1995 Cover: 2.95 **NM** value: **Cover or less**
A: Marvin P. Mann; C.P. Smith **W:** Phil Adams
3 ❑ Jan 1995 Cover: 2.95 **NM** value: **Cover or less**
• indicia is for issue #2 **A:** Marvin P. Mann; C.P. Smith **W:** Phil Adams

TAPESTRY — Superior Junk

1 ❑ b&w Cover: 1.50 **NM** value: **Cover or less**
1-2 ❑ Apr 1995 Cover: 1.50 **NM** value: **Cover or less**
2 ❑ Apr 1994, b&w Cover: 1.95 **NM** value: **Cover or less**
3 ❑ Jun 1994, b&w Cover: 1.95 **NM** value: **Cover or less**
4 ❑ Oct 1994, b&w Cover: 2.25 **NM** value: **Cover or less**
5 ❑ b&w Cover: 2.25 **NM** value: **Cover or less**

TAPPING THE VEIN — Eclipse

1 ❑ Cover: 6.95 **NM** value: **7.50**
Circ: CapCity orders: **6,475**
• prestige format. • foil-embossed logo **A:** John Bolton(cover)
2 ❑ Cover: 6.95 **NM** value: **7.00**
Circ: CapCity orders: **5,950**
• prestige format. 📖 Skins of the Fathers; In the Hills, the Cities • foil-embossed logo **A:** John Bolton; Klaus Janson **W:** Charles Wagner
3 ❑ Cover: 6.95 **NM** value: **7.00**
Circ: CapCity orders: **8,586**
• prestige format. • foil-embossed logo **A:** John Bolton(cover)
4 ❑ Cover: 7.95 **NM** value: **Cover or less**
Circ: CapCity orders: **10,250**
• prestige format. • foil-embossed logo **A:** John Bolton(cover)
5 ❑ Cover: 7.95 **NM** value: **Cover or less**
Circ: CapCity orders: **11,050**
A: John Bolton(cover)

TARGET: AIRBOY — Eclipse

1 ❑ Mar 1988 Cover: 1.95 **NM** value: **2.00**
Circ: CapCity orders: **5,375**
cardstock cover. **A:** Sam Kieth; Sam De La Rosa **W:** Chuck Dixon; Don Chin ★ Appearance of Clint from A.R.B.B.H..

TARGET COMICS — Novelty Press

Target Comics emerged in the heyday of the Golden Age, featuring a credible lineup of masked heroes, comic strip-style adventure stories, and humorous filler. Leading talents such as Jack Cole (creator of Plastic Man), Bill Everett (Sub-Mariner), and Carl Burgos (The Human Torch) contributed to its pages, but Target is today best known as the showcase for Space Hawk, the classic, science-fiction strip by comic art genius Basil Wolverton. Space Hawk appeared in the first several issues, but by the mid-1940s, Target slipped back into the pack as an average-quality anthology title. In 1949, it was bought, along with Novelty's other books including Blue Bolt, by L. B. Cole's Star Publications. Cole contributed a few of his lurid poster-painted covers, but reader interest continued to wane and Target folded before 1950.

1 ❑ Feb 1940 Cover: 0.10 **NM** value: **3200.00**
2 ❑ Mar 1940 Cover: 0.10 **NM** value: **1450.00**
3 ❑ Apr 1940 Cover: 0.10 **NM** value: **1000.00**
• **CGC:** 1 graded, best 9.0
4 ❑ May 1940 Cover: 0.10 **NM** value: **1000.00**
5 ❑ Jun 1940 Cover: 0.10 **NM** value: **2800.00**
• **CGC:** 1 graded, best 9.2
• Spacehawk begins **A:** Basil Wolverton
6 ❑ Jul 1940 Cover: 0.10 **NM** value: **1300.00**
A: Bill Everett ★ 1st Appearance of The Chameleon (Golden Age).
7 ❑ Aug 1940 Cover: 0.10 **NM** value: **3000.00**
• **CGC:** 2 graded, best 8.5
Spacehawk cover. **A:** Basil Wolverton
8 ❑ Sep 1940 Cover: 0.10 **NM** value: **1000.00**
A: Basil Wolverton
9 ❑ Oct 1940 Cover: 0.10 **NM** value: **1000.00**
A: Basil Wolverton
10 ❑ Nov 1940 Cover: 0.10 **NM** value: **1250.00**
A: Basil Wolverton ★ 1st Appearance of The Target.
11 ❑ Dec 1940 Cover: 0.10 **NM** value: **1100.00**
A: Basil Wolverton ★ Origin of The Target.
12 ❑ Jan 1941 Cover: 0.10 **NM** value: **1000.00**
A: Basil Wolverton
13 ❑ Mar 1941 Cover: 0.10 **NM** value: **550.00**
• **CGC:** 1 graded, best 3.5
A: Basil Wolverton
14 ❑ Apr 1941 Cover: 0.10 **NM** value: **525.00**
A: Basil Wolverton
15 ❑ May 1941 Cover: 0.10 **NM** value: **450.00**
A: Basil Wolverton
16 ❑ Jun 1941 Cover: 0.10 **NM** value: **450.00**
A: Basil Wolverton
17 ❑ Jul 1941 Cover: 0.10 **NM** value: **450.00**
A: Basil Wolverton
18 ❑ Aug 1941 Cover: 0.10 **NM** value: **450.00**
• **CGC:** 1 graded, best 8.5
A: Basil Wolverton
19 ❑ Sep 1941 Cover: 0.10 **NM** value: **450.00**
A: Basil Wolverton
20 ❑ Oct 1941 Cover: 0.10 **NM** value: **450.00**
A: Basil Wolverton
21 ❑ Nov 1941 Cover: 0.10 **NM** value: **450.00**
A: Basil Wolverton
22 ❑ Dec 1941 Cover: 0.10 **NM** value: **450.00**
• **CGC:** 1 graded, best 7.5
A: Basil Wolverton
23 ❑ Jan 1942 Cover: 0.10 **NM** value: **450.00**
A: Basil Wolverton
24 ❑ Feb 1942 Cover: 0.10 **NM** value: **450.00**
• **CGC:** 1 graded, best 7.0
A: Basil Wolverton
25 ❑ Mar 1942 Cover: 0.10 **NM** value: **400.00**
A: Basil Wolverton
26 ❑ Apr 1942 Cover: 0.10 **NM** value: **400.00**
A: Basil Wolverton
27 ❑ May 1942 Cover: 0.10 **NM** value: **400.00**
A: Basil Wolverton
28 ❑ Jun 1942 Cover: 0.10 **NM** value: **400.00**
A: Basil Wolverton
29 ❑ Jul 1942 Cover: 0.10 **NM** value: **400.00**
A: Basil Wolverton
30 ❑ Aug 1942 Cover: 0.10 **NM** value: **400.00**
A: Basil Wolverton
31 ❑ Sep 1942 Cover: 0.10 **NM** value: **400.00**
A: Basil Wolverton
32 ❑ Oct 1942 Cover: 0.10 **NM** value: **400.00**
• **CGC:** 1 graded, best 8.0
A: Basil Wolverton
33 ❑ Nov 1942 Cover: 0.10 **NM** value: **400.00**
• **CGC:** 1 graded, best 7.0
A: Basil Wolverton
34 ❑ Dec 1942 Cover: 0.10 **NM** value: **400.00**
• Last Wolverton Spacehawk issue **A:** Basil Wolverton
35 ❑ Jan 1943 Cover: 0.10 **NM** value: **85.00**
36 ❑ Feb 1943 Cover: 0.10 **NM** value: **85.00**
📖 The Cadet; 18 Men and a Boat; Speck Spot and Sis…; Candid Charlie; The Target and The Targeteers; Paper Hero (Text Story); Dan'l Flannel; The Chameleon
37 ❑ Mar 1943 Cover: 0.10 **NM** value: **60.00**
38 ❑ Apr 1943 Cover: 0.10 **NM** value: **60.00**
• **CGC:** 1 graded, best 9.6
39 ❑ May 1943 Cover: 0.10 **NM** value: **60.00**
40 ❑ Jun 1943 Cover: 0.10 **NM** value: **60.00**
41 ❑ Aug 1943 Cover: 0.10 **NM** value: **60.00**
42 ❑ Sep 1943 Cover: 0.10 **NM** value: **60.00**
• **CGC:** 1 graded, best 9.6
43 ❑ Nov 1943 Cover: 0.10 **NM** value: **60.00**
• **CGC:** 1 graded, best 9.6
44 ❑ Dec 1943 Cover: 0.10 **NM** value: **60.00**
• **CGC:** 1 graded, best 9.4
45 ❑ Jan 1944 Cover: 0.10 **NM** value: **60.00**
• **CGC:** 1 graded, best 9.8
46 ❑ Feb 1944 Cover: 0.10 **NM** value: **60.00**
47 ❑ Mar 1944 Cover: 0.10 **NM** value: **60.00**
48 ❑ Apr 1944 Cover: 0.10 **NM** value: **60.00**
49 ❑ May 1944 Cover: 0.10 **NM** value: **50.00**
50 ❑ Jun 1944 Cover: 0.10 **NM** value: **50.00**
51 ❑ Jul 1944 Cover: 0.10 **NM** value: **50.00**
52 ❑ Sep 1944 Cover: 0.10 **NM** value: **50.00**
• **CGC:** 1 graded, best 9.6
53 ❑ Nov 1944 Cover: 0.10 **NM** value: **50.00**
54 ❑ Dec 1944 Cover: 0.10 **NM** value: **50.00**
55 ❑ Jan 1945 Cover: 0.10 **NM** value: **50.00**
56 ❑ Feb 1945 Cover: 0.10 **NM** value: **50.00**
57 ❑ Mar 1945 Cover: 0.10 **NM** value: **45.00**
58 ❑ Apr 1945 Cover: 0.10 **NM** value: **45.00**
59 ❑ May 1945 Cover: 0.10 **NM** value: **45.00**
60 ❑ Jun 1945 Cover: 0.10 **NM** value: **45.00**
61 ❑ Jul 1945 Cover: 0.10 **NM** value: **45.00**
62 ❑ Sep 1945 Cover: 0.10 **NM** value: **45.00**
• **CGC:** 1 graded, best 9.6
63 ❑ Oct 1945 Cover: 0.10 **NM** value: **45.00**
64 ❑ Nov 1945 Cover: 0.10 **NM** value: **45.00**
65 ❑ Dec 1945 Cover: 0.10 **NM** value: **45.00**
66 ❑ Feb 1946 Cover: 0.10 **NM** value: **45.00**
67 ❑ Mar 1946 Cover: 0.10 **NM** value: **40.00**
68 ❑ Apr 1946 Cover: 0.10 **NM** value: **40.00**
📖 The Cadet, featuring Kit **A:** Art Helfant; Milt Hammer; Nina Albright; Schrotter; Vincent **W:** Art Helfant; Milt Hammer; Nina Albright; Robert Plate
69 ❑ May 1946 Cover: 0.10 **NM** value: **40.00**

CGC-graded: Multiply prices above by **33 for 9.9 M** • **16 for 9.8 NM/M** • **7 for 9.6 NM+** • **5 for 9.4 NM** • **2.5 for 9.2 NM-** • **1.5 for 9.0 VF/NM**

70 ❑ Jun 1946 Cover: 0.10 **NM** value: **40.00**
71 ❑ Jul 1946 Cover: 0.10 **NM** value: **40.00**
72 ❑ Aug 1946 Cover: 0.10 **NM** value: **40.00**
• **CGC:** 1 graded, best 8.0
73 ❑ Sep 1946 Cover: 0.10 **NM** value: **40.00**
74 ❑ Oct 1946 Cover: 0.10 **NM** value: **40.00**
75 ❑ Nov 1946 Cover: 0.10 **NM** value: **40.00**
• **CGC:** 1 graded, best 8.0
76 ❑ Dec 1946 Cover: 0.10 **NM** value: **40.00**
77 ❑ Jan 1947 Cover: 0.10 **NM** value: **40.00**
78 ❑ Feb 1947 Cover: 0.10 **NM** value: **40.00**
79 ❑ Mar 1947 Cover: 0.10 **NM** value: **40.00**
80 ❑ Apr 1947 Cover: 0.10 **NM** value: **40.00**
81 ❑ May 1947 Cover: 0.10 **NM** value: **40.00**
82 ❑ Jun 1947 Cover: 0.10 **NM** value: **40.00**
83 ❑ Jul 1947 Cover: 0.10 **NM** value: **40.00**
84 ❑ Aug 1947 Cover: 0.10 **NM** value: **40.00**
85 ❑ Sep 1947 Cover: 0.10 **NM** value: **40.00**
86 ❑ Oct 1947 Cover: 0.10 **NM** value: **40.00**
87 ❑ Nov 1947 Cover: 0.10 **NM** value: **40.00**
88 ❑ Dec 1947 Cover: 0.10 **NM** value: **40.00**
89 ❑ Jan 1948 Cover: 0.10 **NM** value: **40.00**
90 ❑ Feb 1948 Cover: 0.10 **NM** value: **40.00**
91 ❑ Mar 1948 Cover: 0.10 **NM** value: **35.00**
• **CGC:** 1 graded, best 9.2
92 ❑ Apr 1948 Cover: 0.10 **NM** value: **35.00**
93 ❑ May 1948 Cover: 0.10 **NM** value: **35.00**
94 ❑ Jun 1948 Cover: 0.10 **NM** value: **35.00**
95 ❑ Jul 1948 Cover: 0.10 **NM** value: **35.00**
96 ❑ Aug 1948 Cover: 0.10 **NM** value: **35.00**
97 ❑ Sep 1948 Cover: 0.10 **NM** value: **35.00**
98 ❑ Oct 1948 Cover: 0.10 **NM** value: **35.00**
99 ❑ Nov 1948 Cover: 0.10 **NM** value: **35.00**
100 ❑ Dec 1948 Cover: 0.10 **NM** value: **35.00**
101 ❑ Jan 1949 Cover: 0.10 **NM** value: **35.00**
102 ❑ Feb 1949 Cover: 0.10 **NM** value: **35.00**
103 ❑ Apr 1949 Cover: 0.10 **NM** value: **30.00**
104 ❑ Jun 1949 Cover: 0.10 **NM** value: **30.00**
105 ❑ Aug 1949 Cover: 0.10 **NM** value: **30.00**
final issue.

TARGET WESTERN ROMANCES — Star

106 ❑ Oct 1949 Cover: 0.10 **NM** value: **250.00**
107 ❑ Dec 1949 Cover: 0.10 **NM** value: **200.00**

TARGITT — Atlas-Seaboard

1 ❑ Mar 1975 Cover: 0.25 **NM** value: **2.00**
📖 Boston Tea Party **W:** Mary Jo Duffy ★ Origin of Targitt.
2 ❑ Jun 1975 Cover: 0.25 **NM** value: **1.50**
3 ❑ Jul 1975 Cover: 0.25 **NM** value: **1.50**

TAROT: WITCH OF THE BLACK ROSE — Broadsword

1 ❑ Mar 2000 Cover: 2.95 **NM** value: **Cover or less**
Circ: Diamd. preorders: **13,969**
A: Jim Balent **W:** Jim Balent
2 ❑ May 2000 Cover: 2.95 **NM** value: **Cover or less**
Circ: Diamd. preorders: **12,593**
A: Jim Balent **W:** Jim Balent
3 ❑ Jul 2000 Cover: 2.95 **NM** value: **Cover or less**
Circ: Diamd. preorders: **12,375**
A: Jim Balent **W:** Jim Balent
4 ❑ Sep 2000 Cover: 2.95 **NM** value: **Cover or less**
Circ: Diamd. preorders: **11,284**
A: Jim Balent **W:** Jim Balent
5 ❑ Nov 2000 Cover: 2.95 **NM** value: **Cover or less**
Circ: Diamd. preorders: **11,123**
6 ❑ Jan 2001 Cover: 2.95 **NM** value: **Cover or less**
Circ: Diamd. preorders: **9,991**
7 ❑ Mar 2001 Cover: 2.95 **NM** value: **Cover or less**
Circ: Diamd. preorders: **10,134**
8 ❑ May 2001 Cover: 2.95 **NM** value: **Cover or less**
Circ: Diamd. preorders: **10,399**
9 ❑ Jul 2001 Cover: 2.95 **NM** value: **Cover or less**
Circ: Diamd. preorders: **11,018**

TARZAN (DELL) — Dell

This Tarzan series spanned several decades, beginning with Dell's Tarzan #1, published in 1948, then moving to Dell's Gold Key label 13 years later, and finally to DC.

Dell's run of Tarzan was probably the truest to Edgar Rice Burroughs' original vision of the character. A white baby, raised by apes, Tarzan eventually became the jungle's lord and protector. In this series, he had not yet met future love interest Jane, although he did have a kid sidekick, simply called "Boy." For the most part, his adventures centered around fending off poachers, aiding his friends among the tribes, and stopping various plots launched by both white hunters and black tribesmen.

Many issues of this series included a backup storyline, "Brothers of the Spear," a buddy-comic starring white Dan-El (Daniel) and Natongo, an African. These two friends embarked on adventures exploring the mysterious jungle.

1 ❑ Jan 1948 Cover: 0.10 **NM** value: **900.00**
• **CGC:** 6 graded, best 8.0
2 ❑ Mar 1948 Cover: 0.10 **NM** value: **525.00**
• **CGC:** 3 graded, best 9.0
3 ❑ May 1948 Cover: 0.10 **NM** value: **385.00**
• **CGC:** 1 graded, best 8.0
4 ❑ Jul 1948 Cover: 0.10 **NM** value: **385.00**
• **CGC:** 1 graded, best 9.2
5 ❑ Sep 1948 Cover: 0.10 **NM** value: **385.00**
• **CGC:** 2 graded, best 9.6
6 ❑ Nov 1948 Cover: 0.10 **NM** value: **290.00**
• **CGC:** 1 graded, best 9.4
7 ❑ Jan 1949 Cover: 0.10 **NM** value: **290.00**
• **CGC:** 1 graded, best 9.0
8 ❑ Mar 1949 Cover: 0.10 **NM** value: **290.00**
• **CGC:** 1 graded, best 9.0
9 ❑ May 1949 Cover: 0.10 **NM** value: **290.00**
• **CGC:** 1 graded, best 9.0
10 ❑ Jul 1949 Cover: 0.10 **NM** value: **260.00**
11 ❑ Sep 1949 Cover: 0.10 **NM** value: **235.00**
• **CGC:** 1 graded, best 9.2
12 ❑ Nov 1949 Cover: 0.10 **NM** value: **220.00**
13 ❑ Jan 1950 Cover: 0.10 **NM** value: **220.00**
Photo cover.
14 ❑ Mar 1950 Cover: 0.10 **NM** value: **220.00**
Photo cover.
15 ❑ May 1950 Cover: 0.10 **NM** value: **220.00**
Photo cover.
16 ❑ Jul 1950 Cover: 0.10 **NM** value: **160.00**
Photo cover.
17 ❑ Sep 1950 Cover: 0.10 **NM** value: **160.00**
Photo cover.
18 ❑ Nov 1950 Cover: 0.10 **NM** value: **160.00**
Photo cover.
19 ❑ Jan 1951 Cover: 0.10 **NM** value: **160.00**
Photo cover.
20 ❑ Mar 1951 Cover: 0.10 **NM** value: **160.00**
Photo cover.
21 ❑ May 1951 Cover: 0.10 **NM** value: **135.00**
Photo cover.
22 ❑ Jul 1951 Cover: 0.10 **NM** value: **135.00**
Photo cover.
23 ❑ Aug 1951 Cover: 0.10 **NM** value: **135.00**
Photo cover.
24 ❑ Sep 1951 Cover: 0.10 **NM** value: **135.00**
Photo cover.
25 ❑ Oct 1951 Cover: 0.10 **NM** value: **135.00**
• **CGC:** 2 graded, best 9.0
Photo cover.
26 ❑ Nov 1951 Cover: 0.10 **NM** value: **135.00**
Photo cover.
27 ❑ Dec 1951 Cover: 0.10 **NM** value: **135.00**
Photo cover.
28 ❑ Jan 1952 Cover: 0.10 **NM** value: **135.00**
• **CGC:** 1 graded, best 9.0
Photo cover.
29 ❑ Feb 1952 Cover: 0.10 **NM** value: **135.00**
Photo cover.
30 ❑ Mar 1952 Cover: 0.10 **NM** value: **135.00**
Photo cover.
31 ❑ Apr 1952 Cover: 0.10 **NM** value: **80.00**
Photo cover.
32 ❑ May 1952 Cover: 0.10 **NM** value: **80.00**
Photo cover.
33 ❑ Jun 1952 Cover: 0.10 **NM** value: **80.00**
Photo cover.
34 ❑ Jul 1952 Cover: 0.10 **NM** value: **80.00**
Photo cover.
35 ❑ Aug 1952 Cover: 0.10 **NM** value: **80.00**
Photo cover.
36 ❑ Sep 1952 Cover: 0.10 **NM** value: **80.00**
Photo cover.
37 ❑ Oct 1952 Cover: 0.10 **NM** value: **80.00**
Photo cover.
38 ❑ Nov 1952 Cover: 0.10 **NM** value: **80.00**
Photo cover.
39 ❑ Dec 1952 Cover: 0.10 **NM** value: **80.00**
Photo cover.
40 ❑ Jan 1953 Cover: 0.10 **NM** value: **80.00**
Photo cover.
41 ❑ Feb 1953 Cover: 0.10 **NM** value: **80.00**
Photo cover.
42 ❑ Mar 1953 Cover: 0.10 **NM** value: **80.00**
Photo cover.
43 ❑ Apr 1953 Cover: 0.10 **NM** value: **80.00**
Photo cover.
44 ❑ May 1953 Cover: 0.10 **NM** value: **80.00**
Photo cover.
45 ❑ Jun 1953 Cover: 0.10 **NM** value: **80.00**
Photo cover.
46 ❑ Jul 1953 Cover: 0.10 **NM** value: **80.00**
Photo cover.
47 ❑ Aug 1953 Cover: 0.10 **NM** value: **80.00**
Photo cover.
48 ❑ Sep 1953 Cover: 0.10 **NM** value: **80.00**
Photo cover.
49 ❑ Oct 1953 Cover: 0.10 **NM** value: **80.00**
Photo cover.
50 ❑ Nov 1953 Cover: 0.10 **NM** value: **80.00**
Photo cover.
51 ❑ Dec 1953 Cover: 0.10 **NM** value: **80.00**
Photo cover.
52 ❑ Jan 1954 Cover: 0.10 **NM** value: **80.00**
Photo cover.
53 ❑ Feb 1954 Cover: 0.10 **NM** value: **80.00**
Photo cover.
54 ❑ Mar 1954 Cover: 0.10 **NM** value: **80.00**
Photo cover.
55 ❑ Apr 1954 Cover: 0.10 **NM** value: **50.00**
56 ❑ May 1954 Cover: 0.10 **NM** value: **50.00**
57 ❑ Jun 1954 Cover: 0.10 **NM** value: **50.00**
58 ❑ Jul 1954 Cover: 0.10 **NM** value: **50.00**
59 ❑ Aug 1954 Cover: 0.10 **NM** value: **50.00**
60 ❑ Sep 1954 Cover: 0.10 **NM** value: **50.00**
61 ❑ Oct 1954 Cover: 0.10 **NM** value: **50.00**
62 ❑ Nov 1954 Cover: 0.10 **NM** value: **50.00**
63 ❑ Dec 1954 Cover: 0.10 **NM** value: **50.00**
• **CGC:** 1 graded, best 7.0
64 ❑ Jan 1955 Cover: 0.10 **NM** value: **50.00**
65 ❑ Feb 1955 Cover: 0.10 **NM** value: **50.00**
66 ❑ Mar 1955 Cover: 0.10 **NM** value: **50.00**
67 ❑ Apr 1955 Cover: 0.10 **NM** value: **50.00**
• **CGC:** 1 graded, best 7.0
68 ❑ May 1955 Cover: 0.10 **NM** value: **50.00**
69 ❑ Jun 1955 Cover: 0.10 **NM** value: **50.00**
70 ❑ Jul 1955 Cover: 0.10 **NM** value: **50.00**
• **CGC:** 1 graded, best 7.0
71 ❑ Aug 1955 Cover: 0.10 **NM** value: **42.00**
• **CGC:** 1 graded, best 6.0
72 ❑ Sep 1955 Cover: 0.10 **NM** value: **42.00**
• **CGC:** 1 graded, best 8.5
73 ❑ Oct 1955 Cover: 0.10 **NM** value: **42.00**
74 ❑ Nov 1955 Cover: 0.10 **NM** value: **42.00**
• **CGC:** 1 graded, best 8.0
📖 The White Bull; The Winged Men; Brothers of the Spear; A New Undertaking (text)
75 ❑ Dec 1955 Cover: 0.10 **NM** value: **42.00**
• **CGC:** 1 graded, best 9.0
76 ❑ Jan 1956 Cover: 0.10 **NM** value: **42.00**
77 ❑ Feb 1956 Cover: 0.10 **NM** value: **42.00**
• **CGC:** 1 graded, best 7.0
78 ❑ Mar 1956 Cover: 0.10 **NM** value: **42.00**
79 ❑ Apr 1956 Cover: 0.10 **NM** value: **42.00**
• **CGC:** 1 graded, best 9.0
80 ❑ May 1956 Cover: 0.10 **NM** value: **30.00**
• **CGC:** 2 graded, best 9.0
Photo cover.
81 ❑ Jun 1956 Cover: 0.10 **NM** value: **30.00**
Photo cover.
82 ❑ Jul 1956 Cover: 0.10 **NM** value: **30.00**
• **CGC:** 1 graded, best 7.5
Photo cover.
83 ❑ Aug 1956 Cover: 0.10 **NM** value: **30.00**
Photo cover.
84 ❑ Sep 1956 Cover: 0.10 **NM** value: **30.00**
Photo cover.
85 ❑ Oct 1956 Cover: 0.10 **NM** value: **30.00**
Photo cover.
86 ❑ Nov 1956 Cover: 0.10 **NM** value: **30.00**
Photo cover.
87 ❑ Dec 1956 Cover: 0.10 **NM** value: **30.00**
Photo cover.
88 ❑ Jan 1957 Cover: 0.10 **NM** value: **30.00**
Photo cover.
89 ❑ Feb 1957 Cover: 0.10 **NM** value: **30.00**
Photo cover.
90 ❑ Mar 1957 Cover: 0.10 **NM** value: **30.00**
Photo cover.
91 ❑ Apr 1957 Cover: 0.10 **NM** value: **30.00**
Photo cover.
92 ❑ May 1957 Cover: 0.10 **NM** value: **30.00**
Photo cover.
93 ❑ Jun 1957 Cover: 0.10 **NM** value: **30.00**
Photo cover.
94 ❑ Jul 1957 Cover: 0.10 **NM** value: **30.00**
Photo cover.
95 ❑ Aug 1957 Cover: 0.10 **NM** value: **30.00**
Photo cover.
96 ❑ Sep 1957 Cover: 0.10 **NM** value: **30.00**
Photo cover.
97 ❑ Oct 1957 Cover: 0.10 **NM** value: **30.00**
Photo cover.
98 ❑ Nov 1957 Cover: 0.10 **NM** value: **30.00**
Photo cover.
99 ❑ Dec 1957 Cover: 0.10 **NM** value: **30.00**
Photo cover.
100 ❑ Jan 1958 Cover: 0.10 **NM** value: **40.00**
Photo cover.
101 ❑ Feb 1958 Cover: 0.10 **NM** value: **28.00**
Photo cover.
102 ❑ Mar 1958 Cover: 0.10 **NM** value: **28.00**
Photo cover.
103 ❑ Apr 1958 Cover: 0.10 **NM** value: **28.00**
Photo cover.
104 ❑ May 1958 Cover: 0.10 **NM** value: **28.00**
Photo cover.
105 ❑ Jun 1958 Cover: 0.10 **NM** value: **28.00**
Photo cover.
106 ❑ Jul 1958 Cover: 0.10 **NM** value: **28.00**
• **CGC:** 1 graded, best 9.6
Photo cover.
107 ❑ Aug 1958 Cover: 0.10 **NM** value: **28.00**
Photo cover.
108 ❑ Sep 1958 Cover: 0.10 **NM** value: **28.00**
Photo cover.
109 ❑ Nov 1958 Cover: 0.10 **NM** value: **28.00**
Photo cover.
110 ❑ Jan 1959 Cover: 0.10 **NM** value: **28.00**
Photo cover.
111 ❑ Mar 1959 Cover: 0.10 **NM** value: **25.00**
112 ❑ May 1959 Cover: 0.10 **NM** value: **25.00**
113 ❑ Jul 1959 Cover: 0.10 **NM** value: **25.00**
• **CGC:** 1 graded, best 5.0
114 ❑ Sep 1959 Cover: 0.10 **NM** value: **25.00**
115 ❑ Nov 1959 Cover: 0.10 **NM** value: **25.00**
116 ❑ Jan 1960 Cover: 0.10 **NM** value: **25.00**
117 ❑ Mar 1960 Cover: 0.10 **NM** value: **25.00**
📖 Challenges The Ape King
118 ❑ May 1960 Cover: 0.10 **NM** value: **25.00**
119 ❑ Jul 1960 Cover: 0.10 **NM** value: **25.00**
120 ❑ Sep 1960 Cover: 0.10 **NM** value: **25.00**
121 ❑ Nov 1960 Cover: 0.10 **NM** value: **20.00**
122 ❑ Jan 1961 Cover: 0.10 **NM** value: **20.00**
123 ❑ Mar 1961 Cover: 0.15 **NM** value: **20.00**

Other grades: Multiply prices above by **1.5 for Mint • 2/3 for Very Fine • 1/3 for Fine • 1/5 for Very Good • 1/8 for Good**

124 ☐ May 1961 Cover: 0.15 **NM** value: **20.00**
125 ☐ Jul 1961 Cover: 0.15 **NM** value: **20.00**
📖 Jungle Revolt
126 ☐ Sep 1961 Cover: 0.15 **NM** value: **20.00**
127 ☐ Nov 1961 Cover: 0.15 **NM** value: **20.00**
128 ☐ Jan 1962 Cover: 0.15 **NM** value: **20.00**
129 ☐ Mar 1962 Cover: 0.15 **NM** value: **20.00**
130 ☐ May 1962 Cover: 0.15 **NM** value: **20.00**
131 ☐ Jul 1962 Cover: 0.15 **NM** value: **20.00**
• Series continued in Tarzan (Gold Key) #132

TARZAN (GOLD KEY) — Gold Key

132 ☐ Nov 1962 Cover: 0.12 **NM** value: **14.00**
• Continued from Tarzan (Dell) #131 **A:** Russ Manning
133 ☐ Jan 1963 Cover: 0.12 **NM** value: **14.00**
Circ: Statement: **332,460**
134 ☐ Mar 1963 Cover: 0.12 **NM** value: **14.00**
Circ: Statement: **332,460**
135 ☐ May 1963 Cover: 0.12 **NM** value: **14.00**
Circ: Statement: **332,460**
136 ☐ Jul 1963 Cover: 0.12 **NM** value: **14.00**
Circ: Statement: **332,460**
137 ☐ Aug 1963 Cover: 0.12 **NM** value: **14.00**
Circ: Statement: **332,460**
138 ☐ Oct 1963 Cover: 0.12 **NM** value: **14.00**
Circ: Statement: **332,460**
139 ☐ Dec 1963 Cover: 0.12 **NM** value: **14.00**
Circ: Statement: **332,460**
140 ☐ Feb 1964 Cover: 0.12 **NM** value: **14.00**
Circ: Statement: **353,237**
141 ☐ Apr 1964 Cover: 0.12 **NM** value: **14.00**
Circ: Statement: **353,237**
142 ☐ Jun 1964 Cover: 0.12 **NM** value: **14.00**
Circ: Statement: **353,237**
143 ☐ Jul 1964 Cover: 0.12 **NM** value: **14.00**
Circ: Statement: **353,237**
144 ☐ Aug 1964 Cover: 0.12 **NM** value: **14.00**
Circ: Statement: **353,237**
145 ☐ Sep 1964 Cover: 0.12 **NM** value: **14.00**
Circ: Statement: **353,237**
146 ☐ Oct 1964 Cover: 0.12 **NM** value: **14.00**
Circ: Statement: **353,237**
147 ☐ Dec 1964 Cover: 0.12 **NM** value: **14.00**
Circ: Statement: **353,237**
148 ☐ Feb 1965 Cover: 0.12 **NM** value: **14.00**
Circ: Statement: **356,699**
149 ☐ Apr 1965 Cover: 0.12 **NM** value: **14.00**
Circ: Statement: **356,699**
150 ☐ Jun 1965 Cover: 0.12 **NM** value: **14.00**
Circ: Statement: **356,699**
151 ☐ Aug 1965 Cover: 0.12 **NM** value: **14.00**
Circ: Statement: **356,699**
152 ☐ Sep 1965 Cover: 0.12 **NM** value: **14.00**
Circ: Statement: **356,699**
153 ☐ Oct 1965 Cover: 0.12 **NM** value: **14.00**
Circ: Statement: **356,699**
154 ☐ Nov 1965 Cover: 0.12 **NM** value: **14.00**
Circ: Statement: **356,699**
155 ☐ Dec 1965 Cover: 0.12 **NM** value: **18.00**
Circ: Statement: **356,699**
• adapts Tarzan of the Apes **A:** Russ Manning ★ Origin of Tarzan.
156 ☐ Feb 1966 Cover: 0.12 **NM** value: **10.00**
Circ: Statement: **338,052**
• adapts Return of Tarzan **A:** Russ Manning
157 ☐ Apr 1966 Cover: 0.12 **NM** value: **10.00**
Circ: Statement: **338,052**
📖 The Beasts Of Tarzan • adapts Beasts of Tarzan **A:** Russ Manning
158 ☐ Jun 1966 Cover: 0.12 **NM** value: **10.00**
Circ: Statement: **338,052**
• adapts Son of Tarzan **A:** Russ Manning
159 ☐ Aug 1966 Cover: 0.12 **NM** value: **10.00**
Circ: Statement: **338,052**
• adapts Jewels of Opar **A:** Russ Manning
160 ☐ Sep 1966 Cover: 0.12 **NM** value: **10.00**
Circ: Statement: **338,052**
• adapts Jewels of Opar **A:** Russ Manning
161 ☐ Oct 1966 Cover: 0.12 **NM** value: **10.00**
Circ: Statement: **338,052**
• adapts Jewels of Opar **A:** Russ Manning
162 ☐ Dec 1966 Cover: 0.12 **NM** value: **10.00**
Circ: Statement: **338,052**
TV Adventures on cover.
163 ☐ Jan 1967 Cover: 0.12 **NM** value: **8.00**
Circ: Statement: **384,450**
• adapts Tarzan the Untamed **A:** Russ Manning
164 ☐ Feb 1967 Cover: 0.12 **NM** value: **8.00**
Circ: Statement: **384,450**
• adapts Tarzan the Untamed; Has 1967 Statement, filed 9/28/67; avg print run 725,307; avg sales 383,240; avg subs 1,210; avg total paid 384,450; samples 597; max existent 385,047; 47% of run returned **A:** Russ Manning
165 ☐ Mar 1967 Cover: 0.12 **NM** value: **10.00**
Circ: Statement: **384,450**
Photo cover.
166 ☐ Apr 1967 Cover: 0.12 **NM** value: **8.00**
Circ: Statement: **384,450**
• adapts Tarzan the Terrible **A:** Russ Manning
167 ☐ May 1967 Cover: 0.12 **NM** value: **8.00**
Circ: Statement: **384,450**
• adapts Tarzan the Terrible **A:** Russ Manning
168 ☐ Jun 1967 Cover: 0.12 **NM** value: **10.00**
Circ: Statement: **384,450**
Photo cover.
169 ☐ Jul 1967 Cover: 0.12 **NM** value: **8.00**
Circ: Statement: **384,450**
• adapts Jungle Tales of Tarzan
170 ☐ Aug 1967 Cover: 0.12 **NM** value: **8.00**
Circ: Statement: **384,450**
• adapts Jungle Tales of Tarzan
171 ☐ Sep 1967 Cover: 0.12 **NM** value: **10.00**
Circ: Statement: **384,450**
Photo cover.
172 ☐ Oct 1967 Cover: 0.12 **NM** value: **7.00**
Circ: Statement: **384,450**
• adapts Tarzan and the Golden Lion **A:** Russ Manning
173 ☐ Dec 1967 Cover: 0.12 **NM** value: **7.00**
Circ: Statement: **384,450**
• adapts Tarzan and the Golden Lion **A:** Russ Manning
174 ☐ Feb 1968 Cover: 0.12 **NM** value: **7.00**
• adapts Tarzan and the Ant Men **A:** Russ Manning
175 ☐ Apr 1968 Cover: 0.12 **NM** value: **7.00**
• adapts Tarzan and the Ant Men **A:** Russ Manning
176 ☐ Jun 1968 Cover: 0.12 **NM** value: **7.00**
• adapts Tarzan; Lord of the Jungle **A:** Russ Manning
177 ☐ Jul 1968 Cover: 0.12 **NM** value: **7.00**
• adapts Tarzan; Lord of the Jungle **A:** Russ Manning
178 ☐ Aug 1968 Cover: 0.15 **NM** value: **7.00**
• reprints issue #155
179 ☐ Sep 1968 Cover: 0.15 **NM** value: **7.00**
• adapts Tarzan at the Earth's Core
180 ☐ Oct 1968 Cover: 0.15 **NM** value: **7.00**
• **CGC:** 1 graded, best 6.5
• adapts Tarzan at the Earth's Core
181 ☐ Dec 1968 Cover: 0.15 **NM** value: **7.00**
• adapts Tarzan at the Earth's Core
182 ☐ Feb 1969 Cover: 0.15 **NM** value: **7.00**
• adapts Tarzan the Invincible
183 ☐ Apr 1969 Cover: 0.15 **NM** value: **7.00**
• adapts Tarzan the Invincible
184 ☐ Jun 1969 Cover: 0.15 **NM** value: **7.00**
• adapts Tarzan Triumphant
185 ☐ Jul 1969 Cover: 0.15 **NM** value: **7.00**
• adapts Tarzan Triumphant
186 ☐ Aug 1969 Cover: 0.15 **NM** value: **7.00**
• adapts Tarzan and the City of Gold
187 ☐ Sep 1969 Cover: 0.15 **NM** value: **7.00**
• adapts Tarzan and the City of Gold
188 ☐ Oct 1969 Cover: 0.15 **NM** value: **7.00**
• adapts Tarzan's Quest
189 ☐ Dec 1969 Cover: 0.15 **NM** value: **7.00**
• adapts Tarzan's Quest
190 ☐ Feb 1970 Cover: 0.15 **NM** value: **7.00**
• adapts Tarzan ahd the Forbidden City; adapts Tarzan and the Forbidden City
191 ☐ Apr 1970 Cover: 0.15 **NM** value: **7.00**
• adapts Tarzan ahd the Forbidden City; adapts Tarzan and the Forbidden City
192 ☐ Jun 1970 Cover: 0.15 **NM** value: **7.00**
• adapts Tarzan and the Foreign Legion
193 ☐ Jul 1970 Cover: 0.15 **NM** value: **7.00**
• adapts Tarzan and the Foreign Legion
194 ☐ Aug 1970 Cover: 0.15 **NM** value: **7.00**
• adapts Tarzan and the Lost Empire
195 ☐ Sep 1970 Cover: 0.15 **NM** value: **7.00**
• adapts Tarzan and the Lost Empire
196 ☐ Oct 1970 Cover: 0.15 **NM** value: **7.00**
• adapts Tarzan and the Tarzan Twins
197 ☐ Dec 1970 Cover: 0.15 **NM** value: **7.00**
198 ☐ Feb 1971 Cover: 0.15 **NM** value: **7.00**
Circ: Statement: **241,713**
199 ☐ Apr 1971 Cover: 0.15 **NM** value: **7.00**
Circ: Statement: **241,713**
200 ☐ Jun 1971 Cover: 0.15 **NM** value: **7.00**
Circ: Statement: **241,713**
201 ☐ Jul 1971 Cover: 0.15 **NM** value: **6.00**
Circ: Statement: **241,713**
202 ☐ Aug 1971 Cover: 0.15 **NM** value: **6.00**
Circ: Statement: **241,713**
• astronauts land in jungle **A:** Russ Manning
203 ☐ Sep 1971 Cover: 0.15 **NM** value: **6.00**
Circ: Statement: **241,713**
204 ☐ Oct 1971 Cover: 0.15 **NM** value: **6.00**
Circ: Statement: **241,713**
205 ☐ Dec 1971 Cover: 0.15 **NM** value: **6.00**
Circ: Statement: **209,064**
206 ☐ Feb 1972 Cover: 0.15 **NM** value: **6.00**
Circ: Statement: **209,064**
📖 Tarzan and the Lion Man • moves to DC; Series continued in Tarzan (DC) #207; Has 1971 Statement; avg print run 363,916; avg total paid circ 241,713

TARZAN (DC) — DC

Edgar Rice Burroughs' jungle man, Tarzan, has been one of the best-loved and most enduring heroes of American literature. This series had a phenomenally long run as well, starting in 1948 as a Dell book and ending almost thirty years later, in 1977, as a DC title.

The DC run of this title picked up from Tarzan (Gold Key) #206 in 1972. During its run, art legends Jesse Marsh, Joe Kubert, and Russ Manning drew the Lord of the Jungle and his adventures.

207 ☐ Apr 1972 Cover: 0.25 **NM** value: **8.00**
Circ: Statement: **209,064** • **CGC:** 18 graded, best 9.8
• Giant-size. 📖 Origin Of The Ape-Man • John Carter of Mars back-up; Series continued from Tarzan (Dell) **A:** Joe Kubert ★ Origin of Tarzan.
208 ☐ May 1972 Cover: 0.25 **NM** value: **4.00**
Circ: Statement: **209,064** • **CGC:** 2 graded, best 9.6
• John Carter of Mars back-up **A:** Joe Kubert ★ Origin of Tarzan.
209 ☐ Jun 1972 Cover: 0.25 **NM** value: **4.00**
Circ: Statement: **209,064**
• John Carter of Mars back-up continues in Weird Worlds #1 **A:** Joe Kubert ★ Origin of Tarzan.
210 ☐ Jul 1972 Cover: 0.20 **NM** value: **4.00**
Circ: Statement: **209,064** • **CGC:** 2 graded, best 7.0
A: Joe Kubert ★ Origin of Tarzan.
211 ☐ Aug 1972 Cover: 0.20 **NM** value: **3.00**
Circ: Statement: **209,064**
A: Joe Kubert
212 ☐ Sep 1972 Cover: 0.20 **NM** value: **3.00**
Circ: Statement: **209,064**
A: Joe Kubert
213 ☐ Oct 1972 Cover: 0.20 **NM** value: **3.00**
Circ: Statement: **209,064**
A: Joe Kubert
214 ☐ Nov 1972 Cover: 0.20 **NM** value: **3.00**
Circ: Statement: **209,064**
• Beyond the Farthest Star back-up **A:** Joe Kubert
215 ☐ Dec 1972 Cover: 0.20 **NM** value: **3.00**
Circ: Statement: **209,064**
• Beyond the Farthest Star back-up **A:** Joe Kubert
216 ☐ Jan 1973 Cover: 0.20 **NM** value: **3.00**
Circ: Statement: **209,790**
• Beyond the Farthest Star back-up **A:** Joe Kubert
217 ☐ Feb 1973 Cover: 0.20 **NM** value: **3.00**
Circ: Statement: **209,790** • **CGC:** 1 graded, best 9.0
• Beyond the Farthest Star back-up **A:** Joe Kubert
218 ☐ Mar 1973 Cover: 0.20 **NM** value: **3.00**
Circ: Statement: **209,790**
• Beyond the Farthest Star back-up; Has 1972 Statement; avg total paid circ 209,064 **A:** Joe Kubert
219 ☐ May 1973 Cover: 0.20 **NM** value: **3.00**
Circ: Statement: **209,790**
A: Joe Kubert
220 ☐ Jun 1973 Cover: 0.20 **NM** value: **3.00**
Circ: Statement: **209,790**
A: Joe Kubert
221 ☐ Jul 1973 Cover: 0.20 **NM** value: **3.00**
Circ: Statement: **209,790**
A: Joe Kubert
222 ☐ Aug 1973 Cover: 0.20 **NM** value: **3.00**
Circ: Statement: **209,790** • **CGC:** 1 graded, best 9.4
A: Joe Kubert
223 ☐ Sep 1973 Cover: 0.20 **NM** value: **3.00**
Circ: Statement: **209,790**
A: Joe Kubert
224 ☐ Oct 1973 Cover: 0.20 **NM** value: **3.00**
Circ: Statement: **209,790**
A: Joe Kubert
225 ☐ Nov 1973 Cover: 0.20 **NM** value: **3.00**
Circ: Statement: **209,790**
A: Joe Kubert
226 ☐ Dec 1973 Cover: 0.20 **NM** value: **3.00**
Circ: Statement: **209,790**
A: Joe Kubert
227 ☐ Jan 1974 Cover: 0.20 **NM** value: **3.00**
Circ: Statement: **223,710**
A: Joe Kubert
228 ☐ Feb 1974 Cover: 0.20 **NM** value: **3.00**
Circ: Statement: **223,710**
A: Joe Kubert
229 ☐ Mar 1974 Cover: 0.20 **NM** value: **3.00**
Circ: Statement: **223,710**
230 ☐ May 1974 Cover: 0.60 **NM** value: **5.00**
Circ: Statement: **223,710** • **CGC:** 4 graded, best 9.6
• Has 1974 Statement; avg total paid circ 209,790
231 ☐ Jul 1974 Cover: 0.60 **NM** value: **5.00**
Circ: Statement: **223,710** • **CGC:** 1 graded, best 9.0
232 ☐ Sep 1974 Cover: 0.60 **NM** value: **5.00**
Circ: Statement: **223,710** • **CGC:** 2 graded, best 8.5
233 ☐ Nov 1974 Cover: 0.60 **NM** value: **5.00**
Circ: Statement: **223,710** • **CGC:** 1 graded, best 9.2
234 ☐ Jan 1975 Cover: 0.60 **NM** value: **5.00**
Circ: Statement: **145,000** • **CGC:** 2 graded, best 9.0
235 ☐ Mar 1975 Cover: 0.60 **NM** value: **5.00**
Circ: Statement: **145,000** • **CGC:** 2 graded, best 9.4
236 ☐ Apr 1975 Cover: 0.25 **NM** value: **2.50**
Circ: Statement: **145,000**
237 ☐ May 1975 Cover: 0.25 **NM** value: **2.50**
Circ: Statement: **145,000**
• Has 1974 Statement; avg total paid circ 223,710 **A:** Russ Manning
C: Joe Kubert
238 ☐ Jun 1975 Cover: 0.50 **NM** value: **2.50**
Circ: Statement: **145,000**
239 ☐ Jul 1975 Cover: 0.50 **NM** value: **2.50**
Circ: Statement: **145,000**
A: Joe Kubert
240 ☐ Aug 1975 Cover: 0.25 **NM** value: **2.50**
Circ: Statement: **145,000**
• adapts The Castaways **A:** Joe Kubert
241 ☐ Sep 1975 Cover: 0.25 **NM** value: **2.50**
Circ: Statement: **145,000**
242 ☐ Oct 1975 Cover: 0.25 **NM** value: **2.50**
Circ: Statement: **145,000**
243 ☐ Nov 1975 Cover: 0.25 **NM** value: **2.50**
Circ: Statement: **145,000**
244 ☐ Dec 1975 Cover: 0.25 **NM** value: **2.50**
Circ: Statement: **145,000**
245 ☐ Jan 1976 Cover: 0.25 **NM** value: **2.50**
246 ☐ Feb 1976 Cover: 0.25 **NM** value: **2.50**
247 ☐ Mar 1976 Cover: 0.30 **NM** value: **2.50**
248 ☐ Apr 1976 Cover: 0.30 **NM** value: **2.50**
249 ☐ May 1976 Cover: 0.30 **NM** value: **2.50**
250 ☐ Jun 1976 Cover: 0.30 **NM** value: **2.50**
251 ☐ Jul 1976 Cover: 0.30 **NM** value: **2.50**
252 ☐ Aug 1976 Cover: 0.30 **NM** value: **2.50**
253 ☐ Sep 1976 Cover: 0.30 **NM** value: **2.50**

CGC-graded: Multiply prices above by **33 for 9.9 M • 16 for 9.8 NM/M • 7 for 9.6 NM+ • 5 for 9.4 NM • 2.5 for 9.2 NM- • 1.5 for 9.0 VF/NM**

254 ❑ Oct 1976 Cover: 0.30 **NM** value: **2.50**
255 ❑ Nov 1976 Cover: 0.30 **NM** value: **2.50**
256 ❑ Dec 1976 Cover: 0.30 **NM** value: **2.50**
• adapts Tarzan the Untamed **A:** Joe Kubert
257 ❑ Jan 1977 Cover: 0.30 **NM** value: **2.50**
📖 The Nightmare! **A:** Joe Kubert **W:** Joe Kubert
258 ❑ Feb 1977 Cover: 0.30 **NM** value: **2.50**
final issue.

TARZAN AND THE JEWELS OF OPAR (EDGAR RICE BURROUGHS'...) Dark Horse

1 ❑ Jun 1999 Cover: 10.95 **NM** value: **Cover or less**
No issue number. • digest. • collects stories from Dell's Tarzan #159-161 plus pin-ups **A:** Russ Manning **W:** Gaylord DuBois

TARZAN: A TALE OF MUGAMBI (EDGAR RICE BURROUGHS'...) Dark Horse

1 ❑ Jun 1995 Cover: 2.95 **NM** value: **Cover or less**
Circ: CapCity orders: **5,675**
No issue number. One-shot.

TARZAN/CARSON OF VENUS Dark Horse

1 ❑ May 1998 Cover: 2.95 **NM** value: **Cover or less**
Circ: Diamd. preorders: **8,607**
A: Igor Kordey **W:** Darko Macan
2 ❑ Jun 1998 Cover: 2.95 **NM** value: **Cover or less**
Circ: Diamd. preorders: **8,297**
A: Igor Kordey **W:** Darko Macan
3 ❑ Jul 1998 Cover: 2.95 **NM** value: **Cover or less**
Circ: Diamd. preorders: **7,964**
A: Igor Kordey **W:** Darko Macan
4 ❑ Aug 1998 Cover: 2.95 **NM** value: **Cover or less**
Circ: Diamd. preorders: **7,880**
A: Igor Kordey **W:** Darko Macan
Bk 1 ❑ Aug 1999 Cover: 12.95 **NM** value: **Cover or less**
A: Igor Kordey **W:** Darko Macan

TARZAN (DARK HORSE) Dark Horse

There's something about Tarzan, the legendary jungle king created by Edgar Rice Burroughs, that brings out the best in comics. Indeed, there's rarely been a bad version of Tarzan since Hal Foster started doing the Sunday strip in 1930, and the latest incarnation from Dark Horse follows in that hallowed tradition of excellence.

This new Tarzan series is broken into several shorter arcs, such as "The Modern Prometheus," a two-part story following the adventures of the now-civilized ape-man in the New York City of 1909. It's populated by such luminaries as Thomas Edison and his rival Nicholas Tesla (their rivalry is the centerpiece of the story), with cameos by Arthur Conan Doyle, Mark Twain, and others. The creative teams consistently deliver a literate, exciting, and beautifully illustrated version of the classic adventure hero.

1 ❑ Jul 1996 Cover: 2.95 **NM** value: **3.00**
📖 Tarzan's Jungle Fury, Part 1 **A:** Christopher Schenck **W:** Bruce Jones
2 ❑ Aug 1996 Cover: 2.95 **NM** value: **3.00**
📖 Tarzan's Jungle Fury, Part 2 **A:** Christopher Schenck **W:** Bruce Jones
3 ❑ Aug 1996 Cover: 2.95 **NM** value: **3.00**
Circ: Diamd. preorders: **15,360**
📖 Tarzan's Jungle Fury, Part 3 **A:** Christopher Schenck **W:** Bruce Jones
4 ❑ Sep 1996 Cover: 2.95 **NM** value: **3.00**
Circ: Diamd. preorders: **13,890**
📖 Tarzan's Jungle Fury, Part 4 **A:** Christopher Schenck **W:** Bruce Jones
5 ❑ Nov 1996 Cover: 2.95 **NM** value: **3.00**
Circ: Diamd. preorders: **12,694**
📖 Tarzan's Jungle Fury, Part 5 **A:** Christopher Schenck **W:** Bruce Jones
6 ❑ Nov 1996 Cover: 2.95 **NM** value: **3.00**
Circ: Diamd. preorders: **11,671**
📖 Tarzan's Jungle Fury, Part 6 **A:** Christopher Schenck **W:** Bruce Jones
7 ❑ Jan 1997 Cover: 2.95 **NM** value: **3.00**
Circ: Diamd. preorders: **10,804**
📖 Legion of Hate, Part 1; Friend of Foe? **A:** Christopher Schenck **W:** Allan Gross
8 ❑ Feb 1997 Cover: 2.95 **NM** value: **3.00**
Circ: Diamd. preorders: **10,244**
📖 Legion of Hate, Part 2; Flesh and Mud **A:** Christopher Schenck **W:** Allan Gross
9 ❑ Mar 1997 Cover: 2.95 **NM** value: **3.00**
Circ: Diamd. preorders: **9,847**
📖 Legion of Hate, Part 3; Today Your Love Tomorrow The World **A:** Christopher Schenck **W:** Allan Gross
10 ❑ Apr 1997 Cover: 2.95 **NM** value: **3.00**
Circ: Diamd. preorders: **9,492**
📖 Legion of Hate, Part 4
11 ❑ May 1997 Cover: 2.95 **NM** value: **3.00**
Circ: Diamd. preorders: **10,041**
📖 Le Monstre, Part 1; Le Monstre **A:** Stan Manoukian; Vince Roucher **W:** Lovern Kindzierski
12 ❑ Jun 1997 Cover: 2.95 **NM** value: **Cover or less**
Circ: Diamd. preorders: **9,369**
📖 Le Monstre, Part 2; Le Monstre **A:** Stan Manoukian; Vince Roucher **W:** Lovern Kindzierski
13 ❑ Aug 1997 Cover: 2.95 **NM** value: **Cover or less**
Circ: Diamd. preorders: **10,147**
📖 The Modern Prometheus, Part 1 **A:** Stan Manoukian **W:** Lovern Kindzierski
14 ❑ Sep 1997 Cover: 2.95 **NM** value: **Cover or less**
Circ: Diamd. preorders: **9,340**
📖 The Modern Prometheus, Part 2 **A:** Stan Manoukian; Vince Roucher **W:** Lovern Kindzierski
15 ❑ Sep 1997 Cover: 2.95 **NM** value: **Cover or less**
Circ: Diamd. preorders: **9,397**
📖 Tooth and Nail, Part 1 **A:** Stan Manoukian; Vince Roucher **W:** Lovern Kindzierski
16 ❑ Oct 1997 Cover: 2.95 **NM** value: **Cover or less**
Circ: Diamd. preorders: **8,949**
📖 Tooth and Nail, Part 2
17 ❑ Dec 1997 Cover: 2.95 **NM** value: **Cover or less**
Circ: Diamd. preorders: **9,317**
📖 Versus The Moon Men, Part 1; Tarzan vs. The Moon Men **A:** Tom Yeates **W:** Tim Truman
18 ❑ Jan 1998 Cover: 2.95 **NM** value: **Cover or less**
Circ: Diamd. preorders: **8,845**
📖 Versus The Moon Men, Part 2
19 ❑ Feb 1998 Cover: 2.95 **NM** value: **Cover or less**
Circ: Diamd. preorders: **8,273**
📖 Versus The Moon Men, Part 3
20 ❑ Mar 1998 Cover: 2.95 **NM** value: **Cover or less**
📖 Versus The Moon Men, Part 4

TARZAN DIGEST DC

1 ❑ Aut 1972 Cover: 0.50 **NM** value: **3.00**

TARZAN (DISNEY'S...) Dark Horse

1 ❑ Jul 1999 Cover: 2.95 **NM** value: **Cover or less**
A: Mario Cortes **W:** Greg Ehrbar
2 ❑ Jul 1999 Cover: 2.95 **NM** value: **Cover or less**
A: Mario Cortes **W:** Greg Ehrbar

TARZAN FAMILY, THE DC

60 ❑ Dec 1975 Cover: 0.50 **NM** value: **5.00**
Circ: Statement: **103,000**
61 ❑ Feb 1976 Cover: 0.50 **NM** value: **5.00**
62 ❑ Apr 1976 Cover: 0.50 **NM** value: **4.00**
63 ❑ Jun 1976 Cover: 0.50 **NM** value: **4.00**
64 ❑ Aug 1976 Cover: 0.50 **NM** value: **4.00**
• **CGC:** 1 graded, best 9.2
65 ❑ Sep 1976 Cover: 0.50 **NM** value: **4.00**
66 ❑ Nov 1976 Cover: 0.50 **NM** value: **4.00**

TARZAN IN THE LAND THAT TIME FORGOT AND THE POOL OF TIME (EDGAR RICE BURROUGHS'...) Dark Horse

Bk 1 ❑ Jun 1996 Cover: 12.95 **NM** value: **Cover or less**
• collects two stories **A:** Russ Manning **W:** Russ Manning

TARZAN/JOHN CARTER: WARLORDS OF MARS Dark Horse

1 ❑ Jan 1996 Cover: 2.50 **NM** value: **Cover or less**
📖 Red Awakening **A:** Bret Blevin **W:** Simon Revelstroke; Bruce Jones
2 ❑ Apr 1996 Cover: 2.50 **NM** value: **Cover or less**
indicia says #3, cover says #2. ★ Appearance of Dejah Thoris, Cathoris, Tars Tarkas, Dejah Thoris, Tars Tarkas, Cathoris.
3 ❑ May 1996 Cover: 2.50 **NM** value: **Cover or less**
★ Versus John Carter.
4 ❑ Jul 1996 Cover: 2.50 **NM** value: **Cover or less**
final issue. ★ Death of Taka.

TARZAN, LORD OF THE JUNGLE (GOLD KEY) Gold Key

1 ❑ Sep 1965 Cover: 0.25 **NM** value: **40.00**
• **CGC:** 5 graded, best 9.6

TARZAN: LOVE, LIES AND THE LOST CITY Malibu

1 ❑ Aug 1992 Cover: 3.95 **NM** value: **Cover or less**
Circ: CapCity orders: **8,100**
• Flip-book. 📖 Tarzan's First Love, Tarzan: The Scar **A:** Teddy Kristiansen; Peter Snejbjerg; Walt Simonson **W:** Matt Wagner; Walt Simonson
2 ❑ Sep 1992 Cover: 2.50 **NM** value: **3.95**
Circ: CapCity orders: **5,400**
3 ❑ Oct 1992 Cover: 2.50 **NM** value: **3.95**
Circ: CapCity orders: **5,100**

TARZAN (MARVEL) Marvel

In this 1977 adventure series, Marvel brings us its version of Tarzan, the world's most famous jungle dweller.

John Buscema did a great job of presenting the tales of Edgar Rice Burroughs' legendary character. What's more, he managed to bring a new sense of adventure to a character whose exploits had been covered heavily in comics, books, and films.

The adventures were set in the post-World War I era with Tarzan being menaced by biplanes and, later, dinosaurs at the center of the Earth.

1 ❑ Jun 1977 Cover: 0.30 **NM** value: **3.00**
• **CGC:** 7 graded, best 9.6
📖 Tarzan And The Jewels Of Opar **A:** John Buscema **W:** Roy Thomas
2 ❑ Jul 1977 Cover: 0.30 **NM** value: **2.00**
• **CGC:** 2 graded, best 9.8
3 ❑ Aug 1977 Cover: 0.30 **NM** value: **2.00**
4 ❑ Sep 1977 Cover: 0.30 **NM** value: **2.00**
5 ❑ Oct 1977 Cover: 0.30 **NM** value: **2.00**
• **CGC:** 1 graded, best 9.6
6 ❑ Nov 1977 Cover: 0.35 **NM** value: **1.50**
7 ❑ Dec 1977 Cover: 0.35 **NM** value: **1.50**
8 ❑ Jan 1978 Cover: 0.35 **NM** value: **1.50**
9 ❑ Feb 1978 Cover: 0.35 **NM** value: **1.50**
10 ❑ Mar 1978 Cover: 0.35 **NM** value: **1.50**
11 ❑ Apr 1978 Cover: 0.35 **NM** value: **1.50**
12 ❑ May 1978 Cover: 0.35 **NM** value: **1.50**
13 ❑ Jun 1978 Cover: 0.35 **NM** value: **1.50**
14 ❑ Jul 1978 Cover: 0.35 **NM** value: **1.50**
15 ❑ Aug 1978 Cover: 0.35 **NM** value: **1.50**
16 ❑ Sep 1978 Cover: 0.35 **NM** value: **1.50**
17 ❑ Oct 1978 Cover: 0.35 **NM** value: **1.50**
18 ❑ Nov 1978 Cover: 0.35 **NM** value: **1.50**
• **CGC:** 1 graded, best 9.6
19 ❑ Dec 1978 Cover: 0.35 **NM** value: **1.50**
20 ❑ Jan 1979 Cover: 0.35 **NM** value: **1.50**
21 ❑ Feb 1979 Cover: 0.35 **NM** value: **1.50**
22 ❑ Mar 1979 Cover: 0.35 **NM** value: **1.50**
23 ❑ Apr 1979 Cover: 0.35 **NM** value: **1.50**
24 ❑ May 1979 Cover: 0.40 **NM** value: **1.50**
25 ❑ Jun 1979 Cover: 0.40 **NM** value: **1.50**
26 ❑ Jul 1979 Cover: 0.40 **NM** value: **1.50**
27 ❑ Aug 1979 Cover: 0.40 **NM** value: **1.50**
28 ❑ Sep 1979 Cover: 0.40 **NM** value: **1.50**
29 ❑ Oct 1979 Cover: 0.40 **NM** value: **1.50**
Anl 1 ❑ ca. 1977 Cover: 0.50 **NM** value: **2.00**
Anl 2 ❑ ca. 1978 Cover: 0.60 **NM** value: **1.50**
Anl 3 ❑ ca. 1979 Cover: 0.60 **NM** value: **1.50**

TARZAN OF THE APES Marvel

1 ❑ Jul 1984 Cover: 0.60 **NM** value: **3.00**
A: Dan Spiegle **W:** Mark Evanier; Edgar Rice Burroughs; Sharman DiVono ★ Origin of Tarzan.
2 ❑ Aug 1984 Cover: 0.60 **NM** value: **3.00**
A: Dan Spiegle **W:** Mark Evanier; Edgar Rice Burroughs; Sharman DiVono ★ Origin of Tarzan.

TARZAN OF THE APES (EDGAR RICE BURROUGHS'...) Dark Horse

1 ❑ May 1999 Cover: 12.95 **NM** value: **Cover or less**
No issue number. • digest. • collects stories from Dell's Tarzan #155-158 and spot illustrations from Tarzan #154-156 **A:** Russ Manning

TARZAN'S JUNGLE ANNUAL Dell

1 ❑ ca. 1952 Cover: 0.25 **NM** value: **200.00**
2 ❑ ca. 1953 Cover: 0.25 **NM** value: **150.00**
3 ❑ ca. 1954 Cover: 0.25 **NM** value: **125.00**

TARZAN: THE BECKONING Malibu

1 ❑ Nov 1992 Cover: 2.50 **NM** value: **Cover or less**
Circ: CapCity orders: **7,250**
A: Tom Yeates **W:** Tom Yeates; Henning Kure
2 ❑ Dec 1992 Cover: 2.50 **NM** value: **Cover or less**
Circ: CapCity orders: **5,975**
A: Tom Yeates **W:** Tom Yeates; Henning Kure
3 ❑ Jan 1993 Cover: 2.50 **NM** value: **Cover or less**
Circ: CapCity orders: **5,225**
A: Tom Yeates **W:** Tom Yeates; Henning Kure
4 ❑ Feb 1993 Cover: 2.50 **NM** value: **Cover or less**
Circ: CapCity orders: **4,850**
A: Tom Yeates **W:** Tom Yeates; Henning Kure
5 ❑ Mar 1993 Cover: 2.50 **NM** value: **Cover or less**
Circ: CapCity orders: **4,125**
A: Tom Yeates **W:** Tom Yeates; Henning Kure
6 ❑ Apr 1993 Cover: 2.50 **NM** value: **Cover or less**
Circ: CapCity orders: **3,825**
A: Tom Yeates **W:** Tom Yeates; Henning Kure
7 ❑ Jun 1993 Cover: 2.50 **NM** value: **Cover or less**
Circ: CapCity orders: **3,775**
A: Tom Yeates **W:** Tom Yeates; Henning Kure

TARZAN: THE LOST ADVENTURE (EDGAR RICE BURROUGHS'...) Dark Horse

1 ❑ Jan 1995, b&w Cover: 2.95 **NM** value: **Cover or less**
Circ: CapCity orders: **9,550**
📖 Tarzan: The Lost Adventure; John Carter Of Mars • squarebound **A:** Tom Yeates; John Coleman Burroughs **W:** John Coleman Burroughs; Edgar Rice Burroughs
2 ❑ Feb 1995, b&w Cover: 2.95 **NM** value: **Cover or less**
Circ: CapCity orders: **7,775**
• squarebound **A:** Tom Yeates; John Coleman Burroughs **W:** John Coleman Burroughs; Edgar Rice Burroughs
3 ❑ Mar 1995, b&w Cover: 2.95 **NM** value: **Cover or less**
Circ: CapCity orders: **7,250**
• squarebound **A:** Tom Yeates; John Coleman Burroughs **W:** John Coleman Burroughs; Edgar Rice Burroughs
4 ❑ Apr 1995, b&w Cover: 2.95 **NM** value: **Cover or less**
Circ: CapCity orders: **6,150**
• squarebound **A:** Tom Yeates; John Coleman Burroughs **W:** John Coleman Burroughs; Edgar Rice Burroughs

TARZAN: THE RIVERS OF BLOOD (EDGAR RICE BURROUGHS' ...) Dark Horse

1 ❑ Nov 1999 Cover: 2.95 **NM** value: **Cover or less**
Circ: Diamd. preorders: **7,995**
A: Igor Kordey **W:** Igor Kordey; Neven Anticevic
2 ❑ Dec 1999 Cover: 2.95 **NM** value: **Cover or less**
Circ: Diamd. preorders: **7,877**
A: Igor Kordey **W:** Igor Kordey; Neven Anticevic

Other grades: Multiply prices above by **1.5 for Mint • 2/3 for Very Fine • 1/3 for Fine • 1/5 for Very Good • 1/8 for Good**

3 ❑ Jan 2000 Cover: 2.95 **NM value: Cover or less**
Circ: Diamd. preorders: **7,269**
A: Igor Kordey **W:** Igor Kordey; Neven Anticevic
4 ❑ Feb 2000 Cover: 2.95 **NM value: Cover or less**
Circ: Diamd. preorders: **6,904**
• final issue of eight-issue mini-series **A:** Igor Kordey **W:** Igor Kordey; Neven Anticevic

TARZAN: THE SAVAGE HEART — Dark Horse

1 ❑ Apr 1999 Cover: 2.95 **NM value: Cover or less**
Circ: Diamd. preorders: **8,740**
A: Mike Grell **W:** Allan Gross
2 ❑ May 1999 Cover: 2.95 **NM value: Cover or less**
Circ: Diamd. preorders: **7,760**
A: Mike Grell **W:** Allan Gross
3 ❑ Jun 1999 Cover: 2.95 **NM value: Cover or less**
Circ: Diamd. preorders: **7,826**
A: Mike Grell **W:** Allan Gross
4 ❑ Jul 1999 Cover: 2.95 **NM value: Cover or less**
Circ: Diamd. preorders: **7,762**
A: Mike Grell **W:** Allan Gross

TARZAN THE WARRIOR — Malibu

1 ❑ Mar 1992 Cover: 2.50 **NM value: Cover or less**
Circ: CapCity orders: **11,180**
A: Neil Vokes **W:** Mark Wheatley
2 ❑ May 1992 Cover: 2.50 **NM value: Cover or less**
Circ: CapCity orders: **9,790**
A: Neil Vokes **W:** Mark Wheatley
3 ❑ Jun 1992 Cover: 2.50 **NM value: Cover or less**
Circ: CapCity orders: **8,000**
A: Neil Vokes **W:** Mark Wheatley
4 ❑ Aug 1992 Cover: 2.50 **NM value: Cover or less**
Circ: CapCity orders: **8,025**
A: Neil Vokes **W:** Mark Wheatley
5 ❑ Sep 1992 Cover: 2.50 **NM value: Cover or less**
Circ: CapCity orders: **7,270**
A: Neil Vokes **W:** Mark Wheatley

TARZAN VS. PREDATOR AT THE EARTH'S CORE — Dark Horse

1 ❑ Jan 1996 Cover: 2.50 **NM value: Cover or less**
Circ: CapCity orders: **17,575**
📖 Worlds Within Worlds **A:** Lee Weeks **W:** Walt Simonson
2 ❑ Feb 1996 Cover: 2.50 **NM value: Cover or less**
Circ: CapCity orders: **12,975**
A: Lee Weeks **W:** Walt Simonson
3 ❑ Mar 1996 Cover: 2.50 **NM value: Cover or less**
A: Lee Weeks **W:** Walt Simonson
4 ❑ Jun 1996 Cover: 2.50 **NM value: Cover or less**
final issue. **A:** Lee Weeks **W:** Walt Simonson ★ Death of Mahar Queen.
Bk 1 ❑ Oct 1997 Cover: 12.95 **NM value: Cover or less**

TARZAN WEEKLY — Byblos

1 ❑ Cover: 0.12 **NM value: 5.00**

T.A.S.E.R. — Comicreations

1 ❑ Sep 1992, b&w Cover: 2.00 **NM value: Cover or less**
2 ❑ Jun 1993, b&w Cover: 2.00 **NM value: Cover or less**

TASMANIAN DEVIL AND HIS TASTY FRIENDS — Gold Key

1 ❑ Nov 1962 Cover: 0.10 **NM value: 70.00**
• **CGC:** 2 graded, best 9.2

TASTY BITS — Avalon

1 ❑ Jul 1999 Cover: 2.95 **NM value: Cover or less**
📖 Frame 137; Shadows; Upon thy Belly Thou Shalt Go… **A:** James O'Barr **W:** James O'Barr

TATTERED BANNERS — DC / Vertigo

1 ❑ Nov 1998 Cover: 2.95 **NM value: Cover or less**
Circ: Diamd. preorders: **8,198**
📖 Real Men Don't Klik **A:** Mike McMahon **W:** Keith Giffen; Alan Grant
2 ❑ Dec 1998 Cover: 2.95 **NM value: Cover or less**
Circ: Diamd. preorders: **6,377**
A: Mike McMahon **W:** Keith Giffen; Alan Grant
3 ❑ Jan 1999 Cover: 2.95 **NM value: Cover or less**
Circ: Diamd. preorders: **6,155**
📖 Escape From New York **A:** Mike McMahon **W:** Alan Grant
4 ❑ Feb 1999 Cover: 2.95 **NM value: Cover or less**
Circ: Diamd. preorders: **5,263**
A: Mike McMahon **W:** Keith Giffen; Alan Grant

TATTOO — Caliber

1 ❑ Cover: 2.95 **NM value: Cover or less**
📖 Zombie Slayer **A:** Jake Jacobsen **W:** Ralph Griffith; Stuart Kerr
2 ❑ Cover: 2.95 **NM value: Cover or less**

TATTOO MAN — Fantagraphics

1 ❑ b&w Cover: 2.75 **NM value: Cover or less**

TAXX, THE — Express / Parody

0.5 ❑ Cover: 1.50 **NM value: Cover or less**
A: Bill Maus **W:** Bill Maus; Don Chin
1 ❑ b&w Cover: 2.75 **NM value: Cover or less**

T-BIRD CHRONICLES — Me Comix

1 ❑ b&w Cover: 1.50 **NM value: Cover or less**
2 ❑ b&w Cover: 1.50 **NM value: Cover or less**

TEAM 7 — Image

1 ❑ Oct 1994 Cover: 2.50 **NM value: 3.00**
Circ: CapCity orders: **60,800**
📖 Gone Animal **A:** Aron Wiesenfeld **W:** Chuck Dixon
1/A ❑ Oct 1994 Cover: 2.50 **NM value: 3.00**
Variant cover by Whilce Portacio. 📖 Gone Animal **A:** Aron Wiesenfeld; Whilce Portacio(cover) **W:** Chuck Dixon
2 ❑ Nov 1994 Cover: 2.50 **NM value: Cover or less**
Circ: CapCity orders: **43,600**
A: Aron Wiesenfeld **W:** Chuck Dixon
3 ❑ Dec 1994 Cover: 2.50 **NM value: Cover or less**
Circ: CapCity orders: **41,800**
A: Aron Wiesenfeld **W:** Chuck Dixon
4 ❑ Feb 1995 Cover: 2.50 **NM value: Cover or less**
Circ: CapCity orders: **41,775**
A: Aron Wiesenfeld **W:** Chuck Dixon
Ash 1 ❑ Oct 1994, b&w **NM value: 1.00**
• ashcan promo edition.
Bk 1 ❑ Jun 1995 Cover: 9.95 **NM value: Cover or less**

TEAM 7: DEAD RECKONING — Image

This four-issue, 1996 mini-series is the third Team 7 series, and the one which finally explains how the members of a special forces team became the super-heroes Grifter, Backlash, and Deathblow as they are known as today.

The series begins with a fateful last mission for the Team 7 strike force. They had infiltrated into Leningrad and were charged with recovering a scientist working on experimental genetic weapons. As always, they managed to complete their seemingly impossible mission, but in doing so an encounter with a genetically altered being cost team leader John "Topkick" Lynch his right eye. A week later, the team was back in the U.S. where they discovered who it was that had ordered the mission — their old enemy and now new boss Miles Craven. Several of the team immediately rebelled, preferring to dissolve rather than serve under Craven. Team 7 was no more — but Craven's machinations were just beginning...

1 ❑ Jan 1996 Cover: 2.50 **NM value: Cover or less**
📖 Don't Look Back **A:** Jason Johnson **W:** Chuck Dixon
2 ❑ Feb 1996 Cover: 2.50 **NM value: Cover or less**
A: Jason Johnson **W:** Chuck Dixon
3 ❑ Mar 1996 Cover: 2.50 **NM value: Cover or less**
A: Jason Johnson **W:** Chuck Dixon
4 ❑ Apr 1996 Cover: 2.50 **NM value: Cover or less**
A: Jason Johnson **W:** Chuck Dixon

TEAM 7-OBJECTIVE: HELL — Image

1 ❑ May 1995 Cover: 2.50 **NM value: Cover or less**
Circ: CapCity orders: **37,050**
📖 The Wolves • with card **A:** Chris Warner **W:** Chuck Dixon
2 ❑ Jun 1995 Cover: 2.50 **NM value: Cover or less**
Circ: CapCity orders: **29,975**
A: Chris Warner **W:** Chuck Dixon
3 ❑ Jul 1995 Cover: 2.50 **NM value: Cover or less**
Circ: CapCity orders: **29,075**
A: Chris Warner **W:** Chuck Dixon

TEAM AMERICA — Marvel

One of Marvel's few toy licenses not to call forth pangs of nostalgia in Generation X-ers, Team America is based on a line of motorcycle toys from Ideal — sort of the second coming of the Evel Knievel stunt-cycles.

In the Marvel universe, Team America first appears in Captain America #269. Honcho, Lobo, and R.U. Reddy are bike-riding stunt riders and racers who fight crime in their spare time. They're later joined by Cowboy and Wrench, and the series' big mystery is the identity of The Marauder, the black-clad rider who always shows up to save them in the nick of time. The mystery is resolved in the final issue, and before fading out entirely, the Team turns up, of all places, in Chris Claremont's The New Mutants! — JJM

1 ❑ Jun 1982 Cover: 0.60 **NM value: 1.00**
📖 The Origin Of Team America. **A:** Mike Vosburg **W:** Jim Shooter ★ Origin of Team America.
2 ❑ Jul 1982 Cover: 0.60 **NM value: 1.00**
A: Luke McDonnell
3 ❑ Aug 1982 Cover: 0.60 **NM value: 1.00**
A: Luke McDonnell
4 ❑ Sep 1982 Cover: 0.60 **NM value: 1.00**
A: Luke McDonnell
5 ❑ Oct 1982 Cover: 0.60 **NM value: 1.00**
6 ❑ Nov 1982 Cover: 0.60 **NM value: 1.00**
7 ❑ Dec 1982 Cover: 0.60 **NM value: 1.00**
8 ❑ Jan 1983 Cover: 0.60 **NM value: 1.00**
9 ❑ Feb 1983 Cover: 0.60 **NM value: 1.00**
★ Appearance of Iron Man.
10 ❑ Mar 1983 Cover: 0.60 **NM value: 1.00**
11 ❑ Apr 1983 Cover: 0.60 **NM value: 1.00**
★ Appearance of Ghost Rider.
12 ❑ May 1983 Cover: 1.00 **NM value: Cover or less**
• Double-size. • Marauder unmasked **A:** Don Perlin

TEAM ANARCHY — Dagger

1 ❑ Cover: 2.75 **NM value: Cover or less**
Circ: CapCity orders: **4,350**
2 ❑ Cover: 2.50 **NM value: Cover or less**
Circ: CapCity orders: **3,555**
3 ❑ Cover: 2.50 **NM value: Cover or less**
Circ: CapCity orders: **2,640**
4 ❑ Cover: 2.50 **NM value: Cover or less**
Circ: CapCity orders: **2,455**
5 ❑ Cover: 2.50 **NM value: Cover or less**
6 ❑ Cover: 2.50 **NM value: Cover or less**
7 ❑ May 1994 Cover: 2.50 **NM value: Cover or less**
A: Mark Schmitz **W:** Dan Danner

TEAM NIPPON — Aircel

1 ❑ b&w Cover: 1.95 **NM value: Cover or less**
A: Barry Blair **W:** Barry Blair ★ Origin of Team Nippon. ★ 1st Appearance of Team Nippon.
2 ❑ b&w Cover: 1.95 **NM value: Cover or less**
3 ❑ b&w Cover: 1.95 **NM value: Cover or less**
4 ❑ b&w Cover: 1.95 **NM value: Cover or less**
5 ❑ b&w Cover: 1.95 **NM value: Cover or less**
6 ❑ b&w Cover: 1.95 **NM value: Cover or less**
7 ❑ b&w Cover: 1.95 **NM value: Cover or less**
final issue.

TEAM ONE: STORMWATCH — Image

1 ❑ Jun 1995 Cover: 2.50 **NM value: Cover or less**
Circ: CapCity orders: **25,125**
cover says Jul, indicia says Jun. **A:** Tom Raney **W:** Steven Seagle
2 ❑ Aug 1995 Cover: 2.50 **NM value: Cover or less**
Circ: CapCity orders: **19,925**

TEAM ONE: WILDC.A.T.S — Image

1 ❑ Jul 1995 Cover: 2.50 **NM value: Cover or less**
Circ: CapCity orders: **29,675**
A: Richard Johnson **W:** James Robinson
2 ❑ Sep 1995 Cover: 2.50 **NM value: Cover or less**
Circ: CapCity orders: **24,000**
A: Richard Johnson **W:** James Robinson

TEAM SUPERMAN — DC

1 ❑ Jul 1999 Cover: 2.95 **NM value: Cover or less**
Circ: Diamd. preorders: **30,180**
📖 They Died With Their Capes On **A:** Georges Jeanty **W:** Mark Millar

TEAM SUPERMAN SECRET FILES — DC

1 ❑ May 1998 Cover: 4.95 **NM value: Cover or less**
Circ: Diamd. preorders: **32,190**
• biographical info on Superboy, Supergirl, Steel, and respective villains

TEAM TITANS — DC

Donna Troy, one of the Titans, though never trained to use her powers, met and married Terrance Long, a professor of mythology. Troy is now expecting her first child, although she doesn't know that it is destined to become the insane god Chaos — a being who eventually would destroy the world.

A resistance force called Team Titans has formed to kill Donna Troy before she gives birth. Chaos follows them through time in order to assure his birth — though he cares little whether his mother lives or dies afterwards. When the resistance force runs across the Titans, and when both of them in turn meet Lord Chaos, it's a three-way conflict in order to save — or kill — Donna Troy and/or her newborn child in the opening story arc of this ongoing series.

1/A ❑ Sep 1992 Cover: 1.75 **NM value: 2.00**
Circ: CapCity orders: **30,250**
Comes in five different covers. 📖 Total Chaos, Part 3 **A:** Michael Netzer **W:** Marv Wolfman ★ Origin of Killowat.
1/B ❑ Sep 1992 Cover: 1.75 **NM value: 2.00**
Circ: CapCity orders: **30,250**
Comes in five different covers. 📖 Total Chaos, Part 3 **A:** Michael Netzer **W:** Marv Wolfman ★ Origin of Mirage.
1/C ❑ Sep 1992 Cover: 1.75 **NM value: 2.00**
Circ: CapCity orders: **30,250**
Comes in five different covers. 📖 Total Chaos, Part 3 **A:** Michael Netzer **W:** Marv Wolfman ★ Origin of Nightrider.
1/D ❑ Sep 1992 Cover: 1.75 **NM value: 2.00**
Circ: CapCity orders: **30,750**
Comes in five different covers. 📖 Total Chaos, Part 3 **A:** Michael Netzer **W:** Marv Wolfman ★ Origin of Redwing.
1/E ❑ Sep 1992 Cover: 1.75 **NM value: 2.00**
Circ: CapCity orders: **34,400**
Comes in five different covers. 📖 Total Chaos, Part 3 **A:** Michael Netzer **W:** Marv Wolfman ★ Origin of Terra.
2 ❑ Oct 1992 Cover: 1.75 **NM value: Cover or less**
Circ: CapCity orders: **28,200**
📖 Total Chaos, Part 6 ★ 1st Appearance of Battalion.
3 ❑ Nov 1992 Cover: 1.75 **NM value: Cover or less**
Circ: CapCity orders: **26,150**
📖 Total Chaos, Part 9
4 ❑ Dec 1992 Cover: 1.75 **NM value: Cover or less**
Circ: CapCity orders: **24,300**
📖 Judge and Jury ★ 1st Appearance of Judge & Jury.
5 ❑ Feb 1993 Cover: 1.75 **NM value: Cover or less**
Circ: CapCity orders: **21,400**
6 ❑ Mar 1993 Cover: 1.75 **NM value: Cover or less**
Circ: CapCity orders: **20,500**
7 ❑ Apr 1993 Cover: 1.75 **NM value: Cover or less**
Circ: CapCity orders: **19,100**
8 ❑ May 1993 Cover: 1.75 **NM value: Cover or less**
Circ: CapCity orders: **17,750**
★ 1st Appearance of Deathwing.

CGC-graded: Multiply prices above by **33 for 9.9 M • 16 for 9.8 NM/M • 7 for 9.6 NM+ • 5 for 9.4 NM • 2.5 for 9.2 NM- • 1.5 for 9.0 VF/NM**

9 ❑ Jun 1993 Cover: 1.75 **NM** value: **Cover or less**
Circ: CapCity orders: **16,700**

10 ❑ Jul 1993 Cover: 1.75 **NM** value: **Cover or less**
Circ: CapCity orders: **15,500**

11 ❑ Aug 1993 Cover: 1.75 **NM** value: **Cover or less**
Circ: CapCity orders: **16,050**

12 ❑ Sep 1993 Cover: 1.75 **NM** value: **Cover or less**
Circ: CapCity orders: **14,500**

13 ❑ Oct 1993 Cover: 1.75 **NM** value: **Cover or less**
Circ: CapCity orders: **14,250**

14 ❑ Nov 1993 Cover: 1.75 **NM** value: **Cover or less**
Circ: CapCity orders: **13,350**

15 ❑ Dec 1993 Cover: 1.75 **NM** value: **Cover or less**
Circ: CapCity orders: **12,450**
🕮 The Hardest Copy or Truth and Consequences **A:** Phil Jimenez; Steve Crespo; Jeff Jensen **W:** Phil Jimenez; Jeff Jensen

16 ❑ Jan 1994 Cover: 1.75 **NM** value: **Cover or less**
Circ: CapCity orders: **11,650**
🕮 To Sleep, Perchance to Dream... **A:** Phil Jimenez; Jeff Jensen; Jon Regis **W:** Phil Jimenez; Jeff Jensen

17 ❑ Feb 1994 Cover: 1.75 **NM** value: **Cover or less**
Circ: CapCity orders: **10,950**
🕮 You Can't Go Home Again, Part 1 **A:** Terry Dodson **W:** Phil Jimenez; Jeff Jensen

18 ❑ Mar 1994 Cover: 1.75 **NM** value: **Cover or less**
Circ: CapCity orders: **10,350**

19 ❑ Apr 1994 Cover: 1.75 **NM** value: **Cover or less**
Circ: CapCity orders: **9,450**

20 ❑ May 1994 Cover: 1.75 **NM** value: **Cover or less**
Circ: CapCity orders: **10,400**

21 ❑ Jun 1994 Cover: 1.75 **NM** value: **Cover or less**
Circ: CapCity orders: **9,550**
🕮 Facing the Future **A:** Bryan Hitch **W:** Phil Jimenez; Jeff Jensen

22 ❑ Jul 1994 Cover: 1.95 **NM** value: **Cover or less**
Circ: CapCity orders: **9,550**

23 ❑ Aug 1994 Cover: 1.95 **NM** value: **Cover or less**
Circ: CapCity orders: **9,550**

24 ❑ Sep 1994 Cover: 1.95 **NM** value: **Cover or less**
Circ: CapCity orders: **11,050**
final issue. • Zero Hour

Anl 1❑ Cover: 3.50 **NM** value: **Cover or less**
Circ: CapCity orders: **18,700**
🕮 Bloodlines • Bloodlines ★ 1st Appearance of Chimera.

Anl 2❑ Cover: 3.50 **NM** value: **Cover or less**
Circ: CapCity orders: **11,800**
• Elseworlds

TEAM X — Marvel

2000❑ Feb 1999 Cover: 3.50 **NM** value: **Cover or less**
Circ: Diamd. preorders: **42,734**
A: Kevin Lau **W:** Sean Ruffner ★ Appearance of Bishop, Shi'Ar, Morlocks, Deathbird.

TEAM X/TEAM 7 — Marvel

1 ❑ Jan 1997 Cover: 4.95 **NM** value: **Cover or less**
Circ: Direct Market orders: **79,500**
No issue number. 🕮 All Sold Out • crossover with Image; squarebound **A:** Steve Epting **W:** Larry Hama

TEAM YANKEE — First

1 ❑ Jan 1989 Cover: 1.95 **NM** value: **Cover or less**
Circ: CapCity orders: **8,875**
🕮 Zero Hour **A:** Rod Whigham **W:** David Drake

2 ❑ Jan 1989 Cover: 1.95 **NM** value: **Cover or less**
Circ: CapCity orders: **7,375**
A: Rod Whigham **W:** David Drake

3 ❑ Jan 1989 Cover: 1.95 **NM** value: **Cover or less**
Circ: CapCity orders: **6,975**
🕮 Spearhead **A:** Rod Whigham **W:** David Drake

4 ❑ Feb 1989 Cover: 1.95 **NM** value: **Cover or less**
Circ: CapCity orders: **5,550**

5 ❑ Feb 1989 Cover: 1.95 **NM** value: **Cover or less**
Circ: CapCity orders: **5,525**

6 ❑ Feb 1989 Cover: 1.95 **NM** value: **Cover or less**
Circ: CapCity orders: **5,525**

TEAM YOUNGBLOOD — Image

When super-powered villain Giger took over the Liberty II space station, the government turned to its own super-heroes for help. But Youngblood's "home team" were already up to their necks in other troubles, so it was up to the "away team" to save the day.

The new team consists of veteran Youngblood members Riptide, Cougar, and Photon, along with new additions Masada and Dutch. Under the command of team-leader Sentinel, this new team was ready to take on any menace, any time, any place (which is fortunate since the very first mission took them into space to fight one of Youngblood's deadliest enemies!).

This series was the brainchild of Rob Liefeld, who resurrected some of his earliest Youngblood comic characters for use in it. Pencilling duties were handled by newcomer Chap Yaep, who also contributed the character of "Dutch."

1 ❑ Sep 1993 Cover: 1.95 **NM** value: **Cover or less**
Circ: CapCity orders: **100,300**
🕮 Blackout **A:** Chap Yaep **W:** Rob Liefeld ★ 1st Appearance of Dutch, Masada.

2 ❑ Oct 1993 Cover: 1.95 **NM** value: **Cover or less**
Circ: CapCity orders: **67,075**

3 ❑ Nov 1993 Cover: 1.95 **NM** value: **Cover or less**
Circ: CapCity orders: **54,125**

4 ❑ Dec 1993 Cover: 1.95 **NM** value: **Cover or less**
Circ: CapCity orders: **42,775**

5 ❑ Jan 1994 Cover: 1.95 **NM** value: **Cover or less**
Circ: CapCity orders: **36,650**
★ 1st Appearance of Lynx.

6 ❑ Feb 1994 Cover: 1.95 **NM** value: **Cover or less**
Circ: CapCity orders: **31,875**

7 ❑ Mar 1994 Cover: 1.95 **NM** value: **Cover or less**
Circ: CapCity orders: **31,700**
🕮 Extreme Prejudice, Part 1 ★ 1st Appearance of Quantum.

8 ❑ Apr 1994 Cover: 1.95 **NM** value: **Cover or less**
Circ: CapCity orders: **29,525**
🕮 Extreme Prejudice, Part 5

9 ❑ May 1994 Cover: 1.95 **NM** value: **Cover or less**
Circ: CapCity orders: **32,575**

10 ❑ Jun 1994 Cover: 2.50 **NM** value: **Cover or less**
Circ: CapCity orders: **31,150**

11 ❑ Jul 1994 Cover: 2.50 **NM** value: **Cover or less**
Circ: CapCity orders: **28,825**

12 ❑ Aug 1994 Cover: 2.50 **NM** value: **Cover or less**
Circ: CapCity orders: **28,350**

13 ❑ Sep 1994 Cover: 2.50 **NM** value: **Cover or less**
Circ: CapCity orders: **27,150**

14 ❑ Oct 1994 Cover: 2.50 **NM** value: **Cover or less**
Circ: CapCity orders: **24,500**
• Riptide poses nude

15 ❑ Nov 1994 Cover: 2.50 **NM** value: **Cover or less**
Circ: CapCity orders: **22,200**
🕮 New Blood part 2

16 ❑ Dec 1994 Cover: 2.50 **NM** value: **Cover or less**
Circ: CapCity orders: **21,300**
• polybagged with trading card

17 ❑ Jan 1995 Cover: 2.50 **NM** value: **Cover or less**
Circ: CapCity orders: **21,250**
🕮 Extreme Sacrifice, Part 7; Extreme Sacrifice, Part 5 • polybagged with trading card

18 ❑ May 1995 Cover: 2.50 **NM** value: **Cover or less**
Circ: CapCity orders: **14,825**
🕮 Extreme 3000

19 ❑ Jun 1995 Cover: 2.50 **NM** value: **Cover or less**
Circ: CapCity orders: **15,075**

20 ❑ Jul 1995 Cover: 2.50 **NM** value: **Cover or less**
Circ: CapCity orders: **16,000**

21 ❑ Mar 1996 Cover: 2.50 **NM** value: **Cover or less**
Circ: CapCity orders: **14,850**
★ Appearance of Angela and Glory.

22 ❑ Apr 1996 Cover: 2.50 **NM** value: **Cover or less**
🕮 Shadowhunt final issue.

TEARS — Boneyard Press

1 ❑ Oct 1992, b&w Cover: 2.95 **NM** value: **Cover or less**
🕮 Symphony of Pain **A:** Paul Tisdale **W:** William J. Harms

2 ❑ Dec 1992, b&w Cover: 2.95 **NM** value: **Cover or less**
🕮 Journey of the Holy **A:** Paul Tisdale **W:** William J. Harms

TEASER AND THE BLACKSMITH — Fantagraphics

All issues are adults only.

1 ❑ b&w Cover: 3.50 **NM** value: **Cover or less**

TECH HIGH — Virtually Real Enterprises

1 ❑ Fal 1996, b&w Cover: 2.50 **NM** value: **Cover or less**
• **CGC:** 1 graded, best 9.9

2 ❑ Win 1996, b&w Cover: 2.50 **NM** value: **Cover or less**
• **CGC:** 1 graded, best 9.8

3 ❑ Spr 1997, b&w Cover: 2.50 **NM** value: **Cover or less**
• **CGC:** 1 graded, best 9.8

TECHNO MANIACS — Independent

1 ❑ Cover: 1.95 **NM** value: **Cover or less**

TECHNOPOLIS — Caliber

1 ❑ Cover: 2.95 **NM** value: **Cover or less**
🕮 Inceptum **A:** Adrie Van Viersen **W:** Patrick Sauriol; Peter Taylor

2 ❑ Cover: 2.95 **NM** value: **Cover or less**

3 ❑ Cover: 2.95 **NM** value: **Cover or less**

4 ❑ Cover: 2.95 **NM** value: **Cover or less**

TEDDY ROOSEVELT AND HIS ROUGH RIDERS — Avon

1 ❑ ca. 1950 **NM** value: **125.00**
• **CGC:** 1 graded, best 9.4

TEEN-AGE BRIDES — Home

1 ❑	Aug 1953	Cover: 0.10	**NM** value: **40.00**
2 ❑	Oct 1953	Cover: 0.10	**NM** value: **25.00**
3 ❑	Dec 1953	Cover: 0.10	**NM** value: **20.00**
4 ❑	Feb 1954	Cover: 0.10	**NM** value: **20.00**
5 ❑	Apr 1954	Cover: 0.10	**NM** value: **20.00**
6 ❑	Jun 1954	Cover: 0.10	**NM** value: **20.00**

🕮 The Greatest Gift; Wedding-Ring Blues; Unfaithful to my Vows; Stormy Marriage

7 ❑ Aug 1954 Cover: 0.10 **NM** value: **20.00**

TEEN-AGE CONFIDENTIAL CONFESSIONS — Charlton

1 ❑ Jul 1960 Cover: 0.10 **NM** value: **20.00**
• **CGC:** 2 graded, best 8.0

2 ❑	Sep 1960	Cover: 0.10	**NM** value: **12.00**
3 ❑	Nov 1960	Cover: 0.10	**NM** value: **10.00**
4 ❑	Jan 1961	Cover: 0.10	**NM** value: **10.00**

🕮 Date with a Teen-Age Idol; The Small Town Scandal; Those Harmless Kisses!; My Heart Betrayed Me!; Personal Sex Attraction (text); Love Revisited!; High School Hot Shot **A:** Chasal

5 ❑	Mar 1961	Cover: 0.10	**NM** value: **10.00**
6 ❑	May 1961	Cover: 0.10	**NM** value: **8.00**
7 ❑	Jul 1961	Cover: 0.10	**NM** value: **8.00**
8 ❑	Sep 1961	Cover: 0.10	**NM** value: **8.00**
9 ❑	Nov 1961	Cover: 0.10	**NM** value: **8.00**
10 ❑	Jan 1962	Cover: 0.10	**NM** value: **6.00**
11 ❑	ca. 1962	Cover: 0.12	**NM** value: **6.00**
12 ❑	Jun 1962	Cover: 0.12	**NM** value: **6.00**
13 ❑	Aug 1962	Cover: 0.12	**NM** value: **6.00**
14 ❑	ca. 1962	Cover: 0.12	**NM** value: **6.00**
15 ❑	Jan 1963	Cover: 0.12	**NM** value: **6.00**
16 ❑	Feb 1963	Cover: 0.12	**NM** value: **6.00**
17 ❑	Apr 1963	Cover: 0.12	**NM** value: **6.00**
18 ❑	Jun 1963	Cover: 0.12	**NM** value: **6.00**
19 ❑	Aug 1963	Cover: 0.12	**NM** value: **6.00**
20 ❑	Oct 1963	Cover: 0.12	**NM** value: **6.00**
21 ❑	Dec 1963	Cover: 0.12	**NM** value: **6.00**
22 ❑	ca. 1964	Cover: 0.12	**NM** value: **6.00**

TEEN-AGED DOPE SLAVES AND REFORM SCHOOL GIRLS — Eclipse

1 ❑ Cover: 9.95 **NM** value: **Cover or less**
🕮 Reform School Girl; Trapped!; The Bobby Sox Bandit Queen; Lucky Fights it Through; Gun Happy; I Worked for the Fence; Teen-Aged Dope Slaves; The Deadly Needle **A:** Joe Simon; Harvey Kurtzman; Jack Kirby; Frank Edgington; Louis Zansky; Martin Bradley **W:** Joe Simon; Harvey Kurtzman; Jack Kirby; Frank Edgington; Louis Zansky; Martin Bradley

TEEN-AGE DIARY SECRETS — St. John

4 ❑	Oct 1949	Cover: 0.10	**NM** value: **200.00**
5 ❑	Dec 1949	Cover: 0.10	**NM** value: **175.00**
6 ❑	Feb 1950	Cover: 0.10	**NM** value: **175.00**
7 ❑	Apr 1950	Cover: 0.10	**NM** value: **175.00**
8 ❑	Jun 1950	Cover: 0.10	**NM** value: **150.00**
9 ❑	Aug 1950	Cover: 0.10	**NM** value: **150.00**

TEENAGE MUTANT NINJA TURTLES (1ST SERIES) — Mirage

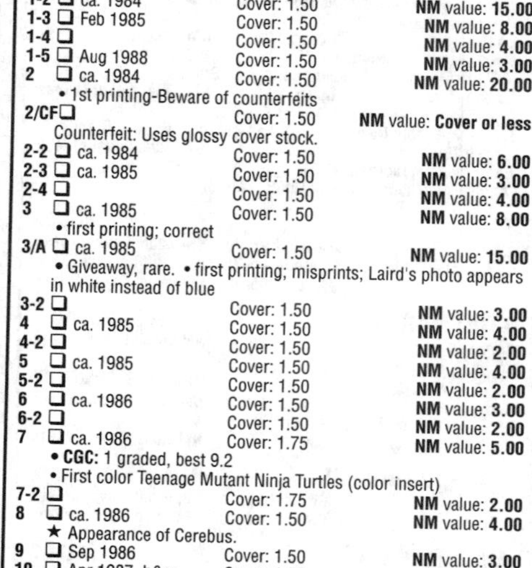

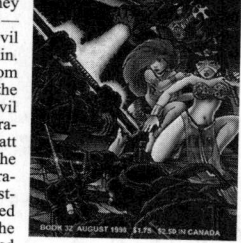

Kevin Eastman and Peter Laird set out to do what amounted to a parody of the work of Frank Miller, whose work was brilliant, distinctive, and popular. So they combined two Miller concepts—his work on Marvel's Daredevil and his work on DC's Ronin. They then extrapolated from what had happened during the event that had created Daredevil in the first place: the drum of radioactive material striking Matt Murdock and blinding him in the street. What happened to that radioactive material? asked Eastman and Laird. Why, it drained into the sewer and affected the turtles that had been flushed there. And what did they get? "Teenage Mutant Ninja Turtles"! They could never have expected that their joke would develop a cult of devoted fans and attract the attention of a merchandiser, eventually turning them into an international phenomenon.

The Turtles: Donatello, Raphael, Michelangelo, and Leonardo, along with their rat sensei Splinter, became one of the hottest tickets in town. Stars of stage, screen, and countless comics (including this, the original), they combine humor and action in a way that appeals to young children and hip intellectuals.

1 ❑ ca. 1984 Cover: 1.50 **NM** value: **150.00**
• 1st printing-Beware of counterfeits ★ 1st Appearance of Teenage Mutant Ninja Turtles.

1/CF❑ Cover: 1.50 **NM** value: **Cover or less**
• Counterfeit of first printing; Most counterfeit copies have streak or scratch marks across center of back cover, black part of cover is slightly bluish instead of black-Info from Overstreet guide

1-2 ❑	ca. 1984	Cover: 1.50	**NM** value: **15.00**
1-3 ❑	Feb 1985	Cover: 1.50	**NM** value: **8.00**
1-4 ❑		Cover: 1.50	**NM** value: **4.00**
1-5 ❑	Aug 1988	Cover: 1.50	**NM** value: **3.00**
2 ❑	ca. 1984	Cover: 1.50	**NM** value: **20.00**

• 1st printing-Beware of counterfeits

2/CF❑ Cover: 1.50 **NM** value: **Cover or less**
Counterfeit: Uses glossy cover stock.

2-2 ❑	ca. 1984	Cover: 1.50	**NM** value: **6.00**
2-3 ❑	ca. 1985	Cover: 1.50	**NM** value: **3.00**
2-4 ❑		Cover: 1.50	**NM** value: **4.00**
3 ❑	ca. 1985	Cover: 1.50	**NM** value: **8.00**

• first printing; correct

3/A ❑ ca. 1985 Cover: 1.50 **NM** value: **15.00**
• Giveaway, rare. • first printing; misprints; Laird's photo appears in white instead of blue

3-2 ❑		Cover: 1.50	**NM** value: **3.00**
4 ❑	ca. 1985	Cover: 1.50	**NM** value: **4.00**
4-2 ❑		Cover: 1.50	**NM** value: **2.00**
5 ❑	ca. 1985	Cover: 1.50	**NM** value: **4.00**
5-2 ❑		Cover: 1.50	**NM** value: **2.00**
6 ❑	ca. 1986	Cover: 1.50	**NM** value: **3.00**
6-2 ❑		Cover: 1.50	**NM** value: **2.00**
7 ❑	ca. 1986	Cover: 1.75	**NM** value: **5.00**

• **CGC:** 1 graded, best 9.2
• First color Teenage Mutant Ninja Turtles (color insert)

7-2 ❑ Cover: 1.75 **NM** value: **2.00**

8 ❑ ca. 1986 Cover: 1.50 **NM** value: **4.00**
★ Appearance of Cerebus.

9 ❑	Sep 1986	Cover: 1.50	**NM** value: **3.00**
10 ❑	Apr 1987, b&w	Cover: 1.50	**NM** value: **3.00**
11 ❑	Jun 1987, b&w	Cover: 1.50	**NM** value: **4.00**

Other grades: Multiply prices above by **1.5 for Mint • 2/3 for Very Fine • 1/3 for Fine • 1/5 for Very Good • 1/8 for Good**

12 ❑ Sep 1987 Cover: 1.50 **NM** value: **3.00**
A: Frank Fosco W: Gary Carlson
13 ❑ Feb 1988 Cover: 1.50 **NM** value: **3.00**
A: Frank Fosco W: Gary Carlson
14 ❑ May 1988 Cover: 1.50 **NM** value: **3.00**
cover says Feb, indicia says May.
15 ❑ Sum 1988 Cover: 1.50 **NM** value: **3.00**
16 ❑ Sep 1988 Cover: 1.50 **NM** value: **2.00**
cover says Jul, indicia says Sep.
17 ❑ Jan 1989 Cover: 1.50 **NM** value: **2.00**
cover says Nov, indicia says Jan.
18 ❑ Feb 1989, b&w Cover: 1.50 **NM** value: **2.00**
Circ: CapCity orders: **10,325**
18-2❑ full color Cover: 1.50 **NM** value: **2.00**
19 ❑ Mar 1989 Cover: 1.75 **NM** value: **2.00**
• Return to NY
20 ❑ Apr 1989 Cover: 1.75 **NM** value: **2.00**
• Return to NY
21 ❑ May 1989 Cover: 1.75 **NM** value: **2.00**
• Return to NY
22 ❑ Jun 1989 Cover: 1.75 **NM** value: **2.00**
A: Mark Martin
23 ❑ Aug 1989 Cover: 1.75 **NM** value: **2.00**
cover says Jul, indicia says Aug. A: Mark Martin
24 ❑ ca. 1989 Cover: 1.75 **NM** value: **2.00**
A: Rick Veitch
25 ❑ ca. 1989 Cover: 1.75 **NM** value: **2.00**
A: Rick Veitch
26 ❑ Dec 1989 Cover: 1.75 **NM** value: **2.00**
cover says Oct, indicia says Dec. A: Rick Veitch
27 ❑ Dec 1989 Cover: 1.75 **NM** value: **2.00**
cover says Nov, indicia says Dec.
28 ❑ ca. 1990 Cover: 1.75 **NM** value: **2.00**
29 ❑ May 1990 Cover: 1.75 **NM** value: **2.00**
cover says Mar, indicia says May.
30 ❑ Jun 1990 Cover: 1.75 **NM** value: **2.00**
cover says Apr, indicia says Jun.
31 ❑ Jul 1990 Cover: 1.75 **NM** value: **2.00**
32 ❑ Aug 1990 Cover: 1.75 **NM** value: **2.00**
A: Mark Bode W: Mark Bode
33 ❑ 1990full color Cover: 1.95 **NM** value: **2.00**
A: Richard Corben
34 ❑ 1991 Cover: 1.75 **NM** value: **2.00**
35 ❑ Mar 1991 Cover: 2.00 **NM** value: **Cover or less**
36 ❑ Aug 1991 Cover: 2.00 **NM** value: **Cover or less**
37 ❑ Jun 1991 Cover: 2.00 **NM** value: **Cover or less**
38 ❑ Jul 1991 Cover: 2.00 **NM** value: **Cover or less**
39 ❑ Sep 1991 Cover: 2.00 **NM** value: **Cover or less**
40 ❑ Oct 1991 Cover: 2.00 **NM** value: **Cover or less**
41 ❑ Nov 1991 Cover: 2.00 **NM** value: **Cover or less**
Circ: CapCity orders: **12,275**
42 ❑ Dec 1991 Cover: 2.00 **NM** value: **Cover or less**
Circ: CapCity orders: **10,975**
43 ❑ Jan 1992 Cover: 2.00 **NM** value: **Cover or less**
Circ: CapCity orders: **9,600**
44 ❑ Feb 1992 Cover: 2.00 **NM** value: **Cover or less**
Circ: CapCity orders: **8,600**
45 ❑ Mar 1992 Cover: 2.00 **NM** value: **Cover or less**
46 ❑ Apr 1992 Cover: 2.00 **NM** value: **Cover or less**
Circ: CapCity orders: **8,175**
47 ❑ May 1992 Cover: 2.00 **NM** value: **Cover or less**
Circ: CapCity orders: **7,850**
48 ❑ Jun 1992 Cover: 2.00 **NM** value: **Cover or less**
Circ: CapCity orders: **8,100**
49 ❑ Jul 1992 Cover: 2.00 **NM** value: **Cover or less**
Circ: CapCity orders: **7,725**
50 ❑ Aug 1992, b&w Cover: 2.00 **NM** value: **Cover or less**
• City At War A: Kevin Eastman; Peter Laird
51 ❑ Sep 1992, b&w Cover: 2.00 **NM** value: **Cover or less**
Circ: CapCity orders: **9,825**
📖 City At War; City At War, Part 1
52 ❑ Oct 1992, b&w Cover: 2.25 **NM** value: **Cover or less**
Circ: CapCity orders: **8,850**
📖 City At War; City At War, Part 2
53 ❑ Nov 1992, b&w Cover: 2.25 **NM** value: **Cover or less**
Circ: CapCity orders: **9,250**
📖 City At War; City At War, Part 3
54 ❑ Dec 1992, b&w Cover: 2.25 **NM** value: **Cover or less**
Circ: CapCity orders: **9,275**
📖 City At War; City At War, Part 4
55 ❑ Jan 1993, b&w Cover: 2.25 **NM** value: **Cover or less**
Circ: CapCity orders: **8,250**
📖 City At War; City At War, Part 5
56 ❑ Feb 1993, b&w Cover: 2.25 **NM** value: **Cover or less**
Circ: CapCity orders: **8,400**
📖 City At War; City At War, Part 6
57 ❑ Mar 1993, b&w Cover: 2.25 **NM** value: **Cover or less**
Circ: CapCity orders: **7,750**
📖 City At War; City At War, Part 7
58 ❑ Apr 1993, b&w Cover: 2.25 **NM** value: **Cover or less**
Circ: CapCity orders: **7,375**
📖 City At War; City At War, Part 8
59 ❑ May 1993, b&w Cover: 2.25 **NM** value: **Cover or less**
Circ: CapCity orders: **7,300**
📖 City At War; City At War, Part 9
60 ❑ Jun 1993, b&w Cover: 2.25 **NM** value: **Cover or less**
Circ: CapCity orders: **7,425**
📖 City At War; City At War, Part 10
61 ❑ Jul 1993, b&w Cover: 2.25 **NM** value: **Cover or less**
Circ: CapCity orders: **6,875**
📖 City At War; City At War, Part 11 A: Jim Lawson W: Jim Lawson; Kevin Eastman; Peter Laird
62 ❑ Aug 1993, b&w Cover: 2.25 **NM** value: **Cover or less**
Circ: CapCity orders: **6,550**
📖 City At War; City At War, Part 12 final issue.
Bk 1❑ b&w Cover: 6.95 **NM** value: **Cover or less**
Bk 1/HC❑ Cover: 75.00 **NM** value: **Cover or less**
Limited hardcover.
Bk 1/LE❑ Cover: 40.00 **NM** value: **Cover or less**
Limited softcover.
Bk 2❑ b&w Cover: 6.95 **NM** value: **Cover or less**
Bk 3❑ b&w Cover: 6.95 **NM** value: **Cover or less**
Bk 4❑ b&w Cover: 6.95 **NM** value: **Cover or less**

TEENAGE MUTANT NINJA TURTLES (2ND SERIES)

Mirage

1 ❑ Oct 1993, full color Cover: 2.75 **NM** value: **3.00**
Circ: CapCity orders: **11,950**
2 ❑ Dec 1993, full color Cover: 2.75 **NM** value: **3.00**
Circ: CapCity orders: **6,350**
3 ❑ Feb 1994, full color Cover: 2.75 **NM** value: **3.00**
Circ: CapCity orders: **5,430**
4 ❑ Apr 1994 Cover: 2.75 **NM** value: **3.00**
Circ: CapCity orders: **4,650**
5 ❑ Jun 1994 Cover: 2.75 **NM** value: **3.00**
Circ: CapCity orders: **4,090**
6 ❑ Aug 1994 Cover: 2.75 **NM** value: **Cover or less**
Circ: CapCity orders: **3,485**
7 ❑ Oct 1994 Cover: 2.75 **NM** value: **Cover or less**
Circ: CapCity orders: **3,150**
8 ❑ Nov 1994 Cover: 2.75 **NM** value: **Cover or less**
Circ: CapCity orders: **3,215**
📖 Bog, Part 1
9 ❑ Aug 1995 Cover: 2.75 **NM** value: **Cover or less**
Circ: CapCity orders: **1,990**
10 ❑ Aug 1995 Cover: 2.75 **NM** value: **Cover or less**
Circ: CapCity orders: **1,990**
📖 Bog, Part 2
11 ❑ Sep 1995 Cover: 2.75 **NM** value: **Cover or less**
Circ: CapCity orders: **1,710**
📖 Bog, Part 3
12 ❑ Sep 1995 Cover: 2.75 **NM** value: **Cover or less**
Circ: CapCity orders: **1,700**
📖 Bog, Part 4
13 ❑ Oct 1995 Cover: 2.75 **NM** value: **Cover or less**
final issue.
SE 1❑ Jan 1993 Cover: 2.95 **NM** value: **Cover or less**
📖 The Maltese Turtle • Special A: Romano W: Hedden; McWeeney

TEENAGE MUTANT NINJA TURTLES (3RD SERIES)

Image

1 ❑ Jun 1996 Cover: 1.95 **NM** value: **3.50**
A: Frank Fosco W: Gary Carlson
2 ❑ Jul 1996 Cover: 1.95 **NM** value: **3.25**
A: Frank Fosco W: Gary Carlson
3 ❑ Sep 1996 Cover: 1.95 **NM** value: **3.25**
A: Frank Fosco W: Gary Carlson
4 ❑ Oct 1996 Cover: 1.95 **NM** value: **3.00**
Circ: Diamd. preorders: **16,558**
A: Frank Fosco W: Gary Carlson
5 ❑ Dec 1996 Cover: 2.50 **NM** value: **3.00**
Circ: Diamd. preorders: **14,728**
A: Frank Fosco W: Gary Carlson
6 ❑ Jan 1997 Cover: 2.50 **NM** value: **3.00**
Circ: Diamd. preorders: **13,129**
A: Frank Fosco W: Gary Carlson
7 ❑ Feb 1997 Cover: 2.50 **NM** value: **3.00**
Circ: Diamd. preorders: **12,321**
A: Frank Fosco W: Gary Carlson
8 ❑ Apr 1997 Cover: 2.50 **NM** value: **3.00**
Circ: Diamd. preorders: **11,421**
A: Frank Fosco W: Gary Carlson
9 ❑ May 1997 Cover: 2.95 **NM** value: **3.00**
Circ: Diamd. preorders: **11,053**
A: Frank Fosco W: Gary Carlson ★ Appearance of Knight Watchman.
10 ❑ Jul 1997 Cover: 2.95 **NM** value: **3.00**
Circ: Diamd. preorders: **10,144**
A: Frank Fosco W: Gary Carlson
11 ❑ Oct 1997 Cover: 2.95 **NM** value: **Cover or less**
Circ: Diamd. preorders: **8,844**
A: Frank Fosco W: Gary Carlson
12 ❑ Dec 1997 Cover: 2.95 **NM** value: **Cover or less**
Circ: Diamd. preorders: **8,546**
A: Frank Fosco W: Gary Carlson
13 ❑ Feb 1998 Cover: 2.95 **NM** value: **Cover or less**
Circ: Diamd. preorders: **8,615**
A: Frank Fosco W: Gary Carlson
14 ❑ Apr 1998 Cover: 2.95 **NM** value: **Cover or less**
Circ: Diamd. preorders: **8,303**
A: Frank Fosco W: Gary Carlson
15 ❑ May 1998 Cover: 2.95 **NM** value: **Cover or less**
Circ: Diamd. preorders: **7,727**
A: Frank Fosco W: Gary Carlson
16 ❑ Jul 1998 Cover: 2.95 **NM** value: **Cover or less**
Circ: Diamd. preorders: **6,838**
A: Frank Fosco W: Gary Carlson
17 ❑ Sep 1998 Cover: 2.95 **NM** value: **Cover or less**
Circ: Diamd. preorders: **6,424**
A: Frank Fosco W: Gary Carlson
18 ❑ Oct 1998 Cover: 2.95 **NM** value: **Cover or less**
Circ: Diamd. preorders: **6,084**
A: Frank Fosco W: Gary Carlson
19 ❑ Jan 1999 Cover: 2.95 **NM** value: **Cover or less**
Circ: Diamd. preorders: **5,443**
A: Frank Fosco W: Gary Carlson
20 ❑ Mar 1999 Cover: 2.95 **NM** value: **Cover or less**
Circ: Diamd. preorders: **5,241**
A: Frank Fosco W: Gary Carlson
21 ❑ May 1999 Cover: 2.95 **NM** value: **Cover or less**
Circ: Diamd. preorders: **5,179**
A: Frank Fosco W: Gary Carlson
22 ❑ Jul 1999 Cover: 2.95 **NM** value: **Cover or less**
Circ: Diamd. preorders: **4,764**
A: Frank Fosco W: Gary Carlson
23 ❑ Oct 1999 Cover: 2.95 **NM** value: **Cover or less**
Circ: Diamd. preorders: **4,647**
A: Frank Fosco W: Gary Carlson
Bk 1❑ Cover: 9.95 **NM** value: **Cover or less**
• A New Beginning; collects issues #1-5

TEENAGE MUTANT NINJA TURTLES ADVENTURES (1ST SERIES)

Archie

1 ❑ Aug 1988 Cover: 1.00 **NM** value: **3.00**
Circ: CapCity orders: **27,675**
📖 Heroes in a Half-Shell! A: Michael Dooney W: Michael Dooney; David Weiss; Pati Howeth
2 ❑ Oct 1988 Cover: 1.00 **NM** value: **2.50**
Circ: CapCity orders: **19,925**
3 ❑ Dec 1988 Cover: 1.00 **NM** value: **2.50**
Circ: CapCity orders: **15,925**
Bk 1❑ full color Cover: 6.95 **NM** value: **Cover or less**
📖 Heroes in a Half-Shell! A: Michael Dooney W: Michael Dooney; David Weiss; Pati Howeth
Bk 2❑ full color Cover: 6.95 **NM** value: **Cover or less**
📖 Wild Things; Codename: Chameleon; Going Down? A: Jim Lawson; Ken Mitchroney W: Ryan Brown; Steve Lavigne; Dean Clarrain ★ Appearance of Cudley the Cowlick.
Bk 3❑ Cover: 6.95 **NM** value: **Cover or less**
Bk 4❑ Cover: 6.95 **NM** value: **Cover or less**

TEENAGE MUTANT NINJA TURTLES ADVENTURES (2ND SERIES)

Archie

Archie Comics adapted their version of the pizza-loving sewer-dwelling reptiles from the TV series, leaving behind the satire of the original Teenage Mutant Ninja Turtles comic book.

In this series, Michelangelo, Raphael, Donatello, and Leonardo are sillier than ever. They're still doing their part to stop crime and thwart the bad guys, but they're getting more laughs than kicks in the process now. And TV reporter April O'Neil has little competition in getting the scoop on the action, since the staff at her station is more concerned with chipped fingernails and vicious poodles. Splinter remains the same father figure he has always been, though, in this title, he bears more resemblance to a dog than a rat.

1 ❑ Mar 1989 Cover: 1.00 **NM** value: **3.00**
Circ: CapCity orders: **20,375**
📖 Return of the Shredder A: Dave Garcia W: Christy Marx; David Wise
2 ❑ May 1989 Cover: 1.00 **NM** value: **2.50**
Circ: CapCity orders: **16,400**
📖 Return of the Shredder A: Dave Garcia W: Christy Marx; David Wise
3 ❑ Jul 1989 Cover: 1.00 **NM** value: **2.50**
Circ: CapCity orders: **16,175**
4 ❑ Sep 1989 Cover: 1.00 **NM** value: **2.00**
5 ❑ Oct 1989 Cover: 1.00 **NM** value: **2.00**
Circ: CapCity orders: **13,550**
6 ❑ Nov 1989 Cover: 1.00 **NM** value: **2.00**
Circ: CapCity orders: **12,050**
📖 Something Fishy Goes Down A: Ken Mitchroney W: Ryan Brown; Dean Clarrain
7 ❑ Dec 1989 Cover: 1.00 **NM** value: **2.00**
Circ: CapCity orders: **12,825**
8 ❑ Feb 1990 Cover: 1.00 **NM** value: **2.00**
Circ: CapCity orders: **10,850**
9 ❑ Mar 1990 Cover: 1.00 **NM** value: **2.00**
Circ: CapCity orders: **11,300**
10 ❑ May 1990 Cover: 1.00 **NM** value: **2.00**
Circ: CapCity orders: **11,725**
11 ❑ Jun 1990 Cover: 1.00 **NM** value: **1.50**
Circ: CapCity orders: **15,000**
12 ❑ Jul 1990 Cover: 1.00 **NM** value: **1.50**
Circ: CapCity orders: **21,725**
13 ❑ Oct 1990 Cover: 1.00 **NM** value: **1.50**
Circ: CapCity orders: **23,600**
14 ❑ Nov 1990 Cover: 1.00 **NM** value: **1.50**
Circ: CapCity orders: **24,575**
15 ❑ Dec 1990 Cover: 1.00 **NM** value: **1.50**
Circ: CapCity orders: **24,375**
📖 The Howling of Distant Shadows A: Ken Mitchroney W: Dean Clarrain
16 ❑ Jan 1991 Cover: 1.00 **NM** value: **1.50**
Circ: CapCity orders: **18,350**
17 ❑ Feb 1991 Cover: 1.00 **NM** value: **1.50**
Circ: CapCity orders: **18,575**
18 ❑ Mar 1991 Cover: 1.00 **NM** value: **1.50**
Circ: CapCity orders: **16,525**
19 ❑ Apr 1991 Cover: 1.25 **NM** value: **1.50**
Circ: CapCity orders: **15,300**
★ 1st Appearance of Mighty Mutanimals.
20 ❑ May 1991 Cover: 1.25 **NM** value: **1.50**
Circ: CapCity orders: **13,200**
21 ❑ Jun 1991 Cover: 1.25 **NM** value: **1.50**
Circ: CapCity orders: **13,075**
22 ❑ Jul 1991 Cover: 1.25 **NM** value: **1.50**
Circ: CapCity orders: **13,775**
23 ❑ Aug 1991 Cover: 1.25 **NM** value: **1.50**
Circ: CapCity orders: **13,325**
24 ❑ Sep 1991 Cover: 1.25 **NM** value: **1.50**
Circ: CapCity orders: **11,425**
25 ❑ Oct 1991 Cover: 1.25 **NM** value: **1.50**
Circ: CapCity orders: **10,750**
26 ❑ Nov 1991 Cover: 1.25 **NM** value: **1.50**
Circ: CapCity orders: **10,125**
27 ❑ Dec 1991 Cover: 1.25 **NM** value: **1.50**
Circ: CapCity orders: **9,250**
28 ❑ Jan 1992 Cover: 1.25 **NM** value: **1.50**
Circ: CapCity orders: **8,925**
29 ❑ Feb 1992 Cover: 1.25 **NM** value: **1.50**
Circ: CapCity orders: **8,375**
30 ❑ Mar 1992 Cover: 1.25 **NM** value: **1.50**
Circ: CapCity orders: **7,600**
31 ❑ Apr 1992 Cover: 1.25 **NM** value: **1.50**
Circ: CapCity orders: **6,725**

CGC-graded: Multiply prices above by **33 for 9.9 M • 16 for 9.8 NM/M • 7 for 9.6 NM+ • 5 for 9.4 NM • 2.5 for 9.2 NM- • 1.5 for 9.0 VF/NM**

32 ❑ May 1992 Cover: 1.25 **NM** value: **1.50**
Circ: CapCity orders: **6,200**
A: Kevin Eastman; Eric Talbot **W:** Mark Bodé
33 ❑ Jun 1992 Cover: 1.25 **NM** value: **1.50**
Circ: CapCity orders: **5,825**
34 ❑ Aug 1992 Cover: 1.25 **NM** value: **1.50**
Circ: CapCity orders: **5,875**
35 ❑ Jul 1992 Cover: 1.25 **NM** value: **1.50**
Circ: CapCity orders: **5,625**
36 ❑ Sep 1992 Cover: 1.25 **NM** value: **1.50**
Circ: CapCity orders: **5,350**
37 ❑ Oct 1992 Cover: 1.25 **NM** value: **1.50**
Circ: CapCity orders: **4,675**
38 ❑ Nov 1992 Cover: 1.25 **NM** value: **1.50**
Circ: CapCity orders: **4,400**
39 ❑ Dec 1992 Cover: 1.25 **NM** value: **1.50**
Circ: CapCity orders: **4,200**
40 ❑ Jan 1993 Cover: 1.25 **NM** value: **1.50**
Circ: CapCity orders: **4,025**
41 ❑ Feb 1993 Cover: 1.25 **NM** value: **1.50**
Circ: CapCity orders: **4,000**
42 ❑ Mar 1993 Cover: 1.25 **NM** value: **1.50**
43 ❑ Apr 1993 Cover: 1.25 **NM** value: **1.50**
Circ: CapCity orders: **3,775**
44 ❑ May 1993 Cover: 1.25 **NM** value: **1.50**
Circ: CapCity orders: **3,775**
45 ❑ Jun 1993 Cover: 1.25 **NM** value: **1.50**
Circ: CapCity orders: **3,825**
46 ❑ Jul 1993 Cover: 1.25 **NM** value: **1.50**
Circ: CapCity orders: **3,750**
47 ❑ Aug 1993 Cover: 1.25 **NM** value: **1.50**
Circ: CapCity orders: **3,825**
48 ❑ Sep 1993 Cover: 1.25 **NM** value: **1.50**
Circ: CapCity orders: **4,200**
49 ❑ Oct 1993 Cover: 1.25 **NM** value: **1.50**
Circ: CapCity orders: **3,750**
50 ❑ Nov 1993 Cover: 1.25 **NM** value: **1.50**
Circ: CapCity orders: **5,525**
51 ❑ Dec 1993 Cover: 1.25 **NM** value: **1.50**
Circ: CapCity orders: **3,375**
52 ❑ Jan 1994 Cover: 1.25 **NM** value: **1.50**
Circ: CapCity orders: **3,450**
53 ❑ Feb 1994 Cover: 1.25 **NM** value: **1.50**
Circ: CapCity orders: **3,150**
54 ❑ Mar 1994 Cover: 1.25 **NM** value: **1.50**
Circ: CapCity orders: **3,175**
55 ❑ Apr 1994 Cover: 1.25 **NM** value: **1.50**
Circ: CapCity orders: **3,150**
Terracide, Part 1
56 ❑ May 1994 Cover: 1.25 **NM** value: **1.50**
Circ: CapCity orders: **2,575**
57 ❑ Jun 1994 Cover: 1.25 **NM** value: **1.50**
Circ: CapCity orders: **2,650**
58 ❑ Jul 1994 Cover: 1.25 **NM** value: **1.50**
Circ: CapCity orders: **2,400**
59 ❑ Aug 1994 Cover: 1.50 **NM** value: **Cover or less**
Circ: CapCity orders: **2,625**
60 ❑ Sep 1994 Cover: 1.50 **NM** value: **Cover or less**
61 ❑ Oct 1994 Cover: 1.50 **NM** value: **Cover or less**
62 ❑ Nov 1994 Cover: 1.75 **NM** value: **Cover or less**
63 ❑ Dec 1994 Cover: 1.50 **NM** value: **Cover or less**
64 ❑ Jan 1995 Cover: 1.50 **NM** value: **Cover or less**
65 ❑ Feb 1995 Cover: 1.50 **NM** value: **Cover or less**
66 ❑ Mar 1995 Cover: 1.50 **NM** value: **Cover or less**
67 ❑ Apr 1995 Cover: 1.50 **NM** value: **Cover or less**
68 ❑ May 1995 Cover: 1.50 **NM** value: **Cover or less**
69 ❑ Jun 1995 Cover: 1.50 **NM** value: **Cover or less**
70 ❑ Jul 1995 Cover: 1.50 **NM** value: **Cover or less**
71 ❑ Sep 1995 Cover: 1.50 **NM** value: **Cover or less**
The Early Years, Part 1
72 ❑ Oct 1995 Cover: 1.50 **NM** value: **Cover or less**
The Early Years, Part 2 final issue.
Bk 1❑ **NM** value: **3.00**
Return of the Shredder • Reprints TNMT Adv. #1-2 **A:** Dave Garcia **W:** Christy Marx; David Wise
Bk 1-2❑ **NM** value: **3.00**
Bk 1-3❑ **NM** value: **3.00**
Bk 1-4❑ **NM** value: **3.00**
SE 1❑ Spr 1991 Cover: 2.50 **NM** value: **Cover or less**
Circ: CapCity orders: **5,125**
No issue number. Green Legs and Gams; Red Sails in the Sunset; Storm Drain Savers; Origin of the Species • Teenage Mutant Ninja Turtles Meet Archie **A:** Jim Lawson; Stan Goldberg; Donald Simpson; Ken Mitchroney; Dave Garcia **W:** Ryan Brown; Dean Clarrain; Stephen Murphy
SE 2❑ Cover: 2.50 **NM** value: **Cover or less**
Circ: CapCity orders: **3,275**
SE 3❑ Cover: 2.50 **NM** value: **Cover or less**
Circ: CapCity orders: **3,925**
SE 4❑ Cover: 2.50 **NM** value: **Cover or less**
Circ: CapCity orders: **2,700**
SE 5❑ Cover: 2.50 **NM** value: **Cover or less**
Circ: CapCity orders: **2,700**
SE 6❑ Cover: 1.95 **NM** value: **2.00**
• Giant-Size Special #6.
SE 7❑ Cover: 1.95 **NM** value: **2.00**
SE 8❑ Cover: 1.95 **NM** value: **2.00**
SE 9❑ Cover: 1.95 **NM** value: **2.00**
SE 10❑ Cover: 2.00 **NM** value: **Cover or less**
SE 11❑ Cover: 2.00 **NM** value: **Cover or less**
• Teenage Mutant Ninja Turtles Special #11

TEENAGE MUTANT NINJA TURTLES ADVENTURES (3RD SERIES) Archie

1 ❑ Jan 1996 Cover: 1.50 **NM** value: **Cover or less**
The Year of the Turtle **A:** Hugh Haynes **W:** Dan Slott
2 ❑ Feb 1996 Cover: 1.50 **NM** value: **Cover or less**
The Year of the Turtle **A:** Hugh Haynes **W:** Dan Slott
3 ❑ Mar 1996 Cover: 1.50 **NM** value: **Cover or less**
The Year of the Turtle **A:** Hugh Haynes **W:** Dan Slott

TEENAGE MUTANT NINJA TURTLES AUTHORIZED MARTIAL ARTS TRAINING MANUAL Solson

1 ❑ Cover: 2.25 **NM** value: **2.50**
A: Rich Buckler; Jason Rodgers **W:** Rich Buckler
2 ❑ Cover: 2.25 **NM** value: **2.50**
3 ❑ Cover: 2.25 **NM** value: **2.50**
4 ❑ Cover: 2.25 **NM** value: **2.50**

TEENAGE MUTANT NINJA TURTLES CLASSICS DIGEST Archie

1 ❑ ca. 1993 Cover: 1.75 **NM** value: **2.00**
2 ❑ ca. 1993 Cover: 1.75 **NM** value: **Cover or less**
3 ❑ ca. 1994 Cover: 1.75 **NM** value: **Cover or less**
4 ❑ ca. 1994 Cover: 1.75 **NM** value: **Cover or less**
5 ❑ ca. 1994 Cover: 1.75 **NM** value: **Cover or less**
6 ❑ ca. 1994 Cover: 1.75 **NM** value: **Cover or less**
7 ❑ Dec 1994 Cover: 1.75 **NM** value: **Cover or less**
• digest.
8 ❑ Cover: 1.75 **NM** value: **Cover or less**

TEENAGE MUTANT NINJA TURTLES/FLAMING CARROT CROSSOVER Mirage

1 ❑ Nov 1993 Cover: 2.75 **NM** value: **3.00**
Circ: CapCity orders: **6,900**
Land Of Green Fire **A:** Jim Lawson **W:** Bob Burden
2 ❑ Dec 1993 Cover: 2.75 **NM** value: **3.00**
Circ: CapCity orders: **5,350**
A: Neil Vokes **W:** Bob Burden
3 ❑ Jan 1994 Cover: 2.75 **NM** value: **3.00**
Circ: CapCity orders: **4,900**
4 ❑ Feb 1994 Cover: 2.75 **NM** value: **3.00**
Circ: CapCity orders: **4,405**

TEENAGE MUTANT NINJA TURTLES III THE MOVIE: THE TURTLES ARE BACK...IN TIME Archie

1 ❑ Cover: 2.50 **NM** value: **Cover or less**
No issue number. • newsstand **A:** Chris Allan **W:** Dean Clarrain; Stuart Gillard
1/PR❑ Cover: 4.95 **NM** value: **Cover or less**
• Prestige edition. **A:** Chris Allan **W:** Dean Clarrain; Stuart Gillard

TEENAGE MUTANT NINJA TURTLES II: THE SECRET OF THE OOZE Mirage

1 ❑ Cover: 5.95 **NM** value: **Cover or less**
Circ: CapCity orders: **3,400**
A: Jim Lawson **W:** Dean Clarrain

TEENAGE MUTANT NINJA TURTLES MEET THE CONSERVATION CORPS Archie

1 ❑ Cover: 2.50 **NM** value: **Cover or less**

TEENAGE MUTANT NINJA TURTLES MICHAELANGELO CHRISTMAS SPECIAL Mirage

1 ❑ Cover: 1.75 **NM** value: **Cover or less**
Michaelangelo: The Christmas Aliens; Raphael: A Christmas Carol **A:** Kevin Eastman; Peter Laird **W:** Kevin Eastman; Peter Laird

TEENAGE MUTANT NINJA TURTLES MOVIE II Archie

1 ❑ Jun 1991 Cover: 2.50 **NM** value: **Cover or less**
Circ: CapCity orders: **15,025**
No issue number. The Secret of the Ooze **A:** Jim Larson **W:** Dean Clarrain

TEENAGE MUTANT NINJA TURTLES MUTANT UNIVERSE SOURCEBOOK Archie

1 ❑ Cover: 1.95 **NM** value: **2.00**
2 ❑ Cover: 1.95 **NM** value: **2.00**
3 ❑ Cover: 1.95 **NM** value: **2.00**

TEENAGE MUTANT NINJA TURTLES PRESENTS: APRIL O'NEIL Archie

1 ❑ Apr 1993 Cover: 1.25 **NM** value: **Cover or less**
Circ: CapCity orders: **4,225**
May East Saga; The May East Saga, Part 1, You're Fired! **A:** Bob Fingerman **W:** Stanley Wiater
2 ❑ Cover: 1.25 **NM** value: **Cover or less**
Circ: CapCity orders: **2,575**
May East Saga; The May East Saga, Part 2 **A:** Bob Fingerman **W:** Stanley Wiater
3 ❑ Cover: 1.25 **NM** value: **Cover or less**
Circ: CapCity orders: **2,825**
May East Saga; The May East Saga, Part 3 **A:** Bob Fingerman **W:** Stanley Wiater

TEENAGE MUTANT NINJA TURTLES PRESENTS: DONATELLO AND LEATHERHEAD Archie

1 ❑ Jul 1993 Cover: 1.25 **NM** value: **Cover or less**
Circ: CapCity orders: **3,425**
Hassles in Hollow Earth! **A:** Garrett Ho **W:** Stanley Wiater
2 ❑ Aug 1993 Cover: 1.25 **NM** value: **Cover or less**
Circ: CapCity orders: **2,650**
Found-One Lost World! **A:** Garrett Ho **W:** Stanley Wiater
3 ❑ Sep 1993 Cover: 1.25 **NM** value: **Cover or less**
A: Garrett Ho **W:** Stanley Wiater

TEENAGE MUTANT NINJA TURTLES PRESENTS MERDUDE AND MICHAELANGELO Archie

1 ❑ Oct 1993 Cover: 1.25 **NM** value: **Cover or less**
2 ❑ Nov 1993 Cover: 1.25 **NM** value: **Cover or less**
3 ❑ Dec 1993 Cover: 1.25 **NM** value: **Cover or less**

TEENAGE MUTANT NINJA TURTLES-SAVAGE DRAGON CROSSOVER Mirage

1 ❑ Aug 1995 Cover: 2.75 **NM** value: **3.00**
Circ: CapCity orders: **42,100**
A: Michael Dooney **W:** Michael Dooney

TEENAGE MUTANT NINJA TURTLES: THE MOVIE (ARCHIE) Archie

1 ❑ Sum 1990 Cover: 2.50 **NM** value: **Cover or less**
Circ: CapCity orders: **17,050**
• newsstand **A:** Jim Lawson **W:** Kevin Eastman; Peter Laird
1/DM❑ Sum 1990 Cover: 4.95 **NM** value: **Cover or less**
Circ: CapCity orders: **21,100**
• prestige format.
1/PR❑ Cover: 5.95 **NM** value: **Cover or less**
• Prestige edition. **A:** Jim Lawson **W:** Kevin Eastman; Peter Laird

TEENAGE MUTANT NINJA TURTLES: THE MOVIE (MIRAGE) Mirage

1 ❑ b&w Cover: 5.95 **NM** value: **Cover or less**
No issue number.

TEENAGENTS (JACK KIRBY'S...) Topps

The Teenagents consist of Seera, a psychic; Kreech, a shapeshifter; Dijit, a smart-aleck technical genius; and their leader, the mighty Aurik. In truth, these are merely the latest of a long line of Teenagents, legends of whom this team hopes someday to be worthy.

The team is based in the miraculous Inner City, a place inside the Earth which can be reached only by means of the Agents' Omni-Bus. Their job is to act as policemen of sorts, stopping bad guys like the monstrous Blood Legion from threatening the "upper world," where we live.

The Teenagents were created by the legendary Jack Kirby. With Kurt Busiek (Marvels) scripting, they became a four-issue mini-series for Topps. Although Kirby was not directly involved with this series, it bears his hallmarks: action, adventure, and a sense of fun (all too rare in many comics).

1 ❑ Aug 1993 Cover: 2.95 **NM** value: **Cover or less**
Circ: CapCity orders: **13,025**
Here be Monsters! • three trading cards **A:** Neil Vokes **W:** Kurt Busiek
2 ❑ Sep 1993 Cover: 2.95 **NM** value: **Cover or less**
Circ: CapCity orders: **9,075**
• trading cards **W:** Kurt Busiek
3 ❑ Oct 1993 Cover: 2.95 **NM** value: **Cover or less**
Circ: CapCity orders: **6,350**
• trading cards **W:** Kurt Busiek ★ Appearance of Liberty Project.
4 ❑ Nov 1993 Cover: 2.95 **NM** value: **Cover or less**
Circ: CapCity orders: **4,750**
• cards; Zorro preview **W:** Kurt Busiek

TEEN-AGE ROMANCES St. John

1 ❑ Jan 1949 Cover: 0.10 **NM** value: **300.00**
2 ❑ Apr 1949 Cover: 0.10 **NM** value: **150.00**
3 ❑ Jul 1949 Cover: 0.10 **NM** value: **150.00**
4 ❑ Aug 1949 Cover: 0.10 **NM** value: **150.00**
5 ❑ Sep 1949 Cover: 0.10 **NM** value: **125.00**
6 ❑ Oct 1949 Cover: 0.10 **NM** value: **125.00**
I Was Caught Stealing Kisses **A:** Matt Baker
7 ❑ Nov 1949 Cover: 0.10 **NM** value: **125.00**
8 ❑ Feb 1950 Cover: 0.10 **NM** value: **125.00**
9 ❑ Apr 1950 Cover: 0.10 **NM** value: **125.00**
10 ❑ Jun 1950 Cover: 0.10 **NM** value: **125.00**
11 ❑ Aug 1950 Cover: 0.10 **NM** value: **125.00**
12 ❑ Oct 1950 Cover: 0.10 **NM** value: **125.00**
13 ❑ Nov 1950 Cover: 0.10 **NM** value: **125.00**
14 ❑ Dec 1950 Cover: 0.10 **NM** value: **125.00**
15 ❑ Feb 1951 Cover: 0.10 **NM** value: **125.00**
I Was an Army Camp Pick-Up
16 ❑ ca. 1951 Cover: 0.10 **NM** value: **125.00**
17 ❑ ca. 1951 Cover: 0.10 **NM** value: **125.00**
18 ❑ ca. 1951 Cover: 0.10 **NM** value: **125.00**
19 ❑ ca. 1951 Cover: 0.10 **NM** value: **125.00**
20 ❑ ca. 1951 Cover: 0.10 **NM** value: **125.00**
21 ❑ ca. 1952 Cover: 0.10 **NM** value: **100.00**
22 ❑ Feb 1952 Cover: 0.10 **NM** value: **100.00**
23 ❑ ca. 1952 Cover: 0.10 **NM** value: **100.00**
24 ❑ ca. 1952 Cover: 0.10 **NM** value: **100.00**
25 ❑ ca. 1952 Cover: 0.10 **NM** value: **100.00**
26 ❑ ca. 1952 Cover: 0.10 **NM** value: **100.00**
27 ❑ ca. 1952 Cover: 0.10 **NM** value: **100.00**
Vacation Love
28❑ ca. 1952 Cover: 0.10 **NM** value: **100.00**
29 ❑ ca. 1953 Cover: 0.10 **NM** value: **100.00**
30 ❑ Feb 1953 Cover: 0.10 **NM** value: **100.00**
31 ❑ ca. 1953 Cover: 0.10 **NM** value: **100.00**
32 ❑ ca. 1953 Cover: 0.10 **NM** value: **100.00**
33 ❑ ca. 1953 Cover: 0.10 **NM** value: **100.00**
34 ❑ ca. 1953 Cover: 0.10 **NM** value: **100.00**
Asking for Trouble **C:** Matt Baker

Other grades: Multiply prices above by **1.5 for Mint • 2/3 for Very Fine • 1/3 for Fine • 1/5 for Very Good • 1/8 for Good**

35 ❑ Jan 1954 Cover: 0.10 **NM** value: **100.00**
36 ❑ ca. 1954 Cover: 0.10 **NM** value: **100.00**
37 ❑ ca. 1954 Cover: 0.10 **NM** value: **100.00**
38 ❑ ca. 1954 Cover: 0.10 **NM** value: **100.00**
39 ❑ ca. 1954 Cover: 0.10 **NM** value: **100.00**
40 ❑ ca. 1954 Cover: 0.10 **NM** value: **100.00**
41 ❑ ca. 1955 Cover: 0.10 **NM** value: **75.00**
42 ❑ ca. 1955 Cover: 0.10 **NM** value: **75.00**
43 ❑ ca. 1955 Cover: 0.10 **NM** value: **75.00**
44 ❑ ca. 1955 Cover: 0.10 **NM** value: **75.00**
45 ❑ Dec 1955 Cover: 0.10 **NM** value: **75.00**

TEEN-AGE TEMPTATIONS — St. John

1 ❑ ca. 1952 Cover: 0.10 **NM** value: **350.00**
2 ❑ ca. 1953 Cover: 0.10 **NM** value: **150.00**
3 ❑ ca. 1953 Cover: 0.10 **NM** value: **150.00**
4 ❑ ca. 1953 Cover: 0.10 **NM** value: **125.00**
5 ❑ ca. 1953 Cover: 0.10 **NM** value: **125.00**
6 ❑ ca. 1954 Cover: 0.10 **NM** value: **125.00**
7 ❑ ca. 1954 Cover: 0.10 **NM** value: **125.00**
8 ❑ ca. 1954 Cover: 0.10 **NM** value: **125.00**
9 ❑ ca. 1954 Cover: 0.10 **NM** value: **125.00**
I Dated the Wrong Boy

TEEN ANGST — Eternity

Bk 1❑ b&w Cover: 14.95 **NM value: Cover or less**

TEEN COMICS — Personality

1 ❑ Cover: 2.50 **NM value: Cover or less**
2 ❑ Cover: 2.50 **NM value: Cover or less**
3 ❑ Cover: 2.50 **NM value: Cover or less**
4 ❑ Cover: 2.50 **NM value: Cover or less**

TEEN CONFESSIONS — Charlton

1 ❑ ca. 1959 Cover: 0.10 **NM** value: **50.00**
2 ❑ 1959 Cover: 0.10 **NM** value: **35.00**
3 ❑ Jan 1960 Cover: 0.10 **NM** value: **20.00**
4 ❑ Mar 1960 Cover: 0.10 **NM** value: **20.00**
5 ❑ May 1960 Cover: 0.10 **NM** value: **20.00**
6 ❑ Jul 1960 Cover: 0.10 **NM** value: **20.00**
7 ❑ Sep 1960 Cover: 0.10 **NM** value: **20.00**
8 ❑ Nov 1960 Cover: 0.10 **NM** value: **20.00**
9 ❑ Jan 1961 Cover: 0.10 **NM** value: **20.00**
10 ❑ Mar 1961 Cover: 0.10 **NM** value: **20.00**
11 ❑ May 1961 Cover: 0.10 **NM** value: **15.00**
12 ❑ Jul 1961 Cover: 0.10 **NM** value: **15.00**
13 ❑ Sep 1961 Cover: 0.10 **NM** value: **15.00**
14 ❑ Nov 1961 Cover: 0.10 **NM** value: **15.00**
15 ❑ Jan 1962 Cover: 0.10 **NM** value: **15.00**
Circ: Statement: **112,441** • **CGC:** 2 graded, best 8.5
16 ❑ Mar 1962 Cover: 0.12 **NM** value: **15.00**
Circ: Statement: **112,441**
17 ❑ May 1962 Cover: 0.12 **NM** value: **15.00**
Circ: Statement: **112,441**
18 ❑ Jul 1962 Cover: 0.12 **NM** value: **15.00**
Circ: Statement: **112,441**
19 ❑ Sep 1962 Cover: 0.12 **NM** value: **15.00**
Circ: Statement: **112,441**
20 ❑ Nov 1962 Cover: 0.12 **NM** value: **15.00**
Circ: Statement: **112,441**
21 ❑ Feb 1963 Cover: 0.12 **NM** value: **15.00**
22 ❑ Apr 1963 Cover: 0.12 **NM** value: **15.00**
23 ❑ Jun 1963 Cover: 0.12 **NM** value: **15.00**
24 ❑ Aug 1963 Cover: 0.12 **NM** value: **15.00**
25 ❑ Oct 1963 Cover: 0.12 **NM** value: **15.00**
26 ❑ Dec 1963 Cover: 0.12 **NM** value: **15.00**
27 ❑ ca. 1964 Cover: 0.12 **NM** value: **15.00**
28 ❑ May 1964 Cover: 0.12 **NM** value: **15.00**
29 ❑ Jul 1964 Cover: 0.12 **NM** value: **15.00**
30 ❑ ca. 1964 Cover: 0.12 **NM** value: **15.00**
31 ❑ ca. 1965 Cover: 0.12 **NM** value: **15.00**
32 ❑ ca. 1965 Cover: 0.12 **NM** value: **15.00**
33 ❑ May 1965 Cover: 0.12 **NM** value: **15.00**
34 ❑ Jul 1965 Cover: 0.12 **NM** value: **15.00**
35 ❑ Sep 1965 Cover: 0.12 **NM** value: **15.00**
36 ❑ Nov 1965 Cover: 0.12 **NM** value: **15.00**
37 ❑ Jan 1966 Cover: 0.12 **NM** value: **15.00**
38 ❑ May 1966 Cover: 0.12 **NM** value: **15.00**
39 ❑ Jul 1966 Cover: 0.12 **NM** value: **15.00**
40 ❑ ca. 1966 Cover: 0.12 **NM** value: **15.00**
41 ❑ Nov 1966 Cover: 0.12 **NM** value: **15.00**
42 ❑ Jan 1967 Cover: 0.12 **NM** value: **15.00**
Circ: Statement: **111,410**
43 ❑ Mar 1967 Cover: 0.12 **NM** value: **15.00**
Circ: Statement: **111,410**
44 ❑ May 1967 Cover: 0.12 **NM** value: **15.00**
Circ: Statement: **111,410**
45 ❑ Jul 1967 Cover: 0.12 **NM** value: **15.00**
Circ: Statement: **111,410**
46 ❑ Sep 1967 Cover: 0.12 **NM** value: **15.00**
Circ: Statement: **111,410**
47 ❑ Nov 1967 Cover: 0.12 **NM** value: **15.00**
Circ: Statement: **111,410**
48 ❑ Jan 1968 Cover: 0.12 **NM** value: **15.00**
49 ❑ Mar 1968 Cover: 0.12 **NM** value: **15.00**
50 ❑ Jul 1968 Cover: 0.12 **NM** value: **15.00**
51 ❑ Sep 1968 Cover: 0.12 **NM** value: **10.00**
52 ❑ Nov 1968 Cover: 0.12 **NM** value: **10.00**
53 ❑ Jan 1968 Cover: 0.12 **NM** value: **10.00**
54 ❑ Mar 1969 Cover: 0.12 **NM** value: **10.00**
55 ❑ ca. 1969 Cover: 0.12 **NM** value: **10.00**
56 ❑ ca. 1969 Cover: 0.12 **NM** value: **10.00**
57 ❑ Aug 1969 Cover: 0.12 **NM** value: **10.00**
58 ❑ Nov 1969 Cover: 0.15 **NM** value: **10.00**
59 ❑ Dec 1969 Cover: 0.15 **NM** value: **10.00**
Circ: Statement: **140,023** Back From Hippyland
60 ❑ ca. 1970 Cover: 0.15 **NM** value: **10.00**
Circ: Statement: **140,023**
61 ❑ ca. 1970 Cover: 0.15 **NM** value: **10.00**
Circ: Statement: **140,023**
62 ❑ ca. 1970 Cover: 0.15 **NM** value: **10.00**
Circ: Statement: **140,023**
63 ❑ ca. 1970 Cover: 0.15 **NM** value: **10.00**
Circ: Statement: **140,023**
64 ❑ Oct 1970 Cover: 0.15 **NM** value: **10.00**
Circ: Statement: **140,023**
65 ❑ Dec 1970 Cover: 0.15 **NM** value: **10.00**
Circ: Statement: **140,023**
66 ❑ Feb 1971 Cover: 0.15 **NM** value: **10.00**
67 ❑ Apr 1971 Cover: 0.15 **NM** value: **10.00**
68 ❑ Jun 1971 Cover: 0.15 **NM** value: **10.00**
• Has 1970 Statement; avg total paid circ 140,023
69 ❑ Aug 1971 Cover: 0.15 **NM** value: **10.00**
70 ❑ Oct 1971 Cover: 0.20 **NM** value: **10.00**
71 ❑ Dec 1971 Cover: 0.20 **NM** value: **10.00**
72 ❑ Feb 1972 Cover: 0.20 **NM** value: **10.00**
Circ: Statement: **110,032**
73 ❑ Apr 1972 Cover: 0.20 **NM** value: **10.00**
Circ: Statement: **110,032**
74 ❑ Jun 1972 Cover: 0.20 **NM** value: **10.00**
Circ: Statement: **110,032**
75 ❑ Aug 1972 Cover: 0.20 **NM** value: **10.00**
Circ: Statement: **110,032**
76 ❑ Oct 1972 Cover: 0.20 **NM** value: **10.00**
Circ: Statement: **110,032**
77 ❑ Dec 1972 Cover: 0.20 **NM** value: **10.00**
Circ: Statement: **110,032**
78 ❑ Feb 1973 Cover: 0.20 **NM** value: **10.00**
Circ: Statement: **124,035**
79 ❑ Apr 1973 Cover: 0.20 **NM** value: **10.00**
Circ: Statement: **124,035**
• Has 1972 Statement; avg total paid circ 110,032
80 ❑ Jun 1973 Cover: 0.20 **NM** value: **10.00**
Circ: Statement: **124,035**
81 ❑ Jul 1973 Cover: 0.20 **NM** value: **10.00**
Circ: Statement: **124,035**
82 ❑ Sep 1973 Cover: 0.20 **NM** value: **10.00**
Circ: Statement: **124,035**
83 ❑ Nov 1973 Cover: 0.20 **NM** value: **10.00**
Circ: Statement: **124,035**
84 ❑ Jan 1974 Cover: 0.20 **NM** value: **10.00**
Circ: Statement: **130,660**
85 ❑ Sep 1974 Cover: 0.25 **NM** value: **10.00**
Circ: Statement: **130,660**
• Has 1973 Statement; avg total paid circ 124,035
86 ❑ ca. 1974 Cover: 0.25 **NM** value: **10.00**
Circ: Statement: **130,660**
87 ❑ Feb 1975 Cover: 0.25 **NM** value: **10.00**
Circ: Statement: **102,166**
88 ❑ Apr 1975 Cover: 0.25 **NM** value: **10.00**
Circ: Statement: **102,166**
89 ❑ Jun 1975 Cover: 0.25 **NM** value: **10.00**
Circ: Statement: **102,166**
• Has 1974 Statement; avg total paid circ 130,660
90 ❑ Aug 1975 Cover: 0.25 **NM** value: **10.00**
Circ: Statement: **102,166**
91 ❑ Oct 1975 Cover: 0.25 **NM** value: **10.00**
Circ: Statement: **102,166**
92 ❑ Dec 1975 Cover: 0.25 **NM** value: **10.00**
Circ: Statement: **102,166**
93 ❑ Feb 1976 Cover: 0.25 **NM** value: **10.00**
94 ❑ Apr 1976 Cover: 0.25 **NM** value: **10.00**
95 ❑ Jun 1976 Cover: 0.25 **NM** value: **10.00**
96 ❑ Aug 1976 Cover: 0.25 **NM** value: **10.00**
97 ❑ Oct 1976 Cover: 0.25 **NM** value: **10.00**

TEENIE WEENIES, THE — Ziff-Davis

10 ❑ ca. 1951 Cover: 0.10 **NM** value: **125.00**
11 ❑ Apr 1951 Cover: 0.10 **NM** value: **125.00**

TEEN TALES: THE LIBRARY COMIC — David G. Brown Studios

1 ❑ Oct 1997 **NM** value: **1.00**
No issue number. • promotional comic book done for the L.A. Public Library

TEEN TITANS, THE — DC

In The Brave and The Bold #54, Robin, Kid Flash, and Aqualad banded together to fight the threat of Mr. Twister in a seaside town. Although not officially known as The Teen Titans yet, the group proved popular enough for a second try-out and then their own series.

In addition to the founding trio the early line-up also included Wonder Girl, and Speedy. Over the next few years other members came and went through the Titans' ranks, including Hawk and Dove, street kid Mal Duncan, the Joker's daughter, Harlequin, and the original Bat-Girl.

Featuring art by Nick Cardy, the series went on hiatus in the early '70s, was revived for a short run in the later 1970s, and revamped as The New Teen Titans in the early 1980s. — Brent

1 ❑ Feb 1966 Cover: 0.12 **NM** value: **150.00**
• **CGC:** 22 graded, best 9.6
• Peace Corps **A:** Nick Cardy
2 ❑ Apr 1966 Cover: 0.12 **NM** value: **80.00**
• **CGC:** 7 graded, best 9.2
A: Nick Cardy
3 ❑ Jun 1966 Cover: 0.12 **NM** value: **45.00**
• **CGC:** 3 graded, best 7.5
A: Nick Cardy
4 ❑ Aug 1966 Cover: 0.12 **NM** value: **45.00**
• **CGC:** 4 graded, best 9.2
A: Nick Cardy
5 ❑ Oct 1966 Cover: 0.12 **NM** value: **45.00**
• **CGC:** 3 graded, best 9.4
A: Nick Cardy; Frank Fosco **W:** Gary Carlson
6 ❑ Dec 1966 Cover: 0.12 **NM** value: **30.00**
• **CGC:** 2 graded, best 9.4
7 ❑ Feb 1967 Cover: 0.12 **NM** value: **30.00**
• **CGC:** 2 graded, best 9.0
The Mad Mod, Merchant of Menace!
8 ❑ Apr 1967 Cover: 0.12 **NM** value: **30.00**
• **CGC:** 2 graded, best 9.6
9 ❑ Jun 1967 Cover: 0.12 **NM** value: **30.00**
• **CGC:** 4 graded, best 9.6
10 ❑ Aug 1967 Cover: 0.12 **NM** value: **30.00**
• **CGC:** 3 graded, best 9.0
11 ❑ Oct 1967 Cover: 0.12 **NM** value: **22.00**
• **CGC:** 2 graded, best 9.4
12 ❑ Dec 1967 Cover: 0.12 **NM** value: **22.00**
• **CGC:** 2 graded, best 9.2
13 ❑ Feb 1968 Cover: 0.12 **NM** value: **22.00**
• **CGC:** 1 graded, best 8.0
14 ❑ Apr 1968 Cover: 0.12 **NM** value: **22.00**
• **CGC:** 2 graded, best 9.2
15 ❑ Jun 1968 Cover: 0.12 **NM** value: **22.00**
• **CGC:** 3 graded, best 9.6
16 ❑ Aug 1968 Cover: 0.12 **NM** value: **22.00**
• **CGC:** 1 graded, best 9.0
17 ❑ Oct 1968 Cover: 0.12 **NM** value: **22.00**
• **CGC:** 3 graded, best 9.4
18 ❑ Dec 1968 Cover: 0.12 **NM** value: **25.00**
• **CGC:** 4 graded, best 9.4
★ 1st Appearance of Starfire.
19 ❑ Feb 1969 Cover: 0.12 **NM** value: **22.00**
• **CGC:** 3 graded, best 9.4
20 ❑ Apr 1969 Cover: 0.12 **NM** value: **25.00**
• **CGC:** 3 graded, best 9.0
A: Neal Adams; Nick Cardy
21 ❑ Jun 1969 Cover: 0.12 **NM** value: **25.00**
• **CGC:** 2 graded, best 9.6
A: Neal Adams; Nick Cardy
22 ❑ Aug 1969 Cover: 0.15 **NM** value: **25.00**
• **CGC:** 6 graded, best 9.4
A: Neal Adams; Nick Cardy ★ Origin of Wonder Girl.
23 ❑ Oct 1969 Cover: 0.15 **NM** value: **14.00**
• **CGC:** 3 graded, best 9.2
The Rock 'n' Roll Rogue **A:** Gil Kane **W:** Dick Giordano; Bob Haney
24 ❑ Dec 1969 Cover: 0.15 **NM** value: **14.00**
• **CGC:** 1 graded, best 9.6
Skis of Death **A:** Gil Kane **W:** Dick Giordano; Bob Haney
25 ❑ Feb 1970 Cover: 0.15 **NM** value: **14.00**
The Titans Kill a Saint? **A:** Nick Cardy **W:** Dick Giordano; Robert Kanigher ★ 1st Appearance of Lilith.
26 ❑ Apr 1970 Cover: 0.15 **NM** value: **12.00**
A Penny for a Black Star **A:** Nick Cardy **W:** Dick Giordano; Robert Kanigher
27 ❑ Jun 1970 Cover: 0.15 **NM** value: **12.00**
• **CGC:** 2 graded, best 9.2
Nightmare in Space • in space **A:** Carmine Infantino; George Tuska **W:** Dick Giordano; Robert Kanigher
28 ❑ Aug 1970 Cover: 0.15 **NM** value: **12.00**
Blindspot **A:** Nick Cardy **W:** Dick Giordano; Steve Skeates
29 ❑ Oct 1970 Cover: 0.15 **NM** value: **12.00**
Captives! **A:** Nick Cardy **W:** Dick Giordano; Steve Skeates ★ Appearance of Hawk & Dove.
30 ❑ Dec 1970 Cover: 0.15 **NM** value: **12.00**
• **CGC:** 2 graded, best 9.2
Greed...Kills!; Whirlwind; Some Call it Noise **A:** Carmine Infantino; Sal Amendola; Nick Cardy **W:** Dick Giordano; Steve Skeates ★ Appearance of Aquagirl.
31 ❑ Feb 1971 Cover: 0.15 **NM** value: **10.00**
To Order is to Destroy; From One to Twenty **A:** George Tuska **W:** Dick Giordano; Steve Skeates
32 ❑ Apr 1971 Cover: 0.15 **NM** value: **10.00**
• **CGC:** 1 graded, best 9.2
A Mystical Realm, a World Gone Mad **A:** Nick Cardy **W:** Dick Giordano; Steve Skeates; Murray Boltinoff
33 ❑ Jun 1971 Cover: 0.15 **NM** value: **10.00**
Less than Human? • Robin returns **A:** George Tuska **W:** Dick Giordano; Bob Haney; Murray Boltinoff
34 ❑ Aug 1971 Cover: 0.15 **NM** value: **10.00**
The Demon of Dog Island **A:** George Tuska **W:** Bob Haney; Murray Boltinoff
35 ❑ Oct 1971 Cover: 0.25 **NM** value: **10.00**
• Giant-size. Intruders of the Forbidden Crypt; A Titan is Born; The Doom Hunters; Have Arrow-Will Travel! **A:** George Tuska **W:** Bob Haney; Murray Boltinoff ★ 1st Appearance of Think Freak.
36 ❑ Dec 1971 Cover: 0.25 **NM** value: **10.00**
• Giant-size. The Tomb Be Their Destiny; The Girl of the Shadows; Superboy Meets Robin the Boy Wonder; The Teen-Ager from Nowhere **A:** George Tuska; Nick Cardy; Jim Aparo **W:** Steve Skeates; Bob Haney; Murray Boltinoff
37 ❑ Feb 1972 Cover: 0.25 **NM** value: **10.00**
• Giant-size. Scourge of the Skeletal Riders; Superboy Meets the Young Green Arrow **A:** George Tuska **W:** Bob Haney; Murray Boltinoff
38 ❑ Apr 1972 Cover: 0.25 **NM** value: **10.00**
• **CGC:** 1 graded, best 9.4
• Giant-size. Through These Doors Pass the Bravest Titans of Them All; Nameless, Wader I; Green Arrow's New Partner; Aqualad Goes to School **A:** George Tuska **W:** Bob Haney; Murray Boltinoff
39 ❑ Jun 1972 Cover: 0.25 **NM** value: **10.00**
• Giant-size. Awake, Barbaric Titan; After the Cat **A:** George Tuska **W:** Bob Haney; Murray Boltinoff
40 ❑ Aug 1972 Cover: 0.20 **NM** value: **10.00**
• **CGC:** 1 graded, best 9.4

CGC-graded: Multiply prices above by **33 for 9.9 M • 16 for 9.8 NM/M • 7 for 9.6 NM+ • 5 for 9.4 NM • 2.5 for 9.2 NM- • 1.5 for 9.0 VF/NM**

The Spawn of the Sinister Sea **A:** Art Saaf **W:** Bob Haney; Murray Boltinoff ★ 1st Appearance of Black Moray. ★ Appearance of Aqualad.

41 ❑ Oct 1972 Cover: 0.20 **NM** value: **10.00**
• **CGC:** 1 graded, best 9.6
What Lies in Litchburg Graveyard?; Her Brother's Keeper **A:** Bob Brown **W:** Bob Haney; Murray Boltinoff

42 ❑ Dec 1972 Cover: 0.20 **NM** value: **10.00**
Slaves of the Emperor Bug **A:** Art Saaf **W:** Bob Haney; Murray Boltinoff

43 ❑ Feb 1973 Cover: 0.20 **NM** value: **10.00**
Inherit the Howling Night; Please Tell Me My Name • series goes on hiatus **A:** Ernie Chan; Art Saaf **W:** Bob Haney; Murray Boltinoff

44 ❑ Nov 1976 Cover: 0.30 **NM** value: **8.00**
• **CGC:** 1 graded, best 9.6
The Man Who Toppled the Titans • Series begins again (1976); New team: Kid Flash, Wonder Girl, Robin, Speedy, Mal **A:** Pablo Marcos **W:** Joe Orlando; Paul Levitz; Bob Rozakis ★ 1st Appearance of Guardian. ★ Versus Doctor Light.

45 ❑ Dec 1976 Cover: 0.30 **NM** value: **8.00**
You Cant Say No The To Angel Of Death! (Or Can You?) **A:** Irv Novick; Vince Colletta(inks) **W:** Bob Rozakis; Julius Schwartz

46 ❑ Feb 1977 Cover: 0.30 **NM** value: **8.00**
• **CGC:** 1 graded, best 8.5
The Fiddler's Concert of Crime **A:** Irv Novick **W:** Bob Rozakis; Julius Schwartz ★ Versus Fiddler.

47 ❑ Apr 1977 Cover: 0.30 **NM** value: **8.00**
Trouble-Which Rhymes with Double **A:** Bob Brown **W:** Bob Rozakis; Julius Schwartz ★ 1st Appearance of Darklight I, Flamesplasher I, Sizematic I, Darklight II, Flamesplasher II, Sizematic II.

48 ❑ Jun 1977 Cover: 0.35 **NM** value: **15.00**
Daddy's Little Crimefighter **A:** Jose Delbo **W:** Bob Rozakis; Julius Schwartz ★ 1st Appearance of Harlequin, The Bumblebee.

49 ❑ Aug 1977 Cover: 0.35 **NM** value: **8.00**
Raid of the Rocket-Rollers **A:** Jose Delbo **W:** Bob Rozakis; Julius Schwartz ★ 1st Appearance of Bryan the Brain.

50 ❑ Oct 1977 Cover: 0.35 **NM** value: **18.00**
• **CGC:** 2 graded, best 9.2
The Coast-to-Coast Calamities • Bat-Girl returns **A:** Don Heck **W:** Bob Rozakis; Julius Schwartz

51 ❑ Nov 1977 Cover: 0.35 **NM** value: **8.00**
Titans East! Titans West! And Never (?) the Teens Shall Meet! **A:** Don Heck **W:** Bob Rozakis; Jack Harris; Julius Schwartz ★ Appearance of Titans West.

52 ❑ Dec 1977 Cover: 0.35 **NM** value: **8.00**
When Titans Clash **A:** Don Heck **W:** Bob Rozakis; Jack Harris; Julius Schwartz ★ Appearance of Titans West.

53 ❑ Feb 1978 Cover: 0.35 **NM** value: **8.00**
In the Beginning… final issue. **A:** Juan Ortiz **W:** Bob Rozakis; Jack Harris ★ Origin of Teen Titans. ★ 1st Appearance of The Antithesis.

TEEN TITANS (2ND SERIES) — DC

After a long period of decline, the Teen Titans were relaunched in 1996 with a whole new team and title. This time out, the Titans consisted of Joto, Risk, Argent, Prysm, and classic hero Atom. Roy Palmer — The Atom — was de-aged during Zero Hour and is now only 17 years old. Although this makes him perfect for the new team, it makes him very out of place in a world where former crimefighters like Barry Allen (the second Flash), and Oliver Queen (Green Arrow) are dead.

The new team was created when the H'San Natall — aliens so terrible that even Darkseid is said to avoid them — kidnapped them and took them onto their spacecraft. It was there that the four youths discovered their powers and decided to band together to escape.

1 ❑ Oct 1996 Cover: 1.95 **NM** value: **4.00**
Titan's Children, Part 1 **A:** George Pérez; Dan Jurgens **W:** Dan Jurgens ★ Origin of New team of four teen-agers led by Atom.

2 ❑ Nov 1996 Cover: 1.95 **NM** value: **3.00**
Circ: Diamd. preorders: **40,950**
Titan's Children, Part 2 **A:** George Pérez; Dan Jurgens **W:** Dan Jurgens

3 ❑ Dec 1996 Cover: 1.95 **NM** value: **3.00**
Circ: Diamd. preorders: **38,970**
Titan's Children, Part 3 • team gets new costumes **A:** George Pérez; Dan Jurgens **W:** Dan Jurgens ★ Appearance of Mr. Jupiter, Mad Mod. ★ Versus Jugular.

4 ❑ Jan 1997 Cover: 1.95 **NM** value: **2.50**
Circ: Diamd. preorders: **38,924**
Coming Out, Part 1 **A:** Dan Jurgens **W:** Dan Jurgens ★ Appearance of Captain Marvel Jr., Nightwing, Robin.

5 ❑ Feb 1997 Cover: 1.95 **NM** value: **2.50**
Circ: Diamd. preorders: **36,594**
Coming Out, Part 2 **A:** Dan Jurgens **W:** Dan Jurgens ★ Appearance of Captain Marvel Jr., Supergirl, Nightwing, Robin.

6 ❑ Mar 1997 Cover: 1.95 **NM** value: **2.50**
Circ: Diamd. preorders: **34,101**
Moving Daze **A:** George Pérez; Dan Jurgens **W:** Dan Jurgens

7 ❑ Apr 1997 Cover: 1.95 **NM** value: **2.50**
Circ: Diamd. preorders: **32,639**
A: Dan Jurgens **W:** Dan Jurgens

8 ❑ May 1997 Cover: 1.95 **NM** value: **2.50**
Circ: Diamd. preorders: **31,960**
A: Dan Jurgens **W:** Dan Jurgens

9 ❑ Jun 1997 Cover: 1.95 **NM** value: **2.50**
Circ: Diamd. preorders: **32,005**
A: Dan Jurgens **W:** Dan Jurgens ★ Appearance of Warlord.

10 ❑ Jul 1997 Cover: 1.95 **NM** value: **2.50**
Circ: Diamd. preorders: **30,429**
• in Skartaris **A:** Dan Jurgens **W:** Dan Jurgens

11 ❑ Aug 1997 Cover: 1.95 **NM** value: **2.00**
Circ: Diamd. preorders: **29,713**
A: Dan Jurgens **W:** Dan Jurgens

12 ❑ Sep 1997 Cover: 2.95 **NM** value: **Cover or less**
Circ: Diamd. preorders: **30,846**
Then & Now, Part 1 • flashback with original Titans **A:** Dan Jurgens **W:** Dan Jurgens

13 ❑ Oct 1997 Cover: 1.95 **NM** value: **2.00**
Circ: Diamd. preorders: **31,830**
Then & Now, Part 2 • flashback with original Titans **A:** Dan Jurgens **W:** Dan Jurgens

14 ❑ Nov 1997 Cover: 1.95 **NM** value: **2.00**
Circ: Diamd. preorders: **29,396**
Then & Now, Part 3 • identity of Omen revealed **A:** George Pérez; Dan Jurgens; Larry Stucker **W:** Dan Jurgens

15 ❑ Jan 1998 Cover: 1.95 **NM** value: **2.00**
Circ: Diamd. preorders: **32,109**
Then & Now, Part 4 • real identity of Omen revealed **A:** George Pérez; Dan Jurgens; Larry Stucker **W:** Dan Jurgens ★ Death of Joto.

16 ❑ Feb 1998 Cover: 1.95 **NM** value: **2.00**
Circ: Diamd. preorders: **30,419**
Then & Now, Part 5 **A:** Dan Jurgens; Joe Rubinstein **W:** Dan Jurgens

17 ❑ Mar 1998 Cover: 1.95 **NM** value: **2.00**
Circ: Diamd. preorders: **31,330**
• new members join

18 ❑ Apr 1998 Cover: 1.95 **NM** value: **2.00**
Circ: Diamd. preorders: **29,836**
Night of the Beast **A:** Phil Jimenez; Dan Jurgens **W:** Dan Jurgens

19 ❑ Apr 1998 Cover: 1.95 **NM** value: **2.00**
Circ: Diamd. preorders: **31,910**
• Millennium Giants ★ Appearance of Superman.

20 ❑ May 1998 Cover: 1.95 **NM** value: **2.00**
Circ: Diamd. preorders: **28,965**

21 ❑ Jun 1998 Cover: 1.95 **NM** value: **2.00**
Circ: Diamd. preorders: **28,837**
Titans Hunt, Part 1

22 ❑ Jul 1998 Cover: 1.95 **NM** value: **2.00**
Circ: Diamd. preorders: **27,414**
Titans Hunt, Part 2 ★ Appearance of Changeling.

23 ❑ Aug 1998 Cover: 1.95 **NM** value: **Cover or less**
Circ: Diamd. preorders: **26,728**
Titans Hunt, Part 3 ★ Appearance of Superman.

24 ❑ Sep 1998 Cover: 1.95 **NM** value: **Cover or less**
Circ: Diamd. preorders: **25,760**
Titans Hunt, Part 4 final issue.

Anl 1❑ca. 1997 Cover: 3.95 **NM** value: **Cover or less**
Circ: Diamd. preorders: **25,771**
• Pulp Heroes

Anl 1999❑ca. 1999 Cover: 4.95 **NM** value: **Cover or less**
Circ: CapCity orders: **28,150** Diamd. preorders: **18,969**
cardstock cover. • published in 1999 in style of '60s Annual

TEEN TITANS SPOTLIGHT — DC

1 ❑ Aug 1986 Cover: 0.75 **NM** value: **1.25**
Circ: CapCity orders: **27,000**
Starfire: Black and White • Starfire **A:** Denys Cowan **W:** Marv Wolfman

2 ❑ Sep 1986 Cover: 0.75 **NM** value: **1.25**
Circ: CapCity orders: **24,650**
• Starfire

3 ❑ Oct 1986 Cover: 0.75 **NM** value: **1.25**
Circ: CapCity orders: **20,600**
Jericho: The Past is Prologue • Jericho **A:** Ross Andru **W:** Marv Wolfman

4 ❑ Nov 1986 Cover: 0.75 **NM** value: **1.25**
Circ: CapCity orders: **20,100**
• Jericho

5 ❑ Dec 1986 Cover: 0.75 **NM** value: **1.25**
Circ: CapCity orders: **16,550**
• Jericho

6 ❑ Jan 1987 Cover: 0.75 **NM** value: **1.00**
Circ: CapCity orders: **15,600**
Conflagration! • Jericho **A:** R.J.M. Lofficier **W:** Marv Wolfman

7 ❑ Feb 1987 Cover: 0.75 **NM** value: **1.00**
Circ: CapCity orders: **15,250**

8 ❑ Mar 1987 Cover: 0.75 **NM** value: **1.00**
Circ: CapCity orders: **14,550**
Queen of Hives • Hawk **A:** Jackson Guice **W:** Mike Baron

9 ❑ Apr 1987 Cover: 0.75 **NM** value: **1.00**
Circ: CapCity orders: **15,750**
• Changeling ★ Appearance of Robotman.

10 ❑ May 1987 Cover: 0.75 **NM** value: **1.00**
Circ: CapCity orders: **12,350**
• Aqualad

11 ❑ Jun 1987 Cover: 0.75 **NM** value: **1.00**
Circ: CapCity orders: **12,300**
• Brotherhood of Evil

12 ❑ Jul 1987 Cover: 0.75 **NM** value: **1.00**
Circ: CapCity orders: **11,950**
• Wonder Girl

13 ❑ Aug 1987 Cover: 0.75 **NM** value: **1.00**
Circ: CapCity orders: **12,850**

14 ❑ Sep 1987 Cover: 0.75 **NM** value: **1.00**
Circ: CapCity orders: **13,850**
• Nightwing, Batman

15 ❑ Oct 1987 Cover: 0.75 **NM** value: **1.00**
Circ: CapCity orders: **12,600**
• Omega Men

16 ❑ Nov 1987 Cover: 0.75 **NM** value: **1.00**
Circ: CapCity orders: **12,500**

17 ❑ Dec 1987 Cover: 0.75 **NM** value: **1.00**
Circ: CapCity orders: **11,900**

18 ❑ Jan 1988 Cover: 0.75 **NM** value: **1.00**
Circ: CapCity orders: **16,450**
Millennium: Week 4 • Millennium; Aqualad

19 ❑ Feb 1988 Cover: 0.75 **NM** value: **1.00**
Circ: CapCity orders: **16,550**
Millennium: Week 8 • Millennium; Starfire

20 ❑ Mar 1988 Cover: 0.75 **NM** value: **1.00**
Circ: CapCity orders: **12,400**
• Cyborg; Changeling

21 ❑ Apr 1988 Cover: 0.75 **NM** value: **1.00**
Circ: CapCity orders: **12,500**
final issue. • original Titans

TEK KNIGHTS — Artline

1 ❑ b&w Cover: 2.95 **NM** value: **Cover or less**

TEKNO*COMIX HANDBOOK — Tekno

1 ❑ May 1996 Cover: 3.95 **NM** value: **Cover or less**
• information on various Tekno characters

TEKNOPHAGE (NEIL GAIMAN'S…) — Tekno

1 ❑ Aug 1995 Cover: 1.95 **NM** value: **Cover or less**
Circ: CapCity orders: **18,000**

1/SC❑Jul 1995 **NM** value: **3.00**
enhanced cover. • Steel Edition.

2 ❑ Sep 1995 Cover: 1.95 **NM** value: **Cover or less**
Circ: CapCity orders: **12,675**

3 ❑ Oct 1995 Cover: 1.95 **NM** value: **Cover or less**
Circ: CapCity orders: **11,150**
Feed the Machine **A:** Bryan Talbot **W:** Rick Veitch

4 ❑ Nov 1995 Cover: 1.95 **NM** value: **Cover or less**
Circ: CapCity orders: **10,300**

5 ❑ Dec 1995 Cover: 1.95 **NM** value: **Cover or less**
Circ: CapCity orders: **8,450**

6 ❑ Dec 1995 Cover: 1.95 **NM** value: **Cover or less**
Circ: CapCity orders: **6,975**

7 ❑ Jan 1996 Cover: 2.25 **NM** value: **Cover or less**

8 ❑ Feb 1996 Cover: 2.25 **NM** value: **Cover or less**

9 ❑ Feb 1996 Cover: 2.25 **NM** value: **Cover or less**

10 ❑ Mar 1996 Cover: 2.25 **NM** value: **Cover or less**

TEKNOPHAGE VERSUS ZEERUS — Big

1 ❑ Jul 1996 Cover: 3.25 **NM** value: **Cover or less**
One-shot. **A:** Fred Harper **W:** Paul Jenkins

TEKQ — Gauntlet

1 ❑ b&w Cover: 2.95 **NM** value: **Cover or less**
A: Brent Dorian Carpenter **W:** Brent Dorian Carpenter

2 ❑ b&w Cover: 2.95 **NM** value: **Cover or less**
A: Brent Dorian Carpenter **W:** Brent Dorian Carpenter

3 ❑ b&w Cover: 2.95 **NM** value: **Cover or less**
A: Brent Dorian Carpenter **W:** Brent Dorian Carpenter

4 ❑ b&w Cover: 2.95 **NM** value: **Cover or less**
A: Brent Dorian Carpenter **W:** Brent Dorian Carpenter

TEKWORLD — Marvel / Epic

Former police officer Jake Cardigan made only one mistake, but it was a big one. He became addicted to Tek — a sort of virtual-reality technology that makes wishes seem to come true. When Teklords no longer want him around, they simply frame him, and Jake ends up in a cryogenic prison. It takes his best friend, Sid Gomez, four years of pulling strings and collecting favors to get him out.

Gomez needs a partner in his business as a private eye, and Cardigan is perfect for the job. His investigative and crime-fighting skills come naturally, but, then, so does putting on the Tek headgear and chips and fading into a fantasy world.

Created by Star Trek actor William Shatner, this comic-book series scripted by Ron Goulart gives a unique and futuristic twist to the classic private eye story. It also appeared as a series of books and a TV show.

1 ❑ Sep 1992 Cover: 1.75 **NM** value: **2.50**
Circ: CapCity orders: **23,100**

2 ❑ Oct 1992 Cover: 1.75 **NM** value: **2.00**
Circ: CapCity orders: **14,100**

3 ❑ Nov 1992 Cover: 1.75 **NM** value: **2.00**
Circ: CapCity orders: **12,400**

4 ❑ Dec 1992 Cover: 1.75 **NM** value: **2.00**
Circ: CapCity orders: **13,000**

5 ❑ Jan 1993 Cover: 1.75 **NM** value: **2.00**
Circ: CapCity orders: **13,300**

6 ❑ Feb 1993 Cover: 1.75 **NM** value: **2.00**
Circ: CapCity orders: **13,700**

7 ❑ Mar 1993 Cover: 1.75 **NM** value: **2.00**
Circ: CapCity orders: **13,600**

8 ❑ Apr 1993 Cover: 1.75 **NM** value: **2.00**
Circ: CapCity orders: **14,000**

9 ❑ May 1993 Cover: 1.75 **NM** value: **2.00**
Circ: CapCity orders: **13,000**

10 ❑ Jun 1993 Cover: 1.75 **NM** value: **2.00**
Circ: CapCity orders: **12,400**

11 ❑ Jul 1993 Cover: 1.75 **NM** value: **Cover or less**
Circ: CapCity orders: **11,400**

12 ❑ Aug 1993 Cover: 1.75 **NM** value: **Cover or less**
Circ: CapCity orders: **11,350**

13 ❑ Sep 1993 Cover: 1.75 **NM** value: **Cover or less**
Circ: CapCity orders: **9,450**

14 ❑ Oct 1993 Cover: 1.75 **NM** value: **Cover or less**
Circ: CapCity orders: **8,700**
• Begins adaptation of TekLords **A:** Lee Sullivan **W:** Ron Goulart ★ Appearance of Jake Cardigan.

15 ❑ Nov 1993 Cover: 1.75 **NM** value: **Cover or less**
Circ: CapCity orders: **8,100**

16 ❑ Dec 1993 Cover: 1.75 **NM** value: **Cover or less**
Circ: CapCity orders: **7,800**

Other grades: Multiply prices above by **1.5 for Mint • 2/3 for Very Fine • 1/3 for Fine • 1/5 for Very Good • 1/8 for Good**

17 ❑ Jan 1994 Cover: 1.75 **NM** value: **Cover or less**
Circ: CapCity orders: **7,200**
18 ❑ Feb 1994 Cover: 1.75 **NM** value: **Cover or less**
Circ: CapCity orders: **6,750**
19 ❑ Mar 1994 Cover: 1.75 **NM** value: **Cover or less**
Circ: CapCity orders: **6,500**
20 ❑ Apr 1994 Cover: 1.75 **NM** value: **Cover or less**
Circ: CapCity orders: **5,800**
21 ❑ May 1994 Cover: 1.75 **NM** value: **Cover or less**
Circ: CapCity orders: **5,800**
22 ❑ Jun 1994 Cover: 1.75 **NM** value: **Cover or less**
Circ: CapCity orders: **5,700**
23 ❑ Jul 1994 Cover: 1.75 **NM** value: **Cover or less**
Circ: CapCity orders: **5,800**
24 ❑ Aug 1994 Cover: 1.75 **NM** value: **Cover or less**
Circ: CapCity orders: **5,600**
final issue.

TELEVISION PUPPET SHOW — Avon

1 ❑ ca. 1950 Cover: 0.10 **NM** value: **125.00**
2 ❑ ca. 1950 Cover: 0.10 **NM** value: **100.00**

TELL IT TO THE MARINES — Toby

1 ❑ Mar 1952 Cover: 0.10 **NM** value: **125.00**
2 ❑ May 1952 Cover: 0.10 **NM** value: **75.00**
3 ❑ Jul 1952 Cover: 0.10 **NM** value: **50.00**
4 ❑ Sep 1952 Cover: 0.10 **NM** value: **50.00**
5 ❑ Nov 1952 Cover: 0.10 **NM** value: **50.00**
6 ❑ Jan 1953 Cover: 0.10 **NM** value: **50.00**
7 ❑ Mar 1953 Cover: 0.10 **NM** value: **50.00**
8 ❑ May 1953 Cover: 0.10 **NM** value: **50.00**
9 ❑ Jul 1953 Cover: 0.10 **NM** value: **50.00**
10 ❑ Sep 1954 Cover: 0.10 **NM** value: **50.00**
11 ❑ Nov 1954 Cover: 0.10 **NM** value: **35.00**
Panther Patrol
12 ❑ Jan 1955 Cover: 0.10 **NM** value: **35.00**
13 ❑ Mar 1955 Cover: 0.10 **NM** value: **35.00**
14 ❑ May 1955 Cover: 0.10 **NM** value: **35.00**
15 ❑ Jul 1955 Cover: 0.10 **NM** value: **35.00**

TELLOS — Image

Anthropomorphic frog soldiers with lisps are in pursuit of Koj, a humanoid tiger in buccaneer garb and his protege, Jarek, a human child. Outwitting the fatuous, self-important frogs is not much of a challenge to this wily team, but there is the matter of the malevolent living shadows that lurk just outside of their perception. When a statuesque female pirate named Serra runs afoul of some more of the frog soldiers chasing her for the mysterious green amulet she possesses, Koj and Jarek are naturally inclined to help her.

Todd Dezago and Mike Wieringo, who previously teamed on The Sensational Spider-Man, return in this creator-owned fantasy featuring all the traditional elements of adventure fiction (as well as gnomes, giants, and griffins), told with clean, clear, vivid art and a nonstop narrative. And there's a resolution to the adventure that adds a powerful twist to all that precedes it.

1 ❑ May 1999 Cover: 2.50 **NM** value: **Cover or less**
Circ: Diamd. preorders: **34,256 • CGC:** 2 graded, best 9.6
A: Mike Wieringo **W:** Todd Dezago
2 ❑ Jun 1999 Cover: 2.50 **NM** value: **Cover or less**
Circ: Diamd. preorders: **30,849**
A: Mike Wieringo **W:** Todd Dezago
3 ❑ Jul 1999 Cover: 2.50 **NM** value: **Cover or less**
Circ: Diamd. preorders: **27,689**
A: Mike Wieringo **W:** Todd Dezago
4 ❑ Oct 1999 Cover: 2.50 **NM** value: **Cover or less**
Circ: Diamd. preorders: **37,828**
A: Mike Wieringo **W:** Todd Dezago
4/A ❑ Oct 1999 Cover: 2.50 **NM** value: **Cover or less**
alternate cover w/moon in background. **A:** Mike Wieringo **W:** Todd Dezago
4/B ❑ Oct 1999 Cover: 2.50 **NM** value: **Cover or less**
alternate cover w/skeletons in bottom left. **A:** Mike Wieringo **W:** Todd Dezago
5 ❑ Dec 1999 Cover: 2.50 **NM** value: **Cover or less**
Circ: Diamd. preorders: **29,231**
A: Mike Wieringo **W:** Todd Dezago
6 ❑ Feb 2000 Cover: 2.50 **NM** value: **Cover or less**
Circ: Diamd. preorders: **25,612**
A: Mike Wieringo **W:** Todd Dezago
7 ❑ Apr 2000 Cover: 2.50 **NM** value: **Cover or less**
Circ: Diamd. preorders: **24,139**
A: Mike Wieringo **W:** Todd Dezago
8 ❑ Aug 2000 Cover: 2.50 **NM** value: **Cover or less**
Circ: Diamd. preorders: **28,529**
The Sleeping Giant **A:** Mike Wieringo **W:** Todd Dezago
9 ❑ Sep 2000 Cover: 2.50 **NM** value: **Cover or less**
Circ: Diamd. preorders: **21,680**
Rites of Darkness **A:** Mike Wieringo **W:** Todd Dezago
10 ❑ Nov 2000 Cover: 2.50 **NM** value: **Cover or less**
Circ: Diamd. preorders: **21,025**
A: Mike Wieringo **W:** Todd Dezago
Ash 1 ❑ Cover: 2.50 **NM** value: **Cover or less**
• Dynamic Forces preview **A:** Mike Wieringo **W:** Todd Dezago
Bk 1 ❑ Nov 1999 Cover: 8.95 **NM** value: **Cover or less**
• The Joining; Collects Tellos #1-3 **A:** Mike Wieringo **W:** Todd Dezago
Bk 2 ❑ Cover: 17.95 **NM** value: **Cover or less**
• Reluctant Heroes **A:** Mike Wieringo **W:** Todd Dezago

TELLTALE HEART, THE — Mojo Press

1 ❑ b&w Cover: 4.95 **NM** value: **Cover or less**
No issue number. • prestige format. • adapts Poe stories

TELL TALE HEART AND OTHER STORIES — Fantagraphics

1 ❑ b&w Cover: 2.50 **NM** value: **Cover or less**

TELLURIA — Zub

1 ❑ Cover: 2.50 **NM** value: **Cover or less**
Yonna **A:** Analise Hairabedian **W:** Kevin Bowman
2 ❑ Cover: 2.50 **NM** value: **Cover or less**
The Orb, Part 1 **A:** Analise Hairabedian **W:** Kevin Bowman
3 ❑ Cover: 2.50 **NM** value: **Cover or less**
The Orb, Part 2 **A:** Analise Hairabedian **W:** Kevin Bowman

TEMPEST — DC

1 ❑ Nov 1996 Cover: 1.75 **NM** value: **Cover or less**
Circ: Diamd. preorders: **31,442**
Prophets And Kings, Part 1 • Tula returns **A:** Phil Jimenez **W:** Phil Jimenez
2 ❑ Dec 1996 Cover: 1.75 **NM** value: **Cover or less**
Circ: Diamd. preorders: **23,881**
Prophets And Kings, Part 2 **A:** Phil Jimenez **W:** Phil Jimenez
3 ❑ Jan 1997 Cover: 1.75 **NM** value: **Cover or less**
Circ: Diamd. preorders: **22,346**
Prophets And Kings, Part 3 • Aqualad's true origin revealed **A:** Phil Jimenez **W:** Phil Jimenez
4 ❑ Feb 1997 Cover: 1.75 **NM** value: **Cover or less**
Circ: Diamd. preorders: **20,783**
Prophets And Kings, Part 4 **A:** Phil Jimenez **W:** Phil Jimenez

TEMPLATE — Head Press

0 ❑ Cover: 2.95 **NM** value: **Cover or less**
• flip-book with Max Damage #0 **A:** Robert Luedke **W:** Robert Luedke
1 ❑ Dec 1995, b&w Cover: 2.50 **NM** value: **Cover or less**
A Mind is a Terrible Thing **A:** Robert Luedke **W:** Robert Luedke
2 ❑ Feb 1996, b&w Cover: 2.50 **NM** value: **Cover or less**
A: Robert Luedke **W:** Robert Luedke
3 ❑ Apr 1996, b&w Cover: 2.50 **NM** value: **Cover or less**
A: Robert Luedke **W:** Robert Luedke
4 ❑ Jun 1996, b&w Cover: 2.50 **NM** value: **Cover or less**
A: Robert Luedke **W:** Robert Luedke
5 ❑ Aug 1996, b&w Cover: 2.50 **NM** value: **Cover or less**
A: Robert Luedke **W:** Robert Luedke
6 ❑ Nov 1996, b&w Cover: 2.50 **NM** value: **Cover or less**
Ism By Thy Name, Part 2 **A:** Robert Luedke **W:** Robert Luedke
7 ❑ Jul 1997, b&w Cover: 2.50 **NM** value: **Cover or less**
A: Robert Luedke **W:** Robert Luedke
SE 1 ❑ Feb 1997, b&w Cover: 2.95 **NM** value: **Cover or less**
A: Bill Maus; Robert Luedke; David BlueStein; Jenni Gregory; Michael Lagocki **W:** Robert Luedke
SE 1/Ash ❑ Feb 1997 Cover: 1.00 **NM** value: **Cover or less**
• Ashcan preview of special #1 **A:** Robert Luedke **W:** Robert Luedke
SE 1/SC ❑ Feb 1997 Cover: 2.95 **NM** value: **Cover or less**
alternate cover. **A:** Bill Maus; Robert Luedke; David BlueStein; Jenni Gregory; Michael Lagocki **W:** Robert Luedke

TEMPLE SNARE — Mu

1 ❑ b&w Cover: 2.25 **NM** value: **Cover or less**
No issue number.

TEMPTRESS: THE BLOOD OF EVE — Caliber

1 ❑ Cover: 2.95 **NM** value: **Cover or less**
Forever and a Day, Part 1 **A:** Eric Powell **W:** Tom Sniegoski

TEMPUS FUGITIVE — DC

1 ❑ ca. 1990 Cover: 4.95 **NM** value: **Cover or less**
Circ: CapCity orders: **11,950**
A: Ken Steacy **W:** Ken Steacy
2 ❑ ca. 1990 Cover: 4.95 **NM** value: **Cover or less**
Circ: CapCity orders: **9,300**
A: Ken Steacy **W:** Ken Steacy
3 ❑ ca. 1990 Cover: 5.95 **NM** value: **Cover or less**
Circ: CapCity orders: **8,800**
A: Ken Steacy **W:** Ken Steacy
4 ❑ ca. 1990 Cover: 5.95 **NM** value: **Cover or less**
Circ: CapCity orders: **6,250**
A: Ken Steacy **W:** Ken Steacy

TENCHI MUYO! — Pioneer

1 ❑ Mar 1997 Cover: 2.95 **NM** value: **Cover or less**
Circ: Diamd. preorders: **6,108**
2 ❑ Mar 1997 Cover: 2.95 **NM** value: **Cover or less**
Circ: Diamd. preorders: **4,882**
3 ❑ May 1997 Cover: 2.95 **NM** value: **Cover or less**
Circ: Diamd. preorders: **5,009**
4 ❑ Jul 1997 Cover: 2.95 **NM** value: **Cover or less**
Circ: Diamd. preorders: **5,360**
5 ❑ Aug 1997 Cover: 2.95 **NM** value: **Cover or less**
Circ: Diamd. preorders: **5,074**

TENDER ROMANCE — Key

1 ❑ Dec 1953 Cover: 0.10 **NM** value: **125.00**
2 ❑ Feb 1954 Cover: 0.10 **NM** value: **60.00**

TENTH, THE — Image

0 ❑ Aug 1997 **NM** value: **3.00**
• American Entertainment exclusive
0.5 ❑ Aug 1997 **NM** value: **5.00**
• Wizard promotional edition with certificate of authenticity.
1 ❑ Jan 1997 Cover: 2.50 **NM** value: **3.00**
Circ: Diamd. preorders: **52,203**
cover says Mar, indicia says Jan.
1/A ❑ Jan 1997 Cover: 2.50 **NM** value: **4.00**
American Entertainment exclusive cover.
2 ❑ Feb 1997 Cover: 2.50 **NM** value: **Cover or less**
cover says Apr, indicia says Feb.
3 ❑ May 1997 Cover: 2.50 **NM** value: **Cover or less**
4 ❑ Jun 1997 Cover: 2.50 **NM** value: **Cover or less**
Bk 1 ❑ Sep 1997 Cover: 10.95 **NM** value: **11.95**
• Abuse Of Humanity; Collects The Tenth Mini-Series #1-4
Bk 1-2 ❑ Oct 1998 Cover: 11.95 **NM** value: **Cover or less**

TENTH, THE (2ND SERIES) — Image

This series continues the saga of The Tenth, the 10th monster created by the evil Rhazes Darkk as part of his plot to alter all life on Earth into a twisted Darkk Earth.

The series features an imaginative cast of characters, caught in a complex plot. Victor, the man reshaped into The Tenth, must drink human blood to avoid turning into a crazed beast. The beautiful Espy befriends The Tenth, just as her telekinetic powers blossom. Gozza, the kid super-monster, believes he is the rightful heir to Darkk's legacy. And Adrenalynn is an android clone killing machine, packaged in the body of a teen-age schoolgirl.

Now The Tenth has joined Gozza, and both Adrenalynn and Espy are searching for them. Gozza is holed up in the ruins of the city of Springdale. What are his plans? And can anyone stop Gozza, if The Tenth has joined him?

0 ❑ Aug 1997 Cover: 2.95 **NM** value: **3.00**
A: Tony Daniel **W:** Beau Smith ★ Origin of The Tenth.
0/A ❑ Aug 1997 **NM** value: **8.00**
A: Tony Daniel **W:** Beau Smith ★ Origin of The Tenth.
0/AE ❑ Aug 1997 **NM** value: **4.00**
• American Entertainment exclusive **A:** Tony Daniel **W:** Beau Smith ★ Origin of The Tenth.
1 ❑ Sep 1997 Cover: 2.50 **NM** value: **3.00**
Circ: Diamd. preorders: **53,991**
Abuse of Humanity **A:** Tony Daniel **W:** Beau Smith
1/AE ❑ Sep 1997 Cover: 2.50 **NM** value: **4.00**
American Entertainment exclusive cover (logo at bottom right). Abuse of Humanity **A:** Tony Daniel **W:** Beau Smith
2 ❑ Oct 1997 Cover: 2.50 **NM** value: **3.00**
Circ: Diamd. preorders: **43,217**
A: Tony Daniel **W:** Tony Daniel; Beau Smith
3 ❑ Nov 1997 Cover: 2.50 **NM** value: **Cover or less**
Circ: Diamd. preorders: **47,013**
A: Tony Daniel **W:** Beau Smith
3/A ❑ Nov 1997 Cover: 2.50 **NM** value: **3.00**
Alternate "Adrenalyn" cover. **A:** Tony Daniel **W:** Beau Smith
3/B ❑ Nov 1997 Cover: 2.50 **NM** value: **8.00**
Circ: Diamd. preorders: **3,666**
• Wizard "Certified Authentic" limited edition. **A:** Tony Daniel **W:** Beau Smith
4 ❑ Dec 1997 Cover: 2.50 **NM** value: **Cover or less**
Circ: Diamd. preorders: **42,120**
A: Tony Daniel **W:** Tony Daniel; Beau Smith
5 ❑ Jan 1998 Cover: 2.50 **NM** value: **Cover or less**
Circ: Diamd. preorders: **40,576**
A: Tony Daniel **W:** Tony Daniel; Beau Smith
6 ❑ Feb 1998 Cover: 2.50 **NM** value: **Cover or less**
Circ: Diamd. preorders: **38,407**
A: Tony Daniel **W:** Beau Smith
7 ❑ Mar 1998 Cover: 2.50 **NM** value: **Cover or less**
Circ: Diamd. preorders: **43,020 • CGC:** 1 graded, best 9.8
A: Tony Daniel **W:** Tony Daniel; Beau Smith
8 ❑ Apr 1998 Cover: 2.50 **NM** value: **Cover or less**
Circ: Diamd. preorders: **38,130 • CGC:** 1 graded, best 9.8
A: Tony Daniel **W:** Tony Daniel; Beau Smith
9 ❑ Jun 1998 Cover: 2.50 **NM** value: **Cover or less**
Circ: Diamd. preorders: **35,876 • CGC:** 1 graded, best 9.6
No Sweets After Dark **A:** Tony Daniel **W:** Tony Daniel; Beau Smith
10 ❑ Jul 1998 Cover: 2.50 **NM** value: **Cover or less**
Circ: Diamd. preorders: **40,733**
Killcrow **A:** Tony Daniel **W:** Tony Daniel
10/A ❑ Jul 1998 Cover: 2.50 **NM** value: **Cover or less**
alternate cover (logo on right). **A:** Tony Daniel **W:** Tony Daniel
11 ❑ Aug 1998 Cover: 2.50 **NM** value: **Cover or less**
Circ: Diamd. preorders: **37,100**
Gathering of the Children **A:** Tony Daniel **W:** Tony Daniel
11/A ❑ Aug 1998 Cover: 2.50 **NM** value: **Cover or less**
alternate cover (white background). **A:** Tony Daniel **W:** Tony Daniel
12 ❑ Oct 1998 Cover: 2.50 **NM** value: **Cover or less**
Circ: Diamd. preorders: **33,627**
A: Tony Daniel **W:** Tony Daniel
13 ❑ Nov 1998 Cover: 2.50 **NM** value: **Cover or less**
Circ: Diamd. preorders: **34,523**
A: Tony Daniel **W:** Tony Daniel
14 ❑ Jan 1999 Cover: 2.50 **NM** value: **Cover or less**
Circ: Diamd. preorders: **33,018**
A: Tony Daniel **W:** Tony Daniel
14/A ❑ Jan 1999 Cover: 2.50 **NM** value: **Cover or less**
alternate cover (solo face). **A:** Tony Daniel **W:** Tony Daniel
Bk 1 ❑ May 1998 Cover: 4.95 **NM** value: **Cover or less**
Circ: Diamd. preorders: **5,837**
• prestige format. • collects issues #1 and 2; no indicia **A:** Tony Daniel **W:** Beau Smith

TENTH, THE (3RD SERIES) — Image

1 ❑ Feb 1999 Cover: 2.95 **NM** value: **Cover or less**
Circ: Diamd. preorders: **34,484 • CGC:** 1 graded, best 9.8
A: Tony Daniel **W:** Scott Lobdell; Tony Daniel
1/A ❑ Feb 1999 Cover: 2.95 **NM** value: **Cover or less**
alternate cover. The Black Embrace **A:** Tony Daniel **W:** Scott Lobdell; Tony Daniel

CGC-graded: Multiply prices above by **33 for 9.9 M • 16 for 9.8 NM/M • 7 for 9.6 NM+ • 5 for 9.4 NM • 2.5 for 9.2 NM- • 1.5 for 9.0 VF/NM**

1/B ❑ Feb 1999 Cover: 2.95 **NM** value: **10.00**
• **CGC:** 4 graded, best 9.8
alternate cover. • DFE chromium edition. **A:** Tony Daniel **W:** Scott Lobdell; Tony Daniel
2 ❑ Apr 1999 Cover: 2.95 **NM** value: **Cover or less**
Circ: Diamd. preorders: **29,805**
A: Tony Daniel **W:** Scott Lobdell; Tony Daniel
3 ❑ May 1999 Cover: 2.95 **NM** value: **Cover or less**
Circ: Diamd. preorders: **28,283**
A: Tony Daniel **W:** Scott Lobdell; Tony Daniel
4 ❑ Jun 1999 Cover: 2.95 **NM** value: **Cover or less**
Circ: Diamd. preorders: **27,945**
A: Tony Daniel **W:** Scott Lobdell; Tony Daniel

TENTH, THE (4TH SERIES) Image

1 ❑ Sep 1999 Cover: 2.95 **NM** value: **Cover or less**
Circ: Diamd. preorders: **33,140**
A: Tony Daniel **W:** Tony Daniel
1/A ❑ Sep 1999 Cover: 2.95 **NM** value: **6.00**
Girl wearing shirt and panties on cover. **A:** Tony Daniel **W:** Tony Daniel
1/B ❑ Sep 1999 Cover: 2.95 **NM** value: **3.00**
Another Universe exclusive cover. **A:** Tony Daniel **W:** Tony Daniel
2 ❑ Oct 1999 Cover: 2.50 **NM** value: **Cover or less**
Circ: Diamd. preorders: **26,857**
📖 Evil's Child **A:** Tony Daniel **W:** Tony Daniel
3 ❑ Nov 1999 Cover: 2.50 **NM** value: **Cover or less**
Circ: Diamd. preorders: **27,236**
A: Tony Daniel **W:** Tony Daniel
4 ❑ Dec 1999 Cover: 2.50 **NM** value: **Cover or less**
Circ: Diamd. preorders: **27,430**
A: Tony Daniel **W:** Tony Daniel

TENTH CONFIGURATION, THE Image

1 ❑ Aug 1998 Cover: 2.50 **NM** value: **Cover or less**
Circ: Diamd. preorders: **27,479**
A: Tony Daniel **W:** Tony Daniel

10TH MUSE Image

1 ❑ Nov 2000 Cover: 2.95 **NM** value: **Cover or less**
Circ: Diamd. preorders: **73,301**
2/A ❑ Jan 2001 Cover: 2.95 **NM** value: **Cover or less**
Circ: Diamd. preorders: **31,535**
Character leaping from right on cover. **A:** Ken Lashley **W:** Marv Wolfman
2/B ❑ Jan 2001 Cover: 2.95 **NM** value: **Cover or less**
Character leaping from left on cover. **A:** Ken Lashley **W:** Marv Wolfman
2/C ❑ Jan 2001 Cover: 2.95 **NM** value: **Cover or less**
Photo cover. **A:** Ken Lashley **W:** Marv Wolfman
3/A ❑ Mar 2001 Cover: 2.95 **NM** value: **Cover or less**
Circ: Diamd. preorders: **28,802**
Drawn cover with woman summoning lightning. **A:** Ken Lashley **W:** Marv Wolfman
3/B ❑ Mar 2001 Cover: 2.95 **NM** value: **Cover or less**
Photo cover with green border. **A:** Ken Lashley **W:** Marv Wolfman
3/C ❑ Mar 2001 Cover: 2.95 **NM** value: **Cover or less**
Drawn cover with woman leaping forward. **A:** Ken Lashley **W:** Marv Wolfman
3/D ❑ Mar 2001 Cover: 2.95 **NM** value: **Cover or less**
Wraparound Tower Records photo cover with red border. **A:** Ken Lashley **W:** Marv Wolfman
4 ❑ ca. 2001 Cover: 2.95 **NM** value: **Cover or less**
Circ: Diamd. preorders: **22,441**
5 ❑ ca. 2001 Cover: 2.95 **NM** value: **Cover or less**
Circ: Diamd. preorders: **13,272**
6 ❑ ca. 2001 Cover: 2.95 **NM** value: **Cover or less**
Circ: Diamd. preorders: **11,646**

TENTH, THE: RESURRECTED Dark Horse

1/A ❑ Jul 2001 Cover: 2.99 **NM** value: **Cover or less**
Circ: Diamd. preorders: **22,379**
Lady standing in front of glowing skulls in background on cover. **A:** Romano! **W:** Tony Daniel
1/B ❑ Jul 2001 Cover: 2.99 **NM** value: **Cover or less**
Circ: Diamd. preorders: **2,087**
Hulking figure on cover. **A:** Romano! **W:** Tony Daniel

TEN YEARS OF LOVE & ROCKETS Fantagraphics

1 ❑ Sep 1992, b&w Cover: 1.50 **NM** value: **Cover or less**
Circ: CapCity orders: **4,950**
No issue number. 📖 Heart Break Soup: Space Case; Is It 10 Years Already?; At the Drawing Board with Jaime; Who's Who in Love in Love & Rockets; Locas Tambien; At the Drawing Board With Gilbert; Las Monjas Asesinas **A:** Gilbert & Jaime Hernandez **W:** Gilbert & Jaime Hernandez

TERMINAL CITY DC / Vertigo

Terminal City is a stylish nine-issue mini-series featuring an assortment of unusual characters set in a future that writer Dean Motter calls "Antique Futurism. The world of tomorrow from yesterday's point of view." The Art Deco style that artist Michael Lark employs is a prominent part of the charm of this unusual story, which depicts hover cars with 1950s-style fins and robot desk clerks capable of independent thought in spite of whirring and clicking like obsolete machinery.

Former daredevil, now window-washer, Cosmo Quinn; Li'l Big Lil, albino gang boss; and the mysterious Lady in Red are just a few of the intriguing characters whose lives intersect at the formerly posh hotel, The Herculean Arms, in a town that is a living anachronism: Terminal City.

1 ❑ Jul 1996 Cover: 2.50 **NM** value: **3.50**
📖 On the Wall **A:** Michael Lark **W:** Dean Motter
1/Aut ❑ Jul 1996 **NM** value: **5.00**
📖 On the Wall • Limited to 75 copies **A:** Michael Lark **W:** Dean Motter
2 ❑ Aug 1996 Cover: 2.50 **NM** value: **3.00**
📖 On the Wall **A:** Michael Lark **W:** Dean Motter
3 ❑ Sep 1996 Cover: 2.50 **NM** value: **3.00**
📖 On the Wall **A:** Michael Lark **W:** Dean Motter
4 ❑ Oct 1996 Cover: 2.50 **NM** value: **Cover or less**
📖 On the Wall **A:** Michael Lark **W:** Dean Motter
5 ❑ Nov 1996 Cover: 2.50 **NM** value: **Cover or less**
Circ: Diamd. preorders: **21,499**
📖 On the Wall **A:** Michael Lark **W:** Dean Motter
6 ❑ Dec 1996 Cover: 2.50 **NM** value: **Cover or less**
Circ: Diamd. preorders: **20,486**
📖 On the Wall **A:** Michael Lark **W:** Dean Motter
7 ❑ Jan 1997 Cover: 2.50 **NM** value: **Cover or less**
Circ: Diamd. preorders: **19,438**
📖 On the Wall **A:** Michael Lark **W:** Dean Motter
8 ❑ Feb 1997 Cover: 2.50 **NM** value: **Cover or less**
Circ: Diamd. preorders: **18,336**
📖 On the Wall **A:** Michael Lark **W:** Dean Motter
9 ❑ Mar 1997 Cover: 2.50 **NM** value: **Cover or less**
Circ: Diamd. preorders: **17,632**
📖 On the Wall final issue. **A:** Michael Lark **W:** Dean Motter
Bk 1 ❑ Cover: 19.95 **NM** value: **Cover or less**
📖 On the Wall **A:** Michael Lark **W:** Dean Motter

TERMINAL CITY: AERIAL GRAFFITI DC / Vertigo

1 ❑ Nov 1997 Cover: 2.50 **NM** value: **Cover or less**
Circ: Diamd. preorders: **17,574**
A: Michael Lark **W:** Dean Motter
2 ❑ Dec 1997 Cover: 2.50 **NM** value: **Cover or less**
Circ: Diamd. preorders: **15,458**
A: Michael Lark **W:** Dean Motter
3 ❑ Jan 1998 Cover: 2.50 **NM** value: **Cover or less**
Circ: Diamd. preorders: **14,489**
A: Michael Lark **W:** Dean Motter
4 ❑ Feb 1998 Cover: 2.50 **NM** value: **Cover or less**
Circ: Diamd. preorders: **13,559**
A: Michael Lark **W:** Dean Motter
5 ❑ Mar 1998 Cover: 2.50 **NM** value: **Cover or less**
Circ: Diamd. preorders: **12,953**
A: Michael Lark **W:** Dean Motter

TERMINAL POINT Dark Horse

1 ❑ Feb 1993, b&w Cover: 2.50 **NM** value: **Cover or less**
Circ: CapCity orders: **12,525**
A: Bruce Zick **W:** Bruce Zick
2 ❑ Mar 1993, b&w Cover: 2.50 **NM** value: **Cover or less**
Circ: CapCity orders: **6,300**
A: Bruce Zick **W:** Bruce Zick
3 ❑ Apr 1993, b&w Cover: 2.50 **NM** value: **Cover or less**
Circ: CapCity orders: **4,575**
A: Bruce Zick **W:** Bruce Zick

TERMINATOR, THE (1ST SERIES) Now

In 1988, Now Comics began publishing the first of many comic titles based on the science-fiction blockbuster, "The Terminator." That epic told of how in August, 1997, a computer defense system called Skynet would gain consciousness and turn on its creators. Within weeks, it had used its control of the nuclear arsenal to all but destroy mankind. Then this machine intelligence began spawning other mechanical creations whose purpose was to annihilate the few human survivors.

By 2031, the leader of humanity, John Connor, was leading his forces toward victory. That's when Skynet decided to change history and send a killing machine — a Terminator — back through time to kill Connor's mother Sarah and prevent John from being born. The movie covered Sarah's struggle for survival, while the 18 issues of this Now Comics series go back to the future to tell the tale of mankind's battle against the machines.

1 ❑ Sep 1988 Cover: 1.75 **NM** value: **2.00**
Circ: CapCity orders: **9,200** • **CGC:** 3 graded, best 9.6
• movie tie-in **A:** Thomas Tenney **W:** Tony Caputo
2 ❑ Oct 1988 Cover: 1.75 **NM** value: **Cover or less**
Circ: CapCity orders: **5,975**
A: Thomas Tenney **W:** Tony Caputo
3 ❑ Nov 1988 Cover: 1.75 **NM** value: **Cover or less**
Circ: CapCity orders: **5,675**
4 ❑ Jan 1989 Cover: 1.75 **NM** value: **Cover or less**
Circ: CapCity orders: **6,400**
5 ❑ Feb 1989 Cover: 1.75 **NM** value: **Cover or less**
Circ: CapCity orders: **6,975**
📖 The Bee Stings **A:** Thomas Tenney **W:** Jack Herman
6 ❑ Mar 1989 Cover: 1.75 **NM** value: **Cover or less**
Circ: CapCity orders: **7,100**
📖 Goin' Back to Miami **A:** Thomas Tenney **W:** Jack Herman
7 ❑ Apr 1989 Cover: 1.75 **NM** value: **Cover or less**
Circ: CapCity orders: **7,075**
8 ❑ May 1989 Cover: 1.75 **NM** value: **Cover or less**
Circ: CapCity orders: **6,475**
📖 In The Belly Of The Beast • Comics Code **A:** Thomas Tenney **W:** Jack Herman
9 ❑ Jun 1989 Cover: 1.75 **NM** value: **Cover or less**
Circ: CapCity orders: **6,475**
• Comics Code
10 ❑ Jul 1989 Cover: 1.75 **NM** value: **Cover or less**
Circ: CapCity orders: **6,775**
• Comics Code
11 ❑ Aug 1989 Cover: 1.75 **NM** value: **Cover or less**
Circ: CapCity orders: **6,350**
• Comics Code
12 ❑ Sep 1989 Cover: 1.75 **NM** value: **Cover or less**
Circ: CapCity orders: **6,025**
• Comics Code
13 ❑ Oct 1989 Cover: 1.75 **NM** value: **Cover or less**
Circ: CapCity orders: **5,525**
• Comics Code
14 ❑ Nov 1989 Cover: 1.75 **NM** value: **Cover or less**
Circ: CapCity orders: **5,275**
📖 Into The Deep Blue Sea • Comics Code **A:** Thomas Tenney **W:** Ron Fortier
15 ❑ Dec 1989 Cover: 1.75 **NM** value: **Cover or less**
Circ: CapCity orders: **5,675**
• Comics Code
16 ❑ Jan 1990 Cover: 1.75 **NM** value: **Cover or less**
Circ: CapCity orders: **5,425**
• Comics Code
17 ❑ Feb 1990 Cover: 1.75 **NM** value: **Cover or less**
Circ: CapCity orders: **5,050**
final issue. • Comics Code

TERMINATOR 2: JUDGMENT DAY Marvel

1 ❑ Sep 1991 Cover: 1.00 **NM** value: **2.00**
Circ: CapCity orders: **22,500**
📖 Arrival **A:** Klaus Janson **W:** Greg Wright; James Cameron; William Wisher
2 ❑ Sep 1991 Cover: 1.00 **NM** value: **2.00**
Circ: CapCity orders: **20,400**
A: Klaus Janson **W:** Greg Wright; James Cameron; William Wisher
3 ❑ Oct 1991 Cover: 1.00 **NM** value: **2.00**
Circ: CapCity orders: **2,100**
📖 Departure **A:** Klaus Janson **W:** Greg Wright; James Cameron; William Wisher

TERMINATOR 2: JUDGMENT DAY (MAGAZINE) Marvel

1 ❑ Sep 1991, b&w Cover: 2.25 **NM** value: **3.00**
No issue number. • magazine.

TERMINATOR, THE (2ND SERIES) Dark Horse

1 ❑ Aug 1990 Cover: 2.50 **NM** value: **3.00**
Circ: CapCity orders: **40,950** • **CGC:** 3 graded, best 9.6
📖 Tempest, Part 1 **A:** Chris Warner; Paul Guinan **W:** John Arcudi
2 ❑ Sep 1990 Cover: 2.50 **NM** value: **3.00**
Circ: CapCity orders: **29,750**
📖 Tempest, Part 2 **A:** Chris Warner; Paul Guinan **W:** John Arcudi
3 ❑ Oct 1990 Cover: 2.50 **NM** value: **3.00**
Circ: CapCity orders: **31,800**
📖 Tempest, Part 3 **A:** Chris Warner; Paul Guinan **W:** John Arcudi
4 ❑ Nov 1990 Cover: 2.50 **NM** value: **3.00**
Circ: CapCity orders: **30,500**
📖 Tempest, Part 4 **A:** Chris Warner; Paul Guinan **W:** John Arcudi

TERMINATOR, THE (3RD SERIES) Dark Horse

1 ❑ ca. 1991 Cover: 2.95 **NM** value: **Cover or less**
No issue number. • leads into 1998 series

TERMINATOR, THE (4TH SERIES) Dark Horse

1 ❑ Sep 1998 Cover: 2.95 **NM** value: **Cover or less**
Circ: Diamd. preorders: **15,705**
• no month of publication **A:** Steve Pugh **W:** Alan Grant
2 ❑ Oct 1998 Cover: 2.95 **NM** value: **Cover or less**
Circ: Diamd. preorders: **11,898**
A: Steve Pugh **W:** Alan Grant
3 ❑ Nov 1998 Cover: 2.95 **NM** value: **Cover or less**
Circ: Diamd. preorders: **10,184**
📖 The Kiss of Death! **A:** Steve Pugh **W:** Alan Grant
4 ❑ Dec 1998 Cover: 2.95 **NM** value: **Cover or less**
Circ: Diamd. preorders: **9,536**
📖 Cyborg Showdown **A:** Steve Pugh **W:** Alan Grant

TERMINATOR, THE: ALL MY FUTURES PAST Now

1 ❑ Aug 1990 Cover: 1.75 **NM** value: **2.50**
Circ: CapCity orders: **3,475**
A: Diego **W:** Chuck Dixon
2 ❑ Sep 1990 Cover: 1.75 **NM** value: **2.50**
A: Diego **W:** Chuck Dixon

TERMINATOR: ENDGAME Dark Horse

1 ❑ Sep 1992 Cover: 2.50 **NM** value: **Cover or less**
Circ: CapCity orders: **32,300**
A: Jackson Guice **W:** James Robinson
2 ❑ Oct 1992 Cover: 2.50 **NM** value: **Cover or less**
Circ: CapCity orders: **25,900**
A: Jackson Guice **W:** James Robinson
3 ❑ Oct 1992 Cover: 2.50 **NM** value: **Cover or less**
Circ: CapCity orders: **25,725**
A: Jackson Guice **W:** James Robinson
Bk 1 ❑ Jan 1999 Cover: 9.95 **NM** value: **Cover or less**
No issue number. • Trade Paperback. • collects mini-series **A:** Jackson Guice **W:** James Robinson

TERMINATOR: HUNTERS AND KILLERS Dark Horse

1 ❑ Mar 1992 Cover: 2.50 **NM** value: **Cover or less**
Circ: CapCity orders: **36,525**
A: Bill Jaaska **W:** Adam Warren; Chris Warner; Toren Smith
2 ❑ Apr 1992 Cover: 2.50 **NM** value: **Cover or less**
Circ: CapCity orders: **30,450**
A: Bill Jaaska **W:** Adam Warren; Chris Warner; Toren Smith

Other grades: Multiply prices above by **1.5 for Mint • 2/3 for Very Fine • 1/3 for Fine • 1/5 for Very Good • 1/8 for Good**

3 ❑ May 1992 Cover: 2.50 **NM** value: **Cover or less**
Circ: CapCity orders: **30,150**
A: Bill Jaaska **W:** Adam Warren; Chris Warner; Toren Smith
Bk 1❑ **NM** value: **10.00**
• Star System Exclusive (Diamond); Collects mini-series **A:** Bill Jaaska **W:** Adam Warren; Chris Warner; Toren Smith

TERMINATOR, THE (MAGAZINE) — Trident
1 ❑ Cover: 1.00 **NM** value: **3.00**
2 ❑ Cover: 1.00 **NM** value: **3.00**
3 ❑ Cover: 1.00 **NM** value: **3.00**
4 ❑ Cover: 1.00 **NM** value: **3.00**

TERMINATOR, THE: ONE SHOT — Dark Horse
1 ❑ Jul 1991 Cover: 5.95 **NM** value: **Cover or less**
Circ: CapCity orders: **21,100**
No issue number. • prestige format. • pop-up **A:** Matt Wagner **W:** James Robinson

TERMINATOR: SECONDARY OBJECTIVES — Dark Horse
1 ❑ Jul 1991 Cover: 2.50 **NM** value: **Cover or less**
Circ: CapCity orders: **39,900**
A: Paul Gulacy **W:** James Robinson
2 ❑ Aug 1991 Cover: 2.50 **NM** value: **Cover or less**
Circ: CapCity orders: **32,775**
A: Paul Gulacy **W:** James Robinson
3 ❑ Sep 1991 Cover: 2.50 **NM** value: **Cover or less**
Circ: CapCity orders: **34,875**
A: Paul Gulacy **W:** James Robinson
4 ❑ Oct 1991 Cover: 2.50 **NM** value: **Cover or less**
Circ: CapCity orders: **36,675**
A: Paul Gulacy **W:** James Robinson
Bk 1❑ Cover: 13.95 **NM** value: **Cover or less**
A: Paul Gulacy **W:** James Robinson

TERMINATOR: TEMPEST — Dark Horse
Bk 1❑ Cover: 12.95 **NM** value: **Cover or less**

TERMINATOR, THE: THE BURNING EARTH — Now
1 ❑ Mar 1990 Cover: 1.75 **NM** value: **7.50**
Circ: CapCity orders: **10,525** • **CGC:** 10 graded, best 9.8
• 1st comics work by Alex Ross **A:** Alex Ross **W:** Ron Fortier
2 ❑ Apr 1990 Cover: 1.75 **NM** value: **5.00**
Circ: CapCity orders: **9,275**
A: Alex Ross **W:** Ron Fortier
3 ❑ May 1990 Cover: 1.75 **NM** value: **5.00**
Circ: CapCity orders: **8,100** • **CGC:** 1 graded, best 9.4
A: Alex Ross **W:** Ron Fortier
4 ❑ Jun 1990 Cover: 1.75 **NM** value: **6.00**
Circ: CapCity orders: **8,500** • **CGC:** 1 graded, best 9.4
A: Alex Ross **W:** Ron Fortier
5 ❑ Jul 1990 Cover: 1.75 **NM** value: **6.00**
Circ: CapCity orders: **9,650**
A: Alex Ross **W:** Ron Fortier
Bk 1❑ Cover: 9.95 **NM** value: **Cover or less**
A: Alex Ross **W:** Ron Fortier

TERMINATOR, THE: THE DARK YEARS — Dark Horse
1 ❑ Sep 1999 Cover: 2.95 **NM** value: **Cover or less**
Circ: Diamd. preorders: **9,815**
A: Mel Rubi **W:** Alan Grant
2 ❑ Oct 1999 Cover: 2.95 **NM** value: **Cover or less**
Circ: Diamd. preorders: **8,662**
A: Mel Rubi **W:** Alan Grant
3 ❑ Nov 1999 Cover: 2.95 **NM** value: **Cover or less**
Circ: Diamd. preorders: **7,765**
A: Mel Rubi **W:** Alan Grant
4 ❑ Dec 1999 Cover: 2.95 **NM** value: **Cover or less**
Circ: Diamd. preorders: **7,552**
A: Mel Rubi **W:** Alan Grant

TERMINATOR, THE: THE ENEMY WITHIN — Dark Horse
1 ❑ Nov 1991 Cover: 2.50 **NM** value: **Cover or less**
Circ: CapCity orders: **48,575**
A: Vince Giarrano; Simon Bisley(cover) **W:** Ian Edginton
2 ❑ Dec 1991 Cover: 2.50 **NM** value: **Cover or less**
Circ: CapCity orders: **36,350**
A: Vince Giarrano; Simon Bisley(cover) **W:** Ian Edginton
3 ❑ Jan 1992 Cover: 2.50 **NM** value: **Cover or less**
Circ: CapCity orders: **30,825**
A: Vince Giarrano; Simon Bisley(cover) **W:** Ian Edginton
4 ❑ Feb 1992 Cover: 2.50 **NM** value: **Cover or less**
Circ: CapCity orders: **28,550**
A: Vince Giarrano; Simon Bisley(cover) **W:** Ian Edginton

TERRAFORMERS — Wonder Color
1 ❑ Apr 1987 Cover: 1.95 **NM** value: **Cover or less**
Circ: CapCity orders: **5,825**
🕮 ...and on the Eighth Day... **A:** Kelley Jones **W:** Peter Quinones; Peter Quinones
2 ❑ 1987 Cover: 1.95 **NM** value: **Cover or less**
Circ: CapCity orders: **4,525**
A: Kelley Jones **W:** Peter Quinones; Peter Quinones

TERRANAUTS — Fantasy General
1 ❑ ca. 1986 Cover: 1.75 **NM** value: **Cover or less**
Circ: CapCity orders: **4,350**
A: Paul Daly **W:** Don Secrease

TERRARISTS — Marvel / Epic
1 ❑ Nov 1993 Cover: 2.50 **NM** value: **Cover or less**
Circ: CapCity orders: **4,900**
🕮 Summertime Blues **A:** John Erasmus **W:** Pat Mills; Tony Skinner
2 ❑ Dec 1993 Cover: 2.50 **NM** value: **Cover or less**
Circ: CapCity orders: **3,200**
🕮 Sign O'the Times **A:** John Erasmus **W:** Pat Mills; Tony Skinner
3 ❑ Jan 1994 Cover: 2.50 **NM** value: **Cover or less**
Circ: CapCity orders: **2,500**
A: John Erasmus **W:** Pat Mills; Tony Skinner
4 ❑ Feb 1994 Cover: 2.50 **NM** value: **Cover or less**
Circ: CapCity orders: **2,200**
🕮 Death and the Maiden **A:** John Erasmus **W:** Pat Mills; Tony Skinner

TERRIFIC COMICS (AJAX) — Ajax
14 ❑ Dec 1954 Cover: 0.10 **NM** value: **200.00**
• **CGC:** 1 graded, best 8.5
15 ❑ ca. 1955 Cover: 0.10 **NM** value: **200.00**
• < Never published?>
16 ❑ Mar 1955 Cover: 0.10 **NM** value: **150.00**
🕮 Midnight Showdown; Mister Creepers; Ace of Hearts; Accidents Do Happen... (Text Story); Wonder Boy • Series continued as Wonder Boy

TERRIFIC COMICS (CONTINENTAL) — Continental
1 ❑ Jan 1944 Cover: 0.10 **NM** value: **3000.00**
• **CGC:** 2 graded, best 7.5
2 ❑ Mar 1944 Cover: 0.10 **NM** value: **2000.00**
• **CGC:** 1 graded, best 5.5
3 ❑ May 1944 Cover: 0.10 **NM** value: **2000.00**
4 ❑ Jul 1944 Cover: 0.10 **NM** value: **2000.00**
• **CGC:** 2 graded, best 8.5
5 ❑ Sep 1944 Cover: 0.10 **NM** value: **2000.00**
• **CGC:** 3 graded, best 9.2
6 ❑ Nov 1944 Cover: 0.10 **NM** value: **1500.00**
• **CGC:** 3 graded, best 9.0

TERRIFYING TALES — Star
11 ❑ Jan 1953 Cover: 0.10 **NM** value: **400.00**
• **CGC:** 1 graded, best 9.2
12 ❑ Apr 1953 Cover: 0.10 **NM** value: **400.00**
• **CGC:** 3 graded, best 9.2
13 ❑ Jun 1953 Cover: 0.10 **NM** value: **400.00**
14 ❑ Sep 1953 Cover: 0.10 **NM** value: **350.00**
15 ❑ Apr 1954 Cover: 0.10 **NM** value: **350.00**
• **CGC:** 1 graded, best 8.0

TERRITORY, THE — Dark Horse
1 ❑ Jan 1999 Cover: 2.95 **NM** value: **Cover or less**
Circ: Diamd. preorders: **6,928**
A: David Lloyd **W:** Jamie Delano
2 ❑ Feb 1999 Cover: 2.95 **NM** value: **Cover or less**
Circ: Diamd. preorders: **5,219**
A: David Lloyd **W:** Jamie Delano
3 ❑ Mar 1999 Cover: 2.95 **NM** value: **Cover or less**
Circ: Diamd. preorders: **4,645**
A: David Lloyd **W:** Jamie Delano
4 ❑ Apr 1999 Cover: 2.95 **NM** value: **Cover or less**
Circ: Diamd. preorders: **4,393**
A: David Lloyd **W:** Jamie Delano

TERROR, THE — Leadslinger
1 ❑ b&w Cover: 2.50 **NM** value: **Cover or less**

TERRORESS — Helpless Anger
All issues are adults only.
1 ❑ Dec 1990, b&w Cover: 2.50 **NM** value: **Cover or less**
🕮 An Act of Insanity **A:** K.L. Roberts **W:** K.L. Roberts

TERROR ILLUSTRATED — E.C.
In an attempt to follow the success of Mad in making the transition from comic book to pictorial magazine (and avoiding the restrictions of the Comics Code), E.C. tried four magazines in its "Picto-Fiction" line, on some covers labeled "a new form of adult entertainment." Each had panels in which an illustration was accompanied by typeset captions. They were: Confessions Illustrated, Crime Illustrated, Shock Illustrated — and Terror Illustrated. All but one lasted only two issues.

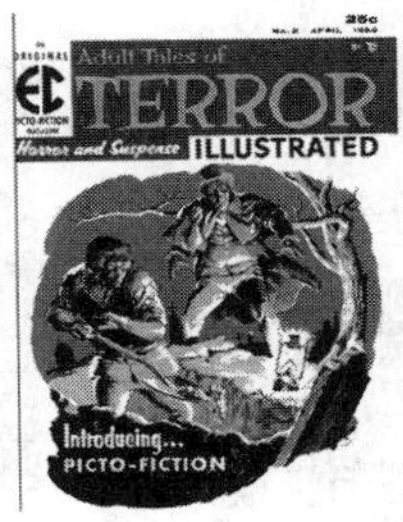

Artists for the horror stories included Reed Crandall and Graham Ingels. — Maggie
1 ❑ Nov 1955 Cover: 0.25 **NM** value: **100.00**
2 ❑ Apr 1956 Cover: 0.25 **NM** value: **75.00**

TERROR, INC. — Marvel
One of the most bizarre "heroes" that Marvel has ever introduced, Terror is a supernatural private detective that seemingly cannot be killed. That doesn't mean, however, that he's the picture of eternal youth. Rather, he's a walking corpse who uses body parts of others to replace the ones that wear out. And when he attaches a limb to himself, he inherits the memories and abilities of its previous owner.

A gruesome hero set in a dark world of monsters and black sorcery, Terror, Inc. bears a strong likeness to a Lovecraft novel. It's scary, it's gory, but once you're hooked, you can't put it down.

1 ❑ Jul 1992 Cover: 1.75 **NM** value: **2.00**
Circ: CapCity orders: **39,300**
🕮 Caveat Emptor **A:** Jorge Zaffino **W:** D.G. Chichester ★ 1st Appearance of Terror.
2 ❑ Aug 1992 Cover: 1.75 **NM** value: **Cover or less**
Circ: CapCity orders: **23,100**
🕮 Deal With the Devil **A:** Jorge Zaffino **W:** D.G. Chichester ★ 1st Appearance of Hellfire.
3 ❑ Sep 1992 Cover: 1.75 **NM** value: **Cover or less**
Circ: CapCity orders: **18,400**
A: Jorge Zaffino **W:** D.G. Chichester
4 ❑ Oct 1992 Cover: 1.75 **NM** value: **Cover or less**
Circ: CapCity orders: **16,000**
🕮 Hostile Takeover **A:** Jorge Zaffino **W:** D.G. Chichester
5 ❑ Nov 1992 Cover: 1.75 **NM** value: **Cover or less**
Circ: CapCity orders: **13,900**
A: Jorge Zaffino **W:** D.G. Chichester
6 ❑ Dec 1992 Cover: 1.75 **NM** value: **Cover or less**
Circ: CapCity orders: **13,700**
A: Jorge Zaffino **W:** D.G. Chichester ★ Appearance of Punisher.
7 ❑ Jan 1993 Cover: 1.75 **NM** value: **Cover or less**
Circ: CapCity orders: **11,000**
A: Jorge Zaffino **W:** D.G. Chichester ★ Appearance of Punisher.
8 ❑ Feb 1993 Cover: 1.75 **NM** value: **Cover or less**
Circ: CapCity orders: **9,400**
9 ❑ Mar 1993 Cover: 1.75 **NM** value: **Cover or less**
Circ: CapCity orders: **13,500**
★ Appearance of Wolverine.
10 ❑ Apr 1993 Cover: 1.75 **NM** value: **Cover or less**
Circ: CapCity orders: **10,700**
★ Appearance of Wolverine.
11 ❑ May 1993 Cover: 1.75 **NM** value: **Cover or less**
Circ: CapCity orders: **10,500**
🕮 For Love Nor Money, Part 1 ★ Appearance of Punisher, Silver Sable.
12 ❑ Jun 1993 Cover: 1.75 **NM** value: **Cover or less**
Circ: CapCity orders: **9,700**
🕮 For Love Nor Money, Part 4
13 ❑ Jul 1993 Cover: 1.75 **NM** value: **Cover or less**
Circ: CapCity orders: **13,400**
🕮 Infinity Crusade final issue. ★ Appearance of Ghost Rider.

TERROR ON THE PLANET OF THE APES — Adventure
1 ❑ 1991b&w Cover: 2.50 **NM** value: **Cover or less**
🕮 The Lawgiver **A:** Mike Ploog; Frank Chiaramonte **W:** Doug Moench
2 ❑ 1991b&w Cover: 2.50 **NM** value: **Cover or less**
3 ❑ Aug 1991, b&w Cover: 2.50 **NM** value: **Cover or less**
🕮 Spawn Of The Mutant-Pits • reprints Planet of the Apes (Marvel) #3 **A:** Mike Ploog; Frank Chiaramonte **W:** Doug Moench
4 ❑ Dec 1991, b&w Cover: 2.50 **NM** value: **Cover or less**
🕮 A Riverboat Named Simian • reprints Planet of the Apes (Marvel) #4

TERRORS OF THE JUNGLE — Star
17 ❑ May 1952 Cover: 0.10 **NM** value: **200.00**
• **CGC:** 1 graded, best 7.5
18 ❑ Aug 1952 Cover: 0.10 **NM** value: **200.00**
• **CGC:** 3 graded, best 9.0
19 ❑ Oct 1952 Cover: 0.10 **NM** value: **200.00**
• **CGC:** 1 graded, best 8.0
20 ❑ Dec 1952 Cover: 0.10 **NM** value: **200.00**
• **CGC:** 3 graded, best 9.2
21 ❑ Feb 1953 Cover: 0.10 **NM** value: **200.00**
• **CGC:** 1 graded, best 7.5
4 ❑ Apr 1953 Cover: 0.10 **NM** value: **400.00**
• **CGC:** 1 graded, best 7.5
5 ❑ Jun 1953 Cover: 0.10 **NM** value: **250.00**
• **CGC:** 1 graded, best 8.0
6 ❑ Sep 1953 Cover: 0.10 **NM** value: **250.00**
7 ❑ Dec 1953 Cover: 0.10 **NM** value: **250.00**
8 ❑ Mar 1954 Cover: 0.10 **NM** value: **250.00**
• **CGC:** 1 graded, best 7.5
9 ❑ Jun 1954 Cover: 0.10 **NM** value: **250.00**
• **CGC:** 1 graded, best 8.5
10 ❑ Sep 1954 Cover: 0.10 **NM** value: **250.00**
• **CGC:** 4 graded, best 8.0

TERROR TALES — Eternity
1 ❑ b&w Cover: 2.50 **NM** value: **Cover or less**

TERRY AND THE PIRATES (AVALON) — Avalon
1 ❑ b&w Cover: 2.95 **NM** value: **Cover or less**
• strip reprints **A:** George Wunder **W:** George Wunder
2 ❑ Cover: 2.95 **NM** value: **Cover or less**
A: George Wunder **W:** George Wunder

TERRY AND THE PIRATES COMICS — Harvey
Milton Caniff's Terry and the Pirates ran as a newspaper strip from 1935 to 1946 (and continued for years under other hands), blazing a trail so influential that it has to stand as the supreme achievement of sequential art in the 20th century. Young Terry and his mentor Pat Ryan set off for adventure in the Far East in 1935, encountering memorable characters like the Dragon Lady, and finding danger at every turn. Terry grew up, joined the Air Force, and fought valiantly against the Japanese in World War II. Characters loved, lost, and died, as the nation waited breathlessly for each new episode.

CGC-graded: Multiply prices above by **33 for 9.9 M • 16 for 9.8 NM/M • 7 for 9.6 NM+ • 5 for 9.4 NM • 2.5 for 9.2 NM- • 1.5 for 9.0 VF/NM**

Caniff's cinematic approach to storytelling combined an effortless mastery of angle, shadow, and characterization with an uncanny sense of timing and composition. Scenes throbbed with drama and tension and exploded in action and excitement. Will Eisner, Alex Toth, and Frank Miller among others drew obvious inspiration from Caniff's work. While it obviously did not reprint the entirety of the strip, Harvey made available a chunk of this classic work to kids around the country.

3 ❑ Apr 1947 Cover: 0.10 **NM** value: **285.00**
• **CGC:** 1 graded, best 6.0
A: Milton Caniff **W:** Milton Caniff ★ 1st Appearance of The Dragon Lady.
4 ❑ Jun 1947 Cover: 0.10 **NM** value: **160.00**
• **CGC:** 1 graded, best 5.0
A: Milton Caniff **W:** Milton Caniff
5 ❑ Aug 1947 Cover: 0.10 **NM** value: **100.00**
A: Milton Caniff **W:** Milton Caniff
6 ❑ Oct 1947 Cover: 0.10 **NM** value: **65.00**
• **CGC:** 1 graded, best 9.2
A: Milton Caniff **W:** Milton Caniff
7 ❑ Dec 1947 Cover: 0.10 **NM** value: **65.00**
• **CGC:** 1 graded, best 9.4
A: Milton Caniff **W:** Milton Caniff
8 ❑ Feb 1948 Cover: 0.10 **NM** value: **65.00**
• **CGC:** 2 graded, best 9.0
A: Milton Caniff **W:** Milton Caniff
9 ❑ Apr 1948 Cover: 0.10 **NM** value: **65.00**
• **CGC:** 1 graded, best 9.4
A: Milton Caniff **W:** Milton Caniff
10 ❑ Jun 1948 Cover: 0.10 **NM** value: **65.00**
🕮 Call To Action; The Trick Works; Plan of Attack; Unknown Identity; Taffy's Dilemma; Jap Treachery; Catching a Spy; Observation Flight; Reporting For Duty; Raging Destruction **A:** Milton Caniff **W:** Milton Caniff
11 ❑ Aug 1948 Cover: 0.10 **NM** value: **55.00**
A: Milton Caniff **W:** Milton Caniff
12 ❑ Oct 1948 Cover: 0.10 **NM** value: **55.00**
• **CGC:** 1 graded, best 9.2
A: Milton Caniff **W:** Milton Caniff
13 ❑ Dec 1948 Cover: 0.10 **NM** value: **55.00**
• **CGC:** 2 graded, best 9.2
A: Milton Caniff **W:** Milton Caniff
14 ❑ Feb 1949 Cover: 0.10 **NM** value: **55.00**
• **CGC:** 1 graded, best 8.5
🕮 Fearless Rough-Rider (text story); Plane Talk; Tommy Tween's Fishing Escapade (text story) **A:** Milton Caniff; Bob Powell **W:** Milton Caniff; Bob Powell
15 ❑ Apr 1949 Cover: 0.10 **NM** value: **55.00**
A: Milton Caniff **W:** Milton Caniff
16 ❑ Jun 1949 Cover: 0.10 **NM** value: **55.00**
• **CGC:** 1 graded, best 9.2
A: Milton Caniff **W:** Milton Caniff
17 ❑ Aug 1949 Cover: 0.10 **NM** value: **55.00**
A: Milton Caniff **W:** Milton Caniff
18 ❑ Oct 1949 Cover: 0.10 **NM** value: **55.00**
A: Milton Caniff **W:** Milton Caniff
19 ❑ Dec 1949 Cover: 0.10 **NM** value: **55.00**
• **CGC:** 1 graded, best 9.4
A: Milton Caniff **W:** Milton Caniff
20 ❑ Feb 1950 Cover: 0.10 **NM** value: **55.00**
A: Milton Caniff **W:** Milton Caniff
21 ❑ Apr 1950 Cover: 0.10 **NM** value: **45.00**
A: Milton Caniff **W:** Milton Caniff
22 ❑ Aug 1950 Cover: 0.10 **NM** value: **45.00**
A: Milton Caniff **W:** Milton Caniff
23 ❑ Oct 1950 Cover: 0.10 **NM** value: **45.00**
• **CGC:** 1 graded, best 9.2
A: Milton Caniff **W:** Milton Caniff
24 ❑ Dec 1950 Cover: 0.10 **NM** value: **45.00**
A: Milton Caniff **W:** Milton Caniff
25 ❑ Feb 1951 Cover: 0.10 **NM** value: **45.00**
A: Milton Caniff **W:** Milton Caniff
26 ❑ Apr 1951 Cover: 0.10 **NM** value: **28.00**
27 ❑ Jun 1955 Cover: 0.10 **NM** value: **28.00**
28 ❑ Oct 1955 Cover: 0.10 **NM** value: **28.00**
final issue.

TERRY-BEARS COMICS — St. John

1 ❑ ca. 1952 Cover: 0.10 **NM** value: **50.00**
2 ❑ ca. 1952 Cover: 0.10 **NM** value: **35.00**
3 ❑ ca. 1953 Cover: 0.10 **NM** value: **35.00**

TERRY-TOONS COMICS (TIMELY) — Timely

The funny animals went to war, at least on the covers of early issues of this series.

Begun in 1942 by Timely (which later became Marvel), the series starred characters created by Paul Terry for animation including Gandy Goose and Sourpuss (a cat). In addition to the war-related covers with Sourpuss as a sergeant, other issues featured typical gags and practical jokes.

With #38, the series added the adventures of Terry's best-known character Mighty Mouse and, with #60, the series moved to St. John.

A second series by St. John, and later Pines, was also published. The characters can also be found in Paul Terry's Comics. — Brent

1 ❑ Oct 1942 Cover: 0.10 **NM** value: **1250.00**
• **CGC:** 1 graded, best 6.0
2 ❑ Nov 1942 Cover: 0.10 **NM** value: **750.00**
3 ❑ Dec 1942 Cover: 0.10 **NM** value: **600.00**
4 ❑ Jan 1943 Cover: 0.10 **NM** value: **500.00**
5 ❑ Feb 1943 Cover: 0.10 **NM** value: **400.00**
6 ❑ Mar 1943 Cover: 0.10 **NM** value: **350.00**
7 ❑ Apr 1943 Cover: 0.10 **NM** value: **350.00**
8 ❑ May 1943 Cover: 0.10 **NM** value: **300.00**
9 ❑ Jun 1943 Cover: 0.10 **NM** value: **300.00**
10 ❑ Jul 1943 Cover: 0.10 **NM** value: **300.00**
• **CGC:** 1 graded, best 4.5
11 ❑ Aug 1943 Cover: 0.10 **NM** value: **175.00**
12 ❑ Sep 1943 Cover: 0.10 **NM** value: **175.00**
13 ❑ Oct 1943 Cover: 0.10 **NM** value: **175.00**
14 ❑ Nov 1943 Cover: 0.10 **NM** value: **175.00**
15 ❑ Dec 1943 Cover: 0.10 **NM** value: **175.00**
16 ❑ Jan 1944 Cover: 0.10 **NM** value: **175.00**
17 ❑ Feb 1944 Cover: 0.10 **NM** value: **175.00**
18 ❑ Mar 1944 Cover: 0.10 **NM** value: **175.00**
19 ❑ Apr 1944 Cover: 0.10 **NM** value: **175.00**
20 ❑ May 1944 Cover: 0.10 **NM** value: **175.00**
21 ❑ Jun 1944 Cover: 0.10 **NM** value: **150.00**
22 ❑ Jul 1944 Cover: 0.10 **NM** value: **150.00**
23 ❑ Aug 1944 Cover: 0.10 **NM** value: **150.00**
24 ❑ Sep 1944 Cover: 0.10 **NM** value: **150.00**
25 ❑ Oct 1944 Cover: 0.10 **NM** value: **150.00**
26 ❑ Nov 1944 Cover: 0.10 **NM** value: **150.00**
27 ❑ Dec 1944 Cover: 0.10 **NM** value: **150.00**
28 ❑ Jan 1945 Cover: 0.10 **NM** value: **150.00**
29 ❑ Feb 1945 Cover: 0.10 **NM** value: **150.00**
30 ❑ Mar 1945 Cover: 0.10 **NM** value: **150.00**
31 ❑ Apr 1945 Cover: 0.10 **NM** value: **150.00**
32 ❑ May 1945 Cover: 0.10 **NM** value: **150.00**
33 ❑ Jun 1945 Cover: 0.10 **NM** value: **150.00**
34 ❑ Jul 1945 Cover: 0.10 **NM** value: **150.00**
35 ❑ Aug 1945 Cover: 0.10 **NM** value: **150.00**
36 ❑ Sep 1945 Cover: 0.10 **NM** value: **150.00**
37 ❑ Oct 1945 Cover: 0.10 **NM** value: **150.00**
38 ❑ Nov 1945 Cover: 0.10 **NM** value: **150.00**
• **CGC:** 1 graded, best 7.0
39 ❑ Dec 1945 Cover: 0.10 **NM** value: **150.00**
40 ❑ Jan 1946 Cover: 0.10 **NM** value: **150.00**
41 ❑ Feb 1946 Cover: 0.10 **NM** value: **125.00**
42 ❑ Mar 1946 Cover: 0.10 **NM** value: **125.00**
43 ❑ Apr 1946 Cover: 0.10 **NM** value: **125.00**
44 ❑ May 1946 Cover: 0.10 **NM** value: **125.00**
• **CGC:** 1 graded, best 8.5
45 ❑ Jun 1946 Cover: 0.10 **NM** value: **125.00**
46 ❑ Jul 1946 Cover: 0.10 **NM** value: **125.00**
47 ❑ Aug 1946 Cover: 0.10 **NM** value: **125.00**
48 ❑ Sep 1946 Cover: 0.10 **NM** value: **125.00**
49 ❑ Oct 1946 Cover: 0.10 **NM** value: **125.00**
50 ❑ Nov 1946 Cover: 0.10 **NM** value: **125.00**
51 ❑ Dec 1946 Cover: 0.10 **NM** value: **125.00**
52 ❑ Jan 1947 Cover: 0.10 **NM** value: **125.00**
53 ❑ Feb 1947 Cover: 0.10 **NM** value: **125.00**
54 ❑ Mar 1947 Cover: 0.10 **NM** value: **125.00**
55 ❑ Apr 1947 Cover: 0.10 **NM** value: **125.00**
56 ❑ May 1947 Cover: 0.10 **NM** value: **125.00**
57 ❑ Jun 1947 Cover: 0.10 **NM** value: **125.00**
58 ❑ Jul 1947 Cover: 0.10 **NM** value: **125.00**
59 ❑ Aug 1947 Cover: 0.10 **NM** value: **125.00**

TERRY-TOONS COMICS (ST. JOHN) — St. John

60 ❑ Sep 1947 Cover: 0.10 **NM** value: **75.00**
61 ❑ Oct 1947 Cover: 0.10 **NM** value: **60.00**
62 ❑ Nov 1947 Cover: 0.10 **NM** value: **60.00**
63 ❑ Dec 1947 Cover: 0.10 **NM** value: **60.00**
64 ❑ ca. 1948 Cover: 0.10 **NM** value: **60.00**
65 ❑ ca. 1948 Cover: 0.10 **NM** value: **60.00**
66 ❑ ca. 1948 Cover: 0.10 **NM** value: **60.00**
67 ❑ ca. 1948 Cover: 0.10 **NM** value: **60.00**
68 ❑ ca. 1948 Cover: 0.10 **NM** value: **60.00**
69 ❑ ca. 1948 Cover: 0.10 **NM** value: **60.00**
70 ❑ ca. 1948 Cover: 0.10 **NM** value: **60.00**
71 ❑ ca. 1948 Cover: 0.10 **NM** value: **60.00**
72 ❑ ca. 1949 Cover: 0.10 **NM** value: **60.00**
73 ❑ ca. 1949 Cover: 0.10 **NM** value: **60.00**
74 ❑ ca. 1949 Cover: 0.10 **NM** value: **60.00**
75 ❑ ca. 1949 Cover: 0.10 **NM** value: **60.00**
76 ❑ ca. 1949 Cover: 0.10 **NM** value: **60.00**
77 ❑ ca. 1949 Cover: 0.10 **NM** value: **60.00**
78 ❑ ca. 1950 Cover: 0.10 **NM** value: **60.00**
79 ❑ ca. 1950 Cover: 0.10 **NM** value: **60.00**
80 ❑ ca. 1950 Cover: 0.10 **NM** value: **60.00**
81 ❑ ca. 1950 Cover: 0.10 **NM** value: **60.00**
82 ❑ ca. 1950 Cover: 0.10 **NM** value: **60.00**
83 ❑ ca. 1950 Cover: 0.10 **NM** value: **60.00**
84 ❑ ca. 1951 Cover: 0.10 **NM** value: **60.00**
85 ❑ ca. 1951 Cover: 0.10 **NM** value: **60.00**
86 ❑ ca. 1951 Cover: 0.10 **NM** value: **60.00**

TERRY-TOONS COMICS (PINES) — Pines

1 ❑ ca. 1952 Cover: 0.10 **NM** value: **125.00**
2 ❑ ca. 1952 Cover: 0.10 **NM** value: **60.00**
3 ❑ ca. 1952 Cover: 0.10 **NM** value: **60.00**
4 ❑ ca. 1952 Cover: 0.10 **NM** value: **50.00**
5 ❑ ca. 1953 Cover: 0.10 **NM** value: **50.00**
6 ❑ ca. 1953 Cover: 0.10 **NM** value: **50.00**
7 ❑ ca. 1953 Cover: 0.10 **NM** value: **50.00**
8 ❑ ca. 1953 Cover: 0.10 **NM** value: **50.00**
9 ❑ ca. 1953 Cover: 0.10 **NM** value: **50.00**

TESSIE THE TYPIST — Marvel / ACG

Timely, the precursor to Marvel Comics, offered Tessie the Typist as a romantic comedy and teen humor offering during the 1940s.

Tessie is a feisty, blond working girl whose misadventures in the world of men and romance generates most of the laughs.

As usual with many Timely titles, more interesting than the title character's adventures herself were some of the backup features that also appeared. Several issues include Powerhouse Pepper features by the inimitable and deeply weird Basil Wolverton, and Hey Look!, the early signature strip of Mad genius Harvey Kurtzman.

1 ❑ Sum 1944 Cover: 0.10 **NM** value: **360.00**
• **CGC:** 1 graded, best 7.0
A: Basil Wolverton
2 ❑ Win 1944 Cover: 0.10 **NM** value: **210.00**
A: Basil Wolverton
3 ❑ Mar 1945 Cover: 0.10 **NM** value: **65.00**
4 ❑ Fal 1945 Cover: 0.10 **NM** value: **135.00**
🕮 Powerhouse Pepper; Ribticklers; **A:** Basil Wolverton
5 ❑ Win 1945 Cover: 0.10 **NM** value: **135.00**
A: Basil Wolverton
6 ❑ Sep 1946 Cover: 0.10 **NM** value: **135.00**
A: Basil Wolverton
7 ❑ ca. 1946 Cover: 0.10 **NM** value: **135.00**
A: Basil Wolverton
8 ❑ ca. 1947 Cover: 0.10 **NM** value: **135.00**
A: Basil Wolverton
9 ❑ ca. 1947 Cover: 0.10 **NM** value: **150.00**
A: Basil Wolverton
10 ❑ ca. 1947 Cover: 0.10 **NM** value: **150.00**
A: Basil Wolverton
11 ❑ ca. 1948 Cover: 0.10 **NM** value: **150.00**
🕮 A Night at the Fights!; Rusty: Shocking Shopping!; A Quiet Saturday Afternoon (text story); Tessie the Typist: Where's Skidsy's Hair?; Powerhouse Pepper: The Big Breeze!; Tessie the Typist: Psychology for Skidsy! **A:** Basil Wolverton **W:** Morris Weiss
12 ❑ ca. 1948 Cover: 0.10 **NM** value: **150.00**
A: Basil Wolverton
13 ❑ ca. 1948 Cover: 0.10 **NM** value: **150.00**
A: Basil Wolverton
14 ❑ ca. 1948 Cover: 0.10 **NM** value: **45.00**
15 ❑ ca. 1948 Cover: 0.10 **NM** value: **45.00**
16 ❑ ca. 1948 Cover: 0.10 **NM** value: **45.00**
17 ❑ ca. 1948 Cover: 0.10 **NM** value: **45.00**
18 ❑ ca. 1948 Cover: 0.10 **NM** value: **45.00**
19 ❑ ca. 1949 Cover: 0.10 **NM** value: **45.00**
20 ❑ ca. 1949 Cover: 0.10 **NM** value: **45.00**
21 ❑ ca. 1949 Cover: 0.10 **NM** value: **45.00**
22 ❑ ca. 1949 Cover: 0.10 **NM** value: **45.00**
23 ❑ ca. 1949 Cover: 0.10 **NM** value: **45.00**
final issue.

TEST DIRT — Fantagraphics

1 ❑ b&w Cover: 2.50 **NM** value: **Cover or less**

TEST DRIVE — M.A.I.N.

1 ❑ Cover: 3.00 **NM** value: **Cover or less**
🕮 (Side A)Symbol; Night Storm; He's All Head; Rednecks in Zombieland; Warrior Nun Areala; (Side B) Judgement Day; Whisper Ribbons, Stanley the Mole; Nightstriker, Kuniochi; Local Justice; Sin; (Side B) Judgement Day • Flip Book Previews (Side A & B) **A:** James Lyle; Grant Vetter; Joanne S; John Orlando; Mike Leonard; Rusty Gilligan **W:** James Lyle; Grant Vetter; Joanne S; John Orlando; Mike Leonard; Rusty Gilligan

TEXAN, THE — St. John

1 ❑ Aug 1948 Cover: 0.10 **NM** value: **60.00**
2 ❑ Oct 1948 Cover: 0.10 **NM** value: **40.00**
3 ❑ Jan 1949 Cover: 0.10 **NM** value: **24.00**
4 ❑ May 1949 Cover: 0.10 **NM** value: **35.00**
5 ❑ Aug 1949 Cover: 0.10 **NM** value: **35.00**
6 ❑ Nov 1949 Cover: 0.10 **NM** value: **35.00**
7 ❑ Feb 1950 Cover: 0.10 **NM** value: **35.00**
8 ❑ May 1950 Cover: 0.10 **NM** value: **35.00**
9 ❑ Aug 1950 Cover: 0.10 **NM** value: **35.00**
10 ❑ Oct 1950 Cover: 0.10 **NM** value: **24.00**
11 ❑ Dec 1950 Cover: 0.10 **NM** value: **35.00**
12 ❑ Mar 1951 Cover: 0.10 **NM** value: **60.00**
13 ❑ May 1951 Cover: 0.10 **NM** value: **35.00**
14 ❑ Jul 1951 Cover: 0.10 **NM** value: **35.00**
🕮 A Talisman Tames the Trail (text); Hawk Knife…Ambush at Buffalo Trail; Comanche Courage Strikes Back!; Prarie Guns…Death's Roundup! • Continues in Fightin' Marines #15

TEXAS KID — Leading

1 ❑ Jan 1951 Cover: 0.10 **NM** value: **95.00**
★ Origin of The Texas Kid.
2 ❑ Mar 1951 Cover: 0.10 **NM** value: **60.00**
3 ❑ May 1951 Cover: 0.10 **NM** value: **50.00**
4 ❑ Jul 1951 Cover: 0.10 **NM** value: **50.00**
5 ❑ Sep 1951 Cover: 0.10 **NM** value: **50.00**
6 ❑ Nov 1951 Cover: 0.10 **NM** value: **40.00**
🕮 Texas Kid; Loco Kid with a Gun (text); Blind Man's Bluff; Ghost Town; Sheriff "Empty Holsters" Cashwell; Robber's Roost!
7 ❑ Jan 1952 Cover: 0.10 **NM** value: **40.00**
8 ❑ Mar 1952 Cover: 0.10 **NM** value: **40.00**
9 ❑ May 1952 Cover: 0.10 **NM** value: **40.00**
10 ❑ Jul 1952 Cover: 0.10 **NM** value: **40.00**

Other grades: Multiply prices above by **1.5 for Mint • 2/3 for Very Fine • 1/3 for Fine • 1/5 for Very Good • 1/8 for Good**

TEXAS RANGERS IN ACTION — Charlton

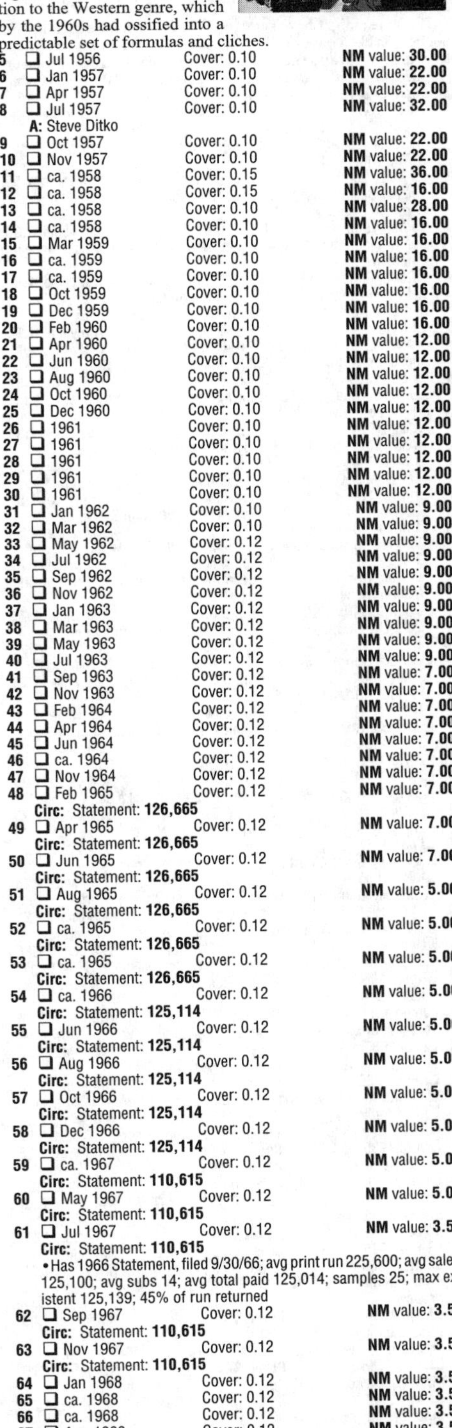

Texas Rangers in Action focuses on the adventures of lawmen on the Texas-Mexico border during the 1840s to 1870s. Ranger Mark Kincaid uses his fists and six-guns to handle outlaws, banditos, and corrupt men while keeping the Texas plains safe for ranchers, cattlemen, and their families. Later issues feature another hero, "The Man Called Loco."

Taking a little bit from Zorro, a little bit from the Cisco Kid, and a little bit of "remember the Alamo" folklore, Charlton here wove together a satisfactory contribution to the Western genre, which by the 1960s had ossified into a predictable set of formulas and cliches.

5 ❑ Jul 1956 Cover: 0.10 **NM** value: **30.00**
6 ❑ Jan 1957 Cover: 0.10 **NM** value: **22.00**
7 ❑ Apr 1957 Cover: 0.10 **NM** value: **22.00**
8 ❑ Jul 1957 Cover: 0.10 **NM** value: **32.00**
A: Steve Ditko
9 ❑ Oct 1957 Cover: 0.10 **NM** value: **22.00**
10 ❑ Nov 1957 Cover: 0.10 **NM** value: **22.00**
11 ❑ ca. 1958 Cover: 0.15 **NM** value: **36.00**
12 ❑ ca. 1958 Cover: 0.15 **NM** value: **16.00**
13 ❑ ca. 1958 Cover: 0.10 **NM** value: **28.00**
14 ❑ ca. 1958 Cover: 0.10 **NM** value: **16.00**
15 ❑ Mar 1959 Cover: 0.10 **NM** value: **16.00**
16 ❑ ca. 1959 Cover: 0.10 **NM** value: **16.00**
17 ❑ ca. 1959 Cover: 0.10 **NM** value: **16.00**
18 ❑ Oct 1959 Cover: 0.10 **NM** value: **16.00**
19 ❑ Dec 1959 Cover: 0.10 **NM** value: **16.00**
20 ❑ Feb 1960 Cover: 0.10 **NM** value: **16.00**
21 ❑ Apr 1960 Cover: 0.10 **NM** value: **12.00**
22 ❑ Jun 1960 Cover: 0.10 **NM** value: **12.00**
23 ❑ Aug 1960 Cover: 0.10 **NM** value: **12.00**
24 ❑ Oct 1960 Cover: 0.10 **NM** value: **12.00**
25 ❑ Dec 1960 Cover: 0.10 **NM** value: **12.00**
26 ❑ 1961 Cover: 0.10 **NM** value: **12.00**
27 ❑ 1961 Cover: 0.10 **NM** value: **12.00**
28 ❑ 1961 Cover: 0.10 **NM** value: **12.00**
29 ❑ 1961 Cover: 0.10 **NM** value: **12.00**
30 ❑ 1961 Cover: 0.10 **NM** value: **12.00**
31 ❑ Jan 1962 Cover: 0.10 **NM** value: **9.00**
32 ❑ Mar 1962 Cover: 0.10 **NM** value: **9.00**
33 ❑ May 1962 Cover: 0.12 **NM** value: **9.00**
34 ❑ Jul 1962 Cover: 0.12 **NM** value: **9.00**
35 ❑ Sep 1962 Cover: 0.12 **NM** value: **9.00**
36 ❑ Nov 1962 Cover: 0.12 **NM** value: **9.00**
37 ❑ Jan 1963 Cover: 0.12 **NM** value: **9.00**
38 ❑ Mar 1963 Cover: 0.12 **NM** value: **9.00**
39 ❑ May 1963 Cover: 0.12 **NM** value: **9.00**
40 ❑ Jul 1963 Cover: 0.12 **NM** value: **9.00**
41 ❑ Sep 1963 Cover: 0.12 **NM** value: **7.00**
42 ❑ Nov 1963 Cover: 0.12 **NM** value: **7.00**
43 ❑ Feb 1964 Cover: 0.12 **NM** value: **7.00**
44 ❑ Apr 1964 Cover: 0.12 **NM** value: **7.00**
45 ❑ Jun 1964 Cover: 0.12 **NM** value: **7.00**
46 ❑ ca. 1964 Cover: 0.12 **NM** value: **7.00**
47 ❑ Nov 1964 Cover: 0.12 **NM** value: **7.00**
48 ❑ Feb 1965 Cover: 0.12 **NM** value: **7.00**
Circ: Statement: **126,665**
49 ❑ Apr 1965 Cover: 0.12 **NM** value: **7.00**
Circ: Statement: **126,665**
50 ❑ Jun 1965 Cover: 0.12 **NM** value: **7.00**
Circ: Statement: **126,665**
51 ❑ Aug 1965 Cover: 0.12 **NM** value: **5.00**
Circ: Statement: **126,665**
52 ❑ ca. 1965 Cover: 0.12 **NM** value: **5.00**
Circ: Statement: **126,665**
53 ❑ ca. 1965 Cover: 0.12 **NM** value: **5.00**
Circ: Statement: **126,665**
54 ❑ ca. 1966 Cover: 0.12 **NM** value: **5.00**
Circ: Statement: **125,114**
55 ❑ Jun 1966 Cover: 0.12 **NM** value: **5.00**
Circ: Statement: **125,114**
56 ❑ Aug 1966 Cover: 0.12 **NM** value: **5.00**
Circ: Statement: **125,114**
57 ❑ Oct 1966 Cover: 0.12 **NM** value: **5.00**
Circ: Statement: **125,114**
58 ❑ Dec 1966 Cover: 0.12 **NM** value: **5.00**
Circ: Statement: **125,114**
59 ❑ ca. 1967 Cover: 0.12 **NM** value: **5.00**
Circ: Statement: **110,615**
60 ❑ May 1967 Cover: 0.12 **NM** value: **5.00**
Circ: Statement: **110,615**
61 ❑ Jul 1967 Cover: 0.12 **NM** value: **3.50**
Circ: Statement: **110,615**
• Has 1966 Statement, filed 9/30/66; avg print run 225,600; avg sales 125,100; avg subs 14; avg total paid 125,014; samples 25; max existent 125,139; 45% of run returned
62 ❑ Sep 1967 Cover: 0.12 **NM** value: **3.50**
Circ: Statement: **110,615**
63 ❑ Nov 1967 Cover: 0.12 **NM** value: **3.50**
Circ: Statement: **110,615**
64 ❑ Jan 1968 Cover: 0.12 **NM** value: **3.50**
65 ❑ ca. 1968 Cover: 0.12 **NM** value: **3.50**
66 ❑ ca. 1968 Cover: 0.12 **NM** value: **3.50**
67 ❑ Aug 1968 Cover: 0.12 **NM** value: **3.50**
68 ❑ Oct 1968 Cover: 0.12 **NM** value: **3.50**
69 ❑ Dec 1968 Cover: 0.12 **NM** value: **3.50**
70 ❑ Feb 1969 Cover: 0.12 **NM** value: **3.50**
Circ: Statement: **136,378**
71 ❑ Apr 1969 Cover: 0.12 **NM** value: **2.00**
Circ: Statement: **136,378**
72 ❑ Jun 1969 Cover: 0.12 **NM** value: **2.00**
Circ: Statement: **136,378**
73 ❑ Aug 1969 Cover: 0.12 **NM** value: **2.00**
Circ: Statement: **136,378**
74 ❑ Oct 1969 Cover: 0.15 **NM** value: **2.00**
Circ: Statement: **136,378**
75 ❑ Dec 1969 Cover: 0.15 **NM** value: **2.00**
Circ: Statement: **136,378**
76 ❑ Feb 1970 Cover: 0.15 **NM** value: **2.00**
📖 The Man Called Loco: Guns of Evil; The Toughest Man in Texas; The Fallen Star; Tarnished Badge
77 ❑ Apr 1970 Cover: 0.15 **NM** value: **2.00**
78 ❑ Jun 1970 Cover: 0.15 **NM** value: **2.00**
• Has 1969 Statement; avg print run 205,000; avg sales 136,350; avg subs 28; avg total paid 136,378; samples 125; max existent 136,503; 33% of run returned
79 ❑ Aug 1970 Cover: 0.15 **NM** value: **2.00**
final issue.

TEX BENSON (3-D ZONE) — 3-D Zone

1 ❑ Cover: 2.50 **NM** value: **Cover or less**
• b&w (not 3-D)
2 ❑ Cover: 2.50 **NM** value: **Cover or less**
• b&w (not 3-D)

TEX BENSON (METRO) — Metro

1 ❑ b&w Cover: 2.00 **NM** value: **Cover or less**
📖 The World Within The Mirror, Part 1 **A:** Chuck Roblin **W:** Chuck Roblin
2 ❑ Cover: 2.00 **NM** value: **Cover or less**
📖 The World Within The Mirror, Part 2 **A:** Chuck Roblin **W:** Chuck Roblin
3 ❑ Cover: 2.00 **NM** value: **Cover or less**
A: Chuck Roblin **W:** Chuck Roblin
4 ❑ Cover: 2.00 **NM** value: **Cover or less**
A: Chuck Roblin **W:** Chuck Roblin

TEX DAWSON, GUNSLINGER — Marvel

1 ❑ Jan 1973 Cover: 0.20 **NM** value: **15.00**
• **CGC:** 2 graded, best 9.0

TEX FARRELL — D.S.

1 ❑ 1948 Cover: 0.10 **NM** value: **75.00**

TEX MORGAN — Marvel

1 ❑ Aug 1948 Cover: 0.10 **NM** value: **200.00**
• **CGC:** 1 graded, best 9.4
2 ❑ Oct 1948 Cover: 0.10 **NM** value: **125.00**
3 ❑ Dec 1948 Cover: 0.10 **NM** value: **100.00**
4 ❑ Feb 1949 Cover: 0.10 **NM** value: **100.00**
5 ❑ Apr 1949 Cover: 0.10 **NM** value: **100.00**
6 ❑ Jun 1949 Cover: 0.10 **NM** value: **100.00**
7 ❑ Aug 1949 Cover: 0.10 **NM** value: **75.00**
8 ❑ Nov 1949 Cover: 0.10 **NM** value: **75.00**
9 ❑ ca. 1950 Cover: 0.10 **NM** value: **75.00**

TEX RITTER WESTERN — Charlton

By the time Charlton got around to licensing a real-world singing cowboy for its comic line, many of the major names (Roy Rogers, Gene Autry, Hopalong Cassidy, even Gabby Hayes) were taken. Charlton readers were treated to Tex Ritter Western, a shoot-em-up, ride-em-in cowboy title featuring the narrow-eyed Ritter in colorful sheriff's garb, busting up bad guys along the sagebrush-speckled plains. Goofy lawman Sam the Sheriff held down the back of the book with four-page humor stories.

Ritter's adventures were drawn by Stan Campbell, a capable artist who made generous use of Zipatone shading to add depth and complexity to the panels. Though his best efforts were undone by Charlton's notoriously cheap printing process, his draftsmanship helped elevate Ritter above other more pedestrian 1950s western strips.

1 ❑ Oct 1950 Cover: 0.10 **NM** value: **450.00**
• **CGC:** 1 graded, best 3.5
2 ❑ Dec 1950 Cover: 0.10 **NM** value: **200.00**
3 ❑ Feb 1951 Cover: 0.10 **NM** value: **145.00**
4 ❑ Apr 1951 Cover: 0.10 **NM** value: **100.00**
5 ❑ Jun 1951 Cover: 0.10 **NM** value: **100.00**
6 ❑ Aug 1951 Cover: 0.10 **NM** value: **80.00**
7 ❑ Oct 1951 Cover: 0.10 **NM** value: **80.00**
8 ❑ Dec 1951 Cover: 0.10 **NM** value: **80.00**
9 ❑ Feb 1952 Cover: 0.10 **NM** value: **80.00**
10 ❑ Apr 1952 Cover: 0.10 **NM** value: **80.00**
11 ❑ Jun 1952 Cover: 0.10 **NM** value: **65.00**
12 ❑ Aug 1952 Cover: 0.10 **NM** value: **65.00**
• **CGC:** 2 graded, best 8.0
13 ❑ Oct 1952 Cover: 0.10 **NM** value: **65.00**
14 ❑ Dec 1952 Cover: 0.10 **NM** value: **65.00**
15 ❑ ca. 1953 Cover: 0.10 **NM** value: **65.00**
16 ❑ ca. 1953 Cover: 0.10 **NM** value: **65.00**
17 ❑ ca. 1953 Cover: 0.10 **NM** value: **65.00**
18 ❑ ca. 1953 Cover: 0.10 **NM** value: **65.00**
19 ❑ ca. 1953 Cover: 0.10 **NM** value: **65.00**
20 ❑ Jan 1954 Cover: 0.10 **NM** value: **65.00**
21 ❑ Mar 1954 Cover: 0.10 **NM** value: **40.00**
22 ❑ ca. 1954 Cover: 0.10 **NM** value: **65.00**
• Charlton begins as publisher
23 ❑ ca. 1954 Cover: 0.10 **NM** value: **40.00**
24 ❑ ca. 1954 Cover: 0.10 **NM** value: **40.00**
25 ❑ ca. 1955 Cover: 0.10 **NM** value: **40.00**
26 ❑ ca. 1955 Cover: 0.10 **NM** value: **40.00**
27 ❑ ca. 1955 Cover: 0.10 **NM** value: **40.00**
28 ❑ ca. 1955 Cover: 0.10 **NM** value: **40.00**
📖 Black Gold; Gopher Face: Quarrelsome Type!; The Kid Comes Back (text story); Dead Man's Diamonds; Sam the Sheriff: The Hard Luck Story; The Coward; Ten Gallon Tex: Spills It! **A:** Stan Campbell **W:** Westbrook Wilson
29 ❑ ca. 1956 Cover: 0.10 **NM** value: **40.00**
30 ❑ ca. 1956 Cover: 0.10 **NM** value: **40.00**
31 ❑ ca. 1956 Cover: 0.10 **NM** value: **30.00**
32 ❑ ca. 1956 Cover: 0.10 **NM** value: **30.00**
33 ❑ ca. 1956 Cover: 0.10 **NM** value: **30.00**
34 ❑ ca. 1957 Cover: 0.10 **NM** value: **30.00**
35 ❑ ca. 1957 Cover: 0.10 **NM** value: **30.00**
36 ❑ ca. 1957 Cover: 0.10 **NM** value: **30.00**
37 ❑ ca. 1957 Cover: 0.10 **NM** value: **30.00**
38 ❑ ca. 1957 Cover: 0.10 **NM** value: **30.00**
39 ❑ ca. 1958 Cover: 0.10 **NM** value: **30.00**
40 ❑ ca. 1958 Cover: 0.10 **NM** value: **30.00**
41 ❑ Jun 1958 Cover: 0.10 **NM** value: **30.00**
42 ❑ Aug 1958 Cover: 0.10 **NM** value: **30.00**
43 ❑ Oct 1958 Cover: 0.10 **NM** value: **30.00**
44 ❑ Jan 1959 Cover: 0.10 **NM** value: **30.00**
45 ❑ Mar 1959 Cover: 0.10 **NM** value: **30.00**
46 ❑ May 1959 Cover: 0.10 **NM** value: **30.00**
final issue.

TEX TAYLOR — Marvel

1 ❑ Sep 1948 Cover: 0.10 **NM** value: **200.00**
• **CGC:** 1 graded, best 7.5
2 ❑ Nov 1948 Cover: 0.10 **NM** value: **125.00**
3 ❑ Jan 1949 Cover: 0.10 **NM** value: **100.00**
4 ❑ Mar 1949 Cover: 0.10 **NM** value: **100.00**
5 ❑ May 1949 Cover: 0.10 **NM** value: **100.00**
6 ❑ Jul 1949 Cover: 0.10 **NM** value: **100.00**
7 ❑ Oct 1949 Cover: 0.10 **NM** value: **75.00**
8 ❑ Dec 1949 Cover: 0.10 **NM** value: **75.00**
9 ❑ ca. 1950 Cover: 0.10 **NM** value: **75.00**

TEYKWA — Gemstone

1 ❑ Oct 1988, b&w Cover: 1.75 **NM** value: **Cover or less**

THACKER'S REVENGE — Explorer

1 ❑ b&w Cover: 2.95 **NM** value: **Cover or less**
• Archie parody

THANE OF BAGARTH — Avalon

1 ❑ Cover: 2.95 **NM** value: **Cover or less**
A: Jim Aparo **W:** Steve Skeates

THANOS QUEST, THE — Marvel

This two-issue prestige format limited series finds the godlike Thanos seeking the Soul Gems in his quest for infinite power.

Individually, these jewels belong to some of the most formidable players in the Marvel universe — the In-Betweener, the Gardner, and Champion, among others. Gathering them together, Thanos knows, would give him the power he seeks — the power to destroy everything.

Written by Jim Starlin and drawn by Ron Lim and John Beatty, The Thanos Quest ties into events in the pages of Starlin's Silver Surfer and his later trilogy of limited series: Infinity Gauntlet, The Infinity War, and The Infinity Crusade. It is a tale of mad, insatiable evil, and it's well-told.

1 ❑ Sep 1990 Cover: 4.95 **NM** value: **Cover or less**
Circ: CapCity orders: **23,000** • **CGC:** 3 graded, best 9.8
📖 Schemes and Dreams **A:** Ron Lim; Jim Starlin(cover) **W:** Jim Starlin
1-2 ❑ 1990 Cover: 4.95 **NM** value: **Cover or less**
Circ: CapCity orders: **10,800**
2 ❑ Oct 1990 Cover: 4.95 **NM** value: **Cover or less**
Circ: CapCity orders: **19,300** • **CGC:** 2 graded, best 9.8

THAT CHEMICAL REFLEX — CFD

1 ❑ Cover: 2.50 **NM** value: **Cover or less**
Circ: CapCity orders: **2,235**
A: Dan Brereton **W:** Mike Kennedy
2 ❑ Cover: 2.50 **NM** value: **Cover or less**
A: Dan Brereton **W:** Mike Kennedy
3 ❑ Cover: 2.50 **NM** value: **Cover or less**
A: Dan Brereton **W:** Mike Kennedy

THAT WILKIN BOY — Archie

1 ❑ Jan 1969 Cover: 0.12 **NM** value: **15.00**
2 ❑ Apr 1969 Cover: 0.12 **NM** value: **9.00**
3 ❑ Jun 1969 Cover: 0.12 **NM** value: **6.00**
4 ❑ Aug 1969 Cover: 0.15 **NM** value: **6.00**
5 ❑ Oct 1969 Cover: 0.15 **NM** value: **6.00**
6 ❑ Jan 1970 Cover: 0.15 **NM** value: **5.00**
7 ❑ Apr 1970 Cover: 0.15 **NM** value: **5.00**
8 ❑ Jul 1970 Cover: 0.15 **NM** value: **5.00**
9 ❑ Sep 1970 Cover: 0.15 **NM** value: **5.00**
• **CGC:** 1 graded, best 9.4
10 ❑ Oct 1970 Cover: 0.15 **NM** value: **5.00**
11 ❑ Jan 1971 Cover: 0.15 **NM** value: **4.00**

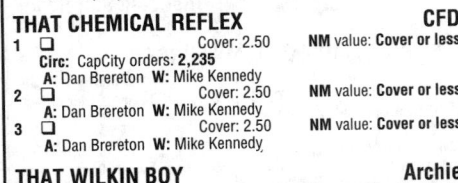

CGC-graded: Multiply prices above by **33 for 9.9 M** • **16 for 9.8 NM/M** • **7 for 9.6 NM+** • **5 for 9.4 NM** • **2.5 for 9.2 NM-** • **1.5 for 9.0 VF/NM**

12 ❑ Apr 1971 Cover: 0.25 **NM** value: **6.00**
13 ❑ Jul 1971 Cover: 0.25 **NM** value: **6.00**
14 ❑ Sep 1971 Cover: 0.25 **NM** value: **6.00**
15 ❑ Nov 1971 Cover: 0.25 **NM** value: **6.00**
16 ❑ Jan 1972 Cover: 0.25 **NM** value: **6.00**
17 ❑ Apr 1972 Cover: 0.25 **NM** value: **6.00**
18 ❑ Jul 1972 Cover: 0.25 **NM** value: **6.00**
19 ❑ Sep 1972 Cover: 0.25 **NM** value: **6.00**
20 ❑ Nov 1972 Cover: 0.25 **NM** value: **6.00**
21 ❑ Jan 1973 Cover: 0.25 **NM** value: **5.00**
📖 Help From Beyond; An Eye Popper; The Price of Advice; Responsibility; The Bees are for the Birds; Dinner Belle; Mum's the Word; Strong Finish
22 ❑ Apr 1973 Cover: 0.25 **NM** value: **5.00**
23 ❑ Jul 1973 Cover: 0.25 **NM** value: **5.00**
24 ❑ Sep 1973 Cover: 0.25 **NM** value: **5.00**
25 ❑ Oct 1973 Cover: 0.25 **NM** value: **5.00**
26 ❑ Jan 1974 Cover: 0.25 **NM** value: **5.00**
27 ❑ Apr 1974 Cover: 0.25 **NM** value: **4.00**
28 ❑ Jul 1974 Cover: 0.25 **NM** value: **4.00**
29 ❑ Sep 1974 Cover: 0.25 **NM** value: **4.00**
30 ❑ Oct 1974 Cover: 0.25 **NM** value: **4.00**
31 ❑ 1975 Cover: 0.25 **NM** value: **3.00**
32 ❑ Jul 1975 Cover: 0.25 **NM** value: **3.00**
33 ❑ Sep 1975 Cover: 0.25 **NM** value: **3.00**
34 ❑ Oct 1975 Cover: 0.25 **NM** value: **3.00**
35 ❑ Jan 1976 Cover: 0.25 **NM** value: **3.00**
36 ❑ Apr 1976 Cover: 0.25 **NM** value: **3.00**
37 ❑ Jul 1976 Cover: 0.30 **NM** value: **3.00**
38 ❑ Sep 1976 Cover: 0.30 **NM** value: **3.00**
39 ❑ Oct 1976 Cover: 0.30 **NM** value: **3.00**
40 ❑ Jan 1977 Cover: 0.30 **NM** value: **3.00**
41 ❑ Aug 1977 Cover: 0.35 **NM** value: **2.50**
📖 The Protectors; Li'l Jinx: On the Ball!; Work of Art; What a Waste; The Rebel Yell
42 ❑ Oct 1977 Cover: 0.35 **NM** value: **2.50**
43 ❑ ca. 1978 Cover: 0.35 **NM** value: **2.50**
44 ❑ ca. 1978 Cover: 0.35 **NM** value: **2.50**
45 ❑ ca. 1979 Cover: 0.40 **NM** value: **2.50**
46 ❑ ca. 1979 Cover: 0.40 **NM** value: **2.50**
47 ❑ ca. 1980 Cover: 0.50 **NM** value: **2.50**
48 ❑ ca. 1980 Cover: 0.50 **NM** value: **2.50**
49 ❑ ca. 1981 Cover: 0.50 **NM** value: **2.50**
50 ❑ ca. 1981 Cover: 0.50 **NM** value: **2.50**
51 ❑ ca. 1982 Cover: 0.60 **NM** value: **2.50**
52 ❑ ca. 1982 Cover: 0.60 **NM** value: **2.50**

THB — Horse Press

1 ❑ Oct 1994, b&w Cover: 2.95 **NM** value: **8.00**
A: Paul Pope **W:** Paul Pope
1-2 ❑ b&w Cover: 5.50 **NM** value: **Cover or less**
• reprints THB #1 with revised and additional material **A:** Paul Pope **W:** Paul Pope
2 ❑ ca. 1994, b&w Cover: 2.95 **NM** value: **6.00**
A: Paul Pope **W:** Paul Pope
3 ❑ Jan 1995, b&w Cover: 2.95 **NM** value: **5.00**
A: Paul Pope **W:** Paul Pope
4 ❑ Feb 1995, b&w Cover: 2.95 **NM** value: **5.00**
A: Paul Pope **W:** Paul Pope
5 ❑ Mar 1995, b&w Cover: 2.95 **NM** value: **4.00**
A: Paul Pope **W:** Paul Pope
6 ❑ 1996 Cover: 2.95 **NM** value: **4.00**
Circ: Diamd. preorders: **5,048**
A: Paul Pope **W:** Paul Pope
69 ❑ Oct 1994, b&w **NM** value: **3.00**
No issue number. no cover price. • promo edition. **A:** Paul Pope **W:** Paul Pope

T.H.E. CAT — Gold Key

T.H.E. Cat was a TV series in the 1966-7 season starring Robert Loggia (1930-) as Thomas Hewitt Edward Cat, a retired cat burglar. Though retired from burgling, he protected clients who'd been threatened with death. The comic book ended when the series did. — Maggie

1 ❑ Mar 1967 Cover: 0.12 **NM** value: **12.00**
Photo cover.
2 ❑ Apr 1967 Cover: 0.12 **NM** value: **10.00**
Photo cover.
3 ❑ Jun 1967 Cover: 0.12 **NM** value: **10.00**
Photo cover.
4 ❑ Oct 1967 Cover: 0.12 **NM** value: **10.00**
Photo cover.

THECOMICSTORE.COM PRESENTS — TheComicStore.com

1 ❑ **NM** value: **1.00**

THERE'S A MADMAN IN MY MIRROR — Bench Press

1 ❑ Mar 1999 Cover: 3.50 **NM** value: **Cover or less**
No issue number. cardstock cover.

THESPIAN — Dark Moon

1 ❑ Apr 1995 Cover: 2.50 **NM** value: **Cover or less**
A: Zoe Rochelle **W:** Steve Kendrick

THEY CALL ME...THE SKUL — Virtual

1 ❑ May 1996 Cover: 3.99 **NM** value: **Cover or less**
• digest. 📖 From the Depths, Part 1 • Only issue published **A:** Ron Lim **W:** Danny Fingeroth ★ 1st Appearance of Skul.
1/A ❑ Oct 1996 Cover: 3.99 **NM** value: **Cover or less**
Circ: Diamd. preorders: **5,895**
• digest.

THEY CAME FROM THE 50S — Eternity

1 ❑ b&w Cover: 9.95 **NM** value: **Cover or less**
📖 De

THEY WERE 11 — Viz

1 ❑ b&w Cover: 2.75 **NM** value: **Cover or less**
Circ: CapCity orders: **2,925**
A: Moto Hagio **W:** Moto Hagio
2 ❑ b&w Cover: 2.75 **NM** value: **Cover or less**
Circ: CapCity orders: **2,925**
A: Moto Hagio **W:** Moto Hagio
3 ❑ b&w Cover: 2.75 **NM** value: **Cover or less**
Circ: CapCity orders: **2,200**
A: Moto Hagio **W:** Moto Hagio
4 ❑ b&w Cover: 2.75 **NM** value: **Cover or less**
Circ: CapCity orders: **2,000**
A: Moto Hagio **W:** Moto Hagio

THEY WERE CHOSEN TO BE THE SURVIVORS — Spectrum

1 ❑ Jun 1983 Cover: 0.60 **NM** value: **2.00**
📖 Siege **A:** Steve Woron; Bob Lewis **W:** Tom Woron
2 ❑ Sep 1983 Cover: 1.00 **NM** value: **2.00**
📖 A Hunter's Rage **A:** Steve Woron; Bob Lewis **W:** Steve Woron
3 ❑ Dec 1983 Cover: 1.00 **NM** value: **2.00**
4 ❑ Mar 1984 Cover: 1.00 **NM** value: **2.00**

THIEF — Penguin Palace

1 ❑ Jul 1995, b&w Cover: 2.50 **NM** value: **Cover or less**

THIEF OF SHERWOOD — A-Plus

1 ❑ b&w Cover: 2.25 **NM** value: **Cover or less**

THIEVES — Silverwolf

1 ❑ Cover: 1.50 **NM** value: **Cover or less**

THIEVES & KINGS — I Box Publishing

1 ❑ Sep 1994 Cover: 2.35 **NM** value: **4.00**
1-2 ❑ Cover: 2.35 **NM** value: **2.50**
2 ❑ Nov 1994 Cover: 2.35 **NM** value: **3.00**
2-2 ❑ Cover: 2.35 **NM** value: **2.50**
3 ❑ Jan 1995 Cover: 2.35 **NM** value: **3.00**
3-2 ❑ Cover: 2.35 **NM** value: **Cover or less**
4 ❑ Mar 1995 Cover: 2.35 **NM** value: **3.00**
5 ❑ May 1995 Cover: 2.35 **NM** value: **3.00**
6 ❑ Jul 1995 Cover: 2.35 **NM** value: **2.75**
7 ❑ Sep 1995 Cover: 2.35 **NM** value: **2.75**
8 ❑ Cover: 2.35 **NM** value: **2.75**
9 ❑ Cover: 2.35 **NM** value: **2.75**
10 ❑ Cover: 2.35 **NM** value: **2.75**
11 ❑ Cover: 2.35 **NM** value: **2.50**
12 ❑ Cover: 2.35 **NM** value: **2.50**
13 ❑ Sep 1996 Cover: 2.35 **NM** value: **2.50**
Circ: Diamd. preorders: **3,847**
14 ❑ Nov 1996 Cover: 2.35 **NM** value: **2.50**
Circ: Diamd. preorders: **3,707**
15 ❑ Jan 1997 Cover: 2.35 **NM** value: **2.50**
Circ: Diamd. preorders: **3,426**
16 ❑ Mar 1997 Cover: 2.35 **NM** value: **2.50**
Circ: Diamd. preorders: **3,404**
17 ❑ May 1997 Cover: 2.35 **NM** value: **2.50**
Circ: Diamd. preorders: **3,442**
18 ❑ 1997 Cover: 2.35 **NM** value: **2.50**
19 ❑ 1997 Cover: 2.35 **NM** value: **2.50**
20 ❑ Cover: 2.35 **NM** value: **2.50**
21 ❑ 1998 Cover: 2.35 **NM** value: **Cover or less**
22 ❑ May 1998 Cover: 2.35 **NM** value: **Cover or less**
Circ: Diamd. preorders: **2,991**
23 ❑ Jul 1998 Cover: 2.35 **NM** value: **Cover or less**
Circ: Diamd. preorders: **2,804**
24 ❑ Sep 1998 Cover: 2.35 **NM** value: **Cover or less**
Circ: Diamd. preorders: **2,698**
25 ❑ Nov 1998 Cover: 2.50 **NM** value: **Cover or less**
Circ: Diamd. preorders: **2,677**
26 ❑ Jan 1999 Cover: 2.50 **NM** value: **Cover or less**
Circ: Diamd. preorders: **2,628**
27 ❑ Mar 1999 Cover: 2.50 **NM** value: **Cover or less**
Circ: Diamd. preorders: **2,622**
28 ❑ Jul 1999 Cover: 2.50 **NM** value: **Cover or less**
Circ: Diamd. preorders: **2,384**
29 ❑ Oct 1999 Cover: 2.50 **NM** value: **Cover or less**
Circ: Diamd. preorders: **2,425**
30 ❑ Cover: 2.50 **NM** value: **Cover or less**
31 ❑ Mar 2000 Cover: 2.50 **NM** value: **Cover or less**
Circ: Diamd. preorders: **2,328**
32 ❑ May 2000 Cover: 2.50 **NM** value: **Cover or less**
Circ: Diamd. preorders: **2,297**
33 ❑ Aug 2000 Cover: 2.50 **NM** value: **Cover or less**
Circ: Diamd. preorders: **2,286**
34 ❑ Nov 2000 Cover: 2.50 **NM** value: **Cover or less**
Circ: Diamd. preorders: **2,287**
35 ❑ Feb 2001 Cover: 2.50 **NM** value: **Cover or less**
Circ: Diamd. preorders: **2,204**
36 ❑ Jul 2001 Cover: 2.50 **NM** value: **Cover or less**
Circ: Diamd. preorders: **2,221**
Bk 1 ❑ b&w Cover: 12.00 **NM** value: **12.99**
• collects issues #1-6
Bk 2 ❑ b&w Cover: 14.00 **NM** value: **15.99**
• collects issues #7-16

The CGC numbers printed in individual listings above represent the **number of copies examined** and given a **Universal** grade by CGC and the **best such copy** graded at press time. For current populations, watch for special ***Comics Buyer's Guide*** issues or check **www.cgccomics.com.**

THING, THE — Marvel

Marvel killed its less popular (but often interesting) team-up title, Marvel Two-In-One, in 1983, replacing it with a series starring Two-in-One's stock player, The Thing.

John Byrne, who had revived sales on Fantastic Four, took on writing chores for the foursome's strongman, resulting in a few stories that would actually take on larger issues in the F.F.'s continuity. "Monsters" in #4 involved Quicksilver and Crystal's baby, Luna, and famously (or infamously) revealed that the Inhumans' trusty dog, Lockjaw, was actually another Inhuman who could talk but just never had anything to say.

The series might have survived Byrne's departure, had its life not been sucked out of it when, thanks to events in Marvel Super Heroes Secret Wars, The Thing was abandoned on a distant planet. He spent a bunch of issues wandering around, and the series ended a little over a year later. — JJM

1 ❑ Jul 1983 Cover: 0.60 **NM** value: **2.00**
• **CGC:** 3 graded, best 9.8
📖 Lifelines **A:** Ron Wilson; John Byrne **W:** John Byrne ★ Origin of The Thing.
2 ❑ Aug 1983 Cover: 0.60 **NM** value: **1.50**
📖 For Beauty Passed Away **A:** Ron Wilson; John Byrne **W:** John Byrne ★ Origin of The Thing.
3 ❑ Sep 1983 Cover: 0.60 **NM** value: **1.50**
📖 Turning Point **A:** Ron Wilson **W:** John Byrne ★ Appearance of Inhumans.
4 ❑ Oct 1983 Cover: 0.60 **NM** value: **1.50**
📖 I, Monster! **A:** Ron Wilson; Brent Anderson(cover) **W:** John Byrne ★ Appearance of Inhumans.
5 ❑ Nov 1983 Cover: 0.60 **NM** value: **1.50**
📖 With Friends Like These **A:** Ron Wilson **W:** John Byrne ★ Appearance of She-Hulk, Spider-Man.
6 ❑ Dec 1983 Cover: 0.60 **NM** value: **1.50**
📖 Mindscape • all-black issue **A:** Ron Wilson; Brent Anderson(cover) **W:** John Byrne ★ Versus Puppet Master.
7 ❑ Jan 1984 Cover: 0.60 **NM** value: **1.50**
• Asst. Editor Month **A:** Brent Anderson(cover)
8 ❑ Feb 1984 Cover: 0.60 **NM** value: **1.50**
📖 Ancient Evenings Ancient Pain! **A:** Ron Wilson **W:** John Byrne
9 ❑ Mar 1984 Cover: 0.60 **NM** value: **1.50**
📖 What Price A Soul? **A:** Ron Wilson **W:** John Byrne
10 ❑ Apr 1984 Cover: 0.60 **NM** value: **1.50**
📖 Marking Time • Secret Wars **A:** Ron Wilson **W:** John Byrne
11 ❑ May 1984 Cover: 0.60 **NM** value: **1.25**
📖 Rocky Grimm, Part 1 • Secret Wars aftermath **A:** Ron Wilson **W:** John Byrne
12 ❑ Jun 1984 Cover: 0.60 **NM** value: **1.25**
📖 Rocky Grimm, Part 2 **A:** Ron Wilson **W:** John Byrne
13 ❑ Jul 1984 Cover: 0.60 **NM** value: **1.25**
📖 Rocky Grimm, Part 3 **A:** Ron Wilson **W:** John Byrne
14 ❑ Aug 1984 Cover: 0.60 **NM** value: **1.25**
📖 Rocky Grimm, Part 4
15 ❑ Sep 1984 Cover: 0.60 **NM** value: **1.25**
📖 Rocky Grimm, Part 5 **A:** Ron Wilson **W:** Mike Carlin
16 ❑ Oct 1984 Cover: 0.60 **NM** value: **1.25**
📖 Rocky Grimm, Part 6 **A:** Ron Wilson **W:** Mike Carlin
17 ❑ Nov 1984 Cover: 0.60 **NM** value: **1.25**
📖 Rocky Grimm, Part 7 **A:** Ron Wilson **W:** Mike Carlin
18 ❑ Dec 1984 Cover: 0.60 **NM** value: **1.25**
📖 Rocky Grimm, Part 8 **A:** Ron Wilson **W:** Bob Harras
19 ❑ Jan 1985 Cover: 0.60 **NM** value: **1.25**
📖 Rocky Grimm, Part 9 **A:** Ron Wilson **W:** John Byrne
20 ❑ Feb 1985 Cover: 0.60 **NM** value: **1.25**
📖 Rocky Grimm, Part 10 **A:** Ron Wilson **W:** John Byrne
21 ❑ Mar 1985 Cover: 0.60 **NM** value: **1.25**
📖 Revelations **A:** Ron Wilson **W:** John Byrne
22 ❑ Apr 1985 Cover: 0.65 **NM** value: **1.25**
📖 Remembrances • returns to Earth **A:** Ron Wilson **W:** Mike Carlin
23 ❑ May 1985 Cover: 0.65 **NM** value: **1.25**
• quits Fantastic Four
24 ❑ Jun 1985 Cover: 0.65 **NM** value: **1.25**
★ Death of Miracle Man (Marvel). ★ Versus Rhino.
25 ❑ Jul 1985 Cover: 0.65 **NM** value: **1.25**
📖 Legends **A:** Ron Wilson **W:** Mike Carlin
26 ❑ Aug 1985 Cover: 0.65 **NM** value: **1.25**
📖 Runaways **A:** Ron Wilson **W:** Mike Carlin ★ Versus Taskmaster.
27 ❑ Sep 1985 Cover: 0.65 **NM** value: **1.25**
📖 The Thing And The Thunderiders **A:** Ron Wilson **W:** Mike Carlin
28 ❑ Oct 1985 Cover: 0.65 **NM** value: **1.25**
★ 1st Appearance of Demolition Dunphy (later becomes D-Man).
29 ❑ Nov 1985 Cover: 0.65 **NM** value: **1.25**
30 ❑ Dec 1985 Cover: 0.65 **NM** value: **1.25**
📖 Secret Wars II • Secret Wars II
31 ❑ Jan 1986 Cover: 0.75 **NM** value: **1.25**
32 ❑ Feb 1986 Cover: 0.75 **NM** value: **1.25**
33 ❑ Mar 1986 Cover: 0.75 **NM** value: **1.25**
Circ: CapCity orders: **12,900**
★ Death of Titania.
34 ❑ Apr 1986 Cover: 0.75 **NM** value: **1.25**
Circ: CapCity orders: **11,250**
★ Death of The Sphinx.
35 ❑ May 1986 Cover: 0.75 **NM** value: **1.25**
Circ: CapCity orders: **12,700**
36 ❑ Jun 1986 Cover: 0.75 **NM** value: **1.25**
Circ: CapCity orders: **12,300**
final issue.

Other grades: Multiply prices above by **1.5 for Mint • 2/3 for Very Fine • 1/3 for Fine • 1/5 for Very Good • 1/8 for Good**

THING FROM ANOTHER WORLD, THE
Dark Horse

1 ❑ ca. 1993 Cover: 2.95 **NM** value: **Cover or less**
Circ: CapCity orders: **20,175**
cardstock cover. **A:** John Higgins **W:** Chuck Pfarrer
2 ❑ ca. 1993 Cover: 2.95 **NM** value: **Cover or less**
Circ: CapCity orders: **13,125**
cardstock cover. **A:** John Higgins **W:** Chuck Pfarrer

THING FROM ANOTHER WORLD: CLIMATE OF FEAR
Dark Horse

1 ❑ ca. 1994 Cover: 2.50 **NM** value: **Cover or less**
Circ: CapCity orders: **12,550**
A: Jim Somerville **W:** John Arcudi
2 ❑ ca. 1994 Cover: 2.50 **NM** value: **Cover or less**
Circ: CapCity orders: **10,475**
A: Jim Somerville **W:** John Arcudi
3 ❑ ca. 1994 Cover: 2.50 **NM** value: **Cover or less**
Circ: CapCity orders: **9,775**
A: Jim Somerville **W:** John Arcudi
4 ❑ ca. 1994 Cover: 2.50 **NM** value: **Cover or less**
Circ: CapCity orders: **9,075**
A: Jim Somerville **W:** John Arcudi

THING FROM ANOTHER WORLD, THE: ETERNAL VOWS
Dark Horse

1 ❑ Dec 1993 Cover: 2.50 **NM** value: **Cover or less**
Circ: CapCity orders: **7,775**
📖 From This Day Forth **A:** Paul Gulacy **W:** Dave DeVries
2 ❑ Jan 1994 Cover: 2.50 **NM** value: **Cover or less**
Circ: CapCity orders: **5,800**
📖 In Sickness Or In Health **A:** Paul Gulacy **W:** Dave DeVries
3 ❑ Feb 1994 Cover: 2.50 **NM** value: **Cover or less**
Circ: CapCity orders: **5,800**
📖 Climate of Fear **A:** Jim Somerville **W:** John Arcudi
4 ❑ Mar 1994 Cover: 2.50 **NM** value: **Cover or less**
Circ: CapCity orders: **4,775**

THING: PEGASUS PROJECT
Marvel

Bk 1 ❑ Jun 1988 Cover: 6.95 **NM** value: **Cover or less**
A: George Pérez; John Byrne

THING, THE (CHARLTON)
Charlton

1 ❑ Feb 1952 Cover: 0.10 **NM** value: **700.00**
• **CGC:** 2 graded, best 8.5
2 ❑ Apr 1952 Cover: 0.10 **NM** value: **500.00**
• **CGC:** 2 graded, best 9.0
3 ❑ Jun 1952 Cover: 0.10 **NM** value: **500.00**
• **CGC:** 2 graded, best 9.4
4 ❑ Aug 1952 Cover: 0.10 **NM** value: **400.00**
• **CGC:** 1 graded, best 5.5
5 ❑ Oct 1952 Cover: 0.10 **NM** value: **400.00**
• **CGC:** 4 graded, best 9.4
6 ❑ Jan 1953 Cover: 0.10 **NM** value: **400.00**
• **CGC:** 1 graded, best 9.2
7 ❑ Mar 1953 Cover: 0.10 **NM** value: **350.00**
• **CGC:** 4 graded, best 8.0
8 ❑ May 1953 Cover: 0.10 **NM** value: **350.00**
• **CGC:** 1 graded, best 9.6
9 ❑ Jul 1953 Cover: 0.10 **NM** value: **350.00**
• **CGC:** 1 graded, best 6.0
10 ❑ Sep 1953 Cover: 0.10 **NM** value: **300.00**
11 ❑ Nov 1953 Cover: 0.10 **NM** value: **300.00**
• **CGC:** 2 graded, best 7.5
12 ❑ Feb 1954 Cover: 0.10 **NM** value: **300.00**
• **CGC:** 3 graded, best 9.2
13 ❑ Apr 1954 Cover: 0.10 **NM** value: **300.00**
14 ❑ Jun 1954 Cover: 0.10 **NM** value: **300.00**
• **CGC:** 3 graded, best 9.2
15 ❑ Jul 1954 Cover: 0.10 **NM** value: **300.00**
• **CGC:** 4 graded, best 9.4
16 ❑ Sep 1954 Cover: 0.10 **NM** value: **300.00**
• **CGC:** 29 graded, best 9.6
17 ❑ Nov 1954 Cover: 0.10 **NM** value: **300.00**
• **CGC:** 3 graded, best 8.5

THIRD EYE (DARK ONE'S...)
Sirius

1 ❑ 1998 Cover: 4.95 **NM** value: **Cover or less**
No issue number. • prestige format. • pin-ups
2 ❑ Dec 1998 Cover: 4.95 **NM** value: **Cover or less**
cardstock cover. • pin-ups and stories

THIRD WORLD WAR
Fleetway-Quality

1 ❑ Cover: 2.50 **NM** value: **Cover or less**
Circ: CapCity orders: **3,175**
2 ❑ Cover: 2.50 **NM** value: **Cover or less**
Circ: CapCity orders: **2,475**
3 ❑ Cover: 2.50 **NM** value: **Cover or less**
Circ: CapCity orders: **2,200**
📖 The Killing Yields **A:** Carlos Ezquerra **W:** Pat Mills
4 ❑ Cover: 2.50 **NM** value: **Cover or less**
Circ: CapCity orders: **2,050**
5 ❑ Cover: 2.50 **NM** value: **Cover or less**
Circ: CapCity orders: **1,825**
6 ❑ Cover: 2.50 **NM** value: **Cover or less**
Circ: CapCity orders: **1,825**

The prices seen above do not represent the highest possible prices seen in online auctions, but rather the prices we have seen these issues reliably fetch in a variety of environments (storefront retail, mail order, auction and convention).

THIRTEEN
Dell

Thirteen (subtitled "...Going on Eighteen") had, believe it or not, a young female, target audience. The main character is Val, a thirteen-year-old girl who lives with her family, including an older sister whom she strives to emulate. Val's best friend is a heavy-set girl named Judy, who's down-to-earth and always has the right advice to help solve Val's many teenage troubles.

Each issue contains several short stories about the many wacky situations in which the girls find themselves. If Val isn't trying to wear makeup too soon, or trying to date the grocery delivery boy, she is thinking up ways to make her friend, Stu, stop following her. In some, Judy has a story of her own.

The series debuted in 1961 and came out sporadically for 29 issues until it was canceled in 1971.

1 ❑ 1961 **NM** value: **35.00**
2 ❑ Feb 1962 Cover: 0.15 **NM** value: **24.00**
3 ❑ May 1962 **NM** value: **20.00**
4 ❑ Sep 1962 Cover: 0.12 **NM** value: **20.00**
5 ❑ Jan 1963 Cover: 0.12 **NM** value: **18.00**
6 ❑ Apr 1963 Cover: 0.12 **NM** value: **18.00**
7 ❑ Jul 1963 Cover: 0.12 **NM** value: **18.00**
8 ❑ Sep 1963 Cover: 0.12 **NM** value: **18.00**
9 ❑ Jan 1964 Cover: 0.12 **NM** value: **18.00**
10 ❑ Apr 1964 Cover: 0.12 **NM** value: **18.00**
11 ❑ Jul 1964 Cover: 0.12 **NM** value: **14.00**
12 ❑ Sep 1964 Cover: 0.12 **NM** value: **14.00**
13 ❑ Jan 1965 Cover: 0.12 **NM** value: **14.00**
Circ: Statement: **175,169**
14 ❑ Apr 1965 Cover: 0.12 **NM** value: **14.00**
Circ: Statement: **175,169**
15 ❑ Jul 1965 Cover: 0.12 **NM** value: **14.00**
Circ: Statement: **175,169**
16 ❑ Sep 1965 Cover: 0.12 **NM** value: **14.00**
Circ: Statement: **175,169**
17 ❑ Jan 1966 Cover: 0.12 **NM** value: **14.00**
Circ: Statement: **161,231**
18 ❑ Apr 1966 Cover: 0.12 **NM** value: **14.00**
Circ: Statement: **161,231**
19 ❑ Jul 1966 Cover: 0.12 **NM** value: **14.00**
Circ: Statement: **161,231**
• Has 1965 Statement, filed 10/1/65; avg print run 306,758; avg sales 175,035; avg subs 134; avg total paid 175,169; samples 130; max existent 175,299; 43% of run returned
20 ❑ Sep 1966 Cover: 0.12 **NM** value: **14.00**
Circ: Statement: **161,231**
21 ❑ Jan 1967 Cover: 0.12 **NM** value: **14.00**
22 ❑ Apr 1967 Cover: 0.12 **NM** value: **14.00**
23 ❑ Jul 1967 Cover: 0.12 **NM** value: **14.00**
• Has 1966 Statement, filed 10/1/66; avg print run 300,632; avg sales 161,151; avg subs 80; avg total paid 161,231; samples 293; max existent 161,524; 46% of run returned
24 ❑ Sep 1967 Cover: 0.12 **NM** value: **14.00**
25 ❑ Jan 1968 Cover: 0.12 **NM** value: **14.00**
26 ❑ ca. 1969 Cover: 0.12 **NM** value: **8.00**
📖 Beginner's Luck...
27 ❑ ca. 1970 Cover: 0.12 **NM** value: **8.00**
28 ❑ ca. 1970 Cover: 0.12 **NM** value: **8.00**
29 ❑ ca. 1971 Cover: 0.12 **NM** value: **8.00**
final issue.

13: ASSASSIN COMICS MODULE
TSR

1 ❑ Cover: 2.95 **NM** value: **Cover or less**
Circ: CapCity orders: **1,344**
📖 The Wakening Storm **A:** Robb Phipps **W:** Mike W. Barr
2 ❑ Cover: 2.95 **NM** value: **Cover or less**
Circ: CapCity orders: **1,152**
3 ❑ Cover: 2.95 **NM** value: **Cover or less**
📖 How Dead is Dead?; Who are the Brotherhood? **A:** Robb Phipps; Juan Muro **W:** Buzz Dixon; Roger Slifer
4 ❑ Cover: 2.95 **NM** value: **Cover or less**
5 ❑ Cover: 2.95 **NM** value: **Cover or less**
📖 The Search for Maggie Darr, Part 1; Weapon **A:** Robb Phipps; Frank Springer **W:** Roger Slifer; Scott Haring
6 ❑ Cover: 2.95 **NM** value: **Cover or less**
📖 The Search for Maggie Darr, Part 2 **A:** Robb Phipps **W:** Roger Slifer
7 ❑ Cover: 2.95 **NM** value: **Cover or less**
📖 The Search for Maggie Darr, Part 3 **A:** Robb Phipps **W:** Roger Slifer
8 ❑ Cover: 2.95 **NM** value: **Cover or less**
📖 The Search for Maggie Darr, Part 4 **A:** Robb Phipps **W:** Roger Slifer

13 DAYS OF CHRISTMAS, THE: A TALE OF THE LOST LUNAR BESTIARY
Sirius

1 ❑ b&w Cover: 2.95 **NM** value: **Cover or less**
wraparound cover.

THIRTEEN O'CLOCK
Dark Horse

1 ❑ b&w Cover: 2.95 **NM** value: **Cover or less**
Circ: CapCity orders: **2,500**
No issue number.

THIRTEEN SOMETHING!
Global

1 ❑ Cover: 1.95 **NM** value: **Cover or less**

39 SCREAMS, THE
Thunder Baas

1 ❑ Cover: 2.00 **NM** value: **Cover or less**

2 ❑ Cover: 2.00 **NM** value: **Cover or less**
📖 Oh to be Desired for Just One Day; The Man Who Experimented on Animals; The Ghoul **A:** Kevin Walsh; Stephen Blickenstaff; Bob Kathman **W:** Ed Colby
3 ❑ Cover: 2.00 **NM** value: **Cover or less**
4 ❑ Cover: 2.00 **NM** value: **Cover or less**
5 ❑ Cover: 2.00 **NM** value: **Cover or less**
6 ❑ Cover: 2.00 **NM** value: **Cover or less**

32 PAGES
Sirius

1 ❑ Jan 2001 Cover: 2.95 **NM** value: **Cover or less**
📖 To Be Continued...; Man Whole; Escalator; Breakfast on the Run **A:** Mark Crilley **W:** Mark Crilley

THIS IS HEAT
Aeon

1 ❑ b&w Cover: 2.50 **NM** value: **Cover or less**
No issue number.

THIS IS NOT AN EXIT
Draculina

1 ❑ Cover: 2.95 **NM** value: **Cover or less**
2 ❑ Cover: 2.95 **NM** value: **Cover or less**
📖 Food **A:** David Watkins **W:** David Watkins

THIS IS SICK!
Silver Skull

1 ❑ b&w Cover: 2.95 **NM** value: **Cover or less**
foil cover. • Zen
2 ❑ Cover: 2.95 **NM** value: **Cover or less**

THIS IS WAR
Standard

5 ❑ Jul 1952 Cover: 0.10 **NM** value: **75.00**
• **CGC:** 1 graded, best 7.5
6 ❑ Sep 1952 Cover: 0.10 **NM** value: **50.00**
7 ❑ Jan 1953 Cover: 0.10 **NM** value: **50.00**
8 ❑ Mar 1953 Cover: 0.10 **NM** value: **45.00**
• **CGC:** 1 graded, best 9.4
9 ❑ May 1953 Cover: 0.10 **NM** value: **45.00**

THIS MAGAZINE IS HAUNTED (1ST SERIES)
Fawcett

1 ❑ Oct 1951 Cover: 0.10 **NM** value: **350.00**
• **CGC:** 1 graded, best 7.0
2 ❑ Dec 1951 Cover: 0.10 **NM** value: **265.00**
3 ❑ Feb 1952 Cover: 0.10 **NM** value: **200.00**
• **CGC:** 1 graded, best 9.0
4 ❑ Apr 1952 Cover: 0.10 **NM** value: **175.00**
• **CGC:** 2 graded, best 7.5
5 ❑ Jun 1952 Cover: 0.10 **NM** value: **175.00**
• **CGC:** 2 graded, best 7.0
6 ❑ Aug 1952 Cover: 0.10 **NM** value: **150.00**
7 ❑ Oct 1952 Cover: 0.10 **NM** value: **150.00**
• **CGC:** 1 graded, best 9.2
8 ❑ Dec 1952 Cover: 0.10 **NM** value: **150.00**
📖 The House in the Web; The Aged Curse!; Lost Chords (text); The Dance of the Dead! **W:** John Martin
9 ❑ Feb 1953 Cover: 0.10 **NM** value: **125.00**
10 ❑ Apr 1953 Cover: 0.10 **NM** value: **200.00**
• **CGC:** 4 graded, best 9.2
Gore cover.
11 ❑ Jun 1953 Cover: 0.10 **NM** value: **125.00**
• **CGC:** 2 graded, best 8.5
12 ❑ Aug 1953 Cover: 0.10 **NM** value: **125.00**
• **CGC:** 2 graded, best 8.5
13 ❑ Oct 1953 Cover: 0.10 **NM** value: **200.00**
• **CGC:** 1 graded, best 9.0
Gore cover.
14 ❑ Dec 1953 Cover: 0.10 **NM** value: **125.00**
15 ❑ Feb 1954 Cover: 0.10 **NM** value: **100.00**
16 ❑ Apr 1954 Cover: 0.10 **NM** value: **225.00**
A: Steve Ditko
17 ❑ May 1954 Cover: 0.10 **NM** value: **250.00**
• **CGC:** 2 graded, best 8.0
A: Steve Ditko
18 ❑ Jul 1954 Cover: 0.10 **NM** value: **225.00**
• **CGC:** 1 graded, best 7.5
A: Steve Ditko
19 ❑ Aug 1954 Cover: 0.10 **NM** value: **215.00**
• **CGC:** 1 graded, best 9.4
A: Steve Ditko
20 ❑ Sep 1954 Cover: 0.10 **NM** value: **100.00**
• **CGC:** 1 graded, best 9.0
21 ❑ Nov 1954 Cover: 0.10 **NM** value: **200.00**
• Series continued in Danger & Adventure #22 **A:** Steve Ditko(cover)

THIS MAGAZINE IS HAUNTED (2ND SERIES)
Charlton

12 ❑ 1957 **NM** value: **300.00**
13 ❑ 1957 **NM** value: **300.00**
14 ❑ Dec 1957 **NM** value: **300.00**
• **CGC:** 1 graded, best 9.4
15 ❑ Feb 1958 **NM** value: **200.00**
16 ❑ May 1958 **NM** value: **200.00**
• **CGC:** 2 graded, best 7.5

There are two different pricing tiers in the modern comic-book hobby. **The prices seen above** are the prices we have seen **loose copies** of these issues reliably fetch in a variety of environments. Condition alters the price by the fractions seen on the bar on the bottom of left-hand pages of this book. **Comics graded by CGC** usually sell for more. Use the guide on the bottom of right-hand pages of this book to estimate what copies have brought on eBay.

CGC-graded: Multiply prices above by **33 for 9.9 M • 16 for 9.8 NM/M • 7 for 9.6 NM+ • 5 for 9.4 NM • 2.5 for 9.2 NM- • 1.5 for 9.0 VF/NM**

THOR

Marvel

In Journey into Mystery #83, Dr. Don Blake discovered the cane that transformed him into Thor, the Asgardian god of thunder — and readers would come to know that Odin had banished his prideful son into Blake's oblivious form. Armed with his mystical uru hammer Mjolnir, Thor battled foes on Earth and in Asgard, and made Journey into Mystery his own title in 1966.

Jack Kirby's work remains the most memorable part of the series early years, with Walter Simonson's reinterpretation reinvigorating the title in the 1980s. It's a title that often needed reinvigorating, with a dull alter ego for Thor and such overworn polot devices as Thor losing his hammer and turning back into Blake. In the mid-1990s, while Thor was off in "Heroes Reborn," the series returned to being Journey Into Mystery, Vol. 1 — there had been a Volume 2 in between! — JJM

126 ❑ Mar 1966 Cover: 0.12 **NM** value: **110.00**
Circ: Statement: **296,251** • **CGC:** 33 graded, best 9.8
Whom the Gods Would Destroy!; The Summons • Has 1965 Statement, filed 10/1/65; avg print run 377,663; avg sales 231,904; avg subs 740; avg total paid 232,644; samples 60; max existent 232,704; 38% of run returned **A:** Jack Kirby; Stan Lee **W:** Jack Kirby; Stan Lee ★ Versus Hercules.

127 ❑ Apr 1966 Cover: 0.12 **NM** value: **45.00**
Circ: Statement: **296,251** • **CGC:** 8 graded, best 9.6
The Hammer and the Holocaust; The Meaning of Ragnarok **A:** Jack Kirby; Stan Lee **W:** Jack Kirby; Stan Lee ★ 1st Appearance of Volla, Midgard Serpent, Pluto.

128 ❑ May 1966 Cover: 0.12 **NM** value: **45.00**
Circ: Statement: **296,251** • **CGC:** 8 graded, best 9.4
The Power of Pluto; Aftermath **A:** Jack Kirby; Stan Lee **W:** Jack Kirby; Stan Lee

129 ❑ Jun 1966 Cover: 0.12 **NM** value: **45.00**
Circ: Statement: **296,251** • **CGC:** 6 graded, best 9.6
The Verdict of Zeus; The Hordes of Harokin **A:** Jack Kirby; Stan Lee **W:** Jack Kirby; Stan Lee ★ 1st Appearance of Ares, Hela, Tana Nile (disguised).

130 ❑ Jul 1966 Cover: 0.12 **NM** value: **45.00**
Circ: Statement: **296,251** • **CGC:** 10 graded, best 9.6
Thunder in the Netherworld!; The Fateful Change **A:** Jack Kirby; Stan Lee **W:** Jack Kirby; Stan Lee ★ 1st Appearance of Tana Nile (in real form).

131 ❑ Aug 1966 Cover: 0.12 **NM** value: **45.00**
Circ: Statement: **296,251** • **CGC:** 6 graded, best 9.8
They Strike From Space; The Warlock's Eye **A:** Jack Kirby; Stan Lee **W:** Jack Kirby; Stan Lee

132 ❑ Sep 1966 Cover: 0.12 **NM** value: **45.00**
Circ: Statement: **296,251** • **CGC:** 66 graded, best 9.8
Rigel Where Gods May Fear to Tread!; The Dark Horse of Death! **A:** Jack Kirby; Stan Lee **W:** Jack Kirby; Stan Lee ★ 1st Appearance of Recorder, Ego. ★ Versus Ego, the Living Planet.

133 ❑ Oct 1966 Cover: 0.12 **NM** value: **45.00**
Circ: Statement: **296,251** • **CGC:** 15 graded, best 9.4
Behold the Living Planet; Valhalla **A:** Jack Kirby; Stan Lee **W:** Jack Kirby; Stan Lee

134 ❑ Nov 1966 Cover: 0.12 **NM** value: **50.00**
Circ: Statement: **296,251** • **CGC:** 9 graded, best 9.6
The People-Breeders; When Speaks the Dragon **A:** Jack Kirby; Stan Lee **W:** Jack Kirby; Stan Lee ★ Origin of Man-Beast. ★ 1st Appearance of Man-Beast, High Evolutionary.

135 ❑ Dec 1966 Cover: 0.12 **NM** value: **45.00**
Circ: Statement: **296,251** • **CGC:** 10 graded, best 9.6
The Maddening Menace of the Man-Beast; The Fiery Breath of Fafnir **A:** Jack Kirby; Stan Lee **W:** Jack Kirby; Stan Lee ★ Origin of High Evolutionary.

136 ❑ Jan 1967 Cover: 0.12 **NM** value: **45.00**
Circ: Statement: **298,219** • **CGC:** 8 graded, best 9.4
To Become An Immortal; There Shall Come A Miracle • Jane Foster denied immortality **A:** Jack Kirby; Stan Lee **W:** Jack Kirby; Stan Lee ★ 1st Appearance of Sif.

137 ❑ Feb 1967 Cover: 0.12 **NM** value: **45.00**
Circ: Statement: **298,219** • **CGC:** 6 graded, best 9.4
The Thunder God and The Troll; The Trajedy of Hogun **A:** Jack Kirby; Stan Lee **W:** Jack Kirby; Stan Lee ★ 1st Appearance of Ulik.

138 ❑ Mar 1967 Cover: 0.12 **NM** value: **45.00**
Circ: Statement: **298,219** • **CGC:** 14 graded, best 9.6
The Flames of Battle; The Quest for the Mystic Mountain • Has 1966 Statement, filed 10/1/66; avg print run 488,526; avg sales 294,851; avg subs 1,400; avg total paid 296,251; samples 60; max existent 296,311; 39% of run returned **A:** Jack Kirby; Stan Lee **W:** Jack Kirby; Stan Lee

139 ❑ Apr 1967 Cover: 0.12 **NM** value: **45.00**
Circ: Statement: **298,219** • **CGC:** 15 graded, best 9.4
To Die Like a God; The Secret of the Mystic Mountain **A:** Jack Kirby; Stan Lee **W:** Jack Kirby; Stan Lee

140 ❑ May 1967 Cover: 0.12 **NM** value: **45.00**
Circ: Statement: **298,219** • **CGC:** 13 graded, best 9.6
The Growing Man; The Battle Begins **A:** Jack Kirby; Stan Lee **W:** Jack Kirby; Stan Lee ★ 1st Appearance of Growing Man. ★ Versus Growing Man.

141 ❑ Jun 1967 Cover: 0.12 **NM** value: **28.00**
Circ: Statement: **298,219** • **CGC:** 7 graded, best 9.6
The Wrath of Replicus; Alibar and the Forty Deemons **A:** Jack Kirby; Stan Lee **W:** Jack Kirby; Stan Lee

142 ❑ Jul 1967 Cover: 0.12 **NM** value: **28.00**
Circ: Statement: **298,219** • **CGC:** 9 graded, best 9.6
The Scourge of the Super Skrull; We, Who Are About to Die **A:** Jack Kirby; Stan Lee **W:** Jack Kirby; Stan Lee

143 ❑ Aug 1967 Cover: 0.12 **NM** value: **28.00**
Circ: Statement: **298,219** • **CGC:** 8 graded, best 9.6
And Soon Shall Come the Enchanters; To The Death **A:** Jack Kirby; Stan Lee **W:** Jack Kirby; Stan Lee

144 ❑ Sep 1967 Cover: 0.12 **NM** value: **28.00**
Circ: Statement: **298,219** • **CGC:** 6 graded, best 9.4
This Battleground Earth; The Beginning of the End **A:** Jack Kirby; Stan Lee **W:** Jack Kirby; Stan Lee

145 ❑ Oct 1967 Cover: 0.12 **NM** value: **28.00**
Circ: Statement: **298,219** • **CGC:** 12 graded, best 9.8
Abandoned On Earth; The End • Tales of Asgard back-up story **A:** Jack Kirby; Stan Lee **W:** Jack Kirby; Stan Lee

146 ❑ Oct 1967 Cover: 0.12 **NM** value: **28.00**
Circ: Statement: **298,219** • **CGC:** 14 graded, best 9.6
If The Thunder Be Gone; The Origin of the Incomparable Inhumans • Origins of the Inhumans backup story **A:** Jack Kirby; Stan Lee **W:** Jack Kirby; Stan Lee ★ Origin of Inhumans. ★ Appearance of Ringmaster, Circus of Crime.

147 ❑ Dec 1967 Cover: 0.12 **NM** value: **28.00**
Circ: Statement: **298,219** • **CGC:** 11 graded, best 9.8
The Wrath of Odin; The Reason Why • Origins of the Inhumans backup story **A:** Jack Kirby; Stan Lee **W:** Jack Kirby; Stan Lee ★ Origin of Inhumans.

148 ❑ Jan 1968 Cover: 0.12 **NM** value: **28.00**
Circ: Statement: **295,371** • **CGC:** 14 graded, best 9.8
Let There Be Chaos; And Finally: Black Bolt • Origins of the Inhumans backup story **A:** Jack Kirby; Stan Lee **W:** Jack Kirby; Stan Lee ★ Origin of The Wrecker III, Black Bolt. ★ 1st Appearance of The Wrecker III.

149 ❑ Feb 1968 Cover: 0.12 **NM** value: **28.00**
Circ: Statement: **295,371** • **CGC:** 15 graded, best 9.6
When Falls a Hero; Silence or Death • Origins of the Inhumans backup story **A:** Jack Kirby; Stan Lee **W:** Jack Kirby; Stan Lee ★ Origin of Maximus, Medusa, Black Bolt.

150 ❑ Mar 1968 Cover: 0.12 **NM** value: **28.00**
Circ: Statement: **295,371** • **CGC:** 10 graded, best 9.6
Even in Death; Triton • Origins of the Inhumans backup story; Has 1967 Statement, filed 10/1/67; avg print run 497,708; avg sales 296,719; avg subs 1,500; avg total paid 289,219; samples 95; max existent 298,314; 40% of run returned **A:** Jack Kirby; Stan Lee **W:** Jack Kirby; Stan Lee ★ Appearance of Inhumans.

151 ❑ Apr 1968 Cover: 0.12 **NM** value: **28.00**
Circ: Statement: **295,371** • **CGC:** 8 graded, best 9.4
To Rise Again; Inhuman at Large • Origins of the Inhumans backup story **A:** Jack Kirby; Stan Lee **W:** Jack Kirby; Stan Lee ★ Appearance of Inhumans.

152 ❑ May 1968 Cover: 0.12 **NM** value: **28.00**
Circ: Statement: **295,371** • **CGC:** 18 graded, best 9.6
The Dilemma of Dr. Blake; While the City Sleeps • Origins of the Inhumans backup story **A:** Jack Kirby; Stan Lee **W:** Jack Kirby; Stan Lee

153 ❑ Jun 1968 Cover: 0.12 **NM** value: **28.00**
Circ: Statement: **295,371** • **CGC:** 12 graded, best 9.6
But Dr. Blake Can Die **A:** Jack Kirby; Stan Lee **W:** Jack Kirby; Stan Lee

154 ❑ Jul 1968 Cover: 0.12 **NM** value: **28.00**
Circ: Statement: **295,371** • **CGC:** 20 graded, best 9.8
To Wake the Mangog **A:** Jack Kirby; Stan Lee **W:** Jack Kirby; Stan Lee ★ Versus Mangog.

155 ❑ Aug 1968 Cover: 0.12 **NM** value: **28.00**
Circ: Statement: **295,371** • **CGC:** 19 graded, best 9.8
Now Ends the Universe **A:** Jack Kirby; Stan Lee **W:** Jack Kirby; Stan Lee

156 ❑ Sep 1968 Cover: 0.12 **NM** value: **28.00**
Circ: Statement: **295,371** • **CGC:** 39 graded, best 10.0
The Hammer and the Holocaust **A:** Jack Kirby; Stan Lee **W:** Jack Kirby; Stan Lee

157 ❑ Oct 1968 Cover: 0.12 **NM** value: **28.00**
Circ: Statement: **295,371** • **CGC:** 13 graded, best 9.6
Behind Him…Ragnarok! **A:** Jack Kirby; Stan Lee **W:** Jack Kirby; Stan Lee

158 ❑ Nov 1968 Cover: 0.12 **NM** value: **55.00**
Circ: Statement: **295,371** • **CGC:** 26 graded, best 9.6
The Way it Was **A:** Jack Kirby; Stan Lee **W:** Jack Kirby; Stan Lee ★ Origin of Don Blake, Thor.

159 ❑ Dec 1968 Cover: 0.12 **NM** value: **28.00**
Circ: Statement: **295,371** • **CGC:** 10 graded, best 9.6
The Answer at Last **A:** Jack Kirby; Stan Lee

160 ❑ Jan 1969 Cover: 0.12 **NM** value: **28.00**
Circ: Statement: **266,368** • **CGC:** 4 graded, best 9.4
And Now Galactus! • Galactus **A:** Jack Kirby; Stan Lee ★ Versus Galactus.

161 ❑ Feb 1969 Cover: 0.12 **NM** value: **18.00**
Circ: Statement: **266,368** • **CGC:** 6 graded, best 9.6
Shall A God Prevail? **A:** Jack Kirby; Stan Lee ★ Versus Galactus.

162 ❑ Mar 1969 Cover: 0.12 **NM** value: **32.00**
Circ: Statement: **266,368** • **CGC:** 8 graded, best 9.6
Galactus Is Born! • Has 1968 Statement, filed 10/1/68; avg print run 470,600; avg sales 293,843; avg subs 1,528X; avg total paid 295,371; samples 400; max existent 295,771; 37% of run returned **A:** Jack Kirby; Stan Lee ★ Origin of Galactus.

163 ❑ Apr 1969 Cover: 0.12 **NM** value: **18.00**
Circ: Statement: **266,368** • **CGC:** 5 graded, best 9.4
Where Dwell the Demons **A:** Jack Kirby; Stan Lee

164 ❑ May 1969 Cover: 0.12 **NM** value: **18.00**
Circ: Statement: **266,368** • **CGC:** 7 graded, best 9.6
Lest Mankind Fall! **A:** Jack Kirby; Stan Lee

165 ❑ Jun 1969 Cover: 0.15 **NM** value: **30.00**
Circ: Statement: **266,368** • **CGC:** 14 graded, best 9.6
Him • Warlock **A:** Jack Kirby; Stan Lee ★ Appearance of Him (Warlock).

166 ❑ Jul 1969 Cover: 0.15 **NM** value: **25.00**
Circ: Statement: **266,368** • **CGC:** 10 graded, best 9.6
A God Berserk **A:** Jack Kirby; Stan Lee ★ Appearance of Him (Warlock).

167 ❑ Aug 1969 Cover: 0.15 **NM** value: **15.00**
Circ: Statement: **266,368** • **CGC:** 5 graded, best 9.6
This World Renounced **A:** Jack Kirby; Stan Lee ★ Appearance of Sif.

168 ❑ Sep 1969 Cover: 0.15 **NM** value: **30.00**
Circ: Statement: **266,368** • **CGC:** 4 graded, best 9.2
Galactus Found **A:** Jack Kirby; Stan Lee ★ Origin of Galactus.

169 ❑ Oct 1969 Cover: 0.15 **NM** value: **30.00**
Circ: Statement: **266,368** • **CGC:** 6 graded, best 9.2
The Aawesome Answer • Origin of Galactus **A:** Jack Kirby; Stan Lee ★ Origin of Galactus.

170 ❑ Nov 1969 Cover: 0.15 **NM** value: **15.00**
Circ: Statement: **266,368** • **CGC:** 8 graded, best 9.4
The Thunder God and the Termal Man

171 ❑ Dec 1969 Cover: 0.15 **NM** value: **15.00**
Circ: Statement: **266,368** • **CGC:** 5 graded, best 9.6
The Wrath of the Wrecker

172 ❑ Jan 1970 Cover: 0.15 **NM** value: **15.00**
Circ: Statement: **232,058** • **CGC:** 5 graded, best 9.8
The Immortal and the Mind-Slave

173 ❑ Feb 1970 Cover: 0.15 **NM** value: **15.00**
Circ: Statement: **232,058** • **CGC:** 4 graded, best 9.4
Ulik Unleashed

174 ❑ Mar 1970 Cover: 0.15 **NM** value: **15.00**
Circ: Statement: **232,058** • **CGC:** 4 graded, best 9.4
The Carnage of the Crypto-Man • Has 1969 Statement, filed 10/1/69; avg print run 446,828; avg sales 264,897; avg subs 1,471; avg total paid 266,368; samples 110; max existent 266,478; 40% of run returned

175 ❑ Apr 1970 Cover: 0.15 **NM** value: **15.00**
Circ: Statement: **232,058** • **CGC:** 4 graded, best 9.6
The Fall of Asgard!

176 ❑ May 1970 Cover: 0.15 **NM** value: **15.00**
Circ: Statement: **232,058** • **CGC:** 5 graded, best 9.4
Inferno! ★ Versus Surtur the Fire Demon.

177 ❑ Jun 1970 Cover: 0.15 **NM** value: **15.00**
Circ: Statement: **232,058** • **CGC:** 3 graded, best 9.4
To End In Flames!

178 ❑ Jul 1970 Cover: 0.15 **NM** value: **15.00**
Circ: Statement: **232,058** • **CGC:** 3 graded, best 9.6
No More Thunder God!

179 ❑ Aug 1970 Cover: 0.15 **NM** value: **15.00**
Circ: Statement: **232,058** • **CGC:** 3 graded, best 9.2
No More the Thunder God

180 ❑ Sep 1970 Cover: 0.15 **NM** value: **13.00**
Circ: Statement: **232,058** • **CGC:** 6 graded, best 9.6
When Gods Go Mad **A:** Neal Adams ★ Versus Mephisto.

181 ❑ Oct 1970 Cover: 0.15 **NM** value: **13.00**
Circ: Statement: **232,058** • **CGC:** 4 graded, best 9.4
One God Must Fall **A:** Neal Adams ★ Versus Mephisto. ★ Versus Loki.

182 ❑ Nov 1970 Cover: 0.15 **NM** value: **6.00**
Circ: Statement: **232,058** • **CGC:** 3 graded, best 9.8
The Prisoner, the Power and Dr. Doom

183 ❑ Dec 1970 Cover: 0.15 **NM** value: **6.00**
Circ: Statement: **232,058** • **CGC:** 3 graded, best 9.4
Trapped in Doomsland

184 ❑ Jan 1971 Cover: 0.15 **NM** value: **6.00**
Circ: Statement: **229,492** • **CGC:** 5 graded, best 9.4
The World Beyond ★ 1st Appearance of Infinity (as force).

185 ❑ Feb 1971 Cover: 0.15 **NM** value: **6.00**
Circ: Statement: **229,492** • **CGC:** 4 graded, best 9.4
In the Grip of Infinity

186 ❑ Mar 1971 Cover: 0.15 **NM** value: **6.00**
Circ: Statement: **229,492** • **CGC:** 4 graded, best 9.4
Worlds at War • Has 1970 Statement, filed 10/1/70; avg print run 412,505; avg sales 230,928; avg subs 1,130; avg total paid 232,058; samples 110; max existent 232,168; 44% of run returned

187 ❑ Apr 1971 Cover: 0.15 **NM** value: **6.00**
Circ: Statement: **229,492** • **CGC:** 4 graded, best 9.6
The World Is Lost

188 ❑ May 1971 Cover: 0.15 **NM** value: **6.00**
Circ: Statement: **229,492** • **CGC:** 5 graded, best 9.6
The End of Infinity

189 ❑ Jun 1971 Cover: 0.15 **NM** value: **6.00**
Circ: Statement: **229,492** • **CGC:** 3 graded, best 9.4
The Icy Touch of Death

190 ❑ Jul 1971 Cover: 0.15 **NM** value: **6.00**
Circ: Statement: **229,492** • **CGC:** 2 graded, best 9.2
And So, To Die

191 ❑ Aug 1971 Cover: 0.15 **NM** value: **6.00**
Circ: Statement: **229,492** • **CGC:** 2 graded, best 9.0
A Time of Evil

192 ❑ Sep 1971 Cover: 0.15 **NM** value: **6.00**
Circ: Statement: **229,492** • **CGC:** 2 graded, best 9.2
Conflagration

193 ❑ Oct 1971 Cover: 0.25 **NM** value: **35.00**
Circ: Statement: **229,492** • **CGC:** 16 graded, best 9.6
What Power Unleashed? **A:** John Buscema; Sal Buscema ★ Appearance of Silver Surfer.

194 ❑ Nov 1971 Cover: 0.20 **NM** value: **4.00**
Circ: Statement: **229,492**
This Fatal Fury

195 ❑ Dec 1971 Cover: 0.20 **NM** value: **4.00**
Circ: Statement: **229,492** • **CGC:** 1 graded, best 9.4
In the Shadow of Mangog

196 ❑ Jan 1972 Cover: 0.20 **NM** value: **4.00**
Circ: Statement: **207,179** • **CGC:** 1 graded, best 9.4
Within the Realm of Kartag

197 ❑ Feb 1972 Cover: 0.20 **NM** value: **4.00**
Circ: Statement: **207,179**
The Well at the Edge of the World

198 ❑ Mar 1972 Cover: 0.20 **NM** value: **4.00**
Circ: Statement: **207,179** • **CGC:** 1 graded, best 9.6
And Odin Dies

199 ❑ Apr 1972 Cover: 0.20 **NM** value: **4.00**
Circ: Statement: **207,179** • **CGC:** 2 graded, best 9.2

Other grades: Multiply prices above by **1.5 for Mint • 2/3 for Very Fine • 1/3 for Fine • 1/5 for Very Good • 1/8 for Good**

📖 If This Be Death • Has 1971 Statement, filed 9/23/71; avg print run 373,623; avg sales 228,412; avg subs 1,080; avg total paid 229,492; samples 0; office use 2,140; max existent 231,632; 38% of run returned
200 ❑ Jun 1972 Cover: 0.20 **NM** value: **8.00**
Circ: Statement: **207,179** • **CGC:** 5 graded, best 9.6
📖 Beware, If This Be Ragnarok • Ragnarok **A:** John Buscema
201 ❑ Jul 1972 Cover: 0.20 **NM** value: **3.00**
Circ: Statement: **207,179**
📖 Resurrection **A:** John Buscema
202 ❑ Aug 1972 Cover: 0.20 **NM** value: **3.00**
Circ: Statement: **207,179**
📖 And None Dare Stand 'Gainst Ego-Prime **A:** John Buscema
203 ❑ Sep 1972 Cover: 0.20 **NM** value: **3.00**
Circ: Statement: **207,179**
📖 They Walk Like Gods **A:** John Buscema
204 ❑ Oct 1972 Cover: 0.20 **NM** value: **3.00**
Circ: Statement: **207,179**
📖 Exiled on Earth **A:** John Buscema
205 ❑ Nov 1972 Cover: 0.20 **NM** value: **3.00**
Circ: Statement: **207,179**
📖 A World Gone Mad! **A:** John Buscema
206 ❑ Dec 1972 Cover: 0.20 **NM** value: **3.00**
Circ: Statement: **207,179**
📖 Rebirth **A:** John Buscema
207 ❑ Jan 1973 Cover: 0.20 **NM** value: **3.00**
Circ: Statement: **195,239**
📖 Firesword **A:** John Buscema
208 ❑ Feb 1973 Cover: 0.20 **NM** value: **3.00**
Circ: Statement: **195,239**
📖 The Fourth-Dimensional Man **A:** John Buscema
209 ❑ Mar 1973 Cover: 0.20 **NM** value: **3.00**
Circ: Statement: **195,239**
📖 Warriors in the Night • Has 1972 Statement, filed 9/21/72; avg print run 374,159; avg sales 205,488; avg subs 1,691; avg total paid 207,179; samples 110; office use 1,566; max existent 208,855; 44% of run returned **A:** John Buscema ★ 1st Appearance of Ultimus.
210 ❑ Apr 1973 Cover: 0.20 **NM** value: **3.00**
Circ: Statement: **195,239**
📖 The Hammer and the Hellfire **A:** John Buscema
211 ❑ May 1973 Cover: 0.20 **NM** value: **3.00**
Circ: Statement: **195,239**
📖 The End of the Battle **A:** John Buscema
212 ❑ Jun 1973 Cover: 0.20 **NM** value: **3.00**
Circ: Statement: **195,239**
📖 Journey to the Golden Star **A:** John Buscema
213 ❑ Jul 1973 Cover: 0.20 **NM** value: **3.00**
Circ: Statement: **195,239**
📖 The Demon Brigade **A:** John Buscema
214 ❑ Aug 1973 Cover: 0.20 **NM** value: **3.00**
Circ: Statement: **195,239**
📖 Into the Dark Nebula
215 ❑ Sep 1973 Cover: 0.20 **NM** value: **3.00**
Circ: Statement: **195,239**
📖 The God in the Jewel
216 ❑ Oct 1973 Cover: 0.20 **NM** value: **3.00**
Circ: Statement: **195,239** • **CGC:** 1 graded, best 9.4
📖 Where Chaos Rules
217 ❑ Nov 1973 Cover: 0.20 **NM** value: **3.00**
Circ: Statement: **195,239**
📖 All Swords Against Them
218 ❑ Dec 1973 Cover: 0.20 **NM** value: **3.00**
Circ: Statement: **195,239**
📖 WherePass the Black Stars, There Also Passes Death
219 ❑ Jan 1974 Cover: 0.20 **NM** value: **3.00**
Circ: Statement: **205,838**
📖 A Galaxy Consumed
220 ❑ Feb 1974 Cover: 0.20 **NM** value: **3.00**
Circ: Statement: **205,838**
📖 Behold the Land of Doom
221 ❑ Mar 1974 Cover: 0.20 **NM** value: **3.00**
Circ: Statement: **205,838**
📖 Hercules Enraged
222 ❑ Apr 1974 Cover: 0.20 **NM** value: **3.00**
Circ: Statement: **205,838**
📖 Before the Gates of Hell
223 ❑ May 1974 Cover: 0.25 **NM** value: **3.00**
Circ: Statement: **205,838** • **CGC:** 2 graded, best 9.4
📖 Hellfire Across the World • Has 1973 Statement; avg sales 194,013; avg subs 1,226; avg total paid 195,239; max existent 195,239
224 ❑ Jun 1974 Cover: 0.25 **NM** value: **3.00**
Circ: Statement: **205,838**
📖 No One Can Stop the Destroyer
225 ❑ Jul 1974 Cover: 0.25 **NM** value: **4.00**
Circ: Statement: **205,838** • **CGC:** 2 graded, best 9.2
📖 The Coming of the Firelord ★ 1st Appearance of Firelord.
226 ❑ Aug 1974 Cover: 0.25 **NM** value: **2.50**
Circ: Statement: **205,838**
📖 The Battle Beyond
227 ❑ Sep 1974 Cover: 0.25 **NM** value: **2.50**
Circ: Statement: **205,838** • **CGC:** 1 graded, best 9.0
📖 In Search of Ego
228 ❑ Oct 1974 Cover: 0.25 **NM** value: **2.50**
Circ: Statement: **205,838** • **CGC:** 1 graded, best 9.2
📖 Ego: Beginning and End
229 ❑ Nov 1974 Cover: 0.25 **NM** value: **2.50**
Circ: Statement: **205,838**
📖 Where Darkness Dwells, Dwell I
230 ❑ Dec 1974 Cover: 0.25 **NM** value: **2.50**
Circ: Statement: **205,838**
📖 The Sky Above, the Pits Below
231 ❑ Jan 1975 Cover: 0.25 **NM** value: **2.50**
Circ: Statement: **197,216**
📖 A Spectre From the Past
232 ❑ Feb 1975 Cover: 0.25 **NM** value: **2.50**
Circ: Statement: **197,216**
📖 Lo, the Raging Battle
233 ❑ Mar 1975 Cover: 0.25 **NM** value: **2.50**
Circ: Statement: **197,216**
📖 Midgard Aflame
234 ❑ Apr 1975 Cover: 0.25 **NM** value: **2.50**
Circ: Statement: **197,216** • **CGC:** 1 graded, best 9.6
📖 O, Bitter Victory; The Assault; Decision at Dawn; Sixty Seconds to Die
235 ❑ May 1975 Cover: 0.25 **NM** value: **2.50**
Circ: Statement: **197,216**
📖 Who Lurks Beyond the Labyrinth; A Time of Waiting; The Man Behind the Maze; The Pathos and the Power • Has 1974 Statement; avg print run 387,083; avg sales 204,723; avg subs 1,115; avg total paid 205,838; max existent 205,838; 0% of run returned ★ 1st Appearance of The Possessor.
236 ❑ Jun 1975 Cover: 0.25 **NM** value: **2.50**
Circ: Statement: **197,216** • **CGC:** 1 graded, best 9.0
📖 One Life to Give; Crisis; Lo, This Hidden Mystery; Resurrection
237 ❑ Jul 1975 Cover: 0.25 **NM** value: **2.50**
Circ: Statement: **197,216**
📖 Ulik Unchained; Those Who Watch; Interlude; Night War
238 ❑ Aug 1975 Cover: 0.25 **NM** value: **2.50**
Circ: Statement: **197,216**
📖 Night of the Troll; A River at the Heart of the World; The Song of Battle; The Troll Supreme **A:** John Buscema; Joe Sinnott
239 ❑ Sep 1975 Cover: 0.25 **NM** value: **2.50**
Circ: Statement: **197,216**
📖 Time-Quake ★ 1st Appearance of Osiris, Horus.
240 ❑ Oct 1975 Cover: 0.25 **NM** value: **2.50**
Circ: Statement: **197,216**
📖 When the Gods Make War ★ 1st Appearance of Isis (Marvel), Seth.
241 ❑ Nov 1975 Cover: 0.25 **NM** value: **2.50**
Circ: Statement: **197,216**
📖 The Death-Ship Sails the Stars **A:** John Buscema
242 ❑ Dec 1975 Cover: 0.25 **NM** value: **2.50**
Circ: Statement: **197,216**
A: John Buscema
243 ❑ Jan 1976 Cover: 0.25 **NM** value: **2.50**
Circ: Statement: **172,389**
A: John Buscema
244 ❑ Feb 1976 Cover: 0.25 **NM** value: **2.50**
Circ: Statement: **172,389**
A: John Buscema
245 ❑ Mar 1976 Cover: 0.25 **NM** value: **2.50**
Circ: Statement: **172,389**
A: John Buscema
246 ❑ Apr 1976 Cover: 0.25 **NM** value: **2.50**
Circ: Statement: **172,389** • **CGC:** 2 graded, best 9.4
📖 The Fury of the Firelord • Has 1975 Statement; avg print run 388,446; avg sales 195,606; avg subs 1,606; avg total paid 197,216; samples 0; office use 3,081; max existent 200,293; 48% of run returned **A:** John Buscema ★ Appearance of Firelord.
247 ❑ May 1976 Cover: 0.25 **NM** value: **2.50**
Circ: Statement: **172,389** • **CGC:** 1 graded, best 8.0
📖 The Flame and the Hammer **A:** John Buscema
248 ❑ Jun 1976 Cover: 0.25 **NM** value: **2.50**
Circ: Statement: **172,389**
📖 There Shall Come a Revolution **A:** John Buscema
249 ❑ Jul 1976 Cover: 0.25 **NM** value: **2.50**
Circ: Statement: **172,389**
📖 The Throne and the Fury • Sif trades places with Jane **A:** John Buscema
250 ❑ Aug 1976 Cover: 0.25 **NM** value: **2.50**
Circ: Statement: **172,389** • **CGC:** 2 graded, best 9.4
📖 If Asgard Should Perish **A:** John Buscema
251 ❑ Sep 1976 Cover: 0.30 **NM** value: **2.50**
Circ: Statement: **172,389**
📖 To Hela and Back
252 ❑ Oct 1976 Cover: 0.30 **NM** value: **2.50**
Circ: Statement: **172,389** • **CGC:** 1 graded, best 9.4
📖 A Dragon at the Gates
253 ❑ Nov 1976 Cover: 0.30 **NM** value: **2.50**
Circ: Statement: **172,389** • **CGC:** 2 graded, best 9.4
📖 Chaos in the Kingdom of the Trolls
254 ❑ Dec 1976 Cover: 0.30 **NM** value: **2.50**
Circ: Statement: **172,389** • **CGC:** 2 graded, best 9.4
📖 The Answer at Last • Reprinted from Thor #159
255 ❑ Jan 1977 Cover: 0.30 **NM** value: **2.50**
Circ: Statement: **158,985** • **CGC:** 1 graded, best 9.4
📖 Lo, the Quest Begins
256 ❑ Feb 1977 Cover: 0.30 **NM** value: **2.50**
Circ: Statement: **158,985** • **CGC:** 1 graded, best 9.4
257 ❑ Mar 1977 Cover: 0.30 **NM** value: **2.50**
Circ: Statement: **158,985**
• Has 1976 Statement; avg total paid circ 172,389
258 ❑ Apr 1977 Cover: 0.30 **NM** value: **2.50**
Circ: Statement: **158,985** • **CGC:** 2 graded, best 9.4
259 ❑ May 1977 Cover: 0.30 **NM** value: **2.50**
Circ: Statement: **158,985**
📖 Escape Into Oblivion
260 ❑ Jun 1977 Cover: 0.30 **NM** value: **2.50**
Circ: Statement: **158,985** • **CGC:** 1 graded, best 8.0
A: Walt Simonson
261 ❑ Jul 1977 Cover: 0.30 **NM** value: **2.50**
Circ: Statement: **158,985**
A: Walt Simonson
262 ❑ Aug 1977 Cover: 0.30 **NM** value: **2.50**
Circ: Statement: **158,985**
📖 Even An Immortal Can Die! **A:** Tony DeZuniga; Walt Simonson **W:** Len Wein
263 ❑ Sep 1977 Cover: 0.30 **NM** value: **2.50**
Circ: Statement: **158,985**
📖 Holocaust and Homecoming **A:** Walt Simonson
264 ❑ Oct 1977 Cover: 0.30 **NM** value: **2.50**
Circ: Statement: **158,985**
A: Walt Simonson
265 ❑ Nov 1977 Cover: 0.35 **NM** value: **2.50**
Circ: Statement: **158,985**
A: Walt Simonson
266 ❑ Dec 1977 Cover: 0.35 **NM** value: **2.50**
Circ: Statement: **158,985**
A: Walt Simonson
267 ❑ Jan 1978 Cover: 0.35 **NM** value: **2.50**
Circ: Statement: **135,748**
A: Walt Simonson
268 ❑ Feb 1978 Cover: 0.35 **NM** value: **2.50**
Circ: Statement: **135,748**
A: Walt Simonson
269 ❑ Mar 1978 Cover: 0.35 **NM** value: **2.50**
Circ: Statement: **135,748**
• Has 1977 Statement; avg print run 364,827; avg sales 155,773; avg subs 3,212; avg total paid 158,985; samples 150; office use 1,940X; max existent 161,075; 56% of run returned **A:** Walt Simonson
270 ❑ Apr 1978 Cover: 0.35 **NM** value: **2.50**
Circ: Statement: **135,748**
A: Walt Simonson
271 ❑ May 1978 Cover: 0.35 **NM** value: **2.50**
Circ: Statement: **135,748**
A: Walt Simonson ★ Appearance of Iron Man.
272 ❑ Jun 1978 Cover: 0.35 **NM** value: **2.50**
Circ: Statement: **135,748**
A: Walt Simonson
273 ❑ Jul 1978 Cover: 0.35 **NM** value: **2.50**
Circ: Statement: **135,748**
★ 1st Appearance of Red Norvell.
274 ❑ Aug 1978 Cover: 0.35 **NM** value: **2.50**
Circ: Statement: **135,748**
★ 1st Appearance of Sigyn, Frigga. ★ Death of Balder.
275 ❑ Sep 1978 Cover: 0.35 **NM** value: **2.50**
Circ: Statement: **135,748**
★ 1st Appearance of Hermod.
276 ❑ Oct 1978 Cover: 0.35 **NM** value: **2.50**
Circ: Statement: **135,748**
• Red Norvell named Thor
277 ❑ Nov 1978 Cover: 0.35 **NM** value: **2.50**
Circ: Statement: **135,748**
278 ❑ Dec 1978 Cover: 0.35 **NM** value: **2.50**
Circ: Statement: **135,748**
279 ❑ Jan 1979 Cover: 0.35 **NM** value: **2.50**
Circ: Statement: **179,915**
280 ❑ Feb 1979 Cover: 0.35 **NM** value: **2.50**
Circ: Statement: **179,915**
281 ❑ Mar 1979 Cover: 0.35 **NM** value: **2.00**
Circ: Statement: **179,915**
• Has 1978 Statement; avg print run 346,479; avg sales 128,916; avg subs 6,832; avg total paid 135,748; samples 210; office use 1,250; max existent 137,208; 60% of run returned ★ Appearance of Immortus.
282 ❑ Apr 1979 Cover: 0.35 **NM** value: **2.00**
Circ: Statement: **179,915**
283 ❑ May 1979 Cover: 0.40 **NM** value: **2.00**
Circ: Statement: **179,915**
★ Appearance of Celestials.
284 ❑ Jun 1979 Cover: 0.40 **NM** value: **2.00**
Circ: Statement: **179,915**
★ Appearance of Externals.
285 ❑ Jul 1979 Cover: 0.40 **NM** value: **2.00**
Circ: Statement: **179,915**
286 ❑ Aug 1979 Cover: 0.40 **NM** value: **2.00**
Circ: Statement: **179,915**
287 ❑ Sep 1979 Cover: 0.40 **NM** value: **2.00**
Circ: Statement: **179,915** • **CGC:** 1 graded, best 9.8
288 ❑ Oct 1979 Cover: 0.40 **NM** value: **2.00**
Circ: Statement: **179,915** • **CGC:** 1 graded, best 9.6
289 ❑ Nov 1979 Cover: 0.40 **NM** value: **2.00**
Circ: Statement: **179,915**
290 ❑ Dec 1979 Cover: 0.40 **NM** value: **2.00**
Circ: Statement: **179,915**
★ Versus El Toro Rojo.
291 ❑ Jan 1980 Cover: 0.40 **NM** value: **2.00**
Circ: Statement: **179,842**
292 ❑ Feb 1980 Cover: 0.40 **NM** value: **2.00**
Circ: Statement: **179,842**
293 ❑ Mar 1980 Cover: 0.40 **NM** value: **2.00**
Circ: Statement: **179,842**
• Has 1979 Statement; avg print run 360,580; avg sales 174,296; avg subs 174,296; avg total paid 5,619; samples 500; office use 1,583; max existent 181,998; 51% of run returned
294 ❑ Apr 1980 Cover: 0.40 **NM** value: **2.00**
Circ: Statement: **179,842**
A: Keith Pollard ★ Origin of Asgard, Odin. ★ 1st Appearance of Frey.
295 ❑ May 1980 Cover: 0.40 **NM** value: **2.00**
Circ: Statement: **179,842**
A: Keith Pollard
296 ❑ Jun 1980 Cover: 0.40 **NM** value: **2.00**
Circ: Statement: **179,842**
A: Keith Pollard
297 ❑ Jul 1980 Cover: 0.40 **NM** value: **2.00**
Circ: Statement: **179,842**
• Thor as Siegfried **A:** Keith Pollard
298 ❑ Aug 1980 Cover: 0.40 **NM** value: **2.00**
Circ: Statement: **179,842**
A: Keith Pollard
299 ❑ Sep 1980 Cover: 0.50 **NM** value: **2.00**
Circ: Statement: **179,842**
A: Keith Pollard
300 ❑ Oct 1980 Cover: 0.75 **NM** value: **5.00**
Circ: Statement: **179,842** • **CGC:** 1 graded, best 9.6
• giant; Balder revived **A:** Keith Pollard ★ Origin of The Destroyer, Odin. ★ Death of Zuras (physical death).
301 ❑ Nov 1980 Cover: 0.50 **NM** value: **2.00**
Circ: Statement: **179,842**
• Thor meets other pantheons
302 ❑ Dec 1980 Cover: 0.50 **NM** value: **2.00**
Circ: Statement: **179,842**
303 ❑ Jan 1981 Cover: 0.50 **NM** value: **2.00**
Circ: Statement: **171,000**

CGC-graded: Multiply prices above by **33 for 9.9 M • 16 for 9.8 NM/M • 7 for 9.6 NM+ • 5 for 9.4 NM • 2.5 for 9.2 NM- • 1.5 for 9.0 VF/NM**

304 ☐ Feb 1981 Cover: 0.50 **NM** value: **2.00**
Circ: Statement: **171,000**
★ Versus Wrecking Crew.
305 ☐ Mar 1981 Cover: 0.50 **NM** value: **2.00**
Circ: Statement: **171,000** • **CGC:** 1 graded, best 9.4
🕮 Hark, The Herald Angel Lives! **A:** Keith Pollard; Chic Stone **W:** Ralph Macchio; Mark Gruenwald
306 ☐ Apr 1981 Cover: 0.50 **NM** value: **2.00**
Circ: Statement: **171,000**
🕮 Fury Of The Firelord! • Has 1980 Statement; avg print run 354,041; avg sales 173,831; avg subs 6,011; avg total paid 179,842; samples 590; office use 2,935; max existent 183,367; 48% of run returned **A:** Keith Pollard **W:** Ralph Macchio; Mark Gruenwald ★ Origin of Firelord. ★ 1st Appearance of Air-Walker (real form). ★ Death of Air-Walker (real form).
307 ☐ May 1981 Cover: 0.50 **NM** value: **2.00**
Circ: Statement: **171,000**
🕮 Wings In The Night! **A:** Alan Kupperberg **W:** Ralph Macchio; Mark Gruenwald
308 ☐ Jun 1981 Cover: 0.50 **NM** value: **2.00**
Circ: Statement: **171,000**
🕮 The Snow Giant **A:** Keith Pollard **W:** Doug Moench
309 ☐ Jul 1981 Cover: 0.50 **NM** value: **2.00**
Circ: Statement: **171,000**
🕮 Beware The Bombardiers! **A:** Rick Leonardi **W:** Bill Mantlo
310 ☐ Aug 1981 Cover: 0.50 **NM** value: **2.00**
Circ: Statement: **171,000**
★ Versus Mephisto.
311 ☐ Sep 1981 Cover: 0.50 **NM** value: **2.00**
Circ: Statement: **171,000**
312 ☐ Oct 1981 Cover: 0.50 **NM** value: **2.00**
Circ: Statement: **171,000**
🕮 The Judgement Of Tyr **A:** Keith Pollard **W:** Doug Moench ★ Versus Tyr.
313 ☐ Nov 1981 Cover: 0.50 **NM** value: **2.00**
Circ: Statement: **171,000**
314 ☐ Dec 1981 Cover: 0.50 **NM** value: **2.00**
Circ: Statement: **171,000**
🕮 Acts Of Destruction **A:** Keith Pollard **W:** Doug Moench ★ 1st Appearance of Shawna Lynde.
315 ☐ Jan 1982 Cover: 0.60 **NM** value: **2.00**
Circ: Statement: **156,391**
🕮 The Thunderbolt God And The Bi-Beast **A:** Keith Pollard **W:** Doug Moench
316 ☐ Feb 1982 Cover: 0.60 **NM** value: **2.00**
Circ: Statement: **156,391**
317 ☐ Mar 1982 Cover: 0.60 **NM** value: **2.00**
Circ: Statement: **156,391**
🕮 Chaos At Canaveral **A:** Keith Pollard **W:** Doug Moench
318 ☐ Apr 1982 Cover: 0.60 **NM** value: **2.00**
Circ: Statement: **156,391**
🕮 A Kingdom Lost **A:** Gil Kane **W:** Doug Moench
319 ☐ May 1982 Cover: 0.60 **NM** value: **2.00**
Circ: Statement: **156,391**
🕮 The Zaniac Craves Blood! **A:** Keith Pollard **W:** Doug Moench
320 ☐ Jun 1982 Cover: 0.60 **NM** value: **2.00**
Circ: Statement: **156,391**
🕮 Blake's Menagerie **A:** Keith Pollard **W:** Doug Moench
321 ☐ Jul 1982 Cover: 0.60 **NM** value: **2.00**
Circ: Statement: **156,391**
🕮 Magick's Menace! **A:** Alan Kupperberg **W:** Doug Moench
322 ☐ Aug 1982 Cover: 0.60 **NM** value: **2.00**
Circ: Statement: **156,391**
🕮 The Wrath And The Power! **A:** Alan Kupperberg **W:** Doug Moench ★ Death of Darkoth.
323 ☐ Sep 1982 Cover: 0.60 **NM** value: **2.00**
Circ: Statement: **156,391**
324 ☐ Oct 1982 Cover: 0.60 **NM** value: **2.00**
Circ: Statement: **156,391**
325 ☐ Nov 1982 Cover: 0.60 **NM** value: **2.00**
Circ: Statement: **156,391**
326 ☐ Dec 1982 Cover: 0.60 **NM** value: **2.00**
Circ: Statement: **156,391**
A: Brent Anderson(cover)
327 ☐ Jan 1983 Cover: 0.60 **NM** value: **2.00**
Circ: Statement: **147,735**
328 ☐ Feb 1983 Cover: 0.60 **NM** value: **2.00**
Circ: Statement: **147,735**
★ 1st Appearance of Megatak.
329 ☐ Mar 1983 Cover: 0.60 **NM** value: **2.00**
Circ: Statement: **147,735**
330 ☐ Apr 1983 Cover: 0.60 **NM** value: **2.00**
Circ: Statement: **147,735**
🕮 The Coming Of The Crusader! • Has 1982 Statement, filed 10/1/82; avg print run 325,628; avg sales 147,623; avg subs 8,768; avg total paid 156,391; max existent 156,391; 51% of run returned **A:** Bob Hall **W:** Alan Zelentz ★ Origin of Crusader II (Arthur Blackwood). ★ 1st Appearance of Crusader II (Arthur Blackwood).
331 ☐ May 1983 Cover: 0.60 **NM** value: **2.00**
Circ: Statement: **147,735**
332 ☐ Jun 1983 Cover: 0.60 **NM** value: **2.00**
Circ: Statement: **147,735**
333 ☐ Jul 1983 Cover: 0.60 **NM** value: **2.00**
Circ: Statement: **147,735**
🕮 ...Like A Bat Out Of Heaven **A:** Mark D. Bright **W:** Alan Zelentz ★ Versus Dracula.
334 ☐ Aug 1983 Cover: 0.60 **NM** value: **2.00**
Circ: Statement: **147,735** • **CGC:** 1 graded, best 9.2
335 ☐ Sep 1983 Cover: 0.60 **NM** value: **2.00**
Circ: Statement: **147,735** • **CGC:** 1 graded, best 9.4
🕮 Runequest's End! **A:** Mark D. Bright **W:** Alan Zelentz ★ 1st Appearance of The Possessor.
336 ☐ Oct 1983 Cover: 0.60 **NM** value: **2.00**
Circ: Statement: **147,735**
🕮 Of Gods And Men **A:** Herb Trimpe **W:** Alan Zelentz
337 ☐ Nov 1983 Cover: 0.60 **NM** value: **4.00**
Circ: Statement: **147,735** • **CGC:** 13 graded, best 9.8
• 1st Simonson Thor **A:** Walt Simonson ★ Origin of Beta Ray Bill. ★ 1st Appearance of Beta Ray Bill.
338 ☐ Dec 1983 Cover: 0.60 **NM** value: **3.00**
Circ: Statement: **147,735** • **CGC:** 2 graded, best 9.8
A: Walt Simonson ★ Appearance of Beta Ray Bill.
339 ☐ Jan 1984 Cover: 0.60 **NM** value: **2.50**
Circ: Statement: **171,290** • **CGC:** 2 graded, best 9.6
A: Walt Simonson ★ 1st Appearance of Lorelei. ★ Appearance of Beta Ray Bill.
340 ☐ Feb 1984 Cover: 0.60 **NM** value: **2.50**
Circ: Statement: **171,290**
A: Walt Simonson ★ Appearance of Beta Ray Bill.
341 ☐ Mar 1984 Cover: 0.60 **NM** value: **2.00**
Circ: Statement: **171,290** • **CGC:** 3 graded, best 9.6
A: Walt Simonson ★ 1st Appearance of Sigurd Jarlson.
342 ☐ Apr 1984 Cover: 0.60 **NM** value: **2.00**
Circ: Statement: **171,290**
A: Walt Simonson **W:** Walt Simonson
343 ☐ May 1984 Cover: 0.60 **NM** value: **2.00**
Circ: Statement: **171,290**
A: Walt Simonson
344 ☐ Jun 1984 Cover: 0.60 **NM** value: **2.00**
Circ: Statement: **171,290**
A: Walt Simonson ★ 1st Appearance of Malekith the Dark Elf.
345 ☐ Jul 1984 Cover: 0.60 **NM** value: **2.00**
Circ: Statement: **171,290**
• Has 1983 Statement, filed 10/1/83; avg print run 310,214; avg sales 138,948; avg subs 8,787; avg total paid 147,735; samples 805; office use 3,268; max existent 151,808; 51% of run returned **A:** Walt Simonson
346 ☐ Aug 1984 Cover: 0.60 **NM** value: **2.00**
Circ: Statement: **171,290**
A: Walt Simonson
347 ☐ Sep 1984 Cover: 0.60 **NM** value: **2.00**
Circ: Statement: **171,290**
A: Walt Simonson ★ 1st Appearance of Algrim.
348 ☐ Oct 1984 Cover: 0.60 **NM** value: **2.00**
Circ: Statement: **171,290**
A: Walt Simonson
349 ☐ Nov 1984 Cover: 0.60 **NM** value: **2.00**
Circ: Statement: **171,290**
A: Walt Simonson ★ Origin of Odin.
350 ☐ Dec 1984 Cover: 0.60 **NM** value: **2.00**
Circ: Statement: **171,290**
A: Walt Simonson ★ Appearance of Beta Ray Bill.
351 ☐ Jan 1985 Cover: 0.60 **NM** value: **2.00**
Circ: Statement: **234,795**
A: Walt Simonson ★ Appearance of Fantastic Four.
352 ☐ Feb 1985 Cover: 0.60 **NM** value: **2.00**
Circ: Statement: **234,795**
A: Walt Simonson ★ Appearance of Fantastic Four, Beta Ray Bill, Avengers.
353 ☐ Mar 1985 Cover: 0.60 **NM** value: **2.00**
Circ: Statement: **234,795**
A: Walt Simonson
354 ☐ Apr 1985 Cover: 0.65 **NM** value: **2.00**
Circ: Statement: **234,795**
• Has 1984 Statement, filed 9/28/84; avg print run 303,055; avg sales 164,041; avg subs 7,247; avg total paid 171,290; samples 190; office use 3,152; max existent 174,630; 42% of run returned **A:** Walt Simonson
355 ☐ May 1985 Cover: 0.65 **NM** value: **2.00**
Circ: Statement: **234,795** CapCity orders: **20,900**
A: Walt Simonson
356 ☐ Jun 1985 Cover: 0.65 **NM** value: **2.00**
Circ: Statement: **234,795** CapCity orders: **20,200**
A: Jackson Guice **W:** Bob Harras
357 ☐ Jul 1985 Cover: 0.65 **NM** value: **2.00**
Circ: Statement: **234,795** CapCity orders: **21,800**
A: Walt Simonson
358 ☐ Aug 1985 Cover: 0.65 **NM** value: **2.00**
Circ: Statement: **234,795** CapCity orders: **21,000**
• Beta Ray Bill vs. Titanium Man **A:** Walt Simonson
359 ☐ Sep 1985 Cover: 0.65 **NM** value: **2.00**
Circ: Statement: **234,795** CapCity orders: **20,900**
A: Walt Simonson ★ Appearance of Loki. ★ Death of Megatak.
360 ☐ Oct 1985 Cover: 0.65 **NM** value: **2.00**
Circ: Statement: **234,795** CapCity orders: **23,600**
A: Walt Simonson
361 ☐ Nov 1985 Cover: 0.65 **NM** value: **2.00**
Circ: Statement: **234,795** CapCity orders: **19,700**
A: Walt Simonson
362 ☐ Dec 1985 Cover: 0.65 **NM** value: **2.00**
Circ: Statement: **234,795** CapCity orders: **19,400**
A: Walt Simonson
363 ☐ Jan 1986 Cover: 0.65 **NM** value: **2.00**
Circ: Statement: **188,474** CapCity orders: **25,500**
🕮 Secret Wars II • Secret Wars II; Thor's face scarred **A:** Walt Simonson
364 ☐ Feb 1986 Cover: 0.75 **NM** value: **2.00**
Circ: Statement: **188,474** CapCity orders: **20,900**
A: Walt Simonson
365 ☐ Mar 1986 Cover: 0.75 **NM** value: **2.00**
Circ: Statement: **188,474** CapCity orders: **20,400**
• Thor turned into frog **A:** Walt Simonson
366 ☐ Apr 1986 Cover: 0.75 **NM** value: **2.00**
Circ: Statement: **188,474** CapCity orders: **21,400**
• Has 1985 Statement, filed 10/1/85; avg print run 389,108; avg sales 225,387; avg subs 9,408; avg total paid 234,795; samples 140; office use 1,321; max existent 236,256; 39% of run returned **A:** Walt Simonson
367 ☐ May 1986 Cover: 0.75 **NM** value: **2.00**
Circ: Statement: **188,474** CapCity orders: **21,600**
A: Walt Simonson
368 ☐ Jun 1986 Cover: 0.75 **NM** value: **2.00**
Circ: Statement: **188,474** CapCity orders: **20,500**
A: Walt Simonson
369 ☐ Jul 1986 Cover: 0.75 **NM** value: **2.00**
Circ: Statement: **188,474** CapCity orders: **20,400**
A: Walt Simonson
370 ☐ Aug 1986 Cover: 0.75 **NM** value: **2.00**
Circ: Statement: **188,474** CapCity orders: **20,500**
A: Walt Simonson
371 ☐ Sep 1986 Cover: 0.75 **NM** value: **2.00**
Circ: Statement: **188,474** CapCity orders: **19,300**
A: Walt Simonson ★ Appearance of Justice Peace.
372 ☐ Oct 1986 Cover: 0.75 **NM** value: **2.00**
Circ: Statement: **188,474** CapCity orders: **19,500**
A: Walt Simonson
373 ☐ Nov 1986 Cover: 0.75 **NM** value: **2.00**
Circ: Statement: **188,474** CapCity orders: **25,100**
• Mutant Massacre **A:** Walt Simonson
374 ☐ Dec 1986 Cover: 0.75 **NM** value: **3.00**
Circ: Statement: **188,474** CapCity orders: **25,700**
🕮 Mutant Massacre • Mutant Massacre **A:** Walt Simonson ★ Appearance of X-Factor.
375 ☐ Jan 1987 Cover: 0.75 **NM** value: **2.00**
Circ: Statement: **190,600** CapCity orders: **19,400**
A: Walt Simonson
376 ☐ Feb 1987 Cover: 0.75 **NM** value: **2.00**
Circ: Statement: **190,600** CapCity orders: **19,900**
A: Walt Simonson
377 ☐ Mar 1987 Cover: 0.75 **NM** value: **2.00**
Circ: Statement: **190,600** CapCity orders: **20,200**
• Has 1986 Statement, filed 10/6/86; avg print run 345,109; avg sales 180,441; avg subs 8,033; avg total paid 188,474; samples 225; office use 3,057; max existent 191,756; 44% of run returned **A:** Walt Simonson
378 ☐ Apr 1987 Cover: 0.75 **NM** value: **2.00**
Circ: Statement: **190,600** CapCity orders: **20,800**
A: Walt Simonson
379 ☐ May 1987 Cover: 0.75 **NM** value: **2.00**
Circ: Statement: **190,600** CapCity orders: **19,900**
A: Walt Simonson
380 ☐ Jun 1987 Cover: 0.75 **NM** value: **2.00**
Circ: Statement: **190,600** CapCity orders: **20,900**
A: Walt Simonson
381 ☐ Jul 1987 Cover: 0.75 **NM** value: **1.50**
Circ: Statement: **190,600** CapCity orders: **22,200**
382 ☐ Aug 1987 Cover: 1.25 **NM** value: **2.00**
Circ: Statement: **190,600** CapCity orders: **22,200**
• 300th Thor issue
383 ☐ Sep 1987 Cover: 0.75 **NM** value: **1.50**
Circ: Statement: **190,600** CapCity orders: **23,500**
• Secret Wars II
384 ☐ Oct 1987 Cover: 0.75 **NM** value: **1.50**
Circ: Statement: **190,600** CapCity orders: **23,600**
★ 1st Appearance of Dargo (future Thor).
385 ☐ Nov 1987 Cover: 0.75 **NM** value: **1.50**
Circ: Statement: **190,600** CapCity orders: **23,900**
★ Appearance of Hulk.
386 ☐ Dec 1987 Cover: 0.75 **NM** value: **1.50**
Circ: Statement: **190,600** CapCity orders: **24,000**
★ 1st Appearance of Leir.
387 ☐ Jan 1988 Cover: 0.75 **NM** value: **1.50**
Circ: Statement: **187,665** CapCity orders: **25,200**
388 ☐ Feb 1988 Cover: 0.75 **NM** value: **1.50**
Circ: Statement: **187,665** CapCity orders: **26,500**
389 ☐ Mar 1988 Cover: 0.75 **NM** value: **1.50**
Circ: Statement: **187,665** CapCity orders: **26,200**
390 ☐ Apr 1988 Cover: 0.75 **NM** value: **1.50**
Circ: Statement: **187,665** CapCity orders: **26,950**
• Has 1987 Statement; avg print run 314,449; avg sales 184,258; avg subs 6,342; avg total paid 190,600; samples 132; office use 850; max existent 191,582; 39% of run returned
391 ☐ May 1988 Cover: 0.75 **NM** value: **2.00**
Circ: Statement: **187,665** CapCity orders: **27,300**
★ 1st Appearance of Eric Masterson. ★ Appearance of Spider-Man.
392 ☐ Jun 1988 Cover: 0.75 **NM** value: **1.50**
Circ: Statement: **187,665** CapCity orders: **25,500**
★ 1st Appearance of Quicksand.
393 ☐ Jul 1988 Cover: 0.75 **NM** value: **1.50**
Circ: Statement: **187,665** CapCity orders: **27,700**
394 ☐ Aug 1988 Cover: 0.75 **NM** value: **1.50**
Circ: Statement: **187,665** CapCity orders: **27,000**
395 ☐ Sep 1988 Cover: 0.75 **NM** value: **1.50**
Circ: Statement: **187,665** CapCity orders: **26,800**
★ Origin of Earth-Lord, Wind Warrior. ★ 1st Appearance of Earth-Lord, Wind Warrior.
396 ☐ Oct 1988 Cover: 0.75 **NM** value: **1.50**
Circ: Statement: **187,665** CapCity orders: **26,700**
397 ☐ Nov 1988 Cover: 0.75 **NM** value: **1.50**
Circ: Statement: **187,665** CapCity orders: **25,800**
398 ☐ Dec 1988 Cover: 0.75 **NM** value: **1.50**
Circ: Statement: **187,665** CapCity orders: **25,900**
★ 1st Appearance of Caber.
399 ☐ Jan 1989 Cover: 0.75 **NM** value: **1.50**
Circ: Statement: **183,720** CapCity orders: **25,700**
400 ☐ Feb 1989 Cover: 1.75 **NM** value: **2.00**
Circ: Statement: **183,720** CapCity orders: **33,000**
• giant★ Appearance of Avengers. ★ Versus Seth and Surtur.
401 ☐ Mar 1989 Cover: 0.75 **NM** value: **1.00**
Circ: Statement: **183,720** CapCity orders: **25,700**
• Has 1988 Statement, filed 10/1/88; avg print run 296,380; avg sales 181,525; avg subs 6,140; avg total paid 187,665; samples 130; office use 860; max existent 188,655; 36% of run returned
402 ☐ Apr 1989 Cover: 0.75 **NM** value: **1.00**
Circ: Statement: **183,720** CapCity orders: **26,800**
403 ☐ May 1989 Cover: 0.75 **NM** value: **1.00**
Circ: Statement: **183,720** CapCity orders: **26,700**
404 ☐ Jun 1989 Cover: 0.75 **NM** value: **1.00**
Circ: Statement: **183,720** CapCity orders: **26,400**
405 ☐ Jul 1989 Cover: 0.75 **NM** value: **1.00**
Circ: Statement: **183,720** CapCity orders: **25,700**
406 ☐ Aug 1989 Cover: 0.75 **NM** value: **1.00**
Circ: Statement: **183,720** CapCity orders: **26,100**
407 ☐ Sep 1989 Cover: 1.00 **NM** value: **Cover or less**
Circ: Statement: **183,720** CapCity orders: **25,400**

Other grades: Multiply prices above by **1.5 for Mint • 2/3 for Very Fine • 1/3 for Fine • 1/5 for Very Good • 1/8 for Good**

408 ❑ Oct 1989 Cover: 1.00 **NM** value: **Cover or less**
Circ: Statement: **183,720** CapCity orders: **24,800**
• Eric Masterson absorbs Thor's essence; series continues as The Mighty Thor through #490

409 ❑ Nov 1989 Cover: 1.00 **NM** value: **Cover or less**
Circ: Statement: **183,720** CapCity orders: **25,200**
• Title changes to The Mighty Thor

410 ❑ Nov 1989 Cover: 1.00 **NM** value: **Cover or less**
Circ: Statement: **183,720** CapCity orders: **26,100**

411 ❑ Dec 1989 Cover: 1.00 **NM** value: **3.00**
Circ: Statement: **183,720** CapCity orders: **27,500** • **CGC:** 1 graded, best 9.0
Acts of Vengeance, Part 4 • Acts of Vengeance ★ 1st Appearance of Night Thrasher, New Warriors (cameo appearance), Chord. ★ Versus Juggernaut.

412 ❑ Dec 1989 Cover: 1.00 **NM** value: **2.00**
Circ: Statement: **183,720** CapCity orders: **29,000**
Acts of Vengeance, Part 13 • Acts of Vengeance ★ 1st Appearance of New Warriors (full appearance). ★ Versus Juggernaut.

413 ❑ Jan 1990 Cover: 1.00 **NM** value: **Cover or less**
Circ: Statement: **169,916** CapCity orders: **26,300**
Acts of Vengeance

414 ❑ Feb 1990 Cover: 1.00 **NM** value: **Cover or less**
Circ: Statement: **169,916** CapCity orders: **26,100**

415 ❑ Mar 1990 Cover: 1.00 **NM** value: **Cover or less**
Circ: Statement: **169,916** CapCity orders: **28,400**
★ Origin of Thor.

416 ❑ Apr 1990 Cover: 1.00 **NM** value: **Cover or less**
Circ: Statement: **169,916** CapCity orders: **25,400**

417 ❑ May 1990 Cover: 1.00 **NM** value: **Cover or less**
Circ: Statement: **169,916** CapCity orders: **25,000**
• Has 1989 Statement, filed 11/1/89; avg print run 291,480; avg sales 177,270; avg subs 6,450; avg total paid 183,720; samples 125; office use 600; max existent 184,445; 37% of run returned

418 ❑ Jun 1990 Cover: 1.00 **NM** value: **Cover or less**
Circ: Statement: **169,916** CapCity orders: **24,700**

419 ❑ Jul 1990 Cover: 1.00 **NM** value: **Cover or less**
Circ: Statement: **169,916** CapCity orders: **25,000**
★ Origin of Stellaris. ★ 1st Appearance of Stellaris, Black Galaxy.

420 ❑ Aug 1990 Cover: 1.00 **NM** value: **Cover or less**
Circ: Statement: **169,916** CapCity orders: **23,700**
Black Galaxy ★ Origin of Nobilus. ★ 1st Appearance of Nobilus (partial appearance).

421 ❑ Aug 1990 Cover: 1.00 **NM** value: **Cover or less**
Circ: Statement: **169,916** CapCity orders: **23,700**
Black Galaxy

422 ❑ Sep 1990 Cover: 1.00 **NM** value: **Cover or less**
Circ: Statement: **169,916** CapCity orders: **23,100**
Black Galaxy ★ Origin of Nobilus. ★ 1st Appearance of Analyzer.

423 ❑ Sep 1990 Cover: 1.00 **NM** value: **Cover or less**
Circ: Statement: **169,916** CapCity orders: **23,100**
Black Galaxy ★ 1st Appearance of Nobilus (full appearance).

424 ❑ Oct 1990 Cover: 1.00 **NM** value: **Cover or less**
Circ: Statement: **169,916** CapCity orders: **22,400**
Black Galaxy

425 ❑ Oct 1990 Cover: 1.00 **NM** value: **Cover or less**
Circ: Statement: **169,916** CapCity orders: **22,600**

426 ❑ Nov 1990 Cover: 1.00 **NM** value: **Cover or less**
Circ: Statement: **169,916** CapCity orders: **22,300**

427 ❑ Dec 1990 Cover: 1.00 **NM** value: **Cover or less**
Circ: Statement: **169,916** CapCity orders: **23,300**
★ Appearance of Excalibur.

428 ❑ Jan 1991 Cover: 1.00 **NM** value: **Cover or less**
Circ: Statement: **164,708** CapCity orders: **23,500**
★ Appearance of Excalibur.

429 ❑ Feb 1991 Cover: 1.00 **NM** value: **Cover or less**
Circ: Statement: **164,708** CapCity orders: **36,000**
★ Appearance of Ghost Rider.

430 ❑ Mar 1991 Cover: 1.00 **NM** value: **Cover or less**
Circ: Statement: **164,708** CapCity orders: **36,800** • **CGC:** 1 graded, best 8.0
• Has 1990 Statement, filed 10/1/90; avg print run 295,049; avg sales 164,250; avg subs 5,666; avg total paid 169,916; samples 100; office use 600; max existent 170,616; 42% of run returned ★ Appearance of Ghost Rider.

431 ❑ Apr 1991 Cover: 1.00 **NM** value: **Cover or less**
Circ: Statement: **164,708** CapCity orders: **23,800**

432 ❑ May 1991 Cover: 1.00 **NM** value: **2.00**
Circ: Statement: **164,708** CapCity orders: **39,000**
• Giant size. **A:** Jack Kirby ★ Origin of Thor. ★ 1st Appearance of Thor II (Eric Masterson), Thor. ★ Appearance of 300th. ★ Death of Loki.

433 ❑ Jun 1991 Cover: 1.00 **NM** value: **2.00**
Circ: Statement: **164,708** CapCity orders: **37,600** • **CGC:** 1 graded, best 9.2

434 ❑ Jul 1991 Cover: 1.00 **NM** value: **Cover or less**
Circ: Statement: **164,708** CapCity orders: **30,200** • **CGC:** 1 graded, best 9.2

435 ❑ Aug 1991 Cover: 1.00 **NM** value: **Cover or less**
Circ: Statement: **164,708** CapCity orders: **31,200**

436 ❑ Sep 1991 Cover: 1.00 **NM** value: **Cover or less**
Circ: Statement: **164,708** CapCity orders: **31,900**

437 ❑ Oct 1991 Cover: 1.00 **NM** value: **Cover or less**
Circ: Statement: **164,708** CapCity orders: **32,300**

438 ❑ Nov 1991 Cover: 1.00 **NM** value: **Cover or less**
Circ: Statement: **164,708** CapCity orders: **31,500**
Thor War, Part 1 ★ Versus Zarrko.

439 ❑ Nov 1991 Cover: 1.00 **NM** value: **Cover or less**
Circ: Statement: **164,708** CapCity orders: **31,100**
Thor War, Part 2

440 ❑ Dec 1991 Cover: 1.00 **NM** value: **Cover or less**
Circ: Statement: **164,708** CapCity orders: **32,800**
Thor War, Part 3 ★ 1st Appearance of Thor Corps (Dargo, Beta Ray Bill, Eric Masterson).

441 ❑ Dec 1991 Cover: 1.00 **NM** value: **Cover or less**
Circ: Statement: **164,708** CapCity orders: **30,900**
Thor War, Part 4

442 ❑ Jan 1992 Cover: 1.00 **NM** value: **Cover or less**
Circ: CapCity orders: **32,400**
• Return of Don Blake

443 ❑ Jan 1992 Cover: 1.00 **NM** value: **Cover or less**
Circ: CapCity orders: **32,000**
★ Appearance of Doctor Strange, Silver Surfer. ★ Versus Mephisto.

444 ❑ Feb 1992 Cover: 1.25 **NM** value: **Cover or less**
Circ: CapCity orders: **29,100**

445 ❑ Mar 1992 Cover: 1.25 **NM** value: **Cover or less**
Circ: CapCity orders: **36,300**
Operation: Galactic Storm, Part 7 • Galactic Storm; Has 1991 Statement, filed 10/1/91; avg print run 256,992; avg sales 161,033; avg subs 3,675; avg total paid 164,708; samples 125; office use 250; max existent 165,083; 36% of run returned ★ Versus Gladiator.

446 ❑ Apr 1992 Cover: 1.25 **NM** value: **Cover or less**
Circ: CapCity orders: **34,200**
Operation: Galactic Storm, Part 14 • Galactic Storm **A:** Patrick Olliffe **W:** Tom DeFalco ★ Appearance of Avengers.

447 ❑ May 1992 Cover: 1.25 **NM** value: **Cover or less**
Circ: CapCity orders: **28,500**
★ Appearance of Spider-Man, Absorbing Man.

448 ❑ Jun 1992 Cover: 1.25 **NM** value: **Cover or less**
Circ: CapCity orders: **31,500**
★ Appearance of Spider-Man.

449 ❑ Jul 1992 Cover: 1.25 **NM** value: **Cover or less**
Circ: CapCity orders: **29,700**
★ Origin of Bloodaxe. ★ 1st Appearance of Bloodaxe.

450 ❑ Aug 1992 Cover: 2.50 **NM** value: **Cover or less**
Circ: CapCity orders: **49,000** • **CGC:** 2 graded, best 9.2
• Giant-size anniversary special. ★ Origin of Loki.

451 ❑ Sep 1992 Cover: 1.25 **NM** value: **Cover or less**
Circ: CapCity orders: **30,400**
★ Versus Bloodaxe.

452 ❑ Oct 1992 Cover: 1.25 **NM** value: **Cover or less**
Circ: CapCity orders: **27,700**

453 ❑ Nov 1992 Cover: 1.25 **NM** value: **Cover or less**
Circ: CapCity orders: **26,300**

454 ❑ Nov 1992 Cover: 1.25 **NM** value: **Cover or less**
Circ: CapCity orders: **26,200**

455 ❑ Dec 1992 Cover: 1.25 **NM** value: **Cover or less**
Circ: CapCity orders: **26,200**

456 ❑ Dec 1992 Cover: 1.25 **NM** value: **Cover or less**
Circ: Statement: **170,917** CapCity orders: **26,300**

457 ❑ Jan 1993 Cover: 1.25 **NM** value: **Cover or less**
Circ: Statement: **170,917** CapCity orders: **30,300**
Final Gauntlet! • Original Thor returns **A:** Ron Frenz **W:** Tom DeFalco

458 ❑ Jan 1993 Cover: 1.25 **NM** value: **Cover or less**
Circ: Statement: **170,917** CapCity orders: **28,900**

459 ❑ Feb 1993 Cover: 1.25 **NM** value: **Cover or less**
Circ: Statement: **170,917** CapCity orders: **32,700**

460 ❑ Mar 1993 Cover: 1.25 **NM** value: **Cover or less**
Circ: Statement: **170,917** CapCity orders: **41,200**
Painted cover. Fragments **A:** Bruce Zick **W:** Jim Starlin; Ron Marz

461 ❑ Apr 1993 Cover: 1.25 **NM** value: **Cover or less**
Circ: Statement: **170,917** CapCity orders: **32,000**

462 ❑ May 1993 Cover: 1.25 **NM** value: **Cover or less**
Circ: Statement: **170,917** CapCity orders: **31,300**

463 ❑ Jun 1993 Cover: 1.25 **NM** value: **Cover or less**
Circ: Statement: **170,917** CapCity orders: **36,800**

464 ❑ Jul 1993 Cover: 1.25 **NM** value: **Cover or less**
Circ: Statement: **170,917** CapCity orders: **34,300**

465 ❑ Aug 1993 Cover: 1.25 **NM** value: **Cover or less**
Circ: Statement: **170,917** CapCity orders: **32,900**

466 ❑ Sep 1993 Cover: 1.25 **NM** value: **Cover or less**
Circ: Statement: **170,917** CapCity orders: **29,500**

467 ❑ Oct 1993 Cover: 1.25 **NM** value: **Cover or less**
Circ: Statement: **170,917** CapCity orders: **27,700**
• Infinity Crusade crossover **A:** Bruce Zick **W:** Ron Marz ★ Appearance of Lady Sif, Valkyrie, Pluto.

468 ❑ Nov 1993 Cover: 1.25 **NM** value: **Cover or less**
Circ: Statement: **170,917** CapCity orders: **25,500**

469 ❑ Dec 1993 Cover: 1.25 **NM** value: **Cover or less**
Circ: Statement: **108,792** CapCity orders: **26,400**

470 ❑ Jan 1994 Cover: 1.25 **NM** value: **Cover or less**
Circ: Statement: **108,792** CapCity orders: **24,200**

471 ❑ Feb 1994 Cover: 1.25 **NM** value: **Cover or less**
Circ: Statement: **108,792** CapCity orders: **24,300**
Blood and Thunder; Blood and Thunder, Part 13 • Has 1993 Statement, filed 10/1/93; avg print run 259,383; avg sales 167,483; avg subs 3,434; avg total paid 170,917; samples 125; office use 500; max existent 171,542; 34% of run returned

472 ❑ Mar 1994 Cover: 1.25 **NM** value: **Cover or less**
Circ: Statement: **108,792** CapCity orders: **21,850**

473 ❑ Apr 1994 Cover: 1.25 **NM** value: **Cover or less**
Circ: Statement: **108,792** CapCity orders: **20,950**

474 ❑ May 1994 Cover: 1.50 **NM** value: **Cover or less**
Circ: Statement: **108,792** CapCity orders: **20,350**

475 ❑ Jun 1994 Cover: 2.00 **NM** value: **Cover or less**
• Giant-size. Survival Of The Fiercest **A:** M.C. Wyman **W:** Roy Thomas ★ Origin of Thor.

475/SC❑Jun 1994 Cover: 2.50 **NM** value: **Cover or less**
Circ: Statement: **108,792** CapCity orders: **31,450**
foil cover. • Giant-size. Survival Of The Fiercest **A:** M.C. Wyman **W:** Roy Thomas ★ Origin of Thor.

476 ❑ Jul 1994 Cover: 1.50 **NM** value: **Cover or less**
Circ: Statement: **108,792** CapCity orders: **20,650**

477 ❑ Aug 1994 Cover: 1.50 **NM** value: **Cover or less**
Circ: Statement: **108,792** CapCity orders: **18,800**

478 ❑ Sep 1994 Cover: 1.50 **NM** value: **Cover or less**
Circ: Statement: **108,792** CapCity orders: **18,450**
★ Appearance of Red Norvell.

479 ❑ Oct 1994 Cover: 1.50 **NM** value: **Cover or less**
Circ: Statement: **108,792** CapCity orders: **17,950**

480 ❑ Nov 1994 Cover: 1.50 **NM** value: **Cover or less**
Circ: Statement: **108,792** CapCity orders: **17,050**

481 ❑ Dec 1994 Cover: 1.50 **NM** value: **Cover or less**
Circ: Statement: **70,125** CapCity orders: **16,550**
★ Versus Grotesk.

482 ❑ Jan 1995 Cover: 2.95 **NM** value: **Cover or less**
Circ: Statement: **70,125** CapCity orders: **16,025**
• Giant-size.

483 ❑ Feb 1995 Cover: 1.50 **NM** value: **Cover or less**
Circ: Statement: **70,125** CapCity orders: **16,225**

484 ❑ Mar 1995 Cover: 1.50 **NM** value: **Cover or less**
Circ: Statement: **70,125** CapCity orders: **13,950**
• Has 1994 Statement, filed 10/1/94; avg print run 188,725; avg sales 105,983; avg subs 2,808; avg total paid 108,792; samples 125; office use 500; max existent 109,416; 42% of run returned

485 ❑ Apr 1995 Cover: 1.50 **NM** value: **Cover or less**
Circ: Statement: **70,125** CapCity orders: **13,800**

486 ❑ May 1995 Cover: 1.50 **NM** value: **Cover or less**
Circ: Statement: **70,125** CapCity orders: **13,450**

487 ❑ Jun 1995 Cover: 1.50 **NM** value: **Cover or less**
Circ: Statement: **70,125** CapCity orders: **13,125**

488 ❑ Jul 1995 Cover: 1.50 **NM** value: **Cover or less**
Circ: Statement: **70,125** CapCity orders: **13,050**

489 ❑ Aug 1995 Cover: 1.50 **NM** value: **Cover or less**
Circ: Statement: **70,125**
★ Versus Hulk.

490 ❑ Sep 1995 Cover: 1.50 **NM** value: **Cover or less**
Circ: Statement: **70,125**
★ Versus Absorbing Man.

491 ❑ Oct 1995 Cover: 1.50 **NM** value: **Cover or less**
Circ: Statement: **111,529**
• Title returns to Thor

492 ❑ Nov 1995 Cover: 1.50 **NM** value: **Cover or less**
Circ: Statement: **111,529**
★ Appearance of Enchantress.

493 ❑ Dec 1995 Cover: 1.50 **NM** value: **Cover or less**
Circ: Statement: **111,529**
A: Mike Deodato **W:** Warren Ellis ★ Appearance of Enchantress.

494 ❑ Jan 1996 Cover: 1.50 **NM** value: **Cover or less**
Circ: Statement: **111,529**
• Has 1995 Statement, filed 10/1/95; avg print run 123,725; avg sales 67,325; avg subs 2,800; avg total paid 70,125; samples 750; office use 500; max existent 71,375; 42% of run returned

495 ❑ Feb 1996 Cover: 1.50 **NM** value: **Cover or less**
Circ: Statement: **111,529**

496 ❑ Mar 1996 Cover: 1.50 **NM** value: **Cover or less**
Circ: Statement: **111,529**
First Sign; First Sign, Part 2 **A:** Mike Deodato Jr. **W:** William Messner-Loebs ★ Appearance of Captain America.

497 ❑ Apr 1996 Cover: 1.50 **NM** value: **Cover or less**
Circ: Statement: **111,529**
Thor Must Die **A:** Mike Deodato Jr. **W:** William Messner-Loebs

498 ❑ May 1996 Cover: 1.50 **NM** value: **Cover or less**
Circ: Statement: **111,529**

499 ❑ Jun 1996 Cover: 1.50 **NM** value: **Cover or less**
Circ: Statement: **111,529**

500 ❑ Jul 1996 Cover: 2.50 **NM** value: **Cover or less**
Circ: Statement: **111,529**
wraparound cover. • Giant-size.

501 ❑ Aug 1996 Cover: 1.50 **NM** value: **Cover or less**
Circ: Statement: **111,529**
★ Appearance of Red Norvell.

502 ❑ Sep 1996 Cover: 1.50 **NM** value: **Cover or less**
• **CGC:** 2 graded, best 9.6
★ Origin of Thor.

Anl 2❑Sep 1966 Cover: 0.25 **NM** value: **45.00**
• **CGC:** 10 graded, best 9.6
• Cover reads "King Size Special". If Asgard Falls…; Defying the Magic of Mad Merlin!; Menaced By The Enchantress and the Executioner! • reprints from Journey into Mystery #96 and #103 **A:** Jack Kirby; R. Berns **W:** Stan Lee

Anl 3❑Jan 1971 Cover: 0.25 **NM** value: **10.00**
• **CGC:** 2 graded, best 9.6
A World Gone Mad!; Balder Must Die!; Trapped by the Trolls!; Banished from Asgard!; The Defeat of Odin!; The Stronger I Am, The Sooner I Die! • reprints Thor stories from Journey into Mystery #113 and #114; reprints Tales of Asgard from Journey into Mystery #107-110 **A:** Jack Kirby ★ Appearance of Grey Gargoyle, Absorbing Man.

Anl 4❑ Cover: 0.25 **NM** value: **9.00**
• Cover reads "King Size Special". They Strike From Space!: Rigel Where The Gods May Fear To Tread; The Boyhood of Loki • reprints stories from Thor #131 and 132, and Journey Into Mystery #113 **A:** Jack Kirby

Anl 5❑ca. 1976 Cover: 0.50 **NM** value: **7.50**
The War of the Gods; Dawn of the Gods; The Thunder God; When Gods Collide; The Spoils of War **A:** John Buscema; Jack Kirby ★ 1st Appearance of Apollo.

Anl 6❑ca. 1977 Cover: 0.50 **NM** value: **7.50**
Thunder in the 31st Century; And They Shall Be Guardians of the Galaxy; The Master Plan of Korvac; This Battleground Paradise **A:** John Buscema; Jack Kirby

Anl 7❑ca. 1978 Cover: 0.60 **NM** value: **7.50**

Anl 8❑ca. 1979 Cover: 0.75 **NM** value: **6.00**

Anl 9❑ca. 1981 Cover: 0.75 **NM** value: **3.50**
The Great Game! **A:** Luke McDonnell; Vince Colletta **W:** Chris Claremont

Anl 10❑ca. 1982 Cover: 1.00 **NM** value: **3.50**
A Time To Die! **A:** Bob Hall **W:** Alan Zelentz ★ Origin of Chthon. ★ 1st Appearance of Ahpuch, Erishkegal, Yama.

Anl 11❑ca. 1983 Cover: 1.00 **NM** value: **3.50**

Anl 12❑ca. 1984 Cover: 1.00 **NM** value: **3.50**
★ 1st Appearance of Vidar.

Anl 13❑ Cover: 1.25 **NM** value: **3.00**
Circ: CapCity orders: **14,600**
★ Versus Mephisto.

Anl 14❑ca. 1989 Cover: 2.00 **NM** value: **2.50**
Circ: CapCity orders: **36,100**
Atlantis Attacks, Part 13 • Title changes to The Mighty Thor Annual

Anl 15❑ca. 1990 Cover: 2.00 **NM** value: **2.50**
Circ: CapCity orders: **30,800**
The Terminus Factor, Part 3 ★ Origin of Terminus.

Anl 16❑ca. 1991 Cover: 2.50 **NM** value: **Cover or less**
Korvac Quest; Korvac Quest, Part 2

Anl 17❑ca. 1992 Cover: 2.25 **NM** value: **2.50**
Circ: CapCity orders: **26,200**

CGC-graded: Multiply prices above by **33 for 9.9 M • 16 for 9.8 NM/M • 7 for 9.6 NM+ • 5 for 9.4 NM • 2.5 for 9.2 NM- • 1.5 for 9.0 VF/NM**

📖 Citizen Kang, Part 2; The Ten Most Heinous Enemies of the Mighty Thor; Paradise Lost • Citizen Kang **A:** Kirk Jarvinen; Rich Yanizeski; Geof Isherwood; Dan Panosian; Tom Raney; Kevin Kobasic **W:** George Caragonne; Roy Thomas; John Lewandowski; Peter Sanderson

Anl 18❑ca. 1993 Cover: 2.95 **NM** value: **Cover or less**
Circ: CapCity orders: **30,100**
• trading card

Anl 19❑ca. 1994 Cover: 2.95 **NM** value: **Cover or less**
Circ: CapCity orders: **14,050**

GS 1❑ca. 1975 Cover: 0.50 **NM** value: **5.00**
📖 If Asgard Falls…; When Titans Clash; When Heimdall Failed • reprints stories from Thor Annual #2, Journey Into Mystery #105 and JIM Annual #1

THOR (VOL. 2) — Marvel

Amazingly, a #1 issue had never been published for Thor, the mightiest hero in the Marvel Universe, until the late 1990s. Finally, the celestial guardian of Midgard received a premiere issue, and Marvel Comics assembled exceptional talent for it. Dan Jurgens, known for his Superman stories, was easily able to adapt to relating the adventures of one of Marvel's most powerful characters, and quickly established a solid foundation upon timeless themes attributed to countless ancient Nordic myths: ambition, bravery, isolation, and sacrifice. John Romita Jr.'s clean artwork contributed greatly to the relaunch.

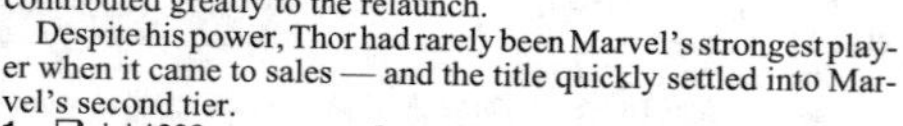

Despite his power, Thor had rarely been Marvel's strongest player when it came to sales — and the title quickly settled into Marvel's second tier.

1 ❑ Jul 1998 Cover: 3.50 **NM** value: **Cover or less**
Circ: Diamd. preorders: **134,677** • **CGC:** 6 graded, best 9.8
• Giant-size. **A:** John Romita Jr. **W:** Dan Jurgens

1/A ❑ Jul 1998 Cover: 2.99 **NM** value: **20.00**
• **CGC:** 21 graded, best 9.9
sketch cover. • gatefold summary.

1/B ❑ Jul 1998 Cover: 2.99 **NM** value: **5.00**
• **CGC:** 2 graded, best 9.6
Sunburst cover.

1/C ❑ Jul 1998 Cover: 10.00 **NM** value: **Cover or less**
• **CGC:** 1 graded, best 9.6
DFE alternate cover.

1/D ❑ Jul 1998 Cover: 24.95 **NM** value: **Cover or less**
• **CGC:** 1 graded, best 9.6
DFE alternate cover.

2 ❑ Aug 1998 Cover: 1.99 **NM** value: **2.50**
Circ: Diamd. preorders: **100,607** • **CGC:** 1 graded, best 9.6
• gatefold summary. • Thor receives new mortal identity **A:** John Romita Jr. **W:** Dan Jurgens

2/A ❑ Aug 1998 Cover: 1.99 **NM** value: **2.50**
variant cover. **A:** John Romita Jr. **W:** Dan Jurgens

3 ❑ Sep 1998 Cover: 1.99 **NM** value: **2.00**
Circ: Diamd. preorders: **81,314**
• gatefold summary. **A:** John Romita Jr. **W:** Dan Jurgens ★ Versus Sedna.

4 ❑ Oct 1998 Cover: 1.99 **NM** value: **2.00**
Circ: Statement: **91,957** Diamd. preorders: **78,245**
• gatefold summary. **A:** John Romita Jr. **W:** Dan Jurgens ★ Appearance of Namor.

5 ❑ Nov 1998 Cover: 1.99 **NM** value: **2.00**
Circ: Statement: **91,957** Diamd. preorders: **74,237**
• gatefold summary. **A:** John Romita Jr. **W:** Dan Jurgens

6 ❑ Dec 1998 Cover: 1.99 **NM** value: **2.00**
Circ: Statement: **91,957** Diamd. preorders: **73,253**
• gatefold summary. **A:** John Romita Jr. **W:** Dan Jurgens ★ Appearance of Hercules.

7 ❑ Jan 1999 Cover: 1.99 **NM** value: **2.00**
Circ: Statement: **91,957** Diamd. preorders: **71,155**
• gatefold summary. **A:** John Romita Jr. **W:** Dan Jurgens ★ Appearance of Hercules.

8 ❑ Feb 1999 Cover: 1.99 **NM** value: **2.00**
Circ: Statement: **91,957** Diamd. preorders: **70,729**
• gatefold summary. • concludes in Peter Parker; Spider-Man #2 **A:** John Romita Jr. **W:** Dan Jurgens ★ Appearance of Spider-Man.

9 ❑ Mar 1999 Cover: 1.99 **NM** value: **2.00**
Circ: Statement: **91,957** Diamd. preorders: **67,866**
A: John Buscema **W:** Dan Jurgens

10 ❑ Apr 1999 Cover: 1.99 **NM** value: **2.00**
Circ: Statement: **91,957** Diamd. preorders: **67,396**
A: John Romita Jr. **W:** Dan Jurgens ★ Versus Perrikus.

11 ❑ May 1999 Cover: 1.99 **NM** value: **Cover or less**
Circ: Statement: **91,957** Diamd. preorders: **66,730**
W: Dan Jurgens ★ Appearance of Volstagg. ★ Versus Perrikus.

12 ❑ Jun 1999 Cover: 2.99 **NM** value: **Cover or less**
Circ: Statement: **91,957** Diamd. preorders: **68,798**
wraparound cover. **W:** Dan Jurgens ★ Appearance of Hercules, Destroyer, Warriors Three, Replicus. ★ Versus Perrikus.

13 ❑ Jul 1999 Cover: 1.99 **NM** value: **Cover or less**
Circ: Statement: **91,957** Diamd. preorders: **66,272**
W: Dan Jurgens ★ Versus Marnot.

14 ❑ Aug 1999 Cover: 1.99 **NM** value: **Cover or less**
Circ: Statement: **91,957** Diamd. preorders: **65,858**
W: Dan Jurgens ★ Appearance of Iron Man. ★ Versus Absorbing Man.

15 ❑ Sep 1999 Cover: 1.99 **NM** value: **Cover or less**
Circ: Statement: **91,957** Diamd. preorders: **65,407**
W: Dan Jurgens ★ Appearance of Warriors Three.

16 ❑ Oct 1999 Cover: 1.99 **NM** value: **Cover or less**
Circ: Diamd. preorders: **61,935**
W: Dan Jurgens

17 ❑ Nov 1999 Cover: 1.99 **NM** value: **Cover or less**
Circ: Diamd. preorders: **61,822**
📖 The Eighth Day **W:** Dan Jurgens

18 ❑ Dec 1999 Cover: 1.99 **NM** value: **Cover or less**
Circ: Diamd. preorders: **58,575**
W: Dan Jurgens

19 ❑ Jan 2000 Cover: 1.99 **NM** value: **Cover or less**
Circ: Diamd. preorders: **57,214**
W: Dan Jurgens

20 ❑ Feb 2000 Cover: 1.99 **NM** value: **2.25**
Circ: Diamd. preorders: **55,217**

21 ❑ Mar 2000 Cover: 1.99 **NM** value: **2.25**
Circ: Diamd. preorders: **55,964**

22 ❑ Apr 2000 Cover: 1.99 **NM** value: **2.25**
Circ: Diamd. preorders: **51,856**

23 ❑ May 2000 Cover: 1.99 **NM** value: **2.25**
Circ: Diamd. preorders: **52,489**

24 ❑ Jun 2000 Cover: 2.25 **NM** value: **Cover or less**
Circ: Diamd. preorders: **51,907**

25 ❑ Jul 2000 Cover: 2.25 **NM** value: **Cover or less**

26 ❑ Aug 2000 Cover: 2.25 **NM** value: **Cover or less**
Circ: Diamd. preorders: **51,425**

27 ❑ Sep 2000 Cover: 2.25 **NM** value: **Cover or less**
Circ: Diamd. preorders: **50,641**

28 ❑ Oct 2000 Cover: 2.25 **NM** value: **Cover or less**
Circ: Statement: **57,174** Diamd. preorders: **46,607**

29 ❑ Nov 2000 Cover: 2.25 **NM** value: **Cover or less**
Circ: Statement: **57,174** Diamd. preorders: **46,868**
📖 Whence Comes Death **A:** Andy Kubert ★ Appearance of Wrecking Crew.

30 ❑ Dec 2000 Cover: 2.25 **NM** value: **Cover or less**
Circ: Statement: **57,174** Diamd. preorders: **46,469**
📖 Maximum Security; Winter's Edge **A:** Andy Kubert **W:** Dan Jurgens ★ Appearance of Malekith, Beta Ray Bill.

31 ❑ Jan 2001 Cover: 2.25 **NM** value: **Cover or less**
Circ: Statement: **57,174** Diamd. preorders: **44,209**
A: Andy Kubert

32 ❑ Feb 2001 Cover: 3.50 **NM** value: **Cover or less**
Circ: Statement: **57,174** Diamd. preorders: **44,102**
📖 Forever Kursed **A:** Andy Kubert **W:** Dan Jurgens

33 ❑ Mar 2001 Cover: 2.25 **NM** value: **Cover or less**
Circ: Statement: **57,174** Diamd. preorders: **43,229**
📖 The Million Dollar Debut of Thor Girl! **A:** Stuart Immonen **W:** Dan Jurgens ★ 1st Appearance of Thor Girl.

34 ❑ Apr 2001 Cover: 2.25 **NM** value: **Cover or less**
Circ: Statement: **57,174** Diamd. preorders: **42,643**
📖 Man of Tomorrow **A:** Andy Kubert **W:** Dan Jurgens ★ Appearance of Gladiator.

35 ❑ May 2001 Cover: 2.99 **NM** value: **Cover or less**
Circ: Statement: **57,174** Diamd. preorders: **42,326**
📖 Across All Worlds **A:** Andy Kubert **W:** Dan Jurgens ★ Appearance of Gladiator.

36 ❑ Jun 2001 Cover: 2.25 **NM** value: **Cover or less**
Circ: Statement: **57,174** Diamd. preorders: **42,432**

37 ❑ Jul 2001 Cover: 2.25 **NM** value: **Cover or less**
Circ: Statement: **57,174** Diamd. preorders: **43,497**

38 ❑ Aug 2001 Cover: 2.25 **NM** value: **Cover or less**
Circ: Statement: **57,174** Diamd. preorders: **43,170**

39 ❑ Sep 2001 Cover: 2.25 **NM** value: **Cover or less**
Circ: Statement: **57,174** Diamd. preorders: **44,538**

40 ❑ Oct 2001 Cover: 2.25 **NM** value: **Cover or less**
Circ: Diamd. preorders: **44,862** • **CGC:** 2 graded, best 9.6

41 ❑ Nov 2001 Cover: 2.25 **NM** value: **Cover or less**
Circ: Diamd. preorders: **41,078** • **CGC:** 2 graded, best 9.6

42 ❑ Dec 2001 Cover: 2.25 **NM** value: **Cover or less**
Circ: Diamd. preorders: **39,139**

43 ❑ Jan 2002 Cover: 2.25 **NM** value: **Cover or less**
Circ: Diamd. preorders: **39,493**

44 ❑ Feb 2002 Cover: 2.25 **NM** value: **Cover or less**
Circ: Diamd. preorders: **38,766**
• Has 2001 Statement, filed 10/1/2001; avg print run 79,300; avg sales 55,354; avg subs 1,820; avg total paid 57,174; samples 600; max existent 57,774; 27% of run returned

45 ❑ Mar 2002 Cover: 2.25 **NM** value: **Cover or less**
Circ: Diamd. preorders: **37,888**

Anl 1999❑Mar 1999 Cover: 3.50 **NM** value: **Cover or less**
Circ: Diamd. preorders: **47,859**
wraparound cover. 📖 Tears of a God • set between Heroes Reborn and Heroes Return **A:** Dan Jurgens **W:** Dan Jurgens ★ Versus Doom.

Anl 2001❑Mar 2001 Cover: 3.50 **NM** value: **Cover or less**
Circ: Diamd. preorders: **31,469**
📖 When Fall the Gods! **A:** Tom Grummett **W:** Dan Jurgens ★ Appearance of Hercules, Beta Ray Bill.

Bk 1❑ Cover: 5.99 **NM** value: **Cover or less**
Circ: CapCity orders: **3,700**
• Collects issues #1-2 **A:** John Romita Jr. **W:** Dan Jurgens

THOR BATTLEBOOK — Marvel

1 ❑ Cover: 3.99 **NM** value: **Cover or less**

THOR CORPS — Marvel

1 ❑ Sep 1993 Cover: 1.75 **NM** value: **Cover or less**
Circ: CapCity orders: **36,200**
📖 A Gathering Of Heroes-! **A:** Patrick Olliffe **W:** Tom DeFalco

2 ❑ Oct 1993 Cover: 1.75 **NM** value: **Cover or less**
Circ: CapCity orders: **25,200**
📖 Gather Chaos! **A:** Patrick Olliffe **W:** Tom DeFalco ★ Appearance of Midnight Wreckers, Franklin Richards, Invaders, Machine Man 2020.

3 ❑ Nov 1993 Cover: 1.75 **NM** value: **Cover or less**
Circ: CapCity orders: **23,400**
A: Patrick Olliffe **W:** Tom DeFalco

4 ❑ Dec 1993 Cover: 1.75 **NM** value: **Cover or less**
Circ: CapCity orders: **21,900**
A: Patrick Olliffe **W:** Tom DeFalco

THOR: GODSTORM — Marvel

1 ❑ Nov 2001 Cover: 3.50 **NM** value: **Cover or less**
Circ: Diamd. preorders: **36,386**

2 ❑ Dec 2001 Cover: 3.50 **NM** value: **Cover or less**
Circ: Diamd. preorders: **32,179**

3 ❑ Jan 2002 Cover: 3.50 **NM** value: **Cover or less**
Circ: Diamd. preorders: **30,865**

THORION OF THE NEW ASGODS — Marvel / Amalgam

1 ❑ Jun 1997 Cover: 1.95 **NM** value: **Cover or less**
Circ: Diamd. preorders: **121,660**
📖 Thorion The Hunter! **A:** John Romita Jr. **W:** Keith Giffen

THORR-SVERD — Vincent

1 ❑ b&w Cover: 1.00 **NM** value: **Cover or less**
2 ❑ b&w Cover: 1.00 **NM** value: **Cover or less**
3 ❑ b&w Cover: 1.00 **NM** value: **Cover or less**

THOR: THE LEGEND — Marvel

1 ❑ Sep 1996 Cover: 3.95 **NM** value: **Cover or less**
One-shot. wraparound cover. • information on Thor's career and supporting cast

THOSE ANNOYING POST BROS. — Vortex

1 ❑ Cover: 1.75 **NM** value: **3.00**
📖 Dopplekiller; Bugtown Is Anywhere It Wants to Be! **A:** Matt Howarth **W:** Matt Howarth; Lou Stathis

2 ❑ Cover: 1.75 **NM** value: **2.00**
A: Matt Howarth **W:** Matt Howarth

3 ❑ Cover: 1.75 **NM** value: **2.00**
A: Matt Howarth **W:** Matt Howarth

4 ❑ Cover: 1.75 **NM** value: **2.00**
📖 Consummation Day **A:** Matt Howarth **W:** Matt Howarth; Lou Stathis

5 ❑ Cover: 1.75 **NM** value: **2.00**
A: Matt Howarth **W:** Matt Howarth

6 ❑ Cover: 1.75 **NM** value: **2.00**
A: Matt Howarth **W:** Matt Howarth

7 ❑ Cover: 1.75 **NM** value: **2.00**
A: Matt Howarth **W:** Matt Howarth

8 ❑ Cover: 1.75 **NM** value: **2.00**
A: Matt Howarth **W:** Matt Howarth

9 ❑ Cover: 1.75 **NM** value: **2.00**
A: Matt Howarth **W:** Matt Howarth

10 ❑ Cover: 1.75 **NM** value: **2.00**
A: Matt Howarth **W:** Matt Howarth

11 ❑ Cover: 1.75 **NM** value: **2.00**
A: Matt Howarth **W:** Matt Howarth

12 ❑ Cover: 1.75 **NM** value: **2.00**
A: Matt Howarth **W:** Matt Howarth

13 ❑ Cover: 1.75 **NM** value: **2.00**
A: Matt Howarth **W:** Matt Howarth

14 ❑ Cover: 1.75 **NM** value: **2.00**
A: Matt Howarth **W:** Matt Howarth

15 ❑ Cover: 2.00 **NM** value: **Cover or less**
A: Matt Howarth **W:** Matt Howarth

16 ❑ Cover: 2.00 **NM** value: **Cover or less**
A: Matt Howarth **W:** Matt Howarth

17 ❑ Cover: 2.00 **NM** value: **Cover or less**
A: Matt Howarth **W:** Matt Howarth

18 ❑ Cover: 2.00 **NM** value: **Cover or less**
• Series continues as Post Brothers **A:** Matt Howarth **W:** Matt Howarth

39 ❑ Aug 1994, b&w Cover: 2.50 **NM** value: **Cover or less**
• Series continued from "Post Brothers" #38 **A:** Matt Howarth **W:** Matt Howarth

40 ❑ Oct 1994, b&w Cover: 2.50 **NM** value: **Cover or less**
A: Matt Howarth **W:** Matt Howarth

41 ❑ Dec 1994, b&w Cover: 2.50 **NM** value: **Cover or less**
A: Matt Howarth **W:** Matt Howarth

42 ❑ Feb 1995, b&w Cover: 2.50 **NM** value: **Cover or less**
A: Matt Howarth **W:** Matt Howarth

43 ❑ Jun 1995, b&w Cover: 2.50 **NM** value: **Cover or less**
📖 Turf **A:** Matt Howarth **W:** Matt Howarth

44 ❑ Jul 1995, b&w Cover: 2.50 **NM** value: **Cover or less**
A: Matt Howarth **W:** Matt Howarth

45 ❑ Aug 1995, b&w Cover: 2.95 **NM** value: **Cover or less**
A: Matt Howarth **W:** Matt Howarth

46 ❑ Oct 1995, b&w Cover: 2.95 **NM** value: **Cover or less**
A: Matt Howarth **W:** Matt Howarth

47 ❑ Nov 1995, b&w Cover: 2.95 **NM** value: **Cover or less**
A: Matt Howarth **W:** Matt Howarth

48 ❑ Feb 1996, b&w Cover: 2.95 **NM** value: **Cover or less**
A: Matt Howarth **W:** Matt Howarth

Anl 1❑Aug 1995, b&w Cover: 4.95 **NM** value: **Cover or less**
cardstock cover. **A:** Matt Howarth **W:** Matt Howarth

Bk 1❑ Aug 1995 Cover: 14.95 **NM** value: **Cover or less**
• Das Loot

Bk 2❑ Sep 1995, b&w Cover: 9.99 **NM** value: **Cover or less**
• Disturb The Neighbors; collects #6-9

THOSE CRAZY PECKERS — U.S.Comics

1 ❑ Feb 1987 Cover: 2.00 **NM** value: **Cover or less**
📖 Hard Days Night **A:** Kent Bivens **W:** James Hallett

THOSE UNSTOPPABLE ROGUES — Original Syndicate

1 ❑ Mar 1995 Cover: 3.95 **NM** value: **Cover or less**
A: Michael Aushenker **W:** Michael Aushenker

THRAX — Event

1 ❑ Nov 1996 Cover: 2.95 **NM** value: **Cover or less**
Circ: Diamd. preorders: **13,982**
📖 Hardwired for Action **A:** Dave Ross **W:** Dave Ross; Mike Baron

2 ❑ Jan 1997 Cover: 2.95 **NM** value: **Cover or less**
Circ: Diamd. preorders: **6,378**

Other grades: Multiply prices above by **1.5 for Mint • 2/3 for Very Fine • 1/3 for Fine • 1/5 for Very Good • 1/8 for Good**

THREAT! — Fantagraphics

1 ❑ b&w Cover: 2.25 **NM** value: **Cover or less**
2 ❑ Cover: 2.25 **NM** value: **Cover or less**
3 ❑ Cover: 2.25 **NM** value: **Cover or less**
4 ❑ Cover: 2.25 **NM** value: **Cover or less**
5 ❑ Cover: 2.25 **NM** value: **Cover or less**
6 ❑ Cover: 2.25 **NM** value: **Cover or less**
7 ❑ Cover: 2.25 **NM** value: **Cover or less**
8 ❑ Jan 1987 Cover: 2.25 **NM** value: **Cover or less**
📖 Zone: As the Crow Flies; The Holo Brothers: Blue Brawls; Enigma Funnies: Rasslin' & Hasslin'; Usagi Yojimbo **A:** Jim Rohn; Gary Fields; Stan Sakai; Michael Kraiger **W:** Jim Rohn; Gary Fields; Stan Sakai; Michael Kraiger
9 ❑ 1987 Cover: 2.25 **NM** value: **Cover or less**
10 ❑ 1987 Cover: 2.25 **NM** value: **Cover or less**

THREE — Invincible

1 ❑ Cover: 2.00 **NM** value: **Cover or less**
📖 Love; City of Assassins, Part 1; Rough Beginnings, Part 1 **A:** Chris Higginson; Marc Brueland; Brian J. Hernandez **W:** Chris Higginson; Marc Brueland
2 ❑ Cover: 2.00 **NM** value: **Cover or less**
3 ❑ Cover: 2.00 **NM** value: **Cover or less**
4 ❑ Cover: 2.00 **NM** value: **Cover or less**
📖 City of Assassins-Chapter 4; Griffons; Lost and Found-Chapter 3 **A:** Chris Higginson; Gagriel Zetheniah; Rayel Friesen **W:** Chris Higginson; Gagriel Zetheniah; Rayel Friesen

3-D ADVENTURE COMICS — Stats Etc.

1 ❑ Aug 1986 Cover: 1.50 **NM** value: **2.00**

3-D ALIEN TERROR — Eclipse

1 ❑ Jun 1986 Cover: 2.50 **NM** value: **Cover or less**
📖 The Wishing World; Oral Hygienist; It ...was just a Matter of Time; Now You see It... **A:** Gray Morrow; John Pound; Jordi Diaz Castrillo; Keith Tucker; Mark Evanier **W:** Bruce Jones; John Pound; Keith Tucker; Mark Evanier; Jake Lincoln

3-D-ELL — Dell

1 ❑ ca. 1953 Cover: 0.25 **NM** value: **200.00**
📖 Flukey Luke • Rootie Kazootie
2 ❑ ca. 1953 Cover: 0.25 **NM** value: **150.00**
• Rootie Kazootie
3 ❑ ca. 1953 Cover: 0.25 **NM** value: **150.00**
• Flukey Luke

3-D EXOTIC BEAUTIES — 3-D Zone

1 ❑ Cover: 3.50 **NM** value: **Cover or less**
No issue number. **A:** L.B. Cole

3-D HEROES — Blackthorne

1 ❑ Cover: 2.00 **NM** value: **2.50**
📖 Rescue • In 3-D, glasses not included **A:** Steve Huston **W:** Cliff MacGillivray

3-D HOLLYWOOD — 3-D Zone

1 ❑ Cover: 2.95 **NM** value: **Cover or less**
• paper dolls

THREE DIMENSIONAL E.C. CLASSICS — E.C.

1 ❑ Spr 1954 **NM** value: **750.00**
• **CGC:** 9 graded, best 9.0

3-D SHEENA, JUNGLE QUEEN — Real Adventures

1 ❑ Cover: 0.25 **NM** value: **400.00**
• in 3-D, glasses included

3-D SPACE ZOMBIES — 3-D Zone

1 ❑ Cover: 3.95 **NM** value: **Cover or less**
No issue number.

3-D SUBSTANCE — 3-D Zone

1 ❑ Cover: 2.95 **NM** value: **Cover or less**
No issue number. **A:** Steve Ditko
2 ❑ Cover: 3.95 **NM** value: **Cover or less**

3-D THREE STOOGES — Eclipse

1 ❑ Cover: 2.50 **NM** value: **Cover or less**
📖 Men In The Moon • Stuntgirl backup feature **A:** Norman Maurer **W:** Norman Maurer
2 ❑ Cover: 2.50 **NM** value: **Cover or less**
📖 The Bandit Moons **A:** Norman Maurer **W:** Norman Maurer
3 ❑ Cover: 2.50 **NM** value: **Cover or less**
📖 Uncivil Warriors; Dee-Fective Comics **A:** Norman Maurer **W:** Norman Maurer

3-D TRUE CRIME — 3-D Zone

1 ❑ Cover: 3.95 **NM** value: **Cover or less**

3-D ZONE, THE — 3-D Zone

1 ❑ ca. 1986 Cover: 2.50 **NM** value: **Cover or less**
Circ: CapCity orders: **3,000**
2 ❑ ca. 1986 Cover: 2.50 **NM** value: **Cover or less**
Circ: CapCity orders: **2,375**
3 ❑ ca. 1987 Cover: 2.50 **NM** value: **Cover or less**
Circ: CapCity orders: **1,800**
4 ❑ ca. 1987 Cover: 2.50 **NM** value: **Cover or less**
Circ: CapCity orders: **1,325**
📖 Electric Fear • Electric Fear
5 ❑ ca. 1987 Cover: 2.50 **NM** value: **Cover or less**
• Krazy Kat
6 ❑ ca. 1987 Cover: 2.50 **NM** value: **Cover or less**
• Rat Fink
7 ❑ ca. 1987 Cover: 2.50 **NM** value: **Cover or less**
• Hollywood **A:** Joe Kubert
8 ❑ ca. 1987 Cover: 2.50 **NM** value: **Cover or less**
• High Seas **A:** Joe Kubert
9 ❑ ca. 1987 Cover: 2.50 **NM** value: **Cover or less**
• Red Mask
10 ❑ ca. 1987 Cover: 2.50 **NM** value: **Cover or less**
Circ: CapCity orders: **1,500**
• Jet **A:** Al Williamson
11 ❑ ca. 1987 Cover: 2.50 **NM** value: **Cover or less**
Circ: CapCity orders: **1,350**
• Matt Fox
12 ❑ ca. 1987 Cover: 2.50 **NM** value: **Cover or less**
• Presidents
13 ❑ ca. 1988 Cover: 2.50 **NM** value: **Cover or less**
Circ: CapCity orders: **2,500**
• Flash Gordon
14 ❑ ca. 1988 Cover: 2.50 **NM** value: **Cover or less**
Circ: CapCity orders: **1,025**
• Tyranostar
15 ❑ ca. 1988 Cover: 2.50 **NM** value: **Cover or less**
• humor **A:** Harvey Kurtzman
16 ❑ ca. 1988 Cover: 2.50 **NM** value: **Cover or less**
• space vixens **A:** Dan Spiegle
17 ❑ ca. 1988 Cover: 2.50 **NM** value: **Cover or less**
📖 My Marriage was Doomed!; I Was a Stepmother at Twenty; Make Him Love Me!; My Secret Husband, My Second-Hand Proposal; I Was a Spoiled Brat; Too Late For Love • Thrilling Love **A:** Al Feldstein; Frank Frazetta; Wally Wood; Ross Andru; Jack Kamen; Mike Esposito; Tony Alderson
18 ❑ ca. 1988 Cover: 2.50 **NM** value: **Cover or less**
19 ❑ ca. 1989 Cover: 2.50 **NM** value: **Cover or less**
• Cracked
20 ❑ ca. 1989 Cover: 2.50 **NM** value: **Cover or less**
• Atomic Sub

.357! — Mu

1 ❑ b&w Cover: 2.25 **NM** value: **2.50**

3 GEEKS, THE — 3 Finger Prints

1 ❑ Sep 1997 Cover: 2.50 **NM** value: **3.50**
• **CGC:** 1 graded, best 9.6
📖 Going to the Con, Part 1 **A:** Rich Koslowski **W:** Rich Koslowski
1-2 ❑ Cover: 2.50 **NM** value: **Cover or less**
2 ❑ Oct 1997 Cover: 2.50 **NM** value: **2.75**
• **CGC:** 1 graded, best 9.6
📖 Going to the Con, Part 2 **A:** Rich Koslowski **W:** Rich Koslowski
3 ❑ Nov 1997 Cover: 2.50 **NM** value: **2.75**
• **CGC:** 2 graded, best 9.8
📖 Going to the Con, Part 3 • Brain Boy back-up **A:** Rich Koslowski **W:** Rich Koslowski
4 ❑ Jan 1998 Cover: 2.50 **NM** value: **3.50**
• **CGC:** 1 graded, best 9.4
• Brain Boy back-up **A:** Rich Koslowski **W:** Rich Koslowski
5 ❑ ca. 1998 Cover: 2.50 **NM** value: **3.50**
📖 The Collector City Club, Part 1 **A:** Rich Koslowski **W:** Rich Koslowski
6 ❑ ca. 1998 Cover: 2.50 **NM** value: **3.50**
📖 The Collector City Club, Part 2 **A:** Rich Koslowski **W:** Rich Koslowski
7 ❑ ca. 1998 Cover: 2.50 **NM** value: **3.50**
📖 Mission Jimpossible **A:** Rich Koslowski **W:** Rich Koslowski
8 ❑ Sep 1998 Cover: 3.50 **NM** value: **Cover or less**
Circ: Diamd. preorders: **1,875** • **CGC:** 1 graded, best 9.4
📖 Get A Job! **A:** Rich Koslowski **W:** Rich Koslowski
9 ❑ Feb 1999 Cover: 2.50 **NM** value: **Cover or less**
Circ: Diamd. preorders: **1,756**
📖 Marvelous Movie Marathon; Close Call!; Sky; Comic Survival Tip #64 • movie night **A:** Rich Koslowski; Eddy Newell; Jason Asala **W:** Rich Koslowski
10 ❑ Apr 1999 Cover: 2.50 **NM** value: **Cover or less**
Circ: Diamd. preorders: **1,656**
📖 Happy Birthday Allen!, Part 1 • Allen's birthday **A:** Rich Koslowski **W:** Rich Koslowski
11 ❑ Jun 1999 Cover: 2.50 **NM** value: **Cover or less**
Circ: Diamd. preorders: **1,706**
📖 Happy Birthday Allen!, Part 2 • Allen's redemption **A:** Rich Koslowski **W:** Rich Koslowski

300 — Dark Horse

1 ❑ May 1998 Cover: 2.95 **NM** value: **3.50**
Circ: Diamd. preorders: **48,986**
📖 Honor **A:** Frank Miller **W:** Frank Miller
2 ❑ Jun 1998 Cover: 2.95 **NM** value: **3.50**
Circ: Diamd. preorders: **43,110**
3 ❑ Jul 1998 Cover: 2.95 **NM** value: **3.25**
Circ: Diamd. preorders: **41,152**
📖 Glory **A:** Frank Miller **W:** Frank Miller
4 ❑ Aug 1998 Cover: 2.95 **NM** value: **3.25**
Circ: Diamd. preorders: **43,646**
📖 Combat **A:** Frank Miller **W:** Frank Miller
5 ❑ Sep 1998 Cover: 3.95 **NM** value: **Cover or less**
Circ: Diamd. preorders: **45,426**
📖 Victory **A:** Frank Miller **W:** Frank Miller
Bk 1/HC❑ **NM** value: **30.00**
Hardcover collection of series. **A:** Frank Miller **W:** Frank Miller

Diamond preorders are the estimated number of comics sold, prior to their release, to comics shops in North America by Diamond Comic Distributors, the largest distributor. These figures underreport the actual number of circulating copies by the amount of reorders Diamond took (usually 5-10% again of the preorders) and sales by publishers to newsstand and bookstore distributors. For many independent publishers, Diamond's preorders may be quite close to the actual number of copies in circulation.

THREE MOUSEKETEERS — DC

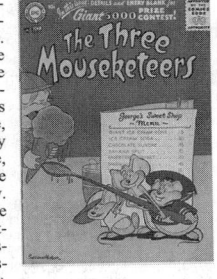

Sheldon Mayer created this funny-animal team as well as the classics Scribbly and Sugar and Spike. The team here consists of three mice, a fat one (Fatsy, ostensibly the head of the gang), a tall, skinny, not-quite-bright one (Patsy), and Minus (the most active, the most aware, and the most easily upset). They meet in a vegetable-can clubhouse, where they often decide on the project that will occupy the story. This is not to be confused with the Mouse Musketeers, which consisted of Jerry and Tuffy Mouse as musketeers and Tom as a royal guardsman during the French aristocracy.

The last issue showed a cat's hand pulling the plug out of a sink, with the three mice (two of them so far oblivious to the danger) about to go down the drain. Yikes. — Maggie

1 ❑ Mar 1956 Cover: 0.10 **NM** value: **150.00**
• **CGC:** 1 graded, best 7.0
2 ❑ May 1956 Cover: 0.10 **NM** value: **75.00**
3 ❑ Aug 1956 Cover: 0.10 **NM** value: **75.00**
4 ❑ Oct 1956 Cover: 0.10 **NM** value: **75.00**
5 ❑ Dec 1956 Cover: 0.10 **NM** value: **75.00**
6 ❑ Feb 1957 Cover: 0.10 **NM** value: **50.00**
7 ❑ Apr 1957 Cover: 0.10 **NM** value: **50.00**
8 ❑ Jun 1957 Cover: 0.10 **NM** value: **50.00**
9 ❑ Jul 1957 Cover: 0.10 **NM** value: **50.00**
10 ❑ Aug 1957 Cover: 0.10 **NM** value: **50.00**
11 ❑ Oct 1957 Cover: 0.10 **NM** value: **40.00**
12 ❑ Dec 1957 Cover: 0.10 **NM** value: **40.00**
13 ❑ Jan 1958 Cover: 0.10 **NM** value: **40.00**
14 ❑ Feb 1958 Cover: 0.10 **NM** value: **40.00**
15 ❑ ca. 1958 Cover: 0.10 **NM** value: **40.00**
16 ❑ May 1958 Cover: 0.10 **NM** value: **35.00**
17 ❑ Jul 1958 Cover: 0.10 **NM** value: **35.00**
18 ❑ Aug 1958 Cover: 0.10 **NM** value: **35.00**
19 ❑ Oct 1958 Cover: 0.10 **NM** value: **35.00**
20 ❑ Nov 1958 Cover: 0.10 **NM** value: **35.00**
21 ❑ Feb 1959 Cover: 0.10 **NM** value: **25.00**
22 ❑ Apr 1959 Cover: 0.10 **NM** value: **25.00**
23 ❑ Jun 1959 Cover: 0.10 **NM** value: **25.00**
24 ❑ ca. 1959 Cover: 0.10 **NM** value: **25.00**
25 ❑ ca. 1960 Cover: 0.10 **NM** value: **25.00**
26 ❑ Dec 1960 Cover: 0.10 **NM** value: **25.00**

THREE MUSKETEERS (ETERNITY) — Eternity

1 ❑ Dec 1988, b&w Cover: 1.95 **NM** value: **Cover or less**
2 ❑ Feb 1989, b&w Cover: 1.95 **NM** value: **Cover or less**
3 ❑ Apr 1989, b&w Cover: 1.95 **NM** value: **Cover or less**
Bk 1❑ Cover: 9.95 **NM** value: **Cover or less**

THREE MUSKETEERS (MARVEL) — Marvel

1 ❑ Cover: 1.50 **NM** value: **Cover or less**
Circ: CapCity orders: **5,600**
2 ❑ Cover: 1.50 **NM** value: **Cover or less**
Circ: CapCity orders: **5,400**

3 NINJAS KICK BACK — Now

1 ❑ Jun 1994 Cover: 1.95 **NM** value: **Cover or less**
📖 Curveballs and Goofballs **A:** Rafael Navarro **W:** Clint McElroy
2 ❑ Cover: 1.95 **NM** value: **Cover or less**
3 ❑ Cover: 1.95 **NM** value: **Cover or less**

THREE STOOGES, THE — Gold Key

6 ❑ Nov 1961 Cover: 0.15 **NM** value: **65.00**
• Previous issues published as Four Color #1043, #1078, #1127, #1170, and #1187.
7 ❑ Jan 1962 Cover: 0.15 **NM** value: **48.00**
8 ❑ Mar 1962 Cover: 0.15 **NM** value: **40.00**
9 ❑ Aug 1962 Cover: 0.15 **NM** value: **40.00**
10 ❑ Oct 1962 **NM** value: **40.00**
11 ❑ 1963 Cover: 0.12 **NM** value: **28.00**
Circ: Statement: **354,785**
12 ❑ ca. 1963 Cover: 0.12 **NM** value: **28.00**
Circ: Statement: **354,785**
13 ❑ Jul 1963 Cover: 0.12 **NM** value: **28.00**
Circ: Statement: **354,785** • **CGC:** 1 graded, best 9.0
14 ❑ ca. 1963 Cover: 0.12 **NM** value: **28.00**
Circ: Statement: **354,785**
15 ❑ Jan 1964 Cover: 0.12 **NM** value: **28.00**
Circ: Statement: **322,860**
16 ❑ Mar 1964 Cover: 0.12 **NM** value: **28.00**
Circ: Statement: **322,860**
17 ❑ May 1964 Cover: 0.12 **NM** value: **28.00**
Circ: Statement: **322,860**
18 ❑ Jul 1964 Cover: 0.12 **NM** value: **28.00**
Circ: Statement: **322,860**
19 ❑ Sep 1964 Cover: 0.12 **NM** value: **28.00**
Circ: Statement: **322,860**
20 ❑ Nov 1964 Cover: 0.12 **NM** value: **28.00**
Circ: Statement: **322,860**
21 ❑ Jan 1965 Cover: 0.12 **NM** value: **22.00**
Circ: Statement: **288,967**
22 ❑ Mar 1965 Cover: 0.12 **NM** value: **22.00**
Circ: Statement: **288,967**
23 ❑ May 1965 Cover: 0.12 **NM** value: **22.00**
Circ: Statement: **288,967**
24 ❑ Jul 1965 Cover: 0.12 **NM** value: **22.00**
Circ: Statement: **288,967**
25 ❑ Sep 1965 Cover: 0.12 **NM** value: **22.00**
Circ: Statement: **288,967**
26 ❑ 1965 Cover: 0.12 **NM** value: **22.00**
Circ: Statement: **288,967**

CGC-graded: Multiply prices above by **33 for 9.9 M** • **16 for 9.8 NM/M** • **7 for 9.6 NM+** • **5 for 9.4 NM** • **2.5 for 9.2 NM-** • **1.5 for 9.0 VF/NM**

27 ❑ Mar 1966 Cover: 0.12 **NM** value: **22.00**
Circ: Statement: **266,701**
28 ❑ May 1966 Cover: 0.12 **NM** value: **22.00**
Circ: Statement: **266,701**
29 ❑ Jul 1966 Cover: 0.12 **NM** value: **22.00**
Circ: Statement: **266,701**
30 ❑ Sep 1966 Cover: 0.12 **NM** value: **22.00**
Circ: Statement: **266,701**
31 ❑ Jan 1967 Cover: 0.12 **NM** value: **18.00**
Circ: Statement: **253,384**
32 ❑ Mar 1967 Cover: 0.12 **NM** value: **18.00**
Circ: Statement: **253,384**
33 ❑ May 1967 Cover: 0.12 **NM** value: **18.00**
Circ: Statement: **253,384**
• Has 1966 Statement; avg print run 386,993; avg sales 266,360; avg subs 341; avg total paid 266,701; samples 566; max existent 267,267; 31% of run returned
34 ❑ Jul 1967 Cover: 0.12 **NM** value: **18.00**
Circ: Statement: **253,384**
35 ❑ Sep 1967 Cover: 0.12 **NM** value: **18.00**
Circ: Statement: **253,384**
36 ❑ Nov 1967 Cover: 0.12 **NM** value: **18.00**
Circ: Statement: **253,384**
37 ❑ Dec 1967 Cover: 0.12 **NM** value: **18.00**
Circ: Statement: **253,384**
38 ❑ Mar 1968 Cover: 0.12 **NM** value: **18.00**
39 ❑ Jun 1968 Cover: 0.12 **NM** value: **18.00**
40 ❑ Sep 1968 Cover: 0.15 **NM** value: **18.00**
41 ❑ Dec 1968 Cover: 0.15 **NM** value: **15.00**
• **CGC:** 1 graded, best 8.5
42 ❑ Mar 1969 Cover: 0.15 **NM** value: **15.00**
43 ❑ Jun 1969 Cover: 0.15 **NM** value: **15.00**
44 ❑ Sep 1969 Cover: 0.15 **NM** value: **15.00**
45 ❑ Dec 1969 Cover: 0.15 **NM** value: **15.00**
46 ❑ Mar 1970 Cover: 0.15 **NM** value: **15.00**
47 ❑ Jun 1970 Cover: 0.15 **NM** value: **15.00**
48 ❑ Sep 1970 Cover: 0.15 **NM** value: **15.00**
49 ❑ Dec 1970 Cover: 0.15 **NM** value: **15.00**
50 ❑ Mar 1971 Cover: 0.15 **NM** value: **15.00**
Circ: Statement: **177,111**
• as ape-men; Little Monsters back-up
51 ❑ Jun 1971 Cover: 0.15 **NM** value: **15.00**
Circ: Statement: **177,111**
52 ❑ Sep 1971 Cover: 0.15 **NM** value: **15.00**
Circ: Statement: **177,111**
53 ❑ Dec 1971 Cover: 0.15 **NM** value: **15.00**
Circ: Statement: **177,111**
54 ❑ Mar 1972 Cover: 0.15 **NM** value: **15.00**
55 ❑ Jun 1972 Cover: 0.15 **NM** value: **15.00**
• Has 1971 Statement; avg print run 283,877;avg total paid 177,111

THREE STOOGES IN 3-D — Eternity
1 ❑ Cover: 3.95 **NM** value: **Cover or less**
Circ: CapCity orders: **1,500**

THREE STOOGES IN FULL COLOR — Eternity
1 ❑ Cover: 5.95 **NM** value: **Cover or less**
Circ: CapCity orders: **1,430**

THREE STOOGES MEET HERCULES, THE — Dell
1 ❑ Aug 1962 Cover: 0.15 **NM** value: **75.00**
• **CGC:** 1 graded, best 9.4

THREE STOOGES (ST. JOHN) — St. John
1 ❑ Sep 1953 Cover: 0.10 **NM** value: **1000.00**
2 ❑ Oct 1953 Cover: 0.10 **NM** value: **750.00**
• **CGC:** 2 graded, best 8.5
3 ❑ Nov 1953 Cover: 0.10 **NM** value: **600.00**
• **CGC:** 2 graded, best 8.5
4 ❑ Mar 1954 Cover: 0.10 **NM** value: **400.00**
5 ❑ May 1954 Cover: 0.10 **NM** value: **350.00**
6 ❑ Aug 1954 Cover: 0.10 **NM** value: **350.00**
7 ❑ Oct 1954 Cover: 0.10 **NM** value: **350.00**

THREE STOOGES: THE KNUCKLEHEADS RETURN — Eternity
Bk 1❑ b&w Cover: 14.95 **NM** value: **Cover or less**

3X3 EYES — Innovation
1 ❑ b&w Cover: 2.25 **NM** value: **2.50**
• Japanese **A:** Yuzo Takada **W:** Yuzo Takada
2 ❑ b&w Cover: 2.25 **NM** value: **Cover or less**
• Japanese **A:** Yuzo Takada **W:** Yuzo Takada
3 ❑ b&w Cover: 2.25 **NM** value: **Cover or less**
• Japanese **A:** Yuzo Takada **W:** Yuzo Takada
4 ❑ b&w Cover: 2.25 **NM** value: **Cover or less**
• Japanese **A:** Yuzo Takada **W:** Yuzo Takada
5 ❑ b&w Cover: 2.25 **NM** value: **Cover or less**
• Japanese **A:** Yuzo Takada **W:** Yuzo Takada
Bk 1❑ Cover: 12.95 **NM** value: **Cover or less**
• House of Demons trade paperback **A:** Yuzo Takada **W:** Yuzo Takada

3X3 EYES: CURSE OF THE GESU — Dark Horse / Manga
1 ❑ Oct 1995, b&w Cover: 2.95 **NM** value: **Cover or less**
2 ❑ Nov 1995, b&w Cover: 2.95 **NM** value: **Cover or less**
3 ❑ Dec 1995, b&w Cover: 2.95 **NM** value: **Cover or less**
4 ❑ Jan 1996, b&w Cover: 2.95 **NM** value: **Cover or less**
5 ❑ Feb 1996, b&w Cover: 2.95 **NM** value: **Cover or less**
final issue. **A:** Yuzo Takada **W:** Yuzo Takada
Bk 1❑ Feb 1997, b&w Cover: 12.95 **NM** value: **Cover or less**
• Collects Curse of the Gesu #1-5 **A:** Yuzo Takada **W:** Yuzo Takada

THRESHOLD (1ST SERIES) — Sleeping Giant
1 ❑ Oct 1996, b&w Cover: 2.50 **NM** value: **Cover or less**
2 ❑ Nov 1996, b&w Cover: 2.50 **NM** value: **Cover or less**
final issue.

THRESHOLD (2ND SERIES) — Sleeping Giant
1 ❑ Dec 1997, b&w Cover: 2.50 **NM** value: **Cover or less**
📖 Nico-Teen **A:** David Yurkovich **W:** David Yurkovich
2 ❑ Mar 1998, b&w Cover: 2.50 **NM** value: **Cover or less**
📖 The Hair Club **A:** David Yurkovich **W:** David Yurkovich
3 ❑ 1998 Cover: 2.50 **NM** value: **Cover or less**
📖 The Demolition **A:** David Yurkovich **W:** David Yurkovich
3/Aut❑ 1998 Cover: 2.50 **NM** value: **Cover or less**
📖 The Demolition **A:** David Yurkovich **W:** David Yurkovich

THRESHOLD (3RD SERIES) — Avatar
1 ❑ Feb 1998 Cover: 4.95 **NM** value: **Cover or less**
2 ❑ Mar 1998 Cover: 4.95 **NM** value: **Cover or less**
3 ❑ Apr 1998 Cover: 4.95 **NM** value: **Cover or less**
4 ❑ May 1998 Cover: 4.95 **NM** value: **Cover or less**
📖 Donna Mia; Black Reign; Journeymen; Lookers **A:** Shelby Robertson; Albert Holaso; Brock Hor Jr.; Trevlin Utz **W:** Shelby Robertson; Trevlin Utz; Barry Gregory
5 ❑ Jun 1998 Cover: 4.95 **NM** value: **Cover or less**
6 ❑ Jul 1998 Cover: 4.95 **NM** value: **Cover or less**
7 ❑ Aug 1998 Cover: 4.95 **NM** value: **Cover or less**
8 ❑ Sep 1998 Cover: 4.95 **NM** value: **Cover or less**
Circ: Diamd. preorders: **3,036**
9 ❑ Oct 1998 Cover: 4.95 **NM** value: **Cover or less**
Circ: Diamd. preorders: **1,897**
10 ❑ Nov 1998 Cover: 4.95 **NM** value: **Cover or less**
11 ❑ Dec 1998 Cover: 4.95 **NM** value: **Cover or less**
Circ: Diamd. preorders: **2,119**
12 ❑ Jan 1999 Cover: 4.95 **NM** value: **Cover or less**
Circ: Diamd. preorders: **1,917**
13 ❑ Feb 1999 Cover: 4.95 **NM** value: **Cover or less**
Circ: Diamd. preorders: **1,802**
14 ❑ Mar 1999 Cover: 4.95 **NM** value: **Cover or less**
Circ: Diamd. preorders: **2,152**
15 ❑ Apr 1999 Cover: 4.95 **NM** value: **Cover or less**
Circ: Diamd. preorders: **1,869**
16 ❑ May 1999 Cover: 4.95 **NM** value: **Cover or less**
17 ❑ Jun 1999 Cover: 4.95 **NM** value: **Cover or less**
Circ: Diamd. preorders: **1,970**
18 ❑ Jul 1999 Cover: 4.95 **NM** value: **Cover or less**
Circ: Diamd. preorders: **1,749**
19 ❑ Aug 1999 Cover: 4.95 **NM** value: **Cover or less**
20 ❑ Sep 1999 Cover: 4.95 **NM** value: **Cover or less**
21 ❑ Oct 1999 Cover: 4.95 **NM** value: **Cover or less**
22 ❑ Nov 1999 Cover: 4.95 **NM** value: **Cover or less**
23 ❑ Dec 1999 Cover: 4.95 **NM** value: **Cover or less**
24 ❑ Jan 2000 Cover: 4.95 **NM** value: **Cover or less**
Circ: Diamd. preorders: **2,151**
25 ❑ Feb 2000 Cover: 4.95 **NM** value: **Cover or less**
Circ: Diamd. preorders: **3,244**
26 ❑ Mar 2000 Cover: 4.95 **NM** value: **Cover or less**
Circ: Diamd. preorders: **2,751**
27 ❑ Apr 2000 Cover: 4.95 **NM** value: **Cover or less**
Circ: Diamd. preorders: **2,727**
28 ❑ May 2000 Cover: 4.95 **NM** value: **Cover or less**
Circ: Diamd. preorders: **2,710**
29 ❑ Jun 2000 Cover: 4.95 **NM** value: **Cover or less**
Circ: Diamd. preorders: **2,680**
30 ❑ Jul 2000 Cover: 4.95 **NM** value: **Cover or less**
Circ: Diamd. preorders: **2,721**
31 ❑ Aug 2000 Cover: 4.95 **NM** value: **Cover or less**
32 ❑ Sep 2000 Cover: 4.95 **NM** value: **Cover or less**
33 ❑ Oct 2000 Cover: 4.95 **NM** value: **Cover or less**
34 ❑ Nov 2000 Cover: 4.95 **NM** value: **Cover or less**
Circ: Diamd. preorders: **1,448**
35 ❑ Dec 2000 Cover: 4.95 **NM** value: **Cover or less**
Circ: Diamd. preorders: **1,392**
36 ❑ Jan 2001 Cover: 4.95 **NM** value: **Cover or less**
Circ: Diamd. preorders: **1,329**
37 ❑ Feb 2001 Cover: 4.95 **NM** value: **Cover or less**
Circ: Diamd. preorders: **1,312**
38 ❑ Mar 2001 Cover: 4.95 **NM** value: **Cover or less**
Circ: Diamd. preorders: **1,342**
39 ❑ Apr 2001 Cover: 4.95 **NM** value: **Cover or less**
Circ: Diamd. preorders: **1,527**
40 ❑ May 2001 Cover: 4.95 **NM** value: **Cover or less**
Circ: Diamd. preorders: **1,347**
41 ❑ Jun 2001 Cover: 4.95 **NM** value: **Cover or less**
Circ: Diamd. preorders: **1,410**
42 ❑ Jul 2001 Cover: 4.95 **NM** value: **Cover or less**
Circ: Diamd. preorders: **1,399**

THRESHOLD OF REALITY — Maintech
1 ❑ Sep 1986 Cover: 1.00 **NM** value: **Cover or less**
2 ❑ Cover: 1.00 **NM** value: **Cover or less**
3 ❑ Cover: 1.00 **NM** value: **Cover or less**

THRESHOLD: THE STAMP COLLECTOR — Sleeping Giant
1 ❑ Mar 1997, b&w Cover: 2.50 **NM** value: **Cover or less**
2 ❑ May 1997, b&w Cover: 2.50 **NM** value: **Cover or less**

THRILLER — DC
1 ❑ Nov 1983 Cover: 1.25 **NM** value: **2.00**
📖 Downtime, Part 1 **A:** Trevor Von Eeden **C:** Trevor Von Eeden **W:** Robert Loren Flemming
2 ❑ Dec 1983 Cover: 1.25 **NM** value: **1.75**
★ Origin of Thriller.
3 ❑ Jan 1984 Cover: 1.25 **NM** value: **1.75**
4 ❑ Feb 1984 Cover: 1.25 **NM** value: **1.50**
5 ❑ Mar 1984 Cover: 1.25 **NM** value: **1.50**
• Elvis satire
6 ❑ Apr 1984 Cover: 1.25 **NM** value: **1.50**
• Elvis satire
7 ❑ May 1984 Cover: 1.25 **NM** value: **1.50**
8 ❑ Jun 1984 Cover: 1.25 **NM** value: **1.50**
9 ❑ Jul 1984 Cover: 1.25 **NM** value: **1.50**
10 ❑ Aug 1984 Cover: 1.25 **NM** value: **1.50**
11 ❑ Sep 1984 Cover: 1.25 **NM** value: **1.50**
12 ❑ Oct 1984 Cover: 1.25 **NM** value: **1.50**

THRILLING ADVENTURE STORIES — Atlas-Seaboard
1 ❑ Feb 1975, b&w Cover: 0.75 **NM** value: **5.00**
• magazine. 📖 Tigerman and the Flesh Peddlers; The Sting of Death; Kromag the Killer; Lawrence of Arabia; Escape from Nine by 1 **A:** Frank Thorne; Ernie Colon; Russ Heath; Jack Sparling; Leo Summers **W:** Russ Heath; Jack Sparling; John Albano; Gabe Levy; Jeff Rovin
2 ❑ Aug 1975 Cover: 0.75 **NM** value: **4.00**

THRILLING ADVENTURE STRIPS — Dragon Lady
5 ❑ 1986 Cover: 2.95 **NM** value: **Cover or less**
• (formerly Best of Tribune Company)
6 ❑ 1986 Cover: 2.95 **NM** value: **Cover or less**
7 ❑ 1986 Cover: 2.95 **NM** value: **Cover or less**
8 ❑ 1987 Cover: 2.95 **NM** value: **Cover or less**
9 ❑ Mar 1987 Cover: 2.95 **NM** value: **Cover or less**
10 ❑ 1987 Cover: 2.95 **NM** value: **Cover or less**

THRILLING COMICS (1ST SERIES) — Better
Years before Stephen Strange would study the mystic arts to become Doctor Strange, Sorcerer Supreme, there was another Doc Strange.

This incarnation was a thinly disguised Doc Savage clone with dark hair piled high in a pompadour, blue or green johdpurs and a red muscle shirt.

In addition to Doc Strange, Thrilling Comics also featured the adventures of The American Crusader and The Commando Cubs.

In the years following World War II, Thrilling shifted focus to jungle-based adventure, then, when tastes changed again, to Westerns. — Brent

1 ❑ Feb 1940 Cover: 0.10 **NM** value: **2250.00**
• **CGC:** 2 graded, best 8.5
2 ❑ Mar 1940 Cover: 0.10 **NM** value: **1500.00**
• **CGC:** 2 graded, best 9.2
3 ❑ Apr 1940 Cover: 0.10 **NM** value: **1000.00**
• **CGC:** 2 graded, best 9.4
4 ❑ May 1940 Cover: 0.10 **NM** value: **750.00**
• **CGC:** 2 graded, best 8.5
5 ❑ Jun 1940 Cover: 0.10 **NM** value: **500.00**
• **CGC:** 5 graded, best 9.2
6 ❑ Jul 1940 Cover: 0.10 **NM** value: **500.00**
• **CGC:** 1 graded, best 9.4
7 ❑ Aug 1940 Cover: 0.10 **NM** value: **500.00**
• **CGC:** 2 graded, best 9.6
8 ❑ Sep 1940 Cover: 0.10 **NM** value: **500.00**
• **CGC:** 1 graded, best 9.4
9 ❑ Oct 1940 Cover: 0.10 **NM** value: **500.00**
• **CGC:** 1 graded, best 9.6
10 ❑ Nov 1940 Cover: 0.10 **NM** value: **500.00**
• **CGC:** 1 graded, best 9.6
11 ❑ Dec 1940 Cover: 0.10 **NM** value: **400.00**
• **CGC:** 1 graded, best 9.6
12 ❑ Jan 1941 Cover: 0.10 **NM** value: **400.00**
• **CGC:** 1 graded, best 9.4
13 ❑ Feb 1941 Cover: 0.10 **NM** value: **400.00**
• **CGC:** 1 graded, best 9.4
14 ❑ Mar 1941 Cover: 0.10 **NM** value: **400.00**
• **CGC:** 2 graded, best 9.6
15 ❑ Apr 1941 Cover: 0.10 **NM** value: **400.00**
• **CGC:** 2 graded, best 9.4
16 ❑ May 1941 Cover: 0.10 **NM** value: **400.00**
• **CGC:** 1 graded, best 9.6
17 ❑ Jun 1941 Cover: 0.10 **NM** value: **400.00**
• **CGC:** 1 graded, best 9.4
18 ❑ Jul 1941 Cover: 0.10 **NM** value: **400.00**
• **CGC:** 1 graded, best 9.0
19 ❑ Aug 1941 Cover: 0.10 **NM** value: **400.00**
• **CGC:** 2 graded, best 9.6
20 ❑ Sep 1941 Cover: 0.10 **NM** value: **400.00**
• **CGC:** 1 graded, best 8.5
21 ❑ Oct 1941 Cover: 0.10 **NM** value: **350.00**
22 ❑ Nov 1941 Cover: 0.10 **NM** value: **350.00**
• **CGC:** 1 graded, best 9.2
23 ❑ Dec 1941 Cover: 0.10 **NM** value: **350.00**
• **CGC:** 1 graded, best 6.0
24 ❑ Jan 1942 Cover: 0.10 **NM** value: **350.00**
25 ❑ Feb 1942 Cover: 0.10 **NM** value: **350.00**
26 ❑ Apr 1942 Cover: 0.10 **NM** value: **350.00**
27 ❑ May 1942 Cover: 0.10 **NM** value: **350.00**
28 ❑ Jun 1942 Cover: 0.10 **NM** value: **350.00**
• **CGC:** 1 graded, best 8.0
29 ❑ Aug 1942 Cover: 0.10 **NM** value: **350.00**
30 ❑ Oct 1942 Cover: 0.10 **NM** value: **350.00**
31 ❑ Nov 1942 Cover: 0.10 **NM** value: **350.00**
32 ❑ Jan 1943 Cover: 0.10 **NM** value: **350.00**
• **CGC:** 1 graded, best 9.6
33 ❑ Feb 1943 Cover: 0.10 **NM** value: **350.00**
34 ❑ Mar 1943 Cover: 0.10 **NM** value: **350.00**
35 ❑ May 1943 Cover: 0.10 **NM** value: **350.00**
• **CGC:** 1 graded, best 7.0
36 ❑ Jul 1943 Cover: 0.10 **NM** value: **350.00**
37 ❑ Aug 1943 Cover: 0.10 **NM** value: **350.00**
• **CGC:** 2 graded, best 9.4
38 ❑ Oct 1943 Cover: 0.10 **NM** value: **350.00**
• **CGC:** 1 graded, best 8.5

Other grades: Multiply prices above by **1.5 for Mint • 2/3 for Very Fine • 1/3 for Fine • 1/5 for Very Good • 1/8 for Good**

39 ❑ Dec 1943 Cover: 0.10 **NM** value: **350.00**
• **CGC:** 2 graded, best 9.4
40 ❑ Feb 1944 Cover: 0.10 **NM** value: **350.00**
41 ❑ Apr 1944 Cover: 0.10 **NM** value: **250.00**
• **CGC:** 3 graded, best 9.2
42 ❑ Jun 1944 Cover: 0.10 **NM** value: **250.00**
43 ❑ Aug 1944 Cover: 0.10 **NM** value: **250.00**
• **CGC:** 1 graded, best 9.4
44 ❑ Oct 1944 Cover: 0.10 **NM** value: **250.00**
• **CGC:** 1 graded, best 6.0
45 ❑ Dec 1944 Cover: 0.10 **NM** value: **250.00**
46 ❑ Feb 1945 Cover: 0.10 **NM** value: **250.00**
• **CGC:** 1 graded, best 6.5
47 ❑ Apr 1945 Cover: 0.10 **NM** value: **250.00**
48 ❑ Jun 1945 Cover: 0.10 **NM** value: **250.00**
• **CGC:** 2 graded, best 9.2
49 ❑ Aug 1945 Cover: 0.10 **NM** value: **250.00**
• **CGC:** 1 graded, best 6.0
50 ❑ Oct 1945 Cover: 0.10 **NM** value: **250.00**
• **CGC:** 1 graded, best 9.0
51 ❑ Dec 1945 Cover: 0.10 **NM** value: **250.00**
52 ❑ Feb 1946 Cover: 0.10 **NM** value: **250.00**
• **CGC:** 1 graded, best 9.6
53 ❑ Apr 1946 Cover: 0.10 **NM** value: **250.00**
• **CGC:** 1 graded, best 9.0
54 ❑ Jun 1946 Cover: 0.10 **NM** value: **250.00**
• **CGC:** 2 graded, best 8.0
55 ❑ Aug 1946 Cover: 0.10 **NM** value: **250.00**
56 ❑ Oct 1946 Cover: 0.10 **NM** value: **250.00**
• **CGC:** 1 graded, best .5
57 ❑ Dec 1946 Cover: 0.10 **NM** value: **250.00**
58 ❑ Feb 1947 Cover: 0.10 **NM** value: **250.00**
• **CGC:** 1 graded, best 8.0
59 ❑ Apr 1947 Cover: 0.10 **NM** value: **250.00**
• **CGC:** 1 graded, best 5.5
60 ❑ Jun 1947 Cover: 0.10 **NM** value: **250.00**
• **CGC:** 2 graded, best 9.2
61 ❑ Aug 1947 Cover: 0.10 **NM** value: **200.00**
• **CGC:** 1 graded, best 9.2
62 ❑ Oct 1947 Cover: 0.10 **NM** value: **200.00**
• **CGC:** 2 graded, best 9.4
63 ❑ Dec 1947 Cover: 0.10 **NM** value: **200.00**
• **CGC:** 5 graded, best 9.4
64 ❑ Feb 1948 Cover: 0.10 **NM** value: **200.00**
• **CGC:** 3 graded, best 9.4
65 ❑ Apr 1948 Cover: 0.10 **NM** value: **200.00**
• **CGC:** 4 graded, best 8.5
66 ❑ Jun 1948 Cover: 0.10 **NM** value: **200.00**
67 ❑ Aug 1948 Cover: 0.10 **NM** value: **200.00**
• **CGC:** 1 graded, best 8.5
68 ❑ Oct 1948 Cover: 0.10 **NM** value: **200.00**
• **CGC:** 6 graded, best 9.0
69 ❑ Dec 1948 Cover: 0.10 **NM** value: **200.00**
• **CGC:** 3 graded, best 9.2
70 ❑ Feb 1949 Cover: 0.10 **NM** value: **200.00**
• **CGC:** 3 graded, best 9.4
71 ❑ Apr 1949 Cover: 0.10 **NM** value: **200.00**
• **CGC:** 3 graded, best 9.4
72 ❑ Jun 1949 Cover: 0.10 **NM** value: **200.00**
73 ❑ Aug 1949 Cover: 0.10 **NM** value: **200.00**
74 ❑ Oct 1949 Cover: 0.10 **NM** value: **200.00**
• **CGC:** 1 graded, best 6.5
75 ❑ Dec 1949 Cover: 0.10 **NM** value: **200.00**
76 ❑ Feb 1950 Cover: 0.10 **NM** value: **200.00**
77 ❑ Cover: 0.10 **NM** value: **200.00**
78 ❑ Cover: 0.10 **NM** value: **200.00**
79 ❑ Cover: 0.10 **NM** value: **200.00**
80 ❑ Apr 1951 Cover: 0.10 **NM** value: **200.00**

THRILLING COMICS (2ND SERIES) — DC

1 ❑ May 1999 Cover: 1.99 **NM** value: **2.00**
Circ: Diamd. preorders: **42,461**
📖 No More Tomorrows • Manhunter apperance **A:** Russ Heath **W:** Chuck Dixon ★ Appearance of Wildcat, Tigress, Hawkman.

THRILLING CRIME CASES — Star Publications

41 ❑ Jun 1950 Cover: 0.10 **NM** value: **100.00**
• Series continued from 4Most #40
42 ❑ Oct 1950 Cover: 0.10 **NM** value: **58.00**
A: L.B. Cole(cover)
43 ❑ Jan 1951 Cover: 0.10 **NM** value: **58.00**
44 ❑ Apr 1951 Cover: 0.10 **NM** value: **58.00**
45 ❑ Jul 1951 Cover: 0.10 **NM** value: **58.00**
46 ❑ Oct 1951 Cover: 0.10 **NM** value: **50.00**
• **CGC:** 1 graded, best 5.0
47 ❑ Jan 1952 Cover: 0.10 **NM** value: **50.00**
48 ❑ Apr 1952 Cover: 0.10 **NM** value: **50.00**
49 ❑ Jul 1952 Cover: 0.10 **NM** value: **140.00**
• **CGC:** 3 graded, best 8.0
• Series continued in Shocking Mystery Cases #50 **A:** L.B. Cole(cover)

THRILLING PLANET TALES — AC

Bk 1❑ Cover: 9.95 **NM** value: **Cover or less**
• some b&w

THRILLING ROMANCES — Standard

5 ❑ Dec 1949 Cover: 0.10 **NM** value: **75.00**
6 ❑ Feb 1950 Cover: 0.10 **NM** value: **40.00**
📖 Honeymoon for three; Pricetag on Love; My Father was Fickle
7 ❑ May 1950 Cover: 0.10 **NM** value: **40.00**
8 ❑ Jul 1950 Cover: 0.10 **NM** value: **40.00**
9 ❑ ca. 1950 Cover: 0.10 **NM** value: **40.00**
10 ❑ ca. 1951 Cover: 0.10 **NM** value: **40.00**
11 ❑ ca. 1951 Cover: 0.10 **NM** value: **35.00**
12 ❑ ca. 1951 Cover: 0.10 **NM** value: **35.00**
13 ❑ ca. 1951 Cover: 0.10 **NM** value: **35.00**
14 ❑ ca. 1951 Cover: 0.10 **NM** value: **35.00**
15 ❑ ca. 1952 Cover: 0.10 **NM** value: **35.00**
16 ❑ ca. 1952 Cover: 0.10 **NM** value: **30.00**
17 ❑ ca. 1952 Cover: 0.10 **NM** value: **30.00**
18 ❑ ca. 1952 Cover: 0.10 **NM** value: **30.00**
19 ❑ ca. 1952 Cover: 0.10 **NM** value: **30.00**
20 ❑ ca. 1953 Cover: 0.10 **NM** value: **30.00**
21 ❑ ca. 1953 Cover: 0.10 **NM** value: **25.00**
22 ❑ ca. 1953 Cover: 0.10 **NM** value: **25.00**
23 ❑ ca. 1953 Cover: 0.10 **NM** value: **25.00**
24 ❑ ca. 1954 Cover: 0.10 **NM** value: **25.00**
25 ❑ ca. 1954 Cover: 0.10 **NM** value: **25.00**
26 ❑ ca. 1954 Cover: 0.10 **NM** value: **25.00**

THRILLING SCIENCE FICTION — Paragon

1 ❑ Cover: 9.95 **NM** value: **Cover or less**
Circ: CapCity orders: **2,475**
📖 Space Magnet; Lost World; Jealousy on Kano; Mars: God of War; Gale Allen and the Girl Squadron; Captain Science: The Martian Slavers; Mysta of the Moon; Mars: God of War: Cerebex **A:** George Evans; Henry C. Kiefer; Joe Orlando; Matt Baker; Wally Wood; Bernie Krigstein; Reed Crandall; Bill Benelus; Joe Doolin; Ray Willner **W:** Douglas McKee; Ross Gallun; Thornliffe Herrick

THRILLING SCIENCE TALES — AC

1 ❑ Cover: 3.50 **NM** value: **3.95**
A: Al Williamson; Frank Frazetta; Wally Wood **C:** Michael W. Kaluta
2 ❑ Cover: 3.50 **NM** value: **3.95**
📖 Stormy Tempest; Captain Video: The Missiles of Doom; Mysta of the Moon; Captain Science: The Martian Slavers **A:** George Evans; Joe Orlando; Wally Wood; Mark Heike; Robimor **W:** George Evans; Joe Orlando; Wally Wood; Mark Heike; John Dell; Ruben Moreira; John Skurulis

THRILLING TRUE STORY OF THE BASEBALL GIANTS, THE — Fawcett

1 ❑ ca. 1952 Cover: 0.10 **NM** value: **600.00**
• **CGC:** 1 graded, best 8.5

THRILLING TRUE STORY OF THE BASEBALL YANKEES, THE — Fawcett

1 ❑ ca. 1952 Cover: 0.10 **NM** value: **500.00**
• **CGC:** 1 graded, best 7.5

THRILLING WONDER TALES — AC

1 ❑ Spr 1991, b&w Cover: 2.95 **NM** value: **Cover or less**
No issue number. **A:** Joe Kubert; Wally Wood; Bob Powell

THRILL KILL — Caliber

1 ❑ b&w Cover: 2.50 **NM** value: **Cover or less**
A: Mark Winfrey **W:** Mark Winfrey

THRILLKILLER — DC

1 ❑ Jan 1997 Cover: 2.50 **NM** value: **Cover or less**
Circ: Diamd. preorders: **51,124** • **CGC:** 1 graded, best 9.4
• Elseworlds story **A:** Dan Brereton **W:** Howard Chaykin
2 ❑ Feb 1997 Cover: 2.50 **NM** value: **Cover or less**
Circ: Diamd. preorders: **41,105**
• Elseworlds story **A:** Dan Brereton **W:** Howard Chaykin
3 ❑ Mar 1997 Cover: 2.50 **NM** value: **Cover or less**
Circ: Diamd. preorders: **39,380**
• Elseworlds story **A:** Dan Brereton **W:** Howard Chaykin

THRILLKILLER '62 — DC

1 ❑ Apr 1998 Cover: 4.95 **NM** value: **Cover or less**
Circ: Diamd. preorders: **32,312**
No issue number. One-shot. • prestige format. • Elseworlds; sequel to Thrillkiller

THRILLOGY — Pacific

1 ❑ Cover: 1.50 **NM** value: **Cover or less**
📖 Prometheus Primeval; All That Glitters…; Red Rover, Red Rover **A:** Tim Conrad **W:** Tim Conrad

THRILL-O-RAMA — Harvey

1 ❑ Oct 1965 Cover: 0.12 **NM** value: **25.00**
📖 The Man in Black Called Fate; This is How it Might have Happened Part 1-2; Six Hours of Doom; When Time Ran Out; The Old Hulk
2 ❑ Sep 1966 Cover: 0.12 **NM** value: **16.00**
3 ❑ Cover: 0.12 **NM** value: **14.00**

THRILLS OF TOMORROW — Harvey

17 ❑ Oct 1954 Cover: 0.10 **NM** value: **100.00**
• **CGC:** 2 graded, best 9.2
18 ❑ Dec 1954 Cover: 0.10 **NM** value: **75.00**
• **CGC:** 1 graded, best 7.5
19 ❑ Feb 1955 Cover: 0.10 **NM** value: **75.00**
• **CGC:** 2 graded, best 9.0
20 ❑ Apr 1955 Cover: 0.10 **NM** value: **75.00**
• **CGC:** 4 graded, best 9.0

THROUGH THE HABITRAILS — Bad Habit

Bk 1❑ Feb 1994, b&w Cover: 9.95 **NM** value: **Cover or less**
• collection of Jeff Nicholson short stories

THUMB SCREW — Caliber

1 ❑ b&w Cover: 3.50 **NM** value: **Cover or less**
2 ❑ b&w Cover: 3.50 **NM** value: **Cover or less**

THUMP'N GUTS — Kitchen Sink

1 ❑ Cover: 2.95 **NM** value: **Cover or less**
• Poly-bag reads Project X, includes poster and trading card **A:** Kevin Eastman; Simon Bisley **W:** Kevin Eastman; Simon Bisley

THUN'DA COMICS — Magazine Enterprises

Thun'da was technically part of the series A-1 Comics, an anthology title with a different feature in each issue, but the six Thun'da issues are generally considered to be a standalone run of their own. Thun'da, King of the Congo, was a brazen Tarzan clone of the kind extremely pervasive on the comic stands during the 1940s and 1950s. He made a living contending with greedy ivory poachers and rescuing hapless maidens from the grip of unruly natives. Unremarkable stuff generally, except for the landmark first issue which bears the unique distinction of being the only comic book illustrated cover to cover by the great fantasy artist Frank Frazetta. Through Frazetta's masterful craftsmanship, the jungles teem with life and details; graceful human forms pour across the pages; eyes sunk in moody, shadow-lined faces convey depth far beyond the simplistic stories. Thun'da #1 was later reprinted as Thun'da Tales.

1 ❑ ca. 1952 Cover: 0.10 **NM** value: **685.00**
• **CGC:** 8 graded, best 8.5
📖 King of the Lost Lands; The Monsters from the Mists; Gods of the Jungle • A-1 Comics #47; All-Frazetta issue **A:** Frank Frazetta **W:** Gardner Fox ★ Origin of Thun'da.
2 ❑ ca. 1952 Cover: 0.10 **NM** value: **120.00**
• **CGC:** 1 graded, best 8.0
• A-1 Comics #56
3 ❑ ca. 1953 Cover: 0.10 **NM** value: **100.00**
• A-1 Comics #73
4 ❑ ca. 1953 Cover: 0.10 **NM** value: **75.00**
• A-1 Comics #78
5 ❑ ca. 1953 Cover: 0.10 **NM** value: **75.00**
• A-1 Comics #83
6 ❑ ca. 1953 Cover: 0.10 **NM** value: **75.00**
• A-1 Comics #86

THUN'DA, KING OF THE CONGO — AC

1 ❑ b&w Cover: 2.50 **NM** value: **Cover or less**
A: Bob Powell

THUN'DA TALES (FRANK FRAZETTA'S...) — Fantagraphics

1 ❑ ca. 1986 Cover: 2.00 **NM** value: **Cover or less**
Circ: CapCity orders: **4,050**
📖 King of the Lost Lands; The Monsters from the Mists; Gods of the Jungle **A:** Frank Frazetta **W:** Gardner Fox ★ Origin of Thun'da.

T.H.U.N.D.E.R. — Solson

1 ❑ Cover: 1.95 **NM** value: **Cover or less**
📖 Rumble! **A:** James E. Lyle; Michael Sawyer **W:** James E. Lyle; Michael Sawyer

THUNDER AGENTS — Tower

Their name stands for The Higher United Nations Defense Enforcement Reserves — THUNDER. They are a group of super-heroes who are sent out to stop threats to world peace.

The THUNDER agents include Lightning, a Flash clone with super-speed; Menthor, whose helmet gives him mentally-enhanced super-powers; NoMan, whose multiple android bodies house the consciousness of a dead scientist, and whose cape makes him invisible. They are led by Dynamo, a man who gains incredible strength and near-invulnerability whenever he twists a dial on the belt of his costume.

Although this series had a relatively brief run from 1967-1969, it is remembered fondly today, due to its classic art by Wally Wood, Steve Ditko, and Gil Kane, and its high-flying stories of adventure.

1 ❑ Nov 1965 Cover: 0.25 **NM** value: **110.00**
• **CGC:** 7 graded, best 9.4
📖 Dynamo **A:** Wally Wood ★ Origin of Dynamo, The THUNDER Squad, Menthor, NoMan. ★ 1st Appearance of Dynamo, Iron Maiden, The THUNDER Squad, Menthor, NoMan.
2 ❑ Jan 1966 Cover: 0.25 **NM** value: **65.00**
• **CGC:** 6 graded, best 9.4
A: Wally Wood ★ 1st Appearance of Lightning. ★ Death of Egghead.
3 ❑ Mar 1966 Cover: 0.25 **NM** value: **45.00**
• **CGC:** 3 graded, best 8.0
A: Wally Wood
4 ❑ Apr 1966 Cover: 0.25 **NM** value: **40.00**
• **CGC:** 4 graded, best 9.6
A: Wally Wood ★ Origin of Lightning.
5 ❑ Jun 1966 Cover: 0.25 **NM** value: **40.00**
• **CGC:** 3 graded, best 9.4
A: Wally Wood
6 ❑ Jul 1966 Cover: 0.25 **NM** value: **30.00**
• **CGC:** 2 graded, best 9.4
A: Wally Wood
7 ❑ Aug 1966 Cover: 0.25 **NM** value: **30.00**
• **CGC:** 2 graded, best 9.4
A: Wally Wood ★ Death of Menthor.
8 ❑ Sep 1966 Cover: 0.25 **NM** value: **30.00**
• **CGC:** 2 graded, best 9.4
A: Wally Wood ★ Origin of Raven. ★ 1st Appearance of Raven.

CGC-graded: Multiply prices above by **33 for 9.9 M • 16 for 9.8 NM/M • 7 for 9.6 NM+ • 5 for 9.4 NM • 2.5 for 9.2 NM- • 1.5 for 9.0 VF/NM**

9 ❑ Oct 1966 Cover: 0.25 **NM** value: **24.00**
• **CGC:** 2 graded, best 9.2
10 ❑ Nov 1966 Cover: 0.25 **NM** value: **24.00**
• **CGC:** 4 graded, best 9.4
11 ❑ Mar 1967 Cover: 0.25 **NM** value: **26.00**
• **CGC:** 1 graded, best 9.4
A: Wally Wood
12 ❑ Apr 1967 Cover: 0.25 **NM** value: **26.00**
• **CGC:** 1 graded, best 9.2
A: Wally Wood
13 ❑ Jun 1967 Cover: 0.25 **NM** value: **26.00**
• **CGC:** 2 graded, best 8.5
A: Wally Wood ★ Appearance of Undersea Agent.
14 ❑ Jul 1967 Cover: 0.25 **NM** value: **26.00**
• **CGC:** 1 graded, best 9.2
A: Wally Wood
15 ❑ Sep 1967 Cover: 0.25 **NM** value: **26.00**
• **CGC:** 2 graded, best 9.0
A: Wally Wood
16 ❑ Oct 1967 Cover: 0.25 **NM** value: **15.00**
• **CGC:** 1 graded, best 8.0
A: Wally Wood
17 ❑ Dec 1967 Cover: 0.25 **NM** value: **15.00**
• **CGC:** 1 graded, best 8.0
A: Wally Wood
18 ❑ Sep 1968 Cover: 0.25 **NM** value: **15.00**
• **CGC:** 1 graded, best 9.2
A: Wally Wood
19 ❑ Nov 1968 Cover: 0.25 **NM** value: **15.00**
• **CGC:** 2 graded, best 9.4
A: Wally Wood
20 ❑ Jan 1966 Cover: 0.25 **NM** value: **10.00**
• **CGC:** 1 graded, best 9.4
final issue. **A:** Wally Wood ★ Origin of Dynamo.

T.H.U.N.D.E.R. AGENTS (VOL. 2) J.C.

1 ❑ May 1983 Cover: 1.00 **NM** value: **2.00**
The Invasion Begins **A:** Will Blyberg; Lou Manna **W:** Chris Adams
2 ❑ Jan 1984 Cover: 1.00 **NM** value: **2.00**

THUNDER AGENTS (WALLY WOOD'S...) Deluxe

1 ❑ Nov 1984 Cover: 2.00 **NM** value: **Cover or less**
A: Keith Giffen; George Pérez; Dave Cockrum
2 ❑ Jan 1985 Cover: 2.00 **NM** value: **Cover or less**
A: Keith Giffen; George Pérez; Dave Cockrum
3 ❑ Nov 1985 Cover: 2.00 **NM** value: **Cover or less**
Circ: CapCity orders: **8,050**
A: Keith Giffen; George Pérez; Dave Cockrum
4 ❑ Feb 1986 Cover: 2.00 **NM** value: **Cover or less**
Circ: CapCity orders: **7,775**
A: Keith Giffen; George Pérez; Dave Cockrum
5 ❑ Oct 1986 Cover: 2.00 **NM** value: **Cover or less**
Circ: CapCity orders: **6,650**
A: Keith Giffen; Jerry Ordway

THUNDERBOLT Charlton

1 ❑ Jan 1966 Cover: 0.12 **NM** value: **16.00**
• **CGC:** 2 graded, best 9.6
★ Origin of Thunderbolt. ★ 1st Appearance of Thunderbolt.
51 ❑ Mar 1966 Cover: 0.12 **NM** value: **10.00**
• Series continues after hiatus (Son of Vulcan #50?)
52 ❑ Jun 1966 Cover: 0.12 **NM** value: **9.00**
53 ❑ Aug 1966 Cover: 0.12 **NM** value: **9.00**
54 ❑ Oct 1966 Cover: 0.12 **NM** value: **9.00**
This One's for Tabu!; Behold...The Sentinels **A:** Sam Grainger **W:** Gary Friedrich
55 ❑ Dec 1966 Cover: 0.12 **NM** value: **9.00**
56 ❑ Feb 1967 Cover: 0.12 **NM** value: **9.00**
57 ❑ May 1967 Cover: 0.12 **NM** value: **9.00**
58 ❑ Jul 1967 Cover: 0.12 **NM** value: **9.00**
59 ❑ Sep 1967 Cover: 0.12 **NM** value: **9.00**
60 ❑ Nov 1967 Cover: 0.12 **NM** value: **9.00**
final issue.

THUNDERBOLTS Marvel

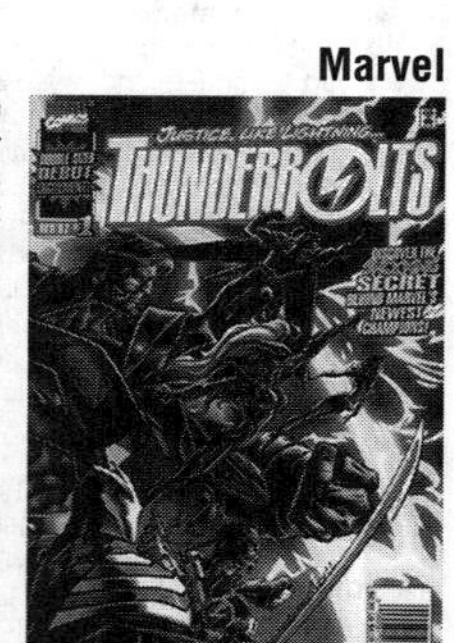

The disappearance of The Avengers and The Fantastic Four due to Onslaught left the citizens of New York concerned about who would protect them from the villains that seem to infect the city. Into the breach came The Thunderbolts, six new heroes professing to take up the mantle for their fallen comrades. They were: Atlas, Mach-1, Meteorite, Songbird, and Techno, and their leader, Citizen V. The Thunderbolts first appeared in The Incredible Hulk #449, where they bravely engaged the gamma ray-spawned monster.

Debuting to the acclaim of the media and the populace by rousting a band of scavengers called The Rat Pack, and then soundly defeating The Wrecking Crew, the city government sought to give them an official sanction and whatever assistance they need. There is no doubt that The Thunderbolts seem to be exactly what New York needs. But things are not always what they seem...

-1 ❑ Jul 1997 Cover: 1.99 **NM** value: **2.00**
Distant Rumblings! • Flashback **A:** Steve Epting **W:** Kurt Busiek ★ Appearance of Baron Zemo, Namor.
0 ❑ Jan 1997 **NM** value: **1.00**
Circ: Statement: **77,986**
A Rare Niight Off • Free **A:** Mark Bagley **W:** Kurt Busiek
1 ❑ Apr 1997 Cover: 2.99 **NM** value: **4.00**
Circ: Statement: **77,986** Direct Market orders: **64,750** • **CGC:** 6 graded, best 9.6
• Giant-size. Justice...Like Lightning! • Identities of Thunderbolts revealed **A:** Mark Bagley **W:** Kurt Busiek
2 ❑ May 1997 Cover: 1.99 **NM** value: **3.00**
Circ: Statement: **77,986** Diamd. preorders: **59,589**
Deceiving Appearances **A:** Mark Bagley **W:** Kurt Busiek ★ Versus Mad Thinker.
3 ❑ Jun 1997 Cover: 1.99 **NM** value: **3.00**
Circ: Statement: **77,986** Diamd. preorders: **46,068**
A: Mark Bagley **W:** Kurt Busiek
4 ❑ Jul 1997 Cover: 1.99 **NM** value: **2.50**
Circ: Statement: **77,986** Diamd. preorders: **46,415**
• Jolt joins team; 1st appearacе of Jolt **A:** Mark Bagley **W:** Kurt Busiek ★ 1st Appearance of Jolt.
5 ❑ Aug 1997 Cover: 1.99 **NM** value: **2.50**
Circ: Statement: **77,986** Diamd. preorders: **47,184**
• gatefold summary. • Atlas vs. Growing Man **A:** Mark Bagley **W:** Kurt Busiek
6 ❑ Sep 1997 Cover: 1.99 **NM** value: **2.00**
Circ: Statement: **77,986** Diamd. preorders: **46,871**
• gatefold summary. **A:** Mark Bagley **W:** Kurt Busiek
7 ❑ Oct 1997 Cover: 1.99 **NM** value: **2.00**
Circ: Statement: **53,467** Diamd. preorders: **47,302**
• gatefold summary. **A:** Mark Bagley **W:** Kurt Busiek ★ Versus Elements of Doom.
8 ❑ Nov 1997 Cover: 1.99 **NM** value: **2.00**
Circ: Statement: **53,467** Diamd. preorders: **47,367**
• gatefold summary. **A:** Mark Bagley **W:** Kurt Busiek
9 ❑ Dec 1997 Cover: 1.99 **NM** value: **2.00**
Circ: Statement: **53,467** Diamd. preorders: **47,297**
• gatefold summary. **A:** Mark Bagley **W:** Kurt Busiek ★ Appearance of Black Widow.
10 ❑ Jan 1998 Cover: 1.99 **NM** value: **2.00**
Circ: Statement: **53,467** Diamd. preorders: **46,336**
• gatefold summary. • Thunderbolts revealed as Masters of Evil; Has 1997 Statement; avg total paid circ 77,986 **A:** Mark Bagley **W:** Kurt Busiek
11 ❑ Feb 1998 Cover: 1.99 **NM** value: **2.00**
Circ: Statement: **53,467** Diamd. preorders: **45,573**
• gatefold summary. **A:** Mark Bagley **W:** Kurt Busiek
12 ❑ Mar 1998 Cover: 2.99 **NM** value: **6.00**
Circ: Statement: **53,467** Diamd. preorders: **50,014**
wraparound cover. • gatefold summary. **A:** Mark Bagley **W:** Kurt Busiek ★ Appearance of Fantastic Four, Avengers.
13 ❑ Apr 1998 Cover: 1.99 **NM** value: **2.00**
Circ: Statement: **53,467** Diamd. preorders: **46,977**
• gatefold summary. **A:** Mark Bagley **W:** Kurt Busiek
14 ❑ May 1998 Cover: 1.99 **NM** value: **2.00**
Circ: Statement: **53,467** Diamd. preorders: **49,551**
• gatefold summary. **A:** Mark Bagley **W:** Kurt Busiek
15 ❑ Jun 1998 Cover: 1.99 **NM** value: **2.00**
Circ: Statement: **53,467** Diamd. preorders: **52,288**
• gatefold summary. **A:** Mark Bagley **W:** Kurt Busiek
16 ❑ Jul 1998 Cover: 1.99 **NM** value: **2.00**
Circ: Statement: **53,467** Diamd. preorders: **50,321**
• gatefold summary. Thunder & Lightning **A:** Mark Bagley **W:** Kurt Busiek ★ Versus Lightning Rods (formerly Great Lakes Avengers).
17 ❑ Aug 1998 Cover: 1.99 **NM** value: **2.00**
Circ: Statement: **53,467** Diamd. preorders: **49,021**
• gatefold summary. **A:** Mark Bagley **W:** Kurt Busiek ★ Versus Graviton.
18 ❑ Sep 1998 Cover: 1.99 **NM** value: **2.00**
Circ: Diamd. preorders: **46,360**
• gatefold summary. **A:** Mark Bagley **W:** Kurt Busiek
19 ❑ Oct 1998 Cover: 1.99 **NM** value: **2.00**
Circ: Diamd. preorders: **44,818**
• gatefold summary. **A:** Mark Bagley **W:** Kurt Busiek ★ 1st Appearance of Charcoal.
20 ❑ Nov 1998 Cover: 1.99 **NM** value: **2.00**
Circ: Diamd. preorders: **44,532**
• gatefold summary. • Has 1998 Statement, filed 10/1/98; avg print run 56,608; avg sales 52,935; avg subs 532; avg total paid 53,467; samples 117; office use 125; max existent 53,709; 5% of run returned **A:** Mark Bagley **W:** Kurt Busiek ★ Versus new Masters of Evil.
21 ❑ Dec 1998 Cover: 1.99 **NM** value: **2.00**
Circ: Diamd. preorders: **44,084**
• gatefold summary. **A:** Mark Bagley **W:** Kurt Busiek ★ Appearance of Hawkeye.
22 ❑ Jan 1999 Cover: 1.99 **NM** value: **2.00**
Circ: Diamd. preorders: **50,007**
• gatefold summary. • Hercules vs. Atlas **A:** Mark Bagley **W:** Kurt Busiek
23 ❑ Feb 1999 Cover: 1.99 **NM** value: **2.00**
Circ: Diamd. preorders: **43,064**
A: Mark Bagley **W:** Kurt Busiek ★ Appearance of U.S. Agent.
24 ❑ Mar 1999 Cover: 1.99 **NM** value: **2.00**
Circ: Diamd. preorders: **43,492**
The Eye of the Storm **A:** Mark Bagley **W:** Kurt Busiek ★ Appearance of Citizen V.
25 ❑ Apr 1999 Cover: 2.99 **NM** value: **Cover or less**
Circ: Diamd. preorders: **44,978**
wraparound cover. • double-sized. **A:** Mark Bagley **W:** Kurt Busiek ★ Appearance of Masters of Evil. ★ Versus Masters of Evil.
25/Aut❑Apr 1999 Cover: 2.99 **NM** value: **12.00**
Circ: Diamd. preorders: **43,980**
A: Mark Bagley **W:** Kurt Busiek ★ Appearance of Masters of Evil.
26 ❑ May 1999 Cover: 1.99 **NM** value: **Cover or less**
Circ: Diamd. preorders: **43,980**
• Mach-1 in prison
27 ❑ Jun 1999 Cover: 1.99 **NM** value: **Cover or less**
Circ: Diamd. preorders: **45,874**
★ Appearance of Archangel.
28 ❑ Jul 1999 Cover: 1.99 **NM** value: **Cover or less**
Circ: Diamd. preorders: **45,515**
★ Appearance of Archangel. ★ Versus Graviton.
29 ❑ Aug 1999 Cover: 1.99 **NM** value: **Cover or less**
Circ: Diamd. preorders: **45,074**
★ Appearance of Machine Man. ★ Versus Graviton.
30 ❑ Sep 1999 Cover: 1.99 **NM** value: **Cover or less**
Circ: Diamd. preorders: **45,000**
• Hawkeye and Moonstone caught in clinch
31 ❑ Oct 1999 Cover: 1.99 **NM** value: **Cover or less**
Circ: Statement: **68,837** Diamd. preorders: **43,333**
32 ❑ Nov 1999 Cover: 1.99 **NM** value: **Cover or less**
Circ: Statement: **68,837** Diamd. preorders: **41,958**
33 ❑ Dec 1999 Cover: 1.99 **NM** value: **Cover or less**
Circ: Statement: **68,837** Diamd. preorders: **42,268**
34 ❑ Jan 2000 Cover: 1.99 **NM** value: **Cover or less**
Circ: Statement: **68,837** Diamd. preorders: **40,333**
35 ❑ Feb 2000 Cover: 2.25 **NM** value: **Cover or less**
Circ: Statement: **68,837** Diamd. preorders: **41,640**
36 ❑ Mar 2000 Cover: 2.25 **NM** value: **Cover or less**
Circ: Statement: **68,837** Diamd. preorders: **38,259**
37 ❑ Apr 2000 Cover: 2.25 **NM** value: **Cover or less**
Circ: Statement: **68,837** Diamd. preorders: **36,570**
38 ❑ May 2000 Cover: 2.25 **NM** value: **Cover or less**
Circ: Statement: **68,837** Diamd. preorders: **37,435**
39 ❑ Jun 2000 Cover: 2.25 **NM** value: **Cover or less**
Circ: Statement: **68,837** Diamd. preorders: **38,261**
40 ❑ Jul 2000 Cover: 2.25 **NM** value: **Cover or less**
Circ: Statement: **68,837** Diamd. preorders: **37,353**
41 ❑ Aug 2000 Cover: 2.25 **NM** value: **Cover or less**
Circ: Statement: **68,837** Diamd. preorders: **38,560**
Tug of War! **A:** Mark Bagley **W:** Fabian Nicieza ★ Appearance of Sandman.
42 ❑ Sep 2000 Cover: 2.25 **NM** value: **Cover or less**
Circ: Statement: **68,837** Diamd. preorders: **39,250**
Two Ships **A:** Mark Bagley **W:** Fabian Nicieza ★ Appearance of Wonder Man.
43 ❑ Oct 2000 Cover: 2.25 **NM** value: **Cover or less**
Circ: Statement: **42,434** Diamd. preorders: **38,050**
Chasing Your Own Tail! **A:** Mark Bagley **W:** Fabian Nicieza ★ Appearance of Black Widow.
44 ❑ Nov 2000 Cover: 2.25 **NM** value: **Cover or less**
Circ: Statement: **42,434** Diamd. preorders: **40,214**
Keeping an Ion the Crowd! **A:** Mark Bagley **W:** Fabian Nicieza ★ Appearance of Nefaria, Avengers.
45 ❑ Dec 2000 Cover: 2.25 **NM** value: **Cover or less**
Circ: Statement: **42,434** Diamd. preorders: **39,258**
Maximum Security; Heroic Tendencies, Part 1: The Inside Job • Has 2000 Statement, filed 10/0/2000; avg print run 69,692; avg sales 68,066; avg subs 771; avg total paid 68,837; samples 600; office use 125; max existent 69,562; 0% of run returned **A:** Patrick Zircher **W:** Fabian Nicieza
46 ❑ Jan 2001 Cover: 2.25 **NM** value: **Cover or less**
Circ: Statement: **42,434** Diamd. preorders: **38,385**
Heroic Tendencies, Part 2: Heart and Soul • return of Jolt **A:** Mark Bagley **W:** Fabian Nicieza
47 ❑ Feb 2001 Cover: 2.25 **NM** value: **Cover or less**
Circ: Statement: **42,434** Diamd. preorders: **38,345**
Heroic Tendencies, Part 3: Big Problems! **A:** Mark Bagley **W:** Fabian Nicieza ★ Appearance of Captain Marvel.
48 ❑ Mar 2001 Cover: 2.25 **NM** value: **Cover or less**
Circ: Statement: **42,434** Diamd. preorders: **37,675**
Revelations! The Beginning of the End ... **A:** Mark Bagley **W:** Fabian Nicieza
49 ❑ Apr 2001 Cover: 2.25 **NM** value: **Cover or less**
Circ: Statement: **42,434** Diamd. preorders: **37,315**
Explanations! The End of the Beginning ... **A:** Mark Bagley **W:** Patrick Zircher; Fabian Nicieza
50 ❑ May 2001 Cover: 2.99 **NM** value: **Cover or less**
Circ: Statement: **42,434** Diamd. preorders: **38,945**
• double-sized. Redemption? **A:** Mark Bagley **W:** Fabian Nicieza ★ Appearance of Citizen V.
51 ❑ Jun 2001 Cover: 2.25 **NM** value: **Cover or less**
Circ: Statement: **42,434** Diamd. preorders: **37,628**
52 ❑ Jul 2001 Cover: 2.25 **NM** value: **Cover or less**
Circ: Statement: **42,434** Diamd. preorders: **37,742**
53 ❑ Aug 2001 Cover: 2.25 **NM** value: **Cover or less**
Circ: Statement: **42,434** Diamd. preorders: **37,848**
54 ❑ Sep 2001 Cover: 2.25 **NM** value: **Cover or less**
Circ: Statement: **42,434** Diamd. preorders: **38,763**
55 ❑ Oct 2001 Cover: 2.25 **NM** value: **Cover or less**
Circ: Diamd. preorders: **38,373**
56 ❑ Nov 2001 Cover: 2.25 **NM** value: **Cover or less**
Circ: Diamd. preorders: **34,852**
57 ❑ Dec 2001 Cover: 2.25 **NM** value: **Cover or less**
Circ: Diamd. preorders: **33,447**
58 ❑ Jan 2002 Cover: 2.25 **NM** value: **Cover or less**
Circ: Diamd. preorders: **33,375**
59 ❑ Feb 2002 Cover: 2.25 **NM** value: **Cover or less**
Circ: Diamd. preorders: **33,082**
• Has 2001 Statement, filed 10/1/2001; avg print run 43,625; avg sales 41,642; avg subs 792; avg total paid 42,434; samples 600; office use 591; max existent 43,625; 1% of run returned
60 ❑ Mar 2002 Cover: 2.25 **NM** value: **Cover or less**
Circ: Diamd. preorders: **32,106**
Anl 1997❑Aug 1997 Cover: 2.99 **NM** value: **3.00**
Circ: Diamd. preorders: **39,910**
wraparound cover. • 1997 Annual **A:** Mark Bagley **W:** Kurt Busiek ★ Origin of Thunderbolts.
Ash 1❑ **NM** value: **2.50**
• Ashcan preview; American Entertainment
Ash 1/Aut❑ **NM** value: **4.00**
• Ashcan preview **A:** Mark Bagley
Bk 1❑ Jul 1997 Cover: 4.99 **NM** value: **Cover or less**
First Strikes • collects issues #1 and 2; Collects Thunderbolts #1-2 **A:** Mark Bagley **W:** Kurt Busiek

THUNDERBOLTS: LIFE SENTENCES Marvel

1 ❑ Jul 2001 Cover: 3.50 **NM** value: **Cover or less**
Circ: Diamd. preorders: **29,197**

Other grades: Multiply prices above by **1.5 for Mint • 2/3 for Very Fine • 1/3 for Fine • 1/5 for Very Good • 1/8 for Good**

THUNDERBUNNY (1ST SERIES)

Archie / Red Circle

1 ❑ Jan 1984 Cover: 1.00 **NM** value: **2.00**
📖 Rabbit Trapped! **A:** Brian Buniak **W:** Martin Greim

THUNDERBUNNY (2ND SERIES) **Warp**

Bobby Caswell loved comic books and dreamed some day of having "powers beyond those of mere mortal man." While vacationing in Vermont, he saw a strange light on Bald Mountain and went to investigate. What he found was a space craft containing a box marked with symbols for energy. Placing his hands on the box revealed to his mind that a dying world chose to send the energy force of their greatest super hero into space so that another world might benefit from their existence. So now whenever help is needed, young Bobby has but to clap his hands together and picture the image of Thunder Bunny in his mind and he becomes that lost world's hero.

Thunder Bunny began in Charlton Bullseye #6 and continued in Blue-Ribbon Comics #13. Warp Graphics finally picked the character up as a black and white in 1985.

1 ❑ Jun 1985 Cover: 1.50 **NM** value: **2.00**
• Warp publishes **A:** Brian Buniak **W:** Martin Greim ★ Origin of retold.
2 ❑ Aug 1985 Cover: 1.50 **NM** value: **2.00**
A: Brian Buniak **W:** Martin Greim
3 ❑ Oct 1985 Cover: 1.50 **NM** value: **2.00**
A: Brian Buniak **W:** Martin Greim
4 ❑ Dec 1985 Cover: 1.50 **NM** value: **2.00**
A: Brian Buniak **W:** Martin Greim
5 ❑ Feb 1986 Cover: 1.50 **NM** value: **2.00**
A: Brian Buniak **W:** Martin Greim
6 ❑ 1986b&w Cover: 1.50 **NM** value: **2.00**
📖 Thunderbunny Vs. Thunderrabbit • Apple begins publishing **A:** Brian Buniak **W:** Martin Greim
7 ❑ 1986b&w Cover: 1.50 **NM** value: **2.00**
A: Brian Buniak **W:** Martin Greim
8 ❑ 1987 Cover: 1.75 **NM** value: **Cover or less**
A: Brian Buniak **W:** Martin Greim
9 ❑ 1987 Cover: 1.75 **NM** value: **Cover or less**
A: Brian Buniak **W:** Martin Greim
10 ❑ Jul 1987 Cover: 1.75 **NM** value: **Cover or less**
A: Brian Buniak **W:** Martin Greim
11 ❑ Sep 1987 Cover: 1.75 **NM** value: **Cover or less**
A: Brian Buniak **W:** Martin Greim ★ Appearance of THUNDER Agents.
12 ❑ Nov 1987 Cover: 1.75 **NM** value: **Cover or less**
• last **A:** Brian Buniak **W:** Martin Greim

THUNDERCATS **Marvel / Star**

In the mid-1980s, "ThunderCats" was a very popular animated and toy series about a group of cat-people — Lion-O, Tygra, Panthro, Cheetara, Wilykat, and Wilykit — who fought the evil forces of the sinister Mumm-Ra. This series from Marvel's Star Comics imprint, a line of comics aimed specifically at young children, offered an origin for the feline furies and added to their adventures in the same style and tone as the television series.

In 2002, DC announced plans to revive the series.

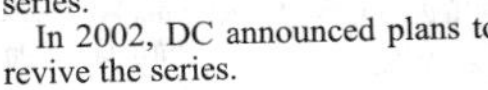

1 ❑ Dec 1985 Cover: 0.65 **NM** value: **2.50**
Circ: CapCity orders: **4,300** • **CGC:** 4 graded, best 9.4
2 ❑ Feb 1956 Cover: 0.65 **NM** value: **1.50**
Circ: CapCity orders: **4,200**
3 ❑ Apr 1986 Cover: 0.75 **NM** value: **1.50**
Circ: CapCity orders: **10,150** • **CGC:** 1 graded, best 9.4
4 ❑ Jun 1986 Cover: 0.75 **NM** value: **1.50**
Circ: CapCity orders: **9,350** • **CGC:** 1 graded, best 9.6
5 ❑ Aug 1986 Cover: 0.75 **NM** value: **1.50**
Circ: CapCity orders: **9,100**
6 ❑ Oct 1986 Cover: 0.75 **NM** value: **1.50**
Circ: CapCity orders: **9,300**
7 ❑ Dec 1986 Cover: 0.75 **NM** value: **1.00**
Circ: CapCity orders: **7,800**
8 ❑ Feb 1987 Cover: 0.75 **NM** value: **1.00**
Circ: Statement: **112,230** CapCity orders: **6,900**
9 ❑ Mar 1987 Cover: 0.75 **NM** value: **1.00**
Circ: Statement: **112,230** CapCity orders: **5,885**
10 ❑ Apr 1987 Cover: 0.75 **NM** value: **1.00**
Circ: Statement: **112,230**
11 ❑ May 1987 Cover: 1.00 **NM** value: **Cover or less**
Circ: Statement: **112,230** CapCity orders: **4,850**
12 ❑ Jun 1987 Cover: 1.00 **NM** value: **Cover or less**
Circ: Statement: **112,230** CapCity orders: **4,600**
13 ❑ Jul 1987 Cover: 1.00 **NM** value: **Cover or less**
Circ: Statement: **112,230** CapCity orders: **4,350**
14 ❑ Aug 1987 Cover: 1.00 **NM** value: **Cover or less**
Circ: Statement: **112,230** CapCity orders: **4,100**
15 ❑ Sep 1987 Cover: 1.00 **NM** value: **Cover or less**
Circ: Statement: **112,230** CapCity orders: **4,350**
16 ❑ Oct 1987 Cover: 1.00 **NM** value: **Cover or less**
Circ: Statement: **112,230** CapCity orders: **4,150**
17 ❑ Nov 1987 Cover: 1.00 **NM** value: **Cover or less**
Circ: Statement: **112,230** CapCity orders: **3,750**
18 ❑ Dec 1987 Cover: 1.00 **NM** value: **Cover or less**
Circ: Statement: **112,230** CapCity orders: **3,500**
19 ❑ Jan 1988 Cover: 1.00 **NM** value: **Cover or less**
Circ: CapCity orders: **3,200**
20 ❑ Feb 1988 Cover: 1.00 **NM** value: **Cover or less**
21 ❑ Mar 1988 Cover: 1.00 **NM** value: **Cover or less**
Circ: CapCity orders: **3,075**
22 ❑ Apr 1988 Cover: 1.00 **NM** value: **Cover or less**
Circ: CapCity orders: **3,250**
23 ❑ May 1988 Cover: 1.00 **NM** value: **Cover or less**
Circ: CapCity orders: **2,700**
24 ❑ Jun 1988 Cover: 1.00 **NM** value: **Cover or less**
Circ: CapCity orders: **2,500**
final issue.

THUNDER GIRLS **Pin & Ink Press**

1 ❑ Sum 1997 Cover: 2.95 **NM** value: **Cover or less**
2 ❑ Sum 1999 Cover: 2.95 **NM** value: **Cover or less**
3 ❑ Fal 1999 Cover: 2.95 **NM** value: **Cover or less**

THUNDERGOD **Crusade**

1 ❑ Aug 1996, b&w Cover: 2.95 **NM** value: **Cover or less**
A: Albert Debnam **W:** Christopher Golden
2 ❑ Oct 1996, b&w Cover: 2.95 **NM** value: **Cover or less**
A: Albert Debnam **W:** Christopher Golden
3 ❑ Dec 1996, b&w Cover: 2.95 **NM** value: **Cover or less**
Circ: Diamd. preorders: **8,520**

THUNDERMACE **Rak**

1 ❑ Mar 1986, b&w Cover: 1.50 **NM** value: **2.00**
• **CGC:** 1 graded, best 9.6
📖 Origin **A:** Rick Sellers; Robert Krause **W:** Robert Kraus; Steve Simshauser
2 ❑ 1986 Cover: 1.75 **NM** value: **Cover or less**
3 ❑ Apr 1987 Cover: 1.75 **NM** value: **Cover or less**
4 ❑ 1987 Cover: 1.75 **NM** value: **Cover or less**
5 ❑ 1987 Cover: 2.00 **NM** value: **Cover or less**
6 ❑ 1987 Cover: 2.00 **NM** value: **Cover or less**
7 ❑ 1987 Cover: 2.00 **NM** value: **Cover or less**
Bk 1❑ b&w Cover: 6.00 **NM** value: **Cover or less**
• The Telling Of The Legend

THUNDERSAURS: THE BODACIOUS ADVENTURES OF BIFF THUNDERSAUR

Innovation

1 ❑ b&w Cover: 2.75 **NM** value: **Cover or less**
A: Cline Siegenthaler **W:** George Broderick Jr.

THUNDERSKULL! (SIDNEY MELLON'S...)

Slave Labor

1 ❑ Aug 1989, b&w Cover: 1.95 **NM** value: **Cover or less**

THUNDERSTRIKE **Marvel**

Eric Masterson was a good friend of the thunder god, Thor, and had even filled in for him on occasion. When Thor finally had to return home to Valhalla, he gave Eric a gift to express his appreciation. The gift, a strange walking stick, becomes a mace called Thunderstrike when it is struck against the ground. Just as Thor's hammer, Mjolner, gives its owner the powers of the thunder god, Thunderstrike turns Eric Masterson into living powerhouse. For lack of a better name, Eric calls his super-powered self Thunderstrike- after his mace.

In terms of raw power, Thunderstrike is not Thor's equal. That means he has to fight smarter in order to prevail. Eric is also more a part of the mortal world than Thor ever was, leading to action which is less cosmic in scope and more concerned with combating earthly problems.

1 ❑ Jun 1993 Cover: 2.95 **NM** value: **Cover or less**
Circ: CapCity orders: **76,200**
Prism cover. 📖 Blood Without Glory! **A:** Ron Frenz **W:** Tom DeFalco ★ 1st Appearance of Carjack. ★ Appearance of Bloodaxe.
2 ❑ Nov 1993 Cover: 1.25 **NM** value: **Cover or less**
Circ: CapCity orders: **42,400**
3 ❑ Dec 1993 Cover: 1.25 **NM** value: **Cover or less**
Circ: CapCity orders: **34,100**
4 ❑ Jan 1994 Cover: 1.25 **NM** value: **Cover or less**
Circ: Statement: **123,940** CapCity orders: **29,000**
5 ❑ Feb 1994 Cover: 1.25 **NM** value: **Cover or less**
Circ: Statement: **123,940** CapCity orders: **27,700**
6 ❑ Mar 1994 Cover: 1.25 **NM** value: **Cover or less**
Circ: Statement: **123,940** CapCity orders: **23,650**
7 ❑ Apr 1994 Cover: 1.25 **NM** value: **Cover or less**
Circ: Statement: **123,940** CapCity orders: **21,700**
8 ❑ May 1994 Cover: 1.50 **NM** value: **Cover or less**
Circ: Statement: **123,940** CapCity orders: **20,650**
9 ❑ Jun 1994 Cover: 1.50 **NM** value: **Cover or less**
Circ: Statement: **123,940** CapCity orders: **20,000**
10 ❑ Jul 1994 Cover: 1.50 **NM** value: **Cover or less**
Circ: Statement: **123,940** CapCity orders: **20,000**
★ Appearance of Thor.
11 ❑ Aug 1994 Cover: 1.50 **NM** value: **Cover or less**
Circ: Statement: **123,940** CapCity orders: **18,200**
12 ❑ Sep 1994 Cover: 1.50 **NM** value: **Cover or less**
Circ: Statement: **123,940** CapCity orders: **17,250**
13 ❑ Oct 1994 Cover: 1.50 **NM** value: **Cover or less**
Circ: Statement: **123,940** CapCity orders: **13,050**
13/A❑ Oct 1994 Cover: 2.50 **NM** value: **Cover or less**
Circ: CapCity orders: **11,850**
• flip-book with Code Blue back-up; second indicia gives title as Marvel Double Feature ... Thunderstrike/Code Blue
14 ❑ Nov 1994 Cover: 1.50 **NM** value: **Cover or less**
Circ: Statement: **123,940** CapCity orders: **12,750**
📖 Home-Wrecker; Up From Below **A:** Al Milgrom; Ron Frenz **W:** Ron Frenz; Roy Thomas; Tom DeFalco
14/A❑ Nov 1994 Cover: 2.50 **NM** value: **Cover or less**
Circ: CapCity orders: **8,550**
• flip-book with Code Blue back-up; second indicia gives title as Marvel Double Feature ... Thunderstrike/Code Blue
15 ❑ Dec 1994 Cover: 1.50 **NM** value: **Cover or less**
Circ: Statement: **123,940** CapCity orders: **12,100**
15/A❑ Dec 1994 Cover: 2.50 **NM** value: **Cover or less**
Circ: CapCity orders: **7,350**
• flip-book with Code Blue back-up; second indicia gives title as Marvel Double Feature ... Thunderstrike/Code Blue
16 ❑ Jan 1995 Cover: 1.50 **NM** value: **Cover or less**
Circ: CapCity orders: **10,300**
16/A❑ Jan 1995 Cover: 2.50 **NM** value: **Cover or less**
Circ: CapCity orders: **6,475**
• flip-book with Code Blue back-up; second indicia gives title as Marvel Double Feature ... Thunderstrike/Code Blue
17 ❑ Feb 1995 Cover: 1.50 **NM** value: **Cover or less**
Circ: CapCity orders: **12,250**
18 ❑ Mar 1995 Cover: 1.50 **NM** value: **Cover or less**
Circ: CapCity orders: **11,075**
19 ❑ Apr 1995 Cover: 1.50 **NM** value: **Cover or less**
Circ: CapCity orders: **10,400**
20 ❑ May 1995 Cover: 1.50 **NM** value: **Cover or less**
Circ: CapCity orders: **10,300**
21 ❑ Jun 1995 Cover: 1.50 **NM** value: **Cover or less**
Circ: CapCity orders: **10,300**
Avengers #1 homage cover.
22 ❑ Jul 1995 Cover: 1.50 **NM** value: **Cover or less**
Circ: CapCity orders: **9,875**
• Identity of Bloodaxe revealed
23 ❑ Aug 1995 Cover: 1.50 **NM** value: **Cover or less**
★ Versus Seth. ★ Versus Thor. ★ Versus Avengers. ★ Versus Seth, Avengers, Thor.
24 ❑ Sep 1995 Cover: 1.50 **NM** value: **Cover or less**
final issue. ★ Death of Eric Masterson.

TICK, THE **NEC**

the plot thicks...

He's strong! He's powerful! He's nigh invulnerable! He's a great, big, oversized super-hero with the I.Q. of topsoil. Oh yes, and to his fans, he's known as the Tick.

Written and drawn by Ben Edlund at tiny New England Comics Press, the Tick has become one of the most beloved of the independent comics. Its star is a grinning idiot who dances across rooftops scanning for crime with his Secret Crime Viewfinder (a ViewMaster(tm)). The only thing that saves him from certain destruction due to his own folly is his tick-like "nigh invulnerability." So when he meets up with the neighborhood Ninja, their throwing stars and knives simply bounce right off. It's a good thing, too, as readers everywhere would mourn if anything were to happen to their favorite bug wannabee.

1 ❑ Jun 1988 Cover: 1.75 **NM** value: **15.00**
• **CGC:** 7 graded, best 9.2
Black background on cover. **A:** Ben Edlund **W:** Ben Edlund
1-2 ❑ Cover: 1.95 **NM** value: **3.00**
1-3 ❑ Cover: 1.95 **NM** value: **2.50**
1-4 ❑ Cover: 2.25 **NM** value: **Cover or less**
1-5 ❑ Cover: 2.75 **NM** value: **Cover or less**
A: Ben Edlund **W:** Ben Edlund
2 ❑ Sep 1988 Cover: 1.75 **NM** value: **8.00**
• **CGC:** 2 graded, best 9.0
Die-cut cover. **A:** Ben Edlund **W:** Ben Edlund
2/SC❑ **NM** value: **15.00**
Without die-cut cover. **A:** Ben Edlund **W:** Ben Edlund
2-2 ❑ Cover: 1.95 **NM** value: **3.00**
2-3 ❑ Cover: 2.25 **NM** value: **Cover or less**
2-4 ❑ Cover: 2.25 **NM** value: **Cover or less**
2-5 ❑ Cover: 2.75 **NM** value: **Cover or less**
A: Ben Edlund **W:** Ben Edlund
3 ❑ Cover: 1.95 **NM** value: **6.00**
A: Ben Edlund **W:** Ben Edlund
3-2 ❑ Nov 1989 Cover: 2.25 **NM** value: **3.00**
3-3 ❑ Cover: 2.75 **NM** value: **Cover or less**
A: Ben Edlund **W:** Ben Edlund
3-4 ❑ Cover: 2.75 **NM** value: **Cover or less**
A: Ben Edlund **W:** Ben Edlund
4 ❑ Apr 1989 Cover: 1.95 **NM** value: **8.00**
A: Ben Edlund **W:** Ben Edlund ★ 1st Appearance of Paul the Samurai.
4-2 ❑ Cover: 2.25 **NM** value: **Cover or less**
4-3 ❑ Cover: 2.75 **NM** value: **Cover or less**
A: Ben Edlund **W:** Ben Edlund ★ 1st Appearance of Paul the Samurai.
4-4 ❑ Cover: 2.75 **NM** value: **Cover or less**
A: Ben Edlund **W:** Ben Edlund ★ 1st Appearance of Paul the Samurai.
4-5 ❑ Cover: 2.75 **NM** value: **Cover or less**
A: Ben Edlund **W:** Ben Edlund ★ 1st Appearance of Paul the Samurai.
5 ❑ Aug 1989 Cover: 1.95 **NM** value: **8.00**
• Scarcer **A:** Max Banks **W:** Ben Edlund
5-2 ❑ Cover: 2.75 **NM** value: **Cover or less**
A: Max Banks **W:** Ben Edlund
6 ❑ Nov 1989 Cover: 2.25 **NM** value: **5.00**
A: Ben Edlund **W:** Ben Edlund
6-2 ❑ Cover: 2.75 **NM** value: **Cover or less**
A: Ben Edlund **W:** Ben Edlund

CGC-graded: Multiply prices above by **33 for 9.9 M** • **16 for 9.8 NM/M** • **7 for 9.6 NM+** • **5 for 9.4 NM** • **2.5 for 9.2 NM-** • **1.5 for 9.0 VF/NM**

6-3 ❑ Cover: 2.75 **NM** value: **Cover or less**
A: Ben Edlund W: Ben Edlund
7 ❑ Feb 1990 Cover: 2.25 **NM** value: **5.00**
A: Ben Edlund W: Ben Edlund
7-2 ❑ Cover: 2.75 **NM** value: **Cover or less**
A: Ben Edlund W: Ben Edlund
8 ❑ Jul 1990 Cover: 2.25 **NM** value: **8.00**
• Has logo A: Ben Edlund W: Ben Edlund
8/SC❑ **NM** value: **8.00**
No logo on cover. A: Ben Edlund W: Ben Edlund
8-2 ❑ Cover: 2.75 **NM** value: **Cover or less**
A: Ben Edlund W: Ben Edlund
9 ❑ Mar 1991 Cover: 2.75 **NM** value: **3.00**
A: Ben Edlund W: Ben Edlund ★ 1st Appearance of The Chainsaw Vigilante.
10 ❑ Oct 1991 Cover: 2.75 **NM** value: **3.00**
A: Ben Edlund W: Ben Edlund
11 ❑ Aug 1992 Cover: 2.75 **NM** value: **3.00**
A: Ben Edlund W: Ben Edlund
12 ❑ May 1993 Cover: 2.75 **NM** value: **3.00**
Circ: CapCity orders: **6,600**
A: Ben Edlund W: Ben Edlund
12/LE❑ **NM** value: **20.00**
• Gold spider foil on front
13 ❑ Nov 2000 Cover: 3.50 **NM** value: **Cover or less**
• Pseudo-Tick edition. A: Mychailo Kazybrid W: Marc Silvia
Bk 1❑ Cover: 12.95 **NM** value: **Cover or less**
• The Tick Omnibus
SE 1❑ Jul 1997 Cover: 4.50 **NM** value: **50.00**
Circ: Diamd. preorders: **11,222** • CGC: 3 graded, best 9.6
• Special edition. ★ 1st Appearance of The Tick.
SE 2❑ **NM** value: **25.00**
• CGC: 2 graded, best 9.4
• Special edition. ★ 2nd Appearance of The Tick.

TICK & ARTHUR, THE — NEC

1 ❑ Apr 1999 Cover: 3.50 **NM** value: **Cover or less**
Circ: Diamd. preorders: **9,390**
A: Sean Wang W: Sean Wang

TICK BIG BLUE DESTINY, THE — NEC

1 ❑ Nov 1997 Cover: 2.95 **NM** value: **Cover or less**
Circ: Diamd. preorders: **14,958**
Arthur and Tick with #1 posing on cover. • Keen Edition. A: Eli Stone W: Eli Stone ★ Origin of The Impressionist. ★ 1st Appearance of The Impressionist.
1/A ❑ Nov 1997 Cover: 4.95 **NM** value: **Cover or less**
Circ: Diamd. preorders: **6,506**
Die-cut cover. • Wicked Keen Edition. 📖 Fear No Art (Unless It's Out To Get You) A: Eli Stone W: Eli Stone ★ Origin of The Impressionist. ★ 1st Appearance of The Impressionist.
1/Ash❑ca. 1997 Cover: 2.95 **NM** value: **Cover or less**
• ashcan edition. A: Eli Stone W: Eli Stone ★ Origin of The Impressionist. ★ 1st Appearance of The Impressionist.
1/B ❑ Nov 1997 Cover: 19.00 **NM** value: **Cover or less**
• Wicked Keen Edition without Die-Cut Cover. 📖 Fear No Art (Unless It's Out To Get You) • (500 printed); (500 printed) A: Eli Stone W: Eli Stone ★ Origin of The Impressionist. ★ 1st Appearance of The Impressionist.
2 ❑ Jan 1998 Cover: 2.95 **NM** value: **Cover or less**
A: Eli Stone W: Eli Stone
2/SC❑Jan 1998 Cover: 2.95 **NM** value: **Cover or less**
Circ: Diamd. preorders: **15,906**
Tick-buster cover. A: Eli Stone W: Eli Stone
3 ❑ Mar 1998 Cover: 3.50 **NM** value: **Cover or less**
Circ: Diamd. preorders: **13,290**
A: Eli Stone W: Eli Stone
4 ❑ May 1998 Cover: 3.50 **NM** value: **Cover or less**
Circ: Diamd. preorders: **11,817**
Justice Cover. A: Eli Stone W: Eli Stone
4/A ❑ May 1998 Cover: 3.50 **NM** value: **Cover or less**
Ocean cover. A: Eli Stone W: Eli Stone
5 ❑ Aug 1998 Cover: 3.50 **NM** value: **Cover or less**
Circ: Diamd. preorders: **11,440**
A: Eli Stone W: Eli Stone

TICK BIG SUMMER ANNUAL, THE — NEC

1 ❑ Jul 1999 Cover: 3.50 **NM** value: **Cover or less**
📖 The Enemy of My Enemy is My Enemy! A: Gabe Crate; Tak Toyoshima W: Marc Silva

TICK, THE: CIRCUS MAXIMUS — NEC

1 ❑ Mar 2000 Cover: 3.50 **NM** value: **Cover or less**
Circ: Diamd. preorders: **5,888**
2 ❑ Apr 2000 Cover: 3.50 **NM** value: **Cover or less**
Circ: Diamd. preorders: **5,074**
3 ❑ May 2000 Cover: 3.50 **NM** value: **Cover or less**
Circ: Diamd. preorders: **5,173**
4 ❑ Jun 2000 Cover: 3.50 **NM** value: **Cover or less**
Circ: Diamd. preorders: **4,862**

TICK, THE: HEROES OF THE CITY — NEC

1 ❑ Feb 1999 Cover: 3.50 **NM** value: **Cover or less**
Circ: Diamd. preorders: **9,171**
📖 Prologue; Arthur; The Tick; Myndi A: Gabe Crate; Nathan MacDicken; Sean Wang W: Clay Griffith; Marc Silvia

TICK, THE: KARMA TORNADO — NEC

1 ❑ Oct 1993 Cover: 3.25 **NM** value: **4.00**
A: Bill Nevill W: Ben Edlund; Chris McCulloch
1-2 ❑ Jan 1997 Cover: 2.95 **NM** value: **Cover or less**
2 ❑ Jan 1994 Cover: 2.75 **NM** value: **3.50**
📖 Electric Boogaloo A: Bill Nevill W: Ben Edlund; Chris McCulloch
2-2 ❑ Feb 1997 Cover: 2.95 **NM** value: **Cover or less**
3 ❑ May 1994 Cover: 2.75 **NM** value: **5.00**
• Scarce A: Bill Nevill W: Ben Edlund; Chris McCulloch
3-2 ❑ Mar 1997 Cover: 2.95 **NM** value: **Cover or less**
4 ❑ Jul 1994 Cover: 2.75 **NM** value: **5.00**
• Scarce A: Bill Nevill W: Ben Edlund; Chris McCulloch
4-2 ❑ Apr 1997 Cover: 2.95 **NM** value: **Cover or less**
5 ❑ Aug 1994 Cover: 2.75 **NM** value: **5.00**
• Scarce A: Bill Nevill W: Ben Edlund; Chris McCulloch
5-2 ❑ Cover: 2.95 **NM** value: **Cover or less**
6 ❑ Oct 1994 Cover: 2.75 **NM** value: **4.00**
A: Bill Nevill W: Ben Edlund; Chris McCulloch
6-2 ❑ Cover: 2.95 **NM** value: **Cover or less**
7 ❑ 1994 Cover: 2.75 **NM** value: **4.00**
A: Bill Nevill W: Ben Edlund; Chris McCulloch
7-2 ❑ Cover: 2.95 **NM** value: **Cover or less**
8 ❑ 1995 Cover: 2.75 **NM** value: **4.00**
A: Bill Nevill W: Ben Edlund; Chris McCulloch
8-2 ❑ Cover: 2.95 **NM** value: **Cover or less**
9 ❑ 1995 Cover: 2.75 **NM** value: **3.00**
A: Bill Nevill W: Ben Edlund; Chris McCulloch
9-2 ❑ Cover: 2.95 **NM** value: **Cover or less**
Bk 1❑ **NM** value: **16.00**
A: Bill Nevill W: Ben Edlund; Chris McCulloch
Bk 1-2❑ Cover: 13.95 **NM** value: **Cover or less**
Bk 2❑ Cover: 11.95 **NM** value: **Cover or less**
A: Bill Nevill W: Ben Edlund; Chris McCulloch

TICK: LUNY BIN TRILOGY — NEC

1 ❑ Oct 1998 Cover: 3.50 **NM** value: **Cover or less**
Circ: Diamd. preorders: **10,748**

TICK'S BACK, THE — NEC

0 ❑ Aug 1997 Cover: 2.95 **NM** value: **Cover or less**
Circ: Diamd. preorders: **18,411**
Red cover.
0/A ❑ Aug 1997 Cover: 5.00 **NM** value: **Cover or less**
Green Cover.
0/B ❑ Aug 1997 Cover: 7.50 **NM** value: **Cover or less**
Gold Tick Cover.
0/C ❑ Aug 1997 Cover: 10.00 **NM** value: **Cover or less**
No logo, Gold cover.

TICK'S BIG BACK TO SCHOOL SPECIAL, THE — NEC

1 ❑ ca. 1998 Cover: 3.50 **NM** value: **Cover or less**
Circ: Diamd. preorders: **10,450**
📖 Back to School! A: Sean Wang W: Sean Wang

TICK'S BIG CRUISE SHIP VACATION SPECIAL, THE — NEC

1 ❑ Sep 2000 Cover: 3.50 **NM** value: **Cover or less**
Circ: Diamd. preorders: **5,030**

TICK'S BIG FATHER'S DAY SPECIAL, THE — NEC

1 ❑ Jun 2000 Cover: 3.50 **NM** value: **Cover or less**
Circ: Diamd. preorders: **5,717**
📖 Enter: Kid Tick! A: Gabe Crate W: Clay Griffith; Susan Griffith ★ 1st Appearance of Kid Tick.

TICK'S BIG HALLOWEEN SPECIAL, THE — NEC

1 ❑ Oct 1999 Cover: 3.50 **NM** value: **Cover or less**
Circ: Diamd. preorders: **7,354**
📖 Haunted Halloween Hootenanny A: Nathan MacDicken W: Clay Griffith; Susan Griffith

TICK'S BIG ROMANTIC ADVENTURE, THE — NEC

1 ❑ Feb 1998 Cover: 2.95 **NM** value: **Cover or less**
Circ: Diamd. preorders: **13,142**
📖 Bad Chemistry A: Sean Wang W: Sean Wang

TICK'S BIG YULE LOG SPECIAL — NEC

1 ❑ Dec 1997, b&w Cover: 3.50 **NM** value: **Cover or less**
1998❑Feb 1998 Cover: 3.50 **NM** value: **Cover or less**
Circ: Diamd. preorders: **13,975**
1999❑Jan 1999 Cover: 3.50 **NM** value: **Cover or less**
Circ: Diamd. preorders: **9,192**

TICK'S GIANT CIRCUS OF THE MIGHTY, THE — NEC

1 ❑ Sum 1992 Cover: 2.75 **NM** value: **Cover or less**
A: Dave Garcia; Ben Edlund; Allan Hopkins; Clay Griffith W: Dave Garcia; Ben Edlund; Allan Hopkins; Clay Griffith
2 ❑ Sum 1992 Cover: 2.75 **NM** value: **Cover or less**
A: Dave Garcia; Ben Edlund; Allan Hopkins; Clay Griffith W: Dave Garcia; Ben Edlund; Allan Hopkins; Clay Griffith

TICK-TOCK FOLLIES — Slave Labor

1 ❑ Dec 1996 Cover: 2.95 **NM** value: **Cover or less**
A: Chris Hogg W: Chris Butler

TICK TOCK TALES — Magazine Enterprises

1 ❑ Jan 1946 Cover: 0.10 **NM** value: **75.00**
2 ❑ Feb 1946 Cover: 0.10 **NM** value: **60.00**
3 ❑ Mar 1946 Cover: 0.10 **NM** value: **45.00**
4 ❑ Apr 1946 Cover: 0.10 **NM** value: **45.00**
5 ❑ May 1946 Cover: 0.10 **NM** value: **45.00**
6 ❑ Jun 1946 Cover: 0.10 **NM** value: **40.00**
7 ❑ Jul 1946 Cover: 0.10 **NM** value: **40.00**
8 ❑ Aug 1946 Cover: 0.10 **NM** value: **40.00**
9 ❑ Sep 1946 Cover: 0.10 **NM** value: **40.00**
10 ❑ Oct 1946 Cover: 0.10 **NM** value: **40.00**
11 ❑ Nov 1946 Cover: 0.10 **NM** value: **30.00**
12 ❑ Dec 1946 Cover: 0.10 **NM** value: **30.00**
13 ❑ Jan 1947 Cover: 0.10 **NM** value: **30.00**
14 ❑ Feb 1947 Cover: 0.10 **NM** value: **30.00**
15 ❑ Mar 1947 Cover: 0.10 **NM** value: **30.00**
16 ❑ Apr 1947 Cover: 0.10 **NM** value: **30.00**
17 ❑ May 1947 Cover: 0.10 **NM** value: **30.00**
18 ❑ Jun 1947 Cover: 0.10 **NM** value: **30.00**
19 ❑ Jul 1947 Cover: 0.10 **NM** value: **30.00**
20 ❑ Aug 1947 Cover: 0.10 **NM** value: **30.00**
21 ❑ Sep 1947 Cover: 0.10 **NM** value: **25.00**
22 ❑ Oct 1947 Cover: 0.10 **NM** value: **25.00**
23 ❑ Nov 1947 Cover: 0.10 **NM** value: **25.00**
24 ❑ Dec 1947 Cover: 0.10 **NM** value: **25.00**
25 ❑ Jan 1948 Cover: 0.10 **NM** value: **25.00**
26 ❑ Mar 1948 Cover: 0.10 **NM** value: **25.00**
Note: Koko and Kola cover
27 ❑ 1948 Cover: 0.10 **NM** value: **25.00**
28 ❑ 1948 Cover: 0.10 **NM** value: **25.00**
29 ❑ 1948 Cover: 0.10 **NM** value: **25.00**
30 ❑ 1948 Cover: 0.10 **NM** value: **25.00**
31 ❑ 1948 Cover: 0.10 **NM** value: **25.00**
32 ❑ 1948 Cover: 0.10 **NM** value: **25.00**
33 ❑ 1948 Cover: 0.10 **NM** value: **25.00**

TIC TOC TOM — Detonator Canada

1 ❑ Aut 1995, b&w Cover: 2.95 **NM** value: **Cover or less**
2 ❑ Win 1995, b&w Cover: 2.95 **NM** value: **Cover or less**
3 ❑ Spr 1996, b&w Cover: 2.95 **NM** value: **Cover or less**

TIGER — King

1 ❑ Jan 1970 Cover: 0.15 **NM** value: **10.00**
1-2 ❑ **NM** value: **6.00**
2 ❑ Mar 1970 Cover: 0.15 **NM** value: **5.00**
3 ❑ May 1970 Cover: 0.15 **NM** value: **4.00**
4 ❑ Sep 1970 Cover: 0.15 **NM** value: **4.00**
5 ❑ Nov 1970 Cover: 0.15 **NM** value: **4.00**
6 ❑ Jan 1971 Cover: 0.15 **NM** value: **4.00**

TIGER GIRL — Gold Key

1 ❑ Sep 1968 Cover: 0.15 **NM** value: **25.00**
• CGC: 3 graded, best 9.4

TIGERMAN — Atlas-Seaboard

1 ❑ Sep 1975 Cover: 0.25 **NM** value: **2.00**
• CGC: 4 graded, best 9.4
★ Origin of Tigerman. ★ 1st Appearance of Tigerman.
2 ❑ Jun 1975 Cover: 0.25 **NM** value: **1.50**
• CGC: 1 graded, best 9.4
A: Steve Ditko
3 ❑ Sep 1975 Cover: 0.25 **NM** value: **1.50**
A: Steve Ditko

TIGERS OF TERRA — Mind-Visions

1 ❑ ca. 1992 Cover: 3.00 **NM** value: **Cover or less**
2 ❑ ca. 1992 Cover: 3.00 **NM** value: **Cover or less**
3 ❑ ca. 1992 Cover: 3.00 **NM** value: **Cover or less**
4 ❑ ca. 1992 Cover: 3.50 **NM** value: **Cover or less**
5 ❑ ca. 1992 Cover: 3.50 **NM** value: **Cover or less**
6 ❑ ca. 1992 Cover: 3.50 **NM** value: **Cover or less**
7 ❑ ca. 1992 Cover: 3.50 **NM** value: **Cover or less**
8 ❑ ca. 1993 Cover: 3.75 **NM** value: **Cover or less**
9 ❑ ca. 1993 Cover: 3.75 **NM** value: **Cover or less**
two covers: a and b.
10 ❑ ca. 1993, b&w Cover: 3.75 **NM** value: **Cover or less**
11 ❑ ca. 1993, b&w Cover: 3.95 **NM** value: **Cover or less**
12 ❑ Jul 1993, b&w Cover: 3.95 **NM** value: **Cover or less**

TIGERS OF TERRA: TECHNICAL MANUAL — Antarctic

1 ❑ b&w Cover: 2.95 **NM** value: **Cover or less**
A: Ted Nomura W: Ted Nomura
2 ❑ Jun 1996, b&w Cover: 2.95 **NM** value: **Cover or less**

TIGERS OF TERRA (VOL. 2) — Antarctic

0 ❑ Aug 1993 Cover: 2.95 **NM** value: **Cover or less**
1 ❑ Oct 1993 Cover: 2.75 **NM** value: **3.00**
📖 Tigers of Burma A: Ted Nomura W: Ted Nomura
2 ❑ Dec 1993 Cover: 2.75 **NM** value: **3.00**
📖 Roses of Red Phoenix A: Ted Nomura W: Ted Nomura
3 ❑ Feb 1994 Cover: 2.75 **NM** value: **3.00**
A: Ted Nomura W: Ted Nomura
4 ❑ Apr 1994 Cover: 2.75 **NM** value: **3.00**
A: Ted Nomura W: Ted Nomura
5 ❑ Jul 1994 Cover: 2.75 **NM** value: **3.00**
📖 The Third Yamato A: Ted Nomura W: Ted Nomura
6 ❑ Sep 1994 Cover: 2.75 **NM** value: **3.00**
A: Ted Nomura W: Ted Nomura
7 ❑ Dec 1994 Cover: 2.75 **NM** value: **3.00**
A: Ted Nomura W: Ted Nomura
8 ❑ Jan 1995 Cover: 2.75 **NM** value: **3.00**
📖 Projekt: Mars A: Ted Nomura W: Ted Nomura
9 ❑ Mar 1995 Cover: 2.75 **NM** value: **3.00**
📖 Tiger III, Part 1 A: Ted Nomura W: Ted Nomura
10 ❑ Apr 1995 Cover: 2.75 **NM** value: **3.00**
📖 Tiger III, Part 2 A: Ted Nomura W: Ted Nomura
11 ❑ May 1995 Cover: 2.75 **NM** value: **Cover or less**
📖 Tiger III, Part 3 A: Ted Nomura W: Ted Nomura
12 ❑ Jun 1995 Cover: 2.75 **NM** value: **Cover or less**
A: Ted Nomura W: Ted Nomura
13 ❑ Jul 1995 Cover: 2.75 **NM** value: **Cover or less**
A: Ted Nomura W: Ted Nomura
14 ❑ Aug 1995 Cover: 2.75 **NM** value: **Cover or less**
A: Ted Nomura W: Ted Nomura
15 ❑ Sep 1995 Cover: 2.75 **NM** value: **Cover or less**
A: Ted Nomura W: Ted Nomura
16 ❑ Oct 1995 Cover: 2.75 **NM** value: **Cover or less**
A: Ted Nomura W: Ted Nomura
17 ❑ Nov 1995 Cover: 2.75 **NM** value: **Cover or less**
A: Ted Nomura W: Ted Nomura
18 ❑ Dec 1996 Cover: 2.75 **NM** value: **2.95**
A: Ted Nomura W: Ted Nomura
19 ❑ Jan 1996 Cover: 2.75 **NM** value: **2.95**
A: Ted Nomura W: Ted Nomura
20 ❑ Mar 1996 Cover: 2.95 **NM** value: **Cover or less**
A: Ted Nomura W: Ted Nomura

21 ❑ May 1996 Cover: 2.95 **NM** value: **Cover or less**
A: Ted Nomura W: Ted Nomura
22 ❑ Jul 1996 Cover: 2.95 **NM** value: **Cover or less**
A: Ted Nomura W: Ted Nomura
23 ❑ Sep 1996 Cover: 2.95 **NM** value: **Cover or less**
A: Ted Nomura W: Ted Nomura
24 ❑ Nov 1996 Cover: 3.95 **NM** value: **Cover or less**
📖 The Flying Cosmotigers A: Ted Nomura W: Ted Nomura
25 ❑ Jan 1997 Cover: 2.95 **NM** value: **Cover or less**
📖 Revelation A: Ted Nomura W: Ted Nomura
Bk 1❑ Aug 1993 Cover: 9.95 **NM** value: **Cover or less**
• collects first two issues
Bk 2❑ Cover: 9.95 **NM** value: **Cover or less**
Bk 3❑ Cover: 9.95 **NM** value: **Cover or less**
Bk 4❑ Cover: 9.95 **NM** value: **Cover or less**
Bk 5❑ Dec 1996 Cover: 9.95 **NM** value: **Cover or less**

TIGERS OF TERRA (VOL. 3) — Antarctic
1 ❑ Jul 2000 Cover: 2.95 **NM** value: **Cover or less**
📖 War Against the Sun A: Ted Nomura W: Ted Nomura

TIGER WOMAN, THE — Millennium
1 ❑ Sep 1994 Cover: 2.95 **NM** value: **Cover or less**
Circ: CapCity orders: **4,305**
• no indicia A: Donnie Jupiter; Donald Marquez W: Donnie Jupiter
2 ❑ Apr 1995 Cover: 2.95 **NM** value: **Cover or less**
cover says Quest of the Tiger Woman #1. • no indicia; but title page says Tiger Woman #2

TIGER WOMAN, THE: THE LAST PLACE ON EARTH — Caliber
1 ❑ Cover: 2.95 **NM** value: **Cover or less**
📖 The Last Place on Earth A: Donald Marquez W: Donald Maruez

TIGER-X — Eternity
1 ❑ 1988b&w Cover: 1.95 **NM** value: **Cover or less**
• Story continued from Tiger-X Special #1 A: Ben Dunn W: Ben Dunn
2 ❑ 1988b&w Cover: 1.95 **NM** value: **Cover or less**
A: Ben Dunn W: Ben Dunn
3 ❑ 1988b&w Cover: 1.95 **NM** value: **Cover or less**
A: Ben Dunn W: Ben Dunn
Bk 1❑ Cover: 9.95 **NM** value: **Cover or less**
• The Adventure Begins
SE 1❑ 1988b&w Cover: 2.25 **NM** value: **Cover or less**
SE 1-2❑ Dec 1988 Cover: 2.25 **NM** value: **Cover or less**

TIGER-X BOOK II — Eternity
1 ❑ 1989b&w Cover: 1.95 **NM** value: **2.00**
📖 Stalking Horse A: Juan Muro W: Paul O'Conner
2 ❑ 1989b&w Cover: 1.95 **NM** value: **2.00**
3 ❑ 1989b&w Cover: 1.95 **NM** value: **2.00**
4 ❑ 1989b&w Cover: 1.95 **NM** value: **2.00**

TIGRESS, THE — Hero
1 ❑ Aug 1992, b&w Cover: 2.95 **NM** value: **Cover or less**
📖 The Return of the Tigress A: Paul Abrams W: Dennis Mallonee
★ Appearance of Flare.
2 ❑ Oct 1992, b&w Cover: 2.95 **NM** value: **Cover or less**
★ Appearance of Flare.
3 ❑ Dec 1992, b&w Cover: 2.95 **NM** value: **Cover or less**
★ 1st Appearance of Mudpie.
4 ❑ Feb 1993, b&w Cover: 2.95 **NM** value: **Cover or less**
5 ❑ Apr 1993, b&w Cover: 2.95 **NM** value: **Cover or less**
6 ❑ Jun 1993 Cover: 3.95 **NM** value: **Cover or less**

TIGRESS (BASEMENT) — Basement
1 ❑ Jul 1998 Cover: 2.95 **NM** value: **Cover or less**
Circ: Diamd. preorders: **3,528**

TIJUANA BIBLE, THE — Starhead
All issues are adults only.
1 ❑ b&w Cover: 3.95 **NM** value: **Cover or less**
2 ❑ b&w Cover: 3.95 **NM** value: **Cover or less**
📖 Blondie; Clock For Sale; Big Game Hunter; Sadie Steps Out; The Judge; Heavy Duty; Joe Palooka VII; The Rescue; Tsk-Tsk; Oh-Oh; Andy Gump
3 ❑ b&w Cover: 3.95 **NM** value: **Cover or less**
4 ❑ b&w Cover: 3.95 **NM** value: **Cover or less**
📖 The Traveling Salesman And The Farmers Daughter; Schnazle Durante; Clark Gable At The Girls' • Bluesie Toons
5 ❑ Cover: 2.50 **NM** value: **Cover or less**
📖 The Sensation Of The Aquacade; It Happened On The Flying Trapeze; She Didn't Miss; Jitterbug Contest; Zonga The Dove Dan • World's Fair
6 ❑ Cover: 2.50 **NM** value: **Cover or less**
📖 The Adventures Of A Fuller Brush Man; Obliging Lady; Ain't Nature Grand; Easy Pickins • Fuller Brush Man
7 ❑ Cover: 2.50 **NM** value: **Cover or less**
📖 Wally And The King; Wally And The Sultan; Wally And The French Ambassador; Wally And The Page Boy; Wally In The Bath; Andy Gump: Dreaming • Royalty issue
8 ❑ Cover: 2.50 **NM** value: **Cover or less**
📖 Get A Li'l Like The Fishes Do; Filling A Large Cavity; The Open Road; Purple Passion In The South Seas; Cert Gabbo • Hollywood women
9 ❑ Cover: 2.50 **NM** value: **Cover or less**
• An Artist's Affaire
Bk 1❑ Cover: 12.95 **NM** value: **Cover or less**
A: Pat Moriarty(cover) W: R.C. Harvey
Bk 2❑ Cover: 12.95 **NM** value: **Cover or less**
A: Pat Moriarty(cover) W: R.C. Harvey
Bk 3❑ Mar 1998, b&w Cover: 12.95 **NM** value: **Cover or less**
• The Tijuana Bibles; Fantagraphics publishes

TILAZEUS MEETS THE MESSIAH — Aiiie
1 ❑ Cover: 2.50 **NM** value: **Cover or less**
A: Herb Apon W: Scott Allie

TIMBER WOLF — DC
In a faraway future, Brin's father wanted him to become a man quickly, so he pumped Brin full of chemicals. The chemicals hurt, but made Brin strong and swift, and allowed him to become a Legionnaire.

Then Brin met Aria, a twelve-year-old in a woman's body. She transported him one thousand years back to our time and turned him into Timber Wolf. Side effects of the time travel include an ever-raging anger that Timber Wolf struggles to contain, and an almost feral, wolf-like form. The fur flies when the Wolf fights, although he's capable of compassion and curiosity as well.

Outside of this five-issue mini-series, Timber Wolf is also known from his exploits with The Legion of Super-Heroes.

1 ❑ Nov 1992 Cover: 1.25 **NM** value: **1.50**
Circ: CapCity orders: **22,000**
📖 Twentieth Century Wolf A: Joe Phillips W: Al Gordon
2 ❑ Dec 1992 Cover: 1.25 **NM** value: **1.50**
Circ: CapCity orders: **14,850**
3 ❑ Jan 1993 Cover: 1.25 **NM** value: **1.50**
Circ: CapCity orders: **13,250**
★ Versus Creeper.
4 ❑ Feb 1993 Cover: 1.25 **NM** value: **1.50**
Circ: CapCity orders: **13,550**
5 ❑ Mar 1993 Cover: 1.25 **NM** value: **1.50**
Circ: CapCity orders: **12,400**

TIME BANDITS — Marvel
1 ❑ Feb 1982 Cover: 1.00 **NM** value: **1.50**

TIME BREAKERS — DC / Helix
1 ❑ Jan 1997 Cover: 2.25 **NM** value: **Cover or less**
Circ: Diamd. preorders: **17,317**
📖 Lives of Our Time A: Chris Weston W: Rachel Pollack
2 ❑ Feb 1997 Cover: 2.50 **NM** value: **Cover or less**
Circ: Diamd. preorders: **12,849**
📖 Mind Out of Time A: Chris Weston W: Rachel Pollack
3 ❑ Mar 1997 Cover: 2.50 **NM** value: **Cover or less**
Circ: Diamd. preorders: **11,973**
📖 Again and Again Time A: Chris Weston W: Rachel Pollack
4 ❑ Apr 1997 Cover: 2.50 **NM** value: **Cover or less**
Circ: Diamd. preorders: **10,154**
📖 Challenge for a Time A: Chris Weston W: Rachel Pollack
5 ❑ May 1997 Cover: 2.50 **NM** value: **Cover or less**
Circ: Diamd. preorders: **9,728**
📖 The Day has Come to Time A: Chris Weston W: Rachel Pollack

TIMECOP — Dark Horse
1 ❑ Sep 1994 Cover: 2.50 **NM** value: **Cover or less**
Circ: CapCity orders: **4,175**
A: Ron Randall W: Mark Verheiden
2 ❑ Sep 1994 Cover: 2.50 **NM** value: **Cover or less**
Circ: CapCity orders: **4,075**
A: Ron Randall W: Mark Verheiden

TIMEDRIFTER (GERARD JONES'...) — Innovation
1 ❑ Dec 1990, b&w Cover: 2.25 **NM** value: **Cover or less**
📖 Right Place, Wrong Time A: Dean Hubenig; Gerald Jones W: Gerald Jones
2 ❑ b&w Cover: 2.25 **NM** value: **Cover or less**
3 ❑ b&w Cover: 2.25 **NM** value: **Cover or less**

TIME FOR LOVE — Charlton
1 ❑ Oct 1967 Cover: 0.12 **NM** value: **7.00**
📖 By Love Inspired
2 ❑ Dec 1967 Cover: 0.12 **NM** value: **5.00**
3 ❑ Mar 1968 Cover: 0.12 **NM** value: **5.00**
4 ❑ May 1968 Cover: 0.12 **NM** value: **5.00**
5 ❑ Jul 1968 Cover: 0.12 **NM** value: **5.00**
6 ❑ Sep 1968 Cover: 0.12 **NM** value: **4.00**
📖 Everybody's Idol and Me
7 ❑ Nov 1968 Cover: 0.12 **NM** value: **4.00**
📖 The Trouble With Annie
8 ❑ Feb 1969 Cover: 0.12 **NM** value: **4.00**
9 ❑ Mar 1969 Cover: 0.12 **NM** value: **4.00**
10 ❑ May 1969 Cover: 0.12 **NM** value: **4.00**
11 ❑ Jul 1969 Cover: 0.15 **NM** value: **3.00**
12 ❑ Sep 1969 Cover: 0.15 **NM** value: **3.00**
13 ❑ Nov 1969 Cover: 0.15 **NM** value: **3.00**
14 ❑ Jan 1970 Cover: 0.15 **NM** value: **3.00**
15 ❑ Mar 1970 Cover: 0.15 **NM** value: **3.00**
16 ❑ May 1970 Cover: 0.15 **NM** value: **3.00**
17 ❑ Jul 1970 Cover: 0.15 **NM** value: **3.00**
18 ❑ Sep 1970 Cover: 0.15 **NM** value: **3.00**
19 ❑ Nov 1970 Cover: 0.15 **NM** value: **3.00**
20 ❑ Jan 1971 Cover: 0.15 **NM** value: **3.00**
21 ❑ Mar 1971 Cover: 0.15 **NM** value: **2.50**
22 ❑ May 1971 Cover: 0.15 **NM** value: **2.50**
23 ❑ Jul 1971 Cover: 0.15 **NM** value: **2.50**
24 ❑ Sep 1971 Cover: 0.15 **NM** value: **2.50**
25 ❑ Nov 1971 Cover: 0.20 **NM** value: **2.50**
26 ❑ Jan 1972 Cover: 0.20 **NM** value: **2.50**
Circ: Statement: **116,030**
27 ❑ Mar 1972 Cover: 0.20 **NM** value: **2.50**
Circ: Statement: **116,030**
28 ❑ May 1972 Cover: 0.20 **NM** value: **2.50**
Circ: Statement: **116,030**
29 ❑ ca. 1972 Cover: 0.20 **NM** value: **2.50**
Circ: Statement: **116,030**
30 ❑ Oct 1972 Cover: 0.20 **NM** value: **2.50**
Circ: Statement: **116,030**
31 ❑ Dec 1972 Cover: 0.20 **NM** value: **2.00**
Circ: Statement: **116,030**
32 ❑ Feb 1973 Cover: 0.20 **NM** value: **2.00**
Circ: Statement: **127,045**
33 ❑ Apr 1973 Cover: 0.20 **NM** value: **2.00**
Circ: Statement: **127,045**
• Has 1972 Statement; avg total paid circ 116,030
34 ❑ Jun 1973 Cover: 0.20 **NM** value: **2.00**
Circ: Statement: **127,045**
35 ❑ Aug 1973 Cover: 0.20 **NM** value: **2.00**
Circ: Statement: **127,045**
36 ❑ ca. 1973 Cover: 0.20 **NM** value: **2.00**
Circ: Statement: **127,045**
37 ❑ Dec 1973 Cover: 0.20 **NM** value: **2.00**
Circ: Statement: **127,045**
38 ❑ ca. 1974 Cover: 0.25 **NM** value: **2.00**
Circ: Statement: **110,089**
📖 Dream Became A Nightmare!; A Rainy Afternoon; Paradise Now?
• Has 1973 Statement; avg total paid circ 127,045
39 ❑ ca. 1974 Cover: 0.25 **NM** value: **2.00**
Circ: Statement: **110,089**
40 ❑ ca. 1974 Cover: 0.25 **NM** value: **2.00**
Circ: Statement: **110,089**
41 ❑ Apr 1975 Cover: 0.25 **NM** value: **2.00**
Circ: Statement: **99,152**
42 ❑ Jun 1975 Cover: 0.25 **NM** value: **2.00**
Circ: Statement: **99,152**
• Has 1974 Statement; avg total paid circ 110.089
43 ❑ Aug 1975 Cover: 0.25 **NM** value: **2.00**
Circ: Statement: **99,152**
44 ❑ Oct 1975 Cover: 0.25 **NM** value: **2.00**
Circ: Statement: **99,152**
45 ❑ Jan 1976 Cover: 0.25 **NM** value: **2.00**
46 ❑ Mar 1976 Cover: 0.25 **NM** value: **2.00**
47 ❑ May 1976 Cover: 0.30 **NM** value: **2.00**
final issue.

TIME GATES — Double Edge
1 ❑ Cover: 1.95 **NM** value: **Cover or less**
2 ❑ Cover: 1.95 **NM** value: **Cover or less**
3 ❑ Cover: 1.95 **NM** value: **Cover or less**

TIMEJUMP WAR, THE — Apple
1 ❑ Oct 1989, b&w Cover: 2.25 **NM** value: **Cover or less**
A: Enrique Villagran W: Chuck Dixon
2 ❑ b&w Cover: 2.25 **NM** value: **Cover or less**
A: Enrique Villagran W: Chuck Dixon
3 ❑ b&w Cover: 2.25 **NM** value: **Cover or less**
A: Enrique Villagran W: Chuck Dixon

TIME KILLERS — Fleetway-Quality
1 ❑ Cover: 2.95 **NM** value: **Cover or less**
Circ: CapCity orders: **3,150**
📖 Killing Time • Tales From Beyond Space: The Men In Red A: Chris Weston; Richard Elson W: John Smith; Peter Milligan
2 ❑ Cover: 2.95 **NM** value: **Cover or less**
3 ❑ Cover: 2.95 **NM** value: **Cover or less**
4 ❑ Cover: 2.95 **NM** value: **Cover or less**
5 ❑ Cover: 2.95 **NM** value: **Cover or less**
6 ❑ Cover: 2.95 **NM** value: **Cover or less**
📖 Tales From Beyond Science: Secrets of the Organism; Shadows; Dry Run
7 ❑ Cover: 2.95 **NM** value: **Cover or less**

TIMELESS TALES (BOB POWELL'S...) — Eclipse
1 ❑ Mar 1989, b&w Cover: 2.00 **NM** value: **Cover or less**
📖 Gotta Match?; Supreme Penalty; The Scarlet Arrow

TIMELY PRESENTS: ALL-WINNERS — Marvel
1 ❑ Dec 1999 Cover: 3.99 **NM** value: **Cover or less**
Circ: Diamd. preorders: **14,873**
No issue number. 📖 The Crime of the Ages! • Reprints All-Winners Comics #19 A: Ray Lago W: Roy Thomas

TIMELY PRESENTS: HUMAN TORCH — Marvel
1 ❑ Feb 1999 Cover: 3.99 **NM** value: **Cover or less**
Painted cover by Ray Lago. 📖 Human Torch, Part 1; Human Torch, Part 2; Human Torch, Part 3 • Reprinted from Human Torch Comics #5 A: Bill Everett W: Carl Burgos ★ Appearance of Sub-Mariner.

TIME MACHINE, THE — Eternity
1 ❑ Apr 1990, b&w Cover: 2.50 **NM** value: **Cover or less**
• Based on the story by H.G. Wells A: John Ross W: Bill Sprangler
2 ❑ 1990b&w Cover: 2.50 **NM** value: **Cover or less**
3 ❑ 1990b&w Cover: 2.50 **NM** value: **Cover or less**
Bk 1❑ Cover: 9.95 **NM** value: **Cover or less**

TIME MASTERS — DC
1 ❑ Feb 1990 Cover: 1.75 **NM** value: **2.00**
Circ: CapCity orders: **22,450**
📖 Time Won't Let Me A: Art Thibert W: Bob Wayne; Lewis Shiner
2 ❑ Mar 1990 Cover: 1.75 **NM** value: **Cover or less**
Circ: CapCity orders: **16,650**
📖 No Time To Live A: Art Thibert W: Bob Wayne; Lewis Shiner
3 ❑ Apr 1990 Cover: 1.75 **NM** value: **Cover or less**
Circ: CapCity orders: **14,700**
A: Art Thibert W: Bob Wayne; Lewis Shiner
4 ❑ May 1990 Cover: 1.75 **NM** value: **Cover or less**
Circ: CapCity orders: **14,200**
📖 Time is on my Side A: Art Thibert W: Bob Wayne; Lewis Shiner
5 ❑ Jun 1990 Cover: 1.75 **NM** value: **Cover or less**
Circ: CapCity orders: **13,600**
A: Art Thibert W: Bob Wayne; Lewis Shiner ★ Appearance of Viking Prince.
6 ❑ Jul 1990 Cover: 1.75 **NM** value: **Cover or less**
Circ: CapCity orders: **13,250**

CGC-graded: Multiply prices above by **33 for 9.9 M • 16 for 9.8 NM/M • 7 for 9.6 NM+ • 5 for 9.4 NM • 2.5 for 9.2 NM- • 1.5 for 9.0 VF/NM**

A: Art Thibert W: Bob Wayne; Lewis Shiner ★ Appearance of Dr. Fate, Doctor Fate.
7 ❑ Aug 1990 Cover: 1.75 **NM** value: **Cover or less**
Circ: CapCity orders: **12,750**
A: Art Thibert **W:** Bob Wayne; Lewis Shiner ★ Appearance of Arion.
8 ❑ Sep 1990 Cover: 1.75 **NM** value: **Cover or less**
Circ: CapCity orders: **11,950**
A: Art Thibert **W:** Bob Wayne; Lewis Shiner

TIME OUT OF MIND — Graphic Serials

1 ❑ Cover: 1.85 **NM** value: **2.00**
Circ: CapCity orders: **1,305**
2 ❑ Cover: 1.75 **NM** value: **Cover or less**
3 ❑ Cover: 1.75 **NM** value: **Cover or less**
Circ: CapCity orders: **900**

TIMESLIP COLLECTION — Marvel

1 ❑ Nov 1998 Cover: 2.99 **NM** value: **Cover or less**
Circ: Diamd. preorders: **10,635**
wraparound cover. • collects short features from Marvel Vision **A:** Tim Sale; Scott McDaniel; John Paul Leon; Mike Allred; Guy Davis; Kelly Jones; Vinc **W:** Jim Krueger

TIMESLIP SPECIAL — Marvel

1 ❑ Oct 1998 Cover: 5.99 **NM** value: **Cover or less**
cardstock cover. 📖 The Coming of the Avengers

TIMESPELL — Club 408 Graphics

0 ❑ ca. 1997, b&w Cover: 2.95 **NM** value: **Cover or less**
cardstock cover. **A:** Rich Henn **W:** Rich Henn; Russ Colchamiro
1 ❑ ca. 1998, b&w Cover: 2.95 **NM** value: **Cover or less**
cardstock cover. 📖 Blood on the Moon **A:** Rich Henn **W:** Rich Henn; Russ Colchamiro
2 ❑ ca. 1998, b&w Cover: 2.95 **NM** value: **Cover or less**
cardstock cover. 📖 Domestic Oblivion **A:** Rich Henn **W:** Rich Henn; Russ Colchamiro
3 ❑ ca. 1998, b&w Cover: 2.95 **NM** value: **Cover or less**
cardstock cover. 📖 The Soul Cage **A:** Rich Henn **W:** Rich Henn; Russ Colchamiro
4 ❑ ca. 1998, b&w Cover: 2.95 **NM** value: **Cover or less**
cardstock cover. 📖 Childermas **A:** Rich Henn **W:** Rich Henn; Russ Colchamiro
Ash 1❑ca. 1997 **NM** value: **1.00**
No issue number. no cover price. • ashcan preview of upcoming series **A:** Rich Henn **W:** Rich Henn; Russ Colchamiro

TIMESPELL: THE DIRECTOR'S CUT — Club 408 Graphics

1 ❑ ca. 1998, b&w Cover: 2.95 **NM** value: **Cover or less**
no price on cover. 📖 Blood on the Moon • reprints #1 with revisions and additions **A:** Rich Henn **W:** Rich Henn; Russ Colchamiro

TIMESPIRITS — Marvel / Epic

1 ❑ Oct 1984 Cover: 1.50 **NM** value: **2.00**
📖 Indian Spring **A:** Tom Yeates **W:** Steve Perry
2 ❑ Dec 1984 Cover: 1.50 **NM** value: **1.75**
3 ❑ Feb 1985 Cover: 1.50 **NM** value: **1.75**
4 ❑ Apr 1985 Cover: 1.50 **NM** value: **1.75**
Circ: CapCity orders: **6,900**
A: Al Williamson
5 ❑ Jul 1985 Cover: 1.50 **NM** value: **1.75**
Circ: CapCity orders: **6,450**
6 ❑ Sep 1985 Cover: 1.50 **NM** value: **1.75**
Circ: CapCity orders: **6,000**
7 ❑ Dec 1985 Cover: 1.50 **NM** value: **1.75**
Circ: CapCity orders: **5,700**
8 ❑ Mar 1986 Cover: 1.50 **NM** value: **1.75**
Circ: CapCity orders: **5,500**

TIME TRAVELER AI — CPM Manga

1 ❑ Oct 1999, b&w Cover: 2.95 **NM** value: **Cover or less**
Circ: Diamd. preorders: **5,019**
2 ❑ Nov 1999, b&w Cover: 2.95 **NM** value: **Cover or less**
Circ: Diamd. preorders: **3,861**
3 ❑ Dec 1999, b&w Cover: 2.95 **NM** value: **Cover or less**
Circ: Diamd. preorders: **3,292**
4 ❑ Jan 2000, b&w Cover: 2.95 **NM** value: **Cover or less**
Circ: Diamd. preorders: **3,288**
5 ❑ Feb 2000, b&w Cover: 2.95 **NM** value: **Cover or less**
Circ: Diamd. preorders: **2,975**
6 ❑ Mar 2000, b&w Cover: 2.95 **NM** value: **Cover or less**
Circ: Diamd. preorders: **2,920**
Bk 1❑ Aug 2000, b&w Cover: 15.95 **NM** value: **Cover or less**
• collects #1-6

TIME TRAVELER HERBIE — Avalon

1 ❑ Cover: 2.95 **NM** value: **Cover or less**
📖 Herbie goes Nap-Happy; Christopher Columbus Popnecker!; Pirate Gold! **A:** Ogden Whitney **W:** Shane O'Shea

TIME TUNNEL, THE — Gold Key

1 ❑ Feb 1967 Cover: 0.12 **NM** value: **25.00**
• **CGC:** 1 graded, best 8.5
📖 The Assassins; Mars Countdown
2 ❑ Jul 1967 Cover: 0.12 **NM** value: **25.00**
• **CGC:** 1 graded, best 8.0

TIME TWISTED TALES — Rip Off

1 ❑ Cover: 2.00 **NM** value: **Cover or less**
📖 The Year is 3711(2nd story) **A:** Dave Sheridan **W:** Dave Sheridan

TIME TWISTERS — Fleetway-Quality

Wedged in between Judge Dredd, Psi-Judge Anderson, or any of the other serials that ran through Britain's 2000 A.D., readers often found a short, ironic science-fiction story. These usually ran under the header "Tharg's Time Twisters" or "Tharg's Future Shocks" in honor of Tharg the Mighty, the fictional alien master of 2000 A.D. magazine.

Often these Time Twisters were a way for Fleetway to break in new writers and artists. This is not to say that they were a mediocre lot — indeed, many were written by Alan Moore (Watchmen) and drawn by such notables as Garry Leach, Alan Davis, and Dave Gibbons. Page for page, these stories were often the best thing about 2000 A.D. Begun in 1986, this series collects and colorizes the best of the stories, letting new readers experience their strange charm for themselves.

1 ❑ Cover: 1.25 **NM** value: **1.50**
Circ: CapCity orders: **5,050**
📖 Tharg's Time Twisters: The Hyper-Historic Headbang; Tharg' **A:** Dave Gibbons; Gary Leach **W:** Alan Moore
2 ❑ Cover: 1.25 **NM** value: **1.50**
Circ: CapCity orders: **3,625**
📖 Tharg's Fu **A:** Dave Gibbons; John Ridgway; Geoff Senior; Steve Dillon; Jesus Redondo; Trevor Goring; John Stokes **W:** Grant Morrison; Peter Milligan; Alan Moore
3 ❑ Cover: 1.25 **NM** value: **1.50**
Circ: CapCity orders: **3,275**
📖 Tharg's Future Shocks The Wages of Sin; Tharg's Future Shocks Salad Days; The Great Infinity Inc. Foul-Up; Tharg's Future Shocks Doing Time; Breathless; Tharg's Future Shocks All of Them Were Empty **A:** John Ridgway; Bryan Talbot; Paul Neary; Jesus Redondo; R. Brant **W:** Jack Adrian; Alan Hebden; Alan Moore; Pat Milligan
4 ❑ Cover: 1.25 **NM** value: **1.50**
Circ: CapCity orders: **2,925**
📖 Tharg's Future Shocks Bad Timing; Tharg's Future Shocks The End of the Universe; Tharg's Future Shocks Sacrifice; Tharg's Future Shocks Together; Spirit of Vengeance; Tharg's Future Shocks The Last Man; Ro Jaw's Robo Tales **A:** Dave Gibbons; John Higgins; Brett Ewins; Mike White; José Casanovas **W:** John Higgins; Alan Hebden; Alan Moore; Gary Rice; Oleh Stepaniuk
5 ❑ Cover: 1.25 **NM** value: **1.50**
Circ: CapCity orders: **1,825**
📖 Tharg's Future Shocks: Bad Maxwell; Extra! Extra!; Slashman Kowalski and Rat; Tharg's Future-Shocks But is it Art?; The Skinner Snack; Tharg's Future-Shocks the Collector; Bad Vibrations **A:** Massimo Belardinelli; Eric Bradbury; Ian Kennedy; J. Roberts; Jack Adrian; Jeff Anderson; Mike White; José Casanovas **W:** Steve Moore; Alan Hebden; Kelvin Gosnell; Pat Milligan
6 ❑ Cover: 1.25 **NM** value: **1.50**
Circ: CapCity orders: **1,800**
📖 Dr. Dales Diary; The Pioneer; Tharg's Future Shocks: Scrambled Eggs; Rogan's Run; Dr. Dibworthy's Disappointing Day **A:** Massimo Belardinelli; John Higgins; Eric Bradbury; Gary Leach; Alan Langford; Boluda; Redondo **W:** Alan Grant; Alan Hebden; Alan Moore; Stavros
7 ❑ Cover: 1.25 **NM** value: **1.50**
Circ: CapCity orders: **1,625**
📖 Tharg's Future Shocks: Twist Ending; Superbean; Tharg's Future Shocks: The Beastly Beliefs of Benjamin Blint; 60 Hours That Shook the World; The Search for Spot; The Return of the Two-storey Brain; Ring Road; Old Quagmires Never Die; The Jigsaw Man **A:** Paul Neary; Mike McMahon; Eric Bradbury; Jeff Anderson; Johnstone Fram; Mike White; R. Jones; Redondo **W:** Alan Moore; Murdoch McKenzie; Pat Milligan; Qirqx 1V
8 ❑ Cover: 1.25 **NM** value: **1.50**
Circ: CapCity orders: **1,475**
📖 Eureka; Horn of Plenty; The Invisible Etchings of Salvador Dali; Now You See It...; the Regrettable Ruse of Rocket Redglare; Fish in a Barrel; Skirmish; Nigel Goes A-Hunting **A:** Dave Gibbons; John Higgins; Eric Bradbury; Mike White; Redondo **W:** Grant Morrison; Steve Moore; Alan Hebden; Alan Moore; Kelvin Gosnell; Staccato
9 ❑ Cover: 1.25 **NM** value: **1.50**
Circ: CapCity orders: **1,400**
📖 The Big Clock; Tharg's **A:** John Higgins; Eric Bradbury; Gary Leach; Mike Dorey; Redondo **W:** Alan Moore; Kelvin Gosnell; W. Gosnell
10 ❑ Cover: 1.25 **NM** value: **1.50**
Circ: CapCity orders: **1,225**
📖 The Message; Tharg's Future Shocks: Fair's Fare; The Machine; Tharg's Future Shocks: Bait!; Seeing is Believing!; Tharg's Birthday Party; The Lanulos Run **A:** Massimo Belardinelli; Cliff Robinson; Jesus Redondo; Eric Bradbury; A. Haddersley; Colin Wilson **W:** Dave Perry; Alan Hebden; Alex Stewart; Jamie Delano; Kelvin Gosnell; T.M.O.
11 ❑ Cover: 1.50 **NM** value: **Cover or less**
Circ: CapCity orders: **1,225**
📖 Tharg's Future Shocks: Sid; Tharg's F **A:** Brett Ewins; Cliff Robinson; Eric Bradbury; Jaimie Ortiz; Redondo **W:** Alan Hebden; Kelvin Gosnell; Pat Milligan; Stavros; T.M. Hebden
12 ❑ Cover: 1.50 **NM** value: **Cover or less**
Circ: CapCity orders: **1,225**
📖 Time Twisters: The Avenging Kong Meets Laur **A:** Ron Tiner; Carlos Ezquerra; Eric Bradbury; Gary Leach; G. Anderson; Mike White; T. Jozwiak **W:** Peter Milligan; Steve Moore; Alan Hebden; Mike Cruden; Oleh Stepaniuk; Stavros; Tharg; W. Gosmore
13 ❑ Cover: 1.50 **NM** value: **Cover or less**
Circ: CapCity orders: **1,175**

📖 T.R.A.I.N.; Tharg's Future Shocks: And So to Bed...; Tharg's Future Shocks: Night Shift; The Invisible Man; Tharg's Future Shocks: His Name Was Janus; Tharg's Future Shocks: Resentment; Hap Hazard; Eric the Wild; Tharg's Future Shocks: Killer Rhythms **A:** Massimo Belardinelli; Steve Dillon; Bill Simpson; Dave D'Antiquis; T. Jozwiak **W:** Mike Collins; Steve Dillon; Peter Milligan; Alan Hebden; Soanes
14 ❑ Cover: 1.50 **NM** value: **Cover or less**
Circ: CapCity orders: **1,175**
📖 Tharg the Mighty: The D **A:** Brian Bolland; Carlos Ezquerra; Trevor Goring; Colin Wilson; Ewan Smith; Mike White; José Casanovas **W:** Steve Parkhouse; Jack Adrian; Alan Moore; Chris Lowder; Gary Rice; T.B. Grover
15 ❑ Cover: 1.50 **NM** value: **Cover or less**
Circ: CapCity orders: **1,075**
📖 T **A:** Dave Gibbons; John Higgins; Brett Ewins; Frisano; John Cooper; Mike White **W:** Grant Morrison; Jack Adrian; Gary Rice; P. Wildebeest; Robert Flynn
16 ❑ Cover: 1.50 **NM** value: **Cover or less**
Circ: CapCity orders: **1,050**
📖 Exit the Wally; Tharg's Future Shocks Car Wars; Zrag Law; Eggravation; The Castaway; Judge Grexnix; Project Salvation; Enter the Beast; Tharg's Future Shocks Speak No Evil **A:** John Higgins; Geoff Senior; Carlos Ezquerra; Eric Bradbury; T. Jozwiak **W:** Oleh Stepaniuk; Pat Milligan; T.M.O.
17 ❑ Cover: 1.50 **NM** value: **Cover or less**
Circ: CapCity orders: **1,000**
📖 Curse Your Lucky Star; Tharg's Future Shocks Daffy Daffid; Tharg's Future Shocks Ten; Conversation Piece; Tharg's Future Shocks You're Never Alone With a Phone; A Change of Scenery; Tharg's Future Shocks The Ship That Liked to Dance; Blood Sport **A:** Barry Kitson; David Pugh; John Hicklenton; Nik Williams **W:** Grant Morrison; John Smith; Jamie Delano; Mark Rogan; Neil Gaiman; Oleh Stepaniuk
18 ❑ Cover: 1.50 **NM** value: **Cover or less**
Circ: CapCity orders: **950**
📖 Wally Saves the Day; Tharg's Future Shocks Disconnected; Tharg's Future Shocks of Glooking Globs and Gloins; Plastic Surgeon; Tharg's Future Shocks Care; I'm a Believer; Tharg's Future Shocks One Man's Meat **A:** Massimo Belardinelli; Glenn Fabry; Richard Elson **W:** Steve Dillon; John Smith; C. Smith; Corderoy; Jon Murphy; McKenzie; Neil Gaiman
19 ❑ Cover: 1.50 **NM** value: **Cover or less**
Circ: CapCity orders: **1,050**
📖 It's the Thought that Counts!; Tharg's Time Twisters; What's Up, Dock?; Tharg's Future Shocks: Uncommon Sense; Working on a Chain Gang; The Ghost Outside the Machine; The Art of Advertising; Tharg's Future Shocks: You Win Some, You Lose Some **A:** Massimo Belardinelli; Mike Collins; Steve Dillon; Ian Gibson; Mark Farmer; José Casanovas **W:** Jack Adrian; Peter Milligan; Alan Hebden; Ben Haldean; Kelvin Gosnell
20 ❑ Cover: 1.50 **NM** value: **Cover or less**
Circ: CapCity orders: **1,000**
📖 Bill Tompkins meets...Bill Tompkins; The Real Right Stuff; Tharg's Future Shocks Bad Timing; Food Fo **A:** Massimo Belardinelli; Geoff Senior; John Stokes; Jeff Anderson; Nevio Zeccara; Tony O'Donnell; José Casanovas **W:** Grant Morrison; Peter Milligan; Alan Hebden; Dean Behnal; Oleh Stepaniuk
21 ❑ Cover: 1.50 **NM** value: **Cover or less**
Circ: CapCity orders: **950**
📖 It's a Mad, Mad, Mad, World; Tharg's Future Shocks Sud's Law; Time, Gentlemen Please; Tharg's Future Shocks Brief Encounter; Beware Planet Earth; Tharg's Future Shocks Some People Never Listen; Say "Aaaagh!"; Tharg's Head final issue. **A:** Alan Davis; Dave Gibbons; Geoff Senior; Barry Kitson; Cam Kennedy; Eric Bradbury; Alan Langford; Dave Wyatt; Kim Raymond; Kevin O'Neill **W:** Mike Collins; Grant Morrison; John Smith; Alan Moore; Oleh Stepaniuk; Steve McManus; T.M.O.

TIMEWALKER — Acclaim / Valiant

Ivar is the third of a group of nearly immortal brothers. The others are Gilad (The Eternal Warrior) and Aram ("Armstrong" of Archer & Armstrong).

Although his brothers have done their share of time travel, it's something of a specialty for Ivar, who jumps in and out of the time stream as casually as most of us board buses. These transitions are eased by a tachyon compass (sometimes nonfunctional) which guides his way, and a translator device which lets him learn local languages in a matter of days.

In his adventures, Ivar might go from being a Roman Legionnaire one instant to masquerading as a Nazi officer the next. Worse yet, he constantly encounters the side-effects of his time tripping. For instance, he's always bumping in to people who reminisce with him about things he hasn't done yet.

0 ❑ Mar 1996 Cover: 2.50 **NM** value: **Cover or less**
Circ: CapCity orders: **7,675**
📖 Child of Time **A:** Don Perlin **W:** Bob Hall ★ Origin of Ivar.
1 ❑ Jan 1995 Cover: 2.50 **NM** value: **Cover or less**
Circ: CapCity orders: **24,575**
cover has Dec 94 coverdate. 📖 Ivar The Traveler **A:** Don Perlin **W:** Bob Hall
2 ❑ Feb 1995 Cover: 2.50 **NM** value: **Cover or less**
Circ: CapCity orders: **14,725**
cover has Jan coverdate. 📖 The Enemy is There **A:** Don Perlin **W:** Bob Hall
3 ❑ Mar 1995 Cover: 2.50 **NM** value: **Cover or less**
Circ: CapCity orders: **12,625**
cover has Feb coverdate.
4 ❑ Apr 1995 Cover: 2.50 **NM** value: **Cover or less**
Circ: CapCity orders: **10,525**

Other grades: Multiply prices above by **1.5 for Mint • 2/3 for Very Fine • 1/3 for Fine • 1/5 for Very Good • 1/8 for Good**

cover has Mar coverdate. 📖 Mac! **A:** Don Perlin **W:** Bob Hall; Susan Wright

5 ❑ Apr 1995 Cover: 2.50 **NM** value: **Cover or less**
Circ: CapCity orders: **9,225**

6 ❑ May 1995 Cover: 2.50 **NM** value: **Cover or less**
Circ: CapCity orders: **8,175**
📖 Harbinger Wars Pt 1

7 ❑ Jun 1995 Cover: 2.50 **NM** value: **Cover or less**
Circ: CapCity orders: **7,200**
📖 Harbinger Wars Pt 2

8 ❑ Jul 1995 Cover: 2.50 **NM** value: **Cover or less**
Circ: CapCity orders: **7,000**
📖 Harbinger Wars Pt 3 • Birthquake

9 ❑ Jul 1995 Cover: 2.50 **NM** value: **Cover or less**
Circ: CapCity orders: **6,950**
• Birthquake **A:** Don Perlin

10 ❑ Aug 1995 Cover: 2.50 **NM** value: **Cover or less**
Circ: CapCity orders: **6,500**
📖 The Last God Of Dura Europus **A:** Howard Simpson **W:** Debra Doyle; James MacDonald

11 ❑ Aug 1995 Cover: 2.50 **NM** value: **Cover or less**
Circ: CapCity orders: **6,500**

12 ❑ Sep 1995 Cover: 2.50 **NM** value: **Cover or less**
Circ: CapCity orders: **6,200**
A: Don Perlin

13 ❑ Sep 1995 Cover: 2.50 **NM** value: **Cover or less**
Circ: CapCity orders: **6,200**

14 ❑ Oct 1995 Cover: 2.50 **NM** value: **Cover or less**
Circ: CapCity orders: **5,950**

15 ❑ Oct 1995 Cover: 2.50 **NM** value: **Cover or less**
Circ: CapCity orders: **5,925**
final issue.

YB 1❑May 1995 Cover: 2.95 **NM** value: **Cover or less**
Circ: CapCity orders: **6,775**
wraparound cover. • Yearbook. ★ Appearance of H.A.R.D. Corps.

TIME WANKERS — Fantagraphics / Eros

All issues are adults only.

1 ❑ Sep 1996, b&w Cover: 2.25 **NM** value: **Cover or less**
A: Stephen Sullivan **W:** Stephen Sullivan

2 ❑ b&w Cover: 2.25 **NM** value: **Cover or less**
A: Stephen Sullivan **W:** Stephen Sullivan

3 ❑ b&w Cover: 2.25 **NM** value: **Cover or less**
A: Stephen Sullivan **W:** Stephen Sullivan

4 ❑ b&w Cover: 2.25 **NM** value: **Cover or less**
A: Stephen Sullivan **W:** Stephen Sullivan

5 ❑ b&w Cover: 2.25 **NM** value: **Cover or less**
A: Stephen Sullivan **W:** Stephen Sullivan

TIME WARP — DC

Most science-fiction comics promise "startling space fiction" while delivering up the same tired cliches. Somehow, Time Warp managed to go beyond this. The ground it covered was familiar to fans of the genre, filled with space aliens and post-apocalypse survival tales. Nevertheless, the writers (including Mike W. Barr, Denny O'Neil, J.M. DeMatteis, and others) made each giant-sized issue of this series a genuine surprise. Undoubtedly, much of the credit belongs to editor Joe Orlando, a longtime veteran of E.C. titles Weird Science and Weird Fantasy.

Unfortunately, Time Warp's $1 price doomed it to low sales when other comics were selling for around 25 cents. The series ran for only five issues, although one is left with the impression that it deserved better.

1 ❑ Nov 1979 Cover: 1.00 **NM** value: **1.25**
• **CGC:** 2 graded, best 9.4
📖 If The World Had To End Twice…; The Mating Game; The Righteous Ones; The Survivors; Forecast; The Monsters; Rescue; The Man Who Could See Yesterday! **A:** Don Newton; Tom Sutton; Rich Buckler; Steve Ditko; Dick Giordano; Jim Aparo; Dan Adkins; Jerry Grandienetti **W:** Paul Levitz; Bob Rozakis; Denny O'Neil; George Kashdan; Jack Harris; Michael Fleisher; Mike W. Barr

2 ❑ Jan 1980 Cover: 1.00 **NM** value: **1.25**
• **CGC:** 1 graded, best 9.4

3 ❑ Mar 1980 Cover: 1.00 **NM** value: **1.25**
• **CGC:** 1 graded, best 9.0

4 ❑ May 1980 Cover: 1.00 **NM** value: **1.25**

5 ❑ Jul 1980 Cover: 1.00 **NM** value: **1.25**
final issue.

TIME WARRIOR — Blazing

1 ❑ Cover: 2.50 **NM** value: **Cover or less**
Circ: CapCity orders: **4,500**

TIME WARRIORS: THE BEGINNING — Fantasy General

1 ❑ Cover: 1.50 **NM** value: **Cover or less**
Circ: CapCity orders: **2,650**

TIM HOLT — Magazine Enterprises

1 ❑ ca. 1948 Cover: 0.10 **NM** value: **500.00**
• **CGC:** 1 graded, best 7.0

2 ❑ ca. 1948 Cover: 0.10 **NM** value: **250.00**
3 ❑ ca. 1948 Cover: 0.10 **NM** value: **200.00**
4 ❑ Jan 1949 Cover: 0.10 **NM** value: **150.00**
5 ❑ Mar 1949 Cover: 0.10 **NM** value: **150.00**
6 ❑ May 1949 Cover: 0.10 **NM** value: **125.00**
7 ❑ Jul 1949 Cover: 0.10 **NM** value: **125.00**
8 ❑ Aug 1949 Cover: 0.10 **NM** value: **125.00**
9 ❑ Sep 1949 Cover: 0.10 **NM** value: **125.00**
10 ❑ Oct 1949 Cover: 0.10 **NM** value: **125.00**
11 ❑ Nov 1949 Cover: 0.10 **NM** value: **100.00**
12 ❑ Dec 1949 Cover: 0.10 **NM** value: **100.00**
13 ❑ Jan 1950 Cover: 0.10 **NM** value: **100.00**
14 ❑ Feb 1950 Cover: 0.10 **NM** value: **100.00**
15 ❑ Mar 1950 Cover: 0.10 **NM** value: **100.00**
16 ❑ Apr 1950 Cover: 0.10 **NM** value: **100.00**
17 ❑ May 1950 Cover: 0.10 **NM** value: **100.00**
• **CGC:** 4 graded, best 8.5
18 ❑ Jul 1950 Cover: 0.10 **NM** value: **100.00**
19 ❑ Sep 1950 Cover: 0.10 **NM** value: **100.00**
20 ❑ Nov 1950 Cover: 0.10 **NM** value: **100.00**
• **CGC:** 1 graded, best 7.0 ★ 1st Appearance of Red Mask
21 ❑ Dec 1950 Cover: 0.10 **NM** value: **75.00**
• **CGC:** 1 graded, best 9.0 • Ghost Rider, Red Mask
22 ❑ Mar 1951 Cover: 0.10 **NM** value: **75.00**
23 ❑ May 1951 Cover: 0.10 **NM** value: **75.00**
24 ❑ Jul 1951 Cover: 0.10 **NM** value: **75.00**
25 ❑ Sep 1951 Cover: 0.10 **NM** value: **75.00**
26 ❑ Nov 1951 Cover: 0.10 **NM** value: **75.00**
27 ❑ Jan 1952 Cover: 0.10 **NM** value: **75.00**
28 ❑ Mar 1952 Cover: 0.10 **NM** value: **75.00**
29 ❑ May 1952 Cover: 0.10 **NM** value: **75.00**
30 ❑ Jul 1952 Cover: 0.10 **NM** value: **75.00**
31 ❑ Sep 1952 Cover: 0.10 **NM** value: **60.00**
32 ❑ Nov 1952 Cover: 0.10 **NM** value: **60.00**
33 ❑ Jan 1953 Cover: 0.10 **NM** value: **60.00**
34 ❑ Mar 1953 Cover: 0.10 **NM** value: **60.00**
35 ❑ May 1953 Cover: 0.10 **NM** value: **60.00**
36 ❑ Jul 1953 Cover: 0.10 **NM** value: **60.00**
37 ❑ Sep 1953 Cover: 0.10 **NM** value: **60.00**
38 ❑ Nov 1953 Cover: 0.10 **NM** value: **60.00**
39 ❑ Dec 1953 Cover: 0.10 **NM** value: **60.00**
40 ❑ Feb 1953 Cover: 0.10 **NM** value: **60.00**
41 ❑ Apr 1953 Cover: 0.10 **NM** value: **60.00**

TIM HOLT WESTERN ANNUAL — AC

1 ❑ b&w Cover: 2.95 **NM** value: **Cover or less**

TIMMY THE TIMID GHOST (1ST SERIES) — Charlton

3 ❑ ca. 1956 Cover: 0.10 **NM** value: **60.00**
4 ❑ ca. 1956 Cover: 0.10 **NM** value: **30.00**
5 ❑ ca. 1956 Cover: 0.10 **NM** value: **30.00**
6 ❑ ca. 1956 Cover: 0.10 **NM** value: **25.00**
7 ❑ ca. 1957 Cover: 0.10 **NM** value: **25.00**
8 ❑ ca. 1957 Cover: 0.10 **NM** value: **25.00**
9 ❑ ca. 1957 Cover: 0.10 **NM** value: **25.00**
10 ❑ ca. 1957 Cover: 0.10 **NM** value: **25.00**
11 ❑ Apr 1958 Cover: 0.25 **NM** value: **20.00**
• **CGC:** 2 graded, best 5.5
12 ❑ Oct 1958 Cover: 0.25 **NM** value: **20.00**
13 ❑ Feb 1959 Cover: 0.10 **NM** value: **20.00**
14 ❑ Apr 1959 Cover: 0.10 **NM** value: **20.00**
15 ❑ Jun 1959 Cover: 0.10 **NM** value: **20.00**
16 ❑ Aug 1959 Cover: 0.10 **NM** value: **20.00**
17 ❑ Oct 1959 Cover: 0.10 **NM** value: **20.00**
18 ❑ Dec 1959 Cover: 0.10 **NM** value: **20.00**
19 ❑ Feb 1960 Cover: 0.10 **NM** value: **20.00**
20 ❑ Apr 1960 Cover: 0.10 **NM** value: **20.00**
21 ❑ Jun 1960 Cover: 0.10 **NM** value: **15.00**
22 ❑ Aug 1960 Cover: 0.10 **NM** value: **15.00**
23 ❑ Oct 1960 Cover: 0.10 **NM** value: **15.00**
24 ❑ Dec 1960 Cover: 0.10 **NM** value: **15.00**
25 ❑ Feb 1961 Cover: 0.10 **NM** value: **15.00**
26 ❑ Apr 1961 Cover: 0.10 **NM** value: **15.00**
27 ❑ ca. 1961 Cover: 0.10 **NM** value: **15.00**
28 ❑ ca. 1961 Cover: 0.10 **NM** value: **15.00**
29 ❑ ca. 1962 Cover: 0.10 **NM** value: **15.00**
30 ❑ ca. 1962 Cover: 0.10 **NM** value: **15.00**
31 ❑ Sep 1962 Cover: 0.10 **NM** value: **12.50**
32 ❑ ca. 1963 Cover: 0.12 **NM** value: **12.50**
33 ❑ Jul 1963 Cover: 0.12 **NM** value: **12.50**
34 ❑ Sep 1963 Cover: 0.12 **NM** value: **12.50**
35 ❑ Nov 1963 Cover: 0.12 **NM** value: **12.50**
36 ❑ Jan 1964 Cover: 0.12 **NM** value: **12.50**
37 ❑ Mar 1964 Cover: 0.12 **NM** value: **12.50**
38 ❑ May 1964 Cover: 0.12 **NM** value: **12.50**
39 ❑ Jun 1964 Cover: 0.12 **NM** value: **12.50**
40 ❑ Jul 1964 Cover: 0.12 **NM** value: **12.50**
41 ❑ Aug 1964 Cover: 0.12 **NM** value: **10.00**
42 ❑ Sep 1964 Cover: 0.12 **NM** value: **10.00**
43 ❑ Oct 1964 Cover: 0.12 **NM** value: **10.00**
44 ❑ Nov 1964 Cover: 0.12 **NM** value: **10.00**
45 ❑ Sep 1966 Cover: 0.12 **NM** value: **10.00**

TIMMY THE TIMID GHOST (2ND SERIES) — Charlton

1 ❑ ca. 1967 Cover: 0.12 **NM** value: **15.00**
2 ❑ Feb 1968 Cover: 0.12 **NM** value: **10.00**
3 ❑ Apr 1968 Cover: 0.12 **NM** value: **10.00**
4 ❑ Jun 1968 Cover: 0.12 **NM** value: **10.00**
5 ❑ Aug 1968 Cover: 0.12 **NM** value: **10.00**
6 ❑ Oct 1968 Cover: 0.12 **NM** value: **10.00**
7 ❑ Dec 1968 Cover: 0.12 **NM** value: **10.00**
8 ❑ Feb 1969 Cover: 0.12 **NM** value: **10.00**
9 ❑ Apr 1969 Cover: 0.12 **NM** value: **10.00**
10 ❑ Jun 1969 Cover: 0.12 **NM** value: **10.00**
11 ❑ Aug 1969 Cover: 0.15 **NM** value: **7.50**
12 ❑ Oct 1969 Cover: 0.15 **NM** value: **7.50**
13 ❑ Dec 1969 Cover: 0.15 **NM** value: **7.50**
14 ❑ Jan 1970 Cover: 0.15 **NM** value: **7.50**
15 ❑ Mar 1970 Cover: 0.15 **NM** value: **7.50**
16 ❑ May 1970 Cover: 0.15 **NM** value: **7.50**
17 ❑ Jul 1970 Cover: 0.15 **NM** value: **7.50**
18 ❑ Sep 1970 Cover: 0.15 **NM** value: **7.50**
19 ❑ Nov 1970 Cover: 0.15 **NM** value: **7.50**
20 ❑ Jan 1971 Cover: 0.15 **NM** value: **7.00**
21 ❑ Mar 1971 Cover: 0.15 **NM** value: **5.00**
22 ❑ May 1971 Cover: 0.15 **NM** value: **5.00**
23 ❑ Jul 1971 Cover: 0.15 **NM** value: **5.00**
24 ❑ Sep 1985 Cover: 0.75 **NM** value: **5.00**
25 ❑ Nov 1986 Cover: 0.75 **NM** value: **5.00**
26 ❑ Jan 1986 Cover: 0.75 **NM** value: **5.00**

TIM TYLER — Standard

11 ❑ **NM** value: **Cover or less**
12 ❑ **NM** value: **Cover or less**
• **CGC:** 1 graded, best 8.5
13 ❑ **NM** value: **Cover or less**
14 ❑ **NM** value: **Cover or less**
15 ❑ **NM** value: **Cover or less**
16 ❑ **NM** value: **Cover or less**
17 ❑ **NM** value: **Cover or less**
18 ❑ **NM** value: **Cover or less**

TINCAN MAN — Image / Valiant

1 ❑ Jan 2000 Cover: 2.95 **NM** value: **Cover or less**
Circ: Diamd. preorders: **10,236**
A: Dietrich Smith **W:** Jim Thornton

2 ❑ Feb 2000 Cover: 2.95 **NM** value: **Cover or less**
Circ: Diamd. preorders: **6,459**
A: Dietrich Smith **W:** Jim Thornton

Ash 1❑Dec 1999 Cover: 2.95 **NM** value: **Cover or less**
Circ: Diamd. preorders: **4,558**
📖 Hitting Bottom • Preview issue **A:** Dietrich Smith **W:** Jim Thornton

TINY DEATHS — YUGP

1 ❑ Cover: 1.75 **NM** value: **Cover or less**
2 ❑ Jan 1997 Cover: 1.75 **NM** value: **Cover or less**
📖 Wrench in my Monkey; My Brain; Kristi; Things She Said to Me; 500 Club; the Sea and Cake; Tales O' the Folds: Questions the Customers Asked Me; Grandma; Carta de Amor **A:** Dan Strachota **W:** Dan Strachota

TINY TESSIE — Marvel

24 ❑ Oct 1949 Cover: 0.10 **NM** value: **50.00**

TINY TOON ADVENTURES — DC

1 ❑ 1994 Cover: 1.95 **NM** value: **2.00**
Circ: CapCity orders: **6,500**
• magazine.

2 ❑ 1994 Cover: 1.95 **NM** value: **2.00**
Circ: CapCity orders: **3,400**
• magazine.

3 ❑ 1994 Cover: 1.95 **NM** value: **2.00**
Circ: CapCity orders: **1,550**
• magazine.

4 ❑ 1994 Cover: 1.95 **NM** value: **2.00**
• magazine.

5 ❑ 1994 Cover: 1.95 **NM** value: **2.00**
• magazine.

6 ❑ 1994 Cover: 1.95 **NM** value: **2.00**
• magazine.

7 ❑ 1994 Cover: 1.95 **NM** value: **2.00**
• magazine.

TINY TOT COMICS — E.C.

This title was one of those early E.C. comics that began the company's diversification beyond educational comics (despite the "Educational Comic" logo on the cover). It aimed at young readers, with the cover declaration "Your FIRST Comic Magazine," and almost all of the contents were written and drawn by Ruth and Burton Geller and edited by Katherine Hutchinson.

Characters included Dunny the Flying Donkey, Peter and Pinky, Smoky the Snake, and Clippety Clop. — Maggie

1❑Mar 1946Cover: 0.10**NM** value: **200.00**
• **CGC:** 2 graded, best 8.5
📖 Dunny the Flying Donkey; Peter and Pinky in Ice Cream Land; Vegetable Village; Smoky the Snake; Lee and His Kite; Sleeping Beauty; Clippety clop

2 ❑ May 1946 Cover: 0.10 **NM** value: **135.00**
• **CGC:** 3 graded, best 7.5
📖 Dunny the Flying Donkey; Peter and Pinky in Chocolate Land; Vegetable Village; Smoky the Snake; Pepe and His Burro; Let's Make a Basket!; The Talking Teddy; Cinderella; Clippety Clop

3 ❑ Jul 1946 Cover: 0.10 **NM** value: **110.00**
📖 Dunny the Flying Donkey; Peter and Pinky in Bakery Land; Vegetable Village; Smoky the Snake; A Sled for Kulee; The Talking Teddy; Jack and the Beanstalk; Clippety Clop

4 ❑ Sep 1946 Cover: 0.10 **NM** value: **110.00**
• **CGC:** 4 graded, best 6.5
📖 Dunny the Flying Donkey; Peter and Pinky Go Fishing; Vegetable Village; Smoky the Snake; Alem and His Camel; Billy and the Magic Raindrop; Tom Thumb; Clippety Clop

5 ❑ Win 1946 Cover: 0.10 **NM** value: **110.00**
• **CGC:** 3 graded, best 5.0
📖 Dunny the Flying Donkey; Peter and Pinky visit Milk Land; Smoky the Snake; Winter Pajamas; The Ugly Duckling; Clippety Clop

6 ❑ Spr 1947 Cover: 0.10 **NM** value: **85.00**
• **CGC:** 1 graded, best 6.0
📖 Peter and Pinky in Dairy Land; Smoky the Snake; The Elves and the Shoemaker; Betty's Doll House; Pierre and Marie; Vegetable Village

CGC-graded: Multiply prices above by **33 for 9.9 M • 16 for 9.8 NM/M • 7 for 9.6 NM+ • 5 for 9.4 NM • 2.5 for 9.2 NM- • 1.5 for 9.0 VF/NM**

7 ❑ Sum 1947 Cover: 0.10 **NM** value: **85.00**
• **CGC:** 3 graded, best 6.5
📖 Dunny the Flying Donkey; Peter and Pinky in Meat Land; Smoky the Snake; The Children's Railroad; Town and Country Stories; Clippety Clop

8 ❑ Jul 1947 Cover: 0.10 **NM** value: **85.00**
• **CGC:** 2 graded, best 5.0
📖 Dunny the Flying Donkey; Smoky the Snake; Carmen and Carlos of Brazil; Jumpy Bean of Vegetable Village; Breakfast at the Farm; The Brave Tin Soldier

9 ❑ Sep 1947 Cover: 0.10 **NM** value: **85.00**
• **CGC:** 5 graded, best 7.5
📖 Dunny the Flying Donkey; Peter and Pinky go Flying; Smoky the Snake; Soli and the Doctor; Watching Breakfast Grow; Jumpy Bean of Vegetable Village

10 ❑ Nov 1947 Cover: 0.10 **NM** value: **85.00**
• **CGC:** 2 graded, best 6.0
📖 Dunny, the Flying Donkey; Puzzle Page (activity); Clifton Catt; Petey Pig; Baby Bruin; The Spirit of Christmas (text); Clippety Clop **W:** Katherine Hutchinson

TIPPER GORE'S COMICS AND STORIES

Revolutionary

1 ❑ Oct 1989, b&w Cover: 1.95 **NM** value: **Cover or less**
2 ❑ Jan 1990, b&w Cover: 1.95 **NM** value: **Cover or less**
📖 Think or Die; Coaster Maniac!; Death by Beaurocracy; There are Things Worse than DeathFor the Love of Money **A:** Landgraf; Lyndal Ferguson; Mike Cliff; PCS **W:** Herb Shapiro; Todd Loren
3 ❑ Mar 1990, b&w Cover: 1.95 **NM** value: **Cover or less**
4 ❑ May 1990, b&w Cover: 1.95 **NM** value: **Cover or less**
5 ❑ Jul 1990, b&w Cover: 1.95 **NM** value: **Cover or less**
📖 Rhoads Beyond; Behind Blue Eyes **A:** Don Roberts; Scott Jackson **C:** Robert Williams **W:** Jason Hecht; Spike Steffenhagen; Todd Loren

TIPPY TEEN

Tower

1 ❑ Nov 1965 Cover: 0.25 **NM** value: **20.00**
2 ❑ Jan 1966 Cover: 0.25 **NM** value: **10.00**
3 ❑ Mar 1966 Cover: 0.25 **NM** value: **6.00**
4 ❑ Apr 1966 Cover: 0.25 **NM** value: **4.00**
5 ❑ May 1966 Cover: 0.25 **NM** value: **4.00**
6 ❑ Jul 1966 Cover: 0.25 **NM** value: **3.00**
7 ❑ Aug 1966 Cover: 0.25 **NM** value: **3.00**
8 ❑ Sep 1966 Cover: 0.25 **NM** value: **3.00**
9 ❑ Oct 1966 Cover: 0.25 **NM** value: **3.00**
10 ❑ Dec 1966 Cover: 0.25 **NM** value: **3.00**
• Anniversary Issue
11 ❑ ca. 1967 Cover: 0.25 **NM** value: **3.00**
12 ❑ ca. 1967 Cover: 0.25 **NM** value: **3.00**
• Valentine's Issue
13 ❑ ca. 1967 Cover: 0.25 **NM** value: **3.00**
• Monkees feature
14 ❑ Jul 1967 Cover: 0.25 **NM** value: **3.00**
15 ❑ Sep 1967 Cover: 0.25 **NM** value: **3.00**
16 ❑ Oct 1967 Cover: 0.25 **NM** value: **3.00**
17 ❑ ca. 1968 Cover: 0.25 **NM** value: **3.00**
18 ❑ ca. 1968 Cover: 0.25 **NM** value: **3.00**
19 ❑ ca. 1968 Cover: 0.25 **NM** value: **3.00**
20 ❑ ca. 1968 Cover: 0.25 **NM** value: **3.00**
21 ❑ Nov 1968 Cover: 0.25 **NM** value: **3.00**
22 ❑ ca. 1969 Cover: 0.25 **NM** value: **3.00**
23 ❑ ca. 1969 Cover: 0.25 **NM** value: **3.00**
24 ❑ Sep 1969 Cover: 0.25 **NM** value: **3.00**
25 ❑ Oct 1969 Cover: 0.25 **NM** value: **3.00**
26 ❑ ca. 1970 Cover: 0.25 **NM** value: **3.00**
27 ❑ ca. 1970 Cover: 0.25 **NM** value: **3.00**

TIP TOP COMICS

St. John

Tip Top Comics packaged reprints of United Features newspaper comic strips. Ernie Bushmiller's "simple to the point of being an archetype" art on his quintessential strip "Nancy," was one of the comic strips that found a second home in comic books.

Nancy was certainly an acquired taste. Her quaint adventures predated the saccharine-laden type of gags perfected by "The Family Circus."

Also featured were reprints of "The Captain and The Kids," an iteration of "The Katzenjammer Kids" by Rudolf Dirks who relinquished his original creation when he went to another syndicate.

One of the most pertinent strips to be found in this title however, is a very early version of "Peanuts." Charles Schultz had not yet refined these characters as the familiar images that enjoy international recognition today, and it is a treat to view the genesis of an icon.

1 ❑ Apr 1936 Cover: 0.10 **NM** value: **5800.00**
• **CGC:** 1 graded, best 5.5
★ 1st Appearance of Tarzan (in comics).
2 ❑ Jun 1936 Cover: 0.10 **NM** value: **1800.00**
3 ❑ Jul 1936 Cover: 0.10 **NM** value: **1250.00**
4 ❑ Aug 1936 Cover: 0.10 **NM** value: **850.00**
5 ❑ Sep 1936 Cover: 0.10 **NM** value: **850.00**
6 ❑ Oct 1936 Cover: 0.10 **NM** value: **600.00**
7 ❑ Nov 1936 Cover: 0.10 **NM** value: **600.00**
• **CGC:** 1 graded, best 9.0
8 ❑ Dec 1936 Cover: 0.10 **NM** value: **600.00**
9 ❑ Jan 1937 Cover: 0.10 **NM** value: **600.00**
Circ: ABC: **308,083**
10 ❑ Feb 1937 Cover: 0.10 **NM** value: **600.00**
Circ: ABC: **320,366**
11 ❑ Mar 1937 Cover: 0.10 **NM** value: **435.00**
Circ: ABC: **297,684**
12 ❑ Apr 1937 Cover: 0.10 **NM** value: **435.00**
Circ: ABC: **286,310**
13 ❑ May 1937 Cover: 0.10 **NM** value: **435.00**
Circ: ABC: **287,258**
14 ❑ Jun 1937 Cover: 0.10 **NM** value: **435.00**
Circ: ABC: **269,938**
15 ❑ Jul 1937 Cover: 0.10 **NM** value: **435.00**
Circ: ABC: **351,196**
16 ❑ Aug 1937 Cover: 0.10 **NM** value: **435.00**
Circ: ABC: **381,762**
17 ❑ Sep 1937 Cover: 0.10 **NM** value: **435.00**
Circ: ABC: **404,793**
18 ❑ Oct 1937 Cover: 0.10 **NM** value: **435.00**
Circ: ABC: **358,464**
19 ❑ Nov 1937 Cover: 0.10 **NM** value: **435.00**
Circ: ABC: **379,834**
20 ❑ Dec 1937 Cover: 0.10 **NM** value: **435.00**
Circ: ABC: **364,756**
21 ❑ Jan 1938 Cover: 0.10 **NM** value: **290.00**
Circ: ABC: **354,822**
22 ❑ Feb 1938 Cover: 0.10 **NM** value: **290.00**
Circ: ABC: **354,432**
23 ❑ Mar 1938 Cover: 0.10 **NM** value: **290.00**
Circ: ABC: **347,751**
24 ❑ Apr 1938 Cover: 0.10 **NM** value: **290.00**
Circ: ABC: **324,717**
25 ❑ May 1938 Cover: 0.10 **NM** value: **290.00**
Circ: ABC: **322,364**
26 ❑ Jun 1938 Cover: 0.10 **NM** value: **290.00**
Circ: ABC: **265,336**
27 ❑ Jul 1938 Cover: 0.10 **NM** value: **290.00**
Circ: ABC: **316,315**
28 ❑ Aug 1938 Cover: 0.10 **NM** value: **290.00**
Circ: ABC: **366,104**
29 ❑ Sep 1938 Cover: 0.10 **NM** value: **290.00**
Circ: ABC: **424,781**
30 ❑ Oct 1938 Cover: 0.10 **NM** value: **290.00**
Circ: ABC: **333,340**
31 ❑ Nov 1938 Cover: 0.10 **NM** value: **210.00**
Circ: ABC: **318,812**
32 ❑ Dec 1938 Cover: 0.10 **NM** value: **210.00**
Circ: ABC: **320,556**
33 ❑ Jan 1939 Cover: 0.10 **NM** value: **210.00**
Circ: ABC: **354,845** • **CGC:** 2 graded, best 5.0
34 ❑ Feb 1939 Cover: 0.10 **NM** value: **210.00**
Circ: ABC: **341,378**
35 ❑ Mar 1939 Cover: 0.10 **NM** value: **210.00**
Circ: ABC: **386,103**
36 ❑ Apr 1939 Cover: 0.10 **NM** value: **210.00**
Circ: ABC: **347,569** • **CGC:** 1 graded, best 4.5
37 ❑ May 1939 Cover: 0.10 **NM** value: **210.00**
Circ: ABC: **342,227** • **CGC:** 1 graded, best 4.0
38 ❑ Jun 1939 Cover: 0.10 **NM** value: **210.00**
Circ: ABC: **326,893**
39 ❑ Jul 1939 Cover: 0.10 **NM** value: **210.00**
Circ: ABC: **420,351**
• Tarzan cover
40 ❑ Aug 1939 Cover: 0.10 **NM** value: **210.00**
Circ: ABC: **441,351**
41 ❑ Sep 1939 Cover: 0.10 **NM** value: **165.00**
Circ: ABC: **441,618**
42 ❑ Oct 1939 Cover: 0.10 **NM** value: **165.00**
Circ: ABC: **409,269**
43 ❑ Nov 1939 Cover: 0.10 **NM** value: **165.00**
Circ: ABC: **333,833**
44 ❑ Dec 1939 Cover: 0.10 **NM** value: **165.00**
Circ: ABC: **348,630**
45 ❑ Jan 1940 Cover: 0.10 **NM** value: **165.00**
46 ❑ Feb 1940 Cover: 0.10 **NM** value: **165.00**
47 ❑ Mar 1940 Cover: 0.10 **NM** value: **165.00**
48 ❑ Apr 1940 Cover: 0.10 **NM** value: **165.00**
49 ❑ May 1940 Cover: 0.10 **NM** value: **165.00**
50 ❑ Jun 1940 Cover: 0.10 **NM** value: **165.00**
51 ❑ Jul 1940 Cover: 0.10 **NM** value: **110.00**
52 ❑ Aug 1940 Cover: 0.10 **NM** value: **110.00**
53 ❑ Sep 1940 Cover: 0.10 **NM** value: **110.00**
54 ❑ Oct 1940 Cover: 0.10 **NM** value: **110.00**
55 ❑ Nov 1940 Cover: 0.10 **NM** value: **110.00**
56 ❑ Dec 1940 Cover: 0.10 **NM** value: **110.00**
57 ❑ Jan 1941 Cover: 0.10 **NM** value: **110.00**
58 ❑ Feb 1941 Cover: 0.10 **NM** value: **110.00**
59 ❑ Mar 1941 Cover: 0.10 **NM** value: **110.00**
60 ❑ Apr 1941 Cover: 0.10 **NM** value: **110.00**
61 ❑ May 1941 Cover: 0.10 **NM** value: **110.00**
62 ❑ Jun 1941 Cover: 0.10 **NM** value: **85.00**
63 ❑ Jul 1941 Cover: 0.10 **NM** value: **85.00**
64 ❑ Aug 1941 Cover: 0.10 **NM** value: **85.00**
65 ❑ Sep 1941 Cover: 0.10 **NM** value: **85.00**
66 ❑ Oct 1941 Cover: 0.10 **NM** value: **85.00**
67 ❑ Nov 1941 Cover: 0.10 **NM** value: **85.00**
68 ❑ Dec 1941 Cover: 0.10 **NM** value: **85.00**
69 ❑ Jan 1942 Cover: 0.10 **NM** value: **85.00**
70 ❑ Feb 1942 Cover: 0.10 **NM** value: **85.00**
71 ❑ Mar 1942 Cover: 0.10 **NM** value: **85.00**
72 ❑ Apr 1942 Cover: 0.10 **NM** value: **85.00**
73 ❑ May 1942 Cover: 0.10 **NM** value: **85.00**
74 ❑ Jun 1942 Cover: 0.10 **NM** value: **85.00**
75 ❑ Jul 1942 Cover: 0.10 **NM** value: **85.00**
• Fritz: Ritz swimsuit cover
76 ❑ Aug 1942 Cover: 0.10 **NM** value: **85.00**
77 ❑ Sep 1942 Cover: 0.10 **NM** value: **85.00**
78 ❑ Oct 1942 Cover: 0.10 **NM** value: **85.00**
79 ❑ Nov 1942 Cover: 0.10 **NM** value: **85.00**
80 ❑ Dec 1942 Cover: 0.10 **NM** value: **85.00**
81 ❑ ca. 1943 Cover: 0.10 **NM** value: **65.00**
82 ❑ ca. 1943 Cover: 0.10 **NM** value: **65.00**
83 ❑ ca. 1943 Cover: 0.10 **NM** value: **65.00**
84 ❑ ca. 1943 Cover: 0.10 **NM** value: **65.00**
85 ❑ ca. 1943 Cover: 0.10 **NM** value: **65.00**
86 ❑ ca. 1943 Cover: 0.10 **NM** value: **65.00**
87 ❑ ca. 1943 Cover: 0.10 **NM** value: **65.00**
88 ❑ ca. 1943 Cover: 0.10 **NM** value: **65.00**
89 ❑ ca. 1943 Cover: 0.10 **NM** value: **65.00**
90 ❑ ca. 1943 Cover: 0.10 **NM** value: **65.00**
91 ❑ ca. 1943 Cover: 0.10 **NM** value: **65.00**
92 ❑ ca. 1944 Cover: 0.10 **NM** value: **65.00**
93 ❑ ca. 1944 Cover: 0.10 **NM** value: **65.00**
94 ❑ ca. 1944 Cover: 0.10 **NM** value: **65.00**
95 ❑ ca. 1944 Cover: 0.10 **NM** value: **65.00**
96 ❑ Jun 1944 Cover: 0.10 **NM** value: **65.00**
• **CGC:** 1 graded, best 5.5
97 ❑ Jul 1944 Cover: 0.10 **NM** value: **65.00**
98 ❑ Aug 1944 Cover: 0.10 **NM** value: **65.00**
99 ❑ Sep 1944 Cover: 0.10 **NM** value: **65.00**
100 ❑ Oct 1944 Cover: 0.10 **NM** value: **65.00**
101 ❑ Nov 1944 Cover: 0.10 **NM** value: **50.00**
102 ❑ Dec 1944 Cover: 0.10 **NM** value: **50.00**
103 ❑ ca. 1945 Cover: 0.10 **NM** value: **50.00**
104 ❑ ca. 1945 Cover: 0.10 **NM** value: **50.00**
105 ❑ ca. 1945 Cover: 0.10 **NM** value: **50.00**
106 ❑ ca. 1945 Cover: 0.10 **NM** value: **50.00**
107 ❑ ca. 1945 Cover: 0.10 **NM** value: **50.00**
108 ❑ ca. 1945 Cover: 0.10 **NM** value: **50.00**
109 ❑ Aug 1945 Cover: 0.10 **NM** value: **50.00**
110 ❑ Sep 1945 Cover: 0.10 **NM** value: **50.00**
111 ❑ Oct 1945 Cover: 0.10 **NM** value: **40.00**
112 ❑ Nov 1945 Cover: 0.10 **NM** value: **40.00**
113 ❑ Dec 1945 Cover: 0.10 **NM** value: **40.00**
114 ❑ Jan 1946 Cover: 0.10 **NM** value: **40.00**
115 ❑ Feb 1946 Cover: 0.10 **NM** value: **40.00**
116 ❑ Mar 1946 Cover: 0.10 **NM** value: **40.00**
117 ❑ Apr 1946 Cover: 0.10 **NM** value: **40.00**
118 ❑ May 1946 Cover: 0.10 **NM** value: **40.00**
119 ❑ Jun 1946 Cover: 0.10 **NM** value: **40.00**
120 ❑ Jul 1946 Cover: 0.10 **NM** value: **40.00**
121 ❑ Aug 1946 Cover: 0.10 **NM** value: **35.00**
122 ❑ Sep 1946 Cover: 0.10 **NM** value: **35.00**
123 ❑ Oct 1946 Cover: 0.10 **NM** value: **35.00**
124 ❑ Nov 1946 Cover: 0.10 **NM** value: **35.00**
125 ❑ Dec 1946 Cover: 0.10 **NM** value: **35.00**
126 ❑ Jan 1947 Cover: 0.10 **NM** value: **35.00**
127 ❑ Feb 1947 Cover: 0.10 **NM** value: **35.00**
128 ❑ Mar 1947 Cover: 0.10 **NM** value: **35.00**
129 ❑ Apr 1947 Cover: 0.10 **NM** value: **35.00**
130 ❑ May 1947 Cover: 0.10 **NM** value: **35.00**
131 ❑ Jun 1947 Cover: 0.10 **NM** value: **32.00**
132 ❑ Jul 1947 Cover: 0.10 **NM** value: **32.00**
133 ❑ Aug 1947 Cover: 0.10 **NM** value: **32.00**
134 ❑ Sep 1947 Cover: 0.10 **NM** value: **32.00**
135 ❑ Oct 1947 Cover: 0.10 **NM** value: **32.00**
136 ❑ Nov 1947 Cover: 0.10 **NM** value: **32.00**
137 ❑ Dec 1947 Cover: 0.10 **NM** value: **32.00**
138 ❑ Jan 1948 Cover: 0.10 **NM** value: **32.00**
139 ❑ Feb 1948 Cover: 0.10 **NM** value: **32.00**
140 ❑ Mar 1948 Cover: 0.10 **NM** value: **32.00**
141 ❑ Apr 1948 Cover: 0.10 **NM** value: **32.00**
• Katzenjammer kids cover
142 ❑ May 1948 Cover: 0.10 **NM** value: **32.00**
143 ❑ Jun 1948 Cover: 0.10 **NM** value: **32.00**
144 ❑ Jul 1948 Cover: 0.10 **NM** value: **32.00**
145 ❑ Aug 1948 Cover: 0.10 **NM** value: **32.00**
146 ❑ Sep 1948 Cover: 0.10 **NM** value: **32.00**
147 ❑ Oct 1948 Cover: 0.10 **NM** value: **32.00**
148 ❑ Nov 1948 Cover: 0.10 **NM** value: **32.00**
149 ❑ Dec 1948 Cover: 0.10 **NM** value: **32.00**
150 ❑ Jan 1949 Cover: 0.10 **NM** value: **32.00**
151 ❑ ca. 1949 Cover: 0.10 **NM** value: **28.00**
152 ❑ ca. 1949 Cover: 0.10 **NM** value: **28.00**
153 ❑ ca. 1949 Cover: 0.10 **NM** value: **28.00**
154 ❑ ca. 1949 Cover: 0.10 **NM** value: **28.00**
155 ❑ ca. 1949 Cover: 0.10 **NM** value: **28.00**
156 ❑ ca. 1949 Cover: 0.10 **NM** value: **28.00**
157 ❑ ca. 1949 Cover: 0.10 **NM** value: **28.00**
158 ❑ ca. 1949 Cover: 0.10 **NM** value: **28.00**
159 ❑ ca. 1949 Cover: 0.10 **NM** value: **28.00**
160 ❑ ca. 1950 Cover: 0.10 **NM** value: **28.00**
161 ❑ ca. 1950 Cover: 0.10 **NM** value: **28.00**
162 ❑ ca. 1950 Cover: 0.10 **NM** value: **28.00**
163 ❑ ca. 1950 Cover: 0.10 **NM** value: **28.00**
164 ❑ ca. 1950 Cover: 0.10 **NM** value: **28.00**
165 ❑ ca. 1950 Cover: 0.10 **NM** value: **28.00**
166 ❑ ca. 1950 Cover: 0.10 **NM** value: **28.00**
167 ❑ ca. 1950 Cover: 0.10 **NM** value: **28.00**
168 ❑ ca. 1950 Cover: 0.10 **NM** value: **28.00**
169 ❑ ca. 1950 Cover: 0.10 **NM** value: **28.00**
170 ❑ ca. 1951 Cover: 0.10 **NM** value: **28.00**
171 ❑ ca. 1951 Cover: 0.10 **NM** value: **28.00**
172 ❑ ca. 1951 Cover: 0.10 **NM** value: **28.00**
173 ❑ ca. 1951 Cover: 0.10 **NM** value: **28.00**
174 ❑ ca. 1952 Cover: 0.10 **NM** value: **28.00**
175 ❑ ca. 1952 Cover: 0.10 **NM** value: **28.00**
176 ❑ ca. 1952 Cover: 0.10 **NM** value: **28.00**
177 ❑ ca. 1952 Cover: 0.10 **NM** value: **28.00**
178 ❑ ca. 1952 Cover: 0.10 **NM** value: **28.00**
179 ❑ ca. 1953 Cover: 0.10 **NM** value: **28.00**
180 ❑ ca. 1953 Cover: 0.10 **NM** value: **28.00**
181 ❑ ca. 1953 Cover: 0.10 **NM** value: **25.00**
182 ❑ ca. 1953 Cover: 0.10 **NM** value: **25.00**
183 ❑ ca. 1953 Cover: 0.10 **NM** value: **25.00**
184 ❑ ca. 1954 Cover: 0.10 **NM** value: **25.00**
185 ❑ ca. 1954 Cover: 0.10 **NM** value: **25.00**
186 ❑ ca. 1954 Cover: 0.10 **NM** value: **25.00**
187 ❑ ca. 1954 Cover: 0.10 **NM** value: **25.00**
188 ❑ ca. 1954 Cover: 0.10 **NM** value: **25.00**
• First St. John issue
189 ❑ ca. 1955 Cover: 0.10 **NM** value: **25.00**

Other grades: Multiply prices above by **1.5 for Mint • 2/3 for Very Fine • 1/3 for Fine • 1/5 for Very Good • 1/8 for Good**

190 ❑ ca. 1955 Cover: 0.10 **NM** value: **25.00**
191 ❑ ca. 1955 Cover: 0.10 **NM** value: **25.00**
192 ❑ ca. 1955 Cover: 0.10 **NM** value: **25.00**
📖 Nancy; The Captain and the Kids; Peanuts; Bingo **A:** Charles Schulz; Ernie Bushmiller **W:** Charles Schulz; Ernie Bushmiller
193 ❑ Dec 1955 Cover: 0.10 **NM** value: **25.00**
194 ❑ ca. 1956 Cover: 0.10 **NM** value: **25.00**
195 ❑ ca. 1956 Cover: 0.10 **NM** value: **25.00**
196 ❑ ca. 1956 Cover: 0.10 **NM** value: **25.00**
197 ❑ ca. 1956 Cover: 0.10 **NM** value: **25.00**
198 ❑ ca. 1956 Cover: 0.10 **NM** value: **25.00**
199 ❑ ca. 1956 Cover: 0.10 **NM** value: **25.00**
200 ❑ ca. 1956 Cover: 0.10 **NM** value: **25.00**
201 ❑ ca. 1956 Cover: 0.10 **NM** value: **20.00**
202 ❑ ca. 1956 Cover: 0.10 **NM** value: **20.00**
203 ❑ ca. 1956 Cover: 0.10 **NM** value: **20.00**
204 ❑ ca. 1956 Cover: 0.10 **NM** value: **20.00**
205 ❑ ca. 1957 Cover: 0.10 **NM** value: **20.00**
206 ❑ ca. 1957 Cover: 0.10 **NM** value: **20.00**
207 ❑ ca. 1957 Cover: 0.10 **NM** value: **20.00**
208 ❑ ca. 1957 Cover: 0.10 **NM** value: **20.00**
209 ❑ ca. 1957 Cover: 0.10 **NM** value: **20.00**
210 ❑ ca. 1957 Cover: 0.10 **NM** value: **20.00**
211 ❑ Jan 1958 Cover: 0.10 **NM** value: **20.00**
212 ❑ Apr 1958 Cover: 0.10 **NM** value: **20.00**
• Peanuts
213 ❑ Jul 1958 Cover: 0.10 **NM** value: **20.00**
214 ❑ Oct 1958 Cover: 0.10 **NM** value: **20.00**
215 ❑ Jan 1959 Cover: 0.10 **NM** value: **20.00**
216 ❑ Apr 1959 Cover: 0.10 **NM** value: **20.00**
217 ❑ Jul 1959 Cover: 0.10 **NM** value: **20.00**
218 ❑ Oct 1959 Cover: 0.10 **NM** value: **20.00**
219 ❑ Jan 1960 Cover: 0.10 **NM** value: **20.00**
220 ❑ Apr 1960 Cover: 0.10 **NM** value: **20.00**
221 ❑ Jul 1960 Cover: 0.10 **NM** value: **20.00**
• Peanuts, Nancy, Katzenjammer kid's cover
222 ❑ Oct 1960 Cover: 0.10 **NM** value: **20.00**
223 ❑ Jan 1961 Cover: 0.10 **NM** value: **20.00**
224 ❑ Apr 1961 Cover: 0.15 **NM** value: **20.00**
225 ❑ Jul 1961 Cover: 0.15 **NM** value: **20.00**

TIP-TOPPER COMICS — United Features

1 ❑ ca. 1949 Cover: 0.10 **NM** value: **38.00**
A: Ernie Bushmiller **W:** Ernie Bushmiller
2 ❑ ca. 1949 Cover: 0.10 **NM** value: **25.00**
A: Ernie Bushmiller **W:** Ernie Bushmiller
3 ❑ ca. 1950 Cover: 0.10 **NM** value: **20.00**
A: Ernie Bushmiller **W:** Ernie Bushmiller
4 ❑ ca. 1950 Cover: 0.10 **NM** value: **20.00**
A: Ernie Bushmiller **W:** Ernie Bushmiller
5 ❑ ca. 1950 Cover: 0.10 **NM** value: **20.00**
A: Ernie Bushmiller **W:** Ernie Bushmiller
6 ❑ ca. 1950 Cover: 0.10 **NM** value: **14.00**
A: Ernie Bushmiller **W:** Ernie Bushmiller
7 ❑ ca. 1950 Cover: 0.10 **NM** value: **14.00**
A: Ernie Bushmiller **W:** Ernie Bushmiller
8 ❑ ca. 1950 Cover: 0.10 **NM** value: **14.00**
A: Ernie Bushmiller **W:** Ernie Bushmiller
9 ❑ ca. 1950 Cover: 0.10 **NM** value: **14.00**
A: Ernie Bushmiller **W:** Ernie Bushmiller
10 ❑ ca. 1951 Cover: 0.10 **NM** value: **14.00**
A: Ernie Bushmiller **W:** Ernie Bushmiller
11 ❑ ca. 1951 Cover: 0.10 **NM** value: **12.00**
A: Ernie Bushmiller **W:** Ernie Bushmiller
12 ❑ ca. 1951 Cover: 0.10 **NM** value: **12.00**
A: Ernie Bushmiller **W:** Ernie Bushmiller
13 ❑ ca. 1951 Cover: 0.10 **NM** value: **12.00**
A: Ernie Bushmiller **W:** Ernie Bushmiller
14 ❑ ca. 1951 Cover: 0.10 **NM** value: **12.00**
A: Ernie Bushmiller; Mik; Sam Leff **W:** Ernie Bushmiller; Mik; Sam Leff
15 ❑ ca. 1951 Cover: 0.10 **NM** value: **12.00**
A: Ernie Bushmiller **W:** Ernie Bushmiller
16 ❑ ca. 1951 Cover: 0.10 **NM** value: **12.00**
A: Ernie Bushmiller **W:** Ernie Bushmiller
17 ❑ ca. 1952 Cover: 0.10 **NM** value: **12.00**
A: Ernie Bushmiller **W:** Ernie Bushmiller
18 ❑ ca. 1952 Cover: 0.10 **NM** value: **12.00**
A: Ernie Bushmiller **W:** Ernie Bushmiller
19 ❑ ca. 1952 Cover: 0.10 **NM** value: **12.00**
A: Ernie Bushmiller **W:** Ernie Bushmiller
20 ❑ ca. 1952 Cover: 0.10 **NM** value: **12.00**
A: Ernie Bushmiller **W:** Ernie Bushmiller
21 ❑ ca. 1952 Cover: 0.10 **NM** value: **12.00**
A: Ernie Bushmiller **W:** Ernie Bushmiller
22 ❑ ca. 1952 Cover: 0.10 **NM** value: **12.00**
A: Ernie Bushmiller **W:** Ernie Bushmiller
23 ❑ ca. 1953 Cover: 0.10 **NM** value: **12.00**
A: Ernie Bushmiller **W:** Ernie Bushmiller
24 ❑ ca. 1953 Cover: 0.10 **NM** value: **12.00**
A: Ernie Bushmiller **W:** Ernie Bushmiller
25 ❑ ca. 1953 Cover: 0.10 **NM** value: **12.00**
A: Ernie Bushmiller **W:** Ernie Bushmiller
26 ❑ ca. 1953 Cover: 0.10 **NM** value: **12.00**
A: Ernie Bushmiller **W:** Ernie Bushmiller
27 ❑ ca. 1953 Cover: 0.10 **NM** value: **12.00**
A: Ernie Bushmiller **W:** Ernie Bushmiller
28 ❑ ca. 1953 Cover: 0.10 **NM** value: **12.00**
A: Ernie Bushmiller **W:** Ernie Bushmiller

TITAN A.E. — Dark Horse

1 ❑ May 2000 Cover: 2.95 **NM** value: **Cover or less**
Circ: Diamd. preorders: **12,815**
A: Al Rio **W:** Scott Allie
2 ❑ Jun 2000 Cover: 2.95 **NM** value: **Cover or less**
Circ: Diamd. preorders: **10,836**
A: Al Rio **W:** Scott Allie
3 ❑ Jul 2000 Cover: 2.95 **NM** value: **Cover or less**
Circ: Diamd. preorders: **10,158**
A: Al Rio **W:** Scott Allie

TITANS, THE — DC

It's back to the basics with this version of DC's team of former sidekicks. The Teen Titans first appeared in the 1960s, but really achieved fan-favorite status rivaling that of the X-Men as The New Teen Titans in the 1980s, under the helm of writer Marv Wolfman and artist George Perez. After four years the title became The New Titans, dropping the teen designation.

In 1996, a year after The New Titans ended, Teen Titans (2nd Series) returned with all-new, younger members. These characters were largely unknowns except for The Atom, who due to the events of Zero Hour, had been "de-aged" to a teenager.

After that series was cancelled, DC decided that the old team still had some life in it. Most of the original members of The New Teen Titans were brought back in this series, hoping to re-capture that elusive chemistry that makes fans care about the characters.

1 ❑ Mar 1999 Cover: 2.50 **NM** value: **3.00**
Circ: Diamd. preorders: **60,707** • **CGC:** 1 graded, best 9.8
📖 That Strange Buzzing Sound • new team **A:** Mark Buckingham **W:** Devin Grayson ★ Appearance of H.I.V.E..
1/Aut ❑ Mar 1999 Cover: 2.50 **NM** value: **15.95**
📖 That Strange Buzzing Sound **A:** Mark Buckingham **W:** Devin Grayson ★ Appearance of H.I.V.E..
2 ❑ Apr 1999 Cover: 2.50 **NM** value: **Cover or less**
Circ: Diamd. preorders: **46,986**
A: Mark Buckingham **W:** Devin Grayson ★ Appearance of Superman, H.I.V.E..
3 ❑ May 1999 Cover: 2.50 **NM** value: **Cover or less**
Circ: Diamd. preorders: **47,444**
A: Mark Buckingham **W:** Devin Grayson ★ Versus Goth.
4 ❑ Jun 1999 Cover: 2.50 **NM** value: **Cover or less**
Circ: Diamd. preorders: **49,032**
📖 The Dissing **A:** Justiniano **W:** Devin Grayson ★ Versus Goth.
5 ❑ Jul 1999 Cover: 2.50 **NM** value: **Cover or less**
Circ: Diamd. preorders: **46,643**
📖 Hydrophobia **A:** Mark Buckingham **W:** Devin Grayson
6 ❑ Aug 1999 Cover: 2.50 **NM** value: **Cover or less**
Circ: Diamd. preorders: **45,483**
📖 Heritage **A:** Mark Buckingham **W:** Devin Grayson ★ Appearance of Green Lantern. ★ Versus Red Panzer.
7 ❑ Sep 1999 Cover: 2.50 **NM** value: **Cover or less**
Circ: Diamd. preorders: **43,321**
📖 Need for Speed Part 1 **A:** Mark Buckingham **W:** Devin Grayson
8 ❑ Oct 1999 Cover: 2.50 **NM** value: **Cover or less**
Circ: Diamd. preorders: **41,186**
📖 Need for Speed Part 2 **A:** Mark Buckingham **W:** Devin Grayson
9 ❑ Nov 1999 Cover: 2.50 **NM** value: **Cover or less**
Circ: Diamd. preorders: **41,740**
A: Mark Buckingham **W:** Devin Grayson
10 ❑ Dec 1999 Cover: 2.50 **NM** value: **Cover or less**
Circ: Diamd. preorders: **39,157**
📖 The Immortal Coil, Part 1 **A:** Mark Buckingham **W:** Devin Grayson
11 ❑ Jan 2000 Cover: 2.50 **NM** value: **Cover or less**
Circ: Diamd. preorders: **37,073**
📖 The Immortal Coil, Part 2 **A:** Mark Buckingham **W:** Devin Grayson
12 ❑ Feb 2000 Cover: 2.50 **NM** value: **Cover or less**
Circ: Diamd. preorders: **38,395**
13 ❑ Mar 2000 Cover: 2.50 **NM** value: **Cover or less**
Circ: Diamd. preorders: **35,466**
14 ❑ Apr 2000 Cover: 2.50 **NM** value: **Cover or less**
Circ: Diamd. preorders: **33,312**
📖 Chain of Command **A:** Cully Hamner **W:** Brian K. Vaughan
15 ❑ May 2000 Cover: 2.50 **NM** value: **Cover or less**
Circ: Diamd. preorders: **34,157**
📖 Survival **A:** Mark Buckingham **W:** Devin Grayson
16 ❑ Jun 2000 Cover: 2.50 **NM** value: **Cover or less**
Circ: Diamd. preorders: **34,016**
17 ❑ Jul 2000 Cover: 2.50 **NM** value: **Cover or less**
Circ: Diamd. preorders: **33,413**
18 ❑ Aug 2000 Cover: 2.50 **NM** value: **Cover or less**
Circ: Diamd. preorders: **34,272**
19 ❑ Sep 2000 Cover: 2.50 **NM** value: **Cover or less**
Circ: Diamd. preorders: **34,259**
📖 The Price of Victory **A:** Adam DeKraker **W:** Devin Grayson; Jay Faerber
20 ❑ Oct 2000 Cover: 2.50 **NM** value: **Cover or less**
Circ: Diamd. preorders: **31,908**
📖 Transitions **A:** Adam DeKraker **W:** Devin Grayson; Jay Faerber
21 ❑ Nov 2000 Cover: 2.50 **NM** value: **Cover or less**
Circ: Diamd. preorders: **31,755**
📖 The Trial of Cheshire, Part 1 **A:** Paul Pelletier **W:** Jay Faerber
22 ❑ Dec 2000 Cover: 2.50 **NM** value: **Cover or less**
Circ: Diamd. preorders: **31,011**
📖 The Trial of Cheshire, Part 2 **A:** Paul Pelletier **W:** Jay Faerber
23 ❑ Jan 2001 Cover: 2.50 **NM** value: **Cover or less**
Circ: Diamd. preorders: **31,255**
📖 Who is Troia?, Part 1 **A:** Paul Pelletier **W:** Jay Faerber
24 ❑ Feb 2001 Cover: 2.50 **NM** value: **Cover or less**
Circ: Diamd. preorders: **30,806**
📖 Who is Troia?, Part 2 **A:** Paul Pelletier **W:** Jay Faerber
25 ❑ Mar 2001 Cover: 3.95 **NM** value: **Cover or less**
Circ: Diamd. preorders: **32,870**
• Giant-size. 📖 Who is Troia?, Part 3 **A:** Terry Dodson; Paul Pelletier; Phil Jimenez; George Pérez; Tom Grummett; Nick Cardy **W:** Jay Faerber; Marv Wolfman
26 ❑ Apr 2001 Cover: 2.50 **NM** value: **Cover or less**
Circ: Diamd. preorders: **30,859**
📖 Nothing Personal,Just Business **A:** Paul Pelletier **W:** Jay Faerber
27 ❑ May 2001 Cover: 2.50 **NM** value: **Cover or less**
Circ: Diamd. preorders: **30,785**
📖 Desperate Measures **A:** Paul Pelletier **W:** Jay Faerber
28 ❑ Jun 2001 Cover: 2.50 **NM** value: **Cover or less**
Circ: Diamd. preorders: **31,327**
29 ❑ Jul 2001 Cover: 2.50 **NM** value: **Cover or less**
Circ: Diamd. preorders: **30,488**
30 ❑ Aug 2001 Cover: 2.50 **NM** value: **Cover or less**
Circ: Diamd. preorders: **30,417**
31 ❑ Sep 2001 Cover: 2.50 **NM** value: **Cover or less**
Circ: Diamd. preorders: **30,959**

TITANS/LEGION OF SUPER-HEROES: UNIVERSE ABLAZE — DC

1 ❑ Mar 2000 Cover: 4.95 **NM** value: **Cover or less**
Circ: Diamd. preorders: **26,784**
A: Phil Jimenez; Dan Jurgens **W:** Dan Jurgens
2 ❑ Apr 2000 Cover: 4.95 **NM** value: **Cover or less**
Circ: Diamd. preorders: **23,623**
A: Phil Jimenez; Dan Jurgens **W:** Dan Jurgens
3 ❑ May 2000 Cover: 4.95 **NM** value: **Cover or less**
Circ: Diamd. preorders: **25,292**
A: Phil Jimenez; Dan Jurgens **W:** Dan Jurgens
4 ❑ Jun 2000 Cover: 4.95 **NM** value: **Cover or less**
Circ: Diamd. preorders: **25,060**
A: Phil Jimenez; Dan Jurgens **W:** Dan Jurgens

TITAN SPECIAL — Dark Horse

1 ❑ Jun 1994 Cover: 3.95 **NM** value: **Cover or less**
Circ: CapCity orders: **7,950**
One-shot. 📖 Chosen People **A:** Chris Sprouse; Tim Hamilton **W:** Michael Eury; Pete Ford ★ Death of Golden Boy.

TITANS: SCISSORS, PAPER, STONE — DC

1 ❑ May 1997 Cover: 4.95 **NM** value: **Cover or less**
Circ: Diamd. preorders: **21,065**
No issue number. • prestige format. • manga-style; Elseworlds **A:** Adam Warren **W:** Adam Warren

TITANS SECRET FILES, THE — DC

1 ❑ Mar 1999 Cover: 4.95 **NM** value: **Cover or less**
Circ: Diamd. preorders: **26,512**
A: Paul Pelletier **W:** Devin Grayson
2 ❑ Oct 2000 Cover: 4.95 **NM** value: **Cover or less**
Circ: Diamd. preorders: **20,538**
📖 Interludes; Shifting Gears; The 1,000: Titans Surveillance Database; Who is Tara Markov; Super Friends **A:** Paul Pelletier; Mark Buckingham; Justiniano; Drew Johnson; Ben Herrera; Derec Aucoin; Georges Jeanty; Adam DeKraker; Dusty Abell **W:** Scott Beatty; Ben Raab; Geoff Johns; Jay Faerber

TITANS SELL-OUT! SPECIAL — DC

1 ❑ Nov 1992 Cover: 3.50 **NM** value: **Cover or less**
Circ: CapCity orders: **24,400**
One-shot.

TIYU — Express / Entity

1 ❑ Oct 1996 Cover: 2.95 **NM** value: **9.95**
Special picture-only cover. **A:** Ken Lashley; Jean-Marc Guillemette **W:** Ken Lashley; Russ Tinkess

T-MINUS-1 — Renegade

1 ❑ b&w Cover: 2.00 **NM** value: **Cover or less**

TMNT MUTANT UNIVERSE SOURCEBOOK — Archie

1 ❑ Cover: 1.95 **NM** value: **2.00**
• A-M **A:** A.C. Farley **W:** Dean Clarrain
2 ❑ Cover: 1.95 **NM** value: **2.00**
• N-Z

TO BE ANNOUNCED — Strawberry Jam

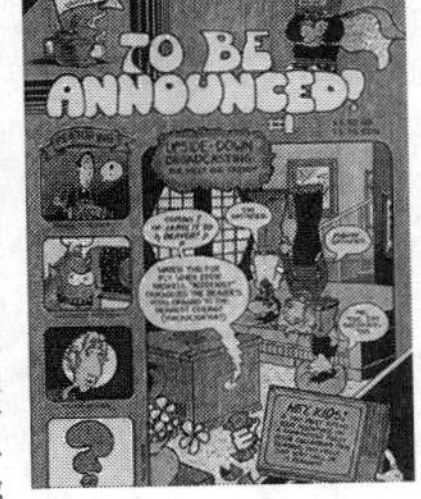

Mike Bannon came to comics fans' attention in Cerebus the Aardvark, first with his funny letters and later with a "Unique Stories" backup there. As the black-and-white comics boom entered full swing, Bannon teamed with Rob and Derek McCullough to produce one of the funniest series of the 1980s.

SCTV in comic-book form, To Be Announced followed a programming day at an absurd television network. Bannon and company came up with many inspired one-page and extended bits, including the children's crime drama "Sesame Street Vice," the bizarre cartoon "It's a Municipal Holiday, Charlie Brown," and more. News bulletins were scorched, too: One zany bit found terrorists taking over the embassy of Iceland, "voted the most innocuous member of the United Nations." (Discovering that their intended blow against Ireland had been foiled by a typographical error, the confused terrorists ask the news crews to follow them over to the Irish embassy.)

To Be Announced ran seven funny issues before falling in the black-and-white comics crash. Bannon went on to apply his unique wit as an occasional cartoonist for Comics Buyer's Guide. — JJM

1 ❑ ca. 1986 Cover: 1.50 **NM** value: **Cover or less**
2 ❑ ca. 1986 Cover: 1.50 **NM** value: **Cover or less**
3 ❑ ca. 1986 Cover: 1.50 **NM** value: **Cover or less**
4 ❑ ca. 1986 Cover: 1.50 **NM** value: **Cover or less**
5 ❑ ca. 1986 Cover: 1.50 **NM** value: **Cover or less**
6 ❑ Feb 1987 Cover: 1.50 **NM** value: **Cover or less**

CGC-graded: Multiply prices above by **33 for 9.9 M • 16 for 9.8 NM/M • 7 for 9.6 NM+ • 5 for 9.4 NM • 2.5 for 9.2 NM- • 1.5 for 9.0 VF/NM**

7 ❑ ca. 1987 Cover: 1.50 **NM** value: **Cover or less**

TODAY'S BRIDES — Ajax

1 ❑ ca. 1955 Cover: 0.10 **NM** value: **50.00**
2 ❑ ca. 1955 Cover: 0.10 **NM** value: **30.00**
3 ❑ ca. 1956 Cover: 0.10 **NM** value: **30.00**
4 ❑ ca. 1956 Cover: 0.10 **NM** value: **30.00**

TODAY'S ROMANCE — Standard

5 ❑ Mar 1952 Cover: 0.10 **NM** value: **30.00**
Photo cover.
6 ❑ May 1952 Cover: 0.10 **NM** value: **24.00**
Photo cover.
7 ❑ Jul 1952 Cover: 0.10 **NM** value: **15.00**
Photo cover. 🕮 I Was No Angel; This Can't Be You!; Moonlight and Problems; Second-Best Love; From Marilee...with Love (text); Dutch Treat; Table Tips; The Little Things; Lips that Lied; Love Problems; Ride a Hobby Horse **W:** Terry Hendryx
8 ❑ Sep 1952 Cover: 0.10 **NM** value: **15.00**
Photo cover.

TODD MCFARLANE PRESENTS: KISS PSYCHO CIRCUS — Image

1 ❑ Oct 1998 Cover: 6.95 **NM** value: **Cover or less**
• magazine. • reprints #1-3 of comic book **A:** Angel Medina **W:** Brian Holguin
2 ❑ Apr 1999 Cover: 4.95 **NM** value: **Cover or less**
A: Angel Medina **W:** Brian Holguin
3 ❑ Aug 1999 Cover: 4.95 **NM** value: **Cover or less**
A: Angel Medina **W:** Brian Holguin
4 ❑ Nov 1999 Cover: 4.95 **NM** value: **Cover or less**
A: Angel Medina **W:** Brian Holguin
5 ❑ Apr 2000 Cover: 4.95 **NM** value: **Cover or less**
🕮 Destroyer, Part 1; Destroyer, Part 2 **A:** Angel Medina **W:** Brian Holguin

TODD MCFARLANE PRESENTS: OZZY OSBOURNE — Image

1 ❑ Jun 1999 Cover: 4.95 **NM** value: **Cover or less**
• magazine. 🕮 Picking the Brain of Ozzy Osbourne; Biography of a Madman; Ozzy photo album; OZZfest '99; OZZY! Speak of the Devil; OZZY Discography **A:** Dean Ormston **W:** Paul Jenkins

TODD MCFARLANE PRESENTS: THE CROW MAGAZINE — Image

1 ❑ Mar 2000 Cover: 4.95 **NM** value: **Cover or less**
🕮 Resurrection; Shadows **A:** Jamie Tolagson **W:** Jon J Muth

TO DIE FOR — Blackthorne

1 ❑ b&w Cover: 2.50 **NM** value: **Cover or less**
A: Edgar Martiarena
1/3D❑ Cover: 2.50 **NM** value: **Cover or less**

TOKA — Dell

1 ❑ Oct 1964 Cover: 0.12 **NM** value: **20.00**
★ Origin of Toka. ★ 1st Appearance of Toka.
2 ❑ Jan 1965 Cover: 0.12 **NM** value: **10.00**
🕮 Toka's Magic Shield
3 ❑ Apr 1965 Cover: 0.12 **NM** value: **8.00**
4 ❑ Jul 1965 Cover: 0.12 **NM** value: **8.00**
5 ❑ Oct 1965 Cover: 0.12 **NM** value: **8.00**
6 ❑ Jan 1966 Cover: 0.12 **NM** value: **8.00**
7 ❑ Apr 1966 Cover: 0.12 **NM** value: **8.00**
8 ❑ Jul 1966 Cover: 0.12 **NM** value: **8.00**
9 ❑ Oct 1966 Cover: 0.12 **NM** value: **8.00**
10 ❑ Jan 1967 Cover: 0.12 **NM** value: **8.00**
final issue.

TOMAHAWK — DC

Tomahawk made his first appearance in Star Spangled Comics #69. Adventures of Tomahawk and his sidekick, Dan Hunter, at the time of America's Revolutionary War were an immediate hit, and Tomahawk received his own series in 1950. In its 22-year run, Tomahawk and the Rangers starred in countless adventures, some of them (in Comics Code days) featuring dinosaurs, fantasy aliens, and the like.

The buckskin-clad Tom Hawk had been raised by Indians and used what he'd learned to fight the British. However, time finally caught up with him, and he settled down to a quiet life. His son, Hawk, took over the starring role in the series, and the cover bore the name Son of Tomahawk for the last 10 issues of its 140-issue run.

1 ❑ Sep 1950 Cover: 0.10 **NM** value: **1050.00**
• **CGC:** 5 graded, best 9.6
2 ❑ Nov 1950 Cover: 0.10 **NM** value: **500.00**
• **CGC:** 3 graded, best 6.5
3 ❑ Jan 1951 Cover: 0.10 **NM** value: **325.00**
• **CGC:** 2 graded, best 9.6
4 ❑ Mar 1951 Cover: 0.10 **NM** value: **325.00**
• **CGC:** 1 graded, best 8.5
5 ❑ May 1951 Cover: 0.10 **NM** value: **325.00**
• **CGC:** 3 graded, best 9.4
6 ❑ Jul 1951 Cover: 0.10 **NM** value: **225.00**
• **CGC:** 1 graded, best 8.0
7 ❑ Sep 1951 Cover: 0.10 **NM** value: **225.00**
• **CGC:** 2 graded, best 9.6
8 ❑ Nov 1951 Cover: 0.10 **NM** value: **225.00**
• **CGC:** 2 graded, best 8.5
9 ❑ Jan 1952 Cover: 0.10 **NM** value: **225.00**
• **CGC:** 1 graded, best 9.0
10 ❑ Mar 1952 Cover: 0.10 **NM** value: **225.00**
• **CGC:** 1 graded, best 7.5
11 ❑ May 1952 Cover: 0.10 **NM** value: **150.00**
• **CGC:** 1 graded, best 9.2
12 ❑ Jul 1952 Cover: 0.10 **NM** value: **150.00**
• **CGC:** 1 graded, best 5.0
13 ❑ Sep 1952 Cover: 0.10 **NM** value: **150.00**
• **CGC:** 1 graded, best 4.0
14 ❑ Nov 1952 Cover: 0.10 **NM** value: **150.00**
• **CGC:** 1 graded, best 7.0
15 ❑ Jan 1953 Cover: 0.10 **NM** value: **150.00**
• **CGC:** 1 graded, best 6.0
16 ❑ Mar 1953 Cover: 0.10 **NM** value: **150.00**
• **CGC:** 1 graded, best 6.5
17 ❑ May 1953 Cover: 0.10 **NM** value: **150.00**
• **CGC:** 1 graded, best 8.0
18 ❑ Jul 1953 Cover: 0.10 **NM** value: **150.00**
• **CGC:** 1 graded, best 4.5
19 ❑ Sep 1953 Cover: 0.10 **NM** value: **150.00**
• **CGC:** 1 graded, best 7.0
20 ❑ Nov 1953 Cover: 0.10 **NM** value: **150.00**
• **CGC:** 1 graded, best 8.0
21 ❑ Jan 1954 Cover: 0.10 **NM** value: **110.00**
• **CGC:** 1 graded, best 4.0
22 ❑ Feb 1954 Cover: 0.10 **NM** value: **110.00**
• **CGC:** 1 graded, best 7.5
23 ❑ Mar 1954 Cover: 0.10 **NM** value: **110.00**
• **CGC:** 1 graded, best 7.0
24 ❑ May 1954 Cover: 0.10 **NM** value: **110.00**
• **CGC:** 1 graded, best 7.5
25 ❑ Jul 1954 Cover: 0.10 **NM** value: **110.00**
• **CGC:** 1 graded, best 8.0
26 ❑ Aug 1954 Cover: 0.10 **NM** value: **110.00**
• **CGC:** 1 graded, best 8.0
27 ❑ Sep 1954 Cover: 0.10 **NM** value: **110.00**
• **CGC:** 1 graded, best 6.0
28 ❑ Nov 1954 Cover: 0.10 **NM** value: **125.00**
• **CGC:** 1 graded, best 6.5
★ 1st Appearance of Lord Shilling.
29 ❑ Jan 1955 Cover: 0.10 **NM** value: **160.00**
• **CGC:** 1 graded, best 7.0
A: Frank Frazetta
30 ❑ Feb 1955 Cover: 0.10 **NM** value: **95.00**
• **CGC:** 1 graded, best 8.0
31 ❑ Mar 1955 Cover: 0.10 **NM** value: **75.00**
• **CGC:** 1 graded, best 7.0
32 ❑ May 1955 Cover: 0.10 **NM** value: **75.00**
• **CGC:** 1 graded, best 8.0
33 ❑ Jul 1955 Cover: 0.10 **NM** value: **75.00**
• **CGC:** 1 graded, best 7.5
34 ❑ Aug 1955 Cover: 0.10 **NM** value: **75.00**
• **CGC:** 1 graded, best 8.0
35 ❑ Sep 1955 Cover: 0.10 **NM** value: **75.00**
• **CGC:** 1 graded, best 7.0
36 ❑ Nov 1955 Cover: 0.10 **NM** value: **75.00**
• **CGC:** 1 graded, best 7.0
37 ❑ Jan 1956 Cover: 0.10 **NM** value: **75.00**
• **CGC:** 1 graded, best 8.0
38 ❑ Feb 1956 Cover: 0.10 **NM** value: **75.00**
• **CGC:** 1 graded, best 8.0
39 ❑ Mar 1956 Cover: 0.10 **NM** value: **75.00**
• **CGC:** 1 graded, best 8.0
40 ❑ May 1956 Cover: 0.10 **NM** value: **75.00**
• **CGC:** 1 graded, best 8.0
41 ❑ Jul 1956 Cover: 0.10 **NM** value: **60.00**
• **CGC:** 1 graded, best 7.5
42 ❑ Aug 1956 Cover: 0.10 **NM** value: **60.00**
• **CGC:** 2 graded, best 9.0
43 ❑ Sep 1956 Cover: 0.10 **NM** value: **60.00**
• **CGC:** 1 graded, best 5.5
44 ❑ Nov 1956 Cover: 0.10 **NM** value: **60.00**
• **CGC:** 1 graded, best 8.0
45 ❑ Jan 1957 Cover: 0.10 **NM** value: **60.00**
• **CGC:** 1 graded, best 7.5
46 ❑ Feb 1957 Cover: 0.10 **NM** value: **60.00**
• **CGC:** 1 graded, best 8.0
47 ❑ Mar 1957 Cover: 0.10 **NM** value: **60.00**
• **CGC:** 1 graded, best 8.0
48 ❑ May 1957 Cover: 0.10 **NM** value: **60.00**
• **CGC:** 1 graded, best 8.0
49 ❑ Jul 1957 Cover: 0.10 **NM** value: **60.00**
• **CGC:** 1 graded, best 7.5
50 ❑ Aug 1957 Cover: 0.10 **NM** value: **60.00**
• **CGC:** 1 graded, best 8.5
51 ❑ Sep 1957 Cover: 0.10 **NM** value: **48.00**
• **CGC:** 1 graded, best 9.0
52 ❑ Nov 1957 Cover: 0.10 **NM** value: **48.00**
• **CGC:** 1 graded, best 8.0
53 ❑ Jan 1958 Cover: 0.10 **NM** value: **48.00**
• **CGC:** 1 graded, best 9.0
54 ❑ Feb 1958 Cover: 0.10 **NM** value: **48.00**
• **CGC:** 1 graded, best 8.0
55 ❑ Mar 1958 Cover: 0.10 **NM** value: **48.00**
• **CGC:** 1 graded, best 9.2
56 ❑ May 1958 Cover: 0.10 **NM** value: **48.00**
• **CGC:** 1 graded, best 9.0
57 ❑ Jul 1958 Cover: 0.10 **NM** value: **90.00**
• **CGC:** 1 graded, best 8.5
A: Frank Frazetta
58 ❑ Sep 1958 Cover: 0.10 **NM** value: **42.00**
• **CGC:** 1 graded, best 7.5
59 ❑ Nov 1958 Cover: 0.10 **NM** value: **42.00**
• **CGC:** 1 graded, best 8.5
60 ❑ Jan 1959 Cover: 0.10 **NM** value: **42.00**
• **CGC:** 1 graded, best 9.0
61 ❑ Mar 1959 Cover: 0.10 **NM** value: **34.00**
62 ❑ May 1959 Cover: 0.10 **NM** value: **34.00**
• **CGC:** 1 graded, best 9.2
63 ❑ Jul 1959 Cover: 0.10 **NM** value: **34.00**
• **CGC:** 1 graded, best 8.5
64 ❑ Sep 1959 Cover: 0.10 **NM** value: **34.00**
• **CGC:** 1 graded, best 9.2
65 ❑ Nov 1959 Cover: 0.10 **NM** value: **34.00**
66 ❑ Jan 1960 Cover: 0.10 **NM** value: **34.00**
Circ: Statement: **180,000** • **CGC:** 1 graded, best 9.2
67 ❑ Mar 1960 Cover: 0.10 **NM** value: **34.00**
Circ: Statement: **180,000** • **CGC:** 1 graded, best 7.5
68 ❑ May 1960 Cover: 0.10 **NM** value: **34.00**
Circ: Statement: **180,000** • **CGC:** 1 graded, best 7.5
69 ❑ Jul 1960 Cover: 0.10 **NM** value: **34.00**
Circ: Statement: **180,000** • **CGC:** 1 graded, best 8.5
70 ❑ Sep 1960 Cover: 0.10 **NM** value: **34.00**
Circ: Statement: **180,000** • **CGC:** 3 graded, best 9.0
71 ❑ Nov 1960 Cover: 0.10 **NM** value: **34.00**
Circ: Statement: **180,000** • **CGC:** 1 graded, best 8.0
72 ❑ Jan 1961 Cover: 0.10 **NM** value: **34.00**
• **CGC:** 2 graded, best 9.2
73 ❑ Mar 1961 Cover: 0.10 **NM** value: **34.00**
• **CGC:** 1 graded, best 9.0
74 ❑ May 1961 Cover: 0.10 **NM** value: **34.00**
• **CGC:** 1 graded, best 9.0
75 ❑ Jul 1961 Cover: 0.10 **NM** value: **34.00**
• **CGC:** 1 graded, best 9.0
76 ❑ Sep 1961 Cover: 0.10 **NM** value: **34.00**
• **CGC:** 1 graded, best 9.2
77 ❑ Nov 1961 Cover: 0.10 **NM** value: **34.00**
• **CGC:** 1 graded, best 7.5
78 ❑ Jan 1962 Cover: 0.10 **NM** value: **34.00**
• **CGC:** 2 graded, best 9.2
79 ❑ Mar 1962 Cover: 0.10 **NM** value: **34.00**
80 ❑ May 1962 Cover: 0.10 **NM** value: **34.00**
81 ❑ Jul 1962 Cover: 0.12 **NM** value: **26.00**
• **CGC:** 1 graded, best 9.0
★ 1st Appearance of Miss Liberty.
82 ❑ Sep 1962 Cover: 0.12 **NM** value: **26.00**
83 ❑ Nov 1962 Cover: 0.12 **NM** value: **26.00**
84 ❑ Jan 1963 Cover: 0.12 **NM** value: **26.00**
85 ❑ Mar 1963 Cover: 0.12 **NM** value: **26.00**
86 ❑ May 1963 Cover: 0.12 **NM** value: **26.00**
87 ❑ Jul 1963 Cover: 0.12 **NM** value: **26.00**
88 ❑ Sep 1963 Cover: 0.12 **NM** value: **26.00**
89 ❑ Nov 1963 Cover: 0.12 **NM** value: **26.00**
90 ❑ Jan 1964 Cover: 0.12 **NM** value: **26.00**
91 ❑ Mar 1964 Cover: 0.12 **NM** value: **16.00**
92 ❑ May 1964 Cover: 0.12 **NM** value: **16.00**
93 ❑ Jul 1964 Cover: 0.12 **NM** value: **16.00**
94 ❑ Sep 1964 Cover: 0.12 **NM** value: **16.00**
• **CGC:** 2 graded, best 9.4
95 ❑ Nov 1964 Cover: 0.12 **NM** value: **16.00**
96 ❑ Jan 1965 Cover: 0.12 **NM** value: **16.00**
Circ: Statement: **229,979**
97 ❑ Mar 1965 Cover: 0.12 **NM** value: **16.00**
Circ: Statement: **229,979**
98 ❑ May 1965 Cover: 0.12 **NM** value: **16.00**
Circ: Statement: **229,979**
99 ❑ Jul 1965 Cover: 0.12 **NM** value: **16.00**
Circ: Statement: **229,979**
100 ❑ Sep 1965 Cover: 0.12 **NM** value: **16.00**
Circ: Statement: **229,979**
101 ❑ Nov 1965 Cover: 0.12 **NM** value: **10.00**
Circ: Statement: **229,979**
102 ❑ Jan 1966 Cover: 0.12 **NM** value: **10.00**
Circ: Statement: **212,954**
103 ❑ Mar 1966 Cover: 0.12 **NM** value: **10.00**
Circ: Statement: **212,954**
104 ❑ May 1966 Cover: 0.12 **NM** value: **10.00**
Circ: Statement: **212,954**
105 ❑ Jul 1966 Cover: 0.12 **NM** value: **10.00**
Circ: Statement: **212,954**
106 ❑ Sep 1966 Cover: 0.12 **NM** value: **10.00**
Circ: Statement: **212,954**
107 ❑ Nov 1966 Cover: 0.12 **NM** value: **10.00**
Circ: Statement: **212,954**
108 ❑ Jan 1967 Cover: 0.12 **NM** value: **10.00**
Circ: Statement: **165,700** • **CGC:** 2 graded, best 9.4
109 ❑ Mar 1967 Cover: 0.12 **NM** value: **10.00**
Circ: Statement: **165,700**
110 ❑ May 1967 Cover: 0.12 **NM** value: **10.00**
Circ: Statement: **165,700**
111 ❑ Jul 1967 Cover: 0.12 **NM** value: **8.00**
Circ: Statement: **165,700**
112 ❑ Sep 1967 Cover: 0.12 **NM** value: **8.00**
Circ: Statement: **165,700**
113 ❑ Nov 1967 Cover: 0.12 **NM** value: **8.00**
Circ: Statement: **165,700** • **CGC:** 1 graded, best 8.0
114 ❑ Jan 1968 Cover: 0.12 **NM** value: **8.00**
Circ: Statement: **157,250** • **CGC:** 1 graded, best 9.4
115 ❑ Mar 1968 Cover: 0.12 **NM** value: **8.00**
Circ: Statement: **157,250** • **CGC:** 1 graded, best 8.5
116 ❑ May 1968 Cover: 0.12 **NM** value: **8.00**
Circ: Statement: **157,250**
117 ❑ Jul 1968 Cover: 0.12 **NM** value: **8.00**
Circ: Statement: **157,250**
118 ❑ Sep 1968 Cover: 0.12 **NM** value: **8.00**
Circ: Statement: **157,250**
119 ❑ Nov 1968 Cover: 0.12 **NM** value: **8.00**
Circ: Statement: **157,250**
120 ❑ Jan 1969 Cover: 0.12 **NM** value: **8.00**
121 ❑ Mar 1969 Cover: 0.12 **NM** value: **6.00**
• Has 1968 Statement, filed 10/1/68; avg print run 298,000; avg sales 157,000; avg subs 250; avg total paid 157,250; samples 386; max existent 157,386; 47% of run returned
122 ❑ May 1969 Cover: 0.12 **NM** value: **6.00**
123 ❑ Jul 1969 Cover: 0.15 **NM** value: **6.00**
124 ❑ Sep 1969 Cover: 0.15 **NM** value: **6.00**
125 ❑ Nov 1969 Cover: 0.15 **NM** value: **6.00**

Other grades: Multiply prices above by **1.5 for Mint • 2/3 for Very Fine • 1/3 for Fine • 1/5 for Very Good • 1/8 for Good**

126 ❑ Jan 1970 Cover: 0.15 **NM** value: **6.00**
Circ: Statement: **139,555**
127 ❑ Mar 1970 Cover: 0.15 **NM** value: **6.00**
Circ: Statement: **139,555**
128 ❑ May 1970 Cover: 0.15 **NM** value: **6.00**
Circ: Statement: **139,555**
129 ❑ Jul 1970 Cover: 0.15 **NM** value: **6.00**
Circ: Statement: **139,555**
130 ❑ Sep 1970 Cover: 0.15 **NM** value: **6.00**
Circ: Statement: **139,555** • **CGC:** 1 graded, best 8.5
131 ❑ Nov 1970 Cover: 0.15 **NM** value: **6.00**
Circ: Statement: **139,555** • **CGC:** 1 graded, best 9.4
• Series becomes "Son of Tomahawk" **A:** Frank Frazetta
132 ❑ Jan 1971 Cover: 0.15 **NM** value: **6.00**
Circ: Statement: **141,865**
133 ❑ Mar 1971 Cover: 0.15 **NM** value: **4.50**
Circ: Statement: **141,865**
🕮 Scalp Hunter; The Way It Was! **A:** Frank Thorne **W:** Robert Kanigher
134 ❑ May 1971 Cover: 0.15 **NM** value: **4.50**
Circ: Statement: **141,865**
• Has 1970 Statement, filed 10/1/70; avg print run 287,240; avg sales 139,437; avg subs 118; avg total paid 139,555; samples 122; max existent 139,677; 51% of run returned
135 ❑ Jul 1971 Cover: 0.15 **NM** value: **4.50**
Circ: Statement: **141,865**
🕮 Death On Ghost Mountain **A:** Frank Thorne **W:** Robert Kanigher
136 ❑ Sep 1971 Cover: 0.25 **NM** value: **4.50**
Circ: Statement: **141,865**
137 ❑ Nov 1971 Cover: 0.25 **NM** value: **4.50**
Circ: Statement: **141,865**
138 ❑ Jan 1972 Cover: 0.25 **NM** value: **4.50**
139 ❑ Mar 1972 Cover: 0.25 **NM** value: **4.50**
says Son of Tomahawk on cover. • Has 1971 Statement, filed 10/1/71; avg print run 279,166; avg sales 141,865; no subscriptions; avg total paid and max existent 141,865; 49% of run returned **A:** Frank Frazetta
140 ❑ May 1972 Cover: 0.25 **NM** value: **4.50**
says Son of Tomahawk on cover. final issue.

TOM & JERRY 50TH ANNIVERSARY SPECIAL
Harvey

1 ❑ Oct 1991 Cover: 2.50 **NM** value: **Cover or less**
Circ: CapCity orders: **3,425**
A: Carl Barks

TOM & JERRY ADVENTURES
Harvey

1 ❑ May 1992 Cover: 1.25 **NM** value: **Cover or less**

TOM & JERRY AND FRIENDS
Harvey

1 ❑ Dec 1991 Cover: 1.25 **NM** value: **Cover or less**
Circ: CapCity orders: **3,700**
2 ❑ Feb 1992 Cover: 1.25 **NM** value: **Cover or less**
Circ: CapCity orders: **2,000**
3 ❑ Apr 1992 Cover: 1.25 **NM** value: **Cover or less**
4 ❑ Jul 1992 Cover: 1.25 **NM** value: **Cover or less**

TOM & JERRY BIG BOOK
Harvey

1 ❑ Sep 1992 Cover: 1.95 **NM** value: **Cover or less**
2 ❑ Cover: 1.95 **NM** value: **Cover or less**

TOM & JERRY COMICS
Dell

Tom and Jerry were one of the funniest and most popular cartoon teams, the product of another major cartoon team, William Hanna and Joseph Barbera. "Puss Gets the Boot" called the cat Jasper, but the 1940 short was clearly the start of their cat and mouse frolics. Some of the shorts even won an Oscar award during their career on the big screen. Tom and Jerry's adventures in print were chronicled by Dell, the kings of movie and television tie-ins, whose high standards of quality and kid-friendly approach guaranteed good reading for young tykes every time out.

Tom, the perpetually scheming (and perpetually frustrated) housecat, and his adversary Jerry, the mouse, lean heavily on violent, Three Stooges-like slapstick for their comedy. The original comic-book version captures all the fun and excitement of Tom and Jerry that kids have enjoyed for more than 50 years. Appearing as an additional feature in Our Gang Comics initially, Tom and Jerry eventually took over the title.

60 ❑ Jul 1949 Cover: 0.10 **NM** value: **50.00**
• Series continued from Our Gang #59
61 ❑ Aug 1949 Cover: 0.10 **NM** value: **40.00**
• **CGC:** 1 graded, best 9.4
62 ❑ Sep 1949 Cover: 0.10 **NM** value: **40.00**
63 ❑ Oct 1949 Cover: 0.10 **NM** value: **40.00**
64 ❑ Nov 1949 Cover: 0.10 **NM** value: **40.00**
65 ❑ Dec 1949 Cover: 0.10 **NM** value: **40.00**
66 ❑ Jan 1950 Cover: 0.10 **NM** value: **36.00**
67 ❑ Feb 1950 Cover: 0.10 **NM** value: **36.00**
68 ❑ Mar 1950 Cover: 0.10 **NM** value: **36.00**
69 ❑ Apr 1950 Cover: 0.10 **NM** value: **36.00**
70 ❑ May 1950 Cover: 0.10 **NM** value: **36.00**
71 ❑ Jun 1950 Cover: 0.10 **NM** value: **28.00**
72 ❑ Jul 1950 Cover: 0.10 **NM** value: **28.00**
73 ❑ Aug 1950 Cover: 0.10 **NM** value: **28.00**
74 ❑ Sep 1950 Cover: 0.10 **NM** value: **28.00**
75 ❑ Oct 1950 Cover: 0.10 **NM** value: **28.00**
76 ❑ Nov 1950 Cover: 0.10 **NM** value: **28.00**
77 ❑ Dec 1950 Cover: 0.10 **NM** value: **28.00**
• **CGC:** 1 graded, best 9.4
78 ❑ Jan 1951 Cover: 0.10 **NM** value: **28.00**
• **CGC:** 1 graded, best 9.4
79 ❑ Feb 1951 Cover: 0.10 **NM** value: **28.00**
80 ❑ Mar 1951 Cover: 0.10 **NM** value: **28.00**
81 ❑ Apr 1951 Cover: 0.10 **NM** value: **24.00**
82 ❑ May 1951 Cover: 0.10 **NM** value: **24.00**
83 ❑ Jun 1951 Cover: 0.10 **NM** value: **24.00**
84 ❑ Jul 1951 Cover: 0.10 **NM** value: **24.00**
• **CGC:** 2 graded, best 9.4
85 ❑ Aug 1951 Cover: 0.10 **NM** value: **24.00**
86 ❑ Sep 1951 Cover: 0.10 **NM** value: **24.00**
87 ❑ Oct 1951 Cover: 0.10 **NM** value: **24.00**
• **CGC:** 1 graded, best 9.6
88 ❑ Nov 1951 Cover: 0.10 **NM** value: **24.00**
89 ❑ Dec 1951 Cover: 0.10 **NM** value: **24.00**
90 ❑ Jan 1952 Cover: 0.10 **NM** value: **24.00**
91 ❑ Feb 1952 Cover: 0.10 **NM** value: **18.00**
92 ❑ Mar 1952 Cover: 0.10 **NM** value: **18.00**
93 ❑ Apr 1952 Cover: 0.10 **NM** value: **18.00**
94 ❑ May 1952 Cover: 0.10 **NM** value: **18.00**
95 ❑ Jun 1952 Cover: 0.10 **NM** value: **18.00**
96 ❑ Jul 1952 Cover: 0.10 **NM** value: **18.00**
97 ❑ Aug 1952 Cover: 0.10 **NM** value: **18.00**
98 ❑ Sep 1952 Cover: 0.10 **NM** value: **18.00**
99 ❑ Oct 1952 Cover: 0.10 **NM** value: **18.00**
100 ❑ Nov 1952 Cover: 0.10 **NM** value: **18.00**
• **CGC:** 1 graded, best 9.0
101 ❑ Dec 1952 Cover: 0.10 **NM** value: **14.00**
102 ❑ Jan 1953 Cover: 0.10 **NM** value: **14.00**
103 ❑ Feb 1953 Cover: 0.10 **NM** value: **14.00**
104 ❑ Mar 1953, four-color Cover: 0.10 **NM** value: **14.00**
105 ❑ Apr 1953 Cover: 0.10 **NM** value: **14.00**
106 ❑ May 1953 Cover: 0.10 **NM** value: **14.00**
107 ❑ Jun 1953 Cover: 0.10 **NM** value: **14.00**
108 ❑ Jul 1953 Cover: 0.10 **NM** value: **14.00**
109 ❑ Aug 1953 Cover: 0.10 **NM** value: **14.00**
110 ❑ Sep 1953 Cover: 0.10 **NM** value: **14.00**
111 ❑ Oct 1953 Cover: 0.10 **NM** value: **12.00**
• **CGC:** 1 graded, best 9.0
112 ❑ Nov 1953 Cover: 0.10 **NM** value: **12.00**
113 ❑ Dec 1953 Cover: 0.10 **NM** value: **12.00**
114 ❑ Jan 1954 Cover: 0.10 **NM** value: **12.00**
115 ❑ Feb 1954 Cover: 0.10 **NM** value: **12.00**
116 ❑ Mar 1954 Cover: 0.10 **NM** value: **12.00**
117 ❑ Apr 1954 Cover: 0.10 **NM** value: **12.00**
118 ❑ May 1954 Cover: 0.10 **NM** value: **12.00**
119 ❑ Jun 1954 Cover: 0.10 **NM** value: **12.00**
120 ❑ Jul 1954 Cover: 0.10 **NM** value: **12.00**
121 ❑ Aug 1954 Cover: 0.10 **NM** value: **9.00**
122 ❑ Sep 1954 Cover: 0.10 **NM** value: **9.00**
123 ❑ Oct 1954 Cover: 0.10 **NM** value: **9.00**
124 ❑ Nov 1954 Cover: 0.10 **NM** value: **9.00**
125 ❑ Dec 1954 Cover: 0.10 **NM** value: **9.00**
126 ❑ Jan 1955 Cover: 0.10 **NM** value: **9.00**
127 ❑ Feb 1955 Cover: 0.10 **NM** value: **9.00**
128 ❑ Mar 1955 Cover: 0.10 **NM** value: **9.00**
129 ❑ Apr 1955 Cover: 0.10 **NM** value: **9.00**
130 ❑ May 1955 Cover: 0.10 **NM** value: **9.00**
131 ❑ Jun 1955 Cover: 0.10 **NM** value: **7.00**
132 ❑ Jul 1955 Cover: 0.10 **NM** value: **7.00**
133 ❑ Aug 1955 Cover: 0.10 **NM** value: **7.00**
134 ❑ Sep 1955 Cover: 0.10 **NM** value: **7.00**
135 ❑ Oct 1955 Cover: 0.10 **NM** value: **7.00**
136 ❑ Nov 1955 Cover: 0.10 **NM** value: **7.00**
137 ❑ Dec 1955 Cover: 0.10 **NM** value: **7.00**
138 ❑ Jan 1956 Cover: 0.10 **NM** value: **7.00**
139 ❑ Feb 1956 Cover: 0.10 **NM** value: **7.00**
140 ❑ Mar 1956 Cover: 0.10 **NM** value: **7.00**
141 ❑ Apr 1956 Cover: 0.10 **NM** value: **7.00**
142 ❑ May 1956 Cover: 0.10 **NM** value: **7.00**
143 ❑ Jun 1956 Cover: 0.10 **NM** value: **7.00**
144 ❑ Jul 1956 Cover: 0.10 **NM** value: **7.00**
145 ❑ Aug 1956 Cover: 0.10 **NM** value: **7.00**
146 ❑ Sep 1956 Cover: 0.10 **NM** value: **7.00**
147 ❑ Oct 1956 Cover: 0.10 **NM** value: **7.00**
148 ❑ Nov 1956 Cover: 0.10 **NM** value: **7.00**
149 ❑ Dec 1956 Cover: 0.10 **NM** value: **7.00**
150 ❑ Jan 1957 Cover: 0.10 **NM** value: **7.00**
151 ❑ Feb 1957 Cover: 0.10 **NM** value: **6.00**
152 ❑ Mar 1957 Cover: 0.10 **NM** value: **6.00**
153 ❑ Apr 1957 Cover: 0.10 **NM** value: **6.00**
154 ❑ May 1957 Cover: 0.10 **NM** value: **6.00**
155 ❑ Jun 1957 Cover: 0.10 **NM** value: **6.00**
156 ❑ Jul 1957 Cover: 0.10 **NM** value: **6.00**
157 ❑ Aug 1957 Cover: 0.10 **NM** value: **6.00**
158 ❑ Sep 1957 Cover: 0.10 **NM** value: **6.00**
159 ❑ Oct 1957 Cover: 0.10 **NM** value: **6.00**
160 ❑ Nov 1957 Cover: 0.10 **NM** value: **6.00**
161 ❑ Dec 1957 Cover: 0.10 **NM** value: **6.00**
162 ❑ Jan 1958 Cover: 0.10 **NM** value: **6.00**
163 ❑ Feb 1958 Cover: 0.10 **NM** value: **6.00**
164 ❑ Mar 1958 Cover: 0.10 **NM** value: **6.00**
165 ❑ Apr 1958 Cover: 0.10 **NM** value: **6.00**
166 ❑ May 1958 Cover: 0.10 **NM** value: **6.00**
167 ❑ Jun 1958 Cover: 0.10 **NM** value: **6.00**
168 ❑ Jul 1958 Cover: 0.10 **NM** value: **6.00**
169 ❑ Aug 1958 Cover: 0.10 **NM** value: **6.00**
170 ❑ Sep 1958 Cover: 0.10 **NM** value: **6.00**
171 ❑ Oct 1958 Cover: 0.10 **NM** value: **5.00**
172 ❑ Nov 1958 Cover: 0.10 **NM** value: **5.00**
173 ❑ Dec 1958 Cover: 0.10 **NM** value: **5.00**
174 ❑ Jan 1959 Cover: 0.10 **NM** value: **5.00**
175 ❑ Feb 1959 Cover: 0.10 **NM** value: **5.00**
176 ❑ Mar 1959 Cover: 0.10 **NM** value: **5.00**
177 ❑ Apr 1959 Cover: 0.10 **NM** value: **5.00**
178 ❑ May 1959 Cover: 0.10 **NM** value: **5.00**
179 ❑ Jun 1959, four-color Cover: 0.10 **NM** value: **5.00**
🕮 Moving Madness (text piece)
180 ❑ Jul 1959, four-color Cover: 0.10 **NM** value: **5.00**
181 ❑ Aug 1959, four-color Cover: 0.10 **NM** value: **5.00**
182 ❑ Sep 1959, four-color Cover: 0.10 **NM** value: **5.00**
183 ❑ Oct 1959, four-color Cover: 0.10 **NM** value: **5.00**
184 ❑ Nov 1959, four-color Cover: 0.10 **NM** value: **5.00**
185 ❑ Dec 1959, four-color Cover: 0.10 **NM** value: **5.00**
186 ❑ Jan 1960, four-color Cover: 0.10 **NM** value: **5.00**
187 ❑ Feb 1960, four-color Cover: 0.10 **NM** value: **5.00**
188 ❑ Mar 1960, four-color Cover: 0.10 **NM** value: **5.00**
189 ❑ Apr 1960, four-color Cover: 0.10 **NM** value: **5.00**
190 ❑ May 1960, four-color Cover: 0.10 **NM** value: **5.00**
191 ❑ Jun 1960 Cover: 0.10 **NM** value: **4.00**
192 ❑ Jul 1960 Cover: 0.10 **NM** value: **4.00**
193 ❑ Aug 1960 Cover: 0.10 **NM** value: **4.00**
194 ❑ Sep 1960 Cover: 0.10 **NM** value: **4.00**
195 ❑ Oct 1960 Cover: 0.10 **NM** value: **4.00**
196 ❑ Nov 1960 Cover: 0.10 **NM** value: **4.00**
197 ❑ Dec 1960 Cover: 0.10 **NM** value: **4.00**
198 ❑ Jan 1961 Cover: 0.10 **NM** value: **4.00**
199 ❑ Feb 1961 Cover: 0.15 **NM** value: **4.00**
200 ❑ Mar 1961 Cover: 0.15 **NM** value: **4.00**
201 ❑ Apr 1961, four-color Cover: 0.15 **NM** value: **3.00**
🕮 The Log Lifters; Hobby Helper; Bandit Badgers; Spring Zing
202 ❑ May 1961 Cover: 0.15 **NM** value: **3.00**
203 ❑ Jun 1961 Cover: 0.15 **NM** value: **3.00**
204 ❑ Jul 1961 Cover: 0.15 **NM** value: **3.00**
205 ❑ Aug 1961 Cover: 0.15 **NM** value: **3.00**
206 ❑ Sep 1961 Cover: 0.15 **NM** value: **3.00**
207 ❑ Oct 1961 Cover: 0.15 **NM** value: **3.00**
208 ❑ Nov 1961 Cover: 0.15 **NM** value: **3.00**
209 ❑ Jan 1962 Cover: 0.15 **NM** value: **3.00**
210 ❑ Mar 1962 Cover: 0.15 **NM** value: **3.00**
211 ❑ May 1962 Cover: 0.15 **NM** value: **3.00**
212 ❑ Aug 1962 Cover: 0.15 **NM** value: **3.00**
213 ❑ Nov 1962 Cover: 0.25 **NM** value: **3.00**
• **CGC:** 1 graded, best 9.6
214 ❑ Mar 1963 Cover: 0.25 **NM** value: **3.00**
215 ❑ May 1963 Cover: 0.12 **NM** value: **3.00**
216 ❑ Aug 1963 Cover: 0.12 **NM** value: **3.00**
217 ❑ Nov 1963 Cover: 0.12 **NM** value: **3.00**
218 ❑ Feb 1964 Cover: 0.12 **NM** value: **3.00**
Circ: Statement: **293,564**
219 ❑ May 1964 Cover: 0.12 **NM** value: **3.00**
Circ: Statement: **293,564**
220 ❑ Aug 1964 Cover: 0.12 **NM** value: **3.00**
Circ: Statement: **293,564**
221 ❑ Nov 1964 Cover: 0.12 **NM** value: **3.00**
Circ: Statement: **293,564**
222 ❑ Feb 1965 Cover: 0.12 **NM** value: **3.00**
Circ: Statement: **276,980**
223 ❑ Apr 1965 Cover: 0.12 **NM** value: **3.00**
Circ: Statement: **276,980**
224 ❑ Jun 1965 Cover: 0.12 **NM** value: **3.00**
Circ: Statement: **276,980**
225 ❑ Aug 1965 Cover: 0.12 **NM** value: **3.00**
Circ: Statement: **276,980**
226 ❑ Oct 1965 Cover: 0.12 **NM** value: **3.00**
Circ: Statement: **276,980**
227 ❑ Dec 1965 Cover: 0.12 **NM** value: **3.00**
Circ: Statement: **276,980**
228 ❑ Feb 1966 Cover: 0.12 **NM** value: **3.00**
Circ: Statement: **271,920**
229 ❑ Apr 1966 Cover: 0.12 **NM** value: **3.00**
Circ: Statement: **271,920**
230 ❑ Jun 1966 Cover: 0.12 **NM** value: **3.00**
Circ: Statement: **271,920**
231 ❑ Aug 1966 Cover: 0.12 **NM** value: **2.00**
Circ: Statement: **271,920**
232 ❑ Oct 1966 Cover: 0.12 **NM** value: **2.00**
Circ: Statement: **271,920**
233 ❑ Dec 1966 Cover: 0.12 **NM** value: **2.00**
Circ: Statement: **271,920**
234 ❑ Feb 1967 Cover: 0.12 **NM** value: **2.00**
Circ: Statement: **256,448**
• Has 1966 Statement, filed 9/28/66; avg print run 403,375; avg sales 270,933; avg subs 987; avg total paid 271,920; samples 582; max existent 272,502; 32% of run returned
235 ❑ Apr 1967 Cover: 0.12 **NM** value: **2.00**
Circ: Statement: **256,448**
236 ❑ Jun 1967 Cover: 0.12 **NM** value: **2.00**
Circ: Statement: **256,448**
237 ❑ Aug 1967 Cover: 0.12 **NM** value: **2.00**
Circ: Statement: **256,448**
238 ❑ Nov 1967 Cover: 0.12 **NM** value: **2.00**
Circ: Statement: **256,448**
239 ❑ Feb 1968 Cover: 0.12 **NM** value: **2.00**
240 ❑ May 1968 Cover: 0.12 **NM** value: **2.00**
• Has 1967 Statement, filed 9/28/67; avg print run 430,030; avg sales 255,698; avg subs 750; avg total paid 256,448; samples 520; max existent 256,968; 40% of run returned
241 ❑ Aug 1968 Cover: 0.12 **NM** value: **2.00**
242 ❑ Nov 1968 Cover: 0.15 **NM** value: **2.00**
243 ❑ Feb 1969 Cover: 0.15 **NM** value: **2.00**
244 ❑ Apr 1969 Cover: 0.15 **NM** value: **2.00**
245 ❑ Jun 1969 Cover: 0.15 **NM** value: **2.00**
246 ❑ Aug 1969 Cover: 0.15 **NM** value: **2.00**
247 ❑ Oct 1969 Cover: 0.15 **NM** value: **2.00**
248 ❑ Dec 1969 Cover: 0.15 **NM** value: **2.00**
249 ❑ Feb 1970 Cover: 0.15 **NM** value: **2.00**
250 ❑ Apr 1970 Cover: 0.15 **NM** value: **2.00**
251 ❑ Jun 1970 Cover: 0.15 **NM** value: **2.00**
252 ❑ Aug 1970 Cover: 0.15 **NM** value: **2.00**
253 ❑ Oct 1970 Cover: 0.15 **NM** value: **2.00**
254 ❑ Dec 1970 Cover: 0.15 **NM** value: **2.00**
255 ❑ Feb 1971 Cover: 0.15 **NM** value: **2.00**
Circ: Statement: **255,132**
256 ❑ Apr 1971 Cover: 0.15 **NM** value: **2.00**

CGC-graded: Multiply prices above by **33 for 9.9 M** • **16 for 9.8 NM/M** • **7 for 9.6 NM+** • **5 for 9.4 NM** • **2.5 for 9.2 NM-** • **1.5 for 9.0 VF/NM**

Circ: Statement: **255,132**
257 ☐ Jun 1971 Cover: 0.15 **NM** value: **2.00**
Circ: Statement: **255,132**
258 ☐ Aug 1971 Cover: 0.15 **NM** value: **2.00**
Circ: Statement: **255,132**
259 ☐ Sep 1971 Cover: 0.15 **NM** value: **2.00**
Circ: Statement: **255,132**
260 ☐ Dec 1971 Cover: 0.15 **NM** value: **2.00**
Circ: Statement: **255,132**
261 ☐ Dec 1971 Cover: 0.15 **NM** value: **2.00**
Circ: Statement: **255,132**
262 ☐ Feb 1972 Cover: 0.15 **NM** value: **2.00**
• Has 1971 Statement, filed 9/30/71; avg print run 375,584; avg sales 253,825; avg subs 1,307; avg total paid 255,132; samples 488; office use 198; max existent 255,818; 32% of run returned
263 ☐ Apr 1972 Cover: 0.15 **NM** value: **2.00**
264 ☐ Jun 1972 Cover: 0.15 **NM** value: **2.00**
265 ☐ Aug 1972 Cover: 0.15 **NM** value: **2.00**
266 ☐ Sep 1972 Cover: 0.15 **NM** value: **2.00**
267 ☐ Oct 1972 Cover: 0.15 **NM** value: **2.00**
268 ☐ Dec 1972 Cover: 0.15 **NM** value: **2.00**
269 ☐ Feb 1973 Cover: 0.15 **NM** value: **2.00**
270 ☐ Apr 1973 Cover: 0.15 **NM** value: **2.00**
271 ☐ Jun 1973 Cover: 0.20 **NM** value: **1.50**
272 ☐ Jul 1973 Cover: 0.20 **NM** value: **1.50**
273 ☐ Aug 1973 Cover: 0.20 **NM** value: **1.50**
📖 The Curious Cat; Unwelcome Guest; Lights, Action, Camera; Tusk! Tusk!
274 ☐ Sep 1973 Cover: 0.20 **NM** value: **1.50**
275 ☐ Oct 1973 Cover: 0.20 **NM** value: **1.50**
276 ☐ Nov 1973 Cover: 0.20 **NM** value: **1.50**
277 ☐ Dec 1973 Cover: 0.20 **NM** value: **1.50**
278 ☐ Jan 1974 Cover: 0.20 **NM** value: **1.50**
279 ☐ Feb 1974 Cover: 0.20 **NM** value: **1.50**
280 ☐ Mar 1974 Cover: 0.20 **NM** value: **1.50**
281 ☐ Apr 1974 Cover: 0.20 **NM** value: **1.50**
282 ☐ May 1974 Cover: 0.20 **NM** value: **1.50**
283 ☐ Jun 1974 Cover: 0.20 **NM** value: **1.50**
284 ☐ Jul 1974 Cover: 0.25 **NM** value: **1.50**
285 ☐ Aug 1974 Cover: 0.25 **NM** value: **1.50**
286 ☐ Sep 1974 Cover: 0.25 **NM** value: **1.50**
287 ☐ Oct 1974 Cover: 0.25 **NM** value: **1.50**
288 ☐ Nov 1974 Cover: 0.25 **NM** value: **1.50**
289 ☐ Dec 1974 Cover: 0.25 **NM** value: **1.50**
290 ☐ Jan 1975 Cover: 0.25 **NM** value: **1.50**
291 ☐ Feb 1975 Cover: 0.25 **NM** value: **1.50**
292 ☐ Mar 1977 Cover: 0.30 **NM** value: **1.50**
293 ☐ Apr 1977 Cover: 0.30 **NM** value: **1.50**
294 ☐ May 1977 Cover: 0.30 **NM** value: **1.50**
295 ☐ Jun 1977 Cover: 0.30 **NM** value: **1.50**
296 ☐ Jul 1977 Cover: 0.30 **NM** value: **1.50**
297 ☐ Aug 1977 Cover: 0.30 **NM** value: **1.50**
298 ☐ Sep 1977 Cover: 0.30 **NM** value: **1.50**
299 ☐ Oct 1977 Cover: 0.30 **NM** value: **1.50**
300 ☐ Nov 1977 Cover: 0.30 **NM** value: **1.50**
301 ☐ Dec 1977 Cover: 0.35 **NM** value: **1.00**
302 ☐ Jan 1978 Cover: 0.35 **NM** value: **1.00**
303 ☐ Feb 1978 Cover: 0.35 **NM** value: **1.00**
304 ☐ Mar 1978 Cover: 0.35 **NM** value: **1.00**
305 ☐ Apr 1978 Cover: 0.35 **NM** value: **1.00**
306 ☐ May 1978 Cover: 0.35 **NM** value: **1.00**
307 ☐ Jun 1978 Cover: 0.35 **NM** value: **1.00**
308 ☐ Jul 1978 Cover: 0.35 **NM** value: **1.00**
309 ☐ Aug 1978 Cover: 0.35 **NM** value: **1.00**
310 ☐ Sep 1978 Cover: 0.35 **NM** value: **1.00**
311 ☐ Oct 1978 Cover: 0.35 **NM** value: **1.00**
312 ☐ Nov 1978 Cover: 0.35 **NM** value: **1.00**
313 ☐ Dec 1978 Cover: 0.35 **NM** value: **1.00**
314 ☐ Jan 1979 Cover: 0.35 **NM** value: **1.00**
315 ☐ Feb 1979 Cover: 0.35 **NM** value: **1.00**
316 ☐ Mar 1979 Cover: 0.35 **NM** value: **1.00**
317 ☐ Apr 1979 Cover: 0.40 **NM** value: **1.00**
318 ☐ May 1979 Cover: 0.40 **NM** value: **1.00**
319 ☐ Jun 1979 Cover: 0.40 **NM** value: **1.00**
320 ☐ Jul 1979 Cover: 0.40 **NM** value: **1.00**
321 ☐ Aug 1979 Cover: 0.40 **NM** value: **1.00**
322 ☐ Sep 1979 Cover: 0.40 **NM** value: **1.00**
323 ☐ Oct 1979 Cover: 0.40 **NM** value: **1.00**
324 ☐ Nov 1979 Cover: 0.40 **NM** value: **1.00**
325 ☐ Dec 1979 Cover: 0.40 **NM** value: **1.00**
326 ☐ Jan 1980 Cover: 0.40 **NM** value: **1.00**
327 ☐ Feb 1980 Cover: 0.40 **NM** value: **1.00**
328 ☐ Apr 1980 Cover: 0.40 **NM** value: **1.00**
329 ☐ Jun 1980 Cover: 0.40 **NM** value: **1.00**
330 ☐ Aug 1980 Cover: 0.40 **NM** value: **1.00**
331 ☐ Oct 1980 Cover: 0.40 **NM** value: **1.00**
332 ☐ Dec 1980 Cover: 0.40 **NM** value: **1.00**
333 ☐ Feb 1981 Cover: 0.50 **NM** value: **1.00**
334 ☐ Apr 1981 Cover: 0.50 **NM** value: **1.00**
335 ☐ ca. 1981 Cover: 0.50 **NM** value: **1.00**
336 ☐ ca. 1981 Cover: 0.50 **NM** value: **1.00**
337 ☐ ca. 1981 Cover: 0.50 **NM** value: **1.00**
338 ☐ ca. 1982 Cover: 0.50 **NM** value: **1.00**
339 ☐ ca. 1982 Cover: 0.50 **NM** value: **1.00**
340 ☐ ca. 1982 Cover: 0.60 **NM** value: **1.00**
341 ☐ ca. 1982 Cover: 0.60 **NM** value: **1.00**
342 ☐ ca. 1982 Cover: 0.60 **NM** value: **1.00**
343 ☐ ca. 1983 Cover: 0.60 **NM** value: **1.00**
344 ☐ ca. 1983 Cover: 0.60 **NM** value: **1.00**
final issue.

TOM & JERRY DIGEST — Harvey
1 ☐ ca. 1992 Cover: 1.75 **NM** value: **Cover or less**

TOM & JERRY GIANT SIZE — Harvey
1 ☐ Cover: 1.95 **NM** value: **Cover or less**
2 ☐ Cover: 2.25 **NM** value: **Cover or less**

TOM & JERRY PICNIC TIME — Dell
1 ☐ Jul 1958 Cover: 0.25 **NM** value: **150.00**
• **CGC:** 2 graded, best 9.6

TOM & JERRY'S BACK TO SCHOOL — Dell
1 ☐ Sep 1956 Cover: 0.25 **NM** value: **200.00**
• **CGC:** 2 graded, best 8.0

TOM & JERRY'S TOY FAIR — Dell
1 ☐ Jun 1958 Cover: 0.25 **NM** value: **150.00**
• **CGC:** 3 graded, best 9.6

TOM & JERRY SUMMER FUN — Gold Key
1 ☐ Oct 1967 Cover: 0.25 **NM** value: **35.00**
• Droopy reprinted from Tom and Jerry Summer Fun (Dell) #1

TOM & JERRY SUMMER FUN (DELL) — Dell
1 ☐ Jul 1954 Cover: 0.25 **NM** value: **250.00**
• **CGC:** 1 graded, best 9.6
• Droopy
2 ☐ Jul 1955 Cover: 0.25 **NM** value: **125.00**
• **CGC:** 1 graded, best 9.0
3 ☐ Jul 1956 Cover: 0.25 **NM** value: **125.00**
• **CGC:** 2 graded, best 9.2
4 ☐ Jul 1957 Cover: 0.25 **NM** value: **125.00**
• **CGC:** 2 graded, best 9.4

TOM & JERRY'S WINTER FUN — Dell
3 ☐ Dec 1954 Cover: 0.25 **NM** value: **100.00**
• **CGC:** 1 graded, best 7.0
4 ☐ Dec 1955 Cover: 0.25 **NM** value: **75.00**
• **CGC:** 2 graded, best 9.4
5 ☐ Dec 1956 Cover: 0.25 **NM** value: **75.00**
• **CGC:** 2 graded, best 9.6
6 ☐ Nov 1957 Cover: 0.25 **NM** value: **75.00**
• **CGC:** 1 graded, best 9.4
7 ☐ Nov 1958 Cover: 0.25 **NM** value: **75.00**
• **CGC:** 1 graded, best 9.4

TOM & JERRY (VOL. 2) — Harvey
1 ☐ Sep 1991 Cover: 1.25 **NM** value: **1.50**
Circ: CapCity orders: **5,925**
2 ☐ Nov 1991 Cover: 1.25 **NM** value: **Cover or less**
📖 At the Circus; What a Parrot; The Title Match
3 ☐ Jan 1992 Cover: 1.25 **NM** value: **Cover or less**
4 ☐ Mar 1992 Cover: 1.25 **NM** value: **Cover or less**
5 ☐ Jun 1992 Cover: 1.25 **NM** value: **Cover or less**
6 ☐ Jan 1993 Cover: 1.25 **NM** value: **Cover or less**
📖 The Karate Mouse; The Mixed -Up **A:** Oscar Martin
7 ☐ ca. 1993 Cover: 1.25 **NM** value: **Cover or less**
8 ☐ ca. 1993 Cover: 1.25 **NM** value: **Cover or less**
9 ☐ ca. 1993 Cover: 1.50 **NM** value: **Cover or less**
10 ☐ Dec 1993 Cover: 1.50 **NM** value: **Cover or less**
11 ☐ Jan 1994 Cover: 1.50 **NM** value: **Cover or less**
12 ☐ Feb 1994 Cover: 1.50 **NM** value: **Cover or less**
13 ☐ Mar 1994 Cover: 1.50 **NM** value: **Cover or less**
14 ☐ Apr 1994 Cover: 1.50 **NM** value: **Cover or less**
15 ☐ May 1994 Cover: 1.50 **NM** value: **Cover or less**
16 ☐ Jun 1994 Cover: 1.50 **NM** value: **Cover or less**
17 ☐ Jul 1994 Cover: 1.50 **NM** value: **Cover or less**
18 ☐ Aug 1994 Cover: 1.50 **NM** value: **Cover or less**
Anl 1 ☐ Sep 1994 Cover: 2.25 **NM** value: **Cover or less**

TOM & JERRY WINTER CARNIVAL — Dell
1 ☐ Dec 1952 Cover: 0.25 **NM** value: **350.00**
• **CGC:** 1 graded, best 9.2
• Droopy
2 ☐ Dec 1953 Cover: 0.25 **NM** value: **250.00**
• **CGC:** 2 graded, best 9.6
• Droopy

TOMATO — Starhead
All issues are adults only.
1 ☐ Apr 1994, b&w Cover: 2.75 **NM** value: **Cover or less**
📖 My Date with Camille Paglia **A:** Ellen Forney **W:** Ellen Forney
2 ☐ Feb 1995, b&w Cover: 2.75 **NM** value: **Cover or less**

TOMB OF DARKNESS — Marvel
9 ☐ Jul 1974 Cover: 0.25 **NM** value: **4.00**
• Series continued from Beware #8
10 ☐ Sep 1974 Cover: 0.25 **NM** value: **4.00**
• **CGC:** 1 graded, best 9.0
11 ☐ Nov 1974 Cover: 0.25 **NM** value: **4.00**
12 ☐ Jan 1975 Cover: 0.25 **NM** value: **4.00**
13 ☐ Mar 1975 Cover: 0.25 **NM** value: **4.00**
14 ☐ May 1975 Cover: 0.25 **NM** value: **4.00**
15 ☐ Jul 1975 Cover: 0.25 **NM** value: **4.00**
• **CGC:** 1 graded, best 9.4
16 ☐ Sep 1975 Cover: 0.25 **NM** value: **4.00**
📖 Back From The Dead!; The Last Of Mr. Mordeaux; We Can't All Be Human!;
17 ☐ Nov 1975 Cover: 0.25 **NM** value: **4.00**
18 ☐ Jan 1976 Cover: 0.25 **NM** value: **4.00**
• **CGC:** 1 graded, best 9.4
19 ☐ Mar 1976 Cover: 0.25 **NM** value: **4.00**
• **CGC:** 1 graded, best 9.4
20 ☐ May 1976 Cover: 0.25 **NM** value: **4.00**
21 ☐ Jul 1976 Cover: 0.25 **NM** value: **4.00**
• **CGC:** 1 graded, best 9.4
📖 The Day Before Doomsday!; Five Fingers; You Can't Kill Me!
22 ☐ Sep 1976 Cover: 0.25 **NM** value: **4.00**
23 ☐ Nov 1976 Cover: 0.25 **NM** value: **4.00**
final issue.

TOMB OF DRACULA — Marvel
Vlad Dracula, who had been bloodthirsty in life, became more so in death. Born as a prince of Wallachia, he grew into a fierce warrior given to impaling his enemies on stakes. This cruel practice earned him the name "Vlad the Impaler." Eventually Dracula's army was defeated and he was mortally wounded. He was taken to a gypsy woman to be healed, but little did anyone know that, in reality, the woman was a vampire. Three days after his lifeless body was buried, Dracula rose again as a vampire.

Tomb of Dracula was a remarkable horror series which enjoyed a long and well-deserved run. Written by Marv Wolfman and featuring the distinctive art of Gene Colan, it was a great example of a horror comic book done right. The plots were dark but not obsessive, and the characters were well-developed. Ultimately, it was hard to know whether to cheer for Dracula's assailants or to hope he would triumph again to bring horror to next month's issue.

1 ☐ Apr 1972 Cover: 0.20 **NM** value: **40.00**
• **CGC:** 77 graded, best 9.6
📖 Dracula • Dracula revived **A:** Gene Colan **W:** Gerry Conway ★ Origin of Frank Drake. ★ 1st Appearance of Frank Drake, Dracula (Marvel).
2 ☐ May 1972 Cover: 0.20 **NM** value: **18.00**
• **CGC:** 10 graded, best 9.6
A: Gene Colan
3 ☐ Jul 1972 Cover: 0.20 **NM** value: **14.00**
• **CGC:** 8 graded, best 9.6
📖 Who Stalks The Vampire? **A:** Gene Colan **W:** Archie Goodwin ★ 1st Appearance of Rachel Van Helsing.
4 ☐ Sep 1972 Cover: 0.20 **NM** value: **14.00**
• **CGC:** 5 graded, best 9.6
📖 Through A Mirror Darkly! **A:** Gene Colan **W:** Archie Goodwin
5 ☐ Nov 1972 Cover: 0.20 **NM** value: **14.00**
• **CGC:** 4 graded, best 9.6
📖 Death To A Vampire Slayer! **A:** Gene Colan **W:** Gardner Fox
6 ☐ Jan 1973 Cover: 0.20 **NM** value: **10.00**
• **CGC:** 3 graded, best 9.8
A: Gene Colan
7 ☐ Mar 1973 Cover: 0.20 **NM** value: **10.00**
• **CGC:** 2 graded, best 9.6
A: Gene Colan ★ 1st Appearance of Edith Harker.
8 ☐ May 1973 Cover: 0.20 **NM** value: **10.00**
• **CGC:** 1 graded, best 9.6
A: Gene Colan
9 ☐ Jun 1973 Cover: 0.20 **NM** value: **10.00**
• **CGC:** 2 graded, best 9.6
📖 Death From The Sea! **A:** Gene Colan **W:** Marv Wolfman ★ 1st Appearance of Lucas Brand.
10 ☐ Jul 1973 Cover: 0.20 **NM** value: **40.00**
• **CGC:** 25 graded, best 9.6
A: Gene Colan ★ 1st Appearance of Blade the Vampire Slayer.
11 ☐ Aug 1973 Cover: 0.20 **NM** value: **8.00**
📖 The Voodoo-Man **A:** Gene Colan **W:** Marv Wolfman
12 ☐ Sep 1973 Cover: 0.20 **NM** value: **10.00**
• **CGC:** 1 graded, best 9.8
📖 Night Of The Screaming House! **A:** Gene Colan **W:** Marv Wolfman ★ Appearance of Blade, Blade the Vampire Slayer.
13 ☐ Oct 1973 Cover: 0.20 **NM** value: **20.00**
• **CGC:** 2 graded, best 9.4
📖 To Kill A Vampire **A:** Gene Colan **W:** Marv Wolfman ★ Origin of Blade the Vampire Slayer. ★ 1st Appearance of Deacon Frost.
14 ☐ Nov 1973 Cover: 0.20 **NM** value: **10.00**
📖 Dracula Is Dead! **A:** Gene Colan **W:** Marv Wolfman ★ Appearance of Blade the Vampire Slayer.
15 ☐ Dec 1973 Cover: 0.20 **NM** value: **8.00**
• **CGC:** 2 graded, best 9.4
📖 Fear Is The Name Of The Game! **A:** Gene Colan **W:** Marv Wolfman
16 ☐ Jan 1974 Cover: 0.20 **NM** value: **8.00**
• **CGC:** 1 graded, best 9.2
📖 Return From The Grave! **A:** Gene Colan **W:** Marv Wolfman
17 ☐ Feb 1974 Cover: 0.20 **NM** value: **10.00**
• **CGC:** 1 graded, best 9.4
📖 Death Rides The Rails! **A:** Gene Colan **W:** Marv Wolfman ★ Appearance of Blade the Vampire Slayer.
18 ☐ Mar 1974 Cover: 0.20 **NM** value: **8.00**
• **CGC:** 2 graded, best 9.4
📖 Enter: Werewolf By Night **A:** Gene Colan **W:** Marv Wolfman ★ Versus Werewolf by Night.
19 ☐ Apr 1974 Cover: 0.20 **NM** value: **10.00**
• **CGC:** 2 graded, best 9.8
📖 Snowbound In Hell! **A:** Gene Colan **W:** Marv Wolfman ★ Appearance of Blade the Vampire Slayer.
20 ☐ May 1974 Cover: 0.25 **NM** value: **8.00**
• **CGC:** 1 graded, best 9.6
📖 The Coming Of Doctor Sun **A:** Gene Colan **W:** Marv Wolfman ★ 1st Appearance of Doctor Sun.
21 ☐ Jun 1974 Cover: 0.25 **NM** value: **8.00**
📖 Deathknell **A:** Gene Colan **W:** Marv Wolfman ★ Origin of Doctor Sun. ★ Appearance of Blade the Vampire Slayer.
22 ☐ Jul 1974 Cover: 0.25 **NM** value: **7.00**
📖 ...In Death Do We Join **A:** Gene Colan **W:** Marv Wolfman
23 ☐ Aug 1974 Cover: 0.25 **NM** value: **7.00**
📖 Shadows In The Night **A:** Gene Colan **W:** Marv Wolfman
24 ☐ Sep 1974 Cover: 0.25 **NM** value: **7.00**
📖 A Night For The Living...A Morning For The Dead **A:** Gene Colan **W:** Marv Wolfman
25 ☐ Oct 1974 Cover: 0.25 **NM** value: **7.00**
📖 Night of the Blood Stalker **A:** Gene Colan **W:** Marv Wolfman ★ Origin of Hannibal King. ★ 1st Appearance of Hannibal King.

Other grades: Multiply prices above by **1.5 for Mint • 2/3 for Very Fine • 1/3 for Fine • 1/5 for Very Good • 1/8 for Good**

25-2❑ **NM** value: **1.50**
26 ❑ Nov 1974 Cover: 0.25 **NM** value: **7.00**
Where Lurks The Chimera! **A:** Gene Colan **W:** Marv Wolfman
27 ❑ Dec 1974 Cover: 0.25 **NM** value: **7.00**
Night-Fire! **A:** Gene Colan; Tom Palmer **W:** Marv Wolfman
28 ❑ Jan 1975 Cover: 0.25 **NM** value: **7.00**
• **CGC:** 1 graded, best 9.0
Madness In the Mind! **A:** Gene Colan; Tom Palmer **W:** Marv Wolfman ★ 1st Appearance of Adri Nitall.
29 ❑ Feb 1975 Cover: 0.25 **NM** value: **7.00**
Vengeance Is Mine! Sayeth The Vampire **A:** Gene Colan; Tom Palmer **W:** Marv Wolfman
30 ❑ Mar 1975 Cover: 0.25 **NM** value: **8.00**
A: Gene Colan ★ Appearance of Blade the Vampire Slayer.
31 ❑ Apr 1975 Cover: 0.25 **NM** value: **6.00**
• **CGC:** 2 graded, best 9.6
Ten Lords A Dying! **A:** Gene Colan; Tom Palmer **W:** Marv Wolfman
32 ❑ May 1975 Cover: 0.25 **NM** value: **6.00**
A: Gene Colan
33 ❑ Jun 1975 Cover: 0.25 **NM** value: **6.00**
Blood On My Hands! **A:** Gene Colan; Tom Palmer **W:** Marv Wolfman
34 ❑ Jul 1975 Cover: 0.25 **NM** value: **6.00**
Showdown Of Blood! **A:** Gene Colan; Tom Palmer **W:** Marv Wolfman ★ Appearance of Brother Voodoo.
35 ❑ Aug 1975 Cover: 0.25 **NM** value: **6.00**
Hell Hath No Fury **A:** Gene Colan; Tom Palmer **W:** Marv Wolfman ★ Appearance of Brother Voodoo.
36 ❑ Sep 1975 Cover: 0.25 **NM** value: **6.00**
A: Gene Colan ★ Appearance of Brother Voodoo.
37 ❑ Oct 1975 Cover: 0.25 **NM** value: **6.00**
The Vampire Is Coming! **A:** Gene Colan; Tom Palmer **W:** Marv Wolfman ★ 1st Appearance of Harold H. Harold.
38 ❑ Nov 1975 Cover: 0.25 **NM** value: **6.00**
Blood-Rush! **A:** Gene Colan; Tom Palmer **W:** Marv Wolfman ★ Appearance of Doctor Sun.
39 ❑ Dec 1975 Cover: 0.25 **NM** value: **6.00**
The Death Of Dracula **A:** Gene Colan; Tom Palmer **W:** Marv Wolfman ★ Death of Dracula.
40 ❑ Jan 1976 Cover: 0.25 **NM** value: **6.00**
Nightmares Of A Living Deadman! **A:** Gene Colan; Tom Palmer **W:** Marv Wolfman
41 ❑ Feb 1976 Cover: 0.25 **NM** value: **6.00**
A: Gene Colan ★ Appearance of Blade the Vampire Slayer.
42 ❑ Mar 1976 Cover: 0.25 **NM** value: **5.00**
A: Gene Colan ★ Appearance of Blade the Vampire Slayer. ★ Versus Doctor Sun.
43 ❑ Apr 1976 Cover: 0.25 **NM** value: **5.00**
A: Gene Colan
44 ❑ May 1976 Cover: 0.25 **NM** value: **5.00**
A: Gene Colan ★ Appearance of Hannibal King, Blade the Vampire Slayer. ★ Versus Doctor Strange.
45 ❑ Jun 1976 Cover: 0.25 **NM** value: **5.00**
• Blade vs. Hannibal King **A:** Gene Colan ★ Appearance of Hannibal King.
46 ❑ Jul 1976 Cover: 0.25 **NM** value: **5.00**
• Wedding of Dracula **A:** Gene Colan ★ Appearance of Blade, Blade the Vampire Slayer.
47 ❑ Aug 1976 Cover: 0.25 **NM** value: **5.00**
A: Gene Colan ★ Appearance of Blade the Vampire Slayer.
48 ❑ Sep 1976 Cover: 0.30 **NM** value: **5.00**
A: Gene Colan ★ Appearance of Hannibal King, Blade the Vampire Slayer.
49 ❑ Oct 1976 Cover: 0.30 **NM** value: **5.00**
• **CGC:** 1 graded, best 9.6
A: Gene Colan ★ Appearance of Zorro, Tom Sawyer, D'Artagnan, Frankenstein, Blade, Blade the Vampire Slayer.
50 ❑ Nov 1976 Cover: 0.30 **NM** value: **8.00**
• **CGC:** 3 graded, best 9.4
A: Gene Colan ★ Appearance of Blade the Vampire Slayer, Silver Surfer.
51 ❑ Dec 1976 Cover: 0.30 **NM** value: **5.00**
The Wildest Party • Blade vs. Hannibal King **A:** Gene Colan; Tom Palmer **W:** Marv Wolfman ★ 1st Appearance of Janus.
52 ❑ Jan 1977 Cover: 0.30 **NM** value: **5.00**
A: Gene Colan
53 ❑ Feb 1977 Cover: 0.30 **NM** value: **5.00**
• Blade vs. Hannibal King and Deacon Frost **A:** Gene Colan ★ Appearance of Son of Satan.
54 ❑ Mar 1977 Cover: 0.30 **NM** value: **5.00**
'Twas The Night Before Christmas • birth of Dracula's son **A:** Gene Colan; Tom Palmer **W:** Marv Wolfman ★ Origin of Janus. ★ Appearance of Blade.
55 ❑ Apr 1977 Cover: 0.30 **NM** value: **5.00**
A: Gene Colan
56 ❑ May 1977 Cover: 0.30 **NM** value: **5.00**
A: Gene Colan
57 ❑ Jun 1977 Cover: 0.30 **NM** value: **5.00**
The Forever Man **A:** Gene Colan; Tom Palmer **W:** Marv Wolfman
58 ❑ Jul 1977 Cover: 0.30 **NM** value: **5.00**
• **CGC:** 2 graded, best 9.4
A: Gene Colan
59 ❑ Aug 1977 Cover: 0.30 **NM** value: **5.00**
A: Gene Colan
60 ❑ Sep 1977 Cover: 0.30 **NM** value: **5.00**
• **CGC:** 1 graded, best 9.6
The Wrath Of Dracula! **A:** Gene Colan; Tom Palmer **W:** Marv Wolfman
61 ❑ Nov 1977 Cover: 0.35 **NM** value: **4.00**
A: Gene Colan ★ Origin of Janus.
62 ❑ Jan 1978 Cover: 0.35 **NM** value: **4.00**
• **CGC:** 1 graded, best 9.6
A: Gene Colan
63 ❑ Mar 1978 Cover: 0.35 **NM** value: **4.00**
A: Gene Colan
64 ❑ May 1978 Cover: 0.35 **NM** value: **4.00**
Life After Undeath **A:** Gene Colan; Tom Palmer **W:** Marv Wolfman
65 ❑ Jul 1978 Cover: 0.35 **NM** value: **4.00**
Where No Vampire Has Gone Before! **A:** Gene Colan; Tom Palmer **W:** Marv Wolfman
66 ❑ Sep 1978 Cover: 0.35 **NM** value: **4.00**
Showdown Greenwich Village! **A:** Gene Colan; Tom Palmer **W:** Marv Wolfman
67 ❑ Nov 1978 Cover: 0.35 **NM** value: **4.00**
At Long Last Lilith! **A:** Gene Colan; Tom Palmer **W:** Marv Wolfman ★ Appearance of Lilith.
68 ❑ Feb 1979 Cover: 0.35 **NM** value: **4.00**
A: Gene Colan
69 ❑ Apr 1979 Cover: 0.35 **NM** value: **4.00**
Batwings Over Transylvania! **A:** Gene Colan; Tom Palmer **W:** Marv Wolfman
70 ❑ Aug 1979 Cover: 0.60 **NM** value: **6.00**
• **CGC:** 4 graded, best 9.6
• Double-size. ★ Death of Dracula.
GS 2❑ Cover: 0.50 **NM** value: **5.00**
GS 3❑ Cover: 0.50 **NM** value: **5.00**
• Reprints Uncanny Tales #6

TOMB OF DRACULA (LTD. SERIES) Marvel / Epic

1 ❑ Nov 1991 Cover: 4.95 **NM** value: **5.00**
Day Of Blood! Night Of Redemption!, Part 1 **A:** Al Williamson; Gene Colan **W:** Marv Wolfman
2 ❑ Dec 1991 Cover: 4.95 **NM** value: **5.00**
Circ: CapCity orders: **17,400**
Day Of Blood! Night Of Redemption!, Part 2 **A:** Al Williamson; Gene Colan **W:** Marv Wolfman
3 ❑ Jan 1992 Cover: 4.95 **NM** value: **5.00**
Circ: CapCity orders: **11,850**
Day Of Blood! Night Of Redemption!, Part 3 **A:** Al Williamson; Gene Colan **W:** Marv Wolfman
4 ❑ Feb 1992 Cover: 4.95 **NM** value: **5.00**
Circ: CapCity orders: **10,900**
Day Of Blood! Night Of Redemption!, Part 4 **A:** Al Williamson; Gene Colan **W:** Marv Wolfman

TOMB OF DRACULA (MAGAZINE) Marvel

1 ❑ Oct 1979, b&w Cover: 1.25 **NM** value: **4.00**
Circ: CapCity orders: **9,800**
• magazine. Black Genesis; The Newest Dracula; Love at First Bite; Legend: According to The Movies **A:** Gene Colan; Joel Thomas; Tom Rogers **W:** Joel Thomas; Tom Rogers; Marv Wolfman
2 ❑ Dec 1979 Cover: 1.25 **NM** value: **3.00**
A: Steve Ditko
3 ❑ Feb 1980 Cover: 1.25 **NM** value: **3.00**
A: Gene Colan; Frank Miller; Tom Palmer
4 ❑ Apr 1980 Cover: 1.25 **NM** value: **3.00**
A: Gene Colan; Tom Palmer; John Busecma
5 ❑ Jun 1980 Cover: 1.25 **NM** value: **3.00**
A: Gene Colan; John Buscema; Tom Palmer
6 ❑ Aug 1980 Cover: 1.25 **NM** value: **3.00**
A House Divided; Violets for a Vampire; Vampires 'Round the World; Chelsea Quinn Yarbro An Alternate Reality; In a Literary Vein; Shadow Shows **A:** Gene Colan; Marie Severin; Dave Simons **W:** Ralph Macchio; Jim Shooter; Tom Rogers; Gil Fitzgerald; Lora Byrne; Lynn Graeme

TOMB OF LIGEIA Dell

1 ❑ Jun 1965 Cover: 0.12 **NM** value: **12.00**
• Adapts movie Tomb of the Cat

TOMB OF TERROR Harvey

1 ❑ Jun 1952 Cover: 0.10 **NM** value: **300.00**
• **CGC:** 2 graded, best 5.5
2 ❑ Jul 1952 Cover: 0.10 **NM** value: **175.00**
• **CGC:** 3 graded, best 9.0
3 ❑ Aug 1952 Cover: 0.10 **NM** value: **175.00**
4 ❑ Sep 1952 Cover: 0.10 **NM** value: **150.00**
5 ❑ Oct 1952 Cover: 0.10 **NM** value: **150.00**
• **CGC:** 1 graded, best 9.0
6 ❑ Nov 1952 Cover: 0.10 **NM** value: **150.00**
• **CGC:** 1 graded, best 6.5
7 ❑ Jan 1953 Cover: 0.10 **NM** value: **150.00**
8 ❑ Mar 1953 Cover: 0.10 **NM** value: **150.00**
• **CGC:** 4 graded, best 9.0
9 ❑ May 1953 Cover: 0.10 **NM** value: **150.00**
• **CGC:** 1 graded, best 9.0
10 ❑ Jul 1953 Cover: 0.10 **NM** value: **150.00**
• **CGC:** 2 graded, best 9.2
11 ❑ Sep 1953 Cover: 0.10 **NM** value: **125.00**
12 ❑ Nov 1953 Cover: 0.10 **NM** value: **125.00**
• **CGC:** 5 graded, best 9.0
13 ❑ Jan 1954 Cover: 0.10 **NM** value: **125.00**
• **CGC:** 6 graded, best 9.4
14 ❑ Mar 1954 Cover: 0.10 **NM** value: **125.00**
• **CGC:** 2 graded, best 9.2
15 ❑ May 1954 Cover: 0.10 **NM** value: **125.00**
• **CGC:** 10 graded, best 9.2
16 ❑ Jul 1954 Cover: 0.10 **NM** value: **125.00**
• **CGC:** 5 graded, best 9.0

TOMB RAIDER GALLERY, THE Image

1 ❑ Dec 2000 Cover: 2.95 **NM** value: **Cover or less**
Circ: Diamd. preorders: **20,182**
A: Adam Hughes; Chris Cross; Humberto Ramos; Gary Frank; Jerry Ordway; Mark Pajarillo; Dan Jurgens; Clayton Crain; Randy Green; Andy Park; Marc Silvestri; Keu Cha; Michael Turner; Joe Weems; Jonathan Sibal; Talent Caldwell

TOMB RAIDER: THE SERIES Image

The non-stop action, exotic locales, and supernatural aspects of Indiana Jones coupled with an extremely healthy young woman became a winning combination in the video game Tomb Raider. In this comic-book incarnation, Lara Croft, the star of the video game, is a little more fleshed out (in more ways than one) than in her original state. Her background as the daughter of an English lord and the introduction of her confidant and bodyguard, Hartford Compton, serve to give the character substance and reality beyond the flickering images of a computer monitor.

Written by Superman alumnus Dan Jurgens and pencilled by Andy Park, whose command of the female form was displayed in Vogue and Avengelyne, Croft finds herself escaping from underwater assassins and man-eating sharks as well as the occasional hired killer one naturally expects to encounter as an archeologist.

1/A ❑ Dec 1999 Cover: 2.50 **NM** value: **Cover or less**
Circ: Diamd. preorders: **189,454** • **CGC:** 62 graded, best 9.8
• Lara Croft crouching on rock with setting sun **A:** Andy Park; Andy Park(cover) **W:** Dan Jurgens
1/B ❑ Dec 1999 Cover: 2.50 **NM** value: **Cover or less**
• Lara in tree with temple in background **A:** Andy Park; David Finch(cover); Joe Weems(cover) **W:** Dan Jurgens
1/C ❑ Dec 1999 Cover: 2.50 **NM** value: **Cover or less**
• Lara climbing mountain **A:** Andy Park; Miichael Turner(cover) **W:** Dan Jurgens
1/D ❑ Dec 1999 Cover: 2.50 **NM** value: **Cover or less**
• Lara standing in front of ruins **A:** Andy Park; Andy Park(cover) **W:** Dan Jurgens
1/E ❑ Dec 1999 **NM** value: **7.00**
• **CGC:** 38 graded, best 9.8
Holofoil cover. • Lara on rock, no sun in background **A:** Andy Park **W:** Dan Jurgens
1/F ❑ Dec 1999 **NM** value: **5.00**
• **CGC:** 17 graded, best 9.8
• Another Universe Exclusive; **A:** Andy Park; Marc Silvestri(cover) **W:** Dan Jurgens
1/G ❑ Dec 1999 **NM** value: **3.00**
• **CGC:** 4 graded, best 9.6
• Tower Records exclusive; Gold foil Tomb Raider logo; Lara on rock, no sun in background **A:** Andy Park **W:** Dan Jurgens
1/H ❑ Dec 1999 **NM** value: **5.00**
• **CGC:** 6 graded, best 9.8
• Tower records exclusive w/o gold logo **A:** Andy Park **W:** Dan Jurgens
2 ❑ Jan 2000 Cover: 2.50 **NM** value: **Cover or less**
Circ: Diamd. preorders: **105,620** • **CGC:** 8 graded, best 9.9
A: Andy Park **W:** Dan Jurgens
2/A ❑ Jan 2000 **NM** value: **5.00**
• **CGC:** 15 graded, best 9.8
Santa cover with blue background. • Tower records **A:** Andy Park **W:** Dan Jurgens
2/B ❑ Jan 2000 **NM** value: **6.50**
• **CGC:** 4 graded, best 9.8
Santa cover with yellowish holo-foil background. • Tower Records **A:** Andy Park **W:** Dan Jurgens
3 ❑ Feb 2000 Cover: 2.50 **NM** value: **Cover or less**
Circ: Diamd. preorders: **63,902** • **CGC:** 1 graded, best 9.4
A: Andy Park **W:** Dan Jurgens
3/A ❑ Feb 2000 **NM** value: **7.00**
• Monster Mart Edition. • Lara kneeling on ruins, Monster Mart logo in lower right **A:** Andy Park **W:** Dan Jurgens
3/B ❑ Feb 2000 **NM** value: **6.00**
• **CGC:** 9 graded, best 9.8
• Gold Monster Mart edition. • Lara kneeling on ruins, Monster Mart logo in lower right **A:** Andy Park **W:** Dan Jurgens
4 ❑ Apr 2000 Cover: 2.50 **NM** value: **Cover or less**
Circ: Diamd. preorders: **58,404**
• Lara sitting on troot of tree, man standing, flames behind **A:** Andy Park **W:** Dan Jurgens
4/A ❑ Apr 2000 **NM** value: **4.00**
• **CGC:** 2 graded, best 9.8
• Lara in tree, DF logo at bottom left. **A:** Andy Park **W:** Dan Jurgens
4/B ❑ Apr 2000 **NM** value: **8.00**
Similar cover to 4, with Certificate of Authenticity. **A:** Andy Park **W:** Dan Jurgens
5 ❑ May 2000 Cover: 2.50 **NM** value: **Cover or less**
Circ: Diamd. preorders: **56,395**
• Lara standing, dinosaur skeleton in background **A:** Andy Park **W:** Dan Jurgens
5/A ❑ May 2000 **NM** value: **6.00**
• **CGC:** 2 graded, best 9.8
• Dynamic Forces variant, Tomb Raider logo in upper right, DF logo below, Lara standing on Triceratops skull **A:** Andy Park **W:** Dan Jurgens
6 ❑ Jul 2000 Cover: 2.50 **NM** value: **Cover or less**
Circ: Diamd. preorders: **56,515**
A: Andy Park; Joe Jusko(cover) **W:** Dan Jurgens
7 ❑ Jul 2000 Cover: 2.50 **NM** value: **Cover or less**
Circ: Diamd. preorders: **52,092**
Dead Center, Part 1 **A:** Andy Park; Billy Tan; Hak Kang; Matt Masilla **W:** Dan Jurgens
7/A ❑ Jul 2000 **NM** value: **125.00**
• Museum edition, limited to 25 copies.. **A:** Andy Park; Billy Tan; Hak Kang; Matt Masilla **W:** Dan Jurgens
8 ❑ Oct 2000 Cover: 2.50 **NM** value: **Cover or less**
Circ: Diamd. preorders: **48,402**
Dead Center, Part 2 **A:** Andy Park; Billy Tan; Hak Kang; Matt Masilla **W:** Dan Jurgens

CGC-graded: Multiply prices above by **33 for 9.9 M • 16 for 9.8 NM/M • 7 for 9.6 NM+ • 5 for 9.4 NM • 2.5 for 9.2 NM- • 1.5 for 9.0 VF/NM**

9 ❑ Dec 2000 Cover: 2.50 **NM** value: **Cover or less**
Circ: Diamd. preorders: **51,583**
• Lara sitting, faces in background **A:** Andy Park **W:** Dan Jurgens
9/A ❑ Dec 2000 **NM** value: **4.00**
• **CGC:** 3 graded, best 10.0
• White background, holding two guns **A:** Andy Park **W:** Dan Jurgens
9/B ❑ Dec 2000 **NM** value: **6.00**
• **CGC:** 1 graded, best 9.9
• Lara fighting crocodile, DF logo at top left **A:** Andy Park **W:** Dan Jurgens
9/C ❑ Dec 2000 **NM** value: **6.00**
• **CGC:** 3 graded, best 9.8
• Lara fighting crocodile, blue foil around DF logo at top left **A:** Andy Park **W:** Dan Jurgens
9/D ❑ Dec 2000 **NM** value: **10.00**
• **CGC:** 1 graded, best 9.8
Sketch cover, black and white. **A:** Andy Park **W:** Dan Jurgens
10 ❑ Jan 2001 Cover: 2.50 **NM** value: **Cover or less**
Circ: Diamd. preorders: **43,568**
A: Andy Park **W:** Dan Jurgens
10/A❑ Jan 2001 **NM** value: **10.00**
• Gold foil around Tomb Raider logo, includes Certificate of Authenticity **A:** Andy Park **W:** Dan Jurgens
10/B❑ Jan 2001 **NM** value: **10.00**
• Red foil around Tomb Raider logo, includes Certificate of Authenticity **A:** Andy Park **W:** Dan Jurgens
11 ❑ Mar 2001 Cover: 2.50 **NM** value: **Cover or less**
Circ: Diamd. preorders: **41,845**
A: Billy Tan **W:** Dan Jurgens
12 ❑ Apr 2001 Cover: 2.50 **NM** value: **Cover or less**
Circ: Diamd. preorders: **40,554**
A: Billy Tan **W:** Dan Jurgens
13 ❑ May 2001 Cover: 2.50 **NM** value: **Cover or less**
Circ: Diamd. preorders: **40,744**
A: Andy Park **W:** Dan Jurgens
14 ❑ Jul 2001 Cover: 2.50 **NM** value: **Cover or less**
Circ: Diamd. preorders: **39,795**
15 ❑ Sep 2001 Cover: 2.50 **NM** value: **Cover or less**
Circ: Diamd. preorders: **41,199**
15/A❑ Sep 2001 Cover: 14.99 **NM** value: **Cover or less**
• **CGC:** 1 graded, best 9.8
DFE red foil cover.
Ash 1❑ **NM** value: **5.00**
• Preview edition. **A:** Andy Park **W:** Dan Jurgens
ASH 1/A❑ **NM** value: **5.00**
• Convention edition. • Preview cover, with second outer cover (black & white) with Lara Croft on front, logo with white space on back **A:** Andy Park **W:** Dan Jurgens
Bk 1❑ Cover: 9.95 **NM** value: **Cover or less**
• Saga of the Medusa Mask **A:** Andy Park **W:** Dan Jurgens
Bk 2❑ Cover: 14.95 **NM** value: **Cover or less**
A: Andy Park **W:** Dan Jurgens

TOMB RAIDER/WITCHBLADE — Image

1 ❑ Dec 1997 **NM** value: **6.00**
• **CGC:** 18 graded, best 9.8
Green Cover. **A:** Michael Turner
1/A ❑ Dec 1997 **NM** value: **6.00**
• **CGC:** 6 graded, best 9.6
Brown cover. **A:** Michael Turner
1/B ❑ Dec 1997 **NM** value: **20.00**
A: Michael Turner

TOMB RAIDER/WITCHBLADE REVISITED — Image

1 ❑ Dec 1998 Cover: 2.95 **NM** value: **Cover or less**
Circ: Diamd. preorders: **61,488**
A: Michael Turner **W:** Michael Turner

TOMB TALES — Cryptic Entertainment

1 ❑ b&w cardstock cover. Cover: 3.00 **NM** value: **Cover or less**
2 ❑ Jun 1997, b&w cardstock cover. Cover: 3.00 **NM** value: **Cover or less**

TOM CORBETT — Eternity

1 ❑ ca. 1990, b&w Cover: 2.25 **NM** value: **Cover or less**
2 ❑ ca. 1990, b&w Cover: 2.25 **NM** value: **Cover or less**
3 ❑ ca. 1990, b&w Cover: 2.25 **NM** value: **Cover or less**
4 ❑ ca. 1990, b&w Cover: 2.25 **NM** value: **Cover or less**

TOM CORBETT BOOK TWO — Eternity

1 ❑ ca. 1990, b&w Cover: 2.25 **NM** value: **Cover or less**
2 ❑ ca. 1990, b&w Cover: 2.25 **NM** value: **Cover or less**
3 ❑ ca. 1990, b&w Cover: 2.25 **NM** value: **Cover or less**
4 ❑ ca. 1990, b&w Cover: 2.25 **NM** value: **Cover or less**

TOM CORBETT, SPACE CADET (DELL) — Dell

4 ❑ Jan 1953 Cover: 0.10 **NM** value: **75.00**
5 ❑ Apr 1953 Cover: 0.10 **NM** value: **75.00**
6 ❑ Jul 1953 Cover: 0.10 **NM** value: **75.00**
7 ❑ Oct 1953 Cover: 0.10 **NM** value: **75.00**
8 ❑ Jan 1954 Cover: 0.10 **NM** value: **75.00**
9 ❑ Apr 1954 Cover: 0.10 **NM** value: **75.00**
10 ❑ Jul 1954 Cover: 0.10 **NM** value: **75.00**
11 ❑ Nov 1954 Cover: 0.10 **NM** value: **75.00**

TOM CORBETT, SPACE CADET (PRIZE) — Prize

1 ❑ May 1955 Cover: 0.10 **NM** value: **200.00**
2 ❑ Jul 1955 Cover: 0.10 **NM** value: **150.00**
• **CGC:** 1 graded, best 9.0
3 ❑ Sep 1955 Cover: 0.10 **NM** value: **150.00**
• **CGC:** 1 graded, best 7.5

TOM LANDRY — Spire

1 ❑ ca. 1973 Cover: 0.49 **NM** value: **3.00**
No issue number.

TOMMI GUNN — London Night

1 ❑ May 1996 Cover: 3.00 **NM** value: **Cover or less**
A: Georges Jeanty **W:** Everette Hartsoe

TOMMI GUNN: KILLER'S LUST — London Night

1 ❑ Feb 1997 Cover: 3.00 **NM** value: **Cover or less**
Circ: Diamd. preorders: **5,898** • **CGC:** 1 graded, best 8.5
1/Nude❑ Feb 1997 Cover: 3.00 **NM** value: **Cover or less**
chromium cover.

TOM MIX WESTERN (1ST SERIES) — Fawcett

1 ❑ Jan 1948 Cover: 0.10 **NM** value: **500.00**
• **CGC:** 1 graded, best 4.5
2 ❑ Feb 1948 Cover: 0.10 **NM** value: **300.00**
• **CGC:** 1 graded, best 8.5
3 ❑ Mar 1948 Cover: 0.10 **NM** value: **200.00**
• **CGC:** 2 graded, best 9.0
4 ❑ Apr 1948 Cover: 0.10 **NM** value: **200.00**
5 ❑ May 1948 Cover: 0.10 **NM** value: **200.00**
• **CGC:** 1 graded, best 8.0
6 ❑ Jun 1948 Cover: 0.10 **NM** value: **200.00**
• **CGC:** 2 graded, best 8.0
7 ❑ Jul 1948 Cover: 0.10 **NM** value: **200.00**
• **CGC:** 1 graded, best 9.0
8 ❑ Aug 1948 Cover: 0.10 **NM** value: **200.00**
• **CGC:** 2 graded, best 9.4
9 ❑ Sep 1948 Cover: 0.10 **NM** value: **200.00**
10 ❑ Oct 1948 Cover: 0.10 **NM** value: **200.00**
11 ❑ Nov 1948 Cover: 0.10 **NM** value: **150.00**
• **CGC:** 2 graded, best 8.5
12 ❑ Dec 1948 Cover: 0.10 **NM** value: **150.00**
13 ❑ Jan 1949 Cover: 0.10 **NM** value: **150.00**
14 ❑ Feb 1949 Cover: 0.10 **NM** value: **150.00**
• **CGC:** 1 graded, best 9.0
15 ❑ Mar 1949 Cover: 0.10 **NM** value: **150.00**
• **CGC:** 1 graded, best 9.0
16 ❑ Apr 1949 Cover: 0.10 **NM** value: **150.00**
17 ❑ May 1949 Cover: 0.10 **NM** value: **150.00**
18 ❑ Jun 1949 Cover: 0.10 **NM** value: **150.00**
19 ❑ Jul 1949 Cover: 0.10 **NM** value: **150.00**
• **CGC:** 1 graded, best 9.0
20 ❑ Aug 1949 Cover: 0.10 **NM** value: **150.00**
21 ❑ Sep 1949 Cover: 0.10 **NM** value: **125.00**
22 ❑ Oct 1949 Cover: 0.10 **NM** value: **125.00**
• **CGC:** 1 graded, best 5.5
23 ❑ Nov 1949 Cover: 0.10 **NM** value: **125.00**
24 ❑ Dec 1949 Cover: 0.10 **NM** value: **125.00**
25 ❑ Jan 1950 Cover: 0.10 **NM** value: **125.00**
• **CGC:** 1 graded, best 9.0
26 ❑ Feb 1950 Cover: 0.10 **NM** value: **100.00**
27 ❑ Mar 1950 Cover: 0.10 **NM** value: **100.00**
28 ❑ Apr 1950 Cover: 0.10 **NM** value: **100.00**
29 ❑ May 1950 Cover: 0.10 **NM** value: **100.00**
30 ❑ Jun 1950 Cover: 0.10 **NM** value: **100.00**
31 ❑ Jul 1950 Cover: 0.10 **NM** value: **100.00**
32 ❑ Aug 1950 Cover: 0.10 **NM** value: **100.00**
33 ❑ Sep 1950 Cover: 0.10 **NM** value: **100.00**
34 ❑ Oct 1950 Cover: 0.10 **NM** value: **100.00**
35 ❑ Nov 1950 Cover: 0.10 **NM** value: **100.00**
36 ❑ Dec 1950 Cover: 0.10 **NM** value: **100.00**
37 ❑ Jan 1951 Cover: 0.10 **NM** value: **100.00**
38 ❑ Feb 1951 Cover: 0.10 **NM** value: **100.00**
39 ❑ Mar 1951 Cover: 0.10 **NM** value: **100.00**
40 ❑ Apr 1951 Cover: 0.10 **NM** value: **100.00**
41 ❑ May 1951 Cover: 0.10 **NM** value: **75.00**
42 ❑ Jun 1951 Cover: 0.10 **NM** value: **75.00**
43 ❑ Jul 1951 Cover: 0.10 **NM** value: **75.00**
44 ❑ Aug 1951 Cover: 0.10 **NM** value: **75.00**
45 ❑ Sep 1951 Cover: 0.10 **NM** value: **75.00**
46 ❑ Oct 1951 Cover: 0.10 **NM** value: **75.00**
47 ❑ Nov 1951 Cover: 0.10 **NM** value: **75.00**
48 ❑ Dec 1951 Cover: 0.10 **NM** value: **75.00**
49 ❑ Jan 1952 Cover: 0.10 **NM** value: **75.00**
50 ❑ Feb 1952 Cover: 0.10 **NM** value: **75.00**
51 ❑ Mar 1948 Cover: 0.10 **NM** value: **60.00**
52 ❑ Apr 1948 Cover: 0.10 **NM** value: **60.00**
53 ❑ May 1948 Cover: 0.10 **NM** value: **60.00**
54 ❑ Jun 1948 Cover: 0.10 **NM** value: **60.00**
55 ❑ Jul 1948 Cover: 0.10 **NM** value: **60.00**
56 ❑ Aug 1948 Cover: 0.10 **NM** value: **60.00**
57 ❑ Sep 1952 Cover: 0.10 **NM** value: **60.00**
58 ❑ Oct 1952 Cover: 0.10 **NM** value: **60.00**
59 ❑ Nov 1952 Cover: 0.10 **NM** value: **60.00**
60 ❑ Dec 1952 Cover: 0.10 **NM** value: **60.00**
61 ❑ May 1953 Cover: 0.10 **NM** value: **60.00**

TOM MIX WESTERN — AC

1 ❑ Cover: 2.95 **NM** value: **Cover or less**
Circ: CapCity orders: **1,375**
2 ❑ b&w Cover: 2.50 **NM** value: **Cover or less**

TOMMY AND THE MONSTERS — New Comics

1 ❑ b&w Cover: 1.95 **NM** value: **Cover or less**
Circ: CapCity orders: **2,825**
📖 The Gibbering Thralls **A:** David Williams **C:** Arthur Adams **W:** Will Jacobs; Gerald Jones

TOMMY OF THE BIG TOP — Best

10 ❑ 1948 Cover: 0.10 **NM** value: **30.00**
11 ❑ Dec 1948 Cover: 0.10 **NM** value: **24.00**
12 ❑ Mar 1949 Cover: 0.10 **NM** value: **24.00**
• **CGC:** 1 graded, best 8.5
📖 Opening Night!; Kidnap Crisis!; Phony Fisticuffs; Murder on His Mind **A:** John Lehti

TOMOE — Crusade

The warriors of Nara retained their honor through the centuries and never succumbed to the seductions of politics and power. But today, even the most honorable individuals sometimes have to make compromises. For the sake of vengeance, the Nara ally themselves with the Yakuza, Japan's powerful criminal overlords.

One woman, Tomoe, desires the leadership of the Nara warriors, and her fighting skills are such that none can challenge her. But skill alone is not enough to lead. She learns, with difficulty, that the Nara only follow whomever, and whenever, they choose. Before she can bring the Nara, and their corrupt allies, to victory against their common foes, she must earn their respect.

This mini-series interacts with Crusade's other main character, Shi. Tomoe's story strongly influences events in that series, beginning with Shi: The Way of the Warrior #6.

0 ❑ Mar 1996 Cover: 2.95 **NM** value: **3.00**
A: Amanda Conner **W:** Bill Tucci; Dan Mishkin
0/LE❑ Mar 1996 **NM** value: **4.00**
• Limited edition (5,000 printed). **A:** Amanda Conner **W:** Bill Tucci; Dan Mishkin
0/SC❑ Mar 1996 Cover: 2.95 **NM** value: **3.00**
variant cover. **A:** Amanda Conner **W:** Bill Tucci; Dan Mishkin
1 ❑ Apr 1996 Cover: 2.95 **NM** value: **3.00**
Circ: Diamd. preorders: **20,773**
A: Amanda Conner **W:** Bill Tucci; Dan Mishkin
1/LE❑ Apr 1996 **NM** value: **4.00**
• Limited edition (5,000 printed). **A:** Amanda Conner **W:** Bill Tucci; Dan Mishkin
1-2 ❑ Cover: 2.95 **NM** value: **3.00**
• Fan Appreciation Edition. • contains preview of Manga Shi 2000
2 ❑ May 1996 Cover: 2.95 **NM** value: **3.00**
A: Amanda Conner **W:** Bill Tucci; Dan Mishkin
3 ❑ Jun 1996 Cover: 2.95 **NM** value: **3.00**
A: Amanda Conner **W:** Bill Tucci; Dan Mishkin
Bk 1❑ Cover: 14.95 **NM** value: **Cover or less**
• collects issues #0-3; Collects Tomoe #0-3 **A:** Amanda Conner **W:** Bill Tucci; Dan Mishkin

TOMOE: UNFORGETTABLE FIRE — Crusade

1 ❑ Jun 1997 Cover: 2.95 **NM** value: **Cover or less**
Circ: Diamd. preorders: **22,716**
• prequel to Shi: The Series **A:** J.G. Jones **W:** Tony Bedard
1/LE❑ Jun 1997 **NM** value: **3.50**
no cover price. • American Entertainment Exclusive Edition. • prequel to Shi: The Series

TOMOE/WITCHBLADE: FIRE SERMON — Crusade

1 ❑ Sep 1996 Cover: 3.95 **NM** value: **Cover or less**
📖 Fire Sermon • one-shot crossover with Image **A:** Jamal Igle **W:** Jamal Igle; Peter Gutierrez; Christina Z.; Gary Cohn; Marc Patten
1/A ❑ Sep 1996 Cover: 5.00 **NM** value: **Cover or less**
no cover price. • Avalon edition.

TOMORROW KNIGHTS — Marvel / Epic

1 ❑ Jun 1990 Cover: 1.95 **NM** value: **Cover or less**
Circ: CapCity orders: **10,200**
📖 Working Class Stiffs **A:** Rod Whigham **W:** Roy Richardson
2 ❑ Jul 1990 Cover: 1.50 **NM** value: **Cover or less**
Circ: CapCity orders: **8,300**
3 ❑ Sep 1990 Cover: 1.50 **NM** value: **Cover or less**
Circ: CapCity orders: **7,200**
4 ❑ Nov 1990 Cover: 1.50 **NM** value: **Cover or less**
Circ: CapCity orders: **5,900**
5 ❑ Jan 1991 Cover: 1.50 **NM** value: **Cover or less**
Circ: CapCity orders: **4,700**
6 ❑ Mar 1991 Cover: 1.50 **NM** value: **Cover or less**
Circ: CapCity orders: **3,900**

TOMORROW MAN — Antarctic

1 ❑ Aug 1993, b&w foil cover. Cover: 2.95 **NM** value: **Cover or less**

TOMORROW MAN & KNIGHT HUNTER: LAST RITES — Antarctic

1 ❑ Jul 1994, b&w Cover: 2.75 **NM** value: **Cover or less**
2 ❑ Oct 1994, b&w Cover: 2.75 **NM** value: **Cover or less**
3 ❑ Dec 1994, b&w Cover: 2.75 **NM** value: **Cover or less**
4 ❑ Feb 1995, b&w Cover: 2.75 **NM** value: **Cover or less**
📖 Resurrection **A:** Bobee Padilla **W:** Bobee Padilla
5 ❑ Apr 1995, b&w Cover: 2.75 **NM** value: **Cover or less**
A: Bobee Padilla **W:** Bobee Padilla
6 ❑ Jun 1995, b&w Cover: 2.75 **NM** value: **Cover or less**
📖 Vendetta **A:** Bobee Padilla **W:** Bobee Padilla

Capital City orders are the actual sales of comic books by Capital City Distribution, once one of the largest U.S. sellers of comics to comics shops. Capital City's share of comics shop sales, while not known exactly, increases from around 10-20% in the mid-1980s to 30-35% in the mid-1990s. Capital City's share of comic books sold on newsstands (most Marvels and DCs) will be less.

Other grades: Multiply prices above by **1.5 for Mint • 2/3 for Very Fine • 1/3 for Fine • 1/5 for Very Good • 1/8 for Good**

TOMORROW STORIES
DC / America's Best Comics

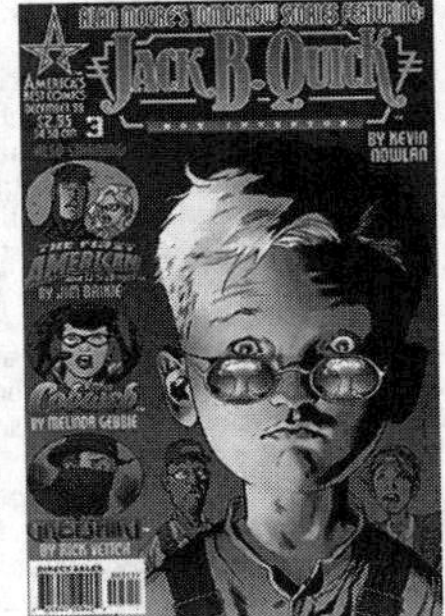

Showcasing the stories of Alan Moore, Tomorrow Stories carries the tongue-in-cheek adventures of First American (and his sidekick U.S.Angel), well-dressed hero Greyshirt, boy inventor Jack B. Quick, and female heroine Cobweb, among others.

With such a varied mix, there's always something to everyone's liking in every issue, even with frequent delays in publication.

Moore's satirical look at superheroes, crimestoppers, and brainy kids is a fine addition to any collection.

1 ❑ Oct 1999 Cover: 3.50 **NM** value: **4.00**
Circ: Diamd. preorders: **43,919 • CGC:** 2 graded, best 9.6
📖 Smalltown Stardom, Amnesia, The First American and U.S.Angel, The Cobweb **A:** Rick Veitch; Kevin Nowlan; Jim Baikie; Melinda Gebbie **W:** Alan Moore

2 ❑ Nov 1999 Cover: 2.95 **NM** value: **3.00**
Circ: Diamd. preorders: **33,988 • CGC:** 1 graded, best 9.4
📖 How Things Work Out; Jack B. Quick: The Unbearableness of Being Light; The Cobweb: Waltztime; The First American and U.S.Angel: The Curse of the Reverse! **A:** Rick Veitch; Jim Baikie; Kevin Nolan; Melinda Gebbie **W:** Alan Moore

3 ❑ Dec 1999 Cover: 2.95 **NM** value: **Cover or less**
Circ: Diamd. preorders: **32,166 • CGC:** 1 graded, best 9.6
📖 Jack B. Quick: Pet Theory; The Cobweb; The First American and U.S.Angel: The Peril of the Pediatric Perpetrators; The Making of Greyshirt **A:** Rick Veitch; Kevin Nowlan; Jim Baikie; Melinda Gibbons **W:** Alan Moore

4 ❑ Jan 2000 Cover: 2.95 **NM** value: **Cover or less**
Circ: Diamd. preorders: **28,533 • CGC:** 1 graded, best 9.6
📖 The First American and U.S.Angel: the bitter Crumbs of Defeat!?!; Li'l Cobweb; Tempus Fugitive!; Jack B. Quick: A Brief Geography of Time **A:** Rick Veitch; Kevin Nowlan; Jim Baikie; Melinda Gebbie **W:** Alan Moore

5 ❑ Feb 2000 Cover: 2.95 **NM** value: **Cover or less**
Circ: Diamd. preorders: **30,016**

6 ❑ Apr 2000 Cover: 2.95 **NM** value: **Cover or less**
Circ: Diamd. preorders: **25,117**

7 ❑ Jun 2000 Cover: 2.95 **NM** value: **Cover or less**
Circ: Diamd. preorders: **22,396**
📖 A Bigger Splash!; Grooveweb; The First American: The 20th Century: My Struggle **A:** Rick Veitch; Jim Baikie; Hilary Barta; Melinda Gebbie **W:** Alan Moore

8 ❑ Jan 2001 Cover: 2.95 **NM** value: **Cover or less**
Circ: Diamd. preorders: **19,274**
📖 Justice in Tights!; Cobweb; Thinx **A:** Jim Baikie **W:** Rick Veitch; Alan Moore; Mel Gebbie

9 ❑ Feb 2001 Cover: 2.95 **NM** value: **Cover or less**
Circ: Diamd. preorders: **19,121**
📖 Farewell, My Lullabye; The Origin of The First American; Greyshirt the Musical; Splash Brannigan: Splash of Two Worlds **A:** Rick Veitch; Jim Baikie; Hilary Barta; Dame Darcy **W:** Alan Moore ★ Origin of The First American.

10 ❑ Apr 2001 Cover: 2.95 **NM** value: **Cover or less**
Circ: Diamd. preorders: **18,299**

11 ❑ Jul 2001 Cover: 2.95 **NM** value: **Cover or less**
Circ: Diamd. preorders: **17,406**

12 ❑ Dec 2001 Cover: 2.95 **NM** value: **Cover or less**
Circ: Diamd. preorders: **17,117**

TOM STRONG
DC / America's Best Comics

Tom Strong was born in 1899 on the secluded island of Attabar Teru. His father, a brilliant, eccentric inventor, had sought out this island for its isolation. There, Tom was reared in a pressure chamber that simulated five gravities. His parents wore pressure suits when they brought him his meals, which consisted primarily of Goloka root, noted for promoting longevity and cognitive awareness. He was essentially another of his father's experiments.

The earthquake that killed his parents when he was nine released him from the chamber. Using his mental acumen, Tom mirrored his father's affinity for innovation. His superb physical conditioning served him well when he left Attabar Teru to become a super-hero in Millennium City. Considering his bizarre childhood, he seems surprisingly well-adjusted, if somewhat slow in matters of affection.

He eventually marries Dhalua, the daughter of the native chief.

Strong's intellectual expertise and superb physique conveys a "Doc Savage" quality, which is bolstered by his feuding partners, a robot named Pnueman and King Solomon, an educated ape. But however uncomplicated the storyline may seem, writer Alan Moore's reputation for multi-layered stories should not be discounted.

1 ❑ Jun 1999 Cover: 2.95 **NM** value: **4.00**
Circ: Diamd. preorders: **57,549 • CGC:** 7 graded, best 9.9
📖 How Tom Strong Got Started **A:** Chris Sprouse **W:** Alan Moore ★ Origin of Tom Strong.

2 ❑ Jul 1999 Cover: 2.95 **NM** value: **3.00**
Circ: Diamd. preorders: **43,056 • CGC:** 1 graded, best 9.6
📖 Return of the Modular Man **A:** Chris Sprouse **W:** Alan Moore

3 ❑ Aug 1999 Cover: 2.95 **NM** value: **Cover or less**
Circ: Diamd. preorders: **44,138 • CGC:** 1 graded, best 9.8
📖 Aztech Nights **A:** Chris Sprouse **W:** Alan Moore

4 ❑ Oct 1999 Cover: 2.95 **NM** value: **Cover or less**
Circ: Diamd. preorders: **42,347 • CGC:** 1 graded, best 9.6
📖 Swastika Girls! **A:** Chris Sprouse **W:** Alan Moore

5 ❑ Dec 1999 Cover: 2.95 **NM** value: **Cover or less**
Circ: Diamd. preorders: **40,048**
📖 Memories of Pangaea **A:** Chris Sprouse **W:** Chris Sprouse; Alan Moore

6 ❑ Jan 2000 Cover: 2.95 **NM** value: **Cover or less**
Circ: Diamd. preorders: **38,862**
A: Chris Sprouse **W:** Alan Moore

7 ❑ Mar 2000 Cover: 2.95 **NM** value: **Cover or less**
Circ: Diamd. preorders: **35,206**
📖 Sons and Heirs **A:** Chris Sprouse; Gary Frank **W:** Alan Moore

8 ❑ May 2000 Cover: 2.95 **NM** value: **Cover or less**
Circ: Diamd. preorders: **34,122**
W: Alan Moore

9 ❑ Sep 2000 Cover: 2.95 **NM** value: **Cover or less**
Circ: Diamd. preorders: **33,381**
📖 Terror Temple of Tayasal! **A:** Paul Chadwick **W:** Alan Moore

10 ❑ Nov 2000 Cover: 2.95 **NM** value: **Cover or less**
Circ: Diamd. preorders: **31,187**
📖 Tom Strong and his Phantom Autogyro; Funnyland! **A:** Chris Sprouse; Gary Gianni **W:** Alan Moore

11 ❑ Jan 2001 Cover: 2.95 **NM** value: **Cover or less**
Circ: Diamd. preorders: **30,420**
📖 Strange Reunion **A:** Chris Sprouse **W:** Alan Moore

TOM TERRIFIC
Pines

1 ❑ Sum 1957 Cover: 0.10 **NM** value: **150.00**
2 ❑ Fal 1957 Cover: 0.10 **NM** value: **125.00**
3 ❑ Win 1958 Cover: 0.10 **NM** value: **125.00**
4 ❑ Spr 1958 Cover: 0.10 **NM** value: **100.00**
5 ❑ Sum 1958 Cover: 0.10 **NM** value: **100.00**
6 ❑ Fal 1958 Cover: 0.10 **NM** value: **100.00**

TONGUE*LASH
Dark Horse

1 ❑ Aug 1996 Cover: 2.95 **NM** value: **Cover or less**
📖 The Serpent's Tooth, Part 1 **A:** David Taylor **W:** R.J.M. Lofficier

2 ❑ Sep 1996 Cover: 2.95 **NM** value: **Cover or less**
Circ: Diamd. preorders: **13,318**
📖 The Serpent's Tooth, Part 2 **A:** David Taylor **W:** R.J.M. Lofficier

TONGUE*LASH II
Dark Horse

1 ❑ Feb 1999 Cover: 2.95 **NM** value: **Cover or less**
Circ: Diamd. preorders: **7,844**
A: David Taylor **W:** R.J.M. Lofficier

2 ❑ Mar 1999 Cover: 2.95 **NM** value: **Cover or less**
Circ: Diamd. preorders: **6,981**
A: David Taylor **W:** R.J.M. Lofficier

TONY BRAVADO, TROUBLE-SHOOTER
Renegade

1 ❑ b&w Cover: 2.00 **NM** value: **Cover or less**
2 ❑ b&w Cover: 2.00 **NM** value: **Cover or less**
3 ❑ b&w Cover: 2.50 **NM** value: **Cover or less**
4 ❑ b&w Cover: 2.50 **NM** value: **Cover or less**

TOOL & DIE
Flashpoint

1 ❑ Mar 1994 Cover: 2.50 **NM** value: **Cover or less**

TOO MUCH COFFEE MAN
Adhesive

A cult favorite, Too Much Coffee Man appeals to everyone who can get through the day only with the aid of heavy doses of hot, steaming, caffeine-in-a-cup. Too Much Coffee Man (TMCM to his fans) is a sort of heroic Everyman with a coffee habit and a huge cup of coffee for a hat. He can't leap tall buildings, run faster than a speeding bullet, or, for that matter, do any of the standard super-things. Still, he is ready to fly to Mars on a minute's notice, if the need arises: a positive mental attitude attributable to the power of caffeine.

Now if only he could shake that edgy, paranoid feeling.

Shannon Wheeler published the early adventures of TMCM in a series of mini-comics. Although scarcely four inches tall with only eight story pages, they packed a surprising amount of fun into their shrunken size. The series won the 1995 Eisner for Best New Series.

1 ❑ ca. 1993, b&w Cover: 2.50 **NM** value: **12.00**
📖 Too Much Coffee Man vs. Trademark Copyright Man **A:** Shannon Wheeler **W:** Shannon Wheeler

2 ❑ b&w Cover: 2.50 **NM** value: **8.00**
📖 ClichT **A:** Shannon Wheeler **W:** Shannon Wheeler

3 ❑ b&w Cover: 2.50 **NM** value: **6.00**
A: Shannon Wheeler **W:** Shannon Wheeler

4 ❑ b&w Cover: 2.50 **NM** value: **5.00**
Circ: CapCity orders: **2,710**
A: Shannon Wheeler **W:** Shannon Wheeler

5 ❑ b&w Cover: 2.50 **NM** value: **5.00**
📖 The Death of Too Much Coffee Man **A:** Shannon Wheeler **W:** Shannon Wheeler

6 ❑ **NM** value: **3.00**
A: Shannon Wheeler **W:** Shannon Wheeler

7 ❑ **NM** value: **3.00**
A: Shannon Wheeler **W:** Shannon Wheeler

8 ❑ Feb 1998 Cover: 2.95 **NM** value: **3.00**
Circ: Diamd. preorders: **7,686**
A: Shannon Wheeler **W:** Shannon Wheeler

Bk 1❑ May 1998, b&w Cover: 10.95 **NM** value: **Cover or less**
• Too Much Coffee Man's Guide for the Perplexed; collects stories from Jab #1-3, Too Much Coffee Man Special, and others

MC 1❑ Cover: 1.00 **NM** value: **10.00**
• Mini-comic **A:** Shannon Wheeler **W:** Shannon Wheeler

MC 1-2❑ Cover: 1.00 **NM** value: **3.00**

MC 2❑ Cover: 1.00 **NM** value: **8.00**
• Mini-comic **A:** Shannon Wheeler **W:** Shannon Wheeler

MC 2-2❑ Cover: 1.00 **NM** value: **3.00**

MC 3❑ Cover: 1.00 **NM** value: **8.00**
• Mini-comic **A:** Shannon Wheeler **W:** Shannon Wheeler

MC 3-2❑ Cover: 1.00 **NM** value: **3.00**

MC 4❑ Cover: 1.00 **NM** value: **6.00**
• Mini-comic **A:** Shannon Wheeler **W:** Shannon Wheeler

MC 4-2❑ Cover: 1.00 **NM** value: **3.00**

SE 1❑ Jul 1997, b&w Cover: 2.95 **NM** value: **3.00**
No issue number. 📖 Too Much Coffee Man Meets His Coffee Maker **A:** Shannon Wheeler **W:** Shannon Wheeler

SE 2❑ Cover: 2.95 **NM** value: **3.00**
• Full-Color Special Edition. **A:** Shannon Wheeler **W:** Shannon Wheeler

TOO MUCH COFFEE MAN'S GUIDE FOR THE PERPLEXED
Dark Horse

Bk 1❑ May 1998, b&w Cover: 10.95 **NM** value: **Cover or less**
• Limited edition hardcover. • collects stories from Jab #1-3, Too Much Coffee Man Special, and others **A:** Shannon Wheeler **W:** Shannon Wheeler

Bk 1/HC❑Jun 1998, b&w Cover: 49.95 **NM** value: **Cover or less**
• collects stories from Jab #1-3, Too Much Coffee Man Special, and others **A:** Shannon Wheeler **W:** Shannon Wheeler

TOON WARZ: THE FANDOM MENACE
Sirius

1/A ❑ Jul 1999 Cover: 2.95 **NM** value: **Cover or less**
Believe This Man cover.

1/B ❑ Jul 1999 Cover: 2.95 **NM** value: **Cover or less**
Vain Affair cover.

1/C ❑ Jul 1999 Cover: 2.95 **NM** value: **Cover or less**
Newspeak cover.

1/D ❑ Jul 1999 Cover: 2.95 **NM** value: **Cover or less**
Primear cover.

TOOTH AND CLAW
Image

1 ❑ Aug 1999 Cover: 2.95 **NM** value: **Cover or less**
Circ: Diamd. preorders: **9,827**
A: Mark Pacella **W:** Mark Pacella

2 ❑ Sep 1999 Cover: 2.95 **NM** value: **Cover or less**
Circ: Diamd. preorders: **8,507**
Woman-cat holding skull on cover. **A:** Mark Pacella **W:** Mark Pacella

2/A ❑ Sep 1999 Cover: 2.95 **NM** value: **Cover or less**
alternate cover. **A:** Mark Pacella **W:** Mark Pacella

3 ❑ Oct 1999 Cover: 2.95 **NM** value: **Cover or less**
Circ: Diamd. preorders: **5,609**
A: Mark Pacella **W:** Mark Pacella

Ash 1❑1999 Cover: 5.00 **NM** value: **Cover or less**
• DF Exclusive preview book **A:** Mark Pacella **W:** Mark Pacella

TOP 10
DC / America's Best Comics

Does the average person have what it takes to be a hero? If suddenly given powers and a flashy costume, would the average man or woman rise to the occasion, and realize their heroic destiny? Welcome to Neopolis, where everyone, from the sweet old lady next door to the hooker on the corner, has a power, a costume, and a code-name. Most of them just want to live so-called normal lives, but there are always a few who feel the need to make trouble.

As you may imagine, the members of the Neopolis PD face some very unique situations, especially when they, the suspects, and the victims all have one or more special abilities. Creators Alan Moore (of Watchman fame) and Gene Ha make this fantasy town realistic, with three-dimensional characters and gritty dialog that many readers find reminiscent of the TV police drama, "Homicide: Life on the Streets."

1 ❑ Sep 1999 Cover: 3.50 **NM** value: **Cover or less**
Circ: Diamd. preorders: **55,056 • CGC:** 8 graded, best 9.8
A: Gene Ha; Zander Cannon **W:** Alan Moore

2 ❑ Oct 1999 Cover: 2.95 **NM** value: **Cover or less**
Circ: Diamd. preorders: **39,501 • CGC:** 2 graded, best 9.4
A: Gene Ha; Zander Cannon **W:** Alan Moore

3 ❑ Nov 1999 Cover: 2.95 **NM** value: **Cover or less**
Circ: Diamd. preorders: **37,986 • CGC:** 1 graded, best 9.6
📖 Eight Miles High **A:** Gene Ha; Zander Cannon **W:** Alan Moore

4 ❑ Dec 1999 Cover: 2.95 **NM** value: **Cover or less**
Circ: Diamd. preorders: **36,268 • CGC:** 1 graded, best 9.4
📖 Great Infestations **A:** Gene Ha; Zander Cannon **W:** Alan Moore

5 ❑ Jan 2000 Cover: 2.95 **NM** value: **Cover or less**
Circ: Diamd. preorders: **34,028**
A: Gene Ha; Zander Cannon **W:** Alan Moore

6 ❑ Feb 2000 Cover: 2.95 **NM** value: **Cover or less**
Circ: Diamd. preorders: **36,967**
W: Alan Moore

7 ❑ Apr 2000 Cover: 2.95 **NM** value: **Cover or less**
Circ: Diamd. preorders: **30,701**
📖 Mythdemeanors **A:** Gene Ha; Zander Cannon **W:** Alan Moore

8 ❑ Jun 2000 Cover: 2.95 **NM** value: **Cover or less**
Circ: Diamd. preorders: **31,510**
W: Alan Moore

9 ❑ Oct 2000 Cover: 2.95 **NM** value: **Cover or less**
Circ: Diamd. preorders: **31,580**
📖 Rules of Engagement **A:** Gene Ha; Zander Cannon **W:** Alan Moore

10 ❑ Jan 2001 Cover: 2.95 **NM** value: **Cover or less**
Circ: Diamd. preorders: **31,151**
📖 Music for the Dead **A:** Gene Ha; Zander Cannon **W:** Alan Moore

11 ❑ May 2001 Cover: 2.95 **NM** value: **Cover or less**
Circ: Diamd. preorders: **31,078**
📖 His First Day on the New Job **A:** Gene Ha; Zander Cannon **W:** Alan Moore

12 ❑ Sep 2001 Cover: 2.95 **NM** value: **Cover or less**
Circ: Diamd. preorders: **32,712**

Bk 1❑ Cover: 24.95 **NM** value: **Cover or less**
• Collects Top 10 #1-7 **A:** Gene Ha; Zander Cannon **W:** Alan Moore

TOP CAT — Charlton

1 ❑ Nov 1970 Cover: 0.15 **NM** value: **18.00**
2 ❑ Jan 1971 Cover: 0.15 **NM** value: **10.00**
3 ❑ Mar 1971 Cover: 0.15 **NM** value: **6.00**
4 ❑ May 1971 Cover: 0.15 **NM** value: **6.00**
5 ❑ Jul 1971 Cover: 0.15 **NM** value: **6.00**
6 ❑ Sep 1971 Cover: 0.15 **NM** value: **4.00**
7 ❑ Nov 1971 Cover: 0.20 **NM** value: **4.00**
8 ❑ Dec 1971 Cover: 0.20 **NM** value: **4.00**
9 ❑ Feb 1972 Cover: 0.20 **NM** value: **4.00**
10 ❑ Apr 1972 Cover: 0.20 **NM** value: **4.00**
11 ❑ Jun 1972 Cover: 0.20 **NM** value: **3.00**
12 ❑ Aug 1972 Cover: 0.20 **NM** value: **3.00**
13 ❑ Oct 1972 Cover: 0.20 **NM** value: **3.00**
14 ❑ Nov 1972 Cover: 0.20 **NM** value: **3.00**
15 ❑ Feb 1973 Cover: 0.20 **NM** value: **3.00**
16 ❑ Mar 1973 Cover: 0.20 **NM** value: **3.00**
17 ❑ May 1973 Cover: 0.20 **NM** value: **3.00**
18 ❑ Jul 1973 Cover: 0.20 **NM** value: **3.00**
19 ❑ Sep 1973 Cover: 0.20 **NM** value: **3.00**
20 ❑ Nov 1973 Cover: 0.20 **NM** value: **3.00**

TOP CAT (1ST SERIES) — Dell

1 ❑ Dec 1961 Cover: 0.15 **NM** value: **100.00**
• **CGC:** 2 graded, best 9.0
2 ❑ Mar 1962 Cover: 0.15 **NM** value: **50.00**
• **CGC:** 1 graded, best 8.0
3 ❑ Jun 1962 Cover: 0.15 **NM** value: **35.00**
4 ❑ Oct 1962 Cover: 0.12 **NM** value: **35.00**
5 ❑ Jan 1963 Cover: 0.12 **NM** value: **35.00**
6 ❑ Apr 1963 Cover: 0.12 **NM** value: **35.00**
• Has 1962 Statement, filed 10/1/62; only sub sales printed; avg subs 123
7 ❑ Jul 1963 Cover: 0.12 **NM** value: **35.00**
8 ❑ Oct 1963 Cover: 0.12 **NM** value: **35.00**
9 ❑ Jan 1964 Cover: 0.12 **NM** value: **35.00**
Circ: Statement: **266,253**
10 ❑ Apr 1964 Cover: 0.12 **NM** value: **35.00**
Circ: Statement: **266,253**
11 ❑ Jul 1964 Cover: 0.12 **NM** value: **20.00**
Circ: Statement: **266,253**
12 ❑ Oct 1964 Cover: 0.12 **NM** value: **20.00**
Circ: Statement: **266,253**
13 ❑ Jan 1965 Cover: 0.12 **NM** value: **20.00**
14 ❑ Apr 1965 Cover: 0.12 **NM** value: **20.00**
• Has 1964 Statement, filed 9/28/1964; avg print run 414,878; avg sales 265,832; avg subs 421; avg total paid 266,253; samples 602; max existent 266,855; 36% of run returned
15 ❑ Jul 1965 Cover: 0.12 **NM** value: **20.00**
16 ❑ Oct 1965 Cover: 0.12 **NM** value: **20.00**
17 ❑ Jan 1966 Cover: 0.12 **NM** value: **20.00**
18 ❑ 1966 Cover: 0.12 **NM** value: **20.00**
19 ❑ 1966 Cover: 0.12 **NM** value: **20.00**
20 ❑ 1967 Cover: 0.12 **NM** value: **20.00**
21 ❑ Dec 1967 Cover: 0.12 **NM** value: **15.00**
22 ❑ ca. 1968 Cover: 0.12 **NM** value: **15.00**
23 ❑ ca. 1968 Cover: 0.15 **NM** value: **15.00**
24 ❑ Dec 1968 Cover: 0.15 **NM** value: **15.00**
• **CGC:** 1 graded, best 8.0
25 ❑ Mar 1969 Cover: 0.15 **NM** value: **15.00**
26 ❑ Jun 1969 Cover: 0.15 **NM** value: **15.00**
• **CGC:** 1 graded, best 8.5
27 ❑ Sep 1969 Cover: 0.15 **NM** value: **15.00**
28 ❑ Dec 1969 Cover: 0.15 **NM** value: **15.00**
29 ❑ Mar 1970 Cover: 0.15 **NM** value: **15.00**
30 ❑ Jun 1970 Cover: 0.15 **NM** value: **15.00**
31 ❑ Sep 1970 Cover: 0.15 **NM** value: **15.00**

TOP COW CLASSICS IN BLACK AND WHITE: APHRODITE IX — Image

1 ❑ Sep 2000 **NM** value: **2.95**
A: Dave Finch **W:** David Wohl

TOP COW CLASSICS IN BLACK AND WHITE: ASCENSCION — Image

1 ❑ Apr 2000 Cover: 2.95 **NM** value: **Cover or less**
Circ: Diamd. preorders: **3,487**

TOP COW CLASSICS IN BLACK AND WHITE: FATHOM — Image

1 ❑ May 2000 Cover: 2.95 **NM** value: **Cover or less**
Circ: Diamd. preorders: **7,938**

TOP COW CLASSICS IN BLACK AND WHITE: MIDNIGHT NATION — Image

1 ❑ Mar 2001 Cover: 2.95 **NM** value: **Cover or less**
Circ: Diamd. preorders: **4,066** • **CGC:** 15 graded, best 9.9
A: Gary Frank **W:** J. Michael Straczynski

TOP COW CLASSICS IN BLACK AND WHITE: RISING STARS — Image

1 ❑ Aug 2000 Cover: 2.95 **NM** value: **Cover or less**
Circ: Diamd. preorders: **7,436** • **CGC:** 4 graded, best 9.8
📖 Nova Placenta **A:** Keu Cha **W:** J. Michael Straczynski

TOP COW CLASSICS IN BLACK AND WHITE: THE DARKNESS — Image

Hitman Jackie Estacado turns 21 and discovers he has inherited a phenomenal power known as The Darkness. With it, he can do almost anything. But he is soon to learn the price for such power brings a feeling of responsibility he has never known before.

Garth Ennis' story, Marc Silvestri's pencilling, Dennis Heisler's lettering, Batt's inks all under the editing of David Wohl bring the characters to life with realism and conflicts galore.

Top Cow highlights the inks, stories, and lettering with this black-and-white reprint of the first issue of The Darkness. Also included is a brief plot summary up to #25 that is enough to induce first-time readers to seek past issues from their local comic-book stores.

1 ❑ Mar 2000 Cover: 2.95 **NM** value: **Cover or less**
Circ: Diamd. preorders: **7,807**
📖 Coming of Age **A:** Marc Silvestri **W:** Garth Ennis

TOP COW CLASSICS IN BLACK AND WHITE: TOMB RAIDER — Image

1 ❑ Dec 2000 Cover: 2.95 **NM** value: **Cover or less**
A: Andy Park **W:** Dan Jurgens

TOP COW CLASSICS IN BLACK AND WHITE: WITCHBLADE — Image

1 ❑ Feb 2000 Cover: 2.95 **NM** value: **Cover or less**
Circ: Diamd. preorders: **10,876** • **CGC:** 1 graded, best 9.6

TOP COW PRODUCTIONS INC./BALLISTIC STUDIOS SWIMSUIT SPECIAL — Image

1 ❑ May 1995 Cover: 2.95 **NM** value: **Cover or less**
Circ: CapCity orders: **16,900**

TOP COW SECRETS — Image

WS 1❑Jan 1996 Cover: 2.95 **NM** value: **Cover or less**
• Special Winter Lingerie Edition. 📖 Blind Justice • pin-ups **A:** Billy Tan Mung Khoy; Bill Sienkiewicz; Randy Green; Brandon Peterson; Adam McDaniel; Marc Silvestri; Randy Queen; Anthony Winn; Brian Haberlin **W:** Brian Selzer

TOP DOG — Marvel / Star

1 ❑ Apr 1985 Cover: 0.65 **NM** value: **1.00**
📖 The Dog-Gone Beginning **A:** Warren Kremer **W:** Lennie Herman
★ 1st Appearance of Top Dog.
2 ❑ Jun 1985 Cover: 0.65 **NM** value: **1.00**
Circ: CapCity orders: **3,600**
A: Warren Kremer **W:** Lennie Herman
3 ❑ Aug 1985 Cover: 0.65 **NM** value: **1.00**
Circ: CapCity orders: **2,900**
📖 The Mad Biter; Caged; Ghost Story; A Fight To The Finish **A:** Warren Kremer **W:** Lennie Herman
4 ❑ Oct 1985 Cover: 0.65 **NM** value: **1.00**
Circ: CapCity orders: **2,200**
A: Warren Kremer **W:** Lennie Herman
5 ❑ Dec 1985 Cover: 0.65 **NM** value: **1.00**
Circ: CapCity orders: **1,800**
A: Warren Kremer **W:** Lennie Herman
6 ❑ Feb 1986 Cover: 0.65 **NM** value: **1.00**
Circ: CapCity orders: **1,600**
📖 Frank 'n' Stein **A:** Warren Kremer **W:** Lennie Herman
7 ❑ Apr 1986 Cover: 0.75 **NM** value: **1.00**
Circ: CapCity orders: **1,500**
8 ❑ Jun 1986 Cover: 0.75 **NM** value: **1.00**
Circ: CapCity orders: **2,250**
9 ❑ Aug 1986 Cover: 0.75 **NM** value: **1.00**
Circ: CapCity orders: **1,500**
10 ❑ Oct 1986 Cover: 0.75 **NM** value: **1.00**
Circ: CapCity orders: **3,050**
11 ❑ Dec 1986 Cover: 0.75 **NM** value: **1.00**
Circ: CapCity orders: **1,450**
12 ❑ Feb 1987 Cover: 0.75 **NM** value: **1.00**
Circ: CapCity orders: **1,700**
13 ❑ Apr 1987 Cover: 0.75 **NM** value: **1.00**
Circ: CapCity orders: **1,550**
14 ❑ Jun 1987 Cover: 1.00 **NM** value: **Cover or less**
Circ: CapCity orders: **1,200**
final issue.

TOP FLIGHT COMICS — St. John

1 ❑ Dec 1952 Cover: 0.10 **NM** value: **50.00**

The prices seen above do not represent the highest possible prices seen in online auctions, but rather the prices we have seen these issues reliably fetch in a variety of environments (storefront retail, mail order, auction and convention).

TOPIX — Catechetical Guild

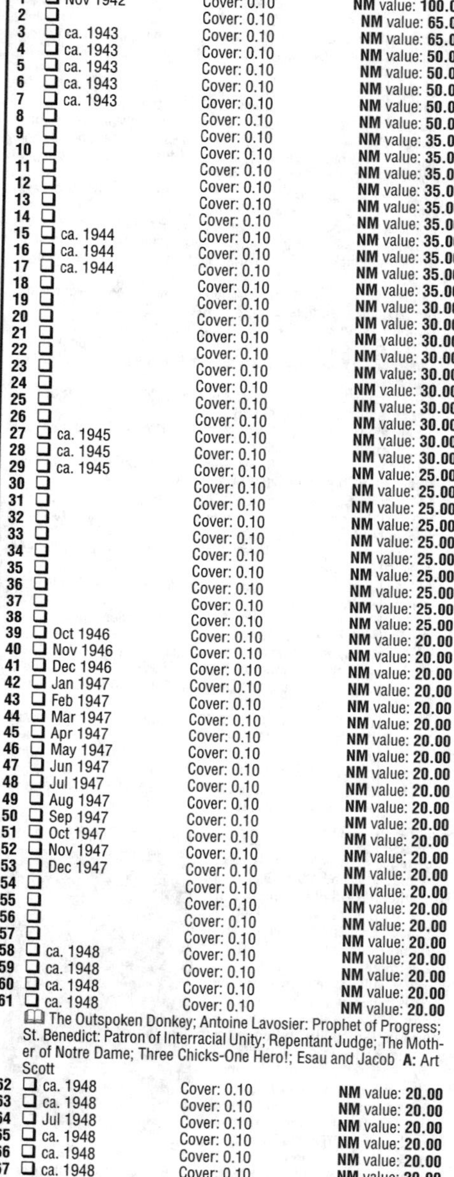

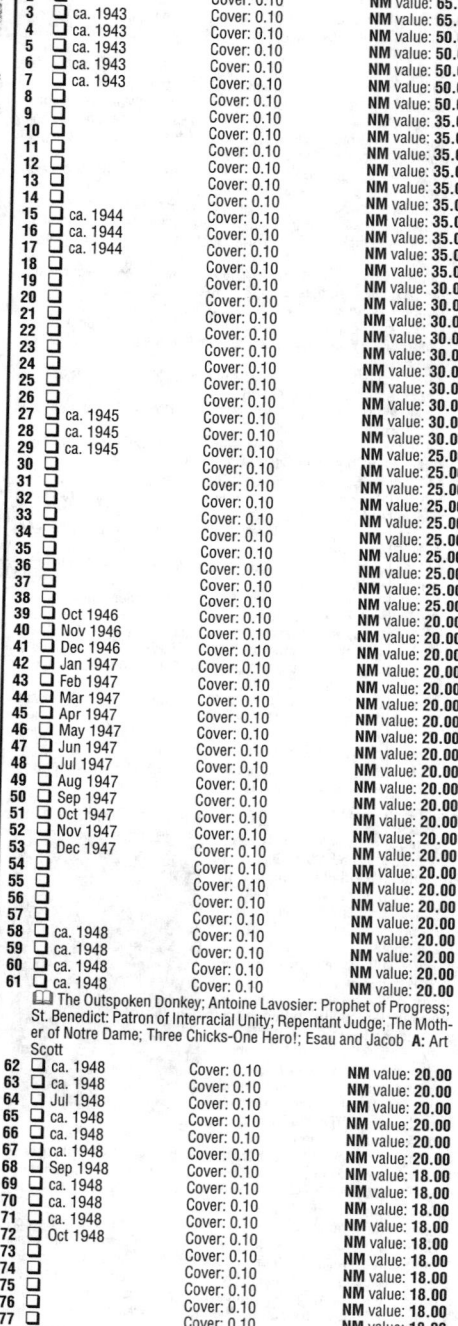

The Catechetical Guild of St. Paul, Minn., published Topix for 10 years between 1942 and 1952. Directed at children — particularly those in Catholic schools — it featured a combination of inspirational fables, profiles of saints and Church notables, adaptations of Biblical stories, and the odd cartoon strip with a strong moral tale. Ads inside each issue encouraged youngsters to sell subscriptions to their friends, and it even ran ads offering "authentically styled nun dolls — dressed like your own teacher!"

From its newsprint covers to its less-memorable stories to its 10-cent cover price, Topix was a weaker imitation of the more popular (and free!) Treasure Chest, another parochial comic book series with higher production values.

1 ❑ Nov 1942 Cover: 0.10 **NM** value: **100.00**
2 ❑ Cover: 0.10 **NM** value: **65.00**
3 ❑ ca. 1943 Cover: 0.10 **NM** value: **65.00**
4 ❑ ca. 1943 Cover: 0.10 **NM** value: **50.00**
5 ❑ ca. 1943 Cover: 0.10 **NM** value: **50.00**
6 ❑ ca. 1943 Cover: 0.10 **NM** value: **50.00**
7 ❑ ca. 1943 Cover: 0.10 **NM** value: **50.00**
8 ❑ Cover: 0.10 **NM** value: **50.00**
9 ❑ Cover: 0.10 **NM** value: **35.00**
10 ❑ Cover: 0.10 **NM** value: **35.00**
11 ❑ Cover: 0.10 **NM** value: **35.00**
12 ❑ Cover: 0.10 **NM** value: **35.00**
13 ❑ Cover: 0.10 **NM** value: **35.00**
14 ❑ Cover: 0.10 **NM** value: **35.00**
15 ❑ ca. 1944 Cover: 0.10 **NM** value: **35.00**
16 ❑ ca. 1944 Cover: 0.10 **NM** value: **35.00**
17 ❑ ca. 1944 Cover: 0.10 **NM** value: **35.00**
18 ❑ Cover: 0.10 **NM** value: **35.00**
19 ❑ Cover: 0.10 **NM** value: **30.00**
20 ❑ Cover: 0.10 **NM** value: **30.00**
21 ❑ Cover: 0.10 **NM** value: **30.00**
22 ❑ Cover: 0.10 **NM** value: **30.00**
23 ❑ Cover: 0.10 **NM** value: **30.00**
24 ❑ Cover: 0.10 **NM** value: **30.00**
25 ❑ Cover: 0.10 **NM** value: **30.00**
26 ❑ Cover: 0.10 **NM** value: **30.00**
27 ❑ ca. 1945 Cover: 0.10 **NM** value: **30.00**
28 ❑ ca. 1945 Cover: 0.10 **NM** value: **30.00**
29 ❑ ca. 1945 Cover: 0.10 **NM** value: **25.00**
30 ❑ Cover: 0.10 **NM** value: **25.00**
31 ❑ Cover: 0.10 **NM** value: **25.00**
32 ❑ Cover: 0.10 **NM** value: **25.00**
33 ❑ Cover: 0.10 **NM** value: **25.00**
34 ❑ Cover: 0.10 **NM** value: **25.00**
35 ❑ Cover: 0.10 **NM** value: **25.00**
36 ❑ Cover: 0.10 **NM** value: **25.00**
37 ❑ Cover: 0.10 **NM** value: **25.00**
38 ❑ Cover: 0.10 **NM** value: **25.00**
39 ❑ Oct 1946 Cover: 0.10 **NM** value: **20.00**
40 ❑ Nov 1946 Cover: 0.10 **NM** value: **20.00**
41 ❑ Dec 1946 Cover: 0.10 **NM** value: **20.00**
42 ❑ Jan 1947 Cover: 0.10 **NM** value: **20.00**
43 ❑ Feb 1947 Cover: 0.10 **NM** value: **20.00**
44 ❑ Mar 1947 Cover: 0.10 **NM** value: **20.00**
45 ❑ Apr 1947 Cover: 0.10 **NM** value: **20.00**
46 ❑ May 1947 Cover: 0.10 **NM** value: **20.00**
47 ❑ Jun 1947 Cover: 0.10 **NM** value: **20.00**
48 ❑ Jul 1947 Cover: 0.10 **NM** value: **20.00**
49 ❑ Aug 1947 Cover: 0.10 **NM** value: **20.00**
50 ❑ Sep 1947 Cover: 0.10 **NM** value: **20.00**
51 ❑ Oct 1947 Cover: 0.10 **NM** value: **20.00**
52 ❑ Nov 1947 Cover: 0.10 **NM** value: **20.00**
53 ❑ Dec 1947 Cover: 0.10 **NM** value: **20.00**
54 ❑ Cover: 0.10 **NM** value: **20.00**
55 ❑ Cover: 0.10 **NM** value: **20.00**
56 ❑ Cover: 0.10 **NM** value: **20.00**
57 ❑ Cover: 0.10 **NM** value: **20.00**
58 ❑ ca. 1948 Cover: 0.10 **NM** value: **20.00**
59 ❑ ca. 1948 Cover: 0.10 **NM** value: **20.00**
60 ❑ ca. 1948 Cover: 0.10 **NM** value: **20.00**
61 ❑ ca. 1948 Cover: 0.10 **NM** value: **20.00**
📖 The Outspoken Donkey; Antoine Lavosier: Prophet of Progress; St. Benedict: Patron of Interracial Unity; Repentant Judge; The Mother of Notre Dame; Three Chicks-One Hero!; Esau and Jacob **A:** Art Scott
62 ❑ ca. 1948 Cover: 0.10 **NM** value: **20.00**
63 ❑ ca. 1948 Cover: 0.10 **NM** value: **20.00**
64 ❑ Jul 1948 Cover: 0.10 **NM** value: **20.00**
65 ❑ ca. 1948 Cover: 0.10 **NM** value: **20.00**
66 ❑ ca. 1948 Cover: 0.10 **NM** value: **20.00**
67 ❑ ca. 1948 Cover: 0.10 **NM** value: **20.00**
68 ❑ Sep 1948 Cover: 0.10 **NM** value: **18.00**
69 ❑ ca. 1948 Cover: 0.10 **NM** value: **18.00**
70 ❑ ca. 1948 Cover: 0.10 **NM** value: **18.00**
71 ❑ ca. 1948 Cover: 0.10 **NM** value: **18.00**
72 ❑ Oct 1948 Cover: 0.10 **NM** value: **18.00**
73 ❑ Cover: 0.10 **NM** value: **18.00**
74 ❑ Cover: 0.10 **NM** value: **18.00**
75 ❑ Cover: 0.10 **NM** value: **18.00**
76 ❑ Cover: 0.10 **NM** value: **18.00**
77 ❑ Cover: 0.10 **NM** value: **18.00**
78 ❑ Cover: 0.10 **NM** value: **18.00**
79 ❑ Cover: 0.10 **NM** value: **18.00**
80 ❑ Cover: 0.10 **NM** value: **18.00**
81 ❑ Cover: 0.10 **NM** value: **18.00**

Other grades: Multiply prices above by **1.5 for Mint • 2/3 for Very Fine • 1/3 for Fine • 1/5 for Very Good • 1/8 for Good**

82 ❑ Apr 1949 Cover: 0.10 NM value: 18.00
83 ❑ ca. 1949 Cover: 0.10 NM value: 18.00
84 ❑ ca. 1949 Cover: 0.10 NM value: 18.00
85 ❑ ca. 1949 Cover: 0.10 NM value: 18.00
86 ❑ ca. 1949 Cover: 0.10 NM value: 18.00
87 ❑ Jun 1949 Cover: 0.10 NM value: 18.00
88 ❑ ca. 1949 Cover: 0.10 NM value: 18.00
89 ❑ ca. 1949 Cover: 0.10 NM value: 18.00
90 ❑ ca. 1949 Cover: 0.10 NM value: 18.00
91 ❑ ca. 1949 Cover: 0.10 NM value: 18.00
92 ❑ ca. 1949 Cover: 0.10 NM value: 18.00
93 ❑ ca. 1949 Cover: 0.10 NM value: 18.00
94 ❑ ca. 1949 Cover: 0.10 NM value: 18.00
95 ❑ ca. 1949 Cover: 0.10 NM value: 18.00
96 ❑ ca. 1949 Cover: 0.10 NM value: 18.00
97 ❑ ca. 1949 Cover: 0.10 NM value: 18.00
98 ❑ Dec 1949 Cover: 0.10 NM value: 18.00
99 ❑ Cover: 0.10 NM value: 18.00
100 ❑ Cover: 0.10 NM value: 18.00
101 ❑ Cover: 0.10 NM value: 18.00
102 ❑ Cover: 0.10 NM value: 18.00
103 ❑ Cover: 0.10 NM value: 18.00
104 ❑ Cover: 0.10 NM value: 18.00
105 ❑ Cover: 0.10 NM value: 18.00
106 ❑ Cover: 0.10 NM value: 18.00
107 ❑ Cover: 0.10 NM value: 18.00
108 ❑ Cover: 0.10 NM value: 18.00
109 ❑ Cover: 0.10 NM value: 18.00
110 ❑ Cover: 0.10 NM value: 18.00
111 ❑ Cover: 0.10 NM value: 18.00
112 ❑ Cover: 0.10 NM value: 18.00
113 ❑ Cover: 0.10 NM value: 18.00
114 ❑ Cover: 0.10 NM value: 18.00
115 ❑ Cover: 0.10 NM value: 18.00
116 ❑ Cover: 0.10 NM value: 18.00
117 ❑ May 1950 Cover: 0.10 NM value: 18.00
118 ❑ ca. 1950 Cover: 0.10 NM value: 15.00
119 ❑ Cover: 0.10 NM value: 15.00
120 ❑ Cover: 0.10 NM value: 15.00
121 ❑ Cover: 0.10 NM value: 15.00
122 ❑ Cover: 0.10 NM value: 15.00
123 ❑ Cover: 0.10 NM value: 15.00
124 ❑ Cover: 0.10 NM value: 15.00
125 ❑ Cover: 0.10 NM value: 15.00
126 ❑ Cover: 0.10 NM value: 15.00
127 ❑ Cover: 0.10 NM value: 15.00
128 ❑ Cover: 0.10 NM value: 15.00
129 ❑ Cover: 0.10 NM value: 15.00
130 ❑ Cover: 0.10 NM value: 15.00
131 ❑ Cover: 0.10 NM value: 15.00
132 ❑ Cover: 0.10 NM value: 15.00
133 ❑ Cover: 0.10 NM value: 15.00
134 ❑ Cover: 0.10 NM value: 15.00
135 ❑ Cover: 0.10 NM value: 15.00
136 ❑ Cover: 0.10 NM value: 15.00
137 ❑ Cover: 0.10 NM value: 15.00
138 ❑ Cover: 0.10 NM value: 15.00
139 ❑ Cover: 0.10 NM value: 15.00
140 ❑ Cover: 0.10 NM value: 15.00
141 ❑ Cover: 0.10 NM value: 15.00
142 ❑ Cover: 0.10 NM value: 15.00
143 ❑ Cover: 0.10 NM value: 15.00
144 ❑ Cover: 0.10 NM value: 15.00
145 ❑ Cover: 0.10 NM value: 15.00
146 ❑ Cover: 0.10 NM value: 15.00
147 ❑ Cover: 0.10 NM value: 15.00
148 ❑ ca. 1951 Cover: 0.10 NM value: 15.00
149 ❑ ca. 1951 Cover: 0.10 NM value: 15.00
150 ❑ ca. 1951 Cover: 0.10 NM value: 15.00
151 ❑ ca. 1951 Cover: 0.10 NM value: 15.00
152 ❑ Oct 1951 Cover: 0.10 NM value: 15.00
153 ❑ ca. 1951 Cover: 0.10 NM value: 15.00
154 ❑ ca. 1951 Cover: 0.10 NM value: 15.00
155 ❑ ca. 1951 Cover: 0.10 NM value: 15.00
156 ❑ ca. 1951 Cover: 0.10 NM value: 15.00
157 ❑ Dec 1951 Cover: 0.10 NM value: 15.00
158 ❑ Cover: 0.10 NM value: 15.00
159 ❑ Cover: 0.10 NM value: 15.00
160 ❑ Cover: 0.10 NM value: 15.00
161 ❑ Cover: 0.10 NM value: 15.00
162 ❑ Jan 1952 Cover: 0.10 NM value: 15.00

TOP LOVE STORIES — Star

3 ❑ May 1951 Cover: 0.10 NM value: 150.00
• CGC: 1 graded, best 9.4
4 ❑ Aug 1951 Cover: 0.10 NM value: 125.00
5 ❑ Nov 1951 Cover: 0.10 NM value: 125.00
6 ❑ Feb 1952 Cover: 0.10 NM value: 125.00
7 ❑ Jul 1952 Cover: 0.10 NM value: 125.00
8 ❑ Sep 1952 Cover: 0.10 NM value: 125.00
9 ❑ Nov 1952 Cover: 0.10 NM value: 125.00
10 ❑ Jan 1953 Cover: 0.10 NM value: 125.00
• CGC: 1 graded, best 7.0
11 ❑ Mar 1953 Cover: 0.10 NM value: 100.00
12 ❑ May 1953 Cover: 0.10 NM value: 100.00
13 ❑ Jul 1953 Cover: 0.10 NM value: 100.00
14 ❑ Sep 1953 Cover: 0.10 NM value: 100.00
15 ❑ Nov 1953 Cover: 0.10 NM value: 100.00
16 ❑ Jan 1954 Cover: 0.10 NM value: 100.00
17 ❑ Mar 1954 Cover: 0.10 NM value: 100.00

TOP-NOTCH COMICS — M.L.J.

1 ❑ Dec 1939 Cover: 0.10 NM value: 5000.00
• CGC: 5 graded, best 8.5
2 ❑ Jan 1940 Cover: 0.10 NM value: 2500.00
• CGC: 1 graded, best 9.6
3 ❑ Feb 1940 Cover: 0.10 NM value: 1500.00
• CGC: 2 graded, best 9.6
4 ❑ Apr 1940 Cover: 0.10 NM value: 1000.00
• CGC: 2 graded, best 9.2
5 ❑ May 1940 Cover: 0.10 NM value: 1000.00
• CGC: 2 graded, best 9.2
6 ❑ Jun 1940 Cover: 0.10 NM value: 750.00
• CGC: 1 graded, best 9.4
7 ❑ Aug 1940 Cover: 0.10 NM value: 750.00
• CGC: 2 graded, best 9.8
8 ❑ Sep 1940 Cover: 0.10 NM value: 750.00
• CGC: 2 graded, best 9.6
9 ❑ Oct 1940 Cover: 0.10 NM value: 750.00
• CGC: 6 graded, best 9.6
10 ❑ Dec 1940 Cover: 0.10 NM value: 750.00
• CGC: 3 graded, best 9.6
11 ❑ Jan 1941 Cover: 0.10 NM value: 600.00
• CGC: 1 graded, best 9.6
12 ❑ Feb 1941 Cover: 0.10 NM value: 600.00
• CGC: 1 graded, best 9.2
13 ❑ Mar 1941 Cover: 0.10 NM value: 600.00
• CGC: 1 graded, best 9.2
14 ❑ Apr 1941 Cover: 0.10 NM value: 600.00
• CGC: 2 graded, best 8.5
15 ❑ May 1941 Cover: 0.10 NM value: 600.00
• CGC: 1 graded, best 9.6
16 ❑ Jun 1941 Cover: 0.10 NM value: 600.00
• CGC: 1 graded, best 9.6
17 ❑ Jul 1941 Cover: 0.10 NM value: 600.00
• CGC: 1 graded, best 9.6
18 ❑ Aug 1941 Cover: 0.10 NM value: 600.00
• CGC: 3 graded, best 9.6
19 ❑ Sep 1941 Cover: 0.10 NM value: 600.00
• CGC: 2 graded, best 9.6
20 ❑ Oct 1941 Cover: 0.10 NM value: 600.00
• CGC: 2 graded, best 9.2
21 ❑ Nov 1941 Cover: 0.10 NM value: 450.00
• CGC: 2 graded, best 9.2
22 ❑ Dec 1941 Cover: 0.10 NM value: 450.00
• CGC: 1 graded, best 9.4
23 ❑ Jan 1942 Cover: 0.10 NM value: 450.00
• CGC: 1 graded, best 9.8
24 ❑ Feb 1942 Cover: 0.10 NM value: 450.00
• CGC: 2 graded, best 9.2
25 ❑ Mar 1942 Cover: 0.10 NM value: 450.00
• CGC: 1 graded, best 9.6
26 ❑ Apr 1942 Cover: 0.10 NM value: 450.00
• CGC: 1 graded, best 9.2
27 ❑ May 1942 Cover: 0.10 NM value: 450.00
• CGC: 1 graded, best 9.4
28 ❑ Jul 1942 Cover: 0.10 NM value: 450.00
• CGC: 1 graded, best 9.0
29 ❑ Sep 1942 Cover: 0.10 NM value: 450.00
• CGC: 1 graded, best 9.4
30 ❑ Nov 1942 Cover: 0.10 NM value: 450.00
• CGC: 1 graded, best 9.2
31 ❑ Dec 1942 Cover: 0.10 NM value: 300.00
• CGC: 1 graded, best 9.8
32 ❑ Jan 1943 Cover: 0.10 NM value: 300.00
• CGC: 1 graded, best 9.6
33 ❑ Feb 1943 Cover: 0.10 NM value: 300.00
• CGC: 1 graded, best 9.8
34 ❑ Mar 1943 Cover: 0.10 NM value: 300.00
• CGC: 1 graded, best 9.2
35 ❑ Apr 1943 Cover: 0.10 NM value: 300.00
• CGC: 1 graded, best 8.0
36 ❑ May 1943 Cover: 0.10 NM value: 300.00
• CGC: 1 graded, best 9.2
37 ❑ Jul 1943 Cover: 0.10 NM value: 300.00
• CGC: 1 graded, best 9.6
38 ❑ Aug 1943 Cover: 0.10 NM value: 300.00
• CGC: 1 graded, best 9.2
39 ❑ Sep 1943 Cover: 0.10 NM value: 300.00
• CGC: 1 graded, best 9.4
40 ❑ Oct 1943 Cover: 0.10 NM value: 300.00
• CGC: 1 graded, best 9.6
41 ❑ Nov 1943 Cover: 0.10 NM value: 300.00
42 ❑ Dec 1943 Cover: 0.10 NM value: 300.00
• CGC: 1 graded, best 8.0
43 ❑ Feb 1944 Cover: 0.10 NM value: 300.00
44 ❑ Apr 1944 Cover: 0.10 NM value: 300.00
• CGC: 1 graded, best 9.2
45 ❑ May 1944 Cover: 0.10 NM value: 300.00
• CGC: 1 graded, best 8.5

TOPPS COMICS PRESENTS — Topps

0 ❑ Jul 1949 Cover: 0.25 NM value: 1.50
• Previewed Teenagents, Silver Star, Jack Kirby's Secret City Saga, Bill the Galactic Hero, etc.
1 ❑ Sep 1949 Cover: 0.25 NM value: 1.00
• giveaway.

TOP SECRET — Hillman

1 ❑ Jan 1952 Cover: 0.10 NM value: 100.00

TOP SECRETS — Street & Smith

1 ❑ Nov 1947 Cover: 0.10 NM value: 250.00
• CGC: 1 graded, best 6.5
2 ❑ Feb 1948 Cover: 0.10 NM value: 175.00
• CGC: 1 graded, best 6.5
3 ❑ May 1948 Cover: 0.10 NM value: 175.00
• CGC: 1 graded, best 5.5
4 ❑ Aug 1948 Cover: 0.10 NM value: 175.00
• CGC: 1 graded, best 6.5
5 ❑ Sep 1948 Cover: 0.10 NM value: 175.00
6 ❑ Nov 1948 Cover: 0.10 NM value: 150.00
7 ❑ Jan 1949 Cover: 0.10 NM value: 150.00
8 ❑ Mar 1949 Cover: 0.10 NM value: 150.00
• CGC: 2 graded, best 8.5
9 ❑ May 1949 Cover: 0.10 NM value: 150.00
10 ❑ Jul 1949 Cover: 0.10 NM value: 150.00

TOP SHELF (PRIMAL GROOVE) — Primal Groove Press

1 ❑ Win 1995, b&w Cover: 5.00 NM value: Cover or less

TOP SHELF (TOP SHELF) — Top Shelf

1 ❑ ca. 1996 Cover: 6.95 NM value: Cover or less
2 ❑ ca. 1997 Cover: 6.95 NM value: Cover or less
3 ❑ ca. 1997 Cover: 6.95 NM value: Cover or less
4 ❑ ca. 1997 Cover: 6.95 NM value: Cover or less
5 ❑ ca. 1998 Cover: 6.95 NM value: Cover or less
6 ❑ ca. 1998 Cover: 6.95 NM value: Cover or less
7 ❑ ca. 1998 Cover: 6.95 NM value: Cover or less
📖 On Parade

TOPS IN ADVENTURE — Ziff-Davis

1 ❑ Spr 1952 Cover: 0.25 NM value: 350.00

TOR 3-D — Eclipse

1 ❑ Cover: 1.50 NM value: 2.50
Circ: CapCity orders: 4,075
📖 Tor; Animals of 1,000,000 Years Ago-Triceratops; The Wizard of Ugghh; Animals of 1,000,000 Years Ago-Brontosaurus; Danny Dreams! A: Joe Kubert W: Joe Kubert
2 ❑ Cover: 1.50 NM value: 2.50
Circ: CapCity orders: 3,850
📖 Killer-man!; The Story of Evolution!; Danny Dreams; Giant-One!!; the Run-a-Way! A: Joe Kubert W: Joe Kubert

TORCH OF LIBERTY SPECIAL — Dark Horse

1 ❑ Jan 1995 Cover: 2.50 NM value: Cover or less
Circ: CapCity orders: 7,075
No issue number. One-shot. A: Kieron Dwyer; John Byrne W: John Byrne

TORCHY — Quality

1 ❑ Nov 1949 Cover: 0.10 NM value: 700.00
• CGC: 2 graded, best 4.5
2 ❑ Jan 1950 Cover: 0.10 NM value: 350.00
• CGC: 3 graded, best 9.2
3 ❑ Mar 1950 Cover: 0.10 NM value: 350.00
• CGC: 1 graded, best 8.5
4 ❑ May 1950 Cover: 0.10 NM value: 350.00
• CGC: 2 graded, best 9.0
5 ❑ Jul 1950 Cover: 0.10 NM value: 300.00
• CGC: 4 graded, best 9.0
6 ❑ Sep 1950 Cover: 0.10 NM value: 300.00
• CGC: 3 graded, best 8.5

TORCHY (INNOVATION) — Innovation

1 ❑ b&w Cover: 2.50 NM value: Cover or less
A: Bill Ward
2 ❑ b&w Cover: 2.50 NM value: Cover or less
A: Bill Ward
3 ❑ b&w Cover: 2.50 NM value: Cover or less
A: Bill Ward
4 ❑ b&w Cover: 2.50 NM value: Cover or less
A: Bill Ward
5 ❑ b&w Cover: 2.50 NM value: Cover or less
A: Bill Ward
9 ❑ b&w Cover: 2.50 NM value: Cover or less
1st Olivia cover. A: Bill Ward C: Olivia
Bk 1 ❑ b&w Cover: 6.95 NM value: Cover or less
A: Bill Ward
Smr 1 ❑ b&w Cover: 2.50 NM value: Cover or less
• Summer Fun Special

TOR (DC) — DC

Tor is a caveman who lives in the savage world of a million years ago. In that time, he is a fierce fighter who possesses the strength necessary for survival. But even in that savage world there is a place for honor, wisdom, and learning that sometimes the best way to overcome an enemy is not to smash him over the head with a stone axe.

Joe Kubert is famous for his work on Tarzan, but even that is not as powerful as his work on his own creation, Tor. The idea for Tor came to him while on a troop ship heading to Korea. It seemed to him that, throughout history, mankind has had violence flowing through its veins and that history has always been a struggle to overcome the urge to kill one another. In creating Tor, he shows readers a world in which the lessons of history are reduced to their primal elements.

1 ❑ Jun 1975 Cover: 0.25 NM value: 3.00
• CGC: 7 graded, best 9.4
📖 The Beating A: Joe Kubert W: Joe Kubert ★ Origin of Tor.
2 ❑ Aug 1975 Cover: 0.25 NM value: 2.00
A: Joe Kubert W: Joe Kubert
3 ❑ Oct 1975 Cover: 0.25 NM value: 2.00
A: Joe Kubert W: Joe Kubert
4 ❑ Dec 1975 Cover: 0.25 NM value: 2.00
A: Joe Kubert W: Joe Kubert
5 ❑ Feb 1976 Cover: 0.25 NM value: 2.00
A: Joe Kubert W: Joe Kubert
6 ❑ Apr 1976 Cover: 0.25 NM value: 2.00
final issue. A: Joe Kubert W: Joe Kubert

CGC-graded: Multiply prices above by **33 for 9.9 M • 16 for 9.8 NM/M • 7 for 9.6 NM+ • 5 for 9.4 NM • 2.5 for 9.2 NM- • 1.5 for 9.0 VF/NM**

TOR (EPIC) — Marvel / Epic

1 ❑ Jun 1993 Cover: 5.95 **NM** value: **Cover or less**
Circ: CapCity orders: **7,750**
• large size. **A:** Joe Kubert **W:** Joe Kubert ★ Origin of Tor.

2 ❑ Jul 1993 Cover: 5.95 **NM** value: **Cover or less**
Circ: CapCity orders: **5,400**
• large size. 📖 The Chosen One **A:** Joe Kubert **W:** Joe Kubert

3 ❑ 1993 Cover: 5.95 **NM** value: **Cover or less**
Circ: CapCity orders: **4,650**
• large size. **A:** Joe Kubert **W:** Joe Kubert

4 ❑ 1993 Cover: 5.95 **NM** value: **Cover or less**
Circ: CapCity orders: **3,450**
• large size. **A:** Joe Kubert **W:** Joe Kubert

TORG — Adventure

1 ❑ b&w Cover: 2.50 **NM** value: **Cover or less**
Circ: CapCity orders: **2,660**

2 ❑ Mar 1992, b&w Cover: 2.50 **NM** value: **Cover or less**

3 ❑ Apr 1992, b&w Cover: 2.50 **NM** value: **Cover or less**

4 ❑ May 1992, b&w Cover: 2.50 **NM** value: **Cover or less**

TORI DO — Penguin Palace

1 ❑ Aug 1994, b&w Cover: 2.25 **NM** value: **Cover or less**

1-2 ❑ Mar 1995 Cover: 2.25 **NM** value: **Cover or less**

TO RIVERDALE AND BACK AGAIN — Archie

1 ❑ ca. 1990 Cover: 2.50 **NM** value: **Cover or less**
No issue number. **A:** Gene Colan **C:** John Byrne

TOR JOHNSON: HOLLYWOOD STAR — Monster

1 ❑ b&w Cover: 2.50 **NM** value: **Cover or less**

TOR LOVE BETTY — Fantagraphics / Eros

All issues are adults only.

1 ❑ b&w Cover: 2.75 **NM** value: **Cover or less**

TORMENT — Aircel

All issues are adults only.

1 ❑ b&w Cover: 2.95 **NM** value: **Cover or less**

2 ❑ b&w Cover: 2.95 **NM** value: **Cover or less**

3 ❑ b&w Cover: 2.95 **NM** value: **Cover or less**

TORPEDO — Hard Boiled

1 ❑ b&w Cover: 2.95 **NM** value: **Cover or less**
📖 Triple Cross **A:** Jordi Bernet **W:** E. Sanchéz Abuli

2 ❑ b&w Cover: 2.95 **NM** value: **Cover or less**
A: Jordi Bernet **W:** E. Sanchéz Abuli

3 ❑ b&w Cover: 2.95 **NM** value: **Cover or less**
A: Jordi Bernet **W:** E. Sanchéz Abuli

4 ❑ b&w Cover: 2.95 **NM** value: **Cover or less**
A: Jordi Bernet **W:** E. Sanchéz Abuli

TORRID AFFAIRS — Eternity

1 ❑ 1988b&w Cover: 2.25 **NM** value: **Cover or less**

2/A ❑ Feb 1989 Cover: 2.25 **NM** value: **Cover or less**
tame cover.

2/B ❑ Feb 1989 Cover: 2.25 **NM** value: **Cover or less**
sexy cover.

3 ❑ 1989 Cover: 2.95 **NM** value: **Cover or less**

4 ❑ 1989 Cover: 2.95 **NM** value: **Cover or less**

5 ❑ 1989 Cover: 2.95 **NM** value: **Cover or less**

TORSO — Image

1 ❑ 1999 Cover: 3.95 **NM** value: **Cover or less**
A: Marc Andreyko **W:** Brian Michael Bendis

2 ❑ 1999 Cover: 3.95 **NM** value: **Cover or less**
A: Marc Andreyko **W:** Brian Michael Bendis

3 ❑ 1999 Cover: 3.95 **NM** value: **4.95**
A: Marc Andreyko **W:** Brian Michael Bendis

4 ❑ 1999 Cover: 4.95 **NM** value: **Cover or less**
A: Marc Andreyko **W:** Brian Michael Bendis

5 ❑ Jun 1999 Cover: 4.95 **NM** value: **Cover or less**
A: Brian Michael Bendis **W:** Brian Michael Bendis; Marc Andreyko

6 ❑ 1999 Cover: 4.95 **NM** value: **Cover or less**
A: Brian Michael Bendis **W:** Brian Michael Bendis; Marc Andreyko

Bk 1❑ Cover: 24.95 **NM** value: **Cover or less**
• Collects series **A:** Brian Michael Bendis **W:** Brian Michael Bendis; Marc Andreyko

Bk 1/HC❑ Cover: 49.95 **NM** value: **Cover or less**
• Hardcover edition. • Collects Series **A:** Brian Michael Bendis **W:** Brian Michael Bendis; Marc Andreyko

TORTOISE AND THE HARE, THE — Last Gasp

1 ❑ Cover: 0.50 **NM** value: **3.00**
📖 Back-up stories: The Phantom Roar-Shock's; The Early Adventures of Roger Rabbit; Dirty Duck; Trots and Bonnie; Tales of Ezekiel Wolf **A:** Gary Hallgren **W:** Gary Hallgren

> To find the median price offered on eBay at press time for pre-1990 **CGC-graded comics**, multiply by:
>
> | | |
> |---|---|
> | 9.9 (M): **33** | 8.5 (VF+): **1.25** |
> | 9.8(NM/M): **16** | 8.0 (VF): **0.85** |
> | 9.6 (NM+): **7** | 7.5 (VF-): **0.6** |
> | 9.4 (NM): **5** | 7.0 (F/VF): **0.5** |
> | 9.2 (NM-): **2.5** | 6.5 (F+): **0.4** |
> | 9.0 (VF/NM): **1.5** | 6.0 (F-): **0.33** |
>
> These are median prices of all CGC comics auctioned on eBay; prices for individual issues will vary.

TOTAL ECLIPSE — Eclipse

This five-issue series was created in celebration of Eclipse Comics' tenth anniversary. The story begins with a total eclipse that took place millennia ago. At that moment, a baby was born and was commanded to be sacrificed. The primitive people complied, only to be stunned when the sacrifice...failed.

Since that day, the boy called Zzed has been immortal. But while he once cherished his longevity, he now seeks oblivion destruction above all else. Sadly for him, knives, bullets, bombs, and even dissection are unable to cause him permanent harm. He simply reincorporates, and his life drags on. Finally, he has decided that the only way to destroy himself is to destroy the entire world.

To stop him, Eclipse gathers all of its modern characters, including Miracleman, the Prowler, Strike!, Aztec Ace, and others in an incredible anniversary event.

1 ❑ May 1988 Cover: 3.95 **NM** value: **Cover or less**
Circ: CapCity orders: **9,675**
📖 Zzed **A:** Brent Anderson; Bill Sienkiewicz(cover) **C:** Bill Sienkiewicz **W:** Marv Wolfman ★ Appearance of Sgt. Strike, Black Angel, Airboy, Skywolf, New Wave, Strike, Prowler, Valkyrie. ★ Versus Z. ★ Versus Misery.

2 ❑ Aug 1988 Cover: 3.95 **NM** value: **Cover or less**
Circ: CapCity orders: **6,950**
📖 Danny Dreams **A:** Joe Kubert **C:** Bill Sienkiewicz ★ Appearance of Miracle, Sgt. Strike, Liberty Project, Airboy, Skywolf, New Wave, Strike, Prowler, Valkyrie.

3 ❑ Dec 1988 Cover: 3.95 **NM** value: **Cover or less**
Circ: CapCity orders: **6,525**
C: Bill Sienkiewicz ★ Appearance of Sgt. Strike, Liberty Project, Airboy, Skywolf, New Wave, Strike, Beanish, Prowler, Valkyrie.

4 ❑ Jan 1989 Cover: 3.95 **NM** value: **Cover or less**
Circ: CapCity orders: **6,650**
C: Bill Sienkiewicz ★ 1st Appearance of Doctor Eclipse. ★ Appearance of Sgt. Strike, Airboy, Skywolf, New Wave, Beanish, Prowler, Valkyrie. ★ Death of Strike!.

5 ❑ Apr 1989 Cover: 3.95 **NM** value: **Cover or less**
Circ: CapCity orders: **5,500**
C: Bill Sienkiewicz ★ Appearance of Sgt. Strike, Airboy, Skywolf, New Wave, Beanish, Prowler, Heap, Aztec Ace, Valkyrie. ★ Versus Misery.

TOTAL ECLIPSE: THE SERAPHIM OBJECTIVE — Eclipse

1 ❑ Nov 1988 Cover: 1.95 **NM** value: **Cover or less**
Circ: CapCity orders: **5,725**
A: James W. Fry **W:** Kurt Busiek ★ Appearance of Liberty Project, Airboy, Heap.

TOTAL JUSTICE — DC

1 ❑ Oct 1996 Cover: 2.25 **NM** value: **Cover or less**
Circ: Diamd. preorders: **39,085**
📖 Tim • based on Kenner action figures **A:** Ramon Bernado **W:** Christopher Priest

2 ❑ Nov 1996 Cover: 2.25 **NM** value: **Cover or less**
Circ: Diamd. preorders: **35,245**
📖 Mike • based on Kenner action figures **A:** Tom Morgan **W:** Christopher Priest

3 ❑ Nov 1996 Cover: 2.25 **NM** value: **Cover or less**
Circ: Diamd. preorders: **34,420**
📖 Kyle • based on Kenner action figures **A:** Denys Cowan **W:** Christopher Priest

TOTALLY ALIEN — Trigon

1 ❑ b&w Cover: 2.50 **NM** value: **Cover or less**

2 ❑ b&w Cover: 2.50 **NM** value: **Cover or less**

3 ❑ b&w Cover: 2.50 **NM** value: **Cover or less**

4 ❑ b&w Cover: 2.50 **NM** value: **Cover or less**

5 ❑ b&w Cover: 2.50 **NM** value: **Cover or less**

TOTALLY HORSES! — Painted Pony

1 ❑ Cover: 1.95 **NM** value: **Cover or less**
• magazine. • horse stories

2 ❑ Spr 1997 Cover: 1.95 **NM** value: **Cover or less**
• magazine. • horse stories

3 ❑ Cover: 1.95 **NM** value: **Cover or less**
• magazine. • horse stories

4 ❑ Cover: 1.95 **NM** value: **Cover or less**
• magazine. • horse stories

5 ❑ Sum 1998 Cover: 1.95 **NM** value: **Cover or less**
• magazine. • horse stories

TOTAL RECALL — DC

1 ❑ ca. 1990 Cover: 2.95 **NM** value: **Cover or less**
Circ: CapCity orders: **8,950**
A: Tom Lyle **W:** Dan O'Bannon; Elliott S! Maggin; Gary Goldman; Phillip K. Dick; Ronald Shusett

TOTAL WAR — Gold Key

1 ❑ Jul 1965 Cover: 0.12 **NM** value: **20.00**
• **CGC:** 1 graded, best 6.0

2 ❑ Oct 1965 Cover: 0.12 **NM** value: **15.00**
• Series continued in M.A.R.S. Patrol #3

TOTEMS (CARTOON FROLICS) — Cartoon Frolics

1 ❑ Cover: 2.95 **NM** value: **Cover or less**

2 ❑ Cover: 2.95 **NM** value: **Cover or less**

3 ❑ Cover: 2.95 **NM** value: **Cover or less**
📖 Pawns **A:** Paul F. Chabot **W:** Paul F. Chabot; R. Bentley

TOTEM: SIGN OF THE WARDOG (1ST SERIES) — Alpha Productions

1 ❑ b&w Cover: 2.25 **NM** value: **Cover or less**

2 ❑ b&w Cover: 2.25 **NM** value: **Cover or less**

TOTEM: SIGN OF THE WARDOG (2ND SERIES) — Alpha Productions

1 ❑ b&w Cover: 2.50 **NM** value: **Cover or less**

2 ❑ b&w Cover: 2.50 **NM** value: **Cover or less**

Anl 1❑ Cover: 3.50 **NM** value: **Cover or less**
📖 No Safe Haven; The Mother Of Mayhem, Databank, Boys Will Be Boys **A:** Paul Pelletier; Derec Aucoin; Steve Reman; D. Kevin Wiggins **W:** Bryan Stratton; Ron Fortier; Scott French

TOTEMS (VERTIGO) — DC / Vertigo

1 ❑ Feb 2000 Cover: 5.95 **NM** value: **Cover or less**
Circ: Diamd. preorders: **15,502**
A: Duncan Fegredo; Richard Case; Dean Ormston **W:** Tom Peyer

TO THE HEART OF THE STORM (DC) — DC

1 ❑ Sep 2000 Cover: 14.95 **NM** value: **Cover or less**
A: Will Eisner **W:** Will Eisner

TOUCH OF SILK, A TASTE OF LEATHER, A — Boneyard

1 ❑ Mar 1994, b&w Cover: 2.95 **NM** value: **Cover or less**
No issue number.

TOUCH OF SILVER, A — Image

Jim Valentino's lovingly crafted story of a young comic-book fan in the early 1960s evokes nostalgia from many middle-aged fans. But Valentino strikes a chord familiar to more than baby-boomers in this slice-of-life narrative about a boy who's a little self-conscious, who's not very athletic, and who doesn't have a stable family life. Through it all, the one refuge he clings to are those four-color wonders of escapism: comic books. This title stands out all the more for its unusual quality among others in the Image line. The story of Timothy B. Silver illustrates the universality of comics fans, regardless of the decade in which they were born or the specifics of their lives.

1 ❑ Jan 1997, b&w Cover: 2.95 **NM** value: **Cover or less**
📖 Birthday • semi-autobiographical **A:** Jim Valentino **W:** Jim Valentino

2 ❑ Mar 1997, b&w Cover: 2.95 **NM** value: **Cover or less**
📖 Dance • semi-autobiographical **A:** Jim Valentino **W:** Jim Valentino

3 ❑ May 1997, b&w Cover: 2.95 **NM** value: **Cover or less**
📖 Bullies • semi-autobiographical **A:** Jim Valentino **W:** Jim Valentino

4 ❑ Jul 1997, b&w Cover: 2.95 **NM** value: **Cover or less**
📖 Separation • semi-autobiographical **A:** Jim Valentino **W:** Jim Valentino

5 ❑ Sep 1997 Cover: 2.95 **NM** value: **Cover or less**
📖 Fantasy • b&w with color section; semi-autobiographical **A:** Jim Valentino **W:** Jim Valentino

6 ❑ Nov 1997, b&w Cover: 2.95 **NM** value: **Cover or less**
Circ: Diamd. preorders: **6,338**
• semi-autobiographical **A:** Jim Valentino **W:** Jim Valentino

Bk 1❑ Dec 1997 Cover: 12.95 **NM** value: **Cover or less**
• A Sociopath In Training; collects first five issues **A:** Jim Valentino **W:** Jim Valentino

TOUGH GUYS AND WILD WOMEN — Eternity

1 ❑ Mar 1989, b&w Cover: 2.25 **NM** value: **Cover or less**
📖 The Saint Dective Cases: Suite 13; Blackmail Beauty; The Diamond of Death; The Saint Breaks a Spell • Saint reprints **A:** Walter Johnson **W:** Walter Johnson

2 ❑ b&w Cover: 2.25 **NM** value: **Cover or less**
• Saint reprints

TOUGH KID SQUAD — Timely

1 ❑ Mar 1942 Cover: 0.10 **NM** value: **8000.00**
• **CGC:** 3 graded, best 7.0

TOWER OF SHADOWS — Marvel

1 ❑ Sep 1969 Cover: 0.15 **NM** value: **15.00**
• **CGC:** 4 graded, best 9.6
📖 At the Stroke of Midnight!; From Beyond the Brink!; A Time to Die! **A:** John Buscema; Johnny Craig; Jim Steranko **W:** Johnny Craig; Jim Steranko; Stan Lee

2 ❑ Nov 1969 Cover: 0.15 **NM** value: **10.00**
• **CGC:** 2 graded, best 9.8
A: Neal Adams

3 ❑ Jan 1970 Cover: 0.15 **NM** value: **10.00**
• **CGC:** 1 graded, best 9.4
A: Barry Windsor-Smith

4 ❑ Jan 1970 Cover: 0.15 **NM** value: **8.00**
• **CGC:** 2 graded, best 9.6

5 ❑ May 1970 Cover: 0.15 **NM** value: **8.00**
• **CGC:** 2 graded, best 9.4
A: Barry Windsor-Smith; Wally Wood

6 ❑ Jul 1970 Cover: 0.15 **NM** value: **8.00**
• **CGC:** 1 graded, best 9.2

Other grades: Multiply prices above by **1.5 for Mint • 2/3 for Very Fine • 1/3 for Fine • 1/5 for Very Good • 1/8 for Good**

📖 Man in the Rat-Hole!; The Ghost-Beast!; Contact!; The Scream from Beyond! **A:** Tom Sutton; Steve Ditko; Gene Colan; Wally Wood **W:** Tom Sutton; Stan Lee; Steve Skeates
7 ❑ Sep 1970 Cover: 0.15 **NM** value: **8.00**
• **CGC:** 3 graded, best 9.4
📖 I Was Trapped By Titano The Monster That Time Forgot!; The Scream Of Things; Of Swords And Sorcery!; **A:** Barry Windsor-Smith; Wally Wood **W:** Allyn Brodsky
8 ❑ Nov 1970 Cover: 0.15 **NM** value: **8.00**
• **CGC:** 1 graded, best 9.6
A: Steve Ditko; Wally Wood
9 ❑ Nov 1970 Cover: 0.15 **NM** value: **6.00**
• **CGC:** 1 graded, best 9.0
• Series continued in Creatures On the Loose #10
SE 1 ❑ Dec 1971 Cover: 0.25 **NM** value: **8.00**
• **CGC:** 1 graded, best 7.5

TOXIC! — Apocalypse
1 ❑ Cover: 2.50 **NM** value: **Cover or less**
• Marshal Law
2 ❑ Cover: 2.50 **NM** value: **Cover or less**
• Marshal Law
3 ❑ Cover: 2.50 **NM** value: **Cover or less**
• Marshal Law
4 ❑ Cover: 2.50 **NM** value: **Cover or less**
• Marshal Law
5 ❑ Cover: 2.50 **NM** value: **Cover or less**
📖 Accident Man: Confessions of a Teenage Sociopath • Marshal Law; Mutomatic; The Driver ★ Origin of Accident Man. ★ Appearance of The Bogie Man.
6 ❑ Cover: 2.50 **NM** value: **Cover or less**
• Marshal Law
7 ❑ Cover: 2.50 **NM** value: **Cover or less**
• Marshal Law
8 ❑ Cover: 2.50 **NM** value: **Cover or less**
• Marshal Law
9 ❑ Cover: 2.50 **NM** value: **Cover or less**
• Marshal Law
10 ❑ Cover: 2.50 **NM** value: **Cover or less**
• Marshal Law
11 ❑ Cover: 2.50 **NM** value: **Cover or less**
• Marshal Law
12 ❑ Cover: 2.50 **NM** value: **Cover or less**
• Marshal Law
13 ❑ Cover: 2.50 **NM** value: **Cover or less**
• Marshal Law
14 ❑ Cover: 2.50 **NM** value: **Cover or less**
• Marshal Law
15 ❑ Cover: 2.50 **NM** value: **Cover or less**
• Marshal Law
16 ❑ Cover: 2.50 **NM** value: **Cover or less**
• Marshal Law
17 ❑ Cover: 2.50 **NM** value: **Cover or less**
• Marshal Law
18 ❑ Cover: 2.50 **NM** value: **Cover or less**
• Marshal Law
19 ❑ Cover: 2.50 **NM** value: **Cover or less**
• Marshal Law

TOXIC AVENGER — Marvel
1 ❑ Apr 1991 Cover: 1.50 **NM** value: **2.00**
Circ: CapCity orders: **25,200**
📖 A Hideously Deformed Creature of Superhuman Size and Strength is Born **A:** Rodney Ramos **W:** Doug Moench ★ Origin of Toxic Avenger. ★ 1st Appearance of Toxic Avenger.
2 ❑ May 1991 Cover: 1.50 **NM** value: **Cover or less**
Circ: CapCity orders: **17,200**
A: Rodney Ramos **W:** Doug Moench
3 ❑ Jun 1991 Cover: 1.50 **NM** value: **Cover or less**
Circ: CapCity orders: **16,200**
A: Rodney Ramos **W:** Doug Moench
4 ❑ Jul 1991 Cover: 1.50 **NM** value: **Cover or less**
Circ: CapCity orders: **16,400**
📖 Lethal Linda And The Legend Of Sludgeface **A:** Rodney Ramos **W:** Doug Moench
5 ❑ Aug 1991 Cover: 1.50 **NM** value: **Cover or less**
Circ: CapCity orders: **14,800**
A: Rodney Ramos **W:** Doug Moench
6 ❑ Sep 1991 Cover: 1.50 **NM** value: **Cover or less**
Circ: CapCity orders: **11,400**
A: Rodney Ramos **W:** Doug Moench
7 ❑ Oct 1991 Cover: 1.50 **NM** value: **Cover or less**
Circ: CapCity orders: **9,400**
A: Rodney Ramos **W:** Doug Moench
8 ❑ Nov 1991 Cover: 1.50 **NM** value: **Cover or less**
Circ: CapCity orders: **8,300**
📖 The Souvlaki Sewer Syndrome, Part 2 **A:** Rodney Ramos **W:** Doug Moench
9 ❑ Dec 1991 Cover: 1.50 **NM** value: **Cover or less**
Circ: CapCity orders: **7,500**
A: Rodney Ramos **W:** Doug Moench
10 ❑ Jan 1992 Cover: 1.50 **NM** value: **Cover or less**
Circ: CapCity orders: **6,400**
Photo cover. 📖 Die Yuppie Scum **A:** Rodney Ramos **W:** Doug Moench
11 ❑ Feb 1992 Cover: 1.50 **NM** value: **Cover or less**
Circ: CapCity orders: **5,400**
📖 Nukin' Weasels **A:** Val Mayerik; Rodney Ramos **W:** Doug Moench

TOXIC CRUSADERS — Marvel
1 ❑ May 1992 Cover: 1.25 **NM** value: **Cover or less**
Circ: CapCity orders: **6,800**
📖 The Making of Toxie **A:** Derek Yaniger; Sam Kieth(cover) **W:** Simon Furman ★ Origin of Toxic Avenger.
2 ❑ Jun 1992 Cover: 1.25 **NM** value: **Cover or less**
Circ: CapCity orders: **4,500**
📖 The Big Broadcast of 1992 **A:** Joe Staton **W:** Hilary Barta; Doug Rice
3 ❑ Jul 1992 Cover: 1.25 **NM** value: **Cover or less**
Circ: CapCity orders: **3,300**
4 ❑ Aug 1992 Cover: 1.25 **NM** value: **Cover or less**
Circ: CapCity orders: **3,000**
5 ❑ Sep 1992 Cover: 1.25 **NM** value: **Cover or less**
6 ❑ Oct 1992 Cover: 1.25 **NM** value: **Cover or less**
7 ❑ Nov 1992 Cover: 1.25 **NM** value: **Cover or less**
8 ❑ Dec 1992 Cover: 1.25 **NM** value: **Cover or less**

TOXIC GUMBO — DC / Vertigo
1 ❑ May 1998 Cover: 5.95 **NM** value: **Cover or less**
Circ: Diamd. preorders: **11,982**
No issue number. One-shot. • prestige format. **A:** Ted McKeever **W:** Lydia Lunch

TOXIC PARADISE — Slave Labor
1 ❑ b&w Cover: 4.95 **NM** value: **Cover or less**
cardstock cover. 📖 Love and Romance; Loser; Warming Up Antarctica; Caveman; Freight Train of Love; Fuck Love; True Wedding Funnies; First Date; One Night; Faith, Hope and Love; Love Song; Hasshahat in Love • Love & Romance **A:** Jim Hill; Michael Bresnahan; Gene Yang; Jeff Levine; Ariel Schrag; Andi Watson; Stephanie Gladden; Leslee Parker; Scott Mills; Tim Lowery; Tony Consiglio **W:** Jim Hill; Michael Bresnahan; Gene Yang; Jeff Levine; Ariel Schrag; Andi Watson; Stephanie Gladden; Leslee Parker; Scott Mills; Tim Lowery; Tony Consiglio

TOXINE — Nose
1 ❑ Cover: 3.00 **NM** value: **Cover or less**

TOYBOY — Continuity
1 ❑ Oct 1986 Cover: 2.00 **NM** value: **Cover or less**
Circ: CapCity orders: **5,950**
A: Neal Adams **W:** Neal Adams
2 ❑ Aug 1987 Cover: 2.00 **NM** value: **Cover or less**
Circ: CapCity orders: **4,475**
A: Neal Adams **W:** Neal Adams
3 ❑ Nov 1987 Cover: 2.00 **NM** value: **Cover or less**
Circ: CapCity orders: **3,275**
A: Neal Adams **W:** Neal Adams
4 ❑ Feb 1988 Cover: 2.00 **NM** value: **Cover or less**
Circ: CapCity orders: **3,350**
A: Neal Adams **W:** Neal Adams
5 ❑ Jun 1988 Cover: 2.00 **NM** value: **Cover or less**
Circ: CapCity orders: **3,025**
A: Neal Adams **W:** Neal Adams
6 ❑ 1988 Cover: 2.00 **NM** value: **Cover or less**
Circ: CapCity orders: **2,325**
A: Neal Adams **W:** Neal Adams
7 ❑ Mar 1989 Cover: 2.00 **NM** value: **Cover or less**
A: Neal Adams **W:** Neal Adams

TOYLAND COMICS — Fiction House
1 ❑ Jan 1947 Cover: 0.10 **NM** value: **150.00**
2 ❑ Mar 1947 Cover: 0.10 **NM** value: **100.00**
3 ❑ Jul 1947 Cover: 0.10 **NM** value: **100.00**

TOY STORY (DISNEY'S...) — Marvel
1 ❑ Dec 1995 Cover: 4.95 **NM** value: **Cover or less**
W: Bob Foster

TOY TOWN COMICS — Toytown
1 ❑ ca. 1945 Cover: 0.10 **NM** value: **150.00**
• **CGC:** 1 graded, best 8.5
2 ❑ Cover: 0.10 **NM** value: **90.00**
3 ❑ Cover: 0.10 **NM** value: **75.00**
4 ❑ Oct 1946 Cover: 0.10 **NM** value: **75.00**
5 ❑ Dec 1946 Cover: 0.10 **NM** value: **75.00**
6 ❑ Mar 1947 Cover: 0.10 **NM** value: **75.00**
7 ❑ May 1947 Cover: 0.10 **NM** value: **75.00**

TRACI LORDS: THE OUTLAW YEARS — Boneyard
1 ❑ Cover: 2.75 **NM** value: **3.00**
A: Hart Fisher; Alain Renauld; Larry Saunders **W:** Hart Fisher

TRACKER — Blackthorne
1 ❑ May 1988, b&w Cover: 2.00 **NM** value: **Cover or less**
A: William Van Horn
2 ❑ b&w Cover: 2.00 **NM** value: **Cover or less**
A: William Van Horn

TRAGG AND THE SKY GODS — Whitman
1 ❑ Jun 1975 Cover: 0.25 **NM** value: **5.00**
• **CGC:** 2 graded, best 9.4
📖 Death-Duel **A:** Dan Spiegle **W:** Don Glut
2 ❑ Sep 1975 Cover: 0.25 **NM** value: **3.00**
3 ❑ Dec 1975 Cover: 0.25 **NM** value: **2.50**
4 ❑ Feb 1976 Cover: 0.25 **NM** value: **2.50**
5 ❑ Apr 1976 Cover: 0.25 **NM** value: **2.50**
6 ❑ Sep 1976 Cover: 0.25 **NM** value: **2.50**
7 ❑ Nov 1976 Cover: 0.30 **NM** value: **2.50**
8 ❑ Feb 1977 Cover: 0.30 **NM** value: **2.50**
9 ❑ May 1982 Cover: 0.60 **NM** value: **2.50**

TRAGICAL COMEDY OR COMICAL TRAGEDY OF MR. PUNCH, THE — DC / Vertigo
1 ❑ Cover: 24.95 **NM** value: **Cover or less**
hardcover. • British softcover edition. **A:** Dave McKean **W:** Neil Gaiman
1/HC ❑ Cover: 29.95 **NM** value: **Cover or less**
• Hardcover edition. **A:** Dave McKean **W:** Neil Gaiman

TRAIL BLAZERS — Street & Smith
1 ❑ ca. 1942 Cover: 0.10 **NM** value: **250.00**
2 ❑ ca. 1942 Cover: 0.10 **NM** value: **150.00**
3 ❑ ca. 1942 Cover: 0.10 **NM** value: **125.00**
4 ❑ ca. 1942 Cover: 0.10 **NM** value: **125.00**

TRAILER TRASH — Tundra
All issues are adults only.
1 ❑ b&w Cover: 2.00 **NM** value: **Cover or less**
4 ❑ b&w Cover: 2.95 **NM** value: **Cover or less**
7 ❑ Jun 1996, b&w Cover: 2.95 **NM** value: **Cover or less**
8 ❑ Nov 1996, b&w Cover: 2.95 **NM** value: **Cover or less**

TRANCERS — Eternity
1 ❑ Aug 1991, full color Cover: 2.50 **NM** value: **Cover or less**
Circ: CapCity orders: **2,300**
A: Cariello **W:** S.A. Bennett
2 ❑ full color Cover: 2.50 **NM** value: **Cover or less**
A: Cariello **W:** S.A. Bennett
Bk 1 ❑ Aug 1991 Cover: 4.95 **NM** value: **Cover or less**

TRANQUILITY — Dreamsmith
1 ❑ Sep 1998, b&w Cover: 2.50 **NM** value: **Cover or less**
Circ: Diamd. preorders: **1,995**
2 ❑ Oct 1998, b&w Cover: 2.50 **NM** value: **Cover or less**
3 ❑ Nov 1998, b&w Cover: 2.50 **NM** value: **Cover or less**

TRANQUILIZER — Luxurious
1 ❑ Cover: 2.95 **NM** value: **Cover or less**
2 ❑ Cover: 2.95 **NM** value: **Cover or less**

TRANSFORMERS, THE — Marvel
On a faraway world in the Alpha Centauri system, there exists a world known as Cybertron. There, through a strange process of carbon-bonding, a race of mechanical beings called Autobots has evolved, eventually transforming their world into a paradise.

But one group, the Decepticons, are not content with their peaceful life and launch a deadly war for control of Cybertron. After a terrible global conflict, the Decepticons are on the verge of total defeat when they change plans suddenly and flee to Earth. There, they disguise themselves in other forms, such as cars and planes. But at a moment's notice, they can once again transform into terrible machines of destruction. To save Earth from their ravages, the Autobots are also forced to come to Earth to battle their age-old enemy.

The Transformers derived from a popular line of Hasbro toys.

1 ❑ Sep 1984 Cover: 0.75 **NM** value: **2.50**
• **CGC:** 21 graded, best 9.8
• "Limited Series #1" ★ 1st Appearance of Transformers.
2 ❑ Nov 1984 Cover: 0.75 **NM** value: **2.00**
• **CGC:** 2 graded, best 9.4
• "Limited Series #2"
3 ❑ Jan 1985 Cover: 0.75 **NM** value: **2.00**
• **CGC:** 3 graded, best 9.2
• Spider-Man; "Limited Series #3"
4 ❑ Mar 1985 Cover: 0.75 **NM** value: **1.50**
• **CGC:** 2 graded, best 9.2
• "Limited Series #4"
5 ❑ Jun 1985 Cover: 0.75 **NM** value: **1.50**
Circ: CapCity orders: **15,300** • **CGC:** 2 graded, best 9.0
6 ❑ Jul 1985 Cover: 0.75 **NM** value: **1.50**
Circ: CapCity orders: **15,100**
7 ❑ Aug 1985 Cover: 0.75 **NM** value: **1.50**
Circ: CapCity orders: **15,500**
8 ❑ Sep 1985 Cover: 0.75 **NM** value: **1.50**
Circ: CapCity orders: **16,100** • **CGC:** 2 graded, best 9.8
★ Appearance of Dinobots.
9 ❑ Oct 1985 Cover: 0.75 **NM** value: **1.50**
Circ: CapCity orders: **15,200**
10 ❑ Nov 1985 Cover: 0.75 **NM** value: **1.50**
Circ: CapCity orders: **15,100** • **CGC:** 2 graded, best 9.8
★ Versus Devastator.
11 ❑ Dec 1985 Cover: 0.75 **NM** value: **1.50**
Circ: CapCity orders: **15,000** • **CGC:** 1 graded, best 9.6
★ Versus Jetfire.
12 ❑ Jan 1986 Cover: 0.75 **NM** value: **1.50**
Circ: Statement: **300,982** CapCity orders: **15,400** • **CGC:** 1 graded, best 9.6
13 ❑ Feb 1986 Cover: 0.75 **NM** value: **1.50**
Circ: Statement: **300,982** CapCity orders: **14,300**
14 ❑ Mar 1986 Cover: 0.75 **NM** value: **1.50**
Circ: Statement: **300,982** CapCity orders: **15,800**
15 ❑ Apr 1986 Cover: 0.75 **NM** value: **1.50**
Circ: Statement: **300,982** CapCity orders: **16,700** • **CGC:** 1 graded, best 9.2
16 ❑ May 1986 Cover: 0.75 **NM** value: **1.50**
Circ: Statement: **300,982** CapCity orders: **17,200** • **CGC:** 1 graded, best 8.5
17 ❑ Jun 1986 Cover: 0.75 **NM** value: **1.50**
Circ: Statement: **300,982** CapCity orders: **16,900** • **CGC:** 3 graded, best 9.8
18 ❑ Jul 1986 Cover: 0.75 **NM** value: **1.50**
Circ: Statement: **300,982** CapCity orders: **16,900** • **CGC:** 1 graded, best 9.4
19 ❑ Aug 1986 Cover: 0.75 **NM** value: **1.50**
Circ: Statement: **300,982** CapCity orders: **16,700** • **CGC:** 1 graded, best 8.5
20 ❑ Sep 1986 Cover: 0.75 **NM** value: **1.50**
Circ: Statement: **300,982** CapCity orders: **116,400** • **CGC:** 1 graded, best 8.5

21 ❑ Oct 1986 Cover: 0.75 **NM** value: **1.25**
Circ: Statement: **300,982** CapCity orders: **16,700 • CGC:** 1 graded, best 8.5
★ 1st Appearance of Aerialbots.

22 ❑ Nov 1986 Cover: 0.75 **NM** value: **1.25**
Circ: Statement: **300,982** CapCity orders: **15,900 • CGC:** 1 graded, best 9.4

23 ❑ Dec 1986 Cover: 0.75 **NM** value: **1.25**
Circ: Statement: **300,982** CapCity orders: **16,400 • CGC:** 1 graded, best 9.0

24 ❑ Jan 1987 Cover: 0.75 **NM** value: **1.25**
Circ: Statement: **217,275** CapCity orders: **15,700**

25 ❑ Feb 1987 Cover: 0.75 **NM** value: **1.25**
Circ: Statement: **217,275** CapCity orders: **15,300 • CGC:** 1 graded, best 9.6

26 ❑ Mar 1987 Cover: 0.75 **NM** value: **1.25**
Circ: Statement: **217,275** CapCity orders: **16,900 • CGC:** 1 graded, best 9.2

27 ❑ Apr 1987 Cover: 0.75 **NM** value: **1.25**
Circ: Statement: **217,275** CapCity orders: **17,300**

28 ❑ May 1987 Cover: 1.00 **NM** value: **1.25**
Circ: Statement: **217,275** CapCity orders: **16,300**

29 ❑ Jun 1987 Cover: 1.00 **NM** value: **1.25**
Circ: Statement: **217,275** CapCity orders: **16,200**

30 ❑ Jul 1987 Cover: 1.00 **NM** value: **1.25**
Circ: Statement: **217,275** CapCity orders: **16,400**

31 ❑ Aug 1987 Cover: 1.00 **NM** value: **1.25**
Circ: Statement: **217,275** CapCity orders: **15,800**

32 ❑ Sep 1987 Cover: 1.00 **NM** value: **1.25**
Circ: Statement: **217,275** CapCity orders: **16,900**

33 ❑ Oct 1987 Cover: 1.00 **NM** value: **1.25**
Circ: Statement: **217,275** CapCity orders: **16,800**

34 ❑ Nov 1987 Cover: 1.00 **NM** value: **1.25**
Circ: Statement: **217,275** CapCity orders: **16,700 • CGC:** 1 graded, best 9.4

35 ❑ Dec 1987 Cover: 1.00 **NM** value: **1.25**
Circ: Statement: **217,275** CapCity orders: **15,700 • CGC:** 1 graded, best 9.0

36 ❑ Jan 1988 Cover: 1.00 **NM** value: **1.25**
Circ: Statement: **149,975** CapCity orders: **15,200 • CGC:** 1 graded, best 9.0

37 ❑ Feb 1988 Cover: 1.00 **NM** value: **1.25**
Circ: Statement: **149,975** CapCity orders: **14,700 • CGC:** 1 graded, best 8.0

38 ❑ Mar 1988 Cover: 1.00 **NM** value: **1.25**
Circ: Statement: **149,975** CapCity orders: **14,100**

39 ❑ Apr 1988 Cover: 1.00 **NM** value: **1.25**
Circ: Statement: **149,975** CapCity orders: **13,400 • CGC:** 1 graded, best 9.4

40 ❑ May 1988 Cover: 1.00 **NM** value: **1.25**
Circ: Statement: **149,975** CapCity orders: **12,800**

41 ❑ Jun 1988 Cover: 1.00 **NM** value: **Cover or less**
Circ: Statement: **149,975** CapCity orders: **11,500**

42 ❑ Jul 1988 Cover: 1.00 **NM** value: **Cover or less**
Circ: Statement: **149,975** CapCity orders: **11,400**

43 ❑ Aug 1988 Cover: 1.00 **NM** value: **Cover or less**
Circ: Statement: **149,975** CapCity orders: **11,250**

44 ❑ Sep 1988 Cover: 1.00 **NM** value: **Cover or less**
Circ: Statement: **149,975** CapCity orders: **10,800**

45 ❑ Oct 1988 Cover: 1.00 **NM** value: **Cover or less**
Circ: Statement: **149,975** CapCity orders: **11,000**

46 ❑ Nov 1988 Cover: 1.00 **NM** value: **Cover or less**
Circ: Statement: **149,975** CapCity orders: **11,200 • CGC:** 1 graded, best 9.2

47 ❑ Dec 1988 Cover: 1.00 **NM** value: **Cover or less**
Circ: Statement: **149,975** CapCity orders: **10,700**

48 ❑ Jan 1989 Cover: 1.00 **NM** value: **Cover or less**
Circ: Statement: **96,380** CapCity orders: **9,800**

49 ❑ Feb 1989 Cover: 1.00 **NM** value: **Cover or less**
Circ: Statement: **96,380** CapCity orders: **3,100**

50 ❑ Mar 1989 Cover: 1.50 **NM** value: **Cover or less**
Circ: Statement: **96,380** CapCity orders: **3,200**

51 ❑ Apr 1989 Cover: 1.00 **NM** value: **Cover or less**
Circ: Statement: **96,380** CapCity orders: **3,200**

52 ❑ May 1989 Cover: 1.00 **NM** value: **Cover or less**
Circ: Statement: **96,380** CapCity orders: **8,700**

53 ❑ Jun 1989 Cover: 1.00 **NM** value: **Cover or less**
Circ: Statement: **96,380** CapCity orders: **8,500 • CGC:** 1 graded, best 9.0

54 ❑ Jul 1989 Cover: 1.00 **NM** value: **Cover or less**
Circ: Statement: **96,380** CapCity orders: **8,500**

55 ❑ Aug 1989 Cover: 1.00 **NM** value: **Cover or less**
Circ: Statement: **96,380** CapCity orders: **8,300**

56 ❑ Sep 1989 Cover: 1.00 **NM** value: **Cover or less**
Circ: Statement: **96,380** CapCity orders: **8,300**

57 ❑ Oct 1989 Cover: 1.00 **NM** value: **Cover or less**
Circ: Statement: **96,380** CapCity orders: **7,800**

58 ❑ Nov 1989 Cover: 1.00 **NM** value: **Cover or less**
Circ: Statement: **96,380** CapCity orders: **7,700**

59 ❑ Nov 1989 Cover: 1.00 **NM** value: **Cover or less**
Circ: Statement: **96,380** CapCity orders: **7,200**

60 ❑ Dec 1989 Cover: 1.00 **NM** value: **Cover or less**
Circ: Statement: **96,380** CapCity orders: **7,300**

61 ❑ Dec 1989 Cover: 1.00 **NM** value: **Cover or less**
Circ: Statement: **96,380** CapCity orders: **7,300**

62 ❑ Jan 1990 Cover: 1.00 **NM** value: **Cover or less**
Circ: Statement: **69,833** CapCity orders: **7,300**

63 ❑ Feb 1990 Cover: 1.00 **NM** value: **Cover or less**
Circ: Statement: **69,833** CapCity orders: **7,100**

64 ❑ Mar 1990 Cover: 1.00 **NM** value: **Cover or less**
Circ: Statement: **69,833** CapCity orders: **7,000**

65 ❑ Apr 1990 Cover: 1.00 **NM** value: **Cover or less**
Circ: Statement: **69,833** CapCity orders: **6,800**

66 ❑ May 1990 Cover: 1.00 **NM** value: **Cover or less**
Circ: Statement: **69,833** CapCity orders: **6,900**

67 ❑ Jun 1990 Cover: 1.00 **NM** value: **Cover or less**
Circ: Statement: **69,833** CapCity orders: **6,800**

68 ❑ Jul 1990 Cover: 1.00 **NM** value: **Cover or less**
Circ: Statement: **69,833** CapCity orders: **6,800**

69 ❑ Aug 1990 Cover: 1.00 **NM** value: **Cover or less**
Circ: Statement: **69,833** CapCity orders: **6,700**

70 ❑ Sep 1990 Cover: 1.00 **NM** value: **Cover or less**
Circ: Statement: **69,833** CapCity orders: **6,700**

71 ❑ Oct 1990 Cover: 1.00 **NM** value: **Cover or less**
Circ: Statement: **69,833** CapCity orders: **6,400 • CGC:** 2 graded, best 9.4

72 ❑ Nov 1990 Cover: 1.00 **NM** value: **Cover or less**
Circ: Statement: **69,833** CapCity orders: **6,300 • CGC:** 2 graded, best 7.5

73 ❑ Dec 1990 Cover: 1.00 **NM** value: **Cover or less**
Circ: Statement: **69,833** CapCity orders: **6,400 • CGC:** 1 graded, best 9.2

74 ❑ Jan 1991 Cover: 1.00 **NM** value: **Cover or less**
Circ: CapCity orders: **6,500 • CGC:** 1 graded, best 9.0

75 ❑ Feb 1991 Cover: 1.50 **NM** value: **Cover or less**
Circ: CapCity orders: **6,900**
• Double-size.

76 ❑ Mar 1991 Cover: 1.00 **NM** value: **Cover or less**
Circ: CapCity orders: **6,500 • CGC:** 1 graded, best 9.4

77 ❑ Apr 1991 Cover: 1.00 **NM** value: **Cover or less**
Circ: CapCity orders: **6,400 • CGC:** 1 graded, best 9.2

78 ❑ May 1991 Cover: 1.00 **NM** value: **15.00**
Circ: CapCity orders: **6,800 • CGC:** 1 graded, best 9.2

79 ❑ Jun 1991 Cover: 1.00 **NM** value: **15.00**
Circ: CapCity orders: **6,900 • CGC:** 2 graded, best 9.6

80 ❑ Jul 1991 Cover: 1.00 **NM** value: **25.00**
Circ: CapCity orders: **7,500 • CGC:** 6 graded, best 9.4
final issue.

TRANSFORMERS COMICS MAGAZINE — Marvel

1 ❑ Jan 1987 Cover: 1.50 **NM** value: **Cover or less**
• digest.
2 ❑ Mar 1987 Cover: 1.50 **NM** value: **Cover or less**
3 ❑ May 1987 Cover: 1.50 **NM** value: **Cover or less**
4 ❑ Jul 1987 Cover: 1.50 **NM** value: **Cover or less**
5 ❑ Sep 1987 Cover: 1.50 **NM** value: **Cover or less**
6 ❑ Nov 1987 Cover: 1.50 **NM** value: **Cover or less**
7 ❑ Jan 1988 Cover: 1.50 **NM** value: **Cover or less**
8 ❑ Mar 1988 Cover: 1.50 **NM** value: **Cover or less**
9 ❑ May 1988 Cover: 1.50 **NM** value: **Cover or less**
10 ❑ Jul 1988 Cover: 1.50 **NM** value: **Cover or less**

TRANSFORMERS: GENERATION 2 — Marvel

1 ❑ Nov 1993 Cover: 1.75 **NM** value: **Cover or less**
Circ: CapCity orders: **25,900**
★ Origin of Transformers.

1/SC❑ Nov 1993 Cover: 2.95 **NM** value: **Cover or less**
Circ: CapCity orders: **8,350 • CGC:** 3 graded, best 9.8
foil fold-out cover. ★ Origin of Transformers.

2 ❑ Dec 1993 Cover: 1.75 **NM** value: **Cover or less**
Circ: CapCity orders: **15,000**

3 ❑ Jan 1994 Cover: 1.75 **NM** value: **Cover or less**
Circ: CapCity orders: **13,100**

4 ❑ Feb 1994 Cover: 1.75 **NM** value: **Cover or less**
Circ: CapCity orders: **12,600**
★ Appearance of Dinobots.

5 ❑ Mar 1994 Cover: 1.75 **NM** value: **Cover or less**
Circ: CapCity orders: **12,800**

6 ❑ Apr 1994 Cover: 1.75 **NM** value: **Cover or less**
Circ: CapCity orders: **11,700**

7 ❑ May 1994 Cover: 1.75 **NM** value: **Cover or less**
Circ: CapCity orders: **11,400**

8 ❑ Jun 1994 Cover: 1.75 **NM** value: **Cover or less**
Circ: CapCity orders: **10,750**

9 ❑ Jul 1994 Cover: 1.75 **NM** value: **Cover or less**
Circ: CapCity orders: **10,150**

10 ❑ Aug 1994 Cover: 1.75 **NM** value: **Cover or less**
Circ: CapCity orders: **9,600**

11 ❑ Sep 1994 Cover: 1.75 **NM** value: **Cover or less**
Circ: CapCity orders: **8,900**

12 ❑ Oct 1994 Cover: 2.25 **NM** value: **Cover or less**
Circ: CapCity orders: **8,500**
• double-sized. final issue.

TRANSFORMERS, THE: HEADMASTERS — Marvel

1 ❑ Jul 1987 Cover: 1.00 **NM** value: **Cover or less**
Circ: CapCity orders: **23,700**

2 ❑ Sep 1987 Cover: 1.00 **NM** value: **Cover or less**
Circ: CapCity orders: **19,800**
📖 Broken Glass **A:** Frank Springer **W:** Bob Budiansky

3 ❑ Nov 1987 Cover: 1.00 **NM** value: **Cover or less**
Circ: CapCity orders: **18,600**

4 ❑ Jan 1988 Cover: 0.75 **NM** value: **1.00**
Circ: CapCity orders: **16,700**

TRANSFORMERS IN 3-D, THE — Blackthorne

1 ❑ Cover: 2.50 **NM** value: **Cover or less**
📖 The Test
2 ❑ Dec 1987 Cover: 2.50 **NM** value: **Cover or less**
3 ❑ Apr 1988 Cover: 2.50 **NM** value: **Cover or less**
Circ: CapCity orders: **2,300**

TRANSFORMERS MOVIE — Marvel

1 ❑ Dec 1986 Cover: 0.75 **NM** value: **1.00**
• **CGC:** 1 graded, best 9.6

2 ❑ Jan 1987 Cover: 0.75 **NM** value: **1.00**
• **CGC:** 1 graded, best 9.6

3 ❑ Feb 1987 Cover: 0.75 **NM** value: **1.00**
Circ: CapCity orders: **14,000**

TRANSFORMERS UNIVERSE — Marvel

1 ❑ Dec 1986 Cover: 1.25 **NM** value: **Cover or less**
Circ: CapCity orders: **16,900**

2 ❑ Jan 1987 Cover: 1.25 **NM** value: **Cover or less**
Circ: CapCity orders: **20,700**

3 ❑ Feb 1987 Cover: 1.25 **NM** value: **Cover or less**
Circ: CapCity orders: **14,400**

4 ❑ Mar 1987 Cover: 1.25 **NM** value: **Cover or less**
Circ: CapCity orders: **18,200**

Bk 1❑ Mar 1988 Cover: 5.95 **NM** value: **Cover or less**
Circ: CapCity orders: **2,275**

TRANSIT — Vortex

1 ❑ Mar 1987 Cover: 1.75 **NM** value: **Cover or less**
2 ❑ May 1987 Cover: 1.75 **NM** value: **Cover or less**
3 ❑ Jul 1987 Cover: 1.75 **NM** value: **Cover or less**
4 ❑ Sep 1987 Cover: 1.75 **NM** value: **Cover or less**
5 ❑ Nov 1987 Cover: 1.75 **NM** value: **Cover or less**

TRANSMETROPOLITAN — DC / Helix

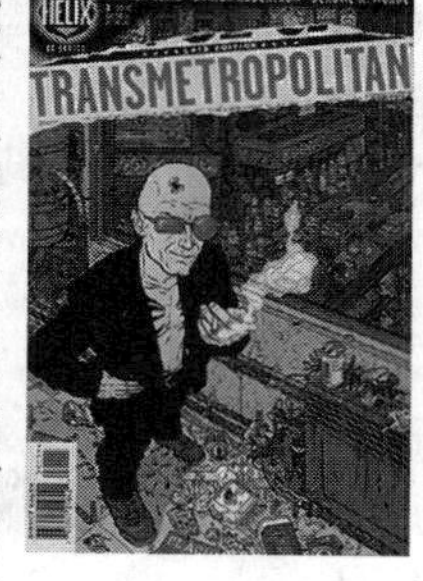

Taking its title from a rowdy song by Irish rockers the Pogues and basing its main character on legendary "gonzo journalist" Dr. Hunter S. Thompson (author of Fear and Loathing in Las Vegas and the model for another famous comic strip character, Doonesbury's Uncle Duke), Transmetropolitan positions itself squarely at the acid-etched edge of 1990s hip culture. Transmetropolitan follows the adventures of psychotic writer Spider Jerusalem in a nightmarish near-future, cyber-nightmare world of drugs, aliens, androids, mutants, technology gone mad, and lots more drugs. High-octane writing by Warren Ellis is augmented by lush, compulsively detail-rich art by Darick Robertson. Transmetropolitan was an adrenaline-charged jumpstart to the science-fiction Helix imprint from DC, which later merged with Vertigo.

1 ❑ Sep 1997 Cover: 2.50 **NM** value: **6.00**
Circ: Diamd. preorders: **18,151 • CGC:** 8 graded, best 9.6
A: Darick Robertson **W:** Warren Ellis

2 ❑ Oct 1997 Cover: 2.50 **NM** value: **5.00**
Circ: Diamd. preorders: **14,445**
A: Darick Robertson **W:** Warren Ellis

3 ❑ Nov 1997 Cover: 2.50 **NM** value: **4.00**
Circ: Diamd. preorders: **15,332**
📖 Up on the Roof **A:** Darick Robertson **W:** Warren Ellis

4 ❑ Dec 1997 Cover: 2.50 **NM** value: **4.00**
Circ: Diamd. preorders: **15,823**
📖 On the Stump **A:** Darick Robertson **W:** Warren Ellis

5 ❑ Jan 1998 Cover: 2.50 **NM** value: **4.00**
Circ: Diamd. preorders: **15,779**
A: Darick Robertson **W:** Warren Ellis

6 ❑ Feb 1998 Cover: 2.50 **NM** value: **3.00**
Circ: Diamd. preorders: **15,107**
A: Darick Robertson **W:** Warren Ellis

7 ❑ Mar 1998 Cover: 2.50 **NM** value: **3.00**
Circ: Diamd. preorders: **14,808**
A: Darick Robertson **W:** Warren Ellis

8 ❑ Apr 1998 Cover: 2.50 **NM** value: **3.00**
Circ: Diamd. preorders: **14,284**
A: Darick Robertson **W:** Warren Ellis

9 ❑ May 1998 Cover: 2.50 **NM** value: **3.00**
Circ: Diamd. preorders: **14,140**
A: Darick Robertson **W:** Warren Ellis

10 ❑ Jun 1998 Cover: 2.50 **NM** value: **3.00**
Circ: Diamd. preorders: **15,012**
A: Darick Robertson **W:** Warren Ellis

11 ❑ Jul 1998 Cover: 2.50 **NM** value: **3.00**
Circ: Diamd. preorders: **14,620**
A: Darick Robertson **W:** Warren Ellis

12 ❑ Aug 1998 Cover: 2.50 **NM** value: **3.00**
Circ: Diamd. preorders: **14,827**
A: Darick Robertson **W:** Warren Ellis

13 ❑ Sep 1998 Cover: 2.50 **NM** value: **Cover or less**
Circ: Diamd. preorders: **15,405**
📖 Year of the Bastard, Part 1 **A:** Darick Robertson **W:** Warren Ellis

14 ❑ Oct 1998 Cover: 2.50 **NM** value: **Cover or less**
Circ: Diamd. preorders: **15,637**
📖 Year of the Bastard, Part 2 **A:** Darick Robertson **W:** Warren Ellis

15 ❑ Nov 1998 Cover: 2.50 **NM** value: **Cover or less**
Circ: Diamd. preorders: **15,907**
📖 Year of the Bastard, Part 3 **A:** Darick Robertson **W:** Warren Ellis

16 ❑ Dec 1998 Cover: 2.50 **NM** value: **Cover or less**
Circ: Diamd. preorders: **18,112**
📖 Year of the Bastard, Part 4 **A:** Darick Robertson **W:** Warren Ellis

17 ❑ Jan 1999 Cover: 2.50 **NM** value: **Cover or less**
Circ: Diamd. preorders: **16,286**
📖 Year of the Bastard, Part 5 **A:** Darick Robertson **W:** Warren Ellis

18 ❑ Feb 1999 Cover: 2.50 **NM** value: **Cover or less**
Circ: Diamd. preorders: **16,444**
📖 Year of the Bastard, Part 6 **A:** Darick Robertson **W:** Warren Ellis

19 ❑ Mar 1999 Cover: 2.50 **NM** value: **Cover or less**
Circ: Diamd. preorders: **16,854**
📖 The New Scum, Part 1 **A:** Darick Robertson **W:** Warren Ellis

20 ❑ Apr 1999 Cover: 2.50 **NM** value: **Cover or less**
Circ: Diamd. preorders: **16,439**
📖 The New Scum, Part 2 **A:** Darick Robertson **W:** Warren Ellis

21 ❑ May 1999 Cover: 2.50 **NM** value: **Cover or less**
Circ: Diamd. preorders: **16,837**
📖 The New Scum, Part 3 **A:** Darick Robertson **W:** Warren Ellis

22 ❑ Jun 1999 Cover: 2.50 **NM** value: **Cover or less**
Circ: Diamd. preorders: **17,694**
📖 The New Scum, Part 4, New Streets **A:** Darick Robertson **W:** Warren Ellis

23 ❑ Jul 1999 Cover: 2.50 **NM** value: **Cover or less**
Circ: Diamd. preorders: **17,725**
📖 The New Scum, Part 5, New Boss • 100 Bullets preview **A:** Darick Robertson **W:** Warren Ellis

24 ❑ Aug 1999 Cover: 2.50 **NM** value: **Cover or less**
Circ: Diamd. preorders: **17,897**
A: Darick Robertson **W:** Warren Ellis

Other grades: Multiply prices above by **1.5 for Mint • 2/3 for Very Fine • 1/3 for Fine • 1/5 for Very Good • 1/8 for Good**

25 ☐ Sep 1999 Cover: 2.50 **NM value: Cover or less**
Circ: Diamd. preorders: **18,646**
Here To Go **A:** Darick Robertson **W:** Warren Ellis

26 ☐ Oct 1999 Cover: 2.50 **NM value: Cover or less**
Circ: Diamd. preorders: **17,970**
21 Days in the City **A:** Darick Robertson **W:** Warren Ellis

27 ☐ Nov 1999 Cover: 2.50 **NM value: Cover or less**
Circ: Diamd. preorders: **18,137**
A: Darick Robertson **W:** Warren Ellis

28 ☐ Dec 1999 Cover: 2.50 **NM value: Cover or less**
Circ: Diamd. preorders: **18,679**
Lonely Ciy, Part 1 **A:** Darick Robertson **W:** Warren Ellis

29 ☐ Jan 2000 Cover: 2.50 **NM value: Cover or less**
Circ: Diamd. preorders: **18,377**
Lonely Ciy, Part 2 **A:** Darick Robertson **W:** Warren Ellis

30 ☐ Feb 2000 Cover: 2.50 **NM value: Cover or less**
Circ: Diamd. preorders: **18,391**
Lonely Ciy, Part 3 **A:** Darick Robertson **W:** Warren Ellis

31 ☐ Mar 2000 Cover: 2.50 **NM value: Cover or less**
Circ: Diamd. preorders: **18,230**
A: Darick Robertson **W:** Warren Ellis

32 ☐ Apr 2000 Cover: 2.50 **NM value: Cover or less**
Circ: Diamd. preorders: **17,614**
A: Darick Robertson **W:** Warren Ellis

33 ☐ May 2000 Cover: 2.50 **NM value: Cover or less**
Circ: Diamd. preorders: **18,237**
Dancing in the Here and Now **A:** Darick Robertson **W:** Warren Ellis

34 ☐ 2000 Cover: 2.50 **NM value: Cover or less**
Circ: Diamd. preorders: **18,517**
A: Darick Robertson **W:** Warren Ellis

35 ☐ 2000 Cover: 2.50 **NM value: Cover or less**
Circ: Diamd. preorders: **19,142**
A: Darick Robertson **W:** Warren Ellis

36 ☐ 2000 Cover: 2.50 **NM value: Cover or less**
Circ: Diamd. preorders: **19,385**
A: Darick Robertson **W:** Warren Ellis

37 ☐ Oct 2000 Cover: 2.50 **NM value: Cover or less**
Circ: Diamd. preorders: **18,517**
Back to Basics, Part 1 **A:** Darick Robertson **W:** Warren Ellis

38 ☐ Nov 2000 Cover: 2.50 **NM value: Cover or less**
Circ: Diamd. preorders: **19,024**
Back to Basics, Part 2 **A:** Darick Robertson **W:** Warren Ellis

39 ☐ Dec 2000 Cover: 2.50 **NM value: Cover or less**
Circ: Diamd. preorders: **18,973**
Back to Basics, Part 3 **A:** Darick Robertson; Tim Bradstreet(cover) **W:** Warren Ellis

40 ☐ Jan 2001 Cover: 2.50 **NM value: Cover or less**
Circ: Diamd. preorders: **19,350**
Business **A:** Rodney Ramos; Darick Robertson **W:** Warren Ellis

41 ☐ Feb 2001 Cover: 2.50 **NM value: Cover or less**
Circ: Diamd. preorders: **19,168**
There is a Reason **A:** Rodney Ramos; Darick Robertson **W:** Warren Ellis

42 ☐ Mar 2001 Cover: 2.50 **NM value: Cover or less**
Circ: Diamd. preorders: **18,913**
Spider's Thrash **A:** Rodney Ramos; Darick Robertson **W:** Warren Ellis

43 ☐ Apr 2001 Cover: 2.50 **NM value: Cover or less**
Circ: Diamd. preorders: **18,870**
Dirge, Part 1 **A:** Darick Robertson **W:** Warren Ellis

44 ☐ May 2001 Cover: 2.50 **NM value: Cover or less**
Circ: Diamd. preorders: **18,840**
Dirge, Part 2 **A:** Darick Robertson **W:** Warren Ellis

45 ☐ Jun 2001 Cover: 2.50 **NM value: Cover or less**
Circ: Diamd. preorders: **18,903**
Dirge, Part 3 **A:** Darick Robertson **W:** Warren Ellis

46 ☐ 2001 Cover: 2.50 **NM value: Cover or less**
Circ: Diamd. preorders: **19,168**

47 ☐ 2001 Cover: 2.50 **NM value: Cover or less**
Circ: Diamd. preorders: **20,499**

Bk 1☐ Cover: 7.95 **NM value: Cover or less**
Back on the Street • Back On The Street; collects issues #1-3 **A:** Darick Robertson **W:** Warren Ellis

Bk 2☐ Cover: 14.95 **NM value: Cover or less**
Lust for Life • Lust For Life; collects #4-12 **A:** Darick Robertson **W:** Warren Ellis

Bk 3☐ Cover: 12.95 **NM value: Cover or less**
• Year of the Bastard; collects #13-18 and Vertigo: Winter's Edge #2

TRANSMETROPOLITAN: I HATE IT HERE — DC / Vertigo

1 ☐ Jun 2000 Cover: 5.95 **NM value: Cover or less**
Circ: Diamd. preorders: **14,860**
A: Danijel Zezelj; Tim Bradstreet; Bryan Talbot; Gary Erskine; Phil Jimenez; Paul Gulacy; Steve Dillon; David Mack; Glenn Fabry; Dave Johnson; Lea Hernandez; James Romberger; Dave Daylor; Eduardo Risso; J.H. Wi; John Casaday **W:** Warren Ellis

TRANSMUTATION OF IKE GARUDA, THE — Marvel / Epic

1 ☐ Cover: 3.95 **NM value: Cover or less**
Circ: CapCity orders: **4,200**
A: James Sherman **W:** Elaine Lee

2 ☐ Cover: 3.95 **NM value: Cover or less**
Circ: CapCity orders: **3,000**
A: James Sherman **W:** Elaine Lee

TRANS NUBIANS — Adeola

1 ☐ Cover: 2.95 **NM value: Cover or less**

TRASH — Fleetway-Quality

1 ☐ Cover: 2.95 **NM value: Cover or less**
How Green Is My Computer **A:** Nigel Dobbyn **W:** Paul Kupperberg

2 ☐ Cover: 2.95 **NM value: Cover or less**
A: Nigel Dobbyn **W:** Paul Kupperberg

TRAUMA CORPS — Anubis

1 ☐ Feb 1994 Cover: 2.75 **NM value: Cover or less**
A: Tom Simonton **W:** Tom Simonton

TRAVELERS, THE — South Jersey Rebellion Productions

1 ☐ b&w Cover: 2.25 **NM value: Cover or less**
• no indicia

TRAVELLER'S TALE, A — Antarctic

1 ☐ b&w Cover: 2.50 **NM value: Cover or less**
2 ☐ Aug 1992, b&w Cover: 2.50 **NM value: Cover or less**
3 ☐ Oct 1992, b&w Cover: 2.50 **NM value: Cover or less**

TREASURE CHESTS — Eros

1 ☐ Jun 1999 Cover: 2.95 **NM value: Cover or less**
Circ: Diamd. preorders: **1,888**
A: Art Wetherell **W:** Art Wetherell

2 ☐ 1999 Cover: 2.95 **NM value: Cover or less**
A: Art Wetherell **W:** Art Wetherell

3 ☐ Cover: 2.95 **NM value: Cover or less**
A: Art Wetherell **W:** Art Wetherell

4 ☐ Feb 2000 Cover: 2.95 **NM value: Cover or less**
Circ: Diamd. preorders: **1,624**
A: Art Wetherell **W:** Art Wetherell

5 ☐ Jul 2000 Cover: 2.95 **NM value: Cover or less**
Dental Men Prefer Blondes; I See London, I See France...; Thumb Like it Hot **A:** Art Wetherell **W:** Art Wetherell

TREASURE CHEST SUMMER (VOL. 1) — George A. Pflaum

1 ☐ Mar 1946 Cover: 0.12 **NM value: 5.00**
• **CGC:** 1 graded, best 8.0
2 ☐ Cover: 0.12 **NM value: 5.00**
3 ☐ Cover: 0.12 **NM value: 5.00**
4 ☐ Cover: 0.12 **NM value: 5.00**
5 ☐ Cover: 0.12 **NM value: 5.00**
6 ☐ Cover: 0.12 **NM value: 5.00**
Humpty Dumpty; So Long Sayers; What Happened To The Mary Celeste?; Hannibal Bear; Bush Pilots; Journey To The Moon **A:** Fran Matera **W:** Frank Moss

TREASURY OF DOGS, A — Dell

1 ☐ 1956 Cover: 0.25 **NM value: 25.00**
• **CGC:** 1 graded, best 9.0
• Dell Giant

TREASURY OF HORSES, A — Dell

1 ☐ 1955 Cover: 0.25 **NM value: 25.00**
• **CGC:** 1 graded, best 9.4
• Dell Giant

TREASURY OF VICTORIAN MURDER THE BORDEN TRAGEDY — NBM

Bk 1☐ Cover: 8.95 **NM value: Cover or less**

TREEHOUSE OF HORROR (BART SIMPSON'S...) — Bongo

Bart Simpson's Treehouse of Horror is an annual Halloween treat for fans of the Simpsons, Matt Groening's dysfunctional television cartoon family. The spooky stories covered here mimic those on the annual TV series episode of the same name.

Examples include "Little Shop Of Homers," in which a man-eating plant has been merged with Homer Simpson's DNA. As a result, the strange plant feeds on donuts (or in a pinch, people), and begins to devour every donut in Springfield. Other stories spoof Moby Dick ("Call Me Homer") and Cat People ("Bart People").

The anthology also allows other creators, including Jeff Smith, Sergio Aragones, Jill Thompson, and Stan Sakai, to try their hands at Springfield's residents.

1 ☐ 1995 Cover: 2.95 **NM value: 3.50**
Circ: CapCity orders: **10,675**
Call Me Homer; Little Shop of Homers; Bart People • Halloween stories **A:** Mike Allred; Bill Morrison; Luis Escobar; Jeff Smith; Chris Roman; Stephanie Gladden **W:** James Robinson; Mike Allred; Jeff Smith

2 ☐ 1996 Cover: 2.50 **NM value: Cover or less**
infinity cover. • Halloween stories **A:** Peter Bagge **W:** Paul Dini

3 ☐ 1997 Cover: 2.50 **NM value: Cover or less**
The Immigration of the Body Snatchers; Fatal Reception • Halloween story **A:** Evan Dorkin; Bill Morrison; Phil Ortiz; Stephanie Gladden **W:** Evan Dorkin; Bill Morrison; Matt Groening; Scott Gimple

4 ☐ 1998 Cover: 2.50 **NM value: Cover or less**
• Halloween stories **A:** Geof Darrow; Batton Lash; Chuck Dixon

5 ☐ 1999 Cover: 3.50 **NM value: Cover or less**
• Halloween stories; Eisner award winner **A:** Sergio Aragonés; Jill Thompson; Doug TenNapel; Scott Shaw!

6 ☐ 2000 Cover: 4.50 **NM value: Cover or less**
Hell-o-Ween; Metamorphsimpsons; Young Frinkenstein; From Duffs Till Dawn • Halloween stories **A:** Stan Sakai; Jim Mahfood; Peter Kuper; Dan DeCarlo; Scott Morse **W:** Bill Morrison; Peter Kuper; Jim Mahfood; Scott Morse

TREKKER (DARK HORSE) — Dark Horse

1 ☐ May 1987, b&w Cover: 1.50 **NM value: Cover or less**
Circ: CapCity orders: **4,425**
Smuggler's Blues **A:** Ron Randall **W:** Ron Randall

2 ☐ Jul 1987, b&w Cover: 1.50 **NM value: Cover or less**
A: Ron Randall **W:** Ron Randall

3 ☐ Sep 1987 Cover: 1.75 **NM value: Cover or less**
A: Ron Randall **W:** Ron Randall

4 ☐ Nov 1987 Cover: 1.75 **NM value: Cover or less**
A: Ron Randall **W:** Ron Randall

5 ☐ Jan 1988 Cover: 1.75 **NM value: Cover or less**
A: Ron Randall **W:** Ron Randall

6 ☐ Mar 1988 Cover: 1.50 **NM value: Cover or less**
A: Ron Randall **W:** Ron Randall

Bk 1☐ b&w Cover: 5.95 **NM value: Cover or less**
SE 1☐ Cover: 2.95 **NM value: Cover or less**
Sins Of The Fathers • Color Special **A:** Ron Randall **W:** Ron Randall

TREKKER (IMAGE) — Image

SE 1☐ Jun 1999 Cover: 2.50 **NM value: 2.95**
Circ: Diamd. preorders: **11,888**
Trial by Fire **A:** Ron Randall **W:** Ron Randall

TREK TEENS — Parody Press

1 ☐ Feb 1993, b&w Cover: 2.50 **NM value: Cover or less**
A: Ross Turner **W:** Ross Turner

1/A ☐ Feb 1993, b&w Cover: 2.50 **NM value: Cover or less**
alternate cover. **A:** Ross Turner **W:** Ross Turner

TRENCHCOAT BRIGADE — DC / Vertigo

1 ☐ Mar 1999 Cover: 2.50 **NM value: Cover or less**
Circ: Diamd. preorders: **23,149**
A: John Ridgway **W:** John Ney Rieber

2 ☐ Apr 1999 Cover: 2.50 **NM value: Cover or less**
Circ: Diamd. preorders: **18,630**
A: John Ridgway **W:** John Ney Rieber

3 ☐ May 1999 Cover: 2.50 **NM value: Cover or less**
Circ: Diamd. preorders: **20,355**
A: John Ridgway **W:** John Ney Rieber

4 ☐ Jun 1999 Cover: 2.50 **NM value: Cover or less**
Circ: Diamd. preorders: **21,007**
A: John Ridgway **W:** John Ney Rieber

TRENCHER — Image

1 ☐ May 1993 Cover: 1.95 **NM value: 2.00**
Circ: CapCity orders: **106,000**
Life Sucks...And Then You Come Back **A:** Keith Giffen **W:** Keith Giffen

2 ☐ Jun 1993 Cover: 1.95 **NM value: 2.00**
Circ: CapCity orders: **74,650**
A: Keith Giffen

3 ☐ Jul 1993 Cover: 1.95 **NM value: 2.00**
Circ: CapCity orders: **45,875**
A: Keith Giffen

4 ☐ Oct 1993 Cover: 1.95 **NM value: 2.00**
Circ: CapCity orders: **34,375**
A: Keith Giffen

TRENCHER X-MAS BITES HOLIDAY BLOW-OUT — Blackball

1 ☐ Dec 1993 Cover: 2.50 **NM value: Cover or less**
A: Keith Giffen

TRESPASSERS, THE — Amazing Montage

1 ☐ Cover: 2.50 **NM value: Cover or less**
2 ☐ Cover: 2.50 **NM value: Cover or less**
3 ☐ Cover: 2.50 **NM value: Cover or less**
4 ☐ Cover: 2.50 **NM value: Cover or less**
5 ☐ Cover: 2.50 **NM value: Cover or less**

TREVOR-THE SAGA OF THE RED BOOTS — McClellan Falk

Bk 1☐ Dec 1994, b&w Cover: 8.99 **NM value: Cover or less**
• collection of illustrated prose

TRIAD UNIVERSE — Triad

1 ☐ Jul 1994 Cover: 2.25 **NM value: Cover or less**
2 ☐ Aug 1994, b&w Cover: 2.25 **NM value: Cover or less**

TRIAL OF SUPERMAN, THE — DC

Bk 1☐ Cover: 14.95 **NM value: Cover or less**
• collects Action Comics #716-717, Adventures of Superman #529-531, Superman #106-108, Superman: The Man of Steel #50-52, and Superman: The Man of Tomorrow #3

TRIAL RUN — Miller

1 ☐ b&w Cover: 2.00 **NM value: Cover or less**
2 ☐ b&w Cover: 2.00 **NM value: Cover or less**
3 ☐ b&w Cover: 2.00 **NM value: Cover or less**
4 ☐ b&w Cover: 2.00 **NM value: Cover or less**
5 ☐ b&w Cover: 2.00 **NM value: Cover or less**
6 ☐ b&w Cover: 2.00 **NM value: Cover or less**
7 ☐ b&w Cover: 2.00 **NM value: Cover or less**
14 ☐ Cover: 2.50 **NM value: Cover or less**
15 ☐ Cover: 2.50 **NM value: Cover or less**

TRIARCH — Caliber

1 ☐ b&w Cover: 2.50 **NM value: Cover or less**
2 ☐ b&w Cover: 2.50 **NM value: Cover or less**

The prices seen above do not represent the highest possible prices seen in online auctions, but rather the prices we have seen these issues reliably fetch in a variety of environments (storefront retail, mail order, auction and convention).

CGC-graded: Multiply prices above by **33 for 9.9 M • 16 for 9.8 NM/M • 7 for 9.6 NM+ • 5 for 9.4 NM • 2.5 for 9.2 NM- • 1.5 for 9.0 VF/NM**

TRIBE — Image

Set in the midst of Brooklyn's culture of club openings, back-alley boxing matches, and underground business deals, Tribe opens just as a corporation called Europan makes its move. Standing against Europan is Ellison Murdock, known as Blindspot, who uses the firm's own "stealth" technology to fight it. Joining him is a colorful group of individuals, codenamed Shift, Hannibal, the Front, Steel Pulse, Fly Girl, Short Order, and Out Cold. Together they fight back against Europan's web of political and underworld connections.

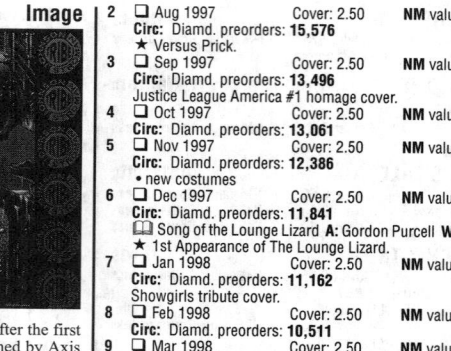

Tribe's creative team and their original publisher, Image Comics, had a falling out after the first issue. A second and third issue of Tribe were published by Axis Comics.

1 ❑ Mar 1993 Cover: 2.95 **NM** value: **Cover or less**
Circ: CapCity orders: **220,900**
Embossed cover. 📖 Blindspot • Only issue published by Image **A:** Larry Stroman **W:** Larry Stroman; Todd Johnson
1/A ❑ Mar 1993 Cover: 2.95 **NM** value: **Cover or less**
foil cover. • Special edition.
1/B ❑ Mar 1993 Cover: 2.95 **NM** value: **Cover or less**
cover says Apr, indicia says Mar. • Special edition. • gold logo
1/C ❑ Mar 1993 Cover: 2.95 **NM** value: **Cover or less**
White cover. • gold logo
2 ❑ ca. 1993 Cover: 1.95 **NM** value: **Cover or less**
Circ: CapCity orders: **144,025**
• Axis begins publishing **A:** Larry Stroman **W:** Larry Stroman; Todd Johnson
3 ❑ Apr 1994 Cover: 1.95 **NM** value: **Cover or less**
Circ: CapCity orders: **117,300**
final issue. **A:** Larry Stroman **W:** Larry Stroman; Todd Johnson

TRIBE (VOL. 2) — Good

0 ❑ Oct 1996 Cover: 2.95 **NM** value: **Cover or less**
Circ: Diamd. preorders: **5,510**

TRICKSTER KING MONKEY — Eastern

1 ❑ Cover: 1.75 **NM** value: **Cover or less**
A: Hyun-jung Choi **W:** Hyun-jung Choi

TRIDENT — Trident

All issues are adults only.

1 ❑ 1989b&w Cover: 3.50 **NM** value: **Cover or less**
2 ❑ 1989b&w Cover: 3.50 **NM** value: **Cover or less**
3 ❑ 1989b&w Cover: 3.50 **NM** value: **Cover or less**
4 ❑ 1990b&w Cover: 3.50 **NM** value: **Cover or less**
5 ❑ Apr 1990, b&w Cover: 3.50 **NM** value: **Cover or less**
6 ❑ 1990b&w Cover: 3.50 **NM** value: **Cover or less**
7 ❑ 1990b&w Cover: 3.50 **NM** value: **Cover or less**
8 ❑ 1990b&w Cover: 3.50 **NM** value: **Cover or less**

TRIGGERMAN — Caliber

1 ❑ Cover: 2.95 **NM** value: **Cover or less**
A: Mark Bloodworth **W:** Malcolm Bourne
2 ❑ Cover: 2.95 **NM** value: **Cover or less**
A: Mark Bloodworth **W:** Malcolm Bourne

TRIGGER TWINS — DC

1 ❑ Mar 1973 Cover: 0.20 **NM** value: **5.00**
📖 Code of the Trigger Twins!; Pow-Wow Smith: The Bandit and the Bracelet!; The Unknown Hero of Rocky City! • Reprints from All-Star Western #94, 81, 103 **A:** Carmine Infantino; Ross Andru; Joe Giella **W:** Bob Kanigher; Gardner Fox

TRILOGY TOUR — Cartoon

1 ❑ Sum 1997, b&w Cover: 1.50 **NM** value: **Cover or less**
• promotional comic for Summer 1997 tour

TRILOGY TOUR II — Cartoon

1 ❑ Jun 1998, b&w and colorCover: 4.95 **NM** value: **Cover or less**
• promotional comic for Summer 1998 tour **A:** Mark Crilley; Linda Medley; Charles Vess; Jill Thompson; Jeff Smith; Stan Sakai

TRINITY ANGELS — Acclaim / Valiant

The Barbelli sisters were regular folks, living out on Long Island, until they woke up one day to find themselves transformed. They had become something like angels, with perfect bodies, wings, and the powers of earth, air, and fire.

Naturally, trouble soon followed in the form of the Ninety-Nine. These are humans who were transformed into demonic beings, and whose souls were being gathered to usher in some great apocalypse. Although the series is intentionally vague on the overall form of their conflict, it's full of nicely written characters and stylish art by Kevin Maguire and Dan Panosian.

1 ❑ Jul 1997 Cover: 2.50 **NM** value: **Cover or less**
Circ: Diamd. preorders: **23,070**
📖 Trinity Angels **A:** Dan Panosian **W:** Kevin Maguire ★ 1st Appearance of Rubberneck, Teresa Angelina Barbella, Trenchmouth, Gianna Barbella, Maria Barbella.
1/SC❑Jul 1997 Cover: 2.50 **NM** value: **Cover or less**
alternate painted cover.
2 ❑ Aug 1997 Cover: 2.50 **NM** value: **Cover or less**
Circ: Diamd. preorders: **15,576**
★ Versus Prick.
3 ❑ Sep 1997 Cover: 2.50 **NM** value: **Cover or less**
Circ: Diamd. preorders: **13,496**
Justice League America #1 homage cover.
4 ❑ Oct 1997 Cover: 2.50 **NM** value: **Cover or less**
Circ: Diamd. preorders: **13,061**
5 ❑ Nov 1997 Cover: 2.50 **NM** value: **Cover or less**
Circ: Diamd. preorders: **12,386**
• new costumes
6 ❑ Dec 1997 Cover: 2.50 **NM** value: **Cover or less**
Circ: Diamd. preorders: **11,841**
📖 Song of the Lounge Lizard **A:** Gordon Purcell **W:** Kevin Maguire ★ 1st Appearance of The Lounge Lizard.
7 ❑ Jan 1998 Cover: 2.50 **NM** value: **Cover or less**
Circ: Diamd. preorders: **11,162**
Showgirls tribute cover.
8 ❑ Feb 1998 Cover: 2.50 **NM** value: **Cover or less**
Circ: Diamd. preorders: **10,511**
9 ❑ Mar 1998 Cover: 2.50 **NM** value: **Cover or less**
Circ: Diamd. preorders: **9,943**
10 ❑ Apr 1998 Cover: 2.50 **NM** value: **Cover or less**
Circ: Diamd. preorders: **9,549**
11 ❑ Jan 1998 Cover: 2.50 **NM** value: **Cover or less**
Circ: Diamd. preorders: **8,967**
no cover date. • indicia says Jan
12 ❑ Feb 1998 Cover: 2.50 **NM** value: **Cover or less**
Circ: Diamd. preorders: **8,152**
no cover date. final issue. • indicia says Feb
Ash 1❑Mar 1997, b&w **NM** value: **1.00**
no cover price. • preview of upcoming series

TRIPLE DARE — Alternative

1 ❑ May 1998, b&w Cover: 2.95 **NM** value: **Cover or less**

TRIPLE THREAT — Holyoke

1 ❑ Win 1946 Cover: 0.10 **NM** value: **200.00**
• **CGC:** 1 graded, best 9.4

TRIPLE•X — Dark Horse

1 ❑ Dec 1994 Cover: 3.95 **NM** value: **Cover or less**
📖 Amsterdam, Part 1 **A:** Arnold Pander; Jacob Pander **W:** Arnold Pander; Jacob Pander
2 ❑ Jan 1995 Cover: 3.95 **NM** value: **Cover or less**
📖 Amsterdam, Part 2 **A:** Arnold Pander; Jacob Pander **W:** Arnold Pander; Jacob Pander
3 ❑ Feb 1995 Cover: 3.95 **NM** value: **Cover or less**
A: Arnold Pander; Jacob Pander **W:** Arnold Pander; Jacob Pander
4 ❑ Mar 1995 Cover: 3.95 **NM** value: **Cover or less**
A: Arnold Pander; Jacob Pander **W:** Arnold Pander; Jacob Pander
5 ❑ Apr 1995 Cover: 3.95 **NM** value: **Cover or less**
A: Arnold Pander; Jacob Pander **W:** Arnold Pander; Jacob Pander
6 ❑ May 1995 Cover: 4.95 **NM** value: **Cover or less**
A: Arnold Pander; Jacob Pander **W:** Arnold Pander; Jacob Pander
7 ❑ Jul 1995 Cover: 4.95 **NM** value: **Cover or less**
A: Arnold Pander; Jacob Pander **W:** Arnold Pander; Jacob Pander
Bk 1❑ Apr 1997 Cover: 24.95 **NM** value: **Cover or less**

TRIPLE-X CINEMA: A CARTOON HISTORY — Re-Visionary

All issues are adults only.

1 ❑ Mar 1997, b&w Cover: 3.50 **NM** value: **Cover or less**
Circ: Diamd. preorders: **2,494**
A: Kevin Breyfogle **W:** Jay Allen Sanford; Bill Margold
2 ❑ Apr 1997, b&w Cover: 3.50 **NM** value: **Cover or less**
A: Kevin Breyfogle **W:** Jay Allen Sanford; Bill Margold
3 ❑ May 1997, b&w Cover: 3.50 **NM** value: **Cover or less**
A: Kevin Breyfogle **W:** Jay Allen Sanford; Bill Margold
Bk 1❑ b&w Cover: 14.95 **NM** value: **Cover or less**
A: Kevin Breyfogle **W:** Jay Allen Sanford; Bill Margold

TRIUMPH — DC

Triumph, written by Christopher Priest and illustrated by Mike Miller, follows Billy Mac, whose father once drove for the super-villain Doctor Cobalt. Due to his father's nefarious work, Billy led a lonely childhood, moving from place to place. That could be why, as Triumph, a grown Billy surrounds himself with a team of assistants — despite the fact that someone of his unique powers could easily work alone.

In this mini-series, Triumph spots Doctor Cobalt at a funeral. Triumph sets his people to work, and so begins his quest for vengeance against the man that corrupted his father and ruined his childhood.

1 ❑ Jun 1995 Cover: 1.75 **NM** value: **Cover or less**
Circ: CapCity orders: **10,050**
A: Mike Miller **W:** Christopher Priest
2 ❑ Jul 1995 Cover: 1.75 **NM** value: **Cover or less**
Circ: CapCity orders: **6,725**
A: Mike Miller **W:** Christopher Priest
3 ❑ Aug 1995 Cover: 1.75 **NM** value: **Cover or less**
Circ: CapCity orders: **6,325**
A: Mike Miller **W:** Christopher Priest
4 ❑ Sep 1995 Cover: 1.75 **NM** value: **Cover or less**
Circ: CapCity orders: **5,275**
A: Mike Miller **W:** Christopher Priest

TRIUMPHANT UNLEASHED — Triumphant

0 ❑ ca. 1993 Cover: 2.50 **NM** value: **Cover or less**
Circ: CapCity orders: **7,645**
• Unleashed Prologue
0/A ❑ ca. 1993 **NM** value: **1.00**
• free; Unleashed Prologue
0/SC❑ca. 1993 Cover: 2.50 **NM** value: **4.00**
no cover price. • Mail-in special-cover edition. Given as promo from coupons in first 9 Triumphant books. • Unleashed Prologue; red logo; mail-away version
1 ❑ ca. 1993 Cover: 2.50 **NM** value: **Cover or less**
Circ: CapCity orders: **6,630**

TRIUMVIRATE — Catacomb

1 ❑ b&w Cover: 2.50 **NM** value: **Cover or less**
• flipbook with Pinnacle #1

TROLL — Image

1 ❑ Dec 1993 Cover: 2.50 **NM** value: **Cover or less**
Circ: CapCity orders: **57,375**

TROLL: HALLOWEEN SPECIAL — Image

1 ❑ Oct 1994 Cover: 2.95 **NM** value: **Cover or less**
Circ: CapCity orders: **19,050**
★ Appearance of The Maxx.

TROLL II — Image

1 ❑ Jul 1994 Cover: 3.95 **NM** value: **Cover or less**
Circ: CapCity orders: **21,175**
A: Karl Altstaetter **W:** Robert Napton; Karl Altstaetter

TROLL: ONCE A HERO — Image

1 ❑ Aug 1994 Cover: 2.50 **NM** value: **Cover or less**
Circ: CapCity orders: **24,325**
A: Gabe Alberola **W:** Eldon Asp

TROLLORDS: DEATH AND KISSES — Apple

1 ❑ 1989b&w Cover: 2.25 **NM** value: **Cover or less**
2 ❑ 1989b&w Cover: 2.25 **NM** value: **Cover or less**
3 ❑ 1989b&w Cover: 2.25 **NM** value: **Cover or less**
4 ❑ 1989b&w Cover: 2.25 **NM** value: **Cover or less**
5 ❑ 1989b&w Cover: 2.25 **NM** value: **Cover or less**
6 ❑ Cover: 2.50 **NM** value: **Cover or less**

TROLLORDS (VOL. 1) — Tru Studios

1 ❑ Feb 1986, b&w Cover: 1.50 **NM** value: **2.00**
★ 1st Appearance of Trollords.
1-2 ❑ Cover: 1.50 **NM** value: **Cover or less**
2 ❑ ca. 1986 Cover: 1.50 **NM** value: **Cover or less**
3 ❑ ca. 1986 Cover: 1.50 **NM** value: **Cover or less**
4 ❑ ca. 1986 Cover: 1.50 **NM** value: **Cover or less**
5 ❑ ca. 1986 Cover: 1.50 **NM** value: **Cover or less**
6 ❑ ca. 1986 Cover: 1.50 **NM** value: **Cover or less**
7 ❑ ca. 1986 Cover: 1.50 **NM** value: **Cover or less**
8 ❑ ca. 1987 Cover: 1.50 **NM** value: **Cover or less**
9 ❑ ca. 1987 Cover: 1.50 **NM** value: **Cover or less**
10 ❑ ca. 1987 Cover: 1.50 **NM** value: **Cover or less**
11 ❑ ca. 1987 Cover: 1.50 **NM** value: **Cover or less**
12 ❑ ca. 1987 Cover: 1.50 **NM** value: **Cover or less**
13 ❑ ca. 1987 Cover: 1.50 **NM** value: **Cover or less**
14 ❑ ca. 1987 Cover: 1.50 **NM** value: **Cover or less**
15 ❑ Feb 1988 Cover: 1.50 **NM** value: **Cover or less**
Bk 1❑ Cover: 11.95 **NM** value: **Cover or less**
• Trollords Classics; collects issues #1-3 and new story
SE 1❑Feb 1987, full color Cover: 1.75 **NM** value: **2.00**
Circ: CapCity orders: **5,050**
📖 One Fearful Night; Remember Me; Remote Possibility • Jerry's Big Fun Book **A:** Ken Holewczynski; Guy Davis **W:** Brian Augustyn; Len Strazewski

TROLLORDS (VOL. 2) — Comico

1 ❑ ca. 1988 Cover: 1.95 **NM** value: **2.00**
Circ: CapCity orders: **4,375**
2 ❑ ca. 1988 Cover: 1.95 **NM** value: **2.00**
Circ: CapCity orders: **3,000**
3 ❑ ca. 1989 Cover: 1.95 **NM** value: **2.00**
Circ: CapCity orders: **2,450**
4 ❑ ca. 1989 Cover: 1.95 **NM** value: **2.50**
Circ: CapCity orders: **1,750**

TROLL PATROL — Harvey

1 ❑ Jan 1993 Cover: 1.95 **NM** value: **Cover or less**
📖 The Legend of Troll Town; The Great Troll Hunt; Where's Trolldo; Trollevision; Terror in Playland; Running on Empty **A:** Dave Mannak **W:** Angelo Decesare

TROMBONE — Knockabout

All issues are adults only.

1 ❑ Cover: 2.50 **NM** value: **Cover or less**

TROPO — Blackbird

1 ❑ b&w Cover: 2.75 **NM** value: **Cover or less**
2 ❑ b&w Cover: 2.75 **NM** value: **Cover or less**
3 ❑ b&w Cover: 2.75 **NM** value: **Cover or less**
4 ❑ b&w Cover: 2.75 **NM** value: **Cover or less**
5 ❑ b&w Cover: 2.75 **NM** value: **Cover or less**

TROUBLE EXPRESS — Radio

1 ❑ Nov 1998 Cover: 2.95 **NM** value: **Cover or less**
Circ: Diamd. preorders: **2,566**
📖 The Hustler **A:** Will Allison **C:** Will Allison **W:** Will Allison
1/A ❑ Nov 1998 Cover: 2.95 **NM** value: **Cover or less**
Adam Warren cover. 📖 The Hustler **A:** Will Allison; Adam Warren(cover) **C:** Adam Warren **W:** Will Allison
2 ❑ Jan 1999 Cover: 2.95 **NM** value: **Cover or less**
Circ: Diamd. preorders: **1,335**
C: Will Allison

Other grades: Multiply prices above by **1.5 for Mint • 2/3 for Very Fine • 1/3 for Fine • 1/5 for Very Good • 1/8 for Good**

TROUBLE MAGNET — DC

1 ❑ Feb 2000 Cover: 2.50 **NM value: Cover or less**
Circ: Diamd. preorders: **9,159**
A: Kilian Plunkett **W:** Ryder Windham
2 ❑ Mar 2000 Cover: 2.50 **NM value: Cover or less**
Circ: Diamd. preorders: **7,381**
A: Kilian Plunkett **W:** Ryder Windham
3 ❑ Apr 2000 Cover: 2.50 **NM value: Cover or less**
Circ: Diamd. preorders: **5,917**
A: Kilian Plunkett **W:** Ryder Windham
4 ❑ May 2000 Cover: 2.50 **NM value: Cover or less**
Circ: Diamd. preorders: **5,442**
📖 The Memory Conflict **A:** Kilian Plunkett **W:** Ryder Windham

TROUBLEMAKERS — Acclaim / Valiant

Pharmaceutical giant G&G accepted volunteers from among their most gifted young employees, and turned their offspring into a new phase of human evolution. The program, called ZEUS: Control, consists of four teenagers- Christine and Zachary Helvin, Parker Matthews and Jane Ngo.

Unlike the angst-ridden superpowered outcasts from titles in the same vein, like Gen13 and Excalibur, the ZEUS youth have believable, boy-and-girl-next-door personalities, with the kind of interaction and camaraderie you'd expect from normal teenagers. Troublemakers is a winning series from writer Fabian Nicieza.

1 ❑ Apr 1997 Cover: 2.50 **NM value: Cover or less**
Circ: Diamd. preorders: **20,080**
cover says Mar, indicia says Apr. 📖 The Age of Innocence **A:** Kenny Martinez **W:** Kenny Martinez; Fabian Nicieza ★ 1st Appearance of Troublemakers, Calamity, XL, Rebound, Blur.
1/SC ❑ Apr 1997 Cover: 2.50 **NM value: Cover or less**
indicia and cover dates match.
2 ❑ May 1997 Cover: 2.50 **NM value: Cover or less**
Circ: Diamd. preorders: **13,921**
cover says Apr, indicia says May.
3 ❑ Jun 1997 Cover: 2.50 **NM value: Cover or less**
Circ: Diamd. preorders: **12,233**
4 ❑ Jun 1997 Cover: 2.50 **NM value: Cover or less**
Circ: Diamd. preorders: **11,535**
5 ❑ Aug 1997 Cover: 2.50 **NM value: Cover or less**
Circ: Diamd. preorders: **11,697**
6 ❑ Sep 1997 Cover: 2.50 **NM value: Cover or less**
Circ: Diamd. preorders: **10,924**
7 ❑ Oct 1997 Cover: 2.50 **NM value: Cover or less**
Circ: Diamd. preorders: **10,306**
8 ❑ Nov 1997 Cover: 2.50 **NM value: Cover or less**
Circ: Diamd. preorders: **9,599**
Cover swipe from X-Men (1st Series) #100. 📖 Controled Chaos **A:** Chuck Wojtkiewicz **W:** Fabian Nicieza
9 ❑ Dec 1997 Cover: 2.50 **NM value: Cover or less**
Circ: Diamd. preorders: **9,407**
• teen sex issue
10 ❑ Jan 1998 Cover: 2.50 **NM value: Cover or less**
Circ: Diamd. preorders: **8,507**
11 ❑ Feb 1998 Cover: 2.50 **NM value: Cover or less**
Circ: Diamd. preorders: **8,187**
12 ❑ Mar 1998 Cover: 2.50 **NM value: Cover or less**
Circ: Diamd. preorders: **8,029**
13 ❑ Apr 1998 Cover: 2.50 **NM value: Cover or less**
Circ: Diamd. preorders: **7,553**
14 ❑ Jan 1998 Cover: 2.50 **NM value: Cover or less**
Circ: Diamd. preorders: **7,051**
no cover date. • indicia says Jan
15 ❑ Feb 1998 Cover: 2.50 **NM value: Cover or less**
Circ: Diamd. preorders: **6,497**
no cover date. final issue. • indicia says Feb
16 ❑ Mar 1998 Cover: 2.50 **NM value: Cover or less**
Circ: Diamd. preorders: **6,350**
• month of publication repeated
17 ❑ Mar 1998 Cover: 2.50 **NM value: Cover or less**
Circ: Diamd. preorders: **6,318**
• month of publication repeated
18 ❑ Mar 1998 Cover: 2.50 **NM value: Cover or less**
Circ: Diamd. preorders: **6,128**
• month of publication repeated
19 ❑ Jun 1998 Cover: 2.50 **NM value: Cover or less**
Circ: Diamd. preorders: **5,539**
Ash 1 ❑ Nov 1996, b&w **NM value: 1.00**
no cover price. • preview of upcoming series

TROUBLEMAN — Image / Motown

1 ❑ Jun 1996 Cover: 2.25 **NM value: Cover or less**
2 ❑ Jul 1996 Cover: 2.25 **NM value: Cover or less**
3 ❑ Aug 1996 Cover: 2.25 **NM value: Cover or less**

TROUBLESHOOTERS INC. — Nightwolf Graphics

1 ❑ Win 1995, b&w Cover: 2.50 **NM value: Cover or less**
A: Reggie Golden **W:** Joni White; Rich White
2 ❑ Spr 1995, b&w Cover: 2.50 **NM value: Cover or less**
A: Reggie Golden **W:** Joni White; Rich White

TROUBLE WITH GIRLS, THE: THE NIGHT OF THE LIZARD — Marvel / Epic

1 ❑ Jun 1993 Cover: 2.50 **NM value: Cover or less**
Circ: CapCity orders: **13,600**
Embossed cover.
2 ❑ Jul 1993 Cover: 1.95 **NM value: 2.25**
Circ: CapCity orders: **7,400**
3 ❑ Aug 1993 Cover: 1.95 **NM value: 2.25**
Circ: CapCity orders: **7,000**
4 ❑ Sep 1993 Cover: 1.95 **NM value: 2.25**
Circ: CapCity orders: **6,600**

TROUBLE WITH GIRLS, THE (VOL. 1) — Malibu

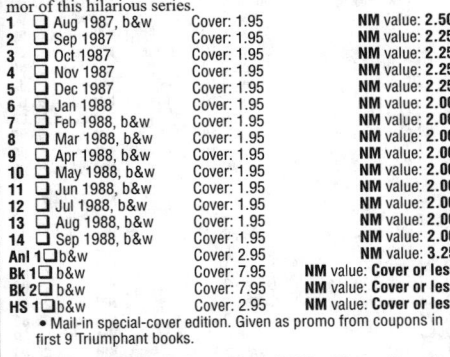

The fourteen issues (and various annuals and specials) of this series started the legend of Lester Girls. It's a tragic tale, as Lester- cursed with dashing good looks, immense wealth, unbelievable sexual escapades, and a life of adventure- tries to cope. The trouble with Girls is that Lester really wants just a quiet life of contentment and enough time to catch up on his reading.

Lester is joined in his adventures by Maxie Scoops, the girl he sweetly loves, but whom he never seems to give more than a peck on the cheek. The Lascivious Lizard Lady, on the other hand, is Lester's arch nemesis- although the call of duty sometimes requires the he make the ultimate sacrifice and bed her (brilliantly, of course). Then there's his comrade Apache Dick, a sex-crazed fiend and scoundrel. The mere name of the team-up between him and Girls is characteristic of the tongue-in-cheek humor of this hilarious series.

1 ❑ Aug 1987, b&w Cover: 1.95 **NM value: 2.50**
2 ❑ Sep 1987 Cover: 1.95 **NM value: 2.25**
3 ❑ Oct 1987 Cover: 1.95 **NM value: 2.25**
4 ❑ Nov 1987 Cover: 1.95 **NM value: 2.25**
5 ❑ Dec 1987 Cover: 1.95 **NM value: 2.25**
6 ❑ Jan 1988 Cover: 1.95 **NM value: 2.00**
7 ❑ Feb 1988, b&w Cover: 1.95 **NM value: 2.00**
8 ❑ Mar 1988, b&w Cover: 1.95 **NM value: 2.00**
9 ❑ Apr 1988, b&w Cover: 1.95 **NM value: 2.00**
10 ❑ May 1988, b&w Cover: 1.95 **NM value: 2.00**
11 ❑ Jun 1988, b&w Cover: 1.95 **NM value: 2.00**
12 ❑ Jul 1988, b&w Cover: 1.95 **NM value: 2.00**
13 ❑ Aug 1988, b&w Cover: 1.95 **NM value: 2.00**
14 ❑ Sep 1988, b&w Cover: 1.95 **NM value: 2.00**
Anl 1 ❑ b&w Cover: 2.95 **NM value: 3.25**
Bk 1 ❑ b&w Cover: 7.95 **NM value: Cover or less**
Bk 2 ❑ b&w Cover: 7.95 **NM value: Cover or less**
HS 1 ❑ b&w Cover: 2.95 **NM value: Cover or less**
• Mail-in special-cover edition. Given as promo from coupons in first 9 Triumphant books.

TROUBLE WITH GIRLS, THE (VOL. 2) — Comico

1 ❑ ca. 1989, full color Cover: 1.95 **NM value: 2.50**
Circ: CapCity orders: **6,200**
📖 Glamour Girls • Comico begins publishing **A:** Tim Hamilton **W:** Will Jacobs; Gerard Jones
2 ❑ ca. 1989, full color Cover: 1.95 **NM value: 2.00**
Circ: CapCity orders: **4,500**
3 ❑ ca. 1989, full color Cover: 1.95 **NM value: 2.00**
Circ: CapCity orders: **4,700**
4 ❑ ca. 1989, full color Cover: 1.95 **NM value: 2.00**
Circ: CapCity orders: **4,850**
5 ❑ ca. 1989, b&w Cover: 1.95 **NM value: Cover or less**
• Eternity begins publishing; Black & white format begins
6 ❑ ca. 1989, b&w Cover: 1.95 **NM value: Cover or less**
7 ❑ ca. 1989, b&w Cover: 1.95 **NM value: Cover or less**
8 ❑ ca. 1989, b&w Cover: 1.95 **NM value: Cover or less**
9 ❑ ca. 1990, b&w Cover: 1.95 **NM value: Cover or less**
10 ❑ ca. 1990, b&w Cover: 1.95 **NM value: Cover or less**
📖 Dreaming of a White Girls **A:** Tim Hamilton **W:** Will Jacobs; Gerard Jones
11 ❑ ca. 1990, b&w Cover: 1.95 **NM value: Cover or less**
12 ❑ ca. 1990, b&w Cover: 1.95 **NM value: Cover or less**
13 ❑ ca. 1990, b&w Cover: 1.95 **NM value: Cover or less**
📖 The Lost City of Girls, Part 1
14 ❑ ca. 1990, b&w Cover: 1.95 **NM value: Cover or less**
📖 The Lost City of Girls, Part 2
15 ❑ ca. 1990, b&w Cover: 1.95 **NM value: 2.25**
📖 The Lost City of Girls, Part 3
16 ❑ ca. 1990 Cover: 2.25 **NM value: Cover or less**
📖 The Lost City of Girls, Part 4
17 ❑ ca. 1991 Cover: 2.25 **NM value: Cover or less**
18 ❑ ca. 1991 Cover: 2.25 **NM value: Cover or less**
19 ❑ ca. 1991 Cover: 2.25 **NM value: Cover or less**
20 ❑ ca. 1991 Cover: 2.25 **NM value: Cover or less**
21 ❑ ca. 1991 Cover: 2.25 **NM value: Cover or less**
22 ❑ ca. 1991 Cover: 2.25 **NM value: Cover or less**
23 ❑ ca. 1991 Cover: 2.25 **NM value: Cover or less**

TROUBLE WITH TIGERS — Antarctic

1 ❑ Jan 1992, b&w Cover: 2.50 **NM value: Cover or less**
2 ❑ Feb 1992, b&w Cover: 2.50 **NM value: Cover or less**

TROUT FISSION — Tall Tale

1 ❑ Jul 1998, b&w Cover: 1.95 **NM value: Cover or less**
2 ❑ Oct 1998, b&w Cover: 2.95 **NM value: Cover or less**

TROY — Tome

1 ❑ Cover: 2.95 **NM value: Cover or less**
A: Philip Xavier **W:** Gary Reed

TRS-80 COMPUTER WHIZ KIDS — Archie

1 ❑ **NM value: 2.00**
No issue number. • giveaway.

TRUCKIN' — Print Mint

1 ❑ Cover: 0.50 **NM value: 3.00**
2 ❑ Cover: 0.50 **NM value: 3.00**
📖 Treasure Trove; Sasquatch; Airships; The Cartoonist Dilemma • Flip Book, Ice Age **A:** George Metzger **W:** George Metzger

TRUE ADVENTURES OF ADAM AND BRYON, THE — American Mule

1 ❑ May 1998, b&w Cover: 2.50 **NM value: Cover or less**
2 ❑ 1998 Cover: 2.50 **NM value: Cover or less**
3 ❑ 1998 Cover: 2.50 **NM value: Cover or less**

TRUE COMICS — Parents' Magazine Institute

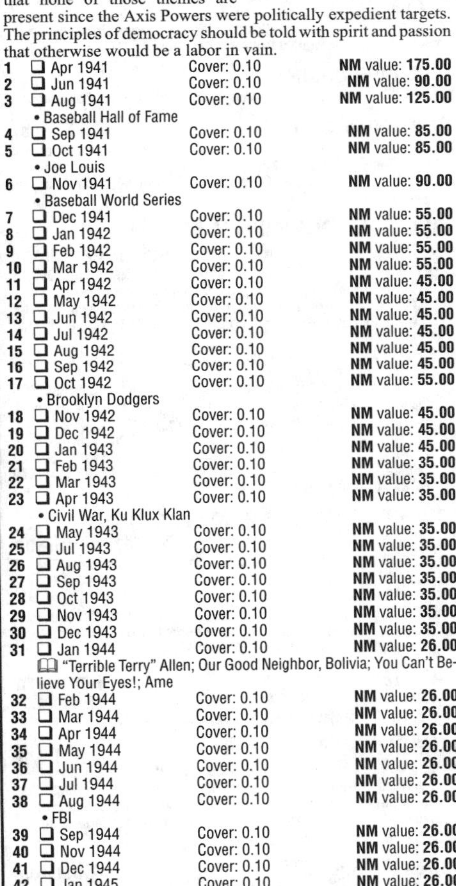

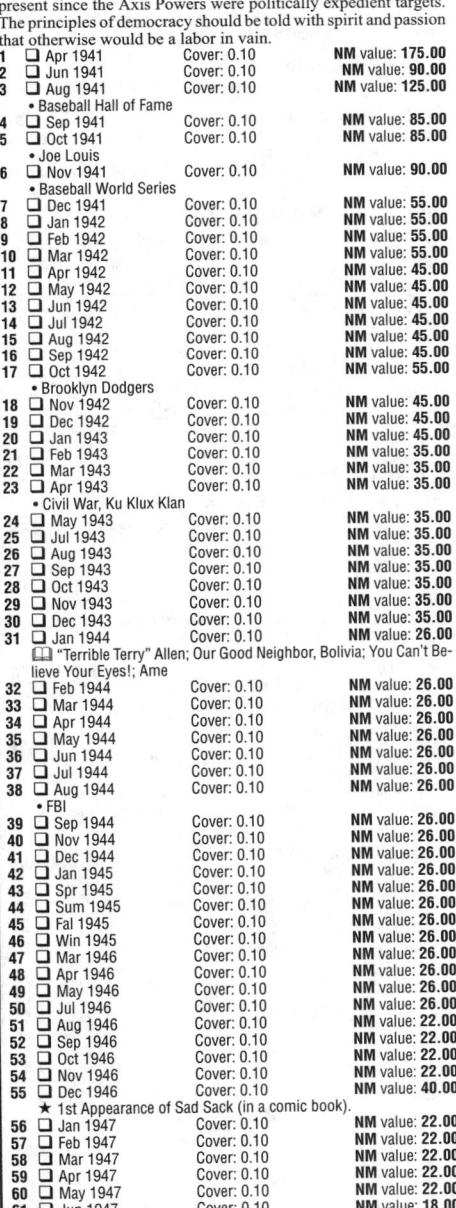

This title boldly promises, "Truth is stranger and thousand times more thrilling than fiction!" Fact stranger than fiction? Yes. A thousand times more thrilling? Not exactly since its narration using a documentary-style point of view that wrings emotions out of the story. Published during World War II, it feels like news correspondence from the front. Initially, one would expect jingoism or propaganda rallying the home front to stay the course during that fateful time in our nation's history. Be assured that none of those themes are present since the Axis Powers were politically expedient targets. The principles of democracy should be told with spirit and passion that otherwise would be a labor in vain.

1 ❑ Apr 1941 Cover: 0.10 **NM value: 175.00**
2 ❑ Jun 1941 Cover: 0.10 **NM value: 90.00**
3 ❑ Aug 1941 Cover: 0.10 **NM value: 125.00**
• Baseball Hall of Fame
4 ❑ Sep 1941 Cover: 0.10 **NM value: 85.00**
5 ❑ Oct 1941 Cover: 0.10 **NM value: 85.00**
• Joe Louis
6 ❑ Nov 1941 Cover: 0.10 **NM value: 90.00**
• Baseball World Series
7 ❑ Dec 1941 Cover: 0.10 **NM value: 55.00**
8 ❑ Jan 1942 Cover: 0.10 **NM value: 55.00**
9 ❑ Feb 1942 Cover: 0.10 **NM value: 55.00**
10 ❑ Mar 1942 Cover: 0.10 **NM value: 55.00**
11 ❑ Apr 1942 Cover: 0.10 **NM value: 45.00**
12 ❑ May 1942 Cover: 0.10 **NM value: 45.00**
13 ❑ Jun 1942 Cover: 0.10 **NM value: 45.00**
14 ❑ Jul 1942 Cover: 0.10 **NM value: 45.00**
15 ❑ Aug 1942 Cover: 0.10 **NM value: 45.00**
16 ❑ Sep 1942 Cover: 0.10 **NM value: 45.00**
17 ❑ Oct 1942 Cover: 0.10 **NM value: 55.00**
• Brooklyn Dodgers
18 ❑ Nov 1942 Cover: 0.10 **NM value: 45.00**
19 ❑ Dec 1942 Cover: 0.10 **NM value: 45.00**
20 ❑ Jan 1943 Cover: 0.10 **NM value: 45.00**
21 ❑ Feb 1943 Cover: 0.10 **NM value: 35.00**
22 ❑ Mar 1943 Cover: 0.10 **NM value: 35.00**
23 ❑ Apr 1943 Cover: 0.10 **NM value: 35.00**
• Civil War, Ku Klux Klan
24 ❑ May 1943 Cover: 0.10 **NM value: 35.00**
25 ❑ Jul 1943 Cover: 0.10 **NM value: 35.00**
26 ❑ Aug 1943 Cover: 0.10 **NM value: 35.00**
27 ❑ Sep 1943 Cover: 0.10 **NM value: 35.00**
28 ❑ Oct 1943 Cover: 0.10 **NM value: 35.00**
29 ❑ Nov 1943 Cover: 0.10 **NM value: 35.00**
30 ❑ Dec 1943 Cover: 0.10 **NM value: 35.00**
31 ❑ Jan 1944 Cover: 0.10 **NM value: 26.00**
📖 "Terrible Terry" Allen; Our Good Neighbor, Bolivia; You Can't Believe Your Eyes!; Ame
32 ❑ Feb 1944 Cover: 0.10 **NM value: 26.00**
33 ❑ Mar 1944 Cover: 0.10 **NM value: 26.00**
34 ❑ Apr 1944 Cover: 0.10 **NM value: 26.00**
35 ❑ May 1944 Cover: 0.10 **NM value: 26.00**
36 ❑ Jun 1944 Cover: 0.10 **NM value: 26.00**
37 ❑ Jul 1944 Cover: 0.10 **NM value: 26.00**
38 ❑ Aug 1944 Cover: 0.10 **NM value: 26.00**
• FBI
39 ❑ Sep 1944 Cover: 0.10 **NM value: 26.00**
40 ❑ Nov 1944 Cover: 0.10 **NM value: 26.00**
41 ❑ Dec 1944 Cover: 0.10 **NM value: 26.00**
42 ❑ Jan 1945 Cover: 0.10 **NM value: 26.00**
43 ❑ Spr 1945 Cover: 0.10 **NM value: 26.00**
44 ❑ Sum 1945 Cover: 0.10 **NM value: 26.00**
45 ❑ Fal 1945 Cover: 0.10 **NM value: 26.00**
46 ❑ Win 1945 Cover: 0.10 **NM value: 26.00**
47 ❑ Mar 1946 Cover: 0.10 **NM value: 26.00**
48 ❑ Apr 1946 Cover: 0.10 **NM value: 26.00**
49 ❑ May 1946 Cover: 0.10 **NM value: 26.00**
50 ❑ Jul 1946 Cover: 0.10 **NM value: 26.00**
51 ❑ Aug 1946 Cover: 0.10 **NM value: 22.00**
52 ❑ Sep 1946 Cover: 0.10 **NM value: 22.00**
53 ❑ Oct 1946 Cover: 0.10 **NM value: 22.00**
54 ❑ Nov 1946 Cover: 0.10 **NM value: 22.00**
55 ❑ Dec 1946 Cover: 0.10 **NM value: 40.00**
★ 1st Appearance of Sad Sack (in a comic book).
56 ❑ Jan 1947 Cover: 0.10 **NM value: 22.00**
57 ❑ Feb 1947 Cover: 0.10 **NM value: 22.00**
58 ❑ Mar 1947 Cover: 0.10 **NM value: 22.00**
59 ❑ Apr 1947 Cover: 0.10 **NM value: 22.00**
60 ❑ May 1947 Cover: 0.10 **NM value: 22.00**
61 ❑ Jun 1947 Cover: 0.10 **NM value: 18.00**
62 ❑ Jul 1947 Cover: 0.10 **NM value: 18.00**
63 ❑ Aug 1947 Cover: 0.10 **NM value: 18.00**
64 ❑ Sep 1947 Cover: 0.10 **NM value: 18.00**
65 ❑ Oct 1947 Cover: 0.10 **NM value: 18.00**

CGC-graded: Multiply prices above by **33 for 9.9 M • 16 for 9.8 NM/M • 7 for 9.6 NM+ • 5 for 9.4 NM • 2.5 for 9.2 NM- • 1.5 for 9.0 VF/NM**

66 ❑ Nov 1947 Cover: 0.10 **NM** value: **18.00**
67 ❑ Dec 1947 Cover: 0.10 **NM** value: **18.00**
68 ❑ Jan 1948 Cover: 0.10 **NM** value: **18.00**
69 ❑ Feb 1948 Cover: 0.10 **NM** value: **18.00**
70 ❑ Mar 1948 Cover: 0.10 **NM** value: **18.00**
71 ❑ May 1948 Cover: 0.10 **NM** value: **35.00**
• Joe DiMaggio
72 ❑ Jul 1948 Cover: 0.10 **NM** value: **26.00**
• Jackie Robinson
73 ❑ Oct 1948 Cover: 0.10 **NM** value: **26.00**
• Walt Disney
74 ❑ Dec 1948 Cover: 0.10 **NM** value: **18.00**
75 ❑ Feb 1949 Cover: 0.10 **NM** value: **18.00**
📖 The Story Behind the U.S. State Department; You're the Detective; The Case of the Barefoot Bandit; King of Reporters; My Most Interesting True Experience (text); Tips on Championship Basketball (text) • U.S. State Department; Jack Robbins; Special Agent; Jane Wyman; Adolph Rupp; Tommy Dorsey; Floyd Gibbons
76 ❑ Apr 1949 Cover: 0.10 **NM** value: **18.00**
77 ❑ Jun 1949 Cover: 0.10 **NM** value: **18.00**
• Lou Boudeau, FBI
78 ❑ Aug 1949 Cover: 0.10 **NM** value: **26.00**
• Stan Musial
79 ❑ Oct 1949 Cover: 0.10 **NM** value: **18.00**
80 ❑ Dec 1949 Cover: 0.10 **NM** value: **65.00**
• Distributed to subscribers only
81 ❑ Feb 1950 Cover: 0.10 **NM** value: **65.00**
• Distributed to subscribers only
82 ❑ Apr 1950 Cover: 0.10 **NM** value: **65.00**
• Distributed to subscribers only
83 ❑ Jun 1950 Cover: 0.10 **NM** value: **65.00**
• Distributed to subscribers only
84 ❑ Aug 1950 Cover: 0.10 **NM** value: **65.00**
final issue. • Distributed to subscribers only

TRUE CONFUSIONS — Fantagraphics
1 ❑ b&w Cover: 2.50 **NM** value: **Cover or less**

TRUE CRIME COMICS — Eclipse
1 ❑ b&w Cover: 2.95 **NM** value: **Cover or less**
Circ: CapCity orders: **3,200**
2 ❑ b&w Cover: 2.95 **NM** value: **Cover or less**
• Amy Fisher story

TRUE CRIME COMICS (1ST SERIES) — Magazine Village
2 ❑ May 1947 Cover: 0.10 **NM** value: **1000.00**
📖 True Crime Comics Offers $100.00 Reward for Information Leading to the Capture of James Kent; Demons Dance on Galloway Moore; A Match for Satan; Boston's Bloody Gang War **A:** Jack Cole **W:** Jack Cole
3 ❑ Jul 1948 Cover: 0.10 **NM** value: **900.00**
• **CGC:** 3 graded, best 8.0
📖 Murder, Morphine, and Me; Meet the Split Benny Dickson; Vengeance of the Mounted • "Injury to the eye" panel cited in Seduction of the Innocent **A:** Jack Cole **W:** Jack Cole
4 ❑ Feb 1949 Cover: 0.10 **NM** value: **800.00**
5 ❑ Apr 1949 Cover: 0.10 **NM** value: **500.00**
6 ❑ May 1949 Cover: 0.10 **NM** value: **400.00**
• **CGC:** 1 graded, best 9.0

TRUE CRIME COMICS (2ND SERIES) — Magazine Village
1 ❑ Sep 1949 Cover: 0.10 **NM** value: **700.00**

TRUE FAITH — DC
1 ❑ Cover: 12.95 **NM** value: **Cover or less**
No issue number. • squarebound; reprints Garth Ennis' first story from 1990 **A:** Warren Pleece **W:** Garth Ennis

TRUE GEIN — Boneyard
1 ❑ May 1993 Cover: 2.75 **NM** value: **3.00**
📖 Ed! **A:** Pat Gabriele **W:** Pat Gabriele

TRUE GLITZ — Rip Off
1 ❑ Cover: 2.50 **NM** value: **Cover or less**
📖 Life in the Bagel Belt with Didi Glitz; Rubberware; I'd Rather be Doing Something Else; Don't Ask; Stupid Cupid; Mix & Match; A Blonde Grows in Brooklyn; Didi has an Orgasm; **A:** Diane Noomin **W:** Diane Noomin

TRUE LIFE SECRETS — Charlton
1 ❑ Mar 1951 Cover: 0.10 **NM** value: **50.00**
2 ❑ ca. 1951 Cover: 0.10 **NM** value: **25.00**
3 ❑ ca. 1951 Cover: 0.10 **NM** value: **18.00**
4 ❑ ca. 1951 Cover: 0.10 **NM** value: **18.00**
5 ❑ ca. 1951 Cover: 0.10 **NM** value: **18.00**
6 ❑ ca. 1952 Cover: 0.10 **NM** value: **15.00**
7 ❑ ca. 1952 Cover: 0.10 **NM** value: **15.00**
8 ❑ ca. 1952 Cover: 0.10 **NM** value: **15.00**
9 ❑ ca. 1952 Cover: 0.10 **NM** value: **15.00**
10 ❑ ca. 1952 Cover: 0.10 **NM** value: **15.00**
11 ❑ ca. 1952 Cover: 0.10 **NM** value: **12.00**
12 ❑ ca. 1953 Cover: 0.10 **NM** value: **12.00**
13 ❑ ca. 1953 Cover: 0.10 **NM** value: **12.00**
14 ❑ ca. 1953 Cover: 0.10 **NM** value: **12.00**
15 ❑ ca. 1953 Cover: 0.10 **NM** value: **12.00**
16 ❑ ca. 1953 Cover: 0.10 **NM** value: **12.00**
17 ❑ ca. 1954 Cover: 0.10 **NM** value: **12.00**
A: Art Cappello
18 ❑ ca. 1954 Cover: 0.10 **NM** value: **12.00**
19 ❑ May 1954 Cover: 0.10 **NM** value: **12.00**
• **CGC:** 1 graded, best 9.0
20 ❑ ca. 1954 Cover: 0.10 **NM** value: **12.00**
21 ❑ ca. 1954 Cover: 0.10 **NM** value: **9.00**
22 ❑ Oct 1954 Cover: 0.10 **NM** value: **9.00**
• **CGC:** 2 graded, best 9.6
23 ❑ Nov 1954 Cover: 0.10 **NM** value: **9.00**
• **CGC:** 5 graded, best 9.2
24 ❑ Jan 1955 Cover: 0.10 **NM** value: **9.00**
25 ❑ ca. 1955 Cover: 0.10 **NM** value: **9.00**
26 ❑ ca. 1955 Cover: 0.10 **NM** value: **9.00**
27 ❑ ca. 1955 Cover: 0.10 **NM** value: **9.00**
28 ❑ ca. 1956 Cover: 0.10 **NM** value: **9.00**
29 ❑ ca. 1956 Cover: 0.10 **NM** value: **9.00**
final issue.

TRUE LOVE — Eclipse
1 ❑ Cover: 1.50 **NM** value: **2.00**
📖 Stars in my Eyes; Wrong Way to Happiness; Heart Divided; Chained to My Past • Reprints stories from New Romances #17, Thrilling Romances #22, #24, and Intimate Love #20 **A:** Alex Toth; Nick Cardy; Mike Peppe; Vince Colletta **C:** Dave Stevens
2 ❑ Cover: 1.50 **NM** value: **2.00**
📖 Blinded by Love; Unwanted Love; Two-Timer; My Other Love • Reprints stories from Popular Romance #22, New Romances #13, #15, and Thrilling Romances #24 **A:** Alex Toth; Nick Cardy; Mike Peppe; Ralph Mayo; Vince Colletta

TRUE LOVE PROBLEMS & ADVICE ILLUSTRATED — Harvey
1 ❑ Jun 1949 Cover: 0.10 **NM** value: **75.00**
2 ❑ Aug 1949 Cover: 0.10 **NM** value: **50.00**
3 ❑ Oct 1949 Cover: 0.10 **NM** value: **40.00**
4 ❑ Dec 1949 Cover: 0.10 **NM** value: **40.00**
5 ❑ Feb 1950 Cover: 0.10 **NM** value: **40.00**
6 ❑ Apr 1950 Cover: 0.10 **NM** value: **40.00**
7 ❑ Jan 1951 Cover: 0.10 **NM** value: **40.00**
8 ❑ Mar 1951 Cover: 0.10 **NM** value: **40.00**
9 ❑ May 1951 Cover: 0.10 **NM** value: **40.00**
10 ❑ Jul 1951 Cover: 0.10 **NM** value: **40.00**
11 ❑ Sep 1951 Cover: 0.10 **NM** value: **25.00**
12 ❑ Nov 1951 Cover: 0.10 **NM** value: **25.00**
13 ❑ Jan 1952 Cover: 0.10 **NM** value: **25.00**
14 ❑ Mar 1952 Cover: 0.10 **NM** value: **25.00**
15 ❑ May 1952 Cover: 0.10 **NM** value: **25.00**
16 ❑ Jul 1952 Cover: 0.10 **NM** value: **25.00**
17 ❑ Sep 1952 Cover: 0.10 **NM** value: **25.00**
• **CGC:** 1 graded, best 3.0
18 ❑ Nov 1952 Cover: 0.10 **NM** value: **25.00**
19 ❑ Jan 1953 Cover: 0.10 **NM** value: **25.00**
20 ❑ Mar 1953 Cover: 0.10 **NM** value: **25.00**
21 ❑ May 1953 Cover: 0.10 **NM** value: **25.00**
22 ❑ Jul 1953 Cover: 0.10 **NM** value: **25.00**
23 ❑ Sep 1953 Cover: 0.10 **NM** value: **25.00**
24 ❑ Nov 1953 Cover: 0.10 **NM** value: **25.00**
25 ❑ Jan 1954 Cover: 0.10 **NM** value: **25.00**
26 ❑ Mar 1954 Cover: 0.10 **NM** value: **25.00**
27 ❑ May 1954 Cover: 0.10 **NM** value: **25.00**
28 ❑ Jul 1954 Cover: 0.10 **NM** value: **25.00**
29 ❑ Sep 1954 Cover: 0.10 **NM** value: **25.00**
30 ❑ Nov 1954 Cover: 0.10 **NM** value: **25.00**
31 ❑ Jan 1955 Cover: 0.10 **NM** value: **20.00**
32 ❑ Mar 1955 Cover: 0.10 **NM** value: **20.00**
33 ❑ May 1955 Cover: 0.10 **NM** value: **20.00**
34 ❑ Jul 1955 Cover: 0.10 **NM** value: **20.00**
35 ❑ Sep 1955 Cover: 0.10 **NM** value: **20.00**
36 ❑ Nov 1955 Cover: 0.10 **NM** value: **20.00**
37 ❑ Jan 1956 Cover: 0.10 **NM** value: **20.00**
38 ❑ Mar 1956 Cover: 0.10 **NM** value: **20.00**
39 ❑ May 1956 Cover: 0.10 **NM** value: **20.00**
40 ❑ Jul 1956 Cover: 0.10 **NM** value: **20.00**
41 ❑ Sep 1956 Cover: 0.10 **NM** value: **20.00**
42 ❑ Nov 1956 Cover: 0.10 **NM** value: **20.00**
43 ❑ Jan 1957 Cover: 0.10 **NM** value: **20.00**
44 ❑ Mar 1957 Cover: 0.10 **NM** value: **20.00**

TRUE NORTH, THE — Comic Legends Defense Fund
1 ❑ ca. 1988, b&w Cover: 3.50 **NM** value: **Cover or less**
No issue number. cardstock cover. • benefit comic

TRUE NORTH II, THE — Comic Legends Defense Fund
1 ❑ ca. 1990 Cover: 4.50 **NM** value: **Cover or less**
No issue number. cardstock foldout cover.

TRUE SIN — Boneyard
1 ❑ Cover: 2.95 **NM** value: **Cover or less**

TRUE SPORT PICTURE STORIES — Street & Smith
1st Series
5❑ Feb 1942Cover: 0.10 **NM** value: **250.00**
6 ❑ Apr 1942 Cover: 0.10 **NM** value: **150.00**
7 ❑ Jun 1942 Cover: 0.10 **NM** value: **150.00**
8 ❑ Aug 1942 Cover: 0.10 **NM** value: **150.00**
9 ❑ Oct 1942 Cover: 0.10 **NM** value: **150.00**
10 ❑ Dec 1942 Cover: 0.10 **NM** value: **150.00**
• Frankie Sinkwich, Whitlow Wyatt
11 ❑ Feb 1943 Cover: 0.10 **NM** value: **150.00**
12 ❑ Apr 1943 Cover: 0.10 **NM** value: **150.00**

TRUE SPORT PICTURE STORIES — Street & Smith
2nd Series
1 ❑ Jun 1943 Cover: 0.10 **NM** value: **125.00**
2 ❑ Aug 1943 Cover: 0.10 **NM** value: **125.00**
3 ❑ Oct 1943 Cover: 0.10 **NM** value: **125.00**
4 ❑ Dec 1943 Cover: 0.10 **NM** value: **125.00**
5 ❑ Feb 1944 Cover: 0.10 **NM** value: **125.00**
6 ❑ Apr 1944 Cover: 0.10 **NM** value: **125.00**
7 ❑ Jun 1944 Cover: 0.10 **NM** value: **125.00**
8 ❑ Aug 1944 Cover: 0.10 **NM** value: **125.00**
9 ❑ Oct 1944 Cover: 0.10 **NM** value: **125.00**
10 ❑ Dec 1944 Cover: 0.10 **NM** value: **125.00**
11 ❑ Feb 1945 Cover: 0.10 **NM** value: **125.00**
12 ❑ Apr 1945 Cover: 0.10 **NM** value: **125.00**

TRUE SPORT PICTURE STORIES — Street & Smith
3rd Series
1 ❑ Jun 1945 Cover: 0.10 **NM** value: **100.00**
2 ❑ Aug 1945 Cover: 0.10 **NM** value: **100.00**
3 ❑ Oct 1945 Cover: 0.10 **NM** value: **100.00**
4 ❑ Nov 1945 Cover: 0.10 **NM** value: **100.00**
5 ❑ Jan 1946 Cover: 0.10 **NM** value: **100.00**
6 ❑ Mar 1946 Cover: 0.10 **NM** value: **100.00**
7 ❑ May 1946 Cover: 0.10 **NM** value: **100.00**
8 ❑ Jul 1946 Cover: 0.10 **NM** value: **100.00**
9 ❑ Sep 1946 Cover: 0.10 **NM** value: **100.00**
10 ❑ Nov 1946 Cover: 0.10 **NM** value: **100.00**
11 ❑ Jan 1947 Cover: 0.10 **NM** value: **100.00**
12 ❑ Mar 1947 Cover: 0.10 **NM** value: **100.00**

TRUE SPORT PICTURE STORIES — Street & Smith
4th Series
1 ❑ May 1947 Cover: 0.10 **NM** value: **100.00**
• Baseball cover
2 ❑ Jul 1947 Cover: 0.10 **NM** value: **100.00**
3 ❑ Sep 1947 Cover: 0.10 **NM** value: **100.00**
• 1947 Super Stars: Joe Fulks, Glenn Dobbs, Cornelius Warmerdam, Gilbert Dodds
4 ❑ Nov 1947 Cover: 0.10 **NM** value: **100.00**
5 ❑ Jan 1948 Cover: 0.10 **NM** value: **100.00**
6 ❑ Mar 1948 Cover: 0.10 **NM** value: **100.00**
7 ❑ May 1948 Cover: 0.10 **NM** value: **100.00**
8 ❑ Jul 1948 Cover: 0.10 **NM** value: **100.00**
9 ❑ Sep 1948 Cover: 0.10 **NM** value: **100.00**
10 ❑ Nov 1948 Cover: 0.10 **NM** value: **100.00**
• Football cover
11 ❑ Jan 1949 Cover: 0.10 **NM** value: **100.00**
• **CGC:** 1 graded, best 5.0
12 ❑ Mar 1949 Cover: 0.10 **NM** value: **100.00**

TRUE SPORT PICTURE STORIES — Street & Smith
5th Series
1 ❑ May 1949 Cover: 0.10 **NM** value: **100.00**
• **CGC:** 1 graded, best 7.5
2 ❑ Jul 1949 Cover: 0.10 **NM** value: **100.00**

TRUE SPY STORIES — Caliber / Tome
1 ❑ b&w Cover: 2.95 **NM** value: **Cover or less**
• bios

TRUE SWAMP — Peristaltic Press
1 ❑ b&w Cover: 2.50 **NM** value: **Cover or less**
A: Jon Lewis **W:** Jon Lewis
2 ❑ May 1994, b&w Cover: 2.50 **NM** value: **Cover or less**
A: Jon Lewis **W:** Jon Lewis
3 ❑ ca. 1994 Cover: 2.50 **NM** value: **Cover or less**
A: Jon Lewis **W:** Jon Lewis
4 ❑ Oct 1994, b&w Cover: 3.00 **NM** value: **Cover or less**
📖 Even Daisies Could Use More White **A:** Jon Lewis **W:** Jon Lewis
5 ❑ Feb 1995, b&w Cover: 2.95 **NM** value: **Cover or less**
Bk 1❑ Apr 1996, b&w Cover: 2.50 **NM** value: **4.95**
• Memoirs Of Lenny The Frog; reprints #1-4

TRUE 3-D — Harvey
1 ❑ Dec 1953 Cover: 0.25 **NM** value: **50.00**
• **CGC:** 3 graded, best 9.4
2 ❑ Feb 1954 Cover: 0.25 **NM** value: **50.00**
• **CGC:** 3 graded, best 9.4

TRUE WAR EXPERIENCES — Harvey
1 ❑ Aug 1952 Cover: 0.10 **NM** value: **75.00**
• **CGC:** 1 graded, best 9.0
2 ❑ Sep 1952 Cover: 0.10 **NM** value: **45.00**
3 ❑ Oct 1952 Cover: 0.10 **NM** value: **45.00**
4 ❑ Dec 1952 Cover: 0.10 **NM** value: **45.00**

TRUFAN ADVENTURES THEATRE — Paragraphics
1 ❑ ca. 1986, b&w Cover: 1.95 **NM** value: **Cover or less**
2 ❑ ca. 1986 Cover: 1.95 **NM** value: **Cover or less**
• 3-D.

TRULY TASTELESS AND TACKY — Caliber
1 ❑ b&w Cover: 2.50 **NM** value: **Cover or less**

TRYPTO THE ACID DOG — Renegade
1 ❑ b&w Cover: 2.00 **NM** value: **Cover or less**

TSC JAMS — TSC
0 ❑ Cover: 3.95 **NM** value: **Cover or less**
📖 TB7 and the Technobeetles; Bushmaster; Bruise Control; Pride and Glory; Ahmon Ra **A:** Doug Gray; Julius Willis; Mark Newman; Patrick Ho; Terry Smith **W:** Doug Gray; Robert Koester
1 ❑ Cover: 3.95 **NM** value: **Cover or less**
No issue number.

Capital City orders are the actual sales of comic books by Capital City Distribution, once one of the largest U.S. sellers of comics to comics shops. Capital City's share of comics shop sales, while not known exactly, increases from around 10-20% in the mid-1980s to 30-35% in the mid-1990s. Capital City's share of comic books sold on newsstands (most Marvels and DCs) will be less.

Other grades: Multiply prices above by **1.5 for Mint • 2/3 for Very Fine • 1/3 for Fine • 1/5 for Very Good • 1/8 for Good**

TSR WORLDS — DC

Billed as an "annual," this one-shot special introduced readers to TSR's various comic worlds, as well as to a new one-the world of the Spelljammers. It begins when Captain Meredith accepts a commission to rescue Pax Ahlmuhn from the spider-pirates known as the Neogi. As part of the payment, Meredith was offered a Crown of Stars. This device allows Spelljammers such as herself to mentally control the organic ships which they use to travel between worlds.

And travel she would. In order to fulfill her quest she would travel to realms of sword and sorcery on the far-off planet of Earth. There she would encounter the casts of Advanced Dungeons & Dragons, Forgotten Realms, and enter the world of Krynn and the Dragonlance. The quest for Pax serves as a framing story for a series of adventures in each of these places, giving readers a firsthand look at the action to be found in those titles.

Anl 1❑ca. 1990 Cover: 3.95 **NM** value: **Cover or less**
Circ: CapCity orders: **13,050**
★ 1st Appearance of The Spelljammers, Meredith.

TSUNAMI GIRL — Image

1 ❑ Feb 1999 Cover: 2.95 **NM** value: **Cover or less**
Circ: Diamd. preorders: **26,863**
• no month of publication **A:** Mark Paniccia **W:** Mark Paniccia
2 ❑ Apr 1999 Cover: 2.95 **NM** value: **Cover or less**
Circ: Diamd. preorders: **16,307**
📖 Even Gods Cry • no month of publication **A:** Mark Paniccia **W:** Mark Paniccia
3 ❑ Jun 1999 Cover: 2.95 **NM** value: **Cover or less**
Circ: Diamd. preorders: **15,677** • **CGC:** 1 graded, best 9.8
A: Mark Paniccia **W:** Mark Paniccia

TSUNAMI, THE IRRESISTIBLE FORCE — Epoch

1 ❑ Cover: 2.00 **NM** value: **Cover or less**
A: Donald McQuay **W:** Donald McQuay

TUBBY AND THE LITTLE MEN FROM MARS (MARGE'S) — Gold Key

1 ❑ Oct 1956 Cover: 0.25 **NM** value: **75.00**
• **CGC:** 1 graded, best 9.2

TUBBY (MARGE'S...) — Dell

Marjorie Henderson Buell, creator of the Little Lulu panel that ran in The Saturday Evening Post, licensed her characters to Dell for comic-book publication. She continued to monitor the material, but it was writer-artist John Stanley who elaborated on her characters and told an ongoing delightful, developed wonderworld of stories for young readers.

Among his most developed characters was Tubby, who became successful enough to support his own series. In these stories, plots focused on such themes as his obsession with the pretty but nasty Gloria (who preferred Wilbur), on his violin playing, and on his adventures with a troupe of tiny men in a flying saucer.

5 ❑ Jul 1953 Cover: 0.10 **NM** value: **45.00**
6 ❑ Oct 1953 Cover: 0.10 **NM** value: **30.00**
7 ❑ Jan 1954 Cover: 0.10 **NM** value: **30.00**
8 ❑ Apr 1954 Cover: 0.10 **NM** value: **30.00**
9 ❑ Jul 1954 Cover: 0.10 **NM** value: **30.00**
10 ❑ Oct 1954 Cover: 0.10 **NM** value: **30.00**
11 ❑ Jan 1955 Cover: 0.10 **NM** value: **26.00**
12 ❑ Apr 1955 Cover: 0.10 **NM** value: **26.00**
13 ❑ Jul 1955 Cover: 0.10 **NM** value: **26.00**
14 ❑ Oct 1955 Cover: 0.10 **NM** value: **26.00**
15 ❑ Mar 1956 Cover: 0.10 **NM** value: **26.00**
16 ❑ May 1956 Cover: 0.10 **NM** value: **26.00**
17 ❑ Jul 1956 Cover: 0.10 **NM** value: **26.00**
18 ❑ Sep 1956 Cover: 0.10 **NM** value: **26.00**
19 ❑ Nov 1956 Cover: 0.10 **NM** value: **26.00**
20 ❑ Jan 1957 Cover: 0.10 **NM** value: **26.00**
21 ❑ Mar 1957 Cover: 0.10 **NM** value: **24.00**
22 ❑ May 1957 Cover: 0.10 **NM** value: **24.00**
23 ❑ Jul 1957 Cover: 0.10 **NM** value: **24.00**
24 ❑ Sep 1957 Cover: 0.10 **NM** value: **24.00**
25 ❑ Nov 1957 Cover: 0.10 **NM** value: **24.00**
26 ❑ Jan 1958 Cover: 0.10 **NM** value: **24.00**
27 ❑ Mar 1958 Cover: 0.10 **NM** value: **24.00**
28 ❑ May 1958 Cover: 0.10 **NM** value: **24.00**
29 ❑ Jul 1958 Cover: 0.10 **NM** value: **24.00**
30 ❑ Sep 1958 Cover: 0.10 **NM** value: **24.00**
📖 Strong Measures; Magic Touch; The Flea Circus; Knotknee Frees his Friend (text story); Alvin
31 ❑ Nov 1958 Cover: 0.10 **NM** value: **24.00**
32 ❑ Jan 1959 Cover: 0.10 **NM** value: **24.00**
33 ❑ Mar 1959 Cover: 0.10 **NM** value: **24.00**
34 ❑ May 1959 Cover: 0.10 **NM** value: **24.00**
35 ❑ Jul 1959 Cover: 0.10 **NM** value: **24.00**
36 ❑ Sep 1959 Cover: 0.10 **NM** value: **24.00**
37 ❑ Nov 1959 Cover: 0.10 **NM** value: **24.00**
38 ❑ Jan 1960 Cover: 0.10 **NM** value: **24.00**
39 ❑ Mar 1960 Cover: 0.10 **NM** value: **24.00**
40 ❑ May 1960 Cover: 0.10 **NM** value: **24.00**
41 ❑ Jul 1960 Cover: 0.10 **NM** value: **20.00**
42 ❑ Sep 1960 Cover: 0.10 **NM** value: **20.00**
43 ❑ Nov 1960 Cover: 0.10 **NM** value: **20.00**
44 ❑ Feb 1961 Cover: 0.15 **NM** value: **20.00**
45 ❑ Apr 1961 Cover: 0.15 **NM** value: **20.00**
46 ❑ Jun 1961 Cover: 0.15 **NM** value: **20.00**
47 ❑ Aug 1961 Cover: 0.15 **NM** value: **20.00**
48 ❑ Oct 1961 Cover: 0.15 **NM** value: **20.00**
49 ❑ Dec 1961 Cover: 0.15 **NM** value: **20.00**

TUFF GHOSTS, STARRING SPOOKY — Harvey

1 ❑ Jul 1962 Cover: 0.12 **NM** value: **65.00**
2 ❑ Sep 1962 Cover: 0.12 **NM** value: **30.00**
3 ❑ Nov 1962 Cover: 0.12 **NM** value: **30.00**
4 ❑ Jan 1963 Cover: 0.12 **NM** value: **30.00**
5 ❑ Mar 1963 Cover: 0.12 **NM** value: **30.00**
6 ❑ May 1963 Cover: 0.12 **NM** value: **25.00**
7 ❑ Jul 1963 Cover: 0.12 **NM** value: **25.00**
8 ❑ Sep 1963 Cover: 0.12 **NM** value: **25.00**
9 ❑ Nov 1963 Cover: 0.12 **NM** value: **25.00**
10 ❑ Jan 1964 Cover: 0.12 **NM** value: **25.00**
11 ❑ May 1964 Cover: 0.12 **NM** value: **20.00**
12 ❑ Jul 1964 Cover: 0.12 **NM** value: **20.00**
13 ❑ Nov 1964 Cover: 0.12 **NM** value: **20.00**
14 ❑ Jan 1965 Cover: 0.12 **NM** value: **20.00**
15 ❑ Mar 1965 Cover: 0.12 **NM** value: **20.00**
16 ❑ May 1965 Cover: 0.12 **NM** value: **20.00**
17 ❑ Jul 1965 Cover: 0.12 **NM** value: **20.00**
18 ❑ Sep 1965 Cover: 0.12 **NM** value: **20.00**
19 ❑ Nov 1965 Cover: 0.12 **NM** value: **20.00**
20 ❑ Jan 1966 Cover: 0.12 **NM** value: **15.00**
21 ❑ Mar 1966 Cover: 0.12 **NM** value: **15.00**
22 ❑ May 1966 Cover: 0.12 **NM** value: **15.00**
23 ❑ Jul 1966 Cover: 0.12 **NM** value: **15.00**
24 ❑ Sep 1966 Cover: 0.12 **NM** value: **15.00**
25 ❑ Nov 1966 Cover: 0.12 **NM** value: **15.00**
26 ❑ Jan 1967 Cover: 0.12 **NM** value: **15.00**
27 ❑ Mar 1967 Cover: 0.12 **NM** value: **15.00**
28 ❑ May 1967 Cover: 0.12 **NM** value: **15.00**
29 ❑ Jul 1967 Cover: 0.12 **NM** value: **15.00**
30 ❑ Sep 1967 Cover: 0.12 **NM** value: **15.00**
31 ❑ Nov 1967 Cover: 0.12 **NM** value: **10.00**
32 ❑ Jan 1968 Cover: 0.12 **NM** value: **10.00**
33 ❑ Jun 1968 Cover: 0.12 **NM** value: **10.00**
34 ❑ Aug 1968 Cover: 0.12 **NM** value: **10.00**
35 ❑ Oct 1968 Cover: 0.15 **NM** value: **10.00**
36 ❑ Nov 1968 Cover: 0.15 **NM** value: **10.00**
37 ❑ Apr 1969 Cover: 0.15 **NM** value: **10.00**
38 ❑ Sep 1969 Cover: 0.15 **NM** value: **10.00**
39 ❑ Nov 1969 Cover: 0.15 **NM** value: **10.00**
40 ❑ Sep 1971 Cover: 0.25 **NM** value: **10.00**
41 ❑ ca. 1972 Cover: 0.25 **NM** value: **10.00**
42 ❑ Jun 1972 Cover: 0.25 **NM** value: **10.00**
43 ❑ Oct 1972 Cover: 0.20 **NM** value: **10.00**

TUFF SH*T — Print Mint

1 ❑ Cover: 0.50 **NM** value: **3.00**
📖 To Have Loved...and Lost!; Tales from the Golden Age of America; The Addictive Personality; Street Corner Daze; Johnny Carter in Tainted Blood; While You're up...Get Me Some Smack **A:** Justin Green; Robert Crumb; Bill Griffith; Jim Osborne **W:** Justin Green; Robert Crumb; Bill Griffith; Jim Osborne

TUG & BUSTER (ART & SOUL) — Art & Soul

1 ❑ Nov 1995 Cover: 2.95 **NM** value: **3.00**
• **CGC:** 1 graded, best 9.4
A: Marc Hempel **W:** Marc Hempel
2 ❑ Jan 1996 Cover: 2.95 **NM** value: **3.00**
A: Marc Hempel **W:** Marc Hempel
3 ❑ Mar 1996 Cover: 2.95 **NM** value: **3.00**
📖 Soiree, Wrong Number **A:** Marc Hempel **W:** Marc Hempel
4 ❑ May 1996 Cover: 2.95 **NM** value: **3.00**
A: Marc Hempel **W:** Marc Hempel
5 ❑ Aug 1996 Cover: 2.95 **NM** value: **3.00**
6 ❑ Cover: 2.95 **NM** value: **3.00**
Circ: Diamd. preorders: **3,682**
7 ❑ Feb 1998 Cover: 2.95 **NM** value: **3.00**
Circ: Diamd. preorders: **2,616**

TUG & BUSTER (IMAGE) — Image

1 ❑ Aug 1998, b&w Cover: 2.95 **NM** value: **Cover or less**
Circ: Diamd. preorders: **5,084**
📖 Now Museum, Now You Don't! **A:** Marc Hempel **W:** Marc Hempel

TUMBLING BOXES — Fantagraphics / Eros

All issues are adults only.
1 ❑ Dec 1994, b&w Cover: 2.95 **NM** value: **Cover or less**

TUROK ADON'S CURSE — Acclaim / Eros

1 ❑ Cover: 4.95 **NM** value: **Cover or less**

TUROK: CHILD OF BLOOD — Acclaim

1 ❑ Jan 1998 Cover: 3.95 **NM** value: **Cover or less**
Circ: Diamd. preorders: **10,888**
One-shot. **A:** Rafael Kayanan **W:** Fabian Nicieza

TUROK, DINOSAUR HUNTER — Acclaim / Valiant

0 ❑ Nov 1995 Cover: 2.50 **NM** value: **Cover or less**
Circ: CapCity orders: **9,000**
📖 Domini Canes **A:** Rags Morales **W:** Tim Truman ★ Origin of Lost Land, Andar, Turok.
1 ❑ Jul 1993 Cover: 3.50 **NM** value: **Cover or less**
Circ: CapCity orders: **378,400** • **CGC:** 3 graded, best 9.8
chromium cover. 📖 Cold Blood Blazing **A:** Bart Sears **W:** David Michelinie
1/GO❑Jul 1993 Cover: 40.00 **NM** value: **Cover or less**
• **CGC:** 1 graded, best 9.6
chromium cover. • Gold edition. **A:** Bart Sears **W:** David Michelinie
2 ❑ Aug 1993 Cover: 2.50 **NM** value: **Cover or less**
Circ: CapCity orders: **120,500**
3 ❑ Sep 1993 Cover: 2.50 **NM** value: **Cover or less**
Circ: CapCity orders: **92,300**
4 ❑ Oct 1993 Cover: 2.50 **NM** value: **Cover or less**
Circ: CapCity orders: **67,600**
5 ❑ Nov 1993 Cover: 2.50 **NM** value: **Cover or less**
Circ: CapCity orders: **56,950**
6 ❑ Dec 1993 Cover: 2.50 **NM** value: **Cover or less**
Circ: CapCity orders: **51,300**
7 ❑ Jan 1994 Cover: 2.50 **NM** value: **Cover or less**
Circ: CapCity orders: **48,150**
A: Tim Truman
8 ❑ Feb 1994 Cover: 2.50 **NM** value: **Cover or less**
Circ: CapCity orders: **39,325**
A: Tim Truman
9 ❑ Mar 1994 Cover: 2.50 **NM** value: **Cover or less**
Circ: CapCity orders: **33,175**
10 ❑ Apr 1994 Cover: 2.50 **NM** value: **Cover or less**
Circ: CapCity orders: **27,400**
11 ❑ May 1994 Cover: 2.50 **NM** value: **Cover or less**
Circ: CapCity orders: **30,425**
• trading card
12 ❑ Jun 1994 Cover: 2.50 **NM** value: **Cover or less**
Circ: CapCity orders: **22,175**
13 ❑ Aug 1994 Cover: 2.50 **NM** value: **Cover or less**
Circ: CapCity orders: **20,900**
📖 Return of Captain Red, Part 1 ★ Versus Captain Red.
14 ❑ Sep 1994 Cover: 2.50 **NM** value: **Cover or less**
Circ: CapCity orders: **20,350**
📖 Return of Captain Red, Part 2 ★ Versus Captain Red.
15 ❑ Oct 1994 Cover: 2.50 **NM** value: **Cover or less**
Circ: CapCity orders: **19,150**
📖 Return of Captain Red, Part 3 ★ Versus Captain Red.
16 ❑ Oct 1994 Cover: 2.50 **NM** value: **Cover or less**
Circ: CapCity orders: **24,125**
📖 The Chaos Effect: Beta, Part 3 • Chaos Effect
17 ❑ Nov 1994 Cover: 2.50 **NM** value: **Cover or less**
Circ: CapCity orders: **17,300**
18 ❑ Dec 1994 Cover: 2.50 **NM** value: **Cover or less**
Circ: CapCity orders: **15,450**
19 ❑ Jan 1995 Cover: 2.50 **NM** value: **Cover or less**
Circ: CapCity orders: **14,325**
★ Appearance of X-O Manowar.
20 ❑ Feb 1995 Cover: 2.50 **NM** value: **Cover or less**
Circ: CapCity orders: **13,300**
21 ❑ Mar 1995 Cover: 2.50 **NM** value: **Cover or less**
Circ: CapCity orders: **11,325**
22 ❑ Apr 1995 Cover: 2.50 **NM** value: **Cover or less**
Circ: CapCity orders: **10,475**
23 ❑ May 1995 Cover: 2.50 **NM** value: **Cover or less**
Circ: CapCity orders: **9,300**
24 ❑ Jun 1995 Cover: 2.50 **NM** value: **Cover or less**
Circ: CapCity orders: **8,425**
• back to the Lost Land **A:** Tim Truman
25 ❑ Jul 1995 Cover: 2.50 **NM** value: **Cover or less**
Circ: CapCity orders: **8,325**
A: Tim Truman
26 ❑ Jul 1995 Cover: 2.50 **NM** value: **Cover or less**
Circ: CapCity orders: **8,275**
• Birthquake **A:** Tim Truman ★ Appearance of Captain Red.
27 ❑ Aug 1995 Cover: 2.50 **NM** value: **Cover or less**
Circ: CapCity orders: **7,700**
A: Tim Truman
28 ❑ Aug 1995 Cover: 2.50 **NM** value: **Cover or less**
Circ: CapCity orders: **7,750**
29 ❑ Sep 1995 Cover: 2.50 **NM** value: **Cover or less**
Circ: CapCity orders: **7,950**
30 ❑ Sep 1995 Cover: 2.50 **NM** value: **Cover or less**
Circ: CapCity orders: **7,950**
31 ❑ Oct 1995 Cover: 2.50 **NM** value: **Cover or less**
Circ: CapCity orders: **2,650**
A: Paul Gulacy; Tim Truman
32 ❑ Oct 1995 Cover: 2.50 **NM** value: **Cover or less**
Circ: CapCity orders: **2,625**
A: Paul Gulacy; Tim Truman
33 ❑ Nov 1995 Cover: 2.50 **NM** value: **Cover or less**
Circ: CapCity orders: **7,725**
34 ❑ Nov 1995 Cover: 2.50 **NM** value: **Cover or less**
Circ: CapCity orders: **7,575**
35 ❑ Dec 1995 Cover: 2.50 **NM** value: **Cover or less**
Circ: CapCity orders: **6,450**
Painted cover.
36 ❑ Dec 1995 Cover: 2.50 **NM** value: **Cover or less**
Circ: CapCity orders: **6,475**
37 ❑ Jan 1996 Cover: 2.50 **NM** value: **Cover or less**
Circ: CapCity orders: **5,625**
A: Tim Truman
38 ❑ Jan 1996 Cover: 2.50 **NM** value: **Cover or less**
Circ: CapCity orders: **5,625**
A: Tim Truman
39 ❑ Feb 1996 Cover: 2.50 **NM** value: **Cover or less**
40 ❑ Mar 1996 Cover: 2.50 **NM** value: **Cover or less**
41 ❑ Apr 1996 Cover: 2.50 **NM** value: **Cover or less**
42 ❑ Apr 1996 Cover: 2.50 **NM** value: **Cover or less**
43 ❑ May 1996 Cover: 2.50 **NM** value: **Cover or less**
44 ❑ May 1996 Cover: 2.50 **NM** value: **Cover or less**
45 ❑ Jun 1996 Cover: 2.50 **NM** value: **Cover or less**
46 ❑ Aug 1996 Cover: 2.50 **NM** value: **Cover or less**
47 ❑ Aug 1996 Cover: 2.50 **NM** value: **Cover or less**
final issue.
Bk 1❑ Cover: 9.95 **NM** value: **Cover or less**
YB 1❑ Cover: 3.95 **NM** value: **Cover or less**
Circ: CapCity orders: **17,850**
• Yearbook 1.

TUROK: SEEDS OF EVIL — Acclaim

1 ❑ Cover: 4.99 **NM** value: **Cover or less**
• newsstand edition.
1/DM❑ Cover: 4.99 **NM** value: **Cover or less**
Direct cover.

TUROK/SHADOWMAN — Acclaim / Valiant

1 ❑ Feb 1999 Cover: 3.95 **NM** value: **Cover or less**
Circ: Diamd. preorders: **5,167**
📖 Army of One **A:** Matt Broome; Ryan Benjamin; Oscar Jimenez **W:** Christopher Priest

TUROK, SON OF STONE — Dell / Gold Key

Out on a hunting trip, Turok and Andar discover a mystical land where dinosaurs still roamed the earth. Soon the duo were trapped there, and had to use their skills to their utmost if they were to survive. Always, the two hoped to someday find the way back home to their families.

First appearing in 1954's Four Color Comics #596, Turok had one more appearance in Four Color Comics before starting this, his first series. Many years later, a revived and updated Turok would become part of the Valiant Universe, with the title "Turok, Dinosaur Hunter."

3 ❑ May 1956 Cover: 0.10 **NM** value: **125.00**
• **CGC:** 4 graded, best 9.4
• Earlier issues were Four Color #596 and #656
4 ❑ Jun 1956 Cover: 0.10 **NM** value: **100.00**
• **CGC:** 1 graded, best 9.2
5 ❑ Sep 1956 Cover: 0.10 **NM** value: **100.00**
• **CGC:** 1 graded, best 9.2
6 ❑ Dec 1956 Cover: 0.10 **NM** value: **90.00**
• **CGC:** 2 graded, best 8.5
7 ❑ Mar 1957 Cover: 0.10 **NM** value: **90.00**
8 ❑ Jun 1957 Cover: 0.10 **NM** value: **90.00**
9 ❑ Sep 1957 Cover: 0.10 **NM** value: **90.00**
10 ❑ Dec 1957 Cover: 0.10 **NM** value: **90.00**
11 ❑ Mar 1958 Cover: 0.10 **NM** value: **60.00**
• Has 1957 Statement, filed 10/1/57; no circ figures published
12 ❑ Jun 1958 Cover: 0.10 **NM** value: **60.00**
• **CGC:** 1 graded, best 7.0
13 ❑ Sep 1958 Cover: 0.10 **NM** value: **60.00**
• **CGC:** 2 graded, best 8.5
14 ❑ Dec 1958 Cover: 0.10 **NM** value: **60.00**
• **CGC:** 2 graded, best 7.5
15 ❑ Mar 1959 Cover: 0.10 **NM** value: **60.00**
• **CGC:** 2 graded, best 7.5
• Has 1958 Statement, filed 10/1/58; no circ figures published
16 ❑ Jun 1959 Cover: 0.10 **NM** value: **60.00**
• **CGC:** 1 graded, best 7.5
17 ❑ Sep 1959 Cover: 0.10 **NM** value: **60.00**
18 ❑ Dec 1959 Cover: 0.10 **NM** value: **60.00**
• **CGC:** 1 graded, best 6.5
19 ❑ Mar 1960 Cover: 0.10 **NM** value: **60.00**
Circ: Statement: **359,013** • **CGC:** 2 graded, best 9.4
• Has 1959 Statement, filed 10/1/59; no circ figures published
20 ❑ Jun 1960 Cover: 0.10 **NM** value: **60.00**
Circ: Statement: **359,013** • **CGC:** 1 graded, best 7.5
21 ❑ Sep 1960 Cover: 0.10 **NM** value: **36.00**
Circ: Statement: **359,013**
22 ❑ Dec 1960 Cover: 0.10 **NM** value: **36.00**
Circ: Statement: **359,013**
23 ❑ Mar 1961 Cover: 0.15 **NM** value: **36.00**
Circ: Statement: **377,145**
• Has 1960 Statement, filed 10/1/60; avg total paid circ 359,013
24 ❑ Jun 1961 Cover: 0.15 **NM** value: **36.00**
Circ: Statement: **377,145**
25 ❑ Sep 1961 Cover: 0.15 **NM** value: **36.00**
Circ: Statement: **377,145** • **CGC:** 1 graded, best 9.4
26 ❑ Dec 1961 Cover: 0.15 **NM** value: **36.00**
Circ: Statement: **377,145** • **CGC:** 1 graded, best 9.6
27 ❑ Mar 1962 Cover: 0.15 **NM** value: **36.00**
• Has 1961 Statement, filed 10/1/61; avg total paid circ 377,145
28 ❑ Jun 1962 Cover: 0.15 **NM** value: **36.00**
29 ❑ Sep 1962 Cover: 0.12 **NM** value: **36.00**
30 ❑ Dec 1962 Cover: 0.12 **NM** value: **36.00**
31 ❑ Jan 1963 Cover: 0.12 **NM** value: **28.00**
Circ: Statement: **276,550**
32 ❑ Mar 1963 Cover: 0.12 **NM** value: **28.00**
Circ: Statement: **276,550**
• Has 1962 Statement, filed 10/1/62; avg subs 3,063
33 ❑ May 1963 Cover: 0.12 **NM** value: **28.00**
Circ: Statement: **276,550**
34 ❑ Jul 1963 Cover: 0.12 **NM** value: **28.00**
Circ: Statement: **276,550**
📖 The Ghostly Terror; Young Earth: The Dinosaur's Day; Andar's Perilous Pet • 10030-307
35 ❑ Sep 1963 Cover: 0.12 **NM** value: **28.00**
Circ: Statement: **276,550**
36 ❑ Nov 1963 Cover: 0.12 **NM** value: **28.00**
Circ: Statement: **276,550**
37 ❑ Jan 1964 Cover: 0.12 **NM** value: **28.00**
Circ: Statement: **274,914**
38 ❑ Mar 1964 Cover: 0.12 **NM** value: **28.00**
Circ: Statement: **274,914**
• Has 1963 Statement, filed 9/27/63; avg print run 408,910; avg sales 274,100; avg subs 2,550; avg total paid 276,550; samples 635; max existent 277,285; 32% of run returned
39 ❑ May 1964 Cover: 0.12 **NM** value: **28.00**
Circ: Statement: **274,914**
40 ❑ Jul 1964 Cover: 0.12 **NM** value: **28.00**
Circ: Statement: **274,914**
41 ❑ Sep 1964 Cover: 0.12 **NM** value: **20.00**
Circ: Statement: **274,914**
42 ❑ Nov 1964 Cover: 0.12 **NM** value: **20.00**
Circ: Statement: **274,914**
43 ❑ Jan 1965 Cover: 0.12 **NM** value: **20.00**
Circ: Statement: **250,316**
44 ❑ Mar 1965 Cover: 0.12 **NM** value: **20.00**
Circ: Statement: **250,316**
• Has 1964 Statement, filed 9/28/64; avg print run 413,285; avg sales 272,617; avg subs 2,297; avg total paid 274,914; samples 508; max existent 275,422; 34% of run returned
45 ❑ May 1965 Cover: 0.12 **NM** value: **20.00**
Circ: Statement: **250,316**
46 ❑ Jul 1965 Cover: 0.12 **NM** value: **20.00**
Circ: Statement: **250,316**
47 ❑ Sep 1965 Cover: 0.12 **NM** value: **20.00**
Circ: Statement: **250,316**
📖 Outcasts of the Flood; Young Earth: The Cro-Magnon Come; Place of No Return • 10030-509
48 ❑ Nov 1965 Cover: 0.12 **NM** value: **20.00**
Circ: Statement: **250,316** • **CGC:** 1 graded, best 7.5
49 ❑ Jan 1966 Cover: 0.12 **NM** value: **20.00**
Circ: Statement: **245,202**
50 ❑ Mar 1966 Cover: 0.12 **NM** value: **20.00**
Circ: Statement: **245,202**
• Has 1965 Statement, filed 9/28/65; avg print run 404,849; avg sales 246,633; avg subs 3,683 avg total paid 250,316; samples 804; max existent 251,120; 38% of run returned
51 ❑ May 1966 Cover: 0.12 **NM** value: **16.00**
Circ: Statement: **245,202**
52 ❑ Jul 1966 Cover: 0.12 **NM** value: **16.00**
Circ: Statement: **245,202**
53 ❑ Sep 1966 Cover: 0.12 **NM** value: **16.00**
Circ: Statement: **245,202** • **CGC:** 1 graded, best 9.4
54 ❑ Nov 1966 Cover: 0.12 **NM** value: **16.00**
Circ: Statement: **245,202**
55 ❑ Jan 1967 Cover: 0.12 **NM** value: **16.00**
Circ: Statement: **232,565**
56 ❑ Mar 1967 Cover: 0.12 **NM** value: **16.00**
Circ: Statement: **232,565**
• Has 1966 Statement, filed 9/28/66; avg print run 375,135; avg sales 244,550; avg subs 652; avg total paid 245,202; samples 573; max existent 245,775; 35% of run returned
57 ❑ May 1967 Cover: 0.12 **NM** value: **16.00**
Circ: Statement: **232,565**
58 ❑ Jul 1967 Cover: 0.12 **NM** value: **16.00**
Circ: Statement: **232,565**
59 ❑ Oct 1967 Cover: 0.12 **NM** value: **16.00**
Circ: Statement: **232,565**
60 ❑ Jan 1968 Cover: 0.12 **NM** value: **16.00**
Circ: Statement: **229,557**
61 ❑ Apr 1968 Cover: 0.12 **NM** value: **12.00**
Circ: Statement: **229,557**
• Has 1967 Statement, filed 9/28/67; avg print run 433,385; avg sales 232,065; avg subs 500; avg total paid 232,565; samples 563; max existent 233,128; 46% of run returned
62 ❑ Jul 1968 Cover: 0.12 **NM** value: **12.00**
Circ: Statement: **229,557**
63 ❑ Oct 1968 Cover: 0.15 **NM** value: **12.00**
Circ: Statement: **229,557**
64 ❑ Jan 1969 Cover: 0.15 **NM** value: **12.00**
Circ: Statement: **209,813**
65 ❑ Apr 1969 Cover: 0.15 **NM** value: **12.00**
Circ: Statement: **209,813** • **CGC:** 1 graded, best 7.0
• Has 1968 Statement, filed 9/27/68; avg print run 358,964; avg sales 229,150; avg subs 407; avg total paid 229,557; samples 499; max existent 230,056; 36% of run returned
66 ❑ Jul 1969 Cover: 0.15 **NM** value: **12.00**
Circ: Statement: **209,813**
67 ❑ Oct 1969 Cover: 0.15 **NM** value: **12.00**
Circ: Statement: **209,813**
68 ❑ Jan 1970 Cover: 0.15 **NM** value: **12.00**
Circ: Statement: **192,381**
69 ❑ Apr 1970 Cover: 0.15 **NM** value: **12.00**
Circ: Statement: **192,381**
• Has 1969 Statement, filed 9/30/69; avg print run 364,961; avg sales 209,500; avg subs 313; avg total paid 209,813; samples 593; max existent 210,406; 42% of run returned
70 ❑ Jul 1970 Cover: 0.15 **NM** value: **12.00**
Circ: Statement: **192,381**
71 ❑ Oct 1970 Cover: 0.15 **NM** value: **8.00**
Circ: Statement: **192,381**
72 ❑ Jan 1971 Cover: 0.15 **NM** value: **8.00**
Circ: Statement: **190,325**
73 ❑ Apr 1971 Cover: 0.15 **NM** value: **8.00**
Circ: Statement: **190,325**
• Has 1970 Statement, filed 9/30/70; avg print run 334,786; avg sales 192,100; avg subs 281; avg total paid 192,381; samples 599; max existent 192,980; 42% of run returned
74 ❑ Jul 1971 Cover: 0.15 **NM** value: **8.00**
Circ: Statement: **190,325**
75 ❑ Oct 1971 Cover: 0.15 **NM** value: **8.00**
Circ: Statement: **190,325**
76 ❑ Jan 1972 Cover: 0.15 **NM** value: **8.00**
77 ❑ Mar 1972 Cover: 0.20 **NM** value: **8.00**
• Has 1971 Statement, filed 9/30/71; avg print run 296,609; avg sales 190,000; avg subs 325; avg total paid 190,325; samples 459; office use 505; max existent 191,289; 36% of run returned
78 ❑ May 1972 Cover: 0.20 **NM** value: **8.00**
79 ❑ Jul 1972 Cover: 0.20 **NM** value: **8.00**
80 ❑ Sep 1972 Cover: 0.20 **NM** value: **8.00**
81 ❑ Nov 1972 Cover: 0.20 **NM** value: **8.00**
82 ❑ Jan 1973 Cover: 0.20 **NM** value: **8.00**
83 ❑ Mar 1973 Cover: 0.20 **NM** value: **8.00**
84 ❑ May 1973 Cover: 0.20 **NM** value: **8.00**
85 ❑ Jul 1973 Cover: 0.20 **NM** value: **8.00**
86 ❑ Sep 1973 Cover: 0.20 **NM** value: **8.00**
87 ❑ Nov 1973 Cover: 0.20 **NM** value: **8.00**
88 ❑ Jan 1974 Cover: 0.20 **NM** value: **8.00**
89 ❑ Mar 1974 Cover: 0.20 **NM** value: **8.00**
90 ❑ May 1974 Cover: 0.20 **NM** value: **8.00**
91 ❑ Jul 1974 Cover: 0.25 **NM** value: **6.00**
92 ❑ Sep 1974 Cover: 0.25 **NM** value: **6.00**
93 ❑ Nov 1974 Cover: 0.25 **NM** value: **6.00**
94 ❑ Jan 1975 Cover: 0.25 **NM** value: **6.00**
95 ❑ Mar 1975 Cover: 0.25 **NM** value: **6.00**
96 ❑ May 1975 Cover: 0.25 **NM** value: **6.00**
97 ❑ Jul 1975 Cover: 0.25 **NM** value: **6.00**
98 ❑ Aug 1975 Cover: 0.25 **NM** value: **6.00**
99 ❑ Sep 1975 Cover: 0.25 **NM** value: **6.00**
100 ❑ Nov 1975 Cover: 0.25 **NM** value: **6.00**
101 ❑ Mar 1976 Cover: 0.25 **NM** value: **6.00**
102 ❑ 1976 Cover: 0.25 **NM** value: **6.00**
103 ❑ 1976 Cover: 0.25 **NM** value: **6.00**
104 ❑ 1976 Cover: 0.25 **NM** value: **6.00**
105 ❑ Sep 1976 Cover: 0.30 **NM** value: **6.00**
• **CGC:** 1 graded, best 9.6
106 ❑ Nov 1976 Cover: 0.30 **NM** value: **6.00**
107 ❑ Jan 1977 Cover: 0.30 **NM** value: **6.00**
108 ❑ Mar 1977 Cover: 0.30 **NM** value: **6.00**
109 ❑ May 1977 Cover: 0.30 **NM** value: **6.00**
110 ❑ Jul 1977 Cover: 0.30 **NM** value: **6.00**
111 ❑ Sep 1977 Cover: 0.30 **NM** value: **5.00**
112 ❑ Nov 1977 Cover: 0.30 **NM** value: **5.00**
113 ❑ Jan 1978 Cover: 0.35 **NM** value: **5.00**
114 ❑ Mar 1978 Cover: 0.35 **NM** value: **5.00**
115 ❑ May 1978 Cover: 0.35 **NM** value: **5.00**
116 ❑ Jul 1978 Cover: 0.35 **NM** value: **5.00**
117 ❑ Sep 1978 Cover: 0.35 **NM** value: **5.00**
118 ❑ Nov 1978 Cover: 0.35 **NM** value: **5.00**
119 ❑ Jan 1979 Cover: 0.35 **NM** value: **5.00**
120 ❑ Mar 1979 Cover: 0.35 **NM** value: **5.00**
121 ❑ May 1979 Cover: 0.40 **NM** value: **5.00**
122 ❑ Jul 1979 Cover: 0.40 **NM** value: **5.00**
123 ❑ Sep 1979 Cover: 0.40 **NM** value: **5.00**
124 ❑ Nov 1979 Cover: 0.40 **NM** value: **5.00**
125 ❑ Jan 1980 Cover: 0.40 **NM** value: **5.00**
126 ❑ Mar 1981 Cover: 0.50 **NM** value: **5.00**
127 ❑ Oct 1981 Cover: 0.50 **NM** value: **5.00**
128 ❑ Dec 1981 Cover: 0.50 **NM** value: **5.00**
129 ❑ Feb 1982 Cover: 0.60 **NM** value: **5.00**
130 ❑ Apr 1982 Cover: 0.60 **NM** value: **5.00**
final issue.
GS 1❑Nov 1966 **NM** value: **65.00**
• **CGC:** 1 graded, best 5.5

TUROK: SPRING BREAK IN THE LOST LAND — Acclaim / Valiant

1 ❑ Jul 1997 Cover: 3.95 **NM** value: **Cover or less**
Circ: Diamd. preorders: **12,552**
One-shot.

TUROK: THE EMPTY SOULS — Acclaim

1 ❑ Apr 1997 Cover: 3.95 **NM** value: **Cover or less**
1/SC❑Apr 1997 Cover: 3.95 **NM** value: **Cover or less**
alternate painted cover.
Ash 1❑Nov 1996, b&w **NM** value: **1.00**
no cover price. • preview of upcoming series

TUROK THE HUNTED — Acclaim / Valiant

1 ❑ Mar 1996 Cover: 2.50 **NM** value: **Cover or less**
A: Mike Deodato; Mozart Couto **W:** Mike Grell; Simon Furman
2 ❑ Mar 1996 Cover: 2.50 **NM** value: **Cover or less**
A: Mike Deodato; Mozart Couto **W:** Mike Grell; Simon Furman

TUROK, TIMEWALKER: SEVENTH SABBATH — Acclaim / Valiant

1 ❑ Aug 1997 Cover: 2.50 **NM** value: **Cover or less**
Circ: Diamd. preorders: **15,631**
covers form diptych.
2 ❑ Sep 1997 Cover: 2.50 **NM** value: **Cover or less**
Circ: Diamd. preorders: **14,016**
covers form diptych.

TURTLE SOUP — Mirage

1 ❑ Nov 1991 Cover: 2.50 **NM** value: **5.00**
Circ: CapCity orders: **14,400**
📖 Toyoduh: The Naked City; Turtles Attack; The Purpose of Fear; The Ring; Luncindra; Turtle Power **A:** Rick McCollum; Jeff Bonivert; Tom McWeeney; Mark Martin; Michael Dooney; Rich Hedden; Rick Arthur **W:** Rick McCollum; Jeff Bonivert; Tom McWeeney; Mark Martin; Michael Dooney; Rich Hedden; Rick Arthur

TURTLE SOUP (2ND SERIES) — Mirage

1 ❑ Nov 1991 Cover: 2.50 **NM** value: **Cover or less**
Circ: CapCity orders: **10,725**
2 ❑ Dec 1991 Cover: 2.50 **NM** value: **Cover or less**
Circ: CapCity orders: **7,575**
3 ❑ Jan 1992 Cover: 2.50 **NM** value: **Cover or less**
Circ: CapCity orders: **6,125**
4 ❑ Feb 1992 Cover: 2.50 **NM** value: **Cover or less**
Circ: CapCity orders: **5,250**

TV FUNNIES (WALTER LANTZ...) — Dell

261 ❑ Cover: 0.10 **NM** value: **3.50**
• Series continued from New Funnies (Walter Lantz...)
262 ❑ Cover: 0.10 **NM** value: **3.50**
263 ❑ Cover: 0.10 **NM** value: **3.50**
📖 Woody Woodpecker; Andy Pandy and Charlie Chicken; Snow Trouble (text story); Chilly Willy; Oswald the Rabbit
264 ❑ Cover: 0.10 **NM** value: **3.50**
265 ❑ Cover: 0.10 **NM** value: **3.50**

Other grades: Multiply prices above by **1.5 for Mint • 2/3 for Very Fine • 1/3 for Fine • 1/5 for Very Good • 1/8 for Good**

266 ❑ Cover: 0.10 **NM** value: **3.50**
267 ❑ ca. 1959 Cover: 0.10 **NM** value: **3.50**
268 ❑ Cover: 0.10 **NM** value: **3.50**
269 ❑ Cover: 0.10 **NM** value: **3.50**
270 ❑ Cover: 0.10 **NM** value: **3.50**
271 ❑ Cover: 0.10 **NM** value: **3.50**
• Series continued in New Funnies (Walter Lantz...)

TV STARS — Marvel

1 ❑ Aug 1978 Cover: 0.35 **NM** value: **6.00**
• **CGC:** 2 graded, best 9.6
★ 1st Appearance of Captain Caveman (in comics), Grape Ape (in comics).
2 ❑ Oct 1978 Cover: 0.35 **NM** value: **4.00**
3 ❑ Dec 1978 Cover: 0.35 **NM** value: **4.00**
4 ❑ Feb 1979 Cover: 0.35 **NM** value: **4.00**
final issue.

TWEETY AND SYLVESTER (1ST SERIES) — Dell

4 ❑ Mar 1954 Cover: 0.10 **NM** value: **20.00**
5 ❑ Jun 1954 Cover: 0.10 **NM** value: **20.00**
6 ❑ Sep 1954 Cover: 0.10 **NM** value: **20.00**
7 ❑ Dec 1954 Cover: 0.10 **NM** value: **20.00**
8 ❑ Mar 1955 Cover: 0.10 **NM** value: **20.00**
9 ❑ Jun 1955 Cover: 0.10 **NM** value: **20.00**
10 ❑ Sep 1955 Cover: 0.10 **NM** value: **20.00**
11 ❑ Dec 1955 Cover: 0.10 **NM** value: **20.00**
12 ❑ Mar 1956 Cover: 0.10 **NM** value: **20.00**
13 ❑ Jun 1956 Cover: 0.10 **NM** value: **20.00**
14 ❑ Sep 1956 Cover: 0.10 **NM** value: **20.00**
15 ❑ Dec 1956 Cover: 0.10 **NM** value: **20.00**
16 ❑ Mar 1957 Cover: 0.10 **NM** value: **20.00**
17 ❑ Jun 1957 Cover: 0.10 **NM** value: **20.00**
18 ❑ Sep 1957 Cover: 0.10 **NM** value: **20.00**
19 ❑ Dec 1957 Cover: 0.10 **NM** value: **20.00**
20 ❑ Mar 1958 Cover: 0.10 **NM** value: **20.00**
21 ❑ Jun 1958 Cover: 0.10 **NM** value: **15.00**
22 ❑ Sep 1958 Cover: 0.10 **NM** value: **15.00**
23 ❑ Dec 1958 Cover: 0.10 **NM** value: **15.00**
24 ❑ Mar 1959 Cover: 0.10 **NM** value: **15.00**
25 ❑ Jun 1959 Cover: 0.10 **NM** value: **15.00**
26 ❑ Sep 1959 Cover: 0.10 **NM** value: **15.00**
27 ❑ Dec 1959 Cover: 0.10 **NM** value: **15.00**
28 ❑ Mar 1960 Cover: 0.10 **NM** value: **15.00**
29 ❑ Jun 1960 Cover: 0.10 **NM** value: **15.00**
30 ❑ Sep 1960 Cover: 0.10 **NM** value: **15.00**
31 ❑ Dec 1960 Cover: 0.10 **NM** value: **15.00**
32 ❑ Mar 1961 Cover: 0.10 **NM** value: **15.00**
33 ❑ Jun 1961 **NM** value: **15.00**
34 ❑ Sep 1961 **NM** value: **15.00**
35 ❑ Dec 1961 Cover: 0.15 **NM** value: **15.00**
36 ❑ Mar 1962 Cover: 0.15 **NM** value: **15.00**
37 ❑ Jun 1962 **NM** value: **15.00**

TWEETY AND SYLVESTER (2ND SERIES) — Gold Key / Whitman

One of the several series featuring Warner Brothers characters spun out of Dell's Four Color, Tweety and Sylvester had a run as a quarterly series before being retired until the late 1960s.

But it's when the canary and the cat came back for their second series that a number of pop-culture savvy stories appeared. Stories from this run tended to focus less on Sylvester and Tweety as predator and prey, and more on Sylvester's life, with Tweety following along as his conscience — and bailing him out of trouble on several occasions. Send-ups of popular movies were frequent, with "The Great Catsby" (with Sylvester in the title role) following Robert Redford's 1974 film. Another great story finds Tweety and Sylvester in a group therapy session (a la The Bob Newhart Show) with other Looney Tunes characters, who each admit their peculiarities, such as Wile E. Coyote's superiority complex and Road Runner's belief that he's a bus.

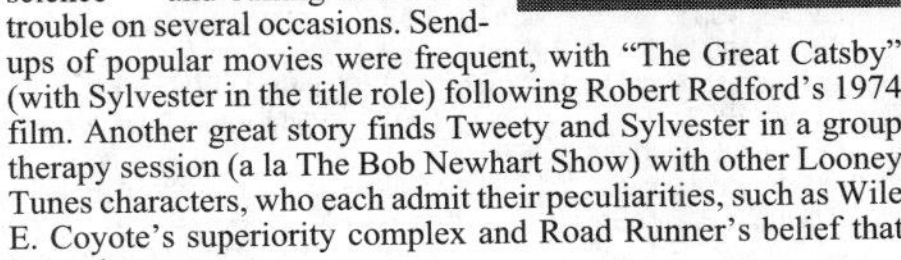

In short, most issues are much better than they probably had to be! — JJM

1 ❑ ca. 1964 Cover: 0.12 **NM** value: **16.00**
2 ❑ Feb 1966 Cover: 0.12 **NM** value: **10.00**
3 ❑ Aug 1966 Cover: 0.12 **NM** value: **8.00**
4 ❑ Nov 1966 Cover: 0.12 **NM** value: **8.00**
5 ❑ Feb 1967 Cover: 0.12 **NM** value: **8.00**
6 ❑ May 1967 Cover: 0.12 **NM** value: **6.00**
7 ❑ Aug 1967 Cover: 0.12 **NM** value: **6.00**
8 ❑ Nov 1967 Cover: 0.12 **NM** value: **6.00**
9 ❑ Oct 1968 Cover: 0.15 **NM** value: **6.00**
10 ❑ Mar 1969 Cover: 0.15 **NM** value: **6.00**
11 ❑ Aug 1969 Cover: 0.15 **NM** value: **5.00**
12 ❑ Nov 1969 Cover: 0.15 **NM** value: **5.00**
13 ❑ Feb 1970 Cover: 0.15 **NM** value: **5.00**
14 ❑ May 1970 Cover: 0.15 **NM** value: **5.00**
15 ❑ Sep 1970 Cover: 0.15 **NM** value: **5.00**
16 ❑ Dec 1970 Cover: 0.15 **NM** value: **5.00**
17 ❑ Mar 1971 Cover: 0.15 **NM** value: **5.00**
Circ: Statement: **237,656**
18 ❑ Jun 1971 Cover: 0.15 **NM** value: **5.00**
Circ: Statement: **237,656**
19 ❑ Aug 1971 Cover: 0.15 **NM** value: **5.00**
Circ: Statement: **237,656**
20 ❑ Oct 1971 Cover: 0.15 **NM** value: **5.00**
Circ: Statement: **237,656**
21 ❑ Dec 1971 Cover: 0.15 **NM** value: **4.00**
Circ: Statement: **237,656**
22 ❑ Jan 1972 Cover: 0.15 **NM** value: **4.00**
• Has 1971 Statement; avg print run 357,475; total paid circ 237,656
23 ❑ Mar 1972 Cover: 0.15 **NM** value: **4.00**
24 ❑ May 1972 Cover: 0.15 **NM** value: **4.00**
25 ❑ Jul 1972 Cover: 0.15 **NM** value: **4.00**
26 ❑ Sep 1972 Cover: 0.15 **NM** value: **4.00**
27 ❑ Nov 1972 Cover: 0.15 **NM** value: **4.00**
28 ❑ Jan 1973 Cover: 0.15 **NM** value: **4.00**
29 ❑ Mar 1973 Cover: 0.15 **NM** value: **4.00**
30 ❑ May 1973 Cover: 0.20 **NM** value: **4.00**
31 ❑ Jul 1973 Cover: 0.20 **NM** value: **4.00**
32 ❑ Aug 1973 Cover: 0.20 **NM** value: **4.00**
33 ❑ Sep 1973 Cover: 0.20 **NM** value: **4.00**
34 ❑ Nov 1973 Cover: 0.20 **NM** value: **4.00**
35 ❑ Jan 1974 Cover: 0.20 **NM** value: **4.00**
36 ❑ Mar 1974 Cover: 0.20 **NM** value: **4.00**
37 ❑ May 1974 Cover: 0.20 **NM** value: **4.00**
38 ❑ Jul 1974 Cover: 0.25 **NM** value: **4.00**
39 ❑ Aug 1974 Cover: 0.25 **NM** value: **4.00**
40 ❑ Sep 1974 Cover: 0.25 **NM** value: **4.00**
41 ❑ Nov 1974 Cover: 0.25 **NM** value: **3.00**
42 ❑ Jan 1975 Cover: 0.25 **NM** value: **3.00**
43 ❑ Mar 1975 Cover: 0.25 **NM** value: **3.00**
44 ❑ Apr 1975 Cover: 0.25 **NM** value: **3.00**
45 ❑ May 1975 Cover: 0.25 **NM** value: **3.00**
46 ❑ Jun 1975 Cover: 0.25 **NM** value: **3.00**
47 ❑ Jul 1975 Cover: 0.25 **NM** value: **3.00**
48 ❑ Aug 1975 Cover: 0.25 **NM** value: **3.00**
49 ❑ Sep 1975 Cover: 0.25 **NM** value: **3.00**
50 ❑ Oct 1975 Cover: 0.25 **NM** value: **3.00**
51 ❑ Nov 1975 Cover: 0.25 **NM** value: **3.00**
52 ❑ Dec 1975 Cover: 0.25 **NM** value: **3.00**
53 ❑ Jan 1976 Cover: 0.25 **NM** value: **3.00**
54 ❑ Feb 1976 Cover: 0.25 **NM** value: **3.00**
55 ❑ Mar 1976 Cover: 0.25 **NM** value: **3.00**
56 ❑ Apr 1976 Cover: 0.25 **NM** value: **3.00**
57 ❑ May 1976 Cover: 0.25 **NM** value: **3.00**
58 ❑ Jun 1976 Cover: 0.25 **NM** value: **3.00**
59 ❑ Jul 1976 Cover: 0.25 **NM** value: **3.00**
60 ❑ Aug 1976 Cover: 0.25 **NM** value: **3.00**
61 ❑ Sep 1976 Cover: 0.30 **NM** value: **3.00**
62 ❑ Oct 1976 Cover: 0.30 **NM** value: **3.00**
63 ❑ Nov 1976 Cover: 0.30 **NM** value: **3.00**
64 ❑ Dec 1976 Cover: 0.30 **NM** value: **3.00**
65 ❑ Jan 1977 Cover: 0.30 **NM** value: **3.00**
66 ❑ Feb 1977 Cover: 0.30 **NM** value: **3.00**
67 ❑ Mar 1977 Cover: 0.30 **NM** value: **3.00**
68 ❑ Apr 1977 Cover: 0.30 **NM** value: **3.00**
69 ❑ May 1977 Cover: 0.30 **NM** value: **3.00**
70 ❑ Jun 1977 Cover: 0.30 **NM** value: **3.00**
71 ❑ Jul 1977 Cover: 0.30 **NM** value: **3.00**
72 ❑ Aug 1977 Cover: 0.30 **NM** value: **3.00**
73 ❑ Sep 1977 Cover: 0.30 **NM** value: **3.00**
74 ❑ Oct 1977 Cover: 0.30 **NM** value: **3.00**
75 ❑ Nov 1977 Cover: 0.30 **NM** value: **3.00**
76 ❑ Dec 1977 Cover: 0.35 **NM** value: **3.00**
77 ❑ Jan 1978 Cover: 0.35 **NM** value: **3.00**
78 ❑ Feb 1978 Cover: 0.35 **NM** value: **3.00**
79 ❑ Mar 1978 Cover: 0.35 **NM** value: **3.00**
80 ❑ Apr 1978 Cover: 0.35 **NM** value: **3.00**
81 ❑ May 1978 Cover: 0.35 **NM** value: **2.50**
82 ❑ Jun 1978 Cover: 0.35 **NM** value: **2.50**
83 ❑ Jul 1978 Cover: 0.35 **NM** value: **2.50**
84 ❑ Aug 1978 Cover: 0.35 **NM** value: **2.50**
85 ❑ Sep 1978 Cover: 0.35 **NM** value: **2.50**
86 ❑ Oct 1978 Cover: 0.35 **NM** value: **2.50**
87 ❑ Nov 1978 Cover: 0.35 **NM** value: **2.50**
88 ❑ Dec 1978 Cover: 0.35 **NM** value: **2.50**
89 ❑ Jan 1979 Cover: 0.35 **NM** value: **2.50**
90 ❑ Feb 1979 Cover: 0.35 **NM** value: **2.50**
91 ❑ Mar 1979 Cover: 0.35 **NM** value: **2.50**
92 ❑ Apr 1979 Cover: 0.40 **NM** value: **2.50**
93 ❑ May 1979 Cover: 0.40 **NM** value: **2.50**
94 ❑ Jun 1979 Cover: 0.40 **NM** value: **2.50**
95 ❑ Jul 1979 Cover: 0.40 **NM** value: **2.50**
96 ❑ Aug 1979 Cover: 0.40 **NM** value: **2.50**
97 ❑ Sep 1979 Cover: 0.40 **NM** value: **2.50**
98 ❑ Oct 1979 Cover: 0.40 **NM** value: **2.50**
99 ❑ Nov 1979 Cover: 0.40 **NM** value: **2.50**
100 ❑ Dec 1979 Cover: 0.40 **NM** value: **2.50**
101 ❑ Jan 1980 Cover: 0.40 **NM** value: **2.00**
102 ❑ Feb 1980 Cover: 0.40 **NM** value: **2.00**
103 ❑ ca. 1980 Cover: 0.40 **NM** value: **2.00**
104 ❑ ca. 1980 Cover: 0.40 **NM** value: **2.00**
105 ❑ ca. 1980 Cover: 0.40 **NM** value: **2.00**
106 ❑ ca. 1980 Cover: 0.40 **NM** value: **2.00**
107 ❑ ca. 1981 Cover: 0.50 **NM** value: **2.00**
108 ❑ ca. 1981 Cover: 0.50 **NM** value: **2.00**
109 ❑ ca. 1981 Cover: 0.50 **NM** value: **2.00**
110 ❑ Aug 1981 Cover: 0.50 **NM** value: **2.00**
111 ❑ Sep 1981 Cover: 0.50 **NM** value: **2.00**
112 ❑ ca. 1981 Cover: 0.50 **NM** value: **2.00**
113 ❑ Feb 1982 Cover: 0.60 **NM** value: **2.00**
114 ❑ Hol 1982 Cover: 0.60 **NM** value: **2.00**
115 ❑ Mar 1982 Cover: 0.60 **NM** value: **2.00**
116 ❑ Apr 1982 Cover: 0.60 **NM** value: **2.00**
117 ❑ ca. 1982 Cover: 0.60 **NM** value: **2.00**
118 ❑ ca. 1982 Cover: 0.60 **NM** value: **2.00**
119 ❑ ca. 1982 Cover: 0.60 **NM** value: **2.00**
120 ❑ Oct 1982 Cover: 0.60 **NM** value: **2.00**
121 ❑ Cover: 0.60 **NM** value: **2.00**

20 NUDE DANCERS 20 YEAR ONE POSTER BOOK — Tundra

Bk 1 ❑ ca. 1991 Cover: 9.95 **NM** value: **Cover or less**
No issue number. **A:** Mark Martin

20 NUDE DANCERS 20 YEAR TWO — Tundra

1 ❑ Cover: 3.50 **NM** value: **Cover or less**
No issue number.

21 — Image

1 ❑ Feb 1996 Cover: 2.50 **NM** value: **Cover or less**
1/A ❑ Feb 1996 Cover: 2.50 **NM** value: **Cover or less**
2 ❑ Mar 1996 Cover: 2.50 **NM** value: **Cover or less**
3 ❑ Apr 1996 Cover: 2.50 **NM** value: **Cover or less**
4 ❑ ca. 1996 Cover: 2.50 **NM** value: **Cover or less**
Bk 1 ❑ Aug 1996 Cover: 9.95 **NM** value: **Cover or less**
• The Saga Begins; collects issues #1-3
5 ❑ ca. 1996 Cover: 2.50 **NM** value: **Cover or less**
6 ❑ ca. 1996 Cover: 2.50 **NM** value: **Cover or less**
Circ: Diamd. preorders: **26,423**

TWICE-TOLD TALES OF UNSUPERVISED EXISTENCE — Rip Off

1 ❑ Apr 1989, b&w Cover: 2.00 **NM** value: **Cover or less**
📖 Sunny and Danny; After Annadette; Hard Night; Bills Band; Dinner at the Dreamtime; Lets do Brunch **A:** Terry Laban **W:** Terry Laban

TWILIGHT (AVATAR) — Avatar

1 ❑ Mar 1997 Cover: 3.00 **NM** value: **Cover or less**
Circ: Diamd. preorders: **1,742**
A: Richard Pollard **W:** Mark Seifert; William A. Christensen
2 ❑ Cover: 3.00 **NM** value: **Cover or less**
A: Richard Pollard **W:** Mark Seifert; William A. Christensen

TWILIGHT AVENGER, THE (ELITE) — Elite

1 ❑ Jul 1986 Cover: 1.75 **NM** value: **Cover or less**
Circ: CapCity orders: **3,350**
A: Terry Tidwell **W:** John Wooley
2 ❑ Oct 1986 Cover: 1.75 **NM** value: **Cover or less**
Circ: CapCity orders: **2,545**
A: Terry Tidwell **W:** John Wooley

TWILIGHT AVENGER, THE (ETERNITY) — Eternity

1 ❑ Jul 1988, b&w Cover: 1.95 **NM** value: **Cover or less**
2 ❑ Aug 1988, b&w Cover: 1.95 **NM** value: **Cover or less**
3 ❑ Sep 1988, b&w Cover: 1.95 **NM** value: **Cover or less**
4 ❑ Nov 1988, b&w Cover: 1.95 **NM** value: **Cover or less**
5 ❑ Feb 1989, b&w Cover: 1.95 **NM** value: **Cover or less**
6 ❑ May 1989, b&w Cover: 1.95 **NM** value: **Cover or less**
7 ❑ Aug 1989, b&w Cover: 1.95 **NM** value: **Cover or less**
8 ❑ Feb 1990, b&w Cover: 1.95 **NM** value: **Cover or less**

TWILIGHT (DC) — DC

1 ❑ ca. 1991 Cover: 4.95 **NM** value: **Cover or less**
Circ: CapCity orders: **14,650**
📖 Last Frontier **A:** José Luis Garcia-Lopez **W:** Howard Chaykin
2 ❑ ca. 1991 Cover: 4.95 **NM** value: **Cover or less**
Circ: CapCity orders: **11,050**
📖 Blood on the Stars **A:** José Luis Garcia-Lopez **W:** Howard Chaykin
3 ❑ ca. 1991 Cover: 4.95 **NM** value: **Cover or less**
Circ: CapCity orders: **10,400**
📖 Lords of the Long Shadow **A:** José Luis Garcia-Lopez **W:** Howard Chaykin

TWILIGHT GIRL — Cross Plains

1 ❑ Nov 2000 Cover: 2.95 **NM** value: **Cover or less**
Circ: Diamd. preorders: **3,966**
A: Helio Guedes **W:** John Calvet
2 ❑ Dec 2000 Cover: 2.95 **NM** value: **Cover or less**
Circ: Diamd. preorders: **2,177**
A: Helio Guedes **W:** John Calvet
3 ❑ Jan 2001 Cover: 2.95 **NM** value: **Cover or less**
Circ: Diamd. preorders: **2,269**
A: Helio Guedes **W:** John Calvet

TWILIGHT MAN — First

1 ❑ Jun 1989 Cover: 2.75 **NM** value: **Cover or less**
Circ: CapCity orders: **4,675**
📖 Wind From the East **A:** Tristan Schane **W:** Steven Grant
2 ❑ Jul 1989 Cover: 2.75 **NM** value: **Cover or less**
Circ: CapCity orders: **3,750**
📖 Bedtime Story **A:** Tristan Schane **W:** Steven Grant
3 ❑ Aug 1989 Cover: 2.75 **NM** value: **Cover or less**
Circ: CapCity orders: **3,650**
📖 Nightmare World **A:** Tristan Schane **W:** Steven Grant
4 ❑ Sep 1989 Cover: 2.75 **NM** value: **Cover or less**
Circ: CapCity orders: **3,900**
📖 Wind Fall **A:** Tristan Schane **W:** Steven Grant

TWILIGHT PEOPLE — Caliber

1 ❑ b&w Cover: 2.95 **NM** value: **Cover or less**
2 ❑ b&w Cover: 2.95 **NM** value: **Cover or less**

TWILIGHT X — Pork Chop Press

1 ❑ b&w Cover: 2.50 **NM** value: **Cover or less**
2 ❑ b&w Cover: 2.50 **NM** value: **Cover or less**
3 ❑ b&w Cover: 2.50 **NM** value: **Cover or less**

TWILIGHT-X: INTERLUDE — Antarctic

1 ❑ Jul 1992, b&w Cover: 2.50 **NM** value: **Cover or less**
2 ❑ Sep 1992, b&w Cover: 2.50 **NM** value: **Cover or less**
3 ❑ Nov 1992, b&w Cover: 2.50 **NM** value: **Cover or less**
4 ❑ Jan 1993, b&w Cover: 2.50 **NM** value: **Cover or less**
5 ❑ Mar 1993, b&w Cover: 2.50 **NM** value: **Cover or less**
6 ❑ May 1993, b&w Cover: 2.50 **NM** value: **Cover or less**

TWILIGHT-X: INTERLUDE (VOL. 2) — Antarctic

1 ❑ Jun 1993, b&w Cover: 2.50 **NM** value: **Cover or less**
2 ❑ Jul 1993, b&w Cover: 2.50 **NM** value: **Cover or less**
3 ❑ Aug 1993, b&w Cover: 2.50 **NM** value: **Cover or less**
4 ❑ Sep 1993, b&w Cover: 2.50 **NM** value: **Cover or less**
5 ❑ Oct 1993, b&w Cover: 2.75 **NM** value: **Cover or less**

CGC-graded: Multiply prices above by **33 for 9.9 M • 16 for 9.8 NM/M • 7 for 9.6 NM+ • 5 for 9.4 NM • 2.5 for 9.2 NM- • 1.5 for 9.0 VF/NM**

TWILIGHT X QUARTERLY — Antarctic

1 ❑ Sep 1994, b&w Cover: 2.95 **NM** value: **Cover or less**
2 ❑ Nov 1994, b&w Cover: 2.95 **NM** value: **Cover or less**
3 ❑ Feb 1995, b&w Cover: 2.95 **NM** value: **Cover or less**
🕮 Ascension 8: Whirlwind Part II; Twilight Knights **A:** Joseph Wight; Dan Morris; Jason Wiebe; Scott Maxwell; Tom Morris **W:** Joseph Wight; Dan Morris; Jason Wiebe; Scott Maxwell; Tom Morris

TWILIGHT X (VOL. 2) — Antarctic

1 ❑ b&w Cover: 2.50 **NM** value: **Cover or less**
2 ❑ b&w Cover: 2.50 **NM** value: **Cover or less**
3 ❑ b&w Cover: 2.50 **NM** value: **Cover or less**
4 ❑ Sep 1993, b&w Cover: 2.50 **NM** value: **Cover or less**
5 ❑ Feb 1994, b&w Cover: 2.75 **NM** value: **Cover or less**

TWILIGHT ZONE 3-D SPECIAL, THE — Now

1 ❑ Apr 1993 Cover: 2.95 **NM** value: **Cover or less**
• glasses

TWILIGHT ZONE PREMIERE, THE — Now

Now Comics ushered in a new era of Twilight Zone comics with this one-shot premiere series. It hit newsstands with a regular edition, a polybagged version, and a special "premiere" edition, making for a confusing start to the new era.

Luckily, the content was top-notch. After an introduction by writer Harlan Ellison, the issue proceeded into the classic Ellison tale "Crazy as a Soup Sandwich." There, a hapless gambler makes a deal with a demon to pick the winning horses at a racetrack, and backs his bet with a large loan from a local "businessman." </PIn the prestige edition, readers are also treated to a second text story by Ellison, Darkness upon the Face of the Deep.

1 ❑ Oct 1991 Cover: 2.50 **NM** value: **Cover or less**
No issue number. 🕮 Crazy as a Soup Sandwich • Introduction by Harlan Ellison **A:** Neal Adams; Neal Adams(cover) **C:** Bill Sienkiewicz **W:** Harlan Ellison
1/CS❑ Cover: 2.50 **NM** value: **2.95**
🕮 Crazy as a Soup Sandwich • Collector's Set (polybagged, gold logo); Not code approved; Introduction by Harlan Ellison **A:** Neal Adams(cover) **W:** Harlan Ellison
1/DM❑ Oct 1991 Cover: 2.95 **NM** value: **Cover or less**
🕮 Crazy as a Soup Sandwich; Wishing Book • Introduction by Harlan Ellison **A:** Neal Adams; Eddy Newell; Bill Sienkiewicz(cover) **W:** Don Glut; Harlan Ellison
1/PR❑ Cover: 4.95 **NM** value: **Cover or less**
• Prestige edition. 🕮 Crazy as a Soup Sandwich; Darkness Upon the Face of the Deep (text story) • Introduction by Harlan Ellison **A:** Neal Adams(cover) **W:** Harlan Ellison
1-2 ❑ Cover: 2.50 **NM** value: **Cover or less**
1/DM-2❑ Cover: 2.50 **NM** value: **Cover or less**
🕮 Crazy as a Soup Sandwich • Not code-approved; Introduction by Harlan Ellison **A:** Neal Adams; Bill Sienkiewicz(cover) **W:** Harlan Ellison

TWILIGHT ZONE, THE (VOL. 1) — Dell

This title, like the 1959-1965 series on which it is based is packed with Done in One fantastic tales about con artists, millionaires, soldiers, and others who find their lives suddenly out of kilter in what they had assumed was reality but which was, instead, the Twilight Zone.

This series published its first issues concurrently with the original television series in 1962 but outlasted its inspiration by several years. Thanks to its being what amounted to a simple short-story anthology, the first volume of The Twilight Zone enjoyed a more-than-10-year run. It would later be revived in subsequent volumes by Now Comics.

1 ❑ Nov 1962 Cover: 0.12 **NM** value: **75.00**
• **CGC:** 4 graded, best 9.8
• published as Dell Four-Color #1173
2 ❑ Feb 1963 Cover: 0.12 **NM** value: **45.00**
• published as Dell Four-Color #1174
3 ❑ May 1963 Cover: 0.12 **NM** value: **35.00**
🕮 The Man from Nowhere; Hard Luck Harvey; Beyond the Window • 01-860-207
4 ❑ Aug 1963 Cover: 0.12 **NM** value: **30.00**
• 01-860-210
5 ❑ Nov 1963 Cover: 0.12 **NM** value: **30.00**
6 ❑ Feb 1964 Cover: 0.12 **NM** value: **30.00**
Circ: Statement: **244,886**
7 ❑ May 1964 Cover: 0.12 **NM** value: **30.00**
Circ: Statement: **244,886**
8 ❑ Aug 1964 Cover: 0.12 **NM** value: **30.00**
Circ: Statement: **244,886**
9 ❑ Nov 1964 Cover: 0.12 **NM** value: **30.00**
Circ: Statement: **244,886**
10 ❑ Feb 1965 Cover: 0.12 **NM** value: **30.00**
Circ: Statement: **256,050**
11 ❑ May 1965 Cover: 0.12 **NM** value: **26.00**
Circ: Statement: **256,050**
12 ❑ Aug 1965 Cover: 0.12 **NM** value: **26.00**
Circ: Statement: **256,050**
🕮 The Shadow With Claws; The Haunted Sentry Box (text story); The Revolt of the Machines
13 ❑ Nov 1965 Cover: 0.12 **NM** value: **26.00**
Circ: Statement: **256,050**
14 ❑ Feb 1966 Cover: 0.12 **NM** value: **26.00**
Circ: Statement: **259,703**
🕮 The Day That Vanished; The Death Car; The Amazing Mr. Home (text story); The Lost Genius; The Lost Oasis; A Nightmare Tale • 10016-602
15 ❑ May 1966 Cover: 0.12 **NM** value: **26.00**
Circ: Statement: **259,703**
🕮 Moment of Decision; Wipe Out The Future; Perfect Preservation; The Vision of Mystir
16 ❑ Jul 1966 Cover: 0.12 **NM** value: **26.00**
Circ: Statement: **259,703**
17 ❑ Sep 1966 Cover: 0.12 **NM** value: **26.00**
Circ: Statement: **259,703**
18 ❑ Nov 1966 Cover: 0.12 **NM** value: **26.00**
Circ: Statement: **259,703**
19 ❑ Jan 1966 Cover: 0.12 **NM** value: **26.00**
Circ: Statement: **236,720**
20 ❑ Mar 1966 Cover: 0.12 **NM** value: **26.00**
Circ: Statement: **236,720**
• Has 1966 Statement, filed 9/28/66; avg print run 405,260; avg sales 259,400; avg subs 303; avg total paid 259,703; samples 576; max existent 260,279; 36% of run returned
21 ❑ May 1967 Cover: 0.12 **NM** value: **13.00**
Circ: Statement: **236,720**
22 ❑ Jul 1967 Cover: 0.12 **NM** value: **13.00**
Circ: Statement: **236,720**
23 ❑ Oct 1967 Cover: 0.12 **NM** value: **13.00**
Circ: Statement: **236,720**
24 ❑ Jan 1968 Cover: 0.12 **NM** value: **13.00**
25 ❑ Apr 1968 Cover: 0.12 **NM** value: **13.00**
🕮 Tombstone Valley; The Ghost in the Drifting Tomb (text story); The Captive; Voices From the Twilight Zone; Doom by Prediction
26 ❑ Jul 1968 Cover: 0.12 **NM** value: **13.00**
🕮 The Bridgegroom; Journeys Into Oblivion; The Visions (text story); The Joiner • 10016-807
27 ❑ Dec 1968 Cover: 0.15 **NM** value: **13.00**
28 ❑ Mar 1969 Cover: 0.15 **NM** value: **8.00**
29 ❑ Jun 1969 Cover: 0.15 **NM** value: **8.00**
🕮 Captain Clegg's Treasure; The Curse of Amne Machen (text story); Past, Present … Eternity; Trapped Between Lives • 10016-906
30 ❑ Sep 1969 Cover: 0.15 **NM** value: **8.00**
🕮 Tall Timber; In The Cards; Made in Hong Kong; The Phantom Balloon
31 ❑ Dec 1969 Cover: 0.15 **NM** value: **6.00**
32 ❑ Mar 1970 Cover: 0.15 **NM** value: **6.00**
🕮 Voice in the Wind!; Secret of the Death-Ship (text story); A Spell in the Night; The Time Machine
33 ❑ Jun 1970 Cover: 0.15 **NM** value: **6.00**
34 ❑ Sep 1970 Cover: 0.15 **NM** value: **6.00**
🕮 Beware the Kewpie Dolls; Dream of Gold (text story); Mirage; The Unseen Thing
35 ❑ Dec 1970 Cover: 0.15 **NM** value: **6.00**
36 ❑ Mar 1971 Cover: 0.15 **NM** value: **6.00**
37 ❑ May 1971 Cover: 0.15 **NM** value: **6.00**
38 ❑ Jul 1971 Cover: 0.15 **NM** value: **6.00**
39 ❑ Sep 1971 Cover: 0.15 **NM** value: **6.00**
40 ❑ Nov 1971 Cover: 0.15 **NM** value: **6.00**
41 ❑ Jan 1972 Cover: 0.15 **NM** value: **5.00**
🕮 Guilt Has A Thousand Eyes; Harbinger of Death; A Matter of Time; The Magic Herb; Long Laugh The King!
42 ❑ Mar 1972 Cover: 0.15 **NM** value: **5.00**
🕮 The Haunted Taxi; Torture Revisited (text story); The Possible Dream; At the End of His Rope; The Day of the Palio • 90016-203
43 ❑ May 1972 Cover: 0.15 **NM** value: **5.00**
44 ❑ Jul 1972 Cover: 0.15 **NM** value: **5.00**
🕮 The Camera Doesn't Lie; The Call; The Swampscott Explosion; The Science Teacher
45 ❑ Sep 1972 Cover: 0.15 **NM** value: **5.00**
46 ❑ Nov 1972 Cover: 0.15 **NM** value: **5.00**
🕮 Dream of the Devil; Passage of the Doomed; The Terrific Ten; Scene of the Crime; The Great Sale
47 ❑ Jan 1973 Cover: 0.15 **NM** value: **5.00**
48 ❑ Mar 1973 Cover: 0.15 **NM** value: **5.00**
🕮 Nightmare in Miniature; Fiery Death (text story); The Numbers Game; The Killer Light; Perfect Partners
49 ❑ May 1973 Cover: 0.20 **NM** value: **5.00**
50 ❑ Jul 1973 Cover: 0.20 **NM** value: **5.00**
51 ❑ Aug 1973 Cover: 0.20 **NM** value: **5.00**
52 ❑ Sep 1973 Cover: 0.20 **NM** value: **4.00**
53 ❑ Nov 1973 Cover: 0.20 **NM** value: **4.00**
54 ❑ Jan 1974 Cover: 0.20 **NM** value: **4.00**
55 ❑ Mar 1974 Cover: 0.20 **NM** value: **4.00**
56 ❑ May 1974 Cover: 0.20 **NM** value: **4.00**
57 ❑ Jul 1974 Cover: 0.25 **NM** value: **4.00**
58 ❑ Aug 1974 Cover: 0.25 **NM** value: **4.00**
59 ❑ Sep 1974 Cover: 0.25 **NM** value: **4.00**
60 ❑ Nov 1974 Cover: 0.25 **NM** value: **4.00**
61 ❑ Jan 1975 Cover: 0.25 **NM** value: **4.00**
62 ❑ Mar 1975 Cover: 0.25 **NM** value: **4.00**
63 ❑ May 1975 Cover: 0.25 **NM** value: **4.00**
64 ❑ Jul 1975 Cover: 0.25 **NM** value: **4.00**
65 ❑ Aug 1975 Cover: 0.25 **NM** value: **4.00**
🕮 The Unseen; Over My Dead Body; The Silver Ghost; Big Foot; The Unmovable Coffin **A:** Rod Serling **W:** Rod Serling
66 ❑ Sep 1975 Cover: 0.25 **NM** value: **4.00**
67 ❑ Nov 1975 Cover: 0.25 **NM** value: **4.00**
68 ❑ Jan 1976 Cover: 0.25 **NM** value: **4.00**
69 ❑ Mar 1976 Cover: 0.25 **NM** value: **4.00**
70 ❑ May 1976 Cover: 0.25 **NM** value: **4.00**
71 ❑ Jul 1976 Cover: 0.25 **NM** value: **3.00**
72 ❑ Aug 1976 Cover: 0.25 **NM** value: **3.00**
🕮 Cave of the Time-Mists; Your Daily Horror-Scope; Sorry, the President Cannot See You Today
73 ❑ Sep 1976 Cover: 0.30 **NM** value: **3.00**
74 ❑ Nov 1976 Cover: 0.30 **NM** value: **3.00**
75 ❑ Jan 1977 Cover: 0.30 **NM** value: **3.00**
76 ❑ Mar 1977 Cover: 0.30 **NM** value: **3.00**
77 ❑ May 1977 Cover: 0.30 **NM** value: **3.00**
78 ❑ Jul 1977 Cover: 0.30 **NM** value: **3.00**
79 ❑ Aug 1977 Cover: 0.30 **NM** value: **3.00**
80 ❑ Sep 1977 Cover: 0.30 **NM** value: **3.00**
81 ❑ Nov 1977 Cover: 0.30 **NM** value: **3.00**
82 ❑ Jan 1978 Cover: 0.35 **NM** value: **3.00**
83 ❑ Apr 1978 Cover: 0.50 **NM** value: **3.00**
84 ❑ Jun 1978 Cover: 0.50 **NM** value: **3.00**
• **CGC:** 1 graded, best 9.2
85 ❑ ca. 1978 Cover: 0.35 **NM** value: **3.00**
86 ❑ ca. 1978 Cover: 0.35 **NM** value: **3.00**
87 ❑ ca. 1978 Cover: 0.35 **NM** value: **3.00**
88 ❑ ca. 1978 Cover: 0.35 **NM** value: **3.00**
89 ❑ Feb 1979 Cover: 0.35 **NM** value: **3.00**
90 ❑ Apr 1979 Cover: 0.40 **NM** value: **3.00**
91 ❑ Jun 1979 Cover: 0.40 **NM** value: **3.00**
92 ❑ ca. 1982 Cover: 0.60 **NM** value: **3.00**
final issue.

TWILIGHT ZONE, THE (VOL. 2) — Now

1 ❑ Nov 1991 Cover: 1.95 **NM** value: **2.50**
Circ: CapCity orders: **9,725** • **CGC:** 1 graded, best 9.0
two covers. 🕮 The Big Dry **A:** Eddy Newell(cover)
1/DM❑ Cover: 1.95 **NM** value: **2.50**
• Direct Market edition. 🕮 The Big Dry **A:** Mitch O'Connell(cover)
2 ❑ Dec 1991 Cover: 1.95 **NM** value: **2.25**
Circ: CapCity orders: **8,300**
🕮 Blind Alley **A:** Todd Fox; Enrique Villagran **W:** J. Michael Straczynski
3 ❑ Jan 1992 Cover: 1.95 **NM** value: **2.25**
Circ: CapCity orders: **7,950**
🕮 Big Shot **A:** Norm Dwyer **W:** Tony Caputo
4 ❑ Feb 1992 Cover: 1.95 **NM** value: **2.00**
Circ: CapCity orders: **7,175**
5 ❑ Mar 1992 Cover: 1.95 **NM** value: **2.00**
Circ: CapCity orders: **6,050**
6 ❑ Apr 1992 Cover: 1.95 **NM** value: **2.00**
Circ: CapCity orders: **5,550**
7 ❑ May 1992 Cover: 1.95 **NM** value: **2.00**
Circ: CapCity orders: **5,350**
A: Steve Lieber
8 ❑ Jun 1992 Cover: 1.95 **NM** value: **2.00**
Circ: CapCity orders: **4,975**
9 ❑ Jul 1992 Cover: 2.95 **NM** value: **Cover or less**
Circ: CapCity orders: **5,725**
Holographic cover. • 3-D. • bagged; hologram; Partial 3-D art
9/PR❑ Jul 1992 Cover: 4.95 **NM** value: **Cover or less**
Holographic cover. • 3-D. • with glasses; hologram; Partial 3-D art; Extra stories
10 ❑ Aug 1992 Cover: 1.95 **NM** value: **Cover or less**
Circ: CapCity orders: **4,850**
11 ❑ Sep 1992 Cover: 1.95 **NM** value: **Cover or less**
Circ: CapCity orders: **4,225**
A: Steve Lieber
12 ❑ Oct 1992 Cover: 1.95 **NM** value: **Cover or less**
Circ: CapCity orders: **4,075**
13 ❑ Nov 1992 Cover: 1.95 **NM** value: **Cover or less**
Circ: CapCity orders: **3,825**
14 ❑ Dec 1992 Cover: 1.95 **NM** value: **Cover or less**
Circ: CapCity orders: **3,450**
15 ❑ Jan 1993 Cover: 1.95 **NM** value: **Cover or less**
Circ: CapCity orders: **3,375**
16 ❑ Feb 1993 Cover: 1.95 **NM** value: **Cover or less**
Circ: CapCity orders: **3,400**
SF 1❑ Mar 1993 Cover: 3.50 **NM** value: **Cover or less**
• hologram button; Science-Fiction Special

TWILIGHT ZONE, THE (VOL. 3) — Now

1 ❑ May 1993 Cover: 2.50 **NM** value: **Cover or less**
Circ: CapCity orders: **2,850**
🕮 Mother, May I Go Out to Play? **A:** Rick Stasi **W:** Len Wein
2 ❑ Jun 1993 Cover: 2.50 **NM** value: **Cover or less**
Circ: CapCity orders: **2,600**
two different covers. 🕮 Pull the Plug • computer special **A:** John Picha **W:** Pat McGreal
3 ❑ Jul 1993 Cover: 2.50 **NM** value: **Cover or less**
Circ: CapCity orders: **2,600**
4 ❑ Aug 1993 Cover: 2.50 **NM** value: **Cover or less**
Anl 1993❑ Apr 1993 Cover: 2.50 **NM** value: **Cover or less**

TWIN EARTHS — R. Susor

1 ❑ b&w Cover: 5.95 **NM** value: **Cover or less**
• strip reprints
2 ❑ b&w Cover: 5.95 **NM** value: **Cover or less**
• strip reprints

TWIST — Kitchen Sink

1 ❑ b&w Cover: 2.00 **NM** value: **Cover or less**
A: Basil Wolverton
2 ❑ May 1988 Cover: 2.00 **NM** value: **Cover or less**
🕮 Greatest Story Ever; The Dope Peddler; Sinister Influence; Scrabble; Origin of Bosko; Untitled; 100 Words; Rural Publishing; Centerfold; Portfolio; Teen Talk; Double Jointed; The Exquisite Corpse; Cool Junk; Twist List **A:** Denis Kitchen; Drew Friedman; Dan Clowes; Peter Bagge; J.D. King; Kaz; Boris Artzybasheff; Dave Schreiner; David Coulson; Fougasse; Jenny Holzer; John Holmstrom; Josh Gosfield; Richard Sala; Steve Fiorilla **W:** Denis Kitchen; Drew Friedman; Dan Clowes; Peter Bagge; J.D. King; Kaz; Boris Artzybasheff; Dave Schreiner; David Coulson; Fougasse; Jenny Holzer; John Holmstrom; Josh Gosfield; Richard Sala; Steve Fiorilla
3 ❑ Cover: 2.00 **NM** value: **Cover or less**

TWISTED — Alchemy

1 ❑ b&w Cover: 3.95 **NM** value: **Cover or less**

Other grades: Multiply prices above by **1.5 for Mint • 2/3 for Very Fine • 1/3 for Fine • 1/5 for Very Good • 1/8 for Good**

TWISTED 3-D TALES — Blackthorne

1 ❑ Cover: 2.50 **NM** value: **Cover or less**

TWISTED SISTERS — Kitchen Sink

1 ❑ b&w Cover: 3.50 **NM** value: **Cover or less**
Boogie Chillun; Impasse; Late; Migrant Mother **A:** Mary Fleener; Carol Tyler; Fiona Smythe; Carel Moisewitsch **W:** Mary Fleener; Carol Tyler; Fiona Smythe; Carel Moisewitsch

2 ❑ Cover: 3.50 **NM** value: **Cover or less**

3 ❑ Cover: 3.50 **NM** value: **Cover or less**

4 ❑ Cover: 3.50 **NM** value: **Cover or less**

Bk 1❑ **NM** value: **10.00**

Bk 2❑ Cover: 15.95 **NM** value: **Cover or less**

Bk 2/HC❑ Cover: 24.95 **NM** value: **Cover or less**
hardcover.

Bk 2/LE❑ Cover: 39.95 **NM** value: **Cover or less**

TWISTED TALES — Pacific

1 ❑ Nov 1982 Cover: 1.50 **NM** value: **3.50**
• **CGC:** 5 graded, best 9.8
Infected; Out of His Depth; A Walk in the Woods; All Hallows • Pacific publishes **A:** Richard Corben; Alfredo Alcala; Bret Blevins; Tim Conrad **W:** Bruce Jones

2 ❑ Apr 1983 Cover: 1.50 **NM** value: **2.50**
• **CGC:** 2 graded, best 9.6
Over His Head; Nightwatch; Infant Terrible; Speed Demons **A:** Rand Holmes; Val Mayerik; Mike Ploog; Ken Steacy **W:** Bruce Jones

3 ❑ Jun 1983 Cover: 1.50 **NM** value: **2.50**
Me an' Ol' Rex; Off Key; With Honor; Sunken Chest **A:** William Wray; Richard Corben; Doug Wildey; Bret Blevins **W:** Bruce Jones

4 ❑ Aug 1983 Cover: 1.50 **NM** value: **2.50**
The Well; Nick of Time; The Secret Place **A:** John Bolton; Don Lomax; Bruce Jones **W:** Bruce Jones

5 ❑ 1983 Cover: 1.50 **NM** value: **2.50**
Terminated; Scritch…Scritch…Scritch; Majority of One; Banjo Lessons **A:** William Wray; Richard Corben; Val Mayerik **W:** Bruce Jones

6 ❑ 1983 Cover: 1.50 **NM** value: **2.50**
You, Illusion; Evening Walk; Home Ties; Roomers **A:** John Bolton; Mike Hoffman; Attilio Micheluzzi; John Totleben **W:** Bruce Jones

7 ❑ 1954 Cover: 1.50 **NM** value: **2.50**

8 ❑ 1954 Cover: 1.50 **NM** value: **2.50**
Way Down There Below the Dark; First Impressions; The Party; • Eclipse publishes **A:** Mike Hoffman; Jackson Guice; Thom Enriquez **W:** Bruce Jones; William F. Nolan

9 ❑ 1954 Cover: 1.50 **NM** value: **2.50**
Warped Panels; Deadlights; Spade the Werewolf and Me; Wet Season **A:** William Wray; Mike Hoffman; Val Mayerik; Thom Enriquez **W:** Bruce Jones; Jan Strnad; Charles Wagner; Dennis Etchison

10 ❑ Dec 1984 Cover: 1.50 **NM** value: **2.50**
Beer; One for the Money…Two for the Show; Hatchet Job; If She Dies; **A:** William Wray; Bernie Wrightson; Gray Morrow; Attilio Micheluzzi **W:** Bruce Jones; David Carren

3D 1❑Aug 1986 Cover: 2.50 **NM** value: **Cover or less**
Circ: CapCity orders: **5,275**
Terminated; Way Down there Below in the Dark; First Impressions; Evening Walk; You, Illusion **A:** John Bolton; Richard Corben; Bruce Guice; John Totleben; Tom Enriquez **W:** Richard Corben; Bruce Jones; Bruce Guice

Bk 1❑ Cover: 4.95 **NM** value: **Cover or less**
Termites From Mars; Fraternity; Night Dive • Eclipse trade paperback **A:** Scott Saavedra; Henry Mayo; Rick Stasi **W:** Bruce Jones

TWISTED TALES OF BRUCE JONES, THE — Eclipse

1 ❑ 1985 Cover: 1.50 **NM** value: **2.00**
Circ: CapCity orders: **4,400**

2 ❑ 1986 Cover: 1.50 **NM** value: **2.00**
Circ: CapCity orders: **4,075**

3 ❑ Mar 1986 Cover: 1.50 **NM** value: **2.00**
Circ: CapCity orders: **3,700**
Morgan; Nudels; Liana; Timmy Tyler's Wonder Book; Birth; Circe; Stalking on Altaria; Girls in Space **A:** Bruce Jones **W:** Bruce Jones

4 ❑ 1986 Cover: 1.50 **NM** value: **2.00**
Circ: CapCity orders: **3,650**

TWISTED TANTRUMS OF THE PURPLE SNIT, THE — Blackthorne

1 ❑ Cover: 1.75 **NM** value: **Cover or less**
A: Dennis Francis **W:** John Stephenson ★ Appearance of Hammy Hamster.

2 ❑ Cover: 1.75 **NM** value: **Cover or less**
A: Dennis Francis **W:** John Stephenson

TWISTER — Harris

1 ❑ Cover: 2.95 **NM** value: **3.00**
Circ: CapCity orders: **2,700**
• trading card

TWITCH (JUSTIN HAMPTON'S...) — Aeon

1 ❑ Cover: 2.75 **NM** value: **Cover or less**

TWO FACES OF TOMORROW, THE — Dark Horse

1 ❑ Aug 1997, b&w Cover: 2.95 **NM** value: **Cover or less**
Circ: Diamd. preorders: **10,545**
A: Yokinobu Hoshino **W:** Yokinobu Hoshino; James P. Hogan

2 ❑ Sep 1997, b&w Cover: 3.95 **NM** value: **Cover or less**
Circ: Diamd. preorders: **7,713**
wraparound cover. **A:** Yokinobu Hoshino **W:** Yokinobu Hoshino; James P. Hogan

3 ❑ Oct 1997, b&w Cover: 3.95 **NM** value: **Cover or less**
Circ: Diamd. preorders: **6,465**
A: Yokinobu Hoshino **W:** Yokinobu Hoshino; James P. Hogan

4 ❑ Nov 1997, b&w Cover: 3.95 **NM** value: **Cover or less**
Circ: Diamd. preorders: **5,854**
A: Yokinobu Hoshino **W:** Yokinobu Hoshino; James P. Hogan

5 ❑ Dec 1997, b&w Cover: 3.95 **NM** value: **Cover or less**
Circ: Diamd. preorders: **5,395**
A: Yokinobu Hoshino **W:** Yokinobu Hoshino; James P. Hogan

6 ❑ Jan 1998, b&w Cover: 3.95 **NM** value: **Cover or less**
Circ: Diamd. preorders: **4,971**
A: Yokinobu Hoshino **W:** Yokinobu Hoshino; James P. Hogan

7 ❑ Feb 1998, b&w Cover: 3.95 **NM** value: **Cover or less**
Circ: Diamd. preorders: **4,483**
A: Yokinobu Hoshino **W:** Yokinobu Hoshino; James P. Hogan

8 ❑ Mar 1998, b&w Cover: 3.95 **NM** value: **Cover or less**
Circ: Diamd. preorders: **4,537**
A: Yokinobu Hoshino **W:** Yokinobu Hoshino; James P. Hogan

9 ❑ Apr 1998, b&w Cover: 3.95 **NM** value: **Cover or less**
Circ: Diamd. preorders: **4,490**
A: Yokinobu Hoshino **W:** Yokinobu Hoshino; James P. Hogan

10 ❑ May 1998, b&w Cover: 3.95 **NM** value: **Cover or less**
Circ: Diamd. preorders: **4,216**
A: Yokinobu Hoshino **W:** Yokinobu Hoshino; James P. Hogan

11 ❑ Jun 1998, b&w Cover: 3.95 **NM** value: **Cover or less**
Circ: Diamd. preorders: **4,153**
A: Yokinobu Hoshino **W:** Yokinobu Hoshino; James P. Hogan

12 ❑ Jul 1998, b&w Cover: 3.95 **NM** value: **Cover or less**
Circ: Diamd. preorders: **4,008**
A: Yokinobu Hoshino **W:** Yokinobu Hoshino; James P. Hogan

13 ❑ Aug 1998, b&w Cover: 3.95 **NM** value: **Cover or less**
Circ: Diamd. preorders: **3,940**
A: Yokinobu Hoshino **W:** Yokinobu Hoshino; James P. Hogan

TWO-FISTED SCIENCE — General Tektronics Labs

1 ❑ b&w Cover: 2.50 **NM** value: **Cover or less**

Bk 1❑ Cover: 10.00 **NM** value: **Cover or less**
A: Steve Lieber; Mark Badger; Scott Saavedra; Bernie Mireault; Scott Roberts; Rob Walton; Colleen Doran; Donna Barr; David Lasky; Lin Lucas; Sean Bieri **C:** Paul Chadwick **W:** Jim Ottaviani

TWO-FISTED TALES (E.C.) — E.C.

The title picked up the numbering of The Haunt of Fear and, with the Frontline Combat title, was E.C.'s outstanding venture into publishing adventure comics. Many of the stories had a focus on stories of army combat (including such armed forces as the Roman army and such battles as Agincourt). Cover logos over the span of issues included "He-Man Adventure," "War and Fighting Men," and simply "Adventure." Two special issues were devoted to the Civil War.

Detailed attention was paid to historic accuracy of story backgrounds, and stories were outstanding. Classic E.C. artists for the title included Johnny Craig, Jack Davis, Reed Crandall, Will Elder, George Evans, Al Feldstein, Bernie Krigstein, Harvey Kurtzman, John Severin, Alex Toth, and Wally Wood. — Maggie

18 ❑ Nov 1950 Cover: 0.10 **NM** value: **700.00**
• **CGC:** 3 graded, best 9.8
Conquest; Hong Kong Intrigue!; Man-Trap (text story); Rescue (text story); Revolution!; Mutiny

19 ❑ Jan 1951 Cover: 0.10 **NM** value: **500.00**
• **CGC:** 3 graded, best 9.8
War Story!; Escape (text story); Decoy (text story); Jivaro Death!; Flight From Danger!; Brutal Capt. Bull!

20 ❑ Mar 1951 Cover: 0.10 **NM** value: **325.00**
• **CGC:** 3 graded, best 9.8
Massacred!; Devils in Baggy Pants!; Army Revolver!; Pirate Gold!

21 ❑ May 1951 Cover: 0.10 **NM** value: **260.00**
• **CGC:** 6 graded, best 9.6
Ambush!; Pigs of the Roman Empire; Dig, You Mutinous Cur! (text story); The Murmansk Run!; Search!

22 ❑ Jul 1951 Cover: 0.10 **NM** value: **260.00**
• **CGC:** 6 graded, best 9.8
Enemy Contact!; Dying City!; Massacre at Agincourt; Chicken!

23 ❑ Sep 1951 Cover: 0.10 **NM** value: **210.00**
• **CGC:** 3 graded, best 9.6
Death Stand!; Old Soldiers Never Die!; Kill!; Dog Fight!

24 ❑ Nov 1951 Cover: 0.10 **NM** value: **210.00**
• **CGC:** 3 graded, best 9.6
Hill 203!; Bug Out!; Boomerang! (text story); Rubble!; Weak Link!

25 ❑ Jan 1952 Cover: 0.10 **NM** value: **210.00**
• **CGC:** 3 graded, best 9.4
Mud!; Bunker Hill!; The Ditch (text story); Corpse on the Imjin!; Buzz Bomb!

26 ❑ Mar 1952 Cover: 0.10 **NM** value: **160.00**
• **CGC:** 4 graded, best 9.8
The Trap!; Hagaru-Ri!; Miracle? (text story); Link-Up!; Hungnam!

27 ❑ May 1952 Cover: 0.10 **NM** value: **160.00**
• **CGC:** 4 graded, best 9.8
Luck!; Custer's Last Stand; D-Day!; Jeep!

28 ❑ Jul 1952 Cover: 0.10 **NM** value: **160.00**
• **CGC:** 4 graded, best 9.6
Checkers!; Pell's Point!; Alamo!; Saipan!

29 ❑ Sep 1952 Cover: 0.10 **NM** value: **160.00**
• **CGC:** 3 graded, best 9.6
Korea!; Red Knight!; Washington!; Fire Mission!

30 ❑ Nov 1952 Cover: 0.10 **NM** value: **160.00**
• **CGC:** 6 graded, best 9.6
Bunker!; Knights!; Wake!; Fledgeling!

31 ❑ Jan 1953 Cover: 0.10 **NM** value: **130.00**
• **CGC:** 5 graded, best 9.4
Blockade!; Campaign!; Donelson!; Grant!

32 ❑ Mar 1953 Cover: 0.10 **NM** value: **130.00**
• **CGC:** 3 graded, best 9.4
Silent Service!; Lost Battalion!; Hannibal!; Tide!

33 ❑ May 1953 Cover: 0.10 **NM** value: **130.00**
• **CGC:** 3 graded, best 9.4
Signal Corps!; Outpost!; Pearl Divers!; Atom Bomber!

34 ❑ Jul 1953 Cover: 0.10 **NM** value: **130.00**
• **CGC:** 2 graded, best 9.6
Betsy!; Trial by Arms!; En Crapaudine!; Guynemer!

35 ❑ Oct 1953 Cover: 0.10 **NM** value: **130.00**
• **CGC:** 3 graded, best 9.0
Robert E. Lee!; New Orleans!; Memphis!; Chancellorsville!

36 ❑ Jan 1954 Cover: 0.10 **NM** value: **115.00**
• **CGC:** 3 graded, best 9.6
Gunfire!; Battle!; Justice!; Dangerous Man!

37 ❑ Apr 1954 Cover: 0.10 **NM** value: **115.00**
• **CGC:** 3 graded, best 9.4
Action!; Warrior!; Homemade Blitz!; Showdown!

38 ❑ Jul 1954 Cover: 0.10 **NM** value: **115.00**
• **CGC:** 3 graded, best 9.2
Lost City!; Warpath!; Bullets!; Stampede! **A:** John Severin **W:** John Severin

39 ❑ Oct 1954 Cover: 0.10 **NM** value: **115.00**
• **CGC:** 3 graded, best 9.6
Uranium Valley!; Oregon Trail!; The Secret!; "Slaughter"!

40 ❑ Dec 1954 Cover: 0.10 **NM** value: **115.00**
• **CGC:** 3 graded, best 9.6
Dien Bien Phu!; Flaming Coffins!; The Last of the Mohicans!; Sharpshooter!

41 ❑ Feb 1955 Cover: 0.10 **NM** value: **115.00**
• **CGC:** 3 graded, best 9.6
Code of Honor!; Mau Mau!; Carl Akeley!; Yellow! final issue.

Anl 1❑ca. 1952 Cover: 0.25 **NM** value: **550.00**
• **CGC:** 1 graded, best 9.0

Anl 2❑ca. 1953 Cover: 0.25 **NM** value: **400.00**
• **CGC:** 6 graded, best 9.0

TWO-FISTED TALES (RCP) — Gemstone

1 ❑ Oct 1992 Cover: 2.00 **NM** value: **Cover or less**
Circ: CapCity orders: **4,000**
Conquest; Hong Kong Intrigue!; Man-Trap (text story); Rescue (text story); Revolution!; Mutiny • Reprints Two-Fisted Tales (EC) #18 **A:** Al Feldstein; Harvey Kurtzman; Johnny Craig; Wally Wood

2 ❑ Jan 1993 Cover: 1.50 **NM** value: **2.00**
Circ: Statement: **19,476** CapCity orders: **3,900**
War Story!; Escape (text story); Decoy (text story); Jivaro Death!; Flight From Danger!; Brutal Capt. Bull! • Reprints Two-Fisted Tales (EC) #19 **A:** Harvey Kurtzman; Johnny Craig; John Severin; Wally Wood; Will Elder

3 ❑ Apr 1993 Cover: 1.50 **NM** value: **2.00**
Circ: Statement: **19,476** CapCity orders: **3,600**
Massacred!; Devils in Baggy Pants!; Army Revolver!; Pirate Gold! • Reprints Two-Fisted Tales (EC) #20 **A:** Harvey Kurtzman; John Severin; Wally Wood; Jack Davis; Will Elder

4 ❑ Jul 1993 Cover: 2.00 **NM** value: **Cover or less**
Circ: Statement: **19,476** CapCity orders: **3,350**
Ambush!; Pigs of the Roman Empire; Dig, You Mutinous Cur! (text story); The Murmansk Run!; Search! • Reprints Two-Fisted Tales (EC) #21 **A:** Harvey Kurtzman; John Severin; Wally Wood; Jack Davis; Will Elder

5 ❑ Oct 1993 Cover: 2.00 **NM** value: **Cover or less**
Circ: Statement: **19,476** CapCity orders: **3,225**
Enemy Contact!; Dying City!; Massacre at Agincourt; Chicken! • Reprints Two-Fisted Tales (EC) #22 **A:** Harvey Kurtzman; John Severin; Wally Wood; Angelo Torres; Jack Davis; Will Elder

6 ❑ Jan 1994 Cover: 2.00 **NM** value: **Cover or less**
Circ: Statement: **8,608** CapCity orders: **2,875**
Death Stand!; Old Soldiers Never Die!; Kill!; Dog Fight! • Reprints Two-Fisted Tales (EC) #23 **A:** Harvey Kurtzman; John Severin; Wally Wood; Jack Davis; Will Elder

7 ❑ Apr 1994 Cover: 2.00 **NM** value: **Cover or less**
Circ: Statement: **8,608** CapCity orders: **2,725**
Hill 203!; Bug Out!; Boomerang! (text story); Rubble!; Weak Link! • Reprints Two-Fisted Tales (EC) #24 **A:** Harvey Kurtzman; John Severin; Wally Wood; Jack Davis; Will Elder

8 ❑ Jul 1994 Cover: 2.00 **NM** value: **Cover or less**
Circ: Statement: **8,608** CapCity orders: **2,675**
Mud!; Bunker Hill!; The Ditch (text story); Corpse on the Imjin!; Buzz Bomb! • Reprints Two-Fisted Tales (EC) #25

9 ❑ Oct 1994 Cover: 2.00 **NM** value: **Cover or less**
Circ: Statement: **8,608** CapCity orders: **2,675**
The Trap!; Hagaru-Ri!; Miracle? (text story); Link-Up!; Hungnam! • Reprints Two-Fisted Tales (EC) #26

10 ❑ Jan 1995 Cover: 2.00 **NM** value: **Cover or less**
Circ: CapCity orders: **2,475**
Luck!; Custer's Last Stand; D-Day!; Jeep! • Reprints Two-Fisted Tales (EC) #27

11 ❑ Apr 1995 Cover: 2.00 **NM** value: **Cover or less**
Circ: CapCity orders: **2,200**
• Reprints Two-Fisted Tales (EC) #28

12 ❑ Jul 1995 Cover: 2.00 **NM** value: **Cover or less**
Circ: CapCity orders: **2,175**
• Reprints Two-Fisted Tales (EC) #29

13 ❑ Oct 1995 Cover: 2.00 **NM** value: **Cover or less**
Circ: CapCity orders: **2,250**
• Reprints Two-Fisted Tales (EC) #30

14 ❑ Jan 1996 Cover: 2.00 **NM** value: **Cover or less**
Circ: Statement: **5,624**
• Reprints Two-Fisted Tales (EC) #31

15 ❑ Apr 1996 Cover: 2.00 **NM** value: **Cover or less**
Circ: Statement: **5,624**
• Reprints Two-Fisted Tales (EC) #32

16 ❑ Jul 1996 Cover: 2.50 **NM** value: **Cover or less**
Circ: Statement: **5,624**
• Reprints Two-Fisted Tales (EC) #33

17 ❑ Oct 1996 Cover: 2.50 **NM** value: **Cover or less**
Circ: Statement: **5,624**
• Reprints Two-Fisted Tales (EC) #34

18 ❑ Jan 1997 Cover: 2.50 **NM** value: **Cover or less**
Circ: Statement: **5,326** Diamd. preorders: **4,818**
• Reprints Two-Fisted Tales (EC) #35; Has 1996 Statement, filed 8/15/96 (not early, title was quarterly); avg print run 7,124; avg sales 5,195; avg subs 429; avg total paid 5,624; office use 1,500; max existent 7,124; no newsstand sales this year

19 ❑ Apr 1997 Cover: 2.50 **NM** value: **Cover or less**
Circ: Statement: **5,326** Diamd. preorders: **4,584**
• Reprints Two-Fisted Tales (EC) #36

CGC-graded: Multiply prices above by **33 for 9.9 M • 16 for 9.8 NM/M • 7 for 9.6 NM+ • 5 for 9.4 NM • 2.5 for 9.2 NM- • 1.5 for 9.0 VF/NM**

20 ❑ Jul 1997 Cover: 2.50 **NM** value: **Cover or less**
Circ: Statement: **5,326** Diamd. preorders: **4,640**
• Reprints Two-Fisted Tales (EC) #37
21 ❑ Oct 1997 Cover: 2.50 **NM** value: **Cover or less**
Circ: Statement: **5,326** Diamd. preorders: **4,832**
📖 Lost City!; Warpath!; Bullets!; Stampede! • Reprints Two-Fisted Tales (EC) #38 **A:** John Severin **W:** John Severin
22 ❑ Jan 1998 Cover: 2.50 **NM** value: **Cover or less**
Circ: Diamd. preorders: **4,344**
• Reprints Two-Fisted Tales (EC) #39
23 ❑ Apr 1998 Cover: 2.50 **NM** value: **Cover or less**
Circ: Diamd. preorders: **4,097**
• Reprints Two-Fisted Tales (EC) #40
24 ❑ Jul 1998 Cover: 2.50 **NM** value: **Cover or less**
Circ: Diamd. preorders: **4,200**
• Reprints Two-Fisted Tales (EC) #41
Anl 1❑ Cover: 8.95 **NM** value: **Cover or less**
• Collects Two-Fisted Tales #1-5
Anl 2❑ Cover: 9.95 **NM** value: **Cover or less**
• Collects Two-Fisted Tales #6-10
Anl 3❑ Cover: 10.95 **NM** value: **Cover or less**
Anl 4❑ Cover: 12.95 **NM** value: **Cover or less**
Anl 5❑ Cover: 13.50 **NM** value: **Cover or less**

TWO-GUN KID — Marvel

In 1948, Marvel Comics saw its super-hero comics in decline. The Next Big Things were romance, crime, and Western comics. Marvel jumped onto the Western bandwagon with Two-Gun Kid, later followed by such titles as Kid Colt Outlaw and the Rawhide Kid.

The Two-Gun Kid was a famed gunslinger who spent much of his time in his secret identity of Matt Hawk, a lawyer. When danger threatened, however, he would don a mask and cowhide vest, strap on his shooting irons, and ride off to stop the bad guys. Like all good Western heroes, however, he avoided killing. Instead, he preferred shooting the guns right out of the villains' hands, then turning them over to the local sheriff.

Issues of this long-running series were written by Larry Lieber (Stan Lee's brother) and included art by Dick Ayers and Bill Everett (creator of the Sub-Mariner).

1 ❑ Mar 1948 Cover: 0.10 **NM** value: **660.00**
• **CGC:** 4 graded, best 9.2
★ 1st Appearance of Two-Gun Kid.
2 ❑ Jun 1948 Cover: 0.10 **NM** value: **300.00**
• **CGC:** 1 graded, best 5.0
3 ❑ Aug 1948 Cover: 0.10 **NM** value: **220.00**
• **CGC:** 1 graded, best 9.4
★ Appearance of Annie Oakley.
4 ❑ Oct 1948 Cover: 0.10 **NM** value: **220.00**
• **CGC:** 2 graded, best 6.0
5 ❑ Dec 1948 Cover: 0.10 **NM** value: **200.00**
• **CGC:** 2 graded, best 7.0
6 ❑ Feb 1949 Cover: 0.10 **NM** value: **165.00**
7 ❑ Apr 1949 Cover: 0.10 **NM** value: **165.00**
• **CGC:** 1 graded, best 2.5
8 ❑ Jun 1949 Cover: 0.10 **NM** value: **165.00**
9 ❑ Aug 1949 Cover: 0.10 **NM** value: **165.00**
10 ❑ Oct 1949 Cover: 0.10 **NM** value: **165.00**
11 ❑ Dec 1953 Cover: 0.10 **NM** value: **125.00**
• **CGC:** 1 graded, best 5.0
12 ❑ Feb 1954 Cover: 0.10 **NM** value: **125.00**
• **CGC:** 1 graded, best 7.0
13 ❑ Apr 1954 Cover: 0.10 **NM** value: **90.00**
14 ❑ Jun 1954 Cover: 0.10 **NM** value: **90.00**
15 ❑ Aug 1954 Cover: 0.10 **NM** value: **90.00**
16 ❑ Oct 1954 Cover: 0.10 **NM** value: **90.00**
17 ❑ Dec 1954 Cover: 0.10 **NM** value: **90.00**
18 ❑ Feb 1955 Cover: 0.10 **NM** value: **90.00**
19 ❑ Apr 1955 Cover: 0.10 **NM** value: **90.00**
20 ❑ Jun 1955 Cover: 0.10 **NM** value: **90.00**
21 ❑ Aug 1955 Cover: 0.10 **NM** value: **80.00**
22 ❑ Sep 1955 Cover: 0.10 **NM** value: **80.00**
23 ❑ Oct 1955 Cover: 0.10 **NM** value: **80.00**
24 ❑ Nov 1955 Cover: 0.10 **NM** value: **80.00**
25 ❑ Dec 1955 Cover: 0.10 **NM** value: **80.00**
26 ❑ Jan 1956 Cover: 0.10 **NM** value: **80.00**
27 ❑ Feb 1956 Cover: 0.10 **NM** value: **80.00**
28 ❑ Mar 1956 Cover: 0.10 **NM** value: **80.00**
29 ❑ Apr 1956 Cover: 0.10 **NM** value: **80.00**
30 ❑ May 1956 Cover: 0.10 **NM** value: **80.00**
31 ❑ Jun 1956 Cover: 0.10 **NM** value: **60.00**
• **CGC:** 1 graded, best 4.5
32 ❑ ca. 1956 Cover: 0.10 **NM** value: **60.00**
33 ❑ ca. 1956 Cover: 0.10 **NM** value: **60.00**
📖 The Gun!; Trapped; (Untitled); Under Arrest; (Untitled); Tenderfoot (text)
34 ❑ ca. 1956 Cover: 0.10 **NM** value: **60.00**
35 ❑ ca. 1957 Cover: 0.10 **NM** value: **60.00**
36 ❑ ca. 1957 Cover: 0.10 **NM** value: **60.00**
37 ❑ ca. 1957 Cover: 0.10 **NM** value: **60.00**
38 ❑ ca. 1958 Cover: 0.10 **NM** value: **60.00**
39 ❑ ca. 1958 Cover: 0.10 **NM** value: **60.00**
40 ❑ ca. 1958 Cover: 0.10 **NM** value: **60.00**
41 ❑ ca. 1959 Cover: 0.10 **NM** value: **60.00**
42 ❑ Jun 1959 Cover: 0.10 **NM** value: **60.00**
43 ❑ Aug 1959 Cover: 0.10 **NM** value: **60.00**
44 ❑ Oct 1959 Cover: 0.10 **NM** value: **60.00**
45 ❑ Dec 1959 Cover: 0.10 **NM** value: **55.00**
A: Jack Davis
46 ❑ Feb 1960 Cover: 0.10 **NM** value: **55.00**
A: Jack Davis
47 ❑ Apr 1960 Cover: 0.10 **NM** value: **45.00**
48 ❑ Jun 1960 Cover: 0.10 **NM** value: **50.00**
49 ❑ Aug 1960 Cover: 0.10 **NM** value: **40.00**
50 ❑ Oct 1960 Cover: 0.10 **NM** value: **40.00**
51 ❑ Dec 1960 Cover: 0.10 **NM** value: **50.00**
52 ❑ Feb 1961 Cover: 0.10 **NM** value: **40.00**
53 ❑ Apr 1961 Cover: 0.10 **NM** value: **20.00**
54 ❑ Jun 1961 Cover: 0.10 **NM** value: **20.00**
55 ❑ Aug 1961 Cover: 0.10 **NM** value: **40.00**
56 ❑ Oct 1961 Cover: 0.10 **NM** value: **20.00**
57 ❑ ca. 1961 Cover: 0.10 **NM** value: **40.00**
58 ❑ ca. 1962 Cover: 0.10 **NM** value: **20.00**
📖 The Monster of Hidden Valley; The Legend of the Two-Gun Kid ★ Origin of Two-Gun Kid.
59 ❑ ca. 1962 Cover: 0.10 **NM** value: **20.00**
📖 At the Mercy of Wolf Waco; Guns Blaze on the Tombstone Trail
60 ❑ Nov 1962 Cover: 0.12 **NM** value: **30.00**
📖 The Beginning of the Two-Gun Kid; I Hate the Two-Gun Kid ★ Origin of Two-Gun Kid.
61 ❑ Jan 1963 Cover: 0.12 **NM** value: **12.00**
📖 The Killer and the Kid; When the Apaches Strike
62 ❑ Mar 1963 Cover: 0.12 **NM** value: **12.00**
63 ❑ May 1963 Cover: 0.12 **NM** value: **12.00**
64 ❑ Jul 1963 Cover: 0.12 **NM** value: **12.00**
65 ❑ Sep 1963 Cover: 0.12 **NM** value: **12.00**
66 ❑ Nov 1963 Cover: 0.12 **NM** value: **12.00**
67 ❑ Jan 1964 Cover: 0.12 **NM** value: **12.00**
68 ❑ Mar 1964 Cover: 0.12 **NM** value: **12.00**
69 ❑ May 1964 Cover: 0.12 **NM** value: **12.00**
70 ❑ Jul 1964 Cover: 0.12 **NM** value: **12.00**
71 ❑ Sep 1964 Cover: 0.12 **NM** value: **12.00**
72 ❑ Nov 1964 Cover: 0.12 **NM** value: **12.00**
★ Versus Geronimo.
73 ❑ Jan 1965 Cover: 0.12 **NM** value: **12.00**
74 ❑ Mar 1965 Cover: 0.12 **NM** value: **12.00**
75 ❑ May 1965 Cover: 0.12 **NM** value: **12.00**
76 ❑ Jul 1965 Cover: 0.12 **NM** value: **12.00**
77 ❑ Sep 1965 Cover: 0.12 **NM** value: **12.00**
• **CGC:** 1 graded, best 9.2
78 ❑ Nov 1965 Cover: 0.12 **NM** value: **12.00**
79 ❑ Jan 1966 Cover: 0.12 **NM** value: **12.00**
• **CGC:** 1 graded, best 9.6
★ Versus Joe Goliath.
80 ❑ Mar 1966 Cover: 0.12 **NM** value: **12.00**
📖 Showdown With Billy The Kid! ★ Versus Billy the Kid.
81 ❑ May 1966 Cover: 0.12 **NM** value: **8.00**
82 ❑ Jul 1966 Cover: 0.12 **NM** value: **8.00**
83 ❑ Sep 1966 Cover: 0.12 **NM** value: **8.00**
• **CGC:** 1 graded, best 9.4
★ Versus Durango.
84 ❑ Nov 1966 Cover: 0.12 **NM** value: **8.00**
85 ❑ Jan 1967 Cover: 0.12 **NM** value: **8.00**
86 ❑ Mar 1967 Cover: 0.12 **NM** value: **8.00**
★ Versus Cole Younger.
87 ❑ May 1967 Cover: 0.12 **NM** value: **8.00**
88 ❑ Jul 1967 Cover: 0.12 **NM** value: **8.00**
★ Versus Rattler.
89 ❑ Sep 1967 Cover: 0.12 **NM** value: **8.00**
• **CGC:** 1 graded, best 9.2
★ Appearance of Rawhide Kid, Kid Colt.
90 ❑ Nov 1967 Cover: 0.12 **NM** value: **8.00**
91 ❑ Jan 1968 Cover: 0.12 **NM** value: **8.00**
• **CGC:** 1 graded, best 9.2
★ Versus Silver Sidewinder.
92 ❑ Mar 1968 Cover: 0.12 **NM** value: **8.00**
• series goes on hiatus
93 ❑ Jul 1970 Cover: 0.15 **NM** value: **4.00**
• Reprints begin
94 ❑ Sep 1970 Cover: 0.15 **NM** value: **4.00**
95 ❑ Nov 1970 Cover: 0.15 **NM** value: **4.00**
96 ❑ Jan 1971 Cover: 0.15 **NM** value: **4.00**
97 ❑ Mar 1971 Cover: 0.15 **NM** value: **4.00**
98 ❑ May 1971 Cover: 0.15 **NM** value: **4.00**
99 ❑ Jul 1971 Cover: 0.15 **NM** value: **4.00**
100 ❑ Sep 1971 Cover: 0.15 **NM** value: **4.00**
101 ❑ Nov 1971 Cover: 0.20 **NM** value: **4.00**
★ Origin of Two Gun Kid.
102 ❑ Jan 1972 Cover: 0.20 **NM** value: **4.00**
103 ❑ Mar 1972 Cover: 0.20 **NM** value: **4.00**
104 ❑ May 1972 Cover: 0.20 **NM** value: **4.00**
105 ❑ Jul 1972 Cover: 0.20 **NM** value: **4.00**
106 ❑ Sep 1972 Cover: 0.20 **NM** value: **4.00**
107 ❑ Nov 1972 Cover: 0.20 **NM** value: **4.00**
108 ❑ Jan 1973 Cover: 0.20 **NM** value: **4.00**
109 ❑ Mar 1973 Cover: 0.20 **NM** value: **4.00**
110 ❑ May 1973 Cover: 0.20 **NM** value: **4.00**
111 ❑ Jul 1973 Cover: 0.20 **NM** value: **4.00**
112 ❑ Sep 1973 Cover: 0.20 **NM** value: **4.00**
113 ❑ Oct 1973 Cover: 0.20 **NM** value: **4.00**
114 ❑ Nov 1973 Cover: 0.20 **NM** value: **4.00**
115 ❑ Dec 1973 Cover: 0.20 **NM** value: **4.00**
116 ❑ Feb 1974 Cover: 0.20 **NM** value: **4.00**
117 ❑ Apr 1974 Cover: 0.20 **NM** value: **4.00**
118 ❑ Jun 1974 Cover: 0.25 **NM** value: **4.00**
119 ❑ Aug 1974 Cover: 0.25 **NM** value: **4.00**
120 ❑ Oct 1974 Cover: 0.25 **NM** value: **4.00**
121 ❑ Dec 1974 Cover: 0.25 **NM** value: **4.00**
122 ❑ Feb 1975 Cover: 0.25 **NM** value: **4.00**
123 ❑ Apr 1975 Cover: 0.25 **NM** value: **4.00**
124 ❑ Jun 1975 Cover: 0.25 **NM** value: **4.00**
125 ❑ Aug 1975 Cover: 0.25 **NM** value: **4.00**
126 ❑ Oct 1975 Cover: 0.25 **NM** value: **4.00**
127 ❑ Dec 1975 Cover: 0.25 **NM** value: **4.00**
128 ❑ Feb 1976 Cover: 0.25 **NM** value: **4.00**
129 ❑ Apr 1976 Cover: 0.25 **NM** value: **4.00**
130 ❑ Jun 1976 Cover: 0.25 **NM** value: **4.00**
131 ❑ Aug 1976 Cover: 0.25 **NM** value: **4.00**
132 ❑ Sep 1976 Cover: 0.30 **NM** value: **4.00**
133 ❑ Oct 1976 Cover: 0.30 **NM** value: **4.00**
134 ❑ Dec 1976 Cover: 0.30 **NM** value: **4.00**
135 ❑ Feb 1977 Cover: 0.30 **NM** value: **4.00**
136 ❑ Apr 1977 Cover: 0.30 **NM** value: **4.00**
final issue.

TWO-GUN KID: SUNSET RIDERS — Marvel

1 ❑ Nov 1995 Cover: 6.95 **NM** value: **Cover or less**
Painted cover. 📖 Biting the Bullet **A:** Christian Gorney; Michael Halbleib **W:** Fabian Nicieza
2 ❑ Dec 1995 Cover: 6.95 **NM** value: **Cover or less**
Painted cover. 📖 Crossing the Golden Gate Bridge **A:** Alex Maleev; Christian Gorney **W:** Fabian Nicieza

2 HOT GIRLS ON A HOT SUMMER NIGHT — Fantagraphics / Eros

All issues are adults only.
1 ❑ b&w Cover: 2.25 **NM** value: **3.00**
2 ❑ b&w Cover: 2.25 **NM** value: **3.00**
3 ❑ b&w Cover: 2.25 **NM** value: **3.00**
4 ❑ b&w Cover: 2.25 **NM** value: **3.00**

2 LIVE CREW COMICS — Fantagraphics / Eros

All issues are adults only.
1 ❑ b&w Cover: 2.95 **NM** value: **Cover or less**

2000 A.D. MONTHLY (1ST SERIES) — Eagle

1 ❑ Apr 1985 Cover: 1.00 **NM** value: **1.50**
📖 Judge Dredd: The Black Plague, Part 1; D.R. & Quinch: Go Straight; Strontium Dog: Death's Head, Part 1 **A:** Alan Davis; Ron Smith; Carlos Ezquerra **W:** Alan Grant; Alan Moore; John Wagner
2 ❑ May 1985 Cover: 1.00 **NM** value: **1.50**
Circ: CapCity orders: **5,650**
📖 Judge Dredd: The Black Plague, Part 2; D.R. & Quinch Go Girl Crazy; Strontium Dog: Death's Head, Part 2 **A:** Alan Davis; Brett Ewins; Carlos Ezquerra **W:** Alan Grant; Alan Moore; John Wagner
3 ❑ Jun 1985 Cover: 1.00 **NM** value: **1.50**
Circ: CapCity orders: **6,150**
📖 Anderson, Psi Division; D.R. & Quinch go to Hollywood, Part 3; Skizz, Part 3 **A:** Alan Davis; Brett Ewins; Jim Baikie **W:** Alan Grant; Alan Moore; John Wagner
4 ❑ Jul 1985 Cover: 1.00 **NM** value: **1.50**
Circ: CapCity orders: **6,550**
📖 Judge Dredd: The Invisible Man; D.R. & Quinch Get Drafted, Part 2; Strontium Dog: Schicklgruber Grab, Part 2 **A:** Alan Davis; Ron Smith; Carlos Ezquerra **W:** Alan Grant; Alan Moore; John Wagner
5 ❑ Aug 1985 Cover: 1.00 **NM** value: **1.50**
Circ: CapCity orders: **6,225**
📖 Judge Dredd: Pirates of the Black Atlantic; D.R. & Quinch Get Drafted, Part 3; Strontium Dog: The Schucklgruber Grab, Part 3 **A:** Alan Davis; Ron Smith **W:** Alan Grant; Alan Moore; John Wagner
6 ❑ Sep 1985 Cover: 1.00 **NM** value: **1.50**
Circ: CapCity orders: **7,000**

2000 A.D. MONTHLY (2ND SERIES) — Eagle

1 ❑ Apr 1986 Cover: 1.25 **NM** value: **1.50**
Circ: CapCity orders: **6,300**
• Judge Anderson, D.R. & Quinch, Skizz
2 ❑ May 1986 Cover: 1.25 **NM** value: **1.50**
Circ: CapCity orders: **5,075**
3 ❑ Jun 1986 Cover: 1.25 **NM** value: **1.50**
Circ: CapCity orders: **4,775**
4 ❑ **NM** value: **1.50**

2000 A.D. PRESENTS — Fleetway-Quality

4 ❑ Jul 1986 Cover: 1.25 **NM** value: **1.50**
Circ: CapCity orders: **4,625**
• Series continued from 2000 A.D. Monthly#3; Title changes to 2000 A.D. Presents; Quality begins publishing
5 ❑ Aug 1986 Cover: 1.25 **NM** value: **1.50**
Circ: CapCity orders: **4,900**
6 ❑ Sep 1986 Cover: 1.25 **NM** value: **1.50**
Circ: CapCity orders: **4,950**
7 ❑ Oct 1986 Cover: 1.25 **NM** value: **1.50**
Circ: CapCity orders: **4,850**
📖 Dan Dare: The Lost Worlds; Skizz **A:** Dave Gibbons; Jim Baikie **W:** Alan Moore; Gerry Finley-Day
8 ❑ Nov 1986 Cover: 1.25 **NM** value: **1.50**
Circ: CapCity orders: **5,250**
9 ❑ Dec 1986 Cover: 1.25 **NM** value: **1.50**
Circ: CapCity orders: **4,325**
10 ❑ Jan 1987 Cover: 1.25 **NM** value: **1.50**
Circ: CapCity orders: **4,250**
11 ❑ Feb 1987 Cover: 1.25 **NM** value: **1.50**
Circ: CapCity orders: **4,050**
📖 Dan Dare: Starship Commander; Harry Twenty on the High Rock **A:** Alan Davis; Dave Gibbons; Brett Ewins **W:** Gerry Finley-Day; Rick Clark
12 ❑ Dec 1987 Cover: 1.50 **NM** value: **Cover or less**
Circ: CapCity orders: **4,100**
📖 Anderson, Psi Division; Dan Dare; Harry Twenty on the High Rock; D.R. & Quinch Have fun on Earth! **A:** Alan Davis; Dave Gibbons; Brett Ewins **W:** Alan Moore; Gerry Finley-Day; Rick Clark
13 ❑ Cover: 1.25 **NM** value: **1.50**
Circ: CapCity orders: **3,450**
📖 Harry 20 on the High Rock; Dan Dare: Star Slayer; Return to Sender **W:** Grant Morrison
14 ❑ Cover: 1.25 **NM** value: **1.50**
Circ: CapCity orders: **2,700**
15 ❑ Cover: 1.25 **NM** value: **1.50**
Circ: CapCity orders: **2,500**
📖 Dan Dare: Waterworld; Harry 20 on the High Rock
16 ❑ Cover: 1.25 **NM** value: **1.50**
Circ: CapCity orders: **2,500**
17 ❑ Cover: 1.25 **NM** value: **1.50**
Circ: CapCity orders: **2,150**

Other grades: Multiply prices above by **1.5 for Mint • 2/3 for Very Fine • 1/3 for Fine • 1/5 for Very Good • 1/8 for Good**

18 ❑ Cover: 1.25 **NM** value: **1.50**
Circ: CapCity orders: **2,175**
19 ❑ Cover: 1.25 **NM** value: **1.50**
Circ: CapCity orders: **1,975**
20 ❑ Cover: 1.25 **NM** value: **1.50**
Circ: CapCity orders: **1,725**
📖 Dan Dare; The VCs **A:** Dave Gibbons; Cam Kennedy; Trevor Goring **W:** Jack Adrian; Gerry Finley-Day; Henry Miller
21 ❑ Cover: 1.25 **NM** value: **1.50**
Circ: CapCity orders: **1,675**
22 ❑ Cover: 1.25 **NM** value: **1.50**
Circ: CapCity orders: **1,600**
23 ❑ Cover: 1.25 **NM** value: **1.50**
Circ: CapCity orders: **1,525**
24 ❑ Cover: 1.25 **NM** value: **1.50**
Circ: CapCity orders: **1,375**
• Series continues as 2000 A.D. Showcase

2000 A.D. SHOWCASE (1ST SERIES) — Fleetway-Quality

25 ❑ Cover: 1.25 **NM** value: **1.50**
Circ: CapCity orders: **1,300**
• Series continued from 2000 A.D. Presents #24
26 ❑ Cover: 1.50 **NM** value: **Cover or less**
Circ: CapCity orders: **1,225**
27 ❑ Cover: 1.50 **NM** value: **Cover or less**
📖 Inferno; Dan Dare; Meltdown Man; Return to Armageddon • double issue #27/28 **A:** Massimo Belardinelli; Dave Gibbons; J. Redondo **W:** Alan Hebden; M. Shaw; Tom Tully
28 ❑ Cover: 1.50 **NM** value: **Cover or less**
Circ: CapCity orders: **1,175**
📖 Inferno; Dan Dare; Meltdown Man; Return to Armageddon • double issue #27/28 **A:** Massimo Belardinelli; Dave Gibbons; J. Redondo **W:** Alan Hebden; M. Shaw; Tom Tully
29 ❑ **NM** value: **1.50**
• double issue #29/30
30 ❑ Cover: 1.50 **NM** value: **Cover or less**
Circ: CapCity orders: **1,150**
• double issue #29/30
31 ❑ Cover: 1.50 **NM** value: **Cover or less**
Circ: CapCity orders: **1,150**
• Zenith
32 ❑ **NM** value: **1.50**
• Zenith
33 ❑ Cover: 1.50 **NM** value: **Cover or less**
Circ: CapCity orders: **1,175**
• Zenith
34 ❑ Cover: 1.50 **NM** value: **Cover or less**
Circ: CapCity orders: **1,225**
• Zenith
35 ❑ Cover: 1.50 **NM** value: **Cover or less**
Circ: CapCity orders: **1,100**
• Zenith
36 ❑ Cover: 1.50 **NM** value: **Cover or less**
Circ: CapCity orders: **1,125**
• Zenith
37 ❑ Cover: 1.50 **NM** value: **Cover or less**
Circ: CapCity orders: **1,150**
• Zenith
38 ❑ Cover: 1.50 **NM** value: **Cover or less**
Circ: CapCity orders: **1,100**
• Zenith
39 ❑ Cover: 1.50 **NM** value: **Cover or less**
Circ: CapCity orders: **1,100**
• Zenith
40 ❑ Cover: 1.50 **NM** value: **Cover or less**
Circ: CapCity orders: **1,100**
• Zenith
41 ❑ Cover: 1.50 **NM** value: **Cover or less**
Circ: CapCity orders: **1,075**
• Zenith
42 ❑ Cover: 1.50 **NM** value: **Cover or less**
Circ: CapCity orders: **1,050**
• Zenith
43 ❑ Cover: 1.50 **NM** value: **Cover or less**
Circ: CapCity orders: **1,050**
• Zenith
44 ❑ Cover: 1.50 **NM** value: **Cover or less**
Circ: CapCity orders: **1,075**
• Zenith
45 ❑ Cover: 1.75 **NM** value: **Cover or less**
Circ: CapCity orders: **1,050**
• Zenith
46 ❑ Cover: 1.75 **NM** value: **Cover or less**
Circ: CapCity orders: **1,025**
47 ❑ Cover: 1.75 **NM** value: **Cover or less**
Circ: CapCity orders: **875**
48 ❑ Cover: 1.75 **NM** value: **Cover or less**
Circ: CapCity orders: **850**
49 ❑ Cover: 1.75 **NM** value: **Cover or less**
50 ❑ Cover: 1.75 **NM** value: **Cover or less**
51 ❑ Cover: 1.75 **NM** value: **Cover or less**
52 ❑ Cover: 1.75 **NM** value: **Cover or less**
53 ❑ Cover: 1.75 **NM** value: **Cover or less**
54 ❑ Cover: 1.75 **NM** value: **Cover or less**
final issue.

2000 A.D. SHOWCASE (2ND SERIES) — Fleetway-Quality

1 ❑ Cover: 2.95 **NM** value: **Cover or less**
📖 Below Zero; Luke Kirby: The Dark Path **A:** John Ridgway; Kev Hopgood; Michael Perkins **W:** Alan McKenzie; John Brosnan
2 ❑ Cover: 2.95 **NM** value: **Cover or less**
📖 Below Zero; Bix Barton **A:** Kev Hopgood; James McCarthy **W:** Peter Milligan; John Brosnan
3 ❑ Cover: 2.95 **NM** value: **Cover or less**
4 ❑ Cover: 2.95 **NM** value: **Cover or less**
• Axa
5 ❑ Cover: 2.95 **NM** value: **Cover or less**
• Axa
6 ❑ Cover: 2.95 **NM** value: **Cover or less**
• Strontium Dogs
7 ❑ Cover: 2.95 **NM** value: **Cover or less**
• Strontium Dogs
8 ❑ Cover: 2.95 **NM** value: **Cover or less**
9 ❑ Cover: 2.95 **NM** value: **Cover or less**
10 ❑ Cover: 2.95 **NM** value: **Cover or less**
11 ❑ Cover: 2.95 **NM** value: **Cover or less**

TWO THOUSAND MANIACS — Aircel

1 ❑ b&w Cover: 2.50 **NM** value: **Cover or less**
A: Nigel Tully **W:** Jack Herman; Herschell Gordon
2 ❑ b&w Cover: 2.50 **NM** value: **Cover or less**
A: Nigel Tully **W:** Jack Herman; Herschell Gordon
3 ❑ b&w Cover: 2.50 **NM** value: **Cover or less**
A: Nigel Tully **W:** Jack Herman; Herschell Gordon

2099 A.D. — Marvel

1 ❑ May 1995 Cover: 3.95 **NM** value: **Cover or less**
Circ: CapCity orders: **22,750**
enhanced cover. **A:** Joe Quesada

2099 A.D. APOCALYPSE — Marvel

1 ❑ Dec 1995 Cover: 4.95 **NM** value: **Cover or less**
enhanced wraparound cover. • continues in 2099 A.D. Genesis #1 ★ Death of Hulk 2099. ★ Death of Punisher 2099.

2099 A.D. GENESIS — Marvel

1 ❑ Jan 1996 Cover: 4.95 **NM** value: **Cover or less**
chromium cover. 📖 Midday Sun **A:** Dale Eaglesham **W:** Warren Ellis ★ 1st Appearance of X-Nation 2099 and Fantastic Four 2099. ★ Appearance of Daredevil 2099.

2099: MANIFEST DESTINY — Marvel

1 ❑ Mar 1998 Cover: 5.99 **NM** value: **Cover or less**
No issue number. One-shot.

2099 SPECIAL: THE WORLD OF DOOM — Marvel

1 ❑ May 1995 Cover: 2.25 **NM** value: **Cover or less**
Circ: CapCity orders: **14,800**

2099 UNLIMITED — Marvel

1 ❑ Jul 1993 Cover: 3.95 **NM** value: **Cover or less**
Circ: CapCity orders: **104,300**
📖 Nothing Ever Changes **A:** Chris Wozniak; Dwayne Turner **W:** Steve Outro ★ 1st Appearance of Hulk 2099. ★ Appearance of Spider-Man 2099.
2 ❑ Oct 1993 Cover: 3.95 **NM** value: **Cover or less**
Circ: CapCity orders: **54,300**
📖 Thirty Mile Mall; Remote Control • Return of Hulk 2099 **A:** Chris Wozniak **W:** Evan Skolnick; Gerard Jones ★ 1st Appearance of R Gang 2099.
3 ❑ Jan 1994 Cover: 3.95 **NM** value: **Cover or less**
Circ: CapCity orders: **32,100**
4 ❑ Apr 1994 Cover: 3.95 **NM** value: **Cover or less**
5 ❑ Jul 1994 Cover: 3.95 **NM** value: **Cover or less**
Circ: CapCity orders: **18,350**
6 ❑ Aug 1994 Cover: 3.95 **NM** value: **Cover or less**
Circ: CapCity orders: **13,750**
7 ❑ Nov 1994 Cover: 3.95 **NM** value: **Cover or less**
Circ: CapCity orders: **10,725**
8 ❑ Apr 1995 Cover: 3.95 **NM** value: **Cover or less**
Circ: CapCity orders: **7,800**
9 ❑ Jul 1995 Cover: 3.95 **NM** value: **Cover or less**
Circ: CapCity orders: **7,950**
10 ❑ Oct 1995 Cover: 3.95 **NM** value: **Cover or less**
Ash 1❑1993 **NM** value: **0.75**
foil cover. • "2099 Limited" ashcan edition from Hero magazine.

2099: WORLD OF TOMORROW — Marvel

1 ❑ Sep 1996 Cover: 2.50 **NM** value: **Cover or less**
wraparound cover. 📖 The World of Tomorrow • 2099 anthology **A:** Pascual Ferry **W:** Joe Kelly; Ben Raab
2 ❑ Oct 1996 Cover: 2.50 **NM** value: **Cover or less**
📖 Revelations **W:** Joe Kelly; Ben Raab
3 ❑ Nov 1996 Cover: 2.50 **NM** value: **Cover or less**
Circ: Diamd. preorders: **35,785**
4 ❑ Dec 1996 Cover: 2.50 **NM** value: **Cover or less**
Circ: Diamd. preorders: **35,626**
📖 De-Evolution **A:** Yancey Labat; Jason Armstrong; Karl Moline **W:** Joe Kelly; Ben Raab ★ Appearance of Doom 2099.
5 ❑ Jan 1997 Cover: 2.50 **NM** value: **Cover or less**
Circ: Diamd. preorders: **31,393**
📖 Finders Keepers **A:** David Brewer; Jason Armstrong **W:** Joe Kelly; Ben Raab
6 ❑ Feb 1997 Cover: 2.50 **NM** value: **Cover or less**
Circ: Diamd. preorders: **26,579**
📖 Final Decision **A:** David Brewer; Jason Armstrong **W:** Joe Kelly; Ben Raab
7 ❑ Mar 1997 Cover: 2.50 **NM** value: **Cover or less**
Circ: Diamd. preorders: **23,331**
📖 Blitzkrieg **A:** David Brewer; Jason Armstrong **W:** Joe Kelly; Ben Raab ★ Appearance of Spider-Man 2099.
8 ❑ Apr 1997 Cover: 2.50 **NM** value: **Cover or less**
Circ: Diamd. preorders: **22,004**
📖 The Quiet Earth final issue. **A:** David Brewer; Jason Armstrong **W:** Joe Kelly; Ben Raab

2001 NIGHTS — Viz

1 ❑ ca. 1990 Cover: 3.75 **NM** value: **4.00**
📖 Night 1, Earthglow; Night 2, Sea Of Fertility; Night 3, Maelstrom III; Night 4, Posterity **A:** Yokinobu Hoshino **W:** Yokinobu Hoshino
2 ❑ ca. 1990 Cover: 3.95 **NM** value: **4.00**
3 ❑ ca. 1990 Cover: 3.95 **NM** value: **4.00**
4 ❑ ca. 1991 Cover: 3.75 **NM** value: **4.00**
5 ❑ ca. 1991 Cover: 3.75 **NM** value: **4.00**
📖 Night 10, Medusa's Throne; Night 11, A Stranger's Footsteps **A:** Yokinobu Hoshino **W:** Yokinobu Hoshino
6 ❑ ca. 1991 Cover: 4.25 **NM** value: **Cover or less**
7 ❑ ca. 1991 Cover: 4.25 **NM** value: **Cover or less**
8 ❑ ca. 1991 Cover: 4.25 **NM** value: **Cover or less**
9 ❑ ca. 1991 Cover: 4.25 **NM** value: **Cover or less**
10 ❑ ca. 1991 Cover: 4.25 **NM** value: **Cover or less**
📖 Children of the Earth final issue. **A:** Yokinobu Hoshino **W:** Yokinobu Hoshino
Bk 1❑ Cover: 16.95 **NM** value: **Cover or less**
Bk 1/HC❑ Cover: 21.95 **NM** value: **Cover or less**
Bk 2❑ Cover: 16.95 **NM** value: **Cover or less**
• Journey Beyond Tomorrow
Bk 3❑ Cover: 16.95 **NM** value: **Cover or less**
• Children of Earth

2001, A SPACE ODYSSEY — Marvel

1 ❑ Dec 1976 Cover: 0.30 **NM** value: **4.00**
📖 Beast-Killer! **A:** Jack Kirby **W:** Jack Kirby
2 ❑ Jan 1977 Cover: 0.30 **NM** value: **2.50**
📖 Vira The She-Demon! **A:** Jack Kirby **W:** Jack Kirby
3 ❑ Feb 1977 Cover: 0.30 **NM** value: **2.50**
📖 Marak! **A:** Jack Kirby **W:** Jack Kirby
4 ❑ Mar 1977 Cover: 0.30 **NM** value: **2.50**
📖 Wheels of Death! **A:** Jack Kirby **W:** Jack Kirby
5 ❑ Apr 1977 Cover: 0.30 **NM** value: **2.50**
📖 Norton Of New York 2040 A.D. **A:** Jack Kirby **W:** Jack Kirby
6 ❑ May 1977 Cover: 0.30 **NM** value: **2.50**
📖 Inter-Galactica, The Ultimate Trip **A:** Jack Kirby **W:** Jack Kirby
7 ❑ Jun 1977 Cover: 0.30 **NM** value: **2.50**
8 ❑ Jul 1977 Cover: 0.30 **NM** value: **2.50**
📖 The Capture of X-51 **A:** Jack Kirby **W:** Jack Kirby ★ Origin of Machine Man (as "Mister Machine").
9 ❑ Aug 1977 Cover: 0.30 **NM** value: **2.50**
10 ❑ Sep 1977 Cover: 0.30 **NM** value: **2.50**
📖 Mister machine **A:** Jack Kirby **W:** Jack Kirby ★ Origin of Machine Man.
GS 1❑ca. 1976 Cover: 1.50 **NM** value: **10.00**
• treasury-sized adaptation of movie. **A:** Jack Kirby

2010 — Marvel

1 ❑ Apr 1984 Cover: 0.75 **NM** value: **1.50**
2 ❑ May 1984 Cover: 0.75 **NM** value: **1.50**

2020 VISIONS — DC / Vertigo

1 ❑ May 1997 Cover: 2.25 **NM** value: **2.50**
Circ: Diamd. preorders: **23,201**
📖 Lust for Life, Part 1 **A:** Frank Quitely **W:** Jamie Delano
2 ❑ Jun 1997 Cover: 2.25 **NM** value: **2.50**
Circ: Diamd. preorders: **19,608**
📖 Lust for Life, Part 2 **A:** Frank Quitely **W:** Jamie Delano
3 ❑ Jul 1997 Cover: 2.25 **NM** value: **2.50**
Circ: Diamd. preorders: **16,301**
📖 Lust for Life, Part 3 **A:** Frank Quitely **W:** Jamie Delano
4 ❑ Aug 1997 Cover: 2.25 **NM** value: **2.50**
Circ: Diamd. preorders: **15,747**
📖 La Tormenta, Part 1 **A:** Warren Pleece **W:** Jamie Delano
5 ❑ Sep 1997 Cover: 2.25 **NM** value: **2.50**
Circ: Diamd. preorders: **15,481**
📖 La Tormenta, Part 2 **A:** Warren Pleece **W:** Jamie Delano
6 ❑ Oct 1997 Cover: 2.25 **NM** value: **2.50**
Circ: Diamd. preorders: **14,979**
📖 La Tormenta, Part 3 **A:** Warren Pleece **W:** Jamie Delano
7 ❑ Nov 1997 Cover: 2.25 **NM** value: **2.50**
Circ: Diamd. preorders: **14,259**
📖 Renegade, Part 1 **A:** James Romberger **W:** Jamie Delano
8 ❑ Dec 1997 Cover: 2.25 **NM** value: **2.50**
Circ: Diamd. preorders: **13,404**
📖 Renegade, Part 2 **A:** James Romberger **W:** Jamie Delano
9 ❑ Jan 1998 Cover: 2.25 **NM** value: **2.50**
Circ: Diamd. preorders: **12,601**
📖 Renegade, Part 3 **A:** James Romberger **W:** Jamie Delano
10 ❑ Feb 1998 Cover: 2.25 **NM** value: **2.50**
Circ: Diamd. preorders: **12,117**
📖 Repro-Man, Part 1 **A:** Steve Pugh **W:** Jamie Delano
11 ❑ Mar 1998 Cover: 2.25 **NM** value: **2.50**
Circ: Diamd. preorders: **11,471**
📖 Repro-Man, Part 2 **A:** Steve Pugh **W:** Jamie Delano
12 ❑ Apr 1998 Cover: 2.25 **NM** value: **2.50**
Circ: Diamd. preorders: **10,774**
📖 Repro-Man, Part 3 **A:** Steve Pugh **W:** Jamie Delano

TWO X JUSTICE — Graphic Serials

1 ❑ Cover: 2.00 **NM** value: **Cover or less**

TYKES — Alternative

1 ❑ Nov 1997 Cover: 2.95 **NM** value: **Cover or less**
Ash 1❑Jul 1997 Cover: 2.95 **NM** value: **Cover or less**
No issue number. • b&w and pink; smaller than normal comic book

TYPHOID — Marvel

1 ❑ Nov 1995 Cover: 3.95 **NM** value: **Cover or less**
wraparound cardstock cover. **A:** John Van Fleet **W:** Ann Nocenti
2 ❑ Dec 1995 Cover: 3.95 **NM** value: **Cover or less**
wraparound cardstock cover. **A:** John Van Fleet **W:** Ann Nocenti ★ Appearance of Cinemaniacs.
3 ❑ Jan 1996 Cover: 3.95 **NM** value: **Cover or less**
wraparound cardstock cover. **A:** John Van Fleet **W:** Ann Nocenti
4 ❑ Feb 1996 Cover: 3.95 **NM** value: **Cover or less**
wraparound cardstock cover. 📖 Red Riding Hood **A:** John Van Fleet **W:** Ann Nocenti

CGC-graded: Multiply prices above by **33 for 9.9 M • 16 for 9.8 NM/M • 7 for 9.6 NM+ • 5 for 9.4 NM • 2.5 for 9.2 NM- • 1.5 for 9.0 VF/NM**

TYRANNOSAURUS TEX — Monster

1 ❑ b&w Cover: 2.50 **NM** value: **Cover or less**
2 ❑ b&w Cover: 2.50 **NM** value: **Cover or less**

TYRANT (S.R. BISSETTE'S...) — Spider Baby

1 ❑ Sep 1994 Cover: 2.95 **NM** value: **3.00**
Circ: CapCity orders: **7,030**
📖 Knock Knock **A:** Stephen R. Bissette **W:** Stephen R. Bissette
2 ❑ ca. 1994 Cover: 2.95 **NM** value: **3.00**
Circ: CapCity orders: **5,200**
A: Stephen R. Bissette **W:** Stephen R. Bissette
3 ❑ Feb 1995 Cover: 2.95 **NM** value: **3.00**
Circ: CapCity orders: **4,550**
A: Stephen R. Bissette **W:** Stephen R. Bissette
3/GO ❑ Feb 1995 **NM** value: **3.50**
A: Stephen R. Bissette **W:** Stephen R. Bissette
4 ❑ ca. 1995 Cover: 2.95 **NM** value: **3.00**
Circ: CapCity orders: **2,845**
A: Stephen R. Bissette **W:** Stephen R. Bissette
5 ❑ ca. 1995 Cover: 2.95 **NM** value: **3.00**
Circ: CapCity orders: **4,390** Diamd. preorders: **7,271**
A: Stephen R. Bissette **W:** Stephen R. Bissette
6 ❑ Dec 1996 Cover: 2.95 **NM** value: **3.00**
Circ: Diamd. preorders: **7,719**
A: Stephen R. Bissette **W:** Stephen R. Bissette

TZU THE REAPER — Murim

1 ❑ Sep 1997 Cover: 2.95 **NM** value: **Cover or less**
Circ: Diamd. preorders: **6,785**
A: C.S. Chun **W:** B.K. Kim; Gary Cohn
2 ❑ Oct 1997 Cover: 2.95 **NM** value: **Cover or less**
Circ: Diamd. preorders: **5,081**
A: C.S. Chun **W:** B.K. Kim; Gary Cohn
3 ❑ Dec 1997 Cover: 2.95 **NM** value: **Cover or less**
Circ: Diamd. preorders: **5,886**

UBERDUB — Caliber

1 ❑ Sep 1991 Cover: 2.50 **NM** value: **Cover or less**
2 ❑ Sep 1991 Cover: 2.50 **NM** value: **Cover or less**
📖 In the Wake of the Call **A:** Matt Howarth **W:** Matt Howarth
3 ❑ Jan 1992 Cover: 2.50 **NM** value: **Cover or less**

UFO & OUTER SPACE — Whitman

14 ❑ Jun 1978 Cover: 0.35 **NM** value: **6.00**
• Reprints UFO Flying Saucers #3
15 ❑ Jul 1978 Cover: 0.35 **NM** value: **4.00**
• Reprints UFO Flying Saucers #4
16 ❑ 1978 Cover: 0.35 **NM** value: **4.00**
17 ❑ 1978 Cover: 0.35 **NM** value: **4.00**
18 ❑ Nov 1978 Cover: 0.35 **NM** value: **4.00**
19 ❑ 1979 Cover: 0.35 **NM** value: **4.00**
20 ❑ Apr 1979 Cover: 0.40 **NM** value: **4.00**
21 ❑ Jun 1979 Cover: 0.40 **NM** value: **3.00**
22 ❑ Aug 1979 Cover: 0.40 **NM** value: **3.00**
23 ❑ Oct 1979 Cover: 0.40 **NM** value: **3.00**
24 ❑ Dec 1979 Cover: 0.40 **NM** value: **3.00**
25 ❑ Feb 1980 Cover: 0.40 **NM** value: **3.00**
• Reprints UFO Flying Saucers #2

UFO ENCOUNTERS — Golden Press

1 ❑ Cover: 1.95 **NM** value: **Cover or less**
📖 The UFOs and Flying Saucers; The UFO R

UFO FLYING SAUCERS — Gold Key

1 ❑ Oct 1968 Cover: 0.25 **NM** value: **20.00**
• giant
2 ❑ Nov 1970 Cover: 0.15 **NM** value: **12.00**
3 ❑ Nov 1972 Cover: 0.15 **NM** value: **12.00**
4 ❑ Nov 1974 Cover: 0.25 **NM** value: **12.00**
5 ❑ Feb 1975 Cover: 0.25 **NM** value: **7.00**
6 ❑ May 1975 Cover: 0.25 **NM** value: **7.00**
7 ❑ Aug 1975 Cover: 0.25 **NM** value: **7.00**
8 ❑ Nov 1975 Cover: 0.25 **NM** value: **7.00**
9 ❑ Jan 1976 Cover: 0.25 **NM** value: **7.00**
10 ❑ 1976 Cover: 0.25 **NM** value: **7.00**
📖 The Phantom Bat Machines; Town in Terror!; The Invisible Menace; The Hoaxmaster: It's All in the Mind!!!; The Geneva Visitors; The Things People See! **A:** Frank Bolle **W:** Pat Fortunato
11 ❑ 1976 Cover: 0.30 **NM** value: **7.00**
12 ❑ Nov 1976 Cover: 0.30 **NM** value: **7.00**
13 ❑ Jan 1977 Cover: 0.30 **NM** value: **7.00**
• series continues as UFO & Outer Space

ULTIMATE MARVEL MAGAZINE — Marvel

1 ❑ Feb 2001 Cover: 3.99 **NM** value: **6.00**
• reprints Ultimate Spider-Man #1 and #2
2 ❑ Mar 2001 Cover: 3.99 **NM** value: **4.00**
• reprints Ultimate Spider-Man #3 and Ultimate X-Men #1
3 ❑ Apr 2001 Cover: 3.99 **NM** value: **4.00**
• reprints Ultimate Spider-Man #4 and Ultimate X-Men #2
4 ❑ May 2001 Cover: 3.99 **NM** value: **Cover or less**
5 ❑ Jun 2001 Cover: 3.99 **NM** value: **Cover or less**
6 ❑ Jul 2001 Cover: 3.99 **NM** value: **Cover or less**
7 ❑ Aug 2001 Cover: 3.99 **NM** value: **Cover or less**
Circ: Diamd. preorders: **3,000**
8 ❑ Sep 2001 Cover: 3.99 **NM** value: **Cover or less**
Circ: Diamd. preorders: **2,833**
9 ❑ Oct 2001 Cover: 3.99 **NM** value: **Cover or less**
Circ: Diamd. preorders: **2,170**
10 ❑ Nov 2001 Cover: 3.99 **NM** value: **Cover or less**
Circ: Diamd. preorders: **2,050**
11 ❑ Dec 2001 Cover: 3.99 **NM** value: **Cover or less**

ULTIMATE MARVEL TEAM-UP — Marvel

1 ❑ Apr 2001 Cover: 2.99 **NM** value: **Cover or less**
• **CGC:** 72 graded, best 9.9
cardstock cover. • Listed in indicia as Ultimate Spider-Man and Wolverine **A:** Matt Wagner **W:** Brian Michael Bendis ★ Appearance of Wolverine, Sabretooth, Spider-Man.
2 ❑ May 2001 Cover: 2.99 **NM** value: **Cover or less**
Circ: Diamd. preorders: **72,643** • **CGC:** 9 graded, best 9.8
3 ❑ Jun 2001 Cover: 2.99 **NM** value: **Cover or less**
• **CGC:** 3 graded, best 9.8
4 ❑ Jul 2001 Cover: 2.99 **NM** value: **Cover or less**
Circ: Diamd. preorders: **66,164**
5 ❑ Aug 2001 Cover: 2.99 **NM** value: **Cover or less**
Circ: Diamd. preorders: **60,444**
6 ❑ Sep 2001 Cover: 2.99 **NM** value: **Cover or less**
Circ: Diamd. preorders: **65,703** • **CGC:** 3 graded, best 9.8
7 ❑ Oct 2001 Cover: 2.25 **NM** value: **Cover or less**
Circ: Diamd. preorders: **61,687** • **CGC:** 2 graded, best 9.8
8 ❑ Nov 2001 Cover: 2.25 **NM** value: **Cover or less**
Circ: Diamd. preorders: **56,737** • **CGC:** 2 graded, best 9.8
9 ❑ Dec 2001 Cover: 2.25 **NM** value: **Cover or less**
Circ: Diamd. preorders: **49,555**
10 ❑ Jan 2002 Cover: 2.25 **NM** value: **Cover or less**
Circ: Diamd. preorders: **48,360**
11 ❑ Feb 2002 Cover: 2.25 **NM** value: **Cover or less**
Circ: Diamd. preorders: **55,845**
12 ❑ Mar 2002 Cover: 2.25 **NM** value: **Cover or less**
Circ: Diamd. preorders: **44,911**

ULTIMATE MELONPOOL, THE — Para-Troop

Bk 1 ❑ Cover: 19.95 **NM** value: **Cover or less**

ULTIMATES — Marvel

1 ❑ Cover: 2.25 **NM** value: **Cover or less**
Circ: Diamd. preorders: **160,243**

ULTIMATE SPIDER-MAN — Marvel

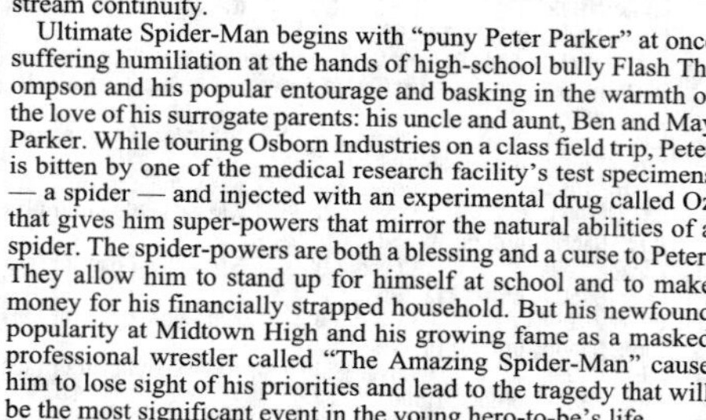

In an effort to make its heroes more accessible to a new audience, Marvel Comics launched its "Ultimate" line with Ultimate Spider-Man in October 2000. The concept is simple: The Ultimate titles — which soon included Ultimate X-Men and a Marvel Team-Up-style series titled Ultimate Marvel: Spider-Man and... — start from scratch. They reintroduce the classic Marvel superheroes with new origins, new or tweaked looks, and refurbished supporting casts and allow readers to get in on the ground floor of a universe that is separate from Marvel's long-running mainstream continuity.

Ultimate Spider-Man begins with "puny Peter Parker" at once suffering humiliation at the hands of high-school bully Flash Thompson and his popular entourage and basking in the warmth of the love of his surrogate parents: his uncle and aunt, Ben and May Parker. While touring Osborn Industries on a class field trip, Peter is bitten by one of the medical research facility's test specimens — a spider — and injected with an experimental drug called Oz that gives him super-powers that mirror the natural abilities of a spider. The spider-powers are both a blessing and a curse to Peter. They allow him to stand up for himself at school and to make money for his financially strapped household. But his newfound popularity at Midtown High and his growing fame as a masked professional wrestler called "The Amazing Spider-Man" cause him to lose sight of his priorities and lead to the tragedy that will be the most significant event in the young hero-to-be's life.

Writer Brian Michael Bendis (Powers) and artist Mark Bagley (Thunderbolts) take Spider-Man back to his roots.

1 ❑ Oct 2000 Cover: 2.99 **NM** value: **30.00**
Circ: Statement: **354,115** Diamd. preorders: **60,540** • **CGC:** 458 graded, best 9.8
📖 Powerless **A:** Mark Bagley **W:** Brian Michael Bendis; Bill Jemas ★ Origin of Spider-Man. ★ Appearance of Mary Jane Watson, Norman Osborn.
1/A ❑ Oct 2000 Cover: 2.50 **NM** value: **60.00**
White background on cover-otherwise same as #1. **A:** Mark Bagley **W:** Brian Michael Bendis; Bill Jemas
1/B ❑ Oct 2000 **NM** value: **40.00**
Dynamic Forces cover. **A:** Mark Bagley **W:** Brian Michael Bendis; Bill Jemas
2 ❑ Dec 2000 Cover: 2.50 **NM** value: **25.00**
Circ: Statement: **354,115** Diamd. preorders: **47,080** • **CGC:** 159 graded, best 9.9
cardstock cover. 📖 Growing Pains **A:** Mark Bagley **W:** Brian Michael Bendis; Bill Jemas
3 ❑ Jan 2001 Cover: 2.50 **NM** value: **20.00**
Circ: Statement: **354,115** Diamd. preorders: **51,898** • **CGC:** 61 graded, best 9.8
cardstock cover. 📖 Wannabe • Spider-Man gets his costume **A:** Mark Bagley **W:** Brian Michael Bendis; Bill Jemas ★ Origin of Green Goblin.
4 ❑ Feb 2001 Cover: 2.50 **NM** value: **15.00**
Circ: Statement: **354,115** Diamd. preorders: **59,361** • **CGC:** 27 graded, best 9.8
cardstock cover. 📖 With Great Power **A:** Mark Bagley **W:** Brian Michael Bendis; Bill Jemas ★ Death of Uncle Ben (off-panel).
5 ❑ Mar 2001 Cover: 2.25 **NM** value: **15.00**
Circ: Statement: **354,115** Diamd. preorders: **59,238** • **CGC:** 35 graded, best 9.8
cardstock cover. 📖 Life Lessons **A:** Mark Bagley **W:** Brian Michael Bendis; Bill Jemas ★ Death of Uncle Ben (revealed).
6 ❑ Apr 2001 Cover: 2.25 **NM** value: **Cover or less**
Circ: Statement: **354,115** Diamd. preorders: **65,343** • **CGC:** 15 graded, best 9.6
cardstock cover. 📖 Big Time Super Hero **A:** Mark Bagley **W:** Brian Michael Bendis; Bill Jemas ★ 1st Appearance of Green Goblin (full).
7 ❑ May 2001 Cover: 2.25 **NM** value: **Cover or less**
Circ: Statement: **354,115** Diamd. preorders: **76,097** • **CGC:** 13 graded, best 9.8
cardstock cover. 📖 Secret Identity **A:** Mark Bagley **W:** Brian Michael Bendis; Bill Jemas ★ Appearance of Green Goblin.
8 ❑ Jun 2001 Cover: 2.25 **NM** value: **Cover or less**
Circ: Statement: **354,115** Diamd. preorders: **84,500** • **CGC:** 8 graded, best 9.8
9 ❑ Jul 2001 Cover: 2.25 **NM** value: **Cover or less**
Circ: Statement: **354,115** Diamd. preorders: **84,723** • **CGC:** 15 graded, best 9.8
10 ❑ Aug 2001 Cover: 2.25 **NM** value: **Cover or less**
Circ: Statement: **354,115** Diamd. preorders: **86,349** • **CGC:** 12 graded, best 9.8
11 ❑ Sep 2001 Cover: 2.25 **NM** value: **Cover or less**
Circ: Statement: **354,115** Diamd. preorders: **89,477** • **CGC:** 8 graded, best 9.8
12 ❑ Oct 2001 Cover: 2.25 **NM** value: **Cover or less**
Circ: Diamd. preorders: **89,153** • **CGC:** 7 graded, best 9.8
13 ❑ Nov 2001 Cover: 2.25 **NM** value: **Cover or less**
Circ: Diamd. preorders: **86,042** • **CGC:** 14 graded, best 9.8
14 ❑ Jan 2002 Cover: 2.25 **NM** value: **Cover or less**
Circ: Diamd. preorders: **84,160** • **CGC:** 12 graded, best 10.0
1st printing. "3-D" cover.
15 ❑ Feb 2002 Cover: 2.25 **NM** value: **Cover or less**
Circ: Diamd. preorders: **86,159** • **CGC:** 3 graded, best 9.8
16 ❑ Mar 2002 Cover: 2.25 **NM** value: **Cover or less**
Circ: Diamd. preorders: **86,921**
• Has 2001 Statement, filed 10/1/01; avg print run 360,425; avg sales 350,566; avg subs 3,549; avg total paid 354,115; samples 600; max existent 354,715; 2% of run returned – heavy newsstand distribution on title
17 ❑ Apr 2002 Cover: 2.25 **NM** value: **Cover or less**
Circ: Diamd. preorders: **85,014**
18 ❑ May 2002 Cover: 2.25 **NM** value: **Cover or less**
Circ: Diamd. preorders: **83,265**
Bk 1 ❑ Jan 2001 Cover: 3.99 **NM** value: **Cover or less**
• collects #1-3 **A:** Mark Bagley **W:** Brian Michael Bendis; Bill Jemas

ULTIMATE X-MEN — Marvel

1 ❑ Feb 2001 Cover: 2.25 **NM** value: **12.00**
Circ: Diamd. preorders: **117,084** • **CGC:** 195 graded, best 9.8
cardstock cover. 📖 The Tomorrow People, Part 1 **A:** Adam Kubert **W:** Mark Millar
1/A ❑ Feb 2001 Cover: 2.25 **NM** value: **10.00**
📖 The Tomorrow People, Part 1 **A:** Adam Kubert **W:** Mark Millar
1/B ❑ Feb 2001 **NM** value: **40.00**
sketch cover. 📖 The Tomorrow People, Part 1 **A:** Adam Kubert **W:** Mark Millar
1/C ❑ Feb 2001 **NM** value: **30.00**
DF alternate (color) cover. 📖 The Tomorrow People, Part 1 • 7000 printed **A:** Adam Kubert **W:** Mark Millar
2 ❑ Mar 2001 Cover: 2.25 **NM** value: **6.00**
Circ: Diamd. preorders: **89,920** • **CGC:** 46 graded, best 9.6
cardstock cover. 📖 The Tomorrow People, Part 2 **A:** Adam Kubert **W:** Mark Millar
3 ❑ Apr 2001 Cover: 2.25 **NM** value: **4.00**
Circ: Diamd. preorders: **98,927** • **CGC:** 29 graded, best 9.8
cardstock cover. 📖 The Tomorrow People, Part 3 **A:** Adam Kubert **W:** Mark Millar
4 ❑ May 2001 Cover: 2.25 **NM** value: **4.00**
Circ: Diamd. preorders: **105,248** • **CGC:** 7 graded, best 9.8
📖 The Tomorrow People, Part 4 **A:** Adam Kubert **W:** Mark Millar
5 ❑ Jun 2001 Cover: 2.25 **NM** value: **4.00**
Circ: Diamd. preorders: **109,670** • **CGC:** 7 graded, best 9.8
📖 The Tomorrow People, Part 5 **A:** Adam Kubert **W:** Mark Millar
6 ❑ Jul 2001 Cover: 2.25 **NM** value: **Cover or less**
Circ: Diamd. preorders: **106,961** • **CGC:** 5 graded, best 9.8
📖 The Tomorrow People, Part 6 **A:** Adam Kubert **W:** Mark Millar
7 ❑ Aug 2001 Cover: 2.25 **NM** value: **Cover or less**
Circ: Diamd. preorders: **107,741** • **CGC:** 8 graded, best 9.8
8 ❑ Sep 2001 Cover: 2.25 **NM** value: **Cover or less**
Circ: Diamd. preorders: **112,348** • **CGC:** 8 graded, best 9.9
9 ❑ Oct 2001 Cover: 2.25 **NM** value: **Cover or less**
Circ: Diamd. preorders: **113,830** • **CGC:** 1 graded, best 9.6
10 ❑ Nov 2001 Cover: 2.25 **NM** value: **Cover or less**
Circ: Diamd. preorders: **107,551** • **CGC:** 5 graded, best 9.9
11 ❑ Dec 2001 Cover: 2.25 **NM** value: **Cover or less**
Circ: Diamd. preorders: **106,578**
12 ❑ Jan 2002 Cover: 2.25 **NM** value: **Cover or less**
Circ: Diamd. preorders: **108,043**
13 ❑ Feb 2002 Cover: 2.25 **NM** value: **Cover or less**
Circ: Diamd. preorders: **107,952**
• Has 2001 Statement of Ownership; appears to be completely in error, having all the same figures that appear in the 2001 Uncanny X-Men Statement; figures for Uncanny do seem to be for that title
Bk 1 ❑ Mar 2001 Cover: 3.99 **NM** value: **Cover or less**
• collects #1-3 **A:** Adam Kubert **W:** Mark Millar

ULTRAFORCE/AVENGERS — Malibu / Ultraverse

1 ❑ Fal 1995 Cover: 3.95 **NM** value: **Cover or less**
📖 Countdown to Black September, Part 5 **A:** George Pérez **W:** George Pérez; Warren Ellis

ULTRAFORCE/AVENGERS PRELUDE — Malibu / Ultraverse

1 ❑ Jul 1995 Cover: 2.50 **NM** value: **Cover or less**
📖 The Sword is Drawn… • a.k.a. UltraForce #11 **A:** John Statema **W:** Terry Kavanaugh

ULTRAFORCE/SPIDER-MAN — Malibu / Ultraverse

1 ❑ Jan 1996 Cover: 3.95 **NM** value: **Cover or less**
alternate covers: 1A and 1B.

Other grades: Multiply prices above by **1.5 for Mint • 2/3 for Very Fine • 1/3 for Fine • 1/5 for Very Good • 1/8 for Good**

ULTRAFORCE (VOL. 1) — Malibu / Ultraverse

UltraForce is the all-out action super-hero team series in Malibu's Ultraverse, featuring big, colorful stars like Prime, Prototype, Hardcase, Topaz, and Contrary. Writer Gerard Jones spends a fair amount of time developing characters and conflicts within the group and providing a firm grounding for the Ultraverse world, while veteran artist George Perez renders it all in his detail-rich and highly controlled style.

The heroes, or "ultras," of UltraForce are sponsored by different entities and compete for acclaim and honor, even as they need to collaborate as a team. Prototype is a teen-age kid in powerful armor; Prime is the "heavy hitter" with more brains than brawn; Hardcase is the reluctant leader, unwilling to assume responsibility for another group after leading a former team member to his death. Together they must tackle the super-villains of the Ultraverse under the intense glare of the media spotlight.

0 ❑ Sep 1994 Cover: 2.50 **NM** value: **Cover or less**
Circ: CapCity orders: **14,550**
Ultra Madness/UltraForce **A:** George Pérez **W:** Gerard Jones
0/SC❑Jul 1994 **NM** value: **1.00**
no cover price. • ashcan-sized. **A:** George Pérez
1 ❑ Aug 1994 Cover: 2.50 **NM** value: **Cover or less**
Circ: CapCity orders: **24,575**
The Force Be With You **A:** George Pérez **W:** Gerard Jones ★ 1st Appearance of Atalon.
1/Hol❑Aug 1994 **NM** value: **5.00**
Hologram cover. The Force Be With You **A:** George Pérez **W:** Gerard Jones
2 ❑ Oct 1994 Cover: 1.95 **NM** value: **Cover or less**
Circ: CapCity orders: **128,000**
Collision Course **A:** George Pérez; John Statema; George Pérez(cover) **W:** Gerard Jones
3 ❑ Nov 1994 Cover: 1.95 **NM** value: **Cover or less**
Circ: CapCity orders: **10,150**
Head to Head **A:** George Pérez **W:** Gerard Jones
4 ❑ Jan 1995 Cover: 1.95 **NM** value: **Cover or less**
Circ: CapCity orders: **9,050**
Ghosts **A:** George Pérez **W:** Gerard Jones
5 ❑ Feb 1995 Cover: 1.95 **NM** value: **Cover or less**
Circ: CapCity orders: **8,100**
Last Stand **A:** George Pérez **W:** Gerard Jones
6 ❑ Mar 1995 Cover: 2.50 **NM** value: **Cover or less**
Circ: CapCity orders: **7,200**
Final Blow **A:** George Pérez; Steven Butler **W:** Gerard Jones
7 ❑ Apr 1995 Cover: 2.50 **NM** value: **Cover or less**
Circ: CapCity orders: **6,400**
Mosh Pit **A:** Steve Erwin; George Pérez **W:** Chris Ulm; Hank Kanalz
8 ❑ May 1995 Cover: 2.50 **NM** value: **Cover or less**
Circ: CapCity orders: **7,625**
Black September, Part 1; Heaven on Earth **A:** George Pérez **W:** Hank Kanalz; Marv Wolfman
9 ❑ 1995 Cover: 2.50 **NM** value: **Cover or less**
Circ: CapCity orders: **7,200**
10 ❑ 1995 Cover: 2.50 **NM** value: **Cover or less**
Ash 1❑ Cover: 0.75 **NM** value: **Cover or less**
• Ashcan

ULTRAFORCE (VOL. 2) — Malibu / Ultraverse

0 ❑ Cover: 1.50 **NM** value: **Cover or less**
Circ: CapCity orders: **14,550**
• #Infinity
0/A ❑ Sep 1995 Cover: 1.50 **NM** value: **Cover or less**
#infinity on cover. Black September
0/B ❑ Sep 1995 Cover: 1.50 **NM** value: **3.50**
alternate cover.
0/SC❑Sep 1995 Cover: 1.50 **NM** value: **Cover or less**
alternate cover. • #Infinity
1 ❑ Oct 1995 Cover: 1.50 **NM** value: **Cover or less**
Shot Down, Part 1 **A:** Steven Butler; Bob Almond; Ken Branch **W:** Warren Ellis
2 ❑ Nov 1995 Cover: 1.50 **NM** value: **Cover or less**
Shot Down, Part 2 • contains reprint of UltraForce #1 **A:** Steven Butler; Bob Almond; Ken Branch **W:** Warren Ellis
3 ❑ Dec 1995 Cover: 1.50 **NM** value: **Cover or less**
Shot Down, Part 3 **A:** Steven Butler; Bob Almond; Ken Branch **W:** Warren Ellis
4 ❑ Jan 1996 Cover: 1.50 **NM** value: **Cover or less**
5 ❑ Feb 1996 Cover: 1.50 **NM** value: **Cover or less**
6 ❑ Mar 1996 Cover: 1.50 **NM** value: **Cover or less**
7 ❑ Apr 1996 Cover: 1.50 **NM** value: **Cover or less**
8 ❑ May 1996 Cover: 1.50 **NM** value: **Cover or less**
9 ❑ Jun 1996 Cover: 1.50 **NM** value: **Cover or less**
10 ❑ 1996 Cover: 1.50 **NM** value: **Cover or less**
11 ❑ Aug 1996 Cover: 1.50 **NM** value: **Cover or less**
12 ❑ Sep 1996 Cover: 1.50 **NM** value: **Cover or less**
Circ: Diamd. preorders: **15,847**
13 ❑ Oct 1996 Cover: 1.50 **NM** value: **Cover or less**
Circ: Diamd. preorders: **14,999**
14 ❑ 1996 Cover: 1.50 **NM** value: **Cover or less**
Circ: Diamd. preorders: **13,713**
15 ❑ Dec 1996 Cover: 1.50 **NM** value: **Cover or less**
Circ: Diamd. preorders: **12,586**
final issue. ★ Death of Ripfire.

ULTRAGIRL — Marvel

1 ❑ Nov 1996 Cover: 1.50 **NM** value: **Cover or less**
Circ: Direct Market orders: **32,250**
Powerhouse of Style **A:** Leonard Kirk **W:** Barbara Kesel
2 ❑ Dec 1996 Cover: 1.50 **NM** value: **Cover or less**
Circ: Direct Market orders: **22,000**
Playing With Fire **A:** Leonard Kirk **W:** Barbara Kesel
3 ❑ Mar 1997 Cover: 1.50 **NM** value: **Cover or less**
Circ: Direct Market orders: **18,250**
Rock My World **A:** Leonard Kirk **W:** Barbara Kesel ★ Appearance of New Warriors.

ULTRAHAWK — D.M.S.

1 ❑ Cover: 1.50 **NM** value: **Cover or less**
The Avenger **A:** Derek McIver **W:** Derek McIver

ULTRA KLUTZ — Onward

1 ❑ Jun 1986 Cover: 1.50 **NM** value: **2.00**
Exile; Deputy Day-shift: Mayhem at the Mall **A:** Jeff Nicholson **W:** Jeff Nicholson
2 ❑ Sep 1986 Cover: 1.50 **NM** value: **2.00**
3 ❑ Oct 1986 Cover: 1.50 **NM** value: **2.00**
4 ❑ Nov 1986 Cover: 1.50 **NM** value: **2.00**
5 ❑ Dec 1986 Cover: 1.50 **NM** value: **2.00**
6 ❑ Jan 1987 Cover: 1.50 **NM** value: **2.00**
7 ❑ Feb 1987 Cover: 1.50 **NM** value: **2.00**
8 ❑ Mar 1987 Cover: 1.50 **NM** value: **2.00**
9 ❑ Apr 1987 Cover: 1.50 **NM** value: **2.00**
10 ❑ May 1987 Cover: 1.50 **NM** value: **2.00**
11 ❑ Jun 1987 Cover: 1.50 **NM** value: **2.00**
12 ❑ Jul 1987 Cover: 1.50 **NM** value: **2.00**
13 ❑ Aug 1987 Cover: 1.50 **NM** value: **2.00**
14 ❑ Sep 1987 Cover: 1.50 **NM** value: **2.00**
15 ❑ Oct 1987 Cover: 1.50 **NM** value: **2.00**
16 ❑ Nov 1987 Cover: 1.50 **NM** value: **Cover or less**
17 ❑ Dec 1987 Cover: 1.50 **NM** value: **Cover or less**
18 ❑ Jan 1988 Cover: 1.75 **NM** value: **Cover or less**
19 ❑ Feb 1988 Cover: 1.75 **NM** value: **Cover or less**
20 ❑ 1988 Cover: 1.75 **NM** value: **Cover or less**
21 ❑ 1988 Cover: 1.75 **NM** value: **Cover or less**
22 ❑ 1988 Cover: 1.75 **NM** value: **Cover or less**
23 ❑ Jul 1988 Cover: 2.00 **NM** value: **Cover or less**
24 ❑ Aug 1988 Cover: 2.00 **NM** value: **Cover or less**
25 ❑ Sep 1988 Cover: 2.00 **NM** value: **Cover or less**
26 ❑ Nov 1988 Cover: 2.00 **NM** value: **Cover or less**
Problem Solving; Hope for the Galaxy; More Problems, More Solutions; A Halloween I'd Just as Soon Forget! **A:** Jeff Nicholson **W:** Jeff Nicholson
27 ❑ Jan 1989 Cover: 2.00 **NM** value: **Cover or less**
28 ❑ 1989 Cover: 2.00 **NM** value: **Cover or less**
29 ❑ Jun 1990 Cover: 2.00 **NM** value: **Cover or less**
30 ❑ 1990 **NM** value: **2.00**
31 ❑ May 1991 Cover: 2.95 **NM** value: **Cover or less**

ULTRA KLUTZ '81 — Onward

1 ❑ ca. 1981 Cover: 1.50 **NM** value: **2.00**

ULTRA KLUTZ DREAMS — Bad Habit

1 ❑ Cover: 2.95 **NM** value: **Cover or less**
Car Trouble; Sea Sick; Sillycybin; Evil Argoll **A:** Jeff Nicholson **W:** Jeff Nicholson

ULTRAMAN CLASSIC: BATTLE OF THE ULTRA-BROTHERS — Viz

1 ❑ b&w Cover: 4.95 **NM** value: **Cover or less**
2 ❑ b&w Cover: 4.95 **NM** value: **Cover or less**
3 ❑ b&w Cover: 4.95 **NM** value: **Cover or less**
4 ❑ b&w Cover: 4.95 **NM** value: **Cover or less**
5 ❑ b&w Cover: 4.95 **NM** value: **Cover or less**

ULTRAMAN (NEMESIS) — Nemesis

-1 ❑ Mar 1994 Cover: 1.75 **NM** value: **2.50**
negative image on cover.
1 ❑ Apr 1994 Cover: 1.75 **NM** value: **2.50**
Split cover.
1/A ❑ Apr 1994 Cover: 2.25 **NM** value: **Cover or less**
alternate cover.
2 ❑ May 1994 Cover: 1.75 **NM** value: **1.95**
3 ❑ Aug 1994 Cover: 1.95 **NM** value: **Cover or less**
4 ❑ Sep 1994 Cover: 1.95 **NM** value: **Cover or less**
5 ❑ 1994 Cover: 1.95 **NM** value: **Cover or less**

ULTRAMAN (ULTRACOMICS) — Harvey / Ultracomics

1 ❑ Jul 1993 Cover: 1.75 **NM** value: **2.00**
Circ: CapCity orders: **38,100**
Revenge of the Gudis, Part 1 • newsstand **A:** Ernie Colon **W:** Dwayne McDuffie ★ Origin of Ultraman.
1/CS❑Jul 1993 Cover: 2.50 **NM** value: **Cover or less**
Circ: CapCity orders: **6,400**
Revenge of the Gudis, Part 1 **A:** Ernie Colon **W:** Dwayne McDuffie
1/DM❑Jul 1993 Cover: 2.50 **NM** value: **3.50**
no type on cover. • trading card
2 ❑ 1993 Cover: 1.75 **NM** value: **Cover or less**
Circ: CapCity orders: **21,300**
Revenge of the Gudis, Part 2 • newsstand **A:** Ernie Colon **W:** Dwayne McDuffie
2/CS❑1993 Cover: 2.50 **NM** value: **Cover or less**
Circ: CapCity orders: **4,550**
Revenge of the Gudis, Part 2 **A:** Ernie Colon **W:** Dwayne McDuffie
2/DM❑1993 Cover: 2.50 **NM** value: **Cover or less**
no cover type. • direct sale; trading card
3 ❑ 1993 Cover: 1.75 **NM** value: **Cover or less**
Circ: CapCity orders: **19,300**
• newsstand
3/CS❑1993 Cover: 2.50 **NM** value: **Cover or less**
Circ: CapCity orders: **2,575**
3/DM❑1993 Cover: 2.50 **NM** value: **Cover or less**
• trading cards

ULTRA MONTHLY — Malibu

1 ❑ Jun 1993 Cover: 0.50 **NM** value: **Cover or less**
Circ: CapCity orders: **35,400**
• actually giveaway.
2 ❑ Jul 1993 Cover: 0.50 **NM** value: **Cover or less**
Circ: CapCity orders: **34,310**
• actually giveaway.
3 ❑ Aug 1993 Cover: 0.50 **NM** value: **Cover or less**
Circ: CapCity orders: **30,283**
cover says Sep, indicia says Aug. • actually giveaway.
4 ❑ Sep 1993 Cover: 0.50 **NM** value: **Cover or less**
Circ: CapCity orders: **13,000**
5 ❑ Oct 1993 Cover: 0.50 **NM** value: **Cover or less**
Circ: CapCity orders: **7,800**
6 ❑ Nov 1993 Cover: 0.50 **NM** value: **Cover or less**
Circ: CapCity orders: **7,670**

ULTRAVERSE/AVENGERS PRELUDE — Malibu / Ultraverse

1 ❑ Jul 1995 Cover: 2.50 **NM** value: **Cover or less**
The Swords are Drawn… **A:** John Statema **W:** Terry Kavanagh

ULTRAVERSE DOUBLE FEATURE: PRIME AND SOLITAIRE — Malibu / Ultraverse

1 ❑ Jan 1995 Cover: 3.95 **NM** value: **Cover or less**
Circ: CapCity orders: **5,175**
Prime: The King of Beasts; Solitaire: No Place Like Home **A:** Joel Thomas; Mark Miragila; Steven Butler(cover) **W:** Gerard Jones

ULTRAVERSE: FUTURE SHOCK — Malibu / Ultraverse

1 ❑ Feb 1997 Cover: 2.50 **NM** value: **Cover or less**
Future Shock • final Ultraverse adventure **A:** Kevin West; Manny Clark; Fabio Laguna **W:** Mark Paniccia

ULTRAVERSE ORIGINS — Malibu / Ultraverse

1993 saw the launch of several different comics universes, including Dark Horse's Comics' Greatest World, Defiant's new line of super-heroes, and Malibu's Ultraverse. The latter was among the most successful of the new comics worlds, owing its success to its strong storytelling, first-class art, and interesting characters.

At the beginning of 1994, Malibu gave new readers a chance to easily get in on that world. This 99-cent one-shot retold the origins of all the major Ultraverse characters. Included are the origin stories of Prototype, The Night Man, The Solution, Warstrike, Hardcase, Rune, Wrath, Sludge, Solitaire, The Strangers, Firearm, Mantra, and Freex. For good measure, this special also throws in a checklist of the Ultraverse titles, listing first appearances and other special issues that had happened by to that time.

1 ❑ Jan 1994 Cover: 0.99 **NM** value: **1.25**
Circ: CapCity orders: **4,925**
• Origin★ Origin of Prime.

ULTRAVERSE PREMIERE — Malibu / Ultraverse

0 ❑ Nov 1993 **NM** value: **1.00**
Circ: CapCity orders: **9,325** • **CGC:** 1 graded, best 9.4
Primal Appearance; From on High; The Last Mission; Once Upon a Bedtime…; Freex **A:** Norm Breyfogle; Rick Hoberg; Kevin Maguire; Gene Ha **W:** Gerard Jones; Len Strazewski; Mike Barr; Steve Englehart

ULTRAVERSE UNLIMITED — Malibu / Ultraverse

1 ❑ Jun 1996 Cover: 2.50 **NM** value: **Cover or less**

ULTRAVERSE YEAR ONE — Malibu / Ultraverse

1 ❑ Sep 1994 Cover: 4.95 **NM** value: **Cover or less**

ULTRAVERSE YEAR TWO — Malibu / Ultraverse

1 ❑ Aug 1995 Cover: 4.95 **NM** value: **Cover or less**

ULTRAVERSE YEAR ZERO: THE DEATH OF THE SQUAD — Malibu / Ultraverse

1 ❑ Apr 1995 Cover: 2.95 **NM** value: **Cover or less**
Circ: CapCity orders: **5,725**
2 ❑ May 1995 Cover: 2.95 **NM** value: **Cover or less**
Circ: CapCity orders: **4,550**
3 ❑ Jun 1995 Cover: 2.95 **NM** value: **Cover or less**
Circ: CapCity orders: **4,425**
4 ❑ Jul 1995 Cover: 2.95 **NM** value: **Cover or less**

UNBOUND — Image

1 ❑ Jan 1998, b&w Cover: 2.95 **NM** value: **Cover or less**
Circ: Diamd. preorders: **4,256**
Chapter One **A:** Mike Peters **W:** Joe Pruett

The CGC numbers printed in individual listings above represent the **number of copies examined** and given a **Universal** grade by CGC and the **best such copy** graded at press time. For current populations, watch for special ***Comics Buyer's Guide*** issues or check **www.cgccomics.com.**

CGC-graded: Multiply prices above by **33 for 9.9 M • 16 for 9.8 NM/M • 7 for 9.6 NM+ • 5 for 9.4 NM • 2.5 for 9.2 NM- • 1.5 for 9.0 VF/NM**

UNCANNY ORIGINS — Marvel

With the standard X-Men storyline groaning under the weight of endless crossovers and spinoffs, and mid-1990s Marvel apparently running away from its 30 years of continuity, the straightforward and non-revisionist approach of Uncanny Origins, X-Men Adventures, and the other animation-based titles, though meant for new readers, was both refreshing and reassuring to longtime fans.

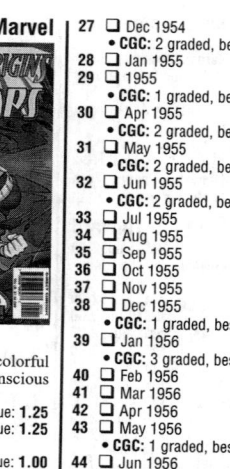

Uncanny Origins presents stories of how The X-Men, beginning with Cyclops, discovered their mutant powers and joined Professor Xavier's team. The stories in Uncanny Origins stick to the standard version developed by Marvel since the 1960s and feature open, colorful art that is diametrically opposed to the dark and Image-conscious style found in more "mainstream" mutant titles.

1 ❑ Sep 1996 Cover: 0.99 **NM** value: **1.25**
1/A ❑ Sep 1996 Cover: 0.99 **NM** value: **1.25**
variant cover. ★ Origin of Cyclops.
2 ❑ Oct 1996 Cover: 0.99 **NM** value: **1.00**
3 ❑ Nov 1996 Cover: 0.99 **NM** value: **1.00**
Circ: Direct Market orders: **39,000**
4 ❑ Dec 1996 Cover: 0.99 **NM** value: **1.00**
Circ: Direct Market orders: **300,250**
Forged in Fire **A:** Dave Hoover **W:** James Felder ★ Origin of Firelord.
5 ❑ Jan 1997 Cover: 0.99 **NM** value: **1.00**
Circ: Direct Market orders: **29,750**
6 ❑ Feb 1997 Cover: 0.99 **NM** value: **1.00**
Circ: Direct Market orders: **27,250**
Lo! A Beast is Born! **A:** Dave Hoover **W:** Michael Higgins ★ Origin of Beast.
7 ❑ Mar 1997 Cover: 0.99 **NM** value: **1.00**
Circ: Direct Market orders: **24,500**
8 ❑ Apr 1997 Cover: 0.99 **NM** value: **1.00**
Circ: Direct Market orders: **23,500**
9 ❑ May 1997 Cover: 0.99 **NM** value: **1.00**
Circ: Diamd. preorders: **23,957**
10 ❑ Jun 1997 Cover: 0.99 **NM** value: **1.00**
Circ: Diamd. preorders: **21,614**
11 ❑ Jul 1997 Cover: 0.99 **NM** value: **1.00**
Circ: Diamd. preorders: **18,119**
12 ❑ Aug 1997 Cover: 0.99 **NM** value: **1.00**
Circ: Diamd. preorders: **17,078**
13 ❑ Sep 1997 Cover: 0.99 **NM** value: **1.00**
Circ: Diamd. preorders: **16,334**
14 ❑ Oct 1997 Cover: 0.99 **NM** value: **1.00**
Circ: Diamd. preorders: **16,821**

UNCANNY TALES (1ST SERIES) — Marvel

1 ❑ Jun 1952 Cover: 0.10 **NM** value: **600.00**
• **CGC:** 2 graded, best 9.2
2 ❑ Aug 1952 Cover: 0.10 **NM** value: **340.00**
3 ❑ Oct 1952 Cover: 0.10 **NM** value: **275.00**
• **CGC:** 1 graded, best 7.5
4 ❑ Dec 1952 Cover: 0.10 **NM** value: **275.00**
• **CGC:** 2 graded, best 8.0
5 ❑ Feb 1953 Cover: 0.10 **NM** value: **275.00**
• **CGC:** 1 graded, best 4.0
6 ❑ Mar 1953 Cover: 0.10 **NM** value: **240.00**
• **CGC:** 1 graded, best 6.0
7 ❑ Apr 1953 Cover: 0.10 **NM** value: **240.00**
• **CGC:** 2 graded, best 7.5
8 ❑ May 1953 Cover: 0.10 **NM** value: **240.00**
9 ❑ Jun 1953 Cover: 0.10 **NM** value: **240.00**
• **CGC:** 2 graded, best 8.5
10 ❑ Jul 1953 Cover: 0.10 **NM** value: **240.00**
• **CGC:** 2 graded, best 6.5
11 ❑ Aug 1953 Cover: 0.10 **NM** value: **185.00**
12 ❑ Sep 1953 Cover: 0.10 **NM** value: **185.00**
• **CGC:** 1 graded, best 8.0
13 ❑ Oct 1953 Cover: 0.10 **NM** value: **185.00**
• **CGC:** 2 graded, best 9.0
14 ❑ Nov 1953 Cover: 0.10 **NM** value: **185.00**
• **CGC:** 1 graded, best 6.0
15 ❑ Dec 1953 Cover: 0.10 **NM** value: **185.00**
• **CGC:** 1 graded, best 5.0
16 ❑ Jan 1954 Cover: 0.10 **NM** value: **185.00**
• **CGC:** 1 graded, best 7.0
17 ❑ Feb 1954 Cover: 0.10 **NM** value: **185.00**
• **CGC:** 2 graded, best 7.0
18 ❑ Mar 1954 Cover: 0.10 **NM** value: **185.00**
One Second Till Doom!; A Favor from Satan (text); The Last Vampire; One Little Man; The Machine Age; The Face in the Mirror **A:** Bob Powell; John Forge **W:** Bob Powell; John Forge
19 ❑ Apr 1954 Cover: 0.10 **NM** value: **185.00**
• **CGC:** 1 graded, best 7.0
20 ❑ May 1954 Cover: 0.10 **NM** value: **185.00**
• **CGC:** 1 graded, best 5.5
21 ❑ Jun 1954 Cover: 0.10 **NM** value: **150.00**
• **CGC:** 2 graded, best 8.0
22 ❑ Jul 1954 Cover: 0.10 **NM** value: **150.00**
• **CGC:** 2 graded, best 8.0
23 ❑ Aug 1954 Cover: 0.10 **NM** value: **150.00**
• **CGC:** 1 graded, best 4.5
24 ❑ Sep 1954 Cover: 0.10 **NM** value: **150.00**
25 ❑ Oct 1954 Cover: 0.10 **NM** value: **150.00**
• **CGC:** 1 graded, best 4.5
26 ❑ Nov 1954 Cover: 0.10 **NM** value: **150.00**
• **CGC:** 2 graded, best 9.0
27 ❑ Dec 1954 Cover: 0.10 **NM** value: **150.00**
• **CGC:** 2 graded, best 8.5
28 ❑ Jan 1955 Cover: 0.10 **NM** value: **150.00**
29 ❑ 1955 Cover: 0.10 **NM** value: **75.00**
• **CGC:** 1 graded, best 8.0
30 ❑ Apr 1955 Cover: 0.10 **NM** value: **75.00**
• **CGC:** 2 graded, best 9.0
31 ❑ May 1955 Cover: 0.10 **NM** value: **75.00**
• **CGC:** 2 graded, best 9.0
32 ❑ Jun 1955 Cover: 0.10 **NM** value: **75.00**
• **CGC:** 2 graded, best 9.2
33 ❑ Jul 1955 Cover: 0.10 **NM** value: **75.00**
34 ❑ Aug 1955 Cover: 0.10 **NM** value: **75.00**
35 ❑ Sep 1955 Cover: 0.10 **NM** value: **75.00**
36 ❑ Oct 1955 Cover: 0.10 **NM** value: **75.00**
37 ❑ Nov 1955 Cover: 0.10 **NM** value: **75.00**
38 ❑ Dec 1955 Cover: 0.10 **NM** value: **75.00**
• **CGC:** 1 graded, best 6.5
39 ❑ Jan 1956 Cover: 0.10 **NM** value: **75.00**
• **CGC:** 3 graded, best 8.5
40 ❑ Feb 1956 Cover: 0.10 **NM** value: **75.00**
41 ❑ Mar 1956 Cover: 0.10 **NM** value: **60.00**
42 ❑ Apr 1956 Cover: 0.10 **NM** value: **60.00**
43 ❑ May 1956 Cover: 0.10 **NM** value: **60.00**
• **CGC:** 1 graded, best 7.5
44 ❑ Jun 1956 Cover: 0.10 **NM** value: **60.00**
• **CGC:** 1 graded, best 7.0
45 ❑ Jul 1956 Cover: 0.10 **NM** value: **60.00**
46 ❑ Aug 1956 Cover: 0.10 **NM** value: **60.00**
47 ❑ Sep 1956 Cover: 0.10 **NM** value: **60.00**
48 ❑ Oct 1956 Cover: 0.10 **NM** value: **60.00**
49 ❑ Nov 1956 Cover: 0.10 **NM** value: **60.00**
• **CGC:** 1 graded, best 7.5
50 ❑ Dec 1956 Cover: 0.10 **NM** value: **60.00**
• **CGC:** 1 graded, best 7.5
51 ❑ Jan 1957 Cover: 0.10 **NM** value: **60.00**
• **CGC:** 1 graded, best 8.5
52 ❑ Feb 1957 Cover: 0.10 **NM** value: **60.00**
• **CGC:** 2 graded, best 9.0
53 ❑ Mar 1957 Cover: 0.10 **NM** value: **60.00**
• **CGC:** 3 graded, best 8.5
54 ❑ Apr 1957 Cover: 0.10 **NM** value: **60.00**
• **CGC:** 2 graded, best 9.0
55 ❑ Jul 1957 Cover: 0.10 **NM** value: **60.00**
• **CGC:** 4 graded, best 8.5
56 ❑ Sep 1957 Cover: 0.10 **NM** value: **60.00**
• **CGC:** 1 graded, best 9.2

UNCANNY TALES (2ND SERIES) — Marvel

1 ❑ Dec 1973 Cover: 0.10 **NM** value: **5.00**
• **CGC:** 1 graded, best 9.6
2 ❑ Feb 1974 Cover: 0.10 **NM** value: **3.50**
• **CGC:** 1 graded, best 9.4
3 ❑ Apr 1974 Cover: 0.10 **NM** value: **3.50**
4 ❑ Jun 1974 Cover: 0.10 **NM** value: **3.50**
5 ❑ Aug 1974 Cover: 0.10 **NM** value: **3.50**
6 ❑ Oct 1974 Cover: 0.10 **NM** value: **3.50**
7 ❑ Dec 1974 Cover: 0.10 **NM** value: **3.50**
8 ❑ Feb 1975 Cover: 0.10 **NM** value: **3.50**
9 ❑ Apr 1975 Cover: 0.10 **NM** value: **3.50**
• **CGC:** 2 graded, best 9.2
10 ❑ Jun 1975 Cover: 0.10 **NM** value: **3.50**
11 ❑ Aug 1975 Cover: 0.10 **NM** value: **3.50**
12 ❑ Oct 1975 Cover: 0.10 **NM** value: **3.50**

UNCANNY X-MEN, THE — Marvel

In the age of the atom, more and more children were being born with strange abilities that set them apart from the rest of humanity. These people were known as mutants, and Professor Charles Xavier decided that he must make it his mission to shelter these mutants from society's fears and teach them to use their abilities for the good of mankind. Thus, he gathered together the heroes that would become known as the X-Men.

The original X-Men (Cyclops, The Beast, The Angel, and Marvel Girl) were eventually replaced by a new team in Giant Size X-Men #1. That team, which added members Thunderbird, Nightcrawler, Colossus, Banshee, Storm, and Wolverine, would become a comic-book sensation.

Readers should note that, with #142, this series, originally known simply as X-Men (1st Series), changed its name officially to "The Uncanny X-Men."

-1 ❑ Jul 1997 Cover: 1.99 **NM** value: **2.00**
• Flashback
142 ❑ Feb 1981 Cover: 0.50 **NM** value: **20.00**
Circ: Statement: **259,007** • **CGC:** 196 graded, best 9.8
Mind Out of Time • Series continued from X-Men (1st Series) #141 **A:** John Byrne; Terry Austin **W:** Chris Claremont ★ Appearance of Rachel Summers (Phoenix III). ★ Death of Colossus (future). ★ Death of Storm (future). ★ Death of Wolverine (future).
143 ❑ Mar 1981 Cover: 0.50 **NM** value: **9.00**
Circ: Statement: **259,007** • **CGC:** 88 graded, best 9.8
Demon • Last Byrne art on X-Men **A:** John Byrne; Terry Austin **W:** Chris Claremont
144 ❑ Apr 1981 Cover: 0.50 **NM** value: **7.00**
Circ: Statement: **259,007** • **CGC:** 32 graded, best 9.8
Even in Death • Has 1980 Statement, filed 10/1/80; avg print run 345,288; avg sales 186,504; avg subs 5,423; avg total paid 191,927; samples 587; office use 1,855; max existent 194,369; 44% of run returned **A:** Brent Anderson **W:** Chris Claremont ★ Appearance of Man-Thing.
145 ❑ May 1981 Cover: 0.50 **NM** value: **7.00**
Circ: Statement: **259,007** • **CGC:** 20 graded, best 9.9
Kidnapped **A:** Dave Cockrum **W:** Chris Claremont
146 ❑ Jun 1981 Cover: 0.50 **NM** value: **7.00**
Circ: Statement: **259,007** • **CGC:** 25 graded, best 9.8
Murderworld **A:** Dave Cockrum **W:** Chris Claremont
147 ❑ Jul 1981 Cover: 0.50 **NM** value: **7.00**
Circ: Statement: **259,007** • **CGC:** 35 graded, best 9.8
Rogue Storm **A:** Dave Cockrum **W:** Chris Claremont
148 ❑ Aug 1981 Cover: 0.50 **NM** value: **7.00**
Circ: Statement: **259,007** • **CGC:** 45 graded, best 9.8
Cry, Mutant **A:** Dave Cockrum **W:** Chris Claremont ★ 1st Appearance of Caliban. ★ Appearance of Dazzler, Spider-Woman.
149 ❑ Sep 1981 Cover: 0.50 **NM** value: **7.00**
Circ: Statement: **259,007** • **CGC:** 39 graded, best 9.8
And the Dead Shall Bury the Living **A:** Dave Cockrum **W:** Chris Claremont
150 ❑ Oct 1981 Cover: 0.75 **NM** value: **8.00**
Circ: Statement: **259,007** • **CGC:** 74 graded, best 9.8
• double-sized. I, Magneto • Cyclops rejoins the X-Men **A:** Dave Cockrum **W:** Chris Claremont ★ Versus Magneto.
151 ❑ Nov 1981 Cover: 0.50 **NM** value: **5.00**
Circ: Statement: **259,007** • **CGC:** 39 graded, best 9.8
X-Men Minus One **A:** Bob McLeod; James Sherman **W:** Chris Claremont
152 ❑ Dec 1981 Cover: 0.50 **NM** value: **5.00**
Circ: Statement: **259,007** • **CGC:** 10 graded, best 9.8
The Hellfire Gambit **A:** Bob McLeod **W:** Chris Claremont
153 ❑ Jan 1982 Cover: 0.60 **NM** value: **5.00**
Circ: Statement: **313,225** • **CGC:** 13 graded, best 9.8
Kitty's Fairy Tale **A:** Dave Cockrum **W:** Chris Claremont
154 ❑ Feb 1982 Cover: 0.60 **NM** value: **5.00**
Circ: Statement: **313,225** • **CGC:** 25 graded, best 9.8
Reunion **A:** Dave Cockrum **W:** Chris Claremont
155 ❑ Mar 1982 Cover: 0.60 **NM** value: **5.00**
Circ: Statement: **313,225** • **CGC:** 10 graded, best 9.8
First Blood **A:** Dave Cockrum **W:** Chris Claremont
156 ❑ Apr 1982 Cover: 0.60 **NM** value: **5.00**
Circ: Statement: **313,225** • **CGC:** 20 graded, best 9.8
Pursuit • Has 1981 Statement, filed 10/1/81; avg print run 414,435; avg sales 248,138; avg subs 10,869; avg total paid 259,007; samples 600; office use 2,622; max existent 262,229; 37% of run returned **A:** Dave Cockrum **W:** Chris Claremont
157 ❑ May 1982 Cover: 0.60 **NM** value: **5.00**
Circ: Statement: **313,225** • **CGC:** 21 graded, best 9.8
Hide-'N-Seek **A:** Dave Cockrum **W:** Chris Claremont ★ Appearance of Phoenix.
158 ❑ Jun 1982 Cover: 0.60 **NM** value: **9.00**
Circ: Statement: **313,225** • **CGC:** 30 graded, best 9.8
The Life That Late I Led **A:** Dave Cockrum **W:** Chris Claremont ★ Appearance of Rogue.
159 ❑ Jul 1982 Cover: 0.60 **NM** value: **6.00**
Circ: Statement: **313,225** • **CGC:** 11 graded, best 9.8
Night Screams **A:** Bill Sienkiewicz **W:** Chris Claremont ★ Appearance of Dracula.
160 ❑ Aug 1982 Cover: 0.60 **NM** value: **6.00**
Circ: Statement: **313,225** • **CGC:** 24 graded, best 9.8
Chutes and Ladders **A:** Brent Anderson **W:** Chris Claremont ★ 1st Appearance of Magik (Illyana Rasputin as teenager).
161 ❑ Sep 1982 Cover: 0.60 **NM** value: **6.00**
Circ: Statement: **313,225** • **CGC:** 18 graded, best 9.8
Gold Rush **A:** Dave Cockrum **W:** Chris Claremont ★ Origin of Professor X, Magneto.
162 ❑ Oct 1982 Cover: 0.60 **NM** value: **8.00**
Circ: Statement: **313,225** • **CGC:** 12 graded, best 9.8
Beyond the Farthest Star • Wolverine solo story **A:** Dave Cockrum **W:** Chris Claremont
163 ❑ Nov 1982 Cover: 0.60 **NM** value: **5.00**
Circ: Statement: **313,225** • **CGC:** 9 graded, best 9.6
Rescue Mission **A:** Dave Cockrum **W:** Chris Claremont
164 ❑ Dec 1982 Cover: 0.60 **NM** value: **5.00**
Circ: Statement: **313,225** • **CGC:** 17 graded, best 9.8
Binary Star **A:** Dave Cockrum **W:** Chris Claremont ★ 1st Appearance of Binary.
165 ❑ Jan 1983 Cover: 0.60 **NM** value: **5.00**
Circ: Statement: **336,824** • **CGC:** 14 graded, best 9.8
Transfigurations **A:** Paul Smith **W:** Chris Claremont
166 ❑ Feb 1983 Cover: 1.00 **NM** value: **5.00**
Circ: Statement: **336,824** • **CGC:** 18 graded, best 9.8
• Double-size. Live Free or Die **A:** Paul Smith **W:** Chris Claremont ★ 1st Appearance of Lockheed.
167 ❑ Mar 1983 Cover: 0.60 **NM** value: **5.00**
Circ: Statement: **336,824** • **CGC:** 12 graded, best 9.8
The Goldilocks Syndrome **A:** Paul Smith **W:** Chris Claremont ★ Appearance of New Mutants.
168 ❑ Apr 1983 Cover: 0.60 **NM** value: **5.00**
Circ: Statement: **336,824** • **CGC:** 11 graded, best 9.8
Professor Xavier is a Jerk! **A:** Paul Smith **W:** Chris Claremont ★ 1st Appearance of Madelyne Pryor.
169 ❑ May 1983 Cover: 0.60 **NM** value: **5.00**
Circ: Statement: **336,824** • **CGC:** 13 graded, best 9.6
Catacombs • Has 1982 Statement, filed 10/11/82; avg print run 507,493; avg sales 311,279; avg subs 1,946; avg total paid 313,225; samples 730; office use 23,558; max existent 337,513; 34% of run returned **A:** Paul Smith **W:** Chris Claremont ★ 1st Appearance of Morlocks, Sunder.
170 ❑ Jun 1983 Cover: 0.60 **NM** value: **5.00**
Circ: Statement: **336,824** • **CGC:** 7 graded, best 9.8
Dancin' in the Dark **A:** Paul Smith **W:** Chris Claremont
171 ❑ Jul 1983 Cover: 0.60 **NM** value: **8.00**
Circ: Statement: **336,824** • **CGC:** 30 graded, best 9.8
Rogue • Rogue joins team **A:** Walt Simonson **W:** Chris Claremont
172 ❑ Aug 1983 Cover: 0.60 **NM** value: **5.00**
Circ: Statement: **336,824** • **CGC:** 21 graded, best 9.8
Scarlet in Glory **A:** Paul Smith **W:** Chris Claremont

Other grades: Multiply prices above by **1.5 for Mint • 2/3 for Very Fine • 1/3 for Fine • 1/5 for Very Good • 1/8 for Good**

173 ❑ Sep 1983 Cover: 0.60 **NM** value: **5.00**
Circ: Statement: **336,824** • **CGC:** 12 graded, best 9.8
📖 To Have and Have Not **A:** Paul Smith **W:** Chris Claremont ★ Origin of Silver Samurai.

174 ❑ Oct 1983 Cover: 0.60 **NM** value: **5.00**
Circ: Statement: **336,824** • **CGC:** 7 graded, best 9.6
📖 Romances **A:** Paul Smith **W:** Chris Claremont

175 ❑ Nov 1983 Cover: 1.00 **NM** value: **6.00**
Circ: Statement: **336,824** • **CGC:** 19 graded, best 9.6
• double-sized. 📖 Phoenix **A:** Paul Smith **W:** Chris Claremont

176 ❑ Dec 1983 Cover: 0.60 **NM** value: **5.00**
Circ: Statement: **336,824** • **CGC:** 17 graded, best 9.8
📖 Decisions **A:** John Romita Jr. **W:** Chris Claremont ★ 1st Appearance of Valerie Cooper.

177 ❑ Jan 1984 Cover: 0.60 **NM** value: **4.00**
Circ: Statement: **378,135** • **CGC:** 6 graded, best 9.8
📖 Sanction **A:** John Romita Jr. **W:** Chris Claremont

178 ❑ Feb 1984 Cover: 0.60 **NM** value: **4.00**
Circ: Statement: **378,135** • **CGC:** 7 graded, best 9.6
📖 Hell Hath No Fury… **A:** John Romita Jr. **W:** Chris Claremont

179 ❑ Mar 1984 Cover: 0.60 **NM** value: **4.00**
Circ: Statement: **378,135** • **CGC:** 11 graded, best 9.8
📖 What Happened to Kitty **A:** John Romita Jr. **W:** Chris Claremont

180 ❑ Apr 1984 Cover: 0.60 **NM** value: **4.00**
Circ: Statement: **378,135** • **CGC:** 10 graded, best 9.6
📖 Whose Life is it, Anyway? **A:** John Romita Jr. **W:** Chris Claremont

181 ❑ May 1984 Cover: 0.60 **NM** value: **4.00**
Circ: Statement: **378,135** • **CGC:** 6 graded, best 9.6
📖 Tokyo Story **A:** John Romita Jr. **W:** Chris Claremont

182 ❑ Jun 1984 Cover: 0.60 **NM** value: **4.00**
Circ: Statement: **378,135** • **CGC:** 8 graded, best 9.6
📖 Madness • Has 1983 Statement, filed 10/5/83; avg print run 546,070; avg sales 313,292; avg subs 23,532; avg total paid 336,824; samples 794; office use 5,739; max existent 343,357; 32% of run returned **A:** John Romita Jr. **W:** Chris Claremont

183 ❑ Jul 1984 Cover: 0.60 **NM** value: **4.00**
Circ: Statement: **378,135** • **CGC:** 8 graded, best 9.8
📖 He'll Never Make Me Cry **A:** John Romita Jr. **W:** Chris Claremont

184 ❑ Aug 1984 Cover: 0.60 **NM** value: **5.00**
Circ: Statement: **378,135** • **CGC:** 12 graded, best 9.8
📖 The Past…of Future Days **A:** John Romita Jr. **W:** Chris Claremont ★ 1st Appearance of Forge. ★ Appearance of Rachel, Selene.

185 ❑ Sep 1984 Cover: 0.60 **NM** value: **4.00**
Circ: Statement: **378,135** • **CGC:** 34 graded, best 9.8
📖 Public Enemy • Storm loses powers **A:** John Romita Jr. **W:** Chris Claremont

186 ❑ Oct 1984 Cover: 1.00 **NM** value: **5.00**
Circ: Statement: **378,135** • **CGC:** 29 graded, best 9.8
• double-sized. 📖 Lifedeath • Storm **A:** Barry Windsor-Smith; Terry Austin **W:** Chris Claremont

187 ❑ Nov 1984 Cover: 0.60 **NM** value: **3.00**
Circ: Statement: **378,135** • **CGC:** 26 graded, best 9.8
📖 Wraithkill **A:** John Romita Jr. **W:** Chris Claremont

188 ❑ Dec 1984 Cover: 0.60 **NM** value: **3.00**
Circ: Statement: **378,135** • **CGC:** 26 graded, best 9.8
📖 Legacy of the Lost **A:** John Romita Jr. **W:** Chris Claremont

189 ❑ Jan 1985 Cover: 0.60 **NM** value: **3.00**
Circ: Statement: **449,870** • **CGC:** 16 graded, best 9.8
📖 Two Girls Out to Have Fun **A:** John Romita Jr. **W:** Chris Claremont

190 ❑ Feb 1985 Cover: 0.60 **NM** value: **3.00**
Circ: Statement: **449,870** • **CGC:** 26 graded, best 9.6
📖 An Age Undreamed Of **A:** John Romita Jr. **W:** Chris Claremont ★ Appearance of Spider-Man, Avengers.

191 ❑ Mar 1985 Cover: 0.60 **NM** value: **3.00**
Circ: Statement: **449,870** • **CGC:** 23 graded, best 9.8
📖 Raiders of the Lost Temple **A:** John Romita Jr. **W:** Chris Claremont ★ Appearance of Captain America, Spider-Man, Avengers.

192 ❑ Apr 1985 Cover: 0.60 **NM** value: **3.00**
Circ: Statement: **449,870** • **CGC:** 29 graded, best 9.9
📖 Fun'n'Games • Magus **A:** John Romita Jr. **W:** Chris Claremont

193 ❑ May 1985 Cover: 1.25 **NM** value: **6.00**
Circ: Statement: **449,870** CapCity orders: **49,800** • **CGC:** 14 graded, best 9.9
• double-sized. 📖 Warhunt 2 • 20th anniv.; 100th New X-Men **A:** John Romita Jr. **W:** Chris Claremont

194 ❑ Jun 1985 Cover: 0.65 **NM** value: **3.00**
Circ: Statement: **449,870** CapCity orders: **44,800** • **CGC:** 11 graded, best 9.6
📖 Juggernaut's Back in Town **A:** John Romita Jr. **W:** Chris Claremont ★ Appearance of Juggernaut. ★ Versus Juggernaut.

195 ❑ Jul 1985 Cover: 0.65 **NM** value: **3.00**
Circ: Statement: **449,870** CapCity orders: **45,500** • **CGC:** 10 graded, best 9.6
📖 It Was a Dark and Stormy Night **A:** John Romita Jr. **W:** Chris Claremont ★ Appearance of Power Pack.

196 ❑ Aug 1985 Cover: 0.65 **NM** value: **3.00**
Circ: Statement: **449,870** CapCity orders: **48,600** • **CGC:** 9 graded, best 9.8
📖 What Was That? • Secret Wars II; Has 1984 Statement, filed 9/28/84; avg print run 560,666; avg sales 354,549; avg subs 23,586; avg total paid 378,135; samples 160; office use 2,652; max existent 380,947; 32% of run returned **A:** John Romita Jr. **W:** Chris Claremont

197 ❑ Sep 1985 Cover: 0.65 **NM** value: **3.00**
Circ: Statement: **449,870** CapCity orders: **44,900** • **CGC:** 14 graded, best 9.8
📖 To Save Arcade? **A:** John Romita Jr. **W:** Chris Claremont

198 ❑ Oct 1985 Cover: 0.65 **NM** value: **3.00**
Circ: Statement: **449,870** CapCity orders: **51,400** • **CGC:** 22 graded, best 9.8
📖 Lifedeath II **A:** Barry Windsor-Smith **W:** Chris Claremont

199 ❑ Nov 1985 Cover: 0.65 **NM** value: **4.00**
Circ: Statement: **449,870** CapCity orders: **46,300** • **CGC:** 8 graded, best 9.8
📖 The Spiral Path **A:** John Romita Jr. **W:** Chris Claremont ★ 1st Appearance of Phoenix III (Rachel Summers).

200 ❑ Dec 1985 Cover: 1.25 **NM** value: **7.00**
Circ: Statement: **449,870** CapCity orders: **57,000** • **CGC:** 18 graded, best 9.8
• Double-size. 📖 Trial of Magneto; The Trial of Magneto **A:** John Romita Jr. **W:** Chris Claremont

201 ❑ Jan 1986 Cover: 0.65 **NM** value: **5.00**
Circ: Statement: **417,350** CapCity orders: **45,900** • **CGC:** 29 graded, best 9.8
📖 Duel • 1st Portacio art in X-Men **A:** Rick Leonardi **W:** Chris Claremont ★ 1st Appearance of Cable (as baby).

202 ❑ Feb 1986 Cover: 0.75 **NM** value: **3.00**
Circ: Statement: **417,350** CapCity orders: **52,300** • **CGC:** 9 graded, best 9.8
📖 X-Men…I've Gone to Kill-The Beyonder! • Secret Wars II **A:** John Romita Jr. **W:** Chris Claremont

203 ❑ Mar 1986 Cover: 0.75 **NM** value: **3.00**
Circ: Statement: **417,350** CapCity orders: **51,300** • **CGC:** 2 graded, best 9.6
📖 Crossroads • Secret Wars II **A:** John Romita Jr. **W:** Chris Claremont

204 ❑ Apr 1986 Cover: 0.75 **NM** value: **3.00**
Circ: Statement: **417,350** CapCity orders: **47,300** • **CGC:** 2 graded, best 9.6
📖 What Happened to Nightcrawler? • Nightcrawler solo story **A:** June Brigman **W:** Chris Claremont

205 ❑ May 1986 Cover: 0.75 **NM** value: **8.00**
Circ: Statement: **417,350** CapCity orders: **52,500** • **CGC:** 28 graded, best 9.8
📖 Wounded Wolf • Wolverine solo story; Has 1985 Statement, filed 10/1/85; avg print run 652,150; avg sales 421,379; avg subs 28,491; avg total paid 449,870; samples 377; office use 2,748; max existent 452,995; 31% of run returned **A:** Barry Windsor-Smith **W:** Chris Claremont ★ Appearance of Power Pack.

206 ❑ Jun 1986 Cover: 0.75 **NM** value: **3.00**
Circ: Statement: **417,350** CapCity orders: **48,800** • **CGC:** 7 graded, best 9.8
📖 Freedom is a Four Letter Word **A:** John Romita Jr. **W:** Chris Claremont ★ Versus Freedom Force.

207 ❑ Jul 1986 Cover: 0.75 **NM** value: **3.00**
Circ: Statement: **417,350** CapCity orders: **49,100** • **CGC:** 12 graded, best 9.6
📖 Ghosts • Wolverine vs. Phoenix **A:** John Romita Jr. **W:** Chris Claremont

208 ❑ Aug 1986 Cover: 0.75 **NM** value: **3.00**
Circ: Statement: **417,350** CapCity orders: **49,500** • **CGC:** 3 graded, best 9.8
📖 Retribution **A:** John Romita Jr. **W:** Chris Claremont

209 ❑ Sep 1986 Cover: 0.75 **NM** value: **3.00**
Circ: Statement: **417,350** CapCity orders: **48,500** • **CGC:** 5 graded, best 9.8
📖 Salvation **A:** John Romita Jr. **W:** Chris Claremont

210 ❑ Oct 1986 Cover: 0.75 **NM** value: **7.00**
Circ: Statement: **417,350** CapCity orders: **50,700** • **CGC:** 40 graded, best 9.8
📖 Mutant Massacre; The Morning After **A:** John Romita Jr. **W:** Chris Claremont ★ 1st Appearance of Marauders.

211 ❑ Nov 1986 Cover: 0.75 **NM** value: **7.00**
Circ: Statement: **417,350** CapCity orders: **55,000** • **CGC:** 67 graded, best 9.8
📖 Mutant Massacre **A:** John Romita Jr. **W:** Chris Claremont

212 ❑ Dec 1986 Cover: 0.75 **NM** value: **8.00**
Circ: Statement: **417,350** CapCity orders: **55,200** • **CGC:** 73 graded, best 9.8
📖 Mutant Massacre; The Last Run • Wolverine vs. Sabretooth **A:** Rick Leonardi **W:** Alan Davis; Chris Claremont ★ Appearance of Sabretooth.

213 ❑ Jan 1987 Cover: 0.75 **NM** value: **8.00**
Circ: Statement: **430,158** CapCity orders: **56,000** • **CGC:** 110 graded, best 9.8
📖 Psylocke • Wolverine vs. Sabretooth **W:** Alan Davis; Chris Claremont

214 ❑ Feb 1987 Cover: 0.75 **NM** value: **3.00**
Circ: Statement: **430,158** CapCity orders: **58,800** • **CGC:** 8 graded, best 9.8
📖 With Malice Toward All **A:** Barry Windsor-Smith **W:** Chris Claremont

215 ❑ Mar 1987 Cover: 0.75 **NM** value: **3.00**
Circ: Statement: **430,158** CapCity orders: **58,400** • **CGC:** 9 graded, best 9.8
📖 Old Soldiers **A:** Alan Davis **W:** Alan Davis; Chris Claremont ★ 1st Appearance of Crimson Commando.

216 ❑ Apr 1987 Cover: 0.75 **NM** value: **3.00**
Circ: Statement: **430,158** CapCity orders: **56,800** • **CGC:** 5 graded, best 9.8
📖 Crucible **A:** Jackson Guice **W:** Chris Claremont

217 ❑ May 1987 Cover: 0.75 **NM** value: **3.00**
Circ: Statement: **430,158** CapCity orders: **55,400** • **CGC:** 2 graded, best 9.6
📖 Folly's Gambit **A:** Jackson Guice **W:** Chris Claremont ★ Appearance of Juggernaut.

218 ❑ Jun 1987 Cover: 0.75 **NM** value: **3.00**
Circ: Statement: **430,158** CapCity orders: **52,700** • **CGC:** 2 graded, best 9.8
📖 Charge of the Light Brigade **A:** Marc Silvestri **W:** Chris Claremont ★ Versus Juggernaut.

219 ❑ Jul 1987 Cover: 0.75 **NM** value: **3.00**
Circ: Statement: **430,158** CapCity orders: **54,700** • **CGC:** 1 graded, best 9.4
📖 Where Duty Lies • Havok joins X-Men **A:** Bret Blevins **W:** Chris Claremont

220 ❑ Aug 1987 Cover: 0.75 **NM** value: **3.00**
Circ: Statement: **430,158** CapCity orders: **59,200** • **CGC:** 1 graded, best 9.6
📖 Unfinished Business **A:** Marc Silvestri **W:** Chris Claremont

221 ❑ Sep 1987 Cover: 0.75 **NM** value: **5.00**
Circ: Statement: **430,158** CapCity orders: **62,900** • **CGC:** 15 graded, best 9.8
📖 Death by Drowning **A:** Marc Silvestri **W:** Chris Claremont ★ 1st Appearance of Mister Sinister. ★ Versus Mr. Sinister.

222 ❑ Oct 1987 Cover: 0.75 **NM** value: **6.00**
Circ: Statement: **430,158** CapCity orders: **62,800** • **CGC:** 41 graded, best 9.8
📖 Heartbreak • Has 1986 Statement, filed 10/6/86; avg print run 630,020; avg sales 392,225; avg subs 24,900; avg total paid 417,350; samples 225; office use 2,681; max existent 420,031; 33% of run returned **A:** Marc Silvestri **W:** Chris Claremont ★ Appearance of Sabretooth. ★ Versus Sabretooth.

223 ❑ Nov 1987 Cover: 0.75 **NM** value: **3.00**
Circ: Statement: **430,158** CapCity orders: **64,000** • **CGC:** 1 graded, best 9.2
📖 Omens and Portents **A:** Kerry Gammill **W:** Chris Claremont

224 ❑ Dec 1987 Cover: 0.75 **NM** value: **3.00**
Circ: Statement: **430,158** CapCity orders: **62,400** • **CGC:** 2 graded, best 9.2
📖 The Dark Before the Dawn • registration card **A:** Marc Silvestri **W:** Chris Claremont

225 ❑ Jan 1988 Cover: 0.75 **NM** value: **5.00**
Circ: Statement: **432,745** CapCity orders: **69,200** • **CGC:** 6 graded, best 9.6
📖 False Dawn • Fall of Mutants **A:** Marc Silvestri **W:** Chris Claremont

226 ❑ Feb 1988 Cover: 1.25 **NM** value: **5.00**
Circ: Statement: **432,745** CapCity orders: **72,800** • **CGC:** 5 graded, best 9.4
• Double-size. 📖 Go Tell the Spartans • Fall of Mutants; Storm regains powers **A:** Marc Silvestri **W:** Chris Claremont

227 ❑ Mar 1988 Cover: 0.75 **NM** value: **5.00**
Circ: Statement: **432,745** CapCity orders: **81,300** • **CGC:** 9 graded, best 9.8
📖 The Belly of the Beast • Fall of Mutants **A:** Marc Silvestri **W:** Chris Claremont

228 ❑ Apr 1988 Cover: 0.75 **NM** value: **3.00**
Circ: Statement: **432,745** CapCity orders: **82,800** • **CGC:** 8 graded, best 9.8
📖 Deadly Games **A:** Rick Leonardi **W:** Chris Claremont

229 ❑ May 1988 Cover: 1.00 **NM** value: **3.00**
Circ: Statement: **432,745** CapCity orders: **71,800** • **CGC:** 5 graded, best 9.8
📖 Down Under • Has 1987 Statement; avg print run 645,041; avg sales 408,625; avg subs 21,533; avg total paid 430,158; samples 132; office use 4,234; max existent 434,524; 33% of run returned **A:** Marc Silvestri **W:** Chris Claremont ★ 1st Appearance of The Reavers.

230 ❑ Jun 1988 Cover: 1.00 **NM** value: **3.00**
Circ: Statement: **432,745** CapCity orders: **67,800** • **CGC:** 3 graded, best 9.6
📖 Twas the Night… **A:** Marc Silvestri **W:** Chris Claremont

231 ❑ Jul 1988 Cover: 1.00 **NM** value: **3.00**
Circ: Statement: **432,745** CapCity orders: **67,200**
📖 … Dressed For Dinner **A:** Rick Leonardi **W:** Chris Claremont

232 ❑ Aug 1988 Cover: 1.00 **NM** value: **3.00**
Circ: Statement: **432,745** CapCity orders: **66,600**
📖 Earthfall **A:** Rick Leonardi **W:** Chris Claremont

233 ❑ Sep 1988 Cover: 1.00 **NM** value: **3.00**
Circ: Statement: **432,745** CapCity orders: **63,400** • **CGC:** 2 graded, best 9.8
📖 Dawn of Blood **A:** Rick Leonardi **W:** Chris Claremont

234 ❑ Sep 1988 Cover: 1.00 **NM** value: **3.00**
Circ: Statement: **432,745** CapCity orders: **63,400** • **CGC:** 7 graded, best 9.6
📖 Glory Day **A:** Rick Leonardi **W:** Chris Claremont

235 ❑ Oct 1988 Cover: 1.00 **NM** value: **3.00**
Circ: Statement: **432,745** CapCity orders: **63,300**
📖 Welcome to Genosha **A:** Rick Leonardi **W:** Chris Claremont

236 ❑ Oct 1988 Cover: 1.00 **NM** value: **3.00**
Circ: Statement: **432,745** CapCity orders: **62,700**
📖 Busting Loose **A:** Marc Silvestri **W:** Chris Claremont

237 ❑ Nov 1988 Cover: 1.00 **NM** value: **3.00**
Circ: Statement: **432,745** CapCity orders: **60,300**
📖 Who's Human **A:** Rick Leonardi **W:** Chris Claremont

238 ❑ Nov 1988 Cover: 1.00 **NM** value: **3.00**
Circ: Statement: **432,745** CapCity orders: **60,500**
📖 Gonna Be a Revolution **A:** Marc Silvestri **W:** Chris Claremont

239 ❑ Dec 1988 Cover: 1.00 **NM** value: **3.00**
Circ: Statement: **432,745** CapCity orders: **70,300** • **CGC:** 1 graded, best 9.2
📖 Vanities • Inferno **A:** Marc Silvestri **W:** Chris Claremont

240 ❑ Jan 1989 Cover: 1.00 **NM** value: **3.00**
Circ: Statement: **408,925** CapCity orders: **68,900** • **CGC:** 2 graded, best 9.8
📖 Strike the Match • Inferno **A:** Marc Silvestri **W:** Chris Claremont ★ Appearance of Sabretooth.

241 ❑ Feb 1989 Cover: 1.00 **NM** value: **3.00**
Circ: Statement: **408,925** CapCity orders: **69,900** • **CGC:** 2 graded, best 9.6
📖 Fan the Flame • Inferno **A:** Marc Silvestri **W:** Chris Claremont

242 ❑ Mar 1989 Cover: 1.00 **NM** value: **3.00**
Circ: Statement: **408,925** CapCity orders: **76,100** • **CGC:** 2 graded, best 8.5
• Double-size. 📖 Burn! • Inferno **A:** Marc Silvestri **W:** Chris Claremont

243 ❑ Apr 1989 Cover: 1.00 **NM** value: **3.00**
Circ: Statement: **408,925** CapCity orders: **75,400** • **CGC:** 2 graded, best 9.4
📖 Ashes • Inferno **A:** Marc Silvestri **W:** Chris Claremont

244 ❑ May 1989 Cover: 1.00 **NM** value: **9.00**
Circ: Statement: **408,925** CapCity orders: **71,200** • **CGC:** 72 graded, best 9.9
📖 Ladies' Night **A:** Marc Silvestri **W:** Chris Claremont ★ 1st Appearance of Jubilee.

245 ❑ Jun 1989 Cover: 1.00 **NM** value: **3.00**
Circ: Statement: **408,925** CapCity orders: **74,400** • **CGC:** 10 graded, best 9.9
📖 Men! **A:** Rob Liefeld **W:** Chris Claremont

246 ❑ Jul 1989 Cover: 1.00 **NM** value: **3.00**
Circ: Statement: **408,925** CapCity orders: **72,800** • **CGC:** 1 graded, best 9.0
📖 The Day of Other Lights • Has 1988 Statement, filed 10/1/88; avg print run 633,760; avg sales 412,745; avg subs 20,000; avg total paid 432,745; samples 130; office use 860; max existent 433,735; 32% of run returned **A:** Marc Silvestri **W:** Chris Claremont

247 ❑ Aug 1989 Cover: 1.00 **NM** value: **3.00**
Circ: Statement: **408,925** CapCity orders: **79,500** • **CGC:** 1 graded, best 9.2
📖 The Light That Failed **A:** Marc Silvestri **W:** Chris Claremont

CGC-graded: Multiply prices above by **33 for 9.9 M** • **16 for 9.8 NM/M** • **7 for 9.6 NM+** • **5 for 9.4 NM** • **2.5 for 9.2 NM-** • **1.5 for 9.0 VF/NM**

248 ❑ Sep 1989 Cover: 1.00 **NM** value: **8.00**
Circ: Statement: **408,925** CapCity orders: **74,400** • **CGC:** 69 graded, best 9.8
The Cradle Will Fall • 1st Jim Lee art on X-Men **A:** Jim Lee **W:** Chris Claremont

248-2 ❑ 1989 Cover: 1.25 **NM** value: **1.50**

249 ❑ Oct 1989 Cover: 1.00 **NM** value: **3.00**
Circ: Statement: **408,925** CapCity orders: **74,700**
The Dane Curse **A:** Marc Silvestri **W:** Chris Claremont

250 ❑ Oct 1989 Cover: 1.00 **NM** value: **3.00**
Circ: Statement: **408,925** CapCity orders: **75,300** • **CGC:** 3 graded, best 9.8
The Shattered Star **A:** Marc Silvestri **W:** Chris Claremont

251 ❑ Nov 1989 Cover: 1.00 **NM** value: **3.00**
Circ: Statement: **408,925** CapCity orders: **77,100**
Fever Dream **A:** Marc Silvestri **W:** Chris Claremont

252 ❑ Nov 1989 Cover: 1.00 **NM** value: **2.50**
Circ: Statement: **408,925** CapCity orders: **77,700**
Where's Wolverine **A:** Rick Leonardi **W:** Chris Claremont

253 ❑ Nov 1989 Cover: 1.00 **NM** value: **2.50**
Circ: Statement: **408,925** CapCity orders: **78,600** • **CGC:** 2 graded, best 9.6
Storm Warnings **A:** Marc Silvestri **W:** Chris Claremont

254 ❑ Dec 1989 Cover: 1.00 **NM** value: **2.50**
Circ: Statement: **408,925** CapCity orders: **78,000**
All-New, All-Different-Here We Go Again **A:** Marc Silvestri **W:** Chris Claremont ★ Death of Sunder.

255 ❑ Dec 1989 Cover: 1.00 **NM** value: **2.50**
Circ: Statement: **408,925** CapCity orders: **80,100**
Crash and Burn **A:** Marc Silvestri **W:** Chris Claremont

256 ❑ Dec 1989 Cover: 1.00 **NM** value: **5.00**
Circ: Statement: **408,925** CapCity orders: **81,300** • **CGC:** 19 graded, best 9.8
The Key That Breaks the Locks • Acts of Vengeance **A:** Jim Lee **W:** Chris Claremont

257 ❑ Jan 1990 Cover: 1.00 **NM** value: **5.00**
Circ: Statement: **415,961** CapCity orders: **85,200** • **CGC:** 8 graded, best 9.6
I am Lady Mandarin • Acts of Vengeance **A:** Jim Lee **W:** Chris Claremont

258 ❑ Feb 1990 Cover: 1.00 **NM** value: **5.00**
Circ: Statement: **415,961** CapCity orders: **85,200** • **CGC:** 11 graded, best 9.8
Broken Chains • Acts of Vengeance **A:** Jim Lee **W:** Chris Claremont

259 ❑ Mar 1990 Cover: 1.00 **NM** value: **3.00**
Circ: Statement: **415,961** CapCity orders: **81,400**
Dream a Little Dream **A:** Marc Silvestri **W:** Chris Claremont

260 ❑ Apr 1990 Cover: 1.00 **NM** value: **3.00**
Circ: Statement: **415,961** CapCity orders: **77,500**
Star 90 **A:** Marc Silvestri; Jim Lee(cover) **W:** Chris Claremont

261 ❑ May 1990 Cover: 1.00 **NM** value: **2.50**
Circ: Statement: **415,961** CapCity orders: **77,800** • **CGC:** 1 graded, best 9.8
Harriers Hunt • Has 1989 Statement, filed 11/1/89; avg print run 592,965; avg sales 392,705; avg subs 16,220; avg total paid 408,925; samples 125; office use 600; max existent 409,650; 31% of run returned **A:** Marc Silvestri; Jim Lee(cover) **W:** Chris Claremont

262 ❑ Jun 1990 Cover: 1.00 **NM** value: **2.50**
Circ: Statement: **415,961** CapCity orders: **78,900**
Scary Monsters **A:** Kieron Dwyer **W:** Chris Claremont

263 ❑ Jul 1990 Cover: 1.00 **NM** value: **2.50**
Circ: Statement: **415,961** CapCity orders: **78,500**
The Lower Depths **A:** Bill Jaaska **W:** Chris Claremont

264 ❑ Jul 1990 Cover: 1.00 **NM** value: **2.50**
Circ: Statement: **415,961** CapCity orders: **77,500** • **CGC:** 1 graded, best 9.6
Hot Pursuit **A:** Mike Collins; Jim Lee(cover) **W:** Chris Claremont

265 ❑ Aug 1990 Cover: 1.00 **NM** value: **2.50**
Circ: Statement: **415,961** CapCity orders: **76,200**
Storm **A:** Bill Jaaska **W:** Chris Claremont

266 ❑ Aug 1990 Cover: 1.00 **NM** value: **25.00**
Circ: Statement: **415,961** CapCity orders: **75,500** • **CGC:** 294 graded, best 9.8
Gambit: Out of the Frying Pan **A:** Mike Collins **W:** Chris Claremont ★ 1st Appearance of Gambit (full appearance).

267 ❑ Sep 1990 Cover: 1.00 **NM** value: **10.00**
Circ: Statement: **415,961** CapCity orders: **73,900** • **CGC:** 20 graded, best 9.8
Nanny: Into the Fire • Captain America, Wolverine, Black Widow team-up **A:** Jim Lee **W:** Chris Claremont

268 ❑ Sep 1990 Cover: 1.00 **NM** value: **10.00**
Circ: Statement: **415,961** CapCity orders: **77,400** • **CGC:** 40 graded, best 9.9
Madripoor Knights **A:** Jim Lee **W:** Chris Claremont

269 ❑ Oct 1990 Cover: 1.00 **NM** value: **4.00**
Circ: Statement: **415,961** CapCity orders: **70,700** • **CGC:** 1 graded, best 9.4
Rogue Redux **A:** Jim Lee **W:** Chris Claremont

270 ❑ Nov 1990 Cover: 1.00 **NM** value: **6.00**
Circ: Statement: **415,961** CapCity orders: **84,800** • **CGC:** 11 graded, best 9.6
X-Tinction; X-Tinction Agenda, Part 1 **A:** Jim Lee **W:** Chris Claremont

270-2 ❑ Nov 1990 Cover: 1.00 **NM** value: **2.00**

271 ❑ Dec 1990 Cover: 1.00 **NM** value: **4.00**
Circ: Statement: **415,961** CapCity orders: **87,000** • **CGC:** 3 graded, best 9.4
X-Tinction; X-Tinction Agenda, Part 4 **A:** Jim Lee **W:** Chris Claremont

272 ❑ Jan 1991 Cover: 1.00 **NM** value: **4.00**
Circ: Statement: **460,625** CapCity orders: **93,100** • **CGC:** 5 graded, best 9.6
X-Tinction; X-Tinction Agenda, Part 7 **A:** Jim Lee **W:** Chris Claremont

273 ❑ Feb 1991 Cover: 1.00 **NM** value: **3.00**
Circ: Statement: **460,625** CapCity orders: **91,500** • **CGC:** 2 graded, best 9.6
Too Many Mutants **A:** Michael Golden; John Byrne; Whilce Portacio; Jim Lee **W:** Chris Claremont

274 ❑ Mar 1991 Cover: 1.00 **NM** value: **3.00**
Circ: Statement: **460,625** CapCity orders: **89,400** • **CGC:** 1 graded, best 9.2
Crossroads • Has 1990 Statement, filed 10/1/89; avg print run 602,581; avg sales 401,868; avg subs 14,093; avg total paid 415,961; samples 150; office use 600; max existent 416,711; 31% of run returned **A:** Jim Lee **W:** Chris Claremont ★ Appearance of Ka-Zar, Magneto, Nick Fury.

275 ❑ Apr 1991 Cover: 1.50 **NM** value: **4.00**
Circ: Statement: **460,625** CapCity orders: **93,200** • **CGC:** 7 graded, best 9.8
• Double-size. The Path Not Taken **A:** Jim Lee **W:** Chris Claremont

275-2 ❑ Apr 1991 Cover: 1.50 **NM** value: **2.00**

276 ❑ May 1991 Cover: 1.00 **NM** value: **2.50**
Circ: Statement: **460,625** CapCity orders: **92,400** • **CGC:** 2 graded, best 9.8
Double Death **A:** Jim Lee **W:** Chris Claremont

277 ❑ Jun 1991 Cover: 1.00 **NM** value: **2.50**
Circ: Statement: **460,625** CapCity orders: **97,800** • **CGC:** 1 graded, best 9.6
Free Charley **A:** Jim Lee **W:** Chris Claremont

278 ❑ Jul 1991 Cover: 1.00 **NM** value: **2.50**
Circ: Statement: **460,625** CapCity orders: **104,100**
The Battle of Muir Isle **A:** Paul Smith **W:** Chris Claremont

279 ❑ Aug 1991 Cover: 1.00 **NM** value: **2.50**
Circ: Statement: **460,625** CapCity orders: **141,000**
Bad to the Bone **A:** Andy Kubert **W:** Fabian Nicieza; Chris Claremont

280 ❑ Sep 1991 Cover: 1.00 **NM** value: **2.50**
Circ: Statement: **460,625** CapCity orders: **129,600** • **CGC:** 1 graded, best 9.6
One Step Back-Two Steps Forward • X-Factor crossover **A:** Andy Kubert **W:** Fabian Nicieza

281 ❑ Oct 1991 Cover: 1.00 **NM** value: **2.00**
Circ: Statement: **460,625** CapCity orders: **196,800** • **CGC:** 62 graded, best 10.0
wraparond cover. Fresh Upstart • new team **A:** Whilce Portacio **W:** John Byrne ★ 1st Appearance of Fitzroy.

281-2 ❑ Oct 1991 Cover: 1.00 **NM** value: **1.50**
wraparound cover. • 2nd printing (red); New team begins **A:** Whilce Portacio ★ 1st Appearance of Fitzroy.

282 ❑ Nov 1991 Cover: 1.00 **NM** value: **3.00**
Circ: Statement: **460,625** CapCity orders: **129,300** • **CGC:** 57 graded, best 9.8
Payback **A:** Whilce Portacio **W:** John Byrne ★ 1st Appearance of Bishop (cameo).

282-2 ❑ Nov 1991 Cover: 1.00 **NM** value: **1.25**

283 ❑ Dec 1991 Cover: 1.00 **NM** value: **4.00**
Circ: Statement: **460,625** CapCity orders: **144,600** • **CGC:** 69 graded, best 9.9
Bishop's Crossing **A:** Whilce Portacio **W:** John Byrne ★ 1st Appearance of Bishop (full).

284 ❑ Jan 1992 Cover: 1.00 **NM** value: **2.50**
Circ: Statement: **731,425** CapCity orders: **153,900** • **CGC:** 1 graded, best 9.8
Into the Void **A:** Whilce Portacio **W:** John Byrne

285 ❑ Feb 1992 Cover: 1.25 **NM** value: **2.50**
Circ: Statement: **731,425** CapCity orders: **142,500**
Down the Rabbit Hole **A:** Whilce Portacio **W:** John Byrne ★ 1st Appearance of Mikhail Rasputin.

286 ❑ Mar 1992 Cover: 1.25 **NM** value: **2.00**
Circ: Statement: **731,425** CapCity orders: **131,700**
Close Call • Has 1991 Statement, filed 10/1/91; avg print run 601,254; avg sales 447,617; avg subs 13,008; avg total paid 460,625; samples 250; office use 500; max existent 461,375; 23% of run returned **A:** Whilce Portacio **W:** Scott Lobdell

287 ❑ Apr 1992 Cover: 1.25 **NM** value: **2.50**
Circ: Statement: **731,425** CapCity orders: **124,500**
Bishop to King's Five **A:** John Romita Jr. **W:** Scott Lobdell ★ Origin of Bishop.

288 ❑ May 1992 Cover: 1.25 **NM** value: **2.00**
Circ: Statement: **731,425** CapCity orders: **126,600**

289 ❑ Jun 1992 Cover: 1.25 **NM** value: **2.00**
Circ: Statement: **731,425** CapCity orders: **124,500** • **CGC:** 2 graded, best 9.6
• Bishop joins X-Men

290 ❑ Jul 1992 Cover: 1.25 **NM** value: **2.00**
Circ: Statement: **731,425** CapCity orders: **127,200** • **CGC:** 2 graded, best 9.6

291 ❑ Aug 1992 Cover: 1.25 **NM** value: **2.00**
Circ: Statement: **731,425** CapCity orders: **128,200** • **CGC:** 1 graded, best 7.0

292 ❑ Sep 1992 Cover: 1.25 **NM** value: **2.00**
Circ: Statement: **731,425** CapCity orders: **118,500**

293 ❑ Oct 1992 Cover: 1.25 **NM** value: **2.00**
Circ: Statement: **731,425** CapCity orders: **113,700**

294/CS ❑ Nov 1992 Cover: 1.50 **NM** value: **2.00**
Circ: Statement: **731,425** CapCity orders: **183,000** • **CGC:** 2 graded, best 8.5
X-Cutioner's Song; X-Cutioner's Song, Part 1

295/CS ❑ Dec 1992 Cover: 1.50 **NM** value: **2.00**
Circ: Statement: **731,425** CapCity orders: **161,100**
X-Cutioner's Song; X-Cutioner's Song, Part 5

296/CS ❑ Jan 1993 Cover: 1.50 **NM** value: **2.00**
Circ: Statement: **714,675** CapCity orders: **169,500**
X-cutioner's Song, Part 9

297 ❑ Feb 1993 Cover: 1.25 **NM** value: **1.50**
Circ: Statement: **714,675** CapCity orders: **120,000**
X-Cutioner's Song aftermath

298 ❑ Mar 1993 Cover: 1.25 **NM** value: **1.50**
Circ: Statement: **714,675** CapCity orders: **114,600**

299 ❑ Apr 1993 Cover: 1.25 **NM** value: **1.50**
Circ: Statement: **714,675** CapCity orders: **123,000**

300 ❑ May 1993 Cover: 3.95 **NM** value: **5.00**
Circ: Statement: **714,675** CapCity orders: **205,400** • **CGC:** 24 graded, best 9.8
holo-foil cover. • Double-size.

301 ❑ Jun 1993 Cover: 1.25 **NM** value: **1.50**
Circ: Statement: **714,675** CapCity orders: **114,100**

302 ❑ Jul 1993 Cover: 1.25 **NM** value: **1.50**
Circ: Statement: **714,675** CapCity orders: **112,500**

303 ❑ Aug 1993 Cover: 1.25 **NM** value: **2.00**
Circ: Statement: **714,675** CapCity orders: **125,700**

304 ❑ Sep 1993 Cover: 3.95 **NM** value: **5.00**
Circ: Statement: **714,675** CapCity orders: **169,800** • **CGC:** 6 graded, best 9.8
• 30th Anniversary Issue. • hologram

305 ❑ Oct 1993 Cover: 1.25 **NM** value: **1.50**
Circ: Statement: **714,675** CapCity orders: **113,400**
The Measure of the Man **A:** Jan Duursema **W:** Scott Lobdell

306 ❑ Nov 1993 Cover: 1.25 **NM** value: **1.50**
Circ: Statement: **714,675** CapCity orders: **115,400**

307 ❑ Dec 1993 Cover: 1.25 **NM** value: **1.50**
Circ: Statement: **714,675** CapCity orders: **139,100**

308 ❑ Jan 1994 Cover: 1.25 **NM** value: **1.50**
Circ: Statement: **552,975** CapCity orders: **120,600**

309 ❑ Feb 1994 Cover: 1.25 **NM** value: **1.50**
Circ: Statement: **552,975** CapCity orders: **108,000**

310 ❑ Mar 1994 Cover: 1.95 **NM** value: **Cover or less**
Circ: Statement: **552,975** CapCity orders: **110,000**

311 ❑ Apr 1994 Cover: 1.25 **NM** value: **1.50**
Circ: Statement: **552,975** CapCity orders: **94,300** • **CGC:** 1 graded, best 9.2

312 ❑ May 1994 Cover: 1.50 **NM** value: **Cover or less**
Circ: Statement: **552,975** CapCity orders: **91,700**

313 ❑ Jun 1994 Cover: 1.50 **NM** value: **Cover or less**
Circ: Statement: **552,975** CapCity orders: **96,950**

314 ❑ Jul 1994 Cover: 1.50 **NM** value: **Cover or less**
Circ: Statement: **552,975** CapCity orders: **98,950**

315 ❑ Aug 1994 Cover: 1.50 **NM** value: **Cover or less**
Circ: Statement: **552,975** CapCity orders: **97,100**

316 ❑ Sep 1994 Cover: 1.50 **NM** value: **Cover or less**
Generation Next, Part 1

316/SC ❑ Sep 1994 Cover: 2.95 **NM** value: **3.00**
Circ: Statement: **552,975** CapCity orders: **113,550** • **CGC:** 5 graded, best 9.8
enhanced cover. Generation Next, Part 1

317 ❑ Oct 1994 Cover: 1.50 **NM** value: **Cover or less**
Generation Next, Part 3

317/SC ❑ Oct 1994 Cover: 2.95 **NM** value: **3.00**
Circ: Statement: **552,975** CapCity orders: **99,250** • **CGC:** 4 graded, best 10.0
enhanced cover. Generation Next, Part 3

318 ❑ Nov 1994 Cover: 1.50 **NM** value: **Cover or less**

318/Dlx ❑ Nov 1994 Cover: 1.95 **NM** value: **2.00**
Circ: Statement: **552,975** CapCity orders: **98,000**
• Deluxe edition.

319 ❑ Dec 1994 Cover: 1.50 **NM** value: **Cover or less**

319/Dlx ❑ Dec 1994 Cover: 1.95 **NM** value: **2.00**
Circ: Statement: **362,128** CapCity orders: **87,800**
• Deluxe edition.

320 ❑ Jan 1995 Cover: 1.50 **NM** value: **Cover or less**
Legion Quest, Part 1 **A:** Roger Cruz **W:** Scott Lobdell; Mark Waid

320/Dlx ❑ Jan 1995 Cover: 1.95 **NM** value: **2.00**
Circ: Statement: **362,128** CapCity orders: **83,225** • **CGC:** 5 graded, best 9.4
• Deluxe edition. Legion Quest, Part 1 **A:** Roger Cruz **W:** Scott Lobdell; Mark Waid

320/GO ❑ Jan 1995 **NM** value: **2.00**
no cover price. • Wizard edition. • gold logo

321 ❑ Feb 1995 Cover: 1.50 **NM** value: **Cover or less**
Legion Quest, Part 3 **W:** Scott Lobdell

321/Dlx ❑ Feb 1995 Cover: 1.95 **NM** value: **2.00**
Circ: Statement: **362,128** CapCity orders: **93,625**
• Deluxe edition. **W:** Scott Lobdell

322 ❑ Jul 1995 Cover: 1.95 **NM** value: **2.00**
Circ: CapCity orders: **86,400** • **CGC:** 1 graded, best 9.4

323 ❑ Aug 1995 Cover: 1.95 **NM** value: **2.00**
Circ: Statement: **362,128** CapCity orders: **88,075**

324 ❑ Sep 1995 Cover: 1.95 **NM** value: **2.00**
Circ: Statement: **362,128**

325 ❑ Oct 1995 Cover: 3.95 **NM** value: **4.00**
Circ: Statement: **362,128** • **CGC:** 5 graded, best 9.8
enhanced gatefold cardstock cover. **W:** Scott Lobdell

326 ❑ Nov 1995 Cover: 1.95 **NM** value: **2.00**
Circ: Statement: **455,570**

327 ❑ Dec 1995 Cover: 1.95 **NM** value: **2.00**
Circ: Statement: **455,570**
The Fate of Magneto Is Revealed **A:** Joe Madureira **W:** Scott Lobdell ★ Appearance of Magneto.

328 ❑ Jan 1996 Cover: 1.95 **NM** value: **2.00**
Circ: Statement: **455,570**
• Psylocke vs. Sabretooth **W:** Scott Lobdell

329 ❑ Feb 1996 Cover: 1.95 **NM** value: **2.00**
Circ: Statement: **455,570**

330 ❑ Mar 1996 Cover: 1.95 **NM** value: **2.00**
Circ: Statement: **455,570**
Quest for the Crimson Dawn **A:** Joe Madureira **W:** Jeph Loeb

331 ❑ Apr 1996 Cover: 1.95 **NM** value: **2.00**
Circ: Statement: **455,570**
The Splinter of our Discontent • Iceman vs. White Queen **A:** Bryan Hitch **W:** Scott Lobdell

332 ❑ May 1996 Cover: 1.95 **NM** value: **2.00**
Circ: Statement: **455,570**

333 ❑ Jun 1996 Cover: 1.95 **NM** value: **2.00**
Circ: Statement: **455,570**

334 ❑ Jul 1996 Cover: 1.95 **NM** value: **2.00**
Circ: Statement: **455,570**

335 ❑ Aug 1996 Cover: 1.95 **NM** value: **2.00**
Circ: Statement: **455,570**
Onslaught: Phase 1 **W:** Scott Lobdell ★ Appearance of Uatu, Apocalypse.

336 ❑ Sep 1996 Cover: 1.95 **NM** value: **2.00**
Circ: Statement: **455,570**
Onslaught: Phase 2 **W:** Scott Lobdell

Other grades: Multiply prices above by **1.5 for Mint • 2/3 for Very Fine • 1/3 for Fine • 1/5 for Very Good • 1/8 for Good**

337 ❑ Oct 1996 Cover: 1.95 **NM** value: **2.00**
Circ: Statement: **300,732**
338 ❑ Nov 1996 Cover: 1.95 **NM** value: **2.00**
Circ: Statement: **300,732** Direct Market orders: **203,750**
• Angel regains his wings **W:** Scott Lobdell
339 ❑ Dec 1996 Cover: 1.95 **NM** value: **2.00**
Circ: Statement: **300,732** Direct Market orders: **200,250**
• Cyclops vs. Havok **W:** Scott Lobdell ★ Appearance of Spider-Man.
340 ❑ Jan 1997 Cover: 1.95 **NM** value: **2.00**
Circ: Statement: **300,732** Direct Market orders: **198,500**
• Has 1996 Statement, filed 10/1/96; avg print run 550,044; avg sales 441,788; avg subs 13,782; avg total paid 455,570; samples 600; office use 125; max existent 456,295; 17% of run returned **W:** Scott Lobdell
341 ❑ Feb 1997 Cover: 1.95 **NM** value: **2.00**
Circ: Statement: **300,732** Direct Market orders: **191,000**
📖 When Strikes a Gladiator! • Cannonball vs. Gladiator **A:** Joe Madureira **W:** Scott Lobdell
342 ❑ Mar 1997 Cover: 1.95 **NM** value: **2.00**
Circ: Statement: **300,732** Direct Market orders: **185,250** • **CGC:** 12 graded, best 9.8
342/A❑ Mar 1997 Cover: 1.95 **NM** value: **12.00**
Variant cover (Rogue). **A:** Joe Madureira **W:** Scott Lobdell
343 ❑ Apr 1997 Cover: 1.95 **NM** value: **2.00**
Circ: Statement: **300,732** Direct Market orders: **171,500**
📖 Where No X-Man Has Gone Before! **A:** Joe Madureira **W:** Scott Lobdell
344 ❑ May 1997 Cover: 1.95 **NM** value: **2.00**
Circ: Statement: **300,732** Diamd. preorders: **175,306**
📖 Casualties of War **A:** Mel Rubi **W:** Scott Lobdell
345 ❑ Jun 1997 Cover: 1.99 **NM** value: **2.00**
Circ: Statement: **300,732** Diamd. preorders: **179,378** • **CGC:** 1 graded, best 9.8
📖 Moving On **A:** Mel Rubi; Joe Madureira **W:** Scott Lobdell; Ben Raab
346 ❑ Aug 1997 Cover: 1.99 **NM** value: **2.00**
Circ: Statement: **300,732** Diamd. preorders: **173,452**
• gatefold summary. 📖 Operation Zero Tolerance ★ Appearance of Spider-Man.
347 ❑ Sep 1997 Cover: 1.99 **NM** value: **2.00**
Circ: Statement: **300,732** Diamd. preorders: **165,832**
• gatefold summary.
348 ❑ Oct 1997 Cover: 1.99 **NM** value: **2.00**
Circ: Diamd. preorders: **163,028**
• gatefold summary.
349 ❑ Nov 1997 Cover: 1.99 **NM** value: **2.00**
Circ: Diamd. preorders: **163,169**
• gatefold summary. ★ Versus Maggot.
350 ❑ Dec 1997 Cover: 1.99 **NM** value: **Cover or less**
• **CGC:** 2 graded, best 9.6
• gatefold summary. • Has 1997 Statement; avg total paid 300,732
350/SC❑ Dec 1997 Cover: 2.99 **NM** value: **Cover or less**
Circ: Diamd. preorders: **171,452** • **CGC:** 15 graded, best 9.8
enhanced cover. • gatefold summary.
351 ❑ Jan 1998 Cover: 1.99 **NM** value: **Cover or less**
Circ: Diamd. preorders: **159,777**
• gatefold summary. • Cecilia joins team ★ Versus Pyro.
352 ❑ Feb 1998 Cover: 1.99 **NM** value: **Cover or less**
Circ: Diamd. preorders: **156,518**
• gatefold summary.
353 ❑ Mar 1998 Cover: 1.99 **NM** value: **Cover or less**
Circ: Diamd. preorders: **154,417** • **CGC:** 1 graded, best 9.6
• gatefold summary. • Rogue vs. Wolverine
354 ❑ Apr 1998 Cover: 1.99 **NM** value: **Cover or less**
Circ: Diamd. preorders: **142,449** • **CGC:** 3 graded, best 9.8
• gatefold summary. ★ Versus Sauron.
355 ❑ May 1998 Cover: 1.99 **NM** value: **Cover or less**
Circ: Diamd. preorders: **143,526**
• gatefold summary. ★ Appearance of Alpha Flight.
356 ❑ Jun 1998 Cover: 1.99 **NM** value: **Cover or less**
Circ: Diamd. preorders: **149,540**
• gatefold summary.
357 ❑ Jul 1998 Cover: 1.99 **NM** value: **Cover or less**
Circ: Diamd. preorders: **142,958**
• gatefold summary.
358 ❑ Aug 1998 Cover: 1.99 **NM** value: **Cover or less**
Circ: Diamd. preorders: **143,672**
• gatefold summary.
359 ❑ Sep 1998 Cover: 1.99 **NM** value: **Cover or less**
Circ: Diamd. preorders: **137,543** • **CGC:** 1 graded, best 9.8
• gatefold summary.
360 ❑ Oct 1998 Cover: 2.99 **NM** value: **Cover or less**
Circ: Statement: **207,381** Diamd. preorders: **29,906** • **CGC:** 2 graded, best 9.6
• double-sized. • Kitty Pryde, Colossus, Nightcrawler rejoin team
360/SC❑ Oct 1998 Cover: 3.99 **NM** value: **Cover or less**
Circ: Diamd. preorders: **142,528** • **CGC:** 2 graded, best 9.8
Special cover. • Kitty Pryde, Colossus, Nightcrawler rejoin team
361 ❑ Nov 1998 Cover: 1.99 **NM** value: **Cover or less**
Circ: Statement: **207,381** Diamd. preorders: **138,138**
• gatefold summary. • Return of Gambit
362 ❑ Dec 1998 Cover: 1.99 **NM** value: **Cover or less**
Circ: Statement: **207,381** Diamd. preorders: **138,548**
• gatefold summary. 📖 The Hunt for Xavier, Part 1
363 ❑ Jan 1999 Cover: 1.99 **NM** value: **Cover or less**
Circ: Statement: **207,381** Diamd. preorders: **136,591**
• gatefold summary. 📖 The Hunt for Xavier, Part 3
364 ❑ Jan 1999 Cover: 1.99 **NM** value: **Cover or less**
Circ: Statement: **207,381** Diamd. preorders: **136,043** • **CGC:** 2 graded, best 9.6
• gatefold summary. 📖 The Hunt for Xavier, Part 5
365 ❑ Mar 1999 Cover: 1.99 **NM** value: **Cover or less**
Circ: Statement: **207,381** Diamd. preorders: **134,676**
cover says Feb, indicia says Mar. • gatefold summary. **A:** Chris Bachalo **W:** Steven Seagle
366 ❑ Apr 1999 Cover: 1.99 **NM** value: **Cover or less**
Circ: Statement: **207,381** Diamd. preorders: **139,010**
367 ❑ Apr 1999 Cover: 1.99 **NM** value: **Cover or less**
Circ: Statement: **207,381** Diamd. preorders: **130,872**
368 ❑ Jun 1999 Cover: 1.99 **NM** value: **Cover or less**
Circ: Statement: **207,381** Diamd. preorders: **131,418**
cover says May, indicia says Jun. • Wolverine vs. Magneto
369 ❑ Jun 1999 Cover: 1.99 **NM** value: **Cover or less**
Circ: Statement: **207,381** Diamd. preorders: **129,900**
370 ❑ Jul 1999 Cover: 1.99 **NM** value: **Cover or less**
Circ: Statement: **207,381** Diamd. preorders: **127,164**
371 ❑ Aug 1999 Cover: 1.99 **NM** value: **Cover or less**
Circ: Statement: **207,381** Diamd. preorders: **125,608**
372 ❑ Sep 1999 Cover: 1.99 **NM** value: **Cover or less**
Circ: Statement: **207,381** Diamd. preorders: **123,144**
373 ❑ Oct 1999 Cover: 1.99 **NM** value: **Cover or less**
Circ: Diamd. preorders: **116,274**
374 ❑ Nov 1999 Cover: 1.99 **NM** value: **Cover or less**
Circ: Diamd. preorders: **110,736**
375 ❑ Dec 1999 Cover: 2.99 **NM** value: **Cover or less**
Circ: Diamd. preorders: **114,868** • **CGC:** 1 graded, best 9.8
• Giant-size. 📖 I am Not Now, Nor Have I Ever Been… **A:** Adam Kubert **W:** Alan Davis; Adam Kubert
376 ❑ Jan 2000 Cover: 1.99 **NM** value: **Cover or less**
Circ: Diamd. preorders: **110,179** • **CGC:** 3 graded, best 9.8
377 ❑ Feb 2000 Cover: 1.99 **NM** value: **Cover or less**
Circ: Diamd. preorders: **111,649** • **CGC:** 1 graded, best 9.4
378 ❑ Mar 2000 Cover: 1.99 **NM** value: **Cover or less**
Circ: Diamd. preorders: **113,703**
379 ❑ Apr 2000 Cover: 1.99 **NM** value: **Cover or less**
Circ: Diamd. preorders: **108,443**
380 ❑ May 2000 Cover: 1.99 **NM** value: **Cover or less**
Circ: Diamd. preorders: **115,158**
381 ❑ Jun 2000 Cover: 1.99 **NM** value: **Cover or less**
Circ: Diamd. preorders: **119,318** • **CGC:** 2 graded, best 9.6
382 ❑ Jul 2000 Cover: 2.25 **NM** value: **Cover or less**
Circ: Diamd. preorders: **114,855**
383 ❑ Aug 2000 Cover: 2.99 **NM** value: **Cover or less**
Circ: Diamd. preorders: **120,671**
• Giant-size. 📖 Moscow Knights **A:** Adam Kubert **W:** Chris Claremont
384 ❑ Sep 2000 Cover: 2.25 **NM** value: **Cover or less**
Circ: Statement: **159,404** Diamd. preorders: **116,651**
385 ❑ Oct 2000 Cover: 2.25 **NM** value: **Cover or less**
Circ: Statement: **159,404** Diamd. preorders: **109,829** • **CGC:** 8 graded, best 9.8
386 ❑ Nov 2000 Cover: 2.25 **NM** value: **Cover or less**
Circ: Statement: **159,404** Diamd. preorders: **111,872**
387 ❑ Dec 2000 Cover: 2.25 **NM** value: **Cover or less**
Circ: Statement: **159,404** Diamd. preorders: **113,695**
📖 Maximum Security; Cry Justice, Cry Vengeance! **A:** Salvador Larroca **W:** Chris Claremont
388 ❑ Jan 2001 Cover: 2.25 **NM** value: **Cover or less**
Circ: Statement: **159,404** Diamd. preorders: **110,873**
389 ❑ Feb 2001 Cover: 2.25 **NM** value: **Cover or less**
Circ: Statement: **159,404** Diamd. preorders: **106,514**
📖 The Good Shepherd **A:** Salvador Larroca **W:** Chris Claremont
390 ❑ Feb 2001 Cover: 2.25 **NM** value: **Cover or less**
Circ: Statement: **159,404** Diamd. preorders: **98,436** • **CGC:** 48 graded, best 9.8
📖 The Cure **A:** Salvador Larroca **W:** Scott Lobdell ★ Death of Colossus.
391 ❑ Mar 2001 Cover: 2.25 **NM** value: **Cover or less**
Circ: Statement: **159,404** Diamd. preorders: **102,427** • **CGC:** 1 graded, best 9.6
📖 Dad **A:** Salvador Larroca **W:** Scott Lobdell
392 ❑ Apr 2001 Cover: 2.25 **NM** value: **Cover or less**
Circ: Statement: **159,404** Diamd. preorders: **103,407**
📖 Eve of Destruction, Part 1 **A:** Salvador Larroca **W:** Scott Lobdell
393 ❑ May 2001 Cover: 2.25 **NM** value: **Cover or less**
Circ: Statement: **159,404** Diamd. preorders: **105,890**
394 ❑ Jun 2001 Cover: 2.25 **NM** value: **Cover or less**
Circ: Statement: **159,404** Diamd. preorders: **136,081** • **CGC:** 55 graded, best 9.8
395 ❑ Jul 2001 Cover: 2.25 **NM** value: **Cover or less**
Circ: Statement: **159,404** Diamd. preorders: **139,358** • **CGC:** 2 graded, best 9.8
396 ❑ Aug 2001 Cover: 2.25 **NM** value: **Cover or less**
Circ: Statement: **159,404** Diamd. preorders: **132,704** • **CGC:** 1 graded, best 9.4
397 ❑ Sep 2001 Cover: 2.25 **NM** value: **Cover or less**
Circ: Statement: **159,404** Diamd. preorders: **132,180** • **CGC:** 1 graded, best 9.6
398 ❑ Oct 2001 Cover: 2.25 **NM** value: **Cover or less**
Circ: Diamd. preorders: **121,425** • **CGC:** 2 graded, best 9.9
399 ❑ Nov 2001 Cover: 2.25 **NM** value: **Cover or less**
Circ: Diamd. preorders: **118,197** • **CGC:** 2 graded, best 9.8
400 ❑ Dec 2001 Cover: 3.50 **NM** value: **Cover or less**
Circ: Diamd. preorders: **134,206**
401 ❑ Jan 2002 Cover: 2.25 **NM** value: **Cover or less**
Circ: Diamd. preorders: **113,545**
• Has 2001 Statement, filed 10/1/01; avg print run 223,017; avg sales 148,399; avg subs 11,005; avg total paid 159,404; samples 600; max existent 160,004; 28% of run returned
402 ❑ Feb 2002 Cover: 2.25 **NM** value: **Cover or less**
Circ: Diamd. preorders: **108,567**
Anl 1❑ Dec 1970 Cover: 0.25 **NM** value: **60.00**
• **CGC:** 32 graded, best 9.8
listed as X-Men in indicia, X-Men Special on cover. • Cover reads "King Size Special". 📖 Enter the Avengers!; The Triumph of Magneto • reprints X-Men #9 and 11
Anl 2❑ Nov 1971 Cover: 0.12 **NM** value: **45.00**
• **CGC:** 10 graded, best 9.6
• Cover reads "King Size Special". 📖 Divided – We Fall; To Save a City • reprints X-Men #22 and 23 **C:** Gil Kane
Anl 3❑ Jan 1980 Cover: 0.75 **NM** value: **20.00**
• **CGC:** 28 graded, best 9.8
📖 A Fire in the Sky; A Rogue in the House; Land of Shadow – Dawn of Death **A:** George Pérez; Frank Miller; Terry Austin; Frank Miller(cover) ★ 1st Appearance of Arkon.
Anl 4❑ Nov 1980 Cover: 0.75 **NM** value: **9.00**
• **CGC:** 6 graded, best 9.6
📖 Nightcrawler's Inferno; Abandon Every Hope, Ye Who Enter • series continues as Uncanny X-Men Annual **A:** John Romita Jr. ★ Appearance of Doctor Strange.
Anl 5❑ Nov 1981 Cover: 0.75 **NM** value: **7.00**
• **CGC:** 2 graded, best 9.6
📖 Ou, La La-Badoon; The Sundered Realm; And Now Armageddon; The Passing of the Dream **A:** Brent Anderson; Bob McLeod **W:** Chris Claremont ★ Appearance of Fantastic Four.
Anl 6❑ Nov 1982 Cover: 1.00 **NM** value: **7.00**
• **CGC:** 4 graded, best 9.4
📖 Blood Feud **A:** Bill Sienkiewicz **W:** Chris Claremont ★ Appearance of Dracula. ★ Death of Rachel Van Helsing.
Anl 7❑ ca. 1983 Cover: 1.00 **NM** value: **5.00**
• **CGC:** 3 graded, best 9.4
📖 Scavenger Hunt **A:** Michael Golden; Bret Blevins **W:** Chris Claremont
Anl 8❑ ca. 1984 Cover: 1.00 **NM** value: **5.00**
• **CGC:** 6 graded, best 9.8
📖 The Adventures of Lockheed the Space Dragon and his Pet Girl, Kitty **A:** Steve Leialoha **W:** Chris Claremont
Anl 9❑ ca. 1985 Cover: 1.25 **NM** value: **12.00**
Circ: CapCity orders: **43,300** • **CGC:** 5 graded, best 9.8
📖 There's No Place Like Home **A:** Arthur Adams; Arthur Adams(cover) **C:** Arthur Adams **W:** Chris Claremont
Anl 10❑ Jan 1986 Cover: 1.25 **NM** value: **10.00**
Circ: CapCity orders: **54,700** • **CGC:** 1 graded, best 9.2
📖 Performance **A:** Arthur Adams **C:** Arthur Adams **W:** Chris Claremont ★ 1st Appearance of Longshot, X-babies.
Anl 11❑ ca. 1987 Cover: 1.25 **NM** value: **4.00**
Circ: CapCity orders: **61,900** • **CGC:** 1 graded, best 9.6
📖 Lost in the Funhouse **A:** Alan Davis **W:** Chris Claremont
Anl 12❑ ca. 1988 Cover: 1.75 **NM** value: **4.00**
Circ: CapCity orders: **68,300** • **CGC:** 3 graded, best 9.6
📖 Resurrection **A:** Arthur Adams **C:** Arthur Adams **W:** Chris Claremont
Anl 13❑ ca. 1989 Cover: 2.00 **NM** value: **3.00**
Circ: CapCity orders: **84,200**
📖 Double Cross • Atlantis Attacks **A:** Mike Vosburg **W:** Terry Austin
Anl 14❑ ca. 1990 Cover: 2.00 **NM** value: **12.00**
Circ: CapCity orders: **76,200** • **CGC:** 41 graded, best 9.9
📖 Future Present; You Must Remember This **A:** Arthur Adams **W:** Chris Claremont ★ 1st Appearance of Gambit (cameo).
Anl 15❑ ca. 1991 Cover: 2.00 **NM** value: **4.00**
Circ: CapCity orders: **104,000**
📖 Kings of Pain; Kings of Pain, Part 3 **A:** Tom Raney **W:** Fabian Nicieza
Anl 16❑ ca. 1992 Cover: 2.25 **NM** value: **Cover or less**
Circ: CapCity orders: **96,000**
📖 Shattershot, Part 2 • Shattershot
Anl 17❑ ca. 1993 Cover: 2.95 **NM** value: **Cover or less**
Circ: CapCity orders: **100,000**
• trading card
Anl 18❑ ca. 1994 Cover: 2.95 **NM** value: **Cover or less**
Circ: CapCity orders: **58,950**
Anl 1995❑ Nov 1995 Cover: 3.95 **NM** value: **Cover or less**
wraparound cover.
Anl 1996❑ ca. 1996 Cover: 2.99 **NM** value: **Cover or less**
wraparound cover.
Anl 1997❑ Oct 1997 Cover: 2.99 **NM** value: **Cover or less**
Circ: Diamd. preorders: **109,168**
wraparound cover.
Anl 1998❑ ca. 1998 Cover: 2.99 **NM** value: **Cover or less**
wraparound cover. • Uncanny X-Men/Fantastic Four '98
Anl 2000❑ Feb 2001 Cover: 3.50 **NM** value: **Cover or less**
Circ: Diamd. preorders: **66,209**
📖 Share **A:** Essad Ribic **W:** Scott Lobdell; Fiona Avery
Bk 1❑ Jul 1984 Cover: 12.95 **NM** value: **Cover or less**
• The Uncanny X-Men Masterworks; X-Men in the Savage Land **A:** Michael Golden **W:** Chris Claremont
Bk 1/HC❑ Cover: 3.95 **NM** value: **Cover or less**
hardcover.
Bk 2❑ Dec 1989 Cover: 3.95 **NM** value: **Cover or less**
📖 Days Of Future Past; From the Ashes • Reprints issues #168-176; Rogue joins X-Men **A:** John Byrne; Paul Smith; John Romita Jr.; Walt Simonson; Terry Austin **W:** Chris Claremont ★ Origin of Silver Samurai. ★ 1st Appearance of Madelyne Pryor, Valerie Cooper, Sunder.
Bk 3❑ Cover: 2.95 **NM** value: **3.50**
• Tor mass-market paperback
GS 1❑ Sum 1975 Cover: 0.50 **NM** value: **600.00**
📖 Second Genesis; And When There Was One; Assault Force; Krakoa… The Island That Walks Like a Man; Call Him Cyclops; I, the Iceman; The Female of the Species • Reprints backup stories from X-Men (1st series) #43, 47 and 57 ★ Origin of Storm, Nightcrawler. ★ 1st Appearance of X-Men (new), Thunderbird, Colossus, Storm, Nightcrawler, Illyana Rasputin.
GS 2❑ Nov 1975 Cover: 0.50 **NM** value: **75.00**
📖 The Sentinels Live; Mission: Murder; Do or Die, Baby • Reprints stories from X-Men (1st series) #57-59

UNCANNY X-MEN IN DAYS OF FUTURE PAST, THE

Marvel

1 ❑ Cover: 3.95 **NM** value: **Cover or less**
📖 Days of Future Past; Mind Out of Time • Reprints Uncanny X-Men #141, 142 **A:** John Byrne **W:** Chris Claremont

UNCENSORED MOUSE, THE — Eternity

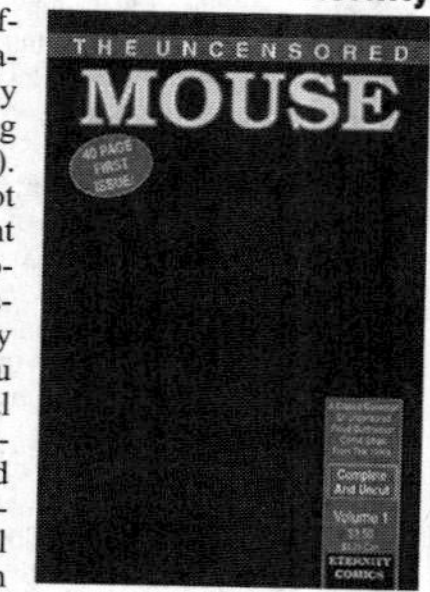

There were no subscriptions offered to this twice-a-month publication that offered reprints of the daily Mickey Mouse comic strip, starting with the first one (Jan. 13, 1930). Since the strips themselves had not been registered with the Copyright Office and Eternity provided the notation, "Mickey Mouse is a registered trademark of Walt Disney Productions," Eternity (a Malibu imprint) hoped there'd be no legal difficulties in the project. Moreover, the strips were accompanied by a wealth of Mickey Mouse historical material provided by Bill Blackbeard, who also provided an article. Fair use arguments did not keep the Disney company from taking action, among its arguments being that much early strip content was based on animated Mickey Mouse material which was in copyright. The April 20, 1989, Entertainment Tonight TV show featured the controversy. Though Eternity solicited issues through #8 (July 1989), the title was quickly pulled — ironically, despite the covers crediting Gottfredson, before it could get to strips Gottfredson drew. (There is Gottfredson work in each but not in the reprinted strips.) — Maggie

1 ❑ Apr 1989, b&w Cover: 2.50 **NM** value: **Cover or less**
• Mickey Mouse **A:** Floyd Gottfredson **W:** Floyd Gottfredson
2 ❑ Apr 1989 Cover: 2.50 **NM** value: **Cover or less**
• Mickey Mouse **A:** Floyd Gottfredson **W:** Floyd Gottfredson

UNCLE CHARLIE'S FABLES — Lev Gleason

1 ❑ Jan 1952 Cover: 0.10 **NM** value: **50.00**
📖 This is a King **W:** Charles Biro
2 ❑ Mar 1952 Cover: 0.10 **NM** value: **30.00**
3 ❑ May 1952 Cover: 0.10 **NM** value: **24.00**
4 ❑ Jul 1952 Cover: 0.10 **NM** value: **24.00**
Painted cover. 📖 Peer Pester the Sad Jester; Priscilla's Patience; A King's Second Chance; A Big Day for Squirrels (text story); Grey Steele **A:** Bob Fujitani; Charles Biro; Dick Rockwell; Hi Makin **W:** Charles Biro
5 ❑ Sep 1952 Cover: 0.10 **NM** value: **24.00**

UNCLE JOE'S COMMIE BOOK FEATURING CUTEY BUNNY — Rip Off

1 ❑ 1995b&w Cover: 2.95 **NM** value: **Cover or less**

UNCLE JOE'S FUNNIES — Centaur

1 ❑ ca. 1938 Cover: 0.10 **NM** value: **250.00**
• **CGC:** 1 graded, best 4.5

UNCLE SAM — DC / Vertigo

1 ❑ ca. 1997 Cover: 4.95 **NM** value: **5.00**
Circ: Diamd. preorders: **70,350** • **CGC:** 3 graded, best 9.8
• prestige format. **A:** Alex Ross
2 ❑ ca. 1997 Cover: 4.95 **NM** value: **5.00**
Circ: Diamd. preorders: **60,996**
• prestige format. **A:** Alex Ross

UNCLE SAM QUARTERLY — Quality

1 ❑ Aut 1941 Cover: 0.10 **NM** value: **750.00**
• **CGC:** 2 graded, best 8.5
2 ❑ Win 1941 Cover: 0.10 **NM** value: **500.00**
3 ❑ Sum 1942 Cover: 0.10 **NM** value: **500.00**
4 ❑ Aut 1942 Cover: 0.10 **NM** value: **500.00**
5 ❑ Win 1942 Cover: 0.10 **NM** value: **500.00**
• **CGC:** 2 graded, best 9.0
6 ❑ Spr 1943 Cover: 0.10 **NM** value: **500.00**
• **CGC:** 2 graded, best 8.5
7 ❑ Sum 1943 Cover: 0.10 **NM** value: **500.00**
• **CGC:** 3 graded, best 8.5
8 ❑ Aut 1943 Cover: 0.10 **NM** value: **500.00**
• **CGC:** 1 graded, best 8.0

UNCLE SCROOGE ADVENTURES — Gladstone

1 ❑ Nov 1987 Cover: 0.95 **NM** value: **5.00**
2 ❑ Dec 1987 Cover: 0.95 **NM** value: **3.00**
3 ❑ Jan 1988 Cover: 0.95 **NM** value: **2.00**
Circ: Statement: **73,028**
4 ❑ Apr 1988 Cover: 0.95 **NM** value: **2.00**
Circ: Statement: **73,028**
5 ❑ Jun 1988 Cover: 0.95 **NM** value: **6.00**
Circ: Statement: **73,028** CapCity orders: **6,125** • **CGC:** 1 graded, best 9.4
6 ❑ Aug 1988 Cover: 0.95 **NM** value: **2.00**
Circ: Statement: **73,028** CapCity orders: **6,000**
7 ❑ Sep 1988 Cover: 0.95 **NM** value: **2.00**
Circ: Statement: **73,028** CapCity orders: **5,900**
8 ❑ Oct 1988 Cover: 0.95 **NM** value: **2.00**
Circ: Statement: **73,028** CapCity orders: **6,450**
9 ❑ Nov 1988 Cover: 0.95 **NM** value: **5.00**
Circ: Statement: **73,028** CapCity orders: **6,100**
10 ❑ Dec 1988 Cover: 0.95 **NM** value: **2.00**
Circ: Statement: **73,028** CapCity orders: **6,150**
11 ❑ Jan 1989 Cover: 0.95 **NM** value: **2.00**
Circ: Statement: **67,321** CapCity orders: **6,050**
12 ❑ Mar 1989 Cover: 0.95 **NM** value: **2.00**
Circ: Statement: **67,321** CapCity orders: **6,300**
13 ❑ Jun 1989 Cover: 0.95 **NM** value: **2.00**
Circ: Statement: **67,321** CapCity orders: **6,500**
14 ❑ Aug 1989 Cover: 0.95 **NM** value: **5.00**
Circ: Statement: **67,321** CapCity orders: **7,800**
15 ❑ Sep 1989 Cover: 0.95 **NM** value: **2.00**
Circ: Statement: **67,321** CapCity orders: **6,700**
16 ❑ Oct 1989 Cover: 0.95 **NM** value: **2.00**
Circ: Statement: **67,321** CapCity orders: **6,750**
17 ❑ Nov 1989 Cover: 0.95 **NM** value: **2.00**
Circ: Statement: **67,321** CapCity orders: **6,800**
18 ❑ Dec 1989 Cover: 0.95 **NM** value: **2.00**
Circ: Statement: **67,321**
19 ❑ Jan 1990 Cover: 0.95 **NM** value: **2.00**
Circ: CapCity orders: **6,900**
20 ❑ Mar 1990 Cover: 1.95 **NM** value: **5.00**
Circ: CapCity orders: **6,350**
• double-sized. **A:** Carl Barks; Don Rosa
21 ❑ May 1990 Cover: 1.95 **NM** value: **5.00**
Circ: CapCity orders: **6,550**
• double-sized. **A:** Carl Barks; Don Rosa
22 ❑ Sep 1993 Cover: 1.50 **NM** value: **Cover or less**
Circ: CapCity orders: **5,425**
23 ❑ Nov 1993 Cover: 2.95 **NM** value: **Cover or less**
Circ: CapCity orders: **5,000**
24 ❑ Jan 1994 Cover: 1.50 **NM** value: **Cover or less**
Circ: CapCity orders: **5,150**
25 ❑ Mar 1994 Cover: 1.50 **NM** value: **Cover or less**
Circ: CapCity orders: **4,825**
26 ❑ May 1994 Cover: 2.95 **NM** value: **Cover or less**
Circ: CapCity orders: **4,600**
📖 Back to the Klondike **A:** Carl Barks
27 ❑ Jul 1994 Cover: 1.50 **NM** value: **Cover or less**
Circ: CapCity orders: **5,150**
28 ❑ Sep 1994 Cover: 2.95 **NM** value: **Cover or less**
Circ: CapCity orders: **4,875**
29 ❑ Nov 1994 Cover: 1.50 **NM** value: **Cover or less**
Circ: CapCity orders: **4,725**
30 ❑ Jan 1995 Cover: 2.95 **NM** value: **Cover or less**
Circ: Statement: **71,884** CapCity orders: **4,650**
31 ❑ Mar 1995 Cover: 1.50 **NM** value: **Cover or less**
Circ: Statement: **71,884** CapCity orders: **4,450**
32 ❑ May 1995 Cover: 1.50 **NM** value: **Cover or less**
Circ: Statement: **71,884** CapCity orders: **4,325**
33 ❑ Jul 1995 Cover: 2.95 **NM** value: **Cover or less**
Circ: Statement: **71,884** CapCity orders: **4,775**
📖 Horsing Around with History • new story **A:** Carl Barks; William Van Horn **C:** William Van Horn **W:** Carl Barks
34 ❑ Sep 1995 Cover: 1.95 **NM** value: **Cover or less**
Circ: Statement: **71,884** CapCity orders: **4,250**
35 ❑ Nov 1995 Cover: 1.95 **NM** value: **Cover or less**
Circ: Statement: **71,884** CapCity orders: **4,175**
36 ❑ Jan 1996 Cover: 1.95 **NM** value: **Cover or less**
Circ: Statement: **38,721**
37 ❑ Mar 1996 Cover: 1.50 **NM** value: **Cover or less**
Circ: Statement: **38,721**
newprint covers begin.
38 ❑ May 1996 Cover: 1.50 **NM** value: **Cover or less**
Circ: Statement: **38,721**
39 ❑ Aug 1996 Cover: 1.50 **NM** value: **Cover or less**
Circ: Statement: **38,721**
40 ❑ Sep 1996 Cover: 1.50 **NM** value: **Cover or less**
Circ: Statement: **38,721**
41 ❑ Nov 1996 Cover: 1.95 **NM** value: **Cover or less**
Circ: Statement: **38,721**
42 ❑ Jan 1997 Cover: 1.50 **NM** value: **1.95**
Circ: Statement: **31,011** Diamd. preorders: **8,205** • **CGC:** 1 graded, best 9.8
43 ❑ Feb 1997 Cover: 1.50 **NM** value: **Cover or less**
Circ: Statement: **31,011**
• reprints The Queen of the Wild Dog Pack from US #62 **A:** Carl Barks
44 ❑ Mar 1997 Cover: 1.50 **NM** value: **Cover or less**
Circ: Statement: **31,011** Diamd. preorders: **7,837**
45 ❑ Apr 1997 Cover: 1.50 **NM** value: **Cover or less**
Circ: Statement: **31,011** Diamd. preorders: **7,554**
46 ❑ May 1997 Cover: 1.95 **NM** value: **Cover or less**
Circ: Statement: **31,011** Diamd. preorders: **7,192**
newprint covers end.
47 ❑ Jun 1997 Cover: 1.95 **NM** value: **Cover or less**
Circ: Statement: **31,011** Diamd. preorders: **7,089**
📖 The Menehune Mystery **A:** Carl Barks
48 ❑ Jul 1997 Cover: 1.95 **NM** value: **Cover or less**
Circ: Statement: **31,011** Diamd. preorders: **7,606**
49 ❑ Aug 1997 Cover: 1.95 **NM** value: **Cover or less**
Circ: Statement: **31,011** Diamd. preorders: **7,008**
50 ❑ Sep 1997 Cover: 1.95 **NM** value: **Cover or less**
Circ: Statement: **31,011** Diamd. preorders: **7,896**
📖 The Secret of Atlantis **A:** Carl Barks
51 ❑ Oct 1997 Cover: 1.95 **NM** value: **Cover or less**
Circ: Statement: **31,011** Diamd. preorders: **7,648**
📖 The Treasure of the Ten Avatars **A:** Don Rosa
52 ❑ Nov 1997 Cover: 1.95 **NM** value: **Cover or less**
Circ: Diamd. preorders: **7,032**
53 ❑ Dec 1997 Cover: 1.95 **NM** value: **Cover or less**
Circ: Diamd. preorders: **6,735**
📖 Secret of the Incas, Part 1
54 ❑ Feb 1998 Cover: 1.95 **NM** value: **Cover or less**
Circ: Diamd. preorders: **5,810**
📖 Secret of the Incas, Part 2 • Has 1997 Statement, filed 9/4/97; avg print run 71,275; avg sales 27,998; avg subs 3,013; avg total paid 31,011; samples 244; office use 1,164; max existent 32,419; 55% of run returned

UNCLE SCROOGE AND DONALD DUCK — Gold Key

1 ❑ Jun 1965 Cover: 0.25 **NM** value: **50.00**
• **CGC:** 4 graded, best 9.8
📖 Only a Poor Old Man; The Mummy's Ring • Reprints stories from Four Color Comics #29 and 386

UNCLE SCROOGE & DONALD DUCK (WALT DISNEY'S...) — Gladstone

Uncle Scrooge enjoyed a tremendously successful comic-book career, due in large measure to the genius of artist-writer Carl Barks. In the 1980s, Don Rosa began his own run on the character of Uncle Scrooge, revisiting the development of the character and fitting new stories into what Barks had established as the Duck mythos, developing the cast of characters, and spinning new tales of high adventure, mystery, and science fiction.

Gladstone began reprinting Rosa's first efforts from the 1980s in this new series from 1998. Donald, his nephews Huey, Dewey, and Louie, and the whole Duckburg gang are here in beautiful full-length, full-color stories.

1 ❑ Jan 1998 Cover: 1.95 **NM** value: **2.00**
📖 Ten-Penny Opera; The Crocodile Collector
2 ❑ Mar 1998 Cover: 1.95 **NM** value: **2.00**

UNCLE SCROOGE AND MONEY — Gold Key

1 ❑ Mar 1967 Cover: 0.12 **NM** value: **6.00**
• Reprints story from Walt Disney's Comics #130; 10167-703 **A:** Carl Barks **W:** Carl Barks

UNCLE SCROOGE CLASSICS (WALT DISNEY'S...) — Whitman

1 ❑ Cover: 0.69 **NM** value: **3.00**
📖 Land beneath the Ground; Back to Long Ago. • #11355-1 **A:** Carl Barks **W:** Carl Barks

UNCLE SCROOGE COMICS DIGEST — Gladstone

1 ❑ Dec 1986 Cover: 1.50 **NM** value: **3.00**
Circ: CapCity orders: **2,325**
• reprints **A:** Carl Barks
2 ❑ Feb 1987 Cover: 1.50 **NM** value: **2.00**
Circ: CapCity orders: **2,350**
• reprints **A:** Carl Barks
3 ❑ Apr 1987 Cover: 1.50 **NM** value: **2.00**
Circ: CapCity orders: **1,825**
• reprints **A:** Carl Barks
4 ❑ Jun 1987 Cover: 1.50 **NM** value: **2.00**
Circ: CapCity orders: **1,350**
📖 The Sunken City & TeaHouse of the Waggin' Dragon (by Barks); The Dime From Uncle; Antique Antics; Super Beagles • reprints **A:** Carl Barks
5 ❑ Aug 1987 Cover: 1.50 **NM** value: **2.00**
Circ: CapCity orders: **1,475**
• reprints **A:** Carl Barks

UNCLE SCROOGE GOES TO DISNEYLAND (WALT DISNEY'S...) — Gladstone

1 ❑ Aug 1985 Cover: 2.50 **NM** value: **275.00**
• **CGC:** 1 graded, best 7.5
• Dell Giant **A:** Carl Barks
1/A ❑ Aug 1985 Cover: 1.50 **NM** value: **5.00**
• digest.
1-2/A❑ Cover: 1.50 **NM** value: **5.00**
• **CGC:** 1 graded, best 9.6
• digest. **A:** Carl Barks
1-2 ❑ Cover: 2.50 **NM** value: **6.00**

UNCLE SCROOGE (WALT DISNEY...) — Dell / Gold Key/Whitman

Uncle Scrooge McDuck is one of the most popular comics characters of all time and was created by the genius artist-writer Carl Barks as a plot device for a Donald Duck story. While the first Scrooge story, "Christmas on Bear Mountain," was cover-featured, that comic book itself was simply another in the tryout Dell Four Color Series. (It was #178, released at the end of 1947). The grumpy rich uncle quickly grew into a fully rounded character, as Barks introduced such plot elements as The Beagle Boys and Scrooge's gigantic money bin.

Scrooge went from being the character who got Donald and Donald's nephews into adventures to being the focal point of a variety of imaginative adventures. — Maggie

4 ❑ Dec 1953 Cover: 0.10 **NM** value: **360.00**
• **CGC:** 1 graded, best 8.0
📖 (Untitled) • Takes place in Hawaii ★ Appearance of Series continued from.
5 ❑ Mar 1954 Cover: 0.10 **NM** value: **265.00**
• **CGC:** 1 graded, best 7.5
📖 Secret of Atlantis
6 ❑ Jun 1954 Cover: 0.10 **NM** value: **225.00**
📖 (Untitled); In the Buying Mood
7 ❑ Sep 1954 Cover: 0.10 **NM** value: **225.00**
• **CGC:** 2 graded, best 9.0
📖 The Seven Cities of Cibola; (Untitled);
8 ❑ Dec 1954 Cover: 0.10 **NM** value: **175.00**
📖 The Mysterious Unfinished Invention; (Untitled)

Other grades: Multiply prices above by **1.5 for Mint • 2/3 for Very Fine • 1/3 for Fine • 1/5 for Very Good • 1/8 for Good**

9 ❑ Mar 1955 Cover: 0.10 **NM** value: **160.00**
🕮 The Lemming With the Locket; The Tuckered Tiger
10 ❑ Jun 1955 Cover: 0.10 **NM** value: **160.00**
• **CGC:** 1 graded, best 8.0
🕮 The Fabulous Philosopher's Stone; Heirloom Watch **A:** Carl Barks
11 ❑ Sep 1955 Cover: 0.10 **NM** value: **125.00**
🕮 The Great Steamboat Race; Riches, Riches, Everywhere!
12 ❑ Dec 1955 Cover: 0.10 **NM** value: **125.00**
🕮 The Golden Fleecing
13 ❑ Mar 1956 Cover: 0.10 **NM** value: **125.00**
🕮 Land Beneath the Ground!; Gyro Gearloose (Untitled) • Gyro Gearloose backup stories begin
14 ❑ Jun 1956 Cover: 0.10 **NM** value: **125.00**
🕮 The Lost Crown of Genghis Khan!Gyro Gearloose (Untitled); Uncle Scrooge (Untitled)
15 ❑ Sep 1956 Cover: 0.10 **NM** value: **125.00**
🕮 The Second-Richest Duck; Gyro Gearloose (Untitled); Uncle Scrooge (Untitled)
16 ❑ Dec 1956 Cover: 0.10 **NM** value: **100.00**
🕮 Back to Long Ago!; Gyro Gearloose (Untitled); Uncle Scrooge (Untitled)
17 ❑ Mar 1957 Cover: 0.10 **NM** value: **100.00**
🕮 A Cold Bargain; Gyro Gearloose (Untitled)
18 ❑ Jun 1957 Cover: 0.10 **NM** value: **100.00**
🕮 Land of the Pygmy Indians; Gyro Gearloose (Untitled)
19 ❑ Sep 1957 Cover: 0.10 **NM** value: **100.00**
🕮 The Mines of King Solomon; Gyro Gearloose (Untitled)
20 ❑ Dec 1957 Cover: 0.10 **NM** value: **100.00**
• **CGC:** 1 graded, best 8.0
🕮 City of Golden Roofs; Gyro Gearloose (Untitled); Uncle Scrooge (Untitled)
21 ❑ Mar 1958 Cover: 0.10 **NM** value: **80.00**
• **CGC:** 1 graded, best 8.0
🕮 The Money Well; Gyro Gearloose (Untitled); Uncle Scrooge (Untitled)
22 ❑ Jun 1958 Cover: 0.10 **NM** value: **80.00**
🕮 The Golden River; Gyro Gearloose (Untitled); Uncle Scrooge (Untitled)
23 ❑ Sep 1958 Cover: 0.10 **NM** value: **80.00**
🕮 The Strange Shipwrecks; Gyro Gearloose (Untitled); Uncle Scrooge and the Fabulous Tycoon; Uncle Scrooge (Untitled)
24 ❑ Dec 1958 Cover: 0.10 **NM** value: **80.00**
🕮 The Twenty-four Carat Moon; Gyro Gearloose (Untitled); Uncle Scrooge and the Magic Ink **A:** Carl Barks **W:** Carl Barks
25 ❑ Mar 1959 Cover: 0.10 **NM** value: **80.00**
🕮 The Flying Dutchman; Gyro Gearloose (Untitled); Uncle Scrooge (Untitled); Uncle Scrooge (Untitled); Uncle Scrooge (Untitled)
26 ❑ Jun 1959 Cover: 0.10 **NM** value: **80.00**
• **CGC:** 1 graded, best 9.0
🕮 The Prize of Pizarro; Krankenstein Gyro; Uncle Scrooge (Untitled)
27 ❑ Sep 1959 Cover: 0.10 **NM** value: **80.00**
🕮 The Money Champ; Firefly Tracker; Uncle Scrooge and His Handy Andy; Uncle Scrooge Crawls for Cash
28 ❑ Dec 1959 Cover: 0.10 **NM** value: **80.00**
🕮 Uncle Scrooge and the "Paul Bunyan" Machine; The Inventor's Contest; The Witching Stick; The Money Hat
29 ❑ Mar 1960 Cover: 0.10 **NM** value: **80.00**
Circ: Statement: **1,040,543**
🕮 Island in the Sky; Oodles of Oomph; Hound of the Whiskervilles
30 ❑ Jun 1960 Cover: 0.10 **NM** value: **80.00**
Circ: Statement: **1,040,543**
🕮 Pipeline to Danger; War Paint; Yoiks! The Fox!
31 ❑ Sep 1960 Cover: 0.10 **NM** value: **65.00**
Circ: Statement: **1,040,543**
🕮 All at Sea; Fishy Warden; Two-way Luck; The Secret Book; The Balmi Swami
32 ❑ Dec 1960 Cover: 0.10 **NM** value: **65.00**
Circ: Statement: **1,040,543** • **CGC:** 1 graded, best 8.0
🕮 That's No Fable!; That Small Feeling; Clothes Make the Duck; The Homey Touch; A Thrift Gift; Turnabout
33 ❑ Mar 1961 Cover: 0.15 **NM** value: **65.00**
Circ: Statement: **853,928**
🕮 Tree Trick; Billions in the Hole; You Can't Win; Bongo on the Congo; The Big Bobber; Thumbs Up
34 ❑ Jun 1961 Cover: 0.15 **NM** value: **65.00**
Circ: Statement: **853,928** • **CGC:** 1 graded, best 9.4
🕮 Mythic Mystery; Wily Rival; Chugwagon Derby;
35 ❑ Sep 1961 Cover: 0.15 **NM** value: **65.00**
Circ: Statement: **853,928**
🕮 The Golden Nugget Boat; Fast Away Castaway; Gift Lion
36 ❑ Dec 1961 Cover: 0.15 **NM** value: **65.00**
Circ: Statement: **853,928** • **CGC:** 1 graded, best 8.5
🕮 The Midas Touch; Duckburg's Day of Peril; Money Bag Goat • Old Number One Dime named as such
37 ❑ Mar 1962 Cover: 0.15 **NM** value: **65.00**
• **CGC:** 1 graded, best 6.5
🕮 Windy Story; Cave of Ali Baba; The Great Pop Up; Deep Down Doings
38 ❑ Jun 1962 Cover: 0.15 **NM** value: **65.00**
• **CGC:** 3 graded, best 9.0
🕮 Monkey Business; The Unsafe Safe; Madcap Inventors; Much Luck McDuck; Collection Day; Seeing Is Believing; Playmates • Has 1961 Statement, filed 10/1/61; avg total paid 853,928
39 ❑ Sep 1962 Cover: 0.12 **NM** value: **65.00**
🕮 Getting the Bird; A Spicy Tale; Finny Fun; Tricky Experiment; Art Appreciation; Nest Egg Collector
40 ❑ Dec 1962 Cover: 0.12 **NM** value: **65.00**
• **CGC:** 1 graded, best 9.0
🕮 Odball Odyssey; Posthasty Postman • Gold Key begins as publisher
41 ❑ Mar 1963 Cover: 0.12 **NM** value: **55.00**
Circ: Statement: **299,155**
🕮 The Status Seeker; Snow Duster
42 ❑ May 1963 Cover: 0.12 **NM** value: **55.00**
Circ: Statement: **299,155** • **CGC:** 2 graded, best 9.4
🕮 The Case of the Sticky Money; Uncle Scrooge (Untitled); Uncle Scrooge (Untitled)
43 ❑ Jul 1963 Cover: 0.12 **NM** value: **55.00**
Circ: Statement: **299,155** • **CGC:** 1 graded, best 6.5
🕮 For Old Dime's Sake
44 ❑ Aug 1963 Cover: 0.12 **NM** value: **55.00**
Circ: Statement: **299,155**
🕮 Crown of the Mayas; The Invisible Intruder
45 ❑ Oct 1963 Cover: 0.12 **NM** value: **55.00**
Circ: Statement: **299,155**
🕮 Isle of Golden Geese; The Travel Tightwad
46 ❑ Dec 1963 Cover: 0.12 **NM** value: **55.00**
Circ: Statement: **299,155** • **CGC:** 1 graded, best 7.5
🕮 Lost Beneath the Sea; A Helper's Helping Hand; The Lemonade Fling
47 ❑ Feb 1964 Cover: 0.12 **NM** value: **55.00**
Circ: Statement: **336,380**
🕮 The Thrifty Spendthrift; Man versus Machine
48 ❑ Mar 1964 Cover: 0.12 **NM** value: **55.00**
Circ: Statement: **336,380**
🕮 The Many Faces of Magica de Spell; Jonah Gyro
49 ❑ May 1964 Cover: 0.12 **NM** value: **55.00**
Circ: Statement: **336,380**
🕮 The Loony Lunar Gold Rush; Clothes Make the Duck
50 ❑ Jul 1964 Cover: 0.12 **NM** value: **55.00**
Circ: Statement: **336,380**
🕮 Rug Riders in the Sky
51 ❑ Aug 1964 Cover: 0.12 **NM** value: **45.00**
Circ: Statement: **336,380**
🕮 How Green Was My Lettuce
52 ❑ Sep 1964 Cover: 0.12 **NM** value: **45.00**
Circ: Statement: **336,380**
🕮 The Great Wig Mystery
53 ❑ Oct 1964 Cover: 0.12 **NM** value: **45.00**
Circ: Statement: **336,380**
🕮 Interplanetary Postman
54 ❑ Dec 1964 Cover: 0.12 **NM** value: **45.00**
Circ: Statement: **336,380**
🕮 The Billion Dollar Safari; Uncle Scrooge (Untitled); Flowers Are Flowers
55 ❑ Feb 1965 Cover: 0.12 **NM** value: **45.00**
Circ: Statement: **330,925**
🕮 McDuck of Arabia
56 ❑ Mar 1965 Cover: 0.12 **NM** value: **45.00**
Circ: Statement: **330,925**
🕮 Mystery of the Ghost Town Railroad
57 ❑ May 1965 Cover: 0.12 **NM** value: **45.00**
Circ: Statement: **330,925**
🕮 The Swamp of No Return
58 ❑ Jul 1965 Cover: 0.12 **NM** value: **45.00**
Circ: Statement: **330,925**
🕮 The Giant Robot Riders
59 ❑ Sep 1965 Cover: 0.12 **NM** value: **45.00**
Circ: Statement: **330,925**
🕮 North of the Yukon
60 ❑ Nov 1965 Cover: 0.12 **NM** value: **45.00**
Circ: Statement: **330,925**
🕮 The Phantom of Notre Duck
61 ❑ Jan 1966 Cover: 0.12 **NM** value: **45.00**
Circ: Statement: **297,516**
🕮 So Far No Safari
62 ❑ Mar 1966 Cover: 0.12 **NM** value: **45.00**
Circ: Statement: **297,516**
🕮 The Queen of the Wild Dog Pack
63 ❑ May 1966 Cover: 0.12 **NM** value: **45.00**
Circ: Statement: **297,516**
🕮 House of Haunts
64 ❑ Jul 1966 Cover: 0.12 **NM** value: **45.00**
Circ: Statement: **297,516**
🕮 Treasure of Marco Polo
65 ❑ Sep 1966 Cover: 0.12 **NM** value: **45.00**
Circ: Statement: **297,516**
🕮 Micro-ducks from Outer Space
66 ❑ Nov 1966 Cover: 0.12 **NM** value: **45.00**
Circ: Statement: **297,516**
🕮 The Heedless Horseman; Gyro Gearloose (Untitled) • Gyro reprinted from Uncle Scrooge (Walt Disney…) #22
67 ❑ Jan 1967 Cover: 0.12 **NM** value: **45.00**
Circ: Statement: **278,901**
🕮 The Fabulous Philosopher's Stone
68 ❑ Mar 1967 Cover: 0.12 **NM** value: **45.00**
Circ: Statement: **278,901**
🕮 Hall of the Mermaid Queen • Has 1966 Statement, filed 9/28/66; avg print run 491,530; avg sales 296,166; avg subs 1,350; avg total paid 297,516; samples 528; max existent 298,044; 39% of run returned
69 ❑ May 1967 Cover: 0.12 **NM** value: **45.00**
Circ: Statement: **278,901**
🕮 The Cattle King
70 ❑ Jul 1967 Cover: 0.12 **NM** value: **45.00**
Circ: Statement: **278,901**
🕮 The Doom Diamond
71 ❑ Oct 1967 Cover: 0.12 **NM** value: **42.00**
Circ: Statement: **278,901**
🕮 King Scrooge the First
72 ❑ Dec 1967 Cover: 0.12 **NM** value: **35.00**
Circ: Statement: **278,901**
🕮 The Great Steamboat Race; Gyro Gearloose (Untitled) • Gyro reprinted from Uncle Scrooge (Walt Disney…) #19
73 ❑ Feb 1968 Cover: 0.12 **NM** value: **35.00**
🕮 Tree Trick; Bongo on the Congo; Duckburg's Day of Peril; Money Bag Goat • Reprints stories from Uncle Scrooge (Walt Disney…) #33 and 36
74 ❑ Apr 1968 Cover: 0.12 **NM** value: **35.00**
75 ❑ Jun 1968 Cover: 0.12 **NM** value: **35.00**
76 ❑ Aug 1968 Cover: 0.15 **NM** value: **35.00**
77 ❑ Oct 1968 Cover: 0.15 **NM** value: **35.00**
78 ❑ Dec 1968 Cover: 0.15 **NM** value: **35.00**
79 ❑ Feb 1969 Cover: 0.15 **NM** value: **35.00**
• **CGC:** 1 graded, best 7.5
80 ❑ Apr 1969 Cover: 0.15 **NM** value: **35.00**
81 ❑ Jun 1969 Cover: 0.15 **NM** value: **35.00**
82 ❑ Aug 1969 Cover: 0.15 **NM** value: **35.00**
🕮 Mythic Mystery • Reprints story from Uncle Scrooge (Walt Disney…) #34
83 ❑ Oct 1969 Cover: 0.15 **NM** value: **35.00**
84 ❑ Dec 1969 Cover: 0.15 **NM** value: **35.00**
🕮 The Lost Crown of Genghis Khan! • Reprints story from Uncle Scrooge (Walt Disney…) #14
85 ❑ Feb 1970 Cover: 0.15 **NM** value: **35.00**
Circ: Statement: **226,614**
🕮 The Great Wig Mystery • Reprints story from Uncle Scrooge (Walt Disney…) #52
86 ❑ Apr 1970 Cover: 0.15 **NM** value: **35.00**
Circ: Statement: **226,614**
🕮 The Golden Nugget Boat • Reprints story from Uncle Scrooge (Walt Disney…) #35
87 ❑ Jun 1970 Cover: 0.15 **NM** value: **35.00**
Circ: Statement: **226,614**
🕮 Uncle Scrooge and the Flying Dutchman • Reprints story from Uncle Scrooge (Walt Disney…) #25
88 ❑ Aug 1970 Cover: 0.15 **NM** value: **35.00**
Circ: Statement: **226,614**
🕮 The Unsafe Safe • Reprints story from Uncle Scrooge (Walt Disney…) #38
89 ❑ Oct 1970 Cover: 0.15 **NM** value: **35.00**
Circ: Statement: **226,614**
🕮 The Second-richest Duck • Reprints story from Uncle Scrooge (Walt Disney…) #15
90 ❑ Dec 1970 Cover: 0.15 **NM** value: **35.00**
Circ: Statement: **226,614**
🕮 Cave of Ali Baba; Gift Lion • Reprints stories from Uncle Scrooge (Walt Disney…) #37 and 35
91 ❑ Feb 1971 Cover: 0.15 **NM** value: **35.00**
Circ: Statement: **222,673**
🕮 Riches, Riches, Everywhere!; Krankenstein Gyro • Reprints stories from Uncle Scrooge (Walt Disney…) #11 and 26; Has 1970 Statement, filed 9/30/70; avg print run 401,762; avg sales 225,500; avg subs 1,114; avg total paid 226,614; samples 589; max existent 227,203; 43% of run returned
92 ❑ Apr 1971 Cover: 0.15 **NM** value: **35.00**
Circ: Statement: **222,673**
🕮 The Magic Ink; Two-way Luck; That Small Feeling • Reprints stories from Uncle Scrooge (Walt Disney…) #24, 31 and 32
93 ❑ Jun 1971 Cover: 0.15 **NM** value: **35.00**
Circ: Statement: **222,673**
🕮 The Midas Touch; Wily Rival • Reprints stories from Uncle Scrooge (Walt Disney…) #34 and 36
94 ❑ Aug 1971 Cover: 0.15 **NM** value: **35.00**
Circ: Statement: **222,673**
🕮 Interplanetary Postman; Fast Away Castaway • Reprints stories from Uncle Scrooge (Walt Disney…) #35 and 53
95 ❑ Oct 1971 Cover: 0.15 **NM** value: **35.00**
Circ: Statement: **222,673**
🕮 How Green Was My Lettuce; War Paint • Reprints stories from Uncle Scrooge (Walt Disney…) #30 and 51
96 ❑ Dec 1971 Cover: 0.15 **NM** value: **35.00**
Circ: Statement: **222,673**
🕮 The Thrifty Spendthrift • Reprints story from Uncle Scrooge (Walt Disney…) #47
97 ❑ Feb 1972 Cover: 0.15 **NM** value: **35.00**
🕮 That's No Fable!; A Thrift Gift • Reprints stories from Uncle Scrooge (Walt Disney…) #32; Has 1971 Statement, filed 9/30/71; avg print run 339,830; avg sales 221,112; avg subs 1,561; avg total paid 222,673; samples 619; office use 298; max existent 223,590; 34% of run returned
98 ❑ Apr 1972 Cover: 0.15 **NM** value: **35.00**
🕮 The Status Seeker • Reprints story from Uncle Scrooge (Walt Disney…) #41
99 ❑ Jun 1972 Cover: 0.15 **NM** value: **35.00**
🕮 The Case of the Sticky Money • Reprints story from Uncle Scrooge (Walt Disney…) #42
100 ❑ Aug 1972 Cover: 0.15 **NM** value: **35.00**
• **CGC:** 4 graded, best 9.6
🕮 Pipeline to Danger • Reprints story from Uncle Scrooge (Walt Disney…) #30
101 ❑ Sep 1972 Cover: 0.15 **NM** value: **20.00**
🕮 Wispy Willie; Old Demontooth • Reprints stories from Walt Disney's Comics #157 and 159
102 ❑ Nov 1972 Cover: 0.15 **NM** value: **20.00**
🕮 A Spicy Tale; Getting the Bird; Nest Egg Collector • Reprints stories from Uncle Scrooge (Walt Disney…) #39
103 ❑ Feb 1973 Cover: 0.15 **NM** value: **20.00**
• **CGC:** 13 graded, best 9.6
🕮 Back to Long Ago • Reprints story from Uncle Scrooge (Walt Disney…) #16
104 ❑ Apr 1973 Cover: 0.15 **NM** value: **20.00**
🕮 The Lemming with the Locket; Uncle Scrooge (Untitled); Uncle Scrooge (Untitled) • Reprints stories from Uncle Scrooge (Walt Disney…) #9 and 42
105 ❑ Jun 1973 Cover: 0.20 **NM** value: **20.00**
🕮 Uncle Scrooge (Untitled); Turnabout • Reprints stories from Four Color Comins #495 (Uncle Scrooge #3) and Uncle Scrooge (Walt Disney…) #32
106 ❑ Aug 1973 Cover: 0.20 **NM** value: **20.00**
🕮 (Untitled Uncle Scrooge stories) • Reprints stories from Uncle Scrooge (Walt Disney…) #6
107 ❑ Sep 1973 Cover: 0.20 **NM** value: **20.00**
🕮 The Money Well • Reprints story from Uncle Scrooge (Walt Disney…) #21
108 ❑ Oct 1973 Cover: 0.20 **NM** value: **20.00**
🕮 The Mines of King Solomon • Reprints story from Uncle Scrooge (Walt Disney…) #19
109 ❑ Dec 1973 Cover: 0.20 **NM** value: **20.00**
🕮 Land Beneath the Ground! • Reprints story from Uncle Scrooge (Walt Disney…) #13
110 ❑ Feb 1974 Cover: 0.20 **NM** value: **20.00**
🕮 Uncle Scrooge and the Golden River • Reprints story from Uncle Scrooge (Walt Disney…) #22
111 ❑ Jun 1974 Cover: 0.20 **NM** value: **20.00**
🕮 The Mysterious Unfinished Invention • Reprints story from Uncle Scrooge (Walt Disney…) #8
112 ❑ Jun 1974 Cover: 0.20 **NM** value: **20.00**
🕮 Land of the Pygmy Indians • Reprints story from Uncle Scrooge (Walt Disney…) #18

CGC-graded: Multiply prices above by **33 for 9.9 M • 16 for 9.8 NM/M • 7 for 9.6 NM+ • 5 for 9.4 NM • 2.5 for 9.2 NM- • 1.5 for 9.0 VF/NM**

113 ❑ Aug 1974 Cover: 0.25 **NM** value: **20.00**
📖 Crown of the Mayas; Gyro Gearloose (Untitled) • Reprints stories from Uncle Scrooge (Walt Disney…) #24 and 44

114 ❑ Sep 1974 Cover: 0.25 **NM** value: **20.00**
📖 The Phantom of Notre Duck • Reprints story from Uncle Scrooge (Walt Disney…) #60

115 ❑ Oct 1974 Cover: 0.25 **NM** value: **20.00**
📖 The Giant Robot Robbers • Reprints story from Uncle Scrooge (Walt Disney…) #58

116 ❑ Dec 1974 Cover: 0.25 **NM** value: **20.00**
📖 Rug Riders in the Sky • Reprints story from Uncle Scrooge (Walt Disney…) #50

117 ❑ Feb 1975 Cover: 0.25 **NM** value: **20.00**
📖 The Loony Lunar Gold Rush; Clothes Make the Duck; The Homey Touch • Reprints stories from Uncle Scrooge (Walt Disney…) #32 and 49

118 ❑ Apr 1975 Cover: 0.25 **NM** value: **20.00**
📖 The Billion Dollar Safari; Uncle Scrooge (Untitled) • Reprints stories from Uncle Scrooge (Walt Disney…) #54

119 ❑ Jun 1975 Cover: 0.25 **NM** value: **20.00**
📖 The Strange Shipwrecks; The Great Pop Up • Reprints stories from Uncle Scrooge (Walt Disney…) #23 and 37

120 ❑ Jul 1975 Cover: 0.25 **NM** value: **20.00**
📖 Billions in the Hole; Chuckwagon Derby • Reprints stories from Uncle Scrooge (Walt Disney…) #33 and 34

121 ❑ Aug 1975 Cover: 0.25 **NM** value: **18.00**
📖 McDuck of Arabia • Reprints story from Uncle Scrooge (Walt Disney…) #55

122 ❑ Sep 1975 Cover: 0.25 **NM** value: **18.00**
📖 Mystery of the Ghost Town Railroad • Reprints story from Uncle Scrooge (Walt Disney…) #56

123 ❑ Oct 1975 Cover: 0.25 **NM** value: **18.00**
📖 The Swamp of No Return • Reprints story from Uncle Scrooge (Walt Disney…) #57

124 ❑ Dec 1975 Cover: 0.25 **NM** value: **18.00**
📖 North of the Yukon • Reprints story from Uncle Scrooge (Walt Disney…) #59

125 ❑ Jan 1976 Cover: 0.25 **NM** value: **18.00**
• **CGC:** 1 graded, best 9.4
📖 Hall of the Mermaid Queen • Reprints story from Uncle Scrooge (Walt Disney…) #68

126 ❑ Mar 1976 Cover: 0.25 **NM** value: **18.00**
• **CGC:** 1 graded, best 9.4
📖 The Cattle King • Reprints story from Uncle Scrooge (Walt Disney…) #69

127 ❑ Apr 1976 Cover: 0.25 **NM** value: **18.00**
• **CGC:** 1 graded, best 8.5
📖 So Far and No Safari • Reprints story from Uncle Scrooge (Walt Disney…) #61

128 ❑ May 1976 Cover: 0.25 **NM** value: **18.00**
• **CGC:** 1 graded, best 9.2
📖 The Queen of the Wild Dog Pack • Reprints story from Uncle Scrooge (Walt Disney…) #62

129 ❑ Jun 1976 Cover: 0.25 **NM** value: **18.00**
📖 House of Haunts • Reprints story from Uncle Scrooge (Walt Disney…) #63

130 ❑ Jul 1976 Cover: 0.25 **NM** value: **18.00**
• **CGC:** 2 graded, best 9.6
📖 Micro-ducks from Outer Space • Reprints story from Uncle Scrooge (Walt Disney…) #65

131 ❑ Aug 1976 Cover: 0.25 **NM** value: **18.00**
• **CGC:** 1 graded, best 9.0
📖 The Heedless Horseman • Reprints story from Uncle Scrooge (Walt Disney…) #66

132 ❑ Sep 1976 Cover: 0.30 **NM** value: **18.00**
📖 The Fabulous Philosopher's Stone • Reprints story from Uncle Scrooge (Walt Disney…) #10

133 ❑ Oct 1976 Cover: 0.30 **NM** value: **18.00**
📖 The Doom Diamond • Reprints story from Uncle Scrooge (Walt Disney…) #70

134 ❑ Nov 1976 Cover: 0.30 **NM** value: **18.00**
📖 Treasure of Marco Polo • Reprints story from Uncle Scrooge (Walt Disney…) #64

135 ❑ Dec 1976 Cover: 0.30 **NM** value: **18.00**
📖 The Twenty-four Carat Moon; The Fabulous Tycoon • Reprints stories from Uncle Scrooge (Walt Disney…) #23 and 24

136 ❑ Jan 1977 Cover: 0.30 **NM** value: **18.00**
📖 Deep Down Doings; Tricky Experiment; Much Luck McDuck • Reprints stories from Uncle Scrooge (Walt Disney…) #37-39

137 ❑ Feb 1977 Cover: 0.30 **NM** value: **18.00**
📖 All at Sea • Reprints story from Uncle Scrooge (Walt Disney…) #31

138 ❑ Mar 1977 Cover: 0.30 **NM** value: **18.00**
📖 The Many Faces of Magica de Spell; The Witching Stick • Reprints stories from Uncle Scrooge (Walt Disney…) #28 and 48

139 ❑ Apr 1977 Cover: 0.30 **NM** value: **18.00**
📖 Isle of the Golden Geese; The Travel Tightwad • Reprints stories from Uncle Scrooge (Walt Disney…) #45

140 ❑ May 1977 Cover: 0.30 **NM** value: **18.00**
📖 For Old Dime's Sake • Reprints story from Uncle Scrooge (Walt Disney…) #43

141 ❑ Jun 1977 Cover: 0.30 **NM** value: **12.00**
📖 The Case of the Sticky Money • Reprints story from Uncle Scrooge (Walt Disney…) #42

142 ❑ Jul 1977 Cover: 0.30 **NM** value: **12.00**
📖 Back to the Klondike • Reprints story from Four Color Comics #456 (Uncle Scrooge #2)

143 ❑ Aug 1977 Cover: 0.30 **NM** value: **12.00**
📖 Island in the Sky; Uncle Scrooge (Untitled) • Reprints stories from Uncle Scrooge (Walt Disney…) #26 and 29

144 ❑ Sep 1977 Cover: 0.30 **NM** value: **12.00**
• **CGC:** 2 graded, best 9.4
📖 The "Paul Bunyan" Machine; The Inventors' Contest • Reprints stories from Uncle Scrooge (Walt Disney…) #28

145 ❑ Oct 1977 Cover: 0.30 **NM** value: **12.00**
📖 King Scrooge the First • Reprints story from Uncle Scrooge (Walt Disney…) #71

146 ❑ Nov 1977 Cover: 0.30 **NM** value: **12.00**
• **CGC:** 1 graded, best 9.4
📖 Pipeline to Danger • Reprints story from Uncle Scrooge (Walt Disney…) #30

147 ❑ Dec 1977 Cover: 0.35 **NM** value: **12.00**
• **CGC:** 1 graded, best 9.4
📖 Mythic Mystery; Money Bag Goat; Gift Lion • Reprints stories from Uncle Scrooge (Walt Disney…) #34-36

148 ❑ Jan 1978 Cover: 0.35 **NM** value: **12.00**
📖 Riches, Riches, Everywhere! • Reprints story from Uncle Scrooge (Walt Disney…) #11

149 ❑ Feb 1978 Cover: 0.35 **NM** value: **12.00**
📖 Lost Beneath the Sea • Reprints story from Uncle Scrooge (Walt Disney…) #46

150 ❑ Mar 1978 Cover: 0.35 **NM** value: **12.00**
• **CGC:** 1 graded, best 9.4
📖 The Money Champ; The Firefly Tracker • Reprints stories from Uncle Scrooge (Walt Disney…) #27

151 ❑ Apr 1978 Cover: 0.35 **NM** value: **12.00**
• **CGC:** 1 graded, best 9.6
📖 The Flying Dutchman; (Uncle Scrooge (Untitled) • Reprints stories from Uncle Scrooge (Walt Disney…) #25

152 ❑ May 1978 Cover: 0.35 **NM** value: **12.00**
📖 The Great Wig Mystery • Reprints story from Uncle Scrooge (Walt Disney…) #52

153 ❑ Jun 1978 Cover: 0.35 **NM** value: **12.00**
📖 The Invisible Intruder • Reprints story from Uncle Scrooge (Walt Disney…) #44

154 ❑ Jul 1978 Cover: 0.35 **NM** value: **12.00**
• **CGC:** 1 graded, best 9.2
📖 Interplanetary Postman; Fast Away Castaway • Reprints stories from Uncle Scrooge (Walt Disney…) #35 and 53

155 ❑ Aug 1978 Cover: 0.35 **NM** value: **12.00**
📖 The Great Steamboat Race; Yoiks! The Fox! • Reprints stories from Uncle Scrooge (Walt Disney…) #11 and 30

156 ❑ Sep 1978 Cover: 0.35 **NM** value: **12.00**
📖 The Unsafe Safe; Somethin' Fishy Here • Reprints stories from Four Color Comics #456 (Uncle Scrooge #2) and Uncle Scrooge (Walt Disney…) #38

157 ❑ Oct 1978 Cover: 0.35 **NM** value: **12.00**
📖 Two-way Luck; The Secret Book • Reprints stories from Uncle Scrooge (Walt Disney…) #31

158 ❑ Nov 1978 Cover: 0.35 **NM** value: **12.00**

159 ❑ Dec 1978 Cover: 0.35 **NM** value: **12.00**
📖 The Golden Nugget Boat • Reprints story from Uncle Scrooge (Walt Disney…) #35

160 ❑ Jan 1979 Cover: 0.35 **NM** value: **12.00**

161 ❑ Feb 1979 Cover: 0.35 **NM** value: **8.00**

162 ❑ Mar 1979 Cover: 0.35 **NM** value: **8.00**

163 ❑ Apr 1979 Cover: 0.40 **NM** value: **8.00**

164 ❑ May 1979 Cover: 0.40 **NM** value: **8.00**

165 ❑ Jun 1979 Cover: 0.40 **NM** value: **8.00**

166 ❑ Jul 1979 Cover: 0.40 **NM** value: **8.00**

167 ❑ Aug 1979 Cover: 0.40 **NM** value: **8.00**

168 ❑ Sep 1979 Cover: 0.40 **NM** value: **8.00**

169 ❑ Oct 1979 Cover: 0.40 **NM** value: **8.00**

170 ❑ Nov 1979 Cover: 0.40 **NM** value: **8.00**

171 ❑ Dec 1979 Cover: 0.40 **NM** value: **8.00**

172 ❑ Jan 1980 Cover: 0.40 **NM** value: **8.00**

173 ❑ Feb 1980 Cover: 0.40 **NM** value: **8.00**

174 ❑ Mar 1980 Cover: 0.40 **NM** value: **8.00**

175 ❑ Apr 1980 Cover: 0.40 **NM** value: **8.00**

176 ❑ May 1980 Cover: 0.40 **NM** value: **8.00**

177 ❑ Jun 1980 Cover: 0.40 **NM** value: **8.00**
• **CGC:** 1 graded, best 7.0

178 ❑ Jul 1980 **NM** value: **8.00**

179 ❑ Sep 1980 **NM** value: **8.00**
• **CGC:** 6 graded, best 9.2

180 ❑ 1980 **NM** value: **8.00**

181 ❑ 1980 **NM** value: **7.00**

182 ❑ Jan 1981 Cover: 0.50 **NM** value: **7.00**

183 ❑ 1981 Cover: 0.50 **NM** value: **7.00**

184 ❑ 1981 Cover: 0.50 **NM** value: **7.00**

185 ❑ Jun 1981 Cover: 0.50 **NM** value: **7.00**

186 ❑ Jul 1981 Cover: 0.50 **NM** value: **7.00**

187 ❑ Aug 1981 Cover: 0.50 **NM** value: **7.00**

188 ❑ Sep 1981 Cover: 0.50 **NM** value: **7.00**

189 ❑ Oct 1981 Cover: 0.50 **NM** value: **7.00**

190 ❑ Nov 1981 Cover: 0.50 **NM** value: **7.00**

191 ❑ Dec 1981 Cover: 0.50 **NM** value: **7.00**

192 ❑ Jan 1982 Cover: 0.50 **NM** value: **7.00**

193 ❑ Feb 1982 Cover: 0.60 **NM** value: **7.00**

194 ❑ Spr 1982 Cover: 0.60 **NM** value: **7.00**

195 ❑ Mar 1982 Cover: 0.60 **NM** value: **7.00**
• **CGC:** 3 graded, best 9.6

196 ❑ Apr 1982 Cover: 0.60 **NM** value: **7.00**
• **CGC:** 4 graded, best 9.4

197 ❑ May 1982 Cover: 0.60 **NM** value: **7.00**
• **CGC:** 2 graded, best 9.6

198 ❑ 1982 Cover: 0.60 **NM** value: **7.00**

199 ❑ 1982 Cover: 0.60 **NM** value: **7.00**

200 ❑ Cover: 0.60 **NM** value: **7.00**
• **CGC:** 2 graded, best 9.6

201 ❑ Cover: 0.60 **NM** value: **6.00**

202 ❑ 1983 Cover: 0.60 **NM** value: **6.00**

203 ❑ 1983 Cover: 0.60 **NM** value: **6.00**

204 ❑ 1983 Cover: 0.60 **NM** value: **6.00**

205 ❑ Cover: 0.60 **NM** value: **6.00**
• **CGC:** 1 graded, best 8.0

206 ❑ 1984 Cover: 0.60 **NM** value: **6.00**
• **CGC:** 1 graded, best 9.4

207 ❑ 1984 Cover: 0.60 **NM** value: **6.00**

208 ❑ 1984 Cover: 0.60 **NM** value: **6.00**

209 ❑ 1984 Cover: 0.60 **NM** value: **6.00**

UNCLE SCROOGE (WALT DISNEY…) Gladstone

210 ❑ Oct 1986 Cover: 0.75 **NM** value: **6.00**
Circ: CapCity orders: **4,325** • **CGC:** 3 graded, best 9.6

211 ❑ Nov 1986 Cover: 0.75 **NM** value: **6.00**
Circ: CapCity orders: **4,175** • **CGC:** 3 graded, best 9.6

212 ❑ Dec 1986 Cover: 0.75 **NM** value: **6.00**
Circ: CapCity orders: **4,075**

213 ❑ Jan 1987 Cover: 0.75 **NM** value: **6.00**
Circ: Statement: **78,935** CapCity orders: **5,550**

214 ❑ Feb 1987 Cover: 0.75 **NM** value: **6.00**
Circ: Statement: **78,935** CapCity orders: **5,550**

215 ❑ Mar 1987 Cover: 0.75 **NM** value: **6.00**
Circ: Statement: **78,935** CapCity orders: **5,975**

216 ❑ Apr 1987 Cover: 0.75 **NM** value: **6.00**
Circ: Statement: **78,935** CapCity orders: **5,600**

217 ❑ May 1987 Cover: 0.75 **NM** value: **6.00**
Circ: Statement: **78,935** CapCity orders: **4,600**

218 ❑ Jun 1987 Cover: 0.95 **NM** value: **6.00**
Circ: Statement: **78,935** CapCity orders: **4,700**

219 ❑ Jul 1987 Cover: 0.95 **NM** value: **6.00**
Circ: Statement: **78,935** CapCity orders: **4,750** • **CGC:** 4 graded, best 9.8
• 1st Rosa Disney story **A:** Don Rosa

220 ❑ Aug 1987 Cover: 0.95 **NM** value: **5.00**
Circ: Statement: **78,935** CapCity orders: **4,925**

221 ❑ Sep 1987 Cover: 0.95 **NM** value: **5.00**
Circ: Statement: **78,935** CapCity orders: **5,025**

222 ❑ Oct 1987 Cover: 0.95 **NM** value: **5.00**
Circ: Statement: **78,935** CapCity orders: **5,375**

223 ❑ Nov 1987 Cover: 0.95 **NM** value: **5.00**
Circ: Statement: **78,935** CapCity orders: **5,250**

224 ❑ Dec 1987 Cover: 0.95 **NM** value: **5.00**
Circ: Statement: **78,935** CapCity orders: **5,425**

225 ❑ Feb 1988 Cover: 0.95 **NM** value: **5.00**
Circ: Statement: **74,092** CapCity orders: **5,200**

226 ❑ May 1988 Cover: 0.95 **NM** value: **5.00**
Circ: Statement: **74,092** CapCity orders: **5,300**

227 ❑ Jul 1988 Cover: 0.95 **NM** value: **5.00**
Circ: Statement: **74,092** CapCity orders: **5,550**

228 ❑ Aug 1988 Cover: 0.95 **NM** value: **5.00**
Circ: Statement: **74,092** CapCity orders: **5,650**

229 ❑ Sep 1988 Cover: 0.95 **NM** value: **5.00**
Circ: Statement: **74,092** CapCity orders: **5,400**

230 ❑ Oct 1988 Cover: 0.95 **NM** value: **5.00**
Circ: Statement: **74,092** CapCity orders: **6,300**

231 ❑ Nov 1988 Cover: 0.95 **NM** value: **5.00**
Circ: Statement: **74,092** CapCity orders: **5,750**

232 ❑ Dec 1988 Cover: 0.95 **NM** value: **5.00**
Circ: Statement: **74,092** CapCity orders: **5,850**

233 ❑ Feb 1989 Cover: 0.95 **NM** value: **5.00**
Circ: Statement: **74,055** CapCity orders: **5,750**

234 ❑ May 1989 Cover: 0.95 **NM** value: **5.00**
Circ: Statement: **74,055** CapCity orders: **6,300**

235 ❑ Jul 1989 Cover: 0.95 **NM** value: **5.00**
Circ: Statement: **74,055** CapCity orders: **7,250**

236 ❑ Aug 1989 Cover: 0.95 **NM** value: **5.00**
Circ: Statement: **74,055** CapCity orders: **6,400**

237 ❑ Sep 1989 Cover: 0.95 **NM** value: **5.00**
Circ: Statement: **74,055** CapCity orders: **6,650**

238 ❑ Oct 1989 Cover: 0.95 **NM** value: **5.00**
Circ: Statement: **74,055** CapCity orders: **6,900**

239 ❑ Nov 1989 Cover: 0.95 **NM** value: **5.00**
Circ: Statement: **74,055** CapCity orders: **6,700**

240 ❑ Dec 1989 Cover: 0.95 **NM** value: **5.00**
Circ: Statement: **74,055** CapCity orders: **6,800**

241 ❑ Feb 1990 Cover: 1.95 **NM** value: **4.00**
Circ: CapCity orders: **6,400**

242 ❑ Apr 1990 Cover: 1.95 **NM** value: **4.00**
Circ: CapCity orders: **6,550**
• double-sized. **A:** Carl Barks

UNCLE SCROOGE (WALT DISNEY…) Disney

243 ❑ Jun 1990 Cover: 1.50 **NM** value: **4.00**
Circ: CapCity orders: **7,950**
📖 Pie in the Sky; The Carpocanth **A:** William Van Horn; Vicar **W:** Bill Riling; J. Sutter

244 ❑ Jul 1990 Cover: 1.50 **NM** value: **4.00**
Circ: CapCity orders: **6,700**

245 ❑ Aug 1990 Cover: 1.50 **NM** value: **4.00**
Circ: CapCity orders: **7,450**

246 ❑ Sep 1990 Cover: 1.50 **NM** value: **4.00**
Circ: CapCity orders: **7,900**

247 ❑ Oct 1990 Cover: 1.50 **NM** value: **4.00**
Circ: CapCity orders: **7,850**

248 ❑ Nov 1990 Cover: 1.50 **NM** value: **4.00**
Circ: CapCity orders: **7,250**

249 ❑ Dec 1990 Cover: 1.50 **NM** value: **4.00**
Circ: CapCity orders: **6,850**

250 ❑ Jan 1991 Cover: 2.25 **NM** value: **4.00**
Circ: CapCity orders: **7,250**

251 ❑ Feb 1991 Cover: 1.50 **NM** value: **4.00**
Circ: CapCity orders: **7,000**

252 ❑ Mar 1991 Cover: 1.50 **NM** value: **4.00**
Circ: CapCity orders: **6,700**

253 ❑ Apr 1991 Cover: 1.50 **NM** value: **4.00**
Circ: CapCity orders: **6,500**
📖 The Fabulous Philosopher's Stone **A:** Carl Barks

254 ❑ May 1991 Cover: 1.50 **NM** value: **4.00**
Circ: CapCity orders: **5,950**

255 ❑ Jun 1991 Cover: 1.50 **NM** value: **4.00**
Circ: CapCity orders: **6,150**

256 ❑ Jul 1991 Cover: 1.50 **NM** value: **4.00**
Circ: CapCity orders: **6,150**

257 ❑ Aug 1991 Cover: 1.50 **NM** value: **4.00**
Circ: CapCity orders: **5,750**

258 ❑ Sep 1991 Cover: 1.50 **NM** value: **4.00**
Circ: CapCity orders: **5,950**

259 ❑ Oct 1991 Cover: 1.50 **NM** value: **4.00**
Circ: CapCity orders: **5,800**
📖 Time Tetrad, Part 3

Other grades: Multiply prices above by **1.5 for Mint • 2/3 for Very Fine • 1/3 for Fine • 1/5 for Very Good • 1/8 for Good**

260 ❑ Nov 1991 Cover: 1.50 **NM** value: **4.00**
Circ: CapCity orders: **5,550**

261 ❑ Dec 1991 Cover: 1.50 **NM** value: **2.50**
Circ: CapCity orders: **7,350**
📖 Return to Xanadu **A:** Don Rosa

262 ❑ Jan 1992 Cover: 1.50 **NM** value: **2.50**
Circ: CapCity orders: **6,700**
📖 Return to Xanadu **A:** Don Rosa

263 ❑ Feb 1992 Cover: 1.50 **NM** value: **2.50**
Circ: CapCity orders: **6,650**

264 ❑ Mar 1992 Cover: 1.50 **NM** value: **2.50**
Circ: CapCity orders: **5,350**

265 ❑ Apr 1992 Cover: 1.50 **NM** value: **2.50**
Circ: CapCity orders: **5,550**

266 ❑ May 1992 Cover: 1.50 **NM** value: **2.50**
Circ: CapCity orders: **5,300**

267 ❑ Jun 1992 Cover: 1.50 **NM** value: **2.50**
Circ: CapCity orders: **5,700**
• contains Duckburg map piece 3 of 9 **A:** Carl Barks

268 ❑ Jul 1992 Cover: 1.50 **NM** value: **2.50**
Circ: CapCity orders: **7,600**
• contains Duckburg map piece 6 of 9 **A:** Carl Barks

269 ❑ Aug 1992 Cover: 1.50 **NM** value: **2.50**
Circ: CapCity orders: **5,600**
• contains Duckburg map piece 9 of 9 **A:** Carl Barks

270 ❑ Sep 1992 Cover: 1.50 **NM** value: **2.50**
Circ: CapCity orders: **5,450**
• Olympics **A:** Carl Barks

271 ❑ Oct 1992 Cover: 1.50 **NM** value: **2.50**
Circ: CapCity orders: **4,850**

272 ❑ Nov 1992 Cover: 1.50 **NM** value: **2.50**
Circ: CapCity orders: **4,900**

273 ❑ Dec 1992 Cover: 1.50 **NM** value: **2.50**
Circ: CapCity orders: **5,050**

274 ❑ Jan 1993 Cover: 1.50 **NM** value: **2.50**
Circ: CapCity orders: **4,800**
📖 Hall of the Mermaid Queen **A:** Carl Barks

275 ❑ Feb 1993 Cover: 1.50 **NM** value: **2.50**
Circ: CapCity orders: **5,000**

276 ❑ Mar 1993 Cover: 1.50 **NM** value: **2.50**
Circ: CapCity orders: **5,850**

277 ❑ Apr 1993 Cover: 1.50 **NM** value: **2.50**
Circ: CapCity orders: **5,800**

278 ❑ May 1993 Cover: 1.50 **NM** value: **2.50**
Circ: CapCity orders: **6,050**

279 ❑ Jun 1993 Cover: 1.50 **NM** value: **2.50**
Circ: CapCity orders: **6,350**

280 ❑ Jul 1993 Cover: 1.50 **NM** value: **2.50**
Circ: CapCity orders: **6,050**

UNCLE SCROOGE (WALT DISNEY...) — Gladstone

281 ❑ Aug 1993 Cover: 1.50 **NM** value: **2.50**
Circ: CapCity orders: **5,500**

282 ❑ Oct 1993 Cover: 1.50 **NM** value: **2.50**
Circ: CapCity orders: **5,550**

283 ❑ Dec 1993 Cover: 1.50 **NM** value: **2.50**
Circ: CapCity orders: **5,575**

284 ❑ Feb 1994 Cover: 1.50 **NM** value: **2.50**
Circ: CapCity orders: **5,125**

285 ❑ Apr 1994 Cover: 1.50 **NM** value: **2.50**
Circ: CapCity orders: **5,550**
📖 Life and Times of Scrooge McDuck, Part 1 **A:** Don Rosa

286 ❑ Jun 1994 Cover: 1.50 **NM** value: **2.50**
Circ: CapCity orders: **5,325**
📖 Life and Times of Scrooge McDuck, Part 2 **A:** Don Rosa

287 ❑ Aug 1994 Cover: 1.50 **NM** value: **2.50**
Circ: CapCity orders: **5,725**
📖 Life and Times of Scrooge McDuck, Part 3 **A:** Don Rosa

288 ❑ Oct 1994 Cover: 1.50 **NM** value: **2.50**
Circ: CapCity orders: **6,050**
📖 Life and Times of Scrooge McDuck, Part 4 **A:** Don Rosa

289 ❑ Dec 1994 Cover: 1.50 **NM** value: **2.50**
Circ: CapCity orders: **5,875**
📖 Life and Times of Scrooge McDuck, Part 5 **A:** Don Rosa

290 ❑ Feb 1995 Cover: 1.50 **NM** value: **2.50**
Circ: Statement: **80,235** CapCity orders: **5,805**
📖 Life and Times of Scrooge McDuck, Part 6 **A:** Don Rosa

291 ❑ Apr 1995 Cover: 1.50 **NM** value: **2.50**
Circ: Statement: **80,235** CapCity orders: **5,325**
📖 Life and Times of Scrooge McDuck, Part 7 **A:** Don Rosa

292 ❑ Jun 1995 Cover: 1.50 **NM** value: **2.50**
Circ: Statement: **80,235** CapCity orders: **5,350**
📖 Life and Times of Scrooge McDuck, Part 8 **A:** Don Rosa

293 ❑ Aug 1995 Cover: 1.95 **NM** value: **2.50**
Circ: Statement: **80,235** CapCity orders: **5,425**
📖 Life and Times of Scrooge McDuck, Part 9 **A:** Don Rosa

294 ❑ Oct 1995 Cover: 1.50 **NM** value: **2.50**
Circ: Statement: **80,235** CapCity orders: **5,650**
newsprint covers begin. 📖 Life and Times of Scrooge McDuck, Part 10 **A:** Don Rosa

295 ❑ Dec 1995 Cover: 1.50 **NM** value: **2.50**
Circ: Statement: **80,235** CapCity orders: **5,075**
📖 Life and Times of Scrooge McDuck, Part 11 **A:** Don Rosa

296 ❑ Feb 1996 Cover: 1.50 **NM** value: **2.50**
Circ: Statement: **41,052**
📖 Life and Times of Scrooge McDuck, Part 12 **A:** Don Rosa

297 ❑ Apr 1996 Cover: 1.50 **NM** value: **2.50**
Circ: Statement: **41,052**
📖 Life and Times of Scrooge McDuck, Part 0 • Has 1995 Statement, filed 10/13/95; avg print run 93,526; avg sales 75,990; avg subs 4,245; avg total paid 80,235; samples 239; office use 1,718; max existent 82,192; 12% of run returned **A:** Don Rosa

298 ❑ Jun 1996 Cover: 1.50 **NM** value: **2.50**
Circ: Statement: **41,052**

299 ❑ Aug 1996 Cover: 1.50 **NM** value: **2.50**
Circ: Statement: **41,052**

300 ❑ Oct 1996 Cover: 2.25 **NM** value: **Cover or less**
Circ: Statement: **41,052**

301 ❑ Dec 1996 Cover: 1.50 **NM** value: **Cover or less**
Circ: Statement: **41,052** Diamd. preorders: **8,933**

302 ❑ Feb 1997 Cover: 1.50 **NM** value: **Cover or less**
Circ: Statement: **33,968**
📖 Monkey Business • reprints from WDC&S #297; Has 1996 Statement, filed 10/1/96; avg print run 80,839; avg sales 36,689; avg subs 4,363; avg total paid 41,052; samples 239; office use 1,301; max existent 42,592; 47% of run returned **A:** Carl Barks

303 ❑ Apr 1997 Cover: 1.50 **NM** value: **Cover or less**
Circ: Statement: **33,968** Diamd. preorders: **8,054**
newsprint covers end.

304 ❑ Jun 1997 Cover: 1.95 **NM** value: **Cover or less**
Circ: Statement: **33,968** Diamd. preorders: **7,604**
📖 Mr. Private Eye **A:** Carl Barks

305 ❑ Aug 1997 Cover: 1.95 **NM** value: **Cover or less**
Circ: Statement: **33,968** Diamd. preorders: **8,148**
📖 Flour Follies; A Matter of Factory; and Fishing Mystery **A:** Carl Barks

306 ❑ Oct 1997 Cover: 1.95 **NM** value: **Cover or less**
Circ: Statement: **33,968** Diamd. preorders: **7,996**
📖 Life and Times of Scrooge McDuck, Part 6.5: The Vigilante of Pizen Bluff **A:** Don Rosa **C:** Don Rosa **W:** Don Rosa

307 ❑ Dec 1997 Cover: 1.95 **NM** value: **Cover or less**
Circ: Statement: **33,968** Diamd. preorders: **7,289**

308 ❑ Feb 1998 Cover: 1.95 **NM** value: **Cover or less**
Circ: Statement: **10,555** Diamd. preorders: **6,207**
• Has 1997 Statement, filed 9/4/97; avg print run 64,938; avg sales 30,121, avg subs 3,847; avg total paid 33,968, samples 244; office use 1,041; max existent 35,253; 46% of run returned

309 ❑ May 1998 Cover: 6.95 **NM** value: **Cover or less**
Circ: Statement: **10,555**
• prestige format begins

310 ❑ Jun 1998 Cover: 6.95 **NM** value: **Cover or less**
Circ: Statement: **10,555**

311 ❑ Jul 1998 Cover: 6.95 **NM** value: **Cover or less**
Circ: Statement: **10,555**

312 ❑ Aug 1998 Cover: 6.95 **NM** value: **Cover or less**
Circ: Statement: **10,555**

313 ❑ Sep 1998 Cover: 6.95 **NM** value: **Cover or less**
Circ: Statement: **10,555**

314 ❑ Oct 1998 Cover: 6.95 **NM** value: **Cover or less**
Circ: Statement: **10,555**

315 ❑ Nov 1998 Cover: 6.95 **NM** value: **Cover or less**
Circ: Statement: **10,555**

316 ❑ Dec 1998 Cover: 6.95 **NM** value: **Cover or less**
• Has 1998 Statement, filed 9/1/98; avg print run 20,430; avg sales 8,397; avg subs 2,158; avg total paid 10,555; samples 247; office use 126; max existent 10,928; 47% of run returned

317 ❑ Jan 1999 Cover: 6.95 **NM** value: **Cover or less**

318 ❑ Feb 1999 Cover: 6.95 **NM** value: **Cover or less**
final issue.

UNCLE SHAM — Print Mint

1 ❑ Cover: 0.50 **NM** value: **4.00**

UNCLE SLAM & FIRE DOG — Action Planet

1 ❑ Cover: 2.95 **NM** value: **Cover or less**
📖 Visiting Yesterday; My Dream Date with Uncle Slam **A:** Ande Parks **W:** Ande Parks

2 ❑ Cover: 2.95 **NM** value: **Cover or less**
📖 The Origin of Me; The Terror of President Binky Dinky Doo **A:** Andy Kuhn; Ande Parks; Phillip Hester **W:** Andy Kuhn; Ande Parks

UNCUT COMICS — Uncut Comics

1 ❑ Apr 1997, b&w **NM** value: **1.00**
No issue number. • free handout; Origins

1/A ❑ Feb 1997, b&w Cover: 1.50 **NM** value: **Cover or less**
non-slick cover.

1/B ❑ Feb 1997, b&w Cover: 1.50 **NM** value: **Cover or less**
non-slick alternate cover.

2 ❑ May 1997, b&w Cover: 1.95 **NM** value: **Cover or less**
flip-book with alternate cover back-up.

UNDERCOVER GIRL — Magazine Enterprises

5 ❑ ca. 1952 Cover: 0.10 **NM** value: **200.00**
• **CGC:** 1 graded, best 9.2

6 ❑ ca. 1952 Cover: 0.10 **NM** value: **200.00**
• **CGC:** 1 graded, best 9.0

7 ❑ ca. 1953 Cover: 0.10 **NM** value: **200.00**
📖 The Man Who Was Yesterday!; The School for Spies; The Puzzle of the Picture!; The Key of Death • Undercover Girl, Fallon of the F.B.I., Roger Wright

UNDERDOG 3-D — Blackthorne

1 ❑ Cover: 2.50 **NM** value: **Cover or less**
Circ: CapCity orders: **1,350**

UNDERDOG (CHARLTON) — Charlton

1 ❑ Jul 1970 Cover: 0.15 **NM** value: **40.00**
• poster

2 ❑ Sep 1970 Cover: 0.15 **NM** value: **24.00**
3 ❑ Nov 1970 Cover: 0.15 **NM** value: **18.00**
4 ❑ Jan 1971 Cover: 0.15 **NM** value: **18.00**
5 ❑ Mar 1971 Cover: 0.15 **NM** value: **18.00**
6 ❑ May 1971 Cover: 0.15 **NM** value: **15.00**
7 ❑ Jul 1971 Cover: 0.15 **NM** value: **15.00**
8 ❑ Sep 1971 Cover: 0.15 **NM** value: **15.00**
9 ❑ Nov 1971 Cover: 0.20 **NM** value: **15.00**
10 ❑ Jan 1972 Cover: 0.20 **NM** value: **15.00**

UNDERDOG (GOLD KEY) — Gold Key

1 ❑ 1975 Cover: 0.25 **NM** value: **25.00**
2 ❑ 1975 Cover: 0.25 **NM** value: **14.00**
3 ❑ 1975 Cover: 0.25 **NM** value: **8.00**
4 ❑ 1975 Cover: 0.25 **NM** value: **6.00**
5 ❑ 1976 Cover: 0.25 **NM** value: **6.00**
6 ❑ 1976 Cover: 0.25 **NM** value: **5.00**
7 ❑ Jun 1976 Cover: 0.25 **NM** value: **5.00**
8 ❑ Aug 1976 Cover: 0.25 **NM** value: **5.00**
9 ❑ Oct 1976 Cover: 0.30 **NM** value: **5.00**
10 ❑ Dec 1976 Cover: 0.30 **NM** value: **5.00**
11 ❑ Feb 1976 Cover: 0.30 **NM** value: **4.00**
12 ❑ Apr 1977 Cover: 0.30 **NM** value: **4.00**
13 ❑ Jun 1977 Cover: 0.30 **NM** value: **4.00**
14 ❑ Aug 1977 Cover: 0.30 **NM** value: **4.00**
15 ❑ Oct 1977 Cover: 0.30 **NM** value: **4.00**
16 ❑ Dec 1977 Cover: 0.30 **NM** value: **4.00**
17 ❑ Feb 1978 Cover: 0.30 **NM** value: **4.00**
18 ❑ Apr 1978 Cover: 0.30 **NM** value: **4.00**
19 ❑ Jun 1978 Cover: 0.30 **NM** value: **4.00**
20 ❑ Aug 1978 Cover: 0.35 **NM** value: **4.00**
21 ❑ Oct 1978 Cover: 0.35 **NM** value: **3.00**
22 ❑ Dec 1978 Cover: 0.35 **NM** value: **3.00**
23 ❑ Feb 1979 Cover: 0.35 **NM** value: **3.00**

UNDERDOG (HARVEY) — Harvey

"Look up in the sky! It's a bird! It's a plane!" It's a frog!"

"No, it's not plane nor bird or even frog, it's just little old me, Underdog!"

In 1993, the much-loved cartoon hero Underdog returned to comics in this Harvey series. Underdog is the super-powered alter-ego of the meek Shoeshine Boy. When danger threatens (usually in the form of peril to Sweet Polly Purebred), he swallows an energy pill hidden in his ring and becomes the super-hero Underdog.

The first issue of this series pits him against his archenemy Simon Bar Sinister, a mad scientist whose schemes include shrinking the world so that he canbe the tallest man alive. A fun-filled and long-running (albeit in repeats) television series, its 1993 comics revival was regrettably short-lived, lasting just five issues.

1 ❑ Nov 1993 Cover: 1.50 **NM** value: **Cover or less**
• **CGC:** 1 graded, best 6.0
• No creator credits listed

2 ❑ Jan 1993 Cover: 1.50 **NM** value: **Cover or less**
• No creator credits listed

3 ❑ Mar 1994 Cover: 1.50 **NM** value: **Cover or less**
📖 Ringer Dinger!; Planet Zot • No creator credits listed

4 ❑ May 1994 Cover: 1.50 **NM** value: **Cover or less**
📖 Whistler's Father • No creator credits listed

5 ❑ Jul 1994 Cover: 1.50 **NM** value: **Cover or less**
• No creator credits listed

Smr 1 ❑ Oct 1993 Cover: 2.25 **NM** value: **Cover or less**

UNDERDOG (SPOTLIGHT) — Spotlight

1 ❑ ca. 1987 Cover: 1.50 **NM** value: **2.00**
Circ: CapCity orders: **3,750**

2 ❑ ca. 1987 Cover: 1.50 **NM** value: **2.00**
Circ: CapCity orders: **2,900**

UNDERGROUND — Aircel

1 ❑ b&w Cover: 1.70 **NM** value: **Cover or less**
No issue number.

UNDERGROUND (ANDREW VACHSS'...) — Dark Horse

1 ❑ Feb 1994 Cover: 3.95 **NM** value: **Cover or less**
Circ: CapCity orders: **3,700**
📖 Into the Underground; There is no Dog; Bum's Rush; My Job; Family; Potions by Isolde; Pooch; 'Way Down **A:** Guy Burwell; John Bergin; Phil Hester; Carol Swain; Harry O. Morris; Jeff Dickinson; Monty Sheldon **W:** John Bergin; Phil Hester; Carol Swain; Andrew Vachss; Bill Crider; Diane Patterson; Steve Rasnic Tem

2 ❑ Mar 1994 Cover: 3.95 **NM** value: **Cover or less**
Circ: CapCity orders: **2,300**

3 ❑ Apr 1994 Cover: 3.95 **NM** value: **Cover or less**
4 ❑ May 1994 Cover: 3.95 **NM** value: **Cover or less**

UNDERGROUND CLASSICS — Rip Off

1 ❑ Dec 1985 Cover: 1.50 **NM** value: **3.00**
• Fabulous Furry Freak Brothers **A:** Gilbert Shelton **W:** Gilbert Shelton

2 ❑ Feb 1986 Cover: 2.00 **NM** value: **2.50**
• Dealer McDope

2-2 ❑ 1986 Cover: 2.00 **NM** value: **Cover or less**
2-3 ❑ 1986 Cover: 2.00 **NM** value: **2.50**
3 ❑ Mar 1986 Cover: 2.00 **NM** value: **2.50**
• Dealer McDope

3-2 ❑ Cover: 2.00 **NM** value: **Cover or less**
4 ❑ Sep 1987 Cover: 2.50 **NM** value: **Cover or less**
5 ❑ Nov 1987 Cover: 2.00 **NM** value: **2.50**
• Wonder Warthog

6 ❑ Feb 1988 Cover: 2.00 **NM** value: **2.50**
7 ❑ Apr 1988 Cover: 2.50 **NM** value: **Cover or less**
8 ❑ Jun 1988 Cover: 2.50 **NM** value: **Cover or less**
📖 The Forty Year Old Hippie: Talks to the Whales; A different Drummer; Gotta Loosen My Load **W:** Ted Richards

9 ❑ Feb 1989 Cover: 2.50 **NM** value: **Cover or less**
• Art of Greg Irons

10 ❑ Cover: 2.50 **NM** value: **Cover or less**
• Jesus

11 ❑ Cover: 2.50 **NM** value: **Cover or less**
• Jesus

12 ❑ Jul 1990 Cover: 2.95 **NM** value: **Cover or less**
• Shelton 3-D

CGC-graded: Multiply prices above by **33 for 9.9 M • 16 for 9.8 NM/M • 7 for 9.6 NM+ • 5 for 9.4 NM • 2.5 for 9.2 NM- • 1.5 for 9.0 VF/NM**

12-2❑ Cover: 2.95 **NM** value: **Cover or less**
13 ❑ Cover: 2.50 **NM** value: **Cover or less**
• Jesus
14 ❑ Cover: 2.50 **NM** value: **Cover or less**
• Jesus
15 ❑ Cover: 2.50 **NM** value: **Cover or less**

UNDERSEA AGENT — Tower

UNDERSEA Agent was designed as a sister title to Tower Comics' THUNDER Agents. UNDERSEA was a particularly tortured acronym that stood for United Nations Department of Experiment and Research SystEms at Atlantis. This was a group of scientists who operated out of a secret underwater base and was charged with peaceful exploration of the oceans. Although there was supposedly a whole squad of agents, the only ones who seemed to see any action were Lt. Jones, kid sidekick Skooby, and the beautiful Renata Del Mar. Jones gained electrical super-powers in #2, when he was zapped by an electric eel while touching an atomic generator.

Of course, there were any number of villains who wanted to abuse the deep for their own ends. These included perennial villain Dr. Fang and the obligatory secret organization of would-be world conquerors known as T.H.E.M. (The Host of Evil Motives).

1 ❑ Jan 1966 Cover: 0.25 **NM** value: **28.00**
• **CGC:** 2 graded, best 9.4
2 ❑ Apr 1966 Cover: 0.25 **NM** value: **20.00**
• **CGC:** 2 graded, best 9.4
• Lt. Jones gains electrical powers
3 ❑ Jun 1966 Cover: 0.25 **NM** value: **16.00**
4 ❑ Aug 1966 Cover: 0.25 **NM** value: **16.00**
• **CGC:** 1 graded, best 9.2
5 ❑ Oct 1966 Cover: 0.25 **NM** value: **16.00**
• **CGC:** 1 graded, best 9.4
6 ❑ Mar 1967 Cover: 0.25 **NM** value: **16.00**
final issue.

UNDERSIDE — Caliber

1 ❑ Cover: 2.95 **NM** value: **Cover or less**

UNDERSTANDING COMICS (1ST EDITION) — Tundra

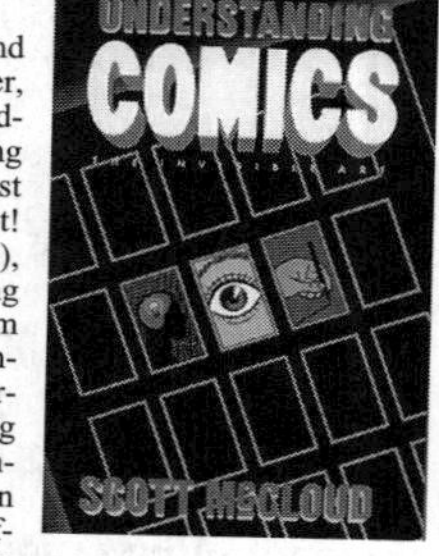

"Anyone interested in this literary form must read it."

So said comic-book legend and creator of The Spirit, Will Eisner, about Scott McCloud's groundbreaking work Understanding Comics. McCloud, the writer-artist known for his creating the Zot! comic book (published by Eclipse), wrote and drew Understanding Comics to analyze the medium known to some students as "sequential art." Narrated by a cartoon version of the author, Understanding Comics intelligently and entertainingly examines comics from both an artistic and cultural perspective. After the success of Understanding Comics, McCloud released his follow-up book, Reinventing Comics, looking at how comics are evolving due to the Internet. Because of his status as an authority in the field of comics, McCloud has been used as an expert witness for the defense in cases of censorship involving comic-book publications.

Bk 1❑ ca. 1993 Cover: 19.95 **NM** value: **Cover or less**
softcover. **A:** Scott McCloud **C:** Scott McCloud **W:** Scott McCloud

UNDERSTANDING COMICS (2ND EDITION) — Paradox

Bk 1/HC❑ Cover: 29.95 **NM** value: **Cover or less**
• Hardover; DC (Paradox Press) 2000 printing **A:** Scott McCloud **W:** Scott McCloud

UNDERTAKER — Chaos

0 ❑ Feb 1999 **NM** value: **3.00**
• Collector's issue; Wizard **A:** Manny Clark **W:** Beau Smith
0.5 ❑ Mar 1999 **NM** value: **4.00**
• **CGC:** 1 graded, best 9.6
1 ❑ Apr 1999 Cover: 2.95 **NM** value: **4.00**
Circ: Diamd. preorders: **34,213**
Drawn cover. 📖 Prophecy of the Dead **A:** Manny Clark **W:** Beau Smith
1/A ❑ Apr 1999 **NM** value: **6.00**
• **CGC:** 1 graded, best 9.8
DFE red foil cover. 📖 Prophecy of the Dead **A:** Manny Clark **W:** Beau Smith
1/B ❑ Apr 1999 **NM** value: **8.00**
DFE red foil cover. 📖 Prophecy of the Dead **A:** Manny Clark **W:** Beau Smith
1/SC❑ Apr 1999 Cover: 2.95 **NM** value: **4.00**
• **CGC:** 1 graded, best 10.0
Photo cover.
2 ❑ May 1999 Cover: 2.95 **NM** value: **Cover or less**
Circ: Diamd. preorders: **33,586**
3 ❑ Jun 1999 Cover: 2.95 **NM** value: **Cover or less**
Circ: Diamd. preorders: **34,458**
4 ❑ Jul 1999 Cover: 2.95 **NM** value: **Cover or less**
Circ: Diamd. preorders: **34,051**
5 ❑ Aug 1999 Cover: 2.95 **NM** value: **Cover or less**
Circ: Diamd. preorders: **31,091**
6 ❑ Sep 1999 Cover: 2.95 **NM** value: **Cover or less**
Circ: Diamd. preorders: **26,851**
7 ❑ Oct 1999 Cover: 2.95 **NM** value: **Cover or less**
Circ: Diamd. preorders: **24,022**
8 ❑ Nov 1999 Cover: 2.95 **NM** value: **Cover or less**
Circ: Diamd. preorders: **23,736**
📖 Streets Paved with Blood **A:** Manny Clark **W:** Beau Smith
9 ❑ Dec 1999 Cover: 2.95 **NM** value: **Cover or less**
Circ: Diamd. preorders: **21,684**
📖 Honeymoon in Hell **A:** Manny Clark **W:** Beau Smith
10 ❑ Jan 2000 Cover: 2.95 **NM** value: **Cover or less**
Circ: Diamd. preorders: **19,930**
📖 Broken Vows. Broken Hearts. Broken Bones. **A:** Manny Clark **W:** Beau Smith
HS 1❑ Oct 1999 Cover: 2.95 **NM** value: **Cover or less**
• digest. **A:** Leonardo Jimenez **W:** Dan Monte; Jim Monte

UNDER TERRA — Predawn

2 ❑ b&w Cover: 2.45 **NM** value: **Cover or less**
3 ❑ b&w Cover: 2.45 **NM** value: **Cover or less**
4 ❑ b&w Cover: 2.45 **NM** value: **Cover or less**
5 ❑ b&w Cover: 2.45 **NM** value: **Cover or less**
6 ❑ b&w Cover: 1.75 **NM** value: **Cover or less**

UNDERTOW — NBM / Amerotica

1 ❑ b&w Cover: 8.95 **NM** value: **Cover or less**
No issue number. • adult graphic novel

UNDERWORLD — D.S.

1 ❑ Feb 1948 Cover: 0.10 **NM** value: **250.00**
2 ❑ Apr 1948 Cover: 0.10 **NM** value: **200.00**
• **CGC:** 1 graded, best 6.5
3 ❑ Jun 1948 Cover: 0.10 **NM** value: **200.00**
4 ❑ Aug 1948 Cover: 0.10 **NM** value: **200.00**
5 ❑ Oct 1948 Cover: 0.10 **NM** value: **200.00**
6 ❑ Dec 1948 Cover: 0.10 **NM** value: **200.00**
7 ❑ Feb 1949 Cover: 0.10 **NM** value: **150.00**
• **CGC:** 1 graded, best 8.0
8 ❑ Apr 1949 Cover: 0.10 **NM** value: **150.00**
9 ❑ Jun 1949 Cover: 0.10 **NM** value: **150.00**

UNDERWORLD CRIME — Fawcett

1 ❑ Jun 1952 Cover: 0.10 **NM** value: **200.00**
2 ❑ Aug 1952 Cover: 0.10 **NM** value: **100.00**
3 ❑ Oct 1952 Cover: 0.10 **NM** value: **100.00**
4 ❑ Dec 1952 Cover: 0.10 **NM** value: **100.00**
• **CGC:** 1 graded, best 7.5
5 ❑ Feb 1953 Cover: 0.10 **NM** value: **100.00**
6 ❑ Apr 1953 Cover: 0.10 **NM** value: **100.00**
7 ❑ Jun 1953 Cover: 0.10 **NM** value: **100.00**
• **CGC:** 3 graded, best 9.0

UNDERWORLD (DC) — DC

1 ❑ Dec 1987 Cover: 1.25 **NM** value: **Cover or less**
Circ: CapCity orders: **19,900**
2 ❑ Jan 1988 Cover: 1.00 **NM** value: **1.25**
Circ: CapCity orders: **15,350**
3 ❑ Feb 1988 Cover: 1.00 **NM** value: **1.25**
Circ: CapCity orders: **14,000**
📖 Saving Grace **A:** Ernie Colon **W:** Robert Loren Flemming
4 ❑ Mar 1988 Cover: 1.00 **NM** value: **1.25**
Circ: CapCity orders: **12,850**

UNDERWORLD (DEATH) — Death

1 ❑ b&w Cover: 2.00 **NM** value: **Cover or less**

UNDERWORLD UNLEASHED — DC

1 ❑ Nov 1995 Cover: 2.95 **NM** value: **3.50**
2 ❑ Dec 1995 Cover: 2.95 **NM** value: **3.25**
3 ❑ Dec 1995 Cover: 2.95 **NM** value: **3.25**
Bk 1❑ Cover: 17.95 **NM** value: **Cover or less**
• collects mini-series and Underworld Unleashed: Abyss – Hell's Sentinel #1

UNDERWORLD UNLEASHED: ABYSS-HELL'S SENTINEL — DC

1 ❑ Dec 1995 Cover: 2.95 **NM** value: **Cover or less**
One-shot.

UNDERWORLD UNLEASHED: APOKOLIPS-DARK UPRISING — DC

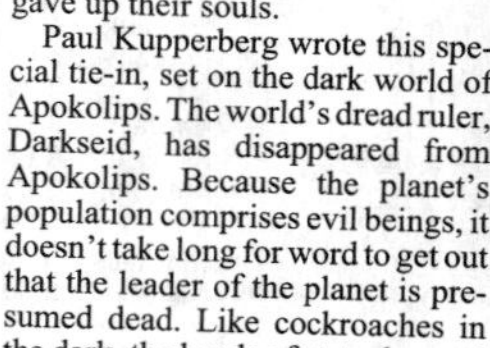

This story is part of DC's Underworld Unleashed crossover that occurred in late 1995. In that saga, about two dozen DC villains were granted their heart's fondest wishes by a strange and evil being named Neron. In exchange, the villains gave up their souls.

Paul Kupperberg wrote this special tie-in, set on the dark world of Apokolips. The world's dread ruler, Darkseid, has disappeared from Apokolips. Because the planet's population comprises evil beings, it doesn't take long for word to get out that the leader of the planet is presumed dead. Like cockroaches in the dark, the heads of state descend on Darkseid's throne, each claiming to be the ruler. But Darkseid's chief scientist and adviser, Desaad, has a better idea. He asks Neron for the ability to look exactly like Darkseid, then uses his newfound appearance to seize control of Apokolips.

1 ❑ Nov 1995 Cover: 1.95 **NM** value: **Cover or less**
One-shot.

UNDERWORLD UNLEASHED: BATMAN-DEVIL'S ASYLUM — DC

1 ❑ 1995 Cover: 2.95 **NM** value: **Cover or less**
One-shot.

UNDERWORLD UNLEASHED: PATTERNS OF FEAR — DC

1 ❑ Dec 1995 Cover: 2.95 **NM** value: **Cover or less**
One-shot. **A:** Anthony Williams; Andy Lanning **W:** Roger Stern ★ Appearance of Oracle.

UNDIE DOG — Halley's

1 ❑ b&w Cover: 1.50 **NM** value: **Cover or less**

UNEARTHLY SPECTACULARS — Harvey

1 ❑ Oct 1965 Cover: 0.12 **NM** value: **18.00**
2 ❑ Dec 1965 Cover: 0.25 **NM** value: **15.00**
3 ❑ Mar 1967 Cover: 0.25 **NM** value: **15.00**
• **CGC:** 1 graded, best 9.0

UNEEDA COMIX — Print Mint

1 ❑ Cover: 0.50 **NM** value: **3.00**
📖 Pud; Bo Bo Bolinski; Mr. Natural Goes to A Meeting of the Minds; Honey Bunch Kominski "The Drug-Crazed Runaway": She's Leaving Home **A:** Robert Crumb **W:** Robert Crumb

UNEXPECTED, THE — DC

105❑ Feb 1968 Cover: 0.12 **NM** value: **26.00**
Circ: Statement: **165,195** • **CGC:** 5 graded, best 9.2
• Series continued from Tales of the Unexpected #104
106❑ Apr 1968 Cover: 0.12 **NM** value: **15.00**
Circ: Statement: **165,195**
• Has 1967 Statement, filed 10/1/67; avg print run 308,000; avg sales 162,000; avg subs 600; avg total paid 162,600; samples 340; max existent 162,940; 47% of run returned
107❑ Jun 1968 Cover: 0.12 **NM** value: **15.00**
Circ: Statement: **165,195** • **CGC:** 1 graded, best 9.4
108❑ Aug 1968 Cover: 0.12 **NM** value: **15.00**
Circ: Statement: **165,195** • **CGC:** 1 graded, best 9.8
109❑ Oct 1968 Cover: 0.12 **NM** value: **15.00**
Circ: Statement: **165,195** • **CGC:** 1 graded, best 9.2
110❑ Dec 1968 Cover: 0.12 **NM** value: **15.00**
Circ: Statement: **165,195**
111❑ Feb 1969 Cover: 0.12 **NM** value: **15.00**
Circ: Statement: **155,110**
112❑ Apr 1969 Cover: 0.12 **NM** value: **15.00**
Circ: Statement: **155,110**
• Has 1968 Statement, filed 10/1/68; avg print run 298,000; avg sales 165,000; avg subs 195; avg total paid 165,195; samples 386; max existent 165,581; 44% of run returned
113❑ Jun 1969 Cover: 0.12 **NM** value: **15.00**
Circ: Statement: **155,110**
114❑ Aug 1969 Cover: 0.15 **NM** value: **10.00**
Circ: Statement: **155,110** • **CGC:** 1 graded, best 9.6
115❑ Oct 1969 Cover: 0.15 **NM** value: **10.00**
Circ: Statement: **155,110** • **CGC:** 1 graded, best 9.2
116❑ Dec 1969 Cover: 0.15 **NM** value: **10.00**
Circ: Statement: **155,110**
117❑ Feb 1970 Cover: 0.15 **NM** value: **10.00**
Circ: Statement: **159,390**
118❑ Apr 1970 Cover: 0.15 **NM** value: **10.00**
Circ: Statement: **159,390**
• Has 1969 Statement, filed 10/1/69; avg print run 292,000; avg sales 155,000; avg subs 110; avg total paid 155,110; samples 346; max existent 155,456; 47% of run returned
119❑ Jun 1970 Cover: 0.15 **NM** value: **12.00**
Circ: Statement: **159,390** • **CGC:** 1 graded, best 9.2
120❑ Aug 1970 Cover: 0.15 **NM** value: **10.00**
Circ: Statement: **159,390**
121❑ Oct 1970 Cover: 0.15 **NM** value: **14.00**
Circ: Statement: **159,390** • **CGC:** 1 graded, best 8.5
122❑ Dec 1970 Cover: 0.15 **NM** value: **10.00**
Circ: Statement: **159,390** • **CGC:** 1 graded, best 9.0
123❑ Feb 1971 Cover: 0.15 **NM** value: **10.00**
Circ: Statement: **178,578** • **CGC:** 1 graded, best 9.6
124❑ Apr 1971 Cover: 0.15 **NM** value: **10.00**
Circ: Statement: **178,578**
• Has 1970 Statement, filed 10/1/70; avg print run 285,935; avg sales 159,308; avg subs 82; avg total paid 159,390; samples 122; max existent 159,512; 44% of run returned
125❑ Jul 1971 Cover: 0.15 **NM** value: **10.00**
Circ: Statement: **178,578**
126❑ Aug 1971 Cover: 0.25 **NM** value: **10.00**
Circ: Statement: **178,578** • **CGC:** 1 graded, best 8.5
127❑ Sep 1971 Cover: 0.25 **NM** value: **10.00**
Circ: Statement: **178,578** • **CGC:** 2 graded, best 9.2
128❑ Oct 1971 Cover: 0.25 **NM** value: **12.00**
Circ: Statement: **178,578** • **CGC:** 2 graded, best 9.2
129❑ Nov 1971 Cover: 0.25 **NM** value: **6.00**
Circ: Statement: **178,578**
130❑ Dec 1971 Cover: 0.25 **NM** value: **6.00**
Circ: Statement: **178,578** • **CGC:** 1 graded, best 9.4
131❑ Jan 1972 Cover: 0.25 **NM** value: **6.00**
Circ: Statement: **168,430** • **CGC:** 1 graded, best 9.4
📖 Run For Your Death; The Beast of Bristol; If Time Runs Out; We Cruised into the Supernatural **A:** Dick Dillin; Frank Giacoia; Nick Cardy; Bob Brown; Mike Esposito **W:** Carl Wessler; Jack Phillips
132❑ Feb 1972 Cover: 0.25 **NM** value: **6.00**
Circ: Statement: **168,430**
133❑ Mar 1972 Cover: 0.25 **NM** value: **6.00**
Circ: Statement: **168,430** • **CGC:** 3 graded, best 9.8

• Has 1971 Statement; avg print run 300,000; avg sales 178,506; avg subs 72; avg total paid 178,578; max existent 178,578; 40% of run returned

134 ❑ Apr 1972 Cover: 0.25 **NM** value: **6.00**
Circ: Statement: **168,430** • **CGC:** 1 graded, best 9.0

135 ❑ May 1972 Cover: 0.25 **NM** value: **6.00**
Circ: Statement: **168,430** • **CGC:** 2 graded, best 9.6

136 ❑ Jun 1972 **NM** value: **6.00**
Circ: Statement: **168,430**

137 ❑ Jul 1972 Cover: 0.20 **NM** value: **6.00**
Circ: Statement: **168,430**

138 ❑ Aug 1972 Cover: 0.20 **NM** value: **6.00**
Circ: Statement: **168,430**

139 ❑ Sep 1972 Cover: 0.20 **NM** value: **6.00**
Circ: Statement: **168,430**

140 ❑ Oct 1972 Cover: 0.20 **NM** value: **6.00**
Circ: Statement: **168,430**

141 ❑ Nov 1972 Cover: 0.20 **NM** value: **6.00**
Circ: Statement: **168,430**

142 ❑ Dec 1972 Cover: 0.20 **NM** value: **6.00**
Circ: Statement: **168,430**

143 ❑ Jan 1973 Cover: 0.20 **NM** value: **6.00**
Circ: Statement: **164,344**

144 ❑ Feb 1973 Cover: 0.20 **NM** value: **6.00**
Circ: Statement: **164,344**

145 ❑ Mar 1973 Cover: 0.20 **NM** value: **6.00**
Circ: Statement: **164,344**
• Has 1972 Statement, filed 10/1/72; avg print run 325,000; avg sales 168,183; avg subs 247; avg total paid 168,430; samples 523; office use 358; max existent 169,311; 48% of run returned

146 ❑ Apr 1973 Cover: 0.20 **NM** value: **6.00**
Circ: Statement: **164,344**

147 ❑ Jun 1973 Cover: 0.20 **NM** value: **6.00**
Circ: Statement: **164,344**

148 ❑ Jul 1973 Cover: 0.20 **NM** value: **6.00**
Circ: Statement: **164,344**

149 ❑ Aug 1973 Cover: 0.20 **NM** value: **6.00**
Circ: Statement: **164,344**

150 ❑ Sep 1973 Cover: 0.20 **NM** value: **6.00**
Circ: Statement: **164,344**

151 ❑ Oct 1973 Cover: 0.20 **NM** value: **6.00**
Circ: Statement: **164,344**

152 ❑ Nov 1973 Cover: 0.20 **NM** value: **6.00**
Circ: Statement: **164,344**

153 ❑ Dec 1973 Cover: 0.20 **NM** value: **6.00**
Circ: Statement: **164,344**

154 ❑ Jan 1974 Cover: 0.20 **NM** value: **6.00**
Circ: Statement: **175,016**

155 ❑ Feb 1974 Cover: 0.20 **NM** value: **6.00**
Circ: Statement: **175,016**

156 ❑ Mar 1974 Cover: 0.20 **NM** value: **6.00**
Circ: Statement: **175,016** • **CGC:** 1 graded, best 9.0

157 ❑ Jun 1974 Cover: 0.60 **NM** value: **10.00**
Circ: Statement: **175,016** • **CGC:** 2 graded, best 9.6
• Has 1973 Statement; avg total paid circ 164,344

158 ❑ Aug 1974 Cover: 0.60 **NM** value: **10.00**
Circ: Statement: **175,016**

159 ❑ Oct 1974 Cover: 0.60 **NM** value: **10.00**
Circ: Statement: **175,016** • **CGC:** 1 graded, best 8.5

160 ❑ Dec 1974 Cover: 0.60 **NM** value: **10.00**
Circ: Statement: **175,016**
📖 The Death of an Exorcist; Over My Dead Body; The Fear Master; Bewitched for a Day; The Riddle of the Glass Bubble; Panic in the Dark; The Wizard of the Diamond World; Doom Was My Inheritance; Rest in Pieces **A:** Mort Meskin; Lee Elias; Rico Rival; Jack Sparling; Bill Ely **W:** Bill Dennehy; Carl Wessler; George Kashdan

161 ❑ Feb 1975 Cover: 0.60 **NM** value: **10.00**
Circ: Statement: **141,000** • **CGC:** 1 graded, best 7.5

162 ❑ Mar 1975 Cover: 0.60 **NM** value: **10.00**
Circ: Statement: **141,000** • **CGC:** 2 graded, best 9.2

163 ❑ Apr 1975 Cover: 0.25 **NM** value: **4.00**
Circ: Statement: **141,000**

164 ❑ May 1975 Cover: 0.25 **NM** value: **4.00**
Circ: Statement: **141,000**
• Has 1974 Statement; avg total paid circ 175,016

165 ❑ Jun 1975 Cover: 0.25 **NM** value: **4.00**
Circ: Statement: **141,000** • **CGC:** 1 graded, best 8.0

166 ❑ Jul 1975 Cover: 0.25 **NM** value: **4.00**
Circ: Statement: **141,000**

167 ❑ Aug 1975 Cover: 0.25 **NM** value: **4.00**
Circ: Statement: **141,000**

168 ❑ Sep 1975 Cover: 0.25 **NM** value: **4.00**
Circ: Statement: **141,000**

169 ❑ 1975 Cover: 0.25 **NM** value: **4.00**
Circ: Statement: **141,000**

170 ❑ Dec 1975 Cover: 0.25 **NM** value: **4.00**
Circ: Statement: **141,000** • **CGC:** 1 graded, best 9.0

171 ❑ Feb 1976 Cover: 0.25 **NM** value: **4.00**
Circ: Statement: **131,000** • **CGC:** 1 graded, best 8.5

172 ❑ Apr 1976 Cover: 0.30 **NM** value: **4.00**
Circ: Statement: **131,000**

173 ❑ Jun 1976 Cover: 0.30 **NM** value: **4.00**
Circ: Statement: **131,000** • **CGC:** 1 graded, best 7.0

174 ❑ Aug 1976 Cover: 0.30 **NM** value: **4.00**
Circ: Statement: **131,000**

175 ❑ Oct 1976 Cover: 0.30 **NM** value: **4.00**
Circ: Statement: **131,000**

176 ❑ Dec 1976 Cover: 0.30 **NM** value: **4.00**
Circ: Statement: **131,000**

177 ❑ Feb 1977 Cover: 0.30 **NM** value: **4.00**
Circ: Statement: **131,315**

178 ❑ Apr 1977 Cover: 0.30 **NM** value: **4.00**
Circ: Statement: **131,315**

179 ❑ Jun 1977 Cover: 0.30 **NM** value: **4.00**
Circ: Statement: **131,315**
• Has 1976 Statement; avg total paid circ 131,000

180 ❑ Aug 1977 Cover: 0.35 **NM** value: **4.00**
Circ: Statement: **131,315**

181 ❑ Oct 1977 Cover: 0.35 **NM** value: **4.00**
Circ: Statement: **131,315**

182 ❑ Dec 1977 Cover: 0.35 **NM** value: **4.00**
Circ: Statement: **131,315**

183 ❑ Feb 1978 Cover: 0.35 **NM** value: **4.00**
184 ❑ Apr 1978 Cover: 0.35 **NM** value: **4.00**
185 ❑ Jun 1978 Cover: 0.35 **NM** value: **4.00**
• Has 1977 Statement; avg total paid circ 131,315
186 ❑ Aug 1978 Cover: 0.35 **NM** value: **4.00**
187 ❑ Oct 1978 Cover: 0.50 **NM** value: **4.00**
188 ❑ Dec 1978 Cover: 0.50 **NM** value: **4.00**
189 ❑ Feb 1979 Cover: 1.00 **NM** value: **4.00**
190 ❑ Apr 1979 Cover: 1.00 **NM** value: **4.00**
191 ❑ Jun 1979 Cover: 1.00 **NM** value: **5.00**
192 ❑ Aug 1979 Cover: 1.00 **NM** value: **3.00**
193 ❑ Oct 1979 Cover: 1.00 **NM** value: **3.00**
194 ❑ Dec 1979 Cover: 1.00 **NM** value: **3.00**
195 ❑ Feb 1980 Cover: 1.00 **NM** value: **3.00**
196 ❑ Mar 1980 Cover: 0.40 **NM** value: **3.00**
197 ❑ Apr 1980 Cover: 0.40 **NM** value: **3.00**
198 ❑ May 1980 Cover: 0.40 **NM** value: **3.00**
199 ❑ Jun 1980 Cover: 0.40 **NM** value: **3.00**
200 ❑ Jul 1980 Cover: 0.40 **NM** value: **3.00**
201 ❑ Aug 1980 Cover: 0.40 **NM** value: **3.00**
202 ❑ Sep 1980 Cover: 0.50 **NM** value: **3.00**
📖 Death Trap; The Creature of the Park **A:** Ken Landgraf; Arthur Geroche; Tenny Henson; Torre Repiso **W:** Carl Wessler; Michael Lislan; Ms. Charlie Seeger; Peter John Palmer
203 ❑ Oct 1980 Cover: 0.50 **NM** value: **3.00**
204 ❑ Nov 1980 Cover: 0.50 **NM** value: **3.00**
205 ❑ Dec 1980 Cover: 0.50 **NM** value: **3.00**
206 ❑ Jan 1981 Cover: 0.50 **NM** value: **3.00**
Circ: Statement: **83,000**

207 ❑ Feb 1981 Cover: 0.50 **NM** value: **3.00**
Circ: Statement: **83,000**

208 ❑ Mar 1981 Cover: 0.50 **NM** value: **3.00**
Circ: Statement: **83,000**

209 ❑ Apr 1981 Cover: 0.50 **NM** value: **3.00**
Circ: Statement: **83,000**

210 ❑ May 1981 Cover: 0.50 **NM** value: **3.00**
Circ: Statement: **83,000**

211 ❑ Jun 1981 Cover: 0.50 **NM** value: **3.00**
Circ: Statement: **83,000**

212 ❑ Jul 1981 Cover: 0.50 **NM** value: **3.00**
Circ: Statement: **83,000**

213 ❑ Aug 1981 Cover: 0.50 **NM** value: **3.00**
Circ: Statement: **83,000**

214 ❑ Sep 1981 Cover: 0.50 **NM** value: **3.00**
Circ: Statement: **83,000**

215 ❑ Oct 1981 Cover: 0.60 **NM** value: **3.00**
Circ: Statement: **83,000**

216 ❑ Nov 1981 Cover: 0.60 **NM** value: **3.00**
Circ: Statement: **83,000**

217 ❑ Dec 1981 Cover: 0.60 **NM** value: **3.00**
Circ: Statement: **83,000**

218 ❑ Jan 1982 **NM** value: **3.00**
219 ❑ Feb 1982 **NM** value: **3.00**
220 ❑ Mar 1982 Cover: 0.60 **NM** value: **3.00**
221 ❑ Apr 1982 **NM** value: **3.00**
222 ❑ May 1982 **NM** value: **3.00**
final issue.

UNEXPURGATED CARL BARKS, THE — Hamilton

Bk 1 ❑ Cover: 9.95 **NM** value: **Cover or less**
• collects Barks cartoons from The Calgary Eye-Opener **A:** Carl Barks

U.N. FORCE — Gauntlet

1 ❑ ca. 1995, full color Cover: 2.95 **NM** value: **Cover or less**
Circ: CapCity orders: **3,280**

2 ❑ ca. 1995, full color Cover: 2.95 **NM** value: **Cover or less**
Circ: CapCity orders: **7,050**

3 ❑ ca. 1995, full color Cover: 2.95 **NM** value: **Cover or less**
Circ: CapCity orders: **6,950**

4 ❑ ca. 1995, full color Cover: 2.95 **NM** value: **Cover or less**
5 ❑ ca. 1995, full color Cover: 2.95 **NM** value: **Cover or less**

UNFORGIVEN, THE — Mythic

1 ❑ Cover: 2.95 **NM** value: **Cover or less**

UNFUNNY X-CONS, THE — Parody Press

1 ❑ Sep 1992 Cover: 2.50 **NM** value: **Cover or less**
three variant covers (X, Y, Z).

1-2 ❑ Cover: 2.50 **NM** value: **Cover or less**
• 2nd Printing with trading card

UNICORN ISLE — Apple

1 ❑ Oct 1986, b&w Cover: 1.50 **NM** value: **2.00**
2 ❑ Nov 1986, b&w Cover: 1.50 **NM** value: **2.00**
3 ❑ Dec 1986, b&w Cover: 1.50 **NM** value: **2.00**
4 ❑ Jan 1987 Cover: 1.75 **NM** value: **2.00**
5 ❑ Feb 1987 Cover: 1.75 **NM** value: **2.00**
6 ❑ Mar 1987 Cover: 1.50 **NM** value: **2.00**
7 ❑ Cover: 1.50 **NM** value: **2.00**
8 ❑ Cover: 1.50 **NM** value: **2.00**
9 ❑ Cover: 1.50 **NM** value: **2.00**
10 ❑ Cover: 1.50 **NM** value: **2.00**
11 ❑ Cover: 1.50 **NM** value: **2.00**
12 ❑ Cover: 1.50 **NM** value: **2.00**

UNICORN KING — Kz Comics

1 ❑ Dec 1986, b&w Cover: 0.95 **NM** value: **2.00**

UNION — Image

1 ❑ Feb 1995 Cover: 2.50 **NM** value: **Cover or less**
Circ: CapCity orders: **22,650**

2 ❑ Mar 1995 Cover: 2.50 **NM** value: **Cover or less**
Circ: CapCity orders: **17,175**

3 ❑ Apr 1995 Cover: 2.50 **NM** value: **Cover or less**
Circ: CapCity orders: **15,725**

4 ❑ May 1995 Cover: 2.50 **NM** value: **Cover or less**
Circ: CapCity orders: **25,400**
• with cards

5 ❑ Jun 1995 Cover: 2.50 **NM** value: **Cover or less**
Circ: CapCity orders: **14,175**

6 ❑ Jul 1995 Cover: 2.50 **NM** value: **Cover or less**
Circ: CapCity orders: **14,525**

7 ❑ Aug 1995 Cover: 2.50 **NM** value: **Cover or less**
Circ: CapCity orders: **14,050**

8 ❑ Oct 1995 Cover: 2.50 **NM** value: **Cover or less**
9 ❑ Feb 1996 Cover: 2.50 **NM** value: **Cover or less**
covers says Dec, indicia says Feb. final issue. • Story continued in Union: Final Vengeance

UNION: FINAL VENGEANCE — Image

1 ❑ Oct 1997 Cover: 2.50 **NM** value: **Cover or less**
Circ: Diamd. preorders: **14,135**
📖 Knight of Faith • concludes story from Union #9 **A:** Carlos Mota **W:** Mike Heisler

UNION JACK — Marvel

Union Jack, the embodiment of the spirit of Great Britain, fights a desperate battle with a group of vampires that dare to seek the Holy Grail. Will his silver accoutrements be sufficient against vampires that are so brazen?

The Union Jack of this three-issue mini-series is the third person to hold that title. Lord Montgomery Falsworth, the first man to wear the colors of England, allied with Captain America and The Submariner as part of The Invaders during World War II. When a battle with the Nazi vampire (and his brother) Baron Blood cost him the use of his legs, his son, Brian Falsworth, took up the mantel of Union Jack until his death in 1953.

Joey Chapman stood in for the first Union Jack in Captain America #254 as a ruse to deceive the resurrected Baron Blood. That masquerade led Chapman to inherit the Union Jack identity, which is the source of resentment from Kenneth Crichton, the grandson of the original Union Jack. Crichton is too sickly to carry on the family tradition but, nevertheless, harbors bitterness for his loss. That bitterness is an underlying theme.

1 ❑ Dec 1998 Cover: 2.99 **NM** value: **Cover or less**
Circ: Diamd. preorders: **21,537**
• gatefold summary. 📖 Tradition **A:** John Cassaday **W:** John Cassaday; Ben Raab

2 ❑ Jan 1999 Cover: 2.99 **NM** value: **Cover or less**
Circ: Diamd. preorders: **17,941**
• gatefold summary. **A:** John Cassaday **W:** John Cassaday; Ben Raab

3 ❑ Feb 1999 Cover: 2.99 **NM** value: **Cover or less**
Circ: Diamd. preorders: **17,704**

UNION JACKS — Anacom

1 ❑ b&w Cover: 2.00 **NM** value: **Cover or less**

UNION (MINI-SERIES) — Image

Ohmen was a brave soldier for the Protectorate, a force for justice from a different world. The Protectorate had long been at war against their enemies, the Directorate. It was in the midst of a battle with two Directorate soldiers, in the middle of a storm, that Ohmen was struck by lightning. The blast, reacting with Ohmen's source of power, the Justice Stone, opened a hole in space and threw Ohmen through it. Much the worse for the wear, he landed on a frozen lake near Jill Monroe's house in Maine.

Jill took Ohmen in and nursed him back to health. In time, Jill fell in love with this strange soldier from another world's war. Unfortunately, as StormWatch discovers, it looks as if the war has come back to haunt him. Directorate soldiers have followed Ohmen and have even been living in secret on Earth for years. Taking on the name "Union" (after his world's name for the cold fusion source of his power), Ohmen begins the fight anew.

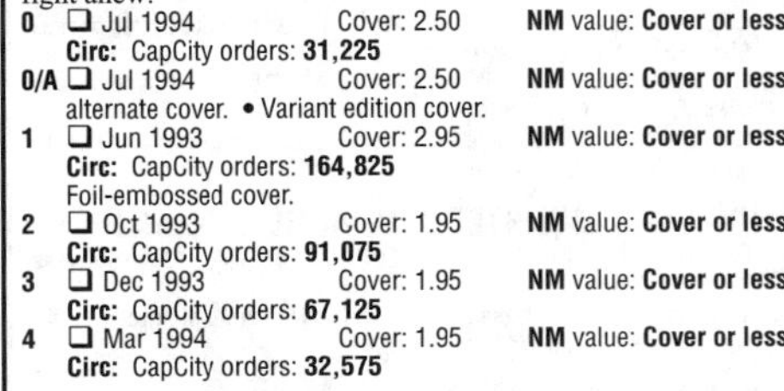

0 ❑ Jul 1994 Cover: 2.50 **NM** value: **Cover or less**
Circ: CapCity orders: **31,225**

0/A ❑ Jul 1994 Cover: 2.50 **NM** value: **Cover or less**
alternate cover. • Variant edition cover.

1 ❑ Jun 1993 Cover: 2.95 **NM** value: **Cover or less**
Circ: CapCity orders: **164,825**
Foil-embossed cover.

2 ❑ Oct 1993 Cover: 1.95 **NM** value: **Cover or less**
Circ: CapCity orders: **91,075**

3 ❑ Dec 1993 Cover: 1.95 **NM** value: **Cover or less**
Circ: CapCity orders: **67,125**

4 ❑ Mar 1994 Cover: 1.95 **NM** value: **Cover or less**
Circ: CapCity orders: **32,575**

UNITED COMICS — United Feature Syndicate

1 ❑ Aug 1940 Cover: 0.10 **NM** value: **100.00**
8 ❑ Jan 1950 Cover: 0.10 **NM** value: **20.00**
9 ❑ Mar 1950 Cover: 0.10 **NM** value: **20.00**

CGC-graded: Multiply prices above by **33 for 9.9 M • 16 for 9.8 NM/M • 7 for 9.6 NM+ • 5 for 9.4 NM • 2.5 for 9.2 NM- • 1.5 for 9.0 VF/NM**

10 ❑ May 1950 Cover: 0.10 **NM** value: **20.00**
• Fritzi Ritz

11 ❑ Jul 1950 Cover: 0.10 **NM** value: **20.00**

12 ❑ Sep 1950 Cover: 0.10 **NM** value: **20.00**
• Fritzi Ritz

13 ❑ Nov 1950 Cover: 0.10 **NM** value: **20.00**

14 ❑ Jan 1951 Cover: 0.10 **NM** value: **20.00**

15 ❑ Mar 1951 Cover: 0.10 **NM** value: **20.00**
📖 Fritzi Ritz; Abbie an' Slats **A:** Raeburn VanBuren; Ernie Bushmiller **W:** Raeburn VanBuren; Ernie Bushmiller

16 ❑ May 1951 Cover: 0.10 **NM** value: **20.00**

17 ❑ Jul 1951 Cover: 0.10 **NM** value: **20.00**

18 ❑ Sep 1951 Cover: 0.10 **NM** value: **20.00**

19 ❑ Nov 1951 Cover: 0.10 **NM** value: **20.00**

20 ❑ Jan 1952 Cover: 0.10 **NM** value: **20.00**

21 ❑ Mar 1952 Cover: 0.10 **NM** value: **16.00**

22 ❑ May 1952 Cover: 0.10 **NM** value: **20.00**

23 ❑ Jul 1952 Cover: 0.10 **NM** value: **16.00**

24 ❑ Sep 1952 Cover: 0.10 **NM** value: **20.00**

25 ❑ Nov 1952 Cover: 0.10 **NM** value: **16.00**

26 ❑ Jan 1953 Cover: 0.10 **NM** value: **16.00**

UNITED STATES MARINES Magazine Enterprises

1 ❑ ca. 1943 Cover: 0.10 **NM** value: **100.00**

2 ❑ ca. 1944 Cover: 0.10 **NM** value: **150.00**
• **CGC:** 1 graded, best 8.0

3 ❑ ca. 1944 Cover: 0.10 **NM** value: **125.00**

4 ❑ ca. 1944 Cover: 0.10 **NM** value: **100.00**

5 ❑ ca. 1952 Cover: 0.10 **NM** value: **40.00**

6 ❑ ca. 1952 Cover: 0.10 **NM** value: **40.00**

7 ❑ ca. 1952 Cover: 0.10 **NM** value: **40.00**

8 ❑ ca. 1952 Cover: 0.10 **NM** value: **40.00**

UNITY Valiant

As a company, Valiant has always been known for its strong continuity — its ability to fit its characters and storylines into a coherent whole. This paid off on a grand scale, when it launched Unity, one of the most ambitious crossovers that has ever been seen in comics.

Unity was the story of how an embittered woman named Erica Pierce appoints herself "Mothergod" in the year 4001. She then launches a project called "Unity" to remake time itself, destroying all reality outside of her tiny realm, then literally remaking the world itself. The Earth itself senses the danger and calls geomancer Geoff McHenry to raise a force to stop Pierce. A truly epic struggle begins, with heroes from all times brought together to stop Pierce.

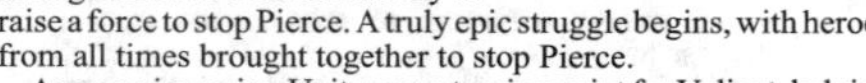

As a comics series, Unity was a turning point for Valiant, helping to transform a fledgling company into an established force in comics.

0 ❑ Aug 1992 **NM** value: **1.00**
• **CGC:** 1 graded, best 9.0
• Blue cover (regular edition). 📖 Unity, Part 1 **A:** Barry Windsor-Smith **W:** Jim Shooter

0/LE ❑ Aug 1992 **NM** value: **3.00**
• **CGC:** 8 graded, best 9.6
• Red cover (limited promotional edition). 📖 Unity, Part 1 **A:** Barry Windsor-Smith **W:** Jim Shooter

1 ❑ Oct 1992 Cover: 1.50 **NM** value: **2.00**
Circ: CapCity orders: **23,927** • **CGC:** 1 graded, best 9.0
📖 Unity, Part 18

1/GO ❑ Oct 1992 **NM** value: **3.00**
• **CGC:** 3 graded, best 9.8
• Gold edition. 📖 Unity, Part 18

1/PL ❑ Oct 1992 **NM** value: **3.00**
• **CGC:** 1 graded, best 9.6
• Platinum edition.

Bk 1 ❑ Cover: 9.95 **NM** value: **Cover or less**

Bk 2 ❑ Cover: 9.95 **NM** value: **Cover or less**
• Collects Unity, Parts 5-9

Bk 3 ❑ Cover: 9.95 **NM** value: **Cover or less**
• Collects Unity, Parts 10-14

Bk 4 ❑ Cover: 9.95 **NM** value: **Cover or less**
• Collects Unity, Parts 15-18 ★ Death of Rai I.

YB 1 ❑ Cover: 3.95 **NM** value: **Cover or less**
cardstock cover. • Yearbook 1. 📖 Yearbook #1; The Lost Chapter • a.k.a. Unity: The Lost Chapter **A:** Michael Bair **W:** Kevin VanHook ★ Appearance of X-O Manowar, Solar.

UNITY 2000 Acclaim

1 ❑ Nov 1999 Cover: 2.50 **NM** value: **Cover or less**
Circ: Diamd. preorders: **12,155**
📖 Absent Friends **A:** Jim Starlin **W:** Jim Shooter

2 ❑ Dec 1999 Cover: 2.50 **NM** value: **Cover or less**
Circ: Diamd. preorders: **10,247**

3 ❑ Jan 2000 Cover: 2.50 **NM** value: **Cover or less**
Circ: Diamd. preorders: **9,609**
📖 Painful Truth or Apocalyptic Consequences • series canceled **A:** Jim Starlin **W:** Jim Shooter

UNIVERSAL MONSTERS: DRACULA Dark Horse

1 ❑ 1993 Cover: 4.95 **NM** value: **Cover or less**
Circ: CapCity orders: **4,500**
No issue number. • Based on the classic Universal pictures film **A:** Jonathan D. Smith **W:** Dan Vado

UNIVERSAL MONSTERS: FRANKENSTEIN Dark Horse

1 ❑ 1993 Cover: 3.95 **NM** value: **Cover or less**
Circ: CapCity orders: **6,175**
No issue number. • Based on the classic Universal pictures film **A:** Denis Beauvais **W:** Denis Beauvais

UNIVERSAL MONSTERS: THE CREATURE FROM THE BLACK LAGOON Dark Horse

1 ❑ Aug 1993 Cover: 4.95 **NM** value: **Cover or less**
No issue number. **A:** Arthur Adams **W:** Steve Moncuse

UNIVERSAL MONSTERS: THE MUMMY Dark Horse

1 ❑ 1993 Cover: 4.95 **NM** value: **Cover or less**
Circ: CapCity orders: **3,675**
No issue number. • Based on the classic Universal pictures film **A:** Tony Harris **W:** Dan Jolley

UNIVERSAL PICTURES PRESENTS DRACULA Dell

1 ❑ Sep 1963 Cover: 0.25 **NM** value: **160.00**
• **CGC:** 3 graded, best 9.4

UNIVERSAL SOLDIER (NOW) Now

1 ❑ Sep 1992 Cover: 1.95 **NM** value: **Cover or less**
📖 The Quick and the Undead • newsstand **A:** Lenin Delsol; Tony DeZuniga **W:** Clint McElroy ★ Origin of Universal Soldiers.

1/DM ❑ Sep 1992 Cover: 2.50 **NM** value: **Cover or less**
Circ: CapCity orders: **8,200**
Hologram cover. 📖 The Quick and the Undead • direct sale **A:** Lenin Delsol; Tony DeZuniga **W:** Clint McElroy ★ Origin of Universal Soldiers.

1/SC ❑ Sep 1992 Cover: 2.50 **NM** value: **Cover or less**
• Waldenbooks; has UPC box and hologram

2 ❑ Oct 1992 Cover: 1.95 **NM** value: **Cover or less**
• newsstand **A:** Lenin Delsol; Tony DeZuniga **W:** Clint McElroy

2/DM ❑ Oct 1992 Cover: 2.50 **NM** value: **Cover or less**
• direct-sale

3 ❑ Nov 1992 Cover: 1.95 **NM** value: **Cover or less**
Photo cover. • newsstand **A:** Lenin Delsol; Tony DeZuniga **W:** Clint McElroy

3/DM ❑ Nov 1992 Cover: 2.50 **NM** value: **Cover or less**
Circ: CapCity orders: **4,325**
• uncensored

UNIVERSE X Marvel

In the wake of the events of Earth X, Captain America has reclaimed Earth for humanity. But he's got a long row to hoe, as he watches over Mar-Vell (the baby who is the key to the world's salvation) and as Reed Richards works to find a cure for the virus that has mutated the human population of Earth into a race of supermen. You see, Virus X made mankind invulnerable to disease or death, and Mar-Vell and Richards' efforts will spark the return of humanity and mortality to a populace that doesn't necessarily want to...um...devolve. Still, Captain America knows that Mar-Vell — the perfect child of Him and Her — is mankind's last, best hope. As the living symbol of all that is good and pure, he will protect the child from scorn and attack.

This sequel limited series finds the Marvel universe of the future struggling to regain some semblance of order. Since it's the work of Jim Krueger (Footsoldiers), Alex Ross (Kingdom Come), and Dougie Braithwaite (Green Arrow), it's one heckuva story.

0 ❑ Sep 2000 Cover: 3.99 **NM** value: **Cover or less**
Circ: Diamd. preorders: **60,038**
cardstock cover. • follows events of Earth X **A:** Dougie Braithwaite; Alex Ross(cover) **C:** Alex Ross **W:** Alex Ross; Jim Krueger

1 ❑ Oct 2000 Cover: 3.50 **NM** value: **Cover or less**
Circ: Diamd. preorders: **60,725**
cardstock cover. **A:** Dougie Braithwaite; Alex Ross(cover) **C:** Alex Ross **W:** Alex Ross; Jim Krueger

2 ❑ Nov 2000 Cover: 3.50 **NM** value: **Cover or less**
Circ: Diamd. preorders: **54,347**
cardstock cover. **A:** Dougie Braithwaite; Alex Ross(cover) **C:** Alex Ross **W:** Alex Ross; Jim Krueger

3 ❑ Dec 2000 Cover: 3.50 **NM** value: **Cover or less**
Circ: Diamd. preorders: **54,142** • **CGC:** 1 graded, best 9.4
cardstock cover. **A:** Dougie Braithwaite; Alex Ross(cover) **C:** Alex Ross **W:** Alex Ross; Jim Krueger

4 ❑ Jan 2001 Cover: 3.50 **NM** value: **Cover or less**
Circ: Diamd. preorders: **53,808**
cardstock cover. **A:** Dougie Braithwaite **C:** Alex Ross **W:** Jim Krueger

5 ❑ Feb 2001 Cover: 3.50 **NM** value: **Cover or less**
Circ: Diamd. preorders: **52,180**
cardstock cover. **A:** Dougie Braithwaite **C:** Alex Ross **W:** Jim Krueger

6 ❑ Mar 2001 Cover: 3.50 **NM** value: **Cover or less**
Circ: Diamd. preorders: **49,746**
cardstock cover. **A:** Dougie Braithwaite **C:** Alex Ross **W:** Jim Krueger

7 ❑ Apr 2001 Cover: 3.50 **NM** value: **Cover or less**
Circ: Diamd. preorders: **48,610**
cardstock cover. **A:** Dougie Braithwaite **C:** Alex Ross **W:** Jim Krueger

8 ❑ May 2001 Cover: 3.50 **NM** value: **Cover or less**
Circ: Diamd. preorders: **47,397**
cardstock cover. **A:** Dougie Braithwaite **C:** Alex Ross **W:** Jim Krueger

9 ❑ Jun 2001 Cover: 3.50 **NM** value: **Cover or less**
Circ: Diamd. preorders: **46,967**

10 ❑ Jul 2001 Cover: 3.50 **NM** value: **Cover or less**
Circ: Diamd. preorders: **45,473**

11 ❑ Aug 2001 Cover: 3.50 **NM** value: **Cover or less**
Circ: Diamd. preorders: **45,169**

12 ❑ Sep 2001 Cover: 3.50 **NM** value: **Cover or less**
Circ: Diamd. preorders: **46,792**

UNIVERSE X: BEASTS Marvel

1 ❑ Cover: 3.99 **NM** value: **Cover or less**

UNIVERSE X: CAP Marvel

1 ❑ Feb 2001 Cover: 3.99 **NM** value: **Cover or less**
• **CGC:** 10 graded, best 9.8

UNIVERSE X: IRON MEN Marvel

1 ❑ Cover: 3.99 **NM** value: **Cover or less**
Circ: Diamd. preorders: **40,788**

UNIVERSE X: OMNIBUS Marvel

1 ❑ Cover: 3.99 **NM** value: **Cover or less**
Circ: Diamd. preorders: **29,734**

UNIVERSE X: SPIDEY Marvel

1 ❑ Jan 2001 Cover: 3.99 **NM** value: **Cover or less**

1/A ❑ Jan 2001 **NM** value: **6.00**
• Dynamic Forces variant **A:** Jackson Guice **C:** Alex Ross **W:** Jim Krueger

1/B ❑ Jan 2001 **NM** value: **10.00**
Dynamic Forces variant sketch cover. **A:** Jackson Guice **C:** Alex Ross **W:** Jim Krueger

1/C ❑ Jan 2001 Cover: 3.99 **NM** value: **60.00**
• recalled edition with potentially libelous statement in background of one panel. **A:** Jackson Guice **C:** Alex Ross **W:** Jim Krueger

UNIVERSE X: X Marvel

1 ❑ Cover: 3.99 **NM** value: **Cover or less**
Circ: Diamd. preorders: **44,025**

UNKNOWN SOLDIER DC

Although his face was scarred beyond recognition, he continued to fight on against the Axis powers, albeit in a new, unusual role. As The Unknown Soldier, this hero has become a master of disguise — and, with a variety of masks of his own creation, he becomes the most powerful weapon in the Allied arsenal. For him no mission is too risky, no challenge too great. And by working behind the scenes, he proves that one man in the right place can make all the difference.

The concept for The Unknown Soldier was first tried out in Our Fighting Forces #41. The Unknown Soldier made his official appearance in Star Spangled War Stories #151, and that title changed names with issue #205 to Unknown Soldier to reflect the popularity of its new hero.

205 ❑ May 1977 Cover: 0.30 **NM** value: **6.00**
Circ: Statement: **126,071**

206 ❑ Jul 1977 Cover: 0.35 **NM** value: **6.00**
Circ: Statement: **126,071**
• Has 1976 Statement, filed 10/1/76; avg print run 316,000; avg sales 123,000; avg subs 1,000; avg total paid 124,000; samples 1,000; office use 1,000; max existent 126,000; 60% of run returned

207 ❑ Sep 1977 Cover: 0.35 **NM** value: **6.00**
Circ: Statement: **126,071**
📖 Kill the King!; Lt. Larry Rock: Killers All! **A:** Dick Ayers; Gerry Talaoc; Ric Estrada; Al Milgrom(cover) **W:** Steve Skeates; Bob Haney

208 ❑ Oct 1977 Cover: 0.35 **NM** value: **6.00**
Circ: Statement: **126,071**

209 ❑ Nov 1977 Cover: 0.35 **NM** value: **6.00**
Circ: Statement: **126,071**
📖 Tattered Glory!; Real Estate **A:** Frank Thorne; Dick Ayers; Gerry Talaoc; Joe Kubert(cover) **W:** Bob Haney; Robert Kanigher

210 ❑ Dec 1977 Cover: 0.35 **NM** value: **6.00**
Circ: Statement: **126,071**
📖 Sparrows Can't Sing! **A:** Dick Ayers; Gerry Talaoc **W:** Bob Haney

211 ❑ Jan 1978 Cover: 0.35 **NM** value: **5.00**
Circ: Statement: **117,001**
📖 Man of War; In Country **A:** Russ Heath; Joe Kubert(cover) **W:** Larry Hama; Bob Haney

212 ❑ Feb 1978 Cover: 0.35 **NM** value: **5.00**
Circ: Statement: **117,001**
📖 The Traitor in Wolf's Clothing! **A:** Dick Ayers; Gerry Talaoc **W:** Bob Haney

213 ❑ Mar 1978 Cover: 0.35 **NM** value: **5.00**
Circ: Statement: **117,001**
📖 The Ten Year Old Secret Weapon!; Across the Staked Plains! **A:** Dick Ayers; Gerry Talaoc; Warren Satter **W:** Bob Haney; Don Kraar

214 ❑ Apr 1978 Cover: 0.35 **NM** value: **5.00**
Circ: Statement: **117,001**
📖 Deadly Reunion **A:** Dick Ayers; Romeo Tanghal **W:** Robert Kanigher ★ Appearance of Mademoiselle Marie.

215 ❑ May 1978 Cover: 0.35 **NM** value: **5.00**
Circ: Statement: **117,001**
📖 The Savage Sea!; Casualty List • Has 1977 Statement; avg print run 304,886; avg sales 125,529; avg subs 542; avg total paid 126,071; samples 400; office use 747; max existent 126,818; 58% of run returned **A:** Joe Kubert; Dick Ayers; Sandy Plunkett; Gerry Talaoc; Bob Smith; Joe Kubert(cover) **W:** Bob Haney; Bob Toomey

216 ❑ Jun 1978 Cover: 0.35 **NM** value: **5.00**
Circ: Statement: **117,001**
📖 Taps at Arlington; The Silk Umbrella of Death! **A:** Dick Ayers; Alex Saviuk; Romeo Tanghal **W:** Bob Haney; Bob Kanigher

217 ❑ Jul 1978 Cover: 0.35 **NM** value: **5.00**
Circ: Statement: **117,001**
📖 Dictators Never Sleep!; Ants **A:** Dick Ayers; Bill Draut; Gerry Talaoc; Joe Kubert(cover) **W:** Bob Haney; Diverse Hands

218 ❑ Aug 1978 Cover: 0.35 **NM** value: **5.00**
Circ: Statement: **117,001**

Other grades: Multiply prices above by **1.5 for Mint • 2/3 for Very Fine • 1/3 for Fine • 1/5 for Very Good • 1/8 for Good**

The Unknown Soldier Must Die! **A:** Dick Ayers; Gerry Talaoc **W:** Bob Haney
219 ❑ Sep 1978 Cover: 0.50 **NM** value: **5.00**
Circ: Statement: **117,001**
Laughter in Hell!; The Edge of History; Frogman! **A:** Joe Kubert; Frank Miller; Dick Ayers; Danny Bulandi; Fred Carillo; Joe Kubert(cover); Romeo Tanghal **W:** Bob Haney; Elliot S! Maggin; Scott Edelman
220 ❑ Oct 1978 Cover: 0.50 **NM** value: **5.00**
Circ: Statement: **117,001**
The Rubber Band Heroes; Of Blood and Roses **A:** Joe Kubert; Dick Ayers; Gerry Talaoc; Ric Estrada; Joe Kubert(cover) **W:** Bob Haney; Bob Kanigher
221 ❑ Nov 1978 Cover: 0.50 **NM** value: **5.00**
Circ: Statement: **117,001**
Sunset for a Samurai!; The Burning Man! **A:** Dick Ayers; Gerry Talaoc; Romeo Tanghal **W:** Bob Haney; Steve Utley
222 ❑ Dec 1978 Cover: 0.40 **NM** value: **5.00**
Circ: Statement: **117,001**
No Exit From Stalag 19! **A:** Joe Kubert; Dick Ayers; Gerry Talaoc **W:** Bob Haney
223 ❑ Jan 1979 Cover: 0.40 **NM** value: **5.00**
Circ: Statement: **99,046**
Mission: Incredible! **A:** Dick Ayers; Romeo Tanghal **W:** Bob Haney
224 ❑ Feb 1979 Cover: 0.40 **NM** value: **5.00**
Circ: Statement: **99,046**
Welcome to Valhalla!; At the Mercy of Tigers! **A:** Dick Ayers; Dan Adkins; Romeo Tanghal **W:** Bob Haney; Steve Utley
225 ❑ Mar 1979 Cover: 0.40 **NM** value: **5.00**
Circ: Statement: **99,046**
226 ❑ Apr 1979 Cover: 0.40 **NM** value: **5.00**
Circ: Statement: **99,046**
Sink the Kronhorst!; Andy Stewart Combat Nurse: Rendevous • Has 1978 Statement, filed 10/1/78; avg print run 351,374; avg sales 116,590; avg subs 411; avg total paid 117,001; samples 109; office use 2,533; max existent 119,643; 66% of run returned **A:** Fred Carrillo; Dick Ayers; Gerry Talaoc; Joe Kubert(cover) **W:** Bill Kelley; Bob Haney
227 ❑ May 1979 Cover: 0.40 **NM** value: **5.00**
Circ: Statement: **99,046**
The Blind Eye of God!; Andy Stewart Combat Nurse: The Iron Fist **A:** Fred Carrillo; Joe Kubert; Dick Ayers; Gerry Talaoc **W:** Bill Kelley; Bob Kanigher
228 ❑ Jun 1979 Cover: 0.40 **NM** value: **5.00**
Circ: Statement: **99,046**
Heroes Don't Have Crowns; Andy Stewart Combat Nurse: Coward's Debt **A:** Fred Carrillo; Joe Kubert; Dick Ayers; Gerry Talaoc **W:** Bill Kelley; Bob Haney
229 ❑ Jul 1979 Cover: 0.40 **NM** value: **5.00**
Circ: Statement: **99,046**
Get the Desert Fox! **A:** Dick Ayers; Jerry Talaoc; Joe Kubert(cover) **W:** Bob Haney
230 ❑ Aug 1979 Cover: 0.40 **NM** value: **4.00**
Circ: Statement: **99,046**
231 ❑ Sep 1979 Cover: 0.40 **NM** value: **4.00**
Circ: Statement: **99,046**
Bridge of No Return! **A:** Joe Kubert; Dick Ayers; Gerry Talaoc; Joe Kubert(cover) **W:** Bob Haney
232 ❑ Oct 1979 Cover: 0.40 **NM** value: **4.00**
Circ: Statement: **99,046**
The Invisible Traitor! **A:** Dick Ayers; Gerry Talaoc; Joe Kubert(cover) **W:** Bob Haney
233 ❑ Nov 1979 Cover: 0.40 **NM** value: **4.00**
Circ: Statement: **99,046**
Destroy Wolf Lair-And Die! **A:** Joe Kubert; Dick Ayers; Gerry Talaoc; Joe Kubert(cover) **W:** Bob Haney
234 ❑ Dec 1979 Cover: 0.40 **NM** value: **4.00**
Circ: Statement: **99,046**
235 ❑ Jan 1980 Cover: 0.40 **NM** value: **4.00**
Circ: Statement: **93,053**
Death in Blue and Grey!; Return to Beach Red **A:** Dick Ayers; Maurice Whitman; Romeo Tanghal **W:** Bob Haney
236 ❑ Feb 1980 Cover: 0.40 **NM** value: **4.00**
Circ: Statement: **93,053**
An Honorable Betrayal? **A:** Dick Ayers; Gerry Talaoc **W:** Bob Haney
237 ❑ Mar 1980 Cover: 0.40 **NM** value: **4.00**
Circ: Statement: **93,053**
No God in St. Just! **A:** Dick Ayers; Gerry Talaoc **W:** Bob Haney
238 ❑ Apr 1980 Cover: 0.40 **NM** value: **4.00**
Circ: Statement: **93,053**
Operation: Pied Piper! • Has 1979 Statement; avg print run 274,943; avg sales 98,817; avg subs 229; avg total paid 99,046; samples 0; office use 122; max existent 99,168; 64% of run returned **A:** Dick Ayers; Gerry Talaoc **W:** Bob Haney
239 ❑ May 1980 Cover: 0.40 **NM** value: **4.00**
Circ: Statement: **93,053**
The 20 Mile Rabbit Hole! **A:** Dick Ayers; Gerry Talaoc **W:** Bob Haney
240 ❑ Jun 1980 Cover: 0.40 **NM** value: **4.00**
Circ: Statement: **93,053**
The Hammer of Glory! **A:** Dick Ayers; Gerry Talaoc **W:** Bob Haney
241 ❑ Jul 1980 Cover: 0.40 **NM** value: **4.00**
Circ: Statement: **93,053**
Shall Heroes Prevail? **A:** Dick Ayers; Gerry Talaoc; Joe Kubert(cover) **W:** Bob Haney
242 ❑ Aug 1980 Cover: 0.40 **NM** value: **4.00**
Circ: Statement: **93,053**
Red Flows the Don! **A:** Dick Ayers; Gerry Talaoc **W:** Bob Haney
243 ❑ Sep 1980 Cover: 0.50 **NM** value: **4.00**
Circ: Statement: **93,053** • **CGC:** 1 graded, best 8.0
Double Switch!; Dateline: Frontline: The Yanks are Comin' **A:** Dick Ayers; Gerry Talaoc; Ric Estrada **W:** Bob Haney; Cary Burkett
244 ❑ Oct 1980 Cover: 0.50 **NM** value: **4.00**
Circ: Statement: **93,053** • **CGC:** 1 graded, best 9.0
245 ❑ Nov 1980 Cover: 0.50 **NM** value: **4.00**
Circ: Statement: **93,053**
Crack of Doom!; The Vanishing American; Dateline: Frontline **A:** Dick Ayers; Gerry Talaoc; Ric Estrada **W:** Bob Kanigher; Cary Burkett
246 ❑ Dec 1980 Cover: 0.50 **NM** value: **4.00**
Circ: Statement: **93,053** • **CGC:** 1 graded, best 7.0
Only the Desert Wins **A:** Dick Ayers; Gerry Talaoc **W:** Bob Haney
247 ❑ Jan 1981 Cover: 0.50 **NM** value: **4.00**
Circ: Statement: **91,024**
Season in Hell! **A:** Joe Kubert; Dick Ayers; Gerry Talaoc; Joe Kubert(cover) **W:** Bob Haney
248 ❑ Feb 1981 Cover: 0.50 **NM** value: **6.00**
Circ: Statement: **91,024**
249 ❑ Mar 1981 Cover: 0.50 **NM** value: **6.00**
Circ: Statement: **91,024**
Doorway of Destiny!, Mask of a Maqui **A:** Dick Ayers; Gerry Talaoc; Joe Kubert(cover); John Cellardo **W:** Bob Haney; Robert Kanigher ★ Origin of Unknown Soldier.
250 ❑ Apr 1981 Cover: 0.50 **NM** value: **4.00**
Circ: Statement: **91,024**
251 ❑ May 1981 Cover: 0.50 **NM** value: **4.00**
Circ: Statement: **91,024** • **CGC:** 1 graded, best 9.6
• Has 1980 Statement; avg print run 270,642; avg sales 92,369; avg subs 684; avg total paid 93,053; samples 127; office use 3,041; max existent 96,094; 64% of run returned
252 ❑ Jun 1981 Cover: 0.50 **NM** value: **4.00**
Circ: Statement: **91,024**
Bomber's Moon!; War Games; Hell in the Heavens, Part 2 **A:** John Severin; Dick Ayers; Gerry Talaoc **W:** Bob Haney; Robert Kanigher
253 ❑ Jul 1981 Cover: 0.50 **NM** value: **4.00**
Circ: Statement: **91,024**
254 ❑ Aug 1981 Cover: 0.50 **NM** value: **4.00**
Circ: Statement: **91,024**
255 ❑ Sep 1981 Cover: 0.50 **NM** value: **4.00**
Circ: Statement: **91,024**
256 ❑ Oct 1981 Cover: 0.60 **NM** value: **4.00**
Circ: Statement: **91,024**
257 ❑ Nov 1981 Cover: 0.60 **NM** value: **4.00**
Circ: Statement: **91,024**
Til Armageddon Do Us Part!; Blood Brothers!; Capt. Storm: You Can't Bury the Dead!, Part 1 **A:** Joe Kubert; Dick Ayers; Sam Grainger; Gerry Talaoc; Jack Sparling; Adrian Gonzales; Joe Kubert(cover) **W:** Bob Haney; Bob Kanigher ★ Origin of Capt. Storm. ★ Appearance of John F. Kennedy.
258 ❑ Dec 1981 Cover: 0.60 **NM** value: **4.00**
Circ: Statement: **91,024**
His Eye is on the Sparrow!; Swan Song!; Capt. Storm: You Can't Bury the Dead!, Part 2 **A:** Dick Ayers; Dan Spiegle; Sam Grainger; Gerry Talaoc; Adrian Gonzales **W:** Steve Mitchell; Bob Haney; Robert Kanigher ★ Appearance of John F. Kennedy.
259 ❑ Jan 1982 Cover: 0.60 **NM** value: **4.00**
We Who Are About to Die…; Bob Kanigher's Gallery of War:Voices; Capt. Storm: You Can't Bury the Dead!, Part 3 **A:** Dick Ayers; Dan Spiegle; Sam Grainger; Gerry Talaoc; Adrian Gonzales **W:** Bob Haney; Bob Kanigher ★ Appearance of John F. Kennedy.
260 ❑ Feb 1982 Cover: 0.60 **NM** value: **4.00**
The Rustbucket Mutiny!; The Fleet That Failed **A:** Dick Ayers; Gerry Talaoc; Ric Estrada **W:** Bob Haney; J. David Warner
261 ❑ Mar 1982 Cover: 0.60 **NM** value: **4.00**
Hour of the Beast!; They Rode to the Sound of The Guns **A:** Dick Ayers; Gerry Talaoc; Ric Estrada **W:** Bob Haney
262 ❑ Apr 1982 Cover: 0.60 **NM** value: **4.00**
• **CGC:** 1 graded, best 9.6
263 ❑ May 1982 Cover: 0.60 **NM** value: **4.00**
• Has 1981 Statement; avg print run 257,017; avg sales 90,283; avg subs 741; avg total paid 91,024; samples 127; office use 3,532; max existent 94,556; 63% of run returned
264 ❑ Jun 1982 Cover: 0.60 **NM** value: **4.00**
Hell is a Cold Place!; Killers of the Sky!, Part 3; Tomahawk: George Washington Died Here! **A:** Dick Ayers; Dan Spiegle; Jose Delbo; Gerry Talaoc; Andy Mushynsky; Joe Kubert(cover) **W:** Bob Haney; Robert Kanigher
265 ❑ Jul 1982 Cover: 0.60 **NM** value: **4.00**
266 ❑ Aug 1982 Cover: 0.60 **NM** value: **4.00**
267 ❑ Sep 1982 Cover: 0.60 **NM** value: **4.00**
268 ❑ Oct 1982 Cover: 0.60 **NM** value: **5.00**
A Farewell to War final issue. • Fall of Berlin **A:** Dick Ayers; Gerry Talaoc; Joe Kubert(cover) **W:** Bob Haney ★ Death of Chat Noir. ★ Death of Hitler. ★ Death of The Unknown Soldier.

UNKNOWN SOLDIER (MINI-SERIES) DC / Vertigo

1 ❑ Apr 1997 Cover: 2.50 **NM** value: **4.00**
Circ: Diamd. preorders: **46,855**
2 ❑ May 1997 Cover: 2.50 **NM** value: **3.00**
Circ: Diamd. preorders: **38,033**
3 ❑ Jun 1997 Cover: 2.50 **NM** value: **3.00**
Circ: Diamd. preorders: **39,234**
4 ❑ Jul 1997 Cover: 2.50 **NM** value: **3.00**
Circ: Diamd. preorders: **41,038**
Bk 1 ❑ Cover: 12.95 **NM** value: **Cover or less**

UNKNOWN SOLDIER, THE (MINI-SERIES) DC

1 ❑ Win 1988 Cover: 1.50 **NM** value: **3.00**
2 ❑ Hol 1988 Cover: 1.50 **NM** value: **3.00**
Circ: CapCity orders: **10,550**
3 ❑ Jan 1989 Cover: 1.50 **NM** value: **3.00**
Circ: CapCity orders: **9,900**
4 ❑ Mar 1989 Cover: 1.50 **NM** value: **3.00**
Circ: CapCity orders: **9,400**
5 ❑ Apr 1989 Cover: 1.50 **NM** value: **3.00**
Circ: CapCity orders: **8,200**
6 ❑ May 1989 Cover: 1.50 **NM** value: **3.00**
Circ: CapCity orders: **7,400**
The Replacement **A:** Phil Gascoine **W:** James Owlsley
7 ❑ Jul 1989 Cover: 1.50 **NM** value: **3.00**
Circ: CapCity orders: **7,000**
8 ❑ Aug 1989 Cover: 1.75 **NM** value: **3.00**
Circ: CapCity orders: **6,600**
9 ❑ Sep 1989 Cover: 1.75 **NM** value: **3.00**
Circ: CapCity orders: **6,300**
10 ❑ Oct 1989 Cover: 1.75 **NM** value: **3.00**
Circ: CapCity orders: **6,050**
11 ❑ Nov 1989 Cover: 1.75 **NM** value: **3.00**
Circ: CapCity orders: **5,850**
12 ❑ Dec 1989 Cover: 1.75 **NM** value: **3.00**
Circ: CapCity orders: **5,500**

UNKNOWN WORLD Fawcett

1 ❑ Jun 1952 Cover: 0.10 **NM** value: **350.00**
• **CGC:** 1 graded, best 3.5

UNKNOWN WORLDS ACG

The series "Unknown Worlds" was published by the American Comic Group and made its debut in 1960. The series lasted for 57 issues and featured a wide variety of odd stories in the science-fiction, monster, and fantasy genres. It was an offshoot of other of ACG's popular titles: Forbidden Worlds and Adventures into the Unknown.

Since it began in 1960, the series had stories that were handicapped by the constraints of the Comics Code (then very much in force, prohibiting many of the most popular horror and crime themes). It made up for the lack of artistic freedom, in some ways, by the exceptional imagination (and sometimes plain weirdness) of Editor Richard Hughes and his artists, including Ogden Whitney (Herbie), Steve Ditko, Johnny Craig, and Al Williamson, all of whom made contributions to later issues.

1 ❑ Aug 1960 Cover: 0.10 **NM** value: **90.00**
Circ: Statement: **192,000** • **CGC:** 3 graded, best 7.5
2 ❑ Sep 1960 Cover: 0.10 **NM** value: **60.00**
Circ: Statement: **192,000**
3 ❑ Oct 1960 Cover: 0.10 **NM** value: **45.00**
Circ: Statement: **192,000**
4 ❑ Dec 1960 Cover: 0.10 **NM** value: **40.00**
Circ: Statement: **192,000**
5 ❑ Feb 1961 Cover: 0.10 **NM** value: **40.00**
Circ: Statement: **159,000**
6 ❑ Mar 1961 Cover: 0.10 **NM** value: **35.00**
Circ: Statement: **159,000**
7 ❑ Apr 1961 Cover: 0.10 **NM** value: **35.00**
Circ: Statement: **159,000**
8 ❑ Jun 1961 Cover: 0.10 **NM** value: **35.00**
Circ: Statement: **159,000**
9 ❑ Aug 1961 Cover: 0.10 **NM** value: **50.00**
Circ: Statement: **159,000**
• Dinosaurs
10 ❑ Sep 1961 Cover: 0.10 **NM** value: **35.00**
Circ: Statement: **159,000**
Magic Mutt; Souvenir From Crete; Eagle Out of the Past; I Owe it all to Myself **A:** Ogden Whitney; Pete Costanza **W:** Shane O'Shea; Zev Zimmer
11 ❑ Oct 1961 Cover: 0.10 **NM** value: **28.00**
Circ: Statement: **159,000**
12 ❑ Dec 1961 Cover: 0.12 **NM** value: **28.00**
Circ: Statement: **159,000**
Where There's a Will, There's a Way!; No Use to the World!; Spook Detective! **A:** Pete Costanza; Beck Hamilton; Ogden Whitney(cover); Tom Hickey **W:** Kermit Lundgren; L'Afcadio Lee; Zev Zimmer
13 ❑ Feb 1962 Cover: 0.12 **NM** value: **28.00**
Circ: Statement: **159,500**
14 ❑ Mar 1962 Cover: 0.12 **NM** value: **28.00**
Circ: Statement: **159,500**
15 ❑ Apr 1962 Cover: 0.12 **NM** value: **28.00**
Circ: Statement: **159,500**
16 ❑ Jun 1962 Cover: 0.12 **NM** value: **28.00**
Circ: Statement: **159,500**
17 ❑ Aug 1962 Cover: 0.12 **NM** value: **28.00**
Circ: Statement: **159,500**
18 ❑ Sep 1962 Cover: 0.12 **NM** value: **28.00**
Circ: Statement: **159,500**
Witch Hunter of Salem; I Saw it With My Own Eyes; Celestial Jackpot **A:** Chic Stone; Bill Walsh **W:** Brad Everson; Zev Zimmer
19 ❑ Oct 1962 Cover: 0.12 **NM** value: **28.00**
Circ: Statement: **159,500**
Time Treasure; The House That Couldn't Be Wrecked; A Gift From the Spirits; Mysterious Furniture **A:** Pete Costanza; Chic Stone; Tom Hickey **W:** Ace Aquila; Greg Olivetti; Shane O'Shea
20 ❑ Dec 1962 Cover: 0.12 **NM** value: **28.00**
Circ: Statement: **159,500**
21 ❑ Feb 1963 Cover: 0.12 **NM** value: **20.00**
Circ: Statement: **143,468**
22 ❑ Mar 1963 Cover: 0.12 **NM** value: **20.00**
Circ: Statement: **143,468**
My Brother Charlie; I'm Saving the Invention for Myself; Specter From Space **A:** Paul Reinman; Ogden Whitney; Chic Stone **W:** Kurato Osaki; L'Afcadio Lee; Pierre Alonzo
23 ❑ Apr 1963 Cover: 0.12 **NM** value: **20.00**
Circ: Statement: **143,468**
24 ❑ Jun 1963 Cover: 0.12 **NM** value: **20.00**
Circ: Statement: **143,468**
25 ❑ Aug 1963 Cover: 0.12 **NM** value: **20.00**
Circ: Statement: **143,468**
26 ❑ Sep 1963 Cover: 0.12 **NM** value: **20.00**
Circ: Statement: **143,468**
27 ❑ Oct 1963 Cover: 0.12 **NM** value: **20.00**
Circ: Statement: **143,468**

CGC-graded: Multiply prices above by **33 for 9.9 M • 16 for 9.8 NM/M • 7 for 9.6 NM+ • 5 for 9.4 NM • 2.5 for 9.2 NM- • 1.5 for 9.0 VF/NM**

📖 Ghost of a Private Eye; You Can't Flee From fate; Voices From the Past; Strange Little Beast **A:** Ogden Whitney; Pete Costanza; Tom Hickey **W:** Ace Aquila; Kurato Osaki; Zev Zimmer

28 ❑ Dec 1963 Cover: 0.12 **NM** value: **20.00**
Circ: Statement: **143,468**

29 ❑ Feb 1964 Cover: 0.12 **NM** value: **20.00**
Circ: Statement: **174,028**

30 ❑ Mar 1964 Cover: 0.12 **NM** value: **20.00**
Circ: Statement: **174,028**
📖 The Man Who Couldn't be Pushed Around; Motel Unit #13 **A:** Paul Reinman; Citron Costanza **W:** Kurato Osaki; Zev Zimmer

31 ❑ Apr 1964 Cover: 0.12 **NM** value: **16.00**
Circ: Statement: **174,028**
• Has 1963 Statement, filed 10/1/63; avg print run 300,000; avg sales 143,258; avg subs 210; avg total paid 143,468; max existent 143,468; 52% of run returned

32 ❑ Jun 1964 Cover: 0.12 **NM** value: **16.00**
Circ: Statement: **174,028**
📖 The Strange Machine of Dr. Malucci; A Good Mixer; Portrait of Priscilla **A:** Paul Reinman; Pete Costanza **W:** Kurato Osaki; Zev Zimmer

33 ❑ Aug 1964 Cover: 0.12 **NM** value: **16.00**
Circ: Statement: **174,028**
📖 Don't Judge Until You Hear My Story; Unfinished Symphony; If I Had My Life to Live Again; The Phantom Flag **A:** Pete Costanza; Robert Jenney **W:** Brad Everson; Kurato Osaki

34 ❑ Sep 1964 Cover: 0.12 **NM** value: **16.00**
Circ: Statement: **174,028**
📖 The Space Schnook; Message Out of the Unknown; The Toughest Guy in the Unknown **A:** Chic Stone; Robert Jenney **W:** Greg Olivetti; Zev Zimmer

35 ❑ Oct 1964 Cover: 0.12 **NM** value: **16.00**
Circ: Statement: **174,028**

36 ❑ Dec 1964 Cover: 0.12 **NM** value: **16.00**
Circ: Statement: **174,028**

37 ❑ Feb 1965 Cover: 0.12 **NM** value: **16.00**
Circ: Statement: **168,330**
📖 The Black Flight!; Time Can Freeze; The Great Gizmo Machine! **A:** Edd Ashe; John Forte **W:** Kurato Osaki; Pierce Rand

38 ❑ Mar 1965 Cover: 0.12 **NM** value: **16.00**
Circ: Statement: **168,330**

39 ❑ Apr 1965 Cover: 0.12 **NM** value: **16.00**
Circ: Statement: **168,330**

40 ❑ Jun 1965 Cover: 0.12 **NM** value: **16.00**
Circ: Statement: **168,330**
• Has 1964 Statement, filed 10/1/64; avg print run 325,000; avg sales 173,938; avg subs 90; avg total paid 174,028; max existent 174,028; 47% of run returned

41 ❑ Aug 1965 Cover: 0.12 **NM** value: **12.00**
Circ: Statement: **168,330**

42 ❑ Sep 1965 Cover: 0.12 **NM** value: **12.00**
Circ: Statement: **168,330**

43 ❑ Oct 1965 Cover: 0.12 **NM** value: **12.00**
Circ: Statement: **168,330**

44 ❑ Dec 1965 Cover: 0.12 **NM** value: **12.00**
Circ: Statement: **168,330**

45 ❑ Feb 1966 Cover: 0.12 **NM** value: **12.00**
Circ: Statement: **162,684**

46 ❑ Mar 1966 Cover: 0.12 **NM** value: **12.00**
Circ: Statement: **162,684**

47 ❑ Apr 1966 Cover: 0.12 **NM** value: **12.00**
Circ: Statement: **162,684**

48 ❑ Jun 1966 Cover: 0.12 **NM** value: **12.00**
Circ: Statement: **162,684**

49 ❑ Aug 1966 Cover: 0.12 **NM** value: **12.00**
Circ: Statement: **162,684** • **CGC:** 1 graded, best 9.0

50 ❑ Nov 1966 Cover: 0.12 **NM** value: **12.00**
Circ: Statement: **162,684**

51 ❑ Oct 1966 Cover: 0.12 **NM** value: **12.00**
Circ: Statement: **162,684**

52 ❑ Dec 1966 Cover: 0.12 **NM** value: **12.00**
Circ: Statement: **162,684**

53 ❑ Feb 1967 Cover: 0.12 **NM** value: **12.00**
• **CGC:** 1 graded, best 9.4

54 ❑ Mar 1967 Cover: 0.12 **NM** value: **12.00**
55 ❑ Apr 1967 Cover: 0.12 **NM** value: **12.00**
56 ❑ Jun 1967 Cover: 0.12 **NM** value: **12.00**
57 ❑ Aug 1967 Cover: 0.12 **NM** value: **12.00**
final issue.

UNKNOWN WORLDS OF FRANK BRUNNER, THE — Eclipse

1 ❑ Aug 1985 Cover: 1.75 **NM** value: **Cover or less**
Circ: CapCity orders: **4,600**
📖 Harvest of Horror!; What Rough Beast; The Comet's Curse!; Santa Claws **A:** Frank Brunner **W:** Frank Brunner

2 ❑ Aug 1985 Cover: 1.75 **NM** value: **Cover or less**
Circ: CapCity orders: **4,300**
📖 Sword of Dragonus; The Wizard's Venom; Werewolf Goes West; Eye of Newt, Toe of Frog **A:** Frank Brunner **W:** Frank Brunner

UNKNOWN WORLDS OF SCIENCE FICTION — Marvel

1 ❑ Jan 1975, b&w Cover: 1.00 **NM** value: **3.00**
• magazine.

2 ❑ Mar 1975, b&w Cover: 1.00 **NM** value: **3.00**
• magazine.

3 ❑ May 1975, b&w Cover: 1.00 **NM** value: **3.00**
• magazine.

4 ❑ Jul 1975, b&w Cover: 1.00 **NM** value: **3.00**
• magazine.

5 ❑ Sep 1975, b&w Cover: 1.00 **NM** value: **3.00**
• magazine.

6 ❑ Nov 1975, b&w Cover: 1.00 **NM** value: **3.00**
• magazine.

SE 1 ❑ 1976 Cover: 1.25 **NM** value: **3.00**

UNLEASHED! — Triumphant

1 ❑ Cover: 2.50 **NM** value: **Cover or less**

UNLIMITED ACCESS — Marvel

Axel Asher has been given the task of keeping two great universes separate in order to maintain the cosmic balance. He is the Access that has always been given this awesome responsibility. In trying to control his newfound power, Axel begins to pull people with him from one universe to the other. Soon, the Marvel mutants of Future Past are fighting Sentinels alongside the Legion of Super-Heroes, Wonder Woman is battling Juggernaut, Daredevil meets Batman, and the mighty Avengers come into conflict with The Justice League of America. And only Axel knows how it begins and ends, but he keeps just missing himself in time to learn what he must.

If you like time-travel paradoxes para-doctored along with just about every major character from both DC and Marvel, this miniseries will keep you on your toes!

1 ❑ Dec 1997 Cover: 1.99 **NM** value: **2.50**
Circ: Diamd. preorders: **60,133**
• crossover with DC ★ Appearance of Wonder Woman, Spider-Man, Juggernaut.

2 ❑ Jan 1998 Cover: 1.99 **NM** value: **2.00**
Circ: Diamd. preorders: **50,458**
📖 Let's Do the Time Warp Again! • crossover with DC **A:** Pat Olliffe **W:** Karl Kesel ★ Appearance of X-Men, Legion of Super-Heroes.

3 ❑ Feb 1998 Cover: 1.99 **NM** value: **2.00**
Circ: Diamd. preorders: **48,474**
• crossover with DC ★ Appearance of Justice League of America, Avengers.

4 ❑ Mar 1998 Cover: 2.99 **NM** value: **3.00**
Circ: Diamd. preorders: **44,056**
• crossover with DC; new Amalgams

UNSEEN — Standard

5 ❑ Jun 1952 Cover: 0.10 **NM** value: **250.00**
• **CGC:** 1 graded, best 7.5

6 ❑ Sep 1952 Cover: 0.10 **NM** value: **200.00**
• **CGC:** 1 graded, best 5.0

7 ❑ Nov 1952 Cover: 0.10 **NM** value: **200.00**
• **CGC:** 1 graded, best 8.5

8 ❑ Jan 1953 Cover: 0.10 **NM** value: **200.00**
• **CGC:** 1 graded, best 8.5

9 ❑ Mar 1953 Cover: 0.10 **NM** value: **200.00**
10 ❑ May 1953 Cover: 0.10 **NM** value: **200.00**
11 ❑ 1953 Cover: 0.10 **NM** value: **200.00**
12 ❑ Nov 1953 Cover: 0.10 **NM** value: **200.00**
13 ❑ Feb 1954 Cover: 0.10 **NM** value: **200.00**
14 ❑ May 1954 Cover: 0.10 **NM** value: **200.00**

UNSUPERVISED EXISTENCE — Fantagraphics

1 ❑ b&w Cover: 2.00 **NM** value: **Cover or less**
2 ❑ b&w Cover: 2.00 **NM** value: **Cover or less**
3 ❑ Cover: 2.50 **NM** value: **Cover or less**
4 ❑ Cover: 2.50 **NM** value: **Cover or less**
5 ❑ Cover: 2.00 **NM** value: **Cover or less**
6 ❑ Cover: 2.25 **NM** value: **Cover or less**
7 ❑ Cover: 2.25 **NM** value: **Cover or less**
7-2 ❑ Cover: 2.00 **NM** value: **Cover or less**

UNTAMED — Marvel / Epic

1 ❑ Jun 1993 Cover: 2.50 **NM** value: **Cover or less**
Circ: CapCity orders: **20,200**
Embossed cover. 📖 Wounds of Equal People, Part 1 **A:** Neil Hansen **W:** Neil Hansen

2 ❑ Jul 1993 Cover: 1.95 **NM** value: **Cover or less**
Circ: CapCity orders: **8,500**
📖 Wounds of Equal People, Part 2 **A:** Neil Hansen **W:** Neil Hansen

3 ❑ Aug 1993 Cover: 1.95 **NM** value: **Cover or less**
Circ: CapCity orders: **8,700**
📖 Wounds of Equal People, Part 3 **A:** Neil Hansen **W:** Neil Hansen

UNTAMED LOVE (FRANK FRAZETTA'S...) — Fantagraphics

1 ❑ Nov 1987 Cover: 2.00 **NM** value: **Cover or less**
📖 Too Late for Love; The Wrong Road; Empty Heart; Untamed Love **A:** Frank Frazetta

UNTOLD LEGEND OF CAPTAIN MARVEL, THE — Marvel

1 ❑ Apr 1997 Cover: 2.50 **NM** value: **Cover or less**
Circ: Direct Market orders: **27,750**
📖 Soldier **A:** Scott Kolins **W:** Mike Kanterovich; Tom Brevoort ★ Appearance of Galactus, Silver Surfer.

2 ❑ May 1997 Cover: 2.50 **NM** value: **Cover or less**
Circ: Diamd. preorders: **21,411**
📖 Hero **A:** Scott Kolins **W:** Mike Kanterovich; Tom Brevoort ★ Versus Imperial Guard.

3 ❑ Jun 1997 Cover: 2.50 **NM** value: **Cover or less**
Circ: Diamd. preorders: **20,361**
📖 Legend **A:** Scott Kolins **W:** Mike Kanterovich; Tom Brevoort ★ Versus Brood.

UNTOLD LEGEND OF THE BATMAN, THE — DC

1 ❑ Jul 1980 Cover: 0.40 **NM** value: **3.00**
• **CGC:** 2 graded, best 9.4
📖 In The Beginning **A:** John Byrne; Jim Aparo **W:** Len Wein ★ Origin of Batman.

2 ❑ Aug 1980 Cover: 0.40 **NM** value: **2.00**
3 ❑ Sep 1980 Cover: 0.50 **NM** value: **2.00**

UNTOLD ORIGIN OF FEMFORCE — AC

1 ❑ 1989 Cover: 4.95 **NM** value: **Cover or less**
Circ: CapCity orders: **2,150**

UNTOLD ORIGIN OF MS. VICTORY — AC

1 ❑ Dec 1989, b&w Cover: 2.50 **NM** value: **Cover or less**

UNTOLD TALES OF CHASTITY — Chaos

1 ❑ Nov 2000 Cover: 2.95 **NM** value: **Cover or less**

UNTOLD TALES OF LADY DEATH — Chaos

1 ❑ Nov 2000 Cover: 2.95 **NM** value: **Cover or less**
Circ: Diamd. preorders: **16,446** • **CGC:** 8 graded, best 9.8

UNTOLD TALES OF PURGATORI — Chaos

1 ❑ Nov 2000 Cover: 2.95 **NM** value: **Cover or less**
Circ: Diamd. preorders: **13,860** • **CGC:** 1 graded, best 9.6

UNTOLD TALES OF SPIDER-MAN — Marvel

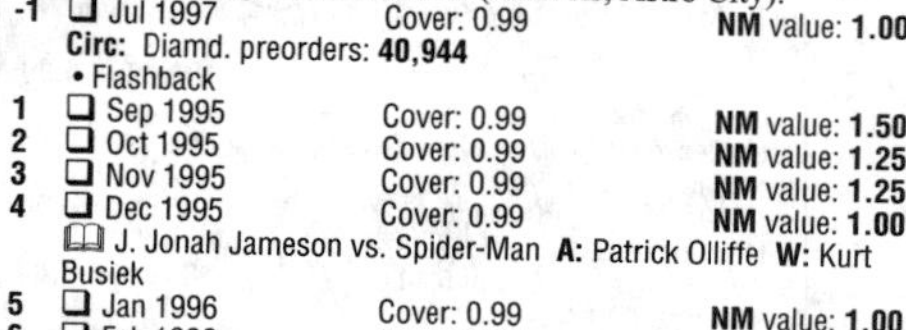

Untold Tales Of Spider-Man is set in the early days of the web-slinger's career as a crimefighting super-hero. Peter Parker is still in high school and is just beginning to adjust to his newfound powers. The series is written in the old, Ditko-Lee style, in which Parker, as Spider-Man, is a wisecracking hero whose only real responsibilities are to get good grades and help his aging Aunt May. The series introduces new villains and brings back some of the classic criminals from Spidey's rogues' gallery.

Since it was released during a veritable flood of Spider-titles in 1995, sales on Untold Tales were slow in the beginning. However, they soon picked up, due to two main factors: the unusually cheap price of 99 cents and the highly entertaining writing of Kurt Busiek (Marvels, Astro City).

-1 ❑ Jul 1997 Cover: 0.99 **NM** value: **1.00**
Circ: Diamd. preorders: **40,944**
• Flashback

1 ❑ Sep 1995 Cover: 0.99 **NM** value: **1.50**
2 ❑ Oct 1995 Cover: 0.99 **NM** value: **1.25**
3 ❑ Nov 1995 Cover: 0.99 **NM** value: **1.25**
4 ❑ Dec 1995 Cover: 0.99 **NM** value: **1.00**
📖 J. Jonah Jameson vs. Spider-Man **A:** Patrick Olliffe **W:** Kurt Busiek

5 ❑ Jan 1996 Cover: 0.99 **NM** value: **1.00**
6 ❑ Feb 1996 Cover: 0.99 **NM** value: **1.00**
7 ❑ Mar 1996 Cover: 0.99 **NM** value: **1.00**
📖 On the Trail of the Amazing Spider-Man **A:** Patrick Olliffe **W:** Kurt Busiek ★ Origin of Electro.

8 ❑ Apr 1996 Cover: 0.99 **NM** value: **1.00**
9 ❑ May 1996 Cover: 0.99 **NM** value: **1.00**
10 ❑ Jun 1996 Cover: 0.99 **NM** value: **1.00**
11 ❑ Jul 1996 Cover: 0.99 **NM** value: **1.00**
12 ❑ Aug 1996 Cover: 0.99 **NM** value: **1.00**
13 ❑ Sep 1996 Cover: 0.99 **NM** value: **1.00**
14 ❑ Oct 1996 Cover: 0.99 **NM** value: **1.00**
15 ❑ Nov 1996 Cover: 0.99 **NM** value: **1.00**
Circ: Direct Market orders: **42,750**

16 ❑ Dec 1996 Cover: 0.99 **NM** value: **1.00**
Circ: Direct Market orders: **43,500**
📖 The Boy Next Door **A:** Patrick Olliffe **W:** Kurt Busiek ★ Appearance of Mary Jane.

17 ❑ Jan 1997 Cover: 0.99 **NM** value: **1.00**
Circ: Direct Market orders: **42,500**
📖 Spidey Battles Hawkeye the Marksman! **A:** Patrick Olliffe; Al Williamson(inks) **W:** Kurt Busiek ★ Origin of Hawkeye. ★ Appearance of Hawkeye. ★ Versus Hawkeye.

18 ❑ Feb 1997 Cover: 0.99 **NM** value: **1.00**
Circ: Direct Market orders: **40,500**
📖 Unseen Dangers **A:** Patrick Olliffe; Al Williamson(inks) **W:** Kurt Busiek ★ Appearance of Headsman. ★ Versus Headsman.

19 ❑ Mar 1997 Cover: 0.99 **NM** value: **1.00**
Circ: Direct Market orders: **38,750**

20 ❑ Apr 1997 Cover: 0.99 **NM** value: **1.00**
Circ: Direct Market orders: **38,750**
📖 Wings of Hatred **A:** Patrick Olliffe; Al Williamson(inks) **W:** Kurt Busiek; G.H. Lawrence ★ Origin of The Vulture. ★ Versus Vulture.

21 ❑ May 1997 Cover: 0.99 **NM** value: **1.00**
Circ: Diamd. preorders: **42,216**

22 ❑ Jun 1997 Cover: 0.99 **NM** value: **1.00**
Circ: Diamd. preorders: **39,039**

23 ❑ Aug 1997 Cover: 0.99 **NM** value: **1.00**
Circ: Diamd. preorders: **36,890**

24 ❑ Sep 1997 Cover: 0.99 **NM** value: **1.00**
Circ: Diamd. preorders: **36,442**

25 ❑ Oct 1997 Cover: 0.99 **NM** value: **1.00**
Circ: Diamd. preorders: **38,100**
cover says Sep, indicia says Oct. final issue. ★ Versus Green Goblin.

Anl 1996 ❑ ca. 1996 Cover: 1.99 **NM** value: **Cover or less**
Circ: Direct Market orders: **44,500**
📖 How Kurt Busiek and Patrick Olliffe Re-Create Untold Tales!; A Guided Tour to the World of Untold Tales! • Untold Tales of Spider-Man '96 **A:** Gil Kane; Patrick Olliffe; Klaus Janson **W:** Kurt Busiek ★ Appearance of Namor, Fantastic Four.

Anl 1997 ❑ ca. 1997 Cover: 1.95 **NM** value: **Cover or less**
Circ: Diamd. preorders: **34,690**
• Untold Tales of Spider-Man '97

Other grades: Multiply prices above by **1.5 for Mint • 2/3 for Very Fine • 1/3 for Fine • 1/5 for Very Good • 1/8 for Good**

UNTOUCHABLES — Caliber

1 ❑ Aug 1997 Cover: 2.95 **NM** value: **Cover or less**
📖 A New Beginning **A:** John Kissee **W:** Joe Pruett
2 ❑ Sep 1997 Cover: 2.95 **NM** value: **Cover or less**
3 ❑ Oct 1997 Cover: 2.95 **NM** value: **Cover or less**
4 ❑ Nov 1997 Cover: 2.95 **NM** value: **Cover or less**

UNTOUCHABLES (DELL) — Dell

3 ❑ Jul 1962 Cover: 0.15 **NM** value: **60.00**
4 ❑ Aug 1962 Cover: 0.12 **NM** value: **60.00**

UNTOUCHABLES (EASTERN) — Eastern

1 ❑ Cover: 0.75 **NM** value: **1.00**
• **CGC:** 2 graded, best 9.4
2 ❑ Cover: 0.75 **NM** value: **1.00**

UNUSUAL TALES — Charlton

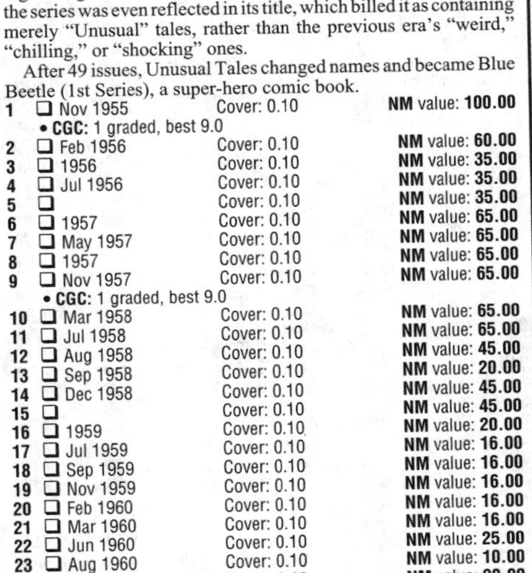

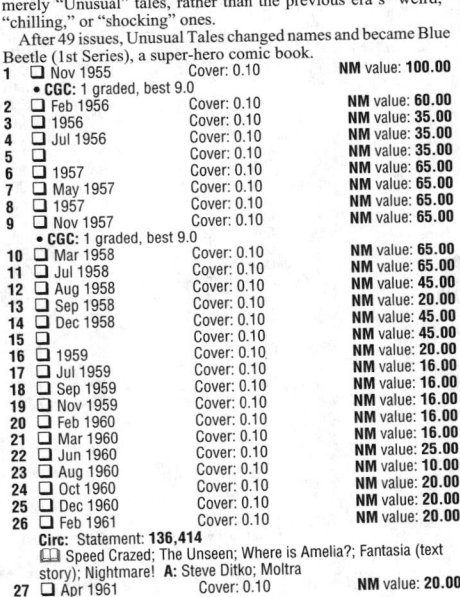

Unusual Tales began its run in 1955, shortly after the dawn of the Comics Code. The Code contained heavy restrictions on the content of comics, but companies often went even further in order to distance themselves from such stellar (but controversial) titles as Tales From the Crypt and Weird Fantasy.

Unusual Tales is symptomatic of just how tame the horror and science-fiction comics had suddenly become. Despite competent work by Steve Ditko, the series was largely a collection of horror and science-fiction story setups without satisfying endings. The tentative nature of the series was even reflected in its title, which billed it as containing merely "Unusual" tales, rather than the previous era's "weird," "chilling," or "shocking" ones.

After 49 issues, Unusual Tales changed names and became Blue Beetle (1st Series), a super-hero comic book.

1 ❑ Nov 1955 Cover: 0.10 **NM** value: **100.00**
• **CGC:** 1 graded, best 9.0
2 ❑ Feb 1956 Cover: 0.10 **NM** value: **60.00**
3 ❑ 1956 Cover: 0.10 **NM** value: **35.00**
4 ❑ Jul 1956 Cover: 0.10 **NM** value: **35.00**
5 ❑ Cover: 0.10 **NM** value: **35.00**
6 ❑ 1957 Cover: 0.10 **NM** value: **65.00**
7 ❑ May 1957 Cover: 0.10 **NM** value: **65.00**
8 ❑ 1957 Cover: 0.10 **NM** value: **65.00**
9 ❑ Nov 1957 Cover: 0.10 **NM** value: **65.00**
• **CGC:** 1 graded, best 9.0
10 ❑ Mar 1958 Cover: 0.10 **NM** value: **65.00**
11 ❑ Jul 1958 Cover: 0.10 **NM** value: **65.00**
12 ❑ Aug 1958 Cover: 0.10 **NM** value: **45.00**
13 ❑ Sep 1958 Cover: 0.10 **NM** value: **20.00**
14 ❑ Dec 1958 Cover: 0.10 **NM** value: **45.00**
15 ❑ Cover: 0.10 **NM** value: **45.00**
16 ❑ 1959 Cover: 0.10 **NM** value: **20.00**
17 ❑ Jul 1959 Cover: 0.10 **NM** value: **16.00**
18 ❑ Sep 1959 Cover: 0.10 **NM** value: **16.00**
19 ❑ Nov 1959 Cover: 0.10 **NM** value: **16.00**
20 ❑ Feb 1960 Cover: 0.10 **NM** value: **16.00**
21 ❑ Mar 1960 Cover: 0.10 **NM** value: **16.00**
22 ❑ Jun 1960 Cover: 0.10 **NM** value: **25.00**
23 ❑ Aug 1960 Cover: 0.10 **NM** value: **10.00**
24 ❑ Oct 1960 Cover: 0.10 **NM** value: **20.00**
25 ❑ Dec 1960 Cover: 0.10 **NM** value: **20.00**
26 ❑ Feb 1961 Cover: 0.10 **NM** value: **20.00**
Circ: Statement: **136,414**
📖 Speed Crazed; The Unseen; Where is Amelia?; Fantasia (text story); Nightmare! **A:** Steve Ditko; Moltra
27 ❑ Apr 1961 Cover: 0.10 **NM** value: **20.00**
Circ: Statement: **136,414**
28 ❑ Jun 1961 Cover: 0.10 **NM** value: **10.00**
Circ: Statement: **136,414**
29 ❑ Aug 1961 Cover: 0.10 **NM** value: **10.00**
Circ: Statement: **136,414**
30 ❑ Oct 1961 Cover: 0.10 **NM** value: **8.00**
Circ: Statement: **136,414**
31 ❑ Dec 1961 Cover: 0.10 **NM** value: **8.00**
Circ: Statement: **136,414** • **CGC:** 1 graded, best 7.5
📖 The Strange Case of Sammy; The Enemy; The World Beyond (text story); The Home of Happiness
32 ❑ Feb 1962 Cover: 0.10 **NM** value: **8.00**
• **CGC:** 3 graded, best 9.6
33 ❑ May 1962 Cover: 0.12 **NM** value: **8.00**
• Has 1961 Statement, filed 9/30/61; avg total paid circ 136,414
34 ❑ Jul 1962 Cover: 0.12 **NM** value: **8.00**
35 ❑ Sep 1962 Cover: 0.12 **NM** value: **8.00**
36 ❑ Nov 1962 Cover: 0.12 **NM** value: **8.00**
37 ❑ Jan 1963 Cover: 0.12 **NM** value: **8.00**
Circ: Statement: **141,083**
📖 Inner Sight; Valley of Life; Empty Paradise; Things to Come; The Treasure of Quebranchcichi; Hand of Fate **A:** Nicholas Alascia
38 ❑ Mar 1963 Cover: 0.12 **NM** value: **8.00**
Circ: Statement: **141,083**
39 ❑ May 1963 Cover: 0.12 **NM** value: **8.00**
Circ: Statement: **141,083**
40 ❑ 1963 Cover: 0.12 **NM** value: **8.00**
Circ: Statement: **141,083**
41 ❑ Nov 1963 Cover: 0.12 **NM** value: **5.00**
Circ: Statement: **141,083**
42 ❑ Dec 1963 Cover: 0.12 **NM** value: **5.00**
Circ: Statement: **141,083**
📖 Prisoner in the Atom; Man From Mars!; Martian Mistake (text story); Macklin's Miracle; Radiation and Space Travel; The Land of Peace **A:** Nicholas Alascia
43 ❑ Jan 1964 Cover: 0.12 **NM** value: **5.00**
Circ: Statement: **136,036**
44 ❑ Mar 1964 Cover: 0.12 **NM** value: **5.00**
Circ: Statement: **136,036**
• Has 1963 Statement, filed 9/30/63; avg print run 234,458; avg sales 141,072; avg subs 11; avg total paid 141,083; samples 25; max existent 141,108; 40% of run returned
45 ❑ 1964 Cover: 0.12 **NM** value: **5.00**
Circ: Statement: **136,036**
46 ❑ 1964 Cover: 0.12 **NM** value: **5.00**
Circ: Statement: **136,036**
47 ❑ Nov 1964 Cover: 0.12 **NM** value: **5.00**
Circ: Statement: **136,036**
📖 The Plan; The Snowman; Invasion; The Legend of Babaru; Yesterday, Today, and Tomorrow; Aladdin's Other Lamp (text); The Unwelcome Guest
48 ❑ Jan 1965 Cover: 0.12 **NM** value: **5.00**
49 ❑ Apr 1965 Cover: 0.12 **NM** value: **5.00**
• Series continued in Blue Beetle (2nd Series) #50

UP FROM BONDAGE — Fantagraphics / Eros

All issues are adults only.

1 ❑ b&w Cover: 2.95 **NM** value: **Cover or less**

UP FROM THE DEEP — Rip Off

1 ❑ ca. 1971 Cover: 1.00 **NM** value: **3.00**
• **CGC:** 1 graded, best 9.4
📖 The Black Saint and the Sinner Lady; When Dreams Collide; The Light in the Distance; Brindlesteen Apparition; Trool Bridge **A:** Jaxon Corben; Kim Deitch **W:** Jaxon Corben; Fowlton Means

URBAN HIPSTER — Alternative

1 ❑ Oct 1998, b&w Cover: 2.95 **NM** value: **Cover or less**
📖 411 UH; Lost in Space; August; Out of Africa; Advertisement; Slob; So Sick of Everything; December; Post-Grunge; Props; October **A:** David Lasky; Greg Stump **W:** David Lasky; Greg Stump

URBAN LEGENDS — Dark Horse

1 ❑ 1993b&w Cover: 2.95 **NM** value: **3.00**
Circ: CapCity orders: **5,100**

UROTSUKIDOJI: LEGEND OF THE OVERFIEND — CPM

1 ❑ Jul 1998 Cover: 2.95 **NM** value: **Cover or less**
Circ: Diamd. preorders: **4,951**
2 ❑ Aug 1998 Cover: 2.95 **NM** value: **Cover or less**
Circ: Diamd. preorders: **3,716**
3 ❑ Sep 1998 Cover: 2.95 **NM** value: **Cover or less**
Circ: Diamd. preorders: **3,587**

URTH 4 — Continuity

1 ❑ May 1989 Cover: 2.00 **NM** value: **Cover or less**
Circ: CapCity orders: **4,150**
2 ❑ Apr 1990 Cover: 2.00 **NM** value: **Cover or less**
Circ: CapCity orders: **2,575**
3 ❑ Oct 1990 Cover: 2.00 **NM** value: **Cover or less**
Circ: CapCity orders: **2,525**
4 ❑ Dec 1990 Cover: 2.00 **NM** value: **Cover or less**
Circ: CapCity orders: **2,525**

URZA-MISHRA WAR ON THE WORLD OF MAGIC: THE GATHERING — Acclaim / Armada

1 ❑ Sep 1996 Cover: 5.95 **NM** value: **Cover or less**
• squarebound; polybagged with Soldevi Steam Beast card
2 ❑ Sep 1996 Cover: 5.95 **NM** value: **Cover or less**
• squarebound; polybagged with Soldevi Steam Beast and Phyrexian War Beast cards

U.S. 1 — Marvel

Ulysses Solomon Archer, known affectionately as U.S., has trucking in his blood. As a child, he loved nothing better than watching the big rigs go by or riding in the cab with his parents, both truckers. Even though he wanted to start trucking right after high school, his adoptive father, Poppa, and his brother put together the money to send him to college. He went on to graduate, magna cum laude, with degrees in computer program design and electronics engineering. But when he finished, he wanted nothing more than to drive a rig down the road.

When the evil Highwayman forced U.S. and his brother (also a truck driver) off the road, only U.S. survived. U.S. vowed to avenge his brother's death and used his knowledge to create a super-cab, fit for the best trucker who ever was.

1 ❑ May 1983 Cover: 0.60 **NM** value: **1.00**
2 ❑ Jun 1983 Cover: 0.60 **NM** value: **1.00**
3 ❑ Jul 1983 Cover: 0.60 **NM** value: **1.00**
4 ❑ Aug 1983 Cover: 0.60 **NM** value: **1.00**
5 ❑ Sep 1983 Cover: 0.60 **NM** value: **1.00**
6 ❑ Oct 1983 Cover: 0.60 **NM** value: **1.00**
7 ❑ Dec 1983 Cover: 0.60 **NM** value: **1.00**
8 ❑ Feb 1984 Cover: 0.60 **NM** value: **1.00**
9 ❑ Apr 1984 Cover: 0.60 **NM** value: **1.00**
10 ❑ Jun 1984 Cover: 0.60 **NM** value: **1.00**
11 ❑ Aug 1984 Cover: 0.60 **NM** value: **1.00**
12 ❑ Oct 1984 Cover: 0.60 **NM** value: **1.00**

USA COMICS — Timely

1 ❑ Aug 1941 Cover: 0.10 **NM** value: **10000.00**
• **CGC:** 6 graded, best 9.0
2 ❑ Nov 1941 Cover: 0.10 **NM** value: **2000.00**
• **CGC:** 2 graded, best 9.4
3 ❑ Jan 1942 Cover: 0.10 **NM** value: **2000.00**
• **CGC:** 1 graded, best 9.4
4 ❑ Jul 1942 Cover: 0.10 **NM** value: **2000.00**
• **CGC:** 3 graded, best 9.2
5 ❑ Sum 1942 Cover: 0.10 **NM** value: **2000.00**
• **CGC:** 2 graded, best 9.2
6 ❑ Dec 1942 Cover: 0.10 **NM** value: **2000.00**
7 ❑ Mar 1943 Cover: 0.10 **NM** value: **2000.00**
• **CGC:** 2 graded, best 7.0
8 ❑ May 1943 Cover: 0.10 **NM** value: **2000.00**
• **CGC:** 1 graded, best 8.5
9 ❑ Jul 1943 Cover: 0.10 **NM** value: **2000.00**
• **CGC:** 2 graded, best 9.2
10 ❑ Sep 1943 Cover: 0.10 **NM** value: **2000.00**
• **CGC:** 1 graded, best 8.5
11 ❑ Jan 1944 Cover: 0.10 **NM** value: **2000.00**
• **CGC:** 1 graded, best 8.5
12 ❑ Spr 1944 Cover: 0.10 **NM** value: **2000.00**
• **CGC:** 1 graded, best 3.0
13 ❑ Sum 1944 Cover: 0.10 **NM** value: **2000.00**
• **CGC:** 1 graded, best 7.0
14 ❑ Fal 1944 Cover: 0.10 **NM** value: **2000.00**
• **CGC:** 1 graded, best 5.0
15 ❑ Spr 1945 Cover: 0.10 **NM** value: **2000.00**
• **CGC:** 1 graded, best 9.4
16 ❑ Sum 1945 Cover: 0.10 **NM** value: **2000.00**
• **CGC:** 2 graded, best 9.0
17 ❑ Fal 1945 Cover: 0.10 **NM** value: **2000.00**
• **CGC:** 2 graded, best 9.0

U.S.AGENT — Marvel

1 ❑ Jun 1993 Cover: 1.75 **NM** value: **2.00**
Circ: CapCity orders: **45,800**
2 ❑ Jul 1993 Cover: 1.75 **NM** value: **2.00**
Circ: CapCity orders: **24,100**
3 ❑ Aug 1993 Cover: 1.75 **NM** value: **2.00**
Circ: CapCity orders: **20,500**
4 ❑ Sep 1993 Cover: 1.75 **NM** value: **2.00**
Circ: CapCity orders: **16,400**

USAGI YOJIMBO (VOL. 1) — Fantagraphics

Stan Sakai's Usagi Yojimbo is a sometimes-lighthearted adventure series starring a rabbit samurai named Usagi. Usagi lives in an alternate-worlds version of Middle Ages Japan, where a collection of animals has grown up in place of humans. These cartoon critters take on the roles of everything from samurai to shopkeepers. These characters, when combined with Sakai's clever storytelling, add up to a cult favorite.

The black-and-white title eventually went color in a second volume published by Mirage Publishing. Usagi has also starred with the Teenage Mutant Ninja Turtles and reached for the stars in the fanciful Space Usagi titles.

1 ❑ Jul 1987, b&w Cover: 2.00 **NM** value: **8.00**
• **CGC:** 1 graded, best 9.6
1-2 ❑ Jul 1987 Cover: 2.00 **NM** value: **2.50**
2 ❑ Sep 1987, b&w Cover: 2.00 **NM** value: **5.00**
3 ❑ Oct 1987, b&w Cover: 2.00 **NM** value: **5.00**
4 ❑ Nov 1987, b&w Cover: 2.00 **NM** value: **3.50**
📖 Bats, The Cat, and The Rabbit **A:** Stan Sakai **W:** Stan Sakai
5 ❑ Jan 1988, b&w Cover: 2.00 **NM** value: **3.50**
6 ❑ Feb 1988, b&w Cover: 2.00 **NM** value: **3.00**
7 ❑ Mar 1988, b&w Cover: 2.00 **NM** value: **3.00**
📖 The Withered Field **A:** Stan Sakai **W:** Stan Sakai
8 ❑ May 1988, b&w Cover: 2.00 **NM** value: **3.00**
📖 The Promise in the Snow **A:** Stan Sakai **W:** Stan Sakai
9 ❑ Jul 1988, b&w Cover: 2.00 **NM** value: **3.00**
📖 The Conspiracy of Eight **A:** Stan Sakai **W:** Stan Sakai
10 ❑ Aug 1988, b&w Cover: 2.00 **NM** value: **3.00**
10-2 ❑ Aug 1988 Cover: 2.00 **NM** value: **Cover or less**
11 ❑ Sep 1988, b&w Cover: 2.00 **NM** value: **2.50**
12 ❑ Oct 1988, b&w Cover: 2.00 **NM** value: **2.50**
13 ❑ Jan 1989, b&w Cover: 2.00 **NM** value: **2.50**
• indicia says Jan 88; a misprint **A:** Stan Sakai **W:** Stan Sakai
14 ❑ Jan 1989, b&w Cover: 2.00 **NM** value: **2.50**
• indicia says Jan 89 **A:** Stan Sakai **W:** Stan Sakai
15 ❑ Mar 1989, b&w Cover: 2.00 **NM** value: **2.50**
16 ❑ May 1989, b&w Cover: 2.00 **NM** value: **2.50**
17 ❑ Jul 1989, b&w Cover: 2.00 **NM** value: **2.50**
18 ❑ Oct 1989, b&w Cover: 2.00 **NM** value: **2.50**
19 ❑ Dec 1989, b&w Cover: 2.00 **NM** value: **2.50**
20 ❑ Feb 1990, b&w Cover: 2.00 **NM** value: **2.50**
21 ❑ Apr 1990, b&w Cover: 2.00 **NM** value: **2.50**
22 ❑ May 1990, b&w Cover: 2.00 **NM** value: **2.50**
23 ❑ Jul 1990, b&w Cover: 2.00 **NM** value: **2.50**
24 ❑ Sep 1990, b&w Cover: 2.00 **NM** value: **2.50**
• Lone Goat & Kid **A:** Stan Sakai **W:** Stan Sakai
25 ❑ Nov 1990, b&w Cover: 2.00 **NM** value: **2.50**
26 ❑ Jan 1991, b&w Cover: 2.00 **NM** value: **2.50**
• indicia says Jan 90; another misprint **A:** Stan Sakai **W:** Stan Sakai
27 ❑ Mar 1991, b&w Cover: 2.00 **NM** value: **2.50**
28 ❑ May 1991, b&w Cover: 2.00 **NM** value: **2.50**
29 ❑ Jul 1991, b&w Cover: 2.00 **NM** value: **2.50**
30 ❑ Sep 1991, b&w Cover: 2.25 **NM** value: **2.50**
back cover reproduces front cover without logos. **A:** Stan Sakai **W:** Stan Sakai
31 ❑ Nov 1991, b&w Cover: 2.25 **NM** value: **2.50**
32 ❑ Feb 1992, b&w Cover: 2.25 **NM** value: **2.50**

CGC-graded: Multiply prices above by **33 for 9.9 M • 16 for 9.8 NM/M • 7 for 9.6 NM+ • 5 for 9.4 NM • 2.5 for 9.2 NM- • 1.5 for 9.0 VF/NM**

33 ❑ Apr 1992, b&w Cover: 2.25 **NM** value: **2.50**
34 ❑ Jun 1992, b&w Cover: 2.25 **NM** value: **2.50**
35 ❑ Aug 1992, b&w Cover: 2.25 **NM** value: **2.50**
36 ❑ Nov 1992, b&w Cover: 2.25 **NM** value: **2.50**
37 ❑ Feb 1993, b&w Cover: 2.25 **NM** value: **2.50**
38 ❑ Mar 1993, b&w Cover: 2.25 **NM** value: **2.50**
Circ: CapCity orders: **3,300**
final issue. **A:** Stan Sakai **W:** Stan Sakai
Bk 1❑ Cover: 12.95 **NM** value: **Cover or less**
Bk 1/HC❑ Cover: 35.00 **NM** value: **Cover or less**
Bk 2❑ Cover: 14.95 **NM** value: **Cover or less**
Bk 2/HC❑ Cover: 35.00 **NM** value: **Cover or less**
Bk 3❑ Cover: 12.95 **NM** value: **Cover or less**
Bk 3/HC❑ Cover: 35.00 **NM** value: **Cover or less**
Bk 4❑ Cover: 14.95 **NM** value: **Cover or less**
Bk 5❑ Cover: 10.95 **NM** value: **Cover or less**
Bk 6❑ Cover: 12.95 **NM** value: **Cover or less**
Bk 6/HC❑ Cover: 39.95 **NM** value: **Cover or less**
Bk 7❑ Cover: 16.95 **NM** value: **Cover or less**
Bk 7/HC❑ Cover: 39.95 **NM** value: **Cover or less**
SE 1❑ Nov 1989 Cover: 2.95 **NM** value: **3.50**
• Color special #1 **A:** Stan Sakai **W:** Stan Sakai
SE 2❑ Oct 1991 Cover: 3.50 **NM** value: **Cover or less**
• Color special #2 **A:** Stan Sakai **W:** Stan Sakai
SE 3❑ Oct 1992 Cover: 3.50 **NM** value: **Cover or less**
• Color special #3 **A:** Stan Sakai **W:** Stan Sakai
Smr 1❑ Oct 1986, b&w Cover: 2.75 **NM** value: **4.00**
• introduction by Mark Evanier **A:** Sergio Aragonés; Stan Sakai **W:** Stan Sakai

USAGI YOJIMBO (VOL. 2) — Mirage

1 ❑ Mar 1993, full color Cover: 2.75 **NM** value: **4.50**
Circ: CapCity orders: **8,950**
2 ❑ May 1993 Cover: 2.75 **NM** value: **3.50**
Circ: CapCity orders: **5,125**
3 ❑ Jul 1993 Cover: 2.75 **NM** value: **3.50**
Circ: CapCity orders: **4,900**
4 ❑ Sep 1993 Cover: 2.75 **NM** value: **3.50**
Circ: CapCity orders: **4,075**
5 ❑ Nov 1993 Cover: 2.75 **NM** value: **3.50**
Circ: CapCity orders: **3,950**
6 ❑ Jan 1994 Cover: 2.75 **NM** value: **3.00**
Circ: CapCity orders: **3,750**
Battlefield, Part 1 **A:** Stan Sakai **W:** Stan Sakai
7 ❑ Apr 1994 Cover: 2.75 **NM** value: **3.00**
Circ: CapCity orders: **3,925**
Battlefield, Part 2 **A:** Stan Sakai **W:** Stan Sakai
8 ❑ Jun 1994 Cover: 2.75 **NM** value: **3.00**
Circ: CapCity orders: **3,645**
9 ❑ Aug 1994 Cover: 2.75 **NM** value: **3.00**
Circ: CapCity orders: **3,480**
Slavers, Part 1 **A:** Stan Sakai **W:** Stan Sakai
10 ❑ Oct 1994 Cover: 2.75 **NM** value: **3.00**
Slavers, Part 2; The Nature of the Serpent **A:** Stan Sakai **W:** Stan Sakai
11 ❑ Dec 1994 Cover: 2.75 **NM** value: **Cover or less**
Circ: CapCity orders: **3,160**
Daisho, Part 1; Mongrels, Part 1 **A:** Stan Sakai **W:** Stan Sakai
12 ❑ Feb 1995 Cover: 2.75 **NM** value: **Cover or less**
Circ: CapCity orders: **2,800**
Daisho, Part 2; Mongrels, Part 2 **A:** Stan Sakai **W:** Stan Sakai
13 ❑ Apr 1995 Cover: 2.75 **NM** value: **Cover or less**
Circ: CapCity orders: **2,980**
Runaways, Part 1; Black Soul **A:** Stan Sakai **W:** Stan Sakai
14 ❑ Jun 1995 Cover: 2.75 **NM** value: **Cover or less**
Circ: CapCity orders: **2,880**
Runaways, Part 2 **A:** Stan Sakai **W:** Stan Sakai
15 ❑ Aug 1995 Cover: 2.75 **NM** value: **Cover or less**
Circ: CapCity orders: **2,845**
Lionheart: Real Heroes, Part 1 **A:** Stan Sakai **W:** Stan Sakai ★ 1st Appearance of Lionheart (in color).
16 ❑ Oct 1995 Cover: 2.75 **NM** value: **Cover or less**
A Meeting of Strangers; Lionheart: Real Heroes, Part 2 final issue. **A:** Stan Sakai **W:** Stan Sakai

USAGI YOJIMBO (VOL. 3) — Dark Horse

1 ❑ Apr 1996 Cover: 2.95 **NM** value: **4.00**
2 ❑ May 1996 Cover: 2.95 **NM** value: **3.00**
3 ❑ Jun 1996 Cover: 2.95 **NM** value: **3.00**
4 ❑ Jul 1996 Cover: 2.95 **NM** value: **3.00**
5 ❑ Aug 1996 Cover: 2.95 **NM** value: **3.00**
The Chrysanthemum Pass **A:** Stan Sakai **W:** Stan Sakai
6 ❑ Oct 1996 Cover: 2.95 **NM** value: **3.00**
Circ: Diamd. preorders: **9,122**
7 ❑ Nov 1996 Cover: 2.95 **NM** value: **3.00**
Circ: Diamd. preorders: **9,156**
8 ❑ Dec 1996 Cover: 2.95 **NM** value: **3.00**
Circ: Diamd. preorders: **8,930**
9 ❑ Jan 1997 Cover: 2.95 **NM** value: **3.00**
Circ: Diamd. preorders: **8,673**
10 ❑ Feb 1997 Cover: 2.95 **NM** value: **3.00**
Circ: Diamd. preorders: **8,754**
11 ❑ Mar 1997 Cover: 2.95 **NM** value: **3.00**
Circ: Diamd. preorders: **8,740**
The Lord of Owls; The First Tenet **A:** Stan Sakai **W:** Stan Sakai
12 ❑ 1997 Cover: 2.95 **NM** value: **3.00**
Circ: Diamd. preorders: **8,980**
The Obakeneko of Geishu Clan **A:** Stan Sakai **W:** Stan Sakai
13 ❑ Aug 1997 Cover: 2.95 **NM** value: **3.00**
Circ: Diamd. preorders: **9,108**
Grasscutter **A:** Stan Sakai **W:** Stan Sakai
14 ❑ Sep 1997 Cover: 2.95 **NM** value: **Cover or less**
Circ: Diamd. preorders: **9,133**
Grasscutter **A:** Stan Sakai **W:** Stan Sakai
15 ❑ Oct 1997 Cover: 2.95 **NM** value: **Cover or less**
Circ: Diamd. preorders: **9,138**
Grasscutter **A:** Stan Sakai **W:** Stan Sakai
16 ❑ Nov 1997 Cover: 2.95 **NM** value: **Cover or less**
Circ: Diamd. preorders: **9,030**
Grasscutter **A:** Stan Sakai **W:** Stan Sakai
17 ❑ Jan 1998 Cover: 2.95 **NM** value: **Cover or less**
Circ: Diamd. preorders: **8,655**
Grasscutter **A:** Stan Sakai **W:** Stan Sakai
18 ❑ Feb 1998 Cover: 2.95 **NM** value: **Cover or less**
Circ: Diamd. preorders: **8,257**
Grasscutter **A:** Stan Sakai **W:** Stan Sakai
19 ❑ Mar 1998 Cover: 2.95 **NM** value: **Cover or less**
Circ: Diamd. preorders: **8,475**
Grasscutter **A:** Stan Sakai **W:** Stan Sakai
20 ❑ 1998 Cover: 2.95 **NM** value: **Cover or less**
Circ: Diamd. preorders: **8,824**
Grasscutter **A:** Stan Sakai **W:** Stan Sakai
21 ❑ Jun 1998 Cover: 2.95 **NM** value: **Cover or less**
Circ: Diamd. preorders: **9,168**
Grasscutter **A:** Stan Sakai **W:** Stan Sakai
22 ❑ Jul 1998 Cover: 2.95 **NM** value: **Cover or less**
Circ: Diamd. preorders: **8,450**
Grasscutter **A:** Stan Sakai **W:** Stan Sakai
23 ❑ Sep 1998 Cover: 2.95 **NM** value: **Cover or less**
Circ: Diamd. preorders: **8,400**
My Father's Swords **A:** Stan Sakai **W:** Stan Sakai
24 ❑ Oct 1998 Cover: 2.95 **NM** value: **Cover or less**
Circ: Diamd. preorders: **8,583**
The Demon Flute **A:** Stan Sakai **W:** Stan Sakai
25 ❑ Nov 1998 Cover: 2.95 **NM** value: **Cover or less**
Circ: Diamd. preorders: **8,757**
Momo-Usagi-Taro • Momo-Usagi-Taro **A:** Stan Sakai **W:** Stan Sakai
26 ❑ Jan 1999 Cover: 2.95 **NM** value: **Cover or less**
The Hairpin Murders **A:** Stan Sakai **W:** Stan Sakai
27 ❑ Feb 1999 Cover: 2.95 **NM** value: **Cover or less**
Circ: Diamd. preorders: **8,160**
The Hairpin Murders **A:** Stan Sakai **W:** Stan Sakai
28 ❑ Apr 1999 Cover: 2.95 **NM** value: **Cover or less**
Circ: Diamd. preorders: **8,610**
The Courtesan **A:** Stan Sakai **W:** Stan Sakai
29 ❑ May 1999 Cover: 2.95 **NM** value: **Cover or less**
Circ: Diamd. preorders: **8,467**
The Courtesan **A:** Stan Sakai **W:** Stan Sakai
30 ❑ Jul 1999 Cover: 2.95 **NM** value: **Cover or less**
Circ: Diamd. preorders: **8,720**
31 ❑ Sep 1999 Cover: 2.95 **NM** value: **Cover or less**
Circ: Diamd. preorders: **8,414**
32 ❑ Oct 1999 Cover: 2.95 **NM** value: **Cover or less**
Circ: Diamd. preorders: **8,846**
33 ❑ Nov 1999 Cover: 2.95 **NM** value: **Cover or less**
Circ: Diamd. preorders: **8,686**
34 ❑ Cover: 2.95 **NM** value: **Cover or less**
Circ: Diamd. preorders: **9,211**
35 ❑ 2000 Cover: 2.95 **NM** value: **Cover or less**
Circ: Diamd. preorders: **8,574**
36 ❑ 2000 Cover: 2.95 **NM** value: **Cover or less**
Circ: Diamd. preorders: **8,323**
37 ❑ Apr 2000 Cover: 2.95 **NM** value: **Cover or less**
Circ: Diamd. preorders: **8,520**
38 ❑ 2000 Cover: 2.95 **NM** value: **Cover or less**
Circ: Diamd. preorders: **8,553**
39 ❑ Jul 2000 Cover: 2.95 **NM** value: **Cover or less**
Circ: Diamd. preorders: **8,901**
Grasscutter II, Part 1 **A:** Stan Sakai **W:** Stan Sakai
40 ❑ Aug 2000 Cover: 2.95 **NM** value: **Cover or less**
Circ: Diamd. preorders: **8,584**
41 ❑ Sep 2000 Cover: 2.95 **NM** value: **Cover or less**
Circ: Diamd. preorders: **8,857**
42 ❑ Oct 2000 Cover: 2.99 **NM** value: **Cover or less**
Circ: Diamd. preorders: **8,930**
43 ❑ Nov 2000 Cover: 2.99 **NM** value: **Cover or less**
Circ: Diamd. preorders: **8,920**
44 ❑ Dec 2000 Cover: 2.99 **NM** value: **Cover or less**
Circ: Diamd. preorders: **8,890**
45 ❑ Jan 2001 Cover: 2.99 **NM** value: **Cover or less**
Circ: Diamd. preorders: **8,728**
Grasscutter II, Part 6 **A:** Stan Sakai **W:** Stan Sakai
46 ❑ Mar 2001 Cover: 2.99 **NM** value: **Cover or less**
Circ: Diamd. preorders: **8,559**
Showdown, Part 1 **A:** Stan Sakai **W:** Stan Sakai
47 ❑ Apr 2001 Cover: 2.99 **NM** value: **Cover or less**
Circ: Diamd. preorders: **8,696**
Showdown, Part 2 **A:** Stan Sakai **W:** Stan Sakai
Bk 1❑ Cover: 55.00 **NM** value: **Cover or less**
• Limited edition hardcover. **A:** Stan Sakai **W:** Stan Sakai
Bk 8❑ Sep 1997 Cover: 14.95 **NM** value: **Cover or less**
Shades of Death **A:** Stan Sakai **W:** Stan Sakai
Bk 9❑ Feb 1998 Cover: 14.95 **NM** value: **Cover or less**
• Daisho **A:** Stan Sakai **W:** Stan Sakai
Bk 10❑ Aug 1998 Cover: 14.95 **NM** value: **Cover or less**
The Brink of Life and Death **A:** Stan Sakai **W:** Stan Sakai
Bk 11❑ Mar 1999 Cover: 14.95 **NM** value: **Cover or less**
Seasons **A:** Stan Sakai **W:** Stan Sakai
Bk 12❑ Aug 1999 Cover: 16.95 **NM** value: **Cover or less**
Grasscutter **A:** Stan Sakai **W:** Stan Sakai

Capital City orders are the actual sales of comic books by Capital City Distribution, once one of the largest U.S. sellers of comics to comics shops. Capital City's share of comics shop sales, while not known exactly, increases from around 10-20% in the mid-1980s to 30-35% in the mid-1990s. Capital City's share of comic books sold on newsstands (most Marvels and DCs) will be less.

U.S. AIR FORCE — Charlton

They don't really make war comics like U.S. Air Force any more. In this Charlton title, the pilots were universally brave, the enemy was stupid and cowardly, and everything always worked out in the end. This was truly a war series of the old school.

This title ran between 1958 and 1965 (after which it changed its name to "Army Attack" and ran two more years). This was a time when the children of those who served in World War II could still ask their fathers how it had been in what may have been the last "great" war. But the war stories that had seemed simple and heroic a few years earlier grew more ambiguous when new readers had to make sense of such battlegrounds as Korea and enemies as communism. Perhaps it was the specter of Vietnam and the change in public mood that doomed war comics like U.S. Air Force.

1 ❑ Oct 1958 Cover: 0.10 **NM** value: **35.00**
2 ❑ Jan 1959 Cover: 0.10 **NM** value: **20.00**
3 ❑ 1959 Cover: 0.10 **NM** value: **12.00**
4 ❑ 1959 Cover: 0.10 **NM** value: **12.00**
5 ❑ 1959 Cover: 0.10 **NM** value: **12.00**
6 ❑ Oct 1959 Cover: 0.10 **NM** value: **10.00**
7 ❑ Dec 1959 Cover: 0.10 **NM** value: **10.00**
8 ❑ Feb 1960 Cover: 0.10 **NM** value: **10.00**
9 ❑ Apr 1960 Cover: 0.10 **NM** value: **10.00**
10 ❑ Jun 1960 Cover: 0.10 **NM** value: **10.00**
11 ❑ Aug 1960 Cover: 0.10 **NM** value: **8.00**
12 ❑ Oct 1960 Cover: 0.10 **NM** value: **8.00**
13 ❑ Dec 1960 Cover: 0.10 **NM** value: **8.00**
14 ❑ Feb 1961 Cover: 0.10 **NM** value: **8.00**
15 ❑ Apr 1961 Cover: 0.10 **NM** value: **8.00**
16 ❑ Jun 1961 Cover: 0.10 **NM** value: **8.00**
17 ❑ Aug 1961 Cover: 0.10 **NM** value: **8.00**
18 ❑ ca. 1961 Cover: 0.10 **NM** value: **8.00**
19 ❑ ca. 1961 Cover: 0.10 **NM** value: **8.00**
20 ❑ 1962 Cover: 0.12 **NM** value: **8.00**
21 ❑ 1962 Cover: 0.12 **NM** value: **7.00**
22 ❑ Jul 1962 Cover: 0.12 **NM** value: **7.00**
23 ❑ 1962 Cover: 0.12 **NM** value: **7.00**
24 ❑ 1962 Cover: 0.12 **NM** value: **7.00**
25 ❑ 1962 Cover: 0.12 **NM** value: **7.00**
26 ❑ ca. 1963 Cover: 0.12 **NM** value: **7.00**
27 ❑ 1963 Cover: 0.12 **NM** value: **7.00**
28 ❑ 1963 Cover: 0.12 **NM** value: **7.00**
29 ❑ 1963 Cover: 0.12 **NM** value: **7.00**
30 ❑ 1963 Cover: 0.12 **NM** value: **7.00**
31 ❑ ca. 1964 Cover: 0.12 **NM** value: **7.00**
32 ❑ ca. 1964 Cover: 0.12 **NM** value: **7.00**
33 ❑ Jun 1964 Cover: 0.12 **NM** value: **7.00**
34 ❑ 1964 Cover: 0.12 **NM** value: **7.00**
35 ❑ Nov 1964 Cover: 0.12 **NM** value: **7.00**
36 ❑ Jan 1965 Cover: 0.12 **NM** value: **7.00**
37 ❑ Mar 1965 Cover: 0.12 **NM** value: **7.00**
final issue.

USER — DC / Vertigo

1 ❑ Cover: 5.95 **NM** value: **Cover or less**
Circ: Diamd. preorders: **13,004**
2 ❑ Cover: 5.95 **NM** value: **Cover or less**
Circ: Diamd. preorders: **10,222**
3 ❑ Cover: 5.95 **NM** value: **Cover or less**
Circ: Diamd. preorders: **8,353**

U.S. FIGHTING AIR FORCE — Superior

1 ❑ Sep 1952 Cover: 0.10 **NM** value: **40.00**
2 ❑ Nov 1952 Cover: 0.10 **NM** value: **24.00**
3 ❑ Jan 1953 Cover: 0.10 **NM** value: **24.00**
Rescue Raider; Crash Hero; Secret Mission (text story); Operation Decoy; Panmunjom Treachery
4 ❑ 1953 Cover: 0.10 **NM** value: **18.00**
5 ❑ Nov 1953 Cover: 0.10 **NM** value: **18.00**
6 ❑ Jan 1954 Cover: 0.10 **NM** value: **15.00**
7 ❑ Mar 1954 Cover: 0.10 **NM** value: **15.00**
8 ❑ May 1954 Cover: 0.10 **NM** value: **15.00**
9 ❑ Jul 1954 Cover: 0.10 **NM** value: **15.00**
10 ❑ Sep 1954 Cover: 0.10 **NM** value: **15.00**
11 ❑ Nov 1954 Cover: 0.10 **NM** value: **12.00**
12 ❑ Jan 1955 Cover: 0.10 **NM** value: **12.00**
13 ❑ Mar 1955 Cover: 0.10 **NM** value: **12.00**
14 ❑ May 1955 Cover: 0.10 **NM** value: **12.00**
15 ❑ Jul 1955 Cover: 0.10 **NM** value: **12.00**
16 ❑ Sep 1955 Cover: 0.10 **NM** value: **12.00**
17 ❑ Oct 1955 Cover: 0.10 **NM** value: **12.00**
18 ❑ Nov 1955 Cover: 0.10 **NM** value: **12.00**
19 ❑ Dec 1955 Cover: 0.10 **NM** value: **12.00**
20 ❑ Jan 1956 Cover: 0.10 **NM** value: **12.00**
21 ❑ Feb 1956 Cover: 0.10 **NM** value: **12.00**
22 ❑ Mar 1956 Cover: 0.10 **NM** value: **12.00**
23 ❑ Apr 1956 Cover: 0.10 **NM** value: **12.00**
24 ❑ May 1956 Cover: 0.10 **NM** value: **12.00**
25 ❑ Jun 1956 Cover: 0.10 **NM** value: **12.00**
26 ❑ Jul 1956 Cover: 0.10 **NM** value: **12.00**
27 ❑ Aug 1956 Cover: 0.10 **NM** value: **12.00**
28 ❑ Sep 1956 Cover: 0.10 **NM** value: **12.00**
final issue.

U.S. WAR MACHINE — Marvel / MAX

1 ❑ 2001 Cover: 1.50 **NM** value: **Cover or less**
Circ: Diamd. preorders: **37,614** • **CGC:** 3 graded, best 9.8

Other grades: Multiply prices above by **1.5 for Mint • 2/3 for Very Fine • 1/3 for Fine • 1/5 for Very Good • 1/8 for Good**

2 ❑ 2001 Cover: 1.50 **NM value: Cover or less**
Circ: Diamd. preorders: **35,895**
3 ❑ 2001 Cover: 1.50 **NM value: Cover or less**
Circ: Diamd. preorders: **35,615**
4 ❑ 2001 Cover: 1.50 **NM value: Cover or less**
Circ: Diamd. preorders: **30,027**
5 ❑ 2001 Cover: 1.50 **NM value: Cover or less**
Circ: Diamd. preorders: **29,907**
6 ❑ 2001 Cover: 1.50 **NM value: Cover or less**
Circ: Diamd. preorders: **29,700**
7 ❑ 2001 Cover: 1.50 **NM value: Cover or less**
Circ: Diamd. preorders: **29,566**
8 ❑ 2001 Cover: 1.50 **NM value: Cover or less**
Circ: Diamd. preorders: **29,432**
9 ❑ 2001 Cover: 1.50 **NM value: Cover or less**
Circ: Diamd. preorders: **29,075**
10 ❑ 2002 Cover: 1.50 **NM value: Cover or less**
Circ: Diamd. preorders: **29,144**
11 ❑ 2002 Cover: 1.50 **NM value: Cover or less**
Circ: Diamd. preorders: **29,031**
12 ❑ 2002 Cover: 1.50 **NM value: Cover or less**
Circ: Diamd. preorders: **28,979**

V — DC

1 ❑ Feb 1985 Cover: 0.75 **NM value: 1.50**
• **CGC:** 4 graded, best 9.6
• Based on TV series **A:** Carmine Infantino
2 ❑ Mar 1985 Cover: 0.75 **NM value: 1.00**
• **CGC:** 4 graded, best 9.6
3 ❑ Apr 1985 Cover: 0.75 **NM value: 1.00**
• **CGC:** 4 graded, best 9.6
Encounter! **A:** Carmine Infantino **W:** Cary Bates
4 ❑ May 1985 Cover: 0.75 **NM value: 1.00**
Circ: CapCity orders: **9,250** • **CGC:** 4 graded, best 9.4
5 ❑ Jun 1985 Cover: 0.75 **NM value: 1.00**
Circ: CapCity orders: **9,250** • **CGC:** 4 graded, best 9.4
The Price of Peace **A:** Tod Smith **W:** Cary Bates
6 ❑ Jul 1985 Cover: 0.75 **NM value: 1.00**
Circ: CapCity orders: **9,200** • **CGC:** 4 graded, best 9.6
Shatterday **A:** Carmine Infantino **W:** Cary Bates
7 ❑ Aug 1985 Cover: 0.75 **NM value: 1.00**
Circ: CapCity orders: **8,800** • **CGC:** 4 graded, best 9.6
8 ❑ Sep 1985 Cover: 0.75 **NM value: 1.00**
Circ: CapCity orders: **8,100**
9 ❑ Oct 1985 Cover: 0.75 **NM value: 1.00**
Circ: CapCity orders: **7,500**
10 ❑ Nov 1985 Cover: 0.75 **NM value: 1.00**
Circ: CapCity orders: **6,800**
11 ❑ Dec 1985 Cover: 0.75 **NM value: 1.00**
Circ: CapCity orders: **6,250**
12 ❑ Jan 1986 Cover: 0.75 **NM value: 1.00**
Circ: CapCity orders: **5,800**
13 ❑ Feb 1986 Cover: 0.75 **NM value: 1.00**
Circ: CapCity orders: **5,650**
14 ❑ Mar 1986 Cover: 0.75 **NM value: 1.00**
Circ: CapCity orders: **5,300**
15 ❑ Apr 1986 Cover: 0.75 **NM value: 1.00**
Circ: CapCity orders: **5,650**
16 ❑ May 1986 Cover: 0.75 **NM value: 1.00**
Circ: CapCity orders: **4,900**
17 ❑ Jun 1986 Cover: 0.75 **NM value: 1.00**
Circ: CapCity orders: **4,700**
18 ❑ Jul 1986 Cover: 0.75 **NM value: 1.00**
Circ: CapCity orders: **4,800**
final issue. **A:** Dick Giordano

VACATION IN DISNEYLAND — Dell

1 ❑ Aug 1958 Cover: 0.25 **NM value: 135.00**
• **CGC:** 4 graded, best 9.6
Mastering the Matterhorn; Trail Tycoon; Dream Planet • Same comic as Four Color Comics #1025

VAGABOND — Image

1/A ❑ Aug 2000 Cover: 2.95 **NM value: Cover or less**
Circ: Diamd. preorders: **14,163**
Pat Lee cover. **A:** Ryan Benjamin **W:** Sean Ruffner
1/B ❑ Aug 2000 Cover: 2.95 **NM value: Cover or less**
Ryan Benjamin cover. **A:** Ryan Benjamin **W:** Sean Ruffner

VALENTINE — Redeye Press

1 ❑ Sep 1997, b&w Cover: 2.95 **NM value: Cover or less**

VALENTINO — Renegade

1 ❑ Apr 1985, b&w Cover: 1.70 **NM value: 2.00**
No issue number. Drafted!; Party!; Fit to be Tied!; The Kid: I Quit Smoking; One For Granny (text story); **A:** Jim Valentino **W:** Jim Valentino
2 ❑ Apr 1987, b&w Cover: 1.70 **NM value: 2.00**
• Valentino Too **A:** Jim Valentino **W:** Jim Valentino
3 ❑ Apr 1988, b&w Cover: 2.00 **NM value: Cover or less**
• Valentino the 3rd **A:** Jim Valentino **W:** Jim Valentino

VALERIAN — Fantasy Flight

1 ❑ Jul 1996, b&w Cover: 2.95 **NM value: Cover or less**
Heroes of the Equinox • Heroes of the Equinox **A:** J.C. Mezieres **W:** P. Christin

Capital City orders are the actual sales of comic books by Capital City Distribution, once one of the largest U.S. sellers of comics to comics shops. Capital City's share of comics shop sales, while not known exactly, increases from around 10-20% in the mid-1980s to 30-35% in the mid-1990s. Capital City's share of comic books sold on newsstands (most Marvels and DCs) will be less.

VALERIA, THE SHE-BAT (CONTINUITY) — Continuity

Valeria, we hardly knew ya ...

A member of the Were-Bred with leather wings, sonar, and deadly claws, Valeria was a perfect character for the complex world of magic and mystery she lived in. This was one of the first titles from Neal Adams' Continuity Comics, but, though the stories and art were excellent, the real story was not to be found in its inside pages.

The first two issues of Valeria were released with great fanfare in the comics boom of 1993. However, Continuity didn't make them available for regular ordering, using them as promotion pieces, instead. Issues #3 and #4 were meant to be star-packed attractions, featuring a collaboration with Spawn's Todd McFarlane. Sadly, these never came to pass. Issue #5 was the first generally released one, followed by new issues #3 and #4. By then, however, the game was up, and Valeria folded.

1 ❑ May 1993 Cover: 2.50 **NM value: 3.00**
• **CGC:** 1 graded, best 9.6
no cover price. • Promotional edition, never available for ordering. Deathwatch 2000 **A:** Neal Adams **W:** Neal Adams; Peter Stone
2 ❑ 1993 Cover: 2.50 **NM value: 3.00**
Circ: CapCity orders: **5,820**
• Promotional edition, never available for ordering.
3 ❑ 1993 Cover: 2.50 **NM value: Cover or less**
Circ: CapCity orders: **3,450**
• Published out of sequence (after #5)
4 ❑ 1993 Cover: 2.50 **NM value: Cover or less**
Circ: CapCity orders: **3,075**
• Published out of sequence
5 ❑ Nov 1993 Cover: 2.50 **NM value: Cover or less**
Circ: CapCity orders: **13,850**
Tyvek wraparound cover. Rise of Magic ★ Appearance of Knighthawk.

VALERIA THE SHE-BAT (WINDJAMMER) — Acclaim / Windjammer

1 ❑ Sep 1995 Cover: 2.50 **NM value: Cover or less**
Circ: CapCity orders: **11,225**
2 ❑ Sep 1995 Cover: 2.50 **NM value: Cover or less**
Circ: CapCity orders: **10,425**

VALHALLA — Antarctic

1 ❑ Feb 1999 Cover: 2.99 **NM value: Cover or less**

VALIANT EFFORTS (VOL. 2) — Valiant Comics

1 ❑ May 1991 Cover: 1.95 **NM value: Cover or less**
Street Fury **A:** Ralph Ellis Miley **W:** Ralph Ellis Miley

VALIANT ERA COLLECTION, THE — Valiant

Bk 1 ❑ ca. 1993 Cover: 13.95 **NM value: Cover or less**
No issue number.

VALIANT READER — Valiant

1 ❑ 1993 Cover: 0.75 **NM value: Cover or less**
Circ: CapCity orders: **10,850**
• background

VALIANT VARMINTS — Shanda Fantasy Arts

1 ❑ b&w Cover: 4.50 **NM value: Cover or less**

VALIANT VISION STARTER KIT — Valiant

Valiant wanted to publish its own 3-D comics, so, naturally, it had to re-create, and improve, the traditional process. One aspect of their version is the fact that it works with full-color comics, so that a publication done in Valiant Vision can be enjoyed with or without the special glasses. Of course, the drawback is that the glasses are still needed to get the three-dimensional effect.

This book details how the process was created and how it works, mostly using pages from Solar, Man of the Atom as examples. Of course, 3-D was way overdue to be improved upon, but that's not what makes this issue worth collecting. Besides a cover by comics legend Neal Adams, the book also features posters, pinups, and other interior art by such talents as Joe Quesada, Bob Layton, and Jimmy Palmiotti.

1 ❑ Jan 1994 Cover: 2.95 **NM value: Cover or less**
• comic book, glasses, poster **A:** Yvel Guichet; Bob Layton; Rodney Ramos; Peter Grau; Andrew Wendel; Scott Friedlander; Stan Drake **C:** Neal Adams **W:** Kevin Van Hook

VALKYR — Ironcat

1 ❑ Cover: 2.95 **NM value: Cover or less**
Circ: Diamd. preorders: **2,838**
2 ❑ Cover: 2.95 **NM value: Cover or less**
Circ: Diamd. preorders: **2,234**
3 ❑ Cover: 2.95 **NM value: Cover or less**
Circ: Diamd. preorders: **1,997**

VALKYRIE (1ST SERIES) — Eclipse

1 ❑ May 1987 Cover: 1.75 **NM value: 2.00**
Circ: CapCity orders: **9,225**
2 ❑ Jun 1987 Cover: 1.75 **NM value: 2.00**
Circ: CapCity orders: **7,475**
3 ❑ Aug 1987 Cover: 1.75 **NM value: 2.00**
Circ: CapCity orders: **7,475**

VALKYRIE (2ND SERIES) — Eclipse

1 ❑ Jul 1988 Cover: 1.75 **NM value: 2.00**
Circ: CapCity orders: **6,100**
2 ❑ Aug 1988 Cover: 1.75 **NM value: 2.00**
Circ: CapCity orders: **5,100**
3 ❑ Sep 1988 Cover: 1.75 **NM value: 2.00**
Circ: CapCity orders: **4,850**

VALKYRIE (3RD SERIES) — Marvel

1 ❑ Jan 1997 Cover: 2.95 **NM value: Cover or less**
Circ: Direct Market orders: **30,750**
Without Wings **A:** Pablo Raimondi; Manny Clark **W:** Len Wein

VALLEY OF THE DINOSAURS — Harvey

1 ❑ Apr 1975 Cover: 2.25 **NM value: 6.00**
Fight the Angry Mountain; Engine Trouble in Space! (text story); The Blind Ones; Legend of Bigfoot **A:** Jim Hanley **W:** Mike Pellowski
2 ❑ Jun 1975 Cover: 0.25 **NM value: 3.00**
3 ❑ Jul 1975 Cover: 0.25 **NM value: 3.00**
4 ❑ Oct 1975 Cover: 0.25 **NM value: 3.00**
5 ❑ Dec 1975 Cover: 0.25 **NM value: 3.00**
6 ❑ Feb 1976 Cover: 0.25 **NM value: 2.50**
7 ❑ Apr 1976 Cover: 0.25 **NM value: 2.50**
8 ❑ Jun 1976 Cover: 0.25 **NM value: 2.50**
9 ❑ Aug 1976 Cover: 0.25 **NM value: 2.50**
10 ❑ Oct 1976 Cover: 0.25 **NM value: 2.50**
11 ❑ Dec 1976 Cover: 0.25 **NM value: 2.50**
final issue.

VALOR (DC) — DC

Valor is Lar Gand, a teen-ager from the planet Daxam who became a super-hero on Earth in the 20th century. He has powers that rival Superman but is still struggling with the problems and inexperience of youth.

As a character, Valor was born of, lived by, and — who knows? — may even die in one crossover series or another. He first appeared as part of the Invasion! series and was joined by The Legion of Super-Heroes who had traveled back almost 1,000 years into their past to recruit him. He then made appearances in such titles as L.E.G.I.O.N., Justice League Quarterly, and the Panic in the Sky storyline that ran through the various Superman titles. Later, he became a key figure in DC's 1992 crossover, Eclipso: The Darkness Within. That last crossover spawned both this title and the Eclipso solo series. Valor then went on to play a major role in Zero Hour, the universe-shattering follow-up to Crisis on Infinite Earths.

1 ❑ Nov 1992 Cover: 1.25 **NM value: 2.00**
Circ: CapCity orders: **29,600** • **CGC:** 5 graded, best 9.8
Eclipso: The Darkness Within aftermath
2 ❑ Dec 1992 Cover: 1.25 **NM value: 1.50**
Circ: CapCity orders: **17,050** • **CGC:** 3 graded, best 9.4
3 ❑ Jan 1993 Cover: 1.25 **NM value: 1.50**
• **CGC:** 3 graded, best 9.6
4 ❑ Feb 1993 Cover: 1.25 **NM value: 1.50**
Circ: CapCity orders: **15,000** • **CGC:** 3 graded, best 9.4
• Lobo
5 ❑ Mar 1993 Cover: 1.25 **NM value: 1.50**
Circ: CapCity orders: **13,800** • **CGC:** 3 graded, best 9.6
6 ❑ Apr 1993 Cover: 1.25 **NM value: 1.50**
Circ: CapCity orders: **14,350**
7 ❑ May 1993 Cover: 1.25 **NM value: 1.50**
Circ: CapCity orders: **13,000**
8 ❑ Jun 1993 Cover: 1.25 **NM value: 1.50**
Circ: CapCity orders: **12,000**
9 ❑ Jul 1993 Cover: 1.25 **NM value: 1.50**
Circ: CapCity orders: **10,850**
10 ❑ Aug 1993 Cover: 1.25 **NM value: 1.50**
11 ❑ Sep 1993 Cover: 1.25 **NM value: 1.50**
Circ: CapCity orders: **9,900**
12 ❑ Oct 1993 Cover: 1.25 **NM value: 1.50**
Circ: CapCity orders: **8,750**
D.O.A., Part 1
13 ❑ Nov 1993 Cover: 1.50 **NM value: Cover or less**
Circ: CapCity orders: **8,250**
D.O.A., Part 2
14 ❑ Dec 1993 Cover: 1.50 **NM value: Cover or less**
Circ: CapCity orders: **8,150**
D.O.A., Part 3
15 ❑ Jan 1994 Cover: 1.50 **NM value: Cover or less**
Circ: CapCity orders: **8,000**
D.O.A., Part 4
16 ❑ Feb 1994 Cover: 1.50 **NM value: Cover or less**
Circ: CapCity orders: **7,750**
D.O.A., Part 5 **A:** Colleen Doran **W:** Mark Waid
17 ❑ Mar 1994 Cover: 1.50 **NM value: Cover or less**
Circ: CapCity orders: **10,850**
D.O.A., Part 6
18 ❑ Apr 1994 Cover: 1.50 **NM value: Cover or less**
Circ: CapCity orders: **11,650**
D.O.A. Aftermath
19 ❑ May 1994 Cover: 1.50 **NM value: Cover or less**
Circ: CapCity orders: **9,850**

CGC-graded: Multiply prices above by **33 for 9.9 M • 16 for 9.8 NM/M • 7 for 9.6 NM+ • 5 for 9.4 NM • 2.5 for 9.2 NM- • 1.5 for 9.0 VF/NM**

20 ❑ Jun 1994 Cover: 1.50 **NM** value: **Cover or less**
Circ: CapCity orders: **10,000**

21 ❑ Jul 1994 Cover: 1.50 **NM** value: **Cover or less**
Circ: CapCity orders: **10,750**

22 ❑ Aug 1994 Cover: 1.50 **NM** value: **Cover or less**
Circ: CapCity orders: **11,750**
📖 End of an Era, Part 2 **W:** Kurt Busiek

23 ❑ Sep 1994 Cover: 1.50 **NM** value: **Cover or less**
Circ: CapCity orders: **12,850**
📖 Zero Hour; End of an Era, Part 5 final issue. **W:** Kurt Busiek

VALOR (E.C.) — E.C.

There were six E.C. titles in its "New Direction," cover-bannered as "an entirely novel and unique reading experience." The cover of each had a frame with the title on top and an identifying icon down the left side. The "New Direction" was one designed to accommodate the Comics Magazine of America's new Comics Code, though the first issue of each did not carry the Code stamp, and all but one lasted for five issues. The six titles were: Aces High, Extra!, Impact, MD, Psychoanalysis — and Valor.

Above Impact's title was the line "Tales of Mortal Combat, and Deeds of ..." and the stories each focused on an act of immense courage, though not necessarily in armed combat. Given the necessities of Code restrictions and the concept of the title, the variety was exceptional and imaginative.

Artists were Al Williamson, Angelo Torres, Bernie Krigstein, Graham Ingels, Wally Wood, Jack Davis, Reed Crandall, Joe Orlando, and George Evans. — Maggie

1 ❑ Apr 1965 Cover: 0.10 **NM** value: **225.00**
📖 The Arena; The Guardians of Empire (text story); Strategy; Revolution; The Return of King Arthur **A:** Al Williamson; Wally Wood; Angelo Torres; Bernie Krigstein; Graham Ingels **W:** Al Williamson; Wally Wood; Angelo Torres; Bernie Krigstein; Graham Ingels

2 ❑ Jun 1965 Cover: 0.10 **NM** value: **175.00**

3 ❑ Aug 1965 Cover: 0.10 **NM** value: **140.00**

4 ❑ Oct 1965 Cover: 0.10 **NM** value: **140.00**

5 ❑ Dec 1955 Cover: 0.10 **NM** value: **125.00**
final issue. **A:** Al Williamson; Wally Wood(cover)

VALOR (RCP) — Gemstone

1 ❑ Oct 1998 Cover: 2.50 **NM** value: **Cover or less**
Circ: Diamd. preorders: **4,610**
📖 The Arena; The Guardians of Empire (text story); Strategy; Revolution; The Return of King Arthur **A:** Al Williamson; Wally Wood; Angelo Torres; Bernie Krigstein; Graham Ingels **W:** Al Williamson; Wally Wood; Angelo Torres; Bernie Krigstein; Graham Ingels

2 ❑ Nov 1998 Cover: 2.50 **NM** value: **Cover or less**
Circ: Diamd. preorders: **3,941**

3 ❑ Dec 1998 Cover: 2.50 **NM** value: **Cover or less**
Circ: Diamd. preorders: **3,800**

4 ❑ Jan 1999 Cover: 2.50 **NM** value: **Cover or less**
Circ: Diamd. preorders: **3,669**

5 ❑ Feb 1999 Cover: 2.50 **NM** value: **Cover or less**
Circ: Diamd. preorders: **3,660**

VALOR THUNDERSTAR AND HIS FIREFLIES — Now

1 ❑ Dec 1986 Cover: 1.50 **NM** value: **Cover or less**
Circ: CapCity orders: **3,375**

2 ❑ 1987 Cover: 1.50 **NM** value: **Cover or less**
Circ: CapCity orders: **2,500**

3 ❑ 1987 Cover: 1.50 **NM** value: **Cover or less**
Circ: CapCity orders: **1,650**

VAMPEROTICA — Brainstorm

All issues are adults only.

1 ❑ b&w Cover: 2.95 **NM** value: **8.00**
📖 Deadly Desire; God's Chariot; Some Things Never Change **A:** Kirk Lindo; Juan Pineda; Mark Hyman **W:** Kirk Lindo; Mark Hyman; Kurt Wimberger

1/GO❑1994 **NM** value: **10.00**
• Gold edition. **A:** Kirk Lindo; Juan Pineda; Mark Hyman **W:** Kirk Lindo; Mark Hyman; Kurt Wimberger

1/PL❑1994 **NM** value: **10.00**
• Platinum edition. **A:** Kirk Lindo; Juan Pineda; Mark Hyman **W:** Kirk Lindo; Mark Hyman; Kurt Wimberger

1-2 ❑ Sep 1994 Cover: 2.95 **NM** value: **4.00**

1-3 ❑ Dec 1994 Cover: 2.95 **NM** value: **3.00**

2 ❑ 1995b&w Cover: 2.95 **NM** value: **5.00**
Circ: CapCity orders: **6,345**

3 ❑ 1995b&w Cover: 2.95 **NM** value: **3.00**
Circ: CapCity orders: **5,050**

4 ❑ 1995b&w Cover: 2.95 **NM** value: **3.00**
Circ: CapCity orders: **4,955**

5 ❑ 1995b&w Cover: 2.95 **NM** value: **3.00**
Circ: CapCity orders: **4,805**

6 ❑ 1995b&w Cover: 2.95 **NM** value: **3.00**
Circ: CapCity orders: **4,490**
📖 Baptism; Sight of Blood; Deadshot **A:** Adam DeKraker; Juan Pineda **W:** Gustavo Pabon; Nancy Kilpatrick; Shane Hawks

7 ❑ 1995b&w Cover: 2.95 **NM** value: **3.00**
Circ: CapCity orders: **4,080**

8 ❑ Oct 1995, b&w Cover: 2.95 **NM** value: **3.00**

9 ❑ Nov 1995, b&w Cover: 2.95 **NM** value: **3.00**

10 ❑ Dec 1995, b&w Cover: 2.95 **NM** value: **3.00**

11 ❑ Jan 1996, b&w Cover: 2.95 **NM** value: **3.00**

12 ❑ Feb 1996, b&w Cover: 2.95 **NM** value: **3.00**

13 ❑ Mar 1996, b&w Cover: 2.95 **NM** value: **3.00**

14 ❑ Apr 1996, b&w Cover: 2.95 **NM** value: **3.00**

15 ❑ May 1996, b&w Cover: 2.95 **NM** value: **3.00**

16 ❑ Jun 1996 Cover: 2.95 **NM** value: **3.00**

16/Nude❑Jun 1996 Cover: 5.00 **NM** value: **Cover or less**
Nude cover.

17 ❑ Jul 1996 Cover: 2.95 **NM** value: **Cover or less**

17/A❑ Jul 1996 Cover: 4.95 **NM** value: **Cover or less**
chromium cover.

18 ❑ Aug 1996 Cover: 2.95 **NM** value: **Cover or less**

18/Nude❑Aug 1996 Cover: 5.00 **NM** value: **Cover or less**
Nude cover.

19 ❑ Sep 1996 Cover: 2.95 **NM** value: **Cover or less**

19/A❑ Sep 1996 Cover: 2.95 **NM** value: **Cover or less**
Circ: Diamd. preorders: **3,928**
variant cover.

19/Nude❑Sep 1996 Cover: 5.00 **NM** value: **Cover or less**
Nude cover.

20 ❑ Oct 1996 Cover: 2.95 **NM** value: **Cover or less**
Circ: Diamd. preorders: **4,781**

20/Nude❑Oct 1996 Cover: 5.00 **NM** value: **Cover or less**
Nude cover.

21 ❑ Nov 1996 Cover: 2.95 **NM** value: **Cover or less**
Circ: Diamd. preorders: **5,123**

22 ❑ Dec 1996 Cover: 2.95 **NM** value: **Cover or less**
Circ: Diamd. preorders: **4,191**

22/Nude❑Dec 1996 Cover: 5.00 **NM** value: **Cover or less**
Circ: Diamd. preorders: **3,846**
Nude cover.

23 ❑ Jan 1997 Cover: 2.95 **NM** value: **3.00**
Circ: Diamd. preorders: **3,742**

24 ❑ Feb 1997 Cover: 2.95 **NM** value: **3.00**
Circ: Diamd. preorders: **3,442**

24/Nude❑Feb 1997 Cover: 2.95 **NM** value: **5.00**
Circ: Diamd. preorders: **3,136**
Nude cover. 📖 Bad Lands **A:** Ronn Sutton **W:** Dan Membiela

25 ❑ Mar 1997 Cover: 3.00 **NM** value: **Cover or less**
Circ: Diamd. preorders: **4,612**

26 ❑ Apr 1997 Cover: 3.00 **NM** value: **Cover or less**
Circ: Diamd. preorders: **3,982**

27 ❑ May 1997 Cover: 3.00 **NM** value: **Cover or less**
Circ: Diamd. preorders: **4,681**

28 ❑ Jun 1997 Cover: 3.00 **NM** value: **Cover or less**
Circ: Diamd. preorders: **3,959**

29 ❑ Jul 1997 Cover: 3.00 **NM** value: **Cover or less**

30 ❑ Aug 1997 Cover: 3.00 **NM** value: **Cover or less**

31 ❑ Sep 1997 Cover: 3.00 **NM** value: **Cover or less**

32 ❑ Oct 1997 Cover: 3.00 **NM** value: **Cover or less**

33 ❑ Nov 1997 Cover: 3.00 **NM** value: **Cover or less**

34 ❑ Dec 1997 Cover: 3.00 **NM** value: **Cover or less**

35 ❑ Jan 1998 Cover: 3.00 **NM** value: **Cover or less**

36 ❑ Feb 1998 Cover: 3.00 **NM** value: **Cover or less**

37 ❑ Mar 1998 Cover: 3.00 **NM** value: **Cover or less**
Circ: Diamd. preorders: **4,070**

38 ❑ Apr 1998 Cover: 3.00 **NM** value: **Cover or less**
Circ: Diamd. preorders: **2,495**

39 ❑ May 1998 Cover: 3.00 **NM** value: **Cover or less**

40 ❑ Jun 1998 Cover: 3.00 **NM** value: **Cover or less**

41 ❑ Jul 1998 Cover: 3.00 **NM** value: **Cover or less**

42 ❑ Aug 1998 Cover: 3.00 **NM** value: **Cover or less**

43 ❑ Sep 1998 Cover: 3.00 **NM** value: **Cover or less**

44 ❑ Oct 1998 Cover: 3.00 **NM** value: **Cover or less**

45 ❑ Nov 1998 Cover: 3.00 **NM** value: **Cover or less**

45/SC❑Nov 1998 Cover: 4.00 **NM** value: **Cover or less**
Photo cover.

46 ❑ Dec 1998 Cover: 3.00 **NM** value: **Cover or less**

47 ❑ Jan 1999 Cover: 3.00 **NM** value: **Cover or less**

48 ❑ Feb 1999 Cover: 3.00 **NM** value: **Cover or less**
Circ: Diamd. preorders: **1,551**

49 ❑ Mar 1999 Cover: 3.00 **NM** value: **Cover or less**
Circ: Diamd. preorders: **1,427**

Anl 1❑ **NM** value: **3.95**
• Annual #1

Anl 1/GO❑ **NM** value: **8.00**
• Annual #1-Gold Edition.

SS 1❑ Cover: 2.95 **NM** value: **4.00**
Circ: CapCity orders: **5,870**
• Blue cover (regular edition).

VAMPEROTICA MAGAZINE — Brainstorm

1 ❑ Cover: 4.95 **NM** value: **Cover or less**
📖 Legend of Ichor; Murder Most Fowl; No Strain No Gain; Masquerade **A:** Kirk Lindo; Harry Langdon; Steven Spencer Ledford **W:** Diane E. Burger; Katrina Bugher

1/Nude❑ **NM** value: **6.00**
Nude cover.

1/SC❑ Cover: 10.00 **NM** value: **Cover or less**
Julie Strain Commemorative cover.

2 ❑ Cover: 4.95 **NM** value: **Cover or less**

2/Nude❑ **NM** value: **6.00**
Nude cover.

2/SC❑ Cover: 5.95 **NM** value: **Cover or less**
Photo cover.

3 ❑ Cover: 4.95 **NM** value: **Cover or less**

3/Nude❑ **NM** value: **6.00**
Nude cover.

3/SC❑ **NM** value: **6.00**
Photo cover.

4 ❑ Cover: 5.95 **NM** value: **Cover or less**

4/Nude❑ **NM** value: **6.00**
Nude cover.

4/SC❑ Cover: 5.95 **NM** value: **Cover or less**
Photo cover.

5 ❑ Cover: 5.95 **NM** value: **Cover or less**

5/Nude❑ **NM** value: **6.00**
Nude cover.

6 ❑ Cover: 5.95 **NM** value: **Cover or less**

6/SC❑ Cover: 5.95 **NM** value: **Cover or less**
Photo cover.

7 ❑ Cover: 5.95 **NM** value: **Cover or less**

7/SC❑ Cover: 5.95 **NM** value: **Cover or less**
Photo cover.

8 ❑ Cover: 5.95 **NM** value: **Cover or less**

8/SC❑ Cover: 5.95 **NM** value: **Cover or less**
Photo cover.

9 ❑ Cover: 5.95 **NM** value: **Cover or less**

9/SC❑ Cover: 5.95 **NM** value: **Cover or less**
Photo cover.

10 ❑ Cover: 5.95 **NM** value: **Cover or less**

10/SC❑ Cover: 5.95 **NM** value: **Cover or less**
Photo cover.

11 ❑ Cover: 2.50 **NM** value: **Cover or less**

11/Nude❑ Cover: 3.00 **NM** value: **Cover or less**
Nude cover.

12 ❑ Cover: 2.50 **NM** value: **Cover or less**

12/Nude❑ Cover: 3.00 **NM** value: **Cover or less**
Nude cover.

VAMPEROTICA PRESENTS COUNTESS VLADIMIRA — Brainstorm

1 ❑ **NM** value: **2.95**

VAMPFIRE — Brainstorm

All issues are adults only.

1 ❑ Sep 1996, b&w Cover: 2.95 **NM** value: **Cover or less**
Circ: Diamd. preorders: **4,790**

VAMPFIRE: EROTIC ECHO — Brainstorm

1 ❑ Cover: 2.95 **NM** value: **Cover or less**
Circ: Diamd. preorders: **3,300**

2 ❑ Feb 1997 Cover: 2.95 **NM** value: **Cover or less**
Circ: Diamd. preorders: **3,124**

2/Nude❑Feb 1997 Cover: 2.95 **NM** value: **Cover or less**
Circ: Diamd. preorders: **2,571**

VAMPFIRE: NECROMANTIQUE — Brainstorm

1 ❑ Aug 1997 Cover: 2.95 **NM** value: **Cover or less**

2 ❑ Cover: 2.95 **NM** value: **Cover or less**

VAMPI — Harris

1 ❑ Aug 2000 **NM** value: **3.00**
red foil cover.

1/A ❑ Aug 2000 **NM** value: **5.00**
Platinum cover.

1/B ❑ Aug 2000 **NM** value: **5.00**
Gold cover.

1/C ❑ Aug 2000 **NM** value: **5.00**
• Royal blue

1/D ❑ Aug 2000 **NM** value: **6.00**
• limited edition.

1/E ❑ Aug 2000 **NM** value: **8.00**
• Convention special (black and white)

1/F ❑ Aug 2000 **NM** value: **15.00**
• Limited Metal-Tex edition cover.

2 ❑ Oct 2000 Cover: 2.95 **NM** value: **3.00**
Circ: Diamd. preorders: **18,240**

3 ❑ Nov 2000 Cover: 2.95 **NM** value: **3.00**
Circ: Diamd. preorders: **18,322**

4 ❑ Dec 2000 Cover: 2.95 **NM** value: **3.00**
Circ: Diamd. preorders: **18,444** • **CGC:** 1 graded, best 9.8

5 ❑ Jan 2001 Cover: 2.95 **NM** value: **3.00**
Circ: Diamd. preorders: **18,940**

Ash 1❑ **NM** value: **4.00**

ASH 1/A❑ **NM** value: **10.00**

VAMPIRE COMPANION, THE — Innovation

1 ❑ Cover: 2.50 **NM** value: **Cover or less**
Circ: CapCity orders: **8,835**
cardstock cover.

2 ❑ Cover: 2.50 **NM** value: **Cover or less**
Circ: CapCity orders: **6,610**
cardstock cover. 📖 The Last Sunrise **A:** Joe Phillips **W:** Cynthy J. Wood

3 ❑ Cover: 2.50 **NM** value: **Cover or less**
Circ: CapCity orders: **4,250**

VAMPIRE GIRLS: BUBBLE GUM & BLOOD — Angel

1 ❑ Cover: 2.95 **NM** value: **Cover or less**

2 ❑ Cover: 2.95 **NM** value: **Cover or less**

VAMPIRE GIRLS: CALIFORNIA 1969 — Angel Entertainment

0 ❑ May 1996, b&w Cover: 2.95 **NM** value: **Cover or less**

0/A ❑ b&w Cover: 20.00 **NM** value: **Cover or less**
No issue number. nude embossed foil cardstock cover. • no indicia

0/Nude❑May 1996, b&w Cover: 10.00 **NM** value: **Cover or less**
Nude cover.

1 ❑ Aug 1996, b&w Cover: 2.95 **NM** value: **Cover or less**

VAMPIRE GIRLS, POETS OF BLOOD: SAN FRANCISCO — Angel

1 ❑ Cover: 5.00 **NM** value: **Cover or less**
📖 The Surreal World **A:** Oclair Albert; Wellington Diaz **W:** Douglas Rociti

1/Nude❑ Cover: 5.00 **NM** value: **Cover or less**
📖 The Surreal World **A:** Oclair Albert; Wellington Diaz **W:** Douglas Rociti

2 ❑ Cover: 5.00 **NM** value: **Cover or less**
• Flipbook Previews of Angel **A:** Oclair Albert; Wellington Diaz **W:** Douglas Rociti

2/Nude❑ Cover: 5.00 **NM** value: **Cover or less**
• Flipbook Previews of Angel **A:** Oclair Albert; Wellington Diaz **W:** Douglas Rociti

Other grades: Multiply prices above by **1.5 for Mint • 2/3 for Very Fine • 1/3 for Fine • 1/5 for Very Good • 1/8 for Good**

VAMPIRE LESTAT, THE (ANNE RICE'S...)
Innovation

1 ❑ Jan 1990 Cover: 2.50 **NM** value: **6.00**
Circ: CapCity orders: **7,450** • **CGC:** 2 graded, best 9.4
1-2 ❑ Cover: 2.50 **NM** value: **3.00**
2 ❑ Cover: 2.50 **NM** value: **4.00**
Circ: CapCity orders: **6,475**
2-2 ❑ Cover: 2.50 **NM** value: **Cover or less**
2-3 ❑ Cover: 2.50 **NM** value: **Cover or less**
3 ❑ May 1990 Cover: 2.50 **NM** value: **4.00**
Circ: CapCity orders: **6,800**
3-2 ❑ Cover: 2.50 **NM** value: **Cover or less**
4 ❑ Jun 1990 Cover: 2.50 **NM** value: **3.00**
Circ: CapCity orders: **10,175**
📖 Vitaicum for the Maquise **A:** Michael Okamoto; Daerick Gröss Sr.; John Bolton(cover) **W:** Anne Rice; Faye Perozich
5 ❑ Sep 1990 Cover: 2.50 **NM** value: **3.00**
Circ: CapCity orders: **12,100**
6 ❑ Nov 1990 Cover: 2.50 **NM** value: **Cover or less**
Circ: CapCity orders: **12,735**
7 ❑ Jan 1991 Cover: 2.50 **NM** value: **Cover or less**
Circ: CapCity orders: **12,540**
8 ❑ Mar 1991 Cover: 2.50 **NM** value: **Cover or less**
Circ: CapCity orders: **12,365**
9 ❑ May 1991 Cover: 2.50 **NM** value: **Cover or less**
Circ: CapCity orders: **11,715**
10 ❑ 1991 Cover: 2.50 **NM** value: **Cover or less**
Circ: CapCity orders: **11,775**
11 ❑ 1991 Cover: 2.50 **NM** value: **Cover or less**
Circ: CapCity orders: **11,875**
12 ❑ 1991 Cover: 2.50 **NM** value: **Cover or less**
Circ: CapCity orders: **11,305**

VAMPIRELLA (MAGAZINE)
Warren

From 1969 until 1983, Warren Publications brought us Vampirella, the sultry female vampire. What had started out as a gag piece first turned into a serious horror comics magazine, then eventually grew into a cult phenomenon.

"Vampi," as she is known to her fans, was the perfect mix of heroine and night creature. She hails from the planet Drakulon, where the rivers flow with blood. Although not one of the classically undead herself, she, nevertheless, needs to drink blood (or a special serum which replaces it) in order to survive.

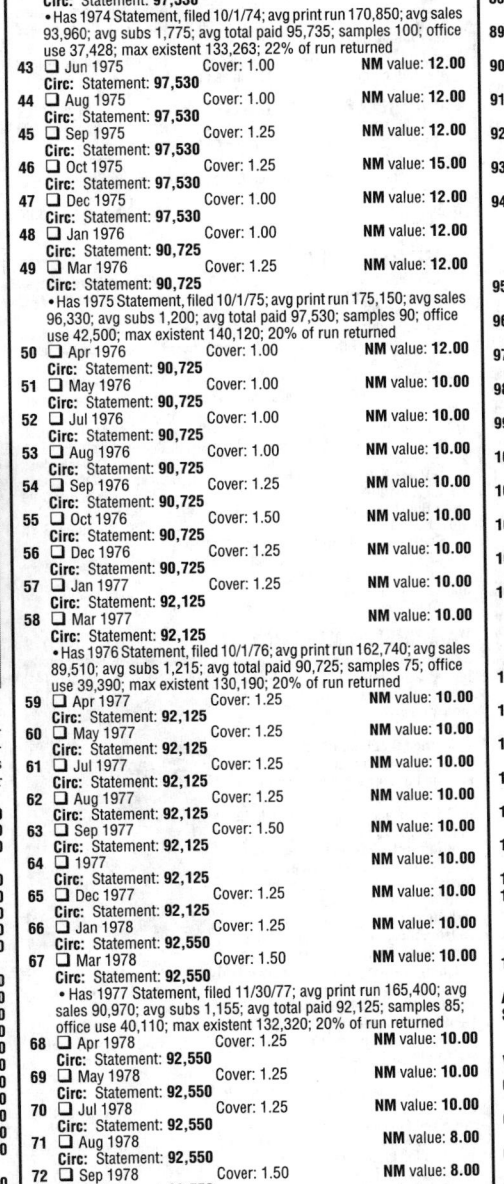

In addition to its thrilling namesake, this adult-oriented black-and-white magazine featured other great tales of horror and science-fiction in each issue. Starlin, Brunner, Wrightson, and others contributed their talents to this unusual and memorable horror comics magazine.

1 ❑ Sep 1969 Cover: 0.50 **NM** value: **290.00**
2 ❑ Nov 1969 Cover: 0.50 **NM** value: **65.00**
3 ❑ Jan 1970 Cover: 0.50 **NM** value: **180.00**
• Scarce
4 ❑ Mar 1970 Cover: 0.50 **NM** value: **50.00**
5 ❑ May 1970 Cover: 0.50 **NM** value: **50.00**
6 ❑ Jul 1970 Cover: 0.50 **NM** value: **40.00**
7 ❑ Sep 1970 Cover: 0.50 **NM** value: **50.00**
8 ❑ Nov 1970 Cover: 0.50 **NM** value: **55.00**
• Horror format begins
9 ❑ Jan 1971 Cover: 0.50 **NM** value: **50.00**
10 ❑ Mar 1971 Cover: 0.50 **NM** value: **20.00**
11 ❑ May 1971 Cover: 0.50 **NM** value: **30.00**
12 ❑ Jul 1971 Cover: 0.50 **NM** value: **30.00**
13 ❑ Sep 1971 Cover: 0.50 **NM** value: **30.00**
14 ❑ Nov 1971 Cover: 0.50 **NM** value: **30.00**
15 ❑ Jan 1972 Cover: 0.50 **NM** value: **30.00**
16 ❑ Apr 1972 Cover: 0.50 **NM** value: **22.00**
17 ❑ Jun 1972 Cover: 0.75 **NM** value: **22.00**
18 ❑ Aug 1972 Cover: 0.75 **NM** value: **22.00**
19 ❑ Sep 1972 Cover: 1.00 **NM** value: **25.00**
• 1973 annual
20 ❑ Oct 1972 **NM** value: **22.00**
21 ❑ Dec 1972 Cover: 0.75 **NM** value: **22.00**
22 ❑ Mar 1973 Cover: 1.00 **NM** value: **22.00**
23 ❑ Apr 1973 Cover: 0.75 **NM** value: **22.00**
24 ❑ May 1973 Cover: 0.75 **NM** value: **22.00**
25 ❑ Jun 1973 Cover: 0.75 **NM** value: **22.00**
26 ❑ Aug 1973 Cover: 0.75 **NM** value: **20.00**
27 ❑ Sep 1973 Cover: 1.00 **NM** value: **22.00**
• 1974 annual
28 ❑ Nov 1973 **NM** value: **15.00**
29 ❑ Dec 1973 **NM** value: **15.00**
30 ❑ Jan 1974 Cover: 0.75 **NM** value: **15.00**
Circ: Statement: **95,735**
31 ❑ Mar 1974 Cover: 1.00 **NM** value: **15.00**
Circ: Statement: **95,735**
32 ❑ Apr 1974 Cover: 1.00 **NM** value: **15.00**
Circ: Statement: **95,735**
33 ❑ May 1974 Cover: 1.00 **NM** value: **15.00**
Circ: Statement: **95,735**
34 ❑ Jun 1974 Cover: 1.00 **NM** value: **15.00**
Circ: Statement: **95,735**
35 ❑ Aug 1974 Cover: 1.00 **NM** value: **15.00**
Circ: Statement: **95,735**
36 ❑ Sep 1974 Cover: 1.25 **NM** value: **15.00**
Circ: Statement: **95,735**
37 ❑ Oct 1974 Cover: 1.25 **NM** value: **20.00**
Circ: Statement: **95,735**
• 1975 annual
38 ❑ Dec 1974 **NM** value: **14.00**
Circ: Statement: **95,735**
39 ❑ Feb 1974 **NM** value: **14.00**
Circ: Statement: **97,530**
40 ❑ Mar 1975 Cover: 1.25 **NM** value: **14.00**
Circ: Statement: **97,530**
41 ❑ Apr 1975 Cover: 1.00 **NM** value: **12.00**
Circ: Statement: **97,530**
42 ❑ May 1975 Cover: 1.00 **NM** value: **12.00**
Circ: Statement: **97,530**
• Has 1974 Statement, filed 10/1/74; avg print run 170,850; avg sales 93,960; avg subs 1,775; avg total paid 95,735; samples 100; office use 37,428; max existent 133,263; 22% of run returned
43 ❑ Jun 1975 Cover: 1.00 **NM** value: **12.00**
Circ: Statement: **97,530**
44 ❑ Aug 1975 Cover: 1.00 **NM** value: **12.00**
Circ: Statement: **97,530**
45 ❑ Sep 1975 Cover: 1.25 **NM** value: **12.00**
Circ: Statement: **97,530**
46 ❑ Oct 1975 Cover: 1.25 **NM** value: **15.00**
Circ: Statement: **97,530**
47 ❑ Dec 1975 Cover: 1.00 **NM** value: **12.00**
Circ: Statement: **97,530**
48 ❑ Jan 1976 Cover: 1.00 **NM** value: **12.00**
Circ: Statement: **90,725**
49 ❑ Mar 1976 Cover: 1.25 **NM** value: **12.00**
Circ: Statement: **90,725**
• Has 1975 Statement, filed 10/1/75; avg print run 175,150; avg sales 96,330; avg subs 1,200; avg total paid 97,530; samples 90; office use 42,500; max existent 140,120; 20% of run returned
50 ❑ Apr 1976 Cover: 1.00 **NM** value: **12.00**
Circ: Statement: **90,725**
51 ❑ May 1976 Cover: 1.00 **NM** value: **10.00**
Circ: Statement: **90,725**
52 ❑ Jul 1976 Cover: 1.00 **NM** value: **10.00**
Circ: Statement: **90,725**
53 ❑ Aug 1976 Cover: 1.00 **NM** value: **10.00**
Circ: Statement: **90,725**
54 ❑ Sep 1976 Cover: 1.25 **NM** value: **10.00**
Circ: Statement: **90,725**
55 ❑ Oct 1976 Cover: 1.50 **NM** value: **10.00**
Circ: Statement: **90,725**
56 ❑ Dec 1976 Cover: 1.25 **NM** value: **10.00**
Circ: Statement: **90,725**
57 ❑ Jan 1977 Cover: 1.25 **NM** value: **10.00**
Circ: Statement: **92,125**
58 ❑ Mar 1977 **NM** value: **10.00**
Circ: Statement: **92,125**
• Has 1976 Statement, filed 10/1/76; avg print run 162,740; avg sales 89,510; avg subs 1,215; avg total paid 90,725; samples 75; office use 39,390; max existent 130,190; 20% of run returned
59 ❑ Apr 1977 Cover: 1.25 **NM** value: **10.00**
Circ: Statement: **92,125**
60 ❑ May 1977 Cover: 1.25 **NM** value: **10.00**
Circ: Statement: **92,125**
61 ❑ Jul 1977 Cover: 1.25 **NM** value: **10.00**
Circ: Statement: **92,125**
62 ❑ Aug 1977 Cover: 1.25 **NM** value: **10.00**
Circ: Statement: **92,125**
63 ❑ Sep 1977 Cover: 1.50 **NM** value: **10.00**
Circ: Statement: **92,125**
64 ❑ 1977 **NM** value: **10.00**
Circ: Statement: **92,125**
65 ❑ Dec 1977 Cover: 1.25 **NM** value: **10.00**
Circ: Statement: **92,125**
66 ❑ Jan 1978 Cover: 1.25 **NM** value: **10.00**
Circ: Statement: **92,550**
67 ❑ Mar 1978 Cover: 1.50 **NM** value: **10.00**
Circ: Statement: **92,550**
• Has 1977 Statement, filed 11/30/77; avg print run 165,400; avg sales 90,970; avg subs 1,155; avg total paid 92,125; samples 85; office use 40,110; max existent 132,320; 20% of run returned
68 ❑ Apr 1978 Cover: 1.25 **NM** value: **10.00**
Circ: Statement: **92,550**
69 ❑ May 1978 Cover: 1.25 **NM** value: **10.00**
Circ: Statement: **92,550**
70 ❑ Jul 1978 Cover: 1.25 **NM** value: **10.00**
Circ: Statement: **92,550**
71 ❑ Aug 1978 **NM** value: **8.00**
Circ: Statement: **92,550**
72 ❑ Sep 1978 Cover: 1.50 **NM** value: **8.00**
Circ: Statement: **92,550**
73 ❑ 1978 **NM** value: **8.00**
Circ: Statement: **92,550**
74 ❑ Dec 1978 Cover: 1.25 **NM** value: **8.00**
Circ: Statement: **92,550**
75 ❑ Jan 1979 Cover: 1.25 **NM** value: **8.00**
Circ: Statement: **90,050**
76 ❑ Mar 1979 Cover: 1.50 **NM** value: **8.00**
Circ: Statement: **90,050**
• Has 1978 Statement, filed 9/30/78; avg print run 166,395; avg sales 95,515; avg subs 1,035; avg total paid 92,550; samples 96; office use 40,469; max existent 137,115; 20% of run returned
77 ❑ 1979 Cover: 1.50 **NM** value: **8.00**
Circ: Statement: **90,050**
78 ❑ 1979 **NM** value: **8.00**
Circ: Statement: **90,050**
79 ❑ 1979 **NM** value: **8.00**
Circ: Statement: **90,050**
80 ❑ 1979 **NM** value: **8.00**
Circ: Statement: **90,050**
81 ❑ 1979 **NM** value: **8.00**
Circ: Statement: **90,050**
82 ❑ 1979 **NM** value: **8.00**
Circ: Statement: **90,050**
83 ❑ Dec 1979 Cover: 1.50 **NM** value: **8.00**
Circ: Statement: **90,050**
84 ❑ Jan 1980 Cover: 1.75 **NM** value: **8.00**
Circ: Statement: **76,468**
85 ❑ Mar 1980 Cover: 2.00 **NM** value: **8.00**
Circ: Statement: **76,468**
• Has 1979 Statement, filed 9/30/79; avg print run 161,745; avg sales 88,960; avg subs 1,090; avg total paid 90,050; samples 109; office use 39,236; max existent 129,395; 20% of run returned
86 ❑ Apr 1980 Cover: 1.75 **NM** value: **8.00**
Circ: Statement: **76,468**
87 ❑ 1980 **NM** value: **8.00**
Circ: Statement: **76,468**
88 ❑ 1980 **NM** value: **8.00**
Circ: Statement: **76,468**
89 ❑ 1980 **NM** value: **8.00**
Circ: Statement: **76,468**
90 ❑ Sep 1980 **NM** value: **8.00**
Circ: Statement: **76,468**
91 ❑ Oct 1980 Cover: 1.75 **NM** value: **8.00**
Circ: Statement: **76,468**
92 ❑ Dec 1980 Cover: 1.75 **NM** value: **8.00**
Circ: Statement: **76,468**
93 ❑ Jan 1981 Cover: 1.75 **NM** value: **8.00**
Circ: Statement: **71,923**
94 ❑ Mar 1981 Cover: 1.95 **NM** value: **8.00**
Circ: Statement: **71,923**
• Has 1980 Statement, filed 9/30/80; avg print run 137,345; avg sales 75,540; avg subs 928; avg total paid 76,468; samples 105; office use 33,303; max existent 109,876; 20% of run returned
95 ❑ Apr 1981 Cover: 2.00 **NM** value: **8.00**
Circ: Statement: **71,923**
96 ❑ May 1981 Cover: 2.00 **NM** value: **8.00**
Circ: Statement: **71,923**
97 ❑ Jul 1981 Cover: 2.00 **NM** value: **8.00**
Circ: Statement: **71,923**
98 ❑ Aug 1981 Cover: 2.00 **NM** value: **8.00**
Circ: Statement: **71,923**
99 ❑ Sep 1981 **NM** value: **8.00**
Circ: Statement: **71,923**
100 ❑ Oct 1981 Cover: 2.25 **NM** value: **8.00**
Circ: Statement: **71,923**
101 ❑ Dec 1981 Cover: 2.00 **NM** value: **7.00**
Circ: Statement: **71,923**
102 ❑ Jan 1982 Cover: 2.00 **NM** value: **7.00**
Circ: Statement: **68,728**
103 ❑ Mar 1982 Cover: 2.25 **NM** value: **7.00**
Circ: Statement: **68,728**
104 ❑ Apr 1982 Cover: 2.00 **NM** value: **7.00**
Circ: Statement: **68,728**
• Has 1981 Statement, filed 9/28/81; avg print run 129,311; avg sales 71,121; avg subs 71,121; avg total paid 71,923; samples 81; office use 31,445; max existent 103,449; 20% of run returned
105 ❑ May 1982 Cover: 2.00 **NM** value: **7.00**
Circ: Statement: **68,728**
106 ❑ 1982 **NM** value: **7.00**
Circ: Statement: **68,728**
107 ❑ 1982 **NM** value: **7.00**
Circ: Statement: **68,728**
108 ❑ 1982 **NM** value: **7.00**
Circ: Statement: **68,728**
109 ❑ 1982 **NM** value: **7.00**
Circ: Statement: **68,728**
110 ❑ 1982 **NM** value: **7.00**
Circ: Statement: **68,728**
111 ❑ 1983 Cover: 1.75 **NM** value: **7.00**
112 ❑ Mar 1983 Cover: 2.50 **NM** value: **7.00**
• Has 1982 Statement, filed 10/1/82; avg print run 123,592; avg sales 67,975; avg subs 753; avg total paid 68,728; samples 257; office use 1,235; max existent 70,220; 43% of run returned
113 ❑ 1983 **NM** value: **180.00**
final issue. • 1st Harris comic; Scarce
Anl 1 ❑ **NM** value: **150.00**
SE 1 ❑ Cover: 1.75 **NM** value: **25.00**
• Special edition.

VAMPIRELLA
Harris

0 ❑ Dec 1994 Cover: 2.95 **NM** value: **5.00**
enhanced cover. • contains Vampirella timeline **C:** Joe Quesada
0/A ❑ Cover: 2.95 **NM** value: **5.00**
• Blue logo
0/GO ❑ **NM** value: **15.00**
• Gold edition.
0/SI ❑ Cover: 2.95 **NM** value: **5.00**
• Silver logo
1 ❑ Nov 1992, full color Cover: 2.95 **NM** value: **15.00**
1-2 ❑ Cover: 2.95 **NM** value: **5.00**
2 ❑ Feb 1993, full color Cover: 2.95 **NM** value: **12.00**
• **CGC:** 1 graded, best 9.6
3 ❑ Mar 1993, full color Cover: 2.95 **NM** value: **10.00**
• **CGC:** 1 graded, best 9.6
4 ❑ Jul 1993, full color Cover: 2.95 **NM** value: **8.00**
5 ❑ Nov 1993, full color Cover: 2.95 **NM** value: **8.00**
Bk 1 ❑ Cover: 4.95 **NM** value: **5.95**
Joe Jusko painted cover. 📖 The Dracula War • The Dracula War trade paperback

VAMPIRELLA 25TH ANNIVERSARY SPECIAL
Harris

1 ❑ Oct 1996 Cover: 5.95 **NM** value: **Cover or less**
Circ: Diamd. preorders: **30,400** • **CGC:** 1 graded, best 9.6
No issue number. One-shot. • prestige format.
1/A ❑ Oct 1996 **NM** value: **6.00**
Silver logo with no words on cover.

VAMPIRELLA 30TH ANNIVERSARY CELEBRATION
Harris

1 ❑ **NM** value: **3.00**
Julie Strain photo cover.

CGC-graded: Multiply prices above by **33 for 9.9 M • 16 for 9.8 NM/M • 7 for 9.6 NM+ • 5 for 9.4 NM • 2.5 for 9.2 NM- • 1.5 for 9.0 VF/NM**

VAMPIRELLA & THE BLOOD RED QUEEN OF HEARTS — Harris

1 ❑ Sep 1996 Cover: 9.95 **NM** value: **Cover or less**
• Collects stories from Vampirella (Magazine) #49, 60, 61, 62, 65, 66, 101, and 102. 📖 The Blood Red Queen of Hearts; The Return of the Blood Red Queen; An Eye for an Eye; Starpatch, Quark & Mother Blitz; The Mad King of Drakulon; To Be a Bride in Death; Attack of the Star Beast; Return of the Blood Red Queen! **A:** Esteban Maroto; Gonzalo Mayo; José Gonzalez **W:** Rich Margopoulos; Bill Dubay; Sean Fernald

VAMPIRELLA: ASCENDING EVIL — Harris

1 ❑ Cover: 2.95 **NM** value: **Cover or less**
Circ: Diamd. preorders: **39,441**
1/AE❑ **NM** value: **5.00**
American Entertainment variant cover.
2 ❑ Cover: 2.95 **NM** value: **Cover or less**
3 ❑ Cover: 2.95 **NM** value: **Cover or less**
4 ❑ Cover: 2.95 **NM** value: **Cover or less**
Bk 1❑ Cover: 7.50 **NM** value: **Cover or less**

VAMPIRELLA: BLOOD LUST — Harris

1 ❑ Jul 1997 Cover: 4.95 **NM** value: **5.00**
Circ: Diamd. preorders: **28,737**
cardstock cover. **A:** Joe Jusko **W:** James Robinson
2 ❑ Aug 1997 Cover: 4.95 **NM** value: **5.00**
Circ: Diamd. preorders: **26,006**
cardstock cover. **A:** Joe Jusko **W:** James Robinson
Bk 1❑ Cover: 39.95 **NM** value: **Cover or less**
hardcover. • Crimson edition. **A:** Joe Jusko **W:** James Robinson

VAMPIRELLA CLASSIC — Harris

Having successfully brought Vampirella back into the public eye with its Vampirella and Vengeance of Vampirella titles, Harris Comics decided the time was right to revisit the classic Vampirella stories of yesteryear. Vampirella Classic reprints stories from the original Vampirella Magazine, beginning with the "serious" Vampirella from #12.

Originally published in black-and-white, the Vampirella stories featured the work of some of the best in the field: Jim Starlin, Archie Goodwin, and Bernie Wrightson among them. This new series colors their black-and-white art, adding up to a total which is much more than the sum of its parts. Vampi has never looked so good.

1 ❑ Feb 1995 Cover: 2.95 **NM** value: **Cover or less**
Circ: CapCity orders: **14,100**
• Reprints Vampirella #12 in color
2 ❑ Apr 1995 Cover: 2.95 **NM** value: **Cover or less**
Circ: CapCity orders: **11,600**
3 ❑ Jun 1995 Cover: 2.95 **NM** value: **Cover or less**
Circ: CapCity orders: **11,925**
4 ❑ Aug 1995 Cover: 2.95 **NM** value: **Cover or less**
Circ: CapCity orders: **9,725**
5 ❑ Oct 1995 Cover: 2.95 **NM** value: **Cover or less**

VAMPIRELLA COMMEMORATIVE EDITION — Harris

1 ❑ Nov 1996 Cover: 2.95 **NM** value: **Cover or less**
• **CGC:** 1 graded, best 9.6

VAMPIRELLA: CROSSOVER GALLERY — Harris

1 ❑ Sep 1997 Cover: 2.95 **NM** value: **Cover or less**
Circ: Diamd. preorders: **18,781**
wraparound cover. • pin-ups; Crossover Pin-up of Hellshock, The Savage Dragon, Kabuki, Monkeyman and O'Brien, Rascals in Paradise, Madman, Pantha, Pain Killer Jane, Shi, Cyberfrog and Salamandroid, Body Bags

VAMPIRELLA: DEATH & DESTRUCTION — Harris

1 ❑ Jul 1996 Cover: 2.95 **NM** value: **Cover or less**
1/A ❑ Jul 1996 **NM** value: **3.00**
Vampirella sitting on cover.
1/LE❑ Jul 1996 **NM** value: **5.00**
Vampirella logo only on cover.
2 ❑ Aug 1996 Cover: 2.95 **NM** value: **Cover or less**
3 ❑ Sep 1996 Cover: 2.95 **NM** value: **Cover or less**
Ash 1❑ **NM** value: **3.00**
Bk 1❑ Sum 1996 Cover: 14.95 **NM** value: **Cover or less**
• collects Vengeance of Vampirella #25 and Vampirella: Death & Destruction #1-3

VAMPIRELLA/DRACULA & PANTHA SHOWCASE — Harris

1 ❑ Aug 1997 Cover: 1.50 **NM** value: **Cover or less**
Circ: Diamd. preorders: **16,844**
Vampirella on cover. • flip-book with previews of Vampirella/Dracula and Pantha **A:** Mark Beachum; Gary Frank; David Mack; Rick Mays **W:** James Robinson; Warren Ellis; Alan Moore
1/A ❑ Aug 1997 Cover: 1.50 **NM** value: **Cover or less**
Pantha on cover. • flip-book with previews of Vampirella/Dracula and Pantha **A:** Mark Beachum; Gary Frank; David Mack; Rick Mays **W:** James Robinson; Warren Ellis; Alan Moore

VAMPIRELLA/DRACULA: THE CENTENNIAL — Harris

1 ❑ Oct 1997 Cover: 5.95 **NM** value: **Cover or less**
Circ: Diamd. preorders: **22,205**
1/A ❑ Oct 1997 Cover: 5.95 **NM** value: **Cover or less**
David Mack cover.
1/B ❑ Oct 1997 Cover: 5.95 **NM** value: **Cover or less**
Gary Frank cover.
2 ❑ Oct 1997 Cover: 5.95 **NM** value: **Cover or less**

VAMPIRELLA: HELL ON EARTH BATTLEBOOK — Harris

1 ❑ Cover: 3.99 **NM** value: **Cover or less**

VAMPIRELLA: JULIE STRAIN SPECIAL — Harris

1 ❑ Cover: 3.95 **NM** value: **Cover or less**
1/A ❑ Cover: 14.95 **NM** value: **Cover or less**
• Chrome version
1/B ❑ Cover: 24.95 **NM** value: **Cover or less**
• Holo-chrome version; 500 copies printed

VAMPIRELLA/LADY DEATH — Harris

1 ❑ Feb 1999 Cover: 3.50 **NM** value: **Cover or less**
Circ: Diamd. preorders: **27,760** • **CGC:** 1 graded, best 9.8
1/A ❑ Feb 1999 **NM** value: **5.00**
• Valentine edition. • Red foil **A:** Louis Small Jr. **W:** Steven Grant; David Conway
1/LE❑ Feb 1999 **NM** value: **10.00**
• **CGC:** 1 graded, best 9.8

VAMPIRELLA LIVES — Harris

1 ❑ Dec 1996 Cover: 3.50 **NM** value: **Cover or less**
white cardstock outer cover with cutout. **A:** Amanda Conner **W:** Warren Ellis
1/A ❑ Dec 1996 **NM** value: **4.00**
Photo cover with Vampirella leaning forward. **A:** Amanda Conner **W:** Warren Ellis
1/B ❑ Dec 1996 **NM** value: **4.00**
Photo cover with Vampirella side view. **A:** Amanda Conner **W:** Warren Ellis
1/C ❑ Dec 1996 **NM** value: **10.00**
Die-cut linen cover. **A:** Amanda Conner **W:** Warren Ellis
2 ❑ Jan 1997 Cover: 2.95 **NM** value: **Cover or less**
• Vampirella bathing in blood **A:** Amanda Conner **W:** Warren Ellis
2/A ❑ Jan 1997 **NM** value: **3.00**
• Blue background **A:** Amanda Conner **W:** Warren Ellis
2/B ❑ Jan 1997 **NM** value: **4.00**
Photo cover. **A:** Amanda Conner **W:** Warren Ellis
3 ❑ Feb 1997 Cover: 2.95 **NM** value: **Cover or less**
Drawn cover. **A:** Amanda Conner **W:** Warren Ellis
3/A ❑ Feb 1997 **NM** value: **4.00**
Photo cover. **A:** Amanda Conner **W:** Warren Ellis

VAMPIRELLA MONTHLY — Harris

Vampirella returned from seeming death, only to find herself stranded in Drakulon, the dimension of her birth. Once, she'd believed it to be an alien planet but later learned that Drakulon is a region of Hell, created by her mother Lilith and sustained by a tributary of the river Styx. But Drakulon is dying: its blood-filled river dry, and the population is being destroyed.

Vampirella has dedicated herself to restoring her homeland to its former glory. She has armed herself with religious talismans, including spiking her bodysuit with barbs taken from the True Cross. In addition, Vampi can now generate an evil-crushing holy light from her own body.

Vampirella has battled hordes of vampires and even her own mother. She has beaten back outside invaders, including Lady Death. But all her previous battles with the creatures of Hell pale in comparison to what lies ahead, as Vampi finds herself facing the forces of Heaven itself.

0 ❑ **NM** value: **4.00**
• Vampirella standing, two figures in background
0/A ❑ **NM** value: **4.00**
• Vampirella bathing in blood
1 ❑ Nov 1997 Cover: 2.95 **NM** value: **4.00**
Gold foil logo on cover. 📖 Ascending Evil, Part 1
1/A ❑ Nov 1997 **NM** value: **5.00**
Vampirella eating something bloody on cover. 📖 Ascending Evil, Part 1
1/B ❑ Nov 1997 **NM** value: **5.00**
Vampirella eating something bloody on cover. 📖 Ascending Evil, Part 1 • Gold marking
1/C ❑ Nov 1997 **NM** value: **5.00**
Vampirella staing on cover, demon-eyed figures in background. 📖 Ascending Evil, Part 1
1/D ❑ Nov 1997 **NM** value: **5.00**
Vampirella standing on cover, black background, blue logo. 📖 Ascending Evil, Part 1
1/E ❑ Nov 1997 **NM** value: **5.00**
• American Entertainment Edition. 📖 Ascending Evil, Part 1 • Vampirella reclining on skull
1/F ❑ Nov 1997 **NM** value: **5.00**
Vampirella standing on cover, black background with foil logo. 📖 Ascending Evil, Part 1
2 ❑ Dec 1997 Cover: 2.95 **NM** value: **3.00**
📖 Ascending Evil, Part 2
2/A ❑ Dec 1997 **NM** value: **3.00**
📖 Ascending Evil, Part 2 • Man shooting gun at Vampirella
3 ❑ Jan 1998 Cover: 2.95 **NM** value: **3.00**
📖 Ascending Evil, Part 3
3/A ❑ Jan 1998 **NM** value: **3.00**
Vampirella on motorcycle (only figure on cover). 📖 Ascending Evil, Part 3
4 ❑ Feb 1998 Cover: 2.95 **NM** value: **3.00**
📖 Holy War, Part 1
4/A ❑ Feb 1998 **NM** value: **4.00**
• Crimson edition. 📖 Holy War, Part 1
4/B ❑ Feb 1998 **NM** value: **3.00**
📖 Holy War, Part 1 • Vampirella holding gun
5 ❑ Mar 1998 Cover: 2.95 **NM** value: **3.00**
• **CGC:** 1 graded, best 9.8
📖 Holy War, Part 2
6 ❑ Apr 1998 Cover: 2.95 **NM** value: **3.00**
📖 Holy War, Part 3
7 ❑ Jun 1998 Cover: 2.95 **NM** value: **3.00**
📖 Queen's Gambit, Part 1 ★ Appearance of Shi.
7/A ❑ Jun 1998 **NM** value: **4.00**
📖 Queen's Gambit, Part 1 • Vampirella with finger to mouth
7/B ❑ Jun 1998 **NM** value: **4.00**
Shi on cover in foreground, Vampirella in background. 📖 Queen's Gambit, Part 1
7/C ❑ Jun 1998 **NM** value: **4.00**
📖 Queen's Gambit, Part 1 • Shi in background, Vampirella in foreground
7/D ❑ Jun 1998 **NM** value: **6.00**
📖 Queen's Gambit, Part 1 • Vampirella and Shi on checkerboard floor, foil logo
7/E ❑ Jun 1998 **NM** value: **4.00**
📖 Queen's Gambit, Part 1 • Vampirella and Shi on checkerboard floor
8 ❑ Jul 1998 Cover: 2.95 **NM** value: **3.00**
📖 Queen's Gambit, Part 2 ★ Appearance of Shi.
9 ❑ Aug 1998 Cover: 2.95 **NM** value: **3.00**
📖 Queen's Gambit, Part 3 ★ Appearance of Shi.
10 ❑ Sep 1998 Cover: 2.95 **NM** value: **3.00**
📖 Hell on Earth, Part 1
10/A❑ Sep 1998 **NM** value: **6.00**
Black-and-white cover. 📖 Hell on Earth, Part 1
10/B❑ Sep 1998 **NM** value: **5.00**
Color cover with no words. 📖 Hell on Earth, Part 1
11 ❑ Oct 1998 Cover: 2.95 **NM** value: **3.00**
📖 Hell on Earth, Part 2
12 ❑ Nov 1998 Cover: 2.95 **NM** value: **3.00**
📖 Hell on Earth, Part 3
12/A❑ Nov 1998 **NM** value: **3.00**
• Vampirella in spiky bodysuit
12/B❑ Nov 1998 Cover: 2.95 **NM** value: **3.00**
📖 Hell on Earth, Part 3 • Vampirella hurling woman
12/SC❑ Nov 1998 Cover: 2.95 **NM** value: **6.00**
Like B cover. 📖 Hell on Earth, Part 3
13 ❑ Mar 1999 Cover: 2.95 **NM** value: **3.00**
📖 World's End, Part 1 **A:** Patrick Zircher **W:** Steven Grant; David Conway
13/A❑ Mar 1999 **NM** value: **3.00**
📖 World's End, Part 1 • Vampirella holding heart
14 ❑ Apr 1999 Cover: 2.95 **NM** value: **Cover or less**
📖 World's End, Part 2
14/A❑ Apr 1999 **NM** value: **3.00**
📖 World's End, Part 2 • Vampirella standing, figure in background
15 ❑ May 1999 Cover: 2.95 **NM** value: **Cover or less**
📖 World's End, Part 3
15/A❑ May 1999 Cover: 2.95 **NM** value: **Cover or less**
📖 World's End, Part 3
15/B❑ May 1999 Cover: 2.95 **NM** value: **Cover or less**
alternate cover (facing away). 📖 World's End, Part 3
16 ❑ Jun 1999 Cover: 2.95 **NM** value: **Cover or less**
16/A❑ Jun 1999 **NM** value: **3.00**
Vampirella ¯ 4 other similarly clad women on cover.
16/B❑ Jun 1999 **NM** value: **4.00**
Pantha photo cover (standing), orange/red background.
16/C❑ Jun 1999 **NM** value: **5.00**
Vampirella photo cover.
16/D❑ Jun 1999 **NM** value: **3.00**
Patha drawn cover.
16/E❑ Jun 1999 **NM** value: **4.00**
Patha photo cover (crawling), white background.
16/F❑ Jun 1999 **NM** value: **4.00**
Pantha photo cover (standing), blue background. 📖 , blue background
17 ❑ Jul 1999 Cover: 2.95 **NM** value: **Cover or less**
📖 Rebirth, Part 1
17/A❑ Jul 1999 **NM** value: **3.00**
Vampirella bound on cover.
17/B❑ Jul 1999 **NM** value: **4.00**
Pantha photo cover (standiing), blue background.
17/C❑ Jul 1999 **NM** value: **4.00**
Vampirella photo cover.
17/D❑ Jul 1999 **NM** value: **3.00**
Two women with giant serpent in background on cover.
17/E❑ Jul 1999 **NM** value: **4.00**
Pantha photo cover (sitting with arm outstretched), blue background.
18 ❑ Aug 1999 Cover: 2.95 **NM** value: **Cover or less**
📖 Rebirth, Part 2 **A:** Tim Sale **W:** Jeph Loeb
18/A❑ Aug 1999 **NM** value: **3.00**
Vampirella with arms outstretched on cover.
18/B❑ Aug 1999 **NM** value: **3.00**
"Chesty" close-up Vampirella cover.
19 ❑ Sep 1999 Cover: 2.95 **NM** value: **Cover or less**
Two Vampirellas on cover. 📖 Rebirth, Part 3; Kust for Life
19/A❑ Sep 1999 **NM** value: **3.00**
Vampirella holding skull on cover.
20 ❑ Oct 1999 Cover: 2.95 **NM** value: **Cover or less**
• Vampirella with gun **A:** Bruce Timm **W:** Ty Templeton
20/A❑ Oct 1999 **NM** value: **3.00**
• Vampirella standing with fangs present
21 ❑ Nov 1999 Cover: 2.95 **NM** value: **Cover or less**
Photo cover, tinted background.
21/A❑ Nov 1999 **NM** value: **3.00**
Drawn cover.
21/B❑ Nov 1999 **NM** value: **4.00**
Photo cover, white background.
22 ❑ Dec 1999 Cover: 2.95 **NM** value: **4.00**
Photo cover, red tinted background.

Other grades: Multiply prices above by **1.5 for Mint • 2/3 for Very Fine • 1/3 for Fine • 1/5 for Very Good • 1/8 for Good**

22/A❑ Dec 1999 NM value: **3.00**
Drawn cover.
22/B❑ Dec 1999 NM value: **4.00**
Photo cover, white background.
23 ❑ Jan 2000 Cover: 2.95 NM value: **Cover or less**
Vampirella fighting Lady Death, cover has words.
23/A❑ Jan 2000 NM value: **7.00**
Wordless cover with Vampirella on knees.
23/B❑ Jan 2000 NM value: **5.00**
Red-logo cover with Vampirella on knees.
23/C❑ Jan 2000 NM value: **3.00**
Silver logo cover with Vampirella on knees.
23/D❑ Jan 2000 NM value: **6.00**
Wordless cover with Vampirella fighting Lady Death.
24 ❑ Feb 2000 Cover: 2.95 NM value: **Cover or less**
Vampirella with gun, fishnet stockings in foreground on cover.
24/A❑ Feb 2000 NM value: **3.00**
Reflections in sunglasses on cover.
24/B❑ Feb 2000 NM value: **3.00**
• Vampirella on motorcycle, other female figure at top
25 ❑ Mar 2000 Cover: 2.95 NM value: **Cover or less**
• Vampirella in chains with male figure
25/A❑ Mar 2000 NM value: **3.00**
• Two women on motorcycles
26 ❑ Apr 2000 Cover: 2.95 NM value: **Cover or less**
Vampirella facing Lady Death on cover. 📖 Vampirella vs. Lady Death: The End **A:** Dorian Cleavenger **W:** David Conway
26/A❑ Apr 2000 NM value: **3.00**
• Vampirella in foreground, Lady Death in background
Ash 1❑ Aug 1997 NM value: **5.00**
"Ascending Evil" on cover.
ASH 1/A❑ NM value: **5.00**
"Holy War" on cover.
Ash 2❑ NM value: **5.00**
Ash 3❑ NM value: **5.00**
Ash 3/A❑ NM value: **15.00**
Leather cover. • Convention exclusive limited to 1000 copies
Ash 4❑ NM value: **3.00**
Ash 5❑ NM value: **3.00**
Ash 6❑ NM value: **3.00**
Bk 1❑ Jun 1998 Cover: 7.50 NM value: **Cover or less**
• Ascending Evil; collects issues #1-3

VAMPIRELLA: MORNING IN AMERICA — Harris

1 ❑ b&w Cover: 3.95 NM value: **Cover or less**
• **CGC:** 3 graded, best 9.8
• distributed by Dark Horse; squarebound
2 ❑ Nov 1991, b&w Cover: 3.95 NM value: **Cover or less**
• squarebound
3 ❑ Jan 1992, b&w Cover: 3.95 NM value: **Cover or less**
• squarebound
4 ❑ Apr 1992, b&w Cover: 3.95 NM value: **Cover or less**
• squarebound

VAMPIRELLA OF DRAKULON — Harris

0 ❑ Cover: 2.95 NM value: **Cover or less**
Circ: Diamd. preorders: **22,915**
📖 The Origin of Vampirella; The High Gloss Egyptian Junk Peddler **A:** Esteban Morato; José Gonzalez **W:** Bill Dubay; Budd Lewis
1 ❑ Jan 1995 Cover: 2.95 NM value: **Cover or less**
📖 Beware, Dreamers **A:** José Gonzalez **W:** T.Casey Brennan
2 ❑ Mar 1995 Cover: 2.95 NM value: **Cover or less**
3 ❑ May 1995 Cover: 2.95 NM value: **Cover or less**
• Poly-bagged

VAMPIRELLA/PAINKILLER JANE — Harris

1 ❑ May 1998 Cover: 3.50 NM value: **Cover or less**
Circ: Diamd. preorders: **20,513**
foil-enhanced cover. • crossover with Event
1/A ❑ May 1998 Cover: 5.00 NM value: **Cover or less**
Variant cover, Vampirella and Painkiller Jane on rooftop.
1/B ❑ May 1998 Cover: 24.95 NM value: **Cover or less**
Blue cover, Vampirella and Painkiller posing (in mid-air!).
1/GO❑ May 1998 Cover: 24.95 NM value: **Cover or less**
• Gold edition.
Ash 1❑ Jan 1998 NM value: **3.00**
no cover price.

VAMPIRELLA PIN-UP SPECIAL — Harris

1 ❑ Oct 1995 Cover: 2.95 NM value: **Cover or less**
Circ: CapCity orders: **12,300**
1/A ❑ Cover: 2.95 NM value: **Cover or less**
White background and snake on cover.

VAMPIRELLA: SAD WINGS OF DESTINY — Harris

1 ❑ Sep 1996 Cover: 3.95 NM value: **Cover or less**
No issue number. One-shot. cardstock cover. • gold edition limited to 5000.
1/GO❑ Sep 1996 NM value: **5.00**
Gold mark on cover.

VAMPIRELLA/SHADOWHAWK: CREATURES OF THE NIGHT — Harris

1 ❑ Feb 1995 Cover: 4.95 NM value: **Cover or less**
• crossover with Image; concludes in Shadowhawk – Vampirella #2 **A:** Jim Valentino **C:** Joe Jusko **W:** Jim Valentino; Len Senecal; Tom Sniegoski
2 ❑ Cover: 4.95 NM value: **Cover or less**
• "ShadowHawk/Vampirella" **A:** Jim Valentino **W:** Jim Valentino; Len Senecal; Tom Sniegoski

VAMPIRELLA/SHI — Harris

1 ❑ Cover: 2.95 NM value: **Cover or less**
Circ: Diamd. preorders: **35,153** • **CGC:** 1 graded, best 9.6
no cover price. 📖 Nine Kinds of Dirt • crossover with Crusade **A:** Louis Small Jr. **W:** Warren Ellis

VAMPIRELLA: SILVER ANNIVERSARY COLLECTION — Harris

1/A ❑ Jan 1997 Cover: 2.50 NM value: **Cover or less**
Circ: Diamd. preorders: **12,859**
Good Girl cover. 📖 The Glorious Return of Sweet Baby Theda **A:** José Gonzalez
1/B ❑ Jan 1997 Cover: 2.50 NM value: **Cover or less**
Circ: Diamd. preorders: **12,094**
Bad Girl cover. 📖 The Glorious Return of Sweet Baby Theda **A:** José Gonzalez
2/A ❑ Feb 1997 Cover: 2.50 NM value: **Cover or less**
Good Girl cover. 📖 The Beauty and the Behemoth; The Blob Beast of Blighter's Boy **A:** José Gonzalez
2/B ❑ Feb 1997 Cover: 2.50 NM value: **Cover or less**
Bad Girl cover. 📖 The Beauty and the Behemoth; The Blob Beast of Blighter's Boy **A:** José Gonzalez
3/A ❑ Mar 1997 Cover: 2.50 NM value: **Cover or less**
Good Girl cover. 📖 Curse of the Pasha's Princess; Down the Earth **A:** Mike Royer; José Gonzalez **W:** Forrest J. Ackerman
3/B ❑ Mar 1997 Cover: 2.50 NM value: **Cover or less**
Bad Girl cover. 📖 Curse of the Pasha's Princess; Down the Earth **A:** Mike Royer; José Gonzalez **W:** Forrest J. Ackerman
4/A ❑ Apr 1997 Cover: 2.50 NM value: **Cover or less**
Circ: Diamd. preorders: **9,764**
Good Girl cover. 📖 Salves of the Alien Amazon; Vampirella and the Alien Amazon **A:** Pablo Marcos
4/B ❑ Apr 1997 Cover: 2.50 NM value: **Cover or less**
Circ: Diamd. preorders: **10,828**
Bad Girl cover. 📖 Salves of the Alien Amazon; Vampirella and the Alien Amazon **A:** Pablo Marcos

VAMPIRELLA'S SUMMER NIGHTS — Harris

This one-shot followed the events of the Morning in America limited series and was a precursor to the 1992 Vampirella monthly series. The main story is at the point in time when Vampirella was just learning that her memories of Drakulon as an alien world were false. She is roaming the country, looking for answers to her past. Her wanderings bring her into contact with two other characters from Warren Publishing's horror magazine days: Uncle Creepy and his twisted cousin Eerie. This 48-page special also explores turning points in the lives of Vampi's erstwhile lover, Adam van Helsing, and her longtime friend, the magician Pendragon.

Fact-keepers and Vampi historians will enjoy the poster insert, which includes a detailed history by Kurt Busiek. Other talent featured in the book includes Steve Englehart, Dave Cockrum, Art Adams, and Steve Leialoha.

1 ❑ b&w Cover: 3.95 NM value: **Cover or less**
• **CGC:** 2 graded, best 9.9
No issue number. 📖 Vampirella Meets Creepy and Eerie; The Reach of the Dead; Magic Tricks; Restless Spirit **A:** J.J. Birch; Richard Howell; James W. Fry III; Dave Cockrum **W:** Kurt Busiek; Steve Englehart

VAMPIRELLA STRIKES — Harris

1 ❑ Oct 1995 Cover: 2.95 NM value: **3.00**
Circ: CapCity orders: **16,950** • **CGC:** 1 graded, best 9.4
Photo cover. 📖 The Prize, Part 1 **A:** Ed McGuinness **W:** Tom Sniegoski
1/A ❑ Oct 1995 Cover: 2.95 NM value: **3.00**
Alternate Photo cover. 📖 The Prize, Part 1 • Marble background **A:** Ed McGuinness **W:** Tom Sniegoski
1/B ❑ Oct 1995 NM value: **3.00**
Photo cover, Vampirella with moon in background.
1/C ❑ Oct 1995 NM value: **3.00**
Photo cover, Vampirella against blue background.
1/LE❑ Oct 1995 NM value: **10.00**
📖 The Prize, Part 1 **A:** Ed McGuinness **W:** Tom Sniegoski
2 ❑ Dec 1995 Cover: 2.95 NM value: **3.00**
📖 The Prize, Part 2 **A:** Mike Deodato Jr.; Ed McGuinness **W:** Tom Sniegoski
3 ❑ Feb 1996 Cover: 2.95 NM value: **3.00**
4 ❑ Apr 1996 Cover: 2.95 NM value: **3.00**
5 ❑ Jun 1996 Cover: 2.95 NM value: **3.00**
6 ❑ Aug 1996 Cover: 2.95 NM value: **3.00**
7 ❑ Oct 1996 Cover: 2.95 NM value: **3.00**
final issue.
Anl 1❑ Dec 1996 Cover: 2.95 NM value: **3.00**
Anl 1/A❑ Dec 1996 Cover: 2.95 NM value: **3.00**
Anl 1/B❑ Dec 1996 Cover: 2.95 NM value: **3.00**

VAMPIRELLA: TRANSCENDING TIME & SPACE — Harris

Bk 1❑ Cover: 12.95 NM value: **Cover or less**
No issue number. • b&w reprint **C:** Dave Stevens

VAMPIRELLA VS HEMORRHAGE — Harris

1 ❑ Apr 1997 Cover: 3.50 NM value: **Cover or less**
Circ: Diamd. preorders: **23,414**
📖 The Red Death part 1 **A:** Michael Bair **W:** Ian Edginton; Tom Sniegoski
1/A ❑ Mar 1997 NM value: **3.50**
Circ: Diamd. preorders: **3,440**
Vampirella with red hand on cover. 📖 The Red Death part 1 **A:** Michael Bair **W:** Ian Edginton; Tom Sniegoski
1/Ash❑ Mar 1997 NM value: **1.00**
no cover price. • ashcan **A:** Michael Bair **W:** Ian Edginton; Tom Sniegoski
2 ❑ May 1997 Cover: 3.50 NM value: **Cover or less**
Circ: Diamd. preorders: **23,327**
📖 The Red Death part 2 **A:** Michael Bair **W:** Ian Edginton; Tom Sniegoski
3 ❑ Jun 1997 Cover: 3.50 NM value: **Cover or less**
📖 The Red Death part 3 **A:** Michael Bair **W:** Ian Edginton; Tom Sniegoski

VAMPIRELLA VS PANTHA — Harris

1/A ❑ Mar 1997 Cover: 3.50 NM value: **Cover or less**
Circ: Diamd. preorders: **18,235**
cardstock cover. • Vampirella standing over body in street with police cars in background **A:** Mark Texeira **W:** Mark Millar
1/B ❑ Mar 1997 Cover: 3.50 NM value: **Cover or less**
Circ: Diamd. preorders: **20,796**
cardstock cover. **A:** Mark Texeira **W:** Mark Millar
1/C ❑ Mar 1997 Cover: 3.50 NM value: **Cover or less**
Pantha on cover with black background. **A:** Mark Texeira **W:** Mark Millar
Ash 1❑ NM value: **3.50**
• "Special Showcase Edition" on cover. **A:** Mark Texeira **W:** Mark Millar

VAMPIRELLA/WETWORKS — Harris

1 ❑ Jun 1997 NM value: **3.00**
Circ: Diamd. preorders: **34,907**

VAMPIRE MIYU — Antarctic

1 ❑ Cover: 2.95 NM value: **3.50**
2 ❑ Cover: 2.95 NM value: **3.00**
3 ❑ Cover: 2.95 NM value: **3.00**
4 ❑ Cover: 2.95 NM value: **3.00**
5 ❑ Cover: 2.95 NM value: **3.00**
6 ❑ Cover: 2.95 NM value: **3.00**
Ash 1❑ NM value: **0.50**
• Ashcan promotional edition from 1995 San Diego Comic-Con. 📖 Spectral Time **A:** Narumi Kakinouchi **W:** Narumi Kakinouchi ★ 1st Appearance of Vampire Miyu.

VAMPIRES LUST — CFD / Boneyard

All issues are adults only.
1 ❑ Sep 1996, b&w Cover: 2.95 NM value: **Cover or less**
1/Nude❑ Sep 1996 Cover: 3.95 NM value: **Cover or less**
nude photo cover.

VAMPIRE'S PRANK — Acid Rain

1 ❑ Cover: 2.95 NM value: **Cover or less**
📖 Morbinjaw **A:** Tavisha Wolfgarth **W:** Rosearik Rikki

VAMPIRE TALES — Marvel

Oversized and stuffed with comics, essays, and film commentary by writers and artists who would later become names in the field, this magazine-style work from Marvel Monster Group takes on all things vampiric.

A comics adaptation of an original vampire story, Lord Ruthven, is offered, along with tales of emotionally tormented vampires in the 1970s and vengeful women vampires. A werewolf tale is tossed in for balance, as is a cautionary story about selling one's soul to Satan. All of them are over the top, and several are delightfully funny. Meanwhile, silly vampire movies are lovingly mocked, and an academic book about the creatures reviewed. Morbius fans should note that the vampire-scientist's first solo adventure took place in #1 of this title.

Not all works are credited, dismaying indexers. Contributors included artists Bill Everett, Pablo Marcos, Esteban Maroto, and Paul Reinman and writers Steve Gerber, Chris Claremont, Mark Evanier, Gardner Fox, Don McGregor, and Ron Goulart. Editorial assists are by Marv Wolfman, Tony Isabella, and Gerry Conway.

1 ❑ Aug 1973 Cover: 0.75 NM value: **15.00**
📖 Morbius; To Kill a Werewolf; The Vampyre; Satan Can Wait; Revenge of the Unliving • 1st full Morbius story **A:** Paul Reinman; Win Mortimer; Bill Everett; Pablo Marcos; Jordi Bernet **W:** Mark Evanier; Roy Thomas; Chris Claremont; Gardner Fox; Ron Goulart; Steve Gerber ★ Appearance of Morbius.
2 ❑ Oct 1973 Cover: 0.75 NM value: **3.50**
3 ❑ Feb 1974 Cover: 0.75 NM value: **3.50**
4 ❑ Apr 1974 Cover: 0.75 NM value: **3.50**
5 ❑ Jun 1974 Cover: 0.75 NM value: **3.50**
6 ❑ Aug 1974 Cover: 0.75 NM value: **3.50**
7 ❑ Oct 1974 Cover: 0.75 NM value: **3.50**
8 ❑ Dec 1974 Cover: 0.75 NM value: **3.50**
9 ❑ Feb 1975 Cover: 0.75 NM value: **3.50**
10 ❑ Apr 1975 Cover: 0.75 NM value: **3.50**
11 ❑ Jun 1975 Cover: 0.75 NM value: **3.50**
final issue.
Anl 1❑ Oct 1975 Cover: 1.25 NM value: **2.00**

VAMPIRE VERSES, THE — CFD

1 ❑ Aug 1995, b&w Cover: 2.95 NM value: **Cover or less**
2 ❑ b&w Cover: 2.95 NM value: **Cover or less**
3 ❑ Jun 1996, b&w Cover: 2.95 NM value: **Cover or less**
3/LE❑ Jun 1996 Cover: 10.00 NM value: **Cover or less**
alternate nude cover. • limited edition of 1000 copies.

VAMPIRE VIXENS — Acid Rain

1 ❑ Cover: 2.75 NM value: **Cover or less**

CGC-graded: Multiply prices above by **33 for 9.9 M • 16 for 9.8 NM/M • 7 for 9.6 NM+ • 5 for 9.4 NM • 2.5 for 9.2 NM- • 1.5 for 9.0 VF/NM**

VAMPIRE WORLD — Acid Rain

1 ❑ Cover: 2.75 **NM** value: **Cover or less**
Upon a Black Spire **A:** Tavisha Wolfgarth **W:** Rosearik Rikki

VAMPIRE YUI — Ironcat

1 ❑ Jul 2000 Cover: 2.95 **NM** value: **Cover or less**

VAMPIRIC JIHAD — Apple

1 ❑ b&w Cover: 4.95 **NM** value: **Cover or less**
No issue number. cardstockcover. • reprints material from Blood of Dracula #14-19

VAMPORNELLA — Adam Post

1 ❑ Cover: 2.95 **NM** value: **Cover or less**
Amori Taylor **W:** Pat Williams

VAMPRESS LUXURA, THE — Brainstorm

1 ❑ Feb 1996 Cover: 2.95 **NM** value: **Cover or less**
wraparound cover. Connoisseur **A:** Kirk Lindo **W:** Kirk Lindo
1/GO ❑ Feb 1996 Cover: 10.00 **NM** value: **Cover or less**
Connoisseur **A:** Kirk Lindo **W:** Kirk Lindo

VAMPS — DC / Vertigo

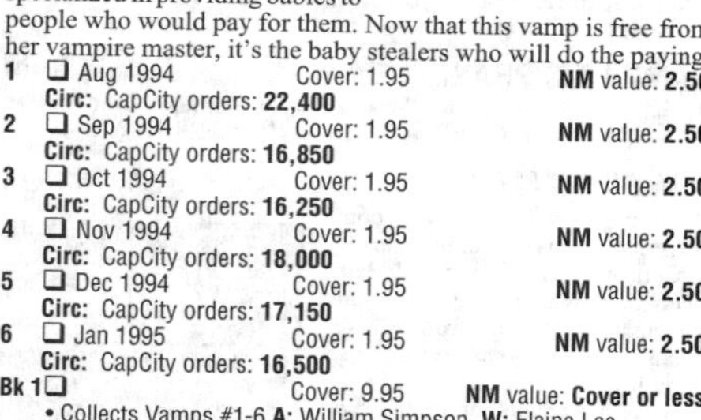

The Vamps are five beautiful women with one trait that makes them even more special: They're vampires. This six-issue mini-series begins, as they turn on their brutal master, Dave, driving a stake through his heart and burying his body in five different graves. After that, the women hit the open road in search of blood and a good time.

But one has something more in mind. She wants to find the people who took her baby away from her while she was still among the living. It was all the work of crooked lawyers and judges, in coordination with a broker who specialized in providing babies to people who would pay for them. Now that this vamp is free from her vampire master, it's the baby stealers who will do the paying.

1 ❑ Aug 1994 Cover: 1.95 **NM** value: **2.50**
Circ: CapCity orders: **22,400**
2 ❑ Sep 1994 Cover: 1.95 **NM** value: **2.50**
Circ: CapCity orders: **16,850**
3 ❑ Oct 1994 Cover: 1.95 **NM** value: **2.50**
Circ: CapCity orders: **16,250**
4 ❑ Nov 1994 Cover: 1.95 **NM** value: **2.50**
Circ: CapCity orders: **18,000**
5 ❑ Dec 1994 Cover: 1.95 **NM** value: **2.50**
Circ: CapCity orders: **17,150**
6 ❑ Jan 1995 Cover: 1.95 **NM** value: **2.50**
Circ: CapCity orders: **16,500**
Bk 1 ❑ Cover: 9.95 **NM** value: **Cover or less**
• Collects Vamps #1-6 **A:** William Simpson **W:** Elaine Lee

VAMPS: HOLLYWOOD & VEIN — DC / Vertigo

1 ❑ Feb 1996 Cover: 2.25 **NM** value: **2.50**
2 ❑ Mar 1996 Cover: 2.25 **NM** value: **2.50**
3 ❑ Apr 1996 Cover: 2.25 **NM** value: **2.50**
Undeath in Venice **A:** William Simpson **W:** Elaine Lee
4 ❑ May 1996 Cover: 2.25 **NM** value: **2.50**
Surfing the Red Wave **A:** William Simpson **W:** Elaine Lee
5 ❑ Jun 1996 Cover: 2.25 **NM** value: **2.50**
6 ❑ Jul 1996 Cover: 2.25 **NM** value: **2.50**
Fire…Earth…Water…Metal…Wood final issue. **A:** William Simpson **W:** Elaine Lee

VAMPS: PUMPKIN TIME — DC / Vertigo

1 ❑ Dec 1998 Cover: 2.50 **NM** value: **Cover or less**
Circ: Diamd. preorders: **17,320**
Midnight Ride **A:** William Simpson **W:** Elaine Lee
2 ❑ Jan 1999 Cover: 2.50 **NM** value: **Cover or less**
Circ: Diamd. preorders: **14,774**
3 ❑ Feb 1999 Cover: 2.50 **NM** value: **Cover or less**
Circ: Diamd. preorders: **13,157**

VAMPURADA — Tavicat

1 ❑ Jul 1995 Cover: 1.95 **NM** value: **Cover or less**

VAMPYRES — Eternity

1 ❑ b&w Cover: 2.25 **NM** value: **Cover or less**
The End of All Vampires; Creatures in the NightThe God of the Dead; Fistfull of Flesh
2 ❑ b&w Cover: 2.25 **NM** value: **Cover or less**
3 ❑ Mar 1989, b&w Cover: 2.25 **NM** value: **Cover or less**
My Flesh Claws; The Voodoo Dead; The Stranger is the Vampire **A:** Ricardo Villamonte; Bob Martin; Paul Pueyo **W:** Alan Hewetson; Paul Pueyo; Joe Dentyn
4 ❑ b&w Cover: 2.25 **NM** value: **Cover or less**
Bk 1 ❑ Cover: 9.95 **NM** value: **Cover or less**

VAMPYRE'S KISS — Aircel

All issues are adults only.

1 ❑ Jun 1990, b&w Cover: 2.50 **NM** value: **Cover or less**
2 ❑ Jul 1990, b&w Cover: 2.50 **NM** value: **Cover or less**
3 ❑ Aug 1990, b&w Cover: 2.50 **NM** value: **Cover or less**
4 ❑ Sep 1990, b&w Cover: 2.50 **NM** value: **Cover or less**
Bk 1 ❑ Cover: 14.95 **NM** value: **Cover or less**

VAMPYRE'S KISS, BOOK II — Aircel

All issues are adults only.

1 ❑ b&w Cover: 2.50 **NM** value: **Cover or less**
2 ❑ Dec 1990, b&w Cover: 2.50 **NM** value: **Cover or less**
3 ❑ Feb 1991, b&w Cover: 2.50 **NM** value: **Cover or less**
4 ❑ Mar 1991, b&w Cover: 2.50 **NM** value: **Cover or less**

VAMPYRE'S KISS, BOOK III — Aircel

All issues are adults only.

1 ❑ Aug 1991, b&w Cover: 2.50 **NM** value: **Cover or less**
2 ❑ b&w Cover: 2.50 **NM** value: **Cover or less**
3 ❑ b&w Cover: 2.50 **NM** value: **Cover or less**
4 ❑ b&w Cover: 2.50 **NM** value: **Cover or less**

VANDALA — Chaos!

1 ❑ Aug 2000 Cover: 2.95 **NM** value: **Cover or less**
Circ: Diamd. preorders: **17,580** • **CGC:** 1 graded, best 9.6
Wings of Fate **A:** David Brewer **C:** Dorian Cleavenger **W:** Len Kaminski

VANGUARD — Image

Vanguard is a Kalyptan, member of an alien race that serves as protector for the planet Earth. Acting somewhat like intergalactic cops, they fight for the peace and freedom of all beings in the entire universe.

Along with high-tech guns and weapons that Earthlings could never imagine, Vanguard possesses great strength and an alien suit that enables him to fly and speak our language. He also has a sidekick in Wally, a tiny robot drone with a personality all his own, Together they battle to protect Earth from any danger, a mission that can occasionally cause him to run afoul of other self-appointed protectors, including the awesomely powerful Supreme.

Vanguard was created more than a decade ago for the series Megaton and was Erik Larsen's first professional assignment in comics. Larsen has since become famous for his work on Amazing Spider-Man and Savage Dragon.

1 ❑ Oct 1993 Cover: 1.95 **NM** value: **2.00**
Circ: CapCity orders: **71,875**
2 ❑ Nov 1993 Cover: 1.95 **NM** value: **2.00**
Circ: CapCity orders: **44,550**
3 ❑ Dec 1993 Cover: 1.95 **NM** value: **2.00**
Circ: CapCity orders: **35,325**
4 ❑ Feb 1994 Cover: 1.95 **NM** value: **2.00**
Circ: CapCity orders: **27,425**
5 ❑ Apr 1994 Cover: 1.95 **NM** value: **2.00**
Circ: CapCity orders: **22,225**
6 ❑ May 1994 Cover: 1.95 **NM** value: **2.00**
Circ: CapCity orders: **19,700**

VANGUARD (2ND SERIES) — Image

1 ❑ Oct 1996, b&w Cover: 2.95 **NM** value: **Cover or less**
Strange Visitors **A:** Scot Eaton **W:** Gary Carlson
2 ❑ Oct 1996, b&w Cover: 2.95 **NM** value: **Cover or less**
Strange Visitors **A:** Scot Eaton **W:** Gary Carlson
3 ❑ Dec 1996, b&w Cover: 2.95 **NM** value: **Cover or less**
Strange Visitors **A:** Scot Eaton **W:** Gary Carlson ★ Appearance of Supreme.
4 ❑ Jan 1997, b&w Cover: 2.95 **NM** value: **Cover or less**
cover says Feb, indicia says Jan. Strange Visitors **A:** Scot Eaton **W:** Gary Carlson ★ Appearance of Super Patriot, Savage Dragon.

VANGUARD: ETHEREAL WARRIORS — Image

1 ❑ Aug 2000 Cover: 5.95 **NM** value: **Cover or less**
Circ: Diamd. preorders: **3,036**

VANGUARD ILLUSTRATED — Pacific

Vanguard Illustrated was a daring (for its time) science-fiction anthology series from independent publisher Pacific Comics. One of the first big independents to emerge from in the 1980s, Pacific aimed for a more adult audience than its mainstream rivals Marvel and DC. As a result, the stories of this series featured occasional nudity and controversial topics in addition to excellent science-fiction.

Mixed with the lot was "Encyclopedias," a four-part tale of door-to-door sales tactics in a post-apocalyptic world. This story was an early team-up between writer Mike Baron and artist Steve Rude, a team who gained prominence for their collaborations on Badger and Nexus. The seventh issue of this series also featured the first appearance of Mr. Monster.

1 ❑ Nov 1983 Cover: 1.50 **NM** value: **Cover or less**
• **CGC:** 2 graded, best 9.8
Libretto; Encyclopedias; A Stranger in Paradise **A:** Steve Rude; Tom Yeates; Brendan McCarthy; Rick Bryant **W:** David Campiti; Mike Baron; Peter Milligan
2 ❑ Jan 1984 Cover: 1.50 **NM** value: **Cover or less**
• **CGC:** 4 graded, best 10.0
3 ❑ Mar 1984 Cover: 1.50 **NM** value: **Cover or less**
• **CGC:** 3 graded, best 9.9
Freak Wave!; Duel With: Dorf Dishware, Part 3; Killer in Orbit!; Be It What It Will, I'll Go To It Laughing **A:** Steve Rude; Tom Yeates; Brendan McCarthy; Peter Milligan **W:** Rex Lindsey; Brendan McCarthy; David Campiti; Mike Baron; Peter Milligan
4 ❑ Apr 1984 Cover: 1.50 **NM** value: **Cover or less**
• **CGC:** 1 graded, best 9.8
Quark; Success, Part 4; A Tangled Web; Low Level Diplomatic Immunity, Student Filmmaker **A:** Mick Austin; Rick Burchett; Ruth Raymond **W:** Paul Neary; Rick Geary; Mike Baron; Ruth Raymond
5 ❑ May 1984 Cover: 1.50 **NM** value: **Cover or less**
Friend in Need; Adventures in Art **A:** Rick Geary; Rick Burchett; Ron Harris **W:** Rick Geary; Ron Harris; Mike Baron
6 ❑ Jun 1984 Cover: 1.50 **NM** value: **Cover or less**
The Struggle's End; The God Run; Hump Hammersmith: Butt-kicker at Large **A:** Vince Argondezzi; George Pérez; George Freeman **W:** Peter Milligan; Bill Dubay; Joey Cavalieri
7 ❑ 1984 Cover: 1.50 **NM** value: **4.00**
The Ballad of Hardcase Bradley; Goldyn; Mr. Monster; The Missed Universe **A:** George Evans; Vince Argondezzi; Michael T. Gilbert; Walter Stuart **W:** Michael T. Gilbert; Walter Stuart; Bill Dubay; Steve Perry ★ 1st Appearance of Mr. Monster.

VANITY — Pacific

1 ❑ Jun 1984 Cover: 1.50 **NM** value: **Cover or less**
Vanity; Escape From Fire; Welcome Home **A:** Will Meugniot; The Joe Kubert School **W:** Will Meugniot; The Joe Kubert School
2 ❑ Aug 1984 Cover: 1.50 **NM** value: **Cover or less**
A Scent of Lilac; Avalone **A:** Will Meugniot; Dave Ross **W:** Will Meugniot; David Campiti

VANITY ANGEL — Antarctic

All issues are adults only.

1 ❑ Sep 1994, b&w Cover: 3.50 **NM** value: **Cover or less**
Circ: CapCity orders: **3,655**
1-2 ❑ May 1995 Cover: 3.50 **NM** value: **Cover or less**
2 ❑ Oct 1994, b&w Cover: 3.50 **NM** value: **Cover or less**
Circ: CapCity orders: **2,785**
2-2 ❑ Jun 1995 Cover: 3.50 **NM** value: **Cover or less**
3 ❑ Nov 1994, b&w Cover: 2.95 **NM** value: **3.50**
Circ: CapCity orders: **2,965**
4 ❑ Dec 1994, b&w Cover: 2.95 **NM** value: **3.50**
5 ❑ Jan 1995, b&w Cover: 2.95 **NM** value: **3.50**
Circ: CapCity orders: **2,600**
6 ❑ Feb 1995, b&w Cover: 2.95 **NM** value: **3.50**
Circ: CapCity orders: **2,615**

VARCEL'S VIXENS — Caliber

1 ❑ b&w Cover: 2.50 **NM** value: **Cover or less**
2 ❑ b&w Cover: 2.50 **NM** value: **Cover or less**
3 ❑ b&w Cover: 2.50 **NM** value: **Cover or less**

VARIATIONS ON THE THEME — Scarlet Rose

1 ❑ Cover: 2.75 **NM** value: **Cover or less**
2 ❑ Cover: 2.75 **NM** value: **Cover or less**
3 ❑ Cover: 2.75 **NM** value: **Cover or less**
4 ❑ Cover: 2.75 **NM** value: **Cover or less**

VARIOGENESIS — Dagger

0 ❑ Jun 1994 Cover: 3.50 **NM** value: **Cover or less**

VARLA VORTEX — Boneyard

1 ❑ Cover: 2.95 **NM** value: **Cover or less**
Babes of Blood

VARMINTS — Blue Comet

1 ❑ Cover: 1.80 **NM** value: **2.00**
SE 1 ❑ Cover: 2.50 **NM** value: **Cover or less**
• Panda Khan

VAST KNOWLEDGE OF GENERAL SUBJECTS, A — Fantagraphics

1 ❑ Sep 1994, b&w Cover: 4.95 **NM** value: **Cover or less**

VAULT OF DOOMNATION, THE — B-Movie

1 ❑ 1986b&w Cover: 1.70 **NM** value: **Cover or less**
Zombie; Valentine's Day; Something Evil; That's My Boy **A:** Ken Holewczynski; Mark A. Paniccia; Paul Fricke; Scott Barker **W:** Ken Holewczynski; Mark A. Paniccia; Scott Barker; Brian Augustyne

VAULT OF EVIL — Marvel

1 ❑ Feb 1973 Cover: 0.20 **NM** value: **5.00**
• **CGC:** 3 graded, best 9.2
2 ❑ Apr 1973 Cover: 0.20 **NM** value: **3.00**
3 ❑ Jun 1973 Cover: 0.20 **NM** value: **3.00**
4 ❑ Aug 1973 Cover: 0.20 **NM** value: **2.50**
The Old Mill; The Face That Followed; Who Is the Master?; The Mystery of the Doomed Derelict!; Till Death Do Us Part **A:** Robert Q. Sale; Al Luster; Vic Carrabotta
5 ❑ Sep 1973 Cover: 0.20 **NM** value: **2.50**
6 ❑ Oct 1973 Cover: 0.20 **NM** value: **2.50**
7 ❑ Nov 1973 Cover: 0.20 **NM** value: **2.50**
8 ❑ Dec 1973 Cover: 0.20 **NM** value: **2.50**
9 ❑ Feb 1974 Cover: 0.20 **NM** value: **2.50**
10 ❑ Apr 1974 Cover: 0.20 **NM** value: **2.50**
11 ❑ Jun 1974 Cover: 0.25 **NM** value: **2.00**
12 ❑ Aug 1974 Cover: 0.25 **NM** value: **2.00**
13 ❑ Sep 1974 Cover: 0.25 **NM** value: **2.00**
14 ❑ Oct 1974 Cover: 0.25 **NM** value: **2.00**

The CGC numbers printed in individual listings above represent the **number of copies examined** and given a **Universal** grade by CGC and the **best such copy** graded at press time. For current populations, watch for special ***Comics Buyer's Guide*** issues or check **www.cgccomics.com.**

Other grades: Multiply prices above by **1.5 for Mint • 2/3 for Very Fine • 1/3 for Fine • 1/5 for Very Good • 1/8 for Good**

15 ❑ Nov 1974 Cover: 0.25 **NM** value: **2.00**

16 ❑ Dec 1974 Cover: 0.25 **NM** value: **2.00**

17 ❑ Feb 1975 Cover: 0.25 **NM** value: **2.00**
• **CGC:** 1 graded, best 9.2

18 ❑ Apr 1975 Cover: 0.25 **NM** value: **2.00**

19 ❑ Jun 1975 Cover: 0.25 **NM** value: **2.00**
• **CGC:** 1 graded, best 9.4

20 ❑ Aug 1975 Cover: 0.25 **NM** value: **2.00**

21 ❑ Sep 1975 Cover: 0.25 **NM** value: **2.00**
• **CGC:** 1 graded, best 9.4

22 ❑ Oct 1975 Cover: 0.25 **NM** value: **2.00**

23 ❑ Nov 1975 Cover: 0.25 **NM** value: **2.00**
final issue.

VAULT OF HORROR (E.C.) — E.C.

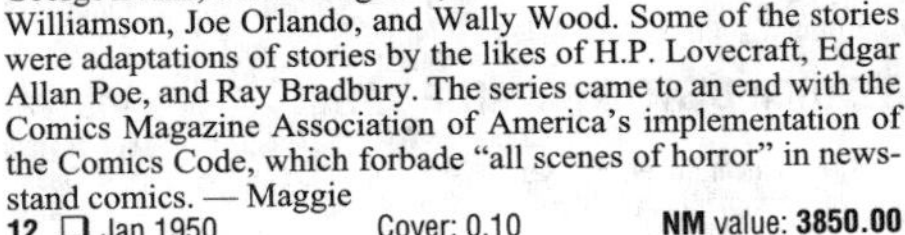

The E.C. line of comics became well-known — in some views, notorious — for its line of horror titles. This was a continuation of the numbering for the crime series War against Crime, and it featured The Vault-Keeper as host. Cover copy for the first three issues read "Introducing a New Trend in Magazines ... Illustrated SuspenStories we dare you to read!"

Artists for whom the E.C. line was known did work in the series: Johnny Craig, Harvey Kurtzman, Al Feldstein, Graham Ingels, Jack Davis, Jack Kamen, Reed Crandall, George Evans, Bernie Krigstein, Al Williamson, Joe Orlando, and Wally Wood. Some of the stories were adaptations of stories by the likes of H.P. Lovecraft, Edgar Allan Poe, and Ray Bradbury. The series came to an end with the Comics Magazine Association of America's implementation of the Comics Code, which forbade "all scenes of horror" in newsstand comics. — Maggie

12 ❑ Jan 1950 Cover: 0.10 **NM** value: **3850.00**
• **CGC:** 14 graded, best 9.4
Bondage cover. 📖 Portrait in Wax!; The Werewolf Legend; Fingers of Death! (text story); Horror in the Night; Terror Train • Series continued from War Against Crime #11; Scarce **A:** Al Feldstein; Harvey Kurtzman; Johnny Craig; Wally Wood; Harrison **W:** Al Feldstein; Harvey Kurtzman; Johnny Craig; Wally Wood; Harrison

13 ❑ Jun 1950 Cover: 0.10 **NM** value: **750.00**
• **CGC:** 9 graded, best 9.8

14 ❑ Aug 1950 Cover: 0.10 **NM** value: **675.00**
• **CGC:** 8 graded, best 9.4

15 ❑ Oct 1950 Cover: 0.10 **NM** value: **550.00**
• **CGC:** 14 graded, best 9.6

16 ❑ Dec 1950 Cover: 0.10 **NM** value: **450.00**
• **CGC:** 8 graded, best 9.6

17 ❑ Feb 1951 Cover: 0.10 **NM** value: **325.00**
• **CGC:** 7 graded, best 9.6
📖 Terror on the Moors!; Baby...It's Cold Inside!; The Beast of the Full Moon!; Voodoo Horror!

18 ❑ Apr 1951 Cover: 0.10 **NM** value: **325.00**
• **CGC:** 9 graded, best 9.8
📖 Sink-Hole!; Lend me a Hand!; The Mask of Horror; Dying to Lose Weight!

19 ❑ Jun 1951 Cover: 0.10 **NM** value: **325.00**
• **CGC:** 7 graded, best 9.8
📖 Southern Hospitality!; The Jellyfish!; Daddy Lost his Head!!; Reunion!

20 ❑ Aug 1951 Cover: 0.10 **NM** value: **250.00**
• **CGC:** 10 graded, best 9.8
📖 About Face; The Reluctant Vampire; Grandma's Ghost; Revenge is the Nuts

21 ❑ Oct 1951 Cover: 0.10 **NM** value: **250.00**
• **CGC:** 7 graded, best 9.8
📖 One Last Fling!; That's a 'Croc'!; Child's Play; Trapped!

22 ❑ Dec 1951 Cover: 0.10 **NM** value: **250.00**
• **CGC:** 9 graded, best 9.6

23 ❑ Feb 1952 Cover: 0.10 **NM** value: **250.00**
• **CGC:** 8 graded, best 9.8

24 ❑ Apr 1952 Cover: 0.10 **NM** value: **250.00**
• **CGC:** 4 graded, best 9.6

25 ❑ Jun 1952 Cover: 0.10 **NM** value: **250.00**
• **CGC:** 6 graded, best 9.2

26 ❑ Aug 1952 Cover: 0.10 **NM** value: **210.00**
• **CGC:** 5 graded, best 9.8
📖 Two of a Kind!; Craft in Concrete!; Half-Way Horrible!; Hook, Line, and Stinker! **A:** George Evans; Johnny Craig; Jack Davis; Graham Ingels **W:** George Evans; Johnny Craig; Jack Davis; Graham Ingels

27 ❑ Oct 1952 Cover: 0.10 **NM** value: **210.00**
• **CGC:** 6 graded, best 9.8

28 ❑ Dec 1952 Cover: 0.10 **NM** value: **210.00**
• **CGC:** 10 graded, best 9.8

29 ❑ Feb 1953 Cover: 0.10 **NM** value: **210.00**
• **CGC:** 4 graded, best 9.6

30 ❑ Apr 1953 Cover: 0.10 **NM** value: **210.00**
• **CGC:** 6 graded, best 9.6

31 ❑ Jun 1953 Cover: 0.10 **NM** value: **175.00**
• **CGC:** 3 graded, best 9.6

32 ❑ Aug 1953 Cover: 0.10 **NM** value: **175.00**
• **CGC:** 6 graded, best 9.8
📖 Whirlpool; Out of His Head!; An Ample Sample; Funereal Disease **A:** George Evans; Johnny Craig; Jack Davis; Graham Ingels **W:** George Evans; Johnny Craig; Jack Davis; Graham Ingels

33 ❑ Oct 1953 Cover: 0.10 **NM** value: **175.00**
• **CGC:** 8 graded, best 9.8

34 ❑ Dec 1953 Cover: 0.10 **NM** value: **175.00**
• **CGC:** 5 graded, best 9.6

35 ❑ Feb 1954 Cover: 0.10 **NM** value: **175.00**
• **CGC:** 7 graded, best 9.6

36 ❑ Apr 1954 Cover: 0.10 **NM** value: **175.00**
• **CGC:** 4 graded, best 9.6

37 ❑ Jun 1954 Cover: 0.10 **NM** value: **175.00**
• **CGC:** 7 graded, best 9.8

38 ❑ Aug 1954 Cover: 0.10 **NM** value: **175.00**
• **CGC:** 5 graded, best 9.8
• Included "Are you a Red Dupe?" anti-censorship ad.

39 ❑ Oct 1954 Cover: 0.10 **NM** value: **175.00**
• **CGC:** 7 graded, best 9.8
Bondage cover.

40 ❑ Dec 1954 Cover: 0.10 **NM** value: **175.00**
• **CGC:** 6 graded, best 9.8
final issue.

VAULT OF HORROR, THE (GLADSTONE) — Gladstone

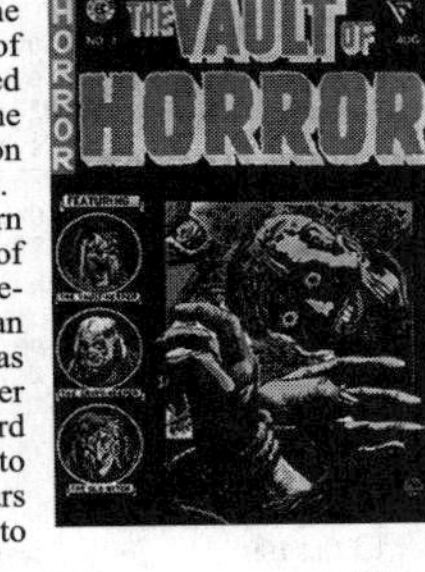

Ever since their original publication, E.C.'s horror titles from the 1950s were hailed as classics of their genre. They've been reprinted in numerous forms, including the definitive hardbound collection costing many hundreds of dollars.

In 1990, Gladstone took its turn reprinting E.C. titles. Its Vault of Horror series ran seven double-sized issues, each reprinting both an issue of Vault of Horror (E.C.) as well as another issue from either E.C.'s The Haunt of Fear or Weird Fantasy. From ghouls to madness to murder, these stories from 40 years ago have lost none of their power to terrify modern readers.

1 ❑ Aug 1990 Cover: 1.95 **NM** value: **2.50**
Circ: CapCity orders: **13,350**
• Reprints The Vault of Horror #34, The Haunt of Fear #1

2 ❑ Oct 1990 Cover: 1.95 **NM** value: **2.50**
Circ: CapCity orders: **12,350**
• Reprints The Vault of Horror #27, The Haunt of Fear #17

3 ❑ Dec 1990 Cover: 1.95 **NM** value: **2.50**
Circ: CapCity orders: **11,850**
• Reprints The Vault of Horror #13, The Haunt of Fear #22

4 ❑ Feb 1991 Cover: 2.00 **NM** value: **2.50**
Circ: CapCity orders: **11,750**
• Reprints The Vault of Horror #23, The Haunt of Fear #13

5 ❑ Apr 1991 Cover: 2.00 **NM** value: **2.50**
Circ: CapCity orders: **9,900**
📖 Southern Hospitality!; The Jelly Fish!; Daddy Lost His Head!!; Reunion!; The Origin of the Species!; It Didn't Matter; The Slave Ship; The Enemies of the Colony • Reprints The Vault of Horror #19, The Haunt of Fear #5 **A:** Al Feldstein; Johnny Craig; Wally Wood; Jack Kamen; Jack Davis; George Roussos; Graham Ingels

6 ❑ Jun 1991 Cover: 2.00 **NM** value: **2.50**
Circ: CapCity orders: **8,550**
• Reprints The Vault of Horror #32, Weird Fantasy #6

7 ❑ Aug 1991 Cover: 2.00 **NM** value: **2.50**
Circ: CapCity orders: **7,400**
• Reprints The Vault of Horror #26, Weird Fantasy #7

VAULT OF HORROR (RCP) — Cochran

1 ❑ Sep 1991 Cover: 2.00 **NM** value: **Cover or less**

2 ❑ Nov 1991 Cover: 2.00 **NM** value: **Cover or less**

3 ❑ Jan 1992 Cover: 2.00 **NM** value: **Cover or less**
📖 Two of a Kind!; Graft in Concrete!; Half-Way Horrible!; Hook, Line, and Stinker!; The Monster From the Fourth Dimension; Something Missing!; ...Gregory Had a Model-T!; The Aliens • Reprints Vault of Horror #26, Weird Science #7 **A:** Al Feldstein; Johnny Craig; Wally Wood; Jack Kamen; Jack Davis; Graham Ingels; Sid Check

4 ❑ Mar 1992 Cover: 2.00 **NM** value: **Cover or less**

5 ❑ May 1992 Cover: 2.00 **NM** value: **Cover or less**

VAULT OF HORROR, THE (RCP) — Gemstone

1 ❑ Oct 1992 Cover: 2.00 **NM** value: **Cover or less**
Circ: Statement: **22,543** CapCity orders: **5,000**
📖 Portrait in Wax!; The Werewolf Legend; Fingers of Death! (text story); Horror in the Night; Terror Train • Reprints The Vault of Horror #12 **A:** Al Feldstein; Harvey Kurtzman; Johnny Craig; Wally Wood; Harrison **W:** Al Feldstein; Harvey Kurtzman; Johnny Craig; Wally Wood; Harrison

2 ❑ Jan 1993 Cover: 2.00 **NM** value: **Cover or less**
Circ: Statement: **22,543** CapCity orders: **4,700**
• Reprints The Vault of Horror #13

3 ❑ Apr 1993 Cover: 2.00 **NM** value: **Cover or less**
Circ: Statement: **22,543** CapCity orders: **4,400**
• Reprints The Vault of Horror #14

4 ❑ Jul 1993 Cover: 2.00 **NM** value: **Cover or less**
Circ: Statement: **22,543** CapCity orders: **4,025**
• Reprints The Vault of Horror #15

5 ❑ Oct 1993 Cover: 2.00 **NM** value: **Cover or less**
Circ: Statement: **18,636** CapCity orders: **3,750**
• Reprints The Vault of Horror #16

6 ❑ Jan 1994 Cover: 2.00 **NM** value: **Cover or less**
Circ: Statement: **18,636** CapCity orders: **3,400**
📖 Terror on the Moors!; Baby...It's Cold Inside!; The Beast of the Full Moon!; Voodoo Horror! • Reprints The Vault of Horror #17

7 ❑ Apr 1994 Cover: 2.00 **NM** value: **Cover or less**
Circ: Statement: **18,636** CapCity orders: **3,125**
📖 Sink-Hole!; Lend me a Hand!; The Mask of Horror; Dying to Lose Weight! • Reprints The Vault of Horror #18

8 ❑ Jul 1994 Cover: 2.00 **NM** value: **Cover or less**
Circ: Statement: **18,636** CapCity orders: **3,150**
📖 Southern Hospitality!; The Jellyfish!; Daddy Lost his Head!!; Reunion! • Reprints The Vault of Horror #19

9 ❑ Oct 1994 Cover: 2.00 **NM** value: **Cover or less**
Circ: Statement: **11,648** CapCity orders: **3,075**
📖 About Face; The Reluctant Vampire; Grandma's Ghost; Revenge is the Nuts • Reprints The Vault of Horror #20

10 ❑ Jan 1995 Cover: 2.00 **NM** value: **Cover or less**
Circ: Statement: **11,648** CapCity orders: **2,925**
📖 One Last Fling!; That's a 'Croc'!; Child's Play; Trapped! • Reprints The Vault of Horror #20

11 ❑ Apr 1995 Cover: 2.00 **NM** value: **Cover or less**
Circ: Statement: **11,648** CapCity orders: **2,675**
• Reprints The Vault of Horror #21

12 ❑ Jul 1995 Cover: 2.00 **NM** value: **Cover or less**
Circ: Statement: **11,648** CapCity orders: **2,700**
• Reprints The Vault of Horror #22

13 ❑ Oct 1995 Cover: 2.00 **NM** value: **Cover or less**
Circ: Statement: **10,264** CapCity orders: **2,650**
• Reprints The Vault of Horror #23

14 ❑ Jan 1996 Cover: 2.00 **NM** value: **Cover or less**
Circ: Statement: **10,264**
• Reprints The Vault of Horror #24; Has 1995 Statement; avg print run 15,116; avg sales 10,760; avg subs 888; avg total paid 11,648

15 ❑ Apr 1996 Cover: 2.00 **NM** value: **Cover or less**
Circ: Statement: **10,264**
• Reprints The Vault of Horror #25

16 ❑ Jul 1996 Cover: 2.50 **NM** value: **Cover or less**
Circ: Statement: **10,264**
• Reprints The Vault of Horror #26

17 ❑ Oct 1996 Cover: 2.50 **NM** value: **Cover or less**
Circ: Statement: **8,070**
• Reprints The Vault of Horror #27

18 ❑ Jan 1997 Cover: 2.50 **NM** value: **Cover or less**
Circ: Statement: **8,070** Diamd. preorders: **5,855**
• Reprints The Vault of Horror #28; Has 1996 Statement, filed 8/15/96; avg print run 11,661; avg sales 9,526; avg subs 738; avg total paid 10,264; office use 1,397; max existent 11,661; no newsstand sales

19 ❑ Apr 1997 Cover: 2.50 **NM** value: **Cover or less**
Circ: Statement: **8,070** Diamd. preorders: **5,515**
• Reprints The Vault of Horror #29

20 ❑ Jul 1997 Cover: 2.50 **NM** value: **Cover or less**
Circ: Statement: **8,070** Diamd. preorders: **5,582**
• Reprints The Vault of Horror #30

21 ❑ Oct 1997 Cover: 2.50 **NM** value: **Cover or less**
Circ: Diamd. preorders: **5,513**
📖 Whirlpool; Out of His Head!; An Ample Sample; Funereal Disease • Reprints The Vault of Horror #31 **A:** George Evans; Johnny Craig; Jack Davis; Graham Ingels **W:** George Evans; Johnny Craig; Jack Davis; Graham Ingels

22 ❑ Jan 1998 Cover: 2.50 **NM** value: **Cover or less**
Circ: Diamd. preorders: **5,241**
• Reprints The Vault of Horror #32; Has 1997 Statement; avg total paid circ 8,070

23 ❑ Apr 1998 Cover: 2.50 **NM** value: **Cover or less**
Circ: Diamd. preorders: **4,715**
• Reprints The Vault of Horror #33

24 ❑ Jul 1998 Cover: 2.50 **NM** value: **Cover or less**
Circ: Diamd. preorders: **4,803**
• Reprints The Vault of Horror #34

25 ❑ Oct 1998 Cover: 2.50 **NM** value: **Cover or less**
Circ: Diamd. preorders: **4,455**

26 ❑ Jan 1999 Cover: 2.50 **NM** value: **Cover or less**
Circ: Diamd. preorders: **4,474**

27 ❑ Apr 1999 Cover: 2.50 **NM** value: **Cover or less**
Circ: Diamd. preorders: **4,034**

28 ❑ Jul 1999 Cover: 2.50 **NM** value: **Cover or less**
Circ: Diamd. preorders: **4,205**

29 ❑ Oct 1999 Cover: 2.50 **NM** value: **Cover or less**
Circ: Diamd. preorders: **3,984**

Anl 1 ❑ Cover: 8.95 **NM** value: **Cover or less**
• Collects The Vault of Horror #1-5

Anl 2 ❑ Cover: 9.95 **NM** value: **Cover or less**
• Collects The Vault of Horror #6-10

Anl 3 ❑ Cover: 10.95 **NM** value: **Cover or less**
📖 Fountains of Youth!; The Monster in the Ice!; Gone Fishing!; What the Dog Dragged In!; A Stitch in Time; 99 44/100 Pure Horror!; Dead Wait!; Staired...In Ho • Collects The Vault of Horror #11-15

Anl 4 ❑ Cover: 12.95 **NM** value: **Cover or less**

Anl 5 ❑ Cover: 13.50 **NM** value: **Cover or less**
📖 Road Hog; Night of the Ghouls; Out of My Head

VAULT OF SCREAMING HORROR — Fantaco

1 ❑ Cover: 3.50 **NM** value: **Cover or less**
📖 Dead Heat!; Mistress of Whorla House; Shana's Secret! **A:** Gurch Singh **W:** Gurch Singh

VAULT OF WHORES — Eros

1 ❑ Cover: 2.95 **NM** value: **Cover or less**
Circ: Diamd. preorders: **2,196**

VC'S, THE — Fleetway-Quality

1 ❑ b&w Cover: 1.95 **NM** value: **Cover or less**

2 ❑ b&w Cover: 1.95 **NM** value: **Cover or less**

3 ❑ b&w Cover: 1.95 **NM** value: **Cover or less**

4 ❑ b&w Cover: 1.95 **NM** value: **Cover or less**

5 ❑ b&w Cover: 1.95 **NM** value: **Cover or less**

VECTOR — Now

1 ❑ Jul 1986 Cover: 1.50 **NM** value: **Cover or less**
Circ: CapCity orders: **5,000**
📖 Happy Birthday from Dimension V **A:** Jim McGreal; Rich Mrozek **W:** Jim McGreal; Rich Mrozek

2 ❑ Sep 1986 Cover: 1.50 **NM** value: **Cover or less**
Circ: CapCity orders: **3,175**
📖 The Menace of Modem **A:** Jim McGreal; Rich Mrozek **W:** Jim McGreal; Rich Mrozek

3 ❑ Nov 1986 Cover: 1.50 **NM** value: **Cover or less**
Circ: CapCity orders: **3,500**
📖 Nite-Flite **A:** Jim McGreal; Rich Mrozek **W:** Jim McGreal; Rich Mrozek

CGC-graded: Multiply prices above by **33 for 9.9 M • 16 for 9.8 NM/M • 7 for 9.6 NM+ • 5 for 9.4 NM • 2.5 for 9.2 NM- • 1.5 for 9.0 VF/NM**

4 ❑ Jan 1987 Cover: 1.75 **NM** value: **Cover or less**
Circ: CapCity orders: **2,800**
Last Stand at Stonehenge **A:** Jim McGreal; Rich Mrozek **W:** Jim McGreal; Rich Mrozek

VEGAS KNIGHTS — Pioneer

1 ❑ Cover: 1.95 **NM** value: **Cover or less**
Circ: CapCity orders: **1,550**

VEGETABLE LOVER — Fantagraphics / Eros

All issues are adults only.
1 ❑ b&w Cover: 2.75 **NM** value: **Cover or less**

VEGMAN — Checker

1 ❑ Spr 1998, b&w Cover: 2.95 **NM** value: **Cover or less**
2 ❑ Sum 1998, b&w Cover: 2.95 **NM** value: **Cover or less**
• indicia for #1 repeated inside

VEILS — DC / Vertigo

This graphic novel from DC's Vertigo imprints is simply beautiful, both in terms of story and art. It is the tale of Vivian Pearse-Packard, a young woman who has just married the alcoholic and abusive son of a British ambassador and who finds herself thousands of miles from home in a mysterious and exotic land. Here, she is invited to enter the Sultan's harem — a world of eroticism and intrigue, where Vivian learns much about the politics of seduction and the power of self-discovery.

This amazing story is written by Pat McGreal (Flashpoint) and illustrated in a variety of forms: photographs by Stephen John Phillips, digital art by Jose Villarrubia, and painted art by Rebecca Guay.

1 ❑ Dec 1999 Cover: 19.95 **NM** value: **Cover or less**
No issue number. One-shot. hardcover. • art and photos **A:** Rebecca Guay; Stephen John Phillips; José Villarrubia **W:** Pat McGreal
1/HC❑ Cover: 19.95 **NM** value: **Cover or less**
No issue number. One-shot. hardcover. • art and photos

VELOCITY (ECLIPSE) — Eclipse

5 ❑ b&w Cover: 2.95 **NM** value: **Cover or less**

VELOCITY (IMAGE) — Image

1 ❑ Nov 1995 Cover: 2.50 **NM** value: **Cover or less**
Circ: CapCity orders: **21,375**
2 ❑ Dec 1995 Cover: 2.50 **NM** value: **Cover or less**
Circ: CapCity orders: **11,875**
3 ❑ Jan 1996 Cover: 2.50 **NM** value: **Cover or less**

VELVET — Adventure

1 ❑ b&w Cover: 2.50 **NM** value: **Cover or less**
Circ: CapCity orders: **3,490**
2 ❑ b&w Cover: 2.50 **NM** value: **Cover or less**
3 ❑ b&w Cover: 2.50 **NM** value: **Cover or less**
4 ❑ b&w Cover: 2.50 **NM** value: **Cover or less**

VELVET ARTICHOKE THEATRE — Velvet Artichoke Press

1 ❑ Sum 1998, b&w Cover: 2.00 **NM** value: **Cover or less**

VELVET TOUCH — Antarctic

All issues are adults only.
1 ❑ Oct 1993 Cover: 3.95 **NM** value: **4.00**
Dino Goddess; Gilligan's Island; Azzurro Spacio (part 1); Valhalla (part 1); No No UFO (part 1); Tiger Tits; Bondage Fairies **A:** Ben Dunn; Fred Perry; Ted Nomura; Joe Rosales; Justin Blanco; Shon Howell **W:** Ben Dunn; Fred Perry; Ted Nomura; Joe Rosales; Justin Blanco; Shon Howell
1/PL❑ Oct 1993, full color Cover: 10.00 **NM** value: **Cover or less**
Dino Goddess; Gilligan's Island; Azzurro Spacio (part 1); Valhalla (part 1); No No UFO (part 1); Tiger Tits; Bondage Fairies • platinum **A:** Ben Dunn; Fred Perry; Ted Nomura; Joe Rosales; Justin Blanco; Shon Howell **W:** Ben Dunn; Fred Perry; Ted Nomura; Joe Rosales; Justin Blanco; Shon Howell
1-2 ❑ Apr 1995 Cover: 3.95 **NM** value: **Cover or less**
2 ❑ Jan 1994 Cover: 2.95 **NM** value: **3.95**
3 ❑ Jul 1994 Cover: 2.95 **NM** value: **3.95**
4 ❑ Aug 1994 Cover: 2.95 **NM** value: **3.95**
5 ❑ Oct 1994 Cover: 2.95 **NM** value: **3.95**
6 ❑ Jan 1995 Cover: 2.95 **NM** value: **3.95**
The Naked Individual's; The B-Squad; Zoo Orgy; The Drums of Mersey **A:** David Watkins; Dan Seneres; Danny Fahl; Jody Wyatt Price; Wade McKenzie **W:** David Watkins; Danny Fahs; Dan Seneres; Jody Wyatt Price; Wade McKenzie

VENDETTA: HOLY VINDICATOR — Red Bullet

1 ❑ b&w Cover: 2.50 **NM** value: **Cover or less**
• first printing limited to 500 copies
2 ❑ b&w Cover: 2.50 **NM** value: **Cover or less**
• first printing limited to 500 copies
3 ❑ b&w Cover: 2.50 **NM** value: **Cover or less**
• first printing limited to 3000 copies
4 ❑ b&w Cover: 2.50 **NM** value: **Cover or less**
final issue.

VENGEANCE OF THE AZTECS — Caliber

1 ❑ b&w Cover: 2.95 **NM** value: **Cover or less**
2 ❑ b&w Cover: 2.95 **NM** value: **Cover or less**
3 ❑ b&w Cover: 2.50 **NM** value: **2.95**

4 ❑ Cover: 2.95 **NM** value: **Cover or less**
5 ❑ Cover: 2.95 **NM** value: **Cover or less**

VENGEANCE OF VAMPIRELLA — Harris

0 ❑ Nov 1995 Cover: 2.95 **NM** value: **Cover or less**
Circ: CapCity orders: **28,375**
The Mystery Walk, Part 0 **A:** Caesar **W:** Tom Sniegoski
0.5 ❑ **NM** value: **Cover or less**
• **CGC:** 5 graded, best 9.8
0.5/A❑ **NM** value: **Cover or less**
1 ❑ Apr 1994 Cover: 2.95 **NM** value: **3.50**
Circ: CapCity orders: **24,925** • **CGC:** 4 graded, best 9.8
red foil wraparound cover. **A:** Joe Quesada(cover) **C:** Joe Quesada; Jimmy Palmiotti
1/A ❑ Apr 1994 **NM** value: **3.00**
• Blue foil
1/GO❑Apr 1994 Cover: 2.95 **NM** value: **10.00**
• Gold promotional edition. **A:** Joe Quesada(cover)
1-2 ❑ Cover: 2.95 **NM** value: **3.00**
2 ❑ May 1994, full color Cover: 2.95 **NM** value: **3.00**
Circ: CapCity orders: **20,425** • **CGC:** 2 graded, best 9.2
3 ❑ Jun 1994 Cover: 2.95 **NM** value: **3.00**
Circ: CapCity orders: **26,025**
4 ❑ Jul 1994 Cover: 2.95 **NM** value: **3.00**
Circ: CapCity orders: **29,375**
Danse with the Undead, Part 1
5 ❑ Aug 1994 Cover: 2.95 **NM** value: **3.00**
Circ: CapCity orders: **26,000**
Danse with the Undead, Part 2 ★ 1st Appearance of The Undead.
6 ❑ Sep 1994 Cover: 2.95 **NM** value: **3.00**
Circ: CapCity orders: **25,575**
6/A ❑ Sep 1994 **NM** value: **4.00**
• Special Limited Edition on cover.
7 ❑ Oct 1994 Cover: 2.95 **NM** value: **3.00**
Circ: CapCity orders: **24,800** • **CGC:** 1 graded, best 9.2
8 ❑ Nov 1994 Cover: 2.95 **NM** value: **3.00**
Circ: CapCity orders: **24,425**
9 ❑ Dec 1994 Cover: 2.95 **NM** value: **3.00**
Circ: CapCity orders: **22,425** • **CGC:** 1 graded, best 7.5
10 ❑ Jan 1995 Cover: 2.95 **NM** value: **3.00**
Circ: CapCity orders: **22,275**
11 ❑ Feb 1995 Cover: 2.95 **NM** value: **3.00**
Circ: CapCity orders: **21,200**
• polybagged with trading card
12 ❑ Mar 1995 Cover: 2.95 **NM** value: **3.00**
Circ: CapCity orders: **22,175**
cover date Feb 95. ★ 1st Appearance of Passion.
13 ❑ Apr 1995 Cover: 2.95 **NM** value: **3.00**
Circ: CapCity orders: **21,750**
14 ❑ May 1995 Cover: 2.95 **NM** value: **3.00**
Circ: CapCity orders: **25,250** • **CGC:** 1 graded, best 9.6
14/A❑ May 1995 **NM** value: **3.00**
• Vampirella sitting, man at top
15 ❑ Jun 1995 Cover: 2.95 **NM** value: **3.00**
Circ: CapCity orders: **24,425** • **CGC:** 1 graded, best 9.8
15/A❑ Jun 1995 **NM** value: **3.00**
• Back-to-back with man holding gun
16 ❑ Jul 1995 Cover: 2.95 **NM** value: **3.00**
Circ: CapCity orders: **20,225**
16/A❑ Jul 1995 **NM** value: **3.00**
• Vampirella springing, fingernails outstretched
17 ❑ Aug 1995 Cover: 2.95 **NM** value: **3.00**
Circ: CapCity orders: **20,900**
17/A❑ Aug 1995 **NM** value: **3.00**
• Woman with sword at right swinging at Vampirella
18 ❑ Sep 1995 Cover: 2.95 **NM** value: **3.00**
Circ: CapCity orders: **17,475**
18/A❑ Sep 1995 **NM** value: **3.00**
• Vampirella against purple-red background
19 ❑ Oct 1995 Cover: 2.95 **NM** value: **3.00**
Circ: CapCity orders: **13,475**
19/A❑ Oct 1995 **NM** value: **3.00**
• Vampirella holding heart
20 ❑ Nov 1995 Cover: 2.95 **NM** value: **3.00**
21 ❑ Dec 1995 Cover: 2.95 **NM** value: **3.00**
22 ❑ Jan 1996 Cover: 2.95 **NM** value: **3.00**
23 ❑ Feb 1996 Cover: 2.95 **NM** value: **3.00**
Strange Days Coming
24 ❑ Mar 1996 Cover: 2.95 **NM** value: **3.00**
Hell in a Handbasket
25 ❑ Apr 1996 Cover: 2.95 **NM** value: **3.00**
• **CGC:** 1 graded, best 9.8
cardstock cover with red foil. The End final issue.
25/A❑ **NM** value: **3.00**
Vampirella with candles on cover.
25/Ash❑Mar 1995 **NM** value: **5.00**
• Preview Ashcan
25/B❑ **NM** value: **5.00**
Blue foil on cover.
25/GO❑ **NM** value: **5.00**
• Gold logo
25/PL❑ **NM** value: **6.00**
• Platinum logo
Bk 1❑ Mar 1995 Cover: 6.95 **NM** value: **Cover or less**
• Bloodshed; collects Vengeance of Vampirella #2 and 3 with other material

VENGEANCE SQUAD — Charlton

1 ❑ Jul 1975 Cover: 0.25 **NM** value: **3.00**
• **CGC:** 1 graded, best 9.6
2 ❑ Sep 1975 Cover: 0.25 **NM** value: **2.00**
3 ❑ Nov 1975 Cover: 0.25 **NM** value: **2.00**
4 ❑ Jan 1976 Cover: 0.25 **NM** value: **2.00**
5 ❑ Mar 1976 Cover: 0.25 **NM** value: **2.00**
6 ❑ May 1976 **NM** value: **2.00**

VENGEFUL SKYE, THE — Davdez

1 ❑ Sum 1998 Cover: 2.95 **NM** value: **Cover or less**

VENGER ROBO — Viz

1 ❑ Cover: 2.75 **NM** value: **Cover or less**
2 ❑ Cover: 2.75 **NM** value: **Cover or less**
Circ: CapCity orders: **2,625**
3 ❑ Cover: 2.75 **NM** value: **Cover or less**
4 ❑ Cover: 2.75 **NM** value: **Cover or less**
5 ❑ Cover: 2.75 **NM** value: **Cover or less**
6 ❑ Cover: 2.75 **NM** value: **Cover or less**
7 ❑ Cover: 2.75 **NM** value: **Cover or less**

VENOM: ALONG CAME A SPIDER — Marvel

1 ❑ Jan 1996 Cover: 2.95 **NM** value: **Cover or less**
2 ❑ Feb 1996 Cover: 2.95 **NM** value: **Cover or less**
3 ❑ Mar 1996 Cover: 2.95 **NM** value: **Cover or less**
4 ❑ Apr 1996 Cover: 2.95 **NM** value: **Cover or less**

VENOM: CARNAGE UNLEASHED — Marvel

1 ❑ Apr 1995 Cover: 2.95 **NM** value: **Cover or less**
Circ: CapCity orders: **30,300**
cardstock cover.
2 ❑ May 1995 Cover: 2.95 **NM** value: **Cover or less**
Circ: CapCity orders: **25,200**
cardstock cover.
3 ❑ Jun 1995 Cover: 2.95 **NM** value: **Cover or less**
Circ: CapCity orders: **24,600**
cardstock cover.
4 ❑ Jul 1995 Cover: 2.95 **NM** value: **Cover or less**
Circ: CapCity orders: **24,350**
cardstock cover.
Bk 1❑ Apr 1996 Cover: 12.95 **NM** value: **Cover or less**
Circ: CapCity orders: **9,150**

VENOM: DEATHTRAP-THE VAULT — Marvel

1 ❑ Cover: 6.95 **NM** value: **Cover or less**
No issue number. • one-shot (also published as Avengers ★ Death of Trap: the Vault).

VENOM: FINALE — Marvel

1 ❑ Nov 1997 Cover: 1.99 **NM** value: **2.00**
Circ: Diamd. preorders: **32,940**
• gatefold summary. The Spider Stratagem **A:** Mark Pajarillo **W:** Larry Hama
2 ❑ Dec 1997 Cover: 1.99 **NM** value: **2.00**
Circ: Diamd. preorders: **29,937**
• gatefold summary. **A:** Mark Pajarillo **W:** Larry Hama ★ Versus Spider-Man.
3 ❑ Jan 1998 Cover: 1.99 **NM** value: **2.00**
Circ: Diamd. preorders: **29,252**
• gatefold summary. **A:** Mark Pajarillo **W:** Larry Hama ★ Versus Spider-Man.

VENOM: FUNERAL PYRE — Marvel

1 ❑ Aug 1993 Cover: 2.95 **NM** value: **Cover or less**
Circ: CapCity orders: **139,700** • **CGC:** 7 graded, best 9.8
foil cover. ★ Appearance of Punisher.
2 ❑ Sep 1993 Cover: 2.95 **NM** value: **Cover or less**
Circ: CapCity orders: **85,500**
3 ❑ Oct 1993 Cover: 2.95 **NM** value: **Cover or less**
Circ: CapCity orders: **74,600**

VENOM: LETHAL PROTECTOR — Marvel

In Marvel Super Heroes Secret Wars, a being known as The Beyonder gave Spider-Man a prize of sorts, in what appeared to be an extraordinary black costume. Eventually, this costume was revealed as an alien symbiote that sought to bond permanently with Spider-Man. When Spider-Man rejected it, the symbiote turned mean and sought out another, which it found with Eddie Brock. Together, as the combined creature known as Venom, they became Spider-Man's deadliest enemy.

Eddie eventually settled his grudge with Spider-Man, agreeing to leave him alone, if Spider-Man would do the same. Unfortunately, extraordinary circumstances leave Spider-Man unable to honor that pact — for someone has found a way to produce new symbiotes and is using them for evil ends. Only by joining forces do Venom and Spider-Man have a prayer of stopping them.

1 ❑ Feb 1993 Cover: 2.95 **NM** value: **3.00**
Circ: CapCity orders: **287,400** • **CGC:** 89 graded, best 10.0
Metallic ink cover.
1/A ❑ Feb 1993 Cover: 2.95 **NM** value: **75.00**
• **CGC:** 12 graded, best 10.0; first 10.0 graded is of this issue black cover. • Black Cover printing error
1/GO❑Feb 1993 **NM** value: **5.00**
• **CGC:** 15 graded, best 9.8
• Gold edition.
2 ❑ Mar 1993 Cover: 2.95 **NM** value: **3.00**
Circ: CapCity orders: **173,800** • **CGC:** 1 graded, best 9.9
War and Pieces! **A:** Mark Bagley **W:** David Michelinie ★ Appearance of Spider-Man.
3 ❑ Apr 1993 Cover: 2.95 **NM** value: **3.00**
Circ: CapCity orders: **150,020**
4 ❑ May 1993 Cover: 2.95 **NM** value: **3.00**
Circ: CapCity orders: **153,300**
5 ❑ Jun 1993 Cover: 2.95 **NM** value: **3.00**
Circ: CapCity orders: **132,700**

Other grades: Multiply prices above by **1.5 for Mint • 2/3 for Very Fine • 1/3 for Fine • 1/5 for Very Good • 1/8 for Good**

6 ❑ Jul 1993 Cover: 2.95 **NM** value: **3.00**
Circ: CapCity orders: **119,900**

VENOM: LICENSE TO KILL — Marvel
1 ❑ Jun 1997 Cover: 1.99 **NM** value: **2.00**
Circ: Diamd. preorders: **38,778**
📖 Dr. Yes! **A:** Derec Aucoin **W:** Larry Hama
2 ❑ Jul 1997 Cover: 1.99 **NM** value: **2.00**
Circ: Diamd. preorders: **32,615**
3 ❑ Aug 1997 Cover: 1.99 **NM** value: **2.00**
Circ: Diamd. preorders: **32,520**
• gatefold summary. **A:** Derec Aucoin **W:** Larry Hama

VENOM: NIGHTS OF VENGEANCE — Marvel
1 ❑ Aug 1994 Cover: 2.95 **NM** value: **Cover or less**
Circ: CapCity orders: **41,450**
red foil cover. **A:** Ron Lim **W:** Howard Mackie
2 ❑ Sep 1994 Cover: 2.95 **NM** value: **Cover or less**
Circ: CapCity orders: **31,950**
cardstock cover. **A:** Ron Lim **W:** Howard Mackie
3 ❑ Oct 1994 Cover: 2.95 **NM** value: **Cover or less**
Circ: CapCity orders: **28,800**
cardstock cover. **A:** Ron Lim **W:** Howard Mackie
4 ❑ Nov 1994 Cover: 2.95 **NM** value: **Cover or less**
Circ: CapCity orders: **27,350**
cardstock cover. **A:** Ron Lim **W:** Howard Mackie

VENOM: ON TRIAL — Marvel
1 ❑ Mar 1997 Cover: 1.99 **NM** value: **2.00**
Circ: Direct Market orders: **42,250**
2 ❑ Apr 1997 Cover: 1.99 **NM** value: **2.00**
Circ: Direct Market orders: **37,750**
📖 Disorder in the Court! **A:** Josh Hood **W:** Larry Hama ★ Appearance of Daredevil, Spider-Man.
3 ❑ May 1997 Cover: 1.99 **NM** value: **2.00**
Circ: Diamd. preorders: **35,828**
📖 Trial and Error! **A:** Josh Hood **W:** Larry Hama ★ Appearance of Daredevil, Carnage, Spider-Man.

VENOM: SEED OF DARKNESS — Marvel
-1 ❑ Jul 1997 Cover: 1.95 **NM** value: **2.00**
Circ: Diamd. preorders: **36,321**
• Flashback

VENOM: SEPARATION ANXIETY — Marvel
1 ❑ Dec 1994 Cover: 2.95 **NM** value: **Cover or less**
Circ: CapCity orders: **33,350**
Embossed cover. 📖 Apart **A:** Ron Randall **W:** Howard Mackie
2 ❑ Jan 1995 Cover: 2.95 **NM** value: **Cover or less**
Circ: CapCity orders: **25,950**
3 ❑ Feb 1995 Cover: 2.95 **NM** value: **Cover or less**
Circ: CapCity orders: **23,675**
4 ❑ Mar 1995 Cover: 2.95 **NM** value: **Cover or less**
Circ: CapCity orders: **22,850**

VENOM: SIGN OF THE BOSS — Marvel
1 ❑ Sep 1997 Cover: 1.99 **NM** value: **2.00**
Circ: Diamd. preorders: **32,561**
• gatefold summary. **A:** Thomas Derenick **W:** Ivan Velez Jr.
2 ❑ Oct 1997 Cover: 1.99 **NM** value: **2.00**
Circ: Diamd. preorders: **30,088**
• gatefold summary. **A:** Thomas Derenick **W:** Ivan Velez Jr.

VENOM: SINNER TAKES ALL — Marvel
1 ❑ Aug 1995 Cover: 2.95 **NM** value: **Cover or less**
📖 Venom: Sinner Takes All, Part 1; The Jury: Trial Run, Part 1 **A:** Greg Luzniak; Jimmy Palmiotti; Ken Branch **W:** Larry Hama ★ 1st Appearance of Sin-Eater III.
2 ❑ Sep 1995 Cover: 2.95 **NM** value: **Cover or less**
📖 Venom: Sinner Takes All, Part 2; The Jury: Trial Run, Part 2 **A:** Greg Luzniak; Jimmy Palmiotti; Ken Branch **W:** Larry Hama
3 ❑ Oct 1995 Cover: 2.95 **NM** value: **Cover or less**
📖 Venom: Sinner Takes All, Part 3; The Jury: Trial Run, Part 3 **A:** Greg Luzniak; Jimmy Palmiotti; Ken Branch **W:** Larry Hama
4 ❑ Nov 1995 Cover: 2.95 **NM** value: **Cover or less**
📖 Venom: Sinner Takes All, Part 4; The Jury: Trial Run, Part 4 **A:** Greg Luzniak; Jimmy Palmiotti; Ken Branch **W:** Larry Hama
5 ❑ Dec 1995 Cover: 2.95 **NM** value: **Cover or less**
📖 Venom: Sinner Takes All, Part 4; The Jury: Trial Run, Part 5 **A:** Greg Luzniak; Jimmy Palmiotti; Ken Branch **W:** Larry Hama

VENOM SUPER SPECIAL — Marvel
1 ❑ Aug 1995 Cover: 3.95 **NM** value: **Cover or less**
Circ: CapCity orders: **25,550**
• Flip-book. • two of the stories continue in Spectacular Spider-Man Super Special #1

VENOM: THE ENEMY WITHIN — Marvel
1 ❑ Feb 1994 Cover: 2.95 **NM** value: **Cover or less**
Circ: CapCity orders: **64,800** • **CGC:** 2 graded, best 9.8
Glow-in-the-dark cover.
2 ❑ Mar 1994 Cover: 2.95 **NM** value: **Cover or less**
Circ: CapCity orders: **47,450**
3 ❑ Apr 1994 Cover: 2.95 **NM** value: **Cover or less**
Circ: CapCity orders: **39,350**

VENOM: THE HUNGER — Marvel
1 ❑ Aug 1996 Cover: 1.95 **NM** value: **2.00**
2 ❑ Sep 1996 Cover: 1.95 **NM** value: **2.00**
3 ❑ Oct 1996 Cover: 1.95 **NM** value: **2.00**
4 ❑ Nov 1996 Cover: 1.95 **NM** value: **2.00**
Circ: Direct Market orders: **40,250**

VENOM: THE HUNTED — Marvel
1 ❑ May 1996 Cover: 2.95 **NM** value: **Cover or less**
2 ❑ Jun 1996 Cover: 2.95 **NM** value: **Cover or less**
3 ❑ Jul 1996 Cover: 2.95 **NM** value: **Cover or less**

VENOM: THE MACE — Marvel
1 ❑ May 1994 Cover: 2.95 **NM** value: **Cover or less**
Circ: CapCity orders: **46,450**
2 ❑ Jun 1994 Cover: 2.95 **NM** value: **Cover or less**
Circ: CapCity orders: **37,850**
3 ❑ Jul 1994 Cover: 2.95 **NM** value: **Cover or less**
Circ: CapCity orders: **35,200**

VENOM: THE MADNESS — Marvel
1 ❑ Nov 1993 Cover: 2.95 **NM** value: **Cover or less**
Circ: CapCity orders: **101,700**
Embossed cover. ★ Versus Juggernaut.
2 ❑ Dec 1993 Cover: 2.95 **NM** value: **Cover or less**
Circ: CapCity orders: **71,900**
3 ❑ Jan 1994 Cover: 2.95 **NM** value: **Cover or less**
Circ: CapCity orders: **59,600**

VENOM: TOOTH AND CLAW — Marvel
Tooth and Claw was ostensibly an excuse to match up Spider-Man foe Venom with claw-wielding mutant Wolverine. It's apparently also an excuse for writer Larry Hama to get really silly and have fun.

The trouble begins in this three-issue mini-series when Venom gets on the trail of Dirt Bag, a mutant shapeshifter who "eats" the souls and forms of his victims. Along the way, he crosses paths with Wolverine, a tough-talking kid named Emmett, a female symbiote, and two kids with skateboards. This whole menagerie chases Dirt Bag while being chased by Chimera, a bondage-gear-clad vixen who commands a crew of plasma wraiths.

Confused? We suspect from the offbeat tone of this series that you were meant to be. With Venom: Tooth and Claw, it might be better to just sit back and enjoy the ride.

1 ❑ Nov 1996 Cover: 1.99 **NM** value: **2.00**
Circ: Direct Market orders: **63,250**
📖 Into the Jaws of Death **A:** Joe St. Pierre **W:** Larry Hama ★ Appearance of Wolverine. ★ Versus Wolverine.
2 ❑ Dec 1996 Cover: 1.99 **NM** value: **2.00**
Circ: Direct Market orders: **53,500**
3 ❑ Jan 1997 Cover: 1.99 **NM** value: **2.00**
Circ: Direct Market orders: **50,250**
final issue. ★ Versus Wolverine.

VENTURE — AC
1 ❑ Aug 1986 Cover: 1.75 **NM** value: **Cover or less**
Circ: CapCity orders: **4,325**
2 ❑ 1986 Cover: 1.75 **NM** value: **Cover or less**
Circ: CapCity orders: **2,825**
3 ❑ 1987 Cover: 1.75 **NM** value: **Cover or less**
Circ: CapCity orders: **2,550**

VENTURE SAN DIEGO COMIC-CON SPECIAL EDITION — Venture
1 ❑ Jul 1994, b&w Cover: 2.50 **NM** value: **Cover or less**

VENUMB — Parody Press
1 ❑ 1993b&w Cover: 2.50 **NM** value: **Cover or less**

VENUS — Marvel
Venus, one of the original "Good Girl" comics of the late 1940s and early '50s, is an interesting example of the changes that comics went through, as the Golden Age came to an end. Venus was originally conceived as a super-heroine: the actual incarnation of Venus, the goddess of love, with powers to charm and beguile her (generally male) antagonists. The series then shifted focus toward "Romantic Tales of Fantasy," continuing the Venus character but putting her in more down-to-earth romantic situations. Finally, the format changed to science fiction and horror. Venus reappeared in later issues as a backup feature in her own comic book.

Venus featured occasional painted covers, above-average art by Bill Everett (creator of Namor, the Sub-Mariner), and stories by the Atlas house writer, one Stan Lee. She was briefly revived in the 1970s in Marvel Premiere.

1 ❑ Aug 1948 Cover: 0.10 **NM** value: **900.00**
• **CGC:** 2 graded, best 8.0
• Romance stories begin★ 1st Appearance of Venus.
2 ❑ Oct 1948 Cover: 0.10 **NM** value: **500.00**
3 ❑ Dec 1948 Cover: 0.10 **NM** value: **400.00**
4 ❑ Apr 1949 Cover: 0.10 **NM** value: **365.00**
5 ❑ Jun 1949 Cover: 0.10 **NM** value: **365.00**
6 ❑ Aug 1949 Cover: 0.10 **NM** value: **350.00**
• **CGC:** 1 graded, best 5.0
7 ❑ Nov 1949 Cover: 0.10 **NM** value: **350.00**
8 ❑ Feb 1950 Cover: 0.10 **NM** value: **350.00**
9 ❑ May 1950 Cover: 0.10 **NM** value: **350.00**
10 ❑ Jul 1950 Cover: 0.10 **NM** value: **450.00**
• **CGC:** 6 graded, best 8.5
• Format changes to science-fiction
11 ❑ Nov 1950 Cover: 0.10 **NM** value: **500.00**
End of the World cover.
12 ❑ Feb 1951 Cover: 0.10 **NM** value: **375.00**
• **CGC:** 1 graded, best 8.5
13 ❑ Apr 1951 Cover: 0.10 **NM** value: **525.00**
• **CGC:** 1 graded, best 6.0
14 ❑ Jun 1951 Cover: 0.10 **NM** value: **525.00**
15 ❑ Aug 1951 Cover: 0.10 **NM** value: **525.00**
16 ❑ Oct 1951 Cover: 0.10 **NM** value: **525.00**
17 ❑ Dec 1951 Cover: 0.10 **NM** value: **525.00**
18 ❑ Feb 1952 Cover: 0.10 **NM** value: **525.00**
19 ❑ Apr 1952 Cover: 0.10 **NM** value: **525.00**
• **CGC:** 1 graded, best 4.5
final issue. **A:** Bill Everett

VENUS DOMINA — Verotik
1 ❑ Cover: 4.95 **NM** value: **Cover or less**
2 ❑ Cover: 4.95 **NM** value: **Cover or less**
Circ: Diamd. preorders: **9,116**
3 ❑ Mar 1997 Cover: 3.95 **NM** value: **4.95**
Circ: Diamd. preorders: **8,714**

VENUS INTERFACE, THE (HEAVY METAL'S...) — HM Communications
1 ❑ Cover: 4.50 **NM** value: **6.00**

VENUS WARS, THE — Dark Horse
1 ❑ Apr 1991, b&w Cover: 2.25 **NM** value: **2.50**
• Japanese; trading cards **A:** Yoshikazu Tasuhiko **W:** Yoshikazu Tasuhiko ★ 1st Appearance of Ken Seno.
2 ❑ May 1991, b&w Cover: 2.25 **NM** value: **Cover or less**
• Japanese; trading cards **A:** Yoshikazu Tasuhiko **W:** Yoshikazu Tasuhiko
3 ❑ Jun 1991, b&w Cover: 2.25 **NM** value: **Cover or less**
• Japanese; trading cards **A:** Yoshikazu Tasuhiko **W:** Yoshikazu Tasuhiko
4 ❑ Jul 1991 Cover: 2.25 **NM** value: **Cover or less**
5 ❑ Aug 1991 Cover: 2.25 **NM** value: **Cover or less**
6 ❑ Sep 1991 Cover: 2.25 **NM** value: **Cover or less**
7 ❑ Oct 1991 Cover: 2.50 **NM** value: **Cover or less**
8 ❑ Nov 1991 Cover: 2.25 **NM** value: **Cover or less**
Circ: CapCity orders: **3,525**
9 ❑ Dec 1991 Cover: 2.25 **NM** value: **Cover or less**
Circ: CapCity orders: **3,250**
10 ❑ Jan 1992 Cover: 2.50 **NM** value: **Cover or less**
Circ: CapCity orders: **3,050**
11 ❑ Feb 1992 Cover: 2.50 **NM** value: **Cover or less**
Circ: CapCity orders: **2,900**
12 ❑ Mar 1992 Cover: 2.75 **NM** value: **Cover or less**
Circ: CapCity orders: **2,800**
13 ❑ Apr 1992 Cover: 2.25 **NM** value: **Cover or less**
14 ❑ May 1992 Cover: 2.25 **NM** value: **Cover or less**
Bk 1❑ Cover: 13.95 **NM** value: **Cover or less**

VENUS WARS II, THE — Dark Horse
1 ❑ Jun 1992 Cover: 2.50 **NM** value: **Cover or less**
Circ: CapCity orders: **3,625**
2 ❑ Jul 1992 Cover: 2.50 **NM** value: **Cover or less**
3 ❑ Aug 1992 Cover: 2.50 **NM** value: **Cover or less**
Circ: CapCity orders: **2,775**
4 ❑ Sep 1992 Cover: 2.50 **NM** value: **Cover or less**
Circ: CapCity orders: **2,675**
5 ❑ Oct 1992, b&w Cover: 2.25 **NM** value: **2.50**
Circ: CapCity orders: **2,650**
6 ❑ Nov 1992, b&w Cover: 2.25 **NM** value: **2.50**
Circ: CapCity orders: **2,650**
7 ❑ Dec 1992, b&w Cover: 2.25 **NM** value: **2.50**
Circ: CapCity orders: **2,525**
8 ❑ Jan 1993, b&w Cover: 2.75 **NM** value: **Cover or less**
Circ: CapCity orders: **2,700**
9 ❑ Feb 1993, b&w Cover: 2.95 **NM** value: **Cover or less**
Circ: CapCity orders: **3,975**
10 ❑ Mar 1993, b&w Cover: 2.95 **NM** value: **Cover or less**
Circ: CapCity orders: **3,975**
11 ❑ Apr 1993, b&w Cover: 2.95 **NM** value: **Cover or less**
Circ: CapCity orders: **2,600**
12 ❑ May 1993, b&w Cover: 2.95 **NM** value: **Cover or less**
Circ: CapCity orders: **2,600**
13 ❑ Jun 1993 Cover: 2.50 **NM** value: **2.95**
14 ❑ Jul 1993 Cover: 2.50 **NM** value: **2.95**
15 ❑ Aug 1993 Cover: 2.50 **NM** value: **2.95**

VERBATIM — Fantagraphics
1 ❑ Apr 1993, b&w Cover: 2.75 **NM** value: **Cover or less**
2 ❑ b&w Cover: 2.75 **NM** value: **Cover or less**

VERDICT, THE — Eternity
1 ❑ Cover: 1.95 **NM** value: **Cover or less**
2 ❑ Cover: 1.95 **NM** value: **Cover or less**
3 ❑ Jun 1988 Cover: 1.95 **NM** value: **Cover or less**
4 ❑ 1988 Cover: 1.95 **NM** value: **Cover or less**
Bk 1❑ b&w Cover: 12.95 **NM** value: **Cover or less**

VERMILLION — DC / Helix
1 ❑ Oct 1996 Cover: 2.25 **NM** value: **Cover or less**
📖 Starlight Drive, Part 1 **A:** Al Davison **W:** Lucius Shepard
2 ❑ Nov 1996 Cover: 2.25 **NM** value: **Cover or less**
Circ: Diamd. preorders: **16,458**
📖 Starlight Drive, Part 2 **A:** Al Davison **W:** Lucius Shepard
3 ❑ Dec 1996 Cover: 2.25 **NM** value: **Cover or less**
Circ: Diamd. preorders: **14,387**
📖 Starlight Drive, Part 3 **A:** Al Davison **W:** Lucius Shepard
4 ❑ Jan 1997 Cover: 2.25 **NM** value: **Cover or less**
Circ: Diamd. preorders: **12,227**
📖 Starlight Drive, Part 4 **A:** Al Davison **W:** Lucius Shepard
5 ❑ Feb 1997 Cover: 2.25 **NM** value: **Cover or less**
Circ: Diamd. preorders: **10,349**
📖 Starlight Drive, Part 5 **A:** Al Davison **W:** Lucius Shepard

CGC-graded: Multiply prices above by **33 for 9.9 M • 16 for 9.8 NM/M • 7 for 9.6 NM+ • 5 for 9.4 NM • 2.5 for 9.2 NM- • 1.5 for 9.0 VF/NM**

6 ❑ Mar 1997 Cover: 2.25 **NM** value: **Cover or less**
Circ: Diamd. preorders: **9,141**
📖 Starlight Drive, Part 6 **A:** Al Davison **W:** Lucius Shepard

7 ❑ Apr 1997 Cover: 2.25 **NM** value: **Cover or less**
Circ: Diamd. preorders: **8,051**

8 ❑ May 1997 Cover: 2.25 **NM** value: **Cover or less**
Circ: Diamd. preorders: **7,514**

9 ❑ Jun 1997 Cover: 2.25 **NM** value: **Cover or less**
Circ: Diamd. preorders: **7,192**

10 ❑ Jul 1997 Cover: 2.25 **NM** value: **Cover or less**
Circ: Diamd. preorders: **6,224**

11 ❑ Aug 1997 Cover: 2.25 **NM** value: **Cover or less**
Circ: Diamd. preorders: **5,792**

12 ❑ Sep 1997 Cover: 2.25 **NM** value: **Cover or less**
Circ: Diamd. preorders: **5,669**

VERONICA — Archie

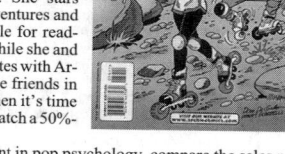

Those famous teenagers Archie Andrews, Jughead Forsythe, and Betty Cooper first showed up in Pep #22. A few months later, Pep #26 introduced Veronica Lodge, the dark-haired rich girl who would become Betty's rival for Archie's affection.

Veronica got her own series in 1989 as part of a relaunch of the Archie Comics line. She stars here in a series of adventures and misadventures suitable for readers of all ages. And while she and Betty may fight for dates with Archie, they'll always be friends in the end-especially when it's time to head to the mall to catch a 50%-off clothing sale.

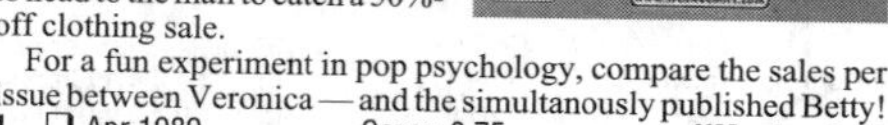

For a fun experiment in pop psychology, compare the sales per issue between Veronica — and the simultanously published Betty!

1 ❑ Apr 1989 Cover: 0.75 **NM** value: **2.00**
• **CGC:** 1 graded, best 9.6

2 ❑ Jul 1989 Cover: 0.95 **NM** value: **1.50**

3 ❑ Sep 1989 Cover: 0.95 **NM** value: **1.50**

4 ❑ Oct 1989 Cover: 0.95 **NM** value: **1.50**

5 ❑ Dec 1989 Cover: 0.95 **NM** value: **1.50**

6 ❑ 1990 Cover: 1.00 **NM** value: **1.50**

7 ❑ Apr 1990 Cover: 1.00 **NM** value: **1.50**

8 ❑ 1990 Cover: 1.00 **NM** value: **1.50**

9 ❑ Jul 1990 Cover: 1.00 **NM** value: **1.50**

10 ❑ Sep 1990 Cover: 1.00 **NM** value: **1.50**

11 ❑ Oct 1990 Cover: 1.00 **NM** value: **1.50**

12 ❑ Dec 1990 Cover: 1.00 **NM** value: **1.50**

13 ❑ Feb 1991 Cover: 1.00 **NM** value: **1.50**

14 ❑ Apr 1991 Cover: 1.00 **NM** value: **1.50**

15 ❑ Jun 1991 Cover: 1.00 **NM** value: **1.50**

16 ❑ Aug 1991 Cover: 1.00 **NM** value: **1.50**

17 ❑ Oct 1991 Cover: 1.00 **NM** value: **1.50**

18 ❑ Dec 1991 Cover: 1.00 **NM** value: **1.50**

19 ❑ Feb 1992 Cover: 1.00 **NM** value: **1.50**
Circ: Statement: **38,236**

20 ❑ Apr 1992 Cover: 1.00 **NM** value: **1.50**
Circ: Statement: **38,236**

21 ❑ Jun 1992 Cover: 1.25 **NM** value: **Cover or less**
Circ: Statement: **38,236**

22 ❑ Aug 1992 Cover: 1.25 **NM** value: **Cover or less**
Circ: Statement: **38,236**

23 ❑ Sep 1992 Cover: 1.25 **NM** value: **Cover or less**
Circ: Statement: **38,236**

24 ❑ Oct 1992 Cover: 1.25 **NM** value: **Cover or less**
Circ: Statement: **38,236**

25 ❑ Dec 1992 Cover: 1.25 **NM** value: **Cover or less**
Circ: Statement: **38,236**

26 ❑ Feb 1993 Cover: 1.25 **NM** value: **Cover or less**
Circ: Statement: **37,035**

27 ❑ Apr 1993 Cover: 1.25 **NM** value: **Cover or less**
Circ: Statement: **37,035**
• Has 1992 Statement, filed 10/1/92; avg print run 134,246; avg sales 35,831; avg subs 2,405; avg total paid 38,236; samples 509; office use 4,293; max existent 43,038; 68% of run returned

28 ❑ Jun 1993 Cover: 1.25 **NM** value: **Cover or less**
Circ: Statement: **37,035**
📖 The Genie is a Teen-i.e.; Mr. Lodge: Jest Request; Looking for Love; Mall in the Family **A:** Stan Goldberg **W:** Angelo Decesare

29 ❑ Aug 1993 Cover: 1.25 **NM** value: **Cover or less**
Circ: Statement: **37,035**

30 ❑ Sep 1993 Cover: 1.25 **NM** value: **Cover or less**
Circ: Statement: **37,035**

31 ❑ Oct 1993 Cover: 1.25 **NM** value: **Cover or less**
Circ: Statement: **37,035**

32 ❑ Dec 1993 Cover: 1.25 **NM** value: **Cover or less**
Circ: Statement: **37,035**

33 ❑ Feb 1994 Cover: 1.25 **NM** value: **Cover or less**
Circ: Statement: **35,640**

34 ❑ Apr 1994 Cover: 1.25 **NM** value: **Cover or less**
Circ: Statement: **35,640**

35 ❑ Jun 1994 Cover: 1.25 **NM** value: **Cover or less**
Circ: Statement: **35,640**

36 ❑ Aug 1994 Cover: 1.50 **NM** value: **Cover or less**
Circ: Statement: **35,640**

37 ❑ Sep 1994 Cover: 1.50 **NM** value: **Cover or less**
Circ: Statement: **35,640**

38 ❑ Oct 1994 Cover: 1.50 **NM** value: **Cover or less**
Circ: Statement: **35,640**

39 ❑ Dec 1994 Cover: 1.50 **NM** value: **Cover or less**
Circ: Statement: **35,640**
📖 Love Showdown, Part 4

40 ❑ Jan 1995 Cover: 1.50 **NM** value: **Cover or less**
Circ: Statement: **29,636**

41 ❑ Mar 1995 Cover: 1.50 **NM** value: **Cover or less**
Circ: Statement: **29,636**

42 ❑ Apr 1995 Cover: 1.50 **NM** value: **Cover or less**
Circ: Statement: **29,636**

43 ❑ Jun 1995 Cover: 1.50 **NM** value: **Cover or less**
Circ: Statement: **29,636**

44 ❑ Jul 1995 Cover: 1.50 **NM** value: **Cover or less**
Circ: Statement: **29,636**

45 ❑ Aug 1995 Cover: 1.50 **NM** value: **Cover or less**
Circ: Statement: **29,636**

46 ❑ Sep 1995 Cover: 1.50 **NM** value: **Cover or less**
Circ: Statement: **29,636**

47 ❑ Oct 1995 Cover: 1.50 **NM** value: **Cover or less**
Circ: Statement: **29,636**

48 ❑ Nov 1995 Cover: 1.50 **NM** value: **Cover or less**
Circ: Statement: **29,636**

49 ❑ Jan 1996 Cover: 1.50 **NM** value: **Cover or less**
Circ: Statement: **29,126**

50 ❑ Feb 1996 Cover: 1.50 **NM** value: **Cover or less**
Circ: Statement: **29,126**

51 ❑ Apr 1996 Cover: 1.50 **NM** value: **Cover or less**
Circ: Statement: **29,126**

52 ❑ Jun 1996 Cover: 1.50 **NM** value: **Cover or less**
Circ: Statement: **29,126**

53 ❑ Jul 1996 Cover: 1.50 **NM** value: **Cover or less**
Circ: Statement: **29,126**

54 ❑ Aug 1996 Cover: 1.50 **NM** value: **Cover or less**
Circ: Statement: **29,126**

55 ❑ Sep 1996 Cover: 1.50 **NM** value: **Cover or less**
Circ: Statement: **29,126**

56 ❑ Oct 1996 Cover: 1.50 **NM** value: **Cover or less**
Circ: Statement: **29,126**

57 ❑ Nov 1996 Cover: 1.50 **NM** value: **Cover or less**
Circ: Statement: **29,126**

58 ❑ Dec 1996 Cover: 1.50 **NM** value: **Cover or less**
Circ: Statement: **29,126** Diamd. preorders: **4,319**
📖 Future Shock; Tooth-Fully Speaking; Sleeping Beauty; Keyless

59 ❑ Jan 1997 Cover: 1.50 **NM** value: **Cover or less**
Circ: Statement: **25,979** Diamd. preorders: **4,466**

60 ❑ Feb 1997 Cover: 1.50 **NM** value: **Cover or less**
Circ: Statement: **25,979** Diamd. preorders: **4,473**

61 ❑ Mar 1997 Cover: 1.50 **NM** value: **Cover or less**
Circ: Statement: **25,979** Diamd. preorders: **4,341**

62 ❑ Apr 1997 Cover: 1.50 **NM** value: **Cover or less**
Circ: Statement: **25,979** Diamd. preorders: **4,096**
• Has 1996 Statement, filed 9/27/96; avg print run 87,530; avg sales 28,529; avg subs 597; avg total paid 29,126; samples 433; office use 1,830; max existent 31,389; 64% of run returned

63 ❑ May 1997 Cover: 1.50 **NM** value: **Cover or less**
Circ: Statement: **25,979** Diamd. preorders: **3,983**

64 ❑ Jun 1997 Cover: 1.50 **NM** value: **Cover or less**
Circ: Statement: **25,979** Diamd. preorders: **3,823**

65 ❑ Jul 1997 Cover: 1.50 **NM** value: **Cover or less**
Circ: Statement: **25,979** Diamd. preorders: **4,043**

66 ❑ Aug 1997 Cover: 1.50 **NM** value: **Cover or less**
Circ: Statement: **25,979** Diamd. preorders: **4,518**

67 ❑ Sep 1997 Cover: 1.50 **NM** value: **Cover or less**
Circ: Statement: **25,979** Diamd. preorders: **4,593**

68 ❑ Oct 1997 Cover: 1.50 **NM** value: **Cover or less**
Circ: Statement: **25,979** Diamd. preorders: **4,581**

69 ❑ Nov 1997 Cover: 1.50 **NM** value: **Cover or less**
Circ: Statement: **25,979** Diamd. preorders: **4,522**

70 ❑ Dec 1997 Cover: 1.50 **NM** value: **Cover or less**
Circ: Statement: **25,979** Diamd. preorders: **4,566**

71 ❑ Jan 1998 Cover: 1.75 **NM** value: **Cover or less**
Circ: Statement: **24,626** Diamd. preorders: **4,794**

72 ❑ Feb 1998 Cover: 1.75 **NM** value: **Cover or less**
Circ: Statement: **24,626** Diamd. preorders: **4,767**

73 ❑ Mar 1998 Cover: 1.75 **NM** value: **Cover or less**
Circ: Statement: **24,626** Diamd. preorders: **4,426**

74 ❑ Apr 1998 Cover: 1.75 **NM** value: **Cover or less**
Circ: Statement: **24,626** Diamd. preorders: **4,190**
• Veronica markets Jughead's beanie; Has 1997 Statement, filed 11/1/97; avg print run 88,638; avg sales 25,568; avg subs 412; avg total paid 25,979; samples 426; office use 1,511; max existent 27,917; 69% of run returned

75 ❑ May 1998 Cover: 1.75 **NM** value: **Cover or less**
Circ: Statement: **24,626** Diamd. preorders: **4,017**

76 ❑ Jun 1998 Cover: 1.75 **NM** value: **Cover or less**
Circ: Statement: **24,626** Diamd. preorders: **4,059**

77 ❑ Jul 1998 Cover: 1.75 **NM** value: **Cover or less**
Circ: Statement: **24,626** Diamd. preorders: **4,099**

78 ❑ Aug 1998 Cover: 1.75 **NM** value: **Cover or less**
Circ: Statement: **24,626** Diamd. preorders: **3,884**

79 ❑ Sep 1998 Cover: 1.75 **NM** value: **Cover or less**
Circ: Statement: **24,626** Diamd. preorders: **4,074**
📖 Shop Around the World; All Washed Up!; My Hiccup Runneth Over **A:** Dan Parent **W:** Dan Parent

80 ❑ Oct 1998 Cover: 1.75 **NM** value: **Cover or less**
Circ: Statement: **24,626** Diamd. preorders: **3,937**

81 ❑ Nov 1998 Cover: 1.75 **NM** value: **Cover or less**
Circ: Statement: **24,626** Diamd. preorders: **3,816**
📖 Another Brilliant Idea • Veronica in Oz **A:** Stan Goldberg **W:** George Gladir

82 ❑ Dec 1998 Cover: 1.75 **NM** value: **Cover or less**
Circ: Statement: **24,626** Diamd. preorders: **3,706**

83 ❑ Jan 1999 Cover: 1.75 **NM** value: **Cover or less**
Circ: Diamd. preorders: **3,886**

84 ❑ Feb 1999 Cover: 1.75 **NM** value: **Cover or less**
Circ: Diamd. preorders: **3,833**

85 ❑ Mar 1999 Cover: 1.75 **NM** value: **Cover or less**
Circ: Diamd. preorders: **3,578**

86 ❑ Apr 1999 Cover: 1.79 **NM** value: **Cover or less**
Circ: Diamd. preorders: **3,440**
📖 Dressed to Chill • Has 1998 Statement, filed 11/1/98; avg print run 77,839; avg sales 24,042; avg subs 584; avg total paid 24,626; samples 421; office use 2,625; max existent 27,672; 64% of run returned

87 ❑ May 1999 Cover: 1.79 **NM** value: **Cover or less**
Circ: Diamd. preorders: **3,293**
📖 Flash in the Pan

88 ❑ Jun 1999 Cover: 1.79 **NM** value: **Cover or less**
Circ: Diamd. preorders: **3,047**

89 ❑ Jul 1999 Cover: 1.79 **NM** value: **Cover or less**
Circ: Diamd. preorders: **3,406**

90 ❑ Aug 1999 Cover: 1.79 **NM** value: **Cover or less**
Circ: Diamd. preorders: **3,082**

91 ❑ Aug 1999 Cover: 1.79 **NM** value: **Cover or less**
Circ: Diamd. preorders: **3,362**

92 ❑ Oct 1999 Cover: 1.79 **NM** value: **Cover or less**
Circ: Diamd. preorders: **3,251**

93 ❑ Nov 1999 Cover: 1.79 **NM** value: **Cover or less**
Circ: Diamd. preorders: **3,172**

94 ❑ Dec 1999 Cover: 1.79 **NM** value: **Cover or less**
Circ: Diamd. preorders: **3,139**

95 ❑ Jan 2000 Cover: 1.79 **NM** value: **Cover or less**
Circ: Diamd. preorders: **3,279**

96 ❑ Feb 2000 Cover: 1.79 **NM** value: **Cover or less**
Circ: Diamd. preorders: **3,280**

97 ❑ Mar 2000 Cover: 1.79 **NM** value: **Cover or less**
Circ: Diamd. preorders: **3,203**

98 ❑ Apr 2000 Cover: 1.79 **NM** value: **Cover or less**
Circ: Diamd. preorders: **3,002**

99 ❑ May 2000 Cover: 1.99 **NM** value: **Cover or less**
Circ: Diamd. preorders: **3,023**

100 ❑ Jun 2000 Cover: 1.99 **NM** value: **Cover or less**
Circ: Diamd. preorders: **3,964**

101 ❑ Jul 2000 Cover: 1.99 **NM** value: **Cover or less**
Circ: Diamd. preorders: **3,066**

102 ❑ Aug 2000 Cover: 1.99 **NM** value: **Cover or less**
Circ: Diamd. preorders: **3,208**

103 ❑ Sep 2000 Cover: 1.99 **NM** value: **Cover or less**
Circ: Diamd. preorders: **3,411**

104 ❑ Oct 2000 Cover: 1.99 **NM** value: **Cover or less**
Circ: Diamd. preorders: **3,221**

105 ❑ Nov 2000 Cover: 1.99 **NM** value: **Cover or less**
Circ: Diamd. preorders: **3,041**

106 ❑ Dec 2000 Cover: 1.99 **NM** value: **Cover or less**
Circ: Diamd. preorders: **2,981**

107 ❑ Jan 2001 Cover: 1.99 **NM** value: **Cover or less**
Circ: Statement: **18,795** Diamd. preorders: **3,035**

108 ❑ Feb 2001 Cover: 1.99 **NM** value: **Cover or less**
Circ: Statement: **18,795** Diamd. preorders: **3,096**

109 ❑ Mar 2001 Cover: 1.99 **NM** value: **Cover or less**
Circ: Statement: **18,795** Diamd. preorders: **2,850**

110 ❑ Apr 2001 Cover: 1.99 **NM** value: **Cover or less**
Circ: Statement: **18,795** Diamd. preorders: **2,796**

111 ❑ May 2001 Cover: 1.99 **NM** value: **Cover or less**
Circ: Statement: **18,795** Diamd. preorders: **3,148**

112 ❑ Jun 2001 Cover: 1.99 **NM** value: **Cover or less**
Circ: Statement: **18,795** Diamd. preorders: **2,722**

113 ❑ Jul 2001 Cover: 1.99 **NM** value: **Cover or less**
Circ: Statement: **18,795** Diamd. preorders: **3,081**

114 ❑ Aug 2001 Cover: 1.99 **NM** value: **Cover or less**
Circ: Statement: **18,795** Diamd. preorders: **2,898**

115 ❑ Sep 2001 Cover: 1.99 **NM** value: **Cover or less**
Circ: Statement: **18,795** Diamd. preorders: **3,308**

116 ❑ Oct 2001 Cover: 1.99 **NM** value: **Cover or less**
Circ: Statement: **18,795** Diamd. preorders: **3,364**

117 ❑ Nov 2001 Cover: 1.99 **NM** value: **Cover or less**
Circ: Statement: **18,795** Diamd. preorders: **3,160**

VERONICA'S DIGEST MAGAZINE — Archie

1 ❑ ca. 1992 Cover: 1.75 **NM** value: **2.00**

2 ❑ ca. 1993 Cover: 1.75 **NM** value: **Cover or less**

3 ❑ ca. 1994 Cover: 1.75 **NM** value: **Cover or less**

4 ❑ Sep 1995 Cover: 1.75 **NM** value: **Cover or less**

5 ❑ Sep 1996 Cover: 1.75 **NM** value: **Cover or less**

6 ❑ Oct 1997 Cover: 1.79 **NM** value: **Cover or less**

VEROTIKA — Verotik

All issues are adults only.

Lest anyone mistakenly believe that all comic-book tales focusing on sex are lighthearted, along comes Verotik Comics to kill that notion with this series featuring stories of sexual horror. In a typical story, a woman meets a mysterious stranger bearing unusual gifts — but will they bring her pleasure or a gruesome kind of pain? In another, a government experiment gone wrong creates thousands of radiation-infected living dead known as "grubs," many of whom endure their hellish existence through depraved sex.

Such tales, in which readers may find themselves briefly aroused and excited before being suddenly repulsed and horrified, are at the heart of this series by various creators, which is published and overseen by Glenn Danzig. Full-color and definitely not for the squeamish or faint of heart.

1 ❑ Cover: 2.95 **NM** value: **4.00**
Circ: CapCity orders: **6,975**

2 ❑ Jan 1995 Cover: 2.95 **NM** value: **3.00**
Circ: CapCity orders: **3,475**

3 ❑ 1995 Cover: 2.95 **NM** value: **3.00**
Circ: CapCity orders: **8,000**

4 ❑ 1995 Cover: 2.95 **NM** value: **3.00**
Circ: CapCity orders: **6,900**

5 ❑ 1995 Cover: 2.95 **NM** value: **3.00**
Circ: CapCity orders: **8,300**

6 ❑ 1995 Cover: 2.95 **NM** value: **3.00**
Circ: CapCity orders: **8,225**

Other grades: Multiply prices above by **1.5 for Mint • 2/3 for Very Fine • 1/3 for Fine • 1/5 for Very Good • 1/8 for Good**

7 ❑ 1995 Cover: 2.95 NM value: **3.00**
8 ❑ Feb 1996 Cover: 2.95 NM value: **3.00**
📖 Grub-Girl; Rococco **A:** JW Chow; Simon Morse **W:** Edward Lee; Graham Masteron
9 ❑ Cover: 2.95 NM value: **3.00**
10 ❑ Cover: 2.95 NM value: **3.00**
11 ❑ Cover: 2.95 NM value: **3.00**
12 ❑ Cover: 2.95 NM value: **3.00**
Circ: Diamd. preorders: **14,084**
13 ❑ Cover: 2.95 NM value: **3.00**
Circ: Diamd. preorders: **12,186**
14 ❑ Cover: 2.95 NM value: **3.00**
Circ: Diamd. preorders: **11,702**
15 ❑ Cover: 3.95 NM value: **Cover or less**
Circ: Diamd. preorders: **10,870**

VEROTIK ILLUSTRATED — Verotik

1 ❑ Aug 1997 Cover: 6.95 NM value: **Cover or less**
2 ❑ Dec 1997 Cover: 6.95 NM value: **Cover or less**
3 ❑ Apr 1998 Cover: 6.95 NM value: **Cover or less**

VEROTIK ROGUES GALLERY OF VILLAINS — Verotik

All issues are adults only.
1 ❑ Nov 1997 Cover: 3.95 NM value: **Cover or less**
Circ: Diamd. preorders: **5,399**
No issue number. • pin-ups

VERSION — Dark Horse

1.1 ❑ Cover: 2.50 NM value: **Cover or less**
Circ: CapCity orders: **2,825**
1.2 ❑ Cover: 2.50 NM value: **Cover or less**
Circ: CapCity orders: **2,525**
1.3 ❑ Cover: 2.50 NM value: **Cover or less**
Circ: CapCity orders: **2,675**
1.4 ❑ Cover: 2.50 NM value: **Cover or less**
Circ: CapCity orders: **2,625**
1.5 ❑ Cover: 2.50 NM value: **Cover or less**
Circ: CapCity orders: **2,450**
1.6 ❑ Cover: 2.50 NM value: **Cover or less**
Circ: CapCity orders: **2,250**
1.7 ❑ Cover: 2.50 NM value: **Cover or less**
1.8 ❑ Cover: 2.50 NM value: **Cover or less**
2.1 ❑ Cover: 2.95 NM value: **Cover or less**
2.2 ❑ Cover: 2.95 NM value: **Cover or less**
2.3 ❑ Cover: 2.95 NM value: **Cover or less**
2.4 ❑ Cover: 2.95 NM value: **Cover or less**
2.5 ❑ Cover: 2.95 NM value: **Cover or less**
2.6 ❑ Cover: 2.95 NM value: **Cover or less**
2.7 ❑ Cover: 2.95 NM value: **Cover or less**

VERTIGO GALLERY, THE: DREAMS AND NIGHTMARES — DC / Vertigo

1 ❑ Cover: 3.50 NM value: **4.00**
• pin-ups **A:** Chas Truog; Dean Motter; Matt Wagner; Geof Darrow; Jon J. Muth; David Lloyd; Bill Sienkiewicz; Alex Toth; Ted McKeever; Duncan Fegredo; Tim Truman; Steve Dillon; Phil Winslade; Michael W. Kaluta; Charles Vess; Glenn Barr; Peter Kuper; Chris Bachalo

VERTIGO JAM — DC / Vertigo

Some compilation titles are little more than collections of castoffs or throw-away stories. This title is nothing of the sort. Just as smart record companies put their best offerings on sampler albums, Vertigo brought out truly great stories for this "Vertigo Jam."

A special line of comics from DC, the Vertigo line specializes in mature, innovative fiction. Vertigo Jam spotlights Vertigo's many bright offerings, including Sandman, Kid Eternity, Shade, the Changing Man, Doom Patrol, Hellblazer, Swamp Thing, and Animal Man. Regular readers of these titles will find real gems here, and new readers will get a chance to pick up on some of the most worthwhile titles being published today.

1 ❑ Aug 1993 Cover: 3.95 NM value: **Cover or less**
Circ: CapCity orders: **26,950**

VERTIGO PREVIEW — DC / Vertigo

One of the more exciting events of late 1992 was the launching of DC's Vertigo line of comics for adult readers. This line became a critical favorite among comics readers, praised for its innovation and strong storytelling.

This one-shot previewed the new Vertigo line, including currently running titles Sandman, Hellblazer, Doom Patrol, Animal Man, Swamp Thing, and Shade, the Changing Man. New Vertigo titles include Sandman Mystery Theatre, a Jazz Age adventure starring Wesley Dodds, the Golden Age Sandman; Kid Eternity, who raises the dead in order to raise humanity's consciousness; Black Orchid, the tales of a beautiful and ephemeral goddess; Enigma, a dark combination of comic books and madness; Mercy, an ethereal entity who changes lives; Death: The High Cost of Living, the story of Death's one day as a mortal; and Sebastian O, a scoundrel who believes the key to high crime is snappy dressing.

1 ❑ Cover: 0.75 NM value: **1.50**
• Previews DC Vertigo titles

VERTIGO RAVE — DC / Vertigo

1 ❑ Aut 1994 Cover: 0.99 NM value: **1.50**

VERTIGO SECRET FILES & ORIGINS: HELLBLAZER — DC / Vertigo

1 ❑ Cover: 3.95 NM value: **Cover or less**

VERTIGO SECRET FILES & ORIGINS: SWAMP THING — DC / Vertigo

1 ❑ Nov 2000 Cover: 4.95 NM value: **Cover or less**
📖 Bitter Fruit: How Tefe's Adventures Began; The DDI Secret Files; The Secret Life of a Planet Elemental; Look Away: It's Not Easy Being a God; Who's Who in the World of Swamp Thing; Lady Arcane: Abby's Past and Future Collide; The Swamp Thing Timeline **A:** Steve Lieber; Michael Zulli; Christopher Jordan; Cliff Chiang **W:** Jon Lewis; Alisa Kwitney; Brian K. Vaughan; Douglas Wolk; Michael Bonner

VERTIGO VERITÉ: THE UNSEEN HAND — DC / Vertigo

1 ❑ Sep 1996 Cover: 2.50 NM value: **Cover or less**
2 ❑ Oct 1996 Cover: 2.50 NM value: **Cover or less**
📖 Ruin, Rape, and Rock 'n' Roll **A:** Ilya **W:** Terry Laban
3 ❑ Nov 1996 Cover: 2.50 NM value: **Cover or less**
Circ: Diamd. preorders: **13,377**
📖 Moscow Underground **A:** Ilya **W:** Terry Laban
4 ❑ Dec 1996 Cover: 2.50 NM value: **Cover or less**
Circ: Diamd. preorders: **12,595**
📖 Hand's Up **A:** Ilya **W:** Terry Laban

VERTIGO VISIONS: DOCTOR OCCULT — DC / Vertigo

1 ❑ Jul 1994 Cover: 3.95 NM value: **Cover or less**
Circ: CapCity orders: **11,250** Diamd. preorders: **8,388**
One-shot.

VERTIGO VISIONS: DR. THIRTEEN — DC / Vertigo

1 ❑ Sep 1998 Cover: 5.95 NM value: **Cover or less**
One-shot. 📖 Do Als Dream of Electric Sleep? **A:** Michael Avon Oeming **W:** Matt Howarth

VERTIGO VISIONS: PREZ — DC / Vertigo

1 ❑ Sep 1995 Cover: 3.95 NM value: **Cover or less**
Circ: CapCity orders: **9,150**
One-shot. 📖 Smells Like Teen President **A:** Eric Shanower **W:** Ed Brubaker

VERTIGO VISIONS: THE GEEK — DC / Vertigo

1 ❑ Cover: 3.95 NM value: **Cover or less**
Circ: CapCity orders: **19,800**

VERTIGO VISIONS: THE PHANTOM STRANGER — DC / Vertigo

1 ❑ Oct 1993 Cover: 3.50 NM value: **Cover or less**
Circ: CapCity orders: **15,100**

VERTIGO VISIONS: TOMAHAWK — DC / Vertigo

1 ❑ Jul 1998 Cover: 4.95 NM value: **Cover or less**
Circ: Diamd. preorders: **11,558**
One-shot.

VERTIGO VOICES: THE EATERS — DC / Vertigo

1 ❑ Cover: 4.95 NM value: **Cover or less**

VERTIGO: WINTER'S EDGE — DC / Vertigo

1 ❑ Jan 1998 Cover: 7.95 NM value: **Cover or less**
wraparound cover. 📖 House of Secrets; The Sandman: The Flowers • prestige format anthology **A:** John Bolton; Paul Pope; Philip Bond; Teddy Kristiansen; Sean Phillips; Duncan Fegredo; Steve Dillon; Phil Winslade; Steve Parkhouse; Peter Hogan **W:** Matt Wagner; Grant Morrison; Peter Milligan; Caitlin R. Kiernan; Garth Ennis; John Ney Rieber; Paul Jenkins; Steve Gerber; Steven Seagle
2 ❑ Jan 1999 Cover: 6.95 NM value: **Cover or less**
Circ: Diamd. preorders: **20,711**
wraparound cover. 📖 The Minx: Stories; Death: Winter's Tale; Transmetropolitan: Edgy Wi **A:** Jason Lutes; Teddy Kristiansen; Phil Jimenez; Sean Phillips; Michael Lark; Jeff Jones; Phil Winslade; Darick Robertson; Glyn Dillon; Paul Rivoche **W:** Warren Ellis; Peter Gross; Ed Brubaker; Grant Morrison; Peter Milligan; Caitlin R. Kiernan; Garth Ennis; Neil Gaiman; Steve Gerber; Steven Seagle
3 ❑ Jan 2000 Cover: 6.95 NM value: **Cover or less**
Circ: Diamd. preorders: **17,545**
📖 The Sandman: Desire: How They Met Themselves; 100 Bullets: Silencer Night; Books **A:** Dave Gibbons; Michael Lark; Richard Case; Michael Zulli; Shawn McManus; Darick Robertson; Goran Sudzuka; Chris Bachalo; Joe Rubinstein; Eduardo Risso **W:** Jeph Loeb; Dave Gibbons; Warren Ellis; Peter Gross; Ed Brubaker; Brian Azzarello; Brian Vaughan; Caitlan R. Kiernan; Jamie Delano; Neil Gaiman

VERY BEST OF DENNIS THE MENACE — Marvel

1 ❑ Apr 1982 Cover: 1.25 NM value: **8.00**
📖 DC logo placed on cover in error by World Color Press • DC logo placed on cover in error by World Color Press; reprints
2 ❑ Jun 1982 Cover: 1.25 NM value: **2.00**
• reprints
3 ❑ Aug 1982 Cover: 1.25 NM value: **2.00**
📖 Ruffing It; Putting on the Dog; The Wing is on the Bird; The Big Question; Flea For Your Life; Mov(ie)ing Along; Just Poolin'; Nobody's Tool; Shower Power; The Pet Patrol; Ruff, The Wet Pett; Hairy Tale • reprints

VERY BEST OF MARVEL COMICS, THE — Marvel

Bk 1❑ Cover: 12.95 NM value: **Cover or less**

VERY MU CHRISTMAS, A — Mu

1 ❑ Nov 1992 Cover: 2.95 NM value: **Cover or less**
No issue number.

VERY VICKY — Iconografix

1 ❑ b&w Cover: 2.95 NM value: **Cover or less**
1-2 ❑ Cover: 2.50 NM value: **Cover or less**
2 ❑ b&w Cover: 2.50 NM value: **Cover or less**
3 ❑ b&w Cover: 2.50 NM value: **Cover or less**
4 ❑ b&w Cover: 2.50 NM value: **Cover or less**
5 ❑ b&w Cover: 2.50 NM value: **Cover or less**
6 ❑ b&w Cover: 2.50 NM value: **Cover or less**
7 ❑ b&w Cover: 2.50 NM value: **Cover or less**
8 ❑ b&w Cover: 2.50 NM value: **Cover or less**

VESPERS — Mars Media Group

1 ❑ Aug 1995 Cover: 2.50 NM value: **Cover or less**

VEXT — DC

1 ❑ Mar 1999 Cover: 2.50 NM value: **Cover or less**
Circ: Diamd. preorders: **16,854**
📖 In the Beginning **A:** Mike McKone **W:** Keith Giffen ★ Origin of Vext. ★ Appearance of Superman, Zauriel.
2 ❑ Apr 1999 Cover: 2.50 NM value: **Cover or less**
Circ: Diamd. preorders: **12,245**
3 ❑ May 1999 Cover: 2.50 NM value: **Cover or less**
Circ: Diamd. preorders: **11,186**
4 ❑ Jun 1999 Cover: 2.50 NM value: **Cover or less**
Circ: Diamd. preorders: **10,537**
📖 Love Hurts! **A:** Mike McKone **W:** Keith Giffen ★ Appearance of Paramour.
5 ❑ Jul 1999 Cover: 2.50 NM value: **Cover or less**
Circ: Diamd. preorders: **9,559**
📖 Love Stinks! **A:** Mike McKone **W:** Keith Giffen
6 ❑ Aug 1999 Cover: 2.50 NM value: **Cover or less**
Circ: Diamd. preorders: **9,036**

V FOR VENDETTA — DC

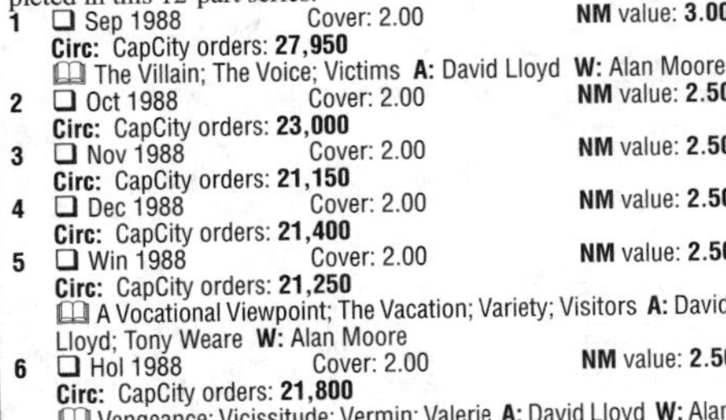

In the nuclear wars of the near future, England narrowly avoids being annihilated. But in the panic that follows, the government falls and is replaced by a totalitarian state. Jews, blacks, homosexuals, intellectuals, and others are rounded up and taken to "resettlement camps," where the lucky ones go into the ovens. The unlucky ones were "experimented" upon. The doors in that part of the facility are labeled with Roman numerals: I, II, III, IV...V.

Now the "experiment" behind door V is back. Dressed in the melodramatic costume of Parliament-bomber Guy Fawkes, he stalks the streets and alleys of totalitarian London. More than revenge, he's out to take down the whole system. He calls himself "V" — "V" for "Vendetta."

Alan Moore once again works his magic in this dark title. Originally begun in England's Warrior magazine, its storyline is completed in this 12-part series.

1 ❑ Sep 1988 Cover: 2.00 NM value: **3.00**
Circ: CapCity orders: **27,950**
📖 The Villain; The Voice; Victims **A:** David Lloyd **W:** Alan Moore
2 ❑ Oct 1988 Cover: 2.00 NM value: **2.50**
Circ: CapCity orders: **23,000**
3 ❑ Nov 1988 Cover: 2.00 NM value: **2.50**
Circ: CapCity orders: **21,150**
4 ❑ Dec 1988 Cover: 2.00 NM value: **2.50**
Circ: CapCity orders: **21,400**
5 ❑ Win 1988 Cover: 2.00 NM value: **2.50**
Circ: CapCity orders: **21,250**
📖 A Vocational Viewpoint; The Vacation; Variety; Visitors **A:** David Lloyd; Tony Weare **W:** Alan Moore
6 ❑ Hol 1988 Cover: 2.00 NM value: **2.50**
Circ: CapCity orders: **21,800**
📖 Vengeance; Vicissitude; Vermin; Valerie **A:** David Lloyd **W:** Alan Moore
7 ❑ Jan 1989 Cover: 2.00 NM value: **2.50**
Circ: CapCity orders: **21,550**
8 ❑ Feb 1989 Cover: 2.00 NM value: **2.50**
Circ: CapCity orders: **21,950**
9 ❑ Mar 1989 Cover: 2.00 NM value: **2.50**
Circ: CapCity orders: **21,100**
10 ❑ May 1989 Cover: 2.00 NM value: **2.50**
Circ: CapCity orders: **20,800**
Bk 1❑ Cover: 14.95 NM value: **19.95**
• Collects V For Vendetta #1-10 **A:** David Lloyd **W:** Alan Moore

VIC & BLOOD — Mad Dog

1 ❑ Oct 1987, b&w Cover: 2.00 NM value: **Cover or less**
2 ❑ Feb 1988, b&w Cover: 2.00 NM value: **Cover or less**

VICIOUS — Brainstorm

All issues are adults only.
1 ❑ b&w Cover: 2.95 NM value: **Cover or less**

VIC JORDAN — Argo

1 ❑ Cover: 0.10 NM value: **60.00**

VICKI — Atlas-Seaboard

1 ❑ Feb 1975 Cover: 0.25 NM value: **20.00**
• **CGC:** 5 graded, best 9.2
• reprints Tippy Teen

CGC-graded: Multiply prices above by **33 for 9.9 M • 16 for 9.8 NM/M • 7 for 9.6 NM+ • 5 for 9.4 NM • 2.5 for 9.2 NM- • 1.5 for 9.0 VF/NM**

2 ❑ Apr 1975 Cover: 0.25 **NM** value: **14.00**
• **CGC:** 9 graded, best 9.2
• reprints Tippy Teen

3 ❑ Jun 1975 Cover: 0.25 **NM** value: **10.00**
• **CGC:** 11 graded, best 9.6
• reprints Tippy Teen

4 ❑ Aug 1975 Cover: 0.25 **NM** value: **10.00**
• **CGC:** 1 graded, best 9.2
• reprints Tippy Teen

VICKI VALENTINE — Renegade

1 ❑ Jul 1985, b&w Cover: 1.70 **NM** value: **Cover or less**
2 ❑ Nov 1985, b&w Cover: 1.70 **NM** value: **Cover or less**
3 ❑ 1986b&w Cover: 1.70 **NM** value: **Cover or less**
4 ❑ 1986b&w Cover: 1.70 **NM** value: **Cover or less**

VICTIM — Silverwolf

1 ❑ Feb 1987 Cover: 1.50 **NM** value: **Cover or less**
📖 Deathborg II **A:** Paul Schultz **W:** Kristoffer A. Silver

VICTIMS — Eternity

1 ❑ 1988 b&w Cover: 1.95 **NM** value: **2.00**
2 ❑ 1988 b&w Cover: 1.95 **NM** value: **2.00**
3 ❑ 1988 b&w Cover: 1.95 **NM** value: **2.00**
4 ❑ Jan 1989, b&w Cover: 1.95 **NM** value: **2.00**
5 ❑ Feb 1989, b&w Cover: 1.95 **NM** value: **2.00**
6 ❑ Cover: 1.95 **NM** value: **2.00**

VICTORIAN, THE — Penny-Farthing

0.5 ❑ Aug 1998 Cover: 1.00 **NM** value: **Cover or less**
• preview of upcoming series; Sketches and notes for series **A:** Courtney Huddleston **W:** Trainor Houghton

1 ❑ Mar 1999 Cover: 2.95 **NM** value: **3.00**
Circ: Diamd. preorders: **4,581**
📖 Self-Realization, Part 1 **A:** Martin Montiel Luna **W:** Trainor Houghton

2 ❑ Apr 1999 Cover: 2.95 **NM** value: **Cover or less**
Circ: Diamd. preorders: **3,069**

3 ❑ May 1999 Cover: 2.95 **NM** value: **Cover or less**
Circ: Diamd. preorders: **2,936**

4 ❑ Jun 1999 Cover: 2.95 **NM** value: **Cover or less**
Circ: Diamd. preorders: **2,653**

5 ❑ Jul 1999 Cover: 2.95 **NM** value: **Cover or less**
Circ: Diamd. preorders: **2,476**

6 ❑ Aug 1999 Cover: 2.95 **NM** value: **Cover or less**
Circ: Diamd. preorders: **2,214**
📖 Ain De Si…cle **A:** Martin Montiel Luna **W:** Lovern Kindzierski; Trainor Houghton

VIC TORRY AND HIS FLYING SAUCER — Fawcett

1 ❑ ca. 1950 Cover: 0.10 **NM** value: **400.00**
• **CGC:** 2 graded, best 9.0

VICTORY COMICS — Hillman

1 ❑ Aug 1941 Cover: 0.10 **NM** value: **2000.00**
• **CGC:** 1 graded, best 7.0
2 ❑ Sep 1941 Cover: 0.10 **NM** value: **1500.00**
3 ❑ Nov 1941 Cover: 0.10 **NM** value: **1000.00**
4 ❑ Dec 1941 Cover: 0.10 **NM** value: **500.00**

VICTORY (TOPPS) — Topps

1 ❑ Jun 1994 Cover: 2.50 **NM** value: **Cover or less**
Circ: CapCity orders: **5,475**
• First and final issue (series cancelled) **A:** Keith Giffen **W:** Kurt Busiek

VIC VERITY — Verity

1 ❑ ca. 1945 Cover: 0.10 **NM** value: **100.00**
2 ❑ ca. 1946 Cover: 0.10 **NM** value: **75.00**
3 ❑ Mar 1946 Cover: 0.10 **NM** value: **75.00**
• **CGC:** 1 graded, best 9.4
4 ❑ ca. 1946 Cover: 0.10 **NM** value: **75.00**
5 ❑ ca. 1946 Cover: 0.10 **NM** value: **50.00**
6 ❑ ca. 1946 Cover: 0.10 **NM** value: **50.00**
7 ❑ Sep 1946 Cover: 0.10 **NM** value: **50.00**
• **CGC:** 1 graded, best 8.5

VIDEO CLASSICS — Eternity

1 ❑ b&w Cover: 3.50 **NM** value: **Cover or less**
• Mighty Mouse
2 ❑ b&w Cover: 3.50 **NM** value: **Cover or less**
• Mighty Mouse

VIDEO HIROSHIMA — Aeon

1 ❑ Aug 1995, b&w Cover: 2.50 **NM** value: **Cover or less**
No issue number. One-shot.

VIDEO JACK — Marvel / Epic

1 ❑ Sep 1987 Cover: 1.25 **NM** value: **Cover or less**
Circ: CapCity orders: **13,700**
📖 Pilot Error **A:** Keith Giffen **W:** Keith Giffen

2 ❑ Nov 1987 Cover: 1.25 **NM** value: **Cover or less**
Circ: CapCity orders: **10,000**

3 ❑ Mar 1988 Cover: 1.25 **NM** value: **Cover or less**
Circ: CapCity orders: **8,600**

4 ❑ May 1988 Cover: 1.25 **NM** value: **Cover or less**
Circ: CapCity orders: **6,100**

5 ❑ Jul 1988 Cover: 1.25 **NM** value: **Cover or less**
Circ: CapCity orders: **4,900**

6 ❑ Sep 1988 Cover: 1.25 **NM** value: **Cover or less**
Circ: CapCity orders: **5,150**

📖 This is Your Life & Death; Space Trek; Sgt. Sitcom; Vidzilla; Singing Slingers; The Grape-Crushers; What's Up Jack?; Jack the Hacker; Da-Mon the Defeated; Welcome Back, Jack **A:** Jose Marzan Jr.; William Wray; Fred Hembeck; Keith Giffen; Michael T. Gilbert; Walt Simonson; Trina Robbins; Dave Hunt **W:** William Wray; Jim Starlin; Fred Hembeck; Keith Giffen; Kevin Maguire; Michael T. Gilbert; Stephen DeStefano; Walt Simonson; Trina Robbins

VIETNAM JOURNAL — Apple

1 ❑ Nov 1987, b&w Cover: 1.75 **NM** value: **2.00**
📖 The Field Jacket **A:** Don Lomax **W:** Don Lomax
1-2 ❑ Cover: 1.75 **NM** value: **2.00**
2 ❑ Jan 1988 Cover: 1.75 **NM** value: **2.00**
3 ❑ Mar 1988 Cover: 1.75 **NM** value: **2.00**
4 ❑ May 1988 Cover: 1.75 **NM** value: **2.00**
5 ❑ Jul 1988 Cover: 1.75 **NM** value: **2.00**
6 ❑ Sep 1988 Cover: 1.95 **NM** value: **2.00**
7 ❑ Nov 1988 Cover: 1.95 **NM** value: **2.00**
8 ❑ Jan 1989 Cover: 1.95 **NM** value: **2.00**
📖 To Face the Beast **A:** Don Lomax **W:** Don Lomax
9 ❑ Mar 1989 Cover: 1.95 **NM** value: **2.00**
10 ❑ May 1989 Cover: 1.95 **NM** value: **2.00**
11 ❑ Jul 1989 Cover: 2.25 **NM** value: **Cover or less**
12 ❑ Sep 1989 Cover: 2.25 **NM** value: **Cover or less**
13 ❑ Nov 1989 Cover: 2.25 **NM** value: **Cover or less**
14 ❑ Jan 1990 Cover: 2.25 **NM** value: **Cover or less**
15 ❑ Mar 1990 Cover: 2.25 **NM** value: **Cover or less**
16 ❑ May 1990 Cover: 2.25 **NM** value: **Cover or less**
final issue. **A:** Don Lomax **W:** Don Lomax
Bk 1 ❑ Cover: 12.95 **NM** value: **Cover or less**
• Indian Country

VIETNAM JOURNAL: BLOODBATH AT KHE SANH — Apple

1 ❑ b&w Cover: 2.75 **NM** value: **Cover or less**
2 ❑ b&w Cover: 2.75 **NM** value: **Cover or less**
3 ❑ b&w Cover: 2.75 **NM** value: **Cover or less**
4 ❑ b&w Cover: 2.75 **NM** value: **Cover or less**

VIETNAM JOURNAL: TET '68 — Apple

1 ❑ b&w Cover: 2.75 **NM** value: **Cover or less**
2 ❑ b&w Cover: 2.75 **NM** value: **Cover or less**
3 ❑ b&w Cover: 2.75 **NM** value: **Cover or less**
4 ❑ b&w Cover: 2.75 **NM** value: **Cover or less**
5 ❑ b&w Cover: 2.75 **NM** value: **Cover or less**
6 ❑ b&w Cover: 2.75 **NM** value: **Cover or less**

VIETNAM JOURNAL: VALLEY OF DEATH — Apple

1 ❑ Jun 1994, b&w Cover: 2.75 **NM** value: **Cover or less**

VIGILANTE, THE — DC

Adrian Chase was an enthusiastic district attorney. He had made quite a name for himself chasing mobsters and was steadily building a case against the infamous Anthony Scarapelli. To stop him, Scarapelli ordered Chase killed. A bomb was planted in Chase's car but, instead of killing Chase, it killed his wife and daughter.

Chase was devastated. Not long after their deaths, he was approached by a member of a strange cult dedicated to punishing evil. They trained him to be their instrument of deadly justice, honing his physical skills to perfection and teaching him to accelerate his healing process. So Chase became The Vigilante. Still, the attorney was never entirely comfortable with his role and attempted to give it up repeatedly, only to have a number of others take up the costume with tragic consequences. Chase was forced back into the role, but the killing (and the revelation of his identity) worked to drive him over the edge of sanity.

1 ❑ Nov 1983 Cover: 1.25 **NM** value: **2.00**
• **CGC:** 1 graded, best 9.8
📖 A Fable For Our Times! **A:** Keith Pollard; Dick Giordano **W:** Marv Wolfman ★ 1st Appearance of Vigilante II (Adrian Chase).
2 ❑ Jan 1984 Cover: 1.25 **NM** value: **1.50**
3 ❑ Feb 1984 Cover: 1.25 **NM** value: **1.50**
4 ❑ Mar 1984 Cover: 1.25 **NM** value: **Cover or less**
5 ❑ Apr 1984 Cover: 1.25 **NM** value: **Cover or less**
6 ❑ May 1984 Cover: 1.25 **NM** value: **Cover or less**
7 ❑ Jun 1984 Cover: 1.25 **NM** value: **Cover or less**
8 ❑ Jul 1984 Cover: 1.25 **NM** value: **Cover or less**
9 ❑ Aug 1984 Cover: 1.25 **NM** value: **Cover or less**
10 ❑ Sep 1984 Cover: 1.25 **NM** value: **Cover or less**
11 ❑ Oct 1984 Cover: 1.25 **NM** value: **Cover or less**
12 ❑ Nov 1984 Cover: 1.25 **NM** value: **Cover or less**
13 ❑ Dec 1984 Cover: 1.25 **NM** value: **Cover or less**
14 ❑ Feb 1985 Cover: 1.25 **NM** value: **Cover or less**
15 ❑ Mar 1985 Cover: 1.25 **NM** value: **Cover or less**
16 ❑ Apr 1985 Cover: 1.25 **NM** value: **Cover or less**
17 ❑ May 1985 Cover: 1.25 **NM** value: **Cover or less**
Circ: CapCity orders: **9,750**
18 ❑ Jun 1985 Cover: 1.25 **NM** value: **Cover or less**
Circ: CapCity orders: **9,200**
19 ❑ Jul 1985 Cover: 1.25 **NM** value: **Cover or less**
Circ: CapCity orders: **9,050**
20 ❑ Aug 1985 Cover: 1.25 **NM** value: **Cover or less**
Circ: CapCity orders: **8,800**
21 ❑ Sep 1985 Cover: 1.25 **NM** value: **Cover or less**
Circ: CapCity orders: **9,150**
22 ❑ Oct 1985 Cover: 1.25 **NM** value: **Cover or less**
Circ: CapCity orders: **9,850**
• Crisis
23 ❑ Nov 1985 Cover: 1.25 **NM** value: **Cover or less**
Circ: CapCity orders: **8,950**
24 ❑ Dec 1985 Cover: 1.50 **NM** value: **Cover or less**
Circ: CapCity orders: **8,700**
25 ❑ Jan 1986 Cover: 1.50 **NM** value: **Cover or less**
Circ: CapCity orders: **8,600**
26 ❑ Feb 1986 Cover: 1.50 **NM** value: **Cover or less**
Circ: CapCity orders: **8,500**
27 ❑ Mar 1986 Cover: 1.50 **NM** value: **Cover or less**
Circ: CapCity orders: **8,300**
28 ❑ Apr 1986 Cover: 1.50 **NM** value: **Cover or less**
Circ: CapCity orders: **8,600**
29 ❑ May 1986 Cover: 1.50 **NM** value: **Cover or less**
Circ: CapCity orders: **8,300**
30 ❑ Jun 1986 Cover: 1.50 **NM** value: **Cover or less**
Circ: CapCity orders: **7,950**
31 ❑ Jul 1986 Cover: 1.50 **NM** value: **Cover or less**
Circ: CapCity orders: **7,850**
32 ❑ Aug 1986 Cover: 1.50 **NM** value: **Cover or less**
Circ: CapCity orders: **7,800**
33 ❑ Sep 1986 Cover: 1.50 **NM** value: **Cover or less**
Circ: CapCity orders: **8,050**
34 ❑ Oct 1986 Cover: 1.50 **NM** value: **Cover or less**
Circ: CapCity orders: **7,900**
35 ❑ Nov 1986 Cover: 1.50 **NM** value: **Cover or less**
Circ: CapCity orders: **8,100**
36 ❑ Dec 1986 Cover: 1.50 **NM** value: **Cover or less**
Circ: CapCity orders: **7,650**
37 ❑ Jan 1987 Cover: 1.50 **NM** value: **Cover or less**
Circ: CapCity orders: **7,500**
38 ❑ Feb 1987 Cover: 1.50 **NM** value: **Cover or less**
Circ: CapCity orders: **7,850**
39 ❑ Mar 1987 Cover: 1.50 **NM** value: **Cover or less**
Circ: CapCity orders: **8,150**
40 ❑ Apr 1987 Cover: 1.50 **NM** value: **Cover or less**
Circ: CapCity orders: **9,050**
41 ❑ May 1987 Cover: 1.50 **NM** value: **Cover or less**
Circ: CapCity orders: **8,300**
42 ❑ Jun 1987 Cover: 1.50 **NM** value: **Cover or less**
Circ: CapCity orders: **8,150**
43 ❑ Jul 1987 Cover: 1.50 **NM** value: **Cover or less**
Circ: CapCity orders: **8,100**
44 ❑ Aug 1987 Cover: 1.50 **NM** value: **Cover or less**
Circ: CapCity orders: **8,900**
45 ❑ Sep 1987 Cover: 1.50 **NM** value: **Cover or less**
Circ: CapCity orders: **8,900**
46 ❑ Oct 1987 Cover: 1.50 **NM** value: **Cover or less**
Circ: CapCity orders: **8,950**
47 ❑ Nov 1987 Cover: 1.50 **NM** value: **Cover or less**
Circ: CapCity orders: **9,950**
48 ❑ Dec 1987 Cover: 1.50 **NM** value: **Cover or less**
Circ: CapCity orders: **8,450**
49 ❑ Jan 1988 Cover: 1.50 **NM** value: **Cover or less**
Circ: CapCity orders: **8,600**
50 ❑ Feb 1988 Cover: 1.50 **NM** value: **Cover or less**
Circ: CapCity orders: **9,800**
• Vigilante commits suicide ★ Death of Vigilante II (Adrian Chase).
Anl 1 ❑ ca. 1985 Cover: 2.00 **NM** value: **Cover or less**
Circ: CapCity orders: **9,950**
Anl 2 ❑ ca. 1986 Cover: 2.00 **NM** value: **Cover or less**
Circ: CapCity orders: **7,800**

VIGILANTE 8: SECOND OFFENSE — Chaos

1 ❑ Dec 1999 Cover: 2.95 **NM** value: **Cover or less**

VIGILANTE: CITY LIGHTS, PRAIRIE JUSTICE — DC

1 ❑ Nov 1995 Cover: 2.50 **NM** value: **Cover or less**
2 ❑ Dec 1995 Cover: 2.50 **NM** value: **Cover or less**
3 ❑ Jan 1996 Cover: 2.50 **NM** value: **Cover or less**
4 ❑ Feb 1996 Cover: 2.50 **NM** value: **Cover or less**

VIGIL: BLOODLINE — Duality

1 ❑ Cover: 2.95 **NM** value: **Cover or less**
📖 Baby Steps **A:** Mike Iverson **W:** Arvin Loudermilk
2 ❑ Cover: 2.95 **NM** value: **Cover or less**
3 ❑ Cover: 2.95 **NM** value: **Cover or less**
📖 Slash ø Burn **A:** Mike Iverson **W:** Arvin Loudermilk
4 ❑ Cover: 2.95 **NM** value: **Cover or less**
📖 Dirt **A:** Mike Iverson **W:** Arvin Loudermilk
5 ❑ Nov 1998 Cover: 2.95 **NM** value: **Cover or less**
📖 Desertion **A:** Mike Iverson **W:** Arvin Loudermilk
6 ❑ Cover: 2.95 **NM** value: **Cover or less**
7 ❑ Cover: 2.95 **NM** value: **Cover or less**
8 ❑ Jul 1999 Cover: 2.95 **NM** value: **Cover or less**
📖 Daddy's Little Girl **A:** Mike Iverson **W:** Arvin Loudermilk

VIGIL: DESERT FOXES — Millennium

1 ❑ Jul 1995, b&w Cover: 3.95 **NM** value: **Cover or less**
2 ❑ Aug 1995, b&w Cover: 3.95 **NM** value: **Cover or less**

VIGIL: ERUPTION — Millennium

1 ❑ Aug 1996, b&w Cover: 3.95 **NM** value: **Cover or less**
2 ❑ Cover: 2.95 **NM** value: **Cover or less**

VIGIL: FALL FROM GRACE — Innovation

1 ❑ Mar 1992, b&w Cover: 2.95 **NM** value: **Cover or less**
2 ❑ b&w Cover: 2.95 **NM** value: **Cover or less**

VIGIL: KUKULKAN — Innovation

1 ❑ Cover: 2.95 **NM** value: **Cover or less**

VIGIL: REBIRTH — Millennium

1 ❑ Nov 1994, b&w Cover: 3.95 **NM** value: **Cover or less**
2 ❑ Dec 1994, b&w Cover: 3.95 **NM** value: **Cover or less**

VIGIL: SCATTERSHOTS — Duality Press

1 ❑ Jul 1997, b&w Cover: 3.95 **NM** value: **Cover or less**
2 ❑ Cover: 3.95 **NM** value: **Cover or less**

VIGIL: THE GOLDEN PARTS — Innovation
1 ❑ b&w Cover: 2.95 **NM** value: **Cover or less**

VIGIL: VAMPORUM ANIMATURI — Millennium
1 ❑ May 1994, b&w Cover: 3.95 **NM** value: **Cover or less**
No issue number.

VIGNETTE COMICS — Harrier
1 ❑ b&w Cover: 1.95 **NM** value: **Cover or less**

VIGNETTES — Eyescream Graphix
Bk 1❑ b&w Cover: 6.95 **NM** value: **Cover or less**
• collects stories from Valentino
Bk 1-2❑b&w Cover: 7.95 **NM** value: **Cover or less**
• collects stories from Valentino

VIKING GLORY-THE VIKING PRINCE — DC
1 ❑ Cover: 14.95 **NM** value: **Cover or less**

VILE — Raging Rhino
1 ❑ Cover: 2.95 **NM** value: **Cover or less**

VILLAINS & VIGILANTES — Eclipse
1 ❑ Dec 1986 Cover: 1.50 **NM** value: **Cover or less**
Circ: CapCity orders: **7,275**
📖 A Charge of Mayhem **A:** Jeff Dee **W:** Jack Herman ★ 1st Appearance of Condor, Shadowman (Eclipse).
2 ❑ Mar 1987 Cover: 1.50 **NM** value: **Cover or less**
Circ: CapCity orders: **4,225**
3 ❑ Apr 1987 Cover: 1.50 **NM** value: **Cover or less**
Circ: CapCity orders: **4,000**
4 ❑ Apr 1987 Cover: 1.50 **NM** value: **Cover or less**
Circ: CapCity orders: **3,900**

VILLA OF THE MYSTERIES — Fantagraphics
1 ❑ b&w Cover: 3.95 **NM** value: **Cover or less**
2 ❑ b&w Cover: 3.95 **NM** value: **Cover or less**
3 ❑ Jul 1998, b&w Cover: 3.95 **NM** value: **Cover or less**

VINCENT J. MIELCAREK JR. MEMORIAL COMIC — Cooper Union
1 ❑ b&w Cover: 3.00 **NM** value: **Cover or less**
No issue number.

VINTAGE COMIC CLASSICS — Recollections
1 ❑ Feb 1990 **NM** value: **2.00**
• Red Demon reprint

VINTAGE MAGNUS ROBOT FIGHTER — Valiant
In the early '90's, Valiant managed to resurrect an assortment of little-known characters from Gold Key, gave them a more modern treatment, and turned them into a fan sensation. Among the bunch were Doctor Solar, Man of the Atom, Turok, and Magnus Robot Fighter.

Having enjoyed huge success with the remake of Magnus, Valiant decided the time was right to revisit the original. This four-issue series from Valiant features the original Magnus Robot Fighter, in which Magnus was a kinder, gentler soul. Rather than smash countless robots to pieces, as he did in the early 1990s version from Valiant, Magnus first attempts to disarm or shut down a robot before resorting to violence. The folks at Valiant Comics did touch-ups on the original work before reprinting the series, including recoloring each issue.

1 ❑ Jan 1992 Cover: 1.95 **NM** value: **2.00**
Circ: CapCity orders: **11,900**
2 ❑ Feb 1992 Cover: 1.95 **NM** value: **2.00**
Circ: CapCity orders: **9,300**
3 ❑ Mar 1992 Cover: 1.95 **NM** value: **2.00**
Circ: CapCity orders: **8,100**
4 ❑ Apr 1992 Cover: 1.95 **NM** value: **2.00**
Circ: CapCity orders: **6,800**

VINTAGE PACK — Marvel
1 ❑ Cover: 19.95 **NM** value: **Cover or less**
No issue number. • 20 Marvel comic books reprinted

VIOLATOR — Image

Violator is Spawn's oldest and most deadly enemy. He appears to be a fat, psychotic clown — dangerous enough in his own right. However, he's also a powerful demon from Hell and can revert to his true form whenever serious carnage is called for.

As this three-issue mini-series begins, however, Violator has been stripped of his powers, his feet encased in concrete, and mobsters are about to dump him into the lake. But for a former demon of Violator's caliber, these are merely minor obstacles. What follows is a horrific, bloody, but strangely engrossing (and sometimes funny) story. Violator runs from mobsters, "The Admonisher" (a gun-crazy parody of The Punisher), and his fellow demons.

This series features a great script by Alan Moore, as well as striking art by rising star Bart Sears.

1 ❑ May 1994 Cover: 1.95 **NM** value: **2.50**
Circ: CapCity orders: **99,200** • **CGC:** 5 graded, best 9.8
2 ❑ Jun 1994 Cover: 1.95 **NM** value: **2.50**
Circ: CapCity orders: **76,025**
3 ❑ Jul 1994 Cover: 1.95 **NM** value: **2.50**
Circ: CapCity orders: **69,200**

VIOLATOR VS. BADROCK — Image
1 ❑ May 1995 Cover: 2.50 **NM** value: **Cover or less**
Circ: CapCity orders: **43,375**
1/A ❑ May 1995 Cover: 2.50 **NM** value: **Cover or less**
2 ❑ Jun 1995 Cover: 2.50 **NM** value: **Cover or less**
Circ: CapCity orders: **36,725**
3 ❑ Jul 1995 Cover: 2.50 **NM** value: **Cover or less**
Circ: CapCity orders: **24,500**
4 ❑ Aug 1995 Cover: 2.50 **NM** value: **Cover or less**
Circ: CapCity orders: **29,000**
Bk 1❑ Dec 1995 Cover: 9.95 **NM** value: **Cover or less**

VIOLENT MESSIAHS — Hurricane
On Rankor Island, a city the size of Manhattan, it's the criminals who live in fear — of a mysterious, hulking vigilante known as Citizen Pain. All police efforts to stop his violent war on crime are hampered by public approval of his actions. Throw in another costumed vigilante known as Scalpel and a serial killer known as Family Man, as well as drug dealers and kidnappers, and you've got a troubled city where no one feels truly safe. Detective Cheri Major, commander of special task force "Violent Messiahs," has her job further complicated, when Citizen Pain contacts her, simultaneously aiding her cause while resisting capture. Pain has secrets he can't share, including a wheelchair-bound father who, nonetheless, exerts control over him.

Writer Joshua Dysart and artist William O'Neill create a gloomy black-and-white world within which it's easy to quickly identify, and sympathize with, the major characters whose motivations and morals are cloudy and uncertain at best.

1 ❑ Jul 1997, b&w Cover: 2.95 **NM** value: **Cover or less**
2 ❑ 1997 Cover: 2.95 **NM** value: **Cover or less**
3 ❑ 1997 Cover: 2.95 **NM** value: **Cover or less**

VIOLENT MESSIAHS (2ND SERIES) — Image
1 ❑ Jun 2000 Cover: 2.95 **NM** value: **Cover or less**
Circ: Diamd. preorders: **30,675** • **CGC:** 3 graded, best 9.6
2 ❑ Aug 2000 Cover: 2.95 **NM** value: **Cover or less**
Circ: Diamd. preorders: **16,498** • **CGC:** 1 graded, best 9.8
3 ❑ Sep 2000 Cover: 2.95 **NM** value: **Cover or less**
Circ: Diamd. preorders: **11,302**
4 ❑ Nov 2000 Cover: 2.95 **NM** value: **Cover or less**
Circ: Diamd. preorders: **10,470**
5 ❑ Jan 2001 Cover: 2.95 **NM** value: **Cover or less**
Circ: Diamd. preorders: **9,982**

VIOLENT TALES — Death
1 ❑ Nov 1997, b&w Cover: 2.95 **NM** value: **Cover or less**

VIP — TV
1 ❑ ca. 2000 Cover: 2.95 **NM** value: **Cover or less**
• **CGC:** 1 graded, best 9.8
📖 Val's Life **A:** Tom Grindberg; Mtom Derenick **W:** Franco Aureliani; C.J. Henderson; Marc Patten

VIPER — DC
1 ❑ Aug 1994 Cover: 1.95 **NM** value: **Cover or less**
Circ: CapCity orders: **6,650**
2 ❑ Sep 1994 Cover: 1.95 **NM** value: **Cover or less**
Circ: CapCity orders: **5,600**
3 ❑ Oct 1994 Cover: 1.95 **NM** value: **Cover or less**
Circ: CapCity orders: **3,900**
4 ❑ Nov 1994 Cover: 1.95 **NM** value: **Cover or less**
Circ: CapCity orders: **3,200**

VIRTEX — Oktomica
0 ❑ Oct 1998 Cover: 1.50 **NM** value: **Cover or less**
Circ: Diamd. preorders: **1,793**
1 ❑ Dec 1998 Cover: 2.50 **NM** value: **Cover or less**
Circ: Diamd. preorders: **2,635**
📖 Divine Intervention, Part 1 **A:** Kano **W:** Mike Baron; Casey Lau; Jeff Kwan
2 ❑ Jan 1999 Cover: 2.50 **NM** value: **Cover or less**
Circ: Diamd. preorders: **2,407**
📖 Divine Intervention, Part 2 **A:** Kano
3 ❑ 1999 Cover: 2.50 **NM** value: **Cover or less**
Circ: Diamd. preorders: **2,648**
📖 Divine Intervention, Part 3 **A:** Kano
Ash 1❑1999 **NM** value: **1.00**

VIRTUA FIGHTER — Marvel
1 ❑ Aug 1995 Cover: 2.95 **NM** value: **Cover or less**

VIRTUAL BANG — Ironcat
1 ❑ Cover: 2.95 **NM** value: **Cover or less**
Circ: Diamd. preorders: **2,955**
2 ❑ Cover: 2.95 **NM** value: **Cover or less**
Circ: Diamd. preorders: **2,207**

VIRUS — Dark Horse
1 ❑ ca. 1993 Cover: 2.50 **NM** value: **Cover or less**
Circ: CapCity orders: **10,675**
2 ❑ ca. 1993 Cover: 2.50 **NM** value: **Cover or less**
Circ: CapCity orders: **7,750**
3 ❑ ca. 1993 Cover: 2.50 **NM** value: **Cover or less**
Circ: CapCity orders: **8,000**
4 ❑ ca. 1994 Cover: 2.50 **NM** value: **Cover or less**
Circ: CapCity orders: **5,700**
Bk 1❑ Jun 1995 Cover: 16.95 **NM** value: **Cover or less**
• Trade Paperback. • Reprints Virus #1-4 **A:** Howard Cobb; Mike Ploog(cover) **W:** Chuck Pfarrer

VISAGE SPECIAL EDITION — Illusion Studios
1 ❑ Aug 1996, b&w Cover: 1.95 **NM** value: **2.00**

VISION, THE — Marvel
1 ❑ Nov 1994 Cover: 1.75 **NM** value: **Cover or less**
Circ: CapCity orders: **19,400**
📖 Dreams and Madmen **A:** Manny Clark **W:** Bob Harras
2 ❑ Dec 1994 Cover: 1.75 **NM** value: **Cover or less**
Circ: CapCity orders: **13,250**
3 ❑ Jan 1995 Cover: 1.75 **NM** value: **Cover or less**
Circ: CapCity orders: **11,450**
📖 Visionary Dreams **A:** Manny Clark **W:** Bob Harras
4 ❑ Feb 1995 Cover: 1.75 **NM** value: **Cover or less**
Circ: CapCity orders: **10,475**

VISION & SCARLET WITCH (VOL. 1) — Marvel
One of Marvel's first wave of limited series, this first Vision and Scarlet Witch series follows the unusual couple on adventures apart from the Avengers — and in suburbia, no less. Problem is, when your life's as convoluted as these characters' are, home life isn't going to be tranquil.

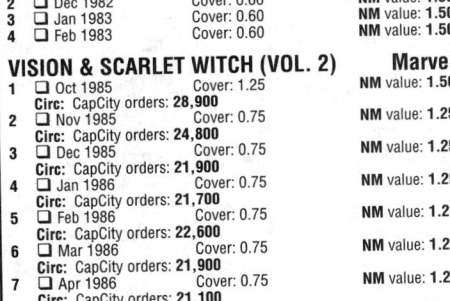

But people expecting these stories to have little effect on continuity were surprised. Issue #4 features a confrontation between the Scarlet Witch, her brother, Quicksilver, and their former leader in the Brotherhood of Evil Mutants, Magneto, and answers a question about the three's relationship that had been lingering for well over a decade. — JJM

1 ❑ Nov 1982 Cover: 0.60 **NM** value: **1.50**
2 ❑ Dec 1982 Cover: 0.60 **NM** value: **1.50**
3 ❑ Jan 1983 Cover: 0.60 **NM** value: **1.50**
4 ❑ Feb 1983 Cover: 0.60 **NM** value: **1.50**

VISION & SCARLET WITCH (VOL. 2) — Marvel
1 ❑ Oct 1985 Cover: 1.25 **NM** value: **1.50**
Circ: CapCity orders: **28,900**
2 ❑ Nov 1985 Cover: 0.75 **NM** value: **1.25**
Circ: CapCity orders: **24,800**
3 ❑ Dec 1985 Cover: 0.75 **NM** value: **1.25**
Circ: CapCity orders: **21,900**
4 ❑ Jan 1986 Cover: 0.75 **NM** value: **1.25**
Circ: CapCity orders: **21,700**
5 ❑ Feb 1986 Cover: 0.75 **NM** value: **1.25**
Circ: CapCity orders: **22,600**
6 ❑ Mar 1986 Cover: 0.75 **NM** value: **1.25**
Circ: CapCity orders: **21,900**
7 ❑ Apr 1986 Cover: 0.75 **NM** value: **1.25**
Circ: CapCity orders: **21,100**
8 ❑ May 1986 Cover: 0.75 **NM** value: **1.25**
Circ: CapCity orders: **20,600**
9 ❑ Jun 1986 Cover: 0.75 **NM** value: **1.25**
Circ: CapCity orders: **19,300**
10 ❑ Jul 1986 Cover: 0.75 **NM** value: **1.25**
Circ: CapCity orders: **18,800**
11 ❑ Aug 1986 Cover: 0.75 **NM** value: **1.25**
Circ: CapCity orders: **18,400**
12 ❑ Sep 1986 Cover: 1.25 **NM** value: **Cover or less**
Circ: CapCity orders: **18,100**

VISIONARIES — Marvel / Star
1 ❑ Jan 1988 Cover: 1.50 **NM** value: **Cover or less**
Circ: CapCity orders: **7,200**
2 ❑ Feb 1988 Cover: 1.00 **NM** value: **Cover or less**
Circ: CapCity orders: **4,200**
3 ❑ Mar 1988 Cover: 1.00 **NM** value: **Cover or less**
Circ: CapCity orders: **5,300**
4 ❑ Apr 1988 Cover: 1.00 **NM** value: **Cover or less**
Circ: CapCity orders: **4,100**
5 ❑ May 1988 Cover: 1.00 **NM** value: **Cover or less**
Circ: CapCity orders: **3,500**
6 ❑ Jun 1988 Cover: 1.00 **NM** value: **Cover or less**
Circ: CapCity orders: **2,700**

VISIONS — Caliber
1 ❑ Cover: 4.95 **NM** value: **Cover or less**

VISIONS: DAVID MACK — Caliber
1 ❑ Cover: 5.95 **NM** value: **Cover or less**

VISIONS OF CURVES — Fantagraphics / Eros
1 ❑ Apr 1994, b&w Cover: 4.95 **NM** value: **Cover or less**
2 ❑ Cover: 4.95 **NM** value: **Cover or less**
3 ❑ May 1995 Cover: 4.95 **NM** value: **Cover or less**
• Sketchbook **A:** Todd Borenstein **W:** Todd Borenstein

CGC-graded: Multiply prices above by **33 for 9.9 M • 16 for 9.8 NM/M • 7 for 9.6 NM+ • 5 for 9.4 NM • 2.5 for 9.2 NM- • 1.5 for 9.0 VF/NM**

VISIONS: R.G. TAYLOR — Caliber

1 ❑ b&w Cover: 2.50 **NM** value: **Cover or less**
No issue number.

VISITATIONS — Image

1 ❑ b&w Cover: 6.95 **NM** value: **Cover or less**
No issue number. • squarebound **A:** C. Scott Morse **W:** C. Scott Morse

VISITOR, THE — Valiant

Who is The Visitor? Why is he here? What does he want?

Those questions follow the mysterious hero throughout this short-lived series, as he deals with people's fears of his alien origins even as he helps mankind in times of direst need. Unlike Superman, who is embraced by Earth's populace in spite of his otherworldly background, The Visitor is not trusted, and his good deeds are only reluctantly accepted by residents of the Valiant Comics universe. Of course, The Visitor's heroics bring him into conflict with the sinister Harada — Valiant's all-around, super-nasty corporate honcho — and his Harbinger Foundation. Entertaining, if somewhat standard, super-hero fare from writer Kevin Van Hook and artist Bernard Chang.

1 ❑ Apr 1995 Cover: 2.50 **NM** value: **Cover or less**
Circ: CapCity orders: **15,700**
📖 Layers Upon Layers **A:** Bernard Chang **W:** Kevin Van Hook
2 ❑ May 1995 Cover: 2.50 **NM** value: **Cover or less**
Circ: CapCity orders: **9,375**
3 ❑ Jun 1995 Cover: 2.50 **NM** value: **Cover or less**
Circ: CapCity orders: **7,500**
• Acclaim begins publishing
4 ❑ Jul 1995 Cover: 2.50 **NM** value: **Cover or less**
Circ: CapCity orders: **6,900**
5 ❑ Jul 1995 Cover: 2.50 **NM** value: **Cover or less**
Circ: CapCity orders: **6,900**
6 ❑ Aug 1995 Cover: 2.50 **NM** value: **Cover or less**
Circ: CapCity orders: **6,225**
7 ❑ Aug 1995 Cover: 2.50 **NM** value: **Cover or less**
Circ: CapCity orders: **6,225**
8 ❑ Sep 1995 Cover: 2.50 **NM** value: **Cover or less**
Circ: CapCity orders: **5,975**
• The Harbinger's identity is revealed
9 ❑ Sep 1995 Cover: 2.50 **NM** value: **Cover or less**
Circ: CapCity orders: **5,925**
10 ❑ Oct 1995 Cover: 2.50 **NM** value: **Cover or less**
Circ: CapCity orders: **5,525**
11 ❑ Oct 1995 Cover: 2.50 **NM** value: **Cover or less**
Circ: CapCity orders: **5,500**
12 ❑ Nov 1995 Cover: 2.50 **NM** value: **Cover or less**
Circ: CapCity orders: **5,825**
13 ❑ Nov 1995 Cover: 2.50 **NM** value: **Cover or less**
Circ: CapCity orders: **5,625**

VISITOR VS. THE VALIANT UNIVERSE, THE — Valiant

1 ❑ Feb 1995 Cover: 2.95 **NM** value: **Cover or less**
Circ: CapCity orders: **14,175**
cardstock cover. 📖 A Stranger in a Strange Land **A:** Bryan Hitch **W:** Kevin VanHook
2 ❑ Mar 1995 Cover: 2.95 **NM** value: **Cover or less**
Circ: CapCity orders: **13,275**
cardstock cover.

VISUAL ASSAULT OMNIBUS — Visual Assault

1 ❑ b&w Cover: 2.50 **NM** value: **Cover or less**
2 ❑ b&w Cover: 2.50 **NM** value: **Cover or less**
3 ❑ b&w Cover: 3.00 **NM** value: **Cover or less**
• Flip-book.

VIXEN 9 — Samson

1 ❑ Cover: 2.50 **NM** value: **Cover or less**
• Flip-book. • no indicia

VIXEN'S KEEP — Mu

Bk 1❑ Nov 1995 Cover: 5.95 **NM** value: **Cover or less**
No issue number. • tpb b&w anthology

VIXEN WARRIOR DIARIES — Raging Rhino

All issues are adults only.

1 ❑ b&w Cover: 2.95 **NM** value: **Cover or less**

VIXEN WARS: VENGEANCE MANIFESTO — Raging Rhino

All issues are adults only.

1 ❑ b&w Cover: 2.95 **NM** value: **Cover or less**
2 ❑ b&w Cover: 2.95 **NM** value: **Cover or less**
3 ❑ b&w Cover: 2.95 **NM** value: **Cover or less**
4 ❑ b&w Cover: 2.95 **NM** value: **Cover or less**
5 ❑ b&w Cover: 2.95 **NM** value: **Cover or less**

VIXEN WARS, WAR WITHOUT WALLS, THE — Raging Rhino

1 ❑ Cover: 2.95 **NM** value: **Cover or less**
2 ❑ Cover: 2.95 **NM** value: **Cover or less**
3 ❑ Cover: 2.95 **NM** value: **Cover or less**
📖 War Without Walls **A:** Rick Lyon **W:** David Cirone

VOGUE — Image

1 ❑ Oct 1995 Cover: 2.50 **NM** value: **Cover or less**
Circ: CapCity orders: **13,300**
1/A ❑ Oct 1995 Cover: 2.50 **NM** value: **Cover or less**
alternate cover. **A:** Marat Mychaels; Andy Park **W:** Jim Valentino; Brian Witten; Cy Voris
2 ❑ Nov 1995 Cover: 2.50 **NM** value: **Cover or less**
3 ❑ Dec 1995 Cover: 2.50 **NM** value: **Cover or less**
4 ❑ Jan 1996 Cover: 2.50 **NM** value: **Cover or less**

VOID INDIGO — Marvel / Epic

Beginning from a story in Marvel Graphic Novel #11, Void Indigo is an intense tale of fantasy and vengeance. It begins before recorded time, when the world was ruled by a race of Dark Lords. In a desperate attempt to stave off a barbarian invasion, the Dark Lords seized the barbarian leader and his wife, brutally torturing and slaying them. Despite their cruel success, the Dark Lords were unable to save their civilization from destruction.

Now, centuries later, the spirit of the slain barbarian leader once again walks the Earth (albeit in an alien's body). The spirit seeks bloody vengeance on the reincarnations of the Dark Lords that slew him and his wife so long ago — no matter whose bodies the miscreants now inhabit.

1 ❑ Nov 1984 Cover: 1.50 **NM** value: **2.00**
• Continued from Marvel Graphic Novel **A:** Val Mayerick
2 ❑ Mar 1985 Cover: 1.50 **NM** value: **2.00**

VOLCANIC NIGHTS — Palliard

All issues are adults only.

1 ❑ b&w Cover: 2.95 **NM** value: **Cover or less**

VOLCANIC REVOLVER — Oni

1 ❑ Jan 1999, b&w Cover: 2.95 **NM** value: **Cover or less**
Circ: Diamd. preorders: **4,218**
2 ❑ Jan 1999, b&w Cover: 2.95 **NM** value: **Cover or less**
Circ: Diamd. preorders: **3,018**
3 ❑ Mar 1999, b&w Cover: 2.95 **NM** value: **Cover or less**
Circ: Diamd. preorders: **3,077**

VOLTRON — Solson

1 ❑ Cover: 0.75 **NM** value: **1.00**
Circ: CapCity orders: **10,125** • **CGC:** 1 graded, best 9.6
2 ❑ Cover: 0.75 **NM** value: **1.00**
Circ: CapCity orders: **8,775**
3 ❑ Cover: 0.75 **NM** value: **1.00**
Circ: CapCity orders: **8,750**

VOLUNTEER COMICS SUMMER LINE-UP '96 — Volunteer

1 ❑ Sum 1996, b&w Cover: 2.95 **NM** value: **Cover or less**
No issue number. • previews

VOLUNTEERS QUEST FOR DREAMS LOST — Literacy

1 ❑ b&w Cover: 2.00 **NM** value: **Cover or less**
• Turtles; Trollords

VON FANGE BROTHERS-GREEN HAIR AND RED "S'S", THE — Mikey-Sized Comics

1 ❑ Jul 1996, b&w Cover: 1.75 **NM** value: **Cover or less**
No issue number.

VON FANGE BROTHERS-THE UNCOMMONS, THE — Mikey-Sized Comics

1 ❑ Oct 1996, b&w Cover: 1.75 **NM** value: **Cover or less**
No issue number.

VONPYRE — Eyeful

1 ❑ Cover: 2.95 **NM** value: **Cover or less**
📖 VonPyre; The Lindy Jax and the Old Tin Box **A:** Randy Zimmerman; Brian Tatge **W:** Randy Zimmerman; Brian Tatge

VOODOO CHILD: THE ILLUSTRATED LEGEND OF JIMI HENDRIX — Kitchen Sink

1 ❑ Cover: 35.00 **NM** value: **Cover or less**
1/LE❑ Cover: 60.00 **NM** value: **Cover or less**
• Limited, slipcased edition. **A:** Bill Sienkiewicz **W:** Martin L. Green

To find the median price offered on eBay at press time for pre-1990 **CGC-graded comics**, multiply by:

9.9 (M): **33**	8.5 (VF+): **1.25**
9.8(NM/M): **16**	8.0 (VF): **0.85**
9.6 (NM+): **7**	7.5 (VF-): **0.6**
9.4 (NM): **5**	7.0 (F/VF): **0.5**
9.2 (NM-): **2.5**	6.5 (F+): **0.4**
9.0 (VF/NM): **1.5**	6.0 (F-): **0.33**

These are median prices of all CGC comics auctioned on eBay; prices for individual issues will vary.

VOODOO (FARRELL) — Farrell

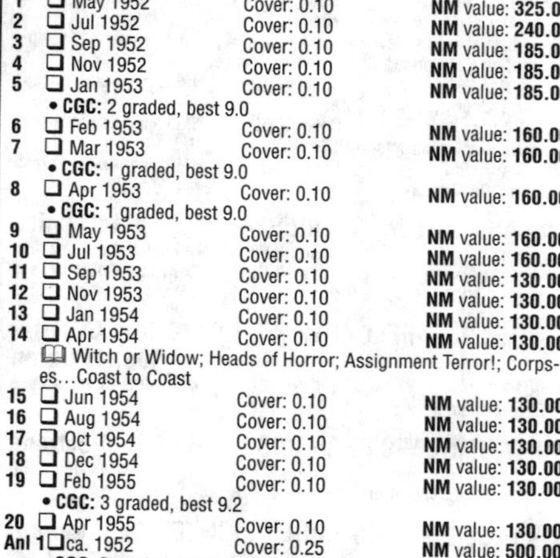

Voodoo is a rarity: a horror anthology series that manages to break out from under the shadow of E.C. titles like Tales from the Crypt, while avoiding the predictable style of storytelling exemplified by Marvel's Tales of Suspense or Monsters on the Prowl. Voodoo is ... well, it's just plain weird.

Take the story "Corpses ... Coast to Coast!" in which a gravedigger strike gives a man the ghoulish idea of having the unburied bodies shipped to him. There, they are transformed into zombies in his service, an ever-growing army which works to raise more zombies under his control. Eventually, the zombies work to sweep the elections! Another ghoulish tale offers an alternate rendition of the "little old lady who lived in a shoe." Then there's "Head of Horror," in which a scientist studying methods of shrinking heads tries his technique on his own faithless wife and her lover.

1 ❑ May 1952 Cover: 0.10 **NM** value: **325.00**
2 ❑ Jul 1952 Cover: 0.10 **NM** value: **240.00**
3 ❑ Sep 1952 Cover: 0.10 **NM** value: **185.00**
4 ❑ Nov 1952 Cover: 0.10 **NM** value: **185.00**
5 ❑ Jan 1953 Cover: 0.10 **NM** value: **185.00**
• **CGC:** 2 graded, best 9.0
6 ❑ Feb 1953 Cover: 0.10 **NM** value: **160.00**
7 ❑ Mar 1953 Cover: 0.10 **NM** value: **160.00**
• **CGC:** 1 graded, best 9.0
8 ❑ Apr 1953 Cover: 0.10 **NM** value: **160.00**
• **CGC:** 1 graded, best 9.0
9 ❑ May 1953 Cover: 0.10 **NM** value: **160.00**
10 ❑ Jul 1953 Cover: 0.10 **NM** value: **160.00**
11 ❑ Sep 1953 Cover: 0.10 **NM** value: **130.00**
12 ❑ Nov 1953 Cover: 0.10 **NM** value: **130.00**
13 ❑ Jan 1954 Cover: 0.10 **NM** value: **130.00**
14 ❑ Apr 1954 Cover: 0.10 **NM** value: **130.00**
📖 Witch or Widow; Heads of Horror; Assignment Terror!; Corpses...Coast to Coast
15 ❑ Jun 1954 Cover: 0.10 **NM** value: **130.00**
16 ❑ Aug 1954 Cover: 0.10 **NM** value: **130.00**
17 ❑ Oct 1954 Cover: 0.10 **NM** value: **130.00**
18 ❑ Dec 1954 Cover: 0.10 **NM** value: **130.00**
19 ❑ Feb 1955 Cover: 0.10 **NM** value: **130.00**
• **CGC:** 3 graded, best 9.2
20 ❑ Apr 1955 Cover: 0.10 **NM** value: **130.00**
Anl 1❑ ca. 1952 Cover: 0.25 **NM** value: **500.00**
• **CGC:** 3 graded, best 7.5

VOODOO (IMAGE) — Image

1 ❑ Nov 1997 Cover: 2.50 **NM** value: **Cover or less**
Circ: Diamd. preorders: **44,715**
📖 Legba **A:** Michael Lopez **W:** Alan Moore
2 ❑ Dec 1997 Cover: 2.50 **NM** value: **Cover or less**
Circ: Diamd. preorders: **41,384**
📖 Erzulie **A:** Al Rio; Michael Lopez **W:** Alan Moore
3 ❑ Jan 1998 Cover: 2.50 **NM** value: **Cover or less**
Circ: Diamd. preorders: **37,470**
📖 Samedi **A:** Al Rio; Michael Lopez **W:** Alan Moore
4 ❑ Mar 1998 Cover: 2.50 **NM** value: **Cover or less**
Circ: Diamd. preorders: **35,496**
📖 Damballa **A:** Al Rio; Michael Lopez **W:** Alan Moore
Bk 1❑ ca. 1999 Cover: 9.95 **NM** value: **Cover or less**
No issue number. • Trade Paperback. • Dancing in the Dark; collects mini-series **A:** Al Rio; Michael Lopez **W:** Alan Moore

VOODOO INK — Deja-Vu

0 ❑ b&w Cover: 1.95 **NM** value: **Cover or less**
1 ❑ b&w Cover: 1.95 **NM** value: **Cover or less**
2 ❑ b&w Cover: 1.95 **NM** value: **Cover or less**
3 ❑ b&w Cover: 1.95 **NM** value: **Cover or less**
4 ❑ b&w Cover: 1.95 **NM** value: **Cover or less**
5 ❑ b&w Cover: 1.95 **NM** value: **Cover or less**

VOODOOM — Oni

1 ❑ Jun 2000, b&w Cover: 4.95 **NM** value: **Cover or less**
Circ: Diamd. preorders: **3,371**
No issue number. • smaller than regular comic book **A:** Jim Mahfood **W:** Scott Morse

VOODOO•ZEALOT: SKIN TRADE — Image

1 ❑ Aug 1995 Cover: 4.95 **NM** value: **Cover or less**
No issue number. One-shot. **A:** Michael Lopez **W:** Steven Seagle

VORTEX (COMICO) — Comico

1 ❑ Cover: 2.50 **NM** value: **Cover or less**
Circ: CapCity orders: **4,950**
2 ❑ Cover: 2.50 **NM** value: **Cover or less**
Circ: CapCity orders: **4,475**
3 ❑ Cover: 2.50 **NM** value: **Cover or less**
Circ: CapCity orders: **3,975**
• Exists?
4 ❑ Cover: 2.50 **NM** value: **Cover or less**
Circ: CapCity orders: **3,775**
• Exists?

VORTEX (ENTITY) — Entity

1 ❑ Jan 1996 Cover: 2.95 **NM** value: **Cover or less**

VORTEX (HALL OF HEROES) — Hall of Heroes

1 ❑ b&w Cover: 2.50 **NM** value: **Cover or less**
2 ❑ Cover: 2.50 **NM** value: **Cover or less**
3 ❑ Dec 1993 Cover: 2.50 **NM** value: **Cover or less**

Other grades: Multiply prices above by **1.5 for Mint • 2/3 for Very Fine • 1/3 for Fine • 1/5 for Very Good • 1/8 for Good**

📖 Run for Cover **A:** Matt Martin **W:** Matt Martin
4 ❑ Feb 1994 Cover: 2.50 **NM** value: **Cover or less**
📖 Drx Kilbourne **A:** Matt Martin **W:** Matt Martin
5 ❑ Apr 1994 Cover: 2.50 **NM** value: **Cover or less**
📖 Into The Dark **A:** Matt Martin **W:** Matt Martin
6 ❑ Dec 1994 Cover: 2.50 **NM** value: **Cover or less**
📖 Machine Gun Messiah **A:** Matt Martin **W:** Matt Martin

VORTEX THE WONDER MULE — Cutting Edge
1 ❑ b&w Cover: 2.95 **NM** value: **Cover or less**
2 ❑ b&w Cover: 2.95 **NM** value: **Cover or less**

VORTEX (VORTEX) — Vortex
1 ❑ Nov 1982 Cover: 1.75 **NM** value: **2.00**
📖 In the Lion's Den; Trip to Glory **A:** Peter Hsu; Don Marshall **W:** Don Marshall; Terry Hanover
2 ❑ Cover: 1.75 **NM** value: **2.00**
3 ❑ May 1983 Cover: 1.95 **NM** value: **2.00**
📖 The Magus; Fantastic Fear; Ice; Eve; Cris, What Crisis? **A:** Nick Poliwko; Bryan Lee; Ken Steacy; Joe Haidar **W:** Nick Poliwko; Bryan Lee; Ken Steacy; Joe Haidar
4 ❑ Cover: 1.75 **NM** value: **2.00**
5 ❑ Cover: 1.75 **NM** value: **2.00**
6 ❑ Cover: 1.75 **NM** value: **2.00**
📖 The Studio; Public Interest; Two Can Play; Hot Mona; The Observer **A:** Michael T. Gilbert; Dave Ross; Dan Day; Don Marshall; Jeff Morgan **W:** Michael T. Gilbert; Dave Ross; Dan Day; Don Marshall; Jeff Morgan
7 ❑ Cover: 1.75 **NM** value: **2.00**
8 ❑ Cover: 1.75 **NM** value: **2.00**
9 ❑ Cover: 1.75 **NM** value: **2.00**
10 ❑ Sep 1984 Cover: 1.75 **NM** value: **2.00**
📖 Elderberry Down; New Ruins for Old; Prologue; The Library; Johny Slaughter **A:** Dean Motter; Gene Day; Dan Day; Ronn Sutton; Don Marshall; Jeff Morgan **W:** Dean Motter; Gene Day; Dan Day; Ronn Sutton; Don Marshall; Jeff Morgan
11 ❑ Cover: 1.75 **NM** value: **Cover or less**
12 ❑ Cover: 1.75 **NM** value: **Cover or less**
13 ❑ Cover: 1.75 **NM** value: **Cover or less**
14 ❑ Cover: 1.75 **NM** value: **Cover or less**
15 ❑ Cover: 1.75 **NM** value: **Cover or less**

VOX — Apple
1 ❑ Jun 1989, b&w Cover: 1.95 **NM** value: **2.00**
📖 Hypehopper **A:** Aaron McClellan; John Byrne(cover) **C:** John Byrne **W:** Angela Harris
2 ❑ Cover: 2.25 **NM** value: **Cover or less**
3 ❑ Cover: 2.25 **NM** value: **Cover or less**
4 ❑ Cover: 2.25 **NM** value: **Cover or less**
5 ❑ Cover: 2.25 **NM** value: **Cover or less**
6 ❑ Cover: 2.25 **NM** value: **Cover or less**
7 ❑ Cover: 2.25 **NM** value: **Cover or less**

VOYAGE TO THE BOTTOM OF THE SEA — Gold Key
1 ❑ Dec 1964 Cover: 0.12 **NM** value: **50.00**
• **CGC:** 1 graded, best 7.0
📖 The Last Survivor
2 ❑ ca. 1965 Cover: 0.12 **NM** value: **40.00**
• **CGC:** 1 graded, best 9.0
3 ❑ Oct 1965 Cover: 0.12 **NM** value: **30.00**
• **CGC:** 1 graded, best 7.5
4 ❑ May 1966 Cover: 0.12 **NM** value: **30.00**
5 ❑ Aug 1966 Cover: 0.12 **NM** value: **30.00**
• **CGC:** 1 graded, best 9.0
6 ❑ Nov 1966 Cover: 0.12 **NM** value: **22.00**
7 ❑ Feb 1967 Cover: 0.12 **NM** value: **22.00**
Circ: Statement: **243,688**
8 ❑ May 1967 Cover: 0.12 **NM** value: **22.00**
Circ: Statement: **243,688**
9 ❑ Aug 1967 Cover: 0.12 **NM** value: **22.00**
Circ: Statement: **243,688**
10 ❑ Nov 1967 Cover: 0.12 **NM** value: **22.00**
Circ: Statement: **243,688**
11 ❑ Feb 1968 Cover: 0.12 **NM** value: **16.00**
12 ❑ May 1968 Cover: 0.12 **NM** value: **16.00**
13 ❑ Aug 1968 Cover: 0.12 **NM** value: **16.00**
14 ❑ Nov 1968 Cover: 0.12 **NM** value: **16.00**
15 ❑ Feb 1969 Cover: 0.12 **NM** value: **10.00**
16 ❑ May 1969 Cover: 0.12 **NM** value: **10.00**
final issue.

VOYAGE TO THE DEEP — Dell
1 ❑ Sep 1962 Cover: 0.12 **NM** value: **28.00**
Painted cover.
2 ❑ May 1963 Cover: 0.12 **NM** value: **14.00**
Painted cover.
3 ❑ Cover: 0.12 **NM** value: **14.00**
Painted cover.
4 ❑ Nov 1964 Cover: 0.12 **NM** value: **14.00**
Painted cover.

VOYEUR, THE — Aircel
All issues are adults only.
1 ❑ b&w Cover: 2.50 **NM** value: **Cover or less**
2 ❑ b&w Cover: 2.50 **NM** value: **Cover or less**
3 ❑ b&w Cover: 2.50 **NM** value: **Cover or less**
4 ❑ Cover: 2.95 **NM** value: **Cover or less**

VROOM SOCKO — Slave Labor
1 ❑ Nov 1993 Cover: 2.50 **NM** value: **Cover or less**
• reprints strips from Deadline U.K. **A:** Evan Dorkin

VULGAR VINCE — Throb
1 ❑ Cover: 1.75 **NM** value: **Cover or less**
📖 Professor Groinwauld's Robot of Death! **A:** Patrick Finney **W:** Patrick Finney

VULTURES OF WHAPETON — Conquest
1 ❑ b&w Cover: 2.95 **NM** value: **Cover or less**

W — Good
1 ❑ Nov 1996 Cover: 2.95 **NM** value: **Cover or less**
Circ: CapCity orders: **6,180** Diamd. preorders: **2,842**

WABBIT WAMPAGE — Amazing
1 ❑ Cover: 1.95 **NM** value: **Cover or less**

WACKY ADVENTURES OF CRACKY — Gold Key
1 ❑ Dec 1972 Cover: 0.15 **NM** value: **8.00**
2 ❑ Mar 1973 Cover: 0.15 **NM** value: **5.00**
3 ❑ Jun 1973 Cover: 0.20 **NM** value: **4.00**
4 ❑ Sep 1973 Cover: 0.20 **NM** value: **4.00**
5 ❑ Dec 1973 Cover: 0.20 **NM** value: **4.00**
6 ❑ Mar 1974 Cover: 0.20 **NM** value: **3.00**
7 ❑ Jun 1974 Cover: 0.20 **NM** value: **3.00**
8 ❑ Sep 1974 Cover: 0.25 **NM** value: **3.00**
9 ❑ Dec 1974 Cover: 0.25 **NM** value: **3.00**
📖 Out of Focus Hocus-Pocus; The Telltale Tattler; The Worst-Aid Kit; The Dirty Jersy
10 ❑ Mar 1975 Cover: 0.25 **NM** value: **3.00**
11 ❑ Jun 1975 Cover: 0.25 **NM** value: **3.00**
12 ❑ Sep 1975 Cover: 0.25 **NM** value: **3.00**

WACKY RACES — Gold Key
1 ❑ Aug 1969 Cover: 0.15 **NM** value: **35.00**
2 ❑ Feb 1971 Cover: 0.15 **NM** value: **22.00**
3 ❑ May 1971 Cover: 0.15 **NM** value: **18.00**
4 ❑ Aug 1971 Cover: 0.15 **NM** value: **18.00**
📖 Beat the Clock Through Yellowrock; Follow Through to Yoo Hoo
5 ❑ Nov 1971 Cover: 0.15 **NM** value: **18.00**
6 ❑ Feb 1972 Cover: 0.15 **NM** value: **18.00**
7 ❑ May 1972 Cover: 0.15 **NM** value: **18.00**

WACKY SQUIRREL — Dark Horse
Wacky Squirrel was a black-and-white humor title published by Dark Horse comics in 1987. The series chronicled the silly adventures of a maniacally slapstick, cartoon squirrel. In the first issue, for instance, Wacky tracks down none other than Boris the Bear, the homicidal cartoon bear who wants to eliminate all comics characters ever created so that he can have the best sales.

Wacky is a lovable character with an interesting supporting cast. The series was written by Dark Horse Publisher Mike Richardson and Jim Bradrick.

1 ❑ 1987b&w Cover: 2.00**NM** value: **Cover or less**
2 ❑ 1988 Cover: 1.75 **NM** value: **2.00**
3 ❑ 1988 Cover: 1.75 **NM** value: **2.00**
4 ❑ Oct 1988 Cover: 1.75 **NM** value: **2.00**
SE 1❑ Oct 1987 Cover: 1.75 **NM** value: **2.00**
• Flip-book. • Halloween Adventure Special **A:** Jim Bradrick **W:** Jim Bradrick; Mike Richardson ★ Appearance of Mr. Monster.
Smr 1❑ Jul 1987 Cover: 2.00 **NM** value: **Cover or less**
• Summer Fun Special

WACKY WITCH — Gold Key
1 ❑ Jan 1971 Cover: 0.15 **NM** value: **12.00**
2 ❑ Apr 1971 Cover: 0.15 **NM** value: **7.00**
3 ❑ Jul 1971 Cover: 0.15 **NM** value: **5.00**
4 ❑ Oct 1971 Cover: 0.15 **NM** value: **5.00**
5 ❑ Jan 1972 Cover: 0.15 **NM** value: **5.00**
6 ❑ Apr 1972 Cover: 0.15 **NM** value: **4.00**
7 ❑ Jul 1972 Cover: 0.15 **NM** value: **4.00**
8 ❑ Oct 1972 Cover: 0.15 **NM** value: **4.00**
9 ❑ Jan 1973 Cover: 0.15 **NM** value: **4.00**
10 ❑ Apr 1973 Cover: 0.15 **NM** value: **4.00**
11 ❑ Jul 1973 Cover: 0.20 **NM** value: **3.00**
12 ❑ Oct 1973 Cover: 0.20 **NM** value: **3.00**
13 ❑ Jan 1974 Cover: 0.20 **NM** value: **3.00**
14 ❑ Apr 1974 Cover: 0.20 **NM** value: **3.00**
15 ❑ Jul 1974 Cover: 0.20 **NM** value: **3.00**
📖 Two Kings on One Throne is Crowded; Sir Turtle's last Battle; The Outside-The-Castle-Caper; Whatsoever a Night Rips... Somebody Must Sew; Squeaky's Medieval Diary;
16 ❑ Oct 1974 Cover: 0.25 **NM** value: **3.00**
17 ❑ Jan 1975 Cover: 0.25 **NM** value: **3.00**
18 ❑ Apr 1975 Cover: 0.25 **NM** value: **3.00**
19 ❑ Jul 1975 Cover: 0.25 **NM** value: **3.00**
20 ❑ Oct 1975 Cover: 0.25 **NM** value: **3.00**
21 ❑ Jan 1976 Cover: 0.25 **NM** value: **3.00**

WAGON TRAIN (DELL) — Dell
4 ❑ Jan 1960 Cover: 0.10 **NM** value: **40.00**
• **CGC:** 1 graded, best 9.2
5 ❑ Apr 1960 Cover: 0.10 **NM** value: **40.00**
• **CGC:** 1 graded, best 8.0
6 ❑ Jul 1960 Cover: 0.10 **NM** value: **40.00**
7 ❑ Oct 1960 Cover: 0.10 **NM** value: **40.00**
8 ❑ Jan 1961 Cover: 0.10 **NM** value: **40.00**
9 ❑ Apr 1961 Cover: 0.10 **NM** value: **40.00**
10 ❑ Jul 1961 Cover: 0.12 **NM** value: **30.00**
11 ❑ Oct 1961 Cover: 0.12 **NM** value: **30.00**
12 ❑ Jan 1962 Cover: 0.12 **NM** value: **30.00**
13 ❑ Apr 1962 Cover: 0.12 **NM** value: **30.00**

WAGON TRAIN (GOLD KEY) — Gold Key
1 ❑ Jan 1964 Cover: 0.12 **NM** value: **30.00**
2 ❑ Apr 1964 Cover: 0.12 **NM** value: **30.00**
3 ❑ Jul 1964 Cover: 0.12 **NM** value: **30.00**
4 ❑ Oct 1964 Cover: 0.12 **NM** value: **30.00**

WAHH — Frank & Hank
1 ❑ b&w Cover: 2.95 **NM** value: **Cover or less**
cardstock cover. • no indicia **A:** Henry Wolyniec **W:** Henry Wolyniec
2 ❑ b&w Cover: 2.95 **NM** value: **Cover or less**
cardstock cover.

WAHOO MORRIS — Too Hip Gott Go Graphics
1 ❑ Jun 1998, b&w Cover: 2.75 **NM** value: **Cover or less**

WAITING FOR THE END OF THE WORLD — Rodent
1 ❑ **NM** value: **1.00**
2 ❑ **NM** value: **1.00**
3 ❑ **NM** value: **1.00**
📖 On the Road to Ragnorak **A:** F. Andrew Taylor **W:** F. Andrew Taylor

WAITING PLACE, THE — Slave Labor
1 ❑ Apr 1997 Cover: 2.95 **NM** value: **Cover or less**
2 ❑ May 1997 Cover: 2.95 **NM** value: **Cover or less**
3 ❑ Jun 1997 Cover: 2.95 **NM** value: **Cover or less**
4 ❑ Jul 1997 Cover: 2.95 **NM** value: **Cover or less**
5 ❑ Aug 1997 Cover: 2.95 **NM** value: **Cover or less**
6 ❑ Sep 1997 Cover: 2.95 **NM** value: **Cover or less**

WALDO WORLD — Fantagraphics
1 ❑ Cover: 2.50 **NM** value: **Cover or less**
📖 Milton in College **A:** Simon Deitch **W:** Simon Deitch
2 ❑ Cover: 2.50 **NM** value: **Cover or less**

WALKING DEAD, THE — Aircel
1 ❑ Cover: 2.25 **NM** value: **Cover or less**
2 ❑ Cover: 2.25 **NM** value: **Cover or less**
3 ❑ Cover: 2.25 **NM** value: **Cover or less**
4 ❑ Cover: 2.25 **NM** value: **Cover or less**
SE 1❑ b&w Cover: 2.25 **NM** value: **Cover or less**
📖 Zombie Special

WALK THROUGH OCTOBER — Caliber
1 ❑ b&w Cover: 2.95 **NM** value: **Cover or less**

WALL OF FLESH — AC
1 ❑ b&w Cover: 2.95 **NM** value: **3.50**

WALLY — Gold Key
1 ❑ Dec 1962 Cover: 0.12 **NM** value: **20.00**
• **CGC:** 1 graded, best 9.2
2 ❑ Mar 1963 Cover: 0.12 **NM** value: **15.00**
3 ❑ Jun 1963 Cover: 0.12 **NM** value: **15.00**
4 ❑ Sep 1963 Cover: 0.12 **NM** value: **15.00**

WALLY THE WIZARD — Marvel / Star
Wally is an apprentice to the great wizard Marlin — not Merlin, mind you: Marlin doesn't believe in most of that sorcerous poppycock that his brother Merlin goes for. Marlin's really more of a scientist, although his apprentice is still fascinated by all things magical.

Wally is a good-hearted sort who befriends dragons and always lends a hand to those in need. Although not a great wizard yet, he uses his bravery and ingenuity to save the kingdom from all manner of nasties, such as the nefarious Vastar the Vile and his mechanized locusts.

This whimsical series was one of the few original Marvel creations that was featured in its Star line of children's comics. (Most others, such as Visionaries or Foofur, were licensed from TV cartoon shows.) Wally the Wizard ran for a dozen issues, concluding in 1986.

1 ❑ Apr 1985 Cover: 0.65 **NM** value: **1.00**
2 ❑ May 1985 Cover: 0.65 **NM** value: **1.00**
Circ: CapCity orders: **4,300**
3 ❑ Jun 1985 Cover: 0.65 **NM** value: **1.00**
Circ: CapCity orders: **3,800**
4 ❑ Jul 1985 Cover: 0.65 **NM** value: **1.00**
Circ: CapCity orders: **3,200**
5 ❑ Aug 1985 Cover: 0.65 **NM** value: **1.00**
Circ: CapCity orders: **2,800**
6 ❑ Sep 1985 Cover: 0.65 **NM** value: **1.00**
Circ: CapCity orders: **2,500**
7 ❑ Oct 1985 Cover: 0.65 **NM** value: **1.00**
Circ: CapCity orders: **2,000**
8 ❑ Nov 1985 Cover: 0.65 **NM** value: **1.00**
Circ: CapCity orders: **2,400**
9 ❑ Dec 1985 Cover: 0.65 **NM** value: **1.00**
Circ: CapCity orders: **1,600**
10 ❑ Jan 1986 Cover: 0.65 **NM** value: **1.00**
Circ: CapCity orders: **1,500**
11 ❑ Feb 1986 Cover: 0.65 **NM** value: **1.00**
Circ: CapCity orders: **1,500**
12 ❑ Mar 1986 Cover: 0.65 **NM** value: **1.00**
Circ: CapCity orders: **1,450**
final issue.

WALT DISNEY GIANT — Gladstone
1 ❑ Sep 1995 Cover: 2.25 **NM** value: **Cover or less**
Circ: CapCity orders: **6,275** • **CGC:** 1 graded, best 9.8
newsprint cover. 📖 Hearts of the Yukon **A:** Don Rosa

CGC-graded: Multiply prices above by **33 for 9.9 M • 16 for 9.8 NM/M • 7 for 9.6 NM+ • 5 for 9.4 NM • 2.5 for 9.2 NM- • 1.5 for 9.0 VF/NM**

2 ❑ Nov 1995 Cover: 2.25 **NM** value: **Cover or less**
Circ: CapCity orders: **3,675**
newsprint cover. 📖 Mines of King Solomon **A:** Carl Barks
3 ❑ Jan 1996 Cover: 2.25 **NM** value: **Cover or less**
newsprint cover. 📖 Super Snooper **A:** Carl Barks
4 ❑ Mar 1996 Cover: 2.25 **NM** value: **Cover or less**
newsprint cover. 📖 The Mysterious Stranger • Mickey Mouse
5 ❑ May 1996 Cover: 2.25 **NM** value: **Cover or less**
newsprint cover. • Mickey and Donald
6 ❑ Jul 1996 Cover: 2.25 **NM** value: **Cover or less**
newsprint cover. • Uncle Scrooge and the Junior Woodchucks
7 ❑ Sep 1996 Cover: 2.25 **NM** value: **Cover or less**
newsprint cover. 📖 Micro-Ducks from Outer Space **A:** Carl Barks

WALT DISNEY'S AUTUMN ADVENTURES Disney

1 ❑ Cover: 2.95 **NM** value: **Cover or less**
2 ❑ Cover: 2.95 **NM** value: **Cover or less**

WALT DISNEY'S CHRISTMAS PARADE (DELL) Dell

1 ❑ ca. 1949 Cover: 0.25 **NM** value: **800.00**
2 ❑ ca. 1950 Cover: 0.25 **NM** value: **600.00**
3 ❑ ca. 1951 Cover: 0.25 **NM** value: **200.00**
4 ❑ ca. 1952 Cover: 0.25 **NM** value: **180.00**
5 ❑ ca. 1953 Cover: 0.25 **NM** value: **160.00**
6 ❑ ca. 1954 Cover: 0.25 **NM** value: **140.00**
7 ❑ ca. 1955 Cover: 0.25 **NM** value: **120.00**
8 ❑ ca. 1956 Cover: 0.25 **NM** value: **300.00**
9 ❑ ca. 1958 Cover: 0.25 **NM** value: **300.00**

WALT DISNEY'S CHRISTMAS PARADE (GLADSTONE) Gladstone

1 ❑ Win 1988 Cover: 2.95 **NM** value: **Cover or less**
cardstock cover. **A:** Carl Barks
2 ❑ Win 1989 Cover: 2.95 **NM** value: **Cover or less**

WALT DISNEY'S CHRISTMAS PARADE (GOLD KEY) Gold Key

1 ❑ ca. 1963 Cover: 0.25 **NM** value: **75.00**
2 ❑ Jan 1964 Cover: 0.12 **NM** value: **50.00**
3 ❑ 1965 **NM** value: **50.00**
4 ❑ 1966 **NM** value: **50.00**
5 ❑ Feb 1967 Cover: 0.25 **NM** value: **50.00**
6 ❑ Feb 1968 Cover: 0.25 **NM** value: **50.00**
7 ❑ **NM** value: **50.00**
8 ❑ Jan 1971 Cover: 0.25 **NM** value: **50.00**
9 ❑ Jan 1972 Cover: 0.15 **NM** value: **50.00**

WALT DISNEY'S COMICS AND STORIES Dell

This title was published off and on for more than 50 years, cycling through numerous publishers, from Dell and Gold Key, to Gladstone, to Disney, and back to Gladstone. What didn't change is the timeless quality of these great stories.

Walt Disney's Comics and Stories featured countless Disney characters, including Winnie the Pooh, Chip 'n' Dale, Mickey Mouse, Dumbo, and Goofy. Of course, many regard the highlight of the entire series as being the legendary "Barks Ducks." These were the stories featuring Donald Duck and his assorted duck friends, drawn by the immortal Carl Barks. Even decades later, they have lost none of their power to delight and inspire readers.

After issue #600, Gladstone took the issue off newsstands and switched to an upscale, prestige format for the title. That move, and publishers' difficulties in making a profit with the license, ended the series.

1 ❑ Oct 1940 Cover: 0.10 **NM** value: **16500.00**
• **CGC:** 6 graded, best 6.5
• Extremely rare
2 ❑ Nov 1940 Cover: 0.10 **NM** value: **5500.00**
3 ❑ Dec 1940 Cover: 0.10 **NM** value: **1900.00**
4 ❑ Jan 1941 Cover: 0.10 **NM** value: **1300.00**
5 ❑ Feb 1941 Cover: 0.10 **NM** value: **950.00**
6 ❑ Mar 1941 Cover: 0.10 **NM** value: **850.00**
7 ❑ Apr 1941 Cover: 0.10 **NM** value: **850.00**
8 ❑ May 1941 Cover: 0.10 **NM** value: **715.00**
9 ❑ Jun 1941 Cover: 0.10 **NM** value: **715.00**
10 ❑ Jul 1941 Cover: 0.10 **NM** value: **675.00**
11 ❑ Aug 1941 Cover: 0.10 **NM** value: **600.00**
• **CGC:** 1 graded, best 4.0
12 ❑ Sep 1941 Cover: 0.10 **NM** value: **600.00**
13 ❑ Oct 1941 Cover: 0.10 **NM** value: **600.00**
14 ❑ Nov 1941 Cover: 0.10 **NM** value: **600.00**
15 ❑ Dec 1941 Cover: 0.10 **NM** value: **600.00**
16 ❑ Jan 1942 Cover: 0.10 **NM** value: **525.00**
17 ❑ Feb 1942 Cover: 0.10 **NM** value: **525.00**
18 ❑ Mar 1942 Cover: 0.10 **NM** value: **500.00**
19 ❑ Apr 1942 Cover: 0.10 **NM** value: **475.00**
20 ❑ May 1942 Cover: 0.10 **NM** value: **475.00**
• **CGC:** 1 graded, best 4.0
21 ❑ Jun 1942 Cover: 0.10 **NM** value: **475.00**
22 ❑ Jul 1942 Cover: 0.10 **NM** value: **475.00**
23 ❑ Aug 1942 Cover: 0.10 **NM** value: **475.00**
24 ❑ Sep 1942 Cover: 0.10 **NM** value: **475.00**
• **CGC:** 1 graded, best 9.4
25 ❑ Oct 1942 Cover: 0.10 **NM** value: **475.00**
26 ❑ Nov 1942 Cover: 0.10 **NM** value: **475.00**
• **CGC:** 1 graded, best 8.5
27 ❑ Dec 1942 Cover: 0.10 **NM** value: **475.00**
• **CGC:** 1 graded, best 9.2
28 ❑ Jan 1943 Cover: 0.10 **NM** value: **475.00**
• **CGC:** 1 graded, best 8.0
29 ❑ Feb 1943 Cover: 0.10 **NM** value: **475.00**
• **CGC:** 1 graded, best 9.2
30 ❑ Mar 1943 Cover: 0.10 **NM** value: **475.00**
• **CGC:** 1 graded, best 9.4
31 ❑ Apr 1943 Cover: 0.10 **NM** value: **2850.00**
• **CGC:** 3 graded, best 7.5
• Donald Duck **A:** Carl Barks
32 ❑ May 1943 Cover: 0.10 **NM** value: **1285.00**
• Donald Duck **A:** Carl Barks
33 ❑ Jun 1943 Cover: 0.10 **NM** value: **900.00**
• **CGC:** 5 graded, best 8.5
• Donald Duck **A:** Carl Barks
34 ❑ Jul 1943 Cover: 0.10 **NM** value: **775.00**
• Donald Duck **A:** Carl Barks
35 ❑ Aug 1943 Cover: 0.10 **NM** value: **660.00**
• **CGC:** 1 graded, best 9.4
• Donald Duck **A:** Carl Barks
36 ❑ Sep 1943 Cover: 0.10 **NM** value: **660.00**
• **CGC:** 1 graded, best 7.0
📖 The Mighty Trapper **A:** Carl Barks
37 ❑ Oct 1943 Cover: 0.10 **NM** value: **335.00**
• **CGC:** 1 graded, best 9.0
38 ❑ Nov 1943 Cover: 0.10 **NM** value: **525.00**
📖 Good Neighbors **A:** Carl Barks
39 ❑ Dec 1943 Cover: 0.10 **NM** value: **475.00**
• **CGC:** 1 graded, best 8.0
📖 Salesman Donald **A:** Carl Barks
40 ❑ Jan 1944 Cover: 0.10 **NM** value: **475.00**
📖 Snow Fun **A:** Carl Barks
41 ❑ Feb 1944 Cover: 0.10 **NM** value: **400.00**
📖 The Duck in the Iron Pants **A:** Carl Barks
42 ❑ Mar 1944 Cover: 0.10 **NM** value: **400.00**
📖 Kite Weather **A:** Carl Barks
43 ❑ Apr 1944 Cover: 0.10 **NM** value: **400.00**
📖 Now Showing "Three Dirty Little Ducks" **A:** Carl Barks
44 ❑ May 1944 Cover: 0.10 **NM** value: **400.00**
📖 This Month the Mad Chemist **A:** Carl Barks
45 ❑ Jun 1944 Cover: 0.10 **NM** value: **400.00**
• **CGC:** 1 graded, best 7.5
📖 This Month's Thriller – Rival Boatmen **A:** Carl Barks
46 ❑ Jul 1944 Cover: 0.10 **NM** value: **400.00**
📖 Camera Crazy **A:** Carl Barks
47 ❑ Aug 1944 Cover: 0.10 **NM** value: **375.00**
• Donald Duck **A:** Carl Barks
48 ❑ Sep 1944 Cover: 0.10 **NM** value: **375.00**
• Donald Duck **A:** Carl Barks
49 ❑ Oct 1944 Cover: 0.10 **NM** value: **375.00**
• Donald Duck **A:** Carl Barks
50 ❑ Nov 1944 Cover: 0.10 **NM** value: **375.00**
• Donald Duck **A:** Carl Barks
51 ❑ Dec 1944 Cover: 0.10 **NM** value: **285.00**
• Donald Duck **A:** Carl Barks
52 ❑ Jan 1945 Cover: 0.10 **NM** value: **285.00**
• Donald Duck **A:** Carl Barks
53 ❑ Feb 1945 Cover: 0.10 **NM** value: **285.00**
• Donald Duck **A:** Carl Barks
54 ❑ Mar 1945 Cover: 0.10 **NM** value: **285.00**
• Donald Duck **A:** Carl Barks
55 ❑ Apr 1945 Cover: 0.10 **NM** value: **285.00**
• Donald Duck **A:** Carl Barks
56 ❑ May 1945 Cover: 0.10 **NM** value: **285.00**
• Donald Duck **A:** Carl Barks
57 ❑ Jun 1945 Cover: 0.10 **NM** value: **285.00**
• Donald Duck **A:** Carl Barks
58 ❑ Jul 1945 Cover: 0.10 **NM** value: **285.00**
• Donald Duck **A:** Carl Barks
59 ❑ Aug 1945 Cover: 0.10 **NM** value: **285.00**
• **CGC:** 1 graded, best 4.5
• Donald Duck **A:** Carl Barks
60 ❑ Sep 1945 Cover: 0.10 **NM** value: **285.00**
• **CGC:** 1 graded, best 7.0
• Donald Duck **A:** Carl Barks
61 ❑ Oct 1945 Cover: 0.10 **NM** value: **220.00**
• Donald Duck **A:** Carl Barks
62 ❑ Nov 1945 Cover: 0.10 **NM** value: **220.00**
• Donald Duck **A:** Carl Barks
63 ❑ Dec 1945 Cover: 0.10 **NM** value: **220.00**
• Donald Duck **A:** Carl Barks
64 ❑ Jan 1946 Cover: 0.10 **NM** value: **220.00**
• Donald Duck **A:** Carl Barks
65 ❑ Feb 1946 Cover: 0.10 **NM** value: **220.00**
• **CGC:** 1 graded, best 8.5
• Donald Duck **A:** Carl Barks
66 ❑ Mar 1946 Cover: 0.10 **NM** value: **220.00**
• Donald Duck **A:** Carl Barks
67 ❑ Apr 1946 Cover: 0.10 **NM** value: **220.00**
• Donald Duck **A:** Carl Barks
68 ❑ May 1946 Cover: 0.10 **NM** value: **220.00**
• Donald Duck **A:** Carl Barks
69 ❑ Jun 1946 Cover: 0.10 **NM** value: **220.00**
70 ❑ Jul 1946 Cover: 0.10 **NM** value: **220.00**
71 ❑ Aug 1946 Cover: 0.10 **NM** value: **165.00**
72 ❑ Sep 1946 Cover: 0.10 **NM** value: **165.00**
• **CGC:** 1 graded, best 9.0
73 ❑ Oct 1946 Cover: 0.10 **NM** value: **165.00**
74 ❑ Nov 1946 Cover: 0.10 **NM** value: **165.00**
75 ❑ Dec 1946 Cover: 0.10 **NM** value: **165.00**
76 ❑ Jan 1947 Cover: 0.10 **NM** value: **165.00**
77 ❑ Feb 1947 Cover: 0.10 **NM** value: **165.00**
78 ❑ Mar 1947 Cover: 0.10 **NM** value: **165.00**
79 ❑ Apr 1947 Cover: 0.10 **NM** value: **165.00**
80 ❑ May 1947 Cover: 0.10 **NM** value: **165.00**
81 ❑ Jun 1947 Cover: 0.10 **NM** value: **140.00**
82 ❑ Jul 1947 Cover: 0.10 **NM** value: **140.00**
83 ❑ Aug 1947 Cover: 0.10 **NM** value: **140.00**
84 ❑ Sep 1947 Cover: 0.10 **NM** value: **140.00**
85 ❑ Oct 1947 Cover: 0.10 **NM** value: **140.00**
86 ❑ Nov 1947 Cover: 0.10 **NM** value: **140.00**
87 ❑ Dec 1947 Cover: 0.10 **NM** value: **140.00**
88 ❑ Jan 1948 Cover: 0.10 **NM** value: **195.00**
• **CGC:** 1 graded, best 9.2
89 ❑ Feb 1948 Cover: 0.10 **NM** value: **135.00**
90 ❑ Mar 1948 Cover: 0.10 **NM** value: **135.00**
91 ❑ Apr 1948 Cover: 0.10 **NM** value: **115.00**
92 ❑ May 1948 Cover: 0.10 **NM** value: **115.00**
93 ❑ Jun 1948 Cover: 0.10 **NM** value: **115.00**
94 ❑ Jul 1948 Cover: 0.10 **NM** value: **115.00**
95 ❑ Aug 1948 Cover: 0.10 **NM** value: **115.00**
96 ❑ Sep 1948 Cover: 0.10 **NM** value: **115.00**
97 ❑ Oct 1948 Cover: 0.10 **NM** value: **115.00**
98 ❑ Nov 1948 Cover: 0.10 **NM** value: **265.00**
• **CGC:** 3 graded, best 9.4
• Uncle Scrooge **A:** Carl Barks
99 ❑ Dec 1948 Cover: 0.10 **NM** value: **115.00**
100 ❑ Jan 1949 Cover: 0.10 **NM** value: **125.00**
• **CGC:** 1 graded, best 9.0
101 ❑ Feb 1949 Cover: 0.10 **NM** value: **85.00**
102 ❑ Mar 1949 Cover: 0.10 **NM** value: **85.00**
103 ❑ Apr 1949 Cover: 0.10 **NM** value: **85.00**
• **CGC:** 1 graded, best 7.5
104 ❑ May 1949 Cover: 0.10 **NM** value: **85.00**
105 ❑ Jun 1949 Cover: 0.10 **NM** value: **85.00**
106 ❑ Jul 1949 Cover: 0.10 **NM** value: **85.00**
• **CGC:** 1 graded, best 7.0
107 ❑ Aug 1949 Cover: 0.10 **NM** value: **85.00**
108 ❑ Sep 1949 Cover: 0.10 **NM** value: **85.00**
109 ❑ Oct 1949 Cover: 0.10 **NM** value: **85.00**
110 ❑ Nov 1949 Cover: 0.10 **NM** value: **85.00**
111 ❑ Dec 1949 Cover: 0.10 **NM** value: **85.00**
📖 Mickey Mouse: The House of the Seven Haunts; The Halloween Party (text) • Donald Duck, Mickey Mouse, the Li'l Bad Wolf, Bucky Bug; Has 1949 Statement, filed 10/1/49; no circ figures published **A:** Carl Barks
112 ❑ Jan 1950 Cover: 0.10 **NM** value: **85.00**
113 ❑ Feb 1950 Cover: 0.10 **NM** value: **40.00**
114 ❑ Mar 1950 Cover: 0.10 **NM** value: **40.00**
115 ❑ Apr 1950 Cover: 0.10 **NM** value: **40.00**
116 ❑ May 1950 Cover: 0.10 **NM** value: **40.00**
117 ❑ Jun 1950 Cover: 0.10 **NM** value: **70.00**
118 ❑ Jul 1950 Cover: 0.10 **NM** value: **36.00**
119 ❑ Aug 1950 Cover: 0.10 **NM** value: **36.00**
120 ❑ Sep 1950 Cover: 0.10 **NM** value: **36.00**
📖 Mickey Mouse: Monarch of Medioka; Jingo: The New Circus Star (text) • Donald Duck, Mickey Mouse, the Li'l Bad Wolf, Bucky Bug
121 ❑ Oct 1950 Cover: 0.10 **NM** value: **36.00**
122 ❑ Nov 1950 Cover: 0.10 **NM** value: **36.00**
123 ❑ Dec 1950 Cover: 0.10 **NM** value: **36.00**
124 ❑ Jan 1951 Cover: 0.10 **NM** value: **70.00**
125 ❑ Feb 1951 Cover: 0.10 **NM** value: **115.00**
126 ❑ Mar 1951 Cover: 0.10 **NM** value: **70.00**
127 ❑ Apr 1951 Cover: 0.10 **NM** value: **70.00**
128 ❑ May 1951 Cover: 0.10 **NM** value: **70.00**
129 ❑ Jun 1951 Cover: 0.10 **NM** value: **70.00**
• **CGC:** 2 graded, best 8.0
130 ❑ Jul 1951 Cover: 0.10 **NM** value: **65.00**
• **CGC:** 1 graded, best 8.0
131 ❑ Aug 1951 Cover: 0.10 **NM** value: **65.00**
132 ❑ Sep 1951 Cover: 0.10 **NM** value: **65.00**
133 ❑ Oct 1951 Cover: 0.10 **NM** value: **65.00**
134 ❑ Nov 1951 Cover: 0.10 **NM** value: **125.00**
• **CGC:** 1 graded, best 8.0
135 ❑ Dec 1951 Cover: 0.10 **NM** value: **52.00**
• **CGC:** 1 graded, best 8.5
136 ❑ Jan 1952 Cover: 0.10 **NM** value: **52.00**
• **CGC:** 1 graded, best 9.4
137 ❑ Feb 1952 Cover: 0.10 **NM** value: **52.00**
• **CGC:** 1 graded, best 9.0
138 ❑ Mar 1952 Cover: 0.10 **NM** value: **52.00**
139 ❑ Apr 1952 Cover: 0.10 **NM** value: **52.00**
140 ❑ May 1952 Cover: 0.10 **NM** value: **150.00**
• **CGC:** 1 graded, best 9.4
141 ❑ Jun 1952 Cover: 0.10 **NM** value: **42.00**
142 ❑ Jul 1952 Cover: 0.10 **NM** value: **42.00**
143 ❑ Aug 1952 Cover: 0.10 **NM** value: **42.00**
144 ❑ Sep 1952 Cover: 0.10 **NM** value: **42.00**
145 ❑ Oct 1952 Cover: 0.10 **NM** value: **42.00**
146 ❑ Nov 1952 Cover: 0.10 **NM** value: **42.00**
147 ❑ Dec 1952 Cover: 0.10 **NM** value: **42.00**
148 ❑ Jan 1953 Cover: 0.10 **NM** value: **42.00**
149 ❑ Feb 1953 Cover: 0.10 **NM** value: **42.00**
150 ❑ Mar 1953 Cover: 0.10 **NM** value: **42.00**
151 ❑ Apr 1953 Cover: 0.10 **NM** value: **38.00**
152 ❑ May 1953 Cover: 0.10 **NM** value: **38.00**
153 ❑ Jun 1953 Cover: 0.10 **NM** value: **38.00**
154 ❑ Jul 1953 Cover: 0.10 **NM** value: **38.00**
155 ❑ Aug 1953 Cover: 0.10 **NM** value: **38.00**
156 ❑ Sep 1953 Cover: 0.10 **NM** value: **38.00**
157 ❑ Oct 1953 Cover: 0.10 **NM** value: **38.00**
158 ❑ Nov 1953 Cover: 0.10 **NM** value: **38.00**
159 ❑ Dec 1953 Cover: 0.10 **NM** value: **38.00**
📖 For Sale; Lens Hunters **A:** Carl Barks
160 ❑ Jan 1954 Cover: 0.10 **NM** value: **38.00**
📖 Bankrupt Sale!; Lens Hunters **A:** Carl Barks
161 ❑ Feb 1954 Cover: 0.10 **NM** value: **38.00**
📖 Donald Duck's Fix-It Shop; The Biggest Bone Ever; Figaro Plays Detective; The Case of the Vanishing Bandit **A:** Carl Barks
162 ❑ Mar 1954 Cover: 0.10 **NM** value: **38.00**
163 ❑ Apr 1954 Cover: 0.10 **NM** value: **38.00**
📖 Charity Bazaar; The Case of the Vanishing Bandit **A:** Carl Barks
164 ❑ May 1954 Cover: 0.10 **NM** value: **38.00**
165 ❑ Jun 1954 Cover: 0.10 **NM** value: **38.00**
166 ❑ Jul 1954 Cover: 0.10 **NM** value: **38.00**
📖 The Rainbow Lunch; The Mysterious Crystal Ball **A:** Carl Barks
167 ❑ Aug 1954 Cover: 0.10 **NM** value: **38.00**
📖 The Circus Rally; The Lost Legion **A:** Carl Barks
168 ❑ Sep 1954 Cover: 0.10 **NM** value: **38.00**
169 ❑ Oct 1954 Cover: 0.10 **NM** value: **38.00**

Other grades: Multiply prices above by **1.5 for Mint • 2/3 for Very Fine • 1/3 for Fine • 1/5 for Very Good • 1/8 for Good**

The Lost Wagon **A:** Carl Barks
170 ❑ Nov 1954 Cover: 0.10 **NM** value: **38.00**
The Magic Rope **A:** Carl Barks
171 ❑ Dec 1954 Cover: 0.10 **NM** value: **30.00**
The Magic Rope **A:** Carl Barks
172 ❑ Jan 1955 Cover: 0.10 **NM** value: **30.00**
The Magic Rope **A:** Carl Barks
173 ❑ Feb 1955 Cover: 0.10 **NM** value: **30.00**
Ridin' The Rails **A:** Carl Barks
174 ❑ Mar 1955 Cover: 0.10 **NM** value: **30.00**
Ridin' The Rails; Panchito's Party (text) • Donald Duck, the Li'l Bad Wolf, Pluto, Mickey Mouse **A:** Carl Barks
175 ❑ Apr 1955 Cover: 0.10 **NM** value: **30.00**
Ridin' The Rails **A:** Carl Barks
176 ❑ May 1955 Cover: 0.10 **NM** value: **30.00**
The Lost City **A:** Carl Barks
177 ❑ Jun 1955 Cover: 0.10 **NM** value: **30.00**
The Lost City **A:** Carl Barks
178 ❑ Jul 1955 Cover: 0.10 **NM** value: **30.00**
The Lost City **A:** Carl Barks
179 ❑ Aug 1955 Cover: 0.10 **NM** value: **30.00**
Yesterday Ranch **A:** Carl Barks
180 ❑ Sep 1955 Cover: 0.10 **NM** value: **30.00**
Yesterday Ranch **A:** Carl Barks
181 ❑ Oct 1955 Cover: 0.10 **NM** value: **30.00**
Yesterday Ranch **A:** Carl Barks
182 ❑ Nov 1955 Cover: 0.10 **NM** value: **30.00**
Mickey Mouse and the Marvelous Magnet **A:** Carl Barks
183 ❑ Dec 1955 Cover: 0.10 **NM** value: **30.00**
Mickey Mouse and the Marvelous Magnet **A:** Carl Barks
184 ❑ Jan 1956 Cover: 0.10 **NM** value: **30.00**
Mickey Mouse and the Marvelous Magnet **A:** Carl Barks
185 ❑ Feb 1956 Cover: 0.10 **NM** value: **30.00**
New Year's Resolutions; The Vanishing Railroad **A:** Carl Barks
186 ❑ Mar 1956 Cover: 0.10 **NM** value: **30.00**
The Vanishing Railroad; The Circus Express (text) • Donald Duck, the Li'l Bad Wolf, Pluto, Mickey Mouse **A:** Carl Barks
187 ❑ Apr 1956 Cover: 0.10 **NM** value: **30.00**
The Vanishing Railroad **A:** Carl Barks
188 ❑ May 1956 Cover: 0.10 **NM** value: **30.00**
The Case of the Hungry Ghost **A:** Carl Barks
189 ❑ Jun 1956 Cover: 0.10 **NM** value: **30.00**
The School Party; The Case of the Hungry Ghost **A:** Carl Barks
190 ❑ Jul 1956 Cover: 0.10 **NM** value: **30.00**
The Case of the Hungry Ghost **A:** Carl Barks
191 ❑ Aug 1956 Cover: 0.10 **NM** value: **30.00**
The Pirates of Tabasco Bay **A:** Carl Barks
192 ❑ Sep 1956 Cover: 0.10 **NM** value: **30.00**
The Supercharged Hero; The Pirates of Tabasco Bay **A:** Carl Barks
193 ❑ Oct 1956 Cover: 0.10 **NM** value: **30.00**
194 ❑ Nov 1956 Cover: 0.10 **NM** value: **30.00**
195 ❑ Dec 1956 Cover: 0.10 **NM** value: **30.00**
196 ❑ Jan 1957 Cover: 0.10 **NM** value: **30.00**
197 ❑ Feb 1957 Cover: 0.10 **NM** value: **30.00**
• **CGC:** 1 graded, best 7.0
198 ❑ Mar 1957 Cover: 0.10 **NM** value: **30.00**
199 ❑ Apr 1957 Cover: 0.10 **NM** value: **30.00**
• **CGC:** 1 graded, best 7.5
200 ❑ May 1957 Cover: 0.10 **NM** value: **30.00**
201 ❑ Jun 1957 Cover: 0.10 **NM** value: **28.00**
202 ❑ Jul 1957 Cover: 0.10 **NM** value: **28.00**
203 ❑ Aug 1957 Cover: 0.10 **NM** value: **28.00**
204 ❑ Sep 1957 Cover: 0.10 **NM** value: **28.00**
205 ❑ Oct 1957 Cover: 0.10 **NM** value: **28.00**
206 ❑ Nov 1957 Cover: 0.10 **NM** value: **28.00**
The Crow's Feat; Message in a Nutshell **A:** Carl Barks
207 ❑ Dec 1957 Cover: 0.10 **NM** value: **28.00**
208 ❑ Jan 1958 Cover: 0.10 **NM** value: **28.00**
209 ❑ Feb 1958 Cover: 0.10 **NM** value: **28.00**
210 ❑ Mar 1958 Cover: 0.10 **NM** value: **28.00**
211 ❑ Apr 1958 Cover: 0.10 **NM** value: **28.00**
212 ❑ May 1958 Cover: 0.10 **NM** value: **28.00**
213 ❑ Jun 1958 Cover: 0.10 **NM** value: **28.00**
214 ❑ Jul 1958 Cover: 0.10 **NM** value: **28.00**
• **CGC:** 1 graded, best 8.0
215 ❑ Aug 1958 Cover: 0.10 **NM** value: **28.00**
216 ❑ Sep 1958 Cover: 0.10 **NM** value: **28.00**
217 ❑ Oct 1958 Cover: 0.10 **NM** value: **28.00**
218 ❑ Nov 1958 Cover: 0.10 **NM** value: **28.00**
219 ❑ Dec 1958 Cover: 0.10 **NM** value: **28.00**
220 ❑ Jan 1959 Cover: 0.10 **NM** value: **28.00**
221 ❑ Feb 1959 Cover: 0.10 **NM** value: **28.00**
222 ❑ Mar 1959 Cover: 0.10 **NM** value: **28.00**
223 ❑ Apr 1959 Cover: 0.10 **NM** value: **28.00**
• **CGC:** 1 graded, best 9.2
224 ❑ May 1959 Cover: 0.10 **NM** value: **28.00**
225 ❑ Jun 1959 Cover: 0.10 **NM** value: **28.00**
226 ❑ Jul 1959 Cover: 0.10 **NM** value: **28.00**
227 ❑ Aug 1959 Cover: 0.10 **NM** value: **28.00**
228 ❑ Sep 1959 Cover: 0.10 **NM** value: **28.00**
229 ❑ Oct 1959 Cover: 0.10 **NM** value: **28.00**
The Good Deeds **A:** Carl Barks
230 ❑ Nov 1959 Cover: 0.10 **NM** value: **28.00**
Black Wednesday **A:** Carl Barks
231 ❑ Dec 1959 Cover: 0.10 **NM** value: **28.00**
The Wax Museum **A:** Carl Barks
232 ❑ Jan 1960 Cover: 0.10 **NM** value: **28.00**
Circ: Statement: **1,004,901**
Under the Polar Ice **A:** Carl Barks
233 ❑ Feb 1960 Cover: 0.10 **NM** value: **28.00**
Circ: Statement: **1,004,901**
Knights of the Flying Sleds **A:** Carl Barks
234 ❑ Mar 1960 Cover: 0.10 **NM** value: **28.00**
Circ: Statement: **1,004,901**
Riding the Pony Express **A:** Carl Barks
235 ❑ Apr 1960 Cover: 0.10 **NM** value: **28.00**
Circ: Statement: **1,004,901**
Want to Buy an Island? **A:** Carl Barks
236 ❑ May 1960 Cover: 0.10 **NM** value: **28.00**
Circ: Statement: **1,004,901**
Froggy Farmer **A:** Carl Barks
237 ❑ Jun 1960 Cover: 0.10 **NM** value: **28.00**
Circ: Statement: **1,004,901**
Mystery of the Loch **A:** Carl Barks
238 ❑ Jul 1960 Cover: 0.10 **NM** value: **28.00**
Circ: Statement: **1,004,901**
The Dog-sitter **A:** Carl Barks
239 ❑ Aug 1960 Cover: 0.10 **NM** value: **28.00**
Circ: Statement: **1,004,901**
The Village Blacksmith **A:** Carl Barks
240 ❑ Sep 1960 Cover: 0.10 **NM** value: **28.00**
Circ: Statement: **1,004,901**
The Fraidy Falcon **A:** Carl Barks
241 ❑ Oct 1960 Cover: 0.10 **NM** value: **22.00**
Circ: Statement: **1,004,901** • **CGC:** 1 graded, best 8.5
Rocks to Riches **A:** Carl Barks
242 ❑ Nov 1960 Cover: 0.10 **NM** value: **22.00**
Circ: Statement: **1,004,901**
Balloonatics **A:** Carl Barks
243 ❑ Dec 1960 Cover: 0.10 **NM** value: **22.00**
Circ: Statement: **1,004,901**
Turkey Trouble **A:** Carl Barks
244 ❑ Jan 1961 Cover: 0.10 **NM** value: **22.00**
Missile Fizzle **A:** Carl Barks
245 ❑ Feb 1961 Cover: 0.10 **NM** value: **22.00**
Sitting High **A:** Carl Barks
246 ❑ Mar 1961 Cover: 0.10 **NM** value: **22.00**
Lost Frontier **A:** Carl Barks
247 ❑ Apr 1961 Cover: 0.10 **NM** value: **22.00**
The Madcap Mariner **A:** Carl Barks
248 ❑ May 1961 Cover: 0.10 **NM** value: **22.00**
Terrible Tourist **A:** Carl Barks
249 ❑ Jun 1961 Cover: 0.10 **NM** value: **22.00**
Stranger Than Fiction **A:** Carl Barks
250 ❑ Jul 1961 Cover: 0.12 **NM** value: **22.00**
Boxed-in • Has 1960 Statement, filed 10/1/60; avg total paid 1,004,901 **A:** Carl Barks
251 ❑ Aug 1961 Cover: 0.12 **NM** value: **22.00**
Duck Luck **A:** Carl Barks
252 ❑ Sep 1961 Cover: 0.12 **NM** value: **22.00**
Mr. Private Eye **A:** Carl Barks
253 ❑ Oct 1961 Cover: 0.12 **NM** value: **22.00**
Hound Hounder **A:** Carl Barks
254 ❑ Nov 1961 Cover: 0.12 **NM** value: **22.00**
Jet Witch **A:** Carl Barks
255 ❑ Dec 1961 Cover: 0.12 **NM** value: **22.00**
Boat Buster **A:** Carl Barks
256 ❑ Jan 1962 Cover: 0.12 **NM** value: **22.00**
Northeaster on Cape Quack **A:** Carl Barks
257 ❑ Feb 1962 Cover: 0.12 **NM** value: **22.00**
• **CGC:** 1 graded, best 9.0
Movie Mad **A:** Carl Barks
258 ❑ Mar 1962 Cover: 0.12 **NM** value: **22.00**
Ten-cent Valentine **A:** Carl Barks
259 ❑ Apr 1962 Cover: 0.12 **NM** value: **22.00**
Jungle Bungle **A:** Carl Barks
260 ❑ May 1962 Cover: 0.12 **NM** value: **22.00**
Merry Ferry **A:** Carl Barks
261 ❑ Jun 1962 Cover: 0.12 **NM** value: **20.00**
Medaling Around **A:** Carl Barks
262 ❑ Jul 1962 Cover: 0.12 **NM** value: **20.00**
Way Out Yonder **A:** Carl Barks
263 ❑ Aug 1962 Cover: 0.12 **NM** value: **20.00**
The Candy Kid **A:** Carl Barks
264 ❑ Sep 1962 Cover: 0.12 **NM** value: **20.00**
Master Wrecker **A:** Carl Barks
265 ❑ Oct 1962 Cover: 0.12 **NM** value: **20.00**
Raven Mad **A:** Carl Barks
266 ❑ Nov 1962 Cover: 0.12 **NM** value: **20.00**
Stalwart Ranger **A:** Carl Barks
267 ❑ Dec 1962 Cover: 0.12 **NM** value: **20.00**
Log Jockey **A:** Carl Barks
268 ❑ Jan 1963 Cover: 0.12 **NM** value: **20.00**
Circ: Statement: **446,000**
Christmas Cheers **A:** Carl Barks
269 ❑ Feb 1963 Cover: 0.12 **NM** value: **20.00**
Circ: Statement: **446,000**
A Matter of Factory **A:** Carl Barks
270 ❑ Mar 1963 Cover: 0.12 **NM** value: **20.00**
Circ: Statement: **446,000**
The Jinxed Jalopy Race **A:** Carl Barks
271 ❑ Apr 1963 Cover: 0.12 **NM** value: **20.00**
Circ: Statement: **446,000**
A Stone's Throw from Ghost Town **A:** Carl Barks
272 ❑ May 1963 Cover: 0.12 **NM** value: **20.00**
Circ: Statement: **446,000**
Spare That Hair **A:** Carl Barks
273 ❑ Jun 1963 Cover: 0.12 **NM** value: **20.00**
Circ: Statement: **446,000**
A Duck's-eye View of Europe **A:** Carl Barks
274 ❑ Jul 1963 Cover: 0.12 **NM** value: **20.00**
Circ: Statement: **446,000**
Gall of the Wild **A:** Carl Barks
275 ❑ Aug 1963 Cover: 0.12 **NM** value: **20.00**
Circ: Statement: **446,000**
Zero Hero **A:** Carl Barks
276 ❑ Sep 1963 Cover: 0.12 **NM** value: **20.00**
Circ: Statement: **446,000**
Beach Boy **A:** Carl Barks
277 ❑ Oct 1963 Cover: 0.12 **NM** value: **20.00**
Circ: Statement: **446,000**
The Duckburg Pet Parade **A:** Carl Barks
278 ❑ Nov 1963 Cover: 0.12 **NM** value: **20.00**
Circ: Statement: **456,425**
Have Gun, Will Dance **A:** Carl Barks
279 ❑ Dec 1963 Cover: 0.12 **NM** value: **20.00**
Circ: Statement: **456,425**
Once Upon a Carnival **A:** Carl Barks
280 ❑ Jan 1964 Cover: 0.12 **NM** value: **20.00**
Circ: Statement: **456,425**
Double Masquerade • Has 1963 Statement, filed 9/27/63; avg print run 625,010; avg sales 289,000; avg subs 157,000; avg total paid 446,000; samples 770; max existent 446,770; 29% of run returned **A:** Carl Barks
281 ❑ Feb 1964 Cover: 0.12 **NM** value: **20.00**
Circ: Statement: **456,425**
Feud and Far Between **A:** Carl Barks
282 ❑ Mar 1964 Cover: 0.12 **NM** value: **20.00**
Circ: Statement: **456,425**
Bubbleweight Champ **A:** Carl Barks
283 ❑ Apr 1964 Cover: 0.12 **NM** value: **20.00**
Circ: Statement: **456,425**
Captain Blight's Mystery Ship **A:** Carl Barks
284 ❑ May 1964 Cover: 0.12 **NM** value: **12.00**
Circ: Statement: **456,425**
285 ❑ Jun 1964 Cover: 0.12 **NM** value: **12.00**
Circ: Statement: **456,425**
286 ❑ Jul 1964 Cover: 0.12 **NM** value: **16.00**
Circ: Statement: **456,425**
The Olympian Torch Bearer **A:** Carl Barks
287 ❑ Aug 1964 Cover: 0.12 **NM** value: **12.00**
Circ: Statement: **456,425**
288 ❑ Sep 1964 Cover: 0.12 **NM** value: **16.00**
Circ: Statement: **456,425**
Hero of the Dike **A:** Carl Barks
289 ❑ Oct 1964 Cover: 0.12 **NM** value: **16.00**
Circ: Statement: **456,425** • **CGC:** 1 graded, best 7.5
Unfriendly Enemies **A:** Carl Barks
290 ❑ Nov 1964 Cover: 0.12 **NM** value: **12.00**
Circ: Statement: **456,425**
291 ❑ Dec 1964 Cover: 0.12 **NM** value: **16.00**
Circ: Statement: **410,209**
Delivery Dilemma **A:** Carl Barks
292 ❑ Jan 1965 Cover: 0.12 **NM** value: **16.00**
Circ: Statement: **410,209**
Instant Hercules **A:** Carl Barks
293 ❑ Feb 1965 Cover: 0.12 **NM** value: **16.00**
Circ: Statement: **410,209**
Grandma Duck's Farm Friends and the Sheepish Cowboys **A:** Carl Barks
294 ❑ Mar 1965 Cover: 0.12 **NM** value: **12.00**
Circ: Statement: **410,209**
Duck Out of Luck
295 ❑ Apr 1965 Cover: 0.12 **NM** value: **12.00**
Circ: Statement: **410,209**
296 ❑ May 1965 Cover: 0.12 **NM** value: **12.00**
Circ: Statement: **410,209**
297 ❑ Jun 1965 Cover: 0.12 **NM** value: **16.00**
Circ: Statement: **410,209**
Monkey Business; Gyro Gearloose (Untitled); Million-dollar Shower • Reprints story from Uncle Scrooge #20 **A:** Carl Barks
298 ❑ Jul 1965 Cover: 0.12 **NM** value: **16.00**
Circ: Statement: **410,209**
The Double Date • Reprints story from Four Color Comics #1055 (Daisy Duck's Diary) **A:** Carl Barks
299 ❑ Aug 1965 Cover: 0.12 **NM** value: **16.00**
Circ: Statement: **410,209**
• Reprints story from Walt Disney's Comics #117 **A:** Carl Barks
300 ❑ Sep 1965 Cover: 0.12 **NM** value: **16.00**
Circ: Statement: **410,209**
Now Showing "Three Dirty Little Ducks" • Reprints story from Walt Disney's Comics #43 **A:** Carl Barks
301 ❑ Oct 1965 Cover: 0.12 **NM** value: **16.00**
Circ: Statement: **346,250**
Too Much Help; This Month The Mad Chemist • Reprints stories from Four Color Comics #1150 (Daisy Duck's Diary) and Walt Disney's Comics #44 **A:** Carl Barks
302 ❑ Nov 1965 Cover: 0.12 **NM** value: **16.00**
Circ: Statement: **346,250**
• Reprints story from Walt Disney's Comics #47 **A:** Carl Barks
303 ❑ Dec 1965 Cover: 0.12 **NM** value: **16.00**
Circ: Statement: **346,250**
• Reprints story from Walt Disney's Comics #49 **A:** Carl Barks
304 ❑ Jan 1966 Cover: 0.12 **NM** value: **16.00**
Circ: Statement: **346,250**
Daringly Different; False Flattery • Reprints stories from Four Color Comics #1150 (Daisy Duck's Diary) and Walt Disney's Comics #63 **A:** Carl Barks
305 ❑ Feb 1966 Cover: 0.12 **NM** value: **16.00**
Circ: Statement: **346,250**
• Reprints stories from Uncle Scrooge #25 andWalt Disney's Comics #70 **A:** Carl Barks
306 ❑ Mar 1966 Cover: 0.12 **NM** value: **16.00**
Circ: Statement: **346,250**
• Reprints story from Walt Disney's Comics #94 **A:** Carl Barks
307 ❑ Apr 1966 Cover: 0.12 **NM** value: **16.00**
Circ: Statement: **346,250**
• Reprints story from Walt Disney's Comics #91 **A:** Carl Barks
308 ❑ May 1966 Cover: 0.12 **NM** value: **16.00**
Circ: Statement: **346,250**
The Beauty Business **A:** Carl Barks
309 ❑ Jun 1966 Cover: 0.12 **NM** value: **12.00**
Circ: Statement: **346,250**
310 ❑ Jul 1966 Cover: 0.12 **NM** value: **12.00**
Circ: Statement: **346,250**
311 ❑ Aug 1966 Cover: 0.12 **NM** value: **12.00**
Circ: Statement: **346,250**
312 ❑ Sep 1966 Cover: 0.12 **NM** value: **16.00**
Circ: Statement: **346,250**
The Big Fetch; The Chipmunk Mobile; The Trail to Treasure; The Not-so-ancient Mariner **A:** Carl Barks
313 ❑ Oct 1966 Cover: 0.12 **NM** value: **8.00**
Circ: Statement: **310,665**
314 ❑ Nov 1966 Cover: 0.12 **NM** value: **8.00**
Circ: Statement: **310,665**

CGC-graded: Multiply prices above by **33 for 9.9 M • 16 for 9.8 NM/M • 7 for 9.6 NM+ • 5 for 9.4 NM • 2.5 for 9.2 NM- • 1.5 for 9.0 VF/NM**

315 ❑ Dec 1966 Cover: 0.12 **NM** value: **8.00**
Circ: Statement: **310,665**
316 ❑ Jan 1967 Cover: 0.12 **NM** value: **8.00**
Circ: Statement: **310,665**
317 ❑ Feb 1967 Cover: 0.12 **NM** value: **8.00**
Circ: Statement: **310,665**
318 ❑ Mar 1967 Cover: 0.12 **NM** value: **8.00**
Circ: Statement: **310,665**
319 ❑ Apr 1967 Cover: 0.12 **NM** value: **8.00**
Circ: Statement: **310,665**
320 ❑ May 1967 Cover: 0.12 **NM** value: **8.00**
Circ: Statement: **310,665**
321 ❑ Jun 1967 Cover: 0.12 **NM** value: **8.00**
Circ: Statement: **310,665**
322 ❑ Jul 1967 Cover: 0.12 **NM** value: **8.00**
Circ: Statement: **310,665**
323 ❑ Aug 1967 Cover: 0.12 **NM** value: **8.00**
Circ: Statement: **310,665**
324 ❑ Sep 1967 Cover: 0.12 **NM** value: **8.00**
Circ: Statement: **310,665**
325 ❑ Oct 1967 Cover: 0.12 **NM** value: **8.00**
326 ❑ Nov 1967 Cover: 0.12 **NM** value: **8.00**
327 ❑ Dec 1967 Cover: 0.12 **NM** value: **8.00**
328 ❑ Jan 1968 Cover: 0.12 **NM** value: **8.00**
• Reprints story from Walt Disney's Comics #148 **A:** Carl Barks
329 ❑ Feb 1968 Cover: 0.12 **NM** value: **8.00**
330 ❑ Mar 1968 Cover: 0.12 **NM** value: **8.00**
331 ❑ Apr 1968 Cover: 0.12 **NM** value: **8.00**
332 ❑ May 1968 Cover: 0.12 **NM** value: **8.00**
333 ❑ Jun 1968 Cover: 0.12 **NM** value: **8.00**
334 ❑ Jul 1968 Cover: 0.12 **NM** value: **8.00**
335 ❑ Aug 1968 Cover: 0.12 **NM** value: **12.00**
• Reprints story from Walt Disney's Comics #129 **A:** Carl Barks
336 ❑ Sep 1968 Cover: 0.15 **NM** value: **8.00**
337 ❑ Oct 1968 Cover: 0.15 **NM** value: **8.00**
338 ❑ Nov 1968 Cover: 0.15 **NM** value: **8.00**
339 ❑ Dec 1968 Cover: 0.15 **NM** value: **8.00**
Circ: Statement: **272,672**
340 ❑ Jan 1969 Cover: 0.15 **NM** value: **8.00**
Circ: Statement: **272,672**
341 ❑ Feb 1969 Cover: 0.15 **NM** value: **8.00**
Circ: Statement: **272,672**
342 ❑ Mar 1969 Cover: 0.15 **NM** value: **12.00**
Circ: Statement: **272,672**
• Reprints story from Walt Disney's Comics #131 **A:** Carl Barks
343 ❑ Apr 1969 Cover: 0.15 **NM** value: **12.00**
Circ: Statement: **272,672**
• Reprints story from Walt Disney's Comics #144 **A:** Carl Barks
344 ❑ May 1969 Cover: 0.15 **NM** value: **12.00**
Circ: Statement: **272,672**
• Reprints story from Walt Disney's Comics #127 **A:** Carl Barks
345 ❑ Jun 1969 Cover: 0.15 **NM** value: **12.00**
Circ: Statement: **272,672**
• Reprints story from Walt Disney's Comics #139 **A:** Carl Barks
346 ❑ Jul 1969 Cover: 0.15 **NM** value: **12.00**
Circ: Statement: **272,672**
• Reprints story from Walt Disney's Comics #140 **A:** Carl Barks
347 ❑ Aug 1969 Cover: 0.15 **NM** value: **12.00**
Circ: Statement: **272,672**
• Reprints story from Walt Disney's Comics #141 **A:** Carl Barks
348 ❑ Sep 1969 Cover: 0.15 **NM** value: **12.00**
Circ: Statement: **272,672**
• Reprints story from Walt Disney's Comics #155 **A:** Carl Barks
349 ❑ Oct 1969 Cover: 0.15 **NM** value: **12.00**
Circ: Statement: **272,672**
• Reprints story from Walt Disney's Comics #92 **A:** Carl Barks
350 ❑ Nov 1969 Cover: 0.15 **NM** value: **12.00**
Circ: Statement: **272,672**
• Reprints story from Walt Disney's Comics #133 **A:** Carl Barks
351 ❑ Dec 1969 Cover: 0.15 **NM** value: **12.00**
• Reprints story from Walt Disney's Comics #147 **A:** Carl Barks
351/A ❑ Jan 1970 Cover: 0.25 **NM** value: **16.00**
352 ❑ Jan 1970 Cover: 0.15 **NM** value: **12.00**
• Reprints story from Walt Disney's Comics #160 **A:** Carl Barks
352/A ❑ Feb 1970 Cover: 0.25 **NM** value: **16.00**
353 ❑ Feb 1970 Cover: 0.15 **NM** value: **12.00**
• Reprints story from Walt Disney's Comics #173 **A:** Carl Barks
353/A ❑ Mar 1970 Cover: 0.25 **NM** value: **16.00**
354 ❑ Mar 1970 Cover: 0.15 **NM** value: **12.00**
• Reprints story from Walt Disney's Comics #197 **A:** Carl Barks
354/A ❑ Apr 1970 Cover: 0.25 **NM** value: **16.00**
355 ❑ Apr 1970 Cover: 0.15 **NM** value: **12.00**
• Reprints story from Walt Disney's Comics #206 **A:** Carl Barks
355/A ❑ May 1970 Cover: 0.25 **NM** value: **16.00**
356 ❑ May 1970 Cover: 0.15 **NM** value: **12.00**
• Reprints story from Walt Disney's Comics #103 **A:** Carl Barks
356/A ❑ Jun 1970 Cover: 0.25 **NM** value: **16.00**
357 ❑ Jun 1970 Cover: 0.15 **NM** value: **12.00**
• Reprints story from Walt Disney's Comics #145 **A:** Carl Barks
357/A ❑ Jul 1970 Cover: 0.25 **NM** value: **16.00**
358 ❑ Jul 1970 Cover: 0.15 **NM** value: **12.00**
• Reprints story from Walt Disney's Comics #146 **A:** Carl Barks
358/A ❑ Aug 1970 Cover: 0.25 **NM** value: **16.00**
359 ❑ Aug 1970 Cover: 0.15 **NM** value: **12.00**
• Reprints story from Walt Disney's Comics #154 **A:** Carl Barks
359/A ❑ Sep 1970 Cover: 0.25 **NM** value: **16.00**
360 ❑ Sep 1970 Cover: 0.15 **NM** value: **12.00**
• Reprints story from Walt Disney's Comics #200 **A:** Carl Barks
360/A ❑ Oct 1970 Cover: 0.25 **NM** value: **16.00**
361 ❑ Oct 1970 Cover: 0.15 **NM** value: **12.00**
• Reprints story from Walt Disney's Comics #158 **A:** Carl Barks
362 ❑ Nov 1970 Cover: 0.15 **NM** value: **12.00**
• Reprints story from Walt Disney's Comics #180 **A:** Carl Barks
363 ❑ Dec 1970 Cover: 0.15 **NM** value: **12.00**
Circ: Statement: **211,846**
• Reprints story from Walt Disney's Comics #126 **A:** Carl Barks
364 ❑ Jan 1971 Cover: 0.15 **NM** value: **12.00**
Circ: Statement: **211,846**
• Reprints story from Walt Disney's Comics #172 **A:** Carl Barks
365 ❑ Feb 1971 Cover: 0.15 **NM** value: **12.00**
Circ: Statement: **211,846**
• Reprints story from Walt Disney's Comics #149 **A:** Carl Barks
366 ❑ Mar 1971 Cover: 0.15 **NM** value: **12.00**
Circ: Statement: **211,846**
• Reprints story from Walt Disney's Comics #150 **A:** Carl Barks
367 ❑ Apr 1971 Cover: 0.15 **NM** value: **12.00**
Circ: Statement: **211,846**
• Reprints story from Walt Disney's Comics #151 **A:** Carl Barks
368 ❑ May 1971 Cover: 0.15 **NM** value: **12.00**
Circ: Statement: **211,846**
• Reprints story from Walt Disney's Comics #156 **A:** Carl Barks
369 ❑ Jun 1971 Cover: 0.15 **NM** value: **12.00**
Circ: Statement: **211,846**
• Reprints story from Walt Disney's Comics #143 **A:** Carl Barks
370 ❑ Jul 1971 Cover: 0.15 **NM** value: **12.00**
Circ: Statement: **211,846**
• Reprints story from Walt Disney's Comics #142 **A:** Carl Barks
371 ❑ Aug 1971 Cover: 0.15 **NM** value: **12.00**
Circ: Statement: **211,846**
• Reprints story from Walt Disney's Comics #153 **A:** Carl Barks
372 ❑ Sep 1971 Cover: 0.15 **NM** value: **12.00**
Circ: Statement: **211,846**
• Reprints story from Walt Disney's Comics #168 **A:** Carl Barks
373 ❑ Oct 1971 Cover: 0.15 **NM** value: **12.00**
Circ: Statement: **211,846**
• Reprints story from Walt Disney's Comics #193 **A:** Carl Barks
374 ❑ Nov 1971 Cover: 0.15 **NM** value: **12.00**
Circ: Statement: **211,846**
• Reprints story from Walt Disney's Comics #203 **A:** Carl Barks
375 ❑ Dec 1971 Cover: 0.15 **NM** value: **12.00**
The Fraidy Falcon • Reprints story from Walt Disney's Comics #240 **A:** Carl Barks
376 ❑ Jan 1972 Cover: 0.15 **NM** value: **12.00**
• Reprints story from Walt Disney's Comics #208 **A:** Carl Barks
377 ❑ Feb 1972 Cover: 0.15 **NM** value: **12.00**
• Reprints story from Walt Disney's Comics #185 **A:** Carl Barks
378 ❑ Mar 1972 Cover: 0.15 **NM** value: **12.00**
• Reprints story from Walt Disney's Comics #196 **A:** Carl Barks
379 ❑ Apr 1972 Cover: 0.15 **NM** value: **12.00**
• Reprints story from Walt Disney's Comics #207 **A:** Carl Barks
380 ❑ May 1972 Cover: 0.15 **NM** value: **12.00**
• Reprints story from Walt Disney's Comics #211 **A:** Carl Barks
381 ❑ Jun 1972 Cover: 0.15 **NM** value: **12.00**
• Reprints story from Walt Disney's Comics #202 **A:** Carl Barks
382 ❑ Jul 1972 Cover: 0.15 **NM** value: **12.00**
• Reprints story from Walt Disney's Comics #213 **A:** Carl Barks
383 ❑ Aug 1972 Cover: 0.15 **NM** value: **12.00**
• Reprints story from Walt Disney's Comics #215 **A:** Carl Barks
384 ❑ Sep 1972 Cover: 0.15 **NM** value: **12.00**
• Reprints story from Walt Disney's Comics #177 **A:** Carl Barks
385 ❑ Oct 1972 Cover: 0.15 **NM** value: **12.00**
• Reprints story from Walt Disney's Comics #187 **A:** Carl Barks
386 ❑ Nov 1972 Cover: 0.15 **NM** value: **12.00**
• Reprints story from Walt Disney's Comics #209 **A:** Carl Barks
387 ❑ Dec 1972 Cover: 0.15 **NM** value: **12.00**
• Reprints story from Walt Disney's Comics #205 **A:** Carl Barks
388 ❑ Jan 1973 Cover: 0.15 **NM** value: **12.00**
• Reprints story from Walt Disney's Comics #136 **A:** Carl Barks
389 ❑ Feb 1973 Cover: 0.15 **NM** value: **12.00**
The Hound Hounder • Reprints story from Walt Disney's Comics #253 **A:** Carl Barks
390 ❑ Mar 1973 Cover: 0.15 **NM** value: **12.00**
The Village Blacksmith • Reprints story from Walt Disney's Comics #239 **A:** Carl Barks
391 ❑ Apr 1973 Cover: 0.15 **NM** value: **12.00**
• Reprints story from Walt Disney's Comics #137 **A:** Carl Barks
392 ❑ May 1973 Cover: 0.20 **NM** value: **12.00**
• Reprints story from Walt Disney's Comics #163 **A:** Carl Barks
393 ❑ Jun 1973 Cover: 0.20 **NM** value: **12.00**
• Reprints story from Walt Disney's Comics #167 **A:** Carl Barks
394 ❑ Jul 1973 Cover: 0.20 **NM** value: **12.00**
• Reprints story from Walt Disney's Comics #176 **A:** Carl Barks
395 ❑ Aug 1973 Cover: 0.20 **NM** value: **12.00**
• Reprints story from Walt Disney's Comics #214 **A:** Carl Barks
396 ❑ Sep 1973 Cover: 0.20 **NM** value: **12.00**
• Reprints story from Walt Disney's Comics #210 **A:** Carl Barks
397 ❑ Oct 1973 Cover: 0.20 **NM** value: **12.00**
• Reprints story from Walt Disney's Comics #218 **A:** Carl Barks
398 ❑ Nov 1973 Cover: 0.20 **NM** value: **12.00**
• Reprints story from Walt Disney's Comics #217 **A:** Carl Barks
399 ❑ Dec 1973 Cover: 0.20 **NM** value: **12.00**
• Reprints story from Walt Disney's Comics #183 **A:** Carl Barks
400 ❑ Jan 1974 Cover: 0.20 **NM** value: **12.00**
• Reprints story from Walt Disney's Comics #171 **A:** Carl Barks
401 ❑ Feb 1974 Cover: 0.20 **NM** value: **8.00**
• Reprints story from Walt Disney's Comics #219 **A:** Carl Barks
402 ❑ Mar 1974 Cover: 0.20 **NM** value: **8.00**
Ten-cent Valentine • Reprints story from Walt Disney's Comics #258 **A:** Carl Barks
403 ❑ Apr 1974 Cover: 0.20 **NM** value: **8.00**
Boat Buster • Reprints story from Walt Disney's Comics #255 **A:** Carl Barks
404 ❑ May 1974 Cover: 0.20 **NM** value: **8.00**
• Reprints story from Walt Disney's Comics #223 **A:** Carl Barks
405 ❑ Jun 1974 Cover: 0.20 **NM** value: **8.00**
Jungle Bungle • Reprints story from Walt Disney's Comics #259 **A:** Carl Barks
406 ❑ Jul 1974 Cover: 0.20 **NM** value: **8.00**
• Reprints story from Walt Disney's Comics #191 **A:** Carl Barks
407 ❑ Aug 1974 Cover: 0.25 **NM** value: **8.00**
• Reprints story from Walt Disney's Comics #221 **A:** Carl Barks
408 ❑ Sep 1974 Cover: 0.25 **NM** value: **8.00**
The Good Deeds • Reprints story from Walt Disney's Comics #229 **A:** Carl Barks
409 ❑ Oct 1974 Cover: 0.25 **NM** value: **8.00**
Stranger Than Fiction; Mechanized Mess • Reprints stories from Four Color Comics #1184 (Gyro Gearloose) and Walt Disney's Comics #249 **A:** Carl Barks
410 ❑ Nov 1974 Cover: 0.25 **NM** value: **8.00**
• Reprints story from Walt Disney's Comics #216 **A:** Carl Barks
411 ❑ Dec 1974 Cover: 0.25 **NM** value: **8.00**
Jet Witch • Reprints story from Walt Disney's Comics #254 **A:** Carl Barks
412 ❑ Jan 1975 Cover: 0.25 **NM** value: **8.00**
• Reprints story from Walt Disney's Comics #220 **A:** Carl Barks
413 ❑ Feb 1975 Cover: 0.25 **NM** value: **8.00**
Duck Out of Luck • Reprints story from Walt Disney's Comics #294 **A:** Carl Barks
414 ❑ Mar 1975 Cover: 0.25 **NM** value: **8.00**
A Matter of Factory • Reprints story from Walt Disney's Comics #269 **A:** Carl Barks
415 ❑ Apr 1975 Cover: 0.25 **NM** value: **8.00**
Raven Mad • Reprints story from Walt Disney's Comics #265 **A:** Carl Barks
416 ❑ May 1975 Cover: 0.25 **NM** value: **8.00**
• Reprints story from Walt Disney's Comics #222 **A:** Carl Barks
417 ❑ Jun 1975 Cover: 0.25 **NM** value: **8.00**
• Reprints story from Walt Disney's Comics #225 **A:** Carl Barks
418 ❑ Jul 1975 Cover: 0.25 **NM** value: **8.00**
Froggy Farmer • Reprints story from Walt Disney's Comics #236 **A:** Carl Barks
419 ❑ Aug 1975 Cover: 0.25 **NM** value: **8.00**
• Reprints story from Walt Disney's Comics #138 **A:** Carl Barks
420 ❑ Sep 1975 Cover: 0.25 **NM** value: **8.00**
• Reprints story from Walt Disney's Comics #65 **A:** Carl Barks
421 ❑ Oct 1975 Cover: 0.25 **NM** value: **8.00**
• **CGC:** 3 graded, best 9.4
• Reprints story from Walt Disney's Comics #152 **A:** Carl Barks
422 ❑ Nov 1975 Cover: 0.25 **NM** value: **8.00**
• Reprints story from Walt Disney's Comics #169 **A:** Carl Barks
423 ❑ Dec 1975 Cover: 0.25 **NM** value: **8.00**
The Wax Museum • Reprints story from Walt Disney's Comics #231 **A:** Carl Barks
424 ❑ Jan 1976 Cover: 0.25 **NM** value: **8.00**
Northeaster on Cape Quack • Reprints story from Walt Disney's Comics #256 **A:** Carl Barks
425 ❑ Feb 1976 Cover: 0.25 **NM** value: **8.00**
Merry Ferry • Reprints story from Walt Disney's Comics #260 **A:** Carl Barks
426 ❑ Mar 1976 Cover: 0.25 **NM** value: **8.00**
Master Wrecker • Reprints story from Walt Disney's Comics #264 **A:** Carl Barks
427 ❑ Apr 1976 Cover: 0.25 **NM** value: **8.00**
A Duck-'s-eye View of Europe • Reprints story from Walt Disney's Comics #273 **A:** Carl Barks
428 ❑ May 1976 Cover: 0.25 **NM** value: **8.00**
Zero Hero • Reprints story from Walt Disney's Comics #275 **A:** Carl Barks
429 ❑ Jun 1976 Cover: 0.25 **NM** value: **8.00**
A Stone's Throw From Ghost Town • Reprints story from Walt Disney's Comics #271 **A:** Carl Barks
430 ❑ Jul 1976 Cover: 0.25 **NM** value: **4.00**
431 ❑ Aug 1976 Cover: 0.25 **NM** value: **6.00**
Hero of the Dike • Reprints story from Walt Disney's Comics #288 **A:** Carl Barks
432 ❑ Sep 1976 Cover: 0.30 **NM** value: **6.00**
Delivery Dilemma • Reprints story from Walt Disney's Comics #291 **A:** Carl Barks
433 ❑ Oct 1976 Cover: 0.30 **NM** value: **4.00**
434 ❑ Nov 1976 Cover: 0.30 **NM** value: **6.00**
• Reprints story from Walt Disney's Comics #199 **A:** Carl Barks
435 ❑ Dec 1976 Cover: 0.30 **NM** value: **6.00**
• Reprints story from Walt Disney's Comics #201 **A:** Carl Barks
436 ❑ Jan 1977 Cover: 0.30 **NM** value: **6.00**
• Reprints story from Walt Disney's Comics #195 **A:** Carl Barks
437 ❑ Feb 1977 Cover: 0.30 **NM** value: **4.00**
438 ❑ Mar 1977 Cover: 0.30 **NM** value: **4.00**
439 ❑ Apr 1977 Cover: 0.30 **NM** value: **6.00**
Instant Hercules • Reprints story from Walt Disney's Comics #292 **A:** Carl Barks
440 ❑ May 1977 Cover: 0.30 **NM** value: **6.00**
Captain Blight's Mystery Ship • Reprints story from Walt Disney's Comics #283 **A:** Carl Barks
441 ❑ Jun 1977 Cover: 0.30 **NM** value: **4.00**
442 ❑ Jul 1977 Cover: 0.30 **NM** value: **5.00**
The Not-so-ancient Mariner • Reprints story from Walt Disney's Comics #312 **A:** Carl Barks
443 ❑ Aug 1977 Cover: 0.30 **NM** value: **5.00**
Monkey Business • Reprints story from Walt Disney's Comics #297 **A:** Carl Barks
444 ❑ Sep 1977 Cover: 0.30 **NM** value: **3.00**
445 ❑ Oct 1977 Cover: 0.30 **NM** value: **3.00**
446 ❑ Nov 1977 Cover: 0.30 **NM** value: **5.00**
The Duckburg Pet Parade • Reprints story from Walt Disney's Comics #277 **A:** Carl Barks
447 ❑ Dec 1977 Cover: 0.35 **NM** value: **5.00**
• Reprints story from Walt Disney's Comics #212 **A:** Carl Barks
448 ❑ Jan 1978 Cover: 0.35 **NM** value: **5.00**
Stalwart Ranger • Reprints story from Walt Disney's Comics #266 **A:** Carl Barks
449 ❑ Feb 1978 Cover: 0.35 **NM** value: **5.00**
Double Masquerade • Reprints story from Walt Disney's Comics #280 **A:** Carl Barks
450 ❑ Mar 1978 Cover: 0.35 **NM** value: **5.00**
The Jinxed Jalopy Race • Reprints story from Walt Disney's Comics #270 **A:** Carl Barks
451 ❑ Apr 1978 Cover: 0.35 **NM** value: **4.00**
Spare That Hair • Reprints story from Walt Disney's Comics #272 **A:** Carl Barks
452 ❑ May 1978 Cover: 0.35 **NM** value: **4.00**
Gall of the Wild • Reprints story from Walt Disney's Comics #274 **A:** Carl Barks
453 ❑ Jun 1978 Cover: 0.35 **NM** value: **4.00**
• Reprints story from Walt Disney's Comics #206 **A:** Carl Barks
454 ❑ Jul 1978 Cover: 0.35 **NM** value: **4.00**

Other grades: Multiply prices above by **1.5 for Mint • 2/3 for Very Fine • 1/3 for Fine • 1/5 for Very Good • 1/8 for Good**

Way Out Yonder • Reprints story from Walt Disney's Comics #262 **A:** Carl Barks

455 ❑ Aug 1978 Cover: 0.35 **NM** value: **4.00**

Rocks to Riches • Reprints story from Walt Disney's Comics #241 **A:** Carl Barks

456 ❑ Sep 1978 Cover: 0.35 **NM** value: **4.00**

Last Frontier • Reprints story from Walt Disney's Comics #246 **A:** Carl Barks

457 ❑ Oct 1978 Cover: 0.35 **NM** value: **4.00**

The Madcap Mariner • Reprints story from Walt Disney's Comics #247 **A:** Carl Barks

458 ❑ Nov 1978 Cover: 0.35 **NM** value: **4.00**

The Candy Kid • Reprints story from Walt Disney's Comics #263 **A:** Carl Barks

459 ❑ Dec 1978 Cover: 0.35 **NM** value: **4.00**

Balloonatics • Reprints story from Walt Disney's Comics #242 **A:** Carl Barks

460 ❑ Jan 1979 Cover: 0.35 **NM** value: **4.00**
461 ❑ Feb 1979 Cover: 0.35 **NM** value: **4.00**
462 ❑ Mar 1979 Cover: 0.35 **NM** value: **4.00**
463 ❑ Apr 1979 Cover: 0.40 **NM** value: **4.00**
464 ❑ May 1979 Cover: 0.40 **NM** value: **4.00**
465 ❑ Jun 1979 Cover: 0.40 **NM** value: **4.00**
466 ❑ Jul 1979 Cover: 0.40 **NM** value: **3.00**
467 ❑ Aug 1979 Cover: 0.40 **NM** value: **4.00**
468 ❑ Sep 1979 Cover: 0.40 **NM** value: **4.00**
469 ❑ Oct 1979 Cover: 0.40 **NM** value: **4.00**
470 ❑ Nov 1979 Cover: 0.40 **NM** value: **4.00**
471 ❑ Dec 1979 Cover: 0.40 **NM** value: **4.00**
472 ❑ Jan 1980 Cover: 0.40 **NM** value: **4.00**
473 ❑ Feb 1980 Cover: 0.40 **NM** value: **4.00**
474 ❑ Mar 1980 Cover: 0.40 **NM** value: **4.00**

• Whitman begins publishing **A:** Carl Barks

475 ❑ Apr 1980 Cover: 0.40 **NM** value: **4.00**
476 ❑ May 1980 Cover: 0.40 **NM** value: **4.00**
477 ❑ Jun 1980 Cover: 0.40 **NM** value: **4.00**
478 ❑ Jul 1980 Cover: 0.40 **NM** value: **4.00**
479 ❑ Aug 1980 Cover: 0.40 **NM** value: **4.00**

• **CGC:** 1 graded, best 9.2

480 ❑ Sep 1980 Cover: 0.40 **NM** value: **4.00**
481 ❑ Oct 1980 Cover: 0.40 **NM** value: **4.00**

• **CGC:** 1 graded, best 8.5

482 ❑ Nov 1980 Cover: 0.40 **NM** value: **4.00**

• **CGC:** 1 graded, best 7.5

483 ❑ Dec 1980 Cover: 0.40 **NM** value: **4.00**
484 ❑ Jan 1981 Cover: 0.50 **NM** value: **4.00**

• **CGC:** 1 graded, best 4.0

485 ❑ Feb 1981 Cover: 0.50 **NM** value: **4.00**
486 ❑ Mar 1981 Cover: 0.50 **NM** value: **4.00**
487 ❑ 1981 Cover: 0.50 **NM** value: **4.00**
488 ❑ 1981 Cover: 0.50 **NM** value: **4.00**
489 ❑ 1981 Cover: 0.50 **NM** value: **4.00**
490 ❑ 1981 Cover: 0.50 **NM** value: **4.00**
491 ❑ Oct 1981 Cover: 0.50 **NM** value: **4.00**
492 ❑ Nov 1981 Cover: 0.50 **NM** value: **4.00**
493 ❑ Dec 1981 Cover: 0.50 **NM** value: **4.00**
494 ❑ Jan 1981 Cover: 0.50 **NM** value: **4.00**
495 ❑ Feb 1982 Cover: 0.50 **NM** value: **4.00**
496 ❑ Feb 1982 Cover: 0.60 **NM** value: **4.00**
497 ❑ Mar 1982 Cover: 0.60 **NM** value: **4.00**
498 ❑ Apr 1982 Cover: 0.60 **NM** value: **4.00**
499 ❑ May 1982 Cover: 0.60 **NM** value: **4.00**
500 ❑ ca. 1983 Cover: 0.60 **NM** value: **4.00**
501 ❑ ca. 1983 Cover: 0.60 **NM** value: **4.00**
502 ❑ ca. 1983 Cover: 0.60 **NM** value: **4.00**
503 ❑ ca. 1983 Cover: 0.60 **NM** value: **4.00**
504 ❑ ca. 1983 Cover: 0.60 **NM** value: **4.00**
505 ❑ ca. 1983 Cover: 0.60 **NM** value: **4.00**

Battle of Petras; The Tragic Magic Touch; Trapped on Wreckers Reef **A:** Carl Barks

506 ❑ ca. 1983 Cover: 0.60 **NM** value: **4.00**
507 ❑ ca. 1984 Cover: 0.60 **NM** value: **4.00**
508 ❑ ca. 1984 Cover: 0.60 **NM** value: **4.00**
509 ❑ ca. 1984 Cover: 0.60 **NM** value: **4.00**
510 ❑ ca. 1984 Cover: 0.60 **NM** value: **4.00**

WALT DISNEY'S COMICS AND STORIES — Gladstone

511 ❑ ca. 1986 Cover: 0.75 **NM** value: **9.00**
Circ: CapCity orders: **3,750** • **CGC:** 1 graded, best 9.4
• Gladstone begins publishing **A:** Carl Barks

512 ❑ Nov 1986 Cover: 0.75 **NM** value: **7.00**
Circ: CapCity orders: **3,600**

513 ❑ Dec 1986 Cover: 0.75 **NM** value: **7.00**
Circ: CapCity orders: **3,775**

514 ❑ Jan 1987 Cover: 0.75 **NM** value: **5.00**
Circ: Statement: **79,129** CapCity orders: **4,825**

515 ❑ Feb 1987 Cover: 0.75 **NM** value: **5.00**
Circ: Statement: **79,129** CapCity orders: **5,375**

516 ❑ Mar 1987 Cover: 0.75 **NM** value: **5.00**
Circ: Statement: **79,129** CapCity orders: **5,275**

517 ❑ Apr 1987 Cover: 0.75 **NM** value: **3.00**
Circ: Statement: **79,129** CapCity orders: **4,975**

518 ❑ May 1987 Cover: 0.75 **NM** value: **3.00**
Circ: Statement: **79,129** CapCity orders: **4,375**

519 ❑ Jun 1987 Cover: 0.75 **NM** value: **8.00**
Circ: Statement: **79,129** CapCity orders: **4,300**

520 ❑ Jul 1987 Cover: 0.95 **NM** value: **4.00**
Circ: Statement: **79,129** CapCity orders: **4,325**

521 ❑ Aug 1987 Cover: 0.95 **NM** value: **4.00**
Circ: Statement: **79,129** CapCity orders: **4,425**

522 ❑ Sep 1987 Cover: 0.95 **NM** value: **4.00**
Circ: Statement: **79,129** CapCity orders: **4,600**

523 ❑ Oct 1987 Cover: 0.95 **NM** value: **4.00**
Circ: Statement: **79,129** CapCity orders: **4,875**
• 1st Rosa 10-page story **A:** Carl Barks; Don Rosa

524 ❑ Nov 1987 Cover: 0.95 **NM** value: **4.00**
Circ: Statement: **79,129** CapCity orders: **4,825**

525 ❑ Dec 1987 Cover: 0.95 **NM** value: **4.00**
Circ: Statement: **79,129** CapCity orders: **4,600**

526 ❑ Jan 1988 Cover: 0.95 **NM** value: **4.00**
Circ: CapCity orders: **5,025**

527 ❑ Mar 1988 Cover: 0.95 **NM** value: **4.00**
Circ: CapCity orders: **4,975**

528 ❑ May 1988 Cover: 0.95 **NM** value: **4.00**
Circ: CapCity orders: **5,300**

529 ❑ Jun 1988 Cover: 0.95 **NM** value: **4.00**
Circ: CapCity orders: **4,925**

530 ❑ Jul 1988 Cover: 0.95 **NM** value: **4.00**
Circ: CapCity orders: **5,000**

531 ❑ Aug 1988 Cover: 0.95 **NM** value: **4.00**
Circ: CapCity orders: **5,050**

532 ❑ Sep 1988 Cover: 0.95 **NM** value: **4.00**
Circ: CapCity orders: **5,150**

533 ❑ Oct 1988 Cover: 0.95 **NM** value: **4.00**
Circ: CapCity orders: **5,250**

534 ❑ Nov 1988 Cover: 0.95 **NM** value: **4.00**
Circ: CapCity orders: **5,350**

535 ❑ Dec 1988 Cover: 0.95 **NM** value: **4.00**
Circ: CapCity orders: **5,300**

536 ❑ Feb 1989 Cover: 0.95 **NM** value: **4.00**
Circ: CapCity orders: **5,175**

537 ❑ Mar 1989 Cover: 0.95 **NM** value: **4.00**
• 1st Wm. Van Horn 10-page story **A:** Carl Barks; William Van Horn

538 ❑ Apr 1989 Cover: 0.95 **NM** value: **4.00**
Circ: CapCity orders: **5,450**

539 ❑ Jun 1989 Cover: 0.95 **NM** value: **4.00**
Circ: CapCity orders: **5,400**

540 ❑ Jul 1989 Cover: 0.95 **NM** value: **4.00**
Circ: CapCity orders: **5,600**

541 ❑ Aug 1989 Cover: 1.50 **NM** value: **4.00**
Circ: CapCity orders: **6,450**
• 48 pgs. **A:** Carl Barks **C:** Walt Kelly

542 ❑ Sep 1989 Cover: 1.50 **NM** value: **4.00**
Circ: CapCity orders: **5,700**

543 ❑ Oct 1989 Cover: 1.50 **NM** value: **4.00**
Circ: CapCity orders: **5,650**

544 ❑ Nov 1989 Cover: 1.50 **NM** value: **4.00**
Circ: CapCity orders: **5,500**

545 ❑ Dec 1989 Cover: 1.50 **NM** value: **4.00**
Circ: CapCity orders: **5,500**

546 ❑ Feb 1990 Cover: 1.95 **NM** value: **4.00**
Circ: CapCity orders: **5,450**

547 ❑ Apr 1990 Cover: 1.95 **NM** value: **4.00**
Circ: CapCity orders: **5,700**

WALT DISNEY'S COMICS AND STORIES — Disney

548 ❑ Jun 1990 Cover: 1.50 **NM** value: **4.00**
Circ: CapCity orders: **7,200**
Home is the Hero • Disney begins publishing **A:** Carl Barks; Vicar **W:** Les Lilley

549 ❑ Jul 1990 Cover: 1.50 **NM** value: **4.00**
Circ: CapCity orders: **6,100**

550 ❑ Aug 1990 Cover: 2.25 **NM** value: **3.00**
Circ: CapCity orders: **9,350**
• Milkman story **A:** Carl Barks

551 ❑ Sep 1990 Cover: 1.50 **NM** value: **2.00**
Circ: CapCity orders: **7,400**

552 ❑ Oct 1990 Cover: 1.50 **NM** value: **2.00**
Circ: CapCity orders: **7,300**

553 ❑ Nov 1990 Cover: 1.50 **NM** value: **2.00**
Circ: CapCity orders: **6,600**

554 ❑ Dec 1990 Cover: 1.50 **NM** value: **2.00**
Circ: CapCity orders: **6,500**

555 ❑ Jan 1991 Cover: 1.50 **NM** value: **Cover or less**
Circ: CapCity orders: **5,900**

556 ❑ Feb 1991 Cover: 1.50 **NM** value: **Cover or less**
Circ: CapCity orders: **5,650**

557 ❑ Mar 1991 Cover: 1.50 **NM** value: **2.00**
Circ: CapCity orders: **5,800**

558 ❑ Apr 1991 Cover: 1.50 **NM** value: **2.00**
Circ: CapCity orders: **5,550**

559 ❑ May 1991 Cover: 1.50 **NM** value: **2.00**
Circ: CapCity orders: **5,350**

560 ❑ Jun 1991 Cover: 1.50 **NM** value: **2.00**
Circ: CapCity orders: **5,550**

561 ❑ Jul 1991 Cover: 1.50 **NM** value: **2.00**
Circ: CapCity orders: **5,350**

562 ❑ Aug 1991 Cover: 1.50 **NM** value: **2.00**
Circ: CapCity orders: **5,250**

563 ❑ Sep 1991 Cover: 1.50 **NM** value: **2.00**
Circ: CapCity orders: **5,150**

564 ❑ Oct 1991 Cover: 1.50 **NM** value: **2.00**
Circ: CapCity orders: **5,100**
Time Tetrad, Part 2 **A:** Carl Barks

565 ❑ Nov 1991 Cover: 1.50 **NM** value: **2.00**
Circ: CapCity orders: **5,050**

566 ❑ Dec 1991 Cover: 2.95 **NM** value: **Cover or less**
Circ: CapCity orders: **4,850**

567 ❑ Jan 1992 Cover: 1.50 **NM** value: **2.00**
Circ: CapCity orders: **4,900**

568 ❑ Feb 1992 Cover: 1.50 **NM** value: **2.00**
Circ: CapCity orders: **5,050**

569 ❑ Mar 1992 Cover: 1.50 **NM** value: **2.00**
Circ: CapCity orders: **4,700**

570 ❑ Apr 1992 Cover: 1.50 **NM** value: **2.00**
Circ: CapCity orders: **5,200**
• Valentine centerfold **A:** Carl Barks

571 ❑ May 1992 Cover: 2.95 **NM** value: **Cover or less**
Circ: CapCity orders: **5,100**

572 ❑ Jun 1992 Cover: 1.50 **NM** value: **2.00**
Circ: CapCity orders: **5,200**
• map piece **A:** Carl Barks

573 ❑ Jul 1992 Cover: 1.50 **NM** value: **2.00**
Circ: CapCity orders: **5,250**
• map piece **A:** Carl Barks

574 ❑ Aug 1992 Cover: 2.95 **NM** value: **Cover or less**
Circ: CapCity orders: **5,200**
• map piece **A:** Carl Barks

575 ❑ Sep 1992 Cover: 2.95 **NM** value: **Cover or less**
Circ: CapCity orders: **4,900**

576 ❑ Oct 1992 Cover: 2.95 **NM** value: **Cover or less**
Circ: CapCity orders: **4,450**

577 ❑ Nov 1992 Cover: 1.50 **NM** value: **2.95**
Circ: CapCity orders: **4,300**

578 ❑ Dec 1992 Cover: 1.50 **NM** value: **Cover or less**
Circ: CapCity orders: **4,550**

579 ❑ Jan 1993 Cover: 1.50 **NM** value: **Cover or less**
Circ: CapCity orders: **4,300**

580 ❑ Feb 1993 Cover: 2.95 **NM** value: **Cover or less**
Circ: CapCity orders: **4,250**
• strip reprint **A:** Carl Barks

581 ❑ Mar 1993 Cover: 1.50 **NM** value: **Cover or less**
Circ: CapCity orders: **4,450**

582 ❑ Apr 1993 Cover: 2.95 **NM** value: **Cover or less**
Circ: CapCity orders: **4,350**
Sky Island **A:** Floyd Gottfredson; Walt Kelly

583 ❑ May 1993 Cover: 2.95 **NM** value: **Cover or less**
Circ: CapCity orders: **4,400**
Sky Island **A:** Floyd Gottfredson; Walt Kelly

584 ❑ Jun 1993 Cover: 1.50 **NM** value: **Cover or less**
Circ: CapCity orders: **4,800**

585 ❑ Jul 1993 Cover: 2.50 **NM** value: **Cover or less**
Circ: CapCity orders: **4,600**

WALT DISNEY'S COMICS AND STORIES — Gladstone

586 ❑ Aug 1993 Cover: 1.50 **NM** value: **Cover or less**
Circ: CapCity orders: **4,900**

587 ❑ Oct 1993 Cover: 1.50 **NM** value: **Cover or less**
Circ: CapCity orders: **4,625**

588 ❑ Dec 1993 Cover: 1.50 **NM** value: **Cover or less**
Circ: CapCity orders: **4,700**

589 ❑ Feb 1994 Cover: 1.50 **NM** value: **Cover or less**
Circ: CapCity orders: **4,500**

590 ❑ Apr 1994 Cover: 1.50 **NM** value: **Cover or less**
Circ: CapCity orders: **4,150**

591 ❑ Jun 1994 Cover: 1.50 **NM** value: **Cover or less**
Circ: CapCity orders: **4,025**

592 ❑ Aug 1994 Cover: 1.50 **NM** value: **Cover or less**
Circ: CapCity orders: **4,125**

593 ❑ Oct 1994 Cover: 1.50 **NM** value: **Cover or less**
Circ: CapCity orders: **3,975**

594 ❑ Dec 1994 Cover: 1.50 **NM** value: **Cover or less**
Circ: CapCity orders: **3,925**

595 ❑ Feb 1995 Cover: 1.50 **NM** value: **Cover or less**
Circ: Statement: **78,132** CapCity orders: **3,955**

596 ❑ Apr 1995 Cover: 1.50 **NM** value: **Cover or less**
Circ: Statement: **78,132** CapCity orders: **3,575**

597 ❑ Jun 1995 Cover: 1.50 **NM** value: **Cover or less**
Circ: Statement: **78,132** CapCity orders: **3,575**

598 ❑ Aug 1995 Cover: 1.50 **NM** value: **2.00**
Circ: Statement: **78,132** CapCity orders: **3,475**

599 ❑ Oct 1995 Cover: 1.95 **NM** value: **2.00**
Circ: Statement: **78,132** CapCity orders: **3,600**

600 ❑ Dec 1995 Cover: 2.95 **NM** value: **Cover or less**
Circ: Statement: **78,132** CapCity orders: **3,650**
• Giant-size. • reprints first Donald Duck stories by trio **A:** Carl Barks; Don Rosa; William Van Horn

601 ❑ Feb 1996 Cover: 5.95 **NM** value: **Cover or less**
Circ: Statement: **14,188** • **CGC:** 2 graded, best 9.6
• upgrades to prestige format

602 ❑ Apr 1996 Cover: 5.95 **NM** value: **Cover or less**
Circ: Statement: **14,188**

603 ❑ Jun 1996 Cover: 5.95 **NM** value: **Cover or less**
Circ: Statement: **14,188**

604 ❑ Aug 1996 Cover: 5.95 **NM** value: **Cover or less**
Circ: Statement: **14,188**

605 ❑ Oct 1996 Cover: 5.95 **NM** value: **Cover or less**
Circ: Statement: **14,188**

606 ❑ Dec 1996 Cover: 5.95 **NM** value: **Cover or less**
Circ: Statement: **14,188** Diamd. preorders: **5,660**

607 ❑ Jan 1996 Cover: 5.95 **NM** value: **Cover or less**
Circ: Diamd. preorders: **5,839**

608 ❑ Feb 1997 Cover: 5.95 **NM** value: **Cover or less**
Circ: Diamd. preorders: **5,361**

609 ❑ Mar 1997 Cover: 5.95 **NM** value: **Cover or less**
610 ❑ Mar 1997 Cover: 6.95 **NM** value: **Cover or less**
611 ❑ Apr 1997 Cover: 6.95 **NM** value: **Cover or less**
612 ❑ May 1997 Cover: 6.95 **NM** value: **Cover or less**
613 ❑ Jun 1997 Cover: 6.95 **NM** value: **Cover or less**
614 ❑ Jul 1997 Cover: 6.95 **NM** value: **Cover or less**
615 ❑ Aug 1997 Cover: 6.95 **NM** value: **Cover or less**
Circ: Diamd. preorders: **4,640**

616 ❑ Sep 1997 Cover: 6.95 **NM** value: **Cover or less**
617 ❑ Oct 1997 Cover: 6.95 **NM** value: **Cover or less**
Circ: Statement: **5,375** Diamd. preorders: **5,706**

618 ❑ Nov 1997 Cover: 6.95 **NM** value: **Cover or less**
Circ: Statement: **5,375** Diamd. preorders: **4,270**

619 ❑ Dec 1997 Cover: 6.95 **NM** value: **Cover or less**
Circ: Statement: **5,375** Diamd. preorders: **4,333**
• Pinocchio features

620 ❑ Jan 1998 Cover: 6.95 **NM** value: **Cover or less**
Circ: Statement: **5,375**

621 ❑ Feb 1998 Cover: 6.95 **NM** value: **Cover or less**
Circ: Statement: **5,375**

622 ❑ Mar 1998 Cover: 6.95 **NM** value: **Cover or less**
Circ: Statement: **5,375**

623 ❑ Apr 1998 Cover: 6.95 **NM** value: **Cover or less**
Circ: Statement: **5,375**

624 ❑ May 1998 Cover: 6.95 **NM** value: **Cover or less**
Circ: Statement: **5,375**

CGC-graded: Multiply prices above by **33 for 9.9 M • 16 for 9.8 NM/M • 7 for 9.6 NM+ • 5 for 9.4 NM • 2.5 for 9.2 NM- • 1.5 for 9.0 VF/NM**

625 ❑ Jun 1998 Cover: 6.95 **NM** value: **Cover or less**
Circ: Statement: **5,375**
626 ❑ Jul 1998 Cover: 6.95 **NM** value: **Cover or less**
Circ: Statement: **5,375**
627 ❑ Aug 1998 Cover: 6.95 **NM** value: **Cover or less**
Circ: Statement: **5,375**
628 ❑ Sep 1998 Cover: 6.95 **NM** value: **Cover or less**
Circ: Statement: **5,375**
629 ❑ Oct 1998 Cover: 6.95 **NM** value: **Cover or less**
630 ❑ Nov 1998 Cover: 6.95 **NM** value: **Cover or less**
631 ❑ Dec 1998 Cover: 6.95 **NM** value: **Cover or less**
632 ❑ Jan 1999 Cover: 6.95 **NM** value: **Cover or less**
633 ❑ Feb 1999 Cover: 6.95 **NM** value: **Cover or less**
final issue.

WALT DISNEY'S COMICS AND STORIES PENNY PINCHER — Gladstone

1 ❑ May 1997 Cover: 0.99 **NM** value: **1.00**
📖 The Purloined Putty **A:** Carl Barks
2 ❑ Jun 1997 Cover: 0.99 **NM** value: **1.00**
Circ: Diamd. preorders: **6,246**
📖 Feud and Far Between • reprints Barks' Feud and Far Between **A:** Carl Barks
3 ❑ Jul 1997 Cover: 0.99 **NM** value: **1.00**
Circ: Diamd. preorders: **6,080**
4 ❑ Aug 1997 Cover: 0.99 **NM** value: **1.00**

WALT DISNEY'S COMICS DIGEST — Gladstone

1 ❑ Dec 1986 Cover: 1.25 **NM** value: **6.00**
📖 Secret of Atlantis • Reprints story from Uncle Scrooge #5 **A:** Carl Barks; Walt Kelly
2 ❑ 1987 Cover: 1.25 **NM** value: **4.00**
📖 Island in the Sky • Reprints story from Uncle Scrooge #29 **A:** Carl Barks
3 ❑ Mar 1987 Cover: 1.25 **NM** value: **4.00**
📖 All at Sea • Reprints story from Uncle Scrooge #31 **A:** Carl Barks
4 ❑ Apr 1987 Cover: 1.25 **NM** value: **4.00**
📖 Donald Duck and the Titanic Ants!; Picnic • Reprints stories from Donald Duck #60 and Picnic Party #8 **A:** Carl Barks
5 ❑ May 1987 Cover: 1.25 **NM** value: **4.00**
📖 The Strange Shipwrecks; Daisy Duck's Diary: The Dainty Daredevil • Reprints story from Uncle Scrooge #23 **A:** Carl Barks
6 ❑ Jun 1987 Cover: 1.25 **NM** value: **4.00**
📖 The Twenty-four Carat Moon • Reprints story from Uncle Scrooge #24 **A:** Carl Barks
7 ❑ Jul 1987 Cover: 1.25 **NM** value: **4.00**
📖 Mastering the Matterhorn; The Dream Planet • Reprints stories from Four Color Comics #1025 (Vacation in Disneyland) **A:** Carl Barks

WALT DISNEY'S COMICS IN COLOR — Gladstone

Bk 1 ❑ Cover: 19.95 **NM** value: **Cover or less**
Bk 2 ❑ Cover: 19.95 **NM** value: **Cover or less**
Bk 3 ❑ Cover: 19.95 **NM** value: **Cover or less**
Bk 4 ❑ Cover: 19.95 **NM** value: **Cover or less**
Bk 5 ❑ Cover: 19.95 **NM** value: **Cover or less**
Bk 6 ❑ Cover: 19.95 **NM** value: **Cover or less**
Bk 7 ❑ Cover: 19.95 **NM** value: **Cover or less**

WALT DISNEY'S HOLIDAY PARADE — Disney

1 ❑ Cover: 2.95 **NM** value: **Cover or less**
Circ: CapCity orders: **5,950**
📖 Three Good Little Ducks; Don We Now Our Prey Apparel; Pluto's Sweater; Santa's Unexpected Visit; Santa Claus Ain't Coming to Town; Shine a Little Light; The Topsy-Turvey Tree; The Moose Head Mystery **A:** Carl Barks; Al Hubbard; Frank McSavage; Julio Ramos; Paul Murray; Tello; Tony Strobl; Cosmé Quartieri **W:** Carl Barks; Cherie Wilkerson; Dave Angus; Don Christensen; Nick George; Vic Lockman
2 ❑ Cover: 2.95 **NM** value: **Cover or less**
Circ: CapCity orders: **4,550**

WALT DISNEY SHOWCASE — Gold Key

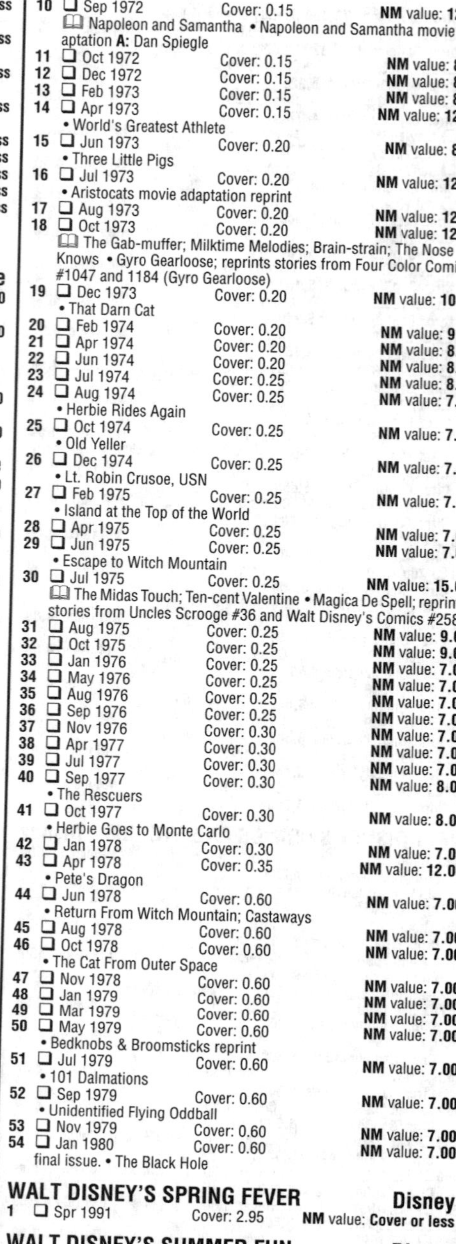

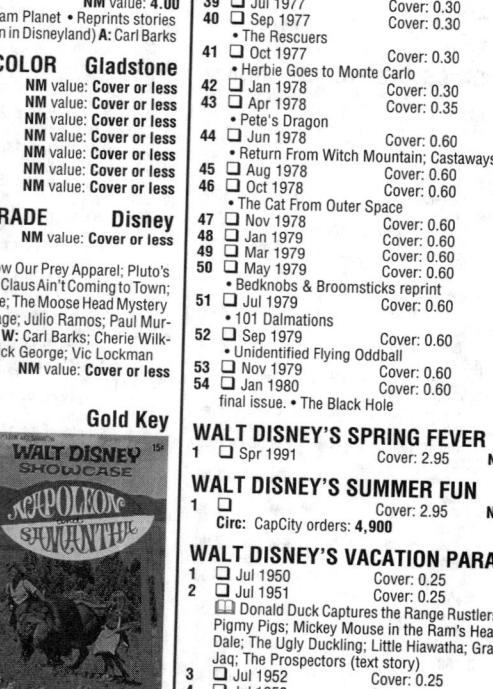

The 1970s were a high point for Walt Disney movie-making, and Walt Disney Showcase threw the spotlight on many of the various productions as they came out. Included were features on Swiss Family Robinson, Bedknobs and Broomsticks, Unidentified Flying Oddball, The Black Hole, and many others.

Naturally, there was always room for Disney's cartoon features, and Mickey Mouse, Goofy, and the rest of the gang were frequent guests in this series. Characters who couldn't support a title all to themselves, such as Pluto and Tinkerbell, would get their own issues here.

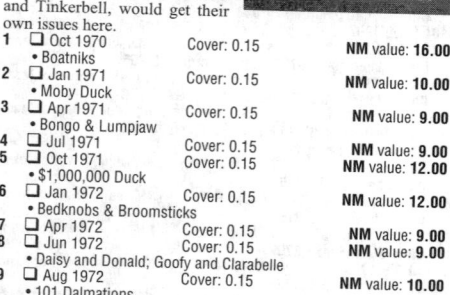

1 ❑ Oct 1970 Cover: 0.15 **NM** value: **16.00**
• Boatniks
2 ❑ Jan 1971 Cover: 0.15 **NM** value: **10.00**
• Moby Duck
3 ❑ Apr 1971 Cover: 0.15 **NM** value: **9.00**
• Bongo & Lumpjaw
4 ❑ Jul 1971 Cover: 0.15 **NM** value: **9.00**
5 ❑ Oct 1971 Cover: 0.15 **NM** value: **12.00**
• $1,000,000 Duck
6 ❑ Jan 1972 Cover: 0.15 **NM** value: **12.00**
• Bedknobs & Broomsticks
7 ❑ Apr 1972 Cover: 0.15 **NM** value: **9.00**
8 ❑ Jun 1972 Cover: 0.15 **NM** value: **9.00**
• Daisy and Donald; Goofy and Clarabelle
9 ❑ Aug 1972 Cover: 0.15 **NM** value: **10.00**
• 101 Dalmations
10 ❑ Sep 1972 Cover: 0.15 **NM** value: **12.00**
📖 Napoleon and Samantha • Napoleon and Samantha movie adaptation **A:** Dan Spiegle
11 ❑ Oct 1972 Cover: 0.15 **NM** value: **8.00**
12 ❑ Dec 1972 Cover: 0.15 **NM** value: **8.00**
13 ❑ Feb 1973 Cover: 0.15 **NM** value: **8.00**
14 ❑ Apr 1973 Cover: 0.15 **NM** value: **12.00**
• World's Greatest Athlete
15 ❑ Jun 1973 Cover: 0.20 **NM** value: **8.00**
• Three Little Pigs
16 ❑ Jul 1973 Cover: 0.20 **NM** value: **12.00**
• Aristocats movie adaptation reprint
17 ❑ Aug 1973 Cover: 0.20 **NM** value: **12.00**
18 ❑ Oct 1973 Cover: 0.20 **NM** value: **12.00**
📖 The Gab-muffer; Milktime Melodies; Brain-strain; The Nose Knows • Gyro Gearloose; reprints stories from Four Color Comics #1047 and 1184 (Gyro Gearloose)
19 ❑ Dec 1973 Cover: 0.20 **NM** value: **10.00**
• That Darn Cat
20 ❑ Feb 1974 Cover: 0.20 **NM** value: **9.00**
21 ❑ Apr 1974 Cover: 0.20 **NM** value: **8.00**
22 ❑ Jun 1974 Cover: 0.20 **NM** value: **8.00**
23 ❑ Jul 1974 Cover: 0.25 **NM** value: **8.00**
24 ❑ Aug 1974 Cover: 0.25 **NM** value: **7.00**
• Herbie Rides Again
25 ❑ Oct 1974 Cover: 0.25 **NM** value: **7.00**
• Old Yeller
26 ❑ Dec 1974 Cover: 0.25 **NM** value: **7.00**
• Lt. Robin Crusoe, USN
27 ❑ Feb 1975 Cover: 0.25 **NM** value: **7.00**
• Island at the Top of the World
28 ❑ Apr 1975 Cover: 0.25 **NM** value: **7.00**
29 ❑ Jun 1975 Cover: 0.25 **NM** value: **7.00**
• Escape to Witch Mountain
30 ❑ Jul 1975 Cover: 0.25 **NM** value: **15.00**
📖 The Midas Touch; Ten-cent Valentine • Magica De Spell; reprints stories from Uncles Scrooge #36 and Walt Disney's Comics #258
31 ❑ Aug 1975 Cover: 0.25 **NM** value: **9.00**
32 ❑ Oct 1975 Cover: 0.25 **NM** value: **9.00**
33 ❑ Jan 1976 Cover: 0.25 **NM** value: **7.00**
34 ❑ May 1976 Cover: 0.25 **NM** value: **7.00**
35 ❑ Aug 1976 Cover: 0.25 **NM** value: **7.00**
36 ❑ Sep 1976 Cover: 0.25 **NM** value: **7.00**
37 ❑ Nov 1976 Cover: 0.30 **NM** value: **7.00**
38 ❑ Apr 1977 Cover: 0.30 **NM** value: **7.00**
39 ❑ Jul 1977 Cover: 0.30 **NM** value: **7.00**
40 ❑ Sep 1977 Cover: 0.30 **NM** value: **8.00**
• The Rescuers
41 ❑ Oct 1977 Cover: 0.30 **NM** value: **8.00**
• Herbie Goes to Monte Carlo
42 ❑ Jan 1978 Cover: 0.30 **NM** value: **7.00**
43 ❑ Apr 1978 Cover: 0.35 **NM** value: **12.00**
• Pete's Dragon
44 ❑ Jun 1978 Cover: 0.60 **NM** value: **7.00**
• Return From Witch Mountain; Castaways
45 ❑ Aug 1978 Cover: 0.60 **NM** value: **7.00**
46 ❑ Oct 1978 Cover: 0.60 **NM** value: **7.00**
• The Cat From Outer Space
47 ❑ Nov 1978 Cover: 0.60 **NM** value: **7.00**
48 ❑ Jan 1979 Cover: 0.60 **NM** value: **7.00**
49 ❑ Mar 1979 Cover: 0.60 **NM** value: **7.00**
50 ❑ May 1979 Cover: 0.60 **NM** value: **7.00**
• Bedknobs & Broomsticks reprint
51 ❑ Jul 1979 Cover: 0.60 **NM** value: **7.00**
• 101 Dalmations
52 ❑ Sep 1979 Cover: 0.60 **NM** value: **7.00**
• Unidentified Flying Oddball
53 ❑ Nov 1979 Cover: 0.60 **NM** value: **7.00**
54 ❑ Jan 1980 Cover: 0.60 **NM** value: **7.00**
final issue. • The Black Hole

WALT DISNEY'S SPRING FEVER — Disney

1 ❑ Spr 1991 Cover: 2.95 **NM** value: **Cover or less**

WALT DISNEY'S SUMMER FUN — Disney

1 ❑ Cover: 2.95 **NM** value: **Cover or less**
Circ: CapCity orders: **4,900**

WALT DISNEY'S VACATION PARADE — Dell

1 ❑ Jul 1950 Cover: 0.25 **NM** value: **500.00**
2 ❑ Jul 1951 Cover: 0.25 **NM** value: **145.00**
📖 Donald Duck Captures the Range Rustlers; Li'l Bad Wolf and the Pigmy Pigs; Mickey Mouse in the Ram's Head Ramblers; Chip 'n' Dale; The Ugly Duckling; Little Hiawatha; Grandma Duck; Gus and Jaq; The Prospectors (text story)
3 ❑ Jul 1952 Cover: 0.25 **NM** value: **80.00**
4 ❑ Jul 1953 Cover: 0.25 **NM** value: **80.00**
📖 Donald Duck: Panama; The Li'l Bad Wolf; Peter Pan and Captain Hook; Mickey Mouse: Whaley Go-Round; Chip 'n' Dale; Robin Hood: The Beards of Little John; Grandma Duck: Livestock Show; Pluto; Bucky Bug; A Summer Vacation (text story); Huey, Dewey, and Louie
5 ❑ Jul 1954 Cover: 0.25 **NM** value: **80.00**

WALTER — Dark Horse

1 ❑ Feb 1996 Cover: 2.50 **NM** value: **Cover or less**
📖 Campaign of Teror **A:** Doug Mahnke **W:** John Arcudi
2 ❑ Mar 1996 Cover: 2.50 **NM** value: **Cover or less**
3 ❑ Apr 1996 Cover: 2.50 **NM** value: **Cover or less**
4 ❑ May 1996 Cover: 2.50 **NM** value: **Cover or less**
final issue. **A:** Doug Mahnke **W:** John Arcudi

WALTER KITTY IN...THE HOLLOW EARTH — Vision

1 ❑ Jul 1996 Cover: 1.95 **NM** value: **Cover or less**
2 ❑ Jul 1996 Cover: 1.95 **NM** value: **Cover or less**

WALT THE WILDCAT — Motion Comics

1 ❑ Sep 1995 Cover: 2.50 **NM** value: **Cover or less**

WAMBI, JUNGLE BOY — Fiction House

1 ❑ Spr 1942 Cover: 0.10 **NM** value: **500.00**
2 ❑ Win 1942 Cover: 0.10 **NM** value: **300.00**
📖 The Hell-Cat Traitior; Slave Beasts for Juju Pygmy; Lair of the Killer Rajah
3 ❑ Spr 1943 Cover: 0.10 **NM** value: **300.00**
4 ❑ Fal 1948 Cover: 0.10 **NM** value: **175.00**
5 ❑ May 1949 Cover: 0.10 **NM** value: **175.00**
6 ❑ Spr 1950 Cover: 0.10 **NM** value: **150.00**
7 ❑ ca. 1950 Cover: 0.10 **NM** value: **150.00**
8 ❑ ca. 1950 Cover: 0.10 **NM** value: **150.00**
9 ❑ ca. 1950 Cover: 0.10 **NM** value: **150.00**
10 ❑ ca. 1950 Cover: 0.10 **NM** value: **150.00**
11 ❑ Spr 1951 Cover: 0.10 **NM** value: **125.00**
12 ❑ Sum 1951 Cover: 0.10 **NM** value: **125.00**
13 ❑ Fal 1951 Cover: 0.10 **NM** value: **125.00**
14 ❑ Win 1951 Cover: 0.10 **NM** value: **125.00**
15 ❑ Spr 1952 Cover: 0.10 **NM** value: **100.00**
16 ❑ Sum 1952 Cover: 0.10 **NM** value: **100.00**
17 ❑ Fal 1952 Cover: 0.10 **NM** value: **100.00**
18 ❑ Win 1952 Cover: 0.10 **NM** value: **100.00**

WANDA LUWAND & THE PIRATE GIRLS — Fantagraphics / Eros

All issues are adults only.
1 ❑ b&w Cover: 2.50 **NM** value: **Cover or less**

WANDERERS, THE — DC

1 ❑ Jun 1988 Cover: 1.25 **NM** value: **1.50**
Circ: CapCity orders: **21,100**
📖 From Graves of Nothing **A:** Dave Hoover; Robert Campanella **W:** Doug Moench ★ Origin of Aviax, The Wanderers, The Elvar, Re-Animage. ★ 1st Appearance of Aviax, The Wanderers, The Elvar, Re-Animage.
2 ❑ Jul 1988 Cover: 1.25 **NM** value: **1.50**
Circ: CapCity orders: **15,400**
📖 The First Mission **A:** Dave Hoover; Robert Campanella **W:** Doug Moench
3 ❑ Aug 1988 Cover: 1.25 **NM** value: **1.50**
Circ: CapCity orders: **14,350**
📖 A Dream of Monsters
4 ❑ Sep 1988 Cover: 1.25 **NM** value: **1.50**
Circ: CapCity orders: **13,650**
5 ❑ Oct 1988 Cover: 1.25 **NM** value: **1.50**
Circ: CapCity orders: **13,350**
6 ❑ Nov 1988 Cover: 1.25 **NM** value: **1.50**
Circ: CapCity orders: **12,300**
7 ❑ Dec 1988 Cover: 1.25 **NM** value: **1.50**
Circ: CapCity orders: **11,400**
8 ❑ Dec 1988 Cover: 1.25 **NM** value: **1.50**
Circ: CapCity orders: **10,450**
9 ❑ Jan 1989 Cover: 1.25 **NM** value: **1.50**
Circ: CapCity orders: **9,500**
10 ❑ Jan 1989 Cover: 1.25 **NM** value: **1.50**
Circ: CapCity orders: **9,050**
11 ❑ Feb 1989 Cover: 1.25 **NM** value: **1.50**
Circ: CapCity orders: **8,650**
12 ❑ Mar 1989 Cover: 1.25 **NM** value: **1.50**
Circ: CapCity orders: **7,950**
13 ❑ Apr 1989 Cover: 1.25 **NM** value: **1.50**
Circ: CapCity orders: **7,700**
final issue.

WANDERING STAR — Pen and Ink

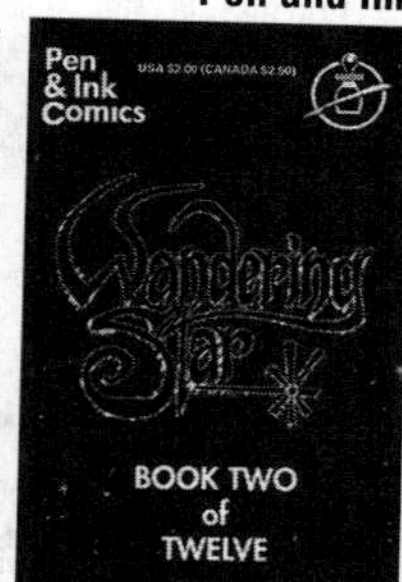

Graikor, Elli, Madison, and Cassandra are the crew of The Wandering Star, an experimental ship being built at the Galactic Academy. In ongoing interludes of flashbacks throughout the series, Cassandra recounts the challenges they faced — challenges that eventually led to their intergalactic fame.

Fighting the Bono Kiro, a species with a ruthless determination and a sinister proclivity to recycle, similar to Star Trek: The Next Generation's Borg, is a grueling process leading to casualties ranging from friends to planets.

Self-publisher Teri Wood is an artist capable of expressing a great range of emotion in humanoid and alien subjects. Her work is also featured in Rhudiprrt, Prince of Fur.

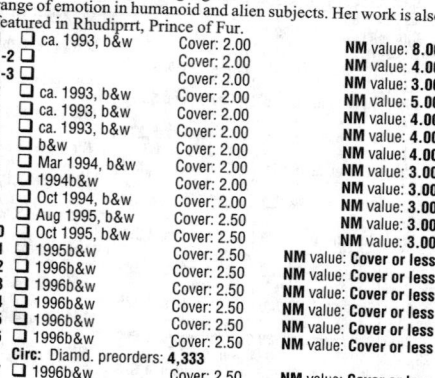

1 ❑ ca. 1993, b&w Cover: 2.00 **NM** value: **8.00**
1-2 ❑ Cover: 2.00 **NM** value: **4.00**
1-3 ❑ Cover: 2.00 **NM** value: **3.00**
2 ❑ ca. 1993, b&w Cover: 2.00 **NM** value: **5.00**
3 ❑ ca. 1993, b&w Cover: 2.00 **NM** value: **4.00**
4 ❑ ca. 1993, b&w Cover: 2.00 **NM** value: **4.00**
5 ❑ b&w Cover: 2.00 **NM** value: **4.00**
6 ❑ Mar 1994, b&w Cover: 2.00 **NM** value: **3.00**
7 ❑ 1994b&w Cover: 2.00 **NM** value: **3.00**
8 ❑ Oct 1994, b&w Cover: 2.00 **NM** value: **3.00**
9 ❑ Aug 1995, b&w Cover: 2.50 **NM** value: **3.00**
10 ❑ Oct 1995, b&w Cover: 2.50 **NM** value: **3.00**
11 ❑ 1995b&w Cover: 2.50 **NM** value: **Cover or less**
12 ❑ 1996b&w Cover: 2.50 **NM** value: **Cover or less**
13 ❑ 1996b&w Cover: 2.50 **NM** value: **Cover or less**
14 ❑ 1996b&w Cover: 2.50 **NM** value: **Cover or less**
15 ❑ 1996b&w Cover: 2.50 **NM** value: **Cover or less**
16 ❑ 1996b&w Cover: 2.50 **NM** value: **Cover or less**
Circ: Diamd. preorders: **4,333**
17 ❑ 1996b&w Cover: 2.50 **NM** value: **Cover or less**
Circ: Diamd. preorders: **4,361**

Other grades: Multiply prices above by **1.5 for Mint • 2/3 for Very Fine • 1/3 for Fine • 1/5 for Very Good • 1/8 for Good**

18 ❑ 1996b&w Cover: 2.50 **NM** value: **Cover or less**
Circ: Diamd. preorders: **3,978**
19 ❑ b&w Cover: 2.50 **NM** value: **Cover or less**
Circ: Diamd. preorders: **3,768**
20 ❑ b&w Cover: 2.50 **NM** value: **Cover or less**
Circ: Diamd. preorders: **3,502**
21 ❑ 1997b&w Cover: 2.50 **NM** value: **Cover or less**
Circ: Diamd. preorders: **3,196**
Bk 1❑ Nov 1994, b&w Cover: 11.95 **NM** value: **Cover or less**
• collects first seven issues **A:** Teri S. Wood **W:** Teri S. Wood
Bk 1-2❑b&w Cover: 11.95 **NM** value: **Cover or less**
Bk 1-3❑Oct 1998, b&w Cover: 14.95 **NM** value: **Cover or less**
Bk 2❑ Nov 1998, b&w Cover: 14.95 **NM** value: **Cover or less**
Bk 3❑ Dec 1998, b&w Cover: 14.95 **NM** value: **Cover or less**

WANDERING STARS — Fantagraphics

1 ❑ Cover: 2.00 **NM** value: **Cover or less**
📖 The Wanderer **A:** Sam Keith **W:** Stuart Hopen

WANTED COMICS — Toytown

9 ❑ Oct 1947 Cover: 0.10 **NM** value: **95.00**
10 ❑ Nov 1947 Cover: 0.10 **NM** value: **58.00**
11 ❑ Jan 1948 Cover: 0.10 **NM** value: **58.00**
12 ❑ Mar 1948 Cover: 0.10 **NM** value: **85.00**
• Cited in Seduction of the Innocent
13 ❑ May 1948 Cover: 0.10 **NM** value: **58.00**
14 ❑ Jul 1948 Cover: 0.10 **NM** value: **52.00**
15 ❑ Sep 1948 Cover: 0.10 **NM** value: **52.00**
📖 The Black Hand; The Tombstone; Sleepy-Eyed Killer; The Badge Bandit
16 ❑ Nov 1948 Cover: 0.10 **NM** value: **48.00**
17 ❑ Jan 1949 Cover: 0.10 **NM** value: **48.00**
18 ❑ Feb 1949 Cover: 0.10 **NM** value: **110.00**
📖 Satan's Cigarettes • Anti-drug story
19 ❑ Mar 1949 Cover: 0.10 **NM** value: **48.00**
20 ❑ May 1949 Cover: 0.10 **NM** value: **48.00**
21 ❑ Jul 1949 Cover: 0.10 **NM** value: **48.00**
22 ❑ Sep 1949 Cover: 0.10 **NM** value: **48.00**
23 ❑ Nov 1949 Cover: 0.10 **NM** value: **38.00**
24 ❑ Jan 1950 Cover: 0.10 **NM** value: **38.00**
25 ❑ Feb 1950 Cover: 0.10 **NM** value: **38.00**
26 ❑ May 1950 Cover: 0.10 **NM** value: **38.00**
27 ❑ Jul 1950 Cover: 0.10 **NM** value: **38.00**
28 ❑ Aug 1950 Cover: 0.10 **NM** value: **38.00**
29 ❑ Sep 1950 Cover: 0.10 **NM** value: **38.00**
30 ❑ Oct 1950 Cover: 0.10 **NM** value: **38.00**
31 ❑ Nov 1950 Cover: 0.10 **NM** value: **32.00**
32 ❑ Dec 1950 Cover: 0.10 **NM** value: **32.00**
33 ❑ Jan 1951 Cover: 0.10 **NM** value: **32.00**
34 ❑ Mar 1951 Cover: 0.10 **NM** value: **32.00**
📖 Hot Money; Wanted: Jon Lewis Carey; Vendetta; Wanted: Fred Tenuto and William Francis Sutton; Crime Lab: The Clue of the Tin Whistle; Smart Boy! (text story); You're the Detective; The Green Parrot Murder Case; **A:** Bob Rogers; Mort Leav **W:** Bob Rogers; Mort Leav
35 ❑ Apr 1951 Cover: 0.10 **NM** value: **52.00**
• Cited in Seduction of the Innocent
36 ❑ May 1951 Cover: 0.10 **NM** value: **32.00**
37 ❑ Jun 1951 Cover: 0.10 **NM** value: **32.00**
38 ❑ Jul 1951 Cover: 0.10 **NM** value: **32.00**
39 ❑ Aug 1951 Cover: 0.10 **NM** value: **85.00**
📖 The Horror Weed • Anti-drug story
40 ❑ Sep 1951 Cover: 0.10 **NM** value: **32.00**
41 ❑ Oct 1951 Cover: 0.10 **NM** value: **32.00**
42 ❑ Nov 1951 Cover: 0.10 **NM** value: **32.00**
43 ❑ Dec 1951 Cover: 0.10 **NM** value: **32.00**
44 ❑ Jan 1952 Cover: 0.10 **NM** value: **32.00**
45 ❑ Feb 1952 Cover: 0.10 **NM** value: **32.00**
46 ❑ Mar 1952 Cover: 0.10 **NM** value: **32.00**
47 ❑ May 1952 Cover: 0.10 **NM** value: **32.00**
48 ❑ Jun 1952 Cover: 0.10 **NM** value: **32.00**
49 ❑ Aug 1952 Cover: 0.10 **NM** value: **32.00**
50 ❑ Oct 1952 Cover: 0.10 **NM** value: **52.00**
51 ❑ Dec 1952 Cover: 0.10 **NM** value: **52.00**
52 ❑ Feb 1953 Cover: 0.10 **NM** value: **52.00**
• **CGC:** 1 graded, best 3.5
53 ❑ Apr 1953 Cover: 0.10 **NM** value: **32.00**
final issue.

WANTED, THE WORLD'S MOST DANGEROUS VILLAINS — DC

1 ❑ Aug 1972 Cover: 0.20 **NM** value: **10.00**
• **CGC:** 1 graded, best 9.0
• reprints stories from Batman #112, World's Finest #111, and Green Lantern #1
2 ❑ Oct 1972 Cover: 0.20 **NM** value: **8.00**
• reprints stories from Batman #25 and Flash #121
3 ❑ Nov 1972 Cover: 0.20 **NM** value: **8.00**
• reprints stories from Action #69, More Fun #65, and Flash #100
4 ❑ Dec 1972 Cover: 0.20 **NM** value: **6.00**
• reprints stories from All-American #61 and Kid Eternity #15★ 1st Appearance of Solomon Grundy.
5 ❑ Jan 1973 Cover: 0.20 **NM** value: **6.00**
• reprints stories from Green Lantern #33 and Doll Man #15
6 ❑ Feb 1973 Cover: 0.20 **NM** value: **6.00**
• reprints stories from Adventure #77 and Sensation Comics #66 and 71
7 ❑ Apr 1973 Cover: 0.20 **NM** value: **6.00**
• reprints stories from More Fun #76, Flash #90, and Adventure #72
8 ❑ Jul 1973 Cover: 0.20 **NM** value: **6.00**
• reprints stories from Flash #114 and More Fun #73
9 ❑ Sep 1973 Cover: 0.20 **NM** value: **6.00**
final issue.

WAR — Charlton

1 ❑ Jul 1975, b&w Cover: 0.25 **NM** value: **5.00**
📖 MiG Country; A Hero I Knew (text); Geronimo's Ghost; The Flying Cowboy **A:** Pat Boyette; Don Perlin; Wally Wood **W:** Joe Gill
2 ❑ Sep 1975 Cover: 0.25 **NM** value: **3.00**
3 ❑ Nov 1975 Cover: 0.25 **NM** value: **3.00**
4 ❑ Jan 1976 Cover: 0.25 **NM** value: **3.00**
5 ❑ Mar 1976 Cover: 0.25 **NM** value: **3.00**
6 ❑ May 1976 Cover: 0.30 **NM** value: **3.00**
7 ❑ Jul 1976 Cover: 0.30 **NM** value: **3.00**
8 ❑ Sep 1976 Cover: 0.30 **NM** value: **3.00**
9 ❑ Nov 1976 Cover: 0.30 **NM** value: **3.00**
10 ❑ Sep 1978 Cover: 0.35 **NM** value: **3.00**
11 ❑ 1978 Cover: 0.35 **NM** value: **2.00**
12 ❑ 1979 Cover: 0.40 **NM** value: **2.00**
13 ❑ 1979 Cover: 0.40 **NM** value: **2.00**
14 ❑ 1979 Cover: 0.40 **NM** value: **2.00**
15 ❑ Aug 1979 Cover: 0.40 **NM** value: **2.00**
16 ❑ Sep 1979 Cover: 0.40 **NM** value: **2.00**
📖 The Enemy Above; The Brothers; Trapped? (text story);
17 ❑ **NM** value: **2.00**
18 ❑ **NM** value: **2.00**
19 ❑ 1980 **NM** value: **2.00**
20 ❑ 1980 **NM** value: **2.00**
21 ❑ 1980 **NM** value: **2.00**
22 ❑ 1980 **NM** value: **2.00**
23 ❑ **NM** value: **2.00**
24 ❑ **NM** value: **2.00**
25 ❑ 1981 Cover: 0.50 **NM** value: **2.00**
26 ❑ 1981 Cover: 0.50 **NM** value: **2.00**
27 ❑ 1981 Cover: 0.50 **NM** value: **2.00**
28 ❑ 1981 Cover: 0.50 **NM** value: **2.00**
29 ❑ 1981 Cover: 0.50 **NM** value: **2.00**
30 ❑ **NM** value: **2.00**
31 ❑ **NM** value: **2.00**
32 ❑ 1982 Cover: 0.60 **NM** value: **2.00**
📖 Lanson's Scow; Navy Guns; Command Decision; One More Chance
33 ❑ 1982 Cover: 0.60 **NM** value: **2.00**
34 ❑ 1982 Cover: 0.60 **NM** value: **2.00**
35 ❑ 1982 Cover: 0.60 **NM** value: **2.00**
36 ❑ 1982 Cover: 0.60 **NM** value: **2.00**
37 ❑ Cover: 0.60 **NM** value: **2.00**
38 ❑ Cover: 0.60 **NM** value: **2.00**
39 ❑ 1983 Cover: 0.60 **NM** value: **2.00**
40 ❑ 1983 Cover: 0.60 **NM** value: **2.00**
41 ❑ 1983 Cover: 0.60 **NM** value: **2.00**
42 ❑ 1983 Cover: 0.60 **NM** value: **2.00**
43 ❑ 1983 Cover: 0.60 **NM** value: **2.00**
44 ❑ Cover: 0.60 **NM** value: **2.00**
45 ❑ Cover: 0.60 **NM** value: **2.00**
46 ❑ 1984 Cover: 0.60 **NM** value: **2.00**
📖 Earning a D.S.C.; Ski's Gun; Recon Squad; The Growth of Fear
47 ❑ **NM** value: **2.00**
48 ❑ **NM** value: **2.00**
49 ❑ **NM** value: **2.00**

WAR, THE — Marvel

1 ❑ Jun 1989 Cover: 3.50 **NM** value: **Cover or less**
Circ: CapCity orders: **16,800**
• Series continued from story in "The Draft"
2 ❑ Jul 1989 Cover: 3.50 **NM** value: **Cover or less**
Circ: CapCity orders: **14,350**
3 ❑ Aug 1989 Cover: 3.50 **NM** value: **Cover or less**
Circ: CapCity orders: **14,000**
4 ❑ Feb 1990 Cover: 3.50 **NM** value: **Cover or less**
Circ: CapCity orders: **10,200**

WAR ACTION — Atlas

1 ❑ Apr 1952 Cover: 0.10 **NM** value: **100.00**
• **CGC:** 1 graded, best 8.5
2 ❑ May 1952 Cover: 0.10 **NM** value: **60.00**
3 ❑ Jun 1952 Cover: 0.10 **NM** value: **60.00**
4 ❑ Jul 1952 Cover: 0.10 **NM** value: **60.00**
5 ❑ Aug 1952 Cover: 0.10 **NM** value: **60.00**
6 ❑ Sep 1952 Cover: 0.10 **NM** value: **60.00**
7 ❑ Oct 1952 Cover: 0.10 **NM** value: **60.00**
C: Russ Heath **A:** Robert Q. Sale
8 ❑ Nov 1952 Cover: 0.10 **NM** value: **60.00**
9 ❑ Dec 1952 Cover: 0.10 **NM** value: **60.00**
10 ❑ Jan 1953 Cover: 0.10 **NM** value: **60.00**
11 ❑ Feb 1953 Cover: 0.10 **NM** value: **60.00**
12 ❑ Mar 1953 Cover: 0.10 **NM** value: **60.00**
13 ❑ Apr 1953 Cover: 0.10 **NM** value: **60.00**
14 ❑ Jun 1953 Cover: 0.10 **NM** value: **60.00**

WAR AGAINST CRIME — E.C.

The first Graham Ingels art for E.C. appeared in the first issue of this Pre-Trend series, a crime comic book that, in its last two issues, introduced a horror element with the introduction of The Vault of Horror and The Vault-Keeper. To that point, however, it was a "crime book," and all but the last cover featured a spine-paralleling blurb "True Crime" and all but the last two carried the cover blurb "Real stories from police records!" Most issues had covers by Johnny Craig.

The last two issues cover-trumpeted stories from "The Vault of Horror," and, with #12, the transformation was complete. It changed its title to The Vault of Horror. — Maggie

1 ❑ Spr 1948 Cover: 0.10 **NM** value: **530.00**
• **CGC:** 2 graded, best 6.5
📖 Public Enemy…the Story of Machine-Gun Kelley!; Portfolio of Death!; The Ruby Stickpin!; Smokin' Six-Guns! **A:** Johnny Craig; Ed Moore; Graham Ingels; Lee Ames **W:** Johnny Craig; Ed Moore; Graham Ingels; Lee Ames
2 ❑ Sum 1948 Cover: 0.10 **NM** value: **325.00**
• **CGC:** 2 graded, best 9.2
📖 Hank "Two-Gun" Corley!; The Crystal Ball Killer; America's First Crime; The Saga of Spotlight John **A:** Frank Bolle; Graham Ingels; Lee Ames; Leonard Starr; Stan Asch **W:** Frank Bolle; Graham Ingels; Lee Ames; Leonard Starr; Stan Asch
3 ❑ Fal 1948 Cover: 0.10 **NM** value: **325.00**
• **CGC:** 3 graded, best 8.0
📖 Frisco Florrie; Strange Strongboy; The Do-It Yourself Kid and the Dimpled Doll **A:** Al Feldstein; Lee Ames; Stan Ash **W:** Al Feldstein; Lee Ames; Stan Ash
4 ❑ Dec 1948 Cover: 0.10 **NM** value: **270.00**
• **CGC:** 5 graded, best 7.0
📖 The Machine-Gun Mad Mobsters; Choo-Choo Jones; The Robbery Ring **A:** Al Feldstein; Howard Larson; Sheldon Moldoff **W:** Al Feldstein; Howard Larson; Sheldon Moldoff
5 ❑ Feb 1949 Cover: 0.10 **NM** value: **270.00**
• **CGC:** 5 graded, best 5.0
📖 Little Miss Mob Marker; Curse of the Pharaoh; The Law's Revenge **A:** Al Feldstein; Johnny Craig; Graham Ingels **W:** Al Feldstein; Johnny Craig; Graham Ingels
6 ❑ Apr 1949 Cover: 0.10 **NM** value: **250.00**
• **CGC:** 2 graded, best 5.5
7 ❑ Jun 1949 Cover: 0.10 **NM** value: **250.00**
• **CGC:** 4 graded, best 8.0
8 ❑ Aug 1949 Cover: 0.10 **NM** value: **250.00**
• **CGC:** 3 graded, best 5.0
9 ❑ Oct 1949 Cover: 0.10 **NM** value: **250.00**
• **CGC:** 6 graded, best 7.5
10 ❑ Dec 1949 Cover: 0.10 **NM** value: **1700.00**
• **CGC:** 8 graded, best 9.8
11 ❑ Nov 1950 Cover: 0.10 **NM** value: **925.00**
• **CGC:** 7 graded, best 9.8
• Series continued in Vault of Horror #12★ 2nd Appearance of The Vault Keeper.

WAR AGAINST CRIME (GEMSTONE) — Gemstone

1 ❑ Apr 2000 Cover: 2.50 **NM** value: **Cover or less**
Circ: Diamd. preorders: **3,085**
📖 Public Enemy…the Story of Machine-Gun Kelley!; Portfolio of Death!; The Ruby Stickpin!; Smokin' Six-Guns! • Reprints War Against Crime #1 **A:** Johnny Craig; Ed Moore; Graham Ingels; Lee Ames **W:** Johnny Craig; Ed Moore; Graham Ingels; Lee Ames
2 ❑ May 2000 Cover: 2.50 **NM** value: **Cover or less**
Circ: Diamd. preorders: **2,706**
📖 Hank "Two-Gun" Corley!; The Crystal Ball Killer; America's First Crime; The Saga of Spotlight John • Reprints War Against Crime #2 **A:** Frank Bolle; Graham Ingels; Lee Ames; Leonard Starr; Stan Asch **W:** Frank Bolle; Graham Ingels; Lee Ames; Leonard Starr; Stan Asch
3 ❑ Jun 2000 Cover: 2.50 **NM** value: **Cover or less**
Circ: Diamd. preorders: **2,808**
📖 Frisco Florrie; Strange Strongboy; The Do-It Yourself Kid and the Dimpled Doll • Reprints War Against Crime #3 **A:** Al Feldstein; Lee Ames; Stan Ash **W:** Al Feldstein; Lee Ames; Stan Ash
4 ❑ Jul 2000 Cover: 2.50 **NM** value: **Cover or less**
Circ: Diamd. preorders: **2,639**
📖 The Machine-Gun Mad Mobsters; Choo-Choo Jones; The Robbery Ring • Reprints War Against Crime #4 **A:** Al Feldstein; Howard Larson; Sheldon Moldoff **W:** Al Feldstein; Howard Larson; Sheldon Moldoff
5 ❑ Aug 2000 Cover: 2.50 **NM** value: **Cover or less**
Circ: Diamd. preorders: **2,685**
📖 Little Miss Mob Marker; Curse of the Pharaoh; The Law's Revenge • Reprints War Against Crime #5 **A:** Al Feldstein; Johnny Craig; Graham Ingels **W:** Al Feldstein; Johnny Craig; Graham Ingels
Anl 1❑ca. 2000 Cover: 13.50 **NM** value: **Cover or less**
• Collects issues #1-5

WAR AND ATTACK — Charlton

1 ❑ ca. 1964 Cover: 0.12 **NM** value: **25.00**
54 ❑ Jun 1966 Cover: 0.12 **NM** value: **6.00**
• Series continued from Fightin' Air Force #53
55 ❑ Aug 1966 Cover: 0.12 **NM** value: **6.00**
56 ❑ Oct 1966 Cover: 0.12 **NM** value: **6.00**
57 ❑ Dec 1966 Cover: 0.12 **NM** value: **6.00**
58 ❑ Feb 1967 Cover: 0.12 **NM** value: **6.00**
59 ❑ Apr 1967 Cover: 0.12 **NM** value: **6.00**
60 ❑ Jun 1967 Cover: 0.12 **NM** value: **6.00**
61 ❑ Aug 1967 Cover: 0.12 **NM** value: **6.00**
62 ❑ Oct 1967 Cover: 0.12 **NM** value: **6.00**
63 ❑ Dec 1967 Cover: 0.12 **NM** value: **6.00**

WARBLADE: ENDANGERED SPECIES — Image

1 ❑ Jan 1995 Cover: 2.50 **NM** value: **Cover or less**
Circ: CapCity orders: **27,375**
Tri-fold cover. **A:** Scott Clark **W:** Steven Seagle
2 ❑ Feb 1995 Cover: 2.50 **NM** value: **Cover or less**
Circ: CapCity orders: **22,475**
3 ❑ Mar 1995 Cover: 2.50 **NM** value: **Cover or less**
Circ: CapCity orders: **19,300**
4 ❑ Apr 1995 Cover: 2.50 **NM** value: **Cover or less**
Circ: CapCity orders: **21,575**

WARCAT — Coconut

Ash 1❑Oct 1997, b&w Cover: 2.95 **NM** value: **Cover or less**
No issue number. • preview of issues #1 and 2; no indicia
SE 1❑ Cover: 2.95 **NM** value: **Cover or less**

WARCHILD — Maximum Press

1/A ❑ Dec 1994 Cover: 2.50 **NM** value: **Cover or less**
Circ: CapCity orders: **16,425**
Warchild charging on cover.
1/B ❑ Dec 1994 Cover: 2.50 **NM** value: **Cover or less**
Variant cover with Warchild standing, red background.

CGC-graded: Multiply prices above by **33 for 9.9 M • 16 for 9.8 NM/M • 7 for 9.6 NM+ • 5 for 9.4 NM • 2.5 for 9.2 NM- • 1.5 for 9.0 VF/NM**

2/A ❑ Jan 1995 Cover: 2.50 **NM** value: **Cover or less**
Circ: CapCity orders: **12,775**
Warchild and woman on cover.
2/B ❑ Jan 1995 Cover: 2.50 **NM** value: **Cover or less**
Warchild alone on cover.
3/A ❑ Jun 1995 Cover: 2.50 **NM** value: **Cover or less**
Circ: CapCity orders: **9,300**
Warchild crouching on cover.
3/B ❑ Jun 1995 Cover: 2.50 **NM** value: **Cover or less**
Warchild standing on cover, white background.
3/C ❑ Jun 1995 Cover: 2.50 **NM** value: **Cover or less**
Warchild standing on cover, red background.
4 ❑ Aug 1995 Cover: 2.50 **NM** value: **Cover or less**
Circ: CapCity orders: **8,975**

WAR COMBAT — Marvel

1 ❑ Mar 1952 Cover: 0.10 **NM** value: **70.00**
2 ❑ May 1952 Cover: 0.10 **NM** value: **40.00**
3 ❑ Jul 1952 Cover: 0.10 **NM** value: **26.00**
4 ❑ Sep 1952 Cover: 0.10 **NM** value: **26.00**
📖 The Raider!; Mig!; Code of the Cavalry!; R.O.K. **A:** Dave Berg **W:** Hank Chapman
5 ❑ Nov 1952 Cover: 0.10 **NM** value: **26.00**
• Series continued in Combat Casey #6

WAR COMICS (ATLAS) — Atlas

1 ❑ Dec 1950 Cover: 0.10 **NM** value: **125.00**
• **CGC:** 1 graded, best 3.5
2 ❑ Feb 1951 Cover: 0.10 **NM** value: **100.00**
3 ❑ Apr 1951 Cover: 0.10 **NM** value: **75.00**
4 ❑ Jun 1951 Cover: 0.10 **NM** value: **60.00**
5 ❑ Aug 1951 Cover: 0.10 **NM** value: **60.00**
6 ❑ Oct 1951 Cover: 0.10 **NM** value: **60.00**
7 ❑ Dec 1951 Cover: 0.10 **NM** value: **60.00**
8 ❑ Feb 1952 Cover: 0.10 **NM** value: **60.00**
9 ❑ Apr 1952 Cover: 0.10 **NM** value: **60.00**
10 ❑ Jun 1952 Cover: 0.10 **NM** value: **40.00**
11 ❑ Aug 1952 Cover: 0.10 **NM** value: **40.00**
12 ❑ Oct 1952 Cover: 0.10 **NM** value: **40.00**
13 ❑ Nov 1952 Cover: 0.10 **NM** value: **40.00**
14 ❑ Dec 1952 Cover: 0.10 **NM** value: **40.00**
15 ❑ Jan 1953 Cover: 0.10 **NM** value: **40.00**
16 ❑ Feb 1953 Cover: 0.10 **NM** value: **40.00**
17 ❑ Mar 1953 Cover: 0.10 **NM** value: **40.00**
18 ❑ Apr 1953 Cover: 0.10 **NM** value: **40.00**
19 ❑ Nov 1953 Cover: 0.10 **NM** value: **40.00**
20 ❑ May 1953 Cover: 0.10 **NM** value: **30.00**
21 ❑ Jun 1953 Cover: 0.10 **NM** value: **30.00**
22 ❑ Jul 1953 Cover: 0.10 **NM** value: **30.00**
23 ❑ Aug 1953 Cover: 0.10 **NM** value: **30.00**
24 ❑ Sep 1953 Cover: 0.10 **NM** value: **30.00**
25 ❑ Nov 1953 Cover: 0.10 **NM** value: **30.00**
26 ❑ Jan 1954 Cover: 0.10 **NM** value: **30.00**
27 ❑ Mar 1954 Cover: 0.10 **NM** value: **30.00**
28 ❑ May 1954 Cover: 0.10 **NM** value: **30.00**
29 ❑ Jul 1954 Cover: 0.10 **NM** value: **30.00**
30 ❑ Sep 1954 Cover: 0.10 **NM** value: **25.00**
31 ❑ Nov 1954 Cover: 0.10 **NM** value: **25.00**
32 ❑ Feb 1955 Cover: 0.10 **NM** value: **25.00**
33 ❑ Jan 1955 Cover: 0.10 **NM** value: **25.00**
34 ❑ Mar 1955 Cover: 0.10 **NM** value: **25.00**
35 ❑ May 1955 Cover: 0.10 **NM** value: **25.00**
36 ❑ Jul 1955 Cover: 0.10 **NM** value: **25.00**
37 ❑ Sep 1955 Cover: 0.10 **NM** value: **25.00**
38 ❑ Nov 1955 Cover: 0.10 **NM** value: **25.00**
39 ❑ Jan 1956 Cover: 0.10 **NM** value: **25.00**
40 ❑ Mar 1956 Cover: 0.10 **NM** value: **20.00**
41 ❑ May 1956 Cover: 0.10 **NM** value: **20.00**
42 ❑ Jul 1956 Cover: 0.10 **NM** value: **20.00**
43 ❑ Sep 1956 Cover: 0.10 **NM** value: **20.00**
A: Angelo Torres; Mort Drucker
44 ❑ Nov 1956 Cover: 0.10 **NM** value: **20.00**
A: Joe Maneely; Paul Reinman; Dick Ayers
45 ❑ Jan 1957 Cover: 0.10 **NM** value: **20.00**
46 ❑ Mar 1957 Cover: 0.10 **NM** value: **20.00**
📖 Breaking the Commie trap!
47 ❑ May 1957 Cover: 0.10 **NM** value: **20.00**
48 ❑ Jul 1957 Cover: 0.10 **NM** value: **20.00**
49 ❑ Sep 1957 Cover: 0.10 **NM** value: **20.00**

WAR COMICS (DELL) — Dell

1 ❑ May 1940 Cover: 0.10 **NM** value: **400.00**
• **CGC:** 1 graded, best 6.0
2 ❑ May 1941 Cover: 0.10 **NM** value: **300.00**
• **CGC:** 1 graded, best 6.5
3 ❑ Jul 1941 Cover: 0.10 **NM** value: **200.00**
4 ❑ ca. 1941 Cover: 0.10 **NM** value: **200.00**

WAR CRIMINALS — Comic Zone

1 ❑ b&w Cover: 2.95 **NM** value: **Cover or less**

WARCRY — Image

1 ❑ Cover: 2.50 **NM** value: **Cover or less**

WAR DANCER — Defiant

1 ❑ Feb 1994 Cover: 2.50 **NM** value: **Cover or less**
Circ: CapCity orders: **23,675**
2 ❑ Mar 1994 Cover: 2.50 **NM** value: **Cover or less**
Circ: CapCity orders: **14,025**
3 ❑ Apr 1994 Cover: 2.50 **NM** value: **Cover or less**
Circ: CapCity orders: **11,100**
4 ❑ May 1994 Cover: 2.50 **NM** value: **3.25**
Circ: CapCity orders: **10,025**
• Giant-size. ★ Origin of War Dancer. ★ Appearance of Charlemagne.
5 ❑ Jun 1994 Cover: 2.50 **NM** value: **Cover or less**
Circ: CapCity orders: **8,350**
6 ❑ Jul 1994 Cover: 2.50 **NM** value: **Cover or less**
Circ: CapCity orders: **7,025**
final issue.

WARFRONT — Harvey

1 ❑ Sep 1951 Cover: 0.10 **NM** value: **75.00**
2 ❑ Nov 1951 Cover: 0.10 **NM** value: **45.00**
3 ❑ Jan 1952 Cover: 0.10 **NM** value: **35.00**
4 ❑ 1952 Cover: 0.10 **NM** value: **35.00**
5 ❑ Apr 1952 Cover: 0.10 **NM** value: **35.00**
• **CGC:** 1 graded, best 7.0
6 ❑ 1952 Cover: 0.10 **NM** value: **32.00**
7 ❑ 1952 Cover: 0.10 **NM** value: **32.00**
8 ❑ 1952 Cover: 0.10 **NM** value: **32.00**
9 ❑ 1952 Cover: 0.10 **NM** value: **32.00**
10 ❑ 1952 Cover: 0.10 **NM** value: **32.00**
11 ❑ Cover: 0.10 **NM** value: **28.00**
12 ❑ Cover: 0.10 **NM** value: **28.00**
13 ❑ Cover: 0.10 **NM** value: **28.00**
📖 The Yalu Story!; Famous Heroes of the U.S. Marine Corps: Major James P.S. Devereux (text); The Innocents; Art Wermuth (text); Red Traitor!
14 ❑ Apr 1953 Cover: 0.10 **NM** value: **28.00**
• **CGC:** 1 graded, best 3.0
15 ❑ Jun 1953 Cover: 0.10 **NM** value: **28.00**
• **CGC:** 1 graded, best 4.0
📖 Timid Hero; Crossfire; Torpedo; Fight for Life
16 ❑ Aug 1953 Cover: 0.10 **NM** value: **28.00**
17 ❑ Oct 1953 Cover: 0.10 **NM** value: **28.00**
📖 Revenge; The fear of Death; Night Shadows; Killed by a Friend
18 ❑ Dec 1953 Cover: 0.10 **NM** value: **28.00**
19 ❑ Feb 1954 Cover: 0.10 **NM** value: **28.00**
20 ❑ Apr 1954 Cover: 0.10 **NM** value: **28.00**
21 ❑ Jun 1954 Cover: 0.10 **NM** value: **24.00**
22 ❑ Aug 1954 Cover: 0.10 **NM** value: **24.00**
23 ❑ Oct 1954 Cover: 0.10 **NM** value: **24.00**
24 ❑ Dec 1954 Cover: 0.10 **NM** value: **24.00**
25 ❑ Feb 1955 Cover: 0.10 **NM** value: **24.00**
26 ❑ 1955 Cover: 0.10 **NM** value: **24.00**
27 ❑ 1955 Cover: 0.10 **NM** value: **24.00**
28 ❑ Jan 1956 Cover: 0.10 **NM** value: **24.00**
29 ❑ Jul 1956 Cover: 0.10 **NM** value: **24.00**
30 ❑ Sep 1957 Cover: 0.10 **NM** value: **24.00**
31 ❑ Nov 1957 Cover: 0.10 **NM** value: **24.00**
• **CGC:** 1 graded, best 3.5
32 ❑ 1958 Cover: 0.10 **NM** value: **24.00**
33 ❑ 1958 Cover: 0.10 **NM** value: **24.00**
34 ❑ Sep 1958 Cover: 0.10 **NM** value: **24.00**
35 ❑ Nov 1958 Cover: 0.10 **NM** value: **24.00**
36 ❑ Oct 1965 Cover: 0.12 **NM** value: **18.00**
37 ❑ 1966 Cover: 0.12 **NM** value: **18.00**
38 ❑ Dec 1966 Cover: 0.12 **NM** value: **18.00**
• Dynamite Joe
39 ❑ Feb 1967 Cover: 0.12 **NM** value: **18.00**
final issue.

WAR FURY — Comic Media

1 ❑ Sep 1952 Cover: 0.10 **NM** value: **80.00**
• **CGC:** 1 graded, best 4.5
2 ❑ Nov 1952 Cover: 0.10 **NM** value: **60.00**
3 ❑ Jan 1953 Cover: 0.10 **NM** value: **60.00**
4 ❑ Mar 1953 Cover: 0.10 **NM** value: **60.00**

WAR GAMES — Bishop Press

1 ❑ b&w Cover: 2.50 **NM** value: **Cover or less**

WARHAMMER MONTHLY — Games Workshop

Britain's Games Workshop is the publisher of such popular fantasy and role-playing games as Warhammer and Warhammer 40,000. Whether to promote its games, or just to extend the line, the company rolled out Warhammer Monthly as an anthology comics series in 1998.

The surprise about this series is just how decent it is. Games Workshop did a fine job of hiring top British creators like Dan Abnett (2000 A.D., The Punisher), Colin MacNeil, and artist Kev Hopgood. The relatively unknown Hopgood was an especially good find, contributing a stylishly rendered "DarkBlade" story which ran through early issues, which used computer-drawn art created with a painter's skill.

0 ❑ Feb 1998 **NM** value: **1.00**
📖 The Bridge; Bloodquest; Shadowfast; Predator & Prey; Titan; The Summoning **A:** Anthony Williams; Colin MacNeil; David Pugh; Simon Coleby; Simon Harrison **W:** Dan Abnett; Gordon Rennie; Michael Browne
1 ❑ Mar 1998 Cover: 2.95 **NM** value: **Cover or less**
Circ: Diamd. preorders: **6,456**
📖 DarkBlade, Part 1; Predator & Prey; Kal Jericho: The Hit; Bloodquest: Beginnings **A:** Kev Hopgood; Colin MacNeil; David Pugh; Karl Kopinski **W:** Dan Abnett; Gordon Rennie
2 ❑ Apr 1998 Cover: 2.95 **NM** value: **Cover or less**
Circ: Diamd. preorders: **5,636**
📖 DarkBlade, Part 2; Titan: Baptism; The Carnival of Change; Bloodquest: Mausoleum **A:** Kev Hopgood; Colin MacNeil; Ant & Andy; Mark Gibbons **W:** Dan Abnett; Gordon Rennie
3 ❑ May 1998 Cover: 2.95 **NM** value: **Cover or less**
Circ: Diamd. preorders: **4,602**
4 ❑ Jun 1998 Cover: 2.95 **NM** value: **Cover or less**
Circ: Diamd. preorders: **4,153**
5 ❑ Jul 1998 Cover: 2.95 **NM** value: **Cover or less**
Circ: Diamd. preorders: **3,418**
6 ❑ Aug 1998 Cover: 2.95 **NM** value: **Cover or less**
Circ: Diamd. preorders: **3,201**
7 ❑ Sep 1998 Cover: 2.95 **NM** value: **Cover or less**
Circ: Diamd. preorders: **3,107**
8 ❑ Oct 1998 Cover: 2.95 **NM** value: **Cover or less**
Circ: Diamd. preorders: **3,079**
9 ❑ Nov 1998 Cover: 2.95 **NM** value: **Cover or less**
Circ: Diamd. preorders: **2,935**
10 ❑ Dec 1998 Cover: 2.95 **NM** value: **Cover or less**
Circ: Diamd. preorders: **2,935**
11 ❑ Jan 1999 Cover: 2.95 **NM** value: **Cover or less**
Circ: Diamd. preorders: **2,762**
12 ❑ Feb 1999 Cover: 2.95 **NM** value: **Cover or less**
Circ: Diamd. preorders: **2,561**
13 ❑ Mar 1999 Cover: 2.95 **NM** value: **Cover or less**
Circ: Diamd. preorders: **2,607**
14 ❑ Apr 1999 Cover: 2.95 **NM** value: **Cover or less**
Circ: Diamd. preorders: **2,648**
15 ❑ May 1999 Cover: 2.95 **NM** value: **Cover or less**
Circ: Diamd. preorders: **2,453**
16 ❑ Jun 1999 Cover: 2.95 **NM** value: **Cover or less**
Circ: Diamd. preorders: **2,327**
17 ❑ Jul 1999 Cover: 2.95 **NM** value: **Cover or less**
Circ: Diamd. preorders: **2,330**
18 ❑ Aug 1999 Cover: 2.95 **NM** value: **Cover or less**
Circ: Diamd. preorders: **1,927**
19 ❑ Sep 1999 Cover: 2.95 **NM** value: **Cover or less**
Circ: Diamd. preorders: **2,208**
20 ❑ Oct 1999 Cover: 2.95 **NM** value: **Cover or less**
21 ❑ Nov 1999 Cover: 2.95 **NM** value: **Cover or less**
22 ❑ Dec 1999 Cover: 2.95 **NM** value: **Cover or less**
23 ❑ Jan 2000 Cover: 2.95 **NM** value: **Cover or less**
24 ❑ Feb 2000 Cover: 2.95 **NM** value: **Cover or less**
25 ❑ Mar 2000 Cover: 2.95 **NM** value: **Cover or less**
26 ❑ Apr 2000 Cover: 2.95 **NM** value: **Cover or less**
Circ: Diamd. preorders: **1,819**
27 ❑ May 2000 Cover: 2.95 **NM** value: **Cover or less**
Circ: Diamd. preorders: **1,648**
28 ❑ Jun 2000 Cover: 2.95 **NM** value: **Cover or less**
29 ❑ Jul 2000 Cover: 2.95 **NM** value: **Cover or less**
30 ❑ Aug 2000 Cover: 2.95 **NM** value: **Cover or less**
31 ❑ Sep 2000 Cover: 2.95 **NM** value: **Cover or less**
32 ❑ Oct 2000 Cover: 2.95 **NM** value: **Cover or less**
33 ❑ Nov 2000 Cover: 2.95 **NM** value: **Cover or less**
34 ❑ Dec 2000 Cover: 2.95 **NM** value: **Cover or less**
35 ❑ Jan 2001 Cover: 2.95 **NM** value: **Cover or less**
36 ❑ Feb 2001 Cover: 2.95 **NM** value: **Cover or less**
Circ: Diamd. preorders: **1,483**
37 ❑ Mar 2001 Cover: 2.95 **NM** value: **Cover or less**
Circ: Diamd. preorders: **1,490**
38 ❑ Apr 2001 Cover: 2.95 **NM** value: **Cover or less**
Circ: Diamd. preorders: **1,466**
39 ❑ May 2001 Cover: 2.95 **NM** value: **Cover or less**
Circ: Diamd. preorders: **1,415**
40 ❑ Jun 2001 Cover: 2.95 **NM** value: **Cover or less**
Circ: Diamd. preorders: **1,397**
41 ❑ Jul 2001 Cover: 2.95 **NM** value: **Cover or less**
Circ: Diamd. preorders: **1,384**
42 ❑ Aug 2001 Cover: 2.95 **NM** value: **Cover or less**
Circ: Diamd. preorders: **1,338**
43 ❑ Sep 2001 Cover: 2.95 **NM** value: **Cover or less**
Circ: Diamd. preorders: **1,313**
44 ❑ Oct 2001 Cover: 2.95 **NM** value: **Cover or less**
Circ: Diamd. preorders: **1,406**

WARHAWKS COMICS MODULE — TSR

1 ❑ ca. 1990 Cover: 2.95 **NM** value: **Cover or less**
Circ: CapCity orders: **4,129**
📖 ...And Let Slip the Hawks of War **A:** Peter Ledger **W:** Roy Thomas; Dann Thomas
2 ❑ ca. 1990 Cover: 2.95 **NM** value: **Cover or less**
Circ: CapCity orders: **3,050**
3 ❑ ca. 1990 Cover: 2.95 **NM** value: **Cover or less**
Circ: CapCity orders: **2,300**
4 ❑ ca. 1990 Cover: 2.95 **NM** value: **Cover or less**
Circ: CapCity orders: **2,050**
5 ❑ ca. 1990 Cover: 2.95 **NM** value: **Cover or less**
Circ: CapCity orders: **1,728**
📖 Court-Martial • Warhawks 2050 **A:** Chuck Wojtkiewicz **W:** Roy Thomas; Dann Thomas
6 ❑ ca. 1990 Cover: 2.95 **NM** value: **Cover or less**
Circ: CapCity orders: **1,536**
• Warhawks 2050
7 ❑ ca. 1990 Cover: 2.95 **NM** value: **Cover or less**
Circ: CapCity orders: **1,536**
📖 Battle of Britain, Part 1 • Warhawks 2050 **A:** Ron Harris **W:** Martin Pasko
8 ❑ ca. 1990 Cover: 2.95 **NM** value: **Cover or less**
Circ: CapCity orders: **1,152**
📖 Battle of Britain, Part 2 • Warhawks 2050 **A:** Ron Harris **W:** Martin Pasko
9 ❑ ca. 1990 Cover: 2.95 **NM** value: **Cover or less**
📖 Battle of Britain, Part 3 • Warhawks 2050 **A:** Ron Harris **W:** Martin Pasko

The CGC numbers printed in individual listings above represent the **number of copies examined** and given a **Universal** grade by CGC and the **best such copy** graded at press time. For current populations, watch for special ***Comics Buyer's Guide*** issues or check **www.cgccomics.com.**

Other grades: Multiply prices above by **1.5 for Mint • 2/3 for Very Fine • 1/3 for Fine • 1/5 for Very Good • 1/8 for Good**

WARHEADS — Marvel

They're the men and women of Kether Troop, heavily armed mercenaries unlike any other. For these mercenaries plunder, not other countries, but other times — other dimensions. In the employ of the sorcerous MyS-TECH corporation, they jump through wormholes in space to bring back weaponry and artifacts to the present day. In this function, Kether Troop and the rest of their time-jumping "Warheads" are some of the most powerful weapons in MyS-TECH's arsenal.

Although the rewards of serving as a Warhead mercenary are high, so are the risks. Even with psionic scouts and hi-tech sensing equipment, they never really know what awaits them, as they enter a new "jump." Sometimes, it's the eerie inhabitants of an alien world; sometimes, it's the familiar face of death from their own past.

1 ❑ Jun 1992 Cover: 1.75 **NM** value: **Cover or less**
Circ: CapCity orders: **41,100**
• Wolverine★ 1st Appearance of Warheads.
2 ❑ Jul 1992 Cover: 1.75 **NM** value: **Cover or less**
Circ: CapCity orders: **25,100**
3 ❑ Aug 1992 Cover: 1.75 **NM** value: **Cover or less**
Circ: CapCity orders: **21,900**
4 ❑ Sep 1992 Cover: 1.75 **NM** value: **Cover or less**
Circ: CapCity orders: **28,400**
5 ❑ Oct 1992 Cover: 1.75 **NM** value: **Cover or less**
Circ: CapCity orders: **24,600**
6 ❑ Nov 1992 Cover: 1.75 **NM** value: **Cover or less**
Circ: CapCity orders: **20,600**
• Death's Head II cameo
7 ❑ Dec 1992 Cover: 1.75 **NM** value: **Cover or less**
Circ: CapCity orders: **20,500**
8 ❑ Jan 1993 Cover: 1.75 **NM** value: **Cover or less**
Circ: CapCity orders: **17,100**
9 ❑ Feb 1993 Cover: 1.75 **NM** value: **Cover or less**
Circ: CapCity orders: **11,000**
10 ❑ Apr 1993 Cover: 1.75 **NM** value: **Cover or less**
Circ: CapCity orders: **10,200**
11 ❑ May 1993 Cover: 1.75 **NM** value: **Cover or less**
Circ: CapCity orders: **11,100**
12 ❑ Jun 1993 Cover: 1.75 **NM** value: **Cover or less**
Circ: CapCity orders: **9,500**
13 ❑ Jul 1993 Cover: 1.75 **NM** value: **Cover or less**
Circ: CapCity orders: **8,300**
14 ❑ Aug 1993 Cover: 1.75 **NM** value: **Cover or less**
Circ: CapCity orders: **7,400**
final issue.

WARHEADS: BLACK DAWN — Marvel

1 ❑ Jul 1993 Cover: 2.95 **NM** value: **Cover or less**
Circ: CapCity orders: **37,800**
foil cover.
2 ❑ 1993 Cover: 1.75 **NM** value: **2.95**
Circ: CapCity orders: **13,100**

WAR HEROES (ACE) — Ace

1 ❑ Jul 1942 Cover: 0.10 **NM** value: **50.00**
2 ❑ Oct 1942 Cover: 0.10 **NM** value: **40.00**
3 ❑ Jan 1943 Cover: 0.10 **NM** value: **40.00**
4 ❑ Apr 1943 Cover: 0.10 **NM** value: **40.00**
5 ❑ Jul 1943 Cover: 0.10 **NM** value: **40.00**
6 ❑ Oct 1943 Cover: 0.10 **NM** value: **40.00**
7 ❑ Jan 1944 Cover: 0.10 **NM** value: **40.00**

WAR HEROES (CHARLTON) — Charlton

1 ❑ Feb 1963 Cover: 0.12 **NM** value: **25.00**
2 ❑ Apr 1963 Cover: 0.12 **NM** value: **25.00**
• PT-109 story★ Appearance of John F. Kennedy.
3 ❑ Jun 1963 Cover: 0.12 **NM** value: **12.00**
4 ❑ Aug 1963 Cover: 0.12 **NM** value: **12.00**
5 ❑ Oct 1963 Cover: 0.12 **NM** value: **12.00**
6 ❑ Dec 1963 Cover: 0.12 **NM** value: **8.00**
7 ❑ Feb 1964 Cover: 0.12 **NM** value: **8.00**
8 ❑ 1964 Cover: 0.12 **NM** value: **8.00**
9 ❑ Jul 1964 Cover: 0.12 **NM** value: **8.00**
10 ❑ Oct 1964 Cover: 0.12 **NM** value: **8.00**
11 ❑ 1964 Cover: 0.12 **NM** value: **8.00**
12 ❑ 1965 Cover: 0.12 **NM** value: **8.00**
13 ❑ 1965 Cover: 0.12 **NM** value: **8.00**
14 ❑ 1965 Cover: 0.12 **NM** value: **8.00**
15 ❑ Sep 1965 Cover: 0.12 **NM** value: **8.00**
16 ❑ Nov 1965 Cover: 0.12 **NM** value: **8.00**
📖 Mulie and the Brain on Murder Mountain; Unfinished Business (text story); Non Combatant; The Beach; The Super Weapon **A:** Nicholas Alascia
17 ❑ Jan 1966 Cover: 0.12 **NM** value: **8.00**
18 ❑ 1966 Cover: 0.12 **NM** value: **8.00**
19 ❑ 1966 Cover: 0.12 **NM** value: **8.00**
20 ❑ Sep 1966 Cover: 0.12 **NM** value: **8.00**
21 ❑ Nov 1966 Cover: 0.12 **NM** value: **5.00**
22 ❑ Jan 1967 Cover: 0.12 **NM** value: **5.00**
23 ❑ Mar 1967 Cover: 0.12 **NM** value: **5.00**
24 ❑ May 1967 Cover: 0.12 **NM** value: **5.00**
25 ❑ Jul 1967 Cover: 0.12 **NM** value: **5.00**
26 ❑ Sep 1967 Cover: 0.12 **NM** value: **5.00**
27 ❑ Nov 1967 Cover: 0.12 **NM** value: **5.00**

WAR HEROES CLASSICS — Recollections

1 ❑ b&w Cover: 2.00 **NM** value: **Cover or less**

WAR HEROES (DELL) — Dell

1 ❑ Jul 1942 Cover: 0.10 **NM** value: **120.00**
2 ❑ Oct 1942 Cover: 0.10 **NM** value: **100.00**
• **CGC:** 1 graded, best 4.0
3 ❑ Jan 1943 Cover: 0.10 **NM** value: **80.00**
4 ❑ Apr 1943 Cover: 0.10 **NM** value: **80.00**
5 ❑ Jul 1943 Cover: 0.10 **NM** value: **80.00**
6 ❑ Oct 1943 Cover: 0.10 **NM** value: **80.00**
7 ❑ Jan 1944 Cover: 0.10 **NM** value: **60.00**
• **CGC:** 2 graded, best 9.6
8 ❑ Apr 1944 Cover: 0.10 **NM** value: **60.00**
9 ❑ Jul 1944 Cover: 0.10 **NM** value: **60.00**
10 ❑ Oct 1944 Cover: 0.10 **NM** value: **60.00**
11 ❑ Jan 1945 Cover: 0.10 **NM** value: **60.00**

WAR IS HELL — Marvel

1 ❑ Jan 1973 Cover: 0.20 **NM** value: **8.00**
• **CGC:** 3 graded, best 9.4
2 ❑ Mar 1973 Cover: 0.20 **NM** value: **5.00**
3 ❑ May 1973 Cover: 0.20 **NM** value: **5.00**
4 ❑ Jul 1973 Cover: 0.20 **NM** value: **5.00**
5 ❑ Sep 1973 Cover: 0.20 **NM** value: **5.00**
6 ❑ Nov 1973 Cover: 0.20 **NM** value: **4.00**
7 ❑ Jun 1974 Cover: 0.25 **NM** value: **4.00**
📖 While the Jungle Sleeps • Reprints Sgt. Fury #17 **A:** Dick Ayers **W:** Stan Lee ★ Appearance of Sgt. Fury.
8 ❑ Aug 1974 Cover: 0.25 **NM** value: **4.00**
9 ❑ Oct 1974 Cover: 0.25 **NM** value: **3.00**
• **CGC:** 1 graded, best 9.6
10 ❑ Dec 1974 Cover: 0.25 **NM** value: **3.00**
11 ❑ Feb 1975 Cover: 0.25 **NM** value: **3.00**
12 ❑ Apr 1975 Cover: 0.25 **NM** value: **3.00**
13 ❑ Jun 1975 Cover: 0.25 **NM** value: **3.00**
14 ❑ Aug 1975 Cover: 0.25 **NM** value: **3.00**
• **CGC:** 1 graded, best 9.0
15 ❑ Oct 1975 Cover: 0.25 **NM** value: **3.00**
final issue.

WARLANDS — Image

1 ❑ Aug 1999 Cover: 2.50 **NM** value: **3.00**
Circ: Diamd. preorders: **56,249** • **CGC:** 2 graded, best 9.8
📖 The Fall of Shal 'Hazar **A:** Adrian Tsang; Patrick Lee **W:** Patrick Lee
1/A ❑ Aug 1999 Cover: 2.50 **NM** value: **3.00**
• **CGC:** 5 graded, best 9.9
alternate cover. 📖 The Fall of Shal 'Hazar **A:** Adrian Tsang; Patrick Lee **W:** Patrick Lee
1/B ❑ Aug 1999 Cover: 2.50 **NM** value: **3.00**
• **CGC:** 7 graded, best 10.0
alternate cover. 📖 The Fall of Shal 'Hazar **A:** Adrian Tsang; Patrick Lee **W:** Patrick Lee
2 ❑ Sep 1999 Cover: 2.50 **NM** value: **Cover or less**
Circ: Diamd. preorders: **36,274** • **CGC:** 1 graded, best 9.8
📖 Homecoming **A:** Adrian Tsang; Patrick Lee **W:** Patrick Lee
2/A ❑ Sep 1999 Cover: 2.50 **NM** value: **Cover or less**
alternate cover. 📖 Homecoming **A:** Adrian Tsang; Patrick Lee **W:** Patrick Lee
3 ❑ Nov 1999 Cover: 2.50 **NM** value: **Cover or less**
Circ: Diamd. preorders: **34,755**
📖 Dataran Rising **A:** Adrian Tsang; Patrick Lee **W:** Patrick Lee
4 ❑ 2000 Cover: 2.50 **NM** value: **Cover or less**
Circ: Diamd. preorders: **36,895**
5 ❑ Mar 2000 Cover: 2.50 **NM** value: **Cover or less**
Circ: Diamd. preorders: **39,327**
📖 A Call to Arms **A:** Adrian Tsang; Patrick Lee **W:** Patrick Lee
6 ❑ 2000 Cover: 2.50 **NM** value: **Cover or less**
Circ: Diamd. preorders: **37,056**
7 ❑ Jun 2000 Cover: 2.50 **NM** value: **Cover or less**
Circ: Diamd. preorders: **34,802**
📖 Fallen Comrades **A:** Adrian Tsang **W:** Adrian Tsang; Patrick Lee
8 ❑ Jul 2000 Cover: 2.50 **NM** value: **Cover or less**
Circ: Diamd. preorders: **35,644**
📖 Fallen Comrades **A:** Adrian Tsang **W:** Adrian Tsang; Patrick Lee
9 ❑ Aug 2000 Cover: 2.50 **NM** value: **Cover or less**
Circ: Diamd. preorders: **34,242**
📖 Aalok's Reckoning **A:** Adrian Tsang **W:** Adrian Tsang; Patrick Lee
10 ❑ Oct 2000 Cover: 2.50 **NM** value: **Cover or less**
Circ: Diamd. preorders: **29,408**
📖 Vampire's Reckoning **A:** Adrian Tsang; Patrick Lee **W:** Adrian Tsang; Patrick Lee
11 ❑ Nov 2000 Cover: 2.50 **NM** value: **Cover or less**
Circ: Diamd. preorders: **29,567**
📖 Into the Teeth of Darkness **A:** Adrian Tsang **W:** Adrian Tsang; Patrick Lee
12 ❑ Feb 2001 Cover: 2.50 **NM** value: **Cover or less**
Circ: Diamd. preorders: **29,158**
📖 Reckoning **A:** Adrian Tsang; James Raiz **W:** Adrian Tsang; Patrick Lee
Bk 1❑ Feb 2000 Cover: 7.95 **NM** value: **Cover or less**
• Warlands Chronicles #1; Collects Warlands #1-3 **A:** Adrian Tsang; Patrick Lee **W:** Patrick Lee
Bk 2❑ Jul 2000 Cover: 7.95 **NM** value: **Cover or less**
• Warlands Chronicles #2; Collects Warlands #4-6 **A:** Adrian Tsang; Patrick Lee **W:** Patrick Lee

WARLANDS EPILOGUE: THREE STORIES — Image

1 ❑ Mar 2001 Cover: 5.95 **NM** value: **Cover or less**
• **CGC:** 1 graded, best 9.8

WARLASH — CFD

1 ❑ Apr 1995 Cover: 2.95 **NM** value: **Cover or less**
📖 The Hardfire Syndrome, Part 1 **A:** Bob Murdock; Frank Forte **W:** Frank Forte

WARLOCK (1ST SERIES) — Marvel

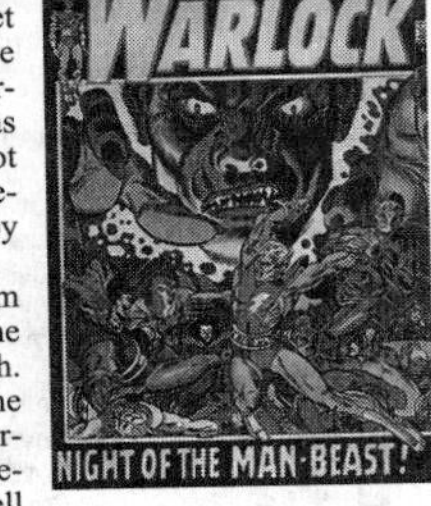

Adam Warlock is one of the more offbeat characters in the Marvel universe. He was created in a secret research project known as The Hive and, at the time of his first appearance in Fantastic Four #67, was known simply as "Him." It was not until Marvel Premiere #1 that he received the name that he is known by today.

In this, his first solo series, Adam Warlock acts as protector of the world known as Counter-Earth. That world had been created by the High Evolutionary as a perfect version of our own world. Nevertheless, it was not long before it fell under the heel of a powerful creature known as The Man-Beast. Warlock conquered The Man-Beast in #2 of this series, thus becoming a hero to the people of Counter-Earth. The series was a complex allegory of saviors and demons, both religious and political, true and false. Sadly, the title's writing was not matched by its sales, and it was canceled suddenly after #8.

1 ❑ Aug 1972 Cover: 0.20 **NM** value: **10.00**
• **CGC:** 16 graded, best 9.6
📖 The Day of the Prophet **A:** Gil Kane **C:** Gil Kane **W:** Roy Thomas ★ Origin of Warlock.
2 ❑ Oct 1972 Cover: 0.20 **NM** value: **5.00**
• **CGC:** 1 graded, best 9.0
📖 Count-Down for Counter-Earth!
3 ❑ Dec 1972 Cover: 0.20 **NM** value: **4.00**
• **CGC:** 2 graded, best 9.6
📖 The Apollo Eclipse
4 ❑ Feb 1973 Cover: 0.20 **NM** value: **4.00**
📖 Come Sing a Searing Song of Vengeance **A:** Gil Kane
5 ❑ Apr 1973 Cover: 0.20 **NM** value: **4.00**
📖 The Day of the Death Birds!
6 ❑ Jun 1973 Cover: 0.20 **NM** value: **4.00**
📖 The Brute!
7 ❑ Aug 1973 Cover: 0.20 **NM** value: **4.00**
📖 Doom: At the Earth's Core
8 ❑ Oct 1973 Cover: 0.20 **NM** value: **4.00**
• **CGC:** 1 graded, best 8.5
📖 Confrontation
9 ❑ Oct 1975 Cover: 0.25 **NM** value: **4.00**
• **CGC:** 2 graded, best 9.4
📖 The Infinity Effect **A:** Jim Starlin ★ Appearance of Thanos.
10 ❑ Dec 1975 Cover: 0.25 **NM** value: **8.00**
• **CGC:** 8 graded, best 9.6
📖 How Strange My Destiny; The Price; Who Is Thanos: Enter the Redemption Principle • Part 1 **A:** Jim Starlin ★ Origin of Thanos.
11 ❑ Feb 1976 Cover: 0.25 **NM** value: **8.00**
• **CGC:** 2 graded, best 9.8
📖 How Strange My Destiny; Escape into the Inner Prison; The Strange Death of Adam Warlock • Part 2 **A:** Jim Starlin ★ Appearance of Thanos.
12 ❑ Apr 1976 Cover: 0.25 **NM** value: **5.00**
• **CGC:** 1 graded, best 9.4
📖 A Trollish Tale **A:** Jim Starlin
13 ❑ Jun 1976 Cover: 0.25 **NM** value: **5.00**
📖 Here Dwells the Star Thief!; The Bizarre Brain of Barry Bauman **A:** Jim Starlin
14 ❑ Aug 1976 Cover: 0.25 **NM** value: **5.00**
📖 Homecoming **A:** Jim Starlin
15 ❑ Nov 1976 Cover: 0.30 **NM** value: **6.00**
• **CGC:** 1 graded, best 9.6
📖 Just a Series of Events **A:** Jim Starlin ★ Appearance of Thanos.

WARLOCK (2ND SERIES) — Marvel

1 ❑ Dec 1982 Cover: 2.00 **NM** value: **3.50**
2 ❑ Jan 1983 Cover: 2.00 **NM** value: **3.00**
3 ❑ Feb 1983 Cover: 2.00 **NM** value: **3.00**
4 ❑ Mar 1983 Cover: 2.00 **NM** value: **3.00**
5 ❑ Apr 1983 Cover: 2.00 **NM** value: **3.00**
6 ❑ May 1983 Cover: 2.00 **NM** value: **3.00**
SE 1❑ ca. 1983 Cover: 2.00 **NM** value: **2.50**

WARLOCK (3RD SERIES) — Marvel

1 ❑ May 1992 Cover: 2.50 **NM** value: **Cover or less**
Circ: CapCity orders: **19,000**
2 ❑ Jun 1992 Cover: 2.50 **NM** value: **Cover or less**
Circ: CapCity orders: **20,400**
📖 The Trial of Adam Warlock
3 ❑ Jul 1992 Cover: 2.50 **NM** value: **Cover or less**
📖 How Strange My Destiny
4 ❑ Aug 1992 Cover: 2.50 **NM** value: **Cover or less**
5 ❑ Sep 1992 Cover: 2.50 **NM** value: **Cover or less**
📖 Just a Series of Events, Part 3; Spider, Spider on the Moon!; The Final Threat
6 ❑ Oct 1992 Cover: 2.50 **NM** value: **Cover or less**

WARLOCK (4TH SERIES) — Marvel

1 ❑ Nov 1998 Cover: 2.99 **NM** value: **3.00**
Circ: Diamd. preorders: **26,221**
• gatefold summary. **A:** Tom Lyle **W:** Tom Lyle
2 ❑ Dec 1998 Cover: 2.99 **NM** value: **3.00**
Circ: Diamd. preorders: **20,821**
• gatefold summary. **A:** Tom Lyle **W:** Tom Lyle ★ Versus Captain Marvel.
3 ❑ Jan 1999 Cover: 2.99 **NM** value: **3.00**
Circ: Diamd. preorders: **20,627**
• gatefold summary. **A:** Tom Lyle **W:** Tom Lyle ★ Versus Drax.
4 ❑ Feb 1999 Cover: 2.99 **NM** value: **3.00**
Circ: Diamd. preorders: **21,160**

CGC-graded: Multiply prices above by **33 for 9.9 M • 16 for 9.8 NM/M • 7 for 9.6 NM+ • 5 for 9.4 NM • 2.5 for 9.2 NM- • 1.5 for 9.0 VF/NM**

WARLOCK 5 — Aircel

1 ❑ 1986b&w Cover: 1.70 **NM** value: **2.00**
2 ❑ 1986b&w Cover: 1.70 **NM** value: **2.00**
3 ❑ Jan 1987, b&w Cover: 1.70 **NM** value: **2.00**
4 ❑ Mar 1987, b&w Cover: 1.70 **NM** value: **2.00**
5 ❑ Apr 1987 Cover: 1.70 **NM** value: **2.00**
robot skull cover.
6 ❑ 1987 Cover: 1.70 **NM** value: **2.00**
woman's face on cover.
7 ❑ 1987 Cover: 1.70 **NM** value: **2.00**
8 ❑ 1987 Cover: 1.70 **NM** value: **2.00**
9 ❑ 1987 Cover: 1.70 **NM** value: **2.00**
10 ❑ 1987 Cover: 1.70 **NM** value: **2.00**
11 ❑ 1987 Cover: 1.70 **NM** value: **2.00**
12 ❑ Dec 1987 Cover: 1.70 **NM** value: **2.00**
13 ❑ Feb 1988 Cover: 1.70 **NM** value: **2.00**
14 ❑ Mar 1988 Cover: 1.70 **NM** value: **2.00**
15 ❑ 1988 Cover: 1.70 **NM** value: **2.00**
16 ❑ 1988 Cover: 1.95 **NM** value: **2.00**
17 ❑ 1988 Cover: 1.95 **NM** value: **2.00**
18 ❑ 1988 Cover: 1.95 **NM** value: **2.00**
19 ❑ 1988 Cover: 1.95 **NM** value: **2.00**
20 ❑ Dec 1988 Cover: 1.95 **NM** value: **2.00**
21 ❑ Jan 1989 Cover: 1.95 **NM** value: **2.00**
22 ❑ Feb 1989 Cover: 1.95 **NM** value: **2.00**
Bk 1❑ Mar 1988, b&w Cover: 5.95 **NM** value: **Cover or less**

WARLOCK 5 BOOK II — Aircel

1 ❑ 1989b&w Cover: 2.00 **NM** value: **Cover or less**
2 ❑ 1989b&w Cover: 2.00 **NM** value: **Cover or less**
3 ❑ 1989b&w Cover: 2.00 **NM** value: **Cover or less**
4 ❑ 1989b&w Cover: 2.00 **NM** value: **Cover or less**
5 ❑ 1989b&w Cover: 2.00 **NM** value: **Cover or less**
6 ❑ 1989b&w Cover: 2.00 **NM** value: **Cover or less**
7 ❑ 1989b&w Cover: 2.00 **NM** value: **Cover or less**

WARLOCK 5 (SIRIUS) — Sirius

1 ❑ Jan 1998 Cover: 2.50 **NM** value: **Cover or less**
2 ❑ Feb 1998 Cover: 2.50 **NM** value: **Cover or less**
3 ❑ Mar 1998 Cover: 2.50 **NM** value: **Cover or less**
4 ❑ Apr 1998 Cover: 2.50 **NM** value: **Cover or less**

WARLOCK (5TH SERIES) — Marvel

1 ❑ Oct 1999 Cover: 1.99 **NM** value: **2.00**
Circ: Diamd. preorders: **40,014**
📖 Cipher **A:** Pascual Ferry **W:** Louise Simonson
2 ❑ Nov 1999 Cover: 1.99 **NM** value: **Cover or less**
3 ❑ Nov 1999 Cover: 1.99 **NM** value: **Cover or less**
Circ: Diamd. preorders: **26,877**
4 ❑ Dec 1999 Cover: 1.99 **NM** value: **Cover or less**
Circ: Diamd. preorders: **25,887**

WARLOCK AND THE INFINITY WATCH — Marvel

1 ❑ Feb 1992 Cover: 1.75 **NM** value: **2.50**
Circ: CapCity orders: **122,000** • **CGC:** 1 graded, best 7.5
• follows events of The Infinity Gauntlet **A:** Angel Medina **W:** Jim Starlin
2 ❑ Mar 1992 Cover: 1.75 **NM** value: **2.00**
Circ: CapCity orders: **73,200**
📖 Gathering the Watch! **A:** Angel Medina **W:** Jim Starlin
3 ❑ Apr 1992 Cover: 1.75 **NM** value: **2.00**
Circ: CapCity orders: **61,500**
4 ❑ May 1992 Cover: 1.75 **NM** value: **2.00**
Circ: CapCity orders: **61,500**
📖 They **A:** Rick Leonardi **W:** Jim Starlin
5 ❑ Jun 1992 Cover: 1.75 **NM** value: **2.00**
Circ: CapCity orders: **63,600**
📖 Old Foes **A:** Angel Medina **W:** Jim Starlin
6 ❑ Jul 1992 Cover: 1.75 **NM** value: **2.00**
Circ: CapCity orders: **60,300**
📖 Revenge of the Beast **A:** Angel Medina **W:** Jim Starlin
7 ❑ Aug 1992 Cover: 1.75 **NM** value: **2.00**
Circ: CapCity orders: **56,700**
8 ❑ Sep 1992 Cover: 1.75 **NM** value: **2.00**
Circ: CapCity orders: **56,700**
9 ❑ Oct 1992 Cover: 1.75 **NM** value: **2.00**
Circ: CapCity orders: **51,300**
📖 Infinity War • Infinity War **A:** Angel Medina **W:** Jim Starlin ★ Origin of Gamora.
10 ❑ Nov 1992 Cover: 1.75 **NM** value: **2.00**
Circ: CapCity orders: **46,800**
📖 Self-Destructive Tendencies **A:** Angel Medina **W:** Jim Starlin
11 ❑ Dec 1992 Cover: 1.75 **NM** value: **Cover or less**
Circ: CapCity orders: **37,500**
📖 The Appeal **A:** Steve Carr; Deryl Skelton **W:** Jim Starlin
12 ❑ Jan 1993 Cover: 1.75 **NM** value: **Cover or less**
Circ: CapCity orders: **36,100**
13 ❑ Feb 1993 Cover: 1.75 **NM** value: **Cover or less**
Circ: CapCity orders: **34,800**
14 ❑ Mar 1993 Cover: 1.75 **NM** value: **Cover or less**
Circ: CapCity orders: **32,700**
15 ❑ Apr 1993 Cover: 1.75 **NM** value: **Cover or less**
Circ: CapCity orders: **32,000**
16 ❑ May 1993 Cover: 1.75 **NM** value: **Cover or less**
Circ: CapCity orders: **30,300**
17 ❑ Jun 1993 Cover: 1.75 **NM** value: **Cover or less**
Circ: CapCity orders: **30,200**
18 ❑ Jul 1993 Cover: 1.75 **NM** value: **Cover or less**
Circ: CapCity orders: **28,900**
19 ❑ Aug 1993 Cover: 1.75 **NM** value: **Cover or less**
Circ: CapCity orders: **30,200**
20 ❑ Sep 1993 Cover: 1.75 **NM** value: **Cover or less**
Circ: CapCity orders: **26,900**
21 ❑ Oct 1993 Cover: 1.75 **NM** value: **Cover or less**
Circ: CapCity orders: **25,600**
• Infinity Crusade crossover **A:** Tom Grindberg **W:** Jim Starlin ★ Appearance of Drax the Destroyer, Thor, Goddess.
22 ❑ Nov 1993 Cover: 1.75 **NM** value: **Cover or less**
Circ: CapCity orders: **23,800**
23 ❑ Dec 1993 Cover: 1.75 **NM** value: **Cover or less**
Circ: CapCity orders: **23,700**
24 ❑ Jan 1994 Cover: 1.75 **NM** value: **Cover or less**
Circ: Statement: **72,876** CapCity orders: **21,500**
25 ❑ Feb 1994 Cover: 2.95 **NM** value: **Cover or less**
Circ: Statement: **72,876** CapCity orders: **20,800**
diecut cover. 📖 Blood and Thunder, Part 12
26 ❑ Mar 1994 Cover: 1.75 **NM** value: **Cover or less**
Circ: Statement: **72,876** CapCity orders: **18,450**
27 ❑ Apr 1994 Cover: 1.75 **NM** value: **Cover or less**
Circ: Statement: **72,876** CapCity orders: **17,650**
28 ❑ May 1994 Cover: 1.95 **NM** value: **Cover or less**
Circ: Statement: **72,876** CapCity orders: **17,700**
29 ❑ Jun 1994 Cover: 1.95 **NM** value: **Cover or less**
Circ: Statement: **72,876** CapCity orders: **16,150**
30 ❑ Jul 1994 Cover: 1.95 **NM** value: **Cover or less**
Circ: Statement: **72,876** CapCity orders: **16,150**
31 ❑ Aug 1994 Cover: 1.95 **NM** value: **Cover or less**
Circ: Statement: **72,876** CapCity orders: **14,200**
32 ❑ Sep 1994 Cover: 1.95 **NM** value: **Cover or less**
Circ: Statement: **72,876** CapCity orders: **13,100**
33 ❑ Oct 1994 Cover: 1.95 **NM** value: **Cover or less**
Circ: Statement: **72,876** CapCity orders: **12,000**
34 ❑ Nov 1994 Cover: 1.95 **NM** value: **Cover or less**
Circ: Statement: **72,876** CapCity orders: **11,300**
35 ❑ Dec 1994 Cover: 1.95 **NM** value: **Cover or less**
Circ: Statement: **72,876** CapCity orders: **10,700**
36 ❑ Jan 1995 Cover: 1.95 **NM** value: **Cover or less**
Circ: CapCity orders: **9,900**
37 ❑ Feb 1995 Cover: 1.95 **NM** value: **Cover or less**
Circ: CapCity orders: **9,350**
38 ❑ Mar 1995 Cover: 1.95 **NM** value: **Cover or less**
Circ: CapCity orders: **8,475**
39 ❑ Apr 1995 Cover: 1.95 **NM** value: **Cover or less**
Circ: CapCity orders: **8,100**
• Has 1994 Statement, filed 10/1/94; avg print run 73,501; avg sales 72,176; avg subs 700; avg total paid 72,876; samples 125; office use 500; no returns (title was direct-market only in this year)
40 ❑ May 1995 Cover: 1.95 **NM** value: **Cover or less**
Circ: CapCity orders: **8,125**
41 ❑ Jun 1995 Cover: 1.95 **NM** value: **Cover or less**
Circ: CapCity orders: **9,375**
📖 Atlantis Rising, Part 3
42 ❑ Jul 1995 Cover: 1.95 **NM** value: **Cover or less**
Circ: CapCity orders: **9,200**
final issue.

WARLOCK CHRONICLES — Marvel

1 ❑ Jul 1993 Cover: 2.95 **NM** value: **Cover or less**
Circ: CapCity orders: **71,100**
Prism cover. 📖 Infinity Crusade; Things Past **A:** Tom Raney **W:** Jim Starlin
2 ❑ Aug 1993 Cover: 2.00 **NM** value: **Cover or less**
Circ: CapCity orders: **35,600**
3 ❑ Sep 1993 Cover: 2.00 **NM** value: **Cover or less**
Circ: CapCity orders: **29,500**
4 ❑ Oct 1993 Cover: 2.00 **NM** value: **Cover or less**
Circ: CapCity orders: **26,000**
• Infinity Crusade crossover **A:** Tom Raney **W:** Jim Starlin ★ Appearance of Goddess, Magus.
5 ❑ Nov 1993 Cover: 2.00 **NM** value: **Cover or less**
Circ: CapCity orders: **23,800**
6 ❑ Dec 1993 Cover: 2.00 **NM** value: **Cover or less**
Circ: CapCity orders: **23,000**
7 ❑ Jan 1994 Cover: 2.00 **NM** value: **Cover or less**
Circ: CapCity orders: **20,500**
8 ❑ Feb 1994 Cover: 2.00 **NM** value: **Cover or less**
Circ: CapCity orders: **19,300**
📖 Blood and Thunder, Part 11 final issue.

WARLOCKS — Aircel

1 ❑ 1988b&w Cover: 1.95 **NM** value: **2.00**
📖 Anarchy Unbound **A:** Barry Blair **W:** Barry Blair
2 ❑ 1988b&w Cover: 1.95 **NM** value: **2.00**
📖 Warlocks in New York **A:** Barry Blair **W:** Barry Blair
3 ❑ 1988b&w Cover: 1.95 **NM** value: **2.00**
📖 Where Angels Fear to Tread **A:** Barry Blair **W:** Barry Blair
4 ❑ 1988b&w Cover: 1.95 **NM** value: **2.00**
5 ❑ 1988b&w Cover: 1.95 **NM** value: **2.00**
6 ❑ Dec 1988, b&w Cover: 1.95 **NM** value: **2.00**
7 ❑ Jan 1989, b&w Cover: 1.95 **NM** value: **2.00**
8 ❑ 1989b&w Cover: 1.95 **NM** value: **2.00**
9 ❑ 1989b&w Cover: 1.95 **NM** value: **2.00**
10 ❑ b&w Cover: 1.95 **NM** value: **2.00**
11 ❑ Mar 1990, b&w Cover: 1.95 **NM** value: **2.00**
12 ❑ b&w Cover: 1.95 **NM** value: **2.00**
SE 1❑ b&w Cover: 2.25 **NM** value: **Cover or less**

WARLORD — DC

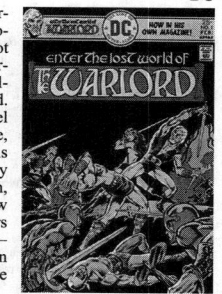

Skartaris is a world in and underneath Earth's crust, ruled by a heroic warrior, former USAF pilot Travis Morgan. Short on fuel, Morgan crashed in this world, eventually becoming the powerful Warlord. A magic mirror allows him to travel through time and, on our surface, have fantastic adventures. He is joined in those adventures by friends and fellow heroes Mariah, Machiste, Aton, Shakira, and Claw the Unconquered. Other characters who have appeared in the series — Arion, Lord of Atlantis, Arak, Son of Thunder, and Conqueror of the Barren Earth — eventually spun off into series of their own.

Rob Liefeld fans will be especially interested in Warlord #131, which features the artist's first professional work in the comic-book field.

1 ❑ Feb 1976 Cover: 0.25 **NM** value: **8.00**
• **CGC:** 8 graded, best 9.4
2 ❑ Apr 1976 Cover: 0.25 **NM** value: **4.00**
• **CGC:** 1 graded, best 8.5
3 ❑ Nov 1976 Cover: 0.30 **NM** value: **3.00**
• **CGC:** 1 graded, best 9.2
4 ❑ Jan 1977 Cover: 0.30 **NM** value: **3.00**
5 ❑ Mar 1977 Cover: 0.30 **NM** value: **3.00**
6 ❑ May 1977 Cover: 0.30 **NM** value: **3.00**
7 ❑ Jul 1977 Cover: 0.35 **NM** value: **2.00**
8 ❑ Sep 1977 Cover: 0.35 **NM** value: **2.00**
• **CGC:** 1 graded, best 9.0
9 ❑ Nov 1977 Cover: 0.35 **NM** value: **2.00**
10 ❑ Jan 1978 Cover: 0.35 **NM** value: **2.00**
• **CGC:** 2 graded, best 9.4
• Deimos **A:** Mike Grell
11 ❑ Mar 1978 Cover: 0.35 **NM** value: **1.50**
• reprints 1st Issue Special **A:** Mike Grell
12 ❑ May 1978 Cover: 0.35 **NM** value: **1.50**
• **CGC:** 1 graded, best 8.5
13 ❑ Jul 1978 Cover: 0.35 **NM** value: **1.50**
14 ❑ Sep 1978 Cover: 0.35 **NM** value: **1.50**
15 ❑ Nov 1978 Cover: 0.50 **NM** value: **1.50**
16 ❑ Dec 1978 Cover: 0.40 **NM** value: **1.50**
17 ❑ Jan 1979 Cover: 0.40 **NM** value: **1.50**
18 ❑ Feb 1979 Cover: 0.40 **NM** value: **1.50**
19 ❑ Mar 1979 Cover: 0.40 **NM** value: **1.50**
20 ❑ Apr 1979 Cover: 0.40 **NM** value: **1.50**
21 ❑ May 1979 Cover: 0.40 **NM** value: **1.50**
22 ❑ Jun 1979 Cover: 0.40 **NM** value: **1.50**
23 ❑ Jul 1979 Cover: 0.40 **NM** value: **1.50**
24 ❑ Aug 1979 Cover: 0.40 **NM** value: **1.50**
• **CGC:** 1 graded, best 9.4
25 ❑ Sep 1979 Cover: 0.40 **NM** value: **1.50**
26 ❑ Oct 1979 Cover: 0.40 **NM** value: **1.50**
27 ❑ Nov 1979 Cover: 0.40 **NM** value: **1.50**
• **CGC:** 1 graded, best 9.0
28 ❑ Dec 1979 Cover: 0.40 **NM** value: **1.50**
29 ❑ Jan 1980 Cover: 0.40 **NM** value: **1.50**
30 ❑ Feb 1980 Cover: 0.40 **NM** value: **1.00**
31 ❑ Mar 1980 Cover: 0.40 **NM** value: **1.00**
32 ❑ Apr 1980 Cover: 0.40 **NM** value: **1.00**
33 ❑ May 1980 Cover: 0.40 **NM** value: **1.00**
34 ❑ Jun 1980 Cover: 0.40 **NM** value: **1.00**
35 ❑ Jul 1980 Cover: 0.40 **NM** value: **1.00**
36 ❑ Aug 1980 Cover: 0.40 **NM** value: **1.00**
37 ❑ Sep 1980 Cover: 0.50 **NM** value: **1.00**
• Omac back-up **A:** Mike Grell ★ Origin of Omac (new origin).
38 ❑ Oct 1980 Cover: 0.50 **NM** value: **1.00**
• **CGC:** 1 graded, best 9.4
• Omac back-up **A:** Mike Grell ★ 1st Appearance of Jennifer Morgan (Warlord's daughter).
39 ❑ Nov 1980 Cover: 0.50 **NM** value: **1.00**
• Omac back-up **A:** Mike Grell
40 ❑ Dec 1980 Cover: 0.50 **NM** value: **1.00**
41 ❑ Jan 1981 Cover: 0.50 **NM** value: **1.00**
Circ: Statement: **109,262**
42 ❑ Feb 1981 Cover: 0.50 **NM** value: **1.00**
Circ: Statement: **109,262**
43 ❑ Mar 1981 Cover: 0.50 **NM** value: **1.00**
Circ: Statement: **109,262**
44 ❑ Apr 1981 Cover: 0.50 **NM** value: **1.00**
Circ: Statement: **109,262**
45 ❑ May 1981 Cover: 0.50 **NM** value: **1.00**
Circ: Statement: **109,262**
46 ❑ Jun 1981 Cover: 0.50 **NM** value: **1.00**
Circ: Statement: **109,262**
47 ❑ Jul 1981 Cover: 0.50 **NM** value: **1.00**
Circ: Statement: **109,262**
• Omac back-up **A:** Mike Grell ★ 1st Appearance of Rostov.
48 ❑ Aug 1981 Cover: 0.50 **NM** value: **1.50**
Circ: Statement: **109,262**
• Giant-size. **A:** Mike Grell; Ernie Colon ★ 1st Appearance of Arak, Son of Thunder, Arak, Claw the Unconquered.
49 ❑ Sep 1981 Cover: 0.50 **NM** value: **1.00**
Circ: Statement: **109,262**
• Claw back-up **A:** Mike Grell ★ 1st Appearance of The Evil One.
50 ❑ Oct 1981 Cover: 0.60 **NM** value: **1.00**
Circ: Statement: **109,262** • **CGC:** 1 graded, best 9.6
51 ❑ Nov 1981 Cover: 0.60 **NM** value: **1.00**
Circ: Statement: **109,262**
• reprints Warlord #1; Dragonsword back-up **A:** Mike Grell
52 ❑ Dec 1981 Cover: 0.60 **NM** value: **1.00**
Circ: Statement: **109,262**
• Dragonsword back-up **A:** Mike Grell
53 ❑ Jan 1982 Cover: 0.60 **NM** value: **1.00**
Circ: Statement: **116,588**
• Dragonsword back-up
54 ❑ Feb 1982 Cover: 0.60 **NM** value: **1.00**
Circ: Statement: **116,588**
55 ❑ Mar 1982 Cover: 0.60 **NM** value: **1.00**
Circ: Statement: **116,588**
• Arion back-up **C:** Mike Grell ★ 1st Appearance of Lady Chian, Arion.
56 ❑ Apr 1982 Cover: 0.60 **NM** value: **1.00**
Circ: Statement: **116,588**
• Arion back-up **C:** Mike Grell
57 ❑ May 1982 Cover: 0.60 **NM** value: **1.00**
Circ: Statement: **116,588**
• Arion back-up; Has 1981 Statement, filed 10/1/81; avg print run 256,587; avg sales 107,398; avg subs 1,864; avg total paid 109,262; samples 127; office use 2,406; max existent 111,795; 56% of run returned **C:** Mike Grell
58 ❑ Jun 1982 Cover: 0.60 **NM** value: **1.00**

Other grades: Multiply prices above by **1.5 for Mint • 2/3 for Very Fine • 1/3 for Fine • 1/5 for Very Good • 1/8 for Good**

Circ: Statement: **116,588**
• Arion back-up **C:** Mike Grell

59 ❑ Jul 1982 Cover: 0.60 **NM** value: **1.00**
Circ: Statement: **116,588**
• Arion back-up **C:** Mike Grell ★ 1st Appearance of Garn Daanuth.

60 ❑ Aug 1982 Cover: 0.60 **NM** value: **1.00**
Circ: Statement: **116,588**
• Arion back-up **C:** Mike Grell

61 ❑ Sep 1982 Cover: 0.60 **NM** value: **1.00**
Circ: Statement: **116,588**
• Arion back-up **C:** Mike Grell

62 ❑ Oct 1982 Cover: 0.60 **NM** value: **1.00**
Circ: Statement: **116,588**
• Arion back-up **C:** Mike Grell

63 ❑ Nov 1982 Cover: 0.60 **NM** value: **1.00**
Circ: Statement: **116,588**
• Arion back-up **C:** Mike Grell ★ 1st Appearance of Conqueror of the Barren Earth.

64 ❑ Dec 1982 Cover: 0.60 **NM** value: **1.00**
Circ: Statement: **116,588**
• Barren Earth back-up; Masters of the Universe preview

65 ❑ Jan 1983 Cover: 0.60 **NM** value: **1.00**
Circ: Statement: **111,922**

66 ❑ Feb 1983 Cover: 0.60 **NM** value: **1.00**
Circ: Statement: **111,922**

67 ❑ Mar 1983 Cover: 0.60 **NM** value: **1.00**
Circ: Statement: **111,922**

68 ❑ Apr 1983 Cover: 0.60 **NM** value: **1.00**
Circ: Statement: **111,922**

69 ❑ May 1983 Cover: 0.60 **NM** value: **1.00**
Circ: Statement: **111,922**
• Has 1982 Statement, filed 10/1/82; avg print run 272,141; avg sales 114,767; avg subs 1,821; avg total paid 116,588; samples 677; office use 2,916; max existent 120,181; 56% of run returned

70 ❑ Jun 1983 Cover: 0.60 **NM** value: **1.00**
Circ: Statement: **111,922**

71 ❑ Jul 1983 Cover: 0.60 **NM** value: **1.00**
Circ: Statement: **111,922**

72 ❑ Aug 1983 Cover: 0.60 **NM** value: **1.00**
Circ: Statement: **111,922**

73 ❑ Sep 1983 Cover: 0.60 **NM** value: **1.00**
Circ: Statement: **111,922**

74 ❑ Oct 1983 Cover: 0.60 **NM** value: **1.00**
Circ: Statement: **111,922**

75 ❑ Nov 1983 Cover: 0.60 **NM** value: **1.00**
Circ: Statement: **111,922**

76 ❑ Dec 1983 Cover: 0.75 **NM** value: **1.00**
Circ: Statement: **111,922**

77 ❑ Jan 1984 Cover: 0.75 **NM** value: **1.00**
Circ: Statement: **101,013**

78 ❑ Feb 1984 Cover: 0.75 **NM** value: **1.00**
Circ: Statement: **101,013**

79 ❑ Mar 1984 Cover: 0.75 **NM** value: **1.00**
Circ: Statement: **101,013**

80 ❑ Apr 1984 Cover: 0.75 **NM** value: **1.00**
Circ: Statement: **101,013**
• Has 1983 Statement, filed 10/1/83; avg print run 271,968; avg sales 110,378; avg subs 1,544; avg total paid 111,922; samples 679; office use 2,533; max existent 115,134; 58% of run returned **A:** Dan Jurgens

81 ❑ May 1984 Cover: 0.75 **NM** value: **1.00**
Circ: Statement: **101,013**

82 ❑ Jun 1984 Cover: 0.75 **NM** value: **1.00**
Circ: Statement: **101,013**

83 ❑ Jul 1984 Cover: 0.75 **NM** value: **1.00**
Circ: Statement: **101,013**

84 ❑ Aug 1984 Cover: 0.75 **NM** value: **1.00**
Circ: Statement: **101,013**

85 ❑ Sep 1984 Cover: 0.75 **NM** value: **1.00**
Circ: Statement: **101,013**

86 ❑ Oct 1984 Cover: 0.75 **NM** value: **1.00**
Circ: Statement: **101,013**

87 ❑ Nov 1984 Cover: 0.75 **NM** value: **1.00**
Circ: Statement: **101,013**

88 ❑ Dec 1984 Cover: 0.75 **NM** value: **1.00**
Circ: Statement: **101,013**

89 ❑ Jan 1985 Cover: 0.75 **NM** value: **1.00**
Circ: Statement: **85,629**

90 ❑ Feb 1985 Cover: 0.75 **NM** value: **1.00**
Circ: Statement: **85,629**

91 ❑ Mar 1985 Cover: 0.75 **NM** value: **1.00**
Circ: Statement: **85,629**

92 ❑ Apr 1985 Cover: 0.75 **NM** value: **1.00**
Circ: Statement: **85,629**

93 ❑ May 1985 Cover: 0.75 **NM** value: **1.00**
Circ: Statement: **85,629** CapCity orders: **6,150**
• Has 1984 Statement, filed 10/1/84; avg print run 251,738; avg sales 99,331; avg subs 1,682; avg total paid 101,013; samples 182; office use 2,853; max existent 104,048; 59% of run returned

94 ❑ Jun 1985 Cover: 0.75 **NM** value: **1.00**
Circ: Statement: **85,629** CapCity orders: **6,300**

95 ❑ Jul 1985 Cover: 0.75 **NM** value: **1.00**
Circ: Statement: **85,629** CapCity orders: **6,300**

96 ❑ Aug 1985 Cover: 0.75 **NM** value: **1.00**
Circ: Statement: **85,629** CapCity orders: **6,200**

97 ❑ Sep 1985 Cover: 0.75 **NM** value: **1.00**
Circ: Statement: **85,629** CapCity orders: **6,300**

98 ❑ Oct 1985 Cover: 0.75 **NM** value: **1.00**
Circ: Statement: **85,629** CapCity orders: **6,050**

99 ❑ Nov 1985 Cover: 0.75 **NM** value: **1.00**
Circ: Statement: **85,629** CapCity orders: **6,100**

100 ❑ Dec 1985 Cover: 1.25 **NM** value: **Cover or less**
Circ: Statement: **85,629** CapCity orders: **7,850**
• Giant-size. 📖 Skartaris Unchained **A:** Adam Kubert **C:** Mike Grell **W:** Michael Fleisher

101 ❑ Jan 1986 Cover: 0.75 **NM** value: **1.00**
Circ: Statement: **71,752** CapCity orders: **6,050**

102 ❑ Feb 1986 Cover: 0.75 **NM** value: **1.00**
Circ: Statement: **71,752** CapCity orders: **6,200**

103 ❑ Mar 1986 Cover: 0.75 **NM** value: **1.00**
Circ: Statement: **71,752** CapCity orders: **6,150**

104 ❑ Apr 1986 Cover: 0.75 **NM** value: **1.00**
Circ: Statement: **71,752** CapCity orders: **6,150**

105 ❑ May 1986 Cover: 0.75 **NM** value: **1.00**
Circ: Statement: **71,752** CapCity orders: **5,950**

106 ❑ Jun 1986 Cover: 0.75 **NM** value: **1.00**
Circ: Statement: **71,752** CapCity orders: **6,300**

107 ❑ Jul 1986 Cover: 0.75 **NM** value: **1.00**
Circ: Statement: **71,752** CapCity orders: **5,850**

108 ❑ Aug 1986 Cover: 0.75 **NM** value: **1.00**
Circ: Statement: **71,752** CapCity orders: **5,950**

109 ❑ Sep 1986 Cover: 0.75 **NM** value: **1.00**
Circ: Statement: **71,752** CapCity orders: **6,000**

110 ❑ Oct 1986 Cover: 0.75 **NM** value: **1.00**
Circ: Statement: **71,752** CapCity orders: **6,150**

111 ❑ Nov 1986 Cover: 0.75 **NM** value: **1.00**
Circ: Statement: **71,752** CapCity orders: **6,000**

112 ❑ Dec 1986 Cover: 0.75 **NM** value: **1.00**
Circ: Statement: **71,752** CapCity orders: **5,950**

113 ❑ Jan 1987 Cover: 0.75 **NM** value: **1.00**
Circ: Statement: **66,961** CapCity orders: **5,800**

114 ❑ Feb 1987 Cover: 0.75 **NM** value: **1.00**
Circ: Statement: **66,961** CapCity orders: **11,450**
• Legends

115 ❑ Mar 1987 Cover: 0.75 **NM** value: **1.00**
Circ: Statement: **66,961** CapCity orders: **10,100**
• Legends

116 ❑ Apr 1987 Cover: 0.75 **NM** value: **1.00**
Circ: Statement: **66,961** CapCity orders: **10,100**

117 ❑ May 1987 Cover: 0.75 **NM** value: **1.00**
Circ: Statement: **66,961** CapCity orders: **6,350**

118 ❑ Jun 1987 Cover: 0.75 **NM** value: **1.00**
Circ: Statement: **66,961** CapCity orders: **7,050**

119 ❑ Jul 1987 Cover: 0.75 **NM** value: **1.00**
Circ: Statement: **66,961** CapCity orders: **6,700**

120 ❑ Aug 1987 Cover: 0.75 **NM** value: **1.00**
Circ: Statement: **66,961** CapCity orders: **7,300**

121 ❑ Sep 1987 Cover: 0.75 **NM** value: **1.00**
Circ: Statement: **66,961** CapCity orders: **7,750**

122 ❑ Oct 1987 Cover: 0.75 **NM** value: **1.00**
Circ: Statement: **66,961** CapCity orders: **8,300**

123 ❑ Nov 1987 Cover: 1.00 **NM** value: **Cover or less**
Circ: Statement: **66,961** CapCity orders: **7,700**

124 ❑ Dec 1987 Cover: 1.00 **NM** value: **Cover or less**
Circ: Statement: **66,961** CapCity orders: **7,500**

125 ❑ Jan 1988 Cover: 1.00 **NM** value: **Cover or less**
Circ: CapCity orders: **7,650**

126 ❑ Feb 1988 Cover: 1.00 **NM** value: **Cover or less**
Circ: CapCity orders: **7,850**

127 ❑ Mar 1988 Cover: 1.00 **NM** value: **Cover or less**
Circ: CapCity orders: **8,000**

128 ❑ Apr 1988 Cover: 1.00 **NM** value: **Cover or less**
Circ: CapCity orders: **7,700**

129 ❑ May 1988 Cover: 1.00 **NM** value: **Cover or less**
Circ: CapCity orders: **7,350**
📖 Maddox's Revenge, Part 1

130 ❑ Jul 1988 Cover: 1.00 **NM** value: **Cover or less**
Circ: CapCity orders: **6,850**
📖 Maddox's Revenge, Part 2

131 ❑ Sep 1988 Cover: 1.00 **NM** value: **2.00**
Circ: CapCity orders: **7,300**
📖 Maddox's Revenge, Part 3 • Bonus Book #6; Rob Liefeld's first work at DC **A:** Rob Liefeld

132 ❑ Nov 1988 Cover: 1.00 **NM** value: **Cover or less**
Circ: CapCity orders: **6,800**

133 ❑ Dec 1988 Cover: 1.50 **NM** value: **Cover or less**
Circ: CapCity orders: **7,400**
• Giant-size. final issue. **A:** Jan Duursema

Anl 1❑ca. 1982 Cover: 1.00 **NM** value: **2.00**
• **CGC:** 2 graded, best 9.8

Anl 2❑ca. 1983 Cover: 1.00 **NM** value: **Cover or less**

Anl 3❑ca. 1984 Cover: 1.25 **NM** value: **Cover or less**

Anl 4❑ca. 1985 Cover: 1.25 **NM** value: **Cover or less**
Circ: CapCity orders: **6,850**

Anl 5❑ca. 1986 Cover: 1.25 **NM** value: **Cover or less**
Circ: CapCity orders: **6,450**

Anl 6❑ca. 1987 Cover: 1.25 **NM** value: **Cover or less**
Circ: CapCity orders: **8,100**

WARLORD (MINI-SERIES) — DC

Travis Morgan left the above-ground world for one within the Earth, called Skartaris. He led its people to victory in the Great Rebellion and ever since then has been known as the leader of men, as the Warlord. Since then, as faithful readers of the regular monthly series know, Morgan has embarked on many an adventure above- and below-ground in a reality that recognizes and uses magic.

This six-part series expands on his origin and delves into the backgrounds of many of the other key characters in the series, including Travis' daughter, Jennifer Morgan.

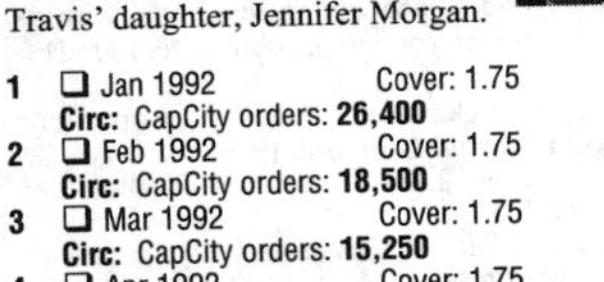

1 ❑ Jan 1992 Cover: 1.75 **NM** value: **2.00**
Circ: CapCity orders: **26,400**

2 ❑ Feb 1992 Cover: 1.75 **NM** value: **2.00**
Circ: CapCity orders: **18,500**

3 ❑ Mar 1992 Cover: 1.75 **NM** value: **2.00**
Circ: CapCity orders: **15,250**

4 ❑ Apr 1992 Cover: 1.75 **NM** value: **2.00**
Circ: CapCity orders: **13,050**

5 ❑ May 1992 Cover: 1.75 **NM** value: **2.00**
Circ: CapCity orders: **12,450**

6 ❑ Jun 1992 Cover: 1.75 **NM** value: **2.00**
Circ: CapCity orders: **12,350**

WARLORD: THE SAVAGE EMPIRE — DC

Bk 1❑ Cover: 19.95 **NM** value: **Cover or less**
• The Savage Empire **A:** Mike Grell

WAR MACHINE — Marvel

1 ❑ Apr 1994 Cover: 2.00 **NM** value: **Cover or less**
• Giant-size. 📖 Something to Believe In • newsstand **A:** Gabriel Gecko **W:** Len Kaminski; Scott Benson

1/SC❑Apr 1994 Cover: 2.95 **NM** value: **Cover or less**
Circ: Statement: **68,627** CapCity orders: **50,100**
Embossed cover. • Giant-size. 📖 Something to Believe In **A:** Gabriel Gecko **W:** Len Kaminski; Scott Benson

2 ❑ May 1994 Cover: 1.50 **NM** value: **Cover or less**
Circ: Statement: **68,627** CapCity orders: **27,250**
📖 Something to Believe In **A:** Gabriel Gecko **W:** Len Kaminski; Scott Benson

3 ❑ Jun 1994 Cover: 1.50 **NM** value: **Cover or less**
Circ: Statement: **68,627** CapCity orders: **24,350**
📖 Contents Under Pressure **A:** Gabriel Gecko **W:** Len Kaminski; Scott Benson

4 ❑ Jul 1994 Cover: 1.50 **NM** value: **Cover or less**
Circ: Statement: **68,627** CapCity orders: **23,500**

5 ❑ Aug 1994 Cover: 1.50 **NM** value: **Cover or less**
Circ: Statement: **68,627** CapCity orders: **20,700**

6 ❑ Sep 1994 Cover: 1.50 **NM** value: **Cover or less**
Circ: Statement: **68,627** CapCity orders: **18,700**

7 ❑ Oct 1994 Cover: 1.50 **NM** value: **Cover or less**
Circ: Statement: **31,716** CapCity orders: **16,850**

8 ❑ Nov 1994 Cover: 1.50 **NM** value: **Cover or less**

8/CS❑Nov 1994 Cover: 2.95 **NM** value: **Cover or less**
Circ: Statement: **31,716** CapCity orders: **18,800**
• polybagged with 16-page Marvel Action Hour preview, acetate print, coupon, sweepstakes entry form

9 ❑ Dec 1994 Cover: 1.50 **NM** value: **Cover or less**
Circ: Statement: **31,716** CapCity orders: **18,500**

10 ❑ Jan 1995 Cover: 1.50 **NM** value: **Cover or less**
Circ: Statement: **31,716** CapCity orders: **15,625**

11 ❑ Feb 1995 Cover: 1.50 **NM** value: **Cover or less**
Circ: Statement: **31,716** CapCity orders: **13,475**

12 ❑ Mar 1995 Cover: 1.50 **NM** value: **Cover or less**
Circ: Statement: **31,716** CapCity orders: **12,600**

13 ❑ Apr 1995 Cover: 1.50 **NM** value: **Cover or less**
Circ: Statement: **31,716** CapCity orders: **11,675**

14 ❑ May 1995 Cover: 1.50 **NM** value: **Cover or less**
Circ: Statement: **31,716** CapCity orders: **10,775**

15 ❑ Jun 1995 Cover: 2.50 **NM** value: **Cover or less**
Circ: Statement: **31,716** CapCity orders: **10,400**
• flip book with War Machine: Brothers in Arms part 2 **W:** Dan Abnett

16 ❑ Jul 1995 Cover: 1.50 **NM** value: **Cover or less**
Circ: Statement: **31,716** CapCity orders: **9,325**

17 ❑ Aug 1995 Cover: 1.50 **NM** value: **Cover or less**
Circ: Statement: **31,716** CapCity orders: **8,725**

18 ❑ Sep 1995 Cover: 1.50 **NM** value: **Cover or less**
Circ: Statement: **31,716**

19 ❑ Oct 1995 Cover: 1.50 **NM** value: **Cover or less**

20 ❑ Nov 1995 Cover: 1.50 **NM** value: **Cover or less**

21 ❑ Dec 1995 Cover: 1.50 **NM** value: **Cover or less**
📖 The Crossing **A:** Fred Haynes **W:** Dan Abnett ★ Appearance of Black Widow, Anachronauts, Hawkeye, U.S.Agent.

22 ❑ Jan 1996 Cover: 1.50 **NM** value: **Cover or less**
• Has 1995 Statement, filed 10/1/95; avg print run 34,104; avg sales 30,783; avg subs 933; avg total paid circ 31,716; samples 750; office use 500; 3% of run returned (series was sold in comics-shops only in this period) **W:** Dan Abnett

23 ❑ Feb 1996 Cover: 1.50 **NM** value: **Cover or less**

24 ❑ Mar 1996 Cover: 1.50 **NM** value: **Cover or less**
📖 Time Will Tell **A:** Yancey Labat; Fred Haynes **W:** Dan Abnett

25 ❑ Apr 1996 Cover: 1.50 **NM** value: **Cover or less**
📖 The Kiss Off! final issue. **A:** Fred Haynes **W:** Dan Abnett

Ash 1❑ca. 1994 Cover: 0.75 **NM** value: **Cover or less**
• ashcan edition.

WAR MAN — Marvel / Epic

1 ❑ Nov 1993 Cover: 2.50 **NM** value: **Cover or less**
Circ: CapCity orders: **5,200**

2 ❑ Dec 1993 Cover: 2.50 **NM** value: **Cover or less**
Circ: CapCity orders: **3,200**

WAR OF THE GODS — DC

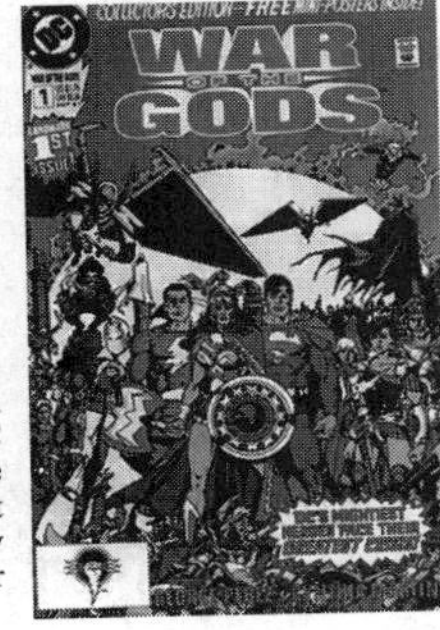

The war begins, when fabled witch Circe manages to pit the Greek gods of legend (Zeus, Hermes, Hades ...) against their Roman counterparts (Jupiter, Mercury, Pluto ...). Previously unknown to each other, they naturally see their own dopplegangers as impostors who must be driven out of New Olympus. The battle that ensues is felt across the dimensions and soon draws in virtually the entire cast of DC characters. Notably involved are those characters who draw at least some of their own history from myth, such as Wonder Woman and Shazam.

War of the Gods was 1991's entry in the DC mega-crossover category. It centered on the four issues of this mini-series but carried into titles as far apart as Animal Man and L.E.G.I.O.N. In total, the story ran across 22 issues.

CGC-graded: Multiply prices above by **33 for 9.9 M • 16 for 9.8 NM/M • 7 for 9.6 NM+ • 5 for 9.4 NM • 2.5 for 9.2 NM- • 1.5 for 9.0 VF/NM**

1 ❑ Sep 1991 Cover: 1.75 **NM** value: **Cover or less**
Circ: CapCity orders: **71,350**
📖 War of the Gods, Part 1 **A:** George Pérez

2 ❑ Oct 1991 Cover: 1.75 **NM** value: **Cover or less**
newsstand cover. 📖 War of the Gods, Part 9 **A:** George Pérez

2/DM❑Oct 1991 Cover: 1.75 **NM** value: **Cover or less**
Circ: CapCity orders: **59,400**
direct sale cover. **A:** George Pérez

3 ❑ Nov 1991 Cover: 1.75 **NM** value: **Cover or less**
newsstand cover. 📖 War of the Gods, Part 17 **A:** George Pérez

3/DM❑Nov 1991 Cover: 1.75 **NM** value: **Cover or less**
Circ: CapCity orders: **55,650**
direct sale cover. **A:** George Pérez

4 ❑ Dec 1991 Cover: 1.75 **NM** value: **Cover or less**
newsstand cover. 📖 War of the Gods, Part 21 **A:** George Pérez

4/DM❑Dec 1991 Cover: 1.75 **NM** value: **Cover or less**
Circ: CapCity orders: **54,400**
direct sale cover. **A:** George Pérez

WAR OF THE WORLDS, THE (CALIBER) Caliber

1 ❑ ca. 1996 Cover: 2.95 **NM** value: **Cover or less**
Circ: Diamd. preorders: **7,267**

2 ❑ ca. 1996 Cover: 2.95 **NM** value: **Cover or less**
Circ: Diamd. preorders: **3,788**

3 ❑ ca. 1996 Cover: 2.95 **NM** value: **Cover or less**
Circ: Diamd. preorders: **3,736**

4 ❑ ca. 1996 Cover: 2.95 **NM** value: **Cover or less**
Circ: Diamd. preorders: **2,715**

5 ❑ ca. 1997 Cover: 2.95 **NM** value: **Cover or less**

WAR OF THE WORLDS (ETERNITY) Eternity

1 ❑ Cover: 1.95 **NM** value: **Cover or less**
2 ❑ Cover: 1.95 **NM** value: **Cover or less**
3 ❑ Cover: 1.95 **NM** value: **Cover or less**
4 ❑ Cover: 1.95 **NM** value: **Cover or less**
5 ❑ Cover: 1.95 **NM** value: **Cover or less**
6 ❑ Cover: 1.95 **NM** value: **Cover or less**
Bk 1❑ Cover: 9.95 **NM** value: **Cover or less**

WAR OF THE WORLDS, THE: THE MEMPHIS FRONT Arrow

1 ❑ b&w Cover: 2.95 **NM** value: **Cover or less**
wrapraound cover.

1/A ❑ b&w Cover: 2.95 **NM** value: **Cover or less**
• expanded page count

2 ❑ Cover: 2.95 **NM** value: **Cover or less**
3 ❑ Cover: 2.95 **NM** value: **Cover or less**
4 ❑ Cover: 2.95 **NM** value: **Cover or less**
5 ❑ Cover: 2.95 **NM** value: **Cover or less**

WARP First

Warp is the story of Danny Carson, a wimpy bank clerk with a strange destiny. Years ago, he was possessed by the spirit of Lord Chaos, who appeared to him in terrifying visions. Things got so bad that Carson was interred in an insane asylum, where he remained until the night that Chaos broke free from him and entered our world. That seemed to cure Danny, but of late he has been having strange headaches — headaches that end when the wizard Lugulbanda calls forth the spirit of Lord Cumulus from within Danny. Danny finds himself on another world, with strange mental powers. Here he is Lord Cumulus, the only one powerful enough to stand against the forces of Chaos.

Warp is notable as the first comic book from independent publisher First Comics. Warp's origin is also unusual in that it began as a daring set of plays, staged beginning in 1971, by Chicago's Organic Theater Company.

1 ❑ Mar 1983 Cover: 2.00 **NM** value: **Cover or less**
• First comic book ever published by First Comics **A:** Frank Brunner
★ 1st Appearance of Lord Cumulus, Chaos.

2 ❑ Apr 1983 Cover: 1.50 **NM** value: **Cover or less**
3 ❑ May 1983 Cover: 1.50 **NM** value: **Cover or less**
4 ❑ Jun 1983 Cover: 1.50 **NM** value: **Cover or less**
5 ❑ Aug 1983 Cover: 1.50 **NM** value: **Cover or less**
6 ❑ Sep 1983 Cover: 1.50 **NM** value: **Cover or less**
7 ❑ Oct 1983 Cover: 1.50 **NM** value: **Cover or less**
8 ❑ Nov 1983 Cover: 1.25 **NM** value: **Cover or less**
9 ❑ Dec 1983 Cover: 1.25 **NM** value: **Cover or less**
10 ❑ Feb 1984 Cover: 1.25 **NM** value: **Cover or less**
11 ❑ Mar 1984 Cover: 1.25 **NM** value: **Cover or less**
12 ❑ Apr 1984 Cover: 1.25 **NM** value: **Cover or less**
13 ❑ May 1984 Cover: 1.25 **NM** value: **Cover or less**
14 ❑ Jul 1984 Cover: 1.25 **NM** value: **Cover or less**
15 ❑ Aug 1984 Cover: 1.25 **NM** value: **Cover or less**
16 ❑ Sep 1984 Cover: 1.25 **NM** value: **Cover or less**
17 ❑ Oct 1984 Cover: 1.25 **NM** value: **Cover or less**
18 ❑ Dec 1984 Cover: 1.25 **NM** value: **Cover or less**
19 ❑ Feb 1985 Cover: 1.25 **NM** value: **Cover or less**
final issue.
SE 1❑Jul 1983 Cover: 1.50 **NM** value: **Cover or less**
SE 2❑Jan 1984 Cover: 1.00 **NM** value: **Cover or less**
SE 3❑Jun 1984 Cover: 1.00 **NM** value: **Cover or less**
• Chaos

WARP-3 Equinox

1 ❑ Mar 1990, b&w Cover: 1.50 **NM** value: **Cover or less**

WAR PARTY Lightning

1 ❑ Oct 1994 Cover: 2.95 **NM** value: **Cover or less**
Circ: CapCity orders: **3,625**

WARP GRAPHICS ANNUAL Warp

1 ❑ full color Cover: 2.95 **NM** value: **3.00**
📖 Elfquest: Courage, b • Elfquest, Panda Khan, Unicorn Isle, Captain Obese, Thunderbunny, MythAdventures **A:** Marc Hempel; Jim Valentino; Don Lomax; Nicholas Koenig; Dave Garcia; Brian Buniak; Colleen Doran; Debbie Hayes **W:** Wendy Pini; Jim Valentino; Don Lomax; Mark Wheatley; Colleen Doran; Phil Foglio; Lee Marrs; Martin Greim; Monica Sharp; Richard Pini; Rick Shanklin; Robert Asprin

WARPWALKING Caliber

1 ❑ b&w Cover: 2.50 **NM** value: **Cover or less**
2 ❑ b&w Cover: 2.50 **NM** value: **Cover or less**
📖 The Quick and the Dead **A:** Mark Ricketts **W:** Mark Ricketts
3 ❑ b&w Cover: 2.50 **NM** value: **Cover or less**
4 ❑ b&w Cover: 2.50 **NM** value: **Cover or less**

WAR REPORT Farrell

1 ❑ Sep 1952 Cover: 0.10 **NM** value: **50.00**
2 ❑ Nov 1952 Cover: 0.10 **NM** value: **25.00**
3 ❑ Jan 1953 Cover: 0.10 **NM** value: **25.00**
4 ❑ May 1953 Cover: 0.10 **NM** value: **25.00**
5 ❑ May 1953 Cover: 0.10 **NM** value: **25.00**
final issue.

WARRIOR COMICS Blackerby

1 ❑ ca. 1945 Cover: 0.10 **NM** value: **100.00**
• CGC: 3 graded, best 7.5

WARRIOR NUN AREALA AND AVENGELYNE Antarctic

1/A ❑ Dec 1996 Cover: 2.95 **NM** value: **Cover or less**
• crossover with Maximum Press

1/B ❑ Dec 1996 Cover: 5.95 **NM** value: **Cover or less**
logoless cover and poster insert. • poster edition.

WARRIOR NUN AREALA AND GLORY Antarctic

1 ❑ Sep 1997 Cover: 2.95 **NM** value: **Cover or less**
• crossover with Awesome **A:** Ben Dunn **W:** Ben Dunn

1/CS❑Sep 1997 Cover: 5.95 **NM** value: **Cover or less**
• limited poster edition. • crossover with Awesome

WARRIOR NUN AREALA/RAZOR: REVENGE Antarctic

1 ❑ Jan 1999 Cover: 2.99 **NM** value: **Cover or less**
📖 Promises to Keep **A:** Ben Dunn; Nathan Lumm **W:** Joe Dunn

1/Dlx❑Jan 1999 Cover: 5.99 **NM** value: **Cover or less**
• Deluxe Edition with painted cover. 📖 Promises to Keep **A:** Ben Dunn; Nathan Lumm; Dorian Cleavenger(cover) **W:** Joe Dunn

WARRIOR NUN AREALA: RESURRECTION Antarctic

1 ❑ Nov 1998 Cover: 2.95 **NM** value: **3.00**
Circ: Diamd. preorders: **6,689**

1/SC❑Sum 1998 Cover: 5.95 **NM** value: **Cover or less**
alternate logoless cover. **A:** Ben Dunn **W:** Ben Dunn; Jim Gelvin

2 ❑ Jan 1999 Cover: 2.95 **NM** value: **3.00**
Circ: Diamd. preorders: **5,040**
📖 Hands of Fate, Fists of Fury **A:** Ben Dunn **W:** Ben Dunn; Jim Gelvin

3 ❑ Mar 1999 Cover: 2.95 **NM** value: **3.00**
Circ: Diamd. preorders: **5,051**

Ash 1❑Nov 1998 Cover: 1.00 **NM** value: **Cover or less**
No issue number. • b&w preview

WARRIOR NUN AREALA: RHEINTÖCHTER Antarctic

1 ❑ Dec 1997, b&w Cover: 2.95 **NM** value: **Cover or less**
2 ❑ Apr 1998, b&w Cover: 2.95 **NM** value: **Cover or less**

WARRIOR NUN AREALA: RITUALS Antarctic

1 ❑ Aug 1995 Cover: 2.95 **NM** value: **Cover or less**
📖 Conspiracy **A:** Ben Dunn **W:** Ben Dunn

1/SC❑Aug 1995 **NM** value: **4.00**
no cover price. 📖 Conspiracy **A:** Ben Dunn **W:** Ben Dunn

2 ❑ Oct 1995 Cover: 2.95 **NM** value: **Cover or less**
📖 Masques **A:** Ben Dunn **W:** Ben Dunn

3 ❑ Dec 1995 Cover: 2.95 **NM** value: **Cover or less**
4 ❑ Feb 1996 Cover: 2.95 **NM** value: **Cover or less**
5 ❑ Apr 1996 Cover: 2.95 **NM** value: **Cover or less**
📖 Treacherous Liaison **A:** Ben Dunn **W:** Ben Dunn
6 ❑ Jun 1996 Cover: 3.50 **NM** value: **Cover or less**

WARRIOR NUN AREALA (VOL. 1) Antarctic

As a rule, nuns oppose evil and the works of the devil through prayer and acts of chastity, charity, and faith. The Warrior Nuns of the Order of Areala take a more hands-on approach. Their habits are decidedly more revealing, allowing the freedom of movement to better oppose demons that seek to overtake society. The mystical nature of this series sets it apart from Evangeline from Comico in the 1980s, which also featured a non-traditional nun set in a space-faring future. This title is a curious mix between "Bad Girl" art, so prevalent in the 1990s, and a Japanese magna style, with its extreme close-ups and prominent, sometimes obtrusive, sound effects and word balloons.

The story and art is by Ben Dunn, whose earlier effort, Ninja High School, introduced a Warrior Nun prototype.

1 ❑ Dec 1994 Cover: 2.95 **NM** value: **5.00**
Circ: CapCity orders: **11,775**
📖 Gods and Beasts **A:** Ben Dunn **W:** Ben Dunn ★ 1st Appearance of Shotgun Mary, Warrior Nun Areala.

1/LE❑ Dec 1994 **NM** value: **5.00**
no cover price. • Limited edition (5000 made). 📖 Gods and Beasts **A:** Ben Dunn **W:** Ben Dunn

1-2 ❑ Mar 1995 Cover: 2.95 **NM** value: **3.00**

2 ❑ Feb 1995 Cover: 2.95 **NM** value: **4.00**
Circ: CapCity orders: **7,650**

3 ❑ Apr 1995 Cover: 2.95 **NM** value: **4.00**
Circ: CapCity orders: **10,500**
📖 Redemption **A:** Ben Dunn **W:** Ben Dunn

3/CS❑Apr 1995 **NM** value: **8.00**
📖 Redemption **A:** Ben Dunn **W:** Ben Dunn

3/Dlx❑Apr 1995 Cover: 7.95 **NM** value: **Cover or less**
cardstock cover. • polybagged with CD

3/LE❑ Apr 1995 Cover: 8.00 **NM** value: **Cover or less**
no cover price. • Limited edition (1000 made). 📖 Redemption **A:** Ben Dunn **W:** Ben Dunn

Bk 1❑ Jun 1995 Cover: 9.95 **NM** value: **Cover or less**
• Collects Warrior Nun Areala #1-3 **A:** Ben Dunn; Pat Kelley; Fred Perry; Joseph Wight; Ted Nomura; Jochen Weltjens; Mike Cogliandro **W:** Ben Dunn

WARRIOR NUN AREALA (VOL. 2) Antarctic

1 ❑ Jun 1997 Cover: 2.95 **NM** value: **3.00**
Circ: CapCity orders: **16,705** Diamd. preorders: **20,180**
📖 The Hammer & The Holocaust, Part 1 **A:** Brian Denham **W:** Barry Lyga

1/SC❑Jun 1997 **NM** value: **6.00**
• Leather edition. 📖 The Hammer & The Holocaust, Part 1 • Print run of 700 **A:** Brian Denham **W:** Barry Lyga

2 ❑ Sep 1997 Cover: 2.95 **NM** value: **3.00**
Circ: Diamd. preorders: **15,002**
📖 The Hammer & The Holocaust, Part 2 **A:** Brian Denham **W:** Barry Lyga

3 ❑ Nov 1997 Cover: 2.95 **NM** value: **3.00**
Circ: Diamd. preorders: **11,841**

4 ❑ Jan 1998 Cover: 2.95 **NM** value: **3.00**
Circ: Diamd. preorders: **9,948**
📖 Holy Man, Holy Terror, Part 1 **A:** Yanick Paquette **W:** Barry Lyga

5 ❑ Mar 1998 Cover: 2.95 **NM** value: **3.00**
Circ: Diamd. preorders: **8,374**
📖 Holy Man, Holy Terror, Part 2 **A:** Yanick Paquette **W:** Barry Lyga

6 ❑ May 1998 Cover: 2.95 **NM** value: **3.00**
Circ: Diamd. preorders: **7,844**
📖 Nor a Liar Run, Aware **A:** Ben Dunn **W:** Barry Lyga

WARRIOR NUN AREALA (VOL. 3) Antarctic

1 ❑ Jul 1999 Cover: 2.50 **NM** value: **Cover or less**
Circ: Diamd. preorders: **3,924**

2 ❑ Aug 1999 Cover: 2.50 **NM** value: **Cover or less**
Circ: Diamd. preorders: **4,896**

WARRIOR NUN: BLACK & WHITE Antarctic

1 ❑ Feb 1997 Cover: 2.95 **NM** value: **3.00**
Circ: Diamd. preorders: **13,405**
📖 Sea Demons, Part 1 **A:** Art Lyon **W:** Herb Mallette

2 ❑ Apr 1997 Cover: 2.95 **NM** value: **3.00**
Circ: Diamd. preorders: **10,275**
cover says Jan, indicia says Apr. 📖 Sea Demons, Part 2 **A:** Art Lyon **W:** Herb Mallette

3 ❑ Jun 1997 Cover: 2.95 **NM** value: **3.00**
Circ: Diamd. preorders: **9,424**
📖 Nemesis **A:** Lee Duhig **W:** Barry Lyga

4 ❑ Aug 1997 Cover: 2.95 **NM** value: **3.00**
Circ: Diamd. preorders: **8,920**
📖 Winter Jade, Part 1 **A:** Michel Lacombe **W:** Derek Kirk

5 ❑ Oct 1997 Cover: 2.95 **NM** value: **3.00**
Circ: Diamd. preorders: **7,337**
📖 Winter Jade, Part 2 **A:** Michel Lacombe **W:** Derek Kirk

6 ❑ Dec 1997 Cover: 2.95 **NM** value: **3.00**
Circ: Diamd. preorders: **6,579**
📖 Winter Jade, Part 3 **A:** Michel Lacombe **W:** Derek Kirk

7 ❑ Feb 1998 Cover: 2.95 **NM** value: **3.00**
Circ: Diamd. preorders: **5,239**

8 ❑ Mar 1998 Cover: 2.95 **NM** value: **3.00**
Circ: Diamd. preorders: **5,250**
📖 Ninja Nun **A:** Jolyon Yates **W:** Jolyon Yates

9 ❑ Apr 1998 Cover: 2.95 **NM** value: **3.00**
Circ: Diamd. preorders: **6,125**
📖 Breaking & Entering **A:** Patrick Blaine **W:** Herb Mallette

10 ❑ May 1998 Cover: 2.95 **NM** value: **3.00**
📖 Dismissal **A:** Patrick Blaine **W:** Herb Mallette

11 ❑ Jun 1998 Cover: 2.95 **NM** value: **3.00**
Circ: Diamd. preorders: **4,673**
📖 The Scenic Route **A:** Patrick Blaine **W:** Herb Mallette

12 ❑ Jul 1998 Cover: 2.95 **NM** value: **3.00**
Circ: Diamd. preorders: **4,246**
📖 Sister Trinity **A:** Langdon Foss **W:** Tom Harris

13 ❑ Sep 1998 Cover: 2.95 **NM** value: **3.00**
Circ: Diamd. preorders: **3,826**
📖 Far West **A:** Richard Moore **W:** Richard Moore

14 ❑ Oct 1998 Cover: 2.95 **NM** value: **3.00**
Circ: Diamd. preorders: **3,772**
📖 Cryptopolis **A:** Jean-Sebastien Duberger; Patrick Blaine **W:** Herb Mallette

15 ❑ Nov 1998 Cover: 2.95 **NM** value: **Cover or less**
Circ: Diamd. preorders: **3,500**
📖 Sister Trinity **A:** Langdon Foss **W:** Tom Harris

16 ❑ Jan 1999 Cover: 2.99 **NM** value: **Cover or less**
Circ: Diamd. preorders: **3,108**
📖 Redeemers, Part 5, End Game **A:** Jean-Sebastien Duberger; Pierre-Andre Derg **W:** Herb Mallette

17 ❑ Feb 1999 Cover: 2.99 **NM** value: **Cover or less**
Circ: Diamd. preorders: **2,886**
📖 Sister Trinity **A:** Langdon Foss **W:** Tom Harris

18 ❑ Mar 1999 Cover: 2.99 **NM** value: **Cover or less**
Circ: Diamd. preorders: **2,904**
📖 Reaction **A:** Lee Duhig **W:** Lee Duhig

Other grades: Multiply prices above by **1.5 for Mint • 2/3 for Very Fine • 1/3 for Fine • 1/5 for Very Good • 1/8 for Good**

19 ❑ Apr 1999 Cover: 2.99 **NM** value: **Cover or less**
Circ: Diamd. preorders: **2,918**

20 ❑ 1999 **NM** value: **2.99**
Circ: Diamd. preorders: **2,848**
📖 A Solemn Duty

21 ❑ Jul 1999 Cover: 2.50 **NM** value: **Cover or less**
Circ: Diamd. preorders: **2,126**

WARRIOR NUN DEI — Antarctic

1 ❑ Cover: 5.95 **NM** value: **Cover or less**
• Comics Cavalcade Commemorative Edition.

WARRIOR NUN DEI: AFTERTIME — Antarctic

1 ❑ Jan 1997 Cover: 2.95 **NM** value: **3.00**
Circ: Diamd. preorders: **17,139**

2 ❑ Cover: 2.95 **NM** value: **3.00**
Circ: Diamd. preorders: **12,791**

3 ❑ Mar 1999 Cover: 2.95 **NM** value: **3.00**
Circ: Diamd. preorders: **4,804**

WARRIOR NUN: FRENZY — Antarctic

1 ❑ Jan 1998 Cover: 2.95 **NM** value: **Cover or less**
Circ: Diamd. preorders: **9,330**

2 ❑ Jun 1998 Cover: 2.95 **NM** value: **Cover or less**
Circ: Diamd. preorders: **6,178**

WARRIOR NUN: SCORPIO ROSE — Antarctic

1 ❑ Sep 1996 Cover: 2.95 **NM** value: **Cover or less**
2 ❑ Nov 1996 Cover: 2.95 **NM** value: **Cover or less**
3 ❑ Jan 1997 Cover: 2.95 **NM** value: **Cover or less**
4 ❑ Mar 1997 Cover: 2.95 **NM** value: **Cover or less**
final issue. **A:** Ben Dunn **W:** Steve Englehart

WARRIOR NUN VS RAZOR — Antarctic

1 ❑ May 1996 Cover: 3.95 **NM** value: **Cover or less**
📖 Deceiver • crossover with London Night Studios **A:** Ben Dunn **W:** Joseph Wolfe

WARRIOR OF WAVERLY STREET, THE — Dark Horse

1 ❑ Nov 1996 Cover: 2.95 **NM** value: **Cover or less**
Circ: Diamd. preorders: **8,106**

2 ❑ Dec 1996 Cover: 2.95 **NM** value: **Cover or less**
Circ: Diamd. preorders: **5,539**
final issue. **A:** John Stokes **W:** Manny Coto

WARRIORS — Adventure

1 ❑ Cover: 1.95 **NM** value: **2.00**
📖 Two Sides of Man; The Twelfth Cup; Sanguis Virginis **A:** Adam Hughes; Sam Inabinet; Brian Guice **W:** Mark Ellis; Brad Freman; Dan Greenburg

2 ❑ Dec 1987 Cover: 1.95 **NM** value: **2.00**
3 ❑ Cover: 1.95 **NM** value: **2.00**

WARRIORS OF PLASM — Defiant

Warriors of Plasm is the first title from Defiant Comics. The Org of Plasm is a strange, savage world which lies in a dimension separated from our own by a split second. Here, all technology is based on biology, and everything from clothing to spaceships are living, genetically designed creatures. Killing someone is incidental — but not recycling the remains is a serious crime.

Biomass — and power — are the only things worth having. Plasm's supreme acquisitor Lorca had a plan to gain both. He found a way to breach the dimension to our world and succeeded in snatching 10,000 Earthlings, whom he intended to mutate into a private army. However, all but five of the subjects died immediately. The remaining few, an unlikely mix including a grandmother, a one-armed giant, and a hawkish army lieutenant, find themselves with strange powers that they must use to save their world from being conquered and "recycled" by Plasm.

1 ❑ Aug 1993 Cover: 2.95 **NM** value: **Cover or less**
Circ: CapCity orders: **134,325**
📖 The Sedition Agenda, Part 1 • First Defiant Comic (not including Warriors of Plasm #0 promotion) **A:** David Lapham **W:** Jim Shooter ★ Origin of Warriors of Plasm. ★ 1st Appearance of Lorca, Warriors of Plasm.

2 ❑ Sep 1993 Cover: 2.95 **NM** value: **Cover or less**
Circ: CapCity orders: **84,050**

3 ❑ Oct 1993 Cover: 2.95 **NM** value: **Cover or less**
Circ: CapCity orders: **53,325**

4 ❑ Nov 1993 Cover: 2.95 **NM** value: **Cover or less**
Circ: CapCity orders: **36,025**

5 ❑ Dec 1993 Cover: 2.50 **NM** value: **Cover or less**
Circ: CapCity orders: **26,900**

6 ❑ Jan 1994 Cover: 2.50 **NM** value: **Cover or less**
Circ: CapCity orders: **20,700**

7 ❑ Feb 1994 Cover: 2.50 **NM** value: **Cover or less**
Circ: CapCity orders: **16,575**

8 ❑ Mar 1994 Cover: 2.75 **NM** value: **Cover or less**
Circ: CapCity orders: **14,075**

9 ❑ Apr 1994 Cover: 2.50 **NM** value: **2.75**
Circ: CapCity orders: **12,200**

10 ❑ May 1994 Cover: 2.50 **NM** value: **Cover or less**
Circ: CapCity orders: **10,975**

11 ❑ Jun 1994 Cover: 2.50 **NM** value: **Cover or less**
Circ: CapCity orders: **9,825**

12 ❑ Jul 1994 Cover: 2.50 **NM** value: **Cover or less**
Circ: CapCity orders: **8,100**

13 ❑ Aug 1994 Cover: 2.50 **NM** value: **Cover or less**
Circ: CapCity orders: **7,200**
• Final issue?

Bk 1❑ Feb 1994 Cover: 9.95 **NM** value: **Cover or less**
• collects Zero issue, Sedition Agenda, and Splatterball.

WARRIORS OF PLASM GRAPHIC NOVEL — Defiant

1 ❑ Cover: 6.95 **NM** value: **Cover or less**
Circ: CapCity orders: **12,150**
• Home for the Holidays

WARRIOR'S WAY — Bench Press

1 ❑ Cover: 2.99 **NM** value: **Cover or less**
2 ❑ Aug 1998 Cover: 2.99 **NM** value: **Cover or less**
2/A ❑ Aug 1998 Cover: 2.99 **NM** value: **Cover or less**
alternate cover.
3 ❑ Cover: 2.99 **NM** value: **Cover or less**

WARRIOR (ULTIMATE CREATIONS) — Ultimate Creations

1 ❑ 1996 Cover: 2.95 **NM** value: **Cover or less**
Circ: Diamd. preorders: **6,714**

2 ❑ 1996 Cover: 2.95 **NM** value: **Cover or less**
Circ: Diamd. preorders: **6,427**

3 ❑ 1997 Cover: 2.95 **NM** value: **Cover or less**
Circ: Diamd. preorders: **3,605**

4 ❑ 1997 Cover: 2.95 **NM** value: **Cover or less**
Circ: Diamd. preorders: **3,416**

Bk 1❑ Cover: 12.95 **NM** value: **Cover or less**
• Warrior Amassment trade paperback; Collects Warrior (Ultimate Creations) #1-4

WAR SIRENS AND LIBERTY BELLES — Recollections

1 ❑ b&w Cover: 4.95 **NM** value: **Cover or less**
cardstock cover.

WAR SLUTS — Pretty Graphic

All issues are adults only.

1 ❑ b&w Cover: 3.95 **NM** value: **Cover or less**
2 ❑ b&w Cover: 3.95 **NM** value: **Cover or less**
cardstock cover.

WARSTRIKE — Malibu / Ultraverse

Warstrike first appeared in Mantra #1. A soldier for hire, he was recruited by Boneyard to help tip the balance against Archimage's men. In fact, it was Warstrike who killed Lukasz, sending him into the body of Mantra. Warstrike, however, is nothing if not smart. So, when he later encounters Lukasz in Mantra's female body, he both recognizes her and decides to help her.

As this series begins, Warstrike (aka Brandon Tark) is once again plying his trade as a super-powered mercenary. He has the ability to quickly heal from any wound and is almost unbelievably skilled with weapons. However, his true power is his intelligence, allowing him to outthink his opponents as well as outfight them. This, along with a little help from trusted friends Shelby and Giz, makes him the equal of just about any challenge.

1 ❑ May 1994 Cover: 1.95 **NM** value: **Cover or less**
Circ: CapCity orders: **20,475**

2 ❑ Jun 1994 Cover: 1.95 **NM** value: **Cover or less**
Circ: CapCity orders: **12,725**
📖 The Darkness **A:** Hoang Nguyen **W:** Dan Danko ★ 1st Appearance of Quixote, Domingo, Gaunt, Backlash (Ultraverse).

3 ❑ Jul 1994 Cover: 1.95 **NM** value: **Cover or less**
Circ: CapCity orders: **10,125**
📖 The Politics of Greed **A:** Hoang Nguyen **W:** Dan Danko

4 ❑ Aug 1994 Cover: 1.95 **NM** value: **Cover or less**
Circ: CapCity orders: **8,600**
📖 Games **A:** Roger Robinson; Hoang Nguyen **W:** Dan Danko ★ 1st Appearance of Captain U.S.A..

5 ❑ Sep 1994 Cover: 1.95 **NM** value: **Cover or less**
Circ: CapCity orders: **7,050**
📖 The Symphony of the Damned **A:** David Wong; Kevin Maguire(cover) **W:** Dan Danko ★ 1st Appearance of Aeon.

6 ❑ Oct 1994 Cover: 1.95 **NM** value: **Cover or less**
Circ: CapCity orders: **6,425**
📖 Fear, Hate, Hope **A:** Hoang Nguyen **W:** Dan Danko ★ Appearance of Rafferty.

7 ❑ Nov 1994 Cover: 1.95 **NM** value: **Cover or less**
Circ: CapCity orders: **5,450**
📖 A Lonely Place of Dying final issue. **A:** Hoang Nguyen **W:** Dan Danko

GS 1❑ Dec 1994 Cover: 2.50 **NM** value: **Cover or less**
Circ: CapCity orders: **5,675**
• Giant-size. 📖 Faith No More; Godwheel (Prelude) • Lord Pumpkin reborn **A:** Keith Conroy **W:** Dan Danko

WAR VICTORY ADVENTURES — Harvey

1 ❑ Sum 1942 Cover: 0.05 **NM** value: **200.00**
2 ❑ Aug 1943 Cover: 0.10 **NM** value: **150.00**
3 ❑ Win 1943 Cover: 0.10 **NM** value: **150.00**
• **CGC:** 1 graded, best 7.0

WARWORLD! — Dark Horse

1 ❑ Feb 1989, b&w Cover: 1.75 **NM** value: **Cover or less**

WARZONE — Express / Entity

1 ❑ ca. 1994, b&w Cover: 2.95 **NM** value: **Cover or less**
enhanced cardstock cover.
2 ❑ ca. 1994, b&w Cover: 2.95 **NM** value: **Cover or less**
enhanced cardstock cover.
3 ❑ ca. 1995, b&w Cover: 2.95 **NM** value: **Cover or less**
enhanced cardstock cover.

WASHMEN — New York

1 ❑ Cover: 1.70 **NM** value: **Cover or less**

WASH TUBBS QUARTERLY — Dragon Lady

1 ❑ Cover: 4.95 **NM** value: **Cover or less**
2 ❑ Cover: 5.95 **NM** value: **Cover or less**
3 ❑ Cover: 5.95 **NM** value: **Cover or less**
4 ❑ Cover: 5.95 **NM** value: **Cover or less**
5 ❑ Cover: 5.95 **NM** value: **Cover or less**

WASTE L.A.: DESCENT — John Gaushell

1 ❑ Jan 1996, b&w Cover: 2.50 **NM** value: **Cover or less**
• fumetti
2 ❑ Mar 1996, b&w Cover: 2.50 **NM** value: **Cover or less**
• fumetti
3 ❑ May 1996, b&w Cover: 2.50 **NM** value: **Cover or less**
• fumetti

WASTELAND — DC

It's like Vertigo before there was Vertigo.

Wasteland is a series of anthologies edited by comics industry legend Mike Gold. The series collects three bizarre stories in each issue, kicking off with a tale by John Ostrander about a drug that will create the highest of highs but will also cause death. One would think that a sure death would be enough of a deterrent to stop people from taking it. But, then again, one never knows. Next comes a story about a futuristic society in which people are married over the phone and abortions are retroactive, up to nine years. The third is a weird autobiographical tale written by Del Close.

Printed in full color, Wasteland first hit the stands in 1987. A critical, if not a commercial, success, it ran for 18 issues.

1 ❑ Dec 1987 Cover: 1.75 **NM** value: **2.00**
Circ: CapCity orders: **16,250**
📖 Foo Goo; R.ab.; Sewer Rat **A:** William Messner-Loebs; David Lloyd; Donald Simpson **W:** Del Close; John Ostrander

2 ❑ Jan 1988 Cover: 1.75 **NM** value: **2.00**
Circ: CapCity orders: **13,150**
📖 That's Entertainment; Ghengis Sings!!; Warning Signals **A:** William Messner-Loebs; David Lloyd; Donald Simpson **W:** Del Close; John Ostrander

3 ❑ Feb 1988 Cover: 1.75 **NM** value: **2.00**
Circ: CapCity orders: **12,400**
📖 American Squalor; Dies Illa; Lotus Blossom **A:** William Messner-Loebs; David Lloyd; Donald Simpson **W:** Del Close; John Ostrander

4 ❑ Mar 1988 Cover: 1.75 **NM** value: **2.00**
Circ: CapCity orders: **12,650**
📖 Sonnet LXVI; A Safe Place; Celebrity Rights **A:** William Messner-Loebs; George Freeman; Donald Simpson; Ty Templeton **W:** Del Close; John Ostrander

5 ❑ Apr 1988 Cover: 1.75 **NM** value: **2.00**
Circ: CapCity orders: **12,050**
correct cover. **A:** William Messner-Loebs; David Lloyd; Donald Simpson **W:** Del Close; John Ostrander

5/A ❑ Apr 1988 Cover: 1.75 **NM** value: **2.00**
cover of #6.

6 ❑ May 1988 Cover: 1.75 **NM** value: **2.00**
Circ: CapCity orders: **10,050**
correct cover. **A:** William Messner-Loebs; David Lloyd; Donald Simpson **W:** Del Close; John Ostrander

6/A ❑ May 1988 Cover: 1.75 **NM** value: **2.00**
blank cover.

7 ❑ Jun 1988 Cover: 1.75 **NM** value: **2.00**
Circ: CapCity orders: **8,800**

8 ❑ Jul 1988 Cover: 1.75 **NM** value: **2.00**
Circ: CapCity orders: **8,400**

9 ❑ Aug 1988 Cover: 1.75 **NM** value: **2.00**
Circ: CapCity orders: **7,800**

10 ❑ Sep 1988 Cover: 1.75 **NM** value: **2.00**
Circ: CapCity orders: **7,300**

11 ❑ Oct 1988 Cover: 1.75 **NM** value: **2.00**
Circ: CapCity orders: **6,850**
📖 Embryo; Revenge of the Swamp Creature!; Dissecting Mister Fleming **A:** William Messner-Loebs; David Lloyd; Donald Simpson; Ty Templeton **W:** Del Close; John Ostrander

12 ❑ Nov 1988 Cover: 1.75 **NM** value: **2.00**
Circ: CapCity orders: **6,050**
📖 After the Dead Detective; Passing Grade; Titty-Tat Breath **A:** William Messner-Loebs; David Lloyd; Joe Orlando; Donald Simpson **W:** Del Close; John Ostrander

13 ❑ Dec 1988 Cover: 1.75 **NM** value: **2.00**
Circ: CapCity orders: **6,050**
📖 Tipped Toes; Astigmata; Message From the Star Worm **A:** William Wray; Joe Orlando; Tim Truman; Donald Simpson **W:** Del Close; John Ostrander

14 ❑ Win 1988 Cover: 1.75 **NM** value: **2.00**
Circ: CapCity orders: **5,500**
📖 Metamorphfloozie; Whistling Past the Graveyard; The Beast **A:** William Wray; Joe Orlando; Donald Simpson; Michael Davis **W:** Del Close; John Ostrander

CGC-graded: Multiply prices above by **33 for 9.9 M** • **16 for 9.8 NM/M** • **7 for 9.6 NM+** • **5 for 9.4 NM** • **2.5 for 9.2 NM-** • **1.5 for 9.0 VF/NM**

15 ❑ Hol 1988 Cover: 1.75 **NM** value: **2.00**
Circ: CapCity orders: **5,200**
📖 Crocophagia, or Hamlet in Aegypt; Zero Hour; Mother's Withered Hands **A:** William Wray; Joe Orlando; Donald Simpson; Rick Magyar **W:** Del Close; John Ostrander

16 ❑ Feb 1989 Cover: 1.75 **NM** value: **2.00**
Circ: CapCity orders: **5,200**
📖 The Woman Who Tried to Find God; All I Want for Christmas is the Head of Idi Amin!; Heartshadow **A:** William Wray; Joe Orlando; Donald Simpson; Michael Davis **W:** Del Close; John Ostrander

17 ❑ Apr 1989 Cover: 2.00 **NM** value: **Cover or less**
Circ: CapCity orders: **5,150**

18 ❑ May 1989 Cover: 2.00 **NM** value: **Cover or less**
Circ: CapCity orders: **4,850**
📖 The Casebook of the Dead Detective: "86" final issue. **A:** William Wray; Joe Orlando; Donald Simpson; Michael Davis **W:** Del Close; John Ostrander

WASTELAND, THE — DC / Piranha

Bk 1❑ b&w Cover: 7.95 **NM** value: **Cover or less**

WATCHCATS — Harrier

1 ❑ Cover: 1.95 **NM** value: **Cover or less**

WATCHMEN — DC

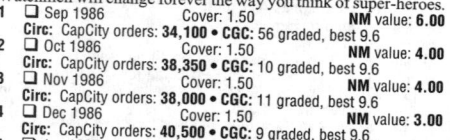

Someone — or something — is stalking costumed crime-fighters. "The Crimebusters" have long been out of action, having been outlawed by the Anti-Vigilante Act. We meet them now in the twilight of their lives, when a closer look also shows that these once-honored heroes were not so heroic, after all. In fact, in many cases, they're borderline psychotics, if not outright insane. And now someone is picking them off, one by one ...

This classic 12-issue maxi-series by writer Alan Moore explores both the darkest and the best in human nature. It has a maturity and insight rarely seen in the world of comics. Watchmen will change forever the way you think of super-heroes.

1 ❑ Sep 1986 Cover: 1.50 **NM** value: **6.00**
Circ: CapCity orders: **34,100** • **CGC:** 56 graded, best 9.6

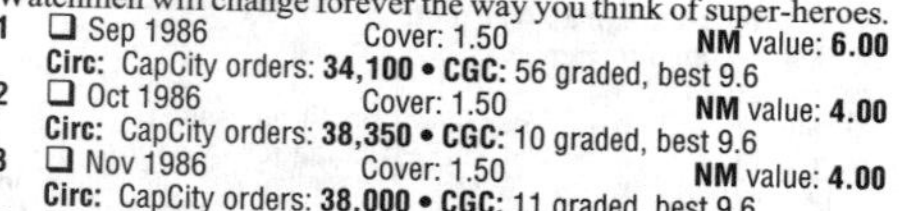

2 ❑ Oct 1986 Cover: 1.50 **NM** value: **4.00**
Circ: CapCity orders: **38,350** • **CGC:** 10 graded, best 9.6
3 ❑ Nov 1986 Cover: 1.50 **NM** value: **4.00**
Circ: CapCity orders: **38,000** • **CGC:** 11 graded, best 9.6
4 ❑ Dec 1986 Cover: 1.50 **NM** value: **3.00**
Circ: CapCity orders: **40,500** • **CGC:** 9 graded, best 9.6
5 ❑ Jan 1987 Cover: 1.50 **NM** value: **3.00**
Circ: CapCity orders: **33,150** • **CGC:** 8 graded, best 9.6
6 ❑ Feb 1987 Cover: 1.50 **NM** value: **3.00**
Circ: CapCity orders: **32,700** • **CGC:** 7 graded, best 9.6
7 ❑ Mar 1987 Cover: 1.50 **NM** value: **3.00**
Circ: CapCity orders: **30,150** • **CGC:** 6 graded, best 9.6
8 ❑ Apr 1987 Cover: 1.50 **NM** value: **3.00**
Circ: CapCity orders: **28,150** • **CGC:** 7 graded, best 9.6
9 ❑ May 1987 Cover: 1.50 **NM** value: **3.00**
Circ: CapCity orders: **28,150** • **CGC:** 6 graded, best 9.2
10 ❑ Jul 1987 Cover: 1.50 **NM** value: **3.00**
Circ: CapCity orders: **26,850** • **CGC:** 5 graded, best 9.8
11 ❑ Aug 1987 Cover: 1.50 **NM** value: **3.00**
Circ: CapCity orders: **28,300** • **CGC:** 7 graded, best 9.6
12 ❑ Oct 1987 Cover: 1.50 **NM** value: **3.00**
Circ: CapCity orders: **34,150** • **CGC:** 12 graded, best 9.6
Bk 1❑ Cover: 14.95 **NM** value: **16.95**
Circ: CapCity orders: **7,650**
• Reprints Watchmen #1-12 **A:** Dave Gibbons **W:** Alan Moore
Bk 1-2❑ Cover: 19.95 **NM** value: **Cover or less**
Circ: CapCity orders: **2,335**

WATERWORLD: CHILDREN OF LEVIATHAN — Acclaim

1 ❑ Aug 1997 Cover: 2.50 **NM** value: **Cover or less**
• no indicia **A:** Kevin Kobasic **W:** Christopher Golden; Tom Sniegoski
2 ❑ Sep 1997 Cover: 2.50 **NM** value: **Cover or less**
3 ❑ Oct 1997 Cover: 2.50 **NM** value: **Cover or less**
4 ❑ Nov 1997 Cover: 2.50 **NM** value: **Cover or less**

WAVEMAKERS — Blind Bat

1 ❑ Cover: 3.00 **NM** value: **Cover or less**

WAVE WARRIORS — Astroboys

1 ❑ full color Cover: 1.00 **NM** value: **2.00**

WAXWORK — Blackthorne

1 ❑ b&w Cover: 2.00 **NM** value: **Cover or less**
3D 1❑ Cover: 2.50 **NM** value: **Cover or less**

WAY OUT STRIPS (FANTAGRAPHICS) — Fantagraphics

1 ❑ 1994b&w Cover: 2.50 **NM** value: **Cover or less**
2 ❑ May 1994, b&w Cover: 2.75 **NM** value: **Cover or less**
3 ❑ Aug 1994, b&w Cover: 2.75 **NM** value: **Cover or less**

WAY OUT STRIPS (TRAGEDY STRIKES) — Tragedy Strikes

1 ❑ b&w Cover: 2.95 **NM** value: **Cover or less**
2 ❑ b&w Cover: 2.95 **NM** value: **Cover or less**
3 ❑ b&w Cover: 2.95 **NM** value: **Cover or less**

WAYWARD WARRIOR — Alpha Productions

1 ❑ b&w Cover: 1.95 **NM** value: **Cover or less**
2 ❑ b&w Cover: 1.95 **NM** value: **Cover or less**
3 ❑ b&w Cover: 1.95 **NM** value: **Cover or less**

WCW WORLD CHAMPIONSHIP WRESTLING — Marvel

1 ❑ Apr 1992 Cover: 1.25 **NM** value: **2.00**
Circ: CapCity orders: **6,600**
2 ❑ May 1992 Cover: 1.25 **NM** value: **1.50**
Circ: CapCity orders: **3,600**
3 ❑ Jun 1992 Cover: 1.25 **NM** value: **1.50**
4 ❑ Jul 1992 Cover: 1.25 **NM** value: **1.50**
5 ❑ Aug 1992 Cover: 1.25 **NM** value: **1.50**
6 ❑ Sep 1992 Cover: 1.25 **NM** value: **1.50**
7 ❑ Oct 1992 Cover: 1.25 **NM** value: **1.50**
8 ❑ Nov 1992 Cover: 1.25 **NM** value: **1.50**
9 ❑ Dec 1992 Cover: 1.25 **NM** value: **1.50**
10 ❑ Jan 1993 Cover: 1.25 **NM** value: **1.50**
11 ❑ Feb 1993 Cover: 1.25 **NM** value: **1.50**
12 ❑ Mar 1993 Cover: 1.25 **NM** value: **1.50**
📖 Bombed!

WEAPON X — Marvel

Marvel Comics created new titles from the X-Men universe for the highly successful X-Men: Age of Apocalypse crossover story. As underground agents committed to peace between humans and mutants, lovers Logan and Jean Grey undertake a suicide mission to steal valuable information from Apocalypse. Apocalypse realizes their termination amnesties are temporary and fights like a man possessed. Their apparent triumph might be a Pyrrhic victory, as leadership struggles within the Human High Council could place mankind on a path of extinction. Logan may have unwittingly provided the means necessary to hasten the Age of Apocalypse instead of leading the final bid for freedom.

1 ❑ Mar 1995 Cover: 1.95 **NM** value: **2.00**
Circ: CapCity orders: **84,250** • **CGC:** 2 graded, best 9.8
📖 Unforgiven Trespasses • Age of Apocalypse **A:** Karl Kesel; Adam Kubert; Dan Green; Chris Warner **W:** Larry Hama
2 ❑ Apr 1995 Cover: 1.95 **NM** value: **2.00**
Circ: CapCity orders: **81,725**
📖 Fire in the Sky! • Age of Apocalypse **A:** Karl Kesel; Adam Kubert; Dan Green; Chris Warner **W:** Larry Hama
3 ❑ May 1995 Cover: 1.95 **NM** value: **2.00**
Circ: CapCity orders: **98,675**
• Age of Apocalypse **A:** Karl Kesel; Adam Kubert; Dan Green; Chris Warner **W:** Larry Hama
4 ❑ Jun 1995 Cover: 1.95 **NM** value: **2.00**
Circ: CapCity orders: **103,800**
• Age of Apocalypse **A:** Karl Kesel; Adam Kubert; Dan Green; Chris Warner **W:** Larry Hama
Bk 1❑ May 1995 Cover: 8.95 **NM** value: **Cover or less**
Gold foil cover. • Ultimate Weapon-X; collects four-issue series
Bk 1/HC❑ Cover: 19.95 **NM** value: **Cover or less**

WEAPON ZERO — Image

Astronaut Tyson Stone's life changed forever after a trip to the moon in which he encountered an extraterrestrial. Since then, he has changed into a not-quite-human being himself, his wife has been murdered, and aliens have invaded his home. Ultimately, he finds himself fighting the awesome power of Lord N'Gloth and his followers in an attempt to protect the entire planet Earth.

When the going gets tough, the not-so-tough materialize a massive battle suit and attempt to save the day. Or at least that's what Stone did, as he escaped with two other humans whom he had met in the enemy fortress. They had been abducted from alternate timestreams by N'Gloth. With the help of his newfound allies, these heroes (as Weapon Zero) might just be able to save the world.

1 ❑ Jun 1995 Cover: 2.50 **NM** value: **3.00**
Circ: CapCity orders: **27,225**
• Issue #T-4 **A:** Joe Benitez **W:** Walt Simonson ★ 1st Appearance of Weapon Zero.
1/GO❑Jun 1995 **NM** value: **2.50**
• Gold edition. • Issue #T-4; 1000 copies produced for Chicago Comicon
2 ❑ Aug 1995 Cover: 2.50 **NM** value: **Cover or less**
Circ: CapCity orders: **24,950**
• Issue #T-3 **A:** Joe Benitez **W:** Walt Simonson
3 ❑ Sep 1995 Cover: 2.50 **NM** value: **Cover or less**
Circ: CapCity orders: **24,025**
• Issue #T-2 **A:** Joe Benitez **W:** Walt Simonson
4 ❑ Oct 1995 Cover: 2.50 **NM** value: **Cover or less**
Circ: CapCity orders: **22,825**
• Issue #T-1 **A:** Joe Benitez **W:** Walt Simonson
5 ❑ Dec 1995 Cover: 2.50 **NM** value: **Cover or less**
Circ: CapCity orders: **14,800**
• Issue #T-O; Issue #T-0 **A:** Joe Benitez **W:** Walt Simonson

WEAPON ZERO (VOL. 2) — Image

1 ❑ Mar 1996 Cover: 2.50 **NM** value: **3.00**
• indicia gives year of publication as 1995
2 ❑ Apr 1996 Cover: 2.50 **NM** value: **3.00**
• indicia gives year of publication as 1995
3 ❑ May 1996 Cover: 2.50 **NM** value: **3.00**
4 ❑ Jun 1996 Cover: 2.50 **NM** value: **3.00**
• indicia gives year of publication as 1995
5 ❑ Jul 1996 Cover: 2.50 **NM** value: **3.00**
• indicia gives year of publication as 1995
6 ❑ Aug 1996 Cover: 2.50 **NM** value: **Cover or less**
7 ❑ Sep 1996 Cover: 2.50 **NM** value: **Cover or less**
8 ❑ Nov 1996 Cover: 2.50 **NM** value: **Cover or less**
Circ: Diamd. preorders: **35,945**
9 ❑ Dec 1996 Cover: 2.50 **NM** value: **Cover or less**
Circ: Diamd. preorders: **34,722**
10 ❑ Feb 1997 Cover: 2.50 **NM** value: **Cover or less**
Circ: Diamd. preorders: **39,177**
📖 Family Feuds **A:** Scott Lee **W:** Walt Simonson
11 ❑ Apr 1997 Cover: 2.50 **NM** value: **Cover or less**
Circ: Diamd. preorders: **34,321**
12 ❑ May 1997 Cover: 2.50 **NM** value: **Cover or less**
Circ: Diamd. preorders: **34,145**
13 ❑ Jun 1997 Cover: 2.50 **NM** value: **Cover or less**
Circ: Diamd. preorders: **32,825**
14 ❑ Sep 1997 Cover: 2.50 **NM** value: **Cover or less**
Circ: Diamd. preorders: **30,276**
15 ❑ Dec 1997 Cover: 3.50 **NM** value: **Cover or less**
Circ: Diamd. preorders: **29,919**

WEAPON ZERO/SILVER SURFER — Top Cow / Image

1 ❑ Jan 1997 Cover: 2.95 **NM** value: **Cover or less**
Circ: Diamd. preorders: **60,496** • **CGC:** 1 graded, best 9.4
📖 Devil's Reign, Part 1; Devil's Reign • crossover with Marvel; continues in Cyblade/Ghost Rider **A:** Kirk Van Wormer; Billy Tan; Marc Silvestri **W:** Walt Simonson
1/A ❑ Jan 1997 Cover: 2.95 **NM** value: **Cover or less**
alternate cover.

WEASEL GUY: ROAD TRIP — Image

1 ❑ Aug 1999 Cover: 2.95 **NM** value: **Cover or less**
Circ: Diamd. preorders: **3,375**
📖 Moving Day **A:** Steve Buccellato **W:** Steve Buccellato
1/A ❑ Aug 1999 Cover: 2.95 **NM** value: **Cover or less**
Circ: Diamd. preorders: **2,487**
alternate cover. 📖 Moving Day **A:** Steve Buccellato **W:** Steve Buccellato
2 ❑ Oct 1999 Cover: 3.50 **NM** value: **Cover or less**
📖 Barn Razing **A:** Steve Buccellato **W:** Steve Buccellato

WEASEL PATROL, THE — Eclipse

1 ❑ b&w Cover: 2.00 **NM** value: **Cover or less**

WEATHER WOMAN — CPM Manga

1 ❑ Aug 2000, b&w Cover: 2.95 **NM** value: **Cover or less**
Circ: Diamd. preorders: **3,251**
1/A ❑ Aug 2000, b&w Cover: 2.95 **NM** value: **Cover or less**
alternate cover. • Weather Woman smoking

WEAVEWORLD — Marvel / Epic

1 ❑ Dec 1991 Cover: 4.95 **NM** value: **Cover or less**
Circ: CapCity orders: **10,700**
• prestige format. **W:** Clive Barker
2 ❑ Jan 1992 Cover: 4.95 **NM** value: **Cover or less**
Circ: CapCity orders: **7,900**
• prestige format. **W:** Clive Barker
3 ❑ Feb 1992 Cover: 4.95 **NM** value: **Cover or less**
Circ: CapCity orders: **6,250**
• prestige format. **W:** Clive Barker

WEB, THE — DC / Impact

Back in the 1950s, a group called the American Crusaders (whose members included the Original Shield) used their super-human abilities to protect the United States. Then, in 1963, they abruptly disappeared.

To fill the gap, the government created a hero known as The Web. In actuality, The Web was a group of people, using special armor and energy to carry out the role of the super-hero. As the Cold War dragged on, the Web's mission expanded from fighting crime to carrying out acts of espionage and political subversion. In time, however, the group lost favor and was eventually disbanded.

Now, they're back — reactivated by the appearance of such super-heroes as The Fly, The Jaguar, and The Comet. Possessing great powers — both physically and politically — they are, indeed, a force to be reckoned with.

1 ❑ Sep 1991 Cover: 1.00 **NM** value: **1.25**
Circ: CapCity orders: **34,700**
2 ❑ Oct 1991 Cover: 1.00 **NM** value: **Cover or less**
Circ: CapCity orders: **22,500**
3 ❑ Nov 1991 Cover: 1.00 **NM** value: **Cover or less**
Circ: CapCity orders: **18,700**
4 ❑ Dec 1991 Cover: 1.00 **NM** value: **Cover or less**
Circ: CapCity orders: **17,650**
5 ❑ Jan 1992 Cover: 1.00 **NM** value: **Cover or less**
Circ: CapCity orders: **13,950**

Other grades: Multiply prices above by **1.5 for Mint • 2/3 for Very Fine • 1/3 for Fine • 1/5 for Very Good • 1/8 for Good**

6 ❑ Feb 1992 Cover: 1.00 **NM** value: **Cover or less**
Circ: CapCity orders: **11,550**
7 ❑ Apr 1992 Cover: 1.00 **NM** value: **Cover or less**
Circ: CapCity orders: **9,750**
8 ❑ Apr 1992 Cover: 1.00 **NM** value: **Cover or less**
Circ: CapCity orders: **8,550**
9 ❑ May 1992 Cover: 1.00 **NM** value: **Cover or less**
Circ: CapCity orders: **8,350**
📖 The Coming Of The Crusaders, Part 5 • trading card
10 ❑ Jun 1992 Cover: 1.25 **NM** value: **Cover or less**
Circ: CapCity orders: **7,800**
11 ❑ Jul 1992 Cover: 1.25 **NM** value: **Cover or less**
Circ: CapCity orders: **7,250**
12 ❑ Aug 1992 Cover: 1.25 **NM** value: **Cover or less**
Circ: CapCity orders: **7,050**
13 ❑ Sep 1992 Cover: 1.25 **NM** value: **Cover or less**
Circ: CapCity orders: **6,200**
14 ❑ Oct 1992 Cover: 1.25 **NM** value: **Cover or less**
Circ: CapCity orders: **5,750**
final issue.
Anl 1❑ca. 1992 Cover: 2.50 **NM** value: **Cover or less**
Circ: CapCity orders: **8,300**
• trading card

WEBBER'S WORLD — Allstar

1 ❑ Cover: 4.95 **NM** value: **Cover or less**

WEB-MAN — Argosy

1 ❑ Cover: 2.50 **NM** value: **Cover or less**
gatefold cover. 📖 The Tentacles of Dr. Kraken **A:** Greg Luzniak **W:** Chuck Dixon

WEB OF EVIL — Quality

1 ❑ Nov 1952 Cover: 0.10 **NM** value: **300.00**
2 ❑ Jan 1953 Cover: 0.10 **NM** value: **250.00**
• **CGC:** 1 graded, best 6.0
3 ❑ Mar 1953 Cover: 0.10 **NM** value: **250.00**
4 ❑ May 1953 Cover: 0.10 **NM** value: **250.00**
5 ❑ Jul 1953 Cover: 0.10 **NM** value: **250.00**
• **CGC:** 1 graded, best 7.5
6 ❑ Sep 1953 Cover: 0.10 **NM** value: **250.00**
7 ❑ Oct 1953 Cover: 0.10 **NM** value: **250.00**
8 ❑ Nov 1953 Cover: 0.10 **NM** value: **250.00**
9 ❑ Dec 1953 Cover: 0.10 **NM** value: **250.00**
10 ❑ Jan 1954 Cover: 0.10 **NM** value: **200.00**
11 ❑ Feb 1954 Cover: 0.10 **NM** value: **200.00**
12 ❑ Mar 1954 Cover: 0.10 **NM** value: **200.00**
13 ❑ Apr 1954 Cover: 0.10 **NM** value: **200.00**
📖 The Ghoul of Ghost Swamp; Demon Inferno; Timepiece of Terror; Prehistoric Beast
14 ❑ May 1954 Cover: 0.10 **NM** value: **200.00**
15 ❑ Jun 1954 Cover: 0.10 **NM** value: **200.00**
16 ❑ Jul 1954 Cover: 0.10 **NM** value: **200.00**
17 ❑ Aug 1954 Cover: 0.10 **NM** value: **200.00**
• **CGC:** 1 graded, best 8.0
18 ❑ Sep 1954 Cover: 0.10 **NM** value: **200.00**
• **CGC:** 1 graded, best 7.0
19 ❑ Oct 1954 Cover: 0.10 **NM** value: **200.00**
20 ❑ Nov 1954 Cover: 0.10 **NM** value: **200.00**
• **CGC:** 1 graded, best 8.5
21 ❑ Dec 1954 Cover: 0.10 **NM** value: **200.00**

WEB OF MYSTERY — Ace

1 ❑ Feb 1951 Cover: 0.10 **NM** value: **250.00**
• **CGC:** 1 graded, best 5.5
2 ❑ Apr 1951 Cover: 0.10 **NM** value: **175.00**
📖 Lorelei of Loon Lake; Legacy of the Accursed; The Unseen Host; Midnight Marauder
3 ❑ Jun 1951 Cover: 0.10 **NM** value: **175.00**
4 ❑ Aug 1951 Cover: 0.10 **NM** value: **175.00**
📖 Stalked by a Nameless Dread; Vengeance of the Undead; Sign of the Smiling Spectre; The Haunted Horse
5 ❑ Oct 1951 Cover: 0.10 **NM** value: **175.00**
6 ❑ Dec 1951 Cover: 0.10 **NM** value: **175.00**
• **CGC:** 2 graded, best 6.5
7 ❑ Feb 1952 Cover: 0.10 **NM** value: **175.00**
• **CGC:** 3 graded, best 9.4
8 ❑ Apr 1952 Cover: 0.10 **NM** value: **175.00**
9 ❑ May 1952 Cover: 0.10 **NM** value: **175.00**
• **CGC:** 1 graded, best 9.2
10 ❑ Jun 1952 Cover: 0.10 **NM** value: **175.00**
11 ❑ Jul 1952 Cover: 0.10 **NM** value: **175.00**
• **CGC:** 1 graded, best 9.2
12 ❑ Aug 1952 Cover: 0.10 **NM** value: **175.00**
• **CGC:** 1 graded, best 8.5
13 ❑ Sep 1952 Cover: 0.10 **NM** value: **175.00**
• **CGC:** 2 graded, best 9.0
14 ❑ Oct 1952 Cover: 0.10 **NM** value: **175.00**
• **CGC:** 1 graded, best 9.4
📖 The Sign of Doom; You Dare not Speak About It; The Dead Dance of Halloween; Haunt of the Iskander Fjord
15 ❑ Nov 1952 Cover: 0.10 **NM** value: **175.00**
• **CGC:** 2 graded, best 9.2
📖 The Famine of Chichen-Itza, The Dreadful Night, Death Never Takes a Furlough; Mirror of Mephisto
16 ❑ Dec 1952 Cover: 0.10 **NM** value: **175.00**
• **CGC:** 1 graded, best 9.2
17 ❑ Feb 1953 Cover: 0.10 **NM** value: **175.00**
• **CGC:** 1 graded, best 7.5
18 ❑ May 1953 Cover: 0.10 **NM** value: **175.00**
19 ❑ Jul 1953 Cover: 0.10 **NM** value: **175.00**
20 ❑ Sep 1953 Cover: 0.10 **NM** value: **175.00**
📖 The Phantom Puppet
21 ❑ Nov 1953 Cover: 0.10 **NM** value: **175.00**
22 ❑ Jan 1954 Cover: 0.10 **NM** value: **125.00**
23 ❑ Mar 1954 Cover: 0.10 **NM** value: **125.00**
24 ❑ May 1954 Cover: 0.10 **NM** value: **125.00**
📖 I Died Laughing; Realm of Lost Faces; She Shrieked with Horror; My Sinister Double
25 ❑ Jul 1954 Cover: 0.10 **NM** value: **125.00**
26 ❑ Sep 1954 Cover: 0.10 **NM** value: **125.00**
27 ❑ Nov 1954 Cover: 0.10 **NM** value: **125.00**
28 ❑ May 1955 Cover: 0.10 **NM** value: **125.00**
29 ❑ Sep 1955 Cover: 0.10 **NM** value: **125.00**

WEB OF SCARLET SPIDER — Marvel

1 ❑ Nov 1995 Cover: 1.95 **NM** value: **2.00**
📖 Virtual Mortality, Part 1 **A:** Paris Karounos **W:** Tom DeFalco; Todd Dezago ★ Origin of Scarlet Spider.
2 ❑ Dec 1995 Cover: 1.95 **NM** value: **2.00**
📖 Cyberwar, Part 1 **A:** Paris Karounos **W:** Tom DeFalco ★ Appearance of Cyber-Slayers.
3 ❑ Jan 1996 Cover: 1.95 **NM** value: **2.00**
📖 Nightmare in Scarlet, Part 1 • continues in New Warriors #67 ★ Appearance of Firestar.
4 ❑ Feb 1996 Cover: 1.95 **NM** value: **2.00**
📖 Nightmare in Scarlet, Part 3 final issue.

WEB OF SPIDER-MAN, THE — Marvel

In 1985, Marvel finally drew the curtains on Marvel Team-Up, known by some as "Trademark Renewal Theater" for its parade of unlikely guest stars into Spider-Man's life. While the series had technically existed as the third ongoing new continuity Spider-title, some Spider-fans didn't take it as seriously as the main titles.

By starting Web of Spider-Man (and moving Team-Up's subscriber base over to it), Marvel moved the series to the same platform as Spectacular and Amazing Spider-Man — and gave itself the opportunity for cross-overs including all three, most notably ones involving the Death of Kraven and Spider-Man in an insane asylum.

Still, it was often considered the 'C' Spider-title, and when the Scarlet Spider storyline ended, Sensational Spider-Man took its place (briefly) as the third Spider-monthly. —JJM

1 ❑ Apr 1985 Cover: 0.65 **NM** value: **5.00**
• **CGC:** 242 graded, best 9.8
2 ❑ May 1985 Cover: 0.65 **NM** value: **3.00**
Circ: CapCity orders: **44,000** • **CGC:** 8 graded, best 9.6
3 ❑ Jun 1985 Cover: 0.65 **NM** value: **3.00**
Circ: CapCity orders: **38,100** • **CGC:** 3 graded, best 9.6
4 ❑ Jul 1985 Cover: 0.65 **NM** value: **3.00**
Circ: CapCity orders: **36,400** • **CGC:** 2 graded, best 9.6
5 ❑ Aug 1985 Cover: 0.65 **NM** value: **3.00**
Circ: CapCity orders: **33,700** • **CGC:** 4 graded, best 9.6
6 ❑ Sep 1985 Cover: 0.65 **NM** value: **3.00**
Circ: CapCity orders: **36,400** • **CGC:** 1 graded, best 9.8
• Secret Wars II
7 ❑ Oct 1985 Cover: 0.65 **NM** value: **3.00**
Circ: CapCity orders: **28,500** • **CGC:** 1 graded, best 9.4
8 ❑ Nov 1985 Cover: 0.65 **NM** value: **3.00**
Circ: CapCity orders: **28,000** • **CGC:** 1 graded, best 9.2
9 ❑ Dec 1985 Cover: 0.65 **NM** value: **3.00**
Circ: CapCity orders: **26,400** • **CGC:** 1 graded, best 9.4
10 ❑ Jan 1986 Cover: 0.65 **NM** value: **3.00**
Circ: Statement: **264,225** CapCity orders: **25,600** • **CGC:** 1 graded, best 8.0
11 ❑ Feb 1986 Cover: 0.75 **NM** value: **2.50**
Circ: Statement: **264,225** CapCity orders: **26,000**
12 ❑ Mar 1986 Cover: 0.75 **NM** value: **2.50**
Circ: Statement: **264,225** CapCity orders: **25,000**
13 ❑ Apr 1986 Cover: 0.75 **NM** value: **2.50**
Circ: Statement: **264,225** CapCity orders: **25,000**
14 ❑ May 1986 Cover: 0.75 **NM** value: **2.50**
Circ: Statement: **264,225** CapCity orders: **25,100**
15 ❑ Jun 1986 Cover: 0.75 **NM** value: **2.50**
Circ: Statement: **264,225** CapCity orders: **24,500**
16 ❑ Jul 1986 Cover: 0.75 **NM** value: **2.50**
Circ: Statement: **264,225** CapCity orders: **25,600**
17 ❑ Aug 1986 Cover: 0.75 **NM** value: **2.50**
Circ: Statement: **264,225** CapCity orders: **25,400**
• red suit destroyed ★ Versus Magma.
18 ❑ Sep 1986 Cover: 0.75 **NM** value: **2.50**
Circ: Statement: **264,225** CapCity orders: **26,600**
• Venom cameo
19 ❑ Oct 1986 Cover: 0.75 **NM** value: **2.50**
Circ: Statement: **264,225** CapCity orders: **25,900**
20 ❑ Nov 1986 Cover: 0.75 **NM** value: **2.50**
Circ: Statement: **264,225** CapCity orders: **28,300**
21 ❑ Dec 1986 Cover: 0.75 **NM** value: **2.50**
Circ: Statement: **264,225** CapCity orders: **26,700**
22 ❑ Jan 1987 Cover: 0.75 **NM** value: **2.50**
Circ: Statement: **242,875** CapCity orders: **25,900**
23 ❑ Feb 1987 Cover: 0.75 **NM** value: **2.50**
Circ: Statement: **242,875** CapCity orders: **27,100**
24 ❑ Mar 1987 Cover: 0.75 **NM** value: **2.50**
Circ: Statement: **242,875** CapCity orders: **27,000**
25 ❑ Apr 1987 Cover: 0.75 **NM** value: **2.50**
Circ: Statement: **242,875** CapCity orders: **26,900**
• Has 1986 Statement, filed 10/6/86; avg print run 460,676, avg sales 251,950, avg subs 12,275, avg total paid 264,225; samples 275; office use 1,985; max existent 266,485; 42% of run returned
26 ❑ May 1987 Cover: 0.75 **NM** value: **2.50**
Circ: Statement: **242,875** CapCity orders: **25,400**
27 ❑ Jun 1987 Cover: 0.75 **NM** value: **2.50**
Circ: Statement: **242,875** CapCity orders: **24,400**
28 ❑ Jul 1987 Cover: 0.75 **NM** value: **2.50**
Circ: Statement: **242,875** CapCity orders: **23,900**
29 ❑ Aug 1987 Cover: 0.75 **NM** value: **4.00**
Circ: Statement: **242,875** CapCity orders: **35,100** • **CGC:** 15 graded, best 9.8
30 ❑ Sep 1987 Cover: 0.75 **NM** value: **3.00**
Circ: Statement: **242,875** CapCity orders: **27,500** • **CGC:** 1 graded, best 9.0
31 ❑ Oct 1987 Cover: 0.75 **NM** value: **4.00**
Circ: Statement: **242,875** CapCity orders: **30,600** • **CGC:** 2 graded, best 9.6
📖 Kraven's Last Hunt, Part 1 ★ Versus Kraven.
32 ❑ Nov 1987 Cover: 0.75 **NM** value: **4.00**
Circ: Statement: **242,875** CapCity orders: **32,500**
📖 Kraven's Last Hunt, Part 4 ★ Versus Kraven.
33 ❑ Dec 1987 Cover: 0.75 **NM** value: **2.50**
Circ: Statement: **242,875** CapCity orders: **29,800**
34 ❑ Jan 1988 Cover: 0.75 **NM** value: **2.50**
Circ: Statement: **238,115** CapCity orders: **29,200**
35 ❑ Feb 1988 Cover: 0.75 **NM** value: **2.50**
Circ: Statement: **238,115** CapCity orders: **30,700**
36 ❑ Mar 1988 Cover: 0.75 **NM** value: **3.00**
Circ: Statement: **238,115** CapCity orders: **31,300**
37 ❑ Apr 1988 Cover: 0.75 **NM** value: **2.50**
Circ: Statement: **238,115** CapCity orders: **31,400**
38 ❑ May 1988 Cover: 1.00 **NM** value: **4.00**
Circ: Statement: **238,115** CapCity orders: **29,000** • **CGC:** 2 graded, best 9.2
39 ❑ Jun 1988 Cover: 1.00 **NM** value: **2.50**
Circ: Statement: **238,115** CapCity orders: **27,700**
📖 Cult of Love • Has 1987 Statement, filed 10/30/87; avg print run 437,255; avg sales 233,008; avg subs 9,867; avg total paid 242,875; samples 132; office use 2,010; max existent 245,017; 44% of run returned
40 ❑ Jul 1988 Cover: 1.00 **NM** value: **2.50**
Circ: Statement: **238,115** CapCity orders: **29,100**
📖 Cult of Love
41 ❑ Aug 1988 Cover: 1.00 **NM** value: **2.50**
Circ: Statement: **238,115** CapCity orders: **29,100**
📖 Cult of Love
42 ❑ Sep 1988 Cover: 1.00 **NM** value: **2.50**
Circ: Statement: **238,115** CapCity orders: **29,200**
📖 Cult of Love
43 ❑ Oct 1988 Cover: 1.00 **NM** value: **2.50**
Circ: Statement: **238,115** CapCity orders: **29,800**
📖 Cult of Love
44 ❑ Nov 1988 Cover: 1.00 **NM** value: **2.00**
Circ: Statement: **238,115** CapCity orders: **29,500**
45 ❑ Dec 1988 Cover: 1.00 **NM** value: **2.00**
Circ: Statement: **238,115** CapCity orders: **28,650**
46 ❑ Jan 1989 Cover: 1.00 **NM** value: **2.00**
Circ: Statement: **199,360** CapCity orders: **28,200**
47 ❑ Feb 1989 Cover: 1.00 **NM** value: **2.00**
Circ: Statement: **199,360** CapCity orders: **32,600**
• Inferno ★ Versus Hobgoblin.
48 ❑ Mar 1989 Cover: 1.00 **NM** value: **6.00**
Circ: Statement: **199,360** CapCity orders: **33,200** • **CGC:** 7 graded, best 9.4
• Inferno ★ Origin of Demogoblin. ★ Versus Hobgoblin.
49 ❑ Apr 1989 Cover: 1.00 **NM** value: **1.50**
Circ: Statement: **199,360** CapCity orders: **29,100**
50 ❑ May 1989 Cover: 1.50 **NM** value: **2.00**
Circ: Statement: **199,360** CapCity orders: **34,300**
• Giant-sized. • Has 1988 Statement, filed 10/1/88; avg print run 409,982; avg sales 230,275; avg subs 7,840; avg total paid 238,115; samples 132; office use 860; max existent 239,107, 42% of run returned
51 ❑ Jun 1989 Cover: 1.00 **NM** value: **1.50**
Circ: Statement: **199,360** CapCity orders: **28,600**
52 ❑ Jul 1989 Cover: 1.00 **NM** value: **1.50**
Circ: Statement: **199,360** CapCity orders: **29,300**
53 ❑ Aug 1989 Cover: 1.00 **NM** value: **1.50**
Circ: Statement: **199,360** CapCity orders: **29,600**
54 ❑ Sep 1989 Cover: 1.00 **NM** value: **1.50**
Circ: Statement: **199,360** CapCity orders: **28,900**
55 ❑ Oct 1989 Cover: 1.00 **NM** value: **1.50**
Circ: Statement: **199,360** CapCity orders: **29,800**
56 ❑ Nov 1989 Cover: 1.00 **NM** value: **1.50**
Circ: Statement: **199,360** CapCity orders: **30,200**
57 ❑ Nov 1989 Cover: 1.00 **NM** value: **1.50**
Circ: Statement: **199,360** CapCity orders: **30,500**
58 ❑ Dec 1989 Cover: 1.00 **NM** value: **2.00**
Circ: Statement: **199,360** CapCity orders: **30,300**
• Acts of Vengeance
59 ❑ Dec 1989 Cover: 1.00 **NM** value: **5.00**
Circ: Statement: **199,360** CapCity orders: **33,600**
📖 Acts of Vengeance • Acts of Vengeance; Spider-Man with cosmic powers
60 ❑ Jan 1990 Cover: 1.00 **NM** value: **2.00**
Circ: Statement: **209,174** CapCity orders: **35,400**
📖 Acts of Vengeance • Acts of Vengeance
61 ❑ Feb 1990 Cover: 1.00 **NM** value: **2.00**
Circ: Statement: **209,174** CapCity orders: **37,300**
📖 Acts of Vengeance • Acts of Vengeance
62 ❑ Mar 1990 Cover: 1.00 **NM** value: **1.50**
Circ: Statement: **209,174** CapCity orders: **32,500**
63 ❑ Apr 1990 Cover: 1.00 **NM** value: **1.50**
Circ: Statement: **209,174** CapCity orders: **33,500**
64 ❑ May 1990 Cover: 1.00 **NM** value: **1.50**
Circ: Statement: **209,174** CapCity orders: **35,000**
• Acts of Vengeance; Has 1989 Statement, filed 11/1/89; avg print run 340,970; avg sales 192,800; avg subs 6,560; avg total paid 199,360; samples 125; office use 600; max existent 200,085; 41% of run returned
65 ❑ Jun 1990 Cover: 1.00 **NM** value: **1.50**
Circ: Statement: **209,174** CapCity orders: **34,400**
• Acts of Vengeance

CGC-graded: Multiply prices above by **33 for 9.9 M** • **16 for 9.8 NM/M** • **7 for 9.6 NM+** • **5 for 9.4 NM** • **2.5 for 9.2 NM-** • **1.5 for 9.0 VF/NM**

66 ❑ Jul 1990 Cover: 1.00 NM value: 1.50
Circ: Statement: 209,174 CapCity orders: 35,900
67 ❑ Aug 1990 Cover: 1.00 NM value: 1.50
Circ: Statement: 209,174 CapCity orders: 35,700
68 ❑ Sep 1990 Cover: 1.00 NM value: 1.50
Circ: Statement: 209,174 CapCity orders: 36,100
69 ❑ Oct 1990 Cover: 1.00 NM value: 1.50
Circ: Statement: 209,174 CapCity orders: 36,900
70 ❑ Nov 1990 Cover: 1.00 NM value: 1.50
Circ: Statement: 209,174 CapCity orders: 36,900
• Spider-Hulk
71 ❑ Dec 1990 Cover: 1.00 NM value: 1.50
Circ: Statement: 209,174 CapCity orders: 34,500
72 ❑ Jan 1991 Cover: 1.00 NM value: 1.50
Circ: Statement: 211,042 CapCity orders: 34,800
73 ❑ Feb 1991 Cover: 1.00 NM value: 1.50
Circ: Statement: 211,042 CapCity orders: 37,400
74 ❑ Mar 1991 Cover: 1.00 NM value: 1.50
Circ: Statement: 211,042 CapCity orders: 35,700
• Has 1990 Statement, filed 10/1/90; avg print run 347,022; avg sales 203,033; avg subs 6,141; avg total paid 209,174; samples 150; office use 600; max existent 209,924; 40% of run returned
75 ❑ Apr 1991 Cover: 1.00 NM value: 1.50
Circ: Statement: 211,042 CapCity orders: 34,500
76 ❑ May 1991 Cover: 1.00 NM value: 1.50
Circ: Statement: 211,042 CapCity orders: 33,600
77 ❑ Jun 1991 Cover: 1.00 NM value: 1.50
Circ: Statement: 211,042 CapCity orders: 33,000
78 ❑ Jul 1991 Cover: 1.00 NM value: 1.50
Circ: Statement: 211,042 CapCity orders: 33,000
79 ❑ Aug 1991 Cover: 1.00 NM value: 1.50
Circ: Statement: 211,042 CapCity orders: 33,900
80 ❑ Sep 1991 Cover: 1.00 NM value: 1.50
Circ: Statement: 211,042 CapCity orders: 33,900
81 ❑ Oct 1991 Cover: 1.00 NM value: 1.50
Circ: Statement: 211,042 CapCity orders: 34,500
82 ❑ Nov 1991 Cover: 1.00 NM value: 1.50
Circ: Statement: 211,042 CapCity orders: 32,700
83 ❑ Dec 1991 Cover: 1.00 NM value: 1.50
Circ: Statement: 211,042 CapCity orders: 33,300
84 ❑ Jan 1992 Cover: 1.00 NM value: 1.50
Circ: CapCity orders: 34,700
🕮 Name of the Rose, Part 1; The Name of the Rose, Part 1 ★ Appearance of Hobgoblin.
85 ❑ Feb 1992 Cover: 1.25 NM value: 1.50
Circ: CapCity orders: 32,100
🕮 Name of the Rose, Part 2; The Name of the Rose, Part 2
86 ❑ Mar 1992 Cover: 1.25 NM value: 1.50
Circ: CapCity orders: 33,000
🕮 Name of the Rose, Part 3; The Name of the Rose, Part 3 • Has 1991 Statement, filed 10/1/91; avg print run 328,225; avg sales 205,050; avg subs 5,992; avg total paid 211,042; samples 125; office use 250; max existent 211,417; 36% of run returned
87 ❑ Apr 1992 Cover: 1.25 NM value: 1.50
Circ: CapCity orders: 31,700
🕮 Name of the Rose, Part 4; The Name of the Rose, Part 4
88 ❑ May 1992 Cover: 1.25 NM value: 1.50
Circ: CapCity orders: 32,600
🕮 Name of the Rose, Part 5; The Name of the Rose, Part 5
89 ❑ Jun 1992 Cover: 1.25 NM value: 1.50
Circ: CapCity orders: 36,100
🕮 Name of the Rose, Part 6; The Name of the Rose, Part 6
90 ❑ Jul 1992 Cover: 2.95 NM value: 4.00
Circ: CapCity orders: 114,000 • CGC: 2 graded, best 9.4
• Double-size. • hologram; Poster
90-2❑Jul 1992 Cover: 1.25 NM value: 2.95
Circ: CapCity orders: 44,600
91 ❑ Aug 1992 Cover: 1.25 NM value: 1.50
Circ: CapCity orders: 37,800
92 ❑ Sep 1992 Cover: 1.25 NM value: 1.50
Circ: CapCity orders: 35,400
93 ❑ Oct 1992 Cover: 1.25 NM value: 1.50
Circ: CapCity orders: 38,300 • CGC: 1 graded, best 9.6
🕮 Hobgoblin Reborn, Part 1
94 ❑ Nov 1992 Cover: 1.25 NM value: 1.50
Circ: CapCity orders: 42,300 • CGC: 1 graded, best 9.2
🕮 Hobgoblin Reborn, Part 2 ★ Versus Hobgoblin.
95 ❑ Dec 1992 Cover: 1.25 NM value: 1.50
Circ: CapCity orders: 61,200 • CGC: 1 graded, best 9.6
🕮 Spirits of Venom, Part 1 ★ Appearance of Ghost Rider, Johnny Blaze. ★ Versus Venom.
96 ❑ Jan 1993 Cover: 1.25 NM value: 1.50
Circ: CapCity orders: 51,400
🕮 Spirits of Venom, Part 3 A: Dan Panosian; Alex Saviuk; Joe Rubinstein W: Howard Mackie ★ Appearance of Ghost Rider, Johnny Blaze. ★ Versus Venom.
97 ❑ Feb 1993 Cover: 1.25 NM value: 1.50
Circ: CapCity orders: 40,300
🕮 My Enemy's Enemy, Part 1
98 ❑ Mar 1993 Cover: 1.25 NM value: 1.50
Circ: CapCity orders: 37,000
🕮 My Enemy's Enemy, Part 2
99 ❑ Apr 1993 Cover: 1.25 NM value: 1.50
Circ: CapCity orders: 38,600
100 ❑ May 1993 Cover: 2.95 NM value: 3.00
Circ: CapCity orders: 146,600 • CGC: 8 graded, best 10.0
foil cover. ★ 1st Appearance of Spider-Armor.
101 ❑ Jun 1993 Cover: 1.25 NM value: 1.50
Circ: CapCity orders: 123,200
🕮 Maximum Carnage, Part 2
102 ❑ Jul 1993 Cover: 1.25 NM value: 1.50
Circ: CapCity orders: 108,300
🕮 Maximum Carnage, Part 6
103 ❑ Aug 1993 Cover: 1.25 NM value: 1.50
Circ: CapCity orders: 108,300
🕮 Maximum Carnage, Part 10
104 ❑ Sep 1993 Cover: 1.25 NM value: 1.50
Circ: CapCity orders: 48,800
105 ❑ Oct 1993 Cover: 1.25 NM value: 1.50
Circ: CapCity orders: 47,400
• Infinity Crusade A: Alex Saviuk W: Terry Kavanagh ★ Appearance of Archangel.
106 ❑ Nov 1993 Cover: 1.25 NM value: 1.50
Circ: CapCity orders: 41,300
• Infinity Crusade
107 ❑ Dec 1993 Cover: 1.25 NM value: 1.50
Circ: CapCity orders: 42,800
108 ❑ Jan 1994 Cover: 1.25 NM value: 1.50
Circ: Statement: 199,708 CapCity orders: 38,500
109 ❑ Feb 1994 Cover: 1.25 NM value: 1.50
Circ: Statement: 199,708 CapCity orders: 36,300
110 ❑ Mar 1994 Cover: 1.25 NM value: 1.50
Circ: Statement: 199,708 CapCity orders: 32,450
111 ❑ Apr 1994 Cover: 1.25 NM value: 1.50
Circ: Statement: 199,708 CapCity orders: 31,250
112 ❑ May 1994 Cover: 1.50 NM value: Cover or less
Circ: Statement: 199,708 CapCity orders: 32,100
🕮 Pursuit, Part 3
113 ❑ Jun 1994 Cover: 1.50 NM value: Cover or less
🕮 Live and Let Die, Part 1 ★ Appearance of Gambit, Black Cat.
113/CS❑Jun 1994 Cover: 2.95 NM value: 3.00
Circ: Statement: 199,708 CapCity orders: 47,500
🕮 Live and Let Die, Part 1 • TV preview; print★ Appearance of Gambit, Black Cat.
114 ❑ Jul 1994 Cover: 1.50 NM value: Cover or less
Circ: Statement: 199,708 CapCity orders: 30,150
115 ❑ Aug 1994 Cover: 1.50 NM value: Cover or less
Circ: Statement: 199,708 CapCity orders: 29,350
116 ❑ Sep 1994 Cover: 1.50 NM value: Cover or less
Circ: Statement: 199,708 CapCity orders: 27,700
117 ❑ Oct 1994 Cover: 1.50 NM value: 2.50
• Flip-book. 🕮 Power & Responsibility; Power and Responsibility, Part 1 ★ Appearance of Ben Reilly.
117/SC❑Oct 1994 Cover: 2.95 NM value: 4.00
Circ: Statement: 199,708 CapCity orders: 43,600
foil cover. • Flip-book. 🕮 Power & Responsibility; Power and Responsibility, Part 1; The Double, Part 1 ★ Origin of Ben Reilly. ★ Appearance of Ben Reilly.
118 ❑ Nov 1994 Cover: 1.50 NM value: 2.50
Circ: Statement: 199,708 CapCity orders: 43,250
119 ❑ Dec 1994 Cover: 1.50 NM value: Cover or less
• Scarlet Spider vs. Venom
119/CS❑Dec 1994 Cover: 6.45 NM value: Cover or less
Circ: Statement: 199,708 CapCity orders: 35,050
• polybagged with Marvel Milestone Edition: Amazing Spider-Man #150 and POP card for Amazing Spider-Ma. • Scarlet Spider vs. Venom
120 ❑ Jan 1995 Cover: 2.25 NM value: 3.00
Circ: Statement: 172,992 CapCity orders: 34,300
• Giant-size. ★ Appearance of Morbius.
121 ❑ Feb 1995 Cover: 1.50 NM value: Cover or less
Circ: Statement: 172,992 CapCity orders: 33,850
🕮 Web of Life, Part 3 ★ Versus Kaine.
122 ❑ Mar 1995 Cover: 1.50 NM value: Cover or less
Circ: Statement: 172,992 CapCity orders: 3,300
🕮 Smoke & Mirrors, Part 1 • Has 1994 Statement, filed 10/1/94; avg print run 346,650; avg sales 195,733; avg subs 3,975; avg total paid 199,708; samples 125; 42% of run returned★ Appearance of Jackal.
123 ❑ Apr 1995 Cover: 1.50 NM value: Cover or less
Circ: Statement: 172,992 CapCity orders: 35,550
🕮 Players & Pawns, Part 2 ★ Appearance of Jackal.
124 ❑ May 1995 Cover: 1.50 NM value: Cover or less
Circ: Statement: 172,992 CapCity orders: 34,300
🕮 The Mark of Kaine, Part 1
125 ❑ Jun 1995 Cover: 2.95 NM value: Cover or less
• Giant-size. 🕮 Lives Unlived; Shining Armor
125/SC❑Jun 1995 Cover: 3.95 NM value: Cover or less
Circ: Statement: 172,992 CapCity orders: 33,875
Hologram on cover. • Giant-size. 🕮 Lives Unlived; Shining Armor
126 ❑ Jul 1995 Cover: 1.50 NM value: Cover or less
Circ: Statement: 172,992 CapCity orders: 33,500
🕮 The Trial of Peter Parker, Part 1
127 ❑ Aug 1995 Cover: 1.50 NM value: Cover or less
Circ: Statement: 172,992 CapCity orders: 37,050
🕮 Maximum Clonage, Part 2
128 ❑ Sep 1995 Cover: 1.50 NM value: Cover or less
Circ: Statement: 172,992
🕮 Exiled, Part 1
129 ❑ Oct 1995 Cover: 1.50 NM value: Cover or less
Circ: Statement: 172,992
🕮 Time Bomb, Part 2 final issue. ★ Appearance of New Warriors.
Anl 1❑ca. 1985 Cover: 1.25 NM value: 5.00
• CGC: 1 graded, best 9.6
Painted cover. ★ Appearance of 4th.
Anl 2❑ca. 1986 Cover: 1.25 NM value: 6.00
Circ: CapCity orders: 31,800
Anl 3❑ca. 1987 Cover: 1.25 NM value: 3.00
Circ: CapCity orders: 22,100
• pin-ups
Anl 4❑ca. 1988 Cover: 1.75 NM value: 3.00
Circ: CapCity orders: 33,300
🕮 Evolutionary War, Part 8 ★ 1st Appearance of Poison.
Anl 5❑ca. 1989 Cover: 2.00 NM value: 2.50
Circ: CapCity orders: 40,500
🕮 Atlantis Attacks, Part 11 • Atlantis Attacks★ Origin of Silver Sable. ★ Appearance of Fantastic Four.
Anl 6❑ca. 1990 Cover: 2.00 NM value: 2.50
• Tiny Spidey★ Versus Psycho-Man.
Anl 7❑ca. 1991 Cover: 2.00 NM value: 2.50
Circ: CapCity orders: 40,400
🕮 Vibranium Vendetta ★ Origin of Hobgoblin, Venom, Green Goblin. ★ Appearance of Iron Man, Black Panther. ★ Versus Ultron.
Anl 8❑ca. 1992 Cover: 2.25 NM value: 3.00
🕮 Hero Killers; The Hero Killers, Part 3 ★ Appearance of New Warriors, Venom. ★ Versus Whiplash. ★ Versus Beetle. ★ Versus Constrictor. ★ Versus Rhino.
Anl 9❑ca. 1993 Cover: 2.95 NM value: Cover or less
Circ: CapCity orders: 51,100
• trading card★ 1st Appearance of The Cadre.
Anl 10❑ca. 1994 Cover: 2.95 NM value: Cover or less
Circ: CapCity orders: 21,600
SS 1❑ca. 1995 Cover: 3.95 NM value: Cover or less
• Flip-book. 🕮 Planet of the Symbiotes, Part 5; Black Cat: Cat & Robbers; Growing Pains, Part 5 • Super Special

WEBSPINNERS: TALES OF SPIDER-MAN Marvel

In an attempt to recharge the Spider-Man family of titles after the frustrating Clone Saga that left the series with a clinging sense of malaise, Marvel canceled titles and started over with new numbering in the last half of 1998. This tactic did not seek to reboot the character from his beginnings; it merely started fresh with new numbering. Additionally, John Byrne retold and embellished Spider-Man's origin in a mini-series, Spider-Man: Chapter One — and this title, Webspinners, retold early episodes of Spider-Man's career, similar to the approach taken with Batman: Legends of the Dark Knight.

The first arc features a fleshed-out origin of Mysterio, illustrating the pathos and insecurities of Quentin Beck (Mysterio's real name) and drawing an eerie parallel to Peter Parker's demeanor, as they both use their costumed alter egos to find comfort behind a mask. With lush art by Michael Zulli, best known for such Vertigo titles as Sandman and Witchcraft, the appearance of the cast is exceedingly expressive.

1 ❑ Jan 1999 Cover: 2.99 NM value: Cover or less
Circ: Diamd. preorders: 73,383
• gatefold summary. 🕮 Webspinners Spider-Man A: Michael Zulli W: J.M. DeMatteis ★ Appearance of Mysterio. ★ Versus Mysterio.
1/Aut❑Jan 1999 Cover: 19.63 NM value: Cover or less
2/A ❑ Feb 1999 Cover: 2.99 NM value: Cover or less
Circ: Diamd. preorders: 64,181
Cover A. A: Michael Zulli; John Romita(inks) W: J.M. DeMatteis
2/B ❑ Feb 1999 Cover: 2.50 NM value: Cover or less
Cover B by Steve Rude. A: Michael Zulli; John Romita(inks) W: J.M. DeMatteis
3 ❑ Mar 1999 Cover: 2.50 NM value: Cover or less
Circ: Diamd. preorders: 47,677
4 ❑ Apr 1999 Cover: 2.50 NM value: Cover or less
Circ: Diamd. preorders: 39,200
5 ❑ May 1999 Cover: 2.50 NM value: Cover or less
Circ: Diamd. preorders: 34,436
6 ❑ Jun 1999 Cover: 2.50 NM value: Cover or less
Circ: Diamd. preorders: 30,859
7 ❑ Jul 1999 Cover: 2.50 NM value: Cover or less
Circ: Diamd. preorders: 29,562
8 ❑ Aug 1999 Cover: 2.50 NM value: Cover or less
Circ: Diamd. preorders: 27,694
9 ❑ Sep 1999 Cover: 2.50 NM value: Cover or less
Circ: Diamd. preorders: 25,740
11 ❑ Nov 1999 Cover: 2.50 NM value: Cover or less
Circ: Diamd. preorders: 23,003

WEDDING OF DRACULA Marvel

1 ❑ Jan 1993 Cover: 2.00 NM value: Cover or less
Circ: CapCity orders: 8,100
• Reprints Tomb of Dracula 30,45, & 46

WEDDING OF POPEYE AND OLIVE, THE Ocean

1 ❑ ca. 1998, b&w Cover: 2.75 NM value: Cover or less

WEEZUL Lightning

1/A ❑ Aug 1996 Cover: 2.75 NM value: Cover or less
1/B ❑ Aug 1996 Cover: 3.00 NM value: Cover or less
alternate cover.

WEIRD Avalon

1 ❑ Cover: 2.99 NM value: Cover or less
2 ❑ Cover: 2.99 NM value: Cover or less
3 ❑ Cover: 2.99 NM value: Cover or less
4 ❑ Cover: 2.99 NM value: Cover or less
Circ: Diamd. preorders: 1,536

WEIRD, THE DC

1 ❑ Apr 1988 Cover: 1.50 NM value: Cover or less
Circ: CapCity orders: 45,150
2 ❑ May 1988 Cover: 1.50 NM value: Cover or less
Circ: CapCity orders: 35,750
3 ❑ Jun 1988 Cover: 1.50 NM value: Cover or less
Circ: CapCity orders: 30,250
4 ❑ Jul 1988 Cover: 1.50 NM value: Cover or less
Circ: CapCity orders: 28,200

WEIRD ADVENTURES P.L. Publishing

1 ❑ May 1951 Cover: 0.10 NM value: 300.00
• CGC: 1 graded, best 8.0
2 ❑ Jul 1951 Cover: 0.10 NM value: 200.00
• CGC: 2 graded, best 9.0
3 ❑ Oct 1951 Cover: 0.10 NM value: 200.00

WEIRD ADVENTURES (ZIFF) Ziff-Davis

10 ❑ Jul 1951 Cover: 0.10 NM value: 225.00
• CGC: 1 graded, best 9.2

Other grades: Multiply prices above by 1.5 for Mint • 2/3 for Very Fine • 1/3 for Fine • 1/5 for Very Good • 1/8 for Good

WEIRD BUSINESS — Mojo

Ash 1❑ Cover: 0.50 **NM** value: **Cover or less**
📖 Green Brother; Chip of Fools; Gorilla Gunslinger; In Repose; Stranger **A:** Brian Biggs; John Lucas; Michael Lark; John Garcia; Chet Williamson **W:** Brian Biggs; Chet Williamson; Joe R. Lansdale; Norman Patridge; Marc Paoletti; Steve Utley

WEIRD CHILLS — Key

1 ❑ Jul 1954 Cover: 0.10 **NM** value: **600.00**
• **CGC:** 7 graded, best 8.0
2 ❑ Sep 1954 Cover: 0.10 **NM** value: **400.00**
• **CGC:** 6 graded, best 9.0
3 ❑ Nov 1954 Cover: 0.10 **NM** value: **400.00**
• **CGC:** 4 graded, best 8.0

WEIRD COMICS — Fox

1 ❑ Apr 1940 Cover: 0.10 **NM** value: **3000.00**
• **CGC:** 5 graded, best 9.0
2 ❑ May 1940 Cover: 0.10 **NM** value: **2500.00**
• **CGC:** 2 graded, best 9.0
3 ❑ Jun 1940 Cover: 0.10 **NM** value: **1400.00**
• **CGC:** 2 graded, best 9.2
4 ❑ Jul 1940 Cover: 0.10 **NM** value: **1400.00**
• **CGC:** 3 graded, best 9.2
5 ❑ Aug 1940 Cover: 0.10 **NM** value: **1400.00**
6 ❑ Sep 1940 Cover: 0.10 **NM** value: **1200.00**
• **CGC:** 2 graded, best 9.2
7 ❑ Oct 1940 Cover: 0.10 **NM** value: **1200.00**
• **CGC:** 1 graded, best 9.2
8 ❑ Nov 1940 Cover: 0.10 **NM** value: **1200.00**
• **CGC:** 1 graded, best 9.4
9 ❑ Dec 1940 Cover: 0.10 **NM** value: **1200.00**
• **CGC:** 1 graded, best 9.2
10 ❑ Jan 1941 Cover: 0.10 **NM** value: **900.00**
• **CGC:** 1 graded, best 9.4
11 ❑ Feb 1941 Cover: 0.10 **NM** value: **900.00**
12 ❑ Mar 1941 Cover: 0.10 **NM** value: **900.00**
• **CGC:** 2 graded, best 9.4
13 ❑ Apr 1941 Cover: 0.10 **NM** value: **750.00**
• **CGC:** 1 graded, best 5.0
14 ❑ May 1941 Cover: 0.10 **NM** value: **750.00**
• **CGC:** 1 graded, best 3.0
15 ❑ Jun 1941 Cover: 0.10 **NM** value: **500.00**
16 ❑ Jul 1941 Cover: 0.10 **NM** value: **500.00**
• **CGC:** 1 graded, best 9.6
17 ❑ Aug 1941 Cover: 0.10 **NM** value: **500.00**
• **CGC:** 2 graded, best 8.5
18 ❑ Sep 1941 Cover: 0.10 **NM** value: **500.00**
19 ❑ Oct 1941 Cover: 0.10 **NM** value: **500.00**
• **CGC:** 1 graded, best 8.5
20 ❑ Jan 1942 Cover: 0.10 **NM** value: **500.00**
• **CGC:** 1 graded, best 9.4

WEIRDFALL — Antarctic

1 ❑ Jul 1995, b&w Cover: 2.75 **NM** value: **Cover or less**
📖 Murphy's War **A:** Matt Howarth **W:** Matt Howarth
2 ❑ Sep 1995, b&w Cover: 2.75 **NM** value: **Cover or less**
3 ❑ Nov 1995, b&w Cover: 2.75 **NM** value: **Cover or less**

WEIRD FANTASY (E.C.) — E.C.

Speaking of weird, how weird was it that the Pre-Trend E.C. title A Moon, a Girl … Romance became Weird Fantasy with #13? While the focus of much of the rest of the New Trend titles was horror, this series was devoted to science-fiction stories, and covers primarily by Feldstein were scenes of rockets, aliens, and people in spacesuits.

The numbering will keep collectors on their toes, because the continued numbering ran from #13 (May 50), #14 (Jul 50), #15 (Sep 50), #16 (Nov 50), and #17 (Jan 51) to #6 (Mar 51); this means there were duplicate numbers. The later dates were #13 (May 52), #14 (Jul 52), #15 (Sep 52), #16 (Nov 52), and #17 (Jan 53).

Artists for whom the E.C. line was known did work in the series: Harvey Kurtzman, Al Feldstein, Jack Kamen, Will Elder, Al Williamson, Joe Orlando, and Wally Wood. Some of the stories were adaptations of stories by the likes of Fritz Leiber, Ward Moore, and Ray Bradbury. The series changed its name and combined with Weird Science to raise its price and become Weird Science-Fantasy. — Maggie

1 ❑ May 1950 Cover: 0.10 **NM** value: **1350.00**
• **CGC:** 11 graded, best 9.6
#13 on cover (1950). 📖 Am I Man or Machine?; Only Time Will Tell; The Men of Tomorrow; ..Trip Into the Unknown
2 ❑ Jul 1950 Cover: 0.10 **NM** value: **575.00**
• **CGC:** 7 graded, best 9.8
#14 on cover (1950). 📖 Cosmic Ray Bomb Explosion; The Black Arts; The Trap of Time!; Atom Bomb Thief!
3 ❑ Sep 1950 Cover: 0.10 **NM** value: **475.00**
• **CGC:** 5 graded, best 9.4
#15 on cover (1950). 📖 Martian Infiltration; Henry and His ...Goon-Child; I Died Tomorrow!; Dark Side of the Moon
4 ❑ Nov 1950 Cover: 0.10 **NM** value: **475.00**
• **CGC:** 3 graded, best 9.2
#16 on cover (1950). 📖 The Last City; The Mysterious Ray from Another Dimension!; Second Childhood; A Trip to a Star;
5 ❑ Jan 1951 Cover: 0.10 **NM** value: **385.00**
• **CGC:** 1 graded, best 9.6
#17 on cover (1951). 📖 Child of Tomorrow!; The Time Machine and the Shmoe!; Deadlock!; Prediction of Disaster! **A:** Al Feldstein; Harvey Kurtzman; Wally Wood; Jack Kamen **W:** Al Feldstein; Harvey Kurtzman; Wally Wood; Jack Kamen
6 ❑ Mar 1951 Cover: 0.10 **NM** value: **275.00**
• **CGC:** 5 graded, best 9.4
📖 Space-Warp; The Dimension Translator; …And Then There Were Two; Rescued
7 ❑ May 1951 Cover: 0.10 **NM** value: **275.00**
• **CGC:** 4 graded, best 9.8
📖 7 Year Old Genius; Come Into My Parlor; Across the Sun; Break-down
8 ❑ Jul 1951 Cover: 0.10 **NM** value: **275.00**
• **CGC:** 5 graded, best 9.6
📖 The Origin of the Species; It Didn't Matter; The Slave Ship; The Enemies of the Colony
9 ❑ Sep 1951 Cover: 0.10 **NM** value: **275.00**
• **CGC:** 4 graded, best 9.6
📖 Spawn of Mars; The Duplicates; The Connection; A Mistake in Multiplication
10 ❑ Nov 1951 Cover: 0.10 **NM** value: **275.00**
• **CGC:** 8 graded, best 9.4
📖 The Secret of Saturn's Ring; A Timely Shock; The Mutants; Not on the Menu
11 ❑ Jan 1952 Cover: 0.10 **NM** value: **215.00**
• **CGC:** 5 graded, best 9.8
📖 The Two-Century Journey!; Shrinking from Abuse!; The 10th at Noon; The Thing in the Jar
12 ❑ Mar 1952 Cover: 0.10 **NM** value: **215.00**
• **CGC:** 2 graded, best 9.8
📖 Project...Survival!; A Lesson in Anatomy!!; The Die is Cast!; A Man's Job!
13 ❑ May 1952 Cover: 0.10 **NM** value: **215.00**
• **CGC:** 5 graded, best 9.2
📖 The End!; The Trip!; Home to Stay!; Don't Count Your Chickens... • "Rocketman" Ray Bradbury adaptation; "Kaleidoscope" Ray Bradbury adaptation
14 ❑ Jul 1952 Cover: 0.10 **NM** value: **340.00**
• **CGC:** 4 graded, best 9.4
📖 The Exile!; The Expert!; The Ad!; Close Call!; Mad Journey! **A:** Frank Frazetta
15 ❑ Sep 1952 Cover: 0.10 **NM** value: **235.00**
• **CGC:** 8 graded, best 9.4
📖 Revulsion!; The Quick Trip; The Long Trip; He Who Waits; By George!! **A:** Al Williamson
16 ❑ Nov 1952 Cover: 0.10 **NM** value: **200.00**
• **CGC:** 8 graded, best 9.6
📖 Mass Meeting!; Skeleton Key!; What He Saw!; The Green Thing! **A:** Al Williamson
17 ❑ Jan 1953 Cover: 0.10 **NM** value: **200.00**
• **CGC:** 3 graded, best 9.4
📖 In the Beginning...; Ahead of the Game!; The Aliens; There will Come Soft Rains.. **A:** Al Williamson
18 ❑ Mar 1953 Cover: 0.10 **NM** value: **200.00**
• **CGC:** 5 graded, best 9.8
📖 Counter-clockwise; Zero Hour; Homesick!; Judgement Day! • "Zero Hour" Ray Bradbury adaptation **W:** Ray Bradbury
19 ❑ May 1953 Cover: 0.10 **NM** value: **200.00**
• **CGC:** 3 graded, best 9.4
📖 King of the Grey Spaces!; Hot-Rod!; Time for a Change!; Brain-Child! **A:** Al Williamson; Joe Orlando; John Severin; Bill Elder; Jack Kamen **W:** Al Williamson; Joe Orlando; John Severin; Bill Elder; Jack Kamen; Ray Bradbury
20 ❑ Jul 1953 Cover: 0.10 **NM** value: **235.00**
• **CGC:** 4 graded, best 9.8
📖 …For Us the Living; I, Rocket; …Conquers All!; The Automaton **A:** Al Williamson; Joe Orlando; John Severin; Bill Elder; Jack Kamen **W:** Al Williamson; Joe Orlando; John Severin; Bill Elder; Jack Kamen; Ray Bradbury
21 ❑ Sep 1953 Cover: 0.10 **NM** value: **325.00**
• **CGC:** 6 graded, best 9.6
📖 My Home…; Saved; Planely Possible; The Million Year Picnic **A:** Al Williamson; Joe Orlando; John Severin; Bill Elder; Jack Kamen **W:** Al Williamson; Joe Orlando; John Severin; Bill Elder; Jack Kamen; Ray Bradbury
22 ❑ Nov 1953 Cover: 0.10 **NM** value: **170.00**
• **CGC:** 4 graded, best 9.6
📖 The Silent Towns; The Freaks; The Fossil; Derelict Ship final issue. **A:** Joe Orlando; Bernie Krigstein; Reed Crandall; Jack Kamen; Ray Bradbury **W:** Joe Orlando; Bernie Krigstein; Reed Crandall; Jack Kamen

WEIRD FANTASY (RCP) — Gemstone

1 ❑ Oct 1992 Cover: 2.00 **NM** value: **2.50**
Circ: Statement: **20,781** CapCity orders: **4,600**
2 ❑ Jan 1993 Cover: 1.50 **NM** value: **2.00**
Circ: Statement: **20,781** CapCity orders: **4,400**
• Reprints Weird Fantasy #14 **A:** Al Feldstein; Harvey Kurtzman; Wally Wood; Jack Kamen
3 ❑ Apr 1993 Cover: 1.50 **NM** value: **2.00**
Circ: Statement: **20,781** CapCity orders: **4,100**
4 ❑ Jul 1993 Cover: 2.00 **NM** value: **Cover or less**
Circ: Statement: **20,781** CapCity orders: **3,900**
5 ❑ Oct 1993 Cover: 2.00 **NM** value: **Cover or less**
Circ: Statement: **9,547** CapCity orders: **3,450**
📖 Child of Tomorrow!; The Time Machine and the Shmoe!; Deadlock!; Prediction of Disaster! **A:** Al Feldstein; Harvey Kurtzman; Wally Wood; Jack Kamen **W:** Al Feldstein; Harvey Kurtzman; Wally Wood; Jack Kamen
6 ❑ Jan 1994 Cover: 2.00 **NM** value: **Cover or less**
Circ: Statement: **9,547** CapCity orders: **3,200**
📖 Space-Warp; The Dimension Translator; …And Then There Were Two; Rescued **A:** Al Feldstein; Harvey Kurtzman; Wally Wood; Jack Kamen
7 ❑ Apr 1994 Cover: 2.00 **NM** value: **Cover or less**
Circ: Statement: **9,547** CapCity orders: **3,000**
📖 7 Year Old Genius; Come Into My Parlor; Across the Sun; Break-down **A:** Al Feldstein; Wally Wood; Jack Kamen
8 ❑ Jul 1994 Cover: 2.00 **NM** value: **Cover or less**
Circ: Statement: **9,547** CapCity orders: **2,975**
📖 The Origin of the Species; It Didn't Matter; The Slave Ship; The Enemies of the Colony
9 ❑ Oct 1994 Cover: 2.00 **NM** value: **Cover or less**
Circ: CapCity orders: **2,925**
📖 Spawn of Mars; The Duplicates; The Connection; A Mistake in Multiplication
10 ❑ Jan 1995 Cover: 2.00 **NM** value: **Cover or less**
Circ: CapCity orders: **2,775**
📖 The Secret of Saturn's Ring; A Timely Shock; The Mutants; Not on the Menu
11 ❑ Apr 1995 Cover: 2.00 **NM** value: **2.50**
Circ: CapCity orders: **2,500**
12 ❑ Jul 1995 Cover: 2.00 **NM** value: **2.50**
Circ: CapCity orders: **2,500**
13 ❑ Oct 1995 Cover: 2.00 **NM** value: **2.50**
Circ: Statement: **6,379** CapCity orders: **2,475**
14 ❑ Jan 1996 Cover: 2.00 **NM** value: **2.50**
Circ: Statement: **6,379**
15 ❑ Apr 1996 Cover: 2.00 **NM** value: **2.50**
Circ: Statement: **6,379**
16 ❑ Jul 1996 Cover: 2.00 **NM** value: **2.50**
Circ: Statement: **6,379**
17 ❑ Oct 1996 Cover: 2.00 **NM** value: **2.50**
Circ: Statement: **6,039**
18 ❑ Jan 1997 Cover: 2.50 **NM** value: **Cover or less**
Circ: Statement: **6,039** Diamd. preorders: **5,442**
• Has 1996 Statement, filed 8/15/96; avg print run 7,523; avg sales 5,883; avg subs 496; avg total paid 6,379; office use 1,144; max existent 7,523; not available on newsstands
19 ❑ Apr 1997 Cover: 2.50 **NM** value: **Cover or less**
Circ: Statement: **6,039** Diamd. preorders: **5,233**
📖 King of the Grey Spaces!; Hot-Rod!; Time for a Change!; Brain-Child! • Reprints Weird Fantasy (EC) #19 **A:** Al Williamson; Joe Orlando; John Severin; Bill Elder; Jack Kamen **W:** Al Williamson; Joe Orlando; John Severin; Bill Elder; Jack Kamen; Ray Bradbury
20 ❑ Jul 1997 Cover: 2.50 **NM** value: **Cover or less**
Circ: Statement: **6,039** Diamd. preorders: **5,324**
📖 …For Us the Living; I, Rocket; …Conquers All!; The Automaton • Reprints Weird Fantasy (EC) #20 **A:** Al Williamson; Joe Orlando; John Severin; Bill Elder; Jack Kamen **W:** Al Williamson; Joe Orlando; John Severin; Bill Elder; Jack Kamen; Ray Bradbury
21 ❑ Oct 1997 Cover: 2.50 **NM** value: **Cover or less**
Circ: Diamd. preorders: **5,401**
📖 My Home…; Saved; Planely Possible; The Million Year Picnic • Reprints Weird Fantasy (EC) #21 **A:** Al Williamson; Joe Orlando; John Severin; Bill Elder; Jack Kamen **W:** Al Williamson; Joe Orlando; John Severin; Bill Elder; Jack Kamen; Ray Bradbury
22 ❑ Jan 1998 Cover: 2.50 **NM** value: **Cover or less**
Circ: Diamd. preorders: **5,080**
📖 The Silent Towns; The Freaks; The Fossil; Derelict Ship • Reprints Weird Fantasy (EC) #22; has 1997 Statement; avg total paid circ 6,039 **A:** Joe Orlando; Bernie Krigstein; Reed Crandall; Jack Kamen; Ray Bradbury **W:** Joe Orlando; Bernie Krigstein; Reed Crandall; Jack Kamen
Anl 1❑ Cover: 8.95 **NM** value: **Cover or less**
• Reprints Weird Fantasy #1-5
Anl 2❑ Cover: 9.95 **NM** value: **Cover or less**
• Reprints Weird Fantasy #6-10
Anl 3❑ Cover: 8.95 **NM** value: **Cover or less**
Anl 4❑ Cover: 9.95 **NM** value: **Cover or less**
Anl 5❑ Cover: 10.95 **NM** value: **Cover or less**
• Reprints Weird Fantasy #19-22

WEIRD HORRORS — St. John

1 ❑ Jun 1952 Cover: 0.10 **NM** value: **225.00**
• **CGC:** 2 graded, best 6.0
2 ❑ 1952 Cover: 0.10 **NM** value: **200.00**
3 ❑ 1952 Cover: 0.10 **NM** value: **200.00**
4 ❑ Nov 1952 Cover: 0.10 **NM** value: **200.00**
• **CGC:** 1 graded, best 8.0
5 ❑ Dec 1952 Cover: 0.10 **NM** value: **200.00**
• **CGC:** 1 graded, best 7.5
6 ❑ Feb 1953 Cover: 0.10 **NM** value: **200.00**
• **CGC:** 2 graded, best 8.0
7 ❑ Apr 1953 Cover: 0.10 **NM** value: **200.00**
• **CGC:** 1 graded, best 7.0
8 ❑ Apr 1953 Cover: 0.10 **NM** value: **200.00**
• **CGC:** 1 graded, best 9.2

WEIRD (MAGAZINE) — DC / Paradox

1 ❑ Sum 1997, b&w Cover: 2.99 **NM** value: **Cover or less**
• magazine. 📖 The Ones That Got Away; Other Osswalds; Syncon-spiracy; Gal Killin'; Killing Castro; Cabal of the Looming Doom; James Garfield: Martyr to Medicine; William Henry Harrison; The Ohio Gang; Presidential Also-Rans; Francis Gary Powers; J. Edgar Hoover • reprints material from Big Book of Conspiracies; Summer 1997 **A:** Joe Sacco; Justin Green; Richard Piers Rayner; Gray Morrow; Randy DuBurke; Ed Hannigan; Gordon Purcell; Glenn Barr; Peter Kuper; Danny Hellman; Graham Manley **W:** Paul Kirchner; Carl Posey; Doug Moench; Joel Rose

WEIRD MELVIN — Marc Hansen Stuff!

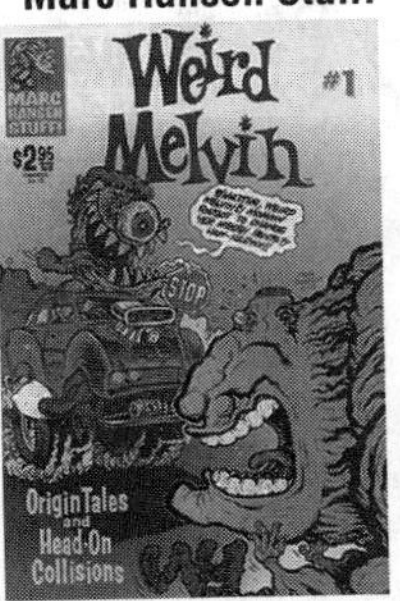

Marc Hansen's Weird Melvin is a zany, surprisingly fun comic book in the tradition of Ralph Snart Adventures. Originally appearing in 1991, it ran as a series of strips in Comics Buyer's Guide. In 1995, this series appeared, giving readers new Melvin adventures, as well as reprinting the old CBG strips in order and uncut.

In the story, Weird Melvin was actually a comic book put out in 1952 by Lloyd Gorpon, starring a Hulk-like monster who later became a monster-slayer. It ran only two issues, after which Gorpon hung himself over the low sales.

CGC-graded: Multiply prices above by **33 for 9.9 M • 16 for 9.8 NM/M • 7 for 9.6 NM+ • 5 for 9.4 NM • 2.5 for 9.2 NM- • 1.5 for 9.0 VF/NM**

However, a crazed fan uses black magic to bring Gorpon back from the dead, forcing him to create new issues. Meanwhile, another fanboy known only as "the Kid" manages to dig up a previously unknown issue which shows Melvin being killed and buried in a familiar place. The Kid then digs up Melvin, who turns out to be surprisingly lively for a fictional and dead monster-slayer!

1 ❑ Feb 1995, b&w Cover: 2.95 **NM** value: **Cover or less**
2 ❑ Apr 1995, b&w Cover: 2.95 **NM** value: **Cover or less**
3 ❑ Jun 1995, b&w Cover: 2.95 **NM** value: **Cover or less**
4 ❑ Aug 1995, b&w Cover: 2.95 **NM** value: **Cover or less**
5 ❑ Oct 1995, b&w Cover: 2.95 **NM** value: **Cover or less**

WEIRD MYSTERIES — Gilmore

1 ❑ Oct 1952 Cover: 0.10 **NM** value: **400.00**
• **CGC:** 2 graded, best 9.0
2 ❑ Dec 1952 Cover: 0.10 **NM** value: **500.00**
• **CGC:** 2 graded, best 9.2
3 ❑ Feb 1953 Cover: 0.10 **NM** value: **400.00**
• **CGC:** 2 graded, best 7.5
4 ❑ Apr 1953 Cover: 0.10 **NM** value: **400.00**
• **CGC:** 5 graded, best 7.5
5 ❑ Jun 1953 Cover: 0.10 **NM** value: **500.00**
• **CGC:** 6 graded, best 7.5
6 ❑ Aug 1953 Cover: 0.10 **NM** value: **400.00**
• **CGC:** 2 graded, best 8.0
7 ❑ Oct 1953 Cover: 0.10 **NM** value: **300.00**
• **CGC:** 1 graded, best 9.2
8 ❑ Jan 1954 Cover: 0.10 **NM** value: **400.00**
• **CGC:** 2 graded, best 8.5
9 ❑ Mar 1954 Cover: 0.10 **NM** value: **300.00**
• **CGC:** 1 graded, best 9.0
10 ❑ May 1954 Cover: 0.10 **NM** value: **300.00**
• **CGC:** 2 graded, best 9.0
11 ❑ Jul 1954 Cover: 0.10 **NM** value: **300.00**
• **CGC:** 2 graded, best 8.5

WEIRD MYSTERY TALES — DC

1 ❑ Jul 1972 Cover: 0.20 **NM** value: **9.00**
• **CGC:** 27 graded, best 9.8
2 ❑ Sep 1972 Cover: 0.20 **NM** value: **6.00**
• **CGC:** 5 graded, best 9.6
3 ❑ Nov 1972 Cover: 0.20 **NM** value: **5.00**
• **CGC:** 1 graded, best 9.6
4 ❑ Jan 1973 Cover: 0.20 **NM** value: **5.00**
• **CGC:** 2 graded, best 9.2
📖 The Devil to Pay; The Secret of Bat Island; To Live Forever **A:** Rico Rival; Romy Gamboa; Rubeny **W:** Steve Skeates; Jack Oleck
5 ❑ Apr 1973 Cover: 0.20 **NM** value: **5.00**
6 ❑ Jul 1973 Cover: 0.20 **NM** value: **4.00**
7 ❑ Sep 1973 Cover: 0.20 **NM** value: **4.00**
• **CGC:** 1 graded, best 9.2
8 ❑ Nov 1973 Cover: 0.20 **NM** value: **4.00**
• **CGC:** 2 graded, best 8.5
9 ❑ Dec 1973 Cover: 0.20 **NM** value: **4.00**
• **CGC:** 2 graded, best 9.0
10 ❑ Mar 1974 Cover: 0.20 **NM** value: **4.00**
11 ❑ Apr 1974 Cover: 0.20 **NM** value: **4.00**
• **CGC:** 2 graded, best 9.2
12 ❑ Jul 1974 Cover: 0.20 **NM** value: **4.00**
13 ❑ Aug 1974 Cover: 0.20 **NM** value: **4.00**
• **CGC:** 1 graded, best 9.0
14 ❑ Oct 1974 Cover: 0.20 **NM** value: **4.00**
• **CGC:** 1 graded, best 9.0
15 ❑ Jan 1975 Cover: 0.20 **NM** value: **4.00**
• **CGC:** 3 graded, best 9.4
16 ❑ Mar 1975 Cover: 0.25 **NM** value: **4.00**
17 ❑ Apr 1975 Cover: 0.25 **NM** value: **4.00**
• **CGC:** 1 graded, best 9.2
18 ❑ May 1975 Cover: 0.25 **NM** value: **4.00**
19 ❑ Jun 1975 Cover: 0.25 **NM** value: **4.00**
• **CGC:** 2 graded, best 9.4
20 ❑ Jul 1975 Cover: 0.25 **NM** value: **4.00**
21 ❑ Aug 1975 Cover: 0.25 **NM** value: **4.00**
• **CGC:** 1 graded, best 7.5
22 ❑ Sep 1975 Cover: 0.25 **NM** value: **4.00**
• **CGC:** 1 graded, best 9.2
23 ❑ Oct 1975 Cover: 0.25 **NM** value: **4.00**
• **CGC:** 2 graded, best 9.2
24 ❑ Nov 1975 Cover: 0.25 **NM** value: **4.00**
final issue.

WEIRDO — Last Gasp

1 ❑ **NM** value: **15.00**
2 ❑ Jun 1981 Cover: 2.25 **NM** value: **10.00**
3 ❑ Cover: 2.25 **NM** value: **8.00**
4 ❑ ca. 1982 Cover: 2.25 **NM** value: **6.00**
5 ❑ ca. 1982 Cover: 2.50 **NM** value: **6.00**
6 ❑ ca. 1982 Cover: 2.50 **NM** value: **6.00**
7 ❑ ca. 1983 Cover: 2.50 **NM** value: **6.00**
8 ❑ ca. 1983 Cover: 2.50 **NM** value: **6.00**
9 ❑ ca. 1983 Cover: 2.50 **NM** value: **6.00**
10 ❑ ca. 1983 Cover: 2.50 **NM** value: **6.00**
11 ❑ Cover: 2.50 **NM** value: **5.00**
12 ❑ Cover: 2.50 **NM** value: **5.00**
13 ❑ Cover: 2.50 **NM** value: **5.00**
14 ❑ ca. 1985 Cover: 2.50 **NM** value: **5.00**
15 ❑ Cover: 2.50 **NM** value: **5.00**
16 ❑ Cover: 2.50 **NM** value: **5.00**
17 ❑ **NM** value: **5.00**
18 ❑ **NM** value: **5.00**
19 ❑ **NM** value: **5.00**
20 ❑ **NM** value: **5.00**
21 ❑ Cover: 2.95 **NM** value: **4.00**
22 ❑ Cover: 2.95 **NM** value: **4.00**
23 ❑ Cover: 2.95 **NM** value: **4.00**
24 ❑ Cover: 2.95 **NM** value: **4.00**
25 ❑ ca. 1989 Cover: 2.95 **NM** value: **4.00**
26 ❑ Cover: 2.95 **NM** value: **4.00**

WEIRDOM COMIX — Weirdom

1 ❑ **NM** value: **3.00**
2 ❑ **NM** value: **2.00**
3 ❑ **NM** value: **2.00**
4 ❑ **NM** value: **2.00**
5 ❑ **NM** value: **2.00**
6 ❑ **NM** value: **2.00**
7 ❑ **NM** value: **2.00**
8 ❑ **NM** value: **2.00**
9 ❑ **NM** value: **2.00**
10 ❑ **NM** value: **2.00**
11 ❑ **NM** value: **2.00**
12 ❑ **NM** value: **2.00**
13 ❑ **NM** value: **2.00**
14 ❑ **NM** value: **2.00**
15 ❑ Cover: 0.50 **NM** value: **2.00**
📖 Once Upon a Planet...; Monsters Rule; Stone Wolf & the 3 Pigs; The Weirder side of Weirdom; What Could Be Worse? **A:** John Williams; Tim Boxell; Richard Corben; Richard Corben(cover); Chuck Rogers; Jerry Firitilli; Jim Garrison; John Williams(back cover); Ken Lodge; Martin Russel; Rudi Granke

WEIRD ROMANCE — Eclipse

1 ❑ ca. 1988, b&w Cover: 2.00 **NM** value: **Cover or less**

WEIRD SCIENCE (E.C.) — E.C.

Speaking of weird, how weird was it that the Pre-Trend E.C. title Saddle Romances became Weird Science with #12? While the focus of much of the rest of the New Trend titles was horror, this series was devoted to science-fiction stories, and covers by Feldstein and by Wood were scenes of rockets, aliens, and people in spacesuits.

The numbering will keep collectors on their toes, because the continued numbering ran from #12 (May 50), #13 (Jul 50), #14 (Sep 50), and #15 (Nov 50) to #5 (Jan 51); this means there were duplicate numbers. The later dates were #12 (Mar 52), #13 (May 52), #14 (Jul 52), and #15 (Sep 52).

Artists for whom the E.C. line was known did work in the series: Johnny Craig, Harvey Kurtzman, Al Feldstein, Graham Ingels, Jack Kamen, Will Elder, George Evans, Al Williamson, Joe Orlando, and Wally Wood. Some of the stories were adaptations of stories by the likes of Anthony Boucher, Donald Wandrei, and Ray Bradbury. The series changed its name and combined with Weird Fantasy to raise its price and become Weird Science-Fantasy. — Maggie

1 ❑ May 1950 Cover: 0.10 **NM** value: **1350.00**
• **CGC:** 13 graded, best 9.4
Cover reads #12 (1950). 📖 Lost in the Microcosm; Dream of Doom; Murder in the 21st Century (text story); Experiment...In Death; By the Dark of the Moon (text story); "Things" From Outer Space! • Series continued from Saddle Romances #11 **A:** Al Feldstein; Harvey Kurtzman; Wally Wood; Jack Kamen **W:** Al Feldstein; Harvey Kurtzman; Wally Wood; Jack Kamen
2 ❑ Jul 1950 Cover: 0.10 **NM** value: **600.00**
• **CGC:** 10 graded, best 9.8
Cover reads #13 (1950). 📖 The Flying Saucer Invasion; The Meteor Monster; Experiment (text story); The Micro Race!; Sands of Time (text story); ...The Man Who Raced Time **A:** Al Williamson; Joe Orlando; Wally Wood; Bernie Krigstein **W:** ...For Posterity; The Pioneer; The Teacher From Mars; Upheaval!
3 ❑ Sep 1950 Cover: 0.10 **NM** value: **550.00**
• **CGC:** 9 graded, best 9.8
Cover reads #14 (1950). 📖 Destruction of the Earth!; The Sounds From Another World!; Machine From Nowhere; The Eternal Man
4 ❑ Nov 1950 Cover: 0.10 **NM** value: **550.00**
• **CGC:** 11 graded, best 9.6
Cover reads #15 (1950). 📖 Panic!; The Radioactive Child!; House, in Time!; Gargantua!
5 ❑ Jan 1951 Cover: 0.10 **NM** value: **350.00**
• **CGC:** 4 graded, best 9.8
📖 Made of the Future!; Return; The Last War on Earth; Killed in Time
6 ❑ Mar 1951 Cover: 0.10 **NM** value: **350.00**
• **CGC:** 6 graded, best 9.6
📖 Spawn of Venus; Man and Superman!; Dilemma (text story); Sinking of the Titanic!; Divide and Conquer
7 ❑ May 1951 Cover: 0.10 **NM** value: **350.00**
• **CGC:** 9 graded, best 9.6
📖 It Was the Monster From the Fourth Dimension; Something Missing!; Miracle! (text story); ...Gregory Had a Model-T!; The Aliens!
8 ❑ Jul 1951 Cover: 0.10 **NM** value: **350.00**
• **CGC:** 6 graded, best 9.8
📖 Seeds of Jupiter!; The Escape; Invasion! (text story); Beyond Repair; The Probers
9 ❑ Sep 1951 Cover: 0.10 **NM** value: **350.00**
• **CGC:** 11 graded, best 9.6
📖 The Gray Cloud of Death!; The Martian Monster; The Invaders; The Slave of Evil!
10 ❑ Nov 1951 Cover: 0.10 **NM** value: **350.00**
• **CGC:** 7 graded, best 9.6
📖 The Maidens Cried; Reducing Costs; Transformation Completed; The Planetoid!
11 ❑ Jan 1952 Cover: 0.10 **NM** value: **225.00**
• **CGC:** 8 graded, best 9.8
📖 The Conquerors of the Moon; Only Human; Why Papa Left Home; The Worm Turns
12 ❑ Mar 1952 Cover: 0.10 **NM** value: **225.00**
• **CGC:** 7 graded, best 9.4
📖 A Goble is a Knog's Best Friend; The Last Man; The Android; Chewed Out
13 ❑ May 1952 Cover: 0.10 **NM** value: **225.00**
• **CGC:** 7 graded, best 9.8
📖 A Weighty Decision; Saving for the Future; He Walked Among Us; Say Your Prayers
14 ❑ Jul 1952 Cover: 0.10 **NM** value: **225.00**
• **CGC:** 8 graded, best 9.8
📖 There'll be Some Changes Made; Inside Story; Strategy; They Shall Inherit
15 ❑ Sep 1952 Cover: 0.10 **NM** value: **250.00**
• **CGC:** 10 graded, best 9.6
📖 The Martians!; Captivity; Miscalculation; Bum Steer **A:** Al Williamson; Joe Orlando; Wally Wood; Jack Kamen **W:** Al Feldstein; William Gaines
16 ❑ Nov 1952 Cover: 0.10 **NM** value: **250.00**
• **CGC:** 9 graded, best 9.8
📖 Down to Earth; Space-Borne!; Given the Heir!; The People's Choice! **A:** Al Williamson
17 ❑ Jan 1953 Cover: 0.10 **NM** value: **250.00**
• **CGC:** 4 graded, best 9.6
📖 Plucked!; The Island Monster; Off Day!; The Long Years! **A:** Al Williamson
18 ❑ Mar 1953 Cover: 0.10 **NM** value: **250.00**
• **CGC:** 5 graded, best 8.5
📖 Mars is Heaven!; Snap Ending!; The Parallel!; Disassembled! **A:** Al Williamson
19 ❑ May 1953 Cover: 0.10 **NM** value: **325.00**
• **CGC:** 6 graded, best 9.8
📖 The Precious Years; The One Who Waits; Right on the Button!; Keyed Up! **A:** Al Williamson; Joe Orlando; Bill Elder; Wally Wood **W:** Al Williamson; Joe Orlando; Bill Elder; Wally Wood
20 ❑ Jul 1953 Cover: 0.10 **NM** value: **325.00**
• **CGC:** 8 graded, best 9.8
📖 The Loathsome!; Surprise Package; The Reformers; 50 Girls 50 **A:** Al Williamson; Joe Orlando; Wally Wood; Jack Kamen **W:** Al Williamson; Joe Orlando; Wally Wood; Jack Kamen
21 ❑ Sep 1953 Cover: 0.10 **NM** value: **325.00**
• **CGC:** 7 graded, best 9.6
📖 EC Confidential; Punishment Without Crime; Two's Company...; The Ugly One **A:** Al Williamson; Joe Orlando; Frank Frazetta; Wally Wood; Jack Kamen **W:** Al Williamson; Joe Orlando; Wally Wood; Jack Kamen
22 ❑ Nov 1953 Cover: 0.10 **NM** value: **325.00**
• **CGC:** 12 graded, best 9.4
📖 A New Beginning; The Headhunters; Outcast of the Stars; My World final issue. **A:** George Evans; Al Williamson; Joe Orlando; Wally Wood **W:** George Evans; Al Williamson; Joe Orlando; Wally Wood

WEIRD SCIENCE-FANTASY (E.C.) — E.C.

E.C. combined the titles Weird Science and Weird Fantasy, picked up from #22 of each, added a nickel to the price, and made Weird Science-Fantasy. (The price dropped back to a dime after two issues at the higher price.) Covers featured a rocket design on the left side and, in the picture space, aliens, other planets, and spaceships. The final issue with that title featured a Frank Frazetta cover originally created as a Buck Rogers cover for Famous Funnies. Issue #26 was entirely devoted to "Flying Saucer Report." Issues #27-29 featured adaptations of Eando Binder's "Adam Link" stories originally published in Amazing Stories. — Maggie

23 ❑ Mar 1954 Cover: 0.15 **NM** value: **225.00**
• **CGC:** 7 graded, best 9.2
📖 The Children; Fish Story; Ninth Wonder; The Flying Machine; Fair Trade • Series continued from Weird Science #22 and Weird Fantasy #22
24 ❑ Jun 1954 Cover: 0.15 **NM** value: **225.00**
• **CGC:** 4 graded, best 9.6
📖 ...For Posterity; The Teacher From Mars; The Pioneer; Upheaval! • "Upheaval" by Harlan Ellison (1st professional work by Harlan Ellison) **A:** Al Williamson; Joe Orlando; Wally Wood; Bernie Krigstein **W:** Al Williamson; Joe Orlando; Wally Wood; Bernie Krigstein; Eando Binder; Harlan Ellison
25 ❑ Sep 1954 Cover: 0.10 **NM** value: **260.00**
• **CGC:** 5 graded, best 9.6
📖 Flying Saucer Report; A Sound of Thunder; Bellyful; Harvest
26 ❑ Dec 1954 Cover: 0.10 **NM** value: **210.00**
• **CGC:** 6 graded, best 9.8
📖 Flying Saucer Report • Flying Saucer Report special issue
27 ❑ Jan 1955 Cover: 0.10 **NM** value: **225.00**
• **CGC:** 8 graded, best 9.8
📖 Adaptability; Close Shave; 4th Degree; I, Robot
28 ❑ Mar 1955 Cover: 0.10 **NM** value: **240.00**
• **CGC:** 6 graded, best 9.8
📖 The Inferiors; Lost in Space; Round Trip; The Trial of Adam Link
29 ❑ May 1955 Cover: 0.10 **NM** value: **400.00**
• **CGC:** 17 graded, best 9.6
Frazetta cover. 📖 The Chosen One; Vicious Circle; Genesis; Adam Link in Business

WEIRD SCIENCE-FANTASY (RCP) — Gemstone

1 ❑ Nov 1992 Cover: 1.50 **NM** value: **2.00**
Circ: Statement: **19,232** CapCity orders: **4,300**
📖 The Children; Fish Story; Ninth Wonder; The Flying Machine; Fair Trade • Reprints Weird Science-Fantasy #23
2 ❑ Feb 1993 Cover: 1.50 **NM** value: **2.00**
Circ: Statement: **19,232** CapCity orders: **4,200**
📖 ...For Posterity; The Teacher From Mars; The Pioneer; Upheaval! • Reprints Weird Science-Fantasy #24; "Upheaval" by Harlan Ellison (1st professional work by Harlan Ellison) **A:** Al Williamson; Joe Or-

lando; Wally Wood; Bernie Krigstein **C:** Al Feldstein **W:** Al Williamson; Joe Orlando; Wally Wood; Bernie Krigstein; Eando Binder; Harlan Ellison

3 ❑ May 1993 Cover: 1.50 **NM value: 2.00**
Circ: Statement: **19,232** CapCity orders: **4,200**
Flying Saucer Report; A Sound of Thunder; Bellyful; Harvest • Reprints Weird Science-Fantasy #25 **A:** Al Williamson; Joe Orlando; Wally Wood; Bernie Krigstein **C:** Al Feldstein

4 ❑ Aug 1993 Cover: 1.50 **NM value: 2.00**
Circ: Statement: **19,232** CapCity orders: **3,900**
Flying Saucer Report • UFO issue; Reprints Weird Science-Fantasy #26; Flying Saucer Report special issue

5 ❑ Nov 1993 Cover: 2.00 **NM** value: **Cover or less**
Circ: Statement: **9,324** CapCity orders: **3,425**
Adaptability; Close Shave; 4th Degree; I, Robot • Reprints Weird Science-Fantasy #27 **A:** Joe Orlando; Wally Wood; Reed Crandall; Jack Kamen

6 ❑ Feb 1994 Cover: 2.00 **NM** value: **Cover or less**
Circ: Statement: **9,324** CapCity orders: **3,175**
• Reprints Weird Science-Fantasy #28 **A:** Al Williamson; Joe Orlando; Wally Wood; Jack Kamen **C:** Al Feldstein

7 ❑ May 1994 Cover: 2.00 **NM** value: **Cover or less**
Circ: Statement: **9,324** CapCity orders: **2,950**
Frazetta cover. • Reprints Weird Science-Fantasy #29 **A:** Al Williamson; Joe Orlando; Wally Wood

8 ❑ Aug 1994 Cover: 2.00 **NM** value: **Cover or less**
Circ: Statement: **9,324**

9 ❑ Nov 1994 Cover: 2.00 **NM** value: **Cover or less**
• Has 1994 Statement, filed 9/15/94; avg print run 12,823; avg sales 8,807; avg subs 517; avg total paid 9,324; office use 3,499; max existent 12,823; not available on newsstands

10 ❑ Feb 1995 Cover: 2.00 **NM** value: **Cover or less**
11 ❑ May 1995 Cover: 2.00 **NM** value: **Cover or less**
Anl 1❑ Cover: 8.95 **NM** value: **Cover or less**
• Collects Weird Science-Fantasy (RCP) #1-5
Anl 2❑ Cover: 12.95 **NM** value: **Cover or less**
• Collects Weird Science-Fantasy (RCP) #?

WEIRD SCIENCE (GLADSTONE) — Gladstone

1 ❑ Sep 1990 Cover: 1.95 **NM value: 2.00**
Circ: CapCity orders: **10,950**
A New Beginning; The Headhunters; My World; Outcast of the Stars; Am I Man or Machine; Only Time Will Tell; The Men of Tomorrow; Trip Into the Unknown • Reprints Weird Science (EC) #22; Weird Fantasy (EC) #1 **A:** Al Feldstein; George Evans; Al Williamson; Harvey Kurtzman; Joe Orlando; Wally Wood; Jack Kamen; Harry Harrison; Ray Bradbury **W:** Al Feldstein; George Evans; Al Williamson; Harvey Kurtzman; Joe Orlando; Wally Wood; Jack Kamen; Harry Harrison; Ray Bradbury

2 ❑ Nov 1990 Cover: 1.95 **NM value: 2.00**
Circ: CapCity orders: **11,400**

3 ❑ Jan 1991 Cover: 2.00 **NM** value: **Cover or less**
Circ: CapCity orders: **9,800**
The Gray Cloud of Death; The Martian Monster; The Invaders; The Slave of Evil; The Cosmic Ray Bomb Explosion; The Black Arts; The Trap of Time; Atom Bomb Thief! • Reprints Weird Science (EC) #9, Weird Fantasy (EC) #14 **A:** Al Feldstein; Harvey Kurtzman; Wally Wood; Jack Kamen

4 ❑ Mar 1991 Cover: 2.00 **NM** value: **Cover or less**
Circ: CapCity orders: **9,550**

WEIRD SCIENCE (RCP) — Gemstone

1 ❑ Sep 1992 Cover: 1.50 **NM value: 2.50**
Circ: Statement: **21,941** CapCity orders: **4,100**
Lost in the Microcosm; Dream of Doom; Murder in the 21st Century (text story); Experiment...In Death; By the Dark of the Moon (text story); "Things" From Outer Space! • Reprints Weird Science (EC) #1 **A:** Al Feldstein; Harvey Kurtzman; Wally Wood; Jack Kamen **W:** Al Feldstein; Harvey Kurtzman; Wally Wood; Jack Kamen

2 ❑ Dec 1992 Cover: 1.50 **NM value: 2.00**
Circ: Statement: **21,941** CapCity orders: **4,800**
The Flying Saucer Invasion; The Meteor Monster; Experiment (text story); The Micro Race!; Sands of Time (text story); ...The Man Who Raced Time • Reprints Weird Science (EC) #2

3 ❑ Mar 1993 Cover: 1.50 **NM value: 2.00**
Circ: Statement: **21,941** CapCity orders: **4,200**
Destruction of the Earth!; The Sounds From Another World!; Machine From Nowhere; The Eternal Man • Reprints Weird Science (EC) #3

4 ❑ Jun 1993 Cover: 2.00 **NM** value: **Cover or less**
Circ: Statement: **21,941**
Panic!; The Radioactive Child!; House, in Time!; Gargantua! • Reprints Weird Science (EC) #4 **A:** Al Feldstein; Harvey Kurtzman; Jack Kamen; Graham Ingels

5 ❑ Sep 1993 Cover: 2.00 **NM** value: **Cover or less**
Circ: Statement: **9,726** CapCity orders: **3,625**
Made of the Future!; Return; The Last War on Earth; Killed in Time • Reprints Weird Science (EC) #5 **A:** Al Feldstein; Harvey Kurtzman; Wally Wood; Jack Kamen

6 ❑ Dec 1993 Cover: 2.00 **NM** value: **Cover or less**
Circ: Statement: **9,726** CapCity orders: **3,475**
Spawn of Venus; Man and Superman!; Dilemma (text story); Sinking of the Titanic!; Divide and Conquer • Reprints Weird Science (EC) #6 **A:** Al Feldstein; Harvey Kurtzman; Wally Wood; Jack Kamen

7 ❑ Mar 1994 Cover: 2.00 **NM** value: **Cover or less**
Circ: Statement: **9,726** CapCity orders: **3,150**
It Was the Monster From the Fourth Dimension; Something Missing!; Miracle! (text story); ...Gregory Had a Model-T!; The Aliens! • Reprints Weird Science (EC) #7 **A:** Al Feldstein; Harvey Kurtzman; Wally Wood; Jack Kamen **C:** Al Feldstein

8 ❑ Jun 1994 Cover: 2.00 **NM** value: **Cover or less**
Circ: Statement: **9,726** CapCity orders: **2,875**
Seeds of Jupiter!; The Escape; Invasion! (text story); Beyond Repair; The Probers • Reprints Weird Science (EC) #8 **A:** Al Feldstein; Wally Wood; Jack Kamen

9 ❑ Sep 1994 Cover: 2.00 **NM** value: **Cover or less**
Circ: Statement: **7,596**
The Gray Cloud of Death!; The Martian Monster; The Invaders; The Slave of Evil! • Reprints Weird Science (EC) #9

10 ❑ Dec 1994 Cover: 2.00 **NM** value: **Cover or less**
Circ: Statement: **7,596** CapCity orders: **2,875**
The Maidens Cried; Reducing Costs; Transformation Completed; The Planetoid! • Reprints Weird Science (EC) #10

11 ❑ Mar 1995 Cover: 2.00 **NM** value: **Cover or less**
Circ: Statement: **7,596** CapCity orders: **2,625**
The Conquerors of the Moon; Only Human; Why Papa Left Home; The Worm Turns • Reprints Weird Science (EC) #11

12 ❑ Jun 1995 Cover: 2.00 **NM** value: **Cover or less**
Circ: Statement: **7,596** CapCity orders: **2,475**
A Goble is a Knog's Best Friend; The Last Man; The Android; Chewed Out • Reprints Weird Science (EC) #12

13 ❑ Sep 1995 Cover: 2.00 **NM** value: **Cover or less**
Circ: Statement: **6,594** CapCity orders: **2,625**
A Weighty Decision; Saving for the Future; He Walked Among Us; Say Your Prayers • Reprints Weird Science (EC) #13

14 ❑ Dec 1995 Cover: 2.00 **NM** value: **Cover or less**
Circ: Statement: **6,594**
There'll be Some Changes Made; Inside Story; Strategy; They Shall Inherit • Reprints Weird Science (EC) #14; has 1995 Statement; avg print run 11,195; avg sales 7,064; avg subs 532; avg total paid 7,596

15 ❑ Mar 1996 Cover: 2.50 **NM** value: **Cover or less**
Circ: Statement: **6,594**
• Reprints Weird Science (EC) #15

16 ❑ Jun 1996 Cover: 2.50 **NM** value: **Cover or less**
Circ: Statement: **6,594**
• Reprints Weird Science (EC) #16

17 ❑ Sep 1996 Cover: 2.50 **NM** value: **Cover or less**
Circ: Statement: **6,157**
• Reprints Weird Science (EC) #17

18 ❑ Dec 1996 Cover: 2.50 **NM** value: **Cover or less**
Circ: Statement: **6,157** Diamd. preorders: **5,566**
• Reprints Weird Science (EC) #18; Has 1996 Statement, filed 7/15/96 (not really early, as title was quarterly); avg print run 8,041; avg sales 6,083; avg subs 511; avg total paid 6,594; office use 1,453; max existent 8,041; not available on newsstands

19 ❑ Mar 1997 Cover: 2.50 **NM** value: **Cover or less**
Circ: Statement: **6,157** Diamd. preorders: **5,430**
The Precious Years; The One Who Waits; Right on the Button!; Keyed Up! • Reprints Weird Science (EC) #19 **A:** Al Williamson; Joe Orlando; Bill Elder; Wally Wood **W:** Al Williamson; Joe Orlando; Bill Elder; Wally Wood

20 ❑ Jun 1997 Cover: 2.50 **NM** value: **Cover or less**
Circ: Statement: **6,157** Diamd. preorders: **5,684**
The Loathsome!; Surprise Package; The Reformers; 50 Girls 50 • Reprints Weird Science (EC) #20 **A:** Al Williamson; Joe Orlando; Wally Wood; Jack Kamen **W:** Al Williamson; Joe Orlando; Wally Wood; Jack Kamen

21 ❑ Sep 1997 Cover: 2.50 **NM** value: **Cover or less**
Circ: Diamd. preorders: **5,461**
EC Confidential; Punishment Without Crime; Two's Company...; The Ugly One • Reprints Weird Science (EC) #21; EC editors put themselves in story **A:** Al Williamson; Joe Orlando; Frank Frazetta; Wally Wood; Jack Kamen **W:** Al Williamson; Joe Orlando; Wally Wood; Jack Kamen

22 ❑ Dec 1997 Cover: 2.50 **NM** value: **Cover or less**
Circ: Diamd. preorders: **5,334**
A New Beginning; The Headhunters; Outcast of the Stars; My World • Reprints Weird Science (EC) #22; Wally Wood puts himself in story; Has 1997 Statement; avg total paid circ 6,157 **A:** George Evans; Al Williamson; Joe Orlando; Wally Wood **W:** George Evans; Al Williamson; Joe Orlando; Wally Wood

Anl 1❑ Cover: 8.95 **NM** value: **Cover or less**
• Reprints Weird Science (EC) #1-5
Anl 2❑ Cover: 9.95 **NM** value: **Cover or less**
• Reprints Weird Science (EC) #6-10
Anl 3❑ Cover: 10.95 **NM** value: **Cover or less**
• Reprints Weird Science (EC) #11-14
Anl 4❑ Cover: 9.95 **NM** value: **Cover or less**
• Reprints Weird Science (EC) #15-18
Anl 5❑ Cover: 10.50 **NM** value: **Cover or less**
• Reprints Weird Science (EC) #19-22

WEIRD SEX — Fantagraphics / Eros

1 ❑ Jan 1999 Cover: 2.95 **NM** value: **Cover or less**
Circ: Diamd. preorders: **1,841**

WEIRD SPACE — Avalon

1 ❑ Cover: 2.95 **NM** value: **Cover or less**
The Brain-Bats of Venus; For As Long As You Live!; This Man is Dangerous! **A:** Basil Wolverton

WEIRD SUSPENSE — Atlas-Seaboard

1 ❑ Feb 1975 Cover: 0.25 **NM value: 1.00**
• **CGC:** 2 graded, best 9.2
2 ❑ Apr 1975 Cover: 0.25 **NM value: 1.00**
3 ❑ Jul 1975 Cover: 0.25 **NM value: 1.00**

WEIRD SUSPENSTORIES — Superior

1 ❑ Oct 1951 Cover: 0.10 **NM value: 300.00**
2 ❑ Nov 1951 Cover: 0.10 **NM value: 300.00**
3 ❑ Dec 1951 Cover: 0.10 **NM value: 300.00**

WEIRDSVILLE — Blindwolf

1 ❑ Feb 1997 Cover: 2.95 **NM** value: **Cover or less**
Welcome to: Weirdsville **A:** Franco Aureliani **W:** Franco Aureliani; Alex Mazzotta; Dino Mazzotta
2 ❑ Apr 1997 Cover: 2.95 **NM** value: **Cover or less**
3 ❑ Jun 1997 Cover: 2.95 **NM** value: **Cover or less**
4 ❑ Aug 1997 Cover: 2.95 **NM** value: **Cover or less**
5 ❑ Sep 1997 Cover: 2.95 **NM** value: **Cover or less**
6 ❑ Dec 1997 Cover: 2.95 **NM** value: **Cover or less**
7 ❑ 1998 Cover: 2.95 **NM** value: **Cover or less**
8 ❑ Mar 1998 Cover: 2.95 **NM** value: **Cover or less**
An American Werewolf in Weirdsville **A:** Franco Aureliani **W:** Franco Aureliani; Alex Mazzotta; Dino Mazzotta
9 ❑ Jun 1998 Cover: 2.95 **NM** value: **Cover or less**
An American Werewolf in Weirdsville **A:** Mike Pascale; Franco Aureliani **W:** Franco Aureliani; Alex Mazzotta; Dino Mazzotta

WEIRD TALES ILLUSTRATED — Millennium

1 ❑ full color Cover: 2.95 **NM** value: **Cover or less**
Circ: CapCity orders: **3,200**
Shattered Like A Glass Goblin; Party Games; Annabel Lee; A Visitor from Egypt **A:** John Bolton; Kelley Jones; P. Craig Russell; Eddy Newell; Paul Davis **W:** Edgar Allan Poe; Faye Perozich; Frank Belknap Long; Harlan Ellison

1/Dlx❑ Cover: 4.95 **NM** value: **Cover or less**
Circ: CapCity orders: **4,225**
• Deluxe edition with extra stories. Shattered Like A Glass Goblin; Party Games; Annabel Lee; A Visitor from Egypt **A:** John Bolton; Kelley Jones; P. Craig Russell; Eddy Newell; Paul Davis **W:** Edgar Allan Poe; Faye Perozich; Frank Belknap Long; Harlan Ellison

2 ❑ Cover: 2.95 **NM** value: **Cover or less**
Circ: CapCity orders: **3,800**

WEIRD TALES OF THE FUTURE — Aragon

1 ❑ Mar 1952 Cover: 0.10 **NM value: 600.00**
• **CGC:** 4 graded, best 9.0
2 ❑ Jun 1952 Cover: 0.10 **NM value: 750.00**
• **CGC:** 7 graded, best 9.4
3 ❑ Sep 1952 Cover: 0.10 **NM value: 600.00**
• **CGC:** 5 graded, best 9.0
4 ❑ Nov 1952 Cover: 0.10 **NM value: 600.00**
• **CGC:** 8 graded, best 9.0
5 ❑ Jan 1953 Cover: 0.10 **NM value: 750.00**
• **CGC:** 2 graded, best 8.0
6 ❑ Mar 1953 Cover: 0.10 **NM value: 600.00**
• **CGC:** 2 graded, best 7.5
7 ❑ May 1953 Cover: 0.10 **NM value: 600.00**
• **CGC:** 7 graded, best 9.4
8 ❑ Jul 1953 Cover: 0.10 **NM value: 500.00**
• **CGC:** 6 graded, best 8.0

WEIRD TALES OF THE MACABRE — Atlas-Seaboard

1 ❑ Apr 1975 Cover: 0.75 **NM value: 3.00**
2 ❑ Apr 1975 Cover: 0.75 **NM value: 3.00**

WEIRD TERROR — Comic Media

1 ❑ Sep 1952 Cover: 0.10 **NM value: 400.00**
• **CGC:** 2 graded, best 8.0
2 ❑ Nov 1952 Cover: 0.10 **NM value: 250.00**
• **CGC:** 1 graded, best 7.5
3 ❑ Jan 1953 Cover: 0.10 **NM value: 250.00**
• **CGC:** 1 graded, best 7.5
4 ❑ Mar 1953 Cover: 0.10 **NM value: 250.00**
• **CGC:** 1 graded, best 3.0
5 ❑ May 1953 Cover: 0.10 **NM value: 250.00**
6 ❑ Jul 1953 Cover: 0.10 **NM value: 250.00**
• **CGC:** 1 graded, best 8.0
7 ❑ Sep 1953 Cover: 0.10 **NM value: 250.00**
• **CGC:** 1 graded, best 9.0
8 ❑ Nov 1953 Cover: 0.10 **NM value: 250.00**
• **CGC:** 1 graded, best 7.5
9 ❑ Jan 1954 Cover: 0.10 **NM value: 250.00**
• **CGC:** 1 graded, best 8.5
"The Fleabite"
10 ❑ Mar 1954 Cover: 0.10 **NM value: 250.00**
• **CGC:** 1 graded, best 8.0
"The Man-Ape"
11 ❑ May 1954 Cover: 0.10 **NM value: 250.00**
• **CGC:** 1 graded, best 8.0
12 ❑ Jul 1954 Cover: 0.10 **NM value: 250.00**
• **CGC:** 1 graded, best 6.0
13 ❑ Sep 1954 Cover: 0.10 **NM value: 250.00**
• **CGC:** 1 graded, best 8.0

WEIRD THRILLERS — Ziff-Davis

1 ❑ Sep 1951 Cover: 0.10 **NM value: 500.00**
• **CGC:** 2 graded, best 9.2
2 ❑ Nov 1951 Cover: 0.10 **NM value: 400.00**
3 ❑ Spr 1952 Cover: 0.10 **NM value: 400.00**
4 ❑ Sum 1952 Cover: 0.10 **NM value: 400.00**
5 ❑ Oct 1952 Cover: 0.10 **NM value: 400.00**

WEIRD TRIPS MAGAZINE — Kitchen Sink

1 ❑ Cover: 0.65 **NM value: 4.00**
Violence and Vegetation in **A:** Evert Geradt **W:** Denis Kitchen; Evert Geradt; Mike Baron; Tom Veitch; Doug Moench; Jane Lynch; Mike Olshan; Pete Poplaski; R.D. Rosen

WEIRD WAR TALES — DC

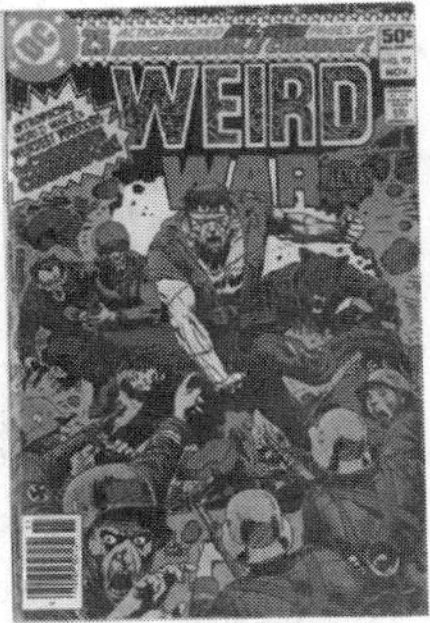

This title took the best of two popular DC genres — war stories and the supernatural — and combined them to create tragedy, comedy, and wonder. The stories range from an odd deja-vu experience to encounters with the supernatural. Moreover, the wartime setting adds tension to these eerie scenes, giving them added effect. In its 124-issue run, Weird War Tales featured many of comicdom's finest artists, including Terry Austin, Keith Giffen, Walt Simonson, Steve Ditko, and Neal Adams.

In its later years, the series did acquire a few ongoing features,

CGC-graded: Multiply prices above by **33 for 9.9 M • 16 for 9.8 NM/M • 7 for 9.6 NM+ • 5 for 9.4 NM • 2.5 for 9.2 NM- • 1.5 for 9.0 VF/NM**

such as The Creature Commandos (a group of G.I.s modeled on horror stereotypes) and the G.I. Robot. Eventually, these two features were combined for several adventures.

1 ❑ Sep 1971 Cover: 0.25 **NM** value: **45.00**
• **CGC:** 29 graded, best 9.6

2 ❑ Nov 1971 Cover: 0.25 **NM** value: **28.00**
• **CGC:** 6 graded, best 9.2
Reef of No Return; The Moon is the Murderer; Behind the Cover; A Promise to Joe; Monsieur Gravedigger; Military Madness; The Face of a Fighter **A:** Mort Drucker **W:** Joe Kubert

3 ❑ Jan 1972 Cover: 0.25 **NM** value: **20.00**
• **CGC:** 6 graded, best 9.4
Been Here Before; The Cloud That Went to War; Kreepy Korps; Combat Size; Pilot for a Sub

4 ❑ Mar 1972 Cover: 0.25 **NM** value: **18.00**
• **CGC:** 5 graded, best 9.4
Time Warp; The Unknown Sentinel **C:** Joe Kubert

5 ❑ May 1972 Cover: 0.25 **NM** value: **18.00**

6 ❑ Jul 1972 Cover: 0.20 **NM** value: **12.00**
• **CGC:** 1 graded, best 9.2

7 ❑ Sep 1972 Cover: 0.20 **NM** value: **12.00**

8 ❑ Nov 1972 Cover: 0.20 **NM** value: **12.00**
The Avenging Grave; Thou Shalt Not Kill; Duel of the Dead **A:** Tony DeZuniga; Adams; Neal Adams(cover) **W:** Harper; Robert Kanigher

9 ❑ Dec 1972 Cover: 0.20 **NM** value: **12.00**
The Promise; Blood Brothers; The Last Battle **A:** Alfredo Alcala; Gerry Talaoc **W:** Robert Kanigher

10 ❑ Jan 1973 Cover: 0.20 **NM** value: **12.00**
• **CGC:** 1 graded, best 8.5
Who is Haunting the Haunted Chateau; The Room That Remembered; Cyrano's Army **A:** Alex Toth; QR **W:** Sheldon Mayer; Len Wein; Raymond Marais

11 ❑ Feb 1973 Cover: 0.20 **NM** value: **8.00**
• **CGC:** 1 graded, best 8.5

12 ❑ Mar 1973 Cover: 0.20 **NM** value: **8.00**
• **CGC:** 1 graded, best 8.5
God of Vengeance; Hand of Hell; The Warrior and the Witch Doctors **A:** Don Perlin; Gerry Talaoc **W:** Arnold Drake; Robert Kanigher

13 ❑ Apr 1973 Cover: 0.20 **NM** value: **8.00**
• **CGC:** 1 graded, best 9.4
The Die-Hards; Old Samurai Never Die; Losers' Luck **A:** Nestor Redondo; Tony DeZuniga **W:** Arnold Drake; George Kashdan; Jack Oleck

14 ❑ Jun 1973 Cover: 0.20 **NM** value: **8.00**
Dream of Disaster; A Phantom for a Co-Pilot; Too Late for the Death March!; The Ghost of McBride's Woman **W:** Sheldon Mayer

15 ❑ Jul 1973 Cover: 0.20 **NM** value: **8.00**
"Ace" King Just Flew in From Hell; The Survivor; The Ultimate Weapon **A:** Don Perlin; Gerry Talaoc **W:** Arnold Drake; Jack Oleck

16 ❑ Aug 1973 Cover: 0.20 **NM** value: **8.00**
• **CGC:** 1 graded, best 9.6
More Dead Than Alive; The Conquerors; Evil Eye **A:** Alfredo Alcala **W:** Arnold Drake; Jack Oleck

17 ❑ Sep 1973 Cover: 0.20 **NM** value: **8.00**
• **CGC:** 1 graded, best 9.2
Dead Man's Hands; A Gun Named Marie! **A:** George Evans; Ernie Chua **W:** E. Nelson Bridwell; Robert Kanigher

18 ❑ Oct 1973 Cover: 0.20 **NM** value: **8.00**
• **CGC:** 1 graded, best 7.0
Captain Dracula; Whim of a Phantom! **A:** Tony DeZuniga; Gerry Talaoc **W:** Arnold Drake; Shelly Meyer

19 ❑ Nov 1973 Cover: 0.20 **NM** value: **8.00**
• **CGC:** 1 graded, best 8.0
The Platoon That Wouldn't Die! **A:** Gerry Talaoc **W:** Arnold Drake

20 ❑ Dec 1973 Cover: 0.20 **NM** value: **8.00**
• **CGC:** 1 graded, best 9.2

21 ❑ Jan 1974 Cover: 0.20 **NM** value: **6.00**
One Hour to Kill; When Death Took a Hand **A:** Frank Robbins; Bernard Baily **W:** Sheldon Mayer; Jack Oleck

22 ❑ Feb 1974 Cover: 0.20 **NM** value: **6.00**
Wings of Death; Last Rites for the Living **A:** George Evans; Tony DeZuniga **W:** Arnold Drake; Jack Oleck

23 ❑ Mar 1974 Cover: 0.20 **NM** value: **6.00**
The Bird of Death; Day After Doomsday **A:** Alfredo Alcala **W:** John Albano

24 ❑ Apr 1974 Cover: 0.20 **NM** value: **6.00**

25 ❑ May 1974 Cover: 0.20 **NM** value: **6.00**
Black Magic White Death!; The Unseen Warrior **A:** Alfredo Alcala **W:** George Kashdan

26 ❑ Jun 1974 Cover: 0.20 **NM** value: **6.00**

27 ❑ Jul 1974 Cover: 0.20 **NM** value: **6.00**
• **CGC:** 1 graded, best 9.4

28 ❑ Aug 1974 Cover: 0.20 **NM** value: **6.00**
Isle of Forgotten Warriors **A:** Alfredo Alcala **W:** George Kashdan

29 ❑ Sep 1974 Cover: 0.20 **NM** value: **6.00**
Breaking Point; The Hunted; The Phantom Bowmen of Crecy **A:** Ernie Chua; Gerry Talaoc **W:** Jack Oleck

30 ❑ Oct 1974 Cover: 0.20 **NM** value: **6.00**

31 ❑ Nov 1974 Cover: 0.20 **NM** value: **6.00**

32 ❑ Dec 1974 Cover: 0.20 **NM** value: **5.00**

33 ❑ Jan 1975 Cover: 0.25 **NM** value: **5.00**
Circ: Statement: **159,000**

34 ❑ Feb 1975 Cover: 0.25 **NM** value: **5.00**
Circ: Statement: **159,000**
The Common Enemy; The Flying Coffins; To His Rescue Came a Maiden **A:** Ricardo Villamonte; Jack Sparling; Rubeny **W:** Arnold Drake; George Kashdan; Robert Kanigher

35 ❑ Mar 1975 Cover: 0.25 **NM** value: **5.00**
Circ: Statement: **159,000**

36 ❑ Apr 1975 Cover: 0.50 **NM** value: **5.00**
Circ: Statement: **159,000** • **CGC:** 2 graded, best 9.6

37 ❑ May 1975 Cover: 0.25 **NM** value: **5.00**
Circ: Statement: **159,000**

38 ❑ Jun 1975 Cover: 0.25 **NM** value: **5.00**
Circ: Statement: **159,000**

39 ❑ Jul 1975 Cover: 0.25 **NM** value: **5.00**
Circ: Statement: **159,000**

40 ❑ Aug 1975 Cover: 0.25 **NM** value: **5.00**
Circ: Statement: **159,000**

41 ❑ Sep 1975 Cover: 0.25 **NM** value: **5.00**
Circ: Statement: **159,000**

42 ❑ Oct 1975 Cover: 0.25 **NM** value: **5.00**
Circ: Statement: **159,000**
Old Soldiers Never Die; Twice Dead; The Day After Doomsday **A:** Ernie Chua; Ricardo Villamonte; Alfredo Alcala; Quico Redondo **W:** Sheldon Mayer; Jack Oleck

43 ❑ Nov 1975 Cover: 0.25 **NM** value: **5.00**
Circ: Statement: **159,000**

44 ❑ Jan 1976 Cover: 0.25 **NM** value: **5.00**
Circ: Statement: **136,000**

45 ❑ Mar 1976 **NM** value: **5.00**
Circ: Statement: **136,000**

46 ❑ May 1976 Cover: 0.30 **NM** value: **5.00**
Circ: Statement: **136,000**

47 ❑ Jul 1976 Cover: 0.30 **NM** value: **5.00**
Circ: Statement: **136,000**

48 ❑ Sep 1976 Cover: 0.30 **NM** value: **5.00**
Circ: Statement: **136,000**

49 ❑ Nov 1976 Cover: 0.30 **NM** value: **5.00**
Circ: Statement: **136,000**
The Face of the Enemy; A Rite to Die; The Day After Doomsday; Mark of the Conqueror **A:** Ernie Chua; Ricardo Villamonte; Steve Ditko; Bill Draut; Vince Colletta; Leopoldo Durañona **W:** Steve Skeates; George Kashdan; Jack Oleck

50 ❑ Jan 1977 Cover: 0.30 **NM** value: **5.00**
Circ: Statement: **122,284**

51 ❑ Mar 1977 Cover: 0.30 **NM** value: **4.00**
Circ: Statement: **122,284**

52 ❑ Apr 1977 Cover: 0.30 **NM** value: **4.00**
Circ: Statement: **122,284**

53 ❑ May 1977 Cover: 0.30 **NM** value: **4.00**
Circ: Statement: **122,284**
• Has 1976 Statement; avg total paid 136,000

54 ❑ Jul 1977 Cover: 0.35 **NM** value: **4.00**
Circ: Statement: **122,284**

55 ❑ Sep 1977 Cover: 0.35 **NM** value: **4.00**
Circ: Statement: **122,284**

56 ❑ Oct 1977 Cover: 0.35 **NM** value: **4.00**
Circ: Statement: **122,284**

57 ❑ Nov 1977 Cover: 0.35 **NM** value: **4.00**
Circ: Statement: **122,284**

58 ❑ Dec 1977 Cover: 0.35 **NM** value: **4.00**
Circ: Statement: **122,284**

59 ❑ Jan 1978 Cover: 0.35 **NM** value: **4.00**

60 ❑ Feb 1978 Cover: 0.35 **NM** value: **4.00**

61 ❑ Mar 1978 Cover: 0.35 **NM** value: **4.00**
Mind War; The Mercenary **A:** Dave Morris; Howard Chaykin; Alex Ni±o **W:** Robert Kanigher; Roger McKenzie

62 ❑ Apr 1978 Cover: 0.35 **NM** value: **4.00**

63 ❑ May 1978 Cover: 0.35 **NM** value: **4.00**
• Has 1977 Statement, filed 10/1/77; avg print run 308,478; avg sales 121,697; avg subs 587; avg total paid 122,284; samples 200; office use 75; max existent 122,559; 60% of run returned

64 ❑ Jun 1978 Cover: 0.35 **NM** value: **4.00**
Deliver Me From D-Day; Beachhead; The Day After Doomsday; The Sand-in **A:** Frank Miller; Juan Ortiz; Dan Bulanadi **C:** Joe Kubert **W:** Roger McKenzie; Wyatt Gwyon

65 ❑ Jul 1978 Cover: 0.35 **NM** value: **4.00**

66 ❑ Aug 1978 Cover: 0.35 **NM** value: **4.00**
The Iron Star **A:** Tom Sutton **W:** Bob Toomey

67 ❑ Sep 1978 Cover: 0.50 **NM** value: **4.00**

68 ❑ Oct 1978 Cover: 0.50 **NM** value: **4.00**
Rotirra-The Monster-Weapon!; Batman and the Corsair of Crime; The Life and Death of Charlie Golem; The Greatest Story Never Told **A:** Frank Miller **W:** Bob Rozakis

69 ❑ Nov 1978 Cover: 0.50 **NM** value: **4.00**

70 ❑ Dec 1978 Cover: 0.40 **NM** value: **4.00**

71 ❑ Jan 1979 Cover: 0.40 **NM** value: **4.00**

72 ❑ Feb 1979 **NM** value: **4.00**

73 ❑ Mar 1979 **NM** value: **4.00**

74 ❑ Apr 1979 **NM** value: **4.00**

75 ❑ May 1979 **NM** value: **4.00**

76 ❑ Jun 1979 Cover: 0.40 **NM** value: **4.00**

77 ❑ Jul 1979 Cover: 0.40 **NM** value: **4.00**

78 ❑ Aug 1979 Cover: 0.40 **NM** value: **4.00**

79 ❑ Sep 1979 Cover: 0.40 **NM** value: **4.00**

80 ❑ Oct 1979 Cover: 0.40 **NM** value: **4.00**
An Old Man's Profession; Heads Up; Ring of Fire!; Technology … 13th Century Style **A:** Ric Estrada; Romeo Tanghal; Sid Greene; Jess Jodloman; Ruben Yandoc **W:** Paul Kupperberg; Robert Kanigher; Steve Gerber

81 ❑ Nov 1979 Cover: 0.40 **NM** value: **4.00**

82 ❑ Dec 1979 Cover: 0.40 **NM** value: **4.00**
Funeral By Fire; The Toy Battle; An Outbreak of Peace **A:** Don Newton; Howard Chaykin; Dave Hunt; Rubeny **W:** George Kashdan

83 ❑ Jan 1980 Cover: 0.40 **NM** value: **4.00**

84 ❑ Feb 1980 Cover: 0.40 **NM** value: **4.00**

85 ❑ Mar 1980 Cover: 0.40 **NM** value: **4.00**

86 ❑ Apr 1980 Cover: 0.40 **NM** value: **4.00**

87 ❑ May 1980 Cover: 0.40 **NM** value: **4.00**

88 ❑ Jun 1980 Cover: 0.40 **NM** value: **4.00**

89 ❑ Jul 1980 Cover: 0.40 **NM** value: **4.00**

90 ❑ Aug 1980 Cover: 0.40 **NM** value: **4.00**

91 ❑ Sep 1980 Cover: 0.50 **NM** value: **4.00**

92 ❑ Oct 1980 Cover: 0.50 **NM** value: **4.00**

93 ❑ Nov 1980 Cover: 0.50 **NM** value: **5.00**

94 ❑ Dec 1980 Cover: 0.50 **NM** value: **4.00**

95 ❑ Jan 1981 Cover: 0.50 **NM** value: **4.00**
Circ: Statement: **80,000**

96 ❑ Feb 1981 Cover: 0.50 **NM** value: **4.00**
Circ: Statement: **80,000**

97 ❑ Mar 1981 Cover: 0.50 **NM** value: **4.00**
Circ: Statement: **80,000**

98 ❑ Apr 1981 Cover: 0.50 **NM** value: **4.00**
Circ: Statement: **80,000**

99 ❑ May 1981 Cover: 0.50 **NM** value: **4.00**
Circ: Statement: **80,000**

100 ❑ Jun 1981 Cover: 0.50 **NM** value: **4.00**
Circ: Statement: **80,000**
• Creature Commandos in War That Time Forgot **C:** Joe Kubert

101 ❑ Jul 1981 Cover: 0.50 **NM** value: **4.00**
Circ: Statement: **80,000**

102 ❑ Aug 1981 Cover: 0.50 **NM** value: **3.00**
Circ: Statement: **80,000**
• Creature Commandos captured by Hitler

103 ❑ Sep 1981 Cover: 0.50 **NM** value: **3.00**
Circ: Statement: **80,000**

104 ❑ Oct 1981 Cover: 0.60 **NM** value: **3.00**
Circ: Statement: **80,000**

105 ❑ Nov 1981 Cover: 0.60 **NM** value: **3.00**
Circ: Statement: **80,000**
• Creature Commandos

106 ❑ Dec 1981 Cover: 0.60 **NM** value: **3.00**
Circ: Statement: **80,000**

107 ❑ Jan 1982 Cover: 0.60 **NM** value: **3.00**
Circ: Statement: **67,978**

108 ❑ Feb 1982 Cover: 0.60 **NM** value: **3.00**
Circ: Statement: **67,978**
• Creature Commandos, G.I. Robot

109 ❑ Mar 1982 Cover: 0.60 **NM** value: **3.00**
Circ: Statement: **67,978**
• Creature Commandos

110 ❑ Apr 1982 Cover: 0.60 **NM** value: **3.00**
Circ: Statement: **67,978**

111 ❑ May 1982 Cover: 0.60 **NM** value: **3.00**
Circ: Statement: **67,978**
• G.I. Robot teams with Creature Commandos

112 ❑ Jun 1982 Cover: 0.60 **NM** value: **3.00**
Circ: Statement: **67,978**
• Creature Commandos

113 ❑ Jul 1982 Cover: 0.60 **NM** value: **3.00**
Circ: Statement: **67,978**

114 ❑ Aug 1982 Cover: 0.60 **NM** value: **3.00**
Circ: Statement: **67,978** • **CGC:** 1 graded, best 9.0
• Creature Commandos ★ Appearance of Hitler.

115 ❑ Sep 1982 Cover: 0.60 **NM** value: **3.00**
Circ: Statement: **67,978**
• G.I. Robot II and Creature Commandos

116 ❑ Oct 1982 Cover: 0.60 **NM** value: **3.00**
Circ: Statement: **67,978**
Doorway to Hell; The Lonely Robot • G.I. Robot II and Creature Commandos **A:** Carmine Infantino; Fred Carrillo **W:** Robert Kanigher

117 ❑ Nov 1982 Cover: 0.60 **NM** value: **3.00**
Circ: Statement: **67,978**
• G.I. Robot II and Creature Commandos

118 ❑ Dec 1982 Cover: 0.60 **NM** value: **3.00**
Circ: Statement: **67,978**

119 ❑ Jan 1983 Cover: 0.60 **NM** value: **3.00**
• Creature Commandos

120 ❑ Feb 1983 Cover: 0.60 **NM** value: **3.00**
• G.I. Robot

121 ❑ Mar 1983 Cover: 0.60 **NM** value: **3.00**
• Creature Commandos

122 ❑ Apr 1983 Cover: 0.60 **NM** value: **3.00**
• G.I. Robot vs. Sumo Robot

123 ❑ May 1983 Cover: 0.60 **NM** value: **3.00**
• Has 1982 Statement, filed 10/1/82; avg print run 220,120; avg sales 67,278, avg subs 700; avg total paid 67,978; samples 677; office use 2,073; max existent 70,728; 68% of run returned

124 ❑ Jun 1983 Cover: 0.60 **NM** value: **3.00**
final issue.

WEIRD WAR TALES (MINI-SERIES) DC

1 ❑ Jun 1997 Cover: 2.50 **NM** value: **Cover or less**
Circ: Diamd. preorders: **37,598**
The Survivor; Ares; The Willow Warriors; Tunnel Rats **A:** Richard Corben; Randy DuBurke; James Romberger; Eric Shanower **W:** Simon Revelstroke; Brian Azzarello; Gordon Rennie; Ian Edginton

2 ❑ Jul 1997 Cover: 2.50 **NM** value: **Cover or less**
Circ: Diamd. preorders: **28,699**
Looking Good, Feeling Great; Mightier; The Elopement **A:** David Lloyd; Sam Glanzman; Peter Kuper **W:** David Lloyd; Peter Kuper; Joe Lansdale

3 ❑ Aug 1997 Cover: 2.50 **NM** value: **Cover or less**
Circ: Diamd. preorders: **27,575**
New Toys; Sniper's Alley; Run **A:** Frank Quitely; George Pratt; Eric Cherry **W:** Grant Morrison; Joel Rose; Paul Jenkins

4 ❑ Sep 1997 Cover: 2.50 **NM** value: **Cover or less**
Circ: Diamd. preorders: **25,889**

SE 1 ❑ Apr 2000 Cover: 4.95 **NM** value: **Cover or less**
Circ: Diamd. preorders: **13,493**
Noah and Barry and Eddie and Joe; The Isihlangu; The Spoils of War; Mind Field; Esprit de Corps; A Prayer to the Sun **A:** Danijel Zezelj; Paul Pope; Frank Teran; Jim Lee; Quique Alcatena; Darko Macan **W:** Edvin Biukovic; Bruce Jones; Chuck Dixon; Garth Ennis; Greg Rucka; Robert Rodi

WEIRD WEST Fantaco

1 ❑ Cover: 2.95 **NM** value: **Cover or less**

2 ❑ Cover: 2.95 **NM** value: **Cover or less**

3 ❑ Cover: 2.95 **NM** value: **Cover or less**

Other grades: Multiply prices above by **1.5 for Mint • 2/3 for Very Fine • 1/3 for Fine • 1/5 for Very Good • 1/8 for Good**

WEIRD WESTERN TALES — DC

The series started staidly enough, with old timer Pow Wow Smith and the title All-Star Western. Stories soon featured Gray Morrow's El Diablo, a mysterious gun-fighter with supernatural powers. Though Billy the Kid roamed the pages, when the grotesque and lethal Jonah Hex was introduced in #10, it quickly became clear that more unusual changes were in the works.

Stories involved adventure and mystery set in the old West. Scalphunter showed up in #39, a light-skinned Indian who faced persecution by both white settlers and his own people. The romps of Bat Lash sometimes lightened the mood, but the title was designed to attract fans of, yes, weird Westerns.

12 ❑ Jun 1972 Cover: 0.25 **NM** value: **30.00**
• **CGC:** 7 graded, best 9.6
• Series continued from All-Star Western #11 **A:** Bernie Wrightson; Neal Adams
13 ❑ Aug 1972 Cover: 0.20 **NM** value: **25.00**
• **CGC:** 1 graded, best 9.4
14 ❑ Oct 1972 Cover: 0.20 **NM** value: **20.00**
• **CGC:** 3 graded, best 9.2
15 ❑ Dec 1972 Cover: 0.20 **NM** value: **20.00**
• **CGC:** 1 graded, best 9.0
📖 Never Kill a Demon; Hang Him High; The Ballad of Doc Satan **A:** Neal Adams; Gil Kane **W:** Cary Bates; Jack Oleck
16 ❑ Feb 1973 Cover: 0.20 **NM** value: **12.00**
17 ❑ Apr 1973 Cover: 0.20 **NM** value: **12.00**
18 ❑ Jul 1973 Cover: 0.20 **NM** value: **12.00**
• Jonah Hex issue
19 ❑ Sep 1973 Cover: 0.20 **NM** value: **12.00**
20 ❑ Nov 1973 Cover: 0.20 **NM** value: **12.00**
• **CGC:** 1 graded, best 8.5
21 ❑ Jan 1974 Cover: 0.20 **NM** value: **12.00**
• **CGC:** 1 graded, best 9.6
22 ❑ May 1974 Cover: 0.20 **NM** value: **12.00**
23 ❑ Jul 1974 Cover: 0.20 **NM** value: **12.00**
24 ❑ Sep 1974 Cover: 0.20 **NM** value: **12.00**
• blind Jonah Hex
25 ❑ Nov 1974 Cover: 0.20 **NM** value: **12.00**
• **CGC:** 1 graded, best 9.2
26 ❑ Jan 1975 Cover: 0.25 **NM** value: **12.00**
Circ: Statement: **152,000**
27 ❑ Mar 1975 Cover: 0.25 **NM** value: **12.00**
Circ: Statement: **152,000**
28 ❑ May 1975 Cover: 0.25 **NM** value: **12.00**
Circ: Statement: **152,000**
29 ❑ Jul 1975 Cover: 0.25 **NM** value: **16.00**
Circ: Statement: **152,000**
30 ❑ Sep 1975 Cover: 0.25 **NM** value: **6.00**
Circ: Statement: **152,000**
31 ❑ Nov 1975 Cover: 0.25 **NM** value: **6.00**
Circ: Statement: **152,000**
32 ❑ Jan 1976 Cover: 0.25 **NM** value: **6.00**
33 ❑ Mar 1976 Cover: 0.25 **NM** value: **6.00**
34 ❑ May 1976 Cover: 0.30 **NM** value: **6.00**
35 ❑ Jul 1976 Cover: 0.30 **NM** value: **6.00**
36 ❑ Sep 1976 Cover: 0.30 **NM** value: **6.00**
37 ❑ Nov 1976 Cover: 0.30 **NM** value: **6.00**
38 ❑ Jan 1977 Cover: 0.30 **NM** value: **6.00**
Circ: Statement: **107,334**
39 ❑ Mar 1977 Cover: 0.30 **NM** value: **6.00**
Circ: Statement: **107,334** • **CGC:** 1 graded, best 9.6
40 ❑ Jun 1977 Cover: 0.30 **NM** value: **6.00**
Circ: Statement: **107,334**
41 ❑ Aug 1977 Cover: 0.35 **NM** value: **6.00**
Circ: Statement: **107,334**
42 ❑ Oct 1977 Cover: 0.35 **NM** value: **6.00**
Circ: Statement: **107,334**
43 ❑ Dec 1977 Cover: 0.35 **NM** value: **6.00**
Circ: Statement: **107,334**
44 ❑ Feb 1978 Cover: 0.35 **NM** value: **6.00**
Circ: Statement: **100,414**
45 ❑ Apr 1978 Cover: 0.35 **NM** value: **6.00**
Circ: Statement: **100,414**
46 ❑ Jun 1978 Cover: 0.35 **NM** value: **6.00**
Circ: Statement: **100,414**
• Has 1977 Statement; avg total paid circ 107,334
47 ❑ Aug 1978 Cover: 0.35 **NM** value: **6.00**
Circ: Statement: **100,414**
48 ❑ Oct 1978 Cover: 0.50 **NM** value: **6.00**
Circ: Statement: **100,414**
49 ❑ Nov 1978 Cover: 0.50 **NM** value: **6.00**
Circ: Statement: **100,414**
50 ❑ Dec 1978 Cover: 0.40 **NM** value: **6.00**
Circ: Statement: **100,414**
51 ❑ Jan 1979 Cover: 0.40 **NM** value: **5.00**
52 ❑ Feb 1979 Cover: 0.40 **NM** value: **5.00**
53 ❑ Mar 1979 Cover: 0.40 **NM** value: **5.00**
54 ❑ Apr 1979 Cover: 0.40 **NM** value: **5.00**
55 ❑ May 1979 Cover: 0.40 **NM** value: **5.00**
56 ❑ Jun 1979 Cover: 0.40 **NM** value: **5.00**
57 ❑ Jul 1979 Cover: 0.40 **NM** value: **5.00**
58 ❑ Aug 1979 Cover: 0.40 **NM** value: **5.00**
59 ❑ Sep 1979 Cover: 0.40 **NM** value: **5.00**
60 ❑ Oct 1979 Cover: 0.40 **NM** value: **5.00**
• **CGC:** 1 graded, best 9.8
61 ❑ Nov 1979 Cover: 0.40 **NM** value: **5.00**
62 ❑ Dec 1979 Cover: 0.40 **NM** value: **5.00**
• **CGC:** 1 graded, best 9.6
63 ❑ Jan 1980 Cover: 0.40 **NM** value: **5.00**
• **CGC:** 1 graded, best 9.6
64 ❑ Feb 1980 Cover: 0.40 **NM** value: **5.00**
65 ❑ Mar 1980 Cover: 0.40 **NM** value: **5.00**
66 ❑ Apr 1980 Cover: 0.40 **NM** value: **5.00**
67 ❑ May 1980 Cover: 0.40 **NM** value: **5.00**
• **CGC:** 1 graded, best 9.8
68 ❑ Jun 1980 Cover: 0.40 **NM** value: **5.00**
69 ❑ Jul 1980 Cover: 0.40 **NM** value: **5.00**
70 ❑ Aug 1980 Cover: 0.40 **NM** value: **5.00**
final issue.

WEIRD WESTERN TALES (MINI-SERIES) — DC / Vertigo

1 ❑ Apr 2001 Cover: 2.50 **NM** value: **Cover or less**
Circ: Diamd. preorders: **13,113**
📖 Tall Tale; Serial Hero; This Gun for Hire **A:** Dave Gibbons; Paul Pope; Rich Burchett **W:** Dave Gibbons; Paul Pope; Greg Rucka
2 ❑ May 2001 Cover: 2.50 **NM** value: **Cover or less**
Circ: Diamd. preorders: **11,441**
📖 First Among Men; Palomino; Devil's Sombrero **A:** Marcelo Frusin; Sam Glanzman; Paul Gulacy **W:** Darko Macan; Joe Pruett; Joe R. Lansdale
3 ❑ Jun 2001 Cover: 2.50 **NM** value: **Cover or less**
Circ: Diamd. preorders: **11,191**
📖 Settlers; The Confession of Gabriel Winters; Once Upon a Time in the Future **A:** Danijel Zezelj; Doug Wheatley; Eduardo Risso **W:** Scott Cunningham; Brett Lewis; Nicholas Burns
4 ❑ Jul 2001 Cover: 2.50 **NM** value: **Cover or less**
Circ: Diamd. preorders: **10,902**

WEIRD WONDER TALES — Marvel

1 ❑ Dec 1973 Cover: 0.20 **NM** value: **4.00**
• **CGC:** 1 graded, best 8.0
• Reprints Mystic #6 (Eye of Doom)
2 ❑ Feb 1974 Cover: 0.20 **NM** value: **2.50**
3 ❑ Apr 1974 Cover: 0.20 **NM** value: **2.50**
• **CGC:** 1 graded, best 9.4
4 ❑ Jun 1974 Cover: 0.25 **NM** value: **2.50**
5 ❑ Aug 1974 Cover: 0.25 **NM** value: **2.50**
6 ❑ Oct 1974 Cover: 0.25 **NM** value: **2.50**
7 ❑ Dec 1974 Cover: 0.25 **NM** value: **2.50**
8 ❑ Feb 1975 Cover: 0.25 **NM** value: **2.50**
9 ❑ Apr 1975 Cover: 0.25 **NM** value: **2.50**
• **CGC:** 1 graded, best 9.4
10 ❑ Jun 1975 Cover: 0.25 **NM** value: **2.50**
11 ❑ Aug 1975 Cover: 0.25 **NM** value: **2.50**
12 ❑ Oct 1975 Cover: 0.25 **NM** value: **2.50**
13 ❑ Dec 1975 Cover: 0.25 **NM** value: **2.50**
• **CGC:** 1 graded, best 8.5
14 ❑ Feb 1976 Cover: 0.25 **NM** value: **2.50**
• **CGC:** 1 graded, best 8.5
15 ❑ Apr 1976 Cover: 0.25 **NM** value: **2.50**
• **CGC:** 2 graded, best 9.4
16 ❑ Jun 1976 Cover: 0.25 **NM** value: **2.50**
• **CGC:** 1 graded, best 7.0
17 ❑ Aug 1976 Cover: 0.25 **NM** value: **2.50**
• **CGC:** 1 graded, best 9.0
18 ❑ Oct 1976 Cover: 0.30 **NM** value: **2.50**
19 ❑ Dec 1976 Cover: 0.30 **NM** value: **2.50**
📖 I Am Dr. Druid!; I Challend...Groot!; The Hypnotist! • Doctor Druid; Reprints from Tales to Astonish #13, Astonishing Tales #47 **A:** Bernie Krigstein
20 ❑ Jan 1977 Cover: 0.30 **NM** value: **2.50**
• Doctor Druid
21 ❑ Mar 1977 Cover: 0.30 **NM** value: **2.50**
• **CGC:** 1 graded, best 9.2
• Doctor Druid
22 ❑ May 1977 Cover: 0.30 **NM** value: **2.50**
• Doctor Druid

WEIRD WORLDS — DC

Edgar Rice Burroughs created heroic fiction in more than one setting. Best-known for his jungle tales of Tarzan (first appearing in 1912), he also wrote stories set on Barsoom (Mars, in stories also with a 1912 debut), featuring John Carter, and Pellucidar (starting in 1914, set in the interior of the planet Earth, where dinosaurs still roamed). Their pulp-fiction origins were translated to swashbuckling stories featuring sword-wielding heroes and gorgeous women in peril, obvious elements that work well in comics.

The first issue made a simple transition from the earlier back-ups in Gold Key's Tarzan and Korak titles. The Burroughs influences can be felt in later comic-book series, even after this title was long gone. — Maggie

1 ❑ Sep 1972 Cover: 0.20 **NM** value: **4.00**
• **CGC:** 3 graded, best 9.4
📖 The Arena of Sudden Death; Trial of Fear • continues John Carter of Mars from Tarzan #209 and Pellucidar from Korak **A:** Alan Weiss **W:** Len Wein
2 ❑ Nov 1972 Cover: 0.20 **NM** value: **3.00**
• **CGC:** 1 graded, best 9.6
• adapts Burroughs' Pellucidar and Martian novels
3 ❑ Jan 1973 Cover: 0.20 **NM** value: **3.00**
• adapts Burroughs' Pellucidar and Martian novels
4 ❑ Mar 1973 Cover: 0.20 **NM** value: **2.50**
• **CGC:** 1 graded, best 9.6
• adapts Burroughs' Pellucidar and Martian novels
5 ❑ May 1973 Cover: 0.20 **NM** value: **2.50**
• **CGC:** 1 graded, best 9.6
• adapts Burroughs' Pellucidar and Martian novels
6 ❑ Aug 1973 Cover: 0.20 **NM** value: **2.00**
• adapts Burroughs' Pellucidar and Martian novels
7 ❑ Oct 1973 Cover: 0.20 **NM** value: **2.00**
• **CGC:** 1 graded, best 9.2
• adapts Burroughs' Pellucidar and Martian novels; John Carter, Warlord of Mars ends
8 ❑ Dec 1973 Cover: 0.20 **NM** value: **2.00**
9 ❑ Feb 1974 Cover: 0.20 **NM** value: **2.00**
• Iron Wolf **A:** Howard Chaykin
10 ❑ Nov 1974 Cover: 0.20 **NM** value: **2.00**
final issue. • Iron Wolf **A:** Howard Chaykin

WELCOME BACK, KOTTER — DC

Actor John Travolta got his break as one of the young "Sweathogs" in the 1975-79 television series which also enjoyed a 10-issue run as a comic book. Gabriel Kotter returns as a teacher to the inner-city Brooklyn high school he'd attended as a teen. His class consists of a variety of young Sweathogs (a nickname for incorrigible students), including slow-witted pretty boy Vinnie Barbarino; deadbeat liar Juan Epstein; perpetually disruptive Freddy "Boom Boom" Washington; and the sometimes weird and always unintelligible Arnold Horshack. These rascals immediately take to their new teacher, a wise-cracking joker himself.

Technically, Kotter is supposed to be teaching the Sweathogs social studies, but little traditional teaching goes on in his classroom. On the other hand, some might consider his lighthearted banter — and the real-life issues his students discuss — social studies of another sort.

1 ❑ Nov 1976 Cover: 0.30 **NM** value: **4.00**
• **CGC:** 5 graded, best 9.6
• based on ABC TV series
2 ❑ Jan 1977 Cover: 0.30 **NM** value: **2.50**
3 ❑ Mar 1977 Cover: 0.30 **NM** value: **2.50**
4 ❑ May 1977 Cover: 0.30 **NM** value: **2.50**
5 ❑ Jul 1977 Cover: 0.35 **NM** value: **2.50**
6 ❑ Sep 1977 Cover: 0.35 **NM** value: **2.50**
7 ❑ Nov 1977 Cover: 0.35 **NM** value: **2.50**
• **CGC:** 1 graded, best 9.2
8 ❑ Jan 1978 Cover: 0.35 **NM** value: **2.50**
9 ❑ Feb 1978 Cover: 0.35 **NM** value: **2.50**
10 ❑ Mar 1978 Cover: 0.35 **NM** value: **2.50**
final issue.

WELCOME BACK TO THE HOUSE OF MYSTERY — DC / Vertigo

1 ❑ Jul 1998 Cover: 5.95 **NM** value: **Cover or less**
Circ: Diamd. preorders: **14,229** • **CGC:** 1 graded, best 9.6
📖 The Gourmet; Nightmare; The Secret of the Egyptian Cat; The House of Endless Years; The Demon Within!; The Burning!; His Name is Kane; Oh, Mom! Oh, Dad!, You've Sent Me Away to Summer Camp and I'm So Sad!; Molded in Evil • collects stories from House of Mystery and Plop **A:** Berni Wrightson; Sergio Aragonés; Gil Kane; Mike Sekowsky; Alex N; John Albano; Wally Wood(inks) **W:** Joe Orlando; Steve Skeates; Jack Oleck; Maxene Fabe; Michael Fleisher; Mike Friedrich; Neil Gaiman

WELCOME TO THE LITTLE SHOP OF HORRORS — Roger Corman's Cosmic Comics

1 ❑ May 1995 Cover: 2.50 **NM** value: **Cover or less**
Circ: CapCity orders: **2,675**
2 ❑ Jun 1995 Cover: 2.50 **NM** value: **Cover or less**
3 ❑ Jul 1995 Cover: 2.50 **NM** value: **Cover or less**

WELCOME TO THE ZONE — Kitchen Sink

1 ❑ Cover: 9.95 **NM** value: **Cover or less**

WENDEL — Kitchen Sink

All issues are adults only.
1 ❑ b&w Cover: 2.95 **NM** value: **Cover or less**

WENDY, THE GOOD LITTLE WITCH (VOL. 1) — Harvey

Wendy, the Good Little Witch, doesn't fit the stereotype of the bad fairy-tale witch. A kindhearted little girl, Wendy only performs good deeds with her magic. This causes great disappointment for her aunts, the traditionally haggard-looking Witch Sisters. As a result, they frequently arrange for nasty tricks for Wendy and her friends. Wendy's good nature always wins out in the end, however, with a little help from her own magic.

Originally a television character appearing in episodes of the adventures of Casper the Friendly Ghost, Wendy's adventures translate well to comic-book form. Casper also makes frequent appearances in this series.

1 ❑ Aug 1960 Cover: 0.10 **NM** value: **60.00**
• **CGC:** 1 graded, best 9.0
2 ❑ Oct 1960 Cover: 0.10 **NM** value: **40.00**
• **CGC:** 1 graded, best 9.0
3 ❑ Dec 1960 Cover: 0.10 **NM** value: **28.00**
• **CGC:** 1 graded, best 8.0

CGC-graded: Multiply prices above by **33 for 9.9 M • 16 for 9.8 NM/M • 7 for 9.6 NM+ • 5 for 9.4 NM • 2.5 for 9.2 NM- • 1.5 for 9.0 VF/NM**

4 ❑ Feb 1961 Cover: 0.10 NM value: 28.00
5 ❑ Apr 1961 Cover: 0.10 NM value: 28.00
6 ❑ Jun 1961 Cover: 0.10 NM value: 22.00
7 ❑ Aug 1961 Cover: 0.10 NM value: 22.00
8 ❑ Oct 1961 Cover: 0.10 NM value: 22.00
9 ❑ Dec 1961 Cover: 0.10 NM value: 22.00
10 ❑ Feb 1962 Cover: 0.10 NM value: 22.00
11 ❑ Apr 1962 Cover: 0.10 NM value: 14.00
12 ❑ Jun 1962 Cover: 0.12 NM value: 14.00
13 ❑ Aug 1962 Cover: 0.12 NM value: 14.00
14 ❑ Oct 1962 Cover: 0.12 NM value: 14.00
15 ❑ Dec 1962 Cover: 0.12 NM value: 14.00
16 ❑ Feb 1963 Cover: 0.12 NM value: 12.00
17 ❑ Apr 1963 Cover: 0.12 NM value: 12.00
18 ❑ Jun 1963 Cover: 0.12 NM value: 12.00
19 ❑ Aug 1963 Cover: 0.12 NM value: 12.00
20 ❑ Oct 1963 Cover: 0.12 NM value: 12.00
21 ❑ Dec 1963 Cover: 0.12 NM value: 8.00
22 ❑ Feb 1964 Cover: 0.12 NM value: 8.00
23 ❑ Apr 1964 Cover: 0.12 NM value: 8.00
24 ❑ Jun 1964 Cover: 0.12 NM value: 8.00
25 ❑ Aug 1964 Cover: 0.12 NM value: 8.00
26 ❑ Oct 1964 Cover: 0.12 NM value: 6.00
27 ❑ Dec 1964 Cover: 0.12 NM value: 6.00
28 ❑ Feb 1965 Cover: 0.12 NM value: 6.00
29 ❑ Apr 1965 Cover: 0.12 NM value: 6.00
30 ❑ Jun 1965 Cover: 0.12 NM value: 6.00
31 ❑ Aug 1965 Cover: 0.12 NM value: 5.00
32 ❑ Oct 1965 Cover: 0.12 NM value: 5.00
33 ❑ Dec 1965 Cover: 0.12 NM value: 5.00
34 ❑ Feb 1966 Cover: 0.12 NM value: 5.00
📖 House in Town; Brooms Are Better; I Don't Scare Anybody; Casper: Call the Witch Doctor (text); Spooky: Wish and Wish Again
35 ❑ Apr 1966 Cover: 0.12 NM value: 5.00
36 ❑ Jun 1966 Cover: 0.12 NM value: 5.00
37 ❑ Aug 1966 Cover: 0.12 NM value: 5.00
38 ❑ Oct 1966 Cover: 0.12 NM value: 5.00
39 ❑ Dec 1966 Cover: 0.12 NM value: 5.00
40 ❑ Feb 1967 Cover: 0.12 NM value: 5.00
41 ❑ Apr 1967 Cover: 0.12 NM value: 4.00
42 ❑ Jun 1967 Cover: 0.12 NM value: 4.00
43 ❑ Aug 1967 Cover: 0.12 NM value: 4.00
44 ❑ Oct 1967 Cover: 0.12 NM value: 4.00
45 ❑ Dec 1967 Cover: 0.12 NM value: 4.00
46 ❑ Feb 1968 Cover: 0.12 NM value: 4.00
47 ❑ Apr 1968 Cover: 0.12 NM value: 4.00
48 ❑ Jun 1968 Cover: 0.12 NM value: 4.00
49 ❑ 1968 Cover: 0.12 NM value: 4.00
50 ❑ Dec 1968 Cover: 0.12 NM value: 4.00
51 ❑ Jan 1969 Cover: 0.12 NM value: 3.00
52 ❑ Feb 1969 Cover: 0.12 NM value: 3.00
53 ❑ 1969 Cover: 0.12 NM value: 3.00
54 ❑ 1969 Cover: 0.12 NM value: 3.00
55 ❑ Jul 1969 Cover: 0.12 NM value: 3.00
• CGC: 1 graded, best 8.5
56 ❑ Sep 1969 Cover: 0.15 NM value: 3.00
57 ❑ Nov 1969 Cover: 0.15 NM value: 3.00
58 ❑ Jan 1970 Cover: 0.15 NM value: 3.00
59 ❑ Mar 1970 Cover: 0.15 NM value: 3.00
60 ❑ May 1970 Cover: 0.15 NM value: 3.00
61 ❑ Jul 1970 Cover: 0.15 NM value: 2.00
62 ❑ Sep 1970 Cover: 0.15 NM value: 2.00
63 ❑ Nov 1970 Cover: 0.15 NM value: 2.00
64 ❑ Jan 1971 Cover: 0.15 NM value: 2.00
65 ❑ Feb 1971 Cover: 0.15 NM value: 2.00
66 ❑ Apr 1971 Cover: 0.15 NM value: 2.00
67 ❑ Jun 1971 Cover: 0.15 NM value: 2.00
68 ❑ Aug 1971 Cover: 0.15 NM value: 2.00
69 ❑ Sep 1971 Cover: 0.15 NM value: 2.00
70 ❑ Nov 1971 Cover: 0.25 NM value: 2.50
71 ❑ Feb 1972 Cover: 0.25 NM value: 2.50
Circ: Statement: 150,308
72 ❑ Apr 1972 Cover: 0.25 NM value: 2.50
Circ: Statement: 150,308
73 ❑ Jun 1972 Cover: 0.25 NM value: 2.50
Circ: Statement: 150,308
74 ❑ Aug 1972 Cover: 0.25 NM value: 2.50
Circ: Statement: 150,308
75 ❑ Oct 1972 Cover: 0.20 NM value: 2.00
Circ: Statement: 150,308
76 ❑ Dec 1972 Cover: 0.20 NM value: 2.00
Circ: Statement: 150,308
77 ❑ Jan 1973 Cover: 0.20 NM value: 2.00
78 ❑ Mar 1973 Cover: 0.20 NM value: 2.00
79 ❑ May 1973 Cover: 0.20 NM value: 2.00
80 ❑ Jul 1973 Cover: 0.20 NM value: 2.00
• Has 1972 Statement; avg total paid circ 150,308
81 ❑ Sep 1973 Cover: 0.20 NM value: 2.00
82 ❑ Nov 1973 Cover: 0.20 NM value: 2.00
83 ❑ Aug 1974 Cover: 0.25 NM value: 2.00
Circ: Statement: 138,917
84 ❑ Oct 1974 Cover: 0.25 NM value: 2.00
Circ: Statement: 138,917
85 ❑ Dec 1974 Cover: 0.25 NM value: 2.00
Circ: Statement: 138,917
86 ❑ Feb 1975 Cover: 0.25 NM value: 2.00
Circ: Statement: 138,917
87 ❑ Apr 1975 Cover: 0.25 NM value: 2.00
88 ❑ Jun 1975 Cover: 0.25 NM value: 2.00
89 ❑ Aug 1975 Cover: 0.25 NM value: 2.00
• Has 1974 Statement; avg total paid circ 138,917
90 ❑ Oct 1975 Cover: 0.25 NM value: 2.00
91 ❑ Dec 1975 Cover: 0.25 NM value: 2.00
92 ❑ Feb 1976 Cover: 0.25 NM value: 2.00
93 ❑ Apr 1976 Cover: 0.25 NM value: 2.00
94 ❑ Sep 1990 Cover: 1.00 NM value: 1.25
• Series begins again (1990)
95 ❑ Oct 1990 Cover: 1.00 NM value: 1.25
96 ❑ Nov 1990 Cover: 1.00 NM value: 1.25
97 ❑ Dec 1990 Cover: 1.00 NM value: 1.25
final issue.

WENDY IN 3-D — Blackthorne

1 ❑ Cover: 2.50 NM value: Cover or less

WENDY THE GOOD LITTLE WITCH (VOL. 2) — Harvey

1 ❑ Apr 1991 Cover: 1.25 NM value: 2.00
Circ: CapCity orders: 2,150
2 ❑ 1991 Cover: 1.25 NM value: 1.50
Circ: CapCity orders: 1,125
3 ❑ 1991 Cover: 1.25 NM value: 1.50
4 ❑ 1991 Cover: 1.25 NM value: 1.50
5 ❑ 1992 Cover: 1.25 NM value: 1.50
6 ❑ 1992 Cover: 1.25 NM value: 1.50
7 ❑ 1992 Cover: 1.25 NM value: 1.50
📖 The Lost Monster; He's Really a Nice Monster; Casper: The Strange Power of Paul Payne; Casper: The Man They Couldn't Catch
8 ❑ Oct 1992 Cover: 1.25 NM value: 1.50
9 ❑ Jan 1993 Cover: 1.25 NM value: 1.50
10 ❑ May 1993 Cover: 1.25 NM value: 1.50
11 ❑ 1993 Cover: 1.25 NM value: 1.50
12 ❑ Dec 1993 Cover: 1.50 NM value: Cover or less
📖 Snarlboro Country; A Sick World; Casper: Boo Am I?; Spooky: Strange Ghosts • Marty Taras, Warren Kremer, and Ernie Colon art credits
13 ❑ Mar 1994 Cover: 1.50 NM value: Cover or less
📖 Eitisoppo; Wendy Makes a Discovery; The Ghost Road; Spooky: High Midnight • Marty Taras and Dom Sileo art credits
14 ❑ 1994 Cover: 1.50 NM value: Cover or less
15 ❑ Aug 1994 Cover: 1.50 NM value: Cover or less

WENDY WHITEBREAD, UNDERCOVER SLUT — Fantagraphics / Eros

All issues are adults only.
1 ❑ b&w Cover: 2.50 NM value: Cover or less
Circ: CapCity orders: 3,370
1-2 ❑ b&w NM value: 2.95
1-3 ❑ b&w NM value: 2.95
1-4 ❑ b&w NM value: 2.95
1-5 ❑ Nov 1990, b&w Cover: 3.95 NM value: Cover or less
2 ❑ b&w Cover: 2.50 NM value: Cover or less

WEREWOLF — Dell

1 ❑ b&w Cover: 2.00 NM value: 8.00
• TV show
2 ❑ b&w Cover: 2.00 NM value: 5.00
📖 Werewolf: The Call of the Sea; The Chinese Water Devils; Reunion at Sea • TV show
3 ❑ b&w Cover: 2.00 NM value: 5.00
📖 Jump to Danger; The Day the World Almost Ended • TV show ★ Origin of Werewolf (Major Wiley Wolf).
4 ❑ b&w Cover: 2.00 NM value: 5.00
• TV show
5 ❑ b&w Cover: 2.00 NM value: 5.00
• TV show

WEREWOLF AT LARGE — Eternity

1 ❑ b&w Cover: 2.25 NM value: Cover or less
2 ❑ b&w Cover: 2.25 NM value: Cover or less
3 ❑ b&w Cover: 2.25 NM value: Cover or less

WEREWOLF BY NIGHT — Marvel

When the moon is full and the wolfsbane blooms, luckless Jack Russell transforms from a quiet young man into the vicious Werewolf by Night. Much like The Incredible Hulk, Jack has little control or memories of his behavior when he goes hairy, and his knack for transforming into a man-beast with a penchant for causing mayhem and fear wreaks havoc with his personal relationships.

Werewolf by Night made his first appearance in Marvel Spotlight #2 and soon graduated to his own series, which came out around the same time as other Marvel monster titles of the '70s Tomb of Dracula and Frankenstein. He crossed over into other series such as Marvel Team-Up and appeared in a few giant-sized specials. The title also introduced Moon Knight, who would go on to become a popular star feature in his own right.

1 ❑ Sep 1972 Cover: 0.20 NM value: 35.00
• CGC: 40 graded, best 9.6
2 ❑ Nov 1972 Cover: 0.20 NM value: 16.00
• CGC: 6 graded, best 9.6
3 ❑ Jan 1973 Cover: 0.20 NM value: 10.00
• CGC: 3 graded, best 9.4
4 ❑ Mar 1973 Cover: 0.20 NM value: 10.00
• CGC: 1 graded, best 9.2
5 ❑ May 1973 Cover: 0.20 NM value: 9.00
• CGC: 2 graded, best 9.6
6 ❑ Jun 1973 Cover: 0.20 NM value: 9.00
7 ❑ Jul 1973 Cover: 0.20 NM value: 9.00
8 ❑ Aug 1973 Cover: 0.20 NM value: 9.00
• CGC: 2 graded, best 9.2
9 ❑ Sep 1973 Cover: 0.20 NM value: 9.00
10 ❑ Oct 1973 Cover: 0.20 NM value: 9.00
• CGC: 1 graded, best 9.2
11 ❑ Nov 1973 Cover: 0.20 NM value: 7.00
12 ❑ Dec 1973 Cover: 0.20 NM value: 7.00
13 ❑ Jan 1974 Cover: 0.20 NM value: 7.00
14 ❑ Feb 1974 Cover: 0.20 NM value: 7.00
15 ❑ Mar 1974 Cover: 0.20 NM value: 7.00
• CGC: 1 graded, best 9.6
16 ❑ Apr 1974 Cover: 0.20 NM value: 7.00
• CGC: 1 graded, best 9.2
17 ❑ May 1974 Cover: 0.25 NM value: 7.00
• CGC: 2 graded, best 9.4
18 ❑ Jun 1974 Cover: 0.25 NM value: 7.00
19 ❑ Jul 1974 Cover: 0.25 NM value: 7.00
20 ❑ Aug 1974 Cover: 0.25 NM value: 7.00
21 ❑ Sep 1974 Cover: 0.25 NM value: 6.00
22 ❑ Oct 1974 Cover: 0.25 NM value: 6.00
23 ❑ Nov 1974 Cover: 0.25 NM value: 6.00
24 ❑ Dec 1974 Cover: 0.25 NM value: 6.00
25 ❑ Jan 1975 Cover: 0.25 NM value: 6.00
26 ❑ Feb 1975 Cover: 0.25 NM value: 6.00
27 ❑ Mar 1975 Cover: 0.25 NM value: 6.00
28 ❑ Apr 1975 Cover: 0.25 NM value: 6.00
29 ❑ May 1975 Cover: 0.25 NM value: 6.00
30 ❑ Jun 1975 Cover: 0.25 NM value: 6.00
• CGC: 2 graded, best 9.2
31 ❑ Jul 1975 Cover: 0.25 NM value: 6.00
32 ❑ Aug 1975 Cover: 0.25 NM value: 40.00
• CGC: 42 graded, best 9.6
33 ❑ Sep 1975 Cover: 0.25 NM value: 20.00
• CGC: 13 graded, best 9.8
34 ❑ Oct 1975 Cover: 0.25 NM value: 4.00
📖 Not All the Shades of Death nor Evil's Majesty A: Don Perlin W: Doug Moench
35 ❑ Nov 1975 Cover: 0.25 NM value: 4.00
📖 Evil in Every Stone No Longer Hiding A: Don Perlin W: Doug Moench
36 ❑ Jan 1976 Cover: 0.25 NM value: 4.00
37 ❑ Mar 1976 Cover: 0.25 NM value: 6.00
• CGC: 11 graded, best 9.6
38 ❑ May 1976 Cover: 0.25 NM value: 3.00
39 ❑ Jul 1976 Cover: 0.25 NM value: 3.00
• CGC: 1 graded, best 9.4
40 ❑ Sep 1976 Cover: 0.30 NM value: 3.00
41 ❑ Nov 1976 Cover: 0.30 NM value: 3.00
42 ❑ Jan 1977 Cover: 0.30 NM value: 3.00
43 ❑ Mar 1977 Cover: 0.30 NM value: 3.00
final issue.

WEREWOLF BY NIGHT (VOL. 2) — Marvel

1 ❑ Feb 1998 Cover: 2.99 NM value: 3.00
Circ: Diamd. preorders: 33,762
📖 Somewhere South of Heaven A: Leonardo Manco W: Paul Jenkins
2 ❑ Mar 1998 Cover: 2.99 NM value: 3.00
Circ: Diamd. preorders: 28,563
• gatefold summary. 📖 Life in the Fast Lane A: Leonardo Manco W: Paul Jenkins
3 ❑ Apr 1998 Cover: 2.99 NM value: 3.00
Circ: Diamd. preorders: 18,831
• gatefold summary.
4 ❑ May 1998 Cover: 2.99 NM value: 3.00
Circ: Diamd. preorders: 17,376
• gatefold summary.
5 ❑ Jun 1998 Cover: 2.99 NM value: 3.00
Circ: Diamd. preorders: 15,960
• gatefold summary.
6 ❑ Jul 1998 Cover: 2.99 NM value: 3.00
Circ: Diamd. preorders: 14,168
• gatefold summary. ★ Appearance of Ghost Rider.

WEREWOLF IN 3-D — Blackthorne

1 ❑ Cover: 2.50 NM value: Cover or less
Circ: CapCity orders: 1,550

WEST COAST AVENGERS — Marvel

Founded by the super-archer Hawkeye, the group called West Coast Avengers was an offshoot of The Avengers, formed to meet challenges that face the country's western portion. Originally founded by super-archer Hawkeye, the original team combined his abilities with those of Mockingbird, Iron Man, Wonder Man, and Tigra. Like its East Coast cousin, Avengers West Coast has seen a continual change in its lineup, with the membership at one time or another including Spider-Woman, U.S.Agent, Hank Pym (aka Yellowjacket), The Vision, and The Scarlet Witch.

Following #46, this title became known as Avengers West Coast.

1 ❑ Oct 1985 Cover: 1.25 NM value: 2.00
Circ: CapCity orders: 40,600
2 ❑ Nov 1985 Cover: 0.65 NM value: 1.50
Circ: CapCity orders: 30,500
3 ❑ Dec 1985 Cover: 0.65 NM value: 1.50
Circ: CapCity orders: 28,300
4 ❑ Jan 1986 Cover: 0.65 NM value: 1.00
Circ: Statement: 244,958 CapCity orders: 27,600
5 ❑ Feb 1986 Cover: 0.75 NM value: 1.00
Circ: Statement: 244,958 CapCity orders: 29,400
6 ❑ Mar 1986 Cover: 0.75 NM value: 1.00
Circ: Statement: 244,958 CapCity orders: 28,200
7 ❑ Apr 1986 Cover: 0.75 NM value: 1.00
Circ: Statement: 244,958 CapCity orders: 28,200
8 ❑ May 1986 Cover: 0.75 NM value: 1.00
Circ: Statement: 244,958 CapCity orders: 27,100

9 ❑ Jun 1986 Cover: 0.75 **NM** value: **1.00**
Circ: Statement: **244,958** CapCity orders: **26,100**
10 ❑ Jul 1986 Cover: 0.75 **NM** value: **1.00**
Circ: Statement: **244,958** CapCity orders: **25,900**
11 ❑ Aug 1986 Cover: 0.75 **NM** value: **1.00**
Circ: Statement: **244,958** CapCity orders: **25,200**
12 ❑ Sep 1986 Cover: 0.75 **NM** value: **1.00**
Circ: Statement: **244,958** CapCity orders: **25,000**
13 ❑ Oct 1986 Cover: 0.75 **NM** value: **1.00**
Circ: Statement: **244,958** CapCity orders: **25,300**
14 ❑ Nov 1986 Cover: 0.75 **NM** value: **1.00**
Circ: Statement: **244,958** CapCity orders: **26,100**
📖 Tigra, Tigra Burning Bright! **A:** Al Milgrom **W:** Steve Englehart ★ 1st Appearance of Hellstorm.
15 ❑ Dec 1986 Cover: 0.75 **NM** value: **1.00**
Circ: Statement: **244,958** CapCity orders: **24,900**
16 ❑ Jan 1987 Cover: 0.75 **NM** value: **1.00**
Circ: Statement: **205,792** CapCity orders: **24,200**
17 ❑ Feb 1987 Cover: 0.75 **NM** value: **1.00**
Circ: Statement: **205,792** CapCity orders: **25,200**
18 ❑ Mar 1987 Cover: 0.75 **NM** value: **1.00**
Circ: Statement: **205,792** CapCity orders: **25,400**
19 ❑ Apr 1987 Cover: 0.75 **NM** value: **1.00**
Circ: Statement: **205,792** CapCity orders: **26,300**
20 ❑ May 1987 Cover: 0.75 **NM** value: **1.00**
Circ: Statement: **205,792** CapCity orders: **23,300**
• Has 1986 Statement, filed 10/6/86; avg print run 442,635; avg sales 240,216; avg subs 4,742; avg total paid 244,958; samples 225; office use 2,770; max existent 247,953; 44% of run returned
21 ❑ Jun 1987 Cover: 0.75 **NM** value: **1.00**
Circ: Statement: **205,792** CapCity orders: **23,700**
📖 Lost in Space-Time, Part 5 **A:** Al Milgrom; Joe Sinnott **W:** Steve Englehart ★ Appearance of Moon Knight.
22 ❑ Jul 1987 Cover: 0.75 **NM** value: **1.00**
Circ: Statement: **205,792** CapCity orders: **23,800**
23 ❑ Aug 1987 Cover: 0.75 **NM** value: **1.00**
Circ: Statement: **205,792** CapCity orders: **25,700**
24 ❑ Sep 1987 Cover: 0.75 **NM** value: **1.00**
Circ: Statement: **205,792** CapCity orders: **26,500**
25 ❑ Oct 1987 Cover: 0.75 **NM** value: **1.00**
Circ: Statement: **205,792** CapCity orders: **26,400**
26 ❑ Nov 1987 Cover: 0.75 **NM** value: **1.00**
Circ: Statement: **205,792** CapCity orders: **27,700**
27 ❑ Dec 1987 Cover: 0.75 **NM** value: **1.00**
Circ: Statement: **205,792** CapCity orders: **26,200**
28 ❑ Jan 1988 Cover: 0.75 **NM** value: **1.00**
Circ: Statement: **178,125** CapCity orders: **26,600**
📖 Double-Crossed **A:** Al Milgrom; Dave Hunt **W:** Steve Englehart ★ Versus Zodiac.
29 ❑ Feb 1988 Cover: 0.75 **NM** value: **1.00**
Circ: Statement: **178,125** CapCity orders: **27,200**
30 ❑ Mar 1988 Cover: 0.75 **NM** value: **1.00**
Circ: Statement: **178,125** CapCity orders: **26,800**
31 ❑ Apr 1988 Cover: 0.75 **NM** value: **1.00**
Circ: Statement: **178,125** CapCity orders: **27,400**
32 ❑ May 1988 Cover: 0.75 **NM** value: **1.00**
Circ: Statement: **178,125** CapCity orders: **25,900**
33 ❑ Jun 1988 Cover: 0.75 **NM** value: **1.00**
Circ: Statement: **178,125** CapCity orders: **25,100**
• Has 1987 Statement; avg print run 383,072; avg sales 197,067; avg subs 8,725; avg total paid 205,792 samples 132; office use 915; max existent 206,839; 46% of run returned
34 ❑ Jul 1988 Cover: 0.75 **NM** value: **1.00**
Circ: Statement: **178,125** CapCity orders: **25,200**
35 ❑ Aug 1988 Cover: 0.75 **NM** value: **1.00**
Circ: Statement: **178,125** CapCity orders: **24,900**
36 ❑ Sep 1988 Cover: 0.75 **NM** value: **1.00**
Circ: Statement: **178,125** CapCity orders: **24,800**
37 ❑ Oct 1988 Cover: 0.75 **NM** value: **1.00**
Circ: Statement: **178,125** CapCity orders: **24,900**
38 ❑ Nov 1988 Cover: 0.75 **NM** value: **1.00**
Circ: Statement: **178,125** CapCity orders: **24,000**
39 ❑ Dec 1988 Cover: 0.75 **NM** value: **1.00**
Circ: Statement: **178,125** CapCity orders: **29,700**
📖 Upset! **A:** Al Milgrom **W:** Steve Englehart
40 ❑ Jan 1989 Cover: 0.75 **NM** value: **1.00**
Circ: Statement: **181,165**
📖 Night Shift! **A:** Al Milgrom **W:** Mark Gruenwald
41 ❑ Feb 1989 Cover: 0.75 **NM** value: **1.00**
Circ: Statement: **181,165** CapCity orders: **24,000**
📖 When Ghosts Can Die, Even Gods Must Fear! **A:** Tom Morgan **W:** Ralph Macchio; Tom DeFalco
42 ❑ Mar 1989 Cover: 0.75 **NM** value: **1.00**
Circ: Statement: **181,165** CapCity orders: **40,200**
📖 Vision Quest **A:** John Byrne **W:** John Byrne
43 ❑ Apr 1989 Cover: 0.75 **NM** value: **1.00**
Circ: Statement: **181,165** CapCity orders: **36,500**
📖 Vision Quest **A:** John Byrne **W:** John Byrne
44 ❑ May 1989 Cover: 0.75 **NM** value: **1.00**
Circ: Statement: **181,165** CapCity orders: **36,700**
📖 Vision Quest **A:** John Byrne **W:** John Byrne ★ 1st Appearance of U.S.Agent.
45 ❑ Jun 1989 Cover: 0.75 **NM** value: **1.00**
Circ: Statement: **181,165** CapCity orders: **37,200**
📖 Vision Quest • Has 1988 Statement, filed 10/1/88; avg print run 306,775; avg sales 172,150; avg subs 5,975; avg total paid 178,125; samples 130; office use 860; max existent 179,115; 42% of run returned **A:** John Byrne **W:** John Byrne
46 ❑ Jul 1989 Cover: 0.75 **NM** value: **1.00**
Circ: Statement: **181,165** CapCity orders: **39,800**
📖 Franchise **A:** John Byrne **W:** John Byrne ★ 1st Appearance of Great Lakes Avengers, Big Bertha.
47 ❑ Aug 1989 Cover: 0.75 **NM** value: **1.00**
Circ: Statement: **181,165** CapCity orders: **39,300**
• Series continues as Avengers West Coast
Anl 1❑ca. 1986 Cover: 1.25 **NM** value: **2.00**
Circ: CapCity orders: **26,000**
📖 One of Our Own! **A:** Mark D. Bright **W:** Mark D. Bright; Steve Englehart ★ Versus Quicksilver.
Anl 2❑ca. 1987 Cover: 1.25 **NM** value: **2.00**
Circ: CapCity orders: **28,700**
Anl 3❑ca. 1988 Cover: 1.75 **NM** value: **2.00**
Circ: CapCity orders: **29,300**
📖 Evolutionary War, Part 9 • series continues as Avengers West Coast Annual **A:** Al Milgrom **W:** Steve Englehart

WEST COAST AVENGERS (LTD. SERIES) Marvel

1 ❑ Sep 1984 Cover: 0.75 **NM** value: **2.50**
• **CGC:** 3 graded, best 9.6
2 ❑ Oct 1984 Cover: 0.75 **NM** value: **2.00**
3 ❑ Nov 1984 Cover: 0.75 **NM** value: **2.00**
4 ❑ Dec 1984 Cover: 0.75 **NM** value: **2.00**

WESTERN ACTION Atlas-Seaboard

1 ❑ Jun 1975 Cover: 0.25 **NM** value: **4.00**

WESTERN COMICS DC

1 ❑ Jan 1948 Cover: 0.10 **NM** value: **625.00**
• **CGC:** 2 graded, best 9.4
2 ❑ Mar 1948 Cover: 0.10 **NM** value: **300.00**
• **CGC:** 1 graded, best 9.6
3 ❑ May 1948 Cover: 0.10 **NM** value: **225.00**
• **CGC:** 1 graded, best 9.4
4 ❑ Jul 1948 Cover: 0.10 **NM** value: **200.00**
• **CGC:** 1 graded, best 9.2
5 ❑ Sep 1948 Cover: 0.10 **NM** value: **200.00**
• **CGC:** 2 graded, best 9.2
6 ❑ Nov 1948 Cover: 0.10 **NM** value: **165.00**
7 ❑ Jan 1949 Cover: 0.10 **NM** value: **165.00**
• **CGC:** 1 graded, best 6.0
• Wyoming Kid, Rodeo Rick, Nighthawk, Cowboy Marshal
8 ❑ Mar 1949 Cover: 0.10 **NM** value: **200.00**
• **CGC:** 1 graded, best 9.8
9 ❑ May 1949 Cover: 0.10 **NM** value: **165.00**
10 ❑ Jul 1949 Cover: 0.10 **NM** value: **165.00**
• **CGC:** 2 graded, best 9.6
11 ❑ Sep 1949 Cover: 0.10 **NM** value: **110.00**
• **CGC:** 1 graded, best 9.8
12 ❑ Dec 1949 Cover: 0.10 **NM** value: **110.00**
• **CGC:** 2 graded, best 9.6
13 ❑ Feb 1950 Cover: 0.10 **NM** value: **110.00**
• **CGC:** 1 graded, best 9.6
• Wyoming Kid
14 ❑ Apr 1950 Cover: 0.10 **NM** value: **110.00**
• **CGC:** 1 graded, best 7.0
15 ❑ Jun 1950 Cover: 0.10 **NM** value: **110.00**
• **CGC:** 1 graded, best 9.6
16 ❑ Aug 1950 Cover: 0.10 **NM** value: **110.00**
• **CGC:** 1 graded, best 9.0
17 ❑ Oct 1950 Cover: 0.10 **NM** value: **110.00**
18 ❑ Dec 1950 Cover: 0.10 **NM** value: **110.00**
• **CGC:** 1 graded, best 9.6
19 ❑ Jan 1951 Cover: 0.10 **NM** value: **110.00**
• **CGC:** 1 graded, best 8.0
20 ❑ Feb 1951 Cover: 0.10 **NM** value: **110.00**
• **CGC:** 1 graded, best 9.6
21 ❑ Mar 1951 Cover: 0.10 **NM** value: **85.00**
22 ❑ Apr 1951 Cover: 0.10 **NM** value: **85.00**
• **CGC:** 1 graded, best 9.6
23 ❑ May 1951 Cover: 0.10 **NM** value: **85.00**
24 ❑ Jun 1951 Cover: 0.10 **NM** value: **85.00**
• **CGC:** 1 graded, best 9.4
25 ❑ Jul 1951 Cover: 0.10 **NM** value: **85.00**
26 ❑ Aug 1951 Cover: 0.10 **NM** value: **85.00**
• **CGC:** 1 graded, best 9.8
27 ❑ Sep 1951 Cover: 0.10 **NM** value: **85.00**
28 ❑ Oct 1951 Cover: 0.10 **NM** value: **85.00**
• **CGC:** 1 graded, best 9.4
29 ❑ Nov 1951 Cover: 0.10 **NM** value: **85.00**
30 ❑ Dec 1951 Cover: 0.10 **NM** value: **85.00**
31 ❑ Jan 1952 Cover: 0.10 **NM** value: **60.00**
• **CGC:** 1 graded, best 9.6
32 ❑ Mar 1952 Cover: 0.10 **NM** value: **60.00**
• **CGC:** 1 graded, best 9.6
33 ❑ May 1952 Cover: 0.10 **NM** value: **60.00**
34 ❑ Jul 1952 Cover: 0.10 **NM** value: **60.00**
35 ❑ Sep 1952 Cover: 0.10 **NM** value: **60.00**
36 ❑ Nov 1952 Cover: 0.10 **NM** value: **60.00**
37 ❑ Jan 1953 Cover: 0.10 **NM** value: **60.00**
38 ❑ Mar 1953 Cover: 0.10 **NM** value: **60.00**
39 ❑ May 1953 Cover: 0.10 **NM** value: **60.00**
40 ❑ Jul 1953 Cover: 0.10 **NM** value: **60.00**
41 ❑ Sep 1953 Cover: 0.10 **NM** value: **45.00**
42 ❑ Nov 1953 Cover: 0.10 **NM** value: **45.00**
43 ❑ Jan 1954 Cover: 0.10 **NM** value: **45.00**
44 ❑ Mar 1954 Cover: 0.10 **NM** value: **45.00**
45 ❑ May 1954 Cover: 0.10 **NM** value: **45.00**
46 ❑ Jul 1954 Cover: 0.10 **NM** value: **45.00**
47 ❑ Sep 1954 Cover: 0.10 **NM** value: **45.00**
48 ❑ Nov 1954 Cover: 0.10 **NM** value: **45.00**
49 ❑ Jan 1955 Cover: 0.10 **NM** value: **45.00**
50 ❑ Mar 1955 Cover: 0.10 **NM** value: **45.00**
51 ❑ May 1955 Cover: 0.10 **NM** value: **38.00**
52 ❑ Jul 1955 Cover: 0.10 **NM** value: **38.00**
53 ❑ Sep 1955 Cover: 0.10 **NM** value: **38.00**
54 ❑ Nov 1955 Cover: 0.10 **NM** value: **38.00**
• **CGC:** 1 graded, best 9.2
55 ❑ Jan 1956 Cover: 0.10 **NM** value: **38.00**
• **CGC:** 1 graded, best 9.0
56 ❑ Mar 1956 Cover: 0.10 **NM** value: **38.00**
57 ❑ May 1956 Cover: 0.10 **NM** value: **38.00**
• Pow-Wow Smith, The nighthawk, Rodeo Rick, Wyoming Kid **A:** Gil Kane
58 ❑ Jul 1956 Cover: 0.10 **NM** value: **38.00**
59 ❑ Sep 1956 Cover: 0.10 **NM** value: **38.00**
60 ❑ Nov 1956 Cover: 0.10 **NM** value: **38.00**
61 ❑ Jan 1957 Cover: 0.10 **NM** value: **35.00**
62 ❑ Mar 1957 Cover: 0.10 **NM** value: **35.00**
63 ❑ May 1957 Cover: 0.10 **NM** value: **35.00**
64 ❑ Jul 1957 Cover: 0.10 **NM** value: **35.00**
65 ❑ Sep 1957 Cover: 0.10 **NM** value: **35.00**
66 ❑ Nov 1957 Cover: 0.10 **NM** value: **35.00**
67 ❑ Jan 1958 Cover: 0.10 **NM** value: **35.00**
68 ❑ Mar 1958 Cover: 0.10 **NM** value: **35.00**
69 ❑ May 1958 Cover: 0.10 **NM** value: **35.00**
70 ❑ Jul 1958 Cover: 0.10 **NM** value: **35.00**
71 ❑ Sep 1958 Cover: 0.10 **NM** value: **35.00**
• **CGC:** 1 graded, best 7.5
72 ❑ Nov 1958 Cover: 0.10 **NM** value: **35.00**
73 ❑ Jan 1959 Cover: 0.10 **NM** value: **35.00**
74 ❑ Mar 1959 Cover: 0.10 **NM** value: **35.00**
• **CGC:** 1 graded, best 7.0
75 ❑ May 1959 Cover: 0.10 **NM** value: **35.00**
76 ❑ Jul 1959 Cover: 0.10 **NM** value: **35.00**
• Tom Mix; Monte Hale; Hopalong Cassidy; Gabby Hayes
77 ❑ Sep 1959 Cover: 0.10 **NM** value: **35.00**
78 ❑ Nov 1959 Cover: 0.10 **NM** value: **35.00**
79 ❑ Jan 1960 Cover: 0.10 **NM** value: **35.00**
80 ❑ Mar 1960 Cover: 0.10 **NM** value: **35.00**
81 ❑ May 1960 Cover: 0.10 **NM** value: **35.00**
82 ❑ Jul 1960 Cover: 0.10 **NM** value: **35.00**
83 ❑ Sep 1960 Cover: 0.10 **NM** value: **35.00**
84 ❑ Nov 1960 Cover: 0.10 **NM** value: **35.00**
85 ❑ Jan 1961 Cover: 0.10 **NM** value: **35.00**

WESTERN CRIME CASES Star

9 ❑ Dec 1951 Cover: 0.10 **NM** value: **125.00**

WESTERNER Toytown

14 ❑ Jun 1948 Cover: 0.10 **NM** value: **75.00**
15 ❑ Aug 1948 Cover: 0.10 **NM** value: **50.00**
16 ❑ Oct 1948 Cover: 0.10 **NM** value: **50.00**
17 ❑ Dec 1948 Cover: 0.10 **NM** value: **50.00**
18 ❑ Feb 1949 Cover: 0.10 **NM** value: **50.00**
19 ❑ Mar 1949 Cover: 0.10 **NM** value: **50.00**
20 ❑ Apr 1949 Cover: 0.10 **NM** value: **50.00**
21 ❑ Jun 1949 Cover: 0.10 **NM** value: **50.00**
22 ❑ Aug 1949 Cover: 0.10 **NM** value: **50.00**
23 ❑ Oct 1949 Cover: 0.10 **NM** value: **50.00**
24 ❑ Dec 1949 Cover: 0.10 **NM** value: **50.00**
25 ❑ Feb 1950 Cover: 0.10 **NM** value: **50.00**
26 ❑ Apr 1950 Cover: 0.10 **NM** value: **75.00**
27 ❑ Jun 1950 Cover: 0.10 **NM** value: **50.00**
28 ❑ Aug 1950 Cover: 0.10 **NM** value: **50.00**
29 ❑ Oct 1950 Cover: 0.10 **NM** value: **50.00**
30 ❑ Dec 1950 Cover: 0.10 **NM** value: **50.00**
31 ❑ Jan 1951 Cover: 0.10 **NM** value: **40.00**
32 ❑ Feb 1951 Cover: 0.10 **NM** value: **40.00**
33 ❑ Mar 1951 Cover: 0.10 **NM** value: **40.00**
34 ❑ Apr 1951 Cover: 0.10 **NM** value: **40.00**
35 ❑ May 1951 Cover: 0.10 **NM** value: **40.00**
36 ❑ Jun 1951 Cover: 0.10 **NM** value: **40.00**
37 ❑ Jul 1951 Cover: 0.10 **NM** value: **40.00**
38 ❑ Aug 1951 Cover: 0.10 **NM** value: **40.00**
39 ❑ Sep 1951 Cover: 0.10 **NM** value: **40.00**
40 ❑ Oct 1951 Cover: 0.10 **NM** value: **40.00**
• **CGC:** 1 graded, best 7.5
41 ❑ Dec 1951 Cover: 0.10 **NM** value: **40.00**

WESTERN FIGHTERS Hillman

Volume 1
1 ❑ Apr 1948 Cover: 0.10 **NM** value: **165.00**
• **CGC:** 2 graded, best 9.0
2 ❑ Jun 1948 Cover: 0.10 **NM** value: **48.00**
3 ❑ Aug 1948 Cover: 0.10 **NM** value: **48.00**
4 ❑ Oct 1948 Cover: 0.10 **NM** value: **55.00**
5 ❑ Jan 1949 Cover: 0.10 **NM** value: **32.00**
6 ❑ Mar 1949 Cover: 0.10 **NM** value: **32.00**
7 ❑ May 1949 Cover: 0.10 **NM** value: **55.00**
8 ❑ Jul 1949 Cover: 0.10 **NM** value: **32.00**
9 ❑ Aug 1949 Cover: 0.10 **NM** value: **32.00**
10 ❑ Sep 1949 Cover: 0.10 **NM** value: **55.00**
11 ❑ Oct 1949 Cover: 0.10 **NM** value: **125.00**
12 ❑ Nov 1949 Cover: 0.10 **NM** value: **30.00**
Volume 2
1 ❑ Dec 1949 Cover: 0.10 **NM** value: **45.00**
2 ❑ Jan 1950 Cover: 0.10 **NM** value: **24.00**
3 ❑ Feb 1950 Cover: 0.10 **NM** value: **24.00**
4 ❑ Mar 1950 Cover: 0.10 **NM** value: **24.00**
5 ❑ Apr 1950 Cover: 0.10 **NM** value: **24.00**
6 ❑ May 1950 Cover: 0.10 **NM** value: **24.00**
7 ❑ Jun 1950 Cover: 0.10 **NM** value: **24.00**
8 ❑ Jul 1950 Cover: 0.10 **NM** value: **24.00**
9 ❑ Aug 1950 Cover: 0.10 **NM** value: **24.00**
10 ❑ Sep 1950 Cover: 0.10 **NM** value: **24.00**
11 ❑ Oct 1950 Cover: 0.10 **NM** value: **24.00**
12 ❑ Nov 1950 Cover: 0.10 **NM** value: **24.00**
Volume 3
1 ❑ Dec 1950 Cover: 0.10 **NM** value: **20.00**
2 ❑ Jan 1951 Cover: 0.10 **NM** value: **20.00**
3 ❑ Feb 1951 Cover: 0.10 **NM** value: **20.00**
4 ❑ Mar 1951 Cover: 0.10 **NM** value: **20.00**
📖 The Grass Grows High…; The Arab of Lonesome Pass; Soapy Six-Gun; Trixie Comes to Town; Scared (text story); The Wonderful Squawk Box; Frontier Facts; Buckskin Benson; Soapy Six-Gun; Trixie Comes to Town; Scared (text story); The Wonderful Squawk Box **A:** Ross Andru
5 ❑ Apr 1951 Cover: 0.10 **NM** value: **20.00**
6 ❑ May 1951 Cover: 0.10 **NM** value: **20.00**
7 ❑ Jun 1951 Cover: 0.10 **NM** value: **20.00**
8 ❑ Jul 1951 Cover: 0.10 **NM** value: **20.00**

CGC-graded: Multiply prices above by **33 for 9.9 M • 16 for 9.8 NM/M • 7 for 9.6 NM+ • 5 for 9.4 NM • 2.5 for 9.2 NM- • 1.5 for 9.0 VF/NM**

9 ❑ Aug 1951 Cover: 0.10 **NM** value: **20.00**
10 ❑ Sep 1951 Cover: 0.10 **NM** value: **20.00**
11 ❑ Oct 1951 Cover: 0.10 **NM** value: **20.00**
12 ❑ Nov 1951 Cover: 0.10 **NM** value: **35.00**

Volume 4

1 ❑ Dec 1951 Cover: 0.10 **NM** value: **35.00**
2 ❑ 1952 Cover: 0.10 **NM** value: **30.00**
3 ❑ 1952 Cover: 0.10 **NM** value: **30.00**
4 ❑ 1952 Cover: 0.10 **NM** value: **30.00**
5 ❑ Dec 1952 Cover: 0.10 **NM** value: **30.00**
• **CGC:** 1 graded, best 6.5
6 ❑ 1953 Cover: 0.10 **NM** value: **30.00**
7 ❑ Mar 1953 Cover: 0.10 **NM** value: **30.00**
8 ❑ ca. 1953 Cover: 0.25 **NM** value: **160.00**
• 3-D.

WESTERN GUNFIGHTERS (1ST SERIES) Atlas

20 ❑ Jun 1956 Cover: 0.10 **NM** value: **50.00**
• picks up numbering from Apache Kid
21 ❑ Aug 1956 Cover: 0.10 **NM** value: **50.00**
22 ❑ Oct 1956 Cover: 0.10 **NM** value: **50.00**
23 ❑ Dec 1956 Cover: 0.10 **NM** value: **50.00**
24 ❑ Feb 1957 Cover: 0.10 **NM** value: **50.00**
25 ❑ Apr 1957 Cover: 0.10 **NM** value: **35.00**
26 ❑ Jun 1957 Cover: 0.10 **NM** value: **35.00**
27 ❑ Aug 1957 Cover: 0.10 **NM** value: **35.00**

WESTERN GUNFIGHTERS (2ND SERIES) Marvel

The heyday of the Westerns was during the 1950s and '60s, when it seemed a generation of kids grew up playing Cisco Kid. Western comics were at their peak then, too, although they have since all but disappeared.

In the 1970s, Marvel reprised the Western comics of yesteryear with Western Gunfighters. This series reprinted the adventures of everyone from Ghost Rider (the original Western hero, since renamed Night Rider) to Kid Colt Outlaw. However, the most interesting hero of the lot was The Apache Kid. This hero spent most of his time dressed as your average sun-reddened cowpoke. But, when trouble arose, he would slip away to put on war paint and Indian garb and change to speaking in pidgin-English. (It was reminiscent of the Straight Arrow radio character of the late 1940s, who also appeared in comics.) Then, after trouncing the bad guys, he would change back, speak his normal, fluent English, and say, "The Apache Kid must have decked the bad guy — I didn't see a thing." Unbelievably, nobody suspected a thing!

1 ❑ Aug 1970 Cover: 0.20 **NM** value: **10.00**
• giant
2 ❑ Oct 1970 Cover: 0.20 **NM** value: **6.00**
• giant★ Origin of Nightwind (The Apache Kid's horse).
3 ❑ Dec 1970 Cover: 0.20 **NM** value: **6.00**
• giant
4 ❑ Mar 1971 Cover: 0.20 **NM** value: **6.00**
• giant
5 ❑ Jun 1971 Cover: 0.25 **NM** value: **6.00**
• giant
6 ❑ Sep 1971 Cover: 0.25 **NM** value: **6.00**
• giant★ Death of Ghost Rider.
7 ❑ Jan 1972 Cover: 0.25 **NM** value: **8.00**
• giant★ Origin of Night Rider ("Ghost Rider"). ★ 1st Appearance of Lincoln Slade as Ghost Rider. ★ Death of Phantom Rider I (Carter Slade).
8 ❑ Mar 1972 Cover: 0.20 **NM** value: **5.00**
9 ❑ May 1972 Cover: 0.20 **NM** value: **5.00**
10 ❑ Jul 1972 Cover: 0.20 **NM** value: **5.00**
11 ❑ Sep 1972 Cover: 0.20 **NM** value: **5.00**
12 ❑ Nov 1972 Cover: 0.20 **NM** value: **5.00**
13 ❑ Jan 1973 Cover: 0.20 **NM** value: **5.00**
14 ❑ Mar 1973 Cover: 0.20 **NM** value: **5.00**
15 ❑ May 1973 Cover: 0.20 **NM** value: **5.00**
16 ❑ Jul 1973 Cover: 0.20 **NM** value: **5.00**
17 ❑ Sep 1973 Cover: 0.20 **NM** value: **4.00**
18 ❑ Oct 1973 Cover: 0.20 **NM** value: **4.00**
19 ❑ Nov 1973 Cover: 0.20 **NM** value: **4.00**
20 ❑ Jan 1974 Cover: 0.20 **NM** value: **4.00**
21 ❑ Mar 1974 Cover: 0.20 **NM** value: **4.00**
22 ❑ May 1974 Cover: 0.25 **NM** value: **4.00**
23 ❑ Jul 1974 Cover: 0.25 **NM** value: **4.00**
24 ❑ Sep 1974 Cover: 0.25 **NM** value: **4.00**
25 ❑ Oct 1974 Cover: 0.25 **NM** value: **4.00**
26 ❑ Nov 1974 Cover: 0.25 **NM** value: **4.00**
27 ❑ Jan 1975 Cover: 0.25 **NM** value: **4.00**
28 ❑ Mar 1975 Cover: 0.25 **NM** value: **4.00**
29 ❑ May 1975 Cover: 0.25 **NM** value: **4.00**
30 ❑ Jul 1975 Cover: 0.25 **NM** value: **4.00**
31 ❑ Sep 1975 Cover: 0.25 **NM** value: **4.00**
32 ❑ Nov 1975 Cover: 0.25 **NM** value: **4.00**
33 ❑ Jan 1976 Cover: 0.25 **NM** value: **4.00**
final issue.

WESTERN HERO Fawcett

76 ❑ Mar 1949 Cover: 0.10 **NM** value: **150.00**
• Tom Mix, Monte Hale, Hopalong Cassidy, Gabby Hayes
77 ❑ Apr 1949 Cover: 0.10 **NM** value: **100.00**
78 ❑ May 1949 Cover: 0.10 **NM** value: **100.00**
79 ❑ Jun 1949 Cover: 0.10 **NM** value: **100.00**
80 ❑ Jul 1949 Cover: 0.10 **NM** value: **100.00**
81 ❑ Aug 1949 Cover: 0.10 **NM** value: **100.00**
82 ❑ Sep 1949 Cover: 0.10 **NM** value: **100.00**
83 ❑ Oct 1949 Cover: 0.10 **NM** value: **75.00**
84 ❑ Nov 1949 Cover: 0.10 **NM** value: **75.00**
85 ❑ Dec 1949 Cover: 0.10 **NM** value: **75.00**
86 ❑ Jan 1950 Cover: 0.10 **NM** value: **75.00**
87 ❑ Feb 1950 Cover: 0.10 **NM** value: **75.00**
88 ❑ Mar 1950 Cover: 0.10 **NM** value: **75.00**
89 ❑ Apr 1950 Cover: 0.10 **NM** value: **75.00**
90 ❑ May 1950 Cover: 0.10 **NM** value: **75.00**
91 ❑ Jun 1950 Cover: 0.10 **NM** value: **75.00**
92 ❑ Jul 1950 Cover: 0.10 **NM** value: **75.00**
93 ❑ Aug 1950 Cover: 0.10 **NM** value: **75.00**
94 ❑ Sep 1950 Cover: 0.10 **NM** value: **75.00**
95 ❑ Oct 1950 Cover: 0.10 **NM** value: **75.00**
96 ❑ Nov 1950 Cover: 0.10 **NM** value: **60.00**
97 ❑ Dec 1950 Cover: 0.10 **NM** value: **60.00**
98 ❑ Jan 1951 Cover: 0.10 **NM** value: **60.00**
99 ❑ Feb 1951 Cover: 0.10 **NM** value: **60.00**
100 ❑ Mar 1951 Cover: 0.10 **NM** value: **60.00**
101 ❑ Apr 1951 Cover: 0.10 **NM** value: **60.00**
102 ❑ May 1951 Cover: 0.10 **NM** value: **60.00**
103 ❑ Jun 1951 Cover: 0.10 **NM** value: **60.00**
104 ❑ Jul 1951 Cover: 0.10 **NM** value: **60.00**
105 ❑ Aug 1951 Cover: 0.10 **NM** value: **60.00**
106 ❑ Sep 1951 Cover: 0.10 **NM** value: **60.00**
107 ❑ Oct 1951 Cover: 0.10 **NM** value: **60.00**
108 ❑ Nov 1951 Cover: 0.10 **NM** value: **60.00**
109 ❑ Dec 1951 Cover: 0.10 **NM** value: **60.00**
• **CGC:** 1 graded, best 9.2
110 ❑ Jan 1952 Cover: 0.10 **NM** value: **60.00**
111 ❑ Feb 1952 Cover: 0.10 **NM** value: **60.00**
112 ❑ Mar 1952 Cover: 0.10 **NM** value: **60.00**

WESTERN KID, THE (2ND SERIES) Marvel

1 ❑ Dec 1971 Cover: 0.20 **NM** value: **9.00**
📖 Boot Hill Vengeance! **W:** The Hidden Trail; The Return of the Badmen!
2 ❑ Feb 1972 Cover: 0.20 **NM** value: **6.00**
3 ❑ Apr 1972 Cover: 0.20 **NM** value: **6.00**
4 ❑ Jun 1972 Cover: 0.20 **NM** value: **6.00**
5 ❑ Aug 1972 Cover: 0.20 **NM** value: **6.00**

WESTERN LIFE ROMANCES Marvel

1 ❑ ca. 1949 Cover: 0.10 **NM** value: **125.00**
2 ❑ ca. 1950 Cover: 0.10 **NM** value: **125.00**

WESTERN LOVE Prize

1 ❑ Jul 1949 Cover: 0.10 **NM** value: **300.00**
2 ❑ Sep 1949 Cover: 0.10 **NM** value: **250.00**
• **CGC:** 1 graded, best 8.0
📖 Sworn Enemies – In Love
3 ❑ Nov 1949 Cover: 0.10 **NM** value: **200.00**
4 ❑ Jan 1950 Cover: 0.10 **NM** value: **200.00**
5 ❑ Mar 1950 Cover: 0.10 **NM** value: **200.00**
📖 Lillie's Last Stand

WESTERN OUTLAWS AND SHERIFFS Marvel

60 ❑ Dec 1949 Cover: 0.10 **NM** value: **100.00**
• Series continued from Best Western #59
61 ❑ Mar 1951 Cover: 0.10 **NM** value: **75.00**
62 ❑ 1951 Cover: 0.10 **NM** value: **75.00**
63 ❑ 1951 Cover: 0.10 **NM** value: **75.00**
64 ❑ 1951 Cover: 0.10 **NM** value: **75.00**
65 ❑ 1951 Cover: 0.10 **NM** value: **75.00**
66 ❑ 1951 Cover: 0.10 **NM** value: **75.00**
67 ❑ 1951 Cover: 0.10 **NM** value: **75.00**
68 ❑ 1951 Cover: 0.10 **NM** value: **75.00**
69 ❑ 1951 Cover: 0.10 **NM** value: **75.00**
70 ❑ 1952 Cover: 0.10 **NM** value: **75.00**
71 ❑ 1952 Cover: 0.10 **NM** value: **75.00**
📖 El Toro Bianca: The Mexican Madman; Bank Robbers Revenge (text story); Six Finger Cassidy!; The Headless Horror; Matt "Swivel-Gun" Snide **A:** Bill Walton; Joe Maneely(cover)
72 ❑ 1952 Cover: 0.10 **NM** value: **75.00**
73 ❑ Jun 1952 Cover: 0.10 **NM** value: **75.00**

WESTERN ROUNDUP Dell

1 ❑ ca. 1952 Cover: 0.25 **NM** value: **200.00**
• Giant Size for entire series
2 ❑ Feb 1953 Cover: 0.25 **NM** value: **100.00**
• **CGC:** 1 graded, best 9.2
• Roy Rogers, Gene Autry, Rex Allen, Johnny Mack Brown, and Bill Elliot photo cover
3 ❑ Jul 1953 Cover: 0.25 **NM** value: **100.00**
• **CGC:** 1 graded, best 9.0
📖 Plan for Murder; Indian Fire Making (text story); The No-Good Brother; The Cowboy's Rope (text story); The 13th Knot; Indian Name Writing (text story); The Last Trick; Surprise Witness (text story); An Album of Famouse Ranches (text story); The Bullet Tip-Off; Indian Bow and Arrow Making (text story); The Cold-Blooded Frame-Up; Oh Bury Me Not (music page); Rex Allen and The Ghost • Gene Autry, Roy Rogers, Johnny Mack Brown, Bill Elliott, and Rex Allen photo cover
4 ❑ Oct 1953 Cover: 0.25 **NM** value: **100.00**
📖 The Disappearing Boulder; As I Went Walking Down the Street (music page); Champion Ropes a Killer; Guns and Gun Fighters of the Frontier West (text story); The Pussy-Footin' Prowlers; Trigger and Bullet Trap a Trickster; The Mysterious Stage Robberies (text story); Johnny Mack Brown Corners a Killer; Famous Horsemen of the World (text story); The Teller's Holdout; Good-bye Old Paint (music page); The Bounty Hunter • Roy Rogers, Gene Autry, Johnny Mack Brown, Bill Elliott, and Rex Allen photo cover
5 ❑ Jan 1954 Cover: 0.25 **NM** value: **100.00**
📖 Cover-Up; Indian Wigwam (text story); Money Buys Trouble; Indian Sand Paintings; The Robin Hood Mystery; Gold is Where You Find It (text story); Race Against Death; Famous Women of the West (text story); An Album of Good Badmen (text story); A Process of Elimination; Great Grand-Dad (music page); Wild Bill Elliott Plays a Hunch; The Big Rock Candy Mountain (music page); The Rustler's Ruse • Gene Autry, Roy Rogers, Bill Elliott, Johnny Mack Brown, and Rex Allen photo cover
6 ❑ Apr 1954 Cover: 0.25 **NM** value: **100.00**
• **CGC:** 1 graded, best 9.0
📖 The Disintegrator Gun; Indian Picture Writings (text story); Rustler's Roundup; The Indian's Cookbook; The Cracked-Up Getaway; The Message in the Springs (text story); Trigger Joins the Boys' Club; Indian Dictionary; The Vengeful Roustabout; The Gal I Left Behind Me (music page); A Lucky Flood; The Little Mohee (music page); A Neat Twist • Gene Autry, Roy Rogers, Bill Elliot, Rex Allen, and Johnny Mack Brown photo cover
7 ❑ Jul 1954 Cover: 0.25 **NM** value: **100.00**
• **CGC:** 1 graded, best 9.0
📖 Double for Murder; Indian Inventions (text story); Trouble for Texas; Heroes in Petticoats; The Right Trail; The New Teacher (text story); Colt Trouble; Colorful National Parks (text story); A Lucky Switch; Indian Inventions (text story); The Feather River Gang; Indian Inventions (text story); Desert Fury • Gene Autry, Roy Rogers, Bill Elliott, Rex Allen, and Johnny Mack Brown photo cover
8 ❑ Oct 1954 Cover: 0.25 **NM** value: **100.00**
• **CGC:** 1 graded, best 9.2
📖 The Bighorn Hunt; Indian Guess Game (puzzle page); Freelance Lawmen; Indian Quiz (puzzle page); Trouble on the Line; When Gramps was a Boy (text story); Trigger and Bullet Trap a Wild One; A Picture Map of Western History (text story); The Clue of the Unfired Gun; The Coyote; Indian Wildlife Homes Game (activity page); The Frame-Up • Gene Autry, Roy Rogers, Bill Elliot, Rex Allen, and Johnny Mack Brown photo cover
9 ❑ Jan 1955 Cover: 0.25 **NM** value: **100.00**
• **CGC:** 1 graded, best 9.2
📖 The Golden Scar; Indian Quiz (puzzle page); The Eagle's Prey; Indian Strategy; Killer at Large; So Blamed Ignorant (text story); The Showdown; Ghost Towns of the West (text story); Whispering Mountain; Rangeland Puzzlers (activity page); Dangerous Decoy; Indian Canoe Travois (text page); X Marks the Spot • Gene Autry, Roy Rogers, Bill Elliott, Rex Allen, and Johnny Mack Brown photo cover
10 ❑ Apr 1955 Cover: 0.25 **NM** value: **100.00**
• **CGC:** 2 graded, best 9.2
11 ❑ Jul 1955 Cover: 0.25 **NM** value: **100.00**
• **CGC:** 2 graded, best 8.0
12 ❑ Oct 1955 Cover: 0.25 **NM** value: **100.00**
• **CGC:** 3 graded, best 9.4
📖 The Killer Gang; Superstition Mountains (text story); The Boom-Town Mystery; Trigger and Bullet Meet Crooked Horse; Guilt Rides the Trail; Indian Quiz; Johnny on the Spot; Luke Sherman's Fortune (text story); Troubled Waters; Petrified Gravity (text story); The Salt Water Broncs (text story); Pecos Bill's Match (text story); The Fur-Bearing Trout (text story); The Trapper and the Bear (text story); Bear George's Ride (text story); The Mugwump (text story); Day of Reckoning; The Fugitive • Roy Rogers, Dale Evans, Rex Allen, Johnny Mack Brown, Wild Bill Elliot, and Gene Autry photo cover
13 ❑ Jan 1956 Cover: 0.25 **NM** value: **100.00**
• **CGC:** 1 graded, best 9.2
14 ❑ Apr 1956 Cover: 0.25 **NM** value: **100.00**
• **CGC:** 1 graded, best 9.2
15 ❑ Jul 1956 Cover: 0.25 **NM** value: **100.00**
• **CGC:** 3 graded, best 9.6
• Dale Evans, Roy Rogers, Rex Allen, Gene Autry, Wild Bill Elliot, and Johnny Mack Brown photo cover
16 ❑ Oct 1956 Cover: 0.25 **NM** value: **100.00**
• Roy Rogers, Dale Evans, Gene Autry, Rex Allen, Johnny Mack Brown, and Wild Bill Elliot cover photo; Dale Evans back cover portrait.
17 ❑ Jan 1957 Cover: 0.25 **NM** value: **100.00**
• **CGC:** 3 graded, best 9.6
• Dale Evans, Roy Rogers, Rex Allen, Gene Autry, Champion, Wild Bill Elliot, and Johnny Mack Brown photo cover
18 ❑ Apr 1957 Cover: 0.25 **NM** value: **100.00**
• **CGC:** 1 graded, best 9.2
• Gene Autry, Rex Allen, Roy Rogers, and Dale Evans photo cover
19 ❑ Jul 1957 Cover: 0.25 **NM** value: **100.00**
• **CGC:** 2 graded, best 9.6
20 ❑ Oct 1957 Cover: 0.25 **NM** value: **100.00**
• **CGC:** 1 graded, best 9.2
21 ❑ Jan 1958 Cover: 0.25 **NM** value: **100.00**
• **CGC:** 1 graded, best 9.6
22 ❑ Apr 1958 Cover: 0.25 **NM** value: **100.00**
• **CGC:** 1 graded, best 9.4
• Wagon Train story; Wells Fargo story
23 ❑ Jul 1958 Cover: 0.25 **NM** value: **100.00**
24 ❑ Oct 1958 Cover: 0.25 **NM** value: **100.00**
• Giant Size; Wagon Train story; Wells Fargo story

WESTERN TEAM-UP Marvel

1 ❑ Nov 1973 Cover: 0.20 **NM** value: **8.00**
• **CGC:** 2 graded, best 9.4

WESTERN THRILLERS Atlas

1 ❑ Nov 1954 Cover: 0.10 **NM** value: **100.00**
2 ❑ Dec 1954 Cover: 0.10 **NM** value: **100.00**
3 ❑ Jan 1955 Cover: 0.10 **NM** value: **100.00**
4 ❑ Feb 1955 Cover: 0.10 **NM** value: **100.00**
• **CGC:** 1 graded, best 3.0

WESTERN WINNERS Marvel

5 ❑ Jun 1949 Cover: 0.10 **NM** value: **150.00**
• Two-Gun Kid, Kid Colt, Black Rider
6 ❑ Sep 1949 Cover: 0.10 **NM** value: **150.00**
7 ❑ Dec 1949 Cover: 0.10 **NM** value: **150.00**
• **CGC:** 1 graded, best 8.0

WESTSIDE Antarctic

1 ❑ Mar 2000 Cover: 2.50 **NM** value: **Cover or less**
📖 Blind Raise **A:** Dean Hsieh; Eric Satrum **W:** Dean Hsieh

WETWORKS — Image

Wetworks is the story of Team 7, a special operations team under the command of Colonel Dane. Usually a hostage rescue unit, they were sent to Transylvania in the Balkans to destroy a biological warfare agent that a losing faction in the war there was threatening to use to trigger doomsday. In reality, the team was being sent to die.

When the team arrived, they discovered a research complex full of slaughtered scientists and guards, as well as containers filled with strange, silicon-based lifeforms. The creatures were symbiotes, exposure to which gave one of Dane's men near-invulnerability and enhanced strength. No sooner had this happened than they were attacked by "the Night Tribe," latter-day vampires that were the real focus of the mission. To escape, the rest of the team merged with the other symbiotes. Now, this well-trained team is a well-trained, invincible team -and they're just a little angry at having been set up.

1 ❑ Jun 1994 Cover: 1.95 **NM** value: **3.00**
Circ: CapCity orders: **93,075**
1/3D❑Jun 1994 Cover: 4.95 **NM** value: **Cover or less**
• 3-D edition. **A:** Whilce Portacio **W:** Whilce Portacio; Brandon Choi ★ Origin of Wetworks. ★ 1st Appearance of Dozer, Dane, Jester, Wetworks.
1/LE❑ Jun 1994 Cover: 1.95 **NM** value: **4.00**
• Special promotional edition distributed at the 1994 Chicago Comicon. **A:** Whilce Portacio **W:** Whilce Portacio; Brandon Choi ★ Origin of Wetworks. ★ 1st Appearance of Dozer, Jester, Wetworks.
2 ❑ Aug 1994 Cover: 1.95 **NM** value: **2.50**
Circ: CapCity orders: **72,350**
Standard cover. • Beast attacking man **A:** Whilce Portacio; Scott Williams(cover) **W:** Whilce Portacio; Brandon Choi
2/A ❑ Aug 1994 Cover: 1.95 **NM** value: **3.00**
alternate cover. • Variant edition cover with whole team posing. **A:** Whilce Portacio; Alex Garner(cover) **W:** Whilce Portacio; Brandon Choi
3 ❑ Sep 1994 Cover: 1.95 **NM** value: **2.50**
Circ: CapCity orders: **66,450**
4 ❑ Nov 1994 Cover: 2.50 **NM** value: **Cover or less**
Circ: CapCity orders: **62,475**
5 ❑ Jan 1995 Cover: 2.50 **NM** value: **Cover or less**
Circ: CapCity orders: **51,575**
6 ❑ Mar 1995 Cover: 2.50 **NM** value: **Cover or less**
Circ: CapCity orders: **45,175**
7 ❑ Apr 1995 Cover: 2.50 **NM** value: **Cover or less**
Circ: CapCity orders: **41,925**
8 ❑ May 1995 Cover: 2.50 **NM** value: **Cover or less**
Circ: CapCity orders: **42,600**
📖 WildStorm Rising, Part 7 • bound-in trading cards
8/SC❑May 1995 Cover: 2.50 **NM** value: **Cover or less**
9 ❑ Aug 1995 Cover: 2.50 **NM** value: **Cover or less**
Circ: CapCity orders: **36,075**
10 ❑ Aug 1995 Cover: 2.50 **NM** value: **Cover or less**
Circ: CapCity orders: **32,475**
11 ❑ Sep 1995 Cover: 2.50 **NM** value: **Cover or less**
Circ: CapCity orders: **28,325**
12 ❑ Nov 1995 Cover: 2.50 **NM** value: **Cover or less**
indicia says Nov, cover says Dec. ★ 1st Appearance of Pilgrim.
13 ❑ Jan 1996 Cover: 2.50 **NM** value: **Cover or less**
14 ❑ Feb 1996 Cover: 2.50 **NM** value: **Cover or less**
15 ❑ Mar 1996 Cover: 2.50 **NM** value: **Cover or less**
16 ❑ Apr 1996 Cover: 2.50 **NM** value: **Cover or less**
📖 Fire from Heaven, Part 4
17 ❑ May 1996 Cover: 2.50 **NM** value: **Cover or less**
📖 Fire from Heaven, Part 11
18 ❑ Jul 1996 Cover: 2.50 **NM** value: **Cover or less**
19 ❑ Aug 1996 Cover: 2.50 **NM** value: **Cover or less**
20 ❑ Aug 1996 Cover: 2.50 **NM** value: **Cover or less**
21 ❑ Sep 1996 Cover: 2.50 **NM** value: **Cover or less**
Circ: Diamd. preorders: **45,372**
22 ❑ Oct 1996 Cover: 2.50 **NM** value: **Cover or less**
Circ: Diamd. preorders: **42,981**
23 ❑ Nov 1996 Cover: 2.50 **NM** value: **Cover or less**
Circ: Diamd. preorders: **39,473**
24 ❑ Dec 1996 Cover: 2.50 **NM** value: **Cover or less**
Circ: Diamd. preorders: **36,451**
25 ❑ Jan 1997 Cover: 3.95 **NM** value: **Cover or less**
Circ: Diamd. preorders: **35,637**
wraparound cover. • Giant-size. **A:** Mel Rubi; Jason Johnson **W:** Francis Takenaga
25/A❑Jan 1997 Cover: 3.95 **NM** value: **Cover or less**
alternate wraparound cover (previous covers in background).
26 ❑ Feb 1997 Cover: 2.50 **NM** value: **Cover or less**
Circ: Diamd. preorders: **32,086**
27 ❑ Mar 1997 Cover: 2.50 **NM** value: **Cover or less**
Circ: Diamd. preorders: **32,152**
28 ❑ Apr 1997 Cover: 2.50 **NM** value: **Cover or less**
Circ: Diamd. preorders: **31,543**
29 ❑ May 1997 Cover: 2.50 **NM** value: **Cover or less**
Circ: Diamd. preorders: **29,932**
30 ❑ Jun 1997 Cover: 2.50 **NM** value: **Cover or less**
Circ: Diamd. preorders: **29,010**
31 ❑ Jul 1997 Cover: 2.50 **NM** value: **Cover or less**
Circ: Diamd. preorders: **27,464**
32 ❑ Aug 1997 Cover: 2.50 **NM** value: **Cover or less**
Circ: Diamd. preorders: **23,079**
📖 Sacraments of Damnation, Part 1 **W:** Steven Grant
32/A❑Aug 1997 Cover: 2.50 **NM** value: **Cover or less**
alternate cover (mostly b&w). • Voyager pack
33 ❑ Sep 1997 Cover: 2.50 **NM** value: **Cover or less**
Circ: Diamd. preorders: **28,077**
📖 Sacraments of Damnation, Part 2 **W:** Steven Grant
34 ❑ Oct 1997 Cover: 2.50 **NM** value: **Cover or less**
Circ: Diamd. preorders: **26,808**
📖 Sacraments of Damnation, Part 3 **A:** Michael Ryan **W:** Steven Grant
35 ❑ Nov 1997 Cover: 2.50 **NM** value: **Cover or less**
Circ: Diamd. preorders: **25,951**
📖 Sacraments of Damnation, Part 4 **A:** Michael Ryan **W:** Steven Grant
36 ❑ Jan 1998 Cover: 2.50 **NM** value: **Cover or less**
Circ: Diamd. preorders: **23,520**
📖 Maximum Security **A:** Michael Ryan **W:** Steven Grant
37 ❑ Feb 1998 Cover: 2.50 **NM** value: **Cover or less**
Circ: Diamd. preorders: **21,638**
📖 Diversionary Tactics, Part 1 **A:** Ken Lashley **W:** Steven Grant
38 ❑ Mar 1998 Cover: 2.50 **NM** value: **Cover or less**
Circ: Diamd. preorders: **21,552**
📖 Diversionary Tactics, Part 3 **A:** Ken Lashley **W:** Steven Grant
39 ❑ Apr 1998 Cover: 2.50 **NM** value: **Cover or less**
Circ: Diamd. preorders: **21,383**
📖 Diversionary Tactics, Part 2 **A:** Ken Lashley **W:** Steven Grant
40 ❑ May 1998 Cover: 2.50 **NM** value: **Cover or less**
Circ: Diamd. preorders: **19,955**
📖 Drawn Swords, Part 1 **A:** Ken Lashley **W:** Steven Grant ★ Appearance of StormWatch.
41 ❑ Jun 1998 Cover: 2.50 **NM** value: **Cover or less**
Circ: Diamd. preorders: **19,792**
📖 Drawn Swords, Part 2 **A:** Ken Lashley **W:** Steven Grant
42 ❑ Jul 1998 Cover: 2.50 **NM** value: **Cover or less**
Circ: Diamd. preorders: **18,567**
📖 Flashback, Part 1 **A:** Ken Lashley **W:** Steven Grant
43 ❑ Aug 1998 Cover: 2.50 **NM** value: **Cover or less**
Circ: Diamd. preorders: **18,090**
📖 Flashback, Part 2 **A:** Ken Lashley **W:** Steven Grant
3D 1❑Feb 1998 Cover: 4.95 **NM** value: **Cover or less**
wraparound cover. • with glasses
Bk 1❑ Oct 1996 Cover: 9.95 **NM** value: **Cover or less**
• Rebirth; collects issues #1-3

WETWORKS SOURCEBOOK — Image

1 ❑ Oct 1994 Cover: 2.50 **NM** value: **Cover or less**
Circ: CapCity orders: **37,150**

WETWORKS/VAMPIRELLA — Image

1 ❑ Jul 1997 Cover: 2.95 **NM** value: **Cover or less**
Circ: Diamd. preorders: **38,387**
• crossover with Harris
1/A ❑ Jul 1997 Cover: 2.95 **NM** value: **Cover or less**
alternate cover. • crossover with Harris **C:** Gil Kane

WHACK — St. John

1 ❑ Oct 1953 Cover: 0.25 **NM** value: **150.00**
• **CGC:** 1 graded, best 7.5
• 3-D Issue
2 ❑ Dec 1953 Cover: 0.10 **NM** value: **100.00**
3 ❑ Feb 1954 Cover: 0.10 **NM** value: **100.00**

WHACKED! — River Group

1 ❑ Mar 1994 Cover: 2.50 **NM** value: **Cover or less**
No issue number. wraparound cover. • Tonya Harding case parody

WHAM — Centaur

1 ❑ Nov 1940 Cover: 0.10 **NM** value: **900.00**
• **CGC:** 3 graded, best 9.2
2 ❑ Dec 1940 Cover: 0.10 **NM** value: **900.00**

WHAT IF THIS WERE HEAVEN, WOULDN'T THAT BE HELL? — DC / Piranha

Bk 1❑ b&w Cover: 14.95 **NM** value: **Cover or less**

WHAT IF...? (VOL. 1) — Marvel

One of the most imaginative titles to come from Marvel, What If... was a more engaging, serious take on DC's "imaginary stories." As series host, The Watcher reminded readers each issue of one or more events from Marvel's history — and then told the story of an alternate reality in which things happened differently.

Some were silly — such as the Marvel Bullpen becoming the Fantastic Four or Sgt. Fury fighting World War II in space — but others were poignant. "What If The Avengers Had Become the Pawns of Korvac" in #32 stands as one of the bleakest, most horrifying tales ever to come from Marvel. (A follow-up later appeared in Classic X-Men.) The story of the survival of Spider-Man's clone in #30 is better than the entire "Clone Saga" that appeared in later Spidey comics. And Tony Isabella's "What If Gwen Stacy Had Lived" in #24 has torn at the heartstrings of many Spidey fans over the years.

Too many stories would follow the "let's kill all the super-heroes" mold, but many from this first series, which is far superior to the second volume, are among Marvel's best. Look for #34's all-humor issue, which remains one of the funniest comics ever published by Marvel. — JJM

1 ❑ Feb 1977 Cover: 0.50 **NM** value: **12.00**
• **CGC:** 73 graded, best 9.8
📖 ...Spider-Man Joined the Fantastic Four? • Spider-Man **A:** Jim Craig **W:** Roy Thomas
2 ❑ Apr 1977 Cover: 0.50 **NM** value: **6.00**
• **CGC:** 9 graded, best 9.8
📖 ...The Hulk Had the Brain of Bruce Banner? • Hulk **C:** Gil Kane
3 ❑ Jun 1977 Cover: 0.50 **NM** value: **5.00**
• **CGC:** 6 graded, best 9.6
📖 ...The Avengers Had Never Been? • Avengers **A:** Gil Kane; Klaus Janson **W:** Jim Shooter; Gil Kane
4 ❑ Aug 1977 Cover: 0.50 **NM** value: **5.00**
• **CGC:** 3 graded, best 9.8
📖 ...The Invaders had stayed together after World War II? • Invaders **C:** Gil Kane
5 ❑ Oct 1977 Cover: 0.50 **NM** value: **5.00**
• **CGC:** 2 graded, best 9.4
📖 ...Captain America Hadn't Vanished During World War II? • Captain America ★ Origin of Bucky II (Fred Davis). ★ 1st Appearance of Captain America II (William Nasland), Captain America III (Jeffrey Mace). ★ Death of Captain America II (William Nasland).
6 ❑ Dec 1977 Cover: 0.60 **NM** value: **4.00**
• **CGC:** 1 graded, best 9.6
📖 ...The Fantastic Four Had Different Super-Powers? • Fantastic Four
7 ❑ Feb 1978 Cover: 0.60 **NM** value: **4.00**
• **CGC:** 2 graded, best 9.4
📖 ...Someone else besides Spider-Man had been bitten by the radioactive spider? • Spider-Man **C:** Gil Kane
8 ❑ Apr 1978 Cover: 0.60 **NM** value: **4.00**
• **CGC:** 3 graded, best 9.4
📖 ...The World Knew That Daredevil is blind? • Daredevil **C:** Gil Kane; John Romita
9 ❑ Jun 1978 Cover: 0.60 **NM** value: **4.00**
• **CGC:** 1 graded, best 9.6
📖 ...Avengers had fought evil during the 1950's? • Avengers **A:** Alan Kupperberg; Bill Black **C:** Jack Kirby **W:** Don Glut ★ Origin of Marvel Boy, Human Robot, 3-D Man, Venus, Gorilla-Man.
10 ❑ Aug 1978 Cover: 0.60 **NM** value: **4.00**
• **CGC:** 3 graded, best 9.6
📖 ...Jane Foster had found the hammer of Thor? • Thor **A:** Rick Hoberg
11 ❑ Oct 1978 Cover: 0.60 **NM** value: **3.00**
• **CGC:** 1 graded, best 9.6
📖 ...The original Marvel bullpen had become the Fantastic Four? • Marvel Bullpen as Fantastic Four **A:** Jack Kirby
12 ❑ Dec 1978 Cover: 0.60 **NM** value: **3.00**
📖 ...Rick Jones had become the Hulk? • Rick Jones as Hulk **A:** Sal Buscema **W:** Don Glut
13 ❑ Feb 1979 Cover: 0.60 **NM** value: **4.00**
Circ: Statement: **134,746**
📖 ...Conan the Barbarian walked the earth today? • Conan **A:** John Buscema
14 ❑ Apr 1979 Cover: 0.60 **NM** value: **3.00**
Circ: Statement: **134,746**
📖 ...Sgt. Fury had fought World War II in outer space? • Sgt. Fury
15 ❑ Jun 1979 Cover: 0.60 **NM** value: **3.00**
Circ: Statement: **134,746**
📖 ...Nova had been four other people? • Nova **A:** John Buscema; Joe Sinnott
16 ❑ Aug 1979 Cover: 0.60 **NM** value: **2.50**
Circ: Statement: **134,746**
📖 ...Shang-Chi, Master of Kung Fu fought on the side of Fu Manchu? • Fu Manchu
17 ❑ Oct 1979 Cover: 0.60 **NM** value: **3.00**
Circ: Statement: **134,746** • **CGC:** 1 graded, best 9.4
📖 ...Ghost Rider, Spider-Woman, Captain Marvel Were Villains • Ghost Rider, Captain Marvel, Spider-Woman **A:** Carmine Infantino
18 ❑ Dec 1979 Cover: 0.75 **NM** value: **2.50**
Circ: Statement: **134,746**
📖 ...Dr. Strange were a disciple of Dormammu? • Doctor Strange **A:** Tom Sutton
19 ❑ Feb 1980 Cover: 0.75 **NM** value: **2.50**
Circ: Statement: **122,402**
📖 ...Spider-Man had never become a crimefighter? • Spider-Man **A:** Pat Broderick
20 ❑ Apr 1980 Cover: 0.75 **NM** value: **2.50**
Circ: Statement: **122,402**
📖 ...The Avengers fought the Kree-Skrull War without Rick Jones? • Avengers; Has 1979 Statement, filed 10/1/79; avg print run 276,176; avg sales 133,625; avg subs 1,121; avg total paid 134,746; samples 635; office use 1,013; max existent 136,394; 51% of run returned **A:** Alan Kupperberg **W:** Tom DeFalco
21 ❑ Jun 1980 Cover: 0.75 **NM** value: **2.50**
Circ: Statement: **122,402**
📖 ...The Invisible Girl of the Fantastic Four had married the Sub-Mariner? • Sub-Mariner **A:** Gene Colan
22 ❑ Aug 1980 Cover: 0.75 **NM** value: **2.50**
Circ: Statement: **122,402**
📖 ...Doctor Doom had become a hero? • Doctor Doom
23 ❑ Oct 1980 Cover: 0.75 **NM** value: **2.50**
Circ: Statement: **122,402**
📖 ...The Hulk had become a barbarian? • Hulk **A:** Herb Trimpe
24 ❑ Dec 1980 Cover: 0.75 **NM** value: **2.50**
Circ: Statement: **122,402**
📖 ...Spider-Man had rescued Gwen Stacy? • Spider-Man
25 ❑ Feb 1981 Cover: 0.75 **NM** value: **2.50**
Circ: Statement: **119,159**
📖 ...Thor and the Avengers battled the gods? • Thor, Avengers ★ Origin of Uni-Mind.
26 ❑ Apr 1981 Cover: 0.75 **NM** value: **2.50**
Circ: Statement: **119,159**
📖 ...Captain America had been elected president? • Captain America; Has 1980 Statement, filed 10/1/80; avg print run 265,877; avg sales 120,933; avg subs 1,469; avg total paid 122,402; samples 623; office use 1,029; max existent 124,054; 53% of run returned **C:** John Byrne
27 ❑ Jul 1981 Cover: 0.75 **NM** value: **4.00**
Circ: Statement: **119,159** • **CGC:** 8 graded, best 9.8
📖 ...Phoenix had not died? • X-Men **A:** Jerry Bingham; Frank Miller(cover) **C:** Frank Miller **W:** Mary Jo Duffy
28 ❑ Aug 1981 Cover: 0.75 **NM** value: **5.00**
Circ: Statement: **119,159** • **CGC:** 3 graded, best 9.6
📖 ...Daredevil became an agent of S.H.I.E.L.D.? • Daredevil **A:** Frank Miller **W:** Frank Miller

CGC-graded: Multiply prices above by **33 for 9.9 M • 16 for 9.8 NM/M • 7 for 9.6 NM+ • 5 for 9.4 NM • 2.5 for 9.2 NM- • 1.5 for 9.0 VF/NM**

29 ❑ Oct 1981 Cover: 0.75 **NM** value: **2.50**
Circ: Statement: **119,159**
📖 ...The Avengers defeated everybody? • Avengers **C:** Michael Golden

30 ❑ Dec 1981 Cover: 0.75 **NM** value: **5.00**
Circ: Statement: **119,159** • **CGC:** 1 graded, best 8.0
📖 ...Spider-Man's clone lived? • Spider-Man clone, Inhumans **A:** Rich Buckler

31 ❑ Feb 1982 Cover: 1.00 **NM** value: **5.00**
Circ: Statement: **160,205** • **CGC:** 10 graded, best 9.8
📖 ...Wolverine had killed the Hulk? • Wolverine **A:** Bob Budiansky **W:** Rich Margopoulos

32 ❑ Apr 1982 Cover: 1.00 **NM** value: **2.50**
Circ: Statement: **160,205**
📖 ...The Avengers had become pawns of Korvac? • Avengers; Has 1981 Statement, filed 10/1/81; avg print run 262,341, avg sales 116,907; avg subs 2,252; avg total paid 119,159; samples 492; office use 2,107; max existent 121,758; 54% of run returned **A:** Greg Laroque; Frank Miller(inks)

33 ❑ Jun 1982 Cover: 1.00 **NM** value: **2.50**
Circ: Statement: **160,205**
📖 ...Dazzler had become the herald of Galactus?; ...Iron Man was trapped in the time of King Arthur? • Dazzler **A:** Don Perlin; Mike Vosberg

34 ❑ Aug 1982 Cover: 1.00 **NM** value: **2.50**
Circ: Statement: **160,205**
• comedy issue **A:** Bill Sienkiewicz; Fred Hembeck; John Byrne; Frank Miller

35 ❑ Oct 1982 Cover: 1.00 **NM** value: **4.00**
Circ: Statement: **160,205** • **CGC:** 15 graded, best 9.8
📖 ...Elektra had lived? • Elektra **A:** Frank Miller **W:** Frank Miller

36 ❑ Dec 1982 Cover: 1.00 **NM** value: **2.50**
Circ: Statement: **160,205** • **CGC:** 1 graded, best 9.6
📖 ...The Fantastic Four had not gained their super-powers? • Fantastic Four; Nova **A:** John Byrne

37 ❑ Feb 1983 Cover: 1.00 **NM** value: **2.50**
📖 ...The Beast and the King continued to mutate? • Beast; Thing; Silver Surfer

38 ❑ Apr 1983 Cover: 1.00 **NM** value: **2.50**
• Daredevil, Captain America, Vision, Scarlet Witch; Has 1982 Statement; filed 10/11/82; avg print run 283,279; avg sales 156,550; avg subs 3,655; avg total paid 160,205; samples 558; office use 2,221; 43% of run returned

39 ❑ Jun 1983 Cover: 1.00 **NM** value: **2.50**
📖 ...Thor battled Conan the Barbarian? • Thor vs. Conan

40 ❑ Aug 1983 Cover: 1.00 **NM** value: **2.50**
📖 ...Dr. Strange had not become master of the mystic arts? • Doctor Strange

41 ❑ Oct 1983 Cover: 1.00 **NM** value: **2.50**
📖 ...The Sub-Mariner had saved Atlantis from its destiny? • Sub-Mariner

42 ❑ Dec 1983 Cover: 1.00 **NM** value: **2.50**
📖 ...The Invisible Girl had died? • Fantastic Four

43 ❑ Feb 1984 Cover: 1.00 **NM** value: **2.50**
📖 ...Conan the Barbarian were stranded in the 20th century? • Conan

44 ❑ Apr 1984 Cover: 1.00 **NM** value: **2.50**
📖 ...Captain America were revived today? • Captain America

45 ❑ Jun 1984 Cover: 1.00 **NM** value: **2.50**
📖 ...The Hulk went berserk? • Hulk

46 ❑ Aug 1984 Cover: 1.00 **NM** value: **3.00**
📖 ...Spider-Man's Uncle Ben had lived? • Spider-Man

47 ❑ Oct 1984 Cover: 1.00 **NM** value: **2.50**
📖 ...Loki had found the hammer of Thor? final issue. • Thor, Loki

SE 1 ❑ Jun 1988 Cover: 1.50 **NM** value: **2.50**
Circ: CapCity orders: **22,000**
• Iron Man

WHAT IF...? (VOL. 2) Marvel

Ah, what if...? This second series of the popular comic follows up on many of the variations on that popular theme. How would life be different if this had not happened, or had happened differently?

For instance, if Frank Castle had stopped a few steps shorter in retrieving his child's lost kite in Central Park, the gang there might never have seen him-and as a result never killed his family. If so, would we have had a Punisher today? And if not, how would the world be different?

And what changes might have occurred if the Avengers had won the Evolutionary War? Would the High Evolutionary have succeeded in affecting the evolution of mankind? And if so, what effect would such a massive change have had on the universe?

Generally weaker than the first series — due to the churn-em-out monthly pace — there are still some interesting stories here and there.

-1 ❑ Jul 1997 Cover: 1.99 **NM** value: **2.00**
• Flashback; Bishop

1 ❑ Jul 1989 Cover: 1.25 **NM** value: **4.00**
Circ: CapCity orders: **38,600** • **CGC:** 1 graded, best 8.0
📖 ...The Avengers had lost the Evolutionary War? • Avengers

2 ❑ Aug 1989 Cover: 1.25 **NM** value: **3.00**
Circ: CapCity orders: **34,300**
• Daredevil

3 ❑ Sep 1989 Cover: 1.25 **NM** value: **3.00**
Circ: CapCity orders: **30,000**
• Captain America

4 ❑ Oct 1989 Cover: 1.25 **NM** value: **3.00**
Circ: CapCity orders: **31,500**
• Spider-Man

5 ❑ Nov 1989 Cover: 1.25 **NM** value: **3.00**
Circ: CapCity orders: **29,900**
• Avengers

6 ❑ Nov 1989 Cover: 1.25 **NM** value: **3.00**
Circ: CapCity orders: **42,700**
• X-Men

7 ❑ Dec 1989 Cover: 1.25 **NM** value: **3.00**
Circ: CapCity orders: **52,500** • **CGC:** 1 graded, best 8.0
• Wolverine **A:** Rob Liefeld

8 ❑ Dec 1989 Cover: 1.25 **NM** value: **2.50**
Circ: CapCity orders: **32,400**
• Iron Man

9 ❑ Jan 1990 Cover: 1.25 **NM** value: **2.50**
Circ: Statement: **203,199** CapCity orders: **45,600** • **CGC:** 4 graded, best 9.8
• X-Men

10 ❑ Feb 1990 Cover: 1.25 **NM** value: **2.50**
Circ: Statement: **203,199** CapCity orders: **53,500**
📖 ...The Punisher's family hadn't been killed? • Punisher

11 ❑ Mar 1990 Cover: 1.25 **NM** value: **2.50**
Circ: Statement: **203,199** CapCity orders: **32,400**
• Fantastic Four

12 ❑ Apr 1990 Cover: 1.25 **NM** value: **2.50**
Circ: Statement: **203,199** CapCity orders: **40,800**
• X-Men

13 ❑ May 1990 Cover: 1.25 **NM** value: **2.50**
Circ: Statement: **203,199** CapCity orders: **39,300**
• X-Men **W:** Kurt Busiek

14 ❑ Jun 1990 Cover: 1.25 **NM** value: **2.50**
Circ: Statement: **203,199** CapCity orders: **32,100**
• Captain Marvel

15 ❑ Jul 1990 Cover: 1.25 **NM** value: **2.50**
Circ: Statement: **203,199** CapCity orders: **42,000**
• Fantastic Four, Galactus

16 ❑ Aug 1990 Cover: 1.25 **NM** value: **3.00**
Circ: Statement: **203,199** CapCity orders: **42,300**
📖 ...Wolverine battled Conan? • Wolverine; Conan

17 ❑ Sep 1990 Cover: 1.25 **NM** value: **2.50**
Circ: Statement: **203,199** CapCity orders: **37,900**

18 ❑ Oct 1990 Cover: 1.25 **NM** value: **2.50**
Circ: Statement: **203,199** CapCity orders: **28,200**
• Fantastic Four, Doctor Doom

19 ❑ Nov 1990 Cover: 1.25 **NM** value: **2.50**
Circ: Statement: **203,199** CapCity orders: **27,900**
• Avengers

20 ❑ Dec 1990 Cover: 1.25 **NM** value: **2.50**
Circ: Statement: **203,199** CapCity orders: **33,900**
• Spider-Man

21 ❑ Jan 1991 Cover: 1.25 **NM** value: **2.25**
Circ: Statement: **178,300** CapCity orders: **33,000**
• Spider-Man ★ Death of Black Cat.

22 ❑ Feb 1991 Cover: 1.25 **NM** value: **2.25**
Circ: Statement: **178,300** CapCity orders: **27,900**
• Silver Surfer

23 ❑ Mar 1991 Cover: 1.25 **NM** value: **2.25**
Circ: Statement: **178,300** CapCity orders: **35,100**
• X-Men; Has 1990 Statement, filed 10/1/90; avg print run 320,410; avg sales 201,391, avg subs 1,808; avg total paid 203,199; samples 100; office use 600; max existent 203,899; 36% of run returned **W:** Kurt Busiek

24 ❑ Apr 1991 Cover: 1.25 **NM** value: **3.50**
Circ: Statement: **178,300** CapCity orders: **39,000**
• vampire Wolverine

25 ❑ May 1991 Cover: 1.25 **NM** value: **3.25**
Circ: Statement: **178,300** CapCity orders: **30,600**
• Atlantis Attacks

26 ❑ Jun 1991 Cover: 1.25 **NM** value: **2.00**
Circ: Statement: **178,300** CapCity orders: **37,400**
• Punisher **W:** Kurt Busiek

27 ❑ Jul 1991 Cover: 1.25 **NM** value: **2.00**
Circ: Statement: **178,300** CapCity orders: **28,500**
• Namor, Fantastic Four

28 ❑ Aug 1991 Cover: 1.25 **NM** value: **2.00**
Circ: Statement: **178,300** CapCity orders: **26,700**
• Captain America

29 ❑ Sep 1991 Cover: 1.25 **NM** value: **2.00**
Circ: Statement: **178,300** CapCity orders: **29,700**
• Captain America, Avengers

30 ❑ Oct 1991 Cover: 1.75 **NM** value: **2.00**
Circ: Statement: **178,300** CapCity orders: **26,100**
• Fantastic Four

31 ❑ Nov 1991 Cover: 1.25 **NM** value: **2.00**
Circ: Statement: **178,300** CapCity orders: **32,100**
• Spider-Man with cosmic powers

32 ❑ Dec 1991 Cover: 1.25 **NM** value: **2.00**
Circ: Statement: **178,300** CapCity orders: **38,200**
• Phoenix

33 ❑ Jan 1992 Cover: 1.25 **NM** value: **2.00**
Circ: Statement: **166,584** CapCity orders: **36,900**
• Phoenix

34 ❑ Feb 1992 Cover: 1.25 **NM** value: **2.00**
Circ: Statement: **166,584** CapCity orders: **24,300**
📖 ...No One Was Watching The Watcher? • parody issue **A:** Tom Morgan **W:** Scott Gimple

35 ❑ Mar 1992 Cover: 1.25 **NM** value: **2.00**
Circ: Statement: **166,584** CapCity orders: **25,800**
📖 Timequake, Part 1 • Fantastic Four; Spider-Man; Doctor Doom

36 ❑ Apr 1992 Cover: 1.25 **NM** value: **2.00**
Circ: Statement: **166,584** CapCity orders: **24,000**
📖 Timequake, Part 2 • Avengers vs. Guardians of the Galaxy

37 ❑ May 1992 Cover: 1.25 **NM** value: **2.00**
Circ: Statement: **166,584** CapCity orders: **26,100**
📖 Timequake, Part 3 • Wolverine

38 ❑ Jun 1992 Cover: 1.25 **NM** value: **2.00**
Circ: Statement: **166,584** CapCity orders: **23,700**
📖 Timequake, Part 4 • Thor

39 ❑ Jul 1992 Cover: 1.25 **NM** value: **2.00**
Circ: Statement: **166,584** CapCity orders: **23,200**
📖 Timequake, Part 5 • Watcher

40 ❑ Aug 1992 Cover: 1.25 **NM** value: **2.00**
Circ: Statement: **166,584**
• X-Men

41 ❑ Sep 1992 Cover: 1.75 **NM** value: **2.00**
Circ: Statement: **166,584** CapCity orders: **24,200**
• Avengers vs. Galactus

42 ❑ Oct 1992 Cover: 1.25 **NM** value: **2.00**
Circ: Statement: **166,584** CapCity orders: **24,600**
• Spider-Man

43 ❑ Nov 1992 Cover: 1.25 **NM** value: **2.00**
Circ: Statement: **166,584** CapCity orders: **26,100**
• Wolverine

44 ❑ Dec 1992 Cover: 1.25 **NM** value: **2.00**
Circ: Statement: **166,584** CapCity orders: **32,600**
• Venom, Punisher **W:** Kurt Busiek

45 ❑ Jan 1993 Cover: 1.25 **NM** value: **2.00**
Circ: Statement: **140,850** CapCity orders: **23,300**
• Ghost Rider

46 ❑ Feb 1993 Cover: 1.25 **NM** value: **2.00**
Circ: Statement: **140,850** CapCity orders: **32,400**
📖 ...Cable Had Destroyed the X-Men?, Part 1 • Cable **W:** Kurt Busiek

47 ❑ Mar 1993 Cover: 1.25 **NM** value: **2.00**
Circ: Statement: **140,850** CapCity orders: **26,000**
📖 ...Cable Had Destroyed the X-Men?, Part 2 • Magneto; Has 1992 Statement, filed 10/4/91; avg print run 270,308; avg sales 163,767; avg subs 2,817; avg total paid 166,584; samples 250; office use 500; max existent 167,334; 38% of run returned **W:** Kurt Busiek

48 ❑ Apr 1993 Cover: 1.25 **NM** value: **2.00**
Circ: Statement: **140,850** CapCity orders: **21,200**
• Daredevil

49 ❑ May 1993 Cover: 1.25 **NM** value: **2.00**
Circ: Statement: **140,850** CapCity orders: **25,600**
• Silver Surfer

50 ❑ Jun 1993 Cover: 2.95 **NM** value: **Cover or less**
Circ: Statement: **140,850** CapCity orders: **56,900** • **CGC:** 3 graded, best 9.6
silver sculpted cover. • Hulk, Wolverine

51 ❑ Jul 1993 Cover: 1.25 **NM** value: **2.00**
Circ: Statement: **140,850** CapCity orders: **23,200**
• Punisher, Captain America

52 ❑ Aug 1993 Cover: 1.25 **NM** value: **2.00**
Circ: Statement: **140,850** CapCity orders: **28,700**
• Doctor Doom

53 ❑ Sep 1993 Cover: 1.25 **NM** value: **2.00**
Circ: Statement: **140,850** CapCity orders: **23,200**
• Spider-Man, Hulk, Iron Man 2020

54 ❑ Oct 1993 Cover: 1.25 **NM** value: **2.00**
Circ: Statement: **140,850** CapCity orders: **19,600**
📖 ...Death's Head I Had Lived? • Death's Head **A:** Geoff Senior **W:** Simon Furman ★ Appearance of Reed Richards, Fantastic Four, Cage, Death's Head II, War Machine, Captain America, Death's Head, Charnel.

55 ❑ Nov 1993 Cover: 1.25 **NM** value: **2.00**
Circ: Statement: **140,850**
• Avengers

56 ❑ Dec 1993 Cover: 1.25 **NM** value: **2.00**
Circ: Statement: **108,608** CapCity orders: **20,300**
• Avengers

57 ❑ Jan 1994 Cover: 1.25 **NM** value: **2.00**
Circ: Statement: **108,608** CapCity orders: **18,700**
• Punisher

58 ❑ Feb 1994 Cover: 1.25 **NM** value: **2.00**
Circ: Statement: **108,608** CapCity orders: **24,450**
📖 ...The Punisher had Killed Spider-Man? • Punisher, Spider-Man

59 ❑ Mar 1994 Cover: 1.25 **NM** value: **2.00**
Circ: Statement: **108,608** CapCity orders: **23,650**
📖 ...Wolverine Led Alpha Flight? • Wolverine/Alpha Flight

60 ❑ Apr 1994 Cover: 1.25 **NM** value: **2.00**
Circ: Statement: **108,608** CapCity orders: **25,100**
• X-Men wedding **W:** Kurt Busiek

61 ❑ May 1994 Cover: 1.50 **NM** value: **2.00**
Circ: Statement: **108,608** CapCity orders: **20,100**
• Spider-Man **W:** Kurt Busiek

62 ❑ Jun 1994 Cover: 1.50 **NM** value: **2.00**
Circ: Statement: **108,608** CapCity orders: **27,250**
• Wolverine **W:** Kurt Busiek

63 ❑ Jul 1994 Cover: 1.50 **NM** value: **2.00**
Circ: Statement: **108,608** CapCity orders: **17,850**
• War Machine

64 ❑ Aug 1994 Cover: 2.00 **NM** value: **Cover or less**
Circ: Statement: **108,608** CapCity orders: **17,050**
📖 ...Iron Man Sold Out? • Iron Man

65 ❑ Sep 1994 Cover: 1.50 **NM** value: **1.75**
Circ: Statement: **108,608** CapCity orders: **19,550**

66 ❑ Oct 1994 Cover: 1.50 **NM** value: **1.75**
Circ: Statement: **108,608** CapCity orders: **19,350**
📖 ...Rogue Possessed the Power of Thor? • Rogue

67 ❑ Nov 1994 Cover: 1.50 **NM** value: **1.75**
Circ: Statement: **88,931** CapCity orders: **14,850**
• Captain America

68 ❑ Dec 1994 Cover: 1.50 **NM** value: **1.75**
Circ: Statement: **88,931** CapCity orders: **14,450**
• Captain America

69 ❑ Jan 1995 Cover: 1.50 **NM** value: **1.75**
Circ: Statement: **88,931** CapCity orders: **18,125**
• X-Men

70 ❑ Feb 1995 Cover: 1.50 **NM** value: **1.75**
Circ: Statement: **88,931** CapCity orders: **13,875**
• Silver Surfer

71 ❑ Mar 1995 Cover: 1.50 **NM** value: **Cover or less**
Circ: Statement: **88,931** CapCity orders: **12,525**
• Hulk

72 ❑ Apr 1995 Cover: 1.50 **NM** value: **Cover or less**
Circ: Statement: **88,931** CapCity orders: **14,300**
• Spider-Man

73 ❑ May 1995 Cover: 1.50 **NM** value: **Cover or less**
Circ: Statement: **88,931** CapCity orders: **11,700**
• Daredevil

Other grades: Multiply prices above by **1.5 for Mint • 2/3 for Very Fine • 1/3 for Fine • 1/5 for Very Good • 1/8 for Good**

74 ❑ Jun 1995 Cover: 1.50 **NM** value: **Cover or less**
Circ: Statement: **88,931** CapCity orders: **19,825**
• Mr. Sinister forms The X-Men
75 ❑ Jul 1995 Cover: 1.50 **NM** value: **Cover or less**
Circ: Statement: **88,931** CapCity orders: **16,400**
• Generation X
76 ❑ Aug 1995 Cover: 1.50 **NM** value: **Cover or less**
Circ: Statement: **88,931** CapCity orders: **13,950**
• Flash Thompson as Spider-Man; last Watcher
77 ❑ Sep 1995 Cover: 1.50 **NM** value: **Cover or less**
Circ: Statement: **88,931**
• Legion
78 ❑ Oct 1995 Cover: 1.50 **NM** value: **Cover or less**
Circ: Statement: **68,529**
• New Fantastic Four remains a team
79 ❑ Nov 1995 Cover: 1.50 **NM** value: **Cover or less**
Circ: Statement: **68,529**
• Storm becomes Phoenix
80 ❑ Dec 1995 Cover: 1.50 **NM** value: **Cover or less**
Circ: Statement: **68,529**
...the Hulk Got Himself Cured? • Hulk becomes The Maestro **A:** Kerry Gammill **W:** James Felder ★ Appearance of Maestro.
81 ❑ Jan 1996 Cover: 1.50 **NM** value: **Cover or less**
Circ: Statement: **68,529**
• Age of Apocalypse didn't end; Has 1995 Statement, filed 10/1/95; avg print run 149,076; avg sales 87,131; avg subs 1,800; avg total paid 88,931; samples 750; office use 500; max existent 90,181; 40% of run returned
82 ❑ Feb 1996 Cover: 1.50 **NM** value: **Cover or less**
Circ: Statement: **68,529**
...J. Jonah Jameson Adopted Spider-Man? • J. Jonah Jameson adopts Peter Parker
83 ❑ Mar 1996 Cover: 1.50 **NM** value: **Cover or less**
Circ: Statement: **68,529**
...Daredevil was the Disciple of Doctor Strange? • Daredevil was the disciple of Doctor Strange
84 ❑ Apr 1996 Cover: 1.50 **NM** value: **Cover or less**
Circ: Statement: **68,529**
...Shard had Lived Instead of Bishop? • Shard lived instead of Bishop **A:** Mark Pacella **W:** Gerard Jones
85 ❑ May 1996 Cover: 1.50 **NM** value: **Cover or less**
Circ: Statement: **68,529**
• Magneto ruled all mutants
86 ❑ Jun 1996 Cover: 1.50 **NM** value: **Cover or less**
Circ: Statement: **68,529**
• Scarlet Spider kills Spider-Man
87 ❑ Jul 1996 Cover: 1.50 **NM** value: **Cover or less**
Circ: Statement: **68,529**
• Sabretooth
88 ❑ Aug 1996 Cover: 1.50 **NM** value: **Cover or less**
Circ: Statement: **68,529**
• Spider-Man
89 ❑ Sep 1996 Cover: 1.50 **NM** value: **Cover or less**
Circ: Statement: **68,529**
• Fantastic Four
90 ❑ Oct 1996 Cover: 1.50 **NM** value: **Cover or less**
Circ: Statement: **69,970**
• Cyclops and Havok
91 ❑ Nov 1996 Cover: 1.50 **NM** value: **Cover or less**
Circ: Statement: **69,970** Direct Market orders: **40,000**
• Hulk
92 ❑ Dec 1996 Cover: 1.50 **NM** value: **Cover or less**
Circ: Statement: **69,970** Direct Market orders: **46,250**
• Joshua Guthrie and a Sentinel
93 ❑ Jan 1997 Cover: 1.50 **NM** value: **Cover or less**
Circ: Statement: **69,970** Direct Market orders: **56,750**
Wolverine: A Man...No More • Wolverine
94 ❑ Feb 1997 Cover: 1.50 **NM** value: **Cover or less**
Circ: Statement: **69,970** Direct Market orders: **41,250**
Juggernaut: Wanderings • Juggernaut **A:** Jim Calafiore **W:** Jorge Gonzalez
95 ❑ Mar 1997 Cover: 1.95 **NM** value: **Cover or less**
Circ: Statement: **69,970** Direct Market orders: **29,500**
Ghost Rider: Broken Soul • Ghost Rider **A:** Eric Battle **W:** Ivan Velez Jr.
96 ❑ Apr 1997 Cover: 1.95 **NM** value: **Cover or less**
Circ: Statement: **69,970** Direct Market orders: **36,000**
Quicksilver: They Grow up so Quickly • Quicksilver **A:** Chris Wozniak **W:** Chris Wozniak
97 ❑ May 1997 Cover: 1.95 **NM** value: **Cover or less**
Circ: Statement: **69,970** Diamd. preorders: **29,476**
Black Knight: Last Light • Black Knight **A:** Leonardo Manco **W:** James Felder ★ Appearance of Doctor Doom.
98 ❑ Jun 1997 Cover: 1.95 **NM** value: **Cover or less**
Circ: Statement: **69,970** Diamd. preorders: **38,528**
Rogue: Seeds of Yesterday • Rogue, Nightcrawler **A:** Leonardo Manco **W:** Bill Rosemann
99 ❑ Aug 1997 Cover: 1.99 **NM** value: **Cover or less**
Circ: Statement: **69,970** Diamd. preorders: **29,293**
• gatefold summary. • Spider-Man
100 ❑ Sep 1997 Cover: 2.99 **NM** value: **Cover or less**
Circ: Diamd. preorders: **44,948**
• double-sized. • Gambit
101 ❑ Oct 1997 Cover: 1.99 **NM** value: **Cover or less**
Circ: Diamd. preorders: **34,498**
• gatefold summary. • Archangel
102 ❑ Nov 1997 Cover: 1.99 **NM** value: **Cover or less**
Circ: Diamd. preorders: **28,306**
• gatefold summary. • Daredevil
103 ❑ Dec 1997 Cover: 1.99 **NM** value: **Cover or less**
Circ: Diamd. preorders: **30,201**
• gatefold summary. • Has 1997 Statement, filed 10/1/97; avg print run 128,457; avg sales 68,812; avg subs 1,158; avg total paid 69,970; samples 116; office use 125; max existent 70,211; 45% of run returned
104 ❑ Jan 1998 Cover: 1.99 **NM** value: **Cover or less**
Circ: Diamd. preorders: **27,586**
• gatefold summary. • Impossible Man with Infinity Gauntlet
105 ❑ Feb 1998 Cover: 1.99 **NM** value: **15.00**
Circ: Diamd. preorders: **29,192** • **CGC:** 21 graded, best 9.8
• gatefold summary. • leads into Marvel 2 ★ Origin of Spider-Girl. ★ 1st Appearance of Spider-Girl.
106 ❑ Mar 1998 Cover: 1.99 **NM** value: **Cover or less**
Circ: Diamd. preorders: **33,591**
• gatefold summary.
107 ❑ Apr 1998 Cover: 1.99 **NM** value: **Cover or less**
Circ: Diamd. preorders: **25,191**
• gatefold summary. • Thor as ruler of Asgard ★ Versus Destroyer.
108 ❑ May 1998 Cover: 1.99 **NM** value: **Cover or less**
Circ: Diamd. preorders: **27,610**
• gatefold summary. • Avengers vs. Carnage
109 ❑ Jun 1998 Cover: 1.99 **NM** value: **Cover or less**
Circ: Diamd. preorders: **25,935**
• gatefold summary. • Thing in Liddleville
110 ❑ Jul 1998 Cover: 1.99 **NM** value: **Cover or less**
Circ: Diamd. preorders: **32,498**
• gatefold summary. • X-Men
111 ❑ Aug 1998 Cover: 1.99 **NM** value: **Cover or less**
Circ: Diamd. preorders: **35,540**
• gatefold summary. • Wolverine as War
112 ❑ Sep 1998 Cover: 1.99 **NM** value: **Cover or less**
Circ: Diamd. preorders: **23,170**
• gatefold summary. • Ka-Zar
113 ❑ Oct 1998 Cover: 1.99 **NM** value: **Cover or less**
Circ: Diamd. preorders: **24,561**
• gatefold summary. • Tony Stark as Sorcerer Supreme
114 ❑ Nov 1998 Cover: 2.50 **NM** value: **Cover or less**
Circ: Diamd. preorders: **29,328** • **CGC:** 1 graded, best 9.8
• gatefold summary. final issue. • Secret Wars 25 years later

WHAT IS...THE FACE? Ace

1 ❑ Dec 1986 Cover: 1.75 **NM** value: **Cover or less**
The Ransomed City; The Two Bottles of Relish **A:** Steve Ditko; Lord Dunsany **W:** Steve Ditko; Lord Dunsany
2 ❑ May 1987 Cover: 1.75 **NM** value: **Cover or less**
The Death Factory; The 5 Durin Brothers **A:** Steve Ditko; George Tuska **W:** Joe Gill
3 ❑ Aug 1987 Cover: 1.75 **NM** value: **Cover or less**

WHAT'S MICHAEL: LIVING TOGETHER Dark Horse

1 ❑ Jul 1997 Cover: 5.95 **NM** value: **Cover or less**
Circ: Diamd. preorders: **4,087**

WHAT'S MICHAEL: MICHAEL'S ALBUM Dark Horse

1 ❑ Apr 1997 Cover: 5.95 **NM** value: **Cover or less**
Circ: Diamd. preorders: **4,529**

WHAT'S MICHAEL: MICHAEL'S MAMBO Dark Horse

1 ❑ Jan 1998 Cover: 5.95 **NM** value: **Cover or less**

WHAT'S MICHAEL: OFF THE DEEP END Dark Horse

1 ❑ Oct 1997 Cover: 5.95 **NM** value: **Cover or less**
Circ: Diamd. preorders: **3,927**

WHAT'S NEW?- THE COLLECTED ADVENTURES OF PHIL & DIXIE Palliard

1 ❑ Oct 1991 Cover: 7.95 **NM** value: **Cover or less**
• color and b&w; The Collected Adventures of Phil and Dixie **A:** Phil Foglio **W:** Phil Foglio
2 ❑ full color Cover: 7.95 **NM** value: **Cover or less**
• prestige format.

WHAT'S NEW? WITH PHIL AND DIXIE Studio Foglio

3 ❑ Apr 2000 Cover: 10.95 **NM** value: **Cover or less**
• prestige format. The Magic Years • collects strips from The Duelist **A:** Phil Foglio **W:** Phil Foglio

WHAT THE-?! Marvel

Leave it to Marvel to spoof itself in its own series. Though most comic book manufacturers take it easy on their own characters, Marvel laughs at everything, from its own tendency to liberally rewrite scripts, to blatant commercialism, to crossovers, to chronological absurdities and all the inherent silliness of some of its heroes. It's thrown in a few really bad puns (is there any other kind?) and also pulled in a few non-Marvel characters to-boot in this occasionally hilarious send-up of the Marvel Universe.

It's not Not Brand Ecch, but that doesn't make it entirely Ecch. Look for a story written, but not drawn(!) by comics funnyman Fred Hembeck.

1 ❑ Aug 1988 Cover: 1.25 **NM** value: **4.00**
Circ: CapCity orders: **18,200**
2 ❑ Sep 1988 Cover: 1.25 **NM** value: **2.50**
Circ: CapCity orders: **17,500**
3 ❑ Oct 1988 Cover: 1.25 **NM** value: **3.00**
Circ: CapCity orders: **15,400** • **CGC:** 1 graded, best 9.4
4 ❑ Nov 1988 Cover: 1.25 **NM** value: **2.50**
Circ: CapCity orders: **15,100**
5 ❑ Jul 1989 Cover: 1.50 **NM** value: **2.50**
Circ: CapCity orders: **17,800**
6 ❑ Jan 1990 Cover: 1.00 **NM** value: **2.50**
Circ: CapCity orders: **24,900**
• Acts of Vengeance parody **A:** John Byrne; Terry Austin
7 ❑ Apr 1990 Cover: 1.25 **NM** value: **2.50**
Circ: CapCity orders: **20,600**
8 ❑ Jul 1990 Cover: 1.25 **NM** value: **2.50**
Circ: CapCity orders: **18,800** • **CGC:** 1 graded, best 9.8
9 ❑ Oct 1990 Cover: 1.25 **NM** value: **1.75**
Circ: CapCity orders: **17,000**
wraparound cover. **C:** John Byrne
10 ❑ Jan 1991 Cover: 1.25 **NM** value: **1.75**
Circ: CapCity orders: **16,500**
• prestige format. **C:** John Byrne
11 ❑ Mar 1991 Cover: 1.25 **NM** value: **1.50**
Circ: CapCity orders: **15,300**
12 ❑ May 1991 Cover: 1.25 **NM** value: **1.50**
Circ: CapCity orders: **15,000**
13 ❑ Jul 1991 Cover: 1.25 **NM** value: **1.50**
Circ: CapCity orders: **15,000**
14 ❑ Sep 1991 Cover: 1.25 **NM** value: **1.50**
Circ: CapCity orders: **13,300**
15 ❑ Nov 1991 Cover: 1.25 **NM** value: **1.50**
Circ: CapCity orders: **12,100**
Strange Young fighting Frogs; Land Shark; So How Goes The War?; You Know You've Been Reading Too Many Comics **A:** Keith Wilson **W:** Charles Santino
16 ❑ Jan 1992 Cover: 1.25 **NM** value: **1.50**
Circ: CapCity orders: **11,600**
EC parody cover. Ock Around the Christmas Tree; The Grinch Who Swiped Chanuka; Marble Superheroes Got for X-Mas; Someone to Watch Over Me; The House of Misery; Monstrous Marble Mirth **A:** Keith Wilson; Rurik Tyler; Darren Alick **W:** Darren Alick; Barry Dutter; Sholly Fisch
17 ❑ Mar 1992 Cover: 1.25 **NM** value: **1.50**
Circ: CapCity orders: **10,400**
18 ❑ May 1992 Cover: 1.25 **NM** value: **1.50**
Circ: CapCity orders: **9,400**
19 ❑ Jul 1992 Cover: 1.25 **NM** value: **1.50**
Circ: CapCity orders: **9,900**
20 ❑ Aug 1992 Cover: 1.25 **NM** value: **1.50**
Circ: CapCity orders: **11,000**
21 ❑ Sep 1992 Cover: 1.25 **NM** value: **1.50**
Circ: CapCity orders: **9,100**
• Weapon X parody
22 ❑ Oct 1992 Cover: 1.25 **NM** value: **1.50**
Circ: CapCity orders: **9,900**
23 ❑ Nov 1992 Cover: 1.25 **NM** value: **1.50**
24 ❑ Dec 1992 Cover: 1.25 **NM** value: **1.50**
25 ❑ Sum 1993 Cover: 2.50 **NM** value: **Cover or less**
26 ❑ Fal 1993 Cover: 2.50 **NM** value: **Cover or less**
27 ❑ Win 1993 Cover: 2.50 **NM** value: **Cover or less**

WHEELIE AND THE CHOPPER BUNCH Charlton

1 ❑ May 1975 Cover: 5.00 **NM** value: **8.00**
• **CGC:** 6 graded, best 9.6
2 ❑ Jul 1975 Cover: 3.00 **NM** value: **5.00**
3 ❑ Sep 1975 Cover: 3.00 **NM** value: **4.00**
4 ❑ Nov 1975 Cover: 2.00 **NM** value: **4.00**
5 ❑ Jan 1976 Cover: 2.00 **NM** value: **4.00**
6 ❑ Mar 1976 Cover: 2.00 **NM** value: **4.00**
7 ❑ May 1976 Cover: 2.00 **NM** value: **4.00**
Medical Mischief; The Basher Crasher; The Friend; The Picnic Poopers; Stick-Shift in the Mud (text story) final issue.

WHEEL OF WORLDS (NEIL GAIMAN'S...) Tekno

Neil Gaiman, one of the most popular comics writers of the 1990s, was commissioned to design a line of comics and characters for newcomer Tekno Comics. Gaiman's concepts were introduced to readers in this one-shot, which presented the background of the shared universe and related the origins of the characters.

As the stories begin, Adam Cain and Mr. Hero (a robot, or "Newmatic Man") have traveled to the dessicated Redchapel, on an alternate Earth called Albion, in search of Mr. Hero's lost hand. Not long after, the lizard-like ruler of worlds known as the Teknophage arrives, intent on finally humbling the pair. The only thing saving them from certain destruction is the timely appearance of Lady Justice, who spins a tale so compelling that even the almighty Teknophage is moved to spare them.

0 ❑ Apr 1995 Cover: 2.95 **NM** value: **Cover or less**
Circ: CapCity orders: **3,450**
• Direct Market edition. • poster **A:** Shea Anton Pensa; Bryan Talbot; Michael Netzer; C.J. Henderson **W:** Rick Veitch; James Vance; John Ney Rieber; Neil Gaiman ★ Appearance of Adam Cain, Lady Justice, Teknophage, Mr. Hero.
0/CS ❑ Apr 1995 Cover: 2.95 **NM** value: **Cover or less**
Circ: CapCity orders: **17,100**
• poster **A:** Shea Anton Pensa; Bryan Talbot; Michael Netzer; C.J. Henderson **W:** Rick Veitch; James Vance; John Ney Rieber; Neil Gaiman ★ Appearance of Adam Cain, Lady Justice, Teknophage, Mr. Hero.
1 ❑ May 1996 Cover: 3.25 **NM** value: **Cover or less**
The Highest Bidder; the Big Bang, Chapter 1 **A:** Rich Buckler; Paul Abrams; Jose Delbo **W:** Bruce Jones; Neil Gaiman; Ron Fortier ★ Origin of Lady Justice.

WHEN BEANIES ATTACK Blatant

1 ❑ Mar 1999 Cover: 2.95 **NM** value: **Cover or less**

1/SC❑Mar 1999 Cover: 4.95 NM value: **Cover or less**
Violent cover. **A:** Erich Owen **W:** Tony Furtado

WHERE CREATURES ROAM — Marvel

1 ❑ Jul 1970 Cover: 0.15 NM value: **8.00**
• **CGC:** 6 graded, best 9.4
2 ❑ Sep 1970 Cover: 0.15 NM value: **5.00**
• **CGC:** 1 graded, best 9.2
3 ❑ Nov 1970 Cover: 0.15 NM value: **5.00**
4 ❑ Jan 1971 Cover: 0.15 NM value: **5.00**
5 ❑ Mar 1971 Cover: 0.15 NM value: **5.00**
• **CGC:** 1 graded, best 9.4
6 ❑ May 1971 Cover: 0.15 NM value: **5.00**
7 ❑ Jul 1971 Cover: 0.15 NM value: **5.00**
8 ❑ Sep 1971 Cover: 0.15 NM value: **5.00**

WHERE IN THE WORLD IS CARMEN SANDIEGO? — DC

1 ❑ Jun 1996 Cover: 1.75 NM value: **Cover or less**
Shop till you Drop!!! • based on computer game series **A:** S.M. Taggart **W:** Barry Liebmann
2 ❑ Sep 1996 Cover: 1.75 NM value: **Cover or less**
3 ❑ Nov 1996 Cover: 1.75 NM value: **Cover or less**
Room with a Deja Vu **A:** S.M. Taggart **W:** Barry Liebmann
4 ❑ Jan 1997 Cover: 1.75 NM value: **Cover or less**
Circ: Diamd. preorders: **2,779**
Stealer by Starlight • all-alien issue **A:** S.M. Taggart **W:** Barry Liebmann

WHERE MONSTERS DWELL — Marvel

1 ❑ Jan 1970 Cover: 0.15 NM value: **10.00**
• **CGC:** 8 graded, best 9.4
2 ❑ Mar 1970 Cover: 0.15 NM value: **6.00**
• **CGC:** 1 graded, best 9.4
3 ❑ May 1970 Cover: 0.15 NM value: **4.00**
4 ❑ Jul 1970 Cover: 0.15 NM value: **4.00**
5 ❑ Sep 1970 Cover: 0.15 NM value: **4.00**
6 ❑ Nov 1970 Cover: 0.15 NM value: **3.00**
7 ❑ Jan 1971 Cover: 0.15 NM value: **3.00**
8 ❑ Mar 1971 Cover: 0.15 NM value: **3.00**
9 ❑ May 1971 Cover: 0.15 NM value: **3.00**
10 ❑ Jul 1971 Cover: 0.15 NM value: **3.00**
Gigantuss, The Monster That Walked Like a Man!; The Frog-Man; Barker's Body Shop!; Dinner Time on Deimos! **A:** Steve Ditko; Larry Lieber; Sol Brodsky **W:** Steve Ditko; Larry Lieber; Stan Lee
11 ❑ Sep 1971 Cover: 0.15 NM value: **3.00**
12 ❑ Nov 1971 Cover: 0.20 NM value: **4.00**
• Giant-size.
13 ❑ Jan 1972 Cover: 0.20 NM value: **3.00**
14 ❑ Mar 1972 Cover: 0.20 NM value: **3.00**
15 ❑ May 1972 Cover: 0.20 NM value: **3.00**
16 ❑ Jul 1972 Cover: 0.20 NM value: **3.00**
17 ❑ Sep 1972 Cover: 0.20 NM value: **3.00**
18 ❑ Nov 1972 Cover: 0.20 NM value: **3.00**
19 ❑ Jan 1973 Cover: 0.20 NM value: **3.00**
20 ❑ Mar 1973 Cover: 0.20 NM value: **3.00**
21 ❑ May 1973 Cover: 0.20 NM value: **3.00**
22 ❑ Jul 1973 Cover: 0.20 NM value: **3.00**
23 ❑ Sep 1973 Cover: 0.20 NM value: **3.00**
24 ❑ Oct 1973 Cover: 0.20 NM value: **3.00**
25 ❑ Nov 1973 Cover: 0.20 NM value: **3.00**
26 ❑ Jan 1974 Cover: 0.20 NM value: **3.00**
27 ❑ Mar 1974 Cover: 0.20 NM value: **3.00**
28 ❑ May 1974 Cover: 0.25 NM value: **3.00**
29 ❑ Jul 1974 Cover: 0.25 NM value: **3.00**
30 ❑ Sep 1974 Cover: 0.25 NM value: **3.00**
31 ❑ Oct 1974 Cover: 0.25 NM value: **3.00**
32 ❑ Nov 1974 Cover: 0.25 NM value: **3.00**
33 ❑ Jan 1975 Cover: 0.25 NM value: **3.00**
34 ❑ Mar 1975 Cover: 0.25 NM value: **3.00**
• **CGC:** 1 graded, best 8.5
35 ❑ May 1975 Cover: 0.25 NM value: **3.00**
36 ❑ Jul 1975 Cover: 0.25 NM value: **3.00**
• **CGC:** 1 graded, best 9.4
37 ❑ Sep 1975 Cover: 0.25 NM value: **3.00**
38 ❑ Oct 1975 Cover: 0.25 NM value: **3.00**
• **CGC:** 1 graded, best 9.0
final issue.

WHILE FIFTY MILLION DIED — Tome Press

1 ❑ b&w Cover: 2.95 NM value: **Cover or less**
• World War II **A:** WW II

WHIP WILSON — Bell Features

9 ❑ ca. 1950 Cover: 0.10 NM value: **400.00**
10 ❑ ca. 1950 Cover: 0.10 NM value: **400.00**
11 ❑ ca. 1950 Cover: 0.10 NM value: **300.00**

WHIRLWIND COMICS — Nita

1 ❑ Jun 1940 Cover: 0.10 NM value: **1250.00**
• **CGC:** 2 graded, best 9.0
2 ❑ Jul 1940 Cover: 0.10 NM value: **1000.00**
3 ❑ Sep 1940 Cover: 0.10 NM value: **1000.00**
• **CGC:** 1 graded, best 3.0

WHISPERS AND SHADOWS — Oasis

1 ❑ b&w Cover: 1.50 NM value: **Cover or less**
2 ❑ b&w Cover: 1.50 NM value: **Cover or less**
3 ❑ b&w Cover: 1.50 NM value: **Cover or less**
4 ❑ b&w Cover: 1.50 NM value: **Cover or less**
5 ❑ b&w Cover: 1.50 NM value: **Cover or less**
6 ❑ b&w Cover: 1.50 NM value: **Cover or less**
7 ❑ b&w Cover: 1.50 NM value: **Cover or less**
8 ❑ b&w Cover: 1.50 NM value: **Cover or less**

WHISPER (VOL. 1) — Capital

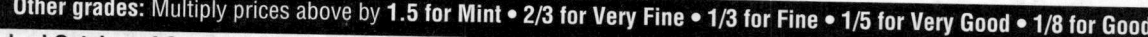

Alexis Devin is an American woman raised by her Japanese stepfather, who trained her in Aikido and Ninjitsu. Many years later, they would have a reunion in Japan, but their joy would be interrupted by the intrusion of Yakuza — the Japanese mob. In order to surprise their attackers, Alexis masks her face and sets out to rescue her stepfather. But, in doing so, she learns that he was a member of the mob and had been the person responsible for her natural father's death. Torn by this new revelation, she flees Japan.

Soon thereafter, Alexis' stepfather is ordered to slay the costumed Ninja the mob calls Whisper. Little does he dream that Whisper is actually his own stepdaughter, Alexis!

1 ❑ Dec 1983 Cover: 1.75 NM value: **2.50**
2 ❑ Mar 1984 Cover: 1.75 NM value: **2.00**

WHISPER (VOL. 2) — First

1 ❑ Jun 1986 Cover: 1.25 NM value: **2.00**
Circ: CapCity orders: **10,050**
Datapanik in the Year Zero; Datapanik in the Year Zero, Part 1 **A:** Dell Barras; Tim Burgard **W:** Steven Grant
2 ❑ Aug 1986 Cover: 1.25 NM value: **1.50**
Circ: CapCity orders: **8,000**
Datapanik in the Year Zero, Part 2 **A:** Rico Rival; Dell Barras **W:** Steven Grant
3 ❑ Oct 1986 Cover: 1.25 NM value: **1.50**
Circ: CapCity orders: **7,825**
Datapanik in the Year Zero, Part 3 **A:** Norm Breyfogle **W:** Steven Grant
4 ❑ Dec 1986 Cover: 1.25 NM value: **1.50**
Circ: CapCity orders: **6,750**
5 ❑ Feb 1987 Cover: 1.25 NM value: **1.50**
Circ: CapCity orders: **5,750**
6 ❑ Apr 1987 Cover: 1.25 NM value: **1.50**
Circ: CapCity orders: **5,375**
7 ❑ Jun 1987 Cover: 1.25 NM value: **1.50**
Circ: CapCity orders: **5,025**
8 ❑ Aug 1987 Cover: 1.75 NM value: **Cover or less**
Circ: CapCity orders: **4,875**
9 ❑ Oct 1987 Cover: 1.25 NM value: **1.75**
Circ: CapCity orders: **5,000**
10 ❑ Dec 1987 Cover: 1.75 NM value: **Cover or less**
Circ: CapCity orders: **4,600**
11 ❑ Feb 1988 Cover: 1.75 NM value: **Cover or less**
Circ: CapCity orders: **4,450**
12 ❑ Apr 1988 Cover: 1.75 NM value: **Cover or less**
Circ: CapCity orders: **4,950**
13 ❑ Jun 1988 Cover: 1.75 NM value: **Cover or less**
Circ: CapCity orders: **3,900**
14 ❑ Jul 1988 Cover: 1.75 NM value: **Cover or less**
Circ: CapCity orders: **4,075**
15 ❑ Aug 1988 Cover: 1.75 NM value: **Cover or less**
Circ: CapCity orders: **4,225**
16 ❑ Sep 1988 Cover: 1.75 NM value: **Cover or less**
Circ: CapCity orders: **3,925**
17 ❑ Oct 1988 Cover: 1.75 NM value: **Cover or less**
Circ: CapCity orders: **4,025**
18 ❑ Nov 1988 Cover: 1.95 NM value: **Cover or less**
Circ: CapCity orders: **3,875**
19 ❑ Dec 1988 Cover: 1.95 NM value: **Cover or less**
Circ: CapCity orders: **3,975**
20 ❑ Jan 1989 Cover: 1.95 NM value: **Cover or less**
Circ: CapCity orders: **4,250**
21 ❑ Feb 1989 Cover: 1.95 NM value: **Cover or less**
Circ: CapCity orders: **3,600**
22 ❑ Mar 1989 Cover: 1.95 NM value: **Cover or less**
Circ: CapCity orders: **3,700**
23 ❑ Apr 1989 Cover: 1.95 NM value: **Cover or less**
Circ: CapCity orders: **3,775**
24 ❑ May 1989 Cover: 1.95 NM value: **Cover or less**
Circ: CapCity orders: **3,600**
25 ❑ Jun 1989 Cover: 1.95 NM value: **Cover or less**
Circ: CapCity orders: **3,525**
26 ❑ Jul 1989 Cover: 1.95 NM value: **Cover or less**
Circ: CapCity orders: **3,525**
27 ❑ Aug 1989 Cover: 1.95 NM value: **Cover or less**
Circ: CapCity orders: **3,450**
28 ❑ Sep 1989 Cover: 1.95 NM value: **Cover or less**
Circ: CapCity orders: **3,525**
29 ❑ Oct 1989 Cover: 1.95 NM value: **Cover or less**
Circ: CapCity orders: **3,575**
30 ❑ Nov 1989 Cover: 1.95 NM value: **Cover or less**
Circ: CapCity orders: **3,550**
31 ❑ Dec 1989 Cover: 1.95 NM value: **Cover or less**
Circ: CapCity orders: **3,475**
32 ❑ Jan 1990 Cover: 1.95 NM value: **Cover or less**
Circ: CapCity orders: **3,500**
33 ❑ Feb 1990 Cover: 1.95 NM value: **Cover or less**
Circ: CapCity orders: **3,300**
34 ❑ Mar 1990 Cover: 1.95 NM value: **Cover or less**
Circ: CapCity orders: **3,350**
35 ❑ Apr 1990 Cover: 1.95 NM value: **Cover or less**
Circ: CapCity orders: **3,175**
36 ❑ May 1990 Cover: 1.95 NM value: **Cover or less**
Circ: CapCity orders: **3,225**
37 ❑ Jun 1990 Cover: 1.95 NM value: **Cover or less**
Circ: CapCity orders: **2,975**
SE 1❑ Nov 1985 Cover: 2.50 NM value: **Cover or less**
Circ: CapCity orders: **7,525**
• Giant-size. **A:** Rich Larson **W:** Steven Grant

WHITE DEVIL — Eternity

All issues are adults only.
1 ❑ b&w Cover: 2.50 NM value: **Cover or less**
2 ❑ b&w Cover: 2.50 NM value: **Cover or less**
3 ❑ b&w Cover: 2.50 NM value: **Cover or less**
4 ❑ b&w Cover: 2.50 NM value: **Cover or less**
5 ❑ b&w Cover: 2.50 NM value: **Cover or less**
6 ❑ b&w Cover: 2.50 NM value: **Cover or less**
7 ❑ b&w Cover: 2.50 NM value: **Cover or less**
8 ❑ b&w Cover: 2.50 NM value: **Cover or less**

WHITE FANG — Disney

1 ❑ ca. 1990 Cover: 2.95 NM value: **Cover or less**
No issue number. • newsstand version
1/DM❑ca. 1990 Cover: 5.95 NM value: **Cover or less**
No issue number.

WHITE LIKE SHE — Dark Horse

1 ❑ May 1994, b&w Cover: 2.95 NM value: **Cover or less**
Circ: CapCity orders: **3,475**
2 ❑ Jun 1994, b&w Cover: 2.95 NM value: **Cover or less**
Circ: CapCity orders: **2,900**
3 ❑ Jul 1994, b&w Cover: 2.95 NM value: **Cover or less**
4 ❑ Aug 1994, b&w Cover: 2.95 NM value: **Cover or less**

WHITE ORCHID — Atlantis

1 ❑ Cover: 2.95 NM value: **Cover or less**

WHITEOUT — Oni Press

It starts with a dead body, as all great mysteries do, found on the ice of Antarctica. With the victim's face bludgeoned beyond recognition, Deputy U.S. Marshal Stetko has her work cut out for her. The clock is ticking, as the winter exodus draws near and with it the likelihood that the murderer will ship out with the majority of the inhabitants. To make matters worse, forces are at work to keep Stetko from learning the truth. She has survived this long by letting the ice harden her heart, but will that be enough, when she's trapped in Victoria Station with the murderer during a blinding snow storm? This Machiavellian suspense-thriller is presented as a four-issue limited series that is sure to leave your teeth chattering.

1 ❑ Jul 1998 Cover: 2.95 NM value: **Cover or less**
Circ: Diamd. preorders: **5,617**
2 ❑ Aug 1998 Cover: 2.95 NM value: **Cover or less**
Circ: Diamd. preorders: **3,940**
3 ❑ Sep 1998 Cover: 2.95 NM value: **Cover or less**
Circ: Diamd. preorders: **4,055**
4 ❑ Nov 1998 Cover: 2.95 NM value: **Cover or less**
Circ: Diamd. preorders: **3,877**
Bk 1❑ May 1999 Cover: 10.95 NM value: **Cover or less**
• Trade Paperback. • collects mini-series

WHITEOUT: MELT — Oni Press

1 ❑ Sep 1999 Cover: 2.95 NM value: **Cover or less**
Circ: Diamd. preorders: **5,409** • **CGC:** 1 graded, best 8.5
2 ❑ Oct 1999 Cover: 2.95 NM value: **Cover or less**
Circ: Diamd. preorders: **4,882**
3 ❑ Nov 1999 Cover: 2.95 NM value: **Cover or less**
Circ: Diamd. preorders: **4,689**
4 ❑ Dec 1999 Cover: 2.95 NM value: **Cover or less**
Circ: Diamd. preorders: **4,572**

WHITE RAVEN — Visionary

1 ❑ Cover: 2.95 NM value: **Cover or less**

WHITE RIDER AND SUPER HORSE — Star

4 ❑ Sep 1950 Cover: 0.10 NM value: **100.00**
5 ❑ Dec 1950 Cover: 0.10 NM value: **80.00**
6 ❑ Mar 1951 Cover: 0.10 NM value: **80.00**

WHITE TRASH — Tundra

1 ❑ Cover: 2.50 NM value: **Cover or less**
No issue number.
2 ❑ Cover: 3.95 NM value: **Cover or less**

WHIZ COMICS — Fawcett

Whiz Comics was Fawcett Publications' first comic-book title. It was an anthology series, featuring one story each about such characters as Ibis the Invincible, Lance O'Casey, Golden Arrow, Spy Smasher, Dan Dare, Scoop Smith, and Dr. Voodoo. There was never an issue numbered #1, although an ashcan exists; the first to hit the newsstand was #2, and it cover-featured the character for whom it's best known: Captain Marvel. The story of how Billy Batson became The Big Red Cheese by shouting, "Shazam!" was first told in this issue, and in #25 the series featured the origin story of another Marvel Family member: Captain Marvel Jr. (Freddy Freeman, no relation to Billy). ("Shazam," by the way, was an acronym for the names of those from whom Captain Marvel

Other grades: Multiply prices above by **1.5 for Mint • 2/3 for Very Fine • 1/3 for Fine • 1/5 for Very Good • 1/8 for Good**

drew his powers: Solomon, Hercules, Atlas, Zeus, Achilles, and Mercury.)

The Marvel Family's career went on hiatus in a consent decree in the 1950s and, by the time the field was eager to read new adventures, the name of Captain Marvel had been usurped by Marvel Comics. As a result, the version from the Silver Age to today appears in titles like Shazam!, rather than in a Captain Marvel-titled series. — Maggie

1 ❑ Feb 1940 Cover: 0.10 **NM** value: **65000.00**
• **CGC:** 1 graded, best 8.5
No number on cover, listed as #2 in indicia. ★ Origin of Captain Marvel (Fawcett). ★ 1st Appearance of Ibis the Invincible, Golden Arrow, Spy Smasher, Captain Marvel (Fawcett).
2 ❑ Feb 1940 Cover: 0.10 **NM** value: **4100.00**
• **CGC:** 2 graded, best 4.5
No number on cover, listed as #3 in indicia.
3 ❑ Mar 1940 Cover: 0.10 **NM** value: **2600.00**
• **CGC:** 1 graded, best 4.5
Listed as #3 on cover, #4 in indicia.
4 ❑ May 1940 Cover: 0.10 **NM** value: **2150.00**
• **CGC:** 1 graded, best 4.0
Listed as #4 on cover, #5 in indicia.
5 ❑ Jun 1940 Cover: 0.10 **NM** value: **1750.00**
• **CGC:** 1 graded, best 4.0
6 ❑ Jul 1940 Cover: 0.10 **NM** value: **1350.00**
• **CGC:** 3 graded, best 6.5
7 ❑ Aug 1940 Cover: 0.10 **NM** value: **1400.00**
• **CGC:** 3 graded, best 8.5
• Doctor Voodoo stories begin
8 ❑ Sep 1940 Cover: 0.10 **NM** value: **1350.00**
• **CGC:** 3 graded, best 7.5
9 ❑ Oct 1940 Cover: 0.10 **NM** value: **1350.00**
10 ❑ Nov 1940 Cover: 0.10 **NM** value: **1050.00**
• **CGC:** 3 graded, best 6.0
11 ❑ Dec 1940 Cover: 0.10 **NM** value: **950.00**
• **CGC:** 1 graded, best 5.0
12 ❑ Jan 1941 Cover: 0.10 **NM** value: **950.00**
13 ❑ Feb 1941 Cover: 0.10 **NM** value: **900.00**
14 ❑ Mar 1941 Cover: 0.10 **NM** value: **900.00**
• **CGC:** 1 graded, best 1.0
15 ❑ Mar 1941 Cover: 0.10 **NM** value: **1000.00**
16 ❑ Apr 1941 Cover: 0.10 **NM** value: **950.00**
• **CGC:** 1 graded, best 4.0
17 ❑ May 1941 Cover: 0.10 **NM** value: **950.00**
• **CGC:** 1 graded, best 6.0
18 ❑ Jun 1941 Cover: 0.10 **NM** value: **950.00**
19 ❑ Jul 1941 Cover: 0.10 **NM** value: **650.00**
20 ❑ Aug 1941 Cover: 0.10 **NM** value: **650.00**
21 ❑ Sep 1941 Cover: 0.10 **NM** value: **700.00**
22 ❑ Aug 1941 Cover: 0.10 **NM** value: **510.00**
• **CGC:** 1 graded, best 8.5
23 ❑ Oct 1941 Cover: 0.10 **NM** value: **510.00**
• **CGC:** 2 graded, best 9.0
24 ❑ Nov 1941 Cover: 0.10 **NM** value: **510.00**
• **CGC:** 1 graded, best 5.0
25 ❑ Dec 1941 Cover: 0.10 **NM** value: **4900.00**
• **CGC:** 9 graded, best 9.0
• Part of 3-issue crossover featuring Captain Marvel, Bulletman, and Captain Nazi; Continued in Master Comics #22★ Origin of Captain Marvel Jr.. ★ 1st Appearance of Captain Marvel Jr..
26 ❑ Jan 1942 Cover: 0.10 **NM** value: **475.00**
27 ❑ Feb 1942 Cover: 0.10 **NM** value: **450.00**
• **CGC:** 1 graded, best 9.2
28 ❑ Mar 1942 Cover: 0.10 **NM** value: **450.00**
• **CGC:** 1 graded, best 7.0
29 ❑ Apr 1942 Cover: 0.10 **NM** value: **450.00**
• **CGC:** 1 graded, best 9.2
30 ❑ May 1942 Cover: 0.10 **NM** value: **450.00**
31 ❑ Jun 1942 Cover: 0.10 **NM** value: **400.00**
MacArthur Defense Stamps cover.
32 ❑ Jul 1942 Cover: 0.10 **NM** value: **400.00**
33 ❑ Aug 1942 Cover: 0.10 **NM** value: **450.00**
• **CGC:** 3 graded, best 9.0
34 ❑ Sep 1942 Cover: 0.10 **NM** value: **325.00**
35 ❑ Oct 1942 Cover: 0.10 **NM** value: **375.00**
• **CGC:** 4 graded, best 9.4
36 ❑ Oct 1942 Cover: 0.10 **NM** value: **325.00**
• **CGC:** 1 graded, best 8.0
37 ❑ Nov 1942 Cover: 0.10 **NM** value: **325.00**
38 ❑ Dec 1942 Cover: 0.10 **NM** value: **325.00**
• **CGC:** 1 graded, best 3.0
39 ❑ Jan 1943 Cover: 0.10 **NM** value: **325.00**
• **CGC:** 1 graded, best 9.2
40 ❑ Feb 1943 Cover: 0.10 **NM** value: **325.00**
41 ❑ Apr 1943 Cover: 0.10 **NM** value: **225.00**
• **CGC:** 1 graded, best 9.6
42 ❑ Jan 1943 Cover: 0.10 **NM** value: **225.00**
43 ❑ Jun 1943 Cover: 0.10 **NM** value: **225.00**
• **CGC:** 2 graded, best 9.4
44 ❑ Jul 1943 Cover: 0.10 **NM** value: **265.00**
• The Life Story of Captain Marvel
45 ❑ Aug 1943 Cover: 0.10 **NM** value: **225.00**
• **CGC:** 1 graded, best 5.5
46 ❑ Sep 1943 Cover: 0.10 **NM** value: **225.00**
• **CGC:** 1 graded, best 9.0
47 ❑ Oct 1943 Cover: 0.10 **NM** value: **225.00**
• **CGC:** 2 graded, best 8.0
48 ❑ Nov 1943 Cover: 0.10 **NM** value: **225.00**
49 ❑ Dec 1943 Cover: 0.10 **NM** value: **225.00**
• **CGC:** 1 graded, best 9.4
50 ❑ Jan 1944 Cover: 0.10 **NM** value: **225.00**
• **CGC:** 2 graded, best 7.5
51 ❑ Feb 1944 Cover: 0.10 **NM** value: **185.00**
• **CGC:** 1 graded, best 9.6
52 ❑ Mar 1944 Cover: 0.10 **NM** value: **185.00**
• **CGC:** 1 graded, best 7.5
53 ❑ Apr 1944 Cover: 0.10 **NM** value: **185.00**
• **CGC:** 1 graded, best 8.0
54 ❑ May 1944 Cover: 0.10 **NM** value: **185.00**
55 ❑ Jun 1944 Cover: 0.10 **NM** value: **185.00**
56 ❑ Jul 1944 Cover: 0.10 **NM** value: **185.00**
• **CGC:** 2 graded, best 9.0
57 ❑ Aug 1944 Cover: 0.10 **NM** value: **185.00**
• **CGC:** 2 graded, best 7.5
58 ❑ Sep 1944 Cover: 0.10 **NM** value: **185.00**
59 ❑ Oct 1944 Cover: 0.10 **NM** value: **185.00**
60 ❑ Nov 1944 Cover: 0.10 **NM** value: **185.00**
61 ❑ Jan 1945 Cover: 0.10 **NM** value: **155.00**
• **CGC:** 3 graded, best 9.4
62 ❑ Feb 1945 Cover: 0.10 **NM** value: **155.00**
• **CGC:** 3 graded, best 7.5
63 ❑ Mar 1945 Cover: 0.10 **NM** value: **155.00**
64 ❑ Apr 1945 Cover: 0.10 **NM** value: **155.00**
65 ❑ May 1945 Cover: 0.10 **NM** value: **155.00**
66 ❑ Jul 1945 Cover: 0.10 **NM** value: **155.00**
• **CGC:** 1 graded, best 6.0
67 ❑ Sep 1945 Cover: 0.10 **NM** value: **155.00**
• **CGC:** 1 graded, best 5.0
68 ❑ Nov 1945 Cover: 0.10 **NM** value: **155.00**
• **CGC:** 2 graded, best 8.5
69 ❑ Dec 1945 Cover: 0.10 **NM** value: **155.00**
• **CGC:** 6 graded, best 9.4
70 ❑ Jan 1946 Cover: 0.10 **NM** value: **155.00**
• **CGC:** 1 graded, best 8.5
71 ❑ Feb 1946 Cover: 0.10 **NM** value: **130.00**
• **CGC:** 3 graded, best 6.5
72 ❑ Mar 1946 Cover: 0.10 **NM** value: **130.00**
• Contains 2 Captain Marvel stories
73 ❑ Apr 1946 Cover: 0.10 **NM** value: **130.00**
• Contains 2 Captain Marvel stories
74 ❑ May 1946 Cover: 0.10 **NM** value: **130.00**
• Contains 2 Captain Marvel stories
75 ❑ Jun 1946 Cover: 0.10 **NM** value: **130.00**
• **CGC:** 2 graded, best 9.2
• Contains 2 Captain Marvel stories
76 ❑ Jul 1946 Cover: 0.10 **NM** value: **130.00**
• **CGC:** 1 graded, best 9.0
• Contains 2 Captain Marvel stories; Spy Smasher becomes Crime Smasher★ 1st Appearance of Crime Smasher.
77 ❑ Aug 1946 Cover: 0.10 **NM** value: **130.00**
• **CGC:** 1 graded, best 8.0
78 ❑ Sep 1946 Cover: 0.10 **NM** value: **130.00**
79 ❑ Oct 1946 Cover: 0.10 **NM** value: **130.00**
• **CGC:** 1 graded, best 8.5
80 ❑ Nov 1946 Cover: 0.10 **NM** value: **130.00**
• **CGC:** 1 graded, best 6.0
81 ❑ Dec 1946 Cover: 0.10 **NM** value: **130.00**
• **CGC:** 1 graded, best 8.5
82 ❑ Feb 1947 Cover: 0.10 **NM** value: **130.00**
83 ❑ Mar 1947 Cover: 0.10 **NM** value: **115.00**
84 ❑ Apr 1947 Cover: 0.10 **NM** value: **115.00**
85 ❑ May 1947 Cover: 0.10 **NM** value: **115.00**
86 ❑ Jun 1947 Cover: 0.10 **NM** value: **115.00**
• **CGC:** 1 graded, best 8.0
87 ❑ Jul 1947 Cover: 0.10 **NM** value: **115.00**
88 ❑ Aug 1947 Cover: 0.10 **NM** value: **115.00**
89 ❑ Sep 1947 Cover: 0.10 **NM** value: **115.00**
90 ❑ Oct 1947 Cover: 0.10 **NM** value: **115.00**
• **CGC:** 2 graded, best 6.5
91 ❑ Nov 1947 Cover: 0.10 **NM** value: **115.00**
92 ❑ Dec 1947 Cover: 0.10 **NM** value: **115.00**
93 ❑ Jan 1948 Cover: 0.10 **NM** value: **115.00**
94 ❑ Feb 1948 Cover: 0.10 **NM** value: **115.00**
95 ❑ Mar 1948 Cover: 0.10 **NM** value: **115.00**
• **CGC:** 1 graded, best 9.0
96 ❑ Apr 1948 Cover: 0.10 **NM** value: **115.00**
• **CGC:** 2 graded, best 9.2
97 ❑ May 1948 Cover: 0.10 **NM** value: **115.00**
• **CGC:** 1 graded, best 7.0
98 ❑ Jun 1948 Cover: 0.10 **NM** value: **115.00**
• **CGC:** 1 graded, best 7.5
99 ❑ Jul 1948 Cover: 0.10 **NM** value: **115.00**
100 ❑ Aug 1948 Cover: 0.10 **NM** value: **115.00**
• **CGC:** 4 graded, best 9.4
• 100th anniversary issue.
101 ❑ Sep 1948 Cover: 0.10 **NM** value: **100.00**
102 ❑ Oct 1948 Cover: 0.10 **NM** value: **100.00**
103 ❑ Nov 1948 Cover: 0.10 **NM** value: **100.00**
104 ❑ Dec 1948 Cover: 0.10 **NM** value: **100.00**
• **CGC:** 1 graded, best 9.4
105 ❑ Jan 1949 Cover: 0.10 **NM** value: **100.00**
• **CGC:** 1 graded, best 9.0
106 ❑ Feb 1949 Cover: 0.10 **NM** value: **100.00**
107 ❑ Mar 1949 Cover: 0.10 **NM** value: **100.00**
White House on cover.
108 ❑ Apr 1949 Cover: 0.10 **NM** value: **100.00**
109 ❑ May 1949 Cover: 0.10 **NM** value: **100.00**
110 ❑ Jun 1949 Cover: 0.10 **NM** value: **100.00**
111 ❑ Jul 1949 Cover: 0.10 **NM** value: **100.00**
112 ❑ Aug 1949 Cover: 0.10 **NM** value: **100.00**
113 ❑ Sep 1949 Cover: 0.10 **NM** value: **100.00**
114 ❑ Oct 1949 Cover: 0.10 **NM** value: **100.00**
115 ❑ Nov 1949 Cover: 0.10 **NM** value: **100.00**
116 ❑ Dec 1949 Cover: 0.10 **NM** value: **100.00**
117 ❑ Jan 1950 Cover: 0.10 **NM** value: **100.00**
118 ❑ Feb 1950 Cover: 0.10 **NM** value: **100.00**
119 ❑ Mar 1950 Cover: 0.10 **NM** value: **100.00**
120 ❑ Apr 1950 Cover: 0.10 **NM** value: **100.00**
• **CGC:** 1 graded, best 5.5
121 ❑ May 1950 Cover: 0.10 **NM** value: **95.00**
122 ❑ Jun 1950 Cover: 0.10 **NM** value: **95.00**
123 ❑ Jul 1950 Cover: 0.10 **NM** value: **95.00**
124 ❑ Aug 1950 Cover: 0.10 **NM** value: **95.00**
125 ❑ Sep 1950 Cover: 0.10 **NM** value: **95.00**
126 ❑ Oct 1950 Cover: 0.10 **NM** value: **95.00**
127 ❑ Nov 1950 Cover: 0.10 **NM** value: **95.00**
128 ❑ Dec 1950 Cover: 0.10 **NM** value: **95.00**
129 ❑ Jan 1951 Cover: 0.10 **NM** value: **95.00**
130 ❑ Feb 1951 Cover: 0.10 **NM** value: **95.00**
131 ❑ Mar 1951 Cover: 0.10 **NM** value: **95.00**
132 ❑ Apr 1951 Cover: 0.10 **NM** value: **95.00**
133 ❑ May 1951 Cover: 0.10 **NM** value: **95.00**
134 ❑ Jun 1951 Cover: 0.10 **NM** value: **95.00**
135 ❑ Jul 1951 Cover: 0.10 **NM** value: **95.00**
136 ❑ Aug 1951 Cover: 0.10 **NM** value: **95.00**
137 ❑ Sep 1951 Cover: 0.10 **NM** value: **95.00**
138 ❑ Oct 1951 Cover: 0.10 **NM** value: **95.00**
139 ❑ Nov 1951 Cover: 0.10 **NM** value: **95.00**
140 ❑ Dec 1951 Cover: 0.10 **NM** value: **95.00**
141 ❑ Jan 1952 Cover: 0.10 **NM** value: **95.00**
142 ❑ Feb 1952 Cover: 0.10 **NM** value: **95.00**
143 ❑ Mar 1952 Cover: 0.10 **NM** value: **95.00**
144 ❑ Apr 1952 Cover: 0.10 **NM** value: **95.00**
145 ❑ May 1952 Cover: 0.10 **NM** value: **95.00**
146 ❑ Jun 1952 Cover: 0.10 **NM** value: **95.00**
147 ❑ Jul 1952 Cover: 0.10 **NM** value: **95.00**
148 ❑ Aug 1952 Cover: 0.10 **NM** value: **95.00**
149 ❑ Sep 1952 Cover: 0.10 **NM** value: **95.00**
150 ❑ Oct 1952 Cover: 0.10 **NM** value: **95.00**
151 ❑ Jan 1953 Cover: 0.10 **NM** value: **95.00**
152 ❑ Feb 1953 Cover: 0.10 **NM** value: **95.00**
153 ❑ Mar 1953 Cover: 0.10 **NM** value: **175.00**
• **CGC:** 1 graded, best 8.5
• Scarcer
154 ❑ Apr 1953 Cover: 0.10 **NM** value: **175.00**
• **CGC:** 1 graded, best 9.0
• Scarcer
155 ❑ Cover: 0.10 **NM** value: **175.00**
• Scarcer

WHOA, NELLIE! — Fantagraphics

1 ❑ Jul 1996, b&w Cover: 2.95 **NM** value: **Cover or less**
2 ❑ Aug 1996, b&w Cover: 2.95 **NM** value: **Cover or less**
3 ❑ Sep 1996, b&w Cover: 2.95 **NM** value: **Cover or less**

WHODUNNIT? — Eclipse

This short-lived 1986 series had a great gimmick. It combined traditional detective fiction with a contest which promised to reward $1,000 cash to the first person to correctly solve the mystery in each issue. Of course, it wasn't enough merely to name the killer — readers had to prove they'd really gotten to the bottom of things by unraveling the whole case, citing motives of the characters involved and, in some cases, pointing out how key pieces of evidence were known to be phony. This was no contest for the sloppy sleuth or lazy reader.

What made it all work was the crisp writing of Mark Evanier. Known for his high standards, this comics and television veteran could be counted on not to employ cheap plot devices or do something totally illogical simply in order to confound readers. Although not a commercial success, the issues of this series are as enjoyable to puzzle out today as they were in 1986.

1 ❑ Jun 1986 Cover: 2.00 **NM** value: **Cover or less**
Circ: CapCity orders: **7,475**
📖 Who Shot Danny Scott? **A:** Dan Spiegle; Brent Anderson(cover); Carrie Spiegle **W:** Dan Spiegle; Mark Evanier
2 ❑ Nov 1986 Cover: 2.00 **NM** value: **Cover or less**
Circ: CapCity orders: **4,625**
📖 Who Slew Kangaroo? **A:** Dan Spiegle; Brent Anderson(cover); Carrie Spiegle **W:** Dan Spiegle; Mark Evanier
3 ❑ Apr 1987 Cover: 2.00 **NM** value: **Cover or less**
Circ: CapCity orders: **2,675**
📖 Who Offed Henry Croft? **A:** Dan Spiegle; Carrie Spiegle **W:** Dan Spiegle; Mark Evanier

WHO IS NEXT? — Standard

5 ❑ Jan 1953 Cover: 0.10 **NM** value: **100.00**
• **CGC:** 1 graded, best 7.5

WHO IS THE CROOKED MAN — Crusade

1 ❑ Sep 1996 Cover: 3.50 **NM** value: **Cover or less**
Circ: Diamd. preorders: **3,965**
📖 The Matyr; Scarlet 7; Garrison **A:** Chris Knowles; John Hazard; Paul Schuurmans **W:** Brian David-Marshall; Paul M. Yellovich; Rob Conroy

WHO REALLY KILLED JFK — Revolutionary

1 ❑ Oct 1993, b&w Cover: 2.50 **NM** value: **Cover or less**
📖 The Kennedy Conspiracy; Who Was Lee Harvey Oswald?; The Cover Up; Who Was Jack Ruby?; The New Orleans Connection **A:** Hugh Fleming; Pete Mullins **W:** Herb Shapiro

WHO'S WHO IN STAR TREK — DC

1 ❑ Mar 1987 Cover: 1.50 **NM** value: **Cover or less**
Circ: CapCity orders: **13,550**
2 ❑ Apr 1987 Cover: 1.50 **NM** value: **Cover or less**
Circ: CapCity orders: **11,750**
• McGivers-Vulcans **A:** George Pérez; John Byrne; Howard Chaykin

CGC-graded: Multiply prices above by **33 for 9.9 M • 16 for 9.8 NM/M • 7 for 9.6 NM+ • 5 for 9.4 NM • 2.5 for 9.2 NM- • 1.5 for 9.0 VF/NM**

WHO'S WHO IN THE DC UNIVERSE — DC

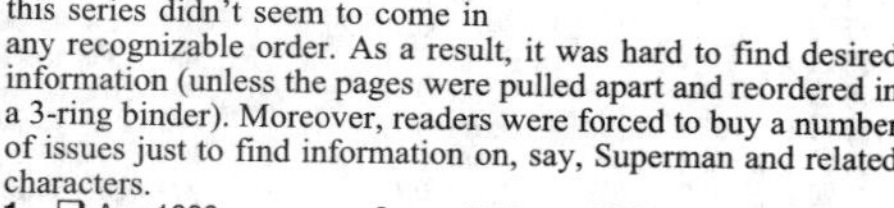

In 1990, DC began issuing this updated index of their various characters. The last such effort had been 1985-1987's Who's Who: The Definitive Directory of the DC Universe, along with the Who's Who Updates in 1987 and 1988. While these had been worthy efforts at the time, changes since (especially Crisis on Infinite Earths) necessitated a major overhaul.

This time out, DC decided to use a looseleaf format, a generally good idea, since new pages could conceivably be put in as needed. Unfortunately, the assorted "issues" of this series didn't seem to come in any recognizable order. As a result, it was hard to find desired information (unless the pages were pulled apart and reordered in a 3-ring binder). Moreover, readers were forced to buy a number of issues just to find information on, say, Superman and related characters.

1 ❑ Aug 1990 Cover: 4.95 **NM** value: **Cover or less**
Circ: CapCity orders: **17,000**
2 ❑ Sep 1990 Cover: 4.95 **NM** value: **Cover or less**
Circ: CapCity orders: **13,400**
3 ❑ Oct 1990 Cover: 4.95 **NM** value: **Cover or less**
Circ: CapCity orders: **13,150**
4 ❑ Nov 1990 Cover: 4.95 **NM** value: **Cover or less**
Circ: CapCity orders: **13,400**
5 ❑ Dec 1990 Cover: 4.95 **NM** value: **Cover or less**
Circ: CapCity orders: **14,750**
6 ❑ Jan 1991 Cover: 4.95 **NM** value: **Cover or less**
Circ: CapCity orders: **1,400**
7 ❑ Feb 1991 Cover: 4.95 **NM** value: **Cover or less**
Circ: CapCity orders: **13,950**
8 ❑ Apr 1991 Cover: 4.95 **NM** value: **Cover or less**
Circ: CapCity orders: **13,700**
9 ❑ May 1991 Cover: 4.95 **NM** value: **Cover or less**
Circ: CapCity orders: **13,050**
10 ❑ Jun 1991 Cover: 4.95 **NM** value: **Cover or less**
Circ: CapCity orders: **12,950**
11 ❑ Jul 1991 Cover: 4.95 **NM** value: **Cover or less**
Circ: CapCity orders: **12,250**
12 ❑ Aug 1991 Cover: 4.95 **NM** value: **Cover or less**
Circ: CapCity orders: **11,850**
13 ❑ Oct 1991 Cover: 4.95 **NM** value: **Cover or less**
Circ: CapCity orders: **12,350**
14 ❑ Nov 1991 Cover: 4.95 **NM** value: **Cover or less**
Circ: CapCity orders: **11,400**
15 ❑ Jan 1992 Cover: 4.95 **NM** value: **Cover or less**
Circ: CapCity orders: **10,900**
16 ❑ Feb 1992 Cover: 4.95 **NM** value: **Cover or less**
Circ: CapCity orders: **10,450**
final issue.

WHO'S WHO IN THE DC UNIVERSE UPDATE 1993 — DC

1 ❑ Dec 1992 Cover: 5.95 **NM** value: **Cover or less**
Circ: CapCity orders: **6,700**
2 ❑ Jan 1993 Cover: 5.95 **NM** value: **Cover or less**
Circ: CapCity orders: **6,550**

WHO'S WHO IN THE IMPACT UNIVERSE — DC / Impact

1 ❑ Sep 1991 Cover: 4.95 **NM** value: **Cover or less**
2 ❑ Dec 1991 Cover: 4.95 **NM** value: **Cover or less**
3 ❑ May 1992 Cover: 4.95 **NM** value: **Cover or less**

WHO'S WHO IN THE LEGION OF SUPER-HEROES — DC

1 ❑ Apr 1988 Cover: 1.25 **NM** value: **1.50**
Circ: CapCity orders: **17,500**
• Absorbancy Boy through Doctor Gym'll; Absorbancy Boy through Dr. Gym'll **A:** Karl Kesel; Jim Valentino; George Pérez; Rob Liefeld; Dan Jurgens; Dave Cockrum; Greg LaRocque; Joe Staton; Grant Miehm; Keith Wilson; Curt Swan; Rick Stasi; Arne Starr; Mike DeCarlo; Robert Campanella; Jonathan Peterson
2 ❑ Jun 1988 Cover: 1.25 **NM** value: **1.50**
Circ: CapCity orders: **13,400**
• Doctor Mayavile through High Seer; Dr. Mayavile through High Seer
3 ❑ Jul 1988 Cover: 1.25 **NM** value: **1.50**
Circ: CapCity orders: **12,150**
• Heroes of Lallor through Legion of Super-Rejects; plus Planets of the 30th Century
4 ❑ Aug 1988 Cover: 1.25 **NM** value: **1.50**
Circ: CapCity orders: **12,150**
5 ❑ Sep 1988 Cover: 1.25 **NM** value: **1.50**
Circ: CapCity orders: **11,350**
• Mordru through Science Police Officer Quav; Plus Tour of Legion Headquarters
6 ❑ Oct 1988 Cover: 1.25 **NM** value: **1.50**
Circ: CapCity orders: **11,050**
7 ❑ Nov 1988 Cover: 1.25 **NM** value: **1.50**
Circ: CapCity orders: **10,200**

WHO'S WHO: THE DEFINITIVE DIRECTORY OF THE DC UNIVERSE — DC

1 ❑ Mar 1985 Cover: 1.00 **NM** value: **1.50**
2 ❑ Apr 1985 Cover: 1.00 **NM** value: **1.50**
3 ❑ May 1985 Cover: 1.00 **NM** value: **1.50**
Circ: CapCity orders: **35,750**
4 ❑ Jun 1985 Cover: 1.00 **NM** value: **1.50**
Circ: CapCity orders: **29,100**
5 ❑ Jul 1985 Cover: 1.00 **NM** value: **1.50**
Circ: CapCity orders: **30,000**
6 ❑ Aug 1985 Cover: 1.00 **NM** value: **1.50**
Circ: CapCity orders: **28,750**
7 ❑ Sep 1985 Cover: 1.00 **NM** value: **1.50**
Circ: CapCity orders: **27,450**
8 ❑ Oct 1985 Cover: 1.00 **NM** value: **1.50**
Circ: CapCity orders: **25,150**
• Fatal Five-Garguax **A:** Todd Dezuniga; Jerry Ordway; George Pérez; Jack Kirby; Gil Kane
9 ❑ Nov 1985 Cover: 1.00 **NM** value: **1.50**
Circ: CapCity orders: **23,950**
10 ❑ Dec 1985 Cover: 1.00 **NM** value: **1.50**
Circ: CapCity orders: **22,000**
11 ❑ Jan 1986 Cover: 1.00 **NM** value: **1.50**
Circ: CapCity orders: **21,100**
12 ❑ Feb 1986 Cover: 1.00 **NM** value: **1.50**
Circ: CapCity orders: **21,100**
13 ❑ Mar 1986 Cover: 1.00 **NM** value: **1.50**
Circ: CapCity orders: **20,550**
• Krona-Losers **A:** Jim Starlin; George Pérez; Jack Kirby; Gil Kane
14 ❑ Apr 1986 Cover: 1.00 **NM** value: **1.50**
Circ: CapCity orders: **20,400**
15 ❑ May 1986 Cover: 1.00 **NM** value: **1.50**
Circ: CapCity orders: **19,250**
16 ❑ Jun 1986 Cover: 1.00 **NM** value: **1.50**
Circ: CapCity orders: **19,550**
17 ❑ Jul 1986 Cover: 1.00 **NM** value: **1.50**
Circ: CapCity orders: **19,050**
18 ❑ Aug 1986 Cover: 1.00 **NM** value: **1.50**
Circ: CapCity orders: **19,200**
19 ❑ Sep 1986 Cover: 1.00 **NM** value: **1.50**
Circ: CapCity orders: **18,150**
20 ❑ Oct 1986 Cover: 1.00 **NM** value: **1.50**
Circ: CapCity orders: **18,050**
21 ❑ Nov 1986 Cover: 1.00 **NM** value: **1.50**
Circ: CapCity orders: **17,900**
22 ❑ Dec 1986 Cover: 1.00 **NM** value: **1.50**
Circ: CapCity orders: **17,800**
23 ❑ Jan 1987 Cover: 1.00 **NM** value: **1.50**
Circ: CapCity orders: **17,450**
24 ❑ Feb 1987 Cover: 1.00 **NM** value: **1.50**
Circ: CapCity orders: **17,250**
• Tim Trench-Universo
25 ❑ Mar 1987 Cover: 1.00 **NM** value: **1.50**
Circ: CapCity orders: **17,250**
• Unknown Soldier-Witch Boy
26 ❑ Apr 1987 Cover: 1.00 **NM** value: **1.50**
Circ: CapCity orders: **17,450**

WHO'S WHO UPDATE '87 — DC

1 ❑ Aug 1987 Cover: 1.25 **NM** value: **1.50**
Circ: CapCity orders: **19,550**
2 ❑ Sep 1987 Cover: 1.25 **NM** value: **1.50**
Circ: CapCity orders: **18,800**
3 ❑ Oct 1987 Cover: 1.25 **NM** value: **1.50**
Circ: CapCity orders: **18,550**
4 ❑ Nov 1987 Cover: 1.25 **NM** value: **1.50**
Circ: CapCity orders: **18,000**
5 ❑ Dec 1987 Cover: 1.25 **NM** value: **1.50**
Circ: CapCity orders: **17,650**

WHO'S WHO UPDATE '88 — DC

1 ❑ Aug 1988 Cover: 1.25 **NM** value: **1.50**
Circ: CapCity orders: **17,250**
• Amazing Man to Harlequin II
2 ❑ Sep 1988 Cover: 1.25 **NM** value: **1.50**
Circ: CapCity orders: **15,650**
• Icemaiden to Nightwing
3 ❑ Oct 1988 Cover: 1.25 **NM** value: **1.50**
Circ: CapCity orders: **14,800**
• Parliament of Trees to Trident
4 ❑ Nov 1988 Cover: 1.25 **NM** value: **1.50**
Circ: CapCity orders: **13,800**
• Ultra-Humanite to Zuggernaut plus Supporting Characters (Abby Cable to Wade Eiling)

WHOTNOT — Fantagraphics

1 ❑ b&w Cover: 2.50 **NM** value: **Cover or less**
2 ❑ b&w Cover: 2.50 **NM** value: **Cover or less**
3 ❑ b&w Cover: 2.50 **NM** value: **Cover or less**

WHY DID PETE DUEL KILL HIMSELF? — Fantagraphics

Bk 1 ❑ Apr 1997, b&w Cover: 8.95 **NM** value: **Cover or less**

WHY I HATE SATURN — DC / Piranha

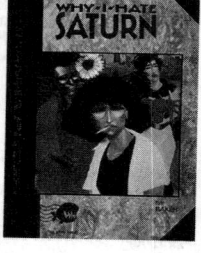

Why I Hate Saturn is a critically acclaimed (and very funny) book by Kyle Baker. More than 200 pages in length, it's the story of Anne, an engagingly neurotic writer for one of New York's hyper-trendy magazines. She's made a career out of being amusingly miserable — something she knows a lot about. She's even gone so far as to get herself signed to a book contract, based entirely on the success of her column. (It certainly wasn't based on the title "Man, is that grapefruit" or any sort of outline or sample chapters.) Truth be told, she hasn't actually gotten around to writing anything — and the book is due. To Anne, it seems like a good time to get really drunk.

That's when her sister Laura shows up at her apartment. Laura fancies herself the queen of the Leather Astro Girls of Saturn and, for all her craziness, is a great deal happier than Anne. But that'ss just one of the many reasons Anne has for hating Saturn ...

1 ❑ Cover: 14.95 **NM** value: **Cover or less**

WICKED — Millennium

1 ❑ 1994 Cover: 2.50 **NM** value: **Cover or less**
2 ❑ 1995 Cover: 2.50 **NM** value: **Cover or less**
3 ❑ Apr 1995, b&w cover dated Mar. Cover: 2.50 **NM** value: **Cover or less**

WICKED, THE — Image

1 ❑ Dec 1999 Cover: 2.95 **NM** value: **Cover or less**
Circ: Diamd. preorders: **33,638**
Man, demoin on cover. **A:** Roy Martinez **W:** Francis Takenaga
1/A ❑ Dec 1999 Cover: 2.95 **NM** value: **Cover or less**
Figure against red background on cover.
1/B ❑ Dec 1999 Cover: 2.95 **NM** value: **Cover or less**
Girl with glowing book on cover.
2 ❑ Feb 2000 Cover: 2.95 **NM** value: **Cover or less**
Circ: Diamd. preorders: **19,010**
3 ❑ 2000 Cover: 2.95 **NM** value: **Cover or less**
Circ: Diamd. preorders: **16,776**
4 ❑ 2000 Cover: 2.95 **NM** value: **Cover or less**
Circ: Diamd. preorders: **17,536**
5 ❑ Jun 2000 Cover: 2.95 **NM** value: **Cover or less**
Circ: Diamd. preorders: **15,310**
6 ❑ Jun 2000 Cover: 2.95 **NM** value: **Cover or less**
Circ: Diamd. preorders: **13,471**
7 ❑ Aug 2000 Cover: 2.95 **NM** value: **Cover or less**
Circ: Diamd. preorders: **12,836**
Ash 1 ❑ Jul 1999 Cover: 5.00 **NM** value: **Cover or less**
• Preview edition. **A:** Roy Martinez **W:** Francis Takenaga

WICKED, THE: MEDUSA'S TALE — Image

1 ❑ Nov 2000 Cover: 3.95 **NM** value: **Cover or less**

WIDOW — Avatar

0 ❑ Cover: 3.95 **NM** value: **Cover or less**

WIDOW: FLESH AND BLOOD — Ground Zero

1 ❑ Cover: 2.50 **NM** value: **Cover or less**
2 ❑ Cover: 2.50 **NM** value: **Cover or less**
3 ❑ Mar 1993 Cover: 2.50 **NM** value: **Cover or less**
Bk 1 ❑ b&w Cover: 5.95 **NM** value: **Cover or less**
No issue number.

WIDOW: METAL GYPSIES — London Night

1 ❑ Cover: 3.95 **NM** value: **Cover or less**
Circ: CapCity orders: **11,430**

WIINDOWS — Cult

1 ❑ Mar 1993, b&w Cover: 2.50 **NM** value: **3.50**
Partial prism cover.
2 ❑ Apr 1993, b&w Cover: 2.50 **NM** value: **3.00**
3 ❑ May 1993, b&w Cover: 2.50 **NM** value: **3.00**
4 ❑ Jun 1993, b&w Cover: 2.50 **NM** value: **Cover or less**
5 ❑ Jul 1993, b&w Cover: 2.50 **NM** value: **Cover or less**
📖 Masterpiece in Bone **A:** James Lyle **W:** Mike Leonard
6 ❑ Aug 1993, b&w Cover: 2.50 **NM** value: **Cover or less**
7 ❑ Sep 1993, b&w Cover: 2.50 **NM** value: **Cover or less**
8 ❑ Oct 1993, b&w Cover: 2.50 **NM** value: **Cover or less**
9 ❑ Nov 1993, b&w Cover: 2.50 **NM** value: **Cover or less**
10 ❑ Dec 1993, b&w Cover: 2.50 **NM** value: **Cover or less**
11 ❑ Jan 1994, b&w Cover: 2.50 **NM** value: **Cover or less**
12 ❑ Feb 1994, b&w Cover: 2.50 **NM** value: **Cover or less**
13 ❑ Mar 1994, b&w Cover: 2.50 **NM** value: **Cover or less**
14 ❑ Apr 1994, b&w Cover: 2.50 **NM** value: **Cover or less**
15 ❑ May 1994, b&w Cover: 2.50 **NM** value: **Cover or less**
16 ❑ Jun 1994, b&w Cover: 2.50 **NM** value: **Cover or less**
17 ❑ Jun 1994, b&w Cover: 2.50 **NM** value: **Cover or less**

WILBUR — Archie

This title bears more than a striking resemblance to Archie, another teen-age comics sensation from Archie Comics. The title character is a perpetual teen, good-natured and slightly girl-crazy. Laurie Lake is the popular blonde who can wrap him around her little finger with a single kiss. Even so, Wilbur wouldn't mind so much, if he wasn't always sparring for her affections with Slats, his worst enemy. The two often play pranks on each other, but, whenever anything truly mean is planned, it inevitably backfires. Probably the high point of this series is #3's introduction of comics favorite Katy Keene, who went on to appear frequently in the following issues.

This humor comic book kicked off in 1944 and proved remarkably popular, running 15 years before its conclusion. Even then, it was revived for an encore briefly in 1963.

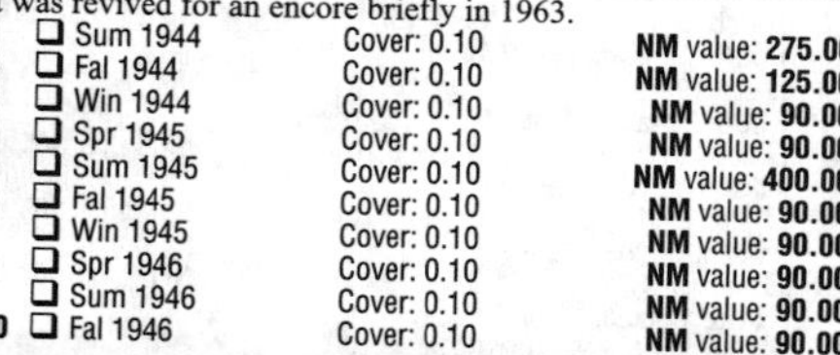

1 ❑ Sum 1944 Cover: 0.10 **NM** value: **275.00**
2 ❑ Fal 1944 Cover: 0.10 **NM** value: **125.00**
3 ❑ Win 1944 Cover: 0.10 **NM** value: **90.00**
4 ❑ Spr 1945 Cover: 0.10 **NM** value: **90.00**
5 ❑ Sum 1945 Cover: 0.10 **NM** value: **400.00**
6 ❑ Fal 1945 Cover: 0.10 **NM** value: **90.00**
7 ❑ Win 1945 Cover: 0.10 **NM** value: **90.00**
8 ❑ Spr 1946 Cover: 0.10 **NM** value: **90.00**
9 ❑ Sum 1946 Cover: 0.10 **NM** value: **90.00**
10 ❑ Fal 1946 Cover: 0.10 **NM** value: **90.00**

Other grades: Multiply prices above by **1.5 for Mint • 2/3 for Very Fine • 1/3 for Fine • 1/5 for Very Good • 1/8 for Good**

11 ❑ Win 1946 Cover: 0.10 **NM** value: **55.00**
12 ❑ Apr 1947 Cover: 0.10 **NM** value: **55.00**
13 ❑ Jun 1947 Cover: 0.10 **NM** value: **55.00**
14 ❑ Aug 1947 Cover: 0.10 **NM** value: **55.00**
15 ❑ Oct 1947 Cover: 0.10 **NM** value: **55.00**
16 ❑ Dec 1947 Cover: 0.10 **NM** value: **55.00**
17 ❑ Feb 1948 Cover: 0.10 **NM** value: **55.00**
18 ❑ Apr 1948 Cover: 0.10 **NM** value: **55.00**
19 ❑ Jun 1948 Cover: 0.10 **NM** value: **55.00**
20 ❑ Aug 1948 Cover: 0.10 **NM** value: **55.00**
21 ❑ Oct 1948 Cover: 0.10 **NM** value: **55.00**
22 ❑ Dec 1948 Cover: 0.10 **NM** value: **38.00**
23 ❑ Feb 1949 Cover: 0.10 **NM** value: **38.00**
24 ❑ Apr 1949 Cover: 0.10 **NM** value: **38.00**
25 ❑ Jun 1949 Cover: 0.10 **NM** value: **38.00**
26 ❑ Aug 1949 Cover: 0.10 **NM** value: **38.00**
27 ❑ Oct 1949 Cover: 0.10 **NM** value: **38.00**
28 ❑ Dec 1949 Cover: 0.10 **NM** value: **38.00**
29 ❑ Feb 1950 Cover: 0.10 **NM** value: **38.00**
30 ❑ Apr 1950 Cover: 0.10 **NM** value: **38.00**
31 ❑ Jun 1950 Cover: 0.10 **NM** value: **25.00**
32 ❑ Aug 1950 Cover: 0.10 **NM** value: **25.00**
33 ❑ Oct 1950 Cover: 0.10 **NM** value: **25.00**
34 ❑ Dec 1950 Cover: 0.10 **NM** value: **25.00**
35 ❑ Feb 1951 Cover: 0.10 **NM** value: **25.00**
36 ❑ Apr 1951 Cover: 0.10 **NM** value: **25.00**
37 ❑ Jun 1951 Cover: 0.10 **NM** value: **25.00**
38 ❑ Aug 1951 Cover: 0.10 **NM** value: **25.00**
39 ❑ Oct 1951 Cover: 0.10 **NM** value: **25.00**
40 ❑ Dec 1951 Cover: 0.10 **NM** value: **25.00**
41 ❑ Feb 1952 Cover: 0.10 **NM** value: **25.00**
42 ❑ Apr 1952 Cover: 0.10 **NM** value: **25.00**
43 ❑ Jun 1952 Cover: 0.10 **NM** value: **25.00**
44 ❑ Aug 1952 Cover: 0.10 **NM** value: **25.00**
45 ❑ Oct 1952 Cover: 0.10 **NM** value: **25.00**
46 ❑ Dec 1952 Cover: 0.10 **NM** value: **25.00**
47 ❑ Feb 1953 Cover: 0.10 **NM** value: **25.00**
48 ❑ Apr 1953 Cover: 0.10 **NM** value: **25.00**
49 ❑ Jun 1953 Cover: 0.10 **NM** value: **25.00**
50 ❑ Aug 1953 Cover: 0.10 **NM** value: **16.00**
51 ❑ Oct 1953 Cover: 0.10 **NM** value: **16.00**
52 ❑ Dec 1953 Cover: 0.10 **NM** value: **16.00**
53 ❑ Feb 1954 Cover: 0.10 **NM** value: **16.00**
54 ❑ Apr 1954 Cover: 0.10 **NM** value: **16.00**
55 ❑ Jun 1954 Cover: 0.10 **NM** value: **16.00**
56 ❑ Aug 1954 Cover: 0.10 **NM** value: **16.00**
57 ❑ Oct 1954 Cover: 0.10 **NM** value: **16.00**
58 ❑ Jan 1955 Cover: 0.10 **NM** value: **16.00**
59 ❑ Mar 1955 Cover: 0.10 **NM** value: **16.00**
60 ❑ May 1955 Cover: 0.10 **NM** value: **16.00**
61 ❑ Jul 1955 Cover: 0.10 **NM** value: **12.00**
62 ❑ Sep 1955 Cover: 0.10 **NM** value: **12.00**
63 ❑ Nov 1955 Cover: 0.10 **NM** value: **12.00**
64 ❑ Jan 1956 Cover: 0.10 **NM** value: **12.00**
65 ❑ Mar 1956 Cover: 0.10 **NM** value: **12.00**
66 ❑ May 1956 Cover: 0.10 **NM** value: **12.00**
67 ❑ Jul 1956 Cover: 0.10 **NM** value: **12.00**
68 ❑ Sep 1956 Cover: 0.10 **NM** value: **12.00**
69 ❑ Nov 1956 Cover: 0.10 **NM** value: **12.00**
70 ❑ Jan 1957 Cover: 0.10 **NM** value: **12.00**
71 ❑ Mar 1957 Cover: 0.10 **NM** value: **9.00**
72 ❑ May 1957 Cover: 0.10 **NM** value: **9.00**
73 ❑ Jul 1957 Cover: 0.10 **NM** value: **9.00**
74 ❑ Sep 1957 Cover: 0.10 **NM** value: **9.00**
75 ❑ Nov 1957 Cover: 0.10 **NM** value: **9.00**
76 ❑ Jan 1958 Cover: 0.10 **NM** value: **9.00**
77 ❑ Mar 1958 Cover: 0.10 **NM** value: **9.00**
78 ❑ May 1958 Cover: 0.10 **NM** value: **9.00**
79 ❑ Jul 1958 Cover: 0.10 **NM** value: **9.00**
80 ❑ Sep 1958 Cover: 0.10 **NM** value: **9.00**
81 ❑ Nov 1958 Cover: 0.10 **NM** value: **9.00**
82 ❑ Jan 1959 Cover: 0.10 **NM** value: **9.00**
83 ❑ Mar 1959 Cover: 0.10 **NM** value: **9.00**
84 ❑ May 1959 Cover: 0.10 **NM** value: **9.00**
85 ❑ Jul 1959 Cover: 0.10 **NM** value: **9.00**
86 ❑ Sep 1959 Cover: 0.10 **NM** value: **9.00**
87 ❑ Nov 1959 Cover: 0.10 **NM** value: **9.00**
88 ❑ Sep 1963 Cover: 0.12 **NM** value: **9.00**
• Last issue of original run
89 ❑ ca. 1964 Cover: 0.12 **NM** value: **4.00**
• Series begins again
90 ❑ Oct 1965 Cover: 0.12 **NM** value: **4.00**
final issue.

WILD, THE — Eastern

1 ❑ Cover: 1.50 **NM** value: **Cover or less**

WILD ANIMALS — Pacific

1 ❑ ca. 1982 Cover: 1.50 **NM** value: **Cover or less**

WILD BILL ELLIOTT — Dell

2 ❑ Nov 1950 Cover: 0.10 **NM** value: **100.00**
• **CGC:** 1 graded, best 9.0
3 ❑ Jan 1951 Cover: 0.10 **NM** value: **100.00**
4 ❑ Apr 1951 Cover: 0.10 **NM** value: **60.00**
5 ❑ Jul 1951 Cover: 0.10 **NM** value: **60.00**
6 ❑ Oct 1951 Cover: 0.10 **NM** value: **60.00**
7 ❑ Jan 1952 Cover: 0.10 **NM** value: **60.00**
8 ❑ Apr 1952 Cover: 0.10 **NM** value: **60.00**
9 ❑ Jul 1952 Cover: 0.10 **NM** value: **60.00**
10 ❑ Oct 1952 Cover: 0.10 **NM** value: **100.00**
13 ❑ Apr 1954 Cover: 0.10 **NM** value: **40.00**
14 ❑ Jul 1954 Cover: 0.10 **NM** value: **40.00**
15 ❑ Oct 1954 Cover: 0.10 **NM** value: **40.00**
• **CGC:** 1 graded, best 9.2
16 ❑ Jan 1955 Cover: 0.10 **NM** value: **40.00**
17 ❑ ca. 1955 Cover: 0.10 **NM** value: **40.00**

WILD BILL HICKOK — Avon

1 ❑ Sep 1949 Cover: 0.10 **NM** value: **200.00**
• **CGC:** 2 graded, best 7.5
2 ❑ Dec 1949 Cover: 0.10 **NM** value: **100.00**
3 ❑ Feb 1950 Cover: 0.10 **NM** value: **75.00**
4 ❑ Jul 1950 Cover: 0.10 **NM** value: **75.00**
5 ❑ 1950 Cover: 0.10 **NM** value: **75.00**
6 ❑ 1951 Cover: 0.10 **NM** value: **50.00**
7 ❑ 1951 Cover: 0.10 **NM** value: **50.00**
8 ❑ 1951 Cover: 0.10 **NM** value: **50.00**
9 ❑ Nov 1951 Cover: 0.10 **NM** value: **50.00**
10 ❑ Jan 1952 Cover: 0.10 **NM** value: **40.00**
11 ❑ Mar 1952 Cover: 0.10 **NM** value: **40.00**
12 ❑ May 1952 Cover: 0.10 **NM** value: **40.00**
13 ❑ Jul 1952 Cover: 0.10 **NM** value: **40.00**
14 ❑ Sep 1952 Cover: 0.10 **NM** value: **40.00**
15 ❑ Nov 1952 Cover: 0.10 **NM** value: **30.00**
16 ❑ Jan 1953 Cover: 0.10 **NM** value: **30.00**
17 ❑ Mar 1953 Cover: 0.10 **NM** value: **30.00**
18 ❑ May 1953 Cover: 0.10 **NM** value: **30.00**
19 ❑ Jul 1953 Cover: 0.10 **NM** value: **30.00**
20 ❑ Sep 1953 Cover: 0.10 **NM** value: **30.00**
21 ❑ Nov 1953 Cover: 0.10 **NM** value: **20.00**
22 ❑ 1954 Cover: 0.10 **NM** value: **20.00**
23 ❑ 1954 Cover: 0.10 **NM** value: **20.00**
24 ❑ Aug 1954 Cover: 0.10 **NM** value: **20.00**
25 ❑ 1954 Cover: 0.10 **NM** value: **20.00**
26 ❑ 1955 Cover: 0.10 **NM** value: **15.00**
27 ❑ 1955 Cover: 0.10 **NM** value: **15.00**
28 ❑ 1956 Cover: 0.10 **NM** value: **15.00**

WILD BILL PECOS — AC

1 ❑ ca. 1989 Cover: 3.50 **NM** value: **Cover or less**

WILDB.R.A.T.S — Fantagraphics

1 ❑ Cover: 2.95 **NM** value: **3.25**

WILDCARDS — Marvel / Epic

On the far-off world of Takhisis, the inhabitants have been battling each other for centuries using psionic powers. Seeking an edge, they developed a virus that could be used to mutate themselves into more powerful beings. But they needed a place to test it — so they they chose our world for this test.

In 1946, a bomb containing the virus was exploded over New York City. This virus — nicknamed the "Wildcard Virus," due to its unpredictable effects — killed 90% of the people it came into contact with. Of those remaining, nine out of 10 became "jokers": hideously mutated beings. Only one in 100 "drew an ace" and wound up with a useful mutation. These aces become the new super-heroes, although they are despised by those less fortunate.

This series is drawn from the George R.R. Martin-edited best-selling set of Bantam science-fiction books by the same name.

1 ❑ Sep 1990 Cover: 4.50 **NM** value: **Cover or less**
• prestige format. • based on prose anthology series
2 ❑ Oct 1990 Cover: 4.50 **NM** value: **Cover or less**
Circ: CapCity orders: **10,050**
• prestige format. • based on prose anthology series
3 ❑ Nov 1990 Cover: 4.50 **NM** value: **Cover or less**
Circ: CapCity orders: **9,250**
• prestige format. • based on prose anthology series
4 ❑ Dec 1990 Cover: 4.50 **NM** value: **Cover or less**
Circ: CapCity orders: **9,350**
• prestige format. • based on prose anthology series

WILDC.A.T.S — Image

Jacob Marlowe was one of many homeless people with a past but with no hope for the future — until Void appeared to bring Jacob back to his proper place as the champion of mankind. Now, he has assembled a squadron of super-heroes into a Covert Action Team (C.A.T.) against the evil Cabal organization and the alien Daemonites.

Created by former Marvel star artist Jim Lee, the WildC.A.T.s include Void, a teleporter; Voodoo, the human-Kherubim hybrid who can exorcise Daemonites from human hosts; Warblade, who can form his metal body into almost any form; Maul, who uses his gigantic size and enormous strength to the team's advantage; Grifter, a deadly marksman; and team leader Spartan, a synthetic being with a human consciousness.

0 ❑ Jun 1993 Cover: 1.95 **NM** value: **3.00**
1 ❑ Aug 1992 Cover: 1.95 **NM** value: **4.00**
Circ: CapCity orders: **281,850** • **CGC:** 29 graded, best 9.8
📖 Resurrection Day **A:** Jim Lee **W:** Jim Lee; Brandon Choi ★ 1st Appearance of Maul, Grifter, Spartan, Gnome, Tri-Ad, Helspont, Pike, WildC.A.T.s., Hightower.
1/3D ❑ Aug 1997 Cover: 4.95 **NM** value: **Cover or less**
• 3-D edition. 📖 Resurrection Day **A:** Jim Lee **W:** Jim Lee; Brandon Choi
1/GO ❑ Aug 1992 **NM** value: **10.00**
• **CGC:** 3 graded, best 9.8
• Gold edition. 📖 Resurrection Day **A:** Jim Lee **W:** Jim Lee; Brandon Choi
1/SC ❑ Aug 1992 **NM** value: **5.00**
• Wizard Ace edition.
2 ❑ Sep 1992 Cover: 2.50 **NM** value: **4.00**
Circ: CapCity orders: **151,875** • **CGC:** 29 graded, best 10.0
Prism cover. • Coupon for Image Comics #0 enclosed **A:** Jim Lee ★ 1st Appearance of Black Razor, Wetworks.
3 ❑ Dec 1992 Cover: 1.95 **NM** value: **3.00**
Circ: CapCity orders: **128,250** • **CGC:** 2 graded, best 9.8
4 ❑ Mar 1993 Cover: 1.95 **NM** value: **3.00**
Circ: CapCity orders: **100,875** • **CGC:** 2 graded, best 9.6
4/A ❑ Mar 1993 Cover: 2.50 **NM** value: **3.00**
• bagged; red trading card **A:** Jim Lee
5 ❑ Nov 1993 Cover: 1.95 **NM** value: **2.50**
Circ: CapCity orders: **100,225**
6 ❑ Dec 1993 Cover: 1.95 **NM** value: **2.50**
Circ: CapCity orders: **82,675**
📖 Killer Instinct, Part 1 **A:** Jim Lee
6/GO ❑ Dec 1993 Cover: 1.95 **NM** value: **3.00**
• Gold edition.
7 ❑ Jan 1994 Cover: 1.95 **NM** value: **2.50**
Circ: CapCity orders: **68,400**
📖 Killer Instinct, Part 3 **A:** Jim Lee
7/PL ❑ Jan 1994 **NM** value: **3.00**
• Platinum edition.
8 ❑ Feb 1994 Cover: 2.50 **NM** value: **Cover or less**
Circ: CapCity orders: **58,950** • **CGC:** 1 graded, best 9.6
9 ❑ Mar 1994 Cover: 2.50 **NM** value: **Cover or less**
Circ: CapCity orders: **56,875**
10 ❑ Apr 1994 Cover: 2.50 **NM** value: **Cover or less**
Circ: CapCity orders: **64,800**
• series becomes WildC.A.T.S **A:** Jim Lee
11 ❑ Jun 1994 Cover: 2.50 **NM** value: **Cover or less**
Circ: CapCity orders: **58,650**
• Title changes to WildC.A.T.S **A:** Jim Lee
11/A ❑ Jun 1994 Cover: 2.50 **NM** value: **Cover or less**
variant cover.
12 ❑ Aug 1994 Cover: 2.50 **NM** value: **Cover or less**
Circ: CapCity orders: **64,725**
13 ❑ Sep 1994 Cover: 2.50 **NM** value: **Cover or less**
Circ: CapCity orders: **65,650**
14 ❑ Sep 1994 Cover: 2.50 **NM** value: **Cover or less**
Circ: CapCity orders: **65,550**
15 ❑ Nov 1994 Cover: 1.95 **NM** value: **2.50**
Circ: CapCity orders: **57,575**
16 ❑ Dec 1994 Cover: 2.50 **NM** value: **Cover or less**
Circ: CapCity orders: **51,925**
17 ❑ Jan 1995 Cover: 2.50 **NM** value: **Cover or less**
Circ: CapCity orders: **46,325**
18 ❑ Mar 1995 Cover: 2.50 **NM** value: **Cover or less**
Circ: CapCity orders: **42,675**
19 ❑ Apr 1995 Cover: 2.50 **NM** value: **Cover or less**
Circ: CapCity orders: **39,175**
20 ❑ May 1995 Cover: 2.50 **NM** value: **Cover or less**
Circ: CapCity orders: **41,950**
📖 Wildstorm Rising, Part 2 • with cards
21 ❑ Jul 1995 Cover: 2.50 **NM** value: **Cover or less**
Circ: CapCity orders: **40,050**
• 1st Moore-written issue **A:** Travis Charest; Jim Lee(cover) **W:** Alan Moore
22 ❑ Aug 1995 Cover: 2.50 **NM** value: **Cover or less**
Circ: CapCity orders: **40,200**
📖 Cat's Cradle **A:** Kevin Maguire **W:** Alan Moore
23 ❑ Sep 1995 Cover: 2.50 **NM** value: **Cover or less**
Circ: CapCity orders: **36,725**
📖 Cat's Eyes **A:** Jason Johnson; Ryan Benjamin **W:** Alan Moore
24 ❑ Nov 1995 Cover: 2.50 **NM** value: **Cover or less**
📖 Catacombs **A:** Jason Johnson; Ryan Benjamin **W:** Alan Moore
25 ❑ Dec 1995 Cover: 4.95 **NM** value: **Cover or less**
enhanced wraparound cover. 📖 On Earth…As It Is In Heaven **A:** Travis Charest; Dave Johnson **W:** Alan Moore
26 ❑ Feb 1996 Cover: 2.50 **NM** value: **Cover or less**
📖 Cat'spaws **A:** Travis Charest; Dave Johnson **W:** Alan Moore
27 ❑ Mar 1996 Cover: 2.50 **NM** value: **Cover or less**
📖 Catastrophe **A:** Dave Johnson; Scott Clark **W:** Alan Moore
28 ❑ Apr 1996 Cover: 2.50 **NM** value: **Cover or less**
📖 Cataclysm **A:** Travis Charest; Dave Johnson; Aron Wiesenfeld **W:** Alan Moore
29 ❑ May 1996 Cover: 2.50 **NM** value: **Cover or less**
cover says Apr, indicia says May. 📖 Fire from Heaven, Part 7; Fire From Heaven, Chapter 7 **A:** Travis Charest; Ryan Benjamin **W:** Alan Moore
30 ❑ Jun 1996 Cover: 2.50 **NM** value: **Cover or less**
📖 Fire from Heaven, Part 13; Fire From Heaven, Chapter 13 **A:** Travis Charest; Ryan Benjamin **W:** Alan Moore
31 ❑ Sep 1996 Cover: 2.50 **NM** value: **Cover or less**
📖 Cats & Dogs **A:** Travis Charest **W:** Alan Moore
32 ❑ Jan 1997 Cover: 2.50 **NM** value: **Cover or less**
📖 Catharsis **A:** Matt Broome; Jim Lee; Patrick Lee **W:** Alan Moore
33 ❑ Feb 1997 Cover: 2.50 **NM** value: **Cover or less**
Circ: Diamd. preorders: **66,275**
📖 Belling the Cat **A:** Matt Broome **W:** Alan Moore
34 ❑ Feb 1997 Cover: 2.50 **NM** value: **Cover or less**
Circ: Diamd. preorders: **56,980**
📖 Catechism **A:** Matt Broome; Rob Stotz **W:** Alan Moore
35 ❑ Mar 1997 Cover: 2.50 **NM** value: **Cover or less**
Circ: Diamd. preorders: **54,841**
36 ❑ Mar 1997 Cover: 2.50 **NM** value: **Cover or less**
Circ: Diamd. preorders: **53,235**
37 ❑ Apr 1997 Cover: 2.50 **NM** value: **Cover or less**
Circ: Diamd. preorders: **50,354**
38 ❑ May 1997 Cover: 2.50 **NM** value: **Cover or less**
Circ: Diamd. preorders: **47,076**
39 ❑ Jun 1997 Cover: 2.50 **NM** value: **Cover or less**
Circ: Diamd. preorders: **44,077**

CGC-graded: Multiply prices above by **33 for 9.9 M • 16 for 9.8 NM/M • 7 for 9.6 NM+ • 5 for 9.4 NM • 2.5 for 9.2 NM- • 1.5 for 9.0 VF/NM**

40 ❑ Jul 1997 Cover: 2.50 **NM** value: **Cover or less**
Circ: Diamd. preorders: **32,231**
40/A❑ Jul 1997 Cover: 2.50 **NM** value: **Cover or less**
alternate mostly b&w cover.
40/B❑ Jul 1997 Cover: 2.50 **NM** value: **Cover or less**
alternate mostly b&w cover.
41 ❑ Aug 1997 Cover: 2.50 **NM** value: **Cover or less**
Circ: Diamd. preorders: **39,894**
42 ❑ Sep 1997 Cover: 2.50 **NM** value: **Cover or less**
Circ: Diamd. preorders: **38,222**
📖 Brothers in Arms **A:** Matt Broome; Mike Miller **W:** Brandon Choi; Jonathan Peterson
43 ❑ Oct 1997 Cover: 2.50 **NM** value: **Cover or less**
Circ: Diamd. preorders: **37,534**
📖 The High Road to China **A:** Anthony Winn **W:** Brandon Choi; Jonathan Peterson
44 ❑ Nov 1997 Cover: 2.50 **NM** value: **Cover or less**
Circ: Diamd. preorders: **34,915**
📖 Paradise Lost **A:** Ed Benés **W:** Brandon Choi; Jonathan Peterson
45 ❑ Jan 1998 Cover: 2.50 **NM** value: **Cover or less**
Circ: Diamd. preorders: **31,486**
📖 Endangered Species, Part 5
46 ❑ Feb 1998 Cover: 2.50 **NM** value: **Cover or less**
Circ: Diamd. preorders: **29,446**
📖 Endangered Species, Part 6 **A:** Ed Benés **W:** Brandon Choi; Jonathan Peterson
47 ❑ Mar 1998 Cover: 2.50 **NM** value: **Cover or less**
Circ: Diamd. preorders: **29,953**
47/A❑ Mar 1998 Cover: 2.50 **NM** value: **Cover or less**
alternate cover with Grifter. 📖 Memories of Tomorrow **A:** Mike Deodato; Al Vey(cover); Ed Benés **W:** Brandon Choi; Jonathan Peterson
47/B❑ Mar 1998 Cover: 2.50 **NM** value: **Cover or less**
alternate cover with Grifter. 📖 Memories of Tomorrow **A:** Mike Deodato; Joe Madureira(cover); Ed Benés **W:** Brandon Choi; Jonathan Peterson
48 ❑ Apr 1998 Cover: 2.50 **NM** value: **Cover or less**
Circ: Diamd. preorders: **29,170**
📖 When Worlds Collide, Part 1 **A:** Ed Benés **W:** Brandon Choi; Jonathan Peterson
49 ❑ May 1998 Cover: 2.50 **NM** value: **Cover or less**
Circ: Diamd. preorders: **27,168**
📖 When Worlds Collide, Part 2 **A:** Ed Benés **W:** Brandon Choi; Jonathan Peterson
50 ❑ Jun 1998 Cover: 3.50 **NM** value: **Cover or less**
Circ: Diamd. preorders: **40,352**
• Giant-size. 📖 Old Feelings; The Last Goodbye; Reincarnation **A:** Travis Charest; Jim Lee; Ed Benés **W:** James Robinson; Alan Moore; Brandon Choi; Jonathan Peterson
50/SC❑ Jun 1998 **NM** value: **3.50**
chromium cover.
Anl 1❑ Feb 1998 Cover: 2.95 **NM** value: **Cover or less**
Circ: Diamd. preorders: **24,646**
Bk 1❑ Cover: 9.95 **NM** value: **Cover or less**
Bk 1/A❑ Jun 1993 Cover: 9.95 **NM** value: **Cover or less**
• collects issues #0-4
Bk 1/B❑ Jun 1993 Cover: 9.95 **NM** value: **Cover or less**
cover has blue sidebar instead of purple. • Diamond Edition.
Bk 1/HC❑ Jun 1993 Cover: 49.95 **NM** value: **Cover or less**
hardcover. • collects issues #0-4
Bk 2❑ Aug 1998 Cover: 19.95 **NM** value: **Cover or less**
📖 Killer Instinct • Homecoming; collects WildC.A.T.S #21-27
Bk 3❑ Nov 1998 Cover: 16.95 **NM** value: **19.95**
📖 Homecoming • Gang War; collects #28-#34
Bk 4❑ Cover: 16.95 **NM** value: **Cover or less**
📖 Gang War • Collects issues #28-34
SE 1❑ Nov 1993 Cover: 3.50 **NM** value: **Cover or less**

WILDCATS (2ND SERIES) DC / Wildstorm

Mysterious troubles have caused dissent among the WildC.A.T.s crew, and the members have supposedly gone their separate ways. Of course, as the old saying almost goes: Once a covert action team, always a covert action team. So, even though Grifter keeps insisting they're not a team any more, he and the others still find themselves working together.

The most pressing problem of the WildC.A.T.s seems to be the ongoing war between two alien races, the Kherubim and the Daemonites. They are trying to find Kenyan, a renegade human who's been playing both groups against each other to gain more power for himself. Unfortunately, the team's problems extend beyond the battlefield. Tension and distrust have eroded the bonds of friendship and loyalty that have always held them together. And, without trust, even the best soldiers are doomed to failure.

1/A ❑ Mar 1999 Cover: 2.50 **NM** value: **Cover or less**
Circ: Diamd. preorders: **82,453**
1/B ❑ Mar 1999 Cover: 2.50 **NM** value: **Cover or less**
1/C ❑ Mar 1999 Cover: 2.50 **NM** value: **Cover or less**
1/D ❑ Mar 1999 Cover: 2.50 **NM** value: **Cover or less**
1/E ❑ Mar 1999 Cover: 2.50 **NM** value: **Cover or less**
1/F ❑ Mar 1999 Cover: 2.50 **NM** value: **Cover or less**
1/G ❑ Mar 1999 Cover: 6.95 **NM** value: **Cover or less**
1/H ❑ Mar 1999 Cover: 6.95 **NM** value: **Cover or less**
DFE alternate cover. **A:** Travis Charest **W:** Scott Lobdell
1/I ❑ Mar 1999 **NM** value: **10.00**
• Euro-Edition sketch cover. **A:** Travis Charest **W:** Scott Lobdell
1/J ❑ Mar 1999 **NM** value: **29.95**
• Euro-Edition sketch cover. **A:** Travis Charest **W:** Scott Lobdell
2 ❑ May 1999 Cover: 2.50 **NM** value: **Cover or less**
Circ: Diamd. preorders: **60,466**
3 ❑ Jul 1999 Cover: 2.50 **NM** value: **Cover or less**
Circ: Diamd. preorders: **60,247**
4 ❑ Sep 1999 Cover: 2.50 **NM** value: **Cover or less**
Circ: Diamd. preorders: **58,554**
📖 Firefight **A:** Travis Charest **W:** Scott Lobdell
5 ❑ Nov 1999 Cover: 2.50 **NM** value: **Cover or less**
Circ: Diamd. preorders: **52,001**
📖 Coda-Fied **A:** Bryan Hitch **W:** Joe Casey; Scott Lobdell
6 ❑ Dec 1999 Cover: 2.50 **NM** value: **Cover or less**
Circ: Diamd. preorders: **47,041**
📖 The Chase **A:** Scott Benefiel **W:** Joe Casey; Scott Lobdell
7 ❑ 2000 Cover: 2.50 **NM** value: **Cover or less**
Circ: Diamd. preorders: **39,274**
8 ❑ 2000 Cover: 2.50 **NM** value: **Cover or less**
Circ: Diamd. preorders: **36,154**
9 ❑ May 2000 Cover: 2.50 **NM** value: **Cover or less**
Circ: Diamd. preorders: **32,784**
📖 Set my Soul on Fire **A:** Sean Phillips **W:** Joe Casey
10 ❑ Jun 2000 Cover: 2.50 **NM** value: **Cover or less**
Circ: Diamd. preorders: **31,071**
📖 Deal of the Century **A:** Sean Phillips **W:** Joe Casey
11 ❑ Jul 2000 Cover: 2.50 **NM** value: **Cover or less**
Circ: Diamd. preorders: **29,811**
12 ❑ Aug 2000 Cover: 2.50 **NM** value: **Cover or less**
Circ: Diamd. preorders: **27,914**
13 ❑ Sep 2000 Cover: 2.50 **NM** value: **Cover or less**
Circ: Diamd. preorders: **26,788**
14 ❑ Oct 2000 Cover: 2.50 **NM** value: **Cover or less**
Circ: Diamd. preorders: **24,129**
📖 Black Action Falls; Serial Boxes, Part 1 **A:** Sean Phillips **W:** Joe Casey
15 ❑ Nov 2000 Cover: 2.50 **NM** value: **Cover or less**
Circ: Diamd. preorders: **23,612**
📖 Serial Boxes, Part 2 **A:** Sean Phillips **W:** Joe Casey
16 ❑ Dec 2000 Cover: 2.50 **NM** value: **Cover or less**
Circ: Diamd. preorders: **22,309**
📖 Serial Boxes, Part 3 **A:** Sean Phillips **W:** Joe Casey
17 ❑ Jan 2001 Cover: 2.50 **NM** value: **Cover or less**
Circ: Diamd. preorders: **21,553**
📖 Serial Boxes, Part 4 **A:** Sean Phillips **W:** Joe Casey
18 ❑ Feb 2001 Cover: 2.50 **NM** value: **Cover or less**
Circ: Diamd. preorders: **20,760**
📖 Serial Boxes, Part 5 **A:** Sean Phillips **W:** Joe Casey
19 ❑ Mar 2001 Cover: 2.50 **NM** value: **Cover or less**
Circ: Diamd. preorders: **19,526**
📖 Serial Boxes, Part 6 **A:** Sean Phillips **W:** Joe Casey
20 ❑ Apr 2001 Cover: 2.50 **NM** value: **Cover or less**
Circ: Diamd. preorders: **19,921** • **CGC:** 1 graded, best 9.6
📖 Sodom and Modem, Part 1 **A:** Steve Dillon **W:** Joe Casey
21 ❑ May 2001 Cover: 2.50 **NM** value: **Cover or less**
Circ: Diamd. preorders: **19,261** • **CGC:** 2 graded, best 9.8
📖 Sodom and Modem, Part 2 **A:** Steve Dillon **W:** Joe Casey
22 ❑ Jun 2001 Cover: 2.50 **NM** value: **Cover or less**
Circ: Diamd. preorders: **18,846**
📖 Unberable Likeness **A:** Sean Phillips **W:** Joe Casey
23 ❑ Jul 2001 Cover: 2.50 **NM** value: **Cover or less**
Circ: Diamd. preorders: **18,641**
24 ❑ Aug 2001 Cover: 2.50 **NM** value: **Cover or less**
Circ: Diamd. preorders: **18,043**
25 ❑ Sep 2001 Cover: 3.50 **NM** value: **Cover or less**
Circ: Diamd. preorders: **18,998**
Anl 2000❑ Dec 2000 Cover: 3.50 **NM** value: **Cover or less**
Circ: Diamd. preorders: **19,315**
📖 Condition Dead **A:** Lee Bermejo **W:** Joe Casey

WILDC.A.T.S ADVENTURES Image

1 ❑ Sep 1994 Cover: 1.95 **NM** value: **2.00**
Circ: CapCity orders: **38,900**
2 ❑ Nov 1994 Cover: 1.95 **NM** value: **2.00**
Circ: CapCity orders: **30,100**
3 ❑ Nov 1994 Cover: 1.95 **NM** value: **2.00**
Circ: CapCity orders: **23,100**
4 ❑ Dec 1994 Cover: 2.50 **NM** value: **Cover or less**
Circ: CapCity orders: **15,400**
5 ❑ Jan 1995 Cover: 2.50 **NM** value: **Cover or less**
Circ: CapCity orders: **11,375**
6 ❑ Feb 1995 Cover: 2.50 **NM** value: **Cover or less**
Circ: CapCity orders: **8,400**
7 ❑ Mar 1995 Cover: 2.50 **NM** value: **Cover or less**
Circ: CapCity orders: **7,375**
8 ❑ Apr 1995 Cover: 2.50 **NM** value: **Cover or less**
Circ: CapCity orders: **5,825**
9 ❑ May 1995 Cover: 2.50 **NM** value: **Cover or less**
Circ: CapCity orders: **4,975**
10 ❑ Jun 1995 Cover: 2.50 **NM** value: **Cover or less**
Circ: CapCity orders: **4,800**

WILDC.A.T.S ADVENTURES SOURCEBOOK Image

1 ❑ Jan 1995 Cover: 2.95 **NM** value: **Cover or less**
Circ: CapCity orders: **9,575**

WILDC.A.T.S/ALIENS Image

1 ❑ Aug 1998 Cover: 4.95 **NM** value: **Cover or less**
Circ: Diamd. preorders: **32,022** • **CGC:** 3 graded, best 9.4
cardstock cover. • crossover with Dark Horse **A:** Chris Sprouse **W:** Warren Ellis
1/A ❑ Aug 1998 Cover: 4.95 **NM** value: **Cover or less**
• **CGC:** 2 graded, best 9.4
alternate cardstock cover (Zealot vs. Alien). • crossover with Dark Horse **A:** Chris Sprouse **W:** Warren Ellis

WILDC.A.T.S: GATHERING OF EAGLES Image

Bk 1❑ Cover: 9.95 **NM** value: **Cover or less**

WILDC.A.T.S (JIM LEE'S...) Image

1 ❑ Apr 1995 **NM** value: **2.00**
no cover price. • informational comic for San Diego Police Dept.

WILDCATS: LADYTRON DC / Wildstorm

1 ❑ Oct 2000 Cover: 5.95 **NM** value: **Cover or less**

WILDCATS: MOSAIC DC / Wildstorm

1 ❑ Feb 2000 Cover: 3.95 **NM** value: **Cover or less**

WILDC.A.T.S SOURCEBOOK Image

1 ❑ Sep 1993 Cover: 2.50 **NM** value: **Cover or less**
Circ: CapCity orders: **146,325**
1/GO❑ Sep 1993 **NM** value: **3.00**
• Gold edition.
2 ❑ Nov 1994 Cover: 2.50 **NM** value: **Cover or less**
Circ: CapCity orders: **31,900**

WILDC.A.T.S TRILOGY Image

1 ❑ Jun 1993 Cover: 2.50 **NM** value: **Cover or less**
Circ: CapCity orders: **182,700** • **CGC:** 4 graded, best 9.9
foil cover. ★ 1st Appearance of Artemis.
2 ❑ Sep 1993 Cover: 1.95 **NM** value: **Cover or less**
Circ: CapCity orders: **118,275**
3 ❑ Nov 1993 Cover: 1.95 **NM** value: **Cover or less**
Circ: CapCity orders: **95,125** • **CGC:** 1 graded, best 9.8
Bk 1❑ Cover: 7.95 **NM** value: **Cover or less**
• Trade Paperback. 📖 The Golden Age; The Silver Age; The Modern Age; The Dark Age • collects mini-series; Collects series **A:** Andrew Robinson; Adam Hughes; Matt Broome; Travis Charest; Jim Lee; Dave Johnson; Lee Bermejo; Aron Wiesenfeld **W:** James Robinson; Warren Ellis; Scott Lobdell

WILDC.A.T.S/X-MEN Image

Bk 1❑ Dec 1998 Cover: 19.95 **NM** value: **Cover or less**
• collects The Golden Age, The Silver Age, and The Modern Age

WILDC.A.T.S/X-MEN: THE DARK AGE Image

1 ❑ Cover: 4.95 **NM** value: **Cover or less**

WILDC.A.T.S/X-MEN: THE GOLDEN AGE Image

1/A ❑ Feb 1997 Cover: 4.50 **NM** value: **5.00**
Circ: Diamd. preorders: **150,475** • **CGC:** 1 graded, best 9.8
cardstock cover. • crossover with Marvel **A:** Travis Charest **C:** Jim Lee **W:** Scott Lobdell
1/B ❑ Feb 1997 Cover: 4.50 **NM** value: **8.00**
scroll cover. • crossover with Marvel **A:** Travis Charest **W:** Scott Lobdell
1/C ❑ Feb 1997 Cover: 4.50 **NM** value: **Cover or less**
cardstock cover. • crossover with Marvel **A:** Travis Charest **W:** Scott Lobdell
1/D ❑ Sep 1997 Cover: 6.50 **NM** value: **Cover or less**
Circ: Diamd. preorders: **25,556**
• crossover with Marvel; with glasses **A:** Travis Charest **W:** Scott Lobdell
1/E ❑ Sep 1997 Cover: 6.50 **NM** value: **Cover or less**
scroll cover. • crossover with Marvel; with glasses **A:** Travis Charest **W:** Scott Lobdell
Bk 1❑ Cover: 19.95 **NM** value: **Cover or less**
📖 The Golden Age; The Silver Age; The Modern Age; The Dark Age **A:** Andrew Robinson; Adam Hughes; Matt Broome; Travis Charest; Jim Lee; Dave Johnson; Lee Bermejo; Aron Wiesenfeld **W:** James Robinson; Warren Ellis; Scott Lobdell

WILDC.A.T.S/X-MEN: THE MODERN AGE Image

1 ❑ Aug 1997 Cover: 4.95 **NM** value: **Cover or less**
Cardstock cover with Wolverine. **A:** Adam Hughes **W:** James Robinson
1/A ❑ Aug 1997 Cover: 4.50 **NM** value: **6.00**
Circ: Diamd. preorders: **94,880**
cardstock cover. • crossover with Marvel **A:** Adam Hughes **C:** Adam Hughes **W:** James Robinson
1/B ❑ Aug 1997 Cover: 4.50 **NM** value: **Cover or less**
cardstock cover. • crossover with Marvel **A:** Adam Hughes **W:** James Robinson
1/C ❑ Nov 1997 Cover: 6.50 **NM** value: **Cover or less**
Circ: Diamd. preorders: **13,593**
• crossover with Marvel **A:** Adam Hughes **W:** James Robinson
1/D ❑ Nov 1997 Cover: 6.50 **NM** value: **Cover or less**
Nightcrawler cover. • crossover with Marvel **A:** Adam Hughes **W:** James Robinson

WILDC.A.T.S/X-MEN: THE SILVER AGE Image

1 ❑ Jun 1997 Cover: 4.95 **NM** value: **Cover or less**
• **CGC:** 1 graded, best 9.2
Jim Lee cover (Grifter standing center). **A:** Jim Lee **W:** Scott Lobdell
1/A ❑ Jun 1997 Cover: 4.50 **NM** value: **4.95**
Circ: Diamd. preorders: **107,506**
Neal Adams cover (Brood attacking). • crossover with Marvel **A:** Neal Adams; Jim Lee **W:** Scott Lobdell
1/B ❑ Jun 1997 Cover: 4.50 **NM** value: **Cover or less**
cardstock cover. • crossover with Marvel
1/C ❑ Jun 1997 Cover: 6.95 **NM** value: **Cover or less**
• 3-D edition. **A:** Jim Lee **W:** Scott Lobdell
1/D ❑ Oct 1997 Cover: 6.50 **NM** value: **Cover or less**
Circ: Diamd. preorders: **18,547**
• crossover with Marvel; has indicia for WildC.A.T.S/X-Men: The Modern Age 3-D

WILDCORE Image

1 ❑ Nov 1997 Cover: 2.50 **NM** value: **Cover or less**
Circ: Diamd. preorders: **60,043**
Three figures fighting on cover. **C:** Tom McWeeney
1/A ❑ Nov 1997 Cover: 2.50 **NM** value: **Cover or less**
White background on cover. • white background **A:** Brett Booth; Travis Charest(cover) **W:** Brett Booth; Sean Ruffner
1/B ❑ Nov 1997 Cover: 2.50 **NM** value: **5.00**
alternate cover. • white background
2 ❑ Dec 1997 Cover: 2.50 **NM** value: **Cover or less**
Circ: Diamd. preorders: **37,920**

Other grades: Multiply prices above by **1.5 for Mint • 2/3 for Very Fine • 1/3 for Fine • 1/5 for Very Good • 1/8 for Good**

Vigor standing on cover. **A:** Brett Booth; Tom McWeeney(cover) **W:** Brett Booth; Sean Ruffner

2/A ❑ Dec 1997 Cover: 2.50 **NM** value: **3.00**
variant cover. **A:** Brett Booth **W:** Brett Booth; Sean Ruffner

3 ❑ Jan 1998 Cover: 2.50 **NM** value: **Cover or less**
Circ: Diamd. preorders: **38,987**

4 ❑ Mar 1998 Cover: 2.50 **NM** value: **Cover or less**
Circ: Diamd. preorders: **33,338**

5 ❑ Jun 1998 Cover: 2.50 **NM** value: **Cover or less**
Circ: Diamd. preorders: **34,556**

6 ❑ Jul 1998 Cover: 2.50 **NM** value: **Cover or less**
Circ: Diamd. preorders: **32,213**
🕮 Paradise Rouge **A:** Brett Booth **W:** Brett Booth; Sean Ruffner

7 ❑ Aug 1998 Cover: 2.50 **NM** value: **Cover or less**
Circ: Diamd. preorders: **29,687**

8 ❑ Oct 1998 Cover: 2.50 **NM** value: **Cover or less**
Circ: Diamd. preorders: **27,524**

9 ❑ Nov 1998 Cover: 2.50 **NM** value: **Cover or less**
Circ: Diamd. preorders: **25,742**

10 ❑ Dec 1998 Cover: 2.50 **NM** value: **Cover or less**
Circ: Diamd. preorders: **23,583**

Ash 1❑ Oct 1997 **NM** value: **3.00**
• Preview edition. **A:** Brett Booth **W:** Sean Ruffner

WILD DOG — DC

This four-issue mini-series is unusual in that the action takes place, not in the big city, but in small-town America. There, a TV news reporter was smiling through a dreary assignment covering the opening of a downtown development, when she suddenly went prime time. On live TV, a man from an organization known as The Committee for Social Change blew up the development. He then took the reporter hostage, holding her for an exclusive interview in a neighboring theater.

Police were reluctant to enter the theater, fearing an on-camera execution of the reporter. However, a mysterious man called Wild Dog has no such qualms. Driving a pick-up whose license plate reads, "Rover," he smashes through police lines and enters the theater. There he takes on the entire terrorist group and saves the reporter. The only question is: Who is Wild Dog?

1 ❑ Sep 1987 Cover: 0.75 **NM** value: **1.50**
Circ: CapCity orders: **27,100**

2 ❑ Oct 1987 Cover: 0.75 **NM** value: **1.50**
Circ: CapCity orders: **19,900**

3 ❑ Nov 1987 Cover: 0.75 **NM** value: **1.50**
Circ: CapCity orders: **18,450**

4 ❑ Dec 1987 Cover: 0.75 **NM** value: **1.50**
Circ: CapCity orders: **16,600**

SE 1❑ Nov 1989 Cover: 2.50 **NM** value: **Cover or less**
Circ: CapCity orders: **9,400**
🕮 Dog Catcher **A:** Terry Beatty **W:** Max Allan Collins

WILDERNESS, THE — 4Winds

Bk 1❑ Cover: 12.95 **NM** value: **Cover or less**
Bk 2❑ Cover: 12.95 **NM** value: **Cover or less**
Dlx 1❑ Cover: 24.95 **NM** value: **Cover or less**
• The Wilderness Parfleche

WILDFLOWER — Sirius

1 ❑ Feb 1998 Cover: 2.50 **NM** value: **Cover or less**
Circ: Diamd. preorders: **3,298**
2 ❑ Apr 1998 Cover: 2.50 **NM** value: **Cover or less**
3 ❑ Jun 1998 Cover: 2.50 **NM** value: **Cover or less**
4 ❑ Aug 1998 Cover: 2.50 **NM** value: **Cover or less**
5 ❑ Oct 1998 Cover: 2.50 **NM** value: **Cover or less**

WILD FRONTIER — Shanda

1 ❑ Jan 2000 Cover: 2.95 **NM** value: **Cover or less**
2 ❑ Cover: 2.95 **NM** value: **Cover or less**

WILD KINGDOM — Mu

All issues are adults only.

1 ❑ Oct 1991, b&w Cover: 2.50 **NM** value: **Cover or less**
2 ❑ May 1993, b&w Cover: 2.95 **NM** value: **Cover or less**
3 ❑ Jan 1995, b&w Cover: 2.95 **NM** value: **Cover or less**
4 ❑ Apr 1995, b&w Cover: 2.95 **NM** value: **Cover or less**
5 ❑ Aug 1995, b&w Cover: 2.95 **NM** value: **Cover or less**
6 ❑ Dec 1995, b&w Cover: 2.95 **NM** value: **Cover or less**

WILD KNIGHTS — Eternity

1 ❑ Mar 1988 Cover: 1.95 **NM** value: **Cover or less**
Circ: CapCity orders: **2,950**
2 ❑ Apr 1988 Cover: 1.95 **NM** value: **Cover or less**
3 ❑ 1988 Cover: 1.95 **NM** value: **Cover or less**
4 ❑ 1988 Cover: 1.95 **NM** value: **Cover or less**
5 ❑ 1988 Cover: 1.95 **NM** value: **Cover or less**
6 ❑ 1988 Cover: 1.95 **NM** value: **Cover or less**
7 ❑ 1988 Cover: 1.95 **NM** value: **Cover or less**
8 ❑ 1988 Cover: 1.95 **NM** value: **Cover or less**
9 ❑ Dec 1988 Cover: 1.95 **NM** value: **Cover or less**
10 ❑ Feb 1989 Cover: 1.95 **NM** value: **Cover or less**

WILD LIFE (ANTARCTIC) — Antarctic

1 ❑ Feb 1993, b&w Cover: 2.50 **NM** value: **Cover or less**
2 ❑ May 1993, b&w Cover: 2.50 **NM** value: **Cover or less**
3 ❑ Jul 1993, b&w Cover: 2.50 **NM** value: **Cover or less**
4 ❑ Nov 1993, b&w Cover: 2.75 **NM** value: **Cover or less**
5 ❑ Feb 1994, b&w Cover: 2.75 **NM** value: **Cover or less**
6 ❑ Apr 1994, b&w Cover: 2.75 **NM** value: **Cover or less**
7 ❑ Jun 1994, b&w Cover: 2.75 **NM** value: **Cover or less**
8 ❑ Aug 1994, b&w Cover: 2.75 **NM** value: **Cover or less**
9 ❑ Oct 1994, b&w Cover: 2.75 **NM** value: **Cover or less**
10 ❑ Dec 1994, b&w Cover: 2.75 **NM** value: **Cover or less**
11 ❑ Feb 1995, b&w Cover: 2.75 **NM** value: **Cover or less**
🕮 M.E.I.; Uni-Universe; Young Teen Cats; One-sided Conversation; The Sophistikats; Null-n-Void; Jaux the Lion; Bye-Bye Gramps; 3 Lil Kittens go to Summer Camp **A:** Pat Kelley; Brigitte Sleiertin; Chris Whalen; Conrad Wong; D.A.C. Crowell; Don Newsome; Paul Castiglia; Phil Morrissey; Shon Howell; Stephan Peregrine **W:** Pat Kelley; Brigitte Sleiertin; Chris Whalen; Conrad Wong; D.A.C. Crowell; Don Newsome; Paul Castiglia; Phil Morrissey; Shon Howell; Stephan Peregrine

12 ❑ Apr 1995, b&w Cover: 2.75 **NM** value: **Cover or less**
🕮 Your Cake Goes Straight to My Hips; Misanthrope; The Sophistikats; Uni-Universe; Bresi's Better World, How I Survived the Big One; By The Clock final issue. **A:** Mark Bodé; Bill Fitts; Carl Gafford; Brigitte Sleiertin; Chris Whalen; Paul Castiglia; Stephan Peregrine; Taff; Van Buren; L'Amazing Prods **W:** Mark Bodé; Bill Fitts; Carl Gafford; Brigitte Sleiertin; Chris Whalen; Paul Castiglia; Stephan Peregrine; Taff; Van Buren; L'Amazing Prods

WILD LIFE (FANTAGRAPHICS) — Fantagraphics

1 ❑ Aug 1994, b&w Cover: 2.75 **NM** value: **Cover or less**
2 ❑ Aug 1994, b&w Cover: 2.75 **NM** value: **Cover or less**

WILDLIFERS — Radio

1 ❑ Cover: 4.95 **NM** value: **Cover or less**

WILDMAN — Miller

1 ❑ Cover: 1.85 **NM** value: **2.00**
2 ❑ Cover: 1.85 **NM** value: **2.00**
3 ❑ b&w Cover: 1.85 **NM** value: **2.00**
4 ❑ b&w Cover: 1.85 **NM** value: **2.00**
5 ❑ b&w Cover: 1.85 **NM** value: **2.00**
6 ❑ b&w Cover: 1.85 **NM** value: **2.00**
7 ❑ b&w Cover: 1.85 **NM** value: **2.00**
8 ❑ b&w Cover: 1.85 **NM** value: **2.00**
9 ❑ Cover: 2.00 **NM** value: **Cover or less**
10 ❑ Cover: 2.00 **NM** value: **Cover or less**
11 ❑ Cover: 2.00 **NM** value: **Cover or less**

WILDMAN (GRASS GREEN'S...) — Megaton

1 ❑ Cover: 1.50 **NM** value: **Cover or less**
2 ❑ Cover: 1.50 **NM** value: **Cover or less**

WILD PARTY, THE — Kitchen Sink

1 ❑ Cover: 22.00 **NM** value: **Cover or less**

WILD PERSON IN THE WOODS — G.T. Labs

1 ❑ 1999 Cover: 2.50 **NM** value: **Cover or less**

WILD SIDE — United Publications

1 ❑ Jan 1998, b&w Cover: 3.95 **NM** value: **Cover or less**
🕮 The King of Han's Bride; Zen Zebras...Stars & Stripes; Lark & Key...Partners, Part 1; Third Eye, Part 1 **W:** Paul Kidd; Mark Barnard; Talis Kimberly

WILDSTAR — Image

1 ❑ Sep 1995 Cover: 2.50 **NM** value: **Cover or less**
🕮 Born to be Wild **A:** Chris Marrinan **W:** Al Gordon
1/A ❑ Sep 1995 Cover: 2.50 **NM** value: **Cover or less**
2 ❑ Nov 1995 Cover: 2.50 **NM** value: **Cover or less**
3 ❑ Jan 1996 Cover: 2.50 **NM** value: **Cover or less**
Circ: CapCity orders: **58,350**
4 ❑ Mar 1996 Cover: 2.50 **NM** value: **Cover or less**
Circ: CapCity orders: **57,025**

WILD STARS — Collector's

1 ❑ Sum 1984, b&w Cover: 1.00 **NM** value: **Cover or less**
• **CGC:** 2 graded, best 9.9

WILDSTAR: SKY ZERO — Image

The 25-year-old WildStar has been running through a time loop all his life, always hunted down by the same group of super-powered beings. But this time, WildStar makes a break from the loop, traveling through time to the current day. Unfortunately, so do his pursuers!

The most unusual thing about this series is the origin of the participants' super-powers. A bit like Venom and Carnage from The Amazing Spider-Man, people in WildStar's world receive their powers from living creatures that symbiotically bind with them. Yes, those glowing eye patches and starfish-like chest badges are actually other creatures (as is gruesomely demonstrated when they're ripped off).

1 ❑ Mar 1993 Cover: 2.50 **NM** value: **3.00**
Circ: CapCity orders: **157,050** • **CGC:** 1 graded, best 9.8
Embossed cover. • silver foil **A:** Jerry Ordway **W:** Al Gordon

1/GO❑ Mar 1993 Cover: 2.50 **NM** value: **4.00**
Embossed cover. • gold **A:** Jerry Ordway **W:** Al Gordon

2 ❑ May 1993 Cover: 1.95 **NM** value: **2.00**
Circ: CapCity orders: **107,575**

3 ❑ Sep 1993 Cover: 1.95 **NM** value: **2.50**
Circ: CapCity orders: **142,275**

4 ❑ Nov 1993 Cover: 1.95 **NM** value: **2.50**
Circ: CapCity orders: **122,250**

Bk 1❑ Jul 1994 Cover: 12.95 **NM** value: **Cover or less**
• Collects WildStar: Sky Zero #1-4 **A:** Jerry Ordway

WILDSTORM! — Image

1 ❑ Aug 1995 Cover: 2.50 **NM** value: **Cover or less**
Circ: CapCity orders: **21,675**
• color and b&w; Gen13, Grifter, Deathblow, Union, Spartan **A:** Mike Zeck; Walt Simonson; Mark Pacella; Aron Wiesenfeld; Allen Im **W:** Walt Simonson; Aron Wiesenfeld; Louise Simonson; Simon Furman

2 ❑ Oct 1995 Cover: 2.50 **NM** value: **Cover or less**
Circ: CapCity orders: **17,125**
cover says Sep, indicia says Oct. • color and b&w

3 ❑ Nov 1995 Cover: 2.50 **NM** value: **Cover or less**
Circ: CapCity orders: **11,025**

4 ❑ Dec 1995 Cover: 2.50 **NM** value: **Cover or less**
🕮 Salvage Operation; Head Problems; Fire Flight • StormWatch Showcase **A:** Randy Green; Ryan Odagawa; Tom Raney **W:** Michael Jan Friedman; Merv; Sarah Becker

WILDSTORM ANNUAL — DC / Wildstorm

2000❑ Dec 2000 Cover: 3.50 **NM** value: **Cover or less**
🕮 Soul Sacrifices **A:** Jeff Moy **W:** Ben Raab

WILDSTORM ARCHIVES: GENESIS THE #1 COLLECTION — Image

Bk 1❑ Jun 1998, b&w Cover: 9.99 **NM** value: **Cover or less**
• collects Wildstorm first issues

WILDSTORM CHAMBER OF HORRORS — Image

1 ❑ Oct 1995 Cover: 3.50 **NM** value: **Cover or less**
Circ: CapCity orders: **9,375**
🕮 Warblade; Lord Emp; Tapestry; Savant **A:** Bernie Wrightson; Jason Johnson; Trevor Scott; Tom Raney; Aaron Wiesen feld **W:** Steven Grant; Jeff Mariotte; Merv; Ron Marz

WILDSTORM FINE ARTS: THE GALLERY COLLECTION — Image

1 ❑ Dec 1998 Cover: 19.95 **NM** value: **Cover or less**
• collects pin-up books and other art

WILDSTORM HALLOWEEN '97 — Image

1 ❑ Oct 1997 Cover: 2.50 **NM** value: **Cover or less**
Circ: Diamd. preorders: **21,794**
🕮 Team 7, In Blood and Faith; Gen 13, ...When all the Freaks Come Out; Wetworks: Berserker **A:** Chris Warner; Ryan Odagawa; Ed Benés **W:** Peter Gutierrez; Christopher Golden; Tom Sniegoski

WILDSTORM RARITIES — Image

1 ❑ Dec 1994 Cover: 4.95 **NM** value: **Cover or less**
Circ: CapCity orders: **18,700**

WILDSTORM RISING — Image

A product of Jim Lee's WildStorm Studios, WildStorm Rising is part of a larger storyline that ran through many of the label's books, including WildC.A.T.s, Wetworks, and Gen13. Fans of WildStorm mainstays Hightower, Void, Maul, and the StormWatch team should have no trouble picking up the plot already in progress, as the WildStorm Rising two-issue mini-series kicks off.

WildStorm Rising teams the talents of Barry Windsor-Smith, James Robinson, and inkers Alex Bialy and John Floyd in a colorful, action-packed comic book. Fans of Windsor-Smith's work on Conan the Barbarian and Storyteller, among others, may be surprised to see his usually spacious and detail-rich style applied to a more conventional super-hero action setting, chock-full of costumed titans and rich with super-saturated computer coloring.

1 ❑ May 1995 Cover: 2.50 **NM** value: **Cover or less**
Circ: CapCity orders: **41,575**
🕮 Wildstorm Rising, Part 1 • with cards **A:** Barry Windsor-Smith; Windsor-Smith Studio **W:** James Robinson; Barry Windsor-Smith

2 ❑ Jun 1995 Cover: 2.50 **NM** value: **Cover or less**
Circ: CapCity orders: **38,850**
🕮 Wildstorm Rising, Part 11 • bound-in trading cards

Bk 1❑ Jun 1996 Cover: 19.95 **NM** value: **Cover or less**
• Trade Paperback. 🕮 Wildstorm Rising • collects 10-part crossover; Reprints Wildstorm Rising

WILDSTORM SAMPLER — Image

1 ❑ **NM** value: **1.00**
No issue number. no cover price. • giveaway.

WILDSTORMS PLAYER'S GUIDE — Image

1 ❑ Mar 1996 Cover: 1.95 **NM** value: **Cover or less**
• tips on WildStorms card game

WILDSTORM SPOTLIGHT — Image

1 ❑ Feb 1997 Cover: 2.50 **NM** value: **Cover or less**
Circ: Diamd. preorders: **25,218**
• Majestic

2 ❑ Mar 1997 Cover: 2.50 **NM** value: **Cover or less**
Circ: Diamd. preorders: **18,008**
• Loner

3 ❑ Apr 1997 Cover: 2.50 **NM** value: **Cover or less**
Circ: Diamd. preorders: **15,576**
• Loner

4 ❑ May 1997 Cover: 2.50 **NM** value: **Cover or less**
Circ: Diamd. preorders: **14,396**
• StormWatch; no indicia

CGC-graded: Multiply prices above by **33 for 9.9 M • 16 for 9.8 NM/M • 7 for 9.6 NM+ • 5 for 9.4 NM • 2.5 for 9.2 NM- • 1.5 for 9.0 VF/NM**

WILDSTORM SWIMSUIT SPECIAL — Image

1 ❑ Dec 1994 Cover: 2.95 **NM** value: **Cover or less**
Circ: CapCity orders: **24,775** • **CGC:** 2 graded, best 9.6
2 ❑ Aug 1995 Cover: 2.50 **NM** value: **Cover or less**
Circ: CapCity orders: **30,475** • **CGC:** 1 graded, best 9.8
• pin-ups
1997❑May 1997 Cover: 2.50 **NM** value: **Cover or less**
Circ: Diamd. preorders: **31,471**
• pin-ups; WildStorm Swimsuits '97 **A:** Oscar Jimenez; Michael Lopez; Sal

WILDSTORM THUNDERBOOK — DC / Wildstorm

1 ❑ Oct 2000 Cover: 6.95 **NM** value: **Cover or less**
Circ: Diamd. preorders: **11,730**
📖 Wham!; Professionals; Family Matters; Cybernary 2.0; Down and Out with the Deviants **A:** Adam Hughes; Dustin Nguyen; Steve Ellis; David Boller; Jeff Moy **W:** Adam Hughes; Andy Lanning; Tommy Yune; Dan Abnett; Joe Harris; John Layman

WILDSTORM ULTIMATE SPORTS OFFICIAL PROGRAM — Image

1 ❑ Aug 1997 Cover: 2.50 **NM** value: **Cover or less**
Circ: Diamd. preorders: **9,108**
• pin-ups

WILDSTORM UNIVERSE 97 — Image

1 ❑ Dec 1996 Cover: 2.50 **NM** value: **Cover or less**
Circ: Diamd. preorders: **21,154**
• information on various Wildstorm characters **A:** Arthur Adams(cover)
2 ❑ Jan 1997 Cover: 2.50 **NM** value: **Cover or less**
Circ: Diamd. preorders: **22,129**
• information on various Wildstorm characters **A:** Arthur Adams(cover)
3 ❑ Feb 1997 Cover: 2.50 **NM** value: **Cover or less**
Circ: Diamd. preorders: **20,072**
• information on various Wildstorm characters

WILDSTORM UNIVERSE SOURCEBOOK — Image

1 ❑ May 1995 Cover: 2.50 **NM** value: **Cover or less**
Circ: CapCity orders: **18,425**
2 ❑ Cover: 2.50 **NM** value: **Cover or less**

WILD THING — Marvel

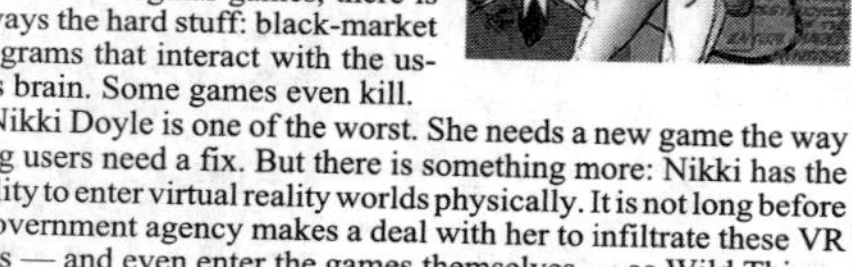

Strap on a headset, put on a special sensor glove, and users of virtual-reality systems are ready to enter another, computer-generated world. Today, these systems are simple, perhaps allowing the user to walk or fly through a computer-generated room. In the future — or at least, Wild Thing's future — virtual reality (VR) simulations have become a popular alternative for life. The VR games have become so intense that many people have become literal addicts. When they tired of the regular games, there is always the hard stuff: black-market programs that interact with the user's brain. Some games even kill.

Nikki Doyle is one of the worst. She needs a new game the way drug users need a fix. But there is something more: Nikki has the ability to enter virtual reality worlds physically. It is not long before a government agency makes a deal with her to infiltrate these VR dens — and even enter the games themselves — as Wild Thing.

1 ❑ Apr 1993 Cover: 2.50 **NM** value: **Cover or less**
Circ: CapCity orders: **87,200**
Embossed cover. ★ 1st Appearance of Wild Thing.
2 ❑ May 1993 Cover: 1.75 **NM** value: **Cover or less**
Circ: CapCity orders: **43,300**
3 ❑ Jun 1993 Cover: 1.75 **NM** value: **Cover or less**
Circ: CapCity orders: **23,100**
4 ❑ Jul 1993 Cover: 1.75 **NM** value: **Cover or less**
Circ: CapCity orders: **21,200**
5 ❑ Aug 1993 Cover: 1.75 **NM** value: **Cover or less**
Circ: CapCity orders: **16,200**
6 ❑ Sep 1993 Cover: 1.75 **NM** value: **Cover or less**
Circ: CapCity orders: **12,000**
7 ❑ Oct 1993 Cover: 1.75 **NM** value: **Cover or less**
Circ: CapCity orders: **9,300**

WILD THING (2ND SERIES) — Marvel

1 ❑ Oct 1999 Cover: 1.99 **NM** value: **Cover or less**
Circ: Diamd. preorders: **47,464**
📖 Crash Course **A:** Ron Lim **W:** Larry Hama
2 ❑ Nov 1999 Cover: 1.99 **NM** value: **Cover or less**
Circ: Diamd. preorders: **38,560**
3 ❑ Dec 1999 Cover: 1.99 **NM** value: **Cover or less**
Circ: Diamd. preorders: **32,250**
📖 Awakening **A:** Ron Lim **W:** Larry Hama
4 ❑ Jan 1999 Cover: 1.99 **NM** value: **Cover or less**
Circ: Diamd. preorders: **28,999**

WILD THINGS — Metro

1 ❑ Cover: 2.00 **NM** value: **Cover or less**
2 ❑ Cover: 2.00 **NM** value: **Cover or less**
3 ❑ Cover: 2.00 **NM** value: **Cover or less**

WILD THINGZ — ABC Studios

0/A ❑ Cover: 3.00 **NM** value: **Cover or less**
Circ: Diamd. preorders: **2,614**
0/B ❑ Cover: 5.95 **NM** value: **Cover or less**
swimsuit cover.

0/PL❑ Cover: 3.00 **NM** value: **Cover or less**
• Virgin Special Preview; limited to 300 copies

WILD THINK — Wild Think

1 ❑ Apr 1987 Cover: 2.00 **NM** value: **Cover or less**

WILD TIMES: DEATHBLOW — DC / Wildstorm

1 ❑ Aug 1999 Cover: 2.50 **NM** value: **Cover or less**
📖 Death Rides a Horse! • set in 1899 **A:** Tommy Lee Edwards **W:** Norman Patridge ★ Appearance of Bat Lash.

WILD TIMES: DV8 — DC / Wildstorm

1 ❑ Aug 1999 Cover: 2.50 **NM** value: **Cover or less**
Circ: Diamd. preorders: **18,626**
📖 D-Day • set in 1944 **A:** Kevin Altieri **W:** Kevin Altieri ★ Appearance of Sgt. Rock and Easy Co..

WILD TIMES: GEN13 — DC / Wildstorm

1 ❑ Aug 1999 Cover: 2.50 **NM** value: **Cover or less**
Circ: Diamd. preorders: **24,135**
📖 All New All Fab • set in 1969, 1972, and 1973 **A:** Jason Johnson **W:** Joe Casey ★ Appearance of Teen Titans.

WILD TIMES: GRIFTER — DC / Wildstorm

1 ❑ Aug 1999 Cover: 2.50 **NM** value: **Cover or less**
Circ: Diamd. preorders: **19,744**
📖 just another chicago grifter • set in 1920s **A:** Paul Smith **W:** Max Allan Collins

WILD TIMES: WETWORKS — DC / Wildstorm

1 ❑ Aug 1999 Cover: 2.50 **NM** value: **Cover or less**
Circ: Diamd. preorders: **19,128**
📖 Still Waters Run Deep **A:** Aaron Lopresti **W:** Mark Waid ★ Appearance of Superman.

WILD WEST C.O.W.-BOYS OF MOO MESA, THE — Archie

1 ❑ Mar 1993 Cover: 1.25 **NM** value: **Cover or less**
2 ❑ May 1993 Cover: 1.25 **NM** value: **Cover or less**
3 ❑ Jul 1993 Cover: 1.25 **NM** value: **Cover or less**

WILD, WILD WEST, THE (GOLD KEY) — Gold Key

Combining James Bond-like spy thrills with Old West adventure and a smattering of pulp science-fiction, the CBS TV show (which ran from 1965 to 1970) starred Robert Conrad as government agent James West and Ross Martin as his master-of-disguise sidekick Artemus Gordon.

The duo reported directly to President Ulysses S. Grant and had their own private, gadget-filled train in which they were quickly whisked across the country to their next mission.

Like many of its other series, Gold Key's comics based on the show had beautiful photo covers and stories that attempted to capture the flavor of the show but had a difficult time doing so, especially the cliffhanger endings of each chapter. — Brent

1 ❑ Jun 1966 Cover: 0.12 **NM** value: **55.00**
• **CGC:** 2 graded, best 9.2
Photo cover. 📖 Outlaw Empire • 10174-606
2 ❑ Aug 1966 Cover: 0.12 **NM** value: **35.00**
• **CGC:** 2 graded, best 9.0
Photo cover.
3 ❑ Jun 1968 Cover: 0.12 **NM** value: **30.00**
• **CGC:** 1 graded, best 7.0
Photo cover.
4 ❑ Dec 1968 Cover: 0.12 **NM** value: **30.00**
• **CGC:** 2 graded, best 9.4
Photo cover.
5 ❑ Apr 1969 Cover: 0.12 **NM** value: **30.00**
Photo cover.
6 ❑ Jul 1969 Cover: 0.15 **NM** value: **30.00**
Photo cover.
7 ❑ Oct 1969 Cover: 0.15 **NM** value: **30.00**
• **CGC:** 3 graded, best 9.6
Photo cover.

WILD, WILD WEST, THE (MILLENNIUM) — Millennium

1 ❑ ca. 1990 Cover: 2.95 **NM** value: **Cover or less**
Circ: CapCity orders: **4,600**
📖 The Night of the Iron Tyrants, Part 1 • TV **A:** John Hebert; Mark Menendez(cover); Robert Lewis; Chris Leidenfrost
2 ❑ ca. 1990 Cover: 2.95 **NM** value: **Cover or less**
Circ: CapCity orders: **3,350**
📖 The Night of the Iron Tyrants, Part 2 • TV **A:** John Hebert; Mark Menendez(cover); Robert Lewis; Chris Leidenfrost
3 ❑ ca. 1991 Cover: 2.95 **NM** value: **Cover or less**
Circ: CapCity orders: **3,425**
📖 The Night of the Iron Tyrants, Part 3 • TV **A:** John Hebert; Mark Menendez(cover); Robert Lewis; Chris Leidenfrost **W:** Mark Ellis; Paul Davis
4 ❑ ca. 1991 Cover: 2.95 **NM** value: **Cover or less**
Circ: CapCity orders: **3,400**
📖 The Night of the Iron Tyrants, Part 4 • TV **A:** John Hebert; Mark Menendez(cover); Robert Lewis; Chris Leidenfrost

Do you have changes or corrections for the **Standard Catalog**? Send your original research to us at **allcomics@krause.com**

WILL EISNER PRESENTS — Eclipse

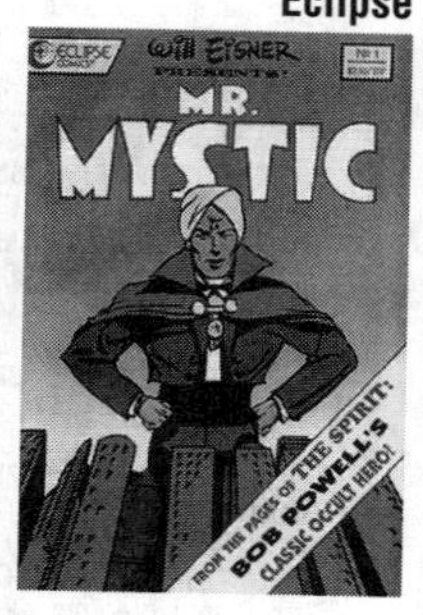

This one-shot brought to a new audience the first five stories of Mr. Mystic, reprinted in black and white from their original publication as back-up features in Will Eisner's "Spirit" newspaper sections. Drawn by Bob Powell (whose work Eclipse also reprinted in Bob Powell's Timeless Tales), who eventually took over scripting the feature, it featured fantasy action and gorgeous women. In the first installment, "Ken" ends up in the Himalayas, is grabbed by seven lamas, branded with a mystic symbol and named "ruler of magic, disciple of the seven lamas and knight of righteousness." Told that his every wish will come true, he quickly discovers that that's the case.

Moreover, a booming voice from the sky tells him, "You will be known as Mr. Mystic, endowed with unlimited powers to combat the forces of evil plaguing the Earth." The young American diplomat stars in stories bylined W. Morgan Thomas, and Eclipse has added graytones to some of the scanned art. The stories feature wish-fulfillment fantasies drawn by one of the top artists of his day — though these specific installments come before the adventures at the top of Powell's — and Mystic's — form.

— Maggie

1 ❑ Dec 1990, b&w Cover: 2.50 **NM** value: **Cover or less**
• Mr. Mystic **A:** Bob Powell ★ Origin of Mr. Mystic. ★ 1st Appearance of Mr. Mystic.

WILL EISNER READER — DC

1 ❑ Oct 2000 Cover: 9.95 **NM** value: **Cover or less**
📖 A Sunset in Sunshine City; The Telephone; Detective Story; The Long Hit; Winning; The Appeal; Humans **A:** Will Eisner **W:** Will Eisner

WILL EISNER'S 3-D CLASSICS: SPIRIT — Kitchen Sink

1 ❑ Dec 1985 Cover: 2.00 **NM** value: **Cover or less**

WILL EISNER'S QUARTERLY — Kitchen Sink

1 ❑ Nov 1983 Cover: 2.95 **NM** value: **Cover or less**
2 ❑ Feb 1984 Cover: 3.50 **NM** value: **Cover or less**
3 ❑ Aug 1984 Cover: 2.00 **NM** value: **Cover or less**
4 ❑ 1985 Cover: 2.00 **NM** value: **Cover or less**
Circ: Statement: **7,619**
5 ❑ 1985 Cover: 2.00 **NM** value: **Cover or less**
Circ: Statement: **7,619**
6 ❑ 1985 Cover: 2.00 **NM** value: **Cover or less**
Circ: Statement: **7,619**
7 ❑ 1985 Cover: 2.00 **NM** value: **Cover or less**
Circ: Statement: **7,619**
8 ❑ Mar 1986 Cover: 2.00 **NM** value: **Cover or less**

WILLIAM SHATNER — Celebrity

1 ❑ Cover: 5.95 **NM** value: **Cover or less**

WILLOW (ANGEL) — Angel

0 ❑ Jun 1996, b&w Cover: 2.95 **NM** value: **Cover or less**
0/Nude❑Jun 1996 Cover: 10.00 **NM** value: **Cover or less**
nude cardstock cover.

WILLOW (MARVEL) — Marvel

1 ❑ Aug 1988 Cover: 1.00 **NM** value: **1.50**
Circ: CapCity orders: **8,100**
2 ❑ Sep 1988 Cover: 1.00 **NM** value: **1.50**
Circ: CapCity orders: **7,300**
3 ❑ Oct 1988 Cover: 1.00 **NM** value: **1.50**
Circ: CapCity orders: **7,000**
Bk 1❑ ca. 1988 Cover: 6.95 **NM** value: **Cover or less**
Circ: CapCity orders: **3,400**

WILLOW: THE ILLUSTRATED VERSION — Marvel

Bk 1❑ ca. 1988 Cover: 4.95 **NM** value: **Cover or less**
• Del Rey mass-market paperback

WILL ROGERS — Fox

5 ❑ Jun 1950 Cover: 0.10 **NM** value: **150.00**
• **CGC:** 1 graded, best 5.0

WILL TO POWER — Dark Horse

1 ❑ Jun 1994 Cover: 1.00 **NM** value: **1.50**
Circ: CapCity orders: **12,800**
2 ❑ Jun 1994 Cover: 1.00 **NM** value: **Cover or less**
Circ: CapCity orders: **12,125**
3 ❑ Jun 1994 Cover: 1.00 **NM** value: **Cover or less**
Circ: CapCity orders: **12,025**
4 ❑ Jul 1994 Cover: 1.00 **NM** value: **Cover or less**
Circ: CapCity orders: **11,800**
5 ❑ Jul 1994 Cover: 1.00 **NM** value: **Cover or less**
Circ: CapCity orders: **9,470**
6 ❑ Jul 1994 Cover: 1.00 **NM** value: **Cover or less**
Circ: CapCity orders: **9,400**
7 ❑ Jul 1994 Cover: 1.00 **NM** value: **Cover or less**
Circ: CapCity orders: **9,375**
8 ❑ Aug 1994 Cover: 1.00 **NM** value: **Cover or less**
Circ: CapCity orders: **9,350**
9 ❑ Aug 1994 Cover: 1.00 **NM** value: **Cover or less**
Circ: CapCity orders: **8,100**
10 ❑ Aug 1994 Cover: 1.00 **NM** value: **Cover or less**
Circ: CapCity orders: **8,100**
11 ❑ Aug 1994 Cover: 1.00 **NM** value: **Cover or less**
Circ: CapCity orders: **8,100**
12 ❑ Aug 1994 Cover: 1.00 **NM** value: **Cover or less**

Other grades: Multiply prices above by **1.5 for Mint • 2/3 for Very Fine • 1/3 for Fine • 1/5 for Very Good • 1/8 for Good**

Circ: CapCity orders: **8,100**
final issue.

WIMMEN'S COMIX — Renegade

All issues are adults only.

1 ❑ Cover: 0.50 **NM** value: **10.00**
📖 Goldie: A Neurotic Woman; A Teenage Abortion; All in a Day's Work; Can This Marriage be Saved?; Sandy Comes Out; There I Was…; Tales of Sativa; Frog; The Cyborgs **A:** Trina Robbins; Aline Kominsky-Crumb; Janet Wolfe Stanley; Karen Marie Haskell; Lee Marrs; Lora Fountain; Michelle Brand; Sharon Rudahl; Shelby **W:** Trina Robbins; Aline Kominsky-Crumb; Janet Wolfe Stanley; Karen Marie Haskell; Lee Marrs; Lora Fountain; Michelle Brand; Sharon Rudahl; Shelby
2 ❑ **NM** value: **8.00**
3 ❑ **NM** value: **8.00**
4 ❑ Cover: 0.75 **NM** value: **8.00**
📖 Didi Glitz: She Chose Crime; Dolly Divine: Hot to Trot; The Blood-Clot Frog: In a Paranoid Vein; **A:** Trina Robbins; Roberta Gregory; Diane Noomin; Aline Kominsky-Crumb; Dot Bucher; Lee Marrs; Barb Brown; Rainy Day Blues Studios; Sharon Banks; Terry Richards **W:** Trina Robbins; Roberta Gregory; Diane Noomin; Aline Kominsky-Crumb; Dot Bucher; Lee Marrs; Barb Brown; Rainy Day Blues Studios; Sharon Banks; Terry Richards
5 ❑ **NM** value: **5.00**
6 ❑ **NM** value: **5.00**
7 ❑ **NM** value: **5.00**
8 ❑ **NM** value: **5.00**
9 ❑ **NM** value: **4.00**
10 ❑ **NM** value: **4.00**
11 ❑ 1987b&w Cover: 2.00 **NM** value: **3.00**
12 ❑ Apr 1987 Cover: 2.50 **NM** value: **3.00**
• 3-D.
13 ❑ Cover: 2.00 **NM** value: **3.00**
14 ❑ Feb 1989, b&w Cover: 2.50 **NM** value: **Cover or less**
📖 Magda Meets the Little Men in the Woods; 1st Crushed • Disastrous Relationships **A:** Mary Fleener; Trina Robbins; Roberta Gregory; Diane Noomin; Angela Bocage; Carol Tyler; Joey Epstein; Kate Worley; Phoebe Gloeckner; Sharon Rudahl; Caryn Leschen; Jackie Urbanovich; Jennifer Camper; Kathryn LeMieux; Lee Binswanger; Leslie Ewing **W:** Tr
15 ❑ Aug 1989, b&w Cover: 2.50 **NM** value: **Cover or less**
📖 Latency Come Lately; Baby Butch Dyke; The Day Kenedy was Shot!; Rooge & Pu; Coming **A:** Angela Bocage; Carol Tyler; Leslie Ew; Phoebe Gloeckner **W:** Angela Bocage; Carol Tyler; Leslie Ew; Phoebe Gloeckner
16 ❑ Nov 1990, b&w Cover: 2.50 **NM** value: **Cover or less**
📖 Men; Sweet Delusions, or The Date from Hell **A:** Donna Barr **W:** Donna Barr
17 ❑ Aug 1992, b&w Cover: 2.50 **NM** value: **Cover or less**
18 ❑ **NM** value: **2.50**

WINDBURNT PLAINS OF WONDER, THE — Lohman Hills

1 ❑ Fal 1996 Cover: 11.95 **NM** value: **Cover or less**
No issue number. • b&w Emma Davenport one-shot

WIND IN THE WILLOWS, THE — NBM

1 ❑ Cover: 15.95 **NM** value: **Cover or less**
2 ❑ Feb 1999 Cover: 15.95 **NM** value: **Cover or less**

WINDRAVEN — Heroic / Blue Comet

1 ❑ b&w Cover: 2.95 **NM** value: **Cover or less**

WINDSOR — Win-Mil / Blue Comet

1 ❑ Cover: 1.95 **NM** value: **Cover or less**
2 ❑ Cover: 1.95 **NM** value: **Cover or less**
Flip-cover format.

WINDY AND WILLY — DC

1 ❑ May 1969 Cover: 0.12 **NM** value: **20.00**
• **CGC:** 1 graded, best 8.5
2 ❑ Jul 1969 Cover: 0.15 **NM** value: **20.00**
3 ❑ Sep 1969 Cover: 0.15 **NM** value: **20.00**
4 ❑ Nov 1969 Cover: 0.15 **NM** value: **20.00**

WINGBIRD AKUMA-SHE — Verotik

All issues are adults only.

1 ❑ Jan 1998 Cover: 3.95 **NM** value: **Cover or less**
Circ: Diamd. preorders: **7,674**
cardstock cover.

WINGBIRD RETURNS — Verotik

All issues are adults only.

1 ❑ Oct 1997 Cover: 9.95 **NM** value: **Cover or less**
No issue number. • prestige format.

WINGDING ORGY — Eros

1 ❑ Cover: 3.95 **NM** value: **Cover or less**
Circ: Diamd. preorders: **5,713**
2 ❑ Cover: 3.95 **NM** value: **Cover or less**
Circ: Diamd. preorders: **5,343**
📖 Wingding Mix **A:** Toshiki Yui **W:** Toshiki Yui

WINGED TIGER, THE — Cartoonists Across America

3 ❑ Sum 1999 Cover: 2.95 **NM** value: **Cover or less**
Circ: Diamd. preorders: **5,410**

WINGING IT — Solo

1 ❑ Cover: 2.00 **NM** value: **Cover or less**

WINGS — Mu

1 ❑ Sep 1992 Cover: 2.50 **NM** value: **Cover or less**

WINGS COMICS — Fiction House

Fiction House was a pulp magazine publisher that entered the comic-book field by adapting its magazine genres to four-color formats: war stories, jungle stories, and science fiction. In the course of that adaptation, the company tossed in plentiful samples of cheesecake art. Wings Comics dealt with stories of (occasionally interchangeable) fighting pilots. The ongoing characters included Suicide Smith (aka Blitzkrieg Buster), Jane Martin (war nurse), Clipper Kirk, Greasemonkey Griffin, The Skull Squad, Captain Wings — and so on. And the "Ghost Squadron" stories, introduced as the war came to an end, injected a fantasy element into issues featuring more straightforward air adventures.

Its competition consisted of titles like Blackhawk and Airboy Comics, and it was DC that took the genre over with long-running series, including taking over Blackhawk, in later decades — Maggie

1 ❑ Sep 1940 Cover: 0.10 **NM** value: **1500.00**
• **CGC:** 7 graded, best 9.8
2 ❑ Oct 1940 Cover: 0.10 **NM** value: **800.00**
• **CGC:** 3 graded, best 8.5
3 ❑ Nov 1940 Cover: 0.10 **NM** value: **460.00**
• **CGC:** 1 graded, best 9.0
4 ❑ Dec 1940 Cover: 0.10 **NM** value: **460.00**
• **CGC:** 2 graded, best 9.4
5 ❑ Jan 1941 Cover: 0.10 **NM** value: **460.00**
• **CGC:** 1 graded, best 9.6
6 ❑ Feb 1941 Cover: 0.10 **NM** value: **365.00**
• **CGC:** 1 graded, best 9.6
7 ❑ Mar 1941 Cover: 0.10 **NM** value: **365.00**
• **CGC:** 1 graded, best 9.2
8 ❑ Apr 1941 Cover: 0.10 **NM** value: **365.00**
• **CGC:** 1 graded, best 6.5
9 ❑ May 1941 Cover: 0.10 **NM** value: **365.00**
📖 The Divers of Doom; Fools for Glory; Ace of Vengeance
10 ❑ Jun 1941 Cover: 0.10 **NM** value: **365.00**
• **CGC:** 1 graded, best 9.0
11 ❑ Jul 1941 Cover: 0.10 **NM** value: **320.00**
• **CGC:** 1 graded, best 9.6
12 ❑ Aug 1941 Cover: 0.10 **NM** value: **320.00**
• **CGC:** 1 graded, best 9.6
13 ❑ Sep 1941 Cover: 0.10 **NM** value: **320.00**
📖 Coffin-Slugs for the Luftwaffe; Sky Hellion
14 ❑ Oct 1941 Cover: 0.10 **NM** value: **320.00**
• **CGC:** 1 graded, best 9.0
15 ❑ Nov 1941 Cover: 0.10 **NM** value: **320.00**
• **CGC:** 1 graded, best 9.4
16 ❑ Dec 1941 Cover: 0.10 **NM** value: **275.00**
• **CGC:** 1 graded, best 8.5
17 ❑ Jan 1942 Cover: 0.10 **NM** value: **275.00**
• **CGC:** 1 graded, best 9.8
18 ❑ Feb 1942 Cover: 0.10 **NM** value: **275.00**
• **CGC:** 1 graded, best 8.5
19 ❑ Mar 1942 Cover: 0.10 **NM** value: **275.00**
• **CGC:** 1 graded, best 9.6
20 ❑ Apr 1942 Cover: 0.10 **NM** value: **275.00**
• **CGC:** 1 graded, best 9.6
21 ❑ May 1942 Cover: 0.10 **NM** value: **215.00**
• **CGC:** 1 graded, best 9.6
22 ❑ Jun 1942 Cover: 0.10 **NM** value: **215.00**
• **CGC:** 2 graded, best 9.0
23 ❑ Jul 1942 Cover: 0.10 **NM** value: **215.00**
24 ❑ Aug 1942 Cover: 0.10 **NM** value: **215.00**
• **CGC:** 1 graded, best 9.2
25 ❑ Sep 1942 Cover: 0.10 **NM** value: **215.00**
• **CGC:** 1 graded, best 8.0
26 ❑ Oct 1942 Cover: 0.10 **NM** value: **215.00**
• **CGC:** 1 graded, best 9.2
27 ❑ Nov 1942 Cover: 0.10 **NM** value: **215.00**
• **CGC:** 1 graded, best 9.4
28 ❑ Dec 1942 Cover: 0.10 **NM** value: **215.00**
• **CGC:** 1 graded, best 9.0
29 ❑ Jan 1943 Cover: 0.10 **NM** value: **215.00**
• **CGC:** 1 graded, best 8.5
30 ❑ Feb 1943 Cover: 0.10 **NM** value: **215.00**
• **CGC:** 1 graded, best 8.5
31 ❑ Mar 1943 Cover: 0.10 **NM** value: **175.00**
32 ❑ Apr 1943 Cover: 0.10 **NM** value: **175.00**
33 ❑ May 1943 Cover: 0.10 **NM** value: **175.00**
• **CGC:** 2 graded, best 9.0
34 ❑ Jun 1943 Cover: 0.10 **NM** value: **175.00**
35 ❑ Jul 1943 Cover: 0.10 **NM** value: **175.00**
• **CGC:** 1 graded, best 8.0
36 ❑ Aug 1943 Cover: 0.10 **NM** value: **175.00**
• **CGC:** 1 graded, best 9.6
37 ❑ Sep 1943 Cover: 0.10 **NM** value: **175.00**
• **CGC:** 1 graded, best 9.2
38 ❑ Oct 1943 Cover: 0.10 **NM** value: **175.00**
• **CGC:** 1 graded, best 9.6
39 ❑ Nov 1943 Cover: 0.10 **NM** value: **175.00**
• **CGC:** 1 graded, best 8.5
40 ❑ Dec 1943 Cover: 0.10 **NM** value: **175.00**
📖 Captain Wings an **A:** Ace Atkins; Capt. A. E. Carruthers; Capt. Derek West; Cliff DuBois; F. E. Lincoln; Kip Beales; Major T. E. Bowen **W:** Ace Atkins; Capt. A. E. Carruthers; Capt. Derek West; Cliff DuBois; F. E. Lincoln; Kip Beales; Major T. E. Bowen; Spud Taylor
41 ❑ Jan 1944 Cover: 0.10 **NM** value: **135.00**
42 ❑ Feb 1944 Cover: 0.10 **NM** value: **135.00**
• **CGC:** 1 graded, best 9.2
43 ❑ Mar 1944 Cover: 0.10 **NM** value: **135.00**
44 ❑ Apr 1944 Cover: 0.10 **NM** value: **135.00**
45 ❑ May 1944 Cover: 0.10 **NM** value: **135.00**
46 ❑ Jun 1944 Cover: 0.10 **NM** value: **135.00**
47 ❑ Jul 1944 Cover: 0.10 **NM** value: **135.00**
48 ❑ Aug 1944 Cover: 0.10 **NM** value: **135.00**
49 ❑ Sep 1944 Cover: 0.10 **NM** value: **135.00**
50 ❑ Oct 1944 Cover: 0.10 **NM** value: **135.00**
51 ❑ Nov 1944 Cover: 0.10 **NM** value: **110.00**
52 ❑ Dec 1944 Cover: 0.10 **NM** value: **110.00**
• **CGC:** 1 graded, best 9.6
53 ❑ Jan 1945 Cover: 0.10 **NM** value: **110.00**
📖 Robot Death Over Manhattan
54 ❑ Feb 1945 Cover: 0.10 **NM** value: **110.00**
55 ❑ Mar 1945 Cover: 0.10 **NM** value: **110.00**
• **CGC:** 1 graded, best 9.6
56 ❑ Apr 1945 Cover: 0.10 **NM** value: **110.00**
57 ❑ May 1945 Cover: 0.10 **NM** value: **110.00**
• **CGC:** 2 graded, best 9.4
58 ❑ Jun 1945 Cover: 0.10 **NM** value: **110.00**
59 ❑ Jul 1945 Cover: 0.10 **NM** value: **110.00**
• **CGC:** 1 graded, best 9.6
60 ❑ Aug 1945 Cover: 0.10 **NM** value: **110.00**
• **CGC:** 1 graded, best 9.2
61 ❑ Sep 1945 Cover: 0.10 **NM** value: **100.00**
62 ❑ Oct 1945 Cover: 0.10 **NM** value: **100.00**
📖 The Twilight of the Gods
63 ❑ Nov 1945 Cover: 0.10 **NM** value: **100.00**
64 ❑ Dec 1945 Cover: 0.10 **NM** value: **100.00**
65 ❑ Jan 1946 Cover: 0.10 **NM** value: **100.00**
66 ❑ Feb 1946 Cover: 0.10 **NM** value: **100.00**
• **CGC:** 1 graded, best 9.8
67 ❑ Mar 1946 Cover: 0.10 **NM** value: **100.00**
• **CGC:** 2 graded, best 9.4
68 ❑ Apr 1946 Cover: 0.10 **NM** value: **100.00**
• **CGC:** 1 graded, best 9.0
69 ❑ May 1946 Cover: 0.10 **NM** value: **100.00**
• **CGC:** 1 graded, best 9.0
70 ❑ Jun 1946 Cover: 0.10 **NM** value: **100.00**
• **CGC:** 1 graded, best 9.2
71 ❑ Jul 1946 Cover: 0.10 **NM** value: **100.00**
72 ❑ Aug 1946 Cover: 0.10 **NM** value: **100.00**
73 ❑ Sep 1946 Cover: 0.10 **NM** value: **100.00**
• **CGC:** 1 graded, best 9.0
74 ❑ Oct 1946 Cover: 0.10 **NM** value: **100.00**
• **CGC:** 1 graded, best 9.4
75 ❑ Nov 1946 Cover: 0.10 **NM** value: **100.00**
76 ❑ Dec 1946 Cover: 0.10 **NM** value: **100.00**
• **CGC:** 1 graded, best 8.5
77 ❑ Jan 1947 Cover: 0.10 **NM** value: **100.00**
78 ❑ Feb 1947 Cover: 0.10 **NM** value: **100.00**
• **CGC:** 1 graded, best 8.0
79 ❑ Mar 1947 Cover: 0.10 **NM** value: **100.00**
80 ❑ Apr 1947 Cover: 0.10 **NM** value: **100.00**
• **CGC:** 1 graded, best 6.5
81 ❑ May 1947 Cover: 0.10 **NM** value: **90.00**
• **CGC:** 2 graded, best 9.4
82 ❑ Jun 1947 Cover: 0.10 **NM** value: **90.00**
83 ❑ Jul 1947 Cover: 0.10 **NM** value: **90.00**
• **CGC:** 1 graded, best 8.0
84 ❑ Aug 1947 Cover: 0.10 **NM** value: **90.00**
• **CGC:** 1 graded, best 8.5
85 ❑ Sep 1947 Cover: 0.10 **NM** value: **90.00**
• **CGC:** 1 graded, best 9.2
86 ❑ Oct 1947 Cover: 0.10 **NM** value: **90.00**
• **CGC:** 1 graded, best 9.2
87 ❑ Nov 1947 Cover: 0.10 **NM** value: **90.00**
• **CGC:** 3 graded, best 9.4
88 ❑ Dec 1947 Cover: 0.10 **NM** value: **90.00**
• **CGC:** 1 graded, best 8.5
89 ❑ Jan 1948 Cover: 0.10 **NM** value: **90.00**
90 ❑ Feb 1948 Cover: 0.10 **NM** value: **90.00**
91 ❑ Mar 1948 Cover: 0.10 **NM** value: **90.00**
92 ❑ Apr 1948 Cover: 0.10 **NM** value: **90.00**
93 ❑ May 1948 Cover: 0.10 **NM** value: **90.00**
94 ❑ Jun 1948 Cover: 0.10 **NM** value: **90.00**
95 ❑ Jul 1948 Cover: 0.10 **NM** value: **90.00**
96 ❑ Aug 1948 Cover: 0.10 **NM** value: **90.00**
• **CGC:** 1 graded, best 9.0
97 ❑ Sep 1948 Cover: 0.10 **NM** value: **90.00**
• **CGC:** 1 graded, best 6.5
98 ❑ Oct 1948 Cover: 0.10 **NM** value: **90.00**
• **CGC:** 1 graded, best 7.0
99 ❑ Nov 1948 Cover: 0.10 **NM** value: **90.00**
100 ❑ Dec 1948 Cover: 0.10 **NM** value: **90.00**
• **CGC:** 1 graded, best 9.2
101 ❑ Jan 1949 Cover: 0.10 **NM** value: **75.00**
102 ❑ Feb 1949 Cover: 0.10 **NM** value: **75.00**
103 ❑ Mar 1949 Cover: 0.10 **NM** value: **75.00**
104 ❑ Apr 1949 Cover: 0.10 **NM** value: **75.00**
105 ❑ May 1949 Cover: 0.10 **NM** value: **75.00**
106 ❑ Jun 1949 Cover: 0.10 **NM** value: **75.00**
107 ❑ Jul 1949 Cover: 0.10 **NM** value: **75.00**
108 ❑ Aug 1949 Cover: 0.10 **NM** value: **75.00**
109 ❑ Sep 1949 Cover: 0.10 **NM** value: **75.00**
110 ❑ Win 1949 Cover: 0.10 **NM** value: **75.00**
111 ❑ Spr 1950 Cover: 0.10 **NM** value: **75.00**
112 ❑ ca. 1950 Cover: 0.10 **NM** value: **75.00**
113 ❑ Win 1951 Cover: 0.10 **NM** value: **75.00**
114 ❑ Sum 1951 Cover: 0.10 **NM** value: **75.00**
📖 The Red-Star Robots; D-Day for Death Rays
115 ❑ Fal 1951 Cover: 0.10 **NM** value: **75.00**
116 ❑ ca. 1952 Cover: 0.10 **NM** value: **75.00**
117 ❑ Fal 1952 Cover: 0.10 **NM** value: **75.00**
118 ❑ Win 1952 Cover: 0.10 **NM** value: **75.00**
• **CGC:** 1 graded, best 8.5
119 ❑ Spr 1953 Cover: 0.10 **NM** value: **75.00**
120 ❑ ca. 1953 Cover: 0.10 **NM** value: **75.00**
📖 The Curse of Squadron 3; Doomsday Mission

CGC-graded: Multiply prices above by **33 for 9.9 M • 16 for 9.8 NM/M • 7 for 9.6 NM+ • 5 for 9.4 NM • 2.5 for 9.2 NM- • 1.5 for 9.0 VF/NM**

121 ❑ ca. 1953 Cover: 0.10 **NM** value: **75.00**
📖 Robot in the Cockpit; Aces of Spyways
122 ❑ Win 1954 Cover: 0.10 **NM** value: **75.00**
📖 Last Kill in Korea
123 ❑ Spr 1954 Cover: 0.10 **NM** value: **75.00**
📖 The Cat and the Canaries
124 ❑ Sum 1954 Cover: 0.10 **NM** value: **75.00**

WINGS COMICS (A-LIST) — A-List

1 ❑ Spr 1997, b&w Cover: 2.95 **NM** value: **Cover or less**
📖 Lucky Wings: The Atomic Blondshell; The Golden Ghouls • Golden Age reprint **A:** Robert Webb **W:** Robert Webb
2 ❑ Fal 1997, b&w Cover: 2.95 **NM** value: **Cover or less**
• Golden Age reprint
3 ❑ Cover: 2.95 **NM** value: **Cover or less**
📖 Shark Brodie; Ace of the Newsreel; Atlas the Mighty; ZX-5; **A:** Major Thorpe; Paul Powers **W:** Major Thorpe; Paul Powers
4 ❑ Cover: 2.95 **NM** value: **Cover or less**

WINNIE THE POOH (WALT DISNEY...) — Whitman

1 ❑ Jan 1977 Cover: 0.30 **NM** value: **12.00**
• **CGC:** 3 graded, best 9.4
2 ❑ May 1977 Cover: 0.30 **NM** value: **6.00**
3 ❑ Sep 1977 Cover: 0.30 **NM** value: **4.00**
4 ❑ **NM** value: **4.00**
5 ❑ **NM** value: **4.00**
6 ❑ Cover: 0.35 **NM** value: **3.00**
7 ❑ **NM** value: **3.00**
8 ❑ **NM** value: **3.00**
9 ❑ **NM** value: **3.00**
10 ❑ **NM** value: **3.00**
11 ❑ **NM** value: **2.50**
12 ❑ **NM** value: **2.50**
13 ❑ **NM** value: **2.50**
14 ❑ **NM** value: **2.50**
15 ❑ **NM** value: **2.50**
16 ❑ **NM** value: **2.50**
17 ❑ **NM** value: **2.50**
18 ❑ **NM** value: **2.50**
19 ❑ **NM** value: **2.50**
20 ❑ **NM** value: **2.50**
21 ❑ **NM** value: **2.50**
22 ❑ **NM** value: **2.50**
23 ❑ **NM** value: **2.50**
24 ❑ **NM** value: **2.50**
25 ❑ **NM** value: **2.50**
26 ❑ **NM** value: **2.50**
27 ❑ Feb 1982 Cover: 0.60 **NM** value: **2.50**
📖 Tumbleweed Trouble; Birthday Blues; The Well-Wishers; The Mysterious Map
28 ❑ ca. 1982 Cover: 0.60 **NM** value: **2.50**
29 ❑ ca. 1982 Cover: 0.60 **NM** value: **2.50**
30 ❑ ca. 1983 Cover: 0.60 **NM** value: **2.50**
31 ❑ ca. 1983 Cover: 0.60 **NM** value: **2.50**
32 ❑ ca. 1984 Cover: 0.60 **NM** value: **2.50**
33 ❑ ca. 1984 Cover: 0.60 **NM** value: **2.50**

WINNIE WINKLE — Dell

1 ❑ ca. 1948 Cover: 0.10 **NM** value: **40.00**
• **CGC:** 1 graded, best 9.4
2 ❑ Jun 1948 Cover: 0.10 **NM** value: **24.00**
3 ❑ Sep 1948 Cover: 0.10 **NM** value: **24.00**
4 ❑ Dec 1948 Cover: 0.10 **NM** value: **18.00**
5 ❑ Mar 1949 Cover: 0.10 **NM** value: **18.00**
6 ❑ Jun 1949 Cover: 0.10 **NM** value: **18.00**
7 ❑ Sep 1949 Cover: 0.10 **NM** value: **18.00**

WINNING IN THE DESERT — Apple

1 ❑ Cover: 2.95 **NM** value: **Cover or less**
• booklet
2 ❑ Cover: 2.95 **NM** value: **Cover or less**
• booklet

WINTERSTAR — Echo

1 ❑ Dec 1996, b&w Cover: 2.95 **NM** value: **Cover or less**

WINTERWORLD — Eclipse

1 ❑ Sep 1987 Cover: 1.75 **NM** value: **2.00**
Circ: CapCity orders: **5,450**
2 ❑ Dec 1987 Cover: 1.75 **NM** value: **2.00**
Circ: CapCity orders: **4,400**
3 ❑ Mar 1988 Cover: 1.75 **NM** value: **2.00**
Circ: CapCity orders: **4,200**

WISE SON: THE WHITE WOLF — DC / Milestone

1 ❑ Nov 1996 Cover: 2.50 **NM** value: **Cover or less**
Circ: Diamd. preorders: **7,488**
2 ❑ Dec 1996 Cover: 2.50 **NM** value: **Cover or less**
Circ: Diamd. preorders: **5,720**
📖 Woman in Chains **A:** Ho Che Anderson **W:** Ho Che Anderson
3 ❑ Jan 1997 Cover: 2.50 **NM** value: **Cover or less**
Circ: Diamd. preorders: **5,069**
📖 Once, When I Was Lost **A:** Ho Che Anderson **W:** Ho Che Anderson
4 ❑ Feb 1997 Cover: 2.50 **NM** value: **Cover or less**
Circ: Diamd. preorders: **4,413**

WISH UPON A STAR — Warp

1 ❑ May 1994 **NM** value: **1.00**
• giveaway. • no price

WITCH — Eternity

1 ❑ b&w Cover: 1.95 **NM** value: **Cover or less**
📖 The Love Witch **A:** Ernie Colon **W:** Marv Wolfman

WITCHBLADE — Image

Witchblade, created by Marc Silvestri and published by Image Comics, began in December 1995. Police Detective Sara Pezzini's life was changed forever, when she discovered the Witchblade, a bio-mechanical weapon. At first, Sara was afraid of the Witchblade but soon became accustomed, if not addicted, to the powerful killing tool. Finding herself haunted by nightmares concerning friends who were murdered, she decides to use the Witchblade to avenge those senseless crimes. But she must keep the knowledge of the Witchblade secret from her friends as well as those who know of its existence and would kill to acquire it.

Although Image co-founder and artist Marc Silvestri created Witchblade, he did not write or draw the issues. Nevertheless, Witchblade managed to combine hints of sex and violence into a collector's phenomenon, with a fury of bidding driving up the prices of early issues.

0 ❑ **NM** value: **5.00**
0.5 ❑ **NM** value: **30.00**
• **CGC:** 34 graded, best 9.8
• Overstreet Fan promotional edition. **A:** Michael Turner **W:** Brian Haberlin; David Wohl
1 ❑ Nov 1995 Cover: 2.50 **NM** value: **20.00**
Circ: CapCity orders: **23,925** • **CGC:** 186 graded, best 9.8
1/A ❑ Nov 1995 Cover: 2.50 **NM** value: **5.00**
Sketch cover variant. • Wizard Ace edition.
1/B ❑ Nov 1995 Cover: 2.50 **NM** value: **15.00**
• Wizard Ace edition.
2 ❑ Jan 1996 Cover: 2.50 **NM** value: **18.00**
• **CGC:** 48 graded, best 9.9
• Relatively scarce **A:** Michael Turner **W:** Brian Haberlin; David Wohl
2/A ❑ Jan 1996 Cover: 2.50 **NM** value: **15.00**
• Wizard Ace edition.
2-2 ❑ Cover: 2.50 **NM** value: **4.00**
3 ❑ Mar 1996 Cover: 2.50 **NM** value: **10.00**
• **CGC:** 25 graded, best 9.8
4 ❑ Apr 1996 Cover: 2.50 **NM** value: **8.00**
• **CGC:** 14 graded, best 9.8
5 ❑ May 1996 Cover: 2.50 **NM** value: **8.00**
• **CGC:** 9 graded, best 9.8
6 ❑ Jun 1996 Cover: 2.50 **NM** value: **6.00**
• **CGC:** 7 graded, best 9.8
7 ❑ Jul 1996 Cover: 2.50 **NM** value: **6.00**
• **CGC:** 5 graded, best 9.4
8 ❑ Aug 1996 Cover: 2.50 **NM** value: **5.00**
• **CGC:** 3 graded, best 9.8
9 ❑ Sep 1996 Cover: 2.50 **NM** value: **5.00**
• **CGC:** 4 graded, best in 9.6
9/A ❑ Sep 1996 Cover: 2.50 **NM** value: **5.00**
• **CGC:** 3 graded, best 9.6
10 ❑ Nov 1996 Cover: 2.50 **NM** value: **5.00**
Circ: Diamd. preorders: **92,391**
10/A ❑ Nov 1996 Cover: 2.50 **NM** value: **20.00**
Alternate cover sold through Dynamic Forces. • Shows two characters back-to-back **A:** Michael Turner **W:** Christina Z.; David Wohl ★ 1st Appearance of The Darkness. ★ Appearance of Darkness.
10/AUT ❑ Nov 1996 Cover: 27.95 **NM** value: **Cover or less**
• limited to 2,500 copies **A:** Michael Turner **W:** Christina Z.; David Wohl ★ 1st Appearance of The Darkness.
10/B ❑ Nov 1996 Cover: 2.50 **NM** value: **8.00**
alternate cover. • American Entertainment alternate ★ Appearance of Darkness.
10/C ❑ Nov 1996 Cover: 2.50 **NM** value: **8.00**
• Dynamic Forces alternate; American Entertainment alternate ★ Appearance of Darkness.
10/D ❑ Nov 1996 Cover: 2.50 **NM** value: **8.00**
• Dynamic Forces alternate ★ Appearance of Darkness.
11 ❑ Dec 1996 Cover: 2.50 **NM** value: **4.00**
Circ: Diamd. preorders: **81,509** • **CGC:** 1 graded, best 9.8
12 ❑ Mar 1997 Cover: 2.50 **NM** value: **4.00**
Circ: Diamd. preorders: **83,623** • **CGC:** 1 graded, best 9.6
13 ❑ Apr 1997 Cover: 2.50 **NM** value: **3.50**
Circ: Diamd. preorders: **90,927** • **CGC:** 1 graded, best 9.6
14 ❑ May 1997 Cover: 2.50 **NM** value: **3.50**
Circ: Diamd. preorders: **93,303** • **CGC:** 3 graded, best 9.8
14/GO ❑ May 1997 Cover: 2.50 **NM** value: **6.00**
• **CGC:** 1 graded, best 9.6
• Gold logo edition. **A:** Michael Turner **W:** Christina Z.; David Wohl
15 ❑ Jul 1997 Cover: 2.50 **NM** value: **3.50**
Circ: Diamd. preorders: **92,432** • **CGC:** 1 graded, best 9.2
16 ❑ Aug 1997 Cover: 2.50 **NM** value: **3.00**
Circ: Diamd. preorders: **89,302**
17 ❑ Sep 1997 Cover: 2.50 **NM** value: **3.00**
Circ: Diamd. preorders: **89,660**
18 ❑ Nov 1997 Cover: 2.50 **NM** value: **3.00**
Circ: Diamd. preorders: **134,571**
📖 Family Ties, Part 1 • continues in The Darkness #9 **A:** Michael Turner **W:** Christina Z.; David Wohl
18/A ❑ Nov 1997 Cover: 2.50 **NM** value: **Cover or less**
variant cover. 📖 Family Ties, Part 1 **A:** Michael Turner **W:** Christina Z.; David Wohl
18/AE ❑ Nov 1997 **NM** value: **5.00**
• **CGC:** 2 graded, best 9.6
Green variant cover. • American Entertainment Edition. 📖 Family Ties, Part 1 **A:** Michael Turner; Michael Turner(cover) **W:** Christina Z.; David Wohl
19 ❑ Dec 1997 Cover: 2.50 **NM** value: **3.00**
Circ: Diamd. preorders: **106,807**
📖 Family Ties, Part 4 **A:** Michael Turner **W:** Michael Turner; Christina Z.; David Wohl
20 ❑ Feb 1998 Cover: 2.50 **NM** value: **3.00**
Circ: Diamd. preorders: **97,147**
21 ❑ Mar 1998 Cover: 2.50 **NM** value: **Cover or less**
Circ: Diamd. preorders: **91,311**
22 ❑ May 1998 Cover: 2.50 **NM** value: **Cover or less**
Circ: Diamd. preorders: **90,350**
23 ❑ Jun 1998 Cover: 2.50 **NM** value: **Cover or less**
Circ: Diamd. preorders: **82,303**
24 ❑ Jul 1998 Cover: 2.50 **NM** value: **Cover or less**
Circ: Diamd. preorders: **80,472**
25 ❑ Aug 1998 Cover: 2.95 **NM** value: **Cover or less**
Circ: Diamd. preorders: **116,796**
26 ❑ Oct 1998 Cover: 2.50 **NM** value: **Cover or less**
Circ: Diamd. preorders: **70,808**
27 ❑ Nov 1998 Cover: 2.50 **NM** value: **Cover or less**
Circ: Diamd. preorders: **80,309** • **CGC:** 2 graded, best 9.8
28 ❑ Feb 1999 Cover: 2.50 **NM** value: **Cover or less**
Circ: Diamd. preorders: **67,557** • **CGC:** 1 graded, best 9.6
29 ❑ Mar 1999 Cover: 2.50 **NM** value: **Cover or less**
Circ: Diamd. preorders: **62,221**
30 ❑ Apr 1999 Cover: 2.50 **NM** value: **Cover or less**
Circ: Diamd. preorders: **58,668**
31 ❑ May 1999 Cover: 2.50 **NM** value: **Cover or less**
Circ: Diamd. preorders: **57,684**
32 ❑ Jul 1999 Cover: 2.50 **NM** value: **Cover or less**
Circ: Diamd. preorders: **54,025**
33 ❑ Aug 1999 Cover: 2.50 **NM** value: **Cover or less**
Circ: Diamd. preorders: **53,309**
34 ❑ Sep 1999 Cover: 2.50 **NM** value: **Cover or less**
Circ: Diamd. preorders: **49,645**
35 ❑ Oct 1999 Cover: 2.50 **NM** value: **Cover or less**
Circ: Diamd. preorders: **49,441**
36 ❑ Dec 1999 Cover: 2.50 **NM** value: **Cover or less**
Circ: Diamd. preorders: **50,419**
37 ❑ 2000 Cover: 2.50 **NM** value: **Cover or less**
Circ: Diamd. preorders: **42,144**
38 ❑ 2000 Cover: 2.50 **NM** value: **Cover or less**
Circ: Diamd. preorders: **39,565**
39 ❑ May 2000 Cover: 2.50 **NM** value: **Cover or less**
Circ: Diamd. preorders: **40,520**
40 ❑ Jun 2000 Cover: 2.50 **NM** value: **Cover or less**
Circ: Diamd. preorders: **41,116**
41 ❑ Jul 2000 Cover: 2.50 **NM** value: **Cover or less**
Circ: Diamd. preorders: **39,908**
41/A ❑ Jul 2000 Cover: 2.50 **NM** value: **3.00**
e-Wanted alternate cover (Pezzini sitting). **A:** Keu Cha **W:** Rick Veitch; Paul Jenkins
42 ❑ Sep 2000 Cover: 2.50 **NM** value: **Cover or less**
Circ: Diamd. preorders: **38,654**
43 ❑ Nov 2000 Cover: 2.50 **NM** value: **Cover or less**
Circ: Diamd. preorders: **38,203**
44 ❑ Jan 2001 Cover: 2.50 **NM** value: **Cover or less**
Circ: Diamd. preorders: **38,311**
45 ❑ Mar 2001 Cover: 2.50 **NM** value: **Cover or less**
Circ: Diamd. preorders: **36,985**
46 ❑ May 2001 Cover: 2.50 **NM** value: **Cover or less**
Circ: Diamd. preorders: **35,492**
47 ❑ Jun 2001 Cover: 2.50 **NM** value: **Cover or less**
Circ: Diamd. preorders: **33,788**
48 ❑ Jul 2001 Cover: 2.50 **NM** value: **Cover or less**
Circ: Diamd. preorders: **32,655**
49 ❑ Aug 2001 Cover: 2.50 **NM** value: **Cover or less**
Circ: Diamd. preorders: **33,023**
50 ❑ Sep 2001 Cover: 4.95 **NM** value: **Cover or less**
Circ: Diamd. preorders: **48,875**
• Giant-size.
50/A ❑ Sep 2001 Cover: 14.99 **NM** value: **Cover or less**
Circ: Diamd. preorders: **31,931**
DFE alternate cover.
50/B ❑ Sep 2001 Cover: 29.99 **NM** value: **Cover or less**
500 ❑ ca. 1998 **NM** value: **5.00**
• **CGC:** 22 graded, best 9.8
• Limited edition foil cover. • Given away as premium for subscription to Wizard
Bk 1 ❑ Jul 1996 Cover: 4.95 **NM** value: **Cover or less**
• prestige format. • reprints Witchblade #1 and 2 **A:** Michael Turner **W:** Christina Z.; David Wohl
Bk 2 ❑ Sep 1996 Cover: 4.95 **NM** value: **Cover or less**
• prestige format. • reprints Witchblade #3 and 4 **A:** Michael Turner **W:** Christina Z.; David Wohl
Bk 3 ❑ Oct 1996 Cover: 4.95 **NM** value: **Cover or less**
• prestige format. • reprints Witchblade #5 and 6 **A:** Michael Turner **W:** Christina Z.; David Wohl
Bk 4 ❑ Nov 1996 Cover: 4.95 **NM** value: **Cover or less**
• prestige format. • reprints Witchblade #7 and 8 **A:** Michael Turner **W:** Christina Z.; David Wohl
Bk 4/Dlx ❑ Oct 1996 Cover: 10.95 **NM** value: **Cover or less**
• prestige format. • reprints Witchblade #7 and 8; with slipcase
Bk 4/HC ❑ Oct 1996 Cover: 29.95 **NM** value: **Cover or less**
• prestige format. • reprints Witchblade #7 and 8; with slipcase and issues #1-4
Bk 5 ❑ Nov 1997 Cover: 4.95 **NM** value: **Cover or less**
• prestige format. • reprints Witchblade #9 and 10 **A:** Michael Turner **W:** Christina Z.; David Wohl
Bk 6 ❑ Jan 1998 Cover: 4.95 **NM** value: **Cover or less**
• prestige format. • reprints Witchblade #11 and 12 **A:** Michael Turner **W:** Christina Z.; David Wohl
Bk 7 ❑ Jan 1998 Cover: 4.95 **NM** value: **Cover or less**
• prestige format. • reprints Witchblade #13 and 14 **A:** Michael Turner **W:** Christina Z.; David Wohl
Bk 8 ❑ Jan 1998 Cover: 4.95 **NM** value: **Cover or less**
• prestige format. • reprints Witchblade #15 and 16 **A:** Michael Turner **W:** Christina Z.; David Wohl
Dlx 1 ❑ Cover: 24.95 **NM** value: **Cover or less**
• Deluxe Collected Edition. • Collects Witchblade #1-8 **A:** Michael Turner **W:** Christina Z.; David Wohl

Other grades: Multiply prices above by **1.5 for Mint • 2/3 for Very Fine • 1/3 for Fine • 1/5 for Very Good • 1/8 for Good**

Dlx 2 ❑ Oct 2000 Cover: 24.95 NM value: **Cover or less**
• Revelations Collected Edition. • Collects Witchblade #9-17 **A:** Michael Turner **W:** Christina Z.; David Wohl
Dlx 3 ❑ Oct 2000 Cover: 14.95 NM value: **Cover or less**
• Prevailing; Collects Witchblade #20-25 **A:** Michael Turner **W:** Christina Z.; David Wohl

WITCHBLADE/ALIENS/THE DARKNESS/ PREDATOR — Dark Horse

1 ❑ Nov 2000 Cover: 2.99 NM value: **Cover or less**
Circ: Diamd. preorders: **37,928** • **CGC:** 1 graded, best 9.8
📖 Mindhunter **A:** Mel Rubi **W:** David Quinn
2 ❑ Dec 2000 Cover: 2.99 NM value: **Cover or less**
Circ: Diamd. preorders: **35,760**
📖 Mindhunter **A:** Mel Rubi **W:** David Quinn
3 ❑ Jan 2001 Cover: 2.99 NM value: **Cover or less**
Circ: Diamd. preorders: **27,938**
📖 Mindhunter **A:** Mel Rubi **W:** David Quinn

WITCHBLADE/DARKCHYLDE — Image

1 ❑ Sep 2000 Cover: 2.50 NM value: **Cover or less**
• **CGC:** 1 graded, best 9.6

WITCHBLADE/DARKNESS SPECIAL — Image

0.5/PI ❑ Sep 2000 NM value: **35.00**
• **CGC:** 45 graded, best 9.9
• Promotional giveaway when applying for Wizard credit card. **A:** Randy Queen **W:** Randy Queen
1 ❑ Dec 1999 Cover: 3.95 NM value: **Cover or less**

WITCHBLADE: DESTINY'S CHILD — Image

1 ❑ May 2000 Cover: 2.95 NM value: **Cover or less**
Circ: Diamd. preorders: **34,669**
2 ❑ Jul 2000 Cover: 2.95 NM value: **Cover or less**
Circ: Diamd. preorders: **32,819**
3 ❑ Sep 2000 Cover: 2.95 NM value: **Cover or less**
Circ: Diamd. preorders: **30,960**

WITCHBLADE/ELEKTRA — Marvel

1 ❑ Mar 1997 Cover: 2.95 NM value: **Cover or less**
• **CGC:** 2 graded, best 9.6
📖 Devil's Reign, Part 6 • crossover with Image; continues in Elektra/Cyblade #1
1/AE ❑ Mar 1997 NM value: **5.00**
• American Entertainment Edition. **A:** Joe Benitez(cover)

WITCHBLADE GALLERY — Image

1 ❑ Nov 2000 Cover: 2.95 NM value: **Cover or less**
Circ: Diamd. preorders: **19,297**

WITCHBLADE INFINITY — Image

1 ❑ May 1999 Cover: 3.50 NM value: **Cover or less**
Circ: Diamd. preorders: **51,946**

WITCHBLADE ORIGIN — Image

1/AE ❑ Oct 1997 NM value: **3.00**
• American Entertainment Edition. **A:** Marc Silvestri; Michael Turner(cover)

WITCHBLADE/THE DARKNESS: FAMILY TIES — Image

Bk 1 ❑ Oct 1998 Cover: 9.95 NM value: **Cover or less**
📖 Family Ties • collects storyline from Witchblade #18 and #19 and The Darkness #9 and #10 **A:** Clarence Lansang; Joe Benitez; Marc Silvestri; Michael Turner **W:** Christina Z.; David Wohl

WITCHBLADE/TOMB RAIDER — Image

0.5 ❑ Jul 2000 Cover: 2.95 NM value: **5.00**
1/A ❑ Dec 1998 Cover: 2.95 NM value: **4.00**
Circ: Diamd. preorders: **190,720**
1/B ❑ Dec 1998 Cover: 2.95 NM value: **5.00**
alternate cover (white background). **A:** Michael Turner **W:** Michael Turner; Bill O'Neil
1/C ❑ Dec 1998 Cover: 2.95 NM value: **5.00**
Croft standing on top of Pezzini with guns crossed on cover. **A:** Michael Turner **W:** Michael Turner; Bill O'Neil

WITCHCRAFT — DC / Vertigo

The three witches are characters who appear frequently throughout legend, including in the pages of Neil Gaiman's Sandman. The trio — Cynthia, Morgana, and Mildred — are featured in this three-part mini-series of their own.

It begins in ancient Britain, when their priestess is murdered. Throughout history, each of the trio seeks a mortal to act as her instrument of revenge upon the reincarnated spirit of the murderer. In the first book, the young witch Cynthia attempts to aid a medieval bride escape a marriage to a sorcerous murderer. In the second, the mother, Morgana, tries to maneuver Sir Richard Burton to kill the murderer incarnation in the late 19th century. Instead, Burton chooses to save his own future. Finally, it is Mildred the Crone who brings the quest to its bloody conclusion in modern London. It's an interesting saga, but not one recommended for young readers.

1 ❑ Jun 1994 Cover: 2.95 NM value: **Cover or less**
Circ: CapCity orders: **17,200**
covers form triptych. 📖 Maiden **A:** Teddy Kristiansen; Peter Snejbjerg **W:** James Robinson
2 ❑ Jul 1994 Cover: 2.95 NM value: **Cover or less**
Circ: CapCity orders: **13,250**
• Sex, violence-recommended for mature readers. **A:** Teddy Kristiansen; Michael Zulli **W:** James Robinson
3 ❑ Aug 1994 Cover: 2.95 NM value: **Cover or less**
Circ: CapCity orders: **12,600**
Bk 1 ❑ Cover: 14.95 NM value: **Cover or less**

WITCHCRAFT (AVON) — Avon

1 ❑ Mar 1952 Cover: 0.10 NM value: **400.00**
• **CGC:** 7 graded, best 9.0
2 ❑ May 1952 Cover: 0.10 NM value: **400.00**
• **CGC:** 2 graded, best 9.0
3 ❑ Jul 1952 Cover: 0.10 NM value: **400.00**
• **CGC:** 2 graded, best 9.0
4 ❑ Oct 1952 Cover: 0.10 NM value: **400.00**

WITCHCRAFT: LA TERREUR — DC / Vertigo

1 ❑ Apr 1998 Cover: 2.50 NM value: **Cover or less**
covers form triptych. 📖 Winter into April **A:** Michael Zulli **W:** James Robinson
2 ❑ May 1998 Cover: 2.50 NM value: **Cover or less**
covers form triptych. **A:** Michael Zulli **W:** James Robinson
3 ❑ Jun 1998 Cover: 2.50 NM value: **Cover or less**
covers form triptych. 📖 September **A:** Teddy Kristiansen; Steve Yeowell; Michael Zulli **W:** James Robinson

WITCHES' CAULDRON: THE BATTLE OF THE CHERKASSY POCKET — Heritage Collection

1 ❑ b&w Cover: 3.50 NM value: **Cover or less**
No issue number.

WITCHES TALES — Harvey

1 ❑ Jan 1951 Cover: 0.10 NM value: **300.00**
• **CGC:** 1 graded, best 8.5
2 ❑ Mar 1951 Cover: 0.10 NM value: **250.00**
• **CGC:** 3 graded, best 9.2
3 ❑ May 1951 Cover: 0.10 NM value: **200.00**
• **CGC:** 4 graded, best 9.2
4 ❑ Jul 1951 Cover: 0.10 NM value: **160.00**
• **CGC:** 1 graded, best 9.0
5 ❑ Sep 1951 Cover: 0.10 NM value: **140.00**
6 ❑ Nov 1951 Cover: 0.10 NM value: **120.00**
7 ❑ Jan 1952 Cover: 0.10 NM value: **100.00**
• **CGC:** 1 graded, best 9.0
8 ❑ Mar 1952 Cover: 0.10 NM value: **100.00**
• **CGC:** 2 graded, best 8.0
9 ❑ Apr 1952 Cover: 0.10 NM value: **100.00**
• **CGC:** 1 graded, best 8.5
10 ❑ May 1952 Cover: 0.10 NM value: **100.00**
• **CGC:** 2 graded, best 9.2
11 ❑ Jun 1952 Cover: 0.10 NM value: **100.00**
12 ❑ Jul 1952 Cover: 0.10 NM value: **100.00**
13 ❑ Aug 1952 Cover: 0.10 NM value: **100.00**
• **CGC:** 3 graded, best 9.2
14 ❑ Sep 1952 Cover: 0.10 NM value: **100.00**
15 ❑ Oct 1952 Cover: 0.10 NM value: **100.00**
• **CGC:** 2 graded, best 9.0
16 ❑ Dec 1952 Cover: 0.10 NM value: **100.00**
• **CGC:** 1 graded, best 8.5
17 ❑ Feb 1953 Cover: 0.10 NM value: **100.00**
18 ❑ Apr 1953 Cover: 0.10 NM value: **100.00**
• **CGC:** 1 graded, best 8.0
19 ❑ Jun 1953 Cover: 0.10 NM value: **100.00**
📖 The Pact; Jungle; Honeymoon; A Matter of Taste
20 ❑ Aug 1953 Cover: 0.10 NM value: **100.00**
• **CGC:** 1 graded, best 8.0
21 ❑ Oct 1953 Cover: 0.10 NM value: **100.00**
• **CGC:** 2 graded, best 9.0
22 ❑ Dec 1953 Cover: 0.10 NM value: **100.00**
23 ❑ Feb 1954 Cover: 0.10 NM value: **100.00**
• **CGC:** 1 graded, best 5.0
24 ❑ Apr 1954 Cover: 0.10 NM value: **100.00**
25 ❑ Jun 1954 Cover: 0.10 NM value: **100.00**
• **CGC:** 3 graded, best 9.2
26 ❑ Aug 1954 Cover: 0.10 NM value: **100.00**
• **CGC:** 1 graded, best 7.5
27 ❑ Oct 1954 Cover: 0.10 NM value: **100.00**
📖 Murder Mansion; Green horror; The Thing That Grew!
28 ❑ Dec 1954 Cover: 0.10 NM value: **100.00**

WITCHES' WESTERN TALES — Harvey

29 ❑ Feb 1955 Cover: 0.10 NM value: **100.00**
30 ❑ Apr 1955 Cover: 0.10 NM value: **100.00**
• **CGC:** 2 graded, best 7.5

WITCHFINDER, THE — Image

1 ❑ Sep 1999 Cover: 2.95 NM value: **Cover or less**
Circ: Diamd. preorders: **20,128**
Man with torch on cover facing forward. **A:** Romano **W:** Matthew Scott; Robert Lugibihl; Sharon Scott
1/A ❑ Sep 1999 Cover: 2.95 NM value: **Cover or less**
1/B ❑ Sep 1999 Cover: 2.95 NM value: **Cover or less**
alternate cover. **A:** Romano **W:** Matthew Scott; Robert Lugibihl; Sharon Scott
2 ❑ Nov 1999 Cover: 2.95 NM value: **Cover or less**
Circ: Diamd. preorders: **14,023**

WITCH HUNTER — Malibu / Ultraverse

1 ❑ Apr 1996 Cover: 2.50 NM value: **Cover or less**

WITCHING HOUR — DC

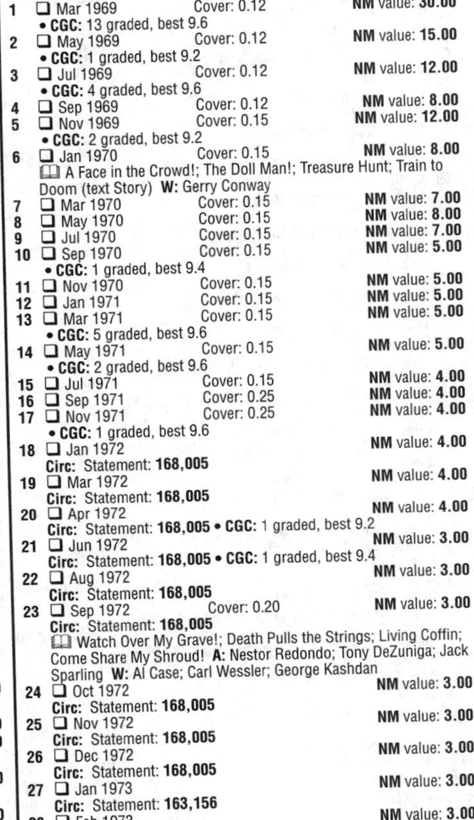

Witches narrate stories involving witchcraft and deceit, many of which have their climax near midnight ... the witching hour. Featured in the pages of this 85-issue series were stories such as "The Killer Came Slithering," about a witch who cures a boy of his illness in exchange for his ripping up the mortgage on the witch's church. When the boy's father reneges on his promise, the snake-charming sorceress gets her own revenge in a subtle and clever way — at midnight.

After almost 10 years of bewitching readers, the witch's lease must have run out, because in 1978 this series became part of The Unexpected, a series hosted by Abel in his own home, the House of Secrets.

1 ❑ Mar 1969 Cover: 0.12 NM value: **30.00**
• **CGC:** 13 graded, best 9.6
2 ❑ May 1969 Cover: 0.12 NM value: **15.00**
• **CGC:** 1 graded, best 9.2
3 ❑ Jul 1969 Cover: 0.12 NM value: **12.00**
• **CGC:** 4 graded, best 9.6
4 ❑ Sep 1969 Cover: 0.12 NM value: **8.00**
5 ❑ Nov 1969 Cover: 0.15 NM value: **12.00**
• **CGC:** 2 graded, best 9.2
6 ❑ Jan 1970 Cover: 0.15 NM value: **8.00**
📖 A Face in the Crowd!; The Doll Man!; Treasure Hunt; Train to Doom (text Story) **W:** Gerry Conway
7 ❑ Mar 1970 Cover: 0.15 NM value: **7.00**
8 ❑ May 1970 Cover: 0.15 NM value: **8.00**
9 ❑ Jul 1970 Cover: 0.15 NM value: **7.00**
10 ❑ Sep 1970 Cover: 0.15 NM value: **5.00**
• **CGC:** 1 graded, best 9.4
11 ❑ Nov 1970 Cover: 0.15 NM value: **5.00**
12 ❑ Jan 1971 Cover: 0.15 NM value: **5.00**
13 ❑ Mar 1971 Cover: 0.15 NM value: **5.00**
• **CGC:** 5 graded, best 9.6
14 ❑ May 1971 Cover: 0.15 NM value: **5.00**
• **CGC:** 2 graded, best 9.6
15 ❑ Jul 1971 Cover: 0.15 NM value: **4.00**
16 ❑ Sep 1971 Cover: 0.25 NM value: **4.00**
17 ❑ Nov 1971 Cover: 0.25 NM value: **4.00**
• **CGC:** 1 graded, best 9.6
18 ❑ Jan 1972 NM value: **4.00**
Circ: Statement: **168,005**
19 ❑ Mar 1972 NM value: **4.00**
Circ: Statement: **168,005**
20 ❑ Apr 1972 NM value: **4.00**
Circ: Statement: **168,005** • **CGC:** 1 graded, best 9.2
21 ❑ Jun 1972 NM value: **3.00**
Circ: Statement: **168,005** • **CGC:** 1 graded, best 9.4
22 ❑ Aug 1972 NM value: **3.00**
Circ: Statement: **168,005**
23 ❑ Sep 1972 Cover: 0.20 NM value: **3.00**
Circ: Statement: **168,005**
📖 Watch Over My Grave!; Death Pulls the Strings; Living Coffin; Come Share My Shroud! **A:** Nestor Redondo; Tony DeZuniga; Jack Sparling **W:** Al Case; Carl Wessler; George Kashdan
24 ❑ Oct 1972 NM value: **3.00**
Circ: Statement: **168,005**
25 ❑ Nov 1972 NM value: **3.00**
Circ: Statement: **168,005**
26 ❑ Dec 1972 NM value: **3.00**
Circ: Statement: **168,005**
27 ❑ Jan 1973 NM value: **3.00**
Circ: Statement: **163,156**
28 ❑ Feb 1973 NM value: **3.00**
Circ: Statement: **163,156**
29 ❑ Mar 1973 NM value: **3.00**
Circ: Statement: **163,156**
30 ❑ Apr 1973 Cover: 0.20 NM value: **3.00**
Circ: Statement: **163,156**
• Has 1972 Statement, filed 10/1/72; avg print run 316,069; avg sales 167,900; avg subs 105; avg total paid 168,005; samples 134; office use 1,583; max existent 169,722; 46% of run returned
31 ❑ Jun 1973 Cover: 0.20 NM value: **2.50**
Circ: Statement: **163,156**
32 ❑ Jul 1973 Cover: 0.20 NM value: **2.50**
Circ: Statement: **163,156**
33 ❑ Aug 1973 Cover: 0.20 NM value: **2.50**
Circ: Statement: **163,156**
34 ❑ Sep 1973 Cover: 0.20 NM value: **2.50**
Circ: Statement: **163,156**
35 ❑ Oct 1973 Cover: 0.20 NM value: **2.50**
Circ: Statement: **163,156**
36 ❑ Nov 1973 Cover: 0.20 NM value: **2.50**
Circ: Statement: **163,156**
37 ❑ Dec 1973 Cover: 0.20 NM value: **2.50**
Circ: Statement: **163,156**
38 ❑ Jan 1974 Cover: 0.50 NM value: **5.00**
Circ: Statement: **175,787** • **CGC:** 5 graded, best 9.2
39 ❑ Feb 1974 Cover: 0.20 NM value: **2.50**
Circ: Statement: **175,787**
40 ❑ Mar 1974 Cover: 0.20 NM value: **2.50**
Circ: Statement: **175,787**
41 ❑ Apr 1974 Cover: 0.20 NM value: **2.50**
Circ: Statement: **175,787**
• Has 1973 Statement, filed 10/1/73; avg print run 334,454; avg sales 162,934; avg subs 222; avg total paid 163,156; samples 100; office use 1,172; max existent 164,428; 51% of run returned
42 ❑ May 1974 NM value: **2.50**
Circ: Statement: **175,787**
43 ❑ Jun 1974 NM value: **2.50**
Circ: Statement: **175,787**

CGC-graded: Multiply prices above by **33 for 9.9 M • 16 for 9.8 NM/M • 7 for 9.6 NM+ • 5 for 9.4 NM • 2.5 for 9.2 NM- • 1.5 for 9.0 VF/NM**

44 ❑ Jul 1974 NM value: 2.50
Circ: Statement: 175,787

45 ❑ Aug 1974 NM value: 2.50
Circ: Statement: 175,787

46 ❑ Sep 1974 Cover: 0.20 NM value: 2.50
Circ: Statement: 175,787
📖 The Killer Game Slithering; Burial Insurance **A:** Lee Elias **W:** George Kashdan

47 ❑ Oct 1974 NM value: 2.50
Circ: Statement: 175,787

48 ❑ Nov 1974 NM value: 2.50
Circ: Statement: 175,787

49 ❑ Dec 1974 NM value: 2.50
Circ: Statement: 175,787

50 ❑ Jan 1975 NM value: 2.50
Circ: Statement: 188,000

51 ❑ Feb 1975 NM value: 2.00
Circ: Statement: 188,000

52 ❑ Mar 1975 NM value: 2.00
Circ: Statement: 188,000

53 ❑ Apr 1975 NM value: 2.00
Circ: Statement: 188,000 • **CGC:** 1 graded, best 9.2

54 ❑ May 1975 NM value: 2.00
Circ: Statement: 188,000
• Has 1974 Statement; avg total paid 175,787

55 ❑ Jun 1975 NM value: 2.00
Circ: Statement: 188,000 • **CGC:** 1 graded, best 9.4

56 ❑ Jul 1975 NM value: 2.00
Circ: Statement: 188,000

57 ❑ Aug 1975 NM value: 2.00
Circ: Statement: 188,000

58 ❑ Sep 1975 NM value: 2.00
Circ: Statement: 188,000

59 ❑ Oct 1975 NM value: 2.00
Circ: Statement: 188,000

60 ❑ Nov 1975 NM value: 2.00
Circ: Statement: 188,000

61 ❑ Jan 1976 NM value: 2.00
Circ: Statement: 134,000

62 ❑ Mar 1976 NM value: 2.00
Circ: Statement: 134,000

63 ❑ May 1976 NM value: 2.00
Circ: Statement: 134,000

64 ❑ Jun 1976 NM value: 2.00
Circ: Statement: 134,000 • **CGC:** 1 graded, best 9.4

65 ❑ Aug 1976 NM value: 2.00
Circ: Statement: 134,000 • **CGC:** 1 graded, best 9.2

66 ❑ Nov 1976 NM value: 2.00
Circ: Statement: 134,000

67 ❑ Jan 1977 NM value: 2.00
Circ: Statement: 115,157

68 ❑ Feb 1977 NM value: 2.00
Circ: Statement: 115,157

69 ❑ Mar 1977 NM value: 2.00
Circ: Statement: 115,157 • **CGC:** 1 graded, best 9.4

70 ❑ Apr 1977 NM value: 2.00
Circ: Statement: 115,157

71 ❑ May 1977 NM value: 2.00
Circ: Statement: 115,157
• Has 1976 Statement; avg total paid 134,000

72 ❑ Jul 1977 NM value: 2.00
Circ: Statement: 115,157 • **CGC:** 1 graded, best 9.2

73 ❑ Sep 1977 NM value: 2.00
Circ: Statement: 115,157

74 ❑ Oct 1977 NM value: 2.00
Circ: Statement: 115,157

75 ❑ Nov 1977 NM value: 2.00
Circ: Statement: 115,157

76 ❑ Jan 1978 Cover: 0.35 NM value: 2.00
77 ❑ Feb 1978 NM value: 2.00
78 ❑ Mar 1978 NM value: 2.00
79 ❑ Apr 1978 NM value: 2.00
80 ❑ May 1978 NM value: 2.00
• Has 1977 Statement; avg total paid 115,157
81 ❑ Jun 1978 NM value: 2.00
82 ❑ Jul 1978 NM value: 2.00
83 ❑ Aug 1978 NM value: 2.00
84 ❑ Sep 1978 NM value: 2.00
85 ❑ Oct 1978 NM value: 2.00
final issue.

WITCHING HOUR, THE (ANNE RICE'S...) Millennium

Horror novelist Anne Rice was made famous by her Vampire Lestat novels including Interview With the Vampire and Queen of the Damned. Her grasp of horror goes beyond mere vampires, however, as shown in this adaptation of her novel The Witching Hour.

The lushly painted story focuses on an antebellum mansion in New Orleans. Within that house, three maiden aunts care for a strangely quiet girl named Deirdre. Deirdre sits nearly catatonic on the porch, never speaking to anyone, although a succession of nurses have quit, citing vague "attacks." She has a regimen of thorazine injections that would kill someone unaccustomed to the drugs, and her aunts seem content to leave her that way. Her only visitor is a strange man who seems to disappear into the mist moments after he was seen.

1 ❑ 1992 Cover: 2.50 NM value: Cover or less
Circ: CapCity orders: 16,975

2 ❑ 1993 Cover: 2.50 NM value: Cover or less
• bound-in Talamasca business card **A:** Duncan Eagleson; John Bolton(cover) **C:** John Bolton **W:** Anne Rice; Terry Collins

3 ❑ 1993 Cover: 2.50 NM value: Cover or less
Circ: CapCity orders: 9,700

4 ❑ 1993 Cover: 2.50 NM value: Cover or less
Circ: CapCity orders: 6,325

5 ❑ Cover: 2.50 NM value: Cover or less
Circ: CapCity orders: 4,505

6 ❑ Cover: 2.50 NM value: Cover or less
Circ: CapCity orders: 4,490

7 ❑ Cover: 2.50 NM value: Cover or less
Circ: CapCity orders: 4,465

8 ❑ Cover: 2.50 NM value: Cover or less
Circ: CapCity orders: 5,150

9 ❑ Cover: 2.50 NM value: Cover or less
10 ❑ Cover: 2.50 NM value: Cover or less
11 ❑ Cover: 2.50 NM value: Cover or less
12 ❑ Cover: 2.50 NM value: Cover or less
13 ❑ Cover: 2.50 NM value: Cover or less

WITCHING HOUR, THE (VERTIGO) DC / Vertigo

1 ❑ Jan 2000 Cover: 5.95 NM value: Cover or less
Circ: Diamd. preorders: 21,485

2 ❑ Feb 2000 Cover: 5.95 NM value: Cover or less
Circ: Diamd. preorders: 18,119

3 ❑ Mar 2000 Cover: 5.95 NM value: Cover or less
Circ: Diamd. preorders: 19,055

Bk 1/HC❑ NM value: 29.95
no cover price. **A:** Chris Bachalo **W:** Jeph Loeb

WITHIN OUR REACH Star*Reach

1 ❑ Cover: 7.95 NM value: Cover or less
Circ: CapCity orders: 4,700
No issue number. 📖 Spider-Man: A Wolf at the Door; The Happy Prince; Brother Elf: A Gift of Peace; The Season of Forgiveness; Santa's Ashram; Gift of the Magi; So This is Christmas; Van Gogh: The Man Suicided by Society; Hom for Christmas; Concrete: American Christmas • Spider-Man, Concrete, Gift of the Magi; Christmas benefit comic **A:** Norm Breyfogle; Tim Sale; Rafael Kayanan; Jeff Butler; P. Craig Russell; Patrick Olliffe; Gary Kato; Eric Shanower; Paul Chadwick **W:** Norm Breyfogle; P. Craig Russell; Paul Chadwick; Lovern Kindzierski; Roy Thomas; Antonin Artaud; Dann Thomas; Martin Powell; O. Henry; Oscar Wilde; Ron Fortier; Shair

WITH THE MARINES ON THE BATTLEFRONTS OF THE WORLD Toby

1 ❑ ca. 1953 Cover: 0.10 NM value: 70.00
• **CGC:** 1 graded, best 8.0
• John Wayne story

2 ❑ ca. 1954 Cover: 0.10 NM value: 40.00
📖 The Man-Eating Idol; Kangaroo Court!; Trojan Camel **A:** Mel Keefer

WITNESS Marvel

1 ❑ Sep 1948 Cover: 0.10 NM value: 1250.00
• **CGC:** 2 graded, best 8.5

WITTY COMICS Chicago Nite Life News

1 ❑ ca. 1945 Cover: 0.10 NM value: 90.00
2 ❑ ca. 1945 Cover: 0.10 NM value: 55.00
📖 Pioneer; Michael Morgan; Poopsies; Dick Royce; Sir Gallagher; Circus Disaster (Text Story); Steve Hagen; Weeny and Pop **A:** Louis Ferstadt **W:** Louis Ferstadt; Sophie Freedman

WIZARD OF 4TH STREET, THE (DARK HORSE) Dark Horse

1 ❑ ca. 1987, b&w Cover: 1.75 NM value: 2.00
📖 Caper **A:** Phil Normand **W:** Simon Hawke
2 ❑ ca. 1987, b&w Cover: 1.75 NM value: 2.00
3 ❑ Cover: 1.75 NM value: 2.00
4 ❑ Cover: 1.75 NM value: 2.00
5 ❑ Cover: 1.75 NM value: 2.00
6 ❑ Cover: 1.75 NM value: 2.00

WIZARD OF 4TH STREET, THE (DAVID P. HOUSE) David P. House

1 ❑ Cover: 1.50 NM value: Cover or less
2 ❑ Cover: 1.50 NM value: Cover or less
3 ❑ Cover: 1.50 NM value: Cover or less

WIZARD OF TIME, THE DPH

1 ❑ Cover: 1.50 NM value: Cover or less
2 ❑ Oct 1986 Cover: 1.50 NM value: Cover or less

WIZARDS OF THE LAST RESORT Blackthorne

1 ❑ Feb 1987 Cover: 1.75 NM value: Cover or less
📖 The Odyssey of the Grey Beret **A:** Dok Rarity **W:** Dok Rarity
2 ❑ Apr 1987 Cover: 1.75 NM value: Cover or less
3 ❑ Jun 1987 Cover: 1.75 NM value: Cover or less
4 ❑ Aug 1987 Cover: 1.75 NM value: Cover or less

WIZARD'S TALE, THE Image

1 ❑ ca. 1997 Cover: 19.95 NM value: Cover or less
1/HC❑ Cover: 29.95 NM value: Cover or less

WIZARD WORKS Fantasy General

1 ❑ Cover: 1.70 NM value: Cover or less
📖 Sorcerer of the Black Void; The Sunshine Wizard; Terranauts **A:** Paul Daly; Francis J. Mao; Kalyn Shaible; Mickey Ritter; Tom Romano **W:** Don Secrease; Grant Fausey
2 ❑ Cover: 1.70 NM value: Cover or less
3 ❑ Cover: 1.70 NM value: Cover or less
4 ❑ Cover: 1.70 NM value: Cover or less

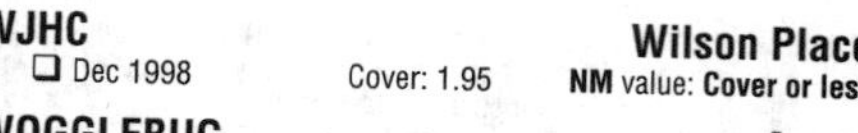

WJHC Wilson Place

1 ❑ Dec 1998 Cover: 1.95 NM value: Cover or less

WOGGLEBUG Arrow

1 ❑ Cover: 2.75 NM value: Cover or less

WOLF & RED Dark Horse

1 ❑ Apr 1995 Cover: 2.50 NM value: Cover or less
Circ: CapCity orders: 7,650
📖 Woo-ful Wolf; Lovestruck Lumberjacks • based on Tex Avery cartoons; Droopy back-up **A:** Jim Massara; Stephanie Gladden **W:** Henry Gilroy

2 ❑ May 1995 Cover: 2.50 NM value: Cover or less
Circ: CapCity orders: 6,050
• based on Tex Avery cartoons; Screwball Squirrel back-up

3 ❑ Jun 1995 Cover: 2.50 NM value: Cover or less
Circ: CapCity orders: 5,575
• based on Tex Avery cartoons; Droopy back-up

WOLFF & BYRD, COUNSELORS OF THE MACABRE Exhibit A Press

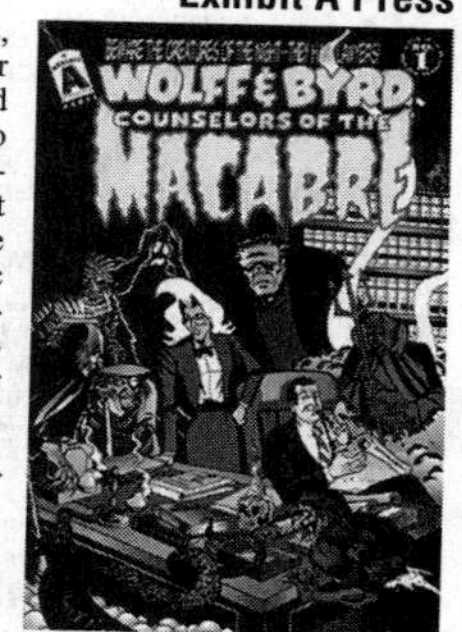

Who can swamp creatures, vampires, and ghouls turn to for legal help, when even spells and potions can't make lawsuits go away? Leave it to the intrepid legal team of Wolff & Byrd to fight for monsters' rights in court. The clever title transposes classic tales and characters of the supernatural into the context of the current litigious world. Like another comic-book lawyer, the Sensational She-Hulk, Wolff and Byrd have a well-developed sense of humor, which probably comes in handy when they have such cases as a light-sensitive demon complaining about being left in the dark on his legal case and a story about a living undead dog titled "Tails from the Crypt."

Batton Lash's Wolff & Byrd, Counselors of the Macabre had long appeared as a strip in Comics Buyer's Guide and The National Law Journal. This series marks its debut as a regular comic book.

1 ❑ May 1994 Cover: 2.50 NM value: 4.00
2 ❑ Jul 1994 Cover: 2.50 NM value: 3.00
3 ❑ Sep 1994 Cover: 2.50 NM value: 3.00
4 ❑ Nov 1994 Cover: 2.50 NM value: 3.00
5 ❑ Feb 1995 Cover: 2.50 NM value: 3.00
6 ❑ Apr 1995 Cover: 2.50 NM value: Cover or less
7 ❑ Jun 1995 Cover: 2.50 NM value: Cover or less
8 ❑ Sep 1995 Cover: 2.50 NM value: Cover or less
9 ❑ Nov 1995 Cover: 2.50 NM value: Cover or less
10 ❑ Feb 1996 Cover: 2.50 NM value: Cover or less
11 ❑ Apr 1996 Cover: 2.50 NM value: Cover or less
12 ❑ Aug 1996 Cover: 2.50 NM value: Cover or less
13 ❑ Oct 1996 Cover: 2.50 NM value: Cover or less
cover purposely upside down and backwards. **A:** Batton Lash **W:** Batton Lash
14 ❑ Jan 1997 Cover: 2.50 NM value: Cover or less
• Anne Rice parody **A:** Batton Lash **W:** Batton Lash
15 ❑ Mar 1997 Cover: 2.50 NM value: Cover or less
16 ❑ Jul 1997 Cover: 2.50 NM value: Cover or less
17 ❑ Oct 1997 Cover: 2.50 NM value: Cover or less
• Halloween issue; reprint strips **A:** Batton Lash **W:** Batton Lash
18 ❑ Mar 1998 Cover: 2.50 NM value: Cover or less
19 ❑ Apr 1998 Cover: 2.50 NM value: Cover or less
20 ❑ May 1998 Cover: 2.50 NM value: Cover or less
21 ❑ 1988 Cover: 2.50 NM value: Cover or less
22 ❑ Feb 1999 Cover: 2.50 NM value: Cover or less
Bk 1❑ b&w Cover: 8.95 NM value: 9.95
• Case Files; collects issues #1-4 **A:** Batton Lash **W:** Batton Lash
Bk 2❑ b&w Cover: 8.95 NM value: 9.95
• Case Files; Reprints Wolff & Byrd, Counselors of the Macabre #5-8 **A:** Batton Lash **W:** Batton Lash
Bk 3❑ b&w Cover: 8.95 NM value: 9.95
• Case Files; Reprints Wolff & Byrd, Counselors of the Macabre #9-12 **A:** Batton Lash **W:** Batton Lash
Bk 4❑ Jul 1998, b&w Cover: 10.95 NM value: Cover or less
• Case Files

WOLFF & BYRD, COUNSELORS OF THE MACABRE'S GREATEST WRITS Exhibit A Press

1 ❑ b&w Cover: 2.95 NM value: Cover or less
cardstock cover. 📖 Herbert has Risen from the Gravel; The Monkey's Law; Tail's from the Crypt; Terms of Interment; The Boogeyman • collects three stories **A:** Batton Lash **W:** Batton Lash

WOLFF & BYRD, COUNSELORS OF THE MACABRE'S SECRETARY MAVIS Exhibit A Press

1 ❑ Aug 1998 Cover: 2.95 NM value: Cover or less
2 ❑ Apr 1999 Cover: 2.95 NM value: Cover or less

WOLFF & BYRD: SUPERNATURAL LAW Exhibit A

1 ❑ Cover: 7.95 NM value: Cover or less
📖 Nine Points of the Law; The Rock 'n' Holy Roller; The Invasion of the Law Firm Snatchers; A Song of the Pitiful Poor • Reprints original Wolff & Byrd strips from The National Law Journal, American Fantasy, & The Brooklyn Paper **A:** Batton Lash **W:** Batton Lash

WOLFMAN Dell

1 ❑ Aug 1964 Cover: 0.12 NM value: 40.00
• **CGC:** 1 graded, best 9.2

Other grades: Multiply prices above by **1.5 for Mint • 2/3 for Very Fine • 1/3 for Fine • 1/5 for Very Good • 1/8 for Good**

WOLFPACK — Marvel

1 ❑ Aug 1988 Cover: 0.75 **NM** value: **1.00**
Circ: CapCity orders: **21,900**
📖 Crusade **A:** Ron Wilson **W:** Larry Hama ★ Origin of Wolfpack. ★ 1st Appearance of Wolfpack.

2 ❑ Sep 1988 Cover: 0.75 **NM** value: **1.00**
Circ: CapCity orders: **16,200**

3 ❑ Oct 1988 Cover: 0.75 **NM** value: **1.00**
Circ: CapCity orders: **12,900**

4 ❑ Nov 1988 Cover: 0.75 **NM** value: **1.00**
Circ: CapCity orders: **10,100**

5 ❑ Dec 1988 Cover: 0.75 **NM** value: **1.00**
Circ: CapCity orders: **9,100**

6 ❑ Jan 1989 Cover: 0.75 **NM** value: **1.00**
Circ: CapCity orders: **8,000**

7 ❑ Feb 1989 Cover: 0.75 **NM** value: **1.00**
Circ: CapCity orders: **7,300**

8 ❑ Mar 1989 Cover: 0.75 **NM** value: **1.00**
Circ: CapCity orders: **6,800**

9 ❑ Apr 1989 Cover: 0.75 **NM** value: **1.00**
Circ: CapCity orders: **6,500**

10 ❑ May 1989 Cover: 0.75 **NM** value: **1.00**
Circ: CapCity orders: **5,900**

11 ❑ Jun 1989 Cover: 0.75 **NM** value: **1.00**
Circ: CapCity orders: **5,700**

12 ❑ Jul 1989 Cover: 0.75 **NM** value: **1.00**
Circ: CapCity orders: **5,500**

Bk 1❑ Cover: 7.95 **NM** value: **Cover or less**

WOLF RUN-A KNOWN ASSOCIATES MYSTERY — Known Associates

1 ❑ b&w Cover: 2.50 **NM** value: **Cover or less**
No issue number.

WOLPH — Blackthorne

1 ❑ Cover: 2.00 **NM** value: **Cover or less**

WOLVERBROAD VS. HOBO — Spoof

1 ❑ b&w Cover: 2.95 **NM** value: **Cover or less**
• parody

WOLVERINE — Marvel

"I'm the best at what I do, but what I do isn't very nice."

He's Wolverine, a mutant with an accelerated healing factor who became part of an experiment to turn him into a living weapon. Now he has adamantium bonded to his skeleton and retractable claws that can slice steel like butter. He's a member of The Uncanny X-Men, but his no-holds-barred style of fighting causes constant friction with his more civilized teammates. As a result, he often prefers to handle things on his own.

He's been called both philosopher and psychotic, hero and killer. He's a man and a beast in one, and he's one of the most compelling characters ever to spring from the minds at Marvel.

-1 ❑ Jul 1997 Cover: 1.99 **NM** value: **2.00**
📖 A Wiff of Sartre's Madeleine • Flashback; Flashback issue **A:** Cary Nord; Card Nord **W:** Larry Hama ★ Appearance of Sabretooth, Carol Danvers, Nick Fury.

0.5 ❑ ca. 1997 **NM** value: **3.00**
• Wizard mail-away edition. **W:** Ben Raab

0.5/LE❑ca. 1997 **NM** value: **8.00**
• Blue foil **W:** Ben Raab

1 ❑ Nov 1988 Cover: 1.50 **NM** value: **15.00**
Circ: CapCity orders: **108,800** • **CGC:** 627 graded, best 9.9

2 ❑ Dec 1988 Cover: 1.50 **NM** value: **9.00**
Circ: CapCity orders: **78,700** • **CGC:** 81 graded, best 10.0

3 ❑ Jan 1989 Cover: 1.50 **NM** value: **7.00**
Circ: Statement: **308,675** CapCity orders: **71,100** • **CGC:** 75 graded, best 9.8

4 ❑ Feb 1989 Cover: 1.50 **NM** value: **7.00**
Circ: Statement: **308,675** CapCity orders: **63,100** • **CGC:** 50 graded, best 9.8

5 ❑ Mar 1989 Cover: 1.50 **NM** value: **7.00**
Circ: Statement: **308,675** CapCity orders: **59,500** • **CGC:** 28 graded, best 9.8

6 ❑ Apr 1989 Cover: 1.50 **NM** value: **6.00**
Circ: Statement: **308,675** CapCity orders: **56,500** • **CGC:** 30 graded, best 9.8

7 ❑ May 1989 Cover: 1.50 **NM** value: **6.00**
Circ: Statement: **308,675** CapCity orders: **55,000** • **CGC:** 19 graded, best 9.8

8 ❑ Jun 1989 Cover: 1.50 **NM** value: **6.00**
Circ: Statement: **308,675** CapCity orders: **55,200** • **CGC:** 28 graded, best 9.9

9 ❑ Jul 1989 Cover: 1.50 **NM** value: **6.00**
Circ: Statement: **308,675** CapCity orders: **54,900** • **CGC:** 17 graded, best 9.8

10 ❑ Aug 1989 Cover: 1.50 **NM** value: **10.00**
Circ: Statement: **308,675** CapCity orders: **53,400** • **CGC:** 227 graded, best 9.9
• vs. Sabretooth **A:** Bill Sienkiewicz ★ Versus Sabretooth.

11 ❑ Sep 1989 Cover: 1.50 **NM** value: **5.00**
Circ: Statement: **308,675** CapCity orders: **55,200** • **CGC:** 4 graded, best 9.8
• New Costume

12 ❑ Sep 1989 Cover: 1.50 **NM** value: **5.00**
Circ: Statement: **308,675** CapCity orders: **53,800** • **CGC:** 6 graded, best 9.6

13 ❑ Oct 1989 Cover: 1.50 **NM** value: **5.00**
Circ: Statement: **308,675** CapCity orders: **54,000**

14 ❑ Oct 1989 Cover: 1.50 **NM** value: **5.00**
Circ: Statement: **308,675** CapCity orders: **53,800** • **CGC:** 1 graded, best 9.4

15 ❑ Nov 1989 Cover: 1.50 **NM** value: **5.00**
Circ: Statement: **308,675** CapCity orders: **54,100**

16 ❑ Nov 1989 Cover: 1.50 **NM** value: **5.00**
Circ: Statement: **308,675** CapCity orders: **54,900**

17 ❑ Nov 1989 Cover: 1.50 **NM** value: **5.00**
Circ: Statement: **308,675** CapCity orders: **71,700** • **CGC:** 13 graded, best 9.8

18 ❑ Dec 1989 Cover: 1.50 **NM** value: **5.00**
Circ: Statement: **308,675** CapCity orders: **66,300** • **CGC:** 3 graded, best 9.8

19 ❑ Dec 1989 Cover: 1.50 **NM** value: **5.00**
Circ: Statement: **308,675** CapCity orders: **67,400**
📖 Acts of Vengeance • Acts of Vengeance **A:** John Byrne

20 ❑ Jan 1990 Cover: 1.50 **NM** value: **4.00**
Circ: Statement: **301,459** CapCity orders: **68,900** • **CGC:** 1 graded, best 9.6
📖 Acts of Vengeance • Acts of Vengeance **A:** John Byrne

21 ❑ Feb 1990 Cover: 1.50 **NM** value: **4.00**
Circ: Statement: **301,459** CapCity orders: **65,400** • **CGC:** 1 graded, best 9.6

22 ❑ Mar 1990 Cover: 1.50 **NM** value: **4.00**
Circ: Statement: **301,459** CapCity orders: **63,500**

23 ❑ Apr 1990 Cover: 1.50 **NM** value: **4.00**
Circ: Statement: **301,459** CapCity orders: **61,800**

24 ❑ May 1990 Cover: 1.50 **NM** value: **3.00**
Circ: Statement: **301,459** CapCity orders: **57,100**
• Has 1989 Statement, filed 11/1/89; avg print run 480,653; avg sales 303,520; avg subs 5,155; avg total paid 308,675; samples 125; office use 600; max existent 309,400; 36% of run returned

25 ❑ Jun 1990 Cover: 1.50 **NM** value: **3.00**
Circ: Statement: **301,459** CapCity orders: **58,300**

26 ❑ Jul 1990 Cover: 1.75 **NM** value: **3.00**
Circ: Statement: **301,459** CapCity orders: **58,800**

27 ❑ Jul 1990 Cover: 1.75 **NM** value: **3.00**
Circ: Statement: **301,459** CapCity orders: **58,500**
📖 Lazarus Project

28 ❑ Aug 1990 Cover: 1.75 **NM** value: **3.00**
Circ: Statement: **301,459** CapCity orders: **56,000**
📖 Lazarus Project

29 ❑ Aug 1990 Cover: 1.75 **NM** value: **3.00**
Circ: Statement: **301,459** CapCity orders: **55,700**
📖 Lazarus Project

30 ❑ Sep 1990 Cover: 1.75 **NM** value: **3.00**
Circ: Statement: **301,459** CapCity orders: **54,100**
📖 Lazarus Project

31 ❑ Sep 1990 Cover: 1.75 **NM** value: **2.50**
Circ: Statement: **301,459** CapCity orders: **54,300**

32 ❑ Oct 1990 Cover: 1.75 **NM** value: **2.50**
Circ: Statement: **301,459** CapCity orders: **51,500**

33 ❑ Nov 1990 Cover: 1.75 **NM** value: **2.50**
Circ: Statement: **301,459** CapCity orders: **49,500**

34 ❑ Dec 1990 Cover: 1.75 **NM** value: **2.50**
Circ: Statement: **301,459** CapCity orders: **50,000**

35 ❑ Jan 1991 Cover: 1.75 **NM** value: **2.50**
Circ: CapCity orders: **49,300**

36 ❑ Feb 1991 Cover: 1.75 **NM** value: **2.50**
Circ: CapCity orders: **49,100**

37 ❑ Mar 1991 Cover: 1.75 **NM** value: **2.50**
Circ: CapCity orders: **48,300**

38 ❑ Apr 1991 Cover: 1.75 **NM** value: **2.50**
Circ: CapCity orders: **47,400**
• Has 1990 Statement, filed 10/1/90; avg print run 480,653; avg sales 303,520; avg subs 6,093; avg total paid 301,459; samples 150; office use 600; max existent 302,209; 33% of run returned

39 ❑ May 1991 Cover: 1.75 **NM** value: **2.50**
Circ: CapCity orders: **48,800**

40 ❑ Jun 1991 Cover: 1.75 **NM** value: **2.50**
Circ: CapCity orders: **49,700**

41 ❑ Jul 1991 Cover: 1.75 **NM** value: **4.00**
Circ: CapCity orders: **55,200** • **CGC:** 5 graded, best 9.8

41-2❑Jul 1991 Cover: 1.75 **NM** value: **Cover or less**

42 ❑ Jul 1991 Cover: 1.75 **NM** value: **2.00**
Circ: CapCity orders: **56,100** • **CGC:** 2 graded, best 9.8

42-2❑Jul 1991 Cover: 1.75 **NM** value: **Cover or less**

43 ❑ Aug 1991 Cover: 1.75 **NM** value: **3.00**
Circ: CapCity orders: **79,500**

44 ❑ Aug 1991 Cover: 1.75 **NM** value: **2.00**
Circ: CapCity orders: **71,200**

45 ❑ Sep 1991 Cover: 1.75 **NM** value: **2.50**
Circ: CapCity orders: **71,500**

46 ❑ Sep 1991 Cover: 1.75 **NM** value: **2.50**
Circ: CapCity orders: **74,600**

47 ❑ Oct 1991 Cover: 1.75 **NM** value: **2.50**
Circ: CapCity orders: **65,400**

48 ❑ Nov 1991 Cover: 1.75 **NM** value: **2.50**
Circ: CapCity orders: **73,500** • **CGC:** 1 graded, best 9.8
📖 Weapon X sequel • Logan's past

49 ❑ Dec 1991 Cover: 1.75 **NM** value: **2.50**
Circ: CapCity orders: **80,700**
📖 Weapon X sequel • Logan's past

50 ❑ Jan 1992 Cover: 2.50 **NM** value: **4.00**
Circ: CapCity orders: **198,900** • **CGC:** 25 graded, best 9.8
diecut cover. 📖 Weapon X sequel ★ 1st Appearance of Shiva.

51 ❑ Feb 1992 Cover: 1.75 **NM** value: **2.00**
Circ: CapCity orders: **76,500**

52 ❑ Mar 1992 Cover: 1.75 **NM** value: **2.00**
Circ: CapCity orders: **73,500**

53 ❑ Apr 1992 Cover: 1.75 **NM** value: **2.00**
Circ: CapCity orders: **73,800**

54 ❑ May 1992 Cover: 1.75 **NM** value: **2.00**
Circ: CapCity orders: **76,200**

55 ❑ Jun 1992 Cover: 1.75 **NM** value: **2.00**
Circ: CapCity orders: **81,600**

56 ❑ Jul 1992 Cover: 1.75 **NM** value: **2.00**
Circ: CapCity orders: **81,600**

57 ❑ Jul 1992 Cover: 1.75 **NM** value: **3.00**
Circ: CapCity orders: **82,400**

58 ❑ Aug 1992 Cover: 1.75 **NM** value: **2.00**
Circ: CapCity orders: **83,100**

59 ❑ Aug 1992 Cover: 1.75 **NM** value: **2.00**
Circ: CapCity orders: **80,700**

60 ❑ Sep 1992 Cover: 1.75 **NM** value: **2.00**
Circ: CapCity orders: **84,000** • **CGC:** 4 graded, best 9.8

61 ❑ Sep 1992 Cover: 1.75 **NM** value: **2.00**
Circ: CapCity orders: **82,800**

62 ❑ Oct 1992 Cover: 1.75 **NM** value: **2.00**
Circ: CapCity orders: **81,300**

63 ❑ Nov 1992 Cover: 1.75 **NM** value: **2.00**
Circ: CapCity orders: **82,800**

64 ❑ Dec 1992 Cover: 1.75 **NM** value: **2.00**
Circ: CapCity orders: **74,400**

65 ❑ Jan 1993 Cover: 1.75 **NM** value: **2.00**
Circ: Statement: **396,958** CapCity orders: **70,200**

66 ❑ Feb 1993 Cover: 1.75 **NM** value: **2.00**
Circ: Statement: **396,958** CapCity orders: **73,200**

67 ❑ Mar 1993 Cover: 1.75 **NM** value: **2.00**
Circ: Statement: **396,958** CapCity orders: **71,700**

68 ❑ Apr 1993 Cover: 1.75 **NM** value: **2.00**
Circ: Statement: **396,958** CapCity orders: **75,600**

69 ❑ May 1993 Cover: 1.75 **NM** value: **2.00**
Circ: Statement: **396,958** CapCity orders: **73,700**

70 ❑ Jun 1993 Cover: 1.75 **NM** value: **2.00**
Circ: Statement: **396,958** CapCity orders: **73,000**

71 ❑ Jul 1993 Cover: 1.75 **NM** value: **2.00**
Circ: Statement: **396,958** CapCity orders: **71,400**

72 ❑ Aug 1993 Cover: 1.75 **NM** value: **2.00**
Circ: Statement: **396,958** CapCity orders: **72,500**

73 ❑ Sep 1993 Cover: 1.75 **NM** value: **2.00**
Circ: Statement: **396,958** CapCity orders: **88,900**

74 ❑ Oct 1993 Cover: 1.75 **NM** value: **2.00**
Circ: Statement: **396,958** CapCity orders: **70,000**

75 ❑ Nov 1993 Cover: 3.95 **NM** value: **5.00**
Circ: Statement: **396,958** CapCity orders: **136,500** • **CGC:** 20 graded, best 9.9
• hologram; Wolverine loses adamantium skeleton

76 ❑ Dec 1993 Cover: 1.75 **NM** value: **2.00**
Circ: Statement: **396,958** CapCity orders: **77,400**

77 ❑ Jan 1994 Cover: 1.75 **NM** value: **2.00**
Circ: Statement: **380,383** CapCity orders: **69,800**
📖 The Lady Strikes **A:** Adam Kubert **W:** Larry Hama

78 ❑ Feb 1994 Cover: 1.75 **NM** value: **2.00**
Circ: Statement: **380,383** CapCity orders: **72,200**

79 ❑ Mar 1994 Cover: 1.75 **NM** value: **2.00**
Circ: Statement: **380,383** CapCity orders: **68,450** • **CGC:** 1 graded, best 9.6

80 ❑ Apr 1994 Cover: 1.75 **NM** value: **2.00**
Circ: Statement: **380,383** CapCity orders: **69,200**

81 ❑ May 1994 Cover: 1.95 **NM** value: **2.00**
Circ: Statement: **380,383** CapCity orders: **66,400**

82 ❑ Jun 1994 Cover: 1.95 **NM** value: **2.00**
Circ: Statement: **380,383** CapCity orders: **71,900**

83 ❑ Jul 1994 Cover: 1.95 **NM** value: **2.00**
Circ: Statement: **380,383** CapCity orders: **78,300**

84 ❑ Aug 1994 Cover: 1.95 **NM** value: **2.00**
Circ: Statement: **380,383** CapCity orders: **79,300**

85 ❑ Sep 1994 Cover: 2.50 **NM** value: **Cover or less**
📖 Final Sanction; Final Sanction, Part 1

85/SC❑Sep 1994 Cover: 3.50 **NM** value: **Cover or less**
Circ: Statement: **380,383** CapCity orders: **97,950** • **CGC:** 2 graded, best 9.6
enhanced cover. 📖 Final Sanction, Part 1

86 ❑ Oct 1994 Cover: 1.95 **NM** value: **2.00**
Circ: Statement: **380,383** CapCity orders: **75,050**

87 ❑ Nov 1994 Cover: 1.50 **NM** value: **Cover or less**

87/Dlx❑Nov 1994 Cover: 1.95 **NM** value: **2.00**
Circ: Statement: **380,383** CapCity orders: **74,000**
• Deluxe edition.

88 ❑ Dec 1994 Cover: 1.50 **NM** value: **Cover or less**

88/Dlx❑Dec 1994 Cover: 1.95 **NM** value: **2.00**
Circ: Statement: **334,592** CapCity orders: **76,300**
• Deluxe edition.

89 ❑ Jan 1995 Cover: 1.50 **NM** value: **Cover or less**

89/Dlx❑Jan 1995 Cover: 1.95 **NM** value: **2.00**
Circ: Statement: **334,592** CapCity orders: **72,650**
• Deluxe edition.

90 ❑ Feb 1995 Cover: 1.50 **NM** value: **Cover or less**
• **CGC:** 1 graded, best 9.4

90/Dlx❑Feb 1995 Cover: 1.95 **NM** value: **2.00**
Circ: Statement: **334,592** CapCity orders: **82,325** • **CGC:** 1 graded, best 9.4
• Deluxe edition.

91 ❑ Jul 1995 Cover: 1.95 **NM** value: **2.00**
Circ: Statement: **334,592** CapCity orders: **79,300**
• Has 1994 Statement, filed 10/1/94; avg print run 504,175; avg sales 374,675; avg subs 5,708; avg total paid 380,383; samples 125; office use 500; max existent 381,008; 24% of run returned

92 ❑ Aug 1995 Cover: 1.95 **NM** value: **2.00**
Circ: Statement: **334,592**

93 ❑ Sep 1995 Cover: 1.95 **NM** value: **2.00**
Circ: Statement: **334,592**

94 ❑ Oct 1995 Cover: 1.95 **NM** value: **2.00**
Circ: Statement: **334,592**

95 ❑ Nov 1995 Cover: 1.95 **NM** value: **2.00**
Circ: Statement: **334,592**

96 ❑ Dec 1995 Cover: 1.95 **NM** value: **2.00**
Circ: Statement: **266,815**

97 ❑ Jan 1996 Cover: 1.95 **NM** value: **2.00**
Circ: Statement: **266,815**

98 ❑ Feb 1996 Cover: 1.95 **NM** value: **2.00**
Circ: Statement: **266,815**

CGC-graded: Multiply prices above by **33 for 9.9 M • 16 for 9.8 NM/M • 7 for 9.6 NM+ • 5 for 9.4 NM • 2.5 for 9.2 NM- • 1.5 for 9.0 VF/NM**

Fade to Black • Has 1995 Statement, filed 10/1/95; avg print run 556,200; avg sales 327,122; avg subs 7,470; avg total paid 334,592; samples 750; office use 500; max existent 335,842; 41% of run returned **A:** Ramon Bernado **W:** Larry Hama

99 ❑ Mar 1996 Cover: 1.95 **NM** value: **4.00**
Circ: Statement: **266,815**

100 ❑ Apr 1996 Cover: 2.95 **NM** value: **4.00**
Circ: Statement: **266,815** • **CGC:** 3 graded, best 9.8

100/SC❑Apr 1996 Cover: 3.95 **NM** value: **7.50**
Circ: Statement: **266,815** • **CGC:** 22 graded, best 9.8
enhanced cardstock cover with hologram.

101 ❑ May 1996 Cover: 1.95 **NM** value: **2.00**
Circ: Statement: **266,815**

102 ❑ Jun 1996 Cover: 1.95 **NM** value: **2.00**
Circ: Statement: **266,815**

103 ❑ Jul 1996 Cover: 1.95 **NM** value: **2.00**
Circ: Statement: **266,815**

104 ❑ Aug 1996 Cover: 1.95 **NM** value: **2.00**
Circ: Statement: **266,815**

105 ❑ Sep 1996 Cover: 1.95 **NM** value: **2.00**
Circ: Statement: **251,738**
Onslaught: Impact 2 ★ Appearance of Stick.

106 ❑ Oct 1996 Cover: 1.95 **NM** value: **2.00**
Circ: Statement: **251,738**

107 ❑ Nov 1996 Cover: 1.95 **NM** value: **2.00**
Circ: Statement: **251,738** Direct Market orders: **184,500**
• Has 1996 Statement, filed 10/1/96; avg print run 410,919; avg sales 258,508; avg subs 8,307; avg total paid 266,815; samples 600; office use 125; max existent 267,540; 35% of run returned

108 ❑ Dec 1996 Cover: 1.95 **NM** value: **2.00**
Circ: Statement: **251,738** Direct Market orders: **179,775**

109 ❑ Jan 1997 Cover: 1.95 **NM** value: **2.00**
Circ: Statement: **251,738** Direct Market orders: **172,250**

110 ❑ Feb 1997 Cover: 1.95 **NM** value: **2.00**
Circ: Statement: **251,738** Direct Market orders: **160,250**
Lesser Beasts **A:** Joe Bennett **W:** Tom DeFalco ★ Appearance of Shaman.

111 ❑ Mar 1997 Cover: 1.95 **NM** value: **2.00**
Circ: Statement: **251,738** Direct Market orders: **147,750**
Restoration **A:** Anthony Winn **W:** Larry Hama

112 ❑ Apr 1997 Cover: 1.95 **NM** value: **2.00**
Circ: Statement: **251,738** Direct Market orders: **140,250** • **CGC:** 1 graded, best 9.6

113 ❑ May 1997 Cover: 1.95 **NM** value: **2.00**
Circ: Statement: **251,738** Diamd. preorders: **137,261**
The Wind From The East **A:** Leinil Francis Yu **W:** Larry Hama

114 ❑ Jun 1997 Cover: 1.95 **NM** value: **2.00**
Circ: Statement: **251,738** Diamd. preorders: **139,554**

115 ❑ Aug 1997 Cover: 1.99 **NM** value: **2.00**
Circ: Statement: **251,738** Diamd. preorders: **137,277**
• gatefold summary. Operation Zero Tolerance

116 ❑ Sep 1997 Cover: 1.99 **NM** value: **2.00**
Circ: Diamd. preorders: **132,563**
• gatefold summary. Operation Zero Tolerance

117 ❑ Oct 1997 Cover: 1.99 **NM** value: **2.00**
Circ: Diamd. preorders: **130,482**
• gatefold summary. Operation Zero Tolerance ★ Appearance of Jubilee.

118 ❑ Nov 1997 Cover: 1.99 **NM** value: **2.00**
Circ: Diamd. preorders: **128,317**
• gatefold summary. Operation Zero Tolerance Epilogue ★ Appearance of Jubilee.

119 ❑ Dec 1997 Cover: 1.99 **NM** value: **2.00**
Circ: Diamd. preorders: **127,250**
• gatefold summary. Not Dead Yet, Part 1 • Has 1997 Statement; avg total paid 251,738

120 ❑ Jan 1998 Cover: 1.99 **NM** value: **2.00**
Circ: Diamd. preorders: **125,207**
• gatefold summary. Not Dead Yet, Part 2

121 ❑ Feb 1998 Cover: 1.99 **NM** value: **2.00**
Circ: Diamd. preorders: **121,830**
Not Dead Yet, Part 3

122 ❑ Mar 1998 Cover: 1.99 **NM** value: **2.00**
Circ: Diamd. preorders: **116,702**
• gatefold summary.

123 ❑ Apr 1998 Cover: 1.99 **NM** value: **2.00**
Circ: Diamd. preorders: **107,060**
• gatefold summary.

124 ❑ May 1998 Cover: 1.99 **NM** value: **2.00**
Circ: Diamd. preorders: **105,978**
• gatefold summary. ★ Appearance of Captain America.

125 ❑ Jun 1998 Cover: 2.99 **NM** value: **3.50**
Circ: Diamd. preorders: **122,933**
wraparound cover. • gatefold summary. ★ Appearance of Lady Hydra.

125/A❑Jun 1998 Cover: 10.00 **NM** value: **Cover or less**
DFE alternate cover.

125/B❑Jun 1998 Cover: 19.95 **NM** value: **Cover or less**
DFE alternate cover.

126 ❑ Jul 1998 Cover: 1.99 **NM** value: **Cover or less**
Circ: Diamd. preorders: **107,629** • **CGC:** 1 graded, best 8.5
• gatefold summary. ★ Versus Lady Hydra. ★ Versus Sabretooth.

127 ❑ Aug 1998 Cover: 1.99 **NM** value: **Cover or less**
Circ: Diamd. preorders: **107,617**
• gatefold summary. ★ Versus Sabretooth.

128 ❑ Sep 1998 Cover: 1.99 **NM** value: **Cover or less**
Circ: Diamd. preorders: **104,689**
• gatefold summary. ★ Appearance of Shadow Cat, Viper. ★ Versus Sabretooth.

129 ❑ Oct 1998 Cover: 1.99 **NM** value: **Cover or less**
Circ: Statement: **146,962** Diamd. preorders: **101,540**
• gatefold summary.

130 ❑ Nov 1998 Cover: 1.99 **NM** value: **Cover or less**
Circ: Statement: **146,962** Diamd. preorders: **100,452**
• gatefold summary.

131 ❑ Nov 1998 Cover: 1.99 **NM** value: **Cover or less**
Circ: Statement: **146,962** Diamd. preorders: **102,273** • **CGC:** 5 graded, best 9.6
• gatefold summary. • error on Page 6, issue recalled

131/A❑Nov 1998 Cover: 1.99 **NM** value: **Cover or less**
Circ: Statement: **146,962** • **CGC:** 3 graded, best 9.6
• Corrected edition.

132 ❑ Dec 1998 Cover: 1.99 **NM** value: **Cover or less**
Circ: Statement: **146,962** Diamd. preorders: **100,447**
• gatefold summary.

133 ❑ Jan 1999 Cover: 1.99 **NM** value: **Cover or less**
Circ: Statement: **146,962** Diamd. preorders: **104,097** • **CGC:** 1 graded, best 9.8
• gatefold summary. The Great Escape ★ Appearance of Warbird.

134 ❑ Feb 1999 Cover: 1.99 **NM** value: **Cover or less**
Circ: Statement: **146,962** Diamd. preorders: **95,889**
• gatefold summary. **A:** Jeff Matsuda **W:** Erik Larsen ★ Versus Everybody.

135 ❑ Feb 1999 Cover: 1.99 **NM** value: **Cover or less**
Circ: Statement: **146,962** Diamd. preorders: **94,886**

136 ❑ Mar 1999 Cover: 1.99 **NM** value: **Cover or less**
Circ: Statement: **146,962** Diamd. preorders: **92,169** • **CGC:** 1 graded, best 9.8

137 ❑ Apr 1999 Cover: 1.99 **NM** value: **Cover or less**
Circ: Statement: **146,962** Diamd. preorders: **88,533**

138 ❑ May 1999 Cover: 1.99 **NM** value: **Cover or less**
Circ: Statement: **146,962** Diamd. preorders: **88,075**

139 ❑ Jun 1999 Cover: 1.99 **NM** value: **Cover or less**
Circ: Statement: **146,962** Diamd. preorders: **88,476**

140 ❑ Jul 1999 Cover: 1.99 **NM** value: **Cover or less**
Circ: Statement: **146,962** Diamd. preorders: **85,781**
Vengeance **A:** Leinil Francis Yu **W:** Erik Larsen ★ Appearance of Nightcrawler. ★ Versus Solo. ★ Versus Cardiac.

141 ❑ Aug 1999 Cover: 1.99 **NM** value: **Cover or less**
Circ: Statement: **146,962** Diamd. preorders: **85,752**

142 ❑ Sep 1999 Cover: 1.99 **NM** value: **Cover or less**
Circ: Statement: **146,962** Diamd. preorders: **83,547** • **CGC:** 1 graded, best 9.0

144 ❑ Nov 1999 Cover: 1.99 **NM** value: **Cover or less**
Circ: Diamd. preorders: **80,502**

145 ❑ Dec 1999 Cover: 1.99 **NM** value: **Cover or less**
Circ: Diamd. preorders: **76,598** • **CGC:** 2 graded, best 9.6

146 ❑ Jan 2000 Cover: 1.99 **NM** value: **2.25**
Circ: Diamd. preorders: **83,843** • **CGC:** 1 graded, best 9.6

147 ❑ Feb 2000 Cover: 1.99 **NM** value: **2.25**
Circ: Diamd. preorders: **84,710** • **CGC:** 1 graded, best 9.6

148 ❑ Mar 2000 Cover: 1.99 **NM** value: **2.25**
Circ: Diamd. preorders: **87,851**

149 ❑ Apr 2000 Cover: 1.99 **NM** value: **2.25**
Circ: Diamd. preorders: **81,153**

150 ❑ May 2000 Cover: 2.99 **NM** value: **Cover or less**
Circ: Diamd. preorders: **99,054**
• Giant-size. Blood Debt **A:** Steve Skroce **W:** Steve Skroce

151 ❑ Jun 2000 Cover: 2.25 **NM** value: **Cover or less**
Circ: Diamd. preorders: **83,576**

152 ❑ Jul 2000 Cover: 2.25 **NM** value: **Cover or less**
Circ: Diamd. preorders: **81,365**

153 ❑ Aug 2000 Cover: 2.25 **NM** value: **Cover or less**
Circ: Diamd. preorders: **83,794**

154 ❑ Sep 2000 Cover: 2.25 **NM** value: **Cover or less**
Circ: Diamd. preorders: **81,999**

155 ❑ Oct 2000 Cover: 2.25 **NM** value: **Cover or less**
Circ: Statement: **102,032** Diamd. preorders: **75,775**
All Along the Watchtower, Part 2 **A:** Rob Liefeld **C:** Rob Liefeld **W:** Rob Liefeld ★ Appearance of Deadpool.

156 ❑ Nov 2000 Cover: 2.25 **NM** value: **Cover or less**
Circ: Statement: **102,032** Diamd. preorders: **77,479**
Going Underground **A:** Ian Churchill **W:** Rob Liefeld ★ Appearance of Spider-Man.

157 ❑ Dec 2000 Cover: 2.25 **NM** value: **Cover or less**
Circ: Statement: **102,032** Diamd. preorders: **79,132**

158 ❑ Jan 2001 Cover: 2.25 **NM** value: **Cover or less**
Circ: Statement: **102,032** Diamd. preorders: **77,481**
Manhunt • polybagged with Marvel Online CD-ROM **A:** Sunny Lee **W:** Joe Pruett

159 ❑ Feb 2001 Cover: 2.25 **NM** value: **Cover or less**
Circ: Statement: **102,032** Diamd. preorders: **77,327**
The Best There Is, Part 1 **A:** Sean Chen **W:** Frank Tieri

160 ❑ Mar 2001 Cover: 2.25 **NM** value: **Cover or less**
Circ: Statement: **102,032** Diamd. preorders: **74,789**
The Best There Is, Part 2 **A:** Sean Chen **W:** Frank Tieri

161 ❑ Apr 2001 Cover: 2.25 **NM** value: **Cover or less**
Circ: Statement: **102,032** Diamd. preorders: **73,631**
The Best There Is, Part 3 **A:** Sean Chen **W:** Frank Tieri

162 ❑ May 2001 Cover: 2.25 **NM** value: **Cover or less**
Circ: Statement: **102,032** Diamd. preorders: **72,785**
The Hunted **A:** Sean Chen **W:** Frank Tieri

163 ❑ Jun 2001 Cover: 2.25 **NM** value: **Cover or less**
Circ: Statement: **102,032** Diamd. preorders: **73,052**

164 ❑ Jul 2001 Cover: 2.25 **NM** value: **Cover or less**
Circ: Statement: **102,032** Diamd. preorders: **72,672**

165 ❑ Aug 2001 Cover: 2.25 **NM** value: **Cover or less**
Circ: Statement: **102,032** Diamd. preorders: **73,153**

166 ❑ Sep 2001 Cover: 2.25 **NM** value: **Cover or less**
Circ: Statement: **102,032** Diamd. preorders: **80,069** • **CGC:** 5 graded, best 9.8

166/A❑Sep 2001 Cover: 39.99 **NM** value: **Cover or less**

167 ❑ Oct 2001 Cover: 2.25 **NM** value: **Cover or less**
Circ: Diamd. preorders: **79,865** • **CGC:** 1 graded, best 9.6

168 ❑ Nov 2001 Cover: 2.25 **NM** value: **Cover or less**
Circ: Diamd. preorders: **76,369**

169 ❑ Dec 2001 Cover: 2.25 **NM** value: **Cover or less**
Circ: Diamd. preorders: **76,518**

170 ❑ Jan 2002 Cover: 2.25 **NM** value: **Cover or less**
Circ: Diamd. preorders: **78,776**

171 ❑ Feb 2002 Cover: 2.25 **NM** value: **Cover or less**
Circ: Diamd. preorders: **78,360**
• Has 2001 Statement, filed 10/1/01; avg print run 146,108; avg sales 97,116; avg subs 4,916; avg total paid 102,032; samples 600; max existent 102,632; 30% of run returned

172 ❑ Mar 2002 Cover: 2.25 **NM** value: **Cover or less**
Circ: Diamd. preorders: **76,825**

Anl 1995❑Sep 1995 Cover: 3.95 **NM** value: **Cover or less**

Anl 1996❑Oct 1996 Cover: 2.95 **NM** value: **Cover or less**
No issue number. wraparound cover. ★ Versus Red Ronin.

Anl 1997❑ca. 1997 Cover: 2.99 **NM** value: **Cover or less**
Circ: Diamd. preorders: **86,636**
wraparound cover. • gatefold summary.

Anl 1999❑ca. 1999 Cover: 3.50 **NM** value: **Cover or less**
Circ: Diamd. preorders: **54,004**

Bk 1❑ Cover: 16.95 **NM** value: **Cover or less**
Circ: CapCity orders: **9,450**
Triumphs and Tragedies **A:** John Byrne; Frank Miller; Marc Silvestri **W:** Chris Claremont ★ Appearance of Sabretooth, Hand.

Bk 2❑ Cover: 14.95 **NM** value: **Cover or less**
Not Dead Yet • Collects issues #119-122 ★ Appearance of McLeish.

SE 1❑ Win 1999 Cover: 2.99 **NM** value: **Cover or less**
Circ: Diamd. preorders: **50,854**
• Blue Print edition.

WOLVERINE AND GHOST RIDER IN ACTS OF VENGEANCE — Marvel

Bk 1❑ Cover: 6.95 **NM** value: **Cover or less**
• book reprint

WOLVERINE AND THE PUNISHER: DAMAGING EVIDENCE — Marvel

1 ❑ Oct 1993 Cover: 2.00 **NM** value: **Cover or less**
Circ: CapCity orders: **57,600**

2 ❑ Nov 1993 Cover: 2.00 **NM** value: **Cover or less**
Circ: CapCity orders: **45,000**

3 ❑ Dec 1993 Cover: 2.00 **NM** value: **Cover or less**
Circ: CapCity orders: **40,900**

WOLVERINE BATTLEBOOK — Battlebooks

1 ❑ Cover: 3.99 **NM** value: **Cover or less**

1/A ❑ Cover: 4.95 **NM** value: **Cover or less**
• Blue Print edition. **A:** Bill Tucci

WOLVERINE BATTLES THE INCREDIBLE HULK — Marvel

1 ❑ ca. 1989 Cover: 4.95 **NM** value: **Cover or less**
• **CGC:** 1 graded, best 9.6
No issue number. • reprints Incredible Hulk #180 and #181

WOLVERINE: BLACK RIO — Marvel

1 ❑ Nov 1998 Cover: 5.99 **NM** value: **Cover or less**
Circ: Diamd. preorders: **35,442** • **CGC:** 1 graded, best 9.6

WOLVERINE: BLOOD HUNGRY! — Marvel

1 ❑ ca. 1993 Cover: 6.95 **NM** value: **Cover or less**
No issue number. • reprint stories

WOLVERINE: BLOODLUST — Marvel

1 ❑ Dec 1990 Cover: 4.95 **NM** value: **Cover or less**
Circ: CapCity orders: **37,600**
No issue number. **A:** Alan Davis; Paul Neary **W:** Alan Davis; Paul Neary

WOLVERINE: BLOODY CHOICES — Marvel

1 ❑ ca. 1993 Cover: 7.95 **NM** value: **Cover or less**
Circ: CapCity orders: **9,200**

WOLVERINE: DAYS OF FUTURE PAST — Marvel

1 ❑ Dec 1997 Cover: 2.50 **NM** value: **Cover or less**
Circ: Diamd. preorders: **106,333**
• gatefold summary. • Wolverine in early 21st century

2 ❑ Jan 1998 Cover: 2.50 **NM** value: **Cover or less**
Circ: Diamd. preorders: **86,295**
• gatefold summary. • Wolverine in early 21st century

3 ❑ Feb 1998 Cover: 2.50 **NM** value: **Cover or less**
Circ: Diamd. preorders: **83,194**
• gatefold summary. • Wolverine in early 21st century

WOLVERINE: DOOMBRINGER — Marvel

1 ❑ Nov 1997 Cover: 5.99 **NM** value: **Cover or less**

1/SC❑ Cover: 14.95 **NM** value: **Cover or less**
foil cover. **A:** Michal Dutkiewicz **W:** Doug Moench

WOLVERINE: EVILUTION — Marvel

1 ❑ Sep 1994 Cover: 5.95 **NM** value: **Cover or less**
Circ: CapCity orders: **36,450**
• Direct Edition. **A:** John Royle **W:** Ann Nocenti

WOLVERINE/GAMBIT: VICTIMS — Marvel

1 ❑ Sep 1995 Cover: 2.95 **NM** value: **Cover or less**
enhanced cardstock cover. **A:** Tim Sale **W:** Jeph Loeb

2 ❑ Oct 1995 Cover: 2.95 **NM** value: **Cover or less**
enhanced cardstock cover. **A:** Tim Sale **W:** Jeph Loeb

3 ❑ Nov 1995 Cover: 2.95 **NM** value: **Cover or less**
enhanced cardstock cover. **A:** Tim Sale **W:** Jeph Loeb

4 ❑ Dec 1995 Cover: 2.95 **NM** value: **Cover or less**
enhanced cardstock cover. **A:** Tim Sale **W:** Jeph Loeb ★ Appearance of Mastermind, Arcade.

Bk 1❑ Cover: 12.95 **NM** value: **Cover or less**
• Collects Wolverine/Gambit: Victims #1-4 **A:** Tim Sale **W:** Jeph Loeb ★ Appearance of Mastermind, Arcade.

WOLVERINE: GLOBAL JEOPARDY — Marvel

1 ❑ Dec 1993 Cover: 2.95 **NM** value: **Cover or less**
Circ: CapCity orders: **28,200**
Embossed cover. The Heart of Animals **A:** Richard Howell **W:** Peter David

WOLVERINE: INNER FURY — Marvel

1 ❑ Nov 1992 Cover: 5.95 **NM** value: **Cover or less**
Circ: CapCity orders: **31,000**
No issue number. **A:** Bill Sienkiewicz **W:** D.G. Chichester

Other grades: Multiply prices above by **1.5 for Mint • 2/3 for Very Fine • 1/3 for Fine • 1/5 for Very Good • 1/8 for Good**

WOLVERINE: KILLING — Marvel

1 ❑ Sep 1993 Cover: 5.95 **NM value: Cover or less**
Circ: CapCity orders: **23,200**
No issue number.

WOLVERINE: KNIGHT OF TERRA — Marvel

1 ❑ Aug 1995 Cover: 6.95 **NM value: Cover or less**

WOLVERINE (LTD. SERIES) — Marvel

1 ❑ Sep 1982 Cover: 0.60 **NM value: 20.00**
• **CGC:** 927 graded, best 10.0
2 ❑ Oct 1982 Cover: 0.60 **NM value: 12.00**
• **CGC:** 394 graded, best 9.9
3 ❑ Nov 1982 Cover: 0.60 **NM value: 12.00**
• **CGC:** 404 graded, best 9.9
4 ❑ Dec 1982 Cover: 0.60 **NM value: 12.00**
• **CGC:** 230 graded, best 9.9
Bk 1❑ Cover: 5.95 **NM value: Cover or less**
• Collects issues #1-4 **A:** Frank Miller **W:** Chris Claremont ★ 1st Appearance of Yukio.
Bk 1-2❑ Cover: 4.95 **NM value: 9.95**

WOLVERINE/NICK FURY: THE SCORPIO CONNECTION — Marvel

1 ❑ Cover: 12.95 **NM value: Cover or less**
1/HC❑ Cover: 16.95 **NM value: Cover or less**
hardcover.

WOLVERINE POSTER MAGAZINE — Marvel

1 ❑ Cover: 4.95 **NM value: Cover or less**
• pin-ups

WOLVERINE/PUNISHER REVELATION — Marvel

1 ❑ Jun 1999 Cover: 2.99 **NM value: Cover or less**
Circ: Diamd. preorders: **75,129** • **CGC:** 2 graded, best 9.8
📖 Ladies in Waiting **A:** Patrick Lee **W:** Christopher Golden; Tom Sniegoski
2 ❑ Jul 1999 Cover: 2.99 **NM value: Cover or less**
Circ: Diamd. preorders: **62,950**
📖 Ascension **A:** Patrick Lee **W:** Christopher Golden; Tom Sniegoski
3 ❑ Aug 1999 Cover: 2.99 **NM value: Cover or less**
4 ❑ Sep 1999 Cover: 2.99 **NM value: Cover or less**

WOLVERINE: RAHNE OF TERRA — Marvel

1 ❑ Aug 1991 Cover: 5.95 **NM value: Cover or less**
Circ: CapCity orders: **4,281**
No issue number. • prestige format. **A:** Andy Kubert **W:** Peter David

WOLVERINE SAGA, THE — Marvel

This four-part series attempts to capture and make sense of the life of Wolverine. This series covers it all, from before his first appearance in The Incredible Hulk #180-181 to his adventures in Japan with Kitty Pryde. It's a veritable "life and times" of one of Marvel's most enigmatic characters.

The prestige-format mini-series combines the respective panels from Wolverine's myriad appearances with accompanying text pieces that gives additional data. Other series utilizing the same format include The Marvel Saga and The Spider-Man Saga. — Brent

1 ❑ Sep 1989 Cover: 3.95 **NM value: 4.00**
Circ: CapCity orders: **45,000** • **CGC:** 1 graded, best 7.5
2 ❑ Nov 1989 Cover: 3.95 **NM value: 4.00**
Circ: CapCity orders: **39,000**
3 ❑ Dec 1989 Cover: 3.95 **NM value: 4.00**
Circ: CapCity orders: **38,700**
4 ❑ Dec 1989 Cover: 3.95 **NM value: 4.00**
Circ: CapCity orders: **32,450**

WOLVERINE: SAVE THE TIGER! — Marvel

1 ❑ May 1992 Cover: 2.95 **NM value: Cover or less**
Circ: CapCity orders: **15,800**
No issue number.

WOLVERINE: THE JUNGLE ADVENTURE — Marvel

1 ❑ ca. 1990 Cover: 4.50 **NM value: Cover or less**
• **CGC:** 2 graded, best 9.8
No issue number.

WOLVERINE: THE ORIGIN — Marvel

1 ❑ 2001 Cover: 3.50 **NM value: 25.00**
• **CGC:** 810 graded, best 10.0
2 ❑ 2001 Cover: 3.50 **NM value: 8.00**
• **CGC:** 396 graded, best 9.9
3 ❑ 2002 Cover: 3.50 **NM value: 5.00**
• **CGC:** 86 graded, best 9.9
4 ❑ 2002 Cover: 3.50 **NM value: Cover or less**

WOLVERINE VS. NIGHT MAN — Marvel

0 ❑ **NM value: 15.00**
• limited edition. **A:** Kyle Hotz

WOLVERINE VS. SPIDER-MAN — Marvel

1 ❑ Mar 1995 Cover: 2.50 **NM value: 3.00**
Circ: CapCity orders: **10,150**
No issue number. One-shot. cardstock cover. 📖 Wolverine/Spider-Man: Life's End • collects story arc from Marvel Comics Presents #48-50

WOLVERINE/WITCHBLADE — Image

1 ❑ Mar 1997 Cover: 2.95 **NM value: 4.50**
📖 Devil's Reign, Part 5; Devil's Reign
1/A ❑ Mar 1997 Cover: 2.95 **NM value: Cover or less**
📖 Devil's Reign, Part 5 • crossover with Marvel; continues in Witchblade/Elektra

WOLVERTON IN SPACE — Dark Horse

Bk 1❑ Mar 1997, b&w Cover: 16.95 **NM value: Cover or less**

WOMBLES, THE — Redan

1 ❑ Cover: 1.25 **NM value: 3.00**
2 ❑ Cover: 1.25 **NM value: 3.00**

WOMEN IN FUR — Shanda Fantasy Arts

2 ❑ b&w Cover: 4.50 **NM value: Cover or less**

WOMEN IN ROCK SPECIAL — Revolutionary

1 ❑ Dec 1993, b&w Cover: 2.50 **NM value: Cover or less**

WOMEN ON TOP — Fantagraphics / Eros

All issues are adults only.

1 ❑ b&w Cover: 2.25 **NM value: Cover or less**

WOMEN OUTLAWS — Fox

1 ❑ Jul 1948 Cover: 0.10 **NM value: 400.00**
2 ❑ Sep 1948 Cover: 0.10 **NM value: 300.00**
3 ❑ Nov 1948 Cover: 0.10 **NM value: 300.00**
4 ❑ Jan 1949 Cover: 0.10 **NM value: 300.00**
5 ❑ Mar 1949 Cover: 0.10 **NM value: 300.00**
6 ❑ May 1949 Cover: 0.10 **NM value: 300.00**
7 ❑ Jul 1949 Cover: 0.10 **NM value: 300.00**
8 ❑ Sep 1949 Cover: 0.10 **NM value: 300.00**

WONDER BOY — Ajax

17 ❑ May 1955 Cover: 0.10 **NM value: 250.00**
• **CGC:** 1 graded, best 5.5
18 ❑ Jul 1955 Cover: 0.10 **NM value: 250.00**

WONDER COMICS (BETTER) — Better

Though the title Wonder Comics had been used briefly by another publisher in 1939, it was resurrected in World War II and ran almost until the end of 1948. Like the earlier title, it was an anthology comic book featuring stories of a number of different characters. Ongoing action characters included The Grim Reaper, Spectro, and Jill Trent (science sleuth).

The title also eventually featured a Wonder Man of its own; the Wonder Man of 1939 appeared in that earlier Wonder Comics. When the second version began in 1946, though, the character was named Brad Spencer, Wonder Man.

Not to be confused, if this isn't confusing enough already, with Marvel's Wonder Man... — Maggie

1 ❑ Mar 1944 Cover: 0.10 **NM value: 900.00**
• **CGC:** 2 graded, best 9.6
2 ❑ Aug 1944 Cover: 0.10 **NM value: 500.00**
• **CGC:** 2 graded, best 8.0
3 ❑ Nov 1944 Cover: 0.10 **NM value: 300.00**
• **CGC:** 1 graded, best 7.0
4 ❑ Feb 1945 Cover: 0.10 **NM value: 300.00**
• **CGC:** 1 graded, best 9.4
5 ❑ Jul 1945 Cover: 0.10 **NM value: 300.00**
• **CGC:** 3 graded, best 9.4
6 ❑ Oct 1945 Cover: 0.10 **NM value: 300.00**
7 ❑ Jan 1946 Cover: 0.10 **NM value: 300.00**
• **CGC:** 1 graded, best 7.5
8 ❑ Oct 1946 Cover: 0.10 **NM value: 300.00**
• **CGC:** 1 graded, best 6.5
9 ❑ Dec 1946 Cover: 0.10 **NM value: 300.00**
• **CGC:** 1 graded, best 9.4
10 ❑ Feb 1947 Cover: 0.10 **NM value: 300.00**
• **CGC:** 2 graded, best 9.2
11 ❑ Apr 1947 Cover: 0.10 **NM value: 300.00**
• **CGC:** 3 graded, best 9.4
12 ❑ Jun 1947 Cover: 0.10 **NM value: 300.00**
• **CGC:** 3 graded, best 8.5
13 ❑ Aug 1947 Cover: 0.10 **NM value: 300.00**
• **CGC:** 6 graded, best 9.4
14 ❑ Oct 1947 Cover: 0.10 **NM value: 300.00**
• **CGC:** 3 graded, best 9.6
15 ❑ Dec 1947 Cover: 0.10 **NM value: 300.00**
• **CGC:** 6 graded, best 9.4
16 ❑ Feb 1948 Cover: 0.10 **NM value: 300.00**
• **CGC:** 7 graded, best 9.6
17 ❑ Apr 1948 Cover: 0.10 **NM value: 300.00**
• **CGC:** 4 graded, best 9.4
18 ❑ Jun 1948 Cover: 0.10 **NM value: 300.00**
• **CGC:** 1 graded, best 8.5
19 ❑ Aug 1948 Cover: 0.10 **NM value: 300.00**
• **CGC:** 2 graded, best 9.4
20 ❑ Oct 1948 Cover: 0.10 **NM value: 300.00**
• **CGC:** 4 graded, best 9.4

WONDER COMICS (FOX) — Fox

1 ❑ May 1939 Cover: 0.10 **NM value: 20000.00**
• **CGC:** 3 graded, best 9.2
2 ❑ Jun 1939 Cover: 0.10 **NM value: 7500.00**
• **CGC:** 2 graded, best 3.0

WONDERLAND — Arrow

1 ❑ Sum 1945 Cover: 2.95 **NM value: Cover or less**
2 ❑ Feb 1946 Cover: 2.95 **NM value: Cover or less**
3 ❑ Apr 1946 Cover: 2.95 **NM value: Cover or less**

WONDERLANDERS, THE — Oktomica

1 ❑ Jan 1999 Cover: 2.50 **NM value: Cover or less**
Circ: Diamd. preorders: **4,353**

WONDER MAN — Marvel

Simon Williams, who first appeared in The Avengers #9, was a misguided youth who was recruited by Baron Zemo and The Masters of Evil. He agreed to be a subject for an ionic ray experiment that would give him his extraordinary strength, earning the name Wonder Man. Although initially working for The Masters of Evil, Wonder Man turns against them in the heat of battle, saving the Avengers. However, due to a side-effect of Zemo's treatments, Wonder Man eventually falls ill and goes into a death-like coma. It is only years later that he truly lives again.

In this, his first solo title, Wonder Man has scaled back on his super-hero involvement in order to try launching an acting career. Even so, he still fights crime as a member of the West Coast Avengers.

1 ❑ Sep 1991 Cover: 1.00 **NM value: 1.50**
Circ: CapCity orders: **76,000**
• poster
2 ❑ Oct 1991 Cover: 1.00 **NM value: 1.25**
Circ: CapCity orders: **44,600**
3 ❑ Nov 1991 Cover: 1.00 **NM value: 1.25**
Circ: CapCity orders: **38,700**
4 ❑ Dec 1991 Cover: 1.00 **NM value: 1.25**
Circ: CapCity orders: **35,000**
5 ❑ Jan 1992 Cover: 1.00 **NM value: 1.25**
Circ: CapCity orders: **30,600**
6 ❑ Feb 1992 Cover: 1.25 **NM value: Cover or less**
Circ: CapCity orders: **26,400**
7 ❑ Mar 1992 Cover: 1.25 **NM value: Cover or less**
Circ: CapCity orders: **30,000**
📖 Operation: Galactic Storm, Part 4 • Operation Galactic Storm
8 ❑ Apr 1992 Cover: 1.25 **NM value: Cover or less**
Circ: CapCity orders: **27,300**
📖 Operation: Galactic Storm, Part 11 • Operation Galactic Storm
9 ❑ May 1992 Cover: 1.25 **NM value: Cover or less**
Circ: CapCity orders: **28,200**
📖 Operation: Galactic Storm, Part 18 • Operation Galactic Storm
10 ❑ Jun 1992 Cover: 1.25 **NM value: Cover or less**
Circ: CapCity orders: **24,800**
11 ❑ Jul 1992 Cover: 1.25 **NM value: Cover or less**
Circ: CapCity orders: **23,800**
12 ❑ Aug 1992 Cover: 1.25 **NM value: Cover or less**
Circ: CapCity orders: **23,400**
13 ❑ Sep 1992 Cover: 1.25 **NM value: Cover or less**
Circ: CapCity orders: **32,100**
📖 Infinity War
14 ❑ Oct 1992 Cover: 1.25 **NM value: Cover or less**
Circ: CapCity orders: **29,400**
15 ❑ Nov 1992 Cover: 1.25 **NM value: Cover or less**
Circ: Statement: **81,103** CapCity orders: **25,900**
16 ❑ Dec 1992 Cover: 1.25 **NM value: Cover or less**
Circ: Statement: **81,103** CapCity orders: **17,300**
17 ❑ Jan 1993 Cover: 1.25 **NM value: Cover or less**
Circ: Statement: **81,103** CapCity orders: **16,300**
18 ❑ Feb 1993 Cover: 1.25 **NM value: Cover or less**
Circ: Statement: **81,103** CapCity orders: **15,700**
19 ❑ Mar 1993 Cover: 1.25 **NM value: Cover or less**
Circ: Statement: **81,103** CapCity orders: **14,000**
20 ❑ Apr 1993 Cover: 1.25 **NM value: Cover or less**
Circ: Statement: **81,103** CapCity orders: **15,000**
21 ❑ May 1993 Cover: 1.25 **NM value: Cover or less**
Circ: Statement: **81,103** CapCity orders: **14,000**
22 ❑ Jun 1993 Cover: 1.25 **NM value: Cover or less**
Circ: Statement: **81,103** CapCity orders: **16,800**
23 ❑ Jul 1993 Cover: 1.25 **NM value: Cover or less**
Circ: Statement: **81,103** CapCity orders: **15,300**
24 ❑ Aug 1993 Cover: 1.25 **NM value: Cover or less**
Circ: Statement: **81,103** CapCity orders: **13,400**
25 ❑ Sep 1993 Cover: 2.95 **NM value: Cover or less**
Circ: Statement: **81,103** CapCity orders: **18,750**
Embossed cover.
26 ❑ Oct 1993 Cover: 1.25 **NM value: Cover or less**
Circ: Statement: **81,103** CapCity orders: **12,050**
27 ❑ Nov 1993 Cover: 1.25 **NM value: Cover or less**
Circ: CapCity orders: **11,600**
28 ❑ Dec 1993 Cover: 1.25 **NM value: Cover or less**
Circ: CapCity orders: **10,900**
29 ❑ Jan 1994 Cover: 1.25 **NM value: Cover or less**
Circ: CapCity orders: **9,950**
Anl 1❑ca. 1992 Cover: 2.25 **NM value: Cover or less**
Circ: CapCity orders: **26,800**
📖 System Bytes **W:** Kurt Busiek
Anl 2❑ca. 1993 Cover: 2.95 **NM value: Cover or less**
Circ: CapCity orders: **29,400**
• trading card

WONDER MAN (ONE-SHOT) — Marvel

1 ❑ Mar 1986 Cover: 1.25 **NM value: 1.50**
Circ: CapCity orders: **20,300**

CGC-graded: Multiply prices above by **33 for 9.9 M • 16 for 9.8 NM/M • 7 for 9.6 NM+ • 5 for 9.4 NM • 2.5 for 9.2 NM- • 1.5 for 9.0 VF/NM**

WONDERS AND ODDITIES (RICK GEARY'S...)

Dark Horse

1 ❑ Dec 1988, b&w Cover: 2.00 **NM** value: **Cover or less**
No issue number. 🕮 On the True Composition of Music; Suburban Romance; Now it Can be Told; Excursions; Queen of the Worms; Edison is Back; It Happened this Morning **A:** Rick Geary **W:** Rick Geary

WONDER WART-HOG, HOG OF STEEL

Rip Off Press

1 ❑ b&w Cover: 2.50 **NM** value: **3.00**
2 ❑ b&w Cover: 2.50 **NM** value: **Cover or less**
🕮 Return From the Planet of the Pigs **A:** Gilbert Shelton **W:** Gilbert Shelton
3 ❑ b&w Cover: 2.50 **NM** value: **Cover or less**

WONDER WOMAN (1ST SERIES) DC

In 1942, an Amazonian princess nursed a downed American pilot, Steve Trevor, back to health. Blessed with great strength and agility, she accompanied him back to the U.S. as Wonder Woman, woman warrior against the forces of war and evil.

In addition to her great strength and speed, Wonder Woman has awesome accessories: an invisible plane, Feminium bracelets (which she uses to deflect bullets and shrapnel), and a magical golden lasso. DC's earliest major female superhero reigned for more than 40 years in this, her first series. Ironically, it took her alter-ego, Diana Prince, almost as long to advance from a low-ranking army nurse to a major.

1 ❑ Sum 1942 Cover: 0.10 **NM** value: **18000.00**
• **CGC:** 13 graded, best 8.0
2 ❑ Fal 1942 Cover: 0.10 **NM** value: **2500.00**
• **CGC:** 4 graded, best 8.0
3 ❑ Feb 1943 Cover: 0.10 **NM** value: **1500.00**
• **CGC:** 4 graded, best 7.5
4 ❑ Apr 1943 Cover: 0.10 **NM** value: **1150.00**
5 ❑ Jun 1943 Cover: 0.10 **NM** value: **1100.00**
• **CGC:** 3 graded, best 8.5
6 ❑ Fal 1943 Cover: 0.10 **NM** value: **1000.00**
• **CGC:** 3 graded, best 9.2
7 ❑ Win 1943 Cover: 0.10 **NM** value: **1000.00**
8 ❑ Spr 1944 Cover: 0.10 **NM** value: **1000.00**
• **CGC:** 2 graded, best 9.0
9 ❑ Sum 1944 Cover: 0.10 **NM** value: **1000.00**
• **CGC:** 3 graded, best 9.6
10 ❑ Fal 1944 Cover: 0.10 **NM** value: **1000.00**
• **CGC:** 4 graded, best 9.4
11 ❑ Win 1944 Cover: 0.10 **NM** value: **700.00**
• **CGC:** 2 graded, best 9.4
12 ❑ Spr 1945 Cover: 0.10 **NM** value: **700.00**
• **CGC:** 3 graded, best 6.5
13 ❑ Sum 1945 Cover: 0.10 **NM** value: **700.00**
14 ❑ Fal 1945 Cover: 0.10 **NM** value: **700.00**
• **CGC:** 2 graded, best 9.0
15 ❑ Win 1945 Cover: 0.10 **NM** value: **700.00**
• **CGC:** 3 graded, best 9.6
16 ❑ Mar 1946 Cover: 0.10 **NM** value: **700.00**
• **CGC:** 2 graded, best 9.2
17 ❑ May 1946 Cover: 0.10 **NM** value: **700.00**
• **CGC:** 2 graded, best 9.6
18 ❑ Jul 1946 Cover: 0.10 **NM** value: **700.00**
• **CGC:** 4 graded, best 8.0
19 ❑ Sep 1946 Cover: 0.10 **NM** value: **700.00**
• **CGC:** 5 graded, best 9.2
20 ❑ Nov 1946 Cover: 0.10 **NM** value: **700.00**
• **CGC:** 3 graded, best 7.5
21 ❑ Jan 1947 Cover: 0.10 **NM** value: **625.00**
• **CGC:** 5 graded, best 9.6
22 ❑ Mar 1947 Cover: 0.10 **NM** value: **625.00**
• **CGC:** 4 graded, best 8.5
23 ❑ May 1947 Cover: 0.10 **NM** value: **625.00**
• **CGC:** 4 graded, best 9.2
24 ❑ Jul 1947 Cover: 0.10 **NM** value: **625.00**
• **CGC:** 4 graded, best 7.0
25 ❑ Sep 1947 Cover: 0.10 **NM** value: **625.00**
• **CGC:** 1 graded, best 4.5
26 ❑ Nov 1947 Cover: 0.10 **NM** value: **575.00**
• **CGC:** 1 graded, best 5.5
27 ❑ Jan 1948 Cover: 0.10 **NM** value: **575.00**
• **CGC:** 3 graded, best 9.0
28 ❑ Mar 1948 Cover: 0.10 **NM** value: **575.00**
• **CGC:** 1 graded, best 9.4
29 ❑ May 1948 Cover: 0.10 **NM** value: **575.00**
• **CGC:** 2 graded, best 8.0
30 ❑ Jul 1948 Cover: 0.10 **NM** value: **575.00**
31 ❑ Sep 1948 Cover: 0.10 **NM** value: **475.00**
32 ❑ Nov 1948 Cover: 0.10 **NM** value: **475.00**
• **CGC:** 1 graded, best .5
33 ❑ Jan 1949 Cover: 0.10 **NM** value: **475.00**
• **CGC:** 2 graded, best 9.2
34 ❑ Mar 1949 Cover: 0.10 **NM** value: **475.00**
• **CGC:** 4 graded, best 9.2
35 ❑ May 1949 Cover: 0.10 **NM** value: **475.00**
36 ❑ Jul 1949 Cover: 0.10 **NM** value: **475.00**
37 ❑ Sep 1949 Cover: 0.10 **NM** value: **475.00**
38 ❑ Nov 1949 Cover: 0.10 **NM** value: **475.00**
• **CGC:** 1 graded, best 6.0
39 ❑ Jan 1950 Cover: 0.10 **NM** value: **475.00**
• **CGC:** 1 graded, best 7.5
40 ❑ Mar 1950 Cover: 0.10 **NM** value: **475.00**
41 ❑ May 1950 Cover: 0.10 **NM** value: **340.00**
42 ❑ Jul 1950 Cover: 0.10 **NM** value: **340.00**
• **CGC:** 1 graded, best 4.0
43 ❑ Sep 1950 Cover: 0.10 **NM** value: **340.00**
• **CGC:** 1 graded, best 2.0
44 ❑ Nov 1950 Cover: 0.10 **NM** value: **340.00**
45 ❑ Jan 1951 Cover: 0.10 **NM** value: **500.00**
• **CGC:** 3 graded, best 9.0
46 ❑ Mar 1951 Cover: 0.10 **NM** value: **340.00**
• **CGC:** 1 graded, best 7.5
47 ❑ May 1951 Cover: 0.10 **NM** value: **340.00**
• **CGC:** 1 graded, best 6.0
48 ❑ Jul 1951 Cover: 0.10 **NM** value: **340.00**
49 ❑ Sep 1951 Cover: 0.10 **NM** value: **340.00**
• **CGC:** 2 graded, best 8.5
50 ❑ Nov 1951 Cover: 0.10 **NM** value: **340.00**
51 ❑ Jan 1952 Cover: 0.10 **NM** value: **260.00**
52 ❑ Mar 1952 Cover: 0.10 **NM** value: **260.00**
53 ❑ May 1952 Cover: 0.10 **NM** value: **260.00**
• **CGC:** 1 graded, best 8.0
54 ❑ Jul 1952 Cover: 0.10 **NM** value: **260.00**
55 ❑ Sep 1952 Cover: 0.10 **NM** value: **260.00**
• **CGC:** 1 graded, best 1.5
56 ❑ Nov 1952 Cover: 0.10 **NM** value: **260.00**
• **CGC:** 2 graded, best 8.5
57 ❑ Jan 1953 Cover: 0.10 **NM** value: **260.00**
58 ❑ Mar 1953 Cover: 0.10 **NM** value: **260.00**
59 ❑ May 1953 Cover: 0.10 **NM** value: **260.00**
60 ❑ Jul 1953 Cover: 0.10 **NM** value: **260.00**
• **CGC:** 1 graded, best 7.0
61 ❑ Sep 1953 Cover: 0.10 **NM** value: **200.00**
• **CGC:** 1 graded, best 4.0
62 ❑ Nov 1953 Cover: 0.10 **NM** value: **200.00**
• **CGC:** 2 graded, best 7.5
63 ❑ Jan 1954 Cover: 0.10 **NM** value: **200.00**
64 ❑ Feb 1954 Cover: 0.10 **NM** value: **200.00**
65 ❑ Apr 1954 Cover: 0.10 **NM** value: **200.00**
• **CGC:** 1 graded, best 6.5
66 ❑ May 1954 Cover: 0.10 **NM** value: **200.00**
• **CGC:** 1 graded, best 7.5
67 ❑ Jul 1954 Cover: 0.10 **NM** value: **200.00**
68 ❑ Aug 1954 Cover: 0.10 **NM** value: **200.00**
• **CGC:** 1 graded, best 5.5
69 ❑ Oct 1954 Cover: 0.10 **NM** value: **200.00**
• **CGC:** 1 graded, best 8.5
70 ❑ Nov 1954 Cover: 0.10 **NM** value: **200.00**
71 ❑ Jan 1955 Cover: 0.10 **NM** value: **160.00**
72 ❑ Feb 1955 Cover: 0.10 **NM** value: **160.00**
• **CGC:** 1 graded, best 6.5
73 ❑ Apr 1955 Cover: 0.10 **NM** value: **160.00**
• **CGC:** 1 graded, best 7.0
74 ❑ May 1955 Cover: 0.10 **NM** value: **160.00**
• **CGC:** 1 graded, best 7.0
75 ❑ Jul 1955 Cover: 0.10 **NM** value: **160.00**
• **CGC:** 1 graded, best 6.5
76 ❑ Aug 1955 Cover: 0.10 **NM** value: **160.00**
• **CGC:** 1 graded, best 6.5
77 ❑ Oct 1955 Cover: 0.10 **NM** value: **160.00**
78 ❑ Nov 1955 Cover: 0.10 **NM** value: **160.00**
• **CGC:** 1 graded, best 5.0
79 ❑ Jan 1956 Cover: 0.10 **NM** value: **160.00**
80 ❑ Feb 1956 Cover: 0.10 **NM** value: **130.00**
81 ❑ Apr 1956 Cover: 0.10 **NM** value: **130.00**
82 ❑ May 1956 Cover: 0.10 **NM** value: **130.00**
• **CGC:** 1 graded, best 8.5
83 ❑ Jul 1956 Cover: 0.10 **NM** value: **130.00**
84 ❑ Aug 1956 Cover: 0.10 **NM** value: **130.00**
85 ❑ Oct 1956 Cover: 0.10 **NM** value: **130.00**
• **CGC:** 1 graded, best 7.0
86 ❑ Nov 1956 Cover: 0.10 **NM** value: **130.00**
• **CGC:** 1 graded, best 5.5
87 ❑ Jan 1957 Cover: 0.10 **NM** value: **130.00**
• **CGC:** 1 graded, best 5.5
88 ❑ Feb 1957 Cover: 0.10 **NM** value: **130.00**
89 ❑ Apr 1957 Cover: 0.10 **NM** value: **130.00**
90 ❑ May 1957 Cover: 0.10 **NM** value: **130.00**
• **CGC:** 1 graded, best 3.0
91 ❑ Jul 1957 Cover: 0.10 **NM** value: **100.00**
• **CGC:** 1 graded, best 5.5
92 ❑ Aug 1957 Cover: 0.10 **NM** value: **100.00**
93 ❑ Oct 1957 Cover: 0.10 **NM** value: **100.00**
94 ❑ Nov 1957 Cover: 0.10 **NM** value: **100.00**
95 ❑ Jan 1958 Cover: 0.10 **NM** value: **100.00**
• **CGC:** 1 graded, best 4.5
96 ❑ Feb 1958 Cover: 0.10 **NM** value: **100.00**
• **CGC:** 1 graded, best 6.5
97 ❑ Apr 1958 Cover: 0.10 **NM** value: **100.00**
98 ❑ May 1958 Cover: 0.10 **NM** value: **100.00**
99 ❑ Jul 1958 Cover: 0.10 **NM** value: **100.00**
• **CGC:** 1 graded, best 7.0
100 ❑ Aug 1958 Cover: 0.10 **NM** value: **100.00**
• **CGC:** 1 graded, best 8.0
101 ❑ Oct 1958 Cover: 0.10 **NM** value: **75.00**
102 ❑ Nov 1958 Cover: 0.10 **NM** value: **75.00**
• **CGC:** 1 graded, best 7.5
103 ❑ Jan 1959 Cover: 0.10 **NM** value: **75.00**
• **CGC:** 1 graded, best 8.0
104 ❑ Feb 1959 Cover: 0.10 **NM** value: **75.00**
105 ❑ Apr 1959 Cover: 0.10 **NM** value: **500.00**
• **CGC:** 9 graded, best 8.0
106 ❑ May 1959 Cover: 0.10 **NM** value: **65.00**
107 ❑ Jul 1959 Cover: 0.10 **NM** value: **65.00**
• **CGC:** 1 graded, best 9.0
108 ❑ Aug 1959 Cover: 0.10 **NM** value: **65.00**
109 ❑ Oct 1959 Cover: 0.10 **NM** value: **65.00**
110 ❑ Nov 1959 Cover: 0.10 **NM** value: **65.00**
111 ❑ Jan 1960 Cover: 0.10 **NM** value: **52.00**
Circ: Statement: **213,000**
112 ❑ Feb 1960 Cover: 0.10 **NM** value: **52.00**
Circ: Statement: **213,000**
113 ❑ Apr 1960 Cover: 0.10 **NM** value: **52.00**
Circ: Statement: **213,000**
114 ❑ May 1960 Cover: 0.10 **NM** value: **52.00**
Circ: Statement: **213,000**
115 ❑ Jul 1960 Cover: 0.10 **NM** value: **52.00**
Circ: Statement: **213,000**
116 ❑ Aug 1960 Cover: 0.10 **NM** value: **52.00**
Circ: Statement: **213,000**
117 ❑ Oct 1960 Cover: 0.10 **NM** value: **52.00**
Circ: Statement: **213,000**
118 ❑ Nov 1960 Cover: 0.10 **NM** value: **52.00**
Circ: Statement: **213,000**
119 ❑ Jan 1961 Cover: 0.10 **NM** value: **52.00**
Circ: Statement: **230,000**
120 ❑ Feb 1961 Cover: 0.10 **NM** value: **52.00**
Circ: Statement: **230,000** • **CGC:** 1 graded, best 9.4
• Has 1960 Statement; avg total paid 213,000
121 ❑ Apr 1961 Cover: 0.10 **NM** value: **35.00**
Circ: Statement: **230,000**
122 ❑ May 1961 Cover: 0.10 **NM** value: **35.00**
Circ: Statement: **230,000**
123 ❑ Jul 1961 Cover: 0.10 **NM** value: **35.00**
Circ: Statement: **230,000**
124 ❑ Aug 1961 Cover: 0.10 **NM** value: **35.00**
Circ: Statement: **230,000**
125 ❑ Oct 1961 Cover: 0.10 **NM** value: **35.00**
Circ: Statement: **230,000** • **CGC:** 1 graded, best 8.0
126 ❑ Nov 1961 Cover: 0.10 **NM** value: **35.00**
Circ: Statement: **230,000** • **CGC:** 3 graded, best 8.0
127 ❑ Jan 1962 Cover: 0.12 **NM** value: **30.00**
Circ: Statement: **215,000** • **CGC:** 1 graded, best 7.5
128 ❑ Feb 1962 Cover: 0.12 **NM** value: **30.00**
Circ: Statement: **215,000** • **CGC:** 1 graded, best 7.5
• Has 1961 Statement; avg total paid 230,000★ Origin of Wonder Woman's Invisible Jet.
129 ❑ Apr 1962 Cover: 0.12 **NM** value: **30.00**
Circ: Statement: **215,000** • **CGC:** 2 graded, best 7.0
130 ❑ May 1962 Cover: 0.12 **NM** value: **30.00**
Circ: Statement: **215,000** • **CGC:** 1 graded, best 9.4
131 ❑ Jul 1962 Cover: 0.12 **NM** value: **20.00**
Circ: Statement: **215,000** • **CGC:** 1 graded, best 9.0
132 ❑ Aug 1962 Cover: 0.12 **NM** value: **20.00**
Circ: Statement: **215,000** • **CGC:** 3 graded, best 9.4
133 ❑ Oct 1962 Cover: 0.12 **NM** value: **20.00**
Circ: Statement: **215,000** • **CGC:** 3 graded, best 9.4
134 ❑ Nov 1962 Cover: 0.12 **NM** value: **20.00**
Circ: Statement: **215,000** • **CGC:** 2 graded, best 9.0
135 ❑ Jan 1963 Cover: 0.12 **NM** value: **20.00**
• **CGC:** 2 graded, best 9.4
136 ❑ Feb 1963 Cover: 0.12 **NM** value: **20.00**
• **CGC:** 4 graded, best 9.4
• Has 1962 Statement; avg total paid 215,000
137 ❑ Apr 1963 Cover: 0.12 **NM** value: **20.00**
• **CGC:** 1 graded, best 9.4
138 ❑ May 1963 Cover: 0.12 **NM** value: **20.00**
• **CGC:** 2 graded, best 9.4
139 ❑ Jul 1963 Cover: 0.12 **NM** value: **20.00**
• **CGC:** 2 graded, best 9.6
140 ❑ Aug 1963 Cover: 0.12 **NM** value: **20.00**
• **CGC:** 3 graded, best 9.6
141 ❑ Oct 1963 Cover: 0.12 **NM** value: **20.00**
• **CGC:** 1 graded, best 9.6
142 ❑ Nov 1963 Cover: 0.12 **NM** value: **20.00**
• **CGC:** 1 graded, best 9.4
143 ❑ Jan 1964 Cover: 0.12 **NM** value: **20.00**
• **CGC:** 1 graded, best 8.5
144 ❑ Feb 1964 Cover: 0.12 **NM** value: **20.00**
• **CGC:** 2 graded, best 9.2
145 ❑ Apr 1964 Cover: 0.12 **NM** value: **20.00**
• **CGC:** 2 graded, best 9.6
146 ❑ May 1964 Cover: 0.12 **NM** value: **20.00**
• **CGC:** 3 graded, best 9.4
147 ❑ Jul 1964 Cover: 0.12 **NM** value: **20.00**
• **CGC:** 3 graded, best 9.4
148 ❑ Aug 1964 Cover: 0.12 **NM** value: **20.00**
• **CGC:** 3 graded, best 9.6
149 ❑ Oct 1964 Cover: 0.12 **NM** value: **20.00**
• **CGC:** 2 graded, best 9.4
🕮 The Last Day of the Amazons
150 ❑ Nov 1964 Cover: 0.12 **NM** value: **20.00**
• **CGC:** 2 graded, best 9.6
151 ❑ Jan 1965 Cover: 0.12 **NM** value: **18.00**
Circ: Statement: **209,918** • **CGC:** 1 graded, best 9.2
152 ❑ Feb 1965 Cover: 0.12 **NM** value: **18.00**
Circ: Statement: **209,918** • **CGC:** 4 graded, best 9.4
153 ❑ Apr 1965 Cover: 0.12 **NM** value: **18.00**
Circ: Statement: **209,918** • **CGC:** 1 graded, best 9.4
154 ❑ May 1965 Cover: 0.12 **NM** value: **18.00**
Circ: Statement: **209,918** • **CGC:** 2 graded, best 9.2
155 ❑ Jul 1965 Cover: 0.12 **NM** value: **18.00**
Circ: Statement: **209,918** • **CGC:** 3 graded, best 8.0
156 ❑ Aug 1965 Cover: 0.12 **NM** value: **18.00**
Circ: Statement: **209,918** • **CGC:** 5 graded, best 9.4
157 ❑ Oct 1965 Cover: 0.12 **NM** value: **18.00**
Circ: Statement: **209,918** • **CGC:** 3 graded, best 9.2
158 ❑ Nov 1965 Cover: 0.12 **NM** value: **18.00**
Circ: Statement: **209,918** • **CGC:** 1 graded, best 9.2
159 ❑ Jan 1966 Cover: 0.12 **NM** value: **18.00**
Circ: Statement: **220,168** • **CGC:** 9 graded, best 9.8
160 ❑ Feb 1966 Cover: 0.12 **NM** value: **16.00**
Circ: Statement: **220,168** • **CGC:** 1 graded, best 9.0
161 ❑ Apr 1966 Cover: 0.12 **NM** value: **16.00**
Circ: Statement: **220,168** • **CGC:** 4 graded, best 9.2
162 ❑ May 1966 Cover: 0.12 **NM** value: **16.00**
Circ: Statement: **220,168** • **CGC:** 3 graded, best 9.4
163 ❑ Jul 1966 Cover: 0.12 **NM** value: **16.00**
Circ: Statement: **220,168** • **CGC:** 2 graded, best 9.4

Other grades: Multiply prices above by **1.5 for Mint • 2/3 for Very Fine • 1/3 for Fine • 1/5 for Very Good • 1/8 for Good**

• Has 1965 Statement; avg print run 346,000; avg sales 209,000; avg subs 918; avg total paid 209,918; max existent 209,918; 0% of run returned
164 ☐ Aug 1966 Cover: 0.12 NM value: 16.00
Circ: Statement: 220,168 • CGC: 5 graded, best 9.4
165 ☐ Oct 1966 Cover: 0.12 NM value: 16.00
Circ: Statement: 220,168 • CGC: 3 graded, best 9.4
166 ☐ Nov 1966 Cover: 0.12 NM value: 16.00
Circ: Statement: 220,168 • CGC: 2 graded, best 9.0
167 ☐ Jan 1967 Cover: 0.12 NM value: 16.00
Circ: Statement: 175,000 • CGC: 6 graded, best 9.4
168 ☐ Feb 1967 Cover: 0.12 NM value: 16.00
Circ: Statement: 175,000 • CGC: 3 graded, best 9.4
• Has 1966 Statement; avg print run 368,000; avg sales 219,000; avg subs 1,168; avg total paid 220,168; max existent 220,168; 0% run returned
169 ☐ Apr 1967 Cover: 0.12 NM value: 16.00
Circ: Statement: 175,000 • CGC: 5 graded, best 9.6
170 ☐ Jun 1967 Cover: 0.12 NM value: 16.00
Circ: Statement: 175,000 • CGC: 2 graded, best 9.6
171 ☐ Aug 1967 Cover: 0.12 NM value: 14.00
Circ: Statement: 175,000 • CGC: 1 graded, best 9.6
172 ☐ Oct 1967 Cover: 0.12 NM value: 14.00
Circ: Statement: 175,000 • CGC: 2 graded, best 9.2
173 ☐ Dec 1967 Cover: 0.12 NM value: 14.00
Circ: Statement: 175,000 • CGC: 3 graded, best 9.4
174 ☐ Feb 1968 Cover: 0.12 NM value: 14.00
Circ: Statement: 166,365 • CGC: 4 graded, best 9.4
175 ☐ Apr 1968 Cover: 0.12 NM value: 14.00
Circ: Statement: 166,365 • CGC: 4 graded, best 9.6
• Has 1967 Statement; avg print run 333,000; avg sales 174,000; avg subs 1,000; avg total paid 175,000; max existent 175,000; 0% of run returned
176 ☐ Jun 1968 Cover: 0.12 NM value: 14.00
Circ: Statement: 166,365 • CGC: 3 graded, best 9.6
177 ☐ Aug 1968 Cover: 0.12 NM value: 14.00
Circ: Statement: 166,365 • CGC: 6 graded, best 9.6
178 ☐ Oct 1968 Cover: 0.12 NM value: 14.00
Circ: Statement: 166,365 • CGC: 5 graded, best 9.6
📖 Wonder Woman's Rival
179 ☐ Dec 1968 Cover: 0.12 NM value: 14.00
Circ: Statement: 166,365 • CGC: 3 graded, best 9.4
180 ☐ Feb 1969 Cover: 0.12 NM value: 15.00
Circ: Statement: 166,365 • CGC: 2 graded, best 9.4
181 ☐ Apr 1969 Cover: 0.12 NM value: 10.00
Circ: Statement: 166,365 • CGC: 5 graded, best 9.6
• Has 1968 Statement, filed 10/1/66; avg print run 302,000; avg sales 166,000; avg subs 365; avg total paid 166,365; max existent 166,365; 0% of run returned
182 ☐ Jun 1969 Cover: 0.15 NM value: 10.00
Circ: Statement: 166,365 • CGC: 3 graded, best 9.4
183 ☐ Aug 1969 Cover: 0.15 NM value: 10.00
Circ: Statement: 166,365 • CGC: 4 graded, best 9.6
184 ☐ Oct 1969 Cover: 0.15 NM value: 10.00
Circ: Statement: 166,365 • CGC: 1 graded, best 8.0
185 ☐ Dec 1969 Cover: 0.15 NM value: 10.00
Circ: Statement: 166,365 • CGC: 2 graded, best 9.4
186 ☐ Feb 1969 Cover: 0.15 NM value: 10.00
Circ: Statement: 171,197 • CGC: 2 graded, best 9.0
187 ☐ Apr 1969 Cover: 0.15 NM value: 10.00
Circ: Statement: 171,197 • CGC: 2 graded, best 9.2
• Has 1969 Statement; avg print run 323,000; avg sales 171,000; avg subs 197; avg total paid 171,197; max existent 171,197; 0% of run returned
188 ☐ Jun 1969 Cover: 0.15 NM value: 10.00
Circ: Statement: 171,197 • CGC: 1 graded, best 9.0
189 ☐ Aug 1969 Cover: 0.15 NM value: 10.00
Circ: Statement: 171,197 • CGC: 2 graded, best 9.6
190 ☐ Oct 1969 Cover: 0.15 NM value: 10.00
Circ: Statement: 171,197 • CGC: 1 graded, best 8.5
191 ☐ Dec 1969 Cover: 0.15 NM value: 10.00
Circ: Statement: 171,197 • CGC: 2 graded, best 9.4
192 ☐ Feb 1971 NM value: 10.00
Circ: Statement: 159,263 • CGC: 1 graded, best 9.4
193 ☐ Apr 1971 NM value: 10.00
Circ: Statement: 159,263 • CGC: 2 graded, best 9.0
• Has 1970 Statement; avg print run 325,594; avg sales 172,356; avg subs 180; avg total paid 172,536; max existent 172,536; 0% of run returned
194 ☐ Jun 1971 NM value: 10.00
Circ: Statement: 159,263 • CGC: 3 graded, best 9.2
195 ☐ Aug 1971 NM value: 10.00
Circ: Statement: 159,263 • CGC: 3 graded, best 9.4
196 ☐ Oct 1971 NM value: 10.00
Circ: Statement: 159,263 • CGC: 7 graded, best 9.6
197 ☐ Dec 1971 NM value: 10.00
Circ: Statement: 159,263 • CGC: 7 graded, best 9.0
198 ☐ Feb 1972 Cover: 0.25 NM value: 10.00
Circ: Statement: 133,918 • CGC: 1 graded, best 8.0
199 ☐ Apr 1972 Cover: 0.25 NM value: 10.00
Circ: Statement: 133,918 • CGC: 19 graded, best 9.6
• Has 1971 Statement; avg print run 302,500; avg sales 159,263; no subs; avg total paid 159,263; max existent 159,263; 47% of run returned A: Dick Giordano
200 ☐ Jun 1972 Cover: 0.25 NM value: 10.00
Circ: Statement: 133,918 • CGC: 14 graded, best 9.6
201 ☐ Aug 1972 Cover: 0.20 NM value: 4.00
Circ: Statement: 133,918 • CGC: 2 graded, best 9.0
202 ☐ Oct 1972 Cover: 0.20 NM value: 4.00
Circ: Statement: 133,918 • CGC: 2 graded, best 9.4
• Fafhrd and The Gray Mouser apperance A: Dick Giordano W: Samuel R. Delany
203 ☐ Dec 1972 Cover: 0.20 NM value: 4.00
Circ: Statement: 133,918 • CGC: 1 graded, best 9.4
204 ☐ Feb 1973 NM value: 4.00
Circ: Statement: 145,771 • CGC: 1 graded, best 9.4
205 ☐ Apr 1973 NM value: 4.00
Circ: Statement: 145,771 • CGC: 2 graded, best 9.6

Suggestive cover. 📖 Target Wonder Woman!; The Mystery of Nubia!
• Has 1972 Statement; avg print run 281,000; avg sales 133,705; avg subs 213; avg total paid 133,918; max existent 133,918; 52% of run returned A: Bob Oksner; Don Heck W: Robert Kanigher
206 ☐ Jun 1973 NM value: 4.00
Circ: Statement: 145,771
207 ☐ Aug 1973 NM value: 4.00
Circ: Statement: 145,771 • CGC: 2 graded, best 9.6
208 ☐ Oct 1973 NM value: 4.00
Circ: Statement: 145,771 • CGC: 3 graded, best 9.4
📖 The Titanic Trials; Chessmen of Death! A: Ric Estrada
209 ☐ Dec 1973 Cover: 0.20 NM value: 4.00
Circ: Statement: 145,771 • CGC: 3 graded, best 9.4
210 ☐ Feb 1974 Cover: 0.20 NM value: 4.00
Circ: Statement: 149,917 • CGC: 2 graded, best 9.8
211 ☐ Apr 1974 NM value: 3.00
Circ: Statement: 149,917 • CGC: 5 graded, best 9.4
• Has 1973 Statement; avg print run 313,000; avg sales 145,064; avg subs 717; avg total paid 145,771; max existent 145,781; 53% of run returned
212 ☐ Jun 1974 Cover: 0.20 NM value: 3.00
Circ: Statement: 149,917 • CGC: 2 graded, best 9.4
213 ☐ Aug 1974 Cover: 0.20 NM value: 3.00
Circ: Statement: 149,917
214 ☐ Oct 1974 Cover: 0.60 NM value: 3.00
Circ: Statement: 149,917 • CGC: 5 graded, best 9.4
215 ☐ Dec 1974 Cover: 0.20 NM value: 3.00
Circ: Statement: 149,917
216 ☐ Feb 1975 Cover: 0.25 NM value: 3.00
Circ: Statement: 150,000 • CGC: 1 graded, best 9.8
217 ☐ Apr 1975 Cover: 0.50 NM value: 3.00
Circ: Statement: 150,000 • CGC: 2 graded, best 9.2
218 ☐ Jun 1975 Cover: 0.25 NM value: 3.00
Circ: Statement: 150,000 • CGC: 1 graded, best 9.2
• Has 1974 Statement; avg print run 332,820; avg sales 148,333; avg subs 1,584; avg total paid 149,917; max existent 149,917; 54% of run returned
219 ☐ Aug 1975 Cover: 0.25 NM value: 3.00
Circ: Statement: 150,000
220 ☐ Oct 1975 Cover: 0.25 NM value: 3.00
Circ: Statement: 150,000
221 ☐ Dec 1975 Cover: 0.25 NM value: 3.00
Circ: Statement: 150,000
222 ☐ Feb 1976 Cover: 0.25 NM value: 3.00
Circ: Statement: 150,000
223 ☐ Apr 1976 Cover: 0.30 NM value: 3.00
Circ: Statement: 150,000
• Return of Steve Trevor
224 ☐ Jun 1976 Cover: 0.30 NM value: 3.00
Circ: Statement: 150,000
• Has 1975 Statement; avg print run 309,000; avg sales 148,000; avg subs 2,000; avg total paid 150,000; max existent 150,000; 49% of run returned
225 ☐ Aug 1976 Cover: 0.30 NM value: 3.00
Circ: Statement: 150,000
226 ☐ Oct 1976 Cover: 0.30 NM value: 3.00
Circ: Statement: 150,000
227 ☐ Dec 1976 Cover: 0.30 NM value: 3.00
Circ: Statement: 150,000
228 ☐ Feb 1977 Cover: 0.30 NM value: 3.00
Circ: Statement: 151,954
229 ☐ Mar 1977 Cover: 0.30 NM value: 3.00
Circ: Statement: 151,954
230 ☐ Apr 1977 Cover: 0.30 NM value: 3.00
Circ: Statement: 151,954
231 ☐ May 1977 Cover: 0.30 NM value: 3.00
Circ: Statement: 151,954 • CGC: 1 graded, best 9.6
• Has 1976 Statement; avg print run 350,000; avg sales 147,000; avg subs 3,000; avg total paid 150,000; max existent 150,000; 57% of run returned
232 ☐ Jun 1977 Cover: 0.35 NM value: 3.00
Circ: Statement: 151,954 • CGC: 1 graded, best 9.4
233 ☐ Jul 1977 Cover: 0.35 NM value: 3.00
Circ: Statement: 151,954
234 ☐ Aug 1977 Cover: 0.35 NM value: 3.00
Circ: Statement: 151,954
235 ☐ Sep 1977 Cover: 0.35 NM value: 3.00
Circ: Statement: 151,954
236 ☐ Oct 1977 Cover: 0.35 NM value: 3.00
Circ: Statement: 151,954
237 ☐ Nov 1977 Cover: 0.35 NM value: 3.00
Circ: Statement: 151,954
238 ☐ Dec 1977 Cover: 0.35 NM value: 3.00
Circ: Statement: 151,954
239 ☐ Jan 1978 Cover: 0.35 NM value: 3.00
Circ: Statement: 124,296
240 ☐ Feb 1978 Cover: 0.35 NM value: 3.00
Circ: Statement: 124,296
241 ☐ Mar 1978 Cover: 0.35 NM value: 3.00
Circ: Statement: 124,296
242 ☐ Apr 1978 Cover: 0.35 NM value: 3.00
Circ: Statement: 124,296
243 ☐ May 1978 Cover: 0.35 NM value: 3.00
Circ: Statement: 124,296
• Has 1977 Statement; avg print run 350,899; avg sales 149,235; avg subs 2,719; avg total paid 151,954; max existent 151,954; 56% of run returned
244 ☐ Jun 1978 Cover: 0.35 NM value: 3.00
Circ: Statement: 124,296
245 ☐ Jul 1978 Cover: 0.35 NM value: 3.00
Circ: Statement: 124,296
246 ☐ Aug 1978 Cover: 0.35 NM value: 3.00
Circ: Statement: 124,296
247 ☐ Sep 1978 Cover: 0.50 NM value: 3.00
Circ: Statement: 124,296
248 ☐ Oct 1978 Cover: 0.50 NM value: 3.00
Circ: Statement: 124,296
249 ☐ Nov 1978 Cover: 0.50 NM value: 3.00
Circ: Statement: 124,296

250 ☐ Dec 1978 Cover: 0.40 NM value: 3.00
Circ: Statement: 124,296
251 ☐ Jan 1979 Cover: 0.40 NM value: 3.00
Circ: Statement: 158,678
252 ☐ Feb 1979 Cover: 0.40 NM value: 3.00
Circ: Statement: 158,678
253 ☐ Mar 1979 Cover: 0.40 NM value: 3.00
Circ: Statement: 158,678
254 ☐ Apr 1979 Cover: 0.40 NM value: 3.00
Circ: Statement: 158,678
• Has 1978 Statement; avg print run 365,609; avg sales 122,814; avg subs 1,482; avg total paid 124,296; max existent 124,296; 65% of run returned
255 ☐ May 1979 Cover: 0.40 NM value: 3.00
Circ: Statement: 158,678
256 ☐ Jun 1979 Cover: 0.40 NM value: 3.00
Circ: Statement: 158,678
257 ☐ Jul 1979 Cover: 0.40 NM value: 3.00
Circ: Statement: 158,678
258 ☐ Aug 1979 Cover: 0.40 NM value: 3.00
Circ: Statement: 158,678
259 ☐ Sep 1979 Cover: 0.40 NM value: 3.00
Circ: Statement: 158,678
260 ☐ Oct 1979 Cover: 0.40 NM value: 3.00
Circ: Statement: 158,678
261 ☐ Nov 1979 Cover: 0.40 NM value: 3.00
Circ: Statement: 158,678
262 ☐ Dec 1979 Cover: 0.40 NM value: 3.00
Circ: Statement: 158,678
263 ☐ Jan 1980 Cover: 0.40 NM value: 3.00
Circ: Statement: 94,901
264 ☐ Feb 1980 Cover: 0.40 NM value: 3.00
Circ: Statement: 94,901
265 ☐ Mar 1980 Cover: 0.40 NM value: 3.00
Circ: Statement: 94,901
266 ☐ Apr 1980 Cover: 0.40 NM value: 3.00
Circ: Statement: 94,901
• Has 1979 Statement; avg print run 315,148; avg sales 157,763; avg subs 915; avg total paid 158,678; max existent 158,678; 50% of run returned
267 ☐ May 1980 Cover: 0.40 NM value: 3.00
Circ: Statement: 94,901 • CGC: 1 graded, best 9.2
268 ☐ Jun 1980 Cover: 0.40 NM value: 3.00
Circ: Statement: 94,901 • CGC: 1 graded, best 9.4
269 ☐ Jul 1980 Cover: 0.40 NM value: 2.50
Circ: Statement: 94,901
270 ☐ Aug 1980 Cover: 0.40 NM value: 2.50
Circ: Statement: 94,901
271 ☐ Sep 1980 Cover: 0.50 NM value: 2.50
Circ: Statement: 94,901
272 ☐ Oct 1980 Cover: 0.50 NM value: 2.50
Circ: Statement: 94,901
273 ☐ Nov 1980 Cover: 0.50 NM value: 2.50
Circ: Statement: 94,901
274 ☐ Dec 1980 Cover: 0.50 NM value: 2.50
Circ: Statement: 94,901
275 ☐ Jan 1981 Cover: 0.50 NM value: 2.50
Circ: Statement: 83,796
276 ☐ Feb 1981 Cover: 0.50 NM value: 2.50
Circ: Statement: 83,796
277 ☐ Mar 1981 Cover: 0.50 NM value: 2.50
Circ: Statement: 83,796
278 ☐ Apr 1981 Cover: 0.50 NM value: 2.50
Circ: Statement: 83,796
279 ☐ May 1981 Cover: 0.50 NM value: 2.50
Circ: Statement: 83,796
• Has 1980 Statement; avg print run 259,039; avg sales 93,453; avg subs 1,448; avg total paid 94,901; max existent 94,901; 62% of run returned
280 ☐ Jun 1981 Cover: 0.50 NM value: 2.50
Circ: Statement: 83,796
281 ☐ Jul 1981 Cover: 0.50 NM value: 4.00
Circ: Statement: 83,796
282 ☐ Aug 1981 Cover: 0.50 NM value: 4.00
Circ: Statement: 83,796
283 ☐ Sep 1981 Cover: 0.50 NM value: 4.00
Circ: Statement: 83,796
284 ☐ Oct 1981 Cover: 0.60 NM value: 2.00
Circ: Statement: 83,796
285 ☐ Nov 1981 Cover: 0.60 NM value: 2.00
Circ: Statement: 83,796
286 ☐ Dec 1981 Cover: 0.60 NM value: 2.00
Circ: Statement: 83,796
287 ☐ Jan 1982 Cover: 0.60 NM value: 2.00
Circ: Statement: 96,198 • CGC: 1 graded, best 9.6
288 ☐ Feb 1982 Cover: 0.60 NM value: 2.00
Circ: Statement: 96,198
289 ☐ Mar 1982 Cover: 0.60 NM value: 2.00
Circ: Statement: 96,198
290 ☐ Apr 1982 Cover: 0.60 NM value: 2.00
Circ: Statement: 96,198
291 ☐ May 1982 Cover: 0.60 NM value: 2.00
Circ: Statement: 96,198
• Has 1981 Statement; avg print run 230,591; avg sales 82,202; avg subs 1,594; avg total paid 83,796; max existent 83,796; 62% of run returned
292 ☐ Jun 1982 Cover: 0.60 NM value: 2.00
Circ: Statement: 96,198
293 ☐ Jul 1982 Cover: 0.60 NM value: 2.00
Circ: Statement: 96,198
294 ☐ Aug 1982 Cover: 0.60 NM value: 2.00
Circ: Statement: 96,198
295 ☐ Sep 1982 Cover: 0.60 NM value: 2.00
Circ: Statement: 96,198
296 ☐ Oct 1982 Cover: 0.60 NM value: 2.00
Circ: Statement: 96,198
297 ☐ Nov 1982 Cover: 0.60 NM value: 2.00
Circ: Statement: 96,198

CGC-graded: Multiply prices above by **33 for 9.9 M • 16 for 9.8 NM/M • 7 for 9.6 NM+ • 5 for 9.4 NM • 2.5 for 9.2 NM- • 1.5 for 9.0 VF/NM**

298 ❑ Dec 1982 Cover: 0.60 **NM** value: **2.00**
Circ: Statement: **96,198**

299 ❑ Jan 1983 Cover: 0.60 **NM** value: **2.00**
Circ: Statement: **73,256**

300 ❑ Feb 1983 Cover: 1.50 **NM** value: **3.00**
Circ: Statement: **73,256** • **CGC:** 6 graded, best 9.6
• Giant-size. ★ 1st Appearance of Fury. ★ Appearance of New Teen Titans.

301 ❑ Mar 1983 Cover: 0.60 **NM** value: **2.00**
Circ: Statement: **73,256**

302 ❑ Apr 1983 Cover: 0.60 **NM** value: **2.00**
Circ: Statement: **73,256**

303 ❑ May 1983 Cover: 0.60 **NM** value: **2.00**
Circ: Statement: **73,256**
• Has 1982 Statement; avg print run 242,052; avg sales 94,605; avg subs 1,593; avg total paid 96,198; max existent 96,198; 59% of run returned

304 ❑ Jun 1983 Cover: 0.60 **NM** value: **2.00**
Circ: Statement: **73,256**

305 ❑ Jul 1983 Cover: 0.60 **NM** value: **2.00**
Circ: Statement: **73,256**

306 ❑ Aug 1983 Cover: 0.60 **NM** value: **2.00**
Circ: Statement: **73,256**

307 ❑ Sep 1983 Cover: 0.60 **NM** value: **2.00**
Circ: Statement: **73,256**

308 ❑ Oct 1983 Cover: 0.60 **NM** value: **2.00**
Circ: Statement: **73,256**

309 ❑ Nov 1983 Cover: 0.60 **NM** value: **2.00**
Circ: Statement: **73,256**

310 ❑ Dec 1983 Cover: 0.75 **NM** value: **2.00**
Circ: Statement: **73,256**

311 ❑ Jan 1984 Cover: 0.75 **NM** value: **2.00**
Circ: Statement: **52,145**

312 ❑ Feb 1984 Cover: 0.75 **NM** value: **2.00**
Circ: Statement: **52,145**

313 ❑ Mar 1984 Cover: 0.75 **NM** value: **2.00**
Circ: Statement: **52,145**

314 ❑ Apr 1984 Cover: 0.75 **NM** value: **2.00**
Circ: Statement: **52,145**
• Has 1983 Statement; avg print run 216,401; avg sales 72,106; avg subs 1,150; avg total paid 73,256; max existent 73,256; 66% of run returned **A:** Don Heck

315 ❑ May 1984 Cover: 0.75 **NM** value: **2.00**
Circ: Statement: **52,145**

316 ❑ Jun 1984 Cover: 0.75 **NM** value: **2.00**
Circ: Statement: **52,145**

317 ❑ Jul 1984 Cover: 0.75 **NM** value: **2.00**
Circ: Statement: **52,145**

318 ❑ Aug 1984 Cover: 0.75 **NM** value: **2.00**
Circ: Statement: **52,145**

319 ❑ Sep 1984 Cover: 0.75 **NM** value: **2.00**
Circ: Statement: **52,145**

320 ❑ Oct 1984 Cover: 0.75 **NM** value: **2.00**
Circ: Statement: **52,145**

321 ❑ Nov 1984 Cover: 0.75 **NM** value: **2.00**
Circ: Statement: **52,145**

322 ❑ Dec 1984 Cover: 0.75 **NM** value: **2.00**
323 ❑ Feb 1985 Cover: 0.75 **NM** value: **2.00**
324 ❑ Apr 1985 Cover: 0.75 **NM** value: **2.00**
325 ❑ May 1985 Cover: 0.75 **NM** value: **2.00**
Circ: CapCity orders: **3,050**
• Has 1984 Statement; avg print run 172,868; avg sales 51,001; avg subs 1,144; avg total paid 52,145; 68% of run returned **A:** Don Heck ★ Appearance of Atomic Knight.

326 ❑ Jul 1985 Cover: 0.75 **NM** value: **2.00**
Circ: CapCity orders: **3,200**

327 ❑ Sep 1985 Cover: 0.75 **NM** value: **2.00**
Circ: CapCity orders: **3,350**

328 ❑ Dec 1985 Cover: 0.75 **NM** value: **2.00**
Circ: CapCity orders: **2,900**
• Crisis

329 ❑ Feb 1986 Cover: 1.25 **NM** value: **2.00**
Circ: CapCity orders: **7,250**
• Giant-size. final issue. • Crisis

WONDER WOMAN (2ND SERIES) DC

When the U.S. prepared for battle in the opening days of World War II, the comics industry did its part to keep up morale, introducing a number of patriotic characters. One such character was Wonder Woman: Princess Diana of a woman-ruled island paradise who decided to strike out on her own to fight for justice in the world.

Clad in a star-spangled costume, armed only with bracelets which deflect bullets and a magic lasso which compels those encircled to speak the truth, Wonder Woman doesn't so much fight criminals as try to bring the ways of peace and truth to the world. Of course, in the times of World War II, the most obvious way to accomplish this was to join the Allied forces. Now, in her second series, Diana faces, not the Nazi threat, but more day-to-day troubles, such as crime and victimization.

0 ❑ Oct 1994 Cover: 1.50 **NM** value: **6.00**
Circ: CapCity orders: **16,400**

1 ❑ Feb 1987 Cover: 0.75 **NM** value: **4.00**
Circ: Statement: **118,550** CapCity orders: **39,250** • **CGC:** 18 graded, best 9.8
📖 The Princess and the Power! **A:** George Pérez; George Perez **W:** George Pérez; Greg Potter ★ Origin of Wonder Woman (new origin). ★ 1st Appearance of Ares (DC).

2 ❑ Mar 1987 Cover: 0.75 **NM** value: **3.00**
Circ: Statement: **118,550** CapCity orders: **25,650** • **CGC:** 1 graded, best 9.8

3 ❑ Apr 1987 Cover: 0.75 **NM** value: **3.00**
Circ: Statement: **118,550** CapCity orders: **22,700** • **CGC:** 1 graded, best 9.8

4 ❑ May 1987 Cover: 0.75 **NM** value: **3.00**
Circ: Statement: **118,550** CapCity orders: **23,050**

5 ❑ Jun 1987 Cover: 0.75 **NM** value: **3.00**
Circ: Statement: **118,550** CapCity orders: **21,600**

6 ❑ Jul 1987 Cover: 0.75 **NM** value: **2.50**
Circ: Statement: **118,550** CapCity orders: **22,200**

7 ❑ Aug 1987 Cover: 0.75 **NM** value: **2.50**
Circ: Statement: **118,550** CapCity orders: **23,450**

8 ❑ Sep 1987 Cover: 0.75 **NM** value: **2.50**
Circ: Statement: **118,550** CapCity orders: **24,400**

9 ❑ Oct 1987 Cover: 0.75 **NM** value: **2.50**
Circ: Statement: **118,550** CapCity orders: **24,200**

10 ❑ Nov 1987 Cover: 0.75 **NM** value: **2.50**
Circ: Statement: **118,550** CapCity orders: **24,600**
• gatefold **A:** George Pérez

10/A ❑ Nov 1987 Cover: 0.75 **NM** value: **2.50**
• no gatefold; gatefold **A:** George Pérez

11 ❑ Dec 1987 Cover: 0.75 **NM** value: **2.00**
Circ: Statement: **118,550** CapCity orders: **22,700**

12 ❑ Jan 1988 Cover: 0.75 **NM** value: **2.00**
Circ: CapCity orders: **27,800**
• Millennium **A:** George Pérez

13 ❑ Feb 1988 Cover: 0.75 **NM** value: **2.00**
Circ: CapCity orders: **28,050**
• Millennium **A:** George Pérez

14 ❑ Mar 1988 Cover: 0.75 **NM** value: **2.00**
Circ: CapCity orders: **23,450**

15 ❑ Apr 1988 Cover: 0.75 **NM** value: **2.00**
Circ: CapCity orders: **23,650**
• Has 1987 Statement; avg print run 217,470; avg sales 118,139; avg subs 411; avg total paid 118,550; max existent 118,550; 30% of run returned **A:** George Pérez ★ 1st Appearance of Silver Swan, Ed Indelicato.

16 ❑ May 1988 Cover: 0.75 **NM** value: **2.00**
Circ: CapCity orders: **25,750**

17 ❑ Jun 1988 Cover: 0.75 **NM** value: **2.00**
Circ: CapCity orders: **21,400**

18 ❑ Jul 1988 Cover: 0.75 **NM** value: **2.00**
Circ: CapCity orders: **21,900**
• Bonus Book **A:** George Pérez

19 ❑ Aug 1988 Cover: 0.75 **NM** value: **2.00**
Circ: CapCity orders: **21,100**

20 ❑ Sep 1988 Cover: 0.75 **NM** value: **2.00**
Circ: CapCity orders: **21,000**

21 ❑ Oct 1988 Cover: 1.00 **NM** value: **2.00**
Circ: CapCity orders: **21,250**

22 ❑ Nov 1988 Cover: 1.00 **NM** value: **2.00**
Circ: CapCity orders: **20,100**

23 ❑ Dec 1988 Cover: 1.00 **NM** value: **2.00**
Circ: CapCity orders: **20,850**

24 ❑ Hol 1988 Cover: 1.00 **NM** value: **2.00**
Circ: CapCity orders: **19,150**

25 ❑ Jan 1989 Cover: 1.00 **NM** value: **2.00**
Circ: CapCity orders: **21,550**
• Invasion! **C:** George Pérez

26 ❑ Jan 1989 Cover: 1.00 **NM** value: **2.00**
Circ: CapCity orders: **20,200**
• Invasion! **C:** George Pérez

27 ❑ Feb 1989 Cover: 1.00 **NM** value: **2.00**
Circ: CapCity orders: **18,150**

28 ❑ Mar 1989 Cover: 1.00 **NM** value: **2.00**
Circ: CapCity orders: **17,950**

29 ❑ Apr 1989 Cover: 1.00 **NM** value: **2.00**
Circ: CapCity orders: **17,900**

30 ❑ May 1989 Cover: 1.00 **NM** value: **2.00**
Circ: CapCity orders: **17,450**

31 ❑ Jun 1989 Cover: 1.00 **NM** value: **1.75**
Circ: CapCity orders: **17,000**

32 ❑ Jul 1989 Cover: 1.00 **NM** value: **1.75**
Circ: CapCity orders: **17,450**

33 ❑ Aug 1989 Cover: 1.00 **NM** value: **1.75**
Circ: CapCity orders: **16,300**

34 ❑ Sep 1989 Cover: 1.00 **NM** value: **1.75**
Circ: CapCity orders: **16,100**

35 ❑ Oct 1989 Cover: 1.00 **NM** value: **1.75**
Circ: CapCity orders: **15,650**

36 ❑ Nov 1989 Cover: 1.00 **NM** value: **1.75**
Circ: CapCity orders: **49,900**

37 ❑ Dec 1989 Cover: 1.00 **NM** value: **1.75**
Circ: CapCity orders: **14,650**

38 ❑ Jan 1990 Cover: 1.00 **NM** value: **1.75**
Circ: CapCity orders: **14,600**

39 ❑ Feb 1990 Cover: 1.00 **NM** value: **1.75**
Circ: CapCity orders: **13,950**

40 ❑ Mar 1990 Cover: 1.00 **NM** value: **1.75**
Circ: CapCity orders: **13,400**

41 ❑ Apr 1990 Cover: 1.00 **NM** value: **1.75**
Circ: CapCity orders: **12,600**

42 ❑ May 1990 Cover: 1.00 **NM** value: **1.75**
Circ: CapCity orders: **12,500**

43 ❑ Jun 1990 Cover: 1.00 **NM** value: **1.75**
Circ: CapCity orders: **12,200**

44 ❑ Jul 1990 Cover: 1.00 **NM** value: **1.75**
Circ: CapCity orders: **11,850**

45 ❑ Aug 1990 Cover: 1.00 **NM** value: **1.75**
Circ: CapCity orders: **11,400**

46 ❑ Sep 1990 Cover: 1.00 **NM** value: **1.75**
Circ: CapCity orders: **11,400**

47 ❑ Oct 1990 Cover: 1.00 **NM** value: **1.75**
Circ: CapCity orders: **11,200**

48 ❑ Nov 1990 Cover: 1.00 **NM** value: **1.75**
Circ: CapCity orders: **11,200**

49 ❑ Dec 1990 Cover: 1.00 **NM** value: **1.75**
Circ: CapCity orders: **11,600**

50 ❑ Jan 1991 Cover: 1.50 **NM** value: **1.75**
Circ: CapCity orders: **13,200**
📖 Embrace the Coming Dawn **A:** Adam Hughes; Matt Wagner; Sergio Aragonés; Cynthia Martin; Brian Bolland; Linda Medley; P. Craig Russell; Marie Severin; Kevin Nowlan; Jill Thompson; Chris Bachalo; Romeo Tanghal **C:** George Pérez **W:** George Pérez

51 ❑ Feb 1991 Cover: 1.00 **NM** value: **1.50**
Circ: CapCity orders: **11,450**

52 ❑ Mar 1991 Cover: 1.00 **NM** value: **1.50**
Circ: CapCity orders: **11,050**

53 ❑ Apr 1991 Cover: 1.00 **NM** value: **1.50**
Circ: CapCity orders: **11,050**

54 ❑ May 1991 Cover: 1.00 **NM** value: **1.50**
Circ: CapCity orders: **10,800**

55 ❑ Jun 1991 Cover: 1.00 **NM** value: **1.50**
Circ: CapCity orders: **10,500**

56 ❑ Jul 1991 Cover: 1.00 **NM** value: **1.50**
Circ: CapCity orders: **10,450**

57 ❑ Aug 1991 Cover: 1.00 **NM** value: **1.50**
Circ: CapCity orders: **10,750**

58 ❑ Sep 1991 Cover: 1.00 **NM** value: **1.50**
Circ: CapCity orders: **18,950**
📖 War of the Gods, Part 3 • War of Gods

59 ❑ Oct 1991 Cover: 1.00 **NM** value: **1.50**
Circ: CapCity orders: **16,850**
📖 War of the Gods, Part 11 • War of Gods

60 ❑ Nov 1991 Cover: 1.00 **NM** value: **1.50**
Circ: CapCity orders: **19,750**
📖 War of the Gods, Part 19; Lobo appearance • War of Gods

61 ❑ Jan 1992 Cover: 1.00 **NM** value: **1.50**
Circ: CapCity orders: **21,100**
📖 War of the Gods, Part 22 • War of Gods

62 ❑ Feb 1992 Cover: 1.00 **NM** value: **1.50**
Circ: CapCity orders: **17,100**

63 ❑ Jun 1992 Cover: 1.25 **NM** value: **1.50**
Circ: CapCity orders: **13,550** • **CGC:** 1 graded, best 8.5
📖 Operation: Cheetah, Part 2 **C:** Brian Bolland

64 ❑ Jul 1992 Cover: 1.25 **NM** value: **1.50**
Circ: CapCity orders: **12,050**

65 ❑ Aug 1992 Cover: 1.25 **NM** value: **1.50**
Circ: CapCity orders: **12,050**

66 ❑ Sep 1992 Cover: 1.25 **NM** value: **1.50**
Circ: CapCity orders: **11,450**

67 ❑ Oct 1992 Cover: 1.25 **NM** value: **1.50**
Circ: CapCity orders: **10,950**

68 ❑ Nov 1992 Cover: 1.25 **NM** value: **1.50**
Circ: CapCity orders: **10,000**

69 ❑ Dec 1992 Cover: 1.25 **NM** value: **1.50**
Circ: CapCity orders: **9,400**

70 ❑ Jan 1993 Cover: 1.25 **NM** value: **1.50**
Circ: CapCity orders: **9,100**

71 ❑ Feb 1993 Cover: 1.25 **NM** value: **1.50**
Circ: CapCity orders: **9,350**

72 ❑ Mar 1993 Cover: 1.25 **NM** value: **1.50**
Circ: CapCity orders: **9,400** • **CGC:** 2 graded, best 9.2

73 ❑ Apr 1993 Cover: 1.25 **NM** value: **1.50**
Circ: CapCity orders: **9,650**

74 ❑ May 1993 Cover: 1.25 **NM** value: **1.50**
Circ: CapCity orders: **9,450**

75 ❑ Jun 1993 Cover: 1.25 **NM** value: **1.50**
Circ: CapCity orders: **10,350**

76 ❑ Jul 1993 Cover: 1.25 **NM** value: **1.50**
Circ: CapCity orders: **9,700**

77 ❑ Aug 1993 Cover: 1.25 **NM** value: **1.50**
Circ: CapCity orders: **9,600**

78 ❑ Sep 1993 Cover: 1.25 **NM** value: **1.50**
Circ: CapCity orders: **8,900**

79 ❑ Oct 1993 Cover: 1.25 **NM** value: **1.50**
Circ: CapCity orders: **8,650**

80 ❑ Nov 1993 Cover: 1.25 **NM** value: **1.50**
Circ: CapCity orders: **8,550**
📖 It's Never a Good Day to Die **A:** Steve Carr; Deryl Skelton **C:** Brian Bolland **W:** William Messner-Loebs

81 ❑ Dec 1993 Cover: 1.25 **NM** value: **1.50**
Circ: CapCity orders: **8,600**
📖 And then she Fell to Earth **A:** Lee Moder **C:** Brian Bolland **W:** William Messner-Loebs

82 ❑ Jan 1994 Cover: 1.25 **NM** value: **1.50**
Circ: CapCity orders: **8,375**

83 ❑ Feb 1994 Cover: 1.50 **NM** value: **Cover or less**
Circ: CapCity orders: **8,100**

84 ❑ Mar 1994 Cover: 1.50 **NM** value: **Cover or less**
Circ: CapCity orders: **7,800**
📖 Ares Rising: Amazon Songs **A:** Massengil **C:** Brian Bolland **W:** William Messner-Loebs

85 ❑ Apr 1994 Cover: 1.50 **NM** value: **10.00**
Circ: CapCity orders: **7,400**
• Mike Deodato Jr.'s first U.S. work **A:** Mike Deodato Jr. **C:** Brian Bolland

86 ❑ May 1994 Cover: 1.50 **NM** value: **4.00**
Circ: CapCity orders: **7,600**

87 ❑ Jun 1994 Cover: 1.50 **NM** value: **3.00**
Circ: CapCity orders: **7,500**

88 ❑ Jul 1994 Cover: 1.50 **NM** value: **3.00**
Circ: CapCity orders: **8,050** • **CGC:** 1 graded, best 9.9

89 ❑ Aug 1994 Cover: 1.50 **NM** value: **3.00**
Circ: CapCity orders: **7,600**
📖 Home **A:** John Ross **C:** Brian Bolland **W:** Christopher Priest

90 ❑ Sep 1994 Cover: 1.50 **NM** value: **3.00**
Circ: CapCity orders: **8,750**
📖 The Contest **C:** Brian Bolland

91 ❑ Nov 1994 Cover: 1.50 **NM** value: **3.00**
Circ: CapCity orders: **9,500** • **CGC:** 1 graded, best 9.6

92 ❑ Dec 1994 Cover: 1.50 **NM** value: **3.00**
Circ: CapCity orders: **11,100**

93 ❑ Jan 1995 Cover: 1.50 **NM** value: **3.00**
Circ: CapCity orders: **12,850**

Other grades: Multiply prices above by **1.5 for Mint • 2/3 for Very Fine • 1/3 for Fine • 1/5 for Very Good • 1/8 for Good**

📖 Violent Beginnings **A:** Mike Deodato Jr. **W:** William Messner-Loebs
94 ❑ Feb 1995 Cover: 1.50 **NM** value: **2.00**
Circ: CapCity orders: **12,900**
95 ❑ Mar 1995 Cover: 1.50 **NM** value: **2.00**
Circ: CapCity orders: **14,175**
96 ❑ Apr 1995 Cover: 1.50 **NM** value: **2.00**
Circ: CapCity orders: **15,400** • **CGC:** 1 graded, best 9.6
97 ❑ May 1995 Cover: 1.50 **NM** value: **2.00**
Circ: CapCity orders: **16,200** • **CGC:** 1 graded, best 9.6
98 ❑ Jun 1995 Cover: 1.75 **NM** value: **2.00**
Circ: CapCity orders: **16,100**
99 ❑ Jul 1995 Cover: 1.75 **NM** value: **2.00**
Circ: CapCity orders: **20,200**
100 ❑ Jul 1995 Cover: 2.95 **NM** value: **Cover or less**
• Giant-size. 📖 Fall of an Amazon • Wonder Woman returns to old uniform ★ Death of Athena.
100/SC ❑ Jul 1995 Cover: 3.95 **NM** value: **4.00**
Circ: CapCity orders: **28,825**
enhanced cover. • Giant-size. • Wonder Woman returns to old uniform ★ Death of Athena.
101 ❑ Sep 1995 Cover: 1.95 **NM** value: **Cover or less**
Circ: CapCity orders: **29,800**
102 ❑ Oct 1995 Cover: 1.95 **NM** value: **Cover or less**
Circ: CapCity orders: **20,650**
103 ❑ Nov 1995 Cover: 1.95 **NM** value: **Cover or less**
104 ❑ Dec 1995 Cover: 1.95 **NM** value: **Cover or less**
105 ❑ Jan 1996 Cover: 1.95 **NM** value: **Cover or less**
📖 Lifelines, Part 1 **A:** John Byrne **W:** John Byrne
106 ❑ Feb 1996 Cover: 1.95 **NM** value: **Cover or less**
📖 Lifelines, Part 2 **A:** John Byrne **W:** John Byrne ★ Appearance of Phantom Stranger.
107 ❑ Mar 1996 Cover: 1.95 **NM** value: **Cover or less**
📖 Lifelines, Part 3 **A:** John Byrne **W:** John Byrne ★ Appearance of Demon.
108 ❑ Apr 1996 Cover: 1.95 **NM** value: **Cover or less**
📖 Lifelines, Part 4 **A:** John Byrne **W:** John Byrne
109 ❑ May 1996 Cover: 1.95 **NM** value: **Cover or less**
110 ❑ Jun 1996 Cover: 1.95 **NM** value: **Cover or less**
111 ❑ Jul 1996 Cover: 1.95 **NM** value: **Cover or less**
112 ❑ Aug 1996 Cover: 1.95 **NM** value: **Cover or less**
113 ❑ Sep 1996 Cover: 1.95 **NM** value: **Cover or less**
114 ❑ Oct 1996 Cover: 1.95 **NM** value: **Cover or less**
📖 Nightmare Alley **A:** John Byrne **W:** John Byrne
115 ❑ Nov 1996 Cover: 1.95 **NM** value: **Cover or less**
Circ: Diamd. preorders: **45,247**
📖 The Men Who Moved the World, Part 1 **A:** John Byrne **W:** John Byrne
116 ❑ Dec 1996 Cover: 1.95 **NM** value: **Cover or less**
Circ: Diamd. preorders: **44,851**
📖 The Men Who Moved the World, Part 2 **A:** John Byrne **W:** John Byrne ★ Appearance of Cave Carson.
117 ❑ Jan 1997 Cover: 1.95 **NM** value: **Cover or less**
Circ: Diamd. preorders: **42,361**
📖 The Men Who Moved the World, Part 3 **A:** John Byrne **W:** John Byrne ★ 1st Appearance of Invisible Plane.
118 ❑ Feb 1997 Cover: 1.95 **NM** value: **Cover or less**
Circ: Diamd. preorders: **40,337**
119 ❑ Mar 1997 Cover: 1.95 **NM** value: **Cover or less**
Circ: Diamd. preorders: **38,513**
📖 In the Forest of the Night **A:** John Byrne **W:** John Byrne ★ Versus Cheetah.
120 ❑ Apr 1997 Cover: 2.95 **NM** value: **Cover or less**
Circ: Diamd. preorders: **38,353**
• 10th anniversary issue. **C:** George Pérez
121 ❑ May 1997 Cover: 1.95 **NM** value: **Cover or less**
Circ: Diamd. preorders: **36,926**
122 ❑ Jun 1997 Cover: 1.95 **NM** value: **Cover or less**
Circ: Diamd. preorders: **37,252**
123 ❑ Jul 1997 Cover: 1.95 **NM** value: **Cover or less**
Circ: Diamd. preorders: **37,081**
124 ❑ Aug 1997 Cover: 1.95 **NM** value: **Cover or less**
Circ: Diamd. preorders: **36,705**
125 ❑ Sep 1997 Cover: 1.95 **NM** value: **Cover or less**
Circ: Diamd. preorders: **38,236**
• Diana in intensive care; Martian Manhunter; Batman; Green Lantern; Flash ★ Origin of Demon. ★ Appearance of Superman, Flash, Martian Manhunter, Green Lantern, Batman.
126 ❑ Oct 1997 Cover: 1.95 **NM** value: **Cover or less**
Circ: Diamd. preorders: **39,648**
• Genesis
127 ❑ Nov 1997 Cover: 1.95 **NM** value: **Cover or less**
Circ: Diamd. preorders: **37,132**
📖 Transfiguration • Diana is turned into a goddess and goes to Olympus **A:** John Byrne **W:** John Byrne
128 ❑ Dec 1997 Cover: 1.95 **NM** value: **Cover or less**
Circ: Diamd. preorders: **38,490**
Face cover. **A:** John Byrne **W:** John Byrne
129 ❑ Jan 1998 Cover: 1.95 **NM** value: **Cover or less**
Circ: Diamd. preorders: **38,552**
130 ❑ Feb 1998 Cover: 1.95 **NM** value: **Cover or less**
Circ: Diamd. preorders: **38,705**
131 ❑ Mar 1998 Cover: 1.95 **NM** value: **Cover or less**
Circ: Diamd. preorders: **38,108**
132 ❑ Apr 1998 Cover: 1.95 **NM** value: **Cover or less**
Circ: Diamd. preorders: **37,049**
133 ❑ May 1998 Cover: 1.95 **NM** value: **Cover or less**
Circ: Diamd. preorders: **37,127**
134 ❑ Jun 1998 Cover: 1.95 **NM** value: **Cover or less**
Circ: Diamd. preorders: **39,057**
📖 Who is Donna Troy?
135 ❑ Jul 1998 Cover: 1.95 **NM** value: **Cover or less**
Circ: Diamd. preorders: **37,206**
136 ❑ Aug 1998 Cover: 1.95 **NM** value: **1.99**
Circ: Diamd. preorders: **36,748**
• Diana returns to Earth; Return of Donna Troy
137 ❑ Sep 1998 Cover: 1.99 **NM** value: **Cover or less**
Circ: Diamd. preorders: **34,582**
138 ❑ Oct 1998 Cover: 1.99 **NM** value: **Cover or less**
Circ: Diamd. preorders: **33,490**
139 ❑ Dec 1998 Cover: 1.99 **NM** value: **Cover or less**
Circ: Diamd. preorders: **32,765**
• Diana becomes mortal again
139/LE ❑ Dec 1998 Cover: 14.95 **NM** value: **Cover or less**
140 ❑ Jan 1999 Cover: 1.99 **NM** value: **Cover or less**
Circ: Diamd. preorders: **31,528**
📖 Trinity, Part 1 ★ Appearance of Superman, Batman.
141 ❑ Feb 1999 Cover: 1.99 **NM** value: **Cover or less**
Circ: Diamd. preorders: **30,431**
📖 Trinity, Part 2 **A:** Yanick Paquette ★ Appearance of Superman, Batman, Oblivion.
142 ❑ Mar 1999 Cover: 1.99 **NM** value: **Cover or less**
Circ: Diamd. preorders: **28,487**
143 ❑ Apr 1999 Cover: 1.99 **NM** value: **Cover or less**
Circ: Diamd. preorders: **27,705**
📖 Devastation, Part 1 **A:** Yanick Paquette **W:** Eric Luke ★ 1st Appearance of Devastation.
144 ❑ May 1999 Cover: 1.99 **NM** value: **Cover or less**
Circ: Diamd. preorders: **28,167**
📖 Devastation, Part 2 **A:** Yanick Paquette **W:** Eric Luke ★ Versus Devastation.
145 ❑ Jun 1999 Cover: 1.99 **NM** value: **Cover or less**
Circ: Diamd. preorders: **27,806**
📖 Devastation, Part 3 **A:** Matthew Clark **W:** Eric Luke ★ Versus Devastation.
146 ❑ Jul 1999 Cover: 1.99 **NM** value: **Cover or less**
Circ: Diamd. preorders: **26,568**
📖 Devastation, Part 4 **A:** Yanick Paquette **W:** Eric Luke ★ Versus Devastation.
147 ❑ Aug 1999 Cover: 1.99 **NM** value: **Cover or less**
Circ: Diamd. preorders: **25,620**
📖 Godwar, Part 1: Revolution; Godwar, Part 1 **A:** Yanick Paquette **W:** Eric Luke
148 ❑ Sep 1999 Cover: 1.99 **NM** value: **Cover or less**
Circ: Diamd. preorders: **24,788**
📖 Godwar, Part 2 **A:** Yanick Paquette **W:** Eric Luke
149 ❑ Oct 1999 Cover: 1.99 **NM** value: **Cover or less**
Circ: Diamd. preorders: **24,416**
150 ❑ Nov 1999 Cover: 1.99 **NM** value: **Cover or less**
Circ: Diamd. preorders: **27,084**
📖 The Pandora Virus, Part 1
151 ❑ Dec 1999 Cover: 1.99 **NM** value: **Cover or less**
Circ: Diamd. preorders: **24,990**
📖 The Pandora Virus, Part 2 **A:** Matthew Clark **W:** Eric Luke
152 ❑ Jan 2000 Cover: 1.99 **NM** value: **Cover or less**
Circ: Diamd. preorders: **23,871**
153 ❑ Feb 2000 Cover: 1.99 **NM** value: **Cover or less**
Circ: Diamd. preorders: **25,196**
154 ❑ Mar 2000 Cover: 1.99 **NM** value: **Cover or less**
Circ: Diamd. preorders: **23,593**
155 ❑ Apr 2000 Cover: 1.99 **NM** value: **Cover or less**
Circ: Diamd. preorders: **22,123**
📖 Three Hearts, Part 2 **A:** John McCrea; George Freeman **W:** Doselle Young
156 ❑ May 2000 Cover: 1.99 **NM** value: **Cover or less**
Circ: Diamd. preorders: **22,859**
📖 Devastation: The Return, Part 1 **A:** Matthew Clark **W:** Eric Luke
157 ❑ Jun 2000 Cover: 1.99 **NM** value: **Cover or less**
Circ: Diamd. preorders: **22,637**
158 ❑ Jul 2000 Cover: 1.99 **NM** value: **Cover or less**
Circ: Diamd. preorders: **22,245**
159 ❑ Aug 2000 Cover: 2.25 **NM** value: **Cover or less**
Circ: Diamd. preorders: **22,373**
160 ❑ Sep 2000 Cover: 2.25 **NM** value: **Cover or less**
Circ: Diamd. preorders: **22,427**
📖 A Piece of You, Part 1 **A:** Scott Kolins **W:** Brian K. Vaughan
161 ❑ Oct 2000 Cover: 2.25 **NM** value: **Cover or less**
Circ: Diamd. preorders: **21,275**
📖 A Piece of You, Part 2 **A:** Scott Kolins **W:** Brian K. Vaughan
162 ❑ Nov 2000 Cover: 2.25 **NM** value: **Cover or less**
Circ: Diamd. preorders: **21,355**
📖 God Complex, Part 1 **A:** Derec Aucoin **W:** Ben Raab
163 ❑ Dec 2000 Cover: 2.25 **NM** value: **Cover or less**
Circ: Diamd. preorders: **21,313**
📖 God Complex, Part 2 **A:** Derec Aucoin **W:** Ben Raab
164 ❑ Jan 2001 Cover: 2.25 **NM** value: **Cover or less**
Circ: Diamd. preorders: **25,653** • **CGC:** 3 graded, best 9.8
📖 Gods of Gotham, Part 1 **A:** Phil Jimenez **W:** Phil Jimenez; J.M. DeMatteis
165 ❑ Feb 2001 Cover: 2.25 **NM** value: **Cover or less**
Circ: Diamd. preorders: **25,129**
📖 Gods of Gotham, Part 2 **A:** Phil Jimenez **W:** Phil Jimenez; J.M. DeMatteis
166 ❑ Mar 2001 Cover: 2.25 **NM** value: **Cover or less**
Circ: Diamd. preorders: **24,741**
📖 Gods of Gotham, Part 3 **A:** Phil Jimenez **W:** Phil Jimenez; J.M. DeMatteis ★ Appearance of Batman.
167 ❑ Apr 2001 Cover: 2.25 **NM** value: **Cover or less**
Circ: Diamd. preorders: **26,702** • **CGC:** 1 graded, best 9.6
📖 Gods of Gotham, Part 4 **A:** Phil Jimenez **W:** Phil Jimenez
168 ❑ May 2001 Cover: 2.25 **NM** value: **Cover or less**
Circ: Diamd. preorders: **27,185**
📖 Paradise Island Lost, Part 1 **A:** Phil Jimenez **W:** Phil Jimenez; George Pérez
169 ❑ Jun 2001 Cover: 2.25 **NM** value: **Cover or less**
Circ: Diamd. preorders: **28,793**
170 ❑ Jul 2001 Cover: 2.25 **NM** value: **Cover or less**
Circ: Diamd. preorders: **29,986** • **CGC:** 3 graded, best 9.6
171 ❑ Aug 2001 Cover: 2.25 **NM** value: **Cover or less**
Circ: Diamd. preorders: **33,234** • **CGC:** 1 graded, best 9.8
172 ❑ Sep 2001 Cover: 2.25 **NM** value: **Cover or less**
Circ: Diamd. preorders: **36,725** • **CGC:** 1 graded, best 9.6
1000000 ❑ Nov 1998 Cover: 1.99 **NM** value: **Cover or less**
Circ: Diamd. preorders: **40,471**
📖 Legends **A:** Mike Collins **W:** Christopher Priest
Anl 1 ❑ ca. 1988 Cover: 1.50 **NM** value: **2.00**
Circ: CapCity orders: **23,750**
📖 Amazons; The Diving Bird; The First Statue; Into the World Go Forth; Flight of the Icarus; Testament **A:** Arthur Adams; George Pérez; Brian Bolland; Curt Swan; Ross Andru; Bob McLeod; José Luis García-Lopez **W:** George Pérez
Anl 2 ❑ ca. 1989 Cover: 2.00 **NM** value: **Cover or less**
Circ: CapCity orders: **17,050**
📖 The Game of the Name; Headline; Trademark; Logo; Play Like; Banner; Marquee; Legend; Tribute **A:** Ramona Fradon; Barb Rausch; Carol Lay; Jan Duursema; Cynthia Martin; Trina Robbins; Colleen Doran; Lee Marrs; Cara Sherman-Tereno; George P…rez; Leslie Sternbergh
Anl 3 ❑ ca. 1992 Cover: 2.50 **NM** value: **Cover or less**
Circ: CapCity orders: **17,550**
📖 Eclipso: The Darkness Within, Part 17 • Eclipso
Anl 4 ❑ ca. 1995 Cover: 3.50 **NM** value: **Cover or less**
Circ: CapCity orders: **14,150**
• Year One **A:** Brent Anderson
Anl 5 ❑ ca. 1996 Cover: 2.95 **NM** value: **Cover or less**
Circ: Diamd. preorders: **37,303**
📖 The Unremembered • Legends of the Dead Earth; 1996 Annual **A:** Dave Cockrum **W:** John Byrne
Anl 6 ❑ ca. 1997 Cover: 3.95 **NM** value: **Cover or less**
Circ: Diamd. preorders: **32,609**
📖 City of the Dead • Pulp Heroes **A:** Tom Palmer **W:** John Byrne
Anl 7 ❑ ca. 1998 Cover: 2.95 **NM** value: **Cover or less**
Circ: Diamd. preorders: **27,193**
• Ghosts
Anl 8 ❑ Sep 1999 Cover: 2.95 **NM** value: **Cover or less**
Circ: Diamd. preorders: **26,483**
📖 The Thin Gold Line • JLApe **A:** Brian Denham **W:** Doselle Young
Bk 1 ❑ Cover: 9.95 **NM** value: **Cover or less**
📖 The Contest • collects Wonder Woman #0; 90-93; The Challenge of Artemis
Bk 2 ❑ Cover: 9.95 **NM** value: **Cover or less**
• The Challenge Of Artemis; collects #94-100
Bk 3 ❑ Cover: 9.95 **NM** value: **Cover or less**
📖 Lifelines • collects issues #106-112 **A:** John Byrne
SE 1 ❑ ca. 1992 Cover: 1.75 **NM** value: **Cover or less**
Circ: CapCity orders: **17,400**
📖 Operation: Cheetah, Part 1 ★ Appearance of Deathstroke.

WONDER WOMAN: AMAZONIA — DC

1 ❑ Cover: 7.95 **NM** value: **Cover or less**
No issue number. • Oversized. • Elseworlds

WONDER WOMAN ARCHIVES — DC

1 ❑ Cover: 49.95 **NM** value: **Cover or less**
hardcover. • collects Wonder Woman stories from Sensation Comics #1-2, Wonder Woman (1st Series) #1
2 ❑ Cover: 49.95 **NM** value: **Cover or less**
• Collects Wonder Woman (1st Series) #2-4, Sensation Comics #13-17

WONDER WOMAN: DONNA TROY — DC

1 ❑ Jun 1998 Cover: 1.95 **NM** value: **Cover or less**
Circ: Diamd. preorders: **37,588**
One-shot. 📖 Why • Girlfrenzy **A:** Phil Jimenez **W:** Phil Jimenez

WONDER WOMAN GALLERY — DC

1 ❑ ca. 1996 Cover: 3.50 **NM** value: **Cover or less**
No issue number. One-shot. • pin-ups

WONDER WOMAN PLUS — DC

1 ❑ Jan 1997 Cover: 2.95 **NM** value: **Cover or less**
Circ: Diamd. preorders: **36,132**
📖 Heroes **A:** Mike Collins **W:** Christopher Priest ★ Appearance of Liberty Belle, Jesse Quick.

WONDER WOMAN SECRET FILES — DC

1 ❑ Mar 1998 Cover: 4.95 **NM** value: **Cover or less**
Circ: Diamd. preorders: **30,122**
📖 Secret Origin; Origin Epilogue; Guided Tour: Themyscira; Artifacts & Weapons; Secret Details about Wonder Woman's Invisible Plane! • background on Wonder Woman and supporting cast **A:** Ron Wagner; Randy DuBurke; Ethan Van Sciver; Eric Battle; Phil Jimenez; John Byrne; Dick Giordano; Joe Kubert; Dave Cockrum; Lee Moder; Jill Thompson; Pablo Raimondi; Kieron Grant **W:** John Byrne; Alex Amado; Jason Hernandez-Rosenblatt; Joanna Sandsmark; Ruth Morrison ★ Origin of Wonder Woman.
2 ❑ Jul 1999 Cover: 4.95 **NM** value: **Cover or less**
Circ: Diamd. preorders: **18,885**
📖 Origin of Devastation • background on Wonder Woman and supporting cast **A:** Adam Hughes; Phil Jimenez; Yanick Paquette; Eliot Brown; Matthew Clark **W:** Phil Jimenez; Eliot Brown; Devin Grayson; Eric Luke; Joanna Sandsmark

WONDER WOMAN: THE ONCE AND FUTURE STORY — DC

1 ❑ ca. 1998 Cover: 4.95 **NM** value: **Cover or less**
Circ: Diamd. preorders: **20,777**
No issue number. • prestige format one-shot; domestic violence

There are two different pricing tiers in the modern comic-book hobby. **The prices seen above** are the prices we have seen **loose copies** of these issues reliably fetch in a variety of environments. Condition alters the price by the fractions seen on the bar on the bottom of left-hand pages of this book. **Comics graded by CGC** usually sell for more. Use the guide on the bottom of right-hand pages of this book to estimate what copies have brought on eBay.

CGC-graded: Multiply prices above by **33 for 9.9 M • 16 for 9.8 NM/M • 7 for 9.6 NM+ • 5 for 9.4 NM • 2.5 for 9.2 NM- • 1.5 for 9.0 VF/NM**

WONDERWORLD COMICS Fox

Though the title began as Wonder Comics in 1939, it switched that same year to Wonderworld with #3. Like many other titles of the 1930s and 1940s, it was an anthology comic book featuring stories concerning a number of different characters. Long-running features included those of Patty O'Day (newsreel reporter), Dr. Fung (master sleuth of the Orient), "Spark Stevens" (Navy stories), Tex Maxon (the Phantom Rider), Yarko the Great (master of magic), and The Flame.

Intriguingly, the Wonder Man character, clearly intended to tie to the title, appeared only in the first issue. As a pioneering attempt to benefit from the popularity of Superman (with a reporter who gets super-powers), it was quickly quashed by the possibility of legal action from Superman's owners. When World War II came, Wonderworld went. — Maggie

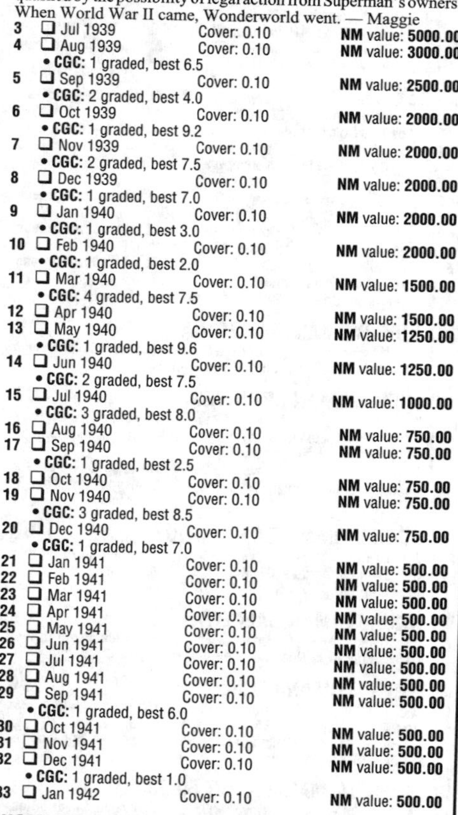

3 ❑ Jul 1939 Cover: 0.10 **NM** value: **5000.00**
4 ❑ Aug 1939 Cover: 0.10 **NM** value: **3000.00**
• **CGC:** 1 graded, best 6.5
5 ❑ Sep 1939 Cover: 0.10 **NM** value: **2500.00**
• **CGC:** 2 graded, best 4.0
6 ❑ Oct 1939 Cover: 0.10 **NM** value: **2000.00**
• **CGC:** 1 graded, best 9.2
7 ❑ Nov 1939 Cover: 0.10 **NM** value: **2000.00**
• **CGC:** 2 graded, best 7.5
8 ❑ Dec 1939 Cover: 0.10 **NM** value: **2000.00**
• **CGC:** 1 graded, best 7.0
9 ❑ Jan 1940 Cover: 0.10 **NM** value: **2000.00**
• **CGC:** 1 graded, best 3.0
10 ❑ Feb 1940 Cover: 0.10 **NM** value: **2000.00**
• **CGC:** 1 graded, best 2.0
11 ❑ Mar 1940 Cover: 0.10 **NM** value: **1500.00**
• **CGC:** 4 graded, best 7.5
12 ❑ Apr 1940 Cover: 0.10 **NM** value: **1500.00**
13 ❑ May 1940 Cover: 0.10 **NM** value: **1250.00**
• **CGC:** 1 graded, best 9.6
14 ❑ Jun 1940 Cover: 0.10 **NM** value: **1250.00**
• **CGC:** 2 graded, best 7.5
15 ❑ Jul 1940 Cover: 0.10 **NM** value: **1000.00**
• **CGC:** 3 graded, best 8.0
16 ❑ Aug 1940 Cover: 0.10 **NM** value: **750.00**
17 ❑ Sep 1940 Cover: 0.10 **NM** value: **750.00**
• **CGC:** 1 graded, best 2.5
18 ❑ Oct 1940 Cover: 0.10 **NM** value: **750.00**
19 ❑ Nov 1940 Cover: 0.10 **NM** value: **750.00**
• **CGC:** 3 graded, best 8.5
20 ❑ Dec 1940 Cover: 0.10 **NM** value: **750.00**
• **CGC:** 1 graded, best 7.0
21 ❑ Jan 1941 Cover: 0.10 **NM** value: **500.00**
22 ❑ Feb 1941 Cover: 0.10 **NM** value: **500.00**
23 ❑ Mar 1941 Cover: 0.10 **NM** value: **500.00**
24 ❑ Apr 1941 Cover: 0.10 **NM** value: **500.00**
25 ❑ May 1941 Cover: 0.10 **NM** value: **500.00**
26 ❑ Jun 1941 Cover: 0.10 **NM** value: **500.00**
27 ❑ Jul 1941 Cover: 0.10 **NM** value: **500.00**
28 ❑ Aug 1941 Cover: 0.10 **NM** value: **500.00**
29 ❑ Sep 1941 Cover: 0.10 **NM** value: **500.00**
• **CGC:** 1 graded, best 6.0
30 ❑ Oct 1941 Cover: 0.10 **NM** value: **500.00**
31 ❑ Nov 1941 Cover: 0.10 **NM** value: **500.00**
32 ❑ Dec 1941 Cover: 0.10 **NM** value: **500.00**
• **CGC:** 1 graded, best 1.0
33 ❑ Jan 1942 Cover: 0.10 **NM** value: **500.00**

WONDERWORLD EXPRESS That Other Comix Co.

1 ❑ Cover: 1.00 **NM** value: **Cover or less**

WONDERWORLDS Innovation

1 ❑ Cover: 3.50 **NM** value: **Cover or less**

WOODSTOCK: THE COMIC Marvel

1 ❑ Cover: 5.95 **NM** value: **Cover or less**

WOODSY OWL Gold Key

1 ❑ Nov 1973 Cover: 0.25 **NM** value: **8.00**
2 ❑ Feb 1974 Cover: 0.25 **NM** value: **5.00**
3 ❑ May 1974 Cover: 0.25 **NM** value: **4.00**
4 ❑ Aug 1974 Cover: 0.25 **NM** value: **4.00**
5 ❑ Nov 1974 Cover: 0.25 **NM** value: **4.00**
6 ❑ Feb 1975 Cover: 0.25 **NM** value: **3.00**
📖 Alias Mother Naure; Operation Hill-Kill; The Power Pig
7 ❑ May 1975 Cover: 0.25 **NM** value: **3.00**
8 ❑ Aug 1975 Cover: 0.25 **NM** value: **3.00**
9 ❑ Nov 1975 Cover: 0.25 **NM** value: **3.00**
10 ❑ Feb 1976 Cover: 0.25 **NM** value: **3.00**

WOODY WOODPECKER 50TH ANNIVERSARY SPECIAL Harvey

1 ❑ Oct 1991 Cover: 2.50 **NM** value: **Cover or less**
Circ: CapCity orders: **3,650**

WOODY WOODPECKER ADVENTURES Harvey

1 ❑ Cover: 1.25 **NM** value: **Cover or less**
📖 The Rain Maker; Charlie Chicken: The Model Farm; Oswald Rabbit; Spooky: The Boo Boob
2 ❑ Cover: 1.25 **NM** value: **Cover or less**
3 ❑ Cover: 1.25 **NM** value: **Cover or less**

WOODY WOODPECKER AND FRIENDS Harvey

1 ❑ Dec 1991 Cover: 1.25 **NM** value: **Cover or less**
Circ: CapCity orders: **3,450**
2 ❑ Feb 1992 Cover: 1.25 **NM** value: **Cover or less**
Circ: CapCity orders: **1,725**
3 ❑ Apr 1992 Cover: 1.25 **NM** value: **Cover or less**
4 ❑ Jun 1992 Cover: 1.25 **NM** value: **Cover or less**

WOODY WOODPECKER DIGEST Harvey

1 ❑ Cover: 1.75 **NM** value: **Cover or less**

WOODY WOODPECKER GIANT SIZE Harvey

1 ❑ Cover: 2.25 **NM** value: **Cover or less**

WOODY WOODPECKER (HARVEY) Harvey

1 ❑ Sep 1991 Cover: 1.25 **NM** value: **1.50**
Circ: CapCity orders: **5,275**
2 ❑ Nov 1991 Cover: 1.25 **NM** value: **Cover or less**
Circ: CapCity orders: **2,650**
3 ❑ Jan 1992 Cover: 1.25 **NM** value: **Cover or less**
📖 The Abominable Snowman; Big Bear & Little Bear: The Natural Expert
4 ❑ Mar 1992 Cover: 1.25 **NM** value: **Cover or less**
5 ❑ Jun 1992 Cover: 1.25 **NM** value: **Cover or less**
6 ❑ Sep 1992 Cover: 1.25 **NM** value: **Cover or less**
7 ❑ Cover: 1.25 **NM** value: **Cover or less**
8 ❑ Jun 1993 Cover: 1.25 **NM** value: **Cover or less**

WOODY WOODPECKER'S BACK TO SCHOOL Dell

6 ❑ Oct 1957 Cover: 0.25 **NM** value: **75.00**
• **CGC:** 1 graded, best 8.0

WOODY WOODPECKER'S CHRISTMAS PARADE Gold Key

1 ❑ Nov 1968 Cover: 0.25 **NM** value: **20.00**
• **CGC:** 1 graded, best 9.4

WOODY WOODPECKER'S COUNTY FAIR Dell

1 ❑ Nov 1958 Cover: 0.25 **NM** value: **60.00**

WOODY WOODPECKER SUMMER SPECIAL Harvey

1 ❑ Oct 1990 Cover: 1.95 **NM** value: **Cover or less**

WOODY WOODPECKER (WALTER LANTZ...) Dell

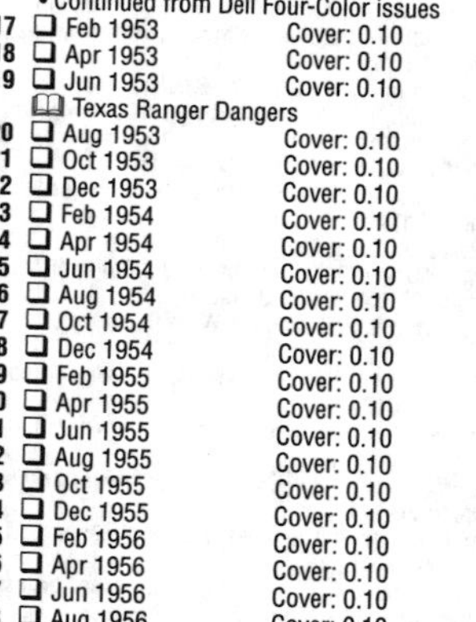

Walter Lantz's Woody Woodpecker was another wacky animal creation to make the jump from animated cartoons to comic books and was featured in a long-running series from Dell Publishing, who owned this segment of the market for many years. The two most memorable aspects of the Woody Woodpecker cartoons — the fast-paced bebop jazz score and Woody's annoying ha-de-de-HAH-hah chuckle — are, of course, absent from the comic-book version, which, instead, focuses on Woody's pranks and mischief. A wily trickster, Woody just as often gets his just deserts in the end, much to his humiliation.

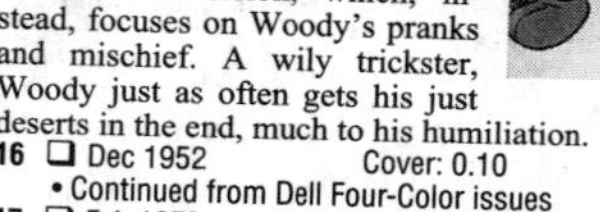

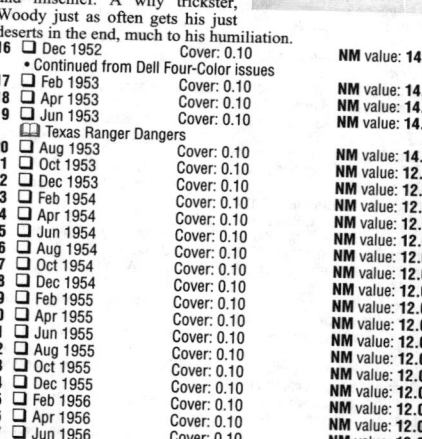

16 ❑ Dec 1952 Cover: 0.10 **NM** value: **14.00**
• Continued from Dell Four-Color issues
17 ❑ Feb 1953 Cover: 0.10 **NM** value: **14.00**
18 ❑ Apr 1953 Cover: 0.10 **NM** value: **14.00**
19 ❑ Jun 1953 Cover: 0.10 **NM** value: **14.00**
📖 Texas Ranger Dangers
20 ❑ Aug 1953 Cover: 0.10 **NM** value: **14.00**
21 ❑ Oct 1953 Cover: 0.10 **NM** value: **12.00**
22 ❑ Dec 1953 Cover: 0.10 **NM** value: **12.00**
23 ❑ Feb 1954 Cover: 0.10 **NM** value: **12.00**
24 ❑ Apr 1954 Cover: 0.10 **NM** value: **12.00**
25 ❑ Jun 1954 Cover: 0.10 **NM** value: **12.00**
26 ❑ Aug 1954 Cover: 0.10 **NM** value: **12.00**
27 ❑ Oct 1954 Cover: 0.10 **NM** value: **12.00**
28 ❑ Dec 1954 Cover: 0.10 **NM** value: **12.00**
29 ❑ Feb 1955 Cover: 0.10 **NM** value: **12.00**
30 ❑ Apr 1955 Cover: 0.10 **NM** value: **12.00**
31 ❑ Jun 1955 Cover: 0.10 **NM** value: **12.00**
32 ❑ Aug 1955 Cover: 0.10 **NM** value: **12.00**
33 ❑ Oct 1955 Cover: 0.10 **NM** value: **12.00**
34 ❑ Dec 1955 Cover: 0.10 **NM** value: **12.00**
35 ❑ Feb 1956 Cover: 0.10 **NM** value: **12.00**
36 ❑ Apr 1956 Cover: 0.10 **NM** value: **12.00**
37 ❑ Jun 1956 Cover: 0.10 **NM** value: **12.00**
38 ❑ Aug 1956 Cover: 0.10 **NM** value: **12.00**
39 ❑ Oct 1956 Cover: 0.10 **NM** value: **12.00**
40 ❑ Dec 1956 Cover: 0.10 **NM** value: **12.00**
41 ❑ Feb 1957 Cover: 0.10 **NM** value: **12.00**
42 ❑ Apr 1957 Cover: 0.10 **NM** value: **12.00**
43 ❑ Jun 1957 Cover: 0.10 **NM** value: **12.00**
44 ❑ Aug 1957 Cover: 0.10 **NM** value: **12.00**
45 ❑ Oct 1957 Cover: 0.10 **NM** value: **12.00**
46 ❑ Dec 1957 Cover: 0.10 **NM** value: **12.00**
47 ❑ Feb 1958 Cover: 0.10 **NM** value: **12.00**
48 ❑ Apr 1958 Cover: 0.10 **NM** value: **12.00**
49 ❑ Jun 1958 Cover: 0.10 **NM** value: **12.00**
50 ❑ Aug 1958 Cover: 0.10 **NM** value: **12.00**
51 ❑ Oct 1958 Cover: 0.10 **NM** value: **9.00**
52 ❑ Dec 1958 Cover: 0.10 **NM** value: **9.00**
53 ❑ Feb 1959 Cover: 0.10 **NM** value: **9.00**
54 ❑ Apr 1959 Cover: 0.10 **NM** value: **9.00**
55 ❑ Jun 1959 Cover: 0.10 **NM** value: **9.00**
56 ❑ Aug 1959 Cover: 0.10 **NM** value: **9.00**
57 ❑ Oct 1959 Cover: 0.10 **NM** value: **9.00**
58 ❑ Dec 1959 Cover: 0.10 **NM** value: **9.00**
59 ❑ Feb 1960 Cover: 0.10 **NM** value: **9.00**
60 ❑ Apr 1960 Cover: 0.10 **NM** value: **9.00**
61 ❑ Jun 1960 Cover: 0.10 **NM** value: **9.00**
62 ❑ Aug 1960 Cover: 0.10 **NM** value: **9.00**
63 ❑ Oct 1960 Cover: 0.10 **NM** value: **9.00**
64 ❑ Dec 1960 Cover: 0.10 **NM** value: **9.00**
65 ❑ Mar 1961 Cover: 0.15 **NM** value: **9.00**
66 ❑ May 1961 Cover: 0.15 **NM** value: **9.00**
67 ❑ Jul 1961 Cover: 0.15 **NM** value: **9.00**
68 ❑ Sep 1961 Cover: 0.15 **NM** value: **9.00**
69 ❑ Nov 1961 Cover: 0.15 **NM** value: **9.00**
70 ❑ Jan 1962 Cover: 0.15 **NM** value: **9.00**
71 ❑ Mar 1962 Cover: 0.15 **NM** value: **9.00**
72 ❑ Jun 1962 Cover: 0.12 **NM** value: **9.00**
73 ❑ Oct 1962 Cover: 0.25 **NM** value: **25.00**
• Giant-size. • Gold Key begins publishing
74 ❑ Dec 1962 Cover: 0.25 **NM** value: **25.00**
• **CGC:** 1 graded, best 7.0
• Giant-size.
75 ❑ Mar 1963 Cover: 0.25 **NM** value: **25.00**
Circ: Statement: **217,350** • **CGC:** 1 graded, best 7.5
• Giant-size.
76 ❑ Jun 1963 Cover: 0.12 **NM** value: **7.00**
Circ: Statement: **217,350**
• Has 1962 Statement, filed 10/1/1962; has subscription figures only; avg subs 3,934
77 ❑ Sep 1963 Cover: 0.12 **NM** value: **7.00**
Circ: Statement: **217,350**
78 ❑ Dec 1963 Cover: 0.12 **NM** value: **7.00**
Circ: Statement: **217,350**
79 ❑ Mar 1964 Cover: 0.12 **NM** value: **7.00**
Circ: Statement: **245,885**
80 ❑ Jun 1964 Cover: 0.12 **NM** value: **7.00**
Circ: Statement: **245,885**
81 ❑ Sep 1964 Cover: 0.12 **NM** value: **7.00**
Circ: Statement: **245,885**
82 ❑ Dec 1964 Cover: 0.12 **NM** value: **7.00**
Circ: Statement: **245,885**
83 ❑ Mar 1965 Cover: 0.12 **NM** value: **7.00**
Circ: Statement: **250,340**
84 ❑ Apr 1965 Cover: 0.12 **NM** value: **7.00**
Circ: Statement: **250,340**
85 ❑ Jun 1965 Cover: 0.12 **NM** value: **7.00**
Circ: Statement: **250,340**
86 ❑ Aug 1965 Cover: 0.12 **NM** value: **7.00**
Circ: Statement: **250,340**
87 ❑ Oct 1965 Cover: 0.12 **NM** value: **7.00**
Circ: Statement: **250,340**
88 ❑ Dec 1965 Cover: 0.12 **NM** value: **7.00**
Circ: Statement: **250,340**
89 ❑ Feb 1966 Cover: 0.12 **NM** value: **7.00**
Circ: Statement: **248,199**
90 ❑ Apr 1966 Cover: 0.12 **NM** value: **7.00**
Circ: Statement: **248,199**
91 ❑ Jun 1966 Cover: 0.12 **NM** value: **7.00**
Circ: Statement: **248,199**
92 ❑ Aug 1966 Cover: 0.12 **NM** value: **7.00**
Circ: Statement: **248,199**
93 ❑ Oct 1966 Cover: 0.12 **NM** value: **7.00**
Circ: Statement: **248,199**
94 ❑ Dec 1966 Cover: 0.12 **NM** value: **7.00**
Circ: Statement: **248,199**
95 ❑ Feb 1967 Cover: 0.12 **NM** value: **7.00**
Circ: Statement: **220,783**
96 ❑ Apr 1967 Cover: 0.12 **NM** value: **7.00**
Circ: Statement: **220,783**
97 ❑ Jun 1967 Cover: 0.12 **NM** value: **7.00**
Circ: Statement: **220,783**
98 ❑ Aug 1967 Cover: 0.12 **NM** value: **7.00**
Circ: Statement: **220,783**
99 ❑ Nov 1967 Cover: 0.12 **NM** value: **7.00**
Circ: Statement: **220,783**
100 ❑ Feb 1968 Cover: 0.12 **NM** value: **7.00**
101 ❑ May 1968 Cover: 0.12 **NM** value: **5.00**
102 ❑ Aug 1968 Cover: 0.12 **NM** value: **5.00**
103 ❑ Nov 1968 Cover: 0.12 **NM** value: **5.00**
104 ❑ Feb 1969 Cover: 0.15 **NM** value: **5.00**
105 ❑ May 1969 Cover: 0.15 **NM** value: **5.00**
106 ❑ Aug 1969 Cover: 0.15 **NM** value: **5.00**
107 ❑ Sep 1969 Cover: 0.15 **NM** value: **5.00**
108 ❑ Nov 1969 Cover: 0.15 **NM** value: **5.00**
109 ❑ Jan 1970 Cover: 0.15 **NM** value: **5.00**
110 ❑ Mar 1970 Cover: 0.15 **NM** value: **5.00**
111 ❑ May 1970 Cover: 0.15 **NM** value: **5.00**
📖 The Timenapper; Getting the Business; Taxi Trouble
112 ❑ Jul 1970 Cover: 0.15 **NM** value: **5.00**
113 ❑ Sep 1970 Cover: 0.15 **NM** value: **5.00**
114 ❑ Nov 1970 Cover: 0.15 **NM** value: **5.00**
115 ❑ Jan 1971 Cover: 0.15 **NM** value: **5.00**
Circ: Statement: **184,699**
116 ❑ Mar 1971 Cover: 0.15 **NM** value: **5.00**
Circ: Statement: **184,699**
117 ❑ May 1971 Cover: 0.15 **NM** value: **5.00**
Circ: Statement: **184,699**
118 ❑ Jul 1971 Cover: 0.15 **NM** value: **5.00**
Circ: Statement: **184,699**
119 ❑ Sep 1971 Cover: 0.15 **NM** value: **5.00**
Circ: Statement: **184,699**
120 ❑ Nov 1971 Cover: 0.15 **NM** value: **5.00**
Circ: Statement: **184,699**
121 ❑ Jan 1972 Cover: 0.15 **NM** value: **4.00**
122 ❑ Mar 1972 Cover: 0.15 **NM** value: **4.00**
• Has 1971 Statement; avg print run 300,066; avg total paid circ 184,699
123 ❑ May 1972 Cover: 0.15 **NM** value: **4.00**

Other grades: Multiply prices above by **1.5 for Mint • 2/3 for Very Fine • 1/3 for Fine • 1/5 for Very Good • 1/8 for Good**

124 ❑ Jul 1972 Cover: 0.15 **NM** value: **4.00**
125 ❑ Sep 1972 Cover: 0.15 **NM** value: **4.00**
126 ❑ Nov 1972 Cover: 0.15 **NM** value: **4.00**
127 ❑ Jan 1973 Cover: 0.15 **NM** value: **4.00**
128 ❑ Mar 1973 Cover: 0.15 **NM** value: **4.00**
129 ❑ May 1973 Cover: 0.20 **NM** value: **4.00**
130 ❑ Jul 1973 Cover: 0.20 **NM** value: **4.00**
131 ❑ Sep 1973 Cover: 0.20 **NM** value: **2.50**
132 ❑ Oct 1973 Cover: 0.20 **NM** value: **2.50**
133 ❑ Nov 1973 Cover: 0.20 **NM** value: **2.50**
134 ❑ Jan 1974 Cover: 0.20 **NM** value: **2.50**
135 ❑ Mar 1974 Cover: 0.20 **NM** value: **2.50**
136 ❑ May 1974 Cover: 0.20 **NM** value: **2.50**
137 ❑ Jul 1974 Cover: 0.25 **NM** value: **2.50**
138 ❑ Sep 1974 Cover: 0.25 **NM** value: **2.50**
139 ❑ Oct 1974 Cover: 0.25 **NM** value: **2.50**
140 ❑ Nov 1974 Cover: 0.25 **NM** value: **2.50**
📖 The Great Brain Robbery; The Maltese Duck; Clictor The Victor; Lot of Trouble
141 ❑ Jan 1975 Cover: 0.25 **NM** value: **2.50**
142 ❑ Mar 1975 Cover: 0.25 **NM** value: **2.50**
143 ❑ May 1975 Cover: 0.25 **NM** value: **2.50**
144 ❑ Jul 1975 Cover: 0.25 **NM** value: **2.50**
145 ❑ Sep 1975 Cover: 0.25 **NM** value: **2.50**
146 ❑ Oct 1975 Cover: 0.25 **NM** value: **2.50**
147 ❑ Nov 1975 Cover: 0.25 **NM** value: **2.50**
148 ❑ Jan 1976 Cover: 0.25 **NM** value: **2.50**
149 ❑ Mar 1976 Cover: 0.25 **NM** value: **2.50**
150 ❑ May 1976 Cover: 0.25 **NM** value: **2.50**
151 ❑ Jul 1976 Cover: 0.25 **NM** value: **2.50**
152 ❑ Aug 1976 Cover: 0.25 **NM** value: **2.50**
153 ❑ Sep 1976 Cover: 0.30 **NM** value: **2.50**
154 ❑ Oct 1976 Cover: 0.30 **NM** value: **2.50**
155 ❑ Dec 1976 Cover: 0.30 **NM** value: **2.50**
156 ❑ Feb 1977 Cover: 0.30 **NM** value: **2.50**
157 ❑ Apr 1977 Cover: 0.30 **NM** value: **2.50**
158 ❑ Jun 1977 Cover: 0.30 **NM** value: **2.50**
159 ❑ Aug 1977 Cover: 0.30 **NM** value: **2.50**
160 ❑ Oct 1977 Cover: 0.30 **NM** value: **2.50**
161 ❑ Dec 1977 Cover: 0.35 **NM** value: **2.50**
162 ❑ Jan 1978 Cover: 0.35 **NM** value: **2.50**
163 ❑ Feb 1978 Cover: 0.35 **NM** value: **2.50**
164 ❑ Mar 1978 Cover: 0.35 **NM** value: **2.50**
165 ❑ Apr 1978 Cover: 0.35 **NM** value: **2.50**
166 ❑ May 1978 Cover: 0.35 **NM** value: **2.50**
167 ❑ Jun 1978 Cover: 0.35 **NM** value: **2.50**
168 ❑ Jul 1978 Cover: 0.35 **NM** value: **2.50**
169 ❑ Aug 1978 Cover: 0.35 **NM** value: **2.50**
170 ❑ Sep 1978 Cover: 0.35 **NM** value: **2.50**
171 ❑ Oct 1978 Cover: 0.35 **NM** value: **2.00**
172 ❑ Nov 1978 Cover: 0.35 **NM** value: **2.00**
173 ❑ Dec 1978 Cover: 0.35 **NM** value: **2.00**
174 ❑ Jan 1979 Cover: 0.35 **NM** value: **2.00**
175 ❑ Feb 1979 Cover: 0.35 **NM** value: **2.00**
176 ❑ Mar 1979 Cover: 0.35 **NM** value: **2.00**
177 ❑ Apr 1979 Cover: 0.40 **NM** value: **2.00**
178 ❑ May 1979 Cover: 0.40 **NM** value: **2.00**
179 ❑ Jun 1979 Cover: 0.40 **NM** value: **2.00**
180 ❑ Jul 1979 Cover: 0.40 **NM** value: **2.00**
181 ❑ Aug 1979 Cover: 0.40 **NM** value: **2.00**
182 ❑ Sep 1979 Cover: 0.40 **NM** value: **2.00**
183 ❑ Oct 1979 Cover: 0.40 **NM** value: **2.00**
184 ❑ Nov 1979 Cover: 0.40 **NM** value: **2.00**
185 ❑ Dec 1979 Cover: 0.40 **NM** value: **2.00**
186 ❑ Jan 1980 Cover: 0.40 **NM** value: **2.00**
187 ❑ Feb 1980 Cover: 0.40 **NM** value: **2.00**
188 ❑ Mar 1980 Cover: 0.40 **NM** value: **2.00**
189 ❑ 1980 **NM** value: **2.00**
190 ❑ 1980 **NM** value: **2.00**
191 ❑ 1980 **NM** value: **2.00**
192 ❑ 1981 **NM** value: **2.00**
193 ❑ 1981 **NM** value: **2.00**
194 ❑ Oct 1981 Cover: 0.50 **NM** value: **2.00**
195 ❑ Dec 1982 **NM** value: **2.00**
196 ❑ Feb 1982 **NM** value: **2.00**
197 ❑ Apr 1982 **NM** value: **2.00**
198 ❑ 1982 **NM** value: **2.00**
199 ❑ 1983 **NM** value: **2.00**
200 ❑ 1984 Cover: 0.60 **NM** value: **2.00**
201 ❑ 1984 **NM** value: **2.00**
final issue.

WOOFERS AND HOOTERS — Fantagraphics / Eros

All issues are adults only.
1 ❑ b&w Cover: 2.50 **NM** value: **Cover or less**

WOOLWORTH'S HAPPY TIME CHRISTMAS BOOK — Whitman

1 ❑ **NM** value: **30.00**
• 1952

WORDS & PICTURES — Maverick Studios

1 ❑ Fal 1994, b&w Cover: 3.95 **NM** value: **Cover or less**
2 ❑ Spr 1995, b&w Cover: 3.95 **NM** value: **Cover or less**
📖 In Vivo: The Waking Dream; Rio Grande; Communication; Deary Diary (Rhizome…Part N-1); Until Dawn **A:** Fernando H. Ramirez; John Picacio **W:** Fernando H. Ramirez; John Picacio

WORDSMITH (CALIBER) — Caliber

1 ❑ 1996 Cover: 2.95 **NM** value: **Cover or less**
2 ❑ 1996 Cover: 2.95 **NM** value: **Cover or less**
3 ❑ 1996 Cover: 2.95 **NM** value: **Cover or less**
4 ❑ 1996 Cover: 2.95 **NM** value: **Cover or less**
5 ❑ 1997 Cover: 2.95 **NM** value: **Cover or less**
6 ❑ 1997 Cover: 2.95 **NM** value: **Cover or less**
Bk 1 ❑ b&w Cover: 14.95 **NM** value: **Cover or less**
Bk 2 ❑ b&w Cover: 14.95 **NM** value: **Cover or less**

WORDSMITH (RENEGADE) — Renegade

Americans trapped in the Great Depression of the 1930s escaped from their troubles by reading the fast-paced, slam-bang action and adventure stories served up in the many pulp magazines of the era — stories written by penny-a-word writers, many aiming at nothing more than earning enough for their next meal.

Wordsmith, a spare black-and-white series created and written by Dave Darrigo and drawn by R.G. Taylor, follows the life and troubles of struggling pulp writer Clay Washburn, as everyday dramas of his life intermingle with the dashing adventures of his pulp heroes. Wordsmith is marinated in the atmosphere of the 1930s, illustrated with an economy of line by Taylor, and told with genuine affection for the pulps and their times. The initial run from Eclipse came to an end because of low sales, with the concluding issue taking Washburn into the early days of the comic-book industry and "his" comic-book story that's a pastiche of a Jack Kirby tale.

1 ❑ Aug 1985, b&w Cover: 1.70 **NM** value: **Cover or less**
2 ❑ Oct 1985, b&w Cover: 1.70 **NM** value: **Cover or less**
3 ❑ Dec 1985, b&w Cover: 1.70 **NM** value: **Cover or less**
4 ❑ Dec 1985, b&w Cover: 1.70 **NM** value: **Cover or less**
5 ❑ May 1986, b&w Cover: 1.70 **NM** value: **Cover or less**
6 ❑ Aug 1986 Cover: 1.70 **NM** value: **Cover or less**
7 ❑ Nov 1986 Cover: 2.00 **NM** value: **Cover or less**
8 ❑ Nov 1986 Cover: 2.00 **NM** value: **Cover or less**
9 ❑ May 1987 Cover: 2.00 **NM** value: **Cover or less**
10 ❑ Aug 1987 Cover: 2.00 **NM** value: **Cover or less**
11 ❑ Nov 1987 Cover: 2.00 **NM** value: **Cover or less**
12 ❑ Jan 1988 Cover: 2.00 **NM** value: **Cover or less**
Bk 1 ❑ b&w Cover: 14.95 **NM** value: **Cover or less**
Bk 2 ❑ b&w Cover: 14.95 **NM** value: **Cover or less**

WORDS WITHOUT PICTURES — Eclipse

Bk 1 ❑ Cover: 8.95 **NM** value: **Cover or less**
• not comics

WORD WARRIORS — Literacy Volunteers

1 ❑ b&w Cover: 1.50 **NM** value: **Cover or less**
• Ms. Tree, Jon Sable **C:** Howard Chaykin **W:** Mark Harris; Dennis Francis; Terry Beatty; Mike Grell; Max Allan Collins

WORGARD: VIKING BERSERKIR — Stronghold Studios

1 ❑ Oct 1997, b&w Cover: 2.95 **NM** value: **Cover or less**

WORKSHOP, THE — Blue Comet

1 ❑ Cover: 2.95 **NM** value: **Cover or less**

WORLD AROUND US, THE — Gilberton

1 ❑ Sep 1958 Cover: 0.25 **NM** value: **35.00**
2 ❑ Oct 1958 Cover: 0.25 **NM** value: **25.00**
3 ❑ Nov 1958 Cover: 0.25 **NM** value: **25.00**
• Horses
4 ❑ Dec 1958 Cover: 0.25 **NM** value: **25.00**
5 ❑ Jan 1959 Cover: 0.25 **NM** value: **25.00**
6 ❑ Feb 1959 Cover: 0.25 **NM** value: **25.00**
7 ❑ Mar 1959 Cover: 0.25 **NM** value: **25.00**
8 ❑ Apr 1959 Cover: 0.25 **NM** value: **25.00**
9 ❑ May 1959 Cover: 0.25 **NM** value: **25.00**
10 ❑ Jun 1959 Cover: 0.25 **NM** value: **25.00**
11 ❑ Jul 1959 Cover: 0.25 **NM** value: **25.00**
12 ❑ Aug 1959 Cover: 0.25 **NM** value: **25.00**
13 ❑ Sep 1959 Cover: 0.25 **NM** value: **40.00**
• Air Force **A:** L.B. Cole(cover)
14 ❑ Oct 1959 Cover: 0.25 **NM** value: **35.00**
15 ❑ Nov 1959 Cover: 0.25 **NM** value: **25.00**
16 ❑ Dec 1959 Cover: 0.25 **NM** value: **25.00**
17 ❑ Jan 1960 Cover: 0.25 **NM** value: **25.00**
18 ❑ Feb 1960 Cover: 0.25 **NM** value: **25.00**
19 ❑ Mar 1960 Cover: 0.25 **NM** value: **25.00**
📖 The Explorer; Island of Mystery (text story); A Soear of Buth Mwon; The Lion and th
20 ❑ Apr 1960 Cover: 0.25 **NM** value: **25.00**
21 ❑ May 1960 Cover: 0.25 **NM** value: **25.00**
22 ❑ Jun 1960 Cover: 0.25 **NM** value: **25.00**
23 ❑ Jul 1960 Cover: 0.25 **NM** value: **25.00**
24 ❑ Aug 1960 Cover: 0.25 **NM** value: **25.00**
25 ❑ Sep 1960 Cover: 0.25 **NM** value: **25.00**
26 ❑ Oct 1960 Cover: 0.25 **NM** value: **35.00**
27 ❑ Nov 1960 Cover: 0.25 **NM** value: **25.00**
28 ❑ Dec 1960 Cover: 0.25 **NM** value: **25.00**
29 ❑ Jan 1961 Cover: 0.25 **NM** value: **25.00**
30 ❑ Feb 1961 Cover: 0.25 **NM** value: **25.00**
📖 Undersea Adventures
31 ❑ Mar 1961 Cover: 0.25 **NM** value: **25.00**
📖 Hunting
32 ❑ Apr 1961 Cover: 0.25 **NM** value: **25.00**
📖 For Gold and Glory
33 ❑ May 1961 Cover: 0.25 **NM** value: **25.00**
34 ❑ Jun 1961 Cover: 0.25 **NM** value: **35.00**
📖 Fishing
35 ❑ Jul 1961 Cover: 0.25 **NM** value: **40.00**
📖 Spies
36 ❑ Oct 1961 Cover: 0.25 **NM** value: **25.00**
📖 Fight for Life

WORLD BANK, THE — Public Services International

1 ❑ Cover: 2.95 **NM** value: **Cover or less**
• educational comic; no indicia

WORLD BELOW, THE — Dark Horse

1 ❑ Mar 1999 Cover: 2.50 **NM** value: **Cover or less**
Circ: Diamd. preorders: **13,462**
📖 The Flock **A:** Paul Chadwick **W:** Paul Chadwick
2 ❑ Apr 1999 Cover: 2.50 **NM** value: **Cover or less**
Circ: Diamd. preorders: **10,252**
3 ❑ May 1999 Cover: 2.50 **NM** value: **Cover or less**
Circ: Diamd. preorders: **9,460**
4 ❑ Jun 1999 Cover: 2.50 **NM** value: **Cover or less**
Circ: Diamd. preorders: **9,155**
📖 The Stove **A:** Paul Chadwick **W:** Paul Chadwick

WORLD BELOW, THE: DEEPER AND STRANGER — Dark Horse

1 ❑ Dec 1999 Cover: 2.95 **NM** value: **Cover or less**
Circ: Diamd. preorders: **8,264**
📖 The Spare! **A:** Paul Chadwick **W:** Paul Chadwick
2 ❑ Jan 2000 Cover: 2.95 **NM** value: **Cover or less**
Circ: Diamd. preorders: **7,320**
📖 Zombies! **A:** Paul Chadwick **W:** Paul Chadwick
3 ❑ Feb 2000 Cover: 2.95 **NM** value: **Cover or less**
Circ: Diamd. preorders: **6,780**
4 ❑ Mar 2000 Cover: 2.95 **NM** value: **Cover or less**
Circ: Diamd. preorders: **6,591**

WORLD FAMOUS HEROES — Centaur

1 ❑ Oct 1941 Cover: 0.10 **NM** value: **1000.00**
• **CGC:** 3 graded, best 7.5
2 ❑ Dec 1941 Cover: 0.10 **NM** value: **600.00**
3 ❑ Feb 1942 Cover: 0.10 **NM** value: **500.00**
4 ❑ Apr 1942 Cover: 0.10 **NM** value: **500.00**
• **CGC:** 1 graded, best 6.0

WORLD HARDBALL LEAGUE — Titus

1 ❑ Aug 1994, b&w Cover: 2.75 **NM** value: **Cover or less**
📖 Widow's Web; Legend of the Ice Bat; Rare Gems **A:** Andy Soliz; Thanh Tran **W:** C.T. Rulander II; Tim Murphy
2 ❑ Jan 1995, b&w Cover: 2.95 **NM** value: **Cover or less**

WORLD OF ARCHIE — Archie

1 ❑ Aug 1992 Cover: 1.25 **NM** value: **2.00**
2 ❑ Nov 1992 Cover: 1.25 **NM** value: **1.50**
3 ❑ Feb 1993 Cover: 1.25 **NM** value: **1.50**
4 ❑ May 1993 Cover: 1.25 **NM** value: **1.50**
5 ❑ Aug 1993 Cover: 1.25 **NM** value: **1.50**
6 ❑ Nov 1993 Cover: 1.25 **NM** value: **1.50**
7 ❑ Feb 1994 Cover: 1.25 **NM** value: **1.50**
Circ: Statement: **26,125**
8 ❑ Apr 1994 Cover: 1.25 **NM** value: **1.50**
Circ: Statement: **26,125**
9 ❑ Jun 1994 Cover: 1.25 **NM** value: **1.50**
Circ: Statement: **26,125**
10 ❑ Aug 1994 Cover: 1.25 **NM** value: **1.50**
Circ: Statement: **26,125**
11 ❑ Sep 1994 Cover: 1.50 **NM** value: **Cover or less**
Circ: Statement: **26,125**
12 ❑ Nov 1994 Cover: 1.50 **NM** value: **Cover or less**
Circ: Statement: **26,125**
13 ❑ Jan 1995 Cover: 1.50 **NM** value: **Cover or less**
📖 When Rhinos Fly **A:** Rex Lindsey; Chain Reaction; Grammar Grapple **W:** Bob Bolling
14 ❑ Mar 1995 Cover: 1.50 **NM** value: **Cover or less**
15 ❑ Jun 1995 Cover: 1.50 **NM** value: **Cover or less**
16 ❑ Sep 1995 Cover: 1.50 **NM** value: **Cover or less**
17 ❑ Dec 1995 Cover: 1.50 **NM** value: **Cover or less**
18 ❑ Mar 1996 Cover: 1.50 **NM** value: **Cover or less**
19 ❑ Jun 1996 Cover: 1.50 **NM** value: **Cover or less**
• Has 1995 Statement, filed 10/1/95; avg print run 95,859; avg sales 24,441; avg subs 1,684; avg total paid 26,125; samples 395; office use 3,620; max existent 30,140; 69% of run returned
20 ❑ Sep 1996 Cover: 1.50 **NM** value: **Cover or less**
21 ❑ Dec 1996 Cover: 1.50 **NM** value: **Cover or less**
Circ: Diamd. preorders: **3,582**
📖 Campaign in the Neck; Not-So-Private Eye; Back to the 70's • Archie and Veronica run for class president
22 ❑ Mar 1997 Cover: 1.50 **NM** value: **Cover or less**
Circ: Diamd. preorders: **3,534**

WORLD OF FANTASY — Atlas

1 ❑ May 1956 Cover: 0.10 **NM** value: **350.00**
• **CGC:** 3 graded, best 7.0
2 ❑ Jul 1956 Cover: 0.10 **NM** value: **300.00**
• **CGC:** 1 graded, best 7.0
📖 Inside the Tunnel; It Stands in the Snow; Midnight on the Mountain; A Cry For Help; One Night
3 ❑ Sep 1956 Cover: 0.10 **NM** value: **250.00**
• **CGC:** 2 graded, best 8.5
4 ❑ Nov 1956 Cover: 0.10 **NM** value: **200.00**
5 ❑ Jan 1957 Cover: 0.10 **NM** value: **160.00**
• **CGC:** 1 graded, best 8.0
6 ❑ Mar 1957 Cover: 0.10 **NM** value: **160.00**
7 ❑ May 1957 Cover: 0.10 **NM** value: **150.00**
• **CGC:** 1 graded, best 9.0
8 ❑ Aug 1957 Cover: 0.10 **NM** value: **150.00**
9 ❑ Oct 1957 Cover: 0.10 **NM** value: **150.00**
10 ❑ Feb 1958 Cover: 0.10 **NM** value: **150.00**
• **CGC:** 1 graded, best 7.5
11 ❑ Apr 1958 Cover: 0.10 **NM** value: **150.00**
12 ❑ Jun 1958 Cover: 0.10 **NM** value: **150.00**
13 ❑ Aug 1958 Cover: 0.10 **NM** value: **125.00**
• **CGC:** 1 graded, best 8.5
14 ❑ Oct 1958 Cover: 0.10 **NM** value: **125.00**
• **CGC:** 1 graded, best 7.5

CGC-graded: Multiply prices above by **33 for 9.9 M • 16 for 9.8 NM/M • 7 for 9.6 NM+ • 5 for 9.4 NM • 2.5 for 9.2 NM- • 1.5 for 9.0 VF/NM**

15 ❑ Dec 1958 Cover: 0.10 **NM** value: **125.00**
16 ❑ Feb 1959 Cover: 0.10 **NM** value: **100.00**
17 ❑ Apr 1959 Cover: 0.10 **NM** value: **100.00**
18 ❑ Jun 1959 Cover: 0.10 **NM** value: **100.00**
19 ❑ Aug 1959 Cover: 0.10 **NM** value: **100.00**

WORLD OF GINGER FOX — Comico

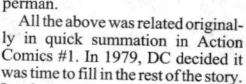

1 ❑ Cover: 6.95 **NM** value: **Cover or less**
Circ: CapCity orders: **1,925**
1/HC❑ Cover: 27.95 **NM** value: **Cover or less**

WORLD OF KRYPTON (1ST SERIES) — DC

The story should be familiar to comics readers everywhere. With his world about to die, the scientist Jor-El of the planet Krypton put his only son, Kal-El, into a tiny spacecraft and sent it blasting on its way mere moments before Krypton exploded. That boy would eventually arrive on the planet Earth, where our world's yellow sun would react with his Kryptonian physiology to give him remarkable powers. Kal-El became known to millions as Superman.

All the above was related originally in quick summation in Action Comics #1. In 1979, DC decided it was time to fill in the rest of the story. In what may have been the first mini-series, DC launched World of Krypton to give readers the full story of the final days of Krypton.

1 ❑ Jul 1979 Cover: 0.40 **NM** value: **2.00**
• **CGC:** 2 graded, best 9.2
2 ❑ Aug 1979 Cover: 0.40 **NM** value: **2.00**
3 ❑ Sep 1979 Cover: 0.40 **NM** value: **2.00**

WORLD OF KRYPTON (2ND SERIES) — DC

1 ❑ Dec 1987 Cover: 0.75 **NM** value: **2.00**
Circ: CapCity orders: **31,850**
📖 Pieces **A:** Mike Mignola; Rick Bryant **C:** John Byrne **W:** John Byrne
2 ❑ Jan 1988 Cover: 0.75 **NM** value: **2.00**
Circ: CapCity orders: **27,750**
3 ❑ Feb 1988 Cover: 0.75 **NM** value: **2.00**
Circ: CapCity orders: **28,650**
4 ❑ Mar 1988 Cover: 0.75 **NM** value: **2.00**
Circ: CapCity orders: **26,700**

WORLD OF METROPOLIS — DC

1 ❑ Aug 1988 Cover: 1.00 **NM** value: **1.50**
Circ: CapCity orders: **23,050**
2 ❑ Sep 1988 Cover: 1.00 **NM** value: **1.50**
Circ: CapCity orders: **19,400**
3 ❑ Oct 1988 Cover: 1.00 **NM** value: **1.50**
Circ: CapCity orders: **17,900**
4 ❑ Nov 1988 Cover: 1.00 **NM** value: **1.50**
Circ: CapCity orders: **15,800**

WORLD OF MYSTERY — Atlas

1 ❑ Jun 1956 Cover: 0.10 **NM** value: **300.00**
• **CGC:** 1 graded, best 6.5
2 ❑ Aug 1956 Cover: 0.10 **NM** value: **200.00**
3 ❑ Oct 1956 Cover: 0.10 **NM** value: **200.00**
4 ❑ Dec 1956 Cover: 0.10 **NM** value: **200.00**
5 ❑ Feb 1957 Cover: 0.10 **NM** value: **150.00**
• **CGC:** 2 graded, best 9.2
6 ❑ Apr 1957 Cover: 0.10 **NM** value: **150.00**
• **CGC:** 1 graded, best 7.5
7 ❑ Jul 1957 Cover: 0.10 **NM** value: **150.00**
• **CGC:** 2 graded, best 8.5

WORLD OF SMALLVILLE — DC

1 ❑ Apr 1988 Cover: 0.75 **NM** value: **1.50**
Circ: CapCity orders: **28,350**
2 ❑ May 1988 Cover: 0.75 **NM** value: **1.50**
Circ: CapCity orders: **22,750**
3 ❑ Jun 1988 Cover: 0.75 **NM** value: **1.50**
Circ: CapCity orders: **19,950**
4 ❑ Jul 1988 Cover: 0.75 **NM** value: **1.50**
Circ: CapCity orders: **18,800**

WORLD OF SUSPENSE — Atlas

1 ❑ Apr 1956 Cover: 0.10 **NM** value: **250.00**
• **CGC:** 1 graded, best 7.0
2 ❑ Jun 1956 Cover: 0.10 **NM** value: **200.00**
3 ❑ Aug 1956 Cover: 0.10 **NM** value: **150.00**
📖 The Man Who Couldn't Be Touched
4 ❑ Oct 1956 Cover: 0.10 **NM** value: **150.00**
5 ❑ Dec 1956 Cover: 0.10 **NM** value: **150.00**
• **CGC:** 1 graded, best 7.0
6 ❑ Feb 1957 Cover: 0.10 **NM** value: **150.00**
• **CGC:** 1 graded, best 8.0
📖 The old Man of the Mountain
7 ❑ Apr 1957 Cover: 0.10 **NM** value: **150.00**
8 ❑ Jul 1957 Cover: 0.10 **NM** value: **150.00**

WORLD OF WHEELS — Charlton

17 ❑ Oct 1967 Cover: 0.12 **NM** value: **12.00**
18 ❑ Cover: 0.12 **NM** value: **12.00**
19 ❑ 1968 Cover: 0.12 **NM** value: **12.00**
20 ❑ 1968 Cover: 0.12 **NM** value: **12.00**
21 ❑ 1968 Cover: 0.12 **NM** value: **8.00**
22 ❑ 1968 Cover: 0.12 **NM** value: **8.00**
23 ❑ Dec 1968 Cover: 0.12 **NM** value: **8.00**
📖 Speedball; Psychological Reconstruction; The Wild Ones (Parents); The Cage of Eagles; The Little Thing **A:** Nicholas Alascia; Jack Keller **W:** Nicholas Alascia; Jack Keller
24 ❑ Feb 1969 Cover: 0.12 **NM** value: **8.00**
25 ❑ Apr 1969 Cover: 0.12 **NM** value: **8.00**
26 ❑ Jun 1969 Cover: 0.12 **NM** value: **8.00**
27 ❑ Aug 1969 Cover: 0.15 **NM** value: **8.00**
28 ❑ Oct 1969 Cover: 0.15 **NM** value: **8.00**
29 ❑ Dec 1969 Cover: 0.15 **NM** value: **8.00**
30 ❑ Feb 1970 Cover: 0.15 **NM** value: **8.00**
31 ❑ Apr 1970 Cover: 0.15 **NM** value: **8.00**
32 ❑ Jun 1970 Cover: 0.15 **NM** value: **8.00**

WORLD OF WOOD — Eclipse

From his early work on The Spirit and E.C.'s science fiction titles (Weird Science, Weird Fantasy) to his 1960s and '70s work on Daredevil, All-Star Squadron, and Stalker, Wally Wood (who died in 1981) was one of the finest illustrators and most distinctive talents in comics. However, because of the restrictive commercial and creative climate in mainstream comics at the time he was working, some of Wood's best material only saw print in small-circulation publications, such as his self-published title, Witzend.

Some of his work featured sword-and-sorcery tales with dark, sexual themes that contrasted brilliantly with the innocent and detail-rich quality of his art. Eclipse's mini-series, The World of Wood, presents under-distributed or previously unpublished science-fiction and fantasy stories by Wood, inked and colored by some of his longtime associates, such as Al Williamson and Marie Severin.

1 ❑ 1986 Cover: 1.75 **NM** value: **2.00**
2 ❑ May 1986 Cover: 1.75 **NM** value: **2.00**
Circ: CapCity orders: **4,775**
📖 The End; The Cosmic AllWar of the Wizards **A:** Wally Wood **W:** Wally Wood
3 ❑ 1986 Cover: 1.75 **NM** value: **2.00**
Circ: CapCity orders: **4,575**
📖 Prelude to Armageddon; The Manhunters; Battle of Britain **A:** Wally Wood **W:** Wally Wood; Nicola Cutii; Gerry Boudreau
4 ❑ 1987 Cover: 1.75 **NM** value: **2.00**
Circ: CapCity orders: **3,975**
📖 Kille Hawk; The Mummy; To Kill a God! **A:** Wally Wood **W:** Wally Wood; Bill Dubay
5 ❑ 1987 Cover: 1.75 **NM** value: **2.00**
Circ: CapCity orders: **4,000**

WORLD OF X-RAY, THE — Pyramid

1 ❑ b&w Cover: 1.80 **NM** value: **Cover or less**

WORLD OF YOUNG MASTER — New Comics

1 ❑ Cover: 1.95 **NM** value: **Cover or less**
📖 Demonblade: Crimson Legacy • Demonblade **A:** Alex Ni±o **W:** Chuck Dixon

WORLD'S BEST COMICS — DC

1 ❑ Spr 1941 Cover: 0.15 **NM** value: **20000.00**
• **CGC:** 13 graded, best 8.0

WORLDS BEYOND — Fawcett

1 ❑ Nov 1951 Cover: 0.10 **NM** value: **250.00**
• **CGC:** 3 graded, best 9.4

WORLDS COLLIDE — DC / Milestone

1 ❑ Jul 1994 Cover: 2.50 **NM** value: **Cover or less**
Circ: CapCity orders: **36,200**
📖 Worlds Collide, Part 7 ★ 1st Appearance of Rift.
1/CS❑ Jul 1994 Cover: 3.95 **NM** value: **4.00**
enhanced cover. 📖 Worlds Collide, Part 7 • vinyl clings; Include press-apply stick-ons ★ 1st Appearance of Rift.
1/PL❑ Jul 1994 **NM** value: **4.00**
• Platinum edition.

WORLD'S FINEST — DC

1 ❑ ca. 1990 Cover: 3.95 **NM** value: **5.00**
Circ: CapCity orders: **55,700** • **CGC:** 1 graded, best 9.6
2 ❑ ca. 1990 Cover: 3.95 **NM** value: **4.50**
Circ: CapCity orders: **41,750** • **CGC:** 1 graded, best 9.4
3 ❑ ca. 1990 Cover: 3.95 **NM** value: **4.50**
Circ: CapCity orders: **38,400**

WORLD'S FINEST ARCHIVES — DC

Bk 1❑ Cover: 49.95 **NM** value: **Cover or less**
• Reprints Superman #76, World's Finest Comics #71-85
Bk 1/Aut❑ **NM** value: **79.95**
• Reprints Superman #76, World's Finest Comics #71-85

Diamond preorders are the estimated number of comics sold, prior to their release, to comics shops in North America by Diamond Comic Distributors, the largest distributor. These figures underreport the actual number of circulating copies by the amount of reorders Diamond took (usually 5-10% again of the preorders) and sales by publishers to newsstand and bookstore distributors. For many independent publishers, Diamond's preorders may be quite close to the actual number of copies in circulation.

WORLD'S FINEST COMICS — DC

World's Finest Comics enjoyed a long and distinguished run from 1941 until 1986. It began as a giant-sized anthology series, featuring stories starring such characters as The Boy Commandos, Green Arrow, Batman, and Superman. What the series is best known for, however, is the ongoing team-ups between Batman and Superman that began in #71.

This pairing of The Man of Steel and The Dark Knight proved greatly popular and eventually squeezed out all other features in the series. The plots generally worked by having Batman solve with detective work the problems that Superman was unable to handle through pure strength. Other plots had Batman tackling villains who used kryptonite to disable Superman. That these stories were often hopelessly forced did little to dampen many fans' enthusiasm for them.

2 ❑ Sum 1941 Cover: 0.15 **NM** value: **3850.00**
• **CGC:** 4 graded, best 6.0
• Series continued from World's Best Comics #1
3 ❑ Fal 1941 Cover: 0.15 **NM** value: **2850.00**
• **CGC:** 7 graded, best 8.0
• Superman, Batman and Robin, Red, White & Blue, Zatara ★ Origin of The Scarecrow (Jonathan Crane). ★ 1st Appearance of The Scarecrow (Jonathan Crane).
4 ❑ Win 1941 Cover: 0.15 **NM** value: **2000.00**
• **CGC:** 6 graded, best 9.0
5 ❑ Spr 1942 Cover: 0.15 **NM** value: **1900.00**
• **CGC:** 8 graded, best 7.0
6 ❑ Sum 1942 Cover: 0.15 **NM** value: **1425.00**
• **CGC:** 2 graded, best 7.0
• Sandman
7 ❑ Fal 1942 Cover: 0.15 **NM** value: **1425.00**
• **CGC:** 8 graded, best 8.0
• Sandman
8 ❑ Win 1942 Cover: 0.15 **NM** value: **1250.00**
• **CGC:** 7 graded, best 9.2
📖 Luck of the Lepparts • Boy Commandos feature begins
9 ❑ Spr 1943 Cover: 0.15 **NM** value: **1275.00**
• **CGC:** 5 graded, best 7.0
10 ❑ Sum 1943 Cover: 0.15 **NM** value: **1050.00**
• **CGC:** 3 graded, best 8.5
11 ❑ Fal 1943 Cover: 0.15 **NM** value: **925.00**
• **CGC:** 6 graded, best 8.5
12 ❑ Win 1943 Cover: 0.15 **NM** value: **925.00**
• **CGC:** 6 graded, best 8.5
13 ❑ Spr 1944 Cover: 0.15 **NM** value: **925.00**
• **CGC:** 4 graded, best 9.4
14 ❑ Sum 1944 Cover: 0.15 **NM** value: **925.00**
• **CGC:** 7 graded, best 9.2
15 ❑ Fal 1944 Cover: 0.15 **NM** value: **925.00**
• **CGC:** 6 graded, best 8.0
16 ❑ Win 1944 Cover: 0.15 **NM** value: **925.00**
• **CGC:** 11 graded, best 8.5
17 ❑ Spr 1945 Cover: 0.15 **NM** value: **900.00**
• **CGC:** 5 graded, best 8.5
18 ❑ Sum 1945 Cover: 0.15 **NM** value: **825.00**
• **CGC:** 11 graded, best 9.2
19 ❑ Fal 1945 Cover: 0.15 **NM** value: **825.00**
• **CGC:** 11 graded, best 9.2
20 ❑ Win 1945 Cover: 0.15 **NM** value: **825.00**
• **CGC:** 10 graded, best 8.5
21 ❑ Mar 1946 Cover: 0.15 **NM** value: **625.00**
• **CGC:** 5 graded, best 9.2
22 ❑ May 1946 Cover: 0.15 **NM** value: **625.00**
• **CGC:** 6 graded, best 9.6
23 ❑ Jul 1946 Cover: 0.15 **NM** value: **625.00**
24 ❑ Sep 1946 Cover: 0.15 **NM** value: **625.00**
• **CGC:** 6 graded, best 9.6
25 ❑ Nov 1946 Cover: 0.15 **NM** value: **625.00**
• **CGC:** 3 graded, best 7.5
26 ❑ Jan 1947 Cover: 0.15 **NM** value: **625.00**
• **CGC:** 7 graded, best 9.0
27 ❑ Mar 1947 Cover: 0.15 **NM** value: **625.00**
• **CGC:** 3 graded, best 7.5
28 ❑ May 1947 Cover: 0.15 **NM** value: **625.00**
• **CGC:** 5 graded, best 9.4
29 ❑ Jul 1947 Cover: 0.15 **NM** value: **625.00**
• **CGC:** 4 graded, best 9.6
30 ❑ Sep 1947 Cover: 0.15 **NM** value: **625.00**
• **CGC:** 5 graded, best 9.2
31 ❑ Nov 1947 Cover: 0.15 **NM** value: **540.00**
• **CGC:** 3 graded, best 9.2
32 ❑ Jan 1948 Cover: 0.15 **NM** value: **540.00**
• **CGC:** 4 graded, best 8.0
33 ❑ Mar 1948 Cover: 0.15 **NM** value: **540.00**
• **CGC:** 2 graded, best 4.0
34 ❑ May 1948 Cover: 0.15 **NM** value: **540.00**
• **CGC:** 2 graded, best 3.0
35 ❑ Jul 1948 Cover: 0.15 **NM** value: **540.00**
• **CGC:** 2 graded, best 5.0
36 ❑ Sep 1948 Cover: 0.15 **NM** value: **540.00**
• **CGC:** 2 graded, best 7.0
37 ❑ Nov 1948 Cover: 0.15 **NM** value: **540.00**
• **CGC:** 1 graded, best 7.0
38 ❑ Jan 1949 Cover: 0.15 **NM** value: **540.00**
• **CGC:** 4 graded, best 8.0
39 ❑ Mar 1949 Cover: 0.15 **NM** value: **540.00**
40 ❑ May 1949 Cover: 0.15 **NM** value: **540.00**
• **CGC:** 2 graded, best 8.0

41 ❑ Jul 1949 Cover: 0.15 **NM** value: **440.00**
• **CGC:** 2 graded, best 7.0
42 ❑ Sep 1949 Cover: 0.15 **NM** value: **440.00**
• **CGC:** 4 graded, best 9.0
43 ❑ Dec 1949 Cover: 0.15 **NM** value: **440.00**
• **CGC:** 1 graded, best 2.5
44 ❑ Feb 1950 Cover: 0.15 **NM** value: **440.00**
45 ❑ Apr 1950 Cover: 0.15 **NM** value: **440.00**
• **CGC:** 1 graded, best 2.5
46 ❑ Jun 1950 Cover: 0.15 **NM** value: **440.00**
• **CGC:** 1 graded, best 4.5
47 ❑ Aug 1950 Cover: 0.15 **NM** value: **440.00**
• **CGC:** 1 graded, best 4.0
48 ❑ Oct 1950 Cover: 0.15 **NM** value: **440.00**
• **CGC:** 1 graded, best 9.0
49 ❑ Dec 1950 Cover: 0.15 **NM** value: **440.00**
• **CGC:** 1 graded, best 7.0
50 ❑ Feb 1951 Cover: 0.15 **NM** value: **440.00**
• **CGC:** 1 graded, best 4.5
51 ❑ Apr 1951 Cover: 0.15 **NM** value: **440.00**
• **CGC:** 1 graded, best 4.0
52 ❑ Jun 1951 Cover: 0.15 **NM** value: **440.00**
• **CGC:** 1 graded, best 8.5
53 ❑ Aug 1951 Cover: 0.15 **NM** value: **440.00**
• **CGC:** 1 graded, best 4.5
54 ❑ Oct 1951 Cover: 0.15 **NM** value: **440.00**
55 ❑ Dec 1951 Cover: 0.15 **NM** value: **440.00**
• **CGC:** 2 graded, best 9.2
56 ❑ Feb 1952 Cover: 0.15 **NM** value: **440.00**
57 ❑ Mar 1952 Cover: 0.15 **NM** value: **440.00**
• **CGC:** 1 graded, best 6.5
58 ❑ May 1952 Cover: 0.15 **NM** value: **440.00**
• **CGC:** 3 graded, best 9.4
59 ❑ Jul 1952 Cover: 0.15 **NM** value: **440.00**
60 ❑ Sep 1952 Cover: 0.15 **NM** value: **440.00**
• **CGC:** 1 graded, best 4.0
61 ❑ Nov 1952 Cover: 0.15 **NM** value: **325.00**
• **CGC:** 1 graded, best 5.0
62 ❑ Jan 1953 Cover: 0.15 **NM** value: **325.00**
63 ❑ Mar 1953 Cover: 0.15 **NM** value: **325.00**
• **CGC:** 2 graded, best 7.5
64 ❑ May 1953 Cover: 0.15 **NM** value: **325.00**
• **CGC:** 1 graded, best 3.0
65 ❑ Jul 1953 Cover: 0.15 **NM** value: **550.00**
• **CGC:** 2 graded, best 8.0
66 ❑ Sep 1953 Cover: 0.15 **NM** value: **375.00**
• **CGC:** 1 graded, best 5.0
67 ❑ Nov 1953 Cover: 0.15 **NM** value: **375.00**
68 ❑ Jan 1954 Cover: 0.15 **NM** value: **375.00**
• **CGC:** 1 graded, best 4.0
69 ❑ Mar 1954 Cover: 0.15 **NM** value: **375.00**
70 ❑ May 1954 Cover: 0.15 **NM** value: **375.00**
71 ❑ Jul 1954 Cover: 0.10 **NM** value: **1000.00**
• **CGC:** 9 graded, best 7.5
📖 Batman – Double for Superman • Superman/Batman team-ups begin **A:** Curt Swan
72 ❑ Sep 1954 Cover: 0.10 **NM** value: **600.00**
• **CGC:** 4 graded, best 4.5
📖 Fort Crime
73 ❑ Nov 1954 Cover: 0.10 **NM** value: **600.00**
• **CGC:** 2 graded, best 7.0
📖 Batman and Superman, Swamis, Inc.
74 ❑ Jan 1955 Cover: 0.10 **NM** value: **400.00**
• **CGC:** 1 graded, best 3.0
📖 The Contest of Heroes
75 ❑ Mar 1955 Cover: 0.10 **NM** value: **400.00**
• **CGC:** 1 graded, best 6.0
📖 Superman and Robin
76 ❑ May 1955 Cover: 0.10 **NM** value: **400.00**
📖 When Gotham City Challenged Metropolis • Superman and Batman switch cities **A:** Curt Swan
77 ❑ Jul 1955 Cover: 0.10 **NM** value: **400.00**
• **CGC:** 3 graded, best 5.5
📖 The Super Bat-Man
78 ❑ Sep 1955 Cover: 0.10 **NM** value: **400.00**
📖 When Superman's Identity Is Exposed
79 ❑ Nov 1955 Cover: 0.10 **NM** value: **400.00**
• **CGC:** 5 graded, best 8.0
📖 The Three Magicians of Bagdad
80 ❑ Jan 1956 Cover: 0.10 **NM** value: **400.00**
• **CGC:** 3 graded, best 9.0
📖 The Super-Newspaper of Gotham City
81 ❑ Mar 1956 Cover: 0.10 **NM** value: **260.00**
📖 The True History of Superman and Batman
82 ❑ May 1956 Cover: 0.10 **NM** value: **260.00**
• **CGC:** 2 graded, best 7.0
📖 The Three Super-Musketeers
83 ❑ Aug 1956 Cover: 0.10 **NM** value: **260.00**
• **CGC:** 3 graded, best 7.5
📖 The Case of the Mother Goose Mystery
84 ❑ Oct 1956 Cover: 0.10 **NM** value: **260.00**
• **CGC:** 2 graded, best 6.0
📖 The Super Mystery of Metropolis
85 ❑ Dec 1956 Cover: 0.10 **NM** value: **260.00**
• **CGC:** 3 graded, best 6.5
📖 The Super-Rivals
86 ❑ Feb 1957 Cover: 0.10 **NM** value: **260.00**
• **CGC:** 2 graded, best 8.0
87 ❑ Apr 1957 Cover: 0.10 **NM** value: **260.00**
• **CGC:** 4 graded, best 7.0
88 ❑ Jun 1957 Cover: 0.10 **NM** value: **260.00**
• **CGC:** 2 graded, best 7.5
• Lex Luthor & The Joker team-up for the first time
89 ❑ Aug 1957 Cover: 0.10 **NM** value: **260.00**
• **CGC:** 2 graded, best 7.5
90 ❑ Oct 1957 Cover: 0.10 **NM** value: **260.00**
📖 The Adventures of the Super Batwoman!
91 ❑ Dec 1957 Cover: 0.10 **NM** value: **185.00**
• **CGC:** 4 graded, best 9.0
92 ❑ Feb 1958 Cover: 0.10 **NM** value: **185.00**
• **CGC:** 1 graded, best 8.0
93 ❑ Apr 1958 Cover: 0.10 **NM** value: **185.00**
• **CGC:** 3 graded, best 8.0
94 ❑ Jun 1958 Cover: 0.10 **NM** value: **600.00**
• **CGC:** 2 graded, best 6.0
95 ❑ Aug 1958 Cover: 0.10 **NM** value: **185.00**
96 ❑ Oct 1958 Cover: 0.10 **NM** value: **185.00**
• **CGC:** 2 graded, best 8.5
97 ❑ Oct 1958 Cover: 0.10 **NM** value: **185.00**
• **CGC:** 3 graded, best 9.0
98 ❑ Dec 1959 Cover: 0.10 **NM** value: **185.00**
• **CGC:** 2 graded, best 8.0
99 ❑ Feb 1959 Cover: 0.10 **NM** value: **185.00**
• **CGC:** 3 graded, best 9.0
100 ❑ Mar 1959 Cover: 0.10 **NM** value: **300.00**
• **CGC:** 6 graded, best 8.5
📖 The Dictator of Krypton City • Luthor conquers Kandor ★ Appearance of Lex Luthor.
101 ❑ May 1959 Cover: 0.10 **NM** value: **100.00**
• **CGC:** 4 graded, best 9.0
102 ❑ Jun 1959 Cover: 0.10 **NM** value: **100.00**
• **CGC:** 3 graded, best 8.0
103 ❑ Aug 1959 Cover: 0.10 **NM** value: **100.00**
• **CGC:** 3 graded, best 6.0
104 ❑ Sep 1959 Cover: 0.10 **NM** value: **100.00**
• **CGC:** 4 graded, best 6.0
105 ❑ Nov 1959 Cover: 0.10 **NM** value: **100.00**
• **CGC:** 2 graded, best 9.0
106 ❑ Dec 1959 Cover: 0.10 **NM** value: **100.00**
Circ: Statement: **476,000** • **CGC:** 1 graded, best 5.5
107 ❑ Feb 1960 Cover: 0.10 **NM** value: **100.00**
Circ: Statement: **476,000** • **CGC:** 2 graded, best 8.5
108 ❑ Mar 1960 Cover: 0.10 **NM** value: **100.00**
Circ: Statement: **476,000** • **CGC:** 2 graded, best 8.5
109 ❑ May 1960 Cover: 0.10 **NM** value: **100.00**
Circ: Statement: **476,000** • **CGC:** 1 graded, best 3.5
110 ❑ Jun 1960 Cover: 0.10 **NM** value: **100.00**
Circ: Statement: **476,000** • **CGC:** 3 graded, best 6.5
111 ❑ Aug 1960 Cover: 0.10 **NM** value: **80.00**
Circ: Statement: **476,000** • **CGC:** 1 graded, best 4.5
112 ❑ Sep 1960 Cover: 0.10 **NM** value: **80.00**
Circ: Statement: **476,000** • **CGC:** 3 graded, best 9.0
113 ❑ Nov 1960 Cover: 0.10 **NM** value: **80.00**
Circ: Statement: **476,000** • **CGC:** 7 graded, best 8.5
114 ❑ Dec 1960 Cover: 0.10 **NM** value: **80.00**
Circ: Statement: **480,000** • **CGC:** 4 graded, best 9.4
115 ❑ Feb 1961 Cover: 0.10 **NM** value: **80.00**
Circ: Statement: **480,000** • **CGC:** 3 graded, best 9.0
• Has 1960 Statement; avg total paid circ 476,000
116 ❑ Mar 1961 Cover: 0.10 **NM** value: **80.00**
Circ: Statement: **480,000** • **CGC:** 1 graded, best 8.5
117 ❑ May 1961 Cover: 0.10 **NM** value: **80.00**
Circ: Statement: **480,000** • **CGC:** 4 graded, best 7.0
118 ❑ Jun 1961 Cover: 0.10 **NM** value: **80.00**
Circ: Statement: **480,000** • **CGC:** 3 graded, best 6.5
119 ❑ Aug 1961 Cover: 0.10 **NM** value: **80.00**
Circ: Statement: **480,000** • **CGC:** 1 graded, best 4.5
120 ❑ Sep 1961 Cover: 0.10 **NM** value: **80.00**
Circ: Statement: **480,000** • **CGC:** 1 graded, best 9.2
121 ❑ Nov 1961 Cover: 0.10 **NM** value: **80.00**
Circ: Statement: **480,000** • **CGC:** 3 graded, best 6.5
122 ❑ Dec 1961 Cover: 0.12 **NM** value: **45.00**
Circ: Statement: **420,000**
123 ❑ Feb 1962 Cover: 0.12 **NM** value: **45.00**
Circ: Statement: **420,000**
• Has 1961 Statement, filed 10/1/61; avg total paid circ 480,000
124 ❑ Mar 1962 Cover: 0.12 **NM** value: **45.00**
Circ: Statement: **420,000**
125 ❑ May 1962 Cover: 0.12 **NM** value: **45.00**
Circ: Statement: **420,000** • **CGC:** 1 graded, best 9.2
126 ❑ Jun 1962 Cover: 0.12 **NM** value: **45.00**
Circ: Statement: **420,000** • **CGC:** 1 graded, best 7.0
127 ❑ Aug 1962 Cover: 0.12 **NM** value: **45.00**
Circ: Statement: **420,000** • **CGC:** 2 graded, best 9.2
128 ❑ Sep 1962 Cover: 0.12 **NM** value: **45.00**
Circ: Statement: **420,000** • **CGC:** 2 graded, best 8.5
129 ❑ Nov 1962 Cover: 0.12 **NM** value: **45.00**
Circ: Statement: **420,000** • **CGC:** 5 graded, best 9.0
130 ❑ Dec 1962 Cover: 0.12 **NM** value: **45.00**
• **CGC:** 3 graded, best 9.2
131 ❑ Feb 1963 Cover: 0.12 **NM** value: **45.00**
• **CGC:** 1 graded, best 4.0
• Has 1962 Statement, filed 10/1/62; avg total paid circ 420,000
132 ❑ Mar 1963 Cover: 0.12 **NM** value: **45.00**
133 ❑ May 1963 Cover: 0.12 **NM** value: **45.00**
• Aqua-Girl tryout
134 ❑ Jun 1963 Cover: 0.12 **NM** value: **45.00**
135 ❑ Aug 1963 Cover: 0.12 **NM** value: **45.00**
• **CGC:** 1 graded, best 9.2
136 ❑ Sep 1963 Cover: 0.12 **NM** value: **45.00**
137 ❑ Nov 1963 Cover: 0.12 **NM** value: **45.00**
138 ❑ Dec 1963 Cover: 0.12 **NM** value: **45.00**
139 ❑ Feb 1964 Cover: 0.12 **NM** value: **45.00**
• **CGC:** 1 graded, best 7.5
• Has 1963 Statement, filed 10/1/63; no circ figures published
140 ❑ Mar 1964 Cover: 0.12 **NM** value: **45.00**
141 ❑ May 1964 Cover: 0.12 **NM** value: **45.00**
• **CGC:** 1 graded, best 4.0
142 ❑ Jun 1964 Cover: 0.12 **NM** value: **45.00**
143 ❑ Aug 1964 Cover: 0.12 **NM** value: **30.00**
• **CGC:** 2 graded, best 9.4
144 ❑ Sep 1964 Cover: 0.12 **NM** value: **30.00**
• **CGC:** 1 graded, best 9.6
145 ❑ Nov 1964 Cover: 0.12 **NM** value: **30.00**
• **CGC:** 2 graded, best 9.4
146 ❑ Dec 1964 Cover: 0.12 **NM** value: **30.00**
• **CGC:** 1 graded, best 9.2
147 ❑ Feb 1965 Cover: 0.12 **NM** value: **30.00**
Circ: Statement: **465,842** • **CGC:** 2 graded, best 9.4
148 ❑ Mar 1965 Cover: 0.12 **NM** value: **30.00**
Circ: Statement: **465,842**
• Has 1964 Statement, filed 10/1/64; no circ figures published **A:** Curt Swan ★ Appearance of Lex Luthor.
149 ❑ May 1965 Cover: 0.12 **NM** value: **30.00**
Circ: Statement: **465,842**
150 ❑ Jun 1965 Cover: 0.12 **NM** value: **30.00**
Circ: Statement: **465,842** • **CGC:** 1 graded, best 9.2
151 ❑ Aug 1965 Cover: 0.12 **NM** value: **24.00**
Circ: Statement: **465,842** • **CGC:** 2 graded, best 9.0
• Congorilla back-up
152 ❑ Sep 1965 Cover: 0.12 **NM** value: **24.00**
Circ: Statement: **465,842** • **CGC:** 2 graded, best 9.2
153 ❑ Nov 1965 Cover: 0.12 **NM** value: **24.00**
Circ: Statement: **465,842**
154 ❑ Dec 1965 Cover: 0.12 **NM** value: **24.00**
Circ: Statement: **465,842** • **CGC:** 3 graded, best 9.2
155 ❑ Feb 1966 Cover: 0.12 **NM** value: **24.00**
Circ: Statement: **513,201** • **CGC:** 1 graded, best 9.0
156 ❑ Mar 1966 Cover: 0.12 **NM** value: **85.00**
Circ: Statement: **513,201** • **CGC:** 1 graded, best 8.5
157 ❑ May 1966 Cover: 0.12 **NM** value: **24.00**
Circ: Statement: **513,201** • **CGC:** 3 graded, best 9.2
• Imaginary story; Supersons
158 ❑ Jun 1966 Cover: 0.12 **NM** value: **24.00**
Circ: Statement: **513,201** • **CGC:** 1 graded, best 7.5
• Has 1965 Statement, filed 10/1/65; avg print run 663,000; avg sales 460,000; avg subs 5,842; avg total paid 465,842; samples 142; max existent 465,984; 30% of run returned **A:** Curt Swan
159 ❑ Aug 1966 Cover: 0.12 **NM** value: **24.00**
Circ: Statement: **513,201** • **CGC:** 1 graded, best 9.0
160 ❑ Sep 1966 Cover: 0.12 **NM** value: **24.00**
Circ: Statement: **513,201** • **CGC:** 1 graded, best 8.5
161 ❑ Nov 1966 Cover: 0.25 **NM** value: **24.00**
Circ: Statement: **513,201** • **CGC:** 6 graded, best 9.6
• Giant-size.
162 ❑ Nov 1966 Cover: 0.12 **NM** value: **16.00**
Circ: Statement: **513,201** • **CGC:** 1 graded, best 9.4
163 ❑ Dec 1966 Cover: 0.12 **NM** value: **16.00**
Circ: Statement: **513,201** • **CGC:** 2 graded, best 9.2
164 ❑ Feb 1967 Cover: 0.12 **NM** value: **16.00**
Circ: Statement: **537,200** • **CGC:** 5 graded, best 9.6
165 ❑ Mar 1967 Cover: 0.12 **NM** value: **16.00**
Circ: Statement: **537,200** • **CGC:** 2 graded, best 9.2
• Has 1966 Statement, filed 10/1/66; avg print run 766,000; avg sales 508,000; avg subs 5,201; avg total paid 513,201; samples 330; max existent 330; 33% of run returned
166 ❑ May 1967 Cover: 0.12 **NM** value: **22.00**
Circ: Statement: **537,200** • **CGC:** 4 graded, best 9.6
167 ❑ Jun 1967 Cover: 0.12 **NM** value: **15.00**
Circ: Statement: **537,200** • **CGC:** 1 graded, best 9.2
• Imaginary story
168 ❑ Aug 1967 Cover: 0.12 **NM** value: **15.00**
Circ: Statement: **537,200** • **CGC:** 1 graded, best 9.2
169 ❑ Sep 1967 Cover: 0.12 **NM** value: **15.00**
Circ: Statement: **537,200** • **CGC:** 2 graded, best 9.2
170 ❑ Nov 1967 Cover: 0.25 **NM** value: **22.00**
Circ: Statement: **537,200** • **CGC:** 2 graded, best 9.4
• Giant-size.
171 ❑ Nov 1967 Cover: 0.12 **NM** value: **15.00**
Circ: Statement: **537,200** • **CGC:** 2 graded, best 9.2
172 ❑ Dec 1967 Cover: 0.12 **NM** value: **15.00**
Circ: Statement: **537,200** • **CGC:** 3 graded, best 9.4
• Imaginary story; Clark and Bruce as brothers **A:** Curt Swan ★ Appearance of Lex Luthor.
173 ❑ Feb 1968 Cover: 0.12 **NM** value: **15.00**
Circ: Statement: **480,115** • **CGC:** 9 graded, best 9.6
• reprints from Action #241 **A:** Curt Swan
174 ❑ Mar 1968 Cover: 0.12 **NM** value: **15.00**
Circ: Statement: **480,115** • **CGC:** 3 graded, best 9.4
• Has 1967 Statement, filed 10/1/67; avg print run 811,000; avg sales 533,000; avg subs 4,200; avg total paid 537,200; samples 340; max existent 537,540; 34% of run returned
175 ❑ May 1968 Cover: 0.12 **NM** value: **22.00**
Circ: Statement: **480,115** • **CGC:** 1 graded, best 9.4
176 ❑ Jun 1968 Cover: 0.12 **NM** value: **22.00**
Circ: Statement: **480,115** • **CGC:** 2 graded, best 9.0
177 ❑ Aug 1968 Cover: 0.12 **NM** value: **22.00**
Circ: Statement: **480,115** • **CGC:** 4 graded, best 9.2
178 ❑ Sep 1968 Cover: 0.12 **NM** value: **9.00**
Circ: Statement: **480,115** • **CGC:** 2 graded, best 9.2
179 ❑ Nov 1968 Cover: 0.25 **NM** value: **9.00**
Circ: Statement: **480,115** • **CGC:** 6 graded, best 9.4
180 ❑ Nov 1968 Cover: 0.12 **NM** value: **9.00**
Circ: Statement: **480,115** • **CGC:** 4 graded, best 9.4
181 ❑ Dec 1968 Cover: 0.12 **NM** value: **9.00**
Circ: Statement: **480,115** • **CGC:** 4 graded, best 9.6
182 ❑ Feb 1969 Cover: 0.12 **NM** value: **9.00**
Circ: Statement: **366,618** • **CGC:** 3 graded, best 9.4
183 ❑ Mar 1969 Cover: 0.12 **NM** value: **9.00**
Circ: Statement: **366,618**
📖 Superman's Crime of the Ages; The Ghost Planet • Reprints story from House of Mystery #80; Has 1968 Statement, filed 10/1/68; avg print run 772,000; avg sales 479,000; avg subs 1,115; avg total paid 480,115; samples 386; max existent 480,501; 38% of run returned **A:** Ross Andru; Mike Esposito **W:** Leo Dorfman ★ Appearance of Lex Luthor, Brainiac.
184 ❑ May 1969 Cover: 0.12 **NM** value: **9.00**
Circ: Statement: **366,618**
185 ❑ Jun 1969 Cover: 0.12 **NM** value: **9.00**
Circ: Statement: **366,618**
186 ❑ Aug 1969 Cover: 0.15 **NM** value: **9.00**
Circ: Statement: **366,618**
187 ❑ Sep 1969 Cover: 0.15 **NM** value: **9.00**
Circ: Statement: **366,618**
188 ❑ Oct 1969 Cover: 0.25 **NM** value: **10.00**
Circ: Statement: **366,618** • **CGC:** 4 graded, best 9.0
• Giant-size.

CGC-graded: Multiply prices above by **33 for 9.9 M • 16 for 9.8 NM/M • 7 for 9.6 NM+ • 5 for 9.4 NM • 2.5 for 9.2 NM- • 1.5 for 9.0 VF/NM**

189 ❑ Nov 1969 Cover: 0.15 **NM** value: **9.00**
Circ: Statement: **366,618** • **CGC:** 1 graded, best 9.2
190 ❑ Dec 1969 Cover: 0.15 **NM** value: **9.00**
Circ: Statement: **366,618** • **CGC:** 2 graded, best 9.4
191 ❑ Feb 1970 Cover: 0.15 **NM** value: **7.00**
Circ: Statement: **333,213**
192 ❑ Mar 1970 Cover: 0.15 **NM** value: **7.00**
Circ: Statement: **333,213**
• Has 1969 Statement, filed 10/1/69; avg print run 624,000; avg sales 366,000; avg subs 618; avg total paid 366,618; samples 346; max existent 366,964; 41% of run returned
193 ❑ May 1970 Cover: 0.15 **NM** value: **7.00**
Circ: Statement: **333,213**
194 ❑ Jun 1970 Cover: 0.15 **NM** value: **7.00**
Circ: Statement: **333,213**
195 ❑ Aug 1970 Cover: 0.15 **NM** value: **7.00**
Circ: Statement: **333,213**
196 ❑ Sep 1970 Cover: 0.15 **NM** value: **7.00**
Circ: Statement: **333,213**
197 ❑ Nov 1970 Cover: 0.25 **NM** value: **9.00**
Circ: Statement: **333,213** • **CGC:** 2 graded, best 9.0
• Giant-size.
198 ❑ Nov 1970 Cover: 0.15 **NM** value: **75.00**
Circ: Statement: **333,213** • **CGC:** 10 graded, best 9.4
• Superman/Flash race
199 ❑ Dec 1970 Cover: 0.15 **NM** value: **75.00**
Circ: Statement: **333,213** • **CGC:** 10 graded, best 9.4
• Superman/Flash race
200 ❑ Feb 1971 Cover: 0.15 **NM** value: **5.00**
Circ: Statement: **312,978** • **CGC:** 3 graded, best 9.2
201 ❑ Mar 1971 Cover: 0.15 **NM** value: **5.00**
Circ: Statement: **312,978** • **CGC:** 1 graded, best 9.2
• Has 1970 Statement, filed 10/1/70; avg print run 606,305; avg sales 322,846; avg subs 367; avg total paid 333,213; samples 122; max existent 323,335; 45% of run returned ★ Appearance of Doctor Fate, Green Lantern.
202 ❑ May 1971 Cover: 0.15 **NM** value: **5.00**
Circ: Statement: **312,978** • **CGC:** 1 graded, best 9.4
203 ❑ Jun 1971 Cover: 0.15 **NM** value: **5.00**
Circ: Statement: **312,978** • **CGC:** 1 graded, best 9.2
204 ❑ Aug 1971 Cover: 0.25 **NM** value: **5.00**
Circ: Statement: **312,978** • **CGC:** 2 graded, best 9.2
• Green Arrow back-up; Captain Comet back-up ★ Appearance of Wonder Woman.
205 ❑ Sep 1971 Cover: 0.25 **NM** value: **5.00**
Circ: Statement: **312,978** • **CGC:** 2 graded, best 9.4
• Shining Knight back-up **A:** Frank Frazetta ★ Appearance of Teen Titans.
206 ❑ Nov 1971 Cover: 0.35 **NM** value: **5.00**
Circ: Statement: **312,978** • **CGC:** 5 graded, best 9.8
• Giant-size.
207 ❑ Nov 1971 Cover: 0.25 **NM** value: **5.00**
Circ: Statement: **312,978** • **CGC:** 3 graded, best 9.0
208 ❑ Dec 1971 Cover: 0.25 **NM** value: **5.00**
Circ: Statement: **312,978** • **CGC:** 2 graded, best 9.4
209 ❑ Feb 1972 Cover: 0.25 **NM** value: **5.00**
Circ: Statement: **234,878** • **CGC:** 7 graded, best 9.8
210 ❑ Mar 1972 Cover: 0.25 **NM** value: **5.00**
Circ: Statement: **234,878** • **CGC:** 2 graded, best 9.4
• Superman, Green Arrow, Black Pirate, The King; Has 1971 Statement, filed 10/1/71; avg print run 556,875; avg sales 312,705; avg subs 273; avg total paid 312,978; office use 227; max existent 313205; 46% of run returned
211 ❑ May 1972 Cover: 0.25 **NM** value: **5.00**
Circ: Statement: **234,878**
212 ❑ Jun 1972 Cover: 0.25 **NM** value: **5.00**
Circ: Statement: **234,878** • **CGC:** 2 graded, best 9.4
213 ❑ Sep 1972 Cover: 0.20 **NM** value: **5.00**
Circ: Statement: **234,878** • **CGC:** 1 graded, best 9.2
214 ❑ Nov 1972 Cover: 0.20 **NM** value: **5.00**
Circ: Statement: **234,878**
215 ❑ Jan 1973 Cover: 0.20 **NM** value: **5.00**
Circ: Statement: **246,871**
216 ❑ Mar 1973 Cover: 0.20 **NM** value: **5.00**
Circ: Statement: **246,871** • **CGC:** 1 graded, best 9.0
217 ❑ May 1973 Cover: 0.20 **NM** value: **5.00**
Circ: Statement: **246,871** • **CGC:** 1 graded, best 9.2
• Has 1972 Statement, filed 10/1/72; avg print run 522,000; avg sales 233,502; avg subs 1,376; avg total paid 234,878; samples 523; office use 503; max existent 235,904; 55% of run returned ★ Appearance of Metamorpho.
218 ❑ Aug 1973 Cover: 0.20 **NM** value: **5.00**
Circ: Statement: **246,871** • **CGC:** 1 graded, best 9.2
219 ❑ Oct 1973 Cover: 0.20 **NM** value: **5.00**
Circ: Statement: **246,871**
220 ❑ Dec 1973 Cover: 0.20 **NM** value: **5.00**
Circ: Statement: **246,871** • **CGC:** 1 graded, best 9.2
221 ❑ Feb 1974 Cover: 0.20 **NM** value: **4.00**
Circ: Statement: **242,726**
222 ❑ Apr 1974 Cover: 0.20 **NM** value: **4.00**
Circ: Statement: **242,726** • **CGC:** 1 graded, best 8.0
223 ❑ Jun 1974 Cover: 0.60 **NM** value: **4.00**
Circ: Statement: **242,726** • **CGC:** 4 graded, best 9.4
• Giant-size. • Has 1973 Statement, filed 10/1/73; avg print run 493,833; avg sales 245,694; avg subs 1,177; avg total paid 246,871; samples 100; office use 3,764; max existent 250,735; 49% of run returned **A:** Neal Adams ★ Origin of Deadman.
224 ❑ Aug 1974 Cover: 0.60 **NM** value: **4.00**
Circ: Statement: **242,726** • **CGC:** 1 graded, best 8.5
• Giant-size.
225 ❑ Oct 1974 Cover: 0.60 **NM** value: **4.00**
Circ: Statement: **242,726** • **CGC:** 11 graded, best 9.6
• Giant-size.
226 ❑ Dec 1974 Cover: 0.60 **NM** value: **4.00**
Circ: Statement: **242,726** • **CGC:** 5 graded, best 9.2
• Giant-size. **A:** Neal Adams ★ Appearance of Metamorpho.
227 ❑ Feb 1975 Cover: 0.60 **NM** value: **4.00**
Circ: Statement: **186,000** • **CGC:** 4 graded, best 9.6
• Giant-size. ★ Appearance of Deadman.
228 ❑ Mar 1975 Cover: 0.60 **NM** value: **4.00**
Circ: Statement: **186,000** • **CGC:** 1 graded, best 6.0
• Giant-size. ★ Appearance of Super-Sons.
229 ❑ Apr 1975 Cover: 0.25 **NM** value: **4.00**
Circ: Statement: **186,000** • **CGC:** 1 graded, best 9.2
230 ❑ May 1975 Cover: 0.50 **NM** value: **4.00**
Circ: Statement: **186,000** • **CGC:** 2 graded, best 9.4
• Giant-size. • Has 1974 Statement; avg total paid circ 242,726
231 ❑ Jul 1975 Cover: 0.25 **NM** value: **4.00**
Circ: Statement: **186,000** • **CGC:** 1 graded, best 7.5
232 ❑ Sep 1975 Cover: 0.25 **NM** value: **4.00**
Circ: Statement: **186,000** • **CGC:** 1 graded, best 8.5
233 ❑ Oct 1975 Cover: 0.25 **NM** value: **4.00**
Circ: Statement: **186,000** • **CGC:** 3 graded, best 9.2
234 ❑ Dec 1975 Cover: 0.25 **NM** value: **4.00**
Circ: Statement: **186,000**
235 ❑ Jan 1976 Cover: 0.25 **NM** value: **4.00**
Circ: Statement: **196,000** • **CGC:** 1 graded, best 8.0
236 ❑ Mar 1976 Cover: 0.30 **NM** value: **4.00**
Circ: Statement: **196,000** • **CGC:** 2 graded, best 9.4
237 ❑ Apr 1976 Cover: 0.30 **NM** value: **4.00**
Circ: Statement: **196,000**
238 ❑ Jun 1976 Cover: 0.30 **NM** value: **4.00**
Circ: Statement: **196,000**
239 ❑ Jul 1976 Cover: 0.30 **NM** value: **4.00**
Circ: Statement: **196,000**
240 ❑ Sep 1976 Cover: 0.30 **NM** value: **4.00**
Circ: Statement: **196,000**
241 ❑ Oct 1976 Cover: 0.30 **NM** value: **4.00**
Circ: Statement: **196,000**
242 ❑ Dec 1976 Cover: 0.30 **NM** value: **4.00**
Circ: Statement: **196,000**
243 ❑ Feb 1977 Cover: 0.30 **NM** value: **4.00**
Circ: Statement: **161,148**
244 ❑ May 1977 Cover: 1.00 **NM** value: **4.00**
Circ: Statement: **161,148**
• Giant-size.
245 ❑ Jul 1977 Cover: 1.00 **NM** value: **4.00**
Circ: Statement: **161,148**
• Giant-size. • Has 1976 Statement, filed 10/1/76; avg print run 440,000; avg sales 194,000; avg subs 2,000; avg total paid 196,000; samples 1,000; max existent 197,000; 55% of run returned
246 ❑ Sep 1977 Cover: 1.00 **NM** value: **4.00**
Circ: Statement: **161,148**
The Prisoner of the Kryptonite Asteroid • JLA **A:** Todd Dezuniga; Mike Nasser; Murphy Anderson; Gray Morrow; Kurt Schaffenberger ★ 1st Appearance of Baron Blitzkrieg. ★ Appearance of Justice League of America.
247 ❑ Nov 1977 Cover: 1.00 **NM** value: **4.00**
Circ: Statement: **161,148**
• Giant-size. Last Hurrah for Superman • JLA **A:** Kurt Schaffenberger
248 ❑ Jan 1978 Cover: 1.00 **NM** value: **4.00**
• Giant-size. **A:** Kurt Schaffenberger
249 ❑ Mar 1978 Cover: 1.00 **NM** value: **6.00**
• Giant-size. • The Creeper begins **A:** Kurt Schaffenberger
250 ❑ May 1978 Cover: 1.00 **NM** value: **4.00**
• Giant-size.
251 ❑ Jul 1978 Cover: 1.00 **NM** value: **3.00**
• Giant-size. • Has 1977 Statement, filed 10/1/77; avg print run 377,678; avg sales 158,956; avg subs 2,192; avg total paid 161,148; samples 400; office use 1,653; max existent 163,201; 57% of run returned ★ 1st Appearance of Count Vertigo.
252 ❑ Sep 1978 Cover: 1.00 **NM** value: **3.00**
• Giant-size.
253 ❑ Nov 1978 Cover: 1.00 **NM** value: **3.00**
• Giant-size. **A:** Kurt Schaffenberger
254 ❑ Jan 1979 Cover: 1.00 **NM** value: **3.00**
• Giant-size. **A:** Kurt Schaffenberger
255 ❑ Mar 1979 Cover: 1.00 **NM** value: **3.00**
256 ❑ May 1979 Cover: 1.00 **NM** value: **3.00**
• Giant-size. Prey of the Harpies **A:** Murphy Anderson **W:** Steve Englehart
257 ❑ Jul 1979 Cover: 1.00 **NM** value: **3.00**
• Giant-size. Attack of the In-and-Out Invaders **A:** Rich Buckler **W:** Gerry Conway
258 ❑ Sep 1979 Cover: 1.00 **NM** value: **3.00**
• **CGC:** 2 graded, best 9.4
• Giant-size. Death Orbit **A:** Rich Buckler **W:** Gerry Conway
259 ❑ Nov 1979 Cover: 1.00 **NM** value: **3.00**
Stake Out Earth **A:** Don Newton; Mike Nasser; Rich Buckler; Dick Giordano; Marshall Rogers; Kurt Schaffenberger **W:** Gerry Conway
260 ❑ Jan 1980 Cover: 1.00 **NM** value: **3.00**
261 ❑ Mar 1980 Cover: 1.00 **NM** value: **3.00**
JLA Databank Dossier: Hawkman **A:** Eduardo Barreto **W:** Bob Rozakis
262 ❑ May 1980 Cover: 1.00 **NM** value: **3.00**
The Ghost of Adam Strange **A:** Ken Landgraf **W:** J.M. DeMatteis
263 ❑ Jul 1980 Cover: 1.00 **NM** value: **3.00**
264 ❑ Sep 1980 Cover: 1.00 **NM** value: **3.00**
Alone **A:** Ken Landgraf **W:** J.M. DeMatteis
265 ❑ Nov 1980 Cover: 1.00 **NM** value: **3.00**
This Hostage World **A:** Ken Landgraf **W:** J.M. DeMatteis
266 ❑ Jan 1981 Cover: 1.00 **NM** value: **3.00**
Circ: Statement: **73,475**
Something Sinister in Sewer Seven **A:** Ken Landgraf **W:** Bob Rozakis ★ 1st Appearance of Lady Lunar.
267 ❑ Mar 1981 Cover: 1.00 **NM** value: **3.00**
Circ: Statement: **73,475**
The Insect Invasion of Midway City **A:** Alex Saviuk **W:** Bob Rozakis ★ Appearance of Challengers of the Unknown.
268 ❑ May 1981 Cover: 1.00 **NM** value: **3.00**
Circ: Statement: **73,475**
Your City or Your Life **A:** Alex Saviuk **W:** Bob Rozakis
269 ❑ Jul 1981 Cover: 1.00 **NM** value: **3.00**
Circ: Statement: **73,475**
... I Must Go Home Again **A:** Alex Saviuk **W:** Bob Rozakis ★ 1st Appearance of Doctor Jymbi Humm.
270 ❑ Aug 1981 Cover: 1.00 **NM** value: **3.00**
Circ: Statement: **73,475**
You and Me Against Our World **A:** Alex Saviuk **W:** Bob Rozakis
271 ❑ Sep 1981 Cover: 1.00 **NM** value: **3.00**
Circ: Statement: **73,475**
272 ❑ Oct 1981 Cover: 1.00 **NM** value: **2.50**
Circ: Statement: **73,475**
Drive Me to the Moon **A:** Alex Saviuk **W:** Bob Rozakis
273 ❑ Nov 1981 Cover: 1.00 **NM** value: **2.50**
Circ: Statement: **73,475**
Victory? **A:** Alex Saviuk **W:** Bob Rozakis
274 ❑ Dec 1981 Cover: 1.00 **NM** value: **2.50**
Circ: Statement: **73,475**
Gone with the Wings **A:** Alex Saviuk **W:** Bob Rozakis
275 ❑ Jan 1982 Cover: 1.00 **NM** value: **2.50**
• **CGC:** 1 graded, best 9.4
Matter... Matter Everywhere **A:** Alex Saviuk **W:** Bob Rozakis
276 ❑ Feb 1982 Cover: 1.00 **NM** value: **2.50**
Stinging in the Rain **A:** Carmine Infantino **W:** Bob Rozakis
277 ❑ Mar 1982 Cover: 1.00 **NM** value: **2.50**
I Have My Wings and I Must Fly **A:** Alex Saviuk **W:** Bob Rozakis
278 ❑ Apr 1982 Cover: 1.00 **NM** value: **2.50**
279 ❑ May 1982 Cover: 1.00 **NM** value: **2.50**
Pirates of the Spaceways **A:** Alex Saviuk **W:** Bob Rozakis ★ Appearance of Kid Eternity.
280 ❑ Jun 1982 Cover: 1.00 **NM** value: **2.50**
Now You Czemm, Now You Don't **A:** Alex Saviuk **W:** Bob Rozakis ★ Appearance of Kid Eternity.
281 ❑ Jul 1982 Cover: 1.00 **NM** value: **2.50**
Out Into Space in Ships **A:** Alex Saviuk **W:** Bob Rozakis
282 ❑ Aug 1982 Cover: 1.00 **NM** value: **2.50**
Doctor Katar and Mister Plert **A:** Carmine Infantino **W:** Bob Rozakis
283 ❑ Sep 1982 Cover: 0.60 **NM** value: **2.50**
284 ❑ Oct 1982 Cover: 0.60 **NM** value: **2.50**
285 ❑ Nov 1982 Cover: 0.60 **NM** value: **2.50**
286 ❑ Dec 1982 Cover: 0.60 **NM** value: **2.50**
287 ❑ Jan 1983 Cover: 0.60 **NM** value: **2.50**
Circ: Statement: **88,928**
288 ❑ Feb 1983 Cover: 0.60 **NM** value: **2.50**
Circ: Statement: **88,928**
289 ❑ Mar 1983 Cover: 0.60 **NM** value: **2.50**
Circ: Statement: **88,928**
290 ❑ Apr 1983 Cover: 0.60 **NM** value: **2.50**
Circ: Statement: **88,928**
291 ❑ May 1983 Cover: 0.60 **NM** value: **2.50**
Circ: Statement: **88,928**
292 ❑ Jun 1983 Cover: 0.60 **NM** value: **2.50**
Circ: Statement: **88,928**
293 ❑ Jul 1983 Cover: 0.60 **NM** value: **2.50**
Circ: Statement: **88,928**
294 ❑ Aug 1983 Cover: 0.60 **NM** value: **2.50**
Circ: Statement: **88,928**
295 ❑ Sep 1983 Cover: 0.60 **NM** value: **2.50**
Circ: Statement: **88,928**
296 ❑ Oct 1983 Cover: 0.60 **NM** value: **2.50**
Circ: Statement: **88,928**
297 ❑ Nov 1983 Cover: 0.60 **NM** value: **2.50**
Circ: Statement: **88,928**
298 ❑ Dec 1983 Cover: 0.75 **NM** value: **2.50**
Circ: Statement: **88,928**
299 ❑ Jan 1984 Cover: 0.75 **NM** value: **2.50**
Circ: Statement: **82,415**
300 ❑ Feb 1984 Cover: 1.25 **NM** value: **3.00**
Circ: Statement: **82,415** • **CGC:** 1 graded, best 9.6
• Giant-size. **A:** Ross Andru ★ Appearance of Justice League of America, Titans, Outsiders.
301 ❑ Mar 1984 Cover: 0.75 **NM** value: **2.00**
Circ: Statement: **82,415**
302 ❑ Apr 1984 Cover: 0.75 **NM** value: **2.00**
Circ: Statement: **82,415**
303 ❑ May 1984 Cover: 0.75 **NM** value: **2.00**
Circ: Statement: **82,415**
304 ❑ Jun 1984 Cover: 0.75 **NM** value: **2.00**
Circ: Statement: **82,415**
305 ❑ Jul 1984 Cover: 0.75 **NM** value: **2.00**
Circ: Statement: **82,415**
306 ❑ Aug 1984 Cover: 0.75 **NM** value: **2.00**
Circ: Statement: **82,415**
307 ❑ Sep 1984 Cover: 0.75 **NM** value: **2.00**
Circ: Statement: **82,415**
308 ❑ Oct 1984 Cover: 0.75 **NM** value: **2.00**
Circ: Statement: **82,415**
309 ❑ Nov 1984 Cover: 0.75 **NM** value: **2.00**
Circ: Statement: **82,415**
The Quantum Inheritance **A:** Mark Texeira **W:** Kurt Busiek
310 ❑ Dec 1984 Cover: 0.75 **NM** value: **2.00**
Circ: Statement: **82,415**
311 ❑ Jan 1985 Cover: 0.75 **NM** value: **2.00**
312 ❑ Feb 1985 Cover: 0.75 **NM** value: **2.00**
313 ❑ Mar 1985 Cover: 0.75 **NM** value: **2.00**
314 ❑ Apr 1985 Cover: 0.75 **NM** value: **2.00**
315 ❑ May 1985 Cover: 0.75 **NM** value: **2.00**
Circ: CapCity orders: **3,750**
316 ❑ Jun 1985 Cover: 0.75 **NM** value: **2.00**
Circ: CapCity orders: **3,600**
317 ❑ Jul 1985 Cover: 0.75 **NM** value: **2.00**
Circ: CapCity orders: **3,700**
318 ❑ Aug 1985 Cover: 0.75 **NM** value: **2.00**
Circ: CapCity orders: **3,800**
319 ❑ Sep 1985 Cover: 0.75 **NM** value: **2.00**
Circ: CapCity orders: **3,750**
320 ❑ Oct 1985 Cover: 0.75 **NM** value: **2.00**
Circ: CapCity orders: **3,650**
321 ❑ Nov 1985 Cover: 0.75 **NM** value: **2.00**
Circ: CapCity orders: **3,550**
322 ❑ Dec 1985 Cover: 0.75 **NM** value: **2.00**
Circ: CapCity orders: **4,100**

323 ❑ Jan 1986 Cover: 0.75 **NM** value: **2.00**
Circ: CapCity orders: **4,450** • **CGC:** 3 graded, best 9.0
final issue.

WORLD'S FUNNIEST COMICS — Moordam

1 ❑ Mar 1998, b&w Cover: 2.95 **NM** value: **Cover or less**
• Cray-Baby Adventures, Mr. Beat

WORLD'S GREATEST SONGS — Atlas

1 ❑ Sep 1954 Cover: 0.10 **NM** value: **250.00**
• **CGC:** 1 graded, best 4.5

WORLDS OF FEAR — Fawcett

2 ❑ Jan 1952 Cover: 0.10 **NM** value: **250.00**
3 ❑ Mar 1952 Cover: 0.10 **NM** value: **250.00**
4 ❑ May 1952 Cover: 0.10 **NM** value: **200.00**
5 ❑ Jul 1952 Cover: 0.10 **NM** value: **200.00**
6 ❑ Sep 1952 Cover: 0.10 **NM** value: **200.00**
• **CGC:** 1 graded, best 6.5
7 ❑ Nov 1952 Cover: 0.10 **NM** value: **200.00**
8 ❑ Jan 1953 Cover: 0.10 **NM** value: **200.00**
9 ❑ Apr 1953 Cover: 0.10 **NM** value: **200.00**
10 ❑ Jun 1953 Cover: 0.10 **NM** value: **400.00**
• **CGC:** 1 graded, best 4.5

WORLDS OF H.P. LOVECRAFT: BEYOND THE WALL OF SLEEP — Tome

1 ❑ Cover: 2.95 **NM** value: **Cover or less**

WORLDS OF H.P. LOVECRAFT, THE: DAGON — Caliber

1 ❑ b&w Cover: 2.95 **NM** value: **Cover or less**

WORLDS OF H.P. LOVECRAFT: THE ALCHEMIST — Tome

1 ❑ Cover: 2.95 **NM** value: **Cover or less**

WORLDS OF H.P. LOVECRAFT, THE: THE MUSIC OF ERICH ZANN — Caliber

1 ❑ b&w Cover: 2.95 **NM** value: **Cover or less**
No issue number.

WORLDS OF H.P. LOVECRAFT, THE: THE PICTURE IN THE HOUSE — Caliber

1 ❑ b&w Cover: 2.95 **NM** value: **Cover or less**
No issue number.

WORLDS UNKNOWN — Marvel

1 ❑ May 1973 Cover: 0.20 **NM** value: **5.00**
• **CGC:** 4 graded, best 9.4
2 ❑ Jul 1973 Cover: 0.20 **NM** value: **4.00**
📖 A Gun for Dinosaur! **A:** Val Mayerik **W:** Roy Thomas
3 ❑ Sep 1973 Cover: 0.20 **NM** value: **4.00**
• **CGC:** 1 graded, best 9.2
4 ❑ Nov 1973 Cover: 0.20 **NM** value: **3.00**
5 ❑ Feb 1974 Cover: 0.20 **NM** value: **3.00**
6 ❑ Apr 1974 Cover: 0.20 **NM** value: **3.00**
• **CGC:** 1 graded, best 9.2
📖 Killdozer! **A:** Dick Ayers **W:** Gerry Conway
7 ❑ Jun 1974 Cover: 0.25 **NM** value: **3.00**
📖 Golden Voyage of Sinbad; Golden Voyage of Sinbad, Part 1
8 ❑ Aug 1974 Cover: 0.25 **NM** value: **3.00**
📖 Golden Voyage of Sinbad; Golden Voyage of Sinbad, Part 2 final issue.

WORLD'S WORST COMICS AWARDS — Kitchen Sink

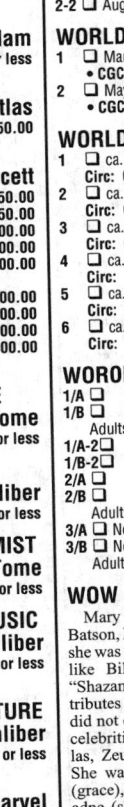

It's about time someone paid tribute to all the horribly corny, tacky, silly, ridiculous, or just plain bad comics published in the last 25 years. In this two-issue "awards show," Rich Larson and James Schumeister do just that. It's a wonderful time, as they hand out awards for "worst costume" (a category so crowded that Mighty Comics' "Vegetable" only scored as runner-up!), "worst name" (Jack Kirby's "Paranex, the Fighting Fetus" didn't win!), "worst team," and more.

There are also special awards for bad ads (remember Sea Monkeys?), bad dialog, and other dubious achievements.

And then there is the piece de resistance: "worst comic of all time" ...

1 ❑ 1990 b&w Cover: 2.50 **NM** value: **Cover or less**
2 ❑ Jan 1991, b&w Cover: 2.50 **NM** value: **Cover or less**

WORLD WAR II: 1946 — Antarctic

1 ❑ Jul 1999 Cover: 2.50 **NM** value: **Cover or less**
Circ: Diamd. preorders: **3,267**
📖 Angels of the Luftwaffe **A:** Ted Nomura **W:** Ted Nomura
2 ❑ Cover: 2.50 **NM** value: **Cover or less**
Circ: Diamd. preorders: **4,102**
📖 Born to Die **A:** Ted Nomura **W:** Ted Nomura

WORLD WAR II: 1946/FAMILIES OF ALTERED WARS — Antarctic

1 ❑ Jul 1998 Cover: 3.95 **NM** value: **Cover or less**
1-2 ❑ Oct 1998 Cover: 3.95 **NM** value: **Cover or less**
2 ❑ Nov 1998 Cover: 3.95 **NM** value: **Cover or less**
• has indicia from #1 **A:** Ted Nomura **W:** Ted Nomura
2-2 ❑ Aug 1998 Cover: 3.95 **NM** value: **Cover or less**

WORLD WAR III — Ace

1 ❑ Mar 1953 Cover: 0.10 **NM** value: **400.00**
• **CGC:** 3 graded, best 9.0
2 ❑ May 1953 Cover: 0.10 **NM** value: **400.00**
• **CGC:** 1 graded, best 9.0

WORLD WITHOUT END — DC

1 ❑ ca. 1990 Cover: 2.50 **NM** value: **Cover or less**
Circ: CapCity orders: **21,450**
2 ❑ ca. 1990 Cover: 2.50 **NM** value: **Cover or less**
Circ: CapCity orders: **14,750**
3 ❑ ca. 1990 Cover: 2.50 **NM** value: **Cover or less**
Circ: CapCity orders: **13,200**
4 ❑ ca. 1990 Cover: 2.50 **NM** value: **Cover or less**
Circ: CapCity orders: **11,650**
5 ❑ ca. 1990 Cover: 2.50 **NM** value: **Cover or less**
Circ: CapCity orders: **1,160**
6 ❑ ca. 1990 Cover: 2.50 **NM** value: **Cover or less**
Circ: CapCity orders: **11,500**

WORON'S WORLDS — Illustration

1/A ❑ Cover: 2.95 **NM** value: **Cover or less**
1/B ❑ Cover: 2.95 **NM** value: **Cover or less**
Adults-only cover. **A:** Steve Woron
1/A-2 ❑ Cover: 3.25 **NM** value: **Cover or less**
1/B-2 ❑ Cover: 3.25 **NM** value: **Cover or less**
2/A ❑ Cover: 2.95 **NM** value: **Cover or less**
2/B ❑ Cover: 2.95 **NM** value: **Cover or less**
Adults-only cover. **A:** Steve Woron
3/A ❑ Nov 1994 Cover: 3.25 **NM** value: **Cover or less**
3/B ❑ Nov 1994 Cover: 3.25 **NM** value: **Cover or less**
Adults-only cover. **A:** Steve Woron

WOW COMICS (FAWCETT) — Fawcett

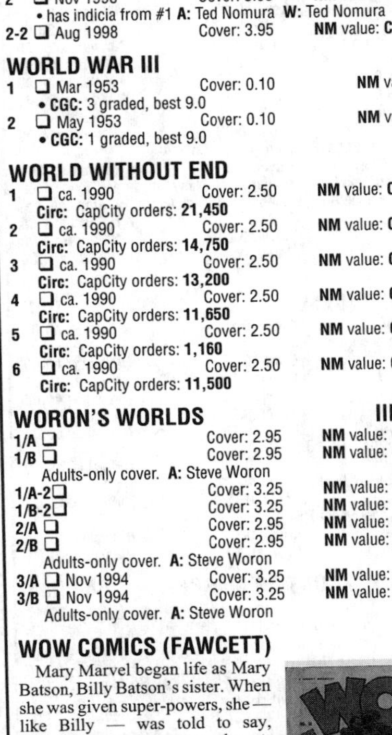

Mary Marvel began life as Mary Batson, Billy Batson's sister. When she was given super-powers, she — like Billy — was told to say, "Shazam!" In her case, the attributes that came to her as a result did not come from his pantheon of celebrities Solomon, Hercules, Atlas, Zeus, Achilles, and Mercury. She was given powers of Selena (grace), Hippolyta (strength), Ariadne (skill), Zephyrus (fleetness), Aurora (beauty), and Minerva (wisdom).

Her outfit featured a short skirt and an adaptation of the rest of Captain Marvel's costume, but she remained looking much like Mary Batson. Her story began in Captain Marvel Adventures in Dec 42, but (as Whiz Comics cover-featured Captain Marvel) her ongoing feature was as the lead in the Wow anthology title, which had begun with characters like Mr. Scarlet, Atom Blake, Rick O'Shay (no relation to the later newspaper strip of the same name), and Jim Dolan. The primary characters for much of the run were Mary, Mr. Scarlet, Phantom Eagle, and Commando Yank. — Maggie

1 ❑ Win 1940 Cover: 0.10 **NM** value: **12000.00**
• Extremely rare
2 ❑ Sum 1941 Cover: 0.10 **NM** value: **1950.00**
• **CGC:** 2 graded, best 9.4
3 ❑ Fal 1941 Cover: 0.10 **NM** value: **1100.00**
• **CGC:** 1 graded, best 9.4
4 ❑ Win 1941 Cover: 0.10 **NM** value: **850.00**
• **CGC:** 1 graded, best 7.5
5 ❑ Spr 1942 Cover: 0.10 **NM** value: **500.00**
6 ❑ Jul 1942 Cover: 0.10 **NM** value: **700.00**
• **CGC:** 1 graded, best 8.0
7 ❑ Oct 1942 Cover: 0.10 **NM** value: **550.00**
• **CGC:** 1 graded, best 5.5
8 ❑ Dec 1942 Cover: 0.10 **NM** value: **550.00**
• **CGC:** 2 graded, best 7.5
9 ❑ Jan 1943 Cover: 0.10 **NM** value: **1000.00**
• **CGC:** 2 graded, best 9.0
• Mary Marvel features begin
10 ❑ Feb 1943 Cover: 0.10 **NM** value: **550.00**
11 ❑ Mar 1943 Cover: 0.10 **NM** value: **300.00**
12 ❑ Apr 1943 Cover: 0.10 **NM** value: **300.00**
13 ❑ May 1943 Cover: 0.10 **NM** value: **300.00**
14 ❑ Jun 1943 Cover: 0.10 **NM** value: **300.00**
15 ❑ Jul 1943 Cover: 0.10 **NM** value: **300.00**
• **CGC:** 1 graded, best 1.5
16 ❑ Aug 1943 Cover: 0.10 **NM** value: **240.00**
17 ❑ Sep 1943 Cover: 0.10 **NM** value: **240.00**
18 ❑ Oct 1943 Cover: 0.10 **NM** value: **275.00**
19 ❑ Nov 1943 Cover: 0.10 **NM** value: **240.00**
20 ❑ Dec 1943 Cover: 0.10 **NM** value: **240.00**
21 ❑ Jan 1944 Cover: 0.10 **NM** value: **165.00**
22 ❑ Feb 1944 Cover: 0.10 **NM** value: **165.00**
23 ❑ Mar 1944 Cover: 0.10 **NM** value: **165.00**
24 ❑ Apr 1944 Cover: 0.10 **NM** value: **165.00**
25 ❑ May 1944 Cover: 0.10 **NM** value: **165.00**
26 ❑ Jun 1944 Cover: 0.10 **NM** value: **165.00**
27 ❑ Jul 1944 Cover: 0.10 **NM** value: **165.00**
28 ❑ Aug 1944 Cover: 0.10 **NM** value: **165.00**
29 ❑ Sep 1944 Cover: 0.10 **NM** value: **165.00**
30 ❑ Oct 1944 Cover: 0.10 **NM** value: **165.00**
31 ❑ Nov 1944 Cover: 0.10 **NM** value: **110.00**
32 ❑ Jan 1945 Cover: 0.10 **NM** value: **110.00**
33 ❑ Feb 1945 Cover: 0.10 **NM** value: **110.00**
• **CGC:** 2 graded, best 9.2
34 ❑ Mar 1945 Cover: 0.10 **NM** value: **110.00**
• **CGC:** 1 graded, best 7.5
35 ❑ Apr 1945 Cover: 0.10 **NM** value: **110.00**
• **CGC:** 1 graded, best 9.6
36 ❑ May 1945 Cover: 0.10 **NM** value: **110.00**
37 ❑ Jul 1945 Cover: 0.10 **NM** value: **110.00**
38 ❑ Sep 1945 Cover: 0.10 **NM** value: **225.00**
• **CGC:** 1 graded, best 7.0
Great cover.
39 ❑ Nov 1945 Cover: 0.10 **NM** value: **110.00**
40 ❑ Jan 1946 Cover: 0.10 **NM** value: **110.00**
• **CGC:** 1 graded, best 7.0
41 ❑ Feb 1946 Cover: 0.10 **NM** value: **75.00**
• **CGC:** 1 graded, best 9.2
42 ❑ Apr 1946 Cover: 0.10 **NM** value: **75.00**
43 ❑ May 1946 Cover: 0.10 **NM** value: **75.00**
44 ❑ Jun 1946 Cover: 0.10 **NM** value: **75.00**
• **CGC:** 1 graded, best 9.6
45 ❑ Jul 1946 Cover: 0.10 **NM** value: **75.00**
• **CGC:** 1 graded, best 9.2
46 ❑ Aug 1946 Cover: 0.10 **NM** value: **75.00**
• **CGC:** 1 graded, best 9.2
47 ❑ Sep 1946 Cover: 0.10 **NM** value: **75.00**
• **CGC:** 1 graded, best 9.2
48 ❑ Oct 1946 Cover: 0.10 **NM** value: **75.00**
49 ❑ Nov 1946 Cover: 0.10 **NM** value: **75.00**
• **CGC:** 1 graded, best 8.5
50 ❑ Dec 1946 Cover: 0.10 **NM** value: **75.00**
51 ❑ Feb 1947 Cover: 0.10 **NM** value: **65.00**
52 ❑ Mar 1947 Cover: 0.10 **NM** value: **65.00**
53 ❑ Apr 1947 Cover: 0.10 **NM** value: **65.00**
54 ❑ May 1947 Cover: 0.10 **NM** value: **65.00**
55 ❑ Jun 1947 Cover: 0.10 **NM** value: **65.00**
56 ❑ Jul 1947 Cover: 0.10 **NM** value: **65.00**
57 ❑ Aug 1947 Cover: 0.10 **NM** value: **65.00**
58 ❑ Sep 1947 Cover: 0.10 **NM** value: **65.00**
• Mary Marvel features end
59 ❑ Oct 1947 Cover: 0.10 **NM** value: **50.00**
60 ❑ Nov 1947 Cover: 0.10 **NM** value: **50.00**
61 ❑ Dec 1947 Cover: 0.10 **NM** value: **40.00**
62 ❑ Jan 1948 Cover: 0.10 **NM** value: **40.00**
63 ❑ Feb 1948 Cover: 0.10 **NM** value: **40.00**
64 ❑ Mar 1948 Cover: 0.10 **NM** value: **40.00**
65 ❑ Apr 1948 Cover: 0.10 **NM** value: **40.00**
• **CGC:** 1 graded, best 8.0
66 ❑ May 1948 Cover: 0.10 **NM** value: **40.00**
67 ❑ Jun 1948 Cover: 0.10 **NM** value: **40.00**
68 ❑ Jul 1948 Cover: 0.10 **NM** value: **40.00**
69 ❑ Fal 1948 Cover: 0.10 **NM** value: **40.00**

W.O.W. THE WORLD OF WARD — Allied American Artists

1 ❑ b&w Cover: 3.95 **NM** value: **Cover or less**

WRATH — Malibu / Ultraverse

1 ❑ Jan 1994 Cover: 1.95 **NM** value: **2.00**
Circ: CapCity orders: **27,225**
1/LE ❑ Jan 1994 **NM** value: **3.00**
• Ultra-limited edition. **W:** Mike W. Barr ★ Appearance of Mantra.
2 ❑ Feb 1994 Cover: 1.95 **NM** value: **2.00**
Circ: CapCity orders: **17,000**
3 ❑ Mar 1994 Cover: 1.95 **NM** value: **2.00**
Circ: CapCity orders: **13,350**
4 ❑ Apr 1994 Cover: 1.95 **NM** value: **Cover or less**
Circ: CapCity orders: **12,200**
5 ❑ May 1994 Cover: 1.95 **NM** value: **Cover or less**
Circ: CapCity orders: **11,150**
6 ❑ Jun 1994 Cover: 1.95 **NM** value: **Cover or less**
Circ: CapCity orders: **10,025**
📖 Interludes **A:** David Ammerman **W:** Mike W. Barr
7 ❑ Jul 1994 Cover: 1.95 **NM** value: **Cover or less**
Circ: CapCity orders: **8,900**
📖 Three Strikes **A:** Aaron Lopresti(cover); Rick Maeys; Rick Mayes **W:** Roland Mann ★ 1st Appearance of Ogre, Pierce, Doc Virtual.
8 ❑ Oct 1994 Cover: 1.95 **NM** value: **Cover or less**
Circ: CapCity orders: **6,675**
📖 Days of Wrath, Part 2 **A:** David Ammerman **W:** David Ammerman; Mike W. Barr ★ 1st Appearance of Project Patriot. ★ Appearance of Warstrike, Mantra.
9 ❑ Dec 1994 Cover: 2.25 **NM** value: **Cover or less**
Circ: CapCity orders: **5,200**
📖 Days of Wrath, Part 3 final issue. **A:** David Ammerman **W:** Mike W. Barr ★ Death of Project Patriot.
GS 1 ❑ Aug 1994 Cover: 2.50 **NM** value: **Cover or less**
Circ: CapCity orders: **7,975**
• Giant-size Wrath #1. 📖 Days of Wrath, Part 1 **A:** David Ammerman **W:** David Ammerman; Mike W. Barr

WRATH OF THE SPECTRE — DC

1 ❑ May 1988 Cover: 2.50 **NM** value: **Cover or less**
Circ: CapCity orders: **13,000**
📖 Wrath of the Spectre; Anguish of the Spectre; The Swami and the Spectre; The Adventurer's Club • Reprints from Adventure Comics #431-433, 426 **A:** Jim Aparo; Russell Carley **W:** Michael Fleisher
2 ❑ Jun 1988 Cover: 2.50 **NM** value: **Cover or less**
Circ: CapCity orders: **10,300**
3 ❑ Jul 1988 Cover: 2.50 **NM** value: **Cover or less**
Circ: CapCity orders: **9,100**
4 ❑ Aug 1988 Cover: 2.50 **NM** value: **Cover or less**
Circ: CapCity orders: **9,500**
• new stories **A:** Jim Aparo

WRETCH, THE — Caliber

1 ❑ Jul 1997, b&w Cover: 2.95 **NM** value: **Cover or less**
📖 The End of the World! **A:** Phil Hester **W:** Phil Hester
2 ❑ Sep 1997, b&w Cover: 2.95 **NM** value: **Cover or less**
📖 Bad Dog **A:** Phil Hester **W:** Phil Hester

CGC-graded: Multiply prices above by **33 for 9.9 M • 16 for 9.8 NM/M • 7 for 9.6 NM+ • 5 for 9.4 NM • 2.5 for 9.2 NM- • 1.5 for 9.0 VF/NM**

3 ❑ Nov 1997, b&w Cover: 2.95 **NM** value: **Cover or less**
📖 Snow; All the Way Down, Part 1 **A:** Mike Worley; Phil Hester **W:** Phil Hester; Paul Tobin
4 ❑ 1998b&w Cover: 2.95 **NM** value: **Cover or less**
📖 The Church Bus; Alarm Clock of the Beast **A:** John Heebink; Phil Hester; Aaron Gillespie; Colin Wales **W:** Phil Hester
5 ❑ May 1998 Cover: 2.95 **NM** value: **Cover or less**
📖 White Lie • Dedicated to Will Eisner **A:** Phil Hester; Andy Brase **W:** Phil Hester
6 ❑ Jul 1998 Cover: 2.95 **NM** value: **Cover or less**
📖 Doomsday **A:** Phil Hester **W:** Phil Hester

WRETCH, THE (VOL. 2) — Slave Labor / Amaze Ink

1 ❑ Jul 1997, b&w Cover: 2.95 **NM** value: **Cover or less**
2 ❑ Sep 1997, b&w Cover: 2.95 **NM** value: **Cover or less**
3 ❑ Nov 1997, b&w Cover: 2.95 **NM** value: **Cover or less**
4 ❑ b&w Cover: 2.95 **NM** value: **Cover or less**

WRITERS' BLOC ANTHOLOGY, THE — Writers' Bloc

1 ❑ **NM** value: **3.00**
Circ: Diamd. preorders: **1,825**
📖 Mis. Candice's Profession; The Gnat; A Walk in the Park-A Prologue; Sundown; Poetry in Motion; Victoriatech **A:** Kaare Andrews; Jack & Scott Purcell; Ruben Cordero; Tom Benham; W. Allen Montgomery **W:** Erik Sirmenis; Fernando Santos; Jack Nolan; Jareth Grealish; Sean Medlock; Shaun Behrens

WULF THE BARBARIAN — Atlas-Seaboard

1 ❑ Feb 1975 Cover: 0.25 **NM** value: **2.00**
• **CGC:** 2 graded, best 9.2
2 ❑ Cover: 0.25 **NM** value: **1.50**
3 ❑ Cover: 0.25 **NM** value: **1.50**
4 ❑ Cover: 0.25 **NM** value: **1.50**

WU WEI — Angus

1 ❑ ca. 1995 Cover: 2.50 **NM** value: **Cover or less**
2 ❑ Cover: 2.50 **NM** value: **Cover or less**
3 ❑ Cover: 2.50 **NM** value: **Cover or less**
4 ❑ Cover: 2.50 **NM** value: **Cover or less**
5 ❑ Cover: 2.50 **NM** value: **Cover or less**
6 ❑ Cover: 2.50 **NM** value: **Cover or less**

WW 2 — NEC

1 ❑ Cover: 3.50 **NM** value: **Cover or less**
2 ❑ Nov 2000 Cover: 3.50 **NM** value: **Cover or less**
📖 Salerno **A:** Ron Ledwell **W:** J. O'Neil

WWF: WORLD WRESTLING FOUNDATION — Valiant

1 ❑ Cover: 2.95 **NM** value: **Cover or less**
Circ: CapCity orders: **3,200**
📖 Ultimate Warrior's Workout • 21841
2 ❑ Cover: 2.95 **NM** value: **Cover or less**
Circ: CapCity orders: **2,000**
📖 Lifestyles of the Brutal & Infamous • 21842
3 ❑ Cover: 2.95 **NM** value: **Cover or less**
📖 Out-of-the-Ring Challenges • 21843
4 ❑ Cover: 2.95 **NM** value: **Cover or less**
📖 Wait Till I Get My Hands on… • 21844

WYATT EARP — Marvel

Marvel played a bit fast and loose with the facts of legendary lawman Wyatt Earp's life in making this series. The real-life version was considerably rougher and shadier than this clean-cut comics hero. Still, what the series may have lacked in historical accuracy it made up for in entertainment. The stories told of how Marshal Wyatt Earp maintained the peace in Dodge City against all manner of ruffians, gunslingers, and murderers. Naturally, this meant using his blazing Colt .45s with great regularity, but Earp's real weapons were his cleverness, and his courage to stand up to any threat.

Stan Lee wrote most of the stories, with art by Dick Ayers, Bill Everett, Jack Kirby, and others. The series ran from 1955 until 1960 and enjoyed a brief revival in 1972, alongside numerous other early Marvel Westerns, reprinting issues from the original run.

1 ❑ Nov 1955 Cover: 0.10 **NM** value: **110.00**
• **CGC:** 1 graded, best 8.5
2 ❑ Jan 1956 Cover: 0.10 **NM** value: **65.00**
• **CGC:** 1 graded, best 8.5
3 ❑ Mar 1956 Cover: 0.10 **NM** value: **48.00**
4 ❑ May 1956 Cover: 0.10 **NM** value: **48.00**
5 ❑ Jul 1956 Cover: 0.10 **NM** value: **48.00**
6 ❑ Sep 1956 Cover: 0.10 **NM** value: **48.00**
7 ❑ Nov 1956 Cover: 0.10 **NM** value: **48.00**
8 ❑ Jan 1957 Cover: 0.10 **NM** value: **48.00**
9 ❑ Mar 1957 Cover: 0.10 **NM** value: **48.00**
10 ❑ Apr 1957 Cover: 0.10 **NM** value: **48.00**
11 ❑ May 1957 Cover: 0.10 **NM** value: **40.00**
12 ❑ Aug 1957 Cover: 0.10 **NM** value: **40.00**
13 ❑ Oct 1957 Cover: 0.10 **NM** value: **40.00**
14 ❑ Dec 1957 Cover: 0.10 **NM** value: **40.00**
15 ❑ Feb 1958 Cover: 0.10 **NM** value: **40.00**
16 ❑ Apr 1958 Cover: 0.10 **NM** value: **40.00**
17 ❑ Jun 1958 Cover: 0.10 **NM** value: **40.00**
18 ❑ Aug 1958 Cover: 0.10 **NM** value: **40.00**
19 ❑ Oct 1958 Cover: 0.10 **NM** value: **40.00**
20 ❑ Dec 1958 Cover: 0.10 **NM** value: **40.00**
21 ❑ Feb 1959 Cover: 0.10 **NM** value: **28.00**
22 ❑ Apr 1959 Cover: 0.10 **NM** value: **28.00**
23 ❑ Jun 1959 Cover: 0.10 **NM** value: **28.00**
24 ❑ Aug 1959 Cover: 0.10 **NM** value: **28.00**
25 ❑ Oct 1959 Cover: 0.10 **NM** value: **28.00**
26 ❑ Dec 1959 Cover: 0.10 **NM** value: **28.00**
27 ❑ Feb 1960 Cover: 0.10 **NM** value: **28.00**
28 ❑ Apr 1960 Cover: 0.10 **NM** value: **28.00**
29 ❑ Jun 1960 Cover: 0.10 **NM** value: **28.00**
• Final issue of original run
30 ❑ Oct 1972 Cover: 0.20 **NM** value: **4.00**
• Revival of old title; Series begins again
31 ❑ Dec 1972 Cover: 0.20 **NM** value: **4.00**
📖 The Man Who Out-Drew Earp; Too Many Murderers; Tenderfoot in Town; Revenge Against a Town! **A:** Dick Ayers **W:** Stan Lee
32 ❑ Feb 1973 Cover: 0.20 **NM** value: **4.00**
33 ❑ Apr 1973 Cover: 0.20 **NM** value: **4.00**
34 ❑ Jun 1973 Cover: 0.20 **NM** value: **4.00**
final issue.

WYATT EARP (DELL) — Dell

4 ❑ Sep 1958 Cover: 0.10 **NM** value: **45.00**
• **CGC:** 1 graded, best 9.0
5 ❑ Dec 1958 Cover: 0.10 **NM** value: **40.00**
6 ❑ Mar 1959 Cover: 0.10 **NM** value: **40.00**
7 ❑ Jun 1959 Cover: 0.10 **NM** value: **40.00**
8 ❑ Sep 1959 Cover: 0.10 **NM** value: **40.00**
9 ❑ Dec 1959 Cover: 0.10 **NM** value: **40.00**
• **CGC:** 1 graded, best 8.5
10 ❑ Mar 1960 Cover: 0.10 **NM** value: **40.00**
• **CGC:** 2 graded, best 9.4
11 ❑ Jun 1960 Cover: 0.10 **NM** value: **40.00**
• **CGC:** 1 graded, best 7.5
12 ❑ Sep 1960 Cover: 0.10 **NM** value: **40.00**
13 ❑ Dec 1960 Cover: 0.10 **NM** value: **40.00**

WYATT EARP, FRONTIER MARSHAL — Charlton

Pretty typical Western fare from Charlton Comics as Wyatt Earp defends the Old West from bank robbers, murderers, horse thieves, etc. The series also features backup stories and prose short stories that relate even more Western tales. The artwork is simplistic, and the colors are a bit garish, but the stories are solid enough for fans of the horse-and-saddle genre.

Of course, Earp is portrayed here as a law-abiding gunslinger and there's no mention of his final days.

12 ❑ Jan 1956 Cover: 0.10 **NM** value: **35.00**
• Continues from Range Busters
13 ❑ 1956 Cover: 0.10 **NM** value: **18.00**
14 ❑ 1956 Cover: 0.10 **NM** value: **18.00**
15 ❑ 1956 Cover: 0.10 **NM** value: **18.00**
16 ❑ 1957 Cover: 0.10 **NM** value: **18.00**
17 ❑ 1957 Cover: 0.10 **NM** value: **18.00**
18 ❑ 1957 Cover: 0.10 **NM** value: **18.00**
19 ❑ 1958 Cover: 0.10 **NM** value: **40.00**
• Giant-size.
20 ❑ Mar 1958 Cover: 0.10 **NM** value: **14.00**
21 ❑ 1958 Cover: 0.10 **NM** value: **14.00**
22 ❑ 1958 Cover: 0.10 **NM** value: **14.00**
23 ❑ Feb 1959 Cover: 0.10 **NM** value: **14.00**
24 ❑ 1959 Cover: 0.10 **NM** value: **14.00**
25 ❑ 1959 Cover: 0.10 **NM** value: **14.00**
26 ❑ 1959 Cover: 0.10 **NM** value: **14.00**
27 ❑ 1959 Cover: 0.10 **NM** value: **14.00**
28 ❑ Jan 1960 Cover: 0.10 **NM** value: **14.00**
29 ❑ Mar 1960 Cover: 0.10 **NM** value: **14.00**
30 ❑ May 1960 Cover: 0.10 **NM** value: **14.00**
31 ❑ Jul 1960 Cover: 0.10 **NM** value: **10.00**
32 ❑ Sep 1960 Cover: 0.10 **NM** value: **10.00**
33 ❑ Nov 1960 Cover: 0.10 **NM** value: **10.00**
34 ❑ Jan 1961 Cover: 0.10 **NM** value: **10.00**
35 ❑ Mar 1961 Cover: 0.10 **NM** value: **10.00**
36 ❑ May 1961 Cover: 0.10 **NM** value: **10.00**
37 ❑ Jul 1961 Cover: 0.10 **NM** value: **10.00**
38 ❑ Sep 1961 Cover: 0.10 **NM** value: **10.00**
39 ❑ Nov 1961 Cover: 0.10 **NM** value: **10.00**
40 ❑ Feb 1962 Cover: 0.12 **NM** value: **10.00**
41 ❑ Apr 1962 Cover: 0.12 **NM** value: **10.00**
42 ❑ Jun 1962 Cover: 0.12 **NM** value: **8.00**
43 ❑ Aug 1962 Cover: 0.12 **NM** value: **8.00**
44 ❑ Oct 1962 Cover: 0.12 **NM** value: **8.00**
45 ❑ Dec 1962 Cover: 0.12 **NM** value: **8.00**
46 ❑ 1963 Cover: 0.12 **NM** value: **8.00**
47 ❑ 1963 Cover: 0.12 **NM** value: **8.00**
📖 Peaceful Citizen; Top Hand; Sheriff Slidell (text); They Made Their Will; The Wrong Bullet **A:** Nicholas Alascia; Ram
48 ❑ 1963 Cover: 0.12 **NM** value: **8.00**
49 ❑ 1963 Cover: 0.12 **NM** value: **8.00**
50 ❑ 1963 Cover: 0.12 **NM** value: **8.00**
51 ❑ 1964 Cover: 0.12 **NM** value: **6.00**
52 ❑ 1964 Cover: 0.12 **NM** value: **6.00**
53 ❑ 1964 Cover: 0.12 **NM** value: **6.00**
54 ❑ Jul 1964 Cover: 0.12 **NM** value: **6.00**
55 ❑ Nov 1964 Cover: 0.12 **NM** value: **6.00**
56 ❑ Jan 1965 Cover: 0.12 **NM** value: **6.00**
57 ❑ 1965 Cover: 0.12 **NM** value: **6.00**
58 ❑ Jun 1965 Cover: 0.12 **NM** value: **6.00**
59 ❑ Aug 1965 Cover: 0.12 **NM** value: **6.00**
60 ❑ 1965 Cover: 0.12 **NM** value: **6.00**
61 ❑ 1965 Cover: 0.12 **NM** value: **6.00**
62 ❑ Mar 1966 Cover: 0.12 **NM** value: **6.00**
63 ❑ May 1966 Cover: 0.12 **NM** value: **6.00**
64 ❑ Jul 1966 Cover: 0.12 **NM** value: **6.00**
65 ❑ Sep 1966 Cover: 0.12 **NM** value: **6.00**
66 ❑ Nov 1966 Cover: 0.12 **NM** value: **6.00**
67 ❑ Jan 1967 Cover: 0.12 **NM** value: **6.00**
68 ❑ Mar 1967 Cover: 0.12 **NM** value: **6.00**
69 ❑ Jun 1967 Cover: 0.12 **NM** value: **6.00**
70 ❑ Aug 1967 Cover: 0.12 **NM** value: **6.00**
71 ❑ Oct 1967 Cover: 0.12 **NM** value: **6.00**
72 ❑ Dec 1967 Cover: 0.12 **NM** value: **6.00**
final issue.

WYNONNA EARP — Image

1 ❑ Dec 1996 Cover: 2.50 **NM** value: **Cover or less**
Circ: Diamd. preorders: **34,459**
2 ❑ Jan 1997 Cover: 2.50 **NM** value: **Cover or less**
Circ: Diamd. preorders: **25,471**
📖 The Bloody Badge of the Law **A:** Joyce Chin **W:** Beau Smith
3 ❑ Feb 1997 Cover: 2.50 **NM** value: **Cover or less**
Circ: Diamd. preorders: **20,832**
cover says Jan, indicia says Feb. **A:** Joyce Chin **W:** Beau Smith
4 ❑ Mar 1997 Cover: 2.50 **NM** value: **Cover or less**
Circ: Diamd. preorders: **20,102**
5 ❑ Apr 1997 Cover: 2.50 **NM** value: **Cover or less**
Circ: Diamd. preorders: **18,580**
final issue. **A:** Pat Lee **W:** Beau Smith ★ Appearance of Beau Smith.

WYOMING TERRITORY — Ark

1 ❑ b&w Cover: 1.95 **NM** value: **Cover or less**

WYRD THE RELUCTANT WARRIOR — Slave Labor

1 ❑ Jul 1999 Cover: 2.95 **NM** value: **Cover or less**
Circ: Diamd. preorders: **3,611**
2 ❑ Aug 1999 Cover: 2.95 **NM** value: **Cover or less**
Circ: Diamd. preorders: **2,383**
3 ❑ Sep 1999 Cover: 2.95 **NM** value: **Cover or less**
4 ❑ Oct 1999 Cover: 2.95 **NM** value: **Cover or less**
Circ: Diamd. preorders: **2,198**
5 ❑ Nov 1999 Cover: 2.95 **NM** value: **Cover or less**
6 ❑ Dec 1999 Cover: 2.95 **NM** value: **Cover or less**
📖 The Final Confrontation! **A:** Jim Starlin **W:** Jim Starlin

X — Dark Horse

The city of Arcadia has long been ruled by the shadowy forces of crime and corruption. Mob bosses have grown comfortable holding the reigns of power, unchallenged by government or police. But lately they have learned about fear from a man they call the X-Killer.

Is he a murdered man seeking revenge from beyond the grave? A rival boss out for control of the gangs? A secret government experiment running loose in the city? Nobody knows who or what he is, but what he does is only too clear: He kills criminals.

Sometimes there is a warning: a single stroke of red. If you are marked with both strokes of the X, it means your life is about to end.

This continuing series was first previewed in the one-shot Comics' Greatest World: X.

1 ❑ Feb 1994 Cover: 2.00 **NM** value: **2.50**
Circ: CapCity orders: **32,400**
embossed cardstock cover.
2 ❑ Mar 1994 Cover: 2.00 **NM** value: **2.50**
Circ: CapCity orders: **15,525**
3 ❑ Apr 1994 Cover: 2.00 **NM** value: **2.50**
Circ: CapCity orders: **12,575**
4 ❑ May 1994 Cover: 2.00 **NM** value: **Cover or less**
Circ: CapCity orders: **14,125**
5 ❑ Jun 1994 Cover: 2.00 **NM** value: **Cover or less**
Circ: CapCity orders: **13,950**
6 ❑ Aug 1994 Cover: 2.00 **NM** value: **Cover or less**
Circ: CapCity orders: **11,900**
7 ❑ Sep 1994 Cover: 2.00 **NM** value: **Cover or less**
Circ: CapCity orders: **10,850**
8 ❑ Oct 1994 Cover: 2.50 **NM** value: **Cover or less**
Circ: CapCity orders: **9,675**
9 ❑ Nov 1994 Cover: 2.50 **NM** value: **Cover or less**
Circ: CapCity orders: **8,025**
10 ❑ Dec 1994 Cover: 2.50 **NM** value: **Cover or less**
Circ: CapCity orders: **7,750**
11 ❑ Jan 1995 Cover: 2.50 **NM** value: **Cover or less**
Circ: CapCity orders: **6,800**
12 ❑ Mar 1995 Cover: 2.50 **NM** value: **Cover or less**
Circ: CapCity orders: **6,475**
13 ❑ Apr 1995 Cover: 2.50 **NM** value: **Cover or less**
Circ: CapCity orders: **6,200**
14 ❑ May 1995 Cover: 2.50 **NM** value: **Cover or less**
Circ: CapCity orders: **5,950**
15 ❑ Jun 1995 Cover: 2.50 **NM** value: **Cover or less**
Circ: CapCity orders: **5,875**
16 ❑ Jul 1995 Cover: 2.50 **NM** value: **Cover or less**
Circ: CapCity orders: **5,850**
17 ❑ Aug 1995 Cover: 2.50 **NM** value: **Cover or less**
Circ: CapCity orders: **5,900**
18 ❑ Sep 1995 Cover: 2.50 **NM** value: **Cover or less**
Circ: CapCity orders: **6,200**
19 ❑ Oct 1995 Cover: 2.50 **NM** value: **Cover or less**
20 ❑ Nov 1995 Cover: 2.50 **NM** value: **Cover or less**
21 ❑ Dec 1995 Cover: 2.50 **NM** value: **Cover or less**
22 ❑ Jan 1996 Cover: 2.50 **NM** value: **Cover or less**
23 ❑ Feb 1996 Cover: 2.50 **NM** value: **Cover or less**

Other grades: Multiply prices above by **1.5 for Mint • 2/3 for Very Fine • 1/3 for Fine • 1/5 for Very Good • 1/8 for Good**

24 ❑ Mar 1996 Cover: 2.50 NM value: Cover or less
25 ❑ Apr 1996 Cover: 2.50 NM value: Cover or less
final issue.
Hero 1❑ Cover: 1.00 NM value: Cover or less
• Included with Hero Illustrated magazine.

X/1999 — Viz

1 ❑ b&w Cover: 2.75 NM value: 3.00
Circ: CapCity orders: 3,775
📖 Homecoming A: Clamp W: Clamp
2 ❑ b&w Cover: 2.75 NM value: Cover or less
Circ: CapCity orders: 2,675
3 ❑ b&w Cover: 2.75 NM value: Cover or less
Circ: CapCity orders: 2,800
4 ❑ b&w Cover: 2.75 NM value: Cover or less
Circ: CapCity orders: 2,475
5 ❑ b&w Cover: 2.75 NM value: Cover or less
Circ: CapCity orders: 2,275
6 ❑ b&w Cover: 2.75 NM value: Cover or less
Bk 1❑ b&w NM value: 15.95
Bk 2❑ Cover: 15.95 NM value: Cover or less
📖 Prelude
Bk 3❑ Cover: 15.95 NM value: Cover or less
• Overture
Bk 4❑ Jan 1998 Cover: 15.95 NM value: Cover or less
• Sonata
Bk 5❑ Mar 1998 Cover: 15.95 NM value: Cover or less
• Intermezzo

X-51 — Marvel

1 ❑ Sep 1999 Cover: 1.99 NM value: Cover or less
📖 The Persistence of Memory A: Joe Bennett W: Karl Bollers; Michael Higgins
2 ❑ Sep 1999 Cover: 1.99 NM value: Cover or less
3 ❑ Oct 1999 Cover: 1.99 NM value: Cover or less
4 ❑ Nov 1999 Cover: 1.99 NM value: Cover or less
5 ❑ Dec 1999 Cover: 1.99 NM value: Cover or less

XANADU (3-D ZONE) — 3-D Zone

1 ❑ b&w Cover: 2.00 NM value: Cover or less
2 ❑ b&w Cover: 2.00 NM value: Cover or less
3 ❑ b&w Cover: 2.00 NM value: Cover or less
4 ❑ b&w Cover: 2.00 NM value: Cover or less

XANADU: ACROSS DIAMOND SEAS — Mu

1 ❑ b&w Cover: 2.50 NM value: Cover or less
2 ❑ Feb 1994, b&w Cover: 2.50 NM value: Cover or less
3 ❑ Mar 1994, b&w Cover: 2.50 NM value: 2.95
4 ❑ Apr 1994, b&w Cover: 2.50 NM value: 2.95
5 ❑ May 1994, b&w Cover: 2.95 NM value: Cover or less
Bk 1❑ Jan 1994 Cover: 12.95 NM value: Cover or less
• Xanadu: Thief of Hearts

XANADU COLOR SPECIAL — Eclipse

1 ❑ Dec 1988 Cover: 2.00 NM value: Cover or less
Circ: CapCity orders: 3,875

XANADU (THOUGHTS & IMAGES) — Thoughts & Images

Xanadu was one of the better anthropomorphic fantasy series to appear in the late 1980s. Drawn by V.M. Wyman, it features clean, uncluttered art that effectively communicates both action and emotion. The story itself is focused on Empress Alicia, who is doing her best to hold together the empire of Xanadu established by her father Allynrud. One of her own nobles, Reginald Plume, resents serving under Alicia, doubly so now that the golden dragon Kinomon is installed as his second in command. Feeling his place at court threatened, he lashes out with a plot of his own to rid himself of Kinomon and to further his own ambitions. Luckily for Alicia, she not only has hidden enemies, but also unexpected allies in the form of an adventure-seeking thief and his sometime partner. Xanadu is an enjoyable story of love, intrigue, and adventure.

1 ❑ May 1988, b&w Cover: 2.00 NM value: Cover or less
2 ❑ Jun 1988, b&w Cover: 2.00 NM value: Cover or less
3 ❑ Jul 1988, b&w Cover: 2.00 NM value: Cover or less
4 ❑ Aug 1988, b&w Cover: 2.00 NM value: Cover or less
5 ❑ Nov 1988, b&w Cover: 2.00 NM value: Cover or less
cover says Part Three of Five. A: Vicky Wyman W: L. X.

XANDER IN LOST UNIVERSE (GENE RODDENBERRY'S...) — Tekno

0 ❑ Nov 1995 Cover: 2.25 NM value: Cover or less
Circ: Statement: 110,805
1 ❑ Dec 1995 Cover: 2.25 NM value: Cover or less
Circ: Statement: 110,805 CapCity orders: 9,125
2 ❑ Dec 1995 Cover: 2.25 NM value: Cover or less
Circ: CapCity orders: 6,550
3 ❑ Jan 1996 Cover: 2.25 NM value: Cover or less
4 ❑ Jan 1996 Cover: 2.25 NM value: Cover or less
• Has 1995 Statement, filed 10/11/95 (Alert: Filed INCREDIBLY early in run; validity suspect); avg print run 261,615; avg sales 110,573; avg subs 232; avg total paid 110,805; samples 7,914; office 8,348; max existent 127,067; 51% of run returned
5 ❑ Feb 1996 Cover: 2.25 NM value: Cover or less
6 ❑ Mar 1996 Cover: 2.25 NM value: Cover or less
7 ❑ Apr 1996 Cover: 2.25 NM value: Cover or less
8 ❑ May 1996 Cover: 2.25 NM value: Cover or less

XANTH GRAPHIC NOVEL — Father Tree

1 ❑ Cover: 9.95 NM value: Cover or less
Circ: CapCity orders: 2,600
📖 Return to Centaur

X-BABIES: MURDERAMA — Marvel

1 ❑ Cover: 2.99 NM value: Cover or less
📖 Murderama A: Arthur Adams W: Chris Claremont

X-BABIES: REBORN — Marvel

1 ❑ Jan 2000 Cover: 3.50 NM value: Cover or less
📖 Beware the Babymaker A: Juvaun Kirby W: Ruben Diaz

X-CALIBRE — Marvel

1 ❑ Mar 1995 Cover: 1.95 NM value: 2.00
Circ: CapCity orders: 60,125
📖 The Infernal Gallop A: Ken Lashley W: Warren Ellis
2 ❑ Apr 1995 Cover: 1.95 NM value: 2.00
Circ: CapCity orders: 60,350
cover says Jun. A: Roger Cruz; Renato Arler W: Warren Ellis
3 ❑ May 1995 Cover: 1.95 NM value: 2.00
Circ: CapCity orders: 76,900
4 ❑ Jun 1995 Cover: 1.95 NM value: 2.00
Circ: CapCity orders: 86,250
Bk 1❑ May 1995 Cover: 8.95 NM value: Cover or less
Gold foil cover. • Ultimate X-Calibre; collects four-issue series

XENA — Brainstorm

1 ❑ Cover: 2.95 NM value: Cover or less

XENA: WARRIOR PRINCESS: AND THE ORIGINAL OLYMPICS — Topps

1 ❑ Jun 1998 Cover: 2.95 NM value: Cover or less
Circ: Diamd. preorders: 27,941
2 ❑ Jul 1998 Cover: 2.95 NM value: Cover or less
Circ: Diamd. preorders: 25,722
3 ❑ Aug 1998 Cover: 2.95 NM value: Cover or less
Circ: Diamd. preorders: 24,488

XENA: WARRIOR PRINCESS: BLOODLINES — Topps

1 ❑ May 1998 Cover: 2.95 NM value: Cover or less
Circ: Diamd. preorders: 28,357
2 ❑ Jun 1998 Cover: 2.95 NM value: Cover or less
Circ: Diamd. preorders: 27,990

XENA: WARRIOR PRINCESS (DARK HORSE) — Dark Horse

This comic takes its cue from the popular television series, continuing the adventures of the bold warrior, her peace-loving sidekick Gabrielle, and a whole slew of gods, goddesses, and enemies they've managed to annoy along the way.

Xena and Gabrielle, captured by the Romans at last, hang dying from crosses on a bleak winter plain. But Xena has one more battle to fight in her mind, a clever trap set by her old enemy Callisto, and its outcome could damn the warrior's soul forever. Only Gabrielle's loving wisdom can save Xena, if she will listen to her heart.

Issues of this series were available with variant art and photo covers.

1 ❑ Sep 1999 Cover: 2.95 NM value: 3.00
Circ: Diamd. preorders: 36,103
📖 The Warrior Way of Death, Part 1 A: Joyce Chin W: John Wagner
1/SC❑Sep 1999 Cover: 2.95 NM value: 3.00
Photo cover. 📖 The Warrior Way of Death, Part 2 A: Joyce Chin W: John Wagner
2 ❑ Oct 1999 Cover: 2.95 NM value: 3.00
Circ: Diamd. preorders: 28,143
📖 In Hell A: Joyce Chin W: John Wagner
2/SC❑Oct 1999 Cover: 2.95 NM value: 3.00
Photo cover. 📖 In Hell A: Joyce Chin W: John Wagner
3 ❑ Nov 1999 Cover: 2.95 NM value: 3.00
Circ: Diamd. preorders: 24,656
📖 Slave A: Mike Deodato Jr.; Ivan Reis W: John Wagner
3/SC❑Nov 1999 Cover: 2.95 NM value: 3.00
Photo cover. 📖 Slave A: Mike Deodato Jr.; Ivan Reis W: John Wagner
4 ❑ Dec 1999 Cover: 2.95 NM value: 3.00
Circ: Diamd. preorders: 24,154
4/SC❑Dec 1999 Cover: 2.95 NM value: 3.00
Photo cover. A: Joyce Chin; Clint Hillman W: John Wagner
5 ❑ Jan 2000 Cover: 2.95 NM value: 3.00
Circ: Diamd. preorders: 20,427
📖 The Slave Trail A: Fabiano Neves W: John Wagner
5/SC❑Jan 2000 Cover: 2.95 NM value: 3.00
Photo cover. 📖 The Slave Trail A: Fabiano Neves W: John Wagner
6 ❑ Feb 2000 Cover: 2.95 NM value: Cover or less
Circ: Diamd. preorders: 18,510
6/SC❑Feb 2000 Cover: 2.95 NM value: Cover or less
Photo cover.
7 ❑ Mar 2000 Cover: 2.95 NM value: Cover or less
Circ: Diamd. preorders: 18,018
7/SC❑Mar 2000 Cover: 2.95 NM value: Cover or less
Photo cover.
8 ❑ Apr 2000 Cover: 2.95 NM value: Cover or less
Circ: Diamd. preorders: 16,934
8/SC❑Apr 2000 Cover: 2.95 NM value: Cover or less
Photo cover.
9 ❑ May 2000 Cover: 2.95 NM value: Cover or less
Circ: Diamd. preorders: 16,744
📖 If You Go Down to the Woods... A: Mike Deodato Jr. W: Ian Edginton
9/SC❑May 2000 Cover: 2.95 NM value: Cover or less
Photo cover. 📖 If You Go Down to the Woods... A: Mike Deodato Jr. W: Ian Edginton
10 ❑ Jun 2000 Cover: 2.95 NM value: Cover or less
Circ: Diamd. preorders: 16,953
📖 The Magnificent Seven A: Mike Deodato Jr. W: Ian Edginton
10/SC❑Jun 2000 Cover: 2.95 NM value: Cover or less
Photo cover. 📖 The Magnificent Seven A: Mike Deodato Jr. W: Ian Edginton
11 ❑ Jul 2000 Cover: 2.95 NM value: Cover or less
Circ: Diamd. preorders: 16,081
📖 Darkness Falls A: Mike Deodato Jr. W: Ian Edginton
11/SC❑Jul 2000 Cover: 2.95 NM value: Cover or less
Photo cover. 📖 Darkness Falls A: Mike Deodato Jr. W: Ian Edginton
12 ❑ Aug 2000 Cover: 2.95 NM value: Cover or less
Circ: Diamd. preorders: 14,849
📖 Darkness Falls, Part 2 A: Mike Deodato Jr. W: Ian Edginton
12/SC❑Aug 2000 Cover: 2.95 NM value: Cover or less
Photo cover. 📖 Darkness Falls, Part 2 A: Mike Deodato Jr. W: Ian Edginton
13 ❑ Sep 2000 Cover: 2.95 NM value: Cover or less
Circ: Diamd. preorders: 14,943
📖 Legion A: Mike Deodato Jr. W: Ian Edginton
13/SC❑Sep 2000 Cover: 2.95 NM value: Cover or less
Photo cover. 📖 Legion A: Mike Deodato Jr. W: Ian Edginton
14 ❑ Oct 2000 Cover: 2.99 NM value: Cover or less
Circ: Diamd. preorders: 14,273
📖 This Year's Model A: Mike Deodato Jr. W: Ian Edginton
14/SC❑Oct 2000 Cover: 2.99 NM value: Cover or less
Photo cover. 📖 This Year's Model A: Mike Deodato Jr. W: Ian Edginton

XENA: WARRIOR PRINCESS/JOXER: WARRIOR PRINCE — Topps

1 ❑ Nov 1997 Cover: 2.95 NM value: Cover or less
1/SC❑Nov 1997 Cover: 2.95 NM value: Cover or less
Photo cover. A: Ron Lim W: Mary Bierbaum; Tom Bierbaum
2 ❑ Dec 1997 Cover: 2.95 NM value: Cover or less
2/SC❑Dec 1997 Cover: 2.95 NM value: Cover or less
Photo cover. A: Ron Lim W: Mary Bierbaum; Tom Bierbaum
3 ❑ Jan 1998 Cover: 2.95 NM value: Cover or less
3/SC❑Jan 1998 Cover: 2.95 NM value: Cover or less
Photo cover. A: Ron Lim W: Mary Bierbaum; Tom Bierbaum

XENA: WARRIOR PRINCESS-THE DRAGON'S TEETH — Topps

1 ❑ Dec 1997 Cover: 2.95 NM value: Cover or less
1/SC❑Dec 1997 Cover: 2.95 NM value: Cover or less
Photo cover.
2 ❑ Jan 1998 Cover: 2.95 NM value: Cover or less
Circ: Diamd. preorders: 35,329
2/SC❑Jan 1998 Cover: 2.95 NM value: Cover or less
Photo cover.
3 ❑ Feb 1998 Cover: 2.95 NM value: Cover or less
3/SC❑Feb 1998 Cover: 2.95 NM value: Cover or less
Photo cover.

XENA: WARRIOR PRINCESS: THE ORPHEUS TRILOGY — Topps

1 ❑ Mar 1998 Cover: 2.95 NM value: Cover or less
Circ: Diamd. preorders: 30,878
1/SC❑Mar 1998 Cover: 2.95 NM value: Cover or less
Photo cover. A: Robert Teranishi W: Mary Bierbaum; Tom Bierbaum
2 ❑ Apr 1998 Cover: 2.95 NM value: Cover or less
Circ: Diamd. preorders: 29,920
2/SC❑Apr 1998 Cover: 2.95 NM value: Cover or less
Photo cover. A: Robert Teranishi W: Mary Bierbaum; Tom Bierbaum
3 ❑ May 1998 Cover: 2.95 NM value: Cover or less
Circ: Diamd. preorders: 27,539
3/SC❑May 1998 Cover: 2.95 NM value: Cover or less
Photo cover. A: Robert Teranishi W: Mary Bierbaum; Tom Bierbaum

XENA: WARRIOR PRINCESS-THE WARRIOR WAY OF DEATH — Dark Horse

1 ❑ Sep 1999 Cover: 2.95 NM value: Cover or less
1/SC❑Sep 1999 Cover: 2.95 NM value: Cover or less
Photo cover.
2 ❑ Oct 1999 Cover: 2.95 NM value: Cover or less
2/SC❑Oct 1999 Cover: 2.95 NM value: Cover or less
Photo cover.

XENA: WARRIOR PRINCESS VS. CALLISTO — Topps

1 ❑ Feb 1998 Cover: 2.95 NM value: Cover or less
Circ: Diamd. preorders: 33,168
1/SC❑Feb 1998 Cover: 2.95 NM value: Cover or less
Photo cover.
2 ❑ Mar 1998 Cover: 2.95 NM value: Cover or less
Circ: Diamd. preorders: 30,867
2/SC❑Mar 1998 Cover: 2.95 NM value: Cover or less
Photo cover.
3 ❑ Mar 1998 Cover: 2.95 NM value: Cover or less
Circ: Diamd. preorders: 30,467
3/SC❑Mar 1998 Cover: 2.95 NM value: Cover or less
Photo cover.

XENA: WARRIOR PRINCESS (VOL. 1) — Topps

0 ❑ Oct 1997 Cover: 2.95 NM value: Cover or less
Photo cover. 📖 The Temple of the Dragon God; Theft of the Young Lovelies, Part 3 A: Aaron Lopresti; Amanda Conner W: Aaron Lopresti; Robert Trebor
1 ❑ Aug 1997 Cover: 2.95 NM value: Cover or less
• CGC: 1 graded, best 9.6

CGC-graded: Multiply prices above by 33 for 9.9 M • 16 for 9.8 NM/M • 7 for 9.6 NM+ • 5 for 9.4 NM • 2.5 for 9.2 NM- • 1.5 for 9.0 VF/NM

• back-up Tales of Salmoneus **A:** Roy Thomas; Bob Trebor **W:** Part 1; Revenge of the Gorgons; Theft of the Young Lovelies ★ Appearance of Hercules.

1/A ❑ Aug 1997 Cover: 2.95 **NM value: Cover or less**
• **CGC:** 3 graded, best 9.4
Photo cover of Xena poised to strike. **A:** Roy Thomas; Bob Trebor **W:** Part 1; Revenge of the Gorgons; Theft of the Young Lovelies

1/AE❑ Aug 1997 **NM value: 7.00**
Photo cover. • American Entertainment **A:** Roy Thomas; Bob Trebor **W:** Part 1; Revenge of the Gorgons; Theft of the Young Lovelies

1/SC❑ Aug 1997 Cover: 2.95 **NM value: Cover or less**
Photo cover of Xena walking hand in hand with Gabrielle. **A:** Roy Thomas; Bob Trebor **W:** Part 1; Revenge of the Gorgons; Theft of the Young Lovelies

2 ❑ Sep 1997 Cover: 2.95 **NM value: Cover or less**
Circ: Diamd. preorders: **35,517**

2/SC❑ Sep 1997 Cover: 2.95 **NM value: Cover or less**
Photo cover.

XENA, WARRIOR PRINCESS: WRATH OF HERA — Topps

1 ❑ Cover: 2.95 **NM value: Cover or less**
Circ: Diamd. preorders: **26,630**

1/SC❑ Cover: 2.95 **NM value: 3.00**
Photo cover.

2 ❑ Cover: 2.95 **NM value: Cover or less**
Circ: Diamd. preorders: **23,661**

2/SC❑ Cover: 2.95 **NM value: 3.00**
Photo cover.

XENA: WARRIOR PRINCES, YEAR ONE — Topps

1 ❑ **NM value: 5.00**
Photo cover of Xena smiling. ★ Origin of Xena.

1/GO❑ **NM value: 10.00**
Gold logo cover. ★ Origin of Xena.

XENE — Eyeball Soup Designs

1 ❑ Jan 1996 Cover: 4.95 **NM value: Cover or less**
cardstock cover.

2 ❑ Mar 1996 Cover: 4.95 **NM value: Cover or less**
cardstock cover.

3 ❑ May 1996 Cover: 4.95 **NM value: Cover or less**
cardstock cover. 📖 The Devil to Pay, Part 2; Hunter's Moon, Part 2 **A:** Gavin Lim; Jon Hoo **W:** Gavin Lim; Elizabeth How

4 ❑ Jul 1996 Cover: 4.95 **NM value: Cover or less**
cardstock cover.

XENOBROOD — DC

0 ❑ Oct 1994 Cover: 1.50 **NM value: Cover or less**
Circ: CapCity orders: **20,150**

1 ❑ Nov 1994 Cover: 1.50 **NM value: Cover or less**
Circ: CapCity orders: **11,950**

2 ❑ Dec 1994 Cover: 1.50 **NM value: Cover or less**
Circ: CapCity orders: **9,300**

3 ❑ Jan 1995 Cover: 1.50 **NM value: Cover or less**
Circ: CapCity orders: **8,350**
📖 The Vimanian Bestiary **A:** Chris Hunter **W:** Doug Moench

4 ❑ Feb 1995 Cover: 1.50 **NM value: Cover or less**
Circ: CapCity orders: **6,525**

5 ❑ Mar 1995 Cover: 1.50 **NM value: Cover or less**
Circ: CapCity orders: **5,075**

6 ❑ Apr 1995 Cover: 1.50 **NM value: Cover or less**
Circ: CapCity orders: **4,350**
final issue.

XENO-MEN — Blackthorne

1 ❑ Cover: 1.75 **NM value: Cover or less**
Circ: CapCity orders: **2,000**

XENON — Eclipse / Viz

1 ❑ Dec 1987 Cover: 1.50 **NM value: 2.00**
📖 Metamorphosis II **A:** Masaomi Kanzaki **W:** Masaomi Kanzaki

2 ❑ Dec 1987 Cover: 1.50 **NM value: 2.00**
📖 Metamorphosis II **A:** Masaomi Kanzaki **W:** Masaomi Kanzaki

3 ❑ Jan 1988 Cover: 1.50 **NM value: 2.00**
📖 Metamorphosis III **A:** Masaomi Kanzaki **W:** Masaomi Kanzaki

4 ❑ Jan 1988 Cover: 1.50 **NM value: 2.00**
5 ❑ Feb 1988 Cover: 1.50 **NM value: 2.00**
6 ❑ Feb 1988 Cover: 1.50 **NM value: 2.00**
7 ❑ Mar 1988 Cover: 1.50 **NM value: 2.00**
8 ❑ Mar 1988 Cover: 1.50 **NM value: 2.00**
9 ❑ Apr 1988 Cover: 1.50 **NM value: 2.00**
10 ❑ Apr 1988 Cover: 1.50 **NM value: 2.00**
11 ❑ May 1988 Cover: 1.50 **NM value: Cover or less**
12 ❑ May 1988 Cover: 1.50 **NM value: Cover or less**
13 ❑ Jun 1988 Cover: 1.50 **NM value: Cover or less**
14 ❑ Jun 1988 Cover: 1.50 **NM value: Cover or less**
15 ❑ Jul 1988 Cover: 1.50 **NM value: Cover or less**
16 ❑ Jul 1988 Cover: 1.50 **NM value: Cover or less**
17 ❑ Aug 1988 Cover: 1.50 **NM value: Cover or less**
18 ❑ Aug 1988 Cover: 1.50 **NM value: Cover or less**
19 ❑ Sep 1988 Cover: 1.50 **NM value: Cover or less**
20 ❑ Sep 1988 Cover: 1.50 **NM value: Cover or less**
21 ❑ Oct 1988 Cover: 1.50 **NM value: Cover or less**
22 ❑ Oct 1988 Cover: 1.50 **NM value: Cover or less**
23 ❑ Nov 1989 Cover: 1.50 **NM value: Cover or less**
final issue. **A:** Masaomi Kanzaki **W:** Masaomi Kanzaki

Bk 1❑ Cover: 12.95 **NM value: Cover or less**
Bk 2❑ Cover: 14.95 **NM value: Cover or less**
Bk 3❑ Cover: 14.95 **NM value: Cover or less**
Bk 4❑ Cover: 12.95 **NM value: Cover or less**

XENO'S ARROW — Cup o' Tea Studios

1 ❑ Feb 1999, b&w Cover: 2.50 **NM value: Cover or less**
📖 In My Garden **A:** Greg Beettam **W:** Greg Beettam; Stephen Geigen-Miller

XENOTECH — Mirage / Next

1 ❑ Aug 1994 Cover: 2.75 **NM value: Cover or less**
Circ: CapCity orders: **6,150**
📖 Fire With Fire **A:** Michael Dooney **W:** Michael Dooney ★ 1st Appearance of Gunner, Xenotech, Haywire (Xenotech), Starker Helm, Pulse, Chunk.

1/A ❑ Aug 1994 Cover: 2.75 **NM value: Cover or less**
Variant cover with monster attacking. 📖 Fire With Fire **A:** Michael Dooney **W:** Michael Dooney ★ 1st Appearance of Gunner, Haywire (Xenotech), Starker Helm, Pulse, Chunk.

2 ❑ Oct 1994 Cover: 2.75 **NM value: Cover or less**
📖 Enter Overblown! **A:** Michael Dooney **W:** Michael Dooney ★ Origin of Xenotech.

XENOZOIC TALES — Kitchen Sink

It is the Xenozoic Era. After a series of cataclysmic upheavals which killed billions, mankind retreated to the bowels of the Earth. After 450 years, humanity returned to the surface and discovered a world populated with dinosaurs. Society has settled into a number of tribes and city-states, each with its own politics. The grudging respect that independent explorer Jack Tenrec and ambassador Hannah Dundee have for each other is fertile territory for tales of adventure and romance.

This title is the brainchild of Mark Schultz, whose keen eye for the human figure is reminiscent of Frank Frazetta, Al Williamson, Alex Raymond, and Wally Wood. It is a series that could be considered self-indulgent, since it features elements that Schultz admires: beautiful women, dinosaurs, and big cars with tailfins. These stories were later collected, colored and reprinted, by Epic under the title Cadillacs and Dinosaurs.

1 ❑ Feb 1987 Cover: 2.00 **NM value: 8.00**
• **CGC:** 8 graded, best 9.8
📖 An Archipelago of Stone **A:** Mark Schultz **W:** Mark Schultz

1-2 ❑ Cover: 2.00 **NM value: 3.00**

2 ❑ Apr 1987 Cover: 2.00 **NM value: 6.00**
• **CGC:** 2 graded, best 9.6

3 ❑ Jun 1987 Cover: 2.00 **NM value: 6.00**
• **CGC:** 2 graded, best 9.6

4 ❑ Nov 1987 Cover: 2.00 **NM value: 6.00**
• **CGC:** 3 graded, best 9.4
📖 History Lesson; Postal Service **A:** Steve Stiles; Mark Schultz **W:** Mark Schultz

5 ❑ Feb 1988 Cover: 2.00 **NM value: 6.00**
• **CGC:** 2 graded, best 9.6
📖 Excursion; Dog's Life **A:** Steve Stiles; Mark Schultz **W:** Mark Schultz

6 ❑ ca. 1988 Cover: 2.00 **NM value: 5.00**
📖 Foundling; Green Air; Intrusion **A:** Mark Schultz **W:** Mark Schultz

7 ❑ ca. 1988 Cover: 2.00 **NM value: 5.00**
• **CGC:** 1 graded, best 9.8
📖 The Growing Pool; Crossed Currents **A:** Mark Schultz **W:** Mark Schultz

8 ❑ ca. 1988 Cover: 2.00 **NM value: 5.00**
📖 In the Dreamtime; Foul Weather **A:** Mark Schultz **W:** Mark Schultz

9 ❑ ca. 1988 Cover: 2.00 **NM value: 5.00**
📖 Last Link in the Chain; The Aqueduct **A:** Mark Schultz **W:** Mark Schultz

10 ❑ ca. 1989 Cover: 2.00 **NM value: 5.00**
📖 Lords of the Earth; Fields of Expertise **A:** Steve Stiles; Mark Schultz **W:** Mark Schultz

11 ❑ ca. 1990 Cover: 2.00 **NM value: 4.00**

12 ❑ ca. 1991 Cover: 2.00 **NM value: 4.00**
📖 Two Cities; A Woman's Work... **A:** Steve Stiles; Mark Schultz **W:** Mark Schultz

13 ❑ Cover: 2.00 **NM value: 4.00**
Circ: CapCity orders: **4,650**

14 ❑ Oct 1996, b&w Cover: 2.95 **NM value: 4.00**
Circ: Diamd. preorders: **7,134**
cardstock cover.

Bk 1❑ Cover: 12.95 **NM value: Cover or less**
• Cadillacs & Dinosaurs

Bk 2❑ Cover: 14.95 **NM value: Cover or less**
• Dinosaur Shaman

XENYA — Sanctuary

1 ❑ Jul 1994 Cover: 2.95 **NM value: Cover or less**
Circ: CapCity orders: **11,795**

2 ❑ ca. 1994 Cover: 2.95 **NM value: Cover or less**
Circ: CapCity orders: **5,150**

3 ❑ ca. 1995 Cover: 2.95 **NM value: Cover or less**
Circ: CapCity orders: **4,475**
no cover price.

XERO — DC

1 ❑ May 1997 Cover: 1.75 **NM value: 2.00**
Circ: Diamd. preorders: **19,001**
📖 The Closer **A:** Chris Cross **W:** Christopher Priest

2 ❑ Jun 1997 Cover: 1.75 **NM value: Cover or less**
Circ: Diamd. preorders: **13,400**

3 ❑ Jul 1997 Cover: 1.75 **NM value: Cover or less**
Circ: Diamd. preorders: **11,491**

4 ❑ Aug 1997 Cover: 1.75 **NM value: Cover or less**
Circ: Diamd. preorders: **10,767**

5 ❑ Sep 1997 Cover: 1.75 **NM value: Cover or less**
Circ: Diamd. preorders: **9,196**

6 ❑ Oct 1997 Cover: 1.75 **NM value: Cover or less**
Circ: Diamd. preorders: **10,598**
📖 The Villain; Genesis • Genesis **A:** Chris Cross **W:** Christopher Priest ★ Versus Polaris.

7 ❑ Nov 1997 Cover: 1.75 **NM value: Cover or less**
Circ: Diamd. preorders: **7,674**
📖 The Soldier, Part 1 **A:** Chris Cross **W:** Christopher Priest

8 ❑ Dec 1997 Cover: 1.95 **NM value: Cover or less**
Circ: Diamd. preorders: **7,332**
Face cover. 📖 The Soldier, Part 2 **A:** Chris Cross **W:** Christopher Priest

9 ❑ Jan 1998 Cover: 1.95 **NM value: Cover or less**
Circ: Diamd. preorders: **6,845**

10 ❑ Feb 1998 Cover: 1.95 **NM value: Cover or less**
Circ: Diamd. preorders: **6,142**

11 ❑ Mar 1998 Cover: 1.95 **NM value: Cover or less**
Circ: Diamd. preorders: **5,630**
📖 The Cowboy **A:** Chris Cross **W:** Christopher Priest

12 ❑ Apr 1998 Cover: 1.95 **NM value: Cover or less**
Circ: Diamd. preorders: **5,180**
final issue. **A:** Eric Battle **W:** Christopher Priest

X-FACTOR — Marvel

X-Factor started with a couple of really bad ideas — three if you considered there to already be too many X-titles. John Byrne preferred the original X-Men cast and wanted to bring back Jean Grey, who died in the classic "Dark Phoenix" storyline in X-Men #137. So he retroactively cloned her before that story took place — rendering the classic story meaningless — in an issue of The Avengers and shipped her over to star in the first issue of X-Factor with her former partners.

Bad idea #2 came in the group's cover: Since there was so much mutant paranoia, these heroes posed as mutant-exterminators who, in reality, collected suspected mutants and took them into protection. Some contemporary readers found the concept offensive. Sure, good guys can save people while pretending to be bad guys (see "Schindler's List") — but early X-Factor storylines seemed not to be well-thought through. Later stories would recognize the trouble with the cover story, and steps were taken to put it to rest.

A much-altered X-Factor series finally gave up the ghost in 1998. — JJM

-1 ❑ Jul 1997 Cover: 1.99 **NM value: 2.00**
📖 A Summer's Tale • Flashback **A:** Jeff Matsuda **W:** Howard Mackie

1 ❑ Feb 1986 Cover: 1.25 **NM value: 4.00**
Circ: CapCity orders: **77,800** • **CGC:** 58 graded, best 9.8
• Giant-size. ★ Origin of X-Factor. ★ 1st Appearance of Rusty Collins.

2 ❑ Mar 1986 Cover: 0.75 **NM value: 3.00**
Circ: CapCity orders: **58,700** • **CGC:** 1 graded, best 9.6

3 ❑ Apr 1986 Cover: 0.75 **NM value: 3.00**
Circ: CapCity orders: **58,500**

4 ❑ May 1986 Cover: 0.75 **NM value: 3.00**
Circ: CapCity orders: **56,800**

5 ❑ Jun 1986 Cover: 0.75 **NM value: 4.00**
Circ: CapCity orders: **49,700** • **CGC:** 1 graded, best 9.6

6 ❑ Jul 1986 Cover: 0.75 **NM value: 7.00**
Circ: CapCity orders: **47,200** • **CGC:** 29 graded, best 9.8

7 ❑ Aug 1986 Cover: 0.75 **NM value: 3.00**
Circ: CapCity orders: **40,100**

8 ❑ Sep 1986 Cover: 0.75 **NM value: 3.00**
Circ: CapCity orders: **43,300**

9 ❑ Oct 1989 Cover: 0.75 **NM value: 3.00**
Circ: CapCity orders: **44,500**
📖 Spots! • Mutant Massacre

10 ❑ Nov 1989 Cover: 0.75 **NM value: 3.00**
Circ: CapCity orders: **48,700**
📖 Falling Angel • Mutant Massacre

11 ❑ Dec 1989 Cover: 0.75 **NM value: 3.00**
Circ: CapCity orders: **46,600**
📖 Redemption! • Mutant Massacre **A:** Walt Simonson

12 ❑ Jan 1987 Cover: 0.75 **NM value: 2.50**
Circ: Statement: **340,850** CapCity orders: **43,800**

13 ❑ Feb 1987 Cover: 0.75 **NM value: 2.50**
Circ: Statement: **340,850** CapCity orders: **45,700**

14 ❑ Mar 1987 Cover: 0.75 **NM value: 2.50**
Circ: Statement: **340,850** CapCity orders: **44,300**

15 ❑ Apr 1987 Cover: 0.75 **NM value: 2.50**
Circ: Statement: **340,850** CapCity orders: **45,500**

16 ❑ May 1987 Cover: 0.75 **NM value: 2.50**
Circ: Statement: **340,850** CapCity orders: **38,700**

17 ❑ Jun 1987 Cover: 0.75 **NM value: 2.50**
Circ: Statement: **340,850** CapCity orders: **43,400**

18 ❑ Jul 1987 Cover: 0.75 **NM value: 2.50**
Circ: Statement: **340,850** CapCity orders: **43,300**

19 ❑ Aug 1987 Cover: 0.75 **NM value: 2.50**
Circ: Statement: **340,850** CapCity orders: **45,600**

20 ❑ Sep 1987 Cover: 0.75 **NM value: 2.50**
Circ: Statement: **340,850** CapCity orders: **48,200**

21 ❑ Oct 1987 Cover: 0.75 **NM value: 2.50**
Circ: Statement: **340,850** CapCity orders: **49,100**

22 ❑ Nov 1987 Cover: 0.75 **NM value: 2.50**
Circ: Statement: **340,850** CapCity orders: **49,000**

23 ❑ Dec 1987 Cover: 0.75 **NM value: 6.00**
Circ: Statement: **340,850** CapCity orders: **46,600** • **CGC:** 4 graded, best 9.6
• registration card ★ 1st Appearance of Archangel (cameo).

24 ❑ Jan 1988 Cover: 0.75 **NM value: 10.00**
Circ: Statement: **311,600** CapCity orders: **48,400** • **CGC:** 36 graded, best 9.8

Other grades: Multiply prices above by **1.5 for Mint • 2/3 for Very Fine • 1/3 for Fine • 1/5 for Very Good • 1/8 for Good**

📖 Fall of the Mutants, Part 1 • Fall of Mutants ★ Origin of Apocalypse. ★ 1st Appearance of Archangel (full appearance).

25 ❑ Feb 1988 Cover: 1.25 **NM** value: **3.00**
Circ: Statement: **311,600** CapCity orders: **52,300**
📖 Fall of the Mutants • Fall of Mutants

26 ❑ Mar 1988 Cover: 0.75 **NM** value: **3.00**
Circ: Statement: **311,600** CapCity orders: **59,500**
📖 Fall of the Mutants • Fall of Mutants

27 ❑ Apr 1988 Cover: 0.75 **NM** value: **2.00**
Circ: Statement: **311,600** CapCity orders: **51,000**

28 ❑ May 1988 Cover: 1.00 **NM** value: **2.00**
Circ: Statement: **311,600** CapCity orders: **49,100**
• Has 1987 Statement; avg print run 568,382; avg sales 326,450; avg subs 13,400; avg total paid 340,850; samples 132; office use 4,890; max existent 344,872; 39% of run returned

29 ❑ Jun 1988 Cover: 1.00 **NM** value: **2.00**
Circ: Statement: **311,600** CapCity orders: **48,500**

30 ❑ Jul 1988 Cover: 1.00 **NM** value: **2.00**
Circ: Statement: **311,600** CapCity orders: **48,200**

31 ❑ Aug 1988 Cover: 1.00 **NM** value: **2.00**
Circ: Statement: **311,600** CapCity orders: **47,900**

32 ❑ Sep 1988 Cover: 1.00 **NM** value: **2.00**
Circ: Statement: **311,600** CapCity orders: **45,600**

33 ❑ Oct 1988 Cover: 1.00 **NM** value: **2.00**
Circ: Statement: **311,600** CapCity orders: **46,600**

34 ❑ Nov 1988 Cover: 1.00 **NM** value: **2.00**
Circ: Statement: **311,600** CapCity orders: **44,900**

35 ❑ Dec 1988 Cover: 1.00 **NM** value: **2.00**
Circ: Statement: **311,600** CapCity orders: **50,100**

36 ❑ Jan 1989 Cover: 1.00 **NM** value: **2.00**
Circ: Statement: **297,575** CapCity orders: **50,900**
• Inferno

37 ❑ Feb 1989 Cover: 1.00 **NM** value: **2.00**
Circ: Statement: **297,575** CapCity orders: **50,800**
• Inferno

38 ❑ Mar 1989 Cover: 1.50 **NM** value: **2.00**
Circ: Statement: **297,575** CapCity orders: **54,100**
• Giant-size. • Inferno ★ Death of Madelyn Pryor.

39 ❑ Apr 1989 Cover: 1.00 **NM** value: **2.00**
Circ: Statement: **297,575** CapCity orders: **55,900** • **CGC:** 1 graded, best 9.8
• Inferno

40 ❑ May 1989 Cover: 1.00 **NM** value: **2.00**
Circ: Statement: **297,575** CapCity orders: **51,600**

41 ❑ Jun 1989 Cover: 1.00 **NM** value: **2.00**
Circ: Statement: **297,575** CapCity orders: **61,400**

42 ❑ Jul 1989 Cover: 1.00 **NM** value: **2.00**
Circ: Statement: **297,575** CapCity orders: **60,500**

43 ❑ Aug 1989 Cover: 1.00 **NM** value: **2.00**
Circ: Statement: **297,575** CapCity orders: **56,700**
📖 Judgment War, Part 1

44 ❑ Sep 1989 Cover: 1.00 **NM** value: **2.00**
Circ: Statement: **297,575** CapCity orders: **56,500**
📖 Judgment War, Part 2

45 ❑ Oct 1989 Cover: 1.00 **NM** value: **2.00**
Circ: Statement: **297,575** CapCity orders: **55,300**
📖 Judgment War, Part 3

46 ❑ Nov 1989 Cover: 1.00 **NM** value: **2.00**
Circ: Statement: **297,575** CapCity orders: **54,000**

47 ❑ Nov 1989 Cover: 1.00 **NM** value: **2.00**
Circ: Statement: **297,575** CapCity orders: **54,600**
• Solo Archangel story

48 ❑ Dec 1989 Cover: 1.00 **NM** value: **2.00**
Circ: Statement: **297,575** CapCity orders: **53,000**
📖 Judgment War, Part 5

49 ❑ Dec 1989 Cover: 1.00 **NM** value: **2.00**
Circ: Statement: **297,575** CapCity orders: **52,500**
📖 Judgment War, Part 6

50 ❑ Jan 1990 Cover: 1.50 **NM** value: **2.50**
Circ: Statement: **268,307** CapCity orders: **55,900**
• Giant-size. 📖 Judgment War, Part 7; Acts of Vengeance **C:** Todd McFarlane

51 ❑ Feb 1990 Cover: 1.00 **NM** value: **2.50**
Circ: Statement: **268,307** CapCity orders: **49,800**

52 ❑ Mar 1990 Cover: 1.00 **NM** value: **2.50**
Circ: Statement: **268,307** CapCity orders: **49,100**

53 ❑ Apr 1990 Cover: 1.00 **NM** value: **2.50**
Circ: Statement: **268,307** CapCity orders: **47,100**

54 ❑ May 1990 Cover: 1.00 **NM** value: **1.50**
Circ: Statement: **268,307**
• Has 1989 Statement, filed 10/1/89; avg print run 436,210; avg sales 288,975; avg subs 8,600; avg total paid 297,575; samples 125; office use 600; max existent 298,000; 32% of run returned ★ 1st Appearance of Crimson.

55 ❑ Jun 1990 Cover: 1.00 **NM** value: **1.50**
Circ: Statement: **268,307** CapCity orders: **47,300**

56 ❑ Jul 1990 Cover: 1.00 **NM** value: **1.50**
Circ: Statement: **268,307** CapCity orders: **47,100**

57 ❑ Aug 1990 Cover: 1.00 **NM** value: **1.50**
Circ: Statement: **268,307** CapCity orders: **45,700**

58 ❑ Sep 1990 Cover: 1.00 **NM** value: **1.50**
Circ: Statement: **268,307** CapCity orders: **44,900**

59 ❑ Oct 1990 Cover: 1.00 **NM** value: **1.50**
Circ: Statement: **268,307** CapCity orders: **44,600**

60 ❑ Nov 1990 Cover: 1.00 **NM** value: **2.50**
Circ: Statement: **268,307** CapCity orders: **58,800**
📖 X-Tinction Agenda, Part 3

60-2❑ Nov 1990 Cover: 1.00 **NM** value: **1.50**

61 ❑ Dec 1990 Cover: 1.00 **NM** value: **2.50**
Circ: Statement: **268,307** CapCity orders: **59,600**
📖 X-Tinction Agenda, Part 6

62 ❑ Jan 1991 Cover: 1.00 **NM** value: **2.50**
Circ: Statement: **265,252** CapCity orders: **65,100**
📖 X-Tinction Agenda, Part 9

63 ❑ Feb 1991 Cover: 1.00 **NM** value: **2.50**
Circ: Statement: **265,252** CapCity orders: **50,400**

64 ❑ Mar 1991 Cover: 1.00 **NM** value: **2.50**
Circ: Statement: **265,252** CapCity orders: **50,400**

65 ❑ Apr 1991 Cover: 1.00 **NM** value: **2.50**
Circ: Statement: **265,252** CapCity orders: **51,900**
📖 Endgame, Part 1 • Has 1990 Statement, filed 10/1/90; avg print run 406,488; avg sales 260,741; avg subs 7,566; avg total paid 268,307; samples 100; office use 600; max existent 269,007; 34% of run returned **A:** Whilce Portacio

66 ❑ May 1991 Cover: 1.00 **NM** value: **2.50**
Circ: Statement: **265,252** CapCity orders: **54,000**
📖 Endgame, Part 2 **A:** Whilce Portacio

67 ❑ Jun 1991 Cover: 1.00 **NM** value: **2.50**
Circ: Statement: **265,252** CapCity orders: **54,900**
📖 Endgame, Part 3 **A:** Whilce Portacio

68 ❑ Jul 1991 Cover: 1.00 **NM** value: **2.50**
Circ: Statement: **265,252** CapCity orders: **61,500**
📖 Endgame, Part 4 • Baby Nathan is sent into future **A:** Whilce Portacio

69 ❑ Aug 1991 Cover: 1.00 **NM** value: **2.50**
Circ: Statement: **265,252** CapCity orders: **93,300**

70 ❑ Sep 1991 Cover: 1.00 **NM** value: **2.00**
Circ: Statement: **265,252** CapCity orders: **95,100**
• Muir Island Epilogue

71 ❑ Oct 1991 Cover: 1.00 **NM** value: **2.00**
Circ: Statement: **265,252** CapCity orders: **129,900**
• new team; Havok, Madrox, Polaris & Wolfsbane

71-2❑ Oct 1991 Cover: 1.00 **NM** value: **1.50**

72 ❑ Nov 1991 Cover: 1.00 **NM** value: **1.50**
Circ: Statement: **265,252** CapCity orders: **93,700**

73 ❑ Dec 1991 Cover: 1.00 **NM** value: **1.50**
Circ: Statement: **265,252** CapCity orders: **87,600**

74 ❑ Jan 1992 Cover: 1.00 **NM** value: **1.50**
Circ: Statement: **448,588** CapCity orders: **93,000**

75 ❑ Feb 1992 Cover: 1.75 **NM** value: **2.00**
Circ: Statement: **448,588** CapCity orders: **92,100**
• Giant-size.

76 ❑ Mar 1992 Cover: 1.25 **NM** value: **1.50**
Circ: Statement: **448,588** CapCity orders: **81,900**

77 ❑ Apr 1992 Cover: 1.25 **NM** value: **1.50**
Circ: Statement: **448,588** CapCity orders: **72,300**

78 ❑ May 1992 Cover: 1.25 **NM** value: **1.50**
Circ: Statement: **448,588** CapCity orders: **74,100**

79 ❑ Jun 1992 Cover: 1.25 **NM** value: **1.50**
Circ: Statement: **448,588** CapCity orders: **72,600**

80 ❑ Jul 1992 Cover: 1.25 **NM** value: **1.50**
Circ: Statement: **448,588** CapCity orders: **75,300**

81 ❑ Aug 1992 Cover: 1.25 **NM** value: **1.50**
Circ: Statement: **448,588** CapCity orders: **74,400**

82 ❑ Sep 1992 Cover: 1.25 **NM** value: **1.50**
Circ: Statement: **448,588** CapCity orders: **67,500**

83 ❑ Oct 1992 Cover: 1.25 **NM** value: **1.50**
Circ: Statement: **448,588** CapCity orders: **72,000**

84/CS❑ Nov 1992 Cover: 1.50 **NM** value: **2.00**
Circ: Statement: **448,588** CapCity orders: **212,800**
📖 X-Cutioner's Song; X-Cutioner's Song, Part 2

85/CS❑ Dec 1992 Cover: 1.50 **NM** value: **2.00**
Circ: Statement: **448,588** CapCity orders: **130,500**
📖 X-Cutioner's Song, Part 6

86/CS❑ Jan 1993 Cover: 1.50 **NM** value: **2.00**
Circ: Statement: **423,808** CapCity orders: **142,200**
📖 X-Cutioner's Song, Part 10

87 ❑ Feb 1993 Cover: 1.25 **NM** value: **1.50**
Circ: Statement: **423,808** CapCity orders: **79,100**

88 ❑ Mar 1993 Cover: 1.25 **NM** value: **1.50**
Circ: Statement: **423,808** CapCity orders: **77,100**
• Has 1992 Statement, filed 10/1/92; avg print run 546,983; avg sales 438,517; avg subs 10,042; avg total paid 448,588; samples 250; office use 500; max existent 449,309; 18% of run returned

89 ❑ Apr 1993 Cover: 1.25 **NM** value: **1.50**
Circ: Statement: **423,808** CapCity orders: **76,700**

90 ❑ May 1993 Cover: 1.25 **NM** value: **1.50**
Circ: Statement: **423,808** CapCity orders: **74,700**

91 ❑ Jun 1993 Cover: 1.25 **NM** value: **1.50**
Circ: Statement: **423,808** CapCity orders: **72,200**

92 ❑ Jul 1993 Cover: 3.50 **NM** value: **4.00**
Circ: Statement: **423,808** CapCity orders: **142,800** • **CGC:** 9 graded, best 9.9
Hologram cover.

93 ❑ Aug 1993 Cover: 1.25 **NM** value: **1.50**
Circ: Statement: **423,808**

94 ❑ Sep 1993 Cover: 1.25 **NM** value: **1.50**
Circ: Statement: **423,808** CapCity orders: **87,700**

95 ❑ Oct 1993 Cover: 1.25 **NM** value: **1.50**
Circ: Statement: **423,808** CapCity orders: **66,500**

96 ❑ Nov 1993 Cover: 1.25 **NM** value: **1.50**
Circ: Statement: **423,808** CapCity orders: **67,000**

97 ❑ Dec 1993 Cover: 1.25 **NM** value: **1.50**
Circ: Statement: **299,700** CapCity orders: **67,400**

98 ❑ Jan 1994 Cover: 1.25 **NM** value: **1.50**
Circ: Statement: **299,700** CapCity orders: **61,900**

99 ❑ Feb 1994 Cover: 1.25 **NM** value: **1.50**
Circ: Statement: **299,700** CapCity orders: **60,800**

100 ❑ Mar 1994 Cover: 1.75 **NM** value: **2.00**
Circ: Statement: **299,700**
• Giant-size. ★ Death of Multiple Man.

100/SC❑ Mar 1994 Cover: 2.95 **NM** value: **3.00**
Circ: CapCity orders: **79,750** • **CGC:** 1 graded, best 9.8
foil cover. • Giant-size. ★ Death of Multiple Man.

101 ❑ Apr 1994 Cover: 1.50 **NM** value: **Cover or less**
Circ: Statement: **299,700** CapCity orders: **54,800**

102 ❑ May 1994 Cover: 1.50 **NM** value: **Cover or less**
Circ: Statement: **299,700** CapCity orders: **51,450**

103 ❑ Jun 1994 Cover: 1.50 **NM** value: **Cover or less**
Circ: Statement: **299,700** CapCity orders: **50,600**

104 ❑ Jul 1994 Cover: 1.50 **NM** value: **Cover or less**
Circ: Statement: **299,700** CapCity orders: **52,550**

105 ❑ Aug 1994 Cover: 1.50 **NM** value: **Cover or less**
Circ: Statement: **299,700** CapCity orders: **50,900**

106 ❑ Sep 1994 Cover: 2.00 **NM** value: **Cover or less**
Circ: Statement: **299,700**
📖 Life Signs; Life Signs, Part 1

106/SC❑ Sep 1994 Cover: 2.95 **NM** value: **Cover or less**
Circ: CapCity orders: **67,550**
enhanced cover. 📖 Life Signs, Part 1

107 ❑ Oct 1994 Cover: 1.50 **NM** value: **Cover or less**
Circ: Statement: **213,745** CapCity orders: **47,500**

108 ❑ Nov 1994 Cover: 1.50 **NM** value: **Cover or less**

108/Dlx❑ Nov 1994 Cover: 1.95 **NM** value: **Cover or less**
Circ: Statement: **213,745** CapCity orders: **46,800**
• Deluxe edition.

109 ❑ Dec 1994 Cover: 1.50 **NM** value: **Cover or less**
📖 Legion Quest

109/Dlx❑ Dec 1994 Cover: 1.95 **NM** value: **Cover or less**
Circ: Statement: **213,745** CapCity orders: **46,150**
• Deluxe edition.

110 ❑ Jan 1995 Cover: 1.50 **NM** value: **Cover or less**

110/Dlx❑ Jan 1995 Cover: 1.95 **NM** value: **Cover or less**
Circ: Statement: **213,745** CapCity orders: **44,925**
• Deluxe edition.

111 ❑ Feb 1995 Cover: 1.50 **NM** value: **Cover or less**

111/Dlx❑ Feb 1995 Cover: 1.95 **NM** value: **Cover or less**
Circ: Statement: **213,745** CapCity orders: **55,125**
• Deluxe edition.

112 ❑ Jul 1995 Cover: 1.95 **NM** value: **Cover or less**
Circ: Statement: **213,745** CapCity orders: **56,950**
• Has 1994 Statement, filed 10/1/94 (appears late due to Age of Apocalypse); avg print run 409,458; avg sales 293,533; avg subs 6,167; avg total paid 299,700; samples 125; office use 500; max existent 300,325; 27% of run returned

113 ❑ Aug 1995 Cover: 1.95 **NM** value: **Cover or less**
Circ: Statement: **213,745** CapCity orders: **56,350**

114 ❑ Sep 1995 Cover: 1.95 **NM** value: **Cover or less**
Circ: Statement: **213,745**

115 ❑ Oct 1995 Cover: 1.95 **NM** value: **Cover or less**
Circ: Statement: **194,652**

116 ❑ Nov 1995 Cover: 1.95 **NM** value: **Cover or less**
Circ: Statement: **194,652**

117 ❑ Dec 1995 Cover: 1.95 **NM** value: **Cover or less**
Circ: Statement: **194,652**

118 ❑ Jan 1996 Cover: 1.95 **NM** value: **Cover or less**
Circ: Statement: **194,652**

119 ❑ Feb 1996 Cover: 1.95 **NM** value: **Cover or less**
Circ: Statement: **194,652**
• Has 1995 Statement, filed 10/1/95; avg print run 301,483; avg sales 210,015; avg subs 3,730; avg total paid 213,745; samples 750; office use 500; max existent 214,995; 29% of run returned ★ Appearance of Shard.

120 ❑ Mar 1996 Cover: 1.95 **NM** value: **Cover or less**
Circ: Statement: **194,652**
📖 Meeting the Maker **A:** Mark D. Bright **W:** Howard Mackie

121 ❑ Apr 1996 Cover: 1.95 **NM** value: **Cover or less**
Circ: Statement: **194,652**
📖 The True Path **A:** Steve Epting **W:** Howard Mackie

122 ❑ May 1996 Cover: 1.95 **NM** value: **Cover or less**
Circ: Statement: **194,652**

123 ❑ Jun 1996 Cover: 1.95 **NM** value: **Cover or less**
Circ: Statement: **194,652**

124 ❑ Jul 1996 Cover: 1.95 **NM** value: **Cover or less**
Circ: Statement: **194,652**

125 ❑ Aug 1996 Cover: 2.95 **NM** value: **Cover or less**
Circ: Statement: **194,652**
📖 Onslaught: Impact 1 **W:** Howard Mackie

126 ❑ Sep 1996 Cover: 1.95 **NM** value: **Cover or less**
Circ: Statement: **143,508**
📖 Onslaught: Impact 2 • real Beast returns **W:** Howard Mackie

127 ❑ Oct 1996 Cover: 1.95 **NM** value: **Cover or less**
Circ: Statement: **143,508**
• bound-in trading cards **W:** Howard Mackie

128 ❑ Nov 1996 Cover: 1.95 **NM** value: **Cover or less**
Circ: Statement: **143,508** Direct Market orders: **122,250**
• Has 1996 Statement, filed 10/1/96 (Alert: Published before filing date); avg print run 248,362; avg sales 191,538; avg subs 3,114; avg total paid 194,652; samples 600; office use 125; max existent 195,377; 21% of run returned **W:** Howard Mackie

129 ❑ Dec 1996 Cover: 1.95 **NM** value: **Cover or less**
Circ: Statement: **143,508** Direct Market orders: **119,750** • **CGC:** 1 graded, best 9.8

130 ❑ Jan 1997 Cover: 1.95 **NM** value: **2.50**
Circ: Statement: **143,508** Direct Market orders: **116,500** • **CGC:** 1 graded, best 9.2

131 ❑ Feb 1997 Cover: 1.95 **NM** value: **Cover or less**
Circ: Statement: **143,508** Direct Market orders: **108,000**
📖 Brotherhood **A:** Jeff Matsuda **W:** Howard Mackie

132 ❑ Mar 1997 Cover: 1.95 **NM** value: **Cover or less**
Circ: Statement: **143,508** Direct Market orders: **101,750**
📖 Breakaway **A:** Jeff Matsuda **W:** Howard Mackie

133 ❑ Apr 1997 Cover: 1.95 **NM** value: **Cover or less**
Circ: Statement: **143,508** Direct Market orders: **100,000**
📖 Down Under **A:** Eric Battle; Art Thibert **W:** Howard Mackie

134 ❑ May 1997 Cover: 1.95 **NM** value: **Cover or less**
Circ: Statement: **143,508** Diamd. preorders: **98,816**
📖 The Child **A:** Eric Battle; Art Thibert **W:** Howard Mackie

135 ❑ Jun 1997 Cover: 1.95 **NM** value: **Cover or less**
Circ: Statement: **143,508** Diamd. preorders: **98,489**
📖 A Virtual Reality • return of Strong Guy **A:** Jeff Matsuda; Art Thibert **W:** Howard Mackie

136 ❑ Aug 1997 Cover: 1.99 **NM** value: **Cover or less**
Circ: Statement: **143,508** Diamd. preorders: **90,294**
• gatefold summary.

137 ❑ Sep 1997 Cover: 1.99 **NM** value: **Cover or less**
Circ: Diamd. preorders: **86,392**
• gatefold summary.

138 ❑ Oct 1997 Cover: 1.99 **NM** value: **Cover or less**
Circ: Diamd. preorders: **85,467**
• gatefold summary. ★ Versus Omega Red.

139 ❑ Nov 1997 Cover: 1.99 **NM** value: **Cover or less**
Circ: Diamd. preorders: **85,187**
• gatefold summary.

140 ❑ Dec 1997 Cover: 1.99 **NM** value: **Cover or less**

CGC-graded: Multiply prices above by **33 for 9.9 M • 16 for 9.8 NM/M • 7 for 9.6 NM+ • 5 for 9.4 NM • 2.5 for 9.2 NM- • 1.5 for 9.0 VF/NM**

Circ: Diamd. preorders: **83,255**
• gatefold summary. • Has 1997 Statement, filed 10/1/97; avg print run 213,083; avg sales 140,760; avg subs 2,748; avg total paid 143,508; samples 275; office use 125; max existent 143,908; 32% of run returned ★ Appearance of Xavier's Underground Enforcers.

141 ❑ Jan 1998 Cover: 1.99 **NM** value: **Cover or less**
Circ: Diamd. preorders: **82,353**
• gatefold summary.

142 ❑ Feb 1998 Cover: 1.99 **NM** value: **Cover or less**
Circ: Diamd. preorders: **77,151**
• gatefold summary.

143 ❑ Mar 1998 Cover: 1.99 **NM** value: **Cover or less**
Circ: Diamd. preorders: **74,250**
• gatefold summary.

144 ❑ Apr 1998 Cover: 1.99 **NM** value: **Cover or less**
Circ: Diamd. preorders: **69,097**
• gatefold summary. ★ Versus Random.

145 ❑ May 1998 Cover: 1.99 **NM** value: **Cover or less**
Circ: Diamd. preorders: **67,352**
• gatefold summary.

146 ❑ Jun 1998 Cover: 1.99 **NM** value: **Cover or less**
Circ: Diamd. preorders: **68,144**
• gatefold summary. • return of Multiple Man

147 ❑ Jul 1998 Cover: 1.99 **NM** value: **Cover or less**
Circ: Diamd. preorders: **63,607**
• gatefold summary.

148 ❑ Aug 1998 Cover: 1.99 **NM** value: **Cover or less**
Circ: Diamd. preorders: **62,209**
• gatefold summary. • return of Polaris ★ Versus Mandroids.

149 ❑ Sep 1998 Cover: 1.99 **NM** value: **Cover or less**
Circ: Diamd. preorders: **58,676**
• gatefold summary. final issue.

Anl 1 ❑ ca. 1986 Cover: 1.25 **NM** value: **3.00**
Circ: CapCity orders: **44,500**

Anl 2 ❑ ca. 1987 Cover: 1.25 **NM** value: **3.00**
Circ: CapCity orders: **44,700**

Anl 3 ❑ ca. 1988 Cover: 1.75 **NM** value: **3.00**
Circ: CapCity orders: **47,200**
Evolutionary War, Part 1 ★ Origin of High Evolutionary.

Anl 4 ❑ ca. 1989 Cover: 2.00 **NM** value: **2.50**
Circ: CapCity orders: **58,500**
Atlantis Attacks, Part 10 • Atlantis Attacks

Anl 5 ❑ ca. 1990 Cover: 2.00 **NM** value: **2.50**
Future Present; Days of Future Present, Part 2 ★ Appearance of Fantastic Four, New Mutants.

Anl 6 ❑ ca. 1991 Cover: 2.00 **NM** value: **2.50**
Circ: CapCity orders: **78,800**
Kings of Pain; Kings of Pain, Part 4 ★ Death of Proteus.

Anl 7 ❑ ca. 1992 Cover: 2.25 **NM** value: **Cover or less**
Circ: CapCity orders: **68,500**
Shattershot, Part 3 • Shattershot

Anl 8 ❑ ca. 1993 Cover: 2.95 **NM** value: **Cover or less**
Circ: CapCity orders: **36,150**
• trading card

Anl 9 ❑ ca. 1994 Cover: 2.95 **NM** value: **Cover or less**
Circ: CapCity orders: **73,100**

X-FACTOR: PRISONER OF LOVE — Marvel

1 ❑ Aug 1990 Cover: 4.95 **NM** value: **Cover or less**
Circ: CapCity orders: **30,150**
No issue number.

X-FARCE — Eclipse

1 ❑ Jan 1992, b&w Cover: 2.50 **NM** value: **Cover or less**
Circ: CapCity orders: **14,575**
• parody

X-FARCE VS. X-CONS: X-TINCTION — Parody Press

1 ❑ Cover: 2.75 **NM** value: **Cover or less**
1.5 ❑ Cover: 2.75 **NM** value: **Cover or less**

X-FILES, THE — Topps

The X-Files is a fictional look into the paranormal, the supernatural, and the just plain weird. Inspired by the Fox TV series, this comic book stars two crack FBI agents who, although crippled by bureaucracy and government cover-ups, set out to investigate "X-Files": cases that seem to point to mysterious phenomena. Agent Fox Mulder is an intrepid investigator who feels compelled to peer into the unknown, since he firmly believes that his own sister was abducted by a UFO when she was a child. His approach is balanced by his more skeptical partner, Dana Scully, who conducts forensic work that seems always to lead to more questions than it answers.

This well-scripted series accurately preserves the pacing and suspense of the Chris Carter television show. Although it may not give any more answers than the television series does, it's every bit as fascinating.

-2 ❑ Sep 1996 Cover: 10.00 **NM** value: **Cover or less**
• **CGC:** 1 graded, best 9.6
no cover price. Trick of the Light; The Pit; The Silent Sword

-1 ❑ Sep 1996 Cover: 10.00 **NM** value: **Cover or less**
• **CGC:** 1 graded, best 9.6
no cover price. A Trick of the Light

0/A ❑ Cover: 3.95 **NM** value: **4.00**
forms diptych with Scully cover. • adapts pilot episode

0/B ❑ Cover: 3.95 **NM** value: **4.00**
forms diptych with Mulder cover. • adapts pilot episode

0/C ❑ Cover: 3.95 **NM** value: **4.00**
Scully and Mulder cover. • adapts pilot episode

0.5 ❑ Cover: 5.00 **NM** value: **10.00**
• **CGC:** 14 graded, best 9.8
• Wizard promotional edition. Tiptoe Through the Tulpa

1 ❑ Jan 1995 Cover: 2.95 **NM** value: **8.00**
Circ: CapCity orders: **16,700** • **CGC:** 23 graded, best 9.8
Do Not Open Until X-Mas **A:** Charles Adlard **W:** Stefan Petrucha

1-2 ❑ Cover: 2.50 **NM** value: **Cover or less**
Do Not Open Until X-Mas **A:** Charles Adlard **W:** Stefan Petrucha

2 ❑ Feb 1995 Cover: 2.95 **NM** value: **5.00**
Circ: CapCity orders: **13,100** • **CGC:** 4 graded, best 9.8
Disremembrance of Things Past **A:** Charles Adlard **W:** Stefan Petrucha

3 ❑ Mar 1995 Cover: 2.95 **NM** value: **4.00**
Circ: CapCity orders: **16,675** • **CGC:** 1 graded, best 9.8
The Return **A:** Charles Adlard **W:** Stefan Petrucha

3-2 ❑ Cover: 2.50 **NM** value: **Cover or less**
The Return **A:** Charles Adlard **W:** Stefan Petrucha

4 ❑ Apr 1995 Cover: 2.95 **NM** value: **3.50**
Circ: CapCity orders: **25,500** • **CGC:** 1 graded, best 9.6
Firebird, Part 1 **A:** Charles Adlard **W:** Stefan Petrucha

4-2 ❑ Cover: 2.50 **NM** value: **Cover or less**
Firebird, Part 2 **A:** Charles Adlard **W:** Stefan Petrucha

5 ❑ May 1995 Cover: 2.95 **NM** value: **3.00**
Circ: CapCity orders: **33,150**
Firebird, Part 2 **A:** Charles Adlard **W:** Stefan Petrucha

6 ❑ Jun 1995 Cover: 2.95 **NM** value: **3.00**
Circ: CapCity orders: **35,575**
Firebird, Part 3 **A:** Charles Adlard **W:** Stefan Petrucha

7 ❑ Jul 1995 Cover: 2.95 **NM** value: **3.00**
Circ: CapCity orders: **36,175**

8 ❑ Aug 1995 Cover: 2.95 **NM** value: **3.00**
Circ: CapCity orders: **33,950**
Silent Cities of the Mind, Part 1 **A:** Charles Adlard **W:** Stefan Petrucha

9 ❑ Sep 1995 Cover: 2.95 **NM** value: **3.00**
Circ: CapCity orders: **29,750**
Silent Cities of the Mind, Part 2 **A:** Charles Adlard **W:** Stefan Petrucha

10 ❑ Oct 1995 Cover: 2.95 **NM** value: **3.00**
Circ: CapCity orders: **24,325**
Feelings of Unreality, Part 1 **W:** Stefan Petrucha

11 ❑ Nov 1995 Cover: 2.95 **NM** value: **3.00**
Circ: CapCity orders: **24,150**
Feelings of Unreality, Part 2 **W:** Stefan Petrucha

12 ❑ Dec 1995 Cover: 2.95 **NM** value: **3.00**
Feelings of Unreality, Part 3 **W:** Stefan Petrucha

13 ❑ Feb 1996 Cover: 2.95 **NM** value: **3.00**
14 ❑ Apr 1996 Cover: 2.95 **NM** value: **3.00**
15 ❑ May 1996 Cover: 2.95 **NM** value: **3.00**
Home of the Brave, Part 1 **W:** Stefan Petrucha

16 ❑ May 1996 Cover: 2.95 **NM** value: **3.00**
Home of the Brave, Part 2 **W:** Stefan Petrucha

17 ❑ May 1996 Cover: 2.95 **NM** value: **3.00**
Thin Air **A:** Gordon Purcell **W:** John Rozum

18 ❑ Jun 1996 Cover: 2.95 **NM** value: **3.00**
Night Lights, Part 1 **W:** John Rozum

19 ❑ Jun 1996 Cover: 2.95 **NM** value: **3.00**
Night Lights, Part 2 **W:** John Rozum

20 ❑ Jul 1996 Cover: 2.95 **NM** value: **3.00**
Family Portrait, Part 1: Gallery **A:** Gordon Purcell **W:** Kevin J. Anderson

21 ❑ Aug 1996 Cover: 2.95 **NM** value: **3.00**
Family Portrait, Part 2: The Camera Eye **A:** Gordon Purcell **W:** Kevin J. Anderson

22 ❑ Sep 1996 Cover: 2.95 **NM** value: **Cover or less**
Circ: Diamd. preorders: **71,832**
The Kanashibari

23 ❑ Nov 1996 Cover: 2.95 **NM** value: **Cover or less**
Circ: Diamd. preorders: **70,749**
Donor • Donor **A:** Charles Adlard **W:** John Rozum

24 ❑ Dec 1996 Cover: 2.95 **NM** value: **Cover or less**
Circ: Diamd. preorders: **67,432**
Silver Lining

25 ❑ Jan 1997 Cover: 2.95 **NM** value: **Cover or less**
Circ: Diamd. preorders: **66,062**
Be Prepared, Part 1

26 ❑ Feb 1997 Cover: 2.95 **NM** value: **Cover or less**
Circ: Diamd. preorders: **63,757**
Be Prepared, Part 2

27 ❑ Mar 1997 Cover: 2.95 **NM** value: **Cover or less**
Circ: Diamd. preorders: **58,488**
Remote Control, Part 1

28 ❑ Apr 1997 Cover: 2.95 **NM** value: **Cover or less**
Circ: Diamd. preorders: **55,832**
Remote Control, Part 2

29 ❑ May 1997 Cover: 2.95 **NM** value: **Cover or less**
Circ: Diamd. preorders: **54,154**
Remote Control Conclusion

30 ❑ Jun 1997 Cover: 2.95 **NM** value: **Cover or less**
Circ: Diamd. preorders: **50,512**
Surrounded, Part 1

31 ❑ Jul 1997 Cover: 2.95 **NM** value: **Cover or less**
Circ: Diamd. preorders: **48,222**
Surrounded, Part 2

32 ❑ Aug 1997 Cover: 2.95 **NM** value: **Cover or less**
Circ: Diamd. preorders: **45,901**

33 ❑ Sep 1997 Cover: 2.95 **NM** value: **Cover or less**
Circ: Diamd. preorders: **44,716**
Soma **A:** Alex Saviuk **W:** John Rozum

33/SC ❑ Sep 1997 Cover: 2.95 **NM** value: **5.00**
Variant photo cover. Soma **A:** Alex Saviuk **W:** John Rozum

34 ❑ Oct 1997 Cover: 2.95 **NM** value: **Cover or less**
35 ❑ Nov 1997 Cover: 2.95 **NM** value: **Cover or less**
Circ: Diamd. preorders: **42,058**

36 ❑ Dec 1997 Cover: 2.95 **NM** value: **Cover or less**
Circ: Diamd. preorders: **39,955**

37 ❑ Jan 1998 Cover: 2.95 **NM** value: **Cover or less**
Circ: Diamd. preorders: **38,773**

38 ❑ Feb 1998 Cover: 2.95 **NM** value: **Cover or less**
Circ: Diamd. preorders: **36,805**
Cam Ranh Bay

39 ❑ Mar 1998 Cover: 2.95 **NM** value: **Cover or less**
Circ: Diamd. preorders: **33,477**
Scum of the Earth

40 ❑ Apr 1998 Cover: 2.95 **NM** value: **Cover or less**
Circ: Diamd. preorders: **37,056**
Devil's Advocate

41 ❑ May 1998 Cover: 2.95 **NM** value: **Cover or less**
Circ: Diamd. preorders: **32,403**

41/SC ❑ Jun 1998 Cover: 2.95 **NM** value: **Cover or less**
Photo cover.

Anl 1 ❑ Aug 1995 Cover: 3.95 **NM** value: **Cover or less**
Circ: CapCity orders: **32,475**

Anl 2 ❑ ca. 1996 Cover: 3.95 **NM** value: **Cover or less**
• E.L.F.s

Ash 1 ❑ Jan 1995 **NM** value: **4.00**
No issue number. no cover price. • polybagged with Star Wars Galaxy #2

Bk 1 ❑ Jul 1995 Cover: 19.95 **NM** value: **Cover or less**
• collects first six issues of series **A:** Charles Adlard **W:** Stefan Petrucha

Bk 2 ❑ Feb 1997 Cover: 19.95 **NM** value: **Cover or less**
• collects issues #7-12 and Annual #1 **W:** Stefan Petrucha

SE 1 ❑ Jun 1995 Cover: 3.95 **NM** value: **4.95**
Circ: CapCity orders: **26,100**
• reprints issues #1 and 2 **A:** Charles Adlard **W:** Stefan Petrucha

SE 2 ❑ ca. 1995 Cover: 3.95 **NM** value: **4.95**
Firebird; Picasso Summer • Reprints X-Files #4-6 **A:** Charles Adlard **W:** Stefan Petrucha

SE 3 ❑ ca. 1996 Cover: 3.95 **NM** value: **4.95**
Trepanning Opera; Silent Cities of the Mind • Reprints X-Files #7-9 **W:** Stefan Petrucha

SE 4 ❑ Nov 1996 Cover: 4.95 **NM** value: **Cover or less**
Feelings of Unreality • reprints Feelings of Unreality **W:** Stefan Petrucha

SE 5 ❑ ca. 1997 Cover: 4.95 **NM** value: **Cover or less**
• Reprints X-Files #13, Annual #1

X-FILES COMICS DIGEST, THE — Topps

1 ❑ Dec 1995 Cover: 3.50 **NM** value: **Cover or less**
Circ: CapCity orders: **22,475**
Big Foot, Warm Heart; The Visitor; Trapdoor; The Foghorn • Bradbury back-up stories **W:** Ray Bradbury; Stefan Petrucha

2 ❑ Apr 1996 Cover: 3.50 **NM** value: **Cover or less**
The Count Saint-Germain Goes West; it Burns Me Up; Touched by Fire; The April Witch • Bradbury back-up stories **A:** Al Williamson; Howard Simpson; Charles Adlard; Jack Davis **W:** Ray Bradbury; Stefan Petrucha

3 ❑ Sep 1996 Cover: 3.95 **NM** value: **Cover or less**
The Wee Folk • Bradbury back-up stories **W:** Ray Bradbury

X-FILES GROUND ZERO, THE — Topps

1 ❑ Dec 1997 Cover: 2.95 **NM** value: **Cover or less**
Circ: Diamd. preorders: **31,517**
• adapts Kevin J. Anderson novel

2 ❑ Jan 1998 Cover: 2.95 **NM** value: **Cover or less**
• adapts Kevin J. Anderson novel

3 ❑ Feb 1998 Cover: 2.95 **NM** value: **Cover or less**
Circ: Diamd. preorders: **26,443**
• adapts Kevin J. Anderson novel

4 ❑ Mar 1998 Cover: 2.95 **NM** value: **Cover or less**
Circ: Diamd. preorders: **24,620**

X-FILES (MAGAZINE), THE — Tops

1 ❑ Cover: 1.25 **NM** value: **4.00**
2 ❑ Sum 1996 Cover: 1.25 **NM** value: **3.00**
3 ❑ Cover: 1.25 **NM** value: **3.00**
4 ❑ Cover: 1.25 **NM** value: **3.00**
5 ❑ Cover: 1.25 **NM** value: **3.00**
6 ❑ Cover: 1.25 **NM** value: **2.50**
7 ❑ Cover: 1.25 **NM** value: **2.50**
8 ❑ Cover: 1.25 **NM** value: **2.50**
9 ❑ Cover: 1.25 **NM** value: **2.50**
10 ❑ Cover: 1.25 **NM** value: **2.50**
Feelings of Unreality, Part 1

11 ❑ **NM** value: **2.50**
Feelings of Unreality, Part 2

12 ❑ **NM** value: **2.50**
13 ❑ **NM** value: **2.50**
14 ❑ **NM** value: **2.50**
15 ❑ **NM** value: **2.50**
16 ❑ **NM** value: **2.50**
17 ❑ **NM** value: **2.50**
18 ❑ **NM** value: **2.50**
19 ❑ **NM** value: **2.50**
20 ❑ **NM** value: **2.50**
21 ❑ **NM** value: **2.50**
22 ❑ **NM** value: **2.50**
Family Portrait, Part 1 **A:** Gordon Purcell **W:** Kevin J. Anderson

23 ❑ Cover: 1.50 **NM** value: **2.50**
Family Portrait, Part 2 **A:** Gordon Purcell **W:** Kevin J. Anderson

X-FILES, THE: SEASON ONE — Topps

1 ❑ Jul 1997 Cover: 4.95 **NM** value: **Cover or less**
• prestige format. Pilot Episode • adapts pilot episode **A:** Jean-Claude St. Aubin; John Van Fleet **W:** Roy Thomas; Chris Carter

2 ❑ Dec 1997 Cover: 4.95 **NM** value: **Cover or less**
• prestige format. Deep Throat

3 ❑ Cover: 3.95 **NM** value: **4.95**
Circ: Diamd. preorders: **55,735**

4 ❑ Cover: 3.95 **NM** value: **4.95**
Circ: Diamd. preorders: **56,235**

5 ❑ Cover: 3.95 **NM** value: **4.95**
Circ: Diamd. preorders: **52,344**

Other grades: Multiply prices above by **1.5 for Mint • 2/3 for Very Fine • 1/3 for Fine • 1/5 for Very Good • 1/8 for Good**

6 ❑ Cover: 3.95 **NM** value: **4.95**
Circ: Diamd. preorders: **50,700**
7 ❑ Cover: 3.95 **NM** value: **4.95**
Circ: Diamd. preorders: **45,284**
8 ❑ Cover: 3.95 **NM** value: **4.95**
Circ: Diamd. preorders: **42,601**

X-FLIES BUG HUNT — Twist and Shout

1 ❑ Dec 1996 Cover: 2.95 **NM** value: **Cover or less**
Circ: Diamd. preorders: **3,918**
📖 Vampires **A:** Richard Johnston **W:** Richard Johnston
2 ❑ Jan 1997 Cover: 2.95 **NM** value: **Cover or less**
📖 Monsters **A:** Richard Johnston **W:** Richard Johnston
3 ❑ Feb 1997 Cover: 2.95 **NM** value: **Cover or less**
📖 Aliens **A:** Richard Johnston **W:** Richard Johnston
4 ❑ Mar 1997 Cover: 2.95 **NM** value: **Cover or less**
📖 The Truth **A:** Richard Johnston **W:** Richard Johnston

X-FLIES CONSPIRACY — Twist and Shout

1 ❑ Mar 1996 Cover: 2.95 **NM** value: **Cover or less**

X-FLIES SPECIAL — Twist and Shout

1 ❑ Sep 1995 Cover: 2.95 **NM** value: **Cover or less**
Circ: CapCity orders: **2,185**
📖 X-Flies; Bobby Ruckers; Life Bytes: Marcie's Underwear; My Life Among the Humans; The Ones We Left Behind; Foetal Attraction **A:** Scott Saavedra; Dan Duncan; Richard Johnston; Bebe William; Dave A. Law; Fabian Nicieza **W:** Scott Saavedra; Dan Duncan; Richard Johnston; Bebe Williams; Dave A. Law; Fabian Nicieza; Mike Meyer

X-FORCE — Marvel

Following the introduction of Cable into the New Mutants, that team took on a decidedly more aggressive role in fighting evil. With Cable as their new leader, the mutants that chose to remain were joined by mysterious new recruits Domino, Shatterstar, and Warpath. Following the conclusion of The New Mutants in #100, this new team became known as X-Force.

Cable led his new team as he would a military strike force. Each operation was carefully planned and run "by the numbers." Even then, danger has a habit of striking without warning, and the new team has suffered its share of defeats. But the battle continues and, as it does, readers uncover more of the secrets of the enigmatic group called X-Force.

-1 ❑ Jul 1997 Cover: 1.99 **NM** value: **2.00**
Circ: Diamd. preorders: **89,914**
📖 The Brothers Proudstar • Flashback; Proudstars team up **A:** Al Milgrom; Adam Pollina; Jon Holdredge; Mark Morales **W:** John Francis Moore
1/A ❑ Aug 1991 Cover: 1.50 **NM** value: **2.00**
Circ: CapCity orders: **806,100** • **CGC:** 20 graded, best 9.8
• with Cable card★ 1st Appearance of G.W. Bridge.
1/B ❑ Aug 1991 Cover: 1.50 **NM** value: **2.00**
• with Deadpool card★ 1st Appearance of G.W. Bridge.
1/C ❑ Aug 1991 Cover: 1.50 **NM** value: **2.00**
• with Shatterstar card★ 1st Appearance of G.W. Bridge.
1/D ❑ Aug 1991 Cover: 1.50 **NM** value: **2.00**
• with Sunspot & Gideon card★ 1st Appearance of G.W. Bridge.
1/E ❑ Aug 1991 Cover: 1.50 **NM** value: **2.00**
• **CGC:** 1 graded, best 8.5
• with X-Force group card★ 1st Appearance of G.W. Bridge.
1-2 ❑ Aug 1991 Cover: 1.50 **NM** value: **Cover or less**
2 ❑ Sep 1991 Cover: 1.00 **NM** value: **2.50**
Circ: CapCity orders: **279,700**
3 ❑ Oct 1991 Cover: 1.00 **NM** value: **2.00**
Circ: CapCity orders: **205,200**
4 ❑ Nov 1991 Cover: 1.00 **NM** value: **2.00**
Circ: CapCity orders: **261,600** • **CGC:** 1 graded, best 9.8
• Sideways printing **W:** Fabian Nicieza ★ Appearance of Spider-Man.
5 ❑ Dec 1991 Cover: 1.00 **NM** value: **2.00**
Circ: CapCity orders: **179,400**
• Return of Brotherhood of Evil Mutants **W:** Fabian Nicieza
6 ❑ Jan 1992 Cover: 1.00 **NM** value: **2.00**
Circ: Statement: **759,125** CapCity orders: **154,800**
7 ❑ Feb 1992 Cover: 1.25 **NM** value: **2.00**
Circ: Statement: **759,125** CapCity orders: **141,900**
8 ❑ Mar 1992 Cover: 1.25 **NM** value: **2.00**
Circ: Statement: **759,125** CapCity orders: **133,800**
9 ❑ Apr 1992 Cover: 1.25 **NM** value: **2.00**
Circ: Statement: **759,125** CapCity orders: **123,600**
10 ❑ May 1992 Cover: 1.25 **NM** value: **2.00**
Circ: Statement: **759,125** CapCity orders: **127,500**
11 ❑ Jun 1992 Cover: 1.25 **NM** value: **2.00**
Circ: Statement: **759,125** CapCity orders: **129,600**
12 ❑ Jul 1992 Cover: 1.25 **NM** value: **2.00**
Circ: Statement: **759,125** CapCity orders: **117,000**
📖 Traitors to the Cause **A:** Mark Pacella **W:** Rob Liefeld; Fabian Nicieza
13 ❑ Aug 1992 Cover: 1.25 **NM** value: **2.00**
Circ: Statement: **759,125** CapCity orders: **124,800**
14 ❑ Sep 1992 Cover: 1.25 **NM** value: **2.00**
Circ: Statement: **759,125** CapCity orders: **116,400**
📖 Payback! **A:** Terry Shoemaker **W:** Fabian Nicieza
15 ❑ Oct 1992 Cover: 1.25 **NM** value: **2.00**
Circ: Statement: **759,125** CapCity orders: **117,200**
📖 To the Pain **A:** Greg Capullo **W:** Fabian Nicieza
16/CS❑ Nov 1992 Cover: 1.50 **NM** value: **2.00**
Circ: Statement: **759,125** CapCity orders: **236,200**
📖 X-Cutioner's Song; X-Cutioner's Song, Part 4 **W:** Fabian Nicieza
17/CS❑ Dec 1992 Cover: 1.50 **NM** value: **2.00**
Circ: Statement: **759,125** CapCity orders: **153,300**
📖 X-Cutioner's Song, Part 8 **W:** Fabian Nicieza ★ Origin of Zero, Stryfe.
18/CS❑ Jan 1993 Cover: 1.50 **NM** value: **2.00**
Circ: Statement: **572,892** CapCity orders: **162,900**
📖 X-Cutioner's Song, Part 12 **A:** Greg Capullo **W:** Fabian Nicieza
19 ❑ Feb 1993 Cover: 1.25 **NM** value: **1.50**
Circ: Statement: **572,892** CapCity orders: **101,400**
📖 The Open Hand, the Closed Fist **A:** Greg Capullo **W:** Fabian Nicieza
20 ❑ Mar 1993 Cover: 1.25 **NM** value: **1.50**
Circ: Statement: **572,892** CapCity orders: **101,700**
📖 Assault on Graymalkin • Has 1992 Statement, filed 10/1/92; avg print run 936,633; avg sales 745,900; avg subs 1,225; avg total paid 759,125; samples 250; office use 500; max existent 747,875; 19% of run returned **A:** Greg Capullo **W:** Fabian Nicieza
21 ❑ Apr 1993 Cover: 1.25 **NM** value: **1.50**
Circ: Statement: **572,892** CapCity orders: **100,400**
22 ❑ May 1993 Cover: 1.25 **NM** value: **1.50**
Circ: Statement: **572,892** CapCity orders: **96,000**
📖 Ordinance Weighed in Blood **A:** Greg Capullo **W:** Fabian Nicieza
23 ❑ Jun 1993 Cover: 1.25 **NM** value: **1.50**
Circ: Statement: **572,892** CapCity orders: **91,500**
📖 Compromising Positions **A:** Greg Capullo **W:** Fabian Nicieza
24 ❑ Jul 1993 Cover: 1.25 **NM** value: **1.50**
Circ: Statement: **572,892** CapCity orders: **90,800**
25 ❑ Aug 1993 Cover: 3.50 **NM** value: **4.00**
Circ: Statement: **572,892** CapCity orders: **138,200** • **CGC:** 2 graded, best 9.8
Hologram cover. **W:** Fabian Nicieza
26 ❑ Sep 1993 Cover: 1.25 **NM** value: **1.50**
Circ: Statement: **572,892** CapCity orders: **87,700**
27 ❑ Oct 1993 Cover: 1.25 **NM** value: **1.50**
Circ: Statement: **572,892** CapCity orders: **82,300**
28 ❑ Nov 1993 Cover: 1.25 **NM** value: **1.50**
Circ: Statement: **572,892** CapCity orders: **87,900**
29 ❑ Dec 1993 Cover: 1.25 **NM** value: **1.50**
Circ: Statement: **572,892** CapCity orders: **83,200**
📖 Toy Soldiers **A:** Matt Broome **W:** Fabian Nicieza ★ Appearance of Arcade.
30 ❑ Jan 1994 Cover: 1.25 **NM** value: **1.50**
Circ: Statement: **572,892** CapCity orders: **74,900**
31 ❑ Feb 1994 Cover: 1.25 **NM** value: **Cover or less**
Circ: Statement: **572,892** CapCity orders: **70,300**
32 ❑ Mar 1994 Cover: 1.25 **NM** value: **Cover or less**
Circ: Statement: **572,892** CapCity orders: **66,350**
📖 Child's Play **A:** Tony Daniel **W:** Fabian Nicieza
33 ❑ Apr 1994 Cover: 1.25 **NM** value: **Cover or less**
Circ: Statement: **572,892** CapCity orders: **60,800**
34 ❑ May 1994 Cover: 1.50 **NM** value: **Cover or less**
Circ: Statement: **572,892** CapCity orders: **57,600**
35 ❑ Jun 1994 Cover: 1.50 **NM** value: **Cover or less**
Circ: Statement: **572,892** CapCity orders: **57,000**
36 ❑ Jul 1994 Cover: 1.50 **NM** value: **Cover or less**
Circ: Statement: **572,892** CapCity orders: **56,900**
37 ❑ Aug 1994 Cover: 1.50 **NM** value: **Cover or less**
Circ: Statement: **572,892** CapCity orders: **55,950**
38 ❑ Sep 1994 Cover: 2.00 **NM** value: **Cover or less**
📖 Life Signs, Part 2
38/SC❑ Sep 1994 Cover: 2.95 **NM** value: **3.00**
Circ: Statement: **572,892** CapCity orders: **70,450**
enhanced cover. 📖 Life Signs, Part 2
39 ❑ Oct 1994 Cover: 1.50 **NM** value: **Cover or less**
Circ: Statement: **572,892** CapCity orders: **52,050**
40 ❑ Nov 1994 Cover: 1.50 **NM** value: **Cover or less**
Circ: Statement: **572,892**
40/Dlx❑ Nov 1994 Cover: 1.95 **NM** value: **Cover or less**
Circ: Statement: **572,892** CapCity orders: **53,100**
• Deluxe edition.
41 ❑ Dec 1994 Cover: 1.50 **NM** value: **Cover or less**
Circ: Statement: **224,293**
41/Dlx❑ Dec 1994 Cover: 1.95 **NM** value: **Cover or less**
Circ: Statement: **224,293** CapCity orders: **49,950**
• Deluxe edition.
42 ❑ Jan 1995 Cover: 1.50 **NM** value: **Cover or less**
42/Dlx❑ Jan 1995 Cover: 1.95 **NM** value: **Cover or less**
Circ: Statement: **224,293** CapCity orders: **48,275**
• Deluxe edition.
43 ❑ Feb 1995 Cover: 1.95 **NM** value: **Cover or less**
43/Dlx❑ Feb 1995 Cover: 1.95 **NM** value: **Cover or less**
Circ: Statement: **224,293** CapCity orders: **56,825**
• Deluxe edition.
44 ❑ Jul 1995 Cover: 1.95 **NM** value: **Cover or less**
Circ: Statement: **224,293** CapCity orders: **58,575**
• Cannonball to join X-Men leaves team
45 ❑ Aug 1995 Cover: 1.95 **NM** value: **Cover or less**
Circ: Statement: **224,293**
46 ❑ Sep 1995 Cover: 1.95 **NM** value: **Cover or less**
Circ: Statement: **224,293**
47 ❑ Oct 1995 Cover: 1.95 **NM** value: **Cover or less**
Circ: Statement: **233,665**
48 ❑ Nov 1995 Cover: 1.95 **NM** value: **Cover or less**
Circ: Statement: **233,665**
49 ❑ Dec 1995 Cover: 1.50 **NM** value: **Cover or less**
49/Dlx❑ Dec 1995 Cover: 1.95 **NM** value: **Cover or less**
Circ: Statement: **233,665**
• Direct Edition. **A:** Terry Dodson **W:** Jeph Loeb
50 ❑ Jan 1996 Cover: 2.95 **NM** value: **Cover or less**
Circ: Statement: **233,665**
wraparound fold-out cover. • Giant-size. 📖 Target: Cable • Has 1995 Statement, filed 10/1/95; avg print run 348,133; avg sales 219,923; avg subs 4,370; avg total paid 224,293; samples 750; office use 500; max existent 225,543; 35% of run returned **A:** Adam Pollina **W:** Jeph Loeb
50/A❑ Jan 1996 Cover: 2.95 **NM** value: **3.00**
Variant cover by Rob Liefeld. • Giant-size. 📖 Target: Cable **A:** Adam Pollina; Rob Liefeld(cover) **W:** Jeph Loeb
50/SC❑ Jan 1996 Cover: 3.95 **NM** value: **5.00**
Special cover. • Giant-size. 📖 Target: Cable **A:** Adam Pollina **W:** Jeph Loeb
51 ❑ Feb 1996 Cover: 1.95 **NM** value: **Cover or less**
Circ: Statement: **233,665**
52 ❑ Mar 1996 Cover: 1.95 **NM** value: **Cover or less**
Circ: Statement: **233,665**
📖 Bad Girls **A:** Adam Pollina **W:** Jeph Loeb ★ Death of Gideon. ★ Versus Blob.
53 ❑ Apr 1996 Cover: 1.95 **NM** value: **Cover or less**
Circ: Statement: **233,665**
54 ❑ May 1996 Cover: 1.95 **NM** value: **Cover or less**
Circ: Statement: **233,665** • **CGC:** 1 graded, best 9.8
55 ❑ Jun 1996 Cover: 1.95 **NM** value: **Cover or less**
Circ: Statement: **233,665**
56 ❑ Jul 1996 Cover: 1.95 **NM** value: **Cover or less**
Circ: Statement: **233,665**
📖 In the Company of Strangers, Part 1 **W:** Jeph Loeb
57 ❑ Aug 1996 Cover: 1.95 **NM** value: **Cover or less**
Circ: Statement: **233,665**
📖 In the Company of Strangers, Part 2; Onslaught: Impact, Part 1 **A:** Anthony Castrillo **W:** Jeph Loeb
58 ❑ Sep 1996 Cover: 1.95 **NM** value: **Cover or less**
Circ: Statement: **155,231**
📖 Onslaught: Impact 2 **W:** Jeph Loeb
59 ❑ Oct 1996 Cover: 1.95 **NM** value: **Cover or less**
Circ: Statement: **155,231**
• bound-in trading cards **W:** Jeph Loeb
60 ❑ Nov 1996 Cover: 1.95 **NM** value: **Cover or less**
Circ: Statement: **155,231** Direct Market orders: **126,250**
• Has 1996 Statement, filed 10/1/96 (Alert: published before filing date); avg print run 268,818; avg sales 230,359; avg subs 3,306; avg total paid 233,665; samples 600; office use 125; max existent 234,390; 13% of run returned **W:** Jeph Loeb
61 ❑ Dec 1996 Cover: 1.95 **NM** value: **Cover or less**
Circ: Statement: **155,231** Direct Market orders: **125,750**
62 ❑ Jan 1997 Cover: 1.95 **NM** value: **Cover or less**
Circ: Statement: **155,231** Direct Market orders: **122,000**
📖 Human Nature **A:** Adam Pollina; Kevin Lau **W:** John Dokes
63 ❑ Feb 1997 Cover: 1.95 **NM** value: **Cover or less**
Circ: Statement: **155,231** Direct Market orders: **113,250**
📖 Wish You Were Here • team invades Doom's castle **A:** Anthony Castrillo **W:** John Francis Moore
64 ❑ Mar 1997 Cover: 1.95 **NM** value: **Cover or less**
Circ: Statement: **155,231** Direct Market orders: **105,500**
📖 The Haunting of Castle Doom! **A:** Anthony Castrillo; Mark Pajarillo **W:** John Francis Moore ★ Appearance of Baron Von Strucker.
65 ❑ Apr 1997 Cover: 1.95 **NM** value: **Cover or less**
Circ: Statement: **155,231** Direct Market orders: **101,000**
📖 Lower East Side Story **A:** Adam Pollina **W:** John Francis Moore
66 ❑ May 1997 Cover: 1.95 **NM** value: **Cover or less**
Circ: Statement: **155,231** Diamd. preorders: **98,421**
📖 Tragic Kingdom **A:** Adam Pollina **W:** John Francis Moore
67 ❑ Jun 1997 Cover: 1.95 **NM** value: **Cover or less**
Circ: Statement: **155,231** Diamd. preorders: **96,440**
• return of Dani Moonstar
68 ❑ Aug 1997 Cover: 1.99 **NM** value: **Cover or less**
Circ: Statement: **155,231** Diamd. preorders: **93,810**
• gatefold summary. 📖 Operation: Zero Tolerance ★ Appearance of Vanisher.
69 ❑ Sep 1997 Cover: 1.99 **NM** value: **Cover or less**
Circ: Diamd. preorders: **87,912**
• gatefold summary. 📖 Operation: Zero Tolerance
70 ❑ Oct 1997 Cover: 1.99 **NM** value: **Cover or less**
Circ: Diamd. preorders: **86,417**
• gatefold summary.
71 ❑ Nov 1997 Cover: 1.99 **NM** value: **Cover or less**
Circ: Diamd. preorders: **86,148**
• gatefold summary.
72 ❑ Dec 1997 Cover: 1.99 **NM** value: **Cover or less**
Circ: Diamd. preorders: **84,814**
• gatefold summary. • Has 1997 Statement, filed 10/1/97; avg print run 242,958; avg sales 152,359; avg subs 2,902; avg total paid 155,261; samples 290; office use 125; max existent 155,676; 36% of run returned
73 ❑ Jan 1998 Cover: 1.99 **NM** value: **Cover or less**
Circ: Diamd. preorders: **82,394**
• gatefold summary. ★ Death of Warpath.
74 ❑ Feb 1998 Cover: 1.99 **NM** value: **Cover or less**
Circ: Diamd. preorders: **78,325**
• gatefold summary. ★ Versus Stryfe.
75 ❑ Mar 1998 Cover: 2.99 **NM** value: **Cover or less**
Circ: Diamd. preorders: **78,961**
wraparound cover. • gatefold summary. ★ Appearance of Cannonball.
76 ❑ Apr 1998 Cover: 1.99 **NM** value: **Cover or less**
Circ: Diamd. preorders: **70,667**
• gatefold summary. • Domino vs. Shatterstar
77 ❑ May 1998 Cover: 1.99 **NM** value: **Cover or less**
Circ: Diamd. preorders: **69,244**
• gatefold summary.
78 ❑ Jun 1998 Cover: 1.99 **NM** value: **Cover or less**
Circ: Diamd. preorders: **69,217**
• gatefold summary.
79 ❑ Jul 1998 Cover: 1.99 **NM** value: **Cover or less**
Circ: Diamd. preorders: **65,494**
• gatefold summary. ★ Origin of Reignfire.
80 ❑ Aug 1998 Cover: 1.99 **NM** value: **Cover or less**
Circ: Diamd. preorders: **63,635**
• gatefold summary.
81 ❑ Sep 1998 Cover: 1.99 **NM** value: **Cover or less**
Circ: Diamd. preorders: **60,033**
• gatefold summary. • poster
82 ❑ Oct 1998 Cover: 1.99 **NM** value: **Cover or less**
Circ: Statement: **76,034** Diamd. preorders: **57,943**
• gatefold summary.
83 ❑ Nov 1998 Cover: 1.99 **NM** value: **Cover or less**
Circ: Statement: **76,034** Diamd. preorders: **57,130**
• gatefold summary.

CGC-graded: Multiply prices above by **33 for 9.9 M • 16 for 9.8 NM/M • 7 for 9.6 NM+ • 5 for 9.4 NM • 2.5 for 9.2 NM- • 1.5 for 9.0 VF/NM**

84 ❑ Dec 1998 Cover: 1.99 **NM** value: **Cover or less**
Circ: Statement: **76,034** Diamd. preorders: **55,602**
• gatefold summary. ★ Versus New Deviants.

85 ❑ Jan 1999 Cover: 1.99 **NM** value: **Cover or less**
Circ: Statement: **76,034** Diamd. preorders: **54,921**
• gatefold summary.

86 ❑ Jan 1999 Cover: 1.99 **NM** value: **Cover or less**
Circ: Statement: **76,034** Diamd. preorders: **54,735**
• gatefold summary.

87 ❑ Feb 1999 Cover: 1.99 **NM** value: **Cover or less**
Circ: Statement: **76,034** Diamd. preorders: **53,181**

88 ❑ Mar 1999 Cover: 1.99 **NM** value: **Cover or less**
Circ: Statement: **76,034** Diamd. preorders: **52,285**

89 ❑ Apr 1999 Cover: 1.99 **NM** value: **Cover or less**
Circ: Statement: **76,034** Diamd. preorders: **49,662**

90 ❑ May 1999 Cover: 1.99 **NM** value: **Cover or less**
Circ: Statement: **76,034** Diamd. preorders: **48,923**

91 ❑ Jun 1999 Cover: 1.99 **NM** value: **Cover or less**
Circ: Statement: **76,034** Diamd. preorders: **49,946**
• Siryn solo tale

92 ❑ Jul 1999 Cover: 1.99 **NM** value: **Cover or less**
Circ: Statement: **76,034** Diamd. preorders: **48,847**
• Domino vs. Halloween Jack

93 ❑ Aug 1999 Cover: 1.99 **NM** value: **Cover or less**
Circ: Statement: **76,034** Diamd. preorders: **48,069**

94 ❑ Sep 1999 Cover: 1.99 **NM** value: **Cover or less**
Circ: Statement: **76,034** Diamd. preorders: **47,810**

96 ❑ Nov 1999 Cover: 1.99 **NM** value: **Cover or less**
Circ: Diamd. preorders: **46,788**

97 ❑ Dec 1999 Cover: 1.99 **NM** value: **Cover or less**
Circ: Diamd. preorders: **44,347**

98 ❑ Jan 2000 Cover: 1.99 **NM** value: **Cover or less**
Circ: Diamd. preorders: **43,933**

99 ❑ Feb 2000 Cover: 1.99 **NM** value: **Cover or less**
Circ: Diamd. preorders: **46,231**

100 ❑ Mar 2000 Cover: 2.99 **NM** value: **Cover or less**
Circ: Diamd. preorders: **46,671**

101 ❑ Apr 2000 Cover: 1.99 **NM** value: **Cover or less**
Circ: Diamd. preorders: **40,572**

102 ❑ May 2000 Cover: 2.25 **NM** value: **Cover or less**
Circ: Diamd. preorders: **54,395 • CGC:** 1 graded, best 9.2

103 ❑ Jun 2000 Cover: 2.25 **NM** value: **Cover or less**
Circ: Diamd. preorders: **47,576**

104 ❑ Jul 2000 Cover: 2.25 **NM** value: **Cover or less**
Circ: Diamd. preorders: **47,297**

105 ❑ Aug 2000 Cover: 2.25 **NM** value: **Cover or less**
Circ: Diamd. preorders: **49,697**

106 ❑ Sep 2000 Cover: 2.25 **NM** value: **Cover or less**
Circ: Diamd. preorders: **49,069**

107 ❑ Oct 2000 Cover: 2.25 **NM** value: **Cover or less**
Circ: Statement: **57,332** Diamd. preorders: **45,440**

108 ❑ Nov 2000 Cover: 2.25 **NM** value: **Cover or less**
Circ: Statement: **57,332** Diamd. preorders: **45,352**
📖 Shockwave, Part 3; Murder Ballads, Part 3 **A:** Whilce Portacio; Ian Medina **W:** Warren Ellis; Ian Edginton

109 ❑ Dec 2000 Cover: 2.25 **NM** value: **Cover or less**
Circ: Statement: **57,332** Diamd. preorders: **44,758**
📖 Shockwave, Part 4; Murder Ballads, Part 4 **A:** Enrique Breccia **W:** Warren Ellis; Ian Edginton

110 ❑ Jan 2001 Cover: 2.25 **NM** value: **Cover or less**
Circ: Statement: **57,332** Diamd. preorders: **44,164**
📖 Rage War, Part 1 **A:** Jorge Lucas **W:** Ian Edginton

111 ❑ Feb 2001 Cover: 2.25 **NM** value: **Cover or less**
Circ: Statement: **57,332** Diamd. preorders: **42,839**
📖 Rage War, Part 2 **A:** Jorge Lucas **W:** Ian Edginton

112 ❑ Mar 2001 Cover: 2.25 **NM** value: **Cover or less**
Circ: Statement: **57,332** Diamd. preorders: **41,258**
📖 Rage War, Part 3 **A:** Jorge Lucas **W:** Ian Edginton

113 ❑ Apr 2001 Cover: 2.25 **NM** value: **Cover or less**
Circ: Statement: **57,332** Diamd. preorders: **39,996**
📖 Rage War, Part 4 **A:** Jorge Lucas **W:** Ian Edginton

114 ❑ May 2001 Cover: 2.25 **NM** value: **Cover or less**
Circ: Statement: **57,332** Diamd. preorders: **38,123**

115 ❑ Jun 2001 Cover: 2.25 **NM** value: **Cover or less**
Circ: Statement: **57,332** Diamd. preorders: **39,377**

116 ❑ Jul 2001 Cover: 2.25 **NM** value: **Cover or less**
Circ: Statement: **57,332** Diamd. preorders: **52,471 • CGC:** 38 graded, best 9.8

117 ❑ Aug 2001 Cover: 2.25 **NM** value: **Cover or less**
Circ: Statement: **57,332** Diamd. preorders: **47,595 • CGC:** 7 graded, best 9.8

118 ❑ Sep 2001 Cover: 2.25 **NM** value: **Cover or less**
Circ: Statement: **57,332** Diamd. preorders: **54,208 • CGC:** 2 graded, best 9.8

119 ❑ Oct 2001 Cover: 2.25 **NM** value: **Cover or less**
Circ: Diamd. preorders: **58,961 • CGC:** 1 graded, best 9.8

120 ❑ Nov 2001 Cover: 2.25 **NM** value: **Cover or less**
Circ: Diamd. preorders: **55,764 • CGC:** 1 graded, best 9.4

121 ❑ Dec 2001 Cover: 2.25 **NM** value: **Cover or less**
Circ: Diamd. preorders: **52,869**

122 ❑ Jan 2002 Cover: 2.25 **NM** value: **Cover or less**
Circ: Diamd. preorders: **52,054**
• Has 2001 Statement, filed 10/1/2001; avg print run 74,525; avg sales 55,762; avg subs 1,570; avg total paid 57,332; samples 600; max existent 57,932; 22% of run returned

123 ❑ Feb 2002 Cover: 2.25 **NM** value: **Cover or less**
Circ: Diamd. preorders: **51,110**

124 ❑ Mar 2002 Cover: 2.25 **NM** value: **Cover or less**
Circ: Diamd. preorders: **49,021**

Anl 1 ❑ ca. 1992 Cover: 2.25 **NM** value: **2.50**
Circ: CapCity orders: **98,600**
📖 Shattershot, Part 4; The Crush • Shattershot **A:** Adam Kubert; Bill Sienkiewicz; Sandu Florea; Tom Raney; Greg Capullo; Gavin Curtis **W:** Fabian Nicieza; Gavin Curtis; Dan Slott

Anl 2 ❑ ca. 1993 Cover: 2.95 **NM** value: **Cover or less**
• Polybagged with trading card **W:** Fabian Nicieza ★ 1st Appearance of Neurotap, X-Treme, Stronghold.

Anl 3 ❑ ca. 1994 Cover: 2.95 **NM** value: **Cover or less**

Anl 1995 ❑ Dec 1995 Cover: 3.95 **NM** value: **Cover or less**
wraparound cover. • X-Force and Cable '95

Anl 1996 ❑ ca. 1996 Cover: 2.99 **NM** value: **Cover or less**
wraparound cover. 📖 Transmission; DTnouement • X-Force and Cable '96 **A:** Luke Ross; Ed Benés **W:** Terry Kavanagh; Ben Raab; John Francis Moore

Anl 1997 ❑ ca. 1997 Cover: 2.99 **NM** value: **Cover or less**
wraparound cover. • X-Force and Cable '97; return of Asgard

Anl 1998 ❑ ca. 1998 Cover: 3.50 **NM** value: **Cover or less**
wraparound cover. • gatefold summary. • X-Force/Champions '98

Anl 1999 ❑ ca. 1999 Cover: 3.50 **NM** value: **Cover or less**
Circ: Diamd. preorders: **34,764**

Bk 1 ❑ Nov 1992 Cover: 6.95 **NM** value: **Cover or less**
• X-Force And Spider-Man: Sabotage; Reprints X-Force #3-4, Spider-Man #16 **A:** Todd McFarlane; Rob Liefeld **W:** Todd McFarlane; Rob Liefeld; Fabian Nicieza

X-FORCE/YOUNGBLOOD — Marvel

1 ❑ Aug 1996 Cover: 4.95 **NM** value: **Cover or less**
• crossover with Image; prestige format one-shot **A:** Ching Lau; Dan Fraga; Stephen Platt; Richard Horie; Andy Park; Marl Pajarillo; Michael Linchang **W:** Robert Napton; Eric Stevenson

XIMOS: VIOLENT PAST — Triumphant

1 ❑ Mar 1994 Cover: 2.50 **NM** value: **Cover or less**
Circ: CapCity orders: **2,760**

2 ❑ Mar 1994 Cover: 2.50 **NM** value: **Cover or less**
Circ: CapCity orders: **2,590**

XIOLA — Xero

0 ❑ Cover: 1.95 **NM** value: **Cover or less**

1 ❑ b&w Cover: 1.95 **NM** value: **Cover or less**
📖 Django; Azhbane; To Move the Shade **A:** Joe Emsle; Josh Gorchov; Will Elder-Groebe **W:** Joe Emsle; Josh Gorchov; Will Elder-Groebe

2 ❑ b&w Cover: 1.95 **NM** value: **Cover or less**
📖 Django; Azhbane; To Move the Shade **A:** Joe Emsle; Josh Gorchov; Will Elder-Groebe **W:** Joe Emsle; Josh Gorchov; Will Elder-Groebe

3 ❑ Cover: 1.95 **NM** value: **Cover or less**
📖 Django; Azhbane; To Move the Shade **A:** Joe Emsle; Josh Gorchov; Will Elder-Groebe **W:** Joe Emsle; Josh Gorchov; Will Elder-Groebe

Ash 1 ❑ b&w **NM** value: **1.00**
no cover price.

XL — Blackthorne

1 ❑ b&w Cover: 3.50 **NM** value: **Cover or less**

X-LAX — Thwack! Pow!

1 ❑ Cover: 1.25 **NM** value: **Cover or less**
📖 It All Comes Out in the End! • Mini-Comic

X-MAN — Marvel

In early 1995, Marvel launched a series of alternate X-Men titles as part of an "Age of Apocalypse" storyline. The story began in a reality in which Professor X had been killed and, thus, had never been able to train a group of young mutants to become The X-Men. In the years that followed, a villainous mutant named Apocalypse gathered his fellow mutants to become the rulers of North America and launched murderous "culls" of the humans that remained.

X-Man is the story of a mutant named Nathan — better known in this reality as Cable — who leads a band of mutants in a challenge to Apocalypse's rule. His crew, which includes several who would otherwise have become notable X-Men villains, fought to stop Apocalypse from mass-murdering both humans and mutants. Remarkably, when the fight is won, Nate actually crosses over into the timestream which today's X-Men occupy.

-1 ❑ Jul 1997 Cover: 1.99 **NM** value: **2.00**
Circ: Diamd. preorders: **96,390**
📖 Breeding Ground • Flashback **A:** Roger Cruz **W:** Terry Kavanagh

1 ❑ Mar 1995 Cover: 1.95 **NM** value: **4.00**
Circ: CapCity orders: **64,425 • CGC:** 3 graded, best 9.8

1-2 ❑ Mar 1995 Cover: 1.95 **NM** value: **2.25**

2 ❑ Apr 1995 Cover: 1.95 **NM** value: **2.50**
Circ: CapCity orders: **64,975**

3 ❑ May 1995 Cover: 1.95 **NM** value: **2.50**
Circ: CapCity orders: **82,300**

4 ❑ Jun 1995 Cover: 1.95 **NM** value: **2.50**
Circ: CapCity orders: **90,150**

5 ❑ Jul 1995 Cover: 1.95 **NM** value: **2.00**
Circ: CapCity orders: **66,550**

6 ❑ Aug 1995 Cover: 1.95 **NM** value: **2.00**
Circ: CapCity orders: **65,425**

7 ❑ Sep 1995 Cover: 1.95 **NM** value: **2.00**

8 ❑ Oct 1995 Cover: 1.95 **NM** value: **2.00**

9 ❑ Nov 1995 Cover: 1.95 **NM** value: **2.00**

10 ❑ Dec 1995 Cover: 1.95 **NM** value: **2.00**

11 ❑ Jan 1996 Cover: 1.95 **NM** value: **Cover or less**

12 ❑ Feb 1996 Cover: 1.95 **NM** value: **Cover or less**

13 ❑ Mar 1996 Cover: 1.95 **NM** value: **Cover or less**
📖 The Hunted Below **A:** Luke Ross **W:** John Ostrander

14 ❑ Apr 1996 Cover: 1.95 **NM** value: **Cover or less**
📖 Fallen From Grace **A:** Steve Skroce **W:** Terry Kavanagh; John Ostrander

15 ❑ May 1996 Cover: 1.95 **NM** value: **2.50**

16 ❑ Jun 1996 Cover: 1.95 **NM** value: **2.00**

17 ❑ Jul 1996 Cover: 1.95 **NM** value: **2.00**

18 ❑ Aug 1996 Cover: 1.95 **NM** value: **Cover or less**

19 ❑ Sep 1996 Cover: 1.95 **NM** value: **Cover or less**
📖 Onslaught: Phase 2 ★ Appearance of Mr. Sinister.

20 ❑ Oct 1996 Cover: 1.95 **NM** value: **Cover or less**
Circ: Statement: **148,203**
• bound-in trading cards ★ Versus Abomination.

21 ❑ Nov 1996 Cover: 1.95 **NM** value: **Cover or less**
Circ: Statement: **148,203** Direct Market orders: **131,750**

22 ❑ Dec 1996 Cover: 1.95 **NM** value: **Cover or less**
Circ: Statement: **148,203** Direct Market orders: **130,500**

23 ❑ Jan 1997 Cover: 1.95 **NM** value: **Cover or less**
Circ: Statement: **148,203** Direct Market orders: **123,250**
📖 Crash Course **A:** Roger Cruz; Manny Clark **W:** Terry Kavanagh

24 ❑ Feb 1997 Cover: 1.95 **NM** value: **Cover or less**
Circ: Statement: **148,203** Direct Market orders: **118,000**
📖 First Noel **A:** Roger Cruz **W:** Terry Kavanagh ★ Appearance of Spider-Man, Morbius. ★ Versus Morbius.

25 ❑ Mar 1997 Cover: 2.99 **NM** value: **Cover or less**
Circ: Statement: **148,203** Direct Market orders: **110,000**
wraparound cover. • Giant-size. 📖 Closer to the Flame **A:** Roger Cruz **W:** Terry Kavanagh ★ Appearance of Madelyne Pryor.

26 ❑ Apr 1997 Cover: 1.95 **NM** value: **Cover or less**
Circ: Statement: **148,203** Direct Market orders: **104,000**
📖 Down to Earth **A:** Pascual Ferry; Roger Cruz(cover) **W:** Terry Kavanagh

27 ❑ May 1997 Cover: 1.95 **NM** value: **Cover or less**
Circ: Statement: **148,203** Diamd. preorders: **104,349**
📖 Blood Brothers **A:** Roger Cruz **W:** Terry Kavanagh

28 ❑ Jun 1997 Cover: 1.95 **NM** value: **Cover or less**
Circ: Statement: **148,203** Diamd. preorders: **103,925**
📖 Dance With the Devil **A:** Roger Cruz **W:** Terry Kavanagh

29 ❑ Aug 1997 Cover: 1.99 **NM** value: **Cover or less**
Circ: Statement: **148,203** Diamd. preorders: **96,018**
• gatefold summary.

30 ❑ Sep 1997 Cover: 1.99 **NM** value: **Cover or less**
Circ: Statement: **148,203** Diamd. preorders: **92,936**
• gatefold summary.

31 ❑ Oct 1997 Cover: 1.99 **NM** value: **Cover or less**
Circ: Diamd. preorders: **91,520**
• gatefold summary.

32 ❑ Nov 1997 Cover: 1.99 **NM** value: **Cover or less**
Circ: Diamd. preorders: **90,246**
• gatefold summary.

33 ❑ Dec 1997 Cover: 1.99 **NM** value: **Cover or less**
Circ: Diamd. preorders: **88,095**
• gatefold summary. • Has 1997 Statement, filed 10/1/97; avg total paid circ 148,203

34 ❑ Jan 1998 Cover: 1.99 **NM** value: **Cover or less**
Circ: Diamd. preorders: **83,934**
• gatefold summary.

35 ❑ Feb 1998 Cover: 1.99 **NM** value: **Cover or less**
Circ: Diamd. preorders: **78,356**
• gatefold summary.

36 ❑ Mar 1998 Cover: 1.99 **NM** value: **Cover or less**
Circ: Diamd. preorders: **74,807**
• gatefold summary.

37 ❑ Apr 1998 Cover: 1.99 **NM** value: **Cover or less**
Circ: Diamd. preorders: **68,890**
• gatefold summary. • Spider-Man

38 ❑ May 1998 Cover: 1.99 **NM** value: **Cover or less**
Circ: Diamd. preorders: **67,357**
• gatefold summary. • Spider-Man

39 ❑ Jun 1998 Cover: 1.99 **NM** value: **Cover or less**
Circ: Diamd. preorders: **66,118**
• gatefold summary.

40 ❑ Jul 1998 Cover: 1.99 **NM** value: **Cover or less**
Circ: Diamd. preorders: **61,614**
• gatefold summary.

41 ❑ Aug 1998 Cover: 1.99 **NM** value: **Cover or less**
Circ: Diamd. preorders: **60,368**
• gatefold summary. ★ Appearance of Madelyne Pryor.

42 ❑ Sep 1998 Cover: 1.99 **NM** value: **Cover or less**
Circ: Diamd. preorders: **56,110**
• gatefold summary.

43 ❑ Oct 1998 Cover: 1.99 **NM** value: **Cover or less**
Circ: Statement: **63,240** Diamd. preorders: **53,761**
• gatefold summary.

44 ❑ Nov 1998 Cover: 1.99 **NM** value: **Cover or less**
Circ: Statement: **63,240** Diamd. preorders: **52,142**
• gatefold summary. ★ Versus Nemesis.

45 ❑ Dec 1998 Cover: 1.99 **NM** value: **Cover or less**
Circ: Statement: **63,240** Diamd. preorders: **51,453**
• gatefold summary. 📖 Blood Brothers

46 ❑ Dec 1998 Cover: 1.99 **NM** value: **Cover or less**
Circ: Statement: **63,240** Diamd. preorders: **51,095**
• gatefold summary. 📖 Blood Brothers

47 ❑ Jan 1999 Cover: 1.99 **NM** value: **Cover or less**
Circ: Statement: **63,240** Diamd. preorders: **50,794**
• gatefold summary. 📖 Blood Brothers

48 ❑ Feb 1999 Cover: 1.99 **NM** value: **Cover or less**
Circ: Statement: **63,240** Diamd. preorders: **48,170**
📖 The Blood of the Righteous **A:** Luke Ross **W:** Mark Bernardo

49 ❑ Mar 1999 Cover: 1.99 **NM** value: **Cover or less**
Circ: Statement: **63,240** Diamd. preorders: **48,436**

50 ❑ Apr 1999 Cover: 2.99 **NM** value: **Cover or less**
Circ: Statement: **63,240** Diamd. preorders: **49,927**
📖 War of the Mutants, part 2 • Story continues from Generation X #50 **A:** Luke Ross **W:** Terry Kavanagh ★ Appearance of Dark Beast, White Queen.

51 ❑ May 1999 Cover: 1.99 **NM** value: **Cover or less**
Circ: Statement: **63,240** Diamd. preorders: **45,331**

52 ❑ Jun 1999 Cover: 1.99 **NM** value: **Cover or less**
Circ: Statement: **63,240** Diamd. preorders: **45,661**

53 ❑ Jul 1999 Cover: 1.99 **NM** value: **Cover or less**
Circ: Statement: **63,240** Diamd. preorders: **44,184**

54 ❑ Aug 1999 Cover: 1.99 **NM** value: **Cover or less**
Circ: Statement: **63,240** Diamd. preorders: **43,833**

Other grades: Multiply prices above by **1.5 for Mint • 2/3 for Very Fine • 1/3 for Fine • 1/5 for Very Good • 1/8 for Good**

55 ☐ Sep 1999 Cover: 1.99 **NM** value: **Cover or less**
Circ: Statement: **63,240** Diamd. preorders: **42,508**
56 ☐ Oct 1999 Cover: 1.99 **NM** value: **Cover or less**
Circ: Diamd. preorders: **41,102**
57 ☐ Nov 1999 Cover: 1.99 **NM** value: **Cover or less**
Circ: Diamd. preorders: **39,211**
58 ☐ Dec 1999 Cover: 1.99 **NM** value: **Cover or less**
Circ: Diamd. preorders: **39,220**
59 ☐ Jan 2000 Cover: 1.99 **NM** value: **Cover or less**
Circ: Diamd. preorders: **37,722**
60 ☐ Feb 2000 Cover: 1.99 **NM** value: **Cover or less**
Circ: Diamd. preorders: **39,877**
61 ☐ Mar 2000 Cover: 1.99 **NM** value: **Cover or less**
Circ: Diamd. preorders: **36,047**
62 ☐ Apr 2000 Cover: 1.99 **NM** value: **Cover or less**
Circ: Diamd. preorders: **34,721**
63 ☐ May 2000 Cover: 1.99 **NM** value: **Cover or less**
Circ: Diamd. preorders: **47,743** • **CGC:** 1 graded, best 9.2
64 ☐ Jun 2000 Cover: 2.25 **NM** value: **Cover or less**
Circ: Diamd. preorders: **40,933**
65 ☐ Jul 2000 Cover: 2.25 **NM** value: **Cover or less**
Circ: Diamd. preorders: **42,184**
66 ☐ Aug 2000 Cover: 2.25 **NM** value: **Cover or less**
Circ: Diamd. preorders: **43,435**
67 ☐ Sep 2000 Cover: 2.25 **NM** value: **Cover or less**
Circ: Diamd. preorders: **42,108**
📖 Shockwave, Part 1; The Infinities of Evil, Part 1: Further Down the Spiral **A:** Ariel Olivetti **W:** Warren Ellis; Steven Grant
68 ☐ Oct 2000 Cover: 2.25 **NM** value: **Cover or less**
Circ: Diamd. preorders: **38,654**
📖 Shockwave, Part 2
69 ☐ Nov 2000 Cover: 2.25 **NM** value: **Cover or less**
Circ: Diamd. preorders: **38,418**
📖 Shockwave, Part 3; The Infinities of Evil, Part 3: Double Vision • polybagged with AOL CD-ROM **A:** Ariel Olivetti **W:** Warren Ellis; Steven Grant
70 ☐ Dec 2000 Cover: 2.25 **NM** value: **Cover or less**
Circ: Diamd. preorders: **37,709**
📖 Shockwave, Part 4; The Infinities of Evil, Part 4: Worlds Without End **A:** Ariel Olivetti **W:** Warren Ellis; Steven Grant
71 ☐ Jan 2001 Cover: 2.25 **NM** value: **Cover or less**
Circ: Diamd. preorders: **36,715**
📖 Fearful Symmetries, Part 1 **A:** Ariel Olivetti **W:** Steven Grant
72 ☐ Feb 2001 Cover: 2.25 **NM** value: **Cover or less**
Circ: Diamd. preorders: **35,825**
📖 Fearful Symmetries, Part 2 **A:** Ariel Olivetti **W:** Steven Grant
73 ☐ Mar 2001 Cover: 2.25 **NM** value: **Cover or less**
Circ: Diamd. preorders: **34,058**
📖 Fearful Symmetries, Part 3 **A:** Ariel Olivetti **W:** Steven Grant
74 ☐ Apr 2001 Cover: 2.25 **NM** value: **Cover or less**
Circ: Diamd. preorders: **32,751**
📖 Fearful Symmetries, Part 4 **A:** Quique Alcatena **W:** Steven Grant
75 ☐ May 2001 Cover: 2.99 **NM** value: **Cover or less**
Circ: Diamd. preorders: **32,321**
• double-sized. 📖 Till the End of the World **A:** Quique Alcatena **W:** Steven Grant
Anl 1996☐ca. 1996 Cover: 2.99 **NM** value: **Cover or less**
Circ: Direct Market orders: **99,000**
No issue number. wraparound cover. 📖 Sins of the Father; Mind Games **A:** Alan Davis; Terry Dodson **W:** Ralph Macchio; Terry Kavanagh
Anl 1997☐ca. 1997 Cover: 2.99 **NM** value: **Cover or less**
Circ: Diamd. preorders: **60,754**
No issue number. wraparound cover. ★ Appearance of Sugar Man, Nemesis, Dark Beast.
Anl 1998☐ca. 1998 Cover: 2.99 **NM** value: **Cover or less**
No issue number. wraparound cover. 📖 Call of the Wild • X-Man/ Hulk '98 **A:** Chris Cross **W:** Terry Kavanagh ★ Versus Thanos.
Bk 1☐ May 1995 Cover: 8.95 **NM** value: **Cover or less**
Gold foil cover. • Ultimate X-Man; collects first four-issues

X-MEN, THE — Marvel

Bk 1☐ Cover: 1.75 **NM** value: **3.00**
• Marvel mass-market paperback

X-MEN (1ST SERIES) — Marvel

Stan Lee co-created the X-Men, one of Marvel's first super-groups, as a youthful counterpart to the full-grown heroes in The Avengers. With membership consisting of Scott Summers (Cyclops), Jean Grey (Marvel Girl), Warren Worthington III (Angel), and Hank McCoy (The Beast), The X-Men are students, enrolled in Professor Xavier's School for Gifted Youngsters. The secret is that these youngsters are mutants. Their genetic structure is different from that of normal people, and they have been blessed with strange superpowers as a result. They are called The X-Men because of that "something X-tra" that each possesses.

Although reasonably popular in its early days, the original run of The X-Men had almost faded from existence when it was suddenly revitalized by the introduction of the "New X-Men" in Giant-Size X-Men #1. It then went on to become one of Marvel's most successful titles.

1 ☐ Sep 1963 Cover: 0.12 **NM** value: **6100.00**
• **CGC:** 237 graded, best 9.8
📖 X-Men **A:** Jack Kirby **W:** Stan Lee ★ Origin of X-Men. ★ 1st Appearance of X-Men, Cyclops, Professor X, Angel II, Marvel Girl, Iceman, Magneto, Beast.
2 ☐ Nov 1963 Cover: 0.12 **NM** value: **1800.00**
• **CGC:** 122 graded, best 9.6
📖 No One Can Stop the Vanisher **A:** Jack Kirby **W:** Stan Lee ★ 1st Appearance of The Vanisher.
3 ☐ Jan 1964 Cover: 0.12 **NM** value: **725.00**
• **CGC:** 90 graded, best 9.8
📖 Beware of the Blob **A:** Jack Kirby **W:** Stan Lee ★ 1st Appearance of The Blob.
4 ☐ Mar 1964 Cover: 0.12 **NM** value: **650.00**
• **CGC:** 80 graded, best 9.6
📖 The Brotherhood of Evil Mutants **A:** Jack Kirby **W:** Stan Lee ★ 1st Appearance of Toad, Mastermind, Scarlet Witch, Quicksilver, Brotherhood of Evil Mutants.
5 ☐ May 1964 Cover: 0.12 **NM** value: **460.00**
• **CGC:** 53 graded, best 9.6
📖 Trapped: One X-Man **A:** Jack Kirby **W:** Stan Lee ★ Appearance of Evil Mutants.
6 ☐ Jul 1964 Cover: 0.12 **NM** value: **340.00**
• **CGC:** 43 graded, best 9.8
📖 Sub-Mariner Joins the Evil Mutants **A:** Jack Kirby **W:** Stan Lee ★ Appearance of Evil Mutants, Sub-Mariner.
7 ☐ Sep 1964 Cover: 0.12 **NM** value: **300.00**
• **CGC:** 65 graded, best 9.6
📖 The Return of the Blob! **A:** Jack Kirby **W:** Stan Lee ★ Appearance of Blob, Evil Mutants.
8 ☐ Nov 1964 Cover: 0.12 **NM** value: **300.00**
• **CGC:** 60 graded, best 9.6
📖 Unas, the Untouchable **A:** Jack Kirby **W:** Stan Lee ★ Origin of Unus the Untouchable. ★ 1st Appearance of Unus the Untouchable.
9 ☐ Jan 1965 Cover: 0.12 **NM** value: **300.00**
• **CGC:** 58 graded, best 9.6
📖 Enter the Avengers! **A:** Jack Kirby **W:** Stan Lee ★ 1st Appearance of Lucifer.
10 ☐ Mar 1965 Cover: 0.12 **NM** value: **300.00**
• **CGC:** 81 graded, best 9.6
📖 The Coming of Ka-Zar! **A:** Jack Kirby **W:** Stan Lee ★ 1st Appearance of Ka-Zar. ★ Appearance of Ka-Zar.
11 ☐ May 1965 Cover: 0.12 **NM** value: **260.00**
• **CGC:** 27 graded, best 9.6
📖 The Triumph of Magneto! **A:** Jack Kirby **W:** Stan Lee ★ 1st Appearance of The Stranger.
12 ☐ Jul 1965 Cover: 0.12 **NM** value: **350.00**
• **CGC:** 71 graded, best 9.6
📖 The Origin of Professor X! **A:** Jack Kirby **W:** Stan Lee ★ Origin of Professor X, Juggernaut. ★ 1st Appearance of Juggernaut.
13 ☐ Sep 1965 Cover: 0.12 **NM** value: **240.00**
• **CGC:** 58 graded, best 9.8
📖 Where Walks the Juggernaut **A:** Jack Kirby **W:** Stan Lee ★ Versus Juggernaut.
14 ☐ Nov 1965 Cover: 0.12 **NM** value: **275.00**
• **CGC:** 93 graded, best 9.6
📖 Among Us Stalk the Sentinels **A:** Jack Kirby **W:** Stan Lee ★ Origin of Sentinels. ★ 1st Appearance of Sentinels.
15 ☐ Dec 1965 Cover: 0.12 **NM** value: **230.00**
• **CGC:** 39 graded, best 9.6
📖 Prisoners of the Mysterious Master Mold **A:** Jack Kirby **W:** Stan Lee ★ Origin of Beast.
16 ☐ Jan 1966 Cover: 0.12 **NM** value: **230.00**
Circ: Statement: **255,070** • **CGC:** 54 graded, best 9.6
📖 The Supreme Sacrifice! **A:** Jack Kirby; Jay Gavin **W:** Stan Lee ★ Appearance of Sentinels, Master Mold.
17 ☐ Feb 1966 Cover: 0.12 **NM** value: **130.00**
Circ: Statement: **255,070** • **CGC:** 29 graded, best 9.8
📖 ...And None Shall Survive! **A:** Jack Kirby; Jay Gavin **W:** Stan Lee ★ Versus Magneto.
18 ☐ Mar 1966 Cover: 0.12 **NM** value: **130.00**
Circ: Statement: **255,070** • **CGC:** 25 graded, best 9.6
📖 If Iceman Should Fail! **A:** Jay Gavin **C:** Jack Kirby **W:** Stan Lee ★ Appearance of Stranger. ★ Versus Magneto.
19 ☐ Apr 1966 Cover: 0.12 **NM** value: **130.00**
Circ: Statement: **255,070** • **CGC:** 56 graded, best 9.6
📖 Lo! Now Shall Appear the Mimic **C:** Jack Kirby ★ Origin of Mimic. ★ 1st Appearance of Mimic.
20 ☐ May 1966 Cover: 0.12 **NM** value: **130.00**
Circ: Statement: **255,070** • **CGC:** 40 graded, best 9.6
📖 I, Lucifer **C:** Jack Kirby ★ Versus Unus. ★ Versus Lucifer.
21 ☐ Jun 1966 Cover: 0.12 **NM** value: **110.00**
Circ: Statement: **255,070** • **CGC:** 62 graded, best 9.8
📖 From Whence Comes Dominus? **C:** Jack Kirby ★ Versus Lucifer.
22 ☐ Jul 1966 Cover: 0.12 **NM** value: **110.00**
Circ: Statement: **255,070** • **CGC:** 31 graded, best 9.6
📖 Divided – We Fall! **A:** Jay Gavin **C:** Jack Kirby **W:** Roy Thomas ★ Versus Count Nefaria.
23 ☐ Aug 1966 Cover: 0.12 **NM** value: **110.00**
Circ: Statement: **255,070** • **CGC:** 55 graded, best 9.8
📖 To Save a City **A:** Werner Roth **W:** Roy Thomas ★ Versus Count Nefaria.
24 ☐ Sep 1966 Cover: 0.12 **NM** value: **110.00**
Circ: Statement: **255,070** • **CGC:** 45 graded, best 9.8
📖 The Plague of the Locust **C:** Jack Kirby
25 ☐ Oct 1966 Cover: 0.12 **NM** value: **110.00**
Circ: Statement: **255,070** • **CGC:** 59 graded, best 9.6
📖 The Power and the Pendant! **A:** Werner Roth **C:** Jack Kirby **W:** Roy Thomas ★ Appearance of El Tigre.
26 ☐ Nov 1966 Cover: 0.12 **NM** value: **110.00**
Circ: Statement: **255,070** • **CGC:** 48 graded, best 9.6
📖 Holocaust **C:** Jack Kirby
27 ☐ Dec 1966 Cover: 0.12 **NM** value: **110.00**
Circ: Statement: **255,070** • **CGC:** 55 graded, best 9.6
📖 Re-enter: The Mimic! • Mimic returns **A:** Werner Roth **C:** Jack Kirby **W:** Roy Thomas ★ Versus Puppet Master.
28 ☐ Jan 1967 Cover: 0.12 **NM** value: **150.00**
Circ: Statement: **266,034** • **CGC:** 70 graded, best 9.8
📖 The Wail of the Banshee **A:** Werner Roth **C:** Jack Kirby **W:** Roy Thomas ★ 1st Appearance of Banshee.
28-2☐ Cover: 0.12 **NM** value: **2.00**
29 ☐ Feb 1967 Cover: 0.12 **NM** value: **110.00**
Circ: Statement: **266,034** • **CGC:** 43 graded, best 9.6
📖 When Titans Clash! **C:** Jack Kirby ★ Versus Super-Adaptoid.
30 ☐ Mar 1967 Cover: 0.12 **NM** value: **110.00**
Circ: Statement: **266,034** • **CGC:** 42 graded, best 9.8
📖 The Warlock Wakes! • Has 1966 Statement, filed 10/1/66; avg print run 412,086; avg sales 253,470; avg subs 1,600; avg total paid 255,070; samples 60; max existent 255,130; 38% of run returned **A:** Jack Sparling **C:** Jack Kirby **W:** Roy Thomas ★ 1st Appearance of Maha Yogi.
31 ☐ Apr 1967 Cover: 0.12 **NM** value: **80.00**
Circ: Statement: **266,034** • **CGC:** 28 graded, best 9.6
📖 We Must Destroy the Cobalt Man **C:** Jack Kirby ★ 1st Appearance of Cobalt Man.
32 ☐ May 1967 Cover: 0.12 **NM** value: **80.00**
Circ: Statement: **266,034** • **CGC:** 55 graded, best 9.6
📖 Beware the Juggernaut, My Son **C:** Jack Kirby ★ Versus Juggernaut.
33 ☐ Jun 1967 Cover: 0.12 **NM** value: **80.00**
Circ: Statement: **266,034** • **CGC:** 29 graded, best 9.6
📖 Into the Crimson Cosmos **C:** Gil Kane ★ Versus Juggernaut.
34 ☐ Jul 1967 Cover: 0.12 **NM** value: **80.00**
Circ: Statement: **266,034** • **CGC:** 36 graded, best 9.6
📖 War in a World of Darkness **A:** Dan Adkins ★ Versus Tyrannus. ★ Versus Mole Man.
35 ☐ Aug 1967 Cover: 0.12 **NM** value: **110.00**
Circ: Statement: **266,034** • **CGC:** 44 graded, best 9.6
📖 Along Came a Spider **C:** Jack Kirby ★ 1st Appearance of Changeling. ★ Appearance of Spider-Man, Banshee.
36 ☐ Sep 1967 Cover: 0.12 **NM** value: **80.00**
Circ: Statement: **266,034** • **CGC:** 39 graded, best 9.6
📖 Mekano Lives **A:** Ross Andru ★ 1st Appearance of Mekano.
37 ☐ Oct 1967 Cover: 0.12 **NM** value: **80.00**
Circ: Statement: **266,034** • **CGC:** 39 graded, best 9.8
📖 We, the Jury **A:** Ross Andru **C:** Don Heck; Jack Kirby ★ Versus Factor Three.
38 ☐ Nov 1967 Cover: 0.12 **NM** value: **100.00**
Circ: Statement: **266,034** • **CGC:** 45 graded, best 9.8
📖 The Sinister Shadow of Doomsday; A Man Called X • The Origins of the X-Men back-ups begin **A:** Don Heck **C:** Dan Adkins ★ Versus Blob, Vanisher. ★ Versus Blob. ★ Versus Vanisher.
39 ☐ Dec 1967 Cover: 0.12 **NM** value: **80.00**
Circ: Statement: **266,034** • **CGC:** 19 graded, best 9.6
📖 The Fateful Finale; Lonely Are the Hunted **A:** Don Heck **C:** George Tuska ★ Death of Mutant-Master.
40 ☐ Jan 1968 Cover: 0.12 **NM** value: **80.00**
Circ: Statement: **273,360** • **CGC:** 60 graded, best 9.6
📖 The Mark of the Monster; The First Evil Mutant **A:** Don Heck **C:** George Tuska ★ Versus Frankenstein.
41 ☐ Feb 1968 Cover: 0.12 **NM** value: **70.00**
Circ: Statement: **273,360** • **CGC:** 26 graded, best 9.9
📖 Now Strikes the Sub-Human; The Living Diamond **A:** Don Heck ★ 1st Appearance of Grotesk the Sub-Human.
42 ☐ Mar 1968 Cover: 0.12 **NM** value: **70.00**
Circ: Statement: **273,360** • **CGC:** 32 graded, best 9.6
📖 If I Should Die; The End or the Beginning • Has 1967 Statement, filed 10/1/67; avg print run 445,763; avg sales 264,434; avg subs 1,600; avg total paid 266,034; samples 95; max existent 266,129; 40% of run returned **A:** Don Heck **C:** John Buscema ★ Death of Changeling (disguised as Professor X). ★ Versus Grotesk.
43 ☐ Apr 1968 Cover: 0.12 **NM** value: **70.00**
Circ: Statement: **273,360** • **CGC:** 37 graded, best 9.6
📖 The Torch is Passed ... !; Call Him Cyclops **A:** George Tuska **C:** John Buscema **W:** Roy Thomas ★ Versus Brotherhood of Evil Mutants.
44 ☐ May 1968 Cover: 0.12 **NM** value: **70.00**
Circ: Statement: **273,360** • **CGC:** 28 graded, best 9.4
📖 Red Raven, Red Raven ...!; The Iceman Cometh • Return of Red Raven **A:** Don Heck; Werner Roth **W:** Gary Friedrich ★ Origin of Red Raven, Iceman. ★ 1st Appearance of Red Raven (in modern age). ★ Appearance of Magneto.
45 ☐ Jun 1968 Cover: 0.12 **NM** value: **70.00**
Circ: Statement: **273,360** • **CGC:** 63 graded, best 9.6
📖 When Mutants Clash; And the Mob Cried Vengeance **A:** Don Heck **C:** John Buscema; George Tuska ★ Origin of Iceman. ★ Versus Evil Mutants.
46 ☐ Jul 1968 Cover: 0.12 **NM** value: **70.00**
Circ: Statement: **273,360** • **CGC:** 16 graded, best 9.8
📖 The End of the X-Men; And Then There Were Two **A:** Don Heck ★ Origin of Iceman. ★ Versus Juggernaut.
47 ☐ Aug 1968 Cover: 0.12 **NM** value: **70.00**
Circ: Statement: **273,360** • **CGC:** 41 graded, best 9.4
📖 The Warlock Wears Three Faces; I, the Iceman **A:** Don Heck ★ Versus Maha Yogi.
48 ☐ Sep 1968 Cover: 0.12 **NM** value: **70.00**
Circ: Statement: **273,360** • **CGC:** 33 graded, best 9.6
📖 Beware Computo Commander of the Robot Hive!; Yours Truly, the Beast **A:** Don Heck; Werner Roth **C:** Sal Buscema **W:** Arnold Drake ★ Versus Quasimodo.
49 ☐ Oct 1968 Cover: 0.12 **NM** value: **75.00**
Circ: Statement: **273,360** • **CGC:** 36 graded, best 9.6
📖 Who Dares Defy the Demi-Men?; A Beast is Born **A:** Don Heck; Jim Steranko ★ 1st Appearance of Mesmero, Lorna Dane, Polaris.
50 ☐ Nov 1968 Cover: 0.12 **NM** value: **75.00**
Circ: Statement: **273,360** • **CGC:** 59 graded, best 9.8
📖 Hail, Queen of Mutants; (Untitled) **A:** Jim Steranko ★ Versus Mesmero.
51 ☐ Dec 1968 Cover: 0.12 **NM** value: **75.00**
Circ: Statement: **273,360** • **CGC:** 48 graded, best 9.6
📖 The Devil Has a Daughter; The Lure of the Beast-Nappers **A:** Jim Steranko ★ Versus Mesmero.
52 ☐ Jan 1969 Cover: 0.12 **NM** value: **50.00**
Circ: Statement: **235,811** • **CGC:** 29 graded, best 9.6
📖 Twilight of the Mutants; The Crimes of the Conquistador **A:** Don Heck ★ Origin of Lorna Dane.
53 ☐ Feb 1969 Cover: 0.12 **NM** value: **60.00**
Circ: Statement: **235,811** • **CGC:** 47 graded, best 9.6
📖 The Rage of Blastaar; Welcome to the Club Beast • Barry Windsor-Smith's 1st comic book art **A:** Barry Windsor-Smith ★ Versus Blastaar.
54 ☐ Mar 1969 Cover: 0.12 **NM** value: **60.00**
Circ: Statement: **235,811** • **CGC:** 50 graded, best 9.8

CGC-graded: Multiply prices above by **33 for 9.9 M** • **16 for 9.8 NM/M** • **7 for 9.6 NM+** • **5 for 9.4 NM** • **2.5 for 9.2 NM-** • **1.5 for 9.0 VF/NM**

Wanted: Dead or Alive – Cyclops; The Million Dollar Angel • Has 1968 Statement, filed 10/1/68; avg print run 415,200; avg sales 272,128; avg subs 1,232; avg total paid 273,360; samples 400; max existent 273,760; 34% of run returned **A:** Don Heck ★ Origin of Havok. ★ 1st Appearance of Alex Summers (Havok), Living Pharaoh.

55 Apr 1969 Cover: 0.12 **NM** value: **60.00**
Circ: Statement: **235,811 • CGC:** 39 graded, best 9.6
The Living Pharoh; Where Angels Fear to Tread **A:** Don Heck ★ Origin of Havok.

56 May 1969 Cover: 0.12 **NM** value: **60.00**
Circ: Statement: **235,811 • CGC:** 45 graded, best 9.6
What Is the Power?; The Flying A-Bomb • Living Pharaoh becomes Living Monolith **A:** Neal Adams ★ 1st Appearance of Living Monolith. ★ Versus Living Monolith.

57 Jun 1969 Cover: 0.12 **NM** value: **60.00**
Circ: Statement: **235,811 • CGC:** 35 graded, best 9.6
The Sentinels Live; The Female of the Species **A:** Neal Adams ★ 1st Appearance of Mark II Sentinels.

58 Jul 1969 Cover: 0.15 **NM** value: **80.00**
Circ: Statement: **235,811 • CGC:** 46 graded, best 9.6
Mission: Murder **A:** Neal Adams ★ 1st Appearance of Havok (in costume).

59 Aug 1969 Cover: 0.15 **NM** value: **55.00**
Circ: Statement: **235,811 • CGC:** 18 graded, best 9.6
Do or Die, Baby **A:** Neal Adams ★ 1st Appearance of Dr. Karl Lykos.

60 Sep 1969 Cover: 0.15 **NM** value: **60.00**
Circ: Statement: **235,811 • CGC:** 31 graded, best 9.6
In the Shadow of Sauron **A:** Neal Adams ★ Origin of Sauron. ★ 1st Appearance of Sauron.

61 Oct 1969 Cover: 0.15 **NM** value: **60.00**
Circ: Statement: **235,811 • CGC:** 27 graded, best 9.8
Monsters Also Weep **A:** Neal Adams ★ Versus Sauron.

62 Nov 1969 Cover: 0.15 **NM** value: **60.00**
Circ: Statement: **235,811 • CGC:** 17 graded, best 9.6
Strangers in a Savage Land! **A:** Neal Adams ★ 1st Appearance of Piper, Lupo, Barbarus. ★ Appearance of Ka-Zar.

62-2 Cover: 0.15 **NM** value: **1.50**
Strangers in a Savage Land! **A:** Neal Adams ★ 1st Appearance of Piper, Lupo, Barbarus. ★ Appearance of Ka-Zar.

63 Dec 1969 Cover: 0.15 **NM** value: **60.00**
Circ: Statement: **235,811 • CGC:** 22 graded, best 9.6
War in the World Below **A:** Neal Adams ★ Origin of Piper, Lupo. ★ Appearance of Ka-Zar. ★ Versus Magneto.

64 Jan 1970 Cover: 0.15 **NM** value: **60.00**
Circ: Statement: **180,589 • CGC:** 24 graded, best 9.8
The Coming of Sunfire **A:** Don Heck **W:** Roy Thomas ★ Origin of Sunfire. ★ 1st Appearance of Sunfire.

65 Feb 1970 Cover: 0.15 **NM** value: **60.00**
Circ: Statement: **180,589 • CGC:** 18 graded, best 9.8
Before I'd Be a Slave **A:** Neal Adams ★ Appearance of Havok, SHIELD, Fantastic Four. ★ Death of Changeling (revealed).

66 Mar 1970 Cover: 0.15 **NM** value: **50.00**
Circ: Statement: **180,589 • CGC:** 24 graded, best 9.6
The Mutants and the Monster • Has 1969 Statement, filed 10/1/69; avg print run 405,115; avg sales 234,745; avg subs 1,066; avg total paid 235,811; samples 110; max existent 235,921; 42% of run returned **A:** Sal Buscema ★ Appearance of Havok, Hulk.

67 Dec 1970 Cover: 0.25 **NM** value: **25.00**
Circ: Statement: **180,589 • CGC:** 16 graded, best 9.4
The Origin of Professor X; Where Walks the Juggernaut • reprints stories from X-Men #12 and 13

68 Feb 1971 Cover: 0.25 **NM** value: **25.00**
• **CGC:** 12 graded, best 9.4
Among Us Stalk the Sentinels; Prisoners of the Mysterious Master Mold • reprints stories from X-Men #14 and 15

69 Apr 1971 Cover: 0.25 **NM** value: **25.00**
• **CGC:** 12 graded, best 9.4
The Supreme Sacrifice; Lo! Now Shall Appear the Mimic • reprints stories from X-Men #16 and 19; Has 1970 Statement, filed 10/1/70; avg print run 339,506; avg sales 179,685; avg subs 904; avg total paid 180,589; max existent 180,699; 47% of run returned

70 Jun 1971 Cover: 0.25 **NM** value: **25.00**
• **CGC:** 11 graded, best 9.6
...And None Shall Survive!; If Iceman Should Fail! • reprints stories from X-Men #17 and 18

71 Aug 1971 Cover: 0.15 **NM** value: **25.00**
• **CGC:** 12 graded, best 9.6
I, Lucifer • reprints X-Men #20

72 Oct 1971 Cover: 0.25 **NM** value: **25.00**
• **CGC:** 8 graded, best 9.6
From Whence Comes Dominus?; The Plague of the Locust • reprints stories from X-Men #21 and 24

73 Dec 1971 Cover: 0.20 **NM** value: **25.00**
• **CGC:** 5 graded, best 9.2
The Power and the Pendant! • reprints X-Men #25

74 Feb 1972 Cover: 0.20 **NM** value: **25.00**
• **CGC:** 7 graded, best 9.6
Holocaust • reprints X-Men #26 **C:** Gil Kane

75 Apr 1972 Cover: 0.20 **NM** value: **25.00**
• **CGC:** 9 graded, best 9.6
Re-enter: The Mimic! • reprints X-Men #27

76 Jun 1972 Cover: 0.20 **NM** value: **25.00**
• **CGC:** 4 graded, best 9.0
The Wail of the Banshee • reprints X-Men #28 **C:** Gil Kane

77 Aug 1972 Cover: 0.20 **NM** value: **25.00**
• **CGC:** 11 graded, best 9.6
When Titans Clash! • reprints X-Men #29

78 Oct 1972 Cover: 0.20 **NM** value: **25.00**
• **CGC:** 13 graded, best 9.2
The Warlock Wakes! • reprints X-Men #30 **C:** Gil Kane

79 Dec 1972 Cover: 0.20 **NM** value: **25.00**
• **CGC:** 6 graded, best 9.2
We Must Destroy the Cobalt Man • reprints X-Men #31 **C:** Gil Kane

80 Feb 1973 Cover: 0.20 **NM** value: **25.00**
Circ: Statement: **127,663 • CGC:** 11 graded, best 9.4
Beware the Juggernaut, My Son • reprints X-Men #32 **C:** Gil Kane

81 Apr 1973 Cover: 0.20 **NM** value: **25.00**
Circ: Statement: **127,663 • CGC:** 7 graded, best 9.2
Into the Crimson Cosmos • reprints X-Men #33

82 Jun 1973 Cover: 0.20 **NM** value: **25.00**
Circ: Statement: **127,663 • CGC:** 6 graded, best 9.4
War in a World of Darkness • reprints X-Men #34

83 Aug 1973 Cover: 0.20 **NM** value: **25.00**
Circ: Statement: **127,663 • CGC:** 7 graded, best 9.4
Along Came a Spider • reprints X-Men #35

84 Oct 1973 Cover: 0.20 **NM** value: **25.00**
Circ: Statement: **127,663 • CGC:** 13 graded, best 9.6
Mekano Lives • reprints X-Men #36

85 Dec 1973 Cover: 0.20 **NM** value: **25.00**
Circ: Statement: **127,663 • CGC:** 10 graded, best 9.6
We, the Jury • reprints X-Men #37

86 Feb 1974 Cover: 0.20 **NM** value: **25.00**
• **CGC:** 13 graded, best 9.6
The Sinister Shadow of Doomsday • reprints stories from X-Men #38 and Amazing Adult Fantasy #2

87 Apr 1974 Cover: 0.20 **NM** value: **25.00**
• **CGC:** 8 graded, best 9.4
The Fateful Finale • reprints stories from X-Men #39 and Amazing Adult Fantasy #10

88 Jun 1974 Cover: 0.25 **NM** value: **25.00**
• **CGC:** 8 graded, best 9.6
The Mark of the Monster • reprints X-Men #40; Has 1973 Statement; avg total paid 127,663

89 Aug 1974 Cover: 0.25 **NM** value: **25.00**
• **CGC:** 14 graded, best 9.8
Now Strikes the Sub-Human • reprints stories from X-Men #41 and Amazing Adult Fantasy #11

90 Oct 1974 Cover: 0.25 **NM** value: **25.00**
• **CGC:** 4 graded, best 9.8
If I Should Die • reprints stories from X-Men #42 and Amazing Adult Fantasy #7

91 Dec 1974 Cover: 0.25 **NM** value: **25.00**
• **CGC:** 7 graded, best 9.2
The Torch is Passed ... ! • reprints stories from X-Men #43 and Amazing Adult Fantasy #7

92 Feb 1975 Cover: 0.25 **NM** value: **25.00**
Circ: Statement: **119,231 • CGC:** 13 graded, best 9.4
Red Raven, Red Raven ...! • reprints stories from X-Men #44 and Mystery Tales #30

93 Apr 1975 Cover: 0.25 **NM** value: **25.00**
Circ: Statement: **119,231 • CGC:** 12 graded, best 9.6
When Mutants Clash • reprints stories from X-Men #45 and Journey Into Mystery #74

94 Aug 1975 Cover: 0.25 **NM** value: **525.00**
Circ: Statement: **119,231 • CGC:** 499 graded, best 9.6
• New X-Men begin (from Giant-Size X-Men #1). The Doomsday Scenario; Death O'er Valhalla High • Old X-Men leave **A:** Dave Cockrum; Bob McLeod **C:** Gil Kane ★ 1st Appearance of New X-Men.

95 Oct 1975 Cover: 0.25 **NM** value: **100.00**
Circ: Statement: **119,231 • CGC:** 181 graded, best 9.8
Warhunt **A:** Dave Cockrum **C:** Gil Kane ★ Death of Thunderbird.

96 Dec 1975 Cover: 0.25 **NM** value: **80.00**
Circ: Statement: **119,231 • CGC:** 147 graded, best 9.6
Night of the Demon **A:** Dave Cockrum ★ 1st Appearance of Moira MacTaggart.

97 Feb 1976 Cover: 0.25 **NM** value: **70.00**
Circ: Statement: **116,992 • CGC:** 108 graded, best 9.8
My Brother, My Enemy • Cyclops vs. Havok **A:** Dave Cockrum **C:** Rich Buckler ★ 1st Appearance of Lilandra Neramani.

98 Apr 1976 Cover: 0.25 **NM** value: **70.00**
Circ: Statement: **116,992 • CGC:** 91 graded, best 9.6
Merry Christmas, X-Men **A:** Dave Cockrum ★ Appearance of Nick Fury, Matt Murdock. ★ Versus Sentinels.

99 Jun 1976 Cover: 0.25 **NM** value: **70.00**
Circ: Statement: **116,992 • CGC:** 123 graded, best 9.8
Deathstar, Rising **A:** Dave Cockrum ★ 1st Appearance of Black Tom Cassidy.

100 Aug 1976 Cover: 0.25 **NM** value: **80.00**
Circ: Statement: **116,992 • CGC:** 192 graded, best 9.6
Greater Love Hath No X-Man • Old X-Men vs. New X-Men **A:** Dave Cockrum

101 Oct 1976 Cover: 0.30 **NM** value: **60.00**
Circ: Statement: **116,992 • CGC:** 135 graded, best 9.8
Like a Phoenix, From the Ashes **A:** Dave Cockrum ★ 1st Appearance of Phoenix II (Jean Grey), Phoenix. ★ Appearance of Juggernaut. ★ Death of Jean Grey.

102 Dec 1976 Cover: 0.30 **NM** value: **30.00**
Circ: Statement: **116,992 • CGC:** 83 graded, best 9.8
Who Will Stop the Juggernaut? **A:** Dave Cockrum ★ Origin of Storm. ★ Versus Juggernaut and Black Tom.

103 Feb 1977 Cover: 0.30 **NM** value: **30.00**
Circ: Statement: **123,725 • CGC:** 45 graded, best 9.8
The Fall of the Tower **A:** Dave Cockrum ★ Versus Black Tom. ★ Versus Juggernaut.

104 Apr 1977 Cover: 0.30 **NM** value: **30.00**
Circ: Statement: **123,725 • CGC:** 63 graded, best 9.8
The Gentleman's Name Is Magneto • Has 1976 Statement; avg total paid 116,992 **A:** Dave Cockrum ★ 1st Appearance of Starjammers (cameo), Muir Island. ★ Versus Magneto.

105 Jun 1977 Cover: 0.30 **NM** value: **30.00**
Circ: Statement: **123,725 • CGC:** 76 graded, best 9.8
Phoenix Unleashed **A:** Dave Cockrum ★ Appearance of Firelord.

106 Aug 1977 Cover: 0.30 **NM** value: **30.00**
Circ: Statement: **123,725 • CGC:** 64 graded, best 9.8
Dark Shroud of the Past **A:** Dave Cockrum ★ Appearance of Firelord.

107 Oct 1977 Cover: 0.30 **NM** value: **30.00**
Circ: Statement: **123,725 • CGC:** 44 graded, best 9.6
Where No X-Man Has Gone Before **A:** Dave Cockrum ★ 1st Appearance of Starjammers.

108 Dec 1977 Cover: 0.35 **NM** value: **55.00**
Circ: Statement: **123,725 • CGC:** 149 graded, best 9.8
Armageddon Now • 1st Byrne art on X-Men **A:** John Byrne; Terry Austin **C:** Dave Cockrum ★ Origin of Polaris. ★ Appearance of Fantastic Four.

109 Feb 1978 Cover: 0.35 **NM** value: **45.00**
Circ: Statement: **115,260 • CGC:** 114 graded, best 9.8
Home Are the Heroes **A:** John Byrne; Terry Austin **C:** Dave Cockrum ★ 1st Appearance of Weapon Alpha, Vindicator (Weapon Alpha).

110 Apr 1978 Cover: 0.35 **NM** value: **28.00**
Circ: Statement: **115,260 • CGC:** 85 graded, best 9.6
The 'X' Sanction • Has 1977 Statement; avg total paid 123,725 **A:** Dave Cockrum; Tony DeZuniga ★ Appearance of Warhawk.

111 Jun 1978 Cover: 0.35 **NM** value: **28.00**
Circ: Statement: **115,260 • CGC:** 63 graded, best 9.8
Mindgames **A:** John Byrne; Terry Austin **C:** Dave Cockrum ★ Appearance of Beast, Magneto. ★ Versus Mesmero.

112 Aug 1978 Cover: 0.35 **NM** value: **25.00**
Circ: Statement: **115,260 • CGC:** 66 graded, best 9.8
Magneto Triumphant **A:** John Byrne; Terry Austin **C:** George Pérez ★ Versus Magneto.

113 Sep 1978 Cover: 0.35 **NM** value: **25.00**
Circ: Statement: **115,260 • CGC:** 56 graded, best 9.9
Showdown **A:** John Byrne; Terry Austin ★ Versus Magneto.

114 Oct 1978 Cover: 0.35 **NM** value: **22.00**
Circ: Statement: **115,260 • CGC:** 60 graded, best 9.6
Desolation **A:** John Byrne; Terry Austin ★ Versus Sauron.

115 Nov 1978 Cover: 0.35 **NM** value: **22.00**
Circ: Statement: **115,260 • CGC:** 64 graded, best 9.6
Visions of Death **A:** John Byrne; Terry Austin ★ 1st Appearance of Nereel. ★ Appearance of Ka-Zar. ★ Versus Sauron.

116 Dec 1978 Cover: 0.35 **NM** value: **22.00**
Circ: Statement: **115,260 • CGC:** 65 graded, best 9.6
To Save the Savage Land **A:** John Byrne; Terry Austin ★ Appearance of Ka-Zar.

117 Jan 1979 Cover: 0.35 **NM** value: **22.00**
Circ: Statement: **171,091 • CGC:** 97 graded, best 9.8
Psi-War **A:** John Byrne; Ric Villamonte **C:** Dave Cockrum ★ Origin of Professor X.

118 Feb 1979 Cover: 0.35 **NM** value: **22.00**
Circ: Statement: **171,091 • CGC:** 113 graded, best 9.8
The Submergence of Japan **A:** John Byrne; Terry Austin **C:** Dave Cockrum ★ 1st Appearance of Mariko Yashida.

119 Mar 1979 Cover: 0.35 **NM** value: **22.00**
Circ: Statement: **171,091 • CGC:** 131 graded, best 9.8
Twas the Night Before Christmas **A:** John Byrne; Terry Austin **C:** Dave Cockrum ★ 1st Appearance of Proteus (voice only).

120 Apr 1979 Cover: 0.35 **NM** value: **40.00**
Circ: Statement: **171,091 • CGC:** 99 graded, best 9.6
Wanted: Wolverine – Dead or Alive **A:** John Byrne; Terry Austin ★ 1st Appearance of Aurora, Alpha Flight (cameo), Snowbird, Northstar, Sasquatch, Vindicator.

121 May 1979 Cover: 0.40 **NM** value: **40.00**
Circ: Statement: **171,091 • CGC:** 164 graded, best 9.8
Shoot-Out at the Stampede **A:** John Byrne; Terry Austin **C:** Dave Cockrum ★ 1st Appearance of Alpha Flight (full). ★ Appearance of Mastermind.

122 Jun 1979 Cover: 0.40 **NM** value: **22.00**
Circ: Statement: **171,091 • CGC:** 60 graded, best 9.6
Cry for the Children **A:** John Byrne; Terry Austin **C:** Dave Cockrum ★ 1st Appearance of Hellfire Club. ★ Versus Arcade.

123 Jul 1979 Cover: 0.40 **NM** value: **22.00**
Circ: Statement: **171,091 • CGC:** 66 graded, best 9.8
Listen-Stop Me If You've Heard It-But This One Will Kill You **A:** John Byrne **W:** Chris Claremont ★ Origin of Colossus. ★ Versus Arcade.

124 Aug 1979 Cover: 0.40 **NM** value: **22.00**
Circ: Statement: **171,091 • CGC:** 75 graded, best 9.8
He Only Laughs When I Hurt **A:** John Byrne **W:** John Byrne; Chris Claremont ★ Origin of Arcade. ★ Appearance of Arcade.

125 Sep 1979 Cover: 0.40 **NM** value: **22.00**
Circ: Statement: **171,091 • CGC:** 97 graded, best 9.8
Phoenix cover. There's Something Awful on Muir Island **A:** John Byrne **W:** Chris Claremont ★ 1st Appearance of Proteus (full appearance).

126 Oct 1979 Cover: 0.40 **NM** value: **22.00**
Circ: Statement: **171,091 • CGC:** 86 graded, best 9.8
How Sharper Than a Serpent's Tooth **A:** John Byrne **W:** Chris Claremont

127 Nov 1979 Cover: 0.40 **NM** value: **22.00**
Circ: Statement: **171,091 • CGC:** 88 graded, best 9.8
The Quality of Hatred **A:** John Byrne **W:** Chris Claremont

128 Dec 1979 Cover: 0.40 **NM** value: **22.00**
Circ: Statement: **171,091 • CGC:** 81 graded, best 9.8
The Action of the Tiger **A:** John Byrne **W:** Chris Claremont ★ Origin of Proteus. ★ Death of Proteus.

129 Jan 1980 Cover: 0.40 **NM** value: **28.00**
Circ: Statement: **191,927 • CGC:** 113 graded, best 9.8
God Spare the Child **A:** John Byrne; Terry Austin **W:** Chris Claremont ★ 1st Appearance of Donald Pierce (the White Bishop). ★ 1st Appearance of White Queen (Emma Frost), Kitty Pryde, Sprite II (Kitty Pryde).

130 Feb 1980 Cover: 0.40 **NM** value: **22.00**
Circ: Statement: **191,927 • CGC:** 119 graded, best 9.8
Dazzler **A:** John Byrne; Terry Austin **C:** John Romita Jr. **W:** Chris Claremont ★ 1st Appearance of Dazzler.

131 Mar 1980 Cover: 0.40 **NM** value: **18.00**
Circ: Statement: **191,927 • CGC:** 78 graded, best 9.8
Run For Your Life • Has 1979 Statement, filed 10/1/79; avg print run 327,387; avg sales 167,641; avg subs 3,450; avg total paid 171,091; office use 1,111; max existent 172,762; 47% of run returned **A:** John Byrne; Terry Austin **W:** Chris Claremont ★ Appearance of Angel, White Queen. ★ Appearance of Dazzler.

132 Apr 1980 Cover: 0.40 **NM** value: **18.00**
Circ: Statement: **191,927 • CGC:** 89 graded, best 9.8
And Hellfire is Their Name **A:** John Byrne; Terry Austin **W:** Chris Claremont ★ 1st Appearance of Hugh Hefner. ★ Appearance of Angel.

133 May 1980 Cover: 0.40 **NM** value: **18.00**
Circ: Statement: **191,927 • CGC:** 88 graded, best 9.8
Wolverine Alone **A:** John Byrne; Terry Austin **W:** Chris Claremont ★ 1st Appearance of Dark Phoenix, Senator Edward Kelly. ★ Appearance of Angel.

134 Jun 1980 Cover: 0.40 **NM** value: **18.00**

Other grades: Multiply prices above by **1.5 for Mint • 2/3 for Very Fine • 1/3 for Fine • 1/5 for Very Good • 1/8 for Good**

Circ: Statement: **191,927** • **CGC:** 97 graded, best 9.8
Too Late, the Heroes **A:** John Byrne; Terry Austin **W:** Chris Claremont ★ Appearance of Dark Phoenix.

135 ❑ Jul 1980 Cover: 0.40 **NM** value: **18.00**
Circ: Statement: **191,927** • **CGC:** 97 graded, best 9.8
Dark Phoenix **A:** John Byrne; Terry Austin **W:** Chris Claremont ★ Appearance of Dark Phoenix. ★ Appearance of Spider-Man.

136 ❑ Aug 1980 Cover: 0.40 **NM** value: **16.00**
Circ: Statement: **191,927** • **CGC:** 91 graded, best 9.8
Child of Light and Darkness **A:** John Byrne; Terry Austin **W:** Chris Claremont

137 ❑ Sep 1980 Cover: 0.75 **NM** value: **22.00**
Circ: Statement: **191,927** • **CGC:** 249 graded, best 9.9
• Giant-size. The Fate of the Phoenix **A:** John Byrne; Terry Austin **W:** Chris Claremont ★ 1st Appearance of Hussar. ★ Appearance of Angel. ★ Death of Phoenix II (Jean Grey).

138 ❑ Oct 1980 Cover: 0.50 **NM** value: **15.00**
Circ: Statement: **191,927** • **CGC:** 124 graded, best 9.8
Elegy **A:** John Byrne; Terry Austin **W:** Chris Claremont ★ Appearance of Angel.

139 ❑ Nov 1980 Cover: 0.50 **NM** value: **25.00**
Circ: Statement: **191,927** • **CGC:** 158 graded, best 9.8
... Something Wicked This Way Comes • Kitty Pryde joins X-Men; New costume for Wolverine **A:** John Byrne; Terry Austin **W:** Chris Claremont ★ 1st Appearance of Stevie Hunter.

140 ❑ Dec 1980 Cover: 0.50 **NM** value: **25.00**
Circ: Statement: **191,927** • **CGC:** 184 graded, best 9.8
Rage **A:** John Byrne; Terry Austin **W:** Chris Claremont ★ Appearance of Alpha Flight.

141 ❑ Jan 1981 Cover: 0.50 **NM** value: **26.00**
Circ: Statement: **259,007** • **CGC:** 208 graded, best 9.8
Days of Future Past • series continues as Uncanny X-Men **A:** John Byrne; Terry Austin **W:** Chris Claremont ★ 1st Appearance of Avalanche, Rachel Summers (Phoenix III), Pyro.

X-MEN (2ND SERIES) Marvel

In 1991, Marvel launched a "mutant genesis," completely transforming its many mutant superhero groups. The New Mutants would become X-Force, and The Uncanny X-Men would split into two teams, each featured in its own title.

This second X-Men series stars the new team consisting of Cyclops, Wolverine, Gambit, Psylocke, Rogue, and The Beast. Although the other X-Men still appear regularly, Marvel's idea was to concentrate this title on a smaller team in order to better craft storylines. With early issues drawn and plotted by Jim Lee, the series was extremely popular.

The first issue of this "adjectiveless" X-Men title was launched in a storm of publicity and sported five different covers. The product of creators Chris Claremont, Jim Lee, and Scott Williams, the issue had an estimated paid circulation of 7,100,000, making it the best-selling — and, if supply is the only important thing, least collectible — comic book of all time.

Marvel would give this series an adjective, "New," in 2001.

-1 ❑ Jul 1997 Cover: 1.99 **NM** value: **2.00**
• Flashback★ Origin of Magneto.

-1/A ❑ Jul 1997 Cover: 1.95 **NM** value: **2.50**
Variant cover: "Magneto's Rage, Xavier's HopeÖI had a Dream!".

1/A ❑ Oct 1991 Cover: 1.50 **NM** value: **3.00**
Circ: CapCity orders: **424,800** • **CGC:** 240 graded, best 9.9
Beast, Storm, etc. on cover. Rubicon **A:** Jim Lee **W:** Jim Lee; Chris Claremont

1/B ❑ Oct 1991 Cover: 1.50 **NM** value: **3.00**
Circ: CapCity orders: **342,600**
Colossus, Rogue, etc. on cover.. Rubicon **A:** Jim Lee **W:** Jim Lee; Chris Claremont

1/C ❑ Oct 1991 Cover: 1.50 **NM** value: **3.00**
Circ: CapCity orders: **365,600**
Cyclops, Wolverine, Iceman on cover. Rubicon **A:** Jim Lee **W:** Jim Lee; Chris Claremont

1/D ❑ Oct 1991 Cover: 1.50 **NM** value: **3.00**
Circ: CapCity orders: **332,800**
Magneto cover. Rubicon **A:** Jim Lee **W:** Jim Lee; Chris Claremont

1/E ❑ Oct 1991 Cover: 3.95 **NM** value: **5.00**
Circ: CapCity orders: **408,300** • **CGC:** 162 graded, best 9.9
gatefold cover. Rubicon **A:** Jim Lee **W:** Jim Lee; Chris Claremont

2 ❑ Nov 1991 Cover: 1.00 **NM** value: **3.00**
Circ: CapCity orders: **325,500** • **CGC:** 22 graded, best 9.9

3 ❑ Dec 1991 Cover: 1.00 **NM** value: **3.00**
Circ: CapCity orders: **244,800** • **CGC:** 6 graded, best 9.8

4 ❑ Jan 1992 Cover: 1.00 **NM** value: **3.00**
Circ: Statement: **967,808** CapCity orders: **212,400** • **CGC:** 4 graded, best 9.6

5 ❑ Feb 1992 Cover: 1.25 **NM** value: **3.00**
Circ: Statement: **967,808** CapCity orders: **184,500** • **CGC:** 4 graded, best 9.8

6 ❑ Mar 1992 Cover: 1.25 **NM** value: **3.00**
Circ: Statement: **967,808** CapCity orders: **162,600** • **CGC:** 3 graded, best 9.6

7 ❑ Apr 1992 Cover: 1.25 **NM** value: **3.00**
Circ: Statement: **967,808** CapCity orders: **150,600** • **CGC:** 3 graded, best 9.8

8 ❑ May 1992 Cover: 1.25 **NM** value: **3.00**
Circ: Statement: **967,808** CapCity orders: **156,301** • **CGC:** 3 graded, best 9.8

9 ❑ Jun 1992 Cover: 1.25 **NM** value: **3.00**
Circ: Statement: **967,808** CapCity orders: **169,500** • **CGC:** 2 graded, best 9.8

10 ❑ Jul 1992 Cover: 1.25 **NM** value: **3.00**
Circ: Statement: **967,808** CapCity orders: **150,600** • **CGC:** 2 graded, best 9.8

11 ❑ Aug 1992 Cover: 1.25 **NM** value: **3.00**
Circ: Statement: **967,808** CapCity orders: **159,900** • **CGC:** 2 graded, best 9.6

12 ❑ Sep 1992 Cover: 1.25 **NM** value: **3.00**
Circ: Statement: **967,808** CapCity orders: **145,200** • **CGC:** 1 graded, best 9.8

13 ❑ Oct 1992 Cover: 1.25 **NM** value: **3.00**
Circ: Statement: **967,808** CapCity orders: **146,100**

14/CS ❑ Nov 1992 Cover: 1.50 **NM** value: **3.00**
Circ: Statement: **967,808** CapCity orders: **198,900**
X-Cutioner's Song; X-Cutioner's Song, Part 3

15/CS ❑ Dec 1992 Cover: 1.50 **NM** value: **3.00**
Circ: Statement: **672,175** CapCity orders: **178,500**
X-Cutioner's Song, Part 7

16/CS ❑ Jan 1993 Cover: 1.50 **NM** value: **3.00**
Circ: Statement: **672,175** CapCity orders: **182,400**
X-Cutioner's Song, Part 11

17 ❑ Feb 1993 Cover: 1.25 **NM** value: **2.50**
Circ: Statement: **672,175** CapCity orders: **130,800**

18 ❑ Mar 1993 Cover: 1.25 **NM** value: **2.50**
Circ: Statement: **672,175** CapCity orders: **129,900**

19 ❑ Apr 1993 Cover: 1.25 **NM** value: **2.50**
Circ: Statement: **672,175** CapCity orders: **129,300**

20 ❑ May 1993 Cover: 1.25 **NM** value: **2.50**
Circ: Statement: **672,175** CapCity orders: **124,700**

21 ❑ Jun 1993 Cover: 1.25 **NM** value: **2.00**
Circ: Statement: **672,175** CapCity orders: **127,200**
The Puzzle Box **A:** Brandon Peterson **W:** Fabian Nicieza

22 ❑ Jul 1993 Cover: 1.25 **NM** value: **2.00**
Circ: Statement: **672,175** CapCity orders: **122,300**

23 ❑ Aug 1993 Cover: 1.25 **NM** value: **2.00**
Circ: Statement: **672,175** CapCity orders: **130,500**

24 ❑ Sep 1993 Cover: 1.25 **NM** value: **2.00**
Circ: Statement: **672,175** CapCity orders: **133,600**

25 ❑ Oct 1993 Cover: 3.50 **NM** value: **8.00**
Circ: Statement: **672,175** CapCity orders: **162,200** • **CGC:** 38 graded, best 9.9
Hologram on cover. • Wolverine loses adamantium skeleton **A:** Andy Kubert **W:** Fabian Nicieza ★ Appearance of Magneto.

25/GO ❑ Oct 1993 **NM** value: **25.00**
• **CGC:** 8 graded, best 9.8
Hologram on cover. • Gold limited edition. • Wolverine loses adamantium skeleton **A:** Andy Kubert **W:** Fabian Nicieza ★ Appearance of Magneto.

25/LE ❑ Oct 1993 **NM** value: **25.00**
• **CGC:** 11 graded, best 9.8
Black and white cover. • Wolverine loses adamantium skeleton **A:** Andy Kubert **W:** Fabian Nicieza ★ Appearance of Magneto.

26 ❑ Nov 1993 Cover: 1.25 **NM** value: **2.00**
Circ: Statement: **672,175** CapCity orders: **150,800**

27 ❑ Dec 1993 Cover: 1.25 **NM** value: **2.00**
Circ: Statement: **614,075** CapCity orders: **128,500**

28 ❑ Jan 1994 Cover: 1.25 **NM** value: **2.00**
Circ: Statement: **614,075** CapCity orders: **126,400** • **CGC:** 1 graded, best 8.5

29 ❑ Feb 1994 Cover: 1.25 **NM** value: **2.00**
Circ: Statement: **614,075** CapCity orders: **115,700**
• Has 1993 Statement, filed 10/1/93; avg print run 902,150; avg sales 651,850; avg subs 20,325; avg total paid 672,175; avg subs 125; office use 500; max existent 672,800; 25% of run returned

30 ❑ Mar 1994 Cover: 1.95 **NM** value: **4.00**
Circ: Statement: **614,075** CapCity orders: **145,750** • **CGC:** 5 graded, best 9.6
• Double-size. • Wedding of Jean Grey and Scott Summers

31 ❑ Apr 1994 Cover: 1.25 **NM** value: **1.75**
Circ: Statement: **614,075** CapCity orders: **104,550**

32 ❑ May 1994 Cover: 1.50 **NM** value: **1.75**
Circ: Statement: **614,075** CapCity orders: **102,650**

33 ❑ Jun 1994 Cover: 1.50 **NM** value: **1.75**
Circ: Statement: **614,075** CapCity orders: **107,750**

34 ❑ Jul 1994 Cover: 1.50 **NM** value: **1.75**
Circ: Statement: **614,075** CapCity orders: **109,200**

35 ❑ Aug 1994 Cover: 1.50 **NM** value: **1.75**
Circ: Statement: **614,075** CapCity orders: **108,650**
Sunset Grace

36 ❑ Sep 1994 Cover: 1.50 **NM** value: **1.75**
Generation Next, Part 2

36/SC ❑ Sep 1994 Cover: 2.95 **NM** value: **4.00**
Circ: Statement: **614,075** CapCity orders: **125,550** • **CGC:** 2 graded, best 9.8
foil cover. Generation Next, Part 2

37 ❑ Oct 1994 Cover: 1.50 **NM** value: **Cover or less**
Generation Next, Part 4

37/SC ❑ Oct 1994 Cover: 2.95 **NM** value: **4.00**
Circ: Statement: **332,889** CapCity orders: **106,800**
enhanced cover. Generation Next, Part 4

38 ❑ Nov 1994 Cover: 1.50 **NM** value: **Cover or less**

38/Dlx ❑ Nov 1994 Cover: 1.95 **NM** value: **2.00**
Circ: Statement: **332,889** CapCity orders: **105,050**
• Deluxe edition.

39 ❑ Dec 1994 Cover: 1.50 **NM** value: **Cover or less**

39/Dlx ❑ Dec 1994 Cover: 1.95 **NM** value: **2.00**
Circ: Statement: **332,889** CapCity orders: **94,850**
• Deluxe edition.

40 ❑ Jan 1995 Cover: 1.50 **NM** value: **Cover or less**

40/Dlx ❑ Jan 1995 Cover: 1.95 **NM** value: **2.00**
Circ: Statement: **332,889** CapCity orders: **95,575**
• Deluxe edition.

41 ❑ Feb 1995 Cover: 1.50 **NM** value: **Cover or less**

41/Dlx ❑ Feb 1995 Cover: 1.95 **NM** value: **2.00**
Circ: Statement: **332,889** CapCity orders: **123,550**
• Deluxe edition.

42 ❑ Jul 1995 Cover: 1.95 **NM** value: **2.00**
Circ: Statement: **332,889** CapCity orders: **89,350**
• Has 1994 Statement, filed 10/1/94; avg print run 800,625; avg sales 593,883; avg subs 20,192; avg total paid 614,075; samples 125; office use 500; max existent 614,700; 23% of run returned

43 ❑ Aug 1995 Cover: 1.95 **NM** value: **2.00**
Circ: Statement: **332,889** CapCity orders: **90,800**

44 ❑ Sep 1995 Cover: 1.95 **NM** value: **2.00**
Circ: Statement: **332,889**

45 ❑ Oct 1995 Cover: 3.95 **NM** value: **4.00**
Circ: Statement: **432,119** • **CGC:** 2 graded, best 9.6
enhanced wraparound gatefold cardstock cover.

46 ❑ Nov 1995 Cover: 1.95 **NM** value: **2.00**
Circ: Statement: **432,119**
• Return of X-Babies

47 ❑ Dec 1995 Cover: 1.95 **NM** value: **2.00**
Circ: Statement: **432,119**

48 ❑ Jan 1996 Cover: 1.95 **NM** value: **2.00**
Circ: Statement: **432,119**

49 ❑ Feb 1996 Cover: 1.95 **NM** value: **2.00**
Circ: Statement: **432,119**
• Has 1995 Statement, filed 10/1/95; avg print run 645,000; avg sales 318,096; avg subs 14,793; avg total paid 332,889; samples 750; office use 500; max existent 334,139; 48% of run returned

50 ❑ Mar 1996 Cover: 2.95 **NM** value: **3.00**
• **CGC:** 1 graded, best 8.0
wraparound cover. • Giant-size. Full Court Press **A:** Andy Kubert **W:** Scott Lobdell

50/SC ❑ Mar 1996 Cover: 3.95 **NM** value: **4.00**
Circ: Statement: **432,119** • **CGC:** 13 graded, best 9.9
foil cover. • Giant-size. Full Court Press **A:** Andy Kubert **W:** Scott Lobdell

51 ❑ Apr 1996 Cover: 1.95 **NM** value: **2.00**
Circ: Statement: **432,119**

52 ❑ May 1996 Cover: 1.95 **NM** value: **2.00**
Circ: Statement: **432,119**

53 ❑ Jun 1996 Cover: 1.95 **NM** value: **2.00**
Circ: Statement: **432,119** • **CGC:** 2 graded, best 9.8
• Jean Grey vs. Onslaught

54 ❑ Jul 1996 Cover: 1.95 **NM** value: **2.00**
Circ: Statement: **432,119** • **CGC:** 3 graded, best 9.8
• Identity of Onslaught revealed

55 ❑ Aug 1996 Cover: 1.95 **NM** value: **2.00**
Circ: Statement: **432,119**

56 ❑ Sep 1996 Cover: 1.95 **NM** value: **2.00**
Circ: Statement: **432,119**
Onslaught: Phase 2

57 ❑ Oct 1996 Cover: 1.95 **NM** value: **2.00**
Circ: Statement: **303,708**

58 ❑ Nov 1996 Cover: 1.95 **NM** value: **2.00**
Circ: Statement: **303,708** Direct Market orders: **203,250**
• Gambit vs. Magneto

59 ❑ Dec 1996 Cover: 1.95 **NM** value: **2.00**
Circ: Statement: **303,708** Direct Market orders: **202,000**

60 ❑ Jan 1997 Cover: 1.95 **NM** value: **2.00**
Circ: Statement: **303,708** Direct Market orders: **197,250** • **CGC:** 1 graded, best 8.5
Night • Has 1996 Statement, filed 10/1/96; avg print run 590,340; avg sales 417,246; avg subs 14,873; avg total paid 432,119; samples 600; office use 125; max existent 432,844; 27% of run returned **A:** Cedric Nocon **W:** Ralph Macchio; Scott Lobdell

61 ❑ Feb 1997 Cover: 1.95 **NM** value: **2.00**
Circ: Statement: **303,708** Direct Market orders: **187,750** • **CGC:** 2 graded, best 8.5
Bolt **W:** Scott Lobdell

62 ❑ Mar 1997 Cover: 1.95 **NM** value: **2.00**
Circ: Statement: **303,708** Direct Market orders: **196,250**
Games of Deceit & Death, Part 1 **A:** Carlos Pacheco **W:** Scott Lobdell; Ben Raab ★ Appearance of Shang-Chi.

62/A ❑ Mar 1997 Cover: 1.95 **NM** value: **2.00**
Circ: Statement: **303,708** • **CGC:** 2 graded, best 9.6
alternate cover. ★ Appearance of Shang-Chi.

63 ❑ Apr 1997 Cover: 1.95 **NM** value: **2.00**
Circ: Statement: **303,708** Direct Market orders: **171,250**
Games of Deceit & Death, Part 2 **A:** Carlos Pacheco **W:** Scott Lobdell ★ Appearance of Kingpin. ★ Appearance of Sebastian Shaw.

64 ❑ May 1997 Cover: 1.95 **NM** value: **2.00**
Circ: Statement: **303,708** Diamd. preorders: **172,821**

65 ❑ Jun 1997 Cover: 1.99 **NM** value: **2.00**
Circ: Statement: **303,708** Diamd. preorders: **177,827**
Operation: Zero Tolerance **A:** Carlos Pacheco **W:** Scott Lobdell

66 ❑ Aug 1997 Cover: 1.99 **NM** value: **2.00**
Circ: Statement: **303,708** Diamd. preorders: **169,677**
• gatefold summary. Operation Zero Tolerance

67 ❑ Sep 1997 Cover: 1.99 **NM** value: **2.00**
Circ: Statement: **303,708** Diamd. preorders: **162,450**
• gatefold summary. Operation Zero Tolerance

68 ❑ Oct 1997 Cover: 1.99 **NM** value: **2.00**
Circ: Diamd. preorders: **160,043**
• gatefold summary. Operation Zero Tolerance

69 ❑ Nov 1997 Cover: 1.99 **NM** value: **2.00**
Circ: Diamd. preorders: **162,599**
• gatefold summary.

70 ❑ Dec 1997 Cover: 2.99 **NM** value: **3.00**
Circ: Diamd. preorders: **166,928**
• gatefold summary. • Has 1997 Statement, filed 10/1/97; avg print run 488,400; avg sales 292,814; avg subs 10,894; avg total paid 303,708; samples 600; office use 125; max existent 304,433; 38% of run returned

71 ❑ Jan 1998 Cover: 1.99 **NM** value: **2.00**
Circ: Diamd. preorders: **155,399**
• gatefold summary. • Cyclops and Phoenix leaves team

72 ❑ Feb 1998 Cover: 1.99 **NM** value: **2.00**
Circ: Diamd. preorders: **151,533**
• gatefold summary.

73 ❑ Mar 1998 Cover: 1.99 **NM** value: **2.00**
Circ: Diamd. preorders: **148,638**
• gatefold summary.

74 ❑ Apr 1998 Cover: 1.99 **NM** value: **2.00**

CGC-graded: Multiply prices above by **33 for 9.9 M** • **16 for 9.8 NM/M** • **7 for 9.6 NM+** • **5 for 9.4 NM** • **2.5 for 9.2 NM-** • **1.5 for 9.0 VF/NM**

Circ: Diamd. preorders: **139,790**
• gatefold summary. ★ Appearance of Abomination.

75 ❑ May 1998 Cover: 2.99 **NM** value: **Cover or less**
Circ: Diamd. preorders: **146,013**
wraparound cover. • gatefold summary.

76 ❑ Jun 1998 Cover: 1.99 **NM** value: **2.00**
Circ: Diamd. preorders: **142,597**
• gatefold summary. ★ Origin of Maggot.

77 ❑ Jul 1998 Cover: 1.99 **NM** value: **2.00**
Circ: Diamd. preorders: **135,239**
• gatefold summary. 📖 Psi-War, Part 1

78 ❑ Aug 1998 Cover: 1.99 **NM** value: **2.00**
Circ: Diamd. preorders: **137,598**
• gatefold summary. 📖 Psi-War, Part 2

79 ❑ Sep 1998 Cover: 1.99 **NM** value: **2.00**
Circ: Diamd. preorders: **131,283**
• gatefold summary.

80 ❑ Oct 1998 Cover: 2.99 **NM** value: **3.00**
Circ: Statement: **200,070** • **CGC:** 1 graded, best 9.2
• double-sized.

81 ❑ Nov 1998 Cover: 1.99 **NM** value: **2.00**
Circ: Statement: **200,070** Diamd. preorders: **132,370**
• gatefold summary.

82 ❑ Dec 1998 Cover: 1.99 **NM** value: **2.00**
Circ: Statement: **200,070** Diamd. preorders: **133,181**
• gatefold summary. 📖 Hunt for Xavier, Part 2

83 ❑ Jan 1999 Cover: 1.99 **NM** value: **2.00**
Circ: Statement: **200,070** Diamd. preorders: **131,752**
• gatefold summary. 📖 Hunt for Xavier, Part 4

84 ❑ Feb 1999 Cover: 1.99 **NM** value: **2.00**
Circ: Statement: **200,070** Diamd. preorders: **131,202**
• gatefold summary. 📖 Hunt for Xavier, Part 6; The Hunt for Xavier **A:** Andy Kubert ★ Appearance of Nina.

85 ❑ Feb 1999 Cover: 1.99 **NM** value: **2.00**
Circ: Statement: **200,070** Diamd. preorders: **135,558**
📖 A Tale of Two Mutants **A:** Alan Davis; Mark Farmer(inks) **W:** Alan Davis; Joe Kelly ★ Appearance of Magneto.

85/Aut❑Feb 1999 **NM** value: **25.00**
📖 The Hunt for Xavier **A:** Alan Davis; Mark Farmer(inks) ★ Appearance of Magneto.

86 ❑ Mar 1999 Cover: 1.99 **NM** value: **Cover or less**
Circ: Statement: **200,070** Diamd. preorders: **136,483**
📖 The Magneto War, part 2 **A:** Alan Davis **W:** Alan Davis ★ Origin of Joseph. ★ Appearance of Astra, Joseph, Acolytes, Magneto.

87 ❑ Apr 1999 Cover: 1.99 **NM** value: **Cover or less**
Circ: Statement: **200,070** Diamd. preorders: **129,408**
cover says Apr. 📖 Magneto War; The Magneto War, part 4 • indicia says May **A:** Alan Davis **W:** Alan Davis ★ Appearance of Joseph, Magneto.

88 ❑ May 1999 Cover: 1.99 **NM** value: **Cover or less**
Circ: Statement: **200,070** Diamd. preorders: **128,424**

89 ❑ Jun 1999 Cover: 1.99 **NM** value: **Cover or less**
Circ: Statement: **200,070** Diamd. preorders: **128,685**

90 ❑ Jul 1999 Cover: 1.99 **NM** value: **Cover or less**
Circ: Statement: **200,070** Diamd. preorders: **124,648**

91 ❑ Aug 1999 Cover: 1.99 **NM** value: **Cover or less**
Circ: Statement: **200,070** Diamd. preorders: **123,280**

92 ❑ Sep 1999 Cover: 1.99 **NM** value: **Cover or less**
Circ: Statement: **200,070** Diamd. preorders: **120,285**

93 ❑ Oct 1999 Cover: 1.99 **NM** value: **Cover or less**
Circ: Diamd. preorders: **113,248**

94 ❑ Nov 1999 Cover: 1.99 **NM** value: **Cover or less**
Circ: Diamd. preorders: **108,543**

95 ❑ Dec 1999 Cover: 1.99 **NM** value: **Cover or less**
Circ: Diamd. preorders: **108,852** • **CGC:** 1 graded, best 9.2

96 ❑ Jan 2000 Cover: 1.99 **NM** value: **Cover or less**
Circ: Diamd. preorders: **106,841**

97 ❑ Feb 2000 **NM** value: **2.25**
Circ: Diamd. preorders: **117,490** • **CGC:** 1 graded, best 9.8

98 ❑ Mar 2000 **NM** value: **2.25**
Circ: Diamd. preorders: **109,675**

99 ❑ Apr 2000 **NM** value: **2.25**
Circ: Diamd. preorders: **104,695**

100/A❑May 2000 Cover: 2.99 **NM** value: **Cover or less**
Circ: Diamd. preorders: **144,877** • **CGC:** 1 graded, best 9.8
📖 End of Days • White background, team charging **A:** Leinil Francis Yu **W:** Chris Claremont

100/B❑May 2000 Cover: 2.99 **NM** value: **Cover or less**
• **CGC:** 6 graded, best 9.8
Nightcrawler vs. villain on cover. 📖 End of Days **A:** Leinil Francis Yu **W:** Chris Claremont

100/C❑May 2000 Cover: 2.99 **NM** value: **Cover or less**
• **CGC:** 4 graded, best 9.8
Nightcrawler, Wolverine, Colossus, Jean Gray, Storm on cover. 📖 End of Days **A:** Leinil Francis Yu **W:** Chris Claremont

100/D❑May 2000 Cover: 2.99 **NM** value: **Cover or less**
• **CGC:** 10 graded, best 9.6
Rogue vs. Villain on cover. 📖 End of Days **A:** Leinil Francis Yu **W:** Chris Claremont

101 ❑ Jun 2000 **NM** value: **2.25**
Circ: Diamd. preorders: **111,182**

102 ❑ Jul 2000 **NM** value: **2.25**
Circ: Diamd. preorders: **111,747**

103 ❑ Aug 2000 **NM** value: **2.25**
Circ: Diamd. preorders: **116,358**

104 ❑ Sep 2000 Cover: 2.25 **NM** value: **Cover or less**
Circ: Diamd. preorders: **113,872**
📖 Painted Ladies **A:** Leinil Francis Yu **W:** Chris Claremont

105 ❑ Oct 2000 Cover: 2.25 **NM** value: **Cover or less**
Circ: Statement: **153,544** Diamd. preorders: **106,815**

106 ❑ Nov 2000 Cover: 2.99 **NM** value: **Cover or less**
Circ: Statement: **153,544** Diamd. preorders: **109,353**
• double-sized. 📖 Search and Rescue, Part 1 **A:** Leinil Francis Yu **W:** Chris Claremont

107 ❑ Dec 2000 Cover: 2.25 **NM** value: **Cover or less**
Circ: Statement: **153,544** Diamd. preorders: **110,786**
📖 Maximum Security; On the Yard! **A:** Leinil Francis Yu **W:** Chris Claremont

108 ❑ Jan 2001 Cover: 2.25 **NM** value: **Cover or less**
Circ: Statement: **153,544** Diamd. preorders: **109,190** • **CGC:** 2 graded, best 9.6
📖 Dream's End, Part 4: The Future is Now! **A:** Leinil Francis Yu **W:** Chris Claremont

109 ❑ Feb 2001 Cover: 2.25 **NM** value: **Cover or less**
Circ: Statement: **153,544** Diamd. preorders: **104,643**

110 ❑ Mar 2001 Cover: 2.25 **NM** value: **Cover or less**
Circ: Statement: **153,544** Diamd. preorders: **100,963**

111 ❑ Apr 2001 Cover: 2.25 **NM** value: **Cover or less**
Circ: Statement: **153,544** Diamd. preorders: **99,712**
📖 Prelude to Destruction **A:** Leinil Francis Yu **W:** Scott Lobdell ★ Appearance of Magneto.

112 ❑ May 2001 Cover: 2.25 **NM** value: **Cover or less**
Circ: Statement: **153,544** Diamd. preorders: **100,353**

113 ❑ Jun 2001 Cover: 2.25 **NM** value: **Cover or less**
Circ: Statement: **153,544** Diamd. preorders: **103,633**

114 ❑ Jul 2001 Cover: 2.25 **NM** value: **Cover or less**
Circ: Statement: **153,544** • **CGC:** 55 graded, best 10.0

115 ❑ Aug 2001 Cover: 2.25 **NM** value: **Cover or less**
Circ: Statement: **153,544** • **CGC:** 3 graded, best 9.6

116 ❑ Sep 2001 Cover: 2.25 **NM** value: **Cover or less**
Circ: Statement: **153,544** • **CGC:** 5 graded, best 9.6

117 ❑ Oct 2001 Cover: 2.25 **NM** value: **Cover or less**
• **CGC:** 4 graded, best 9.8

118 ❑ Nov 2001 Cover: 2.25 **NM** value: **Cover or less**

119 ❑ Dec 2001 Cover: 2.25 **NM** value: **Cover or less**

120 ❑ Jan 2002 Cover: 2.25 **NM** value: **Cover or less**

121 ❑ Feb 2002 Cover: 2.25 **NM** value: **Cover or less**
• Has 2001 Statement, filed 10/1/01; avg print run 212,108; avg sales 144,620; avg subs 8,924; avg total paid 153,544; samples 600; max existent 154,144; 27% of run returned

Anl 1❑ca. 1992 Cover: 2.25 **NM** value: **3.00**
Circ: CapCity orders: **117,400**
📖 Scattershot, Part 1 **A:** Jim **W:** Fabian Nicieza

Anl 2❑ca. 1993 Cover: 2.95 **NM** value: **3.00**
Circ: CapCity orders: **78,725**
• Polybagged **A:** Aron Wiesenfeld **W:** Fabian Nicieza ★ 1st Appearance of Empyrean.

Anl 3❑ca. 1994 Cover: 2.95 **NM** value: **Cover or less**
Circ: CapCity orders: **57,350**

Anl 1995❑Oct 1995 Cover: 3.95 **NM** value: **Cover or less**

Anl 1996❑Nov 1996 Cover: 2.99 **NM** value: **Cover or less**
Circ: Direct Market orders: **141,250**
No issue number. wraparound cover.

Anl 1997❑ca. 1997 Cover: 2.99 **NM** value: **Cover or less**
No issue number. wraparound cover. 📖 Not a Cloud in the Sky **A:** Steve Epting **W:** John Francis Moore

Anl 1998❑ca. 1998 Cover: 2.99 **NM** value: **Cover or less**
No issue number. wraparound cover. • X-Men/Doctor Doom '98

Anl 1999❑Aug 1999 Cover: 3.50 **NM** value: **Cover or less**
Circ: Diamd. preorders: **87,433**

Anl 2001❑ Cover: 3.50 **NM** value: **Cover or less**
• **CGC:** 10 graded, best 9.8
• 2001 Annual

Ash 1❑ Cover: 0.75 **NM** value: **Cover or less**
• **CGC:** 1 graded, best 9.6
• ashcan edition. **W:** Bob Harras

Bk 1❑ Cover: 6.95 **NM** value: **Cover or less**
• X-Men & Ghost Rider: Brood Trouble In The Big Easy

X-MEN ADVENTURES (VOL. 1) Marvel

1 ❑ Nov 1992 Cover: 1.25 **NM** value: **3.00**
Circ: CapCity orders: **103,800**
📖 Night of the Sentinels **A:** Andrew Wildman **W:** Ralph Macchio

2 ❑ Dec 1992 Cover: 1.25 **NM** value: **2.00**
Circ: CapCity orders: **57,900**

3 ❑ Jan 1993 Cover: 1.25 **NM** value: **2.00**
Circ: CapCity orders: **51,000**

4 ❑ Feb 1993 Cover: 1.25 **NM** value: **2.00**
Circ: CapCity orders: **37,800**

5 ❑ Mar 1993 Cover: 1.25 **NM** value: **2.00**
Circ: CapCity orders: **32,700**

6 ❑ Apr 1993 Cover: 1.25 **NM** value: **2.00**
Circ: CapCity orders: **35,400**

7 ❑ May 1993 Cover: 1.25 **NM** value: **2.00**
Circ: CapCity orders: **31,600**

8 ❑ Jun 1993 Cover: 1.25 **NM** value: **2.00**
Circ: CapCity orders: **31,700**

9 ❑ Jul 1993 Cover: 1.25 **NM** value: **2.00**
Circ: CapCity orders: **33,800**

10 ❑ Aug 1993 Cover: 1.25 **NM** value: **2.00**
Circ: CapCity orders: **36,800**

11 ❑ Sep 1993 Cover: 1.25 **NM** value: **1.50**
Circ: CapCity orders: **34,700**

12 ❑ Oct 1993 Cover: 1.25 **NM** value: **1.50**
Circ: CapCity orders: **32,000**

13 ❑ Nov 1993 Cover: 1.25 **NM** value: **1.50**
Circ: CapCity orders: **32,200**

14 ❑ Dec 1993 Cover: 1.25 **NM** value: **1.50**
Circ: CapCity orders: **33,100**

15 ❑ Jan 1994 Cover: 1.75 **NM** value: **Cover or less**
Circ: Statement: **118,525** CapCity orders: **28,600**

Bk 1❑ Cover: 4.95 **NM** value: **Cover or less**
• collects X-Men Adventures #1-4

Bk 2❑ May 1994 Cover: 4.95 **NM** value: **Cover or less**
• Captive Hearts, Slave Island; collects #5-8

Bk 3❑ Oct 1994 Cover: 5.95 **NM** value: **Cover or less**
• The Irrestible Force, The Muir Island Saga; collects #9-12 (adapts first-season episodes)

Bk 4❑ Jul 1995 Cover: 6.95 **NM** value: **Cover or less**
• Days Of Future Past, Final Conflict; collects #13-15 (adapts first season episodes)

X-MEN ADVENTURES (VOL. 2) Marvel

1 ❑ Feb 1994 Cover: 1.25 **NM** value: **2.00**
Circ: Statement: **118,525** CapCity orders: **43,100**

2 ❑ Mar 1994 Cover: 1.25 **NM** value: **Cover or less**
Circ: Statement: **118,525** CapCity orders: **26,850**

3 ❑ Apr 1994 Cover: 1.25 **NM** value: **Cover or less**
Circ: Statement: **118,525** CapCity orders: **24,650**

4 ❑ May 1994 Cover: 1.25 **NM** value: **3.00**
Circ: Statement: **118,525** CapCity orders: **24,350**
• Marvel Mart insert

5 ❑ Jun 1994 Cover: 1.25 **NM** value: **Cover or less**
Circ: Statement: **118,525**

6 ❑ Jul 1994 Cover: 1.25 **NM** value: **Cover or less**
Circ: Statement: **118,525**

7 ❑ Aug 1994 Cover: 1.25 **NM** value: **Cover or less**
Circ: Statement: **118,525**
📖 Time Fugitives, Part 1

8 ❑ Sep 1994 Cover: 1.25 **NM** value: **Cover or less**
Circ: Statement: **118,525**
📖 Time Fugitives, Part 2

9 ❑ Oct 1994 Cover: 1.50 **NM** value: **Cover or less**
Circ: Statement: **118,525**

10 ❑ Nov 1994 Cover: 1.50 **NM** value: **Cover or less**
Circ: Statement: **118,525**

11 ❑ Dec 1994 Cover: 1.50 **NM** value: **Cover or less**
Circ: Statement: **72,907**

12 ❑ Jan 1995 Cover: 1.50 **NM** value: **Cover or less**
Circ: Statement: **72,907**

13 ❑ Feb 1995 Cover: 1.50 **NM** value: **Cover or less**
Circ: Statement: **72,907**

X-MEN ADVENTURES (VOL. 3) Marvel

1 ❑ Mar 1995 Cover: 1.50 **NM** value: **2.00**
Circ: Statement: **72,907**
• Has 1994 Statement, filed 10/1/94; avg print run 207,642; avg sales 117,217; avg subs 1,308; avg total paid 118,525; samples 125; office use 500; max existent 119,150; 43% of run returned ★ Origin of Lady Deathstrike.

2 ❑ Apr 1995 Cover: 1.50 **NM** value: **Cover or less**
Circ: Statement: **72,907** CapCity orders: **10,175**

3 ❑ May 1995 Cover: 1.50 **NM** value: **Cover or less**
Circ: Statement: **72,907** CapCity orders: **9,125**

4 ❑ Jun 1995 Cover: 1.50 **NM** value: **Cover or less**
Circ: Statement: **72,907** CapCity orders: **8,950**

5 ❑ Jul 1995 Cover: 1.50 **NM** value: **Cover or less**
Circ: Statement: **72,907** CapCity orders: **8,925**

6 ❑ Aug 1995 Cover: 1.50 **NM** value: **Cover or less**
Circ: Statement: **72,907** CapCity orders: **8,025**

7 ❑ Sep 1995 Cover: 1.50 **NM** value: **Cover or less**
Circ: Statement: **72,907**

8 ❑ Oct 1995 Cover: 1.50 **NM** value: **Cover or less**
Circ: Statement: **66,165**

9 ❑ Nov 1995 Cover: 1.50 **NM** value: **Cover or less**
Circ: Statement: **66,165**

10 ❑ Dec 1995 Cover: 1.50 **NM** value: **Cover or less**
Circ: Statement: **66,165**
📖 The Dark Phoenix Saga **A:** Ben Herrera **W:** Ralph Macchio ★ Appearance of Dazzler, Hellfire Club, Jason Wyngarde.

11 ❑ Jan 1996 Cover: 1.50 **NM** value: **Cover or less**
Circ: Statement: **66,165**
• Has 1995 Statement, filed 10/1/95; avg print run 144,127; avg sales 70,141; avg subs 2,766; avg total paid 72,907; samples 750; office use 500; max existent 74,157; 49% of run returned

12 ❑ Feb 1996 Cover: 1.50 **NM** value: **Cover or less**
Circ: Statement: **66,165**

13 ❑ Mar 1996 Cover: 1.50 **NM** value: **Cover or less**
Circ: Statement: **66,165**
📖 Crime and Punishment: The Final Fate of Phoenix **A:** Mike Miller; Ben Herrera **W:** Ralph Macchio

X-MEN ALPHA Marvel

1 ❑ Feb 1995 Cover: 3.95 **NM** value: **6.00**
Circ: CapCity orders: **127,225** • **CGC:** 42 graded, best 10.0
One-shot. enhanced cover. ★ 1st Appearance of X-Men (Age of Apocalypse).

1/GO❑ **NM** value: **20.00**
• **CGC:** 7 graded, best 9.8
• Gold edition. ★ 1st Appearance of X-Men (Age of Apocalypse).

X-MEN/ALPHA FLIGHT Marvel

1 ❑ Dec 1985 Cover: 1.50 **NM** value: **4.00**
Circ: CapCity orders: **51,800**

2 ❑ Feb 1986 Cover: 1.50 **NM** value: **4.00**
Circ: CapCity orders: **44,600**

X-MEN/ALPHA FLIGHT (2ND SERIES) Marvel

1 ❑ May 1998 Cover: 2.99 **NM** value: **Cover or less**
Circ: Diamd. preorders: **65,290**
📖 Survivors **A:** John Cassaday **W:** John Cassaday; Ben Raab

2 ❑ Jun 1998 Cover: 2.99 **NM** value: **Cover or less**
Circ: Diamd. preorders: **59,742**

X-MEN/ALPHA FLIGHT: THE GIFT Marvel

1 ❑ May 1998 Cover: 3.99 **NM** value: **Cover or less**
No issue number.

X-MEN & THE MICRONAUTS Marvel

1 ❑ Jan 1984 Cover: 0.60 **NM** value: **2.50**
• Limited Series **A:** Jackson Guice **W:** Bill Mantlo; Chris Claremont

2 ❑ Feb 1984 Cover: 0.60 **NM** value: **2.50**

3 ❑ Mar 1984 Cover: 0.60 **NM** value: **2.50**

4 ❑ Apr 1984 Cover: 0.60 **NM** value: **2.50**

X-MEN ANIMATION SPECIAL: THE PRYDE OF THE X-MEN Marvel

1 ❑ Cover: 10.95 **NM** value: **Cover or less**
Circ: CapCity orders: **7,650**

Other grades: Multiply prices above by **1.5 for Mint • 2/3 for Very Fine • 1/3 for Fine • 1/5 for Very Good • 1/8 for Good**

X-MEN ANNIVERSARY MAGAZINE **Marvel**

1 ❑ Sep 1993 Cover: 3.95 **NM** value: **Cover or less**
• Celebrates 30th anniversary of the X-Men. 📖 Bring Me the Head of Bob Harras; Let There be X-Men; X-Trapolations; X-Men Avengers Crossover; X-Men 2099; X-Men Second Season; Where Are they Now? **W:** Anya Martin; Len Wein; Paula Foye; Roy Thomas; Stan Lee; Chris Claremont; Jaye Gardner; Stephen Vrattos; Steve Saffel

X-MEN ARCHIVES **Marvel**

1 ❑ Jan 1995 Cover: 2.25 **NM** value: **2.50**
cardstock cover. 📖 Legion • Reprints New Mutants #26 **A:** Bill Sienkiewicz **W:** Chris Claremont

2 ❑ Jan 1995 Cover: 2.25 **NM** value: **2.50**
cardstock cover. • Reprints New Mutants #27 **A:** Bill Sienkiewicz **W:** Chris Claremont

3 ❑ Jan 1995 Cover: 2.25 **NM** value: **2.50**
cardstock cover. 📖 Soul War • Reprints New Mutants #28 **A:** Bill Sienkiewicz **W:** Chris Claremont

4 ❑ Jan 1995 Cover: 2.25 **NM** value: **2.50**
cardstock cover. 📖 Gold Rush • Reprints Uncanny X-Men #161 **A:** Dave Cockrum **W:** Chris Claremont

X-MEN ARCHIVES FEATURING CAPTAIN BRITAIN **Marvel**

1 ❑ Jul 1995 Cover: 2.95 **NM** value: **Cover or less**
wraparound cover. • reprints Captain Britain stories from British Marvel Super Heroes #377-383 **A:** Alan Davis **W:** Alan Moore

2 ❑ Aug 1995 Cover: 2.95 **NM** value: **Cover or less**
• reprints Captain Britain stories from British Marvel Super Heroes #384-88 and The Daredevils #1 **A:** Alan Davis **W:** Alan Moore

3 ❑ Sep 1995 Cover: 2.95 **NM** value: **Cover or less**
• reprints stories from The Daredevils #2-5 **A:** Alan Davis **W:** Alan Moore

4 ❑ Oct 1995 Cover: 2.95 **NM** value: **Cover or less**
• reprints stories from The Daredevils #6-8 **A:** Alan Davis **W:** Alan Moore

5 ❑ Nov 1995 Cover: 2.95 **NM** value: **Cover or less**
• reprints stories from The Daredevils #9-11 **A:** Alan Davis **W:** Alan Moore

6 ❑ Dec 1995 Cover: 2.95 **NM** value: **Cover or less**
• reprints stories from The Mighty World of Marvel #7-10 **A:** Alan Davis **W:** Alan Moore

7 ❑ Jan 1996 Cover: 2.95 **NM** value: **Cover or less**
final issue. • reprints stories from The Mighty World of Marvel #11-13 **A:** Alan Davis **W:** Alan Moore

X-MEN ARCHIVES SKETCHBOOK **Marvel**

1 ❑ Dec 2000 Cover: 2.99 **NM** value: **Cover or less**
• character sketches

X-MEN AT THE STATE FAIR **Marvel**

1 ❑ **NM** value: **2.00**
• **CGC:** 15 graded, best 9.8
• Dallas Times-Herald

X-MEN: BOOKS OF THE ASKANI **Marvel**

1 ❑ Cover: 2.95 **NM** value: **Cover or less**
• **CGC:** 2 graded, best 9.8
wraparound cardstock cover. • background info on Askani'son **A:** John Bolton; Bill Sienkiewicz; Larry Stroman; Doug Alexander; Trace Drury **W:** Scott Lobdell

X-MEN: CHILDREN OF THE ATOM **Marvel**

1 ❑ Nov 1999 Cover: 2.99 **NM** value: **Cover or less**
Circ: Diamd. preorders: **64,848**
cardstock cover. 📖 Childhood's End • prequel to X-Men (first series) #1 **A:** Steve Rude **W:** Joe Casey

2 ❑ Dec 1999 Cover: 2.99 **NM** value: **Cover or less**
Circ: Diamd. preorders: **58,011**
cardstock cover. 📖 All Children Wear the Sign • prequel to X-Men (first series) #1 **A:** Steve Rude **W:** Joe Casey

3 ❑ ca. 2000 Cover: 2.99 **NM** value: **Cover or less**
Circ: Diamd. preorders: **53,614**
cardstock cover. • prequel to X-Men (first series) #1

4 ❑ Jul 2000 Cover: 2.99 **NM** value: **Cover or less**
Circ: Diamd. preorders: **55,997**
cardstock cover. 📖 Child's Play • prequel to X-Men (first series) #1 **A:** Michael Ryan; Paul Smith **W:** Joe Casey

5 ❑ Aug 2000 Cover: 2.99 **NM** value: **Cover or less**
Circ: Diamd. preorders: **45,857**
cardstock cover. 📖 Where Your Children Are • prequel to X-Men (first series) #1 **A:** Essad Ribic **W:** Joe Casey

6 ❑ Sep 2000 Cover: 2.99 **NM** value: **Cover or less**
Circ: Diamd. preorders: **40,745**
cardstock cover. 📖 The Great Cathedral Space • prequel to X-Men (first series) #1 **A:** Essad Ribic **W:** Joe Casey

X-MEN CHROMIUM CLASSICS: DAYS OF FUTURE PAST **Marvel**

1 ❑ Cover: 13.50 **NM** value: **Cover or less**

X-MEN CHROMIUM CLASSICS: DEATH OF THE PHOENIX **Marvel**

1 ❑ Cover: 13.50 **NM** value: **Cover or less**
1/A ❑ Cover: 29.99 **NM** value: **Cover or less**

X-MEN CHROMIUM CLASSICS: ORIGIN OF THE X-MEN **Marvel**

1 ❑ Cover: 13.50 **NM** value: **Cover or less**

X-MEN CHRONICLES (MARVEL) **Marvel**

1 ❑ Mar 1995 Cover: 3.95 **NM** value: **Cover or less**
Circ: CapCity orders: **79,225**
📖 Origins • Age of Apocalypse **A:** Terry Dodson **W:** Howard Mackie

2 ❑ Jun 1995 Cover: 3.95 **NM** value: **Cover or less**
Circ: CapCity orders: **82,950**
• Age of Apocalypse

X-MEN: CLANDESTINE **Marvel**

1 ❑ Oct 1996 Cover: 2.95 **NM** value: **Cover or less**
wraparound cover. **A:** Alan Davis **W:** Alan Davis

2 ❑ Nov 1996 Cover: 2.95 **NM** value: **Cover or less**
wraparound cover. 📖 The Destine's Darkest Dreams **A:** Alan Davis **W:** Alan Davis

X-MEN CLASSIC **Marvel**

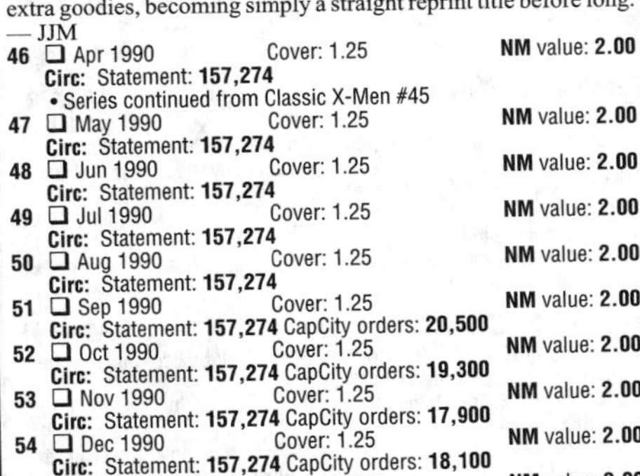

Here's one comic-book name change that can be correctly called "crassly commercial." Classic X-Men had been running along nicely for nearly four years, reprinting wonderful X-Men stories by Chris Claremont, Dave Cockrum, and John Byrne, up to and including the Dark Phoenix saga. A marvelous bonus in that series was new back-up stories by Claremont and John Bolton which fit into the continuity of the issues being re-presented.

Then Marvel's marketers realized that, with many of the retailers in the country racking titles alphabetically, Classic X-Men wound up way down near Conan — not the place to do big X-sales. Hence, a flip-flop.

While the stories X-Men Classic reprinted were still among the best Marvel had to offer, later issues included fewer and fewer extra goodies, becoming simply a straight reprint title before long. — JJM

46 ❑ Apr 1990 Cover: 1.25 **NM** value: **2.00**
Circ: Statement: **157,274**
• Series continued from Classic X-Men #45

47 ❑ May 1990 Cover: 1.25 **NM** value: **2.00**
Circ: Statement: **157,274**

48 ❑ Jun 1990 Cover: 1.25 **NM** value: **2.00**
Circ: Statement: **157,274**

49 ❑ Jul 1990 Cover: 1.25 **NM** value: **2.00**
Circ: Statement: **157,274**

50 ❑ Aug 1990 Cover: 1.25 **NM** value: **2.00**
Circ: Statement: **157,274**

51 ❑ Sep 1990 Cover: 1.25 **NM** value: **2.00**
Circ: Statement: **157,274** CapCity orders: **20,500**

52 ❑ Oct 1990 Cover: 1.25 **NM** value: **2.00**
Circ: Statement: **157,274** CapCity orders: **19,300**

53 ❑ Nov 1990 Cover: 1.25 **NM** value: **2.00**
Circ: Statement: **157,274** CapCity orders: **17,900**

54 ❑ Dec 1990 Cover: 1.25 **NM** value: **2.00**
Circ: Statement: **157,274** CapCity orders: **18,100**

55 ❑ Jan 1991 Cover: 1.25 **NM** value: **2.00**
Circ: CapCity orders: **17,400**

56 ❑ Feb 1991 Cover: 1.25 **NM** value: **2.00**
Circ: CapCity orders: **16,400**

57 ❑ Mar 1991 Cover: 1.25 **NM** value: **2.00**
Circ: CapCity orders: **16,200**

58 ❑ Apr 1991 Cover: 1.25 **NM** value: **2.00**
Circ: CapCity orders: **15,300**

59 ❑ May 1991 Cover: 1.25 **NM** value: **2.00**
Circ: CapCity orders: **15,800**

60 ❑ Jun 1991 Cover: 1.25 **NM** value: **2.00**
Circ: CapCity orders: **15,500**

61 ❑ Jul 1991 Cover: 1.25 **NM** value: **2.00**
Circ: CapCity orders: **15,600**

62 ❑ Aug 1991 Cover: 1.25 **NM** value: **1.75**
Circ: CapCity orders: **15,900**

63 ❑ Sep 1991 Cover: 1.25 **NM** value: **1.75**
Circ: CapCity orders: **16,100**

64 ❑ Oct 1991 Cover: 1.25 **NM** value: **1.75**
Circ: CapCity orders: **15,700**

65 ❑ Nov 1991 Cover: 1.25 **NM** value: **1.75**
Circ: CapCity orders: **15,100**

66 ❑ Dec 1991 Cover: 1.25 **NM** value: **1.75**
Circ: CapCity orders: **16,100**

67 ❑ Jan 1992 Cover: 1.25 **NM** value: **1.75**
Circ: Statement: **169,192** CapCity orders: **15,400**

68 ❑ Feb 1992 Cover: 1.25 **NM** value: **1.75**
Circ: Statement: **169,192** CapCity orders: **14,200**

69 ❑ Mar 1992 Cover: 1.25 **NM** value: **1.75**
Circ: Statement: **169,192** CapCity orders: **13,700**

70 ❑ Apr 1992 Cover: 1.75 **NM** value: **Cover or less**
Circ: Statement: **169,192** CapCity orders: **12,700**
• Giant-size.

71 ❑ May 1992 Cover: 1.25 **NM** value: **1.50**
Circ: Statement: **169,192** CapCity orders: **13,400**

72 ❑ Jun 1992 Cover: 1.25 **NM** value: **1.50**
Circ: Statement: **169,192** CapCity orders: **13,900**

73 ❑ Jul 1992 Cover: 1.25 **NM** value: **1.50**
Circ: Statement: **169,192** CapCity orders: **13,300**

74 ❑ Aug 1992 Cover: 1.25 **NM** value: **1.50**
Circ: Statement: **169,192** CapCity orders: **13,900**

75 ❑ Sep 1992 Cover: 1.25 **NM** value: **1.50**
Circ: Statement: **169,192** CapCity orders: **12,800**

76 ❑ Oct 1992 Cover: 1.25 **NM** value: **1.50**
Circ: Statement: **169,192** CapCity orders: **12,800**

77 ❑ Nov 1992 Cover: 1.25 **NM** value: **1.50**
Circ: Statement: **169,192** CapCity orders: **11,700**

78 ❑ Dec 1992 Cover: 1.25 **NM** value: **1.50**
Circ: Statement: **169,192** CapCity orders: **11,600**

79 ❑ Jan 1993 Cover: 1.75 **NM** value: **Cover or less**
Circ: Statement: **145,392** CapCity orders: **11,500**

80 ❑ Feb 1993 Cover: 1.25 **NM** value: **1.50**
Circ: Statement: **145,392** CapCity orders: **11,500**
📖 Decisions • Reprints Uncanny X-Men #176 **A:** John Romita Jr. **W:** Chris Claremont ★ 1st Appearance of Valerie Cooper.

81 ❑ Mar 1993 Cover: 1.25 **NM** value: **1.50**
Circ: Statement: **145,392** CapCity orders: **11,000**
📖 Sanction • Reprints Uncanny X-Men #177; Has 1992 Statement, filed 10/1/92; avg print run 339,384; avg sales 166,384; avg subs 2,808; avg total paid 169,192; samples 500; max existent 169,692 **A:** John Romita Jr. **W:** Chris Claremont

82 ❑ Apr 1993 Cover: 1.25 **NM** value: **1.50**
Circ: Statement: **145,392** CapCity orders: **12,100**
📖 Hell Hath No Fury… • Reprints Uncanny X-Men #178 **A:** John Romita Jr. **W:** Chris Claremont

83 ❑ May 1993 Cover: 1.25 **NM** value: **1.50**
Circ: Statement: **145,392** CapCity orders: **12,000**
📖 What Happened to Kitty • Reprints Uncanny X-Men #179 **A:** John Romita Jr. **W:** Chris Claremont

84 ❑ Jun 1993 Cover: 1.25 **NM** value: **1.50**
Circ: Statement: **145,392** CapCity orders: **12,700**
📖 Whose Life is it, Anyway? • Reprints Uncanny X-Men #180 **A:** John Romita Jr. **W:** Chris Claremont

85 ❑ Jul 1993 Cover: 1.25 **NM** value: **1.50**
Circ: Statement: **145,392** CapCity orders: **13,300**
📖 Tokyo Story • Reprints Uncanny X-Men #181 **A:** John Romita Jr. **W:** Chris Claremont

86 ❑ Aug 1993 Cover: 1.25 **NM** value: **1.50**
Circ: Statement: **145,392** CapCity orders: **13,700**
📖 Madness • Reprints Uncanny X-Men #182 **A:** John Romita Jr. **W:** Chris Claremont

87 ❑ Sep 1993 Cover: 1.25 **NM** value: **1.50**
Circ: Statement: **145,392** CapCity orders: **13,500**
📖 He'll Never Make Me Cry • Reprints Uncanny X-Men #183 **A:** John Romita Jr. **W:** Chris Claremont

88 ❑ Oct 1993 Cover: 1.25 **NM** value: **1.50**
Circ: Statement: **145,392** CapCity orders: **13,200**
📖 The Past…of Future Days • Reprints Uncanny X-Men #184 **A:** John Romita Jr. **W:** Chris Claremont ★ 1st Appearance of Forge. ★ Appearance of Rachel, Selene.

89 ❑ Nov 1993 Cover: 1.25 **NM** value: **1.50**
Circ: Statement: **145,392** CapCity orders: **13,550**
📖 Public Enemy • Reprints Uncanny X-Men #185; Storm loses powers **A:** John Romita Jr. **W:** Chris Claremont

90 ❑ Dec 1993 Cover: 1.75 **NM** value: **Cover or less**
Circ: Statement: **83,175** CapCity orders: **14,400**
• double-sized. 📖 Lifedeath • Reprints Uncanny X-Men #186 **A:** Barry Windsor-Smith **W:** Chris Claremont

91 ❑ Jan 1994 Cover: 1.25 **NM** value: **1.50**
Circ: Statement: **83,175** CapCity orders: **12,900**
📖 Wraithkill • Reprints Uncanny X-Men #187 **A:** John Romita Jr. **W:** Chris Claremont

92 ❑ Feb 1994 Cover: 1.25 **NM** value: **1.50**
Circ: Statement: **83,175** CapCity orders: **12,350**
📖 Legacy of the Lost • Reprints Uncanny X-Men #188 **A:** John Romita Jr. **W:** Chris Claremont

93 ❑ Mar 1994 Cover: 1.25 **NM** value: **1.50**
Circ: Statement: **83,175** CapCity orders: **11,300**
📖 Two Girls Out to Have Fun • reprints Uncanny X-Men #189 **A:** John Romita Jr. **W:** Chris Claremont

94 ❑ Apr 1994 Cover: 1.25 **NM** value: **1.50**
Circ: Statement: **83,175** CapCity orders: **10,550**
📖 An Age Undreamed Of • Reprints Uncanny X-Men #190 **A:** John Romita Jr. **W:** Chris Claremont ★ Appearance of Spider-Man, Avengers.

95 ❑ May 1994 Cover: 1.25 **NM** value: **1.50**
Circ: Statement: **83,175** CapCity orders: **10,750**
📖 Raiders of the Lost Temple • Reprints Uncanny X-Men #191 **A:** John Romita Jr. **W:** Chris Claremont ★ Appearance of Spider-Man, Avengers.

96 ❑ Jun 1994 Cover: 1.25 **NM** value: **1.50**
Circ: Statement: **83,175** CapCity orders: **10,750**
📖 Fun'n'Games • Reprints Uncanny X-Men #192 **A:** John Romita Jr. **W:** Chris Claremont

97 ❑ Jul 1994 Cover: 1.75 **NM** value: **Cover or less**
Circ: Statement: **83,175** CapCity orders: **11,050**
• double-sized. 📖 Warhunt 2 • giant; Reprints Uncanny X-Men #193; 100th New X-Men **A:** John Romita Jr. **W:** Chris Claremont

98 ❑ Aug 1994 Cover: 1.25 **NM** value: **1.50**
Circ: Statement: **83,175** CapCity orders: **11,150**
📖 Juggernaut's Back in Town • Reprints Uncanny X-Men #194 **A:** John Romita Jr. **W:** Chris Claremont ★ Appearance of Juggernaut.

99 ❑ Sep 1994 Cover: 1.25 **NM** value: **1.50**
Circ: Statement: **83,175** CapCity orders: **10,550**
📖 It Was a Dark and Stormy Night • Reprints Uncanny X-Men #195 **A:** John Romita Jr. **W:** Chris Claremont ★ Appearance of Power-Pack.

100 ❑ Oct 1994 Cover: 1.50 **NM** value: **Cover or less**
Circ: Statement: **83,175** CapCity orders: **10,700**
📖 What Was That? • Reprints Uncanny X-Men #196 **A:** John Romita Jr. **W:** Chris Claremont

101 ❑ Nov 1994 Cover: 1.50 **NM** value: **Cover or less**
Circ: CapCity orders: **9,600**
📖 To Save Arcade? • reprints Uncanny X-Men #197 **A:** John Romita Jr. **W:** Chris Claremont

102 ❑ Dec 1994 Cover: 1.50 **NM** value: **Cover or less**
Circ: CapCity orders: **9,550**
📖 Lifedeath II • reprints Uncanny X-Men #198 **A:** Barry Windsor-Smith **W:** Chris Claremont

103 ❑ Jan 1995 Cover: 1.50 **NM** value: **Cover or less**
Circ: CapCity orders: **9,000**
📖 The Spiral Path • reprints Uncanny X-Men #199 **A:** John Romita Jr. **W:** Chris Claremont ★ 1st Appearance of Phoenix III (Rachel Summers).

104 ❑ Feb 1995 Cover: 1.95 **NM** value: **Cover or less**
Circ: CapCity orders: **7,875**
• Double-size. 📖 The Trial of Magneto • reprints Uncanny X-Men #200 **A:** John Romita Jr. **W:** Chris Claremont

105 ❑ Mar 1995 Cover: 1.50 **NM** value: **Cover or less**
Circ: CapCity orders: **7,950**
📖 Duel • reprints Uncanny X-Men #201; 1st Portacio art in X-Men **A:** Rick Leonardi **W:** Chris Claremont ★ 1st Appearance of Cable (as baby).

106 ❑ Apr 1995 Cover: 1.50 **NM** value: **Cover or less**
Circ: CapCity orders: **7,125**
• reprints Uncanny X-Men #202

CGC-graded: Multiply prices above by **33 for 9.9 M • 16 for 9.8 NM/M • 7 for 9.6 NM+ • 5 for 9.4 NM • 2.5 for 9.2 NM- • 1.5 for 9.0 VF/NM**

107 ❑ May 1995 Cover: 1.50 **NM** value: **Cover or less**
Circ: CapCity orders: **7,025**
• reprints Uncanny X-Men #203
108 ❑ Jun 1995 Cover: 1.50 **NM** value: **Cover or less**
Circ: CapCity orders: **7,000**
• reprints Uncanny X-Men #204
109 ❑ Jul 1995 Cover: 1.50 **NM** value: **Cover or less**
Circ: CapCity orders: **6,975**
• reprints Uncanny X-Men #205
110 ❑ Aug 1995 Cover: 1.50 **NM** value: **Cover or less**
final issue. • reprints Uncanny X-Men #206

X-MEN CLASSICS Marvel
1 ❑ Dec 1983 Cover: 2.00 **NM** value: **3.50**
2 ❑ Jan 1984 Cover: 2.00 **NM** value: **3.50**
3 ❑ Feb 1984 Cover: 2.00 **NM** value: **3.50**

X-MEN COLLECTOR'S EDITION Marvel
2 ❑ **NM** value: **1.00**
contains fold-out poster cover. • Pizza Hut giveaway in 1993.

X-MEN: CROSSROADS Marvel
Bk 1 ❑ Cover: 15.95 **NM** value: **Cover or less**

X-MEN: DAYS OF FUTURE PRESENT Marvel
Bk 1 ❑ Cover: 14.95 **NM** value: **Cover or less**
Circ: CapCity orders: **27,050**

X-MEN: DECLASSIFIED Marvel
1 ❑ Oct 2000 Cover: 3.50 **NM** value: **Cover or less**
Circ: Diamd. preorders: **37,346**

X-MEN: EARTHFALL Marvel
1 ❑ Sep 1996 Cover: 2.95 **NM** value: **Cover or less**
wraparound cover. • reprints The Brood saga

X-MEN: EVOLUTION Marvel
1 ❑ Cover: 2.25 **NM** value: **Cover or less**
Circ: Diamd. preorders: **35,008**
3 ❑ Cover: 2.25 **NM** value: **Cover or less**
Circ: Diamd. preorders: **25,589**
2 ❑ Cover: 2.25 **NM** value: **Cover or less**
Circ: Diamd. preorders: **26,906**

X-MEN FIRSTS Marvel
1 ❑ Feb 1996 Cover: 4.95 **NM** value: **Cover or less**
• reprints Avengers Annual #10, Uncanny X-Men #221 and 266, and Incredible Hulk #181

X-MEN FOREVER Marvel
1 ❑ Jan 2001 Cover: 3.50 **NM** value: **Cover or less**
Circ: Diamd. preorders: **51,743**
cardstock cover. 📖 The Destiny Pact **A:** Kevin Maguire **W:** Fabian Nicieza
2 ❑ Feb 2001 Cover: 3.50 **NM** value: **Cover or less**
Circ: Diamd. preorders: **46,052**
cardstock cover. 📖 Choices Once Made ... **A:** Kevin Maguire **W:** Fabian Nicieza
3 ❑ Mar 2001 Cover: 3.50 **NM** value: **Cover or less**
Circ: Diamd. preorders: **42,965**
cardstock cover. 📖 All of God's Creatures ... **A:** Kevin Maguire **W:** Fabian Nicieza
4 ❑ Apr 2001 Cover: 3.50 **NM** value: **Cover or less**
Circ: Diamd. preorders: **40,742**
cardstock cover. 📖 The Age of Innocence **A:** Kevin Maguire **W:** Fabian Nicieza
5 ❑ May 2001 Cover: 3.50 **NM** value: **Cover or less**
Circ: Diamd. preorders: **39,272**
cardstock cover. 📖 Iceman – Present and Accounted For **A:** Kevin Maguire **W:** Fabian Nicieza

X-MEN: HELLFIRE CLUB Marvel
1 ❑ Jan 2000 Cover: 2.50 **NM** value: **Cover or less**
Circ: Diamd. preorders: **44,080**
📖 Witchhunt **A:** Charles Adlard **W:** Ben Raab
2 ❑ Feb 2000 Cover: 2.50 **NM** value: **Cover or less**
Circ: Diamd. preorders: **40,164**
📖 Toll the Bell Liberty **A:** Charles Adlard **W:** Ben Raab
3 ❑ Mar 2000 Cover: 2.50 **NM** value: **Cover or less**
Circ: Diamd. preorders: **36,388**
📖 For Want of a Soul **A:** Charles Adlard **W:** Ben Raab

X-MEN IN THE SAVAGE LAND Marvel
1 ❑ Cover: 6.95 **NM** value: **Cover or less**

X-MEN: LIBERATORS Marvel
1 ❑ Nov 1998 Cover: 2.99 **NM** value: **Cover or less**
Circ: Diamd. preorders: **60,990**
1/LE ❑ Nov 1998 Cover: 19.99 **NM** value: **Cover or less**
2 ❑ Dec 1998 Cover: 2.99 **NM** value: **Cover or less**
Circ: Diamd. preorders: **54,211**
📖 Home is Where the Heart Is **A:** Phil Jimenez; Andrew Pepoy; Keith Aiken; Leigh **W:** Joseph Harris
3 ❑ Jan 1999 Cover: 2.99 **NM** value: **Cover or less**
Circ: Diamd. preorders: **52,013**
4 ❑ Feb 1999 Cover: 2.99 **NM** value: **Cover or less**
Circ: Diamd. preorders: **49,273**

X-MEN: LOST TALES Marvel
1 ❑ Apr 1997 Cover: 2.99 **NM** value: **3.00**
Circ: Direct Market orders: **36,750**
📖 Mourning; The Big Dare; Prison of the Heart; A Fire in the Night • reprints back-up stories from Classic X-Men #3-5 and 12 **A:** John Bolton **W:** Chris Claremont
2 ❑ Apr 1997 Cover: 2.99 **NM** value: **3.00**
Circ: Direct Market orders: **35,000**
📖 Tag, Sucker; A Taste for Vengeance!; High Adventure; First Love • reprints back-up stories from Classic X-Men #10, 17, 21, and 23 **A:** John Bolton **W:** Chris Claremont

X-MEN: MILLENNIAL VISIONS Marvel
1 ❑ Jul 2000 Cover: 3.99 **NM** value: **Cover or less**

X-MEN MOVIE PREMIERE PREQUEL EDITION Marvel
1 ❑ Jul 2000 **NM** value: **2.00**
• **CGC:** 3 graded, best 9.4
• Toys "R" Us giveaway. **A:** Karl Waller **W:** Jay Faerber

X-MEN MOVIE PREQUEL: MAGNETO Marvel
1 ❑ Aug 2000 Cover: 5.95 **NM** value: **Cover or less**
Circ: Diamd. preorders: **40,955**

X-MEN MOVIE PREQUEL: ROGUE Marvel
1 ❑ Aug 2000 Cover: 5.95 **NM** value: **Cover or less**
Circ: Diamd. preorders: **40,208**
1/SC ❑ Aug 2000 Cover: 5.95 **NM** value: **Cover or less**
Photo cover. **A:** Karl Waller **W:** Jay Faerber

X-MEN MOVIE PREQUEL: WOLVERINE Marvel
1 ❑ Aug 2000 Cover: 5.95 **NM** value: **Cover or less**
Circ: Diamd. preorders: **46,180**
1/SC ❑ Aug 2000 Cover: 5.95 **NM** value: **Cover or less**
Photo cover. **A:** Karl Waller **W:** Jay Faerber

X-MEN MUTANT SEARCH R.U. 1? Marvel
1 ❑ Aug 1998 **NM** value: **2.00**
No issue number. no cover price. • prototype for children's comic

X-MEN OMEGA Marvel
1 ❑ Jun 1995 Cover: 3.95 **NM** value: **6.00**
Circ: CapCity orders: **143,050** • **CGC:** 23 graded, best 10.0
No issue number. enhanced wraparound cover. 📖 Age of Apocalypse • Finale to Age of Apocalypse
1/GO ❑ **NM** value: **25.00**
• **CGC:** 8 graded, best 9.8
chromium cover. • Gold edition. 📖 Age of Apocalypse • Finale to Age of Apocalypse

X-MEN: PHOENIX Marvel
1 ❑ Dec 1999 Cover: 2.50 **NM** value: **Cover or less**
Circ: Diamd. preorders: **50,023**
📖 Askani Rising; Askani Rising, Part 1 **A:** Pascal Alixe **W:** John Francis Moore
2 ❑ Jan 2000 Cover: 2.50 **NM** value: **Cover or less**
📖 Askani Rising, Part 2 **A:** Pascal Alixe **W:** John Francis Moore
3 ❑ Feb 2000 Cover: 2.50 **NM** value: **Cover or less**
📖 Askani Rising, Part 3 **A:** Pascal Alixe **W:** John Francis Moore

X-MEN POSTER MAGAZINE Marvel
1 ❑ Cover: 4.95 **NM** value: **Cover or less**
2 ❑ Cover: 4.95 **NM** value: **Cover or less**
3 ❑ Cover: 4.95 **NM** value: **Cover or less**
4 ❑ Cover: 4.95 **NM** value: **Cover or less**
wraparound cover.

X-MEN PRIME Marvel
1 ❑ Jul 1995 Cover: 4.95 **NM** value: **5.00**
Circ: CapCity orders: **84,925** • **CGC:** 36 graded, best 10.0
No issue number. enhanced wraparound cover with acetate overlay.

X-MEN RARITIES Marvel
1 ❑ Jul 1995 Cover: 5.95 **NM** value: **Cover or less**
No issue number. 📖 Winter Carnival; First Night; Deal With the Devil; The Man in the Sky; Open Volley **A:** John Bolton; Steve Ditko; George Pérez; Alfredo Alcala; Chris Bachalo; Chris Hamilton **W:** Scott Lobdell; Mary Jo Duffy; Stan Lee; Chris Claremont

X-MEN: ROAD TO ONSLAUGHT Marvel
1 ❑ Oct 1996 Cover: 2.50 **NM** value: **Cover or less**
• background on Onslaught's origins

X-MEN: SEARCH FOR CYCLOPS Marvel
1 ❑ Dec 2000 Cover: 2.99 **NM** value: **Cover or less**
Circ: Diamd. preorders: **65,645**
Single figure (red against black background) on cover. 📖 Lost **A:** Tom Raney **W:** Joseph Harris
1/A ❑ Oct 2000 Cover: 2.99 **NM** value: **Cover or less**
Alternate cover: Blue/white split background, man with glowing eyes kneeling at right. 📖 Lost **A:** Tom Raney **W:** Joseph Harris
2 ❑ Jan 2001 Cover: 2.99 **NM** value: **Cover or less**
Circ: Diamd. preorders: **58,326**
📖 Hunted **A:** Tom Raney **W:** Joseph Harris
3 ❑ Feb 2001 Cover: 2.99 **NM** value: **Cover or less**
Circ: Diamd. preorders: **58,633**
📖 Am I Evil? **A:** Tom Raney **W:** Joseph Harris
4 ❑ Mar 2001 Cover: 2.99 **NM** value: **Cover or less**
Circ: Diamd. preorders: **49,746**
📖 Found! **A:** Tom Raney **W:** Joseph Harris

Capital City orders are the actual sales of comic books by Capital City Distribution, once one of the largest U.S. sellers of comics to comics shops. Capital City's share of comics shop sales, while not known exactly, increases from around 10-20% in the mid-1980s to 30-35% in the mid-1990s. Capital City's share of comic books sold on newsstands (most Marvels and DCs) will be less.

X-MEN SPECIAL EDITION Marvel
Published in 1983, this deluxe-format comic book reprints the first adventure of the "all-new all-different" X-Men, as it appeared in Giant-Size X-Men #1. For fans still saving up to buy an original copy of that key comic book, this reprint is an affordable way to see the first appearances of Storm, Colossus, and Nightcrawler, as well as other mutants Professor X gathers in his search to find the original X-Men, who have mysteriously disappeared. The Special Edition also features an original 12-page story by long-time X-Men writer Chris Claremont and artist Dave Cockrum, in which Kitty Pryde reveals the deepest secrets of the X-mansion.
1 ❑ Feb 1983 Cover: 2.00 **NM** value: **4.50**
• reprints Giant-Size X-Men #1. 📖 Second Genesis! **A:** Dave Cockrum **W:** Len Wein ★ Origin of Storm, Nightcrawler. ★ 1st Appearance of X-Men (new), Thunderbird, Colossus, Storm, Nightcrawler, Illyana Rasputin.

X-MEN SPOTLIGHT ON...STARJAMMERS Marvel
1 ❑ May 1990 Cover: 4.50 **NM** value: **Cover or less**
Circ: CapCity orders: **41,300** • **CGC:** 1 graded, best 9.8
📖 Phalkon Quest, Part 1 **A:** Dave Cockrum **W:** Terry Kavanagh
2 ❑ Jun 1990 Cover: 4.50 **NM** value: **Cover or less**
Circ: CapCity orders: **37,550** • **CGC:** 1 graded, best 9.8
📖 Phalkon Quest, Part 2 **A:** Dave Cockrum **W:** Terry Kavanagh

X-MEN: SURVIVAL GUIDE TO THE MANSION Marvel
1 ❑ Aug 1993 Cover: 6.95 **NM** value: **Cover or less**
No issue number. • spiralbound

X-MEN: THE ASGARDIAN WARS Marvel
Bk 1 ❑ Apr 1989 Cover: 14.95 **NM** value: **Cover or less**
Circ: CapCity orders: **6,100**

X-MEN: THE EARLY YEARS Marvel
Marvel's mutant super-team, the X-Men, continue to lead the comic-book industry in terms of, well, just about everything. In any given month, at least two of the "X-family" of titles appears in the top ten sales charts. There are action figures, towels, lunch boxes, clothes, gym shoes, and just about anything thing else that can carry the logo or likeness of the mighty mutants. Fox Television Network even broadcast a cartoon version of X-Men Adventures that enjoyed huge success in the early to mid-'90s.

All of this attention prompted Marvel to reprint the original issues of X-Men (1st Series) in this new title. This gave younger fans a chance to step back in time to view the work of The X-Men's creators, Jack Kirby and Stan Lee. It also featured new covers by some of Marvel's hottest artists.
1 ❑ May 1994 Cover: 1.50 **NM** value: **2.50**
Circ: CapCity orders: **21,800**
• Reprints X-Men (1st Series) #1 **W:** Stan Lee ★ Origin of X-Men.
2 ❑ Jun 1994 Cover: 1.50 **NM** value: **2.00**
Circ: CapCity orders: **17,200**
• Reprints X-Men (1st Series) #2 **W:** Stan Lee
3 ❑ Jul 1994 Cover: 1.50 **NM** value: **2.00**
Circ: CapCity orders: **17,500**
• Reprints X-Men (1st Series) #3 **W:** Stan Lee
4 ❑ Aug 1994 Cover: 1.50 **NM** value: **2.00**
Circ: CapCity orders: **15,500**
• Reprints X-Men (1st Series) #4 **W:** Stan Lee
5 ❑ Sep 1994 Cover: 1.50 **NM** value: **2.00**
Circ: CapCity orders: **13,700**
• Reprints X-Men (1st Series) #5 **W:** Stan Lee
6 ❑ Oct 1994 Cover: 1.50 **NM** value: **2.00**
Circ: CapCity orders: **12,150**
• Reprints X-Men (1st Series) #6 **W:** Stan Lee
7 ❑ Nov 1994 Cover: 1.50 **NM** value: **2.00**
Circ: CapCity orders: **10,700**
• Reprints X-Men (1st Series) #7 **W:** Stan Lee
8 ❑ Dec 1994 Cover: 1.50 **NM** value: **2.00**
Circ: CapCity orders: **10,500**
• Reprints X-Men (1st Series) #8 **W:** Stan Lee
9 ❑ Jan 1995 Cover: 1.50 **NM** value: **2.00**
Circ: CapCity orders: **9,025**
• Reprints X-Men (1st Series) #9 **W:** Stan Lee
10 ❑ Feb 1995 Cover: 1.50 **NM** value: **2.00**
Circ: CapCity orders: **8,325**
• Reprints X-Men (1st Series) #10 **W:** Stan Lee
11 ❑ Mar 1995 Cover: 1.50 **NM** value: **2.00**
Circ: CapCity orders: **7,625**
• Reprints X-Men (1st Series) #11 **W:** Stan Lee
12 ❑ Apr 1995 Cover: 1.50 **NM** value: **2.00**
Circ: CapCity orders: **7,625**
• Reprints X-Men (1st Series) #12 **W:** Stan Lee
13 ❑ May 1995 Cover: 1.50 **NM** value: **2.00**
Circ: CapCity orders: **7,000**
• Reprints X-Men (1st Series) #13 **W:** Stan Lee
14 ❑ Jun 1995 Cover: 1.50 **NM** value: **2.00**

Other grades: Multiply prices above by **1.5 for Mint • 2/3 for Very Fine • 1/3 for Fine • 1/5 for Very Good • 1/8 for Good**

Circ: CapCity orders: **7,100**
• Reprints X-Men (1st Series) #14 **W:** Stan Lee
15 ❑ Jul 1995 Cover: 1.50 **NM** value: **2.00**
Circ: CapCity orders: **6,950**
• Reprints X-Men (1st Series) #15 **W:** Stan Lee
16 ❑ Aug 1995 Cover: 1.50 **NM** value: **2.00**
Circ: CapCity orders: **6,525**
• Reprints X-Men (1st Series) #16 **W:** Stan Lee
17 ❑ Sep 1995 Cover: 2.50 **NM** value: **Cover or less**
• Double-size. 📖 ...And None Shall Survive!; If Iceman Should Fail! final issue. • Reprints X-Men (1st Series) #17 and #18 **A:** Jack Kirby; Jay Gavin; Ande Parks(cover); Phil Hester(cover) **W:** Stan Lee

X-MEN: THE HIDDEN YEARS — Marvel

From #67-93 of the original X-Men series, Marvel reprinted issues #12-45, due to low sales. As a result, fans have discussed for years what happened to the mutant heroes during the lengthy hiatus. The answers are here, as artist John Byrne is joined by original series artist Tom Palmer to fill in the gaps with tales from The X-Men's hidden years.

The adventure begins, as The X-Men manage to awaken Professor Xavier from a deep coma only to discover the professor is not his usual self. Meanwhile, Iceman decides to walk away from the team, and Cyclops, The Beast, Marvel Girl, and Angel must return to The Savage Land to thwart the evil plans of Magneto, who was believed dead.

Each issue captures the magic of the X-Men's early adventures while giving fans a chance to watch two master storytellers at work.

1 ❑ Dec 1999 Cover: 3.50 **NM** value: **Cover or less**
Circ: Diamd. preorders: **68,002**
2 ❑ Jan 2000 Cover: 2.50 **NM** value: **Cover or less**
3 ❑ Feb 2000 Cover: 2.50 **NM** value: **Cover or less**
Circ: Diamd. preorders: **49,135**
4 ❑ Mar 2000 Cover: 2.50 **NM** value: **Cover or less**
Circ: Diamd. preorders: **44,050**
5 ❑ Apr 2000 Cover: 2.75 **NM** value: **Cover or less**
Circ: Diamd. preorders: **39,398**
6 ❑ May 2000 Cover: 2.50 **NM** value: **Cover or less**
Circ: Diamd. preorders: **38,157**
7 ❑ Jun 2000 Cover: 2.50 **NM** value: **Cover or less**
Circ: Diamd. preorders: **36,536**
8 ❑ Jul 2000 Cover: 2.50 **NM** value: **Cover or less**
Circ: Diamd. preorders: **36,884**
9 ❑ Aug 2000 Cover: 2.50 **NM** value: **Cover or less**
Circ: Diamd. preorders: **36,311**
10 ❑ Sep 2000 Cover: 2.50 **NM** value: **Cover or less**
Circ: Diamd. preorders: **35,661**
📖 Home is Where the Hurt Is ... **A:** John Byrne; Tom Palmer **W:** John Byrne
11 ❑ Oct 2000 Cover: 2.50 **NM** value: **Cover or less**
Circ: Diamd. preorders: **33,129**
📖 Destroy All Mutants! **A:** John Byrne; Tom Palmer **W:** John Byrne ★ Appearance of Sentinels.
12 ❑ Nov 2000 Cover: 2.50 **NM** value: **Cover or less**
Circ: Diamd. preorders: **32,662**
13 ❑ Dec 2000 Cover: 2.50 **NM** value: **Cover or less**
Circ: Diamd. preorders: **31,954**
📖 Blood and Circuses **A:** John Byrne; Tom Palmer **W:** John Byrne
14 ❑ Jan 2001 Cover: 2.50 **NM** value: **Cover or less**
Circ: Diamd. preorders: **31,473**
15 ❑ Feb 2001 Cover: 2.50 **NM** value: **Cover or less**
Circ: Diamd. preorders: **30,597**
📖 Death Be Not Proud
16 ❑ Mar 2001 Cover: 2.50 **NM** value: **Cover or less**
Circ: Diamd. preorders: **29,102**
📖 Echoes of a Lost Generation **A:** John Byrne **W:** John Byrne
17 ❑ Apr 2001 Cover: 2.50 **NM** value: **Cover or less**
Circ: Diamd. preorders: **28,354**
📖 Hunter and Hunted **A:** John Byrne; Tom Palmer **W:** John Byrne ★ Appearance of Kraven the Hunter.
18 ❑ May 2001 Cover: 2.50 **NM** value: **Cover or less**
Circ: Diamd. preorders: **27,684**
📖 Promise of a New Tomorrow **A:** John Byrne; Tom Palmer **W:** John Byrne
19 ❑ Jun 2001 Cover: 2.50 **NM** value: **Cover or less**
Circ: Diamd. preorders: **27,834**
20 ❑ Jul 2001 Cover: 2.50 **NM** value: **Cover or less**
Circ: Diamd. preorders: **27,650**
21 ❑ Aug 2001 Cover: 2.50 **NM** value: **Cover or less**
Circ: Diamd. preorders: **27,662**
22 ❑ Sep 2001 Cover: 2.50 **NM** value: **Cover or less**
Circ: Diamd. preorders: **28,741**

X-MEN: THE MAGNETO WAR — Marvel

1 ❑ Mar 1999 Cover: 2.99 **NM** value: **Cover or less**
📖 Savior Complex **A:** Lee Weeks **W:** Alan Davis; Fabian Nicieza
2 ❑ Apr 1999 Cover: 2.99 **NM** value: **Cover or less**
3 ❑ May 1999 Cover: 2.99 **NM** value: **Cover or less**
4 ❑ Jun 1999 Cover: 2.99 **NM** value: **Cover or less**

X-MEN: THE MANGA — Marvel

1 ❑ Mar 1998 Cover: 2.99 **NM** value: **3.00**
Circ: Diamd. preorders: **28,548**
2 ❑ Apr 1998 Cover: 2.99 **NM** value: **Cover or less**
Circ: Diamd. preorders: **19,026**
3 ❑ Apr 1998 Cover: 2.99 **NM** value: **Cover or less**
Circ: Diamd. preorders: **18,323**
4 ❑ Apr 1998 Cover: 2.99 **NM** value: **Cover or less**
Circ: Diamd. preorders: **15,479**
📖 Operation: Rescue, Part 2
5 ❑ May 1998 Cover: 2.99 **NM** value: **Cover or less**
Circ: Diamd. preorders: **15,293**
6 ❑ May 1998 Cover: 2.99 **NM** value: **Cover or less**
Circ: Diamd. preorders: **11,470**
7 ❑ Jun 1998 Cover: 2.99 **NM** value: **Cover or less**
Circ: Diamd. preorders: **11,246**
📖 Inside Sabretooth **A:** Reiji Hagihara **W:** Reiji Hagihara
8 ❑ Jul 1998 Cover: 2.99 **NM** value: **Cover or less**
Circ: Diamd. preorders: **8,412**
cover says Jun, indicia says Jul. **A:** Reiji Hagihara **W:** Reiji Hagihara
9 ❑ Jul 1998 Cover: 2.99 **NM** value: **Cover or less**
Circ: Diamd. preorders: **8,361**
10 ❑ Aug 1998 Cover: 2.99 **NM** value: **Cover or less**
Circ: Diamd. preorders: **6,940**
11 ❑ Aug 1998 Cover: 2.99 **NM** value: **Cover or less**
Circ: Diamd. preorders: **6,921**
12 ❑ Sep 1998 Cover: 2.99 **NM** value: **Cover or less**
Circ: Diamd. preorders: **5,655**
13 ❑ Sep 1998 Cover: 2.99 **NM** value: **Cover or less**
Circ: Diamd. preorders: **5,608**
14 ❑ Oct 1998 Cover: 2.99 **NM** value: **Cover or less**
Circ: Diamd. preorders: **4,646**
15 ❑ Oct 1998 Cover: 2.99 **NM** value: **Cover or less**
Circ: Diamd. preorders: **4,624**
16 ❑ Nov 1998 Cover: 3.99 **NM** value: **Cover or less**
Circ: Diamd. preorders: **4,426**
• Colossus vs. Juggernaut **A:** Reiji Hagihara **W:** Reiji Hagihara
17 ❑ Nov 1998 Cover: 3.99 **NM** value: **Cover or less**
Circ: Diamd. preorders: **4,003**
18 ❑ Dec 1998 Cover: 3.99 **NM** value: **Cover or less**
Circ: Diamd. preorders: **3,922**
19 ❑ Dec 1998 Cover: 3.99 **NM** value: **Cover or less**
Circ: Diamd. preorders: **3,909**
20 ❑ Jan 1999 Cover: 3.99 **NM** value: **Cover or less**
Circ: Diamd. preorders: **3,566**
21 ❑ Jan 1999 Cover: 3.99 **NM** value: **Cover or less**
Circ: Diamd. preorders: **3,269**
22 ❑ Feb 1999 Cover: 3.99 **NM** value: **Cover or less**
Circ: Diamd. preorders: **3,096**
23 ❑ Feb 1999 Cover: 3.99 **NM** value: **Cover or less**
Circ: Diamd. preorders: **2,993**
24 ❑ Mar 1999 Cover: 3.99 **NM** value: **Cover or less**
Circ: Diamd. preorders: **3,022**
25 ❑ Mar 1999 Cover: 3.99 **NM** value: **Cover or less**
Circ: Diamd. preorders: **2,657**
26 ❑ Apr 1999 Cover: 3.99 **NM** value: **Cover or less**
Circ: Diamd. preorders: **2,616**
• Mystique apperance **A:** Kei Amagi **W:** Kei Amagi ★ Appearance of Avalanche, Blob, Brotherhood of Evil Mutants, Pyro.

X-MEN: THE ULTRA COLLECTION — Marvel

1 ❑ Dec 1994 Cover: 2.95 **NM** value: **Cover or less**
Circ: CapCity orders: **21,450**
• Pin-ups
2 ❑ Jan 1995 Cover: 2.95 **NM** value: **Cover or less**
Circ: CapCity orders: **15,625**
• Pin-ups
3 ❑ Feb 1995 Cover: 2.95 **NM** value: **Cover or less**
Circ: CapCity orders: **11,250**
• Pin-ups
4 ❑ Mar 1995 Cover: 2.95 **NM** value: **Cover or less**
Circ: CapCity orders: **7,925**
• Pin-ups
5 ❑ Apr 1995 Cover: 2.95 **NM** value: **Cover or less**
Circ: CapCity orders: **7,250**
• Pin-ups

X-MEN: THE WEDDING ALBUM — Marvel

1 ❑ Cover: 2.95 **NM** value: **3.00**
No issue number.

X-MEN: TRUE FRIENDS — Marvel

1 ❑ Sep 1999 Cover: 2.99 **NM** value: **Cover or less**
Circ: Diamd. preorders: **53,123**
2 ❑ Oct 1999 Cover: 2.99 **NM** value: **Cover or less**
Circ: Diamd. preorders: **46,669**
📖 Royal Hunt **A:** Rick Leonardi **W:** Chris Claremont
3 ❑ Nov 1999 Cover: 2.99 **NM** value: **Cover or less**
Circ: Diamd. preorders: **42,997**

X-MEN 2099 — Marvel

It didn't take long for the world to destroy itself in a paroxysm of greed and selfishness. Following the Corporate Wars, a few huge Mega-Corps would control most of the world's wealth and technology. Once they held that power, they would seldom hesitate to ruthlessly use it to gain their own ends. All this happened about a 100 years from now — in 2099.

In this blasted world, an enclave of outcasts, rebels, mutants, and degens gathered in the supposedly deserted town of Nuevo Sol. They were led by a messianic figure named X'ian who took his inspiration from such 20th century figures as Professor Xavier and Magneto. From the outcasts he formed a group of mutants with special abilities to become his new X-Men. With them, he hoped to forge a better life for all those who didn't want to lead bar-coded existences as pawns of the corporations.

1 ❑ Oct 1993 Cover: 1.75 **NM** value: **2.00**
Circ: CapCity orders: **200,700** • **CGC:** 3 graded, best 9.8
foil cover. **A:** Ron Lim **W:** John Francis Moore ★ 1st Appearance of X-Men 2099.
1/GO❑Oct 1993 **NM** value: **3.00**
• **CGC:** 1 graded, best 9.2
foil cover. • Gold edition. **A:** Ron Lim **W:** John Francis Moore ★ 1st Appearance of X-Men 2099.
1-2 ❑ Cover: 1.75 **NM** value: **Cover or less**
2 ❑ Nov 1993 Cover: 1.25 **NM** value: **1.50**
Circ: CapCity orders: **125,200**
3 ❑ Dec 1993 Cover: 1.25 **NM** value: **1.50**
Circ: Statement: **368,867** CapCity orders: **108,200**
4 ❑ Jan 1994 Cover: 1.25 **NM** value: **1.50**
Circ: Statement: **368,867** CapCity orders: **89,800**
5 ❑ Feb 1994 Cover: 1.25 **NM** value: **1.50**
Circ: Statement: **368,867** CapCity orders: **80,300**
📖 Fall of the Hammer, Part 3
6 ❑ Mar 1994 Cover: 1.25 **NM** value: **Cover or less**
Circ: Statement: **368,867** CapCity orders: **67,050**
7 ❑ Apr 1994 Cover: 1.25 **NM** value: **Cover or less**
Circ: Statement: **368,867** CapCity orders: **62,350**
8 ❑ May 1994 Cover: 1.50 **NM** value: **Cover or less**
Circ: Statement: **368,867** CapCity orders: **59,250**
9 ❑ Jun 1994 Cover: 1.50 **NM** value: **Cover or less**
Circ: Statement: **368,867** CapCity orders: **56,300**
10 ❑ Jul 1994 Cover: 1.50 **NM** value: **Cover or less**
Circ: Statement: **368,867** CapCity orders: **54,800**
11 ❑ Aug 1994 Cover: 1.50 **NM** value: **Cover or less**
Circ: Statement: **368,867** CapCity orders: **51,600**
12 ❑ Sep 1994 Cover: 1.50 **NM** value: **Cover or less**
Circ: Statement: **368,867** CapCity orders: **49,000**
13 ❑ Oct 1994 Cover: 1.50 **NM** value: **Cover or less**
Circ: Statement: **368,867** CapCity orders: **45,800**
14 ❑ Nov 1994 Cover: 1.50 **NM** value: **Cover or less**
Circ: Statement: **368,867** CapCity orders: **42,200**
15 ❑ Dec 1994 Cover: 1.50 **NM** value: **Cover or less**
Circ: Statement: **128,316** CapCity orders: **42,400**
16 ❑ Jan 1995 Cover: 1.50 **NM** value: **Cover or less**
Circ: Statement: **128,316** CapCity orders: **37,150**
17 ❑ Feb 1995 Cover: 1.50 **NM** value: **Cover or less**
Circ: Statement: **128,316** CapCity orders: **34,250**
18 ❑ Mar 1995 Cover: 1.50 **NM** value: **Cover or less**
Circ: Statement: **128,316** CapCity orders: **30,700**
• Has 1994 Statement, filed 10/1/94; avg print run 515,042; avg sales 362,908; avg subs 5,958; avg total paid 368,867; samples 125; office use 500; max existent 369,491; 28% of run returned
19 ❑ Apr 1995 Cover: 1.50 **NM** value: **Cover or less**
Circ: Statement: **128,316** CapCity orders: **28,775**
20 ❑ May 1995 Cover: 1.50 **NM** value: **Cover or less**
Circ: Statement: **128,316** CapCity orders: **29,675**
21 ❑ Jun 1995 Cover: 1.95 **NM** value: **Cover or less**
Circ: Statement: **128,316** CapCity orders: **27,150**
22 ❑ Jul 1995 Cover: 1.95 **NM** value: **Cover or less**
Circ: Statement: **128,316** CapCity orders: **25,150**
23 ❑ Aug 1995 Cover: 1.95 **NM** value: **Cover or less**
Circ: Statement: **128,316** CapCity orders: **23,600**
24 ❑ Sep 1995 Cover: 1.95 **NM** value: **Cover or less**
Circ: Statement: **128,316**
25 ❑ Oct 1995 Cover: 2.50 **NM** value: **Cover or less**
Circ: Statement: **128,316**
25/SC❑Oct 1995 Cover: 3.95 **NM** value: **Cover or less**
enhanced wraparound cardstock cover.
26 ❑ Nov 1995 Cover: 1.50 **NM** value: **1.95**
27 ❑ Dec 1995 Cover: 1.95 **NM** value: **Cover or less**
• Story continued from 2099 Apocalypse and Doom 2099 #36 **A:** Ron Lim **W:** John Francis Moore ★ Appearance of Herod, Doom.
28 ❑ Jan 1996 Cover: 1.95 **NM** value: **Cover or less**
• Has 1995 Statement, filed 10/1/95; avg print run 213,852; avg sales 123,833; avg subs 4,483; avg total paid circ 128,316; samples 750; office use 500; max existent 129,566; 39% of run returned
29 ❑ Feb 1996 Cover: 1.95 **NM** value: **Cover or less**
📖 X-Nation
30 ❑ Mar 1996 Cover: 1.95 **NM** value: **Cover or less**
📖 X-Nation • Story continued in X-Nation #1 **A:** Ron Lim
31 ❑ Apr 1996 Cover: 1.95 **NM** value: **Cover or less**
32 ❑ May 1996 Cover: 1.95 **NM** value: **Cover or less**
33 ❑ Jun 1996 Cover: 1.95 **NM** value: **Cover or less**
34 ❑ Jul 1996 Cover: 1.95 **NM** value: **Cover or less**
35 ❑ Aug 1996 Cover: 1.95 **NM** value: **Cover or less**
final issue. ★ Appearance of Nostromo.
SE 1❑ Oct 1995 Cover: 3.95 **NM** value: **Cover or less**

X-MEN 2099: OASIS — Marvel

1 ❑ Aug 1996 Cover: 5.95 **NM** value: **Cover or less**
No issue number.

X-MEN ULTRA III PREVIEW — Marvel

1 ❑ Nov 1995 Cover: 2.95 **NM** value: **Cover or less**
No issue number. enhanced cardstock cover. • previews Fleer card art

X-MEN UNIVERSE — Marvel

1 ❑ Dec 1999 Cover: 4.99 **NM** value: **Cover or less**
Circ: Diamd. preorders: **9,717**
📖 Beauty & The Beast; Call to Arms!; Another Man's Shoes • contains material originally published as Astonishing X-Men #1, Generation X #55, and Uncanny X-Men #373 **A:** Adam Kubert; Chris Bachalo; Rob Jenson **W:** Alan Davis; Scott Lobdell; Howard Mackie
2 ❑ Jan 2000 Cover: 4.99 **NM** value: **Cover or less**
Circ: Diamd. preorders: **8,853**
3 ❑ Feb 2000 Cover: 4.99 **NM** value: **Cover or less**
Circ: Diamd. preorders: **9,373**
4 ❑ Mar 2000 Cover: 4.99 **NM** value: **Cover or less**
Circ: Diamd. preorders: **6,244**
5 ❑ Apr 2000 Cover: 4.99 **NM** value: **Cover or less**
Circ: Diamd. preorders: **4,911**
6 ❑ May 2000 Cover: 4.99 **NM** value: **Cover or less**
Circ: Diamd. preorders: **4,333**

CGC-graded: Multiply prices above by **33 for 9.9 M • 16 for 9.8 NM/M • 7 for 9.6 NM+ • 5 for 9.4 NM • 2.5 for 9.2 NM- • 1.5 for 9.0 VF/NM**

7 ❑ Jun 2000 Cover: 4.99 **NM** value: **Cover or less**
Circ: Diamd. preorders: **3,587**
8 ❑ Jul 2000 Cover: 4.99 **NM** value: **Cover or less**
Circ: Diamd. preorders: **3,193**
9 ❑ Aug 2000 Cover: 4.99 **NM** value: **Cover or less**
Circ: Diamd. preorders: **3,261**
10 ❑ Sep 2000 Cover: 4.99 **NM** value: **Cover or less**
Circ: Diamd. preorders: **2,755**
11 ❑ Oct 2000 Cover: 4.99 **NM** value: **Cover or less**
Circ: Diamd. preorders: **2,794** • **CGC:** 1 graded, best 9.4
12 ❑ Nov 2000 Cover: 3.99 **NM** value: **Cover or less**
Circ: Diamd. preorders: **2,706**
13 ❑ Dec 2000 Cover: 3.99 **NM** value: **Cover or less**
Circ: Diamd. preorders: **2,514**
14 ❑ Jan 2001 Cover: 3.99 **NM** value: **Cover or less**
Circ: Diamd. preorders: **2,625**
15 ❑ Feb 2001 Cover: 3.99 **NM** value: **Cover or less**
Circ: Diamd. preorders: **2,660**
16 ❑ Cover: 3.99 **NM** value: **Cover or less**
Circ: Diamd. preorders: **2,475**
17 ❑ Cover: 3.99 **NM** value: **Cover or less**
Circ: Diamd. preorders: **2,788**

X-MEN UNIVERSE: PAST, PRESENT AND FUTURE

Marvel

1 ❑ Feb 1999 Cover: 2.99 **NM** value: **Cover or less**
Circ: Diamd. preorders: **33,983**

X-MEN UNLIMITED

Marvel

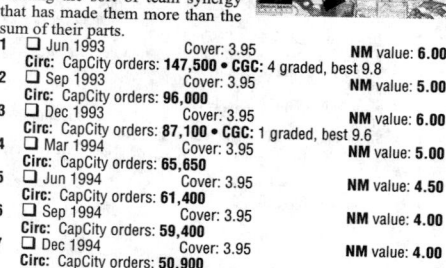

At the time Marvel released X-Men Unlimited, it was already publishing many "X" titles: X-Factor, X-Force, X-Men, Excalibur, The Uncanny X-Men, and X-Men Adventures. Why, then, another title?

To judge by X-Men Unlimited, perhaps the answer was "to do it right!" It does so at a premium price, but X-Men Unlimited uses the best of everything: the best paper, the best art, and, yes, the best stories. In a series of giant-sized issues, X-Men gives fans The X-Men full of life, richly characterized, and exhibiting the sort of team synergy that has made them more than the sum of their parts.

1 ❑ Jun 1993 Cover: 3.95 **NM** value: **6.00**
Circ: CapCity orders: **147,500** • **CGC:** 4 graded, best 9.8
2 ❑ Sep 1993 Cover: 3.95 **NM** value: **5.00**
Circ: CapCity orders: **96,000**
3 ❑ Dec 1993 Cover: 3.95 **NM** value: **6.00**
Circ: CapCity orders: **87,100** • **CGC:** 1 graded, best 9.6
4 ❑ Mar 1994 Cover: 3.95 **NM** value: **5.00**
Circ: CapCity orders: **65,650**
5 ❑ Jun 1994 Cover: 3.95 **NM** value: **4.50**
Circ: CapCity orders: **61,400**
6 ❑ Sep 1994 Cover: 3.95 **NM** value: **4.00**
Circ: CapCity orders: **59,400**
7 ❑ Dec 1994 Cover: 3.95 **NM** value: **4.00**
Circ: CapCity orders: **50,900**
8 ❑ Oct 1995 Cover: 3.95 **NM** value: **4.00**
9 ❑ Dec 1995 Cover: 3.95 **NM** value: **4.00**
10 ❑ Mar 1996 Cover: 3.95 **NM** value: **7.00**
📖 The Beast: Need to Know • Age of Apocalypse Beast imprisons and replaces real Beast **A:** Nick Gnazzo; Frank Toscano **W:** Mark Waid ★ Origin of Beast.
11 ❑ Jun 1996 Cover: 3.95 **NM** value: **5.00**
• Magneto and Rogue
12 ❑ Sep 1996 Cover: 2.95 **NM** value: **4.00**
📖 Onslaught: Impact • Juggernaut imprisoned in Cyttorak Gem ★ Appearance of Doctor Strange.
13 ❑ Dec 1996 Cover: 2.95 **NM** value: **3.00**
Circ: Direct Market orders: **122,750**
📖 Fugitive From Space; Junction ★ Appearance of Silver Surfer.
14 ❑ Mar 1997 Cover: 2.99 **NM** value: **3.00**
Circ: Direct Market orders: **105,000**
📖 Innocence Lost **A:** Jimmy Cheung **W:** Terry Kavanagh ★ Appearance of Franklin Richards.
15 ❑ Jun 1997 Cover: 2.99 **NM** value: **3.00**
Circ: Diamd. preorders: **99,170**
• Wolverine vs. Maverick
16 ❑ Sep 1997 Cover: 2.99 **NM** value: **3.00**
Circ: Diamd. preorders: **86,033**
17 ❑ Dec 1997 Cover: 2.99 **NM** value: **3.00**
Circ: Diamd. preorders: **83,835**
18 ❑ Mar 1998 Cover: 2.99 **NM** value: **3.00**
Circ: Diamd. preorders: **76,958**
19 ❑ Jun 1998 Cover: 2.99 **NM** value: **3.00**
Circ: Diamd. preorders: **72,816**
20 ❑ Sep 1998 Cover: 2.99 **NM** value: **Cover or less**
Circ: Diamd. preorders: **61,057**
21 ❑ Dec 1998 Cover: 2.99 **NM** value: **Cover or less**
Circ: Diamd. preorders: **53,600**
22 ❑ Mar 1999 Cover: 2.99 **NM** value: **Cover or less**
Circ: Diamd. preorders: **51,473**
23 ❑ Jun 1999 Cover: 2.99 **NM** value: **Cover or less**
Circ: Diamd. preorders: **51,898**
24 ❑ Sep 1999 Cover: 2.99 **NM** value: **Cover or less**
Circ: Diamd. preorders: **50,986**
25 ❑ Dec 1999 Cover: 2.99 **NM** value: **Cover or less**
Circ: Diamd. preorders: **53,239**
26 ❑ Mar 2000 Cover: 2.99 **NM** value: **Cover or less**
Circ: Diamd. preorders: **62,097**
27 ❑ Jun 2000 Cover: 2.99 **NM** value: **Cover or less**
Circ: Diamd. preorders: **54,058**
28 ❑ Sep 2000 Cover: 2.99 **NM** value: **Cover or less**
Circ: Diamd. preorders: **52,640**
29 ❑ Dec 2000 Cover: 2.99 **NM** value: **Cover or less**
Circ: Diamd. preorders: **53,437**
📖 Maximum Security; Renewed Acquaintances **A:** Brett Booth **W:** Joe Pruett ★ Appearance of Bishop.
30 ❑ Mar 2001 Cover: 2.99 **NM** value: **Cover or less**
Circ: Diamd. preorders: **50,769**
31 ❑ Jun 2001 **NM** value: **2.99**
Circ: Diamd. preorders: **46,863**
32 ❑ Sep 2001 Cover: 2.50 **NM** value: **Cover or less**
Circ: Diamd. preorders: **48,406**

X-MEN VS. DRACULA

Marvel

1 ❑ Cover: 1.75 **NM** value: **2.00**
Circ: CapCity orders: **40,900**
• Reprints Uncanny X-Men Annual #6

X-MEN VS. EXILES

Malibu

0 ❑ Oct 1995 **NM** value: **3.00**
• limited edition.
0/LE ❑ Oct 1995 **NM** value: **5.00**
• Limited edition with Certificate of Authenticity. • Gold foil

X-MEN VS. THE AVENGERS

Marvel

1 ❑ Apr 1987 Cover: 1.50 **NM** value: **4.00**
• **CGC:** 1 graded, best 9.6
2 ❑ May 1987 Cover: 1.50 **NM** value: **3.00**
• **CGC:** 1 graded, best 9.6
3 ❑ Jun 1987 Cover: 1.50 **NM** value: **3.00**
4 ❑ Jul 1987 Cover: 1.50 **NM** value: **3.00**
• **CGC:** 1 graded, best 9.4
Bk 1 ❑ Cover: 12.95 **NM** value: **Cover or less**

X-MEN VS. THE BROOD

Marvel

1 ❑ Sep 1996 Cover: 2.95 **NM** value: **Cover or less**
wraparound cover. 📖 Brood Day of Wrath part 1 **A:** Bryan Hitch **W:** John Ostrander
2 ❑ Oct 1996 Cover: 2.95 **NM** value: **Cover or less**
wraparound cover. 📖 Brood Day of Wrath part 2 final issue. **A:** Bryan Hitch **W:** John Ostrander

X-MEN/WILDC.A.T.S: THE DARK AGE

Marvel

1/A ❑ May 1998 Cover: 4.50 **NM** value: **Cover or less**
cardstock cover.
1/B ❑ May 1998 Cover: 4.50 **NM** value: **Cover or less**
alternate cardstock cover.

X-MEN: WRATH OF APOCALYPSE

Marvel

1 ❑ Feb 1996 Cover: 4.95 **NM** value: **Cover or less**
📖 Endgame • reprints X-Factor #65-68; Nathan Summers sent into future (becomes Cable) ★ Appearance of Cable (baby).

X-MEN: X-TINCTION AGENDA

Marvel

Bk 1 ❑ Cover: 24.95 **NM** value: **Cover or less**
Foil stamped cover. ★ Appearance of X-Men, Commander Hodge, New Mutants, X-Factor.

X-MEN: YEAR OF THE MUTANTS COLLECTOR'S PREVIEW

Marvel

1 ❑ Feb 1995 Cover: 1.95 **NM** value: **2.00**
Circ: CapCity orders: **20,575**
One-shot.

X-NATION 2099

Marvel

1 ❑ Mar 1996 Cover: 3.95 **NM** value: **Cover or less**
foil cover. **A:** Humberto Ramos; Jimmy Palmiotti(inks) **W:** Tom Peyer
2 ❑ Apr 1996 Cover: 1.95 **NM** value: **Cover or less**
3 ❑ May 1996 Cover: 1.95 **NM** value: **Cover or less**
4 ❑ Jun 1996 Cover: 1.95 **NM** value: **Cover or less**
5 ❑ Jul 1996 Cover: 1.95 **NM** value: **Cover or less**
6 ❑ Aug 1996 Cover: 1.95 **NM** value: **Cover or less**
final issue.

X-O DATABASE

Valiant

1 ❑ **NM** value: **1.00**
no cover price. • polybagged with X-O TPB; armor schematics **A:** Mike Leeke; Bob Layton; Sal Velluto; Jim Calafiore; Joe Quesada; Clifford E. Van Meter; Tom Ryder **W:** Clifford E. Van Meter

X-O MANOWAR

Valiant

X-O Manowar is the name of the most powerful of a line of alien armors. Although the X-O Commando and other armors are formidable, indeed, the wearer of the X-O Manowar becomes one of the most powerful beings in the universe. But there's more: The X-O Manowar armor is more than mere technology — it's actually alive and sentient.

In the Valiant universe, connections between characters over vast periods of time are almost common. As such, it should not be surprising that the futuristic X-O Manowar armor is worn by a barbarian named Aric, who heads a corporation in 1990s America. His adventures cover similar ground, from star-spanning battles with Magnus and Solar to hunting dinosaurs with fellow warrior Turok.

0 ❑ Aug 1993 Cover: 3.50 **NM** value: **Cover or less**
Circ: CapCity orders: **172,900** • **CGC:** 8 graded, best 9.9
chromium cover. ★ Origin of X-O Manowar.
0/GO ❑ **NM** value: **5.00**
• **CGC:** 3 graded, best 9.8
chromium cover. • Gold logo edition. ★ Origin of X-O Manowar.
0.5 ❑ **NM** value: **3.00**
• Mini-comic from Wizard Magazine. 📖 The Wolfbridge Affair
1 ❑ Feb 1992 Cover: 1.95 **NM** value: **2.50**
Circ: CapCity orders: **16,000** • **CGC:** 5 graded, best 9.8
📖 Retribution, Part 1 **A:** Bob Layton; Barry Windsor-Smith; John Holdredge **W:** Jim Shooter; Steve Englehart ★ Origin of X-O Manowar. ★ 1st Appearance of X-O Manowar armor, Aric Dacia.
2 ❑ Mar 1992 Cover: 1.95 **NM** value: **2.50**
Circ: CapCity orders: **10,400** • **CGC:** 3 graded, best 9.6
3 ❑ Apr 1992 Cover: 1.95 **NM** value: **2.00**
Circ: CapCity orders: **9,800** • **CGC:** 1 graded, best 9.0
4 ❑ May 1992 Cover: 1.95 **NM** value: **2.00**
Circ: CapCity orders: **9,800**
5 ❑ Jun 1992 Cover: 1.95 **NM** value: **2.00**
Circ: CapCity orders: **10,100** • **CGC:** 2 graded, best 9.4
6 ❑ Jul 1992 Cover: 2.25 **NM** value: **Cover or less**
Circ: CapCity orders: **12,500**
7 ❑ Aug 1992 Cover: 2.25 **NM** value: **Cover or less**
Circ: CapCity orders: **27,000**
📖 Unity, Part 5 **A:** Frank Miller(cover) **C:** Frank Miller
8 ❑ Sep 1992 Cover: 2.25 **NM** value: **Cover or less**
Circ: CapCity orders: **31,300**
📖 Unity, Part 13 **C:** Walt Simonson
9 ❑ Oct 1992 Cover: 2.25 **NM** value: **Cover or less**
Circ: CapCity orders: **20,500**
10 ❑ Nov 1992 Cover: 2.25 **NM** value: **Cover or less**
Circ: CapCity orders: **18,700**
11 ❑ Dec 1992 Cover: 2.25 **NM** value: **Cover or less**
Circ: CapCity orders: **19,300**
12 ❑ Jan 1993 Cover: 2.25 **NM** value: **Cover or less**
Circ: CapCity orders: **22,500**
📖 Seed of Destruction, Part 2
13 ❑ Feb 1993 Cover: 2.25 **NM** value: **Cover or less**
Circ: CapCity orders: **25,300**
14 ❑ Mar 1993 Cover: 2.25 **NM** value: **Cover or less**
Circ: CapCity orders: **44,100**
15 ❑ Apr 1993 Cover: 2.25 **NM** value: **Cover or less**
Circ: CapCity orders: **60,200**
16 ❑ May 1993 Cover: 2.25 **NM** value: **Cover or less**
Circ: CapCity orders: **50,900**
📖 Family Matters **A:** José Delbo **W:** Jorge Gonzçlez; Jorge Gonzßlez
17 ❑ Jun 1993 Cover: 2.25 **NM** value: **Cover or less**
Circ: CapCity orders: **65,900**
📖 Push and Shove **A:** Jim Calafiore **W:** Jorge Gonzçlez; Jorge Gonzßlez
18 ❑ Jul 1993 Cover: 2.25 **NM** value: **Cover or less**
Circ: CapCity orders: **77,100**
📖 Operation: Deep Freeze, Part 1 **A:** Jim Calafiore **W:** Jorge Gonzçlez; Jorge Gonzßlez
19 ❑ Aug 1993 Cover: 2.25 **NM** value: **Cover or less**
Circ: CapCity orders: **91,000**
📖 Operation: Deep Freeze, Part 2 **A:** Jim Calafiore **W:** Jorge Gonzçlez; Jorge Gonzßlez
20 ❑ Sep 1993 Cover: 2.25 **NM** value: **Cover or less**
Circ: CapCity orders: **61,500**
📖 Operation: Deep Freeze, Part 3 **A:** Paris Karounos **W:** Jorge Gonzçlez; Jorge Gonzßlez
21 ❑ Oct 1993 Cover: 2.25 **NM** value: **Cover or less**
Circ: CapCity orders: **63,000**
📖 Strange Bedfellows **A:** Paris Karounos **W:** Jorge Gonzçlez; Jorge Gonzßlez
22 ❑ Nov 1993 Cover: 2.25 **NM** value: **Cover or less**
Circ: CapCity orders: **49,100**
📖 White Kings and Black Knights, Part 1 **A:** Paris Karounos **W:** Jorge Gonzçlez; Jorge Gonzßlez
23 ❑ Dec 1993 Cover: 2.25 **NM** value: **Cover or less**
Circ: CapCity orders: **44,600**
📖 White Kings and Black Knights, Part 2 **A:** Paris Karounos **W:** Jorge Gonzçlez; Jorge Gonzßlez
24 ❑ Jan 1994 Cover: 2.25 **NM** value: **Cover or less**
Circ: CapCity orders: **41,575**
📖 Homecoming **A:** Paris Karounos **W:** Jorge Gonzçlez; Jorge Gonzßlez
25 ❑ Feb 1994 Cover: 3.50 **NM** value: **Cover or less**
Circ: CapCity orders: **61,850**
📖 Unit, Corps, God, Country, Part 1; Unit, Corps, God, Country, Part 2 • with Armorines #0 **A:** Jim Calafiore; Paris Karounos **W:** Jorge Gonzçlez; Jorge Gonzßlez
26 ❑ Mar 1994 Cover: 2.25 **NM** value: **Cover or less**
Circ: CapCity orders: **31,425**
27 ❑ Apr 1994 Cover: 2.25 **NM** value: **Cover or less**
Circ: CapCity orders: **27,350**
📖 The Hunt ★ Appearance of Turok.
28 ❑ May 1994 Cover: 2.25 **NM** value: **Cover or less**
Circ: CapCity orders: **32,475**
• trading card
29 ❑ Jun 1994 Cover: 2.25 **NM** value: **Cover or less**
Circ: CapCity orders: **23,075**
30 ❑ Aug 1994 Cover: 2.25 **NM** value: **Cover or less**
Circ: CapCity orders: **22,375**
31 ❑ Sep 1994 Cover: 2.25 **NM** value: **Cover or less**
Circ: CapCity orders: **21,500**
• New armor
32 ❑ Oct 1994 Cover: 2.25 **NM** value: **Cover or less**
Circ: CapCity orders: **20,375**
33 ❑ Nov 1994 Cover: 2.25 **NM** value: **Cover or less**
Circ: CapCity orders: **24,825**
📖 The Chaos Effect: Delta, Part 3 • Chaos Effect
34 ❑ Dec 1994 Cover: 2.25 **NM** value: **Cover or less**
Circ: CapCity orders: **17,175**
📖 Vengeance Trail
35 ❑ Jan 1995 Cover: 2.25 **NM** value: **Cover or less**
Circ: CapCity orders: **15,800**
📖 Vengeance Trail
36 ❑ Feb 1995 Cover: 2.25 **NM** value: **Cover or less**
Circ: CapCity orders: **14,700**
📖 Vengeance Trail

Other grades: Multiply prices above by **1.5 for Mint • 2/3 for Very Fine • 1/3 for Fine • 1/5 for Very Good • 1/8 for Good**

37 ❑ Mar 1995 Cover: 2.25 **NM** value: **Cover or less**
Circ: CapCity orders: **13,375**
📖 The Wolfbridge Affair, Part 1

38 ❑ Mar 1995 Cover: 2.25 **NM** value: **Cover or less**
Circ: CapCity orders: **13,225**
📖 The Wolfbridge Affair, Part 2

39 ❑ Mar 1995 Cover: 2.25 **NM** value: **Cover or less**
Circ: CapCity orders: **13,200**
📖 The Wolfbridge Affair, Part 3

40 ❑ Mar 1995 Cover: 2.25 **NM** value: **Cover or less**
Circ: CapCity orders: **13,225**
📖 The Wolfbridge Affair, Part 4

41 ❑ Apr 1995 Cover: 2.25 **NM** value: **Cover or less**
Circ: CapCity orders: **11,975**

42 ❑ May 1995 Cover: 2.25 **NM** value: **Cover or less**
Circ: CapCity orders: **10,825**
• contains Birthquake preview★ Versus Shadowman.

43 ❑ Jun 1995 Cover: 2.25 **NM** value: **Cover or less**
Circ: CapCity orders: **9,725**

44 ❑ Jul 1995 Cover: 2.50 **NM** value: **Cover or less**
Circ: CapCity orders: **13,025**
• Birthquake

45 ❑ Jul 1995 Cover: 2.50 **NM** value: **Cover or less**
Circ: CapCity orders: **12,575**
• Birthquake

46 ❑ Aug 1995 Cover: 2.50 **NM** value: **Cover or less**
Circ: CapCity orders: **10,400**

47 ❑ Aug 1995 Cover: 2.50 **NM** value: **Cover or less**
Circ: CapCity orders: **10,300**

48 ❑ Sep 1995 Cover: 2.50 **NM** value: **Cover or less**
Circ: CapCity orders: **11,050**

49 ❑ Sep 1995 Cover: 2.50 **NM** value: **Cover or less**
Circ: CapCity orders: **10,875**

50 ❑ Oct 1995 Cover: 2.50 **NM** value: **Cover or less**
Circ: CapCity orders: **4,125**
cover forms diptych with X-O Manowar #50-O.

50/A ❑ Oct 1995 Cover: 2.50 **NM** value: **Cover or less**
Circ: CapCity orders: **4,100**
cover forms diptych with X-O Manowar #50-X.

51 ❑ Nov 1995 Cover: 2.50 **NM** value: **Cover or less**
Circ: CapCity orders: **11,300**

52 ❑ Nov 1995 Cover: 2.50 **NM** value: **Cover or less**
Circ: CapCity orders: **10,900**

53 ❑ Dec 1995 Cover: 2.50 **NM** value: **Cover or less**
Circ: CapCity orders: **9,900**

54 ❑ Dec 1995 Cover: 2.50 **NM** value: **Cover or less**
Circ: CapCity orders: **9,670**

55 ❑ Jan 1996 Cover: 2.50 **NM** value: **Cover or less**
Circ: CapCity orders: **8,650**

56 ❑ Jan 1996 Cover: 2.50 **NM** value: **Cover or less**
Circ: CapCity orders: **8,450**

57 ❑ Feb 1996 Cover: 2.50 **NM** value: **Cover or less**
Circ: CapCity orders: **5,925**

58 ❑ Feb 1996 Cover: 2.50 **NM** value: **Cover or less**
Circ: CapCity orders: **5,725**

59 ❑ Mar 1996 Cover: 2.50 **NM** value: **Cover or less**

60 ❑ Mar 1996 Cover: 2.50 **NM** value: **Cover or less**

61 ❑ Apr 1996 Cover: 2.50 **NM** value: **Cover or less**

62 ❑ Apr 1996 Cover: 2.50 **NM** value: **Cover or less**

63 ❑ May 1996 Cover: 2.50 **NM** value: **Cover or less**
• Master Darque acquires X-O armor

64 ❑ May 1996 Cover: 2.50 **NM** value: **Cover or less**

65 ❑ Jun 1996 Cover: 2.50 **NM** value: **Cover or less**
• X-O armor asserts control over itself

66 ❑ Jul 1996 Cover: 2.50 **NM** value: **Cover or less**
• Aric's armor rebels★ Death of Ax. ★ Death of Gamin.

67 ❑ Aug 1996 Cover: 2.50 **NM** value: **Cover or less**

68 ❑ Sep 1996 Cover: 2.50 **NM** value: **Cover or less**
final issue.

Bk 1 ❑ Cover: 9.95 **NM** value: **Cover or less**
• Reprints X-O Manowar #1-4★ 1st Appearance of Shadowman (cameo, out of costume), Aric Dacia, X-O Manowar.

YB 1 ❑ Apr 1995 Cover: 2.95 **NM** value: **Cover or less**
Circ: CapCity orders: **10,250**
• 1995 Yearbook.

X-O MANOWAR/IRON MAN: IN HEAVY METAL
Acclaim / Valiant

1 ❑ Sep 1996 Cover: 2.50 **NM** value: **Cover or less**
📖 The Reality Alchemists • crossover with Marvel; concludes in Iron Man/X-O Manowar: In Heavy Metal **A:** Andy Smith **W:** Fabian Nicieza

X-O MANOWAR (VOL. 2)
Acclaim

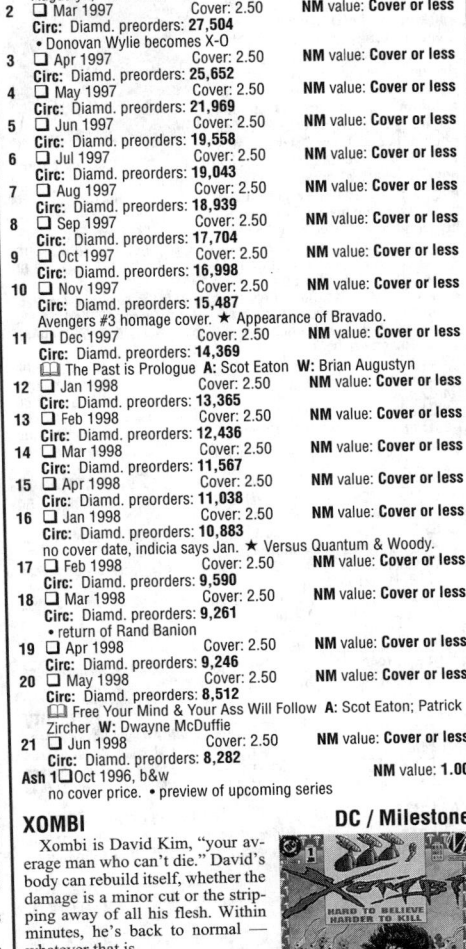

In medieval times, a suit of armor was primarily a defensive weapon. In the early 1960s, Marvel's Iron Man accentuated the offensive capabilities of armor with the addition of repulsor rays and missile-firing mechanisms. Since then, armor-clad heroes have proliferated.

The X-O Manowar armor was supposedly captured from the Nazis 50 years ago, but its secrets were unfathomable until Donovan Wylie, a computer genius, was hired by the government to study it. Rand Banion, who wears the armor, is a fearless war hero whose heroic and selfless attitude make him the ideal subject to be bonded to the armor. Together, he and the armor are X-O Manowar, though the relationship between the man and his armor is not completely harmonious.

1 ❑ Oct 1996 Cover: 2.50 **NM** value: **Cover or less**
Circ: Diamd. preorders: **33,375**
cover says Feb. 📖 Operation: Rebirth, Part 1; Fear Itself • indicia says Oct 96 **A:** Sean Chen; Tom Ryder **W:** Brian Augustyn; Mark Waid ★ Death of Rand Banion.

1/A ❑ Oct 1996 Cover: 2.50 **NM** value: **Cover or less**
alternate cover.

1/SC ❑ Cover: 2.50 **NM** value: **Cover or less**
Painted cover. 📖 Fear Itself **A:** Sean Chen; Tom Ryder **W:** Brian Augustyn; Mark Waid

2 ❑ Mar 1997 Cover: 2.50 **NM** value: **Cover or less**
Circ: Diamd. preorders: **27,504**
• Donovan Wylie becomes X-O

3 ❑ Apr 1997 Cover: 2.50 **NM** value: **Cover or less**
Circ: Diamd. preorders: **25,652**

4 ❑ May 1997 Cover: 2.50 **NM** value: **Cover or less**
Circ: Diamd. preorders: **21,969**

5 ❑ Jun 1997 Cover: 2.50 **NM** value: **Cover or less**
Circ: Diamd. preorders: **19,558**

6 ❑ Jul 1997 Cover: 2.50 **NM** value: **Cover or less**
Circ: Diamd. preorders: **19,043**

7 ❑ Aug 1997 Cover: 2.50 **NM** value: **Cover or less**
Circ: Diamd. preorders: **18,939**

8 ❑ Sep 1997 Cover: 2.50 **NM** value: **Cover or less**
Circ: Diamd. preorders: **17,704**

9 ❑ Oct 1997 Cover: 2.50 **NM** value: **Cover or less**
Circ: Diamd. preorders: **16,998**

10 ❑ Nov 1997 Cover: 2.50 **NM** value: **Cover or less**
Circ: Diamd. preorders: **15,487**
Avengers #3 homage cover. ★ Appearance of Bravado.

11 ❑ Dec 1997 Cover: 2.50 **NM** value: **Cover or less**
Circ: Diamd. preorders: **14,369**
📖 The Past is Prologue **A:** Scot Eaton **W:** Brian Augustyn

12 ❑ Jan 1998 Cover: 2.50 **NM** value: **Cover or less**
Circ: Diamd. preorders: **13,365**

13 ❑ Feb 1998 Cover: 2.50 **NM** value: **Cover or less**
Circ: Diamd. preorders: **12,436**

14 ❑ Mar 1998 Cover: 2.50 **NM** value: **Cover or less**
Circ: Diamd. preorders: **11,567**

15 ❑ Apr 1998 Cover: 2.50 **NM** value: **Cover or less**
Circ: Diamd. preorders: **11,038**

16 ❑ Jan 1998 Cover: 2.50 **NM** value: **Cover or less**
Circ: Diamd. preorders: **10,883**
no cover date, indicia says Jan. ★ Versus Quantum & Woody.

17 ❑ Feb 1998 Cover: 2.50 **NM** value: **Cover or less**
Circ: Diamd. preorders: **9,590**

18 ❑ Mar 1998 Cover: 2.50 **NM** value: **Cover or less**
Circ: Diamd. preorders: **9,261**
• return of Rand Banion

19 ❑ Apr 1998 Cover: 2.50 **NM** value: **Cover or less**
Circ: Diamd. preorders: **9,246**

20 ❑ May 1998 Cover: 2.50 **NM** value: **Cover or less**
Circ: Diamd. preorders: **8,512**
📖 Free Your Mind & Your Ass Will Follow **A:** Scot Eaton; Patrick Zircher **W:** Dwayne McDuffie

21 ❑ Jun 1998 Cover: 2.50 **NM** value: **Cover or less**
Circ: Diamd. preorders: **8,282**

Ash 1 ❑ Oct 1996, b&w **NM** value: **1.00**
no cover price. • preview of upcoming series

XOMBI
DC / Milestone

Xombi is David Kim, "your average man who can't die." David's body can rebuild itself, whether the damage is a minor cut or the stripping away of all his flesh. Within minutes, he's back to normal — whatever that is.

This title began with Xombi #0, which formed part of Milestone's Shadow War crossover series. The series began in its own right a few months later with Xombi #1. That issue told of how David, a promising young research scientist in the field of nanotechnology (microscopic machines), had the bad luck to be working late when his building was overrun by strange, mystical beings. They slaughtered everyone in the building in an effort to steal disks and devices from David's lab. After being critically wounded by the attackers, David begs his assistant to inject him with nanomachines programmed to rebuild his body. Surprisingly, this not only saves his life, but now prevents him from dying at all!

0 ❑ Jan 1994 Cover: 1.95 **NM** value: **2.50**
Circ: CapCity orders: **16,500**
📖 Shadow War, Part 3 • Shadow War★ 1st Appearance of Xombi.

1 ❑ Jun 1994 Cover: 1.75 **NM** value: **2.00**
Circ: CapCity orders: **11,550**
📖 Silent Cathedrals ★ Origin of Xombi. ★ 1st Appearance of Catholic Girl, Nun of the Above.

1/PL ❑ Jun 1994 **NM** value: **3.00**
Platinum cover.

2 ❑ Jul 1994 Cover: 1.75 **NM** value: **Cover or less**
Circ: CapCity orders: **7,150**
📖 Silent Cathedrals ★ 1st Appearance of Knight of the Spoken Fire.

3 ❑ Aug 1994 Cover: 1.75 **NM** value: **Cover or less**
Circ: CapCity orders: **6,250**
📖 Silent Cathedrals

4 ❑ Sep 1994 Cover: 1.75 **NM** value: **Cover or less**
Circ: CapCity orders: **5,900**
📖 Silent Cathedrals

5 ❑ Oct 1994 Cover: 1.75 **NM** value: **Cover or less**
Circ: CapCity orders: **5,400**
📖 Silent Cathedrals

6 ❑ Nov 1994 Cover: 1.75 **NM** value: **Cover or less**
Circ: CapCity orders: **4,650**
📖 Silent Cathedrals

7 ❑ Dec 1994 Cover: 1.75 **NM** value: **Cover or less**
Circ: CapCity orders: **4,350**

8 ❑ Jan 1995 Cover: 1.75 **NM** value: **Cover or less**
Circ: CapCity orders: **3,750**
📖 School of Anguish, Part 2 **A:** J.J. Birch **W:** John Rozum

9 ❑ Feb 1995 Cover: 1.75 **NM** value: **Cover or less**
Circ: CapCity orders: **3,250**

10 ❑ Mar 1995 Cover: 1.75 **NM** value: **Cover or less**
Circ: CapCity orders: **2,900**

11 ❑ Apr 1995 Cover: 1.75 **NM** value: **Cover or less**
Circ: CapCity orders: **2,625**

12 ❑ May 1995 Cover: 1.75 **NM** value: **Cover or less**
Circ: CapCity orders: **2,525**

13 ❑ Jun 1995 Cover: 1.75 **NM** value: **Cover or less**
Circ: CapCity orders: **2,475**

14 ❑ Jul 1995 Cover: 2.50 **NM** value: **Cover or less**
Circ: CapCity orders: **2,475**

15 ❑ Aug 1995 Cover: 2.50 **NM** value: **Cover or less**
Circ: CapCity orders: **2,475**

16 ❑ Sep 1995 Cover: 2.50 **NM** value: **Cover or less**
Circ: CapCity orders: **2,325**

17 ❑ Oct 1995 Cover: 0.99 **NM** value: **Cover or less**
Circ: CapCity orders: **2,075**
📖 Hidden Cities, Part 1

18 ❑ Nov 1995 Cover: 2.50 **NM** value: **Cover or less**
📖 Hidden Cities, Part 2

19 ❑ Dec 1995 Cover: 2.50 **NM** value: **Cover or less**
📖 Hidden Cities, Part 3

20 ❑ Jan 1996 Cover: 2.50 **NM** value: **Cover or less**
📖 Hidden Cities, Part 4

21 ❑ Feb 1996 Cover: 3.50 **NM** value: **Cover or less**
• Giant-size. 📖 Hidden Cities, Part 5 final issue. **A:** J.J. Birch **W:** John Rozum

X: ONE SHOT TO THE HEAD
Dark Horse

1 ❑ Aug 1994 Cover: 2.50 **NM** value: **Cover or less**
Circ: CapCity orders: **8,250**
No issue number. One-shot. **A:** N. Steven Harris; Chris Warner **W:** Jerry Prosser

X-PATROL
Marvel / Amalgam

1 ❑ Apr 1996 Cover: 1.95 **NM** value: **Cover or less**

X-RAY COMICS
Slave Labor / Amalgam

1 ❑ Feb 1998 Cover: 2.95 **NM** value: **Cover or less**
📖 River of Sh*t!; Goth Girls; Telephone; 2-Tone Deaf; The Adventures of Sid the Punk Kid; Sixth Grade **A:** Eric Jones; Landry Quinn Walker **W:** Eric Jones; Landry Quinn Walker

2 ❑ May 1998 Cover: 2.95 **NM** value: **Cover or less**
📖 Redneck U.S.A.; Dead Love; Mystery of the 45 Spider **A:** Eric Jones; Landry Quinn Walker **W:** Eric Jones; Landry Quinn Walker

3 ❑ Apr 1998 Cover: 2.95 **NM** value: **Cover or less**
📖 Strange Air; Satan Strikes!; An Expedition into the Natural Habitat of the Country Western Fan; When Lollapalooza Roamed the Earth; Things not to do with your Band; Hey Skinny! **A:** Eric Jones; Landry Quinn Walker **W:** Eric Jones; Landry Quinn Walker

XSE
Marvel

1 ❑ Nov 1996 Cover: 1.95 **NM** value: **Cover or less**
Circ: Direct Market orders: **172,250**

1/A ❑ **NM** value: **2.50**
variant cover. **A:** Chris Gardner; Mozart Couto **W:** John Ostrander

2 ❑ Dec 1996 Cover: 1.95 **NM** value: **Cover or less**
Circ: Direct Market orders: **96,750**
📖 Future Intense **A:** Mozart Couto **W:** John Ostrander ★ Appearance of Bishop and Shard.

3 ❑ Jan 1997 Cover: 1.95 **NM** value: **Cover or less**
Circ: Direct Market orders: **89,500**
📖 Future Betrayed **A:** Mozart Couto **W:** John Ostrander ★ Appearance of Bishop and Shard.

4 ❑ Feb 1997 Cover: 1.95 **NM** value: **Cover or less**
Circ: Direct Market orders: **72,500**
final issue.★ Appearance of Bishop and Shard.

XSTACY: THE FIRST LOOK EDITION
Fresco

1 ❑ b&w Cover: 2.95 **NM** value: **Cover or less**
No issue number. • promotional comic book sold at convention; also collects cartoons that ran in CBG

XSTACY: THE LIBRETTO
Fresco

1 ❑ b&w Cover: 2.95 **NM** value: **Cover or less**
No issue number.

X-TERMINATORS
Marvel

1 ❑ Oct 1988 Cover: 1.00 **NM** value: **2.00**
Circ: CapCity orders: **65,500**
• Inferno★ 1st Appearance of X-Terminators.

2 ❑ Nov 1988 Cover: 1.00 **NM** value: **2.00**
Circ: CapCity orders: **49,900**
• Inferno

3 ❑ Dec 1988 Cover: 1.00 **NM** value: **2.00**
Circ: CapCity orders: **48,100**
• Inferno

4 ❑ Jan 1989 Cover: 1.00 **NM** value: **2.00**
Circ: CapCity orders: **44,400**
• Inferno

X-TREME X-MEN
Marvel

1 ❑ 2001 Cover: 2.99 **NM** value: **Cover or less**
Circ: Diamd. preorders: **135,219** • **CGC:** 36 graded, best 9.8

2 ❑ 2001 Cover: 2.99 **NM** value: **Cover or less**
Circ: Diamd. preorders: **122,269** • **CGC:** 1 graded, best 9.8

3 ❑ 2001 Cover: 2.99 **NM** value: **Cover or less**
Circ: Diamd. preorders: **110,746**

4 ❑ 2001 Cover: 2.99 **NM** value: **Cover or less**
Circ: Diamd. preorders: **108,527** • **CGC:** 3 graded, best 9.8

5 ❑ 2001 Cover: 2.99 **NM** value: **Cover or less**
Circ: Diamd. preorders: **96,742**

CGC-graded: Multiply prices above by **33 for 9.9 M • 16 for 9.8 NM/M • 7 for 9.6 NM+ • 5 for 9.4 NM • 2.5 for 9.2 NM- • 1.5 for 9.0 VF/NM**

6 ❑ 2001 Cover: 2.99 **NM** value: **Cover or less**
Circ: Diamd. preorders: **93,216** • **CGC:** 2 graded, best 9.8
7 ❑ 2001 Cover: 2.99 **NM** value: **Cover or less**
Circ: Diamd. preorders: **90,504**
8 ❑ 2001 Cover: 2.99 **NM** value: **Cover or less**
Circ: Diamd. preorders: **86,861**
Anl 2001❑2001 Cover: 4.95 **NM** value: **Cover or less**
Circ: Diamd. preorders: **63,210**

X-TREME X-MEN: SAVAGE LAND — Marvel
1 ❑ 2001 Cover: 2.99 **NM** value: **Cover or less**
Circ: Diamd. preorders: **73,984**
2 ❑ 2001 Cover: 2.99 **NM** value: **Cover or less**
Circ: Diamd. preorders: **65,230**
3 ❑ 2001 Cover: 2.99 **NM** value: **Cover or less**
Circ: Diamd. preorders: **62,660**
4 ❑ 2001 Cover: 2.99 **NM** value: **Cover or less**
Circ: Diamd. preorders: **59,044**

X-TV — Comic Zone
All issues are adults only.
1 ❑ b&w Cover: 2.95 **NM** value: **Cover or less**
2 ❑ b&w Cover: 2.95 **NM** value: **Cover or less**

X-UNIVERSE — Marvel
1 ❑ May 1995 Cover: 3.50 **NM** value: **Cover or less**
Circ: CapCity orders: **63,650** • **CGC:** 1 graded, best 9.8
foil cover. 📖 Last Stand **A:** Carlos Pacheco **W:** Terry Kavanagh
2 ❑ Jun 1995 Cover: 3.50 **NM** value: **Cover or less**
Circ: CapCity orders: **64,550**
foil cover. **A:** Carlos Pacheco **W:** Terry Kavanagh

X-VENTURE — Victory
1 ❑ **NM** value: **2.00**
• **CGC:** 2 graded, best 9.4
2 ❑ **NM** value: **2.00**
• **CGC:** 1 graded, best 8.0

XXXENOPHILE — Palliard
All issues are adults only.

XXXenophile covers a wide variety of topics and sexual themes, including aliens, lesbians, zero gravity, curses, deities, fantasy, spies, threesomes, the Olympics, and more. It's a charming and sexy series of stories from Phil Foglio (Angel and the Ape) and others. Although meant for adult readers, Foglio's keen sense of humor makes even the most outlandish sexual situations seem like good clean fun.

1 ❑ Cover: 2.50**NM** value: **5.00**
1-2 ❑ Cover: 2.50**NM** value: **2.95**
2 ❑ Dec 1989 Cover: 2.50**NM** value: **Cover or less**
2-2 ❑ Jun 1991 Cover: 2.50 **NM** value: **2.95**
3 ❑ Jul 1990 Cover: 2.50 **NM** value: **Cover or less**
3-2 ❑ Mar 1992 Cover: 2.50 **NM** value: **3.00**
4 ❑ Cover: 2.50 **NM** value: **Cover or less**
4-2 ❑ Cover: 2.95 **NM** value: **Cover or less**
5 ❑ Cover: 2.95 **NM** value: **Cover or less**
📖 Hoisters **A:** Donna Barr; Phil Foglio **W:** Phil Foglio
6 ❑ Cover: 2.95 **NM** value: **Cover or less**
7 ❑ Cover: 2.95 **NM** value: **Cover or less**
Circ: CapCity orders: **3,415**
8 ❑ Feb 1993 Cover: 2.95 **NM** value: **Cover or less**
9 ❑ Jan 1994 Cover: 2.95 **NM** value: **Cover or less**
Circ: CapCity orders: **3,130**
10 ❑ Jan 1995 Cover: 2.95 **NM** value: **Cover or less**
trading-card game cover. • led to Xxxenophile card game **A:** Phil Foglio **W:** Phil Foglio
11 ❑ Cover: 2.95 **NM** value: **Cover or less**
Bk 1❑ b&w Cover: 14.95 **NM** value: **Cover or less**
• The Xxxenophile Big Book O' Fun; Reprints XXXenophile #1-5 **A:** Phil Foglio **W:** Phil Foglio
Bk 2❑ May 1997, b&w Cover: 9.95 **NM** value: **Cover or less**
• Xxxenophile Collection Book 1; collects previously published material and new stories **A:** Phil Foglio **W:** Phil Foglio
Bk 3❑ Aug 1997, b&w Cover: 9.95 **NM** value: **Cover or less**
• Xxxenophile Collection Book 2; collects previously published material and new stories **A:** Phil Foglio **W:** Phil Foglio
Bk 4❑ Nov 1997, b&w Cover: 9.95 **NM** value: **Cover or less**
• Xxxenophile Collection Book 3; collects previously published material and new stories **A:** Phil Foglio **W:** Phil Foglio
Bk 5❑ Apr 1998, b&w Cover: 9.95 **NM** value: **Cover or less**
• Xxxenophile Collection Book 4; collects previously published material and new stories **A:** Phil Foglio **W:** Phil Foglio
Bk 5-2❑Aug 2000, b&w Cover: 10.95 **NM** value: **Cover or less**

XXXENOPHILE PRESENTS — Palliard
2 ❑ Feb 1993 Cover: 2.95 **NM** value: **Cover or less**
3 ❑ Aug 1994 Cover: 2.95 **NM** value: **Cover or less**
📖 Utopia Unlimited, Part 1
4 ❑ Jul 1995 Cover: 2.95 **NM** value: **Cover or less**
📖 Incubus, Part 2

XXX WOMEN — Fantagraphics / Eros
All issues are adults only.
1 ❑ b&w Cover: 2.95 **NM** value: **Cover or less**
2 ❑ b&w Cover: 2.95 **NM** value: **Cover or less**
3 ❑ b&w Cover: 2.95 **NM** value: **Cover or less**
4 ❑ b&w Cover: 2.95 **NM** value: **Cover or less**

XYZ COMICS — Kitchen Sink
All issues are adults only.

Another study in self-loathing, cynical storytelling, Robert Crumb's XYZ Comics sees the groundbreaking cartoonist lampooning the foibles of Americans in the 1970s. Crumb, known for his often-disturbing and misanthropic depictions of life in the '60s and '70s and arguably best recognized for his creations Fritz the Cat and Mr. Natural, is considered by many to be the father of underground comix. Certainly, he's one of the most famous of the underground cretors. Laying the groundwork for such popular later titles as Peter Bagge's Hate and Roberta Gregory's Bitchy Bitch, in XYZ Comics, Crumb not only satirizes the culture that made him into an underground pop idol but also turns a sardonic eye on some of his most famous work. Mocking his celebrity status created by such iconic work as his well-known "Keep on Truckin'" cartoon, Crumb never shies away from turning a contemptuous introspective eye on himself.

1 ❑ Jun 1972 Cover: 0.50 **NM** value: **10.00**
• **CGC:** 2 graded, best 9.2
📖 Cubist be Bop; Bo Bo Bolinski in Down at the Neighborhood Bar; Comical Comics; Keep on Truckin'; The Many Faces of Robert Crumb; John Public; Fuzzy the Bunny in Nut Factory Blues **A:** Robert Crumb **W:** Robert Crumb
1-2 ❑ b&w **NM** value: **5.00**
1-3 ❑ b&w **NM** value: **4.00**
1-4 ❑ b&w **NM** value: **3.00**
1-5 ❑ b&w **NM** value: **3.00**
1-6 ❑ b&w Cover: 2.95 **NM** value: **3.00**
1-7 ❑ Jan 1987, b&w Cover: 2.00 **NM** value: **3.00**

YAHOO — Fantagraphics
1 ❑ Oct 1988 Cover: 2.00 **NM** value: **2.50**
📖 The Jaded Comix Bistro
2 ❑ Oct 1989 Cover: 2.25 **NM** value: **Cover or less**
• In the Company of Longhair
3 ❑ Apr 1990 Cover: 2.00 **NM** value: **Cover or less**
📖 This Perfect Day
4 ❑ Jan 1991 Cover: 2.50 **NM** value: **Cover or less**
• Airpower Through Victory
5 ❑ Dec 1991 Cover: 2.50 **NM** value: **Cover or less**
📖 How I Loved the War
6 ❑ Aug 1992 Cover: 2.50 **NM** value: **Cover or less**
Take It Off (Topless cover).

YAKUZA — Eternity
1 ❑ Sep 1987 Cover: 1.95 **NM** value: **Cover or less**
2 ❑ Nov 1987 Cover: 1.95 **NM** value: **Cover or less**
3 ❑ Jan 1988 Cover: 1.95 **NM** value: **Cover or less**
4 ❑ Apr 1988 Cover: 1.95 **NM** value: **Cover or less**

YAMARA — Steve Jackson Games
1 ❑ b&w Cover: 9.95 **NM** value: **Cover or less**
No issue number. • magazine-sized. • collects strips from Dragon

YANG — Charlton
1 ❑ Nov 1973 Cover: 0.20 **NM** value: **4.00**
• **CGC:** 2 graded, best 8.0
2 ❑ May 1974 Cover: 0.25 **NM** value: **2.00**
3 ❑ Jul 1974 Cover: 0.25 **NM** value: **2.00**
4 ❑ Sep 1974 Cover: 0.25 **NM** value: **2.00**
5 ❑ Nov 1975 Cover: 0.25 **NM** value: **2.00**
6 ❑ Feb 1975 Cover: 0.25 **NM** value: **2.00**
7 ❑ Apr 1975 Cover: 0.25 **NM** value: **2.00**
8 ❑ Jun 1975 Cover: 0.25 **NM** value: **2.00**
9 ❑ Sep 1975 Cover: 0.25 **NM** value: **2.00**
10 ❑ Nov 1975 Cover: 0.25 **NM** value: **2.00**
11 ❑ Jan 1976 Cover: 0.25 **NM** value: **2.00**
12 ❑ Mar 1976 Cover: 0.25 **NM** value: **2.00**
13 ❑ May 1976 Cover: 0.30 **NM** value: **2.00**
• Final issue of original run
14 ❑ **NM** value: **1.00**
• Series begins again (reprints)
15 ❑ Sep 1985 Cover: 0.75 **NM** value: **1.00**
• reprints #1
16 ❑ Nov 1985 Cover: 0.75 **NM** value: **1.00**
17 ❑ Jan 1986 Cover: 0.75 **NM** value: **1.00**
final issue.

YANKEE COMICS — Harry A. Chesler
1 ❑ Sep 1941 Cover: 0.10 **NM** value: **1250.00**
2 ❑ Nov 1941 Cover: 0.10 **NM** value: **750.00**
3 ❑ Jan 1942 Cover: 0.10 **NM** value: **500.00**
4 ❑ Mar 1942 Cover: 0.10 **NM** value: **500.00**
• **CGC:** 1 graded, best 8.0

YARN MAN — Kitchen Sink
1 ❑ Oct 1989, b&w Cover: 2.00 **NM** value: **Cover or less**

YATTERING AND JACK — Eclipse
1 ❑ Cover: 9.99 **NM** value: **Cover or less**
1/HC❑ Cover: 22.95 **NM** value: **Cover or less**
hardcover. **A:** John Bolton

YAWN — Parody
1 ❑ b&w Cover: 2.50 **NM** value: **Cover or less**
📖 Questionable • Spawn parody **A:** Bill Maus **W:** Bill Maus
1-2 ❑ Cover: 2.50 **NM** value: **Cover or less**

YEAH! — DC / Homage

Krazy, Honey, and Woo-Woo have the hottest band in the universe. Extraterrestrials literally explode with excitement, as the girls of Yeah! belt out the greatest hits ever heard and pay them tons of local currency. Unfortunately, money from other worlds is not yet transferable to banks on Earth, where they're just another so-so rock band not even able to win high-school talent contests. Their parents don't believe their tales of interstellar triumph, while their well-meaning manager, Crusty, still has trouble getting them a show that would make them just as famous at home.

Peter Bagge and Gilbert Hernandez have begun a series putting typical three-girl rock bands of the '70s into an up-to-date situation series for modern young readers.

1 ❑ Oct 1999 Cover: 2.95 **NM** value: **Cover or less**
Circ: Diamd. preorders: **11,506**
📖 Everybody Say Yeah! **A:** Gilbert Hernandez **W:** Peter Bagge
2 ❑ Nov 1999 Cover: 2.95 **NM** value: **Cover or less**
Circ: Diamd. preorders: **9,184**
• all copies destroyed **A:** Gilbert Hernandez **W:** Peter Bagge
3 ❑ Dec 1999 Cover: 2.95 **NM** value: **Cover or less**
Circ: Diamd. preorders: **7,676**
4 ❑ Jan 2000 Cover: 2.95 **NM** value: **Cover or less**
Circ: Diamd. preorders: **5,876**
📖 The Origins of Yeah, Part 1 **A:** Gilbert Hernandez **W:** Peter Bagge
5 ❑ Feb 2000 Cover: 2.95 **NM** value: **Cover or less**
Circ: Diamd. preorders: **5,029**
📖 The Origins of Yeah, Part 2 **A:** Gilbert Hernandez **W:** Peter Bagge
6 ❑ Mar 2000 Cover: 2.95 **NM** value: **Cover or less**
Circ: Diamd. preorders: **4,430**
7 ❑ Apr 2000 Cover: 2.95 **NM** value: **Cover or less**
Circ: Diamd. preorders: **3,953**
📖 Hobo's In Love **A:** Gilbert Hernandez **W:** Peter Bagge
8 ❑ May 2000 Cover: 2.95 **NM** value: **Cover or less**
Circ: Diamd. preorders: **3,746**
📖 Yeah! Goes to War! **A:** Gilbert Hernandez **W:** Peter Bagge

YEAR IN REVIEW: SPIDER-MAN — Marvel
1 ❑ Feb 2000 Cover: 2.99 **NM** value: **Cover or less**

YEAR OF THE MONKEY (AARON WARNER'S...) — Image / Homage
1 ❑ Cover: 2.95 **NM** value: **Cover or less**
2 ❑ Oct 1997 Cover: 2.95 **NM** value: **Cover or less**

YELLOW CLAW — Atlas
1 ❑ Oct 1956 Cover: 0.10 **NM** value: **600.00**
• **CGC:** 3 graded, best 7.0
📖 The Coming of the Yellow Claw; The Yellow Claw Strikes; For Services Rendered; Free Agent (text)
2 ❑ Dec 1956 Cover: 0.10 **NM** value: **450.00**
• **CGC:** 1 graded, best 9.0
📖 Concentrate on Chaos; The Mystery of Cabin 361; The Yellow Claw; Temu-jai, The Golden Goliath!
3 ❑ Feb 1957 Cover: 0.10 **NM** value: **400.00**
• **CGC:** 3 graded, best 9.0
📖 The Microscopic Army; UFO, The Lightning Man; The Yellow Claw Captured; Sleeping City
4 ❑ Apr 1957 Cover: 0.10 **NM** value: **350.00**
• **CGC:** 2 graded, best 8.5
📖 The Living Shadows; The Screemies; Five Million Sleepwalkers; The Yellow Claw and the Thought Master

YELLOW DOG COMIX — Print Mint
1 ❑ Cover: 0.50 **NM** value: **50.00**
• Oversized.
2 ❑ Cover: 0.50 **NM** value: **30.00**
3 ❑ Cover: 0.50 **NM** value: **25.00**
4 ❑ Cover: 0.50 **NM** value: **25.00**
5 ❑ Cover: 0.50 **NM** value: **25.00**
6 ❑ Cover: 0.50 **NM** value: **25.00**
7 ❑ Cover: 0.50 **NM** value: **25.00**
8 ❑ Cover: 0.50 **NM** value: **25.00**
9 ❑ Cover: 0.50 **NM** value: **25.00**
10 ❑ Cover: 0.50 **NM** value: **25.00**
11 ❑ Cover: 0.50 **NM** value: **20.00**
12 ❑ Cover: 0.50 **NM** value: **20.00**
13 ❑ Jul 1969 Cover: 0.50 **NM** value: **30.00**
• First comic-sized issue. • #13 and #14 are one issue **A:** Robert Crumb; Jay Lynch; S. Clay Wilson
15 ❑ Aug 1969 Cover: 0.50 **NM** value: **15.00**
16 ❑ Cover: 0.50 **NM** value: **15.00**
17 ❑ Cover: 0.50 **NM** value: **15.00**
18 ❑ Cover: 0.50 **NM** value: **15.00**
19 ❑ Cover: 0.50 **NM** value: **15.00**
📖 T.V. Channels, Boy Inventor, and his Electric Time Spansules; The Perfect Squelch; Jus' Plain Dick; The Untold Story of Mr. Toad's Childhood Trauma; Office Daze; Killer Weed; Santa Cruz Comics **A:** Trina Robbins; Bill Griffith; Greg Irons; Roger Brand **W:** Trina Robbins; Bill Griffith; Roger Brand
20 ❑ Cover: 0.50 **NM** value: **15.00**
21 ❑ Cover: 0.50 **NM** value: **15.00**
22 ❑ Cover: 0.50 **NM** value: **15.00**
23 ❑ Cover: 0.50 **NM** value: **15.00**
24 ❑ 1973 Cover: 0.50 **NM** value: **15.00**
25 ❑ Cover: 0.50 **NM** value: **15.00**

Other grades: Multiply prices above by **1.5 for Mint • 2/3 for Very Fine • 1/3 for Fine • 1/5 for Very Good • 1/8 for Good**

YELLOWJACKET COMICS — Frank

Yellowjacket Comics would rank as another completely forgettable Golden Age title from a third-string publisher, if not for a storytelling innovation it apparently pioneered in a back-page filler series. "Tales of Terror" is not only an extremely early example of the comic-book horror genre, it also features perhaps the first comic-book appearance of the radio device of a horror "host"- in this case, an old witch who narrates the tale and provides its moral. Considering the staggering influence this device would have on subsequent horror comics, from Tales from the Crypt to House of Mystery, the rest of Yellowjacket is remarkable only in its complete lack of originality. The lead feature is a routine costumed hero ("Yellowjacket"), and the rest of the pages are taken up with the standard assortment of South Seas adventures, second-banana heroes ("Diana the Huntress," "The Filipino Kid"), and humor ("Bee Stings").

1 ❑ Sep 1944 Cover: 0.10 **NM** value: **350.00**
• **CGC:** 4 graded, best 9.0
2 ❑ Oct 1944 Cover: 0.10 **NM** value: **200.00**
3 ❑ Nov 1944 Cover: 0.10 **NM** value: **185.00**
• **CGC:** 1 graded, best 4.5
4 ❑ Dec 1944 Cover: 0.10 **NM** value: **185.00**
5 ❑ Jan 1945 Cover: 0.10 **NM** value: **185.00**
6 ❑ Dec 1945 Cover: 0.10 **NM** value: **165.00**
• **CGC:** 1 graded, best 3.0
7 ❑ Jan 1946 Cover: 0.10 **NM** value: **165.00**
• **CGC:** 4 graded, best 9.2
8 ❑ Feb 1946 Cover: 0.10 **NM** value: **165.00**
• **CGC:** 5 graded, best 9.2
📖 The Adventure of the Mad Architect!; Diana the Huntress; King of the Beasts; Tales of Terror; Bee Stings; Crowning for a Hero (Text Story); Harbor PilotThe Filipino Kid
9 ❑ ca. 1946 Cover: 0.10 **NM** value: **165.00**
10 ❑ Aug 1946 Cover: 0.10 **NM** value: **165.00**

YELLOW SUBMARINE — Gold Key

1 ❑ Feb 1969 Cover: 0.35 **NM** value: **110.00**
• **CGC:** 2 graded, best 9.2
No issue number. • adapts movie; poster **W:** Paul S. Newman

YIKES! (ALTERNATIVE) — Alternative

1 ❑ Nov 1997 Cover: 2.95 **NM** value: **Cover or less**
• green and white
2 ❑ Cover: 2.95 **NM** value: **Cover or less**

YIKES! (WEISSMAN) — Weissman

1 ❑ b&w Cover: 2.50 **NM** value: **Cover or less**
2 ❑ b&w Cover: 2.50 **NM** value: **Cover or less**
3 ❑ b&w Cover: 2.50 **NM** value: **Cover or less**
4 ❑ Win 1995, b&w Cover: 2.50 **NM** value: **Cover or less**
5 ❑ Cover: 2.50 **NM** value: **Cover or less**
• b&w with spot color

YIN FEI THE CHINESE NINJA — Dr. Leung's

1 ❑ ca. 1988 Cover: 1.80 **NM** value: **Cover or less**
2 ❑ Cover: 1.80 **NM** value: **Cover or less**
3 ❑ Cover: 1.80 **NM** value: **Cover or less**
4 ❑ Cover: 1.80 **NM** value: **Cover or less**
5 ❑ Cover: 1.80 **NM** value: **Cover or less**
6 ❑ Cover: 1.80 **NM** value: **Cover or less**
7 ❑ Cover: 2.00 **NM** value: **Cover or less**
8 ❑ Cover: 2.00 **NM** value: **Cover or less**

YOGI BEAR (ARCHIE) — Archie

1 ❑ May 1997 Cover: 1.50 **NM** value: **Cover or less**
Circ: Diamd. preorders: **3,677**

YOGI BEAR BIG BOOK — Harvey

1 ❑ Nov 1992 Cover: 1.95 **NM** value: **Cover or less**
2 ❑ Mar 1993 Cover: 1.95 **NM** value: **Cover or less**

YOGI BEAR (CHARLTON) — Charlton

Yogi Bear is one of the best-loved cartoon characters from Hanna-Barbera. This "smarter-than-average" bear lives in Jellystone Park, where he mooches snacks from picnickers when he's not busy driving Ranger Smith to distraction. Yogi, you see, is a magnet for trouble, and it is only his own good nature (as well as lots of help from girl friend Cindy and little pal Boo-Boo Bear) that gets him out of it.

Begun in 1970, this Charlton series picked up the character from the Dell-Gold Key license and continued to bring readers the ongoing adventures of Yogi, Boo-Boo, and the rest of the gang. Short and humorous, the stories are good, clean fun for all ages.

1 ❑ Nov 1970 Cover: 0.15 **NM** value: **22.00**
• **CGC:** 2 graded, best 9.8
2 ❑ Cover: 0.15 **NM** value: **15.00**
3 ❑ Cover: 0.15 **NM** value: **15.00**
4 ❑ May 1971 Cover: 0.15 **NM** value: **12.00**
5 ❑ 1971 **NM** value: **12.00**
6 ❑ 1971 **NM** value: **12.00**
7 ❑ Sum 1971 Cover: 0.25 **NM** value: **15.00**
8 ❑ **NM** value: **12.00**
9 ❑ Feb 1972 Cover: 0.20 **NM** value: **12.00**
10 ❑ Mar 1972 Cover: 0.20 **NM** value: **12.00**
• **CGC:** 2 graded, best 9.4
📖 The Sleepwalker; Christmas is Coming; Cliff Hanger; Don't Litter Here! **A:** Ray Dirgo
11 ❑ 1972 Cover: 0.20 **NM** value: **8.00**
• **CGC:** 1 graded, best 6.0
12 ❑ 1972 Cover: 0.20 **NM** value: **8.00**
13 ❑ 1972 Cover: 0.20 **NM** value: **8.00**
• **CGC:** 1 graded, best 7.0
14 ❑ 1972 Cover: 0.20 **NM** value: **8.00**
15 ❑ Cover: 0.20 **NM** value: **8.00**
16 ❑ Cover: 0.20 **NM** value: **8.00**
17 ❑ Cover: 0.20 **NM** value: **8.00**
18 ❑ Jun 1973 Cover: 0.20 **NM** value: **8.00**
19 ❑ 1973 Cover: 0.20 **NM** value: **8.00**
20 ❑ Oct 1973 Cover: 0.20 **NM** value: **8.00**
21 ❑ Dec 1973 Cover: 0.20 **NM** value: **6.00**
22 ❑ Sep 1974 Cover: 0.25 **NM** value: **6.00**
Circ: Statement: **124,097**
23 ❑ 1974 Cover: 0.25 **NM** value: **6.00**
Circ: Statement: **124,097**
24 ❑ Feb 1975 Cover: 0.25 **NM** value: **6.00**
Circ: Statement: **98,150**
25 ❑ Apr 1975 Cover: 0.25 **NM** value: **6.00**
Circ: Statement: **98,150**
26 ❑ Jun 1975 Cover: 0.25 **NM** value: **6.00**
Circ: Statement: **98,150**
• Has 1974 Statement; avg total paid circ 124,097
27 ❑ Aug 1975 Cover: 0.25 **NM** value: **6.00**
Circ: Statement: **98,150**
28 ❑ Oct 1975 Cover: 0.25 **NM** value: **6.00**
Circ: Statement: **98,150**
29 ❑ Dec 1975 **NM** value: **6.00**
Circ: Statement: **98,150**
30 ❑ Feb 1976 **NM** value: **6.00**
31 ❑ Apr 1976 Cover: 0.30 **NM** value: **6.00**
32 ❑ 1976 Cover: 0.30 **NM** value: **6.00**
33 ❑ Sep 1976 Cover: 0.30 **NM** value: **6.00**
34 ❑ **NM** value: **6.00**
35 ❑ **NM** value: **6.00**
final issue.

YOGI BEAR GIANT SIZE — Harvey

1 ❑ Oct 1992 Cover: 2.25 **NM** value: **Cover or less**
2 ❑ Apr 1993 Cover: 2.25 **NM** value: **Cover or less**

YOGI BEAR (HARVEY) — Harvey

1 ❑ Sep 1992 Cover: 1.25 **NM** value: **1.50**
• No creator credits listed
2 ❑ Jan 1993 Cover: 1.25 **NM** value: **Cover or less**
• No creator credits listed
3 ❑ Jun 1993 Cover: 1.25 **NM** value: **Cover or less**
• No creator credits listed
4 ❑ Sep 1993 Cover: 1.25 **NM** value: **Cover or less**
📖 The Good Scout; Danger – Disaster Area; I Wish I Was a Tiger; Who's Superstitious? • No creator credits listed
5 ❑ Dec 1993 Cover: 1.50 **NM** value: **Cover or less**
📖 Tunnel Vision; The Dreamers; Time For Lunch; • No creator credits listed
6 ❑ Mar 1994 Cover: 1.50 **NM** value: **Cover or less**
📖 Ranger Topkick; Yogi Versus Goldilocks; Litter; Crash Diet!; The Hypnotist; Caught Red-Handed; • No creator credits listed

YOGI BEAR (MARVEL) — Marvel

1 ❑ Nov 1977 Cover: 0.35 **NM** value: **6.00**
2 ❑ Jan 1978 Cover: 0.35 **NM** value: **4.00**
3 ❑ Mar 1978 Cover: 0.35 **NM** value: **4.00**
4 ❑ May 1978 Cover: 0.35 **NM** value: **4.00**
5 ❑ Jul 1978 Cover: 0.35 **NM** value: **4.00**
• **CGC:** 1 graded, best 9.9
6 ❑ Sep 1978 Cover: 0.35 **NM** value: **3.00**
7 ❑ Nov 1978 Cover: 0.35 **NM** value: **3.00**
8 ❑ Jan 1979 Cover: 0.35 **NM** value: **3.00**
9 ❑ Mar 1979 Cover: 0.35 **NM** value: **3.00**

YOGI BERRA BASEBALL HERO — Fawcett

1 ❑ ca. 1951 Cover: 0.10 **NM** value: **550.00**
• **CGC:** 2 graded, best 9.0

YOSEMITE SAM — Gold Key / Whitman

Yosemite Sam is a pint-sized pirate of the West with an ornery disposition. It doesn't help that one of his neighbors is that rascally rabbit himself, Bugs Bunny. Throughout the 14 years this series ran, Bugs subjected Sam to all manner of mischief. Bugs' stunts ranged from stealing Sam's house while he slept to leading him on wild goose chases with promises of hidden treasure. Inevitably, the diminutive desperado would turn red, puff smoke out of his ears, and hop up and down while storming, "I'll get you ... RABBIT!" By story's end, however, it was usually Bugs who had the last laugh.

1 ❑ Dec 1970 Cover: 0.15 **NM** value: **12.00**
2 ❑ Mar 1971 Cover: 0.15 **NM** value: **9.00**
3 ❑ Jun 1971 Cover: 0.15 **NM** value: **9.00**
4 ❑ Sep 1971 Cover: 0.15 **NM** value: **9.00**
5 ❑ Nov 1971 Cover: 0.15 **NM** value: **9.00**
6 ❑ Mar 1972 Cover: 0.15 **NM** value: **7.50**
7 ❑ 1972 Cover: 0.15 **NM** value: **7.50**
8 ❑ Jun 1972 Cover: 0.15 **NM** value: **7.50**
9 ❑ Aug 1972 Cover: 0.15 **NM** value: **7.50**
10 ❑ Oct 1972 Cover: 0.15 **NM** value: **7.50**
11 ❑ Dec 1972 Cover: 0.15 **NM** value: **5.00**
12 ❑ Feb 1973 Cover: 0.15 **NM** value: **5.00**
13 ❑ Mar 1973 Cover: 0.15 **NM** value: **5.00**
14 ❑ 1973 **NM** value: **5.00**
15 ❑ 1973 Cover: 0.20 **NM** value: **5.00**
16 ❑ 1973 Cover: 0.20 **NM** value: **5.00**
17 ❑ Oct 1973 Cover: 0.20 **NM** value: **5.00**
18 ❑ Dec 1973 Cover: 0.20 **NM** value: **5.00**
19 ❑ Feb 1974 Cover: 0.20 **NM** value: **5.00**
20 ❑ Apr 1974 Cover: 0.20 **NM** value: **5.00**
21 ❑ 1974 **NM** value: **4.00**
22 ❑ 1974 **NM** value: **4.00**
23 ❑ 1974 **NM** value: **4.00**
24 ❑ 1974 Cover: 0.25 **NM** value: **4.00**
25 ❑ Dec 1974 Cover: 0.25 **NM** value: **4.00**
26 ❑ Feb 1975 Cover: 0.25 **NM** value: **4.00**
27 ❑ Apr 1975 Cover: 0.25 **NM** value: **4.00**
28 ❑ Jun 1975 Cover: 0.25 **NM** value: **4.00**
29 ❑ Jul 1975 Cover: 0.25 **NM** value: **4.00**
30 ❑ Aug 1975 Cover: 0.25 **NM** value: **4.00**
31 ❑ Sep 1975 Cover: 0.25 **NM** value: **4.00**
32 ❑ Oct 1975 Cover: 0.25 **NM** value: **4.00**
33 ❑ Dec 1975 Cover: 0.25 **NM** value: **4.00**
34 ❑ Feb 1976 Cover: 0.25 **NM** value: **4.00**
35 ❑ Apr 1976 Cover: 0.25 **NM** value: **4.00**
36 ❑ Jun 1976 Cover: 0.25 **NM** value: **4.00**
37 ❑ Jul 1976, four-color Cover: 0.25 **NM** value: **4.00**
📖 High Seas!
38 ❑ Aug 1976 Cover: 0.25 **NM** value: **4.00**
39 ❑ Sep 1976 Cover: 0.30 **NM** value: **4.00**
40 ❑ Oct 1976 Cover: 0.30 **NM** value: **4.00**
41 ❑ Dec 1976 Cover: 0.30 **NM** value: **4.00**
42 ❑ Feb 1977 Cover: 0.30 **NM** value: **4.00**
43 ❑ Apr 1977 Cover: 0.30 **NM** value: **4.00**
44 ❑ Jun 1977 Cover: 0.30 **NM** value: **4.00**
45 ❑ Jul 1977 Cover: 0.30 **NM** value: **4.00**
46 ❑ Aug 1977 Cover: 0.30 **NM** value: **4.00**
47 ❑ Sep 1977 Cover: 0.30 **NM** value: **4.00**
48 ❑ Oct 1977 Cover: 0.30 **NM** value: **4.00**
49 ❑ Dec 1977 Cover: 0.35 **NM** value: **4.00**
50 ❑ Feb 1978 Cover: 0.35 **NM** value: **4.00**
51 ❑ Apr 1978 Cover: 0.35 **NM** value: **2.50**
52 ❑ Jun 1978 Cover: 0.35 **NM** value: **2.50**
53 ❑ Jul 1978 Cover: 0.35 **NM** value: **2.50**
54 ❑ Aug 1978 Cover: 0.35 **NM** value: **2.50**
55 ❑ Sep 1978 **NM** value: **2.50**
56 ❑ Oct 1978 **NM** value: **2.50**
57 ❑ Dec 1978 **NM** value: **2.50**
58 ❑ Feb 1979 **NM** value: **2.50**
59 ❑ Apr 1979 **NM** value: **2.50**
60 ❑ Jun 1979 Cover: 0.40 **NM** value: **2.50**
61 ❑ Jul 1979 Cover: 0.40 **NM** value: **2.50**
62 ❑ Aug 1979 Cover: 0.40 **NM** value: **2.50**
63 ❑ Sep 1979 Cover: 0.40 **NM** value: **2.50**
64 ❑ Oct 1979 **NM** value: **2.50**
65 ❑ Dec 1979 **NM** value: **2.50**
66 ❑ 1980 **NM** value: **2.50**
67 ❑ 1980 **NM** value: **2.50**
68 ❑ 1980 **NM** value: **2.50**
69 ❑ 1980 **NM** value: **2.50**
70 ❑ 1980 **NM** value: **2.50**
71 ❑ Feb 1981 Cover: 0.50 **NM** value: **2.50**
72 ❑ 1981 Cover: 0.50 **NM** value: **2.50**
73 ❑ Sep 1981 Cover: 0.50 **NM** value: **2.50**
74 ❑ Oct 1981 Cover: 0.50 **NM** value: **2.50**
75 ❑ Jan 1982 Cover: 0.50 **NM** value: **2.50**
76 ❑ Feb 1982 **NM** value: **2.50**
77 ❑ Mar 1982 Cover: 0.60 **NM** value: **2.50**
78 ❑ Apr 1982 Cover: 0.60 **NM** value: **2.50**
79 ❑ Jul 1983 Cover: 0.60 **NM** value: **2.50**
80 ❑ Aug 1983 Cover: 0.60 **NM** value: **2.50**
81 ❑ Feb 1984 Cover: 0.60 **NM** value: **2.50**
final issue.

YOU AND YOUR BIG MOUTH — Fantagraphics

1 ❑ **NM** value: **2.50**
2 ❑ **NM** value: **2.50**
3 ❑ **NM** value: **2.50**
4 ❑ Aug 1994, b&w Cover: 2.50 **NM** value: **Cover or less**

YOU ARE HERE — DC / Vertigo

1 ❑ Cover: 19.95 **NM** value: **Cover or less**

YOUNG ALLIES COMICS — Timely

1 ❑ Sum 1941 Cover: 0.10 **NM** value: **10000.00**
• **CGC:** 6 graded, best 7.0
2 ❑ Win 1941 Cover: 0.10 **NM** value: **2800.00**
• **CGC:** 2 graded, best 9.0
3 ❑ Spr 1942 Cover: 0.10 **NM** value: **2000.00**
• **CGC:** 2 graded, best 7.0
4 ❑ Sum 1942 Cover: 0.10 **NM** value: **2800.00**
• **CGC:** 3 graded, best 8.0
5 ❑ Fal 1942 Cover: 0.10 **NM** value: **1250.00**
• **CGC:** 3 graded, best 9.4
6 ❑ Jan 1943 Cover: 0.10 **NM** value: **850.00**
• **CGC:** 1 graded, best 7.0
7 ❑ Apr 1943 Cover: 0.10 **NM** value: **850.00**
• **CGC:** 2 graded, best 9.2
8 ❑ Jul 1943 Cover: 0.10 **NM** value: **850.00**
• **CGC:** 1 graded, best 9.0
9 ❑ Fal 1943 Cover: 0.10 **NM** value: **875.00**
• **CGC:** 5 graded, best 9.0
• Hitler cover

CGC-graded: Multiply prices above by **33 for 9.9 M • 16 for 9.8 NM/M • 7 for 9.6 NM+ • 5 for 9.4 NM • 2.5 for 9.2 NM- • 1.5 for 9.0 VF/NM**

10 ❑ Dec 1943 Cover: 0.10 **NM** value: **850.00**
• **CGC:** 3 graded, best 9.2
11 ❑ Spr 1944 Cover: 0.10 **NM** value: **700.00**
12 ❑ Spr 1944 Cover: 0.10 **NM** value: **700.00**
13 ❑ Sum 1944 Cover: 0.10 **NM** value: **700.00**
14 ❑ Win 1944 Cover: 0.10 **NM** value: **700.00**
• **CGC:** 2 graded, best 5.5
15 ❑ Spr 1945 Cover: 0.10 **NM** value: **600.00**
• **CGC:** 2 graded, best 7.5
16 ❑ Sum 1945 Cover: 0.10 **NM** value: **600.00**
• **CGC:** 2 graded, best 9.0
17 ❑ Fal 1945 Cover: 0.10 **NM** value: **600.00**
• **CGC:** 3 graded, best 9.2
18 ❑ Win 1945 Cover: 0.10 **NM** value: **600.00**
• **CGC:** 3 graded, best 8.0
19 ❑ Spr 1946 Cover: 0.10 **NM** value: **600.00**
• **CGC:** 2 graded, best 8.5
20 ❑ Oct 1946 Cover: 0.10 **NM** value: **600.00**
• **CGC:** 4 graded, best 9.2
• Series continued in All-Winners #21

YOUNG ALL-STARS, THE — DC

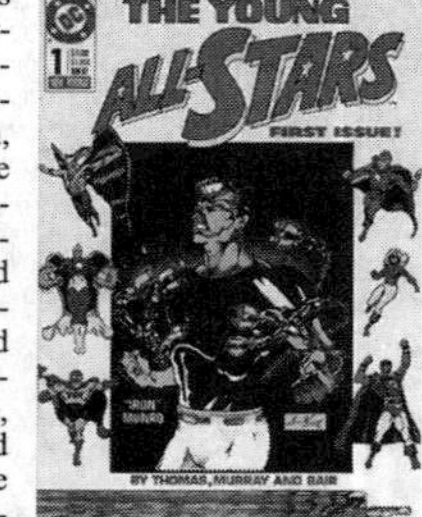

In the wake of the events of Crisis on Infinite Earths, Golden Age versions of several super-heroes, including Superman, Wonder Woman, Batman and Robin, Aquaman, and Green Arrow and Speedy, were wiped from DC continuity, effectively gutting Roy Thomas' All-Star Squadron. Thomas speculated that the "heroic energy" that "created" these heroes was still around and used it to bring several new heroes into being. Arn "Iron" Munroe, The Flying Fox, and Fury joined Dan the Dyna-Mite, Sandy the Golden Boy, Neptune Perkins, Tsunami, and a younger version of later-JSA villainess The Huntress as an offshoot of The All-Star Squadron.

Thomas continued his melding of disparate storylines (later known as retroactive continuity) to create new adventures for the fledgling team and even pulled in such characters from literature as Frankenstein's Monster and Poe's Henry Gordon Pym.

Unfortunately, without more recognizable mainstream heroes, the series couldn't sustain the interest (and sales) of the earlier All-Star Squadron and it was canceled after only 31 issues and one annual that crossed over with Thomas' other series at the time, Infinity Inc.

1 ❑ Jun 1987 Cover: 1.00 **NM** value: **3.00**
📖 The Coming of the Young All-Stars **A:** Michael Bair; Vince Argondezzi; Brian Murray **W:** Roy Thomas; Dann Thomas ★ 1st Appearance of Iron Munroe & Flying Fox.
2 ❑ Jul 1987 Cover: 1.00 **NM** value: **2.50**
Circ: CapCity orders: **14,800**
3 ❑ Aug 1987 Cover: 1.00 **NM** value: **2.50**
Circ: CapCity orders: **16,500**
4 ❑ Sep 1987 Cover: 1.00 **NM** value: **1.75**
Circ: CapCity orders: **15,900**
5 ❑ Oct 1987 Cover: 1.00 **NM** value: **1.75**
Circ: CapCity orders: **15,850**
6 ❑ Nov 1987 Cover: 1.00 **NM** value: **1.75**
Circ: CapCity orders: **15,150**
7 ❑ Dec 1987 Cover: 1.25 **NM** value: **1.50**
Circ: CapCity orders: **13,450**
8 ❑ Jan 1988 Cover: 1.25 **NM** value: **1.50**
Circ: CapCity orders: **17,300**
📖 Millennium • Millennium
9 ❑ Feb 1988 Cover: 1.25 **NM** value: **1.50**
Circ: CapCity orders: **15,550**
📖 Millennium • Millennium
10 ❑ Mar 1988 Cover: 1.25 **NM** value: **1.50**
Circ: CapCity orders: **11,950**
11 ❑ Apr 1988 Cover: 1.25 **NM** value: **1.50**
Circ: CapCity orders: **12,150**
12 ❑ May 1988 Cover: 1.25 **NM** value: **1.50**
Circ: CapCity orders: **11,600**
13 ❑ Jun 1988 Cover: 1.25 **NM** value: **1.50**
Circ: CapCity orders: **10,200**
14 ❑ Jul 1988 Cover: 1.25 **NM** value: **1.50**
Circ: CapCity orders: **10,250**
15 ❑ Aug 1988 Cover: 1.25 **NM** value: **1.50**
Circ: CapCity orders: **9,600**
16 ❑ Sep 1988 Cover: 1.25 **NM** value: **1.50**
Circ: CapCity orders: **9,350**
📖 Dzyan Inheritance
17 ❑ Oct 1988 Cover: 1.25 **NM** value: **1.50**
Circ: CapCity orders: **9,500**
📖 Dzyan Inheritance
18 ❑ Nov 1988 Cover: 1.25 **NM** value: **1.50**
Circ: CapCity orders: **8,800**
📖 Dzyan Inheritance
19 ❑ Dec 1988 Cover: 1.50 **NM** value: **1.75**
Circ: CapCity orders: **8,800**
📖 Dzyan Inheritance
20 ❑ Dec 1988 Cover: 1.50 **NM** value: **1.75**
Circ: CapCity orders: **8,450**
21 ❑ Jan 1988 Cover: 1.50 **NM** value: **1.75**
Circ: CapCity orders: **7,900**
📖 Atom & Evil
22 ❑ Jan 1989 Cover: 1.50 **NM** value: **1.75**
Circ: CapCity orders: **7,950**
📖 Atom & Evil
23 ❑ Mar 1989 Cover: 1.50 **NM** value: **1.75**
Circ: CapCity orders: **7,900**
📖 Atom & Evil
24 ❑ Apr 1989 Cover: 1.50 **NM** value: **1.75**
Circ: CapCity orders: **7,400**
📖 Atom & Evil
25 ❑ May 1989 Cover: 1.50 **NM** value: **1.75**
Circ: CapCity orders: **7,400**
📖 Atom & Evil
26 ❑ Jun 1989 Cover: 1.75 **NM** value: **Cover or less**
Circ: CapCity orders: **7,300**
27 ❑ Jul 1989 Cover: 1.75 **NM** value: **Cover or less**
Circ: CapCity orders: **7,100**
28 ❑ Aug 1989 Cover: 1.75 **NM** value: **Cover or less**
Circ: CapCity orders: **7,200**
29 ❑ Sep 1989 Cover: 1.75 **NM** value: **Cover or less**
Circ: CapCity orders: **6,950**
30 ❑ Oct 1989 Cover: 1.75 **NM** value: **Cover or less**
Circ: CapCity orders: **6,650**
31 ❑ Nov 1989 Cover: 1.75 **NM** value: **Cover or less**
Circ: CapCity orders: **6,400**
final issue.
Anl 1❑ca. 1988 Cover: 2.00 **NM** value: **Cover or less**
Circ: CapCity orders: **10,650**

YOUNGBLOOD — Image

Rob Liefeld is the explosive artist who rose to stardom through Cable and X-Force at Marvel. He later took a bold step by breaking away from Marvel and joining with other famous artists to form Image Comics, which made its debut with this title.

Youngblood features a large cast of characters, including Brahma, Riptide, Photon, Psi-Fire, Sentinel, Cougar, Badrock, Combat, Chapel, Battlestone, Vogue, Diehard, and Shaft. Although these characters are spectacular in their own right, it should come as no surprise that many of them bear a strong resemblance to the characters in Liefeld's earlier creation, X-Force.

The flagship title for Image Comics, Youngblood was also the starting point for many of its titles, bringing readers first appearances of Supreme, Pitt, and ShadowHawk.

0 ❑ Dec 1992 Cover: 1.95 **NM** value: **2.00**
Circ: CapCity orders: **154,000** • **CGC:** 4 graded, best 9.8
0/GO❑Dec 1992 **NM** value: **4.00**
• **CGC:** 1 graded, best 9.8
• gold **A:** Rob Liefeld
1 ❑ Apr 1992 Cover: 2.50 **NM** value: **Cover or less**
Circ: CapCity orders: **78,450** • **CGC:** 10 graded, best 9.6
• Flip-book. • trading card; First comic by Image Comics **A:** Rob Liefeld **W:** Rob Liefeld; Hank Kanalz ★ 1st Appearance of Chapel, Youngblood, The Four.
1-2 ❑ May 1992 Cover: 2.50 **NM** value: **Cover or less**
2 ❑ Jul 1992 Cover: 2.50 **NM** value: **Cover or less**
Circ: CapCity orders: **54,750** • **CGC:** 2 graded, best 9.4
cover says Jun, indicia says Jul. • red logo **A:** Rob Liefeld ★ 1st Appearance of Kirby, Shadowhawk, Darkthorn, Prophet, Berserkers.
2/A ❑ Jul 1992 Cover: 2.50 **NM** value: **Cover or less**
• green logo **A:** Rob Liefeld
3 ❑ Aug 1992 Cover: 2.50 **NM** value: **Cover or less**
Circ: CapCity orders: **86,075**
4 ❑ Feb 1993 Cover: 2.50 **NM** value: **Cover or less**
Circ: CapCity orders: **136,850**
5 ❑ Jul 1993 Cover: 2.50 **NM** value: **Cover or less**
Circ: CapCity orders: **114,750**
• backed with Brigade #4
6 ❑ Jun 1994 Cover: 1.95 **NM** value: **3.50**
Circ: CapCity orders: **47,125**
7 ❑ Jul 1994 Cover: 2.50 **NM** value: **Cover or less**
Circ: CapCity orders: **39,600**
8 ❑ Sep 1994 Cover: 2.50 **NM** value: **Cover or less**
Circ: CapCity orders: **45,225**
9 ❑ Sep 1994 Cover: 2.50 **NM** value: **Cover or less**
Circ: CapCity orders: **42,850**
• Image X-Month
9/A ❑ Sep 1994 Cover: 2.50 **NM** value: **Cover or less**
Circ: CapCity orders: **31,100**
• Image X-Month
10 ❑ Dec 1994 Cover: 2.50 **NM** value: **Cover or less**
Bk 1❑ **NM** value: **45.00**
• Diamond Edition. • collects issues #1-4
Bk 1/LE❑ **NM** value: **100.00**
• limited edition.
SS 1❑ Cover: 2.99 **NM** value: **Cover or less**
• Super Special
YB 1❑Jul 1993 Cover: 2.50 **NM** value: **Cover or less**
Circ: CapCity orders: **143,700**
• Yearbook 1. ★ 1st Appearance of Kanan, Tyrax.

YOUNGBLOOD BATTLEZONE — Image

1 ❑ Apr 1993 Cover: 1.95 **NM** value: **Cover or less**
Circ: CapCity orders: **112,300**
2 ❑ Jul 1994 Cover: 2.95 **NM** value: **Cover or less**
Circ: CapCity orders: **25,125**

YOUNGBLOOD: STRIKEFILE — Image

1 ❑ Apr 1993 Cover: 2.50 **NM** value: **Cover or less**
Circ: CapCity orders: **233,750**
1/GO❑Apr 1993 **NM** value: **2.50**
• Gold edition. **A:** Jae Lee
2 ❑ Jul 1993 Cover: 2.50 **NM** value: **Cover or less**
Circ: CapCity orders: **200,650**
2/GO❑Jul 1993 **NM** value: **2.50**
• Gold edition. **A:** Jae Lee
3 ❑ Sep 1993 Cover: 2.50 **NM** value: **Cover or less**
Circ: CapCity orders: **144,900**
4 ❑ Oct 1993 Cover: 2.50 **NM** value: **Cover or less**
Circ: CapCity orders: **127,425**
5 ❑ Jul 1994 Cover: 2.95 **NM** value: **Cover or less**
Circ: CapCity orders: **26,750**
6 ❑ Aug 1994 Cover: 2.95 **NM** value: **Cover or less**
Circ: CapCity orders: **25,800**
7 ❑ Sep 1994 Cover: 2.95 **NM** value: **Cover or less**
Circ: CapCity orders: **23,750**
8 ❑ Nov 1994 Cover: 2.95 **NM** value: **Cover or less**
Circ: CapCity orders: **21,800**
cover says Oct. **A:** Jae Lee **W:** Kurt Busiek(short story)
9 ❑ Nov 1994 Cover: 2.50 **NM** value: **Cover or less**
Circ: CapCity orders: **18,450**
10 ❑ Dec 1994 Cover: 2.50 **NM** value: **Cover or less**
Circ: CapCity orders: **16,775**
11 ❑ Feb 1995 Cover: 2.50 **NM** value: **Cover or less**
Circ: CapCity orders: **17,725**
📖 Extreme Sacrifice, Part 0 final issue. • polybagged with card **A:** Jae Lee

YOUNGBLOOD TRADE PAPERBACK: BAPTISM BY FIRE — Image

Bk 1❑ Cover: 16.95 **NM** value: **Cover or less**
No issue number. • Trade Paperback. • collects Team Youngblood #9-11 and Youngblood #6-8 and 10

YOUNGBLOOD (VOL. 2) — Image

1 ❑ Sep 1995 Cover: 2.50 **NM** value: **Cover or less**
Circ: CapCity orders: **22,450**
📖 Endings and Beginnings **A:** Roger Cruz **W:** Eric Stephenson
2 ❑ Oct 1995 Cover: 2.50 **NM** value: **Cover or less**
Circ: CapCity orders: **11,175**
2/A ❑ Oct 1995 Cover: 2.50 **NM** value: **Cover or less**
alternate cover.
3 ❑ Nov 1995 Cover: 2.95 **NM** value: **Cover or less**
• Babewatch
3/A ❑ Nov 1995 Cover: 2.50 **NM** value: **Cover or less**
alternate cover. • Babewatch
3/B ❑ Nov 1995 Cover: 2.50 **NM** value: **Cover or less**
alternate cover. • Babewatch
3/C ❑ Nov 1995 Cover: 2.50 **NM** value: **Cover or less**
alternate cover. • Babewatch
4 ❑ Jan 1996 Cover: 2.50 **NM** value: **Cover or less**
📖 Extreme Destroyer, Part 4 • polybagged with Riptide card
5 ❑ Feb 1996 Cover: 2.50 **NM** value: **Cover or less**
5/A ❑ Feb 1996 Cover: 2.50 **NM** value: **Cover or less**
alternate cover. ★ Appearance of Jeriko.
6 ❑ Mar 1996 Cover: 2.50 **NM** value: **Cover or less**
7 ❑ Apr 1996 Cover: 2.50 **NM** value: **Cover or less**
• Shadowhunt
8 ❑ May 1996 Cover: 2.50 **NM** value: **Cover or less**
9 ❑ Jun 1996 Cover: 2.50 **NM** value: **Cover or less**
10 ❑ Jul 1996 Cover: 2.50 **NM** value: **Cover or less**
• flipbook with Blindside #1 preview
11 ❑ Cover: 2.50 **NM** value: **Cover or less**
12 ❑ Cover: 2.50 **NM** value: **Cover or less**
Circ: Diamd. preorders: **23,379**
13 ❑ Cover: 2.50 **NM** value: **Cover or less**
Circ: Diamd. preorders: **21,781**
14 ❑ Cover: 2.50 **NM** value: **Cover or less**
Circ: Diamd. preorders: **20,204**
📖 Bad Intent **A:** Roger Cruz; Richard Horie **W:** Rob Liefeld; Eric Stephenson
15 ❑ Cover: 2.50 **NM** value: **Cover or less**
Circ: Diamd. preorders: **18,616**
final issue.

YOUNGBLOOD (VOL. 3) — Awesome

1/A ❑ Feb 1998 Cover: 2.50 **NM** value: **Cover or less**
Circ: Diamd. preorders: **62,324**
• Blue Awesome logo, Orange Youngblood logo **A:** Steve Skroce **W:** Alan Moore
1/B ❑ Feb 1998 Cover: 2.50 **NM** value: **Cover or less**
• Purple Awesome and Youngblood logos **A:** Steve Skroce **W:** Alan Moore
1/C ❑ Feb 1998 Cover: 2.50 **NM** value: **Cover or less**
• Teal Awesome and Youngblood logos **A:** Steve Skroce **W:** Alan Moore
1/D ❑ Feb 1998 Cover: 2.50 **NM** value: **Cover or less**
• White Awesome logo, Yellow Youngblood logo; Shaft in foreground **A:** Steve Skroce **W:** Alan Moore
1/E ❑ Feb 1998 Cover: 2.50 **NM** value: **Cover or less**
• Blue Awesome logo, White Youngblood logo **A:** Steve Skroce **W:** Alan Moore
1/F ❑ Feb 1998 Cover: 2.50 **NM** value: **Cover or less**
• White Awesome and Youngblood logos **A:** Steve Skroce **W:** Alan Moore
1/G ❑ Feb 1998 Cover: 2.50 **NM** value: **Cover or less**
• White Awesome logo, Yellow Youngblood logo; Suprema in foreground **A:** Steve Skroce **W:** Alan Moore
1/H ❑ Feb 1998 Cover: 2.50 **NM** value: **Cover or less**
Baby Shaft on cover. • Blue Awesome logo **A:** Steve Skroce **W:** Alan Moore
1/I ❑ Feb 1998 Cover: 2.50 **NM** value: **Cover or less**
• Orange Awesome logo, Red Youngblood logo **A:** Steve Skroce **W:** Alan Moore
1/J ❑ Feb 1998 Cover: 2.50 **NM** value: **Cover or less**
• White Awesome logo, Teal Youngblood logo; Suprema in foreground **A:** Steve Skroce **W:** Alan Moore
1/K ❑ Feb 1998 Cover: 2.50 **NM** value: **Cover or less**
3 women on cover. • White Awesome logo, Teal Youngblood logo **A:** Steve Skroce **W:** Alan Moore
1/L ❑ Feb 1998 Cover: 2.50 **NM** value: **Cover or less**
• Teal Awesome logo, Yellow Youngblood logo **A:** Steve Skroce **W:** Alan Moore

Other grades: Multiply prices above by **1.5 for Mint • 2/3 for Very Fine • 1/3 for Fine • 1/5 for Very Good • 1/8 for Good**

1/M ❑ Feb 1998 Cover: 2.50 **NM** value: **3.50**
Three women posing on cover, leaning against wall. • A! List exclusive; Foil logo **A:** Steve Skroce **W:** Alan Moore
1/N ❑ Cover: 2.50 **NM** value: **Cover or less**
• 1+ issue **A:** Steve Skroce **W:** Alan Moore
2 ❑ Aug 1998 Cover: 2.50 **NM** value: **Cover or less**

YOUNGBLOOD/X-FORCE — Image

1/A ❑ Jul 1996 Cover: 4.95 **NM** value: **Cover or less**
• prestige format. • crossover with Marvel
1/B ❑ Jul 1996 Cover: 4.95 **NM** value: **Cover or less**
alternate cover (black background).
1/C ❑ Jul 1996 Cover: 4.95 **NM** value: **Cover or less**
alternate cover.

YOUNG BRIDES — Prize

1 ❑ Sep 1952 Cover: 0.10 **NM** value: **150.00**
2 ❑ Nov 1952 Cover: 0.10 **NM** value: **80.00**
3 ❑ Jan 1953 Cover: 0.10 **NM** value: **70.00**
4 ❑ Mar 1953 Cover: 0.10 **NM** value: **70.00**
5 ❑ May 1953 Cover: 0.10 **NM** value: **70.00**
6 ❑ Jul 1953 Cover: 0.10 **NM** value: **70.00**
7 ❑ Sep 1953 Cover: 0.10 **NM** value: **70.00**
8 ❑ Oct 1953 Cover: 0.10 **NM** value: **70.00**
9 ❑ Nov 1953 Cover: 0.10 **NM** value: **70.00**
10 ❑ Dec 1953 Cover: 0.10 **NM** value: **60.00**
11 ❑ Jan 1954 Cover: 0.10 **NM** value: **60.00**
12 ❑ Feb 1954 Cover: 0.10 **NM** value: **60.00**
13 ❑ Mar 1954 Cover: 0.10 **NM** value: **60.00**
14 ❑ Apr 1954 Cover: 0.10 **NM** value: **60.00**
15 ❑ May 1954 Cover: 0.10 **NM** value: **60.00**
16 ❑ Jun 1954 Cover: 0.10 **NM** value: **60.00**
17 ❑ Jul 1954 Cover: 0.10 **NM** value: **60.00**
18 ❑ Sep 1954 Cover: 0.10 **NM** value: **60.00**
19 ❑ Nov 1954 Cover: 0.10 **NM** value: **30.00**
20 ❑ Jan 1955 Cover: 0.10 **NM** value: **30.00**
21 ❑ Mar 1955 Cover: 0.10 **NM** value: **30.00**
22 ❑ May 1955 Cover: 0.10 **NM** value: **30.00**
23 ❑ Jul 1955 Cover: 0.10 **NM** value: **30.00**
24 ❑ Sep 1955 Cover: 0.10 **NM** value: **30.00**
25 ❑ Nov 1955 Cover: 0.10 **NM** value: **30.00**
26 ❑ Jan 1956 Cover: 0.10 **NM** value: **30.00**
27 ❑ Mar 1956 Cover: 0.10 **NM** value: **30.00**
28 ❑ May 1956 Cover: 0.10 **NM** value: **25.00**
29 ❑ Jul 1956 Cover: 0.10 **NM** value: **25.00**
30 ❑ Sep 1956 Cover: 0.10 **NM** value: **25.00**

YOUNGBROADS: STRIPFILE — Parody Press

1 ❑ Cover: 2.50 **NM** value: **Cover or less**

YOUNG BUG — Zoo Arsonist

1 ❑ Cover: 2.95 **NM** value: **Cover or less**
2 ❑ Cover: 2.95 **NM** value: **Cover or less**
3 ❑ Cover: 2.95 **NM** value: **Cover or less**
📖 Young Bug, Part 4; Good Country Insect, Part 2 **A:** Michael Daedalus Kenny **W:** Michael Daedalus Kenny

YOUNG CYNICS CLUB, THE — Dark Horse

1 ❑ Mar 1993, b&w Cover: 2.50 **NM** value: **Cover or less**
Circ: CapCity orders: **2,575**
No issue number.

YOUNG DEATH — Fleetway-Quality

1 ❑ Cover: 2.95 **NM** value: **Cover or less**
2 ❑ Cover: 2.95 **NM** value: **Cover or less**
3 ❑ Cover: 2.95 **NM** value: **Cover or less**

YOUNG DRACULA — Caliber

1 ❑ b&w Cover: 3.50 **NM** value: **Cover or less**
2 ❑ b&w Cover: 3.50 **NM** value: **Cover or less**
3 ❑ b&w Cover: 3.50 **NM** value: **Cover or less**
• indicia says #2

YOUNG DRACULA: PRAYER OF THE VAMPIRE — Boneyard

1 ❑ Cover: 2.95 **NM** value: **Cover or less**
Circ: CapCity orders: **4,805**
2 ❑ Feb 1998 Cover: 2.95 **NM** value: **Cover or less**
3 ❑ Cover: 2.95 **NM** value: **Cover or less**
4 ❑ Cover: 2.95 **NM** value: **Cover or less**

YOUNG GIRL ON GIRL: PASSION AND FASHION — Angel

1 ❑ Cover: 3.00 **NM** value: **Cover or less**
1/Nude ❑ Cover: 3.95 **NM** value: **Cover or less**
• Nude edition. **A:** Mark Kuettner **W:** Christina

YOUNG GUN — AC

1 ❑ b&w Cover: 2.95 **NM** value: **Cover or less**
• reprints Billy the Kid story **A:** John Severin

YOUNG HERO — AC

1 ❑ Dec 1989, b&w Cover: 2.50 **NM** value: **Cover or less**
• reprints Daredevil #72 (1950) **A:** Norman Maurer; Charles Biro
2 ❑ Aug 1990, b&w Cover: 2.75 **NM** value: **Cover or less**
• reprints Little Wise Guys **A:** Bill Black ★ 1st Appearance of Red Devil.

YOUNG HEROES IN LOVE — DC

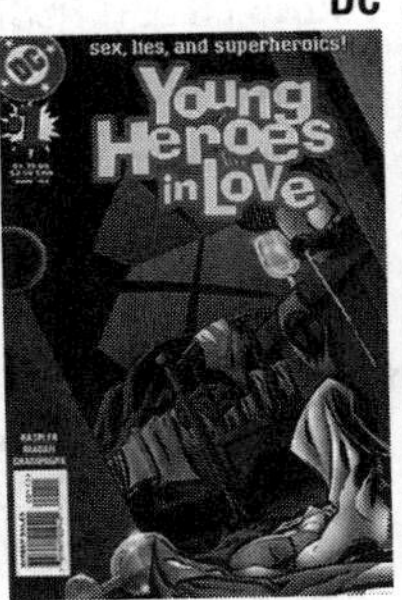

Young Heroes in Love is the story of what happens when seven goofy people find themselves with superpowers and decide to form a club. As group leader Hard Drive puts it, "We want to help, but we're afraid to do it alone." While altruism may be the order of the day, some members are looking forward to the chance to meet cute members of the opposite sex.

The group consists of: ditsy exotherm Bonfire; muscular, but simple-minded Thunderhead; shapeshifter Monstergirl; dimension-hopping Off-Ramp; the tiny man called Junior; ice-powered Frostbite; and leader Hard Drive, a superstrong flier with hypnotic powers. Written by Dan Raspler, the fun-filled series soon gained a loyal following.

1 ❑ Jun 1997 Cover: 1.75 **NM** value: **2.50**
Circ: Diamd. preorders: **26,533**
📖 Your Lips! Your Eyes! Your Nuclear Breath Vision! **A:** Dev Madan **W:** Dan Raspler
1/LE ❑ Jun 1997 **NM** value: **6.00**
• Wizard "Certified Authentic" edition. **W:** Dan Raspler
2 ❑ Jul 1997 Cover: 1.75 **NM** value: **2.00**
Circ: Diamd. preorders: **19,201**
3 ❑ Aug 1997 Cover: 1.75 **NM** value: **2.00**
Circ: Diamd. preorders: **20,474**
4 ❑ Sep 1997 Cover: 1.75 **NM** value: **2.00**
Circ: Diamd. preorders: **19,827**
5 ❑ Oct 1997 Cover: 1.75 **NM** value: **2.00**
Circ: Diamd. preorders: **20,363**
• Genesis
6 ❑ Nov 1997 Cover: 1.75 **NM** value: **2.00**
Circ: Diamd. preorders: **17,613**
📖 You'll Never Walk Alone into the Furnace of Unstable Molecules! **A:** Sergio Cariello **W:** Dan Raspler
7 ❑ Dec 1997 Cover: 1.95 **NM** value: **2.00**
Circ: Diamd. preorders: **16,859**
Face cover. 📖 Young Heroes Unplugged **A:** Dev Madan **W:** Dan Raspler
8 ❑ Jan 1998 Cover: 1.95 **NM** value: **2.00**
Circ: Diamd. preorders: **15,514**
9 ❑ Feb 1998 Cover: 1.95 **NM** value: **2.00**
Circ: Diamd. preorders: **14,570**
10 ❑ Mar 1998 Cover: 1.95 **NM** value: **2.00**
Circ: Diamd. preorders: **13,244**
📖 Tremble in Fear-for the Beast Hunts You! **A:** Christopher Jones **W:** Dan Raspler
11 ❑ Apr 1998 Cover: 1.95 **NM** value: **2.00**
Circ: Diamd. preorders: **12,397**
12 ❑ May 1998 Cover: 1.95 **NM** value: **2.00**
Circ: Diamd. preorders: **11,998**
13 ❑ Jun 1998 Cover: 1.95 **NM** value: **2.00**
Circ: Diamd. preorders: **11,725**
14 ❑ Jul 1998 Cover: 1.95 **NM** value: **2.00**
Circ: Diamd. preorders: **11,137**
15 ❑ Aug 1998 Cover: 1.95 **NM** value: **2.00**
Circ: Diamd. preorders: **10,792**
16 ❑ Sep 1998 Cover: 1.95 **NM** value: **2.00**
Circ: Diamd. preorders: **10,568**
17 ❑ Oct 1998 Cover: 2.50 **NM** value: **Cover or less**
Circ: Diamd. preorders: **10,192**
1000000 ❑ Nov 1998 Cover: 2.50 **NM** value: **Cover or less**
Circ: Diamd. preorders: **17,902**
📖 Happiness is a Warm Nanite final issue. **A:** Dev Madan **W:** Dan Raspler

YOUNG INDIANA JONES CHRONICLES, THE — Dark Horse

Indiana Jones would become a legendary adventurer one day, but how did he get his start? This series supplies part of that answer, as a much older Indiana recounts his childhood adventures in a spinoff of an ambitious — if failed — television series on ABC in the early 1990s. The series was part travelogue and pasrt history lesson, with Young Indy coming into contact with historical figures from World War I.

Another part of Dark Horse's licensing relationship with Lucasfilm, this series saw nowhere near the commercial success in comics shops of its other Star Wars titles — despite the fact that the source material, an ongoing TV show, was relatively fresher. — JJM

1 ❑ Feb 1992 Cover: 2.50 **NM** value: **3.00**
Circ: CapCity orders: **17,700**
📖 Kurt Busiek (text piece) ★ Appearance of T.E. Lawrence.
2 ❑ Mar 1992 Cover: 2.50 **NM** value: **Cover or less**
Circ: CapCity orders: **11,525**
📖 Kurt Busiek (text piece) ★ Appearance of Pancho Villa.
3 ❑ Apr 1992 Cover: 2.50 **NM** value: **Cover or less**
Circ: CapCity orders: **11,500**
📖 Kurt Busiek (text piece) ★ Appearance of Teddy Roosevelt.
4 ❑ May 1992 Cover: 2.50 **NM** value: **Cover or less**
Circ: CapCity orders: **10,800**
📖 Kurt Busiek (text piece)
5 ❑ Jun 1992 Cover: 2.50 **NM** value: **Cover or less**
Circ: CapCity orders: **9,625**
📖 Kurt Busiek (text piece)
6 ❑ Jul 1992 Cover: 2.50 **NM** value: **Cover or less**
Circ: CapCity orders: **7,375**
📖 Kurt Busiek (text piece)
7 ❑ Aug 1992 Cover: 2.50 **NM** value: **Cover or less**
Circ: CapCity orders: **6,425**
📖 Kurt Busiek (text piece)
8 ❑ Sep 1992 Cover: 2.50 **NM** value: **Cover or less**
Circ: CapCity orders: **5,750**
📖 Kurt Busiek (text piece)
9 ❑ Oct 1992 Cover: 2.50 **NM** value: **Cover or less**
Circ: CapCity orders: **5,350**
📖 Kurt Busiek (text piece)
10 ❑ Dec 1992 Cover: 2.50 **NM** value: **Cover or less**
Circ: CapCity orders: **4,625**
📖 Kurt Busiek (text piece)
11 ❑ Jan 1993 Cover: 2.50 **NM** value: **Cover or less**
Circ: CapCity orders: **4,425**
📖 Kurt Busiek (text piece)
12 ❑ Feb 1993 Cover: 2.50 **NM** value: **Cover or less**
Circ: CapCity orders: **4,475**

YOUNG INDIANA JONES CHRONICLES, THE (2ND SERIES) — Hollywood

1 ❑ Cover: 2.50 **NM** value: **Cover or less**
• reprints Dark Horse issues #1 and 2 for newsstand distribution
2 ❑ Cover: 2.50 **NM** value: **Cover or less**
3 ❑ Cover: 2.50 **NM** value: **Cover or less**

YOUNG JUSTICE — DC

In one of the strangest origin stories ever for a team name, the grouping of Impulse, Superboy, Robin, and other heroes was dubbed Young Justice, after reporters misheard the group say, "Just us."

Written by Peter David, the series is rife with puns and in-jokes but also serious looks at such subjects as school violence and racial tolerance.

The spotlight shifts from hero to hero with plenty of character-building in each issue. Where else could a teen-age Lobo go on a date with the daughter of a government agent? Or Impulse and Superboy compete in videogame playoffs? Or the whole team pay a visit to Apokolips where one teammate thinks Darkseid is simply misunderstood? — Brent

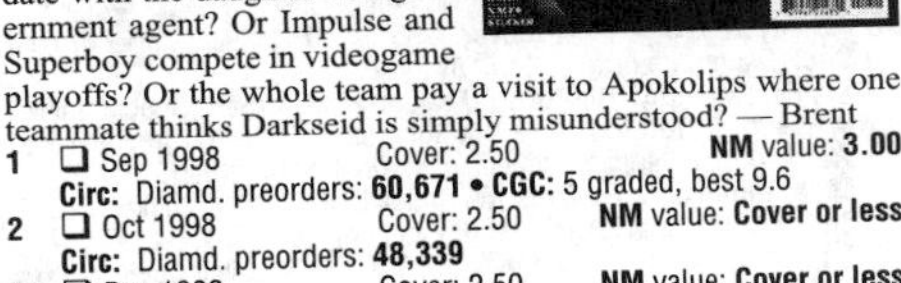

1 ❑ Sep 1998 Cover: 2.50 **NM** value: **3.00**
Circ: Diamd. preorders: **60,671** • **CGC:** 5 graded, best 9.6
2 ❑ Oct 1998 Cover: 2.50 **NM** value: **Cover or less**
Circ: Diamd. preorders: **48,339**
3 ❑ Dec 1998 Cover: 2.50 **NM** value: **Cover or less**
Circ: Diamd. preorders: **46,674**
4 ❑ Jan 1999 Cover: 2.50 **NM** value: **Cover or less**
Circ: Diamd. preorders: **44,096**
5 ❑ Feb 1999 Cover: 2.50 **NM** value: **Cover or less**
Circ: Diamd. preorders: **40,432**
6 ❑ Mar 1999 Cover: 2.50 **NM** value: **Cover or less**
Circ: Diamd. preorders: **39,744**
7 ❑ Apr 1999 Cover: 2.50 **NM** value: **Cover or less**
Circ: Diamd. preorders: **37,357**
• Parent/Teacher conference **A:** Todd Nauck **W:** Peter David ★ Appearance of Nightwing, Max Mercury.
8 ❑ May 1999 Cover: 2.50 **NM** value: **Cover or less**
Circ: Diamd. preorders: **37,024**
9 ❑ Jun 1999 Cover: 2.50 **NM** value: **Cover or less**
Circ: Diamd. preorders: **37,590**
📖 Thug of War **A:** Todd Nauck **W:** Peter David
10 ❑ Jul 1999 Cover: 2.50 **NM** value: **Cover or less**
Circ: Diamd. preorders: **37,084**
📖 Kali'd Away **A:** Todd Nauck **W:** Peter David
11 ❑ Aug 1999 Cover: 2.50 **NM** value: **Cover or less**
Circ: Diamd. preorders: **35,831**
📖 Siege Perilous **A:** Angel Unzuela **W:** Peter David
12 ❑ Sep 1999 Cover: 2.50 **NM** value: **Cover or less**
Circ: Diamd. preorders: **36,081**
📖 Heck's Angels, Part 1 **A:** Todd Nauck **W:** Peter David
13 ❑ Oct 1999 Cover: 2.50 **NM** value: **Cover or less**
Circ: Diamd. preorders: **34,734**
📖 Heck's Angels, Part 3: Dis, Dat and De Other; Heck's Angels, Part 3 **A:** Todd Nauck **W:** Peter David ★ Appearance of Supergirl.
14 ❑ Nov 1999 Cover: 2.50 **NM** value: **Cover or less**
Circ: Diamd. preorders: **35,353**
• Day of Judgment **A:** Todd Nauck **W:** Peter David ★ Appearance of Harm.
15 ❑ Dec 1999 Cover: 2.50 **NM** value: **Cover or less**
Circ: Diamd. preorders: **33,705**
📖 Unstrung **A:** Todd Nauck **W:** Peter David
16 ❑ Jan 2000 Cover: 2.50 **NM** value: **Cover or less**
Circ: Diamd. preorders: **32,615**
📖 Aftermath **A:** Todd Nauck **W:** Peter David
17 ❑ Feb 2000 Cover: 2.50 **NM** value: **Cover or less**
Circ: Diamd. preorders: **31,586**
📖 Stuff Blows Up **A:** Todd Nauck **W:** Peter David
18 ❑ Mar 2000 Cover: 2.50 **NM** value: **Cover or less**
Circ: Diamd. preorders: **30,041**
19 ❑ Apr 2000 Cover: 2.50 **NM** value: **Cover or less**
Circ: Diamd. preorders: **29,076**
20 ❑ Jun 2000 Cover: 2.50 **NM** value: **Cover or less**
Circ: Diamd. preorders: **29,543**
📖 Time Out **A:** Todd Nauck **W:** Peter David

CGC-graded: Multiply prices above by **33 for 9.9 M • 16 for 9.8 NM/M • 7 for 9.6 NM+ • 5 for 9.4 NM • 2.5 for 9.2 NM- • 1.5 for 9.0 VF/NM**

21 ❑ Jul 2000 Cover: 2.50 **NM** value: **Cover or less**
Circ: Diamd. preorders: **30,325**
22 ❑ Aug 2000 Cover: 2.50 **NM** value: **Cover or less**
Circ: Diamd. preorders: **30,965**
23 ❑ Sep 2000 Cover: 2.50 **NM** value: **Cover or less**
Circ: Diamd. preorders: **31,343**
24 ❑ Oct 2000 Cover: 2.50 **NM** value: **Cover or less**
Circ: Diamd. preorders: **29,905**
• Misprinted copies exist with duplicated ad **A:** Todd Nauck **W:** Peter David
25 ❑ Nov 2000 Cover: 2.50 **NM** value: **Cover or less**
Circ: Diamd. preorders: **29,964**
📖 Gold Standard **A:** Todd Nauck **W:** Peter David
26 ❑ Dec 2000 Cover: 2.50 **NM** value: **Cover or less**
Circ: Diamd. preorders: **29,435**
📖 From Myrg With Love **A:** Todd Nauck **W:** Peter David
27 ❑ Jan 2001 Cover: 2.50 **NM** value: **Cover or less**
Circ: Diamd. preorders: **28,914**
📖 Baseball Field: Myrg, or There's a Saga Born Every Minute **A:** Todd Nauck **W:** Peter David
28 ❑ Feb 2001 Cover: 2.50 **NM** value: **Cover or less**
Circ: Diamd. preorders: **28,253**
📖 Hitting for the Cycle **A:** Todd Nauck **W:** Peter David
29 ❑ Mar 2001 Cover: 2.50 **NM** value: **Cover or less**
Circ: Diamd. preorders: **27,089**
📖 Forever and a Day **A:** Todd Nauck **W:** Peter David
30 ❑ Apr 2001 Cover: 2.50 **NM** value: **Cover or less**
Circ: Diamd. preorders: **26,925**
📖 Round Robin **A:** Todd Nauck **W:** Peter David
31 ❑ May 2001 Cover: 2.50 **NM** value: **Cover or less**
Circ: Diamd. preorders: **26,376**
📖 Quiet!!!!! **A:** Todd Nauck **W:** Peter David
32 ❑ Jun 2001 Cover: 2.50 **NM** value: **Cover or less**
Circ: Diamd. preorders: **26,705**
📖 Anita's Date With Lobo **A:** Todd Nauck **W:** Peter David
33 ❑ Jul 2001 Cover: 2.50 **NM** value: **Cover or less**
Circ: Diamd. preorders: **26,294**
34 ❑ Aug 2001 Cover: 2.50 **NM** value: **Cover or less**
Circ: Diamd. preorders: **26,766**
35 ❑ Sep 2001 Cover: 2.50 **NM** value: **Cover or less**
Circ: Diamd. preorders: **32,167**
1000000 ❑ Nov 1998 Cover: 2.50 **NM** value: **Cover or less**
Circ: Diamd. preorders: **51,232**
📖 Just Ice, Cubed **A:** Craig Rousseau; Roberto Flores; Angel Unzueta; Todd Nauck; Larry Stucker; Norm Rapmund; Sean Parsons; Wayne Faucher **W:** Peter David ★ 1st Appearance of Young Justice Legion S.
Bk 1 ❑ Cover: 14.95 **NM** value: **Cover or less**
• A League of their Own; Collects Young Justice #1-7, Young Justice Secret Files #1 **A:** Todd Nauck **W:** Peter David
GS 1 ❑ May 1999 Cover: 4.95 **NM** value: **Cover or less**
Circ: Diamd. preorders: **24,818**
📖 First Memory; The Totally O.K. Corral; My Gun is (Super) Quick; Nosferatu To You Too; Rock 'em Sock 'em... Robot?; Our Justice at War **A:** Sergio Cariello; Justiniano; Keron Grant; Dietrich Smith; Ryan Sook; Tommy Lee Edwards **W:** Chuck Dixon; Larry Stucker; Beau Smith; Jay Faerber; Peter David; Peter Tomasi
SE 1 ❑ Jul 1999 Cover: 3.95 **NM** value: **Cover or less**
📖 Road Trip • Young Justice in No Man's Land **A:** Andy Kuhn **W:** Scott Beatty; Chuck Dixon

YOUNG JUSTICE IN NO MAN'S LAND — DC

1 ❑ Jul 1999 Cover: 3.95 **NM** value: **Cover or less**
Circ: Diamd. preorders: **32,260**
• in Gotham City ★ Appearance of Lagoon Boy.

YOUNG JUSTICE SECRET FILES — DC

1 ❑ Jan 1999 Cover: 4.95 **NM** value: **Cover or less**
Circ: Diamd. preorders: **28,668**
📖 Take Back the Night; Impulse's Trip to the Justice Cave; Mighty Endowed; Tour of the Justice Cave **A:** Ale Garza; Humberto Ramos; Craig Rousseau; Ethan Van Sciver; Dwayne Turner; Mike McKone; Darryl Banks; Tom Grummettt; Todd Nauck **W:** Scott Beatty; D. Curtis Johnson; Joseph Illidge; Matt Brady; Peter David

YOUNG JUSTICE: SINS OF YOUTH — DC

1 ❑ May 2000 Cover: 2.50 **NM** value: **Cover or less**
Circ: Diamd. preorders: **35,595**
📖 Justice for All **A:** Todd Nauck **W:** Peter David
2 ❑ May 2000 Cover: 2.50 **NM** value: **Cover or less**
Circ: Diamd. preorders: **33,525**
📖 Sins of Youth: The Stunning Conclusion **A:** Todd Nauck **W:** Peter David
Bk 1 ❑ Dec 2000 Cover: 19.95 **NM** value: **Cover or less**
• Collects crossover **A:** Todd Nauck **W:** Peter David

YOUNG JUSTICE: THE SECRET — DC

1 ❑ Jun 1998 Cover: 1.95 **NM** value: **Cover or less**
Circ: Diamd. preorders: **38,953**
One-shot. • Girlfrenzy; leads into Young Justice: World Without Grown-Ups

Diamond preorders are the estimated number of comics sold, prior to their release, to comics shops in North America by Diamond Comic Distributors, the largest distributor. These figures underreport the actual number of circulating copies by the amount of reorders Diamond took (usually 5-10% again of the preorders) and sales by publishers to newsstand and bookstore distributors. For many independent publishers, Diamond's preorders may be quite close to the actual number of copies in circulation.

YOUNG LOVE (CRESTWOOD) — Crestwood

This was a companion title to Young Romance (Prize), Joe Simon and Jack Kirby's seminal love comic book. The stories were the standard concerns of romance comics involving love entanglements, dating and relationship problems, and personal life experiences. Also included were traditional advice columns ("Nancy's Hale's Problem Clinic: Treatment for the Troubled Heart"), beauty columns, and stories that asked the readers to write in to solve a particular girl's problem. It's an example of the wide range of comics genres previous decades enjoyed.

1 ❑ Feb 1949 Cover: 0.10 **NM** value: **200.00**
2 ❑ Apr 1949 Cover: 0.10 **NM** value: **100.00**
3 ❑ Jun 1949 Cover: 0.10 **NM** value: **80.00**
4 ❑ Aug 1949 Cover: 0.10 **NM** value: **65.00**
5 ❑ Oct 1949 Cover: 0.10 **NM** value: **65.00**
6 ❑ Dec 1949 Cover: 0.10 **NM** value: **52.00**
7 ❑ Feb 1950 Cover: 0.10 **NM** value: **52.00**
8 ❑ Apr 1950 Cover: 0.10 **NM** value: **52.00**
9 ❑ May 1950 Cover: 0.10 **NM** value: **52.00**
10 ❑ Jun 1950 Cover: 0.10 **NM** value: **52.00**
11 ❑ Jul 1950 Cover: 0.10 **NM** value: **45.00**
12 ❑ Aug 1950 Cover: 0.10 **NM** value: **45.00**
13 ❑ Sep 1950 Cover: 0.10 **NM** value: **45.00**
14 ❑ Oct 1950 Cover: 0.10 **NM** value: **45.00**
15 ❑ Nov 1950 Cover: 0.10 **NM** value: **45.00**
16 ❑ Dec 1950 Cover: 0.10 **NM** value: **45.00**
17 ❑ Jan 1951 Cover: 0.10 **NM** value: **45.00**
18 ❑ Feb 1951 Cover: 0.10 **NM** value: **45.00**
19 ❑ Mar 1951 Cover: 0.10 **NM** value: **45.00**
20 ❑ Apr 1951 Cover: 0.10 **NM** value: **45.00**
21 ❑ May 1951 Cover: 0.10 **NM** value: **36.00**
22 ❑ Jun 1951 Cover: 0.10 **NM** value: **36.00**
23 ❑ Jul 1951 Cover: 0.10 **NM** value: **36.00**
Photo cover. 📖 Maid to Order!; Cradle Robber!; Wrong Number!; Nag, Nag, Nag! **A:** Joe Simon; Jack Kirby

24 ❑ Aug 1951 Cover: 0.10 **NM** value: **36.00**
25 ❑ Sep 1951 Cover: 0.10 **NM** value: **36.00**
26 ❑ Oct 1951 Cover: 0.10 **NM** value: **36.00**
27 ❑ Nov 1951 Cover: 0.10 **NM** value: **36.00**
28 ❑ Dec 1951 Cover: 0.10 **NM** value: **36.00**
29 ❑ Jan 1952 Cover: 0.10 **NM** value: **36.00**
30 ❑ Feb 1952 Cover: 0.10 **NM** value: **36.00**
31 ❑ Mar 1952 Cover: 0.10 **NM** value: **26.00**
32 ❑ Apr 1952 Cover: 0.10 **NM** value: **26.00**
33 ❑ May 1952 Cover: 0.10 **NM** value: **26.00**
34 ❑ Jun 1952 Cover: 0.10 **NM** value: **26.00**
35 ❑ Jul 1952 Cover: 0.10 **NM** value: **26.00**
36 ❑ Aug 1952 Cover: 0.10 **NM** value: **26.00**
37 ❑ Sep 1952 Cover: 0.10 **NM** value: **26.00**
38 ❑ Oct 1952 Cover: 0.10 **NM** value: **26.00**
39 ❑ Nov 1952 Cover: 0.10 **NM** value: **26.00**
40 ❑ Dec 1952 Cover: 0.10 **NM** value: **26.00**
41 ❑ Jan 1953 Cover: 0.10 **NM** value: **20.00**
42 ❑ Feb 1953 Cover: 0.10 **NM** value: **20.00**
43 ❑ Mar 1953 Cover: 0.10 **NM** value: **20.00**
44 ❑ Apr 1953 Cover: 0.10 **NM** value: **20.00**
45 ❑ May 1953 Cover: 0.10 **NM** value: **20.00**
46 ❑ Jun 1953 Cover: 0.10 **NM** value: **20.00**
47 ❑ Jul 1953 Cover: 0.10 **NM** value: **20.00**
48 ❑ Aug 1953 Cover: 0.10 **NM** value: **20.00**
49 ❑ Sep 1953 Cover: 0.10 **NM** value: **20.00**
50 ❑ Oct 1953 Cover: 0.10 **NM** value: **20.00**
51 ❑ Nov 1953 Cover: 0.10 **NM** value: **18.00**
52 ❑ Dec 1953 Cover: 0.10 **NM** value: **18.00**
53 ❑ Jan 1954 Cover: 0.10 **NM** value: **18.00**
54 ❑ Feb 1954 Cover: 0.10 **NM** value: **18.00**
55 ❑ Mar 1954 Cover: 0.10 **NM** value: **18.00**
56 ❑ Apr 1954 Cover: 0.10 **NM** value: **18.00**
57 ❑ May 1954 Cover: 0.10 **NM** value: **18.00**
58 ❑ Jun 1954 Cover: 0.10 **NM** value: **18.00**
59 ❑ Aug 1954 Cover: 0.10 **NM** value: **18.00**
📖 A Stranger to Love!; Love Will Find a Way; No Dream, No Love!; The Truth About Men!
60 ❑ Oct 1954 Cover: 0.10 **NM** value: **18.00**
61 ❑ Dec 1954 Cover: 0.10 **NM** value: **14.00**
62 ❑ Feb 1955 Cover: 0.10 **NM** value: **14.00**
63 ❑ Apr 1955 Cover: 0.10 **NM** value: **14.00**
64 ❑ Jun 1955 Cover: 0.10 **NM** value: **14.00**
65 ❑ Aug 1955 Cover: 0.10 **NM** value: **14.00**
66 ❑ Oct 1955 Cover: 0.10 **NM** value: **14.00**
67 ❑ Dec 1955 Cover: 0.10 **NM** value: **14.00**
68 ❑ Feb 1956 Cover: 0.10 **NM** value: **14.00**
69 ❑ Apr 1956 Cover: 0.10 **NM** value: **14.00**
70 ❑ Jun 1956 Cover: 0.10 **NM** value: **14.00**
71 ❑ Aug 1956 Cover: 0.10 **NM** value: **12.00**
72 ❑ Oct 1956 Cover: 0.10 **NM** value: **12.00**
73 ❑ Dec 1956 Cover: 0.10 **NM** value: **12.00**

YOUNG LOVE (DC) — DC

39 ❑ Oct 1963 Cover: 0.12 **NM** value: **30.00**
40 ❑ Dec 1963 Cover: 0.12 **NM** value: **24.00**
41 ❑ Feb 1964 Cover: 0.12 **NM** value: **24.00**
42 ❑ Apr 1964 Cover: 0.12 **NM** value: **24.00**
43 ❑ Jun 1964 Cover: 0.12 **NM** value: **24.00**
44 ❑ Aug 1964 Cover: 0.12 **NM** value: **24.00**
45 ❑ Oct 1964 Cover: 0.12 **NM** value: **24.00**
46 ❑ Dec 1964 Cover: 0.12 **NM** value: **24.00**
47 ❑ Feb 1965 Cover: 0.12 **NM** value: **24.00**
Circ: Statement: **206,456**
48 ❑ Apr 1965 Cover: 0.12 **NM** value: **24.00**
Circ: Statement: **206,456**
49 ❑ Jun 1965 Cover: 0.12 **NM** value: **24.00**
Circ: Statement: **206,456**
50 ❑ Aug 1965 Cover: 0.12 **NM** value: **24.00**
Circ: Statement: **206,456**
51 ❑ Oct 1965 Cover: 0.12 **NM** value: **20.00**
Circ: Statement: **206,456**
52 ❑ Dec 1965 Cover: 0.12 **NM** value: **20.00**
Circ: Statement: **206,456**
53 ❑ Feb 1966 Cover: 0.12 **NM** value: **20.00**
54 ❑ Apr 1966 Cover: 0.12 **NM** value: **20.00**
55 ❑ Jun 1966 Cover: 0.12 **NM** value: **20.00**
56 ❑ Aug 1966 Cover: 0.12 **NM** value: **20.00**
57 ❑ Oct 1966 Cover: 0.12 **NM** value: **20.00**
58 ❑ Dec 1966 Cover: 0.12 **NM** value: **20.00**
59 ❑ Feb 1967 Cover: 0.12 **NM** value: **20.00**
Circ: Statement: **187,400**
60 ❑ Apr 1967 Cover: 0.12 **NM** value: **20.00**
Circ: Statement: **187,400**
61 ❑ Jun 1967 Cover: 0.12 **NM** value: **20.00**
Circ: Statement: **187,400**
62 ❑ Aug 1967 Cover: 0.12 **NM** value: **20.00**
Circ: Statement: **187,400**
63 ❑ Oct 1967 Cover: 0.12 **NM** value: **20.00**
Circ: Statement: **187,400**
📖 Love is More than This; Happily Ever After; Lets Not Fall in Love
64 ❑ Dec 1967 Cover: 0.12 **NM** value: **20.00**
Circ: Statement: **187,400**
65 ❑ Feb 1968 Cover: 0.12 **NM** value: **20.00**
Circ: Statement: **198,115**
66 ❑ Apr 1968 Cover: 0.12 **NM** value: **20.00**
Circ: Statement: **198,115**
67 ❑ Jun 1968 Cover: 0.12 **NM** value: **20.00**
Circ: Statement: **198,115**
68 ❑ Aug 1968 Cover: 0.12 **NM** value: **20.00**
Circ: Statement: **198,115**
69 ❑ Sep 1968 Cover: 0.25 **NM** value: **20.00**
Circ: Statement: **198,115** • **CGC:** 1 graded, best 6.5
• Giant
70 ❑ Oct 1968 **NM** value: **20.00**
Circ: Statement: **198,115**
71 ❑ Dec 1968 Cover: 0.12 **NM** value: **14.00**
Circ: Statement: **198,115**
72 ❑ Feb 1969 **NM** value: **14.00**
73 ❑ Apr 1969 **NM** value: **14.00**
• Has 1968 Statement; avg print run 357,000; avg sales 198,000; avg subs 115; avg total paid circ 198,115; samples 386; max existent 198,501; 44% of run returned
74 ❑ Jun 1969 **NM** value: **14.00**
75 ❑ Aug 1969 Cover: 0.15 **NM** value: **14.00**
76 ❑ Oct 1969 Cover: 0.15 **NM** value: **14.00**
77 ❑ Dec 1969 Cover: 0.15 **NM** value: **14.00**
78 ❑ Feb 1970 Cover: 0.15 **NM** value: **14.00**
79 ❑ Apr 1970 Cover: 0.15 **NM** value: **14.00**
80 ❑ Jun 1970 Cover: 0.15 **NM** value: **14.00**
81 ❑ Aug 1970 Cover: 0.15 **NM** value: **14.00**
82 ❑ Oct 1970 Cover: 0.15 **NM** value: **14.00**
83 ❑ Dec 1970 Cover: 0.15 **NM** value: **14.00**
84 ❑ Feb 1971 Cover: 0.15 **NM** value: **14.00**
85 ❑ Apr 1971 Cover: 0.15 **NM** value: **14.00**
• **CGC:** 1 graded, best 9.2
86 ❑ Jun 1971 Cover: 0.15 **NM** value: **14.00**
87 ❑ Aug 1971 Cover: 0.15 **NM** value: **14.00**
• **CGC:** 1 graded, best 9.4
88 ❑ Sep 1971 **NM** value: **14.00**
89 ❑ Oct 1971 **NM** value: **14.00**
90 ❑ Dec 1971 **NM** value: **14.00**
91 ❑ Jan 1972 **NM** value: **10.00**
Circ: Statement: **124,326**
92 ❑ Feb 1972 **NM** value: **10.00**
Circ: Statement: **124,326**
93 ❑ Mar 1972 Cover: 0.25 **NM** value: **10.00**
Circ: Statement: **124,326**
94 ❑ Apr 1972 Cover: 0.25 **NM** value: **10.00**
Circ: Statement: **124,326**
95 ❑ May 1972 Cover: 0.25 **NM** value: **10.00**
Circ: Statement: **124,326**
96 ❑ Jun 1972 Cover: 0.25 **NM** value: **10.00**
Circ: Statement: **124,326**
97 ❑ Jul 1972 Cover: 0.20 **NM** value: **10.00**
Circ: Statement: **124,326**
98 ❑ Aug 1972 Cover: 0.20 **NM** value: **10.00**
Circ: Statement: **124,326**
99 ❑ Sep 1972 Cover: 0.20 **NM** value: **10.00**
Circ: Statement: **124,326**
100 ❑ Oct 1972 Cover: 0.20 **NM** value: **10.00**
Circ: Statement: **124,326**
101 ❑ Nov 1972 Cover: 0.20 **NM** value: **7.00**
Circ: Statement: **124,326**
102 ❑ Feb 1973 Cover: 0.20 **NM** value: **7.00**
Circ: Statement: **117,690**
103 ❑ Apr 1973 Cover: 0.20 **NM** value: **7.00**
Circ: Statement: **117,690**
• Has 1972 Statement; avg total paid circ 124,326
104 ❑ Jun 1973 Cover: 0.20 **NM** value: **7.00**
Circ: Statement: **117,690** • **CGC:** 1 graded, best 9.2
105 ❑ Sep 1973 Cover: 0.20 **NM** value: **7.00**
Circ: Statement: **117,690**
106 ❑ Nov 1973 **NM** value: **7.00**
Circ: Statement: **117,690**
107 ❑ Jan 1974 Cover: 0.50 **NM** value: **25.00**
Circ: Statement: **127,972** • **CGC:** 7 graded, best 9.4
108 ❑ Mar 1974 Cover: 0.50 **NM** value: **20.00**
Circ: Statement: **127,972** • **CGC:** 1 graded, best 8.0
109 ❑ May 1974 Cover: 0.60 **NM** value: **20.00**
Circ: Statement: **127,972** • **CGC:** 1 graded, best 9.2
• Has 1973 Statement; avg total paid circ 117,690
110 ❑ Jul 1974 Cover: 0.60 **NM** value: **20.00**
Circ: Statement: **127,972** • **CGC:** 1 graded, best 8.5
111 ❑ Sep 1974 Cover: 0.60 **NM** value: **20.00**
Circ: Statement: **127,972** • **CGC:** 1 graded, best 9.0

Other grades: Multiply prices above by **1.5 for Mint • 2/3 for Very Fine • 1/3 for Fine • 1/5 for Very Good • 1/8 for Good**

112 ☐ Nov 1974 NM value: **20.00**
Circ: Statement: **127,972**
113 ☐ Jan 1975 NM value: **20.00**
114 ☐ Mar 1975 NM value: **20.00**
• **CGC:** 2 graded, best 9.2
115 ☐ May 1975 Cover: 0.25 NM value: **12.00**
• Has 1974 Statement; avg total paid circ 127,972
116 ☐ Jul 1975 Cover: 0.25 NM value: **12.00**
117 ☐ Sep 1975 Cover: 0.25 NM value: **12.00**
118 ☐ Nov 1975 Cover: 0.25 NM value: **12.00**
119 ☐ Jan 1976 Cover: 0.25 NM value: **12.00**
120 ☐ Win 1976 Cover: 0.25 NM value: **12.00**
121 ☐ 1976 NM value: **12.00**
122 ☐ 1976 NM value: **12.00**
123 ☐ 1977 NM value: **12.00**
124 ☐ 1977 NM value: **12.00**
125 ☐ 1977 NM value: **12.00**
126 ☐ Jul 1977 NM value: **12.00**

YOUNG LOVERS — Avalon

1 ☐ Cover: 2.95 NM value: **Cover or less**
📖 Outrageous Flirt; Strength is in the Heart; Blind Love; How Beautiful my Love; A Lamb in Wolf's Clothing; Take Love for Life; Love's Low Road • Indicia reads "Rock and Roll Romance"

YOUNG LUST — Print Mint / Last Gasp

1 ☐ b&w Cover: 0.50 NM value: **5.00**
2 ☐ b&w Cover: 0.50 NM value: **3.00**
3 ☐ full color Cover: 0.75 NM value: **3.00**
4 ☐ full color Cover: 1.00 NM value: **3.00**
📖 5th Grade Confidential; A Dog-Boy and a Geisha; Gilly Conquers His Sex Problem!; Simian Sin; Little Signs of Passion; Claude 'n DiDi: Bottoms-Up!; Smeared Twilight; Raw Meat; Scenic Views from the Griffith Observatory; The Red Hot Romances of Shlub Mugubb • Print Mint publishes **A:** Justin Green; Robert Crumb; Bill Griffith; Jay Kinney; Kim Deitch; Ned Sonntag; Roger Brand; Spain; Spain Rodriguez **W:** Justin Green; Robert Crumb; Diane Noomin; Bill Griffith; Jay Kinney; Kim Deitch; Ned Sonntag; Roger Brand; Spain Rodriguez
5 ☐ b&w Cover: 1.00 NM value: **3.00**
• Kitchen Sink publishes **A:** Paul Mavrides; Bill Griffith; Jay Kinney; Spain
6 ☐ Cover: 1.00 NM value: **3.00**
7 ☐ Cover: 3.50 NM value: **Cover or less**
• 20th Anniversary Issue. **A:** Justin Green; Dan Clowes; Paul Mavrides; Bill Griffith; Jay Kinney; Spain
8 ☐ Cover: 3.95 NM value: **Cover or less**

YOUNG MASTER — New Comics

1 ☐ Nov 1987, b&w Cover: 1.75 NM value: **Cover or less**
2 ☐ Dec 1987, b&w Cover: 1.75 NM value: **Cover or less**
3 ☐ Mar 1988, b&w Cover: 1.75 NM value: **Cover or less**
4 ☐ May 1988, b&w Cover: 1.75 NM value: **Cover or less**
5 ☐ Jul 1988, b&w Cover: 1.75 NM value: **Cover or less**
6 ☐ Oct 1988, b&w Cover: 1.75 NM value: **Cover or less**
7 ☐ Jan 1989 Cover: 1.75 NM value: **Cover or less**
8 ☐ Mar 1989 Cover: 1.95 NM value: **Cover or less**
9 ☐ Cover: 1.95 NM value: **Cover or less**

YOUNG MEN — Marvel

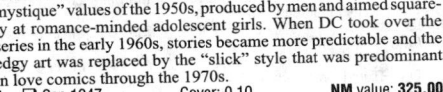

Formerly known as "Cowboy Romances," Young Men was a perfect example of Marvel publisher Martin Goodman's trying to catch hold of whatever type of comics was selling at a given moment. With #12, Young Men took on a war-comics focus and did a modest name change to "Young Men on the Battlefield." Sports and hot-rod issues followed.

The real switch came with #24, when Young Men switched to a super-hero format starring the war-time sensation the Human Torch. Although super-heroes were in a time of decline, #24 brought core Marvel heroes back briefly and retold the origins of Captain America, The Human Torch, and The Sub-Mariner. The effect didn't last, however, and Young Men disappeared with #28. It would not be until six years later that Marvel's age of super-heroes would arrive with the introduction of The Fantastic Four in 1961.

4 ☐ Jun 1950 Cover: 0.10 NM value: **100.00**
📖 The Called Me Shorty; A New Car for Christy; The Movie Queen Murder (text); The Battle Cry; The Champ; The Treachery of Mr. McGoey!
5 ☐ Sep 1950 Cover: 0.10 NM value: **60.00**
6 ☐ Dec 1950 Cover: 0.10 NM value: **60.00**
7 ☐ Feb 1951 Cover: 0.10 NM value: **60.00**
8 ☐ Apr 1951 Cover: 0.10 NM value: **60.00**
9 ☐ Jun 1951 Cover: 0.10 NM value: **60.00**
• **CGC:** 1 graded, best 9.2
10 ☐ Aug 1951 Cover: 0.10 NM value: **60.00**
11 ☐ Oct 1951 Cover: 0.10 NM value: **45.00**
12 ☐ Dec 1951 Cover: 0.10 NM value: **45.00**
13 ☐ Feb 1952 Cover: 0.10 NM value: **45.00**
14 ☐ Mar 1952 Cover: 0.10 NM value: **45.00**
15 ☐ Jun 1952 Cover: 0.10 NM value: **45.00**
16 ☐ Aug 1952 Cover: 0.10 NM value: **45.00**
17 ☐ Oct 1952 Cover: 0.10 NM value: **45.00**
• **CGC:** 1 graded, best 5.5
18 ☐ Dec 1952 Cover: 0.10 NM value: **45.00**
19 ☐ Feb 1953 Cover: 0.10 NM value: **45.00**
20 ☐ Mar 1953 Cover: 0.10 NM value: **45.00**
21 ☐ Jun 1953 Cover: 0.10 NM value: **45.00**
22 ☐ Aug 1953 Cover: 0.10 NM value: **45.00**
23 ☐ Oct 1953 Cover: 0.10 NM value: **45.00**
24 ☐ Dec 1953 Cover: 0.10 NM value: **1600.00**
• **CGC:** 7 graded, best 9.0
25 ☐ Feb 1954 Cover: 0.10 NM value: **775.00**
• **CGC:** 4 graded, best 7.0
📖 The Return of…The Human Torch; Death is Standing By (text story); Captain America: The Executioner; Sub-Mariner **A:** Bill Everett; John Romita
25-2 ☐ Cover: 1.50 NM value: **2.00**
26 ☐ Mar 1954 Cover: 0.10 NM value: **750.00**
27 ☐ Apr 1954 Cover: 0.10 NM value: **750.00**
• **CGC:** 1 graded, best 6.5
28 ☐ Jun 1954 Cover: 0.10 NM value: **25.00**
• **CGC:** 1 graded, best 7.5
final issue.

YOUNG ROMANCE (PRIZE) — Prize

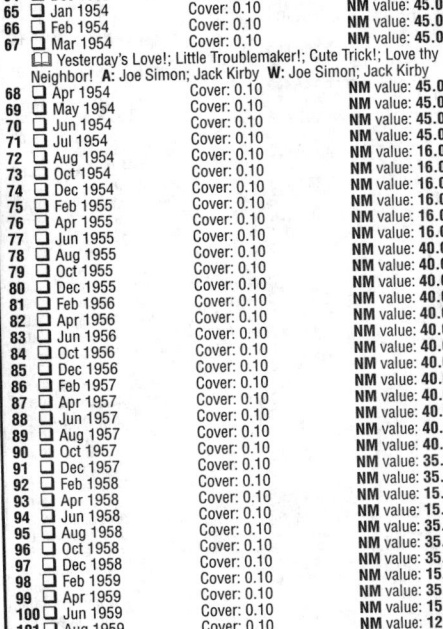

Young Romance was the first legitimate romance comic book in America. Both Young Romance and its sister publication, Young Love, were produced by the innovative team of Simon and Kirby.

In its early days, Young Romance featured a hard-edged melodrama and genuine tension and suspense. Its subjects were often couples from the lower classes, not just well-scrubbed suburban kids, and it dealt with such issues as alcoholism, spousal abuse, infidelity, and serious criminal behavior. Gradually, the title morphed into a tame mouthpiece for the conformist "feminine mystique" values of the 1950s, produced by men and aimed squarely at romance-minded adolescent girls. When DC took over the series in the early 1960s, stories became more predictable and the edgy art was replaced by the "slick" style that was predominant in love comics through the 1970s.

1 ☐ Sep 1947 Cover: 0.10 NM value: **325.00**
• **CGC:** 2 graded, best 8.0
📖 I Was a Pick-Up!; The Farmer's Wife; Misguided Heart; The Plight of the Suspicious Bride Groom; Young Hearts Sing a Summer Song • 1st romance comic **A:** Joe Simon; Jack Kirby; Bill Draut **W:** Joe Simon
2 ☐ Nov 1947 Cover: 0.10 NM value: **200.00**
3 ☐ Jan 1948 Cover: 0.10 NM value: **150.00**
4 ☐ Mar 1948 Cover: 0.10 NM value: **150.00**
• **CGC:** 1 graded, best 6.0
5 ☐ May 1948 Cover: 0.10 NM value: **150.00**
• **CGC:** 1 graded, best 8.0
6 ☐ Jul 1948 Cover: 0.10 NM value: **125.00**
7 ☐ Sep 1948 Cover: 0.10 NM value: **125.00**
• **CGC:** 2 graded, best 9.4
8 ☐ Nov 1948 Cover: 0.10 NM value: **125.00**
9 ☐ Jan 1949 Cover: 0.10 NM value: **125.00**
• **CGC:** 1 graded, best 9.4
10 ☐ Mar 1949 Cover: 0.10 NM value: **125.00**
• **CGC:** 1 graded, best 8.5
11 ☐ May 1949 Cover: 0.10 NM value: **95.00**
12 ☐ Jul 1949 Cover: 0.10 NM value: **95.00**
13 ☐ Sep 1949 Cover: 0.10 NM value: **95.00**
14 ☐ Oct 1949 Cover: 0.10 NM value: **95.00**
15 ☐ Nov 1949 Cover: 0.10 NM value: **95.00**
16 ☐ Dec 1949 Cover: 0.10 NM value: **95.00**
17 ☐ Jan 1950 Cover: 0.10 NM value: **95.00**
18 ☐ Feb 1950 Cover: 0.10 NM value: **95.00**
19 ☐ Mar 1950 Cover: 0.10 NM value: **95.00**
20 ☐ Apr 1950 Cover: 0.10 NM value: **95.00**
21 ☐ May 1950 Cover: 0.10 NM value: **75.00**
22 ☐ Jun 1950 Cover: 0.10 NM value: **75.00**
23 ☐ Jul 1950 Cover: 0.10 NM value: **75.00**
24 ☐ Aug 1950 Cover: 0.10 NM value: **75.00**
25 ☐ Sep 1950 Cover: 0.10 NM value: **75.00**
26 ☐ Oct 1950 Cover: 0.10 NM value: **75.00**
27 ☐ Nov 1950 Cover: 0.10 NM value: **75.00**
28 ☐ Dec 1950 Cover: 0.10 NM value: **75.00**
29 ☐ Jan 1951 Cover: 0.10 NM value: **75.00**
30 ☐ Feb 1951 Cover: 0.10 NM value: **75.00**
31 ☐ Mar 1951 Cover: 0.10 NM value: **60.00**
32 ☐ Apr 1951 Cover: 0.10 NM value: **60.00**
33 ☐ May 1951 Cover: 0.10 NM value: **60.00**
34 ☐ Jun 1951 Cover: 0.10 NM value: **60.00**
📖 Old Fashioned Girl!; Will You Help Me?; The Other Woman!; There's Romance in the Stars; Whistle Bait!; Girl Friday! **A:** Joe Simon; Jack Kirby **W:** Joe Simon; Jack Kirby
35 ☐ Jul 1951 Cover: 0.10 NM value: **60.00**
36 ☐ Aug 1951 Cover: 0.10 NM value: **60.00**
37 ☐ Sep 1951 Cover: 0.10 NM value: **60.00**
38 ☐ Oct 1951 Cover: 0.10 NM value: **60.00**
39 ☐ Nov 1951 Cover: 0.10 NM value: **60.00**
40 ☐ Dec 1951 Cover: 0.10 NM value: **60.00**
41 ☐ Jan 1952 Cover: 0.10 NM value: **55.00**
42 ☐ Feb 1952 Cover: 0.10 NM value: **55.00**
43 ☐ Mar 1952 Cover: 0.10 NM value: **55.00**
44 ☐ Apr 1952 Cover: 0.10 NM value: **55.00**
45 ☐ May 1952 Cover: 0.10 NM value: **55.00**
46 ☐ Jun 1952 Cover: 0.10 NM value: **55.00**
47 ☐ Jul 1952 Cover: 0.10 NM value: **55.00**
48 ☐ Aug 1952 Cover: 0.10 NM value: **24.00**
49 ☐ Sep 1952 Cover: 0.10 NM value: **24.00**
50 ☐ Oct 1952 Cover: 0.10 NM value: **24.00**
51 ☐ Nov 1952 Cover: 0.10 NM value: **55.00**
52 ☐ Dec 1952 Cover: 0.10 NM value: **55.00**
53 ☐ Jan 1953 Cover: 0.10 NM value: **55.00**
54 ☐ Feb 1953 Cover: 0.10 NM value: **55.00**
55 ☐ Mar 1953 Cover: 0.10 NM value: **55.00**
56 ☐ Apr 1953 Cover: 0.10 NM value: **55.00**
57 ☐ May 1953 Cover: 0.10 NM value: **55.00**
58 ☐ Jun 1953 Cover: 0.10 NM value: **55.00**
59 ☐ Jul 1953 Cover: 0.10 NM value: **55.00**
60 ☐ Aug 1953 Cover: 0.10 NM value: **55.00**
61 ☐ Sep 1953 Cover: 0.10 NM value: **45.00**
62 ☐ Oct 1953 Cover: 0.10 NM value: **45.00**
63 ☐ Nov 1953 Cover: 0.10 NM value: **45.00**
64 ☐ Dec 1953 Cover: 0.10 NM value: **45.00**
65 ☐ Jan 1954 Cover: 0.10 NM value: **45.00**
66 ☐ Feb 1954 Cover: 0.10 NM value: **45.00**
67 ☐ Mar 1954 Cover: 0.10 NM value: **45.00**
📖 Yesterday's Love!; Little Troublemaker!; Cute Trick!; Love thy Neighbor! **A:** Joe Simon; Jack Kirby **W:** Joe Simon; Jack Kirby
68 ☐ Apr 1954 Cover: 0.10 NM value: **45.00**
69 ☐ May 1954 Cover: 0.10 NM value: **45.00**
70 ☐ Jun 1954 Cover: 0.10 NM value: **45.00**
71 ☐ Jul 1954 Cover: 0.10 NM value: **45.00**
72 ☐ Aug 1954 Cover: 0.10 NM value: **16.00**
73 ☐ Oct 1954 Cover: 0.10 NM value: **16.00**
74 ☐ Dec 1954 Cover: 0.10 NM value: **16.00**
75 ☐ Feb 1955 Cover: 0.10 NM value: **16.00**
76 ☐ Apr 1955 Cover: 0.10 NM value: **16.00**
77 ☐ Jun 1955 Cover: 0.10 NM value: **16.00**
78 ☐ Aug 1955 Cover: 0.10 NM value: **40.00**
79 ☐ Oct 1955 Cover: 0.10 NM value: **40.00**
80 ☐ Dec 1955 Cover: 0.10 NM value: **40.00**
81 ☐ Feb 1956 Cover: 0.10 NM value: **40.00**
82 ☐ Apr 1956 Cover: 0.10 NM value: **40.00**
83 ☐ Jun 1956 Cover: 0.10 NM value: **40.00**
84 ☐ Oct 1956 Cover: 0.10 NM value: **40.00**
85 ☐ Dec 1956 Cover: 0.10 NM value: **40.00**
86 ☐ Feb 1957 Cover: 0.10 NM value: **40.00**
87 ☐ Apr 1957 Cover: 0.10 NM value: **40.00**
88 ☐ Jun 1957 Cover: 0.10 NM value: **40.00**
89 ☐ Aug 1957 Cover: 0.10 NM value: **40.00**
90 ☐ Oct 1957 Cover: 0.10 NM value: **40.00**
91 ☐ Dec 1957 Cover: 0.10 NM value: **35.00**
92 ☐ Feb 1958 Cover: 0.10 NM value: **35.00**
93 ☐ Apr 1958 Cover: 0.10 NM value: **15.00**
94 ☐ Jun 1958 Cover: 0.10 NM value: **15.00**
95 ☐ Aug 1958 Cover: 0.10 NM value: **35.00**
96 ☐ Oct 1958 Cover: 0.10 NM value: **35.00**
97 ☐ Dec 1958 Cover: 0.10 NM value: **35.00**
98 ☐ Feb 1959 Cover: 0.10 NM value: **15.00**
99 ☐ Apr 1959 Cover: 0.10 NM value: **35.00**
100 ☐ Jun 1959 Cover: 0.10 NM value: **15.00**
101 ☐ Aug 1959 Cover: 0.10 NM value: **12.00**
102 ☐ Oct 1959 Cover: 0.10 NM value: **30.00**
103 ☐ Dec 1959 Cover: 0.10 NM value: **30.00**
104 ☐ Feb 1960 Cover: 0.10 NM value: **30.00**
105 ☐ Apr 1960 Cover: 0.10 NM value: **14.00**
106 ☐ Jun 1960 Cover: 0.10 NM value: **14.00**
107 ☐ Aug 1960 Cover: 0.10 NM value: **14.00**
108 ☐ Oct 1960 Cover: 0.10 NM value: **14.00**
109 ☐ Dec 1960 Cover: 0.10 NM value: **14.00**
110 ☐ Feb 1961 Cover: 0.10 NM value: **14.00**
111 ☐ Apr 1961 Cover: 0.10 NM value: **14.00**
112 ☐ Jun 1961 Cover: 0.10 NM value: **14.00**
113 ☐ Aug 1961 Cover: 0.10 NM value: **14.00**
114 ☐ Oct 1961 Cover: 0.10 NM value: **14.00**
115 ☐ Dec 1961 NM value: **14.00**
116 ☐ Feb 1962 NM value: **14.00**
117 ☐ Apr 1962 NM value: **14.00**
118 ☐ Jun 1962 NM value: **14.00**
119 ☐ Aug 1962 NM value: **14.00**
120 ☐ Oct 1962 NM value: **14.00**
121 ☐ Dec 1962 NM value: **14.00**
122 ☐ Feb 1963 NM value: **14.00**
123 ☐ Apr 1963 NM value: **14.00**
124 ☐ Jun 1963 NM value: **14.00**
• Series continued in Young Romance (DC) #125

YOUNG ROMANCE (DC) — DC

In 1963, DC picked up Young Romance from Prize Comics, which had been publishing it from shortly after World War II. A charmer of a romance series, Young Romance spun tales revolving around the theme of love's overcoming all obstacles. Typical of these were "Dance with Me, Darling" in which a couple grew from childhood as dance partners and eventually found love as adults. Of course, it wouldn't be a true romance unless there was some obstacle to overcome, such as a physical disability or (more commonly) a rival for their love's affections. True love won out in the end, however, and the stories would end with a kiss.

125 ☐ NM value: **42.00**
• Series continued from Young Romance (Prize) #124
126 ☐ NM value: **18.00**
127 ☐ NM value: **18.00**
128 ☐ NM value: **18.00**
129 ☐ NM value: **18.00**
130 ☐ NM value: **18.00**
131 ☐ NM value: **18.00**
132 ☐ NM value: **18.00**
133 ☐ NM value: **18.00**
134 ☐ NM value: **18.00**
135 ☐ NM value: **18.00**
136 ☐ NM value: **18.00**
137 ☐ NM value: **18.00**
138 ☐ Nov 1965 Cover: 0.12 NM value: **18.00**
139 ☐ Jan 1966 Cover: 0.12 NM value: **18.00**
Circ: Statement: **204,613**
140 ☐ Mar 1966 Cover: 0.12 NM value: **18.00**
Circ: Statement: **204,613**
141 ☐ May 1966 NM value: **15.00**
Circ: Statement: **204,613**

CGC-graded: Multiply prices above by **33 for 9.9 M • 16 for 9.8 NM/M • 7 for 9.6 NM+ • 5 for 9.4 NM • 2.5 for 9.2 NM- • 1.5 for 9.0 VF/NM**

142 ❑ Jul 1966 NM value: 15.00
Circ: Statement: 204,613
143 ❑ Sep 1966 NM value: 15.00
Circ: Statement: 204,613
144 ❑ Nov 1966 NM value: 15.00
Circ: Statement: 204,613
145 ❑ Jan 1967 NM value: 15.00
Circ: Statement: 187,400
146 ❑ Mar 1967 NM value: 15.00
Circ: Statement: 187,400
147 ❑ May 1967 NM value: 15.00
Circ: Statement: 187,400
148 ❑ Jul 1967 NM value: 15.00
Circ: Statement: 187,400
149 ❑ Sep 1967 NM value: 15.00
Circ: Statement: 187,400
150 ❑ Nov 1967 NM value: 15.00
Circ: Statement: 187,400
151 ❑ Jan 1968 Cover: 0.12 NM value: 12.00
152 ❑ Mar 1968 Cover: 0.12 NM value: 12.00
153 ❑ May 1968 Cover: 0.12 NM value: 12.00
154 ❑ Jul 1968 Cover: 0.12 NM value: 12.00
155 ❑ Sep 1968 Cover: 0.12 NM value: 12.00
156 ❑ Nov 1968 Cover: 0.12 NM value: 12.00
157 ❑ Jan 1969 Cover: 0.12 NM value: 12.00
158 ❑ Mar 1969 Cover: 0.12 NM value: 12.00
159 ❑ May 1969 Cover: 0.12 NM value: 12.00
160 ❑ Jul 1969 NM value: 10.00
161 ❑ Sep 1969 Cover: 0.15 NM value: 10.00
162 ❑ Nov 1969 Cover: 0.15 NM value: 10.00
163 ❑ Jan 1970 Cover: 0.15 NM value: 10.00
164 ❑ Mar 1970 Cover: 0.15 NM value: 10.00
165 ❑ May 1970 Cover: 0.15 NM value: 10.00
166 ❑ Jul 1970 Cover: 0.15 NM value: 10.00
167 ❑ Sep 1970 Cover: 0.15 NM value: 10.00
168 ❑ Nov 1970 Cover: 0.15 NM value: 10.00
169 ❑ Jan 1971 Cover: 0.15 NM value: 10.00
170 ❑ Mar 1971 Cover: 0.15 NM value: 10.00
171 ❑ May 1971 Cover: 0.15 NM value: 9.00
172 ❑ Jul 1971 Cover: 0.25 NM value: 9.00
173 ❑ Aug 1971 Cover: 0.25 NM value: 9.00
174 ❑ Sep 1971 Cover: 0.25 NM value: 9.00
175 ❑ Oct 1971 Cover: 0.25 NM value: 9.00
176 ❑ Nov 1971 Cover: 0.25 NM value: 9.00
177 ❑ Dec 1971 Cover: 0.25 NM value: 9.00
178 ❑ Jan 1972 Cover: 0.25 NM value: 9.00
Circ: Statement: 124,091
179 ❑ Feb 1972 Cover: 0.25 NM value: 9.00
Circ: Statement: 124,091 • CGC: 1 graded, best 9.0
180 ❑ Mar 1972 Cover: 0.25 NM value: 9.00
Circ: Statement: 124,091
181 ❑ Apr 1972 Cover: 0.25 NM value: 9.00
Circ: Statement: 124,091
182 ❑ May 1972 Cover: 0.25 NM value: 9.00
Circ: Statement: 124,091
183 ❑ Jun 1972 NM value: 9.00
Circ: Statement: 124,091
184 ❑ Jul 1972 NM value: 9.00
Circ: Statement: 124,091
185 ❑ Aug 1972 Cover: 0.20 NM value: 9.00
Circ: Statement: 124,091
186 ❑ Sep 1972 Cover: 0.20 NM value: 9.00
Circ: Statement: 124,091
187 ❑ Oct 1972 Cover: 0.20 NM value: 9.00
Circ: Statement: 124,091
188 ❑ Nov 1972 Cover: 0.20 NM value: 9.00
Circ: Statement: 124,091
189 ❑ Dec 1972 Cover: 0.20 NM value: 9.00
Circ: Statement: 124,091
190 ❑ Jan 1973 Cover: 0.20 NM value: 9.00
Circ: Statement: 119,583
191 ❑ Feb 1973 Cover: 0.20 NM value: 9.00
Circ: Statement: 119,583
192 ❑ Mar 1973 Cover: 0.20 NM value: 9.00
Circ: Statement: 119,583
• Has 1972 Statement; avg total paid circ 124,091
193 ❑ May 1973 Cover: 0.20 NM value: 9.00
Circ: Statement: 119,583
194 ❑ Aug 1973 Cover: 0.20 NM value: 9.00
Circ: Statement: 119,583
195 ❑ Oct 1973 Cover: 0.20 NM value: 9.00
Circ: Statement: 119,583
196 ❑ Dec 1973 Cover: 0.20 NM value: 9.00
Circ: Statement: 119,583
197 ❑ Feb 1974 NM value: 9.00
Circ: Statement: 130,802 • CGC: 5 graded, best 9.4
198 ❑ Apr 1974 Cover: 0.50 NM value: 20.00
Circ: Statement: 130,802 • CGC: 4 graded, best 9.2
199 ❑ Jun 1974 Cover: 0.60 NM value: 20.00
Circ: Statement: 130,802 • CGC: 3 graded, best 9.2
• Has 1973 Statement; avg total paid circ 119,583
200 ❑ Aug 1974 Cover: 0.60 NM value: 20.00
Circ: Statement: 130,802 • CGC: 1 graded, best 8.0
201 ❑ Oct 1974 Cover: 0.60 NM value: 20.00
Circ: Statement: 130,802
202 ❑ Dec 1974 NM value: 8.00
Circ: Statement: 130,802 • CGC: 1 graded, best 8.5
203 ❑ Feb 1975 NM value: 8.00
204 ❑ Apr 1975 NM value: 8.00
• CGC: 1 graded, best 8.0
205 ❑ Jun 1975 NM value: 8.00
• Has 1974 Statement; avg total paid circ 130,802
206 ❑ Aug 1975 NM value: 8.00
207 ❑ Oct 1975 Cover: 0.25 NM value: 8.00
208 ❑ Dec 1975 NM value: 8.00
final issue.

YOUNGSPUD — Spoof

1 ❑ Cover: 2.95 NM value: Cover or less

YOUNG WITCHES, THE — Fantagraphics / Eros

All issues are adults only.

Young Lillian Cunningham belongs to a secret order of witches. Her mother died giving birth to her, and her father (shamed by the birth of the child, when he had met and married the mother only seven months before) took his own life. This left Lillian in the care of strange aunts, who were secretly members of the Cult of Ishtar.

When she reached a proper age, Lillian was placed in "the Institute," where she was indoctrinated with the female-dominant teachings of the Cult of Ishtar. She was also taught to use her latent mental powers — her "talent." Ultimately, the Cult hoped to make her one of their own, because Lillian showed great potential for power. However, she also showed a stubborn streak which rejected the Cult's view that men were unworthy of anything except contempt.

1 ❑ May 1991, b&w Cover: 2.25 NM value: 2.50
2 ❑ Jun 1991, b&w Cover: 2.25 NM value: 2.50
3 ❑ Jul 1991, b&w Cover: 2.25 NM value: 2.50
4 ❑ Sep 1991 Cover: 2.75 NM value: Cover or less

YOUNG WITCHES IV, THE: THE ETERNAL DREAM — Fantagraphics / Eros

1 ❑ Cover: 2.95 NM value: Cover or less
Circ: Diamd. preorders: 2,671
2 ❑ Cover: 2.95 NM value: Cover or less
Circ: Diamd. preorders: 2,378
3 ❑ Cover: 2.95 NM value: Cover or less
Circ: Diamd. preorders: 2,279

YOUNG WITCHES, THE: LONDON BABYLON — Fantagraphics / Eros

1 ❑ Cover: 3.50 NM value: Cover or less
2 ❑ Cover: 3.50 NM value: Cover or less
3 ❑ Cover: 3.50 NM value: Cover or less
4 ❑ Cover: 3.50 NM value: Cover or less
5 ❑ Cover: 3.50 NM value: Cover or less
6 ❑ Cover: 3.50 NM value: Cover or less

YOUNG WITCHES, THE (VOL. 3) — Fantagraphics / Eros

1 ❑ Cover: 2.95 NM value: Cover or less
2 ❑ Cover: 2.95 NM value: Cover or less
3 ❑ Cover: 2.95 NM value: Cover or less

YOUNG ZEN: CITY OF DEATH — Express / Entity

1 ❑ b&w Cover: 3.25 NM value: Cover or less
cardstock cover.

YOUNG ZEN INTERGALACTIC NINJA — Express / Entity

1 ❑ b&w Cover: 3.50 NM value: Cover or less
Circ: CapCity orders: 2,180
• trading card
2 ❑ b&w Cover: 2.95 NM value: Cover or less
Circ: CapCity orders: 19,005

YOU'RE UNDER ARREST! — Dark Horse / Manga

1 ❑ Dec 1995 Cover: 2.95 NM value: Cover or less
2 ❑ Jan 1996 Cover: 2.95 NM value: Cover or less
3 ❑ Feb 1996 Cover: 2.95 NM value: Cover or less
4 ❑ Mar 1996 Cover: 2.95 NM value: Cover or less
5 ❑ Apr 1996 Cover: 2.95 NM value: Cover or less
6 ❑ May 1996 Cover: 2.95 NM value: Cover or less
7 ❑ Jun 1996 Cover: 2.95 NM value: Cover or less
8 ❑ Jul 1996 Cover: 2.95 NM value: Cover or less
Bk 1 ❑ Cover: 12.95 NM value: Cover or less
• Collects series

YOUR HYTONE COMIX — Apex Novelties

1 ❑ Feb 1971, b&w Cover: 0.50 NM value: 8.00
• CGC: 2 graded, best 9.6
Pete the Plumber; Mr. Natural Stops Talking; Horny Harriet Hotpants • underground A: Robert Crumb W: Robert Crumb

Y'S GUYS — October

1 ❑ Jul 1999 Cover: 2.95 NM value: Cover or less

YUMMY FUR — Vortex

All issues are adults only.

Yummy Fur was published by Vortex, the same folks who brought out the enigmatic Mister X. As such, it shouldn't be a surprise that Yummy Fur is both thought-provoking and incredibly hard to describe. It's a blend of slapstick, grotesques, empathy, and scatology. Its stories freely mix secret agents from alternate Earths with spontaneously exploding women and cannibalism. Sometimes, it seems that the whole point of the series is to cheese off the establishment. Its tackling of religion in "Mark" is a prime example of this.

A challenging, and lesser-known series, Yummy Fur comes recommended by such comics cognoscenti as Neil Gaiman.

1 ❑ Dec 1986, b&w Cover: 1.75 NM value: 6.00
• reprint mini-comics #1-3 A: Chester Brown W: Chester Brown
2 ❑ b&w Cover: 1.75 NM value: 5.00
• reprint mini-comics #4-6; no date of publication; says #4 in indicia A: Chester Brown W: Chester Brown
3 ❑ Feb 1987, b&w Cover: 1.75 NM value: 4.00
• reprint mini-comic #7 A: Chester Brown W: Chester Brown
4 ❑ Apr 1987, b&w Cover: 1.75 NM value: 4.00
5 ❑ Jun 1987, b&w Cover: 1.75 NM value: 4.00
6 ❑ Aug 1987, b&w Cover: 1.75 NM value: 3.00
7 ❑ b&w Cover: 1.75 NM value: 3.00
8 ❑ Nov 1987, b&w Cover: 1.75 NM value: 3.00
9 ❑ b&w Cover: 1.75 NM value: 3.00
10 ❑ May 1988, b&w Cover: 1.75 NM value: 3.00
11 ❑ Jul 1988, b&w Cover: 1.75 NM value: 2.50
12 ❑ b&w Cover: 1.75 NM value: 2.50
• no date of publication A: Chester Brown W: Chester Brown
13 ❑ Nov 1988, b&w Cover: 1.75 NM value: 2.50
14 ❑ Jan 1989, b&w Cover: 1.75 NM value: 2.50
15 ❑ Mar 1989, b&w Cover: 2.00 NM value: 2.50
16 ❑ Jun 1989 Cover: 2.00 NM value: 2.50
17 ❑ Aug 1989 Cover: 2.00 NM value: 2.50
18 ❑ Oct 1989 Cover: 2.00 NM value: 2.50
19 ❑ Jan 1990 Cover: 2.00 NM value: 2.50
20 ❑ Apr 1990 Cover: 2.00 NM value: 2.50
21 ❑ Jun 1990 Cover: 2.50 NM value: Cover or less
22 ❑ Sep 1990 Cover: 2.50 NM value: Cover or less
23 ❑ Dec 1990 Cover: 2.50 NM value: Cover or less
24 ❑ 1991 Cover: 2.50 NM value: Cover or less
25 ❑ Jul 1991, b&w Cover: 2.50 NM value: Cover or less
26 ❑ Oct 1991, b&w Cover: 2.50 NM value: Cover or less
27 ❑ b&w Cover: 2.50 NM value: Cover or less
28 ❑ May 1992, b&w Cover: 2.50 NM value: Cover or less
29 ❑ Aug 1992, b&w Cover: 2.50 NM value: Cover or less
30 ❑ Apr 1993, b&w Cover: 2.50 NM value: Cover or less
Circ: CapCity orders: 2,200
31 ❑ 1993 Cover: 2.50 NM value: Cover or less
32 ❑ Jan 1994 Cover: 2.95 NM value: Cover or less
Matthew final issue. • Drawn & Quarterly Publishes A: Chester Brown W: Chester Brown
Bk 1 ❑ Cover: 12.95 NM value: Cover or less
• Ed the Happy Clown A: Chester Brown W: Chester Brown

YUPPIES FROM HELL — Marvel

1 ❑ b&w Cover: 2.95 NM value: Cover or less

YUPPIES, REDNECKS AND LESBIAN BITCHES FROM MARS — Eros

1 ❑ Cover: 2.95 NM value: Cover or less
2 ❑ Cover: 2.95 NM value: Cover or less
3 ❑ Cover: 2.95 NM value: Cover or less
4 ❑ Cover: 2.95 NM value: Cover or less
5 ❑ Cover: 2.95 NM value: Cover or less
6 ❑ Cover: 2.95 NM value: Cover or less
7 ❑ May 1998 Cover: 2.95 NM value: Cover or less

Z — Keystone Graphics

1 ❑ Nov 1994, b&w Cover: 2.75 NM value: Cover or less
2 ❑ Jul 1995, b&w Cover: 2.75 NM value: Cover or less
3 ❑ Nov 1995, b&w Cover: 2.75 NM value: Cover or less

ZAGO — Fox

1 ❑ Sep 1948 Cover: 0.10 NM value: 500.00
• CGC: 2 graded, best 9.4
2 ❑ Nov 1948 Cover: 0.10 NM value: 400.00
• CGC: 2 graded, best 5.0
3 ❑ Jan 1949 Cover: 0.10 NM value: 400.00
4 ❑ Mar 1949 Cover: 0.10 NM value: 300.00
• CGC: 1 graded, best 9.2

ZAIBATSU TEARS — Limelight

1 ❑ b&w Cover: 2.95 NM value: Cover or less
2 ❑ Cover: 2.95 NM value: Cover or less
3 ❑ Cover: 2.95 NM value: Cover or less

ZAP COMIX — Last Gasp

Zap Comix was among the first of the Underground "Comix." It was created by the legendary Robert Crumb in 1967, who reportedly sold his comics from a baby carriage pushed up and down San Francisco's Haight Street.

Topics covered in Zap centered primarily on sex, drugs, and almost overwhelming angst. It was a far cry from the standard super-hero fare the major companies were marketing at the time, and it marked the evolution of comics as a unique, counterculture art form. In addition, Crumb's "do-it-yourself" distribution helped open the way for the independent and small-press comics that would follow.

Zap is also notable as having an early issue numbered at #0. Crumb's original pages for the first issue were stolen before they could be published. By the time he discovered photocopies of the work, a new #1 had already been printed, so Crumb released the original version as #0.

0 ❑ Oct 1967 Cover: 0.35 NM value: 240.00
• CGC: 2 graded, best 9.2
Meatball; Death Valley; City of the Future A: Robert Crumb W: Robert Crumb
0-2 ❑ Cover: 0.35 NM value: 110.00

Other grades: Multiply prices above by **1.5 for Mint • 2/3 for Very Fine • 1/3 for Fine • 1/5 for Very Good • 1/8 for Good**

0-3 ❑ Cover: 0.35 **NM** value: **45.00**
• **CGC:** 1 graded, best 7.5
0-4 ❑ Cover: 0.35 **NM** value: **20.00**
0-5 ❑ Cover: 0.50 **NM** value: **12.00**
0-6 ❑ Cover: 0.50 **NM** value: **6.00**
0-7 ❑ Cover: 0.60 **NM** value: **4.00**
0-8 ❑ Cover: 0.75 **NM** value: **3.00**
0-9 ❑ Cover: 1.50 **NM** value: **3.00**
0-10❑ Cover: 2.95 **NM** value: **3.00**
1 ❑ Nov 1967 Cover: 0.25 **NM** value: **300.00**
• **CGC:** 7 graded, best 9.4
• Often identified as 1st underground comic **A:** Robert Crumb **W:** Robert Crumb
1-2 ❑ Cover: 0.35 **NM** value: **110.00**
1-3 ❑ Cover: 0.35 **NM** value: **70.00**
1-4 ❑ Cover: 0.50 **NM** value: **28.00**
1-5 ❑ Cover: 0.60 **NM** value: **8.00**
1-6 ❑ Cover: 0.75 **NM** value: **6.00**
1-7 ❑ Cover: 1.50 **NM** value: **4.00**
1-8 ❑ Cover: 2.95 **NM** value: **3.00**
2 ❑ ca. 1968 Cover: 0.50 **NM** value: **55.00**
• **CGC:** 2 graded, best 9.6
2-2 ❑ Cover: 0.50 **NM** value: **34.00**
• **CGC:** 2 graded, best 9.4
2-3 ❑ Cover: 0.75 **NM** value: **8.00**
2-4 ❑ Cover: 1.00 **NM** value: **4.00**
2-5 ❑ Cover: 2.95 **NM** value: **3.00**
3 ❑ ca. 1969 Cover: 0.50 **NM** value: **35.00**
• Flip-book. 📖 Captain Pissgums and his Pervert Pirates; Gilded Moments; Dirty Dog; Mr. Goodbar: Off His Rocker; Atomic Comics; Let's Eat; Mr. Natural; Hairy; Come Fix; Wonder War-Hog: Wonder Blows an Easy One…; Street Corner Daze • Wonder Warthog **A:** Gilbert Shelton; Robert Crumb; Rick Griffin; S. Clay Wilson **W:** Gilbert Shelton; Robert Crumb; Rick Griffin; S. Clay Wilson
3-2 ❑ Cover: 0.50 **NM** value: **18.00**
• **CGC:** 1 graded, best 8.5
3-3 ❑ Cover: 0.75 **NM** value: **7.00**
3-4 ❑ Cover: 1.00 **NM** value: **3.00**
3-5 ❑ Cover: 2.95 **NM** value: **3.00**
4 ❑ Cover: 0.50 **NM** value: **28.00**
• **CGC:** 1 graded, best 8.5
📖 Joe Blow; A Ball in the Bunghole; The Supreme Constellation of Dormasintoria; Wonder Wart-Hog Breaks Up the Mutaload Smut Ring; Mr. Natural Takes a Vacation; Mara Mistress of the Void • Wonder Warthog **A:** Gilbert Shelton; Robert Crumb **W:** Gilbert Shelton; Robert Crumb
4-2 ❑ ca. 1971 Cover: 0.50 **NM** value: **8.00**
4-3 ❑ Cover: 0.75 **NM** value: **4.00**
4-4 ❑ Cover: 1.00 **NM** value: **3.00**
4-5 ❑ Cover: 2.95 **NM** value: **3.00**
5 ❑ ca. 1970 Cover: 0.50 **NM** value: **28.00**
• **CGC:** 2 graded, best 9.2
• Freak Bros, Wonder Warthog **A:** Robert Crumb **W:** Robert Crumb
5-2 ❑ Cover: 0.75 **NM** value: **8.00**
5-3 ❑ Cover: 1.00 **NM** value: **4.00**
5-4 ❑ Cover: 2.95 **NM** value: **3.00**
6 ❑ Cover: 0.50 **NM** value: **16.00**
• **CGC:** 1 graded, best 9.0
6-2 ❑ Cover: 0.75 **NM** value: **5.00**
6-3 ❑ Cover: 1.00 **NM** value: **4.00**
6-4 ❑ Cover: 2.95 **NM** value: **3.00**
7 ❑ ca. 1974 Cover: 0.50 **NM** value: **10.00**
• **CGC:** 1 graded, best 9.2
📖 Sangrella; The Adventures of Fat Freddy's Cat; Mr. Natural Meets "The Kid"; Rough Trade Lib; Hookin' and Jabbin' With Zeak the Zuke; Futuristic Glimpse; The Mentor in the Mason Jar; Robert Crumb Presents Robert Crumb **A:** Robert Williams; Gilbert Shelton; Robert Crumb; S. Clay Wilson; Spain Rodriguez **W:** Robert Williams; Gilbert Shelton; Robert Crumb; S. Clay Wilson; Spain Rodriguez
7-2 ❑ Cover: 0.75 **NM** value: **4.00**
7-3 ❑ Cover: 1.00 **NM** value: **3.00**
7-4 ❑ Cover: 2.95 **NM** value: **3.00**
8 ❑ ca. 1975 Cover: 0.75 **NM** value: **10.00**
• **CGC:** 1 graded, best 9.2
📖 What Gives?; The Swap; You Can't Avoid The Void; Field Meet; The Hairmobile; Rumpelstiltskin **A:** Robert Crumb **W:** Robert Crumb
8-2 ❑ Cover: 1.00 **NM** value: **4.00**
8-3 ❑ Cover: 2.95 **NM** value: **3.00**
9 ❑ ca. 1978 Cover: 0.75 **NM** value: **10.00**
• 10th anniversary issue. **A:** Robert Crumb **W:** Robert Crumb
9-2 ❑ Cover: 1.50 **NM** value: **4.00**
• **CGC:** 1 graded, best 9.8
9-3 ❑ Cover: 2.95 **NM** value: **3.00**
10 ❑ Cover: 2.95 **NM** value: **3.50**
11 ❑ ca. 1985 Cover: 2.95 **NM** value: **3.50**
12 ❑ Cover: 2.95 **NM** value: **3.00**
no cover price. **A:** Robert Crumb **W:** Robert Crumb
13 ❑ Cover: 3.95 **NM** value: **Cover or less**
14 ❑ Cover: 3.95 **NM** value: **Cover or less**

ZATANNA — DC

Zatanna is a half-human, half-Atlantean sorceress and onetime lover of John Constantine (Hellblazer). Despite her special abilities, she tries to eke out a relatively normal existence in San Francisco as a booking agent. Over the last few days, however, she has noted a huge increase in the number of darkling spirits in San Francisco and decides to investigate. In doing so, she encounters an ancient enemy and a mystical plan that threatens to spill the darkling realm into our world.

An entertaining mini-series, "Come Together" gives the writers a chance to develop Zatanna. Aside from freeing her from the device of having to speak her spells backward, they add dimension to her personality, turning her into a much stronger character.

1 ❑ Jul 1993 Cover: 1.95 **NM** value: **2.00**
Circ: CapCity orders: **18,600**
2 ❑ Aug 1993 Cover: 1.95 **NM** value: **2.00**
Circ: CapCity orders: **12,000**
• Zatanna gets new costume
3 ❑ Sep 1993 Cover: 1.95 **NM** value: **2.00**
Circ: CapCity orders: **9,600**
4 ❑ Oct 1993 Cover: 1.95 **NM** value: **2.00**
Circ: CapCity orders: **8,550**

ZATANNA SPECIAL — DC

1 ❑ Cover: 2.00 **NM** value: **Cover or less**
Circ: CapCity orders: **11,450**

ZAZA THE MYSTIC (AVALON) — Avalon

1 ❑ Cover: 2.95 **NM** value: **Cover or less**
📖 Double Trouble; No Body, No Case; Lazy Lee…Mind Over Mattress!; Duel at Shallow River; Crushed Crime (text); The Stolen Crystal Ball **A:** Rocke Mastroserio **W:** Rocke Mastroserio

ZEALOT — Image

1 ❑ Aug 1995 Cover: 2.50 **NM** value: **Cover or less**
Circ: CapCity orders: **35,750**
2 ❑ Oct 1995 Cover: 2.50 **NM** value: **Cover or less**
Circ: CapCity orders: **24,125**
3 ❑ Nov 1995 Cover: 2.50 **NM** value: **Cover or less**
Circ: CapCity orders: **14,750**

ZEGRA, JUNGLE EMPRESS — Fox

2 ❑ Oct 1948 Cover: 0.10 **NM** value: **525.00**
• **CGC:** 2 graded, best 9.4
3 ❑ Dec 1948 Cover: 0.10 **NM** value: **450.00**
4 ❑ Feb 1949 Cover: 0.10 **NM** value: **450.00**
5 ❑ Apr 1949 Cover: 0.10 **NM** value: **450.00**

ZELL SWORDDANCER (3-D ZONE) — 3-D Zone

1 ❑ b&w **NM** value: **2.00**

ZELL, SWORDDANCER (THOUGHTS & IMAGES) — Thoughts & Images

1 ❑ Jul 1986, b&w Cover: 2.00 **NM** value: **Cover or less**

ZEN, INTERGALACTIC NINJA (1ST SERIES) — Zen

1 ❑ Nov 1987, b&w Cover: 1.75 **NM** value: **3.00**
1-2 ❑ Cover: 2.00 **NM** value: **Cover or less**
2 ❑ b&w Cover: 1.75 **NM** value: **2.00**
3 ❑ b&w Cover: 1.75 **NM** value: **2.00**
3-2 ❑ Cover: 2.00 **NM** value: **Cover or less**
4 ❑ b&w Cover: 1.75 **NM** value: **2.00**
5 ❑ b&w Cover: 1.75 **NM** value: **2.00**
6 ❑ b&w Cover: 2.00 **NM** value: **Cover or less**

ZEN, INTERGALACTIC NINJA (2ND SERIES) — Zen

1 ❑ b&w Cover: 2.00 **NM** value: **Cover or less**
2 ❑ b&w Cover: 2.00 **NM** value: **Cover or less**
3 ❑ b&w Cover: 2.00 **NM** value: **Cover or less**
4 ❑ b&w Cover: 2.00 **NM** value: **Cover or less**

ZEN, INTERGALACTIC NINJA (3RD SERIES) — Zen

1 ❑ b&w Cover: 2.25 **NM** value: **Cover or less**
2 ❑ b&w Cover: 2.25 **NM** value: **Cover or less**
3 ❑ b&w Cover: 2.25 **NM** value: **Cover or less**
4 ❑ b&w Cover: 2.25 **NM** value: **Cover or less**
5 ❑ b&w Cover: 2.25 **NM** value: **Cover or less**
HS 1❑b&w Cover: 2.95 **NM** value: **Cover or less**
• Flip-book.

ZEN INTERGALACTIC NINJA (4TH SERIES) — Archie

1 ❑ May 1992, full color Cover: 1.25 **NM** value: **Cover or less**
Circ: CapCity orders: **3,950**
📖 Defend the Earth; Defend Earth **A:** Ross Andru; Mike Esposito **W:** Steve Stern
2 ❑ 1992full color Cover: 1.25 **NM** value: **Cover or less**
📖 Defend the Earth
3 ❑ 1992full color Cover: 1.25 **NM** value: **Cover or less**
📖 Defend the Earth

ZEN INTERGALACTIC NINJA (5TH SERIES) — Archie

1 ❑ Sep 1992, full color Cover: 1.25 **NM** value: **Cover or less**
📖 The Untold Origin of Zen **A:** Ross Andru; Mike Esposito; Will Cypser **W:** Steve Stern ★ Origin of Zen Intergalactic Ninja.
2 ❑ Oct 1992, full color Cover: 1.25 **NM** value: **Cover or less**
📖 Rumble in the Rainforest, Part 1
3 ❑ Dec 1992, full color Cover: 1.25 **NM** value: **Cover or less**
📖 Rumble in the Rainforest, Part 2
4 ❑ 1993 Cover: 1.25 **NM** value: **Cover or less**
📖 Rumble in the Rainforest, Part 3
5 ❑ 1993 Cover: 1.25 **NM** value: **Cover or less**
📖 Defend the Earth, Part 1 **A:** Dan Cote; Steve Stern **W:** Dan Cote; Steve Stern
6 ❑ 1993 Cover: 1.25 **NM** value: **Cover or less**
7 ❑ 1993 Cover: 1.25 **NM** value: **Cover or less**

ZEN INTERGALACTIC NINJA (6TH SERIES) — Express / Entity

0 ❑ 1993 Cover: 2.50 **NM** value: **3.00**
Gray trim around outside cover. ★ 1st Appearance of Nira X.
0/A ❑ Jun 1993, b&w Cover: 2.95 **NM** value: **Cover or less**
foil cover.
0/B ❑ Jun 1993, b&w Cover: 3.50 **NM** value: **Cover or less**
chromium cover.
0/LE❑ Cover: 2.50 **NM** value: **3.00**
• Printing limited to 3,000 copies; All-gold trim★ 1st Appearance of Nira X.
1 ❑ b&w Cover: 2.95 **NM** value: **3.00**
📖 A Fire Upon the Earth, Part 1 **A:** Tatsuya Ishida **W:** Steve Stern
1/SC❑ Cover: 3.95 **NM** value: **Cover or less**
Chromium, die-cut cover. 📖 A Fire Upon the Earth, Part 1 **A:** Tatsuya Ishida **W:** Steve Stern
2 ❑ b&w Cover: 2.95 **NM** value: **3.00**
3 ❑ b&w Cover: 2.95 **NM** value: **3.00**
4 ❑ Cover: 2.50 **NM** value: **3.00**
Ash 1❑b&w **NM** value: **1.00**
no cover price. • contains previews of Zen: Hazardous Duty and Zen: Tour of the Universe
Spr 1❑ Cover: 2.95 **NM** value: **Cover or less**
Circ: CapCity orders: **5,380**
• Spring Spectacular **A:** Hearn Cho **W:** Hearn Cho

ZEN INTERGALACTIC NINJA ALL-NEW COLOR SPECIAL — Express / Entity

1 ❑ Cover: 3.50 **NM** value: **Cover or less**
Chronium Cover. **A:** Tatsuya Ishida **W:** Steve Stern ★ Origin of Zen Intergalactic Ninja.

ZEN INTERGALACTIC NINJA COLOR — Express / Entity

1 ❑ Cover: 3.95 **NM** value: **Cover or less**
diecut foil cover.
2 ❑ Cover: 3.95 **NM** value: **Cover or less**
3 ❑ Cover: 3.95 **NM** value: **Cover or less**
4 ❑ Cover: 2.50 **NM** value: **Cover or less**
5 ❑ Cover: 2.50 **NM** value: **Cover or less**
6 ❑ Cover: 2.50 **NM** value: **Cover or less**
7 ❑ Cover: 2.95 **NM** value: **Cover or less**
says #6a on cover. • #7 in indicia

ZEN INTERGALACTIC NINJA COLOR (2ND SERIES) — Express / Entity

1 ❑ Cover: 2.50 **NM** value: **Cover or less**
2 ❑ Cover: 2.50 **NM** value: **Cover or less**

ZEN, INTERGALACTIC NINJA EARTH DAY ANNUAL — Zen

1 ❑ b&w Cover: 2.95 **NM** value: **Cover or less**
No issue number.

ZEN INTERGALACTIC NINJA MILESTONE — Express / Entity

1 ❑ Cover: 2.95 **NM** value: **Cover or less**

ZEN INTERGALACTIC NINJA STARQUEST — Express

1 ❑ b&w Cover: 2.95 **NM** value: **Cover or less**
2 ❑ b&w Cover: 2.95 **NM** value: **Cover or less**
4 ❑ b&w Cover: 2.95 **NM** value: **Cover or less**
cardstock cover.

ZEN INTERGALACTIC NINJA SUMMER SPECIAL: VIDEO WARRIOR — Express

1 ❑ b&w Cover: 2.95 **NM** value: **Cover or less**

ZEN INTERGALACTIC NINJA: TOUR OF THE UNIVERSE SPECIAL, THE AIRBRUSH ART OF DAN COTE — Express / Entity

1 ❑ Cover: 3.95 **NM** value: **Cover or less**
enhanced cardstock cover. **A:** Dan Cote **W:** Dan Cote

ZENITH: PHASE I — Fleetway-Quality

1 ❑ Cover: 1.95 **NM** value: **2.00**
2 ❑ Cover: 1.95 **NM** value: **2.00**
3 ❑ Cover: 1.95 **NM** value: **2.00**

ZENITH: PHASE II — Fleetway-Quality

1 ❑ Cover: 1.95 **NM** value: **Cover or less**
2 ❑ Cover: 1.95 **NM** value: **Cover or less**

ZERO — Zero Comics

All issues are adults only.
1 ❑ Mar 1975, b&w Cover: 0.75 **NM** value: **3.00**
2 ❑ Mar 1975, b&w Cover: 0.75 **NM** value: **3.00**
3 ❑ May 1976, b&w Cover: 0.75 **NM** value: **3.00**

ZERO GIRL — Homage

1 ❑ Feb 2001 Cover: 2.95 **NM** value: **Cover or less**
Circ: Diamd. preorders: **21,067**
2 ❑ Mar 2001 Cover: 2.95 **NM** value: **Cover or less**
Circ: Diamd. preorders: **17,050**
3 ❑ Apr 2001 Cover: 2.95 **NM** value: **Cover or less**
Circ: Diamd. preorders: **15,073**
4 ❑ May 2001 Cover: 2.95 **NM** value: **Cover or less**
Circ: Diamd. preorders: **14,483**
5 ❑ Cover: 2.95 **NM** value: **Cover or less**
Circ: Diamd. preorders: **14,485**

ZERO HOUR — Dog Soup

1 ❑ Apr 1995, b&w Cover: 2.95 **NM** value: **Cover or less**
No issue number. says Pat Leidy's Catfight on cover.

📖 indicates **Story Title** or **Storyline** information.
★ indicates **Character Appearance** information.
W = Writer • A = Artist • C = Cover Artist

CGC-graded: Multiply prices above by **33 for 9.9 M • 16 for 9.8 NM/M • 7 for 9.6 NM+ • 5 for 9.4 NM • 2.5 for 9.2 NM- • 1.5 for 9.0 VF/NM**

ZERO HOUR: CRISIS IN TIME — DC

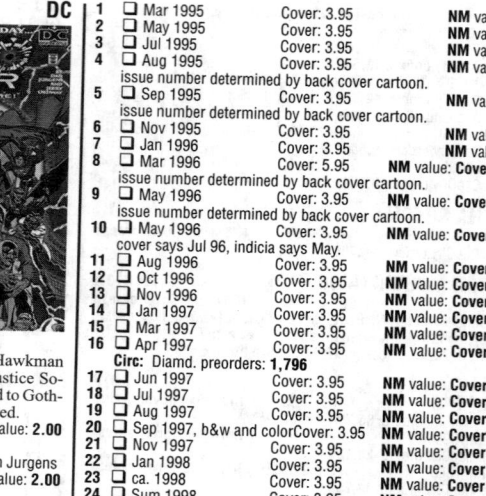

Zero Hour was released in the summer and fall of 1994. Its purpose was to tie up a lot of loose ends caused by the twelve-part Crisis on Infinite Earths storyline from the 1980s.

This latest adventure begins, as a massive crisis in time is causing Earth's time-space continuum to go haywire. All of Earth's super-heroes are called in to help, including the original Justice Society and other older characters. It turns out that Hal Jordan, the Silver-Age Green Lantern, is trying to undo the event that eventually led to his earlier breakdown, the destruction of Coast City. Now, as Parallax, he fights the entire DC hero inventory. As a result of this series, DC's many Hawkman characters were merged into one. The entire original Justice Society (excluding The Spectre) was killed. Batgirl returned to Gotham, and the original Flash and Green Lantern were retired.

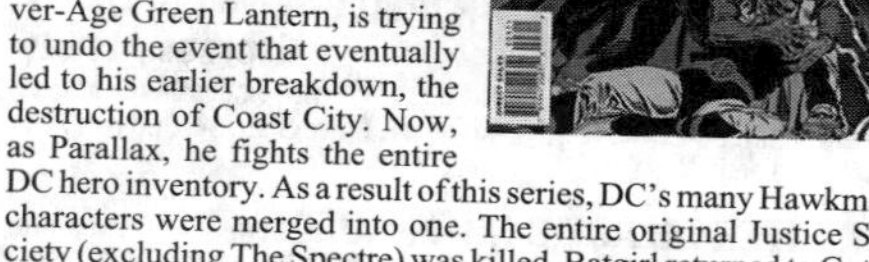

4 ❑ Sep 1994 Cover: 1.50 **NM** value: **2.00**
Circ: CapCity orders: **74,800**
• (#1 in sequence) **A:** Jerry Ordway; Dan Jurgens **W:** Dan Jurgens

3 ❑ Sep 1994 Cover: 1.50 **NM** value: **2.00**
Circ: CapCity orders: **72,750**
• remainder of Justice Society of America aged; (#2 in sequence) **A:** Jerry Ordway; Dan Jurgens **W:** Dan Jurgens ★ Death of Atom. ★ Death of Hourman.

2 ❑ Sep 1994 Cover: 1.50 **NM** value: **2.00**
Circ: CapCity orders: **70,300**
• (#3 in sequence) **A:** Jerry Ordway; Dan Jurgens **W:** Dan Jurgens

1 ❑ Sep 1994 Cover: 1.50 **NM** value: **3.00**
Circ: CapCity orders: **70,450**
• Silver Age Atom de-aged; (#4 in sequence) **A:** Jerry Ordway; Dan Jurgens **W:** Dan Jurgens ★ 1st Appearance of Parallax, David Knight, Jack Knight.

0 ❑ Sep 1994 Cover: 1.50 **NM** value: **2.00**
Circ: CapCity orders: **75,000** • **CGC:** 2 graded, best 9.6
• contains Zero Hour checklist and new DC timeline foldout; (#5 in sequence) **A:** Jerry Ordway; Dan Jurgens **W:** Dan Jurgens ★ Versus Extant.

Ash 1❑ca. 1994 **NM** value: **1.00**
• **CGC:** 2 graded, best 9.6
• Ashcan Preview

Bk 1❑ Cover: 9.95 **NM** value: **Cover or less**
• collects Zero Hour: Crisis in Time #4-0 and related stories from Showcase '94 #8 and 9

ZERO PATROL, THE (1ST SERIES) — Continuity

1 ❑ Nov 1984 Cover: 1.50 **NM** value: **2.00**
2 ❑ Cover: 1.50 **NM** value: **2.00**

ZERO PATROL (2ND SERIES) — Continuity

1 ❑ 1987 Cover: 2.00 **NM** value: **Cover or less**
2 ❑ Nov 1987 Cover: 2.00 **NM** value: **Cover or less**
Circ: CapCity orders: **5,575**
3 ❑ Apr 1988 Cover: 2.00 **NM** value: **Cover or less**
Circ: CapCity orders: **2,975**
4 ❑ Mar 1989 Cover: 2.00 **NM** value: **Cover or less**
Circ: CapCity orders: **2,700**
5 ❑ May 1989 Cover: 2.00 **NM** value: **Cover or less**
Circ: CapCity orders: **2,125**

ZERO STREET — Amaze Ink

1 ❑ 2000 Cover: 2.95 **NM** value: **Cover or less**
📖 Erica **A:** Thomas Hong **W:** Thomas Hong

ZERO TOLERANCE — First

1 ❑ Oct 1990 Cover: 2.25 **NM** value: **Cover or less**
Circ: CapCity orders: **12,200**
2 ❑ Nov 1990 Cover: 2.25 **NM** value: **Cover or less**
Circ: CapCity orders: **7,850**
3 ❑ Dec 1990 Cover: 2.25 **NM** value: **Cover or less**
Circ: CapCity orders: **6,825**
• Vigil **A:** Tim Vigil; Gary Amaro **W:** David Barbour
4 ❑ Jan 1991 Cover: 2.25 **NM** value: **Cover or less**
Circ: CapCity orders: **6,675**

ZERO ZERO — Fantagraphics

Over the years, Marvel and DC have had several "tryout" titles for new artists. Normally, these are anthologies featuring established characters. The more daring ones might even go so far as to let the auditioning team use its own characters and stories. Still, none of these titles comes close to the degree of freedom accorded the artists in Zero Zero.

Begun in 1995, Zero Zero is a spotlight for experimental cartoonists, published by Fantagraphics-one of the most daring comic publishers. The stories contained here are not meant for readers who like super-hero cliches or straightforward storylines. Depending on the artist, illustrations range from stark and angst-ridden to minimalist and surreal. The storylines similarly bounce from one-page black humor to stream-of-consciousness narrative. It's definitely not for everyone, but readers can find exciting surprises inside.

1 ❑ Mar 1995 Cover: 3.95 **NM** value: **4.00**
2 ❑ May 1995 Cover: 3.95 **NM** value: **4.00**
3 ❑ Jul 1995 Cover: 3.95 **NM** value: **4.00**
4 ❑ Aug 1995 Cover: 3.95 **NM** value: **4.00**
issue number determined by back cover cartoon.
5 ❑ Sep 1995 Cover: 3.95 **NM** value: **4.00**
issue number determined by back cover cartoon.
6 ❑ Nov 1995 Cover: 3.95 **NM** value: **4.00**
7 ❑ Jan 1996 Cover: 3.95 **NM** value: **4.00**
8 ❑ Mar 1996 Cover: 5.95 **NM** value: **Cover or less**
issue number determined by back cover cartoon.
9 ❑ May 1996 Cover: 3.95 **NM** value: **Cover or less**
issue number determined by back cover cartoon.
10 ❑ May 1996 Cover: 3.95 **NM** value: **Cover or less**
cover says Jul 96, indicia says May.
11 ❑ Aug 1996 Cover: 3.95 **NM** value: **Cover or less**
12 ❑ Oct 1996 Cover: 3.95 **NM** value: **Cover or less**
13 ❑ Nov 1996 Cover: 3.95 **NM** value: **Cover or less**
14 ❑ Jan 1997 Cover: 3.95 **NM** value: **Cover or less**
15 ❑ Mar 1997 Cover: 3.95 **NM** value: **Cover or less**
16 ❑ Apr 1997 Cover: 3.95 **NM** value: **Cover or less**
Circ: Diamd. preorders: **1,796**
17 ❑ Jun 1997 Cover: 3.95 **NM** value: **Cover or less**
18 ❑ Jul 1997 Cover: 3.95 **NM** value: **Cover or less**
19 ❑ Aug 1997 Cover: 3.95 **NM** value: **Cover or less**
20 ❑ Sep 1997, b&w and colorCover: 3.95 **NM** value: **Cover or less**
21 ❑ Nov 1997 Cover: 3.95 **NM** value: **Cover or less**
22 ❑ Jan 1998 Cover: 3.95 **NM** value: **Cover or less**
23 ❑ ca. 1998 Cover: 3.95 **NM** value: **Cover or less**
24 ❑ Sum 1998 Cover: 3.95 **NM** value: **Cover or less**
25 ❑ Fal 1998 Cover: 3.95 **NM** value: **Cover or less**

ZETRAMAN — Antarctic

Zetraman was inspired by such Japanese live-action super-hero shows as Battle Fever J, Task Force Sun Vulcan, Super-Beast Task Force Liveman, and Dynaman. It's a lighthearted romp of a comic book, combining super-heroes, science-fiction, and goofy humor.

Zetraman, who first appeared in the pages of Ben Dunn's Ninja High School, is a team of three men with super-human abilities. The team consists of Mike ("Zetra Blue"), Howard ("Zetra Red"), and Phrank ("Zetra Yellow") who can fight either by themselves, in robotic armor, or in command of a combined Zetra robot.

In this series, they are attacked by the women of Venus, who seek their genetic ... err ... material to help repopulate the woman-only society on their homeworld. With Ben Dunn handling art duties, this series is a cross between Ultraman and the Mighty Morphin Power Rangers.

1 ❑ Sep 1991, b&w Cover: 1.95 **NM** value: **Cover or less**
📖 Venus Needs Men!! **A:** Ben Dunn **W:** Steve Ross
2 ❑ Oct 1991, b&w Cover: 1.95 **NM** value: **Cover or less**
3 ❑ Feb 1992, b&w Cover: 1.95 **NM** value: **Cover or less**

ZETRAMAN: REVIVAL — Antarctic

1 ❑ Oct 1993 Cover: 2.75 **NM** value: **Cover or less**
📖 Steamanetics **A:** Danny Fahs **W:** Steve Ross
2 ❑ Dec 1993 Cover: 2.75 **NM** value: **Cover or less**
3 ❑ Aug 1995 Cover: 2.75 **NM** value: **Cover or less**

ZIGGY PIG & SILLY SEAL — Timely

1 ❑ Fal 1944 Cover: 0.10 **NM** value: **150.00**
2 ❑ Win 1945 Cover: 0.10 **NM** value: **80.00**
3 ❑ Spr 1946 Cover: 0.10 **NM** value: **80.00**
4 ❑ Sum 1946 Cover: 0.10 **NM** value: **75.00**
5 ❑ Sum 1946 Cover: 0.10 **NM** value: **75.00**
• **CGC:** 1 graded, best 9.4
6 ❑ Sep 1946 Cover: 0.10 **NM** value: **75.00**

ZILLION — Eternity

1 ❑ Apr 1993, b&w Cover: 2.50 **NM** value: **Cover or less**
Circ: CapCity orders: **5,900**
2 ❑ May 1993, b&w Cover: 2.50 **NM** value: **Cover or less**
Circ: CapCity orders: **3,150**
3 ❑ Jun 1993, b&w Cover: 2.50 **NM** value: **Cover or less**
4 ❑ Jul 1993, b&w Cover: 2.50 **NM** value: **Cover or less**

ZIP COMICS — M.L.J.

Zip Comics was the showcase for Steel Sterling, a typical Golden Age costumed adventurer whose exploits gained power from the dynamic art of Irv Novick. Other MLJ stalwarts including The Web, Nevada Jones, and Black Jack also appeared in its pages. Indeed, the standard of art in most MLJ titles was better than average for the 1940s, even down to the backup features. Zip Comics included "The Slap-Happy Applejacks" (hillbilly humor), Senor Banana (racist Mexican humor, though well drawn), Chimpy (funny animals drawn in a Will Eisner style!), and Ginger (female-oriented teen humor). The Red Rube, a humorous takeoff on Captain Marvel who gained the powers of everyone in history ever named Rueben by uttering the words "Hey Rube!" made his debut in issue #39.

1 ❑ Feb 1940 Cover: 0.10 **NM** value: **3500.00**
• **CGC:** 5 graded, best 9.6
2 ❑ Mar 1940 Cover: 0.10 **NM** value: **1600.00**
• **CGC:** 2 graded, best 9.6
3 ❑ Apr 1940 Cover: 0.10 **NM** value: **1250.00**
• **CGC:** 1 graded, best 9.2
4 ❑ May 1940 Cover: 0.10 **NM** value: **900.00**
• **CGC:** 1 graded, best 9.4
5 ❑ Jun 1940 Cover: 0.10 **NM** value: **900.00**
• **CGC:** 2 graded, best 9.4
6 ❑ Jul 1940 Cover: 0.10 **NM** value: **750.00**
• **CGC:** 3 graded, best 9.6
7 ❑ Aug 1940 Cover: 0.10 **NM** value: **750.00**
• **CGC:** 4 graded, best 9.9
8 ❑ Sep 1940 Cover: 0.10 **NM** value: **750.00**
• **CGC:** 1 graded, best 9.4
9 ❑ Nov 1940 Cover: 0.10 **NM** value: **800.00**
• **CGC:** 1 graded, best 8.5
10 ❑ Jan 1941 Cover: 0.10 **NM** value: **750.00**
• **CGC:** 2 graded, best 9.6
11 ❑ Feb 1941 Cover: 0.10 **NM** value: **600.00**
• **CGC:** 2 graded, best 9.4
12 ❑ Mar 1941 Cover: 0.10 **NM** value: **600.00**
• **CGC:** 1 graded, best 9.8
13 ❑ Apr 1941 Cover: 0.10 **NM** value: **600.00**
• **CGC:** 2 graded, best 9.8
14 ❑ May 1941 Cover: 0.10 **NM** value: **600.00**
• **CGC:** 2 graded, best 9.4
15 ❑ Jun 1941 Cover: 0.10 **NM** value: **600.00**
• **CGC:** 3 graded, best 9.6
16 ❑ Jul 1941 Cover: 0.10 **NM** value: **600.00**
• **CGC:** 1 graded, best 9.2
17 ❑ Aug 1941 Cover: 0.10 **NM** value: **600.00**
• **CGC:** 1 graded, best 9.4
18 ❑ Sep 1941 Cover: 0.10 **NM** value: **625.00**
• **CGC:** 1 graded, best 9.6
19 ❑ Oct 1941 Cover: 0.10 **NM** value: **600.00**
• **CGC:** 2 graded, best 9.6
20 ❑ Nov 1941 Cover: 0.10 **NM** value: **900.00**
• **CGC:** 2 graded, best 9.2
21 ❑ Dec 1941 Cover: 0.10 **NM** value: **540.00**
• **CGC:** 2 graded, best 9.0
22 ❑ Jan 1942 Cover: 0.10 **NM** value: **540.00**
• **CGC:** 2 graded, best 9.8
23 ❑ Feb 1942 Cover: 0.10 **NM** value: **540.00**
• **CGC:** 2 graded, best 9.4
24 ❑ Mar 1942 Cover: 0.10 **NM** value: **540.00**
• **CGC:** 1 graded, best 9.4
25 ❑ Apr 1942 Cover: 0.10 **NM** value: **540.00**
• **CGC:** 1 graded, best 9.4
26 ❑ May 1942 Cover: 0.10 **NM** value: **540.00**
• **CGC:** 1 graded, best 9.6
27 ❑ Jul 1942 Cover: 0.10 **NM** value: **800.00**
• **CGC:** 2 graded, best 9.0
• 1st apperance of The Web
28 ❑ Aug 1942 Cover: 0.10 **NM** value: **540.00**
• **CGC:** 1 graded, best 7.5
29 ❑ Sep 1942 Cover: 0.10 **NM** value: **540.00**
30 ❑ Oct 1942 Cover: 0.10 **NM** value: **540.00**
31 ❑ Nov 1942 Cover: 0.10 **NM** value: **375.00**
32 ❑ Dec 1942 Cover: 0.10 **NM** value: **375.00**
• **CGC:** 1 graded, best 9.4
33 ❑ Jan 1943 Cover: 0.10 **NM** value: **375.00**
34 ❑ Feb 1943 Cover: 0.10 **NM** value: **375.00**
35 ❑ Mar 1943 Cover: 0.10 **NM** value: **375.00**
36 ❑ Apr 1943 Cover: 0.10 **NM** value: **375.00**
37 ❑ May 1943 Cover: 0.10 **NM** value: **375.00**
• **CGC:** 1 graded, best 2.0
38 ❑ Jul 1943 Cover: 0.10 **NM** value: **375.00**
• **CGC:** 1 graded, best 9.6
39 ❑ Aug 1943 Cover: 0.10 **NM** value: **375.00**
• **CGC:** 3 graded, best 9.2
📖 Murder out of This World; The Slap Happy Applejacks; Señor Banana; You Can't Get Rich Jerking Sodas (Text Story); Red Rube; Chimpy; Ginger on Vacation; Wilbur; **A:** Irv Novick **W:** Irv Novick; Zenith Gray
40 ❑ Oct 1943 Cover: 0.10 **NM** value: **375.00**
• **CGC:** 1 graded, best 9.6
41 ❑ Nov 1943 Cover: 0.10 **NM** value: **280.00**
• **CGC:** 1 graded, best 9.8
42 ❑ Dec 1943 Cover: 0.10 **NM** value: **280.00**
• **CGC:** 1 graded, best 9.4
43 ❑ Jan 1944 Cover: 0.10 **NM** value: **280.00**
• **CGC:** 2 graded, best 9.2
44 ❑ Feb 1944 Cover: 0.10 **NM** value: **280.00**
• **CGC:** 1 graded, best 9.2
45 ❑ Apr 1944 Cover: 0.10 **NM** value: **280.00**
• **CGC:** 1 graded, best 9.4
46 ❑ May 1944 Cover: 0.10 **NM** value: **280.00**
• **CGC:** 2 graded, best 9.2
47 ❑ Sum 1944 Cover: 0.10 **NM** value: **280.00**
• **CGC:** 1 graded, best 9.0
final issue.

ZIP COMICS (COZMIC) — Cozmic

1 ❑ Cover: 1.00 **NM** value: **4.00**

ZIP JET — St. John

1 ❑ Feb 1953 Cover: 0.10 **NM** value: **650.00**
• **CGC:** 3 graded, best 9.2
2 ❑ Apr 1953 Cover: 0.10 **NM** value: **450.00**

ZIPPY QUARTERLY — Fantagraphics

1 ❑ b&w Cover: 4.95 **NM** value: **Cover or less**
2 ❑ b&w Cover: 4.95 **NM** value: **Cover or less**
3 ❑ Cover: 3.50 **NM** value: **Cover or less**
• strip reprint
4 ❑ Cover: 3.50 **NM** value: **Cover or less**
• strip reprint

Other grades: Multiply prices above by **1.5 for Mint • 2/3 for Very Fine • 1/3 for Fine • 1/5 for Very Good • 1/8 for Good**

5 ❑ Cover: 3.50 **NM** value: **Cover or less**
• strip reprint
7 ❑ Aug 1994, b&w Cover: 3.50 **NM** value: **Cover or less**
• strip reprint
8 ❑ Nov 1994, b&w Cover: 3.50 **NM** value: **Cover or less**
• strip reprint
12 ❑ Dec 1995, b&w Cover: 3.95 **NM** value: **Cover or less**
• strip reprint
13 ❑ Aug 1996, b&w Cover: 3.95 **NM** value: **Cover or less**
cardstock cover. • strip reprint

ZÖLASTRSYA AND THE BARD — Twilight Twins

1 ❑ Jan 1987 Cover: 1.70 **NM** value: **Cover or less**
2 ❑ Cover: 1.70 **NM** value: **Cover or less**
3 ❑ Cover: 1.70 **NM** value: **Cover or less**
wraparound photo cover. **A:** Terry Echterling; ZölastrSya **W:** Terry Echterling; ZölastrSya
4 ❑ Cover: 1.70 **NM** value: **Cover or less**
Photo cover. **A:** Terry Echterling; ZölastrSya **W:** Terry Echterling; ZölastrSya
ZölastrSya
5 ❑ Cover: 1.70 **NM** value: **Cover or less**

ZOMBIE 3-D — 3-D Zone

1 ❑ Cover: 3.95 **NM** value: **Cover or less**
No issue number.

ZOMBIE BOY (ANTARCTIC) — Antarctic

1 ❑ Nov 1996, b&w Cover: 2.95 **NM** value: **Cover or less**
wraparound cover. **A:** Mark Stokes **W:** Mark Stokes
2 ❑ Cover: 2.95 **NM** value: **Cover or less**
3 ❑ Cover: 2.95 **NM** value: **Cover or less**

ZOMBIE BOY RISES AGAIN — Timbuktu

1 ❑ Jan 1994, b&w Cover: 2.50 **NM** value: **Cover or less**
📖 Beverly Hills Corpse; The Nosey Neighbor; The Curse of Rigby the Pygmy; Sticks and Bones; Sombie Boy Meets the Hateful Doppelganger Jasper in Thicker than Water; Duncan's Visit; Zombie Boy Gallery • Collects Zombie Boy #1 and Zombie Boy's Hoodoo Tales #1; Beverly Hillbillies cameo **A:** Mark Stokes **W:** Mark Stokes

ZOMBIE BOY (TIMBUKTU) — Timbuktu

1 ❑ b&w Cover: 1.50 **NM** value: **Cover or less**

ZOMBIE LOVE — ZuZupetal

1 ❑ Cover: 2.50 **NM** value: **Cover or less**
2 ❑ Cover: 2.50 **NM** value: **Cover or less**
3 ❑ Cover: 2.50 **NM** value: **Cover or less**

ZOMBIE WAR: EARTH MUST BE DESTROYED — Fantaco

1 ❑ b&w Cover: 2.95 **NM** value: **Cover or less**
📖 Earth Must be Destroyed! **A:** Jim Whiting **W:** Kevin Eastman; Jim Whiting; Tom Skulan
1/CS ❑ b&w Cover: 3.95 **NM** value: **Cover or less**
• trading card
2 ❑ b&w Cover: 2.95 **NM** value: **Cover or less**
3 ❑ b&w Cover: 2.95 **NM** value: **Cover or less**
4 ❑ b&w Cover: 2.95 **NM** value: **Cover or less**

ZOMBIE WAR (FANTACO) — Fantaco

1 ❑ Cover: 3.50 **NM** value: **Cover or less**
Circ: CapCity orders: **3,370**
2 ❑ Cover: 3.50 **NM** value: **Cover or less**

ZOMBIE WAR (TUNDRA) — Tundra

1 ❑ Cover: 3.50 **NM** value: **Cover or less**

ZOMBIEWORLD: CHAMPION OF THE WORMS — Dark Horse

Nobody has more fun with undead bodies than Mike Mignola and Pat McEown.

Champion of the Worms is a lighthearted tale of ancient evil threatening to wreak destruction on the modern world. It seems that the sarcophagus of the dread Hyperborean necromancer Azzul Gotha has been recovered. Inside, Gotha had been kept alive but immobile and powerless for millenia, held in place by a binding stone. But once archaeologists transported the sarcophagus to a museum, Gotha was able to use what little powers he had to trick a museum guard into removing the stone, freeing him. Now, with a museum full of animated mummies at his disposal, Gotha (aka the Champion of the Worms) intends to raise a new empire of death — unless a motley crew of psychics and bruisers can track Gotha down and put him back in his box.

1 ❑ Sep 1997 Cover: 2.95 **NM** value: **Cover or less**
Circ: Diamd. preorders: **19,044**
2 ❑ Oct 1997 Cover: 2.95 **NM** value: **Cover or less**
Circ: Diamd. preorders: **14,794**
3 ❑ Nov 1997 Cover: 2.95 **NM** value: **Cover or less**
Circ: Diamd. preorders: **13,484**
Bk 1 ❑ Jul 1998 Cover: 8.95 **NM** value: **Cover or less**

ZOMBIEWORLD: DEAD END — Dark Horse

1 ❑ Jan 1998 Cover: 2.95 **NM** value: **Cover or less**
Circ: Diamd. preorders: **8,993**
2 ❑ Cover: 2.95 **NM** value: **Cover or less**
Circ: Diamd. preorders: **7,808**

ZOMBIEWORLD: EAT YOUR HEART OUT — Dark Horse

1 ❑ Apr 1998 Cover: 2.95 **NM** value: **Cover or less**
Circ: Diamd. preorders: **7,964**
No issue number. One-shot. **A:** Kelley Jones **W:** Kelley Jones

ZOMBIEWORLD: HOME FOR THE HOLIDAYS — Dark Horse

1 ❑ Dec 1997 Cover: 2.95 **NM** value: **Cover or less**
Circ: Diamd. preorders: **9,174**
No issue number. One-shot. **A:** Gary Erskine **W:** Gordon Rennie

ZOMBIEWORLD: TREE OF DEATH — Dark Horse

1 ❑ Jun 1999 Cover: 2.95 **NM** value: **Cover or less**
Circ: Diamd. preorders: **6,067**
2 ❑ Aug 1999 Cover: 2.95 **NM** value: **Cover or less**
Circ: Diamd. preorders: **5,377**
3 ❑ Sep 1999 Cover: 2.95 **NM** value: **Cover or less**
Circ: Diamd. preorders: **5,127**
4 ❑ Oct 1999 Cover: 2.95 **NM** value: **Cover or less**

ZOMBIEWORLD: WINTER'S DREGS — Dark Horse

1 ❑ May 1998 Cover: 2.95 **NM** value: **Cover or less**
Circ: Diamd. preorders: **6,750**
2 ❑ Jun 1998 Cover: 2.95 **NM** value: **Cover or less**
Circ: Diamd. preorders: **6,391**
3 ❑ Jul 1998 Cover: 2.95 **NM** value: **Cover or less**
Circ: Diamd. preorders: **5,893**
4 ❑ Aug 1998 Cover: 2.95 **NM** value: **Cover or less**
Circ: Diamd. preorders: **5,426**

ZOMBOY — Inferno

1 ❑ Aug 1996, b&w Cover: 2.95 **NM** value: **Cover or less**

ZOMOID ILLUSTORIES — 3-D Zone

1 ❑ b&w Cover: 2.50 **NM** value: **Cover or less**
• not 3-D

ZONE — Dark Horse

1 ❑ b&w Cover: 1.95 **NM** value: **2.00**

ZONE CONTINUUM, THE — Caliber

1 ❑ b&w Cover: 2.95 **NM** value: **Cover or less**
1/A ❑ **NM** value: **2.00**
no cover price. • Orange background **A:** Bruce Zick **W:** Bruce Zick
1/B ❑ **NM** value: **2.00**
no cover price. • Maroon background **A:** Bruce Zick **W:** Bruce Zick
2 ❑ b&w Cover: 2.95 **NM** value: **Cover or less**

ZONE CONTINUUM (VOL. 2) — Caliber

1 ❑ b&w Cover: 2.95 **NM** value: **Cover or less**
2 ❑ b&w Cover: 2.95 **NM** value: **Cover or less**

ZONE ZERO — Planet Boy

1 ❑ b&w Cover: 2.95 **NM** value: **Cover or less**

ZOO FUNNIES — Children Comics

1 ❑ Nov 1945 Cover: 0.10 **NM** value: **150.00**
2 ❑ Dec 1945 Cover: 0.10 **NM** value: **100.00**
• **CGC:** 5 graded, best 9.6
3 ❑ Jan 1946 Cover: 0.10 **NM** value: **100.00**
4 ❑ Feb 1946 Cover: 0.10 **NM** value: **75.00**
5 ❑ Mar 1946 Cover: 0.10 **NM** value: **75.00**
6 ❑ Apr 1946 Cover: 0.10 **NM** value: **75.00**
7 ❑ May 1946 Cover: 0.10 **NM** value: **65.00**
8 ❑ Jun 1946 Cover: 0.10 **NM** value: **65.00**
9 ❑ Jul 1946 Cover: 0.10 **NM** value: **65.00**
10 ❑ Aug 1946 Cover: 0.10 **NM** value: **50.00**
11 ❑ Sep 1946 Cover: 0.10 **NM** value: **50.00**
12 ❑ Oct 1946 Cover: 0.10 **NM** value: **50.00**
13 ❑ Nov 1946 Cover: 0.10 **NM** value: **45.00**
14 ❑ Dec 1946 Cover: 0.10 **NM** value: **45.00**
15 ❑ Jan 1947 Cover: 0.10 **NM** value: **45.00**

ZOO FUNNIES (2ND SERIES) — Charlton

1 ❑ Jul 1953 Cover: 0.10 **NM** value: **55.00**
📖 Punchy and The Black Crow; Leon the Lyin' Lion: Be Seated Please; Complainin' Time at the Zoo (text story); Nip the Cat; Tubby the Scout; Leon the Lyin' Lion: Big Doings **A:** Al Fago **W:** Al Fago
2 ❑ Jul 1953 Cover: 0.10 **NM** value: **36.00**
• **CGC:** 1 graded, best 9.4
📖 Punchy and The Black Crow; Leon the Lyin' Lion; Zoo's Who: Who's Who in Zoo; Nip the Cat: The Jackpot **A:** Al Fago **W:** Al Fago
3 ❑ Oct 1953 Cover: 0.10 **NM** value: **28.00**
4 ❑ Jan 1954 Cover: 0.10 **NM** value: **24.00**
5 ❑ Apr 1954 Cover: 0.10 **NM** value: **24.00**
6 ❑ Jul 1954 Cover: 0.10 **NM** value: **24.00**
7 ❑ Sep 1954 Cover: 0.10 **NM** value: **24.00**
8 ❑ Nov 1954 Cover: 0.10 **NM** value: **35.00**
9 ❑ Jan 1955 Cover: 0.10 **NM** value: **35.00**
10 ❑ Mar 1955 Cover: 0.10 **NM** value: **35.00**
11 ❑ May 1955 Cover: 0.10 **NM** value: **35.00**
12 ❑ Jul 1955 Cover: 0.10 **NM** value: **35.00**
13 ❑ Sep 1955 Cover: 0.10 **NM** value: **35.00**

ZOO FUNNIES (3RD SERIES) — Charlton

1 ❑ Dec 1984 Cover: 0.75 **NM** value: **2.00**

ZOONIVERSE — Eclipse

1 ❑ Aug 1986 Cover: 1.25 **NM** value: **1.50**
Circ: CapCity orders: **7,400**
2 ❑ Oct 1986 Cover: 1.25 **NM** value: **1.50**
Circ: CapCity orders: **5,000**
📖 Yippo the Magic Zoon **A:** Fil Barlow **W:** Fil Barlow; Michael Logan
3 ❑ Dec 1986 Cover: 1.25 **NM** value: **1.50**
📖 Live at the Hall of Records **A:** Fil Barlow; Chris Johnston **W:** Fil Barlow; Rowena Cory
4 ❑ Feb 1987 Cover: 1.25 **NM** value: **1.50**
Circ: CapCity orders: **3,200**
5 ❑ Apr 1987 Cover: 1.25 **NM** value: **1.50**
Circ: CapCity orders: **2,800**
6 ❑ Jun 1987 Cover: 1.75 **NM** value: **Cover or less**

ZOOT! — Fantagraphics

1 ❑ Nov 1992, b&w Cover: 2.50 **NM** value: **Cover or less**
2 ❑ Mar 1993, b&w Cover: 2.50 **NM** value: **Cover or less**
3 ❑ May 1993, b&w Cover: 2.50 **NM** value: **Cover or less**
4 ❑ Jul 1993, b&w Cover: 2.50 **NM** value: **Cover or less**
5 ❑ Sep 1993, b&w Cover: 2.50 **NM** value: **Cover or less**
6 ❑ Nov 1993, b&w Cover: 2.50 **NM** value: **Cover or less**

ZOOT COMICS — Fox

1 ❑ ca. 1946 Cover: 0.10 **NM** value: **175.00**
• **CGC:** 1 graded, best 5.0
2 ❑ ca. 1946 Cover: 0.10 **NM** value: **150.00**
3 ❑ ca. 1946 Cover: 0.10 **NM** value: **150.00**
4 ❑ ca. 1946 Cover: 0.10 **NM** value: **150.00**
5 ❑ Jan 1947 Cover: 0.10 **NM** value: **150.00**
6 ❑ Mar 1947 Cover: 0.10 **NM** value: **125.00**
7 ❑ Jun 1947 Cover: 0.10 **NM** value: **125.00**
• **CGC:** 1 graded, best 7.0
8 ❑ Aug 1947 Cover: 0.10 **NM** value: **125.00**
• **CGC:** 1 graded, best 7.5
9 ❑ Oct 1947 Cover: 0.10 **NM** value: **125.00**
10 ❑ Nov 1947 Cover: 0.10 **NM** value: **100.00**
• **CGC:** 1 graded, best 8.5
11 ❑ Dec 1947 Cover: 0.10 **NM** value: **100.00**
• **CGC:** 3 graded, best 9.2
12 ❑ Jan 1948 Cover: 0.10 **NM** value: **90.00**
• **CGC:** 2 graded, best 9.0
13 ❑ Feb 1948 Cover: 0.10 **NM** value: **90.00**
• **CGC:** 1 graded, best 8.0
14 ❑ Mar 1948 Cover: 0.10 **NM** value: **90.00**
• **CGC:** 3 graded, best 9.0
15 ❑ May 1948 Cover: 0.10 **NM** value: **85.00**
• **CGC:** 2 graded, best 9.0
16 ❑ Jul 1948 Cover: 0.10 **NM** value: **85.00**
• **CGC:** 1 graded, best 9.2

ZORANN: STAR-WARRIOR! — Blue Comet

0 ❑ May 1994 Cover: 2.95 **NM** value: **Cover or less**
📖 My Enemies Blood! **A:** Dell Barras **W:** Craig Stormon
1 ❑ b&w Cover: 2.00 **NM** value: **Cover or less**

ZORI J'S 3-D BUBBLE BATH — 3-D Zone

1 ❑ b&w Cover: 3.95 **NM** value: **Cover or less**
No issue number.

ZORI J'S SUPER-SWELL BUBBLE BATH ADVENTURE-OH BOY! — 3-D Zone

1 ❑ b&w Cover: 2.95 **NM** value: **Cover or less**
No issue number.

ZORRO (DELL) — Dell

While many fans associate the 1950s Disney-produced TV show with the swashbuckling hero of Old California, Zorro actually got his start in a five-part pulp-magazine story, "The Curse of Capistrano" by Johnston McCulley begun in a 1919 issue of All Story Weekly. The stories became the impetus for a silent film, The Mark of Zorro, starring Douglas Fairbanks Jr., in 1920. (DC even worked the film into Batman's origin about 30 years ago, sending the Waynes to a revival showing of the film on the fateful night when they were killed.)

Zorro's real identity was Don Diego Vega (or sometimes Don Diego de la Vega or variations thereof), the son of a Spanish nobleman who had established himself in California. Vega was outraged by the abuses visited upon the people by Governor Alvarado and donned a black mask, cloak, and hat to help right the wrongs.

The stories are provided comic relief by the bumblings of Alvarado's corpulent sergeant Garcia, whom Zorro often uses as a convenient dupe.

The 1950s TV show, which Dell's comics adventures are based on, starred Guy Williams as Zorro and featured wonderful swashbuckling adventures. In the 1970s, George Hamilton parodied the stories with the film Zorro: The Gay Blade, and, in the late 1990s, Antonio Banderas provided a new look at Zorro with a remake of The Mark of Zorro. — Brent

8 ❑ Dec 1959 Cover: 0.10 **NM** value: **80.00**
• **CGC:** 2 graded, best 9.2
9 ❑ Mar 1960 Cover: 0.10 **NM** value: **80.00**
• **CGC:** 1 graded, best 9.4
10 ❑ Jun 1960 Cover: 0.10 **NM** value: **75.00**
11 ❑ Sep 1960 Cover: 0.10 **NM** value: **75.00**
• **CGC:** 1 graded, best 9.0
12 ❑ Dec 1960 Cover: 0.10 **NM** value: **75.00**
• **CGC:** 3 graded, best 9.4
13 ❑ Mar 1961 Cover: 0.10 **NM** value: **70.00**
14 ❑ Jun 1961 Cover: 0.10 **NM** value: **70.00**
• **CGC:** 1 graded, best 9.4
15 ❑ Sep 1961 Cover: 0.12 **NM** value: **70.00**
• **CGC:** 1 graded, best 9.6

CGC-graded: Multiply prices above by **33 for 9.9 M • 16 for 9.8 NM/M • 7 for 9.6 NM+ • 5 for 9.4 NM • 2.5 for 9.2 NM- • 1.5 for 9.0 VF/NM**

ZORRO (GOLD KEY) — Gold Key

1 ❑ Jan 1966 Cover: 0.12 **NM** value: **75.00**
• **CGC:** 1 graded, best 9.8
2 ❑ May 1966 Cover: 0.12 **NM** value: **40.00**
3 ❑ 1966 Cover: 0.12 **NM** value: **40.00**
4 ❑ 1966 Cover: 0.12 **NM** value: **40.00**
5 ❑ 1967 Cover: 0.12 **NM** value: **35.00**
6 ❑ Jun 1967 Cover: 0.12 **NM** value: **35.00**
7 ❑ 1967 Cover: 0.12 **NM** value: **35.00**
8 ❑ 1967 Cover: 0.12 **NM** value: **30.00**
9 ❑ 1968 Cover: 0.12 **NM** value: **30.00**

ZORRO GRAPHIC ALBUM — Eclipse

Bk 1❑ Cover: 9.95 **NM** value: **Cover or less**
Circ: CapCity orders: **1,236**
Bk 1-2❑Jul 1998 Cover: 15.95 **NM** value: **Cover or less**
Circ: CapCity orders: **183**
• reprints Eclipse tpb
Bk 2❑ Cover: 9.95 **NM** value: **Cover or less**
Bk 2-2❑Aug 1998 Cover: 15.95 **NM** value: **Cover or less**
• reprints Eclipse tpb

ZORRO (MARVEL) — Marvel

1 ❑ Dec 1990 Cover: 1.00 **NM** value: **3.00**
Circ: CapCity orders: **13,000**
2 ❑ Jan 1991 Cover: 1.00 **NM** value: **2.00**
Circ: CapCity orders: **9,400**
3 ❑ Feb 1991 Cover: 1.00 **NM** value: **2.00**
Circ: CapCity orders: **8,100**
4 ❑ Mar 1991 Cover: 1.00 **NM** value: **2.00**
Circ: CapCity orders: **6,800**
5 ❑ Apr 1991 Cover: 1.00 **NM** value: **2.00**
Circ: CapCity orders: **5,600**
6 ❑ May 1991 Cover: 1.00 **NM** value: **2.00**
Circ: CapCity orders: **5,600**
7 ❑ Jun 1991 Cover: 1.00 **NM** value: **2.00**
Circ: CapCity orders: **4,900**
8 ❑ Jul 1991 Cover: 1.00 **NM** value: **2.00**
Circ: CapCity orders: **4,700**
9 ❑ Aug 1991 Cover: 1.00 **NM** value: **2.00**
Circ: CapCity orders: **4,400**
10 ❑ Sep 1991 Cover: 1.00 **NM** value: **2.00**
Circ: CapCity orders: **4,200**
11 ❑ Oct 1991 Cover: 1.00 **NM** value: **2.00**
Circ: CapCity orders: **4,000**
12 ❑ Nov 1991 Cover: 1.00 **NM** value: **2.00**
Circ: CapCity orders: **3,700**
final issue. **C:** Alex Toth

ZORRO: MATANZAS! — Image

Ash 1❑ **NM** value: **1.00**

ZORRO'S RENEGADES — Image

Bk 2❑ Feb 1999, b&w Cover: 14.95 **NM** value: **Cover or less**
No issue number. • Trade Paperback. • collects Topps' Zorro #4-8

ZORRO: THE LADY WEARS RED — Image

Bk 1❑ Dec 1998, b&w Cover: 12.95 **NM** value: **Cover or less**
No issue number. • Trade Paperback. 📖 Prequel in a Hostile Landscape **A:** Mike Mayhew **W:** Don McGregor ★ Appearance of collects Lady Rawhide.

ZORRO (TOPPS) — Topps

0 ❑ Nov 1993 Cover: 1.00 **NM** value: **2.50**
Circ: CapCity orders: **8,425**
1 ❑ Jan 1994 Cover: 2.50 **NM** value: **3.50**
Circ: CapCity orders: **13,475**
📖 Prequel in a Hostile Landscape **A:** Mike Mayhew; Frank Miller(cover) **C:** Frank Miller **W:** Don McGregor ★ 1st Appearance of Machete.
2 ❑ Feb 1994 Cover: 2.50 **NM** value: **8.00**
Circ: CapCity orders: **8,025**
3 ❑ Mar 1994 Cover: 2.50 **NM** value: **3.00**
Circ: CapCity orders: **8,600**
4 ❑ Apr 1994 Cover: 2.50 **NM** value: **3.00**
Circ: CapCity orders: **6,800**
📖 The Man Who Wasn't Felix Quintero **A:** Mike Mayhew; Vince Russell **C:** Mike Grell **W:** Don McGregor ★ 1st Appearance of Moonstalker.
5 ❑ May 1994 Cover: 2.50 **NM** value: **3.00**
Circ: CapCity orders: **6,325**
📖 The Bones Travel to the Ocean **A:** Keith Giffen; Mike Mayhew; Vince Russell **C:** Joe Sinnott **W:** Don McGregor ★ Appearance of Lady Rawhide.
6 ❑ Jun 1994 Cover: 2.50 **NM** value: **3.00**
Circ: CapCity orders: **5,825**
📖 A Whale of a Coffin **A:** Mike Mayhew; Vince Russell **C:** Mike Mignola **W:** Don McGregor
7 ❑ Jul 1994 Cover: 2.50 **NM** value: **Cover or less**
Circ: CapCity orders: **5,675**
📖 Let's Kill the Corpse **A:** Mike Mayhew; Vince Russell **C:** Paul Gulacy **W:** Don McGregor ★ Appearance of Lady Rawhide.
8 ❑ Aug 1994 Cover: 2.50 **NM** value: **Cover or less**
Circ: CapCity orders: **5,000**
📖 As They Die Around You **A:** George Pérez; Mike Mayhew; Vince Russell **C:** George Pérez **W:** Don McGregor ★ Appearance of Lady Rawhide.
9 ❑ Sep 1994 Cover: 2.95 **NM** value: **Cover or less**
Circ: CapCity orders: **4,600**
10 ❑ Oct 1994 Cover: 2.50 **NM** value: **2.95**
Circ: CapCity orders: **6,050**
11 ❑ Nov 1994 Cover: 2.50 **NM** value: **Cover or less**
Circ: CapCity orders: **6,675**
final issue. **W:** Don McGregor ★ Appearance of Lady Rawhide.
Bk 2❑ Feb 1999 Cover: 14.95 **NM** value: **Cover or less**
• Zorro's Renegades trade paperback; Collects Zorro (Topps) #4-8 **A:** Mike Mayhew; Vince Russell **W:** Don McGregor

ZOT! — Eclipse

Zachary T. Paleozogt ("Zot") was a boy who grew up on a more advanced alternate version of Earth. His parents inexplicably abandoned him before he was 10, after which he was cared for by his eccentric uncle Max. Max was a great teacher, and Zot quickly excelled in both school and sports. Most importantly, he became the world arcade marksman champion. He used these skills to become a hero on his home world. He eventually crossed over into our world to stop a robotic rampage. Here, he encountered young Jenny Weaver, a kind teen-ager who would eventually become his girlfriend. The two embarked on a series of high-flying adventures, beginning with the search for the gold key which opens the legendary "Doorway at the Edge of the Universe."

Zot! is delightfully innocent fun by Scott McCloud, best known for his book "Understanding Comics." Later issues also included a backup spoof featuring Matt Feazell's Cynicalman.

1 ❑ Apr 1984, full color Cover: 1.50 **NM** value: **5.00**
• Color issues begin **A:** Scott McCloud **W:** Scott McCloud ★ 1st Appearance of Jenny Weaver, Zot!.
2 ❑ May 1984 Cover: 1.50 **NM** value: **2.50**
3 ❑ Jun 1984 Cover: 1.50 **NM** value: **2.50**
📖 Art & Soul, Part 1 **A:** Scott McCloud **W:** Scott McCloud ★ 1st Appearance of Dekko (full).
4 ❑ Jul 1984 Cover: 1.50 **NM** value: **2.50**
📖 Art & Soul, Part 2 **A:** Scott McCloud **W:** Scott McCloud ★ Origin of Zot!.
5 ❑ Aug 1984 Cover: 1.50 **NM** value: **2.50**
📖 Sirius Business **A:** Scott McCloud **W:** Scott McCloud
6 ❑ Nov 1984 Cover: 1.50 **NM** value: **2.50**
📖 It's Always Darkest… **A:** Scott McCloud **W:** Scott McCloud
7 ❑ Dec 1984 Cover: 1.50 **NM** value: **2.50**
📖 Common Ground; September • The Magic Shop back-up features begin **A:** Dan Spiegle; Scott McCloud **W:** Kurt Busiek; Scott McCloud
8 ❑ Mar 1985 Cover: 1.50 **NM** value: **2.50**
9 ❑ May 1985 Cover: 1.50 **NM** value: **2.50**
📖 Gorilla Warfare! **A:** Scott McCloud **W:** Scott McCloud
10 ❑ Jul 1985 Cover: 1.50 **NM** value: **2.50**
📖 T.K.O. **A:** Scott McCloud **W:** Scott McCloud
10.5❑ Cover: 1.50 **NM** value: **2.50**
11 ❑ Jan 1987 Cover: 2.00 **NM** value: **2.50**
• Black & white issues begin **A:** Scott McCloud **W:** Scott McCloud
12 ❑ Mar 1987 Cover: 2.00 **NM** value: **2.25**
13 ❑ May 1987 Cover: 2.00 **NM** value: **2.25**
14 ❑ Jul 1987 Cover: 2.00 **NM** value: **2.25**
14.5❑ Cover: 2.00 **NM** value: **2.25**
• Adventures of Zot! in Dimension 10 1/2, The **A:** Matt Feazell **W:** Matt Feazell
15 ❑ Oct 1987 Cover: 2.00 **NM** value: **2.25**
16 ❑ Dec 1987 Cover: 2.00 **NM** value: **2.25**
Circ: CapCity orders: **3,350**
17 ❑ Feb 1988 Cover: 2.00 **NM** value: **2.25**
18 ❑ Apr 1988 Cover: 2.00 **NM** value: **2.25**
19 ❑ Jun 1988 Cover: 2.00 **NM** value: **2.25**
20 ❑ Jun 1988 Cover: 2.00 **NM** value: **2.25**
21 ❑ Aug 1988 Cover: 2.00 **NM** value: **2.25**
📖 Can't Buy Me Love, Part 1 **A:** Scott McCloud **W:** Scott McCloud
22 ❑ Oct 1988 Cover: 2.00 **NM** value: **2.25**
📖 Can't Buy Me Love, Part 2; The Adventures of Zot! in Dimension 10 1/2 **A:** Matt Feazell; Scott McCloud **W:** Scott McCloud
23 ❑ Nov 1988 Cover: 2.00 **NM** value: **2.25**
24 ❑ Dec 1988 Cover: 2.00 **NM** value: **2.25**
25 ❑ Feb 1989 Cover: 2.00 **NM** value: **2.25**
26 ❑ Apr 1989 Cover: 2.00 **NM** value: **2.25**
27 ❑ Jun 1989 Cover: 2.00 **NM** value: **2.25**
28 ❑ Sep 1989 Cover: 2.00 **NM** value: **2.25**
29 ❑ Dec 1989 Cover: 2.00 **NM** value: **2.25**
📖 Looking for Crime; Shakedown on Astro Speedway **A:** Matt Feazell; Scott McCloud **W:** Scott McCloud; Ivy Ratafia; Walt Lockley
30 ❑ Mar 1990 Cover: 2.00 **NM** value: **2.25**
31 ❑ May 1990 Cover: 2.00 **NM** value: **2.25**
32 ❑ Jul 1990 Cover: 2.00 **NM** value: **2.25**
33 ❑ Oct 1990 Cover: 2.00 **NM** value: **2.25**
34 ❑ Dec 1990 Cover: 2.00 **NM** value: **2.25**
35 ❑ Mar 1991 Cover: 2.00 **NM** value: **2.25**
36 ❑ Jul 1991 Cover: 2.95 **NM** value: **Cover or less**
final issue.
34973❑ Cover: 1.50 **NM** value: **Cover or less**
Bk 1❑ Cover: 29.95 **NM** value: **Cover or less**
• collects issues #1-10; Reprints Zot! #1-4 **A:** Scott McCloud **W:** Scott McCloud
Bk 1/LE❑ Cover: 30.95 **NM** value: **Cover or less**
• Reprints Zot! #1-4 **A:** Scott McCloud **W:** Scott McCloud
Bk 2❑ Feb 1998, b&w Cover: 19.95 **NM** value: **Cover or less**
• collects issues #11-18
Bk 3/LE❑ Cover: 34.95 **NM** value: **Cover or less**

ZU — Mu

1 ❑ Jan 1995, b&w Cover: 2.95 **NM** value: **Cover or less**
2 ❑ Mar 1995, b&w Cover: 2.95 **NM** value: **Cover or less**
3 ❑ May 1995, b&w Cover: 2.95 **NM** value: **Cover or less**
4 ❑ Jul 1995, b&w Cover: 2.95 **NM** value: **Cover or less**
5 ❑ Sep 1995, b&w Cover: 2.95 **NM** value: **Cover or less**
6 ❑ Nov 1995, b&w Cover: 2.95 **NM** value: **Cover or less**
7 ❑ Jan 1996, b&w Cover: 2.95 **NM** value: **Cover or less**
8 ❑ Cover: 2.95 **NM** value: **Cover or less**
9 ❑ Cover: 2.95 **NM** value: **Cover or less**
10 ❑ Cover: 2.95 **NM** value: **Cover or less**
11 ❑ Cover: 2.95 **NM** value: **Cover or less**
12 ❑ Cover: 2.95 **NM** value: **Cover or less**
13 ❑ Cover: 2.95 **NM** value: **Cover or less**
14 ❑ Cover: 2.95 **NM** value: **Cover or less**
15 ❑ Cover: 2.95 **NM** value: **Cover or less**
16 ❑ Cover: 2.95 **NM** value: **Cover or less**
17 ❑ Cover: 2.95 **NM** value: **Cover or less**
18 ❑ Cover: 2.95 **NM** value: **Cover or less**
19 ❑ Cover: 2.95 **NM** value: **Cover or less**

ZUGAL — Bryan Evans

1 ❑ Cover: 2.95 **NM** value: **Cover or less**
📖 The City **A:** Bryan Evans **W:** Bryan Evans

ZULUNATION — Tome Press

1 ❑ b&w Cover: 2.95 **NM** value: **Cover or less**
2 ❑ b&w Cover: 2.95 **NM** value: **Cover or less**
3 ❑ b&w Cover: 2.95 **NM** value: **Cover or less**

ZU (ONE-SHOT) — Mu

1 ❑ Feb 1992 Cover: 3.95 **NM** value: **Cover or less**
No issue number. One-shot.

ZWANNA, SON OF ZULU — Dark Zulu Lies

1 ❑ Cover: 1.95 **NM** value: **2.00**
Circ: CapCity orders: **7,150**

ZZZ — Alan Bunce

Canadian Alan Bunce neatly handles the dual linguistics of his native country with this whimsical title, which relies solely on pictures to relate its hero's whimsical dreams. In the first issue, the hero, who looks somewhat like one of the Smurfs, falls down a magical, mystery hole into a treasure trove, where he releases a playful genie. Soon, the two are running around, tripping and tumbling in slapstick fashion, made even funner by the genie's magic trickery. It's almost a shame our hero has to wake up at the end.

Zzz is a delightful fantasy title appropriate for kids of all ages-and nationalities.

1 ❑ Mar 2000 Cover: 2.35 **NM** value: **Cover or less**

Other grades: Multiply prices above by **1.5 for Mint • 2/3 for Very Fine • 1/3 for Fine • 1/5 for Very Good • 1/8 for Good**

Suggested reading

Even in a volume this big, there's only so much information we can cram in. Sooner or later, you're going to want to pursue a topic further than we've had room for here. So, as you expand your quest, consider these sources of information. (Some may be out of print, but you should be able to track 'em down, thanks to the wonders of the Internet, right?)

For starters, The ***ComicBase*** CD-ROM contains all the comics found in this edition, as well as many foreign comics. There are summaries for thousands more titles in *ComicBase*, as well. That's *www.human-computing.com* or Human Computing, 4509 Thistle Dr., San Jose, CA 95136.

Then, there's the weekly comics news magazine, ***Comics Buyer's Guide***, 700 E. State St., Iola, WI 54945 (and *www.comicsbuyersguide.com*), which provides the latest news and updates on what's collectible, population reports, pricing reports, and the like — on comics old and new. And no magazine publishes more reviews of new comics each year!

A tireless researcher, one of the world's leading experts on comic books and strips, is Ron Goulart, and all his reference material on comics will make informative *and* entertaining reading on the field. Among his most helpful works is ***The Encyclopedia of American Comics from 1897 to the Present*** (Facts on File, 1990), and, if you yearn for full-color tastes of Golden Age goodies, check out his ***Comic Book Culture: An Illustrated History*** (Collectors Press, 2000). But those are just two; buy anything by Goulart, if you're looking for behind-the-scenes background on Comics That Were

The Overstreet Comic Book Price Guide, one of the leaders in the field of comics collecting, continues to publish an annual update with historical essays; the 2002 edition is its 32nd, and its earliest editions are collectibles themselves. It also has information on many of the precursors to today's comic-book format. Check out *www.gemstonepub.com* or Gemstone Publishing, Inc., 1966 Greenspring Dr., Timonium, MD 21093.

If you'd like to learn more about *Classics Illustrated*, we would encourage you to refer to Dan Malan's definitive two-volume ***The Complete Guide to Classics Illustrated*** available from: Malan Classical Enterprises, 7519 Lindbergh Dr., St. Louis, MO 63117 (314) 781-2319, and there's more info available online at *www.classicscentral.com/hold1/guide.htm*.

Ernst Gerber has put together some incredible compendia of comic-book covers, including valuable information regarding publishing dates and the like. ***The Photo Journal Guide to Comic Books***, for example, is a two-volume set of Golden Age covers and information, packed with beautiful photos. It's not cheap, but it's a major work and rewards the browser.

Fans of Carl Barks' "ducks" comics would do well to consult the work of Michael Barrier, who did the first scholarly work about Barrier's ***Carl Barks and the Art of the Comic Book*** (M. Lilien, 1981) is a valuable resource.

Comic Book Marketplace is a magazine devoted to back-issue scholarship. More information is available from *www.eccrypt.com* and/or Russ Cochran, Publisher, P.O. Box 469, West Plains, MO 65775.

The New York Observer called ***The Comics Journal*** the "tweedy intellectual voice of the industry." That may be, but, between indictments against commercialism, it does publish many excellent long-form interviews with creators. It's available from Fantagraphics Books.

Howard Keltner's ***Golden Age Comic Books Index, 1935-1955***, emphasizing costumed and super-hero titles, is a lifetime's research in a single volume, a complete index to the features in those titles. Completed just before he died, the work is a guide to all the features that appeared in every issue of those comics. Write Bob Klein with a self-addressed, stamped envelope for information at P.O. Box 214, Grafton, MA 01519.

Long out of print but fascinating are the ***Marvel Comics Index*** editions, wherein George Olshevsky sought not only to catalog the events of issues of Marvel series, but to put the characters' appearances in "chronological" order. Pacific distributed the first batch in the early 1980s, and then Olshevsky later did "official" versions for Marvel in comic-book size. Similiar such editions were produced by Eclipse for DC series.

FantaCo's ***Chronicles*** series from the early 1980s provides background on various Marvel super-heroes and some of the better interviews published at that time. There were six comic-book sized editions, which may still be available in comics back-issue bins.

The entire CGC Census is available on the company's website, *www.cgccomics.com*. The information appears at some delay from the company's actual grading, but it still provides valuable information on what's out there and being bought and sold for noticeable bucks. There's more about CGC throughout our **Standard Catalog**.

Prince Namor, the Sub-Mariner from Young Men Comics #26 (Atlas, 1954).
Artwork by Namor's legendary creator Bill Everett. © Atlas/ Marvel.

BUYING
ENTIRE COLLECTIONS!!
Michael Carbonaro's
www.neatstuffcollectibles.com
Buying & Selling EVERYTHING!
INFANTINO
McLAUGHLIN
SPURLOCK
CALL NOW!
800-903-7246
Send correspondence to: NEAT STUFF
FAX 201-569-2272
66 GRAND AVE., STE. 201 ENGLEWOOD, NJ 07631
EMAIL: ebay@neatstuffcollectibles.com
1,000's of items every week on ebay!
Check our weekly auctions on
ebay

Auctioning your comics?

BUYING
ENTIRE COLLECTIONS!!
Michael Carbonaro's
www.neatstuffcollectibles.com
Buying & Selling EVERYTHING!
INFANTINO
McLAUGHLIN
SPURLOCK
CALL NOW!
800-903-7246
Check our weekly auctions on
ebay
Send correspondence to: NEAT STUFF
FAX 201-569-2272
66 GRAND AVE., STE. 201 ENGLEWOOD, NJ 07631
EMAIL: ebay@neatstuffcollectibles.com
1,000's of items every week on ebay!

WANTED
Vintage Collectibles
Motion Picture
FUNNIES
WEEKLY
DON'T WORRY!—I'LL BRING IT RIGHT BACK AGAIN
NOW PLAYING!
TICKETS
Bill Everett
At Jay Parrino's The Mint you will find the absolute best in Vintage Comic Books, Original Comic Book Artwork and Movie Posters. We personally select items that meet the strictest criteria in True Rarity, Unsurpassed Quality and Extreme Desirability. Exemplified in the Ultra-Rare Comic Book pictured above: The Pay Copy of Motion Picture Funnies Weekly #1 featuring the Origin and 1st appearance of Prince Namor, The Sub-Mariner (created by legendary artist Bill Everett in April of 1939). This pedigree book was owned by the publisher himself Martin Goodman, and is by far the finest copy of this super-key Golden-Age comic book in existence. Items such as this, which have True Historical Significance, a Proven Track Record and "Run Away" Potential are the ones on which The Mint has built its reputation for over 50 years.
Seasoned collectors realize that opportunity is the number one most important factor when considering a major purchase. Hopefully, as a future client you will come to realize the Pride of Ownership that comes with acquiring The Rarest and the Finest.
We Never Compromise!
Neither Should You!
© Marvel
Jay Parrino's
The MINT L.L.C.
The Rarest and The Finest
Jay Parrino's The Mint
Post Office Drawer 9326 • Kansas City, MO 64133
Toll Free (866) 355-4591 • (972) 691-8837 Fax
www.JayParrino.com